The National Hockey League

Official Guide & Record Book

2012

THE NATIONAL HOCKEY LEAGUE
Official Guide & Record Book/2012

TERMS & CONDITIONS FOR USING THE DATA CONTAINED IN THIS BOOK

ATTENTION: PLEASE READ THIS DOCUMENT CAREFULLY BEFORE USING THIS BOOK (THE "BOOK") AND/OR THE DATA IT CONTAINS (THE "DATA"). INDIVIDUALS OR ENTITIES USING THE DATA ("END USERS") AGREE TO BE BOUND BY THE TERMS OF THIS LICENSE. IF YOU DO NOT AGREE TO THE TERMS OF THIS LICENSE, DO NOT USE THE DATA AND PROMPTLY RETURN THE UNUSED BOOK AND PROOF OF PAYMENT TO THE FOLLOWING ADDRESS FOR A REFUND:

> Dan Diamond & Associates, Inc.
> 194 Dovercourt Road, Toronto, Ontario, M6J 3C8
> dda.nhl@sympatico.ca.

Dan Diamond & Associates, Inc. (the "Publisher") owns, and retains ownership of, the Data. The Publisher reserves any right not expressly granted to End Users.

1. License. End-Users are granted a limited, non-exclusive license to do only the following, subject to the restrictions set out in Section 2 below:
   (a) End-Users may use the Data for personal, non-commercial purposes.
   (b) End-Users may reproduce individual player records, tables and data panels in connection with bona fide private study and research.
   (c) End-Users who are journalists may reproduce individual player records, tables and data panels for use by the broadcast and print media.

2. Restrictions. End-Users may NOT reproduce the Data, in whole or in part, in any form or by any means, electronic or mechanical, including photocopying, recording, or by any information storage and retrieval system now known or hereafter invented, without written permission from the Publisher. End-Users may NOT sublicense, or assign, or distribute (via the World Wide Web or otherwise) copies of the Data, in whole or in part, to others. END-USERS MAY NOT MODIFY, ADAPT, TRANSLATE, RENT, LEASE, LOAN, RESELL FOR PROFIT, DISTRIBUTE, OR OTHERWISE ASSIGN OR TRANSFER THE DATA, OR CREATE DERIVATIVE WORKS BASED UPON THE DATA OR ANY PART THEREOF, EXCEPT AS PROVIDED ABOVE.

3. Commercial Users. Commercial users (such as sports reference and sports gaming websites) may obtain a license to use customized Data upon payment of a reasonable fee. Please contact the Publisher at the address provided above.

4. Termination. This License is effective until terminated. This License will terminate immediately without notice from the Publisher if the End User fails to comply with any of its provisions. Upon termination End Users must destroy the Data and all copies thereof.

5. General. This License will be governed by and construed in accordance with the laws of the province of Ontario and the laws of Canada applicable therein, and shall inure to the benefit of the Publisher and End-Users and their successors, assigns and legal representatives. If any provision of this License is held by a court of competent jurisdiction to be invalid or unenforceable to any extent under applicable law, that provision will be enforced to the maximum extent permissible and the remaining provisions of this License will remain in full force and effect. Any notices or other communications to be sent to the Publishers must be mailed first class, postage prepaid, to the address provided above. This Agreement constitutes the entire agreement between the parties with respect to the subject matter hereof, and all prior proposals, agreements, representations, statements and undertakings are hereby expressly cancelled and superseded. This Agreement may not be changed or amended except by a written instrument executed by a duly authorized officer of the Publisher.

6. Acknowledgment. BY USING THE DATA, THE END-USER ACKNOWLEDGES THAT IT HAS READ THIS LICENSE, UNDERSTANDS IT, AND AGREES TO BE BOUND BY ITS TERMS AND CONDITIONS. Should you have any questions concerning this License, contact the Publisher at the address provided above.

Copyright © 2011 by the National Hockey League.
Compiled by the NHL Public Relations Department and the 30 NHL Club Public Relations Directors.
Printed in Canada. All rights reserved under the Pan-American and International Copyright Conventions.
Published in Canada by: Dan Diamond and Associates, Inc., 194 Dovercourt Road, Toronto, Ontario M6J 3C8 Canada
ISBN in Canada 978-1-894801-22-5
Published in the United States by: Triumph Books, 542 South Dearborn Street, Chicago, Illinois 60605
ISBN in USA 978-1-60078-592-4

Staff

For the NHL: Dave McCarthy; Supervising Editor: Greg Inglis; Statistician: Benny Ercolani;
Editorial Staff: Dave Baker, John Dellapina, David Keon, Jen Raimondi, Kelley Rosset, Susan Snow, Julie Young.

Senior Managing Editor: Ralph Dinger
Associate Managing Editor: Paul Bontje
Production Editors: John Pasternak, Alex Dubiel, Becky Gowing
Photo Editor: Eric Zweig
Publisher: Dan Diamond
In Memory of Estelle Diamond (1929-2010), Alison McLaughlin (1962-2010)

Data Management and Typesetting: Caledon Data Management, Eden, Ontario
Film Output and Scanning: Astley Gilbert, Etobicoke, Ontario
Printing: Sunrise Consulting Inc.; Webcom Limited, Toronto, Ontario
Production Management: Dan Diamond and Associates, Inc., Toronto, Ontario
Contributors and Photo Credits: see page 663

Distribution

Trade sales and distribution in Canada by:
North 49 Books, 35 Prince Andrew Drive, Toronto, Ontario M3C 2H2   416/449-4000; Fax 416/449-9924
Dan Diamond and Associates, Inc., Toronto   416/531-6535; Fax 416/531-3939   dda.nhl@sympatico.ca   www.nhlofficialguide.com

Trade sales and distribution in the United States by:
Triumph Books, 542 South Dearborn Street, Chicago, Illinois 60605   312/939-3330; Fax 312/663-3557

International representatives:
Igloo Trading Company, Unit 6/7 The Elms Centre, Glaziers Lane, Normandy, Guildford, Surrey GU3 2DF England
Tel 011/441/483/811-971; Fax 011/441/483/811-972   sales@bwwp.co.uk   www.bwwp.co.uk

The National Hockey League
1185 Avenue of the Americas, 14th Floor, New York, New York 10036
1800 McGill College Ave., Suite 2600, Montreal, Quebec H3A 3J6
50 Bay Street, 11th Floor, Toronto, Ontario M5J 2X8

Table of Contents

Table of Contents *continued*

Introduction

WELCOME TO THE **80**TH EDITION OF *THE NATIONAL HOCKEY LEAGUE OFFICIAL GUIDE & RECORD BOOK*, the definitive statistical record of the NHL. This edition contains traces of the DNA of a vest-pocket sized 25-cent 140-pager titled "National Hockey Guide and Record Book Containing Rules and Records of All Leagues 1932-33." Published in New York City and compiled by future Hall of Fame inductee Jim Hendy, this book came out when the NHL was just 15 years old and not long established as the sport's top league. Indeed, 1932-33 would be just the seventh season for the Black Hawks, newly named Red Wings and Rangers; the ninth for the Bruins and the 15th for the Canadiens and Maple Leafs, charter franchises present since the League was formed in 1917. (See each club's Year-by-Year Record, Club Records, All-Time Record vs. Other Clubs, and G.M., Coach and Captain's history beginning on page 15.)

Eighty years later and five years shy of its centennial, the National Hockey League's position atop the hockey foodchain is irrefutable. It attracts the world's best players and tests them through an 82-game regular season and then a playoff campaign that requires winning three best-of-seven series to qualify for the Stanley Cup Final. To win, an organization must possess skill, depth and character in equal measure as the Boston Bruins did in 2011. By the end of game seven of the Final, their players and supporters know that something profound has been accomplished. (Coverage of the 2011 Stanley Cup Playoffs begins on page 239.)

As always, if it has happened in this League, or is about to happen, it's in the *Guide*. The new Winnipeg Jets will begin play in their modern downtown MTS Centre arena against the Montreal Canadiens on October 9, 2011, 15 years and five months after the first edition of the Jets played its final game in the 1996 playoffs. Four pages of detailed Jets information begin on page 131. Note that the new Jets' all-time records include those of the Atlanta Thrashers. The records of the first edition of the Jets – in the NHL from 1979-80 to 1995-96 – are incorporated into those of the Phoenix Coyotes beginning on page 99.

A new feature found on page 13 lists the details of the NHL's recent outdoor games, both Winter Classics played in the USA and Heritage Classics played in Canada. Note that the temperature at game time is listed, and has ranged from 0°F/-18°C at the first Heritage Classic in Edmonton's Commonwealth Stadium in 2003 to 50°F/+10°C at Pittsburgh's Heinz Field in 2011. It is worth noting that these have been the first and only NHL games played outdoors. Even in the League's earliest days, all games were played in covered arenas. In fact no Stanley Cup game going back to the trophy's inception in 1893 was played outdoors.

Also new and also on page 13 is a list of NHL regular-season games played outside North America. The first two of these were played by Vancouver and Anaheim in Tokyo in 1997. Four teams – Anaheim again, Buffalo, Los Angeles and the New York Rangers – will open their 2011-12 campaigns in Europe with games slated for Berlin, Helsinki and Stockholm.

The NHL 2011 Entry Draft (see page 212) yielded 210 new players who require the full treatment in the *NHL Official Guide & Record Book*. This means determining their height, weight, position, shooting side, birthday, birthplace, correct name spelling and phonetic pronunciation in addition to gathering accurate statistics that take them back to age 15 or 16. Social media have been a boon to us here. Players whose early stats prove elusive can be contacted on Twitter, enabling questions like, "Where did you play during that year between high school and college?" to get immediate answers. In years past, this information could be very difficult to source. Similarly late free agent signings often are released on teams' Twitter accounts before a formal press release is issued.

For phonetic pronunciations, almost every player in junior or college or high school hockey now has action clips from game broadcasts or interviews posted on YouTube. When announcers, narrators or interviewers call them by name, this enables us to ensure that guys like Taylor Fedun (*fuh-DOON*, page 293) and Harry Zolnierczyk (*ZOHL-nuhr-chuhk*, page 344) are correct from their first appearance in the Prospect Register (page 275).

As always in the *NHL Guide & Record Book*, every one of the more than 6,700 players who have appeared in an NHL game, plus more than 1,000 prospects who have yet to do so, are in this book, either in the Prospect Register, Active Player Register (345), Goaltender Register (583), Retired Player Index (610), Retired Goaltender Index (651), regular-season or playoff Record Books (166 and 242), Award Winners (204), All-Star Teams (227) or Hockey Hall of Fame sections (235). Photographs of the 2011 inductees to the Hockey Hall of Fame and U.S. Hockey Hall of Fame are found on page 657 and winners of the NHL's Player of the Week and Month Awards for 2010-11 are listed on page 581. A register of free agent signings begins on page 658 and a trade register is found on page 660.

A key to the abbreviations and symbols used in individual player and goaltender data panels, along with useful information on how to use the Registers, is found on page 274. Late additions are found on page 609 and each NHL club's minor-pro affiliates are found on page 14. A list of league abbreviations used in the Prospect, Player and Goaltender Registers is found on page 662 and a useful table on page 216 breaks down U.S. and Canadian-born draftees by state or province of birth. Players from 18 states and nine provinces were drafted in 2011.

And please go to page 663 for a special bonus photograph of 2010-11's NHL Goal of the Year as selected by hockey fans.

As always, our thanks to readers, correspondents and members of the media who take the time to comment on the *Guide & Record Book*. Thanks as well to the people working in the communications departments of the NHL's member clubs and to their counterparts in minor pro, junior, college and European hockey.

Best wishes for an enjoyable 2011-12 season.

ACCURACY REMAINS THE *GUIDE & RECORD BOOK*'S TOP PRIORITY.
We appreciate comments and clarification from our readers. Please direct these to:
- Ralph Dinger — Senior Managing Editor, 194 Dovercourt Road, Toronto, Ontario M6J 3C8. e-mail: ralph.dda@sympatico.ca.
- Greg Inglis — 1185 Avenue of the Americas, New York, New York 10036 . . . or . . .
- David Keon — 50 Bay Street, 11th Floor, Toronto, Ontario, M5J 2X8

Your involvement makes a better book.

NATIONAL HOCKEY LEAGUE

New York
1185 Avenue of the Americas,
New York, NY 10036,
212/789-2000, Fax: 212/789-2020, PR Fax: 212/789-2070

Montréal
1800 McGill College Avenue,
Suite 2600,
Montréal, Québec, H3A 3J6
514/841-9220, Fax: 514/841-1070

Toronto
50 Bay Street,
11th Floor,
Toronto, Ontario, M5J 2X8
416/359-7900, Fax: 416/981-2779

League and Club websites: www.nhl.com

Executive
Commissioner ....Gary B. Bettman
Deputy Commissioner ....William Daly
Chief Operating Officer ....John Collins
Senior Executive Vice President of Hockey Operations ....Colin Campbell

---

Commissioner and League Presidents

Gary B. Bettman

Gary B. Bettman took office as the NHL's first Commissioner on February 1, 1993. Since the League was formed in 1917, there have been five League Presidents.

NHL President	Years in Office
Frank Calder	1917-1943
Mervyn "Red" Dutton	1943-1946
Clarence Campbell	1946-1977
John A. Ziegler, Jr.	1977-1992
Gil Stein	1992-1993

Hockey Hall of Fame

Hockey Hall of Fame
Brookfield Place
30 Yonge Street, Toronto, Ontario M5E 1X8
Phone: 416/360-7735 • Executive Fax: 416/360-1501

William C. Hay – Chairman and Chief Executive Officer
Jeff Denomme – President, C.O.O. and Treasurer
Craig Baines – Vice President, Operations
Peter Jagla – Vice President, Marketing
Ron Ellis – Director, Public Affairs & Asst. to the President
Kelly Massé – Director, Corporate & Media Relations
Sarah Lee – Coordinator, Special Events & Hospitality
Jacqueline Schwartz – Manager, Marketing & Promotions
Darren Boyko – Manager, Business Development

D.K. (Doc) Seaman Resource Centre and Archives
400 Kipling Avenue, Toronto, Ontario M8V 3L1
Phone: 416/360-7735 • Fax: 416/251-5770
www.hhof.com, www.imagesonice.net

Phil Pritchard – Vice President and Curator
Craig Campbell – Manager, Resource Centre
                    & Archives
Izak Westgate – Manager, Outreach & Asst. Curator
Steve Poirier – Coord., HHOF Images & Archival Services
Miragh Bitove – Archivist & Collections Registrar

National Hockey League Players' Association

20 Bay Street, Suite 1700, Toronto, Ontario M5J 2N8
Phone: 416/313-2300 • Fax: 416/313-2301
www.nhlpa.com

Donald Fehr, Executive Director
Mathieu Schneider – Special Asst. to the Exec. Director
Mike Ouellet – Chief of Business Affairs
Roman Stoykewych – Associate Counsel, Labour
Robert DeGregory – Associate Counsel, Labour
Maria Dennis – Associate Counsel, Labour
Roland Lee – Director, Salary Cap and Marketplace
                and Associate Counsel
Adam Larry – Director, Licensing and Associate Counsel
Kim Murdoch – Director, Player Insurance & Pensions
Richard Smit – Director, Finance and HRR
Devin Smith – Director, Marketing & Community Relations
Jonathan Weatherdon – Director, Communications
Tyler Currie – Director, International Affairs
Stephen Frank – Director, Information Technology
Casey Rovinelli – Director, Digital Marketing
Colin Campbell – Director, Corporate Sponsorship

BOARD OF GOVERNORS
CHAIRMAN OF THE BOARD – JEREMY M. JACOBS

Anaheim Ducks
Henry Samueli.. Governor
Susan Samueli ....Alternate Governor
Michael Schulman ....Alternate Governor
Tim Ryan ....Alternate Governor
Bob Murray ....Alternate Governor

Boston Bruins
Jeremy M. Jacobs...................................Governor
Charles Jacobs ....Alternate Governor
Jeremy Jacobs, Jr...........................Alternate Governor
Louis Jacobs ....Alternate Governor
Harry J. Sinden ....Alternate Governor
Cam Neely....................................Alternate Governor
Peter Chiarelli ....Alternate Governor

Buffalo Sabres
Terry Pegula .... Governor
Ted Black ....Alternate Governor
Daniel J. DiPofi ....Alternate Governor
Ken Sawyer ....Alternate Governor
Cliff Benson..................................Alternate Governor

Calgary Flames
N. Murray Edwards ....Governor
Ken King ....Alternate Governor
Alvin Libin ....Alternate Governor

Carolina Hurricanes
Peter Karmanos, Jr. ....Governor
Jim Rutherford..............................Alternate Governor
Michael Amendola ....Alternate Governor
Jason Karmanos ....Alternate Governor

Chicago Blackhawks
W. Rockwell Wirtz ....Governor
Robert J. Pulford...........................Alternate Governor
John A. Ziegler, Jr.........................Alternate Governor
John McDonough...........................Alternate Governor

Colorado Avalanche
Josh Kroenke ....Governor
Pierre Lacroix ....Alternate Governor
Mark Waggoner ....Alternate Governor
Greg Sherman ....Alternate Governor
Joe Sakic ....Alternate Governor

Columbus Blue Jackets
John P. McConnell ....Governor
Mike Priest ....Alternate Governor
Scott Howson ....Alternate Governor

Dallas Stars
Tom Hicks ....Governor
Tom Hicks, Jr................................Alternate Governor
Tony Tavares ....Alternate Governor
Joe Nieuwendyk ....Alternate Governor

Detroit Red Wings
Michael Ilitch ....Governor
Jim Devellano ....Alternate Governor
Ken Holland ....Alternate Governor
Christopher Ilitch ....Alternate Governor
Rob Carr ....Alternate Governor
Tom Wilson ....Alternate Governor

Edmonton Oilers
Daryl Katz..Governor
Patrick LaForge ....Alternate Governor
Kevin Lowe ....Alternate Governor
Bob Black ....Alternate Governor

Florida Panthers
Cliff Viner ....Governor
Bill Torrey ....Alternate Governor
Michael Yormark ....Alternate Governor
Stu Siegel ....Alternate Governor

Los Angeles Kings
Timothy J. Leiweke ....Governor
Philip F. Anschutz..........................Alternate Governor
Luc Robitaille ....Alternate Governor
Dean Lombardi...............................Alternate Governor

Minnesota Wild
Craig Leopold ....Governor
Philip Falcone ....Alternate Governor
Jac Sperling ....Alternate Governor
Chuck Fletcher ....Alternate Governor

Montréal Canadiens
Geoff Molson ....Governor
Kevin Gilmore...............................Alternate Governor
Fred Steer.....................................Alternate Governor
Michael Andlauer ....Alternate Governor
Andrew T. Molson ....Alternate Governor
Pierre Gauthier ....Alternate Governor

Nashville Predators
Joel Dobberpuhl..Governor
Tom Cigarran.................................Alternate Governor
Herbert Fritch ....Alternate Governor
David Polle ....Alternate Governor
Jeff Cogen....................................Alternate Governor
Sean Henry....................................Alternate Governor

New Jersey Devils
Lou Lamoriello ....Governor
Jeff Vanderbeek............................Alternate Governor
Michael Gilfillan............................Alternate Governor

New York Islanders
Charles Wang ....Governor
Roy Reichbach ....Alternate Governor
Arthur J. McCarthy ....Alternate Governor
Michael J. Picker ....Alternate Governor
Garth Snow ....Alternate Governor

New York Rangers
James L. Dolan.. Governor
Glen Sather ....Alternate Governor
Hank Ratner ....Alternate Governor
Scott O'Neil ....Alternate Governor

Ottawa Senators
Eugene Melnyk..Governor
Sheldon Plener ....Alternate Governor
Cyril Leeder ....Alternate Governor
Erin Crowe ....Alternate Governor
Bryan Murray................................Alternate Governor

Philadelphia Flyers
Edward M. Snider ....Governor
Philip I. Weinberg ....Alternate Governor
Peter Luukko ....Alternate Governor
Paul Holmgren...............................Alternate Governor

Phoenix Coyotes
Don Maloney..................................Alternate Governor
Mike Nealy ....Alternate Governor

Pittsburgh Penguins
David Morehouse..Governor
Ronald Burkle ....Alternate Governor
Anthony Liberati ....Alternate Governor
Ray Shero ....Alternate Governor
Travis Williams ....Governor
Mario Lemieux...............................Alternate Governor

St. Louis Blues
Dave Checketts..Governor
John Davidson ....Alternate Governor
Michael McCarthy ....Alternate Governor

San Jose Sharks
Kevin Compton...Governor
Doug Wilson ....Alternate Governor
John Tortora ....Alternate Governor

Tampa Bay Lightning
Jeff Vinik...Governor
Steve Yzerman ....Alternate Governor
Tod Leiweke ....Alternate Governor

Toronto Maple Leafs
Larry Tanenbaum ....Governor
Richard A. Peddie ....Alternate Governor
Dale Lastman.................................Alternate Governor
Erol Uzumeri.................................Alternate Governor
Brian Burke...................................Alternate Governor

Vancouver Canucks
Francesco Aquilini ....Governor
Paolo Aquilini ....Alternate Governor
Roberto Aquilini ....Alternate Governor
Michael Gillis ....Alternate Governor
Victor de Boris ....Alternate Governor

Washington Capitals
Ted Leonsis ....Governor
Richard M. Patrick ....Alternate Governor
George McPhee..............................Alternate Governor

Winnipeg Jets
Mark Chipman...Governor

Two NHL on-ice officials worked their 1,000th regular-season game in 2010-11. Both referee Dennis LaRue (above) and linesman Jay Sharrers (below) reached the 1,000-game milestone in their 21st season.

NHL On-Ice Officials

Total NHL Games and 2010-11 Games columns count regular-season games only.

Referees

#	Name	Birthplace	*Age	First NHL Game	Total NHL Games	2010-11 Games
15	Stephane Auger	Montreal, Que.	41	Apr. 1/00	678	73
44	David Banfield	Halifax, N.S.	32	Mar. 17/08	58	15
42	Darcy Burchell	St. Catharines, Ont.	33	…	…	…
46	Frances Charron	Ottawa, Ont.	28	Apr. 5/10	14	13
10	Paul Devorski	Guelph, Ont.	53	Oct. 14/89	1333	74
19	Gord Dwyer	Halifax, N.S.	34	Nov. 19/05	384	67
27	Eric Furlatt	Trois-Rivieres, Que.	40	Oct. 8/01	611	75
2	Mike Hasenfratz	Regina, Sask.	45	Oct. 21/00	541	0
22	Ghislain Hebert	Bathurst, NB	30	Mar. 2/09	34	23
43	Jean Hebert	Moncton, NB	31	Mar. 30/11	1	1
8	Dave Jackson	Montreal, Que.	47	Dec. 22/90	1144	76
25	Marc Joannette	Verdun, Que.	43	Oct. 1/99	734	75
18	Greg Kimmerly	Toronto, Ont.	47	Nov. 30/96	819	74
32	Tom Kowal	Vernon, B.C.	44	Oct. 29/99	618	74
40	Steve Kozari	Penticton, B.C.	38	Oct. 15/05	345	76
14	Dennis LaRue	Savannah, GA	52	Mar. 26/91	1011	75
17	Frederick L'Ecuyer	Trois-Rivieres, Que.	34	Oct. 11/07	140	75
28	Chris Lee	Saint John, N.B.	41	Apr. 2/00	595	76
3	Mike Leggo	North Bay, Ont.	47	Mar. 3/98	808	76
41	Mark Lemelin	Albequerque, NM	29	…	…	…
26	Rob Martell	Winnipeg, Man.	48	Mar. 14/84	[1] 702	74
4	Wes McCauley	Georgetown, Ont.	39	Jan. 20/03	468	76
34	Brad Meier	Dayton, OH	44	Oct. 23/99	736	76
36	Dean Morton	Peterborough, Ont.	43	Nov. 11/00	294	74
13	Dan O'Halloran	Essex, Ont.	47	Oct. 1/95	889	76
9	Dan O'Rourke	Calgary, Alta.	39	Oct. 2/99	[2] 466	76
20	Tim Peel	Toronto, Ont.	45	Oct. 21/99	743	75
16	Brian Pochmara	Detroit, MI	35	Dec. 23/05	276	75
33	Kevin Pollock	Kincardine, Ont.	41	Mar. 28/00	742	76
37	Kyle Rehman	Stettler, Alta.	33	Jan. 22/08	121	75
5	Chris Rooney	Boston, MA	36	Nov. 22/00	635	75
48	Graham Skilliter	La Ronge, Sask.	26	…	…	…
38	Francois St. Laurent	Greenfield Park, Que.	34	Nov. 10/05	216	74
12	Justin St. Pierre	Dolbeau, Que.	39	Nov. 9/05	380	58
11	Kelly Sutherland	Richmond, BC	40	Dec. 19/00	678	76
21	Don Van Massenhoven	Parkhill, Ont.	51	Nov. 11/93	1092	75
45	Marcus Vinnerborg	Ljungby, Sweden	39	16/11/10	20	20
24	Stephen Walkom	North Bay, Ont.	48	Oct. 18/92	846	77
29	Ian Walsh	Philadelphia, PA	39	Oct. 14/00	580	76
23	Brad Watson	Regina, Sask.	50	Mar. 7/96	840	76

[1] plus 1 game as a linesman.   [2] plus 120 games as a linesman.

Linesmen

#	Name	Birthplace	*Age	First NHL Game	Total NHL Games	2010-11 Games
75	Derek Amell	Port Colborne, Ont.	43	Oct. 11/97	873	76
59	Steve Barton	Vankleek Hill, Ont.	40	Nov. 1/00	652	76
96	David Brisebois	Sudbury, Ont.	35	Oct. 11/99	610	76
74	Lonnie Cameron	Victoria, B.C.	47	Oct. 5/96	986	75
67	Pierre Champoux	Ville St-Pierre, Que.	48	Oct. 8/88	1440	76
50	Scott Cherrey	Drayton, Ont.	35	Oct. 6/07	269	76
76	Michel Cormier	Trois-Rivieres, Que.	37	Oct. 10/03	513	76
88	Mike Cvik	Calgary, Alta.	49	Oct. 8/87	1566	70
54	Greg Devorski	Guelph, Ont.	42	Oct. 9/93	1153	76
68	Scott Driscoll	Seaforth, Ont.	43	Oct. 10/92	1224	76
82	Ryan Galloway	Winnipeg, Man.	39	Oct. 17/02	537	76
66	Darren Gibbs	Edmonton, Alta.	45	Oct. 1/97	839	75
91	Don Henderson	Calgary, Alta.	43	Mar. 11/95	975	76
55	Shane Heyer	Summerland, B.C.	47	Oct. 6/88	[3] 1151	75
71	Brad Kovachik	Woodstock, Ont.	40	Oct. 10/96	949	70
86	Brad Lazarowich	Vancouver, B.C.	49	Oct. 9/86	1666	76
78	Brian Mach	Little Falls, MN	37	Oct. 7/00	715	75
83	Matt MacPherson	Antigonish, N.S.	27	…	…	…
90	Andy McElman	Chicago Heights, IL	50	Oct. 3/93	1157	76
89	Steve Miller	Stratford, Ont.	39	Oct. 11/00	704	76
97	Jean Morin	Sorel, Que.	48	Oct. 5/91	1253	63
93	Brian Murphy	Dover, NH	47	Oct. 7/88	[4] 1353	75
95	Jonny Murray	Beauport, Que.	37	Oct. 7/00	717	76
70	Derek Nansen	Ottawa, Ont.	40	Oct. 11/02	564	77
80	Thor Nelson	Westminister, CA	43	Feb. 16/95	863	68
77	Tim Nowak	Buffalo, NY	44	Oct. 8/93	1159	76
94	Bryan Pancich	Great Falls, MT	29	Oct. 3/09	121	76
65	Pierre Racicot	Verdun, Que.	44	Oct. 12/93	1187	76
73	Vaughan Rody	Winnipeg, Man.	43	Oct. 8/00	687	75
52	Dan Schachte	Madison, WI	53	Oct. 6/82	1961	68
84	Anthony Sericolo	Troy, NY	43	Oct. 21/98	809	76
57	Jay Sharrers	New Westminster, B.C.	44	Oct. 6/90	[5] 1072	75
92	Mark Shewchyk	Waterdown, Ont.	36	Oct. 9/03	514	76
56	Mark Wheler	North Battleford, Sask.	46	Oct. 10/92	1250	75

[3] plus 386 games as a referee.   [4] plus 88 games as a referee.   [5] plus 136 games as a referee.

– Age at start of 2011-12 season

NHL History

1917 — National Hockey League organized November 26 in Montreal following suspension of operations by the National Hockey Association of Canada Limited (NHA). Montreal Canadiens, Montreal Wanderers, Ottawa Senators and Quebec Bulldogs attended founding meeting. Delegates decided to use NHA rules.

Toronto Arenas were later admitted as fifth team; Quebec decided not to operate during the first season. Quebec players allocated to remaining four teams.

Frank Calder elected president and secretary-treasurer.

First NHL games played December 19, with Toronto only arena with artificial ice. Clubs played 22-game split schedule.

1918 — Emergency meeting held January 3 due to destruction by fire of Montreal Arena which was home ice for both Canadiens and Wanderers.

Wanderers withdrew, reducing the NHL to three teams; Canadiens played remaining home games at 3,250-seat Jubilee rink.

Quebec franchise sold to P.J. Quinn of Toronto on October 18 on the condition that the team operate in Quebec City for 1918-19 season. Quinn did not attend the November League meeting and Quebec did not play in 1918-19.

1919-20 — NHL reactivated Quebec Bulldogs franchise. Former Quebec players returned to the club. New Mount Royal Arena became home of Canadiens. Toronto Arenas changed name to St. Patricks. Clubs played 24-game split schedule.

1920-21 — H.P. Thompson of Hamilton, Ontario made application for the purchase of an NHL franchise. Quebec franchise shifted to Hamilton with other NHL teams providing players to strengthen the club.

1921-22 — Split schedule abandoned. First and second place teams at the end of full schedule to play for championship.

1922-23 — Clubs agreed that players could not be sold or traded to clubs in any other league without first being offered to all other clubs in the NHL. Norman Albert made the first broadcast of a hockey game on February 8, 1923. The first NHL game was broadcast on February 14, 1923. Foster Hewitt called his first game on February 16, 1923. All games were broadcast on Toronto radio station CFCA.

1923-24 — Ottawa's new 10,000-seat arena opened. First U.S. franchise granted to Boston for following season.

Dr. Cecil Hart Trophy donated to NHL to be awarded to the player judged most useful to his team.

1924-25 — New franchises granted to Boston and Montreal (later named Maroons). NHL now six team league with two clubs in Montreal. Inaugural game in new Montreal Forum played November 29, 1924 as Canadiens defeated Toronto 7-1. Hamilton finished first in the standings, receiving a bye into the finals. But Hamilton players, demanding $200 each for additional games in the playoffs, went on strike. The NHL suspended all players, fining them $200 each. Stanley Cup finalist to be the winner of NHL semi-final between Toronto and Canadiens.

Lady Byng Trophy donated to NHL.

Clubs played 30-game schedule.

1925-26 — Hamilton club dropped from NHL. Players signed by new New York Americans franchise. Pittsburgh Pirates granted franchise. Prince of Wales Trophy donated to NHL.

Clubs played 36-game schedule.

1926-27 — New York Rangers granted franchise May 15, 1926. Chicago Black Hawks and Detroit Cougars granted franchises September 25, 1926. NHL now ten-team league with an American and a Canadian Division.

Stanley Cup came under the control of NHL. In previous seasons, winners of the now-defunct Western or Pacific Coast leagues would play NHL champion in Cup finals.

Toronto franchise sold to a new company controlled by Hugh Aird and Conn Smythe. Name changed from St. Patricks to Maple Leafs.

Clubs played 44-game schedule.

The Montreal Canadiens donated the Vezina Trophy to be awarded to the team allowing the fewest goals-against in regular season play. The winning team would, in turn, present the trophy to the goaltender playing in the greatest number of games during the season.

1930-31 — Detroit franchise changed name from Cougars to Falcons. Pittsburgh transferred to Philadelphia for one season. Pirates changed name to Philadelphia Quakers. Trading deadline for teams set at February 15 of each year. NHL approved operation of farm teams by Rangers, Americans, Falcons and Bruins. Four-sided electric arena clock first demonstrated.

1931-32 — Philadelphia dropped out. Ottawa withdrew for one season. New Maple Leaf Gardens completed.

Clubs played 48-game schedule.

1932-33 — Detroit franchise changed name from Falcons to Red Wings. Franchise application received from St. Louis but refused because of additional travel costs. Ottawa team resumed play.

1933-34 — First All-Star Game played as a benefit for injured player Ace Bailey. Leafs defeated All-Stars 7-3 in Toronto.

1934-35 — Ottawa franchise transferred to St. Louis. Team called St. Louis Eagles and consisted largely of Ottawa's players.

1935-36 — Ottawa-St. Louis franchise terminated. Montreal Canadiens finished season with very poor record. To strengthen the club, NHL gave Canadiens first call on the services of all French-Canadian players for three seasons.

1937-38 — Second benefit All-Star game staged November 2 in Montreal in aid of the family of the late Canadiens star Howie Morenz.

Montreal Maroons withdrew from the NHL on June 22, 1938, leaving seven clubs in the League.

1938-39 — Expenses for each club regulated at $5 per man per day for meals and $2.50 per man per day for accommodation.

1939-40 — Benefit All-Star Game played October 29, 1939 in Montreal for the children of the late Albert (Babe) Siebert.

1940-41 — Ross-Tyer puck adopted as the official puck of the NHL. Early in the season it was apparent that this puck was too soft. The Spalding puck was adopted in its place.

On May 16, 1941, Arthur Ross, NHL governor from Boston, donated a perpetual trophy to be awarded annually to the player voted outstanding in the league. Due to wartime restrictions, the trophy was never awarded.

1941-42 — New York Americans changed name to Brooklyn Americans.

1942-43 — Brooklyn Americans withdrew from NHL, leaving six teams: Boston, Chicago, Detroit, Montreal, New York and Toronto. Playoff format saw first-place team play third-place team and second play fourth.

Clubs played 50-game schedule.

Frank Calder, president of the NHL since its inception, died in Montreal. Meryn "Red" Dutton, former manager of the New York Americans, became president. The NHL commissioned the Calder Memorial Trophy to be awarded to the League's outstanding rookie each year.

1945-46 — Philadelphia, Los Angeles and San Francisco applied for NHL franchises.

The Philadelphia Arena Company of the American Hockey League applied for an injunction to prevent the possible operation of an NHL franchise in that city.

1946-47 — Mervyn Dutton retired as president of the NHL prior to the start of the season. He was succeeded by Clarence S. Campbell.

Individual trophy winners and all-star team members to receive $1,000 awards.

Playoff guarantees for players introduced.

Clubs played 60-game schedule.

1947-48 — The first annual All-Star Game for the benefit of the players' pension fund was played when the All-Stars defeated the Stanley Cup Champion Toronto Maple Leafs 4-3 in Toronto on October 13, 1947.

Criteria for awarding Art Ross Trophy changed. Now awarded to top scorer. Elmer Lach was its first winner.

Philadelphia and Los Angeles franchise applications refused.

National Hockey League Pension Society formed.

1949-50 — Clubs played 70-game schedule.

First intra-league draft held April 30, 1950. Clubs allowed to protect 30 players. Remaining players available for $25,000 each.

1951-52 — Referees included in the League's pension plan.

1952-53 — In May of 1952, City of Cleveland applied for NHL franchise. Application denied. In March of 1953, the Cleveland Barons of the AHL challenged the NHL champions for the Stanley Cup. The NHL governors did not accept this challenge.

1953-54 — The James Norris Memorial Trophy presented to the NHL for annual presentation to the League's best defenseman.

Intra-league draft rules amended to allow teams to protect 18 skaters and two goaltenders, claiming price reduced to $15,000.

1954-55 — Each arena to operate an "out-of-town" scoreboard.

1956-57 — Referees and linesmen to wear shirts of black and white vertical stripes. Standardized signals for referees and linesmen introduced.

1960-61 — Canadian National Exhibition, City of Toronto and NHL reach agreement for the construction of a Hockey Hall of Fame on the CNE grounds. Hall opens on August 26, 1961.

1963-64 — Player development league established with clubs operated by NHL franchises located in Minneapolis, St. Paul, Indianapolis, Omaha and, beginning in 1964-65, Tulsa. First universal amateur draft took place. All players of qualifying age (17) unaffected by sponsorship of junior teams available to be drafted.

1964-65 — Conn Smythe Trophy presented to the NHL to be awarded annually to the outstanding player in the Stanley Cup playoffs.

Minimum age of players subject to amateur draft changed to 18.

1965-66 — NHL announced expansion plans for a second six-team division to begin play in 1967-68.

1966-67 — Fourteen applications for NHL franchises received.

Lester Patrick Trophy presented to the NHL to be awarded annually for outstanding service to hockey in the United States.

NHL sponsorship of junior teams ceased, making all players of qualifying age not already on NHL-sponsored lists eligible for the amateur draft.

1967-68 — Six new teams added: California Seals, Los Angeles Kings, Minnesota North Stars, Philadelphia Flyers, Pittsburgh Penguins, St. Louis Blues. New teams to play in West Division. Remaining six teams to play in East Division.

Minimum age of players subject to amateur draft changed to 20.

Clubs played 74-game schedule.

Clarence S. Campbell Trophy awarded to team finishing the regular season in first place in West Division.

California Seals change name to Oakland Seals on December 8, 1967.

1968-69 — Clubs played 76-game schedule.

Amateur draft expanded to cover any amateur player of qualifying age throughout the world.

1970-71 — Two new teams added: Buffalo Sabres and Vancouver Canucks. These teams joined East Division: Chicago switched to West Division. Oakland Seals change name to California Golden Seals prior to season.

Clubs played 78-game schedule.

1971-72 — Playoff format amended. In each division, first to play fourth; second to play third.

1972-73 — Soviet Nationals and Canadian NHL stars play eight-game pre-season series. Canadians win 4-3-1.

Two new teams added. Atlanta Flames join West Division; New York Islanders join East Division.

1974-75 — Two new teams added: Kansas City Scouts and Washington Capitals. Teams realigned into two nine-team conferences, the Prince of Wales made up of the Norris and Adams Divisions, and the Clarence Campbell made up of the Smythe and Patrick Divisions.

Clubs played 80-game schedule.

1976-77 — California franchise transferred to Cleveland. Team named Cleveland Barons. Kansas City franchise transferred to Denver. Team named Colorado Rockies.

1977-78 — Clarence S. Campbell retires as NHL president. Succeeded by John A. Ziegler, Jr.

1978-79 — Cleveland and Minnesota franchises merge, leaving NHL with 17 teams. Merged team placed in Adams Division, playing home games in Minnesota.

Minimum age of players subject to amateur draft changed to 19.

1979-80 — Four new teams added: Edmonton Oilers, Hartford Whalers, Quebec Nordiques and Winnipeg Jets.

Minimum age of players subject to entry draft changed to 18.

1980-81 — Atlanta franchise shifted to Calgary, retaining "Flames" name.

1981-82 — Teams realigned within existing divisions. New groupings based on geographical areas. Unbalanced schedule adopted.

1982-83 — Colorado Rockies franchise shifted to East Rutherford, New Jersey. Team named New Jersey Devils. Franchise moved to Patrick Division from Smythe; Winnipeg moved to Smythe Division from Norris.

1991-92 — San Jose Sharks added, making the NHL a 22-team league. NHL celebrates 75th Anniversary Season. The 1991-92 regular season suspended due to a players' strike on April 1, 1992. Play resumed April 12, 1992.

NHL History — continued

1992-93 — Gil Stein named NHL president (October, 1992). Gary Bettman named first NHL Commissioner (February, 1993). Ottawa Senators and Tampa Bay Lightning added, making the NHL a 24-team league. NHL celebrates Stanley Cup Centennial. Clubs played 84-game schedule.

1993-94 — Mighty Ducks of Anaheim and Florida Panthers added, making the NHL a 26-team league. Minnesota franchise shifted to Dallas, team named Dallas Stars. Prince of Wales and Clarence Campbell Conferences renamed Eastern and Western. Adams, Patrick, Norris and Smythe Divisions renamed Northeast, Atlantic, Central and Pacific. Winnipeg moved to Central Division from Pacific; Tampa Bay moved to Atlantic Division from Central; Pittsburgh moved to Northeast Division from Atlantic.

1994-95 — A lockout resulted in the cancellation of 468 games from October 1, 1994 to January 19, 1995. Clubs played a 48-game schedule that began January 20, 1995 and ended May 3, 1995. No inter-conference games were played.

1995-96 — Quebec franchise transferred to Denver. Team named Colorado Avalanche and placed in Pacific Division of Western Conference. Clubs to play 82-game schedule.

1996-97 — Winnipeg franchise transferred to Phoenix. Team named Phoenix Coyotes and placed in Central Division of Western Conference.

1997-98 — Hartford franchise transferred to Raleigh. Team named Carolina Hurricanes and remains in Northeast Division of Eastern Conference.

1998-99 — The addition of the Nashville Predators made the NHL a 27-team league and brought about the creation of two new divisions and a League-wide realignment in preparation for further expansion to 30 teams by 2000-2001. Nashville was added to the Central Division of the Western Conference, while Toronto moved into the Northeast Division of the Eastern Conference. Pittsburgh was shifted from the Northeast to the Atlantic, while Carolina left the Northeast for the newly created Southeast Division of the Eastern Conference. Florida, Tampa Bay and Washington also joined the Southeast. In the Western Conference, Calgary, Colorado, Edmonton and Vancouver make up the new Northwest Division. Dallas and Phoenix moved from the Central to the Pacific Division.

The NHL retired uniform number 99 in honor of all-time scoring leader Wayne Gretzky who retired at the end of the season.

1999-2000 — Atlanta Thrashers added, making the NHL a 28-team league.

2000-01 — Columbus Blue Jackets and Minnesota Wild added, making the NHL a 30-team league.

2003-04 — First outdoor NHL game. 57,167 attend Heritage Classic at Edmonton's Commonwealth Stadium. Montreal defeated Edmonton 4-3, November 22, 2003.

2004-05 — A lockout resulted in the cancellation of the season.

2007-08 — NHL-record crowd of 71,217 fills Buffalo's Ralph Wilson Stadium on New Year's Day for the 2008 Winter Classic, the first NHL outdoor game in the United States. Sidney Crosby's shootout goal gives the Pittsburgh Penguins a 2-1 win over the Buffalo Sabres.

2011-12 — Atlanta franchise transferred to Winnipeg. Team named Winnipeg Jets.

Major Rule Changes

1910-11 — Game changed from two 30-minute periods to three 20-minute periods.

1911-12 — National Hockey Association (forerunner of the NHL) originated six-man hockey, replacing seven-man game.

1917-18 — Goalies permitted to fall to the ice to make saves. Previously a goaltender was penalized for dropping to the ice.

1918-19 — Penalty rules amended. For minor fouls, substitutes not allowed until penalized player had served three minutes. For major fouls, no substitutes for five minutes. For match fouls, no substitutes allowed for the remainder of the game.

With the addition of two lines painted on the ice twenty feet from center, three playing zones were created, producing a forty-foot neutral center ice area in which forward passing was permitted. Kicking the puck was permitted in this neutral zone.

Tabulation of assists began.

1921-22 — Goaltenders allowed to pass the puck forward up to their own blue line.

Overtime limited to twenty minutes.

Minor penalties changed from three minutes to two minutes.

1923-24 — Match foul defined as actions deliberately injuring or disabling an opponent. For such actions, a player was fined not less than $50 and ruled off the ice for the balance of the game. A player assessed a match penalty may be replaced by a substitute at the end of 20 minutes. Match penalty recipients must meet with the League president who can assess additional punishment.

1925-26 — Delayed penalty rules introduced. Each team must have a minimum of four players on the ice at all times.

Two rules were amended to encourage offense: No more than two defensemen permitted to remain inside a team's own blue line when the puck has left the defensive zone. A faceoff to be called for ragging the puck unless shorthanded.

Team captains only players allowed to talk to referees.

Goaltender's leg pads limited to 12-inch width.

Timekeeper's gong to mark end of periods rather than referee's whistle. Teams to dress a maximum of 12 players for each game from a roster of no more than 14 players.

1926-27 — Blue lines repositioned to sixty feet from each goal-line, thereby enlarging the neutral zone and standardizing distance from blue line to goal.

Uniform goal nets adopted throughout NHL with goal posts securely fastened to the ice.

1927-28 — To further encourage offense, forward passes allowed in defending and neutral zones and goaltender's pads reduced in width from 12 to 10 inches.

Game standardized at three twenty-minute periods of stop-time separated by ten-minute intermissions.

Teams to change ends after each period.

Ten minutes of sudden-death overtime to be played if the score is tied after regulation time.

Minor penalty to be assessed to any player other than a goaltender for deliberately picking up the puck while it is in play. Minor penalty to be assessed for deliberately shooting the puck out of play.

The Art Ross goal net adopted as the official net of the NHL.

Maximum length of hockey sticks limited to 53 inches measured from heel of blade to end of handle. No minimum length stipulated.

Home teams given choice of end to defend at start of game.

1928-29 — Forward passing permitted in defensive and neutral zones and into attacking zone if pass receiver is in neutral zone when pass is made. No forward passing allowed inside attacking zone.

Minor penalty to be assessed to any player who delays the game by passing the puck back into his defensive zone.

Ten-minute overtime without sudden-death provision to be played in games tied after regulation time. Games tied after this overtime period declared a draw.

Exclusive of goaltenders, team to dress at least 8 and no more than 12 skaters.

NHL Attendance

Season	Games	Regular Season Attendance	Games	Playoffs Attendance	Total Attendance
1967-68	444	4,938,043	40	495,089	5,433,132
1968-69	456	5,550,613	33	431,739	5,982,352
1969-70	456	5,992,065	34	461,694	6,453,759
1970-71	546	7,257,677	43	707,633	7,965,310
1971-72	546	7,609,368	36	582,666	8,192,034
1972-73	624	8,575,651	38	624,637	9,200,288
1973-74	624	8,640,978	38	600,442	9,241,420
1974-75	720	9,521,536	51	784,181	10,305,717
1975-76	720	9,103,761	48	726,279	9,830,040
1976-77	720	8,563,890	44	646,279	9,210,169
1977-78	720	8,526,564	45	686,634	9,213,198
1978-79	680	7,758,053	45	694,521	8,452,574
1979-80	840	10,533,623	67	976,699	11,510,322
1980-81	840	10,726,198	68	966,390	11,692,588
1981-82	840	10,710,894	71	1,058,948	11,769,842
1982-83	840	11,020,610	66	1,088,222	12,028,832
1983-84	840	11,359,386	70	1,107,400	12,466,786
1984-85	840	11,633,730	70	1,107,500	12,741,230
1985-86	840	11,621,000	72	1,152,503	12,773,503
1986-87	840	11,855,880	87	1,383,967	13,239,847
1987-88	840	12,117,512	83	1,336,901	13,454,413
1988-89	840	12,417,969	82	1,327,214	13,745,183
1989-90	840	12,579,651	85	1,355,593	13,935,244
1990-91	840	12,343,897	92	1,442,203	13,786,100
1991-92	880	12,769,676	86	1,327,920	14,097,596
1992-93	1,008	14,158,177 [1]	83	1,346,034	15,504,211
1993-94	1,092	16,105,604 [2]	90	1,440,095	17,545,699
1994-95	624 [3]	9,233,884	81	1,329,130	10,563,014
1995-96	1,066	17,041,614	86	1,540,140	18,581,754
1996-97	1,066	17,640,529	82	1,494,878	19,135,407
1997-98	1,066	17,264,678	82	1,507,416	18,772,094
1998-99	1,107	18,001,741	86	1,509,411	19,511,152
1999-2000	1,148	18,800,139	83	1,524,629	20,324,768
2000-01	1,230	20,373,379	86	1,584,011	21,957,390
2001-02	1,230	20,614,613	90	1,691,174	22,305,787
2002-03	1,230	20,408,704	89	1,636,120	22,044,824
2003-04	1,230	20,356,199	89	1,708,691	22,064,890
2004-05	.....	.....	....	....	....
2005-06	1,230	20,854,169	83	1,530,405	22,384,574
2006-07	1,230	20,861,787	81	1,496,501	22,358,288
2007-08	1,230	21,236,255	85	1,587,054	22,823,309
2008-09	1,230	21,475,223	87	1,639,602	23,114,825
2009-10	1,230	20,996,455	90	1,702,371	22,698,826
2010-11	1,230	21,112,139	89	1,667,624	22,779,763

NHL Expansion: the NHL operated as a six-team league from 1942-43 to 1966-67. Six teams were added in 1967-68: California (later to move to Cleveland), Los Angeles, Minnesota (later to move to Dallas), Philadelphia, Pittsburgh and St. Louis. In 1970-71: Buffalo and Vancouver. In 1972-73: Atlanta (later to move to Calgary) and NYIslanders. In 1974-75: Kansas City (later to move to Colorado and then to New Jersey) and Washington. In 1979-80, Hartford (later to move to Carolina), Edmonton, Quebec (later to move to Colorado) and Winnipeg (later to move to Phoenix). In 1991-92, San Jose. In 1992-93, Ottawa and Tampa Bay. In 1993-94, Anaheim and Florida. In 1998-99, Nashville. In 1999-2000, Atlanta. In 2000-01, Columbus and Minnesota.

[1] Includes 24 neutral site games • [2] Includes 26 neutral site games
[3] Lockout resulted in the cancellation of 468 regular-season games.

Major Rule Changes — *continued*

1929-30 — Forward passing permitted inside all three zones but not permitted across either blue line.

Kicking the puck allowed, but a goal cannot be scored by kicking the puck in.

No more than three players including the goaltender may remain in their defensive zone when the puck has gone up ice. Minor penalties to be assessed for the first two violations of this rule in a game; major penalties thereafter.

Goaltenders forbidden to hold the puck. Pucks caught must be cleared immediately. For infringement of this rule, a faceoff to be taken ten feet in front of the goal with no player except the goaltender standing between the faceoff spot and the goal-line.

Highsticking penalties introduced.

Maximum number of players in uniform increased from 12 to 15.

December 21, 1929 — Forward passing rules instituted at the beginning of the 1929-30 season more than doubled number of goals scored. Partway through the season, these rules were further amended to read, "No attacking player allowed to precede the play when entering the opposing defensive zone." This is similar to modern offside rule.

1930-31 — A player without a complete stick ruled out of play and forbidden from taking part in further action until a new stick is obtained. A player who has broken his stick must obtain a replacement at his bench.

A further refinement of the offside rule stated that the puck must first be propelled into the attacking zone before any player of the attacking side can enter that zone; for infringement of this rule a faceoff to take place at the spot where the infraction took place.

1931-32 — Though there is no record of a team attempting to play with two goaltenders on the ice, a rule was instituted which stated that each team was allowed only one goaltender on the ice at one time.

Attacking players forbidden to impede the movement or obstruct the vision of opposing goaltenders.

Defending players with the exception of the goaltender forbidden from falling on the puck within 10 feet of the net.

1932-33 — Each team to have captain on the ice at all times. Maximum number of players in uniform reduced to 14 from 15.

If the goaltender is removed from the ice to serve a penalty, the manager of the club to appoint a substitute.

Match penalty with substitution after five minutes instituted for kicking another player.

1933-34 — Number of players permitted to stand in defensive zone restricted to three including goaltender.

Visible time clocks required in each rink.

Two referees replace one referee and one linesman.

1934-35 — Penalty shot awarded when a player is tripped and thus prevented from having a clear shot on goal, having no player to pass to other than the offending player. Shot taken from inside a 10-foot circle located 38 feet from the goal. The goaltender must not advance more than one foot from his goal-line when the shot is taken.

1937-38 — Rules introduced governing icing the puck.

Penalty shot awarded when a player other than a goaltender falls on the puck within 10 feet of the goal.

1938-39 — Penalty shot modified to allow puck carrier to skate in before shooting.

One referee and one linesman replace two referee system.

Blue line widened to 12 inches.

Maximum number of players in uniform increased from 14 to 15.

1939-40 — A substitute replacing a goaltender removed from ice to serve a penalty may use a goaltender's stick and gloves but no other goaltending equipment.

1940-41 — Flooding ice surface between periods made obligatory.

1941-42 — Penalty shots classified as minor and major. Minor shot to be taken from a line 28 feet from the goal. Major shot, awarded when a player is tripped with only the goaltender to beat, permits the player taking the penalty shot to skate right into the goalkeeper and shoot from point-blank range.

One referee and two linesmen employed to officiate games.

For playoffs, standby minor league goaltenders employed by NHL as emergency substitutes.

1942-43 — Because of wartime restrictions on train scheduling, regular-season overtime was discontinued on November 21, 1942.

Player limit reduced from 15 to 14. Minimum of 12 men in uniform abolished.

1943-44 — Red line at center ice introduced to speed up the game and reduce offside calls. This rule is considered to mark the beginning of the modern era in the NHL.

1945-46 — Goal indicator lights synchronized with official time clock required at all rinks.

1946-47 — System of signals by officials to indicate infractions introduced.

Linesmen from neutral cities employed for all games.

1947-48 — Goal awarded when a player with the puck has an open net to shoot at and a thrown stick prevents the shot on goal. Major penalty to any player who throws his stick in any zone other than defending zone. If a stick is thrown by a player in his defending zone but the thrown stick is not considered to have prevented a goal, a penalty shot is awarded.

All playoff games played until a winner determined, with 20-minute sudden-death overtime periods separated by 10-minute intermissions.

1949-50 — Ice surface painted white.

Clubs allowed to dress 17 players exclusive of goaltenders.

Major penalties incurred by goaltenders served by a member of the goaltender's team instead of resulting in a penalty shot.

1950-51 — Each team required to provide an emergency goaltender in attendance with full equipment at each game for use by either team in the event of illness or injury to a regular goaltender.

1951-52 — Home teams to wear basic white uniforms; visiting teams basic colored uniforms.

Goal crease enlarged from 3 × 7 feet to 4 × 8 feet.

Number of players in uniform reduced to 15 plus goaltenders.

Faceoff circles enlarged from 10-foot to 15-foot radius.

1952-53 — Teams permitted to dress 15 skaters on the road and 16 at home.

1953-54 — Number of players in uniform set at 16 plus goaltenders.

1954-55 — Number of players in uniform set at 18 plus goaltenders up to December 1 and 16 plus goaltenders thereafter. Teams agree to wear colored uniforms at home and white uniforms on the road.

1956-57 — Player serving a minor penalty allowed to return to ice when a goal is scored by opposing team.

1959-60 — Players prevented from leaving their benches to enter into an altercation. Substitutions permitted providing substitutes do not enter into altercation.

1960-61 — Number of players in uniform set at 16 plus goaltenders.

1961-62 — Penalty shots to be taken by the player against whom the foul was committed. In the event of a penalty shot called in a situation where a particular player hasn't been fouled, the penalty shot to be taken by any player on the ice when the foul was committed.

1964-65 — No body contact on faceoffs.

In playoff games, each team to have its substitute goaltender dressed in his regular uniform except for leg pads and body protector. All previous rules governing standby goaltenders terminated.

1965-66 — Teams required to dress two goaltenders for each regular-season game. Maximum stick length increased to 55 inches.

1966-67 — Substitution allowed on coincidental major penalties.

Between-periods intermissions fixed at 15 minutes.

1967-68 — If a penalty incurred by a goaltender is a co-incident major, the penalty to be served by a player of the goaltender's team on the ice at the time the penalty was called. Limit of curvature of hockey stick blade set at 1½ inches.

1969-70 — Limit of curvature of hockey stick blade set at 1 inch.

1970-71 — Home teams to wear basic white uniforms; visiting teams to wear basic colored uniforms.

Limit of curvature of hockey stick blade set at ½ inch.

Minor penalty for deliberately shooting the puck out of the playing area.

1971-72 — Number of players in uniform set at 17 plus 2 goaltenders.

Third man to enter an altercation assessed an automatic game misconduct penalty.

1972-73 — Minimum width of stick blade reduced to 2 inches from 2½ inches.

1974-75 — Bench minor penalty imposed if a penalized player does not proceed directly and immediately to the penalty box.

1976-77 — Rule dealing with fighting amended to provide a major and game misconduct penalty for any player who is clearly the instigator of a fight.

1977-78 — Teams requesting a stick measurement to be assessed a minor penalty in the event that the measured stick does not violate the rules.

1979-80 — Wearing of helmets made mandatory for players entering the NHL.

1980-81 — Maximum stick length increased to 58 inches.

1981-82 — If both of a team's listed goaltenders are incapacitated, the team can dress and play any eligible goaltender who is available.

1982-83 — Number of players in uniform set at 18 plus 2 goaltenders.

1983-84 — Five-minute sudden-death overtime to be played in regular-season games that are tied at the end of regulation time.

1985-86 — Substitutions allowed in the event of co-incidental minor penalties. Maximum stick length increased to 60 inches.

1986-87 — Delayed off-side is no longer in effect once the players of the offending team have cleared the opponents' defensive zone.

1990-91 — The goal lines, blue lines, defensive zone face-off circles and markings all moved one foot out from the end boards, creating 11 feet of room behind the nets and shrinking the neutral zone from 60 to 58 feet.

1991-92 — Video replays employed to assist referees in goal/no goal situations. Size of goal crease increased. Crease changed to semi-circular configuration. Time clock to record tenths of a second in last minute of each period and overtime. Major and game misconduct penalty for checking from behind into boards. Penalties added for crease infringement and unnecessary contact with goaltender. Goal disallowed if puck enters net while a player of the attacking team is standing on the goal crease line, is in the goal crease or places his stick in the goal crease.

1992-93 — No substitutions allowed in the event of coincidental minor penalties called when both teams are at full strength. Minor penalty for attempting to draw a penalty ("diving"). Major and game misconduct penalty for checking from behind into goal frame. Game misconduct penalty for instigating a fight. High sticking redefined to include any use of the stick above waist-height. Previous rule stipulated shoulder-height.

1993-94 — High sticking redefined to allow goals scored with a high stick below the height of the crossbar of the goal frame.

1996-97 — Maximum stick length increased to 63 inches. All players must be clear of the attacking zone prior to the puck being shot into that zone. The opportunity to "tag-up" and return into the zone has been removed.

1998-99 — The league instituted a two-referee system with each team to play 20 regular-season games with two referees and a pair of linesmen. Goal line moved to 13 feet from end boards. Goal crease altered to extend one foot beyond each goal post (eight feet across in total. Sides of crease squared off, extending 4'6". Only the top of the crease remains rounded. Only the top of the crease remains rounded.

1999-2000 — Each team to play 25 home and 25 road games using the two-referee system. Crease rule revised to implement a "no harm, no foul, no video review" standard. Teams to play with four skaters and a goaltender in regular-season overtime. If a goal is scored in regular-season overtime, the winner is awarded two points and the loser one point. In no goal is scored in overtime, both teams are awarded one point.

2000-01 — All games to be played using the two-referee system.

2002-03 — "Hurry-up" faceoff and line-change rules implemented.

2003-04 — Home teams to wear basic colored uniforms; visiting teams to wear basic white uniforms. Maximum length of goaltender's pads set at 38 inches.

2005-06 — The NHL adopted a comprehensive package of rule changes that included the following:

Goal line moved to 11 feet from end boards; blue lines moved to 75 feet from end boards, reducing neutral zone from 54 feet to 50 feet. Center red line eliminated for two-line passes. "Tag-up" off-side rule reinstituted. Goaltender not permitted to play the puck outside a designated trapezoid-shaped area behind the net. A team that ices the puck not permitted to make any player substitutions prior to the ensuing faceoff. A player who instigates a fight in the final five minutes of regulation time or at any time of overtime to receive a minor, a major, a misconduct and an automatic one-game suspension. The size of goaltender equipment reduced. If a game remains tied after five minutes of overtime, winner determined by shootout.

2011-12 — Rules and penalties modified to address contact with the head.

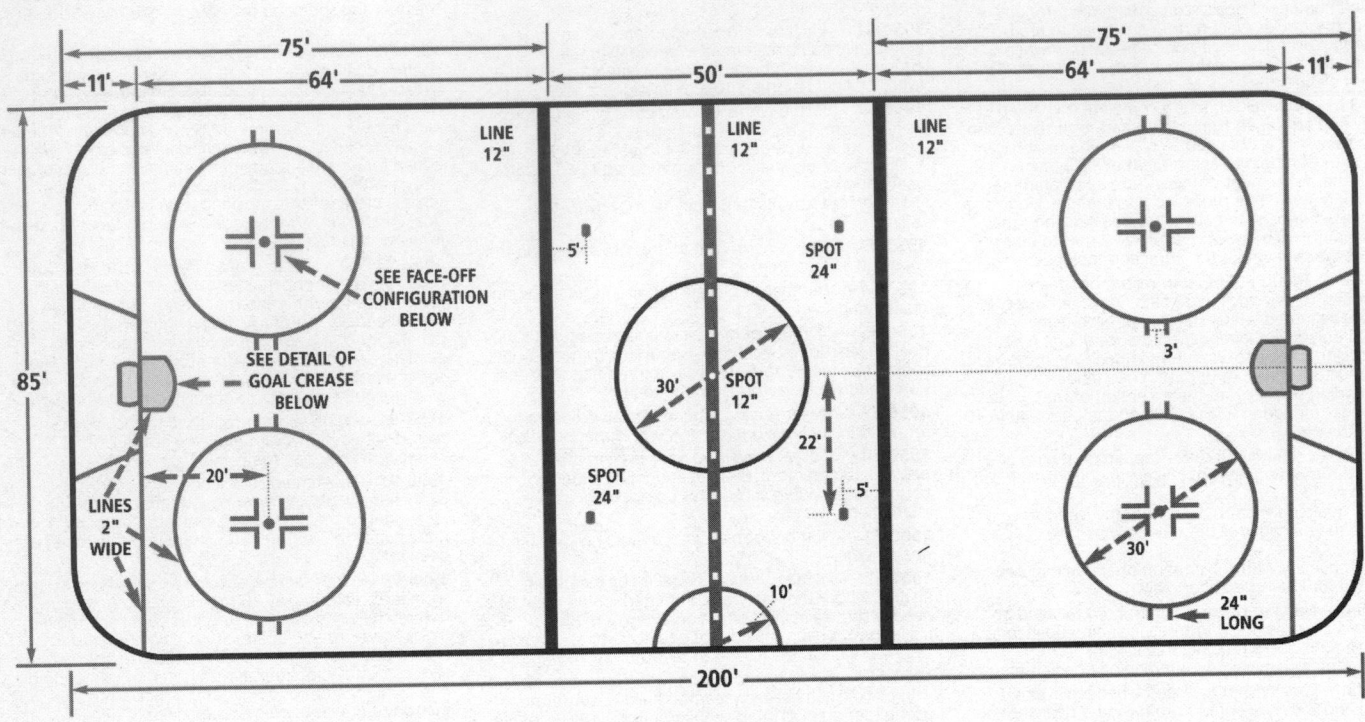

NHL RINK DIMENSIONS

FACEOFF CONFIGURATION

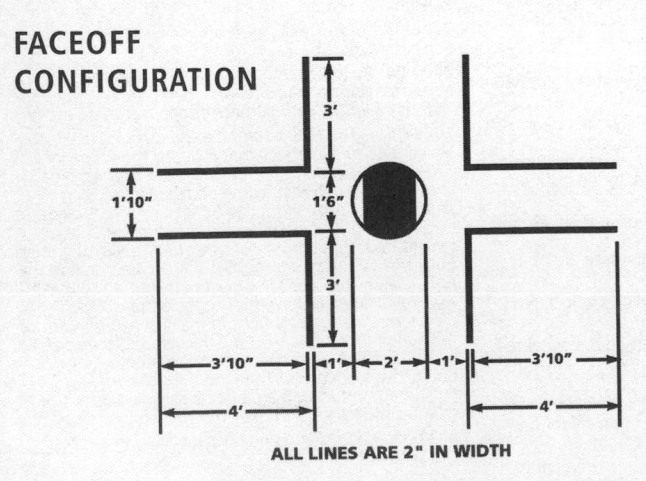

ALL LINES ARE 2" IN WIDTH

CREASE DIMENSIONS

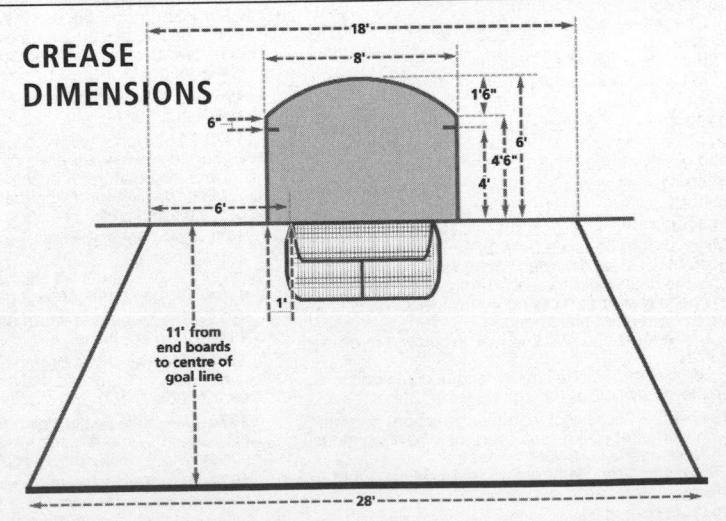

Winter Classic and Heritage Classic Outdoor Games

Date	Location	Venue	Attendance	Final Score				Game-Winning Goal	Time of GWG	Temperature
Nov. 22, 2003**	Edmonton, Alberta	Commonwealth Stadium	57,167	Montreal	4	Edmonton	3	Richard Zednik	14:18 (3rd)	0°F/-18°C
Jan. 1, 2008*	Buffalo, New York	Ralph Wilson Stadium	71,217	Pittsburgh	2	Buffalo	1	Sidney Crosby	Shootout	33°F/+1°C
Jan. 1, 2009*	Chicago, Illinois	Wrigley Field	40,818	Detroit	6	Chicago	4	Brian Rafalski	3:07 (3rd)	32°F/0°C
Jan. 1, 2010*	Boston, Massachusetts	Fenway Park	38,112	Boston	2	Philadelphia	1	Marco Sturm	1:57 (OT)	35°F/+2°C
Jan. 1, 2011*	Pittsburgh, Pennsylvania	Heinz Field	68,111	Washington	3	Pittsburgh	1	Eric Fehr	11:59 (3rd)	50°F/+10°C
Feb. 20, 2011**	Calgary, Alberta	McMahon Stadium	41,022	Calgary	4	Montreal	0	Rene Bourque	8:09 (1st)	18°F/-8°C

*- Winter Classic; ** - Heritage Classic*

Regular-Season Games Played Outside North America

Date	Location	Venue	Attendance	Final Score				Game-Winning Goal	Time of GWG
Oct. 3, 1997	Tokyo, Japan	Yoyogi Arena	10,500	Vancouver	3	Anaheim	2	Pavel Bure	14:41 (2nd)
Oct. 4, 1997	Tokyo, Japan	Yoyogi Arena	10,500	Anaheim	3	Vancouver	2	J.J. Daigneault	13:38 (3rd)
Sept. 29, 2007	London, England	O₂ Arena	17,551	Los Angeles	4	Anaheim	1	Rob Blake	10:15 (2nd)
Sept. 30, 2007	London, England	O₂ Arena	17,300	Anaheim	4	Los Angeles	1	Chris Kunitz	15:19 (1st)
Oct. 4, 2008	Prague, Czech Republic	O₂ Arena	17,085	NY Rangers	2	Tampa Bay	1	Brandon Dubinsky	14:16 (3rd)
Oct. 4, 2008	Stockholm, Sweden	Ericsson Globe Arena	13,699	Pittsburgh	4	Ottawa	3	Tyler Kennedy	4:35 (OT)
Oct. 5, 2008	Prague, Czech Republic	O₂ Arena	17,085	NY Rangers	2	Tampa Bay	1	Scott Gomez	12:12 (2nd)
Oct. 5, 2008	Stockholm, Sweden	Ericsson Globe Arena	13,699	Ottawa	3	Pittsburgh	1	Dany Heatley	12:17 (3rd)
Oct. 2, 2009	Helsinki, Finland	Hartwell Arena	12,056	Florida	4	Chicago	3	Ville Koistinen	Shootout
Oct. 2, 2009	Stockholm, Sweden	Ericsson Globe Arena	13,850	St. Louis	4	Detroit	3	Paul Kariya	17:36 (2nd)
Oct. 3, 2009	Helsinki, Finland	Hartwell Arena	11,526	Chicago	4	Florida	0	Brian Campbell	3:05 (1st)
Oct. 3, 2009	Stockholm, Sweden	Ericsson Globe Arena	13,850	St. Louis	5	Detroit	3	Patrick Berglund	13:37 (2nd)
Oct. 7, 2010	Helsinki, Finland	Hartwell Arena	12,355	Carolina	4	Minnesota	3	Brandon Sutter	18:03 (2nd)
Oct. 8, 2010	Helsinki, Finland	Hartwell Arena	13,465	Carolina	2	Minnesota	1	Jeff Skinner	Shootout
Oct. 8, 2010	Stockholm, Sweden	Ericsson Globe Arena	11,324	San Jose	3	Columbus	2	Logan Couture	10:15 (3rd)
Oct. 9, 2010	Stockholm, Sweden	Ericsson Globe Arena	11,324	Columbus	3	San Jose	2	Ethan Moreau	1:56 (OT)
Oct. 9, 2010	Prague, Czech Republic	O₂ Arena	15,299	Phoenix	5	Boston	2	Scottie Upshall	15:02 (2nd)
Oct. 10, 2010	Prague, Czech Republic	O₂ Arena	12,990	Boston	3	Phoenix	0	Milan Lucic	12:11 (2nd)
Oct. 7, 2011	Helsinki, Finland	Hartwell Arena		Anaheim	@	Buffalo			
Oct. 7, 2011	Stockholm, Sweden	Ericsson Globe Arena		NY Rangers	@	Los Angeles			
Oct. 8, 2011	Stockholm, Sweden	Ericsson Globe Arena		NY Rangers	@	Anaheim			
Oct. 8, 2011	Berlin, Germany	O₂ World		Buffalo	@	Los Angeles			

NHL Clubs' Minor-League Affiliations, 2011-12

NHL CLUB	MINOR-LEAGUE AFFILIATES
Anaheim	Syracuse Crunch (AHL)
	Elmira Jackals (ECHL)
Boston	Providence Bruins (AHL)
	Reading Royals (ECHL)
Buffalo	Rochester Americans (AHL)
Calgary	Abbotsford Heat (AHL)
	Utah Grizzlies (ECHL)
Carolina	Charlotte Checkers (AHL)
	Florida Everblades (ECHL)
Chicago	Rockford IceHogs (AHL)
	Toledo Walleye (ECHL)
Colorado	Lake Erie Monsters (AHL)
Columbus	Springfield Falcons (AHL)
	Chicago Express (ECHL)
Dallas	Texas Stars (AHL)
	Idaho Steelheads (ECHL)
Detroit	Grand Rapids Griffins (AHL)
	Toledo Walleye (ECHL)
Edmonton	Oklahoma City Barons (AHL)
	Stockton Thunder (ECHL)
Florida	San Antonio Rampage (AHL)
	Cincinnati Cyclones (ECHL)
Los Angeles	Manchester Monarchs (AHL)
	Ontario (CA) Reign (ECHL)
Minnesota	Houston Aeros (AHL)
	Bakersfield Condors (ECHL)
Montreal	Hamilton Bulldogs (AHL)
	Wheeling Nailers (ECHL)
Nashville	Milwaukee Admirals (AHL)
	Cincinnati Cyclones (ECHL)

NHL CLUB	MINOR-LEAGUE AFFILIATES
New Jersey	Albany Devils (AHL)
NY Islanders	Bridgeport Sound Tigers (AHL)
	Kalamazoo Wings (ECHL)
	Odessa Jackalopes (CHL)
NY Rangers	Connecticut Whale (AHL)
	Greenville Road Warriors (ECHL)
Ottawa	Binghamton Senators (AHL)
	Elmira Jackals (ECHL)
Philadelphia	Adirondack Phantoms (AHL)
	Trenton Titans (ECHL)
Phoenix	Portland Pirates (AHL)
	Gwinnett Gladiators (ECHL)
Pittsburgh	Wilkes-Barre/Scranton Penguins (AHL)
	Wheeling Nailers (ECHL)
St. Louis	Peoria Rivermen (AHL)
	Alaska Aces (ECHL)
San Jose	Worcester Sharks (AHL)
	Stockton Thunder (ECHL)
Tampa Bay	Norfolk Admirals (AHL)
	Florida Everblades (ECHL)
Toronto	Toronto Marlies (AHL)
	Reading Royals (ECHL)
Vancouver	Chicago Wolves (AHL)
Washington	Hershey Bears (AHL)
	South Carolina Stingrays (ECHL)
Winnipeg	St. John's IceCaps (AHL)
	Colorado Eagles (ECHL)

Anaheim Ducks

Key Off-Season Signings/Acquisitions

2011

June 17 • Re-signed D **Nate Guenin**.

July 1 • Acquired D **Kurtis Foster** from Edmonton for D **Andy Sutton**.

2 • Signed RW **Andrew Gordon**.

5 • Signed D **Bryan Rodney**.

6 • Signed LW **Jean-Francois Jacques**.

7 • Re-signed RW **Brian McGrattan**.

11 • Re-signed RW **Dan Sexton**.

12 • Acquired C **Andrew Cogliano** from Edmonton for a 2nd-round pick in the 2013 Entry Draft.

12 • Signed G **Jeff Deslauriers**.

14 • Signed D **Matt Smaby**.

15 • Re-signed C **Nick Bonino**.

20 • Signed C **Mark Bell**.

2010-11 Results: 47w-30l-3otl-2sol 99pts.
Second, Pacific Division

Year-by-Year Record

Season	GP	Home W	L	T	OL	Road W	L	T	OL	Overall W	L	T	OL	GF	GA	Pts.	Finished	Playoff Result
2010-11	82	26	13	....	2	21	17	....	3	47	30	....	5	239	235	99	2nd, Pacific Div.	Lost Conf. Quarter-Final
2009-10	82	25	11	....	6	14	21	....	6	39	32	....	11	238	251	89	4th, Pacific Div.	Out of Playoffs
2008-09	82	20	18	....	3	22	15	....	4	42	33	....	7	245	238	91	2nd, Pacific Div.	Lost Conf. Semi-Final
2007-08	82	28	9	....	4	19	18	....	4	47	27	....	8	205	191	102	2nd, Pacific Div.	Lost Conf. Quarter-Final
2006-07	**82**	**26**	**6**	**....**	**9**	**22**	**14**	**....**	**5**	**48**	**20**	**....**	**14**	**258**	**208**	**110**	**1st, Pacific Div.**	**Won Stanley Cup**
2005-06*	82	26	10	....	5	17	17	....	7	43	27	....	12	254	229	98	3rd, Pacific Div.	Lost Conf. Championship
2004-05*	....																	
2003-04*	82	19	11	7	4	10	24	3	4	29	35	10	8	184	213	76	4th, Pacific Div.	Out of Playoffs
2002-03*	82	22	10	7	2	18	17	2	4	40	27	9	6	203	193	95	2nd, Pacific Div.	Lost Final
2001-02*	82	15	19	5	2	14	23	3	1	29	42	8	3	175	198	69	5th, Pacific Div.	Out of Playoffs
2000-01*	82	15	20	4	2	10	21	7	3	25	41	11	5	188	245	66	5th, Pacific Div.	Out of Playoffs
1999-2000*	82	19	13	7	2	15	20	5	1	34	33	12	3	217	227	83	5th, Pacific Div.	Out of Playoffs
1998-99*	82	21	14	6	....	14	20	7	....	35	34	13	....	215	206	83	3rd, Pacific Div.	Lost Conf. Quarter-Final
1997-98*	82	12	23	6	....	14	20	7	....	26	43	13	....	205	261	65	6th, Pacific Div.	Out of Playoffs
1996-97*	82	23	12	6	....	13	21	7	....	36	33	13	....	245	233	85	2nd, Pacific Div.	Lost Conf. Semi-Final
1995-96*	82	22	15	4	....	13	24	4	....	35	39	8	....	234	247	78	4th, Pacific Div.	Out of Playoffs
1994-95*	48	11	9	4	....	5	18	1	....	16	27	5	....	125	164	37	6th, Pacific Div.	Out of Playoffs
1993-94*	84	14	26	2	....	19	20	3	....	33	46	5	....	229	251	71	4th, Pacific Div.	Out of Playoffs

* Mighty Ducks of Anaheim

2011-12 Schedule

Oct.	Fri.	7	at Buffalo†
	Sat.	8	NY Rangers††
	Fri.	14	San Jose
	Sun.	16	St. Louis*
	Mon.	17	at San Jose
	Fri.	21	Dallas
	Sun.	23	Phoenix*
	Tue.	25	at Chicago
	Thu.	27	at Minnesota
	Sat.	29	at Nashville
	Sun.	30	at Columbus
Nov.	Tue.	1	at Washington
	Thu.	3	at NY Rangers
	Sat.	5	at Detroit
	Wed.	9	Nashville
	Fri.	11	Vancouver
	Sun.	13	Minnesota*
	Wed.	16	at Los Angeles
	Thu.	17	Los Angeles
	Sun.	20	Detroit*
	Wed.	23	at Phoenix
	Fri.	25	Chicago*
	Sun.	27	Toronto*
	Wed.	30	Montreal
Dec.	Fri.	2	Philadelphia
	Sun.	4	Minnesota*
	Tue.	6	Los Angeles
	Thu.	8	at St. Louis
	Sat.	10	at Nashville
	Wed.	14	Phoenix
	Fri.	16	at Chicago
	Sat.	17	at Winnipeg
	Mon.	19	at Dallas
	Thu.	22	at Los Angeles
	Mon.	26	at San Jose
	Thu.	29	Vancouver
	Sat.	31	Colorado*
Jan.	Wed.	4	San Jose
	Fri.	6	NY Islanders
	Sun.	8	Columbus*
	Tue.	10	Dallas
	Thu.	12	at Calgary
	Fri.	13	at Edmonton
	Sun.	15	at Vancouver
	Wed.	18	Phoenix
	Sat.	21	Ottawa*
	Sun.	22	Colorado*
	Tue.	24	at Dallas
	Tue.	31	at Phoenix
Feb.	Wed.	1	Dallas
	Fri.	3	Columbus
	Mon.	6	Calgary
	Wed.	8	Carolina
	Fri.	10	at Detroit
	Sun.	12	at Columbus
	Tue.	14	at Minnesota
	Wed.	15	at Pittsburgh
	Fri.	17	at New Jersey
	Sun.	19	at Florida
	Tue.	21	at Tampa Bay
	Thu.	23	at Carolina
	Sun.	26	Chicago*
	Mon.	27	at Colorado
	Wed.	29	Buffalo
Mar.	Fri.	2	Calgary
	Sat.	3	at Los Angeles
	Mon.	5	Edmonton
	Thu.	8	at St. Louis
	Sat.	10	at Dallas
	Mon.	12	at Colorado
	Wed.	14	Detroit
	Fri.	16	Los Angeles
	Sun.	18	Nashville*
	Mon.	19	at San Jose
	Wed.	21	St. Louis
	Sun.	25	Boston*
	Wed.	28	San Jose
	Sat.	31	at Phoenix
Apr.	Sun.	1	Edmonton*
	Tue.	3	at Vancouver
	Thu.	5	at Edmonton
	Sat.	7	at Calgary*

* Denotes afternoon game.   † Game played in Helsinki.
†† Game played in Stockholm.

Corey Perry poses with the three pucks he put past Antero Niittymaki in a 6-2 Anaheim victory over San Jose on April 6, 2011. Perry scored 19 goals in the final 16 games of the season to reach 50 on the year and push the Ducks into the playoffs.

PACIFIC DIVISION
19th NHL Season

Franchise date: June 15, 1993

2011-12 Player Personnel

FORWARDS	HT	WT	S	Place of Birth	*Age	2010-11 Club
BELESKEY, Matt	6-0	198	L	Windsor, Ont.	23	Anaheim-Syracuse
BELL, Mark	6-3	220	L	St. Pauls, Ont.	31	Kloten
BLAKE, Jason	5-10	190	L	Moorhead, MN	38	Anaheim
BONINO, Nick	6-1	186	L	Hartford, CT	23	Anaheim-Syracuse
BRITTAIN, Josh	6-5	226	L	Milton, Ont.	21	Syracuse-Elmira
COGLIANO, Andrew	5-10	188	L	Toronto, Ont.	24	Edmonton
DESCHAMPS, Nicolas	6-1	207	L	Lasalle, Que.	21	Syracuse
ETEM, Emerson	6-1	197	L	Long Beach, CA	19	Medicine Hat
GETZLAF, Ryan	6-4	220	R	Regina, Sask.	26	Anaheim
GORDON, Andrew	6-0	194	R	Halifax, N.S.	25	Washington-Hershey
HOLLAND, Peter	6-2	195	L	Toronto, Ont.	20	Guelph-Syracuse
JACQUES, Jean-Francois	6-4	217	L	Montreal, Que.	26	Edmonton-Oklahoma City
KENNEDY, Matt	6-2	202	R	Richmond Hill, Ont.	22	Charlotte-Syracuse
KOIVU, Saku	5-10	182	L	Turku, Finland	36	Anaheim
MACENAUER, Maxime	6-0	205	L	Laval, Que.	22	Syracuse
MAROON, Patrick	6-4	225	L	St Louis, MO	23	Adirondack-Syracuse
McGRATTAN, Brian	6-4	235	R	Hamilton, Ont.	30	Providence (AHL)-Syracuse
McMILLAN, Brandon	5-11	192	L	Richmond, B.C.	21	Anaheim-Syracuse
PALMIERI, Kyle	5-11	193	R	Smithtown, NY	20	Anaheim-Syracuse
PARROS, George	6-5	228	R	Washington, PA	31	Anaheim
PERRY, Corey	6-3	212	R	Peterborough, Ont.	26	Anaheim
RYAN, Bobby	6-2	209	R	Cherry Hill, NJ	24	Anaheim
SCHOFIELD, Rick	6-2	198	L	Pickering, Ont.	24	Lake Superior-Syracuse
SELANNE, Teemu	6-0	199	R	Helsinki, Finland	41	Anaheim
SEXTON, Dan	5-10	174	R	Apple Valley, MN	24	Anaheim-Syracuse
SMITH-PELLY, Devante	6-0	215	R	Scarborough, Ont.	19	St. Michael's
DEFENSEMEN						
BEAUCHEMIN, Francois	6-0	207	L	Sorel, Que.	31	Toronto-Anaheim
BROOKBANK, Sheldon	6-1	202	R	Lanigan, Sask.	31	Anaheim
CARLE, Mathieu	6-0	200	R	Gatineau, Que.	24	Hamilton
CLARK, Mat	6-3	221	R	Wheat Ridge, CO	20	Syracuse
FOSTER, Kurtis	6-5	226	R	Carp, Ont.	29	Edmonton
FOWLER, Cam	6-1	196	L	Windsor, Ont.	19	Anaheim
GUENIN, Nate	6-2	210	R	Sewickley, PA	28	CBJ-Sprfld-Syr
LYDMAN, Toni	6-1	202	L	Lahti, Finland	34	Anaheim
NEWTON, Jake	6-2	218	L	San Jacinto, CA	23	Syracuse
RODNEY, Bryan	6-0	204	R	London, Ont.	27	Carolina-Charlotte
SBISA, Luca	6-2	207	L	Ozieri, Italy	21	Anaheim-Syracuse
SMABY, Matt	6-4	239	L	Minneapolis, MN	26	Tampa Bay
VATANEN, Sami	5-9	163	R	Jyvaskyla, Finland	20	Suomi U20-JYP
VISNOVSKY, Lubomir	5-10	197	L	Topolcany, Czech.	35	Anaheim
ZIMMERMAN, Sean	6-3	205	R	Denver, CO	24	Roch-Prov (AHL)-Syr

GOALTENDERS	HT	WT	C	Place of Birth	*Age	2010-11 Club
BOBKOV, Igor	6-4	192	L	Surgut, USSR	20	London-Syracuse
COUSINEAU, Marco	6-0	195	L	St.Lazare, Que.	21	Elmira
DESLAURIERS, Jeff	6-4	200	R	St-Jean-Richelieu, Que.	27	Oklahoma City
ELLIS, Dan	6-1	191	L	Saskatoon, Sask.	31	Tampa Bay-Anaheim
HILLER, Jonas	6-2	194	R	Felben Wellhausen, Switz.	29	Anaheim
PIELMEIER, Timo	6-0	170	L	Deggendorf, W. Germany	22	Anaheim-Syracuse-Elmira
TARKKI, Iiro	6-2	191		Rauma, Finland	26	Blues

* – Age at start of 2011-12 season

Randy Carlyle

Head Coach

Born: Sudbury, Ont., April 19, 1956.

Randy Carlyle was hired as the head coach in Anaheim on August 1, 2005. In his first season behind the bench in 2005-06, he led the Ducks to the Western Conference Final. He led Anaheim to its first Stanley Cup championship in 2007.

Prior to joining Anaheim, Carlyle had served as the head coach of the Manitoba Moose, the Vancouver Canucks' primary development team. In all, Carlyle spent six seasons between 1996 and 2005 as head coach in Manitoba (both in the International and American Hockey Leagues) with his team posting an overall record of 222-159-52-7. He had the additional duties of general manager of the Moose from 1996 to 2000, and served as club president for the 2001-02 season. Carlyle helped the Moose to a 47-21-14 record for 108 points in 1998-99, for which he was named the IHL's general manager of the year.

Following the 2001-02 season, Carlyle joined the coaching staff of the Washington Capitals. He served as an assistant coach with Washington for two seasons (2002 to 2004), before rejoining Manitoba in 2004–05.

Carlyle played 17 seasons in the NHL with Toronto, Pittsburgh and Winnipeg. He appeared in 1,055 games and had 148 goals and 499 assists for 647 points. Known as a fiery, tough-nosed defenseman, he was selected to play in four NHL All-Star Games, winning the Norris Trophy as the league's top defenseman in 1981. At the conclusion of his playing career in 1993, Carlyle remained with the Winnipeg organization's hockey operations staff, eventually becoming an assistant coach for the 1995-96 season.

2010-11 Scoring

* – rookie

Regular Season

Pos	#	Player	Team	GP	G	A	Pts	TOI	+/-	PIM	PP	SH	GW	S	%
R	10	Corey Perry	ANA	82	50	48	98	22:18	9	104	14	4	11	290	17.2
R	8	Teemu Selanne	ANA	73	31	49	80	17:56	6	49	16	0	5	213	14.6
C	15	Ryan Getzlaf	ANA	67	19	57	76	21:51	14	35	7	0	4	117	16.2
R	9	Bobby Ryan	ANA	82	34	37	71	20:10	15	61	5	1	5	270	12.6
D	17	Lubomir Visnovsky	ANA	81	18	50	68	24:17	18	24	5	0	4	152	11.8
C	11	Saku Koivu	ANA	75	15	30	45	19:08	–8	36	4	0	3	104	14.4
D	4 *	Cam Fowler	ANA	76	10	30	40	22:07	–25	20	6	0	3	123	8.1
L	33	Jason Blake	ANA	76	16	16	32	14:45	–5	41	3	0	3	187	8.6
D	32	Toni Lydman	ANA	78	3	22	25	22:10	32	42	0	0	0	99	3.0
C	64 *	Brandon McMillan	ANA	60	11	10	21	14:04	–5	18	2	2	2	77	14.3
D	23	Francois Beauchemin	TOR	54	2	10	12	23:45	–4	16	0	0	0	76	2.6
			ANA	27	3	2	5	21:42	–4	16	1	0	0	30	10.0
			Total	81	5	12	17	23:04	–8	32	1	0	0	106	4.7
L	19	Brad Winchester	STL	57	9	5	14	10:29	–9	86	3	0	1	67	13.4
			ANA	19	1	1	2	10:28	–9	28	0	0	0	23	4.3
			Total	76	10	6	16	10:29	–18	114	3	0	1	90	11.1
R	42	Dan Sexton	ANA	47	4	9	13	11:35	–6	4	1	0	0	78	5.1
L	37	Jarkko Ruutu	OTT	50	2	8	10	12:28	–2	59	0	0	1	46	4.3
			ANA	23	1	1	2	8:58	0	38	0	0	0	20	5.0
			Total	73	3	9	12	11:22	–2	97	0	0	1	66	4.5
D	5	Luca Sbisa	ANA	68	2	9	11	16:47	–11	43	1	0	0	76	2.6
L	39	Matt Beleskey	ANA	35	3	7	10	12:58	–10	36	0	0	0	58	5.2
C	22	Todd Marchant	ANA	79	1	7	8	13:17	–18	26	0	0	0	63	1.6
D	3	Andreas Lilja	ANA	52	1	6	7	17:25	–15	28	0	0	0	31	3.2
R	16	George Parros	ANA	78	3	1	4	6:24	–4	171	0	0	1	33	9.1
D	25	Andy Sutton	ANA	39	0	4	4	14:45	1	87	0	0	0	31	0.0
C	28	Kyle Chipchura	ANA	40	0	2	2	7:59	1	32	0	0	0	23	0.0
C	51 *	Kyle Palmieri	ANA	10	1	0	1	8:41	–1	0	0	0	0	10	10.0
D	53	Brett Festerling	ANA	1	0	0	0	14:53	–2	0	0	0	0	0	0.0
C	12	Josh Green	ANA	12	0	0	0	10:00	–3	6	0	0	0	10	0.0
L	34	Aaron Voros	ANA	12	0	0	0	5:32	–4	43	0	0	0	8	0.0
C	63 *	Nick Bonino	ANA	26	0	0	0	9:48	–3	4	0	0	0	23	0.0
D	21	Sheldon Brookbank	ANA	40	0	0	0	13:19	–8	63	0	0	0	29	0.0

Goaltending

No.	Goaltender	GPI	Mins	Avg	W	L	OT	EN	SO	GA	SA	S%	G	A	PIM
29	Ray Emery	10	527	2.28	7	2	0	2	0	20	272	.926	0	0	0
38	Dan Ellis	13	729	2.39	8	3	1	0	0	29	348	.917	0	0	0
1	Jonas Hiller	49	2672	2.56	26	16	3	6	5	114	1493	.924	0	1	0
31	Curtis McElhinney	21	996	3.43	6	9	1	0	2	57	516	.890	0	1	0
30	* Timo Pielmeier	1	40	7.50	0	0	0	0	0	5	12	.583	0	0	0
	Totals	**82**	**4993**	**2.80**	**47**	**30**	**5**	**8**	**7**	**233**	**2648**	**.912**			

Playoffs

Pos	#	Player	Team	GP	G	A	Pts	TOI	+/-	PIM	PP	SH	GW	OT	S	%
R	10	Corey Perry	ANA	6	2	6	8	25:15	0	4	1	1	1	0	18	11.1
R	8	Teemu Selanne	ANA	6	6	1	7	18:58	–3	12	4	0	0	0	25	24.0
C	11	Saku Koivu	ANA	6	1	6	7	18:19	–2	6	0	0	0	0	7	14.3
C	15	Ryan Getzlaf	ANA	6	2	4	6	24:01	0	9	0	0	1	0	17	11.8
R	9	Bobby Ryan	ANA	4	3	1	4	20:29	2	2	0	0	0	0	10	30.0
L	33	Jason Blake	ANA	6	3	1	4	13:45	–3	0	2	0	0	0	17	17.6
D	4 *	Cam Fowler	ANA	6	1	3	4	22:13	1	2	1	0	0	0	12	8.3
D	17	Lubomir Visnovsky	ANA	6	0	3	3	21:21	–2	2	0	0	0	0	11	0.0
C	64 *	Brandon McMillan	ANA	6	1	1	2	13:08	0	0	0	0	0	0	8	12.5
D	23	Francois Beauchemin	ANA	6	0	2	2	23:32	1	2	0	0	0	0	2	0.0
L	39	Matt Beleskey	ANA	6	1	0	1	11:14	–1	4	0	0	0	0	8	12.5
C	22	Todd Marchant	ANA	6	0	1	1	14:22	–3	4	0	0	0	0	4	0.0
D	5	Luca Sbisa	ANA	6	0	1	1	16:29	–4	8	0	0	0	0	2	0.0
D	25	Andy Sutton	ANA	1	0	0	0	8:18	0	2	0	0	0	0	0	0.0
R	42	Dan Sexton	ANA	1	0	0	0	8:47	0	2	0	0	0	0	2	0.0
C	51 *	Kyle Palmieri	ANA	1	0	0	0	10:07	0	0	0	0	0	0	1	0.0
L	37	Jarkko Ruutu	ANA	3	0	0	0	5:31	–1	12	0	0	0	0	0	0.0
L	19	Brad Winchester	ANA	3	0	0	0	5:24	0	4	0	0	0	0	2	0.0
D	3	Andreas Lilja	ANA	3	0	0	0	11:02	0	0	0	0	0	0	0	0.0
D	21	Sheldon Brookbank	ANA	4	0	0	0	14:35	–2	14	0	0	0	0	2	0.0
C	63 *	Nick Bonino	ANA	4	0	0	0	11:36	–1	2	0	0	0	0	7	0.0
D	32	Toni Lydman	ANA	6	0	0	0	20:09	–2	2	0	0	0	0	5	0.0
R	16	George Parros	ANA	6	0	0	0	4:06	–1	16	0	0	0	0	3	0.0

Goaltending

No.	Goaltender	GPI	Mins	Avg	W	L	EN	SO	GA	SA	S%	G	A	PIM
29	Ray Emery	6	319	3.20	2	3	1	0	17	165	.897	0	0	0
38	Dan Ellis	1	41	5.85	0	1	0	0	4	24	.833	0	0	0
	Totals	**6**	**362**	**3.65**	**2**	**4**	**1**	**0**	**22**	**190**	**.884**			

Coaching Record

			Regular Season				Playoffs			
Season	Team	League	GC	W	L	O/T	GC	W	L	T
1996-97	Manitoba	IHL	32	16	14	2	....	....	....	....
1997-98	Manitoba	IHL	82	39	36	7	3	0	3	....
1998-99	Manitoba	IHL	82	47	21	14	5	2	3	....
99-2000	Manitoba	IHL	82	37	31	14	2	0	2	....
2000-01	Manitoba	IHL	82	39	31	12	13	6	7	....
2004-05	Manitoba	AHL	80	44	26	10	14	6	8	....
2005-06	**Anaheim**	**NHL**	**82**	**43**	**27**	**12**	**16**	**9**	**7**	....
2006-07♦	**Anaheim**	**NHL**	**82**	**48**	**20**	**14**	**21**	**16**	**5**	....
2007-08	**Anaheim**	**NHL**	**82**	**47**	**27**	**8**	**6**	**2**	**4**	....
2008-09	**Anaheim**	**NHL**	**82**	**42**	**33**	**7**	**13**	**7**	**6**	....
2009-10	**Anaheim**	**NHL**	**82**	**39**	**32**	**11**	....	....	....	....
2010-11	**Anaheim**	**NHL**	**82**	**47**	**30**	**5**	**6**	**2**	**4**	....
	NHL Totals		**492**	**266**	**169**	**57**	**62**	**36**	**26**	....

♦ Stanley Cup win.

Club Records

Team

(Figures in brackets for season records are games played; records for fewest points, wins, ties, losses, goals, goals against are for 70 or more games)

Most Points 110 2006-07 (82)
Most Wins 48 2006-07 (82)
Most Ties 13 1996-97 (82), 1997-98 (82), 1998-99 (82)
Most Losses 46 1993-94 (84)
Most Goals 258 2006-07 (82)
Most Goals Against 261 1997-98 (82)
Fewest Points 65 1997-98 (82)
Fewest Wins 25 2000-01 (82)
Fewest Ties 5 1993-94 (84)
Fewest Losses 20 2006-07 (82)
Fewest Goals 175 2001-02 (82)
Fewest Goals Against 191 2007-08 (82)

Longest Winning Streak
Overall . . . . 7 Feb. 20-Mar. 7/99
Home . . . . 11 Dec. 8/09-Feb. 10/10
Away . . . . 7 Nov. 28-Dec. 13/06

Longest Undefeated Streak
Overall . . . . 12 Feb. 22-Mar. 19/97 (7 wins, 5 ties)
Home . . . . 14 Feb. 12-Apr. 9/97 (10 wins, 4 ties)
Away . . . . 7 Nov. 28-Dec. 13/06 (7 wins)

Longest Losing Streak
Overall . . . . 8 Oct. 12-30/96, Nov. 3-20/05
Home . . . . 8 Jan. 10-Feb. 9/01
Away . . . . 9 Oct. 11-Dec. 11/09

Longest Winless Streak
Overall . . . . 9 Three times
Home . . . . 11 Jan. 5-Feb. 14/01 (8 losses, 3 ties)
Away . . . . 13 Nov. 1-Dec. 27/03 (11 losses, 2 ties)
Most Shutouts, Season 9 2002-03 (82)
Most PIM, Season 1,843 1997-98 (82)
Most Goals, Game . . . . 8 Jan. 21/98 (Fla. 3 at Ana. 8), Mar. 21/04 (Det. 6 at Ana. 8)

Individual

Most Seasons . . . . 12 Teemu Selanne
Most Games . . . . 774 Teemu Selanne
Most Goals, Career . . . . 410 Teemu Selanne
Most Assists, Career . . . . . . 461 Teemu Selanne
Most Points, Career . . . . . . 871 Teemu Selanne (410G, 461A)
Most PIM, Career . . . . 788 Dave Karpa
Most Shutouts, Career . . . . . 32 Jean-Sebastien Giguere

Longest Consecutive Games Streak . . . . 276 Andy McDonald (Oct. 17/03-Dec. 12/07)
Most Goals, Season . . . . 52 Teemu Selanne (1997-98)

Most Assists, Season . . . . 66 Ryan Getzlaf (2008-09)
Most Points, Season . . . . 109 Teemu Selanne (1996-97; 51G, 58A)
Most PIM, Season . . . . 285 Todd Ewen (1995-96)
Most Points, Defenseman, Season . . . . 69 Scott Niedermayer (2006-07; 15G, 54A)
Most Points, Center, Season . . . . 91 Ryan Getzlaf (2008-09; 25G, 66A)
Most Points, Right Wing, Season . . . . 109 Teemu Selanne (1996-97; 51G, 58A)
Most Points, Left Wing, Season . . . . 108 Paul Kariya (1995-96; 50G, 58A)
Most Points, Rookie, Season . . . . 57 Bobby Ryan (2008-09; 31G, 26A)
Most Shutouts, Season . . . . 8 Jean-Sebastien Giguere (2002-03)
Most Goals, Game . . . . 3 Thirty-three times
Most Assists, Game . . . . 5 Dmitri Mironov (Dec. 12/97) Teemu Selanne (Nov. 19/06) Ryan Getzlaf (Oct. 29/08)
Most Points, Game . . . . 5 Fifteen times

General Managers' History

Jack Ferreira, 1993-94 to 1997-98; Pierre Gauthier, 1998-99 to 2001-02; Bryan Murray, 2002-03, 2003-04; Al Coates, 2004-05; Brian Burke, 2005-06 to 2007-08; Brian Burke and Bob Murray, 2008-09; Bob Murray, 2009-10 to date.

Coaching History

Ron Wilson, 1993-94 to 1996-97; Pierre Page, 1997-98; Craig Hartsburg, 1998-99, 1999-2000; Craig Hartsburg and Guy Charron, 2000-01; Bryan Murray, 2001-02; Mike Babcock, 2002-03 to 2004-05; Randy Carlyle, 2005-06 to date.

Captains' History

Troy Loney, 1993-94; Randy Ladouceur, 1994-95, 1995-96; Paul Kariya, 1996-97; Paul Kariya and Teemu Selanne, 1997-98; Paul Kariya, 1998-99 to 2002-03; Steve Rucchin, 2003-04; Scott Niedermayer, 2005-06, 2006-07; Chris Pronger, 2007-08; Scott Niedermayer, 2008-09, 2009-10; Ryan Getzlaf, 2010-11 to date.

All-time Record vs. Other Clubs

Regular Season

	At Home								On Road								Total						
	GP	W	L	T	OL	GF	GA	PTS	GP	W	L	T	OL	GF	GA	PTS	GP	W	L	T	OL	GF	GA	PTS
Atlanta	7	3	3	0	1	22	23	7	6	4	2	0	0	19	13	8	13	7	5	0	1	41	36	15
Boston	11	4	3	2	2	24	28	12	12	6	5	0	1	36	34	13	23	10	8	2	3	60	62	25
Buffalo	12	5	7	0	0	27	37	10	12	3	5	3	1	27	35	10	24	8	12	3	1	54	72	20
Calgary	38	24	8	6	0	126	96	54	37	13	23	1	0	87	107	27	75	37	31	7	0	213	203	81
Carolina	12	6	5	1	0	35	37	13	12	4	7	1	0	27	32	9	24	10	12	2	0	62	69	22
Chicago	34	21	9	3	1	94	69	46	36	17	15	2	2	89	95	38	70	38	24	5	3	183	164	84
Colorado	33	16	12	3	2	91	83	37	33	13	14	4	2	92	91	32	66	29	26	7	4	183	174	69
Columbus	20	10	7	1	2	61	53	23	20	10	9	0	1	49	52	21	40	20	16	1	3	110	105	44
Dallas	48	22	22	3	1	123	131	48	48	12	29	2	5	97	156	31	96	34	51	5	6	220	287	79
Detroit	34	15	15	4	0	87	91	34	34	3	24	3	4	71	123	13	68	18	39	7	4	158	214	47
Edmonton	38	20	15	2	1	109	102	43	37	16	18	0	3	88	89	35	75	36	33	2	4	197	191	78
Florida	12	5	6	1	0	36	36	11	10	4	3	2	1	25	27	11	22	9	9	3	1	59	63	22
Los Angeles	51	26	11	7	7	169	133	66	51	20	25	4	2	129	150	46	102	46	36	11	9	298	283	112
Minnesota	20	12	5	0	3	54	47	27	20	5	9	2	4	38	54	16	40	17	14	2	7	92	101	43
Montreal	10	4	5	0	1	31	32	9	11	5	4	2	0	34	34	12	21	9	9	2	1	65	66	21
Nashville	24	18	3	0	3	75	45	39	24	9	11	2	2	55	61	22	48	27	14	2	5	130	106	61
New Jersey	13	6	6	1	0	35	33	13	10	2	7	0	1	17	35	5	23	8	13	1	1	52	68	18
NY Islanders	12	4	4	3	1	28	33	12	11	4	6	1	0	29	29	9	23	8	10	4	1	57	62	21
NY Rangers	11	7	2	0	2	41	34	16	12	6	4	1	1	32	31	14	23	13	6	1	3	73	65	30
Ottawa	11	5	5	1	0	27	23	13	11	6	4	1	0	29	31	13	22	11	9	2	0	56	54	26
Philadelphia	12	5	4	2	1	43	42	13	11	4	4	3	0	23	29	11	23	9	8	5	1	66	71	24
Phoenix	48	29	13	3	3	145	120	64	47	24	15	2	6	136	133	56	95	53	28	5	9	281	253	120
Pittsburgh	11	7	4	0	0	38	32	14	12	2	8	2	0	34	42	6	23	9	12	2	0	72	74	20
St. Louis	34	17	15	2	0	99	97	36	34	12	15	3	4	91	115	31	68	29	30	5	4	190	212	67
San Jose	51	21	25	2	3	136	150	47	51	24	24	2	1	133	143	51	102	45	49	4	4	269	293	98
Tampa Bay	12	7	4	1	0	38	31	15	11	7	4	0	0	29	21	14	23	14	8	1	0	67	52	29
Toronto	13	6	6	1	0	42	34	13	18	3	11	4	0	37	60	10	31	9	17	5	0	79	94	23
Vancouver	37	13	13	7	4	104	111	37	38	15	20	2	1	96	124	33	75	28	33	9	5	200	235	70
Washington	12	6	4	1	1	41	38	14	12	7	5	0	0	31	23	14	24	13	9	1	1	72	61	28
Totals	**681**	**344**	**239**	**58**	**40**	**1979**	**1821**	**786**	**681**	**260**	**330**	**49**	**42**	**1680**	**1969**	**611**	**1362**	**604**	**569**	**107**	**82**	**3659**	**3790**	**1397**

Playoffs

	Series	W	L	GP	W	L	T	GF	GA	Last Mtg.	Rnd.	Result
Calgary	1	1	0	7	4	3	0	17	16	2006	CQF	W 4-3
Colorado	1	1	0	4	4	0	0	16	4	2006	CSF	W 4-0
Dallas	2	1	1	12	6	6	0	27	34	2008	CQF	L 2-4
Detroit	5	2	3	25	11	14	0	57	75	2009	CSF	L 3-4
Edmonton	1	0	1	5	1	4	0	13	16	2006	CF	L 1-4
Minnesota	2	2	0	9	8	1	0	21	10	2007	CQF	W 4-1
Nashville	1	0	1	6	2	4	0	20	22	2011	CQF	L 2-4
New Jersey	1	0	1	7	3	4	0	12	19	2003	F	L 3-4
Ottawa	1	1	0	5	4	1	0	16	11	2007	F	W 4-1
Phoenix	1	1	0	7	4	3	0	17	17	1997	CQF	W 4-3
San Jose	1	1	0	6	4	2	0	18	10	2009	CQF	W 4-2
Vancouver	1	1	0	5	4	1	0	14	8	2007	CSF	W 4-1
Totals	**18**	**11**	**7**	**98**	**55**	**43**	**0**	**248**	**242**			

Carolina totals include Hartford, 1993-94 to 1996-97.
Colorado totals include Quebec, 1993-94 to 1994-95.
Phoenix totals include Winnipeg, 1993-94 to 1995-96.

Playoff Results 2011-2007

Year	Round	Opponent	Result	GF	GA
2011	CQF	Nashville	L 2-4	20	22
2009	CSF	Detroit	L 3-4	17	22
	CQF	San Jose	W 4-2	18	10
2008	CQF	Dallas	L 2-4	13	20
2007	**F**	**Ottawa**	**W 4-1**	**16**	**11**
	CF	Detroit	W 4-2	16	17
	CSF	Vancouver	W 4-1	14	8
	CQF	Minnesota	W 4-1	12	9

Abbreviations: Round: F - Final; **CF** – conference final; **CSF** – conference semi-final; **CQF** – conference quarter-final

Entry Draft Selections 2011-1997

Name in bold denotes played in NHL.

2011
Pick
30 **Rickard Rakell**
39 John Gibson
53 William Karlsson
65 Joseph Cramarossa
83 Andy Welinski
143 Max Friberg
160 Josh Manson

2010
Pick
12 **Cam Fowler**
29 Emerson Etem
42 Devante Smith-Pelly
122 Chris Wagner
132 Tim Heed
161 Andreas Dahlstrom
177 Kevin Lind
192 Brett Perlini

2009
Pick
15 Peter Holland
26 **Kyle Palmieri**
37 Mat Clark
76 Igor Bobkov
106 Sami Vatanen
136 Radoslav Illo
166 Scott Valentine

2008
Pick
17 Jake Gardiner
35 Nicolas Deschamps
39 Eric O'Dell
43 Justin Schultz
71 Josh Brittain
83 Marco Cousineau
85 **Brandon McMillan**
113 Ryan Hegarty
143 Stefan Warg
208 Nick Pryor

2007
Pick
19 Logan MacMillan
42 **Eric Tangradi**
63 Maxime Macenauer
92 Justin Vaive
93 **Steven Kampfer**
98 Sebastian Stefaniszin
121 Mattias Modig
151 Brett Morrison

2006
Pick
19 Mark Mitera
38 Bryce Swan
83 John de Gray
112 **Matt Beleskey**
172 **Petteri Wirtanen**

2005
Pick
2 **Bobby Ryan**
31 **Brendan Mikkelson**
63 Jason Bailey
127 Bobby Bolt
141 **Brian Salcido**
197 Jean-Philippe Levasseur

2004
Pick
9 **Ladislav Smid**
39 Jordan Smith
74 Kyle Klubertanz
75 **Tim Brent**
172 Matt Auffrey
203 Gabriel Bouthillette
236 Matt Christie
269 **Janne Pesonen**

2003
Pick
19 **Ryan Getzlaf**
28 **Corey Perry**
86 Shane Hynes
90 Juha Alen
119 Nathan Saunders
186 **Drew Miller**
218 Dirk Southern
250 **Shane O'Brien**
280 Ville Mantymaa

2002
Pick
7 **Joffrey Lupul**
37 **Tim Brent**
71 Brian Lee
103 Joonas Vihko
140 George Davis
173 Luke Fritshaw
261 Francois Caron
267 Chris Petrow

2001
Pick
5 **Stanislav Chistov**
35 **Mark Popovic**
69 Joel Stepp
102 **Timo Parssinen**
105 Vladimir Korsunov
118 Brandon Rogers
137 **Joel Perrault**
170 Jan Tabacek
224 **Tony Martensson**
232 **Martin Gerber**
264 **P.A. Parenteau**

2000
Pick
12 **Alexei Smirnov**
44 **Ilya Bryzgalov**
98 **Jonas Ronnqvist**
134 Peter Podhradsky
153 Bill Cass

1999
Pick
44 **Jordan Leopold**
83 **Niclas Havelid**
105 Alexandr Chagodayev
141 Maxim Rybin
173 Jan Sandstrom
230 **Petr Tenkrat**
258 Brian Gornick

1998
Pick
5 **Vitaly Vishnevski**
32 **Stephen Peat**
112 Viktor Wallin
150 **Trent Hunter**
178 **Jesse Fibiger**
205 David Bernier
233 Pelle Prestberg
245 Andreas Andersson

1997
Pick
18 **Michael Holmqvist**
45 **Maxim Balmochnykh**
72 Jay Legault
125 Luc Vaillancourt
178 Tony Mohagen
181 Mat Snesrud
209 Rene Stussi
235 Tommi Degerman

Bob Murray

Executive Vice President and General Manager

Born: Kingston, Ont., November 26, 1954.

Bob Murray was named executive vice president and general manager of the Anaheim Ducks on November 12, 2008 after 3 1/2 years as senior vice president of hockey operations. He was named to that original position on July 14, 2005. Murray's astute judgment of hockey talent and player evaluation were instrumental in several trades and acquisitions the Ducks made over his tenure, highlighted by a Stanley Cup championship in 2007.

Murray's responsibilities include overseeing all aspects of player development, playing a key role in the club's professional scouting efforts, contract negotiations and all matters relating to the National Hockey League. He has been instrumental in the organization's success at both the NHL and AHL level. Both the Ducks and American Hockey League's Portland Pirates made Conference Final appearances in 2006, making Anaheim the only organization to have both their NHL and AHL teams advance to their league's respective Conference Finals.

Prior to joining the Ducks, Murray worked as a professional scout with the Vancouver Canucks from 1999 to 2005 under then-general manager Brian Burke (1998 to 2004). Murray's scouting expertise helped to build teams that recorded 100+ point season two years in a row (2002-03 and 2003-04) and advanced to the Stanley Cup playoffs four seasons in a row (2001 to 2004). Before his stint in Vancouver, he served as a scouting consultant for Anaheim during the 1998-99 season.

Murray was a member of the Chicago Blackhawks organization for 25 years, serving as general manager from 1997 to 1999. He was promoted to the post after serving as assistant general manager under Bob Pulford for two seasons. Before joining upper management, Murray was named the director of player personnel in 1991 and was largely responsible for the club's entry draft selections over eight seasons.

Drafted by the Blackhawks in 1974, Murray spent his entire 1,008-game, 15-year career in a Chicago uniform. He became just the fourth player in Blackhawks history to reach the 1,000-game plateau. In addition, he became the first defenseman in club history to appear in 100 postseason contests, reaching the mark during the 1990 Stanley Cup playoffs. In all, Murray scored had 132 goals and 382 assists for 514 points, and currently ranks second in all-time points among Blackhawk defensemen. He was named to both the 1981 and 1983 NHL All-Star Games. Murray retired at the conclusion of the 1989-90 season. Known for his work ethic, intelligence and determination as a player, Murray remained with the organization as a professional scout following his retirement in 1990.

Club Directory

Honda Center

Anaheim Ducks
Honda Center
2695 E. Katella Ave.
Anaheim, CA 92806
Phone **714/940-2900**
FAX 714/940-2953
Ticket Information 877/WILDWING
www.anaheimducks.com
Capacity: 17,174

Executive Management

Owners	Henry and Susan Samueli
Chief Executive Officer	Michael Schulman
Executive Vice President/General Manager	Bob Murray
Executive Vice President/Chief Operating Officer	Tim Ryan
Senior Vice President, Hockey Operations	David McNab
Chief Financial Officer/Vice President of Finance	Doug Heller
Vice President, Human Resources	Jay Scott
Vice President, Operations, Anaheim Arena	Kevin Starkey
Vice President, Multi-Media & Community Devel.	Aaron Teats
Vice President of Finance, Anaheim Arena	Angela Wergechik
Senior Manager of Hockey Operations	Maureen Nyeholt
Exec. Asst. to the Executive V.P./COO	Cheryl Gorman
Exec. Asst. to the V.P. of Multi-Media & Community Development	Janet Conley

Coaching Staff

Head Coach	Randy Carlyle
Assistant Coaches	Dave Farrish, Mike Foligno
Goaltending Consultant	Pete Peeters
Video Coordinator	Joe Trotta
Strength and Conditioning Coach	Sean Skahan

Hockey Operations

Director of Player Personnel	Rick Paterson
Director of Amateur Scouting	Martin Madden
Director of Player Development	Alain Chainey
Scouting Staff	David Baseggio, Glen Cochrane, Jeff Crisp, Jan-Åke Danielson, Casey Hankinson, Konstantin Krylov, Matt Laatsch, Kevin Murray, Jim Pappin, Jim Sandlak
Manager of Hockey Operations	Ryan Lichtenfels
Coordinator of Minor League Hockey Ops	Jillian Samueli
Video Scouting Analyst	Joe Piscotty
Head Athletic Trainer	Tim Clark
Assistant Athletic Trainer	Rick Burrill
Massage Therapist	James Partida
Equipment Manager	Doug Shearer
Assistant Equipment Manager	Chris Aldrich
Equipment Assistant	Chris Kincaid
Medical Director / Team Physician	Dr. Craig Milhouse / Dr. Orr Limpisvasti
Oral Surgeon	Dr. Bao-Thy Grant

Broadcasting

TV: FSN Prime Ticket (Cable), KDOC-TV	John Ahlers, Brian Hayward
Radio: KLAA AM 830 & Ducks Radio Network	Steve Carroll, Dan Wood
Host/Producer	Kent French
Broadcasting Coordinator	Tiffany Frish

Communications

Director of Media & Communications	Alex Gilchrist
Media & Communications Managers	Steve Hoem, Lauren O'Gorman
Game Night Communications Staff	Lisa Parris, Courtney Strayer, Larry Woodard

Community Relations

Director of Community Relations	Wendy Yamagishi
Community Relations Managers	Jesse Bryson, Jennifer Walker

Entertainment

Director of Production & Entertainment	Rich Cooley
Entertainment Manager	Chris Brown
Arena Vision Editor/Producer	Davin Maske
Producer / Associate Producer	Peter Uvalle / Gabriel Suarez
Production Coordinator	Sarah Montecinos

Fan Development

Director of Fan Development	Matt Savant
Sr Manager of Fan Development, School and Education Programs	Joseph Hwang
Fan Development Manager / Coordinator	Champ Baginski, Mike Hermosa

Finance, Human Resources, Information Technology and Legal

General Counsel	Bernard Schneider
Controller / IT Manager	Melody Martin / Mike Wing
Human Resources Managers	Wendy Mulhall, Donna Vass
Assistant General Counsel	Katie Rodin

Corporate Partnerships

Director of Corporate Partnerships	Greg Rieber
Director of Corporate Partnership Activation	Alex Anderson
Managers	Robert Flanigan, Sara Morales, Erin Moreno, Greg Morrison

Marketing

Director of Marketing	Tracie Jones
Sr. Manager of Signature Programs and Events	Kris Loomis
Senior Media and Marketing Manager	Adam Mendelsohn
Marketing Managers	Jesse Chatfield, Ryan Spillers
Signature Programs and Events Manager	Jamie Minkler
Designers, Senior / Junior	Mariana Stoopen / Ruben Segura

Publications and New Media

Director of Publications and New Media	Adam Brady
Publications & New Media Coordinator	Matt Vevoda
Social Media Producer	Neil Horowitz

Premium Sales and Service

Director of Premium Sales & Service	Jim Panetta
Premium Account Executives	Geoff Matthews, Timothy Thompson
Premium Services Manager	Jana Cannavo

Ticketing

Senior Manager of Ticket Operations	James Bakken
Assistant Managers	Jonas Calicdan, Gina Bulgheroni

Ticket Sales and Customer Service

Director of Ticket Sales and Service	Lisa Johnson
Sr. Manager of Season and Group Sales	Mike Morrow
Inside Sales Manager	Graham Siderius

Boston Bruins

Key Off-Season Signings/Acquisitions

2011

July
- **1** • Signed LW **Benoit Pouliot**.
- **1** • Re-signed C **Trent Whitfield** and G **Anton Khudobin**.
- **5** • Acquired D **Joe Corvo** from Carolina for a 4th-round pick in the 2012 Entry Draft.
- **14** • Re-signed D **Adam McQuaid**.

2010-11 Results: 46W-25L-5OTL-6SOL 103PTS.
First, Northeast Division

2011-12 Schedule

Month	Day	Date	Opponent
Oct.	Thu.	6	Philadelphia
	Sat.	8	Tampa Bay
	Mon.	10	Colorado*
	Wed.	12	at Carolina
	Sat.	15	at Chicago
	Tue.	18	Carolina
	Thu.	20	Toronto
	Sat.	22	San Jose
	Thu.	27	Montreal
	Sat.	29	at Montreal
Nov.	Tue.	1	Ottawa
	Sat.	5	at Toronto
	Mon.	7	NY Islanders
	Thu.	10	Edmonton
	Sat.	12	Buffalo
	Tue.	15	New Jersey
	Thu.	17	Columbus
	Sat.	19	at NY Islanders
	Mon.	21	at Montreal
	Wed.	23	at Buffalo
	Fri.	25	Detroit*
	Sat.	26	Winnipeg
	Wed.	30	at Toronto
Dec.	Sat.	3	Toronto
	Mon.	5	at Pittsburgh
	Tue.	6	at Winnipeg
	Thu.	8	Florida
	Sat.	10	at Columbus
	Tue.	13	Los Angeles
	Wed.	14	at Ottawa
	Sat.	17	at Philadelphia*
	Mon.	19	Montreal
	Fri.	23	Florida
	Wed.	28	at Phoenix
	Sat.	31	at Dallas
Jan.	Wed.	4	at New Jersey
	Thu.	5	Calgary
	Sat.	7	Vancouver*
	Tue.	10	Winnipeg
	Thu.	12	Montreal
	Sat.	14	at Carolina
	Mon.	16	at Florida
	Tue.	17	at Tampa Bay
	Thu.	19	at New Jersey
	Sat.	21	NY Rangers*
	Sun.	22	at Philadelphia*
	Tue.	24	at Washington
	Tue.	31	Ottawa
Feb.	Thu.	2	Carolina
	Sat.	4	Pittsburgh*
	Sun.	5	at Washington*
	Wed.	8	at Buffalo
	Sat.	11	Nashville*
	Tue.	14	NY Rangers
	Wed.	15	at Montreal
	Fri.	17	at Winnipeg
	Sun.	19	at Minnesota*
	Wed.	22	at St. Louis
	Fri.	24	at Buffalo
	Sat.	25	at Ottawa
	Tue.	28	Ottawa
Mar.	Thu.	1	New Jersey
	Sat.	3	NY Islanders*
	Sun.	4	at NY Rangers*
	Tue.	6	at Toronto
	Thu.	8	Buffalo
	Sat.	10	Washington*
	Sun.	11	at Pittsburgh
	Tue.	13	at Tampa Bay
	Thu.	15	at Florida
	Sat.	17	Philadelphia*
	Mon.	19	Toronto
	Thu.	22	at San Jose
	Sat.	24	at Los Angeles
	Sun.	25	at Anaheim*
	Tue.	27	Tampa Bay
	Thu.	29	Washington
	Sat.	31	at NY Islanders*
Apr.	Sun.	1	at NY Rangers*
	Tue.	3	Pittsburgh
	Thu.	5	at Ottawa
	Sat.	7	Buffalo*

* Denotes afternoon game.

Year-by-Year Record

Season	GP	Home W	L	T	OL	Road W	L	T	OL	Overall W	L	T	OL	GF	GA	Pts.	Finished	Playoff Result
2010-11	**82**	**22**	**13**	....	**6**	**24**	**12**	....	**5**	**46**	**25**	....	**11**	**246**	**195**	**103**	**1st, Northeast Div.**	**Won Stanley Cup**
2009-10	82	18	17	....	6	21	13	....	7	39	30	....	13	206	200	91	3rd, Northeast Div.	Lost Conf. Semi-Final
2008-09	82	29	6	....	6	24	13	....	4	53	19	....	10	274	196	116	1st, Northeast Div.	Lost Conf. Semi-Final
2007-08	82	21	16	....	4	20	13	....	8	41	29	....	12	212	222	94	3rd, Northeast Div.	Lost Conf. Quarter-Final
2006-07	82	18	19	....	4	17	22	....	2	35	41	....	6	219	289	76	5th, Northeast Div.	Out of Playoffs
2005-06	82	16	15	....	10	13	22	....	6	29	37	....	16	230	266	74	5th, Northeast Div.	Out of Playoffs
2004-05	....	....	....	....	....	....	....	....	....	....	....	....	....	....	....	....		
2003-04	82	18	12	9	2	23	7	6	5	41	19	15	7	209	188	104	1st, Northeast Div.	Lost Conf. Quarter-Final
2002-03	82	23	11	5	2	13	20	6	2	36	31	11	4	245	237	87	3rd, Northeast Div.	Lost Conf. Quarter-Final
2001-02	82	23	11	2	5	20	13	4	4	43	24	6	9	236	201	101	1st, Northeast Div.	Lost Conf. Quarter-Final
2000-01	82	21	12	5	3	15	18	3	5	36	30	8	8	227	249	88	4th, Northeast Div.	Out of Playoffs
1999-2000	82	12	17	11	1	12	16	8	5	24	33	19	6	210	248	73	5th, Northeast Div.	Out of Playoffs
1998-99	82	22	10	9	....	17	20	4	....	39	30	13	....	214	181	91	3rd, Northeast Div.	Lost Conf. Semi-Final
1997-98	82	19	16	6	....	20	14	7	....	39	30	13	....	221	194	91	2nd, Northeast Div.	Lost Conf. Quarter-Final
1996-97	82	14	20	7	....	12	27	2	....	26	47	9	....	234	300	61	6th, Northeast Div.	Out of Playoffs
1995-96	82	22	14	5	....	18	17	6	....	40	31	11	....	282	269	91	2nd, Northeast Div.	Lost Conf. Quarter-Final
1994-95	48	15	7	2	....	12	11	1	....	27	18	3	....	150	127	57	3rd, Northeast Div.	Lost Conf. Quarter-Final
1993-94	84	20	14	8	....	22	15	5	....	42	29	13	....	289	252	97	2nd, Northeast Div.	Lost Conf. Semi-Final
1992-93	84	29	10	3	....	22	16	4	....	51	26	7	....	332	268	109	1st, Adams Div.	Lost Div. Semi-Final
1991-92	80	23	11	6	....	13	21	6	....	36	32	12	....	270	275	84	2nd, Adams Div.	Lost Conf. Championship
1990-91	80	26	9	5	....	18	15	7	....	44	24	12	....	299	264	100	1st, Adams Div.	Lost Conf. Championship
1989-90	80	23	13	4	....	23	12	5	....	46	25	9	....	289	232	101	1st, Adams Div.	Lost Final
1988-89	80	17	15	8	....	20	14	6	....	37	29	14	....	289	256	88	2nd, Adams Div.	Lost Div. Final
1987-88	80	24	13	3	....	20	17	3	....	44	30	6	....	300	251	94	2nd, Adams Div.	Lost Final
1986-87	80	25	11	4	....	14	23	3	....	39	34	7	....	301	276	85	3rd, Adams Div.	Lost Div. Semi-Final
1985-86	80	24	9	7	....	13	22	5	....	37	31	12	....	311	288	86	3rd, Adams Div.	Lost Div. Semi-Final
1984-85	80	21	15	4	....	15	19	6	....	36	34	10	....	303	287	82	4th, Adams Div.	Lost Div. Semi-Final
1983-84	80	25	12	3	....	24	13	3	....	49	25	6	....	336	261	104	1st, Adams Div.	Lost Div. Semi-Final
1982-83	80	28	6	6	....	22	14	4	....	50	20	10	....	327	228	110	1st, Adams Div.	Lost Conf. Championship
1981-82	80	24	12	4	....	19	15	6	....	43	27	10	....	323	285	96	2nd, Adams Div.	Lost Div. Final
1980-81	80	26	10	4	....	11	20	9	....	37	30	13	....	316	272	87	2nd, Adams Div.	Lost Prelim. Round
1979-80	80	27	9	4	....	19	12	9	....	46	21	13	....	310	234	105	2nd, Adams Div.	Lost Quarter-Final
1978-79	80	25	10	5	....	18	13	9	....	43	23	14	....	316	270	100	1st, Adams Div.	Lost Semi-Final
1977-78	80	29	6	5	....	22	12	6	....	51	18	11	....	333	218	113	1st, Adams Div.	Lost Final
1976-77	80	27	7	6	....	22	16	2	....	49	23	8	....	312	240	106	1st, Adams Div.	Lost Final
1975-76	80	27	5	8	....	21	10	9	....	48	15	17	....	313	237	113	1st, Adams Div.	Lost Semi-Final
1974-75	80	29	5	6	....	11	21	8	....	40	26	14	....	345	245	94	2nd, Adams Div.	Lost Prelim. Round
1973-74	78	33	4	2	....	19	13	7	....	52	17	9	....	349	221	113	1st, East Div.	Lost Final
1972-73	78	27	10	2	....	21	12	3	....	51	22	5	....	330	235	107	2nd, East Div.	Lost Quarter-Final
1971-72	**78**	**28**	**4**	**7**	....	**26**	**9**	**4**	....	**54**	**13**	**11**	....	**330**	**204**	**119**	**1st, East Div.**	**Won Stanley Cup**
1970-71	78	33	4	2	....	24	10	5	....	57	14	7	....	399	207	121	1st, East Div.	Lost Quarter-Final
1969-70	**76**	**27**	**3**	**8**	....	**13**	**14**	**11**	....	**40**	**17**	**19**	....	**277**	**216**	**99**	**2nd, East Div.**	**Won Stanley Cup**
1968-69	76	29	3	6	....	13	15	10	....	42	18	16	....	303	221	100	2nd, East Div.	Lost Semi-Final
1967-68	74	22	9	6	....	15	18	4	....	37	27	10	....	259	216	84	3rd, East Div.	Lost Quarter-Final
1966-67	70	10	21	4	....	7	22	6	....	17	43	10	....	182	253	44	6th,	Out of Playoffs
1965-66	70	15	17	3	....	6	26	3	....	21	43	6	....	174	275	48	5th,	Out of Playoffs
1964-65	70	12	17	6	....	9	26	0	....	21	43	6	....	166	253	48	6th,	Out of Playoffs
1963-64	70	13	15	7	....	5	25	5	....	18	40	12	....	170	212	48	6th,	Out of Playoffs
1962-63	70	7	18	10	....	7	21	7	....	14	39	17	....	198	281	45	6th,	Out of Playoffs
1961-62	70	9	22	4	....	6	25	4	....	15	47	8	....	177	306	38	6th,	Out of Playoffs
1960-61	70	13	17	5	....	2	25	8	....	15	42	13	....	176	254	43	6th,	Out of Playoffs
1959-60	70	21	11	3	....	7	23	5	....	28	34	8	....	220	241	64	5th,	Out of Playoffs
1958-59	70	21	11	3	....	11	18	6	....	32	29	9	....	205	215	73	2nd,	Lost Semi-Final
1957-58	70	15	14	6	....	12	14	9	....	27	28	15	....	199	194	69	4th,	Lost Final
1956-57	70	20	9	6	....	14	15	6	....	34	24	12	....	195	174	80	3rd,	Lost Final
1955-56	70	14	14	7	....	9	20	6	....	23	34	13	....	147	185	59	5th,	Out of Playoffs
1954-55	70	16	10	9	....	7	16	12	....	23	26	21	....	169	188	67	4th,	Lost Semi-Final
1953-54	70	22	8	5	....	10	20	5	....	32	28	10	....	177	181	74	4th,	Lost Semi-Final
1952-53	70	19	10	6	....	9	19	7	....	28	29	13	....	152	172	69	3rd,	Lost Final
1951-52	70	15	12	8	....	10	17	8	....	25	29	16	....	162	176	66	4th,	Lost Semi-Final
1950-51	70	13	12	10	....	9	18	8	....	22	30	18	....	178	197	62	4th,	Lost Semi-Final
1949-50	70	15	12	8	....	7	20	8	....	22	32	16	....	198	228	60	5th,	Out of Playoffs
1948-49	60	18	10	2	....	11	13	6	....	29	23	8	....	178	163	66	2nd,	Lost Semi-Final
1947-48	60	12	8	10	....	11	16	3	....	23	24	13	....	167	168	59	3rd,	Lost Semi-Final
1946-47	60	18	7	5	....	8	16	6	....	26	23	11	....	190	175	63	3rd,	Lost Semi-Final
1945-46	50	11	5	4	....	13	13	4	....	24	18	8	....	167	156	56	2nd,	Lost Final
1944-45	50	11	12	2	....	5	18	2	....	16	30	4	....	179	219	36	4th,	Lost Semi-Final
1943-44	50	15	8	2	....	4	18	3	....	19	26	5	....	223	268	43	5th,	Out of Playoffs
1942-43	50	17	3	5	....	7	14	4	....	24	17	9	....	195	176	57	2nd,	Lost Final
1941-42	48	17	4	3	....	8	13	3	....	25	17	6	....	160	118	56	3rd,	Lost Semi-Final
1940-41	**48**	**15**	**4**	**5**	....	**12**	**4**	**8**	....	**27**	**8**	**13**	....	**168**	**102**	**67**	**1st,**	**Won Stanley Cup**
1939-40	48	20	3	1	....	11	9	4	....	31	12	5	....	170	98	67	1st,	Lost Semi-Final
1938-39	**48**	**20**	**2**	**2**	....	**16**	**8**	**0**	....	**36**	**10**	**2**	....	**156**	**76**	**74**	**1st,**	**Won Stanley Cup**
1937-38	48	18	3	3	....	12	8	4	....	30	11	7	....	142	89	67	1st, Amn. Div.	Lost Semi-Final
1936-37	48	9	11	4	....	14	7	3	....	23	18	7	....	120	110	53	2nd, Amn. Div.	Lost Quarter-Final
1935-36	48	15	8	1	....	7	12	5	....	22	20	6	....	92	83	50	2nd, Amn. Div.	Lost Quarter-Final
1934-35	48	17	7	0	....	9	9	6	....	26	16	6	....	129	112	58	1st, Amn. Div.	Lost Semi-Final
1933-34	48	11	11	2	....	7	14	3	....	18	25	5	....	111	130	41	4th, Amn. Div.	Out of Playoffs
1932-33	48	19	2	3	....	6	13	5	....	25	15	8	....	124	88	58	1st, Amn. Div.	Lost Semi-Final
1931-32	48	11	10	3	....	4	11	9	....	15	21	12	....	122	117	42	4th, Amn. Div.	Out of Playoffs
1930-31	44	16	1	5	....	12	9	1	....	28	10	6	....	143	90	62	1st, Amn. Div.	Lost Semi-Final
1929-30	44	21	1	0	....	17	4	1	....	38	5	1	....	179	98	77	1st, Amn. Div.	Lost Final
1928-29	**44**	**15**	**6**	**1**	....	**11**	**7**	**4**	....	**26**	**13**	**5**	....	**89**	**52**	**57**	**1st, Amn. Div.**	**Won Stanley Cup**
1927-28	44	13	4	5	....	7	9	6	....	20	13	11	....	77	70	51	1st, Amn. Div.	Lost Semi-Final
1926-27	44	15	7	0	....	6	13	3	....	21	20	3	....	97	89	45	2nd, Amn. Div.	Lost Final
1925-26	36	10	7	1	....	7	8	3	....	17	15	4	....	92	85	38	4th,	Out of Playoffs
1924-25	30	3	12	0	....	3	12	0	....	6	24	0	....	49	119	12	6th,	Out of Playoffs

NORTHEAST DIVISION
88th NHL Season

Franchise date: November 1, 1924

2011-12 Player Personnel

FORWARDS	HT	WT	S	Place of Birth	*Age	2010-11 Club
ARNIEL, Jamie	5-11	183	R	Kingston, Ont.	21	Boston-Providence (AHL)
BERGERON, Patrice	6-2	194	R	Ancienne-Lorette, Que.	26	Boston
CAMPBELL, Gregory	6-0	197	L	London, Ont.	27	Boston
CARON, Jordan	6-2	202	L	Sayabec, Que.	20	Boston-Providence (AHL)
HAMILL, Zach	5-11	180	R	Vancouver, B.C.	23	Boston-Providence (AHL)
HENNESSY, Josh	6-0	192	L	Brockton, MA	26	Lugano
HORTON, Nathan	6-2	229	R	Welland, Ont.	26	Boston
KELLY, Chris	6-0	198	L	Toronto, Ont.	30	Ottawa-Boston
KREJCI, David	6-0	177	R	Sternberk, Czech.	25	Boston
LUCIC, Milan	6-4	220	L	Vancouver, B.C.	23	Boston
MacDERMID, Lane	6-3	205	L	Hartford, CT	22	Providence (AHL)
MARCHAND, Brad	5-9	183	L	Halifax, N.S.	23	Boston
PAILLE, Daniel	6-0	200	L	Welland, Ont.	27	Boston
PEVERLEY, Rich	6-0	195	R	Guelph, Ont.	29	Atlanta-Boston
POULIOT, Benoit	6-3	199	L	Alfred, Ont.	25	Montreal
SAUVE, Max	6-0	170	L	Tours, France	21	Providence (AHL)
SAVARD, Marc	5-10	191	L	Ottawa, Ont.	34	Boston
SEGUIN, Tyler	6-1	182	R	Brampton, Ont.	19	Boston
TARDIF, Jamie	6-0	205	R	Welland, Ont.	26	Grand Rapids
THORNTON, Shawn	6-2	217	R	Oshawa, Ont.	34	Boston
WHITFIELD, Trent	5-11	209	L	Estevan, Sask.	34	Providence (AHL)
DEFENSEMEN						
ALEXANDROV, Yury	6-0	185	L	Cherepovets, USSR	23	Providence (AHL)
BARTKOWSKI, Matt	6-1	196	L	Pittsburgh, PA	23	Boston-Providence (AHL)
BODNARCHUK, Andrew	5-11	172	L	Drumheller, Alta.	23	Providence (AHL)
BOYCHUK, Johnny	6-2	225	R	Edmonton, Alta.	27	Boston
CHARA, Zdeno	6-9	255	L	Trencin, Czechoslovakia	34	Boston
COHEN, Colby	6-2	200	R	Villanova, PA	22	Col-Lake Erie-Prov (AHL)
CORVO, Joe	6-1	210	R	Oak Park, IL	34	Carolina
FERENCE, Andrew	5-11	189	L	Edmonton, Alta.	32	Boston
KAMPFER, Steven	5-11	197	R	Ann Arbor, MI	23	Boston-Providence (AHL)
McQUAID, Adam	6-4	197	R	Charlottetown, P.E.I.	24	Boston
SEIDENBERG, Dennis	6-1	210	L	Schwenningen, W. Ger.	30	Boston

GOALTENDERS	HT	WT	C	Place of Birth	*Age	2010-11 Club
HUTCHINSON, Michael	6-3	185	R	Barrie, Ont.	21	Providence (AHL)-Reading
KHUDOBIN, Anton	5-11	203	L	Ust-Kamenogorsk, USSR	25	Min-Houston-Prov (AHL)
RASK, Tuukka	6-3	169	L	Savonlinna, Finland	24	Boston
THOMAS, Tim	5-11	201	L	Flint, MI	37	Boston

* – Age at start of 2011-12 season

Coaching History

Art Ross, 1924-25 to 1927-28; Cy Denneny, 1928-29; Art Ross, 1929-30 to 1933-34; Frank Patrick, 1934-35, 1935-36; Art Ross, 1936-37 to 1938-39; Cooney Weiland, 1939-40, 1940-41; Art Ross, 1941-42 to 1944-45; Dit Clapper, 1945-46 to 1948-49; Georges Boucher, 1949-50; Lynn Patrick, 1950-51 to 1953-54; Lynn Patrick and Milt Schmidt, 1954-55; Milt Schmidt, 1955-56 to 1960-61; Phil Watson, 1961-62; Phil Watson and Milt Schmidt, 1962-63; Milt Schmidt, 1963-64 to 1965-66; Harry Sinden, 1966-67 to 1969-70; Tom Johnson, 1970-71, 1971-72; Tom Johnson and Bep Guidolin, 1972-73; Bep Guidolin, 1973-74; Don Cherry, 1974-75 to 1978-79; Fred Creighton and Harry Sinden, 1979-80; Gerry Cheevers, 1980-81 to 1983-84; Gerry Cheevers and Harry Sinden, 1984-85; Butch Goring, 1985-86; Butch Goring and Terry O'Reilly, 1986-87; Terry O'Reilly, 1987-88, 1988-89; Mike Milbury, 1989-90, 1990-91; Rick Bowness, 1991-92; Brian Sutter, 1992-93 to 1994-95; Steve Kasper, 1995-96, 1996-97; Pat Burns, 1997-98 to 1999-2000; Pat Burns and Mike Keenan, 2000-01; Robbie Ftorek, 2001-02; Robbie Ftorek and Mike O'Connell, 2002-03; Mike Sullivan, 2003-04 to 2005-06; Dave Lewis, 2006-07; Claude Julien, 2007-08 to date.

Claude Julien

Head Coach

Born: Orleans, Ont., April 23, 1960.

The Boston Bruins named Claude Julien the 28th head coach in club history on June 21, 2007. In his first season behind the bench in 2007-08, he guided the Bruins back to the playoffs for the first time since 2003-04. In 2008-09, the Bruins posted the best record in the Eastern Conference and were second overall in the NHL, earning Julien the Jack Adams Award for coach of the year. In 2010-11, he guided the team to a Stanley Cup victory for the first time since 1972.

Julien joined the Bruins with four years of NHL head coaching experience. In his lone season with New Jersey, he held a record of 47-24-8 before being replaced on April 2, 2007 with three games remaining in the 2006-07 regular season. At the time he was replaced by the Devils, Julien's club was in first place in the Atlantic Division. Prior to being named head coach of the Devils, Julien spent three seasons as the head coach of the Montreal Canadiens, serving from January 2003 until January of 2006. During his tenure with Montreal, Julien led the Canadiens to a record of 72-71-16 in 159 games.

Before joining the NHL coaching ranks, Julien spent four seasons with Hull of the Quebec Major Junior Hockey League and three campaigns with Hamilton of the American Hockey League. While with Hamilton, Julien was co-awarded the Louis A. R. Pieri Award as the league's outstanding coach during the 2002-03 season. Julien has also coached at the international level, having served as an assistant coach to Team Canada at the 2006 World Championship after he led Team Canada to a bronze medal as a head coach at the 2000 World Junior Championship.

A defenseman, Julien's professional playing career spanned 12 seasons from 1981 to 1992, highlighted by stints with the Quebec Nordiques between 1984 and 1986.

2010-11 Scoring

* – rookie

Regular Season

Pos	#	Player	Team	GP	G	A	Pts	TOI	+/–	PIM	PP	SH	GW	S	%
L	17	Milan Lucic	BOS	79	30	32	62	16:34	28	121	5	0	7	173	17.3
C	46	David Krejci	BOS	75	13	49	62	18:51	23	28	1	0	2	157	8.3
C	37	Patrice Bergeron	BOS	80	22	35	57	17:53	20	26	3	2	4	211	10.4
R	18	Nathan Horton	BOS	80	26	27	53	16:17	29	85	6	0	2	188	13.8
R	28	Mark Recchi	BOS	81	14	34	48	16:06	13	35	6	0	6	132	10.6
D	12	Tomas Kaberle	TOR	58	3	35	38	22:28	–2	16	0	0	1	99	3.0
			BOS	24	1	8	9	21:14	6	2	0	0	0	31	3.2
			Total	82	4	43	47	22:06	4	18	0	0	1	130	3.1
D	33	Zdeno Chara	BOS	81	14	30	44	25:26	33	88	8	1	2	264	5.3
C	63 *	Brad Marchand	BOS	77	21	20	41	13:59	25	51	2	5	2	149	14.1
R	73	Michael Ryder	BOS	79	18	23	41	14:29	–1	26	8	0	6	165	10.9
C	49	Rich Peverley	ATL	59	14	20	34	19:13	–16	35	6	1	2	161	8.7
			BOS	23	4	3	7	15:46	–1	2	0	1	1	40	10.0
			Total	82	18	23	41	18:15	–17	37	6	2	3	201	9.0
D	44	Dennis Seidenberg	BOS	81	7	25	32	23:32	3	41	1	0	2	166	4.2
C	11	Gregory Campbell	BOS	80	13	16	29	13:26	11	93	1	1	1	98	13.3
C	23	Chris Kelly	OTT	57	12	11	23	15:38	–12	27	0	1	2	89	13.5
			BOS	24	2	3	5	14:51	–1	6	0	0	0	24	8.3
			Total	81	14	14	28	15:24	–13	33	0	1	2	113	12.4
C	19 *	Tyler Seguin	BOS	74	11	11	22	12:12	–4	18	1	0	0	131	8.4
L	22	Shawn Thornton	BOS	79	10	10	20	10:04	8	122	0	0	2	151	6.6
D	55	Johnny Boychuk	BOS	69	3	13	16	20:30	15	45	1	0	1	154	1.9
D	54 *	Adam McQuaid	BOS	67	3	12	15	14:51	30	96	0	0	0	46	6.5
D	21	Andrew Ference	BOS	70	3	12	15	17:58	22	60	0	0	0	78	3.8
L	20	Daniel Paille	BOS	43	6	7	13	11:18	3	28	0	1	0	48	12.5
D	47 *	Steven Kampfer	BOS	38	5	5	10	17:43	9	12	0	0	1	57	8.8
C	91	Marc Savard	BOS	25	2	8	10	15:48	–7	29	0	0	1	50	4.0
R	38 *	Jordan Caron	BOS	23	3	4	7	12:40	3	6	0	0	1	27	11.1
C	52 *	Zach Hamill	BOS	3	0	1	1	10:28	1	0	0	0	0	1	0.0
C	72 *	Jamie Arniel	BOS	1	0	0	0	12:26	–1	0	0	0	0	3	0.0
D	34	Shane Hnidy	BOS	3	0	0	0	14:46	–2	2	0	0	0	3	0.0
D	43 *	Matt Bartkowski	BOS	6	0	0	0	9:10	–1	4	0	0	0	2	0.0

Goaltending

No.	Goaltender	GPI	Mins	Avg	W	L	OT	EN	SO	GA	SA	S%	G	A	PIM
30	Tim Thomas	57	3364	2.00	35	11	9	3	9	112	1811	.938	0	3	13
40	Tuukka Rask	29	1594	2.67	11	14	2	3	2	71	866	.918	0	0	2
	Totals	**82**	**4980**	**2.28**	**46**	**25**	**11**	**6**	**11**	**189**	**2683**	**.930**			

Playoffs

Pos	#	Player	Team	GP	G	A	Pts	TOI	+/–	PIM	PP	SH	GW	OT	S	%
C	46	David Krejci	BOS	25	12	11	23	20:07	8	10	2	0	4	1	57	21.1
C	37	Patrice Bergeron	BOS	23	6	14	20	18:42	15	28	0	2	1	0	67	9.0
C	63 *	Brad Marchand	BOS	25	11	8	19	16:46	12	40	0	1	1	0	61	18.0
R	18	Nathan Horton	BOS	21	8	9	17	16:54	11	35	1	0	3	2	52	15.4
R	73	Michael Ryder	BOS	25	8	9	17	14:34	8	8	2	0	2	1	44	18.2
R	28	Mark Recchi	BOS	25	5	9	14	16:09	7	8	2	0	1	0	40	12.5
C	23	Chris Kelly	BOS	25	5	8	13	15:28	11	6	0	0	0	0	28	17.9
L	17	Milan Lucic	BOS	25	5	7	12	17:54	11	63	1	0	0	0	56	8.9
C	49	Rich Peverley	BOS	25	4	8	12	16:11	6	17	0	0	2	0	42	9.5
D	44	Dennis Seidenberg	BOS	25	1	10	11	27:37	12	31	0	0	0	0	63	1.6
D	12	Tomas Kaberle	BOS	25	0	11	11	16:01	8	4	0	0	0	0	33	0.0
D	21	Andrew Ference	BOS	25	4	6	10	20:36	10	37	1	0	1	0	38	10.5
D	55	Johnny Boychuk	BOS	25	3	6	9	20:38	12	12	0	0	1	0	51	5.9
D	33	Zdeno Chara	BOS	24	2	7	9	27:39	16	34	1	0	0	0	62	3.2
C	19 *	Tyler Seguin	BOS	13	3	4	7	10:35	5	2	0	0	0	0	22	13.6
L	20	Daniel Paille	BOS	25	3	3	6	8:43	2	4	0	1	0	0	25	12.0
C	11	Gregory Campbell	BOS	25	1	3	4	10:59	–2	4	0	0	0	0	24	4.2
D	54 *	Adam McQuaid	BOS	23	0	4	4	13:01	8	14	0	0	0	0	13	0.0
L	22	Shawn Thornton	BOS	18	0	1	1	6:57	–1	24	0	0	0	0	20	0.0
D	34	Shane Hnidy	BOS	3	0	0	0	3:09	0	7	0	0	0	0	0	0.0

Goaltending

No.	Goaltender	GPI	Mins	Avg	W	L	EN	SO	GA	SA	S%	G	A	PIM
30	Tim Thomas	25	1542	1.98	16	9	2	4	51	849	.940	0	0	4
	Totals	**25**	**1551**	**2.05**	**16**	**9**	**2**	**4**	**53**	**851**	**.938**			

Coaching Record

			Regular Season				Playoffs			
Season	Team	League	GC	W	L	O/T	GC	W	L	T
1996-97	Hull	QMJHL	70	48	19	3	14	12	2	....
1996-97	Hull	M-Cup	....	....	....	....	5	3	2	....
1997-98	Hull	QMJHL	70	32	37	1	11	6	5	....
1998-99	Hull	QMJHL	70	23	38	9	23	15	8	....
99-2000	Hull	QMJHL	72	42	24	6	15	9	6	....
2000-01	Hamilton	AHL	80	28	41	11	....	....	....	....
2001-02	Hamilton	AHL	80	37	30	13	15	10	5	....
2002-03	Hamilton	AHL	45	33	9	3	....	....	....	....
2002-03	**Montreal**	**NHL**	**36**	**12**	**16**	**8**	....	....	....	....
2003-04	**Montreal**	**NHL**	**82**	**41**	**30**	**11**	**11**	**4**	**7**	....
2004-05	**Montreal**				SEASON CANCELLED					
2005-06	**Montreal**	**NHL**	**41**	**19**	**16**	**6**	....	....	....	....
2006-07	**New Jersey**	**NHL**	**79**	**47**	**24**	**8**	....	....	....	....
2007-08	**Boston**	**NHL**	**82**	**41**	**29**	**12**	**7**	**3**	**4**	....
2008-09	**Boston**	**NHL**	**82**	**53**	**19**	**19**	**11**	**7**	**4**	....
2009-10	**Boston**	**NHL**	**82**	**39**	**30**	**13**	**13**	**7**	**6**	....
2010-11 ♦	**Boston**	**NHL**	**82**	**46**	**25**	**11**	**25**	**16**	**9**	....
	NHL Totals		**566**	**298**	**189**	**88**	**67**	**37**	**30**	....

♦ Stanley Cup win.
Won Jack Adams Award (2009)

Club Records

Team

(Figures in brackets for season records are games played; records for fewest points, wins, ties, losses, goals, goals against are for 70 or more games)

Most Points	121	1970-71 (78)
Most Wins	57	1970-71 (78)
Most Ties	21	1954-55 (70)
Most Losses	47	1961-62 (70), 1996-97 (82)
Most Goals	399	1970-71 (78)
Most Goals Against	306	1961-62 (70)
Fewest Points	38	1961-62 (70)
Fewest Wins	14	1962-63 (70)
Fewest Ties	5	1972-73 (78)
Fewest Losses	13	1971-72 (78)
Fewest Goals	147	1955-56 (70)
Fewest Goals Against	172	1952-53 (70)
Longest Winning Streak		
Overall	14	Dec. 3/29-Jan. 9/30
Home	*20	Dec. 3/29-Mar. 18/30
Away	8	Feb. 17-Mar. 8/72, Mar. 15-Apr. 14/93
Longest Undefeated Streak		
Overall	23	Dec. 22/40-Feb. 23/41 (15 wins, 8 ties)
Home	27	Nov. 22/70-Mar. 20/71 (26 wins, 1 tie)
Away	15	Dec. 22/40-Mar. 16/41 (9 wins, 6 ties)
Longest Losing Streak		
Overall	11	Dec. 3/24-Jan. 5/25
Home	11	Dec. 8/24-Feb. 17/25
Away	14	Dec. 27/64-Feb. 21/65
Longest Winless Streak		
Overall	20	Jan. 28-Mar. 11/62 (16 losses, 4 ties)
Home	11	Dec. 8/24-Feb. 17/25 (11 losses)
Away	14	Three times
Most Shutouts, Season	15	1927-28 (44)
Most PIM, Season	2,443	1987-88 (80)
Most Goals, Game	14	Jan. 21/45 (NYR 3 at Bos. 14)

Individual

Most Seasons	21	John Bucyk, Raymond Bourque
Most Games	1,518	Raymond Bourque
Most Goals, Career	545	John Bucyk
Most Assists, Career	1,111	Raymond Bourque
Most Points, Career	1,506	Raymond Bourque (395G, 1,111A)
Most PIM, Career	2,095	Terry O'Reilly
Most Shutouts, Career	74	Tiny Thompson
Longest Consecutive Games Streak	418	John Bucyk (Jan. 23/69-Mar. 2/75)
Most Goals, Season	76	Phil Esposito (1970-71)
Most Assists, Season	102	Bobby Orr (1970-71)
Most Points, Season	152	Phil Esposito (1970-71; 76G, 76A)
Most PIM, Season	302	Jay Miller (1987-88)
Most Points, Defenseman, Season	*139	Bobby Orr (1970-71; 37G, 102A)
Most Points, Center, Season	152	Phil Esposito (1970-71; 76G, 76A)
Most Points, Right Wing, Season	105	Ken Hodge (1970-71; 43G, 62A), (1973-74; 50G, 55A) Rick Middleton (1983-84; 47G, 58A)
Most Points, Left Wing, Season	116	John Bucyk (1970-71; 51G, 65A)
Most Points, Rookie, Season	102	Joe Juneau (1992-93; 32G, 70A)
Most Shutouts, Season	15	Hal Winkler (1927-28)
Most Goals, Game	4	Twenty one times
Most Assists, Game	6	Ken Hodge (Feb. 9/71) Bobby Orr (Jan. 1/73)
Most Points, Game	7	Bobby Orr (Nov. 15/73; 3G, 4A) Phil Esposito (Dec. 19/74; 3G, 4A) Barry Pederson (Apr. 4/82; 3G, 4A) Cam Neely (Oct. 16/88; 3G, 4A)

* NHL Record.

Retired Numbers

2	Eddie Shore	1926-1940
3	Lionel Hitchman	1925-1934
4	Bobby Orr	1966-1976
5	Dit Clapper	1927-1947
7	Phil Esposito	1967-1975
8	Cam Neely	1986-1996
9	John Bucyk	1957-1978
15	Milt Schmidt	1936-1955
24	Terry O'Reilly	1971-1985
77	Raymond Bourque	1979-2000

All-time Record vs. Other Clubs

Regular Season

	At Home								On Road								Total							
	GP	W	L	T	OL	GF	GA	PTS	GP	W	L	T	OL	GF	GA	PTS	GP	W	L	T	OL	GF	GA	PTS
Anaheim	12	6	6	0	0	34	36	12	11	5	4	2	0	28	24	12	23	11	10	2	0	62	60	24
Atlanta	22	14	4	2	2	81	68	32	22	12	8	0	2	65	65	26	44	26	12	2	4	146	133	58
Buffalo	128	70	42	14	2	459	377	156	129	46	63	15	5	373	459	112	257	116	105	29	7	832	836	268
Calgary	49	30	12	6	1	173	132	67	47	23	20	4	0	159	167	50	96	53	32	10	1	332	299	117
Carolina	90	52	30	7	1	313	237	112	88	43	35	9	1	302	288	96	178	95	65	16	2	615	525	208
Chicago	288	164	90	34	0	1036	817	362	289	96	145	45	3	778	935	240	577	260	235	79	3	1814	1752	602
Colorado	64	31	23	9	1	243	198	72	69	38	25	6	0	283	244	82	133	69	48	15	1	526	442	154
Columbus	4	2	2	0	0	12	10	4	6	3	1	0	2	21	12	8	10	5	3	0	2	33	22	12
Dallas	63	43	9	10	1	270	152	97	63	31	18	13	1	224	179	76	126	74	27	23	2	494	331	173
Detroit	290	155	91	43	1	1013	771	354	288	80	155	52	1	728	961	213	578	235	246	95	2	1741	1732	567
Edmonton	32	23	6	3	0	131	80	49	32	10	11	3	0	106	104	39	64	41	17	6	0	237	184	88
Florida	34	13	14	4	3	87	84	33	33	18	12	2	1	96	95	39	67	31	26	6	4	183	179	72
Los Angeles	65	44	12	6	3	294	185	97	64	34	22	7	1	235	222	76	129	78	34	13	4	529	407	173
Minnesota	6	0	6	0	0	6	19	0	5	2	3	0	0	10	14	4	11	2	9	0	0	16	33	4
Montreal	356	163	133	56	4	1050	965	386	355	102	203	47	3	835	1195	254	711	265	336	103	7	1885	2160	640
Nashville	7	4	2	1	0	20	12	9	9	4	2	0	3	21	25	11	16	8	4	1	3	41	37	20
New Jersey	68	36	18	8	6	251	203	86	65	31	19	11	4	197	165	77	133	67	37	19	10	448	368	163
NY Islanders	71	40	18	11	2	260	195	93	73	32	29	10	2	231	237	76	144	72	47	21	4	491	432	169
NY Rangers	310	165	99	42	4	1095	860	376	314	118	139	55	2	874	959	293	624	283	238	97	6	1969	1819	669
Ottawa	54	32	16	5	1	183	140	70	52	28	15	3	6	155	126	65	106	60	31	8	7	338	266	135
Philadelphia	88	50	23	11	4	313	247	115	85	40	33	10	2	256	270	92	173	90	56	21	6	569	517	207
Phoenix	33	22	6	4	1	140	101	49	33	16	14	3	0	109	106	35	66	38	20	7	1	249	207	84
Pittsburgh	90	62	19	6	3	383	251	133	92	40	35	15	2	330	315	97	182	102	54	21	5	713	566	230
St. Louis	62	35	15	9	3	253	172	82	62	25	24	9	4	210	196	63	124	60	39	18	7	463	368	145
San Jose	13	7	3	3	0	43	39	17	13	7	4	2	0	42	32	16	26	14	7	5	0	85	71	33
Tampa Bay	35	25	4	6	0	135	82	56	35	18	14	3	0	104	101	39	70	43	18	9	0	239	183	95
Toronto	319	174	95	47	3	1039	852	398	320	104	160	51	5	834	1060	264	639	278	255	98	8	1873	1912	662
Vancouver	54	39	7	7	1	221	127	86	54	29	17	8	0	215	172	66	108	68	24	15	1	436	299	152
Washington	68	40	17	9	2	239	178	91	67	32	20	12	3	221	193	79	135	72	37	21	5	460	371	170
Defunct Clubs	164	112	39	13	0	525	306	237	164	79	67	18	0	496	440	176	328	191	106	31	0	1021	746	413
Totals	**2939**	**1653**	**861**	**376**	**49**	**10302**	**7896**	**3731**	**2939**	**1154**	**1317**	**415**	**53**	**8538**	**9361**	**2776**	**5878**	**2807**	**2178**	**791**	**102**	**18840**	**17257**	**6507**

Playoffs

	Series	W	L	GP	W	L	T	GF	GA	Last Mtg.	Rnd.	Result
Buffalo	8	6	2	45	25	20	0	155	145	2010	CQF	W 4-2
Carolina	4	3	1	26	15	11	0	80	64	2009	CSF	L 3-4
Chicago	6	5	1	22	16	5	1	97	63	1978	QF	W 4-0
Colorado	2	1	1	11	6	5	0	37	36	1983	DSF	W 3-1
Dallas	1	0	1	3	0	3	0	13	20	1981	PRE	L 0-3
Detroit	7	4	3	33	19	14	0	96	98	1957	SF	W 4-1
Edmonton	2	0	2	9	1	8	0	20	41	1990	F	L 1-4
Florida	1	0	1	5	1	4	0	16	22	1996	CQF	L 1-4
Los Angeles	2	2	0	13	8	5	0	56	38	1977	QF	W 4-2
Montreal	33	9	24	170	68	102	0	420	511	2011	CQF	W 4-3
New Jersey	4	1	3	23	8	15	0	60	68	2003	CQF	L 1-4
NY Islanders	2	0	2	11	3	8	0	35	49	1983	CF	L 2-4
NY Rangers	9	6	3	42	22	18	2	114	104	1973	QF	L 1-4
Philadelphia	6	3	3	31	18	13	0	100	86	2011	CSF	W 4-0
Pittsburgh	4	2	2	19	9	10	0	62	67	1992	CF	L 0-4
St. Louis	2	2	0	8	8	0	0	48	15	1972	SF	W 4-0
Tampa Bay	1	1	0	7	4	3	0	21	21	2011	CF	W 4-3
Toronto	13	5	8	62	30	31	1	153	150	1974	QF	W 4-0
Vancouver	1	1	0	7	4	3	0	23	8	2011	F	W 4-3
Washington	2	1	1	10	6	4	0	28	21	1998	CQF	L 2-4
Defunct Clubs	3	1	2	11	4	5	2	20	20			
Totals	**113**	**53**	**60**	**568**	**275**	**287**	**6**	**1654**	**1647**			

Calgary totals include Atlanta Flames, 1972-73 to 1979-80.
Carolina totals include Hartford, 1979-80 to 1996-97.
Colorado totals include Quebec, 1979-80 to 1994-95.
Dallas totals include Minnesota North Stars, 1967-68 to 1992-93.
New Jersey totals include Kansas City, 1974-75, 1975-76, and Colorado Rockies, 1976-77 to 1981-82.
Phoenix totals include Winnipeg, 1979-80 to 1995-96.

Playoff Results 2011-2007

Year	Round	Opponent	Result	GF	GA
2011	**F**	**Vancouver**	**W 4-3**	**23**	**8**
	CF	Tampa Bay	W 4-3	21	21
	CSF	Philadelphia	W 4-0	20	7
	CQF	Montreal	W 4-3	17	17
2010	CSF	Philadelphia	L 3-4	20	22
	CQF	Buffalo	W 4-2	16	15
2009	CSF	Carolina	L 3-4	17	16
	CQF	Montreal	W 4-0	17	6
2008	CQF	Montreal	L 3-4	15	19

Abbreviations: Round: F - Final; **CF** - conference final; **CSF** - conference semi-final; **CQF** - conference quarter-final; **DSF** - division semi-final; **SF** - semi-final; **QF** - quarter-final; **PRE** - preliminary round.

2010-11 Results

Month	Date	Opponent	Score
Oct.	9	Phoenix	2-5
	10	at Phoenix	3-0
	16	at New Jersey	4-1
	19	at Washington	3-1
	21	Washington	4-1
	23	NY Rangers	2-3
	28	Toronto	2-0
	30	at Ottawa	4-0
Nov.	3	at Buffalo	5-2
	5	at Washington	3-5
	6	St. Louis	1-2†
	10	at Pittsburgh	7-4
	11	Montreal	1-3
	13	Ottawa	0-2
	15	New Jersey	3-0
	17	at NY Rangers	3-2
	18	Florida	4-0
	20	Los Angeles	3-4†
	22	at Tampa Bay	1-3
	24	at Florida	3-1
	26	Carolina	0-3
	28	at Atlanta	1-4
Dec.	1	at Philadelphia	3-0
	2	Tampa Bay	8-1
	4	at Toronto	2-3†
	7	Buffalo	3-2*
	9	NY Islanders	5-2
	11	Philadelphia	1-2*
	15	at Buffalo	2-3
	16	at Montreal	3-4
	18	Washington	3-2
	20	Anaheim	0-3
	23	Atlanta	4-1
	27	at Florida	3-2†
	28	at Tampa Bay	4-3
	30	at Atlanta	2-3†
Jan.	1	at Buffalo	6-7†
	3	at Toronto	2-1
	6	Minnesota	1-3
	8	at Montreal	2-3*
	10	at Pittsburgh	4-2
	11	Ottawa	6-0
	13	Philadelphia	7-5
	15	Pittsburgh	2-3
	17	Carolina	7-0
	18	at Carolina	3-2
	20	Buffalo	2-4
	22	at Colorado	6-2
	24	at Los Angeles	0-2
	26	Florida	2-1
Feb.	1	at Carolina	3-2
	3	Dallas	6-3
	5	San Jose	0-2
	9	Montreal	8-6
	11	Detroit	1-6
	13	at Detroit	2-4
	15	Toronto	3-4
	17	at NY Islanders	6-3
	18	at Ottawa	4-2
	22	at Calgary	3-1
	26	at Vancouver	3-1
	27	at Edmonton	3-2
Mar.	1	at Ottawa	1-0
	3	Tampa Bay	2-1
	5	Pittsburgh	2-3*
	8	at Montreal	1-4
	10	Buffalo	3-4*
	11	at NY Islanders	2-4
	15	at Columbus	3-2†
	17	at Nashville	3-4*
	19	at Toronto	2-5
	22	New Jersey	4-1
	24	Montreal	7-0
	26	NY Rangers	0-1
	27	at Philadelphia	2-1
	29	Chicago	3-0
	31	Toronto	3-4†
Apr.	2	Atlanta	3-2
	4	at NY Rangers	3-5
	6	NY Islanders	3-2
	9	Ottawa	3-1
	10	at New Jersey	2-3

* – Overtime † – Shootout

Entry Draft Selections 2011-1997

Name in bold denotes played in NHL.

2011
Pick
9	Dougie Hamilton
40	Alexander Khokhlachev
81	Anthony Camara
121	Brian Ferlin
151	Rob O'Gara
181	Lars Volden

2010
Pick
2	**Tyler Seguin**
32	Jared Knight
45	Ryan Spooner
97	Craig Cunningham
135	Justin Florek
165	Zane Gothberg
195	Maxim Chudinov
210	Zach Trotman

2009
Pick
25	**Jordan Caron**
86	Ryan Button
112	Lane MacDermid
176	Tyler Randell
206	Ben Sexton

2008
Pick
16	Joe Colborne
47	Max Sauve
77	Michael Hutchinson
97	**Jamie Arniel**
173	Nick Tremblay
197	Mark Goggin

2007
Pick
8	**Zach Hamill**
35	Tommy Cross
130	Denis Reul
159	Alain Goulet
169	Radim Ostrcil
189	Jordan Knackstedt

2006
Pick
5	**Phil Kessel**
37	Yury Alexandrov
50	**Milan Lucic**
71	**Brad Marchand**
128	**Andrew Bodnarchuk**
158	Levi Nelson

2005
Pick
22	**Matt Lashoff**
39	Petr Kalus
83	Mikko Lehtonen
100	**Jonathan Sigalet**
106	**Vladimir Sobotka**
154	Wacey Rabbit
172	Lukas Vantuch
217	Brock Bradford

2004
Pick
63	**David Krejci**
64	**Martins Karsums**
108	Ashton Rome
134	**Kris Versteeg**
160	**Ben Walter**
224	**Matt Hunwick**
255	Anton Hedman

2003
Pick
21	**Mark Stuart**
45	**Patrice Bergeron**
66	Masi Marjamaki
107	**Byron Bitz**
118	Frank Rediker
129	Patrik Valcak
153	Mike Brown
183	**Nate Thompson**
247	Benoit Mondou
277	Kevin Regan

2002
Pick
29	**Hannu Toivonen**
56	Vladislav Evseev
130	Jan Kubista
153	Peter Hamerlik
228	Dmitri Utkin
259	**Yan Stastny**
290	Pavel Frolov

2001
Pick
19	**Shaone Morrisonn**
77	Darren McLachlan
111	Matti Kaltiainen
147	Jiri Jakes
179	**Andrew Alberts**
209	**Jordan Sigalet**
241	Milan Jurcina
282	Marcel Rodman

2000
Pick
7	**Lars Jonsson**
27	**Martin Samuelsson**
37	**Andy Hilbert**
59	**Ivan Huml**
66	Tuukka Makela
73	**Sergei Zinovjev**
103	Brett Nowak
174	**Jarno Kultanen**
204	Chris Berti
237	Zdenek Kutlak
268	Pavel Kolarik
279	Andreas Lindstrom

1999
Pick
21	**Nick Boynton**
56	Matt Zultek
89	Kyle Wanvig
118	Jaakko Harikkala
147	Seamus Kotyk
179	Donald Choukalos
207	Greg Barber
236	John Cronin
247	Mikko Eloranta
264	Georgy Pujacs

1998
Pick
48	**Jonathan Girard**
52	Bobby Allen
78	**Peter Nordstrom**
135	**Andrew Raycroft**
165	Ryan Milanovic

1997
Pick
1	**Joe Thornton**
8	**Sergei Samsonov**
27	**Ben Clymer**
54	Mattias Karlin
63	Lee Goren
81	Karol Bartanus
135	Denis Timofeev
162	Joel Trottier
180	Jim Baxter
191	**Antti Laaksonen**
218	Eric Van Acker
246	Jay Henderson

Captains' History

No captain, 1924-25 to 1926-27; Lionel Hitchman, 1927-28 to 1930-31; George Owen, 1931-32; Dit Clapper, 1932-33 to 1937-38; Cooney Weiland, 1938-39; Dit Clapper, 1939-40 to 1945-46; Dit Clapper and John Crawford, 1946-47; John Crawford 1947-48 to 1949-50; Milt Schmidt, 1950-51 to 1953-54; Milt Schmidt, Ed Sanford, 1954-55; Fern Flaman, 1955-56 to 1960-61; Don McKenney, 1961-62, 1962-63; Leo Boivin, 1963-64 to 1965-66; John Bucyk, 1966-67; no captain, 1967-68 to 1972-73; John Bucyk, 1973-74 to 1976-77; Wayne Cashman, 1977-78 to 1982-83; Terry O'Reilly, 1983-84, 1984-85; Raymond Bourque, Rick Middleton (co-captains) 1985-86 to 1987-88; Raymond Bourque, 1988-89 to 1999-2000; Jason Allison, 2000-01; no captain, 2001-02; Joe Thornton, 2002-03, 2003-04; Joe Thornton and no captain, 2005-06; Zdeno Chara, 2006-07 to date.

General Managers' History

Art Ross, 1924-25 to 1953-54; Lynn Patrick, 1954-55 to 1964-65; Hap Emms, 1965-66, 1966-67; Milt Schmidt, 1967-68 to 1971-72; Harry Sinden, 1972-73 to 1999-2000; Harry Sinden and Mike O'Connell, 2000-01; Mike O'Connell, 2001-02 to 2004-05; Mike O'Connell and Jeff Gorton, 2005-06; Peter Chiarelli, 2006-07 to date.

Peter Chiarelli

General Manager

Born: Nepean, Ont., August 5, 1964.

Peter Chiarelli became just the seventh man in club history to hold the position of general manager when he was named to the post on May 26, 2006. He officially began his position in Boston on July 10, 2006 as a result of a league-arbitrated compensation agreement that saw the Bruins surrender a third-round draft pick in the 2006 NHL Entry Draft (Eric Gryba, 68th overall) to the Ottawa Senators. By his third season in Boston in 2008-09, the Bruins posted the best record in the Eastern Conference and were second overall in the NHL. In 2010-11, Boston won the Stanley Cup for the first time since 1972.

Chiarelli came to the Bruins after seven seasons with the Ottawa Senators, five as the director of legal relations and the last two as assistant general manager. He was involved in all aspects of that team's hockey operations, including contract research and negotiations, salary arbitration and all player personnel matters. He was also involved in overseeing Ottawa's top developmental affiliate, the Binghamton Senators of the American Hockey League. The Senators had four 100+ point seasons during his tenure and never finished below 94 points, finished with the NHL's top record in 2002-03 (113 points) and the best record in the Eastern Conference in 2005-06 (113 points).

A native of the Ottawa area, Chiarelli played four seasons of college hockey at Harvard University where he served the team as captain and was a teammate of former Bruin Don Sweeney. He had 21 goals and 28 assists for 49 points with 70 penalty minutes in 109 career college games and earned his degree in Economics in 1987. He played professionally in Europe for one year before returning to school and obtaining his law degree from the University of Ottawa. He was admitted to the Ontario bar in 1993 and spent six years as a lawyer and player agent prior to joining the Senators front office in 1999.

Club Directory

TD Garden

Boston Bruins
TD Garden
100 Legends Way
Boston, MA 02114
Phone **617/624-BEAR (2327)**
FAX 617/523-7184
www.bostonbruins.com
Capacity: 17,565

Ownership
Owner & Governor, Boston Bruins; Chairman, NHL Board of Governors	Jeremy M. Jacobs
Principal, Boston Bruins	Charlie Jacobs
Alternate Governors	Charlie Jacobs, Jeremy Jacobs, Jr., Louis Jacobs, Harry Sinden, Peter Chiarelli, Cam Neely
Senior Advisor to the Owner	Harry Sinden

Executive
President	Cam Neely
Sr. Vice President, Sales & Marketing	Amy Latimer
Vice President, Finance	Jim Bednarek
Vice President, Marketing	Jen Compton
Vice President, Corporate Partnerships	Chris Johnson
Director of Administration	Dale Hamilton-Powers
Executive Secretary	Rita Brandano
Administrative Assistant	Karen Ondo

Hockey Operations
General Manager	Peter Chiarelli
Assistant General Managers	Jim Benning, Don Sweeney
Director of Player Personnel	Scott Bradley
Director of Amateur Scouting	Wayne Smith
Assistant Director of Amateur Scouting	Scott Fitzgerald
Scouting Staff	Mike Chiarelli, Adam Creighton, Keith Gretzky, Jack Higgins, Jukka Holtari, Denis LeBlanc, Dean Malkoc, Mike McGraw, Tom McVie, Svenake Svensson
Director of Hockey Administration & Scout	Ryan Nadeau
Team Road Services Coordinator	John Bucyk

Coaching
Head Coach	Claude Julien
Assistant Coaches	Doug Houda, Geoff Ward, Doug Jarvis
Goaltending Coach	Bob Essensa
Video Analyst	Jeremy Rogalski

Medical, Training and Equipment
Strength & Conditioning Coach	John Whitesides
Athletic Trainer	Don DelNegro
Physical Therapist	Scott Waugh
Assistant Athletic Trainer & Massage Therapist	Derek Repucci
Equipment Manager	Keith Robinson
Assistant Equipment Managers	Jim 'Beets' Johnson, Matt Falconer
Head Team Physician/Orthopedist	Dr. Peter Asnis
Team Psychologists	Dr. Frank Lodato, Dr. Max Offenberger

Communications and Community Relations
Director of Communications	Matthew Chmura
Director of Publications & Information	Heidi Holland
Director of Community Relations	Kerry Collins
Director of Development, Bruins Foundation	Bob Sweeney
Director of Interactive	Darrell Wood
Assistant Director of Media Relations	Eric Tosi
Content Manager, BostonBruins.com	John Bishop
Public Relations Coordinator	Kelly Mohr
Community Relations Coordinator	Cathlin Allen
Boston Bruins Foundation Manager	Erin McEvoy
Boston Bruins Foundation Coordinator	Zack Fitzgerald
Web Video Producer	Jonathan Gotlib
Boston Bruins Alumni Coordinator	Mal Viola

Sales, Marketing and Retail
Vice President, Premium Sales & Service	Leah Leahy
Client Services Manager, The Premium Club	Tamala Levin
Director of Marketing	Chris DiPierro
Director of Ticket Sales	Mark Rodrigues
Retail Director	Lauma Cerlins
Ticket Sales Manager	Sean Cummings
Digital Marketing Manager	Liz d'Entremont
Strategic Marketing Manager	Rachel Markovitz
Youth Hockey Development Manager	Chris Uber
Graphic Designer	Jason Petrie
Promotions Coordinator	Brett Bovio
Marketing Coordinator	Laura Caso
Fan Relations Representatives	John Cadigan, Nick Camara, Mae Larson, Courtney McNeice, Kaitlin Rowe
Season Sales Account Executives	Adam DiVincenzo, Matt Gulley, Chris Silvia, Tina Zettel
Group Sales Account Executives	Charlie Karoly, Briana Lynch, Caillin Miller, Eric Spirko

Finance, Legal, Human Resources and Box Office
Controller	Rick McGlinchey
Staff Accountant	Linda Bartlett
Payroll & Benefits Manager	Botin Bou
Assistant General Counsel	Matt Reece
Legal Assistant	Binnie Hundley
Director of Human Resources	Joe Lawlor
Human Resources Generalist	Kate Gibbon
Director of Ticket Operations	Matthew Whelan
Assistant Director of Ticket Operations	Jim Foley
Ticket Office Receptionist	Jo-Ann Connolly-White
Business Analyst	Matt Synakowski

Broadcasting
TV Rightsholder	New England Sports Network (NESN)
Radio play-by-play / analyst	Jack Edwards / Andy Brickley
Radio Rightsholder	98.5 The Sports Hub (CBS Radio Boston)
Radio play-by-play / analyst	Dave Goucher / Bob Beers

Buffalo Sabres

Key Off-Season Signings/Acquisitions

2011

June 3 • Re-signed RW **Drew Stafford**.

25 • Acquired D **Robyn Regehr**, RW **Ales Kotalik** and a 2nd-round pick in the 2012 Entry Draft from Calgary for D **Chris Butler** and C **Paul Byron**.

29 • Re-signed C **Nathan Gerbe**.

29 • Acquired the rights to negotiate with D **Christian Ehrhoff** from NY Islanders for a 4th-round pick in the 2012 Entry Draft.

30 • Signed D **Christian Ehrhoff**.

July 1 • Signed LW **Ville Leino**.

1 • Re-signed C **Cody McCormick**.

4 • Re-signed D **Mike Weber**.

19 • Re-signed D **Andrej Sekera** and LW **Matt Ellis**.

21 • Re-signed G **Jhonas Enroth**.

Aug. 3 • Named **Kevyn Adams** assistant coach.

2010-11 Results: 43W-29L-9OTL-1SOL 96PTS.
Third, Northeast Division

Drew Stafford established career highs with 31 goals and 52 points for the Sabres in 2010-11 despite playing just 62 games. His plus-minus rating of +13 was the best among Buffalo forwards.

2011-12 Schedule

Oct.	Fri.	7	Anaheim†
	Sat.	8	at Los Angeles††
	Fri.	14	Carolina
	Sat.	15	at Pittsburgh
	Tue.	18	at Montreal
	Thu.	20	at Florida
	Sat.	22	at Tampa Bay
	Tue.	25	Tampa Bay
	Thu.	27	Columbus
	Sat.	29	Florida
Nov.	Wed.	2	Philadelphia
	Fri.	4	Calgary
	Sat.	5	at Ottawa
	Tue.	8	Winnipeg
	Fri.	11	Ottawa
	Sat.	12	at Boston
	Mon.	14	at Montreal
	Wed.	16	New Jersey
	Fri.	18	at Carolina
	Sat.	19	Phoenix
	Wed.	23	Boston
	Fri.	25	at Columbus
	Sat.	26	Washington
	Tue.	29	NY Islanders
Dec.	Fri.	2	Detroit
	Sat.	3	at Nashville
	Wed.	7	Philadelphia
	Fri.	9	Florida
	Sat.	10	NY Rangers
	Tue.	13	Ottawa
	Fri.	16	Toronto
	Sat.	17	at Pittsburgh
	Tue.	20	at Ottawa
	Thu.	22	at Toronto
	Mon.	26	Washington
	Wed.	28	at New Jersey
	Fri.	30	at Washington
	Sat.	31	Ottawa
Jan.	Tue.	3	Edmonton
	Fri.	6	at Carolina
	Sat.	7	Winnipeg

	Tue.	10	at Toronto
	Fri.	13	Toronto
	Sat.	14	at NY Islanders
	Mon.	16	at Detroit
	Wed.	18	at Chicago
	Thu.	19	at Winnipeg
	Sat.	21	at St. Louis
	Tue.	24	at New Jersey
	Tue.	31	at Montreal
Feb.	Wed.	1	NY Rangers
	Sat.	4	at NY Islanders
	Wed.	8	Boston
	Fri.	10	Dallas
	Sat.	11	Tampa Bay
	Tue.	14	New Jersey
	Thu.	16	at Philadelphia
	Fri.	17	Montreal
	Sun.	19	Pittsburgh*
	Tue.	21	NY Islanders
	Fri.	24	Boston
	Sat.	25	at NY Rangers
	Wed.	29	at Anaheim
Mar.	Thu.	1	at San Jose
	Sat.	3	at Vancouver
	Mon.	5	at Winnipeg
	Wed.	7	Carolina
	Thu.	8	at Boston
	Sat.	10	at Ottawa
	Mon.	12	Montreal
	Wed.	14	Colorado
	Sat.	17	at Florida
	Mon.	19	at Tampa Bay
	Wed.	21	Montreal
	Fri.	23	at NY Rangers
	Sat.	24	Minnesota
	Tue.	27	at Washington
	Fri.	30	Pittsburgh
	Sat.	31	at Toronto
Apr.	Tue.	3	Toronto
	Thu.	5	at Philadelphia
	Sat.	7	at Boston*

* Denotes afternoon game.   † Game played in Helsinki.
†† Game played in Berlin.

NORTHEAST DIVISION
42nd NHL Season

Franchise date: May 22, 1970

Year-by-Year Record

Season	GP	Home W	L	T	OL	Road W	L	T	OL	Overall W	L	T	OL	GF	GA	Pts.	Finished	Playoff Result
2010-11	82	21	16	....	4	22	13	....	6	43	29	....	10	245	229	96	3rd, Northeast Div.	Lost Conf. Quarter-Final
2009-10	82	25	10	....	6	20	17	....	4	45	27	....	10	235	207	100	1st, Northeast Div.	Lost Conf. Quarter-Final
2008-09	82	23	15	....	3	18	17	....	6	41	32	....	9	250	234	91	3rd, Northeast Div.	Out of Playoffs
2007-08	82	20	15	....	6	19	16	....	6	39	31	....	12	255	242	90	4th, Northeast Div.	Out of Playoffs
2006-07	82	28	10	....	3	25	12	....	4	53	22	....	7	308	242	113	1st, Northeast Div.	Lost Conf. Championship
2005-06	82	27	11	....	3	25	13	....	3	52	24	....	6	281	239	110	2nd, Northeast Div.	Lost Conf. Championship
2004-05	....			....				....		....		....				....		
2003-04	82	21	13	4	3	16	21	3	1	37	34	7	4	220	221	85	5th, Northeast Div.	Out of Playoffs
2002-03	82	18	16	5	2	9	21	5	6	27	37	10	8	190	219	72	5th, Northeast Div.	Out of Playoffs
2001-02	82	20	16	5	0	15	19	6	1	35	35	11	1	213	200	82	5th, Northeast Div.	Out of Playoffs
2000-01	82	26	12	3	0	20	18	2	1	46	30	5	1	218	184	98	2nd, Northeast Div.	Lost Conf. Semi-Final
1999-2000	82	21	14	5	1	14	18	6	3	35	32	11	4	213	204	85	3rd, Northeast Div.	Lost Conf. Quarter-Final
1998-99	82	23	12	6	....	14	16	11	....	37	28	17	....	207	175	91	4th, Northeast Div.	Lost Final
1997-98	82	20	13	8	....	16	16	9	....	36	29	17	....	211	187	89	3rd, Northeast Div.	Lost Conf. Championship
1996-97	82	24	11	6	....	16	19	6	....	40	30	12	....	237	208	92	1st, Northeast Div.	Lost Conf. Semi-Final
1995-96	82	19	17	5	....	14	25	2	....	33	42	7	....	247	262	73	5th, Northeast Div.	Out of Playoffs
1994-95	48	15	8	1	....	7	11	6	....	22	19	7	....	130	119	51	4th, Northeast Div.	Lost Conf. Quarter-Final
1993-94	84	22	17	3	....	21	15	6	....	43	32	9	....	282	218	95	4th, Northeast Div.	Lost Conf. Quarter-Final
1992-93	84	25	15	2	....	13	21	8	....	38	36	10	....	335	297	86	4th, Adams Div.	Lost Div. Final
1991-92	80	22	13	5	....	9	24	7	....	31	37	12	....	289	299	74	3rd, Adams Div.	Lost Div. Semi-Final
1990-91	80	15	13	12	....	16	17	7	....	31	30	19	....	292	278	81	3rd, Adams Div.	Lost Div. Semi-Final
1989-90	80	27	11	2	....	18	16	6	....	45	27	8	....	286	248	98	2nd, Adams Div.	Lost Div. Semi-Final
1988-89	80	25	12	3	....	13	23	4	....	38	35	7	....	291	299	83	3rd, Adams Div.	Lost Div. Semi-Final
1987-88	80	19	14	7	....	18	18	4	....	37	32	11	....	283	305	85	3rd, Adams Div.	Lost Div. Semi-Final
1986-87	80	18	18	4	....	10	26	4	....	28	44	8	....	280	308	64	5th, Adams Div.	Out of Playoffs
1985-86	80	23	16	1	....	14	21	5	....	37	37	6	....	296	291	80	5th, Adams Div.	Out of Playoffs
1984-85	80	23	10	7	....	15	18	7	....	38	28	14	....	290	237	90	3rd, Adams Div.	Lost Div. Semi-Final
1983-84	80	25	9	6	....	23	16	1	....	48	25	7	....	315	257	103	2nd, Adams Div.	Lost Div. Semi-Final
1982-83	80	25	7	8	....	13	22	5	....	38	29	13	....	318	285	89	3rd, Adams Div.	Lost Div. Final
1981-82	80	23	8	9	....	16	18	6	....	39	26	15	....	307	273	93	3rd, Adams Div.	Lost Div. Semi-Final
1980-81	80	21	7	12	....	18	13	9	....	39	20	21	....	327	250	99	1st, Adams Div.	Lost Quarter-Final
1979-80	80	27	5	8	....	20	12	8	....	47	17	16	....	318	201	110	1st, Adams Div.	Lost Semi-Final
1978-79	80	19	13	8	....	17	15	8	....	36	28	16	....	280	263	88	2nd, Adams Div.	Lost Prelim. Round
1977-78	80	25	7	8	....	19	12	9	....	44	19	17	....	288	215	105	2nd, Adams Div.	Lost Quarter-Final
1976-77	80	27	8	5	....	21	16	3	....	48	24	8	....	301	220	104	2nd, Adams Div.	Lost Quarter-Final
1975-76	80	28	7	5	....	18	14	8	....	46	21	13	....	339	240	105	2nd, Adams Div.	Lost Quarter-Final
1974-75	80	28	6	6	....	21	10	9	....	49	16	15	....	354	240	113	1st, Adams Div.	Lost Final
1973-74	78	23	10	6	....	9	24	6	....	32	34	12	....	242	250	76	5th, East Div.	Out of Playoffs
1972-73	78	30	6	3	....	7	21	11	....	37	27	14	....	257	219	88	4th, East Div.	Lost Quarter-Final
1971-72	78	11	19	9	....	5	24	10	....	16	43	19	....	203	289	51	6th, East Div.	Out of Playoffs
1970-71	78	16	13	10	....	8	26	5	....	24	39	15	....	217	291	63	5th, East Div.	Out of Playoffs

2011-12 Player Personnel

FORWARDS	HT	WT	S	Place of Birth	*Age	2010-11 Club
BOYES, Brad	6-0	204	R	Mississauga, Ont.	29	St. Louis-Buffalo
ELLIS, Matt	6-0	212	L	Welland, Ont.	30	Buffalo-Portland (AHL)
ENNIS, Tyler	5-9	157	L	Edmonton, Alta.	22	Buffalo
GAUSTAD, Paul	6-5	212	L	Fargo, ND	29	Buffalo
GERBE, Nathan	5-5	178	L	Oxford, MI	24	Buffalo
HECHT, Jochen	6-1	198	L	Mannheim, West Germany	34	Buffalo
KALETA, Patrick	6-1	206	R	Buffalo, NY	25	Buffalo
KOTALIK, Ales	6-1	225	R	Jindrichuv Hradec, Czech.	32	Calgary-Abbotsford
LEINO, Ville	6-1	190	L	Savonlinna, Finland	28	Philadelphia
McCORMICK, Cody	6-3	221	R	London, Ont.	28	Buffalo
POMINVILLE, Jason	6-0	185	R	Repentigny, Que.	28	Buffalo
ROY, Derek	5-9	184	L	Ottawa, Ont.	28	Buffalo
STAFFORD, Drew	6-2	214	R	Milwaukee, WI	25	Buffalo
VANEK, Thomas	6-2	205	R	Vienna, Austria	27	Buffalo

DEFENSEMEN						
EHRHOFF, Christian	6-2	203	L	Moers, West Germany	29	Vancouver
GRAGNANI, Marc-Andre	6-2	201	L	Montreal, Que.	24	Buffalo-Portland (AHL)
LEOPOLD, Jordan	6-1	206	L	Golden Valley, MN	31	Buffalo
MORRISONN, Shaone	6-4	210	L	Vancouver, B.C.	28	Buffalo
MYERS, Tyler	6-8	227	R	Houston, TX	21	Buffalo
REGEHR, Robyn	6-3	225	L	Recife, Brazil	31	Calgary
SEKERA, Andrej	6-0	201	L	Bojnice, Czech.	25	Buffalo
WEBER, Mike	6-2	211	L	Pittsburgh, PA	23	Buffalo

GOALTENDERS	HT	WT	C	Place of Birth	*Age	2010-11 Club
ENROTH, Jhonas	5-10	166	L	Stockholm, Sweden	23	Buffalo-Portland (AHL)
MILLER, Ryan	6-2	175	L	East Lansing, MI	31	Buffalo

* – Age at start of 2011-12 season

Coaching History

Punch Imlach, 1970-71; Punch Imlach, Floyd Smith and Joe Crozier, 1971-72; Joe Crozier, 1972-73, 1973-74; Floyd Smith, 1974-75 to 1976-77; Marcel Pronovost, 1977-78; Marcel Pronovost and Billy Inglis, 1978-79; Scotty Bowman, 1979-80; Roger Neilson, 1980-81; Jim Roberts and Scotty Bowman, 1981-82; Scotty Bowman 1982-83 to 1984-85; Jim Schoenfeld and Scotty Bowman, 1985-86; Scotty Bowman, Craig Ramsay and Ted Sator, 1986-87; Ted Sator, 1987-88, 1988-89; Rick Dudley, 1989-90, 1990-91; Rick Dudley and John Muckler, 1991-92; John Muckler, 1992-93 to 1994-95; Ted Nolan, 1995-96, 1996-97; Lindy Ruff, 1997-98 to date.

Lindy Ruff

Head Coach

Born: Warburg, Alta., February 17, 1960.

A former captain of the Sabres, Lindy Ruff was appointed as the club's 15th head coach on July 21, 1997. In 1999, he led the Sabres to the Stanley Cup Finals for just the second time in club history and in 2006 he guided the Sabres to the Eastern Conference Final and was rewarded with the Jack Adams Award as coach of the year. The Sabres won the Presidents' Trophy for finishing first overall in the NHL standings in 2006-07, recording 113 points and a franchise-record 53 wins. Ruff and Toe Blake are the only men in history to win 500 games while coaching just one NHL team. As a player, Ruff was drafted 32nd overall by the Sabres in the 1979 Entry Draft. He played both defense and left wing in an NHL career that spanned 12 seasons including 608 regular-season games with Buffalo. He became a playing assistant coach with Rochester of the AHL in 1991-92 and San Diego of the IHL in 1992-93. Ruff's San Diego club set a pro hockey record with 62 wins. In 1993-94 he became an NHL assistant coach with the Florida Panthers.

Coaching Record

			Regular Season				Playoffs			
Season	Team	League	GC	W	L	O/T	GC	W	L	T
1997-98	Buffalo	NHL	82	36	29	17	15	10	5	....
1998-99	Buffalo	NHL	82	37	28	17	21	14	7	....
99-2000	Buffalo	NHL	82	35	32	15	5	1	4	....
2000-01	Buffalo	NHL	82	46	30	6	13	7	6	....
2001-02	Buffalo	NHL	82	35	35	12	....	....	....	....
2002-03	Buffalo	NHL	82	27	37	18	....	....	....	....
2003-04	Buffalo	NHL	82	37	34	11	....	....	....	....
2004-05	Buffalo				SEASON CANCELLED					
2005-06	Buffalo	NHL	82	52	24	6	18	11	7	....
2006-07	Buffalo	NHL	82	53	22	7	16	9	7	....
2007-08	Buffalo	NHL	82	39	31	12	....	....	....	....
2008-09	Buffalo	NHL	82	41	32	9	....	....	....	....
2009-10	Buffalo	NHL	82	45	27	10	6	2	4	....
2010-11	Buffalo	NHL	82	43	29	10	7	3	4	....
	NHL Totals		1066	526	390	150	101	57	44	....

Jack Adams Award (2006)

Assistant coaches Brian McCutheon and Scott Arniel posted an 0-1-0 record as replacement coach when Lindy Ruff was sidelined due to a family medical emergency, March 20, 2006. Game is credited to Ruff's coaching record.

2010-11 Scoring

* – rookie

Regular Season

Pos	#	Player	Team	GP	G	A	Pts	TOI	+/–	PIM	PP	SH	GW	S	%
L	26	Thomas Vanek	BUF	80	32	41	73	17:21	2	24	11	0	5	238	13.4
R	22	Brad Boyes	STL	62	12	29	41	17:10	11	30	4	0	2	132	9.1
			BUF	21	5	9	14	16:28	2	6	2	0	1	46	10.9
			Total	83	17	38	55	16:59	13	36	6	0	3	178	9.6
R	21	Drew Stafford	BUF	62	31	21	52	16:32	13	34	11	0	4	179	17.3
R	29	Jason Pominville	BUF	73	22	30	52	18:09	1	15	5	1	2	215	10.2
C	63 *	Tyler Ennis	BUF	82	20	29	49	15:40	0	30	5	0	1	210	9.5
C	19	Tim Connolly	BUF	68	13	29	42	16:54	–10	20	6	0	3	151	8.6
D	57	Tyler Myers	BUF	80	10	27	37	22:27	0	40	3	0	5	122	8.2
D	3	Jordan Leopold	BUF	71	13	22	35	23:19	–11	36	5	0	1	134	9.7
C	9	Derek Roy	BUF	35	10	25	35	19:32	–1	16	2	0	1	89	11.2
C	42	Nathan Gerbe	BUF	64	16	15	31	13:19	11	34	2	0	3	171	9.4
C	28	Paul Gaustad	BUF	81	12	19	31	15:08	7	101	1	0	3	117	10.3
C	55	Jochen Hecht	BUF	67	12	17	29	17:04	4	40	0	0	4	172	7.0
D	44	Andrej Sekera	BUF	76	3	26	29	21:05	11	34	0	0	0	88	3.4
D	4	Steve Montador	BUF	73	5	21	26	19:43	16	83	0	0	0	118	4.2
C	8	Cody McCormick	BUF	81	8	12	20	10:57	2	142	0	0	1	104	7.7
C	20	Rob Niedermayer	BUF	71	5	14	19	12:45	–8	22	0	0	1	80	6.3
D	6	Mike Weber	BUF	58	4	13	17	16:53	13	69	0	0	0	53	7.5
R	25	Michael Grier	BUF	73	5	11	16	14:23	0	12	0	0	0	107	4.7
R	36	Patrick Kaleta	BUF	51	4	5	9	10:11	–4	78	0	1	0	65	6.2
D	34	Chris Butler	BUF	49	2	7	9	18:10	8	26	0	0	0	52	3.8
R	12	Mark Mancari	BUF	20	1	7	8	12:19	–1	12	1	0	0	43	2.3
D	27	Shaone Morrisonn	BUF	62	1	4	5	16:10	–2	32	0	0	1	44	2.3
C	72 *	Luke Adam	BUF	19	3	1	4	11:12	–6	12	0	0	1	31	9.7
D	17 *	Marc-Andre Gragnani	BUF	9	1	2	3	15:17	0	2	0	0	1	11	9.1
C	24 *	Paul Byron	BUF	8	1	1	2	10:57	0	2	0	0	0	5	20.0
R	10	Mark Parrish	BUF	2	0	0	0	11:46	–2	0	0	0	0	0	0.0
L	23	Colin Stuart	BUF	3	0	0	0	13:09	1	2	0	0	0	5	0.0
L	37	Matt Ellis	BUF	14	0	0	0	10:02	–4	0	0	0	0	20	0.0

Goaltending

No.	Goaltender	GPI	Mins	Avg	W	L	OT	EN	SO	GA	SA	S%	G	A	PIM
30	Ryan Miller	66	3829	2.59	34	22	8	8	5	165	1964	.916	0	2	6
1	* Jhonas Enroth	14	769	2.73	9	2	2	0	1	35	377	.907	0	0	0
40	Patrick Lalime	7	365	2.96	0	5	0	2	0	18	163	.890	0	1	0
	Totals	**82**	**4999**	**2.74**	**43**	**29**	**10**	**10**	**6**	**228**	**2514**	**.909**			

Playoffs

Pos	#	Player	Team	GP	G	A	Pts	TOI	+/–	PIM	PP	SH	GW	OT	S	%
D	17 *	Marc-Andre Gragnani	BUF	7	1	6	7	21:53	0	4	1	0	0	0	9	11.1
D	57	Tyler Myers	BUF	7	1	5	6	23:52	–4	16	0	0	0	0	9	11.1
L	26	Thomas Vanek	BUF	7	5	0	5	17:10	–7	0	4	0	0	0	20	25.0
C	63 *	Tyler Ennis	BUF	7	2	2	4	16:38	4	4	0	0	1	1	17	11.8
R	29	Jason Pominville	BUF	5	1	3	4	15:51	0	2	0	0	1	0	9	11.1
C	20	Rob Niedermayer	BUF	7	1	3	4	14:06	1	2	0	0	0	0	8	12.5
R	36	Patrick Kaleta	BUF	6	1	2	3	10:58	–1	6	0	0	1	0	8	12.5
R	21	Drew Stafford	BUF	7	1	2	3	20:01	1	2	1	0	0	0	33	3.0
C	42	Nathan Gerbe	BUF	7	2	0	2	13:20	–1	18	0	0	0	0	19	10.5
C	19	Tim Connolly	BUF	6	0	2	2	19:04	–2	2	0	0	0	0	12	0.0
C	28	Paul Gaustad	BUF	7	0	2	2	19:19	–6	13	0	0	0	0	14	0.0
D	44	Andrej Sekera	BUF	2	1	0	1	16:18	–1	4	0	0	0	0	4	25.0
R	22	Brad Boyes	BUF	7	1	0	1	14:23	–2	0	1	0	0	0	14	7.1
C	8	Cody McCormick	BUF	7	1	0	1	8:11	–2	2	0	0	0	0	7	14.3
C	55	Jochen Hecht	BUF	1	0	1	1	15:22	0	0	0	0	0	0	2	0.0
C	9	Derek Roy	BUF	1	0	1	1	20:01	–2	0	0	0	0	0	1	0.0
D	3	Jordan Leopold	BUF	5	0	1	1	20:57	0	4	0	0	0	0	5	0.0
D	4	Steve Montador	BUF	6	0	1	1	15:45	–1	8	0	0	0	0	3	0.0
R	25	Michael Grier	BUF	7	0	1	1	9:29	–3	0	0	0	0	0	5	0.0
D	34	Chris Butler	BUF	7	0	1	1	22:59	–3	10	0	0	0	0	6	0.0
D	6	Mike Weber	BUF	7	0	1	1	15:51	–3	6	0	0	0	0	6	0.0
D	27	Shaone Morrisonn	BUF	1	0	0	0	13:22	0	2	0	0	0	0	0	0.0
L	37	Matt Ellis	BUF	1	0	0	0	11:32	0	0	0	0	0	0	0	0.0
R	12	Mark Mancari	BUF	1	0	0	0	9:50	0	0	0	0	0	0	1	0.0

Goaltending

No.	Goaltender	GPI	Mins	Avg	W	L	EN	SO	GA	SA	S%	G	A	PIM
30	Ryan Miller	7	410	2.93	3	4	1	2	20	242	.917	0	1	2
1	* Jhonas Enroth	1	17	3.53	0	0	0	0	1	8	.875	0	0	0
	Totals	**7**	**430**	**3.07**	**3**	**4**	**1**	**2**	**22**	**251**	**.912**			

Captains' History

Floyd Smith, 1970-71; Gerry Meehan, 1971-72 to 1973-74; Gerry Meehan and Jim Schoenfeld, 1974-75; Jim Schoenfeld, 1975-76, 1976-77; Danny Gare, 1977-78 to 1980-81; Danny Gare and Gilbert Perreault, 1981-82; Gilbert Perreault, 1982-83 to 1985-86; Gilbert Perreault and Lindy Ruff, 1986-87; Lindy Ruff, 1987-88; Lindy Ruff and Mike Foligno, 1988-89; Mike Foligno, 1989-90; Mike Foligno and Mike Ramsey, 1990-91; Mike Ramsey, 1991-92; Mike Ramsey and Pat LaFontaine, 1992-93; Pat LaFontaine and Alexander Mogilny, 1993-94; Pat LaFontaine, 1994-95 to 1996-97; Donald Audette and Michael Peca, 1997-98; Michael Peca, 1998-99, 1999-2000; no captain, 2000-01; Stu Barnes. 2001-02, 2002-03; Miroslav Satan, Chris Drury, James Patrick, J.P. Dumont, Danny Briere, 2003-04; Danny Briere and Chris Drury, 2005-06, 2006-07; Jochen Hecht, Toni Lydman, Brian Campbell, Jaroslav Spacek, Jason Pominville, 2007-08; Craig Rivet, 2008-09 to 2010-11.

Club Records

Team

(Figures in brackets for season records are games played; records for fewest points, wins, ties, losses, goals, goals against are for 70 or more games)

Most Points 113   1974-75 (80), 2006-07 (82)
Most Wins 53   2006-07 (82)
Most Ties 21   1980-81 (80)
Most Losses 44   1986-87 (80)
Most Goals 354   1974-75 (80)
Most Goals Against 308   1986-87 (80)
Fewest Points 51   1971-72 (78)
Fewest Wins 16   1971-72 (78)
Fewest Ties 5   2000-01 (82)
Fewest Losses 16   1974-75 (80)
Fewest Goals 190   2002-03 (82)
Fewest Goals Against 175   1998-99 (82)

Longest Winning Streak
Overall 10   Jan. 4-23/84,
      Oct. 4-26/06
Home 12   Nov. 12/72-Jan. 7/73,
      Oct. 13-Dec. 10/89
Away 10   Dec. 10/83-Jan. 23/84,
      Oct. 4-Nov. 13/06

Longest Undefeated Streak
Overall 14   Mar. 6-Apr. 6/80
      (8 wins, 6 ties)
Home 21   Oct. 8/72-Jan. 7/73
      (18 wins, 3 ties)
Away 10   Dec. 10/83-Jan. 23/84
      (10 wins),
      Oct. 4-Nov. 13/06
      (10 wins)

Longest Losing Streak
Overall 8   Jan. 25-Feb. 13/03
Home 7   Oct. 9-Nov. 5/10
Away 7   Oct. 14-Nov. 7/70,
      Feb. 6-27/71,
      Jan. 10-Feb. 3/96,
      Feb. 19-Mar. 21/09

Longest Winless Streak
Overall 12   Nov. 23-Dec. 20/91
      (8 losses, 4 ties),
      Oct. 25-Nov. 19/02
      (10 losses, 2 ties)
Home 12   Jan. 27-Mar. 10/91
      (7 losses, 5 ties)
Away 23   Oct. 30/71-Feb. 19/72
      (15 losses, 8 ties)

Most Shutouts, Season 13   1997-98 (82)
Most PIM, Season *2,713   1991-92 (80)
Most Goals, Game 14   Jan. 21/75
      (Wsh. 2 at Buf. 14),
      Mar. 19/81
      (Tor. 4 at Buf. 14)

Individual

Most Seasons 17   Gilbert Perreault
Most Games 1,191   Gilbert Perreault
Most Goals, Career 512   Gilbert Perreault
Most Assists, Career 814   Gilbert Perreault
Most Points, Career 1,326   Gilbert Perreault
      (512G, 814A)
Most PIM, Career 3,189   Rob Ray
Most Shutouts, Career 55   Dominik Hasek
Longest Consecutive
  Games Streak 776   Craig Ramsay
      (Mar. 27/73-Feb. 10/83)
Most Goals, Season 76   Alexander Mogilny
      (1992-93)
Most Assists, Season 95   Pat LaFontaine
      (1992-93)

Most Points, Season 148   Pat LaFontaine
      (1992-93; 53G, 95A)
Most PIM, Season 354   Rob Ray
      (1991-92)
Most Points, Defenseman,
  Season 81   Phil Housley
      (1989-90; 21G, 60A)
Most Points, Center,
  Season 148   Pat LaFontaine
      (1992-93; 53G, 95A)
Most Points, Right Wing,
  Season 127   Alexander Mogilny
      (1992-93; 76G, 51A)
Most Points, Left Wing,
  Season 95   Rick Martin
      (1974-75; 52G, 43A)
Most Points, Rookie,
  Season 74   Rick Martin
      (1971-72; 44G, 30A)
Most Shutouts, Season 13   Dominik Hasek (1997-98)
Most Goals, Game 5   Dave Andreychuk
      (Feb. 6/86)
Most Assists, Game 5   Gilbert Perreault
      (Feb. 1/76), (Mar. 9/80),
      (Jan. 4/84)
      Dale Hawerchuk
      (Jan. 15/92)
      Pat LaFontaine
      (Mar. 19/92), (Dec. 31/92),
      (Feb. 10/93)
Most Points, Game 7   Gilbert Perreault
      (Feb. 1/76; 2G, 5A)

* NHL Record.

Retired Numbers

2	Tim Horton	1972-1974
7	Rick Martin	1971-1981
11	Gilbert Perreault	1970-1987
14	Rene Robert	1971-1979
16	Pat Lafontaine	1991-1996
18	Danny Gare	1974-1981

All-time Record vs. Other Clubs

Regular Season

	At Home								On Road								Total						
	GP	W	L	T	OL	GF	GA	PTS	GP	W	L	T	OL	GF	GA	PTS	GP	W	L	T	OL	GF	GA	PTS
Anaheim	12	6	3	3	0	35	27	15	12	7	5	0	0	37	27	14	24	13	8	3	0	72	54	29
Atlanta	22	13	6	0	3	98	60	29	22	7	8	1	6	65	71	21	44	20	14	1	9	163	131	50
Boston	129	68	41	15	5	459	373	156	128	44	66	14	4	377	459	106	257	112	107	29	9	836	832	262
Calgary	47	29	13	5	0	194	134	63	49	18	20	11	0	151	166	47	96	47	33	16	0	345	300	110
Carolina	89	53	28	7	1	353	254	114	90	41	33	11	5	270	261	98	179	94	61	18	6	623	515	212
Chicago	56	34	15	7	0	207	144	75	54	19	29	6	0	145	173	44	110	53	44	13	0	352	317	119
Colorado	65	36	19	9	1	252	211	82	67	23	31	11	2	207	237	59	132	59	50	20	3	459	448	141
Columbus	7	3	4	0	0	19	18	6	5	1	3	1	0	11	16	3	12	4	7	1	0	30	34	9
Dallas	54	30	13	11	0	197	145	71	57	23	28	6	0	163	182	52	111	53	41	17	0	360	327	123
Detroit	56	34	13	8	1	237	166	77	58	19	32	5	2	165	211	45	114	53	45	13	3	402	377	122
Edmonton	32	12	13	7	0	114	114	31	32	8	21	3	0	91	125	19	64	20	34	10	0	205	239	50
Florida	35	23	9	3	0	107	72	49	33	17	15	1	0	94	89	35	68	40	24	4	0	201	161	84
Los Angeles	56	31	16	9	0	236	160	71	56	23	23	9	1	192	197	56	112	54	39	18	1	428	357	127
Minnesota	5	1	4	0	0	10	16	2	6	5	1	0	0	17	11	10	11	6	5	0	0	27	27	12
Montreal	123	66	34	19	4	381	321	155	124	45	66	12	1	357	442	103	247	111	100	31	5	738	763	258
Nashville	7	1	4	1	1	20	26	4	7	5	2	0	0	17	12	10	14	6	6	1	1	37	38	14
New Jersey	66	36	20	8	2	239	193	82	66	32	22	9	2	209	187	74	132	68	42	17	5	448	380	158
NY Islanders	73	40	22	9	2	250	207	91	73	31	31	9	2	203	207	73	146	71	53	18	4	453	414	164
NY Rangers	80	46	22	10	2	316	243	104	78	30	30	15	3	211	246	78	158	76	52	25	5	527	489	182
Ottawa	52	29	19	3	1	161	129	62	54	24	20	7	3	142	147	58	106	53	39	10	4	303	276	120
Philadelphia	75	38	28	8	1	251	216	85	79	23	43	12	1	209	273	59	154	61	71	20	2	460	489	144
Phoenix	34	22	6	5	1	135	84	50	33	17	14	2	0	105	96	36	67	39	20	7	1	240	180	86
Pittsburgh	83	39	22	17	5	303	225	100	83	21	43	18	1	250	308	61	166	60	65	35	6	553	533	161
St. Louis	55	30	19	6	0	207	174	66	52	15	28	7	2	132	186	39	107	45	47	13	2	339	360	105
San Jose	15	14	1	0	0	67	41	28	13	3	5	4	1	45	42	11	28	17	6	4	1	112	83	39
Tampa Bay	35	22	11	2	0	117	96	46	35	24	8	3	0	117	80	51	70	46	19	5	0	234	176	97
Toronto	90	58	25	6	1	353	232	123	88	41	32	12	3	301	258	97	178	99	57	18	4	654	490	220
Vancouver	55	29	18	8	0	199	160	66	54	16	27	11	0	165	200	43	109	45	45	19	0	364	360	109
Washington	68	42	20	6	0	260	176	90	68	38	20	9	1	234	180	86	136	80	40	15	1	494	356	176
Defunct Clubs	23	13	5	5	0	94	63	31	23	12	8	3	0	97	76	27	46	25	13	8	0	191	139	58
Totals	**1599**	**898**	**473**	**197**	**31**	**5871**	**4480**	**2024**	**1599**	**632**	**714**	**212**	**41**	**4779**	**5165**	**1517**	**3198**	**1530**	**1187**	**409**	**72**	**10650**	**9645**	**3541**

Playoffs

	Series	W	L	GP	W	L	T	GF	GA	Last Mtg.	Rnd.	Result
Boston	8	2	6	45	20	25	0	145	155	2010	CQF	L 2-4
Carolina	1	0	1	7	3	4	0	17	22	2006	CF	L 3-4
Chicago	2	2	0	9	8	1	0	36	17	1980	QF	W 4-0
Colorado	2	0	2	8	2	6	0	27	35	1985	DSF	L 2-3
Dallas	3	1	2	13	5	8	0	37	39	1999	F	L 2-4
Montreal	7	3	4	35	17	18	0	111	124	1998	CSF	W 4-0
New Jersey	1	0	1	7	3	4	0	14	14	1994	CQF	L 3-4
NY Islanders	4	1	3	21	8	13	0	62	70	2007	CQF	W 4-1
NY Rangers	2	2	0	9	6	3	0	28	19	2007	CSF	W 4-2
Ottawa	4	3	1	21	13	8	0	52	47	2007	CF	L 1-4
Philadelphia	9	3	6	50	21	29	0	141	146	2011	CQF	L 3-4
Pittsburgh	2	0	2	10	4	6	0	26	26	2001	CSF	L 3-4
St. Louis	1	1	0	3	2	1	0	7	3	1976	PRE	W 2-1
Toronto	1	1	0	5	4	1	0	21	16	1999	CF	W 4-1
Vancouver	2	2	0	7	6	1	0	28	14	1981	PRE	W 3-0
Washington	1	0	1	6	2	4	0	13	13	1998	CF	L 2-4
Totals	**50**	**21**	**29**	**256**	**124**	**132**	**0**	**763**	**765**			

Calgary totals include Atlanta Flames, 1972-73 to 1979-80.
Colorado totals include Quebec, 1979-80 to 1994-95.
New Jersey totals include Kansas City, 1974-75, 1975-76, and Colorado Rockies, 1976-77 to 1981-82.
Phoenix totals include Winnipeg, 1979-80 to 1995-96.
Carolina totals include Hartford, 1979-80 to 1996-97.
Dallas totals include Minnesota North Stars, 1970-71 to 1992-93.

Playoff Results 2011-2007

Year	Round	Opponent	Result	GF	GA
2011	CQF	Philadelphia	L 3-4	18	22
2010	CQF	Boston	L 2-4	15	16
2007	CF	Ottawa	L 1-4	10	15
	CSF	NY Rangers	W 4-2	17	13
	CQF	NY Islanders	W 4-1	17	11

Abbreviations: Round: F - Final; **CF** - conference final; **CSF** - conference semi-final; **CQF** - conference quarter-final; **DSF** - division semi-final; **QF** - quarter-final; **PRE** - preliminary round.

Entry Draft Selections 2011-1997

Name in bold denotes played in NHL.

2011 Pick		2007 Pick		2003 Pick		1999 Pick	
16	Joel Armia	31	T.J. Brennan	5	**Thomas Vanek**	20	**Barrett Heisten**
77	Daniel Catenacci	59	Drew Schiestel	65	Branislav Fabry	35	**Milan Bartovic**
107	Colin Jacobs	89	Corey Tropp	74	**Clarke MacArthur**	55	**Doug Janik**
137	Alex Lepkowski	139	Brad Eidsness	106	**Jan Hejda**	64	**Mike Zigomanis**
167	Nathan Lieuwen	147	Jean-Simon Allard	114	Denis Ezhov	73	Tim Preston
197	Brad Navin	179	**Paul Byron**	150	Thomas Morrow	117	Karel Mosovsky
		187	Nick Eno	172	Pavel Voroshnin	138	**Ryan Miller**
2010 Pick		209	Drew Mackenzie	202	**Nathan Paetsch**	146	Matt Kinch
23	Mark Pysyk			235	Jeff Weber	178	Seneque Hyacinthe
68	Jerome Gauthier-Leduc	**2006 Pick**		266	Louis-Philippe Martin	206	**Bret DeCecco**
75	Kevin Sundher	24	Dennis Persson			235	Brad Self
83	Matt MacKenzie	46	**Jhonas Enroth**	**2002 Pick**		263	Craig Brunel
98	Steven Shipley	57	**Mike Weber**	11	**Keith Ballard**		
143	Gregg Sutch	117	Felix Schutz	20	**Daniel Paille**	**1998 Pick**	
173	Cedrick Henley	147	Alex Biega	76	Michael Tessier	18	**Dmitri Kalinin**
203	Christian Isackson	207	Benjamin Breault	82	John Adams	34	**Andrew Peters**
208	Riley Boychuk			108	Jakub Hulva	47	**Norm Milley**
		2005 Pick		121	Marty Magers	50	**Jaroslav Kristek**
2009 Pick		13	Marek Zagrapan	178	Maxim Scheviev	77	**Mike Pandolfo**
13	Zack Kassian	48	Philip Gogulla	208	**Radoslav Hecl**	137	Aaron Goldade
66	Brayden McNabb	87	**Marc-Andre Gragnani**	241	**Dennis Wideman**	164	**Ales Kotalik**
104	Marcus Foligno	96	**Chris Butler**	271	Martin Cizek	191	**Brad Moran**
134	Mark Adams	142	**Nathan Gerbe**			218	**David Moravec**
164	Connor Knapp	182	Adam Dennis	**2001 Pick**		249	Edo Terglav
194	Maxime Legault	191	Vyacheslav Buravchikov	22	**Jiri Novotny**		
		208	Matt Generous	32	**Derek Roy**	**1997 Pick**	
2008 Pick		227	Andrew Orpik	50	**Chris Thorburn**	21	**Mika Noronen**
12	**Tyler Myers**			55	**Jason Pominville**	48	**Henrik Tallinder**
26	**Tyler Ennis**	**2004 Pick**		155	Michal Vondrka	69	**Maxim Afinogenov**
44	**Luke Adam**	13	**Drew Stafford**	234	Calle Aslund	75	Jeff Martin
81	Corey Fienhage	43	**Michael Funk**	247	Marek Dubec	101	Luc Theoret
101	Justin Jokinen	71	**Andrej Sekera**	279	Ryan Jorde	128	Torrey DiRoberto
104	Jordon Southorn	145	Michal Valent			156	**Brian Campbell**
134	Jacob Lagace	176	**Patrick Kaleta**	**2000 Pick**		184	Jeremy Adduono
164	Nick Crawford	207	**Mark Mancari**	15	Artem Kryukov	212	**Kamil Piros**
		241	**Mike Card**	48	Gerard Dicaire	238	Dylan Kemp
		273	Dylan Hunter	111	Ghyslain Rousseau		
				149	Denis Denisov		
				213	Vasily Bizyayev		
				220	**Paul Gaustad**		
				258	**Sean McMorrow**		
				277	Ryan Courtney		

General Managers' History

Punch Imlach, 1970-71 to 1977-78; Punch Imlach and John Anderson, 1978-79; Scotty Bowman, 1979-80 to 1985-86; Scotty Bowman and Gerry Meehan, 1986-87; Gerry Meehan, 1987-88 to 1992-93; John Muckler, 1993-94 to 1996-97; Darcy Regier, 1997-98 to date.

Darcy Regier
General Manager

Born: Swift Current, Sask., November 27, 1957.

Darcy Regier became the sixth general manager of the Buffalo Sabres on June 11, 1997 after a lengthy management apprenticeship in the New York Islanders organization. As a player, Regier played eight pro seasons, including part of the 1977-78 season with the Cleveland Barons and parts of the 1982-83 and 1983-84 campaigns with the New York Islanders.

He began his career as an administrator with the Islanders in 1984-85 and went on to serve in a variety of capacities including director of administration, assistant director of hockey operations, assistant coach and assistant general manager. He also served as an assistant coach with Hartford in 1991-92.

While with the Islanders, Regier benefited from working with talented managers and coaches including Bill Torrey and Al Arbour. As a minor pro player with Indianapolis of the CHL he became associated with another important influence on his hockey career, current Detroit Red Wing executive Jim Devellano.

Club Directory

HSBC Arena

Buffalo Sabres
HSBC Arena
One Seymour H. Knox III Plaza
Buffalo, NY 14203
Phone 716/855-4100
Fax 716/855-4110
Tickets, U.S.: 888/GO-SABRES
Canada: 888/669-GOAL
www.sabres.com
Capacity: 18,690

Executive
Owner . . . . Terrence M. Pegula
President . . . . Theodore N. Black
Senior Advisors . . . . Ken Sawyer, Clifford Benson
Advisor . . . . Daniel DiPoli

Hockey Department
General Manager . . . . Darcy Regier
Director, Amateur Scouting . . . . Kevin Devine
Director, Pro Scouting . . . . Jon Christiano
Pro Scout / Player Development . . . . Dennis Miller
Amateur Scouts . . . . Bo Berglund, Nik Fattey, Iouri Khmylev, Al MacAdam, Paul Merritt, Craig Benning, Kim Gellert, Eric Weissman, Dave Torrie
Director, Hockey Analytics . . . . Scott Schranz
Hockey Analytics Assistant . . . . Graham Beamish
Assistant to the General Manager . . . . Mark Jakubowski
Coordinator, Hockey Operations . . . . Michael Bermingham
Manager, Hockey Technologies . . . . Kyle Kykiebzak

Coaching Staff
Head Coach . . . . Lindy Ruff
Assistant Coaches . . . . James Patrick, Kevyn Adams
Strength & Conditioning Coach . . . . Doug McKenney
Assistant Strength & Conditioning Coach . . . . . J.T. Allaire
Goaltender Coach . . . . Jim Corsi
Administrative Assistant Coach . . . . Corey Smith
Athletic Trainer / Assistant Trainer . . . . Tim Macre / Bob Mowry
Equipment Managers / Asst. Mgr. . . . . Dave Williams, Rip Simonick / George Babcock
Massage Therapist . . . . Chuck Garlow

Medical
Medical Director . . . . Les Bisson, M.D.
Team Physicians . . . . Nicholas Aquino, M.D., William Hartrich, M.D., Mark Feinberg, M.D.
Oral Surgeon / Team Dentist . . . . Steven Jenson, DDS, David Croglio, DDS
Team Doctor Emeritus . . . . John L. Butsch, M.D.

Legal
V.P., Legal Affairs & Human Resources . . . . Dave Zygaj

Finance and Administration
V.P., Finance & Business Operations . . . . Chuck LaMattina
Assistant Controller / Accounting Manager . . . . . . Kristin Zirnheld / Christine Ivansitz
Payroll & Human Resource Manager / Assistant . . . Birgid Haensel / Ann Pastwick
Accounts Payable Clerk / Executive Assistant . . . . . Kim Binkley / Fay McNamara
IT Systems Engineer . . . . Christian Tabone

Broadcast
V.P., Broadcasting . . . . Chrisanne Bellas
TV Producer / TV Director . . . . Joe Pinter / Matt Gould
Lead Feature Editor / Photographer/Editor . . . . . . Drew Boeing / Mark Blaszak
Editor/Videographer / Production Assistant . . . . . . Jason Holler / Jason Wiese
Scoreboard Director/Editor . . . . Jeff Hill
Broadcast Team . . . . Rick Jeanneret (Play-by-Play), Harry Neale (Commentator), Kevin Sylvester (Studio Host), Mike Robitaille, Rob Ray (Analysts)

Merchandise
Director, Merchandise . . . . Mike Kaminska
Merchandise Mgrs., Inventory / Event Sales . . . . . . Glenn Barker, Jeff Smith
Store Manager / Assistant Manager . . . . Alec Moslow / Mike Fowler

Marketing
Director, Marketing . . . . Rob Kopacz
Game Presentation Director / Coordinator . . . . Jenifer Dunford / Tara Myers
Database Marketing Manager . . . . Tom Matheny
Website Manager . . . . Scott Miner
Web Content Coordinator . . . . TBA
Social Networking Coordinator . . . . Samantha Hicks
Director, Creative Services . . . . Frank Cravotta
Sr. Graphic Designer / Graphic Designer . . . . Vicki Sitek / Melissa Gebhardt

Public and Community Relations
V.P., Public & Community Relations . . . . Michael Gilbert
Director, Media Relations . . . . Chris Bandura
P.R. Assistants / Graduate Assistant . . . . Ian Ott, Marc Heintzman / Jeff Baker
Community Relations Director / Coordinator . . . . . . Rich Jureller / Teresa Balbas
Youth Hockey Coord. / Team Photographer . . . . . . Ed Grudzinski / Bill Wippert
Director, Alumni Relations . . . . Larry Playfair
Corporate & Community Relations Liaison . . . . Gilbert Perreault
Managers, Website / New Media . . . . Scott Miner / Kevin Snow
Social Media Coordinator . . . . Samantha Hicks
Mascot . . . . Sabretooth

Sales and Business Development
V.P. Sales & Business Development . . . . John Livsey
Director, Corporate Sales / Account Executive . . . . . Joe Foy / Rob Nugent
Director, Business Development . . . . Pete Petrella
Corporate Fulfillment Coordinators . . . . Chad Buck, John Latke

Ticket Sales and Operations
V.P., Tickets & Service . . . . John Sinclair
Box Office Manager / Asst. Mgr. / Coord. . . . . Marty Maloney / Paul Barker / Gretchen Knott
Database Mktg. Mgr. / Ticket Administrator . . . . . . Tom Matheney / Melissa Rugg
Account Services Representatives . . . . Roxanne Anderson, Kevin Kennedy, Jessica Kindron, Brad DePuyt, Kristin Debellis
Special Consultant . . . . Joe Crozier
Coordinator, Suite Services . . . . Michelle Mitchell

HSBC Arena
V.P.s, Arena Operations / Booking . . . . Stan Makowski, Jr. / Jennifer Van Rysdam
Directors, Arena Services / Amateur Athletics . . . . . Thomas Ahern / Kevin Sylvester
Managers, Marketing / Events . . . . Tracy Mancini / Beth Giuliani Gatto, Robert Neumann
Managers, Technical Communications . . . . Mike Queeno, Ray Riel
Chief Engineer / Assistant Chief Engineer . . . . Bill Bamberg / Richard Arcangel III
Building Services Manager . . . . Dennis Hooper
Security Manager . . . . Marc Brenner

Calgary Flames

Key Off-Season Signings/Acquisitions

2011

May 16 • Re-signed LW **Curtis Glencross**.

16 • Named **Jay Feaster** general manager.

June 1 • Acquired LW **Roman Horak** and a pair of 2nd-round picks in the 2011 Entry Draft from NY Rangers for D **Tim Erixon** and a 5th-round pick in 2011.

6 • Named **Craig Hartsburg** associate coach.

9 • Re-signed D **Brett Carson**.

20 • Re-signed G **Henrik Karlsson**.

25 • Acquired D **Chris Butler** and C **Paul Byron** from Buffalo for D **Robyn Regehr**, RW **Ales Kotalik** and a 2nd-round pick in the 2012 Entry Draft.

25 • Re-signed LW **Alex Tanguay**.

July 4 • Signed RW **Guillaume Desbiens**.

4 • Re-signed D **Anton Babchuk**.

14 • Acquired RW **Pierre-Luc Letourneau-Leblond** from New Jersey for a 5th-round pick in the 2012 Entry Draft.

14 • Re-signed D **Brendan Mikkelson**.

15 • Re-signed C **Brendan Morrison**.

2010-11 Results: 41w-29L-5OTL-7SOL 94PTS.
Second, Northwest Division

Alex Tanguay congratulates Jarome Iginla after the Calgary captain scored his third goal of the game in a 6-1 win over Edmonton on April 6, 2011. Iginla led the Flames with 43 goals and 86 points while Tanguay was tops with 47 assists.

2011-12 Schedule

Oct.							
Sat.	8	Pittsburgh		Thu.	5	at Boston	
Mon.	10	at St. Louis*		Sat.	7	Minnesota	
Thu.	13	at Montreal		Tue.	10	New Jersey	
Sat.	15	at Toronto		Thu.	12	Anaheim	
Tue.	18	Edmonton		Sat.	14	Los Angeles	
Thu.	20	NY Rangers		Tue.	17	at San Jose	
Sat.	22	Nashville*		Thu.	19	at Los Angeles	
Wed.	26	Colorado		Sat.	21	at Edmonton	
Fri.	28	St. Louis		Tue.	24	San Jose	
Nov. Tue.	1	Vancouver		Tue.	31	Detroit	
Thu.	3	at Detroit		**Feb.** Fri.	3	Chicago	
Fri.	4	at Buffalo		Mon.	6	at Anaheim	
Sun.	6	at Colorado		Wed.	8	at San Jose	
Tue.	8	Minnesota		Thu.	9	at Phoenix	
Fri.	11	at Chicago		Sat.	11	Vancouver	
Sat.	12	at Colorado		Tue.	14	Toronto	
Tue.	15	Ottawa		Thu.	16	at Dallas	
Fri.	18	Chicago		Sat.	18	at Los Angeles	
Mon.	21	at Columbus		Tue.	21	Edmonton	
Wed.	23	at Detroit		Thu.	23	Phoenix	
Fri.	25	at St. Louis		Sat.	25	Philadelphia	
Sun.	27	at Minnesota*		Mon.	27	St. Louis	
Tue.	29	Nashville		**Mar.** Thu.	1	at Phoenix	
Dec. Thu.	1	Columbus		Fri.	2	at Anaheim	
Sat.	3	at Edmonton		Sun.	4	Dallas*	
Sun.	4	at Vancouver		Tue.	6	Montreal	
Tue.	6	Carolina		Fri.	9	Winnipeg	
Thu.	8	Colorado		Sun.	11	at Minnesota*	
Sat.	10	Edmonton		Tue.	13	San Jose	
Tue.	13	at Nashville		Thu.	15	Phoenix	
Thu.	15	at Tampa Bay		Fri.	16	at Edmonton	
Fri.	16	at Florida		Sun.	18	Columbus	
Sun.	18	at Chicago		Tue.	20	at Colorado	
Tue.	20	Minnesota		Thu.	22	at Minnesota	
Thu.	22	Detroit		Sat.	24	at Dallas*	
Fri.	23	at Vancouver		Mon.	26	Dallas	
Tue.	27	at Columbus		Wed.	28	Los Angeles	
Thu.	29	at NY Islanders		Fri.	30	Colorado	
Fri.	30	at Ottawa		Sat.	31	at Vancouver	
Jan. Sun.	1	at Nashville*		**Apr.** Thu.	5	Vancouver	
Tue.	3	at Washington		Sat.	7	Anaheim*	

* Denotes afternoon game.

NORTHWEST DIVISION
40th NHL Season

Franchise date: June 6, 1972

Transferred from Atlanta to Calgary, June 24, 1980.

Year-by-Year Record

Season	GP	Home W	L	T	OL	Road W	L	T	OL	Overall W	L	T	OL	GF	GA	Pts.	Finished	Playoff Result
2010-11	82	23	13	....	5	18	16	....	7	41	29	....	12	250	237	94	2nd, Northwest Div.	Out of Playoffs
2009-10	82	20	17	....	4	20	15	....	6	40	32	....	10	204	210	90	3rd, Northwest Div.	Out of Playoffs
2008-09	82	27	10	....	4	19	20	....	2	46	30	....	6	254	248	98	2nd, Northwest Div.	Lost Conf. Quarter-Final
2007-08	82	21	11	....	9	21	19	....	1	42	30	....	10	229	227	94	3rd, Northwest Div.	Lost Conf. Quarter-Final
2006-07	82	30	9	....	2	13	20	....	8	43	29	....	10	258	226	96	3rd, Northwest Div.	Lost Conf. Quarter-Final
2005-06	82	30	7	....	4	16	18	....	7	46	25	....	11	218	200	103	1st, Northwest Div.	Lost Conf. Quarter-Final
2004-05	....															....		
2003-04	82	21	14	5	1	21	16	2	2	42	30	7	3	200	176	94	3rd, Northwest Div.	Lost Final
2002-03	82	14	16	10	1	15	20	3	3	29	36	13	4	186	228	75	5th, Northwest Div.	Out of Playoffs
2001-02	82	20	14	5	2	12	21	7	1	32	35	12	3	201	220	79	4th, Northwest Div.	Out of Playoffs
2000-01	82	12	18	9	2	15	18	6	2	27	36	15	4	197	236	73	4th, Northwest Div.	Out of Playoffs
1999-2000	82	20	14	6	1	11	22	4	4	31	36	10	5	211	256	77	4th, Northwest Div.	Out of Playoffs
1998-99	82	15	20	6		15	20	6		30	40	12	...	211	234	72	3rd, Northwest Div.	Out of Playoffs
1997-98	82	18	17	6		8	24	9		26	41	15	...	217	252	67	5th, Pacific Div.	Out of Playoffs
1996-97	82	21	18	2		11	23	7		32	41	9	...	214	239	73	5th, Pacific Div.	Out of Playoffs
1995-96	82	18	18	5		16	19	6		34	37	11	...	241	240	79	2nd, Pacific Div.	Lost Conf. Quarter-Final
1994-95	48	15	7	2		9	10	5		24	17	7	...	163	135	55	1st, Pacific Div.	Lost Conf. Quarter-Final
1993-94	84	25	12	5		17	17	8		42	29	13	...	302	256	97	1st, Pacific Div.	Lost Conf. Quarter-Final
1992-93	84	23	14	5		20	16	6		43	30	11	...	322	282	97	2nd, Smythe Div.	Lost Div. Semi-Final
1991-92	80	19	14	7		12	23	5		31	37	12	...	296	305	74	5th, Smythe Div.	Out of Playoffs
1990-91	80	29	8	3		17	18	5		46	26	8	...	344	263	100	2nd, Smythe Div.	Lost Div. Semi-Final
1989-90	80	28	7	5		14	16	10		42	23	15	...	348	265	99	1st, Smythe Div.	Lost Div. Semi-Final
1988-89	**80**	**32**	**4**	**4**		**22**	**13**	**5**		**54**	**17**	**9**	...	**354**	**226**	**117**	**1st, Smythe Div.**	**Won Stanley Cup**
1987-88	80	26	11	3		22	12	6		48	23	9	...	397	305	105	1st, Smythe Div.	Lost Div. Final
1986-87	80	25	13	2		21	18	1		46	31	3	...	318	289	95	2nd, Smythe Div.	Lost Div. Semi-Final
1985-86	80	23	11	6		17	20	3		40	31	9	...	354	315	89	2nd, Smythe Div.	Lost Final
1984-85	80	23	11	6		18	16	6		41	27	12	...	363	302	94	3rd, Smythe Div.	Lost Div. Semi-Final
1983-84	80	22	11	7		12	21	7		34	32	14	...	311	314	82	3rd, Smythe Div.	Lost Div. Final
1982-83	80	21	12	7		11	22	7		32	34	14	...	321	317	78	2nd, Smythe Div.	Lost Div. Final
1981-82	80	20	11	9		9	23	8		29	34	17	...	334	345	75	3rd, Smythe Div.	Lost Div. Semi-Final
1980-81	80	25	5	10		14	22	4		39	27	14	...	329	298	92	3rd, Patrick Div.	Lost Semi-Final
1979-80*	80	18	15	7		17	17	6		35	32	13	...	282	269	83	4th, Patrick Div.	Lost Prelim. Round
1978-79*	80	21	11	4		16	20	4		41	31	8	...	327	280	90	4th, Patrick Div.	Lost Prelim. Round
1977-78*	80	20	13	7		14	14	12		34	27	19	...	274	252	87	3rd, Patrick Div.	Lost Prelim. Round
1976-77*	80	22	13	5		12	21	7		34	34	12	...	264	265	80	3rd, Patrick Div.	Lost Prelim. Round
1975-76*	80	19	14	7		16	19	5		35	33	12	...	262	237	82	3rd, Patrick Div.	Lost Prelim. Round
1974-75*	80	24	9	7		10	22	8		34	31	15	...	243	233	83	4th, Patrick Div.	Out of Playoffs
1973-74*	78	21	14	4		9	19	7		30	34	14	...	214	238	74	4th, West Div.	Lost Quarter-Final
1972-73*	78	16	16	7		9	22	8		25	38	15	...	191	239	65	7th, West Div.	Out of Playoffs

* Atlanta Flames

2011-12 Player Personnel

FORWARDS	HT	WT	S	Place of Birth	*Age	2010-11 Club
BACKLUND, Mikael	6-0	196	L	Vasteras, Sweden	22	Calgary-Abbotsford
BOURQUE, Rene	6-2	213	L	Lac La Biche, Alta.	29	Calgary
GLENCROSS, Curtis	6-1	200	L	Kindersley, Sask.	28	Calgary
HAGMAN, Niklas	6-0	210	L	Espoo, Finland	31	Calgary
IGINLA, Jarome	6-1	207	R	Edmonton, Alta.	34	Calgary
IVANANS, Raitis	6-4	240	L	Riga, Latvia	32	Calgary
JACKMAN, Tim	6-4	220	R	Minot, ND	29	Calgary
JOKINEN, Olli	6-3	215	L	Kuopio, Finland	32	Calgary
KOSTOPOULOS, Tom	6-0	200	R	Mississauga, Ont.	32	Carolina-Calgary
LANGKOW, Daymond	5-10	183	L	Edmonton, Alta.	35	Calgary
MORRISON, Brendan	5-11	185	L	Pitt Meadows, B.C.	36	Calgary
MOSS, Dave	6-3	200	L	Livonia, MI	29	Calgary
STAJAN, Matt	6-1	200	L	Mississauga, Ont.	27	Calgary
TANGUAY, Alex	6-1	195	L	Ste-Justine, Que.	31	Calgary

DEFENSEMEN	HT	WT	S	Place of Birth	*Age	2010-11 Club
BABCHUK, Anton	6-5	212	R	Kiev, USSR	27	Carolina-Calgary
BOUWMEESTER, Jay	6-4	215	L	Edmonton, Alta.	28	Calgary
BUTLER, Chris	6-1	200	L	St. Louis, MO	24	Buffalo
CARSON, Brett	6-4	220	R	Regina, Sask.	25	Car-Charlotte-Cgy
GIORDANO, Mark	6-0	203	L	Toronto, Ont.	28	Calgary
MIKKELSON, Brendan	6-2	202	L	Regina, Sask.	24	Ana-Cgy-Abbotsford
SARICH, Cory	6-4	207	R	Saskatoon, Sask.	33	Calgary

GOALTENDERS	HT	WT	C	Place of Birth	*Age	2010-11 Club
KARLSSON, Henrik	6-5	215	L	Stockholm, Sweden	27	Calgary
KIPRUSOFF, Miikka	6-1	184	L	Turku, Finland	34	Calgary

* – Age at start of 2011-12 season

Coaching History

Bernie Geoffrion, 1972-73, 1973-74; Bernie Geoffrion and Fred Creighton, 1974-75; Fred Creighton, 1975-76 to 1978-79; Al MacNeil, 1979-80 to 1981-82; Bob Johnson, 1982-83 to 1986-87; Terry Crisp, 1987-88 to 1989-90; Doug Risebrough, 1990-91; Doug Risebrough and Guy Charron, 1991-92; Dave King, 1992-93 to 1994-95; Pierre Page, 1995-96, 1996-97; Brian Sutter, 1997-98 to 1999-2000; Don Hay and Greg Gilbert, 2000-01; Greg Gilbert, 2001-02; Greg Gilbert, Al MacNeil and Darryl Sutter, 2002-03; Darryl Sutter, 2003-04 to 2005-06; Jim Playfair, 2006-07; Mike Keenan, 2007-08, 2008-09; Brent Sutter, 2009-10 to date.

Brent Sutter

Head Coach

Born: Viking, Alta., June 10, 1962.

On June 23, 2009 Brent Sutter was named head coach of the Calgary Flames. He joined the Flames after two seasons as the bench boss of the New Jersey Devils compiling a 97-56-11 (.625) record during the regular season, and an Atlantic Division title in 2008-09.

Prior to joining the Devils, Sutter spent eight seasons as owner, president, general manager, and head coach of the Red Deer Rebels of the Western Hockey League. During that time, he led the Rebels to a 314-194-68 (.604) record as the team's head coach. Sutter guided the Rebels to a WHL championship and Memorial Cup title in 2001, and three consecutive WHL Eastern Conference championships from 2001 to 2003. He was named as the WHL's top coach in 2001.

Internationally, Sutter has represented Canada twice as the head coach guiding the national junior team to consecutive 6-0-0 marks and gold medals at the 2005 and 2006 World Junior Championships. As a player, the Viking, Alberta native helped his country win the 1984, 1987, and 1991 Canada Cup titles. Sutter was also a member of Canada's 1986 bronze medal-winning World Championship team.

Sutter played 18 years in the NHL with the New York Islanders and Chicago Blackhawks. Originally the Islanders' first choice (17th overall) in the 1980 NHL Entry Draft, he recorded 363 goals and 466 assists for 829 points and 1,054 penalty minutes in 1,111 career regular-season games. Sutter scored an additional 30 goals and 44 assists for 74 points and 164 penalty minutes in 144 career playoff games. Along with current Flames director of player personnel and brother Duane Sutter, Brent Sutter was a member of New York Islanders 1982 and 1983 Stanley Cup championship teams, and served as captain from 1987 through 1991. Brent was traded to Chicago on October 25, 1991 and played seven more seasons, including three years under his brother Darryl. Brent retired on April 18, 1998.

Brent Sutter is the third youngest of seven Sutter brothers, six of whom played in the NHL. His son Brandon is a member of the Carolina Hurricanes, and was their first choice (11th overall) in the 2007 NHL Entry Draft.

Coaching Record

Season	Team	League	Regular Season				Playoffs			
			GC	W	L	O/T	GC	W	L	T
99-2000	Red Deer	WHL	72	32	31	9	4	0	4	....
2000-01	Red Deer	WHL	72	54	12	6	22	16	6	....
2000-01	Red Deer	M-Cup	....	....	....	....	4	3	1	....
2001-02	Red Deer	WHL	72	46	18	8	23	14	9	....
2002-03	Red Deer	WHL	72	50	17	5	23	14	9	....
2003-04	Red Deer	WHL	72	35	22	15	19	10	9	....
2004-05	Red Deer	WHL	72	36	26	10	7	3	4	....
2005-06	Red Deer	WHL	72	26	40	6				
2006-07	Red Deer	WHL	72	35	28	9	7	3	4	....
2007-08	New Jersey	NHL	82	46	29	7	5	1	4	....
2008-09	New Jersey	NHL	82	51	27	4	7	3	4	....
2009-10	Calgary	NHL	82	40	30	12	....	....	....	....
2010-11	Calgary	NHL	82	41	29	12	....	....	....	....
	NHL Totals		328	178	117	33	12	4	8	

2010-11 Scoring

* – rookie

Regular Season

Pos	#	Player	Team	GP	G	A	Pts	TOI	+/-	PIM	PP	SH	GW	S	%
R	12	Jarome Iginla	CGY	82	43	43	86	20:56	0	40	14	0	6	289	14.9
L	40	Alex Tanguay	CGY	79	22	47	69	19:45	0	24	3	0	2	120	18.3
C	13	Olli Jokinen	CGY	79	17	37	54	17:46	-17	44	5	0	1	208	8.2
R	17	Rene Bourque	CGY	80	27	23	50	17:45	-17	42	6	1	6	218	12.4
L	20	Curtis Glencross	CGY	79	24	19	43	16:14	6	59	3	2	4	149	16.1
C	8	Brendan Morrison	CGY	66	9	34	43	16:41	13	16	3	1	1	89	10.1
D	5	Mark Giordano	CGY	82	8	35	43	23:08	-8	67	5	0	1	165	4.8
D	33	Anton Babchuk	CAR	17	3	5	8	19:06	-4	12	1	0	1	45	6.7
			CGY	65	8	19	27	15:37	18	20	5	1	1	87	9.2
			Total	82	11	24	35	16:20	14	32	6	1	2	132	8.3
C	18	Matt Stajan	CGY	76	6	25	31	14:13	1	32	0	1	0	81	7.4
R	25	David Moss	CGY	58	17	13	30	13:41	9	18	5	0	3	127	13.4
L	10	Niklas Hagman	CGY	71	11	16	27	13:38	-2	24	4	0	0	140	7.9
L	11	* Mikael Backlund	CGY	73	10	15	25	12:04	4	18	2	0	1	144	6.9
D	4	Jay Bouwmeester	CGY	82	4	20	24	25:59	-2	44	1	0	1	121	3.3
R	15	Tim Jackman	CGY	82	10	13	23	9:49	4	86	1	0	1	131	7.6
C	16	Tom Kostopoulos	CAR	17	1	3	4	11:17	-1	30	0	0	0	13	7.7
			CGY	59	7	7	14	12:38	-3	44	2	0	0	66	10.6
			Total	76	8	10	18	12:20	-4	74	2	0	0	79	10.1
D	6	Cory Sarich	CGY	76	4	13	17	17:52	11	75	0	0	1	75	5.3
D	28	Robyn Regehr	CGY	79	2	15	17	21:29	2	58	1	0	1	72	2.8
L	19	Fredrik Modin	ATL	36	7	3	10	11:57	-11	12	0	1	0	51	13.7
			CGY	4	0	0	0	8:28	-3	2	0	0	0	3	0.0
			Total	40	7	3	10	11:36	-14	14	0	1	0	54	13.0
D	27	Steve Staios	CGY	39	3	7	10	14:43	6	24	0	1	0	23	13.0
D	7	Adam Pardy	CGY	30	1	6	7	14:41	3	24	0	0	0	36	2.8
R	26	Ales Kotalik	CGY	26	4	2	6	12:22	-7	8	1	0	2	62	6.5
C	24	Craig Conroy	CGY	18	2	0	2	9:18	-1	8	0	0	1	11	18.2
L	44	* Stefan Meyer	CGY	16	0	2	2	7:45	0	17	0	0	0	12	0.0
D	29	Brendan Mikkelson	ANA	5	0	1	1	19:24	-1	7	0	0	0	4	0.0
			CGY	19	0	1	1	12:52	-5	2	0	0	0	10	0.0
			Total	24	0	2	2	14:13	-6	9	0	0	0	14	0.0
C	22	Daymond Langkow	CGY	4	0	1	1	14:45	3	0	0	0	0	6	0.0
R	48	* Greg Nemisz	CGY	6	0	1	1	5:05	-5	2	0	0	0	9	0.0
L	57	* Lance Bouma	CGY	16	0	1	1	5:52	-1	2	0	0	0	9	0.0
L	41	Raitis Ivanans	CGY	1	0	0	0	8:20	-1	5	0	0	0	0	0.0
D	66	* T.J. Brodie	CGY	3	0	0	0	16:00	-3	2	0	0	0	4	0.0
D	3	Brett Carson	CAR	13	0	0	0	10:49	7	4	0	0	0	8	0.0
			CGY	6	0	0	0	12:46	2	0	0	0	0	4	0.0
			Total	19	0	0	0	11:26	9	4	0	0	0	12	0.0

Goaltending

No.	Goaltender	GPI	Mins	Avg	W	L	OT	EN	SO	GA	SA	S%	G	A	PIM
35	Henrik Karlsson	17	838	2.58	4	5	6	4	0	36	391	.908	0	0	0
34	Miikka Kiprusoff	71	4156	2.63	37	24	6	8	6	182	1935	.906	0	1	2
	Totals	82	5019	2.75	41	29	12	12	6	230	2338	.902			

Miikka Kiprusoff has posted 35 wins or more for six straight seasons in Calgary and enters 2011-12 tied with Mike Vernon for the franchise lead with 262 victories.

Captains' History

Keith McCreary, 1972-73 to 1974-75; Pat Quinn, 1975-76, 1976-77; Tom Lysiak, 1977-78, 1978-79; Jean Pronovost, 1979-80; Brad Marsh, 1980-81; Phil Russell, 1981-82, 1982-83; Lanny McDonald, Doug Risebrough, 1983-84; Lanny McDonald, Doug Risebrough, Jim Peplinski, 1984-85 to 1986-87; Lanny McDonald, Jim Peplinski, 1987-88; Lanny McDonald, Jim Peplinski, Tim Hunter, 1988-89; Brad McCrimmon, 1989-90; alternating captains, 1990-91; Joe Nieuwendyk, 1991-92 to 1994-95; Theoren Fleury, 1995-96, 1996-97; Todd Simpson, 1997-98, 1998-99; Steve Smith, 1999-2000; Steve Smith and Dave Lowry, 2000-01; Dave Lowry; Bob Boughner and Craig Conroy, 2001-02; Bob Boughner and Craig Conroy, 2002-03; Jarome Iginla, 2003-04 to date.

Club Records

Team

(Figures in brackets for season records are games played; records for fewest points, wins, ties, losses, goals, goals against are for 70 or more games)

Most Points **117** 1988-89 (80)
Most Wins **54** 1988-89 (80)
Most Ties **19** 1977-78 (80)
Most Losses **41** 1996-97 (82), 1997-98 (82), 1999-2000 (82)
Most Goals **397** 1987-88 (80)
Most Goals Against **345** 1981-82 (80)
Fewest Points **65** 1972-73 (78)
Fewest Wins **25** 1972-73 (78)
Fewest Ties **3** 1986-87 (80)
Fewest Losses **17** 1988-89 (80)
Fewest Goals **186** 2002-03 (82)
Fewest Goals Against **176** 2003-04 (82)
Longest Winning Streak
Overall .... **10** Oct. 14-Nov. 3/78
Home .... **10** Nov. 7-Dec. 12/06
Away .... **7** Nov. 10-Dec. 4/88
Longest Undefeated Streak
Overall .... **13** Nov. 10-Dec. 8/88 (12 wins, 1 tie)
Home .... **18** Dec. 29/90-Mar. 14/91 (17 wins, 1 tie)
Away .... **9** Feb. 20-Mar. 21/88 (6 wins, 3 ties), Nov. 11-Dec. 16/90 (6 wins, 3 ties)
Longest Losing Streak
Overall .... **11** Dec. 14/85-Jan. 7/86
Home .... **6** Dec. 5-31/98, Jan. 8-25/10
Away .... **9** Dec. 1/85-Jan. 12/86
Longest Winless Streak
Overall .... **11** Dec. 14/85-Jan. 7/86 (11 losses), Jan. 5-26/93 (9 losses, 2 ties)
Home .... **10** Oct. 21-Dec. 4/00 (6 losses, 4 ties)
Away .... **13** Feb. 3-Mar. 29/73 (10 losses, 3 ties)
Most Shutouts, Season **11** 2003-04 (82)
Most PIM, Season **2,643** 1991-92 (80)
Most Goals, Game .... **13** Feb. 10/93 (S.J. 1 at Cgy. 13)

Individual

Most Seasons .... **14** Jarome Iginla
Most Games .... **1,106** Jarome Iginla
Most Goals, Career .... **484** Jarome Iginla
Most Assists, Career .... **609** Al MacInnis
Most Points, Career .... **1,006** Jarome Iginla (484G, 522A)
Most PIM, Career .... **2,405** Tim Hunter
Most Shutouts, Career .... **37** Miikka Kiprusoff
Longest Consecutive Games Streak .... **328** Jarome Iginla (Oct. 4/07-Apr. 9/11)
Most Goals, Season .... **66** Lanny McDonald (1982-83)
Most Assists, Season .... **82** Kent Nilsson (1980-81)
Most Points, Season .... **131** Kent Nilsson (1980-81; 49G, 82A)
Most PIM, Season .... **375** Tim Hunter (1988-89)
Most Points, Defenseman, Season .... **103** Al MacInnis (1990-91; 28G, 75A)
Most Points, Center, Season .... **131** Kent Nilsson (1980-81; 49G, 82A)
Most Points, Right Wing, Season .... **110** Joe Mullen (1988-89; 51G, 59A)
Most Points, Left Wing, Season .... **90** Gary Roberts (1991-92; 53G, 37A)
Most Points, Rookie, Season .... **92** Joe Nieuwendyk (1987-88; 51G, 41A)
Most Shutouts, Season .... **10** Miikka Kiprusoff (2005-06)
Most Goals, Game .... **5** Joe Nieuwendyk (Jan. 11/89)
Most Assists, Game .... **6** Guy Chouinard (Feb. 25/81), Gary Suter (Apr. 4/86)
Most Points, Game .... **7** Sergei Makarov (Feb. 25/90; 2G, 5A)

Records include Atlanta Flames, 1972-73 through 1979-80.

Retired Numbers

9	Lanny McDonald	1981-1989
30	Mike Vernon	1982-1994; 2000-2002

All-time Record vs. Other Clubs

Regular Season

	At Home								On Road								Total							
	GP	W	L	T	OL	GF	GA	PTS	GP	W	L	T	OL	GF	GA	PTS	GP	W	L	T	OL	GF	GA	PTS
Anaheim	37	23	12	1	1	107	87	48	38	8	18	6	6	96	126	28	75	31	30	7	7	203	213	76
Atlanta	5	5	0	0	0	21	8	10	7	1	5	1	0	15	21	3	12	6	5	1	0	36	29	13
Boston	47	20	23	4	0	167	159	44	49	13	30	6	0	132	173	32	96	33	53	10	0	299	332	76
Buffalo	49	20	18	11	0	166	151	51	47	13	26	5	3	134	194	34	96	33	44	16	3	300	345	85
Carolina	31	23	6	2	0	147	93	48	31	14	11	5	1	113	106	34	62	37	17	7	1	260	199	82
Chicago	75	33	27	13	2	230	225	81	73	26	32	13	2	212	242	67	148	59	59	26	4	442	467	148
Colorado	68	33	22	9	4	236	197	79	68	27	28	11	2	217	233	67	136	60	50	20	6	453	430	146
Columbus	20	14	4	0	2	63	44	30	20	6	13	0	1	42	59	13	40	20	17	0	3	105	103	43
Dallas	74	39	19	14	2	238	184	94	74	27	34	11	2	225	260	67	148	66	53	25	4	463	444	161
Detroit	72	39	25	6	2	254	208	86	71	22	37	10	2	213	262	56	143	61	62	16	4	467	470	142
Edmonton	102	59	33	9	1	401	319	128	102	41	49	10	2	320	359	94	204	100	82	19	3	721	678	222
Florida	11	5	4	1	1	28	30	12	11	6	3	2	0	26	23	14	22	11	7	3	1	54	53	26
Los Angeles	106	65	28	12	1	457	335	143	103	42	49	9	3	348	368	96	209	107	77	21	4	805	703	239
Minnesota	31	20	5	3	3	77	64	46	32	15	13	1	3	66	79	34	63	35	18	4	6	143	143	80
Montreal	53	20	26	7	0	163	171	47	50	13	28	8	1	122	177	35	103	33	54	15	1	285	348	82
Nashville	24	12	7	3	2	70	57	29	25	11	13	1	0	62	76	23	49	23	20	4	2	132	133	52
New Jersey	44	29	6	8	1	189	115	67	48	28	16	3	1	169	134	60	92	57	22	11	2	358	249	127
NY Islanders	52	25	15	11	1	183	157	62	53	17	27	9	0	147	197	43	105	42	42	20	1	330	354	105
NY Rangers	51	29	11	10	1	223	152	69	55	24	24	5	2	190	184	55	106	53	35	15	3	413	336	124
Ottawa	15	10	4	1	0	53	31	21	14	5	6	3	0	36	35	13	29	15	10	4	0	89	66	34
Philadelphia	54	25	20	9	0	210	178	59	54	17	33	3	1	145	203	38	108	42	53	12	1	355	381	97
Phoenix	83	45	28	9	1	329	257	100	82	31	37	11	3	277	297	76	165	76	65	20	4	606	554	176
Pittsburgh	48	27	12	8	1	207	146	63	47	11	26	10	0	137	175	32	95	38	38	18	1	344	321	95
St. Louis	74	38	28	5	3	236	200	84	76	33	33	9	1	240	257	76	150	71	61	14	4	476	457	160
San Jose	44	25	14	4	1	153	118	55	46	22	19	4	1	132	147	49	90	47	33	8	2	285	265	104
Tampa Bay	13	7	5	0	1	44	37	15	12	5	5	1	1	42	39	12	25	12	10	1	2	86	76	27
Toronto	65	38	22	5	0	252	201	81	57	20	29	7	1	206	218	48	122	58	51	12	1	458	419	129
Vancouver	119	66	34	15	4	449	348	151	120	53	45	18	4	384	412	128	239	119	79	33	8	833	760	279
Washington	41	25	9	7	0	163	105	57	43	15	22	6	0	146	159	36	84	40	31	13	0	309	264	93
Defunct Clubs	13	8	4	1	0	51	34	17	13	7	3	3	0	43	33	17	26	15	7	4	0	94	67	34
Totals	**1521**	**827**	**471**	**188**	**35**	**5567**	**4411**	**1877**	**1521**	**573**	**714**	**191**	**43**	**4637**	**5248**	**1380**	**3042**	**1400**	**1185**	**379**	**78**	**10204**	**9659**	**3257**

Playoffs

	Series	W	L	GP	W	L	T	GF	GA	Last Mtg.	Rnd.	Result
Anaheim	1	0	1	7	3	4	0	16	17	2006	CQF	L 3-4
Chicago	4	2	2	18	9	9	0	53	54	2009	CQF	L 2-4
Dallas	1	0	1	6	2	4	0	18	25	1981	SF	L 2-4
Detroit	3	1	2	14	6	8	0	26	38	2007	CQF	L 2-4
Edmonton	5	1	4	30	11	19	0	96	132	1991	DSF	L 3-4
Los Angeles	6	2	4	26	13	13	0	112	105	1993	DSF	L 2-4
Montreal	2	1	1	11	5	6	0	32	31	1989	F	W 4-2
NY Rangers	1	0	1	4	1	3	0	8	14	1980	PRE	L 1-3
Philadelphia	2	1	1	11	4	7	0	28	43	1981	QF	W 4-3
Phoenix	3	1	2	13	6	7	0	43	45	1987	DSF	L 2-4
St. Louis	1	1	0	7	4	3	0	28	22	1986	CF	W 4-3
San Jose	3	1	2	20	10	10	0	68	57	2008	CQF	L 3-4
Tampa Bay	1	0	1	7	3	4	0	14	13	2004	F	L 3-4
Toronto	1	0	1	2	0	2	0	5	9	1979	PRE	L 0-2
Vancouver	6	4	2	32	17	15	0	101	96	2004	CQF	W 4-3
Totals	**40**	**15**	**25**	**208**	**94**	**114**	**0**	**648**	**701**			

Carolina totals include Hartford, 1979-80 to 1996-97.
Colorado totals include Quebec, 1979-80 to 1994-95.
Dallas totals include Minnesota North Stars, 1972-73 to 1992-93.
New Jersey totals include Kansas City, 1974-75, 1975-76, and Colorado Rockies, 1976-77 to 1981-82.
Phoenix totals include Winnipeg, 1979-80 to 1995-96.

Playoff Results 2011-2007

Year	Round	Opponent	Result	GF	GA
2009	CQF	Chicago	L 2-4	16	21
2008	CQF	San Jose	L 3-4	17	19
2007	CQF	Detroit	L 2-4	10	18

Abbreviations: Round: F - Final; **CF** - conference final; **CSF** - conference semi-final; **CQF** - conference quarter-final; **DSF** - division semi-final; **SF** - semi-final; **QF** - quarter-final; **PRE** - preliminary round.

2010-11 Results

Month	Day	Opponent	Score	Month	Day	Opponent	Score
Oct.	7	at Edmonton	0-4		7	Detroit	4-5†
	10	Los Angeles	3-1		11	at Carolina	5-6†
	14	Florida	0-3		14	at Ottawa	3-2
	16	Edmonton	5-3		15	at Toronto	2-1†
	19	at Nashville	1-0*		17	at Montreal	4-5*
	21	at Detroit	2-4		19	Minnesota	0-6
	22	at Columbus	6-2		21	Dallas	7-4
	24	San Jose	4-0		22	at Vancouver	4-3†
	26	Edmonton	5-4†		24	Nashville	3-1
	28	Colorado	5-6		26	St. Louis	4-1
	30	Washington	2-7	**Feb.**	1	at Nashville	3-2†
Nov.	3	Detroit	1-2		3	at Atlanta	4-2
	5	at Minnesota	1-2		5	Los Angeles	3-4†
	9	at Colorado	4-2		7	Chicago	3-1
	12	at Phoenix	4-5		9	Ottawa	5-2
	13	at San Jose	3-4		11	Anaheim	4-5*
	17	Phoenix	1-3		12	at Vancouver	2-4
	19	Chicago	7-2		14	at Colorado	9-1
	21	at Detroit	4-5*		16	Dallas	4-2
	22	at NY Rangers	1-2		20	Montreal	4-0
	24	at New Jersey	1-2†		22	Boston	1-3
	26	at Philadelphia	3-2†		25	San Jose	3-4†
	27	at Pittsburgh	1-4		27	St. Louis	1-0
	29	Minnesota	3-0	**Mar.**	1	at St. Louis	6-0
Dec.	1	Vancouver	2-7		2	at Chicago	4-6
	3	at Minnesota	3-2†		4	Columbus	4-3
	5	at Chicago	2-4		6	Nashville	3-2
	7	Tampa Bay	4-2		9	at Dallas	4-3†
	9	at Los Angeles	1-2		10	at Phoenix	0-3
	10	at Anaheim	2-3†		12	Vancouver	3-4
	13	Columbus	3-2*		15	Phoenix	3-4
	16	Toronto	5-2		17	Colorado	5-2
	18	Minnesota	1-3		20	at Anaheim	4-5*
	20	at Minnesota	1-4		21	at Los Angeles	1-2†
	21	at Columbus	1-3		23	at San Jose	3-6
	23	at Dallas	3-2†		26	at Edmonton	5-4†
	27	Buffalo	5-2		30	Anaheim	2-4
	31	Colorado	3-2	**Apr.**	1	at St. Louis	3-2
Jan.	1	at Edmonton	2-1		3	at Colorado	2-1
	3	NY Islanders	2-5		6	Edmonton	6-1
	5	at Vancouver	1-3		9	Vancouver	2-3*

* – Overtime † – Shootout

Entry Draft Selections 2011-1997

Name in bold denotes played in NHL.

2011
Pick
13 Sven Baertschi
45 Markus Granlund
57 Tyler Wotherspoon
104 John Gaudreau
164 Laurent Brossoit

2010
Pick
64 Max Reinhart
73 Joey Leach
103 John Ramage
108 Bill Arnold
133 Michael Ferland
193 Patrick Holland

2009
Pick
23 Tim Erixon
74 Ryan Howse
111 Henrik Bjorklund
141 Spencer Bennett
171 Joni Ortio
201 Gaelan Patterson

2008
Pick
25 **Greg Nemisz**
48 Mitch Wahl
78 **Lance Bouma**
108 Nicholas Larson
114 **T.J. Brodie**
168 Ryley Grantham
198 Alexander Deilert

2007
Pick
24 **Mikael Backlund**
70 **John Negrin**
116 **Keith Aulie**
143 Mickey Renaud
186 C.J. Severyn

2006
Pick
26 Leland Irving
87 John Armstrong
89 Aaron Marvin
118 Hugo Carpentier
149 Juuso Puustinen
179 Jordan Fulton
187 Devin Didiomete
209 Per Jonsson

2005
Pick
26 **Matt Pelech**
69 Gord Baldwin
74 Dan Ryder
111 J.D. Watt
128 Kevin Lalande
158 **Matt Keetley**
179 **Brett Sutter**
221 Myles Rumsey

2004
Pick
24 **Kris Chucko**
70 **Brandon Prust**
98 **Dustin Boyd**
118 Aki Seitsonen
121 Kris Hogg
173 **Adam Pardy**
182 Fred Wikner
200 Matt Schneider
213 James Spratt
279 **Adam Cracknell**

2003
Pick
9 **Dion Phaneuf**
39 **Tim Ramholt**
97 Ryan Donally
112 Jamie Tardif
143 **Greg Moore**
173 Tyler Johnson
206 Thomas Bellemare
240 Cam Cunning
270 Kevin Harvey

2002
Pick
10 **Eric Nystrom**
39 Brian McConnell
90 **Matthew Lombardi**
112 Yuri Artemenkov
141 Jiri Cetkovsky
142 Emanuel Peter
146 Viktor Bobrov
159 Kristofer Persson
176 **Curtis McElhinney**
206 **David Van Der Gulik**
207 Pierre Johnsson
238 Jyri Marttinen

2001
Pick
14 **Chuck Kobasew**
41 Andrei Taratukhin
56 Andrei Medvedev
108 **Tomi Maki**
124 Yegor Shastin
145 James Hakewill
164 Yuri Trubachev
207 Garrett Bembridge
220 **Dave Moss**
233 Joe Campbell
251 Ville Hamalainen

2000
Pick
9 **Brent Krahn**
40 **Kurtis Foster**
46 **Jarret Stoll**
116 Levente Szuper
141 Wade Davis
155 **Travis Moen**
176 **Jukka Hentunen**
239 David Hajek
270 **Micki DuPont**

1999
Pick
11 **Oleg Saprykin**
38 Dan Cavanaugh
77 **Craig Anderson**
106 Roman Rozakov
135 Matt Doman
153 Jesse Cook
166 Cory Pecker
170 **Matt Underhill**
190 Blair Stayzer
252 Dmitri Kirilenko

1998
Pick
6 **Rico Fata**
33 **Blair Betts**
62 **Paul Manning**
102 Shaun Sutter
108 **Dany Sabourin**
120 Brent Gauvreau
192 Radek Duda
206 **Jonas Frogren**
234 Kevin Mitchell

1997
Pick
6 **Daniel Tkaczuk**
32 Evan Lindsay
42 **John Tripp**
51 Dmitri Kokorev
60 Derek Schutz
70 **Erik Andersson**
92 Chris St. Croix
100 **Ryan Ready**
113 Martin Moise
140 Ilja Demidov
167 Jeremy Rondeau
223 Dustin Paul

General Managers' History

Cliff Fletcher, 1972-73 to 1990-91; Doug Risebrough, 1991-92 to 1994-95; Doug Risebrough and Al Coates, 1995-96; Al Coates, 1996-97 to 1999-2000; Craig Button, 2000-01 to 2002-03; Darryl Sutter, 2003-04 to 2009-10; Darryl Sutter and Jay Feaster, 2010-11; Jay Feaster, 2011-12.

Jay Feaster

General Manager

Born: Williamstown, PA, July 30, 1962.

Jay Feaster joined the Calgary Flames in July 2010 as assistant general manager. He was named acting general manager on December 28, 2010 and, on May 16, 2011 was named general manager of the team. Feaster and senior vice president & assistant general manager Michael Holditch are central figures with the Flames hockey management group.

Feaster joined the Flames organization to build on his decorated managerial career that includes a Stanley Cup championship as general manager of the Tampa Bay Lightning in 2004 and a Calder Cup championship as the president of the Hershey Bears (American Hockey League) in 1997. The native of Williamstown, Pennsylvania was originally named general manager of the Lightning on February 10, 2002. In addition to a Stanley Cup championship, the Lightning won back to back Southeast Division titles in 2002-03 and 2003-04.

Feaster was named the 2004 Sporting News NHL Executive of the Year based on a vote of other NHL GMs and hockey executives. Prior to being named general manager, he spent three seasons with the club in the assistant general manager's position. In that capacity, Feaster was responsible for all contractual, collective bargaining and NHL legal issues, as well as the organization's scouting department and its developmental league affiliates.

To join the Lightning, Feaster resigned his post as president of the Hershey Bears and vice president of Hershey Entertainment. In that capacity, Feaster oversaw the operations of the Bears, the Hershey Wildcats professional soccer team and Hersheypark Arena/Stadium, including the star Pavilion. Feaster, who spent nine years with the Bears, led the team to a division title (1993-94) and a Calder Cup Championship (1997), while establishing three consecutive single-season attendance records (1991-92 to 1993-94) and entering into a five-year affiliation agreement with the NHL's Colorado Avalanche. For his work, he was named the AHL's Executive of the Year in 1997. He originally joined Hershey Entertainment as assistant to the president in 1989 and was named general manager of the Bears and Hersheypark Arena/Stadium in 1990.

Prior to joining Hershey Entertainment, Feaster practiced law with the firm of McNees, Wallace & Nurick in Harrisburg, Pennsylvania. Feaster is a Summa Cum Laude graduate of Susquehanna University and a Cum Laude graduate of the Georgetown Law Center in Washington, DC.

Club Directory

Scotiabank Saddledome

Calgary Flames
Scotiabank Saddledome
P.O. Box 1540 Station M
Calgary, Alberta T2P 3B9
Phone **403/777-2177**
FAX 403/777-2195
www.calgaryflames.com
Capacity: 19,289

Owners .... N. Murray Edwards (Chairman), Alvin G. Libin, Allan P. Markin, Jeff McCaig, Clayton H. Riddell

Executive
President & Chief Executive Officer .... Ken King
General Manager .... Jay Feaster
Assistant G.M./Sr. VP of Hockey Admin. .... Michael Holditch
Senior V.P., Finance and Administration .... John Bean
V.P., Building Operations .... Libby Raines
V.P., Advertising, Sponsorship & Marketing....... Jim Bagshaw
V.P., Sales, Customer Service & Ticketing .... Rollie Cyr
V.P., Communications .... Peter Hanlon
V.P., Business Development .... Jim Peplinski
V.P., Food and Beverage..................... Mark Vaillant

Hockey Club Personnel
General Manager .... Jay Feaster
Assistant G.M./Sr. VP of Hockey Admin. .... Michael Holditch
Assistant G.M./Player Personnel .... John Weisbrod
Special Assistant to the G.M. .... Craig Conroy
Director, Hockey Administration .... Mike Burke
Director, Video and Statistical Analysis .... Chris Snow
Director of Amateur Scouting .... Tod Button
Director, Player Development .... Ron Sutter
Head Coach .... Brent Sutter
Associate Coach .... Craig Hartsburg
Assistant Coach .... Dave Lowry
Goalie Coach .... Clint Malarchuk
Senior Video Analyst......................... Jamie Pringle
Mental Development Coach .... Dr. Dave Paskevich
Team Services Manager .... Sean O'Brien
Exec. Asst. to GM and Hockey Operations........ Brenda Koyich
Scouts .... Michael Goulet, Ari Haanpaa, Steve Leach, Bob MacMillan, Fred Parker, Steve Pleau, Blair Reid, Anders Steen, Ritch Thibeau, Tom Webster

Medical/Training Staff
Strength & Conditioning Coach .... Rich Hesketh
Athletic Therapist .... Morris Boyer
Assistant Athletic Therapist................... Schad Richea
Equipment Manager .... Mark DePasquale
Assistant Equipment Manager.................. Corey Osmak
Massage Therapist .... Bryan Lentz
Head Physician .... Dr. Kelly Brett
Team Physician/Sports Medicine .... Dr. Jim Thorne
Team Orthopedic Surgeons.................... Dr. Nicholas Mohtadi, Dr. Richard Boorman
Team Dentist .... Dr. Bill Blair
Team Optometrist........................... Dr. Derek Gaume
Dressing Room Attendant..................... Jules Carriere

Abbotsford Heat
President .... Ryan Walter
Head Coach .... Troy Ward
Assistant Coaches........................... Cail MacLean, Luke Strand
Goaltending Coach.......................... Jordan Sigalet

Communications
Vice-President, Communications............... Peter Hanlon
Manager, Media Relations .... Sean Kelso
Administrative Assistant, Communications .... Bernie Hargrave
Manager, Community Relations .... Candice Goudie

Administration
Senior V.P., Finance and Administration .... John Bean
Exec. Asst. to President/CEO .... Judy O'Brien
Exec. Asst. to V.P. Hockey Admin/CFO .... Anita Cranston
Director, Finance........................... Deniece Kennedy
Manager, Human Resources .... Betty Mah

Marketing/Ticketing
V.P. Advertising, Sponsorship & Marketing .... Jim Bagshaw
V.P. Sales, Customer Service & Ticketing .... Rollie Cyr
V.P. Business Development .... Jim Peplinski
Senior Director, Advertising................... Pat Halls
Director, Corporate Sponsorship .... Kevin Gross
Manager, Key Corporate Accounts .... Mark Stiles
Director, Promotions........................ Scott Matheson
Executive Assistant Marketing.................. Suzanna Chapman
Executive Assistant to V.P. of Sales .... Vicki Rinke
Director, Executive Suites .... Mike Mungiello
Director of Sales .... Mike Franco
Customer Service Manager.................... Marc Leost
Director, Broadcast & Production .... Carlo Petrini
Director, Game Entertainment .... Geordie Macleod
Coordinator, Entertainment .... Steve Edgar
Director, Retail/FanAttic .... Brent Gibbs
Publications Manager .... Laurie Wheeler
Content Manager........................... Mike Board

Scotiabank Saddledome
V.P. Building Operations .... Libby Raines
V.P. Food and Beverage .... Mark Vaillant
Director, Building Operations .... Rob Blanchard
Director, Food Services .... Art Hernandez
Operations Manager......................... George Greenwood
Senior Food Services Manager................. Sheila Parisien
Security/Parking/Loss Prevention Manager........ Bob Godun

Miscellaneous
Radio Affiliate.............................. The FAN 960 (960 AM)
TV Affiliate .... Rogers Sportsnet, CBC-TV, TSN

Carolina Hurricanes

Key Off-Season Signings/Acquisitions

2011

June 7 • Named **Rod Brind'Amour** and **Dave Lewis** assistant coaches.

16 • Re-signed D **Jay Harrison**.

28 • Re-signed D **Joni Pitkanen** and RW **Patrick Dwyer**.

29 • Re-signed RW **Chad LaRose**.

30 • Re-signed LW **Jussi Jokinen**.

July 1 • Re-signed C **Jiri Tlusty**.

1 • Signed G **Brian Boucher**, C **Tim Brent** and LW **Alexei Ponikarovsky**.

2 • Signed RW **Anthony Stewart**.

5 • Signed D **Tomas Kaberle**.

8 • Re-signed D **Derek Joslin**.

13 • Re-signed C **Brandon Sutter**.

2010-11 Results: 40w-31L-6OTL-5SOL 91PTS. Third, Southeast Division

Carolina's Cam Ward was the busiest goalie in the NHL in 2010-11, leading the league with 74 games played and 4,318 minutes. He faced more shots (2,375) and made more saves (2,191) than anyone else in the NHL for a career-best .923 save percentage.

2011-12 Schedule

Oct.	Fri.	7	Tampa Bay	Fri.	6	Buffalo
	Sat.	8	at Washington	Sat.	7	at Nashville
	Mon.	10	at New Jersey*	Tue.	10	Philadelphia
	Wed.	12	Boston	Thu.	12	at Tampa Bay
	Fri.	14	at Buffalo	Sat.	14	Boston
	Tue.	18	at Boston	Sun.	15	at Washington*
	Fri.	21	at St. Louis	Tue.	17	at Pittsburgh
	Sat.	22	at Winnipeg	Fri.	20	Washington
	Tue.	25	Ottawa	Sat.	21	at NY Islanders
	Fri.	28	Chicago	Mon.	23	Winnipeg
	Sat.	29	at Philadelphia	Tue.	31	NY Islanders
Nov.	Tue.	1	Tampa Bay	**Feb.** Thu.	2	at Boston
	Fri.	4	Washington	Sat.	4	Los Angeles
	Sun.	6	Dallas*	Wed.	8	at Anaheim
	Tue.	8	at New Jersey	Fri.	10	at Colorado
	Fri.	11	at NY Rangers	Mon.	13	at Montreal
	Sat.	12	Pittsburgh	Fri.	17	San Jose
	Mon.	14	Philadelphia	Sat.	18	at NY Islanders
	Wed.	16	at Montreal	Mon.	20	Washington
	Fri.	18	Buffalo	Thu.	23	Anaheim
	Sun.	20	Toronto*	Sat.	25	Florida
	Mon.	21	at Philadelphia	Tue.	28	Nashville
	Wed.	23	Montreal	**Mar.** Thu.	1	NY Rangers
	Fri.	25	Winnipeg	Sat.	3	Tampa Bay
	Sun.	27	at Ottawa*	Tue.	6	at Washington
	Tue.	29	Florida	Wed.	7	at Buffalo
Dec.	Thu.	1	NY Rangers	Sat.	10	at Tampa Bay
	Sat.	3	Pittsburgh	Sun.	11	at Florida*
	Tue.	6	at Calgary	Tue.	13	at NY Rangers
	Wed.	7	at Edmonton	Thu.	15	St. Louis
	Fri.	9	at Winnipeg	Sat.	17	at Minnesota*
	Tue.	13	at Toronto	Sun.	18	at Winnipeg
	Thu.	15	Vancouver	Wed.	21	Florida
	Sun.	18	at Florida*	Fri.	23	at Columbus
	Wed.	21	Phoenix	Sat.	24	at Detroit
	Fri.	23	Ottawa	Tue.	27	at Toronto
	Mon.	26	New Jersey	Fri.	30	Winnipeg
	Tue.	27	at Pittsburgh	Sat.	31	New Jersey
	Thu.	29	Toronto	**Apr.** Tue.	3	at Ottawa
	Sat.	31	at Tampa Bay*	Thu.	5	Montreal
Jan.	Tue.	3	NY Islanders	Sat.	7	at Florida

* Denotes afternoon game.

SOUTHEAST DIVISION
33rd NHL Season

Franchise date: June 22, 1979

Transferred from Hartford to Carolina, June 25, 1997.

Year-by-Year Record

Season	GP	Home W	L	T	OL	Road W	L	T	OL	Overall W	L	T	OL	GF	GA	Pts.	Finished	Playoff Result
2010-11	82	22	14	....	5	18	17	....	6	40	31	....	11	236	239	91	3rd, Southeast Div.	Out of Playoffs
2009-10	82	21	17	....	3	14	20	....	7	35	37	....	10	230	256	80	3rd, Southeast Div.	Out of Playoffs
2008-09	82	26	14	....	1	19	16	....	6	45	30	....	7	239	226	97	2nd, Southeast Div.	Lost Conf. Championship
2007-08	82	24	13	....	4	19	20	....	2	43	33	....	6	252	249	92	2nd, Southeast Div.	Out of Playoffs
2006-07	82	21	16	....	4	19	18	....	4	40	34	....	8	241	253	88	3rd, Southeast Div.	Out of Playoffs
2005-06	**82**	**31**	**8**	....	**2**	**21**	**14**	....	**6**	**52**	**22**	....	**8**	**294**	**260**	**112**	**1st, Southeast Div.**	**Won Stanley Cup**
2004-05	....																	
2003-04	82	15	18	8	2	13	16	6	4	28	34	14	6	172	209	76	3rd, Southeast Div.	Out of Playoffs
2002-03	82	12	17	9	3	10	26	3	4	22	43	11	6	171	240	61	5th, Southeast Div.	Out of Playoffs
2001-02	82	15	13	11	2	20	13	5	3	35	26	16	5	217	217	91	1st, Southeast Div.	Lost Final
2000-01	82	23	15	3	0	15	17	6	3	38	32	9	3	212	225	88	2nd, Southeast Div.	Lost Conf. Quarter-Final
1999-2000	82	20	16	5	0	17	19	5	0	37	35	10	0	217	216	84	3rd, Southeast Div.	Out of Playoffs
1998-99	82	20	12	9	....	14	18	9	....	34	30	18	....	210	202	86	1st, Southeast Div.	Lost Conf. Quarter-Final
1997-98	82	16	18	7	....	17	23	1	....	33	41	8	....	200	219	74	6th, Northeast Div.	Out of Playoffs
1996-97*	82	23	15	3	....	9	24	8	....	32	39	11	....	226	256	75	5th, Northeast Div.	Out of Playoffs
1995-96*	82	22	15	4	....	12	24	5	....	34	39	9	....	237	259	77	4th, Northeast Div.	Out of Playoffs
1994-95*	48	12	10	2	....	7	14	3	....	19	24	5	....	127	141	43	5th, Northeast Div.	Out of Playoffs
1993-94*	84	14	22	6	....	13	26	3	....	27	48	9	....	227	288	63	6th, Northeast Div.	Out of Playoffs
1992-93*	84	12	25	5	....	14	27	1	....	26	52	6	....	284	369	58	5th, Adams Div.	Out of Playoffs
1991-92*	80	13	17	10	....	13	24	3	....	26	41	13	....	247	283	65	4th, Adams Div.	Lost Div. Semi-Final
1990-91*	80	18	16	6	....	13	22	5	....	31	38	11	....	238	276	73	4th, Adams Div.	Lost Div. Semi-Final
1989-90*	80	17	18	5	....	21	15	4	....	38	33	9	....	275	268	85	4th, Adams Div.	Lost Div. Semi-Final
1988-89*	80	21	17	2	....	16	21	3	....	37	38	5	....	299	290	79	4th, Adams Div.	Lost Div. Semi-Final
1987-88*	80	21	14	5	....	14	24	2	....	35	38	7	....	249	267	77	4th, Adams Div.	Lost Div. Semi-Final
1986-87*	80	26	9	5	....	17	21	2	....	43	30	7	....	287	270	93	1st, Adams Div.	Lost Div. Semi-Final
1985-86*	80	21	17	2	....	19	19	2	....	40	36	4	....	332	302	84	4th, Adams Div.	Lost Div. Final
1984-85*	80	17	18	5	....	13	23	4	....	30	41	9	....	268	318	69	5th, Adams Div.	Out of Playoffs
1983-84*	80	19	16	5	....	9	26	5	....	28	42	10	....	288	320	66	5th, Adams Div.	Out of Playoffs
1982-83*	80	13	22	5	....	6	32	2	....	19	54	7	....	261	403	45	5th, Adams Div.	Out of Playoffs
1981-82*	80	13	17	10	....	8	24	8	....	21	41	18	....	264	351	60	5th, Adams Div.	Out of Playoffs
1980-81*	80	14	17	9	....	7	24	9	....	21	41	18	....	292	372	60	4th, Norris Div.	Out of Playoffs
1979-80*	80	22	12	6	....	5	22	13	....	27	34	19	....	303	312	73	4th, Norris Div.	Lost Prelim. Round

* Hartford Whalers

NHL EASTERN CONFERENCE

2011-12 Player Personnel

FORWARDS	HT	WT	S	Place of Birth	*Age	2010-11 Club
BOWMAN, Drayson	6-1	190	L	Grand Rapids, MI	22	Carolina-Charlotte
BOYCHUK, Zach	5-10	185	L	Airdrie, Alta.	22	Carolina-Charlotte
BRENT, Tim	6-0	188	R	Cambridge, Ont.	27	Toronto
DALPE, Zac	6-1	195	R	Paris, Ont.	21	Carolina-Charlotte
DURNO, Chris	6-4	223	L	Scarborough, Ont.	30	Norfolk
DWYER, Patrick	5-11	175	R	Spokane, WA	28	Carolina
JOKINEN, Jussi	5-11	198	L	Kalajoki, Finland	28	Carolina
LaROSE, Chad	5-10	181	R	Fraser, MI	29	Carolina
MATSUMOTO, Jon	6-0	184	L	Ottawa, Ont.	24	Carolina-Charlotte
NASH, Riley	6-1	191	R	Consort, Alta.	22	Charlotte
PONIKAROVSKY, Alexei	6-4	226	L	Kiev, USSR	31	Los Angeles
RUUTU, Tuomo	6-0	205	L	Vantaa, Finland	28	Carolina
SAMSON, Jerome	6-0	195	R	Greenfield Park, Que.	24	Carolina-Charlotte
SKINNER, Jeff	5-11	193	L	Markham, Ont.	19	Carolina
STAAL, Eric	6-4	205	L	Thunder Bay, Ont.	26	Carolina
STEWART, Anthony	6-3	230	R	LaSalle, Que.	26	Atlanta
SUTTER, Brandon	6-3	183	R	Huntington, NY	22	Carolina
SUTTER, Brett	6-0	200	L	Viking, Alta.	24	Cgy-Car-Charlotte
TERRY, Chris	5-10	190	L	Brampton, Ont.	22	Charlotte
TLUSTY, Jiri	6-0	209	L	Slany, Czech.	23	Carolina-Charlotte

DEFENSEMEN						
ALLEN, Bryan	6-5	226	L	Kingston, Ont.	31	Florida-Carolina
BELLEMORE, Brett	6-4	205	R	Windsor, Ont.	23	Charlotte
GLEASON, Tim	6-0	217	L	Clawson, MI	28	Carolina
HARRISON, Jay	6-4	211	L	Oshawa, Ont.	28	Carolina
JOSLIN, Derek	6-1	210	L	Richmond Hill, Ont.	24	San Jose-Carolina
KABERLE, Tomas	6-1	214	L	Rakovnik, Czech.	33	Toronto-Boston
McBAIN, Jamie	6-2	200	R	Edina, MN	23	Carolina
PITKANEN, Joni	6-3	210	L	Oulu, Finland	28	Carolina
SANGUINETTI, Bobby	6-3	190	R	Trenton, NJ	23	Charlotte

GOALTENDERS	HT	WT	C	Place of Birth	*Age	2010-11 Club
BOUCHER, Brian	6-2	200	L	Woonsocket, RI	34	Philadelphia
MURPHY, Mike	5-11	172	L	Kingston, Ont.	22	Charlotte
PETERS, Justin	6-1	205	L	Blyth, Ont.	25	Carolina
WARD, Cam	6-1	185	L	Saskatoon, Sask.	27	Carolina

* – Age at start of 2011-12 season

Captains' History

Rick Ley, 1979-80; Rick Ley and Mike Rogers, 1980-81; Dave Keon, 1981-82; Russ Anderson, 1982-83; Mark Johnson, 1983-84; Mark Johnson and Ron Francis, 1984-85; Ron Francis, 1985-86 to 1990-91; Pat Verbeek, 1992-93 to 1994-95; Brendan Shanahan, 1995-96; Kevin Dineen, 1996-97, 1997-98; Keith Primeau, 1998-99; Keith Primeau and Ron Francis, 1999-2000; Ron Francis, 2000-01 to 2003-04; Rod Brind'Amour, 2005-06 to 2008-09; Rod Brind'Amour and Eric Staal, 2009-10; Eric Staal, 2010-11 to date.

Paul Maurice

Head Coach

Born: Sault Ste. Marie, Ont., January 30, 1967.

Paul Maurice was named head coach of the Carolina Hurricanes on December 3, 2008. After coaching the Toronto Maple Leafs for two seasons, he returned to a franchise where he was the winningest coach in history, having amassed 268 wins in his 674 regular-season games coached during first eight-plus seasons with the team from November 6, 1995, until December 15, 2003. After taking over the Hurricanes midway through the 2008-09 season, he led the team to the Eastern Conference Finals.

Maurice guided the Hurricanes to the 2002 Eastern Conference title and two Southeast Division crowns during his first stint as the team's head coach. He led the team to four consecutive winning seasons from 1999 to 2002. Prior to the 2003-04 season, Maurice was the longest-tenured head coach in the NHL after having originally been promoted from a Hartford Whalers assistant coach's position on November 6, 1995. At only 28 years old when he was first hired, Maurice was the league's youngest head coach, a distinction he maintained until the Boston Bruins hired Mike Sullivan on June 23, 2003.

Prior to joining the Whalers as an assistant coach during the summer of 1995, Maurice spent two seasons as head coach of the Ontario Hockey League's Detroit Jr. Red Wings. He led the team to the 1995 OHL championship and an appearance in the Memorial Cup. That season, he finished second in voting to Guelph's Craig Hartsburg for the Matt Leyden Trophy, which is annually awarded to the OHL's Coach of the Year.

Maurice played his junior hockey with the OHL's Windsor Spitfires (1984 to 1988). He was Philadelphia's 12th choice, 252nd overall, in the 1985 NHL Entry Draft but had his career cut short due to an eye injury and began coaching as an assistant with the Jr. Red Wings shortly thereafter.

2010-11 Scoring
* – rookie

Regular Season

Pos	#	Player	Team	GP	G	A	Pts	TOI	+/-	PIM	PP	SH	GW	S	%
C	12	Eric Staal	CAR	81	33	43	76	21:56	–10	72	12	3	8	296	11.1
C	53	* Jeff Skinner	CAR	82	31	32	63	16:43	3	46	6	0	2	215	14.4
R	15	Tuomo Ruutu	CAR	82	19	38	57	16:49	1	54	7	0	1	148	12.8
L	26	Erik Cole	CAR	82	26	26	52	18:27	–1	49	3	1	9	201	12.9
L	36	Jussi Jokinen	CAR	70	19	33	52	17:13	3	24	8	0	1	136	14.0
D	77	Joe Corvo	CAR	82	11	29	40	24:46	–14	18	5	1	1	191	5.8
C	61	Cory Stillman	FLA	44	7	16	23	15:55	3	20	1	0	1	81	8.6
			CAR	21	5	11	16	18:58	2	4	2	0	1	35	14.3
			Total	65	12	27	39	16:54	5	24	3	0	2	116	10.3
D	25	Joni Pitkanen	CAR	72	5	30	35	25:01	–2	60	1	0	1	144	3.5
R	59	Chad Larose	CAR	82	16	15	31	16:00	–21	59	2	1	0	176	9.1
D	4	* Jamie McBain	CAR	76	7	23	30	19:06	–8	32	1	0	2	95	7.4
R	16	Brandon Sutter	CAR	82	14	15	29	16:50	13	25	1	0	3	145	9.7
R	39	Patrick Dwyer	CAR	80	8	10	18	12:34	–6	12	0	1	2	104	7.7
D	5	Bryan Allen	FLA	53	4	8	12	19:12	–5	63	0	0	1	50	8.0
			CAR	19	0	5	5	15:50	4	19	0	0	0	8	0.0
			Total	72	4	13	17	18:19	–1	82	0	0	1	58	6.9
D	6	Tim Gleason	CAR	82	2	14	16	20:57	–11	85	0	0	0	84	2.4
C	19	Jiri Tlusty	CAR	57	6	6	12	9:51	1	14	0	0	1	53	11.3
D	44	Jay Harrison	CAR	72	3	7	10	15:16	5	72	0	0	0	49	6.1
D	33	Derek Joslin	S.J.	17	1	3	4	12:28	–2	8	0	0	0	11	9.1
			CAR	17	1	4	5	18:03	7	2	1	0	1	23	4.3
			Total	34	2	7	9	15:15	5	10	1	0	1	34	5.9
L	11	Zach Boychuk	CAR	23	4	3	7	10:43	–2	4	1	0	1	44	9.1
C	22	* Zac Dalpe	CAR	15	3	1	4	7:56	0	0	0	0	1	16	18.8
R	20	Troy Bodie	ANA	9	0	1	1	9:43	–3	7	0	0	0	5	0.0
			CAR	50	1	2	3	6:18	–4	54	0	0	0	39	2.6
			Total	59	1	3	4	6:49	–7	61	0	0	0	44	2.3
C	18	* Jon Matsumoto	CAR	13	2	0	2	7:04	–4	0	0	0	0	11	18.2
R	71	* Jerome Samson	CAR	23	2	2	2	6:51	0	0	0	0	0	28	0.0
L	42	* Brett Sutter	CGY	4	0	1	1	10:07	–1	5	0	0	0	3	0.0
			CAR	1	0	0	0	4:09	0	0	0	0	0	0	0.0
			Total	5	0	1	1	8:55	–1	5	0	0	0	3	0.0
L	21	* Drayson Bowman	CAR	23	0	1	1	9:48	0	12	0	0	0	28	0.0
D	28	Bryan Rodney	CAR	3	0	0	0	8:44	0	2	0	0	0	3	0.0

Goaltending

No.	Goaltender	GPI	Mins	Avg	W	L	OT	EN	SO	GA	SA	S%	G	A	PIM
30	Cam Ward	74	4318	2.56	37	26	10	7	4	184	2375	.923	0	1	0
60	* Justin Peters	12	648	3.98	3	5	1	0	0	43	343	.875	0	0	4
	Totals	82	4997	2.81	40	31	11	7		4	234	2725	.914			

Brandon Sutter played in all 82 games with Carolina in 2010-11. He is one of three members of the famous family currently in the Hurricanes system, along with cousins Brett and Brody.

Coaching Record

Season	Team	League	GC	W	L	O/T	GC	W	L	T
				Regular Season				Playoffs		
1993-94	Detroit	OHL	66	42	20	4	17	11	6	....
1994-95	Detroit	OHL	44	18	4	....	21	16	5	....
1994-95	Detroit	M-Cup	....	....	....	....	5	3	2	....
1995-96	**Hartford**	**NHL**	70	29	33	8	....	....	....	....
1996-97	**Hartford**	**NHL**	82	32	39	11	....	....	....	....
1997-98	**Carolina**	**NHL**	82	33	41	8	....	....	....	....
1998-99	**Carolina**	**NHL**	82	34	30	18	6	2	4	....
99-2000	**Carolina**	**NHL**	82	37	35	10	....	....	....	....
2000-01	**Carolina**	**NHL**	82	38	32	12	6	2	4	....
2001-02	**Carolina**	**NHL**	82	35	26	21	23	13	10	....
2002-03	**Carolina**	**NHL**	82	22	43	17	....	....	....	....
2003-04	**Carolina**	**NHL**	30	8	12	10	....	....	....	....
2005-06	Toronto	AHL	80	41	29	10	5	1	4	....
2006-07	**Toronto**	**NHL**	82	40	31	11	....	....	....	....
2007-08	**Toronto**	**NHL**	82	36	35	11	....	....	....	....
2008-09	**Carolina**	**NHL**	57	33	19	5	18	8	19	....
2009-10	**Carolina**	**NHL**	82	35	37	10	....	....	....	....
2010-11	**Carolina**	**NHL**	82	40	31	11	....	....	....	....
	NHL Totals		1059	452	444	163	53	25	37	

Club Records

Team

(Figures in brackets for season records are games played; records for fewest points, wins, ties, losses, goals, goals against are for 70 or more games)

Most Points **112** 2005-06 (82)
Most Wins **52** 2005-06 (82)
Most Ties **19** 1979-80 (80)
Most Losses **54** 1982-83 (80)
Most Goals **332** 1985-86 (80)
Most Goals Against **403** 1982-83 (80)
Fewest Points **45** 1982-83 (80)
Fewest Wins **19** 1982-83 (80)
Fewest Ties **4** 1985-86 (80)
Fewest Losses **22** 2005-06 (82)
Fewest Goals **171** 2002-03 (82)
Fewest Goals Against **202** 1998-99 (82)

Longest Winning Streak
Overall .... **9** Oct. 22-Nov. 11/05, Dec. 31/05-Jan. 19/06, Mar. 18-Apr. 07/09
Home .... **12** Feb. 20-Apr. 7/09
Away .... **6** Nov. 10-Dec. 7/90

Longest Undefeated Streak
Overall .... **10** Jan. 20-Feb. 10/82 (6 wins, 4 ties)
Home .... **12** Feb. 20-Apr. 7/09 (12 wins)
Away .... **8** Nov. 11-Dec. 5/96 (4 wins, 4 ties)

Longest Losing Streak
Overall .... **14** Oct. 10-Nov. 13/09
Home .... **7** Dec. 27/02-Jan. 20/03
Away .... **13** Dec. 18/82-Feb. 5/83, Oct. 3-Nov. 28/09

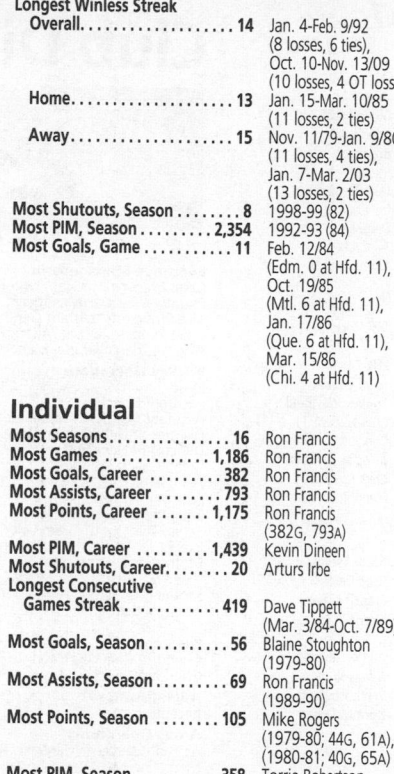

Longest Winless Streak
Overall .... **14** Jan. 4-Feb. 9/92 (8 losses, 6 ties), Oct. 10-Nov. 13/09 (10 losses, 4 OT losses)
Home .... **13** Jan. 15-Mar. 10/85 (11 losses, 2 ties)
Away .... **15** Nov. 11/79-Jan. 9/80 (11 losses, 4 ties), Jan. 7-Mar. 2/03 (13 losses, 2 ties)

Most Shutouts, Season **8** 1998-99 (82)
Most PIM, Season **2,354** 1992-93 (84)
Most Goals, Game .... **11** Feb. 12/84 (Edm. 0 at Hfd. 11), Oct. 19/85 (Mtl. 6 at Hfd. 11), Jan. 17/86 (Que. 6 at Hfd. 11), Mar. 15/86 (Chi. 4 at Hfd. 11)

Individual

Most Seasons .... **16** Ron Francis
Most Games .... **1,186** Ron Francis
Most Goals, Career .... **382** Ron Francis
Most Assists, Career .... **793** Ron Francis
Most Points, Career .... **1,175** Ron Francis (382G, 793A)
Most PIM, Career .... **1,439** Kevin Dineen
Most Shutouts, Career .... **20** Arturs Irbe
Longest Consecutive Games Streak .... **419** Dave Tippett (Mar. 3/84-Oct. 7/89)
Most Goals, Season .... **56** Blaine Stoughton (1979-80)
Most Assists, Season .... **69** Ron Francis (1989-90)
Most Points, Season .... **105** Mike Rogers (1979-80; 44G, 61A), (1980-81; 40G, 65A)
Most PIM, Season .... **358** Torrie Robertson (1985-86)
Most Points, Defenseman, Season .... **69** Dave Babych (1985-86; 14G, 55A)
Most Points, Center, Season .... **105** Mike Rogers (1979-80; 44G, 61A), (1980-81; 40G, 65A)
Most Points, Right Wing, Season .... **100** Blaine Stoughton (1979-80; 56G, 44A)
Most Points, Left Wing, Season .... **89** Geoff Sanderson (1992-93; 46G, 43A)
Most Points, Rookie, Season .... **72** Sylvain Turgeon (1983-84; 40G, 32A)
Most Shutouts, Season .... **6** Arturs Irbe (1998-99), (2000-01) Kevin Weekes (2003-04) Cam Ward (2008-09)
Most Goals, Game .... **4** Jordy Douglas (Feb. 3/80) Ron Francis (Feb. 12/84) Eric Staal (Mar. 7/09)
Most Assists, Game .... **6** Ron Francis (Mar. 5/87)
Most Points, Game .... **6** Paul Lawless (Jan. 4/87; 2G, 4A) Ron Francis (Mar. 5/87; 6A), (Oct. 8/89; 3G, 3A) Eric Staal (Mar. 7/09; 4G, 2A)

Records include Hartford Whalers, 1979-80 through 1996-97.

Retired Numbers

2	Glen Wesley	1994-2008
10	Ron Francis	1981-1991; 1998-2004
17	Rod Brind'Amour	2000-2010

All-time Record vs. Other Clubs

Regular Season

	At Home								On Road								Total							
	GP	W	L	T	OL	GF	GA	PTS	GP	W	L	T	OL	GF	GA	PTS	GP	W	L	T	OL	GF	GA	PTS
Anaheim	12	7	4	1	0	32	27	15	12	5	6	1	0	37	35	11	24	12	10	2	0	69	62	26
Atlanta	34	19	11	1	3	107	106	42	34	24	6	3	1	120	85	52	68	43	17	4	4	227	191	94
Boston	88	36	41	9	2	288	302	83	90	31	52	7	0	237	313	69	178	67	93	16	2	525	615	152
Buffalo	90	38	39	11	2	261	270	89	89	29	52	7	1	254	353	66	179	67	91	18	3	515	623	155
Calgary	31	12	14	5	0	106	113	29	31	6	23	2	0	93	147	14	62	18	37	7	0	199	260	43
Chicago	32	16	12	4	0	106	98	36	32	11	17	3	1	90	125	26	64	27	29	7	1	196	223	62
Colorado	66	27	26	12	1	216	223	67	67	17	41	9	0	197	284	43	133	44	67	21	1	413	507	110
Columbus	7	4	3	0	0	18	20	8	5	2	3	0	0	12	13	4	12	6	6	0	0	30	33	12
Dallas	35	15	16	4	0	112	121	34	33	10	18	2	3	93	127	25	68	25	34	6	3	205	248	59
Detroit	33	19	13	1	0	111	91	39	33	7	18	7	1	89	127	22	66	26	31	8	1	200	218	61
Edmonton	32	13	12	7	0	127	104	33	33	7	21	5	0	95	128	19	65	20	33	12	0	222	232	52
Florida	46	31	11	3	1	149	114	66	47	17	20	8	2	115	147	44	93	48	31	11	3	264	261	110
Los Angeles	33	16	12	5	0	118	121	37	33	11	18	3	1	122	139	26	66	27	30	8	1	240	260	63
Minnesota	5	5	0	0	0	13	7	10	8	2	3	2	1	24	23	7	13	7	3	2	1	37	30	17
Montreal	90	36	40	13	1	265	305	86	87	26	51	7	3	255	338	62	177	62	91	20	4	520	643	148
Nashville	8	3	2	1	2	22	24	9	7	1	6	0	0	11	19	2	15	4	8	1	2	33	43	11
New Jersey	56	24	23	8	1	168	166	57	57	19	31	4	3	167	194	45	113	43	54	12	4	335	360	102
NY Islanders	57	30	20	5	2	204	178	67	56	28	21	4	3	166	162	63	113	58	41	9	5	370	340	130
NY Rangers	55	31	20	3	1	179	163	66	57	19	31	4	3	143	200	45	112	50	51	7	4	322	363	111
Ottawa	39	24	11	4	0	118	95	52	41	17	19	4	1	105	120	39	80	41	30	8	1	223	215	91
Philadelphia	56	16	27	9	4	169	205	45	55	13	32	5	5	138	205	36	111	29	59	14	9	307	410	81
Phoenix	33	15	12	6	0	108	97	36	34	17	15	2	0	127	123	36	67	32	27	8	0	235	220	72
Pittsburgh	60	30	24	5	1	216	207	66	58	23	26	6	3	206	222	55	118	53	50	11	4	422	429	121
St. Louis	34	14	18	2	0	100	105	30	34	11	19	3	1	97	121	26	68	25	37	5	1	197	226	56
San Jose	13	7	6	0	0	41	32	14	14	6	8	0	0	43	59	12	27	13	14	0	0	84	91	26
Tampa Bay	48	28	11	7	2	152	132	65	47	17	23	3	4	132	146	41	95	45	34	10	6	284	278	106
Toronto	49	25	17	6	1	187	162	57	48	25	17	5	1	168	154	56	97	50	34	11	2	355	316	113
Vancouver	31	14	12	5	0	102	104	33	33	10	15	6	2	88	118	28	64	24	27	11	2	190	222	61
Washington	70	27	31	10	2	198	210	66	68	23	37	4	4	178	227	54	138	50	68	14	6	376	437	120
Totals	**1243**	**582**	**488**	**147**	**26**	**3993**	**3902**	**1337**	**1243**	**434**	**649**	**116**	**44**	**3602**	**4454**	**1028**	**2486**	**1016**	**1137**	**263**	**70**	**7595**	**8356**	**2365**

Playoffs

	Series	W	L	GP	W	L	T	GF	GA	Last Mtg.	Rnd.	Result
Boston	4	1	3	26	11	15	0	64	80	2009	CSF	W 4-3
Buffalo	1	1	0	7	4	3	0	22	17	2006	CF	W 4-3
Colorado	2	1	1	9	5	4	0	35	34	1987	DSF	L 2-4
Detroit	1	0	1	5	1	4	0	7	14	2002	F	L 1-4
Edmonton	1	1	0	7	4	3	0	19	16	2006	F	W 4-3
Montreal	7	2	5	39	16	23	0	106	125	2006	CQF	W 4-2
New Jersey	4	3	1	24	14	10	0	51	56	2009	CQF	W 4-3
Pittsburgh	1	0	1	4	0	4	0	9	20	2009	CF	L 0-4
Toronto	1	1	0	6	4	2	0	10	6	2002	CF	W 4-2
Totals	**22**	**10**	**12**	**127**	**59**	**68**	**0**	**323**	**368**			

Calgary totals include Atlanta Flames, 1979-80.
Dallas totals include Minnesota North Stars, 1979-80 to 1992-93.
Phoenix totals include Winnipeg, 1979-80 to 1995-96.

Playoff Results 2011-2007

Year	Round	Opponent	Result	GF	GA
2009	CF	Pittsburgh	L 0-4	9	20
	CSF	Boston	W 4-3	16	17
	CQF	New Jersey	W 4-3	17	15

Abbreviations: Round: F - Final; **CF** - conference final; **CSF** - conference semi-final; **CQF** - conference quarter-final; **DSF** - division semi-final.

Colorado totals include Quebec, 1979-80 to 1994-95.
New Jersey totals include Colorado Rockies, 1979-80 to 1981-82.

2010-11 Results

Oct.	7	at Minnesota	4-3
	8	Minnesota	2-1†
	14	at Ottawa	2-3
	17	at Vancouver	1-5
	19	at San Jose	5-2
	20	at Los Angeles	3-4
	23	at Phoenix	4-3*
	27	Washington	0-3
	29	at NY Rangers	4-3
	30	Pittsburgh	0-3
Nov.	1	at Philadelphia	2-3
	3	NY Islanders	7-2
	5	at Florida	4-7
	6	Florida	3-2
	9	Edmonton	7-1
	11	Philadelphia	1-8
	13	at Montreal	2-7
	17	Ottawa	7-1
	19	at Pittsburgh	4-5†
	20	Nashville	1-2†
	24	Washington	2-3
	26	at Boston	3-0
	28	at Washington	2-3†
	29	Dallas	1-4
Dec.	3	Colorado	2-1*
	4	at Nashville	2-5
	10	at Dallas	1-2†
	11	at St. Louis	2-1†
	15	at Florida	4-3
	16	at Atlanta	3-2†
	18	Anaheim	4-2
	20	at Tampa Bay	1-5
	23	Montreal	2-3
	26	Washington	2-3
	28	at Toronto	4-3
	29	at Ottawa	4-0
Jan.	1	New Jersey	6-3
	3	Florida	3-4*
	5	at NY Rangers	1-2*
	7	at Florida	5-3
	9	Atlanta	4-3*
	11	Calgary	6-5†
	13	at Buffalo	2-3
	15	Tampa Bay	6-4
	17	at Boston	0-7
	18	Boston	2-3
	20	NY Rangers	4-1
	22	at Pittsburgh	2-3
	24	Toronto	6-4
	26	at NY Islanders	4-2
Feb.	1	Boston	2-3
	3	at Toronto	0-3
	5	Atlanta	4-3*
	8	at New Jersey	2-3*
	10	at Philadelphia	1-2
	12	at Tampa Bay	3-4*
	13	at Atlanta	3-2
	16	at New Jersey	2-3
	18	Philadelphia	3-2
	19	New Jersey	1-4
	22	NY Rangers	3-4†
	25	Pittsburgh	4-1
	26	at Montreal	3-4
Mar.	1	Florida	2-1
	3	Buffalo	3-2*
	4	at Chicago	2-5
	9	Atlanta	2-3*
	11	at Washington	1-2
	12	Columbus	2-3
	15	at Buffalo	1-0
	16	Toronto	1-3
	18	NY Islanders	3-2*
	22	Ottawa	4-3
	25	at Tampa Bay	4-3
	26	Tampa Bay	2-4
	29	at Washington	3-2†
	30	Montreal	6-2
Apr.	2	at NY Islanders	4-2
	3	Buffalo	1-2*
	6	Detroit	3-0
	8	at Atlanta	6-1
	9	Tampa Bay	2-6

* – Overtime † – Shootout

Entry Draft Selections 2011-1997

Name in bold denotes played in NHL.

2011

Pick	
12	Ryan Murphy
42	Victor Rask
73	Keegan Lowe
103	Gregory Hofmann
163	Matt Mahalak
193	Brody Sutter

2010

Pick	
7	**Jeff Skinner**
37	Justin Faulk
53	Mark Alt
67	Danny Biega
85	Austin Levi
105	Justin Shugg
167	Tyler Stahl
187	Frederik Andersen

2009

Pick	
27	Philippe Paradis
51	Brian Dumoulin
88	Mattias Lindstrom
131	Matt Kennedy
178	Rasmus Rissanen
208	Tommi Kivisto

2008

Pick	
14	**Zach Boychuk**
45	**Zac Dalpe**
105	Michal Jordan
165	Mike Murphy
195	Samuel Morneau

2007

Pick	
11	**Brandon Sutter**
72	**Drayson Bowman**
102	Justin McCrae
132	Chris Terry
162	Brett Bellemore

2006

Pick	
63	**Jamie McBain**
93	Harrison Reed
123	Bobby Hughes
153	Stefan Chaput
183	Nick Dodge
213	Justin Krueger

2005

Pick	
3	**Jack Johnson**
58	Nate Hagemo
64	Joe Barnes
94	Jakub Vojta
123	Ondrej Otcenas
145	Tim Kunes
159	Risto Korhonen
192	Nicolas Blanchard
198	Kyle Lawson

2004

Pick	
4	**Andrew Ladd**
38	**Justin Peters**
69	**Casey Borer**
109	**Brett Carson**
137	Magnus Akerlund
202	Ryan Pottruff
235	Jonas Fiedler
268	Martin Vagner

2003

Pick	
2	**Eric Staal**
31	**Danny Richmond**
102	Aaron Dawson
126	Kevin Nastiuk
130	Matej Trojovsky
137	**Tyson Strachan**
198	**Shay Stephenson**
230	Jamie Hoffmann
262	Ryan Rorabeck

2002

Pick	
25	**Cam Ward**
91	Jesse Lane
160	Daniel Manzato
224	Adam Taylor

2001

Pick	
15	Igor Knyazev
46	**Mike Zigomanis**
91	Kevin Estrada
110	Rob Zepp
181	Daniel Boisclair
211	Sean Curry
244	Carter Trevisani
274	Peter Reynolds

2000

Pick	
32	**Tomas Kurka**
80	**Ryan Bayda**
97	**Niclas Wallin**
110	Jared Newman
181	J.D. Forrest
212	Magnus Kahnberg
235	Craig Kowalski
276	Troy Ferguson

1999

Pick	
16	**David Tanabe**
49	**Brett Lysak**
84	**Brad Fast**
113	Ryan Murphy
174	**Damian Surma**
202	Jim Baxter
231	David Evans
237	Antti Jokela
259	Yevgeny Kurilin

1998

Pick	
11	**Jeff Heerema**
70	Kevin Holdridge
71	**Erik Cole**
91	**Josef Vasicek**
93	**Tommy Westlund**
97	Chris Madden
184	Don Smith
208	**Jaroslav Svoboda**
211	Mark Kosick
239	Brent McDonald

1997

Pick	
22	**Nikos Tselios**
28	**Brad DeFauw**
80	**Francis Lessard**
88	**Shane Willis**
142	Kyle Dafoe
169	Andrew Merrick
195	**Niklas Nordgren**
199	Randy Fitzgerald
225	**Kent McDonell**

Coaching History

Don Blackburn, 1979-80; Don Blackburn and Larry Pleau, 1980-81; Larry Pleau, 1981-82; Larry Kish, Larry Pleau and John Cuniff, 1982- 83; Jack Evans, 1983-84 to 1986-87; Jack Evans and Larry Pleau, 1987-88; Larry Pleau, 1988-89; Rick Ley, 1989-90, 1990-91; Jim Roberts, 1991-92; Paul Holmgren, 1992-93; Paul Holmgren and Pierre Maguire, 1993-94; Paul Holmgren, 1994-95; Paul Holmgren and Paul Maurice, 1995-96; Paul Maurice, 1996-97 to 2002-03; Paul Maurice and Peter Laviolette, 2003-04; Peter Laviolette, 2004-05 to 2007-08; Peter Laviolette and Paul Maurice, 2008-09; Paul Maurice, 2009-10 to date.

General Managers' History

Jack Kelley, 1979-80; Jack Kelley and Larry Pleau, 1980-81; Larry Pleau, 1981-82, 1982-83; Emile Francis, 1983-84 to 1988-89; Eddie Johnston, 1989-90 to 1991-92; Brian Burke, 1992-93; Paul Holmgren, 1993-94; Jim Rutherford, 1994-95 to date.

Jim Rutherford

President and General Manager

Born: Beeton, Ont., February 17, 1949.

Jim Rutherford, a former NHL goaltender, is the franchise's seventh general manager and the only general manager of the Carolina Hurricanes. Named to his position on June 28, 1994, Rutherford has always taken an aggressive approach towards improving the fortunes of the franchise through trades and the NHL Entry Draft. In 2002, the team reached the Stanley Cup Finals for the first time in history. The Hurricanes won the Stanley Cup in 2006.

A veteran of 13 NHL seasons, Rutherford began his professional goaltending career in 1969 as a first-round selection of the Detroit Red Wings. While playing for Detroit, Pittsburgh, Toronto and Los Angeles, Rutherford collected 14 career shutouts. For five seasons he also served as the Red Wings' player representative. Rutherford also played for Team Canada at the World Championships in Vienna in 1977 and Moscow in 1979.

After his playing days with the Red Wings, Rutherford joined Compuware to serve as the director of hockey operations for Compuware Sports Corporation. Rutherford gained a wealth of experience in youth hockey and junior programs. As a former player, coach, and general manager, his ability to develop players and produce winning programs is widely respected throughout the hockey community.

He started his management career by guiding Compuware Sports Corporation's purchase of the Windsor Spitfires of the Ontario Hockey League in April of 1984. During the next four years, Rutherford acted as general manager of the Spitfires. After the Spitfires advanced to the 1988 Memorial Cup finals, Rutherford led Compuware's efforts to bring the first American-based OHL franchise to Detroit on December 11, 1989. Rutherford was voted the 1987 executive of the year in both the OHL and the Canadian Hockey League and won the OHL executive of the year award again in 1988.

Club Directory

RBC Center

Carolina Hurricanes
1400 Edwards Mill Rd.
Raleigh, NC 27607
Phone **919/467-7825**
FAX 919/462-0123
Tickets 1.866.NHL.CANES
www.carolinahurricanes.com
Capacity: 18,680

Executive Management

Chief Executive Officer/Owner/Governor	Peter Karmanos, Jr.
President/General Manager	Jim Rutherford
Vice President/Assistant General Manager	Jason Karmanos
Chief Financial Officer/Alternate Governor	Mike Amendola
Vice President/General Manager, RBC Center	Davin Olsen

Hockey Operations

Head Coach	Paul Maurice
Assistant Coaches	Dave Lewis, Tom Barrasso
Assistant Coach /Development Coach	Rod Brind'Amour
Director of Defensemen Development	Glen Wesley
Director of Hockey Operations	Ron Francis
Video Coach	Chris Huffine
Head Ath. Trainer/Strength Conditioning Coach	Peter Friesen
Assistant Athletic Trainer	Doug Bennett
Equipment Managers	Wally Tatomir, Skip Cunningham, Bob Gorman
Senior Director of Team Operations	Brian Tatum
Executive Assistant to the President/G.M.	Mari Jeter
Motivational Consultant/Mgr. Community Dev.	Doris E. Barksdale
Video Scouting Coordinator	Darren Yorke
Scouting Directors, Amateur / Pro	Tony MacDonald / Marshall Johnston
Amateur Scouts	Sheldon Ferguson, Robert Kron, Bob Luccini, Bert Marshall
Pro Scouts	Tom Rowe, Greg Stefan
Charlotte Checkers Head Coach/G.M.	Jeff Daniels
Charlotte Checkers Assistant Coach	Geordie Kinnear

Administration

Receptionists	Mary Lou Ruetz, Janet Davis

Arena Operations

Assistant General Manager, RBC Center	Larry Perkins
Marketing Manager	Crystal Pace
Guest Services Coordinator/Executive Assistant	April Keeley
Security Manager / Parking Manager	Clinton Peterson / Mike Alexander
Event Services Manager	Steve Congress
Premium Services and Sales Manager	Suzanne Golden
Operations, Director / Asst. Manager	Dan McGowan / Melvin Terrell
Facility Systems Manager	Alan Wobbleton
Director of Ticket Operations	Bill Nowicki
Managers, Arena Box Office / Office	Joe Sousa / Hilman Huskey
Assistant Managers, Box Office / Ticket Ops	Erin Wallace /

Broadcasters

Television Play-by-Play / Analyst	John Forslund / Tripp Tracy
Radio Play-by-Play	Chuck Kaiton

Communications

Director of Media Relations	Mike Sundheim
Manager of Media Relations/Broadcast Coord.	Kyle Hanlin
Team Photographer	Gregg Forwerck

Finance/Information Technology

General Counsel/Senior Director of Finance	William Traurig
Accountant	David Johnston
Accounts Payable / Receivable	Michael Arrington / Patty Hilliard, Temika Smith-Harris
Payroll/Human Resources Coordinators	Crystal DeDitius, Keitha Stanley
Assistant to the CFO	Stacey Ustin
Director of Information Technology	Glenn Johnson
Client/Server Technologist	Dwight Baptist
Systems Adminstrator / Client/Server Developer	Myatt Williams / Alex Byrd

Food and Beverage

Director of Food and Beverage	Chris Diamond
Chefs	Rick Rhodes , Michael Flood, Dennis Atkinson, Kevin Heintz, Lecan Huynh, Pete Aiello
Managers	Katrina Ryan, Gary Berry, Lori Holtz
Assistant Managers	Barbara Couch, Jim O'Brien, Skip Roach, Frankie McGee

Marketing

Sr Director of Marketing/ Exec. Dir., Kids 'n Community Foundation	Doug Warf
Director of Marketing and Brand Development	Ben Aycock
Dir. of Canesvision and In-Game Marketing	Stephen Rutherford
Dir. of Community Relations and Promotions	Jon Chase
Senior Writer and Digital Media Producer	TBD
Graphic Designers / Marketing Coordinator	Lauren Baxter, Andrew Roman / Coop Elias
Youth and Amateur Hockey Coordinator	TBD
Mascot Coordinator	George Brown
Promotions/Fan Development Coordinator	Ryan O'Quinn
Sr. Coordinator, Community Relations/ Asst. Dir., Kids 'n Community Foundation	Katharine Kelley
Community Relations Coordinator	Kristina Boyce

Gale Force Media, CanesVision and Wolfpack TV

Senior Producers	Charles Graham, Don Sill
Producer	Marshall Alderman,
Graphics Producer	Rachel Cannon

Merchandise

Retail Operations Manager	James Blitch

Sales

Senior Director of Corporate Sponsorships	Jim Ballweg
Senior Corporate Sales Executive	Rick Francis
Corporate Sales Executive	Johnny Gill, Jennifer Pieh
Ticket Sales Director / Assistant	Kyle Prairie / Karen Prince
Manager of Sales and Client Services	Peterson Avetta
Account Executives/Business Development	Brian Chacos, Michael Miller, Greg Perna
Client Relations Representatives	Lauren Barrow, Tim Corrigan, Brian Friedhaber, Matt Horton
Hurricanes Group Sales Manager	Brian Kapusta
RBC Center Group Sales Manager	Brian Slais
Client Services Representative / Coordinator	Rich Davis / Kaitlin Szulik

Chicago Blackhawks

Key Off-Season Signings/Acquisitions

2011

May 19 • Re-signed G **Corey Crawford**.

June 25 • Acquired LW **Rostislav Olesz** from Florida for D **Brian Campbell**.

29 • Acquired the rights to negotiate with D **Steve Montador** from Buffalo for a 7th-round pick in the 2012 or 2013 Entry Draft.

30 • Signed D **Steve Montador**.

July 1 • Signed LW **Andrew Brunette**, RW **Jamal Mayers**, C **Brett McLean**, D **Sean O'Donnell** and LW **Dan Carcillo**.

10 • Re-signed LW **Viktor Stalberg**.

15 • Re-signed LW **Michael Frolik**.

15 • Signed D **Sami Lepisto**.

Aug. 3 • Re-signed C **Patrick Sharp**.

2011-12 Schedule

Month	Day	Date	Opponent
Oct.	Fri.	7	at Dallas
	Sat.	8	Dallas
	Thu.	13	Winnipeg
	Sat.	15	Boston
	Tue.	18	at Phoenix
	Thu.	20	at Colorado
	Sat.	22	Colorado
	Tue.	25	Anaheim
	Fri.	28	at Carolina
	Sat.	29	Columbus
	Mon.	31	Nashville
Nov.	Thu.	3	at Florida
	Fri.	4	at Tampa Bay
	Sun.	6	Vancouver
	Tue.	8	at St. Louis
	Thu.	10	at Columbus
	Fri.	11	Calgary
	Sun.	13	Edmonton
	Wed.	16	at Vancouver
	Fri.	18	at Calgary
	Sat.	19	at Edmonton
	Wed.	23	at San Jose
	Fri.	25	at Anaheim*
	Sat.	26	at Los Angeles
	Tue.	29	Phoenix
Dec.	Fri.	2	NY Islanders
	Sat.	3	at St. Louis
	Mon.	5	Phoenix
	Thu.	8	at NY Islanders
	Sun.	11	San Jose
	Wed.	14	at Minnesota
	Fri.	16	Anaheim
	Sun.	18	Calgary
	Tue.	20	at Pittsburgh
	Wed.	21	Montreal
	Mon.	26	Columbus
	Wed.	28	Los Angeles
	Fri.	30	Detroit
Jan.	Mon.	2	Edmonton
	Thu.	5	at Philadelphia
	Fri.	6	Colorado
	Sun.	8	Detroit
	Tue.	10	Columbus
	Thu.	12	Minnesota
	Sat.	14	at Detroit*
	Sun.	15	San Jose
	Wed.	18	Buffalo
	Fri.	20	Florida
	Sat.	21	at Nashville
	Tue.	24	Nashville
	Tue.	31	at Vancouver
Feb.	Thu.	2	at Edmonton
	Fri.	3	at Calgary
	Tue.	7	at Colorado
	Fri.	10	at San Jose
	Sat.	11	at Phoenix
	Tue.	14	at Nashville
	Thu.	16	at NY Rangers
	Sat.	18	at Columbus*
	Sun.	19	St. Louis*
	Tue.	21	Detroit
	Thu.	23	Dallas
	Sat.	25	at Los Angeles*
	Sun.	26	at Anaheim*
	Wed.	29	Toronto
Mar.	Fri.	2	at Ottawa
	Sun.	4	at Detroit*
	Tue.	6	at St. Louis
	Fri.	9	NY Rangers
	Sun.	11	Los Angeles
	Tue.	13	St. Louis
	Fri.	16	at Dallas
	Sun.	18	Washington
	Tue.	20	at Columbus
	Wed.	21	Vancouver
	Sun.	25	Nashville
	Tue.	27	at New Jersey
	Thu.	29	St. Louis
	Sat.	31	at Nashville
Apr.	Sun.	1	Minnesota
	Thu.	5	at Minnesota
	Sat.	7	at Detroit*

* Denotes afternoon game.

CENTRAL DIVISION
86th NHL Season

Franchise date: September 25, 1926

2010-11 Results: 44W-29L-4OTL-5SOL 97PTS.
Third, Central Division

Year-by-Year Record

		Home				Road				Overall								
Season	**GP**	**W**	**L**	**T**	**OL**	**W**	**L**	**T**	**OL**	**W**	**L**	**T**	**OL**	**GF**	**GA**	**Pts.**	**Finished**	**Playoff Result**
2010-11	82	24	17	....	0	20	12	....	9	44	29	....	9	258	225	97	3rd, Central Div.	Lost Conf. Quarter-Final
2009-10	**82**	**29**	**8**	**....**	**4**	**23**	**14**	**....**	**4**	**52**	**22**	**....**	**8**	**271**	**209**	**112**	**1st, Central Div.**	**Won Stanley Cup**
2008-09	82	24	9	....	8	22	15	....	4	46	24	....	12	264	216	104	2nd, Central Div.	Lost Conf. Championship
2007-08	82	23	16	....	2	17	18	....	6	40	34	....	8	239	235	88	3rd, Central Div.	Out of Playoffs
2006-07	82	17	20	....	4	14	22	....	5	31	42	....	9	201	258	71	5th, Central Div.	Out of Playoffs
2005-06	82	16	19	....	6	10	24	....	7	26	43	....	13	211	285	65	4th, Central Div.	Out of Playoffs
2004-05	....	....	....	....	....	....	....	....	....	....	....	....	....	....	....	....		
2003-04	82	13	17	6	5	7	26	5	3	20	43	11	8	188	259	59	5th, Central Div.	Out of Playoffs
2002-03	82	17	15	7	2	13	18	6	4	30	33	13	6	207	226	79	3rd, Central Div.	Out of Playoffs
2001-02	82	28	7	5	1	13	20	8	0	41	27	13	1	216	207	96	3rd, Central Div.	Lost Conf. Quarter-Final
2000-01	82	14	21	4	2	15	19	4	3	29	40	8	5	210	246	71	4th, Central Div.	Out of Playoffs
1999-2000	82	16	19	5	1	17	18	5	1	33	37	10	2	242	245	78	3rd, Central Div.	Out of Playoffs
1998-99	82	20	17	4	....	9	24	8	....	29	41	12	....	202	248	70	3rd, Central Div.	Out of Playoffs
1997-98	82	14	19	8	....	16	20	5	....	30	39	13	....	192	199	73	5th, Central Div.	Out of Playoffs
1996-97	82	16	21	4	....	18	14	9	....	34	35	13	....	223	210	81	5th, Central Div.	Lost Conf. Quarter-Final
1995-96	82	22	13	6	....	18	15	8	....	40	28	14	....	273	220	94	2nd, Central Div.	Lost Conf. Semi-Final
1994-95	48	11	10	3	....	13	9	2	....	24	19	5	....	156	115	53	3rd, Central Div.	Lost Conf. Championship
1993-94	84	21	16	5	....	18	20	4	....	39	36	9	....	254	240	87	5th, Central Div.	Lost Conf. Quarter-Final
1992-93	84	25	11	6	....	22	14	6	....	47	25	12	....	279	230	106	1st, Norris Div.	Lost Div. Semi-Final
1991-92	80	23	9	8	....	13	20	7	....	36	29	15	....	257	236	87	2nd, Norris Div.	Lost Final
1990-91	80	28	8	4	....	21	15	4	....	49	23	8	....	284	211	106	1st, Norris Div.	Lost Div. Semi-Final
1989-90	80	25	13	2	....	16	20	4	....	41	33	6	....	316	294	88	1st, Norris Div.	Lost Conf. Championship
1988-89	80	16	14	10	....	11	27	2	....	27	41	12	....	297	335	66	4th, Norris Div.	Lost Conf. Championship
1987-88	80	21	17	2	....	9	24	7	....	30	41	9	....	284	328	69	3rd, Norris Div.	Lost Div. Semi-Final
1986-87	80	18	13	9	....	11	24	5	....	29	37	14	....	290	310	72	3rd, Norris Div.	Lost Div. Semi-Final
1985-86	80	23	12	5	....	16	21	3	....	39	33	8	....	351	349	86	1st, Norris Div.	Lost Div. Semi-Final
1984-85	80	22	16	2	....	16	19	5	....	38	35	7	....	309	299	83	2nd, Norris Div.	Lost Conf. Championship
1983-84	80	25	13	2	....	5	29	6	....	30	42	8	....	277	311	68	4th, Norris Div.	Lost Div. Semi-Final
1982-83	80	29	8	3	....	18	15	7	....	47	23	10	....	338	268	104	1st, Norris Div.	Lost Conf. Championship
1981-82	80	20	13	7	....	10	25	5	....	30	38	12	....	332	363	72	4th, Norris Div.	Lost Conf. Championship
1980-81	80	21	11	8	....	10	22	8	....	31	33	16	....	304	315	78	2nd, Smythe Div.	Lost Prelim. Round
1979-80	80	21	12	7	....	13	15	12	....	34	27	19	....	241	250	87	1st, Smythe Div.	Lost Quarter-Final
1978-79	80	18	12	10	....	11	24	5	....	29	36	15	....	244	277	73	1st, Smythe Div.	Lost Quarter-Final
1977-78	80	20	9	11	....	12	20	8	....	32	29	19	....	230	220	83	1st, Smythe Div.	Lost Quarter-Final
1976-77	80	19	16	5	....	7	27	6	....	26	43	11	....	240	298	63	3rd, Smythe Div.	Lost Prelim. Round
1975-76	80	17	15	8	....	15	15	10	....	32	30	18	....	254	261	82	1st, Smythe Div.	Lost Quarter-Final
1974-75	80	24	12	4	....	13	23	4	....	37	35	8	....	268	241	82	3rd, Smythe Div.	Lost Quarter-Final
1973-74	78	20	6	13	....	21	8	10	....	41	14	23	....	272	164	105	2nd, West Div.	Lost Semi-Final
1972-73	78	26	9	4	....	16	18	5	....	42	27	9	....	284	225	93	1st, West Div.	Lost Final
1971-72	78	28	3	8	....	18	14	7	....	46	17	15	....	256	166	107	1st, West Div.	Lost Semi-Final
1970-71	78	30	6	3	....	19	14	6	....	49	20	9	....	277	184	107	1st, West Div.	Lost Final
1969-70	76	26	7	5	....	19	15	4	....	45	22	9	....	250	170	99	1st, East Div.	Lost Semi-Final
1968-69	76	20	14	4	....	14	19	5	....	34	33	9	....	280	246	77	6th, East Div.	Out of Playoffs
1967-68	74	20	13	4	....	12	13	12	....	32	26	16	....	212	222	80	4th, East Div.	Lost Semi-Final
1966-67	70	24	5	6	....	17	12	6	....	41	17	12	....	264	170	94	1st,	Lost Semi-Final
1965-66	70	21	8	6	....	16	17	2	....	37	25	8	....	240	187	82	2nd,	Lost Semi-Final
1964-65	70	20	13	2	....	14	15	6	....	34	28	8	....	224	176	76	3rd,	Lost Final
1963-64	70	26	4	5	....	10	18	7	....	36	22	12	....	218	169	84	2nd,	Lost Semi-Final
1962-63	70	17	9	9	....	15	12	8	....	32	21	17	....	194	178	81	2nd,	Lost Semi-Final
1961-62	70	20	10	5	....	11	16	8	....	31	26	13	....	217	186	75	3rd,	Lost Final
1960-61	**70**	**20**	**6**	**9**	**....**	**9**	**18**	**8**	**....**	**29**	**24**	**17**	**....**	**198**	**180**	**75**	**3rd,**	**Won Stanley Cup**
1959-60	70	18	11	6	....	10	18	7	....	28	29	13	....	191	180	69	3rd,	Lost Semi-Final
1958-59	70	14	12	9	....	14	17	4	....	28	29	13	....	197	208	69	3rd,	Lost Semi-Final
1957-58	70	15	17	3	....	9	22	4	....	24	39	7	....	163	202	55	5th,	Out of Playoffs
1956-57	70	12	15	8	....	4	24	7	....	16	39	15	....	169	225	47	6th,	Out of Playoffs
1955-56	70	9	19	7	....	10	20	5	....	19	39	12	....	155	216	50	6th,	Out of Playoffs
1954-55	70	6	21	8	....	7	19	9	....	13	40	17	....	161	235	43	6th,	Out of Playoffs
1953-54	70	8	21	6	....	4	30	1	....	12	51	7	....	133	242	31	6th,	Out of Playoffs
1952-53	70	14	11	10	....	13	17	5	....	27	28	15	....	169	175	69	4th,	Lost Semi-Final
1951-52	70	9	19	7	....	8	25	2	....	17	44	9	....	158	241	43	6th,	Out of Playoffs
1950-51	70	8	22	5	....	5	25	5	....	13	47	10	....	171	280	36	6th,	Out of Playoffs
1949-50	70	13	18	4	....	9	20	6	....	22	38	10	....	203	244	54	6th,	Out of Playoffs
1948-49	60	13	12	5	....	8	19	3	....	21	31	8	....	173	211	50	5th,	Out of Playoffs
1947-48	60	10	17	3	....	10	17	3	....	20	34	6	....	195	225	46	6th,	Out of Playoffs
1946-47	60	10	17	3	....	9	20	1	....	19	37	4	....	193	274	42	6th,	Out of Playoffs
1945-46	50	15	5	5	....	8	15	2	....	23	20	7	....	200	178	53	3rd,	Lost Semi-Final
1944-45	50	9	14	2	....	4	16	5	....	13	30	7	....	141	194	33	5th,	Out of Playoffs
1943-44	50	15	6	4	....	7	17	1	....	22	23	5	....	178	187	49	4th,	Lost Final
1942-43	50	14	3	8	....	3	15	7	....	17	18	15	....	179	180	49	5th,	Out of Playoffs
1941-42	48	15	8	1	....	7	15	2	....	22	23	3	....	145	155	47	4th,	Lost Quarter-Final
1940-41	48	11	10	3	....	5	15	4	....	16	25	7	....	112	139	39	5th,	Lost Semi-Final
1939-40	48	15	7	2	....	8	12	4	....	23	19	6	....	112	120	52	4th,	Lost Quarter-Final
1938-39	48	5	13	6	....	7	15	2	....	12	28	8	....	91	132	32	7th,	Out of Playoffs
1937-38	**48**	**10**	**10**	**4**	**....**	**4**	**15**	**5**	**....**	**14**	**25**	**9**	**....**	**97**	**139**	**37**	**3rd, Amn. Div.**	**Won Stanley Cup**
1936-37	48	8	13	3	....	6	14	4	....	14	27	7	....	99	131	35	4th, Amn. Div.	Out of Playoffs
1935-36	48	15	7	2	....	6	12	6	....	21	19	8	....	93	92	50	3rd, Amn. Div.	Lost Quarter-Final
1934-35	48	12	9	3	....	14	8	2	....	26	17	5	....	118	88	57	2nd, Amn. Div.	Lost Quarter-Final
1933-34	**48**	**13**	**4**	**7**	**....**	**7**	**13**	**4**	**....**	**20**	**17**	**11**	**....**	**88**	**83**	**51**	**2nd, Amn. Div.**	**Won Stanley Cup**
1932-33	48	12	7	5	....	4	13	7	....	16	20	12	....	88	101	44	4th, Amn. Div.	Out of Playoffs
1931-32	48	13	5	6	....	5	14	5	....	18	19	11	....	86	101	47	2nd, Amn. Div.	Lost Quarter-Final
1930-31	44	13	8	1	....	11	9	2	....	24	17	3	....	108	78	51	2nd, Amn. Div.	Lost Final
1929-30	44	12	9	1	....	9	9	4	....	21	18	5	....	117	111	47	2nd, Amn. Div.	Lost Quarter-Final
1928-29	44	3	13	6	....	4	16	2	....	7	29	8	....	33	85	22	5th, Amn. Div.	Out of Playoffs
1927-28	44	2	18	2	....	5	16	1	....	7	34	3	....	68	134	17	5th, Amn. Div.	Out of Playoffs
1926-27	44	12	8	2	....	7	14	1	....	19	22	3	....	115	116	41	3rd, Amn. Div.	Lost Quarter-Final

2011-12 Player Personnel

FORWARDS	HT	WT	S	Place of Birth	*Age	2010-11 Club
BEACH, Kyle	6-3	202	R	Vancouver, B.C.	21	Rockford
BICKELL, Bryan	6-4	223	L	Bowmanville, Ont.	25	Chicago
BOLLAND, Dave	6-0	181	R	Toronto, Ont.	25	Chicago
BOLLIG, Brandon	6-3	215	L	St. Charles, MO	24	Rockford
BRUNETTE, Andrew	6-1	210	L	Sudbury, Ont.	38	Minnesota
CARCILLO, Daniel	6-0	205	L	King City, Ont.	26	Philadelphia
DIDOMENICO, Chris	5-11	165	R	Toronto, Ont.	22	Rockford-Toledo
FROLIK, Michael	6-1	185	L	Kladno, Czech.	23	Florida-Chicago
HOSSA, Marian	6-1	210	L	Stara Lubovna, Czech.	32	Chicago
KANE, Patrick	5-10	178	L	Buffalo, NY	22	Chicago
KLINKHAMMER, Rob	6-3	206	L	Lethbridge, Alta.	25	Chicago-Rockford
KRUGER, Marcus	5-11	172	L	Stockholm, Sweden	21	Djurgarden-Chicago
MAKAROV, Igor	6-1	195	R	Moscow, USSR	24	Rockford
MAYERS, Jamal	6-1	215	R	Toronto, Ont.	36	San Jose
McLEAN, Brett	5-11	185	L	Comox, B.C.	33	Bern
MORIN, Jeremy	6-1	189	R	Auburn, NY	20	Chicago-Rockford
OLESZ, Rostislav	6-1	214	L	Bilovec, Czech.	25	Florida
PARADIS, Philippe	6-2	212	L	Dolbeau, Que.	20	P.E.I.-Rockford
SHARP, Patrick	6-1	199	R	Winnipeg, Man.	29	Chicago
SMITH, Ben	5-11	205	R	Winston-Salem, NC	23	Chicago-Rockford
STALBERG, Viktor	6-3	210	L	Stockholm, Sweden	25	Chicago
TOEWS, Jonathan	6-2	210	L	Winnipeg, Man.	23	Chicago
DEFENSEMEN						
CONNELLY, Brian	5-10	167	L	Bloomington, MN	25	Rockford
DANIS-PEPIN, Simon	6-6	229	R	Gatineau, Que.	23	Rockford-Toledo
HJALMARSSON, Niklas	6-3	205	L	Eksjo, Sweden	24	Chicago
KEITH, Duncan	6-1	196	L	Winnipeg, Man.	28	Chicago
LALONDE, Shawn	6-1	192	R	Ottawa, Ont.	21	Rockford
LEDDY, Nick	5-11	179	L	Eden Prairie, MN	20	Chicago-Rockford
LEPISTO, Sami	6-0	195	L	Espoo, Finland	26	Phoenix-Columbus
MONTADOR, Steve	6-0	207	R	Vancouver, B.C.	31	Buffalo
O'DONNELL, Sean	6-2	237	L	Ottawa, Ont.	39	Philadelphia
SCOTT, John	6-8	258	L	St. Catharines, Ont.	29	Chicago
SEABROOK, Brent	6-3	218	R	Richmond, B.C.	26	Chicago
STANTON, Ryan	6-2	205	L	St. Albert, Alta.	22	Rockford

GOALTENDERS	HT	WT	C	Place of Birth	*Age	2010-11 Club
CRAWFORD, Corey	6-2	200	L	Montreal, Que.	26	Chicago
RICHARDS, Alec	6-4	210	L	Robbinsdale, MN	24	Rockford
SALAK, Alexander	6-1	189	L	Strakonice, Czech.	24	Farjestad

* – Age at start of 2011-12 season

Joel Quenneville

Head Coach

Born: Windsor, Ont., September 15, 1958.

Joel Quenneville was named the 37th head coach in Chicago Blackhawks history on October 16, 2008 and in 2009-10 he guided the team to its first Stanley Cup championship since 1961. Quenneville originally joined the Blackhawks as a pro scout in September 2008. He has been a proven winner throughout his career as a head coach in the NHL, including seven seasons with the St. Louis Blues (1996 to 2004) and three with the Colorado Avalanche (2005 to 2008). In his first season behind the bench in Chicago, he led the Blackhawks to the Western Conference Final in just their second playoff appearance since the 1996-97 season.

One of only three men in the history of the NHL to have played in and coached 800 or more games, Quenneville is the winningest coach in Blues history, having compiled a 307-191-95 record. He was awarded the 2000 Jack Adams Trophy as the league's top coach. Quenneville was drafted by the Toronto Maple Leafs in the first round (21st overall) of the 1978 NHL Entry Draft. He spent 13 seasons as an NHL defenseman, netting 54 goals, 136 assists, 190 points and 705 penalty minutes in 803 career games with the Toronto Maple Leafs, Colorado Rockies, New Jersey Devils, Hartford Whalers and Washington Capitals.

Quenneville retired as an active player after the 1991-92 season, when he served as a player-coach for the American Hockey League's St. John's Maple Leafs. Quenneville broke into coaching with the AHL's Springfield Indians before serving as an assistant coach for the Quebec Nordiques/Colorado Avalanche organization for two and a half seasons. He helped Colorado capture the 1996 Stanley Cup in that position before accepting his first NHL head coaching job with St. Louis for the 1996-97 campaign.

Coaching Record

			Regular Season				Playoffs			
Season	Team	League	GC	W	L	O/T	GC	W	L	T
1993-94	Springfield	AHL	80	29	38	13	6	2	4	....
1996-97	**St. Louis**	**NHL**	**40**	**18**	**15**	**7**	**6**	**2**	**4**	....
1997-98	**St. Louis**	**NHL**	**82**	**45**	**29**	**8**	**10**	**6**	**4**	....
1998-99	**St. Louis**	**NHL**	**82**	**37**	**32**	**13**	**13**	**6**	**7**	....
99-2000	**St. Louis**	**NHL**	**82**	**51**	**19**	**12**	**7**	**3**	**4**	....
2000-01	**St. Louis**	**NHL**	**82**	**43**	**22**	**17**	**15**	**9**	**6**	....
2001-02	**St. Louis**	**NHL**	**82**	**43**	**27**	**12**	**10**	**5**	**5**	....
2002-03	**St. Louis**	**NHL**	**82**	**41**	**24**	**17**	**7**	**3**	**4**	....
2003-04	**St. Louis**	**NHL**	**61**	**29**	**23**	**9**	....	....	....	....
2004-05	**Colorado**				SEASON CANCELLED					
2005-06	**Colorado**	**NHL**	**82**	**43**	**30**	**9**	**9**	**4**	**5**	....
2006-07	**Colorado**	**NHL**	**82**	**44**	**31**	**7**	....	....	....	....
2007-08	**Colorado**	**NHL**	**82**	**44**	**31**	**7**	**10**	**4**	**6**	....
2008-09	**Chicago**	**NHL**	**78**	**45**	**22**	**11**	**17**	**9**	**8**	....
2009-10♦	**Chicago**	**NHL**	**82**	**52**	**22**	**8**	**22**	**16**	**6**	....
2010-11	**Chicago**	**NHL**	**82**	**44**	**29**	**9**	**7**	**3**	**4**	....
	NHL Totals		**1081**	**579**	**356**	**146**	**133**	**70**	**63**	....

♦ Stanley Cup win.
Won Jack Adams Award (2000)
Assistant coach Mike Haviland posted a 3-1-0 record as replacement coach when Joel Quenneville was sidelined with an ulcer, February 16 to 23, 2011. All games are credited to Quenneville's coaching record.

2010-11 Scoring

* – rookie

Regular Season

Pos	#	Player	Team	GP	G	A	Pts	TOI	+/–	PIM	PP	SH	GW	S	%
C	19	Jonathan Toews	CHI	80	32	44	76	20:45	25	26	10	1	8	233	13.7
R	88	Patrick Kane	CHI	73	27	46	73	19:17	7	28	5	0	2	216	12.5
R	10	Patrick Sharp	CHI	74	34	37	71	19:24	–1	38	12	2	6	268	12.7
R	81	Marian Hossa	CHI	65	25	32	57	19:42	9	32	8	2	2	205	12.2
D	7	Brent Seabrook	CHI	82	9	39	48	24:23	0	47	5	0	1	135	6.7
D	2	Duncan Keith	CHI	82	7	38	45	26:53	–1	22	3	1	1	173	4.0
R	82	Tomas Kopecky	CHI	81	15	27	42	15:19	–13	60	3	0	2	178	8.4
R	67	Michael Frolik	FLA	52	8	21	29	16:01	2	16	1	0	1	158	5.1
			CHI	28	3	6	9	14:46	0	14	0	0	0	93	3.2
			Total	80	11	27	38	15:35	2	30	1	0	1	251	4.4
L	29	* Bryan Bickell	CHI	78	17	20	37	13:50	6	40	2	0	2	130	13.1
C	36	Dave Bolland	CHI	61	15	22	37	17:38	11	34	4	0	1	102	14.7
R	22	Troy Brouwer	CHI	79	17	19	36	15:06	–2	38	7	0	5	122	13.9
D	51	Brian Campbell	CHI	65	5	22	27	22:58	28	6	2	0	1	84	6.0
L	25	Viktor Stalberg	CHI	77	12	12	24	10:41	2	43	0	0	3	135	8.9
C	28	* Jake Dowell	CHI	79	6	15	21	11:48	5	63	0	0	0	74	8.1
D	14	Chris Campoli	OTT	58	3	11	14	18:48	–3	34	0	0	0	59	5.1
			CHI	19	1	6	7	20:07	3	2	1	0	1	25	4.0
			Total	77	4	17	21	19:08	0	36	1	0	1	84	4.8
R	15	Fernando Pisani	CHI	60	7	9	16	12:34	0	10	1	0	1	72	9.7
D	4	Niklas Hjalmarsson	CHI	80	3	7	10	18:28	13	39	0	0	0	64	4.7
D	5	Jassen Cullimore	CHI	36	0	8	8	12:37	4	8	0	0	0	22	0.0
D	8	* Nick Leddy	CHI	46	4	3	7	14:18	–3	4	0	0	0	37	10.8
C	17	Ryan Johnson	CHI	34	1	5	6	10:21	–2	8	0	0	1	25	4.0
L	27	* Jeremy Morin	CHI	9	2	1	3	12:05	2	9	0	0	0	13	15.4
R	57	* Ben Smith	CHI	6	1	0	1	13:46	1	0	0	0	0	6	16.7
D	6	Jordan Hendry	CHI	37	1	0	1	10:41	–2	4	0	0	0	35	2.9
D	32	John Scott	CHI	40	0	1	1	6:15	0	72	0	0	0	15	0.0
L	23	Jeff Taffe	CHI	1	0	0	0	4:05	0	0	0	0	0	0	0.0
C	47	* Evan Brophey	CHI	1	0	0	0	7:09	0	0	0	0	0	1	0.0
C	59	* Rob Klinkhammer	CHI	1	0	0	0	11:36	1	0	0	0	0	1	0.0
C	14	* Brandon Pirri	CHI	1	0	0	0	8:56	–1	0	0	0	0	1	0.0
C	16	* Marcus Kruger	CHI	7	0	0	0	11:57	–4	4	0	0	0	7	0.0

Goaltending

No.	Goaltender	GPI	Mins	Avg	W	L	OT	EN	SO	GA	SA	S%	G	A	PIM
50	* Corey Crawford	57	3337	2.30	33	18	6	6	4	128	1545	.917	0	1	2
30	Marty Turco	29	1631	3.02	11	11	3	4	1	82	799	.897	0	0	6
	Totals	**82**	**5000**	**2.64**	**44**	**29**	**9**	**10**	**5**	**220**	**2354**	**.907**			

Playoffs

Pos	#	Player	Team	GP	G	A	Pts	TOI	+/–	PIM	PP	SH	GW	OT	S	%
D	2	Duncan Keith	CHI	7	4	2	6	26:55	–3	6	1	0	1	0	27	14.8
C	36	Dave Bolland	CHI	4	2	4	6	19:58	6	4	0	0	0	0	9	22.2
R	81	Marian Hossa	CHI	7	2	4	6	18:35	0	2	1	0	1	0	16	12.5
R	88	Patrick Kane	CHI	7	1	5	6	21:50	–1	2	1	0	0	0	22	4.5
R	10	Patrick Sharp	CHI	7	3	2	5	18:55	1	2	3	0	0	0	31	9.7
R	67	Michael Frolik	CHI	7	2	3	5	17:28	3	2	0	0	0	0	18	11.1
L	29	* Bryan Bickell	CHI	5	2	2	4	13:05	4	0	0	0	0	0	6	33.3
C	19	Jonathan Toews	CHI	7	1	3	4	22:31	–4	2	0	1	0	0	19	5.3
R	57	* Ben Smith	CHI	7	3	0	3	14:50	–1	0	0	0	1	1	6	50.0
D	51	Brian Campbell	CHI	7	1	2	3	26:26	2	6	0	0	0	0	11	9.1
D	4	Niklas Hjalmarsson	CHI	7	0	2	2	18:55	4	2	0	0	0	0	5	0.0
L	25	Viktor Stalberg	CHI	7	1	0	1	12:17	0	5	0	0	0	0	10	10.0
D	7	Brent Seabrook	CHI	5	0	1	1	22:57	0	6	0	0	0	0	9	0.0
C	16	* Marcus Kruger	CHI	5	0	1	1	11:51	2	0	0	0	0	0	2	0.0
C	17	Ryan Johnson	CHI	6	0	1	1	9:55	–1	2	0	0	0	0	2	0.0
D	14	Chris Campoli	CHI	7	0	1	1	18:56	3	2	0	0	0	0	4	0.0
R	82	Tomas Kopecky	CHI	1	0	0	0	2:22	0	0	0	0	0	0	1	0.0
C	28	* Jake Dowell	CHI	2	0	0	0	8:23	0	0	0	0	0	0	1	0.0
R	15	Fernando Pisani	CHI	3	0	0	0	7:54	–1	0	0	0	0	0	3	0.0
D	32	John Scott	CHI	4	0	0	0	6:37	1	22	0	0	0	0	2	0.0
R	22	Troy Brouwer	CHI	7	0	0	0	14:25	2	11	0	0	0	0	10	0.0
D	8	* Nick Leddy	CHI	7	0	0	0	14:36	–1	0	0	0	0	0	2	0.0

Goaltending

No.	Goaltender	GPI	Mins	Avg	W	L	EN	SO	GA	SA	S%	G	A	PIM
50	* Corey Crawford	7	435	2.21	3	4	0	1	16	218	.927	0	2	0
	Totals	**7**	**441**	**2.18**	**3**	**4**	**0**	**1**	**16**	**218**	**.927**			

Coaching History

Pete Muldoon, 1926-27; Barney Stanley and Hugh Lehman, 1927-28; Herb Gardiner and Dick Irvin, 1928-29; Tom Shaughnessy and Bill Tobin, 1929-30; Dick Irvin, 1930-31; Bill Tobin, 1931-32; Emil Iverson, Godfrey Matheson and Tommy Gorman, 1932-33; Tommy Gorman, 1933-34; Clem Loughlin, 1934-35 to 1936-37; Bill Stewart, 1937-38; Bill Stewart and Paul Thompson, 1938-39; Paul Thompson, 1939-40 to 1943-44; Paul Thompson and Johnny Gottselig, 1944-45; Johnny Gottselig, 1945-46, 1946-47; Johnny Gottselig and Charlie Conacher, 1947-48; Charlie Conacher, 1948-49, 1949-50; Ebbie Goodfellow, 1950-51, 1951-52; Sid Abel, 1952-53, 1953-54; Frank Eddolls, 1954-55; Dick Irvin, 1955-56; Tommy Ivan, 1956-57; Tommy Ivan and Rudy Pilous, 1957-58; Rudy Pilous, 1958-59 to 1962-63; Billy Reay, 1963-64 to 1975-76; Billy Reay and Bill White, 1976-77; Bob Pulford, 1977-78, 1978-79; Eddie Johnston, 1979-80; Keith Magnuson, 1980-81; Keith Magnuson and Bob Pulford, 1981-82; Orval Tessier, 1982-83, 1983-84; Orval Tessier and Bob Pulford, 1984-85; Bob Pulford, 1985-86, 1986-87; Bob Murdoch, 1987-88; Mike Keenan, 1988-89 to 1991-92; Darryl Sutter, 1992-93 to 1994-95; Craig Hartsburg, 1995-96 to 1997-98; Dirk Graham and Lorne Molleken, 1998-99; Lorne Molleken and Bob Pulford, 1999-2000; Alpo Suhonen, 2000-01; Brian Sutter, 2001-02 to 2004-05; Trent Yawney, 2005-06; Trent Yawney and Denis Savard, 2006-07; Denis Savard, 2007-08; Denis Savard and Joel Quenneville, 2008-09; Joel Quenneville, 2009-10 to date.

Club Records

Team

(Figures in brackets for season records are games played; records for fewest points, wins, ties, losses, goals, goals against are for 70 or more games)

Most Points **112** 2009-10 (82)
Most Wins **52** 2009-10 (82)
Most Ties **23** 1973-74 (78)
Most Losses **56** 2005-06 (82)
Most Goals **351** 1985-86 (80)
Most Goals Against **363** 1981-82 (80)
Fewest Points **31** 1953-54 (70)
Fewest Wins **12** 1953-54 (70)
Fewest Ties **6** 1989-90 (80)
Fewest Losses **14** 1973-74 (78)
Fewest Goals ***133** 1953-54 (70)
Fewest Goals Against **164** 1973-74 (78)
Longest Winning Streak
Overall .... **9** Dec. 7-28/08
Home .... **13** Nov. 11-Dec. 20/70
Away .... **7** Dec. 9-29/64
Longest Undefeated Streak
Overall .... **15** Jan. 14-Feb. 16/67 (12 wins, 3 ties), Oct. 29-Dec. 3/75 (6 wins, 9 ties)
Home .... **18** Oct. 11-Dec. 20/70 (16 wins, 2 ties)
Away .... **12** Nov. 2-Dec. 16/67 (6 wins, 6 ties)
Longest Losing Streak
Overall .... **12** Feb. 25-Mar. 25/51
Home .... **10** Jan. 29-Mar. 21/28
Away .... **19** Nov. 10/03-Jan. 29/04
Longest Winless Streak
Overall .... **21** Dec. 17/50-Jan. 28/51 (18 losses, 3 ties)
Home .... **15** Dec. 16/28-Feb. 28/29 (11 losses, 4 ties)
Away .... **22** Dec. 19/50-Mar. 25/51 (20 losses, 2 ties)
Most Shutouts, Season **15** 1969-70 (76)
Most PIM, Season **2,663** 1991-92 (80)
Most Goals, Game .... **12** Jan. 30/69 (Chi. 12 at Phi. 0)

Individual

Most Seasons .... **22** Stan Mikita
Most Games .... **1,394** Stan Mikita
Most Goals, Career .... **604** Bobby Hull
Most Assists, Career .... **926** Stan Mikita
Most Points, Career ...... **1,467** Stan Mikita (541G, 926A)
Most PIM, Career .... **1,495** Chris Chelios
Most Shutouts, Career .... **74** Tony Esposito
Longest Consecutive Games Streak .... **884** Steve Larmer (Oct. 6/82-Apr. 15/93)
Most Goals, Season .... **58** Bobby Hull (1968-69)
Most Assists, Season .... **87** Denis Savard (1981-82, 1987-88)
Most Points, Season .... **131** Denis Savard (1987-88; 44G, 87A)
Most PIM, Season .... **408** Mike Peluso (1991-92)
Most Points, Defenseman, Season .... **85** Doug Wilson (1981-82; 39G, 46A)
Most Points, Center, Season .... **131** Denis Savard (1987-88; 44G, 87A)
Most Points, Right Wing, Season .... **101** Steve Larmer (1990-91; 44G, 57A)
Most Points, Left Wing, Season .... **107** Bobby Hull (1968-69; 58G, 49A)
Most Points, Rookie, Season .... **90** Steve Larmer (1982-83; 43G, 47A)
Most Shutouts, Season .... **15** Tony Esposito (1969-70)
Most Goals, Game .... **5** Grant Mulvey (Feb. 3/82)
Most Assists, Game .... **6** Pat Stapleton (Mar. 30/69)
Most Points, Game .... **7** Max Bentley (Jan. 28/43; 4G, 3A), Grant Mulvey (Feb. 3/82; 5G, 2A)

* NHL Record.

General Managers' History

Major Frederic McLaughlin, 1926-27 to 1931-32; Major Frederic McLaughlin and Tommy Gorman, 1932-33; Tommy Gorman, 1933-34; Clem Loughlin, 1934-35 to 1935-36; Bill Tobin, 1936-37 to 1953-54; Tommy Ivan, 1954-55 to 1976-77; Bob Pulford, 1977-78 to 1989-90; Mike Keenan, 1990-91, 1991-92; Mike Keenan and Bob Pulford, 1992-93; Bob Pulford, 1993-94 to 1996-97; Bob Murray, 1997-98, 1998-99; Bob Murray and Bob Pulford, 1999-2000; Mike Smith, 2000-01 to 2002-03; Mike Smith and Bob Pulford, 2003-04; Bob Pulford, 2004-05; Dale Tallon, 2005-06 to 2008-09; Stan Bowman, 2009-10 to date.

Retired Numbers

1	Glenn Hall	1957-1967
3	Pierre Pilote	1955-1968
	Keith Magnuson	1969-1980
9	Bobby Hull	1957-1972
18	Denis Savard	1980-1990, 1995-1997
21	Stan Mikita	1958-1980
35	Tony Esposito	1969-1984

All-time Record vs. Other Clubs

Regular Season

	At Home								On Road								Total							
	GP	W	L	T	OL	GF	GA	PTS	GP	W	L	T	OL	GF	GA	PTS	GP	W	L	T	OL	GF	GA	PTS
Anaheim	36	17	17	2	0	95	89	36	34	10	21	3	0	69	94	23	70	27	38	5	0	164	183	59
Atlanta	4	3	1	0	0	13	7	6	7	5	2	0	0	23	23	10	11	8	3	0	0	36	30	16
Boston	289	148	95	45	1	935	778	342	288	90	164	34	0	817	1036	214	577	238	259	79	1	1752	1814	556
Buffalo	54	29	18	6	1	173	145	65	56	15	34	7	0	144	207	37	110	44	52	13	1	317	352	102
Calgary	73	34	26	13	0	242	212	81	75	29	32	13	1	225	230	72	148	63	58	26	1	467	442	153
Carolina	32	18	10	3	1	125	90	40	32	12	16	4	0	98	106	28	64	30	26	7	1	223	196	68
Colorado	53	29	18	3	3	180	161	64	51	17	26	6	2	163	199	42	104	46	44	9	5	343	360	106
Columbus	31	17	11	1	2	94	76	37	32	16	12	1	3	111	109	36	63	33	23	2	5	205	185	73
Dallas	122	71	36	15	0	449	325	157	124	48	57	16	3	379	428	115	246	119	93	31	3	828	753	272
Detroit	359	162	141	51	5	1076	1019	380	356	108	213	33	2	890	1218	251	715	270	354	84	7	1966	2237	631
Edmonton	56	28	17	7	4	208	186	67	57	25	26	5	1	186	195	56	113	53	43	12	5	394	381	123
Florida	13	6	4	2	1	42	37	15	12	7	3	1	1	43	25	16	25	13	7	3	2	85	62	31
Los Angeles	87	44	33	9	1	299	244	98	86	39	37	8	2	281	288	88	173	83	70	17	3	580	532	186
Minnesota	20	8	10	1	1	45	55	18	20	7	9	0	4	53	58	18	40	15	19	1	5	98	113	36
Montreal	275	95	125	55	0	736	764	245	279	54	174	48	3	658	1077	159	554	149	299	103	3	1394	1841	404
Nashville	38	22	13	1	2	109	97	47	37	15	13	3	6	105	115	39	75	37	26	4	8	214	212	86
New Jersey	50	26	13	10	1	189	138	63	50	17	21	11	1	147	153	46	100	43	34	21	2	336	291	109
NY Islanders	51	27	18	5	1	170	168	60	49	14	20	15	0	146	173	43	100	41	38	20	1	316	341	103
NY Rangers	289	130	115	43	1	876	797	304	288	113	120	55	0	812	850	281	577	243	235	98	1	1688	1647	585
Ottawa	11	7	2	2	0	27	23	16	12	7	5	0	0	35	38	14	23	14	7	2	0	62	61	30
Philadelphia	63	27	17	19	0	213	180	73	64	16	37	11	0	164	210	43	127	43	54	30	0	377	390	116
Phoenix	60	33	15	10	2	217	148	78	62	24	29	5	4	191	196	57	122	57	44	15	6	408	344	135
Pittsburgh	63	41	11	10	1	247	165	93	61	24	29	7	1	196	216	56	124	65	40	17	2	443	381	149
St. Louis	139	80	40	18	1	507	397	179	136	51	65	17	3	414	451	122	275	131	105	35	4	921	848	301
San Jose	37	17	16	2	2	116	121	38	38	13	18	3	4	101	112	33	75	30	34	5	6	217	233	71
Tampa Bay	17	10	5	2	0	54	38	22	14	5	4	3	2	38	36	15	31	15	9	5	2	92	74	37
Toronto	320	158	120	42	0	974	834	358	318	100	164	54	0	837	1082	254	638	258	284	96	0	1811	1916	612
Vancouver	83	51	22	7	3	294	199	112	84	26	41	15	2	237	252	69	167	77	63	22	5	531	451	181
Washington	42	23	12	6	1	159	124	53	44	16	22	5	1	136	156	38	86	39	34	11	2	295	280	91
Defunct Clubs	139	79	40	20	0	408	268	178	140	52	67	21	0	316	346	125	279	131	107	41	0	724	614	303
Totals	**2906**	**1440**	**1021**	**410**	**35**	**9272**	**7885**	**3325**	**2906**	**975**	**1481**	**404**	**46**	**8015**	**9679**	**2400**	**5812**	**2415**	**2502**	**814**	**81**	**17287**	**17564**	**5725**

Playoffs

	Series	W	L	GP	W	L	T	GF	GA	Last Mtg.	Rnd.	Result
Boston	6	1	5	22	5	16	1	63	97	1978	QF	L 0-4
Buffalo	2	0	2	9	1	8	0	17	36	1980	QF	L 0-4
Calgary	4	2	2	18	9	9	0	54	53	2009	CQF	W 4-2
Colorado	2	0	2	12	4	8	0	28	49	1997	CQF	L 2-4
Dallas	6	4	2	33	19	14	0	120	118	1991	DSF	L 2-4
Detroit	15	8	7	74	39	35	0	220	209	2009	CF	L 1-4
Edmonton	4	1	3	20	8	12	0	77	102	1992	CF	W 4-0
Los Angeles	1	1	0	5	4	1	0	10	7	1974	QF	W 4-1
Montreal	17	5	12	81	29	50	2	185	261	1976	QF	L 0-4
Nashville	1	1	0	6	4	2	0	17	15	2010	CQF	W 4-2
NY Islanders	2	0	2	6	0	6	0	6	21	1979	QF	L 0-4
NY Rangers	5	4	1	24	14	10	0	66	54	1973	SF	W 4-1
Philadelphia	2	2	0	10	8	2	0	45	30	2010	F	W 4-2
Pittsburgh	2	1	1	8	4	4	0	24	23	1992	F	L 0-4
St. Louis	10	7	3	50	28	22	0	171	142	2002	CQF	L 1-4
San Jose	1	1	0	4	4	0	0	13	7	2010	CF	W 4-0
Toronto	9	3	6	38	15	22	1	89	111	1995	CQF	W 4-3
Vancouver	5	3	2	28	16	12	0	92	77	2011	CQF	L 3-4
Defunct Clubs	4	2	2	9	5	3	1	16	15			
Totals	**98**	**46**	**52**	**457**	**216**	**236**	**5**	**1313**	**1427**			

Calgary totals include Atlanta Flames, 1972-73 to 1979-80. Carolina totals include Hartford, 1979-80 to 1996-97.
Colorado totals include Quebec, 1979-80 to 1994-95. Dallas totals include Minnesota North Stars, 1967-68 to 1992-93.
New Jersey totals include Kansas City, 1974-75, 1975-76, and Colorado Rockies, 1976-77 to 1981-82.
Phoenix totals include Winnipeg, 1979-80 to 1995-96.

Playoff Results 2011-2007

Year	Round	Opponent	Result	GF	GA
2011	CQF	Vancouver	L 3-4	22	16
2010	**F**	**Philadelphia**	**W 4-2**	**25**	**22**
	CF	San Jose	W 4-0	13	7
	CSF	Vancouver	W 4-2	23	18
	CQF	Nashville	W 4-2	17	15
2009	CF	Detroit	L 1-4	10	19
	CSF	Vancouver	W 4-2	23	19
	CQF	Calgary	W 4-2	21	16

Abbreviations: Round: F - Final; **CF** - conference final; **CSF** - conference semi-final; **CQF** - conference quarter-final; **DSF** - division semi-final; **SF** - semi-final; **QF** - quarter-final.

2010-11 Results

Oct.	7	at Colorado	3-4*		5	Dallas	2-4
	9	Detroit	2-3		7	Ottawa	3-2†
	11	at Buffalo	4-3		9	NY Islanders	5-0
	13	Nashville	2-3		12	Colorado	4-0
	15	at Columbus	5-2		15	at Nashville	2-3†
	16	Buffalo	4-3		16	Nashville	6-3
	18	St. Louis	3-2*		22	at Detroit	4-1
	20	Vancouver	2-1†		23	Philadelphia	1-4
	22	at St. Louis	2-4		25	Minnesota	2-4
	23	Columbus	2-3	**Feb.**	1	at Columbus	7-4
	27	Los Angeles	3-1		4	at Vancouver	3-4
	29	Edmonton	4-7		7	at Calgary	1-3
	30	at Minnesota	3-1		9	at Edmonton	4-1
Nov.	1	at NY Rangers	2-3		11	at Dallas	3-4†
	3	New Jersey	3-5		12	at Phoenix	2-3†
	6	at Atlanta	5-4†		16	Minnesota	3-1
	7	Edmonton	1-2		18	Columbus	3-4
	10	Phoenix	1-2		20	Pittsburgh	3-2†
	13	at Nashville	3-4†		21	at St. Louis	5-3
	14	Anaheim	3-2*		24	at Nashville	3-0
	17	at Edmonton	5-0		27	Phoenix	4-3†
	19	at Calgary	2-7		28	at Minnesota	4-2
	20	at Vancouver	7-1	**Mar.**	2	Calgary	6-4
	24	at San Jose	2-5		4	Carolina	5-2
	26	at Anaheim	4-1		5	at Toronto	5-3
	27	at Los Angeles	2-1		8	at Florida	2-3
	30	St. Louis	7-5		9	at Tampa Bay	3-4†
Dec.	3	Vancouver	0-3		13	at Washington	3-4*
	5	Calgary	4-2		14	San Jose	6-3
	8	Dallas	5-3		17	at Dallas	0-5
	11	at San Jose	1-2*		20	at Phoenix	2-1
	13	at Colorado	5-7		23	Florida	4-0
	15	Colorado	3-4		26	Anaheim	1-2
	17	Detroit	4-1		28	at Detroit	3-2*
	19	Los Angeles	3-2		29	at Boston	0-3
	22	Nashville	4-1	**Apr.**	1	at Columbus	4-3†
	26	Columbus	4-1		3	Tampa Bay	0-2
	28	at St. Louis	1-3		5	at Montreal	1-2*
	30	San Jose	3-5		6	St. Louis	4-3*
Jan.	2	at Anaheim	1-2		8	at Detroit	4-2
	3	at Los Angeles	4-3		10	Detroit	3-4

* – Overtime † – Shootout

Entry Draft Selections 2011-1997

Name in bold denotes played in NHL.

2011
Pick
- 18 Mark McNeill
- 26 Phillip Danault
- 36 Adam Clendening
- 43 Brandon Saad
- 70 Michael Paliotta
- 79 Klas Dahlbeck
- 109 Maxim Shalunov
- 139 Andrew Shaw
- 169 Sam Jardine
- 199 Alex Broadhurst
- 211 Johan Mattsson

2010
Pick
- 24 Kevin Hayes
- 35 Ludvig Rensfeldt
- 54 Justin Holl
- 58 Kent Simpson
- 60 Stephen Johns
- 90 Joakim Nordstrom
- 120 Rob Flick
- 151 Mirko Hoefflin
- 180 Nick Mattson
- 191 Mac Carruth

2009
Pick
- 28 Dylan Olsen
- 59 **Brandon Pirri**
- 89 Dan Delisle
- 119 Byron Froese
- 149 **Marcus Kruger**
- 177 David Pacan
- 195 Paul Phillips
- 209 David Gilbert

2008
Pick
- 11 Kyle Beach
- 68 Shawn Lalonde
- 132 Teigan Zahn
- 162 Jonathan Carlsson
- 169 **Ben Smith**
- 179 Braden Birch
- 192 Joe Gleason

2007
Pick
- 1 **Patrick Kane**
- 38 Bill Sweatt
- 56 Akim Aliu
- 69 Maxime Tanguay
- 86 Josh Unice
- 126 Joe Lavin
- 156 Richard Greenop

2006
Pick
- 3 **Jonathan Toews**
- 33 Igor Makarov
- 61 Simon Danis-Pepin
- 76 Tony Lagerstrom
- 95 Ben Shutron
- 96 Joe Palmer
- 156 Jan-Mikael Juutilainen
- 169 Chris Auger
- 186 Peter Leblanc

2005
Pick
- 7 **Jack Skille**
- 43 **Michael Blunden**
- 54 Dan Bertram
- 68 **Evan Brophey**
- 108 **Niklas Hjalmarsson**
- 113 Nathan Davis
- 117 Denis Istomin
- 134 Brennan Turner
- 167 Joe Fallon
- 188 Joe Charlebois
- 202 David Kuchejda
- 203 Adam Hobson

2004
Pick
- 3 **Cam Barker**
- 32 **Dave Bolland**
- 41 **Bryan Bickell**
- 45 Ryan Garlock
- 54 Jakub Sindel
- 68 **Adam Berti**
- 120 Mitch Maunu
- 123 Karel Hromas
- 131 Trevor Kell
- 140 **Jake Dowell**
- 165 Scott McCulloch
- 196 **Petri Kontiola**
- 214 **Troy Brouwer**
- 223 Jared Walker
- 229 Eric Hunter
- 256 Matthew Ford
- 260 Marko Anttila

2003
Pick
- 14 **Brent Seabrook**
- 52 **Corey Crawford**
- 59 **Michal Barinka**
- 151 **Lasse Kukkonen**
- 156 Alexei Ivanov
- 181 Johan Andersson
- 211 **Mike Brodeur**
- 245 **Dustin Byfuglien**
- 275 Michael Grenzy
- 282 **Chris Porter**

2002
Pick
- 21 **Anton Babchuk**
- 54 **Duncan Keith**
- 93 Alexander Kojevnikov
- 128 **Matt Ellison**
- 156 **James Wisniewski**
- 188 Kevin Kantee
- 219 Tyson Kellerman
- 251 Jason Kostadine
- 282 **Adam Burish**

2001
Pick
- 9 **Tuomo Ruutu**
- 29 **Adam Munro**
- 59 **Matt Keith**
- 73 **Craig Anderson**
- 104 Brent MacLellan
- 115 Vladimir Gusev
- 119 Alexei Zotkin
- 142 Tommi Jaminki
- 174 Alexander Golovin
- 186 Petr Puncochar
- 205 Teemu Jaaskelainen
- 216 Oleg Minakov
- 268 Jeff Miles

2000
Pick
- 10 **Mikhail Yakubov**
- 11 **Pavel Vorobiev**
- 49 **Jonas Nordqvist**
- 74 **Igor Radulov**
- 106 Scott Balan
- 117 **Olli Malmivaara**
- 151 Alexander Barkunov
- 177 Michael Ayers
- 193 Joey Martin
- 207 Cliff Loya
- 225 Vladislav Luchkin
- 240 **Adam Berkhoel**
- 262 Peter Flache
- 271 **Reto Von Arx**
- 291 Arne Ramholt

1999
Pick
- 23 **Steve McCarthy**
- 46 Dimitri Levinski
- 63 Stepan Mokhov
- 134 Michael Jacobsen
- 165 **Michael Leighton**
- 194 Mattias Wennerberg
- 195 Yorick Treille
- 223 Andrew Carver

1998
Pick
- 8 **Mark Bell**
- 94 Matthias Trattnig
- 156 **Kent Huskins**
- 158 Jari Viuhkola
- 166 Jonathan Pelletier
- 183 **Tyler Arnason**
- 210 Sean Griffin
- 238 Alexandre Couture
- 240 Andrei Yershov

1997
Pick
- 13 **Dan Cleary**
- 16 **Ty Jones**
- 39 **Jeremy Reich**
- 67 Mike Souza
- 110 **Ben Simon**
- 120 Peter Gardiner
- 130 **Kyle Calder**
- 147 Heath Gordon
- 174 Jerad Smith
- 204 Sergei Shikhanov
- 230 Chris Feil

Captains' History

Dick Irvin, 1926-27 to 1928-29; Duke Dukowski, 1929-30; Ty Arbour, 1930-31; Cy Wentworth, 1931-32; Helge Bostrom, 1932-33; Charlie Gardiner, 1933-34; no captain, 1934-35; Johnny Gottselig, 1935-36 to 1939-40; Earl Seibert, 1940-41, 1941-42; Doug Bentley, 1942-43, 1943-44; Clint Smith 1944-45; John Mariucci, 1945-46; Red Hamill, 1946-47; John Mariucci, 1947-48; Gaye Stewart, 1948-49; Doug Bentley, 1949-50; Jack Stewart, 1950-51, 1951-52; Bill Gadsby, 1952-53, 1953-54; Gus Mortson, 1954-55 to 1956-57; no captain, 1957-58; Ed Litzenberger, 1958-59 to 1960-61; Pierre Pilote, 1961-62 to 1967-68, no captain, 1968-69; Pat Stapleton, 1969-70; no captain, 1970-71 to 1974-75; Stan Mikita and Pit Martin, 1975-76; Stan Mikita, Pit Martin and Keith Magnuson, 1976-77; Keith Magnuson, 1977-78, 1978-79; Keith Magnuson and Terry Ruskowski, 1979-80; Terry Ruskowski, 1980-81, 1981-82; Darryl Sutter, 1982-83 to 1984-85; Darryl Sutter and Bob Murray, 1985-86; Darryl Sutter, 1986-87; no captain, 1987-88; Denis Savard and Dirk Graham, 1988-89; Dirk Graham, 1989-90 to 1994-95; Chris Chelios, 1995-96 to 1998-99; Doug Gilmour, 1999-2000; Tony Amonte, 2000-01, 2001-02; Alex Zhamnov, 2002-03, 2003-04; Adrian Aucoin and Martin Lapointe, 2005-06, 2006-07; no captain, 2007-08; Jonathan Toews, 2008-09 to date.

Stan Bowman

General Manager

Born: Montreal, Que., June 28, 1973.

Stan Bowman was named general manager of the Chicago Blackhawks on July 14, 2009. In his first season on the job in 2009-10, the Blackhawks won the Stanley Cup for the first time since 1961. Prior to being named to the position, Bowman had served for eight years in the Blackhawks operations department.

Bowman originally joined the Blackhawks in 2001, serving for four seasons as special assistant to the G.M. before being promoted to director of hockey operations from 2005 to 2007. As assistant G.M. from 2007 to 2009, Bowman attended to the day-to-day administration of the hockey operations department including contract negotiations, free agency, salary arbitration, player movement and player assignment. He also tracked the progress of the Blackhawks prospects at the club's minor league affiliate in Rockford and assisted with player evaluation, prospect development and scouting.

Bowman graduated from the University of Notre Dame in 1995 with degrees in Finance and Computer Applications. He was born in Montreal where his father, current Blackhawks senior advisor and Hall of Fame member Scotty Bowman, was coaching at the time.

Club Directory

United Center

Chicago Blackhawks
United Center
1901 W. Madison Street
Chicago, IL 60612
Phone **312/455-7000**
FAX 312/455-7041
www.chicagoblackhawks.com
Capacity: 19,717

Management

Chairman	W. Rockwell "Rocky" Wirtz
President/CEO	John F. McDonough
Executive Vice President	Jay Blunk
Vice President/General Manager	Stan Bowman
Assistant General Manager	Marc Bergevin
Vice President/Asst. to the President	Al MacIsaac
Vice President, Ticket Ops and Customer Relations	Chris Werner
Sr. Exec. Asst. to VP/GM and Hockey Operations	Julie Kavanaugh
Sr. Exec. Assts./Special Projects	Jillian Smith, Kayla Kindred

Coaching Staff

Head Coach	Joel Quenneville
Assistant Coaches	Mike Haviland, Mike Kitchen
Goaltending Coach	Stephane Waite
Strength & Conditioning Coach	Paul Goodman
Video Coach	Tim Campbell

Training/Equipment Staff

Athletic Trainers, Head / Assistant	Mike Gapski / Jeff Thomas
Massage Therapist	Pawel Prylinski
Equipment Manager / Asst. Manager / Assistant	Troy Parchman / Clint Reif / Jim Heintzelman

Medical

Head Team Physicians	Drs. Michael Terry, William Harper
Team Physicians	Drs. George Chiampas, Angelo Costas, Ari Levy, Bradley Merk
Team Dentists	Drs. Russ Baer, Martin Marcus, Michael Marcus
Mental Skills Coach	James Gary

Team Security

Team Security	Brian Higgins

Hockey Operations and Scouting

Director, Player Personnel	Norm Maciver
General Manager of Minor League Affiliations	Mark Bernard
Director, Amateur Scouting	Mark Kelley
Director, Player Recruitment	Ron Anderson
Senior Advisor, Hockey Operations	Scotty Bowman
Senior Director, Team Services	Tony Ommen
Coordinators, Hockey Ops / Administration	Ian Gentile / Kyle Davidson
Chief Amateur Scout	Bruce Franklin
Amateur Scouts	Mike Doneghy, Gord Donnelly, Michel Dumas, Darrell May, Jim McKellar, Peter Nevin, Jad Ramsay
Pro Scouts	Bob Berry, Dennis Bonvie, Alex Brooks, Ryan Stewart
European Scouts, Head / Amateur / Pro	Niklas Blomgren / Karel Pavlik / Mats Hallin
European Development Advisor	Barry Smith

Media Relations

Directors, Media Relations / Public Relations	Brandon Faber / Adam Rogowin
Coordinator, Media Relations	Paul Kennedy
Coordinator, Team Photography	Chase Agnello-Dean

Broadcasters

Television Play-By-Play / Analyst	Pat Foley / Ed Olczyk
Radio Play-By-Play / Analyst / Host	John Wiedeman / Troy Murray / Judd Sirott

Community Relations

Sr. Director, Market Dev. and Community Affairs	Pete Hassen
Director / Assistant Youth Hockey	Annie Camins / Ashley Hinton
Manager, Charitable Partnerships	Elizabeth Queen
Mascot Coordinator	Joe Doyle

Finance

Sr. Director, Finance	TJ Skattum
Accounting Mgr. / Payroll Administrator	Michael Dorsch / Patricia Walsh

Human Resources

Human Resources, Sr. Director / Coordinator	Marie Sutera / Kyleen King
Office Coordinator/Receptionist	Leanne Mayville

Marketing / Business Development and Corporate Sponsorships

Sr. Exec. Director, Mktg. and Business Dev.	Dave Knickerbocker
Senior Director, Corporate Sponsorships	Steve Waight
Director, Advertising and Game Promotions	Patrick Dahl
Manager, In-game Presentation and Entertainment	A.J. Dolan
Manager, Client Services	Kelly Smith
Sr. Account Exec., Sponsorships	Sara Bailey
Account Execs., Sponsorships	Ryan Gallante, Sean Keefer, Greg Zinsmeister
Coordinator, Event Marketing	Brian Howe
Coordinator, Market Research and Sponsorship Event	Brian Dahm
Assistant, Marketing	Morgan Sharar-Stoppel
Producer, New Media	Matthew Dominick
Editor/Motion Graphics Designer	Scott Hanson
Production Coordinator	Ryan Linich

New Media and Creative Services

Director, New Media and Creative Services	Adam Kempenaar
Manager, Creative Services	John Sandberg
Coordinator, New Media	Brad Boron
Graphic Designer, Creative Services	Chris Wiebring
Assistant, New Media and Creative Services	Kelsey Peters
Team Historian	Bob Verdi

Tickets

Ticket Operations, Exec. Director / Assistant	Jim Bare / Allison Westfall
Director, Ticket Sales and Service	Dan Rozenblat
Senior Manager, Customer Service	Julie Lovins
Sr. Manager, Group Sales and Special Projects	Steve DiLenardi
Sr. Customer Service Execs.	Liz Breuer, Kathie Raimondi, Aaron Salsbury
Senior Account Executive, Group Sales	Eric Dumais
Customer Service Execs.	Brad Chase, Tracy Cunningham, Lindsay Dresser, T.R. Johnson, Shilpa Rupani
Account Execs., Ticket / Group Sales	Andrew Roan, Jake Tuton, Nick Zombolas

Colorado Avalanche

2010-11 Results: 30w-44L-7OTL-1SOL 68PTS.
Fourth, Northwest Division

Key Off-Season Signings/Acquisitions

2011

May 11 • Re-signed RW **Milan Hejduk**.

June 15 • Signed C **Joakim Lindstrom**.

16 • Named **Adam Deadmarsh** assistant coach.

24 • Selected LW **Gabriel Landeskog** (Kitchener, OHL) with the second overall pick in the 2011 Entry Draft.

29 • Re-signed RW **David Jones**.

30 • Re-signed D **Ryan O'Byrne**.

July 1 • Acquired G **Semyon Varlamov** from Washington for a 1st-round pick in the 2012 Entry Draft and a conditional 2nd-round pick in 2012 or 2013.

1 • Signed D **Jan Hejda**, G **Jean-Sebastien Giguere** and RW **Chuck Kobasew**.

8 • Signed G **Cedrick Desjardins**.

9 • Re-signed C **Kevin Porter** and D **Ryan Wilson**.

12 • Re-signed LW **T.J. Galiardi**.

13 • Signed D **Shane O'Brien**.

2011-12 Schedule

Oct.	Sat. 8	Detroit
	Mon. 10	at Boston*
	Wed. 12	at Columbus
	Thu. 13	at Ottawa
	Sat. 15	at Montreal
	Mon. 17	at Toronto
	Thu. 20	Chicago
	Sat. 22	at Chicago
	Wed. 26	at Calgary
	Fri. 28	Edmonton
	Sun. 30	Los Angeles
Nov.	Wed. 2	Phoenix
	Fri. 4	at Dallas
	Sun. 6	Calgary
	Tue. 8	at Detroit
	Thu. 10	NY Islanders
	Sat. 12	Calgary
	Tue. 15	at Pittsburgh
	Thu. 17	at Minnesota
	Fri. 18	Dallas
	Sun. 20	San Jose
	Wed. 23	Vancouver
	Sat. 26	Edmonton*
	Mon. 28	Dallas
	Wed. 30	New Jersey
Dec.	Fri. 2	St. Louis
	Sun. 4	Detroit
	Tue. 6	at Vancouver
	Thu. 8	at Calgary
	Fri. 9	at Edmonton
	Tue. 13	San Jose
	Thu. 15	at San Jose
	Sat. 17	Washington
	Mon. 19	Philadelphia
	Wed. 21	St. Louis
	Fri. 23	Tampa Bay
	Mon. 26	at Minnesota*
	Tue. 27	Winnipeg
	Thu. 29	Phoenix
	Sat. 31	at Anaheim*
Jan.	Mon. 2	at Los Angeles
	Fri. 6	at Chicago
	Sat. 7	at St. Louis
	Tue. 10	Nashville
	Thu. 12	at Nashville
	Sat. 14	at Dallas*
	Mon. 16	at Phoenix*
	Wed. 18	Florida
	Sat. 21	at Los Angeles
	Sun. 22	at Anaheim*
	Tue. 24	Minnesota
	Tue. 31	at Edmonton
Feb.	Thu. 2	Minnesota
	Sat. 4	Vancouver*
	Tue. 7	Chicago
	Fri. 10	Carolina
	Sat. 11	at St. Louis
	Wed. 15	at Vancouver
	Fri. 17	at Edmonton
	Sun. 19	at Winnipeg
	Wed. 22	Los Angeles
	Fri. 24	at Columbus
	Sat. 25	at Detroit
	Mon. 27	Anaheim
Mar.	Thu. 1	Columbus
	Sat. 3	Pittsburgh
	Sun. 4	at Minnesota
	Tue. 6	Minnesota
	Thu. 8	at Nashville
	Sat. 10	Edmonton*
	Mon. 12	Anaheim
	Wed. 14	at Buffalo
	Thu. 15	at New Jersey
	Sat. 17	at NY Rangers
	Tue. 20	Calgary
	Thu. 22	at Phoenix
	Sat. 24	Vancouver
	Mon. 26	at San Jose
	Wed. 28	at Vancouver
	Fri. 30	at Calgary
Apr.	Thu. 5	Columbus
	Sat. 7	Nashville

* Denotes afternoon game.

Matt Duchene improved on all the scoring numbers from his impressive rookie campaign during the 2010-11 season, leading the Avalanche with 67 points and tying for the team lead in both goals (27) and assists (40).

Year-by-Year Record

		Home				Road				Overall							
Season	GP	W	L	T	OL	W	L	T	OL	W	L	T	OL	GF	GA	Pts.	Finished	Playoff Result
2010-11	82	16	21	....	4	14	23	....	4	30	44	....	8	227	288	68	4th, Northwest Div.	Out of Playoffs
2009-10	82	24	14	....	3	19	16	....	6	43	30	....	9	244	233	95	2nd, Northwest Div.	Lost Conf. Quarter-Final
2008-09	82	18	21	....	2	14	24	....	3	32	45	....	5	199	257	69	5th, Northwest Div.	Out of Playoffs
2007-08	82	27	12	....	2	17	19	....	5	44	31	....	7	231	219	95	2nd, Northwest Div.	Lost Conf. Semi-Final
2006-07	82	22	16	....	3	22	15	....	4	44	31	....	7	272	251	95	4th, Northwest Div.	Out of Playoffs
2005-06	82	25	10	....	6	18	20	....	3	43	30	....	9	283	257	95	2nd, Northwest Div.	Lost Conf. Semi-Final
2004-05	....	....														....		
2003-04	82	19	14	6	2	21	8	7	5	40	22	13	7	236	198	100	2nd, Northwest Div.	Lost Conf. Semi-Final
2002-03	82	21	9	8	3	21	10	5	5	42	19	13	8	251	194	105	1st, Northwest Div.	Lost Conf. Quarter-Final
2001-02	82	24	12	4	1	21	16	7	3	45	28	8	1	212	169	99	1st, Northwest Div.	Lost Conf. Championship
2000-01	**82**	**28**	**6**	**5**	**2**	**24**	**10**	**5**	**2**	**52**	**16**	**10**	**4**	**270**	**192**	**118**	**1st, Northwest Div.**	**Won Stanley Cup**
1999-2000	82	25	12	4	0	17	16	7	1	42	28	11	1	233	201	96	1st, Northwest Div.	Lost Conf. Championship
1998-99	82	21	14	6	....	23	14	4	....	44	28	10	....	239	205	98	1st, Northwest Div.	Lost Conf. Championship
1997-98	82	22	16	10	....	18	16	7	....	39	26	17	....	231	205	95	1st, Pacific Div.	Lost Conf. Quarter-Final
1996-97	82	26	10	5	....	23	14	4	....	49	24	9	....	277	205	107	1st, Pacific Div.	Lost Conf. Championship
1995-96	**82**	**24**	**10**	**7**	**....**	**23**	**15**	**3**	**....**	**47**	**25**	**10**	**....**	**326**	**240**	**104**	**1st, Pacific Div.**	**Won Stanley Cup**
1994-95*	48	19	1	4	....	11	12	1	....	30	13	5	....	185	134	65	1st, Northeast Div.	Lost Conf. Quarter-Final
1993-94*	84	19	17	6	....	15	25	2	....	34	42	8	....	277	292	76	5th, Northeast Div.	Out of Playoffs
1992-93*	84	23	17	2	....	24	10	8	....	47	27	10	....	351	300	104	2nd, Adams Div.	Lost Div. Semi-Final
1991-92*	80	18	19	3	....	2	29	9	....	20	48	12	....	255	318	52	5th, Adams Div.	Out of Playoffs
1990-91*	80	9	23	8	....	7	27	6	....	16	50	14	....	236	354	46	5th, Adams Div.	Out of Playoffs
1989-90*	80	8	26	6	....	4	35	1	....	12	61	7	....	240	407	31	5th, Adams Div.	Out of Playoffs
1988-89*	80	16	20	4	....	11	26	3	....	27	46	7	....	269	342	61	5th, Adams Div.	Out of Playoffs
1987-88*	80	15	23	2	....	17	20	3	....	32	43	5	....	271	306	69	5th, Adams Div.	Out of Playoffs
1986-87*	80	20	13	7	....	11	26	3	....	31	39	10	....	267	276	72	4th, Adams Div.	Lost Div. Final
1985-86*	80	23	13	4	....	20	18	2	....	43	31	6	....	330	289	92	1st, Adams Div.	Lost Div. Semi-Final
1984-85*	80	24	12	4	....	17	18	5	....	41	30	9	....	323	275	91	2nd, Adams Div.	Lost Div. Final
1983-84*	80	24	11	5	....	18	17	5	....	42	28	10	....	360	278	94	3th, Adams Div.	Lost Div. Final
1982-83*	80	23	10	7	....	11	24	5	....	34	34	12	....	343	336	80	4th, Adams Div.	Lost Div. Semi-Final
1981-82*	80	24	13	3	....	9	18	13	....	33	31	16	....	356	345	82	4th, Adams Div.	Lost Conf. Championship
1980-81*	80	18	11	11	....	12	21	7	....	30	32	18	....	314	318	78	4th, Adams Div.	Lost Prelim. Round
1979-80*	80	17	16	7	....	8	28	4	....	25	44	11	....	248	313	61	5th, Adams Div.	Out of Playoffs

* Quebec Nordiques

NORTHWEST DIVISION
33rd NHL Season

Franchise date: June 22, 1979

Transferred from Quebec to Denver, June 21, 1995.

2011-12 Player Personnel

FORWARDS

Player	HT	WT	S	Place of Birth	*Age	2010-11 Club
BORDELEAU, Patrick	6-5	195	L	Montreal, Que.	25	Lake Erie
BROPHEY, Evan	6-2	199	L	Kitchener, Ont.	24	Chicago-Rockford
CARMAN, Mike	6-0	180	L	Augusta, GA	23	Lake Erie
COHEN, Zach	6-3	208	L	Schaumburg, IL	24	Lake Erie
DUCHENE, Matt	5-11	200	L	Haliburton, Ont.	20	Colorado
GALIARDI, T.J.	6-2	190	L	Calgary, Alta.	23	Colorado-Lake Erie
HEJDUK, Milan	6-0	190	R	Usti nad Labem, Czech.	35	Colorado
HISHON, Joey	5-10	175	L	Stratford, Ont.	19	Owen Sound
JONES, David	6-2	210	R	Guelph, Ont.	27	Colorado
KOBASEW, Chuck	6-0	192	R	Vancouver, B.C.	29	Minnesota
LANDESKOG, Gabriel	6-1	204	L	Stockholm, Sweden	18	Kitchener
LINDSTROM, Joakim	6-0	187	L	Skelleftea, Sweden	27	Skelleftea
MALONE, Brad	6-2	207	L	Miramichi, N.B.	22	North Dakota-Lake Erie
MAULDIN, Greg	5-11	195	R	Boston, MA	29	Colorado-Lake Erie
McCLEMENT, Jay	6-1	205	L	Kingston, Ont.	28	St. Louis-Colorado
McLEOD, Cody	6-2	210	L	Binscarth, Man.	27	Colorado
MERCIER, Justin	5-11	190	L	Erie, PA	24	Lake Erie
MUELLER, Peter	6-2	204	R	Bloomington, MN	23	Did Not Play - Injured
OLVER, Mark	5-10	170	L	Burnaby, B.C.	23	Colorado-Lake Erie
O'REILLY, Ryan	6-0	200	L	Clinton, Ont.	20	Colorado
PORTER, Kevin	6-0	190	L	Detroit, MI	25	Colorado
RISSMILLER, Patrick	6-4	225	L	Belmont, MA	32	Atlanta-Chi (AHL)-Lake Erie-Florida-Rochester
STASTNY, Paul	6-0	205	L	Quebec City, Que.	25	Colorado
STOA, Ryan	6-3	200	L	Bloomington, MN	24	Colorado-Lake Erie
VAN DER GULIK, David	5-10	173	L	Abbotsford, B.C.	28	Colorado-Lake Erie
WALKER, Luke	6-1	174	R	New Haven, CT	21	Lake Erie
WINNIK, Daniel	6-2	210	L	Toronto, Ont.	26	Colorado
YIP, Brandon	6-1	195	R	Vancouver, B.C.	26	Colorado

DEFENSEMEN

Player	HT	WT	S	Place of Birth	*Age	2010-11 Club
BARRIE, Tyson	5-10	191	R	Victoria, B.C.	20	Kelowna
CHOUINARD, Joel	6-1	186	L	Longueuil, Que.	21	Lake Erie
CUMISKEY, Kyle	5-10	185	L	Abbotsford, B.C.	24	Colorado
ELLIOTT, Stefan	6-1	192	R	Vancouver, B.C.	20	Saskatoon-Lake Erie
GAUNCE, Cameron	6-1	203	L	Sudbury, Ont.	21	Colorado-Lake Erie
HEJDA, Jan	6-4	237	L	Prague, Czech.	33	Columbus
HOLOS, Jonas	5-11	196	R	Sarpsborg, Norway	24	Colorado-Lake Erie
HUNWICK, Matt	5-11	190	L	Warren, MI	26	Boston-Colorado
JOHNSON, Erik	6-4	232	R	Bloomington, MN	23	St. Louis-Colorado
LIFFITON, David	6-2	210	L	Windsor, Ont.	26	Colorado-Lake Erie
O'BRIEN, Shane	6-3	230	L	Port Hope, Ont.	28	Nashville
O'BYRNE, Ryan	6-5	234	R	Victoria, B.C.	27	Montreal-Colorado
QUINCEY, Kyle	6-2	207	L	Kitchener, Ont.	26	Colorado
SIEMENS, Duncan	6-3	196	L	Edmonton, Alta.	18	Saskatoon
WILSON, Ryan	6-1	207	L	Windsor, Ont.	24	Colorado

GOALTENDERS

Player	HT	WT	C	Place of Birth	*Age	2010-11 Club
CANN, Trevor	5-11	199	L	Oakville, Ont.	22	Lake Erie-Tulsa
DESJARDINS, Cedrick	6-0	192	L	Edmundston, N.B.	26	Tampa Bay-Norfolk
GIGUERE, Jean-Sebastien	6-1	202	L	Montreal, Que.	34	Toronto
PICKARD, Calvin	6-0	197	L	Moncton, N.B.	19	Seattle
VARLAMOV, Semyon	6-2	209	L	Kuybyshev, USSR	23	Washington-Hershey

* – Age at start of 2011-12 season

2010-11 Scoring

*– rookie

Regular Season

Pos	#	Player	Team	GP	G	A	Pts	TOI	+/-	PIM	PP	SH	GW	S	%
C	9	Matt Duchene	COL	80	27	40	67	18:56	-8	33	3	0	2	202	13.4
C	26	Paul Stastny	COL	74	22	35	57	19:44	-7	56	4	1	3	181	12.2
R	23	Milan Hejduk	COL	71	23	34	56	17:55	-23	18	10	0	2	170	12.9
D	4	John-Michael Liles	COL	76	6	40	46	22:00	-9	35	3	0	0	163	3.7
R	54	David Jones	COL	77	27	18	45	17:40	-2	28	6	0	4	153	17.6
L	14	Tomas Fleischmann	WSH	23	4	6	10	14:20	3	10	0	0	1	44	9.1
			COL	22	8	13	21	18:28	-1	8	3	0	1	54	14.8
			Total	45	12	19	31	16:21	2	18	3	0	2	98	12.2
D	6	Erik Johnson	STL	55	5	14	19	22:07	-8	37	1	1	2	108	4.6
			COL	22	3	7	10	24:33	-5	19	2	0	0	53	5.7
			Total	77	8	21	29	22:49	-13	56	3	1	2	161	5.0
C	37	Ryan O'Reilly	COL	74	13	13	26	16:03	-7	16	2	1	0	119	10.9
C	34	Daniel Winnik	COL	80	11	15	26	16:32	-2	35	2	2	1	167	6.6
C	12	Kevin Porter	COL	74	14	11	25	13:49	-11	27	1	0	3	102	13.7
R	18	Brandon Yip	COL	71	12	10	22	13:43	-22	54	3	1	1	127	9.4
C	16	Jay McClement	STL	56	6	10	16	17:08	-13	18	1	0	1	89	6.7
			COL	24	1	3	4	15:39	-8	12	0	0	0	38	0.0
			Total	80	7	13	20	16:41	-21	30	1	0	1	127	5.5
C	11 *	Philippe Dupuis	COL	74	11	17	9:06	-4	40	0	1	0	101	5.9
D	44	Ryan Wilson	COL	67	3	13	19:48	-8	68	1	0	0	62	4.8
D	39	T.J. Galiardi	BOS	35	7	8	16:11	-6	12	0	0	1	62	11.3
D	48	Matt Hunwick	BOS	22	1	2	3	16:12	4	9	0	0	0	26	3.8
			COL	51	0	10	10	19:30	-19	16	0	0	0	74	0.0
			Total	73	1	12	13	18:30	-15	25	0	0	0	100	1.0
C	20	Greg Mauldin	COL	29	5	5	10	10:32	5	8	0	2	1	46	10.9
D	3	Ryan O'Byrne	MTL	3	0	0	0	14:54	0	4	0	0	0	3	0.0
			COL	64	0	10	10	20:24	-7	71	0	0	0	42	0.0
			Total	67	0	10	10	20:09	-7	75	0	0	0	45	0.0
C	40 *	Mark Olver	COL	18	2	9	11:53	-2	18	0	0	0	25	8.0
L	55	Cody McLeod	COL	71	5	3	8	9:46	-7	189	2	0	0	73	6.8
D	10	Kyle Cumiskey	COL	18	1	7	8	19:39	-3	10	0	0	0	21	4.8
D	52	Adam Foote	COL	47	0	8	17:55	-9	33	0	0	0	23	0.0
C	36 *	Jonas Holos	COL	39	0	6	6	18:03	-3	10	0	0	0	36	0.0
C	29 *	Ryan Stoa	COL	25	2	2	4	13:20	-4	20	0	0	1	45	4.4
L	7	David Van Der Gulik	COL	6	1	2	3	6:45	4	2	0	0	0	12	8.3
D	5 *	David Liffiton	COL	4	1	0	7:27	3	17	0	0	0	2	50.0
D	43 *	Cameron Gaunce	COL	11	1	0	12:43	-3	16	0	0	0	4	25.0
D	28	David Koci	COL	35	1	0	4:05	-5	80	0	0	0	9	11.1
D	27	Kyle Quincey	COL	21	0	1	19:34	-5	18	0	0	0	39	0.0
C	21	Peter Forsberg	COL	2	0	0	17:35	-4	4	0	0	0	3	0.0
D	42 *	Ray Macias	COL	2	0	0	15:06	-1	2	0	0	0	4	0.0
D	36 *	Colby Cohen	COL	3	0	0	17:44	-1	4	0	0	0	2	0.0
D	5 *	Shawn Belle	EDM	5	0	0	16:26	-2	0	0	0	0	7	0.0
			COL	4	0	0	18:02	1	2	0	0	0	1	0.0
			Total	9	0	0	17:08	-1	2	0	0	0	8	0.0

Goaltending

No.	Goaltender	GPI	Mins	Avg	W	L	OT	EN	SO	GA	SA	S%	G	A	PIM
31	Peter Budaj	45	2439	3.20	15	21	4	8	1	130	1234	.895	0	1	6
41	Craig Anderson	33	1810	3.28	13	15	3	5	0	99	957	.897	0	1	4
30	Brian Elliott	12	690	3.83	2	8	1	1	0	44	404	.891	0	0	0
	Totals	82	4990	3.45	30	44	8	14	1	287	2609	.890			

Joe Sacco
Head Coach
Born: Medford, MA, February 4, 1969.

Joe Sacco, former head coach of Colorado's American Hockey League affiliate, the Lake Erie Monsters, was named the 13th head coach in franchise history on June 4, 2009. In his first season behind the bench in 2009-10, he led the Avalanche back into the playoffs and was rewarded with a nomination for the Jack Adams Award as coach of the year. Sacco moved into the Avalanche head coach position after four seasons with the organization serving both as assistant coach (Lowell 2005-06; Albany 2006-07) and head coach (Lake Erie 2007-08, 2008-09) with the club's American Hockey League affiliates.

Under Sacco's guidance, the Monsters finished with a 34-38-13 record (76 points) in 2008-09, posting eight more wins and 11 more points than they did in their inaugural season of 2007-08. Following the season, Sacco was tabbed as an assistant coach for Team USA at the 2009 Men's World Championship in Switzerland.

Sacco, a native of Medford, Massachusetts, played college hockey at Boston University where he appeared in 111 games over three seasons with the Terriers. He was a fourth-round draft pick (71st overall) by the Toronto Maple Leafs in the 1987 NHL Entry Draft and went on to play in 738 total games over a 13-year NHL career, which included stints with Toronto, Anaheim, the New York Islanders, Washington and Philadelphia. The right winger finished with 94 goals and 119 assists. Sacco also competed internationally with the United States at the 1992 Olympics in Albertville, France, where the team finished fourth. He would go on to play for Team USA in six World Championships, winning a bronze medal in 1996.

Coaching Record

			Regular Season				Playoffs			
Season	Team	League	GC	W	L	O/T	GC	W	L	T
2007-08	Lake Erie	AHL	80	26	41	13	....	....	....	....
2008-09	Lake Erie	AHL	80	34	38	8	....	....	....	....
2009-10	**Colorado**	**NHL**	82	43	30	9	6	2	4	....
2010-11	**Colorado**	**NHL**	82	30	44	8	....	....	....	....
	NHL Totals		164	73	74	17	6	2	4	....

Coaching History

Jacques Demers, 1979-80; Maurice Filion and Michel Bergeron, 1980-81; Michel Bergeron, 1981-82 to 1986-87; Andre Savard and Ron Lapointe, 1987-88; Ron Lapointe and Jean Perron, 1988-89; Michel Bergeron, 1989-90; Dave Chambers, 1990-91; Dave Chambers and Pierre Page, 1991-92; Pierre Page, 1992-93, 1993-94; Marc Crawford, 1994-95 to 1997-98; Bob Hartley, 1998-99 to 2001-02; Bob Hartley and Tony Granato, 2002-03; Tony Granato, 2003-04; Joel Quenneville, 2004-05 to 2007-08; Tony Granato, 2008-09; Joe Sacco, 2009-10 to date.

Captains' History

Marc Tardif, 1979-80, 1980-81; Robbie Ftorek and Andre Dupont, 1981-82; Mario Marois, 1982-83 to 1984-85; Mario Marois and Peter Stastny, 1985-86; Peter Stastny, 1986-87 to 1989-90; Joe Sakic and Steven Finn, 1990-91; Mike Hough, 1991-92; Joe Sakic, 1992-93 to 2008-09; Adam Foote, 2009-10, 2010-11.

Club Records

Team

(Figures in brackets for season records are games played; records for fewest points, wins, ties, losses, goals, goals against are for 70 or more games)

Most Points	**118**	2000-01 (82)
Most Wins	**52**	2000-01 (82)
Most Ties	**18**	1980-81 (80)
Most Losses	**61**	1989-90 (80)
Most Goals	**360**	1983-84 (80)
Most Goals Against	**407**	1989-90 (80)
Fewest Points	**31**	1989-90 (80)
Fewest Wins	**12**	1989-90 (80)
Fewest Ties	**5**	1987-88 (80)
Fewest Losses	**16**	2000-01 (82)
Fewest Goals	**199**	2008-09 (82)
Fewest Goals Against	**169**	2001-02 (82)
Longest Winning Streak		
Overall	**12**	Jan. 10-Feb. 7/99
Home	**10**	Nov. 26/83-Jan. 10/84, Mar. 6-Apr. 16/95
Away	**7**	Jan. 10-Feb. 7/99
Longest Undefeated Streak		
Overall	**12**	Dec. 23/96-Jan. 20/97 (9 wins, 3 ties), Jan. 10-Feb. 7/99 (12 wins)
Home	**14**	Nov. 19/83-Jan. 21/84 (11 wins, 3 ties)
Away	**10**	Jan. 10-Mar. 3/99 (8 wins, 2 ties)
Longest Losing Streak		
Overall	**14**	Oct. 21-Nov. 19/90
Home	**8**	Oct. 21-Nov. 24/90
Away	**18**	Jan. 18-Apr. 1/90
Longest Winless Streak		
Overall	**17**	Oct. 21-Nov. 25/90 (15 losses, 2 ties)
Home	**11**	Nov. 14-Dec. 26/89 (7 losses, 4 ties)
Away	**33**	Oct. 8/91-Feb. 27/92 (25 losses, 8 ties)
Most Shutouts, Season	**11**	2001-02 (82)
Most PIM, Season	**2,104**	1989-90 (80)
Most Goals, Game	**12**	Feb. 1/83 (Hfd. 3 at Que. 12), Oct. 20/84 (Que. 12 at Tor. 3), Dec. 5/95 (S.J. 2 at Col. 12)

Individual

Most Seasons	**20**	Joe Sakic
Most Games	**1,378**	Joe Sakic
Most Goals, Career	**625**	Joe Sakic
Most Assists, Career	**1,016**	Joe Sakic
Most Points, Career	**1,641**	Joe Sakic (625G, 1,016A)
Most PIM, Career	**1,562**	Dale Hunter
Most Shutouts, Career	**37**	Patrick Roy
Longest Consecutive Games Streak	**312**	Dale Hunter (Oct. 9/80-Mar. 13/84)
Most Goals, Season	**57**	Michel Goulet (1982-83)
Most Assists, Season	**93**	Peter Stastny (1981-82)
Most Points, Season	**139**	Peter Stastny (1981-82; 46G, 93A)
Most PIM, Season	**301**	Gord Donnelly (1987-88)
Most Points, Defenseman, Season	**82**	Steve Duchesne (1992-93; 20G, 62A)
Most Points, Center, Season	**139**	Peter Stastny (1981-82; 46G, 93A)
Most Points, Right Wing, Season	**103**	Jacques Richard (1980-81; 52G, 51A)
Most Points, Left Wing, Season	**121**	Michel Goulet (1983-84; 56G, 65A)
Most Points, Rookie, Season	**109**	Peter Stastny (1980-81; 39G, 70A)
Most Shutouts, Season	**9**	Patrick Roy (2001-02)
Most Goals, Game	**5**	Mats Sundin (Mar. 5/92), Mike Ricci (Feb. 17/94)
Most Assists, Game	**5**	Eight times
Most Points, Game	**8**	Peter Stastny (Feb. 22/81; 4G, 4A), Anton Stastny (Feb. 22/81; 3G, 5A)

Records include Quebec Nordiques, 1979-80 through 1994-95.

Retired Numbers

3	J.C. Tremblay*	1972-1979
8	Marc Tardif*	1979-1983
16	Michel Goulet*	1979-1990
19	Joe Sakic	1988-2009
21	Peter Forsberg	1994-04, 07-08, 2010-11
26	Peter Stastny*	1980-1990
33	Patrick Roy	1995-2003
77	Raymond Bourque	2000-2001

* Quebec Nordiques

All-time Record vs. Other Clubs

Regular Season

	At Home								On Road								Total							
	GP	W	L	T	OL	GF	GA	PTS	GP	W	L	T	OL	GF	GA	PTS	GP	W	L	T	OL	GF	GA	PTS
Anaheim	33	16	12	4	1	91	92	37	33	14	11	3	5	83	91	36	66	30	23	7	6	174	183	73
Atlanta	8	3	3	0	2	26	25	8	7	4	2	1	0	20	15	9	15	7	5	1	2	46	40	17
Boston	69	25	38	6	0	244	283	56	64	24	31	9	0	198	243	57	133	49	69	15	0	442	526	113
Buffalo	67	33	22	11	1	237	207	78	65	20	35	9	1	211	252	50	132	53	57	20	2	448	459	128
Calgary	68	30	26	11	1	233	217	72	68	26	33	9	0	197	236	61	136	56	59	20	1	430	453	133
Carolina	67	41	17	9	0	284	197	91	66	27	26	12	1	223	216	67	133	68	43	21	1	507	413	158
Chicago	51	28	15	6	2	199	163	64	53	21	27	3	2	161	180	47	104	49	42	9	4	360	343	111
Columbus	20	17	3	0	0	76	37	34	20	13	5	1	1	68	41	28	40	30	8	1	1	144	78	62
Dallas	53	29	13	7	4	187	130	69	53	19	27	5	2	150	178	45	106	48	40	12	6	337	308	114
Detroit	54	24	23	4	3	178	180	55	52	20	30	1	1	152	185	42	106	44	53	5	4	330	365	97
Edmonton	68	35	28	4	1	247	233	75	67	29	31	4	3	216	251	65	135	64	59	8	4	463	484	140
Florida	13	6	4	3	0	38	31	15	15	11	2	0	2	60	46	24	28	17	6	3	2	98	77	39
Los Angeles	54	27	23	3	1	213	185	58	55	18	30	5	2	178	216	43	109	45	53	8	3	391	401	101
Minnesota	32	18	11	2	1	90	76	39	31	13	10	1	7	89	86	34	63	31	21	3	8	179	162	73
Montreal	66	34	27	5	0	223	229	73	66	17	39	10	0	206	271	44	132	51	66	15	0	429	500	117
Nashville	24	12	8	2	2	62	55	28	24	9	10	3	2	71	73	23	48	21	18	5	4	133	128	51
New Jersey	37	19	14	4	0	129	103	42	39	15	20	4	0	128	156	34	76	34	34	8	0	257	259	76
NY Islanders	37	21	12	3	1	130	105	46	35	13	21	1	0	117	143	27	72	34	33	4	1	247	248	73
NY Rangers	38	21	14	3	0	153	137	45	37	13	20	4	0	105	142	30	75	34	34	7	0	258	279	75
Ottawa	18	14	3	1	0	81	54	29	20	9	8	3	0	70	57	21	38	23	11	4	0	151	111	50
Philadelphia	38	15	10	12	1	136	129	43	37	11	23	2	1	99	134	25	75	26	33	14	2	235	263	68
Phoenix	53	27	19	5	2	181	174	61	52	23	20	7	2	175	179	55	105	50	39	12	4	356	353	116
Pittsburgh	35	19	13	2	1	152	130	41	39	17	17	5	0	156	153	39	74	36	30	7	1	308	283	80
St. Louis	53	29	16	7	1	189	141	66	52	20	28	4	0	154	183	44	105	49	44	11	1	343	324	110
San Jose	35	20	10	4	1	122	79	45	36	18	15	1	2	113	102	39	71	38	25	5	3	235	181	84
Tampa Bay	16	11	3	2	0	60	34	24	16	6	9	1	0	45	46	13	32	17	12	3	0	105	80	37
Toronto	32	18	9	5	0	123	101	41	37	17	16	4	0	141	120	38	69	35	25	9	0	264	221	79
Vancouver	68	34	24	8	2	221	192	78	68	32	25	7	4	243	220	75	136	66	49	15	6	464	412	153
Washington	36	15	16	5	0	109	127	35	36	13	19	4	0	113	136	30	72	28	35	9	0	222	263	65
Totals	**1243**	**641**	**436**	**138**	**28**	**4414**	**3846**	**1448**	**1243**	**492**	**590**	**123**	**38**	**3942**	**4351**	**1145**	**2486**	**1133**	**1026**	**261**	**66**	**8356**	**8197**	**2593**

Playoffs

	Series	W	L	GP	W	L	T	GF	GA	Last Mtg.	Rnd.	Result
Anaheim	1	0	1	4	0	4	0	4	16	2006	CSF	L 0-4
Boston	2	1	1	11	5	6	0	36	37	1983	DSF	L 1-3
Buffalo	2	2	0	8	6	2	0	35	27	1985	DSF	W 3-2
Carolina	2	1	1	9	4	5	0	34	35	1987	DSF	W 4-2
Chicago	2	2	0	12	8	4	0	49	28	1997	CQF	W 4-2
Dallas	4	2	2	24	14	10	0	66	62	2006	CQF	W 4-1
Detroit	6	3	3	34	17	17	0	88	97	2008	CSF	L 0-4
Edmonton	2	1	1	12	7	5	0	35	30	1998	CQF	L 3-4
Florida	1	1	0	4	4	0	0	15	4	1996	F	W 4-0
Los Angeles	2	2	0	14	8	6	0	33	23	2002	CQF	W 4-3
Minnesota	2	1	1	13	7	6	0	34	28	2008	CQF	W 4-2
Montreal	5	2	3	31	14	17	0	85	105	1993	DSF	L 2-4
New Jersey	1	1	0	7	4	3	0	19	11	2001	F	W 4-3
NY Islanders	1	0	1	4	0	4	0	9	18	1982	CF	L 0-4
NY Rangers	1	0	1	6	2	4	0	19	25	1995	CQF	L 2-4
Philadelphia	2	0	2	11	4	7	0	29	39	1985	CF	L 2-4
Phoenix	1	1	0	5	4	1	0	17	10	2000	CQF	W 4-1
St. Louis	1	1	0	5	4	1	0	17	11	2001	CF	W 4-1
San Jose	4	2	2	25	12	13	0	62	71	2010	CQF	L 2-4
Vancouver	2	2	0	10	8	2	0	40	26	2001	CQF	W 4-0
Totals	**44**	**25**	**19**	**249**	**132**	**117**	**0**	**726**	**703**			

Calgary totals include Atlanta Flames, 1979-80.
Dallas totals include Minnesota North Stars, 1979-80 to 1992-93.
Phoenix totals include Winnipeg, 1979-80 to 1995-96.

Carolina totals include Hartford, 1979-80 to 1996-97.
New Jersey totals include Colorado Rockies, 1979-80 to 1981-82.

Playoff Results 2011-2007

Year	Round	Opponent	Result	GF	GA
2010	CQF	San Jose	L 2-4	11	19
2008	CSF	Detroit	L 0-4	9	21
	CQF	Minnesota	W 4-2	17	12

Abbreviations: Round: F - Final; **CF** - conference final; **CSF** - conference semi-final; **CQF** - conference quarter-final; **DSF** - division semi-final.

2010-11 Results

Oct.	7	Chicago	4-3*		8	NY Islanders	3-4*
	11	at Philadelphia	2-4		10	Detroit	5-4
	12	at Detroit	5-4†		12	at Chicago	0-4
	15	at New Jersey	3-2		14	at Minnesota	4-1
	16	at NY Islanders	2-5		18	Vancouver	4-3*
	18	at NY Rangers	3-1		20	Nashville	1-5
	21	San Jose	2-4		22	Boston	2-6
	23	Los Angeles	4-6		24	St. Louis	4-3
	26	at Vancouver	3-4*		26	Phoenix	2-5
	28	at Calgary	6-5	**Feb.**	3	Minnesota	3-4
	30	Columbus	5-1		5	Anaheim	0-3
Nov.	4	Vancouver	1-3		7	at Phoenix	0-3
	6	Dallas	5-0		9	at Minnesota	2-3
	9	Calgary	2-4		11	at Columbus	1-3
	12	at Columbus	5-1		12	at Nashville	3-5
	13	at Detroit	1-3		14	Calgary	1-9
	15	St. Louis	6-3		16	Pittsburgh	2-3*
	17	San Jose	4-3*		19	at San Jose	0-4
	19	NY Rangers	5-1		22	at St. Louis	4-3
	20	at Dallas	4-3†		23	Edmonton	1-5
	24	at Vancouver	2-4		26	at Los Angeles	3-4
	25	at Edmonton	2-3		27	at Anaheim	2-3
	27	Minnesota	7-4	**Mar.**	1	at San Jose	1-2†
	30	Atlanta	2-3*		5	Edmonton	1-5
Dec.	3	at Carolina	1-2*		8	at Minnesota	2-5
	4	at Tampa Bay	5-6		11	Anaheim	2-6
	7	at Florida	3-4*		12	at Nashville	2-4
	10	at Atlanta	4-2		16	at Vancouver	2-4
	11	at Washington	3-2		17	at Calgary	2-5
	13	Chicago	7-5		19	at Edmonton	3-2†
	15	at Chicago	4-3		22	Columbus	5-4†
	17	Ottawa	6-5*		24	Toronto	3-4
	19	Montreal	3-2		26	at Los Angeles	1-4
	21	Los Angeles	0-5		28	at Anaheim	4-5
	23	Minnesota	1-3		31	Nashville	2-3
	27	Detroit	3-4*	**Apr.**	1	at Phoenix	4-3†
	30	at Edmonton	4-3†		3	Calgary	1-2
	31	at Calgary	2-3		5	at St. Louis	1-3
Jan.	2	Vancouver	1-2		7	at Dallas	2-4
	4	Buffalo	4-3*		8	Dallas	2-3
	6	Phoenix	0-2		10	Edmonton	4-3*

* – Overtime † – Shootout

Entry Draft Selections 2011-1997

Name in bold denotes played in NHL.

2011
Pick
2	Gabriel Landeskog
11	Duncan Siemens
93	Joachim Nermark
123	Garrett Meurs
153	Gabriel Beaupre
183	Dillon Donnelly

2010
Pick
17	Joey Hishon
49	Calvin Pickard
71	Michael Bournival
95	Stephen Silas
107	Sami Aittokallio
137	Troy Rutkowski
139	Luke Walker
197	Luke Moffatt

2009
Pick
3	**Matt Duchene**
33	**Ryan O'Reilly**
49	Stefan Elliott
64	Tyson Barrie
124	Kieran Millan
154	Brandon Maxwell
184	Gus Young

2008
Pick
50	**Cameron Gaunce**
61	Peter Delmas
110	Kelsey Tessier
140	**Mark Olver**
167	Joel Chouinard
170	**Jonas Holos**
200	Nathan Condon

2007
Pick
14	**Kevin Shattenkirk**
45	**Colby Cohen**
49	Trevor Cann
55	**T.J. Galiardi**
105	Brad Malone
113	Kent Patterson
135	Paul Carey
155	Jens Hellgren
195	Johan Alcen

2006
Pick
18	**Chris Stewart**
51	Nigel Williams
59	Codey Burki
81	Mike Carman
110	Kevin Montgomery
201	Billy Sauer

2005
Pick
34	**Ryan Stoa**
44	**Paul Stastny**
47	Tom Fritsche
52	Chris Durand
88	**T.J. Hensick**
124	**Ray Macias**
166	Jason Lynch
168	**Justin Mercier**
222	**Kyle Cumiskey**

2004
Pick
21	**Wojtek Wolski**
55	**Victor Oreskovich**
72	Denis Parshin
154	Richard Demen-Willaume
184	**Derek Peltier**
215	Ian Keserich
239	**Brandon Yip**
249	J.D. Corbin
281	Steve McClellan

2003
Pick
63	**David Liffiton**
131	David Svagrovsky
146	Mark McCutcheon
163	**Brad Richardson**
204	Linus Videll
225	Brett Hemingway
257	Darryl Yacboski
288	**David Jones**

2002
Pick
28	Jonas Johansson
61	Johnny Boychuk
94	Eric Lundberg
107	Mikko Kalteva
129	**Tom Gilbert**
164	**Tyler Weiman**
195	Taylor Christie
227	Ryan Steeves
258	Sergei Shemetov
289	Sean Collins

2001
Pick
63	Peter Budaj
97	Danny Bois
130	Colt King
143	Frantisek Skladany
144	Cody McCormick
149	Mikko Viitanen
165	Pierre-Luc Emond
184	Scott Horvath
196	**Charlie Stephens**
227	**Marek Svatos**

2000
Pick
14	Vaclav Nedorost
47	Jared Aulin
50	Sergei Soin
63	Agris Saviels
88	**Kurt Sauer**
92	Sergei Klyazmin
119	**Brian Fahey**
159	**John-Michael Liles**
189	Chris Bahen
221	Aaron Molnar
252	**Darryl Bootland**
266	Sean Kotary
285	Blake Ward

1999
Pick
25	Mikhail Kuleshov
45	**Martin Grenier**
93	**Branko Radivojevic**
112	Sanny Lindstrom
122	Kristian Kovac
142	Will Magnuson
152	Jordan Krestanovich
158	Anders Lovdahl
183	Riku Hahl
212	Radim Vrbata
240	Jeff Finger

1998
Pick
12	**Alex Tanguay**
17	**Martin Skoula**
19	**Robyn Regehr**
20	**Scott Parker**
28	**Ramzi Abid**
38	**Philippe Sauve**
53	**Steve Moore**
79	Evgeny Lazarev
141	K.C. Timmons
167	Alexander Ryazantsev

1997
Pick
26	Kevin Grimes
53	Graham Belak
55	**Rick Berry**
78	**Ville Nieminen**
87	**Brad Larsen**
133	Aaron Miskovich
161	**David Aebischer**
217	Doug Schmidt
243	Kyle Kidney
245	Stephen Lafleur

General Managers' History

Maurice Filion, 1979-80 to 1987-88; Martin Madden, 1988-89; Martin Madden and Maurice Filion, 1989-90; Pierre Page, 1990-91 to 1993-94; Pierre Lacroix, 1994-95 to 2005-06; Francois Giguere, 2006-07 to 2008-09; Greg Sherman, 2009-10 to date.

Greg Sherman
General Manager/Executive V.P. and Alt. Governor
Born: Scranton, PA, March 30, 1970.

Greg Sherman was named general manager of the Colorado Avalanche on June 3, 2009. At the time of his appointment, he had spent the last seven years as the team's assistant general manager and had been associated with the franchise for 13 years. In his first few weeks on the job, Sherman hired Joe Sacco as the Avalanche's head coach and oversaw the selection of Matt Duchene with the third pick in the NHL Entry Draft. The team showed a 26-point improvement in 2009-10 and returned to the playoffs.

In his previous role in Colorado, Sherman worked on contract negotiations, arbitration cases, salary cap management and matters concerning personnel at all levels of the organization. In addition, Sherman also served as a liaison between the Avalanche and its American Hockey League affiliate, the Lake Erie Monsters. He oversaw and coordinated all financial obligations of both clubs.

Born in Scranton, Pennsylvania and raised in Denver, Colorado, Sherman has spent most of his life in Colorado. He attended the University of San Diego and received his Bachelor in Accountancy in May 1992.

Club Directory

Pepsi Center

Colorado Avalanche
Pepsi Center
1000 Chopper Circle
Denver, CO 80204
Phone 303/405-1100
FAX 303/893-0614
Press Box 303/575-1926
www.coloradoavalanche.com
Capacity: 18,007

Executive
Owner	E. Stanley Kroenke
Governor	Josh Kroenke
President and Alternate Governor	Pierre Lacroix
G.M., Executive V.P. & Alt. Governor	Greg Sherman
Executive Advisor & Alt. Governor	Joe Sakic
Vice President of Player Development	Craig Billington
Vice President of Hockey Administration	Charlotte Grahame
Director of Hockey Operations	Eric Lacroix
Director of Player Personnel	Brad Smith

Coaching Staff
Head Coach	Joe Sacco
Assistant Coaches	Sylvain Lefebvre, Adam Deadmarsh
Assistant Coach/Video	Tim Army
Goaltending Consultant	Kirk McLean

Training Staff
Head Athletic Trainer	Matthew Sokolowski
Assistant Athletic Trainer/Physical Therapist	Scott Woodward
Head Equipment Manager	Mark Miller
Assistant Equipment Managers	Cliff Halstead, Brad Lewkow
Inventory Manager	Wayne Flemming
Strength & Conditioning Coach	Robert McLean
Massage Therapist	Gregorio Pradera

Scouting
Director of Amateur Scouting	Richard Pracey
Assistant Director of Amateur Scouting	Alan Hepple
Scouts	Anders Carlsson, Rick Lanz, Joni Lehto, Don Paarup, Guy Perron, Neil Shea
Pro Scouts	Garth Joy, Dan Laperriere, Terry Martin

Communications/Team Services
Sr. V.P., Communications & Business Operations	Jean Martineau
Sr. Director of Media Services/Internet	Brendan McNicholas
Website/Media Relations Coordinator	Kyle Shohara
Team Services Coordinator	Erin DeGraff

Lake Erie Monsters (AHL affiliate)
Head Coach	David Quinn
Asst. Coach/Director of AHL Operations	David Oliver
Head Athletic Trainer	Brent Woodside
Head Equipment Manager	Dusty Halstead

Team Information
Practice Facility	South Suburban Family Sports Center
Television Outlet	Altitude Sports & Entertainment Network
Radio	Altitude Radio Network

The club's second choice (33rd overall) behind Matt Duchene in the 2009 Entry Draft, Ryan O'Reilly has also spent two full seasons in the NHL after making the team straight out of junior hockey as an 18-year-old.

Columbus Blue Jackets

2010-11 Results: 34w-35l-5otl-8sol 81pts.
Fifth, Central Division

Year-by-Year Record

Season	GP	Home W	L	T	OL	Road W	L	T	OL	Overall W	L	T	OL	GF	GA	Pts.	Finished	Playoff Result
2010-11	82	17	19	....	5	17	16	....	8	34	35	....	13	215	258	81	5th, Central Div.	Out of Playoffs
2009-10	82	20	12	....	9	12	23	....	6	32	35	....	15	216	259	79	5th, Central Div.	Out of Playoffs
2008-09	82	25	13	....	3	16	18	....	7	41	31	....	10	226	230	92	4th, Central Div.	Lost Conf. Quarter-Final
2007-08	82	20	14	....	7	14	22	....	5	34	36	....	12	193	218	80	4th, Central Div.	Out of Playoffs
2006-07	82	18	19	....	4	15	23	....	3	33	42	....	7	201	249	73	4th, Central Div.	Out of Playoffs
2005-06	82	23	18	....	0	12	25	....	4	35	43	....	4	223	279	74	3rd, Central Div.	Out of Playoffs
2004-05	....																	
2003-04	82	17	18	4	2	8	27	4	2	25	45	8	4	177	238	62	4th, Central Div.	Out of Playoffs
2002-03	82	20	14	5	2	9	28	3	1	29	42	8	3	213	263	69	5th, Central Div.	Out of Playoffs
2001-02	82	14	18	5	4	8	29	3	1	22	47	8	5	164	255	57	5th, Central Div.	Out of Playoffs
2000-01	82	19	15	4	3	9	24	5	3	28	39	9	6	190	233	71	5th, Central Div.	Out of Playoffs

2011-12 Schedule

Oct.	Fri.	7	Nashville
	Sat.	8	at Minnesota
	Mon.	10	Vancouver
	Wed.	12	Colorado
	Sat.	15	at Dallas
	Tue.	18	Dallas
	Fri.	21	at Detroit
	Sat.	22	at Ottawa
	Tue.	25	Detroit
	Thu.	27	at Buffalo
	Sat.	29	at Chicago
	Sun.	30	Anaheim
Nov.	Thu.	3	Toronto
	Sat.	5	at Philadelphia
	Thu.	10	Chicago
	Sat.	12	Winnipeg
	Tue.	15	Minnesota
	Thu.	17	at Boston
	Sat.	19	at Nashville
	Mon.	21	Calgary
	Wed.	23	at New Jersey
	Fri.	25	Buffalo
	Sun.	27	St. Louis
	Tue.	29	at Vancouver
Dec.	Thu.	1	at Calgary
	Fri.	2	at Edmonton
	Tue.	6	at Montreal
	Thu.	8	Nashville
	Sat.	10	Boston
	Tue.	13	Vancouver
	Thu.	15	Los Angeles
	Sat.	17	Tampa Bay
	Sun.	18	at St. Louis
	Thu.	22	at Nashville
	Mon.	26	at Chicago
	Tue.	27	Calgary
	Thu.	29	at Dallas
	Sat.	31	Washington
Jan.	Thu.	5	at San Jose
	Sat.	7	at Los Angeles*
	Sun.	8	at Anaheim*
	Tue.	10	at Chicago
	Fri.	13	Phoenix
	Sat.	14	San Jose
	Tue.	17	Edmonton
	Thu.	19	Nashville
	Sat.	21	at Detroit
	Mon.	23	at Nashville
	Tue.	24	at Tampa Bay
	Tue.	31	at San Jose
Feb.	Wed.	1	at Los Angeles
	Fri.	3	at Anaheim
	Tue.	7	Minnesota
	Thu.	9	Dallas
	Sat.	11	at Minnesota
	Sun.	12	Anaheim
	Tue.	14	St. Louis
	Sat.	18	Chicago*
	Sun.	19	at NY Rangers
	Tue.	21	San Jose
	Fri.	24	Colorado
	Sun.	26	at Pittsburgh*
	Tue.	28	Detroit
Mar.	Thu.	1	at Colorado
	Sat.	3	at Phoenix
	Tue.	6	Phoenix
	Thu.	8	Los Angeles
	Sat.	10	at St. Louis
	Sun.	11	St. Louis
	Wed.	14	at Edmonton
	Sat.	17	at Vancouver
	Sun.	18	at Calgary
	Tue.	20	Chicago
	Fri.	23	Carolina
	Sun.	25	Edmonton*
	Mon.	26	at Detroit
	Wed.	28	Detroit
	Fri.	30	Florida
	Sat.	31	at St. Louis
Apr.	Tue.	3	at Phoenix
	Thu.	5	at Colorado
	Sat.	7	NY Islanders

* Denotes afternoon game.

CENTRAL DIVISION
12th NHL Season

Franchise date: June 25, 1997

Rick Nash topped the 30-goal plateau for the sixth time in eight seasons as he led the Blue Jackets with 32 goals and 66 points in 2010-11. He also led the team in assists for just the second time in his career with 34.

2011-12 Player Personnel

FORWARDS	HT	WT	S	Place of Birth	*Age	2010-11 Club
ATKINSON, Cam	5-9	165	R	Riverside, CT	22	Boston College-Springfield
BASS, Cody	6-1	204	R	Owen Sound, Ont.	24	Ottawa-Binghamton
BOLL, Jared	6-2	214	R	Charlotte, NC	25	Columbus
BRASSARD, Derick	6-1	199	L	Hull, Que.	24	Columbus
BYERS, Dane	6-3	204	L	Nipawin, Sask.	25	Connecticut-Springfield-San Antonio
CALVERT, Matt	5-11	189	L	Brandon, Man.	21	Columbus-Springfield
CARTER, Jeff	6-3	200	R	London, Ont.	26	Philadelphia
DORSETT, Derek	6-0	190	R	Kindersley, Sask.	24	Columbus
DRAZENOVIC, Nicholas	6-0	205	L	Prince George, B.C.	24	St. Louis-Peoria
GIROUX, Alexandre	6-3	203	L	Quebec City, Que.	30	Edmonton-Oklahoma City
HUSELIUS, Kristian	6-2	184	L	Osterhaninge, Sweden	32	Columbus
JOHANSEN, Ryan	6-3	202	R	Port Moody, B.C.	19	Portland (WHL)
JOUDREY, Andrew	5-11	185	L	Halifax, N.S.	27	Hershey
KUBALIK, Tomas	6-3	209	R	Plzen, Czech.	21	Columbus-Springfield
MacKENZIE, Derek	5-11	178	L	Sudbury, Ont.	30	Columbus
MAYOROV, Maksim	6-2	202	L	Andizhan, USSR	22	Columbus-Springfield
NASH, Rick	6-4	216	L	Brampton, Ont.	27	Columbus
PAHLSSON, Samuel	6-0	207	L	Ange, Sweden	33	Columbus
PROSPAL, Vinny	6-2	198	L	Ceske Budejovice, Czech.	36	NY Rangers
RUSSELL, Ryan	5-10	180	L	Caroline, Alta.	24	Hamilton
ST. PIERRE, Martin	5-9	187	L	Ottawa, Ont.	28	Nizhnekamsk-Karpat-Salzburg
UMBERGER, R.J.	6-2	220	L	Pittsburgh, PA	29	Columbus
VERMETTE, Antoine	6-1	199	L	St-Agapit, Que.	29	Columbus

DEFENSEMEN						
CLITSOME, Grant	6-0	208	L	Gloucester, Ont.	26	Columbus-Springfield
HOLDEN, Nick	6-4	210	L	St. Albert, Alta.	24	Columbus-Springfield
JOHNSON, Aaron	6-2	211	L	Port Hawkesbury, N.S.	28	Milwaukee
MARTINEK, Radek	6-2	210	R	Havlicko Brod, Czech.	35	NY Islanders
METHOT, Marc	6-3	222	L	Ottawa, Ont.	26	Columbus
MOORE, John	6-3	198	L	Winnetka, IL	20	Columbus-Springfield
PROUT, Dalton	6-3	223	R	LaSalle, Ont.	21	Barrie-Saginaw
RUSSELL, Kris	5-10	174	L	Red Deer, Alta.	24	Columbus
SAVARD, David	6-2	214	R	St. Hyacinthe, Que.	20	Springfield
TYUTIN, Fedor	6-2	214	L	Izhevsk, USSR	28	Columbus
WISNIEWSKI, James	5-11	208	R	Canton, MI	27	NY Islanders-Montreal

GOALTENDERS	HT	WT	C	Place of Birth	*Age	2010-11 Club
DEKANICH, Mark	6-2	190	L	N. Vancouver, B.C.	25	Nashville-Milwaukee
MASON, Steve	6-4	211	R	Oakville, Ont.	23	Columbus
SANFORD, Curtis	5-11	185	L	Owen Sound, Ont.	32	Hamilton
YORK, Allen	6-4	190	L	Wetaskiwin, Alta.	22	RPI-Springfield

* – Age at start of 2011-12 season

2010-11 Scoring

* – rookie

Regular Season

Pos	#	Player	Team	GP	G	A	Pts	TOI	+/-	PIM	PP	SH	GW	S	%
L	61	Rick Nash	CBJ	75	32	34	66	18:55	2	34	6	0	7	305	10.5
C	18	R.J. Umberger	CBJ	82	25	32	57	19:12	3	38	8	3	3	220	11.4
C	50	Antoine Vermette	CBJ	82	19	28	47	18:48	0	60	3	1	3	183	10.4
C	16	Derick Brassard	CBJ	74	17	30	47	17:01	-11	55	6	0	3	183	9.3
R	93	Jakub Voracek	CBJ	80	14	32	46	16:58	-3	26	2	0	2	183	7.7
R	9	Scottie Upshall	PHX	61	16	11	27	13:26	5	42	2	0	2	144	11.1
			CBJ	21	6	1	7	15:45	-12	10	0	0	0	47	12.8
			Total	82	22	12	34	14:02	-7	52	2	0	2	191	11.5
D	51	Fedor Tyutin	CBJ	80	7	20	27	22:41	-12	32	1	0	0	128	5.5
L	20	Kristian Huselius	CBJ	39	14	9	23	16:22	-17	10	6	0	1	94	14.9
C	24	Derek Mackenzie	CBJ	63	9	14	23	10:50	14	22	0	1	1	76	11.8
D	10	Kris Russell	CBJ	73	5	18	23	17:31	-9	37	1	0	0	88	5.7
L	11 *	Matt Calvert	CBJ	42	11	9	20	11:05	3	12	3	0	1	50	22.0
C	26	Samuel Pahlsson	CBJ	82	7	13	20	15:20	-13	30	0	1	1	108	6.5
D	35	Jan Hejda	CBJ	77	5	15	20	21:07	-6	28	0	0	0	79	6.3
D	14 *	Grant Clitsome	CBJ	31	4	15	19	21:16	2	16	2	0	0	50	8.0
D	6	Anton Stralman	CBJ	51	1	17	18	19:44	-11	22	1	0	1	80	1.3
D	15	Derek Dorsett	CBJ	76	4	13	17	13:12	-15	184	0	0	0	112	3.6
D	4	Sami Lepisto	PHX	51	4	7	11	16:38	-7	37	0	0	0	31	12.9
			CBJ	19	0	5	5	20:01	3	18	0	0	0	25	0.0
			Total	70	4	12	16	17:33	10	55	0	0	0	56	7.1
R	71	Chris Clark	CBJ	53	5	10	15	14:38	-3	38	2	0	0	83	6.0
D	3	Marc Methot	CBJ	74	0	15	15	19:53	2	58	0	0	0	58	0.0
R	40	Jared Boll	CBJ	73	5	12	7	7:40	-2	182	0	0	2	66	10.6
C	25 *	Kyle Wilson	CBJ	32	4	7	11	10:38	-3	12	0	0	0	38	10.5
C	17	Andrew Murray	CBJ	29	4	4	8	11:22	2	4	0	0	1	48	8.3
L	28	Nikita Filatov	CBJ	23	0	7	7	12:19	3	8	0	0	0	31	0.0
D	22	Mike Commodore	CBJ	20	2	4	6	18:33	-8	44	0	0	0	32	6.3
D	19	Ethan Moreau	CBJ	37	1	5	6	12:28	-9	24	0	0	1	56	1.8
L	23 *	Tom Sestito	CBJ	9	2	2	4	9:31	-4	40	1	0	0	7	28.6
D	52	Craig Rivet	BUF	23	1	2	3	13:02	-5	12	0	0	0	20	5.0
			CBJ	14	1	0	1	17:21	-7	23	0	0	0	13	7.7
			Total	37	2	2	4	14:40	-12	35	0	0	0	33	6.1
R	33 *	Tomas Kubalik	CBJ	4	0	2	2	14:45	-3	0	0	0	0	5	0.0
R	43 *	Maksim Mayorov	CBJ	5	1	0	1	8:42	0	0	0	0	0	3	33.3
R	12	Mike Blunden	CBJ	1	0	0	0	10:31	-1	0	0	0	0	2	0.0
D	7 *	John Moore	CBJ	2	0	0	0	11:28	0	0	0	0	0	0	0.0
D	2	Nate Guenin	CBJ	3	0	0	0	14:47	-3	2	0	0	0	0	0.0
D	29 *	Nick Holden	CBJ	5	0	0	0	17:11	0	0	0	0	0	6	0.0

Goaltending

No.	Goaltender	GPI	Mins	Avg	W	L	OT	EN	SO	GA	SA	S%	G	A	PIM
32	Mathieu Garon	36	1938	2.72	10	14	6	6	3	88	887	.901	0	1	2
1	Steve Mason	54	3027	3.03	24	21	7	1	3	153	1541	.901	0	1	2
31	David LeNeveu	1	20	6.00	0	0	0	0	0	2	12	.833	0	0	0
	Totals	82	5012	2.99	34	35	13	7	6	250	2447	.898			

Scott Arniel

Head Coach

Born: Kingston, Ont., September 17, 1962.

The Columbus Blue Jackets named Scott Arniel as their new head coach on June 8, 2010. Arniel joined the Blue Jackets after spending four seasons as head coach of the American Hockey League's Manitoba Moose, the top affiliate for the Vancouver Canucks. He led the club to a 181-106-33 record (.617) from 2006 to 2010, including North Division titles during the 2006-07 and 2008-09 seasons, four playoff appearances and a trip to the 2009 Calder Cup Final.

Arniel was named the winner of the 2008-09 A.R. Pieri Memorial Award as the AHL's outstanding coach after guiding the club to a 50-23-7 record, which marked the most successful season in franchise history. The team set franchise records for wins and finished first overall in the AHL for the first time in club history. Prior to his stint in Manitoba, he served as an assistant coach for the Buffalo Sabres for three seasons from 2002 to 2006 and helped the club to a 52-24-6 record and a berth the Eastern Conference Final in 2005-06. He began his coaching career as an assistant coach with the Moose, serving in that capacity from 1999-2002.

Winnipeg's second pick, 22nd overall, in the 1981 Entry Draft, Arniel spent parts of 11 seasons in the NHL from 1981 to 1992 and registered 149 goals and 189 assists for 338 points and 599 penalty minutes in 730 career games with the Sabres, Winnipeg Jets and Boston Bruins. He helped his teams qualify for the Stanley Cup playoffs in eight of those seasons. Arniel set career highs with 21 goals and 35 assists for 56 points in 80 games with Winnipeg during the 1983-84 season.

The Kingston, Ontario native also played eight seasons in the AHL and former International Hockey League, collecting 201 goals, 273 assists (474 points) and 713 penalty minutes in 555 career games with Maine (AHL), New Haven (AHL), San Diego (IHL), Houston (IHL), Utah (IHL) and Manitoba (IHL). He added 25 goals and 17 assists for 42 and 88 penalty minutes in 55 career playoff games and helped the Utah Grizzlies win the Turner Cup in 1995-96. Arniel retired as a player following the 1998-99 season.

Prior to his professional career, Arniel played three seasons of major junior hockey with the Cornwall Royals and tallied 92 goals and 125 assists for 217 points and 196 penalty minutes in 153 career games. He helped the Royals win the Memorial Cup in 1980 and 1981. He also was a member of Team Canada at the 1982 World Junior Championships and helped the team to its first gold medal at the tournament.

Derek MacKenzie spent his first full season in the NHL in 2010-11 and though he played just 63 games his +14 rating was by far the Blue Jackets' best.

Coaching Record

			Regular Season				Playoffs			
Season	Team	League	GC	W	L	O/T	GC	W	L	T
2006-07	Manitoba	AHL	80	45	23	12	13	6	7	....
2007-08	Manitoba	AHL	80	46	27	7	6	2	4	....
2008-09	Manitoba	AHL	80	50	23	7	22	14	8	....
2009-10	Manitoba	AHL	80	40	33	7	6	2	4	....
2010-11	Columbus	NHL	82	34	35	13	....	....	....	....
	NHL Totals		82	34	35	13	....	....	....	....

Coaching History

Dave King, 2000-01, 2001-02; Dave King and Doug MacLean, 2002-03; Doug MacLean and Gerard Gallant, 2003-04; Gerard Gallant, 2004-05, 2005-06; Gerard Gallant, Gary Agnew and Ken Hitchcock, 2006-07; Ken Hitchcock, 2007-08, 2008-09; Ken Hitchcock and Claude Noel, 2009-10; Scott Arniel, 2010-11 to date.

Club Records

Team

(Figures in brackets for season records are games played.)

Most Points	92	2008-09 (82)
Most Wins	41	2008-09 (82)
Most Ties	9	2000-01 (82)
Most Losses	47	2001-02 (82)
Most Goals	226	2008-09 (82)
Most Goals Against	279	2005-06 (82)
Fewest Points	57	2001-02 (82)
Fewest Wins	22	2001-02 (82)
Fewest Ties	8	2001-02 (82), 2002-03 (82), 2003-04 (82)
Fewest Losses	31	2008-09 (82)
Fewest Goals	164	2001-02 (82)
Fewest Goals Against	218	2007-08 (82)

Longest Winning Streak

Overall	6	Mar. 24-Apr. 3/06
Home	6	Dec. 26/07-Jan. 15/08
Away	6	Jan. 19-Feb. 18/11

Longest Undefeated Streak

Overall	6	Mar. 24-Apr. 3/06 (6 wins)
Home	6	Dec. 26/07-Jan. 15/08 (6 wins)
Away	4	Jan. 3-11/03 (3 wins, 1 tie), Dec. 2-12/06 (4 wins)

Longest Losing Streak

Overall	9	Dec. 10-26/09
Home	6	Oct. 12-Nov. 9/01, Mar. 9-27/11
Away	13	Nov. 21/09-Jan. 5/10

Longest Winless Streak

Overall	9	Dec. 4-23/03 (8 losses, 1 tie), Dec. 10-26/09 (7 losses, 2 ties)
Home	8	Oct. 4-Nov. 9/01 (6 losses, 2 ties), Dec. 4-31/03 (7 losses, 1 tie)
Away	14	Oct. 9-Dec. 23/03 (13 losses, 1 tie)

Most Shutouts, Season	11	2007-08 (82), 2008-09 (82)
Most PIM, Season	1,505	2002-03 (82)
Most Goals, Game	8	Mar. 7/09 (CBJ 8 at Det. 2)

Individual

Most Seasons	10	Rostislav Klesla
Most Games	592	Rick Nash
Most Goals, Career	259	Rick Nash
Most Assists, Career	229	David Vyborny
Most Points, Career	488	Rick Nash (259G, 229A)
Most PIM, Career	1,025	Jody Shelley
Most Shutouts, Career	18	Steve Mason

Longest Consecutive

Games Streak	243	Jason Chimera (Oct. 9/05-Apr. 5/08)
Most Goals, Season	41	Rick Nash (2003-04)

Most Assists, Season	52	Ray Whitney (2002-03)
Most Points, Season	79	Rick Nash (2008-09; 40G, 39A)
Most PIM, Season	249	Jody Shelley (2002-03)
Most Points, Defenseman, Season	45	Jaroslav Spacek (2002-03; 9G, 36A)
Most Points, Center, Season	68	Andrew Cassels (2002-03; 20G, 48A)
Most Points, Right Wing, Season	65	David Vyborny (2005-06; 22G, 43A)
Most Points, Left Wing, Season	79	Rick Nash (2008-09; 40G, 39A)
Most Points, Rookie, Season	39	Rick Nash (2002-03; 17G, 22A)
Most Shutouts, Season	10	Steve Mason (2008-09)
Most Goals, Game	4	Geoff Sanderson (Mar. 29/03)
Most Assists, Game	5	Espen Knutsen (Mar. 24/01)
Most Points, Game	5	Espen Knutsen (Mar. 24/01; 5A) Geoff Sanderson (Mar. 29/03; 4G, 1A) Andrew Cassels (Mar. 29/03; 1G, 4A) David Vyborny (Feb. 28/04; 1G, 4A)

Captains' History

Lyle Odelein, 2000-01, 2001-02; Ray Whitney, 2002-03; Luke Richardson, 2003-04; Luke Richardson and Adam Foote, 2005-06; Adam Foote, 2006-07; Adam Foote and Rick Nash, 2007-08; Rick Nash, 2008-09 to date.

All-time Record vs. Other Clubs

Regular Season

	At Home								On Road								Total							
	GP	W	L	T	OL	GF	GA	PTS	GP	W	L	T	OL	GF	GA	PTS	GP	W	L	T	OL	GF	GA	PTS
Anaheim	20	10	9	0	1	52	49	21	20	9	8	1	2	53	61	21	40	19	17	1	3	105	110	42
Atlanta	6	4	2	0	0	16	12	8	7	4	3	0	0	17	13	8	13	8	5	0	0	33	25	16
Boston	6	3	2	0	1	12	21	7	4	2	2	0	0	10	12	4	10	5	4	0	1	22	33	11
Buffalo	5	3	1	1	0	16	11	7	7	4	3	0	0	18	19	8	12	7	4	1	0	34	30	15
Calgary	20	14	4	0	2	59	42	30	20	6	12	0	2	44	63	14	40	20	16	0	4	103	105	44
Carolina	5	3	2	0	0	13	12	6	7	3	4	0	0	20	18	6	12	6	6	0	0	33	30	12
Chicago	32	15	12	1	4	109	111	35	31	13	15	1	2	76	94	29	63	28	27	2	6	185	205	64
Colorado	20	6	13	1	0	41	68	13	20	3	15	0	2	37	76	8	40	9	28	1	2	78	144	21
Dallas	20	7	10	0	3	45	59	17	20	6	12	0	2	42	61	14	40	13	22	0	5	87	120	31
Detroit	32	10	15	1	6	61	99	27	31	7	21	0	3	76	111	17	63	17	36	1	9	137	210	44
Edmonton	20	8	8	3	1	53	66	20	20	5	13	0	2	47	71	12	40	13	21	3	3	100	137	32
Florida	5	3	2	0	0	12	11	6	6	4	2	0	0	18	16	8	11	7	4	0	0	30	27	14
Los Angeles	20	11	7	0	2	54	64	24	20	7	12	1	0	43	60	15	40	18	19	1	2	97	124	39
Minnesota	19	13	5	1	0	54	39	27	20	6	11	0	3	43	59	15	39	19	16	1	3	97	98	42
Montreal	4	2	2	0	0	10	9	4	6	3	2	1	0	12	11	7	10	5	4	1	0	22	20	11
Nashville	31	14	13	0	4	74	85	32	32	4	22	1	5	64	111	14	63	18	35	1	9	138	196	46
New Jersey	7	3	4	0	0	17	20	6	4	0	3	1	0	7	12	1	11	3	7	1	0	24	32	7
NY Islanders	7	5	0	1	1	23	15	12	6	3	1	0	2	19	20	8	13	8	1	1	3	42	35	20
NY Rangers	7	5	2	0	0	24	14	10	4	1	2	1	0	12	16	3	11	6	4	1	0	36	30	13
Ottawa	5	3	1	1	0	18	14	7	5	1	3	1	0	10	16	3	10	4	4	2	0	28	30	10
Philadelphia	6	2	2	2	0	12	11	6	4	0	3	1	0	8	15	1	10	2	5	3	0	20	26	7
Phoenix	20	8	10	1	1	50	52	18	20	5	11	3	1	42	60	14	40	13	21	4	2	92	112	32
Pittsburgh	7	3	1	0	3	25	24	9	6	2	4	0	0	17	22	4	13	5	5	0	3	42	46	13
St. Louis	31	15	10	2	4	88	86	36	32	8	17	1	6	76	114	23	63	23	27	3	10	164	200	59
San Jose	20	10	8	0	2	80	42	22	20	3	15	0	2	35	73	8	40	13	23	0	4	85	115	30
Tampa Bay	5	3	1	0	1	13	9	7	6	1	3	0	2	8	14	4	11	4	4	1	2	21	23	11
Toronto	3	1	2	0	0	9	13	2	6	1	3	0	2	12	16	4	9	3	5	1	0	21	31	7
Vancouver	20	7	9	2	2	51	71	18	20	6	11	1	0	54	76	15	40	13	20	2	5	105	147	33
Washington	7	2	3	0	2	19	22	6	6	2	1	0	1	18	19	6	13	4	3	1	3	37	41	12
Totals	**410**	**193**	**160**	**18**	**39**	**1080**	**1151**	**443**	**410**	**120**	**235**	**15**	**40**	**938**	**1331**	**295**	**820**	**313**	**395**	**33**	**79**	**2018**	**2482**	**738**

Playoffs

	Series	W	L	GP	W	L	T	GF	GA	Last Mtg.	Rnd.	Result
Detroit	1	0	1	4	0	4	0	7	18	2009	CQF	L 0-4
Totals	**1**	**0**	**1**	**4**	**0**	**4**	**0**	**7**	**18**			

Playoff Results 2011-2007

Year	Round	Opponent	Result	GF	GA
2009	CQF	Detroit	L 0-4	7	18

Abbreviations: Round: CQF – conference quarter-final.

2010-11 Results

Oct.	8	San Jose	2-3		8	at Los Angeles	4-6
	9	at San Jose	3-2*		11	Phoenix	3-4
	15	Chicago	2-5		14	Detroit	3-2†
	16	at Minnesota	3-2		15	at Detroit	5-6*
	20	Anaheim	3-1		18	at Tampa Bay	2-3†
	22	Calgary	2-6		19	at Florida	3-2*
	23	at Chicago	3-2		22	at St. Louis	5-2
	25	Philadelphia	2-1		25	Anaheim	2-3
	28	Edmonton	3-2†	Feb.	1	Chicago	4-7
	30	at Colorado	1-5		4	at Detroit	3-0
Nov.	2	Montreal	3-0		5	Edmonton	4-3
	4	at Atlanta	3-0		8	at Pittsburgh	4-1
	6	Minnesota	2-3		9	San Jose	2-3
	10	St. Louis	8-1		11	Colorado	3-1
	12	Colorado	1-5		13	at Dallas	2-1
	17	at Los Angeles	5-3		16	Los Angeles	3-4†
	19	at Anaheim	4-3		18	at Chicago	4-3
	20	at San Jose	3-0		22	Nashville	4-0
	22	Nashville	2-0		25	Phoenix	5-3
	24	at NY Islanders	4-3*		27	at Nashville	2-3
	26	Detroit	1-2	Mar.	1	at Vancouver	1-2†
	28	at Detroit	2-4		3	at Edmonton	2-4
Dec.	1	Nashville	3-4†		4	at Calgary	3-4
	3	at Buffalo	0-5		7	at St. Louis	4-5†
	4	Pittsburgh	2-7		9	St. Louis	3-4*
	6	Dallas	3-2†		11	Los Angeles	2-4
	9	at St. Louis	1-4		12	at Carolina	3-2
	11	NY Rangers	3-1		15	Boston	2-3†
	13	at Calgary	2-3*		17	Detroit	3-4
	15	at Vancouver	2-3*		19	at Minnesota	5-4*
	16	at Edmonton	3-6		20	New Jersey	0-3
	18	Dallas	1-2		22	at Colorado	4-5†
	21	Calgary	3-1		24	at Phoenix	0-3
	23	Vancouver	3-7		27	Vancouver	1-4
	26	at Chicago	1-4		29	Florida	3-2†
	27	Minnesota	4-3†		31	at Washington	3-4*
	30	at Toronto	3-2	Apr.	1	Chicago	3-4†
	31	Ottawa	4-3*		2	St. Louis	1-6
Jan.	2	at Nashville	1-4		5	at Dallas	0-3
	4	at Phoenix	2-4		8	at Nashville	1-4
	7	at Anaheim	0-6		9	Buffalo	4-5

* – Overtime   † – Shootout

Entry Draft Selections 2011-2000

Name in bold denotes played in NHL.

2011
Pick
37 Boone Jenner
66 T.J. Tynan
98 Mike Reilly
128 Seth Ambroz
158 Lukas Sedlak
188 Anton Forsberg

2010
Pick
4 Ryan Johansen
34 Dalton Smith
55 Petr Straka
94 Brandon Archibald
102 Mathieu Corbeil
124 Austin Madaisky
154 Dalton Prout
184 Martin Ouellette

2009
Pick
21 **John Moore**
56 Kevin Lynch
94 David Savard
137 Thomas Larkin
167 Anton Blomqvist
197 Kyle Neuber

2008
Pick
6 **Nikita Filatov**
37 Cody Goloubef
107 Steven Delisle
118 Drew Olson
127 **Matt Calvert**
135 **Tomas Kubalik**
137 Brent Regner
157 Cam Atkinson
187 Sean Collins

2007
Pick
7 **Jakub Voracek**
37 Stefan Legein
53 Will Weber
68 Jake Hansen
94 **Maksim Mayorov**
158 Allen York
211 Trent Vogelhuber

2006
Pick
6 **Derick Brassard**
69 **Steve Mason**
85 **Tom Sestito**
113 Ben Wright
129 Robert Nyholm
136 Nick Sucharski
142 Maxime Frechette
159 Jesse Dudas
189 **Derek Dorsett**
194 Matt Marquardt

2005
Pick
6 **Gilbert Brule**
55 **Adam McQuaid**
67 **Kris Russell**
101 **Jared Boll**
131 **Tomas Popperle**
177 Derek Reinhart
189 Kirill Starkov
201 Trevor Hendrikx

2004
Pick
8 **Alexandre Picard**
46 **Adam Pineault**
59 Kyle Wharton
93 **Dan LaCosta**
96 Andrey Plekhanov
133 Petr Pohl
167 Rob Page
190 Lennart Petrell
198 Justin Vienneau
231 Brian McGuirk
233 Matt Greer
271 **Grant Clitsome**

2003
Pick
4 **Nikolai Zherdev**
46 **Dan Fritsche**
71 Dmitry Kosmachev
103 Kevin Jarman
104 **Philippe Dupuis**
138 Arsi Piispanen
168 **Marc Methot**
200 Alexander Guskov
233 Mathieu Gravel
283 Trevor Hendrikx

2002
Pick
1 **Rick Nash**
41 Joakim Lindstrom
65 Ole-Kristian Tollefsen
96 Jeff Genovy
98 Ivan Tkachenko
119 Jekabs Redlihs
133 **Lasse Pirjeta**
168 Tim Konsorada
184 **Jaroslav Balastik**
199 **Greg Mauldin**
225 **Steven Goertzen**
231 Jaroslav Kracik
263 Sergei Mozyakin

2001
Pick
8 **Pascal Leclaire**
38 **Tim Jackman**
53 Kiel McLeod
85 **Aaron Johnson**
87 Per Mars
141 **Cole Jarrett**
173 Justin Aikins
187 Artem Vostrikov
204 Raffaele Sannitz
236 Ryan Bowness
242 **Andrew Murray**

2000
Pick
4 **Rostislav Klesla**
69 Ben Knopp
133 **Petteri Nummelin**
138 Scott Heffernan
150 Tyler Kolarik
169 Shane Bendera
200 Janne Jokila
231 Peter Zingoni
278 Martin Paroulek
286 **Andrej Nedorost**
292 Louis Mandeville

General Managers' History

Doug MacLean, 2000-01 to 2006-07; Scott Howson, 2007-08 to date.

Scott Howson
Executive V.P., Hockey Operations and General Manager
Born: Toronto, Ont., April 9, 1960.

The Columbus Blue Jackets announced the signing of Scott Howson as the second general manager in franchise history on June 15, 2007. In 2008-09 he led the Blue Jackets to the playoffs for the first time in franchise history. Howson joined the Blue Jackets after spending seven years with the Edmonton Oilers. He joined the Oilers in June 2000 as assistant to the general manager and was named assistant general manager a year later. In that role, he was responsible for all aspects of the club's hockey administration, including player contracts, personnel decisions, the collective bargaining agreement, its American Hockey League affiliates and the salary cap.

During his six seasons with the Oilers, the club posted five-straight winning campaigns from 2000 to 2006, averaged 37 wins and 89 points per season, topped 90 points four times and advanced to the 2006 Stanley Cup Final, where they were defeated in seven games by the Carolina Hurricanes.

Prior to his arrival in Edmonton, Howson spent six years with the club's AHL affiliates. As general manager of the Cape Breton Oilers from 1994 to 1996, he oversaw the franchise's move to Hamilton in 1996 and was the Bulldogs' general manager from 1996 to 2000. During that time, he led Hamilton to a pair of berths in the Calder Cup Finals (1997, 2003) and a conference semifinals appearance in 2002.

Howson played three seasons in the Ontario Hockey League as a forward with the Kingston Canadiens from 1978 to 1981, serving as team captain and earning OHL All-Star honors. Following his junior career, he signed a free agent contract with the New York Islanders and spent the next five years playing at various levels throughout the organization.

During his rookie season in 1981-82, he was named the International Hockey League's rookie of the year after registering 55 goals and 65 assists for 120 points in 71 games with the Toledo Goaldiggers. He was the league's second-leading scorer that year and helped Toledo capture the league championship. Howson also won a Central Hockey League title with the Indianapolis Checkers in 1982-83. He made his NHL debut with the Islanders during the 1984-85 season and tallied 4 goals and one assist in eight games. He added a goal and two assists in 10 games the following season before retiring as a player at the end of the 1985-86 season. Howson received his bachelor's degree in 1987 from York University in Toronto and is a 1990 graduate of the university's Osgoode Hall Law School.

Club Directory

Nationwide Arena

Columbus Blue Jackets
Nationwide Arena
200 W. Nationwide Blvd.
Columbus, Ohio 43215
Phone 614/246-4625
FAX 614/246-4007
www.BlueJackets.com
Capacity: 18,144

Ownership
Majority Owner/Governor . . . . John P. McConnell

Executive Staff
President/Alternate Governor . . . . Mike Priest
Executive Vice President, Business Operations . . . . . Larry Hoepfner
Sr. Vice President/General Counsel . . . . Greg Kirstein
Sr. Vice President, Corporate Development . . . . Cameron Scholvin
Senior Vice President/Chief Marketing Officer . . . . . John Browne
Chief Financial Officer. . . . . T.J. LaMendola
Vice President, Digital Marketing & Media. . . . . Marc Gregory
Vice President, Marketing . . . . J.D. Kershaw
Vice President, Public Relations . . . . Todd Sharrock
Vice President, Ticket Sales and Service . . . . Bob Sivik

Hockey Operations
Executive VP Hockey Operations/General Mgr . . . . . Scott Howson
Assistant General Manager . . . . Chris MacFarland
Dir. of Amateur Scouting & Development Coach . . . Tyler Wright
Amateur Scouting Director / Asst. Director . . . . Paul Castron / John Williams
Amateur Scouts . . . . . Brian Bates, Andrew Dickson, Sam McMaster, Andrew Shaw, Greg Drechsel
Pro Scout / Pro European Scout. . . . . Peter Dineen / Kjell Larsson
Regional Scouts . . . . Artem Telepin, Milan Tichy
Director of Video Scouting . . . . Bryan Stewart
Assistant Video Scout . . . . Scott Harris
Manager of Team Services . . . . Julie Gamble
Manager of Hockey Administration . . . . Josh Flynn
Head Athletic Trainer . . . . Mike Vogt
Assistant Athletic Trainers . . . . Chris Strickland, Mark Teeples
Equipment Manager . . . . Tim LeRoy
Assistant Equipment Manager. . . . . Jamie Healy
Equipment Assistant . . . . Jason Stypinski
Executive Administrative Assistant. . . . . Christina Gest

Coaching Staff
Head Coach . . . . Scott Arniel
Assistant Coaches. . . . . Brad Berry, Dan Hinote, Todd Richards
Goaltending Coach . . . . Ian Clark
Strength & Conditioning Coach . . . . Kevin Collins
Video Assistant Coach . . . . Dan Singleton

Business Operations
Director of Community Relations & Publicity . . . . . . Karen Davis
Director of Game Operations/Event Presentation . . . Derek Dawley
Manager of Communications . . . . Ryan Holtmann
Manager of Multimedia . . . . Ryan Mulcrone
Manager of Marketing . . . . Jim Riley
Partnership Activation Manager . . . . Becky Magaw
Manager of Corporate Development Services . . . . . Craig Smith
Partnership Account Specialists . . . . Josh Hafer, Matt Keller, Amber Krill
Corporate Development Account Executives . . . . . . Jerry Angel, Joe Fisher, Ryan Shirk
Corporate Development Sales Assistant . . . . Julia Wilson
Premium Seating Account Executives . . . . Evan Bollie, Mackenzie Crawford
Premium Seating Relationship Manager . . . . Rachel Mayfield
Manager of Event Presentation . . . . Lynn Truitt
Senior Production Manager. . . . . Jeff Coltoniak
Production Manager . . . . David Traube
Broadcast Engineer . . . . Rick Shepherd
Manager of Fan Development. . . . . Joel Siegman
Manager of Community Development . . . . Kellie Yoskovich
Manger of Mascot Services . . . . Jason Zumpano
Database Marketing Manger. . . . . Jeff Eldersveld
Fan Development/Marketing Coordinator . . . . Mason Fisher
Graphic Designers . . . . Jason Duigan, Nicole Pope

Human Resources and Legal
HumanResources Director / Assistant . . . . Cheryl Sparks / Elizabeth McDougall
Payroll Manager / Paralegal . . . . Christine Parthemore
Paralegal / Legal Admin. Assistant. . . . . Ken Erney / Mendy Cartmill

Finance
Controller / Assistant Controller . . . . Wendy Rohaly / Jason LaPlace
Staff Accountant / A/P Coordinator . . . . Nora Ludwig / Beth Carpenter
Office Coordinator/Receptionist . . . . Beth Carlisle

Information Technology
IT Director / Manager . . . . Jim Connolly / John Gruber
Systems Analyst . . . . Matthew DeStephen

Ticket Sales and Operations
Director of Ticket Operations/Events . . . . Mark Morris
Director of New Business Development . . . . Cory Rowe
Director of Group Sales. . . . . P.J. Keene
Director of Service and Retention . . . . Stephanie Henderson
Inside Sales Supervisor . . . . Drew Ribarchak
Inside Sales Representatives . . . . Ian Bernadas, Heather Crago, Erica Ganyard, Ellen Keough, Corey Mehl, Keith Raynor, Caitlin Reagan, Brooke Schrider, Alexander Siclari, Sean Siebenkittel, Michael Thompson, Michael Vitale

Broadcasting
Director of Broadcasting . . . . Russ Mollohan
FOX Sports Ohio Play-By-Play Announcer / Color . . . Jeff Rimer / Bill Davidge
Radio Play-By-Play Announcer / Color . . . . George Matthews / Bob McElligott

CBJ Arena Management
Operations, Director / Assistant Director . . . . Scott Lofton / Brad Cleveland
Event Services Director / Manager / Coord. . . . . . . Blake Schilling / Amanda Horning / Brian Tarajack
Guest Services Coordinator . . . . Brooke Bockelman
Ticket Office Manager. Cait Schumann
Maintenance Supervisor . . . . Mark Greiner
Conversion Manager . . . . Bill Hunt
Ice Technician . . . . Ian Huffman
Receptionist . . . . Carol Hall

Dallas Stars

Key Off-Season Signings/Acquisitions

2011

June 17 • Named **Glen Gulutzan** head coach.
28 • Named **Paul Jerrard** assistant coach.
28 • Re-signed D **Brad Lukowich**.
July 1 • Signed RW **Michael Ryder**, RW **Radek Dvorak**, C **Vernon Fiddler**, D **Adam Pardy**, D **Sheldon Souray** and C **Jake Dowell**.
12 • Signed RW **Eric Godard**.

2010-11 Results: 42w-29L-4oTL-7sOL 95pTS.
Fifth, Pacific Division

Stars captain Brenden Morrow discusses strategy with Jamie Benn. Morrow led Dallas with a career-high 33 goals in 2010-11 while Benn matched the 22 goals he scored as a rookie the year before despite playing just 69 games.

2011-12 Schedule

Oct.	Fri.	7	Chicago
	Sat.	8	at Chicago
	Mon.	10	Phoenix*
	Thu.	13	St. Louis
	Sat.	15	Columbus
	Tue.	18	at Columbus
	Fri.	21	at Anaheim
	Sat.	22	at Los Angeles
	Tue.	25	at Phoenix
	Thu.	27	Los Angeles
	Sat.	29	New Jersey
Nov.	Fri.	4	Colorado
	Sun.	6	at Carolina*
	Tue.	8	at Washington
	Fri.	11	at Pittsburgh
	Sat.	12	at Detroit
	Tue.	15	Florida
	Fri.	18	at Colorado
	Sat.	19	San Jose
	Mon.	21	Edmonton
	Wed.	23	Los Angeles
	Fri.	25	Toronto
	Sat.	26	at Phoenix
	Mon.	28	at Colorado
Dec.	Thu.	1	Ottawa
	Sat.	3	NY Islanders
	Thu.	8	at San Jose
	Sat.	10	at Los Angeles
	Tue.	13	at NY Rangers
	Thu.	15	at NY Islanders
	Fri.	16	at New Jersey
	Mon.	19	Anaheim
	Wed.	21	Philadelphia
	Fri.	23	Nashville
	Mon.	26	at St. Louis
	Thu.	29	Columbus
	Sat.	31	Boston
Jan.	Tue.	3	Detroit
	Thu.	5	at Nashville
	Sat.	7	Edmonton*
	Tue.	10	at Anaheim

	Thu.	12	at Los Angeles
	Sat.	14	Colorado*
	Mon.	16	at St. Louis
	Tue.	17	Detroit
	Fri.	20	Tampa Bay
	Sat.	21	at Minnesota
	Tue.	24	Anaheim
Feb.	Wed.	1	at Anaheim
	Thu.	2	at San Jose
	Sat.	4	Minnesota
	Tue.	7	Phoenix
	Thu.	9	at Columbus
	Fri.	10	at Buffalo
	Sun.	12	Los Angeles*
	Tue.	14	at Detroit
	Thu.	16	Calgary
	Sat.	18	at Phoenix
	Sun.	19	Nashville
	Tue.	21	at Montreal
	Thu.	23	at Chicago
	Fri.	24	Minnesota
	Sun.	26	Vancouver*
	Wed.	29	Pittsburgh
Mar.	Fri.	2	at Edmonton
	Sun.	4	at Calgary*
	Tue.	6	at Vancouver
	Thu.	8	San Jose
	Sat.	10	Anaheim
	Tue.	13	at Minnesota
	Wed.	14	at Winnipeg
	Fri.	16	Chicago
	Tue.	20	Phoenix
	Thu.	22	Vancouver
	Sat.	24	Calgary*
	Mon.	26	at Calgary
	Wed.	28	at Edmonton
	Fri.	30	at Vancouver
	Sat.	31	at San Jose
Apr.	Tue.	3	San Jose
	Thu.	5	at Nashville
	Sat.	7	St. Louis

* Denotes afternoon game.

PACIFIC DIVISION
45th NHL Season

Franchise date: June 5, 1967

Transferred from Minnesota to Dallas, June 9, 1993.

Year-by-Year Record

| | | Home | | | | Road | | | | Overall | | | | | | |
Season	GP	W	L	T	OL	W	L	T	OL	W	L	T	OL	GF	GA	Pts.	Finished	Playoff Result
2010-11	82	22	11	....	8	20	18	....	3	42	29	....	11	227	233	95	5th, Pacific Div.	Out of Playoffs
2009-10	82	23	11	....	7	14	20	....	7	37	31	....	14	237	254	88	5th, Pacific Div.	Out of Playoffs
2008-09	82	20	16	....	5	16	19	....	6	36	35	....	11	230	257	83	3rd, Pacific Div.	Out of Playoffs
2007-08	82	23	16	....	2	22	14	....	5	45	30	....	7	242	207	97	3rd, Pacific Div.	Lost Conf. Championship
2006-07	82	28	11	....	2	22	14	....	5	50	25	....	7	226	197	107	3rd, Pacific Div.	Lost Conf. Quarter-Final
2005-06	82	28	11	....	2	25	12	....	4	53	23	....	6	265	218	112	1st, Pacific Div.	Lost Conf. Quarter-Final
2004-05	....	....				....				....				....	....	....		
2003 04	82	26	7	8	0	15	19	5	2	41	26	13	2	194	175	82	2nd, Pacific Div.	Lost Conf. Quarter-Final
2002-03	82	28	5	6	2	18	12	9	2	46	17	15	4	245	169	111	1st, Pacific Div.	Lost Conf. Semi-Final
2001-02	82	18	13	6	4	18	15	7	1	36	28	13	5	215	213	90	4th, Pacific Div.	Out of Playoffs
2000-01	82	26	10	5	0	22	14	3	2	48	24	8	2	241	187	106	1st, Pacific Div.	Lost Conf. Semi-Final
1999-2000	82	21	11	5	4	22	12	5	2	43	23	10	6	211	184	102	1st, Pacific Div.	Lost Final
1998-99	**82**	**29**	**8**	**4**		**22**	**11**	**8**		**51**	**19**	**12**		**236**	**168**	**114**	**1st, Pacific Div.**	**Won Stanley Cup**
1997-98	82	26	8	7		23	14	4		49	22	11		242	167	109	1st, Central Div.	Lost Conf. Championship
1996-97	82	25	13	3		23	13	5		48	26	8		252	198	104	1st, Central Div.	Lost Conf. Quarter-Final
1995-96	82	14	18	9		12	24	5		26	42	14		227	280	66	6th, Central Div.	Out of Playoffs
1994-95	48	9	10	5		8	13	3		17	23	8		136	135	42	5th, Central Div.	Lost Conf. Quarter-Final
1993-94	84	23	12	7		19	17	6		42	29	13		286	265	97	3rd, Central Div.	Lost Conf. Semi-Final
1992-93*	84	18	17	7		18	21	3		36	38	10		272	293	82	5th, Norris Div.	Out of Playoffs
1991-92*	80	20	16	4		12	26	2		32	42	6		246	278	70	4th, Norris Div.	Lost Div. Semi-Final
1990-91*	80	19	15	6		8	24	8		27	39	14		256	266	68	4th, Norris Div.	Lost Final
1989-90*	80	26	12	2		10	28	2		36	40	4		284	291	76	4th, Norris Div.	Lost Div. Semi-Final
1988-89*	80	17	15	8		10	22	8		27	37	16		258	278	70	3rd, Norris Div.	Lost Div. Semi-Final
1987-88*	80	10	24	6		9	24	7		19	48	13		242	349	51	5th, Norris Div.	Out of Playoffs
1986-87*	80	17	20	3		13	20	7		30	40	10		296	314	70	5th, Norris Div.	Out of Playoffs
1985-86*	80	21	15	4		17	18	5		38	33	9		327	305	85	2nd, Norris Div.	Lost Div. Semi-Final
1984-85*	80	14	19	7		11	24	5		25	43	12		268	321	62	4th, Norris Div.	Lost Div. Final
1983-84*	80	22	14	4		17	17	6		39	31	10		345	344	88	1st, Norris Div.	Lost Conf. Championship
1982-83*	80	23	6	11		17	18	5		40	24	16		321	290	96	2nd, Norris Div.	Lost Div. Final
1981-82*	80	21	7	12		16	16	8		37	23	20		346	288	94	1st, Norris Div.	Lost Div. Semi-Final
1980-81*	80	23	10	7		12	18	10		35	28	17		291	263	87	3rd, Adams Div.	Lost Final
1979-80*	80	25	8	7		11	20	9		36	28	16		311	253	88	3rd, Adams Div.	Lost Semi-Final
1978-79*	80	19	15	6		9	25	6		28	40	12		257	289	68	4th, Adams Div.	Out Of Playoffs
1977-78*	80	12	24	4		6	29	5		18	53	9		218	325	45	5th, Smythe Div.	Out of Playoffs
1976-77*	80	17	14	9		6	25	9		23	39	18		240	310	64	2nd, Smythe Div.	Lost Prelim. Round
1975-76*	80	15	22	3		5	31	4		20	53	7		195	303	47	4th, Smythe Div.	Out of Playoffs
1974-75*	80	17	20	3		6	30	4		23	50	7		221	341	53	4th, Smythe Div.	Out of Playoffs
1973-74*	78	18	15	6		5	23	11		23	38	17		235	275	63	7th, West Div.	Out of Playoffs
1972-73*	78	26	8	5		11	22	6		37	30	11		254	230	85	3rd, West Div.	Lost Quarter-Final
1971-72*	78	22	11	6		15	18	6		37	29	12		212	191	86	2nd, West Div.	Lost Quarter-Final
1970-71*	78	16	15	8		12	19	8		28	34	16		191	223	72	4th, West Div.	Lost Semi-Final
1969-70*	76	11	16	11		8	19	11		19	35	22		224	257	60	3rd, West Div.	Lost Quarter-Final
1968-69*	76	11	21	6		7	22	9		18	43	15		189	270	51	6th, West Div.	Out of Playoffs
1967-68*	74	17	12	8		10	20	7		27	32	15		191	226	69	4th, West Div.	Lost Semi-Final

* Minnesota North Stars

2011-12 Player Personnel

FORWARDS	HT	WT	S	Place of Birth	*Age	2010-11 Club
BARCH, Krys	6-1	209	L	Hamilton, Ont.	31	Dallas
BENN, Jamie	6-2	208	L	Victoria, B.C.	22	Dallas
BURISH, Adam	6-0	190	R	Madison, WI	28	Dallas
DOWELL, Jake	6-0	199	L	Eau Claire, WI	26	Chicago
DVORAK, Radek	6-2	200	R	Tabor, Czech.	34	Florida-Atlanta
ERIKSSON, Loui	6-3	193	L	Goteborg, Sweden	26	Dallas
FIDDLER, Vernon	5-11	201	L	Edmonton, Alta.	31	Phoenix
GODARD, Eric	6-4	214	R	Vernon, B.C.	31	Pittsburgh
MORROW, Brenden	6-0	209	L	Carlyle, Sask.	32	Dallas
OTT, Steve	6-0	192	L	Summerside, P.E.I.	29	Dallas
PETERSEN, Toby	5-10	197	L	Minneapolis, MN	32	Dallas-Texas
RIBEIRO, Mike	6-0	179	L	Montreal, Que.	31	Dallas
RYDER, Michael	6-0	186	R	St. John's, Nfld.	31	Boston
VINCOUR, Tomas	6-2	199	R	Brno, Czechoslovakia	20	Dallas-Texas
WANDELL, Tom	6-1	197	L	Sodertalje, Sweden	24	Dallas

DEFENSEMEN						
DALEY, Trevor	5-11	205	L	Toronto, Ont.	27	Dallas
FISTRIC, Mark	6-3	231	L	Edmonton, Alta.	25	Dallas-Texas
GOLIGOSKI, Alex	5-11	180	L	Grand Rapids, MN	26	Pittsburgh-Dallas
GROSSMAN, Nicklas	6-3	227	L	Stockholm, Sweden	26	Dallas
LARSEN, Philip	6-1	183	R	Esbjerg, Denmark	21	Dallas-Texas
PARDY, Adam	6-2	220	L	Bonavista, Nfld.	27	Calgary
ROBIDAS, Stephane	5-11	190	R	Sherbrooke, Que.	34	Dallas
SOURAY, Sheldon	6-4	233	L	Elk Point, Alta.	35	Hershey

GOALTENDERS	HT	WT	C	Place of Birth	*Age	2010-11 Club
LEHTONEN, Kari	6-4	215	L	Helsinki, Finland	27	Dallas
RAYCROFT, Andrew	6-1	178	L	Belleville, Ont.	31	Dallas

* – Age at start of 2011-12 season

2010-11 Scoring
* – rookie

Regular Season

Pos	#	Player	Team	GP	G	A	Pts	TOI	+/-	PIM	PP	SH	GW	S	%
C	91	Brad Richards	DAL	72	28	49	77	21:43	1	24	7	0	3	272	10.3
L	21	Loui Eriksson	DAL	79	27	46	73	20:34	10	8	10	1	6	179	15.1
C	63	Mike Ribeiro	DAL	82	19	52	71	19:57	-4	28	7	0	4	161	11.8
L	10	Brenden Morrow	DAL	82	33	23	56	19:14	-3	76	9	1	5	209	15.8
L	14	Jamie Benn	DAL	69	22	34	56	18:00	-5	52	6	4	3	177	12.4
D	33	Alex Goligoski	PIT	60	9	22	31	20:45	20	28	4	0	4	101	8.9
			DAL	23	5	10	15	26:04	0	12	3	0	0	61	8.2
			Total	83	14	32	46	22:14	20	40	7	0	4	162	8.6
C	29	Steve Ott	DAL	12	20	82	32	17:09	7	183	3	2	4	120	10
R	15	Jamie Langenbrunner	N.J.	31	10	14	18:33	-15	16	0	0	2	76	5.3
			DAL	39	5	13	18	16:33	-3	29	1	0	1	77	6.5
			Total	70	9	23	32	17:26	-18	45	1	0	3	153	5.9
D	3	Stephane Robidas	DAL	81	5	25	30	24:31	-7	67	1	0	1	106	4.7
D	6	Trevor Daley	DAL	82	8	19	27	22:29	7	34	2	0	1	131	6.1
R	16	Adam Burish	DAL	63	8	6	14	14:20	2	91	0	0	0	89	9.0
D	44	Jeff Woywitka	DAL	63	2	9	11	17:56	5	24	1	0	0	72	2.8
R	24	Brandon Segal	DAL	46	5	5	10	8:17	0	41	0	0	1	40	12.5
D	2	Nicklas Grossman	DAL	59	1	9	10	18:11	7	35	0	0	0	38	2.6
C	23	Tom Wandell	DAL	75	7	2	9	11:45	-5	14	0	0	1	94	7.4
D	37	Karlis Skrastins	DAL	74	3	5	8	17:57	-1	38	0	0	1	30	10.0
C	17	Toby Petersen	DAL	60	2	4	6	10:02	-7	8	0	2	0	58	3.4
C	27	Jason Williams	DAL	27	2	3	5	8:06	-2	6	0	0	1	18	11.1
D	28	Mark Fistric	DAL	57	2	3	5	14:23	-10	44	0	0	1	32	6.3
C	20	Brian Sutherby	DAL	51	2	2	4	7:24	-10	58	0	0	0	36	5.6
R	13	Krys Barch	DAL	44	2	1	3	5:13	-7	80	0	0	0	16	12.5
C	81	* Tomas Vincour	DAL	24	1	1	2	9:25	-5	4	0	0	0	26	3.8
D	36	* Philip Larsen	DAL	6	0	2	2	13:26	1	0	0	0	0	11	0.0
C	11	* Aaron Gagnon	DAL	19	0	2	2	8:03	-3	0	0	0	0	9	0.0
R	12	* Raymond Sawada	DAL	1	0	0	0	5:50	-1	0	0	0	0	1	0.0
C	22	* Colton Sceviour	DAL	1	0	0	0	5:09	-1	0	0	0	0	0	0.0
L	48	* Francis Wathier	DAL	3	0	0	0	3:55	-2	0	0	0	0	0	0.0
C	39	Travis Morin	DAL	3	0	0	0	8:52	0	0	0	0	2	0	0.0
D	73	Brad Lukowich	DAL	0	0	0	0	10:15	1	0	0	0	0	3	0.0

Goaltending

No.	Goaltender	GPI	Mins	Avg	W	L	OT	EN	SO	GA	SA	S%	G	A	PIM
31	Richard Bachman	1	10	0.00	0	0	0	0	0	0	4	1.000	0	0	0
32	Kari Lehtonen	69	4119	2.55	34	24	11	9	3	175	2043	.914	0	6	6
30	Andrew Raycroft	19	847	2.83	8	5	0	2	2	40	446	.910	0	0	0
	Totals	**82**	**5002**	**2.71**	**42**	**29**	**11**	**11**	**5**	**226**	**2504**	**.910**			

Loui Eriksson established career highs with 46 assists and 73 points in 2010-11 and led the team in plus-minus with a +10 ranking

Glen Gulutzan
Head Coach

Born: The Pas, Man., August 12, 1971.

Glen Gulutzan (pronounced Gull-it-zen) was named as the 21st head coach in Stars franchise history on June 17, 2011. This is Gulutzan's first head coaching job in the National Hockey League, though he is no stranger to the professional ranks and the Stars organization. Gulutzan served as head coach of the Texas Stars, Dallas' primary development affiliate in the American Hockey League (AHL), for the previous two seasons. He led the club to the AHL playoffs in both campaigns and coached the Stars to the Calder Cup Finals in the franchise's inaugural season of 2009-10. Gulutzan posted a cumulative 87-56-17 record (.597 points percentage) during the regular season and a 16-14 (.533 winning percentage) record during the playoffs with Texas.

Born in The Pas, Manitoba but raised in Hudson Bay, Saskatchewan, Gulutzan served as general manager and head coach for the Las Vegas Wranglers of the ECHL from 2003 to 2009. He compiled a record of 254-124-55 for a .650 winning percentage, including 100+ points in three consecutive seasons (2005 to 2008), a first for any team in the 21-year history of the ECHL. Gulutzan took the Wranglers to the Kelly Cup Finals in 2008 and to the Conference Finals in 2009.

In 2005-06, Gulutzan was recognized as the ECHL Coach of the Year. He led Las Vegas to the playoffs in five of six seasons, including their expansion season (2003-04) when the team went 43-22-7 for 93 points. In addition, he was selected to coach in the ECHL All-Star Game three times. He led the Wranglers to the division crown in back-to-back seasons in 2006-07 and 2007-08. Gulutzan missed the playoffs in only one season as a minor league head coach and holds a perfect 5-0 record in game sevens in the playoffs.

Before beginning his coaching career, Gulutzan played professionally in Europe for two seasons and joined Fresno of the West Coast Hockey League in 1996-97, setting a team record with 80 assists and 110 points in 60 games. He spent a total of six seasons with Fresno, including the last four as player-assistant coach from 1999 to 2003. Gulutzan also played in the International Hockey League with Utah and Las Vegas, as well as stints in Finland and Sweden. In 1996, he earned a Bachelor's degree in Education from the University of Saskatchewan. Gulutzan graduated with a major in Kinesiology and minor in Mathematics.

Coaching Record

			Regular Season				Playoffs			
Season	Team	League	GC	W	L	O/T	GC	W	L	T
2003-04	Las Vegas	ECHL	72	43	22	7	5	2	3	....
2004-05	Las Vegas	ECHL	72	31	33	8	....	....	....	....
2005-06	Las Vegas	ECHL	72	53	13	6	13	6	7	....
2006-07	Las Vegas	ECHL	72	46	12	14	10	6	4	....
2007-08	Las Vegas	ECHL	72	47	13	12	21	14	7	....
2008-09	Las Vegas	ECHL	73	34	31	8	18	8	10	....
2009-10	Texas	AHL	80	46	27	7	24	14	10	....
2010-11	Texas	AHL	80	41	29	10	6	2	4	....

Coaching History

Wren Blair, 1967-68; Wren Blair and John Muckler, 1968-69; Wren Blair and Charlie Burns, 1969-70; Jack Gordon, 1970-71 to 1972-73; Jack Gordon and Parker MacDonald, 1973-74; Jack Gordon and Charlie Burns, 1974-75; Ted Harris, 1975-76, 1976-77; Ted Harris, André Beaulieu and Lou Nanne, 1977-78; Harry Howell and Glen Sonmor, 1978-79; Glen Sonmor, 1979-80 to 1981-82; Glen Sonmor and Murray Oliver, 1982-83; Bill Mahoney, 1983-84, 1984-85; Lorne Henning, 1985-86; Lorne Henning and Glen Sonmor, 1986-87; Herb Brooks, 1987-88; Pierre Page, 1988-89, 1989-90; Bob Gainey, 1990-91 to 1994-95; Bob Gainey and Ken Hitchcock, 1995-96; Ken Hitchcock, 1996-97 to 2000-01; Ken Hitchcock and Rick Wilson, 2001-02; Dave Tippett, 2002-03 to 2008-09; Marc Crawford, 2009-10, 2010-11; Glen Gulutzan, 2011-12.

Club Records

Team

(Figures in brackets for season records are games played; records for fewest points, wins, ties, losses, goals, goals against are for 70 or more games)

Record		
Most Points	**114**	1998-99 (82)
Most Wins	**53**	2005-06 (82)
Most Ties	**22**	1969-70 (76)
Most Losses	**53**	1975-76 (80), 1977-78 (80)
Most Goals	**346**	1981-82 (80)
Most Goals Against	**349**	1987-88 (80)
Fewest Points	**45**	1977-78 (80)
Fewest Wins	**18**	1968-69 (76), 1977-78 (80)
Fewest Ties	**4**	1989-90 (80)
Fewest Losses	**19**	1998-99 (82)
Fewest Goals	**189**	1968-69 (76)
Fewest Goals Against	**167**	1997-98 (82)
Longest Winning Streak		
Overall	**7**	Mar. 16-28/80, Mar. 16-Apr. 2/97, Nov. 22-Dec. 5/97, Jan. 29-Feb. 11/08
Home	**11**	Nov. 4-Dec. 27/72
Away	**8**	Dec. 13/10-Jan. 20/11
Longest Undefeated Streak		
Overall	**15**	Dec. 6/98-Jan. 6/99 (12 wins, 3 ties)
Home	**17**	Jan. 23-Mar. 20/04 (13 wins, 4 ties)
Away	**10**	Jan. 12-Mar. 4/99 (8 wins, 2 ties), Dec. 27/02-Feb. 25/03 (7 wins, 3 ties)
Longest Losing Streak		
Overall	**10**	Feb. 1-20/76
Home	**6**	Jan. 17-Feb. 4/70, Feb. 21-Mar. 8/09
Away	**10**	Dec. 12/09-Jan. 21/10
Longest Winless Streak		
Overall	**20**	Jan. 15-Feb. 28/70 (15 losses, 5 ties)
Home	**12**	Jan. 17-Feb. 25/70 (8 losses, 4 ties)
Away	**23**	Oct. 25/74-Jan. 28/75 (19 losses, 4 ties)
Most Shutouts, Season	**11**	2000-01 (82), 2002-03 (82)
Most PIM, Season	**2,313**	1987-88 (80)
Most Goals, Game	**15**	Nov. 11/81 (Wpg. 2 at Min. 15)

Individual

Record		
Most Seasons	**21**	Mike Modano
Most Games	**1,459**	Mike Modano
Most Goals, Career	**557**	Mike Modano
Most Assists, Career	**802**	Mike Modano
Most Points, Career	**1,359**	Mike Modano (557G, 802A)
Most PIM, Career	**1,883**	Shane Churla
Most Shutouts, Career	**40**	Marty Turco
Longest Consecutive Games Streak	**442**	Danny Grant (Dec. 4/68-Apr. 7/74)
Most Goals, Season	**55**	Dino Ciccarelli (1981-82), Brian Bellows (1989-90)
Most Assists, Season	**76**	Neal Broten (1985-86)
Most Points, Season	**114**	Bobby Smith (1981-82; 43G, 71A)
Most PIM, Season	**382**	Basil McRae (1987-88)
Most Points, Defenseman, Season	**77**	Craig Hartsburg (1981-82; 17G, 60A)
Most Points, Center, Season	**114**	Bobby Smith (1981-82; 43G, 71A)
Most Points, Right Wing, Season	**106**	Dino Ciccarelli (1981-82; 55G, 51A)
Most Points, Left Wing, Season	**99**	Brian Bellows (1989-90; 55G, 44A)
Most Points, Rookie, Season	**98**	Neal Broten (1981-82; 38G, 60A)
Most Shutouts, Season	**9**	Ed Belfour (1997-98), Marty Turco (2003-04)
Most Goals, Game	**5**	Tim Young (Jan. 15/79)
Most Assists, Game	**5**	Murray Oliver (Oct. 24/71), Larry Murphy (Oct. 17/89), Brad Richards (Feb. 28/08)
Most Points, Game	**7**	Bobby Smith (Nov. 11/81; 4G, 3A)

Records include Minnesota North Stars, 1967-68 through 1992-93.

Retired Numbers

7	Neal Broten	1980-1995, 1996-1997
8	Bill Goldsworthy*	1967-1976
19	Bill Masterton*	1967-1968

* Minnesota North Stars

All-time Record vs. Other Clubs

Regular Season

	At Home								On Road								Total							
	GP	W	L	T	OL	GF	GA	PTS	GP	W	L	T	OL	GF	GA	PTS	GP	W	L	T	OL	GF	GA	PTS
Anaheim	48	34	10	2	2	156	97	72	48	23	16	3	6	131	123	55	96	57	26	5	8	287	220	127
Atlanta	7	6	1	0	0	19	10	12	6	5	0	0	1	26	18	11	13	11	1	0	1	45	28	23
Boston	63	19	31	13	0	179	224	51	63	10	43	10	0	152	270	30	126	29	74	23	0	331	494	81
Buffalo	57	28	22	6	1	182	163	63	54	13	30	11	0	145	197	37	111	41	52	17	1	327	360	100
Calgary	74	36	22	11	5	260	225	88	74	21	37	14	2	184	238	58	148	57	59	25	7	444	463	146
Carolina	33	21	10	2	0	127	93	44	35	16	15	4	0	121	112	36	68	37	25	6	0	248	205	80
Chicago	124	60	47	16	1	428	379	137	122	36	69	15	2	325	449	89	246	96	116	31	3	753	828	226
Colorado	53	29	16	5	3	178	150	66	53	17	28	7	1	130	187	42	106	46	44	12	4	308	337	108
Columbus	20	14	4	0	2	61	42	30	20	13	4	0	3	59	45	29	40	27	8	0	5	120	87	59
Detroit	118	58	41	18	1	400	352	135	118	43	59	16	0	370	443	102	236	101	100	34	1	770	795	237
Edmonton	57	33	16	7	1	205	155	74	56	23	23	8	2	183	213	56	113	56	39	15	3	388	368	130
Florida	11	4	3	2	2	37	37	12	13	7	4	1	1	37	26	16	24	11	7	3	3	74	63	28
Los Angeles	105	62	28	13	2	378	279	139	103	37	40	19	7	302	337	100	208	99	68	32	9	680	616	239
Minnesota	20	16	2	1	1	77	44	34	20	10	9	0	1	47	52	21	40	26	11	1	2	124	96	55
Montreal	62	19	31	12	0	163	209	50	60	12	39	9	0	149	259	33	122	31	70	21	0	312	468	83
Nashville	24	18	5	0	1	69	33	37	24	10	13	1	0	54	64	21	48	28	18	1	1	123	97	58
New Jersey	49	29	14	6	0	176	124	64	47	20	24	3	0	138	162	43	96	49	38	9	0	314	286	107
NY Islanders	49	19	21	8	1	143	176	47	51	17	25	8	1	147	185	43	100	36	46	16	2	290	361	90
NY Rangers	64	21	31	11	1	201	231	54	65	17	37	11	0	172	221	45	129	38	68	22	1	373	452	99
Ottawa	13	8	5	0	0	51	36	16	12	7	3	0	2	32	28	16	25	15	8	0	2	83	64	32
Philadelphia	69	28	24	16	1	223	220	73	71	10	45	16	0	161	269	36	140	38	69	32	1	384	489	109
Phoenix	76	36	29	9	2	251	218	83	75	39	29	4	3	244	229	85	151	75	58	13	5	495	447	168
Pittsburgh	67	38	22	6	1	255	223	83	65	19	40	6	0	182	246	44	132	57	62	12	1	437	469	127
St. Louis	127	61	42	22	2	423	369	146	129	37	69	21	2	361	458	97	256	98	111	43	4	784	827	243
San Jose	50	23	19	4	4	142	129	54	51	31	17	1	2	138	122	65	101	54	36	5	6	280	251	119
Tampa Bay	13	8	4	1	0	46	36	17	16	11	3	2	0	45	30	24	29	19	7	3	0	91	66	41
Toronto	99	52	36	11	0	372	310	115	104	37	50	17	0	330	363	91	203	89	86	28	0	702	673	206
Vancouver	83	44	27	12	0	285	240	100	83	33	37	10	3	244	294	79	166	77	64	22	3	529	534	179
Washington	44	23	11	8	2	163	118	56	42	18	16	8	0	136	127	44	86	41	27	16	2	299	245	100
Defunct Clubs	33	19	8	6	0	123	86	44	32	10	16	6	0	84	105	26	65	29	24	12	0	207	191	70
Totals	**1712**	**866**	**582**	**228**	**36**	**5773**	**5008**	**1996**	**1712**	**602**	**840**	**231**	**39**	**4829**	**5872**	**1474**	**3424**	**1468**	**1422**	**459**	**75**	**10602**	**10880**	**3470**

Playoffs

	Series	W	L	GP	W	L	T	GF	GA	Last Mtg.	Rnd.	Result
Anaheim	2	1	1	12	6	6	0	34	27	2008	CQF	W 4-2
Boston	1	1	0	3	3	0	0	20	13	1981	PRE	W 3-0
Buffalo	3	2	1	13	8	5	0	39	37	1999	F	W 4-2
Calgary	1	1	0	6	4	2	0	25	18	1981	SF	W 4-2
Chicago	6	2	4	33	14	19	0	118	120	1991	DSF	W 4-2
Colorado	4	2	2	24	10	14	0	62	66	2006	CQF	L 1-4
Detroit	4	0	4	24	8	16	0	50	72	2008	CF	L 2-4
Edmonton	8	6	2	42	27	15	0	118	104	2003	CQF	W 4-2
Los Angeles	1	1	0	7	4	3	0	26	21	1968	QF	W 4-3
Montreal	2	1	1	13	6	7	0	37	48	1980	QF	W 4-3
New Jersey	1	0	1	6	2	4	0	9	15	2000	F	L 2-4
NY Islanders	1	0	1	5	1	4	0	16	26	1981	F	L 1-4
Philadelphia	2	0	2	11	3	8	0	26	41	1980	SF	L 1-4
Pittsburgh	1	0	1	6	2	4	0	16	28	1991	F	L 2-4
St. Louis	12	6	6	66	34	32	0	197	187	2001	CSF	L 0-4
San Jose	3	3	0	17	12	5	0	46	30	2008	CSF	W 4-2
Toronto	2	2	0	7	6	1	0	35	26	1983	DSF	W 3-1
Vancouver	2	0	2	12	4	8	0	23	31	2007	CQF	L 3-4
Totals	**56**	**28**	**28**	**307**	**154**	**153**	**0**	**897**	**910**			

Calgary totals include Atlanta Flames, 1972-73 to 1979-80. Carolina totals include Hartford, 1979-80 to 1996-97.
Colorado totals include Quebec, 1979-80 to 1994-95.
New Jersey totals include Kansas City, 1974-75, 1975-76, and Colorado Rockies, 1976-77 to 1981-82.
Phoenix totals include Winnipeg, 1979-80 to 1995-96.

Playoff Results 2011-2007

Year	Round	Opponent	Result	GF	GA
2008	CF	Detroit	L 2-4	10	17
	CSF	San Jose	W 4-2	15	11
	CQF	Anaheim	W 4-2	20	13
2007	CQF	Vancouver	L 3-4	12	13

Abbreviations: Round: F - Final; **CF** - conference final; **CSF** - conference semi-final; **CQF** - conference quarter-final; **DSF** - division semi-final; **SF** - semi-final; **QF** - quarter-final; **PRE** - preliminary round.

2010-11 Results

Month	Day	Opponent	Score
Oct.	8	at New Jersey	4-3*
	9	at NY Islanders	5-4†
	14	Detroit	4-1
	16	St. Louis	3-2†
	18	at Tampa Bay	4-5
	21	at Florida	4-1
	23	Nashville	0-1
	26	Anaheim	2-5
	28	Los Angeles	2-5
	30	Buffalo	4-0
Nov.	3	Pittsburgh	5-2
	5	Phoenix	6-3
	6	at Colorado	0-5
	11	at Los Angeles	1-3
	12	at Anaheim	2-4
	16	Anaheim	2-1
	18	San Jose	5-4*
	20	Colorado	3-4†
	22	at Toronto	1-4
	24	at Ottawa	2-1
	26	St. Louis	3-2
	27	at St. Louis	2-1
	29	at Carolina	4-1
Dec.	2	Washington	2-1
	4	Minnesota	4-3*
	6	at Columbus	2-3†
	8	at Chicago	3-5
	10	Carolina	2-1†
	11	at Phoenix	2-5
	13	at San Jose	3-2†
	16	San Jose	3-4*
	18	at Columbus	2-1
	19	at Detroit	4-3*
	21	Montreal	5-2
	23	Calgary	2-3†
	26	Phoenix	0-1
	28	at Nashville	4-2
	29	Detroit	3-7
	31	Vancouver	1-4
Jan.	2	at St. Louis	4-2
	5	at Chicago	4-2
	7	NY Rangers	2-3†
	9	at Minnesota	4-0
	11	Edmonton	3-2
	15	Atlanta	6-1
	17	Los Angeles	2-1
	20	at Edmonton	4-2
	21	at Calgary	4-7
	24	at Vancouver	1-7
	26	Edmonton	3-1
Feb.	1	Vancouver	1-4
	3	at Boston	3-6
	5	at Philadelphia	1-3
	9	Phoenix	2-3*
	11	Chicago	4-3†
	13	Columbus	1-2
	15	at Edmonton	1-4
	16	at Calgary	2-4
	19	at Vancouver	2-5
	22	New Jersey	0-1
	24	at Detroit	4-1
	26	Nashville	3-2
Mar.	1	at Phoenix	3-2
	4	at Anaheim	3-4*
	5	at San Jose	3-2
	7	at Los Angeles	4-3*
	9	Calgary	3-4†
	11	Minnesota	4-0
	13	Los Angeles	2-3
	15	San Jose	3-6
	17	Chicago	5-0
	19	Philadelphia	2-3†
	23	Anaheim	3-4*
	26	at Nashville	2-4
	29	at Phoenix	1-2†
	31	at San Jose	0-6
Apr.	2	at Los Angeles	1-3
	3	at Anaheim	4-3
	5	Columbus	3-0
	7	Colorado	4-2
	8	at Colorado	3-2
	10	at Minnesota	3-5

* – Overtime † Shootout

Entry Draft Selections 2011-1997

Name in bold denotes played in NHL.

2011
Pick
14	Jamieson Oleksiak
44	Brett Ritchie
105	Emil Molin
135	Troy Vance
165	Matej Stransky
195	Jyrki Jokipakka

2010
Pick
11	Jack Campbell
41	Patrik Nemeth
77	Alexander Guptill
109	Alex Theriau
131	John Klingberg

2009
Pick
8	Scott Glennie
38	Alex Chiasson
69	Reilly Smith
129	**Tomas Vincour**
159	Curtis McKenzie

2008
Pick
59	Tyler Beskorowany
89	Scott Winkler
149	**Philip Larsen**
176	Matthew Tassone
209	Mike Bergin

2007
Pick
50	Nico Sacchetti
64	Sergei Korostin
112	**Colton Sceviour**
128	Austin Smith
129	**Jamie Benn**
136	Ondrej Roman
149	Michael Neal
172	Luke Gazdic

2006
Pick
27	**Ivan Vishnevskiy**
90	Aaron Snow
120	**Richard Bachman**
138	David McIntyre
150	Max Warn

2005
Pick
28	**Matt Niskanen**
33	**James Neal**
71	**Rich Clune**
75	**Perttu Lindgren**
146	**Tom Wandell**
160	Matt Watkins
223	Pat McGann

2004
Pick
28	**Mark Fistric**
34	Johan Fransson
52	**Raymond Sawada**
56	**Nicklas Grossman**
86	John Lammers
104	Fredrik Naslund
183	Trevor Ludwig
218	Sergei Kukushkin
248	Lukas Vomela
280	Matt McKnight

2003
Pick
33	**Loui Eriksson**
36	**Vojtech Polak**
54	**B.J. Crombeen**
99	Matt Nickerson
134	Alexander Naurov
144	Eero Kilpelainen
165	Gino Guyer
185	**Francis Wathier**
195	**Drew Bagnall**
196	Elias Granath
259	Niko Vainio

2002
Pick
26	Martin Vagner
32	Janos Vas
34	**Tobias Stephan**
42	Marius Holtet
43	**Trevor Daley**
78	Geoff Waugh
110	Jarkko A. Immonen
147	David Bararuk
180	Kirill Sidorenko
210	Bryan Hamm
243	Tuomas Mikkonen
273	Ned Havern

2001
Pick
26	Jason Bacashihua
70	Yared Hagos
92	Anthony Aquino
120	Daniel Volrab
161	**Mike Smith**
167	Michal Blazek
192	**Jussi Jokinen**
255	Marco Rosa
265	Dale Sullivan
285	Marek Tomica

2000
Pick
25	**Steve Ott**
60	**Dan Ellis**
68	**Joel Lundqvist**
91	Alexei Tereschenko
123	Vadim Khomitski
139	Ruslan Bernikov
162	Artem Chernov
192	Ladislav Vlcek
219	Marco Tuokko
224	**Antti Miettinen**

1999
Pick
32	**Michael Ryan**
66	**Dan Jancevski**
96	**Mathias Tjarnqvist**
126	Jeff Bateman
156	Gregor Baumgartner
184	Justin Cox
186	Brett Draney
215	**Jeff MacMillan**
243	Brian Sullivan
265	Jamie Chamberlain
272	Mikhail Donika

1998
Pick
39	**John Erskine**
57	**Tyler Bouck**
86	Gabriel Karlsson
153	**Pavel Patera**
173	**Niko Kapanen**
200	Scott Perry

1997
Pick
25	**Brenden Morrow**
52	**Roman Lyashenko**
77	**Steve Gainey**
105	Marcus Kristoffersson
132	Teemu Elomo
160	Alexei Timkin
189	Jeff McKercher
216	Alexei Komarov
242	**Brett McLean**

American Airlines Center

Club Directory

Dallas Stars
Office Address:
2601 Ave. of the Stars
Frisco, TX 75034
Phone **214/387-5500**
FAX 214/387-5564
Ticket Information 214/GO STARS
www.dallasstars.com
Capacity: 18,532

Executives
President	Tony Tavares
Executive Vice President, Chief Financial Officer	Robert Hutson
Executive Vice President, Business Operations	Randy Locey
Sr. Vice President, Sales & Service	Dan Fine
Vice President, Marketing & Broadcasting	Jason Walsh
Vice President, Corporate Partnerships	Ben Cahalane
Vice President, Communications	Rob Scichili
Vice President, Marketing	John Alexander
Vice President, Dr Pepper StarCenters	Ed Reusch
Assistant to the President	Christine Hill

Hockey Operations
General Manager	Joe Nieuwendyk
Director, Scouting & Player Development	Les Jackson
Assistant General Manager	Frank Provenzano
General Manager, Texas Stars	Scott White
Head Coach	Glen Gulutzan
Associate Coach	Willie Desjardins
Assistant Coach	Paul Jerrard
Goaltending Coach	Mike Valley
Strength and Conditioning Coach	J.J. McQueen
Video Coordinator	Kelly Forbes
Director, Amateur Scouting	Tim Bernhardt
Director, European Scouting	Kari Takko
Director, Professional Scouting	Doug Overton
Regional Scouts	Shane Churla, Jack Foley, Bob Gernander, Dennis Holland, Jiri Hrdina, Jimmy Johnston, Alex LePore, John Markell, Paul McIntosh, Danny O'Brien, Rickard Oquist, Borys Protsenko, Shane Turner, Bobby Vermette.
Head Athletic Trainer	Dave Zeis
Associate Athletic Trainer	Craig Lowry
Head Equipment Manager	Steve Sumner
Assistant Equipment Manager	Dennis Soetaert
Assistant Equipment Manager	Donny White
Massage Therapist	Cleo Bates
Manager, Hockey Administration	Mark Janko
Director, Team Services	Jason Rademan
Executive Assistant, Hockey Operations	Pam Wenzel

Business Operations
Asst. Vice President, Business Operations	Bill Herman
Sr. Director, Dallas Stars Foundation	Lora Farris
Controller	Melissa Embry
Directors, Corporate Partnerships	Rodney Ferrell, Dan Fitzsimmons
Director, Merchandise	Jason Atkinson
Director, New Business Development	Aldo Truden
Director, Group & Suite Sales	John Higgins
Director, Client Relations	Sam Bays
Director, Human Resources	Amy Gomez
Associate Producer, Broadcast Manager	John Sponsler
Animator	Jeff Neal
Lead Editor	Jerry Miranda
Website Producer	Jason Danby
Account Executive, Corporate Partnerships	Brad Cruson
Department Manager, Corporate Partnerships	Ben Young
Account Manager, Corporate Partnerships	Lisa Soloman
Manager, IT Operations	Erwin Chung
Manager, Digital Media	Lane Pate
Manager, Marketing	Trent Morton
Manager, Database Marketing	Ashley Tamez
Manager, Ticket Operations	Jeff Gogerty
Coordinators, Communications	Joe Calvillo, Greg Ramirez
Coordinator, Fan Development & Promotions	Steve Phillips
Coordinator, Human Resources	Kelly Billingham
Coordinator, Community Marketing	Jennifer Petty
Coordinator, Ice Girls	Wendy Dutton

Tom Wandell celebrates a goal against Nashville in a 3-2 Dallas victory on February 26, 2011. Wandell is one of five Dallas draft choices from 2005 to have reached the NHL.

Joe Nieuwendyk
General Manager
Born: Oshawa, Ont., September 10, 1966.

Joe Nieuwendyk was named general manager of the Dallas Stars on May 31, 2009. The former Stars player returned to Dallas from the Toronto Maple Leafs, where he served as special assistant to the general manager in 2008-09. Prior to joining the Leafs and after his 2006 retirement as a player, Nieuwendyk worked as a special consultant to the general manager with the Florida Panthers. He also helped lead Team Canada to a silver medal at the 2009 World Championship as assistant general manager.

A veteran of 20 seasons as a player in the National Hockey League, Nieuwendyk played seven with the Dallas Stars (1995 to 2002). He won the Stanley Cup for three different teams, in three different decades (Calgary in 1989, Dallas in 1999, New Jersey in 2003). Nieuwendyk was awarded the Conn Smythe Trophy as the Stanley Cup playoffs most valuable player in 1999 when he led Dallas in postseason scoring on their way to winning the Stanley Cup. Nieuwendyk played in 1,257 NHL games, scoring 564 goals and 562 assists for 1,126 points. He also appeared in 158 career playoff games, recording 116 points on 66 goals and 50 assists. Nieuwendyk played in 442 games for Dallas, scoring 178 goals and 162 assists for 340 points.

Captains' History
Bob Woytowich, 1967-68; Moose Vasko, 1968-69; Claude Larose, 1969-70; Ted Harris, 1970-71 to 1973-74; Bill Goldsworthy, 1974-75, 1975-76; Bill Hogaboam, 1976-77; Nick Beverley, 1977-78; J.P. Parise, 1978-79; Paul Shmyr, 1979-80, 1980-81; Tim Young, 1981-82; Craig Hartsburg, 1982-83; Craig Hartsburg and Brian Bellows, 1983-84; Craig Hartsburg, 1984-85 to 1987-88; Curt Fraser, Bob Rouse and Curt Giles, 1988-89; Curt Giles, 1989-90, 1990-91; Mark Tinordi, 1991-92 to 1993-94; Neal Broten and Derian Hatcher, 1994-95; Derian Hatcher, 1995-96 to 2002-03; Mike Modano, 2003-04 to 2005-06; Brenden Morrow, 2006-07 to date.

General Managers' History
Wren Blair, 1967-68 to 1973-74; Jack Gordon, 1974-75 to 1976-77; Jack Gordon and Lou Nanne, 1977-78; Lou Nanne, 1978-79 to 1986-87; Lou Nanne and Jack Ferreira, 1987-88; Jack Ferreira, 1988-89, 1989-90; Bob Clarke, 1990-91, 1991-92; Bob Gainey, 1992-93 to 2000-01; Bob Gainey and Doug Armstrong, 2001-02; Doug Armstrong, 2002-03 to 2006-07; Doug Armstrong and Brett Hull/Les Jackson, 2007-08; Brett Hull/Les Jackson, 2008-09; Joe Nieuwendyk, 2009-10 to date.

Detroit Red Wings

Key Off-Season Signings/Acquisitions

2011

- **June 20** • Re-signed D **Nicklas Lidstrom**.
- **July 1** • Re-signed RW **Patrick Eaves**, LW **Drew Miller** and D **Jonathan Ericsson**.
- **1** • Signed D **Mike Commodore**.
- **2** • Signed D **Ian White**.
- **5** • Signed D **Garnet Exelby**.
- **7** • Signed RW **Chris Conner**.
- **11** • Re-signed G **Joey MacDonald**.
- **20** • Signed G **Ty Conklin**.

2011-12 Schedule

Month	Day	Date	Opponent
Oct.	Fri.	7	Ottawa
	Sat.	8	at Colorado
	Thu.	13	Vancouver
	Sat.	15	at Minnesota
	Fri.	21	Columbus
	Sat.	22	at Washington
	Tue.	25	at Columbus
	Fri.	28	San Jose
	Sat.	29	at Minnesota
Nov.	Tue.	1	Minnesota
	Thu.	3	Calgary
	Sat.	5	Anaheim
	Tue.	8	Colorado
	Fri.	11	Edmonton
	Sat.	12	Dallas
	Tue.	15	at St. Louis
	Thu.	17	at San Jose
	Sat.	19	at Los Angeles*
	Sun.	20	at Anaheim*
	Wed.	23	Calgary
	Fri.	25	at Boston*
	Sat.	26	Nashville
	Wed.	30	Tampa Bay
Dec.	Fri.	2	at Buffalo
	Sun.	4	at Colorado
	Tue.	6	at St. Louis
	Thu.	8	Phoenix
	Sat.	10	Winnipeg
	Tue.	13	at Pittsburgh
	Thu.	15	at Nashville
	Sat.	17	Los Angeles
	Mon.	19	at Edmonton
	Wed.	21	at Vancouver
	Thu.	22	at Calgary
	Mon.	26	at Nashville
	Tue.	27	St. Louis
	Fri.	30	at Chicago
	Sat.	31	St. Louis
Jan.	Tue.	3	at Dallas
	Sat.	7	at Toronto
	Sun.	8	at Chicago
	Tue.	10	at NY Islanders
	Thu.	12	Phoenix
	Sat.	14	Chicago*
	Mon.	16	Buffalo
	Tue.	17	at Dallas
	Thu.	19	at Phoenix
	Sat.	21	Columbus
	Mon.	23	St. Louis
	Wed.	25	at Montreal
	Tue.	31	at Calgary
Feb.	Thu.	2	at Vancouver
	Sat.	4	at Edmonton
	Mon.	6	at Phoenix
	Wed.	8	Edmonton
	Fri.	10	Anaheim
	Sun.	12	Philadelphia
	Tue.	14	Dallas
	Fri.	17	Nashville
	Sun.	19	San Jose*
	Tue.	21	at Chicago
	Thu.	23	Vancouver
	Sat.	25	Colorado
	Tue.	28	at Columbus
Mar.	Fri.	2	Minnesota
	Sun.	4	Chicago*
	Tue.	6	at Philadelphia
	Fri.	9	Los Angeles
	Sat.	10	at Nashville
	Tue.	13	at Los Angeles
	Wed.	14	at Anaheim
	Sat.	17	at San Jose
	Mon.	19	Washington
	Wed.	21	at NY Rangers
	Sat.	24	Carolina
	Mon.	26	Columbus
	Wed.	28	at Columbus
	Fri.	30	Nashville
Apr.	Sun.	1	Florida*
	Wed.	4	at St. Louis
	Thu.	5	New Jersey
	Sat.	7	Chicago*

* Denotes afternoon game.

NHL WESTERN CONFERENCE

CENTRAL DIVISION
86th NHL Season

Franchise date: September 25, 1926

2010-11 Results: 47W-25L-6OTL-4SOL 104PTS.
First, Central Division

Year-by-Year Record

		Home				Road				Overall								
Season	GP	W	L	T	OL	W	L	T	OL	W	L	T	OL	GF	GA	Pts.	Finished	Playoff Result
2010-11	82	21	14	....	6	26	11	....	4	47	25	....	10	261	241	104	1st, Central Div.	Lost Conf. Semi-Final
2009-10	82	25	10	....	6	19	14	....	8	44	24	....	14	229	216	102	2nd, Central Div.	Lost Conf. Semi-Final
2008-09	82	27	9	....	5	24	12	....	5	51	21	....	10	295	244	112	1st, Central Div.	Lost Final
2007-08	**82**	**29**	**9**	....	**3**	**25**	**12**	....	**4**	**54**	**21**	....	**7**	**257**	**184**	**115**	**1st, Central Div.**	**Won Stanley Cup**
2006-07	82	29	4	....	8	21	15	....	5	50	19	....	13	254	199	113	1st, Central Div.	Lost Conf. Championship
2005-06	82	27	9	....	5	31	7	....	3	58	16	....	8	305	209	124	1st, Central Div.	Lost Conf. Quarter-Final
2004-05	....	....	....	....	....	....	....	....	....	....	....	....	....	....	....	....		
2003-04	82	30	7	4	0	18	14	7	2	48	21	11	2	255	189	109	1st, Central Div.	Lost Conf. Semi-Final
2002-03	82	28	6	5	2	20	14	5	2	48	20	10	4	269	203	110	1st, Central Div.	Lost Conf. Quarter-Final
2001-02	**82**	**28**	**7**	**5**	**1**	**23**	**10**	**5**	**3**	**51**	**17**	**10**	**4**	**251**	**187**	**116**	**1st, Central Div.**	**Won Stanley Cup**
2000-01	82	27	9	3	2	22	11	6	2	49	20	9	4	253	202	111	1st, Central Div.	Lost Conf. Quarter-Final
1999-2000	82	28	9	3	1	20	13	7	1	48	22	10	2	278	210	108	2nd, Central Div.	Lost Conf. Semi-Final
1998-99	82	27	12	2	....	16	20	5	....	43	32	7	....	245	202	93	1st, Central Div.	Lost Conf. Semi-Final
1997-98	**82**	**25**	**8**	**8**	....	**19**	**15**	**7**	....	**44**	**23**	**15**	....	**250**	**196**	**103**	**2nd, Central Div.**	**Won Stanley Cup**
1996-97	**82**	**20**	**12**	**9**	....	**18**	**14**	**9**	....	**38**	**26**	**18**	....	**253**	**197**	**94**	**2nd, Central Div.**	**Won Stanley Cup**
1995-96	82	36	3	2	....	26	10	5	....	62	13	7	....	325	181	131	1st, Central Div.	Lost Conf. Championship
1994-95	48	17	4	3	....	16	7	1	....	33	11	4	....	180	117	70	1st, Central Div.	Lost Final
1993-94	84	23	13	6	....	23	17	2	....	46	30	8	....	356	275	100	1st, Central Div.	Lost Conf. Quarter-Final
1992-93	84	25	14	3	....	22	14	6	....	47	28	9	....	369	280	103	2nd, Norris Div.	Lost Div. Semi-Final
1991-92	80	24	12	4	....	19	13	8	....	43	25	12	....	320	256	98	1st, Norris Div.	Lost Div. Final
1990-91	80	26	14	0	....	8	24	8	....	34	38	8	....	273	298	76	3rd, Norris Div.	Lost Div. Semi-Final
1989-90	80	20	14	6	....	8	24	8	....	28	38	14	....	288	323	70	5th, Norris Div.	Out of Playoffs
1988-89	80	20	14	6	....	14	20	6	....	34	34	12	....	313	316	80	1st, Norris Div.	Lost Div. Semi-Final
1987-88	80	24	10	6	....	17	18	5	....	41	28	11	....	322	269	93	1st, Norris Div.	Lost Conf. Championship
1986-87	80	20	14	6	....	14	22	4	....	34	36	10	....	260	274	78	2nd, Norris Div.	Lost Conf. Championship
1985-86	80	10	26	4	....	7	31	2	....	17	57	6	....	266	415	40	5th, Norris Div.	Out of Playoffs
1984-85	80	19	14	7	....	8	27	5	....	27	41	12	....	313	357	66	3rd, Norris Div.	Lost Div. Semi-Final
1983-84	80	18	20	2	....	13	22	5	....	31	42	7	....	298	323	69	3rd, Norris Div.	Lost Div. Semi-Final
1982-83	80	14	19	7	....	7	25	8	....	21	44	15	....	263	344	57	5th, Norris Div.	Out of Playoffs
1981-82	80	15	19	6	....	6	28	6	....	21	47	12	....	270	351	54	6th, Norris Div.	Out of Playoffs
1980-81	80	16	15	9	....	3	28	9	....	19	43	18	....	252	339	56	5th, Norris Div.	Out of Playoffs
1979-80	80	14	21	5	....	12	22	6	....	26	43	11	....	268	306	63	5th, Norris Div.	Out of Playoffs
1978-79	80	15	17	8	....	8	24	8	....	23	41	16	....	252	295	62	5th, Norris Div.	Out of Playoffs
1977-78	80	22	11	7	....	10	23	7	....	32	34	14	....	252	266	78	2nd, Norris Div.	Lost Quarter-Final
1976-77	80	12	22	6	....	4	33	3	....	16	55	9	....	183	309	41	5th, Norris Div.	Out of Playoffs
1975-76	80	17	15	8	....	9	29	2	....	26	44	10	....	226	300	62	4th, Norris Div.	Out of Playoffs
1974-75	80	17	17	6	....	6	28	6	....	23	45	12	....	259	335	58	4th, Norris Div.	Out of Playoffs
1973-74	78	21	12	6	....	8	27	4	....	29	39	10	....	255	319	68	6th, East Div.	Out of Playoffs
1972-73	78	22	12	5	....	15	17	7	....	37	29	12	....	265	243	86	5th, East Div.	Out of Playoffs
1971-72	78	25	11	3	....	8	24	7	....	33	35	10	....	261	262	76	5th, East Div.	Out of Playoffs
1970-71	78	17	15	7	....	5	30	4	....	22	45	11	....	209	308	55	7th, East Div.	Out of Playoffs
1969-70	76	20	11	7	....	20	10	8	....	40	21	15	....	246	199	95	3rd, East Div.	Lost Quarter-Final
1968-69	76	23	8	7	....	10	23	5	....	33	31	12	....	239	221	78	5th, East Div.	Out of Playoffs
1967-68	74	18	15	4	....	9	20	8	....	27	35	12	....	245	257	66	6th, East Div.	Out of Playoffs
1966-67	70	21	11	3	....	6	28	1	....	27	39	4	....	212	241	58	5th,	Out of Playoffs
1965-66	70	20	8	7	....	11	19	5	....	31	27	12	....	221	194	74	4th,	Lost Final
1964-65	70	25	7	3	....	15	16	4	....	40	23	7	....	224	175	87	1st,	Lost Semi-Final
1963-64	70	23	9	3	....	7	20	8	....	30	29	11	....	191	204	71	4th,	Lost Final
1962-63	70	19	10	6	....	13	15	7	....	32	25	13	....	200	194	77	4th,	Lost Final
1961-62	70	17	11	7	....	6	22	7	....	23	33	14	....	184	219	60	5th,	Out of Playoffs
1960-61	70	15	13	7	....	10	16	9	....	25	29	16	....	195	215	66	4th,	Lost Final
1959-60	70	18	14	3	....	8	15	12	....	26	29	15	....	186	197	67	4th,	Lost Semi-Final
1958-59	70	13	17	5	....	12	20	3	....	25	37	8	....	167	218	58	6th,	Out of Playoffs
1957-58	70	16	11	8	....	13	18	4	....	29	29	12	....	176	207	70	3rd,	Lost Semi-Final
1956-57	70	23	7	5	....	15	13	7	....	38	20	12	....	198	157	88	1st,	Lost Semi-Final
1955-56	70	21	6	8	....	9	18	8	....	30	24	16	....	183	148	76	2nd,	Lost Final
1954-55	**70**	**25**	**5**	**5**	....	**17**	**12**	**6**	....	**42**	**17**	**11**	....	**204**	**134**	**95**	**1st,**	**Won Stanley Cup**
1953-54	**70**	**24**	**4**	**7**	....	**13**	**15**	**7**	....	**37**	**19**	**14**	....	**191**	**132**	**88**	**1st,**	**Won Stanley Cup**
1952-53	70	20	5	10	....	16	11	8	....	36	16	18	....	222	133	90	1st,	Lost Semi-Final
1951-52	**70**	**24**	**7**	**4**	....	**20**	**7**	**8**	....	**44**	**14**	**12**	....	**215**	**133**	**100**	**1st,**	**Won Stanley Cup**
1950-51	70	25	3	7	....	19	10	6	....	44	13	13	....	236	139	101	1st,	Lost Semi-Final
1949-50	**70**	**19**	**9**	**7**	....	**18**	**10**	**7**	....	**37**	**19**	**14**	....	**229**	**164**	**88**	**1st,**	**Won Stanley Cup**
1948-49	60	21	6	3	....	13	13	4	....	34	19	7	....	195	145	75	1st,	Lost Final
1947-48	60	16	9	5	....	14	9	7	....	30	18	12	....	187	148	72	2nd,	Lost Final
1946-47	60	14	10	6	....	8	17	5	....	22	27	11	....	190	193	55	4th,	Lost Semi-Final
1945-46	50	16	5	4	....	4	15	6	....	20	20	10	....	146	159	50	4th,	Lost Semi-Final
1944-45	50	19	5	1	....	12	9	4	....	31	14	5	....	218	161	67	2nd,	Lost Final
1943-44	50	18	5	2	....	8	13	4	....	26	18	6	....	214	177	58	2nd,	Lost Semi-Final
1942-43	**50**	**16**	**4**	**5**	....	**9**	**10**	**6**	....	**25**	**14**	**11**	....	**169**	**124**	**61**	**1st,**	**Won Stanley Cup**
1941-42	48	14	7	3	....	5	18	1	....	19	25	4	....	140	147	42	5th,	Lost Final
1940-41	48	14	5	5	....	7	11	6	....	21	16	11	....	112	102	53	3rd,	Lost Final
1939-40	48	11	10	3	....	5	16	3	....	16	26	6	....	91	126	38	5th,	Lost Semi-Final
1938-39	48	14	8	2	....	4	16	4	....	18	24	6	....	107	128	42	5th,	Lost Semi-Final
1937-38	48	8	10	6	....	4	15	5	....	12	25	11	....	99	133	35	4th, Amn. Div.	Out of Playoffs
1936-37	**48**	**14**	**5**	**5**	....	**11**	**9**	**4**	....	**25**	**14**	**9**	....	**128**	**102**	**59**	**1st, Amn. Div.**	**Won Stanley Cup**
1935-36	**48**	**14**	**5**	**5**	....	**10**	**11**	**3**	....	**24**	**16**	**8**	....	**124**	**103**	**56**	**1st, Amn. Div.**	**Won Stanley Cup**
1934-35	48	11	8	5	....	8	14	2	....	19	22	7	....	127	114	45	4th, Amn. Div.	Out of Playoffs
1933-34	48	15	5	4	....	9	9	6	....	24	14	10	....	113	98	58	1st, Amn. Div.	Lost Final
1932-33*	48	17	3	4	....	8	12	4	....	25	15	8	....	111	93	58	2nd, Amn. Div.	Lost Semi-Final
1931-32	48	15	3	6	....	3	17	4	....	18	20	10	....	95	108	46	3rd, Amn. Div.	Lost Quarter-Final
1930-31**	44	10	7	5	....	6	14	2	....	16	21	7	....	102	105	39	4th, Amn. Div.	Out of Playoffs
1929-30	44	9	10	3	....	5	14	3	....	14	24	6	....	117	133	34	4th, Amn. Div.	Out of Playoffs
1928-29	44	11	6	5	....	8	10	4	....	19	16	9	....	72	63	47	3rd, Amn. Div.	Lost Quarter-Final
1927-28	44	9	10	3	....	10	9	3	....	19	19	6	....	88	79	44	4th, Amn. Div.	Out of Playoffs
1926-27***	44	5	16	0	....	7	12	4	....	12	28	4	....	76	105	28	5th, Amn. Div.	Out of Playoffs

* Team name changed to Red Wings. ** Team name changed to Falcons. *** Team named Cougars.

2011-12 Player Personnel

FORWARDS	HT	WT	S	Place of Birth	*Age	2010-11 Club
ABDELKADER, Justin	6-1	212	L	Muskegon, MI	24	Detroit
BERTUZZI, Todd	6-3	225	L	Sudbury, Ont.	36	Detroit
CLEARY, Dan	6-0	205	L	Carbonear, Nfld.	32	Detroit
CONNER, Chris	5-8	180	L	Westland, MI	27	Pittsburgh-Wilkes-Barre
DATSYUK, Pavel	5-11	194	L	Sverdlovsk, USSR	33	Detroit
EAVES, Patrick	6-0	191	R	Calgary, Alta.	27	Detroit
EMMERTON, Cory	6-0	190	L	St. Thomas, Ont.	23	Detroit-Grand Rapids
FILPPULA, Valtteri	6-0	193	L	Vantaa, Finland	27	Detroit
FRANZEN, Johan	6-3	222	L	Landsbro, Sweden	31	Detroit
HELM, Darren	5-11	195	L	Winnipeg, Man.	24	Detroit
HOLMSTROM, Tomas	6-0	198	L	Pitea, Sweden	38	Detroit
HUDLER, Jiri	5-10	182	L	Olomouc, Czech.	27	Detroit
MILLER, Drew	6-2	178	L	Dover, NJ	27	Detroit
MURSAK, Jan	5-11	190	R	Maribor, Yugoslavia	23	Detroit-Grand Rapids
TATAR, Tomas	5-11	179	L	Ilava, Slovakia	20	Detroit-Grand Rapids
ZETTERBERG, Henrik	5-11	195	L	Njurunda, Sweden	30	Detroit
DEFENSEMEN						
COMMODORE, Mike	6-4	233	R	Fort Saskatchewan, Alta.	31	Columbus-Springfield
ERICSSON, Jonathan	6-4	220	L	Karlskrona, Sweden	27	Detroit
JANIK, Doug	6-1	214	L	Agawam, MA	31	Detroit-Grand Rapids
KINDL, Jakub	6-3	199	L	Sumperk, Czech.	24	Detroit-Grand Rapids
KRONWALL, Niklas	6-0	192	L	Stockholm, Sweden	30	Detroit
LIDSTROM, Nicklas	6-1	190	L	Vasteras, Sweden	41	Detroit
SMITH, Brendan	6-2	195	L	Toronto, Ont.	22	Grand Rapids
STUART, Brad	6-2	210	L	Rocky Mountain House, Alta.	31	Detroit
WHITE, Ian	5-10	200	R	Steinbach, Man.	27	Cgy-Car-S.J.

GOALTENDERS	HT	WT	C	Place of Birth	*Age	2010-11 Club
CONKLIN, Ty	6-1	192	L	Anchorage, AK	35	St. Louis
HOWARD, Jimmy	6-0	210	L	Syracuse, NY	27	Detroit
MacDONALD, Joey	6-0	197	L	Pictou, N.S.	31	Detroit-Grand Rapids

* – Age at start of 2011-12 season

2010-11 Scoring

* – rookie

Regular Season

Pos	#	Player	Team	GP	G	A	Pts	TOI	+/–	PIM	PP	SH	GW	S	%
L	40	Henrik Zetterberg	DET	80	24	56	80	19:35	–1	40	10	0	3	306	7.8
D	5	Nicklas Lidstrom	DET	82	16	46	62	23:28	–2	20	7	0	1	175	9.1
C	13	Pavel Datsyuk	DET	56	23	36	59	19:19	11	15	6	1	5	137	16.8
C	93	Johan Franzen	DET	76	28	27	55	17:26	5	58	10	0	5	248	11.3
D	28	Brian Rafalski	DET	63	4	44	48	20:25	11	22	0	0	0	106	3.8
R	11	Dan Cleary	DET	68	26	20	46	16:38	–1	20	5	0	8	192	13.5
R	44	Todd Bertuzzi	DET	81	16	29	45	15:57	–7	71	2	0	2	138	11.6
C	51	Valtteri Filppula	DET	71	16	23	39	16:43	–1	22	4	0	5	115	13.9
L	96	Tomas Holmstrom	DET	73	18	19	37	14:48	–6	62	10	0	1	125	14.4
D	55	Niklas Kronwall	DET	77	11	26	37	22:52	5	36	5	0	3	131	8.4
C	26	Jiri Hudler	DET	73	10	27	37	13:39	–7	28	3	0	2	105	9.5
C	43	Darren Helm	DET	82	12	20	32	13:18	9	16	0	2	2	177	6.8
R	17	Patrick Eaves	DET	63	13	7	20	12:41	–2	14	2	1	1	108	12.0
D	23	Brad Stuart	DET	67	3	17	20	21:31	4	40	1	0	1	81	3.7
L	8	Justin Abdelkader	DET	74	7	12	19	12:18	15	61	0	0	1	129	5.4
L	20	Drew Miller	DET	67	10	8	18	11:44	–2	13	0	1	2	85	11.8
C	90	Mike Modano	DET	40	4	11	15	12:26	–4	8	1	0	0	79	5.1
D	52	Jonathan Ericsson	DET	74	3	12	15	18:50	8	87	1	0	0	89	3.4
C	33	Kris Draper	DET	47	6	5	11	10:26	1	12	0	0	1	57	10.5
D	24	Ruslan Salei	DET	75	2	8	10	17:57	0	48	0	0	0	75	2.7
D	4	* Jakub Kindl	DET	48	2	2	4	13:36	–6	36	0	0	0	62	3.2
C	48	* Cory Emmerton	DET	2	1	0	1	8:20	1	0	0	0	0	3	33.3
C	21	* Tomas Tatar	DET	9	1	0	1	9:36	0	0	0	0	0	6	16.7
L	39	* Jan Mursak	DET	19	1	0	1	8:11	–3	4	0	0	0	20	5.0
D	37	Doug Janik	DET	7	0	0	0	13:13	–2	7	0	0	0	8	0.0

Goaltending

No.	Goaltender	GPI	Mins	Avg	W	L	OT	EN	SO	GA	SA	S%	G	A	PIM
31	Joey MacDonald	15	721	2.58	5	5	3	1	1	31	372	.917	0	0	0
30	Chris Osgood	11	629	2.77	5	3	2	1	0	29	298	.903	0	0	4
35	Jimmy Howard	63	3615	2.79	37	17	5	4	2	168	1830	.908	0	1	4
38	* Thomas McCollum	1	15	12.00	0	0	0	0	0	3	8	.625	0	0	0
	Totals	**82**	**5005**	**2.84**	**47**	**25**	**10**	**6**	**3**	**237**	**2514**	**.906**			

Playoffs

Pos	#	Player	Team	GP	G	A	Pts	TOI	+/–	PIM	PP	SH	GW	OT	S	%
C	13	Pavel Datsyuk	DET	11	4	11	15	21:09	10	8	2	0	0	0	38	10.5
D	5	Nicklas Lidstrom	DET	11	4	4	8	21:49	8	4	2	0	0	0	26	15.4
L	40	Henrik Zetterberg	DET	7	3	5	8	21:59	6	2	1	0	0	0	20	15.0
C	51	Valtteri Filppula	DET	11	2	6	8	17:47	5	6	0	0	2	0	24	8.3
L	96	Tomas Holmstrom	DET	11	3	4	7	14:27	7	8	0	0	2	0	25	12.0
C	43	Darren Helm	DET	11	3	3	6	13:28	1	8	0	0	1	0	25	12.0
R	44	Todd Bertuzzi	DET	11	2	4	6	13:42	1	15	0	0	0	0	23	8.7
R	11	Dan Cleary	DET	11	2	4	6	17:09	2	6	0	0	1	0	30	6.7
D	55	Niklas Kronwall	DET	11	2	4	6	23:04	5	4	1	0	0	0	15	13.3
R	17	Patrick Eaves	DET	11	3	1	4	11:24	1	6	0	0	0	0	17	17.6
C	93	Johan Franzen	DET	8	2	1	3	15:47	–1	6	0	0	0	0	21	9.5
D	28	Brian Rafalski	DET	11	2	1	3	21:03	–1	4	2	0	1	0	23	8.7
C	26	Jiri Hudler	DET	10	1	2	3	11:57	–1	6	0	0	0	0	12	8.3
D	52	Jonathan Ericsson	DET	11	1	2	3	18:47	–2	4	0	0	0	0	24	4.2
L	20	Drew Miller	DET	9	1	1	2	10:17	3	4	0	0	0	0	12	8.3
D	23	Brad Stuart	DET	11	0	2	2	21:33	6	8	0	0	0	0	10	0.0
D	24	Ruslan Salei	DET	11	1	0	1	16:40	6	0	0	0	0	0	17	5.9
C	90	Mike Modano	DET	2	0	1	1	10:13	1	0	0	0	0	0	5	0.0
C	33	Kris Draper	DET	8	0	1	1	9:19	2	2	0	0	0	0	3	0.0
L	8	Justin Abdelkader	DET	11	0	0	0	13:27	–4	22	0	0	0	0	17	0.0

Goaltending

No.	Goaltender	GPI	Mins	Avg	W	L	EN	SO	GA	SA	S%	G	A	PIM
35	Jimmy Howard	11	673	2.50	7	4	0	0	28	364	.923	0	0	2
	Totals	**11**	**676**	**2.49**	**7**	**4**	**0**	**0**	**28**	**364**	**.923**			

Mike Babcock

Head Coach

Born: Manitouwadge, Ont., April 29, 1963.

Mike Babcock became the 26th coach in Detroit Red Wings history on July 14, 2005. In 2008, he led the Red Wings to the Stanley Cup. The Red Wings reached the Finals again in 2009 and topped 50 wins during the regular season in each of Babcock's first four years with the team. He coached Canada to an Olympic gold medal in 2010.

Babcock brought a winning track record to Detroit from all levels of play, including college and junior hockey, the American Hockey League, the NHL and international hockey. He is the only man to coach Team Canada to victories at both the World Junior Championship (1997) and the senior World Championship (2004.) Prior to joining the Red Wings, he had spent two seasons with Anaheim, leading the team to the Stanley Cup Finals in his first season behind the bench in 2002-03. He became the first rookie coach to reach the Finals since Florida's Doug MacLean in 1996. With a four-game sweep over Detroit in the first round of the playoffs, the Ducks became the first team since the 1952 Red Wings (over Toronto) to sweep a defending Stanley Cup champion.

Before joining Anaheim, Babcock spent two seasons as head coach of the Cincinnati Mighty Ducks (2000 to 2002), the primary development affiliate for both Detroit and Anaheim in the American Hockey League. He led the club to a franchise-best 41 wins and 95 points in 2000-01. Babcock moved to Cincinnati after a successful six-year run as the head coach of the Spokane Chiefs of the Western Hockey League (1994 through 2000). He was twice named WHL coach of the year (1996 and 2000) after taking the Chiefs to the league finals in both seasons. He began his WHL coaching career with the Moose Jaw Warriors in 1991-92. In Canadian university play, Babcock won a national championship and was named the coach of the year with the Lethbridge Pronghorns in 1993-94. In 1988, he was named head coach at Red Deer College in Red Deer, Alberta. He spent three seasons at the school, winning the Alberta college championship and coach of the year award in 1989.

Babcock played in the WHL for Saskatoon (1980-81) and Kelowna (1982-83), where he was team captain. In between, he spent a year at the University of Saskatoon. Babcock also played four years at McGill University (1983 to 1987), twice being named an All-Star defenseman. He earned his bachelor's degree in physical education and attended graduate school in sports psychology at McGill.

Coaching Record

			Regular Season				Playoffs			
Season	Team	League	GC	W	L	O/T	GC	W	L	T
1991-92	Moose Jaw	WHL	72	33	36	3	4	0	4	....
1992-93	Moose Jaw	WHL	72	27	42	3	....	....	....	....
1993-94	U of Lethbridge	CIAU	28	19	7	2	....	....	....	....
1994-95	Spokane	WHL	72	32	36	4	11	6	5	....
1995-96	Spokane	WHL	72	50	18	4	9	3	6	....
1996-97	Spokane	WHL	72	35	33	4	9	4	5	....
1997-98	Spokane	WHL	72	45	23	4	18	10	8	....
1998-99	Spokane	WHL	72	19	44	9	....	....	....	....
99-2000	Spokane	WHL	72	47	19	6	20	15	5	....
2000-01	Cincinnati	AHL	80	41	26	13	4	1	3	....
2001-02	Cincinnati	AHL	80	33	33	14	3	1	2	....
2002-03	**Anaheim**	**NHL**	**82**	**40**	**27**	**15**	**21**	**15**	**6**	....
2003-04	**Anaheim**	**NHL**	**82**	**29**	**35**	**18**	....	....	....	....
2004-05	**Anaheim**				SEASON CANCELLED					
2005-06	**Detroit**	**NHL**	**82**	**58**	**16**	**8**	**6**	**2**	**4**	....
2006-07	**Detroit**	**NHL**	**82**	**50**	**19**	**13**	**18**	**10**	**8**	....
2007-08 ♦	**Detroit**	**NHL**	**82**	**54**	**21**	**7**	**22**	**16**	**6**	....
2008-09	**Detroit**	**NHL**	**82**	**51**	**21**	**10**	**23**	**15**	**8**	....
2009-10	**Detroit**	**NHL**	**82**	**44**	**24**	**14**	**12**	**5**	**7**	....
2010-11	**Detroit**	**NHL**	**82**	**47**	**25**	**10**	**11**	**7**	**4**	....
	NHL Totals		**656**	**373**	**188**	**95**	**113**	**70**	**43**	....

♦ Stanley Cup win.

Club Records

Team

(Figures in brackets for season records are games played; records for fewest points, wins, ties, losses, goals, goals against are for 70 or more games)

Record		
Most Points	131	1995-96 (82)
Most Wins	*62	1995-96 (82)
Most Ties	18	1952-53 (70), 1980-81 (80), 1996-97 (82)
Most Losses	57	1985-86 (80)
Most Goals	369	1992-93 (84)
Most Goals Against	415	1985-86 (80)
Fewest Points	40	1985-86 (80)
Fewest Wins	16	1976-77 (80)
Fewest Ties	4	1966-67 (70)
Fewest Losses	13	1950-51 (70), 1995-96 (82)
Fewest Goals	167	1958-59 (70)
Fewest Goals Against	132	1953-54 (70)
Longest Winning Streak		
Overall	9	Seven times
Home	14	Jan. 21-Mar. 25/65
Away	*12	Mar. 1-Apr. 15/06
Longest Undefeated Streak		
Overall	15	Nov. 27-Dec. 28/52 (8 wins, 7 ties)
Home	19	Dec. 31/00-Apr.7/01 (17 wins, 2 ties)
Away	15	Oct. 18-Dec. 20/51 (10 wins, 5 ties)
Longest Losing Streak		
Overall	14	Feb. 24-Mar. 25/82
Home	7	Feb. 20-Mar. 25/82
Away	14	Oct. 19-Dec. 21/66
Longest Winless Streak		
Overall	19	Feb. 26-Apr. 3/77 (18 losses, 1 tie)
Home	10	Dec. 11/85-Jan. 18/86 (9 losses, 1 tie)
Away	26	Dec. 15/76-Apr. 3/77 (23 losses, 3 ties)
Most Shutouts, Season	13	1953-54 (70)
Most. PIM, Season	2,393	1985-86 (80)
Most Goals, Game	15	Jan. 23/44 (NYR 0 at Det. 15)

Individual

Record		
Most Seasons	25	Gordie Howe
Most Games	1,687	Gordie Howe
Most Goals, Career	786	Gordie Howe
Most Assists, Career	1,063	Steve Yzerman
Most Points, Career	1,809	Gordie Howe (786G, 1,023A)
Most PIM, Career	2,090	Bob Probert
Most Shutouts, Career	85	Terry Sawchuk
Longest Consecutive Games Streak	548	Alex Delvecchio (Dec. 13/56-Nov. 11/64)
Most Goals, Season	65	Steve Yzerman (1988-89)
Most Assists, Season	90	Steve Yzerman (1988-89)
Most Points, Season	155	Steve Yzerman (1988-89; 65G, 90A)
Most PIM, Season	398	Bob Probert (1987-88)
Most Points, Defenseman, Season	80	Nicklas Lidstrom (2005-06; 16G, 64A)
Most Points, Center, Season	155	Steve Yzerman (1988-89; 65G, 90A)
Most Points, Right Wing, Season	103	Gordie Howe (1968-69; 44G, 59A)
Most Points, Left Wing, Season	105	John Ogrodnick (1984-85; 55G, 50A)
Most Points, Rookie, Season	87	Steve Yzerman (1983-84; 39G, 48A)
Most Shutouts, Season	12	Terry Sawchuk (1951-52), (1953-54), (1954-55) Glenn Hall (1955-56)
Most Goals, Game	6	Syd Howe (Feb. 3/44)
Most Assists, Game	*7	Billy Taylor (Mar. 16/47)
Most Points, Game	7	Carl Liscombe (Nov. 5/42; 3G, 4A), Don Grosso (Feb. 3/44; 1G, 6A), Billy Taylor (Mar. 16/47; 7A)

* NHL Record.

Retired Numbers

1	Terry Sawchuk	1949-55, 57-64, 1968-69
7	Ted Lindsay	1944-57, 64-65
9	Gordie Howe	1946-1971
10	Alex Delvecchio	1951-1973
12	Sid Abel	1938-43, 45-52
19	Steve Yzerman	1983-2006

All-time Record vs. Other Clubs

Regular Season

	At Home								On Road								Total							
	GP	W	L	T	OL	GF	GA	PTS	GP	W	L	T	OL	GF	GA	PTS	GP	W	L	T	OL	GF	GA	PTS
Anaheim	34	28	3	3	0	123	71	59	34	15	13	4	2	91	87	36	68	43	16	7	2	214	158	95
Atlanta	7	5	2	0	0	23	18	10	6	4	2	0	0	32	22	8	13	9	4	0	0	55	40	18
Boston	288	156	80	52	0	961	728	364	290	92	154	43	1	771	1013	228	578	248	234	95	1	1732	1741	592
Buffalo	58	34	18	5	1	211	165	74	56	14	34	8	0	166	237	36	114	48	52	13	1	377	402	110
Calgary	71	39	21	10	1	262	213	89	72	27	39	6	0	208	254	60	143	66	60	16	1	470	467	149
Carolina	33	19	7	7	0	127	89	45	33	13	19	1	0	91	111	27	66	32	26	8	0	218	200	72
Chicago	356	215	104	33	4	1218	890	467	359	146	157	51	5	1019	1076	348	715	361	261	84	9	2237	1966	815
Colorado	52	31	16	1	4	185	152	67	54	26	23	4	1	180	178	57	106	57	39	5	5	365	330	124
Columbus	31	24	5	0	2	111	76	50	32	21	6	1	4	99	61	47	63	45	11	1	6	210	137	97
Dallas	118	59	41	16	2	443	370	136	118	42	55	18	3	352	400	105	236	101	96	34	5	795	770	241
Edmonton	56	33	16	3	4	216	174	73	56	20	20	10	6	195	207	56	112	53	36	13	10	411	381	129
Florida	10	5	1	3	1	36	25	14	12	8	1	2	1	36	25	19	22	13	2	5	2	72	50	33
Los Angeles	91	44	34	13	0	346	306	101	92	33	43	14	2	290	346	82	183	77	77	27	2	636	652	183
Minnesota	20	14	3	1	2	78	46	31	20	13	3	2	2	58	47	30	40	27	6	3	4	136	93	61
Montreal	283	132	98	53	0	812	722	317	284	69	172	43	0	643	997	181	567	201	270	96	0	1455	1719	498
Nashville	38	25	6	2	5	137	89	57	37	18	15	2	2	99	103	40	75	43	21	4	7	236	192	97
New Jersey	43	28	13	2	0	175	133	58	43	12	21	9	1	112	144	34	86	40	34	11	1	287	277	92
NY Islanders	48	26	19	2	1	169	143	55	48	20	24	4	0	141	173	44	96	46	43	6	1	310	316	99
NY Rangers	288	167	76	45	0	1016	708	379	286	94	134	58	0	745	872	246	574	261	210	103	0	1761	1580	625
Ottawa	11	7	4	0	0	39	23	14	13	8	4	1	0	41	38	17	24	15	8	1	0	80	61	31
Philadelphia	62	33	19	10	0	221	190	76	60	13	36	11	0	172	240	37	122	46	55	21	0	393	430	113
Phoenix	63	33	21	8	1	242	206	75	61	27	18	14	2	200	178	70	124	60	39	22	3	442	384	145
Pittsburgh	69	42	13	12	2	269	192	98	69	19	45	4	1	202	287	43	138	61	58	16	3	471	479	141
St. Louis	131	64	47	17	3	474	392	148	131	48	59	20	4	380	423	120	262	112	106	37	7	854	815	268
San Jose	37	29	6	1	1	141	69	60	38	20	15	3	0	144	132	43	75	49	21	4	1	285	201	103
Tampa Bay	14	12	1	1	0	54	23	25	17	12	4	1	0	77	51	25	31	24	5	2	0	131	74	50
Toronto	325	170	107	46	2	979	798	388	318	105	165	47	1	849	1053	258	643	275	272	93	3	1828	1851	646
Vancouver	78	47	20	8	3	310	226	105	77	33	33	10	1	246	273	77	155	80	53	18	4	556	499	182
Washington	50	24	15	11	0	171	142	59	49	21	23	5	0	155	178	47	99	45	38	16	0	326	320	106
Defunct Clubs	141	76	40	25	0	430	307	177	141	49	63	29	0	364	375	127	282	125	103	54	0	794	682	304
Totals	**2906**	**1621**	**856**	**390**	**39**	**9979**	**7686**	**3671**	**2906**	**1042**	**1400**	**425**	**39**	**8158**	**9581**	**2548**	**5812**	**2663**	**2256**	**815**	**78**	**18137**	**17267**	**6219**

Playoffs

	Series	W	L	GP	W	L	T	GF	GA	Last Mtg.	Rnd.	Result
Anaheim	5	3	2	25	14	11	0	75	57	2009	CSF	W 4-3
Boston	7	3	4	33	14	19	0	98	96	1957	SF	L 1-4
Calgary	3	2	1	14	8	6	0	38	26	2007	CQF	W 4-2
Carolina	1	1	0	5	4	1	0	14	7	2002	F	W 4-1
Chicago	15	7	8	74	35	39	0	209	220	2009	CF	W 4-1
Colorado	6	3	3	34	17	17	0	97	88	2008	CSF	W 4-0
Columbus	1	1	0	4	4	0	0	18	7	2009	CQF	W 4-0
Dallas	4	4	0	24	16	8	0	72	50	2008	CF	W 4-2
Edmonton	3	0	3	16	4	12	0	43	58	2006	CQF	L 2-4
Los Angeles	2	1	1	10	6	4	0	32	21	2001	CQF	L 2-4
Montreal	12	7	5	62	29	33	0	149	161	1978	QF	L 1-4
Nashville	2	2	0	12	8	4	0	29	21	2008	CQF	W 4-2
New Jersey	1	0	1	4	0	4	0	7	16	1995	F	L 0-4
NY Rangers	5	4	1	23	13	10	0	57	49	1950	F	W 4-3
Philadelphia	1	1	0	4	4	0	0	16	6	1997	F	W 4-0
Phoenix	4	4	0	23	16	7	0	88	56	2011	CQF	W 4-0
Pittsburgh	2	1	1	13	7	6	0	34	24	2009	F	L 3-4
St. Louis	7	5	2	40	24	16	0	125	103	2002	CSF	W 4-1
San Jose	5	2	3	29	15	14	0	99	69	2011	CSF	L 3-4
Toronto	23	11	12	117	59	58	0	321	311	1993	DSF	L 3-4
Vancouver	1	1	0	6	4	2	0	22	16	2002	CQF	W 4-2
Washington	1	1	0	4	4	0	0	13	7	1998	F	W 4-0
Defunct Clubs	4	3	1	10	7	2	1	21	13			
Totals	**115**	**67**	**48**	**586**	**312**	**273**	**1**	**1677**	**1482**			

Calgary totals include Atlanta Flames, 1972-73 to 1979-80. Carolina totals include Hartford, 1979-80 to 1996-97.
Colorado totals include Quebec, 1979-80 to 1994-95. Dallas totals include Minnesota North Stars, 1967-68 to 1992-93.
New Jersey totals include Kansas City, 1974-75, 1975-76, and Colorado Rockies, 1976-77 to 1981-82.
Phoenix totals include Winnipeg, 1979-80 to 1995-96.

Playoff Results 2011-2007

Year	Round	Opponent	Result	GF	GA
2011	CSF	San Jose	L 3-4	18	18
	CQF	Phoenix	W 4-0	18	10
2010	CSF	San Jose	L 1-4	17	15
	CQF	Phoenix	W 4-3	26	18
2009	F	Pittsburgh	L 3-4	17	14
	CF	Chicago	W 4-1	19	10
	CSF	Anaheim	W 4-3	22	17
	CQF	Columbus	W 4-0	18	7
2008	**F**	**Pittsburgh**	**W 4-2**	**17**	**10**
	CF	Dallas	W 4-2	17	10
	CSF	Colorado	W 4-0	21	9
	CQF	Nashville	W 4-2	17	12
2007	CF	Anaheim	L 2-4	17	16
	CSF	San Jose	W 4-2	13	9
	CQF	Calgary	W 4-2	18	10

Abbreviations: Round: F - Final; **CF** - conference final; **CSF** - conference semi-final; **CQF** - conference quarter-final; **DSF** - division semi-final; **SF** - semi-final; **QF** - quarter-final.

2010-11 Results

Oct.	8	Anaheim	4-0
	9	at Chicago	3-2
	12	Colorado	4-5†
	14	at Dallas	1-4
	16	at Phoenix	2-1*
	21	Calgary	4-2
	23	Anaheim	5-4
	28	Phoenix	2-4
	30	Nashville	5-2
Nov.	3	at Calgary	2-1
	5	at Edmonton	3-1
	6	at Vancouver	4-6
	8	Phoenix	3-2*
	11	Edmonton	6-2
	13	Colorado	3-1
	17	St. Louis	7-3
	19	Minnesota	3-4*
	21	Calgary	5-4*
	24	at Atlanta	1-5
	26	at Columbus	2-1
	28	Columbus	4-2
	30	at San Jose	5-3
Dec.	3	at Anaheim	4-0
	4	at Los Angeles	2-3*
	6	San Jose	2-5
	8	Nashville	2-3
	10	Montreal	4-2
	11	at New Jersey	4-1
	13	Los Angeles	0-5
	15	St. Louis	5-2
	17	at Chicago	1-4
	19	Dallas	3-4*
	22	Vancouver	5-4*
	23	at St. Louis	3-4
	26	at Minnesota	4-1
	27	at Colorado	4-3*
	29	at Dallas	7-3
	31	NY Islanders	3-4*
Jan.	2	Philadelphia	2-3
	4	at Edmonton	5-3
	7	at Calgary	5-4†
	8	at Vancouver	2-1†
	10	at Colorado	4-5
	14	at Columbus	2-3†
	15	Columbus	6-5*
	18	at Pittsburgh	1-4
	20	at St. Louis	4-3*
	22	Chicago	1-4
	26	New Jersey	3-1
Feb.	2	at Ottawa	7-5
	4	Columbus	0-3
	5	at Nashville	0-3
	7	NY Rangers	3-2
	9	Nashville	1-4
	11	at Boston	6-1
	13	Boston	4-2
	17	at Tampa Bay	6-2
	18	at Florida	4-3
	20	at Minnesota	2-1†
	22	San Jose	3-4
	24	Dallas	1-4
	26	at Buffalo	3-2†
	28	at Los Angeles	7-4
Mar.	2	at Anaheim	1-2*
	3	at San Jose	1-3
	5	at Phoenix	4-5†
	9	Los Angeles	1-2
	11	Edmonton	2-1*
	12	at St. Louis	5-3
	16	Washington	3-2
	17	at Columbus	2-0
	19	at Nashville	1-3
	21	Pittsburgh	4-5†
	23	Vancouver	1-2
	26	Toronto	4-2
	28	Chicago	2-3*
	30	St. Louis	3-10
Apr.	2	at Nashville	4-3*
	3	Minnesota	4-2
	6	at Carolina	0-3
	8	Chicago	2-4
	10	at Chicago	4-3

* – Overtime † – Shootout

Entry Draft Selections 2011-1997

Name in bold denotes played in NHL.

2011 Pick		2006 Pick		2002 Pick		1998 Pick	
35	Tomas Jurco	41	**Cory Emmerton**	58	**Jiri Hudler**	25	**Jiri Fischer**
48	Xavier Ouellet	47	**Shawn Matthias**	63	**Tomas Fleischmann**	55	**Ryan Barnes**
55	Ryan Sproul	62	Dick Axelsson	95	**Valtteri Filppula**	56	Tomek Valtonen
85	Alan Quine	92	Daniel Larsson	131	Johan Berggren	84	Jake McCracken
115	Marek Tvrdon	182	**Jan Mursak**	166	Logan Koopmans	111	Brent Hobday
145	Philippe Hudon	191	Nick Oslund	197	Jimmy Cuddihy	142	Calle Steen
146	Mattias Backman	212	Logan Pyett	229	**Derek Meech**	151	Adam DeLeeuw
175	Richard Nedomlel			260	Pierre-Olivier Beaulieu	171	**Pavel Datsyuk**
205	Alexei Marchenko	**2005** Pick		262	Christian Soderstrom	198	Jeremy Goetzinger
		19	**Jakub Kindl**	291	**Jonathan Ericsson**	226	David Petrasek
2010 Pick		42	**Justin Abdelkader**			256	Petja Pietilainen
21	Riley Sheahan	80	Christofer Lofberg	**2001** Pick			
51	Calle Jarnkrok	103	**Mattias Ritola**	62	Igor Grigorenko	**1997** Pick	
81	Louis-Marc Aubry	132	**Darren Helm**	121	**Drew MacIntyre**	49	**Yuri Butsayev**
111	Teemu Pulkkinen	137	Johan Ryno	129	Miroslav Blatak	76	**Petr Sykora**
141	Petr Mrazek	151	Jeff May	157	Andreas Jamtin	102	**Quintin Laing**
171	Brooks Macek	175	Juho Mielonen	195	Nick Pannoni	129	John Wikstrom
201	Ben Marshall	214	Bretton Stamler	258	**Dmitri Bykov**	157	**B.J. Young**
				288	Francois Senez	186	Mike Laceby
2009 Pick		**2004** Pick				213	Steve Willejto
32	Landon Ferraro	97	**Johan Franzen**	**2000** Pick		239	Greg Willers
60	**Tomas Tatar**	128	Evan McGrath	29	**Niklas Kronwall**		
75	Andrej Nestrasil	151	Sergei Kolosov	38	**Tomas Kopecky**		
90	Gleason Fournier	162	Tyler Haskins	102	Stefan Liv		
150	Nick Jensen	192	Anton Axelsson	127	Dmitri Semenov		
180	Mitchell Callahan	226	Steven Covington	128	Alexander Seluyanov		
210	Adam Almqvist	257	Gennady Stolyarov	130	Aaron Van Leusen		
		290	Nils Backstrom	187	Per Backer		
2008 Pick				196	Paul Ballantyne		
30	**Thomas McCollum**	**2003** Pick		228	Jimmie Svensson		
91	Max Nicastro	64	**Jimmy Howard**	251	Todd Jackson		
121	Gustav Nyquist	132	**Kyle Quincey**	260	Yevgeny Bumagin		
151	Julien Cayer	164	Ryan Oulahen				
181	Stephen Johnston	170	Andreas Sundin	**1999** Pick			
211	Jesper Samuelsson	194	Stefan Blom	120	Jari Tolsa		
		226	Tomas Kollar	149	Andrei Maximenko		
2007 Pick		258	Vladimir Kutny	181	**Kent McDonell**		
27	Brendan Smith	289	Mikael Johansson	210	**Henrik Zetterberg**		
88	Joakim Andersson			238	Anton Borodkin		
148	Randy Cameron			266	Ken Davis		
178	Zack Torquato						
208	Bryan Rufenach						

Ken Holland
Executive Vice President and General Manager
Born: Vernon, B.C., November 10, 1955.

Ken Holland has served in the Red Wings front office since 1985, and has been the club's general manager since July 18, 1997. He has established himself as one of the most innovative and aggressive GMs in the National Hockey League. Detroit's Stanley Cup victory in 2008 marked the team's third championship under his leadership. Holland began his tenure as the club's general manager after serving as assistant general manager for the previous three seasons.

Holland oversees all aspects of hockey operations including all matters relating to player personnel, development, contract negotiations and player movements, though he now takes a less prominent role in the NHL draft than he did during his seven years as the club's director of amateur scouting.

At the conclusion of his playing days as a goaltender, spending most of his pro career at the American Hockey League level, Holland began his off-ice career in 1985 as a western Canada scout followed by five years as an amateur scouting director before promotions led to his current position as general manager.

A native of Vernon, British Columbia, Holland played in the junior ranks for Medicine Hat (WHL) in 1974-75. He was Toronto's 13th pick (188th overall) in the 1975 draft but never saw action with the Maple Leafs. Holland twice signed with NHL teams as a free agent — in 1980 with Hartford and 1983 with Detroit. He spent most of his pro career with AHL clubs in Binghamton and Springfield, along with Adirondack, but did appear in four NHL games, making his debut with Hartford in 1980-81 and playing three contests for Detroit in 1983-84.

Club Directory

Joe Louis Arena

Detroit Red Wings
Joe Louis Arena
19 Steve Yzerman Drive
Detroit, MI 48226
Phone **313/394-7000**
FAX PR: 313/567-0296
Media Hotline: 313/396-7599
www.detroitredwings.com
Capacity: 20,066

Owner/Governor	Mike Ilitch
Owner/Secretary-Treasurer	Marian Ilitch
President and CEO, IlitchHoldings/ Alternate Governor Red Wings	Christopher Ilitch
Senior Vice President/Alternate Governor	Jim Devellano
Executive Vice President/General Manager	Ken Holland
Vice President/Assistant General Manager	Jim Nill
Assistant General Manager/HockeyAdmin.	Ryan Martin
Advisor to Hockey Operations	Chris Chelios
Special Assistant to the General Manager	Kris Draper
Alternate Governor Red Wings	Tom Wilson
Vice President Olympia Entertainment/ General Counsel Red Wings	Robert E. Carr
Head Coach	Mike Babcock
Assistant Coaches	Bill Peters, Jeff Blashill
Video Coach	Keith McKittrick
Goaltending Coach	Jim Bedard
Goaltending Development Coach	Chris Osgood
Director of Pro Scouting	Mark Howe
Pro Scouts	Glenn Merkosky, Bruce Haralson, Kirk Maltby
Director of Amateur Scouting	Joe McDonnell
Amateur Scouts	Mark Leach, Jeff Finley, Dave Kolb, Mario Marois, Marty Stein, Sam Lites
Director of EuropeanScouting	Hakan Andersson
European Scouts	Vladimir Havluj, Ari Vouri, Nikolai Vakourov
Director of Player Development	Jiri Fischer
Vice President of Finance	Paul MacDonald
Executive Assistant	Kathi Wyatt
General Accountant	Bridget Merritt
Administrative Assistant	Julie Dailey
Head Athletic Therapist	Piet Van Zant
Head Equipment Manager	Paul Boyer
Assistant Athletic Therapist	Russ Baumann
Assistant Equipment Managers	John Remejes, Adam Sheehan
Team Masseurs	Sergei Tchekmarev, Lynne Newman
Senior Director of Communications	John Hahn
Director, Detroit Red Wings Foundation	Anne Hayes
Media Relations Manager	Todd Beam
Public Relations Coordinator	Richard Bowness
Community Relations Coordinator	Christy Hammond
Medical Director	Dr. Donald Weaver
Team Physicians	Dr. Anthony Colucci, Dr. Doug Plagens
Team Dentists	Dr. Jeffrey Boogren, Dr. Randy Freij
Team Photographer	Dave Reginek
Radio Announcers, 97.1 The Ticket	Ken Kal, Paul Woods
Television Announcers, Fox Sports Detroit	Ken Daniels, Mickey Redmond

Coaching History
Art Duncan and Duke Keats, 1926-27; Jack Adams, 1927-28 to 1946-47; Tommy Ivan, 1947-48 to 1953-54; Jimmy Skinner, 1954-55 to 1956-57; Jimmy Skinner and Sid Abel, 1957-58; Sid Abel, 1958-59 to 1967-68; Bill Gadsby, 1968-69; Bill Gadsby and Sid Abel, 1969-70; Ned Harkness and Doug Barkley, 1970-71; Doug Barkley and Johnny Wilson, 1971-72; Johnny Wilson, 1972-73; Ted Garvin and Alex Delvecchio, 1973-74; Alex Delvecchio, 1974-75; Doug Barkley and Alex Delvecchio, 1975-76; Alex Delvecchio and Larry Wilson, 1976-77; Bobby Kromm, 1977-78, 1978-79; Bobby Kromm and Ted Lindsay, 1979-80; Ted Lindsay and Wayne Maxner, 1980-81; Wayne Maxner and Billy Dea, 1981-82; Nick Polano, 1982-83 to 1984-85; Harry Neale and Brad Park, 1985-86; Jacques Demers, 1986-87 to 1989-90; Bryan Murray, 1990-91 to 1992-93; Scotty Bowman, 1993-94 to 1997-98; Dave Lewis, Barry Smith (co-coaches) and Scotty Bowman, 1998-99; Scotty Bowman, 1999-2000 to 2001-02; Dave Lewis, 2002-03 to 2004-05; Mike Babcock, 2005-06 to date.

General Managers' History
Art Duncan, 1926-27; Jack Adams, 1927-28 to 1961-62; Sid Abel, 1962-63 to 1969-70; Sid Abel and Ned Harkness, 1970-71; Ned Harkness, 1971-72, 1972-73; Ned Harkness and Jimmy Skinner, 1973-74; Alex Delvecchio, 1974-75, 1975-76; Alex Delvecchio and Ted Lindsay, 1976-77; Ted Lindsay, 1977-78 to 1979-80; Jimmy Skinner, 1980-81, 1981-82; Jim Devellano, 1982-83 to 1989-90; Bryan Murray, 1990-91 to 1993-94; Jim Devellano (Senior Vice President/Hockey), 1994-95 to 1996-97; Ken Holland, 1997-98 to date.

Captains' History
Art Duncan, 1926-27; Reg Noble, 1927-28 to 1929-30; George Hay, 1930-31; Carson Cooper, 1931-32; Larry Aurie, 1932-33; Herbie Lewis, 1933-34; Ebbie Goodfellow, 1934-35; Doug Young, 1935-36 to 1937-38; Ebbie Goodfellow, 1938-39 to 1940-41; Ebbie Goodfellow and Syd Howe, 1941-42; Sid Abel, 1942-43; Mud Bruneteau, Flash Hollett, 1943-44; Flash Hollett, 1944-45; Flash Hollett and Sid Abel, 1945-46; Sid Abel, 1946-47 to 1951-52; Ted Lindsay, 1952-53 to 1955-56; Red Kelly, 1956-57, 1957-58; Gordie Howe, 1958-59 to 1961-62; Alex Delvecchio, 1962-63 to 1972-73; Alex Delvecchio, Nick Libett, Red Berenson, Gary Bergman, Ted Harris, Mickey Redmond and Larry Johnston, 1973-74; Marcel Dionne, 1974-75; Danny Grant and Terry Harper, 1975-76; Danny Grant and Dennis Polonich, 1976-77; Dan Maloney and Dennis Hextall, 1977-78; Dennis Hextall, Nick Libett and Paul Woods, 1978-79; Dale McCourt, 1979-80; Errol Thompson and Reed Larson, 1980-81; Reed Larson, 1981-82; Danny Gare, 1982-83 to 1985-86; Steve Yzerman, 1986-87 to 2005-06; Nicklas Lidstrom, 2006-07 to date.

Edmonton Oilers

Key Off-Season Signings/Acquisitions

2011

May 29 • Re-signed LW **Ryan Jones**.

June 24 • Selected C **Ryan Nugent-Hopkins** (Red Deer, WHL) with the first overall selection at the 2011 Entry Draft.

26 • Acquired LW **Ryan Smyth** from Los Angeles for C **Colin Fraser** and a 7th-round pick in the 2012 Entry Draft.

30 • Re-signed D **Ladislav Smid**.

July 1 • Acquired D **Andy Sutton** from Anaheim for D **Kurtis Foster**.

1 • Signed LW **Ben Eager**, LW **Darcy Hordichuk**, D **Cam Barker** and C **Eric Belanger**.

4 • Re-signed D **Theo Peckham**.

15 • Re-signed D **Taylor Chorney** and C **Ryan O'Mara**.

2010-11 Results: 25w-45L-3OTL-9SOL 62PTS.
Fifth, Northwest Division

Year-by-Year Record

Season	GP	Home W	L	T	OL	Road W	L	T	OL	Overall W	L	T	OL	GF	GA	Pts.	Finished	Playoff Result
2010-11	82	13	22	....	6	12	23	....	6	25	45	....	12	193	269	62	5th, Northwest Div.	Out of Playoffs
2009-10	82	18	19	....	4	9	28	....	4	27	47	....	8	214	284	62	5th, Northwest Div.	Out of Playoffs
2008-09	82	18	17	....	6	20	18	....	3	38	35	....	9	234	248	85	4th, Northwest Div.	Out of Playoffs
2007-08	82	23	17	....	1	18	18	....	5	41	35	....	6	235	251	88	4th, Northwest Div.	Out of Playoffs
2006-07	82	19	19	....	3	13	24	....	4	32	43	....	7	195	248	71	5th, Northwest Div.	Out of Playoffs
2005-06	82	20	15	....	6	21	13	....	7	41	28	....	13	256	251	95	3rd, Northwest Div.	Lost Final
2004-05	....	....	....	....	....	....	....	....	....	....	....	....	....	....	....	....		
2003-04	82	22	12	4	3	14	17	8	2	36	29	12	5	221	208	89	4th, Northwest Div.	Out of Playoffs
2002-03	82	20	12	5	4	16	14	6	5	36	26	11	9	231	230	92	4th, Northwest Div.	Lost Conf. Quarter-Final
2001-02	82	23	14	4	0	15	14	8	4	38	28	12	4	205	182	92	3rd, Northwest Div.	Out of Playoffs
2000-01	82	23	9	7	2	16	19	5	1	39	28	12	3	243	222	93	2nd, Northwest Div.	Lost Conf. Quarter-Final
1999-2000	82	18	11	9	3	14	15	7	5	32	26	16	8	226	212	88	2nd, Northwest Div.	Lost Conf. Quarter-Final
1998-99	82	17	19	5	....	16	18	7	....	33	37	12	....	230	226	78	2nd, Northwest Div.	Lost Conf. Quarter-Final
1997-98	82	20	16	5	....	15	21	5	....	35	37	10	....	215	224	80	3rd, Pacific Div.	Lost Conf. Semi-Final
1996-97	82	21	16	4	....	15	21	5	....	36	37	9	....	252	247	81	3rd, Pacific Div.	Lost Conf. Semi-Final
1995-96	82	15	21	5	....	15	23	3	....	30	44	8	....	240	304	68	5th, Pacific Div.	Out of Playoffs
1994-95	48	11	12	1	....	6	15	3	....	17	27	4	....	136	183	38	5th, Pacific Div.	Out of Playoffs
1993-94	84	17	22	3	....	8	23	11	....	25	45	14	....	261	305	64	6th, Pacific Div.	Out of Playoffs
1992-93	84	16	21	5	....	10	29	3	....	26	50	8	....	242	337	60	5th, Smythe Div.	Out of Playoffs
1991-92	80	22	13	5	....	14	21	5	....	36	34	10	....	295	297	82	3rd, Smythe Div.	Lost Conf. Championship
1990-91	80	22	15	3	....	15	22	3	....	37	37	6	....	272	272	80	3rd, Smythe Div.	Lost Conf. Championship
1989-90	**80**	**23**	**11**	**6**	....	**15**	**17**	**8**	....	**38**	**28**	**14**	....	**315**	**283**	**90**	**2nd, Smythe Div.**	**Won Stanley Cup**
1988-89	80	21	16	3	....	17	18	5	....	38	34	8	....	325	306	84	3rd, Smythe Div.	Lost Div. Semi-Final
1987-88	**80**	**28**	**8**	**4**	....	**16**	**17**	**7**	....	**44**	**25**	**11**	....	**363**	**288**	**99**	**2nd, Smythe Div.**	**Won Stanley Cup**
1986-87	**80**	**29**	**6**	**5**	....	**21**	**18**	**1**	....	**50**	**24**	**6**	....	**372**	**284**	**106**	**1st, Smythe Div.**	**Won Stanley Cup**
1985-86	80	32	6	2	....	24	11	5	....	56	17	7	....	426	310	119	1st, Smythe Div.	Lost Div. Final
1984-85	**80**	**26**	**7**	**7**	....	**23**	**13**	**4**	....	**49**	**20**	**11**	....	**401**	**298**	**109**	**1st, Smythe Div.**	**Won Stanley Cup**
1983-84	**80**	**31**	**5**	**4**	....	**26**	**13**	**1**	....	**57**	**18**	**5**	....	**446**	**314**	**119**	**1st, Smythe Div.**	**Won Stanley Cup**
1982-83	80	25	9	6	....	22	12	6	....	47	21	12	....	424	315	106	1st, Smythe Div.	Lost Final
1981-82	80	31	5	4	....	17	12	11	....	48	17	15	....	417	295	111	1st, Smythe Div.	Lost Div. Semi-Final
1980-81	80	17	13	10	....	12	22	6	....	29	35	16	....	328	327	74	4th, Smythe Div.	Lost Quarter-Final
1979-80	80	17	14	9	....	11	25	4	....	28	39	13	....	301	322	69	4th, Smythe Div.	Lost Prelim. Round

2011-12 Schedule

Oct.	Sun.	9	Pittsburgh
	Thu.	13	at Minnesota
	Sat.	15	Vancouver
	Mon.	17	Nashville
	Tue.	18	at Calgary
	Thu.	20	Minnesota
	Sat.	22	NY Rangers
	Tue.	25	Vancouver
	Thu.	27	Washington
	Fri.	28	at Colorado
	Sun.	30	St. Louis
Nov.	Thu.	3	at Los Angeles
	Sat.	5	at Phoenix
	Tue.	8	at Montreal
	Thu.	10	at Boston
	Fri.	11	at Detroit
	Sun.	13	at Chicago
	Thu.	17	Ottawa
	Sat.	19	Chicago
	Mon.	21	at Dallas
	Tue.	22	at Nashville
	Fri.	25	at Minnesota*
	Sat.	26	at Colorado*
	Mon.	28	Nashville
	Wed.	30	Minnesota
Dec.	Fri.	2	Columbus
	Sat.	3	Calgary
	Wed.	7	Carolina
	Fri.	9	Colorado
	Sat.	10	at Calgary
	Thu.	15	at Phoenix
	Sat.	17	at San Jose
	Mon.	19	Detroit
	Thu.	22	Minnesota
	Mon.	26	at Vancouver
	Thu.	29	at Minnesota
	Sat.	31	at NY Islanders*
Jan.	Mon.	2	at Chicago
	Tue.	3	at Buffalo
	Thu.	5	at St. Louis
	Sat.	7	at Dallas*

	Wed.	11	New Jersey
	Fri.	13	Anaheim
	Sun.	15	Los Angeles
	Tue.	17	at Columbus
	Thu.	19	at St. Louis
	Sat.	21	Calgary
	Mon.	23	San Jose
	Tue.	24	at Vancouver
	Tue.	31	Colorado
Feb.	Thu.	2	Chicago
	Sat.	4	Detroit
	Mon.	6	at Toronto
	Wed.	8	at Detroit
	Sat.	11	at Ottawa
	Wed.	15	Toronto
	Fri.	17	Colorado
	Sun.	19	Vancouver
	Tue.	21	at Calgary
	Thu.	23	Philadelphia
	Sat.	25	Phoenix*
	Mon.	27	at Winnipeg
	Wed.	29	St. Louis
Mar.	Fri.	2	Dallas
	Mon.	5	at Anaheim
	Tue.	6	at San Jose
	Thu.	8	Montreal
	Sat.	10	at Colorado*
	Mon.	12	San Jose
	Wed.	14	Columbus
	Fri.	16	Calgary
	Sun.	18	Phoenix
	Tue.	20	at Nashville
	Thu.	22	at Tampa Bay
	Fri.	23	at Florida
	Sun.	25	at Columbus*
	Wed.	28	Dallas
	Fri.	30	Los Angeles
Apr.	Sun.	1	at Anaheim*
	Mon.	2	at Los Angeles
	Thu.	5	Anaheim
	Sat.	7	at Vancouver

Denotes afternoon game.

Jordan Eberle (left) and Taylor Hall share a laugh during a pregame warm-up. The two young teammates enjoyed fine rookie seasons in 2010-11 with Eberle leading the Oilers with 43 points in just 69 games while Hall topped the team with 22 goals in only 65 games.

NORTHWEST DIVISION
33rd NHL Season

Franchise date: June 22, 1979

2011-12 Player Personnel

FORWARDS	HT	WT	S	Place of Birth	*Age	2010-11 Club
BELANGER, Eric	5-11	185	L	Sherbrooke, Que.	33	Phoenix
BRULE, Gilbert	5-11	186	R	Edmonton, Alta.	24	Edmonton
EAGER, Ben	6-2	235	L	Ottawa, Ont.	27	Atlanta-San Jose
EBERLE, Jordan	6-0	185	R	Regina, Sask.	21	Edmonton
GAGNER, Sam	5-11	191	R	London, Ont.	22	Edmonton
GREEN, Josh	6-4	225	L	Camrose, Alta.	33	Anaheim-Syracuse
HALL, Taylor	6-1	194	L	Calgary, Alta.	19	Edmonton
HARTIKAINEN, Teemu	6-1	215	L	Kuopio, Finland	21	Edmonton-Oklahoma City
HEMSKY, Ales	6-0	184	R	Pardubice, Czech.	28	Edmonton
HORCOFF, Shawn	6-1	208	L	Trail, B.C.	33	Edmonton
HORDICHUK, Darcy	6-1	211	L	Kamsack, Sask.	31	Florida
JONES, Ryan	6-0	205	L	Chatham, Ont.	27	Edmonton
NUGENT-HOPKINS, Ryan	6-0	171	L	Burnaby, B.C.	18	Red Deer
OMARK, Linus	5-10	174	L	Overtornea, Sweden	24	Edmonton-Oklahoma City
O'MARRA, Ryan	6-2	220	R	Tokyo, Japan	24	Edmonton-Oklahoma City
PAAJARVI, Magnus	6-3	200	L	Norrkoping, Sweden	20	Edmonton
SMYTH, Ryan	6-2	192	L	Banff, Alta.	35	Los Angeles

DEFENSEMEN						
BARKER, Cam	6-3	215	L	Winnipeg, Man.	25	Minnesota
CHORNEY, Taylor	6-0	193	L	Thunder Bay, Ont.	24	Edmonton-Oklahoma City
GILBERT, Tom	6-3	206	R	Bloomington, MN	28	Edmonton
PECKHAM, Theo	6-2	234	L	Richmond Hill, Ont.	23	Edmonton
PETRY, Jeff	6-3	196	R	Ann Arbor, MI	23	Edmonton-Oklahoma City
SMID, Ladislav	6-3	226	L	Frydlant V Cechach, Czech.	25	Edmonton
SUTTON, Andy	6-6	245	L	Kingston, Ont.	36	Anaheim
WHITNEY, Ryan	6-3	210	L	Boston, MA	28	Edmonton

GOALTENDERS	HT	WT	C	Place of Birth	*Age	2010-11 Club
DUBNYK, Devan	6-6	202	L	Regina, Sask.	25	Edmonton
KHABIBULIN, Nikolai	6-1	206	L	Sverdlovsk, USSR	38	Edmonton

* – Age at start of 2011-12 season

Coaching History

Glen Sather, 1979-80; Bryan Watson and Glen Sather, 1980-81; Glen Sather, 1981-82 to 1988-89; John Muckler, 1989-90, 1990-91; Ted Green, 1991-92, 1992-93; Ted Green and Glen Sather, 1993-94; George Burnett and Ron Low, 1994-95; Ron Low, 1995-96 to 1998-99; Kevin Lowe, 1999-2000; Craig MacTavish, 2000-01 to 2008-09; Pat Quinn, 2009-10; Tom Renney, 2010-11 to date.

Tom Renney
Head Coach

Born: Cranbrook, B.C., March 1, 1955.

General manager Steve Tambellini announced that Tom Renney had become the tenth head coach in franchise history on June 22, 2010. Renney had joined the Oilers on May 26, 2009 as an associate coach for the 2009-10 season.

Prior to joining the Oilers, Renney had spent five seasons as head coach of the New York Rangers. His tenure with the Rangers organization began as director of player personnel before being promoted to vice-president of player development in 2002. Renney was appointed head coach with 20 games left in the 2003-04 season. He led the Rangers into the postseason in each of his first three campaigns following the 2004-05 NHL lockout. The team's three consecutive 40-win seasons were a feat last accomplished in 1974.

Renney began his coaching career in 1990-91 with the Western Hockey League's Kamloops Blazers. He guided the Blazers to consecutive President's Cup championships as WHL champions and was named WHL coach of the year in 1990-91. He captured a Memorial Cup title in 1992.

Following his junior coaching career, Renney joined Hockey Canada in 1992, where he began coaching the Canadian national team. He guided Canada to a silver medal at the 1994 Winter Olympics in Lillehammer, Norway. Renney continued to represent his country, working on Team Canada's coaching staff at the 2004 (gold) and 2005 (silver) World Championships. In total, Tom Renney has coached in a range of capacities in 10 World Championships, capturing two gold, four silver and one bronze medal.

Coaching Record

Season	Team	League	GC	Regular Season W	L	O/T	GC	Playoffs W	L	T
1990-91	Kamloops	WHL	72	50	20	2	12	5	7	....
1991-92	Kamloops	WHL	72	51	17	4	17	12	5	....
1991-92	Kamloops	M-Cup	....	....	....	....	5	4	1	....
1993-94*	Canada	Exhib	63	33	26	4	8	5	2	....
1994-95**	Canada	Exhib	57	37	17	3	8	3	2	....
1995-96***	Canada	Exhib	53	33	12	8	8	4	2	2
1996-97	Vancouver	NHL	82	35	40	7	....	....	....	....
1997-98	Vancouver	NHL	19	4	13	2	....	....	....	....
99-2000	Canada	Exhib	56	27	23	6	....	....	....	....
2003-04	NY Rangers	NHL	20	5	11	4	....	....	....	....
2004-05	NY Rangers				SEASON CANCELLED					
2005-06	NY Rangers	NHL	82	44	26	12	4	0	4	....
2006-07	NY Rangers	NHL	82	42	30	10	10	6	4	....
2007-08	NY Rangers	NHL	82	42	27	13	10	5	5	....
2008-09	NY Rangers	NHL	61	31	23	7	....	....	....	....
2010-11	Edmonton	NHL	82	25	45	12	....	....	....	....
	NHL Totals		510	228	215	67	24	11	13	....

* Olympics (silver medal)
** World Championship (bronze)
*** World Championship (silver)

2010-11 Scoring
* – rookie

Regular Season

Pos	#	Player	Team	GP	G	A	Pts	TOI	+/–	PIM	PP	SH	GW	S	%
C	14	* Jordan Eberle	EDM	69	18	25	43	17:40	-12	22	4	2	5	158	11.4
L	4	* Taylor Hall	EDM	65	22	20	42	18:12	-9	27	8	0	4	186	11.8
C	89	Sam Gagner	EDM	68	15	27	42	17:44	-17	37	3	1	2	138	10.9
R	83	Ales Hemsky	EDM	47	14	28	42	18:16	3	18	1	1	1	100	14.0
C	13	Andrew Cogliano	EDM	82	11	24	35	17:15	-12	64	0	1	3	129	8.5
L	91	* Magnus Paajarvi	EDM	80	15	19	34	15:23	-13	16	3	0	0	180	8.3
C	10	Shawn Horcoff	EDM	47	9	18	27	18:41	-1	46	5	0	1	78	11.5
L	23	* Linus Omark	EDM	51	5	22	27	15:21	-16	26	1	0	0	76	6.6
D	6	Ryan Whitney	EDM	35	2	25	27	25:20	13	33	0	0	0	43	4.7
D	77	Tom Gilbert	EDM	79	6	20	26	24:30	-14	32	3	0	0	106	5.7
L	28	Ryan Jones	EDM	81	18	7	25	13:50	-5	34	2	1	2	126	14.3
D	26	Kurtis Foster	EDM	74	8	14	22	17:39	-12	45	5	0	0	182	4.4
D	2	Jim Vandermeer	EDM	62	2	12	14	18:12	-15	74	0	0	0	57	3.5
D	49	Theo Peckham	EDM	71	3	10	13	18:35	-5	198	0	0	0	41	7.3
L	85	Liam Reddox	EDM	44	1	9	10	14:59	-8	20	0	0	0	85	1.2
D	5	Ladislav Smid	EDM	80	0	10	10	20:16	-10	85	0	0	0	48	0.0
C	67	Gilbert Brule	EDM	41	7	2	9	13:47	-7	41	1	0	1	72	9.7
L	22	Jean-Francois Jacques	EDM	51	4	1	5	7:04	-6	63	0	0	0	28	14.3
C	56	* Teemu Hartikainen	EDM	12	3	2	5	17:24	-3	4	1	0	0	21	14.3
C	16	Colin Fraser	EDM	67	3	2	5	10:16	-2	60	0	1	0	57	5.3
C	42	Ryan O'Marra	EDM	21	1	4	5	11:01	-2	13	0	0	0	13	7.7
D	58	* Jeff Petry	EDM	35	1	4	5	20:22	-12	10	0	0	0	41	2.4
D	41	Taylor Chorney	EDM	12	1	3	4	15:59	-5	4	0	0	0	13	7.7
R	46	Zack Stortini	EDM	32	0	4	4	7:05	-2	76	0	0	0	16	0.0
L	12	Alexandre Giroux	EDM	8	1	1	2	14:45	-2	2	0	0	0	13	7.7
C	54	* Chris Vande Velde	EDM	12	0	2	2	17:16	-6	12	0	0	0	16	0.0
D	43	Jason Strudwick	EDM	43	0	2	2	15:03	-16	23	0	0	0	9	0.0
L	33	Steve MacIntyre	EDM	34	0	1	1	3:32	-1	93	0	0	0	6	0.0
D	37	Richard Petiot	EDM	2	0	0	0	13:05	1	2	0	0	0	1	0.0
D	48	* Alex Plante	EDM	3	0	0	0	15:03	-2	11	0	0	0	5	0.0

Goaltending

No.	Goaltender	GPI	Mins	Avg	W	L	OT	EN	SO	GA	SA	S%	G	A	PIM
29	Martin Gerber	3	185	1.30	3	0	0	0	0	4	95	.958	0	1	0
40	* Devan Dubnyk	35	2061	2.71	12	13	8	4	2	93	1103	.916	0	0	2
35	Nikolai Khabibulin	47	2701	3.40	10	32	4	6	2	153	1389	.890	0	0	12
	Totals	82	4990	3.13	25	45	12	10	4	260	2597	.900			

Magnus Paajarvi made his NHL debut in 2010-11 and was one of just five rookies in the league to play as many as 80 games.

Club Records

Team

(Figures in brackets for season records are games played; records for fewest points, wins, ties, losses, goals, goals against are for 70 or more games)

Most Points	**119**	1983-84 (80), 1985-86 (80)
Most Wins	**57**	1983-84 (80)
Most Ties	**16**	1980-81 (80), 1999-2000 (82)
Most Losses	**50**	1992-93 (84)
Most Goals	***446**	1983-84 (80)
Most Goals Against	**337**	1992-93 (84)
Fewest Points	**60**	1992-93 (84)
Fewest Wins	**25**	1993-94 (84)
Fewest Ties	**5**	1983-84 (80)
Fewest Losses	**17**	1981-82 (80), 1985-86 (80)
Fewest Goals	**195**	2006-07 (82)
Fewest Goals Against	**182**	2001-02 (82)
Longest Winning Streak		
Overall	**9**	Feb. 20-Mar. 13/01
Home	**8**	Jan. 19-Feb. 22/85, Feb. 24-Apr. 2/86
Away	**8**	Dec. 9/86-Jan. 17/87
Longest Undefeated Streak		
Overall	**15**	Oct. 11-Nov. 9/84 (12 wins, 3 ties)
Home	**14**	Nov. 15/89-Jan. 6/90 (11 wins, 3 ties)
Away	**9**	Jan. 17-Mar. 2/82 (6 wins, 3 ties), Nov. 23/82-Jan. 18/83 (7 wins, 2 ties)
Longest Losing Streak		
Overall	**13**	Dec. 31/09-Jan. 30/10
Home	**9**	Oct. 16-Nov. 24/93
Away	**11**	Dec. 23/09-Feb. 10/10
Longest Winless Streak		
Overall	**14**	Oct. 11-Nov. 7/93 (13 losses, 1 tie)
Home	**9**	Oct. 16-Nov. 24/93 (9 losses)
Away	**11**	Dec. 18/01-Feb. 8/02 (7 losses, 4 ties), Dec. 23/09-Feb. 10/10 (11 loses)
Most Shutouts, Season	**8**	1997-98 (82); 2000-01 (82); 2001-02 (82)
Most PIM, Season	**2,173**	1987-88 (80)
Most Goals, Game	**13**	Nov. 19/83 (N.J. 4 at Edm. 13), Nov. 8/85 (Van. 0 at Edm. 13)

Individual

Most Seasons	**15**	Kevin Lowe
Most Games	**1,037**	Kevin Lowe
Most Goals, Career	**583**	Wayne Gretzky
Most Assists, Career	**1,086**	Wayne Gretzky
Most Points, Career	**1,669**	Wayne Gretzky (583G, 1,086A)
Most PIM, Career	**1,747**	Kelly Buchberger
Most Shutouts, Career	**23**	Tommy Salo
Longest Consecutive Games Streak	**518**	Craig MacTavish (Oct. 12/86-Jan. 2/93)
Most Goals, Season	***92**	Wayne Gretzky (1981-82)
Most Assists, Season	***163**	Wayne Gretzky (1985-86)
Most Points, Season	***215**	Wayne Gretzky (1985-86; 52G, 163A)
Most PIM, Season	**286**	Steve Smith (1987-88)
Most Points, Defenseman, Season	**138**	Paul Coffey (1985-86; 48G, 90A)
Most Points, Center, Season	***215**	Wayne Gretzky (1985-86; 52G, 163A)
Most Points, Right Wing, Season	**135**	Jari Kurri (1984-85; 71G, 64A)
Most Points, Left Wing, Season	**106**	Mark Messier (1982-83; 48G, 58A)
Most Points, Rookie, Season	**75**	Jari Kurri (1980-81; 32G, 43A)
Most Shutouts, Season	**8**	Curtis Joseph (1997-98), Tommy Salo (2000-01)
Most Goals, Game	**5**	Wayne Gretzky (Feb. 18/81), (Dec. 30/81), (Dec. 15/84), (Dec. 6/87) Jari Kurri (Nov. 19/83) Pat Hughes (Feb. 3/84)
Most Assists, Game	***7**	Wayne Gretzky (Feb. 15/80), (Dec. 11/85), (Feb. 14/86)
Most Points, Game	**8**	Wayne Gretzky (Nov. 19/83; 3G, 5A), (Jan. 4/84; 4G, 4A) Paul Coffey (Mar. 14/86; 2G, 6A)

* NHL Record.

Captains' History

Ron Chipperfield, 1979-80; Blair MacDonald and Lee Fogolin, Jr., 1980-81; Lee Fogolin, Jr., 1981-82, 1982-83; Wayne Gretzky, 1983-84 to 1987-88; Mark Messier, 1988-89 to 1990-91; Kevin Lowe, 1991-92; Craig MacTavish, 1992-93, 1993-94; Shayne Corson, 1994-95; Kelly Buchberger, 1995-96 to 1998-99; Doug Weight, 1999-2000, 2000-01; Jason Smith, 2001-02 to 2006-07; Ethan Moreau, 2007-08 to 2009-10; Shawn Horcoff, 2010-11.

Retired Numbers

3	Al Hamilton	1972-1980
7	Paul Coffey	1980-1987
9	Glenn Anderson	1980-91, 1996
11	Mark Messier	1980-1991
17	Jari Kurri	1980-1990
31	Grant Fuhr	1981-1991
99	Wayne Gretzky	1979-1988

All-time Record vs. Other Clubs

Regular Season

	At Home								On Road								Total							
	GP	W	L	T	OL	GF	GA	PTS	GP	W	L	T	OL	GF	GA	PTS	GP	W	L	T	OL	GF	GA	PTS
Anaheim	37	21	13	0	3	89	88	45	38	16	20	2	0	102	109	34	75	37	33	2	3	191	197	79
Atlanta	7	4	1	1	1	27	19	10	5	3	2	0	0	14	8	6	12	7	3	1	1	41	27	10
Boston	32	11	16	3	2	104	106	27	32	6	22	3	1	80	131	16	64	17	38	6	3	184	237	43
Buffalo	32	21	8	3	0	125	91	45	32	13	11	7	1	114	114	34	64	34	19	10	1	239	205	79
Calgary	102	51	37	10	4	359	320	116	102	34	58	9	1	319	401	78	204	85	95	19	5	678	721	194
Carolina	33	21	7	5	0	128	95	47	32	12	13	7	0	104	127	31	65	33	20	12	0	232	222	78
Chicago	57	27	25	5	0	195	186	59	56	21	28	7	0	186	208	49	113	48	53	12	0	381	394	108
Colorado	67	34	24	4	5	251	216	77	68	29	32	4	3	233	247	65	135	63	56	8	8	484	463	142
Columbus	20	15	4	0	1	71	47	31	20	9	5	3	3	66	53	24	40	24	9	3	4	137	100	55
Dallas	56	25	18	8	5	213	183	63	57	17	31	7	2	155	205	43	113	42	49	15	7	368	388	106
Detroit	56	26	19	10	1	207	195	63	56	20	30	3	3	174	216	46	112	46	49	13	4	381	411	109
Florida	10	6	3	1	0	31	21	13	11	4	5	2	0	31	29	10	21	10	8	3	0	62	50	23
Los Angeles	89	43	31	15	0	376	310	101	89	41	31	15	2	351	336	99	178	84	62	30	2	727	646	200
Minnesota	32	15	13	3	1	77	77	34	31	10	16	1	4	62	92	25	63	25	29	4	5	139	169	59
Montreal	39	22	17	0	0	136	121	44	34	11	16	4	3	108	120	29	73	33	33	4	3	244	241	73
Nashville	24	10	11	0	3	64	75	23	25	9	12	3	1	75	70	22	49	19	23	3	4	139	145	45
New Jersey	33	15	11	6	1	139	117	37	36	17	13	3	3	118	118	40	69	32	24	9	4	257	235	77
NY Islanders	32	19	8	5	0	116	90	43	33	7	16	9	1	113	134	24	65	26	24	14	1	229	224	67
NY Rangers	30	13	14	3	0	106	100	29	33	15	10	6	2	122	127	38	63	28	24	9	2	228	227	67
Ottawa	15	7	6	2	0	48	42	16	14	6	4	2	2	38	32	16	29	13	10	4	2	86	74	32
Philadelphia	30	16	8	6	0	104	86	38	34	11	21	2	0	94	138	24	64	27	29	8	0	198	224	62
Phoenix	84	53	22	6	3	363	267	115	83	43	30	5	5	347	324	96	167	96	52	11	8	710	591	211
Pittsburgh	32	22	9	1	0	152	105	45	33	13	16	3	1	135	128	30	65	35	25	4	1	287	233	75
St. Louis	56	28	22	4	2	191	182	62	56	22	26	7	1	189	194	52	112	50	48	11	3	380	376	114
San Jose	45	24	13	7	1	142	110	56	44	17	20	5	2	127	145	41	89	41	33	12	3	269	255	97
Tampa Bay	13	9	4	0	0	36	30	18	13	7	4	2	0	41	37	16	26	16	8	2	0	77	67	34
Toronto	47	24	16	6	1	186	151	55	41	17	22	2	0	170	165	36	88	41	38	8	1	356	316	91
Vancouver	102	60	31	7	4	409	314	131	103	46	41	12	4	373	365	108	205	106	72	19	8	782	679	239
Washington	31	16	11	4	0	126	95	36	32	10	19	2	1	102	130	23	63	26	30	6	1	228	225	59
Totals	**1243**	**658**	**422**	**125**	**38**	**4571**	**3839**	**1479**	**1243**	**486**	**574**	**137**	**46**	**4143**	**4503**	**1155**	**2486**	**1144**	**996**	**262**	**84**	**8714**	**8342**	**2634**

Playoffs

	Series	W	L	GP	W	L	T	GF	GA	Last Mtg.	Rnd.	Result
Anaheim	1	1	0	5	4	1	0	16	13	2006	CF	W 4-1
Boston	2	2	0	9	8	1	0	41	20	1990	F	W 4-1
Calgary	5	4	1	30	19	11	0	132	96	1991	DSF	W 4-3
Carolina	1	0	1	7	3	4	0	16	19	2006	F	L 3-4
Chicago	4	3	1	20	12	8	0	102	77	1992	CF	L 0-4
Colorado	2	1	1	12	5	7	0	30	35	1998	CQF	W 4-3
Dallas	8	2	6	42	15	27	0	104	118	2003	CQF	L 2-4
Detroit	3	3	0	16	12	4	0	58	43	2006	CQF	W 4-2
Los Angeles	7	5	2	36	24	12	0	154	127	1992	DSF	W 4-2
Montreal	1	1	0	3	3	0	0	15	6	1981	PRE	W 3-0
NY Islanders	3	1	2	15	6	9	0	47	58	1984	F	W 4-1
Philadelphia	3	2	1	15	8	7	0	49	44	1987	F	W 4-3
Phoenix	6	6	0	26	22	4	0	120	75	1990	DSF	W 4-3
San Jose	1	1	0	6	4	2	0	19	12	2006	CSF	W 4-2
Vancouver	2	2	0	9	7	2	0	35	20	1992	DF	W 4-2
Totals	**49**	**34**	**15**	**251**	**152**	**99**	**0**	**938**	**763**			

Calgary totals include Atlanta Flames, 1979-80.
Colorado totals include Quebec, 1979-80 to 1994-95.
New Jersey totals include Colorado Rockies, 1979-80 to 1981-82.
Carolina totals include Hartford, 1979-80 to 1996-97.
Dallas totals include Minnesota North Stars, 1979-80 to 1992-93.
Phoenix totals include Winnipeg, 1979-80 to 1995-96.

Playoff Results 2011-2007

(Last playoff appearance: 2006)

Abbreviations: Round: F - Final;
CF - conference final; **CSF** - conference semi-final;
CQF - conference quarter-final; **DF** - division final;
DSF - division semi-final; **PRE** - preliminary round.

2010-11 Results

Oct.	7	Calgary	4-0		13	at San Jose	5-2
	10	Florida	3-2		15	at Los Angeles	2-5
	14	at Minnesota	2-4		16	at Anaheim	2-3
	16	at Calgary	3-5		18	Minnesota	1-4
	21	Minnesota	2-4		20	Dallas	2-4
	23	San Jose	1-6		23	Nashville	2-3†
	26	at Calgary	4-5†		25	at Phoenix	4-3
	28	at Columbus	2-3†		26	at Dallas	1-3
	29	at Chicago	7-4	**Feb.**	2	Los Angeles	1-3
Nov.	2	Vancouver	3-4		4	at St. Louis	3-5
	5	Detroit	1-3		5	at Columbus	3-4
	7	at Chicago	2-1		7	at Nashville	4-0
	9	at Carolina	1-7		9	Chicago	1-4
	11	at Detroit	2-6		12	Ottawa	3-5
	12	at New Jersey	3-4*		13	Anaheim	0-4
	14	at NY Rangers	2-8		15	Dallas	4-1
	17	Chicago	0-5		17	Montreal	4-1
	19	Phoenix	3-4†		19	Atlanta	5-3
	21	at Anaheim	4-2		22	at Minnesota	1-4
	23	at Phoenix	0-5		23	at Colorado	5-1
	25	Colorado	3-2		25	St. Louis	0-5
	27	San Jose	3-4		27	Boston	2-3
	29	at Ottawa	4-1	**Mar.**	1	Nashville	2-1†
Dec.	1	at Montreal	4-3*		3	Columbus	4-2
	2	at Toronto	5-0		5	at Colorado	5-1
	4	St. Louis	2-1*		8	at Philadelphia	1-4
	7	Anaheim	2-3†		9	at Washington	0-5
	10	Tampa Bay	4-3†		11	at Detroit	1-2*
	12	Vancouver	1-2		13	at Pittsburgh	1-5
	14	Toronto	1-4		17	Phoenix	1-3
	16	Columbus	6-3		19	Colorado	2-3†
	21	at San Jose	1-2		22	at Nashville	1-3
	23	at Los Angeles	2-3†		24	at St. Louis	0-4
	26	at Vancouver	2-3		26	Calgary	4-5†
	28	Buffalo	2-4		29	Los Angeles	0-2
	30	Colorado	3-4†		31	at Minnesota	2-4
Jan.	1	Calgary	1-2	**Apr.**	2	at Vancouver	4-1
	4	Detroit	3-5		5	Vancouver	2-0
	6	NY Islanders	2-1		6	at Calgary	1-6
	7	at Vancouver	1-6		8	Minnesota	1-3
	11	at Dallas	2-3		10	at Colorado	3-4*

* – Overtime † – Shootout

Entry Draft Selections 2011-1997

Name in bold denotes played in NHL.

2011

Pick	
1	Ryan Nugent-Hopkins
19	Oscar Klefbom
31	David Musil
62	Samu Perhonen
74	Travis Ewanyk
92	Dillon Simpson
114	Tobias Rieder
122	Martin Gernat
182	Frans Tuohimaa

2010

Pick	
1	**Taylor Hall**
31	Tyler Pitlick
46	Martin Marincin
48	Curtis Hamilton
61	Ryan Martindale
91	Jeremie Blain
121	Tyler Bunz
162	Brandon Davidson
166	Drew Czerwonka
181	Kristians Pelss
202	Kellen Jones

2009

Pick	
10	**Magnus Paajarvi**
40	Anton Lander
71	Troy Hesketh
82	Cameron Abney
99	Kyle Bigos
101	Toni Rajala
133	Olivier Roy

2008

Pick	
22	**Jordan Eberle**
103	**Johan Motin**
133	Philippe Cornet
163	**Teemu Hartikainen**
193	Jordan Bendfeld

2007

Pick	
6	**Sam Gagner**
15	**Alex Plante**
21	Riley Nash
97	**Linus Omark**
127	Milan Kytnar
157	William Quist

2006

Pick	
45	**Jeff Petry**
75	**Theo Peckham**
133	Bryan Pitton
140	Cody Wild
170	Alexander Bumagin

2005

Pick	
25	**Andrew Cogliano**
36	**Taylor Chorney**
81	**Danny Syvret**
86	Robby Dee
97	**Chris Vande Velde**
120	Viacheslav Trukhno
157	Fredrik Pettersson
220	Matthew Glasser

2004

Pick	
14	**Devan Dubnyk**
25	**Rob Schremp**
44	Roman Tesliuk
57	Geoff Paukovich
112	**Liam Reddox**
146	**Bryan Young**
177	Max Gordichuk
208	Stephane Goulet
242	Tyler Spurgeon
274	Bjorn Bjurling

2003

Pick	
22	**Marc Pouliot**
51	**Colin McDonald**
68	**Jean-Francois Jacques**
72	Mikhail Zhukov
94	**Zack Stortini**
147	Kalle Olsson
154	David Rohlfs
184	Dragan Umicevic
214	**Kyle Brodziak**
215	**Mathieu Roy**
248	Josef Hrabal
278	**Troy Bodie**

2002

Pick	
15	Jesse Niinimaki
31	**Jeff Deslauriers**
36	**Jarret Stoll**
44	**Matt Greene**
79	Brock Radunske
106	Ivan Koltsov
111	Jonas Almtorp
123	invalid pick
148	Glenn Fisher
181	**Mikko Luoma**
205	J.F. Dufort
211	Patrick Murphy
244	**Dwight Helminen**
245	Tomas Micka
274	Fredrik Johansson

2001

Pick	
13	**Ales Hemsky**
43	**Doug Lynch**
52	Ed Caron
84	Kenny Smith
133	**Jussi Markkanen**
154	Jake Brenk
185	Mikael Svensk
215	Dan Baum
248	**Kari Haakana**
272	**Ales Pisa**
278	**Shay Stephenson**

2000

Pick	
17	**Alexei Mikhnov**
35	**Brad Winchester**
83	Alexander Liubimov
113	Lou Dickenson
152	Paul Flache
184	Shaun Norrie
211	Joe Cullen
215	**Matthew Lombardi**
247	Jason Platt
274	Yevgeny Muratov

1999

Pick	
13	**Jani Rita**
36	**Alexei Semenov**
41	**Tony Salmelainen**
81	**Adam Hauser**
91	**Mike Comrie**
139	Jonathan Fauteux
171	Chris Legg
199	Christian Chartier
256	Tamas Groschl

1998

Pick	
13	Michael Henrich
67	**Alex Henry**
99	**Shawn Horcoff**
113	Kristian Antila
128	Paul Elliott
144	Oleg Smirnov
159	Trevor Ettinger
186	**Mike Morrison**
213	Christian Lefebvre
241	Maxim Spiridonov

1997

Pick	
14	**Michel Riesen**
41	Patrick Dovigi
68	Sergei Yerkovich
94	Jonas Elofsson
121	**Jason Chimera**
141	**Peter Sarno**
176	Kevin Bolibruck
187	Chad Hinz
205	Chris Kerr
231	Alexander Fomichev

General Managers' History

Larry Gordon, 1979-80; Glen Sather, 1980-81 to 1999-2000; Kevin Lowe, 2000-01 to 2007-08; Steve Tambellini, 2008-09 to date.

Steve Tambellini

General Manager

Born: Trail, B.C., May 14, 1958.

Steve Tambellini joined the Edmonton Oilers as general manager on July 31, 2008 after 17 seasons as a member of the Vancouver Canucks management team. During his tenure with Vancouver, which began in 1990-91, Tambellini served in several positions. During his last three years with the club, he was vice president and assistant general manager. In that role, he was involved in all aspects of the team's hockey operations, including contract negotiations, scouting and minor league affiliates.

Tambellini took over in Edmonton from Kevin Lowe, who was promoted to the position of president of hockey operations. Tambellini and Lowe have previously worked together as members of Team Canada's management team, helping lead Canada to success on the international stage. As director of player personnel, Tambellini helped put together the roster that won the gold medal at the 2002 Winter Olympics in Salt Lake City and he was also a member of the management team for Team Canada's gold medal triumph at the 2004 World Cup of Hockey. He also served as the general manager of Team Canada at the 2003 and 2005 World Championships, winning gold in 2003 and silver in 2005.

Inducted into the B.C. Hockey Hall of Fame in 2004, Tambellini played 10 seasons in the NHL after being selected 15th overall in the 1978 NHL Amateur Draft by the New York Islanders. A member of the Islanders' 1980 Stanley Cup championship team, he played 553 career NHL games with five NHL teams between 1978-79 and 1987-88. He had 160 goals and 150 assists for 310 career points with 105 penalty minutes with the Islanders, Colorado Rockies, New Jersey Devils, Calgary Flames and Vancouver Canucks.

Besides his outstanding hockey resume, Tambellini has also been a contributor to the Canucks' off-ice activities. He served as the president of the Canucks for Kids Fund for 12 seasons and was awarded the B.C. Humanitarian of the Year Award by the B.C. Hockey Hall of Fame in 2006. He was also awarded the Jake Milford Plaque in 2004 for his significant and lasting contributions to hockey in his home province of British Columbia.

Club Directory

Rexall Place

Edmonton Oilers
11230 – 110 Street
Edmonton, Alberta T5G 3H7
Phone **780/414-GOAL(4625)**
Press Box 780/409-3780
Media Lounge 780/409-3778
FAX 780/409-5890
www.edmontonoilers.com
Capacity: 16,839

Owner & Governor	Daryl A. Katz (Rexall Sports Corp)
President, COO & Alternate Governor	Patrick LaForge
President of Hockey Ops & Alternate Governor	Kevin Lowe
Manager of Hockey Administration	Connie Hadden
Chief Revenue Officer	Stew MacDonald
Chief Marketing Officer	Steve Katzman
Chief Financial Officer	Darryl Boessenkool
Executive Assistants to the President / CFO	Lisa Nicolson / Bobbie-Jo Dawe
Security	Michael Fluker
Hockey Operations	
General Manager	Steve Tambellini
Asst. G.M & Dir. of Hockey Ops/Legal Affairs	Ricky Olczyk
Head Coach	Tom Renney
Associate Coach	Ralph Krueger
Assistant Coaches	Kelly Buchberger, Steve Smith
Goaltending Coach	Frederic Chabot
Video Coordinator	Myles Fee
Director of Player Development	Mike Sillinger
Coordinator of Player Development	Billy Moores
Skating & Skills Coach	Steve Serdachny
Performance / Fitness Consultants	Kimberley Amirault / Simon Bennett
Dir. of Research, Analysis & Software Development	Sean Draper
Manager of Scouting Information	James McGregor
Head Scouts, Amateur / Pro	Stu MacGregor / Morey Gare
Amateur Scouts	Bob Brown, Bill Dandy, Brad Davis, Kent Hawley, Scott Harlow, Frank Musil, Pelle Eklund, Robert Nordmark, James Crosson, Joseph Cucci, Matti Virmanen, Dave Heinz
Pro Scouts	Michael Abbamont, Dave Semenko, Chris Cichocki
Family Liaison	Jill Metz
Medical and Training Staff	
Head Athletic Therapist	T.D. Forss
Equipment Manager / Assistant Managers	Jeff Lang / Brad Harrison, Chris Hamelin
Assistant Medical Trainer	Chris Davie
Massage Therapist / Assistant Therapist	Steve Lines / Ryan Williams
Team Medical Chief of Staff	Dr. Dhiren Naidu
Medical Staff	Drs. John Clarke, Jeff Robinson, Ben Eastwood, Tony Sneazwell, David Magee, Brent Saik
Communications and Broadcast	
Vice President, Communications	Allan Watt
Director, Communications & Media Relations	J.J. Hebert
Director of Broadcast	Don Metz
Manager, Communications & Team Services	Patrick Garland
Coordinator, Communications & Media Relations	Rob Thomas
Finance and Administration	
Vice President, Business Operations & Development	Jason Quilley
Director, Human Resources	Tandy Kustiak
General Counsel	Keely Brown
Coordinator, Trademark & Licensing	Max Dawson
Vice President, Facility Operations	Tom Cornwall
Manager, Administration & Operations	Sherry Smith
Corporate Controller	Roger Dang
Controller / Assistant Controller	Zeshan Qureshi / Corinne Carey
Accounting	Christine Marceau, Jamie Schenknecht, Michelle Schwendeman, Linda Chong
Managers, Payroll	Shawna Quigley, Lanette Vermeersch
Manager, IT / Analysts	Kevin Flemming / Raphael Caluttung, Mike Heath
Director, Operations & Analysis / Business Analyst	Sharon Lyseng / Jason Lee
Sharepoint Architect	Kelvin Sun
Manager, Ticket Operations	Gavin Morton
Accounting Team Lead	Travis Nielsen
Coordinator, Facility Operations	Gilbert da Silva
Receptionists / Operations Assistant	Sandy Langley, Lynn Berglund / Macy Beley
Corporate Partnerships	
Vice President, Sales	Brad MacGregor
Sr. Directors, Corp. Partnerships	Lisa Munro, Scott Murray
Directors, Partnerships / Suites / Sales	Andrew Hore / Bob Haromy / Abe Hajar
Digital Media Sales	Jessica Butts
Partner Activation Specialists	Angie Zander, Aaron Berman, David Reynar, Kendra Morton, Stephen Rausch, Sara Ripko, Brent Frew, Ashley Johnson
Ticket Sales and Customer Relations	
Director, Ticket Sales and Customer Relationships	Bill Makris
Manager, Customer Relationships	Jody Young
Ticket Accounts, Sr. Exec. / Execs.	Erik Hapke / Cody Osborne, Graham Smith, Ryan Bellerose
Customer Experience Reps.	Angelina Mead, Raelene Dufva, Pierre Farage, Jack Pethybridge, Keenyn Bijou
Inside Sales Reps.	Daniel Troiani, Elizabeth Young, Derek Perchaluk, Natalie Butts
Supervisors, Ticket Services	Tony Bao and Dianne Kalita
Marketing	
Director, Brand Marketing & CRM	Christine McAnally
Director, Website & New Media	Marc Ciampa
Digital Media Producer / Reporter-Host	Nyki Scheuerman / Tom Gazzola
Coordinator, New Media Content	Ryan Dittrick
Sr. Mgr. Brand Integrity / Coord. Brand Mktg., CRM	Debbie George / Avery Grbavac
Director / Coord., Community Partnerships	Trevor Murphy / Dallas Fidierchuk
Director / Manager, Social Media	Jessica McPhee / Ryan Frankson
Lead Designer	Joey Angeles
Event Manager / Coordinators	Kevin Radomski / Jenni Daines, Brad Ellard
Game Night Director / Team Photographer	Ben Broder / Andy Devlin
Community	
Exec. Dir., Oilers Community Foundation	Natalie Minckler
Coordinators	Lindsay Gilbert, Dwain Tomkow, Diane Gurnham, Andrea Goss, Erin Barrett
Community Coordinator	Cheryl Thomas
Radio/TV Broadcasters	
Television Outlets	Sportsnet, CBXT TV and TSN
Radio Flagship Station	630 CHED (AM); Jack Michaels (play-by-play) & Bob Stauffer (color)

Florida Panthers

Key Off-Season Signings/Acquisitions

2011

Apr. 27 • Re-signed D **Keaton Ellerby**.
May 31 • Re-signed RW **Jack Skille**.
June 1 • Named **Kevin Dineen** head coach.
20 • Re-signed LW **Tim Kennedy**.
24 • Selected C **Jonathan Huberdeau** (Saint John, QMJHL) with the third overall pick in the 2011 Entry Draft.
25 • Acquired D **Brian Campbell** from Chicago for LW **Rostislav Olesz**.
27 • Acquired the rights to C **Tomas Kopecky** from Chicago for a conditional 7th-round pick in the 2012 Entry Draft.
29 • Signed C **Tomas Kopecky**.
July 1 • Signed LW **Scottie Upshall**, G **Jose Theodore**, D **Ed Jovanovski**, C **Marcel Goc**, RW **Tomas Fleischmann**, D **Nolan Yonkman** and LW **Sean Bergenheim**.
1 • Acquired RW **Kris Versteeg** from Philadelphia for a conditional 2nd-round pick in the 2012 or 2013 NHL Entry Draft and San Jose's 3rd-round pick in 2012 (previously acquired by Florida).
2 • Signed RW **Matt Bradley**.
6 • Re-signed C **Mike Santorelli**.
7 • Named **Craig Ramsay** assistant coach.
9 • Acquired C **Angelo Esposito** from Winnipeg for LW **Kenndal McArdle**.
9 • Re-signed C **Ryan Carter**.
15 • Signed 2010 1st-round pick (third overall), D **Erik Gudbranson**.

2010-11 Results: 30W-40L-5OTL-7SOL 72PTS.
Fifth, Southeast Division

Year-by-Year Record

Season	GP	Home W	L	T	OL	Road W	L	T	OL	Overall W	L	T	OL	GF	GA	Pts.	Finished	Playoff Result
2010-11	82	16	17	....	8	14	23	....	4	30	40	....	12	195	229	72	5th, Southeast Div.	Out of Playoffs
2009-10	82	16	16	....	9	16	21	....	4	32	37	....	13	208	244	77	5th, Southeast Div.	Out of Playoffs
2008-09	82	22	12	....	7	19	18	....	4	41	30	....	11	234	231	93	3rd, Southeast Div.	Out of Playoffs
2007-08	82	18	15	....	8	20	20	....	1	38	35	....	9	216	226	85	3rd, Southeast Div.	Out of Playoffs
2006-07	82	23	12	....	6	12	19	....	10	35	31	....	16	247	257	86	4th, Southeast Div.	Out of Playoffs
2005-06	82	25	11	....	5	12	23	....	6	37	34	....	11	240	257	85	4th, Southeast Div.	Out of Playoffs
2004-05																		
2003-04	82	16	15	7	3	12	20	8	1	28	35	15	4	188	221	75	4th, Southeast Div.	Out of Playoffs
2002-03	82	8	21	7	5	16	15	6	4	24	36	13	9	176	237	70	4th, Southeast Div.	Out of Playoffs
2001-02	82	11	23	3	4	11	21	7	2	22	44	10	6	180	250	60	4th, Southeast Div.	Out of Playoffs
2000-01	82	12	18	7	4	10	20	6	5	22	38	13	9	200	246	66	3rd, Southeast Div.	Out of Playoffs
1999-2000	82	26	9	4	2	17	18	2	4	43	27	6	6	244	209	98	2nd, Southeast Div.	Lost Conf. Quarter-Final
1998-99	82	17	17	7	....	13	17	11	....	30	34	18	....	210	228	78	2nd, Southeast Div.	Out of Playoffs
1997-98	82	11	24	6	....	13	19	9	....	24	43	15	....	203	256	63	6th, Atlantic Div.	Out of Playoffs
1996-97	82	21	12	8	....	14	16	11	....	35	28	19	....	221	201	89	3rd, Atlantic Div.	Lost Conf. Quarter-Final
1995-96	82	25	12	4	....	16	19	6	....	41	31	10	....	254	234	92	3rd, Atlantic Div.	Lost Final
1994-95	48	9	12	3	....	11	10	3	....	20	22	6	....	115	127	46	5th, Atlantic Div.	Out of Playoffs
1993-94	84	15	18	9	....	18	16	8	....	33	34	17	....	233	233	83	5th, Atlantic Div.	Out of Playoffs

2011-12 Schedule

Oct.			
Sat.	8	at NY Islanders	
Tue.	11	at Pittsburgh	
Sat.	15	Tampa Bay	
Mon.	17	at Tampa Bay	
Tue.	18	at Washington	
Thu.	20	Buffalo	
Sat.	22	NY Islanders	
Mon.	24	at Montreal	
Thu.	27	at Ottawa	
Sat.	29	at Buffalo	
Mon.	31	Winnipeg	
Nov. Thu.	3	Chicago	
Sun.	6	Tampa Bay*	
Tue.	8	at Toronto	
Thu.	10	at Winnipeg	
Sun.	13	Philadelphia*	
Tue.	15	at Dallas	
Thu.	17	at St. Louis	
Sat.	19	Pittsburgh	
Mon.	21	New Jersey	
Wed.	23	NY Rangers	
Fri.	25	Tampa Bay	
Sat.	26	at Tampa Bay	
Tue.	29	at Carolina	
Dec. Thu.	1	at Los Angeles	
Sat.	3	at San Jose	
Mon.	5	Washington	
Thu.	8	at Boston	
Fri.	9	at Buffalo	
Sun.	11	at NY Rangers	
Tue.	13	New Jersey	
Fri.	16	Calgary	
Sun.	18	Carolina*	
Tue.	20	Phoenix	
Thu.	22	at Ottawa	
Fri.	23	at Boston	
Tue.	27	Toronto	
Fri.	30	NY Rangers	
Sat.	31	Montreal	
Jan. Thu.	5	at NY Rangers	
Fri.	6	at New Jersey	
Mon.	9	Vancouver	
Fri.	13	Pittsburgh	
Mon.	16	Boston	
Wed.	18	at Colorado	
Fri.	20	at Chicago	
Sat.	21	at Winnipeg	
Tue.	24	Philadelphia	
Feb. Wed.	1	Washington	
Fri.	3	Winnipeg	
Sat.	4	at Tampa Bay	
Tue.	7	at Washington	
Thu.	9	Los Angeles	
Sat.	11	at New Jersey*	
Sun.	12	at NY Islanders*	
Wed.	15	Ottawa	
Fri.	17	Washington	
Sun.	19	Anaheim	
Thu.	23	Minnesota	
Sat.	25	at Carolina	
Sun.	26	Montreal*	
Tue.	28	at Toronto	
Mar. Thu.	1	at Winnipeg	
Sat.	3	Nashville	
Sun.	4	Ottawa	
Thu.	8	at Philadelphia	
Fri.	9	at Pittsburgh	
Sun.	11	Carolina*	
Tue.	13	Toronto	
Thu.	15	Boston	
Sat.	17	Buffalo	
Tue.	20	at Philadelphia	
Wed.	21	at Carolina	
Fri.	23	Edmonton	
Sun.	25	NY Islanders*	
Tue.	27	at Montreal	
Thu.	29	at Minnesota	
Fri.	30	at Columbus	
Apr. Sun.	1	at Detroit*	
Tue.	3	Winnipeg	
Thu.	5	at Washington	
Sat.	7	Carolina	

* Denotes afternoon game.

SOUTHEAST DIVISION
19th NHL Season

Franchise date: June 14, 1993

After missing 54 games in 2009-10, David Booth returned to play a full 82-game schedule in 2010-11. His 23 goals were tops on the team, as where his eight power-play goals.

2011-12 Player Personnel

FORWARDS	HT	WT	S	Place of Birth	*Age	2010-11 Club
BERGENHEIM, Sean	5-11	200	L	Helsinki, Finland	27	Tampa Bay
BOOTH, David	6-0	212	L	Detroit, MI	26	Florida
BRADLEY, Matt	6-3	201	R	Stittsville, Ont.	33	Washington
CARTER, Ryan	6-2	200	L	White Bear Lake, MN	28	Anaheim-Carolina-Florida
CULLEN, Mark	5-11	182	L	Moorhead, MN	32	Rochester
DADONOV, Evgeny	5-10	178	L	Chelyabinsk, USSR	22	Florida-Rochester
FLEISCHMANN, Tomas	6-1	192	L	Koprivnice, Czech.	27	Washington-Colorado
GOC, Marcel	6-1	202	L	Calw, West Germany	28	Nashville
HOWDEN, Quinton	6-3	183	L	Winnipeg, Man.	19	Moose Jaw
KEARNS, Bracken	6-0	195	R	Vancouver, B.C.	30	San Antonio
KENNEDY, Tim	5-10	173	L	Buffalo, NY	25	Connecticut-Fla-Roch
KOPECKY, Tomas	6-3	203	L	Ilava, Czech.	29	Chicago
MATTHIAS, Shawn	6-2	213	L	Mississauga, Ont.	23	Florida
REINPRECHT, Steve	6-0	195	L	Edmonton, Alta.	35	Florida-Mannheim
REPIK, Michal	5-10	180	L	Vlasim, Czech.	22	Florida-Rochester
SANTORELLI, Mike	6-0	189	R	Vancouver, B.C.	25	Florida
SKILLE, Jack	6-1	215	R	Madison, WI	24	Chicago-Florida
UPSHALL, Scottie	6-0	200	L	Fort McMurray, Alta.	27	Phoenix-Columbus
VERSTEEG, Kris	5-10	182	R	Lethbridge, Alta.	25	Toronto-Philadelphia
WEISS, Stephen	5-11	185	L	Toronto, Ont.	28	Florida

DEFENSEMEN						
CAMPBELL, Brian	6-0	189	L	Strathroy, Ont.	32	Chicago
ELLERBY, Keaton	6-4	186	L	Strathmore, Alta.	22	Florida-Rochester
GARRISON, Jason	6-2	220	L	White Rock, B.C.	26	Florida
GUDBRANSON, Erik	6-4	206	R	Ottawa, Ont.	19	Kingston
JOVANOVSKI, Ed	6-3	221	L	Windsor, Ont.	35	Phoenix
KULIKOV, Dmitry	6-1	183	L	Lipetsk, USSR	20	Florida
STRACHAN, Tyson	6-2	215	R	Melfort, Sask.	26	St. Louis-Peoria
WEAVER, Mike	5-9	186	R	Bramalea, Ont.	33	Florida
YONKMAN, Nolan	6-6	253	R	Punnichy, Sask.	30	Phoenix-San Antonio

GOALTENDERS	HT	WT	C	Place of Birth	*Age	2010-11 Club
CLEMMENSEN, Scott	6-3	205	L	Des Moines, IA	34	Florida
MARKSTROM, Jacob	6-3	178	L	Gavle, Sweden	21	Florida-Rochester
THEODORE, Jose	5-11	185	R	Laval, Que.	35	Minnesota

* – Age at start of 2011-12 season

2010-11 Scoring

* – rookie

Regular Season

Pos	#	Player	Team	GP	G	A	Pts	TOI	+/−	PIM	PP	SH	GW	S	%
C	9	Stephen Weiss	FLA	76	21	28	49	20:05	−9	49	3	2	1	172	12.2
C	13	Mike Santorelli	FLA	82	20	21	41	16:41	−17	20	5	1	1	193	10.4
L	10	David Booth	FLA	82	23	17	40	18:53	−31	26	8	0	3	280	8.2
L	14	Sergei Samsonov	CAR	58	10	16	26	14:09	0	12	4	0	0	87	11.5
			FLA	20	3	11	14	19:13	−2	2	0	0	1	36	8.3
			Total	78	13	27	40	15:27	−2	14	4	0	1	123	10.6
R	11	Niclas Bergfors	ATL	52	11	18	29	14:09	−11	6	3	0	1	99	11.1
			FLA	20	1	6	7	16:18	2	2	0	0	0	53	1.9
			Total	72	12	24	36	14:45	−9	8	3	0	1	152	7.9
C	19	Marty Reasoner	FLA	82	14	18	32	17:09	2	22	0	0	4	124	11.3
D	7	Dmitry Kulikov	FLA	72	6	20	26	19:57	−5	45	1	0	1	83	7.2
R	15	Jack Skille	CHI	49	7	10	17	10:44	3	25	1	0	1	121	5.8
			FLA	13	1	2	3	16:24	−12	4	0	0	0	33	3.0
			Total	62	8	11	19	11:55	−9	29	1	0	1	154	5.2
D	52	Jason Garrison	FLA	73	5	13	18	22:17	−2	26	0	0	3	116	4.3
R	63	* Evgeny Dadonov	FLA	36	8	9	17	14:15	0	14	1	0	0	60	13.3
L	85	Rostislav Olesz	FLA	44	6	11	17	13:52	−1	8	1	0	1	71	8.5
C	18	Shawn Matthias	FLA	51	6	10	16	11:50	0	16	0	0	0	90	6.7
R	26	Steve Bernier	FLA	68	5	10	15	13:01	−14	21	3	0	0	97	5.2
D	43	Mike Weaver	FLA	82	2	11	13	20:48	1	34	0	0	1	53	3.8
D	4	* Keaton Ellerby	FLA	54	2	10	12	16:05	−15	22	0	0	0	56	3.6
C	27	Steve Reinprecht	FLA	29	4	6	10	11:46	−2	6	1	0	1	31	12.9
C	20	Ryan Carter	ANA	18	1	2	3	10:44	−4	22	0	0	0	23	4.3
			CAR	32	0	3	3	8:18	0	22	0	0	0	26	0.0
			FLA	12	2	1	3	13:30	3	22	0	0	0	14	14.3
			Total	62	3	6	9	10:01	−1	66	0	0	0	63	4.8
R	32	* Michal Repik	FLA	31	2	6	8	12:47	−6	22	0	0	0	54	3.7
R	37	William Thomas	FLA	24	4	3	7	8:30	1	6	0	0	2	33	12.1
D	3	Clay Wilson	FLA	15	3	2	5	14:50	4	6	0	0	0	22	13.6
D	2	Alexander Sulzer	NSH	31	1	3	4	17:42	−5	14	0	0	0	30	3.3
			FLA	9	0	1	1	17:00	−3	0	0	0	0	7	0.0
			Total	40	1	4	5	17:32	−8	14	0	0	0	37	2.7
L	16	Darcy Hordichuk	FLA	64	1	4	5	5:04	−1	76	0	0	0	32	3.1
L	75	* Scott Timmins	FLA	19	1	0	1	10:49	−8	8	0	0	0	13	7.7
L	8	Tim Kennedy	FLA	6	0	1	1	10:22	0	0	0	0	0	2	0.0
L	34	Patrick Rissmiller	ATL	1	0	0	0	13:07	−1	0	0	0	0	2	0.0
			FLA	9	0	1	1	10:03	0	0	0	0	0	12	0.0
			Total	10	0	1	1	10:21	−1	0	0	0	0	14	0.0
D	48	Joe Callahan	FLA	27	0	1	1	15:52	−1	12	0	0	0	21	0.0
R	28	Hugh Jessiman	FLA	2	0	0	0	7:21	−1	5	0	0	0	2	0.0
R	6	* Mike Duco	FLA	2	0	0	0	8:33	−1	10	0	0	0	2	0.0
L	17	* Kenndal McArdle	FLA	11	0	0	0	9:56	−3	16	0	0	0	6	0.0

Goaltending

No.	Goaltender	GPI	Mins	Avg	W	L	OT	EN	SO	GA	SA	S%	G	A	PIM
29	Tomas Vokoun	57	3224	2.55	22	28	5	5	6	137	1753	.922	0	1	2
30	Scott Clemmensen	31	1696	2.62	8	11	7	3	1	74	833	.911	0	1	2
33	* Jacob Markstrom	1	40	3.00	0	1	0	1	0	2	14	.857	0	0	0
	Totals	82	5004	2.66	30	40	12	9	7	222	2609	.915			

Kevin Dineen
Head Coach
Born: Quebec City, Que., October 28, 1963.

Kevin Dineen was named to the position as the head coach of the Florida Panthers on June 1, 2011. Dineen had spent the previous six seasons as the head coach of the Portland Pirates (AHL), where he compiled a record of 266-155-59 with a .616 winning percentage, the best in the franchise's history. During this tenure with Portland, his teams won at least 40 games in four out of six seasons, won a pair of division titles (2005-06 and 2010-11) and advanced to the AHL's Eastern Conference Finals twice (2005-06 and 2007-08).

A third-round draft pick of the Hartford Whalers in the 1982 NHL Entry Draft, Dineen played in 1,188 career National Hockey League games with Hartford (1984 to 1991 and 1995 to 1997), Philadelphia (1991 to 1995), Carolina (1997 to 1999), Ottawa (1999-2000) and Columbus (2000 to 2003). Throughout his 19-year NHL playing career, he scored 355 goals with 405 assists and 2,229 penalty minutes. He also served as team captain while playing for Philadelphia, Hartford and Carolina. Dineen appeared in two NHL All-Star Games while playing for Hartford (1988 and 1989). He was named the 1990-91 NHL Man of the Year and was a three-time finalist for the Bill Masterton Memorial Trophy (1995, 2001 and 2002). After retiring as a player on November 5, 2002, Dineen spent two seasons working in the Columbus Blue Jackets hockey operations department.

As a coach for Portland in the AHL for six seasons, Dineen demonstrated the ability to develop young talent. He guided young stars like Corey Perry, Bobby Ryan, Ryan Getzlaf and Dustin Penner before they moved to the NHL with the Anaheim Ducks, then coached the three straight winners of the AHL Rookie of the Year award – Buffalo farmhands Nathan Gerbe, Tyler Ennis and Luke Adam.

Dineen comes from one of the most prominent hockey families. His father, Bill, was a two-time NHL All-Star with the Detroit Red Wings who later was head coach of the Flyers for a season and a half at the time Kevin played for Philadelphia. His brothers Gord and Peter also played in the NHL. Gord is currently an assistant with the Toronto Marlies of the AHL, while Peter is a scout for the Columbus Blue Jackets. Brothers Shawn and Jerry played minor league hockey – Shawn is now a professional scout with the Nashville Predators, where he worked with Panthers assistant general manager Mike Santos; Jerry is the video coach of the New York Rangers.

Coaching Record

Season	Team	League	Regular Season				Playoffs			
			GC	W	L	O/T	GC	W	L	T
2005-06	Portland	AHL	80	53	19	8	19	11	8	.....
2006-07	Portland	AHL	80	37	31	12	.....	.....	.....	.....
2007-08	Portland	AHL	80	45	26	9	18	11	7	.....
2008-09	Portland	AHL	80	39	31	10	5	1	4	.....
2009-10	Portland	AHL	80	45	24	11	4	0	4	.....
2010-11	Portland	AHL	80	47	24	9	12	6	6	.....

Coaching History

Roger Neilson, 1993-94, 1994-95; Doug MacLean, 1995-96, 1996-97; Doug MacLean and Bryan Murray, 1997-98; Terry Murray, 1998-99, 1999-2000; Terry Murray and Duane Sutter, 2000-01; Duane Sutter and Mike Keenan, 2001-02; Mike Keenan, 2002-03; Mike Keenan, Rick Dudley and John Torchetti, 2003-04; Jacques Martin, 2004-05 to 2007-08; Peter DeBoer, 2008-09 to 2010-11; Kevin Dineen, 2011-12.

General Managers' History

Bob Clarke, 1993-94; Bryan Murray, 1994-95 to 1999-2000; Bryan Murray and Bill Torrey, 2000-01; Bill Torrey and Chuck Fletcher, 2001-02; Rick Dudley, 2002-03, 2003-04; Mike Keenan, 2004-05, 2005-06; Jacques Martin, 2006-07 to 2008-09; Randy Sexton, 2009-10; Dale Tallon, 2010-11 to date.

Club Records

Team

(Figures in brackets for season records are games played; records for fewest points, wins, ties, losses, goals, goals against are for 70 or more games)

Most Points	98	1999-2000 (82)	
Most Wins	43	1999-2000 (82)	
Most Ties	19	1996-97 (82)	
Most Losses	44	2001-02 (82)	
Most Goals	254	1995-96 (82)	
Most Goals Against	257	2005-06 (82), 2006-07 (82)	
Fewest Points	60	2001-02 (82)	
Fewest Wins	22	2000-01 (82), 2001-02 (82)	
Fewest Ties	6	1999-2000 (82)	
Fewest Losses	27	1999-2000 (82)	
Fewest Goals	176	2002-03 (82)	
Fewest Goals Against	201	1996-97 (82)	

Longest Winning Streak

Overall...7 Nov. 2-14/95,
Mar. 17-29/06,
Mar. 2-16/08

Home...5 Nov. 5-14/95,
Mar. 17-Apr. 1/06,
Mar. 6-16/08,
Jan. 27-Feb. 13/09,
Jan. 16-31/10

Away...5 Nov. 30-Dec. 12/08

Longest Undefeated Streak

Overall...12 Oct. 5-30/96
(8 wins, 4 ties)

Home...8 Nov. 5-26/95
(7 wins, 1 tie)

Away...7 Dec. 7-29/93
(5 wins, 2 ties),
Oct. 5-29/96
(4 wins, 3 ties)

Longest Losing Streak

Overall...13 Feb. 7-Mar. 23/98
Home...6 Feb. 25-Mar. 23/98
Away...13 Oct. 27-Dec. 17/05

Longest Winless Streak

Overall...15 Feb. 1-Mar. 23/98
(14 losses, 1 tie)

Home...13 Feb. 5-Mar. 24/03
(11 losses, 2 ties)

Away...16 Jan. 2-Mar. 21/98
(12 losses, 4 ties)

Most Shutouts, Season...9 2008-09 (82)
Most PIM, Season...1,994 2001-02 (82)
Most Goals, Game...10 Nov. 26/97
(Bos. 5 at Fla. 10)

Individual

Most Seasons...9 Paul Laus,
Radek Dvorak

Most Games...613 Radek Dvorak
Most Goals, Career...188 Olli Jokinen
Most Assists, Career...231 Olli Jokinen
Most Points, Career...419 Olli Jokinen
(188G, 231A)

Most PIM, Career...1,702 Paul Laus
Most Shutouts, Career...26 Roberto Luongo

Longest Consecutive
Games Streak...376 Olli Jokinen
(Dec. 27/02-Apr. 5/08)

Most Goals, Season...59 Pavel Bure
(2000-01)

Most Assists, Season...53 Viktor Kozlov
(1999-2000)

Most Points, Season...94 Pavel Bure
(1999-2000; 58G, 36A)

Most PIM, Season...354 Peter Worrell
(2001-02)

Most Points, Defenseman,
Season...57 Robert Svehla
(1995-96; 8G, 49A)

Most Points, Center,
Season...91 Olli Jokinen
(2006-07; 39G, 52A)

Most Points, Right Wing,
Season...94 Pavel Bure
(1999-2000; 58G, 36A)

Most Points, Left Wing,
Season...71 Ray Whitney
(1999-2000; 29G, 42A)

Most Points, Rookie,
Season...50 Jesse Belanger
(1993-94; 17G, 33A)

Most Shutouts, Season...7 Roberto Luongo
(2003-04)
Tomas Vokoun
(2009-10)

Most Goals, Game...4 Mark Parrish
(Oct. 30/98)
Pavel Bure
(Jan. 1/00), (Feb. 10/01)

Most Assists, Game...4 Six times
Most Points, Game...6 Olli Jokinen
(Mar. 17/07; 2G, 4A)

Captains' History

Brian Skrudland, 1993-94 to 1996-97; Scott Mellanby, 1997-98 to 2000-01; Pavel Bure, 2001-02; no captain, 2002-03; Olli Jokinen, 2003-04 to 2007-08; no captain, 2008-09; Bryan McCabe, 2009-10, 2010-11.

All-time Record vs. Other Clubs

Regular Season

	At Home							On Road							Total						
	GP	W	L	T	OL	GF	GA	PTS	GP	W	L	T	OL	GF	GA	PTS	GP	W	L	T	OL	GF	GA	PTS
Anaheim	10	4	4	0		27	25	10	12	6	4	1	0	36	34	14	22	10	8	3	1	63	59	24
Atlanta	34	15	15	1	3	86	99	34	34	11	14	4	5	93	112	31	68	26	29	5	8	179	211	65
Boston	33	13	14	2	4	95	96	32	34	17	13	4	0	84	87	38	67	30	27	6	4	179	183	70
Buffalo	33	15	15	1	2	89	94	33	35	9	21	3	2	72	107	23	68	24	36	4	4	161	201	56
Calgary	11	3	4	2	2	23	26	10	11	5	4	1	1	30	28	12	22	8	8	3	3	53	54	22
Carolina	47	22	9	8	8	147	115	60	46	12	28	3	3	114	149	30	93	34	37	11	11	261	264	90
Chicago	12	4	7	1	0	25	43	9	13	5	6	2	0	37	42	12	25	9	13	3	0	62	85	21
Colorado	15	4	10	0	1	46	60	9	13	4	5	3	1	31	38	12	28	8	15	3	2	77	98	21
Columbus	6	2	1	0	3	16	18	7	5	2	2	0	1	11	12	5	11	4	3	0	4	27	30	12
Dallas	13	5	7	1	0	26	37	11	11	5	4	2	0	37	37	12	24	10	11	3	0	63	74	23
Detroit	12	2	6	2	2	25	36	8	10	2	5	3	0	25	36	7	22	4	11	5	2	50	72	15
Edmonton	11	5	2	2	2	29	31	14	10	3	6	1	0	21	31	7	21	8	8	3	2	50	62	21
Los Angeles	10	4	2	3	1	26	25	12	12	4	8	0	0	34	36	8	22	8	10	3	1	60	61	20
Minnesota	6	2	4	0	0	12	18	4	5	1	3	1	0	6	16	3	11	3	7	1	0	18	34	7
Montreal	34	16	13	3	2	95	91	37	33	14	11	3	5	74	86	36	67	30	24	6	7	169	177	73
Nashville	8	5	0	1	2	26	16	13	9	2	4	2	1	16	22	7	17	7	4	3	3	42	38	20
New Jersey	37	13	17	4	3	84	93	33	36	10	21	3	2	71	111	25	73	23	38	7	5	155	204	58
NY Islanders	37	20	10	6	1	118	105	47	37	16	14	2	5	99	97	39	74	36	24	8	6	217	202	86
NY Rangers	37	16	14	2	5	92	99	39	36	13	19	4	0	80	107	30	73	29	33	6	5	172	206	69
Ottawa	34	12	20	1	1	101	112	26	34	14	16	2	2	87	105	32	68	26	36	3	3	188	217	58
Philadelphia	36	11	21	1	3	89	120	26	37	15	15	6	1	96	98	37	73	26	36	7	4	185	218	63
Phoenix	10	4	5	0	1	31	27	9	13	5	4	1	1	37	36	14	23	9	9	3	2	68	63	23
Pittsburgh	34	18	13	1	2	100	85	39	35	12	14	3	6	98	107	33	69	30	27	4	8	198	192	72
St. Louis	12	4	5	2	1	26	26	11	12	3	8	1	0	17	29	7	24	7	13	3	1	43	55	18
San Jose	12	4	3	5	0	33	34	13	11	3	6	2	0	22	34	8	23	7	9	7	0	55	68	21
Tampa Bay	49	33	9	4	5	166	120	71	49	22	19	6	2	140	121	52	98	53	28	10	7	306	241	123
Toronto	29	11	11	5	2	83	80	29	27	9	13	2	3	76	85	23	56	20	24	7	5	159	165	52
Vancouver	10	4	4	1	1	25	33	10	12	1	6	3	2	26	36	8	22	5	9	4	3	51	69	18
Washington	49	22	19	4	4	128	132	52	49	19	23	5	2	125	151	45	98	41	42	9	6	253	283	97
Totals	**681**	**291**	**264**	**65**	**61**	**1869**	**1896**	**708**	**681**	**244**	**315**	**77**	**45**	**1695**	**1990**	**610**	**1362**	**535**	**579**	**142**	**106**	**3564**	**3886**	**1318**

Playoffs

	Series	W	L	GP	W	L	T	GF	GA	Last Mtg.	Rnd.	Result
Boston	1	1	0	5	4	1	0	22	16	1996	CQF	W 4-1
Colorado	1	0	1	4	0	4	0	4	15	1996	F	L 0-4
New Jersey	1	0	1	4	0	4	0	6	12	2000	CQF	L 0-4
NY Rangers	1	0	1	5	1	4	0	10	13	1997	CQF	L 1-4
Philadelphia	1	1	0	6	4	2	0	15	11	1996	CSF	W 4-2
Pittsburgh	1	1	0	7	4	3	0	20	15	1996	CF	W 4-3
Totals	**6**	**3**	**3**	**31**	**13**	**18**	**0**	**77**	**82**			

Colorado totals include Quebec, 1993-94 to 1994-95.
Phoenix totals include Winnipeg, 1993-94 to 1995-96.

Carolina totals include Hartford, 1993-94 to 1996-97.

Playoff Results 2011-2007

(Last playoff appearance: 2000)

Abbreviations: Round: F - Final;
CF - conference final; **CSF** - conference semi-final;
CQF - conference quarter-final.

2010-11 Results

Oct.	10	at Edmonton	2-3	13	Nashville	3-2
	11	at Vancouver	1-2	15	New Jersey	3-2*
	14	at Calgary	3-0	17	Atlanta	2-3†
	16	Tampa Bay	6-0	19	Columbus	2-3*
	21	Dallas	1-4	21	Tampa Bay	1-2†
	23	NY Islanders	4-3	23	at New Jersey	2-5
	26	at Toronto	1-3	25	at NY Rangers	4-3
	28	at Ottawa	3-5	26	at Boston	1-2
	30	at Montreal	3-1	**Feb.** 1	at Toronto	3-4†
Nov.	3	Atlanta	3-4	2	at Montreal	2-3
	5	Carolina	7-4	4	at New Jersey	4-3*
	6	at Carolina	2-3	8	St. Louis	1-2
	10	Toronto	4-1	10	Buffalo	2-3*
	12	Minnesota	2-1	13	San Jose	3-2
	13	at Philadelphia	2-5	16	Philadelphia	2-4
	17	at Atlanta	2-1	18	Detroit	3-4
	18	at Boston	0-4	19	at Tampa Bay	3-2†
	20	at NY Islanders	4-1	21	at NY Islanders	1-5
	22	Pittsburgh	2-3	23	at Ottawa	1-5
	24	Boston	1-3	25	at Atlanta	2-1†
	26	NY Rangers	0-3	27	New Jersey	1-2
	27	at Tampa Bay	4-3†	**Mar.** 1	at Carolina	1-2
Dec.	1	at Anaheim	3-5	3	Montreal	0-4
	2	at Los Angeles	2-3	5	at Atlanta	3-4*
	4	at Phoenix	2-1†	6	Washington	2-3*
	7	Colorado	4-3*	8	Chicago	3-2
	9	at Washington	3-0	10	Ottawa	1-2
	11	at Nashville	0-3	12	Tampa Bay	4-3*
	15	Carolina	3-4	15	Philadelphia	2-3
	17	Buffalo	6-2	17	Toronto	4-0
	20	at Philadelphia	5-0	19	NY Islanders	3-4†
	22	at Pittsburgh	2-5	22	at NY Rangers	0-1
	23	at Buffalo	4-3	23	at Chicago	0-4
	27	Boston	2-3†	25	at Buffalo	0-4
	31	Montreal	2-3*	27	at Pittsburgh	1-2†
Jan.	2	NY Rangers	3-0	29	at Columbus	2-3†
	3	at Carolina	4-3†	31	Ottawa	1-4
	5	Atlanta	2-3	**Apr.** 2	Pittsburgh	2-4
	7	Carolina	3-5	6	at Washington	2-5
	8	at Washington	2-3	8	at Tampa Bay	2-4
	11	Washington	4-3*	9	Washington	1-0

*– Overtime   †– Shootout

Entry Draft Selections 2011-1997

Name in bold denotes played in NHL.

2011
Pick
3	Jonathan Huberdeau
33	Rocco Grimaldi
59	Rasmus Bengtsson
64	Vincent Trocheck
76	Logan Shaw
87	Jonathan Racine
91	Kyle Rau
124	Yaroslav Kosov
154	Eddie Wittchow
184	Iiro Pakarinen

2010
Pick
3	Erik Gudbranson
19	Nick Bjugstad
25	Quinton Howden
33	John McFarland
36	Alex Petrovic
50	Connor Brickley
69	Joe Basaraba
92	Sam Brittain
93	Benjamin Gallacher
99	Joonas Donskoi
123	Zach Hyman
153	Corey Durocher
183	R.J. Boyd

2009
Pick
14	**Dmitry Kulikov**
44	Drew Shore
67	Josh Birkholz
107	Garrett Wilson
135	Corban Knight
138	Wade Megan
165	**Scott Timmins**

2008
Pick
31	**Jacob Markstrom**
46	Colby Robak
80	Adam Comrie
100	A.J. Jenks
190	**Matt Bartkowski**

2007
Pick
10	**Keaton Ellerby**
40	**Michal Repik**
71	**Evgeny Dadonov**
101	Matt Rust
131	John Lee
181	Corey Syvret
191	Ryan Watson
202	Sergei Gayduchenko

2006
Pick
10	**Michael Frolik**
73	Brady Calla
103	Michael Caruso
116	Derrick Lapoint
155	Peter Aston
193	Marc Cheverie

2005
Pick
20	**Kenndal McArdle**
32	Tyler Plante
90	Dan Collins
93	Olivier Legault
104	Matt Duffy
161	Brian Foster
164	Roman Derlyuk
224	Zach Bearson

2004
Pick
7	**Rostislav Olesz**
37	David Shantz
53	**David Booth**
105	Evan Schafer
152	Bret Nasby
267	Spencer Dillon
283	Luke Beaverson

2003
Pick
3	**Nathan Horton**
25	**Anthony Stewart**
38	Kamil Kreps
55	Stefan Meyer
105	**Martin Lojek**
124	James Pemberton
141	Dan Travis
162	Martin Tuma
171	Denis Stasyuk
223	Dany Roussin
234	Petr Kadlec
264	John Hecimovic
265	**Tanner Glass**

2002
Pick
3	**Jay Bouwmeester**
9	**Petr Taticek**
40	**Rob Globke**
67	**Gregory Campbell**
134	Topi Jaakola
158	Vince Bellissimo
169	Jeremy Swanson
196	Mikael Vuorio
200	Denis Yachmenev
232	Peter Hafner

2001
Pick
4	**Stephen Weiss**
24	**Lukas Krajicek**
34	Greg Watson
64	**Tomas Malec**
68	**Grant McNeill**
117	Mike Woodford
136	Billy Thompson
169	Dustin Johner
200	Toni Koivisto
231	Kyle Bruce
263	Jan Blanar
267	**Ivan Majesky**

2000
Pick
58	Vladimir Sapozhnikov
77	Robert Fried
82	Sean O'Connor
115	Chris Eade
120	Davis Parley
190	**Josh Olson**
234	**Janis Sprukts**
253	Mathew Sommerfeld

1999
Pick
12	**Denis Shvidki**
40	**Alex Auld**
70	**Niklas Hagman**
80	Jean-Francois Laniel
103	Morgan McCormick
109	Rod Sarich
169	Brad Woods
198	Travis Eagles
227	Jonathon Charron

1998
Pick
30	**Kyle Rossiter**
61	**Joe DiPenta**
63	**Lance Ward**
89	**Ryan Jardine**
117	**Jaroslav Spacek**
148	Chris Ovington
176	B.J. Ketcheson
203	Ian Jacobs
231	Adrian Wichser

1997
Pick
20	**Mike Brown**
47	**Kristian Huselius**
56	Vratislav Cech
74	**Nick Smith**
95	**Ivan Novoseltsev**
127	Pat Parthenais
155	Keith Delaney
183	Tyler Palmer
211	Doug Schueller
237	Benoit Cote

Club Directory

BankAtlantic Center

Florida Panthers
BankAtlantic Center
One Panther Parkway
Sunrise, FL 33323
Phone **954/835-7000**
FAX 954/835-7700
www.floridapanthers.com
Capacity: 17,040

Ownership
| General Partner/Chairman of the Board/ Chief Executive Officer/Governor | Cliff Viner |
| Partners | Alan Cohen, Steve Cohen, David Epstein, Dr. Elliott Hahn, H. Wayne Huizenga, Bernie Kosar, Richard C. Lehman, M.D., Albert E. Maroone, Michael E. Maroone, James L Nederlander, Stu Siegel, Jordan Zimmerman |

Executive
President/Chief Operating Officer	Michael R. Yormark
Exec. Vice President & G.M., Hockey Ops	Dale Tallon
Exec. Vice President, Chief Marketing Officer	Pedro Goncalves
Exec. Vice President, Finance/CFO	Lowell Heit
Senior Vice President, Human Resources	Carol Duncanson
Vice President, Event Marketing	Matt Bell
Vice President/G.M., Saveology.com Iceplex	Jeff Campol
Vice President, Corporate Development	R.J. Martino
Vice President, Sales and Services	Ryan McCoy
Vice President, Broadcasting & Panthers Alumni	Randy Moller
Vice President / G.M., BankAtlantic Center	Erik Waldman
Vice President, Business Affairs	Ed Wildermuth
Vice President, Marketing & Brand Strategy	Steve Ziff
Vice President, Communications and Public Affairs/Editor, Panthers Insider	Matthew F. Sacco
Executive Assistant to the President / COO / Director VIP Services	Heidi Leigh
Executive Assistant to the Chief Financial Officer	Cathy Stevenson

Hockey Operations
General Manager	Dale Tallon
Assistant General Manager	Mike Santos
Alternate Governor	William Torrey
Executive Assistant to the General Manager	Giselle Seoane
Team Services Manager	Mike Dixon
Director of Amateur Scouting	Scott Luce
Director of Player Development	Brian Skrudland
Pro Scout	Peter Mahovlich, Al Tuer
Amateur Scouts	Fred Bandel, Craig Demetrick, Paul Gallagher, Erin Ginnell, Al Tuer, Kent Nilsson, Vadim Podrezov, Jari Kekalainen, Mike Yandle

Coaching Staff
Head Coach	Kevin Dineen
Assistant Coaches	Gord Murphy, Craig Ramsay
Goaltending Coach	Robb Tallas
Strength & Conditioning Coach	Craig Slaunwhite
Video Coach	P.J. Deluca

Training Staff
Head Athletic Trainer	David Zenobi
Assistant Athletic Trainers	Steve Dischiavi, Tommy Alva
Head Equipment Manager	Chris Scoppetto
Equipment Manager	Chris Moody
Assistant Equipment Manager	Jason MacDonald

Communications and Media Content
| Director, Communications | Justin Copertino |
| Senior Manager, Websites & Social Media | Glenn Odebralski |

Broadcasting
Television	FS Florida
Play-By-Play	Steve Goldstein
Television Analyst	Bill Lindsay
Panthers Preview/Review Host	Allison Williams
Radio	560 WQAM
Radio Play-By-Play	Randy Moller

Dale Tallon
Executive Vice President and General Manager
Born: Noranda, Que., October 19, 1950.

Dale Tallon was named general manager of the Florida Panthers on May 17, 2010. After joining Florida, Tallon conducted a successful 2010 NHL Entry Draft that saw the club stockpile 13 picks, including three first-round selections (No. 3 - D Erik Gudbranson, No. 19 - C Nick Bjugstad and No. 25 - C Quinton Howden).

Prior to joining the Panthers, Tallon spent 33 years with the Blackhawks organization as a front office executive, player and broadcast personality. He served as Chicago's general manager from June of 2005 to July of 2009 after having served as assistant general manager from November of 2003 to June of 2005. Tallon was responsible for drafting or acquiring many of the players who led the Blackhawks to the Stanley Cup in 2010, including Jonathan Toews, Patrick Kane, Marian Hossa, Patrick Sharp, Kris Versteeg, John Madden and Brian Campbell.

As a player, Tallon was the Vancouver Canucks' first-round selection (second overall) in the 1970 NHL Draft. The Rouyn-Noranda, Quebec native played in 642 NHL contests with Vancouver (1970 to 1973), Chicago (1973 to 1978) and Pittsburgh (1978 to 1980) registering 336 points (98 goals, 238 assists) and 568 penalty minutes. Tallon recorded a career-high 17 goals in 69 games with Vancouver during the 1971-72 season and appeared in the 1971 and 1972 NHL All-Star Games. In 1972, Tallon was picked as an alternate for Team Canada for the Summit Series against the Soviet Union. After retiring following the 1979-80 season, Tallon served as a color analyst for Chicago radio and television broadcasts for 16 seasons.

Prior to joining the Panthers, Tallon spent the 2009-10 season serving as a senior advisor of hockey operations for the Blackhawks. He also served four years (1998 to 2002) as director of player personnel before returning to the radio and television booth prior to the 2002-03 season.

Los Angeles Kings

Key Off-Season Signings/Acquisitions

2011

June 23 • Acquired C **Mike Richards** from Philadelphia for RW **Wayne Simmonds**, C **Brayden Schenn** and a 2nd-round pick in the 2012 Entry Draft.

26 • Acquired C **Colin Fraser** and a 7th-round pick in the 2012 Entry Draft from Edmonton for LW **Ryan Smyth**.

July 2 • Signed LW **Simon Gagne**.

8 • Re-signed D **Alec Martinez**.

13 • Re-signed C **Brad Richardson**.

15 • Re-signed C **Trevor Lewis**.

2010-11 Results: 46w-30L-4OTL-2SOL 98PTS.
Fourth, Pacific Division

Kings captain Dustin Brown camps out in front of Ray Emery in the Ducks' net. Brown led Los Angeles with 28 goals in 2010-11 (the fourth straight season he's scored 24 or more) and continued to make significant contributions in the community off the ice.

2011-12 Schedule

Oct.	Fri.	7	NY Rangers†
	Sat.	8	Buffalo††
	Thu.	13	at New Jersey
	Sat.	15	at Philadelphia
	Tue.	18	St. Louis
	Thu.	20	at Phoenix
	Sat.	22	Dallas
	Tue.	25	New Jersey
	Thu.	27	at Dallas
	Sat.	29	at Phoenix
	Sun.	30	at Colorado
Nov.	Thu.	3	Edmonton
	Sat.	5	Pittsburgh
	Mon.	7	at San Jose
	Tue.	8	Nashville
	Thu.	10	Vancouver
	Sat.	12	Minnesota
	Wed.	16	Anaheim
	Thu.	17	at Anaheim
	Sat.	19	Detroit*
	Tue.	22	at St. Louis
	Wed.	23	at Dallas
	Sat.	26	Chicago
	Mon.	28	San Jose
Dec.	Thu.	1	Florida
	Sat.	3	Montreal*
	Tue.	6	at Anaheim
	Thu.	8	Minnesota
	Sat.	10	Dallas
	Tue.	13	at Boston
	Thu.	15	at Columbus
	Sat.	17	at Detroit
	Mon.	19	at Toronto
	Thu.	22	Anaheim
	Fri.	23	at San Jose
	Mon.	26	Phoenix
	Wed.	28	at Chicago
	Thu.	29	at Winnipeg
	Sat.	31	Vancouver
Jan.	Mon.	2	Colorado
	Thu.	5	Phoenix

	Sat.	7	Columbus*
	Mon.	9	Washington
	Thu.	12	Dallas
	Sat.	14	at Calgary
	Sun.	15	at Edmonton
	Tue.	17	at Vancouver
	Thu.	19	Calgary
	Sat.	21	Colorado
	Mon.	23	Ottawa
Feb.	Wed.	1	Columbus
	Fri.	3	at St. Louis
	Sat.	4	at Carolina
	Tue.	7	at Tampa Bay
	Thu.	9	at Florida
	Sat.	11	at NY Islanders*
	Sun.	12	at Dallas*
	Thu.	16	Phoenix
	Sat.	18	Calgary
	Tue.	21	at Phoenix
	Wed.	22	at Colorado
	Sat.	25	Chicago*
	Mon.	27	at Nashville
	Tue.	28	at Minnesota
Mar.	Sat.	3	Anaheim
	Tue.	6	at Nashville
	Thu.	8	at Columbus
	Fri.	9	at Detroit
	Sun.	11	at Chicago
	Tue.	13	at Detroit
	Fri.	16	at Anaheim
	Sat.	17	Nashville
	Tue.	20	San Jose
	Thu.	22	St. Louis
	Sat.	24	Boston
	Mon.	26	at Vancouver
	Wed.	28	at Calgary
	Fri.	30	at Edmonton
	Sat.	31	at Minnesota
Apr.	Mon.	2	Edmonton
	Thu.	5	San Jose
	Sat.	7	at San Jose

* Denotes afternoon game.   † Game played in Stockholm.
†† Game played in Berlin.

PACIFIC DIVISION
45th NHL Season

Franchise date: June 5, 1967

Year-by-Year Record

Season	GP	Home W	L	T	OL	Road W	L	T	OL	Overall W	L	T	OL	GF	GA	Pts.	Finished	Playoff Result
2010-11	82	25	13	....	3	21	17	....	3	46	30	....	6	219	198	98	4th, Pacific Div.	Lost Conf. Quarter-Final
2009-10	82	22	13	....	6	24	14	....	3	46	27	....	9	241	219	101	3rd, Pacific Div.	Lost Conf. Quarter-Final
2008-09	82	18	15	....	8	16	22	....	3	34	37	....	11	207	234	79	5th, Pacific Div.	Out of Playoffs
2007-08	82	17	21	....	3	15	22	....	4	32	43	....	7	231	266	71	5th, Pacific Div.	Out of Playoffs
2006-07	82	16	16	....	9	11	25	....	5	27	41	....	14	227	283	68	4th, Pacific Div.	Out of Playoffs
2005-06	82	26	14	....	1	16	21	....	4	42	35	....	5	249	270	89	4th, Pacific Div.	Out of Playoffs
2004-05	...	...	...	...	...	...	...	...	...	...	...	...	...	...	...	...		
2003-04	82	15	16	9	1	13	13	7	8	28	29	16	9	205	217	81	3rd, Pacific Div.	Out of Playoffs
2002-03	82	19	19	2	1	14	18	4	5	33	37	6	6	203	221	78	3rd, Pacific Div.	Out of Playoffs
2001-02	82	22	12	6	1	18	15	5	3	40	27	11	4	214	190	95	3rd, Pacific Div.	Lost Conf. Quarter-Final
2000-01	82	20	12	8	1	18	16	5	2	38	28	13	3	252	228	92	3rd, Pacific Div.	Lost Conf. Semi-Final
1999-2000	82	21	13	5	2	18	14	7	2	39	27	12	4	245	228	94	2nd, Pacific Div.	Lost Conf. Quater-Final
1998-99	82	18	20	3	....	14	25	2	....	32	45	5	....	189	222	69	5th, Pacific Div.	Out of Playoffs
1997-98	82	22	16	3	....	16	17	8	....	38	33	11	....	227	225	87	2nd, Pacific Div.	Lost Conf. Quater-Final
1996-97	82	18	16	7	....	10	27	4	....	28	43	11	....	214	268	67	6th, Pacific Div.	Out of Playoffs
1995-96	82	16	16	9	....	8	24	9	....	24	40	18	....	256	302	66	6th, Pacific Div.	Out of Playoffs
1994-95	48	7	11	6	....	9	12	3	....	16	23	9	....	142	174	41	4th, Pacific Div.	Out of Playoffs
1993-94	84	18	19	5	....	9	26	7	....	27	45	12	....	294	322	66	5th, Pacific Div.	Out of Playoffs
1992-93	84	22	15	5	....	17	20	5	....	39	35	10	....	338	340	88	3rd, Smythe Div.	Lost Final
1991-92	80	20	11	9	....	15	20	5	....	35	31	14	....	287	296	84	2nd, Smythe Div.	Lost Div. Semi-Final
1990-91	80	26	9	5	....	20	15	5	....	46	24	10	....	340	254	102	1st, Smythe Div.	Lost Div. Final
1989-90	80	21	16	3	....	13	23	4	....	34	39	7	....	338	337	75	4th, Smythe Div.	Lost Div. Final
1988-89	80	25	12	3	....	17	19	4	....	42	31	7	....	376	335	91	2nd, Smythe Div.	Lost Div. Final
1987-88	80	19	18	3	....	11	24	5	....	30	42	8	....	318	359	68	4th, Smythe Div.	Lost Div. Semi-Final
1986-87	80	20	17	3	....	11	24	5	....	31	41	8	....	318	341	70	4th, Smythe Div.	Lost Div. Semi-Final
1985-86	80	9	27	4	....	14	22	4	....	23	49	8	....	284	389	54	5th, Smythe Div.	Out of Playoffs
1984-85	80	20	14	6	....	14	18	8	....	34	32	14	....	339	326	82	4th, Smythe Div.	Lost Div. Semi-Final
1983-84	80	13	19	8	....	10	25	5	....	23	44	13	....	309	376	59	5th, Smythe Div.	Out of Playoffs
1982-83	80	20	13	7	....	7	28	5	....	27	41	12	....	308	365	66	5th, Smythe Div.	Out of Playoffs
1981-82	80	19	15	6	....	5	26	9	....	24	41	15	....	314	369	63	4th, Smythe Div.	Lost Div. Final
1980-81	80	22	11	7	....	21	13	6	....	43	24	13	....	337	290	99	2nd, Norris Div.	Lost Prelim. Round
1979-80	80	18	13	9	....	12	23	5	....	30	36	14	....	290	313	74	2nd, Norris Div.	Lost Prelim. Round
1978-79	80	20	13	7	....	14	21	5	....	34	34	12	....	292	286	80	3rd, Norris Div.	Lost Prelim. Round
1977-78	80	18	16	6	....	13	18	9	....	31	34	15	....	243	245	77	3rd, Norris Div.	Lost Prelim. Round
1976-77	80	20	13	7	....	14	18	8	....	34	31	15	....	271	241	83	2nd, Norris Div.	Lost Quarter-Final
1975-76	80	22	13	5	....	16	20	4	....	38	33	9	....	263	265	85	2nd, Norris Div.	Lost Quarter-Final
1974-75	80	22	7	11	....	20	10	10	....	42	17	21	....	269	185	105	2nd, Norris Div.	Lost Quarter-Final
1973-74	78	22	13	4	....	11	20	8	....	33	33	12	....	233	231	78	3rd, West Div.	Lost Quarter-Final
1972-73	78	21	11	7	....	10	25	4	....	31	36	11	....	232	245	73	6th, West Div.	Out of Playoffs
1971-72	78	14	23	2	....	6	26	7	....	20	49	9	....	206	305	49	7th, West Div.	Out of Playoffs
1970-71	78	17	14	8	....	8	26	5	....	25	40	13	....	239	303	63	5th, West Div.	Out of Playoffs
1969-70	76	12	22	4	....	2	30	6	....	14	52	10	....	168	290	38	6th, West Div.	Out of Playoffs
1968-69	76	19	14	5	....	5	28	5	....	24	42	10	....	185	260	58	4th, West Div.	Lost Semi-Final
1967-68	74	20	13	4	....	11	20	6	....	31	33	10	....	200	224	72	2nd, West Div.	Lost Quarter-Final

2011-12 Player Personnel

FORWARDS	HT	WT	S	Place of Birth	*Age	2010-11 Club
BROWN, Dustin	6-0	209	R	Ithaca, NY	26	Los Angeles
CLUNE, Rich	5-10	199	L	Toronto, Ont.	24	Manchester
FRASER, Colin	6-1	193	L	Surrey, B.C.	26	Edmonton
GAGNE, Simon	6-1	193	L	Ste-Foy, Que.	31	Tampa Bay
KAUNISTO, Ray	6-3	185	L	Sault Ste. Marie, MI	24	Manchester
KOPITAR, Anze	6-3	227	L	Jesenice, Yugoslavia	24	Los Angeles
LEWIS, Trevor	6-1	195	R	Salt Lake City, UT	24	Los Angeles
MOLLER, Oscar	5-10	189	R	Stockholm, Sweden	22	Los Angeles-Manchester
PARSE, Scott	5-11	188	R	Portage, MI	27	Los Angeles
PENNER, Dustin	6-4	245	L	Winkler, Man.	29	Edmonton-Los Angeles
RICHARDS, Mike	5-11	195	L	Kenora, Ont.	26	Philadelphia
RICHARDSON, Brad	5-11	192	L	Belleville, Ont.	26	Los Angeles
STOLL, Jarret	6-1	210	R	Melville, Sask.	29	Los Angeles
WESTGARTH, Kevin	6-4	228	R	Amherstburg, Ont.	27	Los Angeles
WILLIAMS, Justin	6-1	188	R	Cobourg, Ont.	30	Los Angeles
DEFENSEMEN						
DOUGHTY, Drew	6-0	212	R	London, Ont.	21	Los Angeles
DREWISKE, Davis	6-2	218	L	Hudson, WI	26	Los Angeles
FRANSSON, Johan	6-1	192	L	Kalix, Sweden	26	St. Petersburg
GREENE, Matt	6-3	231	R	Grand Ledge, MI	28	Los Angeles
JOHNSON, Jack	6-1	219	L	Indianapolis, IN	24	Los Angeles
MITCHELL, Willie	6-3	212	L	Port McNeill, B.C.	34	Los Angeles
SCUDERI, Rob	6-1	216	L	Syosset, NY	32	Los Angeles

GOALTENDERS	HT	WT	C	Place of Birth	*Age	2010-11 Club
BERNIER, Jonathan	5-11	186	L	Laval, Que.	23	Los Angeles
QUICK, Jonathan	6-1	212	L	Milford, CT	25	Los Angeles

* – Age at start of 2011-12 season

Terry Murray

Head Coach

Born: Shawville, Que., July 20, 1950.

The Los Angeles Kings named Terry Murray their head coach on July 17, 2008. Murray – formerly the head coach of the Washington Capitals, Florida Panthers and the Philadelphia Flyers, where he led that club to the 1997 Stanley Cup Finals – is the 22nd head coach in Kings history. In his second season behind the bench in 2009-10, Murray guided the team to the playoffs for the first time since 2001-02. The Kings tied a club record with 46 wins and their 101 points was the second-best total in franchise history. The team won 46 games again in 2010-11.

Murray spent the four seasons prior to being hired by the Kings as an assistant coach with the Flyers, an organization he had worked for as a head coach, assistant coach, pro scout and player. In 2007-08, he helped the Flyers record 95 points and advance to Eastern Conference Finals after earning just 56 points in 2006-07. Murray compiled a 118-64-30 record as head coach of the Flyers for three seasons from 1994-95 through 1996-97. In addition to the 1997 Stanley Cup Finals / Eastern Conference Championship, Murray coached the team to two Atlantic Division Championships (1995 and 1996).

Murray's NHL head coaching career began with Washington for five seasons (1989-90 through 1993-94), where he compiled a 163-134-28 record. In his first season he helped lead the Capitals to the Eastern Conference Finals. Murray also coached Florida for three seasons (1998-99 through 2000-01), which included a franchise-record 98-point season and a team-record 43 wins in 1999-2000. He has also worked as an assistant coach with the Capitals (1983-84 through 1987-88); as head coach with the Baltimore Skipjacks of the American Hockey League; and as head coach with the Cincinnati Cyclones of the International Hockey League (1993-94).

As an NHL defenseman, Murray played in 302 career NHL regular-season games over eight seasons with Washington, Philadelphia (two stints), the Detroit Red Wings and the California Golden Seals / California Seals, who originally drafted Murray in the seventh-round (88th overall) of the 1970 NHL Amateur Draft. He recorded 80 points (four goals, 76 assists) and 199 penalty minutes during his NHL career and he also played in 18 career NHL playoff games, recording two goals, two assists and 10 penalty minutes.

Coaching Record

			Regular Season				Playoffs			
Season	Team	League	GC	W	L	O/T	GC	W	L	T
1988-89	Baltimore	AHL	80	30	46	4	....	....	....	....
1989-90	Baltimore	AHL	45	26	17	2	....	....	....	....
1989-90	**Washington**	**NHL**	**34**	**18**	**14**	**2**	**15**	**8**	**7**	....
1990-91	**Washington**	**NHL**	**80**	**37**	**36**	**7**	**11**	**5**	**6**	....
1991-92	**Washington**	**NHL**	**80**	**45**	**27**	**8**	**7**	**3**	**4**	....
1992-93	**Washington**	**NHL**	**84**	**43**	**34**	**7**	**6**	**2**	**4**	....
1993-94	Cincinnati	IHL	28	17	7	4	11	6	5	....
1993-94	**Washington**	**NHL**	**47**	**20**	**23**	**4**	....	....	....	....
1994-95	**Philadelphia**	**NHL**	**48**	**28**	**16**	**4**	**15**	**10**	**5**	....
1995-96	**Philadelphia**	**NHL**	**82**	**45**	**24**	**13**	**12**	**6**	**6**	....
1996-97	**Philadelphia**	**NHL**	**82**	**45**	**24**	**13**	**19**	**12**	**7**	....
1998-99	**Florida**	**NHL**	**82**	**30**	**34**	**18**	....	....	....	....
99-2000	**Florida**	**NHL**	**82**	**43**	**27**	**12**	**4**	**0**	**4**	....
2000-01	**Florida**	**NHL**	**36**	**6**	**18**	**12**	....	....	....	....
2008-09	**Los Angeles**	**NHL**	**82**	**34**	**37**	**11**	....	....	....	....
2009-10	**Los Angeles**	**NHL**	**82**	**46**	**27**	**9**	**6**	**2**	**4**	....
2010-11	**Los Angeles**	**NHL**	**82**	**42**	**29**	**11**	**62**	**4**	....	....
	NHL Totals		**983**	**482**	**370**	**131**	**157**	**52**	**47**	....

2010-11 Scoring

* – rookie

Regular Season

Pos	#	Player	Team	GP	G	A	Pts	TOI	+/–	PIM	PP	SH	GW	S	%
C	11	Anze Kopitar	L.A.	75	25	48	73	21:35	25	20	6	1	6	233	10.7
L	23	Dustin Brown	L.A.	82	28	29	57	19:22	17	67	7	0	2	228	12.3
R	14	Justin Williams	L.A.	73	22	35	57	17:15	14	59	5	0	3	213	10.3
L	94	Ryan Smyth	L.A.	82	23	24	47	18:02	–1	35	9	0	2	195	11.8
R	25	Dustin Penner	EDM	62	21	18	39	18:27	–12	45	6	1	3	137	15.3
			L.A.	19	2	4	6	17:00	0	2	0	0	0	36	5.6
			Total	81	23	22	45	18:07	–12	47	6	1	3	173	13.3
C	28	Jarret Stoll	L.A.	82	20	23	43	17:09	–6	42	4	1	5	187	10.7
D	3	Jack Johnson	L.A.	82	5	37	42	23:11	–21	44	3	0	0	153	3.3
D	8	Drew Doughty	L.A.	76	11	29	40	25:38	13	68	5	0	3	139	7.9
R	17	Wayne Simmonds	L.A.	80	14	16	30	13:27	–2	75	1	0	3	117	12.0
C	26	Michal Handzus	L.A.	82	12	18	30	17:20	–5	20	4	0	3	94	12.8
R	15	Brad Richardson	L.A.	68	7	12	19	11:45	–13	47	0	1	1	103	6.8
D	53 *	Alec Martinez	L.A.	60	5	11	16	15:16	11	18	1	0	0	74	6.8
L	27	Alexei Ponikarovsky	L.A.	61	5	10	15	12:35	1	36	1	0	1	94	5.3
D	7	Rob Scuderi	L.A.	82	2	13	15	20:17	1	16	0	0	1	46	4.3
L	13 *	Kyle Clifford	L.A.	76	7	7	14	9:30	–10	141	0	0	0	69	10.1
C	22 *	Trevor Lewis	L.A.	72	3	10	13	11:29	–11	6	0	0	2	105	2.9
D	2	Matt Greene	L.A.	71	2	9	11	16:58	3	70	0	0	1	50	4.0
D	33	Willie Mitchell	L.A.	57	5	5	10	21:48	4	21	0	1	1	59	8.5
C	12 *	Andrei Loktionov	L.A.	19	4	3	7	14:45	2	2	0	0	2	26	15.4
D	44	Davis Drewiske	L.A.	38	0	5	5	14:21	–1	19	0	0	0	27	0.0
R	21	Scott Parse	L.A.	5	1	3	4	13:47	5	0	0	0	0	6	16.7
C	9	Oscar Moller	L.A.	13	1	3	4	14:35	–1	2	0	0	0	27	3.7
D	5	Peter Harrold	L.A.	19	1	3	4	12:15	3	4	0	0	0	12	8.3
R	19	Kevin Westgarth	L.A.	56	0	3	3	5:26	–6	105	0	0	0	20	0.0
C	10 *	Brayden Schenn	L.A.	8	0	2	2	11:14	–1	0	0	0	0	11	0.0
D	6 *	Jake Muzzin	L.A.	11	0	1	1	13:42	–2	0	0	0	0	8	0.0
R	29	John Zeiler	L.A.	4	0	0	0	5:36	–1	0	0	0	0	1	0.0
L	74 *	Dwight King	L.A.	6	0	0	0	11:43	–2	2	0	0	0	3	0.0

Goaltending

No.	Goaltender	GPI	Mins	Avg	W	L	OT	EN	SO	GA	SA	S%	G	A	PIM
32	Jonathan Quick	61	3591	2.24	35	22	3	4	6	134	1631	.918	0	2	0
45	* Jonathan Bernier	25	1378	2.48	11	8	3	1	3	57	652	.913	0	0	0
	Totals	**82**	**4994**	**2.35**	**46**	**30**	**6**	**5**	**9**	**196**	**2288**	**.914**			

Playoffs

Pos	#	Player	Team	GP	G	A	Pts	TOI	+/–	PIM	PP	SH	GW	OT	S	%
L	13 *	Kyle Clifford	L.A.	6	3	2	5	13:17	–2	7	0	0	1	0	9	33.3
L	94	Ryan Smyth	L.A.	6	2	3	5	18:20	3	0	0	0	0	0	14	14.3
R	15	Brad Richardson	L.A.	6	2	3	5	15:37	–4	2	0	0	0	0	17	11.8
D	3	Jack Johnson	L.A.	6	1	4	5	22:48	–2	0	1	0	1	0	16	6.3
R	14	Justin Williams	L.A.	6	3	1	4	16:44	0	2	1	0	0	0	16	18.8
D	8	Drew Doughty	L.A.	6	2	2	4	27:08	0	8	1	0	0	0	12	16.7
C	22 *	Trevor Lewis	L.A.	6	1	3	4	16:39	0	2	1	0	0	0	11	9.1
R	17	Wayne Simmonds	L.A.	6	1	2	3	14:44	–1	20	0	0	0	0	12	8.3
C	28	Jarret Stoll	L.A.	5	0	3	3	18:44	4	0	0	0	0	0	5	0.0
C	26	Michal Handzus	L.A.	6	1	1	2	20:21	–4	0	0	0	0	0	7	14.3
D	33	Willie Mitchell	L.A.	6	1	1	2	24:17	1	4	0	0	0	0	8	12.5
L	23	Dustin Brown	L.A.	6	1	1	2	20:00	–3	6	1	0	0	0	10	10.0
R	25	Dustin Penner	L.A.	6	1	1	2	14:32	–3	4	0	0	0	0	10	10.0
D	7	Rob Scuderi	L.A.	6	0	2	2	20:49	–1	0	0	0	0	0	3	0.0
R	19	Kevin Westgarth	L.A.	6	0	2	2	6:15	2	14	0	0	0	0	3	0.0
L	27	Alexei Ponikarovsky	L.A.	4	1	0	1	10:10	1	0	0	0	0	0	5	20.0
D	53 *	Alec Martinez	L.A.	6	0	1	1	13:29	–1	2	0	0	0	0	5	0.0
C	9	Oscar Moller	L.A.	1	0	0	0	10:37	1	0	0	0	0	0	0	0.0
R	21	Scott Parse	L.A.	2	0	0	0	8:47	–1	0	0	0	0	0	0	0.0
D	2	Matt Greene	L.A.	6	0	0	0	16:44	–3	14	0	0	0	0	6	0.0

Goaltending

No.	Goaltender	GPI	Mins	Avg	W	L	EN	SO	GA	SA	S%	G	A	PIM
32	Jonathan Quick	6	380	3.16	2	4	0	1	20	229	.913	0	0	0
	Totals	**6**	**380**	**3.16**	**2**	**4**	**0**	**1**	**20**	**229**	**.913**			

Captains' History

Bob Wall, 1967-68, 1968-69; Larry Cahan, 1969-70, 1970-71; Bob Pulford, 1971-72, 1972-73; Terry Harper, 1973-74, 1974-75; Mike Murphy, 1975-76 to 1980-81; Dave Lewis, 1981-82, 1982-83; Terry Ruskowski, 1983-84, 1984-85; Dave Taylor, 1985-86 to 1988-89; Wayne Gretzky, 1989-90 to 1991-92; Wayne Gretzky and Luc Robitaille, 1992-93; Wayne Gretzky, 1993-94, 1994-95; Wayne Gretzky and Rob Blake, 1995-96; Rob Blake, 1996-97 to 2000-01; Mattias Norstrom, 2001-02 to 2006-07; Rob Blake, 2007-08; Dustin Brown, 2008-09 to date.

Club Records

Team

(Figures in brackets for season records are games played; records for fewest points, wins, ties, losses, goals, goals against are for 70 or more games)

Most Points **105** 1974-75 (80)
Most Wins **46** 1990-91 (80), 2009-10 (82), 2010-11 (82)
Most Ties **21** 1974-75 (80)
Most Losses **52** 1969-70 (76)
Most Goals **376** 1988-89 (80)
Most Goals Against **389** 1985-86 (80)
Fewest Points **38** 1969-70 (76)
Fewest Wins **14** 1969-70 (76)
Fewest Ties **5** 1998-99 (82)
Fewest Losses **17** 1974-75 (80)
Fewest Goals **168** 1969-70 (76)
Fewest Goals Against **185** 1974-75 (80)
Longest Winning Streak
Overall .... **9** Jan. 21-Feb. 6/10
Home .... **12** Oct. 10-Dec. 5/92
Away .... **8** Dec. 18/74-Jan. 16/75
Longest Undefeated Streak
Overall .... **11** Feb. 28-Mar. 24/74 (9 wins, 2 ties)
Home .... **13** Oct. 10-Dec. 8/92 (12 wins, 1 tie)
Away .... **11** Oct. 10-Dec. 11/74 (6 wins, 5 ties)
Longest Losing Streak
Overall .... **11** Mar. 16-Apr. 4/04
Home .... **9** Feb. 8-Mar. 12/86
Away .... **11** Jan. 11-Feb. 15/70
Longest Winless Streak
Overall .... **17** Jan. 29-Mar. 5/70 (13 losses, 4 ties)
Home .... **9** Jan. 29-Mar. 5/70 (8 losses, 1 tie), Feb. 8-Mar. 12/86 (9 losses)
Away .... **20** Jan. 11-Apr. 3/70 (16 losses, 4 ties)
Most Shutouts, Season **10** 2000-01 (82)
Most PIM, Season **2,247** 1992-93 (84)
Most Goals, Game .... **12** Nov. 29/84 (Van. 1 at L.A. 12)

Individual

Most Seasons .... **17** Dave Taylor
Most Games .... **1,111** Dave Taylor
Most Goals, Career .... **557** Luc Robitaille
Most Assists, Career .... **757** Marcel Dionne
Most Points Career .... **1,307** Marcel Dionne (550G, 757A)
Most PIM, Career .... **1,846** Marty McSorley
Most Shutouts, Career .... **32** Rogie Vachon
Longest Consecutive Games Streak .... **330** Anze Kopitar (Mar. 21/07-Mar. 26/11)
Most Goals, Season .... **70** Bernie Nicholls (1988-89)
Most Assists, Season .... **122** Wayne Gretzky (1990-91)
Most Points, Season .... **168** Wayne Gretzky (1988-89; 54G, 114A)
Most PIM, Season .... **399** Marty McSorley (1992-93)
Most Points, Defenseman, Season .... **76** Larry Murphy (1980-81; 16G, 60A)
Most Points, Center, Season .... **168** Wayne Gretzky (1988-89; 54G, 114A)
Most Points, Right Wing, Season .... **112** Dave Taylor (1980-81; 47G, 65A)
Most Points, Left Wing, Season .... ***125** Luc Robitaille (1992-93; 63G, 62A)
Most Points, Rookie, Season .... **84** Luc Robitaille (1986-87; 45G, 39A)
Most Shutouts, Season .... **8** Rogie Vachon (1976-77)
Most Goals, Game .... **4** Seventeen times
Most Assists, Game .... **6** Bernie Nicholls (Dec. 1/88), Tomas Sandstrom (Oct. 9/93)
Most Points, Game .... **8** Bernie Nicholls (Dec. 1/88; 2G, 6A)

* NHL Record.

Coaching History

Red Kelly, 1967-68, 1968-69; Hal Laycoe and Johnny Wilson, 1969-70; Larry Regan, 1970-71; Larry Regan and Fred Glover, 1971-72; Bob Pulford, 1972-73 to 1976-77; Ron Stewart, 1977-78; Bob Berry, 1978-79 to 1980-81; Parker MacDonald and Don Perry, 1981-82; Don Perry, 1982-83; Don Perry, Rogie Vachon and Roger Neilson, 1983-84; Pat Quinn, 1984-85, 1985-86; Pat Quinn and Mike Murphy 1986-87; Mike Murphy, Rogie Vachon and Robbie Ftorek, 1987-88; Robbie Ftorek, 1988-89; Tom Webster, 1989-90 to 1991-92; Barry Melrose, 1992-93, 1993-94; Barry Melrose and Rogie Vachon, 1994-95; Larry Robinson, 1995-96 to 1998-99; Andy Murray, 1999-2000 to 2004-05; Andy Murray and John Torchetti, 2005-06; Marc Crawford, 2006-07, 2007-08; Terry Murray, 2008-09 to date.

Retired Numbers

16	Marcel Dionne	1975-1987
18	Dave Taylor	1977-1994
20	Luc Robitaille	1986-94, 97-01, 2003-2006
30	Rogie Vachon	1971-1978
99	Wayne Gretzky	1988-1996

All-time Record vs. Other Clubs

Regular Season

	At Home								On Road								Total							
	GP	W	L	T	OL	GF	GA	PTS	GP	W	L	T	OL	GF	GA	PTS	GP	W	L	T	OL	GF	GA	PTS
Anaheim	51	27	15	4	5	150	129	63	51	18	23	7	3	133	169	46	102	45	38	11	8	283	298	109
Atlanta	7	5	0	0	2	35	23	12	6	3	2	0	1	18	20	7	13	8	2	0	3	53	43	19
Boston	64	23	33	7	1	222	235	54	65	15	44	6	0	105	294	36	129	38	77	13	1	407	529	90
Buffalo	56	24	23	9	0	197	192	57	56	16	31	9	0	160	236	41	112	40	54	18	0	357	428	98
Calgary	103	52	42	9	0	368	348	113	106	29	62	12	3	335	457	73	209	81	104	21	3	703	805	186
Carolina	33	19	11	3	0	139	122	41	33	12	14	5	2	121	118	31	66	31	25	8	2	260	240	72
Chicago	86	39	36	8	3	288	281	89	87	34	42	9	2	244	299	79	173	73	78	17	5	532	580	168
Colorado	55	32	17	5	1	216	178	70	54	24	26	3	1	185	213	52	109	56	43	8	2	401	391	122
Columbus	20	12	7	1	0	60	43	25	20	9	8	0	3	64	54	21	40	21	15	1	3	124	97	46
Dallas	103	47	35	19	2	337	302	115	105	30	58	13	4	279	378	77	208	77	93	32	6	616	680	192
Detroit	92	45	32	14	1	346	290	105	91	34	41	13	3	306	346	84	183	79	73	27	4	652	636	189
Edmonton	89	33	35	15	6	336	351	87	89	31	43	15	0	310	376	77	178	64	78	30	6	646	727	164
Florida	12	8	4	0	0	36	34	16	10	3	4	3	0	25	26	9	22	11	8	3	0	61	60	25
Minnesota	20	9	6	2	3	52	50	23	20	9	6	3	2	45	42	23	40	18	12	5	5	97	92	46
Montreal	67	19	39	9	0	203	265	47	67	8	48	11	0	166	300	27	134	27	87	20	0	369	565	74
Nashville	24	11	12	0	1	68	70	23	24	13	7	3	1	68	52	30	48	24	19	3	2	136	122	53
New Jersey	45	30	9	6	0	208	138	66	46	21	19	5	1	157	151	48	91	51	28	11	1	365	289	114
NY Islanders	48	24	17	7	0	173	146	55	48	18	25	5	0	132	164	41	96	42	42	12	0	305	310	96
NY Rangers	63	25	26	10	2	207	221	62	61	18	36	6	1	181	243	43	124	43	62	16	3	388	464	105
Ottawa	12	10	1	1	0	54	24	21	12	5	6	1	0	32	38	11	24	15	7	2	0	86	62	32
Philadelphia	70	22	40	8	0	204	238	52	66	17	41	7	1	159	249	42	136	39	81	15	1	363	487	94
Phoenix	95	39	40	14	2	349	341	94	97	33	50	11	3	309	377	80	192	72	90	25	5	658	718	174
Pittsburgh	71	45	17	8	1	273	189	99	76	25	40	10	1	237	275	61	147	70	57	18	2	510	464	160
St. Louis	90	41	36	12	1	301	260	95	90	22	57	10	1	226	329	55	180	63	93	22	2	527	589	150
San Jose	58	30	22	4	2	166	156	66	58	20	30	3	5	158	195	48	116	50	52	7	7	324	351	114
Tampa Bay	14	2	10	2	0	27	43	6	12	6	5	0	1	26	27	13	26	8	15	2	1	53	70	19
Toronto	68	35	23	10	0	242	199	80	70	24	34	11	1	230	270	60	138	59	57	21	1	472	469	140
Vancouver	111	57	36	16	2	425	340	132	109	36	56	16	1	328	402	89	220	93	92	32	3	753	742	221
Washington	50	29	14	6	1	196	150	65	49	23	18	7	1	183	194	54	99	52	32	13	2	379	344	119
Defunct Clubs	35	27	6	2	0	141	76	56	34	11	14	9	0	91	109	31	69	38	20	11	0	232	185	87
Totals	**1712**	**821**	**644**	**211**	**36**	**6019**	**5434**	**1889**	**1712**	**567**	**890**	**213**	**42**	**5093**	**6403**	**1389**	**3424**	**1388**	**1534**	**424**	**78**	**11112**	**11837**	**3278**

Playoffs

	Series	W	L	GP	W	L	T	GF	GA	Last Mtg.	Rnd.	Result
Boston	2	0	2	13	5	8	0	38	56	1977	QF	L 2-4
Calgary	6	4	2	26	13	13	0	105	112	1993	DSF	W 4-2
Chicago	1	0	1	5	1	4	0	7	10	1974	QF	L 1-4
Colorado	2	0	2	14	6	8	0	23	33	2002	CQF	L 3-4
Dallas	1	0	1	7	3	4	0	21	26	1968	QF	L 3-4
Detroit	2	1	1	10	4	6	0	21	32	2001	CQF	W 4-2
Edmonton	7	2	5	36	12	24	0	127	154	1992	DSF	L 2-4
Montreal	1	0	1	5	1	4	0	12	15	1993	F	L 1-4
NY Islanders	1	0	1	4	1	3	0	10	21	1980	PRE	L 1-3
NY Rangers	2	0	2	6	1	5	0	14	32	1981	PRE	L 1-3
St. Louis	2	0	2	8	0	8	0	13	32	1998	CQF	L 0-4
San Jose	1	0	1	6	2	4	0	20	20	2011	CQF	L 2-4
Toronto	3	1	2	12	5	7	0	31	41	1993	CF	W 4-3
Vancouver	4	2	2	23	11	12	0	84	85	2010	CQF	L 2-4
Defunct Clubs	1	1	0	7	4	3	0	23	25			
Totals	**36**	**11**	**25**	**182**	**69**	**113**	**0**	**549**	**694**			

Calgary totals include Atlanta Flames, 1972-73 to 1979-80. Carolina totals include Hartford, 1979-80 to 1996-97.
Colorado totals include Quebec, 1979-80 to 1994-95. Dallas totals include Minnesota North Stars, 1967-68 to 1992-93.
New Jersey totals include Kansas City, 1974-75, 1975-76, and Colorado Rockies, 1976-77 to 1981-82.
Phoenix totals include Winnipeg, 1979-80 to 1995-96.

Playoff Results 2011-2007

Year	Round	Opponent	Result	GF	GA
2011	CQF	San Jose	L 2-4	20	20
2010	CQF	Vancouver	L 2-4	18	25

Abbreviations: Round: F - Final;
CF - conference final; **CQF** - conference quarter-final;
DF - division final; **DSF** - division semi-final;
QF - quarter-final; **PRE** - preliminary round.

2010-11 Results

Oct.	9	at Vancouver	2-1†		10	Toronto	2-3
	10	at Calgary	1-0		13	St. Louis	1-3
	12	Atlanta	3-1		15	Edmonton	5-2
	15	Vancouver	4-1		17	at Dallas	1-2
	20	Carolina	4-3		18	at St. Louis	1-2
	21	at Phoenix	2-4		20	Phoenix	0-2
	23	at Colorado	6-4		22	at Phoenix	4-3
	25	at Minnesota	3-2†		24	Boston	2-0
	27	at Chicago	1-3		26	San Jose	3-2†
	28	at Dallas	5-2	**Feb.**	1	at Minnesota	0-1†
	30	New Jersey	3-1		2	at Edmonton	3-1
Nov.	4	Tampa Bay	1-0		5	at Calgary	4-3†
	6	Nashville	4-1		10	at Pittsburgh	1-2*
	11	Dallas	3-1		12	at Washington	4-1
	13	NY Islanders	5-1		13	at Philadelphia	1-0
	15	at San Jose	3-6		16	at Columbus	4-3†
	17	Columbus	3-5		17	at NY Rangers	3-4†
	19	at Buffalo	2-4		19	at NY Islanders	0-3
	20	at Boston	4-3†		23	at Anaheim	3-2
	22	at Ottawa	2-3		24	Minnesota	4-2
	24	at Montreal	1-4		26	Colorado	4-3
	27	Chicago	1-2		28	Detroit	4-7
	29	at Anaheim	0-2	**Mar.**	3	Phoenix	1-0
Dec.	2	Florida	3-2		5	Vancouver	1-3
	4	Detroit	3-2*		7	Dallas	3-4*
	9	Calgary	2-1		9	at Detroit	2-1
	11	Minnesota	2-3*		11	at Columbus	4-2
	13	at Detroit	5-0		13	at Dallas	3-2
	16	at St. Louis	4-6		15	at Nashville	4-2
	18	at Nashville	6-1		17	St. Louis	0-4
	19	at Chicago	2-3		19	Anaheim	1-2*
	21	at Colorado	5-0		21	Calgary	2-1†
	23	Edmonton	3-2†		24	San Jose	4-3†
	26	Anaheim	4-1		26	Colorado	4-1
	27	at San Jose	4-0		29	at Edmonton	2-0
	29	at Phoenix	3-6		31	at Vancouver	1-3
	30	Philadelphia	4-7	**Apr.**	2	Dallas	3-1
Jan.	1	San Jose	0-1		4	at San Jose	1-6
	3	Chicago	3-4		6	Phoenix	3-2†
	6	Nashville	2-5		8	at Anaheim	1-2
	8	Columbus	6-4		9	Anaheim	1-3

* – Overtime † – Shootout

Entry Draft Selections 2011-1997

Name in bold denotes played in NHL.

2011 Pick	**2007** Pick	**2003** Pick	**2000** Pick
49 Christopher Gibson	4 Thomas Hickey	13 **Dustin Brown**	20 **Alex Frolov**
80 Andy Andreoff	52 **Oscar Moller**	26 **Brian Boyle**	54 **Andreas Lilja**
82 Nick Shore	61 **Wayne Simmonds**	27 **Jeff Tambellini**	86 **Yanick Lehoux**
110 Michael Mersch	82 Bryan Cameron	44 **Konstantin Pushkarev**	118 **Lubomir Visnovsky**
140 Joel Lowry	95 **Alec Martinez**	82 Ryan Munce	165 Nathan Marsters
200 Michael Schumacher	109 **Dwight King**	152 **Brady Murray**	201 **Yevgeny Fedorov**
	124 Linden Rowat	174 **Esa Pirnes**	206 Tim Eriksson
2010 Pick	137 Joshua Turnbull	231 **Matt Zaba**	218 Craig Olynick
15 Derek Forbort	184 Josh Kidd	244 Mike Sullivan	245 Dan Welch
47 Tyler Toffoli	188 Matt Fillier	274 Marty Guerin	250 Flavien Conne
70 Jordan Weal			282 Carl Grahn
148 Kevin Gravel	**2006** Pick	**2002** Pick	
158 Maxim Kitsyn	11 **Jonathan Bernier**	18 **Denis Grebeshkov**	**1999** Pick
	17 **Trevor Lewis**	50 Sergei Anshakov	43 Andrei Shefer
2009 Pick	48 Joe Ryan	66 **Petr Kanko**	74 Jason Crain
5 **Brayden Schenn**	74 Jeff Zatkoff	104 **Aaron Rome**	76 **Frantisek Kaberle**
35 **Kyle Clifford**	86 Bud Holloway	115 Mark Rooneem	92 Cory Campbell
84 Nicolas Deslauriers	114 Niclas Andersen	152 Greg Hogeboom	104 **Brian McGrattan**
95 Jean-Francois Berube	134 David Meckler	157 Joel Andresen	125 Daniel Johansson
96 Linden Vey	144 Martin Nolet	185 Ryan Murphy	133 Jean-Francois Nogues
126 David Kolomatis	164 Constantin Braun	215 Mikhail Lyubushin	193 Kevin Baker
156 Michael Pelech		248 Tuukka Pulliainen	222 **George Parros**
179 Brandon Kozun	**2005** Pick	279 **Connor James**	250 **Noah Clarke**
186 Jordan Nolan	11 **Anze Kopitar**		
198 Nic Dowd	50 Dany Roussin	**2001** Pick	**1998** Pick
	60 T.J. Fast	18 Jens Karlsson	21 **Mathieu Biron**
2008 Pick	72 **Jonathan Quick**	30 **David Steckel**	46 **Justin Papineau**
2 **Drew Doughty**	139 Patrik Hersley	49 **Michael Cammalleri**	76 Alexei Volkov
13 Colten Teubert	184 Ryan McGinnis	51 Jaroslav Bednar	103 **Kip Brennan**
32 Viatcheslav Voynov	206 Josh Meyers	83 Henrik Juntunen	133 Joe Rullier
63 Robert Czarnik	226 John Seymour	116 **Richard Petiot**	163 **Tomas Zizka**
74 Andrew Campbell		152 Terry Denike	190 Tommi Hannus
88 Geordie Wudrick	**2004** Pick	153 Tuukka Mantyla	217 Jim Henkel
123 **Andrei Loktionov**	11 **Lauri Tukonen**	214 **Cristobal Huet**	248 **Matthew Yeats**
153 Justin Azevedo	95 Paul Baier	237 Mike Gabinet	
183 Garrett Roe	110 Ned Lukacevic	277 Sebastien Laplante	**1997** Pick
	143 Eric Neilson		3 **Olli Jokinen**
	174 **Scott Parse**		15 Matt Zultek
	205 Mike Curry		29 **Scott Barney**
	221 **Daniel Taylor**		83 **Joe Corvo**
	238 **Yutaka Fukufuji**		99 Sean Blanchard
	264 Valtteri Tenkanen		137 Richard Seeley
			150 Jeff Katcher
			193 Jay Kopischke
			220 Konrad Brand

General Managers' History

Larry Regan, 1967-68 to 1972-73; Larry Regan and Jake Milford, 1973-74; Jake Milford, 1974-75 to 1976-77; George Maguire, 1977-78 to 1982-83; George Maguire and Rogie Vachon, 1983-84; Rogie Vachon, 1984-85 to 1991-92; Nick Beverley, 1992-93, 1993-94; Sam McMaster, 1994-95 to 1996-97; Dave Taylor, 1997-98 to 2005-06; Dean Lombardi, 2006-07 to date.

Dean Lombardi
President and General Manager
Born: Holyoke, MA, March 5, 1958.

The Kings entered into a new executive era when the club hired Dean Lombardi as Kings President/General Manager on April 21, 2006. Coming to Los Angeles as a veteran of 20 NHL seasons in the front office as an executive and a pro scout, Lombardi brought a well-earned reputation for being one of hockey's true visionaries while possessing a solid track record of success, building from within, and of development on the ice and infrastructure off the ice. The Kings have made back-to-back playoff appearances in 2010 and 2011 after having previously failed to reach the postseason since 2002.

Lombardi was formerly a member of the San Jose Sharks front office for 13 years, including seven seasons as general manager, followed by three years as a pro scout for the Philadelphia Flyers from 2003 to 2006. As an executive in the San Jose front office beginning in 1990, Lombardi first served as assistant general manager (a post he held the previous two seasons with the Minnesota North Stars) for the expansion Sharks before being elevated to vice president, director of hockey operations in 1992. Four years later, he was promoted to executive vice president and general manager. During his tenure as general manager in San Jose from 1996 to 2003, Lombardi helped build the Sharks into one of the premier teams in the NHL.

Prior to joining the North Stars, Lombardi spent three seasons as a player representative, including the representation of five members of the 1988 United States Olympic team, and at the time he joined Minnesota's front office Lombardi was only the second former player agent to be employed in an NHL front office (Brian Burke/Vancouver Canucks was the other).

Born in Holyoke, Massachusetts, and raised in nearby Ludlow, Lombardi received his undergraduate degree from the University of New Haven where he finished third in his class. On the ice he was the hockey team's captain his final two seasons, and he received a full athletic scholarship and the school's student-athlete of the year award. In 1985, Lombardi earned his Law degree (with honors) from Tulane Law School where he specialized in Labor Law.

Club Directory

Los Angeles Kings
STAPLES Center
1111 South Figueroa Street
Los Angeles, CA 90015
Phone **213/742-7100**
GM FAX 310/535-4525
www.lakings.com
Capacity: 18,118

STAPLES Center

Ownership
Owner . . . . Philip F. Anschutz
Owner . . . . Edward P. Roski, Jr.
Governor . . . . Timothy J. Leiweke
Chief Operating Officer/Chief Financial Officer . . . Dan Beckerman
Executive Administrative Assistant to the Governor . Carla Garcia
Executive Assistant, COO/CFO. . . . . Karen Zamora

Kings Executive
President/General Manager, Alternate Governor . . Dean Lombardi
President, Business Operations, Alt. Governor . . . . . Luc Robitaille
Chief Operating Officer. . . . . Chris McGowan
Executive Assistant, President/General Manager . . . Tiffany Grommon
Executive Assistant, President, Business Ops . . . . . Kehly Sloane
Executive Assistant, Chief Operating Officer . . . . . Alicia Briones

Hockey Operations
Vice President/Assistant General Manager . . . . Ron Hextall
Special Assistant to the General Manager . . . . Jack Ferreira
Vice President/Hockey Ops and Legal Affairs . . . . . Jeff Solomon
Director of Team Operations . . . . Marshall Dickerson

Coaches
Head Coach . . . . Terry Murray
Assistant Coaches. . . . . John Stevens, Jamie Kompon
Goaltending Coach. Bill Ranford
Video Coordinator . . . . Ryan Colville

Player Development
Player Development . . . . Nelson Emerson
Pro Development and Special Assignments . . . . . . Mike O'Connell
Goaltender Development . . . . Kim Dillabaugh

Training Staff – Medical
Head Athletic Trainer . . . . Chris Kingsley
Strength and Conditioning Coach. . . . . Tim Adams
Assistant Athletic Trainer. . . . . Myles Hirayama
Massage Therapist . . . . Chris Pikosky

Training Staff – Equipment
Head Equipment Manager . . . . Darren Granger
Assistant Equipment Managers . . . . Dana Bryson / Denver Wilson

Medical
Team Physician / Internist . . . . Dr. Ronald Kvitne / Dr. Michael Mellman
Team Dentist / Opthalmologist . . . . Dr. Jeffrey Hoy / Dr. Howard Lazerson

Scouts/Hockey Operations
Scouting Operations Coordinator . . . . Lee Callans
Senior Pro Scout / Pro Scouts . . . . Rob Laird / Steve Greeley, Alyn McCauley
Co-Directors of Amateur Scouting . . . . Mark Yannetti, Michael Futa
Amateur Scouts . . . . Brent McEwen, Tony Gasparini, Denis Fugere, Todd Woodcroft, Bob Crocker
Collegiate Scouts . . . . Mike Donnelly, Mark Mullen
Video Technicians . . . . Bob Friedlander, Bill Gurney

Broadcasters
TV Station / Play-by-Play / Analyst . . . . FS West / Bob Miller / Jim Fox
Radio Falgship / Play-by-Play / Analyst . . . . KTLK AM 1150 / Nick Nickson / Daryl Evans

Communications and Content
Vice President, Communications and Content. . . . . Michael Altieri
Senior Director, Communications . . . . Jeff Moeller
Senior Manager, Communications . . . . Mike Kalinowski
Manager, Communications and Broadcasting . . . . . Jeremy Zager
Manager, Content/Host . . . . Heidi Androl
Manager, Production and Feature Producer . . . . . . Aaron Brenner
Beat Writer/Columnist – LAKings.com. . . . . Rich Hammond

Group Sales
Vice President, Group Sales. . . . . Matt Rosenfeld
Fan Development and Community Relations
Director, Fan Development/Community Relations . . James Cefaly

Finance
Vice President, Finance . . . . Peter Mazur

Humans Resources
Human Resources Generalist. . . . . Casey Niehaus

Marketing
Vice President, Marketing . . . . Jonathan Lowe

Sponsorship Sales and Service
Senior Vice President, Corporate Partnerships . . . . . Bill Pedigo
Senior Vice President, Partnership Activation . . . . . Tracy Hartman
Director, Partnership Activation. . . . . Nam McGrail
Director, Corporate Partnerships . . . . Josh Veilleux

Ticket Sales and Service
Vice President, Ticket Sales and Service . . . . Kelly Cheeseman
Director, Ticket Sales and Service. . . . . Josh Bender
Director, Ticket Operations . . . . Elizabeth Hauck

Key Off-Season Signings/Acquisitions

2011

June 17 • Named **Mike Yeo** head coach.

24 • Acquired RW **Devin Setoguchi**, C **Charlie Coyle** and San Jose's 1st-round pick in the 2011 Entry Draft from San Jose for D **Brent Burns** and Minnesota's 2nd-round pick in 2012.

27 • Acquired C **Darroll Powe** from Philadelphia for Minnesota's 3rd-round pick in the 2013 Entry Draft.

30 • Named **Darryl Sydor** assistant coach.

July 1 • Re-signed G **Josh Harding**.

3 • Acquired RW **Dany Heatley** from San Jose for RW **Martin Havlat**.

6 • Re-signed LW **Colton Gillies**.

9 • Signed D **Mike Lundin**.

Minnesota Wild

2010-11 Results: 39w-35l-3otl-5sol 86pts. Third, Northwest Division

Year-by-Year Record

		Home				Road				Overall							
Season	GP	W	L	T	OL	W	L	T	OL	W	L	T	OL	GF	GA	Pts.	Finished	Playoff Result
2010-11	82	19	17	....	5	20	18	....	3	39	35	....	8	206	233	86	3rd, Northwest Div.	Out of Playoffs
2009-10	82	25	12	....	4	13	24	....	4	38	36	....	8	219	246	84	4th, Northwest Div.	Out of Playoffs
2008-09	82	23	11	....	7	17	22	....	2	40	33	....	9	219	200	89	3rd, Northwest Div.	Out of Playoffs
2007-08	82	25	11	....	5	19	17	....	5	44	28	....	10	223	218	98	1st, Northwest Div.	Lost Conf. Quarter-Final
2006-07	82	29	7	....	5	19	19	....	3	48	26	....	8	235	191	104	2nd, Northwest Div.	Lost Conf. Quarter-Final
2005-06	82	23	16	....	2	15	20	....	6	38	36	....	8	231	215	84	5th, Northwest Div.	Out of Playoffs
2004-05	...	...	...	...	...	...	...	...	...	...	...	...	...	...	...	...		
2003-04	82	19	13	7	2	11	16	13	1	30	29	20	3	188	183	83	5th, Northwest Div.	Out of Playoffs
2002-03	82	25	13	3	0	17	16	7	1	42	29	10	1	198	178	95	3rd, Northwest Div.	Lost Conf. Championship
2001-02	82	14	14	8	5	12	21	4	4	26	35	12	9	195	238	73	5th, Northwest Div.	Out of Playoffs
2000-01	82	14	13	10	4	11	26	3	1	25	39	13	5	168	210	68	5th, Northwest Div.	Out of Playoffs

2011-12 Schedule

Oct.	Sat.	8	Columbus
	Mon.	10	at NY Islanders*
	Tue.	11	at Ottawa
	Thu.	13	Edmonton
	Sat.	15	Detroit
	Tue.	18	Pittsburgh
	Thu.	20	at Edmonton
	Sat.	22	at Vancouver*
	Thu.	27	Anaheim
	Sat.	29	Detroit
Nov.	Tue.	1	at Detroit
	Thu.	3	Vancouver
	Sat.	5	St. Louis
	Tue.	8	at Calgary
	Thu.	10	at San Jose
	Sat.	12	at Los Angeles
	Sun.	13	at Anaheim*
	Tue.	15	at Columbus
	Thu.	17	Colorado
	Sat.	19	St. Louis
	Wed.	23	Nashville
	Fri.	25	Edmonton*
	Sun.	27	Calgary*
	Mon.	28	Tampa Bay
	Wed.	30	at Edmonton
Dec.	Fri.	2	New Jersey
	Sun.	4	at Anaheim*
	Tue.	6	at San Jose
	Thu.	8	at Los Angeles
	Sat.	10	at Phoenix
	Tue.	13	at Winnipeg
	Wed.	14	Chicago
	Sat.	17	NY Islanders
	Mon.	19	at Vancouver
	Tue.	20	at Calgary
	Thu.	22	at Edmonton
	Mon.	26	Colorado*
	Wed.	28	at Nashville
	Thu.	29	Edmonton
	Sat.	31	Phoenix*
Jan.	Wed.	4	at Vancouver

	Sat.	7	at Calgary
	Tue.	10	San Jose
	Thu.	12	at Chicago
	Sat.	14	at St. Louis
	Tue.	17	at Philadelphia
	Thu.	19	at Toronto
	Sat.	21	Dallas
	Tue.	24	at Colorado
	Tue.	31	Nashville
Feb.	Thu.	2	at Colorado
	Sat.	4	at Dallas
	Tue.	7	at Columbus
	Thu.	9	Vancouver
	Sat.	11	Columbus
	Tue.	14	Anaheim
	Thu.	16	Winnipeg
	Sat.	18	at St. Louis*
	Sun.	19	Boston*
	Thu.	23	at Florida
	Fri.	24	at Dallas
	Sun.	26	San Jose*
	Tue.	28	Los Angeles
Mar.	Thu.	1	at Montreal
	Fri.	2	at Detroit
	Sun.	4	Colorado
	Tue.	6	at Colorado
	Thu.	8	at Phoenix
	Sun.	11	Calgary*
	Tue.	13	Dallas
	Sat.	17	Carolina*
	Mon.	19	Vancouver
	Thu.	22	Calgary
	Sat.	24	at Buffalo
	Sun.	25	at Washington*
	Tue.	27	NY Rangers
	Thu.	29	Florida
	Sat.	31	Los Angeles
Apr.	Sun.	1	at Chicago
	Tue.	3	at Nashville
	Thu.	5	Chicago
	Sat.	7	Phoenix

* Denotes afternoon game.

Nicklas Backstrom earned the Wild's team award for player of the week six times during the 2010-11 season and was the team's player of the year.

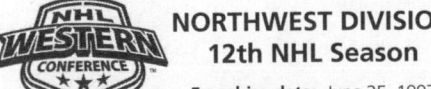

NORTHWEST DIVISION
12th NHL Season

Franchise date: June 25, 1997

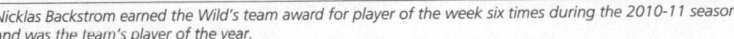

2011-12 Player Personnel

FORWARDS	HT	WT	S	Place of Birth	*Age	2010-11 Club
ALMOND, Cody	6-2	217	L	Calgary, Alta.	22	Minnesota-Houston
BOUCHARD, Pierre-Marc	5-10	178	L	Sherbrooke, Que.	27	Minnesota
BRODZIAK, Kyle	6-2	209	R	St. Paul, Alta.	27	Minnesota
CLUTTERBUCK, Cal	5-11	213	R	Welland, Ont.	23	Minnesota
CULLEN, Matt	6-1	196	L	Virginia, MN	34	Minnesota
GILLIES, Colton	6-4	208	L	White Rock, B.C.	22	Minnesota-Houston
HEATLEY, Dany	6-4	220	L	Freiburg, West Germany	30	San Jose
KASSIAN, Matt	6-5	252	L	Edmonton, Alta.	24	Minnesota-Houston
KOIVU, Mikko	6-2	219	L	Turku, Finland	28	Minnesota
LATENDRESSE, Guillaume	6-2	240	L	Ste-Catherine, Que.	24	Minnesota
McINTYRE, David	6-0	190	L	Oakville, Ont.	24	Albany
McMILLAN, Carson	6-1	193	R	Brandon, Man.	23	Minnesota-Houston
NYSTROM, Eric	6-1	197	L	Syosset, NY	28	Minnesota
ORTMEYER, Jed	6-0	200	R	Omaha, NE	33	San Antonio-Houston-Min
PALMER, Jarod	6-0	200	R	Fridley, MN	25	Houston
PETERS, Warren	6-0	203	L	Saskatoon, Sask.	29	Minnesota-Houston
POWE, Darroll	5-11	212	L	Saskatoon, Sask.	26	Philadelphia
SETOGUCHI, Devin	6-0	200	R	Taber, Alta.	24	San Jose
STAUBITZ, Brad	6-1	205	R	Bright's Grove, Ont.	27	Minnesota
TAFFE, Jeff	6-3	207	L	Hastings, MN	30	Chicago-Rockford
WELLMAN, Casey	6-0	186	R	Brentwood, CA	23	Minnesota-Houston

DEFENSEMEN	HT	WT	S	Place of Birth		2010-11 Club
BAGNALL, Drew	6-3	220	L	Oakbank, Man.	27	Minnesota-Houston
FALK, Justin	6-5	215	L	Snowflake, Man.	22	Minnesota-Houston
LUNDIN, Mike	6-2	191	L	Burnsville, MN	27	Tampa Bay
PROSSER, Nate	6-2	207	R	Elk River, MN	25	Minnesota-Houston
SCANDELLA, Marco	6-3	217	L	Montreal, Que.	21	Minnesota-Houston
SCHULTZ, Nick	6-1	206	L	Strasbourg, Sask.	29	Minnesota
SPURGEON, Jared	5-9	175	R	Edmonton, Alta.	21	Minnesota-Houston
STONER, Clayton	6-3	220	L	Port McNeill, B.C.	26	Minnesota
ZANON, Greg	5-11	201	L	Burnaby, B.C.	31	Minnesota
ZIDLICKY, Marek	5-11	190	R	Most, Czech.	34	Minnesota

GOALTENDERS	HT	WT	C	Place of Birth	*Age	2010-11 Club
BACKSTROM, Niklas	6-1	189	L	Helsinki, Finland	33	Minnesota
HARDING, Josh	6-1	197	R	Regina, Sask.	27	Minnesota

* – Age at start of 2011-12 season

2010-11 Scoring
*– rookie

Regular Season

Pos	#	Player	Team	GP	G	A	Pts	TOI	+/-	PIM	PP	SH	GW	S	%
R	24	Martin Havlat	MIN	78	22	40	62	18:21	-10	52	3	0	4	229	9.6
C	9	Mikko Koivu	MIN	71	17	45	62	19:29	4	50	7	1	3	191	8.9
L	15	Andrew Brunette	MIN	82	18	28	46	16:47	-7	16	8	0	3	117	15.4
D	8	Brent Burns	MIN	80	17	29	46	25:02	-10	98	8	0	3	170	10.0
C	7	Matt Cullen	MIN	78	12	27	39	18:01	-14	34	5	4	2	150	8.0
C	96	Pierre-Marc Bouchard	MIN	59	12	26	38	15:42	-3	14	0	0	2	98	12.2
C	21	Kyle Brodziak	MIN	80	16	21	37	15:46	4	56	2	1	1	126	12.7
R	20	Antti Miettinen	MIN	73	16	19	35	17:01	-3	38	8	0	1	168	9.5
R	22	Cal Clutterbuck	MIN	76	19	15	34	15:50	-5	79	4	0	3	191	9.9
C	11	John Madden	MIN	76	12	13	25	15:20	-9	10	1	1	4	107	11.2
D	3	Marek Zidlicky	MIN	46	7	17	24	21:46	-6	30	3	0	0	53	13.2
D	55	Nick Schultz	MIN	74	3	14	17	20:13	-4	38	0	0	0	46	6.5
R	12	Chuck Kobasew	MIN	63	9	7	16	11:50	-6	19	0	0	1	74	12.2
D	46	*Jared Spurgeon	MIN	53	4	8	12	15:04	-1	2	2	0	1	38	10.5
L	23	Eric Nystrom	MIN	82	4	8	12	13:18	-16	30	1	0	0	83	4.8
L	16	Brad Staubitz	MIN	71	4	5	9	6:30	-5	173	0	0	1	29	13.8
D	4	*Clayton Stoner	MIN	57	2	7	9	16:51	-5	96	0	0	1	40	5.0
C	19	Patrick O'Sullivan	CAR	10	1	0	1	8:51	-1	2	0	0	0	13	7.7
			MIN	21	1	6	7	13:46	-1	2	0	0	0	37	2.7
			Total	31	2	6	8	12:11	-2	4	0	0	0	50	4.0
D	5	Greg Zanon	MIN	82	0	7	7	21:32	-5	48	0	0	0	55	0.0
L	48	*Guillaume Latendresse	MIN	11	3	3	6	12:42	2	8	1	0	1	18	16.7
D	25	Cam Barker	MIN	52	1	4	5	16:24	-10	34	0	0	1	44	2.3
D	41	*Justin Falk	MIN	22	0	3	3	14:09	-4	6	0	0	0	7	0.0
R	45	*Carson McMillan	MIN	4	1	1	2	9:20	1	0	0	0	0	5	20.0
C	17	*Casey Wellman	MIN	15	1	1	2	10:38	-1	4	0	0	1	20	5.0
D	6	*Marco Scandella	MIN	20	0	2	2	14:58	-9	2	0	0	0	13	0.0
D	18	Colton Gillies	MIN	7	1	0	1	10:22	-2	2	0	0	0	3	33.3
D	43	Warren Peters	MIN	11	1	0	1	8:42	-2	4	0	0	0	11	9.1
D	42	Drew Bagnall	MIN	2	0	0	0	13:00	-2	4	0	0	0	1	0.0
D	39	Nate Prosser	MIN	2	0	0	0	14:48	0	0	0	0	0	1	0.0
R	29	Jed Ortmeyer	MIN	4	0	0	0	9:23	-1	2	0	0	0	5	0.0
L	28	*Matt Kassian	MIN	6	0	0	0	5:29	-1	12	0	0	0	1	0.0
L	38	Robbie Earl	MIN	6	0	0	0	8:45	-1	0	0	0	0	6	0.0
C	27	*Cody Almond	MIN	8	0	0	0	7:01	0	2	0	0	0	3	0.0
D	34	*Maxim Noreau	MIN	5	0	0	0	14:17	-1	0	0	0	0	8	0.0

Goaltending

No.	Goaltender	GPI	Mins	Avg	W	L	OT	EN	SO	GA	SA	S%	G	A	PIM
35	*Anton Khudobin	4	189	1.59	2	1	0	1	1	5	86	.942	0	0	0
32	Niklas Backstrom	51	2978	2.66	22	23	5	6	3	132	1566	.916	0	1	2
60	Jose Theodore	32	1793	2.71	15	11	3	3	1	81	963	.916	0	0	2
	Totals	82	4985	2.74	39	35	8	10	5	228	2625	.913			

Kyle Brodziak reached career highs with 16 goals and 37 points for the Wild in 2010-11.

Mike Yeo
Head Coach
Born: North Bay, Ont., July 31, 1973.

Mike Yeo was named head coach of the Minnesota Wild on June 17, 2011. The hiring came 366 days after Yeo had been tabbed to lead the Houston Aeros, the Wild's primary developmental affiliate in the American Hockey League. In his one year as a head coach, he led the Aeros to an appearance in the Calder Cup Finals. Yeo joined the Wild franchise with the Aeros after spending the previous five seasons as assistant coach of the NHL's Pittsburgh Penguins. During Yeo's tenure in Pittsburgh he helped lead the Penguins to the 2008-09 Stanley Cup championship.

Yeo played five seasons with the Aeros (1994 to 1999) and was the captain of Houston's 1999 Turner Cup Championship team. He joined the Aeros in 1994 after playing the previous four seasons with the Sudbury Wolves (Ontario Hockey Leaue). As a left winger, he accumulated 127 points (55 goals, 72 assists) and 511 penalty minutes over 317 games during his Aeros playing career. Yeo enjoyed career-highs of 20 goals, 21 assists, 41 points and 128 penalty minutes during the 1997-98 season while serving as team captain. The native of North Bay, Ontario posted 18 points (six goals, 12 assists) and 65 penalty minutes in 57 games during the 1998-99 season. He also added four assists and 11 penalty minutes in nine games during the Aeros' run to the Turner Cup. Yeo joined the Wilkes-Barre/Scranton Penguins for the 1999-2000 season and played in 19 games before suffering a career-ending knee injury.

After his injury, Yeo joined the Wilkes-Barre/Scranton coaching staff where he spent six seasons as the assistant coach of Pittsburgh's AHL affiliate. During his tenure in Wilkes-Barre/Scranton, Yeo helped the Penguins to a Western Conference championship in 2001, an Eastern Conference championship in 2005, and two trips to the Calder Cup Finals. He made the jump to the NHL's Pittsburgh Penguins under head coach Michel Therrien in December 2005. During his first full season in 2006-07, Yeo helped the Penguins to a 47-point improvement from the previous season, the fourth-largest turnaround from one season to the next in NHL history. In Yeo's second season, he helped lead the Penguins to the Stanley Cup Final for the first time since the 1992 season. Yeo remained on staff in Pittsburgh during the 2008-09 season after Dan Byslma replaced Therrien on February 15, 2009, and the Penguins went on to win their third Stanley Cup championship in franchise history.

Coaching Record

				Regular Season				Playoffs			
Season	Team	League	GC	W	L	O/T		GC	W	L	T
2010-11	Houston	AHL	80	46	28	6		24	14	10	0

Club Records

Team

(Figures in brackets for season records are games played.)

Most Points	104	2006-07 (82)
Most Wins	48	2006-07 (82)
Most Ties	20	2003-04 (82)
Most Losses	39	2000-01 (82)
Most Goals	235	2006-07 (82)
Most Goals Against	246	2009-10 (82)
Fewest Points	68	2000-01 (82)
Fewest Wins	25	2000-01 (82)
Fewest Ties	10	2002-03 (82)
Fewest Losses	26	2006-07 (82)
Fewest Goals	168	2000-01 (82)
Fewest Goals Against	178	2002-03 (82)

Longest Winning Streak
- Overall......9 Mar. 8-24/07
- Home......8 Oct. 5-Nov. 2/06, Dec. 5/06-Jan. 2/07
- Away......5 Mar. 8-17/07

Longest Undefeated Streak
- Overall......9 Dec. 13-30/03 (4 wins, 5 ties) Mar. 8-24/07 (9 wins)
- Home......9 Dec. 13/00-Jan. 10/01 (5 wins, 4 ties)
- Away......7 Dec. 6-30/03 (2 wins, 5 ties)

Longest Losing Streak
- Overall......8 Mar. 10-26/11
- Home......4 Oct. 29-Nov. 15/00
- Away......11 Nov. 20/06-Jan. 9/07

Longest Winless Streak
- Overall......12 Mar. 11-Apr. 4/01 (9 losses, 3 ties)
- Home......8 Feb. 26-Mar. 28/01 (5 losses, 3 ties)
- Away......12 Dec. 18/03-Jan. 31/04 (5 losses, 7 ties)

Most Shutouts, Season	8	
Most PIM, Season	1,209	2001-02 (82), 2005-06 (82)
Most Goals, Game	8	Mar. 25/04 (Min. 8 at Chi. 2) Apr. 10/09 (Nsh. 2 at Min. 8)

Individual

Most Seasons	9	Nick Schultz
Most Games	681	Nick Schultz
Most Goals, Career	219	Marian Gaborik
Most Assists, Career	218	Marian Gaborik
Most Points, Career	437	Marian Gaborik (219G, 218A)
Most PIM, Career	698	Matt Johnson
Most Shutouts, Career	22	Niklas Backstrom

Longest Consecutive Games Streak......288 Antti Laaksonen (Oct. 6/00-Dec. 29/03)

Most Goals, Season	42	Marian Gaborik (2007-08)
Most Assists, Season	50	Pierre-Marc Bouchard (2007-08)
Most Points, Season	83	Marian Gaborik (2007-08; 42G, 41A)
Most PIM, Season	201	Matt Johnson (2002-03)

Most Points, Defenseman,
- Season......46 Brent Burns (2010-11; 17G, 29A)

Most Points, Center,
- Season......71 Mikko Koivu (2009-10; 22G, 49A)

Most Points, Right Wing,
- Season......83 Marian Gaborik (2007-08; 42G, 41A)

Most Points, Left Wing,
- Season......79 Brian Rolston (2005-06; 34G, 45A)

Most Points, Rookie,
- Season......36 Marian Gaborik (2000-01; 18G, 18A)

Most Shutouts, Season......8 Nicklas Backstrom (2008-09)

Most Goals, Game......5 Marian Gaborik (Dec. 20/07)

Most Assists, Game......4 Andrew Brunette (Mar. 10/02) Marian Gaborik (Oct. 26/02) Pascal Dupuis (Mar. 25/04) Eric Belanger (Nov. 15/07) Mikko Koivu (Oct. 16/08, Jan. 2/11)

Most Points, Game......6 Marian Gaborik (Oct. 26/02; 2G, 4A), (Dec. 20/07; 5G, 1A)

Captains' History

Sean O'Donnell, Scott Pellerin, Wes Walz, Brad Bombardir, Darby Hendrickson, 2000-01; Jim Dowd, Filip Kuba, Brad Brown, Andrew Brunette, 2001-02; Brad Bombardir, Matt Johnson, Sergei Zholtok, 2002-03; Brad Brown, Andrew Brunette, Richard Park, Brad Bombardir, Jim Dowd, 2003-04; Alex Henry, Filip Kuba, Willie Mitchell, Brian Rolston, Wes Walz, 2005-06; Brian Rolston, Keith Carney, Mark Parrish, 2006-07; Pavol Demitra, Brian Rolston, Mark Parrish, Nick Schultz, Marian Gaborik, 2007-08; Mikko Koivu, Kim Johnsson, Andrew Brunette, 2008-09; Mikko Koivu, 2009-10 to date.

General Managers' History

Doug Risebrough, 2000-01 to 2008-09; Chuck Fletcher, 2009-10 to date.

Coaching History

Jacques Lemaire, 2000-01 to 2008-09; Todd Richards, 2009-10, 2010-11; Mike Yeo, 2011-12.

All-time Record vs. Other Clubs

Regular Season

	At Home								On Road								Total							
	GP	W	L	T	OL	GF	GA	PTS	GP	W	L	T	OL	GF	GA	PTS	GP	W	L	T	OL	GF	GA	PTS
Anaheim	20	13	4	2	1	54	38	29	20	8	11	0	1	47	54	17	40	21	15	2	2	101	92	46
Atlanta	5	3	1	1	0	15	9	7	5	3	1	0	1	17	16	7	10	6	2	1	1	32	25	14
Boston	5	3	1	0	1	14	10	7	6	6	0	0	0	19	6	12	11	9	1	0	1	33	16	19
Buffalo	6	1	3	0	2	11	17	4	5	4	1	0	0	16	10	8	11	5	4	0	2	27	27	12
Calgary	32	16	9	1	6	79	66	39	31	8	19	3	1	64	77	20	63	24	28	4	7	143	143	59
Carolina	8	4	2	2	0	23	24	10	5	0	3	0	2	7	13	2	13	4	5	2	2	30	37	12
Chicago	20	13	7	0	0	58	53	26	20	11	8	1	0	55	45	23	40	24	15	1	0	113	98	49
Colorado	31	17	10	1	3	86	89	38	32	12	16	2	2	76	90	28	63	29	26	3	5	162	179	66
Columbus	20	14	4	0	2	59	43	30	19	5	10	1	3	39	54	14	39	19	14	1	5	98	97	44
Dallas	20	10	8	0	2	52	47	22	20	3	12	1	4	44	77	11	40	13	20	1	6	96	124	33
Detroit	20	5	8	2	5	47	58	17	20	5	14	1	0	46	78	11	40	10	22	3	5	93	136	28
Edmonton	31	20	9	1	1	92	62	42	32	14	11	3	4	77	77	35	63	34	20	4	5	169	139	77
Florida	5	3	0	1	1	16	6	8	6	4	2	0	0	18	12	8	11	7	2	1	1	34	18	16
Los Angeles	20	8	6	3	3	42	45	22	20	9	7	2	2	50	52	22	40	17	13	5	5	92	97	44
Montreal	5	2	2	0	1	12	18	5	5	2	1	0	2	13	14	5	10	4	4	1	1	25	32	10
Nashville	20	11	6	3	0	68	56	25	20	6	12	2	0	42	61	14	40	17	18	5	0	110	117	39
New Jersey	5	1	2	1	1	13	17	4	6	1	3	1	1	12	21	4	11	2	5	2	2	25	38	8
NY Islanders	6	5	1	0	0	20	15	10	6	3	3	0	0	17	15	6	12	8	4	0	0	37	30	16
NY Rangers	7	3	3	0	1	22	23	7	6	2	4	0	0	12	16	4	13	5	7	0	1	34	39	11
Ottawa	6	1	3	1	1	15	22	4	4	1	3	0	0	8	13	2	10	2	6	1	1	23	35	6
Philadelphia	5	2	2	1	0	9	13	5	7	2	5	0	0	10	20	4	12	4	7	1	0	19	33	9
Phoenix	20	10	7	2	1	56	45	23	20	8	10	1	1	44	53	18	40	18	17	3	2	100	98	41
Pittsburgh	5	3	1	1	0	15	12	7	7	6	1	0	0	25	8	12	12	9	2	1	0	40	20	19
St. Louis	20	12	4	2	2	63	41	28	20	8	8	3	1	42	47	20	40	20	12	5	3	105	88	48
San Jose	20	8	9	1	2	47	51	19	20	7	11	1	1	43	58	16	40	15	20	2	3	90	109	35
Tampa Bay	6	4	2	0	0	20	16	8	7	4	1	1	1	20	15	10	13	8	3	1	1	40	31	18
Toronto	4	2	2	0	0	11	8	4	5	1	4	0	0	11	17	2	9	3	6	0	0	22	25	6
Vancouver	32	16	11	2	3	93	76	37	31	10	13	3	5	73	92	28	63	26	24	5	8	166	168	65
Washington	6	6	0	0	0	15	7	12	5	1	4	0	0	8	14	2	11	7	4	0	0	23	21	14
Totals	**410**	**216**	**127**	**28**	**39**	**1127**	**987**	**499**	**410**	**154**	**199**	**27**	**30**	**955**	**1125**	**365**	**820**	**370**	**326**	**55**	**69**	**2082**	**2112**	**864**

Playoffs

	Series	W	L	GP	W	L	T	GF	GA	Last Mtg.	Rnd.	Result
Anaheim	2	0	2	9	1	8	0	10	21	2007	CQF	L 1-4
Colorado	2	1	1	13	6	7	0	28	34	2008	CQF	L 2-4
Vancouver	1	1	0	7	4	3	0	26	17	2003	CSF	W 4-3
Totals	**5**	**2**	**3**	**29**	**11**	**18**	**0**	**64**	**72**			

Playoff Results 2011-2007

Year	Round	Opponent	Result	GF	GA
2008	CQF	Colorado	L 2-4	12	17
2007	CQF	Anaheim	L 1-4	9	12

Abbreviations: Round: CF – conference final; **CSF** – conference semi-final; **CQF** – conference quarter-final.

2010-11 Results

Oct.	7	Carolina	3-4		9	Dallas	0-4
	8	at Carolina	1-2†		11	at Nashville	1-5
	14	Edmonton	4-2		14	Colorado	1-4
	16	Columbus	2-3		16	Vancouver	4-0
	19	Vancouver	6-2		18	at Edmonton	4-1
	21	at Edmonton	4-2		19	at Calgary	6-0
	22	at Vancouver	1-5		22	at San Jose	3-4
	25	Los Angeles	2-3†		25	at Chicago	4-2
	28	Washington	2-1	Feb. 1	Los Angeles	1-0†
	30	Chicago	1-3		3	at Colorado	4-3
Nov.	2	San Jose	1-0		5	at Phoenix	0-1
	5	Calgary	2-1		9	Colorado	3-2
	6	at Columbus	3-2		11	at St. Louis	5-4†
	11	at Atlanta	1-5		12	St. Louis	3-1
	12	at Florida	1-2		15	Vancouver	1-4
	14	at Tampa Bay	4-1		16	at Chicago	1-3
	17	Anaheim	2-1*		18	Anaheim	5-1
	19	at Detroit	4-3*		20	Detroit	1-2†
	20	NY Rangers	2-5		22	Edmonton	4-1
	24	Philadelphia	1-6		24	at Los Angeles	2-4
	26	Nashville	5-2		25	at Anaheim	3-2*
	27	at Colorado	4-7		28	Chicago	2-4
	29	at Calgary	0-3	Mar. 2	at NY Islanders	1-4
Dec.	1	Phoenix	2-4		3	at NY Rangers	3-1
	3	Calgary	2-3†		6	Buffalo	2-3*
	4	at Dallas	3-4*		8	Colorado	5-2
	9	at Phoenix	3-2		10	at Nashville	0-4
	11	at Los Angeles	3-2*		11	at Dallas	0-4
	12	at Anaheim	2-6		14	at Vancouver	2-4
	16	Ottawa	1-3		17	at San Jose	2-3
	18	at Calgary	3-1		19	Columbus	4-5*
	20	Calgary	4-1		20	Montreal	1-8
	23	at Colorado	3-1		22	Toronto	0-3
	26	Detroit	1-4		26	St. Louis	3-6
	27	at Columbus	3-4†		29	at St. Louis	3-2†
	29	San Jose	5-3		31	Edmonton	4-2
	31	Nashville	1-4	Apr. 2	Tampa Bay	1-3
Jan.	2	Phoenix	6-5*		3	at Detroit	2-4
	4	at New Jersey	2-1		7	at Vancouver	0-5
	6	at Boston	3-1		8	at Edmonton	3-1
	8	at Pittsburgh	4-0		10	Dallas	5-3

* – Overtime † – Shootout

Entry Draft Selections 2011-2000

Name in bold denotes played in NHL.

2011 Pick	2007 Pick	2004 Pick	2002 Pick
10 Jonas Brodin	16 **Colton Gillies**	12 A.J. Thelen	8 **Pierre-Marc Bouchard**
28 Zack Phillips	110 **Justin Falk**	42 Roman Voloshenko	38 **Josh Harding**
60 Mario Lucia	140 **Cody Almond**	78 **Peter Olvecky**	72 Mike Erickson
131 Nick Seeler	170 Harri Ilvonen	79 **Clayton Stoner**	73 **Barry Brust**
161 Stephen Michalek	200 **Carson McMillan**	111 **Ryan Jones**	155 Armands Berzins
191 Tyler Graovac		114 Patrick Bordeleau	175 **Matt Foy**
	2006 Pick	117 Julien Sprunger	204 Niklas Eckerblom
2010 Pick	9 **James Sheppard**	161 Jean-Claude Sawyer	237 **Christoph Brandner**
9 Mikael Granlund	40 Ondrej Fiala	175 Aaron Boogaard	268 Mikhail Tyulyapkin
39 Brett Bulmer	72 **Cal Clutterbuck**	195 Jean-Michel Rizk	269 Mika Hannula
56 Johan Larsson	102 Kyle Medvec	206 **Anton Khudobin**	
59 Jason Zucker	132 Niko Hovinen	272 Kyle Wilson	2001 Pick
159 Johan Gustafsson	162 Julian Walker		6 **Mikko Koivu**
189 Dylen McKinlay	192 Chris Hickey	2003 Pick	36 **Kyle Wanvig**
		20 **Brent Burns**	74 Chris Heid
2009 Pick	2005 Pick	56 **Patrick O'Sullivan**	93 **Stephane Veilleux**
16 **Nick Leddy**	4 **Benoit Pouliot**	78 **Danny Irmen**	103 **Tony Virta**
77 **Matt Hackett**	57 **Matt Kassian**	157 Marcin Kolusz	202 **Derek Boogaard**
103 Kris Foucault	65 Kristofer Westblom	187 Miroslav Kopriva	239 Jake Riddle
116 Alexander Fallstrom	110 Kyle Bailey	207 Georgy Misharin	
161 Darcy Kuemper	122 Morten Madsen	219 Adam Courchaine	2000 Pick
163 Jere Sallinen	129 Anthony Aiello	251 Mathieu Melanson	3 **Marian Gaborik**
182 Erik Haula	199 Riley Emmerson	281 Jean-Michel Bolduc	33 **Nick Schultz**
193 Anthony Hamburg			99 Marc Cavosie
			132 **Maxim Sushinsky**
2008 Pick			170 Erik Reitz
23 Tyler Cuma			199 Brian Passmore
55 **Marco Scandella**			214 **Peter Bartos**
115 Sean Lorenz			232 **Lubomir Sekeras**
145 Eero Elo			255 Eric Johansson

Chuck Fletcher
General Manager
Born: Montreal, Que., April 29, 1967.

The Minnesota Wild announced the hiring of Chuck Fletcher as the second general manager in club history on May 22, 2009. Fletcher has been to the Stanley Cup Finals in management with three different teams (Florida, Anaheim and Pittsburgh). With the Penguins from 2006 to 2009, he worked closely with general manager Ray Shero on all hockey-related matters, including scouting, overseeing the development of young prospects and contract negotiations. Fletcher also managed hockey operations for the club's American Hockey League affiliate, the Wilkes-Barre/Scranton Penguins. Under his leadership, Wilkes-Barre/Scranton reached the AHL's Calder Cup finals in 2007-08, and the division finals in 2008-09.

Fletcher, the son of Hockey Hall of Famer Cliff Fletcher, had extensive NHL management experience before he joined the Penguins in July 2006 – including a four-year stint with the Anaheim Ducks from 2003 to 2006 as director of hockey operations, assistant general manager, and vice president of amateur scouting and player development.

The Montreal native also spent nine years in the front office of the Florida Panthers from 1993 to 2002, working seven seasons as assistant general manager and part of one season (2001-02) as interim general manager. In 1996, the Panthers advanced to the Stanley Cup Finals.

Fletcher graduated from Harvard in 1990 and spent one year as the sales and merchandising coordinator for Hockey Canada and two years as a player representative for Newport Sports Management before making the transition to the front office.

Club Directory

Xcel Energy Center

Minnesota Wild
317 Washington Street
St. Paul, MN 55102
Phone **651/602-6000**
FAX 651/222-1055
Tickets 651/222-9453
www.wild.com
Capacity: 18,064

Board Members . . . . Craig Leipold (Owner/Governor), Philip Falcone (Minority Owner), Mark Falcone, Quinn Martin, Mark Pacchini and Jac Sperling
Investors in MSE . . . . Craig Leipold (Owner/Governor), Philip Falcone (Minority Owner); Limited Partners: Robert Hubbard, Stanley E. Hubbard, Stanley S. Hubbard, Horace H. Irvine III, Robert Marvin, Robert O. Naegele, Jr., Ford Nicholson, Todd Nicholson, Vance Opperman and Michael Reilly
Owner/Governor . . . . Craig Leipold
Minority Owner . . . . Philip Falcone
General Manager . . . . Chuck Fletcher
Executive Vice President, Chief Financial Officer. . . . Jeff Pellegrom
Chief Operating Officer. . . . . Matt Majka
Vice President and General Counsel . . . . Steve Weinreich
Vice President, Facility Admin. / G.M., RiverCentre . . . Jim Ibister
V.P./General Manager, Xcel Energy Center . . . . Jack Larson
Vice President Corp. Partnerships and Retail Mgmt. . . Carin Anderson
Vice President, Brand Marketing . . . . John Maher
Executive Assistant . . . . Stephanie Huseby
Administrative Assistant, Sales and Service,
  Creative Services and Marketing . . . . Tawnya Vidnovic
Administrative Assistant, Communications/Broadcasting,
  Corp. Partnerships, Legal and Human Resources . Deb Hanson
Hockey Operations
Assistant General Manager . . . . Brent Flahr
Assistant to the G.M. and G.M. Houston Aeros. . . . Jim Mill
Head Coach . . . . Mike Yeo
Assistant Coaches. . . . . Rick Wilson, Darryl Sydor, Darby Hendrickson
Goalie Coach . . . . Bob Mason
Strength and Conditioning Coach . . . . Kirk Olson
Coordinator of Amateur Scouting . . . . Guy Lapointe
Director of Player Personnel/Development . . . . Blair Mackasey/Brad Bombardir
Scouts . . . . Marc Chamard, Craig Channell, Paul Charles, Brian Fortin, Christopher Hamel, Jamie Hislop, Brian Hunter, Chris Kelleher, Martin Nanne, Ricard Perrson, Pavel Routa, Ernie Vargas
Head Athletic Trainer / Assistant . . . . Don Fuller / John Worley
Head Equipment Manager / Assistants . . . . Tony DaCosta / Matt Benz, Rick Bronwell
Message Therapist . . . . Travis Green
Director of Hockey Administration . . . . Shep Harder
Hockey Operations Administrator . . . . Cindy Sweiger
Travel Coordinator . . . . Mary Kenna
Medical Staff . . . . Drs. Sheldon Burns, Joel Boyd, Brad Nelson, Dan Peterson
Oral Surgeon / Team Dentists . . . . . . David Hamlar / Kyle Edlund, Mike Nanne, Mike Pelke
Sales and Service
Director, Customer Sales. Matt Cords
Director, Ticket Operations . . . . Chris Turns
Director, Fan Relations . . . . Maria Troje
Retail Operation
Director, Retail Operations . . . . Matt Freiberg
Managers, Retail Operations . . . . Scott Sarkis
Corporate Partnerships
Senior Account Executive . . . . Bryan Bellows
Account Executives . . . . Brandon Latack, Jeff Hunsaker
Communications and Broadcasting
Manager, Media Relations and Team Services . . . . . Aaron Sickman
Coordinator, Media Relations and Team Services. . . Ryan Stanzel
Manager of Broadcasting . . . . Maggie Kukar
Radio Operations Coordinator. . . . . Kevin Falness
Media Relations Intern . . . . Natalie Dillon
Radio Play-By-Play / Analyst. . . . . Bob Kurtz / Tom Reid
Television Play-By-Play / Analyst. . . . . Dan Terhaar / Mike Greenlay
Brand Marketing
Director, Events and Promotions . . . . Wayne Petersen
Director, Marketing Intelligence . . . . Mitch Helgerson
Manager, Game Presentation . . . . Paul Loomis
Manager, Production Facilities Operations . . . . Hank Dolan
Manager, Web and Creative Services . . . . Matt Minnichsoffer
Managing Editor, Web Sites . . . . Glen Andresen
Team Curator . . . . Roger Godin
Community Giving
Sr. Director, Community Partnerships . . . . Brad Bombardir
Manager, Community Relations . . . . Rachel Schuldt
Minnesota Wild Foundation
Executive Director . . . . Amy Woog-Patnode
Finance and Accounting
Controller and Senior Director Finance . . . . Molly Jungbauer
Senior Manager, Accounting Services . . . . Molly McArdle
Human Resources
Specialist, Human Resources . . . . Melissa Orrey
Information Technology
Helpdesk Manager Mike Vevea
Miscellaneous
Radio Network Flagship . . . . KFAN-AM / 100.3 FM
Television Network Fox Sports Net
Team Photographer / Public Address Announcer . . . Bruce Kluckhohn / Adam Abrams

Montreal Canadiens

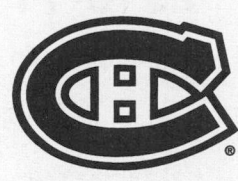

2010-11 Results: 44W-30L-5OTL-3SOL 96PTS.
Second, Northeast Division

Key Off-Season Signings/Acquisitions

2011

June
- **1** • Re-signed D **Hal Gill**.
- **9** • Re-signed LW **Andrei Kostitsyn**.
- **10** • Re-signed LW **Mathieu Darche**.
- **20** • Re-signed LW **Max Pacioretty** and C **David Desharnais**.
- **23** • Re-signed D **Andrei Markov**.
- **29** • Re-signed D **Yannick Weber**.

July
- **1** • Signed LW **Erik Cole** and G **Peter Budaj**.
- **13** • Re-signed C **Ryan White**.
- **22** • Named **Randy Cunneyworth** and **Randy Ladouceur** assistant coaches.
- **22** • Re-signed D **Josh Gorges**.

2011-12 Schedule

Month	Day	Date	Opponent
Oct.	Thu.	6	at Toronto
	Sun.	9	at Winnipeg*
	Thu.	13	Calgary
	Sat.	15	Colorado
	Tue.	18	Buffalo
	Thu.	20	at Pittsburgh
	Sat.	22	Toronto
	Mon.	24	Florida
	Wed.	26	Philadelphia
	Thu.	27	at Boston
	Sat.	29	Boston
Nov.	Fri.	4	at Ottawa
	Sat.	5	at NY Rangers
	Tue.	8	Edmonton
	Thu.	10	at Phoenix
	Sat.	12	at Nashville
	Mon.	14	Buffalo
	Wed.	16	Carolina
	Thu.	17	at NY Islanders
	Sat.	19	NY Rangers
	Mon.	21	Boston
	Wed.	23	at Carolina
	Fri.	25	at Philadelphia*
	Sat.	26	Pittsburgh
	Wed.	30	at Anaheim
Dec.	Thu.	1	at San Jose
	Sat.	3	at Los Angeles*
	Tue.	6	Columbus
	Thu.	8	Vancouver
	Sat.	10	at New Jersey*
	Tue.	13	NY Islanders
	Thu.	15	Philadelphia
	Sat.	17	New Jersey
	Mon.	19	at Boston
	Wed.	21	at Chicago
	Thu.	22	at Winnipeg
	Tue.	27	at Ottawa
	Thu.	29	at Tampa Bay
	Sat.	31	at Florida
Jan.	Wed.	4	Winnipeg
	Sat.	7	Tampa Bay
	Tue.	10	St. Louis
	Thu.	12	at Boston
	Sat.	14	Ottawa
	Sun.	15	NY Rangers
	Wed.	18	Washington
	Fri.	20	at Pittsburgh
	Sat.	21	at Toronto
	Wed.	25	Detroit
	Tue.	31	Buffalo
Feb.	Thu.	2	at New Jersey
	Sat.	4	Washington*
	Sun.	5	Winnipeg*
	Tue.	7	Pittsburgh
	Thu.	9	at NY Islanders
	Sat.	11	at Toronto
	Mon.	13	Carolina
	Wed.	15	Boston
	Fri.	17	at Buffalo
	Sun.	19	New Jersey
	Tue.	21	Dallas
	Fri.	24	at Washington
	Sun.	26	at Florida*
	Tue.	28	at Tampa Bay
Mar.	Thu.	1	Minnesota
	Sat.	3	Toronto
	Tue.	6	at Calgary
	Thu.	8	at Edmonton
	Sat.	10	at Vancouver
	Mon.	12	at Buffalo
	Wed.	14	Ottawa
	Fri.	16	at Ottawa
	Sat.	17	NY Islanders
	Wed.	21	at Buffalo
	Fri.	23	Ottawa
	Sat.	24	at Philadelphia
	Tue.	27	Florida
	Fri.	30	at NY Rangers
	Sat.	31	at Washington
Apr.	Wed.	4	Tampa Bay
	Thu.	5	at Carolina
	Sat.	7	Toronto

* Denotes afternoon game.

NORTHEAST DIVISION
95th NHL Season

Franchise date: November 26, 1917

Year-by-Year Record

		Home				Road				Overall								
Season	**GP**	**W**	**L**	**T**	**OL**	**W**	**L**	**T**	**OL**	**W**	**L**	**T**	**OL**	**GF**	**GA**	**Pts.**	**Finished**	**Playoff Result**
2010-11	82	24	11	....	6	20	19	....	2	44	30	....	8	216	209	96	2nd, Northeast Div.	Lost Conf. Quarter-Final
2009-10	82	20	16	....	5	19	17	....	5	39	33	....	10	217	223	88	4th, Northeast Div.	Lost Conf. Championship
2008-09	82	24	10	....	7	17	20	....	4	41	30	....	11	249	247	93	2nd, Northeast Div.	Lost Conf. Quarter-Final
2007-08	82	22	13	....	6	25	12	....	4	47	25	....	10	262	222	104	1st, Northeast Div.	Lost Conf. Semi-Final
2006-07	82	26	12	....	3	16	22	....	3	42	34	....	6	245	256	90	4th, Northeast Div.	Out of Playoffs
2005-06	82	24	13	....	4	18	18	....	5	42	31	....	9	243	247	93	3rd, Northeast Div.	Lost Conf. Quarter-Final
2004-05	....	....	....	....	....	....	....	....	....	....	....	....	....	....	....	....		
2003-04	82	23	13	4	1	18	17	3	3	41	30	7	4	208	192	93	4th, Northeast Div.	Lost Conf. Semi-Final
2002-03	82	16	16	5	4	14	19	3	5	30	35	8	9	206	234	77	4th, Northeast Div.	Out of Playoffs
2001-02	82	21	13	6	1	15	18	6	2	36	31	12	3	207	209	87	4th, Northeast Div.	Lost Conf. Semi-Final
2000-01	82	15	20	4	2	13	20	4	4	28	40	8	6	206	232	70	5th, Northeast Div.	Out of Playoffs
1999-2000	82	18	17	5	1	17	17	4	3	35	34	9	4	196	194	83	4th, Northeast Div.	Out of Playoffs
1998-99	82	21	15	5	....	11	24	6	....	32	39	11	....	184	209	75	5th, Northeast Div.	Out of Playoffs
1997-98	82	15	17	9	....	22	15	4	....	37	32	13	....	235	208	87	4th, Northeast Div.	Lost Conf. Semi-Final
1996-97	82	17	17	7	....	14	19	8	....	31	36	15	....	249	276	77	4th, Northeast Div.	Lost Conf. Quarter-Final
1995-96	82	23	12	6	....	17	20	4	....	40	32	10	....	265	248	90	3rd, Northeast Div.	Lost Conf. Quarter-Final
1994-95	48	15	5	4	....	3	18	3	....	18	23	7	....	125	148	43	6th, Northeast Div.	Out of Playoffs
1993-94	84	26	12	4	....	15	17	10	....	41	29	14	....	283	248	96	3rd, Northeast Div.	Lost Conf. Quarter-Final
1992-93	**84**	**27**	**13**	**2**	....	**21**	**17**	**4**	....	**48**	**30**	**6**	....	**326**	**280**	**102**	**3rd, Adams Div.**	**Won Stanley Cup**
1991-92	80	27	8	5	....	14	20	6	....	41	28	11	....	267	207	93	1st, Adams Div.	Lost Div. Final
1990-91	80	23	12	5	....	16	18	6	....	39	30	11	....	273	249	89	2nd, Adams Div.	Lost Div. Final
1989-90	80	26	8	6	....	15	20	5	....	41	28	11	....	288	234	93	3rd, Adams Div.	Lost Div. Final
1988-89	80	30	6	4	....	23	12	5	....	53	18	9	....	315	218	115	1st, Adams Div.	Lost Final
1987-88	80	26	8	6	....	19	14	7	....	45	22	13	....	298	238	103	1st, Adams Div.	Lost Div. Final
1986-87	80	27	9	4	....	14	20	6	....	41	29	10	....	277	241	92	2nd, Adams Div.	Lost Conf. Championship
1985-86	**80**	**25**	**11**	**4**	....	**15**	**22**	**3**	....	**40**	**33**	**7**	....	**330**	**280**	**87**	**2nd, Adams Div.**	**Won Stanley Cup**
1984-85	80	24	10	6	....	17	17	6	....	41	27	12	....	309	262	94	1st, Adams Div.	Lost Div. Final
1983-84	80	19	19	2	....	16	21	3	....	35	40	5	....	286	295	75	4th, Adams Div.	Lost Conf. Championship
1982-83	80	25	6	9	....	17	18	5	....	42	24	14	....	350	286	98	2nd, Adams Div.	Lost Div. Semi-Final
1981-82	80	25	6	9	....	21	11	8	....	46	17	17	....	360	223	109	1st, Adams Div.	Lost Div. Semi-Final
1980-81	80	31	7	2	....	14	15	11	....	45	22	13	....	332	232	103	1st, Norris Div.	Lost Prelim. Round
1979-80	80	30	7	3	....	17	13	10	....	47	20	13	....	328	240	107	1st, Norris Div.	Lost Quarter-Final
1978-79	**80**	**29**	**6**	**5**	....	**23**	**11**	**6**	....	**52**	**17**	**11**	....	**337**	**204**	**115**	**1st, Norris Div.**	**Won Stanley Cup**
1977-78	**80**	**32**	**4**	**4**	....	**27**	**6**	**7**	....	**59**	**10**	**11**	....	**359**	**183**	**129**	**1st, Norris Div.**	**Won Stanley Cup**
1976-77	**80**	**33**	**1**	**6**	....	**27**	**7**	**6**	....	**60**	**8**	**12**	....	**387**	**171**	**132**	**1st, Norris Div.**	**Won Stanley Cup**
1975-76	**80**	**32**	**3**	**5**	....	**26**	**8**	**6**	....	**58**	**11**	**11**	....	**337**	**174**	**127**	**1st, Norris Div.**	**Won Stanley Cup**
1974-75	80	27	8	5	....	20	6	14	....	47	14	19	....	374	225	113	1st, Norris Div.	Lost Semi-Final
1973-74	78	24	12	3	....	21	12	6	....	45	24	9	....	293	240	99	2nd, East Div.	Lost Quarter-Final
1972-73	**78**	**29**	**4**	**6**	....	**23**	**6**	**10**	....	**52**	**10**	**16**	....	**329**	**184**	**120**	**1st, East Div.**	**Won Stanley Cup**
1971-72	78	29	3	7	....	17	13	9	....	46	16	16	....	307	205	108	3rd, East Div.	Lost Quarter-Final
1970-71	**78**	**29**	**7**	**3**	....	**13**	**16**	**10**	....	**42**	**23**	**13**	....	**291**	**216**	**97**	**3rd, East Div.**	**Won Stanley Cup**
1969-70	76	21	9	8	....	17	13	8	....	38	22	16	....	244	201	92	5th, East Div.	Out of Playoffs
1968-69	**76**	**26**	**7**	**5**	....	**20**	**12**	**6**	....	**46**	**19**	**11**	....	**271**	**202**	**103**	**1st, East Div.**	**Won Stanley Cup**
1967-68	**74**	**26**	**5**	**6**	....	**16**	**17**	**4**	....	**42**	**22**	**10**	....	**236**	**167**	**94**	**1st, East Div.**	**Won Stanley Cup**
1966-67	70	19	9	7	....	13	16	6	....	32	25	13	....	202	188	77	2nd,	Lost Final
1965-66	**70**	**23**	**11**	**1**	....	**18**	**10**	**7**	....	**41**	**21**	**8**	....	**239**	**173**	**90**	**1st,**	**Won Stanley Cup**
1964-65	**70**	**20**	**8**	**7**	....	**16**	**15**	**4**	....	**36**	**23**	**11**	....	**211**	**185**	**83**	**2nd,**	**Won Stanley Cup**
1963-64	70	22	7	6	....	14	14	7	....	36	21	13	....	209	167	85	1st,	Lost Semi-Final
1962-63	70	15	10	10	....	13	9	13	....	28	19	23	....	225	183	79	3rd,	Lost Semi-Final
1961-62	70	26	2	7	....	16	12	7	....	42	14	14	....	259	166	98	1st,	Lost Semi-Final
1960-61	70	24	6	5	....	17	13	5	....	41	19	10	....	254	188	92	1st,	Lost Semi-Final
1959-60	**70**	**23**	**4**	**8**	....	**17**	**14**	**4**	....	**40**	**18**	**12**	....	**255**	**178**	**92**	**1st,**	**Won Stanley Cup**
1958-59	**70**	**21**	**8**	**6**	....	**18**	**10**	**7**	....	**39**	**18**	**13**	....	**258**	**158**	**91**	**1st,**	**Won Stanley Cup**
1957-58	**70**	**23**	**8**	**4**	....	**20**	**9**	**6**	....	**43**	**17**	**10**	....	**250**	**158**	**96**	**1st,**	**Won Stanley Cup**
1956-57	**70**	**23**	**6**	**6**	....	**12**	**17**	**6**	....	**35**	**23**	**12**	....	**210**	**155**	**82**	**2nd,**	**Won Stanley Cup**
1955-56	**70**	**29**	**5**	**1**	....	**16**	**10**	**9**	....	**45**	**15**	**10**	....	**222**	**131**	**100**	**1st,**	**Won Stanley Cup**
1954-55	70	26	5	4	....	15	13	7	....	41	18	11	....	228	157	93	2nd,	Lost Final
1953-54	70	27	5	3	....	8	19	8	....	35	24	11	....	195	141	81	2nd,	Lost Final
1952-53	**70**	**18**	**12**	**5**	....	**10**	**11**	**14**	....	**28**	**23**	**19**	....	**155**	**148**	**75**	**2nd,**	**Won Stanley Cup**
1951-52	70	22	8	5	....	12	18	5	....	34	26	10	....	195	164	78	2nd,	Lost Final
1950-51	70	17	10	8	....	8	20	7	....	25	30	15	....	173	184	65	3rd,	Lost Final
1949-50	70	17	8	10	....	12	14	9	....	29	22	19	....	172	150	77	2nd,	Lost Semi-Final
1948-49	60	19	8	3	....	9	15	6	....	28	23	9	....	152	126	65	3rd,	Lost Semi-Final
1947-48	60	13	13	4	....	7	16	7	....	20	29	11	....	147	169	51	5th,	Out of Playoffs
1946-47	60	19	6	5	....	15	10	5	....	34	16	10	....	189	138	78	1st,	Lost Final
1945-46	**50**	**16**	**6**	**3**	....	**12**	**11**	**2**	....	**28**	**17**	**5**	....	**172**	**134**	**61**	**1st,**	**Won Stanley Cup**
1944-45	50	21	2	2	....	17	6	2	....	38	8	4	....	228	121	80	1st,	Lost Semi-Final
1943-44	**50**	**22**	**0**	**3**	....	**16**	**5**	**4**	....	**38**	**5**	**7**	....	**234**	**109**	**83**	**1st,**	**Won Stanley Cup**
1942-43	50	14	4	7	....	5	15	5	....	19	19	12	....	181	191	50	4th,	Lost Semi-Final
1941-42	48	12	10	2	....	6	17	1	....	18	27	3	....	134	173	39	6th,	Lost Quarter-Final
1940-41	48	11	9	4	....	5	17	2	....	16	26	6	....	121	147	38	6th,	Lost Quarter-Final
1939-40	48	5	14	5	....	5	19	0	....	10	33	5	....	90	168	25	7th,	Out of Playoffs
1938-39	48	8	11	5	....	7	13	4	....	15	24	9	....	115	146	39	6th,	Lost Quarter-Final
1937-38	48	13	4	7	....	5	13	6	....	18	17	13	....	123	128	49	3rd, Cdn. Div.	Lost Quarter-Final
1936-37	48	16	8	0	....	8	10	6	....	24	18	6	....	115	111	54	1st, Cdn. Div.	Lost Semi-Final
1935-36	48	5	11	8	....	6	15	3	....	11	26	11	....	82	123	33	4th, Cdn. Div.	Out of Playoffs
1934-35	48	11	11	2	....	8	12	4	....	19	23	6	....	110	145	44	3rd, Cdn. Div.	Lost Quarter-Final
1933-34	48	16	6	2	....	6	14	4	....	22	20	6	....	99	101	50	2nd, Cdn. Div.	Lost Quarter-Final
1932-33	48	15	5	4	....	3	20	1	....	18	25	5	....	92	115	41	3rd, Cdn. Div.	Lost Quarter-Final
1931-32	48	18	3	3	....	7	13	4	....	25	16	7	....	128	111	57	1st, Cdn. Div.	Lost Semi-Final
1930-31	**44**	**15**	**3**	**4**	....	**11**	**7**	**4**	....	**26**	**10**	**8**	....	**129**	**89**	**60**	**1st, Cdn. Div.**	**Won Stanley Cup**
1929-30	**44**	**13**	**5**	**4**	....	**8**	**9**	**5**	....	**21**	**14**	**9**	....	**142**	**114**	**51**	**2nd, Cdn. Div.**	**Won Stanley Cup**
1928-29	44	12	4	6	....	10	3	9	....	22	7	15	....	71	43	59	1st, Cdn. Div.	Lost Semi-Final
1927-28	44	12	7	3	....	14	4	4	....	26	11	7	....	116	48	59	1st, Cdn. Div.	Lost Semi-Final
1926-27	44	15	5	2	....	13	9	0	....	28	14	2	....	99	67	58	2nd, Cdn. Div.	Lost Semi-Final
1925-26	36	5	12	1	....	6	12	0	....	11	24	1	....	79	108	23	7th,	Out of Playoffs
1924-25	30	10	5	0	....	7	6	2	....	17	11	2	....	93	56	36	3rd,	Lost Final
1923-24	**24**	**10**	**2**	**0**	....	**3**	**9**	**0**	....	**13**	**11**	**0**	....	**59**	**48**	**26**	**2nd,**	**Won Stanley Cup**
1922-23	24	10	2	0	....	3	7	2	....	13	9	2	....	73	61	28	2nd,	Lost NHL Final
1921-22	24	8	3	1	....	4	8	0	....	12	11	1	....	88	94	25	3rd,	Out of Playoffs
1920-21	24	9	3	0	....	4	8	0	....	13	11	0	....	112	99	26	3rd and 2nd*	Out of Playoffs
1919-20	24	8	4	0	....	5	7	0	....	13	11	0	....	129	113	26	2nd and 3rd*	Out of Playoffs
1918-19	18	7	2	0	....	3	6	0	....	10	8	0	....	88	78	20	1st and 2nd*	Cup Final but no Decision
1917-18	22	8	3	0	....	5	6	0	....	13	9	0	....	115	84	26	1st and 3rd*	Lost NHL Final

* Season played in two halves with no combined standing at end.
From 1917-18 through 1925-26, NHL champions played against PCHA/WCHL champions for Stanley Cup.

2011-12 Player Personnel

FORWARDS	HT	WT	S	Place of Birth	*Age	2010-11 Club
CAMMALLERI, Michael	5-9	182	L	Richmond Hill, Ont.	29	Montreal
COLE, Erik	6-2	205	L	Oswego, NY	32	Carolina
DARCHE, Mathieu	6-1	215	L	St. Laurent, Que.	34	Montreal
DESHARNAIS, David	5-7	177	L	Laurier-Station, Que.	25	Montreal-Hamilton
ELLER, Lars	6-2	198	L	Rodovre, Denmark	22	Montreal
GIONTA, Brian	5-7	173	R	Rochester, NY	32	Montreal
GOMEZ, Scott	5-11	198	L	Anchorage, AK	31	Montreal
KOSTITSYN, Andrei	6-0	214	L	Novopolotsk, USSR	26	Montreal
MOEN, Travis	6-2	215	L	Stewart Valley, Sask.	29	Montreal
PACIORETTY, Max	6-2	196	L	New Canaan, CT	22	Montreal-Hamilton
PLEKANEC, Tomas	5-11	198	L	Kladno, Czech.	28	Montreal
WHITE, Ryan	6-0	193	R	Brandon, Man.	23	Montreal-Hamilton
DEFENSEMEN						
GILL, Hal	6-7	241	L	Concord, MA	36	Montreal
GORGES, Josh	6-1	200	L	Kelowna, B.C.	27	Montreal
MARKOV, Andrei	6-0	207	L	Voskresensk, USSR	32	Montreal
SPACEK, Jaroslav	6-0	210	L	Rokycany, Czech.	37	Montreal
SUBBAN, P.K.	6-0	206	R	Toronto, Ont.	22	Montreal
WEBER, Yannick	5-11	193	R	Morges, Switz.	23	Montreal-Hamilton

GOALTENDERS	HT	WT	C	Place of Birth	*Age	2010-11 Club
BUDAJ, Peter	6-1	200	L	Banska Bystrica, Czech.	29	Colorado
PRICE, Carey	6-3	219	L	Vancouver, B.C.	24	Montreal

* – Age at start of 2011-12 season

2010-11 Scoring

* – rookie

Regular Season

Pos	#	Player	Team	GP	G	A	Pts	TOI	+/-	PIM	PP	SH	GW	S	%
C	14	Tomas Plekanec	MTL	77	22	35	57	20:14	8	60	3	1	4	227	9.7
D	20	James Wisniewski	NYI	32	3	18	21	23:14	–18	18	3	0	0	71	4.2
			MTL	43	7	23	30	22:42	4	20	4	0	2	87	8.0
			Total	75	10	41	51	22:56	–14	38	7	0	2	158	6.3
L	13	Michael Cammalleri	MTL	67	19	28	47	18:28	2	33	7	0	2	193	9.8
R	21	Brian Gionta	MTL	82	29	17	46	19:37	3	24	7	2	6	298	9.7
L	46	Andrei Kostitsyn	MTL	81	20	25	45	15:53	3	36	5	0	6	196	10.2
D	76 *	P.K. Subban	MTL	77	14	24	38	22:16	–8	124	9	0	3	197	7.1
C	11	Scott Gomez	MTL	80	7	31	38	18:33	–15	48	3	0	2	157	4.5
D	44	Roman Hamrlik	MTL	79	5	29	34	22:16	6	81	2	0	0	129	3.9
L	57	Benoit Pouliot	MTL	79	13	17	30	11:32	2	87	1	0	4	129	10.1
L	52	Mathieu Darche	MTL	59	12	14	26	11:16	7	10	2	0	1	90	13.3
C	15	Jeff Halpern	MTL	72	11	15	26	12:43	6	29	0	1	3	62	17.7
L	67	Max Pacioretty	MTL	37	14	10	24	15:53	–1	39	7	0	2	112	12.5
C	58 *	David Desharnais	MTL	43	8	14	22	12:52	–3	12	4	0	0	55	14.5
C	81 *	Lars Eller	MTL	77	7	10	17	11:08	–4	48	0	0	2	79	8.9
L	32	Travis Moen	MTL	79	6	10	16	13:11	–4	96	0	1	0	99	6.1
D	6	Jaroslav Spacek	MTL	59	1	15	16	19:14	9	45	0	0	0	65	1.5
D	68 *	Yannick Weber	MTL	41	1	10	11	16:33	0	14	0	0	0	63	1.6
D	75	Hal Gill	MTL	75	2	7	9	19:49	–9	43	0	0	1	62	3.2
D	45	Alexandre Picard	MTL	43	3	5	8	16:25	0	17	2	0	1	49	6.1
C	94	Tom Pyatt	MTL	61	2	5	7	10:38	–1	9	0	0	0	65	3.1
D	55	Brent Sopel	ATL	59	2	5	7	16:25	7	16	0	0	0	40	5.0
			MTL	12	0	0	0	15:54	–1	0	0	0	0	4	0.0
			Total	71	2	5	7	16:20	6	16	0	0	0	44	4.5
D	26	Josh Gorges	MTL	36	1	6	7	21:10	–3	18	1	0	1	20	5.0
D	22	Paul Mara	ANA	33	1	1	2	20:10	–1	40	0	0	1	34	2.9
			MTL	20	0	4	4	15:09	2	48	0	0	0	16	0.0
			Total	53	1	5	6	18:16	1	88	0	0	1	50	2.0
C	53 *	Ryan White	MTL	27	2	3	5	8:55	5	38	0	0	0	30	6.7
D	79	Andrei Markov	MTL	7	1	2	3	22:54	2	4	0	0	1	20	5.0
C	17	Dustin Boyd	MTL	10	1	0	1	9:50	–6	2	0	0	0	8	12.5
L	34	Nigel Dawes	ATL	9	0	1	1	11:11	–6	0	0	0	0	9	0.0
			MTL	4	0	0	0	6:44	0	0	0	0	0	3	0.0
			Total	13	0	1	1	9:49	–6	0	0	0	0	12	0.0
D	47 *	Brendon Nash	MTL	2	0	0	0	10:11	–1	0	0	0	0	2	0.0
R	51 *	Aaron Palushaj	MTL	3	0	0	0	8:31	1	2	0	0	0	3	0.0
C	63 *	Andreas Engqvist	MTL	3	0	0	0	8:45	0	0	0	0	0	1	0.0

Goaltending

No.	Goaltender	GPI	Mins	Avg	W	L	OT	EN	SO	GA	SA	S%	G	A	PIM
31	Carey Price	72	4206	2.35	38	28	6	7	8	165	2147	.923	0	2	13
35	Alex Auld	16	749	2.64	6	2	2	1	0	33	383	.914	0	1	2
	Totals	**82**	**4974**	**2.48**	**44**	**30**	**8**	**8**	**8**	**206**	**2538**	**.919**			

Playoffs

Pos	#	Player	Team	GP	G	A	Pts	TOI	+/-	PIM	PP	SH	GW	OT	S	%
L	13	Michael Cammalleri	MTL	7	3	7	10	23:35	–5	0	1	0	0	0	24	12.5
R	21	Brian Gionta	MTL	7	3	2	5	22:35	–6	0	1	0	2	0	35	8.6
C	14	Tomas Plekanec	MTL	7	2	3	5	23:20	–1	2	0	1	0	0	24	8.3
D	76 *	P.K. Subban	MTL	7	2	2	4	28:33	–2	2	2	0	0	0	16	12.5
C	11	Scott Gomez	MTL	7	0	4	4	19:42	–6	2	0	0	0	0	21	0.0
D	44	Roman Hamrlik	MTL	7	0	3	3	23:20	–1	6	0	0	0	0	4	0.0
D	68 *	Yannick Weber	MTL	3	2	0	2	8:46	1	0	1	0	0	0	5	40.0
L	46	Andrei Kostitsyn	MTL	6	2	0	2	18:19	0	6	0	0	0	0	15	13.3
L	52	Mathieu Darche	MTL	7	1	1	2	15:42	–1	0	1	0	1	0	12	8.3
D	20	James Wisniewski	MTL	6	0	2	2	22:23	–3	7	0	0	0	0	7	0.0
C	81 *	Lars Eller	MTL	7	0	2	2	13:04	1	4	0	0	0	0	11	0.0
C	15	Jeff Halpern	MTL	4	1	0	1	17:46	–1	0	0	0	0	0	9	11.1
D	55	Brent Sopel	MTL	7	1	0	1	14:51	–2	2	0	0	0	0	4	25.0
C	58 *	David Desharnais	MTL	5	0	1	1	11:03	0	2	0	0	0	0	10	0.0
L	32	Travis Moen	MTL	7	0	1	1	16:33	–1	2	0	0	0	0	13	0.0
D	22	Paul Mara	MTL	1	0	0	0	13:11	0	0	0	0	0	0	0	0.0
L	57	Benoit Pouliot	MTL	3	0	0	0	6:12	0	7	0	0	0	0	0	0.0
D	75	Hal Gill	MTL	7	0	0	0	23:21	–1	2	0	0	0	0	4	0.0
D	6	Jaroslav Spacek	MTL	7	0	0	0	17:42	–3	4	0	0	0	0	5	0.0
C	94	Tom Pyatt	MTL	7	0	0	0	9:54	0	0	0	0	0	0	7	0.0
C	53 *	Ryan White	MTL	7	0	0	0	6:35	0	2	0	0	0	0	3	0.0

Goaltending

No.	Goaltender	GPI	Mins	Avg	W	L	EN	SO	GA	SA	S%	G	A	PIM
31	Carey Price	7	455	2.11	3	4	1	1	16	242	.934	0	0	0
	Totals	**7**	**457**	**2.23**	**3**	**4**	**1**	**1**	**17**	**243**	**.930**			

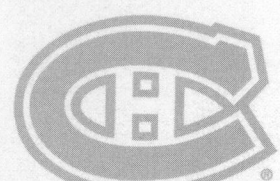

Jacques Martin

Head Coach

Born: St. Pascal, Ont., October 1, 1952.

The Montreal Canadiens announced the appointment of Jacques Martin as the club's new head coach on June 1, 2009. Martin was the Florida Panthers' general manager the previous three seasons (2006 to 2009).He had originally been hired as Panthers coach in 2004 and served in both capacities through the 2007-08 season. In his first season with the Canadiens in 2009-10 he led the club to the Eastern Conference Final.

Midway through the 1995-96 season, Martin was hired as head coach of the Ottawa Senators. In his nine-year tenure with the Senators, he led his team to three division titles and had four seasons of at least 100 points. Martin was nominated for the Jack Adams Trophy as NHL coach of the year four times (1997, 1999, 2001, 2003), winning the award in 1999.

In 1986-87, Martin entered the NHL as head coach of the St. Louis Blues. From 1988 to 1993, Martin worked as an assistant coach with the Chicago Blackhawks and associate coach with the Quebec Nordiques and, following a one-year stint as head coach of the American Hockey League's Cornwall Aces, with the Colorado Avalanche. Martin also has extensive experience on the international level serving as an associate coach with Team Canada for two Winter Olympics (Salt Lake City and Turin), earning a gold medal in 2002. He was also a member of the Canadian Team coaching staff at the 2004 World Cup.

Martin began his coaching career in major junior hockey with the Ontario Hockey League's Peterborough Petes as an assistant to Dick Todd from 1982 to 1984. He then moved on to become Guelph's head coach in 1985-86 season leading the Platers to a Memorial Cup championship and winning the Matt Leyden Trophy as OHL coach of the year. As a player, Martin was a goaltender with the NCAA's St. Lawrence University from 1972 to 1974.

Coaching Record

			Regular Season				Playoffs			
Season	Team	League	GC	W	L	O/T	GC	W	L	T
1985-86	Guelph	OHL	66	41	23	2	20	15	3	2
1985-86	Guelph	M-Cup	....	....	....	....	4	3	1	....
1986-87	**St. Louis**	**NHL**	**80**	**32**	**33**	**15**	**6**	**2**	**4**	....
1987-88	**St. Louis**	**NHL**	**80**	**34**	**38**	**8**	**10**	**5**	**5**	....
1993-94	Cornwall	AHL	80	33	36	22	13	8	5	....
1995-96	**Ottawa**	**NHL**	**38**	**10**	**24**	**4**	....	....	....	....
1996-97	**Ottawa**	**NHL**	**82**	**31**	**36**	**15**	**7**	**3**	**4**	....
1997-98	**Ottawa**	**NHL**	**82**	**34**	**33**	**15**	**11**	**5**	**6**	....
1998-99	**Ottawa**	**NHL**	**82**	**44**	**23**	**15**	**4**	**0**	**4**	....
99-2000	**Ottawa**	**NHL**	**82**	**41**	**28**	**13**	**6**	**2**	**4**	....
2000-01	**Ottawa**	**NHL**	**82**	**48**	**21**	**13**	**4**	**0**	**4**	....
2001-02	**Ottawa**	**NHL**	**80**	**38**	**26**	**16**	**12**	**7**	**5**	....
2002-03	**Ottawa**	**NHL**	**82**	**52**	**21**	**9**	**18**	**11**	**7**	....
2003-04	**Ottawa**	**NHL**	**82**	**43**	**23**	**16**	**7**	**3**	**4**	....
2004-05	**Florida**				SEASON CANCELLED					
2005-06	**Florida**	**NHL**	**82**	**37**	**34**	**11**	....	....	....	....
2006-07	**Florida**	**NHL**	**82**	**35**	**31**	**16**	....	....	....	....
2007-08	**Florida**	**NHL**	**82**	**38**	**35**	**9**	....	....	....	....
2009-10	**Montreal**	**NHL**	**82**	**39**	**33**	**10**	**19**	**9**	**10**	....
2010-11	**Montreal**	**NHL**	**82**	**44**	**30**	**8**	**7**	**3**	**4**	....
	NHL Totals		**1262**	**600**	**469**	**193**	**111**	**50**	**61**	....

Won Jack Adams Award (1999)

Martin stepped aside (with NHL permission) during the final two games of the 2001-02 season in order to allow assistant coach Roger Neilson to reach the 1,000-game plateau, April 11 and 13, 2002.

Coaching History

Jack Laviolette, 1909-10; Adolphe Lecours, 1910-11; Napoleon Dorval, 1911-12, 1912-13; Jimmy Gardner, 1913-14, 1914-15; Newsy Lalonde, 1915-16 to 1920-21; Newsy Lalonde and Léo Dandurand, 1921-22; Léo Dandurand, 1922-23 to 1925-26; Cecil Hart, 1926-27 to 1931-32; Newsy Lalonde, 1932-33, 1933-34; Newsy Lalonde and Léo Dandurand, 1934-35; Sylvio Mantha, 1935-36; Cecil Hart, 1936-37, 1937-38; Cecil Hart and Jules Dugal, 1938-39; Babe Siebert, 1939*; Pit Lepine, 1939-40; Dick Irvin 1940-41 to 1954-55; Toe Blake, 1955-56 to 1967-68; Claude Ruel, 1968-69, 1969-70; Claude Ruel and Al MacNeil, 1970-71; Scotty Bowman, 1971-72 to 1978-79; Bernie Geoffrion and Claude Ruel, 1979-80; Claude Ruel, 1980-81; Bob Berry, 1981-82, 1982-83; Bob Berry and Jacques Lemaire, 1983-84; Jacques Lemaire, 1984-85; Jean Perron, 1985-86 to 1987-88; Pat Burns, 1988-89 to 1991-92; Jacques Demers, 1992-93 to 1994-95; Jacques Demers, Jacques Laperriere, Mario Tremblay, 1995-96; Mario Tremblay, 1996-97; Alain Vigneault, 1997-98 to 1999-2000; Alain Vigneault and Michel Therrien, 2000-01; Michel Therrien, 2001-02; Michel Therrien and Claude Julien, 2002-03; Claude Julien, 2003-04, 2004-05; Claude Julien and Bob Gainey, 2005-06; Guy Carbonneau, 2006-07, 2007-08; Guy Carbonneau and Bob Gainey, 2008-09; Jacques Martin, 2009-10 to date.

* Named coach in summer but died before 1939-40 season began.

Club Records

Team

(Figures in brackets for season records are games played; records for fewest points, wins, ties, losses, goals, goals against are for 70 or more games)

Most Points .... *132 — 1976-77 (80)
Most Wins .... 60 — 1976-77 (80)
Most Ties .... 23 — 1962-63 (70)
Most Losses .... 40 — 1983-84 (80), 2000-01 (82)
Most Goals .... 387 — 1976-77 (80)
Most Goals Against .... 295 — 1983-84 (80)
Fewest Points .... 65 — 1950-51 (70)
Fewest Wins .... 25 — 1950-51 (70)
Fewest Ties .... 5 — 1983-84 (80)
Fewest Losses .... *8 — 1976-77 (80)
Fewest Goals .... 155 — 1952-53 (70)
Fewest Goals Against ...... *131 — 1955-56 (70)

Longest Winning Streak
Overall .... 12 — Jan. 6-Feb. 3/68
Home .... 13 — Nov. 2/43-Jan. 8/44, Jan. 30-Mar. 26/77
Away .... 8 — Dec. 18/77-Jan. 18/78, Jan. 21-Feb. 21/82

Longest Undefeated Streak
Overall .... 28 — Dec. 18/77-Feb. 23/78 (23 wins, 5 ties)
Home .... *34 — Nov. 1/76-Apr. 2/77 (28 wins, 6 ties)
Away .... *23 — Nov. 27/74-Mar. 12/75 (14 wins, 9 ties)

Longest Losing Streak
Overall .... 12 — Feb. 13-Mar. 13/26
Home .... 7 — Dec. 16/39-Jan. 18/40, Oct. 28-Nov. 25/00
Away .... 10 — Jan. 16-Mar. 13/26

Longest Winless Streak
Overall .... 12 — Feb. 13-Mar. 13/26 (12 losses), Nov. 28-Dec. 29/35 (8 losses, 4 ties)
Home .... 15 — Dec. 16/39-Mar. 7/40 (12 losses, 3 ties)
Away .... 12 — Nov. 26/33-Jan. 28/34 (8 losses, 4 ties), Oct. 20-Dec. 13/51 (8 losses, 4 ties)

Most Shutouts, Season ...... *22 — 1928-29 (44)
Most PIM, Season .... 1,847 — 1995-96 (82)
Most Goals, Game .... *16 — Mar. 3/20 (Mtl. 16 at Que. 3)

Individual

Most Seasons .... 20 — Henri Richard, Jean Béliveau
Most Games .... 1,256 — Henri Richard
Most Goals, Career .... 544 — Maurice Richard
Most Assists, Career .... 728 — Guy Lafleur
Most Points, Career .... 1,246 — Guy Lafleur (518G, 728A)
Most PIM, Career .... 2,248 — Chris Nilan
Most Shutouts, Career .... 75 — George Hainsworth
Longest Consecutive Games Streak .... 560 — Doug Jarvis (Oct. 8/75-Apr. 4/82)
Most Goals, Season .... 60 — Steve Shutt (1976-77), Guy Lafleur (1977-78)
Most Assists, Season .... 82 — Pete Mahovlich (1974-75)
Most Points, Season .... 136 — Guy Lafleur (1976-77; 56G, 80A)
Most PIM, Season .... 358 — Chris Nilan (1984-85)
Most Points, Defenseman, Season .... 85 — Larry Robinson (1976-77; 19G, 66A)
Most Points, Center, Season .... 117 — Pete Mahovlich (1974-75; 35G, 82A)
Most Points, Right Wing, Season .... 136 — Guy Lafleur (1976-77; 56G, 80A)
Most Points, Left Wing, Season .... 110 — Mats Naslund (1985-86; 43G, 67A)
Most Points, Rookie, Season .... 71 — Mats Naslund (1982-83; 26G, 45A), Kjell Dahlin (1985-86; 32G, 39A)
Most Shutouts, Season ...... *22 — George Hainsworth (1928-29)
Most Goals, Game .... 6 — Newsy Lalonde (Jan. 10/20)
Most Assists, Game .... 6 — Elmer Lach (Feb. 6/43)
Most Points, Game .... 8 — Maurice Richard (Dec. 28/44; 5G, 3A), Bert Olmstead (Jan. 9/54; 4G, 4A)

* NHL Record.

Retired Numbers

1	Jacques Plante	1952-1963
2	Doug Harvey	1947-1961
3	Butch Bouchard	1941-1956
4	Jean Béliveau	1950-1971
5	Bernard Geoffrion	1950-1964
7	Howie Morenz	1923-1937
9	Maurice Richard	1942-1960
10	Guy Lafleur	1971-1984
12	Dickie Moore	1951-1963
	Yvan Cournoyer	1963-1979
16	Henri Richard	1955-1975
	Elmer Lach	1940-1954
18	Serge Savard	1966-1981
19	Larry Robinson	1972-1989
23	Bob Gainey	1973-1989
29	Ken Dryden	1970-1979
33	Patrick Roy	1984-1996

All-time Record vs. Other Clubs

Regular Season

	At Home								On Road								Total							
	GP	W	L	T	OL	GF	GA	PTS	GP	W	L	T	OL	GF	GA	PTS	GP	W	L	T	OL	GF	GA	PTS
Anaheim	11	4	4	2	1	34	34	11	10	6	4	0	0	32	31	12	21	10	8	2	1	66	65	23
Atlanta	22	15	4	0	3	75	53	33	22	12	6	2	2	56	45	28	44	27	10	2	5	131	98	61
Boston	355	206	100	47	2	1195	835	461	356	137	159	56	4	965	1050	334	711	343	259	103	6	2160	1885	795
Buffalo	124	67	40	12	5	442	357	151	123	38	61	19	5	321	381	100	247	105	101	31	10	763	738	251
Calgary	50	29	13	8	0	177	122	66	53	26	19	7	1	171	163	60	103	55	32	15	1	348	285	126
Carolina	87	54	24	7	2	338	255	117	90	41	34	13	2	305	265	97	177	95	58	20	4	643	520	214
Chicago	279	177	54	48	0	1077	658	402	275	125	95	55	0	764	736	305	554	302	149	103	0	1841	1394	707
Colorado	66	39	16	10	1	271	206	89	66	27	33	5	1	229	223	60	132	66	49	15	2	500	429	149
Columbus	6	2	2	1	1	11	12	6	4	2	1	0	1	9	10	5	10	4	3	1	2	20	22	11
Dallas	60	39	12	9	0	259	149	87	62	31	19	12	0	209	163	74	122	70	31	21	0	468	312	161
Detroit	284	172	68	43	1	997	643	388	283	98	131	53	1	722	812	250	567	270	199	96	2	1719	1455	638
Edmonton	34	19	9	4	2	120	108	44	39	17	20	0	2	121	136	36	73	36	29	4	4	241	244	80
Florida	33	16	12	3	2	86	74	37	34	15	16	3	0	91	95	33	67	31	28	6	2	177	169	70
Los Angeles	67	48	8	11	0	300	166	107	67	39	19	9	0	265	203	87	134	87	27	20	0	565	369	194
Minnesota	5	2	2	1	0	14	13	5	5	3	1	0	1	18	12	7	10	5	3	1	1	32	25	12
Nashville	7	5	1	0	1	22	19	11	6	2	3	1	0	13	21	5	13	7	4	1	1	35	40	16
New Jersey	66	35	23	6	2	200	165	78	66	29	32	4	1	219	198	63	132	64	55	10	3	419	363	141
NY Islanders	72	44	16	9	3	258	196	100	72	32	31	6	3	206	214	73	144	76	47	15	6	464	410	173
NY Rangers	302	198	63	40	1	1171	704	437	302	123	123	54	2	874	874	302	604	321	186	94	3	2045	1578	739
Ottawa	54	28	21	4	1	159	153	61	52	23	24	1	4	147	160	51	106	51	45	5	5	306	313	112
Philadelphia	86	42	29	14	1	291	255	99	85	36	32	16	1	256	255	89	171	78	61	30	2	547	510	188
Phoenix	32	27	3	2	0	154	71	56	31	15	9	7	0	120	98	37	63	42	12	9	0	274	169	93
Pittsburgh	94	67	17	10	0	421	244	144	94	47	32	13	2	327	280	109	188	114	49	23	2	748	524	253
St. Louis	61	41	11	7	2	261	169	91	60	30	15	15	0	203	156	75	121	71	26	22	2	464	325	166
San Jose	14	10	2	2	0	48	25	22	13	4	6	2	1	34	42	11	27	14	8	4	1	82	67	33
Tampa Bay	34	18	13	1	2	96	84	39	35	16	14	5	0	94	85	37	69	34	27	6	2	190	169	76
Toronto	354	209	98	43	4	1233	889	465	354	126	180	45	3	934	1078	300	708	335	278	88	7	2167	1967	765
Vancouver	57	41	11	5	0	252	141	87	59	34	16	8	1	210	165	77	116	75	27	13	1	462	306	164
Washington	72	41	20	8	3	267	164	93	71	29	31	9	2	208	200	69	143	70	51	17	5	475	364	162
Defunct Clubs	231	148	58	25	0	779	469	321	230	98	97	35	0	586	606	231	461	246	155	60	0	1365	1075	552
Totals	**3019**	**1843**	**754**	**382**	**40**	**11008**	**7433**	**4108**	**3019**	**1261**	**1263**	**455**	**40**	**8709**	**8757**	**3017**	**6038**	**3104**	**2017**	**837**	**80**	**19717**	**16190**	**7125**

Playoffs

	Series	W	L	GP	W	L	T	GF	GA	Last Mtg.	Rnd.	Result
Boston	33	24	9	170	102	68	0	511	420	2011	CQF	L 3-4
Buffalo	7	4	3	35	18	17	0	124	111	1998	CSF	L 0-4
Calgary	2	1	1	11	6	5	0	31	32	1989	F	L 2-4
Carolina	7	5	2	39	23	16	0	125	106	2006	CQF	L 2-4
Chicago	17	12	5	81	50	29	2	261	185	1976	QF	W 4-0
Colorado	5	3	2	31	17	14	0	105	85	1993	DSF	W 4-2
Dallas	2	1	1	13	7	6	0	48	37	1980	QF	L 3-4
Detroit	12	5	7	62	33	29	0	161	149	1978	QF	W 4-1
Edmonton	1	0	1	3	0	3	0	6	15	1981	PRE	L 0-3
Los Angeles	1	1	0	5	4	1	0	15	12	1993	F	W 4-1
New Jersey	1	0	1	5	1	4	0	11	22	1997	CQF	L 1-4
NY Islanders	4	3	1	22	14	8	0	64	55	1993	CF	W 4-1
NY Rangers	14	7	7	61	34	25	2	188	158	1996	CQF	L 2-4
Philadelphia	6	3	3	31	16	15	0	93	89	2010	CF	L 1-4
Pittsburgh	2	2	0	13	8	5	0	37	33	2010	CSF	W 4-3
St. Louis	3	3	0	12	12	0	0	42	14	1977	QF	W 4-0
Tampa Bay	1	0	1	4	0	4	0	5	14	2004	CSF	L 0-4
Toronto	15	8	7	71	42	29	0	215	160	1979	QF	W 4-0
Vancouver	1	1	0	5	4	1	0	20	9	1975	QF	W 4-1
Washington	1	1	0	7	4	3	0	20	22	2010	CQF	W 4-3
Defunct Clubs	10*	5	4	28	15	9	4	70	71			
Totals	**145***	**89**	**55**	**709**	**410**	**291**	**8**	**2152**	**1799**			

Calgary totals include Atlanta Flames, 1972-73 to 1979-80.
Colorado totals include Quebec, 1979-80 to 1994-95.
New Jersey totals include Kansas City, 1974-75, 1975-76, and Colorado Rockies, 1976-77 to 1981-82.
Phoenix totals include Winnipeg, 1979-80 to 1995-96.
Carolina totals include Hartford, 1979-80 to 1996-97.
Dallas totals include Minnesota North Stars, 1967-68 to 1992-93.

Playoff Results 2011-2007

Year	Round	Opponent	Result	GF	GA
2011	CQF	Boston	L 3-4	17	17
2010	CF	Philadelphia	L 1-4	7	17
	CSF	Pittsburgh	W 4-3	19	18
	CQF	Washington	W 4-3	20	22
2009	CQF	Boston	L 0-4	6	17
2008	CSF	Philadelphia	L 1-4	14	20
	CQF	Boston	W 4-3	19	15

Abbreviations: Round: F - Final; **CF** - conference final; **CSF** - conference semi-final; **CQF** - conference quarter-final; **DSF** - division semi-final; **QF** - quarter-final; **PRE** - preliminary round.

2010-11 Results

Oct.	7	at Toronto	2-3		8	Boston	3-2*
	9	at Pittsburgh	3-2		11	at NY Rangers	2-1
	13	Tampa Bay	3-4*		12	Pittsburgh	2-5
	15	at Buffalo	2-1		15	NY Rangers	3-2
	16	Ottawa	4-3		17	Calgary	5-4*
	21	New Jersey	0-3		18	at Buffalo	1-2*
	23	at Ottawa	3-0		21	at Ottawa	7-1
	25	Phoenix	3-2*		22	Anaheim	3-4†
	27	NY Islanders	5-3		25	at Philadelphia	2-5
	29	at NY Islanders	3-1	**Feb.**	1	at Washington	3-2†
	30	Florida	1-3		2	Florida	3-2
Nov.	2	at Columbus	0-3		5	NY Rangers	2-0
	5	at Buffalo	3-2		6	New Jersey	1-4
	6	Ottawa	2-3		9	at Boston	6-8
	9	Vancouver	2-0		10	NY Islanders	3-4†
	11	at Boston	3-1		12	Toronto	3-0
	13	Carolina	7-2		15	Buffalo	2-3†
	16	Philadelphia	3-0		17	at Edmonton	1-4
	18	Nashville	0-3		20	at Calgary	0-4
	20	Toronto	2-0		22	at Vancouver	3-2
	22	at Philadelphia	2-3		24	Toronto	4-5
	24	Los Angeles	4-1		26	Carolina	4-3
	26	at Atlanta	0-3	**Mar.**	1	at Atlanta	3-1
	27	Buffalo	3-1		3	at Florida	4-0
Dec.	1	Edmonton	3-4*		5	at Tampa Bay	4-2
	2	at New Jersey	5-1		8	Boston	4-1
	4	San Jose	3-1		10	at St. Louis	1-4
	7	Ottawa	4-1		12	at Pittsburgh	3-0
	10	at Detroit	2-4		15	Washington	2-4
	11	at Toronto	1-3		17	Tampa Bay	3-2†
	15	Philadelphia	3-5		18	at NY Rangers	3-6
	16	Boston	4-3		20	at Minnesota	8-1
	19	at Colorado	2-3		22	Buffalo	0-2
	21	at Dallas	2-5		24	at Boston	0-7
	23	at Carolina	3-2		26	Washington	0-2
	26	at NY Islanders	1-4		29	Atlanta	3-1
	28	at Washington	0-3		30	at Carolina	2-6
	30	at Tampa Bay	1-4	**Apr.**	2	at New Jersey	3-1
	31	at Florida	3-2*		5	Chicago	2-1*
Jan.	2	Atlanta	3-4*		7	at Ottawa	2-3*
	6	Pittsburgh	2-1†		9	at Toronto	4-1

* – Overtime † – Shootout

Entry Draft Selections 2011-1997

Name in bold denotes played in NHL.

2011
Pick
17 Nathan Beaulieu
97 Josiah Didier
108 Olivier Archambault
113 Magnus Nygren
138 Darren Dietz
168 Daniel Pribyl
198 Colin Sullivan

2010
Pick
22 Jarred Tinordi
113 Mark MacMillan
117 Morgan Ellis
147 Brendan Gallagher
207 John Westin

2009
Pick
18 Louis Leblanc
65 Joonas Nattinen
79 Mac Bennett
109 Alexander Avtsin
139 Gabriel Dumont
169 Dustin Walsh
199 Michael Cichy
211 Petteri Simila

2008
Pick
56 Danny Kristo
86 Steve Quailer
116 Jason Missiaen
138 Maxim Trunev
206 Patrick Johnson

2007
Pick
12 **Ryan McDonagh**
22 **Max Pacioretty**
43 **P.K. Subban**
65 Olivier Fortier
73 **Yannick Weber**
133 Joe Stejskal
142 Andrew Conboy
163 Nichlas Torp
192 Scott Kishel

2006
Pick
20 David Fischer
49 **Ben Maxwell**
53 **Mathieu Carle**
66 **Ryan White**
139 Pavel Valentenko
199 Cameron Cepek

2005
Pick
5 **Carey Price**
45 **Guillaume Latendresse**
121 Juraj Mikus
130 Mathieu Aubin
190 **Matt D'Agostini**
200 **Sergei Kostitsyn**
229 Philippe Paquet

2004
Pick
18 **Kyle Chipchura**
84 Alexei Yemelin
100 **James Wyman**
150 **Mikhail Grabovski**
181 Loic Lacasse
212 Jon Gleed
246 **Greg Stewart**
262 **Mark Streit**
278 Alex Dulac-Lemelin

2003
Pick
10 **Andrei Kostitsyn**
40 Cory Urquhart
61 **Maxim Lapierre**
79 **Ryan O'Byrne**
113 **Corey Locke**
123 Danny Stewart
177 Chris Heino-Lindberg
188 **Mark Flood**
217 Oskari Korpikari
241 Jimmy Bonneau
271 **Jaroslav Halak**

2002
Pick
14 **Chris Higgins**
45 Tomas Linhart
99 Michael Lambert
182 **Andre Deveaux**
212 **Jonathan Ferland**
275 Konstantin Korneev

2001
Pick
7 **Mike Komisarek**
25 **Alexander Perezhogin**
37 **Duncan Milroy**
71 **Tomas Plekanec**
109 **Martti Jarventie**
171 Eric Himelfarb
203 Andrew Archer
266 Viktor Ujcik

2000
Pick
13 **Ron Hainsey**
16 **Marcel Hossa**
78 **Jozef Balej**
79 Tyler Hanchuck
109 Johan Eneqvist
114 Christian Larrivee
145 Ryan Glenn
172 Scott Selig
182 Petr Chvojka
243 Joni Puurula
275 Jonathan Gauthier

1999
Pick
39 Alexander Buturlin
58 **Matt Carkner**
97 Chris Dyment
107 Evan Lindsay
136 Dusty Jamieson
145 Marc-Andre Thinel
150 Matt Shasby
167 Sean Dixon
196 Vadim Tarasov
225 Mikko Hyytia
253 Jerome Marois

1998
Pick
16 **Eric Chouinard**
45 **Mike Ribeiro**
75 **Francois Beauchemin**
132 **Andrei Bashkirov**
152 **Gordie Dwyer**
162 **Andrei Markov**
189 Andrei Kruchinin
201 Craig Murray
216 **Michael Ryder**
247 Darcy Harris

1997
Pick
11 **Jason Ward**
37 Gregor Baumgartner
65 Ilkka Mikkola
91 Daniel Tetrault
118 Konstantin Sidulov
122 Gennady Razin
145 Jonathan Desroches
172 **Ben Guite**
197 Petr Kubos
202 Andrei Sidyakin
228 Jarl Espen Ygranes

Captains' History

Jack Laviolette, 1909-10; Newsy Lalonde, 1910-11; Jack Laviolette, 1911-12; Newsy Lalonde, 1912-13; Jimmy Gardner, 1913-14, 1914-15; Howard McNamara, 1915-16; Newsy Lalonde, 1916-17 to 1921-22; Sprague Cleghorn, 1922-23 to 1924-25; Bill Coutu, 1925-26; Sylvio Mantha, 1926-27 to 1931-32; George Hainsworth, 1932-33; Sylvio Mantha, 1933-34 to 1935-36; Babe Siebert, 1936-37 to 1938-39; Walt Buswell, 1939-40; Toe Blake, 1940-41 to 1946-47; Toe Blake and Bill Durnan, 1947-48; Butch Bouchard, 1948-49 to 1955-56; Maurice Richard, 1956-57 to 1959-60; Doug Harvey, 1960-61; Jean Béliveau, 1961-62 to 1970-71; Henri Richard, 1971-72 to 1974-75; Yvan Cournoyer, 1975-76 to 1978-79; Serge Savard, 1979-80, 1980-81; Bob Gainey, 1981-82 to 1988-89; Guy Carbonneau and Chris Chelios, 1989-90; Guy Carbonneau, 1990-91 to 1993-94; Kirk Muller and Mike Keane, 1994-95; Mike Keane and Pierre Turgeon, 1995-96; Pierre Turgeon and Vincent Damphousse, 1996-97; Vincent Damphousse, 1997-98, 1998-99; Saku Koivu, 1999-2000 to 2008-09; no captain, 2009-10; Brian Gionta, 2010-11 to date.

General Managers' History

Jack Laviolette and Joseph Cattarinich, 1909-1910; George Kennedy, 1910-11 to 1920-21; Leo Dandurand, 1921-22 to 1934-35; Ernest Savard, 1935-36; Cecil Hart, 1936-37, 1937-38; Cecil Hart and Jules Dugal, 1938-39; Jules Dugal, 1939-40; Tom P. Gorman, 1940-41 to 1945-46; Frank J. Selke, 1946-47 to 1963-64; Sam Pollock, 1964-65 to 1977-78; Irving Grundman, 1978-79 to 1982-83; Serge Savard, 1983-84 to 1994-95; Serge Savard and Réjean Houle, 1995-96; Réjean Houle, 1996-97 to 1999-2000; Réjean Houle and Andre Savard, 2000-01; Andre Savard, 2001-02, 2002-03; Bob Gainey, 2003-04 to 2008-09; Bob Gainey and Pierre Gauthier, 2009-10; Pierre Gauthier, 2010-11 to date.

Pierre Gauthier

Executive Vice President and General Manager

Born: Montreal, Que., May 28, 1953.

Pierre Gauthier joined the Montreal Canadiens organization as director of professional scouting on July 21, 2003. On February 8, 2010, he was named general manager to replace Bob Gainey while keeping the responsibilities attached to professional scouting. Prior to his promotion, he held the assistant general manager position since June 2006.

Gauthier worked with the Mighty Ducks of Anaheim during six seasons, serving as the team's assistant general manager from 1993 to 1995. Following three seasons as general manager of the Ottawa Senators from 1995 to 1998, he returned to the Mighty Ducks' organization as president and general manager from 1998 to 2002. Gauthier originally came to the Anaheim organization from the Quebec Nordiques where he spent 12 seasons from 1981 to 1993, serving in all areas of scouting.

Gauthier also made his mark on the international hockey scene. Along with Bob Gainey and Bobby Clarke, he was one of three NHL general managers for the Canadian national team at the 1998 Olympic Games in Nagano. He was also Team Canada's general manager for the gold-medal winning team at the 1997 World Championships in Finland, as well as the silver medal-winning team at the 1996 World Championship in Austria.

Club Directory

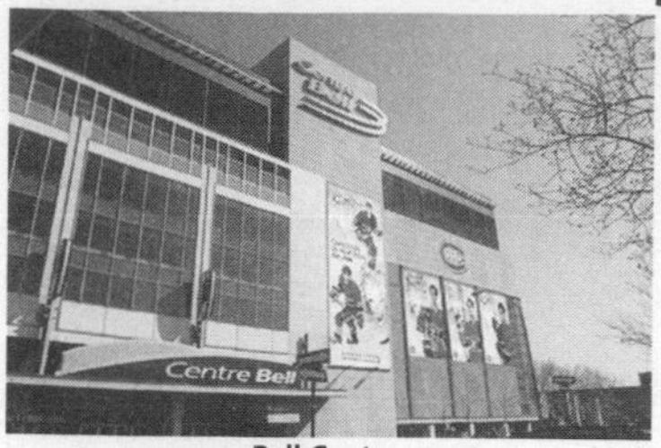
Bell Centre

Club de hockey Canadien
1909, avenue des
Canadiens-de-Montrèal
Montrèal, QC H4B 5G0
Phone: **514/932-2582**
Media Hotline: 514/989-2835
Fax Lines (all area code 514):
Communications 932-8285
Hockey 989-2717
Press Lounge 932-5258
Marketing 925-2145
Community Relations 925-2144
www.canadiens.com
Capacity: 21,273

Executive Management

Owner, President and CEO, Club de hockey Canadien, Bell Centre & evenko	Geoff Molson
Chief Operating Officer	Kevin Gilmore
Executive Vice President Hockey and G.M.	Pierre Gauthier
Chief Financial Officer	Fred Steer
Vice President, Communications and Community Relations	Donald Beauchamp
Vice President, Building Operations	Alain Gauthier
Vice President & General Manager, evenko	Jacques Aubé
President, Effix – Advertising and Sponsorship Sales	François Seigneur
President, Canadiens Alumni	Réjean Houle
Executive Assistant to the President and CEO	Rolande Bernier
Administrative Assistant to COO	Carina Houle

Hockey Operations

Assistant General Manager/Player Personnel	Larry Carrière
Special Advisor to the General Manager	Bob Gainey
Director of Hockey Operations	Patrick Boivin
Head Coach	Jacques Martin
Assistant Coaches	Perry Pearn, Randy Cunneyworth, Randy Ladouceur
Assistant Coach and Goaltending Coach	Pierre Groulx
Video Coach	Mario Leblanc
Director of Player Recruitment and Development	Trevor Timmins
Professional Scouts	Doug Gibson, Vaughn Karpan, Christer Rockstrom
Amateur Scouting Staff	Elmer Benning, Bill Berglund, Serge Boisvert, Ryan Jankowski, Frank Jay, Michal Krupa, Hannu Laine, Pat Westrum
Team Services & Hockey Admin. Manager	Claudine Crépin
Coordinator of Hockey Information	Ken Morin
Team Services Coordinator	Alain Gagnon

Medical and Training Staff

Club Physician and Chief Surgeon	Dr. David Mulder
Assistants to the Chief Surgeon	Dr. Tarek Razek, Dr. Kosar Khwaja
Dentist	Dr. Jean-François Desjardins
Consultant, Ophthalmologist	Dr. John Little
Head Athletic Therapist	Graham Rynbend
Athletic Therapist	Nick Addey-Jibb
Consultant, Osteopathy	Dave Campbell
Consultant, Physiotherapy	Donald Balmforth
Strength & Conditioning Coordinator	Pierre Allard
Equipment Manager	Pierre Gervais
Assistants to the Equipment Manager	Richard Généreux, Patrick Langlois, Pierre Ouellette

Communications

Director of Media Relations	Dominick Saillant
Administrative Asst. to the VP Communications	Sylvie Lambert
Manager, Research and Translation	Carl Lavigne
Communications Coordinator	François Marchand

Communnity Relations

Director of Community Relations / Exec. Dir., Children's Foundation	Geneviève Paquette
Manager, Event and Communications, Children's Foundation	Marie-Christine Boucher
Community Relations Coordinator	Anne-Marie Bégin
Coordinator, fundraising	Ryan Frank
Coordinator, Donations and Administration, Children's Foundation	Sylvie Nadeau
Project Manager, Children's Foundation	Patrick Mahoney

Marketing and Sales

Director, Group Sales	Pierre Constant
Executive Director, Luxury Suites and Services	Richard Primeau
Director, Ticket Sales	Vincent Lucier
Director, Marketing	Jon Trzcienski
Director, Publications and Creative Services	Jean Simard
Group Manager, Game Production	Paul Gallant
Manager, Digital Media	Alexandre Harvey
Manager, Publications and Editorial	Manny Almela
Manager, Creative Services	Marie-Élaine Arbour
Manager, Luxury Suites Services	Sabina D'Ascoli
Managers, Consumer Products	Mathieu Lapointe, Stéphane Lévy
Manager, Event Planning and Logistics	David McGinnis
Manager, Youth Hockey Development	Stéphane Verret

Building Operations

Director of Ticket Office	Cathy D'Ascoli
Assistant Director of Ticket Office	Lucie Masse
Director of Building Operations	Xavier Luydlin
Director of Concessions	Alec Beaudry
Director of Customer Satisfaction	Caroline Hamel
Administrative Assistant to the VP Operations	Maryse Cartwright

Finance

Exec. Dir. Info. and Communication Technology	Pierre-Éric Belzile
Controller	TBC
Assistant Controller	Raymond Lamarche
Administrator, Human Resources	Susan Cryans
Administrative Assistant, Chief Financial Officer	Christine Ouellette

Broadcasting

Play-by-play – Radio/TV	Pierre Houde (RDS), Martin McGuire (CKAC), TBC (TEAM 990)
Colormen – Radio/TV	Marc Denis (RDS), Dany Dubé (CKAC), TBC (TEAM 990)
Radio/television flagships	RDS (Cable 33), CKAC (730 AM), THE TEAM (990 AM)

Nashville Predators

Key Off-Season Signings/Acquisitions

2011

June 9 • Named **Lane Lambert** assistant coach.
15 • Re-signed D **Teemu Laakso**.
July 3 • Signed RW **Niclas Bergfors**.
5 • Signed C **Kyle Wilson** and RW **Zack Stortini**.
7 • Re-signed RW **Matt Halischuk**, LW **Nick Spaling**, C **Cal O'Reilly** and RW **Chris Mueller**.
8 • Re-signed LW **Sergei Kostitsyn**.
29 • Signed D **Tyler Sloan**.
Aug. 3 • D **Shea Weber** awarded one-year contract in arbitration.
8 • Signed D **Jack Hillen**.

2010-11 Results: 44W-27L-7OTL-4SOL 99PTS.
Second, Central Division

Year-by-Year Record

Season	GP	Home W	L	T	OL	Road W	L	T	OL	Overall W	L	T	OL	GF	GA	Pts.	Finished	Playoff Result
2010-11	82	24	9	....	8	20	18	....	3	44	27	....	11	219	194	99	2nd, Central Div.	Lost Conf. Semi-Final
2009-10	82	24	14	....	3	23	15	....	3	47	29	....	6	225	225	100	3rd, Central Div.	Lost Conf. Quarter-Final
2008-09	82	24	13	....	4	16	21	....	4	40	34	....	8	213	233	88	5th, Central Div.	Out of Playoffs
2007-08	82	23	14	....	4	18	18	....	5	41	32	....	9	230	229	91	2nd, Central Div.	Lost Conf. Quarter-Final
2006-07	82	28	8	....	5	23	15	....	3	51	23	....	8	272	212	110	2nd, Central Div.	Lost Conf. Quarter-Final
2005-06	82	32	8	....	1	17	17	....	7	49	25	....	8	259	227	106	2nd, Central Div.	Lost Conf. Quarter-Final
2004-05	....																.....	
2003-04	82	22	10	7	2	16	19	4	2	38	29	11	4	216	217	91	3rd, Central Div.	Lost Conf. Quarter-Final
2002-03	82	18	17	5	1	9	18	8	6	27	35	13	7	183	206	74	4th, Central Div.	Out of Playoffs
2001-02	82	17	16	8	0	11	25	5	0	28	41	13	0	196	230	69	4th, Central Div.	Out of Playoffs
2000-01	82	16	18	7	0	18	18	2	3	34	36	9	3	186	200	80	3rd, Central Div.	Out of Playoffs
1999-2000	82	15	21	3	2	13	19	4	5	28	40	7	7	199	240	70	4th, Central Div.	Out of Playoffs
1998-99	82	15	22	4	....	13	25	3	....	28	47	7	....	190	261	63	4th, Central Div.	Out of Playoffs

2011-12 Schedule

Oct.
Fri. 7 at Columbus
Sat. 8 at St. Louis
Thu. 13 Phoenix
Sat. 15 New Jersey
Mon. 17 at Edmonton
Thu. 20 at Vancouver
Sat. 22 at Calgary*
Tue. 25 San Jose
Thu. 27 Tampa Bay
Sat. 29 Anaheim
Mon. 31 at Chicago

Nov.
Thu. 3 at Phoenix
Sat. 5 at San Jose
Tue. 8 at Los Angeles
Wed. 9 at Anaheim
Sat. 12 Montreal
Tue. 15 Washington
Thu. 17 Toronto
Sat. 19 Columbus
Tue. 22 Edmonton
Wed. 23 at Minnesota
Sat. 26 at Detroit
Mon. 28 at Edmonton
Tue. 29 at Calgary

Dec.
Thu. 1 at Vancouver
Sat. 3 Buffalo
Tue. 6 Phoenix
Thu. 8 at Columbus
Sat. 10 Anaheim
Tue. 13 Calgary
Thu. 15 Detroit
Sat. 17 St. Louis
Tue. 20 at Washington
Thu. 22 Columbus
Fri. 23 at Dallas
Mon. 26 Detroit
Wed. 28 Minnesota
Fri. 30 at St. Louis

Jan.
Sun. 1 Calgary*
Thu. 5 Dallas
Sat. 7 Carolina

Tue. 10 at Colorado
Thu. 12 Colorado
Sat. 14 Philadelphia
Mon. 16 at NY Islanders*
Tue. 17 at NY Rangers
Thu. 19 at Columbus
Sat. 21 Chicago
Mon. 23 Columbus
Tue. 24 at Chicago
Tue. 31 at Minnesota

Feb.
Thu. 2 at Philadelphia
Sat. 4 St. Louis
Tue. 7 Vancouver
Thu. 9 at Ottawa
Sat. 11 at Boston*
Tue. 14 Chicago
Fri. 17 at Detroit
Sun. 19 at Dallas
Tue. 21 Vancouver
Thu. 23 St. Louis
Sat. 25 San Jose
Mon. 27 Los Angeles
Tue. 28 at Carolina

Mar.
Sat. 3 at Florida
Tue. 6 Los Angeles
Thu. 8 Colorado
Sat. 10 Detroit
Mon. 12 at Phoenix
Thu. 15 at San Jose
Sat. 17 at Los Angeles
Sun. 18 at Anaheim*
Tue. 20 Edmonton
Thu. 22 at Pittsburgh
Sat. 24 Winnipeg
Sun. 25 at Chicago
Tue. 27 at St. Louis
Fri. 30 at Detroit
Sat. 31 Chicago

Apr.
Tue. 3 Minnesota
Thu. 5 Dallas
Sat. 7 at Colorado

* Denotes afternoon game.

CENTRAL DIVISION
14th NHL Season

Franchise date: June 25, 1997

Nashville's Pekka Rinne was a Vezina Trophy finalist for the first time after ranking second among NHL goaltenders in save percentage (.930) and third in goals-against average (2.12) in 2010-11. His 33 victories were a career high.

2011-12 Player Personnel

FORWARDS	HT	WT	S	Place of Birth	*Age	2010-11 Club
BECK, Taylor	6-2	203	R	St. Catharines, Ont.	20	Guelph-Milwaukee
BERGFORS, Niclas	6-0	200	R	Sodertalje, Sweden	24	Atlanta-Florida
ERAT, Martin	6-0	200	L	Trebic, Czech.	30	Nashville
FISHER, Mike	6-1	208	R	Peterborough, Ont.	31	Ottawa-Nashville
GEOFFRION, Blake	6-1	192	L	Plantation, FL	23	Nashville-Milwaukee
HALISCHUK, Matt	6-0	185	R	Toronto, Ont.	23	Nashville-Milwaukee
HORNQVIST, Patric	6-0	188	L	Sollentuna, Sweden	24	Nashville
KOSTITSYN, Sergei	6-0	207	L	Novopolotsk, USSR	24	Nashville
LEGWAND, David	6-2	204	L	Detroit, MI	31	Nashville
MUELLER, Chris	5-10	180	R	West Seneca, NY	25	Nashville-Milwaukee
O'REILLY, Cal	6-0	188	L	Toronto, Ont.	25	Nashville
SMITH, Craig	6-1	197	R	Madison, WI	22	U. of Wisconsin
SMITHSON, Jerred	6-3	209	R	Vernon, B.C.	32	Nashville
SPALING, Nick	6-1	198	L	Palmerston, Ont.	23	Nashville-Milwaukee
STORTINI, Zack	6-4	215	R	Elliot Lake, Ont.	26	Edmonton-Oklahoma City
TOOTOO, Jordin	5-9	199	R	Churchill, Man.	28	Nashville
WILSON, Colin	6-1	201	L	Greenwich, CT	21	Nashville
WILSON, Kyle	6-2	205	R	Oakville, Ont.	26	Columbus-Springfield
DEFENSEMEN						
BLUM, Jonathon	6-1	190	R	Long Beach, CA	22	Nashville-Milwaukee
BOUILLON, Francis	5-8	198	L	New York, NY	35	Nashville
EKHOLM, Mattias	6-4	204	L	Borlange, Sweden	21	Brynas
ELLIS, Ryan	5-10	179	R	Hamilton, Ont.	20	Windsor-Milwaukee
HILLEN, Jack	5-10	190	L	Minnetonka, MN	25	NY Islanders
JOSI, Roman	6-2	198	L	Bern, Switzerland	21	Milwaukee
KLEIN, Kevin	6-1	200	R	Kitchener, Ont.	26	Nashville
LAAKSO, Teemu	6-1	215	R	Tuusula, Finland	24	Nashville-Milwaukee
SLOAN, Tyler	6-4	214	L	Calgary, Alta.	30	Washington-Hershey
SUTER, Ryan	6-1	198	L	Madison, WI	26	Nashville
WEBER, Shea	6-4	234	R	Sicamous, B.C.	26	Nashville

GOALTENDERS	HT	WT	C	Place of Birth	*Age	2010-11 Club
LINDBACK, Anders	6-6	205	L	Gavle, Sweden	23	Nashville-Milwaukee
PICKARD, Chet	6-2	206	L	Moncton, N.B.	21	Milwaukee-Cincinnati (ECHL)
RINNE, Pekka	6-5	209	L	Kempele, Finland	28	Nashville
SMITH, Jeremy	6-0	173	L	Dearborn, MI	22	Milwaukee-Cincinnati (ECHL)

* – Age at start of 2011-12 season

Barry Trotz
Head Coach

Born: Winnipeg, Man., July 15, 1962.

The only head coach in the history of the Nashville Predators, Barry Trotz was hired on August 6, 1997. He is the second-longest tenured coach in the NHL behind Buffalo's Lindy Ruff. Trotz was hired after serving four seasons as head coach and director of hockey operations for the American Hockey League's Portland Pirates. He and assistant Paul Gardner spent the 1997-98 season scouting in preparation for the inaugural season of the Predators. In his sixth season behind the bench in 2003-04, Trotz led Nashville into the playoffs for the first time. During the 2006-07 season, Nashville was in contention for first overall in the NHL, setting club records with 51 wins and 110 points.Trotz was nominated for the Jack Adams Award as coach of the year for the first time in 2009-10 and received a second nomination in 2010-11.

Trotz began his coaching career in 1984 as assistant coach with the University of Manitoba for one season, before serving two seasons as the head coach and general manager of the Dauphin Kings Junior Hockey Club from 1985 to 1987. He became head coach of the University of Manitoba during the 1987 season and also served as a scout for the Spokane Chiefs of the Western Hockey League that season. Trotz joined the Washington Capitals organization as their chief western scout during the 1988 season. The Winnipeg, Manitoba native was appointed an assistant coach of the Capitals' American Hockey League affiliate in Baltimore prior to the 1991 season before being named head coach prior to the 1992 season. When the franchise relocated to Portland, he guided the Pirates to two AHL Calder Cup Final appearances in the club's first four seasons. He led the Pirates to a league-best 43-27-10 record, captured the Calder Cup championship and was named the American Hockey League coach of the year following the 1994-95 season.

In 1995, Trotz guided Portland to a new North American professional hockey league record 17-game unbeaten streak (14-0-3) to start the season. He was named head coach for the U.S. team at the American Hockey League All-Star Game in 1996.

Prior to his coaching career, Trotz played junior hockey for the Western Hockey League's Regina Pats from 1979-83. During that time, he recorded 39 goals, 121 assists for 160 points, along with 490 penalty minutes in 204 games.

Coaching Record

			Regular Season				Playoffs			
Season	Team	League	GC	W	L	O/T	GC	W	L	T
1992-93	Baltimore	AHL	80	28	40	12	7	3	4	....
1993-94	Portland	AHL	80	43	27	10	8	6	2	....
1994-95	Portland	AHL	80	46	22	12	7	3	4	....
1995-96	Portland	AHL	80	32	34	14	24	14	10	....
1996-97	Portland	AHL	80	37	26	17	5	2	3	....
1998-99	**Nashville**	**NHL**	**82**	**28**	**47**	**7**	....	....	....	....
99-2000	**Nashville**	**NHL**	**82**	**28**	**40**	**14**	....	....	....	....
2000-01	**Nashville**	**NHL**	**82**	**34**	**36**	**12**	....	....	....	....
2001-02	**Nashville**	**NHL**	**82**	**28**	**41**	**13**	....	....	....	....
2002-03	**Nashville**	**NHL**	**82**	**27**	**35**	**20**	....	....	....	....
2003-04	**Nashville**	**NHL**	**82**	**38**	**29**	**15**	**6**	**2**	**4**	....
2004-05	**Nashville**				SEASON CANCELLED					
2005-06	**Nashville**	**NHL**	**82**	**49**	**25**	**8**	**5**	**1**	**4**	....
2006-07	**Nashville**	**NHL**	**82**	**51**	**23**	**8**	**5**	**1**	**4**	....
2007-08	**Nashville**	**NHL**	**82**	**41**	**32**	**9**	**6**	**2**	**4**	....
2008-09	**Nashville**	**NHL**	**82**	**40**	**34**	**8**	....	....	....	....
2009-10	**Nashville**	**NHL**	**82**	**47**	**29**	**6**	**6**	**2**	**4**	....
2010-11	**Nashville**	**NHL**	**82**	**44**	**27**	**11**	**12**	**6**	**6**	....
	NHL Totals		**984**	**455**	**398**	**131**	**40**	**14**	**26**	....

2010-11 Scoring

* – rookie

Regular Season

Pos	#	Player	Team	GP	G	A	Pts	TOI	+/–	PIM	PP	SH	GW	S	%
L	74	Sergei Kostitsyn	NSH	77	23	27	50	15:11	10	20	4	1	2	93	24.7
R	10	Martin Erat	NSH	64	17	33	50	18:05	14	22	7	0	3	135	12.6
R	27	Patric Hornqvist	NSH	79	21	27	48	15:43	11	47	6	0	5	265	7.9
D	6	Shea Weber	NSH	82	16	32	48	25:19	7	56	6	1	3	254	6.3
C	11	David Legwand	NSH	64	17	24	41	18:48	13	24	0	2	3	130	13.1
D	20	Ryan Suter	NSH	70	4	35	39	25:12	20	54	1	0	1	115	3.5
C	12	Mike Fisher	OTT	55	14	10	24	18:25	–19	33	3	0	1	132	10.6
			NSH	27	5	7	12	18:15	2	10	1	0	1	60	8.3
			Total	82	19	17	36	18:22	–17	43	4	0	2	192	9.9
C	33	Colin Wilson	NSH	82	16	18	34	13:17	9	17	2	0	2	101	15.8
R	29	Joel Ward	NSH	80	10	19	29	17:04	–1	42	5	0	4	157	6.4
D	4	Cody Franson	NSH	80	8	21	29	15:10	10	30	2	0	2	156	5.1
C	9	Marcel Goc	NSH	51	9	15	24	16:02	10	6	0	1	2	111	8.1
L	26	Steve Sullivan	NSH	44	10	12	22	16:01	4	28	3	0	1	79	12.7
R	71	J.P. Dumont	NSH	70	10	9	19	11:10	2	16	1	0	2	89	11.2
R	22	Jordin Tootoo	NSH	54	8	10	18	11:52	8	61	0	0	1	85	9.4
C	16	Cal O'Reilly	NSH	38	6	12	18	16:54	4	2	1	0	1	44	13.6
D	8	Kevin Klein	NSH	81	2	16	18	20:47	9	24	0	0	0	99	2.0
C	13	Nick Spaling	NSH	74	8	6	14	13:55	–10	20	1	0	2	75	10.7
R	25	Jerred Smithson	NSH	82	5	8	13	14:50	–6	34	0	0	0	73	6.8
R	24 *	Matt Halischuk	NSH	27	4	8	12	10:07	5	2	0	0	1	29	13.8
D	51	Francis Bouillon	NSH	44	1	9	10	20:13	–3	27	0	0	0	47	2.1
D	55	Shane O'Brien	NSH	80	2	7	9	17:06	1	83	0	0	0	50	4.0
C	5 *	Blake Geoffrion	NSH	20	6	2	8	8:16	3	7	0	0	1	24	25.0
D	7 *	Jonathon Blum	NSH	23	3	5	8	17:45	8	8	1	0	1	18	16.7
C	53 *	Chris Mueller	NSH	15	0	3	3	8:38	0	2	0	0	0	7	0.0
D	32 *	Teemu Laakso	NSH	1	0	0	0	2:43	0	0	0	0	0	0	0.0
L	28	Steve Begin	NSH	2	0	0	0	9:48	–2	4	0	0	0	2	0.0
C	15	Matthew Lombardi	NSH	2	0	0	0	14:49	–1	0	0	0	0	6	0.0
R	12 *	Andreas Thuresson	NSH	3	0	0	0	10:08	–1	2	0	0	0	2	0.0
L	58 *	Linus Klasen	NSH	4	0	0	0	12:53	–3	0	0	0	0	4	0.0
R	3	Wade Belak	NSH	15	0	0	0	3:46	–1	18	0	0	0	4	0.0

Goaltending

No.	Goaltender	GPI	Mins	Avg	W	L	OT	EN	SO	GA	SA	S%	G	A	PIM
35	Pekka Rinne	64	3789	2.12	33	22	9	4	6	134	1905	.930	0	0	12
39	* Anders Lindback	22	1131	2.60	11	5	2	0	2	49	576	.915	0	0	0
31	* Mark Dekanich	1	50	3.60	0	0	0	0	0	3	25	.880	0	0	0
	Totals	**82**	**4994**	**2.28**	**44**	**27**	**11**	**4**	**8**	**190**	**2510**	**.924**			

Playoffs

Pos	#	Player	Team	GP	G	A	Pts	TOI	+/–	PIM	PP	SH	GW	OT	S	%
R	29	Joel Ward	NSH	12	7	6	13	20:25	4	6	2	0	1	0	28	25.0
C	11	David Legwand	NSH	12	6	3	9	22:06	1	8	1	2	0	0	31	19.4
C	12	Mike Fisher	NSH	12	3	4	7	20:43	–1	11	0	0	1	0	25	12.0
C	13	Nick Spaling	NSH	12	2	4	6	15:19	3	0	0	0	1	0	11	18.2
R	10	Martin Erat	NSH	10	1	5	6	19:15	0	6	1	0	0	0	15	6.7
R	22	Jordin Tootoo	NSH	12	1	5	6	13:26	4	28	0	0	0	0	30	3.3
D	20	Ryan Suter	NSH	12	1	5	6	28:51	2	6	0	0	0	0	23	4.3
D	4	Cody Franson	NSH	12	1	5	6	15:19	0	0	0	0	0	0	22	4.5
D	6	Shea Weber	NSH	12	3	2	5	27:58	3	8	2	0	0	0	38	7.9
L	74	Sergei Kostitsyn	NSH	12	0	5	5	18:21	0	2	0	0	0	0	10	0.0
L	26	Steve Sullivan	NSH	9	2	1	3	9:23	2	2	0	0	1	0	7	28.6
R	27	Patric Hornqvist	NSH	12	2	1	3	15:16	–2	6	1	0	0	0	43	4.7
D	8	Kevin Klein	NSH	12	1	2	3	20:14	3	6	0	0	0	0	15	6.7
R	24 *	Matt Halischuk	NSH	12	2	0	2	11:45	–1	0	0	0	1	1	7	28.6
R	25	Jerred Smithson	NSH	11	1	1	2	14:09	2	8	0	0	1	1	16	6.3
C	5 *	Blake Geoffrion	NSH	12	0	2	2	7:37	1	4	0	0	0	0	12	0.0
D	7 *	Jonathon Blum	NSH	12	0	2	2	18:51	2	0	0	0	0	0	11	0.0
R	71	J.P. Dumont	NSH	3	0	1	1	6:48	–1	2	0	0	0	0	2	0.0
C	33	Colin Wilson	NSH	3	0	0	0	11:37	–1	0	0	0	0	0	2	0.0
D	55	Shane O'Brien	NSH	12	0	0	0	16:47	–2	18	0	0	0	0	6	0.0

Goaltending

No.	Goaltender	GPI	Mins	Avg	W	L	EN	SO	GA	SA	S%	G	A	PIM
39	* Anders Lindback	1	13	0.00	0	0	0	0	0	9	1.000	0	0	0
35	Pekka Rinne	12	748	2.57	6	6	2	0	32	343	.907	0	1	0
	Totals	**12**	**768**	**2.66**	**6**	**6**	**2**	**0**	**34**	**354**	**.904**			

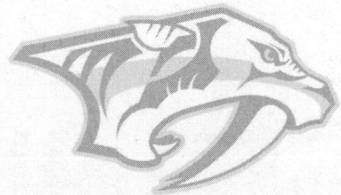

Captains' History

Tom Fitzgerald, 1998-99 to 2001-02; Greg Johnson, 2002-03 to 2005-06; Kimmo Timonen, 2006-07; Jason Arnott, 2007-08 to 2009-10; Shea Weber, 2010-11 to date.

Coaching History

Barry Trotz, 1998-99 to date.

Club Records

Team

(Figures in brackets for season records are games played; records for fewest points, wins, ties, losses, goals, goals against are for 70 or more games)

Most Points	110	2006-07 (82)
Most Wins	51	2006-07 (82)
Most Ties	13	2001-02 (82), 2002-03 (82)
Most Losses	47	1998-99 (82)
Most Goals	272	2006-07 (82)
Most Goals Against	261	1998-99 (82)
Fewest Points	63	1998-99 (82)
Fewest Wins	27	2002-03 (82)
Fewest Ties	7	1998-99 (82)
		1999-2000 (82)
Fewest Losses	23	2006-07 (82)
Fewest Goals	183	2002-03 (82)
Fewest Goals Against	194	2010-11 (82)

Longest Winning Streak
Overall	8	Oct. 5-25/05
Home	8	Jan. 6-Feb. 8/07
Away	7	Oct. 16-Nov. 4/06

Longest Undefeated Streak
Overall	8	Dec. 18/99-Jan. 1/00
		(5 wins, 3 ties),
		Oct. 5-25/05
		(8 wins)
Home	11	Dec. 20/03-Jan. 31/04
		(9 wins, 2 ties),
		Nov. 3-Dec. 23/01
		(8 wins, 3 ties)
Away	7	Oct. 16-Nov. 4/06
		(7 wins)

Longest Losing Streak
Overall	7	Nov. 20-Dec. 2/99
Home	6	Jan. 21-Feb. 15/99,
		Feb. 26-Mar. 21/02,
		Feb. 21-Mar. 20/08
Away	7	Jan. 26-Mar. 5/06,
		Dec. 8/08-Jan. 11/09

Longest Winless Streak
Overall	15	Mar. 10-Apr. 6/03
		(10 losses, 2 OT losses, 3 ties)
Home	9	Jan. 21-Mar. 2/99
		(8 losses, 1 tie)
Away	9	Nov. 2-Dec. 2/01
		(8 losses, 1 tie),
		Oct. 11-Nov. 7/02
		(3 losses, 4 OT losses, 2 ties),
		Mar. 12-Apr. 6/03
		(6 losses, 1 OT loss, 2 ties)

Most Shutouts, Season	11	2006-07 (82)
Most PIM, Season	1,533	2005-06 (82)
Most Goals, Game	9	Mar. 4/04
		(Nsh. 9 at Pit. 4),
		Mar. 18/06
		(Cgy. 4 at Nsh. 9)

Individual

Most Seasons	12	David Legwand
Most Games	768	David Legwand
Most Goals, Career	169	David Legwand
Most Assists, Career	279	David Legwand
Most Points, Career	448	David Legwand
		(169G, 279A)
Most PIM, Career	633	Jordin Tootoo
Most Shutouts, Career	21	Tomas Vokoun
Longest Consecutive Games Streak	269	Karlis Skrastins
		(Feb. 21/00-Apr. 6/03)

Most Goals, Season	33	Jason Arnott (2008-09)
Most Assists, Season	54	Paul Kariya (2005-06)
Most Points, Season	85	Paul Kariya (2005-06; 31G, 54A)
Most PIM, Season	242	Patrick Cote (1998-99)
Most Points, Defenseman, Season	55	Kimmo Timonen (2006-07; 13G, 42A)
Most Points, Center, Season	72	Jason Arnott (2007-08; 28G, 44A)
Most Points, Right Wing, Season	72	J.P. Dumont (2007-08; 29G, 43A)
Most Points, Left Wing, Season	85	Paul Kariya (2005-06; 31G, 54A)
Most Points, Rookie, Season	37	Alexander Radulov (2006-07; 18G, 19A)
Most Shutouts, Season	7	Pekka Rinne (2008-09) (2009-10)
Most Goals, Game	3	Twenty times
Most Assists, Game	5	Marek Zidlicky (Feb. 18/04)
Most Points, Game	5	Marek Zidlicky (Feb. 18/04; 5A)
		Dan Hamhuis (Mar. 4/04; 1G, 4A)
		J.P. Dumont (Oct. 22/09; 1G, 4A)

All-time Record vs. Other Clubs

Regular Season

	At Home								On Road								Total							
	GP	W	L	T	OL	GF	GA	PTS	GP	W	L	T	OL	GF	GA	PTS	GP	W	L	T	OL	GF	GA	PTS
Anaheim	24	13	7	2	2	61	55	30	24	6	15	0	3	45	75	15	48	19	22	2	5	106	130	45
Atlanta	7	5	2	0	0	27	19	10	8	3	2	1	2	21	23	9	15	8	4	1	2	48	42	19
Boston	9	5	4	0	0	25	21	10	7	2	4	1	0	12	20	5	16	7	8	1	0	37	41	15
Buffalo	7	2	4	0	1	12	17	5	7	5	1	1	0	26	20	11	14	7	5	1	1	38	37	16
Calgary	25	13	9	1	2	76	62	29	24	9	9	1	5	57	70	24	49	22	18	4	5	133	132	53
Carolina	7	6	1	0	0	19	11	12	8	4	2	1	1	24	22	10	15	10	3	1	1	43	33	22
Chicago	37	19	12	3	3	115	105	44	38	15	22	1	0	97	109	31	75	34	34	4	3	212	214	75
Colorado	24	12	9	3	0	73	71	27	24	10	11	2	1	55	62	23	48	22	20	5	1	128	133	50
Columbus	32	27	3	1	1	111	64	56	31	17	11	0	3	85	74	37	63	44	14	1	4	196	138	93
Dallas	24	13	10	1	0	64	54	27	24	6	17	0	1	33	69	13	48	19	27	1	1	97	123	40
Detroit	37	17	15	2	3	103	99	39	38	11	20	2	5	89	137	29	75	28	35	4	8	192	236	68
Edmonton	25	13	9	3	0	70	75	29	24	14	7	0	3	75	64	31	49	27	16	3	3	145	139	60
Florida	9	5	2	2	0	22	16	12	8	2	5	1	0	16	26	5	17	7	7	3	0	38	42	17
Los Angeles	24	8	13	3	0	52	68	19	24	13	8	0	3	70	68	29	48	21	21	3	3	122	136	48
Minnesota	20	12	5	2	1	61	42	27	20	6	9	3	2	56	68	17	40	18	14	5	3	117	110	44
Montreal	6	3	1	1	1	21	13	8	7	2	4	1	0	19	22	5	13	5	5	1	2	40	35	13
New Jersey	8	2	5	0	1	16	23	5	8	5	2	0	1	23	24	11	16	7	7	0	2	39	47	16
NY Islanders	8	6	2	0	0	22	17	12	6	3	1	0	2	17	16	8	14	9	3	0	2	39	33	20
NY Rangers	7	2	4	0	1	17	25	5	8	5	2	1	0	20	19	11	15	7	6	1	1	37	44	16
Ottawa	7	3	4	0	0	15	15	6	7	3	4	0	0	19	25	6	14	6	8	0	0	34	40	12
Philadelphia	6	2	2	2	0	12	13	6	8	3	4	1	0	15	26	7	14	5	6	3	0	27	39	13
Phoenix	24	14	7	2	1	68	54	31	24	9	13	0	2	71	72	20	48	23	20	2	3	139	126	51
Pittsburgh	9	6	2	0	1	34	21	13	7	3	2	2	0	22	21	8	16	9	4	2	1	56	42	21
St. Louis	38	20	11	3	4	89	88	47	37	17	17	1	2	79	100	37	75	37	28	4	6	168	188	84
San Jose	24	12	10	1	1	61	64	26	24	8	11	1	4	61	71	21	48	20	21	2	5	122	135	47
Tampa Bay	8	3	4	0	1	20	22	7	7	2	3	2	0	18	22	6	15	5	7	2	1	38	44	13
Toronto	3	2	1	0	0	10	8	4	9	4	4	1	0	25	21	9	12	6	5	1	0	35	29	13
Vancouver	25	10	10	1	4	68	68	25	24	8	15	1	0	55	79	17	49	18	25	2	4	123	147	42
Washington	8	3	2	1	2	21	20	9	7	2	3	0	2	18	19	6	15	5	5	1	4	39	39	15
Totals	**492**	**258**	**170**	**34**	**30**	**1365**	**1230**	**580**	**492**	**197**	**228**	**26**	**41**	**1223**	**1444**	**461**	**984**	**455**	**398**	**60**	**71**	**2588**	**2674**	**1041**

Playoffs

	Series	W	L	GP	W	L	T	GF	GA	Last Mtg.	Rnd.	Result
Anaheim	1	1	0	6	4	2	0	22	20	2011	CQF	W 4-2
Chicago	1	0	1	6	2	4	0	15	17	2010	CQF	L 2-4
Detroit	2	0	2	8	2	6	0	21	29	2008	CQF	L 2-4
San Jose	2	0	2	10	2	8	0	24	33	2007	CQF	L 1-4
Vancouver	1	0	1	6	2	4	0	11	14	2011	CSF	L 2-4
Totals	**7**	**1**	**6**	**40**	**14**	**26**	**0**	**93**	**113**			

Playoff Results 2011-2007

Year	Round	Opponent	Result	GF	GA
2011	CSF	Vancouver	L 2-4	11	14
	CQF	Anaheim	W 4-2	22	20
2010	CQF	Chicago	L 2-4	15	17
2008	CQF	Detroit	L 2-4	12	17
2007	CQF	San Jose	L 1-4	14	16

Abbreviations: Round: CSF - conference semi-final; CQF - conference quarter-final.

2010-11 Results

Oct.	9		Anaheim	4-1		11		Minnesota	5-1
	13	at	Chicago	3-2		13	at	Florida	2-3
	14		St. Louis	4-3		15		Chicago	3-2†
	16		Washington	2-3*		16	at	Chicago	3-6
	19		Calgary	0-1*		18	at	Phoenix	5-2
	21		Pittsburgh	3-4*		20	at	Colorado	5-1
	23	at	Dallas	1-0		23	at	Edmonton	3-2†
	24	at	Tampa Bay	4-3		24	at	Calgary	1-3
	28		St. Louis	0-3		26	at	Vancouver	1-2
	30	at	Detroit	2-5	Feb.	1		Calgary	2-3†
Nov.	3	at	Phoenix	3-4		3	at	Philadelphia	2-3
	6	at	Los Angeles	4-5		5		Detroit	3-0
	7	at	Anaheim	4-5		7		Edmonton	0-4
	11	at	St. Louis	3-2†		9	at	Detroit	4-1
	13		Chicago	4-3†		12		Colorado	5-3
	16	at	Toronto	4-5		15		San Jose	1-2*
	18	at	Montreal	3-0		17		Vancouver	3-1
	20	at	Carolina	2-1†		19		Phoenix	2-3
	22	at	Columbus	0-2		22	at	Columbus	0-4
	24		St. Louis	1-2†		24		Chicago	0-3
	26	at	Minnesota	2-5		26	at	Dallas	2-3
	27		NY Rangers	1-2†		27		Columbus	3-2
	30		Phoenix	3-0	Mar.	1	at	Edmonton	1-2†
Dec.	1	at	Columbus	4-3†		3	at	Vancouver	3-0
	4		Carolina	2-3*		6	at	Calgary	2-3
	6	at	Atlanta	2-3*		8	at	San Jose	2-3*
	8	at	Detroit	3-2		10		Minnesota	4-0
	11		Florida	3-0		12		Colorado	4-2
	13		NY Islanders	5-0		15		Los Angeles	2-4
	15		San Jose	3-2		17		Boston	4-3*
	17	at	New Jersey	3-1		19		Detroit	3-1
	18		Los Angeles	1-6		20	at	Buffalo	4-3*
	22	at	Chicago	1-4		22	at	Edmonton	3-1
	23		Ottawa	1-2		24		Anaheim	5-4
	26	at	St. Louis	0-2		26		Dallas	4-2
	28		Dallas	2-4		29		Vancouver	1-3
	31	at	Minnesota	4-1		31	at	Colorado	4-2
Jan.	2		Columbus	4-1	Apr.	2		Detroit	3-4*
	5	at	Anaheim	4-1		5		Atlanta	6-3
	6	at	Los Angeles	5-2		8		Columbus	4-1
	8	at	San Jose	2-1		9	at	St. Louis	0-2

* – Overtime † – Shootout

Entry Draft Selections 2011-1998

Name in bold denotes played in NHL.

2011 Pick		2007 Pick		2003 Pick		2000 Pick	
38	Magnus Hellberg	23	**Jonathon Blum**	7	**Ryan Suter**	6	**Scott Hartnell**
52	Miikka Salomaki	54	Jeremy Smith	35	Konstantin Glazachev	36	Daniel Widing
94	Josh Shalla	58	**Nick Spaling**	37	**Kevin Klein**	72	Mattias Nilsson
112	Garrett Noonan	81	Ryan Thang	49	**Shea Weber**	89	Libor Pivko
142	Simon Karlsson	114	Ben Ryan	76	Richard Stehlik	131	**Matt Hendricks**
170	Chase Balisy	119	Mark Santorelli	89	Paul Brown	137	**Mike Stuart**
202	Brent Andrews	144	**Andreas Thuresson**	92	**Alexander Sulzer**	154	Matt Koalska
		174	Robert Dietrich	98	Grigory Shafigulin	173	Tomas Harant
2010 Pick		204	Atte Engren	117	Teemu Lassila	197	Zbynek Irgl
18	Austin Watson			133	Rustam Sidikov	203	Jure Penko
78	Taylor Aronson	**2006** Pick		210	Andrei Mukhachev	236	Mats Christeen
126	Patrick Cehlin	56	**Blake Geoffrion**	213	Miroslav Hanuljak	284	Martin Hohener
168	Anthony Bitetto	105	Niko Snellman	268	Lauris Darzins		
194	David Elsner	146	**Mark Dekanich**			**1999** Pick	
198	Joonas Rask	176	Ryan Flynn	**2002** Pick		6	**Brian Finley**
		206	Viktor Sjodin	6	**Scottie Upshall**	33	Jonas Andersson
2009 Pick				102	**Brandon Segal**	52	**Adam Hall**
11	Ryan Ellis	**2005** Pick		138	Patrick Jarrett	54	**Andrew Hutchinson**
41	Zach Budish	18	**Ryan Parent**	172	**Mike McKenna**	61	Ed Hill
42	Charles-Olivier Roussel	78	**Teemu Laakso**	203	Josh Morrow	65	**Jan Lasak**
70	Taylor Beck	79	**Cody Franson**	235	Kaleb Betts	72	Brett Angel
72	Michael Latta	150	**Cal O'Reilly**	264	Matt Davis	121	Yevgeny Pavlov
98	Craig Smith	176	Ryan Maki	266	Steven Spencer	124	Alexandre Krevsun
102	Mattias Ekholm	213	Scott Todd			131	Konstantin Panov
110	Nick Oliver	230	**Patric Hornqvist**	**2001** Pick		162	**Timo Helbling**
132	Gabriel Bourque			12	**Dan Hamhuis**	191	**Martin Erat**
192	Cameron Reid	**2004** Pick		33	**Timofei Shishkanov**	205	Kyle Kettles
		15	**Alexander Radulov**	42	Tomas Slovak	220	Miroslav Durak
2008 Pick		81	Vaclav Meidl	75	Denis Platonov	248	**Darren Haydar**
7	**Colin Wilson**	107	Nick Fugere	76	Oliver Setzinger		
18	Chet Pickard	139	Kyle Moir	98	**Jordin Tootoo**	**1998** Pick	
38	Roman Josi	147	**Janne Niskala**	178	Anton Lavrentiev	2	**David Legwand**
136	Taylor Stefishen	178	**Mike Santorelli**	240	Gustav Grasberg	60	**Denis Arkhipov**
166	Jeff Foss	193	Kevin Schaeffer	271	**Mikko Lehtonen**	85	Geoff Koch
201	Jani Lajunen	209	Stanislav Balan			88	Kent Sauer
207	**Anders Lindback**	243	Denis Kulyash			138	Martin Beauchesne
		258	**Pekka Rinne**			147	Craig Brunel
		275	Craig Switzer			202	Martin Bartek
						230	**Karlis Skrastins**

General Managers' History

David Poile, 1998-99 to date.

David Poile

President of Hockey Operations and General Manager

Born: Toronto, Ont., February 14, 1949.

Hired as the first general manager in franchise history on July 9, 1997, David Poile has been committed to building the team through the NHL Draft. In 2003-04, Nashville reached the playoffs for the first time in franchise history. During the 2006-07 season, the team was in contention for first overall in the NHL, setting club records with 51 wins and 110 points. Though forced to rebuild the roster for 2007-08, the Predators reached the playoffs for the fourth year in a row. Poile has an impressive reputation as an NHL leader and in 2001 he received the Lester Patrick Trophy for his contributions to hockey in the United States. His father, Norman "Bud" Poile, had won the honor in 1989. He served as Associate G.M. for the 2010 U.S. Olympic Team and U.S. squads for the 2009 and 2010 IIHF World Championships. He was a finalist for the NHL's inaugural G.M. of the Year Award in 2010 and was a finalist for the award again in 2011.

Prior to joining Nashville, Poile spent 15 seasons as vice president/general manager of the Washington Capitals. During his tenure in Washington, the Capitals made 14 postseason appearances, winning their only Patrick Division title in 1989 and advancing to the Conference Finals in 1990. During Poile's 15 years in Washington, the Capitals compiled a record of 594-454-132, finished second in the Patrick Division seven times and recorded 90-or-more points seven different seasons.

Poile started his professional hockey career as an administrative assistant for the Atlanta Flames in 1972, shortly after graduating from Northeastern University in Boston. At Northeastern, he was hockey team captain, leading scorer and most valuable player for two years.

In 1977, he was named assistant general manager of the Atlanta Flames (who moved to Calgary in 1980), serving as the manager and coordinator of the Flames farm club.

Poile was instrumental in the NHL's adoption of the instant replay rule in 1991. He was awarded *Inside Hockey's* man of the year for his leadership on the issue. He has also been honored three times as *The Sporting News* NHL executive of the year in 1982-83, 1983-84 and 2006-07. Poile served as general manager of the 1998 and 1999 U.S. national teams for the World Championships.

Club Directory

Bridgestone Arena

Nashville Predators
Bridgestone Arena
501 Broadway
Nashville, TN 37203
Phone **615/770-2300**
FAX 615/770-2309
Ticket Information 615/770-PUCK
www.nashvillepredators.com
Capacity: 17,113

Owner	Predators Holdings LLC
Investor Group	Christopher Cigarran, Thomas Cigarran, Joel and Holly Dobberpuhl, David Freeman, Herbert Fritch, DeWitt Thompson V, John Thompson, Warren Woo.
Chairman and Alternate Governor	Thomas Cigarran
Governor	Joel Dobberpuhl
Pres. of Hockey Ops/G.M./Alt. Gov.	David Poile
Chief Executive Officer	Jeff Cogen
President/COO	Sean Henry
Exec. V.P./Chief Sales & Marketing Officer	Chris Parker
Exec. V.P., General Counsel and Chief Financial Officer	Michelle Kennedy
Sr. V.P., Hockey Communications and P.R.	Gerry Helper
Sr. V.P., Corporate Development	Chris Junghans

Hockey Operations

Assistant General Manager	Paul Fenton
Director of Hockey Operations	Brian Poile
Hockey Operations Manager / Assistant	Brandon Walker / Paul Cook
Hockey Operations Advisor	Brent Peterson
Director of Player Development	Martin Gelinas
Executive Assistant	Connell Crow
Head Coach	Barry Trotz
Associate Coach	Peter Horachek
Assistant Coach	Lane Lambert
Goaltending Coach	Mitch Korn
Strength and Conditioning Coach	David Good
Video Coordinator	Lawrence Feloney
Chief Amateur Scout	Jeff Kealty
Professional Scout	Nick Beverley, Shawn Dineen
North American Amateur Scouts	Jason Bukala, Tom Nolan, Glen Sanders, David Westby
European Scouts	Martin Bakula, Lucas Bergman, Janne Kekalainen
Head Athletic Trainer / Assistant Trainer	Dan Redmond / Andy Hosler
Equipment Manger / Asst. Manager	Pete Rogers / Jeff Camelio
Equipment Assistant / Locker Room Attendant	Brad Peterson / Craig "Partner" Baugh

Medical Staff

Team Doctors	Drs. John E. Kuhn, Paul J. Rummo, Charles L. Cox, Alex Diamond, Daniel S. Weikert, Mark Melson, Joseph L. Fredi, Kevin Hagan, Gary Solomon, Blair Summitt, Wesley Thayer, Jason Wendel, Cristin M. Wallace

Communications/Development

Manager of Hockey Communications	Kevin Wilson
Corporate Communications Coordinator	Jessica Jones
Community Relations Director	Rebecca Ward
Team Photographer	John Russell

Corporate Partnerships

Director, New Business Development	Bob Flynn
Senior Director, Corporate Development	Delmar Smith
Director, Corporate Partnerships	Rock Upchurch
Account Executives, Corporate Partnerships	Jack Burk, Bradford Hollingsworth
Account Service Managers, Corporate Partnerships	Kathryn Cloud, Lauren Yono
Sr. Account Service Mgr., Corporate Partnerships	Jennifer Maxwell
Sales Coordinator	Lindsay Rutledge

Marketing

Marketing Director / Sr. Manager	David Kells / Danny Shacklan
Internet Development Manager	Jay Levin
Marketing Entertainment Manager	Adam DeVault
Director Youth Hockey and Fan Development	Andee Boiman
Youth and Amateur Hockey Coordinator	Mike Dargin
Marketing Associate	Sandy Weaver

Premium Seats

Director, Corporate Development Service	Britt Kincheloe
Senior Manager, Premium Seat Sales	Tim Wilson
Senior Manager, Premium Seats	Chris Burton
Premium Seats Coordinators	Paige Ciuffo, Tasha McAllister

Finance/Administration/Human Resources

Vice Presidents, Finance	Rick Bailey, Beth Snider
Vice President, Human Resources	Allison Simms
Coordinator, Legal and Administrative Affairs	Suzanne Wyatt
Senior Legal and Financial Analyst	Sean Marshall

Event Technology

Event Presentation Senior Director / Manager	Blake Grant / Patrick Abell
Game Presentation Producer / Coordinator	Ron Zolkower / Chris Smith
Information Systems Director	Casey Millar

Broadcast

Broadcasting, Sr. Director / Associate Producer	Bob Kohl / David White
Television Play-by-Play Announcer	Pete Weber
Color Analyst	Terry Crisp
Radio Play-by-Play Announcer	Tom Callahan
Video Production Manager	Mitch Jordan
Videographer/Editor / Assistant	Brett Newkirk / Vickie Chien
Broadcast Services Manager	Kelly Sparks

Ticket Operations

Vice President of Ticket Sales	Nat Harden
Director of Ticket Sales	Marty Mulford
Director of Business Strategy	Jordan Kolosey
Database Research Coordinator	Mike Connolly
Director of Ticket Operations	David Chadwell
Inside Sales Manager	Brad Gillispie
Ticket Operations Manager	Sara Shear
Senior Account Executives	Will Myers, Dan Schaefer
Account Executives	Ben DeHaan, Tim Hazelwood, Travis Laufle, Curry McKeel, Charles Rand

New Jersey Devils

Key Off-Season Signings/Acquisitions

2011

June 24 • Selected D **Adam Larsson** (Sweden) with the fourth overall selection in the 2011 Entry Draft.

July 1 • Re-signed D **Andy Greene** and G **Johan Hedberg**.

14 • Signed RW **Cam Janssen**.

14 • Re-signed D **Matt Corrente**.

15 • Signed LW **Eric Boulton**.

19 • Named **Peter DeBoer** head coach.

26 • Re-signed D **Mark Fraser**.

29 • Re-signed LW **Zach Parise**.

29 • Named **Dave Barr** assistant coach.

2010-11 Results: 38w-39l-3otl-2sol 81pts.
Fourth, Atlantic Division

2011-12 Schedule

Oct.	Sat.	8	Philadelphia
	Mon.	10	Carolina*
	Thu.	13	Los Angeles
	Sat.	15	at Nashville
	Fri.	21	San Jose
	Sat.	22	at Pittsburgh
	Tue.	25	at Los Angeles
	Thu.	27	at Phoenix
	Sat.	29	at Dallas
Nov.	Wed.	2	Toronto
	Thu.	3	at Philadelphia
	Sat.	5	Winnipeg
	Tue.	8	Carolina
	Fri.	11	Washington
	Sat.	12	at Washington
	Tue.	15	at Boston
	Wed.	16	at Buffalo
	Sat.	19	at Tampa Bay
	Mon.	21	at Florida
	Wed.	23	Columbus
	Fri.	25	at NY Islanders*
	Sat.	26	NY Islanders*
	Wed.	30	at Colorado
Dec.	Fri.	2	at Minnesota
	Sat.	3	at Winnipeg
	Tue.	6	at Toronto
	Thu.	8	Ottawa
	Sat.	10	Montreal*
	Mon.	12	at Tampa Bay
	Tue.	13	at Florida
	Fri.	16	Dallas
	Sat.	17	at Montreal
	Tue.	20	NY Rangers
	Fri.	23	Washington
	Mon.	26	at Carolina
	Wed.	28	Buffalo
	Sat.	31	Pittsburgh*
Jan.	Mon.	2	at Ottawa
	Wed.	4	Boston
	Fri.	6	Florida
	Sat.	7	at Pittsburgh

	Tue.	10	at Calgary
	Wed.	11	at Edmonton
	Sat.	14	at Winnipeg*
	Tue.	17	Winnipeg
	Thu.	19	Boston
	Sat.	21	Philadelphia*
	Tue.	24	Buffalo
	Tue.	31	NY Rangers
Feb.	Thu.	2	Montreal
	Sat.	4	at Philadelphia*
	Sun.	5	Pittsburgh*
	Tue.	7	at NY Rangers
	Thu.	9	St. Louis
	Sat.	11	Florida*
	Tue.	14	at Buffalo
	Fri.	17	Anaheim
	Sun.	19	at Montreal
	Tue.	21	at Toronto
	Fri.	24	Vancouver
	Sun.	26	Tampa Bay*
	Mon.	27	at NY Rangers
Mar.	Thu.	1	at Boston
	Fri.	2	at Washington
	Sun.	4	at NY Islanders*
	Tue.	6	NY Rangers
	Thu.	8	NY Islanders
	Sat.	10	at NY Islanders
	Sun.	11	Philadelphia
	Tue.	13	at Philadelphia
	Thu.	15	Colorado
	Sat.	17	Pittsburgh*
	Mon.	19	at NY Rangers
	Tue.	20	at Ottawa
	Fri.	23	Toronto
	Sun.	25	at Pittsburgh
	Tue.	27	Chicago
	Thu.	29	Tampa Bay
	Sat.	31	at Carolina
Apr.	Tue.	3	NY Islanders
	Thu.	5	at Detroit
	Sat.	7	Ottawa*

* Denotes afternoon game.

Patrik Elias was New Jersey's leader with 62 points (21 goals, 41 assists) in 2010-11. Elias is the franchise's all-time leader in assists and points and has led the team in scoring seven times since the 1999-2000 season.

Year-by-Year Record

| | | Home | | | | Road | | | | Overall | | | | | | | |
Season	GP	W	L	T	OL	W	L	T	OL	W	L	T	OL	GF	GA	Pts.	Finished	Playoff Result
2010-11	82	22	16	....	3	16	23	....	2	38	39	....	5	174	209	81	4th, Atlantic Div.	Out of Playoffs
2009-10	82	27	10	....	4	21	17	....	3	48	27	....	7	222	191	103	1st, Atlantic Div.	Lost Conf. Quarter-Final
2008-09	82	28	12	....	1	23	15	....	3	51	27	....	4	244	209	106	1st, Atlantic Div.	Lost Conf. Quarter-Final
2007-08	82	25	14	....	2	21	15	....	5	46	29	....	7	206	197	99	2nd, Atlantic Div.	Lost Conf. Quarter-Final
2006-07	82	25	10	....	6	24	14	....	3	49	24	....	9	216	201	107	1st, Atlantic Div.	Lost Conf. Semi-Final
2005-06	82	27	11	....	4	19	16	....	6	46	27	....	9	242	229	101	1st, Atlantic Div.	Lost Conf. Semi-Final
2004-05	....	....																
2003-04	82	22	13	5	1	21	12	7	1	43	25	12	2	213	164	100	2nd, Atlantic Div.	Lost Conf. Quarter-Final
2002-03	**82**	**25**	**11**	**3**	**2**	**21**	**9**	**7**	**4**	**46**	**20**	**10**	**6**	**216**	**166**	**108**	**1st, Atlantic Div.**	**Won Stanley Cup**
2001-02	82	22	13	4	2	19	15	5	2	41	28	9	4	205	187	95	3rd, Atlantic Div.	Lost Conf. Quarter-Final
2000-01	82	24	11	6	0	24	8	6	3	48	19	12	3	295	195	111	1st, Atlantic Div.	Lost Final
1999-2000	**82**	**28**	**9**	**3**	**1**	**17**	**15**	**5**	**4**	**45**	**24**	**8**	**5**	**251**	**203**	**103**	**2nd, Atlantic Div.**	**Won Stanley Cup**
1998-99	82	19	14	8	....	28	10	3	....	47	24	11	....	248	196	105	1st, Atlantic Div.	Lost Conf. Quarter-Final
1997-98	82	29	10	2	....	19	13	9	....	48	23	11	....	225	166	107	1st, Atlantic Div.	Lost Conf. Semi-Final
1996-97	82	23	9	9	....	22	14	5	....	45	23	14	....	231	182	104	1st, Atlantic Div.	Lost Conf. Semi-Final
1995-96	82	22	17	2	....	15	16	10	....	37	33	12	....	215	202	86	6th, Atlantic Div.	Out of Playoffs
1994-95	**48**	**14**	**4**	**6**	**....**	**8**	**14**	**2**	**....**	**22**	**18**	**8**	**....**	**136**	**121**	**52**	**2nd, Atlantic Div.**	**Won Stanley Cup**
1993-94	84	29	11	2	....	18	14	10	....	47	25	12	....	306	220	106	2nd, Atlantic Div.	Lost Conf. Championship
1992-93	84	24	14	4	....	16	23	3	....	40	37	7	....	308	299	87	4th, Patrick Div.	Lost Div. Semi-Final
1991-92	80	24	12	4	....	14	19	3	....	38	31	11	....	289	259	87	4th, Patrick Div.	Lost Div. Semi-Final
1990-91	80	23	10	7	....	9	23	8	....	32	33	15	....	272	264	79	4th, Patrick Div.	Lost Div. Semi-Final
1989-90	80	22	15	3	....	15	19	6	....	37	34	9	....	295	288	83	2nd, Patrick Div.	Lost Div. Semi-Final
1988-89	80	17	18	5	....	10	23	7	....	27	41	12	....	281	325	66	5th, Patrick Div.	Out of Playoffs
1987-88	80	23	16	1	....	15	20	5	....	38	36	6	....	295	296	82	4th, Patrick Div.	Lost Conf. Championship
1986-87	80	20	17	3	....	9	28	3	....	29	45	6	....	293	368	64	6th, Patrick Div.	Out of Playoffs
1985-86	80	17	21	2	....	11	28	1	....	28	49	3	....	300	374	59	6th, Patrick Div.	Out of Playoffs
1984-85	80	13	21	6	....	9	27	4	....	22	48	10	....	264	346	54	5th, Patrick Div.	Out of Playoffs
1983-84	80	10	28	2	....	7	28	5	....	17	56	7	....	231	350	41	5th, Patrick Div.	Out of Playoffs
1982-83	80	11	20	9	....	6	29	5	....	17	49	14	....	230	338	48	5th, Patrick Div.	Out of Playoffs
1981-82**	80	14	21	5	....	4	28	8	....	18	49	13	....	241	362	49	5th, Smythe Div.	Out of Playoffs
1980-81**	80	15	16	9	....	7	29	4	....	22	45	13	....	258	344	57	5th, Smythe Div.	Out of Playoffs
1979-80**	80	12	20	8	....	7	28	5	....	19	48	13	....	234	308	51	6th, Smythe Div.	Out of Playoffs
1978-79**	80	8	24	8	....	7	29	4	....	15	53	12	....	210	331	42	4th, Smythe Div.	Lost Prelim. Round
1977-78**	80	17	14	9	....	2	26	12	....	19	40	21	....	257	305	59	2nd, Smythe Div.	Out of Playoffs
1976-77**	80	12	20	8	....	8	26	6	....	20	46	14	....	226	307	54	5th, Smythe Div.	Out of Playoffs
1975-76*	80	8	24	8	....	4	32	4	....	12	56	12	....	190	351	36	5th, Smythe Div.	Out of Playoffs
1974-75*	80	12	20	8	....	3	34	3	....	15	54	11	....	184	328	41	5th, Smythe Div.	Out of Playoffs

* Kansas City Scouts. ** Colorado Rockies.

ATLANTIC DIVISION
38th NHL Season

Franchise date: June 11, 1974

Transferred from Denver to New Jersey, June 30, 1982.
Transferred from Kansas City to Denver, August 25, 1976.

2011-12 Player Personnel

FORWARDS	HT	WT	S	Place of Birth	*Age	2010-11 Club
ANDERSON, Matt	5-11	195	R	West Islip, NY	28	Albany
BERUBE, Jean-Sebastien	6-4	210	L	Matane, Que.	21	Albany-Trenton
BOULTON, Eric	6-1	225	L	Halifax, N.S.	35	Atlanta
CLARKSON, David	6-1	200	R	Toronto, Ont.	27	New Jersey
ELIAS, Patrik	6-1	195	L	Trebic, Czech.	35	New Jersey
GIONTA, Stephen	5-7	185	R	Rochester, NY	27	New Jersey-Albany
HENRIQUE, Adam	6-0	200	L	Brantford, Ont.	21	New Jersey-Albany
HOEFFEL, Mike	6-3	205	L	North Oaks, MN	22	U. of Minnesota-Albany
JANSSEN, Cam	6-0	215	R	St. Louis, MO	27	St. Louis
JOSEFSON, Jacob	6-1	190	L	Stockholm, Sweden	20	New Jersey-Albany
KOVALCHUK, Ilya	6-3	230	R	Tver, USSR	28	New Jersey
MILLS, Brad	6-0	195	R	Terrace, B.C.	28	New Jersey-Albany
NAGY, Kory	5-11	195	L	London, Ont.	21	Albany-Trenton
PALMIERI, Nick	6-3	220	R	Utica, NY	22	New Jersey-Albany
PARISE, Zach	5-11	195	L	Minneapolis, MN	27	New Jersey
PELLEY, Rod	5-11	195	L	Kitimat, B.C.	27	New Jersey
PERKOVICH, Nathan	6-5	215	R	Canton, MI	25	Albany
PIETILA, Blake	5-11	190	L	Milford, MI	18	USNTDP
SESTITO, Tim	5-11	195	L	Rome, NY	27	New Jersey-Albany
SISLO, Mike	5-11	190	R	Superior, WI	23	New Hampshire-Albany
STECKEL, David	6-5	215	L	Milwaukee, WI	29	Washington-New Jersey
TEDENBY, Mattias	5-10	175	L	Vetlanda, Sweden	21	New Jersey-Albany
VEILLEUX, Stephane	6-1	190	L	Beauceville, Que.	29	Blues-Ambri
WISEMAN, Chad	6-1	205	L	Burlington, Ont.	30	Albany
ZAJAC, Darcy	6-3	200	R	Winnipeg, Man.	25	Albany-Trenton
ZAJAC, Travis	6-3	200	R	Winnipeg, Man.	26	New Jersey
ZALEWSKI, Steven	6-0	195	L	Utica, NY	25	Worcester-Albany
ZHARKOV, Vladimir	6-1	205	L	Elektrostal, USSR	23	New Jersey-Albany
ZUBRUS, Dainius	6-5	225	L	Elektrenai, USSR	33	New Jersey
DEFENSEMEN						
BURLON, Brandon	6-0	190	L	Nobleton, Ont.	21	U. of Michigan
CORRENTE, Matthew	6-0	205	R	Mississauga, Ont.	23	New Jersey-Albany
FAYNE, Mark	6-3	215	R	Nashua, NH	24	New Jersey-Albany
FRASER, Mark	6-3	220	L	Ottawa, Ont.	25	New Jersey-Albany
GELINAS, Eric	6-4	195	L	Vanier, Ont.	20	Chicoutimi-Saint John
GREENE, Andy	5-11	190	L	Trenton, MI	28	New Jersey
HARROLD, Peter	6-0	185	R	Kirtland Hills, OH	28	Los Angeles
KELLY, Dan	6-1	200	L	Morrisonville, NY	22	Albany
LARSSON, Adam	6-3	210	R	Skelleftea, Sweden	18	Skelleftea
LEACH, Jay	6-5	220	L	Syracuse, NY	32	Wor-N.J.-Alb
NOREAU, Maxim	6-0	195	R	Montreal, Que.	24	Minnesota-Houston
SALVADOR, Bryce	6-3	215	L	Brandon, Man.	35	Did Not Play - Injured
SCARLETT, Reece	6-1	170	R	Edmonton, Alta.	18	Swift Current
SOVA, Joe	6-3	205	L	Berwyn, IL	23	Alaska-Albany
TALLINDER, Henrik	6-4	210	L	Stockholm, Sweden	32	New Jersey
TAORMINA, Matt	5-10	185	L	Warren, MI	24	New Jersey
URBOM, Alexander	6-5	215	L	Stockholm, Sweden	20	New Jersey-Albany
VOLCHENKOV, Anton	6-1	225	L	Moscow, USSR	29	New Jersey
YOUNG, Harry	6-4	215	L	Windsor, Ont.	21	Albany-Trenton

GOALTENDERS	HT	WT	C	Place of Birth	*Age	2010-11 Club
BRODEUR, Martin	6-2	215	L	Montreal, Que.	39	New Jersey
CLERMONT, Maxime	6-1	195	L	Montreal, Que.	19	Gatineau
FRAZEE, Jeff	6-0	195	L	Edina, MN	24	Albany
HEDBERG, Johan	6-0	190	L	Stockholm, Sweden	38	New Jersey
KINKAID, Keith	6-3	180	L	Farmingville, NY	22	Union College
WEDGEWOOD, Scott	6-1	190	L	Etobicoke, Ont.	19	Plymouth

* – Age at start of 2011-12 season

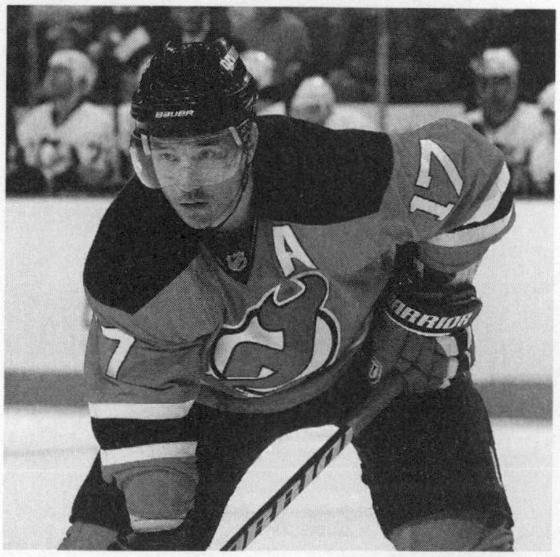

After a slow start to the 2010-11 season, both the Devils and Ilya Kovalchuk got on a roll. Kovalchuk finished the year with a team-leading 31 goals.

Captains' History

Simon Nolet, 1974-75 to 1976-77; Wilf Paiement, 1977-78; Gary Croteau, 1978-79; Mike Christie, Rene Robert and Lanny McDonald, 1979-80; Lanny McDonald, 1980-81; Lanny McDonald and Rob Ramage, 1981-82; Don Lever, 1982-83; Don Lever and Mel Bridgman, 1983-84; Mel Bridgman, 1984-85 to 1986-87; Kirk Muller, 1987-88 to 1990-91; Bruce Driver, 1991-92; Scott Stevens, 1992-93 to 2002-03; Scott Stevens and Scott Neidermayer, 2003-04; no captain, 2005-06; Patrik Elias, 2006-07; Patrik Elias and Jamie Langenbrunner, 2007-08; Jamie Langenbrunner, 2008-09 to 2010-11.

2010-11 Scoring

* – rookie

Regular Season

Pos	#	Player	Team	GP	G	A	Pts	TOI	+/–	PIM	PP	SH	GW	S	%
L	26	Patrik Elias	N.J.	81	21	41	62	18:38	–4	16	7	1	5	204	10.3
L	17	Ilya Kovalchuk	N.J.	81	31	29	60	22:33	–26	28	9	0	9	245	12.7
C	19	Travis Zajac	N.J.	82	13	31	44	19:46	–6	24	2	1	1	173	7.5
R	12	Brian Rolston	N.J.	65	14	20	34	17:36	–6	34	6	0	4	168	8.3
C	8	Dainius Zubrus	N.J.	79	13	17	30	17:09	–11	53	1	0	2	115	11.3
D	6	Andy Greene	N.J.	82	4	19	23	22:21	–23	22	1	0	1	91	4.4
L	21 *	Mattias Tedenby	N.J.	58	8	14	22	12:32	3	14	2	0	2	87	9.2
R	23	David Clarkson	N.J.	82	12	6	18	13:37	–20	116	1	0	1	192	6.3
R	32 *	Nick Palmieri	N.J.	43	9	8	17	14:19	9	6	1	0	2	66	13.6
D	7	Henrik Tallinder	N.J.	82	5	11	16	22:32	–6	40	0	1	2	102	4.9
D	34 *	Mark Fayne	N.J.	57	4	10	14	17:50	10	27	0	0	0	77	5.2
C	25	David Steckel	WSH	57	5	6	11	11:34	–3	24	0	1	1	61	8.2
			N.J.	18	1	0	1	12:50	–3	2	0	0	0	18	5.6
			Total	75	6	6	12	11:52	–6	26	0	1	1	79	7.6
C	16 *	Jacob Josefson	N.J.	28	3	7	10	13:14	5	6	0	0	1	31	9.7
C	10	Rod Pelley	N.J.	74	3	7	10	11:48	–9	27	1	0	0	88	3.4
D	28	Anton Volchenkov	N.J.	57	0	8	8	18:06	3	36	0	0	0	65	0.0
D	29	Anssi Salmela	N.J.	48	1	6	7	17:23	–11	14	0	0	1	57	1.8
L	9	Zach Parise	N.J.	13	3	3	6	19:51	–1	6	0	0	1	49	6.1
D	22 *	Matthew Corrente	N.J.	22	0	6	6	13:35	–5	44	0	0	0	21	0.0
D	5	Colin White	N.J.	69	0	6	6	18:51	–2	48	0	0	0	50	0.0
D	20 *	Matt Taormina	N.J.	17	3	2	5	20:40	–2	2	1	0	0	38	7.9
L	16 *	Alexander Vasyunov	N.J.	18	1	4	5	11:28	0	0	0	0	0	18	5.6
R	18	Vladimir Zharkov	N.J.	38	2	2	4	11:19	3	2	0	0	0	40	5.0
C	11	Adam Mair	N.J.	65	1	3	4	9:05	–16	45	0	0	0	58	1.7
D	2	Mark Fraser	N.J.	26	0	2	2	13:58	2	29	0	0	0	16	0.0
C	14	Tim Sestito	N.J.	36	0	2	2	10:49	–5	9	0	0	0	22	0.0
C	22	Bradley Mills	N.J.	4	1	0	1	8:16	1	5	0	0	0	6	16.7
D	22 *	Alexander Urbom	N.J.	8	1	0	1	12:34	–2	0	0	0	1	5	20.0
C	14 *	Adam Henrique	N.J.	1	0	0	0	13:21	1	0	0	0	0	3	0.0
R	22	Pierre-Luc Letourneau	N.J.	2	0	0	0	3:27	–2	21	0	0	0	0	0.0
D	21 *	Tyler Eckford	N.J.	4	0	0	0	8:43	–1	0	0	0	0	1	0.0
D	33	Jay Leach	N.J.	7	0	0	0	14:14	0	7	0	0	0	2	0.0
R	14	Stephen Gionta	N.J.	12	0	0	0	9:00	–3	6	0	0	0	13	0.0
D	29 *	Olivier Magnan-Grenier	N.J.	18	0	0	0	15:42	–4	4	0	0	0	8	0.0

Goaltending

No.	Goaltender	GPI	Mins	Avg	W	L	OT	EN	SO	GA	SA	S%	G	A	PIM
1	Johan Hedberg	34	1717	2.38	15	12	2	1	3	68	777	.912	0	1	4
30	Martin Brodeur	56	3116	2.45	23	26	3	5	6	127	1313	.903	0	2	2
40	Mike McKenna	2	118	3.05	0	1	0	0	0	6	56	.893	0	0	0
	Totals	**82**	**4976**	**2.50**	**38**	**39**	**5**	**6**	**9**	**207**	**2152**	**.904**			

Peter DeBoer

Head Coach

Born: Dunnville, Ont., June 13, 1968.

New Jersey Devils general manager Lou Lamoriello introduced Peter DeBoer as the 21st coach in franchise history on July 19, 2011. DeBoer was the seventh different head man hired by Lamoriello in seven seasons. He had spent the previous three seasons as head coach of the Florida Panthers.

DeBoer was named coach of the Panthers on June 13, 2008, and would lead the club to the second-best point total in team history in his first season (93 points) and a 41-30-11 mark. It was not enough for the Panthers to qualify for the Stanley Cup playoffs, however, as they finished ninth in the Eastern Conference. DeBoer joined the Panthers following 13 seasons of leading teams in the Ontario Hockey League. The current part-owner of the OHL's Oshawa Generals is a two-time winner of the OHL coach of the year – both coming with the Plymouth Whalers, in 1998-99 and 1999-2000. He coached the Kitchener Rangers to the Memorial Cup twice, winning it in 2003. DeBoer also served as an assistant coach for Team Canada at the 2010 World Championships and was a member of the gold medal-winning Canadian staff at the 2005 World Junior Championship.

As a player, DeBoer won the 1988 Memorial Cup as a member of the Windsor Spitfires. He was a 12th-round selection of the Toronto Maple Leafs in the 1988 NHL Entry Draft and played two full seasons professionally with the Milwaukee Admirals of the International Hockey League. He holds a law degree from the University of Windsor/University of Detroit.

Coaching Record

			Regular Season				Playoffs			
Season	Team	League	GC	W	L	O/T	GC	W	L	T
1995-96	Detroit	OHL	66	40	22	4	17	9	8	....
1996-97	Detroit	OHL	66	26	34	6	5	1	4	....
1997-98	Plymouth	OHL	66	37	22	7	15	8	7	....
1998-99	Plymouth	OHL	66	51	13	4	11	7	4	....
99-2000	Plymouth	OHL	68	45	18	5	23	15	8	....
2000-01	Plymouth	OHL	68	43	15	10	19	14	5	....
2001-02	Kitchener	OHL	68	35	22	11	4	0	4	....
2002-03	Kitchener	OHL	68	46	14	8	21	16	5	....
2002-03	Kitchener	M-Cup	....	....	....	....	4	4	0	....
2003-04	Kitchener	OHL	68	34	26	8	5	1	4	....
2004-05	Kitchener	OHL	68	35	20	13	15	9	6	....
2005-06	Kitchener	OHL	68	47	19	2	5	1	4	....
2006-07	Kitchener	OHL	68	47	17	4	9	5	4	....
2007-08	Kitchener	OHL	68	53	11	4	20	16	4	....
2007-08	Kitchener	M-Cup	....	....	....	....	5	2	3	....
2008-09	**Florida**	**NHL**	**82**	**41**	**30**	**11**	....	....	....	....
2009-10	**Florida**	**NHL**	**82**	**32**	**37**	**13**	....	....	....	....
2010-11	**Florida**	**NHL**	**82**	**30**	**40**	**12**	....	....	....	....
	NHL Totals		**246**	**103**	**107**	**36**	....	....	....	....

Club Records

Team

(Figures in brackets for season records are games played; records for fewest points, wins, ties, losses, goals, goals against are for 70 or more games)

Most Points **111** 2000-01 (82)
Most Wins **51** 2008-09 (82)
Most Ties ***21** 1977-78 (80)
.... **15** 1990-91 (80)
Most Losses **56** 1975-76 (80), 1983-84 (80)
Most Goals **308** 1992-93 (84)
Most Goals Against **374** 1985-86 (80)
Fewest Points ***36** 1975-76 (80)
41 1983-84 (80)
Fewest Wins ***12** 1975-76 (80)
17 1982-83 (80), 1983-84 (80)
Fewest Ties **3** 1985-86 (80)
Fewest Losses **19** 2000-01 (82)
Fewest Goals **174** 2010-11 (82)
Fewest Goals Against **164** 2003-04 (82)
Longest Winning Streak
Overall .... **13** Feb. 26-Mar. 23/01
Home .... **11** Feb. 9-Mar. 20/09
Away .... **10** Feb. 27-Apr. 7/01
Longest Undefeated Streak
Overall .... **13** Four times
Home .... **15** Jan. 8-Mar. 15/97 (9 wins, 6 ties)
Away .... **10** Feb. 27-Apr. 7/01 (10 wins)
Longest Losing Streak
Overall .... ***14** Dec. 30/75-Jan. 29/76
10 Oct. 14-Nov. 4/83
Home .... **9** Dec. 22/85-Feb. 6/86
Away .... **12** Oct. 19-Dec. 1/83
Longest Winless Streak
Overall .... ***27** Feb. 12-Apr. 4/76 (21 losses, 6 ties)
18 Oct. 20-Nov. 26/82 (14 losses 4 ties)
Home .... ***14** Feb. 12-Mar. 30/76 (10 losses, 4 ties), Feb. 4-Mar. 31/79 (12 losses, 2 ties)
9 Dec. 22/85-Feb. 6/86 (9 losses)
Away .... ***32** Nov. 12/77-Mar. 15/78 (22 losses, 10 ties)
14 Dec. 26/82-Mar. 5/83 (13 losses, 1 tie)
Most Shutouts, Season **14** 2003-04 (82)
Most PIM, Season **2,494** 1988-89 (80)
Most Goals, Game .... **9** Nine times

Individual

Most Seasons .... **20** Ken Daneyko
Most Games .... **1,283** Ken Daneyko
Most Goals, Career .... **347** John MacLean
Most Assists, Career .... **481** Patrik Elias
Most Points, Career .... **816** Patrik Elias (335G, 481A)
Most PIM, Career .... **2,519** Ken Daneyko
Most Shutouts, Career ..... ****116** Martin Brodeur
Longest Consecutive Games Streak .... **388** Ken Daneyko (Nov. 4/89-Mar. 29/94)
Most Goals, Season .... **48** Brian Gionta (2005-06)
Most Assists, Season .... **60** Scott Stevens (1993-94)
Most Points, Season .... **96** Patrik Elias (2000-01; 40G, 56A)
Most PIM, Season .... **295** Krzysztof Oliwa (1997-98)
Most Points, Defenseman, Season .... **78** Scott Stevens (1993-94; 18G, 60A)
Most Points, Center, Season .... **94** Kirk Muller (1987-88; 37G, 57A)
Most Points, Right Wing, Season .... **89** Brian Gionta (2005-06; 48G, 41A)
Most Points, Left Wing, Season .... **96** Patrik Elias (2000-01; 40G, 56A)
Most Points, Rookie, Season .... **70** Scott Gomez (1999-2000; 19G, 51A)
Most Shutouts, Season .... **12** Martin Brodeur (2006-07)
Most Goals, Game .... **4** Six times
Most Assists, Game .... **5** Greg Adams (Oct. 10/85), Kirk Muller (Mar. 25/87), Tom Kurvers (Feb. 13/89), Scott Gomez (Mar. 30/03)
Most Points, Game .... **6** Kirk Muller (Oct. 29/86; 3G, 3A)

* Records include Kansas City Scouts and Colorado Rockies, 1974-75 through 1981-82.
** NHL Record.

General Managers' History

Sid Abel, 1974-75; Sid Abel and Baz Bastien, 1975-76; Ray Miron, 1976-77 to 1980-81; Bill MacMillan, 1981-82, 1982-83; Bill MacMillan and Max McNab, 1983-84; Max McNab 1984-85 to 1986-87; Lou Lamoriello, 1987-88 to date.

Retired Numbers

3	Ken Daneyko	1982-2003
4	Scott Stevens	1991-2005

All-time Record vs. Other Clubs

Regular Season

	At Home								On Road								Total							
	GP	W	L	T	OL	GF	GA	PTS	GP	W	L	T	OL	GF	GA	PTS	GP	W	L	T	OL	GF	GA	PTS
Anaheim	10	8	2	0	0	35	17	16	13	6	6	1	0	33	35	13	23	14	8	1	0	68	52	29
Atlanta	22	12	6	1	3	64	49	28	22	14	4	2	2	77	52	32	44	26	10	3	5	141	101	60
Boston	65	23	30	11	1	165	197	58	68	24	34	8	2	203	251	58	133	47	64	19	3	368	448	116
Buffalo	66	25	31	9	1	187	209	60	66	22	34	8	2	193	239	54	132	47	65	17	3	380	448	114
Calgary	48	17	28	3	0	134	169	37	44	7	28	8	1	115	189	23	92	24	56	11	1	249	358	60
Carolina	57	34	19	4	0	194	167	72	56	24	22	8	2	166	168	58	113	58	41	12	2	360	335	130
Chicago	50	22	16	11	1	153	147	56	50	14	25	10	1	138	189	39	100	36	41	21	2	291	336	95
Colorado	39	20	14	4	1	156	128	45	37	14	19	4	0	103	129	32	76	34	33	8	1	259	257	77
Columbus	4	3	0	1	0	12	7	7	7	4	2	0	1	20	17	9	11	7	2	1	1	32	24	16
Dallas	47	24	19	3	1	162	138	52	49	14	28	6	1	124	176	35	96	38	47	9	2	286	314	87
Detroit	43	22	12	9	0	144	112	53	43	13	27	2	1	133	175	29	86	35	39	11	1	277	287	82
Edmonton	36	16	17	3	0	118	118	35	33	12	15	6	0	117	139	30	69	28	32	9	0	235	257	65
Florida	36	23	9	3	1	111	71	50	37	20	12	4	1	93	84	45	73	43	21	7	2	204	155	95
Los Angeles	46	20	21	5	0	151	157	45	45	9	28	6	2	138	208	26	91	29	49	11	2	289	365	71
Minnesota	6	4	1	1	0	21	12	9	5	3	1	1	0	17	13	7	11	7	2	2	0	38	25	16
Montreal	66	33	29	4	0	198	219	70	66	25	34	6	1	165	200	57	132	58	63	10	1	363	419	127
Nashville	8	3	4	0	1	24	23	7	8	6	1	0	1	23	16	13	16	9	5	0	2	47	39	20
NY Islanders	105	48	44	11	2	336	340	109	106	29	63	11	3	293	407	72	211	77	107	22	5	629	747	181
NY Rangers	107	56	41	7	3	352	332	122	105	31	50	20	4	295	376	86	212	87	91	27	7	647	708	208
Ottawa	35	22	11	2	0	99	80	46	36	21	11	3	1	89	84	46	71	43	22	5	1	188	164	92
Philadelphia	104	59	36	8	1	350	325	127	106	32	62	10	2	271	387	76	210	91	98	18	3	621	712	203
Phoenix	32	14	12	6	0	104	93	34	33	7	23	3	0	85	121	17	65	21	35	9	0	189	214	51
Pittsburgh	102	52	36	13	1	352	315	118	100	47	47	4	2	322	348	100	202	99	83	17	3	674	663	218
St. Louis	48	22	19	7	0	148	132	51	49	14	27	7	1	154	201	36	97	36	46	14	1	302	333	87
San Jose	15	10	4	1	0	55	32	21	13	7	4	1	1	38	34	16	28	17	8	2	1	93	66	37
Tampa Bay	38	26	8	2	2	136	80	56	37	20	10	5	2	112	83	47	75	46	18	7	4	248	163	103
Toronto	58	23	17	15	3	197	183	64	60	17	36	5	2	159	207	41	118	40	53	20	5	356	390	105
Vancouver	51	21	22	6	2	156	164	50	50	10	29	11	0	135	186	31	101	31	51	17	2	291	350	81
Washington	91	47	36	7	1	280	260	102	91	31	54	6	0	254	345	68	182	78	90	13	1	534	605	170
Defunct Clubs	8	4	2	2	0	25	19	10	8	2	3	3	0	19	27	7	16	6	5	5	0	44	46	17
Totals	**1443**	**713**	**546**	**159**	**25**	**4619**	**4295**	**1610**	**1443**	**499**	**739**	**169**	**36**	**4084**	**5086**	**1203**	**2886**	**1212**	**1285**	**328**	**61**	**8703**	**9381**	**2813**

Playoffs

	Series	W	L	GP	W	L	T	GF	GA	Last Mtg.	Rnd.	Result
Anaheim	1	1	0	7	4	3	0	19	12	2003	F	W 4-3
Boston	4	3	1	23	15	8	0	68	60	2003	CQF	W 4-1
Buffalo	1	1	0	7	4	3	0	14	14	1994	CQF	W 4-3
Carolina	4	1	3	24	10	14	0	56	51	2009	CQF	L 3-4
Colorado	1	0	1	7	3	4	0	11	19	2001	F	L 3-4
Dallas	1	1	0	6	4	2	0	15	9	2000	F	W 4-2
Detroit	1	1	0	4	4	0	0	16	7	1995	F	W 4-0
Florida	1	1	0	4	4	0	0	12	6	2000	CQF	W 4-0
Montreal	1	1	0	5	4	1	0	22	11	1997	CQF	W 4-1
NY Islanders	1	1	0	6	4	2	0	23	18	1988	DSF	W 4-2
NY Rangers	5	1	4	28	12	16	0	75	79	2008	CQF	L 1-4
Ottawa	3	1	2	18	7	11	0	40	41	2007	CSF	L 1-4
Philadelphia	5	2	3	25	10	15	0	59	64	2010	CQF	L 1-4
Pittsburgh	5	2	3	29	15	14	0	86	80	2001	CF	W 4-1
Tampa Bay	2	2	0	11	8	3	0	33	22	2007	CQF	W 4-2
Toronto	2	2	0	13	8	5	0	37	27	2001	CSF	W 4-3
Washington	2	1	1	13	6	7	0	43	44	1990	DSF	L 2-4
Totals	**40**	**22**	**18**	**230**	**122**	**108**	**0**	**629**	**564**			

Calgary totals include Atlanta Flames, 1974-75 to 1979-80.
Colorado totals include Quebec, 1979-80 to 1994-95.
Phoenix totals include Winnipeg, 1979-80 to 1995-96.
Carolina totals include Hartford, 1979-80 to 1996-97.
Dallas totals include Minnesota North Stars, 1974-75 to 1992-93.

Playoff Results 2011-2007

Year	Round	Opponent	Result	GF	GA
2010	CQF	Philadelphia	L 1-4	9	15
2009	CQF	Carolina	L 3-4	15	17
2008	CQF	NY Rangers	L 1-4	12	19
2007	CSF	Ottawa	L 1-4	11	15
	CQF	Tampa Bay	W 4-2	19	14

Abbreviations: Round: F – Final; **CF** – conference final; **CSF** – conference semi-final; **CQF** – conference quarter-final; **DSF** – division semi-final.

2010-11 Results

Oct.	8	Dallas	3-4*
	9	at Washington	2-7
	11	Pittsburgh	1-3
	13	at Buffalo	1-0*
	15	Colorado	2-3
	16	Boston	1-4
	21	at Montreal	3-0
	23	Buffalo	1-6
	24	at NY Rangers	1-3
	27	at San Jose	2-5
	29	at Anaheim	2-1
	30	at Los Angeles	1-3
Nov.	1	at Vancouver	0-3
	3	at Chicago	5-3
	5	NY Rangers	0-3
	10	Buffalo	4-5†
	12	Edmonton	4-3*
	15	at Boston	0-3
	18	at Toronto	1-3
	20	at St. Louis	2-3
	22	Washington	5-0
	24	Calgary	2-1†
	26	at NY Islanders	0-2
	27	Philadelphia	2-1†
Dec.	2	Montreal	1-5
	4	at Philadelphia	3-5
	6	at Pittsburgh	1-2
	10	at Ottawa	2-3
	11	Detroit	1-4
	15	Phoenix	3-0
	17	Nashville	1-3
	18	at Atlanta	1-7
	21	at Washington	1-5
	23	NY Islanders	1-5
	26	Toronto	1-4
	29	NY Rangers	1-3
	31	Atlanta	3-1
Jan.	1	at Carolina	3-6
	4	Minnesota	1-2
	6	Philadelphia	2-4
	8	at Philadelphia	1-2
	9	Tampa Bay	6-3
	14	at Tampa Bay	5-2
	15	at Florida	2-3*
	17	at NY Islanders	5-2
	20	Pittsburgh	2-0
	22	at Philadelphia	3-1
	23	Florida	5-2
	26	at Detroit	1-3
Feb.	1	Ottawa	2-1
	3	at NY Rangers	3-2
	4	Florida	3-4*
	6	at Montreal	4-1
	8	Carolina	3-2*
	10	at Toronto	2-1*
	11	San Jose	2-1
	16	Carolina	3-2
	18	NY Rangers	1-0
	19	at Carolina	4-1
	22	at Dallas	1-0
	25	at Tampa Bay	1-2
	27	at Florida	2-1
Mar.	2	Tampa Bay	2-1
	4	Pittsburgh	2-1*
	6	at NY Islanders	3-2†
	8	Ottawa	1-2
	11	at Atlanta	3-2*
	12	NY Islanders	3-2*
	15	Atlanta	4-2
	17	at Ottawa	1-3
	18	Washington	0-3
	20	at Columbus	3-0
	22	at Boston	1-4
	25	at Pittsburgh	0-1†
	26	at Buffalo	0-2
	30	NY Islanders	3-2
Apr.	1	Philadelphia	4-2
	2	Montreal	1-3
	5	at Pittsburgh	2-4
	6	Toronto	4-2
	9	at NY Rangers	2-5
	10	Boston	3-2

* – Overtime † – Shootout

Entry Draft Selections 2011-1997

Name in bold denotes played in NHL.

2011
Pick
4	Adam Larsson
69	forfeited
75	Blake Coleman
99	Reid Boucher
129	Blake Pietila
159	Reece Scarlett
189	Patrick Daly

2010
Pick
38	Jonathon Merrill
84	Scott Wedgewood
114	Joe Faust
174	Maxime Clermont
204	Mauro Jorg

2009
Pick
20	**Jacob Josefson**
54	Eric Gelinas
73	**Alexander Urbom**
114	Seth Helgeson
144	Derek Rodwell
174	Ashton Bernard
204	Curtis Gedig

2008
Pick
24	**Mattias Tedenby**
52	Brandon Burlon
54	**Patrice Cormier**
82	**Adam Henrique**
112	Matt Delahey
142	Kory Nagy
172	David Wohlberg
202	Harry Young
205	Jean-Sebastien Berube

2007
Pick
57	Mike Hoeffel
79	**Nick Palmieri**
87	Corbin McPherson
117	**Matt Halischuk**
177	Vili Sopanen
207	Ryan Molle

2006
Pick
30	**Matthew Corrente**
58	**Alexander Vasyunov**
67	Kirill Tulupov
77	**Vladimir Zharkov**
107	Tyler Miller
148	**Olivier Magnan**
178	Tony Romano
208	Kyell Henegan

2005
Pick
23	**Niclas Bergfors**
38	Jeff Frazee
84	**Mark Fraser**
99	**Patrick Davis**
155	**Mark Fayne**
170	Sean Zimmerman
218	Alexander Sundstrom

2004
Pick
20	**Travis Zajac**
155	Alexander Mikhailishin
185	Josh Disher
216	**Pierre-Luc Letourneau-Leblond**
217	Tyler Eckford
250	Nathan Perkovich
282	Valeri Klimov

2003
Pick
17	**Zach Parise**
42	**Petr Vrana**
93	Ivan Khomutov
167	Zach Tarkir
197	Jason Smith
261	**Joey Tenute**
292	Arseny Bondarev

2002
Pick
51	Anton Kadeykin
53	**Barry Tallackson**
64	**Jason Ryznar**
84	Marek Chvatal
85	Ahren Nittel
117	**Cam Janssen**
154	Krisjanis Redlihs
187	Eric Johansson
218	**Ilkka Pikkarainen**
250	Dan Glover
281	Bill Kinkel

2001
Pick
28	Adrian Foster
44	Igor Pohanka
48	**Tuomas Pihlman**
60	Victor Uchevatov
67	Robin Leblanc
72	**Brandon Nolan**
128	Andrei Posnov
163	**Andreas Salomonsson**
194	James Massen
229	**Aaron Voros**
257	Yevgeny Gamalei

2000
Pick
22	**David Hale**
39	Teemu Laine
56	Alexander Suglobov
57	Matt DeMarchi
62	**Paul Martin**
67	Max Birbraer
76	**Mike Rupp**
125	Phil Cole
135	**Mike Danton**
164	Matus Kostur
194	**Deryk Engelland**
198	Ken Magowan
257	Warren McCutcheon

1999
Pick
27	Ari Ahonen
42	**Mike Commodore**
50	Brett Clouthier
95	Andre Lakos
100	Teemu Kesa
185	Scott Cameron
214	Chris Hartsburg
242	Justin Dziama

1998
Pick
26	**Mike Van Ryn**
27	**Scott Gomez**
37	**Christian Berglund**
82	**Brian Gionta**
96	**Mikko Jokela**
105	**Pierre Dagenais**
119	Anton But
143	**Ryan Flinn**
172	Jacques Lariviere
199	Erik Jensen
227	Marko Ahosilta
257	Ryan Held

1997
Pick
24	**Jean-Francois Damphousse**
38	**Stanislav Gron**
104	Lucas Nehrling
131	**Jiri Bicek**
159	**Sascha Goc**
188	Mathieu Benoit
215	**Scott Clemmensen**
241	Jan Srdinko

Coaching History

Bep Guidolin, 1974-75; Bep Guidolin, Sid Abel and Eddie Bush, 1975-76; Johnny Wilson, 1976-77; Pat Kelly, 1977-78; Pat Kelly and Aldo Guidolin, 1978-79; Don Cherry, 1979-80; Bill MacMillan, 1980-81; Bert Marshall and Marshall Johnston, 1981-82; Bill MacMillan, 1982-83; Bill MacMillan and Tom McVie, 1983-84; Doug Carpenter, 1984-85 to 1986-87; Doug Carpenter and Jim Schoenfeld, 1987-88; Jim Schoenfeld, 1988-89; Jim Schoenfeld and John Cunniff, 1989-90; John Cunniff and Tom McVie, 1990-91; Tom McVie, 1991-92; Herb Brooks, 1992-93; Jacques Lemaire, 1993-94 to 1997-98; Robbie Ftorek, 1998-99; Robbie Ftorek and Larry Robinson, 1999-2000; Larry Robinson, 2000-01; Larry Robinson and Kevin Constantine, 2001-02; Pat Burns, 2002-03 to 2004-05; Larry Robinson and Lou Lamoriello, 2005-06; Claude Julien and Lou Lamoriello, 2006-07; Brent Sutter, 2007-08, 2008-09; Jacques Lemaire, 2009-10; John MacLean and Jacques Lemaire, 2010-11; Peter DeBoer, 2011-12.

Lou Lamoriello
CEO, President and General Manager
Born: Providence, RI, October 21, 1942.

Lou Lamoriello has been president and general manager of the Devils since 1987-88 following more than 20 years with Providence College as a player, coach and administrator. He was inducted into the Hockey Hall of Fame's Builder category in November, 2009. His trades, signings and draft choices helped lead the Devils to their first Stanley Cup Championship in 1995 and were followed by victories again in 2000 and 2003. During his tenure, the Devils have had 12 100-point seasons, four Eastern Conference titles and nine Atlantic Division regular-season championships. In 2005-06, Lamoriello took over behind the bench and coached the Devils to first place in the Atlantic Division.

While at Providence, Lamoriello served as hockey coach for 15 seasons, compiling an impressive .578 winning percentage (248-179-13), while guiding the Friars to 12 post-season tournaments in a row. During his last five seasons (1978-83) of coaching, the school compiled a record of 107-58-4 and had more players drafted by the National Hockey League after entering college than any other college team during those years. Lamoriello helped propel numerous players and administrators toward NHL careers during his tenure at Providence. He was hired as president of the Devils on April 30, 1987, and assumed the responsibility of general manager on September 10, 1987. Lamoriello was G.M. of Team USA for the first World Cup of Hockey in 1996 as the U.S. captured the championship. He was also the G.M. for the 1998 U.S. Olympic Team.

NHL Coaching Record

Season	Team	League	Regular Season				Playoffs			
			GC	W	L	O/T	GC	W	L	T
2005-06	New Jersey	NHL	50	32	14	4	9	5	4	....
2006-07	New Jersey	NHL	3	2	0	1	11	5	6	....
	NHL Totals		**53**	**34**	**14**	**5**	**20**	**10**	**10**	....

Posted an 0-1 playoff record as replacement coach when Jim Schoenfeld was suspended, May 10, 1988. Loss is credited to Schoenfeld's coaching record.

Club Directory

Prudential Center

New Jersey Devils
Prudential Center
165 Mulberry Street
Newark, NJ 07102
Phone **973/757-6100**
FAX 973/757-6399
www.newjerseydevils.com
Capacity: 17,625

Owners	Jeff Vanderbeek, Mike Gilfillan, Peter Simon
Chairman/Managing Partner	Jeff Vanderbeek
Vice Chairman	Mike Gilfillan
President/CEO/General Manager	Lou Lamoriello
Exec. Vice President, Hockey Ops/Director, Scouting	David Conte
Exec. Vice President, Operations	Peter McMullen
Sr. Vice President, Hockey Ops/ General Manager, Albany/Scout	Chris Lamoriello
Senior Vice President, Communications	Mike Levine
Vice President, Hockey Operations	Stephen Pellegrini

Hockey Club Personnel
Head Coach	Peter DeBoer
Assistant Coaches	Larry Robinson, Adam Oates, Dave Barr
Goaltending Coach	Chris Terreri
Special Assignment Coaches	Jacques Caron, Jacques Laperriere, Jacques Lemaire, Scott Stevens
Assistant Director, Scouting	Claude Carrier
Scouting Staff	Timo Blomqvist, Glen Dirk, Milt Fisher, Ferny Flaman, Dan Labraaten, Scott Lachance, Pierre Mondou, Gates Orlando, Larry Perris, Marcel Pronovost, Lou Reycroft, Vaclav Slansky, Jr., Steve Smith, Geoff Stevens, Ed Thomlinson, Les Widdifield
Pro Scouting Staff	Bob Hoffmeyer, Jan Ludvig, Andre Boudrias
Hockey Operations Video Coordinator	Taran Singleton
Hockey Operations Video Assistant	Mike Ford
Scouting Staff Assistant	Callie A. Smith
Head Trainer	Richard Stinziano
Equipment Manager	Rich Matthews
Assistant Equipment Managers	Jason McGrath, Mike Thibault
Strength/Conditioning Coordinator	Michael Vasalani
Massage Therapist	Tommy Plasko
Team Orthopedists	Dr. Barry Fisher, Dr. Len Jaffe
Team Cardiologist	Dr. Joseph Niznik
Team Dentist	Dr. H. Hugh Gardy
Team Optometrist	Dr. Paul Berman
Exercise Physiologist	Dr. Garret Caffrey
Physical Therapist	David Feniger
Video Consultant	Mitch Kaufman
Head Coach, Albany	Rick Kowalsky
Assistant Coach, Albany	Tommy Albelin
Video Coordinator, Albany	Matthew DeMado
Athletic Trainer, Albany	Kevin Morley
Equipment Manager, Albany	Stephen Bratspis
Assistant Equipment Manager, Albany	Andrew Schmidt

President's Office
Hockey Operations Executive Assistant to the President/CEO/General Manager	Marie Carnevale
Administrative Assistant	Christine Garcia

Communications
Senior Director, Communications	Jeff Altstadter
Director, Communications	Pete Albietz
Director, Website Content	Eric Marin
Assistant Director, Communications	Daniel Beam

Computer Operations
Director, Programming/Computer Operations	Jack Skelley

Alumni
Alumni Representatives	Ken Daneyko, Bruce Driver, Grant Marshall, Jim Dowd

Television/Radio
Television Outlet	MSG Plus
Television Play-by-Play / Color	TBA / Glenn Resch
Radio Outlet	SportsRadio 66 WFAN
Radio Play-by-Play / Color	Matt Loughlin / Sherry Ross

Key Off-Season Signings/Acquisitions

2011

May 13 • Re-signed RW **Michael Grabner**.

25 • Re-signed RW **Kyle Okposo**.

27 • Named **Doug Weight** assistant coach and special assistant to the GM.

June 19 • Re-signed LW **Trevor Gillies**.

July 1 • Signed C **Marty Reasoner**.

15 • Re-signed D **Ty Wishart**.

28 • Acquired LW **Brian Rolston** and a conditional pick in the 2012 Entry Draft from New Jersey for RW **Trent Hunter**.

Aug. 2 • Re-signed RW **Blake Comeau**.

New York Islanders

2010-11 Results: 30w-39L-7otl-6sol 73pts.
Fifth, Atlantic Division

John Tavares fends off Alex Kovalev behind the Pittsburgh goal. Tavares improved on all the offensive numbers from his 2009-10 rookie campaign with 29 goals and a team-leading 38 assists and 67 points in 2010-11.

2011-12 Schedule

Oct.	Sat.	8	Florida	Sat.	14	Buffalo
	Mon.	10	Minnesota*	Mon.	16	Nashville*
	Thu.	13	Tampa Bay	Tue.	17	at Washington
	Sat.	15	NY Rangers	Thu.	19	at Philadelphia
	Thu.	20	at Tampa Bay	Sat.	21	Carolina
	Sat.	22	at Florida	Mon.	23	at Toronto
	Tue.	25	Pittsburgh	Tue.	24	Toronto
	Thu.	27	at Pittsburgh	Tue.	31	at Carolina
	Sat.	29	San Jose	**Feb.** Fri.	3	at Ottawa
Nov.	Thu.	3	Winnipeg	Sat.	4	Buffalo
	Sat.	5	Washington	Tue.	7	at Philadelphia
	Mon.	7	at Boston	Thu.	9	Montreal
	Thu.	10	at Colorado	Sat.	11	Los Angeles*
	Sun.	13	at Vancouver	Sun.	12	Florida*
	Tue.	15	NY Rangers	Tue.	14	at Winnipeg
	Thu.	17	Montreal	Thu.	16	at St. Louis
	Sat.	19	Boston	Sat.	18	Carolina
	Mon.	21	at Pittsburgh	Mon.	20	Ottawa*
	Wed.	23	Philadelphia	Tue.	21	at Buffalo
	Fri.	25	New Jersey*	Fri.	24	NY Rangers
	Sat.	26	at New Jersey*	Sun.	26	at Ottawa*
	Tue.	29	at Buffalo	Tue.	28	at Washington
Dec.	Fri.	2	at Chicago	**Mar.** Thu.	1	at Philadelphia
	Sat.	3	at Dallas	Sat.	3	at Boston*
	Tue.	6	Tampa Bay	Sun.	4	New Jersey*
	Thu.	8	Chicago	Thu.	8	at New Jersey
	Sat.	10	Pittsburgh	Sat.	10	New Jersey
	Tue.	13	at Montreal	Sun.	11	at NY Rangers
	Thu.	15	Dallas	Tue.	13	Washington
	Sat.	17	at Minnesota	Thu.	15	Philadelphia
	Tue.	20	at Winnipeg	Sat.	17	at Montreal
	Thu.	22	at NY Rangers	Tue.	20	at Toronto
	Fri.	23	Toronto	Sat.	24	at Tampa Bay
	Mon.	26	at NY Rangers	Sun.	25	at Florida*
	Thu.	29	Calgary	Tue.	27	at Pittsburgh
	Sat.	31	Edmonton*	Thu.	29	Pittsburgh
Jan.	Tue.	3	at Carolina	Sat.	31	Boston*
	Fri.	6	at Anaheim	**Apr.** Sun.	1	Ottawa*
	Sat.	7	at Phoenix	Tue.	3	at New Jersey
	Tue.	10	Detroit	Thu.	5	Winnipeg
	Thu.	12	Philadelphia	Sat.	7	at Columbus

* Denotes afternoon game.

ATLANTIC DIVISION
40th NHL Season
Franchise date: June 6, 1972

Year-by-Year Record

Season	GP	Home W	L	T	OL	Road W	L	T	OL	Overall W	L	T	OL	GF	GA	Pts.	Finished	Playoff Result
2010-11	82	17	18	....	6	13	21	....	7	30	39	....	13	229	264	73	5th, Atlantic Div.	Out of Playoffs
2009-10	82	23	14	....	4	11	23	....	7	34	37	....	11	222	264	79	5th, Atlantic Div.	Out of Playoffs
2008-09	82	17	18	....	6	9	29	....	3	26	47	....	9	201	279	61	5th, Atlantic Div.	Out of Playoffs
2007-08	82	18	18	....	5	17	20	....	4	35	38	....	9	194	243	79	5th, Atlantic Div.	Out of Playoffs
2006-07	82	22	13	....	6	18	17	....	6	40	30	....	12	248	240	92	4th, Atlantic Div.	Lost Conf. Quarter-Final
2005-06	82	20	18	....	3	16	22	....	3	36	40	....	6	230	278	78	4th, Atlantic Div.	Out of Playoffs
2004-05	....	....	....	....	....	....	....	....	....	....	....	....	....	....	....	....		
2003-04	82	25	11	4	1	13	18	7	3	38	29	11	4	237	210	91	3rd, Atlantic Div.	Lost Conf. Quarter-Final
2002-03	82	18	18	5	0	17	16	6	2	35	34	11	2	224	231	83	3rd, Atlantic Div.	Lost Conf. Quarter-Final
2001-02	82	21	13	5	2	21	15	3	2	42	28	8	4	239	220	96	2nd, Atlantic Div.	Lost Conf. Quarter-Final
2000-01	82	12	27	1	1	9	24	6	2	21	51	7	3	185	268	52	5th, Atlantic Div.	Out of Playoffs
1999-2000	82	10	25	5	1	14	23	4	0	24	48	9	1	194	275	58	5th, Atlantic Div.	Out of Playoffs
1998-99	82	11	23	7	....	13	25	3	....	24	48	10	....	194	244	58	4th, Atlantic Div.	Out of Playoffs
1997-98	82	17	20	4	....	13	21	7	....	30	41	11	....	212	225	71	4th, Atlantic Div.	Out of Playoffs
1996-97	82	19	18	4	....	10	23	8	....	29	41	12	....	240	250	70	7th, Atlantic Div.	Out of Playoffs
1995-96	82	14	21	6	....	8	29	4	....	22	50	10	....	229	315	54	7th, Atlantic Div.	Out of Playoffs
1994-95	48	10	11	3	....	5	17	2	....	15	28	5	....	126	158	35	7th, Atlantic Div.	Out of Playoffs
1993-94	84	23	15	4	....	13	21	8	....	36	36	12	....	282	264	84	4th, Atlantic Div.	Lost Conf. Quarter-Final
1992-93	84	20	19	3	....	20	18	4	....	40	37	7	....	335	297	87	3rd, Patrick Div.	Lost Conf. Championship
1991-92	80	20	15	5	....	14	20	6	....	34	35	11	....	291	299	79	5th, Patrick Div.	Out of Playoffs
1990-91	80	15	19	6	....	10	26	4	....	25	45	10	....	223	290	60	6th, Patrick Div.	Out of Playoffs
1989-90	80	15	17	8	....	16	21	3	....	31	38	11	....	281	288	73	4th, Patrick Div.	Lost Div. Semi-Final
1988-89	80	19	18	3	....	9	29	2	....	28	47	5	....	265	325	61	6th, Patrick Div.	Out of Playoffs
1987-88	80	24	10	6	....	15	21	4	....	39	31	10	....	308	267	88	1st, Patrick Div.	Lost Div. Semi-Final
1986-87	80	20	15	5	....	15	18	7	....	35	33	12	....	279	281	82	3rd, Patrick Div.	Lost Div. Final
1985-86	80	22	11	7	....	17	18	5	....	39	29	12	....	327	284	90	3rd, Patrick Div.	Lost Div. Semi-Final
1984-85	80	26	11	3	....	14	23	3	....	40	34	6	....	345	312	86	3rd, Patrick Div.	Lost Div. Final
1983-84	80	28	11	1	....	22	15	3	....	50	26	4	....	357	269	104	1st, Patrick Div.	Lost Final
1982-83	**80**	**26**	**11**	**3**	....	**16**	**15**	**9**	....	**42**	**26**	**12**	....	**302**	**226**	**96**	**2nd, Patrick Div.**	**Won Stanley Cup**
1981-82	**80**	**33**	**3**	**4**	....	**21**	**13**	**6**	....	**54**	**16**	**10**	....	**385**	**250**	**118**	**1st, Patrick Div.**	**Won Stanley Cup**
1980-81	**80**	**23**	**6**	**11**	....	**25**	**12**	**3**	....	**48**	**18**	**14**	....	**355**	**260**	**110**	**1st, Patrick Div.**	**Won Stanley Cup**
1979-80	**80**	**26**	**9**	**5**	....	**13**	**19**	**8**	....	**39**	**28**	**13**	....	**281**	**247**	**91**	**2nd, Patrick Div.**	**Won Stanley Cup**
1978-79	80	31	3	6	....	20	12	8	....	51	15	14	....	358	214	116	1st, Patrick Div.	Lost Semi-Final
1977-78	80	29	3	8	....	19	14	7	....	48	17	15	....	334	210	111	1st, Patrick Div.	Lost Quarter-Final
1976-77	80	24	11	5	....	23	10	7	....	47	21	12	....	288	193	106	2nd, Patrick Div.	Lost Semi-Final
1975-76	80	24	8	8	....	18	13	9	....	42	21	17	....	297	190	101	2nd, Patrick Div.	Lost Semi-Final
1974-75	80	22	9	6	12	....	11	19	10	....	33	25	22	264	221	88	3rd, Patrick Div.	Lost Semi-Final
1973-74	78	13	17	9	....	6	24	9	....	19	41	18	....	182	247	56	8th, East Div.	Out of Playoffs
1972-73	78	10	25	4	....	2	35	2	....	12	60	6	....	170	347	30	8th, East Div.	Out of Playoffs

2011-12 Player Personnel

FORWARDS	HT	WT	S	Place of Birth	*Age	2010-11 Club
BAILEY, Josh	6-1	201	L	Bowmanville, Ont.	22	NY Islanders-Bridgeport
COMEAU, Blake	6-0	198	L	Meadow Lake, Sask.	25	NY Islanders
GILLIES, Trevor	6-3	227	L	Cambridge, Ont.	32	NY Islanders
GRABNER, Michael	6-0	170	L	Villach, Austria	24	NY Islanders
HALEY, Micheal	5-10	204	L	Guelph, Ont.	25	NY Islanders-Bridgeport
MARTIN, Matt	6-3	210	L	Windsor, Ont.	22	NY Islanders-Bridgeport
MOULSON, Matt	6-1	210	L	North York, Ont.	27	NY Islanders
NIEDERREITER, Nino	6-2	205	L	Chur, Switzerland	19	NY Islanders-Portland (WHL)
NIELSEN, Frans	6-0	187	L	Herning, Denmark	27	NY Islanders
OKPOSO, Kyle	6-0	210	R	St. Paul, MN	23	NY Islanders
PARENTEAU, P.A.	6-0	198	R	Hull, Que.	28	NY Islanders
REASONER, Marty	6-1	205	L	Honeoye Falls, NY	34	Florida
ROLSTON, Brian	6-2	215	L	Flint, MI	38	New Jersey
TAVARES, John	6-0	202	L	Mississauga, Ont.	21	NY Islanders
WALLACE, Tim	6-1	207	R	Anchorage, AK	27	Pittsburgh-Wilkes-Barre

DEFENSEMEN						
EATON, Mark	6-1	214	L	Wilmington, DE	34	NY Islanders
HAMONIC, Travis	6-2	208	R	Winnipeg, Man.	21	NY Islanders-Bridgeport
JURCINA, Milan	6-4	240	R	Liptovsky Mikulas, Czech.	28	NY Islanders
MacDONALD, Andrew	6-1	201	L	Judique, N.S.	25	NY Islanders
MOTTAU, Mike	6-0	190	L	Quincy, MA	33	NY Islanders
STREIT, Mark	5-11	202	L	Bern, Switz.	33	Did Not Play - Injured
WISHART, Ty	6-4	222	L	Belleville, Ont.	23	Norfolk-NYI-Bridgeport

GOALTENDERS	HT	WT	C	Place of Birth	*Age	2010-11 Club
DiPIETRO, Rick	6-1	190	R	Winthrop, MA	30	NY Islanders
MONTOYA, Al	6-2	195	L	Chicago, IL	26	NY Islanders-San Antonio
NABOKOV, Evgeni	6-0	200	L	Ust-Kamenogorsk, USSR	36	St. Petersburg

* – Age at start of 2011-12 season

2010-11 Scoring
* – rookie

Regular Season

Pos	#	Player	Team	GP	G	A	Pts	TOI	+/-	PIM	PP	SH	GW	S	%
C	91	John Tavares	NYI	79	29	38	67	19:15	-16	53	9	0	4	243	11.9
L	26	Matt Moulson	NYI	82	31	22	53	18:52	-10	24	9	0	3	237	13.1
R	15	P.A. Parenteau	NYI	81	20	33	53	18:13	-8	46	9	0	2	161	12.4
R	40 *	Michael Grabner	NYI	76	34	18	52	15:04	13	10	2	6	3	228	14.9
L	57	Blake Comeau	NYI	77	24	22	46	18:41	-17	43	5	1	3	182	13.2
C	51	Frans Nielsen	NYI	71	13	31	44	17:45	13	38	0	7	1	156	8.3
C	12	Josh Bailey	NYI	70	11	17	28	17:50	-13	57	5	0	2	102	10.8
D	47	Andrew MacDonald	NYI	60	4	23	27	23:24	9	37	1	0	1	72	5.6
D	36 *	Travis Hamonic	NYI	62	5	21	26	21:34	4	103	1	0	0	118	4.2
D	38	Jack Hillen	NYI	64	4	18	22	18:49	-5	45	0	0	1	81	4.9
R	21	Kyle Okposo	NYI	38	5	15	20	16:34	3	40	0	0	2	72	6.9
D	27	Milan Jurcina	NYI	46	4	13	17	18:04	-4	30	1	1	0	76	5.3
D	24	Radek Martinek	NYI	64	3	13	16	20:50	-5	35	1	0	0	97	3.1
L	17 *	Matt Martin	NYI	68	5	9	14	10:57	-13	147	0	0	1	60	8.3
L	58	Jesse Joensuu	NYI	42	6	3	9	11:34	-6	33	0	0	2	41	14.6
C	93	Doug Weight	NYI	18	2	7	9	17:31	-3	10	1	0	0	26	7.7
C	28	Zenon Konopka	NYI	82	2	7	9	10:11	-14	307	0	0	0	56	3.6
D	42	Dylan Reese	NYI	27	0	6	6	14:48	-12	15	0	0	0	23	0.0
D	8	Bruno Gervais	NYI	53	0	6	6	15:40	-14	30	0	0	0	43	0.0
D	6 *	Ty Wishart	NYI	20	1	4	5	16:49	-5	10	1	0	0	23	4.3
R	7	Trent Hunter	NYI	17	1	3	4	12:39	-3	23	0	0	0	30	3.3
L	16	Jon Sim	NYI	34	1	3	4	11:24	-10	22	0	0	0	38	2.6
C	37	Jeremy Colliton	NYI	15	2	1	3	11:53	-7	10	2	0	0	7	28.6
C	59 *	Micheal Haley	NYI	27	2	1	3	8:01	-4	85	0	0	0	13	15.4
D	10	Mike Mottau	NYI	20	0	3	3	20:20	-12	8	0	0	0	21	0.0
D	4	Mark Eaton	NYI	34	0	3	3	20:21	-2	8	0	0	0	29	0.0
L	14	Trevor Gillies	NYI	39	0	2	2	3:04	-3	165	0	0	0	9	22.2
R	25 *	Nino Niederreiter	NYI	9	1	1	2	13:35	-1	8	0	0	0	12	8.3
C	81 *	Justin Dibenedetto	NYI	8	0	1	1	9:03	-2	2	0	0	0	6	0.0
D	71 *	Mark Katic	NYI	11	0	1	1	16:25	-9	4	0	0	0	8	0.0
D	55 *	Shane Sims	NYI	1	0	0	0	6:34	0	0	0	0	0	0	0.0
D	29 *	Jamie Doornbosch	NYI	1	0	0	0	5:21	-1	0	0	0	0	1	0.0
D	55 *	Matt Campanale	NYI	1	0	0	0	8:21	1	2	0	0	0	0	0.0
R	49 *	Rhett Rakhshani	NYI	1	0	0	0	11:42	-1	0	0	0	0	2	0.0

Goaltending

No.	Goaltender	GPI	Mins	Avg	W	L	OT	EN	SO	GA	SA	S%	G	A	PIM
35 *	Al Montoya	20	1154	2.39	9	5	5	1	1	46	585	.921	0	1	2
60 *	Kevin Poulin	10	491	2.44	4	2	1	0	0	20	262	.924	0	0	0
35	Dwayne Roloson	20	1206	2.64	6	13	1	4	0	53	629	.916	0	1	2
39	Rick DiPietro	26	1533	3.44	8	14	4	5	1	88	773	.886	0	1	25
52	Nathan Lawson	10	384	4.06	1	4	2	0	0	26	243	.893	0	0	0
1 *	Mikko Koskinen	4	208	4.33	2	1	0	0	0	15	118	.873	0	0	0
	Totals	82	5013	3.09	30	39	13	10	2	258	2620	.902			

Jack Capuano
Head Coach
Born: Cranston, RI, July 7, 1966.

Jack Capuano was named the interim head coach of the New York Islanders on November 15, 2010. Islanders general manager Garth Snow announced his decision to remove the "interim" title and officially name Capuano the club's head coach on April 12, 2011.

Capuano made his debut in the midst of one of the worst winless streaks in team history and was tasked with turning the season around. Right after Capuano took the reigns, the team posted a 1-8-2 record, but that wouldn't last. After their rough patch, Capuano led the Islanders to a 25-21-8 record in their last 54 games of the season, making the Islanders one of the best teams in the Eastern Conference after December 15. The coach went above .500 with a 15-12-6 record after the All-Star Break.

Capuano joined the Islanders organization in the 2005-06 season as an assistant coach with the Islanders. The native of Cranston, Rhode Island, was named head coach of the Bridgeport Sound Tigers on April 30, 2007. In four seasons he had a 133-100-22 mark as head coach of the Sound Tigers. From 1997 to 2005 he served as the general manager of the Pee Dee Pride of the East Coast Hockey League. Capuano also served as the head coach of the 2005 U.S. Under-18 Select Team at the Five Nations Cup in Slovakia.

Capuano began his coaching career in 1995 as an assistant coach with the Tallahassee Tiger Sharks of the ECHL after ending a pro playing career that included stints with Boston, Vancouver and Toronto of the NHL and Springfield and Maine of the American Hockey League. The former First Team All-American captained the University of Maine to a Hockey East championship and NCAA Frozen Four appearance in 1998.

Coaching Record

			Regular Season				Playoffs			
Season	Team	League	GC	W	L	O/T	GC	W	L	T
1996-97	Knoxville	ECHL	16	7	8	1	....	....	....	....
1997-98	Pee Dee	ECHL	70	34	25	11	8	3	5	....
1998-99	Pee Dee	ECHL	70	51	15	4	13	7	6	....
2000-01	Pee Dee	ECHL	15	9	5	1	....	....	....	....
2007-08	Bridgeport	AHL	80	40	36	4	....	....	....	....
2008-09	Bridgeport	AHL	80	49	23	8	5	1	4	....
2009-10	Bridgeport	AHL	80	38	32	10	5	1	4	....
2010-11	Bridgeport	AHL	15	6	9	0	....	....	....	....
2010-11	**NY Islanders**	**NHL**	65	26	29	10	....	....	....	....
	NHL Totals		65	26	29	10	....	....	....	....

P.A. Parenteau celebrates a goal with young Islanders defensemen Travis Hamonic and Andrew MacDonald.

Coaching History
Phil Goyette and Earl Ingarfield, 1972-73; Al Arbour, 1973-74 to 1985-86; Terry Simpson, 1986-87, 1987-88; Terry Simpson and Al Arbour, 1988-89; Al Arbour, 1989-90 to 1993-94; Lorne Henning, 1994-95; Mike Milbury, 1995-96; Mike Milbury and Rick Bowness, 1996-97; Rick Bowness and Mike Milbury, 1997-98; Mike Milbury and Bill Stewart, 1998-99; Butch Goring, 1999-2000; Butch Goring and Lorne Henning, 2000-01; Peter Laviolette, 2001-02, 2002-03; Steve Stirling, 2003-04, 2004-05; Steve Stirling and Brad Shaw, 2005-06; Ted Nolan, 2006-07, 2007-08; Scott Gordon, 2008-09, 2009-10; Scott Gordon and Jack Capuano, 2010-11; Jack Capuano, 2011-12.

Club Records

Team

(Figures in brackets for season records are games played; records for fewest points, wins, ties, losses, goals, goals against are for 70 or more games)

Most Points	**118**	1981-82 (80)
Most Wins	**54**	1981-82 (80)
Most Ties	**22**	1974-75 (80)
Most Losses	**60**	1972-73 (78)
Most Goals	**385**	1981-82 (80)
Most Goals Against	**347**	1972-73 (78)
Fewest Points	**30**	1972-73 (78)
Fewest Wins	**12**	1972-73 (78)
Fewest Ties	**4**	1983-84 (80)
Fewest Losses	**15**	1978-79 (80)
Fewest Goals	**170**	1972-73 (78)
Fewest Goals Against	**190**	1975-76 (80)
Longest Winning Streak		
Overall	**15**	Jan. 21-Feb. 20/82
Home	**14**	Jan. 2-Feb. 25/82
Away	**8**	Feb. 27-Mar. 29/81
Longest Undefeated Streak		
Overall	**15**	Three times
Home	**23**	Oct. 17/78-Jan. 20/79 (19 wins, 4 ties), Jan. 2-Apr. 3/82 (21 wins, 2 ties)
Away	**8**	Three times
Longest Losing Streak		
Overall	**14**	Oct. 23-Nov. 24/10
Home	**7**	Nov. 13-Dec. 14/99
Away	**15**	Jan. 20-Mar. 31/73
Longest Winless Streak		
Overall	**15**	Nov. 22-Dec. 21/72 (12 losses, 3 ties)
Home	**9**	Mar. 2-Apr. 6/99 (7 losses, 2 ties)
Away	**20**	Nov. 3/72-Jan. 13/73 (19 losses, 1 tie)
Most Shutouts, Season	**10**	1975-76 (80)
Most PIM, Season	**1,857**	1986-87 (80)
Most Goals, Game	**11**	Dec. 20/83 (Pit. 3 at NYI 11), Mar. 3/84 (NYI 11 at Tor. 6)

Individual

Most Seasons	**17**	Billy Smith
Most Games	**1,123**	Bryan Trottier
Most Goals, Career	**573**	Mike Bossy
Most Assists, Career	**853**	Bryan Trottier
Most Points, Career	**1,353**	Bryan Trottier (500G, 853A)
Most PIM, Career	**1,879**	Mick Vukota
Most Shutouts, Career	**25**	Glenn Resch
Longest Consecutive Games Streak	**576**	Billy Harris (Oct. 7/72-Nov. 30/79)
Most Goals, Season	**69**	Mike Bossy (1978-79)
Most Assists, Season	**87**	Bryan Trottier (1978-79)
Most Points, Season	**147**	Mike Bossy (1981-82; 64G, 83A)
Most PIM, Season	**356**	Brian Curran (1986-87)
Most Points, Defenseman, Season	**101**	Denis Potvin (1978-79; 31G, 70A)
Most Points, Center, Season	**134**	Bryan Trottier (1978-79; 47G, 87A)
Most Points, Right Wing, Season	**147**	Mike Bossy (1981-82; 64G, 83A)
Most Points, Left Wing, Season	**100**	John Tonelli (1984-85; 42G, 58A)
Most Points, Rookie, Season	**95**	Bryan Trottier (1975-76; 32G, 63A)
Most Shutouts, Season	**7**	Glenn Resch (1975-76)
Most Goals, Game	**5**	Bryan Trottier (Dec. 23/78), (Feb. 13/82) John Tonelli (Jan. 6/81)
Most Assists, Game	**6**	Mike Bossy (Jan. 6/81)
Most Points, Game	**8**	Bryan Trottier (Dec. 23/78; 5G, 3A)

Captains' History

Ed Westfall, 1972-73 to 1975-76; Ed Westfall and Clark Gillies, 1976-77; Clark Gillies, 1977-78, 1978-79; Denis Potvin, 1979-80 to 1986-87; Brent Sutter, 1987-88 to 1990-91; Brent Sutter and Pat Flatley, 1991-92; Pat Flatley, 1992-93 to 1995-96; no captain, 1996-97; Bryan McCabe and Trevor Linden, 1997-98; Trevor Linden, 1998-99; Kenny Jonsson, 1999-2000, 2000-01; Michael Peca, 2001-02 to 2003-04; Alexei Yashin, 2005-06, 2006-07; Bill Guerin, 2007-08; Bill Guerin and no captain, 2008-09; Doug Weight, 2009-10, 2010-11.

Retired Numbers

5	Denis Potvin	1973-1988
9	Clark Gillies	1974-1986
19	Bryan Trottier	1975-1990
22	Mike Bossy	1977-1987
23	Bob Nystrom	1972-1986
31	Billy Smith	1972-1989

All-time Record vs. Other Clubs

Regular Season

	At Home								On Road								Total							
	GP	W	L	T	OL	GF	GA	PTS	GP	W	L	T	OL	GF	GA	PTS	GP	W	L	T	OL	GF	GA	PTS
Anaheim	11	6	4	1	0	29	29	13	12	5	3	3	1	33	28	14	23	11	7	4	1	62	57	27
Atlanta	22	11	11	0	0	76	62	22	22	12	5	2	3	83	67	29	44	23	16	2	3	159	129	51
Boston	73	31	32	10	0	237	231	72	71	20	37	11	3	195	260	54	144	51	69	21	3	432	491	126
Buffalo	73	33	30	9	1	207	203	76	73	24	38	9	2	207	250	59	146	57	68	18	3	414	453	135
Calgary	53	27	17	9	0	197	147	63	52	16	25	11	0	157	183	43	105	43	42	20	0	354	330	106
Carolina	56	24	27	4	1	162	166	53	57	22	29	5	1	178	204	50	113	46	56	9	2	340	370	103
Chicago	49	20	14	15	0	173	146	55	51	19	27	5	0	168	170	43	100	39	41	20	0	341	316	98
Colorado	35	21	13	1	0	143	117	43	37	13	20	3	1	105	130	30	72	34	33	4	1	248	247	73
Columbus	6	3	2	0	1	20	19	7	7	1	4	1	1	15	23	4	13	4	6	1	2	35	42	11
Dallas	51	26	15	8	2	185	147	62	49	22	19	8	0	176	143	52	100	48	34	16	2	361	290	114
Detroit	48	24	18	4	2	173	141	54	48	20	26	2	0	143	169	42	96	44	44	6	2	316	310	96
Edmonton	33	17	7	9	0	134	113	43	32	8	19	5	0	90	116	21	65	25	26	14	0	224	229	64
Florida	37	19	15	2	1	97	99	41	37	11	19	6	1	105	118	29	74	30	34	8	2	202	217	70
Los Angeles	48	25	17	5	1	164	132	56	48	17	24	7	0	146	173	41	96	42	41	12	1	310	305	97
Minnesota	6	3	3	0	0	15	17	6	6	1	4	0	1	15	20	3	12	4	7	0	1	30	37	9
Montreal	72	34	32	6	0	214	206	74	72	19	43	9	1	196	258	48	144	53	75	15	1	410	464	122
Nashville	6	3	2	0	1	16	17	7	8	2	6	0	0	17	22	4	14	5	8	0	1	33	39	11
New Jersey	106	66	26	11	3	407	293	146	105	46	44	11	4	340	336	107	211	112	70	22	7	747	629	253
NY Rangers	117	62	45	8	2	424	374	134	117	41	64	11	1	338	423	94	234	103	109	19	3	762	797	228
Ottawa	36	10	19	6	1	114	133	27	35	8	20	5	2	86	120	23	71	18	39	11	3	200	253	50
Philadelphia	119	55	47	15	2	406	357	127	116	34	69	11	2	316	417	81	235	89	116	26	4	722	774	208
Phoenix	33	15	9	8	1	122	99	39	33	16	13	4	0	117	111	36	66	31	22	12	1	239	210	75
Pittsburgh	107	57	35	8	7	418	353	129	109	38	54	14	3	358	414	93	216	95	89	22	10	776	767	222
St. Louis	53	27	13	11	2	196	140	67	49	21	18	9	1	160	173	52	102	48	31	20	3	356	313	119
San Jose	13	6	5	2	0	44	41	14	15	6	7	1	1	44	39	14	28	12	12	3	1	88	80	28
Tampa Bay	37	19	16	1	1	107	98	40	38	16	17	2	3	110	109	37	75	35	33	3	4	217	207	77
Toronto	65	38	22	3	2	248	186	81	67	27	34	4	2	216	235	60	132	65	56	7	4	464	421	141
Vancouver	50	27	12	10	1	180	142	65	49	22	23	3	1	160	160	48	99	49	35	13	2	340	302	113
Washington	93	47	41	2	3	333	287	99	93	35	43	11	4	288	305	85	186	82	84	13	7	621	592	184
Defunct Clubs	13	11	0	2	0	75	33	24	13	4	5	4	0	35	41	12	26	15	5	6	0	110	74	36
Totals	**1521**	**767**	**549**	**170**	**35**	**5316**	**4528**	**1739**	**1521**	**546**	**759**	**177**	**39**	**4597**	**5217**	**1308**	**3042**	**1313**	**1308**	**347**	**74**	**9913**	**9745**	**3047**

Playoffs

	Series	W	L	GP	W	L	T	GF	GA	Last Mtg.	Rnd.	Result
Boston	2	2	0	11	8	3	0	49	35	1983	CF	W 4-2
Buffalo	4	3	1	21	13	8	0	70	62	2007	CQF	L 1-4
Chicago	2	2	0	6	6	0	0	21	6	1979	QF	W 4-0
Colorado	1	1	0	4	4	0	0	18	9	1982	CF	W 4-0
Dallas	1	1	0	5	4	1	0	26	16	1981	F	W 4-1
Edmonton	3	2	1	15	9	6	0	58	47	1984	F	L 1-4
Los Angeles	1	1	0	4	3	1	0	21	10	1980	PRE	W 3-1
Montreal	4	1	3	22	8	14	0	55	64	1993	CF	L 1-4
New Jersey	1	0	1	6	2	4	0	18	23	1988	DSF	L 2-4
NY Rangers	8	5	3	39	20	19	0	129	132	1994	CQF	L 0-4
Ottawa	1	0	1	5	1	4	0	7	13	2003	CQF	L 1-4
Philadelphia	4	1	3	25	11	14	0	69	83	1987	DF	L 3-4
Pittsburgh	3	3	0	19	11	8	0	67	58	1993	DF	W 4-3
Tampa Bay	1	0	1	5	1	4	0	5	12	2004	CQF	L 1-4
Toronto	3	1	2	17	9	8	0	54	42	2002	CQF	L 3-4
Vancouver	2	2	0	6	6	0	0	26	14	1982	F	W 4-0
Washington	6	5	1	30	18	12	0	99	88	1993	DSF	W 4-2
Totals	**47**	**30**	**17**	**240**	**134**	**106**	**0**	**792**	**714**			

Calgary totals include Atlanta Flames, 1972-73 to 1979-80. Carolina totals include Hartford, 1979-80 to 1996-97.
Colorado totals include Quebec, 1979-80 to 1994-95. Dallas totals include Minnesota North Stars, 1972-73 to 1992-93.
New Jersey totals include Kansas City, 1974-75, 1975-76, and Colorado Rockies, 1976-77 to 1981-82.
Phoenix totals include Winnipeg, 1979-80 to 1995-96.

Playoff Results 2011-2007

Year	Round	Opponent	Result	GF	GA
2007	CQF	Buffalo	L 1-4	11	17

Abbreviations: Round: F – Final; **CF** – conference final; **CQF** – conference quarter-final; **DF** – division final; **DSF** – division semi-final; **QF** – quarter-final; **PRE** – preliminary round.

2010-11 Results

Oct.	9	Dallas	4-5†		13	Ottawa	4-6
	11	NY Rangers	6-4		15	Buffalo	5-3
	13	at Washington	1-2		17	New Jersey	2-5
	15	at Pittsburgh	2-3*		20	Washington	1-2
	16	Colorado	5-2		21	at Buffalo	5-2
	18	at Toronto	2-1*		23	Buffalo	3-5
	21	at Tampa Bay	3-2*		25	at Pittsburgh	0-1
	23	at Florida	3-4		26	Carolina	2-4
	27	at Montreal	3-5	Feb.	1	at Atlanta	4-1
	29	Montreal	1-3		2	at Pittsburgh	0-3
	30	at Philadelphia	1-6		5	Ottawa	5-3
Nov.	3	at Carolina	2-7		8	Toronto	3-5
	4	at Ottawa	1-4		10	at Montreal	4-3†
	6	Philadelphia	1-2		11	Pittsburgh	9-3
	10	at Anaheim	0-1		13	at Buffalo	7-6*
	11	at San Jose	1-2†		15	at Ottawa	4-3†
	13	at Los Angeles	1-5		17	Boston	3-6
	17	Tampa Bay	2-4		19	Los Angeles	3-0
	20	Florida	1-4		21	Florida	5-1
	21	at Atlanta	1-2*		22	at Toronto	1-2
	24	Columbus	3-4*		24	at Philadelphia	3-4*
	26	New Jersey	2-0		26	Washington	2-3
Dec.	2	NY Rangers	5-6	Mar.	1	at Washington	1-2*
	3	at NY Rangers	0-2		2	Minnesota	4-1
	5	Philadelphia	2-3		5	St. Louis	5-2
	9	at Boston	2-5		6	New Jersey	2-3†
	11	Atlanta	4-5		8	Toronto	4-3*
	13	at Nashville	0-5		11	Boston	4-2
	16	Anaheim	3-2		12	at New Jersey	2-3*
	18	Phoenix	3-4†		15	at NY Rangers	3-6
	22	Tampa Bay	2-1*		18	at Carolina	2-3*
	23	at New Jersey	5-1		19	at Florida	4-3†
	26	Montreal	4-1		22	at Tampa Bay	5-2
	27	at NY Rangers	2-7		24	Atlanta	1-2
	29	Pittsburgh	2-1†		26	Philadelphia	1-4
	31	at Detroit	4-3*		30	at New Jersey	2-3
Jan.	3	at Calgary	5-2		31	NY Rangers	6-2
	6	at Edmonton	1-2	Apr.	2	Carolina	2-4
	8	at Colorado	4-3*		6	at Boston	2-3
	9	at Chicago	0-5		8	Pittsburgh	3-4†
	11	Vancouver	3-4†		9	at Philadelphia	4-7

* – Overtime † – Shootout

Entry Draft Selections 2011-1997

Name in bold denotes played in NHL.

2011
Pick
5	Ryan Strome
34	Scott Mayfield
50	Johan Sundstrom
63	Andrei Pedan
95	Robbie Russo
125	John Persson
127	Brenden Kichton
185	Mitchell Theoret

2010
Pick
5	**Nino Niederreiter**
30	Brock Nelson
65	Kirill Kabanov
82	Jason Clark
125	Tony Dehart
185	Cody Rosen

2009
Pick
1	John Tavares
12	Calvin De Haan
31	Mikko Koskinen
62	Anders Nilsson
92	Casey Cizikas
122	Anton Klementyev
152	Anders Lee

2008
Pick
9	**Josh Bailey**
36	Corey Trivino
40	Aaron Ness
53	**Travis Hamonic**
66	David Toews
72	Jyri Niemi
73	Kirill Petrov
96	Matt Donovan
102	David Ullstrom
126	**Kevin Poulin**
148	**Matt Martin**
156	**Jared Spurgeon**
175	**Justin Dibenedetto**

2007
Pick
62	**Mark Katic**
76	Jason Gregoire
106	Maxim Gratchev
166	Blake Kessel
196	Simon Lacroix

2006
Pick
7	**Kyle Okposo**
60	**Jesse Joensuu**
70	Robin Figren
100	**Rhett Rakhshani**
108	Jase Weslosky
115	Tomas Marcinko
119	Doug Rogers
126	**Shane Sims**
141	Kim Johansson
160	**Andrew MacDonald**
171	Brian Day
173	Stefan Ridderwall
190	Troy Mattila

2005
Pick
15	**Ryan O'Marra**
46	**Dustin Kohn**
76	Shea Guthrie
144	**Masi Marjamaki**
180	Tyrell Mason
196	Nick Tuzzolino
210	Luciano Aquino

2004
Pick
16	**Petteri Nokelainen**
47	**Blake Comeau**
82	Sergei Ogorodnikov
115	**Wes O'Neill**
148	**Steve Regier**
179	Jaroslav Mrazek
210	Emil Axelsson
227	**Chris Campoli**
244	Jason Pitton
276	Sylvain Michaud

2003
Pick
15	**Robert Nilsson**
48	Dmitri Chernykh
53	Evgeny Tunik
58	**Jeremy Colliton**
120	Stefan Blaho
182	**Bruno Gervais**
212	Denis Rehak
238	Cody Blanshan
246	Igor Volkov

2002
Pick
22	**Sean Bergenheim**
87	**Frans Nielsen**
149	Marcus Paulsson
189	Alexei Stonkus
220	Brad Topping
252	Martin Chabada
283	Per Braxenholm

2001
Pick
101	Cory Stillman
132	Dusan Salficky
166	**Andy Chiodo**
197	Jan Holub
228	Mike Bray
260	Bryan Perez
280	Roman Kuhtinov
287	Juha-Pekka Ketola

2000
Pick
1	**Rick DiPietro**
5	**Raffi Torres**
101	Arto Tukio
105	Vladimir Gorbunov
136	Dmitri Upper
148	Kristofer Ottosson
202	**Ryan Caldwell**
264	Dmitri Altarev
267	**Tomi Pettinen**

1999
Pick
5	Tim Connolly
8	Taylor Pyatt
10	Branislav Mezei
28	Kristian Kudroc
78	Mattias Weinhandl
87	Brian Collins
101	Juraj Kolnik
102	Johan Halvardsson
130	Justin Mapletoft
140	Adam Johnson
163	Bjorn Melin
228	Radek Martinek
255	Brett Henning
268	Tyler Scott

1998
Pick
9	**Mike Rupp**
36	**Chris Nielsen**
95	Andy Burnham
123	Jiri Dopita
155	Kevin Clauson
182	**Evgeny Korolev**
209	Frederik Brindamour
237	Ben Blais
242	Jason Doyle
250	Radek Matejovsky

1997
Pick
4	**Roberto Luongo**
5	**Eric Brewer**
31	**Jeff Zehr**
59	Jarrett Smith
79	**Robert Schnabel**
85	**Petr Mika**
115	Adam Edinger
139	Bobby Leavins
166	Kris Knoblauch
196	Jeremy Symington
222	Ryan Clark

General Managers' History

Bill Torrey, 1972-73 to 1991-92; Don Maloney, 1992-93 to 1994-95; Don Maloney, Darcy Regier and Mike Milbury, 1995-96; Mike Milbury, 1996-97 to 2005-06; Neil Smith and Garth Snow, 2006-07; Garth Snow, 2007-08 to date.

Garth Snow
General Manager

Born: Wrentham, MA, June 28, 1969.

Former Islanders' goaltender Garth Snow retired as a player on July 18, 2006 to become the fifth general manager of the New York Islanders. In his first season as general manager, Snow successfully bolstered the lineup with several key additions that helped to propel the Islanders into the postseason for the first time since the 2003–04 season and earned Snow the title of NHL Executive of the Year from *Sports Illustrated*.

Snow spent four seasons with the Islanders and 12 in the NHL. The goaltender was 135-147-44 with a 2.80 goals-against average and .901 save percentage over 368 games with Quebec, Philadelphia, Vancouver, Pittsburgh and the Islanders. Originally selected in the sixth round by Quebec in the 1987 NHL Entry Draft, the native of Wrentham, Massachusetts signed with the Islanders as a free agent on July 1, 2001.

Club Directory

Nassau Veterans Memorial Coliseum

New York Islanders
Executive Office
1255 Hempstead Turnpike
Uniondale, NY 11553
Phone 516/501-6700
FAX 516/501-6850
www.newyorkislanders.com
Arena
Nassau Veterans
Memorial Coliseum
Uniondale, NY 11553
Capacity: 16,234

Owner and Governor	Charles B. Wang
General Manager and Alternate Governor	Garth Snow
Alternate Governors	Art McCarthy, Roy Reichbach
Sr. Vice President & Alternate Governor	Michael Picker
Sr. Vice President of Marketing and Sales	Paul Lancey
President of Bridgeport Sound Tigers (AHL)	Howard Saffan

Hockey Operations
Manager, Hockey Administration	Joanne Holewa
Director of Pro Scouting	Ken Morrow
Sr. Advisor to the G.M. & Assistant Coach	Doug Weight
Assistant to the General Manager	Kerry Gwydir
Head Coach	Jack Capuano
Assistant Coaches	Dean Chynoweth, Scott Allen
Goaltending Coach / Consultant	Mike Dunham / Sudarshan Maharaj
Skill Development Coach	Bernie Cassell
Player Development	Eric Cairns, Trent Klatt, Geoff Sanderson
Equipment Manager / Asst. Manager / Assistant	Scott Boggs / Richard Krouse / Tom Kitz
Head Athletic Trainer / Assistant Trainer	Garrett Timms / Nates Goto
Massage Therapist	Jim Miccio
Strength and Conditioning Coach	Jesse Demers
Director of Sports Performance	Sean Donellan
Video Coordinator	Ryan Ward
Chief European Scout	Vellu-Pekka Kautonen
Scouts	Anders Kallur, Mario Saraceno, Chris O'Sullivan, Tim Maclean, David Hymovitz, Mike Remmerde, Jay Saraceno

Administration
Deputy General Counsel	Stacey Sabo
Human Resources Manager / Coordinator	Michele Finkelstein / Caroline Seiter
IT Manager	Pawel Tauter
Receptionist / Office Attendant	Bonnie Dreher / Todd Aronovich

Corporate Partnerships and Islanders Networking Club
Sr. Vice President, Corporate Partnerships	Justin Johnson
Vice Presidents, Corporate Partnerships	Mike Bossy, Dave Decina
Director, Corporate Partnerships	Marc Arnberg
Manager, Executive Suites	Allison Chin
Managers, Partnership Marketing	Robert Hofmann, Richard Rossi, Jennifer Rothmann, Ryan Thorvaldsen, Dave DiLello, Steven Olwell
Coordinators, Partnership Marketing	Mike Murtha, Stephen Smyth

Ticket Sales and Operations
Vice President of Ticket Operations	Ralph Sellitti
Ticket Manager	Adam Ortiz
Ticket Operations Coordinator / Assistant	Steve Aprill / Alfred Jahn
Customer Service Director / Coordinator	Kerry Cornils / Ashley Piccione
Group Sales Director / Coordinator	Josh Rose / Grant Comarato
Senior Sales Executive, Group Tickets	Cliff Gault
Sales Execs, Group Tickets	Sean Cassin, Scott Einhorn, Tom Giulietti, Scott Hill, Marc Iervolino, Bryce Mitchell, Nick Lombardo, Eric Nadeau, David Sibelman, Chris Stellato, Christopher Ruffe, Maggie Witowski
Senior Sales Executives	Steven Beisel, Marc Gerstein, Jeffrey Guida
Sales Execs, Tickets	Brian Aiello, Vito Cataldo, Brett Cohen, Eric Conway, Bill DeGeorge, Leif Eriksen, Dan Esposito, Kali Fisher, Ariel Greenberg, John Odierna, Meredith Petrecki, Michael Rien, Jerard Roggio, Robert Tolve

Marketing and Client Services
Director of Marketing	Thomas Rakoczy
Marketing Coordinator	Lauren Margiotta
Creative Service Manager	Erik White
Graphic Designer	Cristina Weigel

Media Relations / Communications
Director of Communications	Kimber Auerbach
Manager of Digital Media	Katrina Doell
Corporate Communications Coordinator	David Hochman
Communications Coordinator	Jesse Eisenberg
Website Coordinator	Dyan LeBourdais
Social Media Coordinator	Dani Muccio
Radio Producer and Broadcaster	Chris King

Game Operations
Vice President, Operations	Tim Beach
Assistant to Vice President of Operations	Alexa Conforti
Director of Operations	Ken Zore
Community Relations Manager	Ann Rina
Operations Coordinator	Joe Giarroputo
Game Operations	Erin Willey
Manager, Video Production & Game Ops Coord.	Brian Jones
Manager, Amateur Hockey Development	Michelle Winter

Retail and Merchandise Operations
Director of Retail Operations	Terry Goldstein
Retail Sales Exec. / Pro Shop Manager	Matthew Miller / Tim Murray

Finance
Controller / Accounting Manager	Frank Romano / Chris Vardaro
Payroll Manager / A/P Coordinator	Christine Bowler / Janet Nelson
Staff Accountants	Erica Palladino, Jennifer Penning

New York Rangers

Key Off-Season Signings/Acquisitions

2011

June **1** • Acquired D **Tim Erixon** and a 5th-round pick in the 2011 Entry Draft from Calgary for LW **Roman Horak** and a pair of 2nd-round picks in 2011.

30 • Re-signed C **John Mitchell**.

July **1** • Signed C **Michael Rupp**.

1 • Re-signed LW **Ruslan Fedotenko**.

2 • Signed C **Brad Richards**.

8 • Re-signed D **Michael Sauer** and C **Artem Anisimov**.

15 • Re-signed C **Brian Boyle**.

21 • Re-signed C **Brandon Dubinsky**.

25 • Re-signed D **Steve Eminger**.

27 • Re-signed RW **Ryan Callahan**.

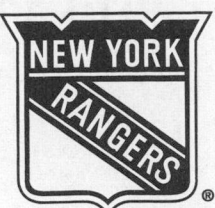

2011-12 Schedule

Month	Day	Date	Opponent
Oct.	Fri.	7	at Los Angeles†
	Sat.	8	at Anaheim†
	Sat.	15	at NY Islanders
	Tue.	18	at Vancouver
	Thu.	20	at Calgary
	Sat.	22	at Edmonton
	Mon.	24	at Winnipeg
	Thu.	27	Toronto
	Sat.	29	Ottawa*
	Mon.	31	San Jose
Nov.	Thu.	3	Anaheim
	Sat.	5	Montreal
	Sun.	6	Winnipeg
	Wed.	9	at Ottawa
	Fri.	11	Carolina
	Tue.	15	at NY Islanders
	Sat.	19	at Montreal
	Wed.	23	at Florida
	Fri.	25	at Washington*
	Sat.	26	Philadelphia*
	Tue.	29	Pittsburgh
Dec.	Thu.	1	at Carolina
	Sat.	3	at Tampa Bay
	Mon.	5	Toronto
	Thu.	8	Tampa Bay
	Sat.	10	at Buffalo
	Sun.	11	Florida
	Tue.	13	Dallas
	Thu.	15	at St. Louis
	Sat.	17	at Phoenix
	Tue.	20	at New Jersey
	Thu.	22	NY Islanders
	Fri.	23	Philadelphia
	Mon.	26	NY Islanders
	Wed.	28	at Washington
	Fri.	30	at Florida
Jan.	Mon.	2	at Philadelphia*
	Thu.	5	Florida
	Fri.	6	at Pittsburgh
	Tue.	10	Phoenix
	Thu.	12	Ottawa
	Sat.	14	at Toronto
	Sun.	15	at Montreal
	Tue.	17	Nashville
	Thu.	19	Pittsburgh
	Sat.	21	at Boston*
	Tue.	24	Winnipeg
	Tue.	31	at New Jersey
Feb.	Wed.	1	at Buffalo
	Sun.	5	Philadelphia*
	Tue.	7	New Jersey
	Thu.	9	Tampa Bay
	Sat.	11	at Philadelphia*
	Sun.	12	Washington*
	Tue.	14	at Boston
	Thu.	16	Chicago
	Sun.	19	Columbus
	Tue.	21	at Pittsburgh
	Fri.	24	at NY Islanders
	Sat.	25	Buffalo
	Mon.	27	New Jersey
Mar.	Thu.	1	at Carolina
	Fri.	2	at Tampa Bay
	Sun.	4	Boston*
	Tue.	6	at New Jersey
	Thu.	8	at Ottawa
	Fri.	9	at Chicago
	Sun.	11	NY Islanders
	Tue.	13	Carolina
	Thu.	15	Pittsburgh
	Sat.	17	Colorado
	Mon.	19	New Jersey
	Wed.	21	Detroit
	Fri.	23	Buffalo
	Sat.	24	at Toronto
	Tue.	27	at Minnesota
	Wed.	28	at Winnipeg
	Fri.	30	Montreal
Apr.	Sun.	1	Boston*
	Tue.	3	at Philadelphia
	Thu.	5	at Pittsburgh
	Sat.	7	Washington*

* Denotes afternoon game. † Games played in Stockholm.

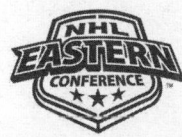

ATLANTIC DIVISION
86th NHL Season

Franchise date: May 15, 1926

2010-11 Results: 44W-33L-2OTL-3SOL 93PTS.
Third, Atlantic Division

Year-by-Year Record

		Home				Road				Overall								
Season	GP	W	L	T	OL	W	L	T	OL	W	L	T	OL	GF	GA	Pts.	Finished	Playoff Result
2010-11	82	20	17	....	4	24	16	....	1	44	33	....	5	233	198	93	3rd, Atlantic Div.	Lost Conf. Quarter-Final
2009-10	82	18	17	....	6	20	16	....	5	38	33	....	11	222	218	87	4th, Atlantic Div.	Out of Playoffs
2008-09	82	26	11	....	4	17	19	....	5	43	30	....	9	210	218	95	4th, Atlantic Div.	Lost Conf. Quarter-Final
2007-08	82	25	13	....	3	17	14	....	10	42	27	....	13	213	199	97	3rd, Atlantic Div.	Lost Conf. Semi-Final
2006-07	82	21	15	....	5	21	15	....	5	42	30	....	10	242	216	94	3rd, Atlantic Div.	Lost Conf. Semi-Final
2005-06	82	25	10	....	6	19	16	....	6	44	26	....	12	257	215	100	3rd, Atlantic Div.	Lost Conf. Quarter-Final
2004-05	....	....	....	....	....	....	....	....	....	....	....	....	....	....	....	....		
2003-04	82	13	21	3	4	14	19	4	4	27	40	7	8	206	250	69	4th, Atlantic Div.	Out of Playoffs
2002-03	82	17	18	4	2	15	18	6	2	32	36	10	4	210	231	78	4th, Atlantic Div.	Out of Playoffs
2001-02	82	19	19	2	1	17	19	2	3	36	38	4	4	227	258	80	4th, Atlantic Div.	Out of Playoffs
2000-01	82	17	20	3	1	16	23	2	0	33	43	5	1	250	290	72	4th, Atlantic Div.	Out of Playoffs
1999-2000	82	15	20	5	1	14	18	7	2	29	38	12	3	218	246	73	4th, Atlantic Div.	Out of Playoffs
1998-99	82	17	19	5	....	16	19	6	....	33	38	11	....	217	227	77	4th, Atlantic Div.	Out of Playoffs
1997-98	82	14	18	9	....	11	21	9	....	25	39	18	....	197	231	68	5th, Atlantic Div.	Out of Playoffs
1996-97	82	21	14	6	....	17	20	4	....	38	34	10	....	258	231	86	4th, Atlantic Div.	Lost Conf. Championship
1995-96	82	22	10	9	....	19	17	5	....	41	27	14	....	272	237	96	2nd, Atlantic Div.	Lost Conf. Semi-Final
1994-95	48	11	10	3	....	11	13	0	....	22	23	3	....	139	134	47	4th, Atlantic Div.	Lost Conf. Semi-Final
1993-94	**84**	**28**	**8**	**6**	....	**24**	**16**	**2**	....	**52**	**24**	**8**	....	**299**	**231**	**112**	**1st, Atlantic Div.**	**Won Stanley Cup**
1992-93	84	20	17	5	....	14	22	6	....	34	39	11	....	304	308	79	6th, Patrick Div.	Out of Playoffs
1991-92	80	28	8	4	....	22	17	1	....	50	25	5	....	321	246	105	1st, Patrick Div.	Lost Div. Final
1990-91	80	22	11	7	....	14	20	6	....	36	31	13	....	297	265	85	2nd, Patrick Div.	Lost Div. Semi-Final
1989-90	80	20	11	9	....	16	20	4	....	36	31	13	....	279	267	85	1st, Patrick Div.	Lost Div. Final
1988-89	80	21	17	2	....	16	18	6	....	37	35	8	....	310	307	82	3rd, Patrick Div.	Lost Div. Semi-Final
1987-88	80	22	13	5	....	14	21	5	....	36	34	10	....	300	283	82	5th, Patrick Div.	Out of Playoffs
1986-87	80	18	18	4	....	16	20	4	....	34	38	8	....	307	323	76	4th, Patrick Div.	Lost Div. Semi-Final
1985-86	80	20	18	2	....	16	20	4	....	36	38	6	....	280	276	78	4th, Patick Div.	Lost Conf. Championship
1984-85	80	16	18	6	....	10	26	4	....	26	44	10	....	295	345	62	4th, Patrick Div.	Lost Div. Semi-Final
1983-84	80	27	12	1	....	15	17	8	....	42	29	9	....	314	304	93	4th, Patrick Div.	Lost Div. Semi-Final
1982-83	80	24	13	3	....	11	22	7	....	35	35	10	....	306	287	80	4th, Patrick Div.	Lost Div. Final
1981-82	80	19	15	6	....	20	12	8	....	39	27	14	....	316	306	92	2nd, Patrick Div.	Lost Div. Final
1980-81	80	17	13	10	....	13	23	4	....	30	36	14	....	312	317	74	4th, Patrick Div.	Lost Semi-Final
1979-80	80	22	10	8	....	16	22	2	....	38	32	10	....	308	284	86	3rd, Patrick Div.	Lost Quarter-Final
1978-79	80	19	13	8	....	21	16	3	....	40	29	11	....	316	292	91	3rd, Patrick Div.	Lost Final
1977-78	80	18	15	7	....	12	22	6	....	30	37	13	....	279	280	73	4th, Patrick Div.	Lost Prelim. Round
1976-77	80	17	18	5	....	12	19	9	....	29	37	14	....	272	310	72	4th, Patrick Div.	Out of Playoffs
1975-76	80	16	16	8	....	13	26	1	....	29	42	9	....	262	333	67	4th, Patrick Div.	Out of Playoffs
1974-75	80	21	11	8	....	16	18	6	....	37	29	14	....	319	276	88	2nd, Patrick Div.	Lost Prelim. Round
1973-74	78	26	7	6	....	14	17	8	....	40	24	14	....	300	251	94	3rd, East Div.	Lost Semi-Final
1972-73	78	26	8	5	....	21	15	3	....	47	23	8	....	297	208	102	3rd, East Div.	Lost Semi-Final
1971-72	78	26	6	7	....	22	11	6	....	48	17	13	....	317	192	109	2nd, East Div.	Lost Final
1970-71	78	30	2	7	....	19	16	4	....	49	18	11	....	259	177	109	2nd, East Div.	Lost Semi-Final
1969-70	76	22	8	8	....	16	14	8	....	38	22	16	....	246	189	92	4th, East Div.	Lost Quarter-Final
1968-69	76	27	7	4	....	14	19	5	....	41	26	9	....	231	196	91	3rd, East Div.	Lost Quarter-Final
1967-68	74	22	8	7	....	17	15	5	....	39	23	12	....	226	183	90	2nd, East Div.	Lost Quarter-Final
1966-67	70	18	12	5	....	12	16	7	....	30	28	12	....	188	189	72	4th,	Lost Semi-Final
1965-66	70	12	16	7	....	6	25	4	....	18	41	11	....	195	261	47	6th,	Out of Playoffs
1964-65	70	8	19	8	....	12	19	4	....	20	38	12	....	179	246	52	5th,	Out of Playoffs
1963-64	70	14	13	8	....	8	25	2	....	22	38	10	....	186	242	54	5th,	Out of Playoffs
1962-63	70	12	17	6	....	10	19	6	....	22	36	12	....	211	233	56	5th,	Out of Playoffs
1961-62	70	16	11	8	....	10	21	4	....	26	32	12	....	195	207	64	4th,	Lost Semi-Final
1960-61	70	15	15	5	....	7	23	5	....	22	38	10	....	204	248	54	5th,	Out of Playoffs
1959-60	70	10	15	10	....	7	23	5	....	17	38	15	....	187	247	49	6th,	Out of Playoffs
1958-59	70	14	16	5	....	12	16	7	....	26	32	12	....	201	217	64	5th,	Out of Playoffs
1957-58	70	14	15	6	....	18	10	7	....	32	25	13	....	195	188	77	2nd,	Lost Semi-Final
1956-57	70	15	12	8	....	11	18	6	....	26	30	14	....	184	227	66	4th,	Lost Semi-Final
1955-56	70	20	7	8	....	12	21	2	....	32	28	10	....	204	203	74	3rd,	Lost Semi-Final
1954-55	70	10	12	13	....	7	23	5	....	17	35	18	....	150	210	52	5th,	Out of Playoffs
1953-54	70	18	12	5	....	11	19	5	....	29	31	10	....	161	182	68	5th,	Out of Playoffs
1952-53	70	11	14	10	....	6	23	6	....	17	37	16	....	152	211	50	6th,	Out of Playoffs
1951-52	70	16	13	6	....	7	21	7	....	23	34	13	....	192	219	59	5th,	Out of Playoffs
1950-51	70	14	11	10	....	6	18	11	....	20	29	21	....	169	201	61	5th,	Out of Playoffs
1949-50	70	19	12	4	....	9	19	7	....	28	31	11	....	170	189	67	4th,	Lost Final
1948-49	60	13	12	5	....	5	19	6	....	18	31	11	....	133	172	47	6th,	Out of Playoffs
1947-48	60	11	12	7	....	10	14	6	....	21	26	13	....	176	201	55	4th,	Lost Semi-Final
1946-47	60	11	14	5	....	11	18	1	....	22	32	6	....	167	186	50	5th,	Out of Playoffs
1945-46	50	8	12	5	....	5	16	4	....	13	28	9	....	144	191	35	6th,	Out of Playoffs
1944-45	50	7	11	7	....	4	18	3	....	11	29	10	....	154	247	32	6th,	Out of Playoffs
1943-44	50	4	17	4	....	2	22	1	....	6	39	5	....	162	310	17	6th,	Out of Playoffs
1942-43	50	7	13	5	....	4	18	3	....	11	31	8	....	161	253	30	6th,	Out of Playoffs
1941-42	48	15	8	1	....	14	9	1	....	29	17	2	....	177	143	60	1st,	Lost Semi-Final
1940-41	48	13	7	4	....	8	12	4	....	21	19	8	....	143	125	50	4th,	Lost Quarter-Final
1939-40	**48**	**17**	**4**	**3**	....	**10**	**7**	**7**	....	**27**	**11**	**10**	....	**136**	**77**	**64**	**2nd,**	**Won Stanley Cup**
1938-39	48	13	8	3	....	13	8	3	....	26	16	6	....	149	105	58	2nd,	Lost Semi-Final
1937-38	48	15	5	4	....	12	10	2	....	27	15	6	....	149	96	60	2nd, Amn. Div.	Lost Quarter-Final
1936-37	48	9	7	8	....	10	13	1	....	19	20	9	....	117	106	47	3rd, Amn. Div.	Lost Final
1935-36	48	11	6	7	....	8	11	5	....	19	17	12	....	91	96	50	4th, Amn. Div.	Out of Playoffs
1934-35	48	11	8	5	....	11	12	1	....	22	20	6	....	137	139	50	3rd, Amn. Div.	Lost Semi-Final
1933-34	48	11	7	6	....	10	12	2	....	21	19	8	....	120	113	50	3rd, Amn. Div.	Lost Quarter-Final
1932-33	**48**	**12**	**7**	**5**	....	**11**	**10**	**3**	....	**23**	**17**	**8**	....	**135**	**107**	**54**	**3rd, Amn. Div.**	**Won Stanley Cup**
1931-32	48	13	7	4	....	10	10	4	....	23	17	8	....	134	112	54	1st, Amn. Div.	Lost Final
1930-31	44	10	9	3	....	9	7	6	....	19	16	9	....	106	87	47	3rd, Amn. Div.	Lost Semi-Final
1929-30	44	11	5	6	....	6	12	4	....	17	17	10	....	136	143	44	3rd, Amn. Div.	Lost Semi-Final
1928-29	44	12	6	4	....	9	7	6	....	21	13	10	....	72	65	52	2nd, Amn. Div.	Lost Final
1927-28	**44**	**10**	**8**	**4**	....	**9**	**8**	**5**	....	**19**	**16**	**9**	....	**94**	**79**	**47**	**2nd, Amn. Div.**	**Won Stanley Cup**
1926-27	44	13	5	4	....	12	8	2	....	25	13	6	....	95	72	56	1st, Amn. Div.	Lost Quarter-Final

2011-12 Player Personnel

FORWARDS	HT	WT	S	Place of Birth	*Age	2010-11 Club
ANISIMOV, Artem	6-4	197	L	Yaroslavl, USSR	23	NY Rangers
AVERY, Sean	5-10	195	L	Pickering, Ont.	31	NY Rangers
BOYLE, Brian	6-7	244	L	Hingham, MA	26	NY Rangers
CALLAHAN, Ryan	5-10	190	R	Rochester, NY	26	NY Rangers
CHRISTENSEN, Erik	6-1	200	L	Edmonton, Alta.	27	NY Rangers
DUBINSKY, Brandon	6-1	210	L	Anchorage, AK	25	NY Rangers
FEDOTENKO, Ruslan	6-1	200	L	Kiev, USSR	32	NY Rangers
GABORIK, Marian	6-1	204	L	Trencin, Czech.	29	NY Rangers
KOLARIK, Chad	5-11	185	R	Abington, PA	25	Sprfld-NYR-Connecticut
MITCHELL, John	6-1	204	L	Oakville, Ont.	26	Tor-Tor (AHL)-Connecticut
NEWBURY, Kris	5-11	213	L	Brampton, Ont.	29	NY Rangers-Connecticut
PRUST, Brandon	6-2	192	L	London, Ont.	27	NY Rangers
RICHARDS, Brad	6-0	195	L	Murray Harbour, P.E.I.	31	Dallas
RUPP, Mike	6-5	230	L	Cleveland, OH	31	Pittsburgh
STEPAN, Derek	6-0	182	R	Hastings, MN	21	NY Rangers
THURESSON, Andreas	6-1	212	R	Kristianstad, Sweden	23	Nashville-Milwaukee
WEISE, Dale	6-2	210	R	Winnipeg, Man.	23	NY Rangers-Connecticut
WOLSKI, Wojtek	6-3	215	L	Zabrze, Poland	25	Phoenix-NY Rangers
ZUCCARELLO, Mats	5-7	174	L	Oslo, Norway	24	NY Rangers-Connecticut
DEFENSEMEN						
DEL ZOTTO, Michael	6-0	193	L	Stouffville, Ont.	21	NY Rangers-Connecticut
EMINGER, Steve	6-2	203	R	Woodbridge, Ont.	27	NY Rangers
ERIXON, Tim	6-2	190	L	Port Chester, NY	20	Skelleftea
GIRARDI, Dan	6-1	206	R	Welland, Ont.	27	NY Rangers
McDONAGH, Ryan	6-1	213	L	St.Paul, MN	22	NY Rangers-Connecticut
SAUER, Michael	6-3	213	R	St. Cloud, MN	24	NY Rangers
STAAL, Marc	6-4	208	L	Thunder Bay, Ont.	24	NY Rangers

GOALTENDERS	HT	WT	C	Place of Birth	*Age	2010-11 Club
BIRON, Martin	6-2	180	L	Lac-St-Charles, Que.	34	NY Rangers
LUNDQVIST, Henrik	6-1	195	L	Are, Sweden	29	NY Rangers

* – Age at start of 2011-12 season

Captains' History

Bill Cook, 1926-27 to 1936-37; Art Coulter, 1937-38 to 1941-42; Ott Heller, 1942-43 to 1944-45; Neil Colville 1945-46 to 1948-49; Buddy O'Connor, 1949-50; Frank Eddolls, 1950-51; Frank Eddolls and Allan Stanley, 1951-52; Allan Stanley, 1952-53; Allan Stanley and Don Raleigh, 1953-54; Don Raleigh, 1954-55; Harry Howell, 1955-56, 1956-57; Red Sullivan, 1957-58 to 1960-61; Andy Bathgate, 1961-62, 1962-63; Andy Bathgate and Camille Henry, 1963-64; Camille Henry and Bob Nevin, 1964-65; Bob Nevin 1965-66 to 1970-71; Vic Hadfield, 1971-72 to 1973-74; Brad Park, 1974-75; Brad Park and Phil Esposito, 1975-76; Phil Esposito, 1976-77, 1977-78; Dave Maloney, 1978-79, 1979-80; Dave Maloney, Walt Tkaczuk and Barry Beck, 1980-81; Barry Beck, 1981-82 to 1985-86; Ron Greschner, 1986-87; Ron Greschner and Kelly Kisio, 1987-88; Kelly Kisio, 1988-89 to 1990-91; Mark Messier, 1991-92 to 1996-97; Brian Leetch, 1997-98 to 1999-2000; Mark Messier, 2000-01 to 2003-04; no captain, 2005-06; Jaromir Jagr, 2006-07, 2007-08; Chris Drury, 2008-09 to 2010-11.

John Tortorella

Head Coach

Born: Boston, MA, June 24, 1958.

John Tortorella was named head coach of the New York Rangers on February 23, 2009. He returned to the organization after serving as head coach of the Tampa Bay Lightning for seven seasons. In 2003-04, Tortorella guided Tampa Bay to the club's first Stanley Cup championship and was awarded the Jack Adams Award as the NHL's coach of the year.

Tortorella joined Tampa Bay following a one-year stint with the Rangers in 1999-2000 where he was an assistant coach and served as head coach for the final four games of the season. Prior to joining the Rangers, he spent two seasons as an assistant coach with the Phoenix Coyotes. He joined Phoenix during the 1997-98 season, after spending the previous eight seasons with the Buffalo Sabres organization. Tortorella served as an assistant coach with the Sabres from 1989-90 to 1994-95 and as head coach with their American Hockey League affiliate, the Rochester Americans, during the 1995-96 and 1996-97 campaigns. He guided the club to the Calder Cup championship in 1995-96.

Prior to joining the coaching ranks, Tortorella played at Salem State College before transferring to the University of Maine Black Bears of the East Coast Athletic Conference, where he skated for three seasons as a right winger and was twice named an ECAC All-Star. After playing in Sweden, he returned to North America to skate in the ACHL with the Hampton Roads Gulls, Erie Golden Blades and Virginia Lancers, recording 98 goals and 160 assists for 258 points, along with 302 penalty minutes in 200 games over four seasons.

Coaching Record

			Regular Season				Playoffs			
Season	Team	League	GC	W	L	O/T	GC	W	L	T
1995-96	Rochester	AHL	80	37	34	9	19	15	4	....
1996-97	Rochester	AHL	80	40	30	10	10	6	4	....
99-2000	**NY Rangers**	**NHL**	**4**	**0**	**3**	**1**	....	....	....	....
2000-01	**Tampa Bay**	**NHL**	**43**	**12**	**27**	**4**	....	....	....	....
2001-02	**Tampa Bay**	**NHL**	**82**	**27**	**40**	**15**	....	....	....	....
2002-03	**Tampa Bay**	**NHL**	**82**	**36**	**25**	**21**	**11**	**5**	**6**	....
2003-04♦	**Tampa Bay**	**NHL**	**82**	**46**	**22**	**14**	**23**	**16**	**7**	....
2004-05	**Tampa Bay**				SEASON CANCELLED					
2005-06	**Tampa Bay**	**NHL**	**82**	**43**	**33**	**6**	**5**	**1**	**4**	....
2006-07	**Tampa Bay**	**NHL**	**82**	**44**	**33**	**5**	**6**	**2**	**4**	....
2007-08	**Tampa Bay**	**NHL**	**82**	**31**	**42**	**9**	....	....	....	....
2008-09	**NY Rangers**	**NHL**	**21**	**12**	**7**	**2**	**7**	**3**	**4**	....
2009-10	**NY Rangers**	**NHL**	**82**	**38**	**33**	**11**	....	....	....	....
2010-11	**NY Rangers**	**NHL**	**82**	**44**	**33**	**5**	**5**	**1**	**4**	....
	NHL Totals		**724**	**333**	**298**	**93**	**57**	**28**	**29**	....

♦ Stanley Cup win.
Won Jack Adams Award (2004)
Jim Schoenfeld posted an 0-1 playoff record as replacement coach when John Tortorella was suspended, April 26, 2009. Loss is credited to Tortorella's coaching record.

2010-11 Scoring

* – rookie

Regular Season

Pos	#	Player	Team	GP	G	A	Pts	TOI	+/–	PIM	PP	SH	GW	S	%
C	17	Brandon Dubinsky	NYR	77	24	30	54	20:13	–3	100	4	2	2	202	11.9
R	24	Ryan Callahan	NYR	60	23	25	48	19:54	–7	46	10	0	5	179	12.8
R	10	Marian Gaborik	NYR	62	22	26	48	18:05	8	18	7	0	4	192	11.5
C	21 *	Derek Stepan	NYR	82	21	24	45	16:26	8	20	3	0	3	166	12.7
C	42	Artem Anisimov	NYR	82	18	26	44	16:12	3	20	3	0	2	190	9.5
C	22	Brian Boyle	NYR	82	21	14	35	15:44	2	74	4	1	2	218	9.6
L	86	Wojtek Wolski	PHX	36	6	10	16	14:41	–6	10	0	0	0	57	10.5
			NYR	37	6	13	19	14:28	12	8	1	0	1	78	7.7
			Total	73	12	23	35	14:34	6	18	1	0	1	135	8.9
D	5	Dan Girardi	NYR	80	4	27	31	24:34	7	37	2	0	1	110	3.6
L	8	Brandon Prust	NYR	82	13	16	29	13:48	2	160	0	5	1	87	14.9
D	18	Marc Staal	NYR	77	7	22	29	25:44	8	50	4	2	2	116	6.0
D	28	Bryan McCabe	FLA	48	5	17	22	21:00	3	28	2	0	0	88	5.7
			NYR	19	2	4	6	15:54	–1	6	2	0	0	34	5.9
			Total	67	7	21	28	19:34	2	34	4	0	0	122	5.7
C	26	Erik Christensen	NYR	63	11	16	27	12:45	3	18	4	0	1	86	12.8
L	19	Ruslan Fedotenko	NYR	66	10	15	25	14:59	9	25	0	1	0	120	8.3
L	16	Sean Avery	NYR	76	3	21	24	11:14	–4	174	0	0	1	137	2.2
L	20	Vinny Prospal	NYR	29	9	14	23	15:19	4	8	2	0	0	61	14.8
C	36 *	Mats Zuccarello	NYR	42	6	17	23	14:10	3	4	0	0	2	74	8.1
L	31	Alex Frolov	NYR	43	7	9	16	14:25	4	8	0	0	2	78	9.0
D	38 *	Michael Sauer	NYR	76	3	12	15	17:31	20	75	1	0	2	54	5.6
D	97	Matt Gilroy	NYR	58	3	8	11	14:10	5	14	0	0	1	75	4.0
D	4	Michael Del Zotto	NYR	47	2	9	11	19:29	–5	20	2	0	0	58	3.4
D	27 *	Ryan McDonagh	NYR	40	1	8	9	18:44	16	14	0	0	1	27	3.7
D	44	Steve Eminger	NYR	65	2	4	6	15:51	–5	22	0	0	1	23	8.7
C	23	Chris Drury	NYR	24	1	4	5	12:00	2	8	0	0	0	26	3.8
C	12	Todd White	NYR	18	1	1	2	7:40	–2	2	0	0	0	11	9.1
L	94	Derek Boogaard	NYR	22	1	1	2	4:32	0	45	0	0	0	4	25.0
C	25 *	Chad Kolarik	NYR	4	0	1	1	9:07	–1	2	0	0	0	4	0.0
C	45	Kris Newbury	NYR	11	0	1	1	7:38	–1	35	0	0	0	6	0.0
R	86	Jeremy Williams	NYR	1	0	0	0	3:43	0	0	0	0	0	0	0.0
L	39 *	Brodie Dupont	NYR	1	0	0	0	5:34	0	0	0	0	0	1	0.0
C	91 *	Evgeny Grachev	NYR	8	0	0	0	7:42	–3	0	0	0	0	3	0.0
R	32 *	Dale Weise	NYR	10	0	0	0	6:30	–1	19	0	0	0	9	0.0

Goaltending

No.	Goaltender	GPI	Mins	Avg	W	L	OT	EN	SO	GA	SA	S%	G	A	PIM
43	Martin Biron	17	928	2.13	8	6	0	4	0	33	426	.923	0	0	0
30	Henrik Lundqvist	68	4007	2.28	36	27	5	4	11	152	1965	.923	0	4	6
29	Chad Johnson	1	20	6.00	0	0	0	0	0	2	11	.818	0	0	0
	Totals	**82**	**4992**	**2.34**	**44**	**33**	**5**	**8**	**11**	**195**	**2410**	**.919**			

Playoffs

Pos	#	Player	Team	GP	G	A	Pts	TOI	+/–	PIM	PP	SH	GW	OT	S	%
C	17	Brandon Dubinsky	NYR	5	2	1	3	24:56	–3	2	0	0	1	0	7	28.6
L	86	Wojtek Wolski	NYR	5	1	2	3	12:16	0	0	0	0	0	0	10	10.0
R	10	Marian Gaborik	NYR	5	1	1	2	23:55	0	2	0	0	0	0	20	5.0
D	28	Bryan McCabe	NYR	5	0	2	2	19:13	0	14	0	0	0	0	6	0.0
L	19	Ruslan Fedotenko	NYR	5	0	2	2	20:55	–1	4	0	0	0	0	5	0.0
L	20	Vinny Prospal	NYR	5	1	0	1	19:30	1	0	0	0	0	0	9	11.1
C	26	Erik Christensen	NYR	5	1	0	1	13:04	0	2	1	0	0	0	10	10.0
C	42	Artem Anisimov	NYR	5	1	0	1	15:10	2	0	0	0	0	0	9	11.1
D	97	Matt Gilroy	NYR	5	1	0	1	15:40	–1	2	0	0	0	0	7	14.3
L	16	Sean Avery	NYR	4	0	1	1	12:22	–1	12	0	0	0	0	7	0.0
C	23	Chris Drury	NYR	5	0	1	1	10:36	0	2	0	0	0	0	3	0.0
L	8	Brandon Prust	NYR	5	0	1	1	16:24	0	4	0	0	0	0	8	0.0
D	18	Marc Staal	NYR	5	0	1	1	28:01	–3	0	0	0	0	0	5	0.0
D	38 *	Michael Sauer	NYR	5	0	1	1	23:16	–1	0	0	0	0	0	2	0.0
C	22	Brian Boyle	NYR	5	0	0	0	21:30	–1	6	0	0	0	0	25	0.0
D	5	Dan Girardi	NYR	5	0	0	0	27:01	–2	0	0	0	0	0	6	0.0
D	27 *	Ryan McDonagh	NYR	5	0	0	0	22:49	0	4	0	0	0	0	4	0.0
C	21 *	Derek Stepan	NYR	5	0	0	0	20:29	–5	2	0	0	0	0	4	0.0

Goaltending

No.	Goaltender	GPI	Mins	Avg	W	L	EN	SO	GA	SA	S%	G	A	PIM
30	Henrik Lundqvist	5	346	2.25	1	4	0	0	13	156	.917	0	0	0
	Totals	**5**	**351**	**2.22**	**1**	**4**	**0**	**0**	**13**	**156**	**.917**			

General Managers' History

Lester Patrick, 1926-27 to 1944-45; Lester Patrick and Frank Boucher, 1945-46; Frank Boucher, 1946-47 to 1954-55; Muzz Patrick, 1955-56 to 1963-64; Muzz Patrick and Emile Francis, 1964-65; Emile Francis, 1965-66 to 1974-75; Emile Francis and John Ferguson, 1975-76; John Ferguson, 1976-77, 1977-78; Fred Shero, 1978-79, 1979-80; Fred Shero and Craig Patrick, 1980-81; Craig Patrick, 1981-82 to 1985-86; Phil Esposito, 1986-87 to 1988-89; Neil Smith, 1989-90 to 1999-2000; Glen Sather, 2000-01 to date.

Coaching History

Lester Patrick, 1926-27 to 1938-39; Frank Boucher, 1939-40 to 1947-48; Frank Boucher and Lynn Patrick, 1948-49; Lynn Patrick, 1949-50; Neil Colville, 1950-51; Neil Colville and Bill Cook, 1951-52; Bill Cook, 1952-53; Frank Boucher and Muzz Patrick, 1953-54; Muzz Patrick, 1954-55; Phil Watson, 1955-56 to 1958-59; Phil Watson, Muzz Patrick and Alf Pike, 1959-60; Alf Pike, 1960-61; Doug Harvey, 1961-62; Muzz Patrick and Red Sullivan, 1962-63; Red Sullivan, 1963-64, 1964-65; Red Sullivan and Emile Francis, 1965-66; Emile Francis, 1966-67, 1967-68; Bernie Geoffrion and Emile Francis, 1968-69; Emile Francis, 1969-70 to 1972-73; Larry Popein and Emile Francis, 1973-74; Emile Francis, 1974-75; Ron Stewart and John Ferguson, 1975-76; John Ferguson, 1976-77; Jean-Guy Talbot, 1977-78; Fred Shero, 1978-79, 1979-80; Fred Shero and Craig Patrick, 1980-81; Herb Brooks, 1981-82 to 1983-84; Herb Brooks and Craig Patrick, 1984-85; Ted Sator, 1985-86; Ted Sator, Tom Webster and Phil Esposito, 1986-87; Michel Bergeron, 1987-88; Michel Bergeron and Phil Esposito, 1988-89; Roger Neilson, 1989-90 to 1991-92; Roger Neilson and Ron Smith, 1992-93; Mike Keenan, 1993-94; Colin Campbell, 1994-95 to 1996-97; Colin Campbell and John Muckler, 1997-98; John Muckler, 1998-99; John Muckler and John Tortorella, 1999-2000; Ron Low, 2000-01, 2001-02; Bryan Trottier and Glen Sather, 2002-03; Glen Sather and Tom Renney, 2003-04; Tom Renney, 2004-05 to 2007-08; Tom Renney and John Tortorella, 2008-09; John Tortorella, 2009-10 to date.

Club Records

Team

(Figures in brackets for season records are games played; records for fewest points, wins, ties, losses, goals, goals against are for 70 or more games)

Most Points	**112**	1993-94 (84)
Most Wins	**52**	1993-94 (84)
Most Ties	**21**	1950-51 (70)
Most Losses	**44**	1984-85 (80)
Most Goals	**321**	1991-92 (80)
Most Goals Against	**345**	1984-85 (80)
Fewest Points	**47**	1965-66 (70)
Fewest Wins	**17**	1952-53 (70), 1954-55 (70), 1959-60 (70)
Fewest Ties	**4**	2001-02 (82)
Fewest Losses	**17**	1971-72 (78)
Fewest Goals	**150**	1954-55 (70)
Fewest Goals Against	**177**	1970-71 (78)
Longest Winning Streak		
Overall	**10**	Dec. 19/39-Jan. 13/40, Jan. 19-Feb. 10/73
Home	**14**	Dec. 19/39-Feb. 25/40
Away	**7**	Jan. 12-Feb. 12/35, Oct. 28-Nov. 29/78
Longest Undefeated Streak		
Overall	**19**	Nov. 23/39-Jan. 13/40 (14 wins, 5 ties)
Home	**24**	Oct. 14/70-Jan. 31/71 (18 wins, 6 ties), Oct. 24/95-Feb.15/96 (18 wins, 6 ties)
Away	**11**	Nov. 5/39-Jan. 13/40 (6 wins, 5 ties)
Longest Losing Streak		
Overall	**11**	Oct. 30-Nov. 27/43
Home	**7**	Oct. 20-Nov. 14/76, Mar. 24-Apr. 14/93
Away	**10**	Oct. 30-Dec. 23/43, Feb. 8-Mar. 15/61
Longest Winless Streak		
Overall	**21**	Jan. 23-Mar. 19/44 (17 losses, 4 ties)
Home	**10**	Jan. 30-Mar. 19/44 (7 losses, 3 ties)
Away	**16**	Oct. 9-Dec. 20/52 (12 losses, 4 ties)
Most Shutouts, Season	**13**	1928-29 (44)
Most PIM, Season	**2,018**	1989-90 (80)
Most Goals, Game	**12**	Nov. 21/71 (Cal. 1 at NYR 12)

Individual

Most Seasons	**18**	Rod Gilbert
Most Games	**1,160**	Harry Howell
Most Goals, Career	**406**	Rod Gilbert
Most Assists, Career	**741**	Brian Leetch
Most Points, Career	**1,021**	Rod Gilbert (406G, 615A)
Most PIM, Career	**1,226**	Ron Greschner
Most Shutouts, Career	**49**	Ed Giacomin
Longest Consecutive Games Streak	**560**	Andy Hebenton (Oct. 7/55-Mar. 24/63)
Most Goals, Season	**54**	Jaromir Jagr (2005-06)
Most Assists, Season	**80**	Brian Leetch (1991-92)
Most Points, Season	**123**	Jaromir Jagr (2005-06; 54G, 69A)
Most PIM, Season	**305**	Troy Mallette (1989-90)
Most Points, Defenseman, Season	**102**	Brian Leetch (1991-92; 22G, 80A)
Most Points, Center, Season	**109**	Jean Ratelle (1971-72; 46G, 63A)
Most Points, Right Wing, Season	**123**	Jaromir Jagr (2005-06; 54G, 69A)
Most Points, Left Wing, Season	**106**	Vic Hadfield (1971-72; 50G, 56A)
Most Points, Rookie, Season	**76**	Mark Pavelich (1981-82; 33G, 43A)
Most Shutouts, Season	**13**	John Ross Roach (1928-29)
Most Goals, Game	**5**	Don Murdoch (Oct. 12/76), Mark Pavelich (Feb. 23/83)
Most Assists, Game	**5**	Walt Tkaczuk (Feb. 12/72), Rod Gilbert (Mar. 2/75), (Mar. 30/75), (Oct. 8/76), Don Maloney (Jan. 3/87), Brian Leetch (Apr. 18/95), Wayne Gretzky (Feb. 15/99)
Most Points, Game	**7**	Steve Vickers (Feb. 18/76; 3G, 4A)

Retired Numbers

1	Ed Giacomin	1965-1975
2	Brian Leetch	1987-2004
3	Harry Howell	1952-1969
7	Rod Gilbert	1960-1977
9	Andy Bathgate	1952-1964
	Adam Graves	1991-2001
11	Mark Messier	1991-97; 2000-04
35	Mike Richter	1989-2003

All-time Record vs. Other Clubs

Regular Season

	At Home								On Road								Total							
	GP	W	L	T	OL	GF	GA	PTS	GP	W	L	T	OL	GF	GA	PTS	GP	W	L	T	OL	GF	GA	PTS
Anaheim	12	5	6	1	0	31	32	11	11	4	7	0	0	34	41	8	23	9	13	1	0	65	73	19
Atlanta	22	7	9	1	5	59	68	20	22	12	6	0	4	71	63	28	44	19	15	1	9	130	131	48
Boston	314	141	118	55	0	959	874	337	310	103	163	42	2	860	1095	250	624	244	281	97	2	1819	1969	587
Buffalo	78	33	27	15	3	246	211	84	80	24	44	10	2	243	316	60	158	57	71	25	5	489	527	144
Calgary	55	26	24	5	0	184	190	57	51	12	29	10	0	152	223	34	106	38	53	15	0	336	413	91
Carolina	57	34	17	4	2	200	143	74	55	21	31	3	0	163	179	45	112	55	48	7	2	363	322	119
Chicago	288	120	113	55	0	850	812	295	289	116	128	43	2	797	876	277	577	236	241	98	2	1647	1688	572
Colorado	37	20	11	4	2	142	105	46	38	14	19	3	2	137	153	33	75	34	30	7	4	279	258	79
Columbus	4	2	1	1	0	16	12	5	7	2	5	0	0	14	24	4	11	4	6	1	0	30	36	9
Dallas	65	37	17	11	0	221	172	85	64	32	20	11	1	231	201	76	129	69	37	22	1	452	373	161
Detroit	286	134	94	58	0	872	745	326	288	76	166	45	1	708	1016	198	574	210	260	103	1	1580	1761	524
Edmonton	33	12	14	6	1	127	122	31	30	14	12	3	1	100	106	32	63	26	26	9	2	227	228	63
Florida	36	19	13	4	0	107	80	42	37	19	12	2	4	99	92	44	73	38	25	6	4	206	172	86
Los Angeles	61	37	18	6	0	243	181	80	63	28	25	10	0	221	207	66	124	65	43	16	0	464	388	146
Minnesota	6	4	2	0	0	16	12	8	7	4	3	0	0	23	22	8	13	8	5	0	0	39	34	16
Montreal	302	125	122	54	1	874	874	305	302	64	196	40	2	704	1171	170	604	189	318	94	3	1578	2045	475
Nashville	8	2	4	1	1	19	20	6	7	5	1	0	1	25	17	11	15	7	5	1	2	44	37	17
New Jersey	105	54	29	20	2	376	295	130	107	44	53	7	3	332	352	98	212	98	82	27	5	708	647	228
NY Islanders	117	65	37	11	4	423	338	145	117	47	61	8	1	374	424	103	234	112	98	19	5	797	762	248
Ottawa	35	14	20	0	1	98	103	29	35	18	13	3	1	94	95	40	70	32	33	3	2	192	198	69
Philadelphia	131	57	47	23	4	413	383	141	130	53	60	14	3	360	408	123	261	110	107	37	7	773	791	264
Phoenix	33	21	10	2	0	142	113	44	33	15	14	4	0	110	113	34	66	36	24	6	0	252	226	78
Pittsburgh	122	64	46	9	3	462	398	140	121	51	51	14	5	418	422	121	243	115	97	23	8	880	820	261
St. Louis	63	45	12	6	0	251	151	96	67	30	27	10	0	211	199	70	130	75	39	16	0	462	350	166
San Jose	12	8	3	1	0	46	37	17	16	11	3	2	0	57	37	24	28	19	6	3	0	103	74	41
Tampa Bay	39	21	13	2	3	130	108	47	37	16	16	3	2	113	118	37	76	37	29	5	5	243	226	84
Toronto	295	127	109	56	3	918	864	313	294	91	161	39	3	775	1006	224	589	218	270	95	6	1693	1870	537
Vancouver	57	39	13	5	0	243	148	83	53	33	17	3	0	205	170	69	110	72	30	8	0	448	318	152
Washington	94	46	37	9	2	352	315	103	96	37	47	9	3	302	347	86	190	83	84	18	5	654	662	189
Defunct Clubs	139	87	30	22	0	460	290	196	139	82	34	23	0	441	291	187	278	169	64	45	0	901	581	383
Totals	**2906**	**1406**	**1016**	**447**	**37**	**9480**	**8196**	**3296**	**2906**	**1078**	**1424**	**361**	**43**	**8374**	**9784**	**2560**	**5812**	**2484**	**2440**	**808**	**80**	**17854**	**17980**	**5856**

Playoffs

	Series	W	L	GP	W	L	T	GF	GA	Last Mtg.	Rnd.	Result
Atlanta	1	1	0	4	4	0	0	17	6	2007	CQF	W 4-0
Boston	9	3	6	42	18	22	2	104	114	1973	QF	W 4-1
Buffalo	2	0	2	9	3	6	0	19	28	2007	CSF	L 2-4
Calgary	1	1	0	4	3	1	0	14	8	1980	PRE	W 3-1
Chicago	5	1	4	24	10	14	0	54	66	1973	SF	L 1-4
Colorado	1	1	0	6	4	2	0	25	19	1995	CQF	W 4-2
Detroit	5	1	4	23	10	13	0	49	57	1950	F	L 3-4
Florida	1	1	0	5	4	1	0	13	10	1997	CQF	W 4-1
Los Angeles	2	2	0	6	5	1	0	32	14	1981	PRE	W 3-1
Montreal	14	7	7	61	25	34	2	158	188	1996	CQF	W 4-2
New Jersey	5	4	1	28	16	12	0	79	75	2008	CQF	W 4-1
NY Islanders	8	3	5	39	19	20	0	132	129	1994	CQF	W 4-0
Philadelphia	10	4	6	47	20	27	0	153	157	1997	CF	L 1-4
Pittsburgh	4	0	4	20	4	16	0	57	79	2008	CSF	L 1-4
St. Louis	1	1	0	6	4	2	0	29	22	1981	QF	W 4-2
Toronto	8	5	3	35	19	16	0	86	86	1971	QF	W 4-2
Vancouver	1	1	0	7	4	3	0	21	19	1994	F	W 4-3
Washington	6	2	4	34	15	19	0	90	107	2011	CQF	L 1-4
Defunct Clubs	9	6	3	22	11	7	4	43	29			
Totals	**93**	**44**	**49**	**422**	**198**	**216**	**8**	**1175**	**1213**			

Calgary totals include Atlanta Flames, 1972-73 to 1979-80.
Colorado totals include Quebec, 1979-80 to 1994-95.
New Jersey totals include Kansas City, 1974-75, 1975-76, and Colorado Rockies, 1976-77 to 1981-82.
Phoenix totals include Winnipeg, 1979-80 to 1995-96.
Carolina totals include Hartford, 1979-80 to 1996-97.
Dallas totals include Minnesota North Stars, 1967-68 to 1992-93.

Playoff Results 2011-2007

Year	Round	Opponent	Result	GF	GA
2011	CQF	Washington	L 1-4	8	13
2009	CQF	Washington	L 3-4	11	19
2008	CSF	Pittsburgh	L 1-4	12	15
	CQF	New Jersey	W 4-1	19	12
2007	CSF	Buffalo	L 2-4	13	17
	CQF	Atlanta	W 4-0	17	6

Abbreviations: Round: F – Final; **CF** – conference final; **CSF** – conference semi final; **CQF** – conference quarter-final; **SF** – semi-final; **QF** – quarter-final; **PRE** – preliminary round.

2010-11 Results

Oct.	9	at Buffalo	6-3
	11	at NY Islanders	4-6
	15	Toronto	3-4*
	18	Colorado	1-3
	21	at Toronto	2-1
	23	at Boston	3-2
	24	New Jersey	3-1
	27	Atlanta	4-6
	29	Carolina	3-4
	30	at Toronto	2-0
Nov.	1	Chicago	3-2
	4	at Philadelphia	1-4
	5	at New Jersey	3-0
	7	St. Louis	0-2
	9	Washington	3-5
	11	Buffalo	3-2*
	14	Edmonton	8-2
	15	at Pittsburgh	3-2*
	17	Boston	2-3
	19	at Colorado	1-5
	20	at Minnesota	5-2
	22	Calgary	2-1
	24	at Tampa Bay	3-5
	26	at Florida	3-0
	27	at Nashville	2-1†
	29	Pittsburgh	1-3
Dec.	2	at NY Islanders	6-5
	3	NY Islanders	2-0
	5	Ottawa	1-3
	9	at Ottawa	5-3
	11	at Columbus	1-3
	12	Washington	7-0
	15	at Pittsburgh	4-1
	16	Phoenix	4-3†
	18	at Philadelphia	1-4
	23	Tampa Bay	3-4†
	27	NY Islanders	7-2
	29	at New Jersey	3-1
Jan.	1	at Tampa Bay	1-2*
	2	at Florida	0-3
	5	Carolina	2-1*
	7	at Dallas	3-2†
	8	at St. Louis	2-1
	11	Montreal	1-2
	13	Vancouver	1-0
	15	at Montreal	2-3
	16	Philadelphia	2-3
	19	Toronto	7-0
	20	at Carolina	1-4
	22	at Atlanta	3-2†
	24	at Washington	2-1†
	25	Florida	3-4
Feb.	1	Pittsburgh	3-4†
	3	New Jersey	2-3
	5	at Montreal	0-2
	7	at Detroit	2-3
	11	at Atlanta	2-3
	13	Pittsburgh	5-3
	17	Los Angeles	4-3†
	18	at New Jersey	0-1
	20	Philadelphia	2-4
	22	at Carolina	4-3†
	25	at Washington	6-0
	27	Tampa Bay	1-2
Mar.	1	Buffalo	2-3
	3	Minnesota	1-3
	4	at Ottawa	4-1
	6	Philadelphia	7-0
	9	at Anaheim	2-5
	12	at San Jose	3-2†
	15	NY Islanders	6-3
	18	Montreal	6-3
	20	at Pittsburgh	5-2
	22	Florida	1-0
	24	Ottawa	1-2†
	26	at Boston	1-0
	30	at Buffalo	0-1
	31	at NY Islanders	2-6
Apr.	3	at Philadelphia	3-2†
	4	Boston	5-3
	7	Atlanta	0-3
	9	New Jersey	5-2

* – Overtime † – Shootout

Entry Draft Selections 2011-1997

Name in bold denotes played in NHL.

2011
Pick
15 J.T. Miller
72 Steven Fogarty
106 Michael St. Croix
134 Shane McColgan
136 Samuel Noreau
172 Peter Ceresnak

2010
Pick
10 Dylan McIlrath
40 Christian Thomas
100 Andrew Yogan
130 Jason Wilson
157 Jesper Fasth
190 Randy McNaught

2009
Pick
19 Chris Kreider
47 Ethan Werek
80 Ryan Bourque
127 Roman Horak
140 Scott Stajcer
170 Dan Maggio
200 Mikhail Pashnin

2008
Pick
20 **Michael Del Zotto**
51 **Derek Stepan**
75 **Evgeny Grachev**
90 Tomas Kundratek
111 **Dale Weise**
141 Chris Doyle
171 Mitch Gaulton

2007
Pick
17 Alexei Cherepanov
48 Antoine Lafleur
138 Max Campbell
168 Carl Hagelin
193 David Skokan
198 Danny Hobbs

2006
Pick
21 **Bobby Sanguinetti**
54 **Artem Anisimov**
84 Ryan Hillier
104 David Kveton
137 Tomas Zaborsky
174 Eric Hunter
204 Lukas Zeliska

2005
Pick
12 **Marc Staal**
40 **Michael Sauer**
56 **Marc-Andre Cliche**
66 **Brodie Dupont**
77 Dalyn Flatt
107 **Tom Pyatt**
147 Trevor Koverko
178 Greg Beller
211 Ryan Russell

2004
Pick
6 **Al Montoya**
19 **Lauri Korpikoski**
36 Darin Olver
48 **Dane Byers**
51 Bruce Graham
60 **Brandon Dubinsky**
73 Zdenek Bahensky
80 Billy Ryan
127 **Ryan Callahan**
135 Roman Psurny
169 Jordan Foote
247 Jonathan Paiement
266 **Jakub Petruzalek**

2003
Pick
12 **Hugh Jessiman**
50 **Ivan Baranka**
75 Ken Roche
122 **Corey Potter**
149 **Nigel Dawes**
176 Ivan Dornic
179 Philippe Furrer
180 **Chris Holt**
209 **Dylan Reese**
243 Jan Marek

2002
Pick
33 Lee Falardeau
81 Marcus Jonasen
127 **Nate Guenin**
143 Mike Walsh
177 Jake Taylor
194 Kim Hirschovits
226 **Joey Crabb**
240 **Petr Prucha**
270 Rob Flynn

2001
Pick
10 **Dan Blackburn**
40 **Fedor Tyutin**
79 **Garth Murray**
113 **Bryce Lampman**
139 Shawn Collymore
176 **Marek Zidlicky**
206 Petr Preucil
226 Pontus Petterstrom
230 Leonid Zhvachkin
238 **Ryan Hollweg**
269 Juris Stals

2000
Pick
64 **Filip Novak**
95 **Dominic Moore**
112 Premysl Duben
140 Nathan Martz
143 Brandon Snee
175 Sven Helfenstein
205 **Henrik Lundqvist**
238 Danny Eberly
269 Martin Richter

1999
Pick
4 **Pavel Brendl**
9 **Jamie Lundmark**
59 David Inman
79 Johan Asplund
90 Patrick Aufiero
137 Garrett Bembridge
177 Jay Dardis
197 Arto Laatikainen
226 Yevgeny Gusakov
251 Petter Henning
254 Alexei Bulatov

1998
Pick
7 **Manny Malhotra**
40 Randy Copley
66 **Jason LaBarbera**
114 **Boyd Kane**
122 **Patrick Leahy**
131 **Tomas Kloucek**
180 Stefan Lundqvist
207 **Johan Witehall**
235 **Jan Mertzig**

1997
Pick
19 Stefan Cherneski
46 Wes Jarvis
73 **Burke Henry**
93 Tomi Kallarsson
126 Jason McLean
134 **Johan Lindbom**
136 **Mike York**
154 Shawn Degagne
175 **Johan Holmqvist**
182 **Mike Mottau**
210 Andrew Proskurnicki
236 Richard Miller

Glen Sather

President and General Manager

Born: High River, Alta., September 2, 1943.

Glen Sather, who spent parts of four seasons with the New York Rangers as a player from 1970 to 1974, became the franchise's 12th president and tenth general manager on June 2, 2000. He also served as coach of the team from January 30, 2003, to February 25, 2004.

Sather joined the Rangers following a 24-year career with the Edmonton Oilers, where he was the architect of five Stanley Cup championships between 1984 and 1990. One of the most respected executives in the National Hockey League, Sather was honored for his tremendous achievements in 1997 by becoming the first member of the Oilers organization to be selected to the Hockey Hall of Fame.

Named coach and vice president of hockey operations for the Oilers when the franchise joined the NHL in June of 1979, Sather became general manager and club president in May of 1980. He coached through the 1988-89 season and also returned for 60 games behind the bench in 1993-94. Sather-coached teams won the Stanley Cup four times in the 1980s. As general manager, Sather was instrumental in the Oilers' fifth Cup triumph in 1990.

He played for six different teams during a 10-year NHL career. He scored 80 goals in 658 games.

NHL Coaching Record

			Regular Season				Playoffs			
Season	**Team**	**League**	**GC**	**W**	**L**	**O/T**	**GC**	**W**	**L**	**T**
1979-80	Edmonton	NHL	80	28	39	13	3	0	3	....
1980-81	Edmonton	NHL	62	25	26	11	9	5	4	....
1981-82	Edmonton	NHL	80	48	17	15	5	2	3	....
1982-83	Edmonton	NHL	80	47	21	12	16	11	5	....
1983-84♦	Edmonton	NHL	80	57	18	5	19	15	4	....
1984-85♦	Edmonton	NHL	80	49	20	11	18	15	3	....
1985-86	Edmonton	NHL	80	56	17	7	10	6	4	....
1986-87♦	Edmonton	NHL	80	50	24	6	21	16	5	....
1987-88♦*	Edmonton	NHL	80	44	25	11	19	16	2	1
1988-89	Edmonton	NHL	80	38	34	8	7	3	4	....
1993-94	Edmonton	NHL	60	22	27	11	....	....	....	....
2002-03	NY Rangers	NHL	28	11	10	7	....	....	....	....
2003-04	NY Rangers	NHL	62	22	29	11	....	....	....	....
	NHL Totals		**932**	**497**	**307**	**128**	**127**	**89**	**37**	**1**

♦ Stanley Cup win.
Won Jack Adams Award (1986)
* Playoff game May 24, 1988 suspended due to power failure. Score tied.

Club Directory

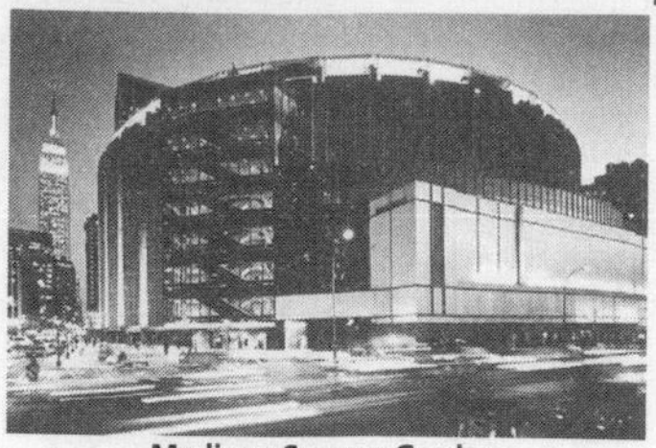

Madison Square Garden

New York Rangers
14th Floor
2 Pennsylvania Plaza
New York, New York 10121
Phone **212/465-6486**
PR FAX 212/465-6494
www.newyorkrangers.com
Capacity: 18,200

Team Executive Management
Exec. Chairman, The Madison Square Garden Company . . James L. Dolan
President & CEO, The Madison Square Garden Company . . Hank J. Ratner
President, MSG Sports . . . Scott O'Neil
President and G.M. . . . Glen Sather
Executive V.P., Business Development & Operations . . . Casey Coffman
Executive V.P., Marketing & Sales . . . Howard Jacobs
Executive V.P., Revenue Performance . . . Greg Economou
Sr. V.P., Finance & Controller . . . John Cudmore
Sr. V.P., Sports Team Operations . . . Mark Piazza
Sr. V.P., Legal & Business Affairs – Sports Ops . . . John Master
Deputy General Counsel & Sr. V.P., Legal & Business Affairs – Team Ops . . . Marc Schoenfeld
Sr. V.P., Marketing . . . Janet Duch
V.P., Public Relations and Player Recruitment . . . John Rosasco

Hockey Club Personnel
Asst. G.M., Player Personnel, Assistant Coach and G.M. – Connecticut Whale . . . Jim Schoenfeld
Asst. G.M. . . . Jeff Gorton
Special Assistant to the President . . . Mark Messier
Head Coach . . . John Tortorella
Assistant Coach . . . Mike Sullivan
Assistant Coach and Goaltending Coach . . . Benoit Allaire
Director, Player Personnel . . . Gordie Clark
Director, Professional Scouting . . . Kevin Maxwell
Senior Advisor to the President and G.M. and Director of U.S. Amateur Scouting . . . Mike Barnett
Hockey and Business Operations . . . Adam Graves
Hockey Consultant . . . Doug Risebrough
Head Professional Scout, Europe . . . Anders Hedberg
European Scouts . . . Jan Gajdosik, Otto Hascak, Vladimir Lutchenko
Amateur Scouts . . . Larry Bernard, Rich Brown, Brendon Clark, Daniel Dore, Ernie Gare, Tom Thompson
Professional Scouts . . . Rick Kehoe, Gilles Leger, Peter Stephan
Head Athletic Trainer . . . Jim Ramsay
Equipment Manager / Assistant Manager . . . Acacio Marques / Jason Levy
Massage Therapist/Assistant Trainer . . . Bruce Lifrieri
Strength and Conditioning Coach . . . Reg Grant
Strength and Conditioning Consultant – Europe . . . Daniel Hedin
Video Coach / Video Analyst . . . Jerry Dineen / Jim Sullivan
Manager, MSG Training Center Operations . . . Alex Case

Sports Team Operations
V.P., Sports Team Operations . . . Jason Vogel
Administrator, Sports Team Operations . . . Brian Wendth
Coordinator, Team Ops and Integrated Marketing . . . Caroline Giglio
Exec. Admin. Assistant to the President, MSG Sports . . . Denise Schuler

Hockey Operations
Managers, Scouting / Hockey Administration . . . Victor Saljanin / TBA
Executive Administrative Assistant . . . Barbara Steppe
Director, Operations, MSG Training Center . . . Miguel Vazquez
Manager, Building Operations, MSG Training Center . . . Kristine DeRosa

Medical Staff
Team Physician and Orthopedic Surgeon . . . Dr. Andrew Feldman
Assistant Team Physician . . . Dr. Anthony Maddalo
Medical Consultants . . . Drs. Ronald Weissman, Ron Preston, Martin Posner
Team Dentists . . . Drs. Don Salomon, Joe Esposito

Public Relations
V.P., Business Public Relations . . . Stacey Escudero
V.P., Publicity, Sports Teams . . . Kaley Hoffman
Public Relations, Director / Manager / Coordinator . . . Brendan McIntyre / Lauren Buchman / Dino Ticinelli

Marketing
V.P., Marketing and Programming . . . Jeanie Baumgartner
Director, Marketing Programs/Brands . . . Leigh Anne Minutoli
Coordinator, Marketing . . . Teanna DiMicco
Marketing Programs, Director / Coordinator . . . Jayne Wise / Nick Brener
Design Director / Art Directors . . . Joanecy Kagalingan / Alex Mount, Brei Stevenson
Sr. Administrative Assistant, MSG Sports . . . Meredith Malaga

Event Presentation
V.P., Event Presentation . . . Ryan Halkett
Director, Event Presentation . . . Greg Kwizak
Music Director, MSG Sports . . . Ray Castoldi
Coordinating Producer, MSG Sports . . . Faith Astrada
Production Assistant . . . Danielle Nardi

Community Relations and Fan Development
V.P., Community Relations . . . Kerryann Tomlinson
Director, Special Projects and Comm. Relations Rep. . . . Rod Gilbert
Director, Fan Development . . . Rick Nadeau
Coordinator, Field Marketing and Fan Development . . . Devin Pacheco
Manager, Community Relations . . . David Martella
Manager, Alumni and Community Relations . . . Anthony Zucconi

MSG Interactive
MSG Interactive, Sr. V.P. and G.M. / V.P. . . . Scott Richman / Heather Pariseau
Manager, MSG Interactive Websites – Teams . . . Dan David

MSG Photo Services
Official Photographer of Madison Square Garden . . . George Kalinsky
MSG Photo Services, V.P. / Manager / Coordinator . . . Rebecca Taylor / Angela Cranford / Zoey Klein

Finance
V.P., Finance . . . Jeanine McGrory
Director, Accounting Suites and Teams . . . Dean Cannizzo
Director, Finance Marketing Partnerships . . . Brandy Champion
Director, Accounting . . . Paul Kohler
Sr. Staff Accountant . . . Marc Weiss
Coordinator, Accounts Payable . . . Dularie Harris
Sr. Administrative Assistant . . . Jen Bianchi

Legal and Business Affairs
V.P.s, Legal & Business Affairs . . . Jamaal Lesane, Christina Song

Additional Information
Television / Radio Network . . . MSG Network / MSG Radio

Ottawa Senators

2010-11 Results: 32w-40L-5OTL-5SOL 74PTS.
Fifth, Northeast Division

Year-by-Year Record

Season	GP	Home W	L	T	OL	Road W	L	T	OL	Overall W	L	T	OL	GF	GA	Pts.	Finished	Playoff Result
2010-11	82	16	20	....	5	16	20	....	5	32	40	....	10	192	250	74	5th, Northeast Div.	Out of Playoffs
2009-10	82	26	11	....	4	18	21	....	2	44	32	....	6	225	238	94	2nd, Northeast Div.	Lost Conf. Quarter-Final
2008-09	82	22	12	....	7	14	23	....	4	36	35	....	11	217	237	83	4th, Northeast Div.	Out of Playoffs
2007-08	82	22	15	....	4	21	16	....	4	43	31	....	8	261	247	94	2nd, Northeast Div.	Lost Conf. Quarter-Final
2006-07	82	25	13	....	3	23	12	....	6	48	25	....	9	288	222	105	2nd, Northeast Div.	Lost Final
2005-06	82	29	9	....	3	23	12	....	6	52	21	....	9	314	211	113	1st, Northeast Div.	Lost Conf. Semi-Final
2004-05	...	...	...	....	...	...	...	....	...	...	...	....	...	....	...	...		
2003-04	82	23	8	5	5	20	15	5	1	43	23	10	6	262	189	102	3rd, Northeast Div.	Lost Conf. Quarter-Final
2002-03	82	28	9	3	1	24	12	5	0	52	21	8	1	263	182	113	1st, Northeast Div.	Lost Conf. Championship
2001-02	82	21	13	3	4	18	14	6	3	39	27	9	7	243	208	94	3rd, Northeast Div.	Lost Conf. Semi-Final
2000-01	82	26	7	5	3	22	14	4	1	48	21	9	4	274	205	109	1st, Northeast Div.	Lost Conf. Quarter-Final
1999-2000	82	24	10	5	2	17	18	6	0	41	28	11	2	244	210	95	2nd, Northeast Div.	Lost Conf. Quarter-Final
1998-99	82	22	11	8	....	22	12	7	....	44	23	15	....	239	179	103	1st, Northeast Div.	Lost Conf. Quarter-Final
1997-98	82	18	16	7	....	16	17	8	....	34	33	15	....	193	200	83	5th, Northeast Div.	Lost Conf. Semi-Final
1996-97	82	16	17	8	....	15	19	7	....	31	36	15	....	226	234	77	3rd, Northeast Div.	Lost Conf. Quarter-Final
1995-96	82	8	28	5	....	10	31	0	....	18	59	5	....	191	291	41	5th, Northeast Div.	Out of Playoffs
1994-95	48	5	16	3	....	4	18	2	....	9	34	5	....	117	174	23	7th, Northeast Div.	Out of Playoffs
1993-94	84	8	30	4	....	6	31	5	....	14	61	9	....	201	397	37	7th, Northeast Div.	Out of Playoffs
1992-93	84	9	29	4	....	1	41	0	....	10	70	4	....	202	395	24	6th, Adams Div.	Out of Playoffs

2011-12 Schedule

Oct.	Fri.	7	at Detroit
	Sat.	8	at Toronto
	Tue.	11	Minnesota
	Thu.	13	Colorado
	Sat.	15	at Washington
	Tue.	18	Philadelphia
	Thu.	20	Winnipeg
	Sat.	22	Columbus
	Tue.	25	at Carolina
	Thu.	27	Florida
	Sat.	29	at NY Rangers*
	Sun.	30	Toronto
Nov.	Tue.	1	at Boston
	Fri.	4	Montreal
	Sat.	5	Buffalo
	Wed.	9	NY Rangers
	Fri.	11	at Buffalo
	Sat.	12	at Toronto
	Tue.	15	at Calgary
	Thu.	17	at Edmonton
	Sun.	20	at Vancouver
	Fri.	25	at Pittsburgh
	Sun.	27	Carolina*
	Tue.	29	at Winnipeg
Dec.	Thu.	1	at Dallas
	Sat.	3	at Washington
	Mon.	5	Tampa Bay
	Wed.	7	Washington
	Thu.	8	at New Jersey
	Sat.	10	Vancouver
	Tue.	13	at Buffalo
	Wed.	14	Boston
	Fri.	16	Pittsburgh
	Tue.	20	Buffalo
	Thu.	22	Florida
	Fri.	23	at Carolina
	Tue.	27	Montreal
	Fri.	30	Calgary
	Sat.	31	at Buffalo
Jan.	Mon.	2	New Jersey
	Thu.	5	Tampa Bay
Feb.	Fri.	3	NY Islanders
	Sat.	4	Toronto
	Tue.	7	St. Louis
	Thu.	9	Nashville
	Sat.	11	Edmonton*
	Tue.	14	at Tampa Bay
	Wed.	15	at Florida
	Mon.	20	at NY Islanders*
	Wed.	22	Washington
	Sat.	25	Boston
	Sun.	26	NY Islanders*
	Tue.	28	at Boston
Mar.	Fri.	2	Chicago
	Sun.	4	at Florida
	Tue.	6	at Tampa Bay
	Thu.	8	NY Rangers
	Sat.	10	Buffalo
	Wed.	14	at Montreal
	Fri.	16	Montreal
	Sat.	17	Toronto
	Tue.	20	New Jersey
	Fri.	23	at Montreal
	Sat.	24	Pittsburgh
	Mon.	26	at Winnipeg
	Sat.	31	at Philadelphia*
Apr.	Sun.	1	at NY Islanders*
	Tue.	3	Carolina
	Thu.	5	Boston
	Sat.	7	at New Jersey*

* Denotes afternoon game.

NORTHEAST DIVISION
20th NHL Season

Franchise date: December 16, 1991

Craig Anderson arrived in Ottawa in a trade with Colorado on February 18, 2011 and provided stellar goaltending the rest of the way. In 18 games with the Senators in 2010-11, Anderson was 11-5-1 with a 2.05 goals-against average and .939 save percentage.

2011-12 Player Personnel

FORWARDS	HT	WT	S	Place of Birth	*Age	2010-11 Club
ALFREDSSON, Daniel	5-11	200	R	Gothenburg, Sweden	38	Ottawa
BUTLER, Bobby	6-0	185	R	Marlborough, MA	24	Ottawa-Binghamton
CONDRA, Erik	6-0	188	R	Trenton, MI	25	Ottawa-Binghamton
DA COSTA, Stephane	5-11	183	R	Paris, France	22	Merrimack-Ottawa
DAUGAVINS, Kaspars	6-1	204	L	Riga, Latvia	23	Binghamton
FILATOV, Nikita	6-0	190	R	Moscow, USSR	21	Columbus-Springfield
FOLIGNO, Nick	6-0	208	L	Buffalo, NY	23	Ottawa
GREENING, Colin	6-3	211	L	St. John's, Nfld.	23	Ottawa-Binghamton
KONOPKA, Zenon	6-0	209	L	Niagara on the Lake, Ont.	30	NY Islanders
MICHALEK, Milan	6-2	217	L	Jindrichuv Hradec, Czech.	26	Ottawa
NEIL, Chris	6-1	215	R	Markdale, Ont.	32	Ottawa
REGIN, Peter	6-2	205	L	Herning, Denmark	25	Ottawa
SMITH, Zack	6-2	210	L	Medicine Hat, Alta.	23	Ottawa-Binghamton
SPEZZA, Jason	6-3	216	R	Mississauga, Ont.	28	Ottawa
WINCHESTER, Jesse	6-1	206	R	Long Sault, Ont.	28	Ottawa

DEFENSEMEN	HT	WT	S	Place of Birth		2010-11 Club
CARKNER, Matt	6-4	238	R	Winchester, Ont.	30	Ottawa
COWEN, Jared	6-5	226	L	Saskatoon, Sask.	20	Spokane-Binghamton
GONCHAR, Sergei	6-2	211	L	Chelyabinsk, USSR	37	Ottawa
KARLSSON, Erik	6-0	175	R	Landsbro, Sweden	21	Ottawa
KUBA, Filip	6-4	229	L	Ostrava, Czech.	34	Ottawa
LEE, Brian	6-3	208	R	Moorhead, MN	24	Ottawa
PHILLIPS, Chris	6-3	220	L	Calgary, Alta.	33	Ottawa
RUNDBLAD, David	6-2	190	R	Lycksele, Sweden	20	Skelleftea

GOALTENDERS	HT	WT	C	Place of Birth	*Age	2010-11 Club
ANDERSON, Craig	6-2	180	L	Park Ridge, IL	30	Colorado-Ottawa
AULD, Alex	6-4	216	L	Cold Lake, Alta.	30	Montreal
LEHNER, Robin	6-4	224	L	Goteborg, Sweden	20	Ottawa-Binghamton

* – Age at start of 2011-12 season

2010-11 Scoring

* – rookie

Regular Season

Pos	#	Player	Team	GP	G	A	Pts	TOI	+/-	PIM	PP	SH	GW	S	%
C	19	Jason Spezza	OTT	62	21	36	57	20:11	–7	28	7	0	2	188	11.2
D	65	Erik Karlsson	OTT	75	13	32	45	23:30	–30	50	4	0	4	182	7.1
L	71	Nick Foligno	OTT	82	14	20	34	15:34	–19	43	5	0	3	149	9.4
L	9	Milan Michalek	OTT	66	18	15	33	18:03	–12	49	1	4	0	167	10.8
R	11	Daniel Alfredsson	OTT	54	14	17	31	19:16	–19	18	7	0	1	96	14.6
R	26	Ryan Shannon	OTT	79	11	16	27	12:55	3	24	5	1	1	118	9.3
D	55	Sergei Gonchar	OTT	67	7	20	27	23:11	–15	20	5	0	0	107	6.5
R	16 *	Bobby Butler	OTT	36	10	11	21	15:25	–16	10	1	0	3	73	13.7
C	13	Peter Regin	OTT	55	3	14	17	13:23	–4	12	0	0	1	87	3.4
R	25	Chris Neil	OTT	80	6	10	16	12:45	–14	210	0	0	2	105	5.7
D	17	Filip Kuba	OTT	64	2	14	16	20:43	–26	16	0	0	1	76	2.6
C	52 *	Colin Greening	OTT	24	6	7	13	15:05	2	10	0	0	2	57	10.5
C	18	Jesse Winchester	OTT	72	4	9	13	10:50	–9	42	0	0	0	118	3.4
R	38 *	Erik Condra	OTT	26	6	5	11	15:52	–1	12	1	0	2	48	12.5
C	15 *	Zack Smith	OTT	55	4	5	9	12:36	–11	120	0	0	1	78	5.1
D	4	Chris Phillips	OTT	82	1	8	9	21:31	–35	32	0	0	1	81	1.2
R	10	Marek Svatos	NSH	9	1	2	3	11:14	1	2	0	0	0	17	5.9
			OTT	19	3	2	5	11:57	–1	8	0	0	0	33	9.1
			Total	28	4	4	8	11:43	0	10	0	0	0	50	8.0
D	39	Matt Carkner	OTT	50	1	6	7	14:53	0	136	0	0	0	40	2.5
D	36	David Hale	OTT	25	1	4	5	16:18	7	6	0	0	1	20	5.0
D	5	Brian Lee	OTT	50	0	3	3	17:11	–10	24	0	0	0	35	0.0
D	46 *	Patrick Wiercioch	OTT	8	0	2	2	13:54	0	4	0	0	0	3	0.0
C	37	Corey Locke	OTT	5	0	1	1	9:10	–1	0	0	0	0	6	0.0
C	47	Andre Benoit	OTT	8	0	1	1	16:50	–1	6	0	0	0	17	0.0
D	51 *	Derek Smith	OTT	9	0	1	1	15:19	3	0	0	0	0	13	0.0
C	58	Cody Bass	OTT	1	0	0	0	7:09	0	0	0	0	0	0	0.0
C	24 *	Stephane Da Costa	OTT	4	0	0	0	11:24	–1	0	0	0	0	9	0.0
C	42 *	Jim O'Brien	OTT	6	0	0	0	9:40	–3	2	0	0	0	11	0.0
R	43 *	Roman Wick	OTT	7	0	0	0	8:37	–4	0	0	0	0	4	0.0
C	21	Ryan Potulny	CHI	3	0	0	0	10:07	–1	0	0	0	0	2	0.0
			OTT	7	0	0	0	6:56	0	0	0	0	0	5	0.0
			Total	10	0	0	0	7:53	–1	0	0	0	0	7	0.0
R	49	Francis Lessard	OTT	24	0	0	0	3:51	0	78	0	0	0	6	0.0

Goaltending

No.	Goaltender	GPI	Mins	Avg	W	L	OT	EN	SO	GA	SA	S%	G	A	PIM
41	Craig Anderson	18	1055	2.05	11	5	1	1	2	36	589	.939	0	0	0
31	Curtis McElhinney	7	399	2.56	3	4	0	1	0	17	205	.917	0	0	0
33	Pascal Leclaire	14	763	2.83	4	7	1	0	0	36	391	.908	0	0	0
30	Brian Elliott	43	2293	3.19	13	19	8	4	3	122	1147	.894	0	0	0
40	* Robin Lehner	8	341	3.52	1	4	0	1	0	20	178	.888	0	0	2
29	Mike Brodeur	4	97	4.33	0	1	0	0	0	7	42	.833	0	0	0
	Totals	82	4972	2.96	32	40	10	7	5	245	2559	.904			

Paul MacLean
Head Coach
Born: Grostenquin, France, March 9, 1958.

Ottawa Senators general manager Bryan Murray announced the hiring of Paul MacLean as the club's head coach on June 14, 2011. MacLean joined the Senators after spending the previous six seasons as assistant coach to Mike Babcock with the Detroit Red Wings. During his tenure with Detroit, the Red Wings finished first in the Central Division five times and made two appearances in the Stanley Cup Final, winning in six games over the Pittsburgh Penguins in 2008 and losing in seven games to Pittsburgh in 2009. During his six seasons with Detroit, the team posted a 304-126-62 record in 492 regular-season games (.681 winning percentage).

Prior to joining Detroit, MacLean was hired in 2002 by Murray, who was then the general manager of the Mighty Ducks of Anaheim. MacLean spent two seasons as an assistant to Babcock, the Mighty Ducks' head coach at that time. In his first season in Anaheim, the club made its first Stanley Cup final appearance and posted a 69-62-33 record (.521) during MacLean's two seasons behind the bench. In his last eight seasons as an assistant coach, MacLean was part of a team that has reached the Stanley Cup Final on three occasions.

Before joining the Anaheim coaching staff in 2002, MacLean, who was born in Grostenquin, France, but grew up in Antigonish, Nova Scotia, was head coach of the Quad City Mallards of the United Hockey League (UHL) from 2000 to 2002. MacLean led the Mallards to a two-season record of 112-27-9 (.787) and the 2001 Colonial Cup championship. MacLean was the head coach of the International Hockey League's Kansas City Blades from 1997 to 2000. He spent one season as an assistant coach with the Phoenix Coyotes in 1996-97 and was head coach at Peoria (IHL) from 1993 to 1996. While with Peoria, MacLean was named The Hockey News Minor League Coach of the Year in 1994 after leading the Rivermen to a 51-24-6 mark and a division title. He was also a scout with the St. Louis Blues for two seasons from 1991 to 1993.

MacLean spent 11 seasons in the National Hockey League as a forward with St. Louis, the Winnipeg Jets and Detroit from 1980-81 to 1990-91. He played in 719 NHL regular-season games, scoring 324 goals and adding 349 assists for 673 points. He recorded eight seasons of 30 or more goals. He also appeared in 53 playoff games, scoring 21 goals and 35 points. MacLean set career highs in goals (41) and points (101) during the 1984-85 season with Winnipeg and was named to the Campbell Conference All-Star Team. MacLean also represented Canada internationally at the 1980 Winter Olympics, held in Lake Placid, New York.

Coaching Record

Season	Team	League	Regular Season GC	W	L	O/T	Playoffs GC	W	L	T
1993-94	Peoria	IHL	81	51	24	6	6	2	4	....
1994-95	Peoria	IHL	81	51	19	11	9	4	5	....
1995-96	Peoria	IHL	82	39	38	5	12	6	6	....
1997-98	Kansas City	IHL	82	41	29	12	11	6	5	....
1998-99	Kansas City	IHL	82	44	31	7	3	1	2	....
99-2000	Kansas City	IHL	82	36	37	9	....	....	....	....
2000-01	Quad City	UHL	74	55	12	7	12	10	2	....
2001-02	Quad City	UHL	74	57	15	2	12	6	6	....

Nick Foligno was one of only two Ottawa players to suit up for all 82 games in 2010-11. He established career highs with 20 assists and 34 points.

Coaching History
Rick Bowness, 1992-93 to 1994-95; Rick Bowness, Dave Allison and Jacques Martin, 1995-96; Jacques Martin, 1996-97 to 2000-01; Jacques Martin and Roger Neilson, 2001-02; Jacques Martin, 2002-03, 2003-04; Bryan Murray, 2004-05 to 2006-07; John Paddock and Bryan Murray, 2007-08; Craig Hartsburg and Cory Clouston, 2008-09; Cory Clouston, 2009-10, 2010-11; Paul MacLean, 2011-12.

Club Records

Team

(Figures in brackets for season records are games played; records for fewest points, wins, ties, losses, goals, goals against are for 70 or more games)

Most Points	113	2002-03 (82), 2005-06 (82)
Most Wins	52	2002-03 (82), 2005-06 (82)
Most Ties	15	1996-97 (82), 1997-98 (82), 1998-99 (82)
Most Losses	70	1992-93 (84)
Most Goals	312	2005-06 (82)
Most Goals Against	397	1993-94 (84)
Fewest Points	24	1992-93 (84)
Fewest Wins	10	1992-93 (84)
Fewest Ties	4	1992-93 (84)
Fewest Losses	21	2000-01 (82), 2002-03 (82), 2005-06 (82)
Fewest Goals	191	1995-96 (82)
Fewest Goals Against	179	1998-99 (82)

Longest Winning Streak

Overall	11	Jan. 14-Feb. 4/10
Home	9	Mar. 5-Apr. 7/09
Away	6	Mar. 18-Apr. 5/03, Jan. 14-Feb. 3/10

Longest Undefeated Streak

Overall	11	Three times
Home	12	Dec. 18/03-Jan. 24/04 (10 wins, 2 ties)
Away	7	Three times

** NHL records do not include neutral site games

Longest Losing Streak

Overall	14	Mar. 2-Apr. 7/93
Home	11	Oct. 27-Dec. 8/93
Away	*38	Oct. 10/92-Apr. 3/93**

Longest Winless Streak

Overall	21	Oct. 10-Nov. 23/92 (20 losses, 1 tie)
Home	*17	Oct. 28/95-Jan. 27/96 (15 losses, 2 ties)
Away	*38	Oct. 10/92-Apr. 3/93 (38 losses)

Most Shutouts, Season	10	2001-02 (82)
Most PIM, Season	1,716	1992-93 (84)
Most Goals, Game	11	Nov. 13/01 (Ott. 11 at Wsh. 5)

Individual

Most Seasons	15	Daniel Alfredsson
Most Games, Career	1,056	Daniel Alfredsson
Most Goals, Career	389	Daniel Alfredsson
Most Assists, Career	634	Daniel Alfredsson
Most Points, Career	1,023	Daniel Alfredsson (389G, 634A)
Most PIM, Career	1,683	Chris Neil
Most Shutouts, Career	30	Patrick Lalime
Longest Consecutive Games Streak	292	Alexei Yashin (Dec. 31/95-Apr. 17/99)
Most Goals, Season	50	Dany Heatley (2005-06), (2006-07)
Most Assists, Season	71	Jason Spezza (2005-06)
Most Points, Season	105	Dany Heatley (2006-07; 50G, 55A)

Most PIM, Season	318	Mike Peluso (1992-93)
Most Points, Defenseman, Season	63	Norm Maciver (1992-93; 17G, 46A)
Most Points, Center, Season	94	Alexei Yashin (1998-99; 44G, 50A)
Most Points, Right Wing, Season	103	Daniel Alfredsson (2005-06; 43G, 60A)
Most Points, Left Wing, Season	105	Dany Heatley (2006-07; 50G, 55A)
Most Points, Rookie, Season	79	Alexei Yashin (1993-94; 30G, 49A)
Most Shutouts, Season	8	Patrick Lalime (2002-03)
Most Goals, Game	4	Marian Hossa (Jan. 2/03) Dany Heatley (Oct. 29/05) Daniel Alfredsson (Nov. 2/05) Martin Havlat (Nov. 2/05) Alex Kovalev (Jan. 3/10)
Most Assists, Game	5	Marian Hossa (Jan. 4/01)
Most Points, Game	7	Daniel Alfredsson (Jan. 24/08; 3G, 4A)

* NHL Record.

General Managers' History

Mel Bridgman, 1992-93; Randy Sexton, 1993-94, 1994-95; Randy Sexton and Pierre Gauthier, 1995-96; Pierre Gauthier, 1996-97, 1997-98; Rick Dudley, 1998-99; Marshall Johnston, 1999-2000 to 2001-02; John Muckler, 2002-03 to 2006-07; Bryan Murray, 2007-08 to date.

Captains' History

Laurie Boschman, 1992-93; Brad Shaw, Mark Lamb and Gord Dineen, 1993-94; Randy Cunneyworth, 1994-95 to 1997-98; Alexei Yashin, 1998-99; Daniel Alfredsson, 1999-2000 to date.

Retired Numbers

8 Frank Finnigan   1924-1934

All-time Record vs. Other Clubs

Regular Season

			At Home								On Road								Total					
	GP	W	L	T	OL	GF	GA	PTS	GP	W	L	T	OL	GF	GA	PTS	GP	W	L	T	OL	GF	GA	PTS
Anaheim	11	4	4	1	2	31	29	11	11	4	5	2	0	23	27	10	22	8	9	3	2	54	56	21
Atlanta	22	13	4	1	4	93	61	31	22	11	8	1	2	79	79	25	44	24	12	2	6	172	140	56
Boston	52	21	26	3	2	126	155	47	54	17	30	5	2	140	183	41	106	38	56	8	4	266	338	88
Buffalo	54	23	18	7	6	147	142	59	52	20	25	3	4	129	161	47	106	43	43	10	10	276	303	106
Calgary	14	6	4	3	1	35	36	16	15	4	9	1	1	31	53	10	29	10	13	4	2	66	89	26
Carolina	41	20	15	4	2	120	105	46	39	11	24	4	0	95	118	26	80	31	39	8	2	215	223	72
Chicago	12	5	5	0	2	38	35	12	11	2	5	2	2	23	27	8	23	7	10	2	4	61	62	20
Colorado	20	8	9	3	0	57	70	19	18	3	12	1	2	54	81	9	38	11	21	4	2	111	151	28
Columbus	5	3	0	1	1	16	10	8	5	1	2	1	1	14	18	4	10	4	2	2	2	30	28	12
Dallas	12	5	7	0	0	28	32	10	13	5	8	0	0	36	51	10	25	10	15	0	0	64	83	20
Detroit	13	4	7	1	1	38	41	10	11	4	6	0	1	23	39	9	24	8	13	1	2	61	80	19
Edmonton	14	6	6	2	0	32	38	14	15	6	7	2	0	42	48	14	29	12	13	4	0	74	86	28
Florida	34	18	12	2	2	105	87	40	34	21	12	1	0	112	101	43	68	39	24	3	2	217	188	83
Los Angeles	12	6	4	1	1	38	32	14	12	1	10	1	0	24	54	3	24	7	14	2	1	62	86	17
Minnesota	4	3	1	0	0	13	8	6	6	4	1	1	0	22	15	9	10	7	2	1	0	35	23	15
Montreal	52	28	21	1	2	160	147	59	54	22	27	4	1	153	159	49	106	50	48	5	3	313	306	108
Nashville	7	4	2	0	1	25	19	9	7	4	3	0	0	15	15	8	14	8	5	0	1	40	34	17
New Jersey	36	12	18	3	3	84	89	30	35	11	18	2	4	80	99	28	71	23	36	5	7	164	188	58
NY Islanders	35	22	7	5	1	120	86	50	36	20	9	6	1	133	114	47	71	42	16	11	2	253	200	97
NY Rangers	35	14	17	3	1	95	94	32	35	21	13	0	1	103	98	43	70	35	30	3	2	198	192	75
Philadelphia	36	18	12	6	0	112	99	42	35	12	21	2	0	95	121	26	71	30	33	8	0	207	220	68
Phoenix	14	7	6	1	0	47	41	15	12	6	5	1	0	44	39	13	26	13	11	2	0	91	80	28
Pittsburgh	39	14	17	5	3	113	127	36	39	14	19	4	2	108	133	34	78	28	36	9	5	221	260	70
St. Louis	12	6	6	0	0	29	40	12	12	5	5	2	0	34	35	12	24	11	11	2	0	63	75	24
San Jose	12	4	4	4	0	37	34	12	11	4	6	0	1	20	26	9	23	8	10	4	1	57	60	21
Tampa Bay	35	24	11	0	0	126	75	48	35	19	11	2	3	121	102	43	70	43	22	2	3	247	177	91
Toronto	41	24	12	1	4	125	111	53	43	21	19	2	1	120	116	45	84	45	31	3	5	245	227	98
Vancouver	14	6	6	1	1	32	38	14	15	5	8	1	1	31	48	12	29	11	14	2	2	63	86	26
Washington	35	20	13	1	1	125	102	42	36	12	18	4	2	101	126	30	71	32	31	5	3	226	228	72
Totals	**723**	**348**	**274**	**60**	**41**	**2147**	**1983**	**797**	**723**	**290**	**346**	**55**	**32**	**2005**	**2286**	**667**	**1446**	**638**	**620**	**115**	**73**	**4152**	**4269**	**1464**

Playoffs

	Series	W	L	GP	W	L	T	GF	GA	Last Mtg.
Anaheim	1	0	1	5	1	4	0	11	16	2007
Buffalo	4	1	3	21	8	13	0	47	52	2007
New Jersey	3	2	1	18	11	7	0	41	40	2007
NY Islanders	1	1	0	5	4	1	0	13	7	2003
Philadelphia	2	2	0	11	8	3	0	28	12	2003
Pittsburgh	3	1	2	15	6	9	0	42	50	2010
Tampa Bay	1	1	0	5	4	1	0	13	7	2003
Toronto	4	0	4	24	8	16	0	42	57	2004
Washington	1	0	1	5	1	4	0	18	7	1998
Totals	**20**	**8**	**12**	**109**	**51**	**58**	**0**	**254**	**265**	

Colorado totals include Quebec, 1992-93 to 1994-95.
Dallas totals include Minnesota North Stars, 1992-93.

Carolina totals include Hartford, 1992-93 to 1996-97.
Phoenix totals include Winnipeg, 1992-93 to 1995-96.

Playoff Results 2011-2007

Year	Round	Opponent	Result	GF	GA
2010	CQF	Pittsburgh	L 2-4	19	24
2008	CQF	Pittsburgh	L 0-4	5	16
2007	F	Anaheim	L 1-4	11	16
	CF	Buffalo	W 4-1	15	10
	CSF	New Jersey	W 4-1	15	11
	CQF	Pittsburgh	W 4-1	18	10

Abbreviations: Round: F - Final; CF – conference final; CSF – conference semi-final; CQF – conference quarter-final.

2010-11 Results

Oct.	8	Buffalo	1-2		8	Tampa Bay	1-2
	9	at Toronto	1-5		11	at Boston	0-6
	11	at Washington	2-3*		13	at NY Islanders	6-4
	14	Carolina	3-2		14	Calgary	2-3
	16	at Montreal	3-4		16	at Washington	1-3
	18	at Pittsburgh	2-5		18	Anaheim	1-2†
	22	at Buffalo	4-2		20	at Philadelphia	2-6
	23	Montreal	0-3		21	Montreal	1-7
	26	Phoenix	5-2		25	Buffalo	2-3*
	28	Florida	5-3	Feb.	1	at New Jersey	1-2
	30	Boston	0-4		2	Detroit	5-7
Nov.	2	at Toronto	3-2		5	at NY Islanders	3-5
	4	NY Islanders	4-1		7	at Vancouver	2-4
	6	at Montreal	3-2		9	at Calgary	2-5
	9	Atlanta	5-2		12	at Edmonton	5-3
	11	Vancouver	2-6		15	NY Islanders	3-4†
	13	at Boston	2-0		18	Boston	2-4
	15	at Philadelphia	1-5		19	at Toronto	1-0†
	17	at Carolina	1-7		23	Florida	5-1
	19	at St. Louis	2-5		25	at Buffalo	2-3
	22	Los Angeles	3-2		26	Philadelphia	4-1
	24	Dallas	1-2	Mar.	1	Boston	0-1
	26	at Pittsburgh	1-2		3	at Atlanta	3-1
	27	Toronto	3-0		4	NY Rangers	1-4
	29	Edmonton	2-3		8	at New Jersey	2-1
Dec.	2	San Jose	0-4		10	at Florida	2-1
	4	Buffalo	0-1†		11	at Tampa Bay	2-1
	5	at NY Rangers	3-1		13	at Buffalo	4-6
	7	at Montreal	1-4		15	Pittsburgh	3-1
	9	NY Rangers	3-5		17	New Jersey	3-1
	10	New Jersey	3-2		19	Tampa Bay	3-2*
	13	Atlanta	3-4*		22	at Carolina	3-4
	16	at Minnesota	3-1		24	at NY Rangers	2-1†
	17	at Colorado	5-6*		25	Washington	2-0
	19	Washington	2-3		27	at Atlanta	4-5†
	23	at Nashville	2-1		29	at Tampa Bay	2-5
	26	Pittsburgh	3-1		31	at Florida	4-1
	29	Carolina	0-4	Apr.	2	Toronto	2-4
	31	at Columbus	3-4*		5	Philadelphia	5-2
Jan.	1	Toronto	1-5		7	Montreal	3-2*
	7	at Chicago	2-3†		9	at Boston	1-3

* – Overtime   † – Shootout

Entry Draft Selections 2011-1997

Name in bold denotes played in NHL.

2011
Pick
- 6 Mika Zibanejad
- 21 Stefan Noesen
- 24 Matt Puempel
- 61 Shane Prince
- 96 Jean-Gabriel Pageau
- 126 Fredrik Claesson
- 156 Darren Kramer
- 171 Max McCormick
- 186 Jordan Fransoo
- 204 Ryan Dzingel

2010
Pick
- 76 Jakub Culek
- 106 Marcus Sorensen
- 178 Mark Stone
- 196 Bryce Aneloski

2009
Pick
- 9 **Jared Cowen**
- 39 Jakob Silfverberg
- 46 **Robin Lehner**
- 100 Chris Wideman
- 130 Mike Hoffman
- 146 Jeff Costello
- 160 Corey Cowick
- 190 Brad Peltz
- 191 Michael Sdao

2008
Pick
- 15 **Erik Karlsson**
- 42 **Patrick Wiercioch**
- 79 **Zack Smith**
- 109 Andre Petersson
- 119 Derek Grant
- 139 Mark Borowiecki
- 199 Emil Sandin

2007
Pick
- 29 **Jim O'Brien**
- 60 Ruslan Bashkirov
- 90 Louie Caporusso
- 120 Ben Blood

2006
Pick
- 28 **Nick Foligno**
- 68 Eric Gryba
- 91 **Kaspars Daugavins**
- 121 Pierre-Luc Lessard
- 151 Ryan Daniels
- 181 Kevin Koopman
- 211 **Erik Condra**

2005
Pick
- 9 **Brian Lee**
- 70 Vitali Anikeyenko
- 95 Cody Bass
- 98 **Ilya Zubov**
- 115 Janne Kolehmainen
- 136 Tomas Kudelka
- 186 Dmitri Megalinsky
- 204 **Colin Greening**

2004
Pick
- 23 **Andrej Meszaros**
- 58 Kirill Lyamin
- 77 Shawn Weller
- 87 **Peter Regin**
- 89 Jeff Glass
- 122 **Alexander Nikulin**
- 141 Jim McKenzie
- 156 **Roman Wick**
- 219 Joe Cooper
- 251 Matthew McIlvane
- 284 John Wikren

2003
Pick
- 29 **Patrick Eaves**
- 67 Igor Mirnov
- 100 Philippe Seydoux
- 135 Mattias Karlsson
- 142 Tim Cook
- 166 Sergei Gimayev
- 228 Will Colbert
- 260 Ossi Louhivaara
- 291 **Brian Elliott**

2002
Pick
- 16 **Jakub Klepis**
- 47 **Alexei Kaigorodov**
- 75 Arttu Luttinen
- 113 Scott Dobben
- 125 Johan Bjork
- 150 Brock Hooton
- 246 Josef Vavra
- 276 Vitali Atyushov

2001
Pick
- 2 **Jason Spezza**
- 23 **Tim Gleason**
- 81 Neil Komadoski
- 99 **Ray Emery**
- 127 **Christoph Schubert**
- 162 Stefan Schauer
- 193 **Brooks Laich**
- 218 Jan Platil
- 223 **Brandon Bochenski**
- 235 Neil Petruic
- 256 Gregg Johnson
- 286 **Toni Dahlman**

2000
Pick
- 21 **Anton Volchenkov**
- 45 **Mathieu Chouinard**
- 55 **Antoine Vermette**
- 87 Jan Bohac
- 122 Derrick Byfuglien
- 156 **Greg Zanon**
- 157 Grant Potulny
- 158 Sean Connolly
- 188 Jason Maleyko
- 283 James Demone

1999
Pick
- 26 **Martin Havlat**
- 48 **Simon Lajeunesse**
- 62 Teemu Sainomaa
- 94 **Chris Kelly**
- 154 Andrew Ianiero
- 164 **Martin Prusek**
- 201 Mikko Ruutu
- 209 **Layne Ulmer**
- 213 **Alexandre Giroux**
- 269 Konstantin Gorovikov

1998
Pick
- 15 **Mathieu Chouinard**
- 44 **Mike Fisher**
- 58 **Chris Bala**
- 74 Julien Vauclair
- 101 **Petr Schastlivy**
- 130 Gavin McLeod
- 161 **Chris Neil**
- 188 Michel Periard
- 223 Sergei Verenikin
- 246 Rastislav Pavlikovsky

1997
Pick
- 12 **Marian Hossa**
- 58 **Jani Hurme**
- 66 **Josh Langfeld**
- 119 **Magnus Arvedson**
- 146 Jeff Sullivan
- 173 Robin Bacul
- 203 Nick Gillis
- 229 **Karel Rachunek**

Club Directory

Scotiabank Place

Ottawa Senators
Scotiabank Place
1000 Palladium Drive
Ottawa, Ontario
K2V 1A5
Phone **613/599-0250**
FAX 613/599-0358
www.ottawasenators.com
Capacity: 19,153

Executive
Owner, Governor and Chairman	Eugene Melnyk
President and Alternate Governor	Cyril Leeder
Exec. V.P., CFO and Alternate Governor	Erin Crowe
Exec. V.P., G.M. and Alternate Governor	Bryan Murray
V.P. and Executive Director, Scotiabank Place	Tom Conroy
Exec. Assistant to the President	Kathy Downs
Exec. Assistant to the Exec. V.P. and CFO	Colette Hiscott

Hockey Operations
Assistant General Manager	Tim Murray
Director of Player Personnel	Pierre Dorion
Director of Hockey Operations and Player Development	Randy Lee
Manager of Hockey Administration	Allison Vaughan
Head Coach	Paul MacLean
Assistant Coaches	Dave Cameron, Mark Reeds, Luke Richardson, Rick Wamsley
Video Coach	Tim Pattyson
Conditioning Coach	Chris Schwarz
Manager, Team Services	Jordan Silmser
Head Athletic Therapist	Gerry Townend
Assistant Athletic Therapist	Domenic Nicoletta
Equipment Manager	Scott Allegrino
Assistant Equipment Manager	Chris Cook
Massage Therapist	Shawn Markwick

Scouts
Scouts	Vaclav Burda, George Fargher, Bob Janecyk, Bob Lowes, Bill McCarthy, Trent Mann, Lew Mongelluzzo, Greg Royce, Mikko Ruutu
Pro Scouts	Jim Clark, Rob Murphy, Nick Polano

Communications and Publications
Director, Communications	Brian Morris
Director, Publications	Karen Ruttan
Communications Coordinator	Chris Moore
Writer/Editorial Manager	Rob Brodie
Translator	Eric Tremblay
Communications & Publications Assistant	Amanda Nigh

Broadcasting
Vice-President, Broadcast	Jim Steel

Legal
Senior Legal Council	Richard Stacey

Corporate & Ticket Sales and Service
Sr, V.P., Corporate & Ticketing Sales	Mark Bonneau
Exec. Ass't. to Sr. V.P., Corp. & Ticketing	Brooke Brown
Director, Corporate Sales	Bill Courchaine
Senior Exec Asst to Director, Corporate Sales	Cheryl Blake
Sr. Corporate Account Managers	Steve Chestnut, Jason Dashnay, Michael Lummack
Director, Business Development	Gina Hillcoat
Director, Ticket Sales	Jim Orban
Manager, Ticket Sales	Chris Atack
Manager, Group Sales	Devon Hogan
Director, Premium Services	Christine Clancy
Manager, Premium Seating Sales	Joe Lowes
Manager, Premium Client Services	Tracey Bonner
Manager, Corporate Services	Kristin Wood

Finance
Controller	Derek Winch
Accounting Manager, Ottawa Senators	Morgan Cranley

Information Technology
Systems Administrator, IT	Robin Zanichkowsky
IT architech	Don Morin
Technical support specialist, IT	Tom Spooner

Marketing
Vice-President, Marketing	Jeff Kyle
Exec. Assistant to the VP, Marketing	Deborah Wilson
Director, Marketing	Isabelle Perrault-Lachapelle
Director, Merchandise Operations	Kevin Lawton
Director, Game Entertainment	Glen Gower
Director, Fan and Community Development	Aaron Robinson
Art Director	Edtmun Jasvins
Director, Promotions & Marketing Services	Lisa Trevisanutto

Operations and Events
Assistant to the V.P. & Executive Director	Linda Julian
Director, Engineering & Operations	Ed Healy
Director, Scotiabank Place Marketing	Krista Galbraith

People Department
Director, People Department	Sandi Horner

Sens Foundation
President	Danielle Robinson

Miscellaneous
Radio	Team 1200 (English), 104,7 FM (French)
Television	Rogers Sportsnet, TVA and RDS
Team Photographer	Freestyle Photography (Andre Ringuette)
Anthem singer	Lyndon Slewidge
Mascot	Spartacat

Bryan Murray
Executive Vice President and General Manager
Born: Shawville, Que., December 5, 1942.

On June 18, 2007, Bryan Murray was appointed as the seventh general manager of the Ottawa Senators. Murray had joined the organization on June 8, 2004, when he was named the club's head coach. Murray resigned as senior vice president and general manager of Anaheim to take the coaching position in Ottawa. As coach in Ottawa in 2006-07, Murray led the Senators to the Stanley Cup Finals for the first time in franchise history, only to lose to his former Anaheim team. He also has previous front office experience as vice president and general manager of the Florida Panthers from 1994 to 2001, assembling a team that reached the Stanley Cup Finals in just its third year of existence in 1996.

Murray, who was back behind the bench in Ottawa briefly in 2007-08, began his NHL career as head coach of the Washington Capitals in 1981. He has served 16+ years behind the bench, coaching more than 1,300 regular-season and playoff games, including 672 wins. He earned the Jack Adams Award as coach of the year in 1983-84. Murray's regular-season coaching record in Ottawa is 107-55-20 and includes winning the 2007 Prince of Wales Trophy as the NHL's Eastern Conference champions.

NHL Coaching Record

Season	Team	League	Regular Season GC	W	L	O/T	Playoffs GC	W	L	T
1981-82	Washington	NHL	66	25	28	13	....			....
1982-83	Washington	NHL	80	39	25	16	4	1	3	....
1983-84	Washington	NHL	80	48	27	5	8	4	4	....
1984-85	Washington	NHL	80	46	25	9	5	2	3	....
1985-86	Washington	NHL	80	50	23	7	9	5	4	....
1986-87	Washington	NHL	80	38	32	10	7	3	4	....
1987-88	Washington	NHL	80	38	33	9	14	7	7	....
1988-89	Washington	NHL	80	41	29	10	6	2	4	....
1989-90	Washington	NHL	46	18	24	4	....			....
1990-91	Detroit	NHL	80	34	38	8	7	3	4	....
1991-92	Detroit	NHL	80	43	25	12	11	4	7	....
1992-93	Detroit	NHL	84	47	28	9	7	3	4	....
1997-98	Florida	NHL	59	17	31	11	....			....
2001-02	Anaheim	NHL	82	29	42	11	....			....
2004-05	Ottawa				SEASON CANCELLED					
2005-06	Ottawa	NHL	82	52	21	9	10	5	5	....
2006-07	Ottawa	NHL	82	48	25	9	20	13	7	....
2007-08	Ottawa	NHL	18	7	9	2	4	0	4	....
NHL Totals			1239	620	465	154	112	52	60	....

Won Jack Adams Award (1984)

Philadelphia Flyers

2010-11 Results: 47w-23l-5otl-7sol 106pts.
First, Atlantic Division

Year-by-Year Record

Season	GP	Home W	L	T	OL	Road W	L	T	OL	Overall W	L	T	OL	GF	GA	Pts.	Finished	Playoff Result
2010-11	82	22	12	....	7	25	11	....	5	47	23	....	12	259	223	106	1st, Atlantic Div.	Lost Conf. Semi-Final
2009-10	82	24	14	....	3	17	21	....	3	41	35	....	6	236	225	88	3rd, Atlantic Div.	Lost Final
2008-09	82	24	13	....	4	20	14	....	7	44	27	....	11	264	238	99	3rd, Atlantic Div.	Lost Conf. Quarter-Final
2007-08	82	21	14	....	6	21	15	....	5	42	29	....	11	248	233	95	4th, Atlantic Div.	Lost Conf. Championship
2006-07	82	10	24	....	7	12	24	....	5	22	48	....	12	214	303	56	5th, Atlantic Div.	Out of Playoffs
2005-06	82	22	13	....	6	23	13	....	5	45	26	....	11	267	259	101	2nd, Atlantic Div.	Lost Conf. Quarter-Final
2004-05	....																	
2003-04	82	24	11	3	3	16	10	12	3	40	21	15	6	229	186	101	1st, Atlantic Div.	Lost Conf. Championship
2002-03	82	21	10	8	2	24	10	5	2	45	20	13	4	211	166	107	2nd, Atlantic Div.	Lost Conf. Semi-Final
2001-02	82	20	13	5	3	22	14	5	0	42	27	10	3	234	192	97	1st, Atlantic Div.	Lost Conf. Quarter-Final
2000-01	82	26	11	4	0	17	14	7	3	43	25	11	3	240	207	100	2nd, Atlantic Div.	Lost Conf. Quarter-Final
1999-2000	82	25	6	7	3	20	16	5	0	45	22	12	3	237	179	105	1st, Atlantic Div.	Lost Conf. Championship
1998-99	82	21	9	11	....	16	17	8	....	37	26	19	....	231	196	93	2nd, Atlantic Div.	Lost Conf. Quarter-Final
1997-98	82	24	11	6	....	18	18	5	....	42	29	11	....	242	193	95	2nd, Atlantic Div.	Lost Conf. Quarter-Final
1996-97	82	23	12	6	....	22	12	7	....	45	24	13	....	274	217	103	2nd, Atlantic Div.	Lost Final
1995-96	82	27	9	5	....	18	15	8	....	45	24	13	....	282	208	103	1st, Atlantic Div.	Lost Conf. Semi-Final
1994-95	48	16	7	1	....	12	9	3	....	28	16	4	....	150	132	60	1st, Atlantic Div.	Lost Conf. Championship
1993-94	84	19	20	3	....	16	19	7	....	35	39	10	....	294	314	80	6th, Atlantic Div.	Out of Playoffs
1992-93	84	23	14	5	....	13	23	6	....	36	37	11	....	319	319	83	5th, Patrick Div.	Out of Playoffs
1991-92	80	22	11	7	....	10	26	4	....	32	37	11	....	252	273	75	6th, Patrick Div.	Out of Playoffs
1990-91	80	18	16	6	....	15	21	4	....	33	37	10	....	252	267	76	5th, Patrick Div.	Out of Playoffs
1989-90	80	17	19	4	....	13	20	7	....	30	39	11	....	290	297	71	6th, Patrick Div.	Out of Playoffs
1988-89	80	22	15	3	....	14	21	5	....	36	36	8	....	307	285	80	4th, Patrick Div.	Lost Conf. Championship
1987-88	80	20	14	6	....	18	19	3	....	38	33	9	....	292	292	85	3rd, Patrick Div.	Lost Div. Semi-Final
1986-87	80	29	9	2	....	17	17	6	....	46	26	8	....	310	245	100	1st, Patrick Div.	Lost Final
1985-86	80	33	6	1	....	20	17	3	....	53	23	4	....	335	241	110	1st, Patrick Div.	Lost Div. Semi-Final
1984-85	80	32	4	4	....	21	16	3	....	53	20	7	....	348	241	113	1st, Patrick Div.	Lost Final
1983-84	80	25	10	5	....	19	16	5	....	44	26	10	....	350	290	98	3rd, Patrick Div.	Lost Div. Semi-Final
1982-83	80	29	8	3	....	20	15	5	....	49	23	8	....	326	240	106	3rd, Patrick Div.	Lost Div. Semi-Final
1981-82	80	25	10	5	....	13	21	6	....	38	31	11	....	325	313	87	3rd, Patrick Div.	Lost Div. Semi-Final
1980-81	80	23	9	8	....	18	15	7	....	41	24	15	....	313	249	97	2nd, Patrick Div.	Lost Quarter-Final
1979-80	80	27	5	8	....	21	7	12	....	48	12	20	....	327	254	116	1st, Patrick Div.	Lost Final
1978-79	80	26	10	4	....	14	15	11	....	40	25	15	....	281	248	95	2nd, Patrick Div.	Lost Quarter-Final
1977-78	80	29	6	5	....	16	14	10	....	45	20	15	....	296	200	105	2nd, Patrick Div.	Lost Semi-Final
1976-77	80	33	6	1	....	15	11	14	....	48	16	16	....	323	213	112	1st, Patrick Div.	Lost Semi-Final
1975-76	80	36	2	2	....	15	11	14	....	51	13	16	....	348	209	118	1st, Patrick Div.	Lost Final
1974-75	**80**	**32**	**6**	**2**	**....**	**19**	**12**	**9**	**....**	**51**	**18**	**11**	**....**	**293**	**181**	**113**	**1st, Patrick Div.**	**Won Stanley Cup**
1973-74	**78**	**28**	**6**	**5**	**....**	**22**	**10**	**7**	**....**	**50**	**16**	**12**	**....**	**273**	**164**	**112**	**1st, West Div.**	**Won Stanley Cup**
1972-73	78	27	8	4	....	10	22	7	....	37	30	11	....	296	256	85	2nd, West Div.	Lost Semi-Final
1971-72	78	19	13	7	....	7	25	7	....	26	38	14	....	200	236	66	5th, West Div.	Out of Playoffs
1970-71	78	20	10	9	....	8	23	8	....	28	33	17	....	207	225	73	3rd, West Div.	Lost Quarter-Final
1969-70	76	11	14	13	....	6	21	11	....	17	35	24	....	197	225	58	5th, West Div.	Out of Playoffs
1968-69	76	14	16	8	....	6	19	13	....	20	35	21	....	174	225	61	3rd, West Div.	Lost Quarter-Final
1967-68	74	17	13	7	....	14	19	4	....	31	32	11	....	173	179	73	1st, West Div.	Lost Quarter-Final

2011-12 Schedule

Oct.						
Thu.	6	at Boston		Thu.	12	at NY Islanders
Sat.	8	at New Jersey		Sat.	14	at Nashville
Wed.	12	Vancouver		Tue.	17	Minnesota
Sat.	15	Los Angeles		Thu.	19	NY Islanders
Tue.	18	at Ottawa		Sat.	21	at New Jersey*
Thu.	20	Washington		Sun.	22	Boston*
Sat.	22	St. Louis		Tue.	24	at Florida
Mon.	24	Toronto		Tue.	31	Winnipeg
Wed.	26	at Montreal	**Feb.** Thu.	2	Nashville
Thu.	27	Winnipeg		Sat.	4	New Jersey
Sat.	29	Carolina		Sun.	5	at NY Rangers*
Nov. Wed.	2	at Buffalo		Tue.	7	NY Islanders
Thu.	3	New Jersey		Thu.	9	Toronto
Sat.	5	Columbus		Sat.	11	NY Rangers*
Wed.	9	at Tampa Bay		Sun.	12	at Detroit
Sun.	13	at Florida*		Thu.	16	Buffalo
Mon.	14	at Carolina		Sat.	18	Pittsburgh*
Thu.	17	Phoenix		Tue.	21	at Winnipeg
Sat.	19	at Winnipeg*		Thu.	23	at Edmonton
Mon.	21	Carolina		Sat.	25	at Calgary
Wed.	23	at NY Islanders		Tue.	28	at San Jose
Fri.	25	Montreal*	**Mar.** Thu.	1	NY Islanders
Sat.	26	at NY Rangers*		Sun.	4	at Washington
Dec. Fri.	2	at Anaheim		Tue.	6	Detroit
Sat.	3	at Phoenix		Thu.	8	Florida
Wed.	7	at Buffalo		Sat.	10	at Toronto
Thu.	8	Pittsburgh		Sun.	11	at New Jersey
Sat.	10	Tampa Bay		Tue.	13	New Jersey
Tue.	13	at Washington		Thu.	15	at NY Islanders
Thu.	15	at Montreal		Sat.	17	at Boston*
Sat.	17	Boston*		Sun.	18	Pittsburgh*
Mon.	19	at Colorado		Tue.	20	Florida
Wed.	21	at Dallas		Thu.	22	Washington
Fri.	23	at NY Rangers		Sat.	24	Montreal
Tue.	27	at Tampa Bay		Mon.	26	Tampa Bay
Thu.	29	at Pittsburgh		Thu.	29	at Toronto
Jan. Mon.	2	NY Rangers*		Sat.	31	Ottawa*
Thu.	5	Chicago	**Apr.** Sun.	1	at Pittsburgh
Sat.	7	Ottawa*		Tue.	3	NY Rangers
Sun.	8	at Ottawa*		Thu.	5	Buffalo
Tue.	10	at Carolina		Sat.	7	at Pittsburgh*

* Denotes afternoon game.

ATLANTIC DIVISION
45th NHL Season

Franchise date: June 5, 1967

Philadelphia's Danny Briere scored a career-high 34 goals in 2010-11. His 68 points ranked him second on the club behind Claude Giroux's team-best 76

2011-12 Player Personnel

FORWARDS	HT	WT	S	Place of Birth	*Age	2010-11 Club
BETTS, Blair	6-3	210	L	Edmonton, Alta.	31	Philadelphia
BRIERE, Danny	5-10	179	R	Gatineau, Que.	34	Philadelphia
GIROUX, Claude	5-11	172	R	Hearst, Ont.	23	Philadelphia
HARTNELL, Scott	6-2	210	L	Regina, Sask.	29	Philadelphia
HOLMSTROM, Ben	6-1	197	R	Colorado Springs, CO	24	Philadelphia-Adirondack
JAGR, Jaromir	6-3	240	L	Kladno, Czech.	39	Omsk
KALINSKI, Jon	6-1	175	L	Bonnyville , Alta.	24	Adirondack
READ, Matt	5-10	185	R	Ilderton, Ont.	25	Bemidji State-Adirondack
RINALDO, Zac	5-11	169	L	Mississauga, Ont.	21	Adirondack-Philadelphia
ROWE, Andrew	6-2	185	L	Muskegon, MI	23	Adirondack-Greenville
SCHENN, Brayden	6-0	193	L	Saskatoon, Sask.	20	L.A.-Bran-Sask-Manchester
SESTITO, Tom	6-5	228	L	Rome, NY	24	CBJ-Sprfld-Adi
SHELLEY, Jody	6-3	230	L	Thompson, Man.	35	Philadelphia
SIMMONDS, Wayne	6-2	183	R	Scarborough, Ont.	23	Los Angeles
TALBOT, Maxime	5-11	190	L	Lemoyne, Que.	27	Pittsburgh
TESTWUIDE, Mike	6-3	210	R	Vail, CO	24	Adirondack
van RIEMSDYK, James	6-3	200	L	Middletown, NJ	22	Philadelphia
VORACEK, Jakub	6-2	214	L	Kladno, Czech.	22	Columbus

DEFENSEMEN	HT	WT	S	Place of Birth	*Age	2010-11 Club
BARTULIS, Oskars	6-2	184	L	Ogre, Latvia	24	Philadelphia-Adirondack
CARLE, Matt	6-0	205	L	Anchorage, AK	27	Philadelphia
COBURN, Braydon	6-5	220	L	Calgary, Alta.	26	Philadelphia
GUSTAFSSON, Erik	5-10	180	L	Kvissleby, Sweden	22	Philadelphia-Adirondack
JANCEVSKI, Dan	6-3	222	L	Windsor, Ont.	30	Adirondack
LILJA, Andreas	6-3	220	L	Helsingborg, Sweden	36	Anaheim
MARSHALL, Kevin	6-1	191	L	Boucherville, Que.	22	Adirondack
MESZAROS, Andrej	6-2	223	L	Povazska Bystrica, Czech.	25	Philadelphia
PRONGER, Chris	6-6	220	L	Dryden, Ont.	36	Philadelphia
TIMONEN, Kimmo	5-10	194	L	Kuopio, Finland	36	Philadelphia
WALKER, Matt	6-4	215	R	Beaverlodge, Alta.	31	Philadelphia-Adirondack

GOALTENDERS	HT	WT	C	Place of Birth	*Age	2010-11 Club
BOBROVSKY, Sergei	6-2	190	L	Novokuznetsk, USSR	23	Philadelphia
BRYZGALOV, Ilya	6-3	213	L	Togliatti, USSR	31	Phoenix
LEIGHTON, Michael	6-3	186	L	Petrolia, Ont.	30	Philadelphia-Adirondack

* – Age at start of 2011-12 season

Peter Laviolette

Head Coach

Born: Norwood, MA, December 7, 1964.

Peter Laviolette was named the 17th coach in Flyers history on December 4, 2009. Taking over the team two months into the season, Laviolette's Flyers would clinch a playoff berth in the final game on the schedule and go on to reach the Stanley Cup Finals before losing to the Chicago Blackhawks. Along the way, they became just the third team in NHL history to rally from a three-games-to-nothing deficit when they beat the Boston Bruins in the second round of the playoffs.

Previously, Laviolette had coached the Carolina Hurricanes from 2003-04 until partway through the 2008-09 season. He 2005-06 he led the Hurricanes to a club-record 52 wins and 112 points in the regular-season and a Stanley Cup championship. Laviolette's career as an NHL head coach began with the New York Islanders in 2001-02. He led the team to the playoffs two years in a row after the club had failed to reach the postseason for seven straight seasons. Prior to joining the Islanders, Laviolette served as an assistant coach with the Boston Bruins after two years of guiding Boston's AHL affiliate, Providence. In 1998-99, Laviolette led the Providence Bruins to a 56-16-8 regular-season record, and a 15-4 playoff record that culminated with Providence hoisting the Calder Cup and Laviolette being named AHL coach of the year.

Laviolette played 11 seasons of professional hockey, mostly in the AHL and IHL, but did play 12 games with the New York Rangers during the 1988-89 season. He was a member of the 1988 and 1994 U.S. Olympic hockey teams, and captained the 1994 Olympic squad.

In the spring of 2004, Laviolette helped assure the United States a spot in the 2006 Olympic Games in Torino, Italy, when he guided Team USA to a bronze medal at the 2004 World Championship in the Czech Republic. He also served as an assistant to San Jose Sharks head coach Ron Wilson behind the bench for Team USA in the 2004 World Cup of Hockey and was head coach again at the 2005 World Championship and 2006 Olympics.

Coaching Record

			Regular Season				Playoffs			
Season	Team	League	GC	W	L	O/T	GC	W	L	T
1997-98	Wheeling	ECHL	70	37	24	9	15	8	7	....
1998-99	Providence	AHL	80	56	16	8	19	15	4	....
99-2000	Providence	AHL	80	33	38	9	14	10	4	....
2001-02	**NY Islanders**	**NHL**	**82**	**42**	**28**	**12**	**7**	**3**	**4**	....
2002-03	**NY Islanders**	**NHL**	**82**	**35**	**34**	**13**	**5**	**1**	**4**	....
2003-04	**Carolina**	**NHL**	**52**	**20**	**22**	**10**	....	....	....	....
2004-05	**Carolina**		SEASON CANCELLED							
2005-06 ♦	**Carolina**	**NHL**	**82**	**52**	**22**	**8**	**25**	**16**	**9**	....
2006-07	**Carolina**	**NHL**	**82**	**40**	**34**	**8**	....	....	....	....
2007-08	**Carolina**	**NHL**	**82**	**43**	**33**	**6**	....	....	....	....
2008-09	**Carolina**	**NHL**	**25**	**12**	**11**	**2**	....	....	....	....
2009-10	**Philadelphia**	**NHL**	**57**	**28**	**24**	**5**	**23**	**14**	**9**	....
2010-11	**Philadelphia**	**NHL**	**82**	**47**	**23**	**12**	**11**	**4**	**7**	....
	NHL Totals		**626**	**319**	**231**	**76**	**71**	**38**	**33**	....

♦ Stanley Cup win.

2010-11 Scoring

* – rookie

Regular Season

Pos	#	Player	Team	GP	G	A	Pts	TOI	+/–	PIM	PP	SH	GW	S	%
R	28	Claude Giroux	PHI	82	25	51	76	19:23	20	47	8	3	5	169	14.8
C	48	Danny Briere	PHI	77	34	34	68	18:18	20	87	6	0	6	246	13.8
C	17	Jeff Carter	PHI	80	36	30	66	18:14	27	39	8	0	7	335	10.7
C	18	Mike Richards	PHI	81	23	43	66	18:52	11	62	5	3	4	184	12.5
L	22	Ville Leino	PHI	81	19	34	53	16:00	14	22	5	0	2	117	16.2
L	19	Scott Hartnell	PHI	82	24	25	49	16:36	14	142	4	0	4	177	13.6
R	10	Kris Versteeg	TOR	53	14	21	35	18:55	–13	29	5	0	0	128	10.9
			PHI	27	7	4	11	15:22	4	24	1	1	0	52	13.5
			Total	80	21	25	46	17:43	–9	53	6	1	0	180	11.7
L	21	James van Riemsdyk	PHI	75	21	19	40	14:31	15	35	3	0	4	173	12.1
D	25	Matt Carle	PHI	82	1	39	40	21:59	30	23	0	0	0	117	0.9
D	44	Kimmo Timonen	PHI	82	6	31	37	22:28	11	36	1	2	0	147	4.1
D	41	Andrej Meszaros	PHI	81	8	24	32	21:07	30	42	3	0	2	144	5.6
D	20	Chris Pronger	PHI	50	4	21	25	22:29	7	44	3	0	1	112	3.6
R	93	Nikolai Zherdev	PHI	56	16	6	22	12:51	5	22	1	0	1	135	11.9
R	15	Andreas Nodl	PHI	67	11	11	22	13:16	14	16	1	1	2	100	11.0
D	6	Sean O'Donnell	PHI	81	1	17	18	15:32	8	87	0	0	0	34	2.9
C	36	Darroll Powe	PHI	81	7	10	17	12:17	–6	41	0	2	2	87	8.0
D	5	Braydon Coburn	PHI	82	2	14	16	21:04	15	53	0	0	0	114	1.8
C	11	Blair Betts	PHI	75	5	7	12	10:27	–3	8	0	1	2	51	9.8
D	24	Nick Boynton	CHI	41	1	7	8	15:43	2	36	0	0	0	42	2.4
			PHI	10	0	0	0	10:14	–3	4	0	0	0	1	0.0
			Total	51	1	7	8	14:38	–1	40	0	0	0	43	2.3
L	13	Daniel Carcillo	PHI	57	4	2	6	7:45	–14	127	0	0	2	56	7.1
L	45	Jody Shelley	PHI	58	2	2	4	6:10	0	127	0	0	0	31	6.5
D	26	Danny Syvret	ANA	6	1	1	2	16:26	–3	4	0	0	0	8	12.5
			PHI	4	0	0	0	12:57	0	2	0	0	0	3	0.0
			Total	10	1	1	2	15:03	–3	6	0	0	0	11	9.1
L	47	* Eric Wellwood	PHI	3	0	1	1	13:25	1	2	0	0	0	8	0.0
C	34	* Ben Holmstrom	PHI	2	0	0	0	9:04	–1	5	0	0	0	0	0.0
D	27	* Erik Gustafsson	PHI	3	0	0	0	10:57	–1	4	0	0	0	2	0.0
D	8	Matt Walker	PHI	4	0	0	0	11:38	0	4	0	0	0	3	0.0
D	3	Oskars Bartulis	PHI	13	0	0	0	13:01	–4	4	0	0	0	7	0.0

Goaltending

No.	Goaltender	GPI	Mins	Avg	W	L	OT	EN	SO	GA	SA	S%	G	A	PIM
33	Brian Boucher	34	1885	2.42	18	10	4	2	0	76	902	.916	0	0	0
35	* Sergei Bobrovsky	54	3017	2.59	28	13	8	4	0	130	1527	.915	0	2	2
49	Michael Leighton	1	60	4.00	1	0	0	0	0	4	36	.889	0	0	0
	Totals	**82**	**4988**	**2.60**	**47**	**23**	**12**	**6**	**0**	**216**	**2471**	**.913**			

Playoffs

Pos	#	Player	Team	GP	G	A	Pts	TOI	+/–	PIM	PP	SH	GW	OT	S	%
R	28	Claude Giroux	PHI	11	1	11	12	21:57	2	8	0	0	0	0	21	4.8
C	48	Danny Briere	PHI	11	7	2	9	19:56	–7	14	2	0	1	0	47	14.9
L	21	James van Riemsdyk	PHI	11	7	0	7	19:23	–3	4	2	0	1	0	70	10.0
C	18	Mike Richards	PHI	11	1	6	7	19:19	–1	15	1	0	0	0	43	2.3
D	41	Andrej Meszaros	PHI	11	2	4	6	26:01	–3	8	0	0	0	0	21	9.5
D	44	Kimmo Timonen	PHI	11	1	5	6	24:53	3	14	0	0	0	0	23	4.3
R	10	Kris Versteeg	PHI	11	1	5	6	15:00	1	12	0	0	0	0	21	4.8
L	22	Ville Leino	PHI	11	3	2	5	16:46	–1	0	1	0	1	1	12	25.0
L	19	Scott Hartnell	PHI	11	1	3	4	16:18	–5	23	0	0	0	0	17	5.9
D	25	Matt Carle	PHI	11	0	4	4	23:24	–8	2	0	0	0	0	19	0.0
L	13	Daniel Carcillo	PHI	11	2	1	3	8:25	2	30	0	0	0	0	14	14.3
R	93	Nikolai Zherdev	PHI	8	1	2	3	11:56	–1	2	0	0	1	0	21	4.8
D	5	Braydon Coburn	PHI	11	1	2	3	24:07	0	6	0	0	0	0	21	4.8
C	17	Jeff Carter	PHI	6	1	1	2	15:15	–3	2	1	0	0	0	18	5.6
D	6	Sean O'Donnell	PHI	11	0	2	2	12:43	–2	5	0	0	0	0	4	0.0
D	20	Chris Pronger	PHI	3	0	1	1	13:55	–3	4	0	0	0	0	4	0.0
C	36	Darroll Powe	PHI	11	0	1	1	12:10	–3	4	0	0	0	0	10	0.0
L	45	Jody Shelley	PHI	2	0	0	0	3:58	0	2	0	0	0	0	1	0.0
R	15	Andreas Nodl	PHI	2	0	0	0	7:25	0	0	0	0	0	0	1	0.0
C	51	* Zac Rinaldo	PHI	2	0	0	0	2:53	–1	12	0	0	0	0	0	0.0
D	26	Danny Syvret	PHI	10	0	0	0	6:49	–3	0	0	0	0	0	6	0.0
C	11	Blair Betts	PHI	11	0	0	0	11:51	–2	0	0	0	0	0	6	0.0

Goaltending

No.	Goaltender	GPI	Mins	Avg	W	L	EN	SO	GA	SA	S%	G	A	PIM
33	Brian Boucher	9	422	3.13	4	4	0	0	22	229	.904	0	0	2
35	* Sergei Bobrovsky	6	186	3.23	0	2	2	0	10	81	.877	0	0	0
49	Michael Leighton	2	70	3.43	0	1	0	0	4	29	.862	0	0	0
	Totals	**11**	**684**	**3.33**	**4**	**7**	**2**	**0**	**38**	**341**	**.889**			

Coaching History

Keith Allen, 1967-68, 1968-69; Vic Stasiuk, 1969-70, 1970-71; Fred Shero, 1971-72 to 1977-78; Bob McCammon and Pat Quinn, 1978-79; Pat Quinn, 1979-80, 1980-81; Pat Quinn and Bob McCammon, 1981-82; Bob McCammon, 1982-83, 1983-84; Mike Keenan, 1984-85 to 1987-88; Paul Holmgren, 1988-89 to 1990-91; Paul Holmgren and Bill Dineen, 1991-92; Bill Dineen, 1992-93; Terry Simpson, 1993-94; Terry Murray, 1994-95 to 1996-97; Wayne Cashman and Roger Neilson, 1997-98; Roger Neilson, 1998-99, 1999-2000; Craig Ramsay and Bill Barber, 2000-01; Bill Barber, 2001-02; Ken Hitchcock, 2002-03 to 2005-06; Ken Hitchcock and John Stevens, 2006-07; John Stevens, 2007-08, 2008-09; John Stevens and Peter Laviolette, 2009-10; Peter Laviolette, 2010-11 to date.

Captains' History

Lou Angotti, 1967-68; Ed Van Impe, 1968-69 to 1971-72; Ed Van Impe and Bobby Clarke, 1972-73; Bobby Clarke, 1973-74 to 1978-79; Mel Bridgman, 1979-80, 1980-81; Bill Barber, 1981-82; Bill Barber and Bobby Clarke, 1982-83; Bobby Clarke, 1983-84; Dave Poulin, 1984-85 to 1988-89; Dave Poulin and Ron Sutter, 1989-90; Ron Sutter, 1990-91; Rick Tocchet, 1991-92; no captain, 1992-93; Kevin Dineen, 1993-94; Eric Lindros, 1994-95 to 1998-99; Eric Lindros and Eric Desjardins, 1999-2000; Eric Desjardins, 2000-01; Eric Desjardins and Keith Primeau, 2001-02; Keith Primeau, 2002-03, 2003-04; Keith Primeau and Derian Hatcher, 2005-06; Peter Forsberg, 2006-07; Jason Smith, 2007-08; Mike Richards, 2008-09 to 2010-11.

Club Records

Team

(Figures in brackets for season records are games played; records for fewest points, wins, ties, losses, goals, goals against are for 70 or more games)

Most Points	**118**	1975-76 (80)
Most Wins	**53**	1984-85 (80), 1985-86 (80)
Most Ties	***24**	1969-70 (76)
Most Losses	**48**	2006-07 (82)
Most Goals	**350**	1983-84 (80)
Most Goals Against	**319**	1992-93 (84)
Fewest Points	**56**	2006-07 (82)
Fewest Wins	**17**	1969-70 (76)
Fewest Ties	**4**	1985-86 (80)
Fewest Losses	**12**	1979-80 (80)
Fewest Goals	**173**	1967-68 (74)
Fewest Goals Against	**164**	1973-74 (78)
Longest Winning Streak		
Overall	**13**	Oct. 19-Nov. 17/85
Home	***20**	Jan. 4-Apr. 3/76
Away	**8**	Dec. 22/82-Jan. 16/83
Longest Undefeated Streak		
Overall	***35**	Oct. 14/79-Jan. 6/80 (25 wins, 10 ties)
Home	**26**	Oct. 11/79-Feb. 3/80 (19 wins, 7 ties)
Away	**16**	Oct. 20/79-Jan. 6/80 (11 wins, 5 ties)
Longest Losing Streak		
Overall	**9**	Dec. 8-27/06
Home	**13**	Nov. 29/06-Feb. 8/07
Away	**8**	Oct. 25-Nov. 26/72, Mar. 3-29/88
Longest Winless Streak		
Overall	**12**	Feb. 24-Mar. 16/99 (8 losses, 4 ties)
Home	**13**	Nov. 29/06-Feb. 8/07 (13 losses)
Away	**19**	Oct. 23/71-Jan. 27/72 (15 losses, 4 ties)
Most Shutouts, Season	**13**	1974-75 (80)
Most PIM, Season	**2,621**	1980-81 (80)
Most Goals, Game	**13**	Mar. 22/84 (Pit. 4 at Phi. 13), Oct. 18/84 (Van. 2 at Phi. 13)

Individual

Most Seasons	**15**	Bobby Clarke
Most Games	**1,144**	Bobby Clarke
Most Goals, Career	**420**	Bill Barber
Most Assists, Career	**852**	Bobby Clarke
Most Points, Career	**1,210**	Bobby Clarke (358G, 852A)
Most PIM, Career	**1,817**	Rick Tocchet
Most Shutouts, Career	**50**	Bernie Parent
Longest Consecutive Game Streak	**484**	Rod Brind'Amour (Feb. 24/93-Apr. 18/99)
Most Goals, Season	**61**	Reggie Leach (1975-76)
Most Assists, Season	**89**	Bobby Clarke (1974-75), (1975-76)
Most Points, Season	**123**	Mark Recchi (1992-93; 53G, 70A)
Most PIM, Season	***472**	Dave Schultz (1974-75)
Most Points, Defenseman, Season	**82**	Mark Howe (1985-86; 24G, 58A)
Most Points, Center, Season	**119**	Bobby Clarke (1975-76; 30G, 89A)
Most Points, Right Wing, Season	**123**	Mark Recchi (1992-93; 53G, 70A)
Most Points, Left Wing, Season	**112**	Bill Barber (1975-76; 50G, 62A)
Most Points, Rookie, Season	**82**	Mikael Renberg (1993-94; 38G, 44A)
Most Shutouts, Season	**12**	Bernie Parent (1973-74), (1974-75)
Most Goals, Game	**4**	Sixteen times
Most Assists, Game	**6**	Eric Lindros (Feb. 26/97)
Most Points, Game	**8**	Tom Bladon (Dec. 11/77; 4G, 4A)

* NHL Record.

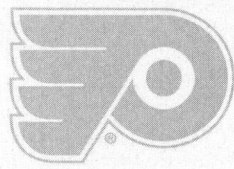

Retired Numbers

1	Bernie Parent	1967-1971, 1973-1979
4	Barry Ashbee	1970-1974
7	Bill Barber	1972-1985
16	Bobby Clarke	1969-1984

All-time Record vs. Other Clubs

Regular Season

	At Home								On Road								Total							
	GP	W	L	T	OL	GF	GA	PTS	GP	W	L	T	OL	GF	GA	PTS	GP	W	L	T	OL	GF	GA	PTS
Anaheim	11	4	3	3	1	29	23	12	12	5	4	2	1	42	43	13	23	9	7	5	2	71	66	25
Atlanta	22	14	4	2	2	85	62	32	22	16	4	1	1	76	49	34	44	30	8	3	3	161	111	66
Boston	85	35	38	10	2	270	256	82	88	27	46	11	4	247	313	69	173	62	84	21	6	517	569	151
Buffalo	79	44	20	12	3	273	209	103	75	29	36	8	2	216	251	68	154	73	56	20	5	489	460	171
Calgary	54	34	15	3	2	203	145	73	54	20	25	9	0	178	210	49	108	54	40	12	2	381	355	122
Carolina	55	37	10	5	3	205	138	82	56	31	15	9	1	205	169	72	111	68	25	14	4	410	307	154
Chicago	64	37	16	11	0	210	164	85	63	17	27	19	0	180	213	53	127	54	43	30	0	390	377	138
Colorado	37	24	9	2	2	134	99	52	38	11	14	12	1	129	136	35	75	35	23	14	3	263	235	87
Columbus	4	3	0	1	0	15	8	7	6	2	2	2	0	11	12	6	10	5	2	3	0	26	20	13
Dallas	71	45	10	16	0	269	161	106	69	25	28	16	0	220	223	66	140	70	38	32	0	489	384	172
Detroit	60	36	13	11	0	240	172	83	62	19	33	10	0	190	221	48	122	55	46	21	0	430	393	131
Edmonton	34	21	11	2	0	138	94	44	30	8	16	6	0	86	104	22	64	29	27	8	0	224	198	66
Florida	37	16	13	6	2	98	96	40	36	24	11	1	0	120	89	49	73	40	24	7	2	218	185	89
Los Angeles	66	42	16	7	1	249	159	92	70	40	21	8	1	238	204	89	136	82	37	15	2	487	363	181
Minnesota	7	5	1	0	1	20	10	11	5	2	2	1	0	13	9	5	12	7	3	1	1	33	19	16
Montreal	85	33	34	16	2	255	256	84	86	30	40	14	2	255	291	76	171	63	74	30	4	510	547	160
Nashville	8	4	2	1	1	26	15	10	6	2	0	2	2	13	12	8	14	6	2	3	3	39	27	18
New Jersey	106	64	28	10	4	387	271	142	104	37	54	8	5	325	350	87	210	101	82	18	9	712	621	229
NY Islanders	116	71	32	11	2	417	316	155	119	49	53	15	2	357	406	115	235	120	85	26	4	774	722	270
NY Rangers	130	63	49	14	4	408	360	144	131	51	54	23	3	383	413	128	261	114	103	37	7	791	773	272
Ottawa	35	21	11	2	1	121	95	45	36	12	16	6	2	99	112	32	71	33	27	8	3	220	207	77
Phoenix	34	24	9	0	1	142	92	49	33	16	15	2	0	107	106	34	67	40	24	2	1	249	198	83
Pittsburgh	127	90	25	8	4	517	331	192	127	47	55	22	3	406	447	119	254	137	80	30	7	923	778	311
St. Louis	69	47	12	10	0	270	157	104	71	36	27	7	1	225	202	80	140	83	39	17	1	495	359	184
San Jose	15	6	5	2	2	48	46	16	15	7	5	2	1	39	39	17	30	13	10	4	3	87	85	33
Tampa Bay	37	18	10	7	2	116	91	45	38	22	15	1	0	117	112	45	75	40	25	8	2	233	203	90
Toronto	79	49	22	8	0	296	189	106	79	35	28	14	2	254	243	86	158	84	50	22	2	550	432	192
Vancouver	56	37	18	1	0	238	167	75	54	31	11	12	0	216	154	74	110	68	29	13	0	454	321	149
Washington	95	58	29	6	2	360	265	124	92	39	36	13	4	294	302	95	187	97	65	19	6	654	567	219
Defunct Clubs	34	24	4	6	0	137	67	54	35	13	14	8	0	102	89	34	69	37	18	14	0	239	156	88
Totals	**1712**	**1006**	**469**	**193**	**44**	**6176**	**4514**	**2249**	**1712**	**703**	**707**	**264**	**38**	**5343**	**5524**	**1708**	**3424**	**1709**	**1176**	**457**	**82**	**11519**	**10038**	**3957**

Playoffs

	Series	W	L	GP	W	L	T	GF	GA	Last Mtg.	Rnd.	Result
Boston	6	3	3	31	13	18	0	86	100	2011	CSF	L 0-4
Buffalo	9	6	3	50	29	21	0	146	141	2011	CQF	W 4-3
Calgary	2	1	1	11	7	4	0	43	28	1981	QF	L 3-4
Chicago	2	0	2	10	2	8	0	30	45	2010	F	L 2-4
Colorado	2	2	0	11	7	4	0	39	29	1985	CF	W 4-2
Dallas	2	2	0	11	8	3	0	41	26	1980	SF	W 4-1
Detroit	1	0	1	4	0	4	0	6	16	1997	F	L 0-4
Edmonton	3	1	2	15	7	8	0	44	49	1987	F	L 3-4
Florida	1	0	1	6	2	4	0	11	15	1996	CSF	L 2-4
Montreal	6	3	3	31	15	16	0	89	93	2010	CF	W 4-1
New Jersey	5	3	2	25	15	10	0	64	59	2010	CQF	W 4-1
NY Islanders	4	3	1	25	14	11	0	83	69	1987	DF	W 4-3
NY Rangers	10	6	4	47	27	20	0	157	153	1997	CF	W 4-1
Ottawa	2	0	2	11	3	8	0	12	28	2003	CSF	L 2-4
Pittsburgh	5	3	2	29	15	14	0	91	89	2009	CQF	L 2-4
St. Louis	2	0	2	11	3	8	0	20	34	1969	QF	L 0-4
Tampa Bay	2	1	1	13	7	6	0	45	34	2004	CF	L 3-4
Toronto	6	5	1	36	22	14	0	119	85	2004	CSF	W 4-2
Vancouver	1	1	0	3	2	1	0	15	9	1979	PRE	W 2-1
Washington	4	2	2	23	11	12	0	78	85	2008	CQF	W 4-3
Totals	**75**	**42**	**33**	**403**	**209**	**194**	**0**	**1219**	**1187**			

Calgary totals include Atlanta Flames, 1972-73 to 1979-80. Carolina totals include Hartford, 1979-80 to 1996-97.
Colorado totals include Quebec, 1979-80 to 1994-95. Dallas totals include Minnesota North Stars, 1967-68 to 1992-93.
New Jersey totals include Kansas City, 1974-75, 1975-76, and Colorado Rockies, 1976-77 to 1981-82.
Phoenix totals include Winnipeg, 1979-80 to 1995-96.

Playoff Results 2011-2007

Year	Round	Opponent	Result	GF	GA
2011	CSF	Boston	L 0-4	7	20
	CQF	Buffalo	W 4-3	22	18
2010	F	Chicago	L 2-4	22	25
	CF	Montreal	W 4-1	17	7
	CSF	Boston	W 4-3	22	20
	CQF	New Jersey	W 4-1	15	9
2009	CQF	Pittsburgh	L 2-4	16	18
2008	CF	Pittsburgh	L 1-4	9	20
	CSF	Montreal	W 4-1	20	14
	CQF	Washington	W 4-3	23	20

Abbreviations: Round: F – Final; **CF** – conference final; **CSF** – conference semi-final; **CQF** – conference quarter-final; **DF** – division final; **SF** – semi-final; **QF** – quarter-final; **PRE** – preliminary round.

2010-11 Results

Oct.	7	at Pittsburgh	3-2		11	at Buffalo	5-2
	9	at St. Louis	1-2*		13	at Boston	5-7
	11	Colorado	4-2		14	at Atlanta	5-2
	14	Tampa Bay	2-3		16	at NY Rangers	3-2
	16	Pittsburgh	1-5		18	Washington	3-2*
	21	Anaheim	2-3		20	Ottawa	6-2
	23	Toronto	5-2		22	New Jersey	1-3
	25	at Columbus	1-2		23	at Chicago	4-1
	26	Buffalo	6-3		25	Montreal	5-2
	29	at Pittsburgh	3-2	**Feb.**	1	at Tampa Bay	0-4
	30	NY Islanders	6-1		3	Nashville	3-2
Nov.	1	Carolina	3-2		5	Dallas	3-1
	4	NY Rangers	4-1		10	Carolina	2-1
	6	at NY Islanders	2-1		13	Los Angeles	0-1
	7	at Washington	2-3*		15	at Tampa Bay	4-3†
	11	at Carolina	8-1		16	at Florida	4-2
	13	Florida	5-2		18	at Carolina	2-3
	15	Ottawa	5-1		20	at NY Rangers	4-2
	16	at Montreal	0-3		22	Phoenix	2-3*
	18	Tampa Bay	7-8		24	NY Islanders	4-3*
	20	at Washington	5-4†		26	at Ottawa	1-4
	22	Montreal	3-2	**Mar.**	3	Toronto	2-3
	24	at Minnesota	6-1		5	Buffalo	3-5
	26	Calgary	2-3†		6	at NY Rangers	0-7
	27	at New Jersey	1-2†		8	Edmonton	4-1
Dec.	1	Boston	0-3		10	at Toronto	3-2
	4	New Jersey	5-3		12	Atlanta	4-5*
	5	at NY Islanders	3-2		15	at Florida	3-2
	8	San Jose	4-5†		17	at Atlanta	3-4†
	9	at Toronto	4-1		19	at Dallas	3-2†
	11	at Boston	2-1*		22	Washington	4-5†
	14	Pittsburgh	3-2		24	Pittsburgh	1-2†
	15	at Montreal	5-3		26	at NY Islanders	4-1
	18	NY Rangers	4-1		27	Boston	1-2
	20	Florida	0-5		29	at Pittsburgh	5-2
	28	at Vancouver	2-6		31	Atlanta	0-1
	30	at Los Angeles	7-4	**Apr.**	1	at New Jersey	2-4
	31	at Anaheim	2-5		3	NY Rangers	2-3†
Jan.	2	at Detroit	3-2		5	at Ottawa	2-5
	6	at New Jersey	4-2		8	at Buffalo	3-4*
	8	New Jersey	2-1		9	NY Islanders	7-4

* – Overtime † – Shootout

Entry Draft Selections 2011-1997

Name in bold denotes played in NHL.

2011
Pick
8	Sean Couturier
68	Nick Cousins
116	Colin Suellentrop
118	Marcel Noebels
176	Petr Placek
206	Derek Mathers

2010
Pick
89	Michael Chaput
119	Tye McGinn
149	Michael Parks
179	Nick Luukko
206	Ricard Blidstrand
209	Brendan Ranford

2009
Pick
81	Adam Morrison
87	Simon Bertilsson
142	Nic Riopel
153	Dave Labrecque
172	**Eric Wellwood**
196	Oliver Lauridsen

2008
Pick
19	**Luca Sbisa**
67	Marc-Andre Bourdon
84	Jacob Deserres
178	**Zac Rinaldo**
196	Joacim Eriksson

2007
Pick
2	**James van Riemsdyk**
41	Kevin Marshall
66	Garrett Klotz
122	Mario Kempe
152	**Jon Kalinski**
161	Patrick Maroon
182	Brad Phillips

2006
Pick
22	**Claude Giroux**
39	**Andreas Nodl**
42	Michael Ratchuk
55	Denis Bodrov
79	**Jon Matsumoto**
101	Joonas Lehtivuori
109	Jakub Kovar
145	Jon Rheault
175	Michael Dupont
205	Andrei Popov

2005
Pick
29	**Steve Downie**
91	**Oskars Bartulis**
119	Jeremy Duchesne
152	Josh Beaulieu
174	John Flatters
215	Matt Clackson

2004
Pick
92	Rob Bellamy
101	R.J. Anderson
124	**David Laliberte**
144	Chris Zarb
149	Gino Pisellini
170	Ladislav Scurko
171	Frederik Cabana
232	**Martin Houle**
253	Travis Gawryletz
286	**Triston Grant**
291	John Carter

2003
Pick
11	**Jeff Carter**
24	**Mike Richards**
69	**Colin Fraser**
81	**Stefan Ruzicka**
85	**Alexandre Picard**
87	**Ryan Potulny**
95	Rick Kozak
108	Kevin Romy
140	David Tremblay
191	Rejean Beauchemin
193	Ville Hostikka

2002
Pick
4	**Joni Pitkanen**
105	Rosario Ruggeri
126	Konstantin Baranov
161	Dov Grumet-Morris
192	Nikita Korovkin
193	**Joey Mormina**
201	Mathieu Brunelle

2001
Pick
27	**Jeff Woywitka**
95	**Patrick Sharp**
146	**Jussi Timonen**
150	Bernd Bruckler
158	Roman Malek
172	**Dennis Seidenberg**
177	Andrei Razin
208	Thierry Douville
225	**David Printz**

2000
Pick
28	**Justin Williams**
94	Alexander Drozdetsky
171	**Roman Cechmanek**
195	Colin Shields
210	John Eichelberger
227	**Guillaume Lefebvre**
259	Regan Kelly
287	Milan Kopecky

1999
Pick
22	**Maxime Ouellet**
119	Jeff Feniak
160	Konstantin Rudenko
200	Pavel Kasparik
208	**Vaclav Pletka**
224	David Nystrom

1998
Pick
22	**Simon Gagne**
42	Jason Beckett
51	Ian Forbes
109	Jean-Philippe Morin
124	**Francis Belanger**
139	Garrett Prosofsky
168	**Antero Niittymaki**
175	Cam Ondrik
195	**Tomas Divisek**
222	Lubomir Pistek
243	**Petr Hubacek**
253	**Bruno St. Jacques**
258	Sergei Skrobot

1997
Pick
30	**Jean-Marc Pelletier**
50	**Pat Kavanagh**
62	Kris Mallette
103	Mikhail Chernov
158	Jordon Flodell
164	**Todd Fedoruk**
214	Marko Kauppinen
240	Par Styf

General Managers' History

Bud Poile, 1967-68, 1968-69; Bud Poile and Keith Allen, 1969-70; Keith Allen, 1970-71 to 1982-83; Bob McCammon, 1983-84; Bob Clarke, 1984-85 to 1989-90; Russ Farwell, 1990-91 to 1993-94; Bob Clarke, 1994-95 to 2005-06; Bob Clarke and Paul Holmgren, 2006-07; Paul Holmgren, 2007-08 to date.

Paul Holmgren
General Manager

Born: St. Paul, MN, December 2, 1955.

Paul Holmgren was named interim general manager of the Philadelphia Flyers on November 11, 2006, replacing Bob Clarke who resigned on October 22. On March 14, 2007, Holmgren was officially announced as the club's new g.m. In his first full season on the job in 2007-08, the Flyers returned to the playoffs after finishing last overall in the NHL the year before. They reached the Stanley Cup Final in 2010. Prior to his promotion, Holmgren had served the previous seven seasons as the team's assistant general manager. He rejoined the Flyers organization as a scout after being replaced as the Hartford Whalers' head coach on November 6, 1995. He had served as a head coach with both the Whalers and the Flyers and also served as general manager in Hartford during the 1993–94 season.

Holmgren retired from playing after the 1984-85 season, having recorded 144 goals and 179 assists for 323 points and 1,684 penalty minutes in 527 career regular season NHL games with the Flyers and the Minnesota North Stars. He recorded 138 goals and 171 assists for 309 points and 1,600 penalty minutes in 500 games over parts of nine seasons with the Flyers (1975-76 to 1983-84). His 1,600 penalty minutes with the Flyers are second all-time in club history. Holmgren was drafted from the University of Minnesota by the Flyers in the sixth round (108th overall) of the 1975 NHL Entry Draft.

NHL Coaching Record

| Season | Team | League | | Regular Season | | | | Playoffs | | | |
			GC	W	L	O/T	GC	W	L	T
1988-89	Philadelphia	NHL	80	36	36	8	19	10	9	....
1989-90	Philadelphia	NHL	80	30	39	11	....	....	....	....
1990-91	Philadelphia	NHL	80	33	37	10	....	....	....	....
1991-92	Philadelphia	NHL	24	8	14	2	....	....	....	....
1992-93	Hartford	NHL	84	26	52	6	....	....	....	....
1993-94	Hartford	NHL	17	4	11	2	....	....	....	....
1994-95	Hartford	NHL	48	19	24	5	....	....	....	....
1995-96	Hartford	NHL	12	5	6	1	....	....	....	....
	NHL Totals		**425**	**161**	**219**	**45**	**19**	**10**	**9**	....

Club Directory

Wells Fargo Center

Philadelphia Flyers
Wells Fargo Center
3601 South Broad Street
Philadelphia, PA 19148-5290
Phone **215/465-4500**
PR FAX 215/218-7837
www.philadelphiaflyers.com
Capacity: 19,537

Executive Management
Chairman	Ed Snider
President and COO of Comcast-Spectacor.	Peter A. Luukko
General Manager	Paul Holmgren
Senior Vice President.	Bob Clarke
Executive Vice President	Keith Allen
Governor	Ed Snider
Alternate Governors	Paul Holmgren, Peter A. Luukko, Phil Weinberg
Senior Vice President, Business Operations	Shawn Tilger
Executive Assistants	Sharon Allison, Cheri Arnao, Ann Marie Nasuti

Hockey Club Personnel
Assistant General Managers	Barry Hanrahan, John Paddock
Director of Hockey Operations	Chris Pryor
Director of Player Development	Don Luce
Director of Player Personnel	Dave Brown
Head Coach	Peter Laviolette
Assistant Coaches	Craig Berube, Kevin McCarthy, Joe Mullen
Goaltending Coach.	Jeff Reese
Player Development Coach	Derian Hatcher
Video Coach	Adam Patterson
Pro Scouts	Patrick Burke, John Chapman, Al Hill
Scouting Staff	Andre Beaulieu, Wade Clarke, Ross Fitzpatrick, Mark Greig, Todd Hearty, Ken Hoodikoff, Matti Kautto, Neil Little, Jack McIlhargey, Simon Nolet, Dennis Patterson, John Riley, Ilkka Sinisalo, Vaclav Slansky
Scouting Consultant	Bill Barber
Director, Team Services	Bryan Hardenbergh
Executive Assistant	Dianna Taylor
Administrative Assistant	Jody Clarke

Medical / Training Staff
Team Physicians	Peter DeLuca, M.D.; Gary Dorshimer, M.D.; Guy Lanzi, D.M.D.; Frank Brady, D.C.
Athletic Trainer/Strength & Conditioning Coach	Jim McCrossin
Assistant Athletic Trainer.	Sal Raffa
Massage Therapist	Brad Smith
Head Equipment Manager	Derek Settlemyre
Equipment Managers	Harry Bricker, Anthony Oratorio, Luke Clarke
Assistant Equipment Trainer	Mike Craytor

Communications
Senior Director, Communications	Zack Hill
Manager, Public Relations.	Joe Siville
Manager, Broadcasting & Media Services	Brian Smith

Community Relations
Director, Community Relations & Special Events	Linda Mantai
Manager, Youth & Amateur Hockey	Rob Baer
Community Relations Coordinator	Jason Tempesta
Youth & Amateur Hockey Coordinator	Eric McQuillan
Ambassador of Hockey	Bob Kelly
Fan Relations Assistant	Jerry Callahan
Ambassadors	Gary Dornhoefer, Joe Kadlec, Bernie Parent

Customer Service
Vice President, Customer Solutions	Cindy Stutman
Director, Customer Service	Lauren Pawlowski
Manager, Client Communications.	Nadine Enders
Senior Customer Service Account Manager	Courtney Sams
Customer Service Account Managers	Vincent Galasso, Tom Griendling, Courtney Sams
Customer Service Coordinator	Shannon Bowes

Game Presentation
Director, Game Presentation	Anthony Gioia
Game Presentation Coordinator	Michaela Sweet
Marketing Coordinator, Flyers Skate Zone	Hung Tran
Producer/Director	Artie Halstead
Graphics Designer / Video Editor	Mike Cahill / Chris Shay
Public Address Announcer / Anthem Singer	Lou Nolan / Lauren Hart

Marketing
Vice President, Marketing	Lindsey Masciangelo
Director, Marketing.	Rob Johnson
Marketing Coordinator	Alicia DeFilippo
Senior Manager, New Media.	Lauren Cochran
Publicist	Rebecca Goodman

Ticket Sales
Vice President, Sales	Jim Willits
Director, Client Development	Bryan Anton
Director, Ticket Sales.	Tim Gobs
Ticket Sales Coordinator	Rachel Meyrowitz
Direct Marketing Coordinator	Megan Bell
Account Executives	Mike Andrews, Paul Haines-Lapenta, Erin Dunn, Austin Foley, Steve Greenblatt, Ilkka Kortesluoma, Dan Ryan, Melissa Sylvester, James Stewart, Josh Wentz
Client Development Executives	James Darlington, Steve Hanson, Lindsay Heck, Travis Kraus, Owen Mullin, Bret Sokirka, Tony Sukanick, Fran Walmsley, Andrew Sherman
Sales Associates	Marty Asalone, Bryan D'Ottavi, Brad Rinehart, Ben Schegel, Andrew Sherman

Ticketing
Vice President, Ticket Operations	Cecilia Baker
Senior Manager, Ticket Operations and Processing	Dan McGinnis
Ticket Office Administration	Joan Kadlec

Finance
Chief Financial Officer.	Angelo Cardone
Controller.	Judy Zdunkiewicz
Staff Accountants	Kim Chuba, Tyler Deane
Payroll Accountant / Accounting Clerk	Renee Eiler / Michele Dominic
Team Consultant	Ron Ryan

Phoenix Coyotes

Key Off-Season Signings/Acquisitions

2011

May 20 • Signed C **Petteri Nokelainen**.

June 6 • Re-signed G **Jason LaBarbera**.

13 • Named **Jim Playfair** associate coach.

July 1 • Signed G **Mike Smith**, LW **Raffi Torres** and C **Boyd Gordon**.

2 • Re-signed RW **Radim Vrbata**.

2 • Signed C **Alex Bolduc**.

4 • Signed G **Curtis McElhinney** and D **Tyler Eckford**.

5 • Re-signed D **Keith Yandle**.

12 • Named **John Anderson** assistant coach.

19 • Re-signed LW **Brett MacLean**.

19 • Signed C **Kyle Chipchura**.

20 • Re-signed LW **Lauri Korpikoski**.

Aug. 5 • Signed C **Patrick O'Sullivan**.

2010-11 Results: 43w-26L-7OTL-6SOL 99PTS.
Third, Pacific Division

Year-by-Year Record

Season	GP	Home W	L	T	OL	Road W	L	T	OL	Overall W	L	T	OL	GF	GA	Pts.	Finished	Playoff Result
2010-11	82	21	13	....	7	22	13	....	6	43	26	....	13	231	226	99	3rd, Pacific Div.	Lost Conf. Quarter-Final
2009-10	82	29	10	....	2	21	15	....	5	50	25	....	7	225	202	107	2nd, Pacific Div.	Lost Conf. Quarter-Final
2008-09	82	23	15	....	3	13	24	....	4	36	39	....	7	208	252	79	4th, Pacific Div.	Out of Playoffs
2007-08	82	17	20	....	4	21	17	....	3	38	37	....	7	214	231	83	4th, Pacific Div.	Out of Playoffs
2006-07	82	18	20	....	3	13	26	....	2	31	46	....	5	216	284	67	5th, Pacific Div.	Out of Playoffs
2005-06	82	19	18	....	4	19	21	....	1	38	39	....	5	246	271	81	5th, Pacific Div.	Out of Playoffs
2004-05																		
2003-04	82	11	19	7	4	11	17	11	2	22	36	18	6	188	245	68	5th, Pacific Div.	Out of Playoffs
2002-03	82	17	16	6	2	14	19	5	3	31	35	11	5	204	230	78	4th, Pacific Div.	Out of Playoffs
2001-02	82	27	8	3	3	13	19	6	3	40	27	9	6	228	210	95	2nd, Pacific Div.	Lost Conf. Quarter-Final
2000-01	82	21	11	7	2	14	16	10	1	35	27	17	3	214	212	90	4th, Pacific Div.	Out of Playoffs
1999-2000	82	22	16	2	1	17	15	6	3	39	31	8	4	232	228	90	3rd, Pacific Div.	Lost Conf. Quarter-Final
1998-99	82	23	13	5	....	16	18	7	....	39	31	12	....	205	197	90	2nd, Pacific Div.	Lost Conf. Quarter-Final
1997-98	82	19	16	6	....	16	19	6	....	35	35	12	....	224	227	82	4th, Central Div.	Lost Conf. Quarter-Final
1996-97	82	15	19	7	....	23	18	0	....	38	37	7	....	240	243	83	3rd, Central Div.	Lost Conf. Quarter-Final
1995-96*	82	22	16	3	....	14	24	3	....	36	40	6	....	275	291	78	5th, Central Div.	Lost Conf. Quarter-Final
1994-95*	48	10	10	4	....	6	15	3	....	16	25	7	....	157	177	39	6th, Central Div.	Out of Playoffs
1993-94*	84	15	23	4	....	9	28	5	....	24	51	9	....	245	344	57	6th, Central Div.	Out of Playoffs
1992-93*	84	23	16	3	....	17	21	4	....	40	37	7	....	322	320	87	4th, Smythe Div.	Lost Div. Semi-Final
1991-92*	80	20	14	6	....	13	18	9	....	33	32	15	....	251	244	81	4th, Smythe Div.	Lost Div. Semi-Final
1990-91*	80	17	18	5	....	9	25	6	....	26	43	11	....	260	288	63	5th, Smythe Div.	Out of Playoffs
1989-90*	80	22	13	5	....	15	19	6	....	37	32	11	....	298	290	85	3rd, Smythe Div.	Lost Div. Semi-Final
1988-89*	80	17	18	5	....	9	24	7	....	26	42	12	....	300	355	64	5th, Smythe Div.	Out of Playoffs
1987-88*	80	20	14	6	....	13	22	5	....	33	36	11	....	292	310	77	3rd, Smythe Div.	Lost Div. Semi-Final
1986-87*	80	25	12	3	....	15	20	5	....	40	32	8	....	279	271	88	3rd, Smythe Div.	Lost Div. Final
1985-86*	80	18	19	3	....	8	28	4	....	26	47	7	....	295	372	59	3rd, Smythe Div.	Lost Div. Semi-Final
1984-85*	80	21	13	6	....	22	14	4	....	43	27	10	....	358	332	96	2nd, Smythe Div.	Lost Div. Final
1983-84*	80	17	15	8	....	14	23	3	....	31	38	11	....	340	374	73	4th, Smythe Div.	Lost Div. Semi-Final
1982-83*	80	22	16	2	....	11	23	6	....	33	39	8	....	311	333	74	4th, Smythe Div.	Lost Div. Semi-Final
1981-82*	80	18	13	9	....	15	20	5	....	33	33	14	....	319	332	80	2nd, Norris Div.	Lost Div. Semi-Final
1980-81*	80	7	25	8	....	2	32	6	....	9	57	14	....	246	400	32	6th, Smythe Div.	Out of Playoffs
1979-80*	80	13	19	8	....	7	30	3	....	20	49	11	....	214	314	51	5th, Smythe Div.	Out of Playoffs

* Winnipeg Jets

2011-12 Schedule

Oct.	Sat.	8	at San Jose
	Mon.	10	at Dallas*
	Thu.	13	at Nashville
	Sat.	15	Winnipeg*
	Tue.	18	Chicago
	Thu.	20	Los Angeles
	Sun.	23	at Anaheim*
	Tue.	25	Dallas
	Thu.	27	New Jersey
	Sat.	29	Los Angeles
Nov.	Wed.	2	at Colorado
	Thu.	3	Nashville
	Sat.	5	Edmonton
	Thu.	10	Montreal
	Sat.	12	at San Jose
	Tue.	15	at Toronto
	Thu.	17	at Philadelphia
	Sat.	19	at Buffalo
	Mon.	21	at Washington
	Wed.	23	Anaheim
	Fri.	25	Vancouver
	Sat.	26	Dallas
	Tue.	29	at Chicago
Dec.	Thu.	1	at Winnipeg
	Sat.	3	Philadelphia
	Mon.	5	at Chicago
	Tue.	6	at Nashville
	Thu.	8	at Detroit
	Sat.	10	Minnesota
	Wed.	14	at Anaheim
	Thu.	15	Edmonton
	Sat.	17	NY Rangers
	Tue.	20	at Florida
	Wed.	21	at Carolina
	Fri.	23	St. Louis
	Mon.	26	at Los Angeles
	Wed.	28	Boston
	Thu.	29	at Colorado
	Sat.	31	at Minnesota*
Jan.	Tue.	3	at St. Louis
	Thu.	5	at Los Angeles

	Sat.	7	NY Islanders
	Tue.	10	at NY Rangers
	Thu.	12	at Detroit
	Fri.	13	at Columbus
	Mon.	16	Colorado*
	Wed.	18	at Anaheim
	Thu.	19	Detroit
	Sat.	21	Tampa Bay
	Tue.	24	Ottawa
	Tue.	31	Anaheim
Feb.	Sat.	4	San Jose
	Mon.	6	Detroit
	Tue.	7	at Dallas
	Thu.	9	Calgary
	Sat.	11	Chicago
	Mon.	13	at Vancouver
	Thu.	16	at Los Angeles
	Sat.	18	Dallas
	Tue.	21	Los Angeles
	Thu.	23	at Calgary
	Sat.	25	at Edmonton*
	Tue.	28	Vancouver
Mar.	Thu.	1	Calgary
	Sat.	3	Columbus
	Mon.	5	at Pittsburgh
	Tue.	6	at Columbus
	Thu.	8	Minnesota
	Sat.	10	San Jose
	Mon.	12	Nashville
	Wed.	14	at Vancouver
	Thu.	15	at Calgary
	Sun.	18	at Edmonton
	Tue.	20	at Dallas
	Thu.	22	Colorado
	Sat.	24	at San Jose
	Sun.	25	St. Louis
	Thu.	29	San Jose
	Sat.	31	Anaheim
Apr.	Tue.	3	Columbus
	Fri.	6	at St. Louis
	Sat.	7	at Minnesota

* Denotes afternoon game.

Keith Yandle and captain Shane Doan celebrate a goal at the Phoenix bench. Yandle scored 11 goals in 2010-11. He ranked second among NHL defensemen with 48 assists and third in points with 59. Doan led the team in scoring (20 goals, 40 assists, 60 points) for the seventh year in a row.

PACIFIC DIVISION
33rd NHL Season

Franchise date: June 22, 1979

Transferred from Winnipeg to Phoenix, July 1, 1996.

2011-12 Player Personnel

FORWARDS	HT	WT	S	Place of Birth	*Age	2010-11 Club
BEAUDOIN, Matt	5-11	190	R	Rock Forest, Que.	27	San Antonio
BISSONNETTE, Paul	6-3	220	L	Welland, Ont.	26	Phoenix
BOEDKER, Mikkel	5-11	202	L	Brondby, Denmark	21	Phoenix-San Antonio
BOLDUC, Alexandre	6-3	200	L	Montreal, Que.	26	Vancouver-Manitoba
CHIPCHURA, Kyle	6-2	206	L	Westlock, Alta.	25	Anaheim
DOAN, Shane	6-1	230	R	Halkirk, Alta.	34	Phoenix
GORDON, Boyd	6-1	200	R	Unity, Sask.	27	Washington
HANZAL, Martin	6-5	220	L	Pisek, Czech.	24	Phoenix
KORPIKOSKI, Lauri	6-1	200	L	Turku, Finland	25	Phoenix
LONG, Colin	5-11	187	R	Santa Ana, CA	22	San Antonio-Las Vegas
MACLEAN, Brett	6-1	200	R	Port Elgin, Ont.	22	Phoenix-San Antonio
MIELE, Andy	5-9	180	L	Grosse Pointe Woods, MI	23	Miami U.
NOKELAINEN, Petteri	6-1	200	R	Imatra, Finland	25	Jokerit
O'SULLIVAN, Patrick	5-11	190	L	Toronto, Ont.	26	Car-Min-Houston
POULIOT, Marc	6-2	193	R	Quebec, Que.	26	Tampa Bay-Norfolk
PYATT, Taylor	6-3	226	L	Thunder Bay, Ont.	30	Phoenix
STEMPNIAK, Lee	6-0	201	R	Buffalo, NY	28	Phoenix
SZWARZ, Jordan	6-0	189	R	Burlington, Ont.	20	Saginaw
TIKHONOV, Viktor	6-2	187	R	Riga, Latvia	23	San Antonio
TORRES, Raffi	6-0	216	L	Toronto, Ont.	29	Vancouver
TURRIS, Kyle	6-1	185	R	New Westminster, B.C.	22	Phoenix-San Antonio
VRBATA, Radim	6-1	197	R	Mlada Boleslav, Czech.	30	Phoenix
WATKINS, Matt	5-10	188	L	Aylesbury, Sask.	24	San Antonio
WEREK, Ethan	6-2	200	L	Markham, Ont.	20	Kingston
WHITNEY, Ray	5-10	180	R	Fort Saskatchewan, Alta.	39	Phoenix
DEFENSEMEN						
ARSENE, Dean	6-2	195	L	Abbotsford, B.C.	31	Peoria
AUCOIN, Adrian	6-2	217	R	Ottawa, Ont.	38	Phoenix
BRODEUR, Mathieu	6-5	230	L	Laval, Que.	21	San Antonio-Las Vegas
ECKFORD, Tyler	6-1	205	L	Vancouver, B.C.	26	New Jersey-Albany
EKMAN-LARSSON, Oliver	6-2	190	L	Karlskrona, Sweden	20	Phoenix-San Antonio
GONCHAROV, Maxim	6-4	208	R	Moscow, USSR	22	San Antonio
GORMLEY, Brandon	6-2	190	L	Charlottetown, P.E.I.	19	Moncton-San Antonio
KLESLA, Rostislav	6-3	221	L	Novy Jicin, Czech.	29	Columbus-Phoenix
MORRIS, Derek	6-0	215	R	Edmonton, Alta.	33	Phoenix
OYSTRICK, Nathan	6-0	210	L	Regina, Sask.	28	St. Louis-Peoria
ROSS, Nick	6-1	196	L	Edmonton, Alta.	22	San Antonio-Las Vegas
ROZSIVAL, Michal	6-2	212	R	Vlasim, Czech.	33	NY Rangers-Phoenix
SCHLEMKO, David	6-1	201	L	Edmonton, Alta.	24	Phoenix-San Antonio
STAFFORD, Garrett	6-1	207	R	Los Angeles, CA	31	Phoenix-San Antonio
STONE, Michael	6-4	207	R	Winnipeg, Man.	21	San Antonio
SUMMERS, Chris	6-2	210	L	Ann Arbor, MI	23	Phoenix-San Antonio
YANDLE, Keith	6-1	195	L	Boston, MA	25	Phoenix

GOALTENDERS	HT	WT	C	Place of Birth	*Age	2010-11 Club
LaBARBERA, Jason	6-3	230	L	Burnaby, B.C.	31	Phoenix
McELHINNEY, Curtis	6-2	193	L	London, Ont.	28	Anaheim-Ottawa
POGGE, Justin	6-3	204	L	Ft. McMurray, Alta.	25	Charlotte
SMITH, Mike	6-4	215	L	Kingston, Ont.	29	Tampa Bay-Norfolk

* – Age at start of 2011-12 season

2010-11 Scoring

* – rookie

Regular Season

Pos	#	Player	Team	GP	G	A	Pts	TOI	+/–	PIM	PP	SH	GW	S	%
R	19	Shane Doan	PHX	72	20	40	60	19:17	5	67	11	0	6	221	9.0
D	3	Keith Yandle	PHX	82	11	48	59	24:22	12	68	3	0	0	199	5.5
L	13	Ray Whitney	PHX	75	17	40	57	16:57	0	24	3	0	1	156	10.9
R	17	Radim Vrbata	PHX	79	19	29	48	16:22	5	20	10	0	2	240	7.9
L	28	Lauri Korpikoski	PHX	79	19	21	40	15:31	17	20	0	2	4	103	18.4
C	20	Eric Belanger	PHX	82	13	27	40	17:20	11	36	1	1	2	127	10.2
R	22	Lee Stempniak	PHX	82	19	19	38	15:15	4	19	2	0	0	199	9.5
L	14	Taylor Pyatt	PHX	76	18	13	31	15:30	11	27	2	0	6	126	14.3
C	11	Martin Hanzal	PHX	61	16	10	26	19:30	4	54	7	0	5	149	10.7
C	91	Kyle Turris	PHX	65	11	14	25	11:16	0	16	0	0	1	116	9.5
L	38	Vernon Fiddler	PHX	71	6	16	22	15:32	3	46	0	1	2	97	6.2
D	33	Adrian Aucoin	PHX	75	3	19	22	21:39	18	52	0	0	0	99	3.0
D	32	Michal Rozsival	NYR	32	3	12	15	22:02	3	22	0	0	1	24	12.5
			PHX	33	3	3	6	19:59	3	20	2	0	2	31	9.7
			Total	65	6	15	21	21:00	6	42	2	0	3	55	10.9
D	53	Derek Morris	PHX	77	5	11	16	21:03	–2	58	1	0	1	83	6.0
D	55	Ed Jovanovski	PHX	50	5	9	14	20:28	4	39	1	0	1	73	6.8
L	89	Mikkel Boedker	PHX	34	4	10	14	10:54	11	8	0	0	0	39	10.3
D	6	* David Schlemko	PHX	43	4	10	14	16:02	8	24	0	0	0	47	8.5
D	16	Rostislav Klesla	CBJ	45	3	7	10	19:18	10	26	0	0	0	45	6.7
			PHX	16	1	0	1	18:23	–6	12	0	0	0	22	4.5
			Total	61	4	7	11	19:04	4	38	0	0	0	67	6.0
D	23	* Oliver Ekman-Larsson	PHX	48	1	10	11	15:02	3	24	0	0	0	50	2.0
C	26	Andrew Ebbett	PHX	33	2	3	5	10:00	–1	4	0	1	1	23	8.7
L	39	* Brett Maclean	PHX	13	2	1	3	8:45	0	2	1	0	2	16	12.5
L	12	Paul Bissonnette	PHX	48	1	0	1	5:15	6	71	0	0	0	18	5.6
R	16	Petr Prucha	PHX	11	0	1	1	11:27	0	4	0	0	0	10	0.0
D	52	Nolan Yonkman	PHX	16	0	1	1	12:07	5	39	0	0	0	8	0.0
D	29	Garrett Stafford	PHX	2	0	0	0	12:24	0	0	0	0	0	2	0.0
D	5	* Chris Summers	PHX	2	0	0	0	13:52	–3	4	0	0	0	0	0.0
L	15	Ryan Hollweg	PHX	3	0	0	0	6:33	–1	0	0	0	0	0	0.0

Goaltending

No.	Goaltender	GPI	Mins	Avg	W	L	OT	EN	SO	GA	SA	S%	G	A	PIM
31	Matt Climie	1	32	1.88	0	0	0	0	0	1	16	.938	0	0	0
30	Ilya Bryzgalov	68	4060	2.48	36	20	10	3	7	168	2125	.921	0	0	2
1	Jason LaBarbera	17	883	3.26	7	6	3	0	2	48	529	.909	0	0	2
	Totals	**82**	**4995**	**2.64**	**43**	**26**	**13**	**3**	**9**	**220**	**2673**	**.918**			

Playoffs

Pos	#	Player	Team	GP	G	A	Pts	TOI	+/–	PIM	PP	SH	GW	OT	S	%
R	19	Shane Doan	PHX	4	3	2	5	21:42	–2	6	2	0	0	0	12	25.0
R	17	Radim Vrbata	PHX	4	2	3	5	19:55	–5	0	1	0	0	0	13	15.4
D	3	Keith Yandle	PHX	4	0	5	5	25:50	–5	0	0	0	0	0	9	0.0
L	13	Ray Whitney	PHX	4	1	2	3	19:24	0	2	1	0	0	0	11	9.1
C	11	Martin Hanzal	PHX	4	1	2	3	19:50	–6	8	1	0	0	0	7	14.3
C	91	Kyle Turris	PHX	4	1	2	3	13:49	1	2	0	0	0	0	8	12.5
L	14	Taylor Pyatt	PHX	4	1	0	1	14:56	–3	0	0	0	0	0	10	10.0
D	6	* David Schlemko	PHX	4	1	0	1	15:54	–3	4	1	0	0	0	4	25.0
D	55	Ed Jovanovski	PHX	4	0	1	1	15:24	–2	2	0	0	0	0	3	0.0
L	28	Lauri Korpikoski	PHX	4	0	1	1	16:33	–6	2	0	0	0	0	3	0.0
L	89	Mikkel Boedker	PHX	4	0	1	1	8:58	–1	2	0	0	0	0	3	0.0
L	12	Paul Bissonnette	PHX	1	0	0	0	4:05	0	0	0	0	0	0	1	0.0
C	26	Andrew Ebbett	PHX	3	0	0	0	7:58	–1	0	0	0	0	0	3	0.0
D	33	Adrian Aucoin	PHX	4	0	0	0	19:17	–4	2	0	0	0	0	3	0.0
C	20	Eric Belanger	PHX	4	0	0	0	15:57	–4	2	0	0	0	0	5	0.0
D	32	Michal Rozsival	PHX	4	0	0	0	19:54	–3	2	0	0	0	0	3	0.0
D	16	Rostislav Klesla	PHX	4	0	0	0	17:43	–2	7	0	0	0	0	7	0.0
L	38	Vernon Fiddler	PHX	4	0	0	0	9:57	–2	0	0	0	0	0	5	0.0
R	22	Lee Stempniak	PHX	4	0	0	0	12:13	–3	0	0	0	0	0	8	0.0

Goaltending

No.	Goaltender	GPI	Mins	Avg	W	L	EN	SO	GA	SA	S%	G	A	PIM
30	Ilya Bryzgalov	4	234	4.36	0	4	1	0	17	140	.879	0	0	0
	Totals	**4**	**240**	**4.50**	**0**	**4**	**1**	**0**	**18**	**140**	**.871**			

Don Maloney

General Manager

Born: Lindsay, Ont., September 5, 1958.

Don Maloney was signed as general manager of the Phoenix Coyotes on May 30, 2007. Maloney has steered the team through turbulent times and guided the Coyotes to the most successful season in franchise history in 2009-10, setting club records with 50 wins and 107 points. He was rewarded for his efforts by being named the inaugural winner of the NHL General Manager of the Year Award in 2010.

Maloney joined the Coyotes from the New York Rangers for whom he served as vice president of player personnel and assistant general manager. He assisted Rangers' president and g.m. Glen Sather in all player transactions and contract negotiations and was involved with the team's professional and amateur scouting operations. Maloney spent 10 seasons in the Rangers' front office. He played a key role in the Rangers' development of several prospects into productive NHL players, including Henrik Lundqvist. Maloney also served as assistant general manager for Team Canada squads that won gold medals at the 2003 and 2004 World Championships.

Maloney's first front office position in the NHL was as assistant general manager of the New York Islanders following his retirement as a player with the club on January 17, 1991. Maloney later served as Islanders' general manager from August 17, 1992 to December 2, 1995. Among the players drafted by the Islanders during Maloney's tenure with the club were Todd Bertuzzi, Bryan McCabe, Ziggy Palffy, Tommy Salo and Darius Kasparaitis. Maloney then served as Eastern professional scout for the San Jose Sharks during the 1996-97 season prior to joining the Rangers' front office.

As a player, Maloney registered 214 goals, 350 assists, and 564 points as well as 815 penalty minutes in 765 regular-season games over 13 NHL campaigns with the Rangers, Hartford Whalers and Islanders. He also collected 22 goals, 35 assists, and 57 points in 94 career playoff games. Maloney spent 11 seasons with the Rangers after being selected by the club in the second round (26th overall) of the 1978 NHL Entry Draft. He helped lead the Rangers to the 1980 Stanley Cup Final by posting 20 points (7 goals, 13 assists) that postseason, a playoff record for rookies at the time. Maloney played in the NHL All-Star Game in 1983 and 1984. He was named MVP of the 1984 game.

General Managers' History

John Ferguson Sr., 1979-80 to 1987-88; John Ferguson Sr. and Mike Smith, 1988-89; Mike Smith, 1989-90 to 1992-93; Mike Smith and John Paddock, 1993-94; John Paddock, 1994-95, 1995-96; John Paddock and Bobby Smith, 1996-97; Bobby Smith, 1997-98 to 1999-2000; Bobby Smith and Cliff Fletcher, 2000-01; Michael Barnett, 2001-02 to 2006-07; Don Maloney, 2007-08 to date.

Coaching History

Tom McVie and Bill Sutherland, 1979-80; Tom McVie, Bill Sutherland and Mike Smith, 1980-81; Tom Watt, 1981-82, 1982-83; Tom Watt and Barry Long, 1983-84; Barry Long, 1984-85; Barry Long and John Ferguson Sr., 1985-86; Dan Maloney, 1986-87, 1987-88; Dan Maloney and Rick Bowness, 1988-89; Bob Murdoch, 1989-90, 1990-91; John Paddock, 1991-92 to 1993-94; John Paddock and Terry Simpson, 1994-95; Terry Simpson, 1995-96; Don Hay, 1996-97; Jim Schoenfeld, 1997-98, 1998-99; Bob Francis, 1999-2000 to 2002-03; Bob Francis and Rick Bowness, 2003-04; Rick Bowness, 2004-05; Wayne Gretzky, 2005-06 to 2008-09; Dave Tippett, 2009-10 to date.

Club Records

Team

(Figures in brackets for season records are games played; records for fewest points, wins, ties, losses, goals, goals against are for 70 or more games)

Record	Value	Details
Most Points	107	2009-10 (82)
Most Wins	50	2009-10 (82)
Most Ties	18	2003-04 (82)
Most Losses	57	1980-81 (80)
Most Goals	358	1984-85 (80)
Most Goals Against	400	1980-81 (80)
Fewest Points	32	1980-81 (80)
Fewest Wins	9	1980-81 (80)
Fewest Ties	6	1995-96 (82)
Fewest Losses	25	2009-10 (82)
Fewest Goals	188	2003-04 (82)
Fewest Goals Against	197	1998-99 (82)
Longest Winning Streak		
Overall	9	Mar. 8-27/85, Mar. 4-21/10
Home	10	Nov. 21-Dec. 29/09
Away	8	Feb. 25-Apr. 6/85
Longest Undefeated Streak		
Overall	14	Oct. 25-Nov. 28/98 (12 wins, 2 ties)
Home	11	Dec. 23/83-Feb. 5/84 (6 wins, 5 ties), Oct. 15-Dec. 20/98 (10 wins, 1 tie)
Away	9	Feb. 25-Apr. 7/85 (8 wins, 1 tie), Dec. 7/03-Jan. 9/04 (5 wins, 4 ties)
Longest Losing Streak		
Overall	10	Nov. 30-Dec. 20/80, Feb. 6-25/94
Home	6	Oct. 6-Nov. 3/07, Jan. 27-Feb. 16/09
Away	13	Jan. 26-Apr. 14/94
Longest Winless Streak		
Overall	*30	Oct. 19-Dec. 20/80 (23 losses, 7 ties)
Home	14	Oct. 19-Dec. 14/80 (9 losses, 5 ties)
Away	18	Oct. 10-Dec. 20/80 (16 losses, 2 ties)
Most Shutouts, Season	9	1998-99 (82)
Most PIM, Season	2,278	1987-88 (80)
Most Goals, Game	12	Feb. 25/85 (Wpg. 12 at NYR 5)

Individual

Record	Value	Details
Most Seasons	15	Teppo Numminen, Shane Doan
Most Games	1,119	Shane Doan
Most Goals, Career	379	Dale Hawerchuk
Most Assists, Career	553	Thomas Steen
Most Points, Career	929	Dale Hawerchuk (379G, 550A)
Most PIM, Career	1,508	Keith Tkachuk
Most Shutouts, Career	21	Nikolai Khabibulin, Ilya Bryzgalov
Longest Consecutive Games Streak	475	Dale Hawerchuk (Dec. 19/82-Dec. 10/88)
Most Goals, Season	76	Teemu Selanne (1992-93)
Most Assists, Season	79	Phil Housley (1992-93)
Most Points, Season	132	Teemu Selanne (1992-93; 76G, 56A)
Most PIM, Season	347	Tie Domi (1993-94)
Most Points, Defenseman, Season	97	Phil Housley (1992-93; 18G, 79A)
Most Points, Center, Season	130	Dale Hawerchuk (1984-85; 53G, 77A)
Most Points, Right Wing, Season	132	Teemu Selanne (1992-93; 76G, 56A)
Most Points, Left Wing, Season	98	Keith Tkachuk (1995-96; 50G, 48A)
Most Points, Rookie, Season	*132	Teemu Selanne (1992-93; 76G, 56A)
Most Shutouts, Season	8	Nikolai Khabibulin (1998-99), Ilya Bryzgalov (2009-10)
Most Goals, Game	5	Willy Lindstrom (Mar. 2/82), Alexei Zhamnov (Apr. 1/95)
Most Assists, Game	5	Dale Hawerchuk (Mar. 6/84), (Mar. 18/89), (Mar. 4/90), Phil Housley (Jan. 18/93), Keith Tkachuk (Feb. 23/01)
Most Points, Game	6	Willy Lindstrom (Mar. 2/82; 5G, 1A), Dale Hawerchuk (Dec. 14/83; 3G, 3A), (Mar. 5/88; 2G, 4A), (Mar. 18/89; 1G, 5A), Thomas Steen (Oct. 24/84; 2G, 4A), Ed Olczyk (Dec. 21/91; 2G, 4A)

* NHL Record.

Records include Winnipeg Jets, 1979-80 through 1995-96.

Winnipeg Jets Retired Numbers

9	Bobby Hull	1972-1980
10	Dale Hawerchuk	1981-1990
25	Thomas Steen	1981-1995
27	Teppo Numminen	1988-2003

Captains' History

Lars-Erik Sjoberg, 1979-80; Morris Lukowich and Scott Campbell, 1980-81; Dave Christian and Barry Long, 1981-82; Dave Christian and Lucien DeBlois, 1982-83; Lucien DeBlois, 1983-84; Dale Hawerchuk, 1984-85 to 1988-89; Randy Carlyle, Dale Hawerchuk and Thomas Steen (tri-captains), 1989-90; Randy Carlyle and Thomas Steen (co-captains), 1990-91; Troy Murray, 1991-92; Troy Murray and Dean Kennedy, 1992-93; Dean Kennedy and Keith Tkachuk, 1993-94; Keith Tkachuk, 1994-95; Kris King, 1995-96; Keith Tkachuk, 1996-97 to 2000-01; Teppo Numminen, 2001-02, 2002-03; Shane Doan, 2003-04 to date.

All-time Record vs. Other Clubs

Regular Season

	At Home								On Road								Total							
	GP	W	L	T	OL	GF	GA	PTS	GP	W	L	T	OL	GF	GA	PTS	GP	W	L	T	OL	GF	GA	PTS
Anaheim	47	21	19	2	5	133	136	49	48	16	26	3	3	120	145	38	95	37	45	5	8	253	281	87
Atlanta	8	7	0	1	0	29	15	15	6	5	1	0	0	20	12	10	14	12	1	1	0	49	27	25
Boston	33	14	16	3	0	106	109	31	33	7	22	4	0	101	140	18	66	21	38	7	0	207	249	49
Buffalo	33	14	16	2	1	96	105	31	34	7	22	5	0	84	135	19	67	21	38	7	1	180	240	50
Calgary	82	40	31	11	0	297	277	91	83	29	44	9	1	257	329	68	165	69	75	20	1	554	606	159
Carolina	34	15	15	2	2	123	127	34	33	12	14	6	1	97	108	31	67	27	29	8	3	220	235	65
Chicago	62	33	22	5	2	196	191	73	60	17	31	10	2	148	217	46	122	50	53	15	4	344	408	119
Colorado	52	22	21	7	2	179	175	53	53	21	24	5	3	174	181	50	105	43	45	12	5	353	356	103
Columbus	20	12	5	3	0	60	42	27	20	11	8	1	0	52	50	23	40	23	13	4	0	112	92	50
Dallas	75	32	36	4	3	229	244	71	76	31	34	9	2	218	251	73	151	63	70	13	5	447	495	144
Detroit	61	20	25	14	2	178	200	56	63	22	31	8	2	206	242	54	124	42	56	22	4	384	442	110
Edmonton	83	35	41	5	2	324	347	77	84	25	51	6	2	267	363	58	167	60	92	11	4	591	710	135
Florida	13	5	3	3	2	36	37	15	10	6	4	0	0	27	31	12	23	11	7	3	2	63	68	27
Los Angeles	97	53	31	11	2	377	309	119	95	42	35	14	4	341	349	102	192	95	66	25	6	718	658	221
Minnesota	20	11	8	1	0	53	44	23	20	8	9	2	1	45	56	19	40	19	17	3	1	98	100	42
Montreal	31	9	15	7	0	98	120	25	32	3	26	2	1	71	154	9	63	12	41	9	1	169	274	34
Nashville	24	15	7	0	2	72	71	32	24	8	10	2	4	54	68	22	48	23	17	2	6	126	139	54
New Jersey	33	23	7	3	0	121	85	49	32	12	14	6	0	93	104	30	65	35	21	9	0	214	189	79
NY Islanders	33	13	15	4	1	111	117	31	33	10	15	8	0	99	122	28	66	23	30	12	1	210	239	59
NY Rangers	33	14	14	4	1	113	110	33	33	10	19	2	2	113	142	24	66	24	33	6	3	226	252	57
Ottawa	12	5	6	1	0	39	44	11	14	6	7	1	0	41	47	13	26	11	13	2	0	80	91	24
Philadelphia	33	15	16	2	0	106	107	32	34	10	23	0	1	92	142	21	67	25	39	2	1	198	249	53
Pittsburgh	34	15	14	3	2	125	119	35	33	11	22	0	0	91	129	22	67	26	36	3	2	216	248	57
St. Louis	63	33	23	7	0	201	195	73	62	21	29	11	1	170	206	54	125	54	52	18	1	371	401	127
San Jose	56	27	22	3	4	165	161	61	53	21	26	4	2	145	175	48	109	48	48	7	6	310	336	109
Tampa Bay	15	7	8	0	0	33	38	14	13	6	7	0	0	41	47	12	28	13	15	0	0	74	85	26
Toronto	42	23	13	6	0	177	147	52	45	23	20	2	0	171	163	48	87	46	33	8	0	348	310	100
Vancouver	81	39	30	10	2	288	280	90	84	23	51	10	0	226	306	56	165	62	81	20	2	514	586	146
Washington	33	17	9	7	0	118	114	41	33	9	18	5	1	90	125	24	66	26	27	12	1	208	239	65
Totals	**1243**	**589**	**488**	**131**	**35**	**4183**	**4066**	**1344**	**1243**	**432**	**643**	**135**	**33**	**3654**	**4539**	**1032**	**2486**	**1021**	**1131**	**266**	**68**	**7837**	**8605**	**2376**

Playoffs

	Series	W	L	GP	W	L	T	GF	GA	Last Mtg.	Rnd.	Result
Anaheim	1	0	1	7	3	4	0	17	17	1997	CQF	L 3-4
Calgary	3	2	1	13	7	6	0	45	43	1987	DSF	W 4-2
Colorado	1	0	1	5	1	4	0	10	17	2000	CQF	L 1-4
Detroit	4	0	4	23	7	16	0	56	88	2011	CQF	L 0-4
Edmonton	6	0	6	26	4	22	0	75	120	1990	DSF	L 3-4
St. Louis	2	0	2	11	4	7	0	29	39	1999	CQF	L 3-4
San Jose	1	0	1	5	1	4	0	7	13	2002	CQF	L 1-4
Vancouver	2	0	2	13	5	8	0	34	50	1993	DSF	L 2-4
Totals	**20**	**2**	**18**	**103**	**32**	**71**	**0**	**273**	**387**			

Calgary totals include Atlanta Flames, 1979-80.
Colorado totals include Quebec, 1979-80 to 1994-95.
New Jersey totals include Colorado Rockies, 1979-80 to 1981-82.
Carolina totals include Hartford, 1979-80 to 1996-97.
Dallas totals include Minnesota North Stars, 1979-80 to 1992-93.

Playoff Results 2011-2007

Year	Round	Opponent	Result	GF	GA
2011	CQF	Detroit	L 0-4	10	18
2010	CQF	Detroit	L 3-4	18	26

Abbreviations: Round: CQF – conference quarter-final; **DSF** – division semi-final.

2010-11 Results

Oct.	9	at Boston	5-2
	10	Boston	0-3
	16	Detroit	1-2*
	17	at Anaheim	2-3
	21	Los Angeles	4-2
	23	Carolina	3-4*
	25	at Montreal	2-3*
	26	at Ottawa	2-5
	28	at Detroit	4-2
	30	Tampa Bay	0-3
Nov.	3	Nashville	4-3
	5	at Dallas	3-6
	6	Pittsburgh	3-4†
	8	at Detroit	2-3*
	10	at Chicago	2-1
	12	Calgary	5-4
	13	St. Louis	5-3
	17	at Calgary	3-1
	19	at Edmonton	4-3†
	21	at Vancouver	3-2
	23	Edmonton	5-0
	27	Anaheim	4-6
	30	at Nashville	0-3
Dec.	1	at Minnesota	4-2
	4	Florida	1-2†
	5	at Anaheim	3-0
	9	Minnesota	2-3
	11	Dallas	5-2
	15	at New Jersey	0-3
	16	at NY Rangers	3-4†
	18	at NY Islanders	4-3†
	20	at Pittsburgh	1-6
	23	at San Jose	1-4
	26	at Dallas	1-0
	28	Anaheim	1-3
	29	Los Angeles	6-3
	31	at St. Louis	3-4
Jan.	2	at Minnesota	5-6*
	4	Columbus	4-2
	6	at Colorado	2-0
	8	Buffalo	1-2*
	10	at St. Louis	4-3
	11	at Columbus	4-3
	13	Toronto	5-1
	15	Anaheim	6-2
	17	San Jose	2-4
	18	Nashville	2-5
	20	at Los Angeles	2-0
	22	Los Angeles	3-4
	25	Edmonton	3-4
	26	at Colorado	5-2
Feb.	1	at San Jose	3-5
	2	Vancouver	0-6
	5	Minnesota	1-0
	7	Colorado	3-0
	9	at Dallas	3-2*
	12	Chicago	3-2†
	14	Washington	3-2
	17	Atlanta	4-3
	19	at Nashville	3-2
	22	at Philadelphia	3-2*
	23	at Tampa Bay	3-8
	25	at Columbus	3-5
	27	at Chicago	3-4†
Mar.	1	Dallas	2-3
	3	at Los Angeles	0-1
	5	Detroit	5-4†
	8	Vancouver	3-4*
	10	Calgary	3-0
	13	at Anaheim	5-2
	15	at Calgary	4-3
	17	at Edmonton	3-1
	18	at Vancouver	3-1
	20	Chicago	1-2
	22	St. Louis	2-1
	24	Columbus	3-0
	26	San Jose	1-4
	29	Dallas	2-1†
Apr.	1	Colorado	3-4†
	6	at Los Angeles	2-3†
	8	San Jose	4-3
	9	at San Jose	1-3

* – Overtime † – Shootout

Entry Draft Selections 2011-1997

Name in bold denotes played in NHL.

2011
Pick
- 20 Connor Murphy
- 51 Alexander Ruuttu
- 56 Lucas Lessio
- 84 Harrison Ruopp
- 111 Kale Kessy
- 141 Darian Dziurzynski
- 155 Andrew Fritsch
- 196 Zac Larraza

2010
Pick
- 13 Brandon Gormley
- 27 Mark Visentin
- 52 Philip Lane
- 57 Oscar Lindberg
- 138 Louis Domingue

2009
Pick
- 6 Oliver Ekman-Larsson
- 36 Chris Brown
- 91 Michael Lee
- 97 Jordan Szwarz
- 105 Jon Weller
- 157 Evan Bloodoff

2008
Pick
- 8 **Mikkel Boedker**
- 28 **Viktor Tikhonov**
- 49 Jared Staal
- 69 Michael Stone
- 76 Mathieu Brodeur
- 99 Colin Long
- 159 Brett Hextall
- 189 Tim Billingsley

2007
Pick
- 3 **Kyle Turris**
- 30 Nick Ross
- 32 **Brett Maclean**
- 36 Joel Gistedt
- 103 Vladimir Ruzicka
- 123 Maxim Goncharov
- 153 Scott Darling

2006
Pick
- 8 **Peter Mueller**
- 29 **Chris Summers**
- 88 Jonas Ahnelov
- 130 Brett Bennett
- 131 Martin Latal
- 152 Jordan Bendfeld
- 188 Chris Frank
- 196 **Benn Ferriero**

2005
Pick
- 17 **Martin Hanzal**
- 59 Pier-Olivier Pelletier
- 105 **Keith Yandle**
- 148 Anton Krysanov
- 212 Pat Brosnihan

2004
Pick
- 5 **Blake Wheeler**
- 35 Logan Stephenson
- 50 **Enver Lisin**
- 103 Roman Tomanek
- 119 **Kevin Porter**
- 168 Kevin Cormier
- 199 **Chad Kolarik**
- 240 **Aaron Gagnon**
- 261 Will Engasser
- 265 **Daniel Winnik**

2003
Pick
- 77 Tyler Redenbach
- 80 Dmitri Pestunov
- 115 Liam Lindstrom
- 178 Ryan Gibbons
- 208 Randall Gelech
- 242 Eduard Lewandowski
- 272 Sean Sullivan
- 290 Loic Burkhalter

2002
Pick
- 19 Jakub Koreis
- 23 **Ben Eager**
- 46 **David LeNeveu**
- 70 **Joe Callahan**
- 80 **Matt Jones**
- 97 Lance Monych
- 132 **John Zeiler**
- 186 Jeff Pietrasiak
- 216 Ladislav Kouba
- 249 Marcus Smith
- 280 Russell Spence

2001
Pick
- 11 **Fredrik Sjostrom**
- 31 **Matthew Spiller**
- 45 Martin Podlesak
- 78 Beat Forster
- 148 David Klema
- 180 Scott Polaski
- 210 Steve Belanger
- 243 Frantisek Lukes
- 273 Severin Blindenbacher

2000
Pick
- 19 **Krys Kolanos**
- 53 Alexander Tatarinov
- 85 **Ramzi Abid**
- 160 Nate Kiser
- 186 Brent Gauvreau
- 217 Igor Samoilov
- 249 Sami Venalainen
- 281 Peter Fabus

1999
Pick
- 15 Scott Kelman
- 19 **Kirill Safronov**
- 53 **Brad Ralph**
- 71 **Jason Jaspers**
- 116 Ryan Lauzon
- 123 Preston Mizzi
- 168 Erik Lewerstrom
- 234 **Goran Bezina**
- 262 Alexei Litvinenko

1998
Pick
- 14 **Patrick DesRochers**
- 43 **Ossi Vaananen**
- 73 Pat O'Leary
- 100 Ryan Vanbuskirk
- 115 **Jay Leach**
- 116 Josh Blackburn
- 129 **Robert Schnabel**
- 160 **Rickard Wallin**
- 187 **Erik Westrum**
- 214 Justin Hansen

1997
Pick
- 43 Juha Gustafsson
- 96 Scott McCallum
- 123 Curtis Suter
- 151 Robert Francz
- 207 Alexander Andreyev
- 233 **Wyatt Smith**

Club Directory

Jobing.com Arena

Phoenix Coyotes
6751 N. Sunset Blvd. #200
Glendale, AZ 85305
Phone **623/772-3200**
FAX 623/872-2000
Tickets 480/563-PUCK

Jobing.com Arena
9400 W. Maryland Avenue
Glendale, AZ 85305
Phone 623/772-3200
FAX 623/772-3201
www.PhoenixCoyotes.com
Capacity: 17,125

Club Officers and Executives
Chief Operating Officer & Alt. Governor	Mike Nealy
Executive Vice President, G.M. & Alt. Gov.	Don Maloney
Vice President of Hockey Ops & Asst. G.M.	Brad Treliving
Executive Assistant to the C.O.O.	Cheryl Taylor

Hockey Operations
Head Coach	Dave Tippett
Associate Coach	Jim Playfair
Assistant Coach	John Anderson
Director, Player Develop./Goaltending Coach	Sean Burke
Development Coach	Dave King
Video Coach	Steve Peters
Power Skating Coach	Mark Ciaccio
Hockey Admin. Director/Manager	Chris O'Hearn
Manager of Hockey Administration	Kimberly Trichel
Head Athletic Trainer / Assistant Trainer	Jason Serbus / Mike Ermatinger
Strength & Conditioning Coordinator	Mike Bahn
Manual Therapist	Mike Griebel
Head Equipment Manager	Stan Wilson
Equipment Manager / Assistant Manager	Tony Silva / Jason Rudee
Manager of Team Services	Rick Braunstein
Scouting Directors, Amateur / Pro	Rick Knickle / Frank Effinger
Professional Scout	David MacLean
European & Amateur Scouts	Norm Gosselin, Rob Pulford, Jeff Twohey, Glen Zacharias
Hockey Operations Video Coordinator	Bob Teofilo
Team Services Coordinator/Security	Jim O'Neal
Team Internist	Robert Luberto, D.O.
Team Orthopedic Surgeons	Gary Waslewski, M.D., Amit Sahasrabudhe, M.D., Brian Shafer, M.D., Doug Freedberg, M.D.
Team Dentists	Byron J. Larsen, DDS, Rick Langrin, DDS, Larry Emmott, DDS
Team Opthamologists	Dr. George Reiss, Dr. Jeffrey Edelstein
Portland (AHL) Head Coach	Ray Edwards
Portland (AHL) Assistant Coach	John Slaney
Portland (AHL) Head Athletic Trainer	Mike Booi
Portland (AHL) Equipment Manager	John Krouse

Broadcasting
TV Play-by-Play Announcer	TBA
TV/Radio Color Analyst / Host	Tyson Nash / Todd Walsh
Radio Play-by-Play Announcer / Host	Bob Heethuis / Luke Lapinski
Director of Broadcasting/Production	Doug Cannon
Video Production Manager	Gannon Hubler
Senior Producer/Editor	Colin Kelly
Producer/Editor	Amanda Flanagan
Video Graphics/Editor	Stephen Mitchell

Communications
Senior Director of Communications	Richard Nairn
Media Relations, Sr. Manager / Manager	Chris Wojcik / Tim Bulmer

Community Relations
Director of Community Relations & Fan Development	Sarah Finecey
Manager, Charities & Community Relations	Maggie Wakeford
Community Relations Coordinator	Kevin West

Corporate Sales & Service
Sales Consultant	Tom Garrity
Corporate Partnerships Account Execs.	Casey Charpio, Brittany Grant, Jenni Hansen
Corporate Partnerships	Stacy Gewecke, Ryan Dastrup, Lindsay Foletta

Finance & Accounting
Vice President of Finance and Controller	Joe Leibfried
Assistant Controller	Burlenti Shaban
Senior Accountant / Purchasing Manager	Stephanie Johnson / John Dickey
Administrators, A/P / Payroll	Kathy Kelly / Marie Welsh

Game Operations
Event Presentation Mgr. / Field Producer	TBA

Human Resources
Vice President of Human Resources	Julie Atherton
Receptionist	Chris Osborne

Legal
Legal Counsel	Courtney Lewis
Exec. Support/Legal & Risk Mgmt. Coord.	Gail Avisar

Marketing
Director of Advertising & Media	Ted Santiago
Managers, New Media / Creative Services	Michael Sharer / Scott Jenner
Production Artist	Kelly Gladden

News Content
Senior Director of News Content	Dave Vest

Ticket Operations
Director of Ticket Operations	Douglas Vanderheyden

Ticket Sales & Service
Senior Director of Business Development	Grant Buckborough
Senior Business Development Executive	Mike Briody
Director of Consumer Development	Sean Ream
Manager of Customer Service	Lindsay Kray
Inside Sales Manager	Justin Brickner

Technology
Senior Director, IT / System Administrator	Jay Gaskin / Lynsey Downing

Arena Management Group
Senior Vice President & General Manager	Jim Foss

Team Information
Regional Sports Network / Radio Station	FOX Sports Arizona / KGME XTRA Sports 910

Dave Tippett
Head Coach

Born: Moosomin, Sask., August 25, 1961.

Dave Tippett was named the 17th head coach in Coyotes/Jets history on September 24, 2009. In his first season with the team in 2009-10, he led the Coyotes to a club-record 50 wins and 107 points and the team's first playoff appearance since 2001-02. Tippett was rewarded with the Jack Adams Award as coach of the year.

Prior to Phoenix, Tippett spent seven seasons as the head coach of the Dallas Stars from 2002-03 to 2008-09. Under Tippett's leadership, the Stars won two Pacific Division titles (2002-03 and 2005-06), made the playoffs in five out of six years and reached the Western Conference Final in 2008. His 271 career regular-season coaching victories rank him second all-time in Stars history.

Tippett joined the Stars organization on May 16, 2002 after serving as an assistant coach with the Los Angeles Kings for three seasons. Prior to becoming a coach, Tippett played 11 years as a forward in the National Hockey League with the Hartford Whalers, Washington Capitals, Pittsburgh Penguins and Philadelphia Flyers. He ended his playing career in 1995 as a player-assistant coach with the Houston Aeros (IHL). Internationally, he captained the 1984 Canadian Olympic team in Sarajevo, Yugoslavia, and he earned a silver medal as a member of the Canadian Olympic team in Albertville, France, in 1992. He was a member of the 1982 NCAA Division I championship squad at the University of North Dakota with former Stars defenseman Craig Ludwig. Tippett became head coach of the Houston Aeros in 1995-96. In 1999, he led the team to the Turner Cup championship and was named the IHL coach of the year.

Coaching Record

Season	Team	League	GC	W	L	O/T	GC	W	L	T
				Regular Season				**Playoffs**		
1995-96	Houston	IHL	42	17	18	7	....	....	....	....
1996-97	Houston	IHL	82	44	30	8	13	8	5	....
1997-98	Houston	IHL	82	50	22	10	4	1	3	....
1998-99	Houston	IHL	82	54	15	13	19	11	8	....
2002-03	Dallas	NHL	82	46	17	19	12	6	6	....
2003-04	Dallas	NHL	82	41	26	15	5	1	4	....
2004-05	Dallas					SEASON CANCELLED				
2005-06	Dallas	NHL	82	53	23	6	5	1	4	....
2006-07	Dallas	NHL	82	50	25	7	7	3	4	....
2007-08	Dallas	NHL	82	45	30	7	18	10	8	....
2008-09	Dallas	NHL	82	36	35	11				
2009-10	Phoenix	NHL	82	50	25	7	7	3	4	....
2010-11	Phoenix	NHL	82	46	30	6	6	2	4	....
NHL Totals			656	367	211	78	60	26	34	....

Won Jack Adams Award (2010)

Posted a 2-1-2 record as replacement coach when Andy Murray was sidelined following a car accident, February 26 to March 6, 2002, All games are credited to Murray's coaching record.

Pittsburgh Penguins

Key Off-Season Signings/Acquisitions

2011

June	9	• Re-signed RW **Craig Adams**.
	28	• Re-signed RW **Pascal Dupuis**.
	29	• Re-signed RW **Arron Asham**.
July	1	• Re-signed C **Tyler Kennedy**.
	1	• Signed LW **Steve Sullivan**.
	3	• Signed D **Boris Valabik**.
	5	• Signed D **Alexandre Picard**.
	12	• Re-signed LW **Dustin Jeffrey**.
	26	• Signed C **Jason Williams**.

2010-11 Results: 49W-25L-5OTL-3SOL 106PTS.
Second, Atlantic Division

Pittsburgh's Kris Letang ranked among the NHL's top defensemen with a career-best 42 assists and 50 points in 2010-11. He led the Penguins in ice time with 24:02 minutes per game and topped all club blueliners with a plus-minus rating of +15.

2011-12 Schedule

Oct.	Thu.	6	at Vancouver
	Sat.	8	at Calgary
	Sun.	9	at Edmonton
	Tue.	11	Florida
	Thu.	13	Washington
	Sat.	15	Buffalo
	Mon.	17	at Winnipeg
	Tue.	18	at Minnesota
	Thu.	20	Montreal
	Sat.	22	New Jersey
	Tue.	25	at NY Islanders
	Thu.	27	NY Islanders
	Sat.	29	at Toronto
Nov.	Thu.	3	at San Jose
	Sat.	5	at Los Angeles
	Fri.	11	Dallas
	Sat.	12	at Carolina
	Tue.	15	Colorado
	Thu.	17	at Tampa Bay
	Sat.	19	at Florida
	Mon.	21	NY Islanders
	Wed.	23	St. Louis
	Fri.	25	Ottawa
	Sat.	26	at Montreal
	Tue.	29	at NY Rangers
Dec.	Thu.	1	at Washington
	Sat.	3	at Carolina
	Mon.	5	Boston
	Thu.	8	at Philadelphia
	Sat.	10	at NY Islanders
	Tue.	13	Detroit
	Fri.	16	at Ottawa
	Sat.	17	Buffalo
	Tue.	20	Chicago
	Fri.	23	at Winnipeg
	Tue.	27	Carolina
	Thu.	29	Philadelphia
	Sat.	31	at New Jersey*
Jan.	Fri.	6	NY Rangers
	Sat.	7	New Jersey
	Tue.	10	Ottawa

	Wed.	11	at Washington
	Fri.	13	at Florida
	Sun.	15	at Tampa Bay*
	Tue.	17	Carolina
	Thu.	19	at NY Rangers
	Fri.	20	Montreal
	Sun.	22	Washington*
	Tue.	24	at St. Louis
	Tue.	31	Toronto
Feb.	Wed.	1	at Toronto
	Sat.	4	at Boston*
	Sun.	5	at New Jersey*
	Tue.	7	at Montreal
	Sat.	11	Winnipeg*
	Sun.	12	Tampa Bay
	Wed.	15	Anaheim
	Sat.	18	at Philadelphia*
	Sun.	19	at Buffalo*
	Tue.	21	NY Rangers
	Sat.	25	Tampa Bay*
	Sun.	26	Columbus*
	Wed.	29	at Dallas
Mar.	Sat.	3	at Colorado
	Mon.	5	Phoenix
	Wed.	7	Toronto
	Fri.	9	Florida
	Sun.	11	Boston
	Thu.	15	at NY Rangers
	Sat.	17	at New Jersey*
	Sun.	18	at Philadelphia*
	Tue.	20	Winnipeg
	Thu.	22	Nashville
	Sat.	24	at Ottawa
	Sun.	25	New Jersey
	Tue.	27	NY Islanders
	Thu.	29	at NY Islanders
	Fri.	30	at Buffalo
Apr.	Sun.	1	Philadelphia
	Tue.	3	at Boston
	Thu.	5	NY Rangers
	Sat.	7	Philadelphia*

* Denotes afternoon game.

Year-by-Year Record

		Home				Road				Overall							
Season	GP	W	L	T	OL	W	L	T	OL	W	L	T	OL	GF	GA	Pts.	Finished	Playoff Result
2010-11	82	25	14	....	2	24	11	....	6	49	25	....	8	238	199	106	2nd, Atlantic Div.	Lost Conf. Quarter-Final
2009-10	82	25	12	....	4	22	16	....	3	47	28	....	7	257	237	101	2nd, Atlantic Div.	Lost Conf. Semi-Final
2008-09	**82**	**25**	**13**	**....**	**3**	**20**	**15**	**....**	**6**	**45**	**28**	**....**	**9**	**264**	**239**	**99**	**2nd, Atlantic Div.**	**Won Stanley Cup**
2007-08	82	26	10	....	5	21	17	....	3	47	27	....	8	247	216	102	1st, Atlantic Div.	Lost Final
2006-07	82	26	10	....	5	21	14	....	6	47	24	....	11	277	246	105	5th, Atlantic Div.	Lost Conf. Quarter-Final
2005-06	82	12	21	....	8	10	25	....	6	22	46	....	14	244	316	58	5th, Atlantic Div.	Out of Playoffs
2004-05	....	....	....	....	....	....	....	....	....	....	....	....	....	....	....	....		
2003-04	82	13	22	6	0	10	25	2	4	23	47	8	4	190	303	58	5th, Atlantic Div.	Out of Playoffs
2002-03	82	15	22	2	2	12	22	4	3	27	44	6	5	189	255	65	5th, Atlantic Div.	Out of Playoffs
2001-02	82	16	20	4	1	12	21	4	4	28	41	8	5	198	249	69	5th, Atlantic Div.	Out of Playoffs
2000-01	82	24	15	2	0	18	13	7	3	42	28	9	3	281	256	96	3rd, Atlantic Div.	Lost Conf. Championship
1999-2000	82	23	11	7	0	14	20	1	6	37	31	8	6	241	236	88	3rd, Atlantic Div.	Lost Conf. Semi-Final
1998-99	82	21	10	10	....	17	20	4	....	38	30	14	....	242	225	90	3rd, Atlantic Div.	Lost Conf. Semi-Final
1997-98	82	21	10	10	....	19	14	8	....	40	24	18	....	228	188	98	1st, Northeast Div.	Lost Conf. Quarter-Final
1996-97	82	25	11	5	....	13	25	3	....	38	36	8	....	285	280	84	2nd, Northeast Div.	Lost Conf. Quarter-Final
1995-96	82	32	9	0	....	17	20	4	....	49	29	4	....	362	284	102	1st, Northeast Div.	Lost Conf. Championship
1994-95	48	18	5	1	....	11	11	2	....	29	16	3	....	181	158	61	2nd, Northeast Div.	Lost Conf. Semi-Final
1993-94	84	25	9	8	....	19	18	5	....	44	27	13	....	299	285	101	1st, Northeast Div.	Lost Conf. Quarter-Final
1992-93	84	32	6	4	....	24	15	3	....	56	21	7	....	367	268	119	1st, Patrick Div.	Lost Div. Final
1991-92	**80**	**21**	**13**	**6**	**....**	**18**	**19**	**3**	**....**	**39**	**32**	**9**	**....**	**343**	**308**	**87**	**3rd, Patrick Div.**	**Won Stanley Cup**
1990-91	**80**	**25**	**12**	**3**	**....**	**16**	**21**	**3**	**....**	**41**	**33**	**6**	**....**	**342**	**305**	**88**	**1st, Patrick Div.**	**Won Stanley Cup**
1989-90	80	22	15	3	....	10	25	5	....	32	40	8	....	318	359	72	5th, Patrick Div.	Out of Playoffs
1988-89	80	24	13	3	....	16	20	4	....	40	33	7	....	347	349	87	2nd, Patrick Div.	Lost Div. Final
1987-88	80	22	12	6	....	14	23	3	....	36	35	9	....	319	316	81	6th, Patrick Div.	Out of Playoffs
1986-87	80	19	15	6	....	11	23	6	....	30	38	12	....	297	290	72	5th, Patrick Div.	Out of Playoffs
1985-86	80	20	15	5	....	14	23	3	....	34	38	8	....	313	305	76	5th, Patrick Div.	Out of Playoffs
1984-85	80	17	20	3	....	7	31	2	....	24	51	5	....	276	385	53	6th, Patrick Div.	Out of Playoffs
1983-84	80	7	29	4	....	9	29	2	....	16	58	6	....	254	390	38	6th, Patrick Div.	Out of Playoffs
1982-83	80	14	22	4	....	4	31	5	....	18	53	9	....	257	394	45	6th, Patrick Div.	Out of Playoffs
1981-82	80	21	11	8	....	10	25	5	....	31	36	13	....	310	337	75	4th, Patrick Div.	Lost Div. Semi-Final
1980-81	80	21	16	3	....	9	21	10	....	30	37	13	....	302	345	73	3rd, Norris Div.	Lost Prelim. Round
1979-80	80	20	13	7	....	10	24	6	....	30	37	13	....	251	303	73	3rd, Norris Div.	Lost Prelim. Round
1978-79	80	23	12	5	....	13	19	8	....	36	31	13	....	281	279	85	2nd, Norris Div.	Lost Quarter-Final
1977-78	80	16	15	9	....	9	22	9	....	25	37	18	....	254	321	68	4th, Norris Div.	Out of Playoffs
1976-77	80	22	12	6	....	12	21	7	....	34	33	13	....	240	252	81	3rd, Norris Div.	Lost Prelim. Round
1975-76	80	23	11	6	....	12	22	6	....	35	33	12	....	339	303	82	3rd, Norris Div.	Lost Prelim. Round
1974-75	80	25	5	10	....	12	23	5	....	37	28	15	....	326	289	89	3rd, Norris Div.	Lost Quarter-Final
1973-74	78	15	18	6	....	13	23	3	....	28	41	9	....	242	273	65	5th, West Div.	Out of Playoffs
1972-73	78	24	11	4	....	8	26	5	....	32	37	9	....	257	265	73	5th, West Div.	Out of Playoffs
1971-72	78	18	15	6	....	8	23	8	....	26	38	14	....	220	258	66	4th, West Div.	Lost Quarter-Final
1970-71	78	18	12	9	....	3	25	11	....	21	37	20	....	221	240	62	6th, West Div.	Out of Playoffs
1969-70	76	17	13	8	....	9	25	4	....	26	38	12	....	182	238	64	2nd, West Div.	Lost Semi-Final
1968-69	76	12	20	6	....	8	25	5	....	20	45	11	....	189	252	51	5th, West Div.	Out of Playoffs
1967-68	74	15	12	10	....	12	22	3	....	27	34	13	....	195	216	67	5th, West Div.	Out of Playoffs

ATLANTIC DIVISION
45th NHL Season

Franchise date: June 5, 1967

2011-12 Player Personnel

FORWARDS	HT	WT	S	Place of Birth	*Age	2010-11 Club
ADAMS, Craig	6-0	197	R	Seria, Brunei	34	Pittsburgh
ASHAM, Arron	5-11	205	R	Portage La Prairie, Man.	33	Pittsburgh
COOKE, Matt	5-11	205	L	Belleville, Ont.	33	Pittsburgh
CRAIG, Ryan	6-1	215	L	Abbotsford, B.C.	29	Pittsburgh-Wilkes-Barre
CROSBY, Sidney	5-11	200	L	Cole Harbour, N.S.	24	Pittsburgh
DUPUIS, Pascal	6-1	205	L	Laval, Que.	32	Pittsburgh
GIBBONS, Brian	5-8	165	L	Braintree, MA	23	Boston College
JEFFREY, Dustin	6-1	205	L	Sarnia, Ont.	23	Pittsburgh-Wilkes-Barre
JOHNSON, Nick	6-1	183	R	Calgary, Alta.	25	Pittsburgh-Wilkes-Barre
KENNEDY, Tyler	5-11	183	R	Sault Ste. Marie, Ont.	25	Pittsburgh
KUNITZ, Chris	6-0	193	L	Regina, Sask.	32	Pittsburgh
LETESTU, Mark	5-11	195	R	Elk Point, Alta.	26	Pittsburgh
MacINTYRE, Steve	6-5	250	L	Brock, Sask.	31	Edmonton
MALKIN, Evgeni	6-3	195	L	Magnitogorsk, USSR	25	Pittsburgh
McDONALD, Colin	6-2	190	R	New Haven, CT	27	Oklahoma City
NEAL, James	6-2	208	L	Whitby, Ont.	24	Dallas-Pittsburgh
PETERSEN, Nick	6-2	186	R	Wakefield, Que.	22	Wilkes-Barre-Wheeling
SILL, Zach	6-0	200	L	Truro, N.S.	23	Wilkes-Barre
STAAL, Jordan	6-4	220	L	Thunder Bay, Ont.	23	Pittsburgh
SULLIVAN, Steve	5-8	161	R	Timmins, Ont.	37	Nashville
TANGRADI, Eric	6-4	221	L	Philadelphia, PA	22	Pittsburgh-Wilkes-Barre
THOMPSON, Paul	6-0	210	R	Melrose, MA	22	New Hampshire-Wilkes-Barre
VEILLEUX, Keven	6-5	218	R	Saint-Renee, Que.	22	Wilkes-Barre
VITALE, Joe	5-11	205	R	St. Louis, MO	26	Pittsburgh-Wilkes-Barre
WILLIAMS, Jason	5-11	192	R	London, Ont.	31	Connecticut-Dallas
DEFENSEMEN						
BORTUZZO, Robert	6-3	196	R	Thunder Bay, Ont.	22	Wilkes-Barre
DESPRES, Simon	6-4	225	L	Laval, Que.	20	Saint John
ENGELLAND, Deryk	6-2	202	R	Edmonton, Alta.	29	Pittsburgh
GRANT, Alex	6-2	185	R	Antigonish, N.S.	22	Wilkes-Barre-Wheeling
LETANG, Kris	6-0	201	R	Montreal, Que.	24	Pittsburgh
LOVEJOY, Ben	6-2	215	R	Concord, NH	27	Pittsburgh
MARTIN, Paul	6-1	200	L	Minneapolis, MN	30	Pittsburgh
MICHALEK, Zbynek	6-2	210	R	Jindrichuv Hradec, Czech.	28	Pittsburgh
NISKANEN, Matt	6-0	200	R	Virginia, MN	24	Dallas-Pittsburgh
ORPIK, Brooks	6-2	219	L	San Francisco, CA	31	Pittsburgh
PICARD, Alexandre	6-3	215	L	Gatineau, Que.	26	Montreal
SAMUELSSON, Philip	6-3	198	L	Leksand, Sweden	20	Boston College
SNEEP, Carl	6-4	210	R	St. Louis Park, MN	23	Wilkes-Barre
STRAIT, Brian	6-1	200	L	Boston, MA	23	Pittsburgh-Wilkes-Barre
VALABIK, Boris	6-7	245	L	Nitra, Czech.	25	Chi (AHL)-Prov (AHL)

GOALTENDERS	HT	WT	C	Place of Birth	*Age	2010-11 Club
FLEURY, Marc-Andre	6-2	180	L	Sorel, Que.	26	Pittsburgh
JOHNSON, Brent	6-3	199	L	Farmington, MI	34	Pittsburgh
KILLEEN, Patrick	6-4	194	L	Almonte, Ont.	21	Wilkes-Barre-Wheeling
MODIG, Mattias	6-0	163	L	Lulea, Sweden	24	Wheeling
MUNROE, Scott	6-2	210	L	Moose Jaw, Sask.	29	Nizhnekamsk
THIESSEN, Brad	6-0	180	L	Aldergrove, B.C.	25	Wilkes-Barre

* – Age at start of 2011-12 season

Ray Shero

Executive Vice President and General Manager

Born: St. Paul, MN, July 28, 1962.

The Pittsburgh Penguins signed Ray Shero to a five-year contract as their new general manager on May 25, 2006. His fresh ideas and calm but firm management style helped transform the Penguins organization in his first year on the job as the team made the playoffs in 2006-07 for the first time since 2000-01. In 2007-08 the team posted the second-best record in the Eastern Conference and advanced to the Stanley Cup Finals. They won the Stanley Cup in 2009. Shero is the son of the late Fred Shero, who coached the Philadelphia Flyers for seven years and led them to back-to-back Stanley Cup championships in 1973-74 and 1974-75. Fred Shero also was g.m. and coach of the New York Rangers from 1978 to 1980. Ray Shero played college hockey at St. Lawrence University, serving twice as team captain, and was drafted by the Los Angeles Kings in 1982. He worked as a player agent for seven years before entering NHL management.

Before joining the Penguins, Shero had been assistant general manager of the Nashville Predators for eight seasons, working closely with Predators g.m. David Poile on all aspects of the club's hockey operations. His specific responsibilities included scouting at the amateur and professional levels, contract negotiations, and personnel matters such as arbitration, in addition to overseeing operations of the Predators top minor-league affiliate, the Milwaukee Admirals of the American Hockey League. Before joining the Predators organization, Shero spent six seasons as assistant general manager of the Ottawa Senators – joining the club in its second year of existence as an expansion team.

Both Ottawa and Nashville made significant improvement during Shero's tenure as assistant g.m., building with youth while adhering to a budget and business plan. The Predators went 49-25-8 and established a club record with 106 points in 2005-06, qualifying for the Stanley Cup playoffs for the second straight season. They had the third-best record in the Western Conference and fifth-best in the NHL.

Shero also played an important role in the success of the Milwaukee Admirals, Nashville's top affiliate in the American Hockey League. In 2003-04, the Admirals led the AHL in wins (43) and points (102) and won the Calder Cup by defeating the Wilkes-Barre/Scranton Penguins in the league final. Milwaukee reached the Calder Cup Final again in 2005-06.

2010-11 Scoring

* – rookie

Regular Season

Pos	#	Player	Team	GP	G	A	Pts	TOI	+/–	PIM	PP	SH	GW	S	%
C	87	Sidney Crosby	PIT	41	32	34	66	21:55	20	31	10	1	3	161	19.9
D	58	Kris Letang	PIT	82	8	42	50	24:02	15	101	4	0	2	236	3.4
L	14	Chris Kunitz	PIT	66	23	25	48	18:16	18	47	7	1	2	133	17.3
L	18	James Neal	DAL	59	21	18	39	17:41	8	60	5	0	3	160	13.1
			PIT	20	1	5	6	16:53	–1	6	0	0	0	52	1.9
			Total	79	22	23	45	17:29	7	66	5	0	3	212	10.4
C	48	Tyler Kennedy	PIT	80	21	24	45	14:31	1	37	7	0	2	234	9.0
L	9	Pascal Dupuis	PIT	81	17	20	37	16:51	16	59	0	4	3	171	9.9
C	71	Evgeni Malkin	PIT	43	15	22	37	19:49	–4	18	5	0	3	182	8.2
R	72	Alex Kovalev	OTT	54	14	13	27	16:16	–9	28	6	0	3	123	11.4
			PIT	20	2	5	7	17:10	3	16	0	0	0	28	7.1
			Total	74	16	18	34	16:30	–6	44	6	0	3	151	10.6
L	24	Matt Cooke	PIT	67	12	18	30	15:38	14	129	0	3	2	95	12.6
C	11	Jordan Staal	PIT	42	11	19	30	21:21	7	24	3	0	4	91	12.1
C	10 *	Mark Letestu	PIT	64	14	13	27	14:15	4	13	4	0	3	128	10.9
D	7	Paul Martin	PIT	77	3	21	24	23:21	9	16	2	0	1	104	2.9
C	25	Maxime Talbot	PIT	82	8	13	21	15:04	–3	66	0	2	2	117	6.8
D	4	Zbynek Michalek	PIT	73	5	14	19	21:50	0	30	1	0	2	104	4.8
C	17	Michael Rupp	PIT	81	9	8	17	10:03	–4	124	0	0	1	81	11.1
D	6	Ben Lovejoy	PIT	47	3	14	17	15:00	11	48	0	0	0	60	5.0
R	16	Chris Conner	PIT	60	7	9	16	11:49	5	10	0	0	3	91	7.7
R	27	Craig Adams	PIT	80	4	11	15	12:11	–5	76	0	2	1	90	4.4
D	44	Brooks Orpik	PIT	63	1	12	13	20:52	12	66	0	0	0	56	1.8
C	15 *	Dustin Jeffrey	PIT	25	7	5	12	12:58	5	4	1	0	1	39	17.9
R	45	Arron Asham	PIT	44	5	6	11	9:33	0	46	0	0	0	60	8.3
D	5	Deryk Engelland	PIT	63	3	7	10	13:20	–5	123	0	0	0	49	6.1
D	2	Matt Niskanen	DAL	45	0	6	6	15:44	–1	30	0	0	0	51	0.0
			PIT	18	1	3	4	18:30	–2	20	0	0	0	26	3.8
			Total	63	1	9	10	16:31	–3	50	0	0	0	77	1.3
C	19	Mike Comrie	PIT	21	1	5	6	11:49	–4	18	0	0	0	25	4.0
L	12	Brett Sterling	PIT	7	3	2	5	15:07	1	16	1	0	0	14	21.4
R	38 *	Nick Johnson	PIT	4	1	2	3	16:44	1	5	0	0	0	10	10
C	26 *	Eric Tangradi	PIT	15	1	2	3	11:12	–4	10	0	0	0	18	5.6
R	28	Eric Godard	PIT	19	0	3	3	5:10	4	105	0	0	0	1	0.0
C	46 *	Joe Vitale	PIT	9	1	1	2	10:34	–1	13	0	0	0	13	7.7
D	8	Andrew Hutchinson	PIT	5	0	1	1	15:18	–3	6	0	0	0	2	0.0
D	42	Corey Potter	PIT	1	0	0	0	16:43	0	0	0	0	0	1	0.0
D	37 *	Brian Strait	PIT	3	0	0	0	13:32	–1	0	0	0	0	0	0.0
R	22	Tim Wallace	PIT	7	0	0	0	8:03	–3	5	0	0	0	1	0.0
C	23	Ryan Craig	PIT	6	0	0	0	9:49	–3	22	0	0	0	7	0.0

Goaltending

No.	Goaltender	GPI	Mins	Avg	W	L	OT	EN	SO	GA	SA	S%	G	A	PIM
1	Brent Johnson	23	1297	2.17	13	5	3	1	1	47	604	.922	0	1	24
29	Marc-Andre Fleury	65	3695	2.32	36	20	5	5	3	143	1742	.918	0	1	10
	Totals	**82**	**5016**	**2.34**	**49**	**25**	**8**	**6**	**5**	**196**	**2352**	**.917**			

Brent Johnson and Marc-Andre Fleury shared a shutout vs. NYI on Feb. 2, 2011

Playoffs

Pos	#	Player	Team	GP	G	A	Pts	TOI	+/–	PIM	PP	SH	GW	OT	S	%
R	45	Arron Asham	PIT	7	3	1	4	10:00	2	2	0	0	0	0	8	37.5
C	25	Maxime Talbot	PIT	7	1	3	4	16:53	1	14	0	0	0	0	9	11.1
D	58	Kris Letang	PIT	7	0	4	4	26:32	0	10	0	0	0	0	28	0.0
C	48	Tyler Kennedy	PIT	7	2	1	3	17:32	0	2	1	0	1	0	33	6.1
C	11	Jordan Staal	PIT	7	1	2	3	21:28	–2	2	0	0	0	0	17	5.9
D	44	Brooks Orpik	PIT	7	0	3	3	24:11	–2	14	0	0	0	0	5	0.0
R	72	Alex Kovalev	PIT	7	1	1	2	16:02	–3	10	0	0	1	0	16	6.3
C	17	Michael Rupp	PIT	7	1	1	2	9:07	4	4	0	0	0	0	15	6.7
L	18	James Neal	PIT	7	1	1	2	17:25	–1	6	0	0	1	1	20	5.0
D	7	Paul Martin	PIT	7	0	2	2	24:42	1	2	0	0	0	0	10	0.0
D	6	Ben Lovejoy	PIT	7	0	2	2	10:54	0	4	0	0	0	0	8	0.0
L	14	Chris Kunitz	PIT	6	1	0	1	17:22	–1	6	0	0	0	0	13	7.7
R	27	Craig Adams	PIT	7	1	0	1	13:06	2	2	0	0	0	0	6	16.7
L	9	Pascal Dupuis	PIT	7	1	0	1	16:36	–2	2	0	0	0	0	16	6.3
R	16	Chris Conner	PIT	7	1	0	1	12:22	1	0	0	0	0	0	9	11.1
D	4	Zbynek Michalek	PIT	7	0	1	1	27:20	1	0	0	0	0	0	21	0.0
D	2	Matt Niskanen	PIT	7	0	1	1	12:58	–3	0	0	0	0	0	5	0.0
C	10 *	Mark Letestu	PIT	7	0	1	1	15:29	–3	0	0	0	0	0	16	0.0
C	26 *	Eric Tangradi	PIT	1	0	0	0	15:12	0	0	0	0	0	0	2	0.0

Goaltending

No.	Goaltender	GPI	Mins	Avg	W	L	EN	SO	GA	SA	S%	G	A	PIM
29	Marc-Andre Fleury	7	405	2.52	3	4	1	1	17	168	.899	0	0	0
1	Brent Johnson	1	34	7.06	0	0	0	0	4	11	.636	0	0	2
	Totals	**7**	**444**	**2.97**	**3**	**4**	**1**	**1**	**22**	**180**	**.878**			

Captains' History

Ab McDonald, 1967-68; Earl Ingarfield, 1968-69; no captain, 1968-69 to 1972-73; Ron Schock, 1973-74 to 1976-77; Jean Pronovost, 1977-78; Orest Kindrachuk, 1978-79 to 1980-81; Randy Carlyle, 1981-82 to 1983-84; Mike Bullard, 1984-85, 1985-86; Mike Bullard and Terry Ruskowski, 1986-87; Dan Frawley and Mario Lemieux, 1987-88; Mario Lemieux, 1988-89 to 1993-94; Ron Francis, 1994-95; Mario Lemieux, 1995-96, 1996-97; Ron Francis, 1997-98; Jaromir Jagr, 1998-99 to 2000-01; Mario Lemieux, 2001-02 to 2004-05; Mario Lemieux and no captain, 2005-06; no captain, 2006-07; Sidney Crosby, 2007-08 to date.

Coaching History

Red Sullivan, 1967-68, 1968-69; Red Kelly, 1969-70 to 1971-72; Red Kelly and Ken Schinkel, 1972-73; Ken Schinkel and Marc Boileau, 1973-74; Marc Boileau, 1974-75; Marc Boileau and Ken Schinkel, 1975-76; Ken Schinkel, 1976-77; Johnny Wilson, 1977-78 to 1979-80; Eddie Johnston, 1980-81 to 1982-83; Lou Angotti, 1983-84; Bob Berry, 1984-85 to 1986-87; Pierre Creamer, 1987-88; Gene Ubriaco, 1988-89; Gene Ubriaco and Craig Patrick, 1989-90; Bob Johnson, 1990-91; Scotty Bowman, 1991-92, 1992-93; Eddie Johnston, 1993-94 to 1995-96; Eddie Johnston and Craig Patrick, 1996-97; Kevin Constantine, 1997-98, 1998-99; Kevin Constantine and Herb Brooks, 1999-2000; Ivan Hlinka, 2000-01; Ivan Hlinka and Rick Kehoe, 2001-02; Rick Kehoe, 2002-03; Ed Olczyk, 2003-04, 2004-05; Ed Olczyk and Michel Therrien, 2005-06; Michel Therrien, 2006-07, 2007-08; Michel Therrien and Dan Bylsma, 2008-09; Dan Bylsma, 2009-10 to date.

Club Records

Team

(Figures in brackets for season records are games played; records for fewest points, wins, ties, losses, goals, goals against are for 70 or more games)

Record		
Most Points	119	1992-93 (84)
Most Wins	56	1992-93 (84)
Most Ties	20	1970-71 (78)
Most Losses	58	1983-84 (80)
Most Goals	367	1992-93 (84)
Most Goals Against	394	1982-83 (80)
Fewest Points	38	1983-84 (80)
Fewest Wins	16	1983-84 (80)
Fewest Ties	4	1995-96 (82)
Fewest Losses	21	1992-93 (84)
Fewest Goals	182	1969-70 (76)
Fewest Goals Against	188	1997-98 (82)
Longest Winning Streak		
Overall	*17	Mar. 9-Apr. 10/93
Home	11	Jan. 5-Mar. 7/91
Away	7	Mar. 14-Apr. 9/93, Oct. 3-Nov. 3/09, Nov. 6-Dec. 11/10
Longest Undefeated Streak		
Overall	18	Mar. 9-Apr. 14/93 (17 wins, 1 tie)
Home	20	Nov. 30/74-Feb. 22/75 (12 wins, 8 ties)
Away	8	Mar. 14-Apr. 14/93 (7 wins, 1 tie)
Longest Losing Streak		
Overall	18	Jan. 13-Feb. 22/04
Home	*14	Dec. 31/03-Feb. 22/04
Away	18	Dec. 23/82-Mar. 4/83
Longest Winless Streak		
Overall	18	Jan. 2-Feb. 10/83 (17 losses, 1 tie), Jan. 13-Feb. 22/04 (18 losses)
Home	16	Dec. 31/03-Mar. 4/04 (15 losses, 1 tie)
Away	18	Oct. 25/70-Jan. 14/71 (11 losses, 7 ties), Dec. 23/82-Mar. 4/83 (18 losses)
Most Shutouts, Season	9	1998-99 (82)
Most PIM, Season	2,670	1988-89 (80)
Most Goals, Game	12	Mar. 15/75 (Wsh. 1 at Pit. 12), Dec. 26/91 (Tor. 1 at Pit. 12)

Individual

Record		
Most Seasons	17	Mario Lemieux
Most Games	915	Mario Lemieux
Most Goals, Career	690	Mario Lemieux
Most Assists, Career	1,033	Mario Lemieux
Most Points, Career	1,723	Mario Lemieux (690G, 1,033A)
Most PIM, Career	1,048	Kevin Stevens
Most Shutouts, Career	22	Tom Barrasso
Longest Consecutive Games Streak	313	Ron Schock (Oct. 24/73-Apr. 3/77)
Most Goals, Season	85	Mario Lemieux (1988-89)
Most Assists, Season	114	Mario Lemieux (1988-89)
Most Points, Season	199	Mario Lemieux (1988-89; 85G, 114A)
Most PIM, Season	409	Paul Baxter (1981-82)
Most Points, Defenseman, Season	113	Paul Coffey (1988-89; 30G, 83A)
Most Points, Center, Season	199	Mario Lemieux (1988-89; 85G, 114A)
Most Points, Right Wing, Season	*149	Jaromir Jagr (1995-96; 62G, 87A)
Most Points, Left Wing, Season	123	Kevin Stevens (1991-92; 54G, 69A)
Most Points, Rookie, Season	102	Sidney Crosby (2005-06; 39G, 63A)
Most Shutouts, Season	7	Tom Barrasso (1997-98)
Most Goals, Game	5	Mario Lemieux (Dec. 31/88), (Apr. 9/93), (Mar. 26/96)
Most Assists, Game	6	Ron Stackhouse (Mar. 8/75); Greg Malone (Nov. 28/79); Mario Lemieux (Oct. 15/88), (Dec. 5/92), (Nov. 1/95)
Most Points, Game	8	Mario Lemieux (Oct. 15/88; 2G, 6A), (Dec. 31/88; 5G, 3A)

* NHL Record.

General Managers' History

Jack Riley, 1967-68 to 1969-70; Red Kelly, 1970-71; Red Kelly and Jack Riley, 1971-72; Jack Riley, 1972-73; Jack Riley and Jack Button, 1973-74; Jack Button, 1974-75; Wren Blair, 1975-76; Wren Blair and Baz Bastien, 1976-77; Baz Bastien, 1977-78 to 1982-83; Eddie Johnston, 1983-84 to 1987-88; Tony Esposito, 1988-89; Tony Esposito and Craig Patrick, 1989-90; Craig Patrick, 1990-91 to 2005-06; Ray Shero, 2006-07 to date.

Retired Numbers

21	Michel Brière	1969-1970
66	Mario Lemieux	1984-2006

All-time Record vs. Other Clubs

Regular Season

	At Home								On Road								Total							
	GP	W	L	T	OL	GF	GA	PTS	GP	W	L	T	OL	GF	GA	PTS	GP	W	L	T	OL	GF	GA	PTS
Anaheim	12	8	2	2	0	42	34	18	11	4	5	0	2	32	38	10	23	12	7	2	2	74	72	28
Atlanta	22	18	3	0	1	88	54	37	22	15	5	0	2	74	61	32	44	33	8	0	3	162	115	69
Boston	92	37	38	15	2	315	330	91	90	22	61	6	1	251	383	51	182	59	99	21	3	566	713	142
Buffalo	83	44	20	18	1	308	250	107	83	27	38	17	1	225	303	72	166	71	58	35	2	533	553	179
Calgary	47	26	11	10	0	175	137	62	48	13	27	8	0	146	207	34	95	39	38	18	0	321	344	96
Carolina	58	29	22	6	1	222	206	65	60	25	26	5	4	207	216	59	118	54	48	11	5	429	422	124
Chicago	61	30	23	7	1	216	196	68	63	12	40	10	1	165	247	35	124	42	63	17	2	381	443	103
Colorado	39	17	17	5	0	153	156	39	35	14	18	2	1	130	152	31	74	31	35	7	1	283	308	70
Columbus	6	4	2	0	0	22	17	8	7	4	2	0	1	24	25	9	13	8	4	0	1	46	42	17
Dallas	65	40	19	6	0	246	182	86	67	23	37	6	1	223	255	53	132	63	56	12	1	469	437	139
Detroit	69	46	19	4	0	287	202	96	69	15	41	12	1	192	269	43	138	61	60	16	1	479	471	139
Edmonton	33	17	13	3	0	128	135	37	32	9	22	1	0	105	152	19	65	26	35	4	0	233	287	56
Florida	35	20	11	3	1	107	98	44	34	15	16	1	2	85	100	33	69	35	27	4	3	192	198	77
Los Angeles	76	41	25	10	0	275	237	92	71	18	44	8	1	189	273	45	147	59	69	18	1	464	510	137
Minnesota	7	1	5	0	1	8	25	3	5	1	3	1	0	12	15	3	12	2	8	1	1	20	40	6
Montreal	94	34	45	13	2	280	327	83	94	17	63	10	4	244	421	48	188	51	108	23	6	524	748	131
Nashville	7	2	2	2	1	21	22	7	9	3	6	0	0	21	34	6	16	5	8	2	1	42	56	13
New Jersey	100	49	43	4	4	348	322	106	102	37	48	13	4	315	352	91	202	86	91	17	8	663	674	197
NY Islanders	109	57	36	14	2	414	358	130	107	42	53	8	4	353	418	96	216	99	89	22	6	767	776	226
NY Rangers	121	56	47	14	4	422	418	130	122	49	60	9	4	398	462	111	243	105	107	23	8	820	880	241
Ottawa	39	21	12	4	2	133	108	48	39	20	14	5	0	127	113	45	78	41	26	9	2	260	221	93
Philadelphia	127	58	47	22	0	447	406	138	127	29	86	8	4	331	517	70	254	87	133	30	4	778	923	208
Phoenix	33	22	11	0	0	129	91	44	34	16	15	3	0	119	125	35	67	38	26	3	0	248	216	79
St. Louis	66	33	21	12	0	244	195	78	67	16	42	6	3	177	254	41	133	49	63	18	3	421	449	119
San Jose	12	5	4	1	2	46	38	13	16	6	8	2	0	57	44	14	28	11	12	3	2	103	82	27
Tampa Bay	35	20	9	3	3	125	89	46	35	14	18	2	1	86	105	31	70	34	27	5	4	211	194	77
Toronto	81	42	32	6	1	323	264	91	79	29	35	11	4	259	312	73	160	71	67	17	5	582	576	164
Vancouver	53	34	12	7	0	233	179	75	52	24	23	4	1	191	187	53	105	58	35	11	1	424	366	128
Washington	95	52	35	7	1	362	303	112	98	39	47	9	3	352	399	90	193	91	82	16	4	714	702	202
Defunct Clubs	35	22	6	7	0	148	93	51	34	13	10	11	0	108	101	37	69	35	16	18	0	256	194	88
Totals	**1712**	**885**	**592**	**205**	**30**	**6267**	**5472**	**2005**	**1712**	**571**	**913**	**178**	**50**	**5198**	**6540**	**1370**	**3424**	**1456**	**1505**	**383**	**80**	**11465**	**12012**	**3375**

Playoffs

	Series	W	L	GP	W	L	T	GF	GA	Last Mtg.	Rnd.	Result
Boston	4	2	2	19	10	9	0	67	62	1992	CF	W 4-0
Buffalo	2	2	0	10	6	4	0	26	26	2001	CSF	W 4-3
Carolina	1	1	0	4	4	0	0	20	9	2009	CF	W 4-0
Chicago	2	1	1	8	4	4	0	23	24	1992	F	W 4-0
Dallas	1	1	0	6	4	2	0	28	16	1991	F	W 4-2
Detroit	2	1	1	13	6	7	0	24	34	2009	F	W 4-3
Florida	1	0	1	7	3	4	0	15	20	1996	CF	L 3-4
Montreal	2	0	2	13	5	8	0	33	37	2010	CSF	L 3-4
New Jersey	5	3	2	29	14	15	0	80	86	2001	CF	L 1-4
NY Islanders	3	0	3	19	8	11	0	58	67	1993	DF	L 3-4
NY Rangers	4	4	0	20	16	4	0	79	57	2008	CSF	W 4-1
Ottawa	3	2	1	15	9	6	0	50	42	2010	CQF	W 4-2
Philadelphia	5	2	3	29	14	15	0	89	91	2009	CQF	W 4-2
St. Louis	3	1	2	13	6	7	0	40	45	1981	PRE	L 2-3
Tampa Bay	1	0	1	7	3	4	0	14	22	2011	CQF	L 3-4
Toronto	3	0	3	12	4	8	0	27	39	1999	CSF	L 2-4
Washington	8	7	1	49	30	19	0	164	143	2009	CSF	W 4-3
Defunct Clubs	1	1	0	4	4	0	0	13	6			
Totals	**51**	**28**	**23**	**277**	**150**	**127**	**0**	**850**	**826**			

Playoff Results 2011-2007

Year	Round	Opponent	Result	GF	GA
2011	CQF	Tampa Bay	L 3-4	14	22
2010	CSF	Montreal	L 3-4	18	19
	CQF	Ottawa	W 4-2	24	19
2009	**F**	**Detroit**	**W 4-3**	**14**	**17**
	CF	Carolina	W 4-0	20	9
	CSF	Washington	W 4-3	27	22
	CQF	Philadelphia	W 4-2	18	16
2008	F	Detroit	L 2-4	10	17
	CF	Philadelphia	W 4-1	20	9
	CSF	NY Rangers	W 4-1	15	12
	CQF	Ottawa	W 4-0	16	5
2007	CQF	Ottawa	L 1-4	10	18

Abbreviations: Round: F – Final; **CF** – conference final; **CSF** – conference semi-final; **CQF** – conference quarter-final; **DF** – division final; **PRE** – preliminary round.

Calgary totals include Atlanta Flames, 1972-73 to 1979-80. Carolina totals include Hartford, 1979-80 to 1996-97.
Colorado totals include Quebec, 1979-80 to 1994-95. Dallas totals include Minnesota North Stars, 1967-68 to 1992-93.
New Jersey totals include Kansas City, 1974-75, 1975-76, and Colorado Rockies, 1976-77 to 1981-82.
Phoenix totals include Winnipeg, 1979-80 to 1995-96.

2010-11 Results

Month	Day	Opponent	Score
Oct.	7	Philadelphia	2-3
	9	Montreal	2-3
	11	at New Jersey	3-1
	13	Toronto	3-4
	15	NY Islanders	3-2*
	16	at Philadelphia	5-1
	18	Ottawa	5-2
	21	at Nashville	4-3*
	23	at St. Louis	0-1*
	27	at Tampa Bay	3-5
	29	Philadelphia	2-3
	30	at Carolina	3-0
Nov.	3	at Dallas	2-5
	5	at Anaheim	2-3
	6	at Phoenix	4-3†
	10	Boston	4-7
	12	Tampa Bay	5-1
	13	at Atlanta	4-2
	15	NY Rangers	2-3*
	17	Vancouver	3-1
	19	Carolina	5-4†
	22	at Florida	3-2
	24	at Buffalo	1-0
	26	Ottawa	2-1
	27	Calgary	4-1
	29	at NY Rangers	3-1
Dec.	2	Atlanta	3-2
	4	at Columbus	7-2
	6	New Jersey	2-1
	8	Toronto	5-2
	11	at Buffalo	5-2
	14	at Philadelphia	2-3
	15	NY Rangers	1-4
	20	Phoenix	6-1
	22	Florida	5-2
	23	at Washington	3-2†
	26	at Ottawa	1-3
	28	Atlanta	6-3
	29	at NY Islanders	1-2†
Jan.	1	Washington	1-3
	5	Tampa Bay	8-1
	6	at Montreal	1-2†
	8	Minnesota	0-4
	10	Boston	2-4
	12	at Montreal	5-2
	15	at Boston	3-2
	18	Detroit	4-1
	20	at New Jersey	0-2
	22	Carolina	3-2
	25	NY Islanders	1-0
Feb.	1	at NY Rangers	4-3†
	2	NY Islanders	3-0
	4	Buffalo	3-2
	6	at Washington	0-3
	8	Columbus	1-4
	10	Los Angeles	2-1*
	11	at NY Islanders	3-9
	13	at NY Rangers	3-5
	16	at Colorado	3-2*
	20	at Chicago	2-3†
	21	Washington	0-1
	23	San Jose	2-3*
	25	at Carolina	1-4
	26	at Toronto	6-5†
Mar.	2	at Toronto	2-3*
	4	at New Jersey	1-2*
	5	at Boston	3-2*
	8	Buffalo	3-1
	12	Montreal	0-3
	13	Edmonton	5-1
	15	at Ottawa	5-1
	20	NY Rangers	2-5
	21	at Detroit	5-4†
	24	at Philadelphia	2-1†
	25	New Jersey	1-0†
	27	Florida	2-1†
	29	Philadelphia	2-5
	31	at Tampa Bay	1-2
Apr.	2	at Florida	4-2
	5	New Jersey	4-2
	8	at NY Islanders	4-3†
	10	at Atlanta	5-2

* – Overtime † – Shootout

Entry Draft Selections 2011-1997

Name in bold denotes played in NHL.

2011
Pick
23 Joe Morrow
54 Scott Harrington
144 Dominik Uher
174 Josh Archibald
209 Scott Wilson

2010
Pick
20 Beau Bennett
80 Bryan Rust
110 Tom Kuhnhackl
140 Kenneth Agostino
152 Joe Rogalski
170 Reid McNeill

2009
Pick
30 Simon Despres
61 Philip Samuelsson
63 Ben Hanowski
121 Nick Petersen
123 Alex Velischek
151 Andy Bathgate
181 Viktor Ekbom

2008
Pick
120 Nathan Moon
150 **Alexander Pechurski**
180 Patrick Killeen
210 Nicholas D'Agostino

2007
Pick
20 Angelo Esposito
51 Keven Veilleux
78 Robert Bortuzzo
80 Casey Pierro-Zabotel
111 **Luca Caputi**
118 Alex Grant
141 **Jake Muzzin**
171 **Dustin Jeffrey**

2006
Pick
2 **Jordan Staal**
32 Carl Sneep
65 **Brian Strait**
125 **Chad Johnson**
185 Timo Seppanen

2005
Pick
1 **Sidney Crosby**
61 Michael Gergen
62 **Kris Letang**
125 Tommi Leinonen
126 Tim Crowder
194 Jean-Philippe Paquet
195 **Joe Vitale**

2004
Pick
2 **Evgeni Malkin**
31 Johannes Salmonsson
61 **Alex Goligoski**
67 **Nick Johnson**
85 Brian Gifford
99 **Tyler Kennedy**
130 Michal Sersen
164 Moises Gutierrez
194 Chris Peluso
222 Jordan Morrison
228 David Brown
259 Brian Ihnacak

2003
Pick
1 **Marc-Andre Fleury**
32 **Ryan Stone**
70 **Jonathan Filewich**
73 **Daniel Carcillo**
121 **Paul Bissonnette**
161 Evgeni Isakov
169 Lukas Bolf
199 **Andy Chiodo**
229 Stephen Dixon
232 **Joe Jensen**
263 **Matt Moulson**

2002
Pick
5 **Ryan Whitney**
35 Ondrej Nemec
69 **Erik Christensen**
101 Daniel Fernholm
136 Andrew Sertich
137 **Cam Paddock**
171 Robert Goepfert
202 Patrik Baertschi
234 **Maxime Talbot**
239 Ryan Lannon
265 Dwight Labrosse

2001
Pick
21 **Colby Armstrong**
54 **Noah Welch**
86 **Drew Fata**
96 Alexandre Rouleau
120 **Tomas Surovy**
131 Ben Eaves
156 Andy Schneider
217 Tomas Duba
250 Brandon Crawford-West

2000
Pick
18 **Brooks Orpik**
52 **Shane Endicott**
84 Peter Hamerlik
124 **Michel Ouellet**
146 **David Koci**
185 Patrick Foley
216 Jim Abbott
248 Steve Crampton
273 **Roman Simicek**
280 Nick Boucher

1999
Pick
18 **Konstantin Koltsov**
51 **Matt Murley**
57 Jeremy Van Hoof
86 **Sebastien Caron**
115 **Ryan Malone**
144 Tomas Skvaridlo
157 Vladimir Malenkykh
176 Doug Meyer
204 **Tom Kostopoulos**
233 Darcy Robinson
261 Andrew McPherson

1998
Pick
23 **Milan Kraft**
54 Alexander Zevakhin
80 David Cameron
110 Scott Myers
134 **Rob Scuderi**
169 Jan Fadrny
196 Joel Scherban
224 Mika Lehto
244 **Toby Petersen**
254 **Matt Hussey**

1997
Pick
17 **Robert Dome**
44 Brian Gaffaney
71 **Josef Melichar**
97 Alexandre Mathieu
124 Harlan Pratt
152 Petr Havelka
179 Mark Moore
208 **Andrew Ference**
234 Eric Lind

Dan Bylsma

Head Coach

Born: Grand Haven, MI, September 19, 1970.

Dan Bylsma was named interim head coach of the Pittsburgh Penguins on February 15, 2009 and had the interim tag removed on April 28. He took over a Penguins team that was six points out of a playoff spot with 25 games to go and guided them to the Stanley Cup. Bylsma was the 14th rookie head coach, and just the fourth in 50 years, to win the Stanley Cup. Of these, only Montreal's Al MacNeil (1970-71) took over in midseason. In 2010-11 he won the Jack Adams Award as coach of the year for guiding an injury-riddled Penguins club to a 49 wins and 106 points.

Bylsma played nine NHL seasons as a right winger with Los Angeles and Anaheim from 1995 to 2004. A role player who excelled at killing penalties and blocking shots, he played 429 NHL regular-season games and also played in the 2003 Stanley Cup Final with Anaheim. He retired as a player following the 2003-04 season. The native of Grand Haven, Michigan began his coaching career as an assistant with the Cincinnati Mighty Ducks of the AHL in 2004-05. He made his NHL coaching debut as an assistant with the New York Islanders in 2005-06.

Bylsma joined the Penguins organization as an assistant to Todd Richards in Wilkes-Barre/Scranton in 2006-07. The Baby Penguins won the AHL East Division and Eastern Conference championships in 2007-08 and advanced to the Calder Cup Final. When Richards accepted the job as an assistant coach with the NHL's San Jose Sharks in the offseason, Bylsma was elevated to head coach at Wilkes-Barre/Scranton.

Bylsma was an outstanding athlete at West Michigan Christian High School, winning a state individual golf championship and starting in left field on a state championship baseball team. He played Junior B hockey for St. Mary's of the Ontario Hockey Association before playing four years of college hockey at Bowling Green. He was twice selected to the Central Collegiate Hockey Association (CCHA) All-Academic Team. Dan and his father, Jay, also have written four books about sports for kids and families, including "So Your Son Wants to Play in the NHL" and "So You Want to Play in the NHL." He operates Dan Bylsma's Western Michigan Hockey Camp and has established the Dan Bylsma Charitable Trust Fund, which provides a means to assist children with the high cost of participating in youth sports, especially hockey.

Coaching Record

			Regular Season				Playoffs			
Season	Team	League	GC	W	L	O/T	GC	W	L	T
2008-09	Wilkes-Barre	AHL	55	36	16	3	....	....	....	....
2008-09♦	**Pittsburgh**	**NHL**	**25**	**18**	**3**	**4**	**24**	**16**	**8**	....
2009-10	**Pittsburgh**	**NHL**	**82**	**47**	**28**	**7**	**13**	**7**	**6**	....
2010-11	**Pittsburgh**	**NHL**	**82**	**49**	**25**	**8**	**7**	**3**	**4**	....
	NHL Totals		**189**	**114**	**56**	**19**	**44**	**26**	**18**	....

♦ Stanley Cup win.
Jack Adams Award (2011)

Club Directory

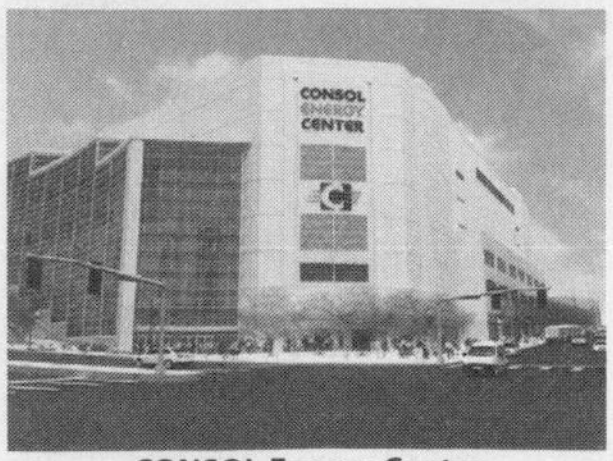

CONSOL Energy Center

Pittsburgh Penguins
CONSOL Energy Center
1001 Fifth Avenue
Pittsburgh, PA 15219
Phone **412/642-1300**
PR FAX 412/255-1988
www.pittsburghpenguins.com
Capacity: 18,087

Executive

CEO/President	David Morehouse
COO/General Council	Travis Williams
Vice President & Controller	Kevin Hart
Vice President, Communications	Tom McMillan
Director, Government Affairs	Abass Kamara
Executive Assistants	Amber Auchey, Kimberly Wood
Shipping/Receiving Coordinator / Receptionist	Brett Hart / Kelly Hart

Hockey Operations

Executive V.P./General Manager	Ray Shero
Assistant General Manager	Jason Botterill
Assistant to the General Manager	Tom Fitzgerald
Head Coach	Dan Bylsma
Assistant Coaches	Tony Granato, Todd Reirden
Goaltending Coach	Gilles Meloche
AHL Head Coach / Assistant Coach	John Hynes / Alain Nasreddine
Strength & Conditioning Coach	Michael Kadar
Player Development Coach	Bill Guerin
Goaltender Development Coach	Mike Bales
Sr. Director, Team Operations	Frank Buonomo
Hockey Operations Assistant	Erik Heasley
Video Coordinator	Jim Britt
Head Athletic Trainer / Asst. Trainer	Chris Stewart / Scott Adams
Head Equipment Manager / Asst. Managers	Dana Heinze / Paul Defazio, Daniel Kroll
Physical Therapist	Mark Mortland

Scouting

Pro Scouting Director	Derek Clancey
Professional Scouts	Andre Savard, Kevin Stevens
Director, Player Personnel	Daniel MacKinnon
Amateur Scouting Director / Asst. Director	Jay Heinbuck / Randy Sexton
Amateur Scouts	David Allison, Brian Fitzgerald, Luc Gauthier, James Madigan, David McNamara, Wayne Meier, Ron Pyette
European Scout	Patrik Allvin

Communications

Communications Director	Jennifer Bullano
Content Director / Manager	Sam Kasan / Michelle Crechiolo
Communications Coordinator	Jason Seidling

Marketing

Vice President, Marketing	James Santilli
Executive Director, Strategic Planning	Rich Hixon
Director, Marketing	Ross Miller
Director, Fan Development & Special Events	Jill Shipley
New Media Director / Coordinator	Jeremy Zimmer / TBD
Director, Community/Alumni Relations	Cindy Himes
Director, Amateur Hockey	Mark Shuttleworth
Creative Director / Graphic Designers	Barbara Pilarski / Erin Halley, Lori Haramia
Manager, Amateur Hockey Development	Max Malone
Marketing Coordinator	Sarah Swartz
Community Relations Coordinator	Kathleen Unger
Community Relations/Alumni Liason	Ed Johnston
Fan Development Coordinator	Laura Spencer

Game Entertainment

Sr. Director, Production and Game Presentation	Rod Murray
Game Night Producer	Billy Wareham
Manager, Arts and Graphics	Dori Minnis
Pens TV Host	Katie O'Malley
Game Entertainment Editors	James Archer, Michael Davenport, Stephen Finerty, Aaron Spiegel, Dave Weldon

Partnership Sales

Sr. Vice President, Sales	David Peart
Sr. Director, Corporate Sales	Kimberly Bogesdorfer
Corporate Sales Media Director	Mark Turley
Senior Managers, Client Services	Lori Wineland, Ron Hay, Julie Klausner
Corporate Sales Managers / Coordinator	Robbie Hofmann, Danny Smith / Kristen Crosby
Coordinator, Client Services	Jeff Harshman
Manager, Special Events & Hospitality Sales	Lindsay Mulvihill
Corporate Sales Liaison	Pierre Larouche

Finance

Assistant Controller / Senior Accountant	Mark Kuczinski / Troy Ussack
Payroll Manager / Accounts Payable	Andrea Winschel / Tawni Love

CONSOL Energy Center Operations

Director, CONSOL Energy Center Project Devel.	Brian Magness
Director, Technology	Erik Watts
Director, Video Production & Technical Ops.	Andrew Warren

Ticketing

Vice President, Ticket Sales	Chad Slencak
Director, Customer Service	Kathy Davis
Database Marketing Director / Manager	Erin Exley / Dana DiCello
Director, Premium Seating	Michael Guiffre
Manager, Box Office Operations	Jason Onufer
Director, Ticket Sales	George Murphy
Box Office Manager / Assistant	Caroline Coulson / Kelly Gabany
Ticket Sales Account Execs	George Birman, Jeff Blizman, Bonnie Golinski, Nicole Kyslinger, Chuck Pukansky
Manager, Group Sales	Michael Zatchey
Premium Services / Seating Representatives	Amanda Gurney / Kyle Lux
Customer Service Representatives	Holly Homistek, Daniel Gardner

Penguins Foundation

President, Penguins Foundation	David Soltesz
Manager, Foundation Programs / Program Coord.	Jaime Greenwald / Michael Grimm

Broadcasting

Executive Producer, Penguins Radio Network	Ray Walker
Radio Broadcasters / HD Radio Host	Phil Bourque, Mike Lange / Steve Mears

St. Louis Blues

Key Off-Season Signings/Acquisitions

2011

May 31 • Re-signed C **Patrik Berglund**.
June 2 • Re-signed D **Roman Polak**.
6 • Re-signed C **T.J. Hensick**.
9 • Re-signed D **Nikita Nikitin**.
13 • Re-signed C **Chris Porter**.
15 • Re-signed C **Vladimir Sobotka**.
22 • Re-signed RW **B.J. Crombeen**.
25 • Acquired C **Evgeny Grachev** from NY Rangers for St. Louis' 3rd-round pick in the 2011 Entry Draft.
30 • Re-signed C **T.J. Oshie**.
July 1 • Re-signed RW **Matt D'Agostini**.
1 • Signed G **Brian Elliott**.
2 • Signed D **Kent Huskins**.
4 • Signed LW **Brett Sterling**.
5 • Signed C **Scott Nichol**.
5 • Re-signed G **Ben Bishop**.
6 • Signed C **Jason Arnott** and RW **Jamie Langenbrunner**.
13 • Signed RW **Jonathan Cheechoo**.
Aug. 8 • Signed D **Danny Syvret**.

2011-12 Schedule

Oct.	Sat.	8	Nashville
	Mon.	10	Calgary*
	Thu.	13	at Dallas
	Sat.	15	at San Jose
	Sun.	16	at Anaheim*
	Tue.	18	at Los Angeles
	Fri.	21	Carolina
	Sat.	22	at Philadelphia
	Wed.	26	at Vancouver
	Fri.	28	at Calgary
	Sun.	30	at Edmonton
Nov.	Fri.	4	Vancouver
	Sat.	5	at Minnesota
	Tue.	8	Chicago
	Thu.	10	Toronto
	Sat.	12	Tampa Bay
	Tue.	15	Detroit
	Thu.	17	Florida
	Sat.	19	at Minnesota
	Tue.	22	Los Angeles
	Wed.	23	at Pittsburgh
	Fri.	25	Calgary
	Sun.	27	at Columbus
	Tue.	29	at Washington
Dec.	Fri.	2	at Colorado
	Sat.	3	Chicago
	Tue.	6	Detroit
	Thu.	8	Anaheim
	Sat.	10	San Jose
	Thu.	15	NY Rangers
	Sat.	17	at Nashville
	Sun.	18	Columbus
	Wed.	21	at Colorado
	Fri.	23	at Phoenix
	Mon.	26	Dallas
	Tue.	27	at Detroit
	Fri.	30	Nashville
	Sat.	31	at Detroit
Jan.	Tue.	3	Phoenix
	Thu.	5	Edmonton
	Sat.	7	Colorado
	Tue.	10	at Montreal
	Thu.	12	Vancouver
	Sat.	14	Minnesota
	Mon.	16	Dallas
	Thu.	19	Edmonton
	Sat.	21	Buffalo
	Mon.	23	at Detroit
	Tue.	24	Pittsburgh
Feb.	Fri.	3	Los Angeles
	Sat.	4	at Nashville
	Tue.	7	at Ottawa
	Thu.	9	at New Jersey
	Sat.	11	Colorado
	Sun.	12	San Jose
	Tue.	14	at Columbus
	Thu.	16	NY Islanders
	Sat.	18	Minnesota*
	Sun.	19	at Chicago*
	Wed.	22	Boston
	Thu.	23	at Nashville
	Sat.	25	at Winnipeg*
	Mon.	27	at Calgary
	Wed.	29	at Edmonton
Mar.	Thu.	1	at Vancouver
	Sat.	3	at San Jose
	Tue.	6	Chicago
	Thu.	8	Anaheim
	Sat.	10	Columbus
	Sun.	11	at Columbus
	Tue.	13	at Chicago
	Thu.	15	at Carolina
	Sat.	17	at Tampa Bay
	Wed.	21	at Anaheim
	Thu.	22	at Los Angeles
	Sun.	25	at Phoenix
	Tue.	27	Nashville
	Thu.	29	at Chicago
	Sat.	31	Columbus
Apr.	Wed.	4	Detroit
	Fri.	6	Phoenix
	Sat.	7	at Dallas

* Denotes afternoon game.

CENTRAL DIVISION
45th NHL Season

Franchise date: June 5, 1967

2010-11 Results: 38w-33l-5otl-6sol 87pts.
Fourth, Central Division

In a debut season split between Colorado and St. Louis, defenseman Kevin Shattenkirk led all NHL rookies with 34 assists in 2010-11. He had two goals and 15 assists in just 26 games with the Blues and had a plus-minus rating of +7.

Year-by-Year Record

| | | Home | | | | Road | | | | Overall | | | | | | | |
Season	GP	W	L	T	OL	W	L	T	OL	W	L	T	OL	GF	GA	Pts.	Finished	Playoff Result
2010-11	82	23	13	....	5	15	20	....	6	38	33	....	11	240	234	87	4th, Central Div.	Out of Playoffs
2009-10	82	18	18	....	5	22	14	....	5	40	32	....	10	225	223	90	4th, Central Div.	Out of Playoffs
2008-09	82	23	13	....	5	18	18	....	5	41	31	....	10	233	233	92	3rd, Central Div.	Lost Conf. Quarter-Final
2007-08	82	20	15	....	6	13	21	....	7	33	36	....	13	205	237	79	5th, Central Div.	Out of Playoffs
2006-07	82	18	19	....	4	16	16	....	9	34	35	....	13	214	254	81	3rd, Central Div.	Out of Playoffs
2005-06	82	12	23	....	6	9	23	....	9	21	46	....	15	197	292	57	5th, Central Div.	Out of Playoffs
2004-05	....																	
2003-04	82	23	11	7	0	16	19	4	2	39	30	11	2	191	198	91	2nd, Central Div.	Lost Conf. Quarter-Final
2002-03	82	23	11	4	3	18	13	7	3	41	24	11	6	253	222	99	2nd, Central Div.	Lost Conf. Quarter-Final
2001-02	82	27	12	1	1	16	15	7	3	43	27	8	4	227	188	98	2nd, Central Div.	Lost Conf. Semi-Final
2000-01	82	28	5	5	3	15	17	7	2	43	22	12	5	249	195	103	2nd, Central Div.	Lost Conf. Championship
1999-2000	82	24	9	7	1	27	10	4	0	51	19	11	1	248	165	114	1st, Central Div.	Lost Conf. Quarter-Final
1998-99	82	18	17	6	....	19	15	7	....	37	32	13	....	237	209	87	2nd, Central Div.	Lost Conf. Semi-Final
1997-98	82	26	10	5	....	19	19	3	....	45	29	8	....	256	204	98	3rd, Central Div.	Lost Conf. Quarter-Final
1996-97	82	17	20	4	....	19	16	6	....	36	35	11	....	236	239	83	4th, Central Div.	Lost Conf. Quarter-Final
1995-96	82	15	17	9	....	17	17	7	....	32	34	16	....	219	248	80	4th, Central Div.	Lost Conf. Semi-Final
1994-95	48	16	6	2	....	12	13	1	....	28	15	5	....	178	135	61	2nd, Central Div.	Lost Conf. Quarter-Final
1993-94	84	23	11	8	....	17	22	3	....	40	33	11	....	270	283	91	4th, Central Div.	Lost Conf. Quarter-Final
1992-93	84	22	13	7	....	15	23	4	....	37	36	11	....	282	278	85	4th, Norris Div.	Lost Div. Final
1991-92	80	25	12	3	....	11	21	8	....	36	33	11	....	279	266	83	3rd, Norris Div.	Lost Div. Semi-Final
1990-91	80	24	9	7	....	23	13	4	....	47	22	11	....	310	250	105	2nd, Norris Div.	Lost Div. Final
1989-90	80	20	15	5	....	17	19	4	....	37	34	9	....	295	279	83	2nd, Norris Div.	Lost Div. Final
1988-89	80	22	11	7	....	11	24	5	....	33	35	12	....	275	285	78	2nd, Norris Div.	Lost Div. Final
1987-88	80	18	17	5	....	16	21	3	....	34	38	8	....	278	294	76	2nd, Norris Div.	Lost Div. Final
1986-87	80	21	12	7	....	11	21	8	....	32	33	15	....	281	293	79	1st, Norris Div.	Lost Div. Semi-Final
1985-86	80	23	11	6	....	14	23	3	....	37	34	9	....	302	291	83	3rd, Norris Div.	Lost Conf. Championship
1984-85	80	21	12	7	....	16	19	5	....	37	31	12	....	299	288	86	1st, Norris Div.	Lost Div. Semi-Final
1983-84	80	23	14	3	....	9	27	4	....	32	41	7	....	293	316	71	2nd, Norris Div.	Lost Div. Final
1982-83	80	16	16	8	....	9	24	7	....	25	40	15	....	285	316	65	4th, Norris Div.	Lost Div. Semi-Final
1981-82	80	22	14	4	....	10	26	4	....	32	40	8	....	315	349	72	3rd Norris Div.	Lost Div. Final
1980-81	80	29	7	4	....	16	11	13	....	45	18	17	....	352	281	107	1st, Smythe Div.	Lost Quarter-Final
1979-80	80	20	13	7	....	14	21	5	....	34	34	12	....	266	278	80	2nd, Smythe Div.	Lost Prelim. Round
1978-79	80	14	20	6	....	4	30	6	....	18	50	12	....	249	348	48	3rd, Smythe Div.	Out of Playoffs
1977-78	80	12	20	8	....	8	27	5	....	20	47	13	....	195	304	53	4th, Smythe Div.	Out of Playoffs
1976-77	80	22	13	5	....	10	26	4	....	32	39	9	....	239	276	73	1st, Smythe Div.	Lost Quarter-Final
1975-76	80	20	12	8	....	9	25	6	....	29	37	14	....	249	290	72	3rd, Smythe Div.	Lost Prelim. Round
1974-75	80	23	13	4	....	12	18	10	....	35	31	14	....	269	267	84	2nd, Smythe Div.	Lost Quarter-Final
1973-74	78	16	16	7	....	10	24	5	....	26	40	12	....	206	248	64	6th, West Div.	Out of Playoffs
1972-73	78	21	11	7	....	11	23	5	....	32	34	12	....	233	251	76	4th, West Div.	Lost Quarter-Final
1971-72	78	17	17	5	....	11	22	6	....	28	39	11	....	208	247	67	3rd, West Div.	Lost Semi-Final
1970-71	78	23	7	9	....	11	18	10	....	34	25	19	....	223	208	87	2nd, West Div.	Lost Quarter-Final
1969-70	76	24	9	5	....	13	18	7	....	37	27	12	....	224	179	86	1st, West Div.	Lost Final
1968-69	76	21	8	9	....	16	17	5	....	37	25	14	....	204	157	88	1st, West Div.	Lost Final
1967-68	74	18	12	7	....	9	19	9	....	27	31	16	....	177	191	70	3rd, West Div.	Lost Final

2011-12 Player Personnel

FORWARDS	HT	WT	S	Place of Birth	*Age	2010-11 Club
ARNOTT, Jason	6-5	220	R	Collingwood, Ont.	36	New Jersey-Washington
BACKES, David	6-3	225	R	Blaine, MN	27	St. Louis
BARRIBALL, Jay	5-9	171	L	Prior Lake, MN	24	U. of Minnesota-Peoria
BERGLUND, Patrik	6-4	218	L	Vasteras, Sweden	23	St. Louis
CHEECHOO, Jonathan	6-1	200	R	Moose Factory, Ont.	31	Worcester
CRACKNELL, Adam	6-2	216	R	Prince Albert, Sask.	26	St. Louis-Peoria
CROMBEEN, B.J.	6-2	214	R	Denver, CO	26	St. Louis
D'AGOSTINI, Matt	6-0	200	R	Sault Ste. Marie, Ont.	24	St. Louis
DELLA ROVERE, Stefan	5-11	200	L	Richmond Hill, Ont.	21	St. Louis-Peoria
GRACHEV, Evgeny	6-4	224	L	Khabarovsk, USSR	21	NY Rangers-Connecticut
HENSICK, T.J.	5-10	190	R	Lansing, MI	25	St. Louis-Peoria
LANGENBRUNNER, Jamie	6-1	205	R	Cloquet, MN	36	New Jersey-Dallas
McDONALD, Andy	5-11	190	L	Strathroy, Ont.	34	St. Louis
McRAE, Philip	6-2	200	L	Minneapolis, MN	21	St. Louis-Peoria
NICHOL, Scott	5-9	180	R	Edmonton, Alta.	36	San Jose
NIGRO, Anthony	5-11	180	L	Vaughan, Ont.	21	Peoria
OSHIE, T.J.	5-11	195	R	Mt. Vernon, WA	24	St. Louis
PERRON, David	6-0	200	R	Sherbrooke, Que.	23	St. Louis
PORTER, Chris	6-1	200	L	Toronto, Ont.	27	St. Louis-Peoria
REAVES, Ryan	6-1	225	R	Winnipeg, Man.	24	St. Louis-Peoria
SHATTOCK, Tyler	6-2	205	L	Vernon, B.C.	21	Peoria
SOBOTKA, Vladimir	5-10	183	L	Trebic, Czech.	24	St. Louis
SONNE, Brett	6-0	201	L	Chilliwack, B.C.	22	Peoria
STEEN, Alex	6-1	209	L	Winnipeg, Man.	27	St. Louis
STERLING, Brett	5-7	175	L	Los Angeles, CA	27	Pittsburgh-Wilkes-Barre
STEWART, Chris	6-2	228	R	Toronto, Ont.	23	Colorado-St. Louis

DEFENSEMEN						
COLAIACOVO, Carlo	6-1	205	L	Toronto, Ont.	28	St. Louis
COLE, Ian	6-1	221	L	Ann Arbour, MI	22	St. Louis-Peoria
CUNDARI, Mark	5-9	200	L	Woodbridge, Ont.	21	Peoria
EVANS, Brennan	6-3	230	L	North Battleford, Sask.	29	Peoria
FAIRCHILD, Cade	5-11	190	L	Duluth, MN	22	U. of Minnesota
HAGEL, Kyle	6-0	205	L	Hamilton, Ont.	26	Rockford
HUSKINS, Kent	6-4	210	L	Ottawa, Ont.	32	San Jose
JACKMAN, Barret	6-0	205	L	Trail, B.C.	30	St. Louis
NIKITIN, Nikita	6-3	217	L	Omsk, USSR	25	St. Louis-Peoria
PELUSO, Anthony	6-3	235	R	North York, Ont.	22	Peoria
PIETRANGELO, Alex	6-3	206	R	King City, Ont.	21	St. Louis
POLAK, Roman	6-1	227	R	Ostrava, Czech.	25	St. Louis
PONICH, Brett	6-7	225	L	Edmonton, Alta.	20	Portland (WHL)
SHATTENKIRK, Kevin	5-11	193	R	Greenwich, CT	22	Col-Lake Erie-StL
SHIELDS, David	6-3	215	R	Buffalo, NY	20	Erie (OHL)
SYVRET, Danny	5-11	203	L	Millgrove, Ont.	26	Ana-Syr-Phi-Adi

GOALTENDERS	HT	WT	C	Place of Birth	*Age	2010-11 Club
ALLEN, Jake	6-2	190	L	Fredericton, N.B.	21	Peoria
BISHOP, Ben	6-7	215	L	Denver, CO	24	St. Louis-Peoria
ELLIOTT, Brian	6-3	201	L	Newmarket, Ont.	26	Ottawa-Colorado
HALAK, Jaroslav	5-11	185	L	Bratislava, Czech.	26	St. Louis

* – Age at start of 2011-12 season

2010-11 Scoring

* – rookie

Regular Season

Pos	#	Player	Team	GP	G	A	Pts	TOI	+/-	PIM	PP	SH	GW	S	%
R	42	David Backes	STL	82	31	31	62	19:42	32	93	5	0	2	211	14.7
R	25	Chris Stewart	COL	36	13	17	30	16:55	-10	38	5	0	3	95	13.7
			STL	26	15	8	23	18:15	4	15	7	0	2	67	22.4
			Total	62	28	25	53	17:29	-6	53	12	0	5	162	17.3
C	21	Patrik Berglund	STL	81	22	30	52	17:11	-3	26	8	0	1	175	12.6
C	20	Alexander Steen	STL	72	20	31	51	19:33	-3	26	1	2	5	218	9.2
C	10	Andy McDonald	STL	58	20	30	50	20:02	18	26	5	1	3	180	11.1
R	36	Matt D'Agostini	STL	82	21	25	46	14:45	8	40	6	0	5	163	12.9
D	27	Alex Pietrangelo	STL	79	11	32	43	22:00	18	19	4	0	1	161	6.8
D	12 *	Kevin Shattenkirk	COL	46	7	19	26	19:50	-11	20	2	0	1	67	10.4
			STL	26	2	15	17	19:50	7	16	1	0	1	41	4.9
			Total	72	9	34	43	19:50	-4	36	3	0	2	108	8.3
C	74	T.J. Oshie	STL	49	12	22	34	19:11	10	15	3	1	3	103	11.7
C	17	Vladimir Sobotka	STL	65	7	22	29	16:10	-4	69	1	1	0	75	9.3
D	28	Carlo Colaiacovo	STL	65	6	20	26	18:08	-4	23	1	0	1	81	7.4
R	26	B.J. Crombeen	STL	80	7	7	14	12:47	-18	154	0	1	0	113	6.2
D	5	Barret Jackman	STL	60	0	13	13	20:48	3	57	0	0	0	65	0.0
D	46	Roman Polak	STL	55	3	9	12	19:57	-4	33	0	0	1	54	5.6
D	64 *	Nikita Nikitin	STL	41	1	8	9	16:23	1	10	0	0	0	46	2.2
D	57	David Perron	STL	10	5	2	7	18:25	7	12	0	0	0	29	17.2
R	79 *	Adam Cracknell	STL	24	3	4	7	8:55	1	8	0	0	0	26	11.5
L	57	Chris Porter	STL	45	3	4	7	10:23	-4	16	0	0	1	55	5.5
R	75	Ryan Reaves	STL	28	2	2	4	6:48	-1	78	0	0	1	16	12.5
D	23 *	Ian Cole	STL	26	1	3	4	17:36	6	35	0	0	0	22	4.5
R	55	Cam Janssen	STL	54	1	3	4	4:52	-6	131	0	0	0	16	6.3
D	37	Nathan Oystrick	STL	9	1	2	3	12:10	1	0	0	0	0	11	9.1
C	77	T.J. Hensick	STL	13	1	2	3	9:05	-5	2	0	0	0	12	8.3
C	38 *	Philip McRae	STL	15	1	2	3	9:02	-10	2	0	0	0	13	7.7
C	38	Dave Scatchard	STL	8	0	1	1	4:45	1	6	0	0	0	6	0.0
D	33	Tyson Strachan	STL	29	0	1	1	12:08	-10	39	0	0	0	28	0.0
C	47 *	Nicholas Drazenovic	STL	3	0	0	0	8:58	-3	0	0	0	0	2	0.0
L	19 *	Stefan Della Rovere	STL	7	0	0	0	6:05	0	11	0	0	0	4	0.0

Goaltending

No.	Goaltender	GPI	Mins	Avg	W	L	OT	EN	SO	GA	SA	S%	G	A	PIM
41	Jaroslav Halak	57	3294	2.48	27	21	7	3	7	136	1518	.910	0	0	6
30	Ben Bishop	7	369	2.76	3	4	0	1	1	17	168	.899	0	0	4
29	Ty Conklin	25	1285	3.22	8	8	4	3	2	69	582	.881	0	0	4
	Totals	82	4988	2.74	38	33	11	6	10	228	2274	.900			

Davis Payne
Head Coach
Born: Port Alberni, B.C., September 24, 1970.

Davis Payne was named the 23rd head coach of the St. Louis Blues on January 2, 2010 after serving as head coach of the team's AHL club, the Peoria Rivermen. Originally named to the position on an interim basis, he was officially confirmed as the head coach on April 14, 2010 and spent his first full season behind the bench in 2010-11.

Payne guided Peoria to a 43-31-6 record in 2008-09 and returned the Rivermen to the postseason following a two-year drought. Prior to joining Peoria before the 2007-08 campaign, Payne had spent a total of seven seasons as a head coach in the ECHL. He established a .691 winning percentage over four years as head coach for the Alaska Aces, the Blues' ECHL affiliate. The 2006-07 ECHL coach of the year, Payne led the Aces to the 2006 ECHL Kelly Cup championship and also guided the club to three consecutive trips to the Conference Finals; it was the first time in 15 years and only the second time in ECHL history that a team advanced to the ECHL's Final Four in three straight seasons. Payne owns a 289-142-45 record (.654) in seven seasons as an ECHL head coach between Alaska and the Pee Dee Pride. He had a record of 50-35 in the postseason.

A graduate of NCAA Division I Michigan Tech, Payne appeared in 22 NHL games with the Boston Bruins and played a total of eight professional seasons. He was originally drafted by the Edmonton Oilers in the seventh round of the 1989 NHL Entry Draft.

Coaching Record

			Regular Season				Playoffs			
Season	Team	League	GC	W	L	O/T	GC	W	L	T
2000-01	Pee Dee	ECHL	44	23	16	5	10	5	5	....
2001-02	Pee Dee	ECHL	72	41	25	6	9	4	5	....
2002-03	Pee Dee	ECHL	72	40	26	6	7	3	4	....
2003-04	Alaska	ECHL	72	38	28	6	7	4	3	....
2004-05	Alaska	ECHL	72	45	19	8	15	9	6	....
2005-06	Alaska	ECHL	72	53	12	7	22	16	6	....
2006-07	Alaska	ECHL	72	49	16	7	15	9	6	....
2008-09	Peoria	AHL	80	43	31	6	7	3	4	....
2009-10	Peoria	AHL	35	19	13	3	....	....	....	....
2009-10	St. Louis	NHL	42	23	15	4	....	....	....	....
2010-11	St. Louis	NHL	82	38	33	11	....	....	....	....
	NHL Totals		124	61	48	15				

General Managers' History
Lynn Patrick, 1967-68; Scotty Bowman, 1968-69 to 1970-71; Lynn Patrick and Sid Abel, 1971-72; Sid Abel, 1972-73; Charles Catto, 1973-74; Gerry Ehman and Dennis Ball, 1974-75; Emile Francis, 1976-77 to 1982-83; Ron Caron, 1983-84 to 1993-94; Mike Keenan, 1994-95, 1995-96; Mike Keenan and Ron Caron, 1996-97; Larry Pleau, 1997-98 to 2009-10; Doug Armstrong, 2010-11 to date.

Coaching History
Lynn Patrick and Scotty Bowman, 1967-68; Scotty Bowman, 1968-69, 1969-70; Al Arbour and Scotty Bowman, 1970-71; Sid Abel, Bill McCreary and Al Arbour, 1971-72; Al Arbour and Jean-Guy Talbot, 1972-73; Jean-Guy Talbot and Lou Angotti, 1973-74; Lou Angotti, Lynn Patrick and Garry Young, 1974-75; Garry Young, Lynn Patrick and Leo Boivin, 1975-76; Emile Francis, 1976-77; Leo Boivin and Barclay Plager, 1977-78; Barclay Plager, 1978-79; Barclay Plager and Red Berenson, 1979-80; Red Berenson, 1980-81; Red Berenson and Emile Francis, 1981-82; Emile Francis and Barclay Plager, 1982-83; Jacques Demers, 1983-84 to 1985-86; Jacques Martin, 1986-87, 1987-88; Brian Sutter, 1988-89 to 1991-92; Bob Plager and Bob Berry, 1992-93; Bob Berry, 1993-94; Mike Keenan, 1994-95, 1995-96; Mike Keenan, Jim Roberts and Joel Quenneville, 1996-97; Joel Quenneville, 1997-98 to 2002-03; Joel Quenneville and Mike Kitchen, 2003-04; Mike Kitchen, 2004-05, 2005-06; Mike Kitchen and Andy Murray, 2006-07; Andy Murray, 2007-08, 2008-09; Andy Murray and Davis Payne, 2009-10; Davis Payne, 2010-11 to date.

Club Records

Team

(Figures in brackets for season records are games played; records for fewest points, wins, ties, losses, goals, goals against are for 70 or more games)

Most Points **114** 1999-2000 (82)
Most Wins **51** 1999-2000 (82)
Most Ties **19** 1970-71 (78)
Most Losses **50** 1978-79 (80)
Most Goals **352** 1980-81 (80)
Most Goals Against **349** 1981-82 (80)
Fewest Points **48** 1978-79 (80)
Fewest Wins **18** 1978-79 (80)
Fewest Ties **7** 1983-84 (80)
Fewest Losses **18** 1980-81 (80)
Fewest Goals **177** 1967-68 (74)
Fewest Goals Against **157** 1968-69 (76)

Longest Winning Streak
- **Overall** .... **10** Jan. 3-23/02
- **Home** .... **9** Jan. 26-Feb. 26/91
- **Away** .... ***10** Jan. 21-Mar. 2/00

Longest Undefeated Streak
- **Overall** .... **12** Nov. 10-Dec. 8/68 (5 wins, 7 ties), Nov. 24-Dec. 26/00 (11 wins, 1 tie)
- **Home** .... **11** Four times
- **Away** .... **11** Jan. 21-Mar. 4/00 (10 wins, 1 tie)

Longest Losing Streak
- **Overall** .... **13** Mar. 16-Apr. 8/06
- **Home** .... **7** Oct. 22-Nov. 26/05, Nov. 25-Dec. 17/06
- **Away** .... **10** Jan. 20-Mar. 8/82, Dec. 29/05-Feb. 1/06, Feb. 16-Mar. 15/08

Longest Winless Streak
- **Overall** .... **13** Mar. 16-Apr. 8/06 (13 losses)
- **Home** .... **7** Dec. 28/82-Jan. 25/83 (5 losses, 2 ties), Oct. 22-Nov. 26/05 (7 losses)
- **Away** .... **17** Jan. 23-Apr. 7/74 (14 losses, 3 ties)

Most Shutouts, Season **13** 1968-69 (76)
Most PIM, Season **2,041** 1990-91 (80)
Most Goals, Game .... **11** Feb. 26/94 (St.L. 11 at Ott. 1)

Individual

Most Seasons .... **13** Bernie Federko
Most Games .... **927** Bernie Federko
Most Goals, Career .... **527** Brett Hull
Most Assists, Career .... **721** Bernie Federko
Most Points, Career .... **1,073** Bernie Federko (352G, 721A)
Most PIM, Career .... **1,786** Brian Sutter
Most Shutouts, Career .... **16** Glenn Hall
Longest Consecutive Games Streak .... **662** Garry Unger (Feb. 7/71-Apr. 8/79)
Most Goals, Season .... **86** Brett Hull (1990-91)
Most Assists, Season .... **90** Adam Oates (1990-91)
Most Points, Season .... **131** Brett Hull (1990-91; 86G, 45A)
Most PIM, Season .... **306** Bob Gassoff (1975-76)
Most Points, Defenseman, Season .... **78** Jeff Brown (1992-93; 25G, 53A)
Most Points, Center, Season .... **115** Adam Oates (1990-91; 25G, 90A)
Most Points, Right Wing, Season .... **131** Brett Hull (1990-91; 86G, 45A)
Most Points, Left Wing, Season .... **102** Brendan Shanahan (1993-94; 52G, 50A)
Most Points, Rookie, Season .... **73** Jorgen Pettersson (1980-81; 37G, 36A)
Most Shutouts, Season .... **8** Glenn Hall (1968-69)
Most Goals, Game .... **6** Red Berenson (Nov. 7/68)
Most Assists, Game .... **5** Brian Sutter (Nov. 22/83), Bernie Federko (Feb. 27/88), Adam Oates (Jan. 26/91), Dallas Drake (Oct. 29/03)
Most Points, Game .... **7** Red Berenson (Nov. 7/68; 6G, 1A), Garry Unger (Mar. 13/71; 3G, 4A)

* NHL Record.

Retired Numbers

2	Al MacInnis	1994-2004
3	Bob Gassoff	1973-1977
8	Barclay Plager	1967-1977
11	Brian Sutter	1976-1988
16	Brett Hull	1987-1998
24	Bernie Federko	1976-1989

All-time Record vs. Other Clubs

Regular Season

	At Home								On Road								Total							
	GP	W	L	T	OL	GF	GA	PTS	GP	W	L	T	OL	GF	GA	PTS	GP	W	L	T	OL	GF	GA	PTS
Anaheim	34	19	8	3	4	115	91	45	34	15	16	2	1	97	99	33	68	34	24	5	5	212	190	78
Atlanta	6	4	1	0	1	19	11	9	8	4	2	1	1	26	23	10	14	8	3	1	2	45	34	19
Boston	62	28	25	9	0	196	210	65	62	18	35	9	0	172	253	45	124	46	60	18	0	368	463	110
Buffalo	52	30	15	7	0	186	132	67	55	19	30	6	0	174	207	44	107	49	45	13	0	360	339	111
Calgary	76	34	31	9	2	257	240	79	74	31	35	5	3	200	236	70	150	65	66	14	5	457	476	149
Carolina	34	20	10	3	1	121	97	44	34	18	14	2	0	105	100	38	68	38	24	5	1	226	197	82
Chicago	136	68	48	17	3	451	414	156	139	41	73	18	7	397	507	107	275	109	121	35	10	848	921	263
Colorado	52	28	18	4	2	183	154	62	53	17	29	7	0	141	189	41	105	45	47	11	2	324	343	103
Columbus	32	23	7	1	1	114	76	48	31	14	13	2	2	86	88	32	63	37	20	3	3	200	164	80
Dallas	129	71	37	21	0	458	361	163	127	44	57	22	4	369	423	114	256	115	94	43	4	827	784	277
Detroit	131	63	46	20	2	423	380	148	131	50	61	17	3	392	474	120	262	113	107	37	5	815	854	268
Edmonton	56	27	19	7	3	194	189	64	56	24	25	4	3	182	191	55	112	51	44	11	6	376	380	119
Florida	12	8	3	1	0	29	17	17	12	6	4	2	0	26	26	14	24	14	7	3	0	55	43	31
Los Angeles	90	58	21	10	1	329	226	127	90	37	41	12	0	260	301	86	180	95	62	22	1	589	527	213
Minnesota	20	9	5	3	3	47	42	24	20	6	10	2	2	41	63	16	40	15	15	5	5	88	105	40
Montreal	60	15	29	15	1	156	203	46	61	13	41	7	0	169	261	33	121	28	70	22	1	325	464	79
Nashville	37	19	13	1	4	100	79	43	38	15	13	3	7	88	89	40	75	34	26	4	11	188	168	83
New Jersey	49	28	13	7	1	201	154	64	48	19	22	7	0	132	148	45	97	47	35	14	1	333	302	109
NY Islanders	49	19	19	9	2	173	160	49	53	15	27	11	0	140	196	41	102	34	46	20	2	313	356	90
NY Rangers	67	27	29	10	1	199	211	65	63	12	44	6	1	151	251	31	130	39	73	16	2	350	462	96
Ottawa	12	5	5	2	0	35	34	12	12	6	6	0	0	40	29	12	24	11	11	2	0	75	63	24
Philadelphia	71	28	34	7	2	202	225	65	69	12	45	10	2	157	270	36	140	40	79	17	4	359	495	101
Phoenix	62	30	21	11	0	206	170	71	63	23	29	7	4	195	201	57	125	53	50	18	4	401	371	128
Pittsburgh	67	45	16	6	0	254	177	96	66	21	32	12	1	195	244	55	133	66	48	18	1	449	421	151
San Jose	40	21	17	1	1	116	103	44	36	22	10	1	3	113	93	48	76	43	27	2	4	229	196	92
Tampa Bay	13	10	3	0	0	51	35	20	16	6	5	3	2	53	50	17	29	16	8	3	2	104	85	37
Toronto	104	59	30	14	1	353	285	133	102	32	58	11	1	305	381	76	206	91	88	25	2	658	666	209
Vancouver	83	48	23	9	3	305	233	108	84	38	34	9	3	262	247	88	167	86	57	18	6	567	480	196
Washington	44	22	14	8	0	174	137	52	42	15	22	4	1	125	148	35	86	37	36	12	1	299	285	87
Defunct Clubs	32	25	4	3	0	131	55	53	33	11	10	12	0	95	100	34	65	36	14	15	0	226	155	87
Totals	**1712**	**891**	**564**	**218**	**39**	**5778**	**4901**	**2039**	**1712**	**604**	**843**	**214**	**51**	**4888**	**5888**	**1473**	**3424**	**1495**	**1407**	**432**	**90**	**10666**	**10789**	**3512**

Playoffs

	Series	W	L	GP	W	L	T	GF	GA	Last Mtg.	Rnd.	Result
Boston	2	0	2	8	0	8	0	15	48	1972	SF	L 0-4
Buffalo	1	0	1	3	1	2	0	8	7	1976	PRE	L 1-2
Calgary	1	0	1	7	3	4	0	22	28	1986	CF	L 3-4
Chicago	10	3	7	50	22	28	0	142	171	2002	CQF	W 4-1
Colorado	1	0	1	5	1	4	0	11	17	2001	CF	L 1-4
Dallas	12	6	6	66	32	34	0	187	197	2001	CSF	W 4-0
Detroit	7	2	5	40	16	24	0	103	125	2002	CSF	L 1-4
Los Angeles	2	2	0	8	8	0	0	32	13	1998	CQF	W 4-0
Montreal	3	0	3	12	0	12	0	14	42	1977	QF	L 0-4
NY Rangers	1	0	1	6	2	4	0	22	29	1981	QF	L 2-4
Philadelphia	2	2	0	11	8	3	0	34	20	1969	QF	W 4-0
Phoenix	2	2	0	11	7	4	0	39	29	1999	CQF	W 4-3
Pittsburgh	3	2	1	13	7	6	0	45	40	1981	PRE	W 3-2
San Jose	3	1	2	18	8	10	0	47	43	2004	CQF	L 1-4
Toronto	5	3	2	31	17	14	0	88	90	1996	CQF	W 4-2
Vancouver	3	0	3	18	6	12	0	53	55	2009	CQF	L 0-4
Totals	**58**	**23**	**35**	**307**	**138**	**169**	**0**	**862**	**954**			

Calgary totals include Atlanta Flames, 1972-73 to 1979-80. Carolina totals include Hartford, 1979-80 to 1996-97.
Colorado totals include Quebec, 1979-80 to 1994-95. Dallas totals include Minnesota North Stars, 1967-68 to 1992-93.
New Jersey totals include Kansas City, 1974-75, 1975-76, and Colorado Rockies, 1976-77 to 1981-82.
Phoenix totals include Winnipeg, 1979-80 to 1995-96.

Playoff Results 2011-2007

Year	Round	Opponent	Result	GF	GA
2009	CQF	Vancouver	L 0-4	5	11

Abbreviations: Round: CF – conference final; **CSF** – conference semi-final; **CQF** – conference quarter-final; **SF** – semi-final; **QF** – quarter-final; **PRE** – preliminary round.

2010-11 Results

Oct.	9	Philadelphia	2-1*
	11	Anaheim	5-1
	14	at Nashville	3-4
	16	at Dallas	2-3†
	18	at Chicago	2-3*
	22	Chicago	4-2
	23	Pittsburgh	1-0*
	28	at Nashville	3-0
	30	Atlanta	4-3†
Nov.	4	San Jose	2-0
	6	at Boston	2-1†
	7	at NY Rangers	2-0
	10	at Columbus	1-8
	11	Nashville	2-3†
	13	at Phoenix	3-5
	15	at Colorado	3-6
	17	at Detroit	3-7
	19	Ottawa	5-2
	20	New Jersey	3-2
	24	at Nashville	2-1†
	26	at Dallas	2-3
	27	Dallas	1-2
	30	at Chicago	5-7
Dec.	1	Washington	1-4
	4	at Edmonton	1-2*
	5	at Vancouver	3-2
	9	Columbus	4-1
	11	Carolina	1-2†
	15	at Detroit	2-5
	16	Los Angeles	6-4
	18	San Jose	1-4
	20	Vancouver	1-3
	21	at Atlanta	4-2
	23	Detroit	4-3
	26	Nashville	2-0
	28	Chicago	3-1
	31	Phoenix	4-3
Jan.	2	Dallas	2-4
	6	at Toronto	5-6†
	8	NY Rangers	1-2
	10	Phoenix	3-4
	12	at Anaheim	4-7
	13	at Los Angeles	3-1
	15	at San Jose	2-4
	18	Los Angeles	2-1
	20	Detroit	3-4*
	22	Columbus	2-5
	24	at Colorado	3-4
	26	at Calgary	1-4
Feb.	4	Edmonton	5-3
	6	at Tampa Bay	3-4*
	8	at Florida	2-1
	11	Minnesota	4-5†
	12	at Minnesota	1-3
	14	Vancouver	3-2
	18	at Buffalo	3-0
	19	Anaheim	9-3
	21	Chicago	3-5
	22	Colorado	3-4
	24	at Vancouver	2-3
	25	at Edmonton	5-0
	27	at Calgary	0-1
Mar.	1	Calgary	0-6
	3	at Washington	2-3
	5	at NY Islanders	2-5
	7	Columbus	5-4†
	9	at Columbus	4-3*
	10	Montreal	4-1
	12	Detroit	3-5
	16	at Anaheim	1-2
	17	at Los Angeles	4-0
	19	at San Jose	3-5
	22	at Phoenix	1-2
	24	Edmonton	4-0
	26	at Minnesota	6-3
	29	Minnesota	2-3†
	30	at Detroit	10-3
Apr.	1	Calgary	2-3
	3	at Columbus	6-1
	5	Colorado	3-1
	6	at Chicago	3-4*
	9	Nashville	2-0

* – Overtime † – Shootout

Entry Draft Selections 2011-1997

Name in bold denotes played in NHL.

2011
Pick
32	Ty Rattie
41	Dmitrij Jaskin
46	**Joel Edmundson**
88	Jordan Binnington
102	Yannick Veilleux
132	Niklas Lundstrom
162	Ryan Tesink
192	Teemu Eronen

2010
Pick
14	Jaden Schwartz
16	Vladimir Tarasenko
44	Sebastian Wannstrom
74	Max Gardiner
104	Jani Hakanpaa
134	Cody Beach
164	Stephen Macaulay

2009
Pick
17	David Rundblad
48	Brett Ponich
78	Sergei Andronov
108	Tyler Shattock
168	David Shields
202	Maxwell Tardy

2008
Pick
4	**Alex Pietrangelo**
33	**Philip McRae**
34	Jake Allen
65	Jori Lehtera
70	James Livingston
87	Ian Schultz
95	David Warsofsky
125	Kristofer Berglund
155	Anthony Nigro
185	Paul Karpowich

2007
Pick
13	**Lars Eller**
18	**Ian Cole**
26	**David Perron**
39	Simon Hjalmarsson
44	**Aaron Palushaj**
85	Brett Sonne
96	Cade Fairchild
100	Travis Erstad
160	Anthony Peluso
190	Trevor Nill

2006
Pick
1	**Erik Johnson**
25	**Patrik Berglund**
31	**Tomas Kana**
64	**Jonas Junland**
94	Ryan Turek
106	Reto Berra
124	Andy Sackrison
154	Matthew McCollem
184	Alexander Hellstrom

2005
Pick
24	**T.J. Oshie**
37	**Scott Jackson**
85	**Ben Bishop**
156	**Ryan Reaves**
169	Mike Gauthier
171	**Nicholas Drazenovic**
219	Nikolai Lemtyugov

2004
Pick
17	**Marek Schwarz**
49	Carl Soderberg
83	Viktor Alexandrov
116	Michal Birner
136	**Nikita Nikitin**
180	**Roman Polak**
211	David Fredriksson
277	Jonathan Michel Boutin

2003
Pick
30	**Shawn Belle**
62	**David Backes**
84	Konstantin Barulin
88	**Zack Fitzgerald**
101	Konstantin Zakharov
127	**Alexandre Bolduc**
148	**Lee Stempniak**
159	**Chris Beckford-Tseu**
189	Jonathan Lehun
221	Evgeny Skachkov
253	Andrei Pervyshin
284	Juhamatti Aaltonen

2002
Pick
48	Alexei Shkotov
62	Andrei Mikhnov
89	Tomas Troliga
120	Robin Jonsson
165	Justin Maiser
190	**D.J. King**
221	Jonas Johnson
253	**Tom Koivisto**
284	Ryan MacMurchy

2001
Pick
57	**Jay McClement**
89	Tuomas Nissinen
122	Igor Valeev
159	Dmitri Semin
190	Brett Scheffelmaier
253	**Petr Cajanek**
270	Grant Jacobsen
283	Simon Skoog

2000
Pick
30	**Jeff Taffe**
65	**Dave Morisset**
75	**Justin Papineau**
96	Antoine Bergeron
129	Troy Riddle
167	**Craig Weller**
229	Brett Lutes
261	**Reinhard Divis**
293	Lauri Kinos

1999
Pick
17	**Barret Jackman**
85	**Peter Smrek**
114	Chad Starling
143	Trevor Byrne
180	Tore Vikingstad
203	Phil Osaer
221	**Colin Hemingway**
232	**Alexander Khavanov**
260	Brian McMeekin
270	James Desmarais

1998
Pick
24	**Christian Backman**
41	Maxim Linnik
83	**Matt Walker**
157	Brad Voth
170	Andrei Troschinsky
197	Brad Twordik
225	Yevgeny Pastukh
255	**John Pohl**

1997
Pick
40	Tyler Rennette
86	Didier Tremblay
98	Jan Horacek
106	**Jame Pollock**
149	Nicholas Bilotto
177	**Ladislav Nagy**
206	Bobby Haglund
232	Dmitri Plekhanov
244	Marek Ivan

Captains' History

Al Arbour, 1967-68 to 1969-70; Red Berenson and Barclay Plager, 1970-71; Barclay Plager, 1971-72 to 1975-76; no captain, 1976-77; Red Berenson, 1977-78; Barry Gibbs, 1978-79; Brian Sutter, 1979-80 to 1987-88; Bernie Federko, 1988-89; Rick Meagher, 1989-90; Scott Stevens, 1990-91; Garth Butcher, 1991-92; Brett Hull, 1992-93 to 1994-95; Brett Hull, Shayne Corson and Wayne Gretzky, 1995-96; no captain, 1996-97; Chris Pronger, 1997-98 to 2001-02; Al MacInnis, 2002-03, 2003-04; Dallas Drake, 2005-06, 2006-07; Eric Brewer, 2007-08 to 2010-11.

Doug Armstrong
Executive Vice President and General Manager

Born: Sarnia, Ont., September 24, 1964.

Doug Armstrong was named the Blues' executive vice president and general manager on July 1, 2010 after serving two seasons with the club as vice president of player personnel. Previously, Armstrong spent 17 years with the Dallas Stars organization and the last six seasons (from January 25, 2002, to 2008) as the club's general manager.

Armstrong was a part of the Stars' organization since the club moved to Dallas in 1993 and helped lead the franchise to two Presidents' Trophies, two Western Conference titles and the 1999 Stanley Cup championship. Prior to being named the team's seventh general manager, Armstrong served nine years as the assistant general manager under Bob Gainey. As Gainey's assistant, Armstrong worked on contract negotiations and season scheduling, and handled the day-to-day operations of the hockey department.

On the international level, Armstrong was the associate director of player personnel for Team Canada at the 2010 Winter Olympics in Vancouver. He also served as general manager for Team Canada and won the silver medal at the 2009 World Championship in Switzerland. He was the assistant general manager for Team Canada at the 2002 World Championship and 2008 World Championship (silver medal) and served as a special advisor to Steve Yzerman for the Canadian team that won gold at the 2007 World Championship. Armstrong is the son of former NHL linesman Neil Armstrong who was inducted into the Hockey Hall of Fame in 1991.

Club Directory

Scottrade Center

St. Louis Blues
Scottrade Center
1401 Clark Avenue
St. Louis, MO 63103
Phone **314/622-2500**
FAX 314/622-2582
www.stlouisblues.com
Capacity: 19,150

SCP Worldwide
Principal Owner and Chairman/Governor/ Chairman, SCP Worldwide	David W. Checketts
CEO, St. Louis Blues /Alternate Governor/ Partner, SCP Worldwide	Michael McCarthy
Partner, SCP Worldwide	Steven Potter
Minority Owner	Tom Stillman

Executive
President of Hockey Operations/Alt. Governor	John Davidson
Exec. V.P., General Manager, St. Louis Blues	Doug Armstrong
Vice President/Senior Consultant to Hockey Ops	Larry Pleau
Vice President, Hockey Operations	Al MacInnis
Exec. V.P., General Manager, Scottrade Center	Marty Brooks
Exec. V.P., Chief Marketing Officer	David Bullock
Exec. V.P., Corporate and Sponsorship Sales	Mark Toffolo
Exec. V.P., Events and New Business, Scottrade Center – Rio Tinto Stadium	John Urban
Sr. V.P., Sales	Todd Lambert
Sr. V.P., Finance and Administration	Phil Siddle
Sr. V.P., Business Development	Eric Stisser
Sr. V.P., Marketing	Karrie Yager
Vice President, Broadcasting and Blues Alumni	Bruce Affleck
Vice President, Public Relations	Mike Caruso
Vice President, Suite Sales	Chris Diiorio
Vice President, Corporate and Sponsorship Sales	Bryan Lucas
Vice President, Entertainment and Event Mktg.	Mark Tamar
Exec. Asst. to the President and G.M.	Donna Lembke
Exec. Asst. to the CEO, St. Louis Blues Enterprises	Amber Daniels
Exec. Asst. to the Chief Marketing Officer	Stephanie Sadler

Hockey Operations
Director, Player Personnel	Dave Taylor
Assistant G.M./Director, Pro Scouting/Peoria G.M.	Kevin McDonald
Director, Amateur Scouting	Bill Armstrong
Director, Player Development	Tim Taylor
Head Coach	Davis Payne
Assistant Coaches	Ray Bennett, Scott Mellanby, Brad Shaw
Goaltending Consultant	Corey Hirsch
Strength and Conditioning Coach	Nelson Ayotte
Video Coach	Scott Masters
Director, Hockey Administration	Ryan Miller
Director, Media Relations	Rich Jankowski
Coordinator, Media Relations	Dan O'Neill

Scouting
Professional Scouts	Rob DiMaio, Tony Feltrin, Jan Vopat
Part-Time Professional Scout	Wayne Mundey
Amateur Scouts	Mike Antonovich, Marshall Davidson, Dan Ginnell, J Niemiec, Ville Siren
Part-Time Amateur Scouts	Basil McRae, Rick Meagher, Blair Nicholson, Michel Picard, Vincent Montalbano

Training
Athletic Trainer / Assistant Trainer	Ray Barile / Mike Hannegan
Equipment Manager / Asst. Manager / Assistant	Bert Godin / Joel Farnsworth / Chad O'Neil
Massage Therapist	Jeff Wright

Medical
Orthopedic Surgeons	Drs. Matt Matava, Rick Wright
Internists	Drs. Aaron Birenbaum, Dr. William Birenbaum
Neurosurgeon	Dr. Ralph Dacey
General / Plastic Surgeons	Dr. Michael Brunt / Dr. Tom Francel
Dentist / Oral Surgeon	Dr. Glenn Edwards / Dr. Ken Kram
Ophthalmologist / Optometrist	Dr. Gill Grand / Dr. David Seibel

Broadcasting
Radio / Television Stations	KMOX, 1120 AM / FS Midwest
Radio Play-by-play / Color & Comm. Relations	Chris Kerber / Kelly Chase
Community Relations and KMOX Radio	Bob Plager
Television Play-by-Play / Color	John Kelly / Darren Pang, Bernie Federko
FS Midwest Analyst / Host	Jim Hayes / Pat Parris

Marketing
Senior Director, Advertising/Promotions	Lisa Kampeter
Senior Director, Digital Media	Beth Schwartz
Director, Event Presentation	Chris Frome
Director, Community Relations/14 Fund	Renah Jones
Manager, Event Marketing / Website	Lamont Buford / Chris Pinkert

Sponsorship
Director, Sponsorship Sales	Deni Allen
Corporate Sales Executive	Matt Poling
Sr. Director, Corporate Sponsorship Services	Julie Drochelman
Marketing/Sponsorship Assistant	Donna Ferguson

Ticket Sales
Director, Client Services	Abby Jones
Managers, Ticket Sales / Suite Sales	Yancey Jones / Nick Wierciak
Coordinator, Suite Sales	Melissa Weissman

Group Ticket Sales
Group Sales Senior Director / Manager	Jennifer Nevins / Kari Takmajian

Finance
Finance Controller	Keith Hegger
Managers, Accounting	Craig Bryant, Mike Tonjes, Kristy Atwater
Manager, IT	Tony Kostansek

Retail
Retail Director / Manager	George Pavlik / Barry Smith

Box Office
Manager, Ticket Operations	Eric Fronczek

San Jose Sharks

Key Off-Season Signings/Acquisitions

2011

June 24 • Acquired D **Brent Burns** and a 2nd-round pick in the 2012 Entry Draft from Minnesota for RW **Devin Setoguchi**, C **Charlie Coyle** and San Jose's 1st-round pick in the 2011 Entry Draft.

30 • Re-signed LW **Jamie McGinn** and LW **Frazer McLaren**.

July 1 • Signed C **Michal Handzus** and D **Jim Vandermeer**.

3 • Acquired RW **Martin Havlat** from Minnesota for RW **Dany Heatley**.

6 • Re-signed G **Thomas Greiss**.

8 • Re-signed C **Benn Ferriero**.

12 • Re-signed LW **John McCarthy**.

19 • Signed C **Andrew Murray**.

Aug. 3 • Signed D **Colin White**.

7 • Acquired C **James Sheppard** from Minnesota for a 3rd-round pick in the 2013 Entry Draft.

2010-11 Results: 48W-25L-4OTL-5SOL 105PTS.
First, Pacific Division

Year-by-Year Record

Season	GP	Home W	L	T	OL	Road W	L	T	OL	Overall W	L	T	OL	GF	GA	Pts.	Finished	Playoff Result
2010-11	82	25	11	....	5	23	14	....	4	48	25	....	9	248	213	105	1st, Pacific Div.	Lost Conf. Championship
2009-10	82	27	6	....	8	24	14	....	3	51	20	....	11	264	215	113	1st, Pacific Div.	Lost Conf. Championship
2008-09	82	32	5	....	4	21	13	....	7	53	18	....	11	257	204	117	1st, Pacific Div.	Lost Conf. Quarter-Final
2007-08	82	22	13	....	6	27	10	....	4	49	23	....	10	222	193	108	1st, Pacific Div.	Lost Conf. Semi-Final
2006-07	82	25	12	....	4	26	14	....	1	51	26	....	5	258	199	107	2nd, Pacific Div.	Lost Conf. Semi-Final
2005-06	82	25	9	....	7	19	18	....	4	44	27	....	11	266	242	99	2nd, Pacific Div.	Lost Conf. Semi-Final
2004-05	....	...	...	...	...	...	...	...	...	...	...	...	...	...	...	...	...	...
2003-04	82	24	8	7	2	19	13	5	4	43	21	12	6	219	183	104	1st, Pacific Div.	Lost Conf. Championship
2002-03	82	17	16	5	3	11	21	4	5	28	37	9	8	214	239	73	5th, Pacific Div.	Out of Playoffs
2001-02	82	25	11	3	2	19	16	5	1	44	27	8	3	248	199	99	1st, Pacific Div.	Lost Conf. Semi-Final
2000-01	82	22	14	4	1	18	13	8	2	40	27	12	3	217	192	95	2nd, Pacific Div.	Lost Conf. Quarter-Final
1999-2000	82	21	14	3	3	14	16	7	4	35	30	10	7	225	214	87	4th, Pacific Div.	Lost Conf. Semi-Final
1998-99	82	17	15	9	....	14	18	9	....	31	33	18	....	196	191	80	4th, Pacific Div.	Lost Conf. Quarter-Final
1997-98	82	17	19	5	....	17	19	5	....	34	38	10	....	210	216	78	4th, Pacific Div.	Lost Conf. Quarter-Final
1996-97	82	14	23	4	....	13	24	4	....	27	47	8	....	211	278	62	7th, Pacific Div.	Out of Playoffs
1995-96	82	12	26	3	....	8	29	4	....	20	55	7	....	252	357	47	7th, Pacific Div.	Out of Playoffs
1994-95	48	10	13	1	....	9	12	3	....	19	25	4	....	129	161	42	3rd, Pacific Div.	Lost Conf. Semi-Final
1993-94	84	19	13	10	....	14	22	6	....	33	35	16	....	252	265	82	3rd, Pacific Div.	Lost Conf. Semi-Final
1992-93	84	8	33	1	....	3	38	1	....	11	71	2	....	218	414	24	6th, Smythe Div.	Out of Playoffs
1991-92	80	14	23	3	....	3	35	2	....	17	58	5	....	219	359	39	6th, Smythe Div.	Out of Playoffs

2011-12 Schedule

Oct.						
Sat.	8	Phoenix		Sun.	15	at Chicago
Fri.	14	at Anaheim		Tue.	17	Calgary
Sat.	15	St. Louis		Thu.	19	Ottawa
Mon.	17	Anaheim		Sat.	21	at Vancouver*
Fri.	21	at New Jersey		Mon.	23	at Edmonton
Sat.	22	at Boston		Tue.	24	at Calgary
Tue.	25	at Nashville		Tue.	31	Columbus
Fri.	28	at Detroit	**Feb.**	Thu.	2	Dallas
Sat.	29	at NY Islanders		Sat.	4	at Phoenix
Mon.	31	at NY Rangers		Wed.	8	Calgary
Nov. Thu.	3	Pittsburgh		Fri.	10	Chicago
Sat.	5	Nashville		Sun.	12	at St. Louis
Mon.	7	Los Angeles		Mon.	13	at Washington
Thu.	10	Minnesota		Thu.	16	at Tampa Bay
Sat.	12	Phoenix		Fri.	17	at Carolina
Thu.	17	Detroit		Sun.	19	at Detroit*
Sat.	19	at Dallas		Tue.	21	at Columbus
Sun.	20	at Colorado		Thu.	23	at Toronto
Wed.	23	Chicago		Sat.	25	at Nashville
Sat.	26	Vancouver		Sun.	26	at Minnesota*
Mon.	28	at Los Angeles		Tue.	28	Philadelphia
Dec. Thu.	1	Montreal	**Mar.**	Thu.	1	Buffalo
Sat.	3	Florida		Sat.	3	St. Louis
Tue.	6	Minnesota		Tue.	6	Edmonton
Thu.	8	Dallas		Thu.	8	at Dallas
Sat.	10	at St. Louis		Sat.	10	at Phoenix
Sun.	11	at Chicago		Mon.	12	at Edmonton
Tue.	13	at Colorado		Tue.	13	at Calgary
Thu.	15	Colorado		Thu.	15	Nashville
Sat.	17	Edmonton		Sat.	17	Detroit
Wed.	21	Tampa Bay		Mon.	19	Anaheim
Fri.	23	Los Angeles		Tue.	20	at Los Angeles
Mon.	26	Anaheim		Thu.	22	Boston
Wed.	28	Vancouver		Sat.	24	Phoenix
Jan. Mon.	2	at Vancouver*		Mon.	26	Colorado
Wed.	4	at Anaheim		Wed.	28	at Anaheim
Thu.	5	Columbus		Thu.	29	at Phoenix
Sat.	7	Washington		Sat.	31	Dallas
Tue.	10	at Minnesota	**Apr.**	Tue.	3	at Dallas
Thu.	12	at Winnipeg		Thu.	5	at Los Angeles
Sat.	14	at Columbus		Sat.	7	Los Angeles

* Denotes afternoon game.

PACIFIC DIVISION
21st NHL Season

Franchise date: May 9, 1990

Dan Boyle reached the 50-point plateau for the third straight season in San Jose in 2010-11, and then led all defensemen in playoff scoring with 16 points (four goals, 12 assists) in 18 postseason games.

2011-12 Player Personnel

FORWARDS	HT	WT	S	Place of Birth	*Age	2010-11 Club
CLOWE, Ryane	6-2	225	L	St. John's, Nfld.	29	San Jose
CONNOLLY, Mike	5-9	180	L	Calgary, Alta.	22	U. Minn-Duluth
COUTURE, Logan	6-1	195	L	Guelph, Ont.	22	San Jose
DESJARDINS, Andrew	6-1	200	R	Lively, Ont.	25	San Jose-Worcester
FERRIERO, Benn	5-11	195	R	Boston, MA	24	San Jose-Worcester
GOGOL, Curt	6-0	185	L	Calgary, Alta.	20	Saskatoon-Chilliwack
GUITE, Ben	6-1	210	R	Montreal, Que.	33	Springfield
HAMILTON, Freddie	6-1	190	R	Toronto, Ont.	19	Niagara
HANDZUS, Michal	6-4	220	L	Banska Bystrica, Czech.	34	Los Angeles
HAVLAT, Martin	6-2	217	L	Mlada Boleslav, Czech.	30	Minnesota
LIVINGSTON, James	6-1	210	R	Halifax, N.S.	21	Plymouth
LUCIA, Tony	6-0	190	L	Wayzata, MN	24	Worcester
MacINTYRE, Cam	6-1	225	R	Sooke, B.C.	26	Worcester
MARCOU, James	5-8	165	R	Huntington, NY	23	Worcester
MARLEAU, Patrick	6-2	220	L	Aneroid, Sask.	32	San Jose
MASHINTER, Brandon	6-4	220	L	Bradford, Ont.	23	San Jose-Worcester
McCARTHY, John	6-1	200	L	Boston, MA	25	San Jose-Worcester
McGINN, Jamie	6-1	205	L	Fergus, Ont.	23	San Jose-Worcester
McLAREN, Frazer	6-5	250	L	Winnipeg, Man.	23	San Jose-Worcester
MITCHELL, Torrey	5-11	190	R	Montreal, Que.	26	San Jose
MURRAY, Andrew	6-2	210	L	Selkirk, Man.	29	Columbus
PAVELSKI, Joe	5-11	195	R	Plover, WI	27	San Jose
REID, Brodie	6-1	195	R	Delta, B.C.	22	Northeastern
SGARBOSSA, Michael	5-11	170	L	Campbellville, Ont.	19	Saginaw-Sudbury
SHEPPARD, James	6-2	210	L	Halifax, N.S.	23	Did Not Play - Injured
THORNTON, Joe	6-4	230	L	London, Ont.	32	San Jose
VIEDENSKY, Marek	6-3	208	R	Handlova, Czechoslovakia	21	Saskatoon
WINGELS, Tommy	6-0	190	R	Evanston, IL	23	San Jose-Worcester
DEFENSEMEN						
ACOLATSE, Sena	5-11	205	R	Hayward, CA	20	Sask-Pr. Geo.-Wor
BOYLE, Dan	5-11	190	R	Ottawa, Ont.	35	San Jose
BRAUN, Justin	6-1	205	R	St. Paul, MN	24	San Jose-Worcester
BURNS, Brent	6-5	219	R	Ajax, Ont.	26	Minnesota
DEMERS, Jason	6-1	195	R	Dorval, Que.	23	San Jose
DOHERTY, Taylor	6-7	230	R	Cambridge, Ont.	20	Kingston-Worcester
IRWIN, Matt	6-2	210	L	Brentwood Bay, B.C.	23	Worcester
MOORE, Mike	6-1	190	L	Calgary, Alta.	26	San Jose-Worcester
MURRAY, Douglas	6-3	240	L	Bromma, Sweden	31	San Jose
PELECH, Matt	6-3	220	R	Toronto, Ont.	24	Abbotsford
PETRECKI, Nicholas	6-3	230	L	Schenectady, NY	22	Worcester
SULLIVAN, Sean	6-0	190	L	Boston, MA	27	Worcester
VANDERMEER, Jim	6-1	215	L	Caroline, Alta.	31	Edmonton
VLASIC, Marc-Edouard	6-1	200	L	Montreal, Que.	24	San Jose
WHITE, Colin	6-4	215	L	New Glasgow, N.S.	33	New Jersey
GOALTENDERS	**HT**	**WT**	**C**	**Place of Birth**	***Age**	**2010-11 Club**
ANDERSON, J.P.	5-11	190	R	Toronto, Ont.	19	St. Michael's
GREISS, Thomas	6-1	210	L	Straubing, West Germany	25	Brynas
HEEMSKERK, Thomas	6-0	195	L	Chilliwack, B.C.	21	Moose Jaw
NIEMI, Antti	6-2	215	L	Vantaa, Finland	28	San Jose
NIITTYMAKI, Antero	6-1	210	L	Turku, Finland	31	San Jose
SATERI, Harri	6-1	210	L	Toijala, Finland	21	Tappara-Worcester
SEXSMITH, Tyson	5-11	210	L	Calgary, Alta.	22	Worcester-Stockton
STALOCK, Alex	6-0	185	L	St. Paul, MN	24	San Jose-Worcester

* – Age at start of 2011-12 season

Todd McLellan

Head Coach

Born: Melville, Sask., October 3, 1967.

The San Jose Sharks introduced Todd McLellan as their new head coach on June 12, 2008. In just three seasons as an NHL head coach, McLellan continues to make remarkable additions to an already impressive coaching resume. McLellan has posted a 152-63-31 record behind the San Jose Sharks bench, tying him with Mike Keenan for the most wins by any NHL head coach in their first three years. During that span, the Sharks have posted three 40-plus win and 100-point seasons, captured a Presidents' Trophy (2009), three consecutive Pacific Division titles and made back-to-back appearances in the Western Conference Final (2010, 2011).

During the 2010-11 campaign, McLellan's Sharks tied for the third-most wins in the NHL (48), were second in power play percentage (23.5%), led the NHL in shots per game (34.5) and were second in faceoff percentage (53.7%). In 2009-10, McLellan's team finished in the top-five among all NHL teams in goals per game (3.13), power play (21.0 percent), penalty killing (85.0), faceoff percentage (55.6) and even-strength goal differential (plus-32). He became just the third coach in NHL history to record 50-plus wins in his first two seasons. In his first season as an NHL head coach, he was named as a finalist for the Jack Adams Award and became just the sixth NHL coach (and first since 1990) to lead his team to the Presidents' Trophy for the best overall regular season record (53-18-11) in his first season behind the bench.

Before joining San Jose, McLellan spent three seasons as an assistant coach under Mike Babcock with the Detroit Red Wings. During that span, no NHL team won more games (162) or earned more points (352) than Detroit. One of McLellan's key responsibilities was working with the Red Wings power play, which finished third in the NHL in 2007-08 (20.7) and first in 2005-06 (22.1). Prior to being hired in Detroit, McLellan spent four seasons as head coach of the Houston Aeros in the American Hockey League, capturing the Calder Cup championship and being named Minor League coach of the year by The Hockey News in 2003. In 2000-01, he was the head coach of the Cleveland Lumberjacks of the International Hockey League. From 1994-95 through 1999-00, McLellan coached the Swift Current Broncos of the Western Hockey League, where he also served as general manager in his final four seasons. He was named 2000 WHL coach of the year and 1997 WHL executive of the year. The team captured division titles in 1996 and 2000. In his 17 years of serving as a head and assistant coach, McLellan's teams have never missed the postseason.

McLellan played his junior hockey with Saskatoon (WHL) and was drafted by the New York Islanders in the fifth round (106th overall) in the 1986 NHL Entry Draft. He played parts of two seasons with Springfield in the AHL and played in five games with the Islanders in 1987-88, posting two points (one goal, one assist) before a shoulder injury ended his career.

2010-11 Scoring

* – rookie

Regular Season

Pos	#	Player	Team	GP	G	A	Pts	TOI	+/–	PIM	PP	SH	GW	S	%
C	12	Patrick Marleau	S.J.	82	37	36	73	20:47	–3	16	11	2	9	279	13.3
C	19	Joe Thornton	S.J.	80	21	49	70	19:52	4	47	9	2	3	149	14.1
C	8	Joe Pavelski	S.J.	74	20	46	66	19:39	10	24	11	1	5	282	7.1
L	15	Dany Heatley	S.J.	80	26	38	64	19:39	8	56	11	1	5	217	12.0
L	29	Ryane Clowe	S.J.	75	24	38	62	17:57	13	100	5	0	2	185	13.0
C	39 *	Logan Couture	S.J.	79	32	24	56	17:49	18	41	10	0	8	253	12.6
D	22	Dan Boyle	S.J.	76	9	41	50	26:14	2	67	4	0	2	199	4.5
R	16	Devin Setoguchi	S.J.	72	22	19	41	15:12	–2	37	4	0	5	199	11.1
D	9	Ian White	CGY	16	2	4	6	21:44	–10	6	1	0	0	34	5.9
			CAR	39	0	10	10	19:18	4	12	0	0	0	53	0.0
			S.J.	23	2	8	10	19:55	9	8	0	0	0	51	3.9
			Total	78	4	22	26	19:59	3	26	1	0	0	138	2.9
D	60	Jason Demers	S.J.	75	2	22	24	19:29	19	28	0	0	0	105	1.9
C	17	Torrey Mitchell	S.J.	66	9	14	23	13:20	10	46	0	0	1	116	7.8
D	44	Marc-Edouard Vlasic	S.J.	80	4	14	18	20:51	14	18	0	0	2	116	3.4
L	55	Ben Eager	ATL	34	3	7	10	12:15	4	77	0	0	1	41	7.3
			S.J.	34	4	3	7	9:01	0	43	0	0	0	43	9.3
			Total	68	7	10	17	10:38	4	120	0	0	1	84	8.3
R	10	Jamal Mayers	S.J.	78	3	11	14	8:52	3	124	0	0	0	62	4.8
D	3	Douglas Murray	S.J.	73	1	13	14	19:36	5	44	0	0	0	102	1.0
C	20	Kyle Wellwood	S.J.	35	5	8	13	13:40	10	0	0	0	0	50	10
D	61 *	Justin Braun	S.J.	28	2	9	11	16:30	–1	2	2	0	0	44	4.5
D	40	Kent Huskins	S.J.	50	2	8	10	16:36	8	12	0	0	0	38	5.3
R	78 *	Benn Ferriero	S.J.	33	5	4	9	13:05	8	9	1	0	1	56	8.9
D	7	Niclas Wallin	S.J.	74	3	5	8	15:50	0	46	0	0	0	86	3.5
C	21	Scott Nichol	S.J.	56	4	3	7	9:44	–3	50	0	0	0	61	6.6
L	64	Jamie McGinn	S.J.	49	1	5	6	11:35	–6	33	0	0	0	63	1.6
L	43 *	John McCarthy	S.J.	37	2	2	4	8:44	–8	8	0	0	0	41	4.9
C	69 *	Andrew Desjardins	S.J.	17	1	2	3	7:08	–1	4	0	0	0	12	8.3
D	55 *	Mike Moore	S.J.	6	1	0	1	10:06	–1	7	0	0	0	5	20.0
C	57 *	Tommy Wingels	S.J.	5	0	0	0	5:06	–1	0	0	0	0	1	0.0
L	68 *	Frazer McLaren	S.J.	9	0	0	0	4:15	–1	22	0	0	0	1	0.0
L	72 *	Brandon Mashinter	S.J.	13	0	0	0	6:22	–2	17	0	0	0	5	0.0

Goaltending

No.	Goaltender	GPI	Mins	Avg	W	L	OT	EN	SO	GA	SA	S%	G	A	PIM
32	* Alex Stalock	1	30	0.00	1	0	0	0	0	0	9	1.000	0	0	0
31	Antti Niemi	60	3524	2.38	35	18	6	2	6	140	1741	.920	0	1	2
30	Antero Niittymaki	24	1414	2.72	12	7	3	2	0	64	615	.896	0	0	2
	Totals	**82**	**4999**	**2.50**	**48**	**25**	**9**	**4**	**6**	**208**	**2369**	**.912**			

Playoffs

Pos	#	Player	Team	GP	G	A	Pts	TOI	+/–	PIM	PP	SH	GW	OT	S	%
C	19	Joe Thornton	S.J.	18	3	14	17	22:15	–5	16	0	0	2	1	48	6.3
D	22	Dan Boyle	S.J.	18	4	12	16	26:10	–7	8	2	0	1	0	67	6.0
L	29	Ryane Clowe	S.J.	17	6	9	15	19:27	5	32	3	0	0	0	39	15.4
C	39 *	Logan Couture	S.J.	18	7	7	14	19:23	2	2	1	0	0	0	64	10.9
C	12	Patrick Marleau	S.J.	18	7	6	13	22:21	–1	9	3	0	1	0	59	11.9
R	16	Devin Setoguchi	S.J.	18	7	3	10	17:26	–7	12	3	0	2	2	65	10.8
C	8	Joe Pavelski	S.J.	18	5	5	10	21:08	1	10	1	0	1	1	58	8.6
L	15	Dany Heatley	S.J.	18	3	6	9	18:56	–2	12	0	0	0	0	47	6.4
D	9	Ian White	S.J.	17	1	8	9	20:04	3	8	1	0	0	0	40	2.5
C	20	Kyle Wellwood	S.J.	18	1	6	7	13:49	6	0	0	0	0	0	18	5.6
C	17	Torrey Mitchell	S.J.	18	1	4	5	15:02	0	10	0	0	0	0	33	3.0
D	7	Niclas Wallin	S.J.	18	1	3	4	16:35	2	10	0	0	1	0	24	4.2
D	60	Jason Demers	S.J.	13	2	1	3	19:56	–1	8	0	0	0	0	20	10.0
D	44	Marc-Edouard Vlasic	S.J.	18	0	3	3	21:45	4	4	0	0	0	0	18	0.0
C	69 *	Andrew Desjardins	S.J.	3	1	0	1	6:48	1	4	0	0	0	0	4	25.0
R	78 *	Benn Ferriero	S.J.	8	1	0	1	6:54	0	6	0	0	1	1	3	33.3
L	55	Ben Eager	S.J.	10	1	0	1	4:53	–2	41	0	0	0	0	11	9.1
D	40	Kent Huskins	S.J.	5	0	1	1	18:48	1	2	0	0	0	0	2	0.0
L	64	Jamie McGinn	S.J.	7	0	1	1	6:33	0	30	0	0	0	0	3	0.0
D	3	Douglas Murray	S.J.	18	0	1	1	19:30	–7	8	0	0	0	0	27	0.0
D	61 *	Justin Braun	S.J.	1	0	0	0	15:32	–1	0	0	0	0	0	1	0.0
R	10	Jamal Mayers	S.J.	12	0	0	0	5:37	–3	12	0	0	0	0	5	0.0
C	21	Scott Nichol	S.J.	15	0	0	0	6:22	–7	26	0	0	0	0	8	0.0

Goaltending

No.	Goaltender	GPI	Mins	Avg	W	L	EN	SO	GA	SA	S%	G	A	PIM
30	Antero Niittymaki	2	91	0.66	1	0	0	0	1	30	.967	0	0	0
31	Antti Niemi	18	1044	3.22	8	9	1	0	56	538	.896	0	0	0
	Totals	**18**	**1147**	**3.03**	**9**	**9**	**1**	**0**	**58**	**569**	**.898**			

Coaching Record

			Regular Season				Playoffs			
Season	Team	League	GC	W	L	O/T	GC	W	L	T
1994-95	Swift Current	WHL	72	31	34	7	6	2	4	....
1995-96	Swift Current	WHL	72	36	31	5	6	2	4	....
1996-97	Swift Current	WHL	72	44	23	5	10	4	4	....
1997-98	Swift Current	WHL	72	44	19	9	12	7	5	....
1998-99	Swift Current	WHL	72	34	32	6	6	2	4	....
99-2000	Swift Current	WHL	72	47	18	7	12	6	6	....
2000-01	Cleveland	IHL	82	43	32	7	4	0	4	....
2001-02	Houston	AHL	80	39	26	15	14	8	6	....
2002-03	Houston	AHL	80	47	23	10	23	15	8	....
2003-04	Houston	AHL	80	28	34	18	2	0	2	....
2004-05	Houston	AHL	80	40	28	12	5	1	4	....
2008-09	**San Jose**	**NHL**	**82**	**53**	**18**	**11**	**6**	**2**	**4**	....
2009-10	**San Jose**	**NHL**	**82**	**51**	**20**	**11**	**15**	**8**	**7**	....
2010-11	**San Jose**	**NHL**	**82**	**48**	**25**	**9**	**18**	**9**	**9**	....
	NHL Totals		**246**	**152**	**63**	**31**	**39**	**19**	**20**	....

Club Records

Team

(Figures in brackets for season records are games played; records for fewest points, wins, ties, losses, goals, goals against are for 70 or more games)

Most Points	**117**	2008-09 (82)
Most Wins	**53**	2008-09 (82)
Most Ties	**18**	1998-99 (82)
Most Losses	***71**	1992-93 (84)
Most Goals	**266**	2005-06 (82)
Most Goals Against	**414**	1992-93 (84)
Fewest Points	**24**	1992-93 (84)
Fewest Wins	**11**	1992-93 (84)
Fewest Ties	***2**	1992-93 (84)
Fewest Losses	**18**	2008-09 (82)
Fewest Goals	**196**	1998-99 (82)
Fewest Goals Against	**183**	2003-04 (82)
Longest Winning Streak		
Overall	**11**	Feb. 21-Mar. 14/08
Home	**9**	Oct. 9-Nov. 8/08
Away	**10**	Nov. 14-Dec. 31/07
Longest Undefeated Streak		
Overall	**10**	Nov. 27-Dec. 19/01 (9 wins, 1 tie)
Home	**11**	Nov. 15-Dec. 29/03 (8 wins, 3 ties)
Away	**10**	Dec. 26/00-Feb. 16/01 (6 wins, 4 ties)
Longest Losing Streak		
Overall	***17**	Jan. 4-Feb. 12/93
Home	**9**	Nov. 19-Dec. 19/92
Away	**19**	Nov. 27/92-Feb. 12/93
Longest Winless Streak		
Overall	**20**	Dec. 29/92-Feb. 12/93 (19 losses, 1 tie)
Home	**9**	Nov. 19-Dec. 19/92 (9 losses), Oct. 16-Nov. 18/03 (4 losses, 5 ties)
Away	**19**	Nov. 27/92-Feb. 12/93 (19 losses)
Most Shutouts, Season	**11**	2003-04 (82), 2006-07 (82)
Most PIM, Season	**2,134**	1992-93 (84)
Most Goals, Game	**10**	Jan. 13/96 (S.J. 10 at Pit. 8), Mar. 30/02 (CBJ 2 at S.J. 10)

Individual

Most Seasons	**13**	Patrick Marleau
Most Games, Career	**1,035**	Patrick Marleau
Most Goals, Career	**357**	Patrick Marleau
Most Assists, Career	**409**	Patrick Marleau
Most Points, Career	**766**	Patrick Marleau (357G, 409A)
Most PIM, Career	**1,001**	Jeff Odgers
Most Shutouts, Career	**50**	Evgeni Nabokov
Longest Consecutive Games Streak	**379**	Joe Thornton (Dec. 1/05-Mar. 27/10)
Most Goals, Season	**56**	Jonathan Cheechoo (2005-06)
Most Assists, Season	**92**	Joe Thornton (2006-07)
Most Points, Season	**114**	Joe Thornton (2006-07; 22G, 92A)
Most PIM, Season	**326**	Link Gaetz (1991-92)
Most Points, Defenseman, Season	**64**	Sandis Ozolinsh (1993-94; 26G, 38A)
Most Points, Center, Season	**114**	Joe Thornton (2006-07; 22G, 92A)
Most Points, Right Wing, Season	**93**	Jonathan Cheechoo (2005-06; 56G, 37A)
Most Points, Left Wing, Season	**83**	Patrick Marleau (2009-10; 44G, 39A)
Most Points, Rookie, Season	**59**	Pat Falloon (1991-92; 25G, 34A)
Most Shutouts, Season	**9**	Evgeni Nabokov (2003-04)
Most Goals, Game	**4**	Owen Nolan (Dec. 19/95)
Most Assists, Game	**4**	Eighteen times
Most Points, Game	**6**	Owen Nolan (Oct. 4/99; 3G, 3A)

* NHL Record.

Captains' History

Doug Wilson, 1991-92, 1992-93; Bob Errey, 1993-94; Bob Errey and Jeff Odgers, 1994-95; Jeff Odgers, 1995-96; Todd Gill, 1996-97, 1997-98; Owen Nolan, 1998-99 to 2002-03; Mike Ricci, Vincent Damphousse, Alyn McCauley, Patrick Marleau, 2003-04; Patrick Marleau, 2005-06 to 2008-09; Rob Blake, 2009-10; Joe Thornton, 2010-11 to date.

Coaching History

George Kingston, 1991-92, 1992-93; Kevin Constantine, 1993-94, 1994-95; Kevin Constantine and Jim Wiley, 1995-96; Al Sims, 1996-97; Darryl Sutter, 1997-98 to 2001-02; Darryl Sutter, Cap Raeder and Ron Wilson, 2002-03; Ron Wilson, 2003-04 to 2007-08; Todd McLellan, 2008-09 to date.

All-time Record vs. Other Clubs

Regular Season

	At Home								On Road								Total							
	GP	W	L	T	OL	GF	GA	PTS	GP	W	L	T	OL	GF	GA	PTS	GP	W	L	T	OL	GF	GA	PTS
Anaheim	51	25	21	2	3	143	133	55	51	28	17	2	4	150	136	62	102	53	38	4	7	293	269	117
Atlanta	7	5	1	1	0	26	15	11	6	4	0	1	1	20	11	10	13	9	1	2	1	46	26	21
Boston	13	4	6	2	1	32	42	11	13	3	7	3	0	39	43	9	26	7	13	5	1	71	85	20
Buffalo	13	6	3	4	0	42	45	16	15	1	13	0	1	41	67	3	28	7	16	4	1	83	112	19
Calgary	46	20	20	4	2	147	132	46	44	15	24	4	1	118	153	35	90	35	44	8	3	265	285	81
Carolina	14	8	5	0	1	59	43	17	13	6	7	0	0	32	41	12	27	14	12	0	1	91	84	29
Chicago	38	22	11	3	2	112	101	49	37	18	13	2	4	121	116	42	75	40	24	5	6	233	217	91
Colorado	36	17	18	1	0	102	113	35	35	11	17	4	3	79	122	29	71	28	35	5	3	181	235	64
Columbus	20	17	1	0	2	73	35	36	20	10	8	0	2	42	50	22	40	27	9	0	4	115	85	58
Dallas	51	19	23	1	8	122	138	47	50	23	21	4	2	129	142	52	101	42	44	5	10	251	280	99
Detroit	38	15	19	3	1	132	144	34	37	7	26	1	3	69	141	18	75	22	45	4	4	201	285	52
Edmonton	44	22	14	5	3	145	127	52	45	14	22	7	2	110	142	37	89	36	36	12	5	255	269	89
Florida	11	6	2	2	1	34	22	15	12	3	4	5	0	34	33	11	23	9	6	7	1	68	55	26
Los Angeles	58	35	18	3	2	195	158	75	58	24	26	4	4	156	166	56	116	59	44	7	6	351	324	131
Minnesota	20	12	5	1	2	58	43	27	20	11	6	1	2	51	47	25	40	23	11	2	4	109	90	52
Montreal	13	7	3	2	1	42	34	17	14	2	10	2	0	25	48	6	27	9	13	4	1	67	82	23
Nashville	24	15	6	1	2	71	61	33	24	11	11	1	1	64	61	24	48	26	17	2	3	135	122	57
New Jersey	13	5	6	1	1	34	38	12	15	4	9	1	1	32	55	10	28	9	15	2	2	66	93	22
NY Islanders	15	8	5	1	1	39	44	18	13	5	6	2	0	41	44	12	28	13	11	3	1	80	88	30
NY Rangers	16	3	10	2	1	37	57	9	12	3	7	1	1	37	46	8	28	6	17	3	2	74	103	17
Ottawa	11	7	4	0	0	26	20	14	12	4	4	4	0	34	37	12	23	11	8	4	0	60	57	26
Philadelphia	15	6	7	2	0	39	39	14	15	7	6	2	0	46	48	16	30	13	13	4	0	85	87	30
Phoenix	53	28	16	4	5	175	145	65	56	26	25	3	2	161	165	57	109	54	41	7	7	336	310	122
Pittsburgh	16	8	6	2	0	44	57	18	12	6	4	1	1	38	46	14	28	14	10	3	1	82	103	32
St. Louis	36	13	19	1	3	93	113	30	40	18	19	1	2	103	116	39	76	31	38	2	5	196	229	69
Tampa Bay	13	6	6	1	0	47	40	13	15	6	7	1	1	40	39	14	28	12	13	2	1	87	79	27
Toronto	18	7	8	3	0	42	48	17	20	6	12	2	0	55	75	14	38	13	20	5	0	97	123	31
Vancouver	46	20	18	5	3	138	135	48	44	17	22	4	1	119	149	39	90	37	40	9	4	257	284	87
Washington	14	10	3	1	0	48	33	21	15	9	6	0	0	42	40	18	29	19	9	1	0	90	73	39
Totals	**763**	**376**	**284**	**58**	**45**	**2297**	**2155**	**855**	**763**	**302**	**359**	**63**	**39**	**2028**	**2379**	**706**	**1526**	**678**	**643**	**121**	**84**	**4325**	**4534**	**1561**

Playoffs

	Series	W	L	GP	W	L	T	GF	GA	Last Mtg.	Rnd.	Result
Anaheim	1	0	1	6	2	4	0	10	18	2009	CQF	L 2-4
Calgary	3	2	1	20	10	10	0	57	68	2008	CQF	W 4-3
Chicago	1	0	1	4	0	4	0	7	13	2010	CF	L 0-4
Colorado	4	2	2	25	13	12	0	71	62	2010	CQF	W 4-2
Dallas	3	0	3	17	5	12	0	30	46	2008	CSF	L 2-4
Detroit	5	3	2	29	14	15	0	69	99	2011	CSF	W 4-3
Edmonton	1	0	1	6	2	4	0	12	19	2006	CSF	L 2-4
Los Angeles	1	1	0	6	4	2	0	20	20	2011	CQF	W 4-2
Nashville	2	2	0	10	8	2	0	33	24	2007	CQF	W 4-1
Phoenix	1	1	0	5	4	1	0	13	7	2002	CQF	W 4-1
St. Louis	3	2	1	18	10	8	0	43	47	2004	CQF	W 4-1
Toronto	1	0	1	7	3	4	0	21	26	1994	CSF	L 3-4
Vancouver	1	0	1	5	1	4	0	13	20	2011	CF	L 1-4
Totals	**27**	**13**	**14**	**158**	**76**	**82**	**0**	**399**	**469**			

Playoff Results 2011-2007

Year	Round	Opponent	Result	GF	GA
2011	CF	Vancouver	L 1-4	13	20
	CSF	Detroit	W 4-3	18	18
	CQF	Los Angeles	W 4-2	20	20
2010	CF	Chicago	L 0-4	7	13
	CSF	Detroit	W 4-1	15	17
	CQF	Colorado	W 4-2	19	11
2009	CQF	Anaheim	L 2-4	10	18
2008	CSF	Dallas	L 2-4	11	15
	CQF	Calgary	W 4-3	19	17
2007	CSF	Detroit	L 2-4	9	13
	CQF	Nashville	W 4-1	16	14

Abbreviations: Round: CF – conference final; **CSF** – conference semi-final; **CQF** – conference quarter-final.

Carolina totals include Hartford, 1991-92 to 1996-97.
Dallas totals include Minnesota North Stars, 1991-92 to 1992-93.

Colorado totals include Quebec, 1991-92 to 1994-95.
Phoenix totals include Winnipeg, 1991-92 to 1995-96.

2010-11 Results

Oct.	8	at Columbus	3-2
	9	Columbus	2-3*
	16	Atlanta	2-4
	19	Carolina	2-5
	21	at Colorado	4-2
	23	at Edmonton	6-1
	24	at Calgary	0-4
	27	New Jersey	5-2
	30	Anaheim	5-2
Nov.	2	at Minnesota	0-1
	4	at St. Louis	0-2
	6	Tampa Bay	5-2
	9	Anaheim	2-3*
	11	NY Islanders	2-1†
	13	Calgary	4-3
	15	Los Angeles	6-3
	17	at Colorado	3-4*
	18	at Dallas	4-5*
	20	Columbus	0-3
	24	Chicago	5-2
	26	at Vancouver	1-6
	27	at Edmonton	4-3
	30	Detroit	3-5
Dec.	2	at Ottawa	4-0
	4	at Montreal	1-3
	6	at Detroit	5-2
	8	at Philadelphia	5-4†
	9	at Buffalo	3-6
	11	Chicago	2-1*
	13	Dallas	2-3†
	15	at Nashville	2-3
	16	at Dallas	4-3*
	18	at St. Louis	4-1
	21	Edmonton	2-1
	23	Phoenix	4-1
	27	Los Angeles	0-4
	29	at Minnesota	3-5
	30	at Chicago	5-3
Jan.	1	at Los Angeles	1-0
	3	Vancouver	3-4
	6	Buffalo	0-3
	8	Nashville	1-2
	9	at Anaheim	0-1
	11	Toronto	2-4
	13	Edmonton	2-5
	15	St. Louis	4-2
	17	at Phoenix	4-2
	20	at Vancouver	2-1†
	22	Minnesota	4-3
	26	at Los Angeles	2-3†
Feb.	1	Phoenix	5-3
	2	at Anaheim	4-3
	5	at Boston	2-0
	8	at Washington	2-0
	9	at Columbus	3-2
	11	at New Jersey	1-2
	13	at Florida	2-3
	15	at Nashville	2-1*
	17	Washington	3-2
	19	Colorado	4-0
	22	at Detroit	4-3
	23	at Pittsburgh	3-2*
	25	at Calgary	4-3†
Mar.	1	Colorado	2-1†
	3	Detroit	3-1
	5	Dallas	2-3
	8	Nashville	3-2*
	10	Vancouver	4-5†
	12	NY Rangers	2-3†
	14	at Chicago	3-6
	15	at Dallas	6-3
	17	Minnesota	3-2
	19	St. Louis	5-3
	23	Calgary	6-3
	24	at Los Angeles	3-4†
	26	at Phoenix	4-1
	31	Dallas	6-0
Apr.	2	Anaheim	4-2
	4	Los Angeles	6-1
	6	at Anaheim	2-6
	8	at Phoenix	3-4
	9	Phoenix	3-1

* – Overtime † – Shootout

Entry Draft Selections 2011-1997

Name in bold denotes played in NHL.

2011
Pick
47 Matthew Nieto
89 Justin Sefton
133 Sean Kuraly
166 Daniil Sobchenko
179 Dylan Demelo
194 Colin Blackwell

2010
Pick
28 Charlie Coyle
88 Max Gaede
127 Cody Ferriero
129 Freddie Hamilton
136 Isaac MacLeod
163 Konrad Abeltshauser
188 Lee Moffie
200 Chris Crane

2009
Pick
43 William Wrenn
57 Taylor Doherty
147 Phil Varone
189 Marek Viedensky
207 Dominik Bielke

2008
Pick
62 Justin Daniels
92 Samuel Groulx
106 Harri Sateri
146 Julien Demers
177 **Tommy Wingels**
186 **Jason Demers**
194 Drew Daniels

2007
Pick
9 **Logan Couture**
28 Nicholas Petrecki
83 **Timo Pielmeier**
91 Tyson Sexsmith
165 Patrick Zackrisson
173 **Nick Bonino**
201 **Justin Braun**
203 **Frazer McLaren**

2006
Pick
16 **Ty Wishart**
36 **Jamie McGinn**
98 James Delory
143 Ashton Rome
202 **John McCarthy**
203 Jay Barriball

2005
Pick
8 **Devin Setoguchi**
35 **Marc-Edouard Vlasic**
112 **Alex Stalock**
140 Taylor Dakers
149 **Derek Joslin**
162 P.J. Fenton
183 Will Colbert
193 Tony Lucia

2004
Pick
22 **Lukas Kaspar**
94 **Thomas Greiss**
126 **Torrey Mitchell**
129 Jason Churchill
153 **Steven Zalewski**
201 **Michael Vernace**
225 David MacDonald
234 Derek MacIntyre
288 Brian Mahoney-Wilson
289 Christian Jensen

2003
Pick
6 **Milan Michalek**
16 **Steve Bernier**
43 **Josh Hennessy**
47 **Matt Carle**
139 Patrick Ehelechner
201 Jonathan Tremblay
205 **Joe Pavelski**
216 Kai Hospelt
236 Alexander Hult
267 Brian O'Hanley
276 Carter Lee

2002
Pick
27 Mike Morris
52 Dan Spang
86 Jonas Fiedler
139 **Kris Newbury**
163 Tom Walsh
217 **Tim Conboy**
288 Michael Hutchins

2001
Pick
20 **Marcel Goc**
106 **Christian Ehrhoff**
107 **Dimitri Patzold**
140 **Tomas Plihal**
175 **Ryane Clowe**
182 **Tom Cavanagh**

2000
Pick
41 Tero Maatta
104 **Jon DiSalvatore**
142 Michal Pinc
166 **Nolan Schaefer**
183 Michal Macho
246 **Chad Wiseman**
256 Pasi Saarinen

1999
Pick
14 **Jeff Jillson**
82 Mark Concannon
111 Willie Levesque
155 **Niko Dimitrakos**
229 Eric Betournay
241 **Douglas Murray**
257 **Hannes Hyvonen**

1998
Pick
3 **Brad Stuart**
29 **Jonathan Cheechoo**
65 Eric Laplante
98 **Rob Davison**
104 **Miroslav Zalesak**
127 Brandon Coalter
145 **Mikael Samuelsson**
185 Robert Mulick
212 **Jim Fahey**

1997
Pick
2 **Patrick Marleau**
23 **Scott Hannan**
82 Adam Colagiacomo
107 Adam Nittel
163 Joe Dusbabek
192 **Cam Severson**
219 **Mark Smith**

Doug Wilson

Executive Vice President and General Manager

Born: Ottawa, Ont., July 5, 1957.

Through strong drafting, shrewd trades and timely free agent signings, Executive Vice President and General Manager Doug Wilson has crafted one of the National Hockey League's most successful on-ice franchises since being named to his post prior to the 2003-04 season.

In his seven seasons in charge of the Sharks hockey department, Wilson, who also serves as the team's alternate governor to the NHL, has guided the team to its most successful era since the franchise's inception, capturing the Presidents' Trophy (2009), five Pacific Division titles (2004, 2008, 2009, 2010, 2011) and advancing to the Western Conference Final in 2004, 2010 and 2011.

In his current role, Wilson has overall authority regarding all hockey-related operations. He oversees all player personnel decisions, negotiates player contracts, coordinates the efforts of the team's scouting department, leads the team in its draft day preparation and administers the club's player evaluation process at all professional, minor and junior levels.

In his previous role as the team's director of pro development (1997-03), the 16-year NHL veteran's responsibilities included evaluating talent at all professional and minor league levels and continuous assessment of the Sharks roster and reserve list.

Working closely with the entire hockey department, Wilson played a major role in creating a positive atmosphere in the dressing room and on-the-ice attractiveness to obtaining and retaining veteran free agents such as Vincent Damphousse, Mike Ricci, Gary Suter, Scott Thornton and Mike Vernon.

Wilson was an integral member of the NHL Players' Association for four years (1993-97) and is a past president of the NHLPA.

Wilson draws on a vast amount of hockey knowledge. He served a consultant to Team Canada, winners of four consecutive World Junior gold medals in the 1990s. His brother Murray was a member of four Stanley Cup championship teams with Montreal in the 1970s. With the Ottawa 67s In junior, Wilson played for Hall of Famer Hec Kilrea, junior hockey's winningest coach.

In 2004, Wilson was named to the NHL Game Committee, a panel of players, coaches, executives and media responsible for examining all aspects of the game. The committee, which initially met during the offseason, included Hall of Fame Coach Scotty Bowman, Pittsburgh's Chairman of the Board Mario Lemieux and former national television analyst/goaltender and current St. Louis President of Hockey Operations John Davidson, among others.

A first round draft choice (sixth overall) by the Blackhawks in 1977 after a stellar junior career with the Ottawa 67s, Wilson played 14 seasons in Chicago and still ranks as the club's highest scoring defenseman in points (779 — fifth overall), goals (225 — 12th overall) and assists (554 — third overall). Wilson ranks fifth all-time in games played (938) for Chicago. In addition, he led all Blackhawks defensemen in scoring for 10 consecutive seasons (1980-81 through 1990-91) and captured the 1982 James Norris Memorial Trophy, symbolic of the League's top defenseman, when he tallied 39 goals and 85 points — still Blackhawks single-season records for goals and points for a defenseman.

General Managers' History

Jack Ferreira, 1991-92; Chuck Grillo (V.P. Director of Player Personnel), 1992-93 to 1995-96; Chuck Grillo and Dean Lombardi, 1996-97; Dean Lombardi, 1997-98 to 2002-03; Doug Wilson, 2003-04 to date.

Club Directory

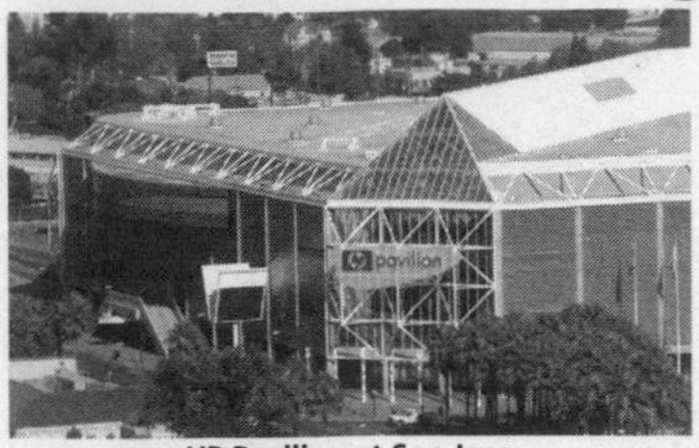
HP Pavilion at San Jose

San Jose Sharks
HP Pavilion at San Jose
525 West Santa Clara Street
San Jose, CA 95113
Phone **408/287-7070**
FAX 408/999-5797
www.sjsharks.com
Capacity: 17,562

San Jose Sports and Entertainment Enterprises Ownership Group
Kevin Compton, Hasso Plattner, Stratton Sclavos, Gary Valenzuela, Gordon Russell, Rudy Staedler, Floyd Kvamme, Greg Jamison, Harvey Armstrong, Tom McEnery, George Gund III

Executive Staff

Executive V.P. of Business Operations	Malcolm Bordelon
Executive V.P. & Chief Financial Officer	Charlie Faas
Executive V.P. & G.M. (HP Pavilion at San Jose)	Jim Goddard
Executive V.P. of Business Development	Michael T. Lehr
Executive V.P. & General Counsel	John Tortora
Executive V.P. & General Manager (Sharks)	Doug Wilson
Vice President of Finance	Ken Caveney
Vice President of Corporate Partnerships	Eric Mastalir
Vice President of Sales & Marketing	Kent Russell
Vice President of Building Operations	Rich Sotelo
Vice President and Assistant G.M. (Sharks)	Wayne Thomas
Executive Assistants	Misty Macias, Mary Grace Miller, Michelle Simmons, Tricia Sullivan-Minsky

Hockey Operations

Director of Hockey Operations	Joe Will
Head Coach	Todd McLellan
Assistant Coaches	Matt Shaw, Jay Woodcroft
Goaltending Development Coach	Corey Schwab
Development Coach	Mike Ricci
Coaching Staff Assistant	Brett Heimlich
Director of Scouting	Tim Burke
Director of Pro Scouting	John Ferguson
Scouts	Gilles Cote, Pat Funk, Jack Gardiner, Dirk Graham, Rob Grillo, Brian Gross, Shin Larsson, Bryan Marchment, Karel Masopust, Jason Rowe
Director of Hockey Administration	Rosemary Tebaldi
Manager of Hockey Technology	Paul Fink
Head Athletic Trainer	Ray Tufts, ATC
Assistant Athletic Trainer	Wes Howard, ATC
Strength & Conditioning Coordinator	Mike Potenza
Massage Therapist	Arnulfo Aguirre, CMT, ART
Equipment Manager	Mike Aldrich
Assistant Equipment Manager	Vinny Ferraiuolo
Equipment Assistant & Equipment Transportation	Roy Sneesby
Cleaning Specialist	Norma Hernandez
Team Physician	Arthur J. Ting, M.D.
Team Internists	Greg Whitley M.D., John Chiu, M.D.
Team Dentists	Don Goudy, D.D.S., Robert Bonahoom, D.D.S.
Team Vision Specialist	Vincent S. Zuccaro, O.D., F.A.A.O.
Medical Staff	Steve Franzino, M.D., Robert Millard, M.D., Mark Sontag, M.D.
Chiropractic Consultant	Mike McMurray, D. C.
Manual Therapy Consultant	Tobe Hanson

SVS&E Business Operations

Senior Director of Communications	Ken Arnold
Director of Broadcasting	Frank Albin
Director of Marketing	Doug Bentz
Director of Ticket Sales	John Castro
Director of Media Relations	Scott Emmert
Director of Event Presentation	Steve Maroni
Director of Suite Sales & Service	Bruce Ross
Director of Communications & Internet Services	Roger Ross
Director of Public Relations	Jim Sparaco
Senior Sales Managers, Corporate Partnerships	Jennifer Birmingham, Bryan Deierling
Senior Ticket Operations Manager	Scott Fitzsimmons
Senior Service Manager, Corporate Partnerships	Heather Hunter
Sales Managers, Corporate Partnerships	Darren O'Donnell, Kevin Hilton, Kevin Chen
Account Sales Managers	Ted Chuba, Mike Hollywood, Patrick Frost, Adam King
Account Service Managers	Sharon Holman, Julie Kennedy, Kayla Chickos
Marketing Manager	Deanna Miller, Nicole Omron-Diep
Internet Services Manager	Alex Aragon
Creative Services Manager	Derik Green
Media Relations Manager	Tom Holy
Suite Sales & Service Managers	Kathy Payne-Tovar
Internet Content and Publications Manager	Tony Khing
Group Sales Manager	Mike Nieves
Mascot Operations Manager	Tim Patnode
Media Relations & Team Services Manager	Ryan Stenn
Service Managers, Corporate Partnerships	Jennifer De Carlo, Reza Wiriaatmadja

Sharks Foundation

Sharks Foundation Manager	Jeff Cafuir
Sharks Foundation Coordinator	Kelly Esrey

Finance

Director of Human Resources	Cathy Chandler
Director of Information Technology	Uy Ut
Controller	Stephanie Reitz

Building Operations

Director of Ticket Operations	Daniel DeBoer
Director of Booking & Events	Steve Kirsner, James Hamnett
Director of Guest Services	David Cahill
Director of Building Services	Monte Chavez
Facilities Technical Director	Greg Carrolan
Chief Engineer	Mark Mullins

Miscellaneous

Television Station	Comcast SportsNet California
Radio Network Flagship	98.5/102.1 FM KFOX (KUFX)
Television Play-By-Play / Color Analyst	Randy Hahn / Drew Remenda
Radio Play-By-Play / Color Analyst	Dan Rusanowsky / Jamie Baker
Radio Reporter	David Maley
P.A. Announcer	Danny Miller
Mascot	S.J. Sharkie

Tampa Bay Lightning

Key Off-Season Signings/Acquisitions

2011

June 13 • Re-signed D **Mike Vernace**.
24 • Re-signed D **Eric Brewer** and C **Blair Jones**.
25 • Acquired D **Bruno Gervais** from NY Islanders for future considerations.
28 • Re-signed D **Marc-Andre Bergeron**.
29 • Re-signed C **Adam Hall**.
30 • Re-signed G **Dwayne Roloson**.
July 1 • Signed G **Mathieu Garon** and RW **Michel Ouellet**.
2 • Signed D **Matt Gilroy**.
6 • Signed C **Tom Pyatt**.
7 • Signed RW **Ryan Shannon**.
19 • Re-signed C **Steven Stamkos**.
20 • Re-signed RW **Teddy Purcell**.

2010-11 Results: 46W-25L-5OTL-6SOL 103PTS.
Second, Southeast Division

Year-by-Year Record

		Home				Road				Overall							
Season	GP	W	L	T	OL	W	L	T	OL	W	L	T	OL	GF	GA	Pts.	Finished	Playoff Result
2010-11	82	25	11	....	5	21	14	....	6	46	25	....	11	247	240	103	2nd, Southeast Div.	Lost Conf. Championship
2009-10	82	21	14	....	6	13	22	....	6	34	36	....	12	217	260	80	4th, Southeast Div.	Out of Playoffs
2008-09	82	12	18	....	11	12	22	....	7	24	40	....	18	210	279	66	5th, Southeast Div.	Out of Playoffs
2007-08	82	20	18	....	3	11	24	....	6	31	42	....	9	223	267	71	5th, Southeast Div.	Out of Playoffs
2006-07	82	22	18	....	1	22	15	....	4	44	33	....	5	253	261	93	2nd, Southeast Div.	Lost Conf. Quarter-Final
2005-06	82	25	14	....	2	18	19	....	4	43	33	....	6	252	260	92	2nd, Southeast Div.	Lost Conf. Quarter-Final
2004-05																		
2003-04	**82**	**24**	**10**	**4**	**3**	**22**	**12**	**4**	**3**	**46**	**22**	**8**	**6**	**245**	**192**	**106**	**1st, Southeast Div.**	**Won Stanley Cup**
2002-03	82	22	9	7	3	14	16	9	2	36	25	16	5	219	210	93	1st, Southeast Div.	Lost Conf. Semi-Final
2001-02	82	16	17	5	3	11	23	6	1	27	40	11	4	178	219	69	3rd, Southeast Div.	Out of Playoffs
2000-01	82	17	19	3	2	7	28	3	3	24	47	6	5	201	280	59	5th, Southeast Div.	Out of Playoffs
1999-2000	82	13	20	4	4	6	27	5	3	19	47	9	7	204	310	54	4th, Southeast Div.	Out of Playoffs
1998-99	82	12	25	4	....	7	29	5	....	19	54	9	....	179	292	47	4th, Southeast Div.	Out of Playoffs
1997-98	82	11	23	7	....	6	32	3	....	17	55	10	....	151	269	44	7th, Atlantic Div.	Out of Playoffs
1996-97	82	15	18	8	....	17	22	2	....	32	40	10	....	217	247	74	6th, Atlantic Div.	Out of Playoffs
1995-96	82	22	14	5	....	16	18	7	....	38	32	12	....	238	248	88	5th, Atlantic Div.	Lost Conf. Quarter-Final
1994-95	48	10	14	0	....	7	14	3	....	17	28	3	....	120	144	37	6th, Atlantic Div.	Out of Playoffs
1993-94	84	14	22	6	....	16	21	5	....	30	43	11	....	224	251	71	7th, Atlantic Div.	Out of Playoffs
1992-93	84	12	27	3	....	11	27	4	....	23	54	7	....	245	332	53	6th, Norris Div.	Out of Playoffs

2011-12 Schedule

Oct.
Fri.	7	at Carolina
Sat.	8	at Boston
Mon.	10	at Washington
Thu.	13	at NY Islanders
Sat.	15	at Florida
Mon.	17	Florida
Thu.	20	NY Islanders
Sat.	22	Buffalo
Tue.	25	at Buffalo
Thu.	27	at Nashville
Sat.	29	Winnipeg

Nov.
Tue.	1	at Carolina
Fri.	4	Chicago
Sun.	6	at Florida*
Wed.	9	Philadelphia
Sat.	12	at St. Louis
Mon.	14	at Winnipeg
Thu.	17	Pittsburgh
Sat.	19	New Jersey
Tue.	22	Toronto
Fri.	25	at Florida
Sat.	26	Florida
Mon.	28	at Minnesota
Wed.	30	at Detroit

Dec.
Sat.	3	NY Rangers
Mon.	5	at Ottawa
Tue.	6	at NY Islanders
Thu.	8	at NY Rangers
Sat.	10	at Philadelphia
Mon.	12	New Jersey
Thu.	15	Calgary
Sat.	17	at Columbus
Wed.	21	at San Jose
Fri.	23	at Colorado
Tue.	27	Philadelphia
Thu.	29	Montreal
Sat.	31	Carolina*

Jan.
Tue.	3	at Toronto
Thu.	5	at Ottawa
Sat.	7	at Montreal
Tue.	10	Vancouver

Thu.	12	Carolina
Fri.	13	at Washington
Sun.	15	Pittsburgh*
Tue.	17	Boston
Fri.	20	at Dallas
Sat.	21	at Phoenix
Tue.	24	Columbus
Tue.	31	Washington

Feb.
Thu.	2	Winnipeg
Sat.	4	Florida
Tue.	7	Los Angeles
Thu.	9	at NY Rangers
Sat.	11	at Buffalo
Sun.	12	at Pittsburgh
Tue.	14	Ottawa
Thu.	16	San Jose
Sat.	18	Washington
Tue.	21	Anaheim
Thu.	23	at Winnipeg
Sat.	25	at Pittsburgh*
Sun.	26	at New Jersey*
Tue.	28	Montreal

Mar.
Fri.	2	NY Rangers
Sat.	3	at Carolina
Tue.	6	Ottawa
Thu.	8	at Washington
Sat.	10	Carolina
Tue.	13	Boston
Thu.	15	Toronto
Sat.	17	St. Louis
Mon.	19	Buffalo
Thu.	22	Edmonton
Sat.	24	NY Islanders
Mon.	26	at Philadelphia
Tue.	27	at Boston
Thu.	29	at New Jersey
Sat.	31	Winnipeg

Apr.
Mon.	2	Washington
Wed.	4	at Montreal
Thu.	5	at Toronto
Sat.	7	at Winnipeg

* Denotes afternoon game.

SOUTHEAST DIVISION
20th NHL Season

Franchise date: December 16, 1991

Tampa Bay's Martin St. Louis finished second in the NHL in scoring in 2010-11. His 99 points represented the second-highest total of his career, while his 68 assists tied a franchise record.

2011-12 Player Personnel

FORWARDS	HT	WT	S	Place of Birth	*Age	2010-11 Club
DOWNIE, Steve	5-11	191	R	Newmarket, Ont.	24	Tampa Bay
HALL, Adam	6-3	213	R	Kalamazoo, MI	31	Tampa Bay
JONES, Blair	6-2	216	R	Central Butte, Sask.	25	Tampa Bay-Norfolk
LECAVALIER, Vincent	6-4	208	L	Ile Bizard, Que.	31	Tampa Bay
MALONE, Ryan	6-4	219	L	Pittsburgh, PA	31	Tampa Bay
MOORE, Dominic	6-0	192	L	Sarnia, Ont.	31	Tampa Bay
OUELLET, Michel	6-0	200	R	Rimouski, Que.	29	Hamburg Freez.
PICARD, Alexandre	6-2	206	L	Les Saules, Que.	25	San Antonio
PURCELL, Teddy	6-2	201	R	St. Johns, Nfld.	26	Tampa Bay
PYATT, Tom	5-11	187	L	Thunder Bay, Ont.	24	Montreal
RITOLA, Mattias	6-0	192	L	Borlange, Sweden	24	Tampa Bay-Norfolk
ST. LOUIS, Martin	5-8	176	L	Laval, Que.	36	Tampa Bay
SHANNON, Ryan	5-9	175	R	Darien, CT	28	Ottawa
SMITH, Trevor	6-1	195	L	North Vancouver, B.C.	26	Syracuse-Springfield
STAMKOS, Steven	6-1	188	R	Markham, Ont.	21	Tampa Bay
THOMPSON, Nate	6-0	210	L	Anchorage, AK	27	Tampa Bay
TYRELL, Dana	5-11	185	L	Airdrie, Alta.	22	Tampa Bay
WRIGHT, James	6-4	200	L	Saskatoon, Sask.	21	Tampa Bay-Norfolk
WYMAN, James	6-2	199	R	Edina, MN	25	Hamilton
DEFENSEMEN						
BERGERON, Marc-Andre	5-9	198	L	St-Louis-de-France, Que.	30	Tampa Bay-Norfolk
BREWER, Eric	6-3	220	L	Vernon, B.C.	32	St. Louis-Tampa Bay
CLARK, Brett	6-0	194	L	Wapella, Sask.	34	Tampa Bay
GERVAIS, Bruno	6-1	200	R	Longueuil, Que.	27	NY Islanders
GILROY, Matt	6-1	201	R	North Bellmore, NY	27	NY Rangers
HEDMAN, Victor	6-6	229	L	Ornskoldsvik, Sweden	20	Tampa Bay
JACKSON, Scott	6-3	219	L	Salmon Arm, B.C.	24	Norfolk
KUBINA, Pavel	6-4	258	R	Celadna, Czech.	34	Tampa Bay
OHLUND, Mattias	6-4	229	L	Pitea, Sweden	35	Tampa Bay
PETIOT, Richard	6-3	215	L	Daysland, Alta.	29	Edmonton-Oklahoma City
VERNACE, Michael	6-0	216	L	Toronto, Ont.	25	Tampa Bay-Norfolk

GOALTENDERS	HT	WT	C	Place of Birth	*Age	2010-11 Club
GARON, Mathieu	6-1	206	R	Chandler, Que.	33	Columbus
ROLOSON, Dwayne	6-1	170	L	Simcoe, Ont.	41	NY Islanders-Tampa Bay

* – Age at start of 2011-12 season

Guy Boucher

Head Coach

Born: Notre-Dame-du-Lac, Que., August 3, 1971.

The Tampa Bay Lightning agreed to terms with Guy Boucher on June 10, 2010 to become the seventh head coach in the organization's history. Boucher joined the Lightning after coaching the Hamilton Bulldogs of the American Hockey League to 52 wins and 115 points in the 2009-10 regular season. In his first season in Tampa Bay in 2010-11, Boucher led the Lightning back into the playoffs for the first time since 2006-07 and all the way to the Eastern Conference Final after tying a club record with 46 wins during the regular season.

Boucher became the youngest coach in the NHL after quickly building a track record of success in the Quebec Major Junior Hockey League and the AHL. In addition to winning the AHL's North Division Championship for 2009-10, Boucher's Bulldogs team allowed just 182 goals during the 80-game regular season, the lowest total in the league. Its 271 goals scored marked the league's third highest total. He was honored with the AHL's Louis A. R. Pieri Award as its coach of the year.

Boucher was named head coach of the Bulldogs for the 2009-10 season after leading the Drummondville Voltigeurs for three seasons. Boucher led Drummondville to QMJHL regular season and playoff championships and a berth in the Memorial Cup in 2008-09. That Voltigeurs team set franchise records with 54 wins and 112 points. He was also awarded the Paul Dumont Trophy as the QMJHL's personality of the year for 2008-09.

Boucher also has extensive experience working for Hockey Canada, most recently serving as an assistant coach under Pat Quinn on the gold medal-winning team for the 2009 World Junior Championship. He was an assistant coach with Canada's national men's under-18 team program three times, also helping that team to the gold medal in 2008.

Boucher is a graduate of Montreal's McGill University where he starred with the Redmen from 1991 to 1995. Boucher also has a unique resume for an NHL coach, with educational studies in four different fields – sports psychology, biosystems engineering, environmental biology and history.

Coaching Record

			Regular Season				Playoffs			
Season	Team	League	GC	W	L	O/T	GC	W	L	T
2006-07	Drummondville	QMJHL	70	37	26	7	12	7	5	....
2007-08	Drummondville	QMJHL	70	14	51	5	....	....	....	....
2008-09	Drummondville	QMJHL	68	54	10	4	19	16	3	....
2008-09	Drummondville	M-Cup	....	....	....	....	4	2	2	....
2009-10	Hamilton	AHL	80	52	11	11	19	11	8	....
2010-11	**Tampa Bay**	**NHL**	**82**	**46**	**25**	**11**	**18**	**11**	**7**	....
	NHL Totals		**82**	**46**	**25**	**11**	**18**	**11**	**7**	....

2010-11 Scoring

* – rookie

Regular Season

Pos	#	Player	Team	GP	G	A	Pts	TOI	+/–	PIM	PP	SH	GW	S	%
R	26	Martin St. Louis	T.B.	82	31	68	99	20:58	0	12	4	0	7	254	12.2
C	91	Steven Stamkos	T.B.	82	45	46	91	20:11	3	74	17	0	8	272	16.5
C	4	Vincent Lecavalier	T.B.	65	25	29	54	18:27	–5	43	12	0	5	210	11.9
R	16	Teddy Purcell	T.B.	81	17	34	51	14:06	5	10	3	0	1	196	8.7
L	12	Simon Gagne	T.B.	63	17	23	40	16:53	–12	20	7	0	3	154	11.0
L	6	Ryan Malone	T.B.	54	14	24	38	16:01	–3	51	9	0	1	149	9.4
C	19	Dominic Moore	T.B.	77	18	14	32	15:35	–12	52	6	0	3	175	10.3
R	9	Steve Downie	T.B.	57	10	22	32	14:31	8	171	2	0	1	83	12.0
D	7	Brett Clark	T.B.	82	9	22	31	18:52	2	14	6	0	1	87	10.3
L	10	Sean Bergenheim	T.B.	80	14	15	29	13:58	0	56	2	0	1	182	7.7
D	77	Victor Hedman	T.B.	79	3	23	26	21:00	3	70	0	0	0	101	3.0
C	44	Nate Thompson	T.B.	79	10	15	25	15:05	–6	29	0	1	2	123	8.1
D	13	Pavel Kubina	T.B.	79	4	19	23	19:13	2	62	1	0	2	78	5.1
R	18	Adam Hall	T.B.	82	7	11	18	14:50	–12	32	0	0	1	167	4.2
D	2	Eric Brewer	STL	54	8	6	14	22:14	1	57	0	0	1	86	9.3
			T.B.	22	1	1	2	21:34	5	24	0	0	0	24	4.2
			Total	76	9	7	16	22:02	6	81	0	0	1	110	8.2
C	42	* Dana Tyrell	T.B.	78	6	9	15	12:03	–5	12	0	0	1	73	8.2
D	8	Randy Jones	T.B.	61	1	12	13	17:03	–4	15	0	0	0	52	1.9
D	39	Mike Lundin	T.B.	69	1	11	12	20:24	–3	12	0	0	0	55	1.8
C	21	* Mattias Ritola	T.B.	31	4	4	8	10:03	–5	11	0	0	2	42	9.5
D	47	Marc-Andre Bergeron	T.B.	23	2	6	8	14:19	–10	8	0	0	1	37	5.4
D	5	Mattias Ohlund	T.B.	72	0	5	5	18:43	–7	70	0	0	0	39	0.0
L	24	* Johan Harju	T.B.	10	1	2	3	8:28	–2	2	0	0	0	14	7.1
C	49	Blair Jones	T.B.	18	1	2	3	8:00	–2	2	0	0	0	20	5.0
D	48	* Michael Vernace	T.B.	10	0	1	1	8:42	–2	2	0	0	0	6	0.0
C	43	James Wright	T.B.	1	0	0	0	4:36	–2	0	0	0	0	0	0.0
C	34	Marc-Antoine Pouliot	T.B.	3	0	0	0	10:46	–2	0	0	0	0	2	0.0
D	28	Mathieu Roy	T.B.	4	0	0	0	4:43	–2	2	0	0	0	1	0.0
D	32	Matt Smaby	T.B.	32	0	0	0	6:59	2	17	0	0	0	9	0.0

Goaltending

No.	Goaltender	GPI	Mins	Avg	W	L	OT	EN	SO	GA	SA	S%	G	A	PIM
30	* Cedrick Desjardin	2	120	1.00	2	0	0	0	0	2	63	.968	0	0	0
35	Dwayne Roloson	34	1993	2.56	18	12	4	3	4	85	967	.912	0	1	6
41	Mike Smith	22	1202	2.90	13	6	1	0	1	58	576	.899	0	1	2
38	Dan Ellis	31	1679	2.93	13	7	6	4	2	82	741	.889	0	1	0
	Totals	**82**	**5013**	**2.80**	**46**	**25**	**11**	**7**	**7**	**234**	**2354**	**.901**			

Playoffs

Pos	#	Player	Team	GP	G	A	Pts	TOI	+/–	PIM	PP	SH	GW	OT	S	%
R	26	Martin St. Louis	T.B.	18	10	10	20	21:11	–8	4	4	0	1	0	50	20.0
C	4	Vincent Lecavalier	T.B.	18	6	13	19	19:51	6	16	3	0	3	1	56	10.7
R	16	Teddy Purcell	T.B.	18	6	11	17	13:42	4	2	1	0	1	0	46	13.0
R	9	Steve Downie	T.B.	17	2	12	14	12:35	7	40	0	0	1	0	27	7.4
C	91	Steven Stamkos	T.B.	18	6	7	13	19:43	–5	6	3	0	1	0	46	13.0
L	12	Simon Gagne	T.B.	15	5	7	12	15:52	6	4	0	0	1	0	21	23.8
L	10	Sean Bergenheim	T.B.	16	9	2	11	14:09	2	8	0	0	1	0	46	19.6
C	19	Dominic Moore	T.B.	18	3	8	11	17:46	–3	18	1	0	0	0	26	11.5
D	2	Eric Brewer	T.B.	18	1	6	7	25:36	–3	14	0	0	0	0	26	3.8
L	6	Ryan Malone	T.B.	18	3	3	6	15:35	–3	24	1	0	1	0	33	9.1
D	77	Victor Hedman	T.B.	18	0	6	6	22:16	0	8	0	0	0	0	24	0.0
R	18	Adam Hall	T.B.	18	1	4	5	13:53	–2	8	0	0	0	0	17	5.9
C	44	Nate Thompson	T.B.	18	1	3	4	15:37	3	4	0	0	0	0	26	3.8
D	13	Pavel Kubina	T.B.	8	2	1	3	15:17	2	10	2	0	0	0	7	28.6
D	47	Marc-Andre Bergeron	T.B.	14	2	1	3	12:58	–2	9	2	0	1	0	24	8.3
D	5	Mattias Ohlund	T.B.	18	1	2	3	20:12	5	8	0	1	0	0	9	11.1
D	7	Brett Clark	T.B.	18	1	2	3	17:35	1	8	0	0	0	0	17	5.9
D	39	Mike Lundin	T.B.	18	0	2	2	14:40	4	2	0	0	0	0	10	0.0
D	8	Randy Jones	T.B.	5	0	1	1	6:58	1	2	0	0	0	0	1	0.0
C	21	* Mattias Ritola	T.B.	1	0	0	0	2:23	0	0	0	0	0	0	0	0.0
C	49	Blair Jones	T.B.	7	0	0	0	6:24	–1	2	0	0	0	0	5	0.0
C	42	* Dana Tyrell	T.B.	7	0	0	0	7:24	–3	2	0	0	0	0	4	0.0

Goaltending

No.	Goaltender	GPI	Mins	Avg	W	L	EN	SO	GA	SA	S%	G	A	PIM
41	Mike Smith	3	120	1.00	1	1	1	0	2	48	.958	0	0	0
35	Dwayne Roloson	17	982	2.51	10	6	1	1	41	541	.924	0	0	0
	Totals	**18**	**1110**	**2.43**	**11**	**7**	**2**	**1**	**45**	**591**	**.924**			

Coaching History

Terry Crisp, 1992-93 to 1996-97; Terry Crisp, Rick Paterson and Jacques Demers, 1997-98; Jacques Demers, 1998-99; Steve Ludzik, 1999-2000; Steve Ludzik and John Tortorella, 2000-01; John Tortorella, 2001-02 to 2007-08; Barry Melrose and Rick Tocchet, 2008-09; Rick Tocchet, 2009-10; Guy Boucher, 2010-11 to date.

Club Records

Team

(Figures in brackets for season records are games played; records for fewest points, wins, ties, losses, goals, goals against are for 70 or more games)

Most Points	**106**	2003-04 (82)
Most Wins	**46**	2003-04 (82), 2010-11 (82)
Most Ties	**16**	2002-03 (82)
Most Losses	**55**	1997-98 (82)
Most Goals	**247**	2010-11 (82)
Most Goals Against	**332**	1992-93 (84)
Fewest Points	**44**	1997-98 (82)
Fewest Wins	**17**	1997-98 (82)
Fewest Ties	**6**	2000-01 (82)
Fewest Losses	**22**	2003-04 (82)
Fewest Goals	**151**	1997-98 (82)
Fewest Goals Against	**192**	2003-04 (82)
Longest Winning Streak		
Overall	**8**	Feb. 23-Mar. 6/04
Home	**8**	Mar. 17-Apr. 8/06
Away	**7**	Jan. 7-Feb. 1/07
Longest Undefeated Streak		
Overall	**13**	Mar. 7-Apr. 2/03 (7 wins, 6 ties)
Home	**10**	Jan. 29-Mar. 12/04 (9 wins, 1 tie)
Away	**7**	Feb. 23-Mar. 10/04 (6 wins, 1 tie), Jan. 7-Feb. 1/07 (7 wins)
Longest Losing Streak		
Overall	**13**	Jan. 3-Feb. 2/98
Home	**10**	Jan. 3-Feb. 26/98
Away	**11**	Oct. 24-Dec. 10/97
Longest Winless Streak		
Overall	**16**	Oct. 10-Nov. 17/97 (15 losses, 1 tie), Jan. 2-Feb. 5/98 (14 losses, 2 ties)
Home	**11**	Jan. 2-Feb. 26/98 (10 losses, 1 tie)
Away	**17**	Dec. 2/99-Feb. 19/00 (14 losses, 3 ties)
Most Shutouts, Season	**9**	2001-02 (82)
Most PIM, Season	**1,823**	1997-98 (82)
Most Goals, Game	**9**	Nov. 8/03 (Pit. 0 at T.B. 9)

Individual

Most Seasons	**12**	Vincent Lecavalier
Most Games, Career	**934**	Vincent Lecavalier
Most Goals, Career	**351**	Vincent Lecavalier
Most Assists, Career	**464**	Martin St. Louis
Most Points, Career	**793**	Vincent Lecavalier (351G, 442A)
Most PIM, Career	**828**	Chris Gratton
Most Shutouts, Career	**14**	Nikolai Khabibulin
Longest Consecutive Games Streak	**472**	Martin St. Louis (Nov. 17/05-to date)
Most Goals, Season	**52**	Vincent Lecavalier (2006-07)
Most Assists, Season	**68**	Brad Richards (2005-06), Martin St. Louis (2010-11)
Most Points, Season	**108**	Vincent Lecavalier (2006-07; 52G, 56A)
Most PIM, Season	**265**	Zenon Konopka (2009-10)
Most Points, Defenseman, Season	**65**	Roman Hamrlik (1995-96; 16G, 49A)
Most Points, Center, Season	**108**	Vincent Lecavalier (2006-07; 52G, 56A)
Most Points, Right Wing, Season	**102**	Martin St. Louis (2006-07; 43G, 59A)
Most Points, Left Wing, Season	**80**	Cory Stillman (2003-04; 25G, 55A), Vaclav Prospal (2005-06; 25G, 55A)
Most Points, Rookie, Season	**62**	Brad Richards (2000-01; 21G, 41A)
Most Shutouts, Season	**7**	Nikolai Khabibulin (2001-02)
Most Goals, Game	**4**	Chris Kontos (Oct. 7/92)
Most Assists, Game	**5**	Mark Recchi (Mar. 1/09), Martin St. Louis (Nov. 18/10)
Most Points, Game	**6**	Doug Crossman (Nov. 7/92; 3G, 3A)

Captains' History

No captain, 1992-93 to 1994-95; Paul Ysebaert, 1995-96, 1996-97; Paul Ysebaert and Mikael Renberg, 1997-98; Rob Zamuner, 1998-99; Bill Houlder, Chris Gratton and Vincent Lecavalier, 1999-2000; Vincent Lecavalier, 2000-01; no captain, 2001-02; Dave Andreychuk, 2002-03 to 2004-05; Dave Andreychuk and no captain, 2005-06; Tim Taylor, 2006-07, 2007-08; Vincent Lecavalier, 2008-09 to date.

All-time Record vs. Other Clubs

Regular Season

	At Home								On Road								Total							
	GP	W	L	T	OL	GF	GA	PTS	GP	W	L	T	OL	GF	GA	PTS	GP	W	L	T	OL	GF	GA	PTS
Anaheim	11	4	6	0	1	21	29	9	12	4	5	1	2	31	38	11	23	8	11	1	3	52	67	20
Atlanta	34	23	8	1	2	126	84	49	34	13	15	3	3	94	109	32	68	36	23	4	5	220	193	81
Boston	35	14	16	3	2	101	104	33	35	4	22	6	3	82	135	17	70	18	38	9	5	183	239	50
Buffalo	35	8	20	3	4	80	117	23	35	11	20	2	2	96	117	26	70	19	40	5	6	176	234	49
Calgary	12	6	5	1	0	39	42	13	13	6	6	0	1	37	44	13	25	12	11	1	1	76	86	26
Carolina	47	27	16	3	1	146	132	58	48	13	24	7	4	132	152	37	95	40	40	10	5	278	284	95
Chicago	14	6	4	3	1	36	38	16	17	5	10	2	0	38	54	12	31	11	14	5	1	74	92	28
Colorado	16	9	4	1	2	46	45	21	16	3	10	2	1	34	60	9	32	12	14	3	3	80	105	30
Columbus	6	5	1	0	0	14	8	10	5	1	3	1	0	9	13	3	11	6	4	1	0	23	21	13
Dallas	16	3	10	2	1	30	45	9	13	4	7	1	1	36	46	10	29	7	17	3	2	66	91	19
Detroit	17	4	11	1	1	51	77	10	14	1	12	1	0	23	54	3	31	5	23	2	1	74	131	13
Edmonton	13	4	6	2	1	37	41	11	13	4	8	0	1	30	36	9	26	8	14	2	2	67	77	20
Florida	49	21	18	6	4	121	140	52	49	14	26	4	5	120	166	37	98	35	44	10	9	241	306	89
Los Angeles	12	6	4	0	2	27	26	14	14	10	2	2	0	43	27	22	26	16	6	2	2	70	53	36
Minnesota	7	2	3	1	1	15	20	6	6	2	4	0	0	16	20	4	13	4	7	1	1	31	40	10
Montreal	35	14	13	5	3	85	94	36	34	15	16	1	2	84	96	33	69	29	29	6	5	169	190	69
Nashville	7	3	2	2	0	22	18	8	8	5	3	0	0	22	20	10	15	8	5	2	0	44	38	18
New Jersey	37	12	17	5	3	83	112	32	38	10	23	2	3	80	136	25	75	22	40	7	6	163	248	57
NY Islanders	38	20	13	2	3	109	110	45	37	17	17	1	2	98	107	37	75	37	30	3	5	207	217	82
NY Rangers	37	18	14	3	2	118	113	41	39	16	20	2	1	108	130	35	76	34	34	5	3	226	243	76
Ottawa	35	14	18	2	1	102	121	31	35	11	20	0	4	75	126	26	70	25	38	2	5	177	247	57
Philadelphia	38	15	20	1	2	112	117	33	37	12	17	7	1	91	116	32	75	27	37	8	3	203	233	65
Phoenix	13	7	6	0	0	47	41	14	15	8	7	0	0	38	33	16	28	15	13	0	0	85	74	30
Pittsburgh	35	19	14	2	0	105	86	40	35	12	18	3	2	89	125	29	70	31	32	5	2	194	211	69
St. Louis	16	7	5	3	1	50	53	18	13	3	9	0	1	35	51	7	29	10	14	3	2	85	104	25
San Jose	15	8	6	1	0	39	40	17	13	6	6	1	0	40	47	13	28	14	12	2	0	79	87	30
Toronto	32	11	18	1	2	77	99	25	33	12	17	1	3	91	117	28	65	23	35	2	5	168	216	53
Vancouver	11	5	5	0	1	38	41	11	12	1	8	2	1	24	51	5	23	6	13	2	2	62	92	16
Washington	50	18	28	2	2	125	158	40	50	14	30	4	2	125	184	34	100	32	58	6	4	250	342	74
Totals	**723**	**313**	**311**	**56**	**43**	**2002**	**2151**	**725**	**723**	**237**	**385**	**56**	**45**	**1821**	**2410**	**575**	**1446**	**550**	**696**	**112**	**88**	**3823**	**4561**	**1300**

Playoffs

	Series	W	L	GP	W	L	T	GF	GA	Last Mtg.	Rnd.	Result
Boston	1	0	1	7	3	4	0	21	21	2011	CF	L 3-4
Calgary	1	1	0	7	4	3	0	13	14	2004	F	W 4-3
Montreal	1	1	0	4	4	0	0	14	5	2004	CSF	W 4-0
New Jersey	2	0	2	11	3	8	0	22	33	2007	CQF	L 2-4
NY Islanders	1	1	0	5	4	1	0	12	5	2004	CQF	W 4-1
Ottawa	1	0	1	5	1	4	0	13	23	2006	CQF	L 1-4
Philadelphia	2	1	1	13	6	7	0	34	45	2004	CF	W 4-3
Pittsburgh	1	1	0	7	4	3	0	22	14	2011	CQF	W 4-3
Washington	2	2	0	10	8	2	0	30	25	2011	CSF	W 4-0
Totals	**12**	**7**	**5**	**69**	**37**	**32**	**0**	**181**	**185**			

Playoff Results 2011-2007

Year	Round	Opponent	Result	GF	GA
2011	CF	Boston	L 3-4	21	21
	CSF	Washington	W 4-0	16	10
	CQF	Pittsburgh	W 4-3	22	14
2007	CQF	New Jersey	L 2-4	14	19

Abbreviations: Round: F – Final; **CF** – conference final; **CSF** – conference semi-final; **CQF** – conference quarter-final.

Carolina totals include Hartford, 1992-93 to 1996-97.
Dallas totals include Minnesota North Stars, 1992-93.
Colorado totals include Quebec, 1992-93 to 1994-95.
Phoenix totals include Winnipeg, 1992-93 to 1995-96.

2010-11 Results

Oct.	9	Atlanta	5-3
	13	at Montreal	4-3*
	14	at Philadelphia	3-2
	16	at Florida	0-6
	18	Dallas	5-4
	21	NY Islanders	2-3*
	22	at Atlanta	5-2
	24	Nashville	3-4
	27	Pittsburgh	5-3
	30	at Phoenix	3-0
Nov.	3	at Anaheim	2-3*
	4	at Los Angeles	0-1
	6	at San Jose	2-5
	9	Toronto	4-0
	11	at Washington	3-6
	12	at Pittsburgh	1-5
	14	Minnesota	1-4
	17	at NY Islanders	4-2
	18	at Philadelphia	8-7
	20	at Buffalo	2-1
	22	Boston	3-1
	24	NY Rangers	5-3
	26	at Washington	0-6
	27	Florida	3-4†
	30	at Toronto	4-3*
Dec.	2	at Boston	1-8
	4	Colorado	6-5
	7	at Calgary	2-4
	10	at Edmonton	3-4†
	11	at Vancouver	5-4*
	15	Atlanta	2-1†
	18	Buffalo	3-1
	20	Carolina	5-1
	22	at NY Islanders	1-2*
	23	at NY Rangers	4-3†
	26	at Atlanta	3-2*
	28	Boston	3-4
	30	Montreal	4-1
Jan.	1	NY Rangers	2-1*
	4	at Washington	1-0*
	5	at Pittsburgh	1-8
	8	at Ottawa	2-1
	9	at New Jersey	3-6
	12	Washington	3-0
	14	New Jersey	2-5
	15	at Carolina	4-6
	18	Columbus	3-2†
	20	at Atlanta	3-2†
	21	at Florida	2-1†
	23	Atlanta	7-1
	25	Toronto	2-0
Feb.	1	Philadelphia	4-0
	4	Washington	2-5
	6	St. Louis	4-3*
	8	Buffalo	4-7
	12	Carolina	4-3*
	15	Philadelphia	3-4†
	17	Detroit	2-6
	19	Florida	2-3†
	23	Phoenix	8-3
	25	New Jersey	2-1
	27	at NY Rangers	2-1
Mar.	2	at New Jersey	1-2
	3	at Boston	1-2
	5	Montreal	2-4
	7	Washington	1-2†
	9	Chicago	4-3†
	11	Ottawa	1-2
	12	at Florida	3-4*
	14	at Toronto	6-2
	17	at Montreal	2-3†
	19	at Ottawa	2-3*
	22	NY Islanders	2-5
	25	Carolina	3-4
	26	at Carolina	4-2
	29	Ottawa	5-2
	31	Pittsburgh	2-1
Apr.	2	at Minnesota	3-1
	3	at Chicago	2-0
	5	at Buffalo	2-4
	8	Florida	4-2
	9	at Carolina	6-2

* – Overtime † – Shootout

Entry Draft Selections 2011-1997

Name in bold denotes played in NHL.

2011
Pick
27 Vladislav Namestnikov
58 Nikita Kucherov
148 Nikita Nesterov
178 Adam Wilcox
201 Matthew Peca
208 Ondrej Palat

2010
Pick
6 Brett Connolly
63 Brock Beukeboom
66 Radko Gudas
72 Adam Janosik
96 Geoffrey Schemitsch
118 Jimmy Mullin
156 Brendan O'Donnell
186 Teigan Zahn

2009
Pick
2 **Victor Hedman**
29 Carter Ashton
52 Richard Panik
93 Alex Hutchings
148 Michael Zador
162 Jaroslav Janus
183 Kirill Gotovets

2008
Pick
1 **Steven Stamkos**
117 **James Wright**
122 **Dustin Tokarski**
147 Kyle DeCoste
152 Mark Barberio
160 Luke Witkowski
182 Matias Sointu
203 David Carle

2007
Pick
47 **Dana Tyrell**
75 Luca Cunti
77 Alexander Killorn
107 Mitch Fadden
150 Matt Marshall
167 **Johan Harju**
183 Torrie Jung
197 Michael Ward
210 Justin Courtnall

2006
Pick
15 **Riku Helenius**
78 **Kevin Quick**
168 Dane Crowley
198 Denis Kazionov

2005
Pick
30 **Vladimir Mihalik**
73 **Radek Smolenak**
89 Chris Lawrence
92 Marek Bartanus
102 **Blair Jones**
133 Stanislav Lascek
163 Marek Kvapil
165 Kevin Beech
225 John Wessbecker

2004
Pick
30 Andy Rogers
65 Mark Tobin
102 **Mike Lundin**
158 Brandon Elliott
163 Dusty Collins
188 Jan Zapletal
191 **Karri Ramo**
245 Justin Keller

2003
Pick
34 Mike Egener
41 **Matt Smaby**
96 Jonathan Boutin
192 **Doug O'Brien**
224 **Gerald Coleman**
227 **Jay Rosehill**
255 Raimonds Danilics
256 Brady Greco
273 Albert Vishnyakov
286 Zbynek Hrdel
287 **Nick Tarnasky**

2002
Pick
60 Adam Henrich
100 Dmitri Kazionov
135 Joe Pearce
162 Gerard Dicaire
170 P.J. Atherton
174 Karri Akkanen
183 **Paul Ranger**
213 **Fredrik Norrena**
233 Vasily Koshechkin
255 **Ryan Craig**
256 **Darren Reid**
286 Alexei Glukhov
287 John Toffey

2001
Pick
3 **Alexander Svitov**
47 Alexander Polushin
61 Andreas Holmqvist
94 **Evgeny Artyukhin**
123 Aaron Lobb
138 Paul Lynch
188 Art Femenella
219 Dennis Packard
222 Jeremy Van Hoof
252 J.F. Soucy
259 Dmitri Bezrukov
261 Vitali Smolyaninov
281 Ilja Solarev
289 Henrik Bergfors

2000
Pick
8 **Nikita Alexeev**
34 Ruslan Zainullin
81 **Alexander Kharitonov**
126 Johan Hagglund
161 Pavel Sedov
191 Aaron Gionet
222 Marek Priechodsky
226 **Brian Eklund**
233 Alexander Polukeyev
263 **Thomas Ziegler**

1999
Pick
47 **Sheldon Keefe**
67 **Evgeny Konstantinov**
75 Brett Scheffelmaier
88 **Jimmie Olvestad**
127 **Kaspars Astashenko**
148 Michal Lanicek
182 **Fedor Fedorov**
187 Ivan Rachunek
216 Erkki Rajamaki
244 Mikko Kuparinen

1998
Pick
1 **Vincent Lecavalier**
64 **Brad Richards**
72 **Dmitry Afanasenkov**
92 **Eric Beaudoin**
121 Curtis Rich
146 Sergei Kuznetsov
174 Brett Allan
194 Oak Hewer
221 Daniel Hulak
229 Chris Lyness
252 **Martin Cibak**

1997
Pick
7 **Paul Mara**
33 Kyle Kos
61 **Matt Elich**
108 Mark Thompson
109 Jan Sulc
112 **Karel Betik**
153 **Andrei Skopintsev**
168 Justin Jack
170 Eero Somervuori
185 Samuel St-Pierre
198 Shawn Skolney
224 **Paul Comrie**

General Managers' History

Phil Esposito, 1992-93 to 1997-98; Phil Esposito and Jacques Demers, 1998-99; Rick Dudley, 1999-2000, 2000-01; Rick Dudley and Jay Feaster, 2001-02; Jay Feaster, 2002-03 to 2007-08; Brian Lawton, 2008-09, 2009-10; Steve Yzerman, 2010-11 to date.

Steve Yzerman

Vice President and General Manager

Born: Cranbrook, B.C., May 9, 1965.

Steve Yzerman – the iconic Detroit Red Wing player and executive – was named the sixth general manager in Lightning history on May 25, 2010. In his first season wih the club in 2010-11 Yzerman was a finalist for the G.M of the Year award as Tampa Bay returned to the playoffs for the first time since 2006-07 and reached the Eastern Conference Final after tying a club record with 46 wins during the regular season.

Before joining the Lightning Yzerman spent five seasons as vice president with the Red Wings, working closely with general manager Ken Holland, senior vice president Jim Devellano and assistant general manager Jim Nill on evaluating talent at both the professional and amateur levels. He also contributed valuable input on trades, free agent signings and at the Entry Draft each summer. Yzerman served as general manager for Canada at the 2007 and 2008 World Championships, bringing home gold and silver respectively. He then led Canada to an Olympic gold medal victory on home ice in Vancouver at the 2010 Winter Olympics as executive director. Yzerman also won an Olympic gold medal as a player with Canada in 2002.

Yzerman is a four-time Stanley Cup champion, winning three as a player (1997, 1998 and 2002) and another as a member of Detroit's management team (2008). Overall he spent 27 seasons with the franchise. He was inducted into the Hockey Hall of Fame in 2009, his first year of eligibility. Recognized as one of the best centers in NHL history, Yzerman retired on July 3, 2006 after a remarkable 22-year NHL career with the Red Wings. He ranks among the NHL's all-time leaders with 1,514 career games, 692 goals, 1,063 assists and 1,755 career points. Even more impressive than his career statistics may be his 20-year run as captain in Detroit, the longest tenure in NHL and major sports history. Yzerman was named captain of the Red Wings prior to the 1986-87 season, making him the youngest captain in franchise history at 21-years-old.

During his illustrious career Yzerman was selected to the NHL All-Star Game on 10 occasions. He also won the Bill Masterton Trophy (perseverance, sportsmanship and dedication to hockey) in 2002, the Frank J. Selke Trophy (best defensive forward) in 2000, the Conn Smythe Trophy (playoff MVP) in 1998, the Lester B. Pearson Trophy (the NHLPA's top player) in 1989 and was also selected to the NHL All-Rookie Team in 1984.

Club Directory

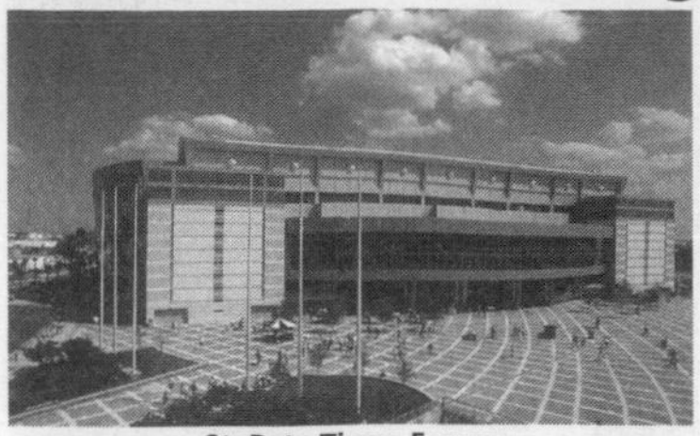
St. Pete Times Forum

Tampa Bay Lightning
St. Pete Times Forum
401 Channelside Drive
Tampa, FL 33602
Phone **813/301-6500**
FAX 813/301-1480
Ticket Info. 813/301-6600
www.tampabaylightning.com
Capacity: 19,758

Executive Staff	
Owner, Governor & Chairman	Jeff Vinik
Chief Executive Officer and Alternate Governor	Tod Leiweke
Chief Operating Officer	Steve Griggs
Chief Financial Officer	Martha Fuller
V.P. and General Manager	Steve Yzerman
Executive V.P., Service & Operations	Brad Lott
Executive V.P., Communications	Bill Wickett
Sr. V.P., Corporate Partnership & Activation	Bill Abercrombie
Sr. V.P., Suite Sales & Service	Patrick Duffy
V.P., Fans	Dave Andreychuk
V.P., Legal Counsel	Paul Davis
V.P., Corporate Partnerships	Kyle Draper
V.P., Corporate Relations	Phil Esposito
V.P., Event Production & Entertainment	John Franzone
V.P., Philanthropy & Community Initiatives	Elizabeth Frazier
V.P., Human Resources	Keith Harris
V.P., Ticket Operations	Jim Mannino
V.P., Operations	Mary Milne
V.P., Partnership Activation & Suite Services	Courtney Simons
V.P., Event Booking	Elmer Straub
Director, Govt. Relations & Community Affairs	Ron Pierce
Executive Assistant to Mr. Vinik	Michele Rooney
Executive Assistant	Wendy Scolaro
Executive V.P., Sales	TBD
Hockey Operations	
Asst. G.M., G.M., Norfolk Admirals	Julien BriseBois
Asst. G.M., Director of Player Personnel	Pat Verbeek
Senior Advisor to the General Manager	Tom Kurvers
Director of Amateur Scouting	Al Murray
Head Scouts, Pro / Amateur	Greg Malone / Darryl Plandowski
Player Development Coordinator	Steve Thomas
Director of Team Services	Ryan Belec
Manager of Hockey Administration	Elizabeth Sylvia
Head Athletic Trainer / Assistant Trainer	Tom Mulligan / Mike Poirier
Massage Therapist / Strength & Conditioning Coach	Christian Rivas / Mark Lambert
Equipment Manager	Ray Thill
Assistant Equipment Managers	Rob Kennedy, Clay Roffer
Statistical Analyst	Michael Peterson
Norfolk Admirals Coach / Trainer / Equip. Mgr.	Jon Cooper / Brad Chavis / JW Aiken
Coaching Staff	
Head Coach	Guy Boucher
Assistant Coaches	Wayne Fleming, Dan Lacroix, Martin Raymond
Goaltending Coach / Video Coach	Frantz Jean / Nigel Kirwan
Accounting/Finance	
Controller	Doug Riefler
Finance Manager / Senior Accountant	Michelle Davidson / Logan Thompson
Managers, Accounts Payable / Receivable	Donna Clark / Angela Edwards
Audio/Video/Game Entertainment	
Director of Game Operations/Creative Services	Greg Von Schottenstein
Audio Visual Manager	JC Kent
Broadcasting	
Director Broadcasting/Programming	Matt Sammon
Radio Broadcaster	David Mishkin
Television Broadcasters / On-Air Reporter	Rick Peckham, Bobby "the Chief" Taylor / Paul Kennedy
Flagship Stations, Radio / Television	WHNZ 1250 / SunSports Network
Public Relations	
Media Relations Manager	Brian Breseman
Media Relations Assistants	Peter Pupello, Nick Colelli
Audio Manager	Tom Gilbert
Community Relations and Lightning Foundation	
Executive Director of Lightning Foundation	Kasey Smith
Director, Fan Development	Brian Bradley
Director, Community Relations/Youth	Mark Sofia
Corporate Communications	
Director of Loyalty Marketing	Chris Kamke
Marketing Manager	Jessica Eckley
Promotions & Entertainment Manager	Heather Chamberlain
Information Technology	
Director of IT Services	Ian Steele
Corporate, Executive, Group, Inside and Suite Sales	
Sr. Director of New Business Development	Ryan Bringger
Sr. Director, Premium Seating Operations	Paul Wallace
Director of Group Sales / Inside Sales	Behn Custard / Ryan Cook
Executive Sales Managers	John Blume, Michael Lopez, Gary Napert
Senior Suite Sales Manager	Matthew Hill
Suite Sales Managers	Mark Beyer, Steven Duffy, Adam Laws, Katie Valone
Client Services (Premium Services and Retention)	
Senior Director, Client Services & Retention	Ryan West
Premium Services Managers	Andrea Khanzadian, Justin Versaggi
Client Services Manager / Assistant Manager	Lakisha Sharpe / Thomas Gregory
Client Sales Managers	Shannon Dixie, Elyse Hopkins, Vince Massi, Dan Schlindwein, Jeff Terry
Executive Suite Services	
Director of Executive Suite Services	Amanda Graul
Corporate Partnerships	
Director of New Business Dev., Strategic Mktg.	Mike Harrison
V.P., Corporate Partnerships	Kyle Draper
Corporate Partnership Consultant	Rob Keith
Corporate Partnership Managers	Joe Fontanetta, Tim Post, Bob Rossi, Jon Werbeck
Partnership Activation	
Director of Corporate Partnership Activation	Sarah Breseman
Senior Partnership Activation Manager	Erik Langner
Partnership Activation Managers	Chrissy Beaulieu, Leah Heiring, Bree Maddocks
Building/Event Operations / Box Office	
Directors, Arena Departments	Tim Friedenberger, Todd Perruccio, Ricardo Collado
Managers, Arena Departments	Tripp Turbiville, Tom Garavaglia, Ashley Desper, Nick Byer, Kevin Alexander, Amy Ford, Stevan Simms, Rhett Blewett
V.P., Design & Construction	Ray Chandler
Box Office Supervisor	Helen Junker
Special Advisors	Michael Deutsch, Michael O'Donnell

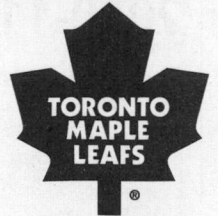

Toronto Maple Leafs

Key Off-Season Signings/Acquisitions

2011

June 9 • Re-signed G **James Reimer**.
14 • Re-signed D **Carl Gunnarsson**.
20 • Named **Scott Gordon** and **Greg Cronin** assistant coaches.
24 • Acquired D **John-Michael Liles** from Colorado for a 2nd-round pick in the 2012 Entry Draft.

July 2 • Signed C **Tim Connolly**.
3 • Acquired D **Cody Franson** and C **Matthew Lombardi** from Nashville for D **Brett Lebda** and LW **Robert Slaney**.
5 • Re-signed LW **Clarke MacArthur**.
6 • Re-signed C **Tyler Bozak**.
7 • Signed C **Philippe Dupuis**.
7 • Re-signed D **Matt Lashoff**.
19 • Re-signed RW **Joey Crabb**.

2011-12 Schedule

Oct.	Thu.	6	Montreal
	Sat.	8	Ottawa
	Sat.	15	Calgary
	Mon.	17	Colorado
	Wed.	19	Winnipeg
	Thu.	20	at Boston
	Sat.	22	at Montreal
	Mon.	24	at Philadelphia
	Thu.	27	at NY Rangers
	Sat.	29	Pittsburgh
	Sun.	30	at Ottawa
Nov.	Wed.	2	at New Jersey
	Thu.	3	at Columbus
	Sat.	5	Boston
	Tue.	8	Florida
	Thu.	10	at St. Louis
	Sat.	12	Ottawa
	Tue.	15	Phoenix
	Thu.	17	at Nashville
	Sat.	19	Washington
	Sun.	20	at Carolina*
	Tue.	22	at Tampa Bay
	Fri.	25	at Dallas
	Sun.	27	at Anaheim*
	Wed.	30	Boston
Dec.	Sat.	3	at Boston
	Mon.	5	at NY Rangers
	Tue.	6	New Jersey
	Fri.	9	at Washington
	Tue.	13	Carolina
	Fri.	16	at Buffalo
	Sat.	17	Vancouver
	Mon.	19	Los Angeles
	Thu.	22	Buffalo
	Fri.	23	at NY Islanders
	Tue.	27	at Florida
	Thu.	29	at Carolina
	Sat.	31	at Winnipeg
Jan.	Tue.	3	Tampa Bay
	Thu.	5	Winnipeg
	Sat.	7	Detroit
	Tue.	10	Buffalo
	Fri.	13	at Buffalo
	Sat.	14	NY Rangers
	Tue.	17	Ottawa
	Thu.	19	Minnesota
	Sat.	21	Montreal
	Mon.	23	NY Islanders
	Tue.	24	at NY Islanders
	Tue.	31	at Pittsburgh
Feb.	Wed.	1	Pittsburgh
	Sat.	4	at Ottawa
	Mon.	6	Edmonton
	Tue.	7	at Winnipeg
	Thu.	9	at Philadelphia
	Sat.	11	Montreal
	Tue.	14	at Calgary
	Wed.	15	at Edmonton
	Sat.	18	at Vancouver*
	Tue.	21	New Jersey
	Thu.	23	San Jose
	Sat.	25	Washington
	Tue.	28	Florida
	Wed.	29	at Chicago
Mar.	Sat.	3	at Montreal
	Tue.	6	Boston
	Wed.	7	at Pittsburgh
	Sat.	10	Philadelphia
	Sun.	11	at Washington*
	Tue.	13	at Florida
	Thu.	15	at Tampa Bay
	Sat.	17	at Ottawa
	Mon.	19	at Boston
	Tue.	20	NY Islanders
	Fri.	23	at New Jersey
	Sat.	24	NY Rangers
	Tue.	27	Carolina
	Thu.	29	Philadelphia
	Sat.	31	Buffalo
Apr.	Tue.	3	at Buffalo
	Thu.	5	Tampa Bay
	Sat.	7	at Montreal

* Denotes afternoon game.

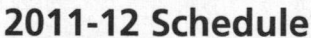

NORTHEAST DIVISION
95th NHL Season

Franchise date: November 26, 1917

2010-11 Results: 37W-34L-5OTL-6SOL 85PTS.
Fourth, Northeast Division

Year-by-Year Record

		Home				Road				Overall								
Season	**GP**	**W**	**L**	**T**	**OL**	**W**	**L**	**T**	**OL**	**W**	**L**	**T**	**OL**	**GF**	**GA**	**Pts.**	**Finished**	**Playoff Result**
2010-11	82	18	15	....	8	19	19	....	3	37	34	....	11	218	251	85	4th, Northeast Div.	Out of Playoffs
2009-10	82	18	17	....	6	12	21	....	8	30	38	....	14	214	267	74	5th, Northeast Div.	Out of Playoffs
2008-09	82	16	16	....	9	18	19	....	4	34	35	....	13	250	293	81	5th, Northeast Div.	Out of Playoffs
2007-08	82	18	17	....	6	18	18	....	5	36	35	....	11	231	260	83	5th, Northeast Div.	Out of Playoffs
2006-07	82	21	15	....	5	19	16	....	6	40	31	....	11	258	269	91	3rd, Northeast Div.	Out of Playoffs
2005-06	82	26	12	....	3	15	21	....	5	41	33	....	8	257	270	90	4th, Northeast Div.	Out of Playoffs
2004-05	....	....	....	....	....	....	....	....	....	....	....	....	....	....	....	....		
2003-04	82	22	14	3	2	23	10	7	1	45	24	10	3	242	204	103	2nd, Northeast Div.	Lost Conf. Semi-Final
2002-03	82	24	13	4	0	20	15	3	3	44	28	7	3	236	208	98	2nd, Northeast Div.	Lost Conf. Quarter-Final
2001-02	82	24	11	6	0	19	14	4	4	43	25	10	4	249	207	100	2nd, Northeast Div.	Lost Conf. Championship
2000-01	82	19	11	7	4	18	18	4	1	37	29	11	5	232	207	90	3rd, Northeast Div.	Lost Conf. Semi-Final
1999-2000	82	24	12	5	0	21	15	2	3	45	27	7	3	246	222	100	1st, Northeast Div.	Lost Conf. Semi-Final
1998-99	82	23	13	5	....	22	17	2	....	45	30	7	....	268	231	97	2nd, Northeast Div.	Lost Conf. Championship
1997-98	82	16	20	5	....	14	23	4	....	30	43	9	....	194	237	69	6th, Central Div.	Out of Playoffs
1996-97	82	18	20	3	....	12	24	5	....	30	44	8	....	230	273	68	6th, Central Div.	Out of Playoffs
1995-96	82	19	15	7	....	15	21	5	....	34	36	12	....	247	252	80	3rd, Central Div.	Lost Conf. Quarter-Final
1994-95	48	15	7	2	....	6	12	6	....	21	19	8	....	135	146	50	4th, Central Div.	Lost Conf. Quarter-Final
1993-94	84	23	15	4	....	20	14	8	....	43	29	12	....	280	243	98	2nd, Central Div.	Lost Conf. Championship
1992-93	84	25	11	6	....	19	18	5	....	44	29	11	....	288	241	99	3rd, Norris Div.	Lost Conf. Championship
1991-92	80	21	16	3	....	9	27	4	....	30	43	7	....	234	294	67	5th, Norris Div.	Out of Playoffs
1990-91	80	15	21	4	....	8	25	7	....	23	46	11	....	241	318	57	5th, Norris Div.	Out of Playoffs
1989-90	80	24	14	2	....	14	24	2	....	38	38	4	....	337	358	80	3rd, Norris Div.	Lost Div. Semi-Final
1988-89	80	15	20	5	....	13	26	1	....	28	46	6	....	259	342	62	5th, Norris Div.	Out of Playoffs
1987-88	80	14	20	6	....	7	29	4	....	21	49	10	....	273	345	52	4th, Norris Div.	Lost Div. Semi-Final
1986-87	80	22	14	4	....	10	28	2	....	32	42	6	....	286	319	70	4th, Norris Div.	Lost Div. Final
1985-86	80	16	21	3	....	9	27	4	....	25	48	7	....	311	386	57	4th, Norris Div.	Lost Div. Final
1984-85	80	10	28	2	....	10	24	6	....	20	52	8	....	253	358	48	5th, Norris Div.	Out of Playoffs
1983-84	80	17	16	7	....	9	29	2	....	26	45	9	....	303	387	61	5th, Norris Div.	Out of Playoffs
1982-83	80	20	15	5	....	8	25	7	....	28	40	12	....	293	330	68	3rd, Norris Div.	Lost Div. Semi-Final
1981-82	80	12	20	8	....	8	24	8	....	20	44	16	....	298	380	56	5th, Norris Div.	Out of Playoffs
1980-81	80	14	21	5	....	14	16	10	....	28	37	15	....	322	367	71	5th, Adams Div.	Lost Prelim. Round
1979-80	80	17	19	4	....	18	21	1	....	35	40	5	....	304	327	75	4th, Adams Div.	Lost Prelim. Round
1978-79	80	20	12	8	....	14	21	5	....	34	33	13	....	267	252	81	3rd, Adams Div.	Lost Quarter-Final
1977-78	80	21	13	6	....	20	16	4	....	41	29	10	....	271	237	92	3rd, Adams Div.	Lost Semi-Final
1976-77	80	18	13	9	....	15	19	6	....	33	32	15	....	301	285	81	3rd, Adams Div.	Lost Quarter-Final
1975-76	80	23	12	5	....	11	19	10	....	34	31	15	....	294	276	83	3rd, Adams Div.	Lost Quarter-Final
1974-75	80	19	12	9	....	12	21	7	....	31	33	16	....	280	309	78	3rd, Adams Div.	Lost Quarter-Final
1973-74	78	21	11	7	....	14	16	9	....	35	27	16	....	274	230	86	4th, East Div.	Lost Quarter-Final
1972-73	78	20	12	7	....	7	29	3	....	27	41	10	....	247	279	64	6th, East Div.	Out of Playoffs
1971-72	78	21	11	7	....	12	20	7	....	33	31	14	....	209	208	80	4th, East Div.	Lost Quarter-Final
1970-71	78	24	9	6	....	13	24	2	....	37	33	8	....	248	211	82	4th, East Div.	Lost Quarter-Final
1969-70	76	18	13	7	....	11	21	6	....	29	34	13	....	222	242	71	6th, East Div.	Out of Playoffs
1968-69	76	20	8	10	....	15	18	5	....	35	26	15	....	234	217	85	4th, East Div.	Lost Quarter-Final
1967-68	74	24	9	4	....	9	22	6	....	33	31	10	....	209	176	76	5th, East Div.	Out of Playoffs
1966-67	**70**	**21**	**8**	**6**	....	**11**	**19**	**5**	....	**32**	**27**	**11**	....	**204**	**211**	**75**	**3rd,**	**Won Stanley Cup**
1965-66	70	22	9	4	....	12	16	7	....	34	25	11	....	208	187	79	3rd,	Lost Semi-Final
1964-65	70	17	15	3	....	13	11	11	....	30	26	14	....	204	173	74	4th,	Lost Semi-Final
1963-64	**70**	**22**	**7**	**6**	....	**11**	**18**	**6**	....	**33**	**25**	**12**	....	**192**	**172**	**78**	**3rd,**	**Won Stanley Cup**
1962-63	**70**	**21**	**8**	**6**	....	**14**	**15**	**6**	....	**35**	**23**	**12**	....	**221**	**180**	**82**	**1st,**	**Won Stanley Cup**
1961-62	**70**	**25**	**5**	**5**	....	**12**	**17**	**6**	....	**37**	**22**	**11**	....	**232**	**180**	**85**	**2nd,**	**Won Stanley Cup**
1960-61	70	21	6	8	....	18	13	4	....	39	19	12	....	234	176	90	2nd,	Lost Semi-Final
1959-60	70	20	9	6	....	15	17	3	....	35	26	9	....	199	195	79	2nd,	Lost Final
1958-59	70	17	13	5	....	10	19	6	....	27	32	11	....	189	201	65	4th,	Lost Final
1957-58	70	12	16	7	....	9	22	4	....	21	38	11	....	192	226	53	6th,	Out of Playoffs
1956-57	70	12	16	7	....	9	18	8	....	21	34	15	....	174	192	57	5th,	Out of Playoffs
1955-56	70	19	10	6	....	5	23	7	....	24	33	13	....	153	181	61	4th,	Lost Semi-Final
1954-55	70	14	10	11	....	10	14	11	....	24	24	22	....	147	135	70	3rd,	Lost Semi-Final
1953-54	70	22	6	7	....	10	18	7	....	32	24	14	....	152	131	78	3rd,	Lost Semi-Final
1952-53	70	17	12	6	....	10	18	7	....	27	30	13	....	156	167	67	5th,	Out of Playoffs
1951-52	70	17	10	8	....	12	15	8	....	29	25	16	....	168	157	74	3rd,	Lost Semi-Final
1950-51	**70**	**22**	**8**	**5**	....	**19**	**8**	**8**	....	**41**	**16**	**13**	....	**212**	**138**	**95**	**2nd,**	**Won Stanley Cup**
1949-50	70	18	9	8	....	13	18	4	....	31	27	12	....	176	173	74	3rd,	Lost Semi-Final
1948-49	**60**	**12**	**8**	**10**	....	**10**	**17**	**3**	....	**22**	**25**	**13**	....	**147**	**161**	**57**	**4th,**	**Won Stanley Cup**
1947-48	**60**	**22**	**3**	**5**	....	**10**	**12**	**8**	....	**32**	**15**	**13**	....	**182**	**143**	**77**	**1st,**	**Won Stanley Cup**
1946-47	**60**	**20**	**8**	**2**	....	**11**	**11**	**8**	....	**31**	**19**	**10**	....	**209**	**172**	**72**	**2nd,**	**Won Stanley Cup**
1945-46	50	10	13	2	....	9	11	5	....	19	24	7	....	174	185	45	5th,	Out of Playoffs
1944-45	**50**	**13**	**9**	**3**	....	**11**	**13**	**1**	....	**24**	**22**	**4**	....	**183**	**161**	**52**	**3rd,**	**Won Stanley Cup**
1943-44	50	13	11	1	....	10	12	3	....	23	23	4	....	214	174	50	3rd,	Lost Semi-Final
1942-43	50	17	6	2	....	5	13	7	....	22	19	9	....	198	159	53	3rd,	Lost Semi-Final
1941-42	**48**	**18**	**6**	**0**	....	**9**	**12**	**3**	....	**27**	**18**	**3**	....	**158**	**136**	**57**	**2nd,**	**Won Stanley Cup**
1940-41	48	16	5	3	....	12	9	3	....	28	14	6	....	145	99	62	2nd,	Lost Semi-Final
1939-40	48	15	3	6	....	10	14	0	....	25	17	6	....	134	110	56	3rd,	Lost Final
1938-39	48	13	8	3	....	6	12	6	....	19	20	9	....	114	107	47	3rd,	Lost Final
1937-38	48	13	6	5	....	11	9	4	....	24	15	9	....	151	127	57	1st, Cdn. Div.	Lost Final
1936-37	48	14	9	1	....	8	12	4	....	22	21	5	....	119	115	49	3rd, Cdn. Div.	Lost Quarter-Final
1935-36	48	15	4	5	....	8	15	1	....	23	19	6	....	126	106	52	2nd, Cdn. Div.	Lost Final
1934-35	48	16	6	2	....	14	8	2	....	30	14	4	....	157	111	64	1st, Cdn. Div.	Lost Final
1933-34	48	19	2	3	....	7	11	6	....	26	13	9	....	174	119	61	1st, Cdn. Div.	Lost Semi-Final
1932-33	48	16	4	4	....	8	14	2	....	24	18	6	....	119	111	54	1st, Cdn. Div.	Lost Final
1931-32	**48**	**17**	**4**	**3**	....	**6**	**14**	**4**	....	**23**	**18**	**7**	....	**155**	**127**	**53**	**2nd, Cdn. Div.**	**Won Stanley Cup**
1930-31	44	15	4	3	....	7	9	6	....	22	13	9	....	118	99	53	2nd, Cdn. Div.	Lost Quarter-Final
1929-30	44	10	8	4	....	7	13	2	....	17	21	6	....	116	124	40	4th, Cdn. Div.	Out of Playoffs
1928-29	44	15	5	2	....	6	13	3	....	21	18	5	....	85	69	47	3rd, Cdn. Div.	Lost Semi-Final
1927-28	44	9	8	5	....	9	10	3	....	18	18	8	....	89	88	44	4th, Cdn. Div.	Out of Playoffs
1926-27*	44	10	10	2	....	5	14	3	....	15	24	5	....	79	94	35	5th, Cdn. Div.	Out of Playoffs
1925-26	36	11	5	2	....	1	16	1	....	12	21	3	....	92	114	27	6th,	Out of Playoffs
1924-25	30	10	5	0	....	9	6	0	....	19	11	0	....	90	84	38	2nd,	Lost NHL S-Final
1923-24	24	7	5	0	....	3	9	0	....	10	14	0	....	59	85	20	3rd,	Out of Playoffs
1922-23	24	10	1	1	....	3	9	0	....	13	10	1	....	82	88	27	3rd,	Out of Playoffs
1921-22	**24**	**8**	**4**	**0**	....	**5**	**6**	**1**	....	**13**	**10**	**1**	....	**98**	**97**	**27**	**2nd,**	**Won Stanley Cup**
1920-21	24	9	3	0	....	6	6	0	....	15	9	0	....	105	100	30	2nd and 1st***	Lost NHL Final
1919-20**	24	8	4	0	....	4	8	0	....	12	12	0	....	119	106	24	3rd and 2nd***	Out of Playoffs
1918-19	18	5	4	0	....	0	9	0	....	5	13	0	....	64	92	10	3rd and 3rd***	Out of Playoffs
1917-18	**22**	**10**	**1**	**0**	....	**3**	**8**	**0**	....	**13**	**9**	**0**	....	**108**	**109**	**26**	**2nd and 1st*** **	**Won Stanley Cup**

* Name changed from St. Patricks to Maple Leafs (February, 1927). ** Name changed from Arenas to St. Patricks.
*** Season played in two halves with no combined standing at end.
From 1917-18 through 1925-26, NHL champions played against PCHA/WCHL champions for Stanley Cup.

2011-12 Player Personnel

FORWARDS	HT	WT	S	Place of Birth	*Age	2010-11 Club
ARMSTRONG, Colby	6-2	195	R	Lloydminster, Sask.	28	Toronto
BOYCE, Darryl	6-0	200	L	Summerside, P.E.I.	27	Toronto-Toronto (AHL)
BOZAK, Tyler	6-1	195	R	Regina, Sask.	25	Toronto
BRENNER, Tyler	6-2	200	R	Linwood, Ont.	23	RIT Tigers-Toronto (AHL)
BROWN, Mike	5-11	205	R	Chicago, IL	26	Toronto
CAPUTI, Luca	6-3	200	L	Toronto, Ont.	23	Toronto-Toronto (AHL)
COLBORNE, Joe	6-5	213	L	Calgary, Alta.	21	Prov (AHL)-Tor-Tor (AHL)
CONNOLLY, Tim	6-1	190	R	Syracuse, NY	30	Buffalo
CRABB, Joey	6-1	190	R	Anchorage, AK	28	Toronto-Toronto (AHL)
D'AMIGO, Jerry	5-11	213	L	Binghamton, NY	20	Toronto (AHL)-Kitchener
DUPUIS, Philippe	6-0	196	R	Laval, Que.	26	Colorado
FRATTIN, Matt	6-0	200	R	Edmonton, Alta.	23	North Dakota-Toronto
GRABOVSKI, Mikhail	5-11	183	L	Potsdam, East Germany	27	Toronto
HAMILTON, Ryan	6-2	230	L	Oshawa, Ont.	26	Toronto (AHL)
KADRI, Nazem	6-0	188	L	London, Ont.	21	Toronto-Toronto (AHL)
KESSEL, Phil	6-0	202	R	Madison, WI	24	Toronto
KULEMIN, Nikolai	6-1	225	L	Magnitogorsk, USSR	25	Toronto
LOMBARDI, Matthew	5-11	195	L	Montreal, Que.	29	Nashville
LUPUL, Joffrey	6-1	206	R	Fort Saskatchewan, Alta.	28	Anaheim-Syracuse-Toronto
MacARTHUR, Clarke	6-0	191	L	Lloydminster, Alta.	26	Toronto
MUELLER, Marcel	6-3	232	L	Berlin, East Germany	23	Toronto-Toronto (AHL)
ORR, Colton	6-3	222	R	Winnipeg, Man.	29	Toronto
ROSEHILL, Jay	6-3	215	L	Olds, Alta.	26	Toronto-Toronto (AHL)
DEFENSEMEN						
AULIE, Keith	6-5	217	L	Rouleau, Sask.	22	Toronto-Toronto (AHL)
BLACKER, Jesse	6-2	190	R	Toronto, Ont.	20	Owen Sound
FINGER, Jeff	6-1	209	R	Houghton, MI	31	Toronto (AHL)
FRANSON, Cody	6-5	213	R	Salmon Arm, B.C.	24	Nashville
GARDINER, Jake	6-2	184	L	Deephaven, MN	21	U. of Wisconsin-Tor (AHL)
GUNNARSSON, Carl	6-2	196	L	Orebro, Sweden	24	Toronto
GYSBERS, Simon	6-4	200	R	Richmond Hill, Ont.	24	Toronto (AHL)
HOLZER, Korbinian	6-3	205	R	Munich, West Germany	23	Toronto-Toronto (AHL)
KOMISAREK, Mike	6-4	243	R	West Islip, NY	29	Toronto
LASHOFF, Matt	6-2	204	L	East Greenbush, NY	25	Toronto-Toronto (AHL)
LILES, John-Michael	5-10	185	L	Indianapolis, IN	30	Colorado
PHANEUF, Dion	6-3	214	L	Edmonton, Alta.	26	Toronto
SCHENN, Luke	6-2	229	R	Saskatoon, Sask.	21	Toronto

GOALTENDERS	HT	WT	C	Place of Birth	*Age	2010-11 Club
GUSTAVSSON, Jonas	6-3	192	L	Danderyd, Sweden	26	Toronto-Toronto (AHL)
REIMER, James	6-2	220	L	Morweena, Man.	23	Toronto-Toronto (AHL)
SCRIVENS, Ben	6-2	192	L	Spruce Grove, Alta.	25	Toronto (AHL)-Reading

* – Age at start of 2011-12 season

Captains' History

Bert Corbeau, 1926-27; Hap Day, 1927-28 to 1936-37; Charlie Conacher, 1937-38; Red Horner, 1938-39, 1939-40; Syl Apps, 1940-41 to 1942-43; Bob Davidson, 1943-44, 1944-45; Syl Apps, 1945-46 to 1947-48; Ted Kennedy, 1948-49 to 1954-55; Sid Smith, 1955-56; Jimmy Thomson, Ted Kennedy, 1956-57; George Armstrong, 1957-58 to 1968-69; Dave Keon, 1969-70 to 1974-75; Darryl Sittler, 1975-76 to 1980-81; Rick Vaive, 1981-82 to 1985-86; no captain, 1986-87 to 1988-89; Rob Ramage, 1989-90, 1990-91; Wendel Clark, 1991-92 to 1993-94; Doug Gilmour, 1994-95 to 1996-97; Mats Sundin, 1997-98 to 2007-08; no captain, 2008-09, 2009-10; Dion Phaneuf, 2010-11 to date.

Ron Wilson

Head Coach

Born: Windsor, Ont., May 28, 1955.

The Toronto Maple Leafs announced on June 10, 2008 that Ron Wilson had been named the 27th head coach in the club's history. Wilson previously held NHL head coaching duties with Anaheim, Washington, and the San Jose Sharks.

Under Wilson's guidance the Sharks were the only NHL team to have won at least one playoff round in each season from 2003-04 through 2007-08. In his four full seasons behind the Sharks bench, the team advanced to the Western Conference Final for the first time ever in 2004, and reached the Conference semifinals in 2006, 2007 and 2008. His Sharks teams garnered two Pacific Division championships (2004 and 2008); twice finished second in their division, and twice posted the second-best point total in the conference. With 206 victories in San Jose, Wilson surpassed Darryl Sutter as the Sharks' all-time wins leader on March 1, 2008.

Wilson coached the Washington Capitals from 1997 until 2002, with his tenure in the United State's capital highlighted by the team's only trip to the Stanley Cup Final in 1998. Prior to spending five seasons with the Capitals, Wilson had served as the first head coach of the expansion Mighty Ducks of Anaheim in 1993, and he led the team to the postseason for the very first time in 1996-97.

Throughout his professional and amateur career, Wilson has enjoyed a long-standing relationship with USA Hockey. He led Team USA to the gold medal in 1996 at the inaugural World Cup of Hockey and he coached the team again at the 2004 tournament. Wilson coached the U.S. team at the World Championship in 1994, 1996 and again in 2009. He also served as head coach for Team USA at the 1998 Nagano Olympics and will do again at the 2010 Vancouver Games.

Wilson was a seventh-round selection of the Toronto Maple Leafs (132nd overall) in the 1975 NHL Amateur Draft. He made his NHL debut by playing in 13 games for Toronto in 1977-78, followed by 46 games in 1978-79 and five games in 1979-80. In 177 career NHL games as a player with Toronto and Minnesota, Wilson recorded 26 goals and 67 assists for 93 points. He is one of 15 individuals that have both played for the Maple Leafs and then went on to coach at least one game for the Original Six franchise. He is the son of Larry Wilson and the nephew of Johnny Wilson, both former players on Stanley Cup winning teams from Detroit.

2010-11 Scoring

* – rookie

Regular Season

Pos	#	Player	Team	GP	G	A	Pts	TOI	+/-	PIM	PP	SH	GW	S	%
C	81	Phil Kessel	TOR	82	32	32	64	19:38	–20	24	12	1	6	325	9.8
L	16	Clarke MacArthur	TOR	82	21	41	62	17:06	–3	37	6	0	3	154	13.6
C	84	Mikhail Grabovski	TOR	81	29	29	58	19:21	14	60	10	0	4	239	12.1
L	41	Nikolai Kulemin	TOR	82	30	27	57	17:19	7	26	5	1	5	173	17.3
C	42	Tyler Bozak	TOR	82	15	17	32	19:16	–29	14	6	1	4	120	12.5
R	19	Joffrey Lupul	ANA	26	5	8	13	13:13	–4	14	2	0	1	54	9.3
			TOR	28	9	9	18	17:51	–7	19	2	0	1	75	12.0
			Total	54	14	17	31	15:37	–11	33	4	0	2	129	10.9
D	3	Dion Phaneuf	TOR	66	8	22	30	25:18	–2	88	3	0	1	190	4.2
R	9	Colby Armstrong	TOR	50	8	15	23	16:07	–1	38	0	0	0	69	11.6
D	2	Luke Schenn	TOR	82	5	17	22	22:22	–7	34	0	0	0	128	3.9
C	37	Tim Brent	TOR	79	8	12	20	11:39	–4	33	0	1	1	60	13.3
D	36	Carl Gunnarsson	TOR	68	4	16	20	18:14	–2	14	1	0	1	69	5.8
R	46	Joey Crabb	TOR	48	3	12	15	12:58	–1	24	0	1	2	51	5.9
C	47	Darryl Boyce	TOR	46	5	8	13	11:22	8	33	0	0	1	27	18.5
C	43 *	Nazem Kadri	TOR	29	3	9	12	15:46	–3	8	0	0	0	51	5.9
D	8	Mike Komisarek	TOR	75	1	9	10	13:37	–8	86	0	0	0	48	2.1
R	18	Mike Brown	TOR	50	3	5	8	10:05	1	69	1	0	0	59	5.1
L	11	Fredrik Sjostrom	TOR	66	2	3	5	11:12	–5	14	0	0	0	62	3.2
D	23	Brett Lebda	TOR	41	1	3	4	13:20	–14	14	0	0	0	34	2.9
C	39	John Mitchell	TOR	23	2	1	3	12:30	–7	12	1	0	1	28	7.1
L	38 *	Jay Rosehill	TOR	26	1	2	3	5:12	–6	71	0	0	0	12	8.3
D	59 *	Keith Aulie	TOR	40	2	0	2	19:07	–1	32	0	0	0	32	6.3
R	28	Colton Orr	TOR	46	2	0	2	5:04	–1	128	0	0	1	14	14.3
C	32 *	Joe Colborne	TOR	1	0	1	1	18:41	1	0	0	0	0	1	0.0
C	26	Michael Zigomanis	TOR	8	0	1	1	6:58	0	4	0	0	0	7	0.0
D	29	Matt Lashoff	TOR	11	0	1	1	13:49	1	6	0	0	0	8	0.0
R	39 *	Matt Frattin	TOR	1	0	0	0	15:34	–1	0	0	0	0	5	0.0
D	55 *	Korbinian Holzer	TOR	2	0	0	0	13:01	–1	2	0	0	0	1	0.0
C	45 *	Marcel Mueller	TOR	3	0	0	0	10:07	0	2	0	0	0	5	0.0
C	20	Christian Hanson	TOR	6	0	0	0	8:26	0	4	0	0	0	2	0.0
L	33 *	Luca Caputi	TOR	7	0	0	0	11:04	–2	4	0	0	0	8	0.0

Goaltending

No.	Goaltender	GPI	Mins	Avg	W	L	OT	EN	SO	GA	SA	S%	G	A	PIM
34	* James Reimer	37	2080	2.60	20	10	5	3	3	90	1134	.921	0	1	2
35	Jean-Sebastien Giguere	33	1633	2.87	11	11	4	5	0	78	777	.900	0	0	4
50	Jonas Gustavsson	23	1242	3.29	6	13	2	1	0	68	620	.890	0	0	0
	Totals	**82**	**4995**	**2.94**	**37**	**34**	**11**	**9**	**3**	**245**	**2540**	**.904**			

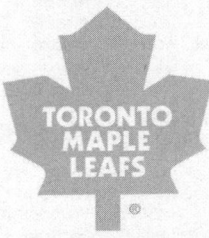

Coaching History

Dick Carroll, 1917-18, 1918-19; Frank Heffernan and Harry Sproule, 1919-20; Frank Carroll, 1920-21; George O'Donohue, 1921-22; George O'Donohue and Charles Querrie, 1922-23; Charles Querrie, 1923-24; Eddie Powers, 1924-25, 1925-26; Charles Querrie, Mike Rodden and Alex Romeril, 1926-27; Conn Smythe, 1927-28 to 1929-30; Conn Smythe and Art Duncan, 1930-31; Art Duncan and Dick Irvin, 1931-32; Dick Irvin, 1932-33 to 1939-40; Hap Day, 1940-41 to 1949-50; Joe Primeau, 1950-51 to 1952-53; King Clancy, 1953-54 to 1955-56; Howie Meeker, 1956-57; Billy Reay, 1957-58; Billy Reay and Punch Imlach, 1958-59; Punch Imlach, 1959-60 to 1968-69; John McLellan, 1969-70 to 1972-73; Red Kelly, 1973-74 to 1976-77; Roger Neilson, 1977-78, 1978-79; Floyd Smith, Dick Duff and Punch Imlach, 1979-80; Joe Crozier and Mike Nykoluk, 1980-81; Mike Nykoluk, 1981-82 to 1983-84; Dan Maloney, 1984-85, 1985-86; John Brophy, 1986-87, 1987-88; John Brophy and George Armstrong, 1988-89; Doug Carpenter, 1989-90; Doug Carpenter and Tom Watt, 1990-91; Tom Watt, 1991-92; Pat Burns, 1992-93 to 1994-95; Pat Burns and Nick Beverley, 1995-96; Mike Murphy, 1996-97, 1997-98; Pat Quinn, 1998-99 to 2005-06; Paul Maurice, 2006-07, 2007-08; Ron Wilson, 2008-09 to date.

Coaching Record

			Regular Season				Playoffs			
Season	**Team**	**League**	**GC**	**W**	**L**	**O/T**	**GC**	**W**	**L**	**T**
1993-94	Anaheim	NHL	84	33	46	5	....	....	....	....
1994-95	Anaheim	NHL	48	16	27	5	....	....	....	....
1995-96	Anaheim	NHL	82	35	39	8	....	....	....	....
1996-97	Anaheim	NHL	82	36	33	13	11	4	7	....
1997-98	Washington	NHL	82	40	30	12	21	12	9	....
1998-99	Washington	NHL	82	31	45	6	....	....	....	....
99-2000	Washington	NHL	82	44	24	14	5	1	4	....
2000-01	Washington	NHL	82	41	27	14	6	2	4	....
2001-02	Washington	NHL	82	36	33	13	....	....	....	....
2002-03	San Jose	NHL	57	19	25	13	....	....	....	....
2003-04	San Jose	NHL	82	43	21	18	17	10	7	....
2004-05	San Jose				SEASON CANCELLED					
2005-06	San Jose	NHL	82	44	27	11	11	6	5	....
2006-07	San Jose	NHL	82	51	26	5	11	6	5	....
2007-08	San Jose	NHL	82	49	23	10	13	6	7	....
2008-09	Toronto	NHL	82	34	35	13	....	....	....	....
2009-10	Toronto	NHL	82	30	38	14	....	....	....	....
2010-11	Toronto	NHL	82	37	34	11	....	....	....	....
	NHL Totals		1337	619	533	185	95	47	48	....

Club Records

Team

(Figures in brackets for season records are games played; records for fewest points, wins, ties, losses, goals, goals against are for 70 or more games)

Most Points 103 2003-04 (82)
Most Wins 45 1998-99 (82), 1999-2000 (82), 2003-04 (82)
Most Ties 22 1954-55 (70)
Most Losses 52 1984-85 (80)
Most Goals 337 1989-90 (80)
Most Goals Against 387 1983-84 (80)
Fewest Points 48 1984-85 (80)
Fewest Wins 20 1981-82 (80), 1984-85 (80)
Fewest Ties 4 1989-90 (80)
Fewest Losses 16 1950-51 (70)
Fewest Goals 147 1954-55 (70)
Fewest Goals Against *131 1953-54 (70)
Longest Winning Streak
Overall .... 10 Oct. 7-28/93
Home .... 9 Nov. 11-Dec. 26/53, Mar. 6-Apr. 7/07
Away .... 7 Three times
Longest Undefeated Streak
Overall .... 11 Oct. 15-Nov. 8/50 (8 wins, 3 ties), Jan. 6-Feb. 1/94 (7 wins, 4 ties)
Home .... 18 Nov. 28/33-Mar. 10/34 (15 wins, 3 ties), Oct. 31/53-Jan. 23/54 (16 wins, 2 ties)
Away .... 9 Nov. 30/47-Jan. 11/48 (4 wins, 5 ties)
Longest Losing Streak
Overall .... 10 Jan. 15-Feb. 8/67
Home .... 7 Nov. 11-Dec. 5/84
Away .... 11 Feb. 20-Apr. 1/88
Longest Winless Streak
Overall .... 15 Dec. 26/87-Jan. 25/88 (11 losses, 4 ties)
Home .... 11 Dec. 19/87-Jan. 25/88 (7 losses, 4 ties)
Away .... 18 Oct. 6/82-Jan. 5/83 (13 losses, 5 ties)
Most Shutouts, Season 13 1953-54 (70)
Most PIM, Season 2,419 1989-90 (80)
Most Goals, Game .... 14 Mar. 16/57 (NYR 1 at Tor. 14)

Individual

Most Seasons .... 21 George Armstrong
Most Games .... 1,187 George Armstrong
Most Goals, Career .... 420 Mats Sundin
Most Assists, Career .... 620 Borje Salming
Most Points, Career .... 987 Mats Sundin (420G, 567A)
Most PIM, Career .... 2,265 Tie Domi
Most Shutouts, Career .... 62 Turk Broda
Longest Consecutive Games Streak .... 486 Tim Horton (Feb. 11/61-Feb. 4/68)
Most Goals, Season .... 54 Rick Vaive (1981-82)
Most Assists, Season .... 95 Doug Gilmour (1992-93)
Most Points, Season .... 127 Doug Gilmour (1992-93; 32G, 95A)
Most PIM, Season .... 365 Tie Domi (1997-98)
Most Points, Defenseman, Season .... 79 Ian Turnbull (1976-77; 22G, 57A)
Most Points, Center, Season .... 127 Doug Gilmour (1992-93; 32G, 95A)
Most Points, Right Wing, Season .... 97 Wilf Paiement (1980-81; 40G, 57A)
Most Points, Left Wing, Season .... 99 Dave Andreychuk (1993-94; 53G, 46A)
Most Points, Rookie, Season .... 66 Peter Ihnacak (1982-83; 28G, 38A)
Most Shutouts, Season .... 13 Harry Lumley (1953-54)
Most Goals, Game .... 6 Corb Denneny (Jan. 26/21), Darryl Sittler (Feb. 7/76)
Most Assists, Game .... 6 Babe Pratt (Jan. 8/44), Doug Gilmour (Feb. 13/93)
Most Points, Game .... *10 Darryl Sittler (Feb. 7/76; 6G, 4A)

* NHL Record.

Retired Numbers

5	Bill Barilko	1946-1951
6	Ace Bailey	1926-1934

Honored Numbers

1	Turk Broda	1936-43, 1945-52
	Johnny Bower	1958-1970
4	Hap Day	1926-1937
	Red Kelly	1959-1967
7	King Clancy	1930-1937
	Tim Horton	1949-50, 1951-70
9	Charlie Conacher	1929-1938
	Ted Kennedy	1942-55, 1956-57
10	Syl Apps	1936-43, 1945-48
	George Armstrong	1949-50, 1951-71
17	Wendel Clark	1985-94, 96-98, 2000
21	Borje Salming	1973-1989
27	Frank Mahovlich	1956-1968
	Darryl Sittler	1970-1982
93	Doug Gilmour	1992-97, 2003

All-time Record vs. Other Clubs

Regular Season

	At Home								On Road								Total							
	GP	W	L	T	OL	GF	GA	PTS	GP	W	L	T	OL	GF	GA	PTS	GP	W	L	T	OL	GF	GA	PTS
Anaheim	18	11	2	4	1	60	37	27	13	6	6	1	0	34	42	13	31	17	8	5	1	94	79	40
Atlanta	21	12	6	1	2	77	60	27	21	13	5	0	3	79	44	29	42	25	11	1	5	156	104	56
Boston	320	165	102	51	2	1060	834	383	319	98	169	47	5	852	1039	248	639	263	271	98	7	1912	1873	631
Buffalo	88	35	37	12	4	258	301	86	90	26	56	6	2	232	353	60	178	61	93	18	6	490	654	146
Calgary	57	30	18	7	2	218	206	69	65	22	36	5	2	201	252	51	122	52	54	12	4	419	458	120
Carolina	48	18	24	5	1	154	168	42	49	18	21	6	4	162	187	46	97	36	45	11	5	316	355	88
Chicago	318	164	99	54	1	1082	837	383	320	120	158	42	0	834	974	282	638	284	257	96	1	1916	1811	665
Colorado	37	16	17	4	0	120	141	36	32	9	18	5	0	101	123	23	69	25	35	9	0	221	264	59
Columbus	6	3	1	1	1	18	12	8	3	2	0	0	1	13	9	5	9	5	1	1	2	31	21	13
Dallas	104	50	37	17	0	363	330	117	99	36	51	11	1	310	372	84	203	86	88	28	1	673	702	201
Detroit	318	166	105	47	0	1053	849	379	325	109	170	46	0	798	979	264	643	275	275	93	0	1851	1828	643
Edmonton	41	22	17	2	0	165	170	46	47	17	23	6	1	151	186	41	88	39	40	8	1	316	356	87
Florida	27	16	8	2	1	85	76	35	29	13	10	5	1	80	83	32	56	29	18	7	2	165	159	67
Los Angeles	70	35	24	11	0	270	230	81	68	23	35	10	0	199	242	56	138	58	59	21	0	469	472	137
Minnesota	5	4	1	0	0	17	11	8	4	2	2	0	0	8	11	4	9	6	3	0	0	25	22	12
Montreal	354	183	120	45	6	1078	934	417	354	102	206	43	3	889	1233	250	708	285	326	88	9	1967	2167	667
Nashville	9	4	4	1	0	21	25	9	3	1	1	0	1	8	10	3	12	5	5	1	1	29	35	12
New Jersey	60	38	15	5	2	207	159	83	58	20	20	15	3	183	197	58	118	58	35	20	5	390	356	141
NY Islanders	67	36	24	4	3	235	216	79	65	24	34	3	4	186	248	55	132	60	58	7	7	421	464	134
NY Rangers	294	164	89	39	2	1006	775	369	295	112	124	56	3	864	918	283	589	276	213	95	5	1870	1693	652
Ottawa	43	20	16	2	5	116	120	47	41	16	21	1	3	111	125	36	84	36	37	3	8	227	245	83
Philadelphia	79	30	34	14	1	243	254	75	79	22	48	8	1	189	296	53	158	52	82	22	2	432	550	128
Phoenix	45	20	23	2	0	163	171	42	42	13	23	6	0	147	177	32	87	33	46	8	0	310	348	74
Pittsburgh	79	39	27	11	2	312	259	91	81	33	41	6	1	264	323	73	160	72	68	17	3	576	582	164
St. Louis	102	59	29	11	3	381	305	132	104	31	59	14	0	285	353	76	206	90	88	25	3	666	658	208
San Jose	20	12	6	2	0	75	55	26	18	8	7	3	0	48	42	19	38	20	13	5	0	123	97	45
Tampa Bay	33	20	10	1	2	117	91	43	32	20	8	1	3	99	77	44	65	40	18	2	5	216	168	87
Vancouver	64	28	24	11	1	228	214	68	68	24	33	11	0	223	240	59	132	52	57	22	1	451	454	127
Washington	60	32	21	6	1	244	199	71	62	22	35	4	1	178	227	49	122	54	56	10	2	422	426	120
Defunct Clubs	232	158	53	21	0	860	515	337	233	84	120	29	0	607	745	197	465	242	173	50	0	1467	1260	534
Totals	**3019**	**1590**	**993**	**393**	**43**	**10286**	**8554**	**3616**	**3019**	**1046**	**1540**	**390**	**43**	**8335**	**10107**	**2525**	**6038**	**2636**	**2533**	**783**	**86**	**18621**	**18661**	**6141**

Playoffs

	Series	W	L	GP	W	L	T	GF	GA	Last Mtg.	Rnd.	Result
Boston	13	8	5	62	31	30	1	150	153	1974	QF	L 0-4
Buffalo	1	0	1	5	1	4	0	16	21	1999	CF	L 1-4
Calgary	1	1	0	2	2	0	0	9	5	1979	PRE	W 2-0
Carolina	1	0	1	6	2	4	0	6	10	2002	CF	L 2-4
Chicago	9	6	3	38	22	15	1	111	89	1995	CQF	L 3-4
Dallas	2	0	2	7	1	6	0	26	35	1983	DSF	L 1-3
Detroit	23	12	11	117	58	59	0	311	321	1993	DSF	W 4-3
Los Angeles	3	2	1	12	7	5	0	41	31	1993	CF	L 3-4
Montreal	15	7	8	71	29	42	0	160	215	1979	QF	L 0-4
New Jersey	2	0	2	13	5	8	0	27	37	2001	CSF	L 3-4
NY Islanders	3	2	1	17	8	9	0	42	54	2002	CQF	W 4-3
NY Rangers	8	3	5	35	16	19	0	86	86	1971	QF	L 2-4
Ottawa	4	4	0	24	16	8	0	57	42	2004	CQF	W 4-3
Philadelphia	6	1	5	36	14	22	0	85	119	2004	CSF	L 2-4
Pittsburgh	3	3	0	12	8	4	0	39	27	1999	CSF	W 4-2
St. Louis	5	2	3	31	14	17	0	90	88	1996	CQF	L 2-4
San Jose	1	1	0	7	4	3	0	26	21	1994	CSF	W 4-3
Vancouver	1	0	1	5	1	4	0	9	16	1994	CF	L 1-4
Defunct Clubs	8	6	2	24	12	10	2	59	57			
Totals	**109**	**58**	**51**	**524**	**251**	**269**	**4**	**1350**	**1427**			

Calgary totals include Atlanta Flames, 1972-73 to 1979-80. Carolina totals include Hartford, 1979-80 to 1996-97.
Colorado totals include Quebec, 1979-80 to 1994-95. Dallas totals include Minnesota North Stars, 1967-68 to 1992-93.
New Jersey totals include Kansas City, 1974-75, 1975-76, and Colorado Rockies, 1976-77 to 1981-82.
Phoenix totals include Winnipeg, 1979-80 to 1995-96.

Playoff Results 2011-2007

(Last playoff appearance: 2004)

Abbreviations: Round: CF – conference final; **CSF** – conference semi-final; **CQF** – conference quarter-final; **DSF** – division semi-final; **QF** – quarter-final; **PRE** – preliminary round.

2010-11 Results

Oct.	7	Montreal	3-2		11	at San Jose	4-2
	9	Ottawa	5-1		13	at Phoenix	1-5
	13	at Pittsburgh	4-3		15	Calgary	1-2†
	15	at NY Rangers	4-3*		19	at NY Rangers	0-7
	18	NY Islanders	1-2*		20	Anaheim	5-2
	21	NY Rangers	1-2		22	Washington	1-4
	23	at Philadelphia	2-5		24	at Carolina	4-6
	26	Florida	3-1		25	at Tampa Bay	0-2
	28	at Boston	0-2	**Feb.**	1	Florida	4-3†
	30	NY Rangers	0-2		3	Carolina	3-0
Nov.	2	Ottawa	2-3		5	at Buffalo	2-6
	3	at Washington	4-5†		7	Atlanta	5-4
	6	Buffalo	2-3†		8	at NY Islanders	5-3
	9	at Tampa Bay	0-4		10	New Jersey	1-2*
	10	at Florida	1-4		12	at Montreal	0-3
	13	Vancouver	3-5		15	at Boston	4-3
	16	Nashville	5-4		16	at Buffalo	2-1
	18	New Jersey	3-1		19	Ottawa	0-1†
	20	at Montreal	0-2		22	NY Islanders	2-1
	22	Dallas	4-1		24	at Montreal	5-4
	26	at Buffalo	1-3		26	Pittsburgh	5-6†
	27	at Ottawa	0-3		27	at Atlanta	2-3*
	30	Tampa Bay	3-4*	**Mar.**	2	Pittsburgh	3-2*
Dec.	2	Edmonton	0-5		3	at Philadelphia	3-2
	4	Boston	3-2†		5	Chicago	3-5
	6	at Washington	5-4†		8	at NY Islanders	3-4*
	8	at Pittsburgh	2-5		10	Philadelphia	2-3
	9	Philadelphia	1-4		12	Buffalo	4-3
	11	Montreal	3-1		14	Tampa Bay	2-6
	14	at Edmonton	4-1		16	at Carolina	3-1
	16	at Calgary	2-5		17	at Florida	0-4
	18	at Vancouver	1-4		19	Boston	5-2
	20	Atlanta	3-6		22	at Minnesota	3-0
	26	at New Jersey	4-1		24	at Colorado	4-3
	28	Carolina	3-4		26	at Detroit	2-4
	30	Columbus	2-3		29	Buffalo	4-3
Jan.	1	at Ottawa	5-1		31	at Boston	4-3†
	3	Boston	1-2	**Apr.**	2	at Ottawa	4-2
	6	St. Louis	6-5†		5	Washington	2-3†
	7	at Atlanta	9-3		6	at New Jersey	2-4
	10	at Los Angeles	3-2		9	Montreal	1-4

* – Overtime † – Shootout

Entry Draft Selections 2011-1997

Name in bold denotes played in NHL.

2011 Pick	2007 Pick	2002 Pick	1999 Pick
22 Tyler Biggs	74 Dale Mitchell	24 **Alex Steen**	24 Luca Cereda
25 **Stuart Percy**	99 **Matt Frattin**	57 **Matt Stajan**	60 Peter Reynolds
86 Josh Leivo	104 Ben Winnett	74 Todd Ford	108 Mirko Murovic
100 Tom Nilsson	134 Juraj Mikus	88 Dominic D'Amour	110 Jon Zion
130 Tony Cameranesi	164 Chris Didomenico	122 David Turon	151 Vaclav Zavoral
152 David Broll	194 **Carl Gunnarsson**	191 **Ian White**	161 Jan Sochor
173 Dennis Robertson		222 Scott May	211 Vladimir Kulikov
190 Garret Sparks	**2006**	254 **Jarkko Immonen**	239 **Pierre Hedin**
203 Max Everson	Pick	285 Staffan Kronwall	267 Peter Metcalf

2010 Pick	2006 Pick	2001 Pick	1998 Pick
43 Brad Ross	13 **Jiri Tlusty**	17 **Carlo Colaiacovo**	10 **Nik Antropov**
62 Greg McKegg	44 **Nikolai Kulemin**	39 Karel Pilar	35 Petr Svoboda
79 Sondre Olden	99 **James Reimer**	65 **Brendan Bell**	69 Jamie Hodson
116 Petter Granberg	111 **Korbinian Holzer**	82 **Jay Harrison**	87 **Alexei Ponikarovsky**
144 Sam Carrick	161 **Viktor Stalberg**	88 Nicolas Corbeil	126 Morgan Warren
146 Daniel Brodin	166 Tyler Ruegsegger	134 Kyle Wellwood	154 **Allan Rourke**
182 Josh Nicholls	180 **Leo Komarov**	168 **Maxim Kondratiev**	181 Jonathan Gagnon
		183 Jaroslav Sklenar	215 Dwight Wolfe
2009	**2005**	198 Ivan Kolozvary	228 Michal Travnicek
Pick	Pick	213 Jan Chovan	236 Sergei Rostov
7 **Nazem Kadri**	21 **Tuukka Rask**	246 **Tomas Mojzis**	
50 Kenny Ryan	82 **Phil Oreskovic**	276 Mike Knoepfli	**1997**
58 Jesse Blacker	153 Alex Berry		Pick
68 Jamie Devane	173 Johan Dahlberg	**2000**	57 **Jeff Farkas**
128 Eric Knodel	216 **Anton Stralman**	Pick	84 **Adam Mair**
158 Jerry D'Amigo	228 Chad Rau	24 **Brad Boyes**	111 Frantisek Mrazek
188 Barron Smith		51 **Kris Vernarsky**	138 Eric Gooldy
	2004	70 **Mikael Tellqvist**	165 Hugo Marchand
2008	Pick	90 Jean-Francois Racine	190 **Shawn Thornton**
Pick	90 **Justin Pogge**	100 Miguel Delisle	194 Russ Bartlett
5 **Luke Schenn**	113 Roman Kukumberg	179 Vadim Sozinov	221 **Jonathan Hedstrom**
60 Jimmy Hayes	157 Dmitri Vorobiev	209 Markus Seikola	
98 Mikhail Stefanovich	187 **Robbie Earl**	223 Lubos Velebny	
128 Greg Pateryn	220 Maxim Semenov	254 Alexander Shinkar	
129 Joel Champagne	252 Jan Steber	265 **Jean-Philippe Cote**	
130 Jerome Flaake	285 Pierce Norton		
158 Grant Rollheiser			
188 Andrew MacWilliam	**2003**		
	Pick		
	57 John Doherty		
	91 Martin Sagat		
	125 Konstantin Volkov		
	158 **John Mitchell**		
	220 **Jeremy Williams**		
	237 Shaun Landolt		

General Managers' History

Charles Querrie, 1917-18 to 1926-27; Conn Smythe, 1927-28 to 1953-54; Hap Day, 1954-55 to 1956-57; Howie Meeker, summer 1957; Stafford Smythe 1957-58; Stafford Smythe and Punch Imlach, 1958-59; Punch Imlach, 1959-60 to 1968-69; Jim Gregory, 1969-70 to 1978-79; Punch Imlach, 1979-80, 1980-81; Punch Imlach and Gerry McNamara, 1981-82; Gerry McNamara, 1982-83 to 1986-87; Gerry McNamara and Gord Stellick, 1987-88; Gord Stellick, 1988-89; Floyd Smith, 1989-90, 1990-91; Cliff Fletcher, 1991-92 to 1996-97; Ken Dryden, 1997-98, 1998-99; Pat Quinn, 1999-2000 to 2002-03; John Ferguson Jr., 2003-04 to 2006-07; John Ferguson Jr. and Cliff Fletcher, 2007-08; Cliff Fletcher and Brian Burke, 2008-09; Brian Burke, 2009-10 to date.

Brian Burke

President and General Manager

Born: Providence, RI, June 30, 1955.

Brian Burke was named president and general manager of the Toronto Maple Leafs on November 29, 2008, bringing over 20 years of National Hockey League experience in various roles to the franchise. Most recently, Burke had served as executive vice president and general manager of the Anaheim Ducks from 2005 to 2008. In just over three seasons in Anaheim, Burke guided the Ducks to their first Stanley Cup (2007), first Pacific Division title (2007), and first-two 100+ point seasons (2006-07 and 2007-08).

Burke received two outstanding honours in the summer of 2008. On June 6, he was chosen by USA Hockey as general manager of the 2010 U.S. Olympic hockey team, and on August 7, he was named a recipient of the 2008 Lester Patrick Award for outstanding service to hockey in the United States. Burke was also ranked number one by The Hockey News in the magazine's Annual GM rankings in March of 2008, and was a finalist for The Hockey News Executive of the Year in 2006. He was named The Sporting News Executive of the Year in 2001, and was a runner-up for the same award following the 2005-06 season.

Burke joined the Ducks after a six-year stint (1998 to 2004) as president and general manager of the Vancouver Canucks where he revitalized the team en route to consecutive 100+ point seasons and the 2004 Northwest Division title. Under Burke's leadership, the Canucks improved their point total in four consecutive years from 1999-2003.

Born in Providence, Rhode Island and raised in Edina, Minnesota, Burke was named the vice president and director of hockey operations by the Vancouver Canucks in June of 1987. Burke left Vancouver to serve as general manager of the Hartford Whalers for one season in 1992, before joining the NHL front office as senior vice president and director of hockey operations in September of 1993.

After earning his Bachelor of Arts in history from Providence College in 1977, Burke signed with the Philadelphia Flyers prior to the 1977-78 season and won a Calder Cup championship with the Flyers' American Hockey League affiliate the Maine Mariners. He then returned to school and graduated from Harvard Law in 1981. Burke practiced law in Boston for the next six years, representing professional hockey players until joining the Canucks in 1987.

Club Directory

Air Canada Centre

Toronto Maple Leafs
Air Canada Centre
40 Bay St., Suite 400
Toronto, Ontario M5J 2X2
Phone 416/815-5700
FAX 416/359-9331
www.mapleleafs.com
Capacity: 18,819

Board of Directors
Lawrence M. Tanenbaum (Chairman of the Board), Glen Silvestri, Robert G. Bertram, Ashvin Malkani, Robert MacLellan, Dale H. Lastman, Richard Peddie, Jane Rowe

Maple Leaf Sports & Entertainment
Chairman, NHL Governor	Lawrence M. Tanenbaum
President, CEO and Alt. Governor	Richard Peddie
Alternate NHL Governor	Brian Burke
Alternate NHL Governor	Dale H. Lastman
Exec. V.P. and Chief Operating Officer	Tom Anselmi
Exec. V.P. and CFO, Business Development	Ian Clarke
Exec. V.P., Venues and Entertainment	Bob Hunter
Exec. V.P., General Counsel and Corp. Secretary	Robin Brudner
Senior Vice-President, People	Mardi Walker
Senior Vice-President, Broadcast and Content	Chris Hebb
Senior Vice-President, Business Partnerships	Dave Hopkinson
Senior Vice-President, Finance	Kevin Nonomura
Senior Vice-President, Ticket Sales and Service	Beth Robertson
Vice-President, Live Entertainment	Patti-Anne Tarlton
Vice-President, Food & Beverage	Michael Doyle

Hockey Operations
President, G.M. and Alternate NHL Governor	Brian Burke
Senior Vice-President of Hockey Operations	David Nonis
Vice-President of Hockey Operations	Dave Poulin
Director, Player Personnel	Rick Dudley
Senior Advisor	Cliff Fletcher
Assistant General Manager	Claude Loiselle
Head Coach	Ron Wilson
Assistant Coaches	Greg Cronin, Scott Gordon, Rob Zettler
Goaltending Consultant	Francois Allaire
Skating Coach	Graeme Townshend
Director of Player Development	Jim Hughes
Director, Hockey and Scouting Administration	Reid Mitchell
Strength and Conditioning Coordinator	Anthony Belza
Manager, Team Services	Dave Griffiths
Video Coach	Chris Dennis
Director of Amateur Scouting	Dave Morrison
Pro Scouts	Rob Cowie, Steve Kasper, Mike Penny, Tom Watt
Amateur Scouts	Scott Carter, Gary Harker, John Lilley, Garth Malarchuk, Mike Palmateer, Allan Power, George Armstrong, Pierre Rioux, Roy Stasiuk, John McMorrow, Dave Starman
European Scouts	Thommie Bergman, Joe Gibbs, Peter Ihnacak, Nikolai Ladygin, Jari Gronstrand
Community Representatives	Wendel Clark, Darryl Sittler
Executive Assistant, Hockey Operations	Sandi Dunn
Exec. Assistant to the President and G.M.	Catherine Grey

Medical and Training Staff
Head Athletic Therapist	Andy Playter
Athletic Therapist	Marty Dudgeon
Equipment Manager	Brian Papineau
Assistant Equipment Managers	Tom Blatchford, Bobby Hastings
Medical Director, Maple Leafs and Marlies	Dr. Noah Forman
Orthopedic Consultant	Dr. John Theodoropoulos
Team Dentists	Dr. Marvin Lean, Dr. Charles Goldberg

Communications
Director, Media Relations	Pat Park
Manager, Media Relations	Craig Downey
Coordinator, Media Relations	Aaron Gogishvili

Broadcasting
Senior Vice-President, Broadcast and Content	Chris Hebb
Senior Director, Broadcast and Networks	Liana Bristol
Director, Content and Networks G.M.	Frank Hayward
Sr. Producer, Networks, Broadcast and Content	Mark Askin
Talent, Leafs TV	Joe Bowen, Paul Hendrick, Bob McGill, Greg Millen, Andi Petrillo
AM 640 Toronto Radio, Play-By-Play	Joe Bowen, Dennis Beyak (mid-week)
AM 640 Toronto Radio, Analyst	Jim Ralph
Television Play-By-Play	Joe Bowen (mid-week)
Television Analysts	Bob McGill, Greg Millen

Vancouver Canucks

2010-11 Results: 54w-19l-4OTL-5SOL 117PTS.
First, Northwest Division

Ryan Kesler and Daniel Sedin celebrate a Canucks goal. The two players tied for the team lead with 41 goals in 2010-11 with Sedin also winning the Art Ross Trophy with 104 points and Kesler winning the Frank Selke Trophy as the NHL's best defensive forward.

2011-12 Schedule

Oct.	Thu.	6	Pittsburgh	Sat.	7	at Boston*
	Mon.	10	at Columbus	Mon.	9	at Florida
	Wed.	12	at Philadelphia	Tue.	10	at Tampa Bay
	Thu.	13	at Detroit	Thu.	12	at St. Louis
	Sat.	15	at Edmonton	Sun.	15	Anaheim
	Tue.	18	NY Rangers	Tue.	17	Los Angeles
	Thu.	20	Nashville	Sat.	21	San Jose*
	Sat.	22	Minnesota*	Tue.	24	Edmonton
	Tue.	25	at Edmonton	Tue.	31	Chicago
	Wed.	26	St. Louis	Feb. Thu.	2	Detroit
	Sat.	29	Washington	Sat.	4	at Colorado*
Nov.	Tue.	1	at Calgary	Tue.	7	at Nashville
	Thu.	3	at Minnesota	Thu.	9	at Minnesota
	Fri.	4	at St. Louis	Sat.	11	at Calgary
	Sun.	6	at Chicago	Mon.	13	Phoenix
	Thu.	10	at Los Angeles	Wed.	15	Colorado
	Fri.	11	at Anaheim	Sat.	18	Toronto*
	Sun.	13	NY Islanders	Sun.	19	at Edmonton
	Wed.	16	Chicago	Tue.	21	at Nashville
	Sun.	20	Ottawa	Thu.	23	at Detroit
	Wed.	23	at Colorado	Fri.	24	at New Jersey
	Fri.	25	at Phoenix	Sun.	26	at Dallas*
	Sat.	26	at San Jose	Tue.	28	at Phoenix
	Tue.	29	Columbus	Mar. Thu.	1	St. Louis
Dec.	Thu.	1	Nashville	Sat.	3	Buffalo
	Sun.	4	Calgary	Tue.	6	Dallas
	Tue.	6	Colorado	Thu.	8	Winnipeg
	Thu.	8	at Montreal	Sat.	10	Montreal
	Sat.	10	at Ottawa	Wed.	14	Phoenix
	Tue.	13	at Columbus	Sat.	17	Columbus
	Thu.	15	at Carolina	Mon.	19	at Minnesota
	Sat.	17	at Toronto	Wed.	21	at Chicago
	Mon.	19	Minnesota	Thu.	22	at Dallas
	Wed.	21	Detroit	Sat.	24	at Colorado
	Fri.	23	Calgary	Mon.	26	Los Angeles
	Mon.	26	Edmonton	Wed.	28	Colorado
	Wed.	28	at San Jose	Fri.	30	Dallas
	Thu.	29	at Anaheim	Sat.	31	Calgary
	Sat.	31	at Los Angeles	Apr. Tue.	3	Anaheim
Jan.	Mon.	2	San Jose*	Thu.	5	at Calgary
	Wed.	4	Minnesota	Sat.	7	Edmonton

* Denotes afternoon game.

Year-by-Year Record

		Home				Road				Overall							
Season	GP	W	L	T	OL	W	L	T	OL	W	L	T	OL	GF	GA	Pts.	Finished	Playoff Result
2010-11	82	27	9	....	5	27	10	....	4	54	19	....	9	262	185	117	1st, Northwest Div.	Lost Final
2009-10	82	30	8	....	3	19	20	....	2	49	28	....	5	272	222	103	1st, Northwest Div.	Lost Conf. Semi-Final
2008-09	82	24	12	....	5	21	15	....	5	45	27	....	10	246	220	100	1st, Northwest Div.	Lost Conf. Semi-Final
2007-08	82	21	15	....	5	18	18	....	5	39	33	....	10	213	215	88	5th, Northwest Div.	Out of Playoffs
2006-07	82	26	11	....	4	23	15	....	3	49	26	....	7	222	201	105	1st, Northwest Div.	Lost Conf. Semi-Final
2005-06	82	25	10	....	6	17	22	....	2	42	32	....	8	256	255	92	4th, Northwest Div.	Out of Playoffs
2004-05	....	....				....				....								
2003-04	82	21	13	7	0	22	11	3	5	43	24	10	5	235	194	101	1st, Northwest Div.	Lost Conf. Quarter-Final
2002-03	82	22	13	6	0	23	10	7	1	45	23	13	1	264	208	104	2nd, Northwest Div.	Lost Conf. Quarter-Final
2001-02	82	23	11	5	2	19	19	2	1	42	30	7	3	254	211	94	2nd, Northwest Div.	Lost Conf. Quarter-Final
2000-01	82	21	12	5	3	15	16	6	4	36	28	11	7	239	238	90	3rd, Northwest Div.	Lost Conf. Quarter-Final
1999-2000	82	16	14	5	6	14	15	10	2	30	29	15	8	227	237	83	3rd, Northwest Div.	Out of Playoffs
1998-99	82	14	21	6	....	9	26	6	....	23	47	12	....	192	258	58	4th, Northwest Div.	Out of Playoffs
1997-98	82	15	22	4	....	10	21	10	....	25	43	14	....	224	273	64	7th, Pacific Div.	Out of Playoffs
1996-97	82	20	17	4	....	15	23	3	....	35	40	7	....	257	273	77	4th, Pacific Div.	Out of Playoffs
1995-96	82	15	19	7	....	17	16	8	....	32	35	15	....	278	278	79	3rd, Pacific Div.	Lost Conf. Quarter-Final
1994-95	48	10	8	6	....	8	10	6	....	18	18	12	....	153	148	48	2nd, Pacific Div.	Lost Conf. Semi-Final
1993-94	84	20	19	3	....	21	21	0	....	41	40	3	....	279	276	85	2nd, Pacific Div.	Lost Final
1992-93	84	27	11	4	....	19	18	5	....	46	29	9	....	346	278	101	1st, Smythe Div.	Lost Div. Final
1991-92	80	23	10	7	....	19	16	5	....	42	26	12	....	285	250	96	1st, Smythe Div.	Lost Div. Final
1990-91	80	18	17	5	....	10	26	4	....	28	43	9	....	243	315	65	4th, Smythe Div.	Lost Div. Semi-Final
1989-90	80	13	16	11	....	12	25	3	....	25	41	14	....	245	306	64	5th, Smythe Div.	Out of Playoffs
1988-89	80	19	15	6	....	14	24	2	....	33	39	8	....	251	253	74	4th, Smythe Div.	Lost Div. Semi-Final
1987-88	80	15	20	5	....	10	26	4	....	25	46	9	....	272	320	59	5th, Smythe Div.	Out of Playoffs
1986-87	80	17	19	4	....	12	24	4	....	29	43	8	....	282	314	66	5th, Smythe Div.	Out of Playoffs
1985-86	80	17	18	5	....	6	26	8	....	23	44	13	....	282	333	59	4th, Smythe Div.	Lost Div. Semi-Final
1984-85	80	15	21	4	....	10	25	5	....	25	46	9	....	284	401	59	5th, Smythe Div.	Out of Playoffs
1983-84	80	20	16	4	....	12	23	5	....	32	39	9	....	306	328	73	3rd, Smythe Div.	Lost Div. Semi-Final
1982-83	80	20	12	8	....	10	23	7	....	30	35	15	....	303	309	75	3rd, Smythe Div.	Lost Div. Semi-Final
1981-82	80	20	8	12	....	10	25	5	....	30	33	17	....	290	286	77	2nd, Smythe Div.	Lost Final
1980-81	80	17	12	11	....	11	20	9	....	28	32	20	....	289	301	76	3rd, Smythe Div.	Lost Prelim. Round
1979-80	80	14	17	9	....	13	20	7	....	27	37	16	....	256	281	70	3rd, Smythe Div.	Lost Prelim. Round
1978-79	80	15	18	7	....	10	24	6	....	25	42	13	....	217	291	63	2nd, Smythe Div.	Lost Prelim. Round
1977-78	80	13	15	12	....	7	28	5	....	20	43	17	....	239	320	57	3rd, Smythe Div.	Out of Playoffs
1976-77	80	13	21	6	....	12	21	7	....	25	42	13	....	235	294	63	4th, Smythe Div.	Out of Playoffs
1975-76	80	22	11	7	....	11	21	8	....	33	32	15	....	271	272	81	2nd, Smythe Div.	Lost Prelim. Round
1974-75	80	23	12	5	....	15	20	5	....	38	32	10	....	271	254	86	1st, Smythe Div.	Lost Quarter-Final
1973-74	78	14	18	7	....	10	25	4	....	24	43	11	....	224	296	59	7th, East Div.	Out of Playoffs
1972-73	78	17	18	4	....	5	29	5	....	22	47	9	....	233	339	53	7th, East Div.	Out of Playoffs
1971-72	78	14	20	5	....	6	30	3	....	20	50	8	....	203	297	48	7th, East Div.	Out of Playoffs
1970-71	78	17	18	4	....	7	28	4	....	24	46	8	....	229	296	56	6th, East Div.	Out of Playoffs

NORTHWEST DIVISION
42nd NHL Season

Franchise date: May 22, 1970

2011-12 Player Personnel

FORWARDS	HT	WT	S	Place of Birth	*Age	2010-11 Club
BITZ, Byron	6-5	215	R	Saskatoon, Sask.	27	Did Not Play - Injured
BURROWS, Alexandre	6-1	199	L	Pincourt, Que.	30	Vancouver
DUCO, Mike	5-10	200	L	Toronto, Ont.	24	Florida-Rochester
EBBETT, Andrew	5-9	174	L	Calgary, Alta.	28	Phoenix-San Antonio
HANSEN, Jannik	6-1	195	R	Herlev, Denmark	25	Vancouver
HIGGINS, Chris	6-0	205	L	Smithtown, NY	28	Florida-Vancouver
HODGSON, Cody	6-0	185	R	Toronto, Ont.	21	Vancouver-Manitoba
KESLER, Ryan	6-2	202	R	Livonia, MI	27	Vancouver
LAPIERRE, Maxim	6-2	207	R	St. Leonard, Que.	26	Mtl-Ana-Van
MALHOTRA, Manny	6-2	208	L	Mississauga, Ont.	31	Vancouver
MANCARI, Mark	6-3	225	R	London, Ont.	26	Buffalo-Portland (AHL)
ORESKOVICH, Victor	6-3	215	R	Whitby, Ont.	25	Vancouver-Manitoba
PINIZZOTTO, Steve	6-1	200	R	Mississauga, Ont.	27	Hershey
RAYMOND, Mason	6-0	185	L	Cochrane, Alta.	26	Vancouver
SAMUELSSON, Mikael	6-1	218	R	Mariefred, Sweden	34	Vancouver
SEDIN, Daniel	6-1	187	L	Ornskoldsvik, Sweden	31	Vancouver
SEDIN, Henrik	6-2	188	L	Ornskoldsvik, Sweden	31	Vancouver
STURM, Marco	6-0	194	L	Dingolfing, West Germany	33	Los Angeles-Washington
VOLPATTI, Aaron	6-0	215	L	Revelstoke, B.C.	26	Vancouver-Manitoba
DEFENSEMEN						
ALBERTS, Andrew	6-5	209	L	Minneapolis, MN	30	Vancouver
BALLARD, Keith	5-11	208	L	Baudette, MN	28	Vancouver
BAUMGARTNER, Nolan	6-2	195	R	Calgary, Alta.	35	Manitoba
BIEKSA, Kevin	6-0	198	R	Grimsby, Ont.	30	Vancouver
EDLER, Alexander	6-4	215	L	Ostersund, Sweden	25	Vancouver
HAMHUIS, Dan	6-0	209	L	Smithers, B.C.	28	Vancouver
PARENT, Ryan	6-3	198	L	Prince Albert, Sask.	24	Vancouver-Manitoba
ROME, Aaron	6-1	218	L	Nesbitt, Man.	28	Vancouver
SALO, Sami	6-3	212	R	Turku, Finland	37	Vancouver-Manitoba
SAUVE, Yann	6-3	209	L	Montreal, Que.	21	Van-Manitoba-Victoria
SULZER, Alexander	6-1	204	L	Kaufbeuren, W. Germany	27	Nashville-Florida
TANEV, Chris	6-2	199	R	Toronto, Ont.	21	Vancouver-Manitoba

GOALTENDERS	HT	WT	C	Place of Birth	*Age	2010-11 Club
CLIMIE, Matt	6-3	194	L	Leduc, Alta.	28	Phoenix-San Antonio
LACK, Eddie	6-4	187	L	Norrtalje, Sweden	23	Manitoba
LUONGO, Roberto	6-3	208	L	Montreal, Que.	32	Vancouver
SCHNEIDER, Cory	6-2	195	L	Marblehead, MA	25	Vancouver

* – Age at start of 2011-12 season

Alain Vigneault

Head Coach

Born: Quebec City, Que., May 14, 1961.

On June 20, 2006, Alain Vigneault became the 16th head coach in Vancouver Canucks history. He previously served in the NHL as head coach of the Montreal Canadiens from 1997 to 2001, becoming the second youngest coach in club history at the age of 36. Vigneault was nominated for the Jack Adams Award as NHL coach of the year following the 1999-2000 season. In 2006-07, he led the Canucks to first place in the Northwest Division by setting new club records with 49 wins and 105 points after the club had missed the playoffs the previous season. Vigneault was rewarded with the Jack Adams Award as NHL coach of the year. In 2010-11, Vigneault led Vancouver to the Presidents' Trophy for the first time after setting franchise records with 54 wins and 117 points and received another nomination for the Jack Adams Award.

Vigneault joined the Canucks from the club's AHL affiliate, the Manitoba Moose, where he led the team to within one game of the conference finals in 2005-06. Prior to joining the Moose, Vigneault spent many years as a head coach in the QMJHL with Trois-Rivieres, Hull, Beauport and PEI. In 1988, Vigneault led the Hull Olympiques into the Memorial Cup and was subsequently named CHL coach of the year. He has also been honoured as coach of the QMJHL's Second All-Star team on three separate occasions. Vigneault has also achieved success on the international stage. He served as an assistant coach with Canada's national junior team in 1989 and 1991, winning a gold medal at the 1991 World Junior Championships in Saskatoon.

As a player, Vigneault was a member of the St. Louis Blues from 1981 to 1983. Drafted by the Blues in the eighth round, 167th overall, in the 1981 Entry Draft, the defenceman recorded two goals, five assists and 82 penalty minutes in his NHL career. Vigneault went on to serve as a scout for the Blues for two seasons and as an assistant coach for the Ottawa Senators from 1992 to 1996.

Coaching Record

			Regular Season				Playoffs			
Season	Team	League	GC	W	L	O/T	GC	W	L	T
1986-87	Trois-Rivieres	QMJHL	70	28	40	2	....	....	....	....
1987-88	Hull	QMJHL	70	43	23	4	19	12	7	....
1987-88	Hull	M-Cup	....	....	....	....	4	1	3	....
1988-89	Hull	QMJHL	70	40	25	5	9	5	4	....
1989-90	Hull	QMJHL	70	36	29	5	11	4	7	....
1990-91	Hull	QMJHL	70	36	27	7	6	2	4	....
1991-92	Hull	QMJHL	70	41	24	5	6	2	4	....
1995-96	Beauport	QMJHL	31	19	7	5	20	13	7	....
1996-97	Beauport	QMJHL	70	24	44	2	4	1	3	....
1997-98	**Montreal**	**NHL**	**82**	**37**	**32**	**13**	**10**	**4**	**6**	....
1998-99	**Montreal**	**NHL**	**82**	**32**	**39**	**11**	....	....	....	....
99-2000	**Montreal**	**NHL**	**82**	**35**	**34**	**13**	....	....	....	....
2000-01	**Montreal**	**NHL**	**20**	**5**	**13**	**2**	....	....	....	....
2003-04	PEI	QMJHL	70	40	19	11	11	6	5	....
2004-05	PEI	QMJHL	70	24	39	7	....	....	....	....
2005-06	Manitoba	AHL	80	44	24	12	13	7	6	....
2006-07	**Vancouver**	**NHL**	**82**	**49**	**26**	**7**	**12**	**5**	**7**	....
2007-08	**Vancouver**	**NHL**	**82**	**39**	**33**	**10**	....	....	....	....
2008-09	**Vancouver**	**NHL**	**82**	**45**	**27**	**10**	**10**	**6**	**4**	....
2009-10	**Vancouver**	**NHL**	**82**	**49**	**28**	**5**	**12**	**6**	**6**	....
2010-11	**Vancouver**	**NHL**	**82**	**54**	**19**	**9**	**25**	**15**	**10**	....
	NHL Totals		**676**	**345**	**251**	**80**	**69**	**36**	**33**	....

Won Jack Adams Award (2007)

2010-11 Scoring

* – rookie

Regular Season

Pos	#	Player	Team	GP	G	A	Pts	TOI	+/–	PIM	PP	SH	GW	S	%
L	22	Daniel Sedin	VAN	82	41	63	104	18:33	30	32	18	0	10	266	15.4
C	33	Henrik Sedin	VAN	82	19	75	94	19:15	26	40	8	0	4	157	12.1
C	17	Ryan Kesler	VAN	82	41	32	73	20:29	24	66	15	3	7	260	15.8
R	26	Mikael Samuelsson	VAN	75	18	32	50	16:37	8	36	5	0	2	215	8.4
D	5	Christian Ehrhoff	VAN	79	14	36	50	23:59	19	52	6	0	3	209	6.7
L	14	Alexandre Burrows	VAN	72	26	22	48	17:01	26	77	1	1	4	152	17.1
L	21	Mason Raymond	VAN	70	15	24	39	15:47	8	10	2	1	5	197	7.6
D	23	Alexander Edler	VAN	51	8	25	33	24:17	13	24	5	0	1	121	6.6
C	27	Manny Malhotra	VAN	72	11	19	30	16:09	9	22	3	1	2	111	9.9
L	13	Raffi Torres	VAN	80	14	15	29	12:29	4	78	3	0	4	115	12.2
R	36	Jannik Hansen	VAN	82	9	20	29	14:42	13	32	0	0	2	113	8.0
L	20	Chris Higgins	FLA	48	11	12	23	16:38	5	10	0	0	0	126	8.7
			VAN	14	2	3	5	15:07	0	6	1	0	0	34	5.9
			Total	62	13	15	28	16:17	5	16	1	0	0	160	8.1
D	2	Dan Hamhuis	VAN	64	6	17	23	22:40	29	34	2	0	1	109	5.5
D	3	Kevin Bieksa	VAN	66	6	16	22	22:28	32	73	1	0	2	105	5.7
L	10	Jeff Tambellini	VAN	62	9	8	17	11:47	10	18	1	0	0	114	7.9
C	40	Maxim Lapierre	MTL	38	5	3	8	11:41	–7	63	0	0	0	78	6.4
			ANA	21	0	3	3	11:34	–6	9	0	0	0	28	0.0
			VAN	19	1	0	1	11:32	–1	8	0	0	0	23	4.3
			Total	78	6	6	12	11:37	–14	80	0	0	0	129	4.7
L	15	Tanner Glass	VAN	73	3	7	10	8:55	–5	72	0	0	1	45	6.7
D	6	Sami Salo	VAN	27	3	4	7	20:20	–3	14	1	0	0	39	7.7
D	4	Keith Ballard	VAN	65	2	5	7	15:54	10	53	0	0	0	53	3.8
D	41	Andrew Alberts	VAN	42	1	6	7	15:09	0	41	0	0	0	21	4.8
D	29	Aaron Rome	VAN	56	1	4	5	17:24	1	53	0	0	0	50	2.0
C	49	Alexandre Bolduc	VAN	24	2	2	4	7:26	1	21	0	0	1	21	9.5
R	38	Victor Oreskovich	VAN	16	0	3	3	7:54	1	8	0	0	0	19	0.0
D	57	* Lee Sweatt	VAN	3	1	1	2	13:23	4	2	0	0	1	4	25.0
C	39	* Cody Hodgson	VAN	8	1	1	2	7:44	1	0	0	0	0	9	11.1
L	54	* Aaron Volpatti	VAN	15	1	1	2	6:49	–1	16	0	0	0	6	16.7
L	18	Peter Schaefer	VAN	16	1	1	2	9:40	–3	2	0	0	0	10	10.0
L	25	* Sergei Shirokov	VAN	2	1	0	1	10:17	1	0	0	0	0	6	16.7
C	62	* Mario Bliznak	VAN	4	1	0	1	6:36	1	0	0	0	0	1	100.0
C	37	Rick Rypien	VAN	9	0	1	1	5:07	–5	31	0	0	0	6	0.0
D	18	* Chris Tanev	VAN	29	0	1	1	13:47	0	0	0	0	0	15	0.0
D	64	* Evan Oberg	VAN	2	0	0	0	9:49	0	0	0	0	0	1	0.0
R	24	Jonas Andersson	VAN	4	0	0	0	6:03	1	0	0	0	0	1	0.0
D	20	Ryan Parent	VAN	4	0	0	0	13:53	–3	0	0	0	0	3	0.0
D	47	* Yann Sauve	VAN	5	0	0	0	13:00	–2	0	0	0	0	6	0.0
C	32	Joel Perrault	VAN	7	0	0	0	7:11	–1	0	0	0	0	3	0.0
R	34	* Guillaume Desbiens	VAN	12	0	0	0	7:21	–3	10	0	0	0	4	0.0

Goaltending

No.	Goaltender	GPI	Mins	Avg	W	L	OT	EN	SO	GA	SA	S%	G	A	PIM
1	Roberto Luongo	60	3590	2.11	38	15	7	3	4	126	1753	.928	0	3	2
35	* Cory Schneider	25	1372	2.23	16	4	2	0	1	51	714	.929	0	3	0
	Totals	**82**	**4985**	**2.17**	**54**	**19**	**9**	**3**	**5**	**180**	**2470**	**.927**			

Playoffs

Pos	#	Player	Team	GP	G	A	Pts	TOI	+/–	PIM	PP	SH	GW	OT	S	%
C	33	Henrik Sedin	VAN	25	3	19	22	20:56	–11	16	2	0	1	0	46	6.5
L	22	Daniel Sedin	VAN	25	9	11	20	20:12	–9	32	5	0	2	0	99	9.1
C	17	Ryan Kesler	VAN	25	7	12	19	22:34	0	47	4	0	2	1	76	9.2
L	14	Alexandre Burrows	VAN	25	9	8	17	20:40	0	34	1	1	2	2	62	14.5
D	5	Christian Ehrhoff	VAN	23	2	10	12	22:26	–13	16	1	0	0	0	50	4.0
D	23	Alexander Edler	VAN	25	2	9	11	24:46	–4	8	0	0	0	0	58	3.4
D	3	Kevin Bieksa	VAN	25	5	5	10	25:40	6	51	1	0	1	1	47	10.6
R	36	Jannik Hansen	VAN	25	3	6	9	15:50	7	18	0	0	0	0	50	6.0
L	20	Chris Higgins	VAN	25	4	4	8	17:08	1	2	1	0	3	0	49	8.2
L	21	Mason Raymond	VAN	24	2	6	8	17:29	–1	6	0	0	0	0	57	3.5
L	13	Raffi Torres	VAN	23	3	4	7	11:51	2	28	0	0	1	0	20	15.0
D	2	Dan Hamhuis	VAN	19	1	5	6	24:50	5	6	1	0	0	0	26	3.8
D	6	Sami Salo	VAN	21	3	2	5	19:13	–4	2	3	0	1	0	33	9.1
C	40	Maxim Lapierre	VAN	25	3	2	5	13:34	2	66	0	0	1	0	42	7.1
R	26	Mikael Samuelsson	VAN	11	1	2	3	16:26	–4	8	0	0	1	0	20	5.0
D	29	Aaron Rome	VAN	14	1	0	1	13:01	3	37	0	0	0	0	10	10.0
C	39	* Cody Hodgson	VAN	12	0	1	1	6:45	–4	2	0	0	0	0	12	0.0
C	49	Alexandre Bolduc	VAN	3	0	0	0	3:38	0	0	0	0	0	0	2	0.0
D	18	* Chris Tanev	VAN	5	0	0	0	14:40	0	0	0	0	0	0	2	0.0
C	27	Manny Malhotra	VAN	6	0	0	0	11:50	–1	0	0	0	0	0	6	0.0
L	10	Jeff Tambellini	VAN	6	0	0	0	7:12	–3	2	0	0	0	0	2	0.0
D	41	Andrew Alberts	VAN	9	0	0	0	12:48	–8	6	0	0	0	0	6	0.0
D	4	Keith Ballard	VAN	10	0	0	0	14:14	–4	6	0	0	0	0	12	0.0
R	38	Victor Oreskovich	VAN	19	0	0	0	6:21	–6	12	0	0	0	0	14	0.0
L	15	Tanner Glass	VAN	20	0	0	0	7:28	–5	18	0	0	0	0	7	0.0

Goaltending

No.	Goaltender	GPI	Mins	Avg	W	L	EN	SO	GA	SA	S%	G	A	PIM
1	Roberto Luongo	25	1427	2.56	15	10	1	4	61	711	.914	0	0	0
35	* Cory Schneider	5	163	2.58	0	0	0	0	7	82	.915	0	0	0
	Totals	**25**	**1597**	**2.59**	**15**	**10**	**1**	**4**	**69**	**794**	**.913**			

Coaching History

Hal Laycoe, 1970-71, 1971-72; Vic Stasiuk, 1972-73; Bill McCreary and Phil Maloney, 1973-74; Phil Maloney, 1974-75, 1975-76; Phil Maloney and Orland Kurtenbach, 1976-77; Orland Kurtenbach, 1977-78; Harry Neale, 1978-79 to 1980-81; Harry Neale and Roger Neilson, 1981-82; Roger Neilson, 1982-83; Roger Neilson and Harry Neale, 1983-84; Bill Laforge and Harry Neale, 1984-85; Tom Watt, 1985-86, 1986-87; Bob McCammon, 1987-88 to 1989-90; Bob McCammon and Pat Quinn, 1990-91; Pat Quinn, 1991-92 to 1993-94; Rick Ley, 1994-95; Rick Ley and Pat Quinn, 1995-96; Tom Renney, 1996-97; Tom Renney and Mike Keenan, 1997-98; Mike Keenan and Marc Crawford, 1998-99; Marc Crawford, 1999-2000 to 2005-06; Alain Vigneault, 2006-07 to date.

Club Records

Team

(Figures in brackets for season records are games played; records for fewest points, wins, ties, losses, goals, goals against are for 70 or more games)

Most Points **117** 2010-11 (82)
Most Wins **54** 2010-11 (82)
Most Ties **20** 1980-81 (80)
Most Losses **50** 1971-72 (78)
Most Goals **346** 1992-93 (84)
Most Goals Against **401** 1984-85 (80)
Fewest Points **48** 1971-72 (78)
Fewest Wins **20** 1971-72 (78), 1977-78 (80)
Fewest Ties **3** 1993-94 (84)
Fewest Losses **19** 2010-11 (82)
Fewest Goals **192** 1998-99 (82)
Fewest Goals Against **185** 2010-11 (82)
Longest Winning Streak
- **Overall** .... **10** Nov. 9-30/02
- **Home** .... **11** Feb. 3-Mar. 19/09
- **Away** .... **9** Mar. 5-29/11

Longest Undefeated Streak
- **Overall** .... **14** Jan.26-Feb. 25/03 (10 wins, 4 ties)
- **Home** .... **18** Nov. 4/92-Jan. 16/93 (16 wins, 2 ties)
- **Away** .... **9** Feb. 4-Mar. 3/03 (6 wins, 3 ties), Mar. 5-29/11 (9 wins)

Longest Losing Streak
- **Overall** .... **10** Oct. 23-Nov. 11/97
- **Home** .... **6** Dec. 18/70-Jan. 20/71
- **Away** .... **12** Nov. 28/81-Feb. 6/82

Longest Winless Streak
- **Overall** .... **13** Nov. 9-Dec. 7/73 (10 losses, 3 ties)
- **Home** .... **11** Dec. 18/70-Feb. 6/71 (10 losses, 1 tie)
- **Away** .... **20** Jan. 2-Apr. 2/86 (14 losses, 6 ties)

Most Shutouts, Season **10** 2008-09 (82)
Most PIM, Season **2,326** 1992-93 (84)
Most Goals, Game .... **11** Mar. 28/71 (Cal. 5 at Van. 11), Nov. 25/86 (L.A. 5 at Van. 11), Mar. 1/92 (Cgy. 0 at Van. 11)

Individual

Most Seasons .... **16** Trevor Linden
Most Games .... **1,140** Trevor Linden
Most Goals, Career .... **346** Markus Naslund
Most Assists, Career .... **509** Henrik Sedin
Most Points, Career .... **756** Markus Naslund (346G, 410A)
Most PIM, Career .... **2,127** Gino Odjick
Most Shutouts, Career .... **28** Roberto Luongo
Longest Consecutive Games Streak .... **534** Brendan Morrison (Mar. 16/00-Dec. 10/07)
Most Goals, Season .... **60** Pavel Bure (1992-93), (1993-94)
Most Assists, Season .... **83** Henrik Sedin (2009-10)
Most Points, Season .... **112** Henrik Sedin (2009-10; 29G, 83A)
Most PIM, Season .... **372** Donald Brashear (1997-98)
Most Points, Defenseman, Season .... **63** Doug Lidster (1986-87; 12G, 51A)
Most Points, Center, Season .... **112** Henrik Sedin (2009-10; 29G, 83A)
Most Points, Right Wing, Season .... **110** Pavel Bure (1992-93; 60G, 50A)
Most Points, Left Wing, Season .... **104** Markus Naslund (2002-03; 48G, 56A), Daniel Sedin (2010-11; 41G, 63A)
Most Points, Rookie, Season .... **60** Ivan Hlinka (1981-82; 23G, 37A), Pavel Bure (1991-92; 34G, 26A)
Most Shutouts, Season .... **9** Roberto Luongo (2008-09)
Most Goals, Game .... **4** Twelve times
Most Assists, Game .... **6** Patrik Sundstrom (Feb. 29/84)
Most Points, Game .... **7** Patrik Sundstrom (Feb. 29/84; 1G, 6A)

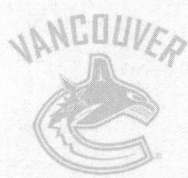

Retired Numbers

12	Stan Smyl	1978-1991
16	Trevor Linden	1988-1998; 2001-2008
19	Markus Naslund	1996-2008

All-time Record vs. Other Clubs

Regular Season

	At Home								On Road								Total							
	GP	W	L	T	OL	GF	GA	PTS	GP	W	L	T	OL	GF	GA	PTS	GP	W	L	T	OL	GF	GA	PTS
Anaheim	38	21	14	2	1	124	96	45	37	17	12	7	1	111	104	42	75	38	26	9	2	235	200	87
Atlanta	5	3	1	1	0	17	9	7	6	4	1	0	1	20	17	9	11	7	2	1	1	37	26	16
Boston	54	17	28	8	1	172	215	43	54	8	38	7	1	127	221	24	108	25	66	15	2	299	436	67
Buffalo	54	27	16	11	0	200	165	65	55	18	27	8	2	160	199	46	109	45	43	19	2	360	364	111
Calgary	120	49	49	18	4	412	384	120	119	38	66	15	0	348	449	91	239	87	115	33	4	760	833	211
Carolina	33	17	10	6	0	118	88	40	31	12	14	5	0	104	102	29	64	29	24	11	0	222	190	69
Chicago	84	43	26	15	0	252	237	101	83	25	48	7	3	199	294	60	167	68	74	22	3	451	531	161
Colorado	68	29	27	7	5	220	243	70	68	26	30	8	4	192	221	64	136	55	57	15	9	412	464	134
Columbus	20	14	3	0	3	76	54	31	20	11	6	2	1	71	51	25	40	25	9	2	4	147	105	56
Dallas	83	40	31	10	2	294	244	92	83	27	42	12	2	240	285	68	166	67	73	22	4	534	529	160
Detroit	77	34	31	10	2	273	246	80	78	23	44	8	3	226	310	57	155	57	75	18	5	499	556	137
Edmonton	103	45	43	12	3	365	373	105	102	35	55	7	5	314	409	82	205	80	98	19	8	679	782	187
Florida	12	6	1	5	0	36	26	17	10	5	3	1	1	33	25	12	22	11	4	6	1	69	51	29
Los Angeles	109	57	33	16	3	402	328	133	111	38	56	16	1	340	425	93	220	95	89	32	4	742	753	226
Minnesota	31	18	5	3	5	92	73	44	32	14	15	2	1	76	93	31	63	32	20	5	6	168	166	75
Montreal	59	17	34	8	0	165	210	42	57	11	41	5	0	141	252	27	116	28	75	13	0	306	462	69
Nashville	24	15	7	1	1	79	55	32	25	14	10	1	0	68	68	29	49	29	17	2	1	147	123	61
New Jersey	50	29	10	11	0	186	135	69	51	24	21	6	0	164	156	54	101	53	31	17	0	350	291	123
NY Islanders	49	24	22	3	0	160	160	51	50	13	25	10	2	142	180	38	99	37	47	13	2	302	340	89
NY Rangers	53	17	33	3	0	170	205	37	57	13	39	5	0	148	243	31	110	30	72	8	0	318	448	68
Ottawa	15	9	5	1	0	48	31	19	14	7	6	1	0	38	32	15	29	16	11	2	0	86	63	34
Philadelphia	54	11	30	12	1	154	216	35	56	18	36	1	1	167	238	38	110	29	66	13	2	321	454	73
Phoenix	84	51	22	10	1	306	226	113	81	32	36	10	3	280	288	77	165	83	58	20	4	586	514	190
Pittsburgh	52	24	23	4	1	187	191	53	53	12	34	7	0	179	233	31	105	36	57	11	1	366	424	84
St. Louis	84	37	38	9	0	247	262	83	83	26	48	9	0	233	305	61	167	63	86	18	0	480	567	144
San Jose	44	23	15	4	2	149	119	52	46	21	19	5	1	135	138	48	90	44	34	9	3	284	257	100
Tampa Bay	12	9	0	2	1	51	24	21	11	6	5	0	0	41	38	12	23	15	5	2	1	92	62	33
Toronto	68	33	22	11	2	240	223	79	64	25	28	11	0	214	228	61	132	58	50	22	2	454	451	140
Washington	41	20	15	5	1	142	127	46	43	16	22	4	1	128	141	37	84	36	37	9	2	270	268	83
Defunct Clubs	19	14	3	2	0	82	48	30	19	10	8	1	0	71	68	21	38	24	11	3	0	153	116	51
Totals	**1599**	**753**	**597**	**210**	**39**	**5419**	**5013**	**1755**	**1599**	**549**	**835**	**181**	**34**	**4710**	**5813**	**1313**	**3198**	**1302**	**1432**	**391**	**73**	**10129**	**10826**	**3068**

Playoffs

	Series	W	L	GP	W	L	T	GF	GA	Last Mtg.	Rnd.	Result
Anaheim	1	0	1	5	1	4	0	8	14	2007	CSF	L 1-4
Boston	1	0	1	7	3	4	0	8	23	2011	F	L 3-4
Buffalo	2	0	2	7	1	6	0	14	28	1981	PRE	L 0-3
Calgary	6	2	4	32	15	17	0	96	101	2004	CQF	L 3-4
Chicago	5	2	3	28	12	16	0	77	92	2011	CQF	W 4-3
Colorado	2	0	2	10	2	8	0	26	40	2001	CQF	L 0-4
Dallas	2	2	0	12	8	4	0	31	23	2007	CQF	W 4-3
Detroit	1	0	1	6	2	4	0	16	22	2002	CQF	L 2-4
Edmonton	2	0	2	9	2	7	0	20	35	1992	DF	L 2-4
Los Angeles	4	2	2	23	12	11	0	85	84	2010	CQF	W 4-2
Minnesota	1	0	1	7	3	4	0	17	26	2003	CSF	L 3-4
Montreal	1	0	1	5	1	4	0	9	20	1975	QF	L 1-4
Nashville	1	1	0	6	4	2	0	14	11	2011	CSF	W 4-2
NY Islanders	2	0	2	6	0	6	0	14	26	1982	F	L 0-4
NY Rangers	1	0	1	7	3	4	0	19	21	1994	F	L 3-4
Philadelphia	1	0	1	3	1	2	0	9	15	1979	PRE	L 1-2
Phoenix	2	2	0	13	8	5	0	50	34	1993	DSF	W 4-2
St. Louis	3	3	0	18	12	6	0	55	53	2009	CQF	W 4-0
San Jose	1	1	0	5	4	1	0	20	13	2011	CF	W 4-1
Toronto	1	1	0	5	4	1	0	16	9	1994	CF	W 4-1
Totals	**40**	**16**	**24**	**214**	**98**	**116**	**0**	**604**	**690**			

Playoff Results 2011-2007

Year	Round	Opponent	Result	GF	GA
2011	F	Boston	L 3-4	8	23
	CF	San Jose	W 4-1	20	13
	CSF	Nashville	W 4-2	14	11
	CQF	Chicago	W 4-3	16	22
2010	CSF	Chicago	L 2-4	18	23
	CQF	Los Angeles	W 4-2	25	18
2009	CSF	Chicago	L 2-4	19	23
	CQF	St. Louis	W 4-0	11	5
2007	CSF	Anaheim	L 1-4	8	14
	CQF	Dallas	W 4-3	13	12

Abbreviations: Round: F – Final; **CF** – conference final; **CSF** – conference semi-final; **CQF** – conference quarter-final; **DF** – division final; **DSF** – division semi-final; **QF** – quarter-final; **PRE** – preliminary round.

Calgary totals include Atlanta Flames, 1972-73 to 1979-80. Carolina totals include Hartford, 1979-80 to 1996-97.
Colorado totals include Quebec, 1979-80 to 1994-95. Dallas totals include Minnesota North Stars, 1970-71 to 1992-93.
New Jersey totals include Kansas City, 1974-75, 1975-76, and Colorado Rockies, 1976-77 to 1981-82.
Phoenix totals include Winnipeg, 1979-80 to 1995-96.

2010-11 Results

Month	Day	Opponent	Score
Oct.	9	Los Angeles	1-2†
	11	Florida	2-1
	13	at Anaheim	3-4
	15	at Los Angeles	1-4
	17	Carolina	5-1
	19	at Minnesota	2-6
	20	at Chicago	1-2†
	22	Minnesota	5-1
	26	Colorado	4-3*
Nov.	1	New Jersey	3-0
	2	at Edmonton	4-3
	4	at Colorado	3-1
	6	Detroit	6-4
	9	at Montreal	0-2
	11	at Ottawa	6-2
	13	at Toronto	5-3
	15	at Buffalo	3-4*
	17	at Pittsburgh	1-3
	20	Chicago	1-7
	21	Phoenix	2-3
	24	Colorado	4-2
	26	San Jose	6-1
Dec.	1	at Calgary	7-2
	3	at Chicago	3-0
	5	St. Louis	2-3
	8	Anaheim	5-4†
	11	Tampa Bay	4-5*
	12	at Edmonton	2-1
	15	Columbus	3-2*
	18	Toronto	4-1
	20	at St. Louis	3-1
	22	at Detroit	4-5*
	23	at Columbus	7-3
	26	Edmonton	3-2
	28	Philadelphia	6-2
	31	at Dallas	4-1
Jan.	2	at Colorado	2-1
	3	at San Jose	4-3
	5	Calgary	3-1
	7	Edmonton	6-1
	8	Detroit	1-2†
	11	at NY Islanders	4-3†
	13	at NY Rangers	0-1
	14	at Washington	4-2
	16	at Minnesota	0-4
	18	at Colorado	3-4*
	20	San Jose	1-2†
	22	Calgary	3-4†
	24	Dallas	7-1
	26	Nashville	2-1
Feb.	1	at Dallas	4-1
	2	at Phoenix	6-0
	4	Chicago	4-3
	7	Ottawa	4-2
	9	Anaheim	3-4
	12	Calgary	4-2
	14	at St. Louis	2-3
	15	at Minnesota	4-1
	17	at Nashville	1-3
	19	Dallas	5-2
	22	Montreal	2-3
	24	St. Louis	3-2
	26	Boston	1-3
Mar.	1	Columbus	2-1†
	3	Nashville	0-3
	5	at Los Angeles	3-1
	6	at Anaheim	3-0
	8	at Phoenix	4-3*
	10	at San Jose	5-4†
	12	at Calgary	4-3
	14	Minnesota	4-2
	16	Colorado	4-2
	18	Phoenix	1-3
	23	at Detroit	2-1
	25	at Atlanta	3-1
	27	at Columbus	4-1
	29	at Nashville	3-1
	31	Los Angeles	3-1
Apr.	2	Edmonton	1-4
	5	at Edmonton	0-2
	7	Minnesota	5-0
	9	at Calgary	3-2*

* – Overtime † – Shootout

Entry Draft Selections 2011-1997

Name in bold denotes played in NHL.

2011
Pick
- 29 Nicklas Jensen
- 71 David Honzik
- 90 Alexandre Grenier
- 101 Joseph Labate
- 120 Ludwig Blomstrand
- 150 Frank Corrado
- 180 Pathrik Westerholm
- 210 Henrik Tommernes

2010
Pick
- 115 Patrick McNally
- 145 Adam Polasek
- 172 Alex Friesen
- 175 Jonathan Iilahti
- 205 Sawyer Hannay

2009
Pick
- 22 Jordan Schroeder
- 53 Anton Rodin
- 83 Kevin Connauton
- 113 Jeremy Price
- 143 Peter Andersson
- 173 Joe Cannata
- 187 Steven Anthony

2008
Pick
- 10 **Cody Hodgson**
- 41 **Yann Sauve**
- 131 Prab Rai
- 161 Mats Froshaug
- 191 Morgan Clark

2007
Pick
- 25 Patrick White
- 33 Taylor Ellington
- 145 Charles-Antoine Messier
- 146 Ilja Kablukov
- 176 Taylor Matson
- 206 Dan Gendur

2006
Pick
- 14 **Michael Grabner**
- 82 Daniel Rahimi
- 163 **Sergei Shirokov**
- 167 Juraj Simek
- 197 Evan Fuller

2005
Pick
- 10 **Luc Bourdon**
- 51 **Mason Raymond**
- 114 Alexandre Vincent
- 138 Matt Butcher
- 185 Kris Fredheim
- 205 **Mario Bliznak**

2004
Pick
- 26 **Cory Schneider**
- 91 **Alexander Edler**
- 125 Andrew Sarauer
- 159 **Mike Brown**
- 189 Julien Ellis
- 254 David Schulz
- 287 **Jannik Hansen**

2003
Pick
- 23 **Ryan Kesler**
- 60 Marc-Andre Bernier
- 111 **Brandon Nolan**
- 128 Ty Morris
- 160 Nicklas Danielsson
- 190 Chad Brownlee
- 222 Francois-Pierre Guenette
- 252 Sergei Topol
- 254 **Nathan McIver**
- 285 Matthew Hansen

2002
Pick
- 49 Kirill Koltsov
- 55 Denis Grot
- 68 **Brett Skinner**
- 83 Lukas Mensator
- 114 John Laliberte
- 151 **Rob McVicar**
- 214 Marc-Andre Roy
- 223 Ilja Krikunov
- 247 Matt Violin
- 277 Thomas Nussli
- 278 Matt Gens

2001
Pick
- 16 **R.J. Umberger**
- 66 **Fedor Fedorov**
- 114 Evgeny Gladskikh
- 151 **Kevin Bieksa**
- 212 **Jason King**
- 245 Konstantin Mikhailov

2000
Pick
- 23 **Nathan Smith**
- 71 Thatcher Bell
- 93 Tim Branham
- 144 Pavel Duma
- 208 **Brandon Reid**
- 241 Nathan Barrett
- 272 Tim Smith

1999
Pick
- 2 **Daniel Sedin**
- 3 **Henrik Sedin**
- 69 Rene Vydareny
- 129 Ryan Thorpe
- 172 Josh Reed
- 189 Kevin Swanson
- 218 Markus Kankaanpera
- 271 Darrell Hay

1998
Pick
- 4 **Bryan Allen**
- 31 **Artem Chubarov**
- 68 **Jarkko Ruutu**
- 81 Justin Morrison
- 90 Regan Darby
- 136 David Ytfeldt
- 140 Rick Bertran
- 149 Paul Cabana
- 177 Vincent Malts
- 204 Greg Mischler
- 219 Curtis Valentine
- 232 Jason Metcalfe

1997
Pick
- 10 **Brad Ference**
- 34 **Ryan Bonni**
- 36 Harold Druken
- 64 Kyle Freadrich
- 90 Chris Stanley
- 114 David Darguzas
- 117 Matt Cockell
- 144 **Matt Cooke**
- 148 Larry Shapley
- 171 Rod Leroux
- 201 Denis Martynyuk
- 227 Peter Brady

General Managers' History

Bud Poile, 1970-71 to 1971-72; Bud Poile and Hal Laycoe, 1972-73; Hal Laycoe and Phil Maloney, 1973-74; Phil Maloney, 1974-75 to 1976-77; Jake Milford, 1977-78 to 1981-82; Harry Neale, 1982-83 to 1984-85; Jack Gordon, 1985-86, 1986-87; Pat Quinn, 1987-88 to 1996-97; Pat Quinn and Mike Keenan, 1997-98; Brian Burke, 1998-99 to 2003-04; David Nonis, 2004-05 to 2007-08; Mike Gillis, 2008-09 to date.

Mike Gillis

President and General Manager

Born: Sudbury, Ont., December 1, 1958.

The Vancouver Canucks announced on April 23, 2008, that Mike Gillis had been named the tenth general manager in club history. Gillis joined the Canucks organization after spending the previous 16 years as a player representative. In his first two seasons with the club, the Canucks won the Northwest Division title. In his third season of 2010-11, Gillis won the NHL's G.M. of the Year Award after Vancouver set new club records with 54 wins and 117 points. The team won the Presidents' Trophy for the first time and reached the seventh game of the Stanley Cup Finals.

Gillis began his NHL career in 1978 as a member of the Colorado Rockies. In 246 NHL regular season games, Gillis recorded 76 points (33 goals, 43 assists) and 186 penalty minutes with Colorado and Boston before a leg injury forced him to retire in 1985. He then returned to Kingston, Ontario, where he had grown up, to obtain his law degree from Queen's University in 1990. Gillis began his career as a NHL player representative in 1992 and became one of the most successful in his industry. His ability to evaluate players, negotiate contracts and his extensive knowledge of the Collective Bargaining Agreement, provided him the opportunity to work with a number of the NHL's most elite players.

Club Directory

Rogers Arena

Vancouver Canucks
Rogers Arena
800 Griffiths Way
Vancouver, B.C. V6B 6G1
Phone **604/899-4600**
FAX 604/899-4640
www.canucks.com
Capacity: 18,860

Executive Directory – Vancouver Canucks Limited Partnership

Chairman, Canucks L.P. and Governor, NHL . . . . . . Francesco Aquilini
Alternate Governors, NHL . . . . Roberto Aquilini, Paolo Aquilini
Executive Office Manager . . . . Cheryl Loveseth
President, G.M. and Alt. Governor, NHL . . . . Mike Gillis
Executive Assistants . . . . Joan Stobbs, Andrea Lobo
Chief Operating Officer and Alt. Governor, NHL . . Victor de Bonis
Executive Vice President, Sales and Service . . . . . . Trent Carroll
Vice President, Hockey Ops and Assistant G.M. . . . . Laurence Gilman
Vice President, Player Personnel and Assistant G.M. . Lorne Henning
Vice President and G.M., Arena Operations . . . . Harvey Jones
Vice President, Business nd General Counsel . . . . . . Chris Gear
Vice President, Finance and CFO . . . . Todd Kobus
Vice President, Communications
  and Community Partnerships. . . . . TC Carling
Vice President, Marketing and Game Presentation. . Ali Gardiner

Hockey Operations

President, G.M. and Alt. Governor, NHL . . . . Mike Gillis
Executive Assistant . . . . Joan Stobbs
Vice President, Player Personnel and Asst. G.M. . . . Lorne Henning
Vice President, Hockey Operations and Asst. G.M. . Laurence Gilman
Senior Advisor to the General Manager. . . . . Stan Smyl
Head Coach . . . . Alain Vigneault
Associate Coach . . . . Rick Bowness
Assistant Coach . . . . Newell Brown
Assistant Coach, Video . . . . Darryl Williams
Goaltending Coach. . . . . Roland Melanson
Strength & Conditioning Coach . . . . Roger Takahashi
Skill Coach . . . . Glenn Carnegie
Director, Player Development . . . . Dave Gagner
Director, Player Personnel . . . . Eric Crawford
Director, Hockey Administration . . . . Jonathan Wall
Head Coach, Chicago Wolves . . . . Craig MacTavish
Assistant Coaches, Chicago Wolves . . . . TBD
Vice President, Communications
  and Community Partnerships. . . . . TC Carling
Director, Media Relations and Team Operations . . . Ben Brown
Manager, Media Relations and Publications . . . . . . Stephanie Maniago
Coordinator, Media Relations and Publications . . . . Jen Rollins
Director, Community Partnerships. . . . . Alex Mitchell
Director of Charitable, Corporate and On-Ice Events . . Karen Christiansen
Program Manager, Community Partnerships . . . . . . Jessica Hoffman
Program Manager, Community Partnerships . . . . . . Tara Clarke
Manager, Hockey Development and Alumni Liaison . . Rod Brathwaite
Coordinator, Comm. Partnerships and
  Mascot Liaison . . . . Paul Buckley

Scouting Staff

Chief Amateur Scout . . . . Ron Delorme
Associate Chief Scout . . . . Thomas Gradin
Amateur Scouts . . . . Brian Chapman, Sergei Chibisov, Frank Kollar, Tim Lenardon, Harold Snepsts, Darrell Young, Judd Brackett, Inge Hammarstrom, Richard Rose, Ken Cook, Mike Gerrits, Edward Hampson, Dan Palango
Director, Player Personnel . . . . Eric Crawford
Professional Scouts . . . . Lucien DeBlois, Lars Lindgren, Brett Henning, Neil Komadoski, Don Granato, Jonathan Bates
Director of Hockey Administration . . . . Jonathan Wall
Scouting Coordinator . . . . Mike Brown

Medical and Training Staff

Head Athletic Trainer . . . . Mike Burnstein
Assistant Athletic Trainers . . . . Jon Sanderson, Dave Zarn
Equipment Manager . . . . Pat O'Neill
Assistant Equipment Manager. . . . . Jamie Hendricks
Equipment Assistant . . . . Brian Hamilton
Game Dressing Room Attendants . . . . John Jukich, Ron Shute, Brian Brumwell, Ferdie De Guzman
Team Physicians . . . . Dr. Bill Regan, Dr. Mike Wilkinson
Team Dentist . . . . Dr. Jeffrey Norden
Team Chiropractor . . . . Dr. Sid Sheard
Team Optometrist. . . . . Dr. Alan R. Boyco

Broadcast

Director, Facilities & In-House Broadcast . . . . Paul Brettell
Executive Producer, Broadcast Media . . . . Mike Hall
Senior Broadcast Technician . . . . Greg Story
Multimedia Senior Producer/Producer . . . . Jason Steensma/Gayla Anderson
Broadcast Business Manager. . . . . Shannon Baker
Production Assistant & Editor . . . . Rory McGarry
Reporter. . . . . Joey Kenward

Captains' History

Orland Kurtenbach, 1970-71 to 1973-74; no captain, 1974-75; Andre Boudrias, 1975-76; Chris Oddleifson, 1976-77; Don Lever, 1977-78; Don Lever and Kevin McCarthy, 1978-79; Kevin McCarthy, 1979-80 to 1981-82; Stan Smyl, 1982-83 to 1989-90; Dan Quinn, Doug Lidster and Trevor Linden, 1990-91; Trevor Linden, 1991-92 to 1996-97; Mark Messier, 1997-98 to 1999-2000; Markus Naslund, 2000-01 to 2007-08; Roberto Luongo, 2008-09, 2009-10; Henrik Sedin, 2010-11 to date.

Washington Capitals

Key Off-Season Signings/Acquisitions

2011

June 24 • Acquired LW **Troy Brouwer** from Chicago for Washington's 1st-round pick in the 2011 Entry Draft.

28 • Re-signed C **Brooks Laich**.

July 1 • Signed RW **Joel Ward**, C **Jeff Halpern** and D **Roman Hamrlik**.

1 • Re-signed D **Sean Collins**.

2 • Signed G **Tomas Vokoun**.

13 • Re-signed C **Mathieu Perreault**.

15 • Re-signed D **Karl Alzner**.

2010-11 Results: 48w-23L-5oTL-6soL 107pts.
First, Southeast Division

Alexander Semin and Alex Ovechkin celebrate a goal during a 7-6 win over Anaheim on February 16, 2011. Washington went 19-5-1 from that night through the end of the season to claim top spot in the Eastern Conference standings.

2011-12 Schedule

Oct.	Sat.	8	Carolina	Fri.	13	Tampa Bay	
	Mon.	10	Tampa Bay	Sun.	15	Carolina*	
	Thu.	13	at Pittsburgh	Tue.	17	NY Islanders	
	Sat.	15	Ottawa	Wed.	18	at Montreal	
	Tue.	18	Florida	Fri.	20	at Carolina	
	Thu.	20	at Philadelphia	Sun.	22	at Pittsburgh*	
	Sat.	22	Detroit	Tue.	24	Boston	
	Thu.	27	at Edmonton	Tue.	31	at Tampa Bay	
	Sat.	29	at Vancouver	**Feb.** Wed.	1	at Florida	
Nov.	Tue.	1	Anaheim	Sat.	4	at Montreal*	
	Fri.	4	at Carolina	Sun.	5	Boston*	
	Sat.	5	at NY Islanders	Tue.	7	Florida	
	Tue.	8	Dallas	Thu.	9	Winnipeg	
	Fri.	11	at New Jersey	Sun.	12	at NY Rangers*	
	Sat.	12	New Jersey	Mon.	13	San Jose	
	Tue.	15	at Nashville	Fri.	17	at Florida	
	Thu.	17	at Winnipeg	Sat.	18	at Tampa Bay	
	Sat.	19	at Toronto	Mon.	20	at Carolina	
	Mon.	21	Phoenix	Wed.	22	at Ottawa	
	Wed.	23	Winnipeg	Fri.	24	Montreal	
	Fri.	25	NY Rangers*	Sat.	25	at Toronto	
	Sat.	26	at Buffalo	Tue.	28	NY Islanders	
	Tue.	29	St. Louis	**Mar.** Fri.	2	New Jersey	
Dec.	Thu.	1	Pittsburgh	Sun.	4	Philadelphia	
	Sat.	3	Ottawa	Tue.	6	Carolina	
	Mon.	5	at Florida	Thu.	8	Tampa Bay	
	Wed.	7	at Ottawa	Sat.	10	at Boston*	
	Fri.	9	Toronto	Sun.	11	Toronto*	
	Tue.	13	Philadelphia	Tue.	13	at NY Islanders	
	Thu.	15	at Winnipeg	Fri.	16	at Winnipeg	
	Sat.	17	at Colorado	Sun.	18	at Chicago	
	Tue.	20	Nashville	Mon.	19	at Detroit	
	Fri.	23	at New Jersey	Thu.	22	at Philadelphia	
	Mon.	26	at Buffalo	Fri.	23	Winnipeg	
	Wed.	28	NY Rangers	Sun.	25	Minnesota*	
	Fri.	30	Buffalo	Tue.	27	Buffalo	
	Sat.	31	at Columbus	Thu.	29	at Boston	
Jan.	Tue.	3	Calgary	Sat.	31	Montreal	
	Sat.	7	at San Jose	**Apr.** Mon.	2	at Tampa Bay	
	Mon.	9	at Los Angeles	Thu.	5	Florida	
	Wed.	11	Pittsburgh	Sat.	7	at NY Rangers*	

* Denotes afternoon game.

Year-by-Year Record

Season	GP	Home W	L	T	OL	Road W	L	T	OL	Overall W	L	T	OL	GF	GA	Pts.	Finished	Playoff Result
2010-11	82	25	8	....	8	23	15	....	3	48	23	....	11	224	197	107	1st, Southeast Div.	Lost Conf. Semi-Final
2009-10	82	30	5	....	6	24	10	....	7	54	15	....	13	318	233	121	1st, Southeast Div.	Lost Conf. Quarter-Final
2008-09	82	29	9	....	3	21	15	....	5	50	24	....	8	272	245	108	1st, Southeast Div.	Lost Conf. Semi-Final
2007-08	82	23	15	....	3	20	16	....	5	43	31	....	8	242	231	94	1st, Southeast Div.	Lost Conf. Quarter-Final
2006-07	82	17	17	....	7	11	23	....	7	28	40	....	14	235	286	70	5th, Southeast Div.	Out of Playoffs
2005-06	82	16	18	....	7	13	23	....	5	29	41	....	12	237	306	70	5th, Southeast Div.	Out of Playoffs
2004-05	....	....		....		....		....		....		....		....	....	....		
2003-04	82	13	20	6	2	10	26	4	1	23	46	10	3	186	253	59	5th, Southeast Div.	Out of Playoffs
2002-03	82	24	13	2	2	15	16	6	4	39	29	8	6	224	220	92	2nd, Southeast Div.	Lost Conf. Quarter-Final
2001-02	82	21	12	6	2	15	21	5	0	36	33	11	2	228	240	85	2nd, Southeast Div.	Out of Playoffs
2000-01	82	24	9	6	2	17	18	4	2	41	27	10	4	233	211	96	1st, Southeast Div.	Lost Conf. Quarter-Final
1999-2000	82	26	5	8	2	18	19	4	0	44	24	12	2	227	194	102	1st, Southeast Div.	Lost Conf. Quarter-Final
1998-99	82	16	23	2	....	15	22	4	....	31	45	6	....	200	218	68	3rd, Southeast Div.	Out of Playoffs
1997-98	82	23	12	6	....	17	18	5	....	40	30	12	....	219	202	92	3rd, Atlantic Div.	Lost Final
1996-97	82	19	17	5	....	14	23	4	....	33	40	9	....	214	231	75	5th, Atlantic Div.	Out of Playoffs
1995-96	82	21	15	5	....	18	17	6	....	39	32	11	....	234	204	89	4th, Atlantic Div.	Lost Conf. Quarter-Final
1994-95	48	15	6	3	....	7	12	5	....	22	18	8	....	136	120	52	3rd, Atlantic Div.	Lost Conf. Quarter-Final
1993-94	84	17	16	9	....	22	19	1	....	39	35	10	....	277	263	88	3rd, Atlantic Div.	Lost Conf. Semi-Final
1992-93	84	21	15	6	....	22	19	1	....	43	34	7	....	325	286	93	2nd, Patrick Div.	Lost Div. Semi-Final
1991-92	80	25	12	3	....	20	15	5	....	45	27	8	....	330	275	98	2nd, Patrick Div.	Lost Div. Semi-Final
1990-91	80	21	14	5	....	16	22	2	....	37	36	7	....	258	258	81	3rd, Patrick Div.	Lost Div. Final
1989-90	80	19	18	3	....	17	20	3	....	36	38	6	....	284	275	78	3rd, Patrick Div.	Lost Conf. Championship
1988-89	80	25	12	3	....	16	17	7	....	41	29	10	....	305	259	92	1st, Patrick Div.	Lost Div. Semi-Final
1987-88	80	22	14	4	....	16	19	5	....	38	33	9	....	281	249	85	2nd, Patrick Div.	Lost Div. Final
1986-87	80	22	15	3	....	16	17	7	....	38	32	10	....	285	278	86	2nd, Patrick Div.	Lost Div. Semi-Final
1985-86	80	30	8	2	....	20	15	5	....	50	23	7	....	315	272	107	2nd, Patrick Div.	Lost Div. Final
1984-85	80	27	11	2	....	19	14	7	....	46	25	9	....	322	240	101	2nd, Patrick Div.	Lost Div. Semi-Final
1983-84	80	26	11	3	....	22	16	2	....	48	27	5	....	308	226	101	2nd, Patrick Div.	Lost Div. Final
1982-83	80	22	12	6	....	17	13	10	....	39	25	16	....	306	283	94	3rd, Patrick Div.	Lost Div. Semi-Final
1981-82	80	16	16	8	....	10	25	5	....	26	41	13	....	319	338	65	5th, Patrick Div.	Out of Playoffs
1980-81	80	16	17	7	....	10	19	11	....	26	36	18	....	286	317	70	5th, Patrick Div.	Out of Playoffs
1979-80	80	20	14	6	....	7	26	7	....	27	40	13	....	261	293	67	5th, Patrick Div.	Out of Playoffs
1978-79	80	15	19	6	....	9	22	9	....	24	41	15	....	273	338	63	4th, Norris Div.	Out of Playoffs
1977-78	80	10	23	7	....	7	26	7	....	17	49	14	....	195	321	48	5th, Norris Div.	Out of Playoffs
1976-77	80	17	15	8	....	7	27	6	....	24	42	14	....	221	307	62	4th, Norris Div.	Out of Playoffs
1975-76	80	6	26	8	....	5	33	2	....	11	59	10	....	224	394	32	5th, Norris Div.	Out of Playoffs
1974-75	80	7	28	5	....	1	39	0	....	8	67	5	....	181	446	21	5th, Norris Div.	Out of Playoffs

SOUTHEAST DIVISION
38th NHL Season

Franchise date: June 11, 1974

2011-12 Player Personnel

FORWARDS	HT	WT	S	Place of Birth	*Age	2010-11 Club
AUCOIN, Keith	5-9	162	R	Waltham, MA	32	Washington-Hershey
BACKSTROM, Nicklas	6-1	210	L	Gavle, Sweden	23	Washington
BEAGLE, Jay	6-3	204	R	Calgary, Alta.	25	Washington-Hershey
BOUCHARD, Francois	6-1	195	L	Sherbrooke, Que.	23	Hershey
BROUWER, Troy	6-2	214	R	Vancouver, B.C.	26	Chicago
CHIMERA, Jason	6-2	216	L	Edmonton, Alta.	32	Washington
HALPERN, Jeff	5-11	198	R	Potomac, MD	35	Montreal
HANSON, Christian	6-4	228	R	Venetia, PA	25	Toronto-Toronto (AHL)
HENDRICKS, Matt	6-0	215	L	Blaine, MN	30	Washington
JOHANSSON, Marcus	5-11	189	L	Landskrona, Sweden	21	Washington-Hershey
KING, D.J.	6-3	230	L	Meadow Lake, Sask.	27	Washington
KNUBLE, Mike	6-3	223	R	Toronto, Ont.	39	Washington
LAICH, Brooks	6-2	200	L	Wawota, Sask.	28	Washington
OVECHKIN, Alex	6-2	233	R	Moscow, USSR	26	Washington
PERREAULT, Mathieu	5-10	174	L	Drummondville, Que.	23	Washington-Hershey
POTULNY, Ryan	6-0	190	L	Grand Forks, ND	27	Chi-Rockford-Ott-Binghamton
SEMIN, Alexander	6-2	208	L	Krasnoyarsk, USSR	27	Washington
SJOGREN, Mattias	6-2	214	L	Landskrona, Sweden	23	Farjestad
WARD, Joel	6-1	218	R	Toronto, Ont.	30	Nashville
DEFENSEMEN						
ALZNER, Karl	6-3	206	L	Burnaby, B.C.	23	Washington
CARLSON, John	6-3	208	R	Natick, MA	21	Washington
COLLINS, Sean	6-1	207	R	Troy, MI	27	Washington-Hershey
ERSKINE, John	6-4	220	L	Kingston, Ont.	31	Washington
GREEN, Mike	6-1	204	R	Calgary, Alta.	25	Washington
HAMRLIK, Roman	6-2	207	L	Zlin, Czech.	37	Montreal
POTI, Tom	6-3	197	L	Worcester, MA	34	Washington
RICHMOND, Danny	6-0	192	L	Chicago, IL	27	Toronto (AHL)
SCHULTZ, Jeff	6-6	230	L	Calgary, Alta.	25	Washington
WIDEMAN, Dennis	6-0	196	R	Kitchener, Ont.	28	Florida-Washington

GOALTENDERS	HT	WT	C	Place of Birth	*Age	2010-11 Club
HOLTBY, Braden	6-1	209	L	Lloydminster, Sask.	22	Washington-Hershey
NEUVIRTH, Michal	6-1	190	L	Usti nad Labem, Czech.	23	Washington
VOKOUN, Tomas	6-0	195	R	Karlovy Vary, Czech.	35	Florida

* – Age at start of 2011-12 season

Bruce Boudreau

Head Coach

Born: Toronto, Ont., January 9, 1955.

Bruce Boudreau became the 14th head coach in Washington Capitals history when he was named to the position on an interim basis on November 22, 2007. He had the interim tag removed on December 26. His tremendously successful first season behind the bench in Washington landed the Capitals a playoff berth and earned Boudreau the Jack Adams Award as the NHL's coach of the year. Boudreau led the Capitals on a remarkable comeback from 30th in the NHL when he took over the team to the Southeast Division championship. The Capitals won a second consecutive Southeast Division title in 2008-09, tying a franchise record with 50 wins and setting a new record with 108 points. They shattered those records with 54 wins and 121 points in 2009-10 and won the Presidents' Trophy for the first time in franchise history.

Boudreau spent nine seasons as a head coach in the American Hockey League, compiling a record of 340-216-99. He won the Calder Cup with the Hershey Bears in 2006 and won the Kelly Cup as head coach and director of hockey operations for the Mississippi Sea Wolves (ECHL) in 1999. He was named coach of the year in the International Hockey League in 1994 after leading the Fort Wayne Komets to the Turner Cup finals.

Boudreau played parts of eight seasons in the NHL with the Toronto Maple Leafs and Chicago Blackhawks, recording 70 points in 141 games. He enjoyed one of the best seasons ever by a Canadian junior player during 1974-75, collecting 165 points for the Toronto Marlboros, a Canadian Hockey League record until Wayne Gretzky surpassed the mark during the 1977-78 season. An outstanding minor league scorer, no AHL player in the 1980s notched more points than Boudreau.

Coaching Record

			Regular Season				Playoffs			
Season	Team	League	GC	W	L	O/T	GC	W	L	T
1992-93	Muskegon	CoHL	60	28	27	5	7	3	4	....
1993-94	Fort Wayne	IHL	81	41	29	11	18	10	8	....
1994-95	Fort Wayne	IHL	39	15	21	3	....	....	....	....
1996-97	Mississippi	ECHL	70	34	26	10	3	0	3	....
1997-98	Mississippi	ECHL	70	34	27	9	....	....	....	....
1998-99	Mississippi	ECHL	70	41	22	7	18	14	4	....
99-2000	Lowell	AHL	80	33	36	11	7	3	4	....
2000-01	Lowell	AHL	80	35	35	10	4	1	3	....
2001-02	Manchester	AHL	80	38	28	14	5	2	3	....
2002-03	Manchester	AHL	80	40	23	17	3	0	3	....
2003-04	Manchester	AHL	80	40	28	12	6	2	4	....
2004-05	Manchester	AHL	80	51	21	8	6	2	4	....
2005-06	Hershey	AHL	80	44	21	15	21	16	5	....
2006-07	Hershey	AHL	80	51	17	12	19	13	6	....
2007-08	Hershey	AHL	15	8	7	0	....	....	....	....
2007-08	**Washington**	**NHL**	**61**	**37**	**17**	**7**	**7**	**3**	**4**	....
2008-09	**Washington**	**NHL**	**82**	**50**	**24**	**8**	**14**	**7**	**7**	....
2009-10	**Washington**	**NHL**	**82**	**54**	**15**	**13**	**7**	**3**	**4**	....
2010-11	**Washington**	**NHL**	**82**	**48**	**23**	**11**	**9**	**4**	**5**	....
	NHL Totals		**307**	**189**	**79**	**39**	**37**	**17**	**20**	....

Jack Adams Award (2008)

2010-11 Scoring

* – rookie

Regular Season

Pos	#	Player	Team	GP	G	A	Pts	TOI	+/–	PIM	PP	SH	GW	S	%
L	8	Alex Ovechkin	WSH	79	32	53	85	21:21	24	41	7	0	11	367	8.7
C	19	Nicklas Backstrom	WSH	77	18	47	65	20:35	24	40	4	1	2	202	8.9
R	28	Alexander Semin	WSH	65	28	26	54	18:04	22	71	6	1	4	196	14.3
L	21	Brooks Laich	WSH	82	16	32	48	18:25	14	46	4	1	3	207	7.7
R	22	Mike Knuble	WSH	79	24	16	40	17:52	10	36	7	1	1	203	11.8
D	6	Dennis Wideman	FLA	61	9	24	33	23:57	–26	33	8	0	1	135	6.7
			WSH	14	1	6	7	24:04	7	6	1	0	0	25	4.0
			Total	75	10	30	40	23:58	–19	39	9	0	1	160	6.3
D	74	* John Carlson	WSH	82	7	30	37	22:38	21	44	1	0	3	144	4.9
C	44	Jason Arnott	N.J.	62	13	11	24	15:27	–9	32	2	0	0	139	9.4
			WSH	11	4	3	7	15:53	3	8	2	0	1	30	13.3
			Total	73	17	14	31	15:31	–6	40	4	0	1	169	10.1
C	90	* Marcus Johansson	WSH	69	13	14	27	14:43	2	10	2	1	2	102	12.7
L	25	Jason Chimera	WSH	81	10	16	26	13:15	–10	64	2	0	1	162	6.2
C	26	Matt Hendricks	WSH	77	9	16	25	11:27	–2	110	1	0	3	113	8.0
D	52	Mike Green	WSH	49	8	16	24	25:11	6	48	5	0	1	115	7.0
R	16	Eric Fehr	WSH	52	10	10	20	12:35	0	16	3	0	1	120	8.3
L	18	Marco Sturm	L.A.	17	4	5	9	14:28	6	17	1	0	0	27	14.8
			WSH	18	1	6	7	14:00	0	6	0	0	1	30	3.3
			Total	35	5	11	16	14:14	6	23	1	0	1	57	8.8
C	85	* Mathieu Perreault	WSH	35	7	7	14	11:52	–3	20	1	0	1	41	17.1
D	27	Karl Alzner	WSH	82	2	10	12	20:00	14	24	0	0	0	64	3.1
R	10	Matt Bradley	WSH	61	4	7	11	10:29	–3	68	0	0	0	58	6.9
D	4	John Erskine	WSH	73	4	7	11	14:49	1	94	0	0	1	58	6.9
D	23	Scott Hannan	COL	23	0	6	6	18:37	1	6	0	0	0	21	0.0
			WSH	55	1	4	5	20:16	3	28	0	0	0	35	2.9
			Total	78	1	10	11	19:47	4	34	0	0	0	56	1.8
D	55	Jeff Schultz	WSH	72	1	9	10	19:46	6	12	0	0	1	34	2.9
C	15	Boyd Gordon	WSH	60	3	6	9	13:02	–5	16	0	1	1	77	3.9
D	3	Tom Poti	WSH	21	2	5	7	18:21	–4	8	0	0	0	20	10.0
D	89	Tyler Sloan	WSH	33	1	5	6	12:30	–6	14	0	0	0	12	8.3
C	83	* Jay Beagle	WSH	31	2	1	3	10:30	–2	8	0	0	2	27	7.4
R	63	* Andrew Gordon	WSH	9	1	1	2	8:40	–2	0	0	0	0	5	20.0
L	17	D.J. King	WSH	16	0	2	2	5:41	–3	30	0	0	0	6	0.0
D	62	Sean Collins	WSH	4	1	0	1	14:44	2	0	0	0	1	4	25.0
R	24	Brian Willsie	WSH	1	0	1	1	6:15	0	0	0	0	0	0	0.0
D	44	Brian Fahey	WSH	7	0	1	1	11:49	–1	2	0	0	0	4	0.0
C	20	Keith Aucoin	WSH	1	0	0	0	11:47	0	0	0	0	0	0	0.0

Goaltending

No.	Goaltender	GPI	Mins	Avg	W	L	OT	EN	SO	GA	SA	S%	G	A	PIM
70	* Braden Holtby	14	736	1.79	10	2	2	0	2	22	332	.934	0	1	0
1	Semyon Varlamov	27	1560	2.23	11	9	5	1	2	58	759	.924	0	0	2
30	* Michal Neuvirth	48	2689	2.45	27	12	4	0	4	110	1283	.914	0	0	0
	Totals	**82**	**5011**	**2.29**	**48**	**23**	**11**	**1**	**8**	**191**	**2375**	**.920**			

Playoffs

Pos	#	Player	Team	GP	G	A	Pts	TOI	+/–	PIM	PP	SH	GW	OT	S	%
L	8	Alex Ovechkin	WSH	9	5	5	10	23:30	–1	10	1	0	1	0	34	14.7
L	21	Brooks Laich	WSH	9	1	6	7	21:54	0	2	0	0	0	0	21	4.8
R	28	Alexander Semin	WSH	9	4	2	6	18:36	2	8	0	0	1	1	28	14.3
C	90	* Marcus Johansson	WSH	9	2	4	6	18:22	–2	0	0	0	0	0	14	14.3
D	52	Mike Green	WSH	8	1	5	6	21:27	0	8	1	0	0	0	23	4.3
C	44	Jason Arnott	WSH	9	1	5	6	16:02	4	2	1	0	0	0	13	7.7
L	25	Jason Chimera	WSH	9	2	2	4	12:53	–3	2	0	0	2	1	15	13.3
D	74	* John Carlson	WSH	9	2	1	3	24:23	–2	4	0	0	0	0	23	8.7
L	18	Marco Sturm	WSH	9	1	2	3	14:38	1	4	1	0	0	0	18	5.6
R	22	Mike Knuble	WSH	6	2	0	2	21:10	2	8	1	0	0	0	12	16.7
D	4	John Erskine	WSH	9	1	1	2	13:26	1	6	0	0	0	0	6	16.7
C	19	Nicklas Backstrom	WSH	9	0	2	2	23:18	0	4	0	0	0	0	25	0.0
R	16	Eric Fehr	WSH	5	1	0	1	13:28	3	0	0	0	0	0	10	10.0
D	23	Scott Hannan	WSH	9	0	1	1	23:37	1	2	0	0	0	0	6	0.0
D	27	Karl Alzner	WSH	9	0	1	1	22:44	–4	0	0	0	0	0	12	0.0
D	62	Sean Collins	WSH	1	0	0	0	6:10	0	0	0	0	0	0	0	0.0
C	26	Matt Hendricks	WSH	7	0	0	0	9:08	–2	4	0	0	0	0	1	0.0
R	10	Matt Bradley	WSH	9	0	0	0	8:48	–3	4	0	0	0	0	6	0.0
C	15	Boyd Gordon	WSH	9	0	0	0	12:54	–1	6	0	0	0	0	13	0.0
D	55	Jeff Schultz	WSH	9	0	0	0	20:45	1	6	0	0	0	0	9	0.0

Goaltending

No.	Goaltender	GPI	Mins	Avg	W	L	EN	SO	GA	SA	S%	G	A	PIM
30	* Michal Neuvirth	9	590	2.34	4	5	1	1	23	261	.912	0	0	0
	Totals	**9**	**597**	**2.41**	**4**	**5**	**1**	**1**	**24**	**262**	**.908**			

Captains' History

Doug Mohns, 1974-75; Bill Clement and Yvon Labre, 1975-76; Yvon Labre, 1976-77, 1977-78; Guy Charron, 1978-79; Ryan Walter, 1979-80 to 1981-82; Rod Langway, 1982-83 to 1991-92; Rod Langway and Kevin Hatcher, 1992-93; Kevin Hatcher, 1993-94; Dale Hunter, 1994-95 to 1998-99; Adam Oates, 1999-2000, 2000-01; Brendan Witt and Steve Konowalchuk, 2001-02; Steve Konowalchuk, 2002-03; Steve Konowalchuk and no captain, 2003-04; Jeff Halpern, 2005-06; Chris Clark, 2006-07 to 2008-09; Chris Clark and Alex Ovechkin, 2009-10; Alex Ovechkin, 2010-11 to date.

Coaching History

Jim Anderson, Red Sullivan and Milt Schmidt, 1974-75; Milt Schmidt and Tom McVie, 1975-76; Tom McVie, 1976-77, 1977-78; Danny Belisle, 1978-79; Danny Belisle and Gary Green, 1979-80; Gary Green, 1980-81; Gary Green, Roger Crozier and Bryan Murray, 1981-82; Bryan Murray, 1982-83 to 1988-89; Bryan Murray and Terry Murray, 1989-90; Terry Murray, 1990-91 to 1992-93; Terry Murray and Jim Schoenfeld, 1993-94; Jim Schoenfeld, 1994-95 to 1996-97; Ron Wilson, 1997-98 to 2001-02; Bruce Cassidy, 2002-03; Bruce Cassidy and Glen Hanlon, 2003-04; Glen Hanlon, 2004-05 to 2006-07; Glen Hanlon and Bruce Boudreau, 2007-08; Bruce Boudreau, 2008-09 to date.

Club Records

Team

(Figures in brackets for season records are games played; records for fewest points, wins, ties, losses, goals, goals against are for 70 or more games)

Most Points **121** 2009-10 (82)
Most Wins **54** 2009-10 (82)
Most Ties **18** 1980-81 (80)
Most Losses **67** 1974-75 (80)
Most Goals **330** 1991-92 (80)
Most Goals Against ***446** 1974-75 (80)
Fewest Points ***21** 1974-75 (80)
Fewest Wins ***8** 1974-75 (80)
Fewest Ties **5** 1974-75 (80), 1983-84 (80)
Fewest Losses **15** 2009-10 (82)
Fewest Goals **181** 1974-75 (80)
Fewest Goals Against **194** 1999-00 (82)

Longest Winning Streak
Overall .... **14** Jan. 13-Feb. 7/10
Home .... **13** Jan. 5-Mar. 6/10
Away .... **6** Feb. 26-Apr. 1/84, Feb. 20-Mar. 15/11

Longest Undefeated Streak
Overall .... **14** Nov. 24-Dec. 23/82 (9 wins, 5 ties), Jan. 17-Feb. 18/84 (13 wins, 1 tie), Jan. 13-Feb. 7/10 (14 wins)
Home .... **13** Nov. 25/92-Jan. 31/93 (9 wins, 4 ties), Dec. 27/99-Feb. 23/00 (11 wins, 2 ties), Jan. 5-Mar. 6/10 (13 wins)
Away .... **10** Nov. 24/82-Jan. 8/83 (6 wins, 4 ties)

Longest Losing Streak
Overall .... ***17** Feb. 18-Mar. 26/75
Home .... **11** Feb. 18-Mar. 30/75
Away .... **37** Oct. 9/74-Mar. 26/75

Longest Winless Streak
Overall .... **25** Nov. 29/75-Jan. 21/76 (22 losses, 3 ties)
Home .... **14** Dec. 3/75-Jan. 21/76 (11 losses, 3 ties)
Away .... **37** Oct. 9/74-Mar. 26/75 (37 losses)

Most Shutouts, Season **9** 1995-96 (82)
Most PIM, Season **2,204** 1989-90 (80)
Most Goals, Game .... **12** Feb. 6/90 (Que. 2 at Wsh. 12), Jan. 11/03 (Fla. 2 at Wsh. 12)

Individual

Most Seasons .... **16** Olaf Kolzig
Most Games .... **983** Calle Johansson
Most Goals, Career .... **472** Peter Bondra
Most Assists, Career .... **418** Michal Pivonka
Most Points, Career .... **825** Peter Bondra (472G, 353A)
Most PIM, Career .... **2,003** Dale Hunter
Most Shutouts, Career .... **35** Olaf Kolzig
Longest Consecutive Games Streak .... **422** Bob Carpenter (Oct. 7/81-Nov. 22/86)
Most Goals, Season .... **65** Alex Ovechkin (2007-08)
Most Assists, Season .... **76** Dennis Maruk (1981-82)
Most Points, Season .... **136** Dennis Maruk (1981-82; 60G, 76A)
Most PIM, Season .... **339** Alan May (1989-90)
Most Points, Defenseman, Season .... **81** Larry Murphy (1986-87; 23G, 58A)
Most Points, Center, Season .... **136** Dennis Maruk (1981-82; 60G, 76A)
Most Points, Right Wing, Season .... **102** Mike Gartner (1984-85; 50G, 52A)
Most Points, Left Wing, Season .... **112** Alex Ovechkin (2007-08; 65G, 47A)
Most Points, Rookie, Season .... **106** Alex Ovechkin (2005-06; 52G, 54A)
Most Shutouts, Season .... **9** Jim Carey (1995-96)
Most Goals, Game .... **5** Bengt Gustafsson (Jan. 8/84), Peter Bondra (Feb. 5/94)
Most Assists, Game .... **6** Mike Ridley (Jan. 7/89)
Most Points, Game .... **7** Dino Ciccarelli (Mar. 18/89; 4G, 3A), Jaromir Jagr (Jan. 11/03; 3G, 4A)

* NHL Record.

Retired Numbers

5	Rod Langway	1982-1993
7	Yvon Labre	1974-1981
11	Mike Gartner	1979-1989
32	Dale Hunter	1987-1999

All-time Record vs. Other Clubs

Regular Season

	At Home								On Road								Total							
	GP	W	L	T	OL	GF	GA	PTS	GP	W	L	T	OL	GF	GA	PTS	GP	W	L	T	OL	GF	GA	PTS
Anaheim	12	5	6	0	1	23	31	11	12	5	6	1	0	38	41	11	24	10	12	1	1	61	72	22
Atlanta	34	22	8	3	1	124	97	48	34	14	14	2	4	100	102	34	68	36	22	5	5	224	199	82
Boston	67	23	28	12	4	193	221	62	68	19	36	9	4	178	239	51	135	42	64	21	8	371	460	113
Buffalo	68	21	36	9	2	180	234	53	68	20	41	6	1	176	260	47	136	41	77	15	3	356	494	100
Calgary	43	22	15	6	0	159	146	50	41	9	25	7	0	105	163	25	84	31	40	13	0	264	309	75
Carolina	68	41	21	4	2	227	178	88	70	33	23	10	4	210	198	80	138	74	44	14	6	437	376	168
Chicago	44	23	15	5	1	156	136	52	42	13	23	6	0	124	159	32	86	36	38	11	1	280	295	84
Colorado	36	19	12	4	1	136	113	43	36	16	15	5	0	127	109	37	72	35	27	9	1	263	222	80
Columbus	6	3	1	1	1	19	18	8	7	5	2	0	0	22	19	10	13	8	3	1	1	41	37	18
Dallas	42	16	17	8	1	127	136	41	44	13	23	8	0	118	163	34	86	29	40	16	1	245	299	75
Detroit	49	23	21	5	0	178	155	51	50	15	22	11	2	142	171	43	99	38	43	16	2	320	326	94
Edmonton	32	20	10	2	0	130	102	42	31	11	16	4	0	95	126	26	63	31	26	6	0	225	228	68
Florida	49	25	14	5	5	151	125	60	49	23	20	4	2	132	128	52	98	48	34	9	7	283	253	112
Los Angeles	49	19	23	7	0	194	183	45	50	15	29	6	0	150	196	36	99	34	52	13	0	344	379	81
Minnesota	5	4	1	0	0	14	8	8	6	0	5	0	1	7	15	1	11	4	6	0	1	21	23	9
Montreal	71	33	28	9	1	200	208	76	72	23	39	8	2	164	267	56	143	56	67	17	3	364	475	132
Nashville	7	5	2	0	0	19	18	10	8	4	3	1	0	20	21	9	15	9	5	1	0	39	39	19
New Jersey	91	54	26	6	5	345	254	119	91	37	43	7	4	260	280	85	182	91	69	13	9	605	534	204
NY Islanders	93	47	33	11	2	305	288	107	93	44	46	2	1	287	333	91	186	91	79	13	3	592	621	198
NY Rangers	96	50	33	9	4	347	302	113	94	39	44	9	2	315	352	89	190	89	77	18	6	662	654	202
Ottawa	36	20	11	4	1	126	101	45	35	14	18	1	2	102	125	31	71	34	29	5	3	228	226	76
Philadelphia	92	40	38	13	1	302	294	94	95	31	56	6	2	265	360	70	187	71	94	19	3	567	654	164
Phoenix	33	19	8	5	1	125	90	44	33	9	17	7	0	114	118	25	66	28	25	12	1	239	208	69
Pittsburgh	98	50	35	9	4	399	352	113	95	36	51	7	1	303	362	80	193	86	86	16	5	702	714	193
St. Louis	42	23	15	4	0	148	125	50	44	14	21	8	1	137	174	37	86	37	36	12	1	285	299	87
San Jose	15	6	8	0	1	40	42	13	14	3	10	1	0	33	48	7	29	9	18	1	1	73	90	20
Tampa Bay	50	32	11	4	3	184	125	71	50	30	16	2	2	158	125	64	100	62	27	6	5	342	250	135
Toronto	62	36	20	4	2	227	178	78	60	22	29	6	3	199	244	53	122	58	49	10	5	426	422	131
Vancouver	43	23	16	4	0	141	128	50	41	16	19	5	1	127	142	38	84	39	35	9	1	268	270	88
Defunct Clubs	10	2	8	0	0	28	42	4	10	4	5	1	0	30	39	9	20	6	13	1	0	58	81	13
Totals	**1443**	**726**	**520**	**153**	**44**	**4947**	**4430**	**1649**	**1443**	**537**	**717**	**150**	**39**	**4238**	**5079**	**1263**	**2886**	**1263**	**1237**	**303**	**83**	**9185**	**9509**	**2912**

Playoffs

	Series	W	L	GP	W	L	T	GF	GA	Last Mtg.	Rnd.	Result
Boston	2	1	1	10	4	6	0	21	28	1998	CQF	W 4-2
Buffalo	1	1	0	6	4	2	0	13	11	1998	CF	W 4-2
Detroit	1	0	1	4	0	4	0	7	13	1998	F	L 0-4
Montreal	1	0	1	7	3	4	0	22	20	2010	CQF	L 3-4
New Jersey	2	1	1	13	7	6	0	44	43	1990	DSF	W 4-2
NY Islanders	6	1	5	30	12	18	0	88	99	1993	DSF	L 2-4
NY Rangers	6	4	2	34	19	15	0	107	90	2011	CQF	W 4-1
Ottawa	1	1	0	5	4	1	0	18	7	1998	CSF	W 4-1
Philadelphia	4	2	2	23	12	11	0	85	78	2008	CQF	L 3-4
Pittsburgh	8	1	7	49	19	30	0	143	164	2009	CSF	L 3-4
Tampa Bay	2	0	2	10	2	8	0	25	30	2011	CSF	L 0-4
Totals	**34**	**12**	**22**	**191**	**86**	**105**	**0**	**573**	**583**			

Calgary totals include Atlanta Flames, 1974-75 to 1979-80. Carolina totals include Hartford, 1979-80 to 1996-97.
Colorado totals include Quebec, 1979-80 to 1994-95. Dallas totals include Minnesota North Stars, 1974-75 to 1992-93.
New Jersey totals include Kansas City, 1974-75, 1975-76, and Colorado Rockies, 1976-77 to 1981-82.
Phoenix totals include Winnipeg, 1979-80 to 1995-96.

Playoff Results 2011-2007

Year	Round	Opponent	Result	GF	GA
2011	CSF	Tampa Bay	L 0-4	10	16
	CQF	NY Rangers	W 4-1	13	8
2010	CQF	Montreal	L 3-4	22	20
2009	CSF	Pittsburgh	L 3-4	22	27
	CQF	NY Rangers	W 4-3	19	11
2008	CQF	Philadelphia	L 3-4	20	23

Abbreviations: Round: F – Final; **CF** – conference final; **CSF** – conference semi-final; **CQF** – conference quarter-final; **DSF** – division semi-final.

2010-11 Results

Month	Date	Opponent	Score	Month	Date	Opponent	Score
Oct.	8	at Atlanta	2-4		8	Florida	3-2
	9	New Jersey	7-2		11	at Florida	3-4*
	11	Ottawa	3-2*		12	at Tampa Bay	0-3
	13	NY Islanders	2-1		14	Vancouver	2-4
	16	at Nashville	3-2*		16	Ottawa	3-1
	19	Boston	1-3		18	at Philadelphia	2-3*
	21	at Boston	1-4		20	at NY Islanders	2-1
	23	Atlanta	4-3*		22	at Toronto	4-1
	27	at Carolina	3-0		24	NY Rangers	1-2†
	28	at Minnesota	1-2		26	at Atlanta	0-1
	30	at Calgary	7-2	Feb.	1	Montreal	2-3†
Nov.	3	Toronto	5-4†		4	at Tampa Bay	5-2
	5	Boston	5-3		6	Pittsburgh	3-0
	7	Philadelphia	3-2*		8	San Jose	0-2
	9	at NY Rangers	5-3		12	Los Angeles	1-4
	11	Tampa Bay	6-3		14	at Phoenix	2-3
	13	at Buffalo	2-3*		16	at Anaheim	7-6
	14	Atlanta	6-4		17	at San Jose	2-3
	17	Buffalo	4-2		20	at Buffalo	2-1
	19	at Atlanta	0-5		21	at Pittsburgh	1-0
	20	Philadelphia	4-5†		25	NY Rangers	0-6
	22	at New Jersey	0-5		26	at NY Islanders	3-2
	24	at Carolina	3-2	Mar.	1	NY Islanders	2-1*
	26	Tampa Bay	6-0		3	St. Louis	3-2
	28	Carolina	3-2†		6	at Florida	3-2*
Dec.	1	at St. Louis	4-1		7	at Tampa Bay	2-1†
	2	at Dallas	1-2		9	Edmonton	5-0
	4	Atlanta	1-3		11	Carolina	2-1
	6	Toronto	4-5†		13	Chicago	4-3*
	9	Florida	0-3		15	at Montreal	4-2
	11	Colorado	2-3		16	at Detroit	2-3
	12	at NY Rangers	0-7		18	at New Jersey	3-0
	15	Anaheim	1-2*		22	at Philadelphia	5-4†
	18	at Boston	2-3		25	at Ottawa	0-2
	19	at Ottawa	3-2		26	at Montreal	2-0
	21	New Jersey	5-1		29	Carolina	2-3†
	23	Pittsburgh	2-3†		31	Columbus	4-3*
	26	at Carolina	3-2	Apr.	2	Buffalo	5-4*
	28	Montreal	3-0		5	at Toronto	3-2†
Jan.	1	at Pittsburgh	3-1		6	Florida	5-2
	4	Tampa Bay	0-1*		9	at Florida	0-1

* – Overtime † – Shootout

Entry Draft Selections 2011-1997

Name in bold denotes played in NHL.

2011
Pick
117 Steffen Soberg
147 Patrick Koudys
177 Travis Boyd
207 Garrett Haar

2010
Pick
26 Evgeny Kuznetsov
86 Stanislav Galiev
112 Philipp Grubauer
142 Caleb Herbert
176 Samuel Carrier

2009
Pick
24 **Marcus Johansson**
55 **Dmitri Orlov**
85 Cody Eakin
115 Patrick Wey
145 Brett Flemming
175 Garrett Mitchell
205 Benjamin Casavant

2008
Pick
21 Anton Gustafsson
27 **John Carlson**
57 Eric Mestery
58 Dmitry Kugryshev
93 **Braden Holtby**
144 Joel Broda
174 Greg Burke
204 **Stefan Della Rovere**

2007
Pick
5 **Karl Alzner**
34 Josh Godfrey
46 Theo Ruth
84 Phil Desimone
108 Brett Bruneteau
125 Brett Leffler
154 Dan Dunn
180 Justin Taylor
185 Nick Larson
199 Andrew Glass

2006
Pick
4 **Nicklas Backstrom**
23 **Semyon Varlamov**
34 **Michal Neuvirth**
35 Francois Bouchard
52 Keith Seabrook
97 **Oskar Osala**
122 Luke Lynes
127 Maxime Lacroix
157 Brent Gwidt
177 **Mathieu Perreault**

2005
Pick
14 Sasha Pokulok
27 Joe Finley
109 Andrew Thomas
118 Patrick McNeill
143 Daren Machesney
181 **Tim Kennedy**
209 Viktor Dovgan

2004
Pick
1 **Alex Ovechkin**
27 **Jeff Schultz**
29 **Mike Green**
33 **Chris Bourque**
62 Mikhail Yunkov
66 **Sami Lepisto**
88 Clayton Barthel
132 Oscar Hedman
138 Pasi Salonen
166 Peter Guggisberg
197 **Andrew Gordon**
230 Justin Mrazek
263 **Travis Morin**

2003
Pick
18 **Eric Fehr**
83 Steve Werner
109 Andreas Valdix
155 Josh Robertson
249 Andrew Joudrey
279 Mark Olafson

2002
Pick
12 **Steve Eminger**
13 **Alexander Semin**
17 **Boyd Gordon**
59 Maxime Daigneault
77 Patrick Wellar
92 Derek Krestanovich
109 Jevon Desautels
118 Petr Dvorak
145 Rob Gherson
179 Marian Havel
209 Joni Lindlof
242 Igor Ignatushkin
272 Patric Blomdahl

2001
Pick
58 **Nathan Paetsch**
90 **Owen Fussey**
125 Jeff Lucky
160 Artem Ternavsky
191 Zbynek Novak
221 **Johnny Oduya**
249 Matt Maglione
254 Peter Polcik
275 Robert Muller
284 Viktor Hubl

2000
Pick
26 **Brian Sutherby**
43 **Matt Pettinger**
61 **Jakub Cutta**
121 Ryan Vanbuskirk
163 Ivan Nepryayev
289 Bjorn Nord

1999
Pick
7 **Kris Beech**
29 **Michal Sivek**
31 Charlie Stephens
34 **Ross Lupaschuk**
37 Nolan Yonkman
132 **Roman Tvrdon**
175 Kyle Clark
192 David Bornhammar
219 Maxim Orlov
249 Igor Shadilov

1998
Pick
49 Jomar Cruz
59 Todd Hornung
106 **Krys Barch**
107 **Chris Corrinet**
118 **Mike Siklenka**
125 Erik Wendell
179 Nate Forster
193 **Rastislav Stana**
220 **Mike Farrell**
251 Blake Evans

1997
Pick
9 **Nick Boynton**
35 **Jean-Francois Fortin**
89 Curtis Cruickshank
116 Kevin Caulfield
143 Henrik Petre
200 Pierre-Luc Therrien
226 Matt Oikawa

General Managers' History

Milt Schmidt, 1974-75; Milt Schmidt and Max McNab, 1975-76; Max McNab, 1976-77 to 1980-81; Max McNab and Roger Crozier, 1981-82; David Poile, 1982-83 to 1996-97; George McPhee, 1997-98 to date.

George McPhee
Vice President and General Manager
Born: Wallaceburg, Ont., July 2, 1958.

On June 9, 1997, George McPhee became the fifth general manager of the Washington Capitals. In his first year on the job, McPhee led the Caps to the Stanley Cup Finals for the first time in franchise history. He has since rebuilt the Capitals with younger players and used the first overall choice at the 2004 NHL Entry Draft to select Alex Ovechkin. In 2007-08 and 2008-09, the Capitals won the Southeast Division. They shattered club records with 54 wins and 121 points in 2009-10 and won the Presidents' Trophy for the first time in franchise history.

Prior to joining the Capitals, McPhee spent five years in the front office of the Vancouver Canucks where he served as vice president of hockey operations and alternate governor. He has earned degrees in both law and business and, while attending law school at Rutgers University, interned at the United States Court of International Trade in 1991.

A back injury forced McPhee to retire as an active player at the conclusion of the 1988-89 season, after a seven year playing career with the New York Rangers and New Jersey Devils. McPhee originally signed as a free agent with the Rangers in July, 1982, after graduating from Bowling Green State University with a business degree. McPhee did not waste any time in college, tallying 40 goals and 48 assists in his freshman season and easily winning CCHA rookie of the year honors. His outstanding collegiate hockey career was capped off when he was named the recipient of the Hobey Baker Award as the top U.S. collegiate player in his senior season. McPhee also earned All-America honors as a senior and finished his career at Bowling Green as the CCHA's all-time leading scorer with 114-153-267. He was the first player in CCHA history to make the Conference's all-academic team three straight seasons.

Club Directory

Verizon Center

Washington Capitals
627 N. Glebe Road, Suite 850
Arlington, VA 22203
Phone **202/266-2200**
PR FAX 202/266-2360
www.washingtoncaps.com
Capacity: 18,506

Ownership (Monumental Sports & Entertainment)
Chairman and Majority Owner . . . . Ted Leonsis
Vice Chairman and President, C.O.O. . . . . Dick Patrick
Vice Chairmen . . . . Raul Fernandez, Sheila Johnson
MSE Partners . . . . Scott Brickman, Albert Cohen, Neil Cohen, Jack Davies, Richard Fairbank, Michelle D. Freeman, Richard Kay, Jeong Kim, Mark D. Lerner, Roger Mody, Anthony Nader, Fred Schaufeld, George Stamas, Earl Stafford, Cliff White

Hockey Operations
Vice President and General Manager . . . . George McPhee
Assistant General Manager, Dir. of Legal Affairs . . . Don Fishman
Head Coach . . . . Bruce Boudreau
Assistant Coaches . . . . Dean Evason, Bob Woods
Assistant Coach/Video . . . . Blaine Forsythe
Goaltending Coach . . . . Dave Prior
Associate Goaltending Coach . . . . Olie Kolzig
Strength and Conditioning Coach . . . . Mark Nemish
Physiologist . . . . Jack Blatherwick
Director, Team Operations . . . . Katy Headman
Hockey Operations Assistants . . . . Eric Garvey, Evan Gold
Manager, Team Services . . . . Ian Anderson
Hershey Bears, Head Coach / Assistant Coach . . . . . Mark French / Troy Mann

Scouting Staff
Assistant General Manager, Player Personnel . . . . . . Brian MacLellan
Director, Player Development . . . . Steve Richmond
Director, Amateur Scouting . . . . Ross Mahoney
Pro Scouts . . . . Jason Fitzsimmons, Chris Patrick, Martin Pouliot
Amateur Scouts . . . . Darrell Baumgartner, Steve Bowman, Alan Haworth, Phil Horner, Ed McColgan, Terry Richardson, A.J. Toews
European Scouts . . . . Vojtech Kucera, Petri Skriko, Mats Weiderstal
Director, Scouting Operations . . . . Kris Wagner

Medical Staff
Head Athletic Trainer / Assistant Trainer . . . . Greg Smith / Ben Reisz
Massage Therapist . . . . Curt Millar
Team Physician / Team Internist . . . . Ben Shaffer, MD / Chris Walsh, MD
Team Ophthalmologist / Team Dentist . . . . Thomas Clinch, MD / Thomas Lenz, DDS, PC

Equipment Staff
Head Equipment Manager . . . . Brock Myles
Assistant Equipment Manager . . . . Craig Leydig
Equipment Assistant . . . . Dave Marin

Business Operations
Vice President, Administration . . . . Michelle Trostle
Senior Director, Information Technology . . . . Brian McPartland
Office Assistant / Receptionist . . . . Valerie Garrett / Chuquita Pettus
Chief Building Engineer . . . . Larry Hollen
Building Engineer . . . . Pedro Pena

Communications
Senior Vice President, Communications and
COO, Monumental Sports & Entertainment . . . . . Kurt Kehl
Director, Media Relations . . . . Sergey Kocharov
Director, Community Relations . . . . Elizabeth Wodatch
Senior Sports Media Producer . . . . Mike Vogel
Media Relations Manager . . . . Ben Guerrero
Community Relations Manager . . . . Nadia Wajid
Website Producer . . . . James Heuser
Communications Coordinator . . . . Kelly Murray

Broadcasting
Radio Rightsholder . . . . WFED 1500 AM
Radio Play-by-Play / Analyst . . . . John Walton / Ken Sabourin
Television Rightsholder . . . . Comcast SportsNet
Television Play-by-Play / Analyst . . . . Joe Beninati / Craig Laughlin
Television Reporters / Studio Analyst . . . . Al Koken / Jill Sorenson / Alan May

Marcus Johansson, John Carlson and Nicklas Backstrom celebrate the game-winning goal against Ottawa on January 16, 2010. All three players were first-round selections by the Capitals in recent years.

Winnipeg Jets

Key Off-Season Signings/Acquisitions

2011

June 8 • Named **Kevin Cheveldayoff** general manager.

24 • Named **Claude Noel** head coach.

July 4 • Signed D **Randy Jones**, LW **Tanner Glass**, D **Derek Meech**, C **Aaron Gagnon** and D **Mark Flood**.

5 • Re-signed LW **Andrew Ladd**.

8 • Acquired RW **Eric Fehr** from Washington for RW **Danick Paquette** and Winnipeg's 4th-round pick in the 2012 Entry Draft.

9 • Acquired LW **Kenndal McArdle** from Florida for C **Angelo Esposito**.

15 • Named **Charlie Huddy** assistant coach.

18 • Re-signed RW **Blake Wheeler**.

22 • Named **Pascal Vincent** assistant coach.

2010-11 Results: 34W-36L-5OTL-7SOL 80PTS.
Fourth, Southeast Division

Year-by-Year Record

Season	GP	Home W	L	T	OL	Road W	L	T	OL	Overall W	L	T	OL	GF	GA	Pts.	Finished	Playoff Result
2010-11*	82	17	17	....	7	17	19	....	5	34	36	....	12	223	269	80	4th, Southeast Div.	Out of Playoffs
2009-10*	82	19	16	....	6	16	18	....	7	35	34	....	13	234	256	83	2nd, Southeast Div.	Out of Playoffs
2008-09*	82	18	21	....	2	17	20	....	4	35	41	....	6	257	280	76	4th, Southeast Div.	Out of Playoffs
2007-08*	82	19	19	....	3	15	21	....	5	34	40	....	8	216	272	76	4th, Southeast Div.	Out of Playoffs
2006-07*	82	23	12	....	6	20	16	....	5	43	28	....	11	246	245	97	1st, Southeast Div.	Lost Conf. Quarter-Final
2005-06*	82	24	13	....	4	17	20	....	4	41	33	....	8	281	275	90	3rd, Southeast Div.	Out of Playoffs
2004-05*																		
2003-04*	82	18	17	4	2	15	20	4	2	33	37	8	4	214	243	78	2nd, Southeast Div.	Out of Playoffs
2002-03*	82	15	19	4	3	16	20	3	2	31	39	7	5	226	284	74	3rd, Southeast Div.	Out of Playoffs
2001-02*	82	11	21	9	0	8	26	2	5	19	47	11	5	187	288	54	5th, Southeast Div.	Out of Playoffs
2000-01*	82	10	23	6	2	13	22	6	0	23	45	12	2	211	289	60	4th, Southeast Div.	Out of Playoffs
1999-2000*	82	9	26	3	3	5	31	4	1	14	57	7	4	170	313	39	5th, Southeast Div.	Out of Playoffs

* Atlanta Thrashers

2011-12 Schedule

Oct.	Sun.	9	Montreal*		Tue.	10	at Boston
	Thu.	13	at Chicago		Thu.	12	San Jose
	Sat.	15	at Phoenix*		Sat.	14	New Jersey*
	Mon.	17	Pittsburgh		Mon.	16	at Ottawa
	Wed.	19	at Toronto		Tue.	17	at New Jersey
	Thu.	20	at Ottawa		Thu.	19	Buffalo
	Sat.	22	Carolina		Sat.	21	Florida
	Mon.	24	NY Rangers		Mon.	23	at Carolina
	Thu.	27	at Philadelphia		Tue.	24	at NY Rangers
	Sat.	29	at Tampa Bay		Tue.	31	at Philadelphia
	Mon.	31	at Florida	**Feb.**	Thu.	2	at Tampa Bay
Nov.	Thu.	3	at NY Islanders		Fri.	3	at Florida
	Sat.	5	at New Jersey		Sun.	5	at Montreal*
	Sun.	6	at NY Rangers		Tue.	7	Toronto
	Tue.	8	at Buffalo		Thu.	9	at Washington
	Thu.	10	Florida		Sat.	11	at Pittsburgh*
	Sat.	12	at Columbus		Tue.	14	NY Islanders
	Mon.	14	Tampa Bay		Thu.	16	at Minnesota
	Thu.	17	Washington		Fri.	17	Boston
	Sat.	19	Philadelphia*		Sun.	19	Colorado
	Wed.	23	at Washington		Tue.	21	Philadelphia
	Fri.	25	at Carolina		Thu.	23	Tampa Bay
	Sat.	26	at Boston		Sat.	25	St. Louis*
	Tue.	29	Ottawa		Mon.	27	Edmonton
Dec.	Thu.	1	Phoenix	**Mar.**	Thu.	1	Florida
	Sat.	3	New Jersey		Mon.	5	Buffalo
	Tue.	6	Boston		Thu.	8	at Vancouver
	Fri.	9	Carolina		Fri.	9	at Calgary
	Sat.	10	at Detroit		Wed.	14	Dallas
	Tue.	13	Minnesota		Fri.	16	Washington
	Thu.	15	Washington		Sun.	18	Carolina
	Sat.	17	Anaheim		Tue.	20	at Pittsburgh
	Tue.	20	NY Islanders		Fri.	23	at Washington
	Thu.	22	Montreal		Sat.	24	at Nashville
	Fri.	23	Pittsburgh		Mon.	26	Ottawa
	Tue.	27	at Colorado		Wed.	28	NY Rangers
	Thu.	29	Los Angeles		Fri.	30	at Carolina
	Sat.	31	Toronto		Sat.	31	at Tampa Bay
Jan.	Wed.	4	at Montreal	**Apr.**	Tue.	3	at Florida
	Thu.	5	at Toronto		Thu.	5	at NY Islanders
	Sat.	7	at Buffalo		Sat.	7	Tampa Bay

* Denotes afternoon game.

SOUTHEAST DIVISION
13th NHL Season

Franchise date: June 25, 1997

Transferred from Atlanta to Winnipeg, June 21, 2011.

Dustin Byfuglien moves to Winnipeg after a big year in 2010-11. Converted from right wing back to defense, Byfuglien led all NHL blueliners with 20 goals and also reached career highs with 33 assists and 53 points.

2011-12 Player Personnel

FORWARDS	HT	WT	S	Place of Birth	*Age	2010-11 Club
ANTROPOV, Nik	6-6	245	L	Ust-Kamenogorsk, USSR	31	Atlanta
BURMISTROV, Alexander	6-1	180	L	Kazan, USSR	19	Atlanta
CORMIER, Patrice	6-2	215	L	Moncton, N.B.	21	Atlanta-Chicago (AHL)
FEHR, Eric	6-4	212	R	Winkler, Man.	26	Washington
GLASS, Tanner	6-1	210	L	Regina, Sask.	27	Vancouver
HOLZAPFEL, Riley	6-2	190	L	Regina, Sask.	23	Chicago (AHL)
JAFFRAY, Jason	6-1	195	L	Olds, Alta.	30	Manitoba
KANE, Evander	6-2	195	L	Vancouver, B.C.	20	Atlanta
LADD, Andrew	6-3	205	L	Maple Ridge, B.C.	25	Atlanta
LITTLE, Bryan	5-11	185	R	Edmonton, Alta.	23	Atlanta
MACHACEK, Spencer	6-1	200	R	Lethbridge, Alta.	22	Atlanta-Chicago (AHL)
MAXWELL, Ben	6-1	195	L	North Vancouver, B.C.	23	Hamilton-Atlanta-Chi (AHL)
McARDLE, Kenndal	5-11	190	L	Toronto, Ont.	24	Florida-Rochester
SLATER, Jim	6-0	200	L	Lapeer, MI	28	Atlanta
THORBURN, Chris	6-3	230	R	Sault Ste. Marie, Ont.	28	Atlanta
WHEELER, Blake	6-5	205	R	Robbinsdale, MN	25	Boston-Atlanta

DEFENSEMEN	HT	WT	S	Place of Birth	*Age	2010-11 Club
BOGOSIAN, Zach	6-3	215	R	Massena, NY	21	Atlanta
BYFUGLIEN, Dustin	6-5	265	R	Minneapolis, MN	26	Atlanta
ENSTROM, Tobias	5-10	180	L	Nordingra, Sweden	26	Atlanta
FESTERLING, Brett	6-1	210	L	Quesnel, B.C.	25	Ana-Syr-Hamilton-Chi (AHL)
HAINSEY, Ron	6-3	210	L	Bolton, CT	30	Atlanta
JONES, Randy	6-2	210	L	Quispamsis, N.B.	30	Tampa Bay
KULDA , Arturs	6-2	215	L	Riga, Latvia	23	Atlanta-Chicago (AHL)
MEECH, Derek	5-11	205	L	Winnipeg, Man.	27	Grand Rapids
ODUYA, Johnny	6-0	190	L	Stockholm, Sweden	30	Atlanta
POSTMA, Paul	6-3	195	R	Red Deer, Alta.	22	Atlanta-Chicago (AHL)
STUART, Mark	6-2	213	L	Rochester, MN	27	Boston-Atlanta

GOALTENDERS	HT	WT	C	Place of Birth	*Age	2010-11 Club
MANNINO, Peter	6-1	195	R	Farmington Hills, MI	27	Atlanta-Chicago (AHL)
MASON, Chris	6-0	195	L	Red Deer, Alta.	35	Atlanta
PAVELEC, Ondrej	6-3	220	L	Kladno, Czech.	24	Atlanta-Chicago (AHL)

* – Age at start of 2011-12 season

2010-11 Scoring

* – rookie

Regular Season

Pos	#	Player	Team	GP	G	A	Pts	TOI	+/-	PIM	PP	SH	GW	S	%
L	16	Andrew Ladd	ATL	81	29	30	59	20:04	-10	39	9	2	2	195	14.9
D	33	Dustin Byfuglien	ATL	81	20	33	53	23:18	-2	93	8	0	6	347	5.8
D	39	Tobias Enstrom	ATL	72	10	41	51	23:41	-10	54	6	0	0	113	8.8
R	10	Bryan Little	ATL	76	18	30	48	18:27	11	33	2	2	1	158	11.4
R	26	Blake Wheeler	BOS	58	11	16	27	15:12	8	32	0	0	2	101	10.9
			ATL	23	7	10	17	18:52	2	14	0	0	0	78	9.0
			Total	81	18	26	44	16:14	10	46	0	0	2	179	10.1
L	9	Evander Kane	ATL	73	19	24	43	17:51	-12	68	4	0	2	234	8.1
C	80	Nik Antropov	ATL	76	16	25	41	15:39	-17	42	5	0	2	105	15.2
C	22	Anthony Stewart	ATL	80	14	25	39	14:58	-10	55	5	0	1	141	9.9
C	13	Rob Schremp	NYI	45	10	12	22	15:02	-19	12	2	0	1	64	15.6
			ATL	18	3	1	4	11:31	-1	4	2	0	2	19	15.8
			Total	63	13	13	26	14:02	-20	16	4	0	3	83	15.7
R	20	Radek Dvorak	FLA	53	7	14	21	16:33	2	20	0	1	3	89	7.9
			ATL	13	0	1	1	14:07	0	4	0	0	0	20	0.0
			Total	66	7	15	22	16:04	2	24	0	1	3	109	6.4
C	8 *	Alexander Burmistrov	ATL	74	6	14	20	13:13	-12	27	0	0	2	92	6.5
R	27	Chris Thorburn	ATL	82	9	10	19	13:47	-4	77	2	0	0	114	7.9
D	6	Ron Hainsey	ATL	82	3	16	19	18:05	3	24	0	0	2	83	3.6
D	4	Zach Bogosian	ATL	71	5	12	17	22:24	-27	29	0	0	1	155	3.2
D	29	Johnny Oduya	ATL	82	2	15	17	20:43	-15	22	0	0	0	90	2.2
C	13	Jim Slater	ATL	36	5	7	12	10:34	4	19	0	0	1	53	9.4
L	36	Eric Boulton	ATL	69	6	4	10	8:57	1	87	0	0	1	51	11.8
R	14	Tim Stapleton	ATL	45	5	7	11	11:06	-10	12	1	0	1	44	11.4
D	5	Mark Stuart	BOS	31	1	4	5	16:15	8	23	0	0	1	20	5.0
			ATL	23	1	0	1	14:50	-8	24	0	0	0	21	4.8
			Total	54	2	4	6	15:39	0	47	0	0	1	41	4.9
C	49	Ben Maxwell	ATL	12	1	1	2	11:59	-7	9	0	0	0	13	7.7
D	24	Freddy Meyer	ATL	15	1	1	2	15:15	-7	8	0	0	0	11	9.1
C	45 *	Patrice Cormier	ATL	21	1	1	2	9:38	-5	4	0	0	0	27	3.7
D	51 *	Andrey Zubarev	ATL	4	0	1	1	20:04	-4	4	0	0	0	2	0.0
D	38 *	Paul Postma	ATL	1	0	0	0	9:55	0	0	0	0	0	1	0.0
C	48 *	Carl Klingberg	ATL	1	0	0	0	10:22	0	0	0	0	0	0	0.0
D	26	Noah Welch	ATL	2	0	0	0	17:33	-1	0	0	0	0	1	0.0
D	44 *	Arturs Kulda	ATL	2	0	0	0	11:06	-2	2	0	0	0	3	0.0
R	46 *	Spencer Machacek	ATL	10	0	0	0	7:40	-2	0	0	0	0	7	0.0

Goaltending

No.	Goaltender	GPI	Mins	Avg	W	L	OT	EN	SO	GA	SA	S%	G	A	PIM
31	Ondrej Pavelec	58	3225	2.73	21	23	9	8	4	147	1705	.914	0	0	4
50	Chris Mason	33	1682	3.39	13	13	3	6	1	95	882	.892	0	0	4
34 *	Peter Mannino	2	73	4.11	0	0	0	1	0	5	36	.861	0	0	0
	Totals	82	5013	3.14	34	36	12	15	5	262	2638	.901			

General Managers' History

Don Waddell, 1999-2000 to 2009-10; Rick Dudley, 2010-11; Kevin Cheveldayoff, 2011-12.

Captains' History

Kelly Buchberger, 1999-2000; Steve Staios, 2000-01; Ray Ferraro, 2001-02; Shawn McEachern, 2002-03, 2003-04; Scott Mellanby, 2005-06, 2006-07; Bobby Holik, 2007-08; no captain and Ilya Kovalchuk, 2008-09; Ilya Kovalchuk, 2009-10; Andrew Ladd, 2010-11.

Coaching History

Curt Fraser, 1999-2000 to 2001-02; Curt Fraser, Don Waddell and Bob Hartley, 2002-03; Bob Hartley, 2003-04 to 2006-07; Bob Hartley and Don Waddell, 2007-08; John Anderson, 2008-09, 2009-10; Craig Ramsay, 2010-11; Claude Noel, 2011-12.

Kevin Cheveldayoff

Executive Vice President and General Manager

Born: Blaine Lake, Sask., February 4, 1970.

Kevin Cheveldayoff was given his first assignment as general manager of an NHL hockey club when he was named to the position by the Winnipeg Jets on June 8, 2011. Prior to joining the Jets, he had spent two seasons with the Chicago Blackhawks and served as the club's assistant general manager/senior director, hockey operations in 2010-11. During Cheveldayoff's tenure, the Blackhawks won the 2010 Stanley Cup championship, the team's first since 1961.

Before joining the Blackhawks on August 3, 2009, Cheveldayoff spent the previous 12 seasons as the general manager of the Chicago Wolves, guiding the franchise to four league championships, which included the 2002 and 2008 Calder Cup titles in the American Hockey League and the 1998 and 2000 1998 International Hockey League's Turner Cup. Overall, Cheveldayoff was a part of seven league championships during his 15-year management career before being hired in Winnipeg, including two Turner Cup titles in three seasons as the assistant vice president of hockey operations and assistant coach for the Denver and Utah Grizzlies (1994 to 1997).

Cheveldayoff was the architect of 12 Wolves teams that compiled a .615 regular-season winning percentage (544-320-114) and ten postseason berths from 1997 to 2009. Eight of those clubs reached the 100-point mark during the regular season while earning four division titles and six postseason conference championships.

Born in Saskatoon but raised in Blaine Lake, Saskatchewan, Cheveldayoff was originally drafted by the New York Islanders with their first pick (16th overall) in the 1988 NHL Entry Draft. He began his career in the AHL with the Capital District Islanders, serving as the alternate captain from 1991 to 1993. He held the same role with the Salt Lake Golden Eagles in 1993-94, earning the team's "Unsung Hero Award" after racking up a career-high 216 penalty minutes in 73 games. Known as a defensive defenseman during his playing days, a knee injury cut his professional career short after five seasons.

Club Records

Team

(Figures in brackets for season records are games played.)

Most Points	97	2006-07 (82)
Most Wins	43	2006-07 (82)
Most Ties	12	2000-01 (82)
Most Losses	57	1999-2000 (82)
Most Goals	281	2005-06 (82)
Most Goals Against	313	1999-2000 (82)
Fewest Points	39	1999-2000 (82)
Fewest Wins	14	1999-2000 (82)
Fewest Ties	7	1999-2000 (82), 2002-03 (82)
Fewest Losses	28	2006-07 (82)
Fewest Goals	170	1999-2000 (82)
Fewest Goals Against	243	2003-04 (82)

Longest Winning Streak

Overall	6	Mar. 6-16/09, Nov. 19-30/10
Home	7	Mar. 2-18/07
Away	4	Jan. 13-Feb. 7/03, Nov. 3-21/07, Feb. 3-16/09, Nov. 12-Dec. 5/09

Longest Undefeated Streak

Overall	6	Mar. 6-16/09 (6 wins), Nov. 19-30/10 (6 wins)
Home	7	Mar. 2-18/07 (7 wins)
Away	7	Oct. 21-Nov. 13/00 (3 wins, 4 ties)

Longest Losing Streak

Overall	12	Jan. 24-Feb. 20/00
Home	11	Jan. 24-Mar. 16/00
Away	10	Oct. 6-Nov. 18/01, Feb. 16-Mar. 18/08

Longest Winless Streak

Overall	16	Jan. 16-Feb. 20/00 (14 losses, 2 ties)
Home	*17	Jan. 19-Mar. 29/00 (15 losses, 2 ties)
Away	10	Oct. 6-Nov. 18/01 (10 losses)

Most Shutouts, Season	5	2005-06 (82), 2007-08 (82), 2010-11 (82)
Most PIM, Season	1,505	2003-04 (82)
Most Goals, Game	9	Nov. 12/05 (Atl. 9 at Car. 0)

Individual

Most Seasons	8	Ilya Kovalchuk
Most Games	594	Ilya Kovalchuk
Most Goals, Career	328	Ilya Kovalchuk
Most Assists, Career	287	Ilya Kovalchuk
Most Points, Career	615	Ilya Kovalchuk (328G, 287A)
Most PIM, Career	639	Eric Boulton
Most Shutouts, Career	14	Kari Lehtonen
Longest Consecutive Games Streak	252	Vyacheslav Kozlov (Jan. 9/07-Jan. 21/10)
Most Goals, Season	52	Ilya Kovalchuk (2005-06), (2007-08)
Most Assists, Season	69	Marc Savard (2005-06)

Most Points, Season	100	Marian Hossa (2006-07; 43G, 57A)
Most PIM, Season	226	Jeff Odgers (2000-01)
Most Points, Defenseman, Season	51	Tobias Enstrom (2010-11; 10G, 41A)
Most Points, Center, Season	97	Marc Savard (2005-06; 28G, 69A)
Most Points, Right Wing, Season	100	Marian Hossa (2006-07; 43G, 57A)
Most Points, Left Wing, Season	98	Ilya Kovalchuk (2005-06; 52G, 46A)
Most Points, Rookie, Season	67	Dany Heatley (2001-02; 26G, 41A)
Most Shutouts, Season	4	Kari Lehtonen (2006-07), (2007-08), Ondrej Pavelec (2010-11)
Most Goals, Game	4	Pascal Rheaume (Jan. 19/02), Ilya Kovalchuk (Nov. 11/05)
Most Assists, Game	4	Seven times
Most Points, Game	5	Seven times

* NHL Record.

Records include Atlanta Thrashers, 1999-2000 through 2010-11.

Captain Andrew Ladd was the team's top scorer in Atlanta in 2010-11 while defenseman Tobias Enstrom led the club with 41 assists.

All-time Record vs. Other Clubs

Regular Season

	At Home								On Road								Total						
	GP	W	L	T	OL	GF	GA	PTS	GP	W	L	T	OL	GF	GA	PTS	GP	W	L	T	OL	GF	GA	PTS
Anaheim	6	2	4	0	0	13	19	4	7	4	3	0	0	23	22	8	13	6	7	0	0	36	41	12
Boston	22	10	11	0	1	65	65	21	22	6	11	2	3	68	81	17	44	16	22	2	4	133	146	38
Buffalo	22	14	4	1	3	71	65	32	22	9	12	0	1	60	98	19	44	23	16	1	4	131	163	51
Calgary	7	5	1	1	0	21	15	11	5	0	5	0	0	8	21	0	12	5	6	1	0	29	36	11
Carolina	34	7	20	3	4	85	120	21	34	14	14	1	5	106	107	34	68	21	34	4	9	191	227	55
Chicago	7	2	3	0	2	23	23	6	4	1	2	0	1	7	13	3	11	3	5	0	3	30	36	9
Colorado	7	2	3	1	1	15	20	6	8	5	2	0	1	25	26	11	15	7	5	1	2	40	46	17
Columbus	7	3	4	0	0	13	17	6	6	2	3	0	1	12	16	5	13	5	7	0	1	25	33	11
Dallas	6	1	4	0	1	18	26	3	7	1	6	0	0	10	19	2	13	2	10	0	1	28	45	5
Detroit	6	2	4	0	0	22	32	4	7	2	3	0	2	18	23	6	13	4	7	0	2	40	55	10
Edmonton	5	2	3	0	0	8	14	4	7	2	4	1	0	19	27	5	12	4	7	1	0	27	41	9
Florida	34	19	8	4	3	112	93	45	34	18	11	1	4	99	86	41	68	37	19	5	7	211	179	86
Los Angeles	6	3	3	0	0	20	18	6	7	2	5	0	0	23	35	4	13	5	8	0	0	43	53	10
Minnesota	5	2	3	0	0	16	17	4	5	1	3	1	0	9	15	3	10	3	6	1	0	25	32	7
Montreal	22	8	10	2	2	45	56	20	22	7	13	0	2	53	75	16	44	15	23	2	4	98	131	36
Nashville	8	4	1	1	2	23	21	11	7	2	5	0	0	19	27	4	15	6	6	1	2	42	48	15
New Jersey	22	6	13	2	1	52	77	15	22	9	11	1	1	49	64	20	44	15	24	3	2	101	141	35
NY Islanders	22	8	11	2	1	67	83	19	22	11	10	0	1	62	76	23	44	19	21	2	2	129	159	42
NY Rangers	22	10	10	0	2	63	71	22	22	14	6	1	1	68	59	30	44	24	16	1	3	131	130	52
Ottawa	22	10	11	1	0	79	79	21	22	8	13	1	0	61	93	17	44	18	24	2	0	140	172	38
Philadelphia	22	5	14	1	2	49	76	13	22	6	13	2	1	62	85	15	44	11	27	3	3	111	161	28
Phoenix	6	1	3	0	2	12	20	4	8	0	6	1	1	15	29	2	14	1	9	1	3	27	49	6
Pittsburgh	22	7	13	0	2	61	74	16	22	4	15	0	3	54	88	11	44	11	28	0	5	115	162	27
St. Louis	8	3	4	1	0	23	26	7	6	2	3	0	1	11	19	5	14	5	7	1	1	34	45	12
San Jose	6	1	4	1	0	11	20	3	7	1	5	1	0	15	26	3	13	2	9	2	0	26	46	6
Tampa Bay	34	18	8	3	5	109	94	44	34	10	17	1	6	84	126	27	68	28	25	4	11	193	220	71
Toronto	21	8	11	0	2	44	79	18	21	8	11	1	1	60	77	18	42	16	22	1	3	104	156	36
Vancouver	6	2	4	0	0	17	20	4	5	1	3	1	0	9	17	3	11	3	7	1	0	26	37	7
Washington	34	18	11	2	2	102	100	40	34	9	18	3	4	97	124	25	68	27	30	5	6	199	224	65
Totals	**451**	**183**	**204**	**26**	**38**	**1259**	**1440**	**430**	**451**	**159**	**233**	**19**	**40**	**1206**	**1574**	**377**	**902**	**342**	**437**	**45**	**78**	**2465**	**3014**	**807**

Playoffs

	Series	W	L	GP	W	L	T	GF	GA	Last Mtg.	Rnd.	Result
NY Rangers	1	0	1	4	0	4	0	6	17	2007	CQF	L 0-4
Totals	**1**	**0**	**1**	**4**	**0**	**4**	**0**	**6**	**17**			

Playoff Results 2011-2007

Year	Round	Opponent	Result	GF	GA
2007	CQF	NY Rangers	L 0-4	6	17

Abbreviations: Round: CQF – conference quarter-final.

2010-11 Results

Oct.	8	Washington	4-2		Jan.	2	at Montreal	4-3*
	9	at Tampa Bay	3-5			5	at Florida	3-2
	12	at Los Angeles	1-3			7	Toronto	3-9
	15	at Anaheim	5-4†			9	at Carolina	3-4*
	16	at San Jose	4-2			14	Philadelphia	2-5
	20	Buffalo	1-4			15	at Dallas	1-6
	22	Tampa Bay	2-5			17	at Florida	3-2†
	23	at Washington	3-4*			20	Tampa Bay	2-3†
	27	at NY Rangers	6-4			22	NY Rangers	2-3†
	29	Buffalo	4-3*			23	at Tampa Bay	1-7
	30	at St. Louis	3-4†			26	Washington	1-0
Nov.	3	at Florida	4-3		Feb.	1	NY Islanders	1-4
	4	Columbus	0-3			3	Calgary	2-4
	6	Chicago	4-5†			5	at Carolina	3-4*
	9	at Ottawa	2-5			7	at Toronto	4-5
	11	Minnesota	5-1			11	NY Rangers	3-2
	13	Pittsburgh	2-3			13	Carolina	2-3
	14	at Washington	4-6			17	at Phoenix	3-4
	17	Florida	1-2			19	at Edmonton	3-5
	19	Washington	5-0			23	at Buffalo	1-4
	21	NY Islanders	2-1*			25	Florida	1-2†
	24	Detroit	5-1			27	Toronto	3-2*
	26	Montreal	3-0		Mar.	1	Montreal	1-3
	28	Boston	4-1			3	Ottawa	1-3
	30	at Colorado	3-2*			5	Florida	4-3*
Dec.	2	at Pittsburgh	2-3			9	at Carolina	3-2*
	4	at Washington	3-1			11	New Jersey	2-3*
	6	Nashville	3-2*			12	at Philadelphia	5-4*
	10	Colorado	2-4			15	at New Jersey	2-4
	11	at NY Islanders	2-3			17	Philadelphia	4-3*
	13	at Ottawa	4-3*			19	at Buffalo	2-8
	15	at Tampa Bay	1-2†			24	at NY Islanders	2-1
	16	Carolina	2-3†			25	Vancouver	1-3
	18	New Jersey	7-1			27	Ottawa	5-4†
	20	at Toronto	6-3			29	at Montreal	1-3
	21	St. Louis	2-4			31	at Philadelphia	1-0
	23	at Boston	1-4		Apr.	2	at Boston	2-3
	26	Tampa Bay	2-3*			5	at Nashville	3-6
	28	at Pittsburgh	3-6			7	at NY Rangers	3-0
	30	Boston	3-2†			8	Carolina	1-6
	31	at New Jersey	1-3			10	Pittsburgh	2-5

* – Overtime † – Shootout

Entry Draft Selections 2011-1999

Name in bold denotes played in NHL.

2011
Pick
7	Mark Scheifele
67	Adam Lowry
78	Brennan Serville
119	Zachary Yuen
149	Austen Brassard
157	Jason Kasdorf
187	Aaron Harstad

2010
Pick
8	**Alexander Burmistrov**
87	Julian Melchiori
101	Ivan Telegin
128	Fredrik Pettersson-Wentzel
150	Yasin Cisse
155	Kendall McFaull
160	Tanner Lane
169	Sebastian Owuya
199	Peter Stoykewych

2009
Pick
4	**Evander Kane**
34	**Carl Klingberg**
45	**Jeremy Morin**
117	Edward Pasquale
120	Ben Chiarot
125	Cody Sol
155	Jimmy Bubnick
185	Levko Koper
203	Jordan Samuels-Thomas

2008
Pick
3	**Zach Bogosian**
29	Daultan Leveille
64	Danick Paquette
94	Vinny Saponari
124	Nicklas Lasu
154	Chris Carrozzi
184	Zach Redmond

2007
Pick
67	**Spencer Machacek**
115	Niclas Lucenius
175	John Albert
205	**Paul Postma**

2006
Pick
12	**Bryan Little**
43	Riley Holzapfel
80	Michael Forney
135	Alex Kangas
165	Jonas Enlund
195	Jesse Martin
200	**Arturs Kulda**
210	Will O'Neill

2005
Pick
16	Alex Bourret
41	**Ondrej Pavelec**
49	Chad Denny
53	Andrew Kozek
116	**Jordan Smotherman**
135	Tomas Pospisil
187	**Andrei Zubarev**
207	Myles Stoesz

2004
Pick
10	**Boris Valabik**
40	**Grant Lewis**
76	**Scott Lehman**
106	Chad Painchaud
142	Juraj Gracik
186	Dan Turple
204	Miikka Tuomainen
237	Mitch Carefoot
270	Matt Siddall

2003
Pick
8	**Braydon Coburn**
110	Jim Sharrow
116	**Guillaume Desbiens**
136	Michael Vannelli
145	**Brett Sterling**
175	Mike Hamilton
203	Denis Loginov
239	**Tobias Enstrom**
269	Rylan Kaip

2002
Pick
2	**Kari Lehtonen**
30	**Jim Slater**
116	**Patrick Dwyer**
124	Lane Manson
144	Paul Flache
167	Brad Schell
198	**Nathan Oystrick**
230	Colton Fretter
236	Tyler Boldt
257	Pauli Levokari

2001
Pick
1	**Ilya Kovalchuk**
80	**Michael Garnett**
100	Brian Sipotz
112	Milan Gajic
135	**Colin Stuart**
189	**Pasi Nurminen**
199	Matt Suderman
201	Colin FitzRandolph
262	Mario Cartelli

2000
Pick
2	**Dany Heatley**
31	Ilja Nikulin
42	Libor Ustrnul
107	Carl Mallette
108	Blake Robson
147	Matt McRae
168	Zdenek Smid
178	Jeff Dwyer
180	**Darcy Hordichuk**
230	Samu Isosalo
242	Evan Nielsen
244	Eric Bowen
288	Mark McRae
290	Simon Gamache

1999
Pick
1	**Patrik Stefan**
30	**Luke Sellars**
68	**Zdenek Blatny**
98	David Kaczowka
99	Rob Zepp
128	**Derek MacKenzie**
159	Yuri Dobryshkin
188	Stephen Baby
217	**Garnet Exelby**
245	**Tommi Santala**
246	Raymond DiLauro

Claude Noel
Coach

Born: Kirkland Lake, Ont., October 31, 1955.

Claude Noel was hired on June 24, 2011, as the first head coach of the Winnipeg Jets and the sixth head coach in the history of the franchise dating back to the inception of the Atlanta Thrashers in 1999. Noel was the former coach of the American Hockey League's Manitoba Moose, where he spent the 2010-11 season. Previously, Noel had spent three seasons with the Columbus Blue Jackets from 2007 to 2010. He began the 2009-10 season as an assistant coach before taking over from Ken Hitchcock as interim head coach on February 3, 2010.

Before his time with the Blue Jackets, Noel spent four seasons as head coach of the Milwaukee Admirals, the AHL affiliate of the Nashville Predators. During that time he recorded three 100-point seasons, won two West Division titles and made two appearances in the Calder Cup Finals. During the 2003-04 season, the club compiled a 46-24-10 record and went 16-6 in the playoffs en route to capturing the organization's first Calder Cup championship. Noel was subsequently named the coach of the year when he was honored with the Louis A.R. Pieri Memorial Award.

Noel made his coaching debut in the ECHL with the Roanoke Valley Rebels in 1990-91 and served as head coach and director of hockey operations for the ECHL's Dayton Bombers from 1991 to 1993. In 1993 he joined the Kalamazoo Wings (later the Michigan K-Wings), the International Hockey League affiliate of the Dallas Stars, as an assistant coach. He succeeded then coach Ken Hitchcock behind the bench during the 1995-96 season and served in that capacity through the 1997-98 campaign. From 1998 to 2002 he was an assistant coach with the Milwaukee Admirals and in 2002-03 was named ECHL coach of the year with the Toledo Storm before returning to Milwaukee as head coach prior to the 2003-04 season.

As a player, Noel appeared in seven games with the Washington Capitals during the 1979-80 season. He spent most of his playing career in the AHL and IHL and was named the IHL's Most Valuable Player in 1982-83 after leading the Toledo Goaldiggers to the Turner Cup championship. He also won a Calder Cup as a member of the Hershey Bears in 1979-80. Noel wrapped up his playing career with Milwaukee in 1987-88. Noel was born in Kirkland Lake, Ontario and was raised in Virginiatown and North Bay, Ontario. He moved away from home at age 20 to play junior hockey for the Kitchener Rangers.

Coaching Record

Season	Team	League	GC	W	L	O/T	GC	W	L	T
			Regular Season				**Playoffs**			
1990-91	Roanoke	ECHL	64	26	31	7	....	....	....	....
1991-92	Dayton	ECHL	64	32	26	6	3	0	3	....
1992-93	Dayton	ECHL	64	35	23	6	3	0	3	....
1995-96	Kalamazoo	IHL	42	21	14	7	10	6	4	....
1996-97	Michigan	IHL	82	31	44	7	4	1	3	....
1997-98	Michigan	IHL	82	36	39	7	4	1	3	....
2002-03	Toledo	ECHL	72	47	15	10	7	4	3	....
2003-04	Milwaukee	AHL	80	46	24	10	22	16	6	....
2004-05	Milwaukee	AHL	80	47	24	9	7	3	4	....
2005-06	Milwaukee	AHL	80	49	21	10	21	14	7	....
2006-07	Milwaukee	AHL	80	41	25	14	4	0	4	....
2009-10	**Columbus**	**NHL**	24	10	8	6	....	....	....	....
2010-11	Manitoba	AHL	80	43	30	7	14	7	7	....
	NHL Totals		24	10	8	6	....	....	....	....

Club Directory

MTS Centre

Winnipeg Jets
MTS Centre
260 Hargrave Street
Winnipeg, Manitoba, R3C 5S5
Phone 204/987-7835
FAX 204/926-5555
www.winnipegjets.com
Twitter @NHLJets
Capacity 15,015

Senior Management
Chairman and Governor	Mark Chipman
President and Chief Executive Officer	Jim Ludlow
Exec. V.P. and Chief Financial Officer	John Olfert
Exec. V.P. and General Manager	Kevin Cheveldayoff
Sr. V.P. and Director Hockey Ops/Asst. G.M.	Craig Heisinger
Sr. V.P. and General Manager – MTS Centre	Kevin Donnelly
Sr. V.P., Sales & Marketing	Norva Riddell

Hockey Operations
Exec. V.P. and General Manager	Kevin Cheveldayoff
Sr. V.P. and Director Hockey Ops/Asst. G.M.	Craig Heisinger
Assistant to the General Manager	Larry Simmons
Executive Assistant, Hockey Ops	Sandra Smith
Head Coach	Claude Noel
Assistant Coaches	Charlie Huddy, Pascal Vincent
Goaltending Coach	Wade Flaherty
Video Coach	Tony Borgford
Head Equipment Manager	Jason McMaster
Assistant Equipment Managers	Mark Grehan, Mike Flaman
Head Athletic Therapist	Rob Milette
Assistant Athletic Therapist	Brad Shaw
Asst. Athletic Therapist/Strength & Conditioning	Lee Stubbs
Manager, Hockey Ops & Team Services	Ryan Bowness

Scouting Staff
Director, Amateur Scouting	Marcel Comeau
Head Scout	Mark Hillier
Pro Scouts	Mark Dobson, John Perpich, Jack Birch, Bruce Southern
Amateur Scouts	Tavis MacMillan, Evgeny Bogdanovich, Freddie Jax, Pat Carmichael, Chris Snell, Keith Sullivan, Scott Scoville
Director, Player Development	Jimmy Roy

Medical Staff
Head Physician	Dr. Peter MacDonald
Assistant Physicians	Dr. Greg Stranges, Dr. Jamie Dubberley
Primary Care	Dr. Mike MacKay, Dr. Swee Teo
Team Dentist	Dr. Gene Solmundson

Marketing & Communications
Senior Director Corporate Communications	Scott Brown
Senior Director Marketing & Brand Management	Dorian Morphy
Director Event Production	Kyle Balharry
Communications Coordinators	Christina Caligiuri, Kalen Qually
Manager Marketing	TBD
Managers, Visual Media	Steve Godkin, Curtis Robson
Manager, Digital Media	Eric Postma
Web Content Coordinator	TBD
Graphic Designers	Josh Dudych, Jesse Greenwood

Sales
Director Ticket Administration & CRM	Mitch Brennan
Director Ticket Sales & Service	Linzy Jones
Director Corporate Partnerships	Jeff Mager

Retail Operations
Director Retail Development	Ryan Rogers
Director Retail Operations	Dave Blackmore
Assistant Manager Retail Operations	Shane Tucker

Finance
Senior Director Finance	Lorna Daniels
Senior Director Business Operations	Audrey Gan
Controller	Lindsay Yurick

Event Management
Director, Event Management & Security	Kim Boulet
Director, Event Marketing	Alayne Nott
Manager, Client Services	Joanne Harder
Sr. Manager Broadcast Services & Event Production	Lloyd Fox
Manager, Professional Audio & Video Services	Brian Johnson
Manager, Event Production	Kevin Clifford

Information Systems
Director Information Technology	Dan Gill
Systems Administrator	Darryl Elyk

Foundation
Foundation Coordinator	Katie Dicks

Building Operations
Senior Director, Facility Operations	Ed Meichsner
Chief Engineer	Derek King

2010-11 Final Standings

Standings

Abbreviations: GP - games played; **W -** wins; **L -** losses; **OTL -** overtime losses; **SOL -** shootout losses; **GF -** goals for; **GA -** goals against; **PTS -** points; **% -** winning percentage.

Note: teams receive two points for a Win (W), one point for an Overtime or Shootout Loss (OT)

EASTERN CONFERENCE

Northeast Division

		GP	W	L	OT	GF	GA	PTS
Boston	(3)	82	46	25	11	246	195	103
Montreal	(6)	82	44	30	8	216	209	96
Buffalo	(7)	82	43	29	10	245	229	96
Toronto		82	37	34	11	218	251	85
Ottawa		82	32	40	10	192	250	74

Atlantic Division

		GP	W	L	OT	GF	GA	PTS
Philadelphia	(2)	82	47	23	12	259	223	106
Pittsburgh	(4)	82	49	25	8	238	199	106
NY Rangers	(8)	82	44	33	5	233	198	93
New Jersey		82	38	39	5	174	209	81
NY Islanders		82	30	39	13	229	264	73

Southeast Division

		GP	W	L	OT	GF	GA	PTS
Washington	(1)	82	48	23	11	224	197	107
Tampa Bay	(5)	82	46	25	11	247	240	103
Carolina		82	40	31	11	236	239	91
Atlanta		82	34	36	12	223	269	80
Florida		82	30	40	12	195	229	72

WESTERN CONFERENCE

Central Division

		GP	W	L	OT	GF	GA	PTS
Detroit	(3)	82	47	25	10	261	241	104
Nashville	(5)	82	44	27	11	219	194	99
Chicago	(8)	82	44	29	9	258	225	97
St. Louis		82	38	33	11	240	234	87
Columbus		82	34	35	13	215	258	81

Pacific Division

		GP	W	L	OT	GF	GA	PTS
San Jose	(2)	82	48	25	9	248	213	105
Anaheim	(4)	82	47	30	5	239	235	99
Phoenix	(6)	82	43	26	13	231	226	99
Los Angeles	(7)	82	46	30	6	219	198	98
Dallas		82	42	29	11	227	233	95

Northwest Division

		GP	W	L	OT	GF	GA	PTS
Vancouver	(1)	82	54	19	9	262	185	117
Calgary		82	41	29	12	250	237	94
Minnesota		82	39	35	8	206	233	86
Colorado		82	30	44	8	227	288	68
Edmonton		82	25	45	12	193	269	62

INDIVIDUAL LEADERS

Goal Scoring

Player	Team	GP	G
Corey Perry	Anaheim	82	50
Steven Stamkos	Tampa Bay	82	45
Jarome Iginla	Calgary	82	43
Daniel Sedin	Vancouver	82	41
Ryan Kesler	Vancouver	82	41
Patrick Marleau	San Jose	82	37
Jeff Carter	Philadelphia	80	36
Patrick Sharp	Chicago	74	34
Michael Grabner*	NY Islanders	76	34
Danny Briere	Philadelphia	77	34
Bobby Ryan	Anaheim	82	34
Eric Staal	Carolina	81	33
Brenden Morrow	Dallas	82	33

Assists

Player	Team	GP	A
Henrik Sedin	Vancouver	82	75
Martin St. Louis	Tampa Bay	82	68
Daniel Sedin	Vancouver	82	63
Ryan Getzlaf	Anaheim	67	57
Henrik Zetterberg	Detroit	80	56
Alex Ovechkin	Washington	79	53
Mike Ribeiro	Dallas	82	52
Claude Giroux	Philadelphia	82	51
Lubomir Visnovsky	Anaheim	81	50
Brad Richards	Dallas	72	49
Teemu Selanne	Anaheim	73	49
David Krejci	Boston	75	49
Joe Thornton	San Jose	80	49

Power-play Goals

Player	Team	GP	PP
Daniel Sedin	Vancouver	82	18
Steven Stamkos	Tampa Bay	82	17
Teemu Selanne	Anaheim	73	16
Ryan Kesler	Vancouver	82	15
Jarome Iginla	Calgary	82	14
Corey Perry	Anaheim	82	14
5 players tied with			12

Shorthand Goals

Player	Team	GP	SH
Frans Nielsen	NY Islanders	71	7
Michael Grabner*	NY Islanders	76	6
Brad Marchand*	Boston	77	5
Brandon Prust	NY Rangers	82	5
5 players tied with			4

Game-winning Goals

Player	Team	GP	GW
Alex Ovechkin	Washington	79	11
Corey Perry	Anaheim	82	11
Daniel Sedin	Vancouver	82	10
Ilya Kovalchuk	New Jersey	81	9
Patrick Marleau	San Jose	82	9
Erik Cole	Carolina	82	9

Shots

Player	Team	GP	S
Alex Ovechkin	Washington	79	367
Dustin Byfuglien	Atlanta	81	347
Jeff Carter	Philadelphia	80	335
Phil Kessel	Toronto	82	325
Henrik Zetterberg	Detroit	80	306

Shooting Percentage

(minimum 82 shots)

Player	Team	GP	G	S	%
Sergei Kostitsyn	Nashville	77	23	93	24.7
Sidney Crosby	Pittsburgh	41	32	161	19.9
Lauri Korpikoski	Phoenix	79	19	103	18.4
Alex Tanguay	Calgary	79	22	120	18.3
David Jones	Colorado	77	27	153	17.6

Plus/Minus

Player	Team	GP	+/-
Zdeno Chara	Boston	81	33
Kevin Bieksa	Vancouver	66	32
Toni Lydman	Anaheim	78	32
David Backes	St. Louis	82	32
Adam McQuaid*	Boston	67	30
Andrej Meszaros	Philadelphia	81	30
Daniel Sedin	Vancouver	82	30
Matt Carle	Philadelphia	82	30

Anaheim's Corey Perry was the NHL's only 50-goal scorer in 2010-11 and he finished third in the league with 98 points. Perry's 11 game-winning goals tied Washington's Alex Ovechkin for top spot in the NHL and he was also among the league leaders in power-play goals.

Individual Leaders

Abbreviations: GP – games played; **G** – goals; **A** – assists; **Pts** – points; **+/–** – difference between Goals For (**GF**) scored when a player is on the ice with his team at even strength or shorthanded and Goals Against (**GA**) scored when the same player is on the ice with his team at even strength or on a power play; **PIM** – penalties in minutes; **PP** – power play goals; **SH** – shorthanded goals; **GW** – game-winning goals; **S** – shots on goal; **%** – percentage of shots on goal resulting in goals.

Individual Scoring Leaders for Art Ross Trophy

Player	Team	GP	G	A	Pts	+/–	PIM	PP	SH	GW	S	%
Daniel Sedin	Vancouver	82	41	63	104	30	32	18	0	10	266	15.4
Martin St. Louis	Tampa Bay	82	31	68	99	0	12	4	0	7	254	12.2
Corey Perry	Anaheim	82	50	48	98	9	104	14	4	11	290	17.2
Henrik Sedin	Vancouver	82	19	75	94	26	40	8	0	4	157	12.1
Steven Stamkos	Tampa Bay	82	45	46	91	3	74	17	0	8	272	16.5
Jarome Iginla	Calgary	82	43	43	86	0	40	14	0	6	289	14.9
Alex Ovechkin	Washington	79	32	53	85	24	41	7	0	11	367	8.7
Teemu Selanne	Anaheim	73	31	49	80	6	49	16	0	5	213	14.6
Henrik Zetterberg	Detroit	80	24	56	80	-1	40	10	0	3	306	7.8
Brad Richards	Dallas	72	28	49	77	1	24	7	0	3	272	10.3
Eric Staal	Carolina	81	33	43	76	-10	72	12	3	8	296	11.1
Jonathan Toews	Chicago	80	32	44	76	25	26	10	1	8	233	13.7
Claude Giroux	Philadelphia	82	25	51	76	20	47	8	3	5	169	14.8
Ryan Getzlaf	Anaheim	67	19	57	76	14	35	7	0	4	117	16.2
Ryan Kesler	Vancouver	82	41	32	73	24	66	15	3	7	260	15.8
Patrick Marleau	San Jose	82	37	36	73	-3	16	11	2	9	279	13.3
Thomas Vanek	Buffalo	80	32	41	73	2	24	11	0	5	238	13.4
Patrick Kane	Chicago	73	27	46	73	7	28	5	0	2	216	12.5
Loui Eriksson	Dallas	79	27	46	73	10	8	10	1	6	179	15.1
Anze Kopitar	Los Angeles	75	25	48	73	25	20	6	1	6	233	10.7
Patrick Sharp	Chicago	74	34	37	71	-1	38	12	2	6	268	12.7
Bobby Ryan	Anaheim	82	34	37	71	15	61	5	1	5	270	12.6
Mike Ribeiro	Dallas	82	19	52	71	-4	28	7	0	4	161	11.8

Defencemen Scoring Leaders

Player	Team	GP	G	A	Pts	+/–	PIM	PP	SH	GW	S	%
Lubomir Visnovsky	Anaheim	81	18	50	68	18	24	5	0	4	152	11.8
Nicklas Lidstrom	Detroit	82	16	46	62	-2	20	7	0	1	175	9.1
Keith Yandle	Phoenix	82	11	48	59	12	68	3	0	0	199	5.5
Dustin Byfuglien	Atlanta	81	20	33	53	-2	93	8	0	6	347	5.8
Tobias Enstrom	Atlanta	72	10	41	51	-10	54	6	0	0	113	8.8
James Wisniewski	NYI-Mtl.	75	10	41	51	-14	38	7	0	2	158	6.3
Christian Ehrhoff	Vancouver	79	14	36	50	19	52	6	0	3	209	6.7
Dan Boyle	San Jose	76	9	41	50	2	67	4	0	2	199	4.5
Kris Letang	Pittsburgh	82	8	42	50	15	101	4	0	2	236	3.4
Shea Weber	Nashville	82	16	32	48	7	56	6	1	3	254	6.3
Brent Seabrook	Chicago	82	9	39	48	0	47	5	0	1	135	6.7
Brian Rafalski	Detroit	63	4	44	48	11	22	0	0	0	106	3.8
Tomas Kaberle	Tor.-Bos.	82	4	43	47	4	18	0	0	1	130	3.1
Brent Burns	Minnesota	80	17	29	46	-10	98	8	0	3	170	10
Alex Goligoski	Pit.-Dal.	83	14	32	46	20	40	7	0	4	162	8.6
John-Michael Liles	Colorado	76	6	40	46	-9	35	3	0	0	163	3.7
Erik Karlsson	Ottawa	75	13	32	45	-30	50	4	0	4	182	7.1
Duncan Keith	Chicago	82	7	38	45	-1	22	3	1	1	173	4.0
Zdeno Chara	Boston	81	14	30	44	33	88	8	1	2	264	5.3
Alex Pietrangelo	St. Louis	79	11	32	43	18	19	4	0	1	161	6.8
Kevin Shattenkirk*	Col.-St.L.	72	9	34	43	-4	36	3	0	2	108	8.3
Mark Giordano	Calgary	82	8	35	43	-8	67	5	0	1	165	4.8

CONSECUTIVE SCORING STREAKS

Goals

Games	Player	Team	G
6	Michael Grabner*	NY Islanders	10
6	Dan Cleary	Detroit	8
6	Jamie Benn	Dallas	6
5	Corey Perry	Anaheim	8
5	Jonathan Toews	Chicago	7
5	Danny Briere	Philadelphia	6
5	Curtis Glencross	Calgary	6
5	Sidney Crosby	Pittsburgh	6
5	Sidney Crosby	Pittsburgh	6
5	Marian Hossa	Chicago	5
5	Brenden Morrow	Dallas	5
5	Patrick Sharp	Chicago	5
5	Sergei Kostitsyn	Nashville	5

Assists

Games	Player	Team	A
9	Keith Yandle	Phoenix	12
9	John-Michael Liles	Colorado	11
9	Loui Eriksson	Dallas	10
8	Daniel Sedin	Vancouver	10
8	R.J. Umberger	Columbus	8
7	Dustin Brown	Los Angeles	9
7	Martin St. Louis	Tampa Bay	8
7	Alex Tanguay	Calgary	8
7	Pavel Datsyuk	Detroit	7

Points

Games	Player	Team	G	A	PTS
25	Sidney Crosby	Pittsburgh	26	24	50
12	Ilya Kovalchuk	New Jersey	7	7	14
11	Henrik Zetterberg	Detroit	6	10	16
11	Mike Ribeiro	Dallas	4	11	15
11	Sergei Kostitsyn	Nashville	7	8	15
11	Nicklas Lidstrom	Detroit	2	12	14
11	Justin Williams	Los Angeles	7	7	14
10	Corey Perry	Anaheim	14	8	22
10	Joe Pavelski	San Jose	6	13	19
10	Keith Yandle	Phoenix	3	12	15
10	Daniel Sedin	Vancouver	4	10	14
10	Jamie Benn	Dallas	8	6	14
10	Pavel Datsyuk	Detroit	4	9	13
10	R.J. Umberger	Columbus	3	10	13
10	Alexandre Burrows	Vancouver	8	4	12
10	Loui Eriksson	Dallas	2	10	12
10	Phil Kessel	Toronto	4	7	11

A year after his brother won the Art Ross Trophy, Daniel Sedin made himself and Henrik just the third set of siblings in NHL history to both lead the league in scoring. They are the first to do so in back-to-back seasons.

Individual Rookie Scoring Leaders

Player	Team	GP	G	A	Pts	+/-	PIM	PP	SH	GW	S	%
Jeff Skinner	Carolina	82	31	32	63	3	46	6	0	2	215	14.4
Logan Couture	San Jose	79	32	24	56	18	41	10	0	8	253	12.6
Michael Grabner	NY Islanders	76	34	18	52	13	10	2	6	3	228	14.9
Tyler Ennis	Buffalo	82	20	29	49	0	30	5	0	1	210	9.5
Derek Stepan	NY Rangers	82	21	24	45	8	20	3	0	3	166	12.7
Jordan Eberle	Edmonton	69	18	25	43	-12	22	4	2	5	158	11.4
Kevin Shattenkirk	Col.-St.L.	72	9	34	43	4-	36	3	0	2	108	8.3
Taylor Hall	Edmonton	65	22	20	42	-9	27	8	0	4	186	11.8
Brad Marchand	Boston	77	21	20	41	25	51	2	5	2	149	14.1
Cam Fowler	Anaheim	76	10	30	40	-25	20	6	0	3	123	8.1
P.K. Subban	Montreal	77	14	24	38	8-	124	9	0	3	197	7.1
Bryan Bickell	Chicago	78	17	20	37	6	40	2	0	2	130	13.1
John Carlson	Washington	82	7	30	37	21	44	1	0	3	144	4.9
Magnus Paajarvi	Edmonton	80	15	19	34	-13	16	3	0	0	180	8.3
Jamie McBain	Carolina	76	7	23	30	8-	32	1	0	2	95	7.4
3 players tied with					27							

Goal Scoring

Player	Team	GP	G
Michael Grabner	NY Islanders	76	34
Logan Couture	San Jose	79	32
Jeff Skinner	Carolina	82	31
Taylor Hall	Edmonton	65	22
Brad Marchand	Boston	77	21
Derek Stepan	NY Rangers	82	21
Tyler Ennis	Buffalo	82	20
Jordan Eberle	Edmonton	69	18
Bryan Bickell	Chicago	78	17

Assists

Player	Team	GP	A
Kevin Shattenkirk	Col.-St.L.	72	34
Jeff Skinner	Carolina	82	32
Cam Fowler	Anaheim	76	30
John Carlson	Washington	82	30
Tyler Ennis	Buffalo	82	29
Jordan Eberle	Edmonton	69	25
P.K. Subban	Montreal	77	24
Logan Couture	San Jose	79	24
Derek Stepan	NY Rangers	82	24

Power-play Goals

Player	Team	GP	PP
Logan Couture	San Jose	79	10
P.K. Subban	Montreal	77	9
Taylor Hall	Edmonton	65	8
Cam Fowler	Anaheim	76	6
Jeff Skinner	Carolina	82	6
Tyler Ennis	Buffalo	82	5

Shorthand Goals

Player	Team	GP	SH
Michael Grabner	NY Islanders	76	6
Brad Marchand	Boston	77	5
Brandon McMillan	Anaheim	60	2
Jordan Eberle	Edmonton	69	2
Marcus Johansson	Washington	69	1
Philippe Dupuis	Colorado	74	1

Game-winning Goals

Player	Team	GP	GW
Logan Couture	San Jose	79	8
Jordan Eberle	Edmonton	69	5
Taylor Hall	Edmonton	65	4
Bobby Butler	Ottawa	36	3
Mark Letestu	Pittsburgh	64	3
Michael Grabner	NY Islanders	76	3
Cam Fowler	Anaheim	76	3
P.K. Subban	Montreal	77	3
John Carlson	Washington	82	3
Derek Stepan	NY Rangers	82	3

Shots

Player	Team	GP	S
Logan Couture	San Jose	79	253
Michael Grabner	NY Islanders	76	228
Jeff Skinner	Carolina	82	215
Tyler Ennis	Buffalo	82	210
P.K. Subban	Montreal	77	197

Shooting Percentage

(minimum 82 shots)

Player	Team	GP	G	S	%
Michael Grabner	NY Islanders	76	34	228	14.9
Jeff Skinner	Carolina	82	31	215	14.4
Brad Marchand	Boston	77	21	149	14.1
Bryan Bickell	Chicago	78	17	130	13.1
Derek Stepan	NY Rangers	82	21	166	12.7
Marcus Johansson	Washington	69	13	102	12.7

Plus/Minus

Player	Team	GP	+/-
Adam McQuaid	Boston	67	30
Brad Marchand	Boston	77	25
John Carlson	Washington	82	21
Michael Sauer	NY Rangers	76	20
Logan Couture	San Jose	79	18

Three-or-More-Goal Games

Player	Team	Date	Final Score	G
Daniel Alfredsson	Ottawa	Oct. 22	Ott. 4 Buf. 2	3
Patrice Bergeron	Boston	Jan. 11	Ott. 0 Bos. 6	3
Eric Boulton	Atlanta	Dec. 18	N.J. 1 Atl. 7	3
Rene Bourque	Calgary	Oct. 22	Cgy. 6 CBJ 2	3
Ryan Callahan	NY Rangers	Mar. 6	Phi. 0 NYR 7	4
Matt Calvert*	Columbus	Feb. 25	Phx. 3 CBJ 5	3
Jeff Carter	Philadelphia	Nov. 11	Phi. 8 Car. 1	3
Zdeno Chara	Boston	Jan. 17	Car. 0 Bos. 7	3
Sidney Crosby	Pittsburgh	Nov. 27	Cgy. 1 Pit. 4	3
Sidney Crosby	Pittsburgh	Dec. 2	Atl. 2 Pit. 3	3
J.P. Dumont	Nashville	Jan. 18	Nsh. 5 Phx. 2	3
Patrick Eaves	Detroit	Dec. 29	Det. 7 Dal. 3	3
Patrik Elias	New Jersey	Apr. 1	Phi. 2 N.J. 4	3
Vernon Fiddler	Phoenix	Nov. 12	Cgy. 4 Phx. 5	3
Tomas Fleischmann	Colorado	Dec. 15	Col. 4 Chi. 3	3
Johan Franzen	Detroit	Feb. 2	Det. 7 Ott. 5	5
Marian Gaborik	NY Rangers	Nov. 14	Edm. 2 NYR 8	3
Marian Gaborik	NY Rangers	Dec. 2	NYR 6 NYI 5	3
Marian Gaborik	NY Rangers	Jan. 19	Tor. 0 NYR 7	4
Blake Geoffrion*	Nashville	Mar. 20	Nsh. 4 Buf. 3	3
Michael Grabner*	NY Islanders	Feb. 13	NYI 7 Buf. 6	3
Taylor Hall*	Edmonton	Feb. 19	Atl. 3 Edm. 5	3
Kristian Huselius	Columbus	Dec. 16	CBJ 3 Edm. 6	3
Jarome Iginla	Calgary	Nov. 19	Chi. 2 Cgy. 7	3
Jarome Iginla	Calgary	Apr. 6	Edm. 1 Cgy. 6	3
Ed Jovanovski	Phoenix	Nov. 3	Nsh. 3 Phx. 4	3
Chris Kelly	Ottawa	Dec. 5	Ott. 3 NYR 1	3
Ryan Kesler	Vancouver	Dec. 15	CBJ 2 Van. 3	3
Ryan Kesler	Vancouver	Jan. 7	Edm. 1 Van. 6	3
Ryan Kesler	Vancouver	Apr. 7	Min. 0 Van. 5	3
Anze Kopitar	Los Angeles	Mar. 11	L.A. 4 CBJ 2	3
Chris Kunitz	Pittsburgh	Jan. 5	T.B. 1 Pit. 8	3
Ville Leino	Philadelphia	Mar. 12	Atl. 5 Phi. 4	3
Nicklas Lidstrom	Detroit	Dec. 15	St.L. 2 Det. 5	3
Milan Lucic	Boston	Nov. 18	Fla. 0 Bos. 4	3
Evgeni Malkin	Pittsburgh	Nov. 13	Pit. 4 Atl. 2	3
Jay McClement	St. Louis	Oct. 30	Atl. 3 St.L. 4	3
Matt Moulson	NY Islanders	Feb. 21	Fla. 1 NYI 5	3
Rick Nash	Columbus	Nov. 20	CBJ 3 S.J. 0	3
Alex Ovechkin	Washington	Jan. 22	Wsh. 4 Tor. 1	3
Corey Perry	Anaheim	Dec. 12	Min. 2 Ana. 6	3
Corey Perry	Anaheim	Feb. 5	Phx. 3 Ana. 6	3
Corey Perry	Anaheim	Apr. 6	S.J. 2 Ana. 6	3
Teddy Purcell	Tampa Bay	Feb. 23	Phx. 3 T.B. 8	3
Mason Raymond	Vancouver	Dec. 1	Van. 7 Cgy. 2	3
Brad Richardson	Los Angeles	Oct. 23	L.A. 6 Col. 4	3
Bobby Ryan	Anaheim	Nov. 27	Ana. 6 Phx. 4	3
Bobby Ryan	Anaheim	Jan. 12	St.L. 4 Ana. 7	3
Teemu Selanne	Anaheim	Mar. 28	Col. 4 Ana. 5	3
Alexander Semin	Washington	Oct. 23	Atl. 3 Wsh. 4	3
Alexander Semin	Washington	Nov. 11	T.B. 3 Wsh. 6	3
Alexander Semin	Washington	Nov. 26	T.B. 0 Wsh. 6	3
Alexander Semin	Washington	Feb. 16	Wsh. 7 Ana. 6	3
Devin Setoguchi	San Jose	Feb. 19	Col. 0 S.J. 4	3
Eric Staal	Carolina	Nov. 17	Ott. 1 Car. 7	3
Eric Staal	Carolina	Dec. 18	Ana. 2 Car. 4	3
Drew Stafford	Buffalo	Dec. 15	Bos. 2 Buf. 3	3
Drew Stafford	Buffalo	Jan. 1	Bos. 6 Buf. 7	3
Drew Stafford	Buffalo	Feb. 8	NYI 7 Buf. 6	3
Drew Stafford	Buffalo	Feb. 13	NYI 7 Buf. 6	3
Steven Stamkos	Tampa Bay	Oct. 22	T.B. 5 Atl. 2	3
Steven Stamkos	Tampa Bay	Nov. 18	I.B. 8 Phi. /	3
Lee Stempniak	Phoenix	Oct. 21	L.A. 2 Phx. 4	3
Derek Stepan*	NY Rangers	Oct. 9	NYR 6 Buf. 3	3
Anthony Stewart	Atlanta	Oct. 15	Atl. 5 Ana. 4	3
Chris Stewart	Colorado	Oct. 28	Col. 6 Cgy. 5	3
P.K. Subban*	Montreal	Mar. 20	Mtl. 8 Min. 1	3
John Tavares	NY Islanders	Oct. 23	NYI 3 Fla. 4	3
John Tavares	NY Islanders	Jan. 15	Buf. 3 NYI 5	3
Joe Thornton	San Jose	Oct. 27	N.J. 2 S.J. 5	3
Jonathan Toews	Chicago	Nov. 17	Chi. 5 Edm. 0	3
Raffi Torres	Vancouver	Nov. 2	Van. 4 Edm. 3	3
James van Riemsdyk	Philadelphia	Mar. 26	Phi. 4 NYI 1	3
Thomas Vanek	Buffalo	Apr. 5	T.B. 2 Buf. 4	3
Lubomir Visnovsky	Anaheim	Mar. 4	Dal. 3 Ana. 4	3
Ray Whitney	Phoenix	Nov. 13	St.L. 3 Phx. 4	3

2010-11 Penalty Shots

(For shootout statistics, see page 143.)

Scored

Evander Kane (Atl.) scored against Michal Neuvirth (Wsh.)
Oct. 8. Final Score: Wsh. 2 at Atl. 4

Alex Ovechkin (Wsh.) scored against Martin Brodeur (N.J.)
Oct. 9. Final Score: N.J. 2 at Wsh. 7

Ryan Callahan (NYR) scored against Jean-Sebastien Giguere (Tor.)
Oct. 30. Final Score: NYR 2 at Tor. 0

David Booth (Fla.) scored against Carey Price (Mtl.)
Oct. 30. Final Score: Fla. 3 at Mtl. 1

Frans Nielsen (NYI) scored against Sergei Bobrovsky (Phi.)
Oct. 30. Final Score: NYI 1 at Phi. 6

David Steckel (Wsh.) scored against Henrik Karlsson (Cgy.)
Oct. 30. Final Score: Wsh. 7 at Cgy. 2

Henrik Sedin (Van.) scored against Martin Brodeur (N.J.)
Nov. 1. Final Score: N.J. 0 at Van. 3

Mike Fisher (Ott.) scored against Jean-Sebastien Giguere (Tor.)
Nov. 2. Final Score: Ott. 3 at Tor. 2

Loui Eriksson (Dal.) scored against Brent Johnson (Pit.)
Nov. 3. Final Score: Pit. 2 at Dal. 5

Dustin Brown (L.A.) scored against Dwayne Roloson (NYI)
Nov. 13. Final Score: NYI 1 at L.A. 5

Mattias Tedenby (N.J.) scored against Braden Holtby (Wsh.)
Nov. 22. Final Score: Wsh. 0 at N.J. 5

Radek Dvorak (Fla.) scored against Dan Ellis (T.B.)
Nov 27. Final Score: Fla. 4 at T.B. 3

Frans Nielsen (NYI) scored against Tuukka Rask (Bos.)
Dec. 9. Final Score: NYI 2 at Bos. 5

Corey Perry (Ana.) scored against Niklas Backstrom (Min.)
Dec 12. Final Score: Min. 2 at Ana. 6

Jason Spezza (Ott.) scored against Ondrej Pavelec (Atl.)
Dec. 13. Final Score: Atl. 4 at Ott. 3

Michael Cammalleri (Mtl.) scored against Tim Thomas (Bos.)
Dec. 16. Final Score: Bos. 3 at Mtl. 4

David Backes (St.L.) scored against Antero Niittymaki (S.J.)
Dec. 18. Final Score: S.J. 4 at St.L. 1

Steven Stamkos (T.B.) scored against Carey Price (Mtl.)
Dec. 30. Final Score: Mtl. 1 at T.B. 4

Chris Conner (Pit.) scored against Joey MacDonald (Det.)
Jan. 18. Final Score: Det. 1 at Pit. 4

Marian Hossa (Chi.) scored against Sergei Bobrovsky (Phi.)
Jan. 23. Final Score: Phi. 4 at Chi. 1

Darroll Powe (Phi.) scored against Dwayne Roloson (T.B.)
Feb 15. Final Score: Phi. 4 at T.B. 3

Bobby Ryan (Ana.) scored against Jimmy Howard (Det.)
Mar. 2. Final Score: Det. 1 at Ana. 2

Jarome Iginla (Cgy.) scored against Pekka Rinne (Nsh.)
Mar. 6. Final Score: Nsh. 2 at Cgy. 3

Mikko Koivu (Min.) scored against Alex Auld (Mtl.)
Mar 20. Final Score: Mtl. 8 at Min. 1

Teemu Selanne (Ana.) scored against Brian Elliott (Col.)
Mar 28. Final Score: Col. 4 at Ana. 5

Michael Ryder (Bos.) scored against Ondrej Pavelec (Atl.)
Apr. 2. Final Score: Atl. 2 at Bos. 3

Vincent Lecavalier (T.B.) scored against Scott Clemmensen (Fla.)
Apr. 8. Final Score: Fla. 2 at T.B. 4

Stopped

Marian Gaborik (NYR) unsuccessful against Rick DiPietro (NYI)
Oct 11. Final Score: NYR 4 at NYI 6

Evgeni Malkin (Pit.) unsuccessful against Jonas Gustavsson (Tor.)
Oct 13. Final Score: Tor. 4 at Pit. 3

Benoit Pouliot (Mtl.) unsuccessful against Dwayne Roloson (NYI)
Oct 27. Final Score: NYI 3 at Mtl. 5

Sean Bergenheim (T.B.) unsuccessful against Marc-Andre Fleury (Pit.)
Oct 27. Final Score: Pit. 3 at T.B. 5

Tom Kostopoulos (Car.) unsuccessful against Devan Dubnyk (Edm.)
Nov. 9. Final Score: Edm. 1 at Car. 7

Mike Modano (Det.) unsuccessful against Nikolai Khabibulin (Edm.)
Nov 11. Final Score: Edm. 2 at Det. 6

Jamie Benn (Dal.) unsuccessful against Jonas Hiller (Ana.)
Nov. 12. Final Score: Dal. 2 at Ana. 4

Jared Boll (CBJ) unsuccessful against Jimmy Howard (Det.)
Nov. 26. Final Score: Det. 2 at CBJ 1

Sidney Crosby (Pit.) unsuccessful against Miikka Kiprusoff (Cgy.)
Nov. 27. Final Score: Cgy. 1 at Pit. 4

Scott Hartnell (Phi.) unsuccessful against Tim Thomas (Bos.)
Dec. 1. Final Score: Bos. 3 at Phi. 0

Tomas Plekanec (Mtl.) unsuccessful against Mike McKenna (N.J.)
Dec. 2. Final Score: Mtl. 5 at N.J. 1

Evander Kane (Atl.) unsuccessful against Rick DiPietro (NYI)
Dec 11. Final Score: Atl. 5 at NYI 4

Magnus Paajarvi (Edm.) unsuccessful against Roberto Luongo (Van.)
Dec 12. Final Score: Van. 2 at Edm. 1

Jarome Iginla (Cgy.) unsuccessful against Jonas Gustavsson (Tor.)
Dec 16. Final Score: Tor. 2 at Cgy. 5

Vincent Lecavalier (T.B.) unsuccessful against Ryan Miller (Buf.)
Dec 18. Final Score: Buf. 1 at T.B. 3

Sean Bergenheim (T.B.) unsuccessful against Justin Peters (Car.)
Dec 20. Final Score: Car. 1 at T.B. 5

Evgeni Malkin (Pit.) unsuccessful against Michal Neuvirth (Wsh.)
Dec 23. Final Score: Pit. 3 at Wsh. 2

Nick Foligno (Ott.) unsuccessful against Marc-Andre Fleury (Pit.)
Dec. 26. Final Score: Pit. 1 at Ott. 3

Jack Skille (Chi.) unsuccessful against Mathieu Garon (CBJ)
Dec. 26. Final Score: CBJ 1 at Chi. 4

Loui Eriksson (Dal.) unsuccessful against Jason LaBarbera (Phx.)
Dec. 26. Final Score: Phx. 1 at Dal. 0

Kris Letang (Pit.) unsuccessful against Rick DiPietro (NYI)
Dec 29. Final Score: Pit. 1 at NYI 2

James Neal (Dal.) unsuccessful against Cory Schneider (Van.)
Dec 31. Final Score: Van. 4 at Dal. 1

Teemu Selanne (Ana.) unsuccessful against Corey Crawford (Chi.)
Jan. 2. Final Score: Chi. 1 at Ana. 2

Steven Stamkos (T.B.) unsuccessful against Marc-Andre Fleury (Pit.)
Jan. 5. Final Score: T.B. 1 at Pit. 8

Viktor Stalberg (Chi.) unsuccessful against Kari Lehtonen (Dal.)
Jan. 5. Final Score: Dal. 4 at Chi. 2

Jack Johnson (L.A.) unsuccessful against Kari Lehtonen (Dal.)
Jan. 17. Final Score: L.A. 1 at Dal. 2

Kevin Porter (Col.) unsuccessful against Roberto Luongo (Van.)
Jan. 18. Final Score: Van. 3 at Col. 4

Vincent Lecavalier (T.B.) unsuccessful against Tomas Vokoun (Fla.)
Jan 21. Final Score: T.B. 2 at Fla. 1

Jarret Stoll (L.A.) unsuccessful against Nikolai Khabibulin (Edm.)
Feb. 2. Final Score: L.A. 3 at Edm. 1

Michael Grabner (NYI) unsuccessful against Brent Johnson (Pit.)
Feb 11. Final Score: Pit. 3 at NYI 9

Marian Gaborik (NYR) unsuccessful against Ondrej Pavelec (Atl.)
Feb 11. Final Score: NYR 2 at Atl. 3

Olli Jokinen (Cgy.) unsuccessful against Curtis McElhinney (Ana.)
Feb 11. Final Score: Ana. 5 at Cgy. 4

Shane Doan (Phx.) unsuccessful against Pekka Rinne (Nsh.)
Feb 19. Final Score: Phx. 3 at Nsh. 2

R.J. Umberger (CBJ) unsuccessful against Ilya Bryzgalov (Phx.)
Feb 25. Final Score: Phx. 3 at CBJ 5

R.J. Umberger (CBJ) unsuccessful against Devan Dubnyk (Edm.)
Mar. 3. Final Score: CBJ 2 at Edm. 4

Matt Calvert (CBJ) unsuccessful against Miikka Kiprusoff (Cgy.)
Mar. 4. Final Score: CBJ 3 at Cgy. 4

Antoine Vermette (CBJ) unsuccessful against Miikka Kiprusoff (Cgy.)
Mar. 4. Final Score: CBJ 3 at Cgy. 4

Mikhail Grabovski (Tor.) unsuccessful against Corey Crawford (Chi.)
Mar. 5. Final Score: Chi. 5 at Tor. 3

Matt Martin (NYI) unsuccessful against James Reimer (Tor.)
Mar. 8. Final Score: Tor. 3 at NYI 4

Brad Marchand (Bos.) unsuccessful against Carey Price (Mtl.)
Mar. 8. Final Score: Bos. 1 at Mtl. 4

Alexandre Burrows (Van.) unsuccessful against Ilya Bryzgalov (Phx.)
Mar. 8. Final Score: Van. 4 at Phx. 3

Andrew Cogliano (Edm.) unsuccessful against Ilya Bryzgalov (Phx.)
Mar 17. Final Score: Phx. 3 at Edm. 1

Evander Kane (Atl.) unsuccessful against Ryan Miller (Buf.)
Mar 19. Final Score: Atl. 2 at Buf. 8

David Booth (Fla.) unsuccessful against Rick DiPietro (NYI)
Mar 19. Final Score: NYI 4 at Fla. 3

Bobby Ryan (Ana.) unsuccessful against Henrik Karlsson (Cgy.)
Mar 20. Final Score: Cgy. 4 at Ana. 5

Daniel Sedin (Van.) unsuccessful against Chris Mason (Atl.)
Mar 25. Final Score: Van. 3 at Atl. 1

Chad Larose (Car.) unsuccessful against Semyon Varlamov (Wsh.)
Mar 29. Final Score: Car. 3 at Wsh. 2

Mikhail Grabovski (Tor.) unsuccessful against Tim Thomas (Bos.)
Mar 31. Final Score: Tor. 4 at Bos. 3

Mattias Tedenby (N.J.) unsuccessful against Carey Price (Mtl.)
Apr. 2. Final Score: Mtl. 3 at N.J. 1

Teemu Hartikainen (Edm.) unsuccessful against Cory Schneider (Van.)
Apr. 2. Final Score: Edm. 4 at Van. 1

Alex Tanguay (Cgy.) unsuccessful against Nikolai Khabibulin (Edm.)
Apr. 6. Final Score: Edm. 1 at Cgy. 6

Total Shots: 78
Total Goals: 27
Total Saves: 51

Alex Ovechkin of Washington puts the puck past New Jersey's Martin Brodeur for a penalty shot goal during the second period of their game on October 9, 2010. Ovechkin had two goals that night in the Capitals' 7-2 win over the Devils.

Goaltending Leaders

Minimum 25 games

Goals Against Average

Goaltender	Team	GPI	MINS	GA	Avg
Tim Thomas	Boston	57	3364	112	2.00
Roberto Luongo	Vancouver	60	3590	126	2.11
Pekka Rinne	Nashville	64	3789	134	2.12
Semyon Varlamov	Washington	27	1560	58	2.23
*Cory Schneider	Vancouver	25	1372	51	2.23
Jonathan Quick	Los Angeles	61	3591	134	2.24
Henrik Lundqvist	NY Rangers	68	4007	152	2.28
*Corey Crawford	Chicago	57	3337	128	2.30
Marc-Andre Fleury	Pittsburgh	65	3695	143	2.32

Save Percentage

Goaltender	Team	GPI	MINS	GA	SA	S%	W	L	OT
Tim Thomas	Boston	57	3364	112	1811	.938	35	11	9
Pekka Rinne	Nashville	64	3789	134	1905	.930	33	22	9
*Cory Schneider	Vancouver	25	1372	51	714	.929	16	4	2
Roberto Luongo	Vancouver	60	3590	126	1753	.928	38	15	7
Jonas Hiller	Anaheim	49	2672	114	1493	.924	26	16	3
Semyon Varlamov	Washington	27	1560	58	759	.924	11	9	5
Cam Ward	Carolina	74	4318	184	2375	.923	37	26	10
Carey Price	Montreal	72	4206	165	2147	.923	38	28	6
Henrik Lundqvist	NY Rangers	68	4007	152	1965	.923	36	27	5

Wins

Goaltender	Team	GPI	MINS	W	L	OT
Roberto Luongo	Vancouver	60	3590	38	15	7
Carey Price	Montreal	72	4206	38	28	6
Jimmy Howard	Detroit	63	3615	37	17	5
Miikka Kiprusoff	Calgary	71	4156	37	24	6
Cam Ward	Carolina	74	4318	37	26	10

Shutouts

Goaltender	Team	GPI	MINS	SO	W	L	OT
Henrik Lundqvist	NY Rangers	68	4007	11	36	27	5
Tim Thomas	Boston	57	3364	9	35	11	9
Carey Price	Montreal	72	4206	8	38	28	6
Jaroslav Halak	St. Louis	57	3294	7	27	21	7
Ilya Bryzgalov	Phoenix	68	4060	7	36	20	10

Team-by-Team Point Totals

2006-07 to 2010-11

(Ranked by five-year point %)

Team	10-11	09-10	08-09	07-08	06-07	Pts%
San Jose	105	113	117	108	107	.671
Detroit	104	102	112	115	113	.666
Vancouver	117	103	100	88	105	.625
Pittsburgh	106	101	99	102	105	.625
Washington	107	121	108	94	70	.610
New Jersey	81	103	106	99	107	.605
Anaheim	99	89	91	102	110	.599
Buffalo	96	100	91	90	113	.598
Nashville	99	100	88	91	110	.595
Boston	103	91	116	94	76	.585
Chicago	97	112	104	88	71	.576
Calgary	94	90	98	94	96	.576
Montreal	96	88	93	104	90	.574
Dallas	95	88	83	97	107	.573
NY Rangers	93	87	95	97	94	.568
Minnesota	86	84	89	98	104	.562
Ottawa	74	94	83	94	105	.549
Carolina	91	80	97	92	88	.546
Philadelphia	106	88	99	95	56	.541
Phoenix	99	107	79	83	67	.530
St. Louis	87	90	92	79	81	.523
Colorado	68	95	69	95	95	.548
Los Angeles	98	101	79	71	68	.509
Toronto	85	74	81	83	91	.505
Tampa Bay	103	80	66	71	93	.504
Florida	72	77	93	85	86	.504
Atlanta	80	83	76	76	97	.502
Columbus	81	79	92	80	73	.494
NY Islanders	73	79	61	79	92	.468
Edmonton	62	62	85	88	71	.449

Team Record When Scoring First Goal of a Game

Team	FG	W	L	OT
Anaheim	46	34	10	2
Atlanta	45	22	14	9
Boston	42	30	6	6
Buffalo	38	25	10	3
Calgary	39	28	8	3
Carolina	37	28	5	4
Chicago	47	32	10	5
Colorado	33	18	11	4
Columbus	36	22	9	5
Dallas	39	32	5	2
Detroit	41	30	5	6
Edmonton	32	18	8	6
Florida	39	23	8	8
Los Angeles	50	36	12	2
Minnesota	39	31	4	4
Montreal	44	32	6	6
Nashville	43	30	5	8
New Jersey	39	27	9	3
NY Islanders	29	20	4	5
NY Rangers	41	28	11	2
Ottawa	38	24	10	4
Philadelphia	50	34	9	7
Phoenix	42	31	5	6
Pittsburgh	41	31	7	3
San Jose	43	32	6	5
St. Louis	46	27	14	5
Tampa Bay	51	32	12	7
Toronto	32	21	4	7
Vancouver	49	41	4	4
Washington	35	25	4	6

Team Plus/Minus Differential

Team	GF	PPGF	Net GF	GA	PPGA	Net GA	Goal Differential
Boston	246	43	203	195	46	149	+54
Vancouver	262	72	190	185	45	140	+50
Philadelphia	259	49	210	223	54	169	+41
Pittsburgh	238	49	189	199	45	154	+35
NY Rangers	233	49	184	198	42	156	+28
Nashville	219	41	178	194	41	153	+25
Washington	224	46	178	197	43	154	+24
Phoenix	231	46	185	226	64	162	+23
San Jose	248	68	180	213	56	157	+23
Chicago	258	64	194	225	53	172	+22
Los Angeles	219	47	172	198	40	158	+14
Buffalo	245	54	191	229	51	178	+13
Detroit	261	67	194	241	53	188	+6
St. Louis	240	52	188	234	51	183	+5
Calgary	250	62	188	237	53	184	+4
Montreal	216	57	159	209	51	158	+1
Anaheim	239	67	172	235	57	178	-6
Dallas	227	55	172	233	55	178	-6
Carolina	236	55	181	239	51	188	-7
Tampa Bay	247	69	178	240	49	191	-13
Columbus	215	42	173	258	62	196	-23
Toronto	218	52	166	251	62	189	-23
Minnesota	206	53	153	233	53	180	-27
Florida	195	35	160	229	41	188	-28
New Jersey	174	34	140	209	40	169	-29
Colorado	227	49	178	288	75	213	-35
NY Islanders	229	52	177	264	52	212	-35
Atlanta	223	53	170	269	64	205	-35
Edmonton	193	44	149	269	74	195	-46
Ottawa	192	45	147	250	48	202	-55

Team Record When Leading, Trailing, Tied

Team	Leading after 1 period W	L	OT	Leading after 2 periods W	L	OT	Trailing after 1 period W	L	OT	Trailing after 2 periods W	L	OT	Tied after 1 period W	L	OT	Tied after 2 periods W	L	OT
Anaheim	25	3	0	30	1	1	8	18	3	3	22	1	14	9	3	14	7	2
Atlanta	13	8	5	20	2	5	7	19	3	6	26	2	14	9	4	8	8	5
Boston	24	4	2	30	2	2	4	14	3	5	16	5	18	7	6	11	7	4
Buffalo	20	6	3	25	2	3	11	12	4	5	24	1	12	11	3	13	3	6
Calgary	19	6	1	25	1	4	7	16	6	5	25	6	15	5	11	3	2	—
Carolina	19	0	1	27	1	0	4	19	4	5	25	5	17	12	6	8	5	6
Chicago	26	8	3	33	4	3	7	11	3	2	15	3	11	10	3	9	10	3
Colorado	15	6	0	17	1	0	4	30	3	5	38	2	11	8	5	8	5	6
Columbus	17	4	1	19	2	2	8	22	6	3	29	5	9	9	6	12	4	6
Dallas	26	2	1	24	0	3	7	15	5	9	21	4	9	12	5	9	8	4
Detroit	20	3	2	28	0	4	10	17	5	8	23	4	17	5	11	2	2	—
Edmonton	15	1	4	15	2	5	5	27	6	4	40	6	5	17	2	6	3	1
Florida	14	8	2	18	3	3	5	22	2	2	26	3	11	10	8	10	11	6
Los Angeles	19	5	2	26	0	1	5	12	2	4	21	2	22	13	2	16	9	3
Minnesota	23	3	3	25	0	1	4	21	2	1	31	1	12	11	3	13	4	6
Montreal	25	3	4	30	1	5	4	22	1	1	27	2	15	6	4	13	2	1
Nashville	25	4	7	31	3	5	8	11	1	6	16	0	11	12	3	7	6	6
New Jersey	19	4	2	22	0	2	4	25	0	4	34	1	15	10	3	12	5	2
NY Islanders	13	4	1	19	3	5	6	29	6	5	34	3	11	6	6	9	4	4
NY Rangers	17	4	2	29	0	0	8	13	1	8	24	4	19	16	2	7	9	1
Ottawa	18	7	2	25	3	1	4	21	5	5	26	5	10	15	3	5	11	4
Philadelphia	25	5	4	38	1	5	8	11	4	1	16	5	14	7	4	8	6	2
Phoenix	18	2	5	32	2	2	9	13	2	7	20	4	16	6	4	4	7	3
Pittsburgh	23	4	2	32	3	1	10	12	1	0	19	1	16	9	5	17	7	6
San Jose	17	5	0	29	4	3	7	12	3	3	15	3	24	8	6	16	6	3
St. Louis	17	8	5	26	4	1	4	15	2	2	20	3	17	10	4	10	9	7
Tampa Bay	21	2	6	34	2	3	7	12	2	4	19	1	18	11	3	8	4	7
Toronto	18	4	4	24	0	4	8	25	0	5	31	3	11	7	7	8	11	3
Vancouver	32	2	1	38	0	3	4	9	4	5	13	3	18	4	11	6	3	—
Washington	21	1	5	29	0	3	15	11	3	8	18	4	12	11	3	11	5	4

Boston's Tim Thomas led the NHL in both goals-against average and save percentage for the second time in three years. His .938 save percentage was the best since the NHL introduced the statistic in 1976-77.

Team Statistics

TEAMS' HOME AND ROAD RECORD

Eastern Conference

Team	GP	W	L	OT	GF	GA	PTS	GP	W	L	OT	GF	GA	PTS
			Home								Road			
WSH	41	25	8	8	124	100	58	41	23	15	3	100	97	49
PHI	41	22	12	7	130	109	51	41	25	11	5	129	114	55
PIT	41	25	14	2	119	94	52	41	24	11	6	119	105	54
BOS	41	22	13	6	124	92	50	41	24	12	5	122	103	53
T.B.	41	25	11	5	137	111	55	41	21	14	6	110	129	48
MTL	41	24	11	6	113	98	54	41	20	19	2	103	111	42
BUF	41	21	16	4	124	111	46	41	22	13	6	121	118	50
NYR	41	20	17	4	127	101	44	41	24	16	1	106	97	49
CAR	41	22	14	5	126	114	49	41	18	17	6	110	125	42
TOR	41	18	15	8	110	119	44	41	19	19	3	108	132	41
N.J.	41	22	16	3	94	101	47	41	16	23	2	80	108	34
ATL	41	17	17	7	106	121	41	41	17	19	5	117	148	39
OTT	41	16	20	5	94	117	37	41	16	20	5	98	133	37
NYI	41	17	18	6	132	128	40	41	13	21	7	97	136	33
FLA	41	16	17	8	105	110	40	41	14	23	4	90	119	32
Totals	615	312	219	84	1765	1626	708	615	296	253	66	1610	1775	658

Western Conference

Team	GP	W	L	OT	GF	GA	PTS	GP	W	L	OT	GF	GA	PTS
VAN	41	27	9	5	135	93	59	41	27	10	4	127	92	58
S.J.	41	25	11	5	130	103	55	41	23	14	4	118	110	50
DET	41	21	14	6	129	129	48	41	26	11	4	132	112	56
ANA	41	26	13	2	127	110	54	41	21	17	3	112	125	45
NSH	41	24	9	8	116	91	56	41	20	18	3	103	103	43
PHX	41	21	13	7	118	110	49	41	22	13	6	113	116	50
L.A.	41	25	13	3	111	96	53	41	21	17	3	108	102	45
CHI	41	24	17	0	132	108	48	41	20	12	9	126	117	49
DAL	41	22	11	8	117	101	52	41	20	18	3	110	132	43
CGY	41	23	13	5	135	117	51	41	18	16	7	115	120	43
ST.L.	41	23	13	5	121	106	51	41	15	20	6	119	128	36
MIN	41	19	17	5	105	118	43	41	20	18	3	101	115	43
CBJ	41	17	19	5	109	126	39	41	17	16	8	106	132	42
COL	41	16	21	4	120	150	36	41	14	23	4	107	138	32
EDM	41	13	22	6	91	125	32	41	12	23	6	102	144	30
Totals	615	326	215	74	1796	1683	726	615	296	246	73	1699	1786	665
	1230	638	434	158	3561	3309	1434	1230	592	499	139	3309	3561	1323

TEAMS' DIVISIONAL RECORD

Northeast Division

Team	GP	W	L	OT	GF	GA	PTS	GP	W	L	OT	GF	GA	PTS
		Against Own Division							Against Other Divisions					
BOS	24	11	8	5	75	64	27	58	35	17	6	171	131	76
MTL	24	14	7	3	69	56	31	58	30	23	5	147	153	65
BUF	24	15	8	1	70	60	31	58	28	21	9	175	169	65
TOR	24	13	9	2	60	60	28	58	24	25	9	158	191	57
OTT	24	7	15	2	40	74	16	58	25	25	8	152	176	58
Totals	120	60	47	13	314	314	133	290	142	111	37	803	820	321

Atlantic Division

Team	GP	W	L	OT	GF	GA	PTS	GP	W	L	OT	GF	GA	PTS
PHI	24	17	4	3	74	58	37	58	30	19	9	185	165	69
PIT	24	12	9	3	56	61	27	58	37	16	5	182	138	79
NYR	24	14	9	1	80	62	29	58	30	24	4	153	136	64
N.J.	24	11	12	1	46	57	23	58	27	27	4	128	152	58
NYI	24	6	13	5	65	83	17	58	24	26	8	164	181	56
Totals	120	60	47	13	321	321	133	290	148	112	30	812	772	326

Southeast Division

Team	GP	W	L	OT	GF	GA	PTS	GP	W	L	OT	GF	GA	PTS
WSH	24	14	7	3	62	54	31	58	34	16	8	162	143	76
T.B.	24	14	6	4	75	68	32	58	32	19	7	172	172	71
CAR	24	12	8	4	71	76	28	58	28	23	7	165	163	63
ATL	24	9	7	8	61	74	26	58	25	29	4	162	195	54
FLA	24	11	9	4	68	65	26	58	19	31	8	127	164	46
Totals	120	60	37	23	337	337	143	290	138	118	34	788	837	310

Central Division

Team	GP	W	L	OT	GF	GA	PTS	GP	W	L	OT	GF	GA	PTS
DET	24	12	10	2	69	77	26	58	35	15	8	192	164	78
NSH	24	13	9	2	55	60	28	58	31	18	9	164	134	71
CHI	24	15	7	2	87	64	32	58	29	22	7	171	161	65
ST.L.	24	12	8	4	81	79	28	58	26	25	7	159	155	59
CBJ	24	8	11	5	66	78	21	58	26	24	8	149	180	60
Totals	120	60	45	15	358	358	135	290	147	104	39	835	794	333

Pacific Division

Team	GP	W	L	OT	GF	GA	PTS	GP	W	L	OT	GF	GA	PTS
S.J.	24	14	5	5	82	61	33	58	34	20	4	166	152	72
ANA	24	14	10	0	66	64	28	58	33	20	5	173	171	71
PHX	24	11	12	1	66	66	23	58	32	14	12	165	160	76
L.A.	24	12	10	2	56	59	26	58	34	20	4	163	139	72
DAL	24	9	10	5	59	79	23	58	33	19	6	168	154	72
Totals	120	60	47	13	329	329	133	290	166	93	31	835	776	363

Northwest Division

Team	GP	W	L	OT	GF	GA	PTS	GP	W	L	OT	GF	GA	PTS
VAN	24	18	4	2	80	54	38	58	36	15	7	182	131	79
CGY	24	13	10	1	74	72	27	58	28	19	11	176	165	67
MIN	24	16	7	1	74	57	33	58	23	28	7	132	176	53
COL	24	7	16	1	61	89	15	58	23	28	7	166	199	53
EDM	24	6	13	5	60	77	17	58	19	32	7	133	192	45
Totals	120	60	50	10	349	349	130	290	129	122	39	789	863	297

San Jose's Logan Couture led all NHL rookies with 10 power-play goals in 2010-11. The Sharks had the NHL's best power-play at home and ranked second overall in the NHL behind the Vancouver Canucks.

TEAM STREAKS

Consecutive Wins

Games	Team	From	To
12	Pittsburgh	Nov. 17	Dec. 11
9	Washington	Feb. 26	Mar. 15
8	Vancouver	Dec. 23	Jan. 7
8	Phoenix	Feb. 5	Feb. 22
8	New Jersey	Feb. 6	Feb. 22
8	San Jose	Feb. 15	Mar. 3
8	Chicago	Feb. 20	Mar. 5
7	St. Louis	Oct. 22	Nov. 7
7	Phoenix	Nov. 10	Nov. 23
7	Boston	Feb. 17	Mar. 3
7	Vancouver	Mar. 5	Mar. 16

Consecutive Home Wins

Games	Team	From	To
8	Los Angeles	Oct. 12	Nov. 13
7	Philadelphia	Oct. 23	Nov. 15
7	Washington	Oct. 23	Nov. 17
7	Pittsburgh	Nov. 17	Dec. 8
7	San Jose	Jan. 15	Mar. 3
7	San Jose	Mar. 17	Apr. 9"
6	St. Louis	Oct. 9	Nov. 4
6	Vancouver	Oct. 11	Nov. 6
6	Atlanta	Nov. 19	Dec. 6
6	Vancouver	Dec. 15	Jan. 7
6	New Jersey	Feb. 8	Mar. 4
6	Chicago	Feb. 20	Mar. 23

Consecutive Road Wins

Games	Team	From	To
9	Vancouver	Mar. 5	Mar. 29
8	Dallas	Dec. 13	Jan. 20
7	Pittsburgh	Nov. 6	Dec. 11
6	Detroit	Dec. 26	Jan. 8
6	Columbus	Jan. 19	Feb. 18
6	Anaheim	Jan. 22	Feb. 13
6	Detroit	Feb. 11	Feb. 28
6	Boston	Feb. 17	Mar. 1
6	Washington	Feb. 20	Mar. 15
6	Los Angeles	Feb. 23	Mar. 29

TEAM PENALTIES

Abbreviations: GP – games played; **PEN** – total penalty minutes including bench minutes; **BMI** – total bench minor minutes; **AVG** – average penalty minutes/game calculated by dividing total penalty minutes by games played

Team	GP	PEN	BMI	AVG	Team	GP	PEN	BMI	AVG
FLA	82	716	22	8.7	TOR	82	985	18	12.0
NSH	82	720	26	8.8	DAL	82	1066	14	13.0
CHI	82	742	22	9.0	COL	82	1077	22	13.1
DET	82	754	6	9.2	NYR	82	1074	14	13.1
N.J.	82	765	18	9.3	MTL	82	1097	28	13.4
CGY	82	836	18	10.2	BOS	82	1115	10	13.6
CAR	82	835	14	10.2	CBJ	82	1113	14	13.6
PHX	82	863	12	10.5	PHI	82	1119	8	13.6
T.B.	82	905	24	11.0	OTT	82	1149	6	14.0
ATL	82	930	22	11.3	ANA	82	1178	20	14.4
WSH	82	926	20	11.3	ST.L.	82	1225	16	14.9
S.J.	82	931	10	11.4	EDM	82	1270	20	15.5
VAN	82	943	10	11.5	PIT	82	1388	16	16.9
BUF	82	958	16	11.7	NYI	82	1515	26	18.5
L.A.	82	962	24	11.7	**Totals**	**1230**	**30140**	**510**	**24.5**
MIN	82	983	14	12.0					

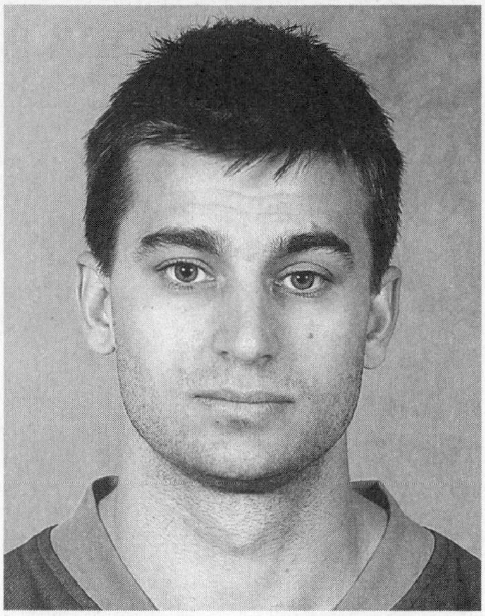

Frans Nielsen of the New York Islanders led the NHL with seven shorthand goals in 2010-11. As a team, the Islanders led the league with a total of 15 shorthand goals.

TEAMS' POWER-PLAY RECORD

Abbreviations: ADV – total advantages; **PPGF** – power-play goals for; **%** – calculated by dividing number of power-play goals by total advantages.

	Home					Road					Overall				
	Team	GP	ADV	PPGF	%	Team	GP	ADV	PPGF	%	Team	GP	ADV	PPGF	%
1	S.J.	41	153	41	26.8	VAN	41	150	42	28.0	VAN	82	296	72	24.3
2	CGY	41	160	41	25.6	DET	41	147	35	23.8	S.J.	82	289	68	23.5
3	ANA	41	149	38	25.5	CHI	41	135	29	21.5	ANA	82	285	67	23.5
4	CHI	41	142	35	24.6	ANA	41	136	29	21.3	CHI	82	277	64	23.1
5	T.B.	41	178	40	22.5	MTL	41	140	28	20.0	DET	82	301	67	22.3
6	BUF	41	139	30	21.6	S.J.	41	136	27	19.9	T.B.	82	336	69	20.5
7	DAL	41	169	36	21.3	ATL	41	147	29	19.7	MTL	82	290	57	19.7
8	DET	41	154	32	20.8	NYI	41	140	27	19.3	CGY	82	318	62	19.5
9	OTT	41	130	27	20.8	T.B.	41	158	29	18.4	BUF	82	279	54	19.4
10	ST.L.	41	151	31	20.5	COL	41	125	22	17.6	ST.L.	82	279	52	18.6
11	VAN	41	146	30	20.5	PIT	41	154	27	17.5	COL	82	265	49	18.5
12	MIN	41	152	30	19.7	BOS	41	122	21	17.2	ATL	82	289	53	18.3
13	COL	41	140	27	19.3	BUF	41	140	24	17.1	MIN	82	292	53	18.2
14	MTL	41	150	29	19.3	MIN	41	140	23	16.4	DAL	82	306	55	18.0
15	WSH	41	145	27	18.6	ST.L.	41	128	21	16.4	OTT	82	257	45	17.5
16	NYR	41	151	28	18.5	L.A.	41	130	21	16.2	WSH	82	263	46	17.5
17	PHX	41	135	24	17.8	WSH	41	118	19	16.1	NYI	82	302	52	17.2
18	PHI	41	163	29	17.8	CBJ	41	135	21	15.6	NYR	82	290	49	16.9
19	CAR	41	181	32	17.7	PHI	41	132	20	15.2	PHI	82	295	49	16.6
20	ATL	41	142	24	16.9	TOR	41	171	26	15.2	BOS	82	265	43	16.2
21	TOR	41	155	26	16.8	NYR	41	139	21	15.1	L.A.	82	292	47	16.1
22	NSH	41	147	24	16.3	N.J.	41	123	18	14.6	TOR	82	326	52	16.0
23	L.A.	41	162	26	16.0	EDM.	41	146	21	14.4	CAR	82	346	55	15.9
24	BOS	41	143	22	15.4	PHX	41	154	22	14.3	PHX	82	289	46	15.9
25	NYI	41	162	25	15.4	OTT	41	127	18	14.2	PIT	82	311	49	15.8
26	EDM	41	158	23	14.6	CAR	41	165	23	13.9	NSH	82	269	41	15.2
27	FLA	41	140	20	14.3	DAL	41	137	19	13.9	EDM.	82	304	44	14.5
28	PIT	41	157	22	14.0	NSH	41	122	17	13.9	N.J.	82	237	34	14.3
29	N.J.	41	114	16	14.0	CGY	41	158	21	13.3	CBJ	82	301	42	14.0
30	CBJ	41	166	21	12.7	FLA	41	127	15	11.8	FLA	82	267	35	13.1
Totals		**1230**	**4534**	**856**	**18.9**		**1230**	**4182**	**715**	**17.1**		**1230**	**8716**	**1571**	**18.0**

TEAMS' PENALTY KILLING RECORD

Abbreviations: TSH – total times shorthanded; **PPGA** – power-play goals against; **%** – calculated by dividing times short minus power-play goals against by times short.

	Home					Road					Overall				
	Team	GP	TSH	PPGA	%	Team	GP	TSH	PPGA	%	Team	GP	TSH	PPGA	%
1	VAN	41	155	18	88.4	MTL	41	168	24	85.7	PIT	82	324	45	86.1
2	NSH	41	139	17	87.8	PIT	41	172	25	85.5	WSH	82	299	43	85.6
3	L.A.	41	136	17	87.5	WSH	41	149	22	85.2	VAN	82	312	45	85.6
4	PIT	41	152	20	86.8	OTT	41	146	22	84.9	L.A.	82	276	40	85.5
5	ST.L.	41	139	19	86.3	NYI	41	159	25	84.3	NSH	82	272	41	84.9
6	WSH	41	150	21	86.0	NYR	41	139	22	84.2	FLA	82	267	41	84.6
7	FLA	41	128	18	85.9	N.J.	41	142	23	83.8	MTL	82	327	51	84.4
8	CAR	41	134	21	84.3	L.A.	41	140	23	83.6	T.B.	82	302	49	83.8
9	T.B.	41	153	24	84.3	BOS	41	134	22	83.6	OTT	82	294	48	83.7
10	BUF	41	138	22	84.1	FLA	41	139	23	83.5	NYR	82	257	42	83.7
11	PHI	41	157	25	84.1	T.B.	41	149	25	83.2	N.J.	82	241	40	83.4
12	CBJ	41	154	25	83.8	DET	41	160	27	83.1	NYI	82	310	52	83.2
13	MIN	41	154	26	83.1	VAN	41	157	27	82.8	BUF	82	300	51	83.0
14	NYR	41	118	20	83.1	MIN	41	154	27	82.5	MIN	82	308	53	82.8
15	MTL	41	159	27	83.0	CHI	41	136	24	82.4	PHI	82	313	54	82.7
16	ANA	41	135	23	83.0	BUF	41	162	29	82.1	BOS	82	265	46	82.6
17	N.J.	41	99	17	82.8	NSH	41	133	24	82.0	DET	82	300	53	82.3
18	OTT	41	148	26	82.4	PHI	41	156	29	81.4	ST.L.	82	279	51	81.7
19	CGY	41	130	23	82.3	COL	41	155	29	81.3	CAR	82	272	51	81.3
20	NYI	41	151	27	82.1	CGY	41	152	30	80.3	ANA	82	305	57	81.3
21	PHX	41	132	24	81.8	S.J.	41	150	30	80.0	CGY	82	282	53	81.2
22	BOS	41	131	24	81.7	ANA	41	170	34	80.0	CBJ	82	314	62	80.3
23	DET	41	140	26	81.4	DAL	41	134	28	79.1	DAL	82	277	55	80.1
24	ATL	41	139	26	81.3	CAR	41	138	30	78.3	S.J.	82	274	56	79.6
25	DAL	41	143	27	81.1	ST.L.	41	140	32	77.1	CHI	82	255	53	79.2
26	EDM.	41	152	29	80.9	CBJ	41	160	37	76.9	PHX	82	296	64	78.4
27	TOR	41	114	22	80.7	PHX	41	164	40	75.6	TOR	82	275	62	77.5
28	S.J.	41	124	26	79.0	TOR	41	161	40	75.2	ATL	82	285	64	77.5
29	CHI	41	119	29	75.6	ATL	41	146	38	74.0	EDM.	82	321	74	76.9
30	COL	41	159	46	71.1	EDM.	41	169	45	73.4	COL	82	314	75	76.1
Totals		**1230**	**4182**	**715**	**82.9**		**1230**	**4534**	**856**	**81.1**		**1230**	**8716**	**1571**	**82.0**

SHORTHAND GOALS FOR

	Home			Road			Overall		
	Team	GP	SHGF	Team	GP	SHGF	Team	GP	SHGF
1	PIT	41	7	NYI	41	10	NYI	82	15
2	EDM	41	6	PHI	41	8	PIT	82	13
3	BOS	41	5	CHI	41	6	PHI	82	13
4	NYI	41	5	DAL	41	6	BOS	82	11
5	WSH	41	5	NYR	41	6	NYR	82	11
6	PHI	41	5	BOS	41	6	DAL	82	10
7	ANA	41	5	PIT	41	6	COL	82	8
8	NYR	41	5	CBJ	41	5	EDM	82	8
9	MIN	41	4	TOR	41	5	MIN	82	7
10	COL	41	4	CAR	41	4	CAR	82	7
11	ST.L.	41	4	OTT	41	4	CGY	82	7
12	CGY	41	4	ATL	41	4	ANA	82	7
13	DAL	41	4	COL	41	4	WSH	82	7
14	CAR	41	3	VAN	41	4	ST.L.	82	7
15	NSH	41	3	CGY	41	3	CHI	82	6
16	S.J.	41	3	S.J.	41	3	CBJ	82	6
17	PHX	41	3	MIN	41	3	S.J.	82	6
18	MTL	41	3	DET	41	3	OTT	82	6
19	DET	41	2	ST.L.	41	3	ATL	82	6
20	OTT	41	2	MTL	41	2	VAN	82	6
21	ATL	41	2	ANA	41	2	TOR	82	5
22	BUF	41	2	WSH	41	2	MTL	82	5
23	VAN	41	2	PHX	41	2	DET	82	5
24	L.A.	41	2	N.J.	41	2	PHX	82	5
25	FLA	41	2	L.A.	41	2	NSH	82	5
26	CBJ	41	1	FLA	41	2	L.A.	82	4
27	N.J.	41	1	NSH	41	2	FLA	82	4
28	T.B.	41	1	EDM	41	2	N.J.	82	3
29	TOR	41	0	BUF	41	0	BUF	82	2
30	CHI	41	0	T.B.	41	0	T.B.	82	1
Totals		**1230**	**95**		**1230**	**111**		**1230**	**206**

SHORTHAND GOALS AGAINST

	Home			Road			Overall		
	Team	GP	SHGA	Team	GP	SHGA	Team	GP	SHGA
1	ST.L.	41	0	PHI	41	1	ST.L.	82	1
2	VAN	41	0	CAR	41	1	EDM	82	2
3	EDM	41	1	BOS	41	1	NSH	82	2
4	OTT	41	1	FLA	41	1	VAN	82	2
5	NSH	41	1	NSH	41	1	CHI	82	4
6	MTL	41	1	ST.L.	41	1	OTT	82	4
7	WSH	41	2	EDM	41	1	PHI	82	5
8	CHI	41	2	CHI	41	2	WSH	82	5
9	PHX	41	2	N.J.	41	2	BOS	82	5
10	ANA	41	2	VAN	41	2	NYR	82	5
11	NYR	41	2	S.J.	41	3	FLA	82	5
12	TOR	41	3	MIN	41	3	MTL	82	6
13	PIT	41	3	WSH	41	3	PIT	82	6
14	NYI	41	3	NYR	41	3	CAR	82	6
15	L.A.	41	3	OTT	41	3	PHX	82	6
16	MIN	41	4	DET	41	3	L.A.	82	6
17	DET	41	4	CBJ	41	3	MIN	82	7
18	ATL	41	4	L.A.	41	3	S.J.	82	7
19	BOS	41	4	PIT	41	3	DET	82	7
20	S.J.	41	4	CGY	41	4	ANA	82	7
21	PHI	41	4	PHX	41	4	NYI	82	7
22	FLA	41	4	COL	41	4	TOR	82	8
23	CAR	41	5	NYI	41	4	N.J.	82	8
24	CGY	41	5	MTL	41	5	CGY	82	9
25	N.J.	41	6	ANA	41	5	ATL	82	10
26	COL	41	7	BUF	41	5	COL	82	11
27	DAL	41	7	T.B.	41	5	CBJ	82	11
28	CBJ	41	8	TOR	41	5	BUF	82	13
29	BUF	41	8	ATL	41	6	DAL	82	15
30	T.B.	41	11	DAL	41	8	T.B.	82	16
Totals		**1230**	**111**		**1230**	**95**		**1230**	**206**

Regular-Season Overtime Results

2010-11 to 1990-91

Team	2010-11 GP	W	L	SO	2009-10 GP	W	L	SO	2008-09 GP	W	L	SO	2007-08 GP	W	L	SO	2006-07 GP	W	L	SO
ANA	18	9	3	6	19	3	3	13	19	5	4	10	20	4	1	15	23	5	4	14
BOS	14	1	5	8	27	4	4	19	17	3	4	10	21	3	5	13	19	4	2	13
BUF	25	10	9	6	20	6	4	10	19	2	4	13	21	5	3	13	22	5	3	14
CGY	23	2	5	16	15	2	3	10	12	3	4	5	16	3	7	6	15	2	5	8
CAR/HFD	22	6	6	10	19	5	5	9	17	7	2	8	13	5	3	5	14	6	3	5
CHI	19	4	4	11	23	6	2	15	22	6	5	11	17	4	4	9	18	3	2	13
COL/QUE	20	6	7	7	18	2	4	12	17	3	1	13	18	4	4	10	15	3	3	9
CBJ	23	5	5	13	20	3	5	12	21	5	3	13	17	2	4	11	16	4	2	10
DAL/MIN	21	5	4	12	23	2	4	17	22	5	5	12	15	3	4	8	22	6	3	13
DET	23	9	6	8	25	5	5	15	19	3	6	10	14	2	2	10	18	3	5	10
EDM	16	2	3	11	17	1	2	14	16	1	5	10	25	4	2	19	11	1	4	6
FLA	22	6	5	11	21	2	3	16	18	4	3	11	18	4	3	11	21	3	8	10
L.A.	17	1	4	12	23	4	1	18	19	3	3	13	14	2	4	8	20	2	8	10
MIN	16	5	3	8	18	5	1	12	17	3	6	8	19	6	2	11	25	7	1	17
MTL	16	5	5	6	25	8	5	12	22	4	4	14	20	5	4	11	14	2	1	11
NSH	19	2	7	10	20	6	2	12	20	6	3	11	17	5	4	8	17	3	3	11
N.J.	15	7	3	5	15	2	2	11	19	9	2	8	22	7	3	12	22	3	1	18
NYI	24	7	7	10	25	6	5	14	15	3	4	8	19	5	6	8	22	2	7	13
NYR	17	3	2	12	15	1	7	7	22	3	3	16	25	4	4	17	22	3	5	14
OTT	14	2	5	7	16	5	1	10	18	3	5	10	14	3	3	8	13	2	3	8
PHI	18	3	5	10	12	2	3	7	21	6	5	10	17	3	5	9	16	3	6	7
PHX/WPG	20	2	7	11	26	5	1	20	11	1	4	6	16	4	1	11	12	2	3	7
PIT	23	5	5	13	21	6	5	10	21	6	3	12	16	1	4	11	27	6	5	16
ST.L.	18	3	5	10	20	3	5	12	20	4	4	12	17	1	8	8	23	4	7	12
S.J.	19	5	4	10	19	1	5	13	21	4	6	11	19	3	4	12	8	1	3	4
T.B.	25	8	5	12	21	5	5	11	23	2	8	13	13	2	8	3	20	5	3	12
TOR	18	2	5	11	23	5	10	8	23	4	6	13	19	5	7	7	19	4	4	11
VAN	17	4	4	9	13	4	1	8	18	5	3	10	20	4	1	15	24	12	3	9
WSH	25	9	5	11	24	6	7	11	18	6	3	9	19	7	4	8	19	4	3	12
WPG/ATL	27	10	5	12	19	2	7	10	17	4	5	8	23	6	2	15	25	7	7	11
Totals	**297**	**148**		**149**	**301**	**117**		**184**	**282**	**123**		**159**	**272**	**116**		**156**	**281**	**117**		**164**

Team	2005-06 GP	W	L	SO	2003-04 GP	W	L	T	2002-03 GP	W	L	T	2001-02 GP	W	L	T	2000-01 GP	W	L	T
ANA	18	3	5	10	22	4	8	10	21	6	6	9	14	3	3	8	20	4	5	11
BOS	22	4	8	10	30	8	7	15	21	6	4	11	24	9	9	6	20	4	8	8
BUF	17	6	1	10	13	2	4	7	21	3	8	10	16	4	1	11	10	4	1	5
CGY	15	2	4	9	13	3	3	7	19	2	6	11	17	2	3	12	22	3	4	15
CAR/HFD	20	4	6	10	25	5	6	14	15	4	3	8	27	6	5	16	18	6	3	9
CHI	22	7	7	8	23	4	8	11	23	6	4	13	17	3	1	13	15	2	5	8
COL/QUE	15	3	3	9	28	8	7	13	23	4	6	13	13	4	1	8	20	6	4	10
CBJ	18	6	1	11	18	6	4	8	28	7	8	13	15	2	5	8	18	3	6	9
DAL/MIN	21	3	5	13	18	3	2	13	24	5	4	15	21	3	5	13	16	6	2	8
DET	15	3	5	7	20	7	2	11	21	7	4	10	24	10	4	10	23	10	4	9
EDM	26	6	4	16	23	6	5	12	27	7	9	11	19	3	4	12	20	5	3	12
FLA	23	8	6	9	24	5	4	15	26	4	9	13	16	0	6	10	24	2	9	13
L.A.	15	4	4	7	27	2	9	16	19	6	7	6	18	3	4	11	19	3	3	13
MIN	14	1	5	8	24	1	3	20	19	8	1	10	21	0	9	12	22	4	5	13
MTL	18	7	6	5	16	5	4	7	19	2	9	8	17	2	3	12	16	2	6	8
NSH	17	3	5	9	22	7	4	11	24	8	6	10	18	5	0	13	17	5	3	9
N.J.	22	4	5	13	21	7	2	12	25	5	7	13	19	6	4	9	20	5	3	12
NYI	18	3	3	12	17	2	4	11	18	5	2	11	18	6	4	8	12	2	3	7
NYR	23	4	8	11	18	3	8	7	20	6	4	10	13	5	4	4	11	5	1	5
OTT	13	2	3	8	19	3	6	10	16	7	1	8	19	3	7	9	16	3	4	9
PHI	22	7	5	10	23	2	6	15	23	6	4	13	16	3	3	10	19	5	3	11
PHX/WPG	15	6	2	7	29	5	6	18	20	4	5	11	19	4	6	9	23	3	3	17
PIT	19	4	8	7	19	7	4	8	14	3	5	6	20	7	5	8	15	3	3	9
ST.L.	22	3	7	12	24	11	2	11	19	2	8	9	18	6	4	8	23	6	5	12
S.J.	21	9	4	8	21	3	6	12	23	6	6	11	13	2	3	8	22	7	3	12
T.B.	18	6	2	10	18	4	6	8	23	2	5	16	19	4	4	11	13	2	5	6
TOR	18	7	1	10	17	4	3	10	17	7	3	7	17	3	4	10	19	3	5	11
VAN	16	4	4	8	26	11	5	10	19	5	1	13	14	4	3	7	23	5	7	11
WSH	21	2	6	13	14	1	3	10	20	6	6	8	19	6	2	11	16	2	4	10
WPG/ATL	18	5	3	10	18	6	4	8	19	7	5	7	19	3	5	11	16	2	2	12
Totals	**281**	**136**		**145**	**315**	**145**		**170**	**313**	**156**		**157**	**270**	**121**		**149**	**274**	**122**		**152**

Team	1999-2000 GP	W	L	T	1998-99 GP	W	L	T	1997-98 GP	W	L	T	1996-97 GP	W	L	T	1995-96 GP	W	L	T
ANA	18	3	3	12	17	1	3	13	20	3	4	13	16	3	0	13	16	6	2	8
BOS	26	1	6	19	17	2	2	13	17	3	1	13	15	3	3	9	19	2	6	11
BUF	20	5	4	11	23	3	3	17	21	3	1	17	21	5	4	12	15	2	6	7
CGY	26	11	5	10	16	3	1	12	22	4	3	15	16	3	4	9	16	2	3	11
CAR/HFD	14	4	0	10	24	1	5	18	12	2	2	8	18	3	4	11	14	2	3	9
CHI	17	5	2	10	15	1	2	12	18	1	4	13	19	1	5	13	19	1	4	14
COL/QUE	17	5	1	11	12	2	0	10	22	2	3	17	15	2	3	10	6	1	0	5
CBJ	...	...	...	...	...	...	...	...	...	...	...	...	...	...	...	...	...	...	...	...
DAL/MIN	19	3	6	10	16	3	1	12	17	5	1	11	15	4	3	8	15	1	0	14
DET	16	4	2	10	10	2	1	7	15	0	0	15	27	7	2	18	11	3	1	7
EDM	27	3	8	16	20	3	5	12	15	3	2	10	16	1	6	9	14	4	2	8
FLA	15	3	6	6	21	1	2	18	20	3	2	15	26	3	4	19	13	0	3	10
L.A.	21	5	4	12	12	5	2	5	16	3	2	11	14	0	3	11	23	3	2	18
MIN	...	...	...	...	...	...	...	...	...	...	...	...	...	...	...	...	...	...	...	...
MTL	17	4	4	9	15	0	4	11	20	3	4	13	21	2	4	15	15	2	3	10
NSH	18	4	7	7	10	1	2	7	...	...	...	...	...	...	...	...	...	...	...	...
N.J.	16	3	5	8	15	3	1	11	16	2	3	11	17	1	2	14	19	7	0	12
NYI	15	5	1	9	17	1	6	10	13	0	2	11	17	3	2	12	17	2	5	10
NYR	21	6	3	12	19	5	3	11	24	2	4	18	13	3	0	10	17	2	1	14
OTT	15	2	2	11	18	1	2	15	17	2	0	15	17	0	2	15	8	0	3	5
PHI	21	6	3	12	24	2	3	19	15	3	1	11	18	3	2	13	20	4	3	13
PHX/WPG	16	4	4	8	15	2	1	12	14	0	2	12	16	5	4	7	8	2	0	6
PIT	17	3	6	8	22	7	1	14	23	3	2	18	13	1	4	8	9	3	2	4
ST.L.	17	5	1	11	15	1	1	13	12	2	2	8	13	1	1	11	18	1	1	16
S.J.	21	4	7	10	21	1	2	18	12	0	2	10	12	3	1	8	9	1	1	7
T.B.	16	0	7	9	12	1	2	9	13	0	3	10	16	4	2	10	18	3	3	12
TOR	17	7	3	7	14	6	1	7	10	1	0	9	10	1	1	8	18	4	2	12
VAN	27	4	8	15	13	0	1	12	17	0	3	14	14	5	2	7	20	1	4	15
WSH	19	5	2	12	11	2	3	6	17	4	1	12	13	2	2	9	16	4	1	11
WPG/ATL	11	0	4	7	...	...	...	...	...	...	...	...	...	...	...	...	...	...	...	...
Totals	**260**	**114**		**146**	**222**	**60**		**162**	**219**	**54**		**165**	**214**	**70**		**144**	**201**	**64**		**137**

Team	1994-95 GP	W	L	T	1993-94 GP	W	L	T	1992-93 GP	W	L	T	1991-92 GP	W	L	T	1990-91 GP	W	L	T
ANA	7	2	0	5	12	2	5	5	...	...	...	...	...	...	...	...	...	...	...	...
BOS	8	2	3	3	17	2	2	13	15	5	3	7	20	6	2	12	17	5	0	12
BUF	9	1	1	7	13	0	4	9	18	4	4	10	16	2	2	12	24	3	2	19
CGY	9	1	1	7	18	3	2	13	19	4	4	11	19	2	5	12	15	3	4	8
CAR/HFD	9	1	1	7	14	4	1	9	18	3	9	6	18	2	3	13	9	1	1	7
CHI	7	2	0	5	16	2	5	9	16	1	3	12	19	2	2	15	12	3	1	8
COL/QUE	8	0	0	8	15	3	3	9	15	4	1	10	17	0	5	12	18	1	3	14
CBJ	...	...	...	...	...	...	...	...	...	...	...	...	...	...	...	...	...	...	...	...
DAL/MIN	9	0	1	8	22	6	3	13	10	0	0	10	8	0	2	6	17	0	3	14
DET	4	0	0	4	15	5	2	8	11	2	0	9	16	3	1	12	14	2	4	8
EDM	7	1	2	4	21	1	6	14	17	5	4	8	12	0	2	10	15	4	5	6
FLA	9	0	3	6	24	2	5	17	...	...	...	...	...	...	...	...	...	...	...	...
L.A.	9	0	0	9	18	3	3	12	13	2	1	10	16	1	1	14	16	4	2	10
MIN	...	...	...	...	...	...	...	...	...	...	...	...	...	...	...	...	...	...	...	...
MTL	10	1	2	7	19	3	2	14	14	5	3	6	20	6	3	11	17	3	3	11
NSH	...	...	...	...	...	...	...	...	...	...	...	...	...	...	...	...	...	...	...	...
N.J.	11	1	2	8	14	1	1	12	11	4	0	7	17	2	4	11	17	1	1	15
NYI	7	1	1	5	19	5	2	12	13	3	3	7	16	3	2	11	15	2	3	10
NYR	3	0	0	3	12	3	1	8	17	2	4	11	11	5	1	5	16	1	2	13
OTT	7	1	1	5	17	4	4	9	10	0	6	4	...	...	...	...	...	...	...	...
PHI	8	3	1	4	18	3	5	10	17	4	2	11	17	2	4	11	11	1	0	10
PHX/WPG	9	0	2	7	15	1	5	9	11	2	2	7	20	1	4	15	14	1	2	11
PIT	5	1	1	3	19	4	2	13	10	3	0	7	12	2	1	9	12	4	2	6
ST.L.	7	1	1	5	17	4	2	11	17	2	4	11	15	2	2	11	18	3	4	11
S.J.	5	1	0	4	19	2	1	16	10	3	5	2	9	1	3	5	...	...	...	...
T.B.	7	2	2	3	18	3	4	11	14	3	4	7	...	...	...	...	...	...	...	...
TOR	8	0	0	8	17	4	1	12	13	1	1	11	11	4	0	7	17	4	2	11
VAN	13	0	1	12	12	5	4	3	10	1	0	9	17	4	1	12	15	3	3	9
WSH	9	0	1	8	14	2	2	10	11	2	2	7	12	2	2	8	14	4	3	7
WPG/ATL	...	...	...	...	...	...	...	...	...	...	...	...	...	...	...	...	...	...	...	...
Totals	**101**	**26**		**75**	**214**	**74**		**140**	**165**	**65**		**100**	**169**	**52**		**117**	**166**	**54**		**112**

Abbreviations: GP – games played; **W** – overtime win; **L** – overtime loss;
SO – game tied after overtime. Game decided in shootout. (2005-06 to date); See page 143.
T – game tied after overtime. (Up to and including 2003-04.)

2010-11 Shootout Summary

Team Shootout Statistics

	GP	W	L	W%	G	S	S%	GA	SA	Sv%
Anaheim	6	4	2	.667	6	24	.250	4	26	.846
Atlanta	12	5	7	.417	12	42	.286	13	41	.683
Boston	8	2	6	.250	6	23	.261	11	24	.542
Buffalo	6	5	1	.833	12	26	.462	9	27	.667
Calgary	16	9	7	.563	19	50	.380	17	52	.673
Carolina	10	5	5	.500	8	29	.276	8	27	.704
Chicago	11	6	5	.545	11	33	.333	10	32	.688
Colorado	7	6	1	.857	7	25	.280	2	27	.926
Columbus	13	5	8	.385	13	46	.283	14	43	.674
Dallas	12	5	7	.417	15	42	.357	15	39	.615
Detroit	8	4	4	.500	6	26	.231	4	26	.846
Edmonton	11	2	9	.182	8	46	.174	15	41	.634
Florida	11	4	7	.364	9	37	.243	14	36	.611
Los Angeles	12	10	2	.833	20	49	.408	11	49	.776
Minnesota	8	3	5	.375	11	29	.379	15	32	.531
Montreal	6	3	3	.500	7	28	.250	7	28	.750
Nashville	10	6	4	.600	9	31	.290	7	34	.794
New Jersey	5	3	2	.600	6	19	.316	5	20	.750
NY Islanders	10	4	6	.400	11	31	.355	14	34	.588
NY Rangers	12	9	3	.750	16	51	.314	9	53	.830
Ottawa	7	2	5	.286	3	22	.136	7	20	.650
Philadelphia	10	3	7	.300	10	35	.286	17	37	.541
Phoenix	11	5	6	.455	13	39	.333	13	37	.649
Pittsburgh	13	10	3	.769	16	49	.327	7	49	.857
St. Louis	10	4	6	.400	16	38	.421	18	40	.550
San Jose	10	5	5	.500	10	34	.294	8	32	.750
Tampa Bay	12	6	6	.500	11	52	.212	12	52	.769
Toronto	11	5	6	.455	12	36	.333	14	35	.600
Vancouver	9	4	5	.444	10	30	.333	12	29	.586
Washington	11	5	6	.455	11	36	.306	12	36	.667
Totals	**149**				**324**	**1058**	**.306**			

Team Shootout Leaders

Wins

	W	L	W%
L.A.	10	2	.833
Pit.	10	3	.769
NYR	9	3	.750
Cgy.	9	7	.563
Col.	6	1	.857
Nsh.	6	4	.600
Chi.	6	5	.545
T.B.	6	6	.500

9 teams tied with 5 wins.

Goals Scored

	G	S	S%
L.A.	20	49	.408
Cgy.	19	50	.380
NYR	16	51	.314
Pit.	16	49	.327
St.L.	16	38	.421
Dal.	15	42	.357
CBJ	13	46	.283
Phx.	13	39	.333
Atl.	12	42	.286
Tor.	12	36	.333
Buf.	12	26	.462

Fewest Goals Against

	GA	SA	Sv%
Col.	2	27	.926
Det.	4	26	.846
Ana.	4	26	.846
N.J.	5	20	.750
Pit.	7	49	.857
Nsh.	7	34	.794
Mtl.	7	28	.750
Ott.	7	20	.650
S.J.	8	32	.750
Car.	8	27	.704

Winning Percentage

	W	L	Win%
Col.	6	1	.857
L.A.	10	2	.833
Buf.	5	1	.833
Pit.	10	3	.769
NYR	9	3	.750
Ana.	4	2	.667
Nsh.	6	4	.600
N.J.	3	2	.600
Cgy.	9	7	.563
Chi.	6	5	.545

5 teams tied at .500.

Shootout Abbreviations

G	Goals Scored
GA	Goals Against
GDG	Game Deciding Goal
S	Shots Taken
SA	Shots Against
S%	Goal Scoring %
Sv%	Save %

Individual Shootout Leaders – Goaltenders

Goaltender Shootout Wins

	Team	W	L
Jonathan Quick	L.A.	10	0
Marc-Andre Fleury	PIT	8	2
Miikka Kiprusoff	Cgy.	8	4
Henrik Lundqvist	NYR	7	3
Pekka Rinne	Nsh.	6	4
Cam Ward	Car.	5	4
Jonas Hiller	Ana.	4	2
Corey Crawford	Chi.	4	3
Ilya Bryzgalov	Phx.	4	5
Steve Mason	CBJ	4	5

Goaltender Shootout Shots Against

	Team	SA	GA	Sv%
Henrik Lundqvist,	NYR	46	7	.848
Jonathan Quick,	L.A.	44	8	.818
Miikka Kiprusoff	Cgy.	41	12	.707
Marc-Andre Fleury	Pit.	38	6	.842
Pekka Rinne	Nsh.	34	7	.794
Kari Lehtonen,	Dal.	33	14	.576
Ilya Bryzgalov	Pho.	32	11	.656
Steve Mason	CBJ	31	10	.677
Jaroslav Halak	St.L.	29	10	.655
Antti Niemi	S.J.	28	8	.714

Goaltender Shootout Save Percentage

(min.20 shots faced)	Team	Sv%	SA	GA
Henrik Lundqvist	NYR	.848	46	7
Jonas Hiller	Ana.	.846	26	4
Marc-Andre Fleury	Pit.	.842	38	6
Jonathan Quick	L.A.	.818	44	8
Pekka Rinne	Nsh.	.794	34	7
Cam Ward	Car.	.760	25	6
Dan Ellis	T.B.-Ana.	.750	24	6
Carey Price	Mtl.	.750	24	6
Antti Niemi	S.J.	.714	28	8
Michal Neuvirth	Wsh.	.714	21	6

Calgary's Alex Tanguay beats Edmonton's Devan Dubnyk for one of his NHL-best 10 shootout goals on 16 shots taken in 2010-11.

Individual Shootout Leaders – Skaters

Shootout Goals Scored

	Team	G	S	S%
Alex Tanguay	Cgy.	10	16	.625
Jarret Stoll	L.A.	9	10	.900
Radim Vrbata	Phx.	7	11	.636
Mike Ribeiro	Dal.	6	10	.600
9 players tied with		5		

Shootout Shots Taken

	Team	G	S	S%
Alex Tanguay	Cgy.	10	16	.625
Kris Letang	Pit.	3	13	.231
Rene Bourque	Cgy.	5	12	.417
Rick Nash	CBJ	5	12	.417
Brad Richards	Dal.	5	12	.417
Radim Vrbata	Phx.	7	11	.636
Jonathan Toews	Chi.	5	11	.455
Mike Santorelli	Fla.	4	11	.364
8 players tied with			10	

Shootout Scoring Percentage

(min. 5 shots taken)	Team	S%	G	S
Jarret Stoll	L.A.	.900	9	10
Thomas Vanek	Buf.	.833	5	6
T.J. Oshie	St.L.	.800	4	5
Pierre-Marc Bouchard	Min.	.667	4	6
Radim Vrbata	Phx.	.636	7	11
Brad Boyes	St.L.-Buf.	.625	5	8
Erik Christensen	NYR	.625	5	8
Frans Nielsen	NYI	.625	5	8
Alex Tanguay	Cgy.	.625	10	16
4 players tied with		.600		

Shootout Game-Deciding Goals

	Team	GDG	G	S
Alex Tanguay	Cgy.	4	10	16
Jarret Stoll	L.A.	4	9	10
Radim Vrbata	Phx.	3	7	11
Mats Zuccarello	NYR	3	5	9
Brad Richards	Dal.	3	5	12
Rene Bourque	Cgy.	3	5	12
Erik Christensen	NYR	3	5	8
Jeff Skinner	Car.	3	4	10
Alex Ovechkin	Wsh.	3	4	10
19 players tied with		2		

Shootout Register, 2010-11

Skaters

Player	Team	S	G	S%	GDG
Daniel Alfredsson	Ott.	3	0	.000	0
Artem Anisimov	NYR	5	1	.200	1
Nik Antropov	Atl.	4	1	.250	0
Colby Armstrong	Tor.	2	2	1.000	1
Jason Arnott	N.J.-Wsh.	2	1	.500	0
David Backes	St.L.	1	0	.000	0
Nicklas Backstrom	Wsh.	9	2	.222	0
Eric Belanger	Phx.	3	1	.333	1
Jamie Benn	Dal.	7	2	.286	0
Sean Bergenheim	T.B.	2	0	.000	0
Patrice Bergeron	Bos.	3	0	.000	0
Niclas Bergfors	Atl.-Fla.	3	0	.000	0
Patrik Berglund	St.L.	3	0	.000	0
Steve Bernier	Fla.	1	1	1.000	1
Todd Bertuzzi	Det.	7	2	.286	1
Jason Blake	Ana.	1	0	.000	0
Mikkel Boedker	Phx.	2	0	.000	0
David Booth	Fla.	5	1	.200	0
Pierre-Marc Bouchard	Min.	6	4	.667	1
Rene Bourque	Cgy.	12	5	.417	3
Jay Bouwmeester	Cgy.	1	0	.000	0
Brad Boyes	St.L.-Buf.	8	5	.625	1
Brian Boyle	NYR	2	0	.000	0
Dan Boyle	S.J.	3	3	1.000	0
Tyler Bozak	Tor.	4	3	.750	1
Derick Brassard	CBJ	1	0	.000	0
Danny Briere	Phi.	9	3	.333	1
Troy Brouwer	Chi.	1	0	.000	0
Dustin Brown	L.A.	7	2	.286	1
Gilbert Brule	Edm.	3	0	.000	0
Andrew Brunette	Min.	1	0	.000	0
Alexander Burmistrov	Atl.	3	1	.333	1
Brent Burns	Min.	3	1	.333	0
Alexandre Burrows	Van.	2	2	1.000	1
Bobby Butler	Ott.	1	0	.000	0
Dustin Byfuglien	Atl.	2	0	.000	0
Paul Byron	Buf.	1	0	.000	0
Ryan Callahan	NYR	4	0	.000	0
Matt Calvert	CBJ	3	0	.000	0
Michael Cammalleri	Mtl.	2	1	.500	1
Jeff Carter	Phi.	2	0	.000	0
Zdeno Chara	Bos.	1	0	.000	0
Erik Christensen	NYR	8	5	.625	3
Danny Cleary	Det.	1	0	.000	0
Ryane Clowe	S.J.	8	3	.375	2
Cal Clutterbuck	Min.	1	0	.000	0
Andrew Cogliano	Edm.	2	0	.000	0
Blake Comeau	NYI	1	0	.000	0
Chris Conner	Pit	1	0	.000	0
Tim Connolly	Buf.	2	0	.000	0
Logan Couture	S.J.	8	2	.250	2
Sidney Crosby	Pit	4	1	.250	0
Matt Cullen	Min.	3	1	.333	0
Matt D'Agostini	St.L.	6	1	.167	0
Evgeny Dadonov	Fla.	1	0	.000	0
Pavel Datsyuk	Det.	4	2	.500	2
Nigel Dawes	Atl.-Mtl.	3	2	.667	1
David Desharnais	Mtl.	2	1	.500	0
Shane Doan	Phx.	3	1	.333	0
Drew Doughty	L.A.	1	0	.000	0
Steve Downie	T.B.	1	0	.000	0
Chris Drury	NYR	1	0	.000	0
Brandon Dubinsky	NYR	4	1	.250	1
Matt Duchene	Col.	6	0	.000	0
Pascal Dupuis	Pit	4	1	.250	1
Jordan Eberle	Edm.	9	4	.444	1
Patrik Elias	N.J.	3	0	.000	0
Tyler Ennis	Buf.	4	3	.750	2
Martin Erat	Nsh.	7	2	.286	1
Loui Eriksson	Dal.	5	1	.200	1
Nikita Filatov	CBJ	2	1	.500	0
Mike Fisher	Ott.-Nsh.	2	0	.000	0
Nick Foligno	Ott.	1	0	.000	0
Kurtis Foster	Edm.	1	0	.000	0
Cam Fowler	Ana.	1	1	1.000	1
Cody Franson	Nsh.	3	1	.333	1
Johan Franzen	Det.	2	0	.000	0
Colin Fraser	Edm.	1	0	.000	0
Michael Frolik	Fla.-Chi.	2	1	.500	1
Alex Frolov	NYR	1	0	.000	0
Marian Gaborik	NYR	1	0	.000	0
Simon Gagne	T.B.	3	1	.333	0
Sam Gagner	Edm.	5	0	.000	0
Nathan Gerbe	Buf.	1	1	1.000	0
Ryan Getzlaf	Ana.	3	1	.333	0
Matt Gilroy	NYR	1	0	.000	0
Brian Gionta	Mtl.	6	1	.167	1
Alexandre Giroux	Edm.	1	0	.000	0
Claude Giroux	Phi.	9	2	.222	0
Curtis Glencross	Cgy.	3	1	.333	1
Marcel Goc	Nsh.	6	2	.333	2
Alex Goligoski	Pit-Dal.	1	0	.000	0
Scott Gomez	Mtl.	1	0	.000	0
Mikhail Grabovski	Tor.	6	2	.333	1
Mike Green	Wsh.	1	0	.000	0
Niklas Hagman	Cgy.	8	1	.125	0
Adam Hall	T.B.	7	2	.286	0
Taylor Hall	Edm.	7	2	.286	0
Michal Handzus	L.A.	9	4	.444	2
Teemu Hartikainen	Edm.	1	0	.000	0
Martin Havlat	Min.	2	0	.000	0
Dany Heatley	S.J.	1	0	.000	0
Jochen Hecht	Buf.	1	1	1.000	1
Victor Hedman	T.B.	6	2	.333	1
Milan Hejduk	Col.	6	2	.333	2
Ales Hemsky	Edm.	3	0	.000	0
Matt Hendricks	Wsh.	4	2	.500	0
Chris Higgins	Fla.-Van.	2	0	.000	0
Shawn Horcoff	Edm.	1	0	.000	0
Nathan Horton	Bos.	1	0	.000	0
Marian Hossa	Chi.	2	0	.000	0
Jiri Hudler	Det.	7	2	.286	1
Kristian Huselius	CBJ	4	1	.250	0
Jarome Iginla	Cgy.	1	0	.000	0
Dustin Jeffrey	Pit	1	1	1.000	1
Marcus Johansson	Wsh.	1	0	.000	0
Erik Johnson	St.L.-Col.	2	0	.000	0
Jack Johnson	L.A.	7	1	.143	0
Olli Jokinen	Cgy.	5	1	.200	1
Jussi Jokinen	Car.	10	2	.200	1
Ryan Jones	Edm.	2	0	.000	0
David Jones	Col.	4	0	.000	0
Jacob Josefson	N.J.	1	0	.000	0
Tomas Kaberle	Tor.-Bos.	1	0	.000	0
Nazem Kadri	Tor.	4	2	.500	1
Evander Kane	Atl.	4	0	.000	0
Patrick Kane	Chi.	10	3	.300	2
Erik Karlsson	Ott.	3	1	.333	1
Tyler Kennedy	Pit	3	0	.000	0
Ryan Kesler	Van.	8	2	.250	1
Phil Kessel	Tor.	8	1	.125	1
Mike Knuble	Wsh.	2	1	.500	1
Saku Koivu	Ana.	2	0	.000	0
Mikko Koivu	Min.	6	3	.500	1
Anze Kopitar	L.A.	10	3	.300	2
Lauri Korpikoski	Phx.	4	0	.000	0
Andrei Kostitsyn	Mtl.	3	0	.000	0
Sergei Kostitsyn	Nsh.	1	0	.000	0
Ales Kotalik	Cgy.	2	1	.500	0
Ilya Kovalchuk	N.J.	5	2	.400	1
Alex Kovalev	Ott.-Pit	10	4	.400	2
David Krejci	Bos.	2	0	.000	0
Tomas Kubalik	CBJ	1	0	.000	0
Pavel Kubina	T.B.	1	0	.000	0
Nikolai Kulemin	Tor.	4	0	.000	0
Chris Kunitz	Pit	5	2	.400	2
Andrew Ladd	Atl.	5	2	.400	1
Brooks Laich	Wsh.	1	0	.000	0
Jamie Langenbrunner	N.J.-Dal.	2	1	.500	0
Vincent Lecavalier	T.B.	5	0	.000	0
David Legwand	Nsh.	3	0	.000	0
Ville Leino	Phi.	4	2	.500	1
Jordan Leopold	Buf.	1	0	.000	0
Kris Letang	Pit	13	3	.231	1
Mark Letestu	Pit	4	1	.250	1
Bryan Little	Atl.	10	3	.300	0
Milan Lucic	Bos.	1	0	.000	0
Joffrey Lupul	Ana.-Tor.	5	1	.200	0
Toni Lydman	Ana.	1	0	.000	0
Clarke MacArthur	Tor.	1	0	.000	0
Derek MacKenzie	CBJ	1	0	.000	0
John Madden	Min.	1	1	1.000	1
Evgeni Malkin	Pit	3	1	.333	0
Ryan Malone	T.B.	3	2	.667	2
Patrick Marleau	S.J.	3	0	.000	0
Matt Martin	NYI	1	0	.000	0
Maksim Mayorov	CBJ	2	1	.500	1
Andy McDonald	St.L.	5	3	.600	1
Antti Miettinen	Min.	4	0	.000	0
John Mitchell	Tor.	1	1	1.000	0
Mike Modano	Det.	2	0	.000	0
Dominic Moore	T.B.	6	3	.500	2
Brendan Morrison	Cgy.	2	0	.000	0
Brenden Morrow	Dal.	1	1	1.000	0
Matt Moulson	NYI	2	0	.000	0
Tyler Myers	Buf.	1	0	.000	0
Rick Nash	CBJ	12	5	.417	1
James Neal	Dal.-Pit	6	3	.500	2
Frans Nielsen	NYI	8	5	.625	2
Cal O'Reilly	Nsh.	6	3	.500	1
Ryan O'Reilly	Col.	2	1	.500	1
Patrick O'Sullivan	Car.-Min.	2	1	.500	0
Kyle Okposo	NYI	2	1	.500	1
Linus Omark	Edm.	5	2	.400	1
T.J. Oshie	St.L.	5	4	.800	1
Steve Ott	Dal.	1	0	.000	0
Alex Ovechkin	Wsh.	10	4	.400	3
Magnus Paajarvi	Edm.	2	0	.000	0
Max Pacioretty	Mtl.	2	1	.500	0
P.A. Parenteau	NYI	8	2	.250	1
Joe Pavelski	S.J.	9	2	.222	1
Dustin Penner	Edm.-L.A.	4	0	.000	0
Mathieu Perreault	Wsh.	2	0	.000	0
Corey Perry	Ana.	6	1	.167	1
Rich Peverley	Atl.-Bos.	5	0	.000	0
Tomas Plekanec	Mtl.	2	1	.500	0
Jason Pominville	Buf.	4	0	.000	0
Kevin Porter	Col.	2	1	.500	1
Benoit Pouliot	Mtl.	4	1	.250	1
Marc-Antoine Pouliot	T.B.	1	0	.000	0
Teddy Purcell	T.B.	4	0	.000	0
Tom Pyatt	Mtl.	1	0	.000	0
Mason Raymond	Van.	6	2	.333	0
Marty Reasoner	Fla.	1	0	.000	0
Steve Reinprecht	Fla.	1	0	.000	0
Michal Repik	Fla.	1	0	.000	0
Mike Ribeiro	Dal.	10	6	.600	1
Brad Richards	Dal.	12	5	.417	3
Michael Richards	Phi.	5	1	.200	0
Mattias Ritola	T.B.	1	0	.000	0
Stephane Robidas	Dal.	1	0	.000	0
Brian Rolston	N.J.	2	1	.500	1
Derek Roy	Buf.	2	1	.500	1
Michal Rozsival	NYR-Phx.	1	0	.000	0
Tuomo Ruutu	Car.	4	1	.250	0
Bobby Ryan	Ana.	3	2	.667	2
Michael Ryder	Bos.	5	1	.200	0
Sergei Samsonov	Car.-Fla.	4	1	.250	1
Mikael Samuelsson	Van.	2	0	.000	0
Mike Santorelli	Fla.	11	4	.364	1
Rob Schremp	NYI-Atl.	7	4	.571	1
Daniel Sedin	Van.	5	1	.200	0
Henrik Sedin	Van.	1	0	.000	0
Brandon Segal	Dal.	1	0	.000	0
Tyler Seguin	Bos.	8	4	.500	1
Teemu Selanne	Ana.	3	0	.000	0
Alexander Semin	Wsh.	6	2	.333	1
Ryan Shannon	Ott.	2	0	.000	0
Patrick Sharp	Chi.	7	1	.143	0
Jeff Skinner	Car.	10	4	.400	3
Vladimir Sobotka	St.L.	1	0	.000	0
Jason Spezza	Ott.	5	1	.200	1
Martin St. Louis	T.B.	5	1	.200	1
Eric Staal	Car.	1	0	.000	0
Marc Staal	NYR	1	0	.000	0
Drew Stafford	Buf.	3	1	.333	0
Viktor Stalberg	Chi.	2	2	1.000	2
Steven Stamkos	T.B.	7	0	.000	0
Tim Stapleton	Atl.	1	1	1.000	1
Alexander Steen	St.L.	5	3	.600	1
Lee Stempniak	Phx.	4	1	.250	0
Derek Stepan	NYR	5	0	.000	0
Chris Stewart	Col.-St.L.	4	1	.250	0
Cory Stillman	Fla.-Car.	2	0	.000	0
Ryan Stoa	Col.	2	1	.500	1
Jarret Stoll	L.A.	10	9	.900	4
P.K. Subban	Mtl.	2	0	.000	0
Steve Sullivan.	Nsh.	4	1	.250	1
Brandon Sutter	Car.	1	0	.000	0
Marek Svatos	Nsh.-Ott.	2	0	.000	0
Jeff Tambellini	Van.	5	2	.400	1
Alex Tanguay	Cgy.	16	10	.625	4
John Tavares	NYI	4	0	.000	0
Mattias Tedenby	N.J.	3	0	.000	0
Kimmo Timonen	Phi.	2	1	.500	1
Jonathan Toews	Chi.	11	5	.454	2
Raffi Torres	Van.	1	1	1.000	1
Kyle Turris	Phx.	4	1	.250	0
Fedor Tyutin	CBJ	3	1	.333	0
R.J. Umberger	CBJ	2	0	.000	0
Scottie Upshall	Phx.-CBJ	4	1	.250	0
Thomas Vanek	Buf.	6	5	.833	1
Antoine Vermette	CBJ	5	2	.400	1
Kris Versteeg	Tor.-Phi.	5	1	.200	0
Lubomir Visnovsky	Ana.	1	0	.000	0
Jakub Voracek	CBJ	3	0	.000	0
Radim Vrbata	Phx.	11	7	.636	3
Stephen Weiss	Fla.	7	2	.286	1
Kyle Wellwood	S.J.	2	0	.000	0
Blake Wheeler	Bos.-Atl.	5	3	.600	1
Ray Whitney	Phx.	5	1	.200	1
Jason Williams	Dal.	1	0	.000	0
Justin Williams	L.A.	4	1	.250	1
Kyle Wilson	CBJ	5	2	.400	2
James Wisniewski	NYI-Mtl.	2	0	.000	0
Wojtek Wolski	Phx.-NYR	9	4	.444	1
Brandon Yip	Col.	1	1	1.000	1
Travis Zajac	N.J.	2	1	.500	1
Henrik Zetterberg	Det.	3	0	.000	0
Nikolai Zherdev	Phi.	2	1	.500	0
Marek Zidlicky	Min.	1	0	.000	0
Mats Zuccarello	NYR	9	5	.556	3

Goaltenders

Goaltender	Team	W	L	SA	GA	Sv %
Craig Anderson	Col.-Ott.	3	1	15	1	.933
Alex Auld	Mtl.	0	1	4	1	.750
Niklas Backstrom	Min.	1	4	17	8	.529
Jonathan Bernier	L.A.	0	2	5	3	.400
Martin Biron	NYR	2	0	7	2	.714
Ben Bishop	St.L.	1	0	4	2	.500
Sergei Bobrovsky	Phi.	1	4	17	9	.471
Brian Boucher	Phi.	2	3	20	8	.600
Martin Brodeur	N.J.	1	1	9	2	.778
Ilya Bryzgalov	Phx.	4	5	32	11	.656
Peter Budaj	Col.	3	0	14	1	.929
Scott Clemmensen	Fla.	2	6	23	12	.478
Ty Conklin	St.L.	0	2	7	6	.143
Corey Crawford	Chi.	4	3	19	3	.842
Rick DiPietro	NYI	2	1	9	3	.667
Devan. Dubnyk	Edm.	0	6	19	10	.474
Brian Elliott	Ott.-Col.	2	5	18	7	.611
Dan Ellis	T.B.-Ana.	2	3	24	6	.750
Jhonas Enroth	Buf.	3	0	19	5	.737
Marc-Andre Fleury	Pit	8	2	38	6	.842
Mathieu Garon	CBJ	1	3	12	4	.667
Martin Gerber	Edm.	1	0	4	1	.750
J-S Giguere	Tor.	2	2	15	7	.533
Jonas Gustavsson	Tor.	2	1	10	4	.600
Jaroslav Halak	St.L.	3	4	29	10	.655
Johan Hedberg	N.J.	2	1	11	3	.727
Jonas Hiller	Ana.	4	2	26	4	.846
Braden Holtby	Wsh.	1	1	7	3	.571
Jimmy Howard	Det.	3	2	17	2	.882
Brent Johnson	Pit	2	1	11	1	.909
Henrik Karlsson	Cgy.	1	3	11	5	.546
Nikolai Khabibulin	Edm.	1	3	18	4	.778
Miikka Kiprusoff	Cgy.	8	4	41	12	.707
Mikko Koskinen	NYI	1	0	4	0	1.000
Jason LaBarbera	Phx.	1	1	5	2	.600
Nathan Lawson	NYI	1	1	6	4	.333
Kari Lehtonen	Dal.	3	7	33	14	.576
Henrik Lundqvist	NYR	7	3	46	7	.848
Roberto Luongo	Van.	3	5	26	12	.538
Joey MacDonald	Det.	1	2	9	2	.778
Chris Mason	Atl.	2	2	17	4	.765
Steve Mason	CBJ	4	5	31	10	.677
Ryan Miller	Buf.	2	1	8	4	.500
Al Montoya	NYI	0	2	9	3	.667
Michal Neuvirth	Wsh.	3	3	21	6	.714
Antti Niemi	S.J.	3	5	28	8	.714
Antero Niittymaki	S.J.	2	0	4	0	1.000
Ondrej Pavelec	Atl.	3	5	24	9	.625
Justin Peters	Car.	0	1	2	2	.000
Kevin Poulin	NYI	0	1	3	2	.333
Carey Price	Mtl.	3	2	24	6	.750
Jonathan Quick	L.A.	10	0	44	8	.818
Tuukka Rask	Bos.	1	1	5	2	.600
Andrew Raycroft	Dal.	2	0	6	1	.833
James Reimer	Tor.	1	3	11	3	.727
Pekka Rinne	Nsh.	6	4	34	7	.794
Dwayne Roloson	NYI-T.B.	3	4	27	8	.704
Cory Schneider	Van.	1	0	3	0	1.000
Mike Smith	T.B.	1	0	4	0	1.000
Jose Theodore	Min.	2	1	15	7	.533
Tim Thomas	Bos.	1	5	19	9	.526
Marty Turco	Chi.	2	2	13	7	.462
Semyon Varlamov	Wsh.	1	2	8	3	.625
Tomas Vokoun	Fla.	2	1	13	2	.846
Cam Ward	Car.	5	4	25	6	.760

NHL Record Book

Year-By-Year Final Standings & Leading Scorers

*Stanley Cup winner

1917-18

First Half

Team	GP	W	L	T	GF	GA	PTS
Montreal	14	10	4	0	81	47	20
Toronto	14	8	6	0	71	75	16
Ottawa	14	5	9	0	67	79	10
**Mtl. Wanderers	6	1	5	0	17	35	2

**Montreal Arena burned down and Wanderers forced to withdraw from League. Montreal Canadiens and Toronto each counted a win for defaulted games with Wanderers.

Second Half

*Toronto	8	5	3	0	37	34	10
Ottawa	8	4	4	0	35	35	8
Montreal	8	3	5	0	34	37	6

Leading Scorers

Player	Team	GP	G	A	PTS	PIM
Joe Malone	Montreal	20	44	4	48	30
Cy Denneny	Ottawa	20	36	10	46	80
Reg Noble	Toronto	20	30	10	40	35
Newsy Lalonde	Montreal	14	23	7	30	51
Corb Denneny	Toronto	21	20	9	29	14
Harry Cameron	Toronto	21	17	10	27	28
Didier Pitre	Montreal	20	17	6	23	29
Eddie Gerard	Ottawa	20	13	7	20	26
Jack Darragh	Ottawa	18	14	5	19	26
Frank Nighbor	Ottawa	10	11	8	19	6
Harry Meeking	Toronto	21	10	9	19	28

1918-19

First Half

Team	GP	W	L	T	GF	GA	PTS
• Montreal	10	7	3	0	57	50	14
Ottawa	10	5	5	0	39	39	10
Toronto	10	3	7	0	42	49	6

Second Half

Ottawa	8	7	1	0	32	14	14
Montreal	8	3	5	0	31	28	6
Toronto	8	2	6	0	22	43	4

• NHL Champion. Stanley Cup not awarded due to influenza epidemic.

Leading Scorers

Player	Team	GP	G	A	PTS	PIM
Newsy Lalonde	Montreal	17	22	10	32	40
Odie Cleghorn	Montreal	17	22	6	28	22
Frank Nighbor	Ottawa	18	19	9	28	27
Cy Denneny	Ottawa	18	18	4	22	58
Didier Pitre	Montreal	17	14	5	19	12
Alf Skinner	Toronto	17	12	4	16	26
Harry Cameron	Tor., Ott.	14	11	3	14	35
Jack Darragh	Ottawa	14	11	3	14	33
Ken Randall	Toronto	15	8	6	14	27
Sprague Cleghorn	Ottawa	18	7	6	13	27

1919-20

First Half

Team	GP	W	L	T	GF	GA	PTS
Ottawa	12	9	3	0	59	23	18
Montreal	12	8	4	0	62	51	16
Toronto	12	5	7	0	52	62	10
Quebec	12	2	10	0	44	81	4

Second Half

*Ottawa	12	10	2	0	62	41	20
Toronto	12	7	5	0	67	44	14
Montreal	12	5	7	0	67	62	10
Quebec	12	2	10	0	47	96	4

Leading Scorers

Player	Team	GP	G	A	PTS	PIM
Joe Malone	Quebec	24	39	10	49	12
Newsy Lalonde	Montreal	23	37	9	46	34
Frank Nighbor	Ottawa	23	26	15	41	18
Corb Denneny	Toronto	24	24	12	36	20
Jack Darragh	Ottawa	23	22	14	36	22
Reg Noble	Toronto	24	24	9	33	52
Amos Arbour	Montreal	22	21	5	26	13
Cully Wilson	Toronto	23	20	6	26	86
Didier Pitre	Montreal	22	14	12	26	6
Punch Broadbent	Ottawa	21	19	6	25	40

1920-21

First Half

Team	GP	W	L	T	GF	GA	PTS
*Ottawa	10	8	2	0	49	23	16
Toronto	10	5	5	0	39	47	10
Montreal	10	4	6	0	37	51	8
Hamilton	10	3	7	0	34	38	6

Second Half

Toronto	14	10	4	0	66	53	20
Montreal	14	9	5	0	75	48	18
Ottawa	14	6	8	0	48	52	12
Hamilton	14	3	11	0	58	94	6

Leading Scorers

Player	Team	GP	G	A	PTS	PIM
Newsy Lalonde	Montreal	24	33	10	43	36
Babe Dye	Ham., Tor.	24	35	5	40	32
Cy Denneny	Ottawa	24	34	5	39	10
Joe Malone	Hamilton	20	28	9	37	6
Frank Nighbor	Ottawa	24	19	10	29	10
Reg Noble	Toronto	24	19	8	27	54
Harry Cameron	Toronto	24	18	9	27	35
Goldie Prodgers	Hamilton	24	18	9	27	8
Corb Denneny	Toronto	20	19	7	26	29
Jack Darragh	Ottawa	24	11	15	26	20

All-Time Standings of NHL Teams

(ranked by percentage)

Active Teams

Team	Games	Wins	Losses	Ties	OT Losses	SO Losses	Goals For	Goals Against	Points	Pts %	First Season
Montreal	6038	3104	2017	837	51	29	19717	16190	7125	.590	1917-18
Philadelphia	3424	1709	1176	457	48	34	11519	10038	3957	.578	1967-68
Buffalo	3198	1530	1187	409	42	30	10650	9645	3541	.554	1970-71
Boston	5878	2807	2178	791	62	40	18840	17257	6507	.554	1924-25
Calgary	3042	1400	1185	379	47	31	10204	9659	3257	.535	1972-73
Detroit	5812	2663	2256	815	45	33	18137	17267	6219	.535	1926-27
Edmonton	2486	1144	996	262	49	35	8714	8342	2634	.530	1979-80
Nashville	984	455	398	60	45	26	2588	2674	1041	.529	1998-99
Minnesota	820	370	326	55	36	33	2082	2112	864	.527	2000-01
Colorado	2486	1133	1026	261	43	23	8356	8197	2593	.522	1979-80
St. Louis	3424	1495	1407	432	54	36	10666	10789	3512	.513	1967-68
Anaheim	1362	604	569	107	45	37	3659	3790	1397	.513	1993-94
San Jose	1526	678	643	121	53	31	4325	4534	1561	.511	1991-92
Toronto	6038	2636	2533	783	51	35	18621	18661	6141	.509	1917-18
Dallas	3424	1468	1422	459	44	31	10602	10880	3470	.507	1967-68
Ottawa	1446	638	620	115	40	33	4152	4269	1464	.506	1992-93
Washington	2886	1263	1237	303	45	38	9185	9509	2912	.505	1974-75
NY Rangers	5812	2484	2440	808	49	31	17854	17980	5856	.504	1926-27
NY Islanders	3042	1313	1308	347	46	28	9913	9745	3047	.501	1972-73
Pittsburgh	3424	1456	1505	383	53	27	11465	12012	3375	.493	1967-68
Chicago	5812	2415	2502	814	46	35	17287	17564	5725	.493	1926-27
New Jersey	2886	1212	1285	328	36	25	8703	9381	2813	.487	1974-75
Florida	1362	535	579	142	62	44	3564	3886	1318	.484	1993-94
Vancouver	3198	1302	1432	391	40	33	10129	10826	3068	.480	1970-71
Los Angeles	3424	1388	1534	424	50	28	11112	11837	3278	.479	1967-68
Phoenix	2486	1021	1131	266	42	26	7837	8605	2376	.478	1979-80
Carolina	2486	1016	1137	263	45	25	7595	8356	2365	.476	1979-80
Columbus	820	313	395	33	38	41	2018	2482	738	.450	2000-01
Tampa Bay	1446	550	696	112	58	30	3823	4561	1300	.450	1992-93
Winnipeg	902	342	437	45	49	29	2465	3014	807	.447	1999-2000

Defunct Teams

Team	Games	Wins	Losses	Ties	Goals For	Goals Against	Points	Pts %	First Season	Last Season
Ottawa Senators	542	258	221	63	1458	1333	579	.534	1917-18	1933-34
Montreal Maroons	622	271	260	91	1474	1405	633	.509	1924-25	1937-38
NY/Brooklyn Americans	784	255	402	127	1643	2182	637	.406	1925-26	1941-42
Hamilton Tigers	126	47	78	1	414	475	95	.377	1920-21	1924-25
Cleveland Barons	160	47	87	26	470	617	120	.375	1976-77	1977-78
Pittsburgh Pirates	212	67	122	23	376	519	157	.370	1925-26	1929-30
Calif./Oakland Seals	698	182	401	115	1826	2580	479	.343	1967-68	1975-76
St. Louis Eagles	48	11	31	6	86	144	28	.292	1934-35	1934-35
Quebec Bulldogs	24	4	20	0	91	177	8	.167	1919-20	1919-20
Montreal Wanderers	6	1	5	0	17	35	2	.167	1917-18	1917-18
Philadelphia Quakers	44	4	36	4	76	184	12	.136	1930-31	1930-31

Calgary totals include Atlanta Flames, 1972-73 to 1979-80.
Carolina totals include Hartford, 1979-80 to 1996-97.
Colorado totals include Quebec, 1979-80 to 1994-95.
Dallas totals include Minnesota North Stars, 1967-68 to 1992-93.
Detroit totals include Cougars, 1926-27 to 1929-30, and Falcons, 1930-31 to 1931-32.
New Jersey totals include Kansas City, 1974-75 to 1975-76, and Colorado Rockies, 1976-77 to 1981-82.
Phoenix totals include Winnipeg, 1979-80 to 1995-96.
Toronto totals include Arenas, 1917-18 to 1918-19, and St. Patricks, 1919-20 to 1925-26.
Winnipeg totals include Atlanta Thrashers, 1999-2000 to 2010-11.

1921-22

Team	GP	W	L	T	GF	GA	PTS
Ottawa	24	14	8	2	106	84	30
*Toronto	24	13	10	1	98	97	27
Montreal	24	12	11	1	88	94	25
Hamilton	24	7	17	0	88	105	14

Leading Scorers

Player	Team	GP	G	A	PTS	PIM
Punch Broadbent	Ottawa	24	32	14	46	28
Cy Denneny	Ottawa	22	27	12	39	20
Babe Dye	Toronto	24	31	7	38	39
Harry Cameron	Toronto	24	18	17	35	22
Joe Malone	Hamilton	24	24	7	31	4
Corb Denneny	Toronto	24	19	9	28	28
Reg Noble	Toronto	24	17	11	28	19
Sprague Cleghorn	Montreal	24	17	9	26	80
Georges Boucher	Ottawa	23	13	12	25	12
Odie Cleghorn	Montreal	23	21	3	24	26

1922-23

Team	GP	W	L	T	GF	GA	PTS
*Ottawa	24	14	9	1	77	54	29
Montreal	24	13	9	2	73	61	28
Toronto	24	13	10	1	82	88	27
Hamilton	24	6	18	0	81	110	12

Leading Scorers

Player	Team	GP	G	A	PTS	PIM
Babe Dye	Toronto	22	26	11	37	19
Cy Denneny	Ottawa	24	23	11	34	28
Billy Boucher	Montreal	24	24	7	31	55
Jack Adams	Toronto	23	19	9	28	42
Mickey Roach	Hamilton	24	17	10	27	8
Odie Cleghorn	Montreal	24	19	6	25	18
Georges Boucher	Ottawa	24	14	9	23	58
Reg Noble	Toronto	24	12	11	23	47
Cully Wilson	Hamilton	23	16	5	21	46
Aurel Joliat	Montreal	24	12	9	21	31

1923-24

Team	GP	W	L	T	GF	GA	PTS
Ottawa	24	16	8	0	74	54	32
*Montreal	24	13	11	0	59	48	26
Toronto	24	10	14	0	59	85	20
Hamilton	24	9	15	0	63	68	18

Leading Scorers

Player	Team	GP	G	A	PTS	PIM
Cy Denneny	Ottawa	22	22	2	24	10
Georges Boucher	Ottawa	21	13	10	23	38
Billy Boucher	Montreal	23	16	6	22	48
Billy Burch	Hamilton	24	16	6	22	4
Aurel Joliat	Montreal	24	15	5	20	27
Babe Dye	Toronto	19	16	3	19	23
Jack Adams	Toronto	22	14	4	18	51
Reg Noble	Toronto	24	12	5	17	79
Frank Nighbor	Ottawa	20	11	6	17	16
Howie Morenz	Montreal	24	13	3	16	20
King Clancy	Ottawa	24	8	8	16	26

1924-25

Team	GP	W	L	T	GF	GA	PTS
Hamilton	30	19	10	1	90	60	39
Toronto	30	19	11	0	90	84	38
• Montreal	30	17	11	2	93	56	36
Ottawa	30	17	12	1	83	66	35
Mtl. Maroons	30	9	19	2	45	65	20
Boston	30	6	24	0	49	119	12

• NHL Champion (Stanley Cup won by Victoria Cougars, WCHL)

Leading Scorers

Player	Team	GP	G	A	PTS	PIM
Babe Dye	Toronto	29	38	6	46	41
Cy Denneny	Ottawa	29	27	15	42	16
Aurel Joliat	Montreal	25	30	11	41	85
Howie Morenz	Montreal	30	28	11	39	46
Red Green	Hamilton	30	19	15	34	81
Jack Adams	Toronto	27	21	10	31	67
Billy Boucher	Montreal	30	17	13	30	92
Billy Burch	Hamilton	27	20	7	27	10
Jimmy Herberts	Boston	30	17	7	24	55
Hooley Smith	Ottawa	30	10	13	23	81

1925-26

Team	GP	W	L	T	GF	GA	PTS
Ottawa	36	24	8	4	77	42	52
*Mtl. Maroons	36	20	11	5	91	73	45
Pittsburgh	36	19	16	1	82	70	39
Boston	36	17	15	4	92	85	38
NY Americans	36	12	20	4	68	89	28
Toronto	36	12	21	3	92	114	27
Montreal	36	11	24	1	79	108	23

Leading Scorers

Player	Team	GP	G	A	PTS	PIM
Nels Stewart	Mtl. Maroons	36	34	8	42	119
Cy Denneny	Ottawa	36	24	12	36	18
Carson Cooper	Boston	36	28	3	31	10
Jimmy Herberts	Boston	36	26	5	31	47
Howie Morenz	Montreal	31	23	3	26	39
Jack Adams	Toronto	36	21	5	26	52
Aurel Joliat	Montreal	35	17	9	26	52
Billy Burch	NY Americans	36	22	3	25	33
Hooley Smith	Ottawa	28	16	9	25	53
Frank Nighbor	Ottawa	35	12	13	25	40

1926-27

Canadian Division

Team	GP	W	L	T	GF	GA	PTS
*Ottawa	44	30	10	4	86	69	64
Montreal	44	28	14	2	99	67	58
Mtl. Maroons	44	20	20	4	71	68	44
NY Americans	44	17	25	2	82	91	36
Toronto	44	15	24	5	79	94	35

American Division

Team	GP	W	L	T	GF	GA	PTS
NY Rangers	44	25	13	6	95	72	56
Boston	44	21	20	3	97	89	45
Chicago	44	19	22	3	115	116	41
Pittsburgh	44	15	26	3	79	108	33
Detroit	44	12	28	4	76	105	28

Leading Scorers

Player	Team	GP	G	A	PTS	PIM
Bill Cook	NY Rangers	44	33	4	37	58
Dick Irvin	Chicago	43	18	18	36	34
Howie Morenz	Montreal	44	25	7	32	49
Frank Fredrickson	Det., Bos.	41	18	13	31	46
Babe Dye	Chicago	41	25	5	30	14
Ace Bailey	Toronto	42	15	13	28	82
Frank Boucher	NY Rangers	44	13	15	28	17
Billy Burch	NY Americans	43	19	8	27	40
Harry Oliver	Boston	42	18	6	24	17
Duke Keats	Bos., Det.	42	16	8	24	52

1927-28

Canadian Division

Team	GP	W	L	T	GF	GA	PTS
Montreal	44	26	11	7	116	48	59
Mtl. Maroons	44	24	14	6	96	77	54
Ottawa	44	20	14	10	78	57	50
Toronto	44	18	18	8	89	88	44
NY Americans	44	11	27	6	63	128	28

American Division

Team	GP	W	L	T	GF	GA	PTS
Boston	44	20	13	11	77	70	51
*NY Rangers	44	19	16	9	94	79	47
Pittsburgh	44	19	17	8	67	76	46
Detroit	44	19	19	6	88	79	44
Chicago	44	7	34	3	68	134	17

Leading Scorers

Player	Team	GP	G	A	PTS	PIM
Howie Morenz	Montreal	43	33	18	51	66
Aurel Joliat	Montreal	44	28	11	39	105
Frank Boucher	NY Rangers	44	23	12	35	15
George Hay	Detroit	42	22	13	35	20
Nels Stewart	Mtl. Maroons	41	27	7	34	104
Art Gagne	Montreal	44	20	10	30	75
Bun Cook	NY Rangers	44	14	14	28	45
Bill Carson	Toronto	32	20	6	26	36
Frank Finnigan	Ottawa	38	20	5	25	34
Bill Cook	NY Rangers	43	18	6	24	42
Duke Keats	Det., Chi.	38	14	10	24	60

1928-29

Canadian Division

Team	GP	W	L	T	GF	GA	PTS
Montreal	44	22	7	15	71	43	59
NY Americans	44	19	13	12	53	53	50
Toronto	44	21	18	5	85	69	47
Ottawa	44	14	17	13	54	67	41
Mtl. Maroons	44	15	20	9	67	65	39

American Division

Team	GP	W	L	T	GF	GA	PTS
*Boston	44	26	13	5	89	52	57
NY Rangers	44	21	13	10	72	65	52
Detroit	44	19	16	9	72	63	47
Pittsburgh	44	9	27	8	46	80	26
Chicago	44	7	29	8	33	85	22

Leading Scorers

Player	Team	GP	G	A	PTS	PIM
Ace Bailey	Toronto	44	22	10	32	78
Nels Stewart	Mtl. Maroons	44	21	8	29	74
Carson Cooper	Detroit	43	18	9	27	14
Howie Morenz	Montreal	42	17	10	27	47
Andy Blair	Toronto	44	12	15	27	41
Frank Boucher	NY Rangers	44	10	16	26	8
Harry Oliver	Boston	43	17	6	23	24
Bill Cook	NY Rangers	43	15	8	23	41
Jimmy Ward	Mtl. Maroons	43	14	8	22	46

Seven players tied with 19 points

1929-30

Canadian Division

Team	GP	W	L	T	GF	GA	PTS
Mtl. Maroons	44	23	16	5	141	114	51
*Montreal	44	21	14	9	142	114	51
Ottawa	44	21	15	8	138	118	50
Toronto	44	17	21	6	116	124	40
NY Americans	44	14	25	5	113	161	33

American Division

Team	GP	W	L	T	GF	GA	PTS
Boston	44	38	5	1	179	98	77
Chicago	44	21	18	5	117	111	47
NY Rangers	44	17	17	10	136	143	44
Detroit	44	14	24	6	117	133	34
Pittsburgh	44	5	36	3	102	185	13

Leading Scorers

Player	Team	GP	G	A	PTS	PIM
Cooney Weiland	Boston	44	43	30	73	27
Frank Boucher	NY Rangers	42	26	36	62	16
Dit Clapper	Boston	44	41	20	61	48
Bill Cook	NY Rangers	44	29	30	59	56
Hec Kilrea	Ottawa	44	36	22	58	72
Nels Stewart	Mtl. Maroons	44	39	16	55	81
Howie Morenz	Montreal	44	40	10	50	72
Normie Himes	NY Americans	44	28	22	50	15
Joe Lamb	Ottawa	44	29	20	49	119
Dutch Gainor	Boston	42	18	31	49	39

1930-31

Canadian Division

Team	GP	W	L	T	GF	GA	PTS
*Montreal	44	26	10	8	129	89	60
Toronto	44	22	13	9	118	99	53
Mtl. Maroons	44	20	18	6	105	106	46
NY Americans	44	18	16	10	76	74	46
Ottawa	44	10	30	4	91	142	24

American Division

Team	GP	W	L	T	GF	GA	PTS
Boston	44	28	10	6	143	90	62
Chicago	44	24	17	3	108	78	51
NY Rangers	44	19	16	9	106	87	47
Detroit	44	16	21	7	102	105	39
Philadelphia	44	4	36	4	76	184	12

Leading Scorers

Player	Team	GP	G	A	PTS	PIM
Howie Morenz	Montreal	39	28	23	51	49
Ebbie Goodfellow	Detroit	44	25	23	48	32
Charlie Conacher	Toronto	37	31	12	43	78
Bill Cook	NY Rangers	43	30	12	42	39
Ace Bailey	Toronto	40	23	19	42	46
Joe Primeau	Toronto	38	9	32	41	18
Nels Stewart	Mtl. Maroons	42	25	14	39	75
Frank Boucher	NY Rangers	44	12	27	39	20
Cooney Weiland	Boston	44	25	13	38	14
Bun Cook	NY Rangers	44	18	17	35	72
Aurel Joliat	Montreal	43	13	22	35	73

1931-32

Canadian Division

Team	GP	W	L	T	GF	GA	PTS
Montreal	48	25	16	7	128	111	57
*Toronto	48	23	18	7	155	127	53
Mtl. Maroons	48	19	22	7	142	139	45
NY Americans	48	16	24	8	95	142	40

American Division

Team	GP	W	L	T	GF	GA	PTS
NY Rangers	48	23	17	8	134	112	54
Chicago	48	18	19	11	86	101	47
Detroit	48	18	20	10	95	108	46
Boston	48	15	21	12	122	117	42

Leading Scorers

Player	Team	GP	G	A	PTS	PIM
Busher Jackson	Toronto	48	28	25	53	63
Joe Primeau	Toronto	46	13	37	50	25
Howie Morenz	Montreal	48	24	25	49	46
Charlie Conacher	Toronto	44	34	14	48	66
Bill Cook	NY Rangers	48	34	14	48	33
Dave Trottier	Mtl. Maroons	48	26	18	44	94
Hooley Smith	Mtl. Maroons	43	11	33	44	49
Babe Siebert	Mtl. Maroons	48	21	18	39	64
Dit Clapper	Boston	48	17	22	39	21
Aurel Joliat	Montreal	48	15	24	39	46

1932-33

Canadian Division

Team	GP	W	L	T	GF	GA	PTS
Toronto	48	24	18	6	119	111	54
Mtl. Maroons	48	22	20	6	135	119	50
Montreal	48	18	25	5	92	115	41
NY Americans	48	15	22	11	91	118	41
Ottawa	48	11	27	10	88	131	32

American Division

Team	GP	W	L	T	GF	GA	PTS
Boston	48	25	15	8	124	88	58
Detroit	48	25	15	8	111	93	58
*NY Rangers	48	23	17	8	135	107	54
Chicago	48	16	20	12	88	101	44

Leading Scorers

Player	Team	GP	G	A	PTS	PIM
Bill Cook	NY Rangers	48	28	22	50	51
Busher Jackson	Toronto	48	27	17	44	43
Baldy Northcott	Mtl. Maroons	48	22	21	43	30
Hooley Smith	Mtl. Maroons	48	20	21	41	66
Paul Haynes	Mtl. Maroons	48	16	25	41	18
Aurel Joliat	Montreal	48	18	21	39	53
Marty Barry	Boston	48	24	13	37	40
Bun Cook	NY Rangers	48	22	15	37	35
Nels Stewart	Boston	47	18	18	36	62
Howie Morenz	Montreal	46	14	21	35	32
Johnny Gagnon	Montreal	48	12	23	35	64
Eddie Shore	Boston	48	8	27	35	102
Frank Boucher	NY Rangers	46	7	28	35	4

1933-34

Canadian Division

Team	GP	W	L	T	GF	GA	PTS
Toronto	48	26	13	9	174	119	61
Montreal	48	22	20	6	99	101	50
Mtl. Maroons	48	19	18	11	117	122	49
NY Americans	48	15	23	10	104	132	40
Ottawa	48	13	29	6	115	143	32

American Division

Team	GP	W	L	T	GF	GA	PTS
Detroit	48	24	14	10	113	98	58
*Chicago	48	20	17	11	88	83	51
NY Rangers	48	21	19	8	120	113	50
Boston	48	18	25	5	111	130	41

Leading Scorers

Player	Team	GP	G	A	PTS	PIM
Charlie Conacher	Toronto	42	32	20	52	38
Joe Primeau	Toronto	45	14	32	46	8
Frank Boucher	NY Rangers	48	14	30	44	4
Marty Barry	Boston	48	27	12	39	12
Cecil Dillon	NY Rangers	48	13	26	39	10
Nels Stewart	Boston	48	21	17	38	68
Busher Jackson	Toronto	38	20	18	38	38
Aurel Joliat	Montreal	48	22	15	37	27
Hooley Smith	Mtl. Maroons	47	18	19	37	58
Paul Thompson	Chicago	48	20	16	36	17

1934-35

Canadian Division

Team	GP	W	L	T	GF	GA	PTS
Toronto	48	30	14	4	157	111	64
*Mtl. Maroons	48	24	19	5	123	92	53
Montreal	48	19	23	6	110	145	44
NY Americans	48	12	27	9	100	142	33
St. Louis	48	11	31	6	86	144	28

American Division

Team	GP	W	L	T	GF	GA	PTS
Boston	48	26	16	6	129	112	58
Chicago	48	26	17	5	118	88	57
NY Rangers	48	22	20	6	137	139	50
Detroit	48	19	22	7	127	114	45

Leading Scorers

Player	Team	GP	G	A	PTS	PIM
Charlie Conacher	Toronto	47	36	21	57	24
Syd Howe	St.L., Det.	50	22	25	47	34
Larry Aurie	Detroit	48	17	29	46	24
Frank Boucher	NY Rangers	48	13	32	45	2
Busher Jackson	Toronto	42	22	22	44	27
Herbie Lewis	Detroit	47	16	27	43	26
Art Chapman	NY Americans	47	9	34	43	4
Marty Barry	Boston	48	20	20	40	33
Sweeney Schriner	NY Americans	48	18	22	40	6
Nels Stewart	Boston	47	21	18	39	45
Paul Thompson	Chicago	48	16	23	39	20

1935-36

Canadian Division

Team	GP	W	L	T	GF	GA	PTS
Mtl. Maroons	48	22	16	10	114	106	54
Toronto	48	23	19	6	126	106	52
NY Americans	48	16	25	7	109	122	39
Montreal	48	11	26	11	82	123	33

American Division

Team	GP	W	L	T	GF	GA	PTS
*Detroit	48	24	16	8	124	103	56
Boston	48	22	20	6	92	83	50
Chicago	48	21	19	8	93	92	50
NY Rangers	48	19	17	12	91	96	50

Leading Scorers

Player	Team	GP	G	A	PTS	PIM
Sweeney Schriner	NY Americans	48	19	26	45	8
Marty Barry	Detroit	48	21	19	40	16
Paul Thompson	Chicago	45	17	23	40	19
Bill Thoms	Toronto	48	23	15	38	29
Charlie Conacher	Toronto	44	23	15	38	74
Hooley Smith	Mtl. Maroons	47	19	19	38	75
Doc Romnes	Chicago	48	13	25	38	6
Art Chapman	NY Americans	47	10	28	38	14
Herbie Lewis	Detroit	45	14	23	37	25
Baldy Northcott	Mtl. Maroons	48	15	21	36	41

1936-37

Canadian Division

Team	GP	W	L	T	GF	GA	PTS
Montreal	48	24	18	6	115	111	54
Mtl. Maroons	48	22	17	9	126	110	53
Toronto	48	22	21	5	119	115	49
NY Americans	48	15	29	4	122	161	34

American Division

Team	GP	W	L	T	GF	GA	PTS
*Detroit	48	25	14	9	128	102	59
Boston	48	23	18	7	120	110	53
NY Rangers	48	19	20	9	117	106	47
Chicago	48	14	27	7	99	131	35

Leading Scorers

Player	Team	GP	G	A	PTS	PIM
Sweeney Schriner	NY Americans	48	21	25	46	17
Syl Apps	Toronto	48	16	29	45	10
Marty Barry	Detroit	48	17	27	44	6
Larry Aurie	Detroit	45	23	20	43	20
Busher Jackson	Toronto	46	21	19	40	12
Johnny Gagnon	Montreal	48	20	16	36	38
Bob Gracie	Mtl. Maroons	47	11	25	36	18
Nels Stewart	Bos., NYA	43	23	12	35	37
Paul Thompson	Chicago	47	17	18	35	28
Bill Cowley	Boston	46	13	22	35	4

1937-38

Canadian Division

Team	GP	W	L	T	GF	GA	PTS
Toronto	48	24	15	9	151	127	57
NY Americans	48	19	18	11	110	111	49
Montreal	48	18	17	13	123	128	49
Mtl. Maroons	48	12	30	6	101	149	30

American Division

Team	GP	W	L	T	GF	GA	PTS
Boston	48	30	11	7	142	89	67
NY Rangers	48	27	15	6	149	96	60
*Chicago	48	14	25	9	97	139	37
Detroit	48	12	25	11	99	133	35

Leading Scorers

Player	Team	GP	G	A	PTS	PIM
Gordie Drillon	Toronto	48	26	26	52	4
Syl Apps	Toronto	47	21	29	50	9
Paul Thompson	Chicago	48	22	22	44	14
Georges Mantha	Montreal	47	23	19	42	12
Cecil Dillon	NY Rangers	48	21	18	39	6
Bill Cowley	Boston	48	17	22	39	8
Sweeney Schriner	NY Americans	49	21	17	38	22
Bill Thoms	Toronto	48	14	24	38	14
Clint Smith	NY Rangers	48	14	23	37	0
Nels Stewart	NY Americans	48	19	17	36	37
Neil Colville	NY Rangers	45	17	19	36	11

1938-39

Team	GP	W	L	T	GF	GA	PTS
*Boston	48	36	10	2	156	76	74
NY Rangers	48	26	16	6	149	105	58
Toronto	48	19	20	9	114	107	47
NY Americans	48	17	21	10	119	157	44
Detroit	48	18	24	6	107	128	42
Montreal	48	15	24	9	115	146	39
Chicago	48	12	28	8	91	132	32

Leading Scorers

Player	Team	GP	G	A	PTS	PIM
Toe Blake	Montreal	48	24	23	47	10
Sweeney Schriner	NY Americans	48	13	31	44	20
Bill Cowley	Boston	34	8	34	42	2
Clint Smith	NY Rangers	48	21	20	41	2
Marty Barry	Detroit	48	13	28	41	4
Syl Apps	Toronto	44	15	25	40	4
Tom Anderson	NY Americans	48	13	27	40	14
Johnny Gottselig	Chicago	48	16	23	39	15
Paul Haynes	Montreal	47	5	33	38	27
Roy Conacher	Boston	47	26	11	37	12
Lorne Carr	NY Americans	46	19	18	37	16
Neil Colville	NY Rangers	48	18	19	37	12
Phil Watson	NY Rangers	48	15	22	37	42

1939-40

Team	GP	W	L	T	GF	GA	PTS
Boston	48	31	12	5	170	98	67
*NY Rangers	48	27	11	10	136	77	64
Toronto	48	25	17	6	134	110	56
Chicago	48	23	19	6	112	120	52
Detroit	48	16	26	6	91	126	38
NY Americans	48	15	29	4	106	140	34
Montreal	48	10	33	5	90	168	25

Leading Scorers

Player	Team	GP	G	A	PTS	PIM
Milt Schmidt	Boston	48	22	30	52	37
Woody Dumart	Boston	48	22	21	43	16
Bobby Bauer	Boston	48	17	26	43	2
Gordie Drillon	Toronto	43	21	19	40	13
Bill Cowley	Boston	48	13	27	40	24
Bryan Hextall	NY Rangers	48	24	15	39	52
Neil Colville	NY Rangers	48	19	19	38	22
Syd Howe	Detroit	46	14	23	37	17
Toe Blake	Montreal	48	17	19	36	48
Murray Armstrong	NY Americans	48	16	20	36	12

1940-41

Team	GP	W	L	T	GF	GA	PTS
*Boston	48	27	8	13	168	102	67
Toronto	48	28	14	6	145	99	62
Detroit	48	21	16	11	112	102	53
NY Rangers	48	21	19	8	143	125	50
Chicago	48	16	25	7	112	139	39
Montreal	48	16	26	6	121	147	38
NY Americans	48	8	29	11	99	186	27

Leading Scorers

Player	Team	GP	G	A	PTS	PIM
Bill Cowley	Boston	46	17	45	62	16
Bryan Hextall	NY Rangers	48	26	18	44	16
Gordie Drillon	Toronto	42	23	21	44	2
Syl Apps	Toronto	41	20	24	44	6
Lynn Patrick	NY Rangers	48	20	24	44	12
Syd Howe	Detroit	48	20	24	44	8
Neil Colville	NY Rangers	48	14	28	42	28
Eddie Wiseman	Boston	48	16	24	40	10
Bobby Bauer	Boston	48	17	22	39	2
Sweeney Schriner	Toronto	48	24	14	38	6
Roy Conacher	Boston	40	24	14	38	7
Milt Schmidt	Boston	44	13	25	38	23

1941-42

Team	GP	W	L	T	GF	GA	PTS
NY Rangers	48	29	17	2	177	143	60
*Toronto	48	27	18	3	158	136	57
Boston	48	25	17	6	160	118	56
Chicago	48	22	23	3	145	155	47
Detroit	48	19	25	4	140	147	42
Montreal	48	18	27	3	134	173	39
Brooklyn	48	16	29	3	133	175	35

Leading Scorers

Player	Team	GP	G	A	PTS	PIM
Bryan Hextall	NY Rangers	48	24	32	56	30
Lynn Patrick	NY Rangers	47	32	22	54	18
Don Grosso	Detroit	48	23	30	53	13
Phil Watson	NY Rangers	48	15	37	52	48
Sid Abel	Detroit	48	18	31	49	45
Toe Blake	Montreal	47	17	28	45	19
Bill Thoms	Chicago	47	15	30	45	8
Gordie Drillon	Toronto	48	23	18	41	6
Syl Apps	Toronto	38	18	23	41	0
Tom Anderson	Brooklyn	48	12	29	41	54

1942-43

Team	GP	W	L	T	GF	GA	PTS
*Detroit	50	25	14	11	169	124	61
Boston	50	24	17	9	195	176	57
Toronto	50	22	19	9	198	159	53
Montreal	50	19	19	12	181	191	50
Chicago	50	17	18	15	179	180	49
NY Rangers	50	11	31	8	161	253	30

Leading Scorers

Player	Team	GP	G	A	PTS	PIM
Doug Bentley	Chicago	50	33	40	73	18
Bill Cowley	Boston	48	27	45	72	10
Max Bentley	Chicago	47	26	44	70	2
Lynn Patrick	NY Rangers	50	22	39	61	28
Lorne Carr	Toronto	50	27	33	60	15
Billy Taylor	Toronto	50	18	42	60	2
Bryan Hextall	NY Rangers	50	27	32	59	28
Toe Blake	Montreal	48	23	36	59	28
Elmer Lach	Montreal	45	18	40	58	14
Buddy O'Connor	Montreal	50	15	43	58	2

1943-44

Team	GP	W	L	T	GF	GA	PTS
*Montreal	50	38	5	7	234	109	83
Detroit	50	26	18	6	214	177	58
Toronto	50	23	23	4	214	174	50
Chicago	50	22	23	5	178	187	49
Boston	50	19	26	5	223	268	43
NY Rangers	50	6	39	5	162	310	17

Leading Scorers

Player	Team	GP	G	A	PTS	PIM
Herb Cain	Boston	48	36	46	82	4
Doug Bentley	Chicago	50	38	39	77	22
Lorne Carr	Toronto	50	36	38	74	9
Carl Liscombe	Detroit	50	36	37	73	17
Elmer Lach	Montreal	48	24	48	72	23
Clint Smith	Chicago	50	23	49	72	4
Bill Cowley	Boston	36	30	41	71	12
Bill Mosienko	Chicago	50	32	38	70	10
Art Jackson	Boston	49	28	41	69	8
Gus Bodnar	Toronto	50	22	40	62	18

1944-45

Team	GP	W	L	T	GF	GA	PTS
Montreal	50	38	8	4	228	121	80
Detroit	50	31	14	5	218	161	67
*Toronto	50	24	22	4	183	161	52
Boston	50	16	30	4	179	219	36
Chicago	50	13	30	7	141	194	33
NY Rangers	50	11	29	10	154	247	32

Leading Scorers

Player	Team	GP	G	A	PTS	PIM
Elmer Lach	Montreal	50	26	54	80	37
Maurice Richard	Montreal	50	50	23	73	36
Toe Blake	Montreal	49	29	38	67	15
Bill Cowley	Boston	49	25	40	65	2
Ted Kennedy	Toronto	49	29	25	54	14
Bill Mosienko	Chicago	50	28	26	54	0
Joe Carveth	Detroit	50	26	28	54	6
Ab DeMarco	NY Rangers	50	24	30	54	10
Clint Smith	Chicago	50	23	31	54	0
Syd Howe	Detroit	46	17	36	53	6

1945-46

Team	GP	W	L	T	GF	GA	PTS
*Montreal	50	28	17	5	172	134	61
Boston	50	24	18	8	167	156	56
Chicago	50	23	20	7	200	178	53
Detroit	50	20	20	10	146	159	50
Toronto	50	19	24	7	174	185	45
NY Rangers	50	13	28	9	144	191	35

Leading Scorers

Player	Team	GP	G	A	PTS	PIM
Max Bentley	Chicago	47	31	30	61	6
Gaye Stewart	Toronto	50	37	15	52	8
Toe Blake	Montreal	50	29	21	50	2
Clint Smith	Chicago	50	26	24	50	2
Maurice Richard	Montreal	50	27	21	48	50
Bill Mosienko	Chicago	40	18	30	48	12
Ab DeMarco	NY Rangers	50	20	27	47	20
Elmer Lach	Montreal	50	13	34	47	34
Alex Kaleta	Chicago	49	19	27	46	17
Billy Taylor	Toronto	48	23	18	41	14
Pete Horeck	Chicago	50	20	21	41	34

1946-47

Team	GP	W	L	T	GF	GA	PTS
Montreal	60	34	16	10	189	138	78
*Toronto	60	31	19	10	209	172	72
Boston	60	26	23	11	190	175	63
Detroit	60	22	27	11	190	193	55
NY Rangers	60	22	32	6	167	186	50
Chicago	60	19	37	4	193	274	42

Leading Scorers

Player	Team	GP	G	A	PTS	PIM
Max Bentley	Chicago	60	29	43	72	12
Maurice Richard	Montreal	60	45	26	71	69
Billy Taylor	Detroit	60	17	46	63	35
Milt Schmidt	Boston	59	27	35	62	40
Ted Kennedy	Toronto	60	28	32	60	27
Doug Bentley	Chicago	52	21	34	55	18
Bobby Bauer	Boston	58	30	24	54	4
Roy Conacher	Detroit	60	30	24	54	6
Bill Mosienko	Chicago	59	25	27	52	2
Woody Dumart	Boston	60	24	28	52	12

1947-48

Team	GP	W	L	T	GF	GA	PTS
*Toronto	60	32	15	13	182	143	77
Detroit	60	30	18	12	187	148	72
Boston	60	23	24	13	167	168	59
NY Rangers	60	21	26	13	176	201	55
Montreal	60	20	29	11	147	169	51
Chicago	60	20	34	6	195	225	46

Leading Scorers

Player	Team	GP	G	A	PTS	PIM
Elmer Lach	Montreal	60	30	31	61	72
Buddy O'Connor	NY Rangers	60	24	36	60	8
Doug Bentley	Chicago	60	20	37	57	16
Gaye Stewart	Tor., Chi.	61	27	29	56	83
Max Bentley	Chi., Tor.	59	26	28	54	14
Bud Poile	Tor., Chi.	58	25	29	54	17
Maurice Richard	Montreal	53	28	25	53	89
Syl Apps	Toronto	55	26	27	53	12
Ted Lindsay	Detroit	60	33	19	52	95
Roy Conacher	Chicago	52	22	27	49	4

1948-49

Team	GP	W	L	T	GF	GA	PTS
Detroit	60	34	19	7	195	145	75
Boston	60	29	23	8	178	163	66
Montreal	60	28	23	9	152	126	65
*Toronto	60	22	25	13	147	161	57
Chicago	60	21	31	8	173	211	50
NY Rangers	60	18	31	11	133	172	47

Leading Scorers

Player	Team	GP	G	A	PTS	PIM
Roy Conacher	Chicago	60	26	42	68	8
Doug Bentley	Chicago	58	23	43	66	38
Sid Abel	Detroit	60	28	26	54	49
Ted Lindsay	Detroit	50	26	28	54	97
Jim Conacher	Det., Chi.	59	26	23	49	43
Paul Ronty	Boston	60	20	29	49	11
Harry Watson	Toronto	60	26	19	45	0
Billy Reay	Montreal	60	22	23	45	33
Gus Bodnar	Chicago	59	19	26	45	14
Johnny Peirson	Boston	59	22	21	43	45

1949-50

Team	GP	W	L	T	GF	GA	PTS
*Detroit	70	37	19	14	229	164	88
Montreal	70	29	22	19	172	150	77
Toronto	70	31	27	12	176	173	74
NY Rangers	70	28	31	11	170	189	67
Boston	70	22	32	16	198	228	60
Chicago	70	22	38	10	203	244	54

Leading Scorers

Player	Team	GP	G	A	PTS	PIM
Ted Lindsay	Detroit	69	23	55	78	141
Sid Abel	Detroit	69	34	35	69	46
Gordie Howe	Detroit	70	35	33	68	69
Maurice Richard	Montreal	70	43	22	65	114
Paul Ronty	Boston	70	23	36	59	8
Roy Conacher	Chicago	70	25	31	56	16
Doug Bentley	Chicago	64	20	33	53	28
Johnny Peirson	Boston	57	27	25	52	49
Metro Prystai	Chicago	65	29	22	51	31
Bep Guidolin	Chicago	70	17	34	51	42

1950-51

Team	GP	W	L	T	GF	GA	PTS
Detroit	70	44	13	13	236	139	101
*Toronto	70	41	16	13	212	138	95
Montreal	70	25	30	15	173	184	65
Boston	70	22	30	18	178	197	62
NY Rangers	70	20	29	21	169	201	61
Chicago	70	13	47	10	171	280	36

Leading Scorers

Player	Team	GP	G	A	PTS	PIM
Gordie Howe	Detroit	70	43	43	86	74
Maurice Richard	Montreal	65	42	24	66	97
Max Bentley	Toronto	67	21	41	62	34
Sid Abel	Detroit	69	23	38	61	30
Milt Schmidt	Boston	62	22	39	61	33
Ted Kennedy	Toronto	63	18	43	61	32
Ted Lindsay	Detroit	67	24	35	59	110
Tod Sloan	Toronto	70	31	25	56	105
Red Kelly	Detroit	70	17	37	54	24
Sid Smith	Toronto	70	30	21	51	10
Cal Gardner	Toronto	66	23	28	51	42

1951-52

Team	GP	W	L	T	GF	GA	PTS
*Detroit	70	44	14	12	215	133	100
Montreal	70	34	26	10	195	164	78
Toronto	70	29	25	16	168	157	74
Boston	70	25	29	16	162	176	66
NY Rangers	70	23	34	13	192	219	59
Chicago	70	17	44	9	158	241	43

Leading Scorers

Player	Team	GP	G	A	PTS	PIM
Gordie Howe	Detroit	70	47	39	86	78
Ted Lindsay	Detroit	70	30	39	69	123
Elmer Lach	Montreal	70	15	50	65	36
Don Raleigh	NY Rangers	70	19	42	61	14
Sid Smith	Toronto	70	27	30	57	6
Bernie Geoffrion	Montreal	67	30	24	54	66
Bill Mosienko	Chicago	70	31	22	53	10
Sid Abel	Detroit	62	17	36	53	32
Ted Kennedy	Toronto	70	19	33	52	33
Milt Schmidt	Boston	69	21	29	50	57
Johnny Peirson	Boston	68	20	30	50	30

1952-53

Team	GP	W	L	T	GF	GA	PTS
Detroit	70	36	16	18	222	133	90
*Montreal	70	28	23	19	155	148	75
Boston	70	28	29	13	152	172	69
Chicago	70	27	28	15	169	175	69
Toronto	70	27	30	13	156	167	67
NY Rangers	70	17	37	16	152	211	50

Leading Scorers

Player	Team	GP	G	A	PTS	PIM
Gordie Howe	Detroit	70	49	46	95	57
Ted Lindsay	Detroit	70	32	39	71	111
Maurice Richard	Montreal	70	28	33	61	112
Wally Hergesheimer	NY Rangers	70	30	29	59	10
Alex Delvecchio	Detroit	70	16	43	59	28
Paul Ronty	NY Rangers	70	16	38	54	20
Metro Prystai	Detroit	70	16	34	50	12
Red Kelly	Detroit	70	19	27	46	8
Bert Olmstead	Montreal	69	17	28	45	83
Fleming Mackell	Boston	65	27	17	44	63
Jim McFadden	Chicago	70	23	21	44	29

1953-54

Team	GP	W	L	T	GF	GA	PTS
*Detroit	70	37	19	14	191	132	88
Montreal	70	35	24	11	195	141	81
Toronto	70	32	24	14	152	131	78
Boston	70	32	28	10	177	181	74
NY Rangers	70	29	31	10	161	182	68
Chicago	70	12	51	7	133	242	31

Leading Scorers

Player	Team	GP	G	A	PTS	PIM
Gordie Howe	Detroit	70	33	48	81	109
Maurice Richard	Montreal	70	37	30	67	112
Ted Lindsay	Detroit	70	26	36	62	110
Bernie Geoffrion	Montreal	54	29	25	54	87
Bert Olmstead	Montreal	70	15	37	52	85
Red Kelly	Detroit	62	16	33	49	18
Dutch Reibel	Detroit	69	15	33	48	18
Ed Sandford	Boston	70	16	31	47	42
Fleming Mackell	Boston	67	15	32	47	60
Ken Mosdell	Montreal	67	22	24	46	64
Paul Ronty	NY Rangers	70	13	33	46	18

1954-55

Team	GP	W	L	T	GF	GA	PTS
*Detroit	70	42	17	11	204	134	95
Montreal	70	41	18	11	228	157	93
Toronto	70	24	24	22	147	135	70
Boston	70	23	26	21	169	188	67
NY Rangers	70	17	35	18	150	210	52
Chicago	70	13	40	17	161	235	43

Leading Scorers

Player	Team	GP	G	A	PTS	PIM
Bernie Geoffrion	Montreal	70	38	37	75	57
Maurice Richard	Montreal	67	38	36	74	125
Jean Béliveau	Montreal	70	37	36	73	58
Dutch Reibel	Detroit	70	25	41	66	15
Gordie Howe	Detroit	64	29	33	62	68
Red Sullivan	Chicago	69	19	42	61	51
Bert Olmstead	Montreal	70	10	48	58	103
Sid Smith	Toronto	70	33	21	54	14
Ken Mosdell	Montreal	70	22	32	54	82
Danny Lewicki	NY Rangers	70	29	24	53	8

1955-56

Team	GP	W	L	T	GF	GA	PTS
*Montreal	70	45	15	10	222	131	100
Detroit	70	30	24	16	183	148	76
NY Rangers	70	32	28	10	204	203	74
Toronto	70	24	33	13	153	181	61
Boston	70	23	34	13	147	185	59
Chicago	70	19	39	12	155	216	50

Leading Scorers

Player	Team	GP	G	A	PTS	PIM
Jean Béliveau	Montreal	70	47	41	88	143
Gordie Howe	Detroit	70	38	41	79	100
Maurice Richard	Montreal	70	38	33	71	89
Bert Olmstead	Montreal	70	14	56	70	94
Tod Sloan	Toronto	70	37	29	66	100
Andy Bathgate	NY Rangers	70	19	47	66	59
Bernie Geoffrion	Montreal	59	29	33	62	66
Dutch Reibel	Detroit	68	17	39	56	10
Alex Delvecchio	Detroit	70	25	26	51	24
Dave Creighton	NY Rangers	70	20	31	51	43
Bill Gadsby	NY Rangers	70	9	42	51	84

1956-57

Team	GP	W	L	T	GF	GA	PTS
Detroit	70	38	20	12	198	157	88
*Montreal	70	35	23	12	210	155	82
Boston	70	34	24	12	195	174	80
NY Rangers	70	26	30	14	184	227	66
Toronto	70	21	34	15	174	192	57
Chicago	70	16	39	15	169	225	47

Leading Scorers

Player	Team	GP	G	A	PTS	PIM
Gordie Howe	Detroit	70	44	45	89	72
Ted Lindsay	Detroit	70	30	55	85	103
Jean Béliveau	Montreal	69	33	51	84	105
Andy Bathgate	NY Rangers	70	27	50	77	60
Ed Litzenberger	Chicago	70	32	32	64	48
Maurice Richard	Montreal	63	33	29	62	74
Don McKenney	Boston	69	21	39	60	31
Dickie Moore	Montreal	70	29	29	58	56
Henri Richard	Montreal	63	18	36	54	71
Norm Ullman	Detroit	64	16	36	52	47

1957-58

Team	GP	W	L	T	GF	GA	PTS
*Montreal	70	43	17	10	250	158	96
NY Rangers	70	32	25	13	195	188	77
Detroit	70	29	29	12	176	207	70
Boston	70	27	28	15	199	194	69
Chicago	70	24	39	7	163	202	55
Toronto	70	21	38	11	192	226	53

Leading Scorers

Player	Team	GP	G	A	PTS	PIM
Dickie Moore	Montreal	70	36	48	84	65
Henri Richard	Montreal	67	28	52	80	56
Andy Bathgate	NY Rangers	65	30	48	78	42
Gordie Howe	Detroit	64	33	44	77	40
Bronco Horvath	Boston	67	30	36	66	71
Ed Litzenberger	Chicago	70	32	30	62	63
Fleming Mackell	Boston	70	20	40	60	72
Jean Béliveau	Montreal	55	27	32	59	93
Alex Delvecchio	Detroit	70	21	38	59	22
Don McKenney	Boston	70	28	30	58	22

1958-59

Team	GP	W	L	T	GF	GA	PTS
*Montreal	70	39	18	13	258	158	91
Boston	70	32	29	9	205	215	73
Chicago	70	28	29	13	197	208	69
Toronto	70	27	32	11	189	201	65
NY Rangers	70	26	32	12	201	217	64
Detroit	70	25	37	8	167	218	58

Leading Scorers

Player	Team	GP	G	A	PTS	PIM
Dickie Moore	Montreal	70	41	55	96	61
Jean Béliveau	Montreal	64	45	46	91	67
Andy Bathgate	NY Rangers	70	40	48	88	48
Gordie Howe	Detroit	70	32	46	78	57
Ed Litzenberger	Chicago	70	33	44	77	37
Bernie Geoffrion	Montreal	59	22	44	66	30
Red Sullivan	NY Rangers	70	21	42	63	56
Andy Hebenton	NY Rangers	70	33	29	62	8
Don McKenney	Boston	70	32	30	62	20
Tod Sloan	Chicago	59	27	35	62	79

1959-60

Team	GP	W	L	T	GF	GA	PTS
*Montreal	70	40	18	12	255	178	92
Toronto	70	35	26	9	199	195	79
Chicago	70	28	29	13	191	180	69
Detroit	70	26	29	15	186	197	67
Boston	70	28	34	8	220	241	64
NY Rangers	70	17	38	15	187	247	49

Leading Scorers

Player	Team	GP	G	A	PTS	PIM
Bobby Hull	Chicago	70	39	42	81	68
Bronco Horvath	Boston	68	39	41	80	60
Jean Béliveau	Montreal	60	34	40	74	57
Andy Bathgate	NY Rangers	70	26	48	74	28
Henri Richard	Montreal	70	30	43	73	66
Gordie Howe	Detroit	70	28	45	73	46
Bernie Geoffrion	Montreal	59	30	41	71	36
Don McKenney	Boston	70	20	49	69	28
Vic Stasiuk	Boston	69	29	39	68	121
Dean Prentice	NY Rangers	70	32	34	66	43

1960-61

Team	GP	W	L	T	GF	GA	PTS
Montreal	70	41	19	10	254	188	92
Toronto	70	39	19	12	234	176	90
*Chicago	70	29	24	17	198	180	75
Detroit	70	25	29	16	195	215	66
NY Rangers	70	22	38	10	204	248	54
Boston	70	15	42	13	176	254	43

Leading Scorers

Player	Team	GP	G	A	PTS	PIM
Bernie Geoffrion	Montreal	64	50	45	95	29
Jean Béliveau	Montreal	69	32	58	90	57
Frank Mahovlich	Toronto	70	48	36	84	131
Andy Bathgate	NY Rangers	70	29	48	77	22
Gordie Howe	Detroit	64	23	49	72	30
Norm Ullman	Detroit	70	28	42	70	34
Red Kelly	Toronto	64	20	50	70	12
Dickie Moore	Montreal	57	35	34	69	62
Henri Richard	Montreal	70	24	44	68	91
Alex Delvecchio	Detroit	70	27	35	62	26

1961-62

Team	GP	W	L	T	GF	GA	PTS
Montreal	70	42	14	14	259	166	98
*Toronto	70	37	22	11	232	180	85
Chicago	70	31	26	13	217	186	75
NY Rangers	70	26	32	12	195	207	64
Detroit	70	23	33	14	184	219	60
Boston	70	15	47	8	177	306	38

Leading Scorers

Player	Team	GP	G	A	PTS	PIM
Bobby Hull	Chicago	70	50	34	84	35
Andy Bathgate	NY Rangers	70	28	56	84	44
Gordie Howe	Detroit	70	33	44	77	54
Stan Mikita	Chicago	70	25	52	77	97
Frank Mahovlich	Toronto	70	33	38	71	87
Alex Delvecchio	Detroit	70	26	43	69	18
Ralph Backstrom	Montreal	66	27	38	65	29
Norm Ullman	Detroit	70	26	38	64	54
Bill Hay	Chicago	60	11	52	63	34
Claude Provost	Montreal	70	33	29	62	22

1962-63

Team	GP	W	L	T	GF	GA	PTS
*Toronto	70	35	23	12	221	180	82
Chicago	70	32	21	17	194	178	81
Montreal	70	28	19	23	225	183	79
Detroit	70	32	25	13	200	194	77
NY Rangers	70	22	36	12	211	233	56
Boston	70	14	39	17	198	281	45

Leading Scorers

Player	Team	GP	G	A	PTS	PIM
Gordie Howe	Detroit	70	38	48	86	100
Andy Bathgate	NY Rangers	70	35	46	81	54
Stan Mikita	Chicago	65	31	45	76	69
Frank Mahovlich	Toronto	67	36	37	73	56
Henri Richard	Montreal	67	23	50	73	57
Jean Béliveau	Montreal	69	18	49	67	68
John Bucyk	Boston	69	27	39	66	36
Alex Delvecchio	Detroit	70	20	44	64	8
Bobby Hull	Chicago	65	31	31	62	27
Murray Oliver	Boston	65	22	40	62	38

1963-64

Team	GP	W	L	T	GF	GA	PTS
Montreal	70	36	21	13	209	167	85
Chicago	70	36	22	12	218	169	84
*Toronto	70	33	25	12	192	172	78
Detroit	70	30	29	11	191	204	71
NY Rangers	70	22	38	10	186	242	54
Boston	70	18	40	12	170	212	48

Leading Scorers

Player	Team	GP	G	A	PTS	PIM
Stan Mikita	Chicago	70	39	50	89	146
Bobby Hull	Chicago	70	43	44	87	50
Jean Béliveau	Montreal	68	28	50	78	42
Andy Bathgate	NYR, Tor.	71	19	58	77	34
Gordie Howe	Detroit	69	26	47	73	70
Kenny Wharram	Chicago	70	39	32	71	18
Murray Oliver	Boston	70	24	44	68	41
Phil Goyette	NY Rangers	67	24	41	65	15
Rod Gilbert	NY Rangers	70	24	40	64	62
Dave Keon	Toronto	70	23	37	60	6

1964-65

Team	GP	W	L	T	GF	GA	PTS
Detroit	70	40	23	7	224	175	87
*Montreal	70	36	23	11	211	185	83
Chicago	70	34	28	8	224	176	76
Toronto	70	30	26	14	204	173	74
NY Rangers	70	20	38	12	179	246	52
Boston	70	21	43	6	166	253	48

Leading Scorers

Player	Team	GP	G	A	PTS	PIM
Stan Mikita	Chicago	70	28	59	87	154
Norm Ullman	Detroit	70	42	41	83	70
Gordie Howe	Detroit	70	29	47	76	104
Bobby Hull	Chicago	61	39	32	71	32
Alex Delvecchio	Detroit	68	25	42	67	16
Claude Provost	Montreal	70	27	37	64	28
Rod Gilbert	NY Rangers	70	25	36	61	52
Pierre Pilote	Chicago	68	14	45	59	162
John Bucyk	Boston	68	26	29	55	24
Ralph Backstrom	Montreal	70	25	30	55	41
Phil Esposito	Chicago	70	23	32	55	44

1965-66

Team	GP	W	L	T	GF	GA	PTS
*Montreal	70	41	21	8	239	173	90
Chicago	70	37	25	8	240	187	82
Toronto	70	34	25	11	208	187	79
Detroit	70	31	27	12	221	194	74
Boston	70	21	43	6	174	275	48
NY Rangers	70	18	41	11	195	261	47

Leading Scorers

Player	Team	GP	G	A	PTS	PIM
Bobby Hull	Chicago	65	54	43	97	70
Stan Mikita	Chicago	68	30	48	78	58
Bobby Rousseau	Montreal	70	30	48	78	20
Jean Béliveau	Montreal	67	29	48	77	50
Gordie Howe	Detroit	70	29	46	75	83
Norm Ullman	Detroit	70	31	41	72	35
Alex Delvecchio	Detroit	70	31	38	69	16
Bob Nevin	NY Rangers	69	29	33	62	10
Henri Richard	Montreal	62	22	39	61	47
Murray Oliver	Boston	70	18	42	60	30

1966-67

Team	GP	W	L	T	GF	GA	PTS
Chicago	70	41	17	12	264	170	94
Montreal	70	32	25	13	202	188	77
*Toronto	70	32	27	11	204	211	75
NY Rangers	70	30	28	12	188	189	72
Detroit	70	27	39	4	212	241	58
Boston	70	17	43	10	182	253	44

Leading Scorers

Player	Team	GP	G	A	PTS	PIM
Stan Mikita	Chicago	70	35	62	97	12
Bobby Hull	Chicago	66	52	28	80	52
Norm Ullman	Detroit	68	26	44	70	26
Kenny Wharram	Chicago	70	31	34	65	21
Gordie Howe	Detroit	69	25	40	65	53
Bobby Rousseau	Montreal	68	19	44	63	58
Phil Esposito	Chicago	69	21	40	61	40
Phil Goyette	NY Rangers	70	12	49	61	6
Doug Mohns	Chicago	61	25	35	60	58
Henri Richard	Montreal	65	21	34	55	28
Alex Delvecchio	Detroit	70	17	38	55	10

1967-68

East Division

Team	GP	W	L	T	GF	GA	PTS
*Montreal	74	42	22	10	236	167	94
NY Rangers	74	39	23	12	226	183	90
Boston	74	37	27	10	259	216	84
Chicago	74	32	26	16	212	222	80
Toronto	74	33	31	10	209	176	76
Detroit	74	27	35	12	245	257	66

West Division

Team	GP	W	L	T	GF	GA	PTS
Philadelphia	74	31	32	11	173	179	73
Los Angeles	74	31	33	10	200	224	72
St. Louis	74	27	31	16	177	191	70
Minnesota	74	27	32	15	191	226	69
Pittsburgh	74	27	34	13	195	216	67
Oakland	74	15	42	17	153	219	47

Leading Scorers

Player	Team	GP	G	A	PTS	PIM
Stan Mikita	Chicago	72	40	47	87	14
Phil Esposito	Boston	74	35	49	84	21
Gordie Howe	Detroit	74	39	43	82	53
Jean Ratelle	NY Rangers	74	32	46	78	18
Rod Gilbert	NY Rangers	73	29	48	77	12
Bobby Hull	Chicago	71	44	31	75	39
Norm Ullman	Det., Tor.	71	35	37	72	28
Alex Delvecchio	Detroit	74	22	48	70	14
John Bucyk	Boston	72	30	39	69	8
Kenny Wharram	Chicago	74	27	42	69	18

1968-69

East Division

Team	GP	W	L	T	GF	GA	PTS
*Montreal	76	46	19	11	271	202	103
Boston	76	42	18	16	303	221	100
NY Rangers	76	41	26	9	231	196	91
Toronto	76	35	26	15	234	217	85
Detroit	76	33	31	12	239	221	78
Chicago	76	34	33	9	280	246	77

West Division

Team	GP	W	L	T	GF	GA	PTS
St. Louis	76	37	25	14	204	157	88
Oakland	76	29	36	11	219	251	69
Philadelphia	76	20	35	21	174	225	61
Los Angeles	76	24	42	10	185	260	58
Pittsburgh	76	20	45	11	189	252	51
Minnesota	76	18	43	15	189	270	51

Leading Scorers

Player	Team	GP	G	A	PTS	PIM
Phil Esposito	Boston	74	49	77	126	79
Bobby Hull	Chicago	74	58	49	107	48
Gordie Howe	Detroit	76	44	59	103	58
Stan Mikita	Chicago	74	30	67	97	52
Ken Hodge	Boston	75	45	45	90	75
Yvan Cournoyer	Montreal	76	43	44	87	31
Alex Delvecchio	Detroit	72	25	58	83	8
Red Berenson	St. Louis	76	35	47	82	43
Jean Béliveau	Montreal	69	33	49	82	55
Frank Mahovlich	Detroit	76	49	29	78	38
Jean Ratelle	NY Rangers	75	32	46	78	26

1969-70

East Division

Team	GP	W	L	T	GF	GA	PTS
Chicago	76	45	22	9	250	170	99
*Boston	76	40	17	19	277	216	99
Detroit	76	40	21	15	246	199	95
NY Rangers	76	38	22	16	246	189	92
Montreal	76	38	22	16	244	201	92
Toronto	76	29	34	13	222	242	71

West Division

Team	GP	W	L	T	GF	GA	PTS
St. Louis	76	37	27	12	224	179	86
Pittsburgh	76	26	38	12	182	238	64
Minnesota	76	19	35	22	224	257	60
Oakland	76	22	40	14	169	243	58
Philadelphia	76	17	35	24	197	225	58
Los Angeles	76	14	52	10	168	290	38

Leading Scorers

Player	Team	GP	G	A	PTS	PIM
Bobby Orr	Boston	76	33	87	120	125
Phil Esposito	Boston	76	43	56	99	50
Stan Mikita	Chicago	76	39	47	86	50
Phil Goyette	St. Louis	72	29	49	78	16
Walt Tkaczuk	NY Rangers	76	27	50	77	38
Jean Ratelle	NY Rangers	75	32	42	74	28
Red Berenson	St. Louis	67	33	39	72	38
Jean-Paul Parise	Minnesota	74	24	48	72	72
Gordie Howe	Detroit	76	31	40	71	58
Frank Mahovlich	Detroit	74	38	32	70	59
Dave Balon	NY Rangers	76	33	37	70	100
John McKenzie	Boston	72	29	41	70	114

1970-71

East Division

Team	GP	W	L	T	GF	GA	PTS
Boston	78	57	14	7	399	207	121
NY Rangers	78	49	18	11	259	177	109
*Montreal	78	42	23	13	291	216	97
Toronto	78	37	33	8	248	211	82
Buffalo	78	24	39	15	217	291	63
Vancouver	78	24	46	8	229	296	56
Detroit	78	22	45	11	209	308	55

West Division

Team	GP	W	L	T	GF	GA	PTS
Chicago	78	49	20	9	277	184	107
St. Louis	78	34	25	19	223	208	87
Philadelphia	78	28	33	17	207	225	73
Minnesota	78	28	34	16	191	223	72
Los Angeles	78	25	40	13	239	303	63
Pittsburgh	78	21	37	20	221	240	62
California	78	20	53	5	199	320	45

Leading Scorers

Player	Team	GP	G	A	PTS	PIM
Phil Esposito	Boston	78	76	76	152	71
Bobby Orr	Boston	78	37	102	139	91
John Bucyk	Boston	78	51	65	116	8
Ken Hodge	Boston	78	43	62	105	113
Bobby Hull	Chicago	78	44	52	96	32
Norm Ullman	Toronto	73	34	51	85	24
Wayne Cashman	Boston	77	21	58	79	100
John McKenzie	Boston	65	31	46	77	120
Dave Keon	Toronto	76	38	38	76	4
Jean Béliveau	Montreal	70	25	51	76	40
Fred Stanfield	Boston	75	24	52	76	12

1971-72

East Division

Team	GP	W	L	T	GF	GA	PTS
*Boston	78	54	13	11	330	204	119
NY Rangers	78	48	17	13	317	192	109
Montreal	78	46	16	16	307	205	108
Toronto	78	33	31	14	209	208	80
Detroit	78	33	35	10	261	262	76
Buffalo	78	16	43	19	203	289	51
Vancouver	78	20	50	8	203	297	48

West Division

Team	GP	W	L	T	GF	GA	PTS
Chicago	78	46	17	15	256	166	107
Minnesota	78	37	29	12	212	191	86
St. Louis	78	28	39	11	208	247	67
Pittsburgh	78	26	38	14	220	258	66
Philadelphia	78	26	38	14	200	236	66
California	78	21	39	18	216	288	60
Los Angeles	78	20	49	9	206	305	49

Leading Scorers

Player	Team	GP	G	A	PTS	PIM
Phil Esposito	Boston	76	66	67	133	76
Bobby Orr	Boston	76	37	80	117	106
Jean Ratelle	NY Rangers	63	46	63	109	4
Vic Hadfield	NY Rangers	78	50	56	106	142
Rod Gilbert	NY Rangers	73	43	54	97	64
Frank Mahovlich	Montreal	76	43	53	96	36
Bobby Hull	Chicago	78	50	43	93	24
Yvan Cournoyer	Montreal	73	47	36	83	15
John Bucyk	Boston	78	32	51	83	4
Bobby Clarke	Philadelphia	78	35	46	81	87
Jacques Lemaire	Montreal	77	32	49	81	26

1972-73

East Division

Team	GP	W	L	T	GF	GA	PTS
*Montreal	78	52	10	16	329	184	120
Boston	78	51	22	5	330	235	107
NY Rangers	78	47	23	8	297	208	102
Buffalo	78	37	27	14	257	219	88
Detroit	78	37	29	12	265	243	86
Toronto	78	27	41	10	247	279	64
Vancouver	78	22	47	9	233	339	53
NY Islanders	78	12	60	6	170	347	30

West Division

Team	GP	W	L	T	GF	GA	PTS
Chicago	78	42	27	9	284	225	93
Philadelphia	78	37	30	11	296	256	85
Minnesota	78	37	30	11	254	230	85
St. Louis	78	32	34	12	233	251	76
Pittsburgh	78	32	37	9	257	265	73
Los Angeles	78	31	36	11	232	245	73
Atlanta	78	25	38	15	191	239	65
California	78	16	46	16	213	323	48

Leading Scorers

Player	Team	GP	G	A	PTS	PIM
Phil Esposito	Boston	78	55	75	130	87
Bobby Clarke	Philadelphia	78	37	67	104	80
Bobby Orr	Boston	63	29	72	101	99
Rick MacLeish	Philadelphia	78	50	50	100	69
Jacques Lemaire	Montreal	77	44	51	95	16
Jean Ratelle	NY Rangers	78	41	53	94	12
Mickey Redmond	Detroit	76	52	41	93	24
John Bucyk	Boston	78	40	53	93	12
Frank Mahovlich	Montreal	78	38	55	93	51
Jim Pappin	Chicago	76	41	51	92	82

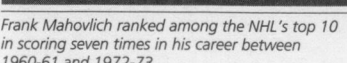

Frank Mahovlich ranked among the NHL's top 10 in scoring seven times in his career between 1960-61 and 1972-73.

1973-74

East Division

Team	GP	W	L	T	GF	GA	PTS
Boston	78	52	17	9	349	221	113
Montreal	78	45	24	9	293	240	99
NY Rangers	78	40	24	14	300	251	94
Toronto	78	35	27	16	274	230	86
Buffalo	78	32	34	12	242	250	76
Detroit	78	29	39	10	255	319	68
Vancouver	78	24	43	11	224	296	59
NY Islanders	78	19	41	18	182	247	56

West Division

Team	GP	W	L	T	GF	GA	PTS
*Philadelphia	78	50	16	12	273	164	112
Chicago	78	41	14	23	272	164	105
Los Angeles	78	33°	33	12	233	231	78
Atlanta	78	30	34	14	214	238	74
Pittsburgh	78	28	41	9	242	273	65
St. Louis	78	26	40	12	206	248	64
Minnesota	78	23	38	17	235	275	63
California	78	13	55	10	195	342	36

Leading Scorers

Player	Team	GP	G	A	PTS	PIM
Phil Esposito	Boston	78	68	77	145	58
Bobby Orr	Boston	74	32	90	122	82
Ken Hodge	Boston	76	50	55	105	43
Wayne Cashman	Boston	78	30	59	89	111
Bobby Clarke	Philadelphia	77	35	52	87	113
Rick Martin	Buffalo	78	52	34	86	38
Syl Apps Jr.	Pittsburgh	75	24	61	85	37
Darryl Sittler	Toronto	78	38	46	84	55
Lowell MacDonald	Pittsburgh	78	43	39	82	14
Brad Park	NY Rangers	78	25	57	82	148
Dennis Hextall	Minnesota	78	20	62	82	138

1974-75

PRINCE OF WALES CONFERENCE
Norris Division

Team	GP	W	L	T	GF	GA	PTS
Montreal	80	47	14	19	374	225	113
Los Angeles	80	42	17	21	269	185	105
Pittsburgh	80	37	28	15	326	289	89
Detroit	80	23	45	12	259	335	58
Washington	80	8	67	5	181	446	21

Adams Division

Team	GP	W	L	T	GF	GA	PTS
Buffalo	80	49	16	15	354	240	113
Boston	80	40	26	14	345	245	94
Toronto	80	31	33	16	280	309	78
California	80	19	48	13	212	316	51

CLARENCE CAMPBELL CONFERENCE
Patrick Division

Team	GP	W	L	T	GF	GA	PTS
*Philadelphia	80	51	18	11	293	181	113
NY Rangers	80	37	29	14	319	276	88
NY Islanders	80	33	25	22	264	221	88
Atlanta	80	34	31	15	243	233	83

Smythe Division

Team	GP	W	L	T	GF	GA	PTS
Vancouver	80	38	32	10	271	254	86
St. Louis	80	35	31	14	269	267	84
Chicago	80	37	35	8	268	241	82
Minnesota	80	23	50	7	221	341	53
Kansas City	80	15	54	11	184	328	41

Leading Scorers

Player	Team	GP	G	A	PTS	PIM
Bobby Orr	Boston	80	46	89	135	101
Phil Esposito	Boston	79	61	66	127	62
Marcel Dionne	Detroit	80	47	74	121	14
Guy Lafleur	Montreal	70	53	66	119	37
Pete Mahovlich	Montreal	80	35	82	117	64
Bobby Clarke	Philadelphia	80	27	89	116	125
Rene Robert	Buffalo	74	40	60	100	75
Rod Gilbert	NY Rangers	76	36	61	97	22
Gilbert Perreault	Buffalo	68	39	57	96	36
Rick Martin	Buffalo	68	52	43	95	72

1975-76

PRINCE OF WALES CONFERENCE
Norris Division

Team	GP	W	L	T	GF	GA	PTS
*Montreal	80	58	11	11	337	174	127
Los Angeles	80	38	33	9	263	265	85
Pittsburgh	80	35	33	12	339	303	82
Detroit	80	26	44	10	226	300	62
Washington	80	11	59	10	224	394	32

Adams Division

Team	GP	W	L	T	GF	GA	PTS
Boston	80	48	15	17	313	237	113
Buffalo	80	46	21	13	339	240	105
Toronto	80	34	31	15	294	276	83
California	80	27	42	11	250	278	65

CLARENCE CAMPBELL CONFERENCE
Patrick Division

Team	GP	W	L	T	GF	GA	PTS
Philadelphia	80	51	13	16	348	209	118
NY Islanders	80	42	21	17	297	190	101
Atlanta	80	35	33	12	262	237	82
NY Rangers	80	29	42	9	262	333	67

Smythe Division

Team	GP	W	L	T	GF	GA	PTS
Chicago	80	32	30	18	254	261	82
Vancouver	80	33	32	15	271	272	81
St. Louis	80	29	37	14	249	290	72
Minnesota	80	20	53	7	195	303	47
Kansas City	80	12	56	12	190	351	36

Leading Scorers

Player	Team	GP	G	A	PTS	PIM
Guy Lafleur	Montreal	80	56	69	125	36
Bobby Clarke	Philadelphia	76	30	89	119	136
Gilbert Perreault	Buffalo	80	44	69	113	36
Bill Barber	Philadelphia	80	50	62	112	104
Pierre Larouche	Pittsburgh	76	53	58	111	33
Jean Ratelle	Bos., NYR	80	36	69	105	18
Pete Mahovlich	Montreal	80	34	71	105	76
Jean Pronovost	Pittsburgh	80	52	52	104	24
Darryl Sittler	Toronto	79	41	59	100	90
Syl Apps Jr.	Pittsburgh	80	32	67	99	24

1976-77

PRINCE OF WALES CONFERENCE
Norris Division

Team	GP	W	L	T	GF	GA	PTS
*Montreal	80	60	8	12	387	171	132
Los Angeles	80	34	31	15	271	241	83
Pittsburgh	80	34	33	13	240	252	81
Washington	80	24	42	14	221	307	62
Detroit	80	16	55	9	183	309	41

Adams Division

Team	GP	W	L	T	GF	GA	PTS
Boston	80	49	23	8	312	240	106
Buffalo	80	48	24	8	301	220	104
Toronto	80	33	32	15	301	285	81
Cleveland	80	25	42	13	240	292	63

CLARENCE CAMPBELL CONFERENCE
Patrick Division

Team	GP	W	L	T	GF	GA	PTS
Philadelphia	80	48	16	16	323	213	112
NY Islanders	80	47	21	12	288	193	106
Atlanta	80	34	34	12	264	265	80
NY Rangers	80	29	37	14	272	310	72

Smythe Division

Team	GP	W	L	T	GF	GA	PTS
St. Louis	80	32	39	9	239	276	73
Minnesota	80	23	39	18	240	310	64
Chicago	80	26	43	11	240	298	63
Vancouver	80	25	42	13	235	294	63
Colorado	80	20	46	14	226	307	54

Leading Scorers

Player	Team	GP	G	A	PTS	PIM
Guy Lafleur	Montreal	80	56	80	136	20
Marcel Dionne	Los Angeles	80	53	69	122	12
Steve Shutt	Montreal	80	60	45	105	28
Rick MacLeish	Philadelphia	79	49	48	97	42
Gilbert Perreault	Buffalo	80	39	56	95	30
Tim Young	Minnesota	80	29	66	95	58
Jean Ratelle	Boston	78	33	61	94	22
Lanny McDonald	Toronto	80	46	44	90	77
Darryl Sittler	Toronto	73	38	52	90	89
Bobby Clarke	Philadelphia	80	27	63	90	71

1977-78

PRINCE OF WALES CONFERENCE
Norris Division

Team	GP	W	L	T	GF	GA	PTS
*Montreal	80	59	10	11	359	183	129
Detroit	80	32	34	14	252	266	78
Los Angeles	80	31	34	15	243	245	77
Pittsburgh	80	25	37	18	254	321	68
Washington	80	17	49	14	195	321	48

Adams Division

Team	GP	W	L	T	GF	GA	PTS
Boston	80	51	18	11	333	218	113
Buffalo	80	44	19	17	288	215	105
Toronto	80	41	29	10	271	237	92
Cleveland	80	22	45	13	230	325	57

CLARENCE CAMPBELL CONFERENCE
Patrick Division

Team	GP	W	L	T	GF	GA	PTS
NY Islanders	80	48	17	15	334	210	111
Philadelphia	80	45	20	15	296	200	105
Atlanta	80	34	27	19	274	252	87
NY Rangers	80	30	37	13	279	280	73

Smythe Division

Team	GP	W	L	T	GF	GA	PTS
Chicago	80	32	29	19	230	220	83
Colorado	80	19	40	21	257	305	59
Vancouver	80	20	43	17	239	320	57
St. Louis	80	20	47	13	195	304	53
Minnesota	80	18	53	9	218	325	45

Leading Scorers

Player	Team	GP	G	A	PTS	PIM
Guy Lafleur	Montreal	78	60	72	132	26
Bryan Trottier	NY Islanders	77	46	77	123	46
Darryl Sittler	Toronto	80	45	72	117	100
Jacques Lemaire	Montreal	76	36	61	97	14
Denis Potvin	NY Islanders	80	30	64	94	81
Mike Bossy	NY Islanders	73	53	38	91	6
Terry O'Reilly	Boston	77	29	61	90	211
Gilbert Perreault	Buffalo	79	41	48	89	20
Bobby Clarke	Philadelphia	71	21	68	89	83
Lanny McDonald	Toronto	74	47	40	87	54
Wilf Paiement	Colorado	80	31	56	87	114

1978-79

PRINCE OF WALES CONFERENCE
Norris Division

Team	GP	W	L	T	GF	GA	PTS
*Montreal	80	52	17	11	337	204	115
Pittsburgh	80	36	31	13	281	279	85
Los Angeles	80	34	34	12	292	286	80
Washington	80	24	41	15	273	338	63
Detroit	80	23	41	16	252	295	62

Adams Division

Team	GP	W	L	T	GF	GA	PTS
Boston	80	43	23	14	316	270	100
Buffalo	80	36	28	16	280	263	88
Toronto	80	34	33	13	267	252	81
Minnesota	80	28	40	12	257	289	68

CLARENCE CAMPBELL CONFERENCE

Patrick Division

Team	GP	W	L	T	GF	GA	PTS
NY Islanders	80	51	15	14	358	214	116
Philadelphia	80	40	25	15	281	248	95
NY Rangers	80	40	29	11	316	292	91
Atlanta	80	41	31	8	327	280	90

Smythe Division

Team	GP	W	L	T	GF	GA	PTS
Chicago	80	29	36	15	244	277	73
Vancouver	80	25	42	13	217	291	63
St. Louis	80	18	50	12	249	348	48
Colorado	80	15	53	12	210	331	42

Leading Scorers

Player	Team	GP	G	A	PTS	PIM
Bryan Trottier	NY Islanders	76	47	87	134	50
Marcel Dionne	Los Angeles	80	59	71	130	30
Guy Lafleur	Montreal	80	52	77	129	28
Mike Bossy	NY Islanders	80	69	57	126	25
Bob MacMillan	Atlanta	79	37	71	108	14
Guy Chouinard	Atlanta	80	50	57	107	14
Denis Potvin	NY Islanders	73	31	70	101	58
Bernie Federko	St. Louis	74	31	64	95	14
Dave Taylor	Los Angeles	78	43	48	91	124
Clark Gillies	NY Islanders	75	35	56	91	68

1979-80

PRINCE OF WALES CONFERENCE

Norris Division

Team	GP	W	L	T	GF	GA	PTS
Montreal	80	47	20	13	328	240	107
Los Angeles	80	30	36	14	290	313	74
Pittsburgh	80	30	37	13	251	303	73
Hartford	80	27	34	19	303	312	73
Detroit	80	26	43	11	268	306	63

Adams Division

Team	GP	W	L	T	GF	GA	PTS
Buffalo	80	47	17	16	318	201	110
Boston	80	46	21	13	310	234	105
Minnesota	80	36	28	16	311	253	88
Toronto	80	35	40	5	304	327	75
Quebec	80	25	44	11	248	313	61

CLARENCE CAMPBELL CONFERENCE

Patrick Division

Team	GP	W	L	T	GF	GA	PTS
Philadelphia	80	48	12	20	327	254	116
*NY Islanders	80	39	28	13	281	247	91
NY Rangers	80	38	32	10	308	284	86
Atlanta	80	35	32	13	282	269	83
Washington	80	27	40	13	261	293	67

Smythe Division

Team	GP	W	L	T	GF	GA	PTS
Chicago	80	34	27	19	241	250	87
St. Louis	80	34	34	12	266	278	80
Vancouver	80	27	37	16	256	281	70
Edmonton	80	28	39	13	301	322	69
Winnipeg	80	20	49	11	214	314	51
Colorado	80	19	48	13	234	308	51

Leading Scorers

Player	Team	GP	G	A	PTS	PIM
Marcel Dionne	Los Angeles	80	53	84	137	32
Wayne Gretzky	Edmonton	79	51	86	137	21
Guy Lafleur	Montreal	74	50	75	125	12
Gilbert Perreault	Buffalo	80	40	66	106	57
Mike Rogers	Hartford	80	44	61	105	10
Bryan Trottier	NY Islanders	78	42	62	104	68
Charlie Simmer	Los Angeles	64	56	45	101	65
Blaine Stoughton	Hartford	80	56	44	100	16
Darryl Sittler	Toronto	73	40	57	97	62
Blair MacDonald	Edmonton	80	46	48	94	6
Bernie Federko	St. Louis	79	38	56	94	24

1980-81

PRINCE OF WALES CONFERENCE

Norris Division

Team	GP	W	L	T	GF	GA	PTS
Montreal	80	45	22	13	332	232	103
Los Angeles	80	43	24	13	337	290	99
Pittsburgh	80	30	37	13	302	345	73
Hartford	80	21	41	18	292	372	60
Detroit	80	19	43	18	252	339	56

Adams Division

Team	GP	W	L	T	GF	GA	PTS
Buffalo	80	39	20	21	327	250	99
Boston	80	37	30	13	316	272	87
Minnesota	80	35	28	17	291	263	87
Quebec	80	30	32	18	314	318	78
Toronto	80	28	37	15	322	367	71

CLARENCE CAMPBELL CONFERENCE

Patrick Division

Team	GP	W	L	T	GF	GA	PTS
*NY Islanders	80	48	18	14	355	260	110
Philadelphia	80	41	24	15	313	249	97
Calgary	80	39	27	14	329	298	92
NY Rangers	80	30	36	14	312	317	74
Washington	80	26	36	18	286	317	70

Smythe Division

Team	GP	W	L	T	GF	GA	PTS
St. Louis	80	45	18	17	352	281	107
Chicago	80	31	33	16	304	315	78
Vancouver	80	28	32	20	289	301	76
Edmonton	80	29	35	16	328	327	74
Colorado	80	22	45	13	258	344	57
Winnipeg	80	9	57	14	246	400	32

Leading Scorers

Player	Team	GP	G	A	PTS	PIM
Wayne Gretzky	Edmonton	80	55	109	164	28
Marcel Dionne	Los Angeles	80	58	77	135	70
Kent Nilsson	Calgary	80	49	82	131	26
Mike Bossy	NY Islanders	79	68	51	119	32
Dave Taylor	Los Angeles	72	47	65	112	130
Peter Stastny	Quebec	77	39	70	109	37
Charlie Simmer	Los Angeles	65	56	49	105	62
Mike Rogers	Hartford	80	40	65	105	32
Bernie Federko	St. Louis	78	31	73	104	47
Jacques Richard	Quebec	78	52	51	103	39
Rick Middleton	Boston	80	44	59	103	16
Bryan Trottier	NY Islanders	73	31	72	103	74

1981-82

CLARENCE CAMPBELL CONFERENCE

Norris Division

Team	GP	W	L	T	GF	GA	PTS
Minnesota	80	37	23	20	346	288	94
Winnipeg	80	33	33	14	319	332	80
St. Louis	80	32	40	8	315	349	72
Chicago	80	30	38	12	332	363	72
Toronto	80	20	44	16	298	380	56
Detroit	80	21	47	12	270	351	54

Smythe Division

Team	GP	W	L	T	GF	GA	PTS
Edmonton	80	48	17	15	417	295	111
Vancouver	80	30	33	17	290	286	77
Calgary	80	29	34	17	334	345	75
Los Angeles	80	24	41	15	314	369	63
Colorado	80	18	49	13	241	362	49

PRINCE OF WALES CONFERENCE

Adams Division

Team	GP	W	L	T	GF	GA	PTS
Montreal	80	46	17	17	360	223	109
Boston	80	43	27	10	323	285	96
Buffalo	80	39	26	15	307	273	93
Quebec	80	33	31	16	356	345	82
Hartford	80	21	41	18	264	351	60

Patrick Division

Team	GP	W	L	T	GF	GA	PTS
*NY Islanders	80	54	16	10	385	250	118
NY Rangers	80	39	27	14	316	306	92
Philadelphia	80	38	31	11	325	313	87
Pittsburgh	80	31	36	13	310	337	75
Washington	80	26	41	13	319	338	65

Leading Scorers

Player	Team	GP	G	A	PTS	PIM
Wayne Gretzky	Edmonton	80	92	120	212	26
Mike Bossy	NY Islanders	80	64	83	147	22
Peter Stastny	Quebec	80	46	93	139	91
Dennis Maruk	Washington	80	60	76	136	128
Bryan Trottier	NY Islanders	80	50	79	129	88
Denis Savard	Chicago	80	32	87	119	82
Marcel Dionne	Los Angeles	78	50	67	117	50
Bobby Smith	Minnesota	80	43	71	114	82
Dino Ciccarelli	Minnesota	76	55	51	106	138
Dave Taylor	Los Angeles	78	39	67	106	130

1982-83

CLARENCE CAMPBELL CONFERENCE

Norris Division

Team	GP	W	L	T	GF	GA	PTS
Chicago	80	47	23	10	338	268	104
Minnesota	80	40	24	16	321	290	96
Toronto	80	28	40	12	293	330	68
St. Louis	80	25	40	15	285	316	65
Detroit	80	21	44	15	263	344	57

Smythe Division

Team	GP	W	L	T	GF	GA	PTS
Edmonton	80	47	21	12	424	315	106
Calgary	80	32	34	14	321	317	78
Vancouver	80	30	35	15	303	309	75
Winnipeg	80	33	39	8	311	333	74
Los Angeles	80	27	41	12	308	365	66

PRINCE OF WALES CONFERENCE

Adams Division

Team	GP	W	L	T	GF	GA	PTS
Boston	80	50	20	10	327	228	110
Montreal	80	42	24	14	350	286	98
Buffalo	80	38	29	13	318	285	89
Quebec	80	34	34	12	343	336	80
Hartford	80	19	54	7	261	403	45

Patrick Division

Team	GP	W	L	T	GF	GA	PTS
Philadelphia	80	49	23	8	326	240	106
*NY Islanders	80	42	26	12	302	226	96
Washington	80	39	25	16	306	283	94
NY Rangers	80	35	35	10	306	287	80
New Jersey	80	17	49	14	230	338	48
Pittsburgh	80	18	53	9	257	394	45

Leading Scorers

Player	Team	GP	G	A	PTS	PIM
Wayne Gretzky	Edmonton	80	71	125	196	59
Peter Stastny	Quebec	75	47	77	124	78
Denis Savard	Chicago	78	35	86	121	99
Mike Bossy	NY Islanders	79	60	58	118	20
Marcel Dionne	Los Angeles	80	56	51	107	22
Barry Pederson	Boston	77	46	61	107	47
Mark Messier	Edmonton	77	48	58	106	72
Michel Goulet	Quebec	80	57	48	105	51
Glenn Anderson	Edmonton	72	48	56	104	70
Kent Nilsson	Calgary	80	46	58	104	10
Jari Kurri	Edmonton	80	45	59	104	22

1983-84

CLARENCE CAMPBELL CONFERENCE

Norris Division

Team	GP	W	L	T	GF	GA	PTS
Minnesota	80	39	31	10	345	344	88
St. Louis	80	32	41	7	293	316	71
Detroit	80	31	42	7	298	323	69
Chicago	80	30	42	8	277	311	68
Toronto	80	26	45	9	303	387	61

Smythe Division

Team	GP	W	L	T	GF	GA	PTS
*Edmonton	80	57	18	5	446	314	119
Calgary	80	34	32	14	311	314	82
Vancouver	80	32	39	9	306	328	73
Winnipeg	80	31	38	11	340	374	73
Los Angeles	80	23	44	13	309	376	59

PRINCE OF WALES CONFERENCE

Adams Division

Team	GP	W	L	T	GF	GA	PTS
Boston	80	49	25	6	336	261	104
Buffalo	80	48	25	7	315	257	103
Quebec	80	42	28	10	360	278	94
Montreal	80	35	40	5	286	295	75
Hartford	80	28	42	10	288	320	66

Patrick Division

Team	GP	W	L	T	GF	GA	PTS
NY Islanders	80	50	26	4	357	269	104
Washington	80	48	27	5	308	226	101
Philadelphia	80	44	26	10	350	290	98
NY Rangers	80	42	29	9	314	304	93
New Jersey	80	17	56	7	231	350	41
Pittsburgh	80	16	58	6	254	390	38

Leading Scorers

Player	Team	GP	G	A	PTS	PIM
Wayne Gretzky	Edmonton	74	87	118	205	39
Paul Coffey	Edmonton	80	40	86	126	104
Michel Goulet	Quebec	75	56	65	121	76
Peter Stastny	Quebec	80	46	73	119	73
Mike Bossy	NY Islanders	67	51	67	118	8
Barry Pederson	Boston	80	39	77	116	64
Jari Kurri	Edmonton	64	52	61	113	14
Bryan Trottier	NY Islanders	68	40	71	111	59
Bernie Federko	St. Louis	79	41	66	107	43
Rick Middleton	Boston	80	47	58	105	14

1984-85

CLARENCE CAMPBELL CONFERENCE

Norris Division

Team	GP	W	L	T	GF	GA	PTS
St. Louis	80	37	31	12	299	288	86
Chicago	80	38	35	7	309	299	83
Detroit	80	27	41	12	313	357	66
Minnesota	80	25	43	12	268	321	62
Toronto	80	20	52	8	253	358	48

Smythe Division

Team	GP	W	L	T	GF	GA	PTS
*Edmonton	80	49	20	11	401	298	109
Winnipeg	80	43	27	10	358	332	96
Calgary	80	41	27	12	363	302	94
Los Angeles	80	34	32	14	339	326	82
Vancouver	80	25	46	9	284	401	59

PRINCE OF WALES CONFERENCE

Adams Division

Team	GP	W	L	T	GF	GA	PTS
Montreal	80	41	27	12	309	262	94
Quebec	80	41	30	9	323	275	91
Buffalo	80	38	28	14	290	237	90
Boston	80	36	34	10	303	287	82
Hartford	80	30	41	9	268	318	69

Patrick Division

Team	GP	W	L	T	GF	GA	PTS
Philadelphia	80	53	20	7	348	241	113
Washington	80	46	25	9	322	240	101
NY Islanders	80	40	34	6	345	312	86
NY Rangers	80	26	44	10	295	345	62
New Jersey	80	22	48	10	264	346	54
Pittsburgh	80	24	51	5	276	385	53

Leading Scorers

Player	Team	GP	G	A	PTS	PIM
Wayne Gretzky	Edmonton	80	73	135	208	52
Jari Kurri	Edmonton	73	71	64	135	30
Dale Hawerchuk	Winnipeg	80	53	77	130	74
Marcel Dionne	Los Angeles	80	46	80	126	46
Paul Coffey	Edmonton	80	37	84	121	97
Mike Bossy	NY Islanders	76	58	59	117	38
John Ogrodnick	Detroit	79	55	50	105	30
Denis Savard	Chicago	79	38	67	105	56
Bernie Federko	St. Louis	76	30	73	103	27
Mike Gartner	Washington	80	50	52	102	71

1985-86
CLARENCE CAMPBELL CONFERENCE
Norris Division

Team	GP	W	L	T	GF	GA	PTS
Chicago	80	39	33	8	351	349	86
Minnesota	80	38	33	9	327	305	85
St. Louis	80	37	34	9	302	291	83
Toronto	80	25	48	7	311	386	57
Detroit	80	17	57	6	266	415	40

Smythe Division

Team	GP	W	L	T	GF	GA	PTS
Edmonton	80	56	17	7	426	310	119
Calgary	80	40	31	9	354	315	89
Winnipeg	80	26	47	7	295	372	59
Vancouver	80	23	44	13	282	333	59
Los Angeles	80	23	49	8	284	389	54

PRINCE OF WALES CONFERENCE
Adams Division

Team	GP	W	L	T	GF	GA	PTS
Quebec	80	43	31	6	330	289	92
*Montreal	80	40	33	7	330	280	87
Boston	80	37	31	12	311	288	86
Hartford	80	40	36	4	332	302	84
Buffalo	80	37	37	6	296	291	80

Patrick Division

Team	GP	W	L	T	GF	GA	PTS
Philadelphia	80	53	23	4	335	241	110
Washington	80	50	23	7	315	272	107
NY Islanders	80	39	29	12	327	284	90
NY Rangers	80	36	38	6	280	276	78
Pittsburgh	80	34	38	8	313	305	76
New Jersey	80	28	49	3	300	374	59

Leading Scorers

Player	Team	GP	G	A	PTS	PIM
Wayne Gretzky	Edmonton	80	52	163	215	52
Mario Lemieux	Pittsburgh	79	48	93	141	43
Paul Coffey	Edmonton	79	48	90	138	120
Jari Kurri	Edmonton	78	68	63	131	22
Mike Bossy	NY Islanders	80	61	62	123	14
Peter Stastny	Quebec	76	41	81	122	60
Denis Savard	Chicago	80	47	69	116	111
Mats Naslund	Montreal	80	43	67	110	16
Dale Hawerchuk	Winnipeg	80	46	59	105	44
Neal Broten	Minnesota	80	29	76	105	47

1986-87
CLARENCE CAMPBELL CONFERENCE
Norris Division

Team	GP	W	L	T	GF	GA	PTS
St. Louis	80	32	33	15	281	293	79
Detroit	80	34	36	10	260	274	78
Chicago	80	29	37	14	290	310	72
Toronto	80	32	42	6	286	319	70
Minnesota	80	30	40	10	296	314	70

Smythe Division

Team	GP	W	L	T	GF	GA	PTS
*Edmonton	80	50	24	6	372	284	106
Calgary	80	46	31	3	318	289	95
Winnipeg	80	40	32	8	279	271	88
Los Angeles	80	31	41	8	318	341	70
Vancouver	80	29	43	8	282	314	66

PRINCE OF WALES CONFERENCE
Adams Division

Team	GP	W	L	T	GF	GA	PTS
Hartford	80	43	30	7	287	270	93
Montreal	80	41	29	10	277	241	92
Boston	80	39	34	7	301	276	85
Quebec	80	31	39	10	267	276	72
Buffalo	80	28	44	8	280	308	64

Patrick Division

Team	GP	W	L	T	GF	GA	PTS
Philadelphia	80	46	26	8	310	245	100
Washington	80	38	32	10	285	278	86
NY Islanders	80	35	33	12	279	281	82
NY Rangers	80	34	38	8	307	323	76
Pittsburgh	80	30	38	12	297	290	72
New Jersey	80	29	45	6	293	368	64

Leading Scorers

Player	Team	GP	G	A	PTS	PIM
Wayne Gretzky	Edmonton	79	62	121	183	28
Jari Kurri	Edmonton	79	54	54	108	41
Mario Lemieux	Pittsburgh	63	54	53	107	57
Mark Messier	Edmonton	77	37	70	107	73
Doug Gilmour	St. Louis	80	42	63	105	58
Dino Ciccarelli	Minnesota	80	52	51	103	92
Dale Hawerchuk	Winnipeg	80	47	53	100	54
Michel Goulet	Quebec	75	49	47	96	61
Tim Kerr	Philadelphia	75	58	37	95	57
Raymond Bourque	Boston	78	23	72	95	36

1987-88
CLARENCE CAMPBELL CONFERENCE
Norris Division

Team	GP	W	L	T	GF	GA	PTS
Detroit	80	41	28	11	322	269	93
St. Louis	80	34	38	8	278	294	76
Chicago	80	30	41	9	284	328	69
Toronto	80	21	49	10	273	345	52
Minnesota	80	19	48	13	242	349	51

Smythe Division

Team	GP	W	L	T	GF	GA	PTS
Calgary	80	48	23	9	397	305	105
*Edmonton	80	44	25	11	363	288	99
Winnipeg	80	33	36	11	292	310	77
Los Angeles	80	30	42	8	318	359	68
Vancouver	80	25	46	9	272	320	59

PRINCE OF WALES CONFERENCE
Adams Division

Team	GP	W	L	T	GF	GA	PTS
Montreal	80	45	22	13	298	238	103
Boston	80	44	30	6	300	251	94
Buffalo	80	37	32	11	283	305	85
Hartford	80	35	38	7	249	267	77
Quebec	80	32	43	5	271	306	69

Patrick Division

Team	GP	W	L	T	GF	GA	PTS
NY Islanders	80	39	31	10	308	267	88
Washington	80	38	33	9	281	249	85
Philadelphia	80	38	33	9	292	292	85
New Jersey	80	38	36	6	295	296	82
NY Rangers	80	36	34	10	300	283	82
Pittsburgh	80	36	35	9	319	316	81

Leading Scorers

Player	Team	GP	G	A	PTS	PIM
Mario Lemieux	Pittsburgh	77	70	98	168	92
Wayne Gretzky	Edmonton	64	40	109	149	24
Denis Savard	Chicago	80	44	87	131	95
Dale Hawerchuk	Winnipeg	80	44	77	121	59
Luc Robitaille	Los Angeles	80	53	58	111	82
Peter Stastny	Quebec	76	46	65	111	69
Mark Messier	Edmonton	77	37	74	111	103
Jimmy Carson	Los Angeles	80	55	52	107	45
Hakan Loob	Calgary	80	50	56	106	47
Michel Goulet	Quebec	80	48	58	106	56

1988-89
CLARENCE CAMPBELL CONFERENCE
Norris Division

Team	GP	W	L	T	GF	GA	PTS
Detroit	80	34	34	12	313	316	80
St. Louis	80	33	35	12	275	285	78
Minnesota	80	27	37	16	258	278	70
Chicago	80	27	41	12	297	335	66
Toronto	80	28	46	6	259	342	62

Smythe Division

Team	GP	W	L	T	GF	GA	PTS
*Calgary	80	54	17	9	354	226	117
Los Angeles	80	42	31	7	376	335	91
Edmonton	80	38	34	8	325	306	84
Vancouver	80	33	39	8	251	253	74
Winnipeg	80	26	42	12	300	355	64

PRINCE OF WALES CONFERENCE
Adams Division

Team	GP	W	L	T	GF	GA	PTS
Montreal	80	53	18	9	315	218	115
Boston	80	37	29	14	289	256	88
Buffalo	80	38	35	7	291	299	83
Hartford	80	37	38	5	299	290	79
Quebec	80	27	46	7	269	342	61

Patrick Division

Team	GP	W	L	T	GF	GA	PTS
Washington	80	41	29	10	305	259	92
Pittsburgh	80	40	33	7	347	349	87
NY Rangers	80	37	35	8	310	307	82
Philadelphia	80	36	36	8	307	285	80
New Jersey	80	27	41	12	281	325	66
NY Islanders	80	28	47	5	265	325	61

Leading Scorers

Player	Team	GP	G	A	PTS	PIM
Mario Lemieux	Pittsburgh	76	85	114	199	100
Wayne Gretzky	Los Angeles	78	54	114	168	26
Steve Yzerman	Detroit	80	65	90	155	61
Bernie Nicholls	Los Angeles	79	70	80	150	96
Rob Brown	Pittsburgh	68	49	66	115	118
Paul Coffey	Pittsburgh	75	30	83	113	193
Joe Mullen	Calgary	79	51	59	110	16
Jari Kurri	Edmonton	76	44	58	102	69
Jimmy Carson	Edmonton	80	49	51	100	36
Luc Robitaille	Los Angeles	78	46	52	98	65

1989-90
CLARENCE CAMPBELL CONFERENCE
Norris Division

Team	GP	W	L	T	GF	GA	PTS
Chicago	80	41	33	6	316	294	88
St. Louis	80	37	34	9	295	279	83
Toronto	80	38	38	4	337	358	80
Minnesota	80	36	40	4	284	291	76
Detroit	80	28	38	14	288	323	70

Smythe Division

Team	GP	W	L	T	GF	GA	PTS
Calgary	80	42	23	15	348	265	99
*Edmonton	80	38	28	14	315	283	90
Winnipeg	80	37	32	11	298	290	85
Los Angeles	80	34	39	7	338	337	75
Vancouver	80	25	41	14	245	306	64

PRINCE OF WALES CONFERENCE
Adams Division

Team	GP	W	L	T	GF	GA	PTS
Boston	80	46	25	9	289	232	101
Buffalo	80	45	27	8	286	248	98
Montreal	80	41	28	11	288	234	93
Hartford	80	38	33	9	275	268	85
Quebec	80	12	61	7	240	407	31

Patrick Division

Team	GP	W	L	T	GF	GA	PTS
NY Rangers	80	36	31	13	279	267	85
New Jersey	80	37	34	9	295	288	83
Washington	80	36	38	6	284	275	78
NY Islanders	80	31	38	11	281	288	73
Pittsburgh	80	32	40	8	318	359	72
Philadelphia	80	30	39	11	290	297	71

Leading Scorers

Player	Team	GP	G	A	PTS	PIM
Wayne Gretzky	Los Angeles	73	40	102	142	42
Mark Messier	Edmonton	79	45	84	129	79
Steve Yzerman	Detroit	79	62	65	127	79
Mario Lemieux	Pittsburgh	59	45	78	123	78
Brett Hull	St. Louis	80	72	41	113	24
Bernie Nicholls	L.A., NYR	79	39	73	112	86
Pierre Turgeon	Buffalo	80	40	66	106	29
Pat LaFontaine	NY Islanders	74	54	51	105	38
Paul Coffey	Pittsburgh	80	29	74	103	95
Joe Sakic	Quebec	80	39	63	102	27
Adam Oates	St. Louis	80	23	79	102	30

1990-91
CLARENCE CAMPBELL CONFERENCE
Norris Division

Team	GP	W	L	T	GF	GA	PTS
Chicago	80	49	23	8	284	211	106
St. Louis	80	47	22	11	310	250	105
Detroit	80	34	38	8	273	298	76
Minnesota	80	27	39	14	256	266	68
Toronto	80	23	46	11	241	318	57

Smythe Division

Team	GP	W	L	T	GF	GA	PTS
Los Angeles	80	46	24	10	340	254	102
Calgary	80	46	26	8	344	263	100
Edmonton	80	37	37	6	272	272	80
Vancouver	80	28	43	9	243	315	65
Winnipeg	80	26	43	11	260	288	63

PRINCE OF WALES CONFERENCE
Adams Division

Team	GP	W	L	T	GF	GA	PTS
Boston	80	44	24	12	299	264	100
Montreal	80	39	30	11	273	249	89
Buffalo	80	31	30	19	292	278	81
Hartford	80	31	38	11	238	276	73
Quebec	80	16	50	14	236	354	46

Patrick Division

Team	GP	W	L	T	GF	GA	PTS
*Pittsburgh	80	41	33	6	342	305	88
NY Rangers	80	36	31	13	297	265	85
Washington	80	37	36	7	258	258	81
New Jersey	80	32	33	15	272	264	79
Philadelphia	80	33	37	10	252	267	76
NY Islanders	80	25	45	10	223	290	60

Leading Scorers

Player	Team	GP	G	A	PTS	PIM
Wayne Gretzky	Los Angeles	78	41	122	163	16
Brett Hull	St. Louis	78	86	45	131	22
Adam Oates	St. Louis	61	25	90	115	29
Mark Recchi	Pittsburgh	78	40	73	113	48
John Cullen	Pit., Hfd.	78	39	71	110	101
Joe Sakic	Quebec	80	48	61	109	24
Steve Yzerman	Detroit	80	51	57	108	34
Theoren Fleury	Calgary	79	51	53	104	136
Al MacInnis	Calgary	78	28	75	103	90
Steve Larmer	Chicago	80	44	57	101	79

1991-92
CLARENCE CAMPBELL CONFERENCE
Norris Division

Team	GP	W	L	T	GF	GA	PTS
Detroit	80	43	25	12	320	256	98
Chicago	80	36	29	15	257	236	87
St. Louis	80	36	33	11	279	266	83
Minnesota	80	32	42	6	246	278	70
Toronto	80	30	43	7	234	294	67

Smythe Division

Team	GP	W	L	T	GF	GA	PTS
Vancouver	80	42	26	12	285	250	96
Los Angeles	80	35	31	14	287	296	84
Edmonton	80	36	34	10	295	297	82
Winnipeg	80	33	32	15	251	244	81
Calgary	80	31	37	12	296	305	74
San Jose	80	17	58	5	219	359	39

PRINCE OF WALES CONFERENCE
Adams Division

Team	GP	W	L	T	GF	GA	PTS
Montreal	80	41	28	11	267	207	93
Boston	80	36	32	12	270	275	84
Buffalo	80	31	37	12	289	299	74
Hartford	80	26	41	13	247	283	65
Quebec	80	20	48	12	255	318	52

Patrick Division

Team	GP	W	L	T	GF	GA	PTS
NY Rangers	80	50	25	5	321	246	105
Washington	80	45	27	8	330	275	98
*Pittsburgh	80	39	32	9	343	308	87
New Jersey	80	38	31	11	289	259	87
NY Islanders	80	34	35	11	291	299	79
Philadelphia	80	32	37	11	252	273	75

Leading Scorers

Player	Team	GP	G	A	PTS	PIM
Mario Lemieux	Pittsburgh	64	44	87	131	94
Kevin Stevens	Pittsburgh	80	54	69	123	254
Wayne Gretzky	Los Angeles	74	31	90	121	34
Brett Hull	St. Louis	73	70	39	109	48
Luc Robitaille	Los Angeles	80	44	63	107	95
Mark Messier	NY Rangers	79	35	72	107	76
Jeremy Roenick	Chicago	80	53	50	103	23
Steve Yzerman	Detroit	79	45	58	103	64
Brian Leetch	NY Rangers	80	22	80	102	26
Adam Oates	St.L., Bos.	80	20	79	99	22

1992-93
CLARENCE CAMPBELL CONFERENCE
Norris Division

Team	GP	W	L	T	GF	GA	PTS
Chicago	84	47	25	12	279	230	106
Detroit	84	47	28	9	369	280	103
Toronto	84	44	29	11	288	241	99
St. Louis	84	37	36	11	282	278	85
Minnesota	84	36	38	10	272	293	82
Tampa Bay	84	23	54	7	245	332	53

Smythe Division

Team	GP	W	L	T	GF	GA	PTS
Vancouver	84	46	29	9	346	278	101
Calgary	84	43	30	11	322	282	97
Los Angeles	84	39	35	10	338	340	88
Winnipeg	84	40	37	7	322	320	87
Edmonton	84	26	50	8	242	337	60
San Jose	84	11	71	2	218	414	24

PRINCE OF WALES CONFERENCE
Adams Division

Team	GP	W	L	T	GF	GA	PTS
Boston	84	51	26	7	332	268	109
Quebec	84	47	27	10	351	300	104
*Montreal	84	48	30	6	326	280	102
Buffalo	84	38	36	10	335	297	86
Hartford	84	26	52	6	284	369	58
Ottawa	84	10	70	4	202	395	24

Patrick Division

Team	GP	W	L	T	GF	GA	PTS
Pittsburgh	84	56	21	7	367	268	119
Washington	84	43	34	7	325	286	93
NY Islanders	84	40	37	7	335	297	87
New Jersey	84	40	37	7	308	299	87
Philadelphia	84	36	37	11	319	319	83
NY Rangers	84	34	39	11	304	308	79

Leading Scorers

Player	Team	GP	G	A	PTS	PIM
Mario Lemieux	Pittsburgh	60	69	91	160	38
Pat LaFontaine	Buffalo	84	53	95	148	63
Adam Oates	Boston	84	45	97	142	32
Steve Yzerman	Detroit	84	58	79	137	44
Teemu Selanne	Winnipeg	84	76	56	132	45
Pierre Turgeon	NY Islanders	83	58	74	132	26
Alexander Mogilny	Buffalo	77	76	51	127	40
Doug Gilmour	Toronto	83	32	95	127	100
Luc Robitaille	Los Angeles	84	63	62	125	100
Mark Recchi	Philadelphia	84	53	70	123	95

1993-94
EASTERN CONFERENCE
Northeast Division

Team		GP	W	L	T	GF	GA	PTS
Pittsburgh	(2)	84	44	27	13	299	285	101
Boston	(4)	84	42	29	13	289	252	97
Montreal	(5)	84	41	29	14	283	248	96
Buffalo	(6)	84	43	32	9	282	218	95
Quebec		84	34	42	8	277	292	76
Hartford		84	27	48	9	227	288	63
Ottawa		84	14	61	9	201	397	37

Atlantic Division

Team		GP	W	L	T	GF	GA	PTS
*NY Rangers	(1)	84	52	24	8	299	231	112
New Jersey	(3)	84	47	25	12	306	220	106
Washington	(7)	84	39	35	10	277	263	88
NY Islanders	(8)	84	36	36	12	282	264	84
Florida		84	33	34	17	233	233	83
Philadelphia		84	35	39	10	294	314	80
Tampa Bay		84	30	43	11	224	251	71

WESTERN CONFERENCE
Central Division

Team		GP	W	L	T	GF	GA	PTS
Detroit	(1)	84	46	30	8	356	275	100
Toronto	(3)	84	43	29	12	280	243	98
Dallas	(4)	84	42	29	13	286	265	97
St. Louis	(5)	84	40	33	11	270	283	91
Chicago	(6)	84	39	36	9	254	240	87
Winnipeg		84	24	51	9	245	344	57

Pacific Division

Team		GP	W	L	T	GF	GA	PTS
Calgary	(2)	84	42	29	13	302	256	97
Vancouver	(7)	84	41	40	3	279	276	85
San Jose	(8)	84	33	35	16	252	265	82
Anaheim		84	33	46	5	229	251	71
Los Angeles		84	27	45	12	294	322	66
Edmonton		84	25	45	14	261	305	64

Leading Scorers

Player	Team	GP	G	A	PTS	PIM
Wayne Gretzky	Los Angeles	81	38	92	130	20
Sergei Fedorov	Detroit	82	56	64	120	34
Adam Oates	Boston	77	32	80	112	45
Doug Gilmour	Toronto	83	27	84	111	105
Pavel Bure	Vancouver	76	60	47	107	86
Jeremy Roenick	Chicago	84	46	61	107	125
Mark Recchi	Philadelphia	84	40	67	107	46
Brendan Shanahan	St. Louis	81	52	50	102	211
Dave Andreychuk	Toronto	83	53	46	99	98
Jaromir Jagr	Pittsburgh	80	32	67	99	61

1994-95
EASTERN CONFERENCE
Northeast Division

Team		GP	W	L	T	GF	GA	PTS
Quebec	(1)	48	30	13	5	185	134	65
Pittsburgh	(3)	48	29	16	3	181	158	61
Boston	(4)	48	27	18	3	150	127	57
Buffalo	(7)	48	22	19	7	130	119	51
Hartford		48	19	24	5	127	141	43
Montreal		48	18	23	7	125	148	43
Ottawa		48	9	34	5	117	174	23

Atlantic Division

Team		GP	W	L	T	GF	GA	PTS
Philadelphia	(2)	48	28	16	4	150	132	60
*New Jersey	(5)	48	22	18	8	136	121	52
Washington	(6)	48	22	18	8	136	120	52
NY Rangers	(8)	48	22	23	3	139	134	47
Florida		48	20	22	6	115	127	46
Tampa Bay		48	17	28	3	120	144	37
NY Islanders		48	15	28	5	126	158	35

WESTERN CONFERENCE
Central Division

Team		GP	W	L	T	GF	GA	PTS
Detroit	(1)	48	33	11	4	180	117	70
St. Louis	(3)	48	28	15	5	178	135	61
Chicago	(4)	48	24	19	5	156	115	53
Toronto	(5)	48	21	19	8	135	146	50
Dallas	(8)	48	17	23	8	136	135	42
Winnipeg		48	16	25	7	157	177	39

Pacific Division

Team		GP	W	L	T	GF	GA	PTS
Calgary	(2)	48	24	17	7	163	135	55
Vancouver	(6)	48	18	18	12	153	148	48
San Jose	(7)	48	19	25	4	129	161	42
Los Angeles		48	16	23	9	142	174	41
Edmonton		48	17	27	4	136	183	38
Anaheim		48	16	27	5	125	164	37

Leading Scorers

Player	Team	GP	G	A	PTS	PIM
Jaromir Jagr	Pittsburgh	48	32	38	70	37
Eric Lindros	Philadelphia	46	29	41	70	60
Alex Zhamnov	Winnipeg	48	30	35	65	20
Joe Sakic	Quebec	47	19	43	62	30
Ron Francis	Pittsburgh	44	11	48	59	18
Theoren Fleury	Calgary	47	29	29	58	112
Paul Coffey	Detroit	45	14	44	58	72
Mikael Renberg	Philadelphia	47	26	31	57	20
John LeClair	Mtl., Phi.	46	26	28	54	30
Mark Messier	NY Rangers	46	14	39	53	40
Adam Oates	Boston	48	12	41	53	8

1995-96
EASTERN CONFERENCE
Northeast Division

Team		GP	W	L	T	GF	GA	PTS
Pittsburgh	(2)	82	49	29	4	362	284	102
Boston	(5)	82	40	31	11	282	269	91
Montreal	(6)	82	40	32	10	265	248	90
Hartford		82	34	39	9	237	259	77
Buffalo		82	33	42	7	247	262	73
Ottawa		82	18	59	5	191	291	41

Atlantic Division

Team		GP	W	L	T	GF	GA	PTS
Philadelphia	(1)	82	45	24	13	282	208	103
NY Rangers	(3)	82	41	27	14	272	237	96
Florida	(4)	82	41	31	10	254	234	92
Washington	(7)	82	39	32	11	234	204	89
Tampa Bay	(8)	82	38	32	12	238	248	88
New Jersey		82	37	33	12	215	202	86
NY Islanders		82	22	50	10	229	315	54

WESTERN CONFERENCE
Central Division

Team		GP	W	L	T	GF	GA	PTS
Detroit	(1)	82	62	13	7	325	181	131
Chicago	(3)	82	40	28	14	273	220	94
Toronto	(4)	82	34	36	12	247	252	80
St. Louis	(5)	82	32	34	16	219	248	80
Winnipeg	(8)	82	36	40	6	275	291	78
Dallas		82	26	42	14	227	280	66

Pacific Division

Team		GP	W	L	T	GF	GA	PTS
*Colorado	(2)	82	47	25	10	326	240	104
Calgary	(6)	82	34	37	11	241	240	79
Vancouver	(7)	82	32	35	15	278	278	79
Anaheim		82	35	39	8	234	247	78
Edmonton		82	30	44	8	240	304	68
Los Angeles		82	24	40	18	256	302	66
San Jose		82	20	55	7	252	357	47

Leading Scorers

Player	Team	GP	G	A	PTS	PIM
Mario Lemieux	Pittsburgh	70	69	92	161	54
Jaromir Jagr	Pittsburgh	82	62	87	149	96
Joe Sakic	Colorado	82	51	69	120	44
Ron Francis	Pittsburgh	77	27	92	119	56
Peter Forsberg	Colorado	82	30	86	116	47
Eric Lindros	Philadelphia	73	47	68	115	163
Paul Kariya	Anaheim	82	50	58	108	20
Teemu Selanne	Wpg., Ana.	79	40	68	108	22
Alexander Mogilny	Vancouver	79	55	52	107	16
Sergei Fedorov	Detroit	78	39	68	107	48

1996-97
EASTERN CONFERENCE
Northeast Division

Team		GP	W	L	T	GF	GA	PTS
Buffalo	(2)	82	40	30	12	237	208	92
Pittsburgh	(6)	82	38	36	8	285	280	84
Ottawa	(7)	82	31	36	15	226	234	77
Montreal	(8)	82	31	36	15	249	276	77
Hartford		82	32	39	11	226	256	75
Boston		82	26	47	9	234	300	61

Atlantic Division

Team		GP	W	L	T	GF	GA	PTS
New Jersey	(1)	82	45	23	14	231	182	104
Philadelphia	(3)	82	45	24	13	274	217	103
Florida	(4)	82	35	28	19	221	201	89
NY Rangers	(5)	82	38	34	10	258	231	86
Washington		82	33	40	9	214	231	75
Tampa Bay		82	32	40	10	217	247	74
NY Islanders		82	29	41	12	240	250	70

WESTERN CONFERENCE
Central Division

Team		GP	W	L	T	GF	GA	PTS
Dallas	(2)	82	48	26	8	252	198	104
*Detroit	(3)	82	38	26	18	253	197	94
Phoenix	(5)	82	38	37	7	240	243	83
St. Louis	(6)	82	36	35	11	236	239	83
Chicago	(8)	82	34	35	13	223	210	81
Toronto		82	30	44	8	230	273	68

Pacific Division

Team		GP	W	L	T	GF	GA	PTS
Colorado	(1)	82	49	24	9	277	205	107
Anaheim	(4)	82	36	33	13	245	233	85
Edmonton	(7)	82	36	37	9	252	247	81
Vancouver		82	35	40	7	257	273	77
Calgary		82	32	41	9	214	239	73
Los Angeles		82	28	43	11	214	268	67
San Jose		82	27	47	8	211	278	62

Leading Scorers

Player	Team	GP	G	A	PTS	PIM
Mario Lemieux	Pittsburgh	76	50	72	122	65
Teemu Selanne	Anaheim	78	51	58	109	34
Paul Kariya	Anaheim	69	44	55	99	6
John LeClair	Philadelphia	82	50	47	97	58
Wayne Gretzky	NY Rangers	82	25	72	97	28
Jaromir Jagr	Pittsburgh	63	47	48	95	40
Mats Sundin	Toronto	82	41	53	94	59
Ziggy Palffy	NY Islanders	80	48	42	90	43
Ron Francis	Pittsburgh	81	27	63	90	20
Brendan Shanahan	Hfd., Det.	81	47	41	88	131

1997-98

EASTERN CONFERENCE

Northeast Division

Team		GP	W	L	T	GF	GA	PTS
Pittsburgh	(2)	82	40	24	18	228	188	98
Boston	(5)	82	39	30	13	221	194	91
Buffalo	(6)	82	36	29	17	211	187	89
Montreal	(7)	82	37	32	13	235	208	87
Ottawa	(8)	82	34	33	15	193	200	83
Carolina		82	33	41	8	200	219	74

Atlantic Division

Team		GP	W	L	T	GF	GA	PTS
New Jersey	(1)	82	48	23	11	225	166	107
Philadelphia	(3)	82	42	29	11	242	193	95
Washington	(4)	82	40	30	12	219	202	92
NY Islanders		82	30	41	11	212	225	71
NY Rangers		82	25	39	18	197	231	68
Florida		82	24	43	15	203	256	63
Tampa Bay		82	17	55	10	151	269	44

WESTERN CONFERENCE

Central Division

Team		GP	W	L	T	GF	GA	PTS
Dallas	(1)	82	49	22	11	242	167	109
*Detroit	(3)	82	44	23	15	250	196	103
St. Louis	(4)	82	45	29	8	256	204	98
Phoenix	(6)	82	35	35	12	224	227	82
Chicago		82	30	39	13	192	199	73
Toronto		82	30	43	9	194	237	69

Pacific Division

Team		GP	W	L	T	GF	GA	PTS
Colorado	(2)	82	39	26	17	231	205	95
Los Angeles	(5)	82	38	33	11	227	225	87
Edmonton	(7)	82	35	37	10	215	224	80
San Jose	(8)	82	34	38	10	210	216	78
Calgary		82	26	41	15	217	252	67
Anaheim		82	26	43	13	205	261	65
Vancouver		82	25	43	14	224	273	64

Leading Scorers

Player	Team	GP	G	A	PTS	PIM
Jaromir Jagr	Pittsburgh	77	35	67	102	64
Peter Forsberg	Colorado	72	25	66	91	94
Pavel Bure	Vancouver	82	51	39	90	48
Wayne Gretzky	NY Rangers	82	23	67	90	28
John LeClair	Philadelphia	82	51	36	87	32
Ziggy Palffy	NY Islanders	82	45	42	87	34
Ron Francis	Pittsburgh	81	25	62	87	20
Teemu Selanne	Anaheim	73	52	34	86	30
Jason Allison	Boston	81	33	50	83	60
Jozef Stumpel	Los Angeles	77	21	58	79	53

1998-99

EASTERN CONFERENCE

Northeast Division

Team		GP	W	L	T	GF	GA	PTS
Ottawa	(2)	82	44	23	15	239	179	103
Toronto	(4)	82	45	30	7	268	231	97
Boston	(6)	82	39	30	13	214	181	91
Buffalo	(7)	82	37	28	17	207	175	91
Montreal		82	32	39	11	184	209	75

Atlantic Division

Team		GP	W	L	T	GF	GA	PTS
New Jersey	(1)	82	47	24	11	248	196	105
Philadelphia	(5)	82	37	26	19	231	196	93
Pittsburgh	(8)	82	38	30	14	242	225	90
NY Rangers		82	33	38	11	217	227	77
NY Islanders		82	24	48	10	194	244	58

Southeast Division

Team		GP	W	L	T	GF	GA	PTS
Carolina	(3)	82	34	30	18	210	202	86
Florida		82	30	34	18	210	228	78
Washington		82	31	45	6	200	218	68
Tampa Bay		82	19	54	9	179	292	47

WESTERN CONFERENCE

Central Division

Team		GP	W	L	T	GF	GA	PTS
Detroit	(3)	82	43	32	7	245	202	93
St Louis	(5)	82	37	32	13	237	209	87
Chicago		82	29	41	12	202	248	70
Nashville		82	28	47	7	190	261	63

Pacific Division

Team		GP	W	L	T	GF	GA	PTS
*Dallas	(1)	82	51	19	12	236	168	114
Phoenix	(4)	82	39	31	12	205	197	90
Anaheim	(6)	82	35	34	13	215	206	83
San Jose	(7)	82	31	33	18	196	191	80
Los Angeles		82	32	45	5	189	222	69

Northwest Division

Team		GP	W	L	T	GF	GA	PTS
Colorado	(2)	82	44	28	10	239	205	98
Edmonton	(8)	82	33	37	12	230	226	78
Calgary		82	30	40	12	211	234	72
Vancouver		82	23	47	12	192	258	58

Leading Scorers

Player	Team	GP	G	A	PTS	PIM
Jaromir Jagr	Pittsburgh	81	44	83	127	66
Teemu Selanne	Anaheim	75	47	60	107	30
Paul Kariya	Anaheim	82	39	62	101	40
Peter Forsberg	Colorado	78	30	67	97	108
Joe Sakic	Colorado	73	41	55	96	29
Alexei Yashin	Ottawa	82	44	50	94	54
Eric Lindros	Philadelphia	71	40	53	93	120
Theoren Fleury	Cgy., Col.	75	40	53	93	86
John LeClair	Philadelphia	76	43	47	90	30
Pavol Demitra	St Louis	82	37	52	89	16

1999-2000

EASTERN CONFERENCE

Northeast Division

Team		GP	W	L	T	OTL	GF	GA	PTS
Toronto	(3)	82	45	27	7	3	246	222	100
Ottawa	(6)	82	41	28	11	2	244	210	95
Buffalo	(8)	82	35	32	11	4	213	204	85
Montreal		82	35	34	9	4	196	194	83
Boston		82	24	33	19	6	210	248	73

Atlantic Division

Team		GP	W	L	T	OTL	GF	GA	PTS
Philadelphia	(1)	82	45	22	12	3	237	179	105
*New Jersey	(4)	82	45	24	8	5	251	203	103
Pittsburgh	(7)	82	37	31	8	6	241	236	88
NY Rangers		82	29	38	12	3	218	246	73
NY Islanders		82	24	48	9	1	194	275	58

Southeast Division

Team		GP	W	L	T	OTL	GF	GA	PTS
Washington	(2)	82	44	24	12	2	227	194	102
Florida	(5)	82	43	27	6	6	244	209	98
Carolina		82	37	35	10	0	217	216	84
Tampa Bay		82	19	47	9	7	204	310	54
Atlanta		82	14	57	7	4	170	313	39

WESTERN CONFERENCE

Central Division

Team		GP	W	L	T	OTL	GF	GA	PTS
St. Louis	(1)	82	51	19	11	1	248	165	114
Detroit	(4)	82	48	22	10	2	278	210	108
Chicago		82	33	37	10	2	242	245	78
Nashville		82	28	40	7	7	199	240	70

Pacific Division

Team		GP	W	L	T	OTL	GF	GA	PTS
Dallas	(2)	82	43	23	10	6	211	184	102
Los Angeles	(5)	82	39	27	12	4	245	228	94
Phoenix	(6)	82	39	31	8	4	232	228	90
San Jose	(8)	82	35	30	10	7	225	214	87
Anaheim		82	34	33	12	3	217	227	83

Northwest Division

Team		GP	W	L	T	OTL	GF	GA	PTS
Colorado	(3)	82	42	28	11	1	233	201	96
Edmonton	(7)	82	32	26	16	8	226	212	88
Vancouver		82	30	29	15	8	227	237	83
Calgary		82	31	36	10	5	211	256	77

Leading Scorers

Player	Team	GP	G	A	PTS	PIM
Jaromir Jagr	Pittsburgh	63	42	54	96	50
Pavel Bure	Florida	74	58	36	94	16
Mark Recchi	Philadelphia	82	28	63	91	50
Paul Kariya	Anaheim	74	42	44	86	24
Teemu Selanne	Anaheim	79	33	52	85	12
Owen Nolan	San Jose	78	44	40	84	110
Tony Amonte	Chicago	82	43	41	84	48
Mike Modano	Dallas	77	38	43	81	48
Joe Sakic	Colorado	60	28	53	81	28
Steve Yzerman	Detroit	78	35	44	79	34

2000-01

EASTERN CONFERENCE

Northeast Division

Team		GP	W	L	T	OTL	GF	GA	PTS
Ottawa	(2)	82	48	21	9	4	274	205	109
Buffalo	(5)	82	46	30	5	1	218	184	98
Toronto	(7)	82	37	29	11	5	232	207	90
Boston		82	36	30	8	8	227	249	88
Montreal		82	28	40	8	6	206	232	70

Atlantic Division

Team		GP	W	L	T	OTL	GF	GA	PTS
New Jersey	(1)	82	48	19	12	3	295	195	111
Philadelphia	(4)	82	43	25	11	3	240	207	100
Pittsburgh	(6)	82	42	28	9	3	281	256	96
NY Rangers		82	33	43	5	1	250	290	72
NY Islanders		82	21	51	7	3	185	268	52

Southeast Division

Team		GP	W	L	T	OTL	GF	GA	PTS
Washington	(3)	82	41	27	10	4	233	211	96
Carolina	(8)	82	38	32	9	3	212	225	88
Florida		82	22	38	13	9	200	246	66
Atlanta		82	23	45	12	2	211	289	60
Tampa Bay		82	24	47	6	5	201	280	59

WESTERN CONFERENCE

Central Division

Team		GP	W	L	T	OTL	GF	GA	PTS
Detroit	(2)	82	49	20	9	4	253	202	111
St. Louis	(4)	82	43	22	12	5	249	195	103
Nashville		82	34	36	9	3	186	200	80
Chicago		82	29	40	8	5	210	246	71
Columbus		82	28	39	9	6	190	233	71

Pacific Division

Team		GP	W	L	T	OTL	GF	GA	PTS
Dallas	(3)	82	48	24	8	2	241	187	106
San Jose	(5)	82	40	27	12	3	217	192	95
Los Angeles	(7)	82	38	28	13	3	252	228	92
Phoenix		82	35	27	17	3	214	212	90
Anaheim		82	25	41	11	5	188	245	66

Northwest Division

Team		GP	W	L	T	OTL	GF	GA	PTS
*Colorado	(1)	82	52	16	10	4	270	192	118
Edmonton	(6)	82	39	28	12	3	243	222	93
Vancouver	(8)	82	36	28	11	7	239	238	90
Calgary		82	27	36	15	4	197	236	73
Minnesota		82	25	39	13	5	168	210	68

Leading Scorers

Player	Team	GP	G	A	PTS	PIM
Jaromir Jagr	Pittsburgh	81	52	69	121	42
Joe Sakic	Colorado	82	54	64	118	30
Patrik Elias	New Jersey	82	40	56	96	51
Alex Kovalev	Pittsburgh	79	44	51	95	96
Jason Allison	Boston	82	36	59	95	85
Martin Straka	Pittsburgh	82	27	68	95	38
Pavel Bure	Florida	82	59	33	92	58
Doug Weight	Edmonton	82	25	65	90	91
Ziggy Palffy	Los Angeles	73	38	51	89	20
Peter Forsberg	Colorado	73	27	62	89	54

2001-02

EASTERN CONFERENCE

Northeast Division

Team		GP	W	L	T	OTL	GF	GA	PTS
Boston	(1)	82	43	24	6	9	236	201	101
Toronto	(4)	82	43	25	10	4	249	207	100
Ottawa	(7)	82	39	27	9	7	243	208	94
Montreal	(8)	82	36	31	12	3	207	209	87
Buffalo		82	35	35	11	1	213	200	82

Atlantic Division

Team		GP	W	L	T	OTL	GF	GA	PTS
Philadelphia	(2)	82	42	27	10	3	234	192	97
NY Islanders	(5)	82	42	28	8	4	239	220	96
New Jersey	(6)	82	41	28	9	4	205	187	95
NY Rangers		82	36	38	4	4	227	258	80
Pittsburgh		82	28	41	8	5	198	249	69

Southeast Division

Team		GP	W	L	T	OTL	GF	GA	PTS
Carolina	(3)	82	35	26	16	5	217	217	91
Washington		82	36	33	11	2	228	240	85
Tampa Bay		82	27	40	11	4	178	219	69
Florida		82	22	44	10	6	180	250	60
Atlanta		82	19	47	11	5	187	288	54

WESTERN CONFERENCE

Central Division

Team		GP	W	L	T	OTL	GF	GA	PTS
*Detroit	(1)	82	51	17	10	4	251	187	116
St. Louis	(4)	82	43	27	8	4	227	188	98
Chicago	(5)	82	41	27	13	1	216	207	96
Nashville		82	28	41	13	0	196	230	69
Columbus		82	22	47	8	5	164	255	57

Pacific Division

Team		GP	W	L	T	OTL	GF	GA	PTS
San Jose	(3)	82	44	27	8	3	248	199	99
Phoenix	(6)	82	40	27	9	6	228	210	95
Los Angeles	(7)	82	40	27	11	4	214	190	95
Dallas		82	36	28	13	5	215	213	90
Anaheim		82	29	42	8	3	175	198	69

Northwest Division

Team		GP	W	L	T	OTL	GF	GA	PTS
Colorado	(2)	82	45	28	8	1	212	169	99
Vancouver	(8)	82	42	30	7	3	254	211	94
Edmonton		82	38	28	12	4	205	182	92
Calgary		82	32	35	12	3	201	220	79
Minnesota		82	26	35	12	9	195	238	73

Leading Scorers

Player	Team	GP	G	A	PTS	PIM
Jarome Iginla	Calgary	82	52	44	96	77
Markus Naslund	Vancouver	81	40	50	90	50
Todd Bertuzzi	Vancouver	72	36	49	85	110
Mats Sundin	Toronto	82	41	39	80	94
Jaromir Jagr	Washington	69	31	48	79	30
Joe Sakic	Colorado	82	26	53	79	18
Pavol Demitra	St. Louis	82	35	43	78	46
Adam Oates	Wsh., Phi.	80	14	64	78	28
Mike Modano	Dallas	78	34	43	77	38
Ron Francis	Carolina	80	27	50	77	18

2002-03
EASTERN CONFERENCE
Northeast Division

Team		GP	W	L	T	OTL	GF	GA	PTS
Ottawa	(1)	82	52	21	8	1	263	182	113
Toronto	(5)	82	44	28	7	3	236	208	98
Boston	(7)	82	36	31	11	4	245	237	87
Montreal		82	30	35	8	9	206	234	77
Buffalo		82	27	37	10	8	190	219	72

Atlantic Division

Team		GP	W	L	T	OTL	GF	GA	PTS
*New Jersey	(2)	82	46	20	10	6	216	166	108
Philadelphia	(4)	82	45	20	13	4	211	166	107
NY Islanders	(8)	82	35	34	11	2	224	231	83
NY Rangers		82	32	36	10	4	210	231	78
Pittsburgh		82	27	44	6	5	189	255	65

Southeast Division

Team		GP	W	L	T	OTL	GF	GA	PTS
Tampa Bay	(3)	82	36	25	16	5	219	210	93
Washington	(6)	82	39	29	8	6	224	220	92
Atlanta		82	31	39	7	5	226	284	74
Florida		82	24	36	13	9	176	237	70
Carolina		82	22	43	11	6	171	240	61

WESTERN CONFERENCE
Central Division

Team		GP	W	L	T	OTL	GF	GA	PTS
Detroit	(2)	82	48	20	10	4	269	203	110
St. Louis	(5)	82	41	24	11	6	253	222	99
Chicago		82	30	33	13	6	207	226	79
Nashville		82	27	35	13	7	183	206	74
Columbus		82	29	42	8	3	213	263	69

Pacific Division

Team		GP	W	L	T	OTL	GF	GA	PTS
Dallas	(1)	82	46	17	15	4	245	169	111
Anaheim	(7)	82	40	27	9	6	203	193	95
Los Angeles		82	33	37	6	6	203	221	78
Phoenix		82	31	35	11	5	204	230	78
San Jose		82	28	37	9	8	214	239	73

Northwest Division

Team		GP	W	L	T	OTL	GF	GA	PTS
Colorado	(3)	82	42	19	13	8	251	194	105
Vancouver	(4)	82	45	23	13	1	264	208	104
Minnesota	(6)	82	42	29	10	1	198	178	95
Edmonton	(8)	82	36	26	11	9	231	230	92
Calgary		82	29	36	13	4	186	228	75

Leading Scorers

Player	Team	GP	G	A	PTS	PIM
Peter Forsberg	Colorado	75	29	77	106	70
Markus Naslund	Vancouver	82	48	56	104	52
Joe Thornton	Boston	77	36	65	101	109
Milan Hejduk	Colorado	82	50	48	98	52
Todd Bertuzzi	Vancouver	82	46	51	97	144
Pavol Demitra	St. Louis	78	36	57	93	32
Glen Murray	Boston	82	44	48	92	64
Mario Lemieux	Pittsburgh	67	28	63	91	43
Dany Heatley	Atlanta	77	41	48	89	58
Ziggy Palffy	Los Angeles	76	37	48	85	47
Mike Modano	Dallas	79	28	57	85	30

2003-04
EASTERN CONFERENCE
Northeast Division

Team		GP	W	L	T	OTL	GF	GA	PTS
Boston	(2)	82	41	19	15	7	209	188	104
Toronto	(4)	82	45	24	10	3	242	204	103
Ottawa	(5)	82	43	23	10	6	262	189	102
Montreal	(7)	82	41	30	7	4	208	192	93
Buffalo		82	37	34	7	4	220	221	85

Atlantic Division

Team		GP	W	L	T	OTL	GF	GA	PTS
Philadelphia	(3)	82	40	21	15	6	229	186	101
New Jersey	(6)	82	43	25	12	2	213	164	100
NY Islanders	(8)	82	38	29	11	4	237	210	91
NY Rangers		82	27	40	7	8	206	250	69
Pittsburgh		82	23	47	8	4	190	303	58

Southeast Division

Team		GP	W	L	T	OTL	GF	GA	PTS
*Tampa Bay	(1)	82	46	22	8	6	245	192	106
Atlanta		82	33	37	8	4	214	243	78
Carolina		82	28	34	14	6	172	209	76
Florida		82	28	35	15	4	188	221	75
Washington		82	23	46	10	3	186	253	59

WESTERN CONFERENCE
Central Division

Team		GP	W	L	T	OTL	GF	GA	PTS
Detroit	(1)	82	48	21	11	2	255	189	109
St. Louis	(7)	82	39	30	11	2	191	198	91
Nashville	(8)	82	38	29	11	4	216	217	91
Columbus		82	25	45	8	4	177	238	62
Chicago		82	20	43	11	8	188	259	59

Pacific Division

Team		GP	W	L	T	OTL	GF	GA	PTS
San Jose	(2)	82	43	21	12	6	219	183	104
Dallas	(5)	82	41	26	13	2	194	175	97
Los Angeles		82	28	29	16	9	205	217	81
Anaheim		82	29	35	10	8	184	213	76
Phoenix		82	22	36	18	6	188	245	68

Northwest Division

Team		GP	W	L	T	OTL	GF	GA	PTS
Vancouver	(3)	82	43	24	10	5	235	194	101
Colorado	(4)	82	40	22	13	7	236	198	100
Calgary	(6)	82	42	30	7	3	200	176	94
Edmonton		82	36	29	12	5	221	208	89
Minnesota		82	30	29	20	3	188	183	83

Leading Scorers

Player	Team	GP	G	A	PTS	PIM
Martin St. Louis	Tampa Bay	82	38	56	94	24
Ilya Kovalchuk	Atlanta	81	41	46	87	63
Joe Sakic	Colorado	81	33	54	87	42
Markus Naslund	Vancouver	78	35	49	84	58
Marian Hossa	Ottawa	81	36	46	82	46
Patrik Elias	New Jersey	82	38	43	81	44
Daniel Alfredsson	Ottawa	77	32	48	80	24
Cory Stillman	Tampa Bay	81	25	55	80	36
Robert Lang	Wsh., Det.	69	30	49	79	24
Brad Richards	Tampa Bay	82	26	53	79	12
Alex Tanguay	Colorado	69	25	54	79	42

2004-05
SEASON CANCELLED

2005-06
EASTERN CONFERENCE
Northeast Division

Team		GP	W	L	OL	GF	GA	PTS
Ottawa	(1)	82	52	21	9	314	211	113
Buffalo	(4)	82	52	24	6	281	239	110
Montreal	(7)	82	42	31	9	243	247	93
Toronto		82	41	33	8	257	270	90
Boston		82	29	37	16	230	266	74

Atlantic Division

Team		GP	W	L	OL	GF	GA	PTS
New Jersey	(3)	82	46	27	9	242	229	101
Philadelphia	(5)	82	45	26	11	267	259	101
NY Rangers	(6)	82	44	26	12	257	215	100
NY Islanders		82	36	40	6	230	278	78
Pittsburgh		82	22	46	14	244	316	58

Southeast Division

Team		GP	W	L	OL	GF	GA	PTS
*Carolina	(2)	82	52	22	8	294	260	112
Tampa Bay	(8)	82	43	33	6	252	260	92
Atlanta		82	41	33	8	281	275	90
Florida		82	37	34	11	240	257	85
Washington		82	29	41	12	237	306	70

WESTERN CONFERENCE
Central Division

Team		GP	W	L	OL	GF	GA	PTS
Detroit	(1)	82	58	16	8	305	209	124
Nashville	(4)	82	49	25	8	259	227	106
Columbus		82	35	43	4	223	279	74
Chicago		82	26	43	13	211	285	65
St. Louis		82	21	46	15	197	292	57

Pacific Division

Team		GP	W	L	OL	GF	GA	PTS
Dallas	(2)	82	53	23	6	265	218	112
San Jose	(5)	82	44	27	11	266	242	99
Anaheim	(6)	82	43	27	12	254	229	98
Los Angeles		82	42	35	5	249	270	89
Phoenix		82	38	39	5	246	271	81

Northwest Division

Team		GP	W	L	OL	GF	GA	PTS
Calgary	(3)	82	46	25	11	218	200	103
Colorado	(7)	82	43	30	9	283	257	95
Edmonton	(8)	82	41	28	13	256	251	95
Vancouver		82	42	32	8	256	255	92
Minnesota		82	38	36	8	231	215	84

Leading Scorers

Player	Team	GP	G	A	PTS	PIM
Joe Thornton	Bos., S.J.	81	29	96	125	61
Jaromir Jagr	NY Rangers	82	54	69	123	72
Alex Ovechkin	Washington	81	52	54	106	52
Dany Heatley	Ottawa	82	50	53	103	86
Daniel Alfredsson	Ottawa	77	43	60	103	50
Sidney Crosby	Pittsburgh	81	39	63	102	110
Eric Staal	Carolina	82	45	55	100	81
Ilya Kovalchuk	Atlanta	78	52	46	98	68
Marc Savard	Atlanta	82	28	69	97	100
Jonathan Cheechoo	San Jose	82	56	37	93	58

2006-07
EASTERN CONFERENCE
Northeast Division

Team		GP	W	L	OL	GF	GA	PTS
Buffalo	(1)	82	53	22	7	308	242	113
Ottawa	(4)	82	48	25	9	288	222	105
Toronto		82	40	31	11	258	269	91
Montreal		82	42	34	6	245	256	90
Boston		82	35	41	6	219	289	76

Atlantic Division

Team		GP	W	L	OL	GF	GA	PTS
New Jersey	(2)	82	49	24	9	216	201	107
Pittsburgh	(5)	82	47	24	11	277	246	105
NY Rangers	(6)	82	42	30	10	242	216	94
NY Islanders	(8)	82	40	30	12	248	240	92
Philadelphia		82	22	48	12	214	303	56

Southeast Division

Team		GP	W	L	OL	GF	GA	PTS
Atlanta	(3)	82	43	28	11	246	245	97
Tampa Bay	(7)	82	44	33	5	253	261	93
Carolina		82	40	34	8	241	253	88
Florida		82	35	31	16	247	257	86
Washington		82	28	40	14	235	286	70

WESTERN CONFERENCE
Central Division

Team		GP	W	L	OL	GF	GA	PTS
Detroit	(1)	82	50	19	13	254	199	113
Nashville	(4)	82	51	23	8	272	212	110
St. Louis		82	34	35	13	214	254	81
Columbus		82	33	42	7	201	249	73
Chicago		82	31	42	9	201	258	71

Pacific Division

Team		GP	W	L	OL	GF	GA	PTS
*Anaheim	(2)	82	48	20	14	258	208	110
San Jose	(5)	82	51	26	5	258	199	107
Dallas	(6)	82	50	25	7	226	197	107
Los Angeles		82	27	41	14	227	283	68
Phoenix		82	31	46	5	216	284	67

Northwest Division

Team		GP	W	L	OL	GF	GA	PTS
Vancouver	(3)	82	49	26	7	222	201	105
Minnesota	(7)	82	48	26	8	235	191	104
Calgary	(8)	82	43	29	10	258	226	96
Colorado		82	44	31	7	272	251	95
Edmonton		82	32	43	7	195	248	71

Leading Scorers

Player	Team	GP	G	A	PTS	PIM
Sidney Crosby	Pittsburgh	79	36	84	120	60
Joe Thornton	San Jose	82	22	92	114	44
Vincent Lecavalier	Tampa Bay	82	52	56	108	44
Dany Heatley	Ottawa	82	50	55	105	74
Martin St. Louis	Tampa Bay	82	43	59	102	28
Marian Hossa	Atlanta	82	43	57	100	49
Joe Sakic	Colorado	82	36	64	100	46
Jaromir Jagr	NY Rangers	82	30	66	96	78
Marc Savard	Boston	82	22	74	96	96
Danny Briere	Buffalo	81	32	63	95	89

2007-08
EASTERN CONFERENCE
Northeast Division

Team		GP	W	L	OL	GF	GA	PTS
Montreal	(1)	82	47	25	10	262	222	104
Ottawa	(7)	82	43	31	8	261	247	94
Boston	(8)	82	41	29	12	212	222	94
Buffalo		82	39	31	12	255	242	90
Toronto		82	36	35	11	231	260	83

Atlantic Division

Team		GP	W	L	OL	GF	GA	PTS
Pittsburgh	(2)	82	47	27	8	247	216	102
New Jersey	(4)	82	46	29	7	206	197	99
NY Rangers	(5)	82	42	27	13	213	199	97
Philadelphia	(6)	82	42	29	11	248	233	95
NY Islanders		82	35	38	9	194	243	79

Southeast Division

Team		GP	W	L	OL	GF	GA	PTS
Washington	(3)	82	43	31	8	242	231	94
Carolina		82	43	33	6	252	249	92
Florida		82	38	35	9	216	226	85
Atlanta		82	34	40	8	216	272	76
Tampa Bay		82	31	42	9	223	267	71

WESTERN CONFERENCE
Central Division

Team		GP	W	L	OL	GF	GA	PTS
*Detroit	(1)	82	54	21	7	257	184	115
Nashville	(8)	82	41	32	9	230	229	91
Chicago		82	40	34	8	239	235	88
Columbus		82	34	36	12	193	218	80
St. Louis		82	33	36	13	205	237	79

Pacific Division

Team		GP	W	L	OL	GF	GA	PTS
San Jose	(2)	82	49	23	10	222	193	108
Anaheim	(4)	82	47	27	8	205	191	102
Dallas	(5)	82	45	30	7	242	207	97
Phoenix		82	38	37	7	214	231	83
Los Angeles		82	32	43	7	231	266	71

Northwest Division

Team		GP	W	L	OL	GF	GA	PTS
Minnesota	(3)	82	44	28	10	223	218	98
Colorado	(6)	82	44	31	7	231	219	95
Calgary	(7)	82	42	30	10	229	227	94
Edmonton		82	41	35	6	235	251	88
Vancouver		82	39	33	10	213	215	88

Leading Scorers

Player	Team	GP	G	A	PTS	PIM
Alex Ovechkin	Washington	82	65	47	112	40
Evgeni Malkin	Pittsburgh	82	47	59	106	78
Jarome Iginla	Calgary	82	50	48	98	83
Pavel Datsyuk	Detroit	82	31	66	97	20
Joe Thornton	San Jose	82	29	67	96	59
Henrik Zetterberg	Detroit	75	43	49	92	34
Vincent Lecavalier	Tampa Bay	81	40	52	92	89
Jason Spezza	Ottawa	76	34	58	92	66
Daniel Alfredsson	Ottawa	70	40	49	89	34
Ilya Kovalchuk	Atlanta	79	52	35	87	52

2008-09
EASTERN CONFERENCE
Northeast Division

Team		GP	W	L	OL	GF	GA	PTS
Boston	(1)	82	53	19	10	274	196	116
Montreal	(8)	82	41	30	11	249	247	93
Buffalo		82	41	32	9	250	234	91
Ottawa		82	36	35	11	217	237	83
Toronto		82	34	35	13	250	293	81

Atlantic Division

Team		GP	W	L	OL	GF	GA	PTS
New Jersey	(3)	82	51	27	4	244	209	106
*Pittsburgh	(4)	82	45	28	9	264	239	99
Philadelphia	(5)	82	44	27	11	264	238	99
NY Rangers	(7)	82	43	30	9	210	218	95
NY Islanders		82	26	47	9	201	279	61

Southeast Division

Team		GP	W	L	OL	GF	GA	PTS
Washington	(2)	82	50	24	8	272	245	108
Carolina	(6)	82	45	30	7	239	226	97
Florida		82	41	30	11	234	231	93
Atlanta		82	35	41	6	257	280	76
Tampa Bay		82	24	40	18	210	279	66

WESTERN CONFERENCE
Central Division

Team		GP	W	L	OL	GF	GA	PTS
Detroit	(2)	82	51	21	10	295	244	112
Chicago	(4)	82	46	24	12	264	216	104
St. Louis	(6)	82	41	31	10	233	233	92
Columbus	(7)	82	41	31	10	226	230	92
Nashville		82	40	34	8	213	233	88

Pacific Division

Team		GP	W	L	OL	GF	GA	PTS
San Jose	(1)	82	53	18	11	257	204	117
Anaheim	(8)	82	42	33	7	245	238	91
Dallas		82	36	35	11	230	257	83
Phoenix		82	36	39	7	208	252	79
Los Angeles		82	34	37	11	207	234	79

Northwest Division

Team		GP	W	L	OL	GF	GA	PTS
Vancouver	(3)	82	45	27	10	246	220	100
Calgary	(5)	82	46	30	6	254	248	98
Minnesota		82	40	33	9	219	200	89
Edmonton		82	38	35	9	234	248	85
Colorado		82	32	45	5	199	257	69

Leading Scorers

Player	Team	GP	G	A	PTS	PIM
Evgeni Malkin	Pittsburgh	82	35	78	113	80
Alex Ovechkin	Washington	79	56	54	110	72
Sidney Crosby	Pittsburgh	77	33	70	103	76
Pavel Datsyuk	Detroit	81	32	65	97	34
Zach Parise	New Jersey	82	45	49	94	24
Ilya Kovalchuk	Atlanta	79	43	48	91	50
Ryan Getzlaf	Anaheim	81	25	66	91	121
Jarome Iginla	Calgary	82	35	54	89	37
Marc Savard	Boston	82	25	63	88	70
Nicklas Backstrom	Washington	82	22	66	88	46

2009-10
EASTERN CONFERENCE
Northeast Division

Team		GP	W	L	OL	GF	GA	PTS
Buffalo	(3)	82	45	27	10	235	207	100
Ottawa	(5)	82	44	32	6	225	238	94
Boston	(6)	82	39	30	13	206	200	91
Montreal	(8)	82	39	33	10	217	223	88
Toronto		82	30	38	14	214	267	74

Atlantic Division

Team		GP	W	L	OL	GF	GA	PTS
New Jersey	(2)	82	48	27	7	222	191	103
Pittsburgh	(4)	82	47	28	7	257	237	101
Philadelphia	(7)	82	41	35	6	236	225	88
NY Rangers		82	38	33	11	222	218	87
NY Islanders		82	34	37	11	222	264	79

Southeast Division

Team		GP	W	L	OL	GF	GA	PTS
Washington	(1)	82	54	15	13	318	233	121
Atlanta		82	35	34	13	234	256	83
Carolina		82	35	37	10	230	256	80
Tampa Bay		82	34	36	12	217	260	80
Florida		82	32	37	13	208	244	77

WESTERN CONFERENCE
Central Division

Team		GP	W	L	OL	GF	GA	PTS
*Chicago	(2)	82	52	22	8	271	209	112
Detroit	(5)	82	44	24	14	229	216	102
Nashville	(7)	82	47	29	6	225	225	100
St. Louis		82	40	32	10	225	223	90
Columbus		82	32	35	15	216	259	79

Pacific Division

Team		GP	W	L	OL	GF	GA	PTS
San Jose	(1)	82	51	20	11	264	215	113
Phoenix	(4)	82	50	25	7	225	202	107
Los Angeles	(6)	82	46	27	9	241	219	101
Anaheim		82	39	32	11	238	251	89
Dallas		82	37	31	14	237	254	88

Northwest Division

Team		GP	W	L	OL	GF	GA	PTS
Vancouver	(3)	82	49	28	5	272	222	103
Colorado	(8)	82	43	30	9	244	233	95
Calgary		82	40	32	10	204	210	90
Minnesota		82	38	36	8	219	246	84
Edmonton		82	27	47	8	214	284	62

Leading Scorers

Player	Team	GP	G	A	PTS	PIM
Henrik Sedin	Vancouver	82	29	83	112	48
Sidney Crosby	Pittsburgh	81	51	58	109	71
Alex Ovechkin	Washington	72	50	59	109	89
Nicklas Backstrom	Washington	82	33	68	101	50
Steven Stamkos	Tampa Bay	82	51	44	95	38
Martin St. Louis	Tampa Bay	82	29	65	94	12
Brad Richards	Dallas	80	24	67	91	14
Joe Thornton	San Jose	79	20	69	89	54
Patrick Kane	Chicago	82	30	58	88	20
Marian Gaborik	NY Rangers	76	42	44	86	37

2010-11
EASTERN CONFERENCE
Northeast Division

Team		GP	W	L	OT	GF	GA	PTS
*Boston	(3)	82	46	25	11	246	195	103
Montreal	(6)	82	44	30	8	216	209	96
Buffalo	(7)	82	43	29	10	245	229	96
Toronto		82	37	34	11	218	251	85
Ottawa		82	32	40	10	192	250	74

Atlantic Division

Team		GP	W	L	OT	GF	GA	PTS
Philadelphia	(2)	82	47	23	12	259	223	106
Pittsburgh	(4)	82	49	25	8	238	199	106
NY Rangers	(8)	82	44	33	5	233	198	93
New Jersey		82	38	39	5	174	209	81
NY Islanders		82	30	39	13	229	264	73

Southeast Division

Team		GP	W	L	OT	GF	GA	PTS
Washington	(1)	82	48	23	11	224	197	107
Tampa Bay	(5)	82	46	25	11	247	240	103
Carolina		82	40	31	11	236	239	91
Atlanta		82	34	36	12	223	269	80
Florida		82	30	40	12	195	229	72

WESTERN CONFERENCE
Central Division

Team		GP	W	L	OT	GF	GA	PTS
Detroit	(3)	82	47	25	10	261	241	104
Nashville	(5)	82	44	27	11	219	194	99
Chicago	(8)	82	44	29	9	258	225	97
St. Louis		82	38	33	11	240	234	87
Columbus		82	34	35	13	215	258	81

Pacific Division

Team		GP	W	L	OT	GF	GA	PTS
San Jose	(2)	82	48	25	9	248	213	105
Anaheim	(4)	82	47	30	5	239	235	99
Phoenix	(6)	82	43	26	13	231	226	99
Los Angeles	(7)	82	46	30	6	219	198	98
Dallas		82	42	29	11	227	233	95

Northwest Division

Team		GP	W	L	OT	GF	GA	PTS
Vancouver	(1)	82	54	19	9	262	185	117
Calgary		82	41	29	12	250	237	94
Minnesota		82	39	35	8	206	233	86
Colorado		82	30	44	8	227	288	68
Edmonton		82	25	45	12	193	269	62

Leading Scorers

Player	Team	GP	G	A	PTS	PIM
Daniel Sedin	Vancouver	82	41	63	104	32
Martin St. Louis	Tampa Bay	82	31	68	99	12
Corey Perry	Anaheim	82	50	48	98	104
Henrik Sedin	Vancouver	82	19	75	94	40
Steven Stamkos	Tampa Bay	82	45	46	91	74
Jarome Iginla	Calgary	82	43	43	86	40
Alex Ovechkin	Washington	79	32	53	85	41
Teemu Selanne	Anaheim	73	31	49	80	49
Henrik Zetterberg	Detroit	80	24	56	80	40
Brad Richards	Dallas	72	28	49	77	24

Note: Detailed statistics for 2010-11 are listed in the Final Statistics, 2010-11 section of the *NHL Guide & Record Book*. **See page 135.**

Former scoring champions Alex Ovechkin and Sidney Crosby shake hands in front of six-time Art Ross Trophy winner Mario Lemieux before the 2011 Winter Classic.

Two of the game's most talented two-way performers, Detroit's Henrik Zetterberg and Pavel Datsyuk have each finished among the top-10 scorers on two occasions.

Team Records

Regular Season

FINAL STANDINGS

MOST POINTS, ONE SEASON:
132 – Montreal Canadiens, 1976-77. 60w-8L-12T. 80GP
131 – Detroit Red Wings, 1995-96. 62w-13L-7T. 82GP
129 – Montreal Canadiens, 1977-78. 59w-10L-11T. 80GP

BEST POINTS PERCENTAGE, ONE SEASON:
.875 – Boston Bruins, 1929-30. 38w-5L-1T. 77PTS in 44GP
.830 – Montreal Canadiens, 1943-44. 38w-5L-7T. 83PTS in 50GP
.825 – Montreal Canadiens, 1976-77. 60w-8L-12T. 132PTS in 80GP
.806 – Montreal Canadiens, 1977-78. 59w-10L-11T. 129PTS in 80GP
.800 – Montreal Canadiens, 1944-45. 38w-8L-4T. 80PTS in 50GP

FEWEST POINTS, ONE SEASON:
8 – Quebec Bulldogs, 1919-20. 4w-20L-0T. 24GP
10 – Toronto Arenas, 1918-19. 5w-13L-0T. 18GP
12 – Hamilton Tigers, 1920-21. 6w-18L-0T. 24GP
– Hamilton Tigers, 1922-23. 6w-18L-0T. 24GP
– Boston Bruins, 1924-25. 6w-24L-0T. 30GP
– Philadelphia Quakers, 1930-31. 4w-36L-4T. 44GP

FEWEST POINTS, ONE SEASON (MINIMUM 70-GAME SCHEDULE):
21 – Washington Capitals, 1974-75. 8w-67L-5T. 80GP
24 – Ottawa Senators, 1992-93. 10w-70L-4T. 84GP
– San Jose Sharks, 1992-93. 11w-71L-2T. 84GP
30 – New York Islanders, 1972-73. 12w-60L-6T. 78GP

WORST POINTS PERCENTAGE, ONE SEASON:
.131 – Washington Capitals, 1974-75. 8w-67L-5T. 21PTS in 80GP
.136 – Philadelphia Quakers, 1930-31. 4w-36L-4T. 12PTS in 44GP
.143 – Ottawa Senators, 1992-93. 10w-70L-4T. 24PTS in 84GP
– San Jose Sharks, 1992-93. 11w-71L-2T. 24PTS in 84GP
.148 – Pittsburgh Pirates, 1929-30. 5w-36L-3T. 13PTS in 44GP

TEAM WINS

Most Wins

MOST WINS, ONE SEASON:
62 – Detroit Red Wings, 1995-96. 82GP
60 – Montreal Canadiens, 1976-77. 80GP
59 – Montreal Canadiens, 1977-78. 80GP

MOST HOME WINS, ONE SEASON:
36 – Philadelphia Flyers, 1975-76. 40GP
– **Detroit Red Wings**, 1995-96. 41GP
33 – Boston Bruins, 1970-71. 39GP
– Boston Bruins, 1973-74. 39GP
– Montreal Canadiens, 1976-77. 40GP
– Philadelphia Flyers, 1976-77. 40GP
– New York Islanders, 1981-82. 40GP
– Philadelphia Flyers, 1985-86. 40GP

MOST ROAD WINS, ONE SEASON:
31 – Detroit Red Wings, 2005-06. 41GP
28 – New Jersey Devils, 1998-99. 41GP
27 – Montreal Canadiens, 1976-77. 40GP
– Montreal Canadiens, 1977-78. 40GP
– St. Louis Blues, 1999-2000. 41GP
– San Jose Sharks, 2007-08. 41GP
– Vancouver Canucks, 2010-11. 41GP
26 – Boston Bruins, 1971-72. 39GP
– Montreal Canadiens, 1975-76. 40GP
– Edmonton Oilers, 1983-84. 40GP
– Detroit Red Wings, 1995-96. 41GP
– San Jose Sharks, 2006-07. 41GP
– Detroit Red Wings, 2010-11. 41GP

Fewest Wins

FEWEST WINS, ONE SEASON:
4 – Quebec Bulldogs, 1919-20. 24GP
– **Philadelphia Quakers**, 1930-31. 44GP
5 – Toronto Arenas, 1918-19. 18GP
Pittsburgh Pirates, 1929-30. 44GP

FEWEST WINS, ONE SEASON (MINIMUM 70-GAME SCHEDULE):
8 – Washington Capitals, 1974-75. 80GP
9 – Winnipeg Jets, 1980-81. 80GP
10 – Ottawa Senators, 1992-93. 84GP

FEWEST HOME WINS, ONE SEASON:
2 – Chicago Blackhawks, 1927-28. 22GP
3 – Boston Bruins, 1924-25. 15GP
– Chicago Blackhawks, 1928-29. 22GP
– Philadelphia Quakers, 1930-31. 22GP

FEWEST HOME WINS, ONE SEASON (MINIMUM 70-GAME SCHEDULE):
6 – Chicago Blackhawks, 1954-55. 35GP
– **Washington Capitals**, 1975-76. 40GP
7 – Boston Bruins, 1962-63. 35GP
– Washington Capitals, 1974-75. 40GP
– Winnipeg Jets, 1980-81. 40GP
– Pittsburgh Penguins, 1983-84. 40GP

FEWEST ROAD WINS, ONE SEASON:
0 – Toronto Arenas, 1918-19. 9GP
– **Quebec Bulldogs**, 1919-20. 12GP
– **Pittsburgh Pirates**, 1929-30. 22GP
1 – Hamilton Tigers, 1921-22. 12GP
– Toronto St. Patricks, 1925-26. 18GP
– Philadelphia Quakers, 1930-31. 22GP
– New York Americans, 1940-41. 24GP
– Washington Capitals, 1974-75. 40GP
* – Ottawa Senators, 1992-93. 41GP

FEWEST ROAD WINS, ONE SEASON (MINIMUM 70-GAME SCHEDULE):
1 – Washington Capitals, 1974-75. 40GP
* – **Ottawa Senators**, 1992-93. 41GP
2 – Boston Bruins, 1960-61. 35GP
– Los Angeles Kings, 1969-70. 38GP
– New York Islanders, 1972-73. 39GP
– California Golden Seals, 1973-74. 39GP
– Colorado Rockies, 1977-78. 40GP
– Winnipeg Jets, 1980-81. 40GP
– Quebec Nordiques, 1991-92. 40GP

TEAM LOSSES

Fewest Losses

FEWEST LOSSES, ONE SEASON:
5 – Ottawa Senators, 1919-20. 24GP
– **Boston Bruins**, 1929-30. 44GP
– **Montreal Canadiens**, 1943-44. 50GP

FEWEST HOME LOSSES, ONE SEASON:
0 – Ottawa Senators, 1922-23. 12GP
– **Montreal Canadiens**, 1943-44. 25GP
1 – Toronto Arenas, 1917-18. 11GP
– Ottawa Senators, 1918-19. 9GP
– Ottawa Senators, 1919-20. 12GP
– Toronto St. Patricks, 1922-23. 12GP
– Boston Bruins, 1929-30. 22GP
– Boston Bruins, 1930-31. 22GP
– Montreal Canadiens, 1976-77. 40GP
– Quebec Nordiques, 1994-95. 24GP

FEWEST ROAD LOSSES, ONE SEASON:
3 – Montreal Canadiens, 1928-29. 22GP
4 – Ottawa Senators, 1919-20. 12GP
– Montreal Canadiens, 1927-28. 22GP
– Boston Bruins, 1929-30. 20GP
– Boston Bruins, 1940-41. 24GP

FEWEST LOSSES, ONE SEASON (MINIMUM 70-GAME SCHEDULE):
8 – Montreal Canadiens, 1976-77. 80GP
10 – Montreal Canadiens, 1972-73. 78GP
– Montreal Canadiens, 1977-78. 80GP
11 – Montreal Canadiens, 1975-76. 80GP

FEWEST HOME LOSSES, ONE SEASON (MINIMUM 70-GAME SCHEDULE):
1 – Montreal Canadiens, 1976-77. 40GP
2 – Montreal Canadiens, 1961-62. 35GP
– New York Rangers, 1970-71. 39GP
– Philadelphia Flyers, 1975-76. 40GP

FEWEST ROAD LOSSES, ONE SEASON (MINIMUM 70-GAME SCHEDULE):
6 – Montreal Canadiens, 1972-73. 39GP
– **Montreal Canadiens**, 1974-75. 40GP
– **Montreal Canadiens**, 1977-78. 40GP
7 – Detroit Red Wings, 1951-52. 35GP
– Montreal Canadiens, 1976-77. 40GP
– Philadelphia Flyers, 1979-80. 40GP
– Boston Bruins, 2003-04. 41GP
– Detroit Red Wings, 2005-06. 41GP

Most Losses

MOST LOSSES, ONE SEASON:
71 – San Jose Sharks, 1992-93. 84GP
70 – Ottawa Senators, 1992-93. 84GP
67 – Washington Capitals, 1974-75. 80GP
61 – Quebec Nordiques, 1989-90. 80GP
– Ottawa Senators, 1993-94. 84GP

MOST HOME LOSSES, ONE SEASON:
***32 – San Jose Sharks**, 1992-93. 41GP
29 – Pittsburgh Penguins, 1983-84. 40GP
* – Ottawa Senators, 1993-94. 41GP

MOST ROAD LOSSES, ONE SEASON:
***40 – Ottawa Senators**, 1992-93. 41GP
39 – Washington Capitals, 1974-75. 40GP
37 – California Golden Seals, 1973-74. 39GP
* – San Jose Sharks, 1992-93. 41GP

* – Does not include neutral site games

TEAM TIES

Most Ties

MOST TIES, ONE SEASON:
24 – **Philadelphia Flyers**, 1969-70. 76GP
23 – Montreal Canadiens, 1962-63. 70GP
– Chicago Blackhawks, 1973-74. 78GP

MOST HOME TIES, ONE SEASON:
13 – **New York Rangers**, 1954-55. 35GP
– **Philadelphia Flyers**, 1969-70. 38GP
– **California Golden Seals**, 1971-72. 39GP
– **California Golden Seals**, 1972-73. 39GP
– **Chicago Blackhawks**, 1973-74. 39GP

MOST ROAD TIES, ONE SEASON:
15 – **Philadelphia Flyers**, 1976-77. 40GP
14 – Montreal Canadiens, 1952-53. 35GP
– Montreal Canadiens, 1974-75. 40GP
– Philadelphia Flyers, 1975-76. 40GP

Fewest Ties

FEWEST TIES, ONE SEASON (Since 1926-27):
1 – **Boston Bruins**, 1929-30. 44GP
2 – Montreal Canadiens, 1926-27. 44GP
– New York Americans, 1926-27. 44GP
– Boston Bruins, 1938-39. 48GP
– New York Rangers, 1941-42. 48GP
– San Jose Sharks, 1992-93. 84GP

FEWEST TIES, ONE SEASON (MINIMUM 70-GAME SCHEDULE):
2 – **San Jose Sharks**, 1992-93. 84GP
3 – New Jersey Devils, 1985-86. 80GP
– Calgary Flames, 1986-87. 80GP
– Vancouver Canucks, 1993-94. 84GP

WINNING STREAKS

LONGEST WINNING STREAK, ONE SEASON:
17 Games – **Pittsburgh Penguins**, Mar. 9 – Apr. 10, 1993.
15 Games – New York Islanders, Jan. 21 – Feb. 20, 1982.
14 Games – Boston Bruins, Dec. 3, 1929 – Jan. 9, 1930.
– Washington Capitals, Jan.13 – Feb. 7, 2010.

LONGEST HOME WINNING STREAK, ONE SEASON:
20 Games – **Boston Bruins**, Dec. 3, 1929 – Mar. 18, 1930.
– **Philadelphia Flyers**, Jan. 4 – Apr. 3, 1976.

LONGEST ROAD WINNING STREAK, ONE SEASON:
12 Games – **Detroit Red Wings**, Mar. 1 – Apr. 15, 2006.
10 Games – Buffalo Sabres, Dec. 10, 1983 – Jan. 23, 1984.
– St. Louis Blues, Jan. 21 – Mar. 2, 2000.
– New Jersey Devils, Feb. 27 – Apr. 7, 2001.
– Buffalo Sabres, Oct. 4 – Nov. 13, 2006.
– San Jose Sharks, Nov. 14 – Dec. 31, 2007.

LONGEST WINNING STREAK FROM START OF SEASON:
10 Games – **Toronto Maple Leafs**, 1993-94.
– **Buffalo Sabres**, 2006-07.
8 Games – Toronto Maple Leafs, 1934-35.
– Buffalo Sabres, 1975-76.
– Nashville Predators, 2005-06.
7 Games – Edmonton Oilers, 1983-84.
– Quebec Nordiques, 1985-86.
– Pittsburgh Penguins, 1986-87.
– Pittsburgh Penguins, 1994-95.

LONGEST HOME WINNING STREAK FROM START OF SEASON:
11 Games – **Chicago Blackhawks**, 1963-64.
10 Games – Ottawa Senators, 1925-26.
9 Games – Montreal Canadiens, 1953-54.
– Chicago Blackhawks, 1971-72.
– San Jose Sharks, 2008-09.

LONGEST ROAD WINNING STREAK FROM START OF SEASON:
10 Games – **Buffalo Sabres**, Oct.4 – Nov. 13, 2006.
9 Games – New Jersey Devils, Oct. 8 – Nov. 12, 2009.
7 Games – Toronto Maple Leafs, Nov. 14 – Dec. 15, 1940.
– Philadelphia Flyers, Oct. 12 – Nov. 16, 1985.
– Detroit Red Wings, Oct. 6 – Nov. 6, 2005.
– Pittsburgh Penguins, Oct. 3 – Nov. 3, 2009.

LONGEST WINNING STREAK, INCLUDING PLAYOFFS:
15 Games – **Detroit Red Wings**, Feb. 27 – Apr. 5, 1955.
(9 regular-season games, 6 playoff games)
– **New Jersey Devils**, Mar. 28 – Apr. 29, 2006.
(11 regular-season games, 4 playoff games)

LONGEST HOME WINNING STREAK, INCLUDING PLAYOFFS:
24 Games – **Philadelphia Flyers**, Jan. 4 – Apr. 25, 1976.
(20 regular-season games, 4 playoff games)

LONGEST ROAD WINNING STREAK, INCLUDING PLAYOFFS:
11 Games – **New Jersey Devils**, Feb. 27 – Apr. 17, 2001.
(10 regular-season games, 1 playoff game)

UNDEFEATED STREAKS

LONGEST UNDEFEATED STREAK, ONE SEASON:
35 Games – **Philadelphia Flyers**, Oct. 14, 1979 – Jan. 6, 1980. 25w-10T
28 Games – Montreal Canadiens, Dec. 18, 1977 – Feb. 23, 1978. 23w-5T

LONGEST HOME UNDEFEATED STREAK, ONE SEASON:
34 Games – **Montreal Canadiens**, Nov. 1, 1976 – Apr. 2, 1977. 28w-6T
27 Games – Boston Bruins, Nov. 22, 1970 – Mar. 20, 1971. 26w-1T

LONGEST ROAD UNDEFEATED STREAK, ONE SEASON:
23 Games – **Montreal Canadiens**, Nov. 27, 1974 – Mar. 12, 1975. 14w-9T
17 Games – Montreal Canadiens, Dec. 18, 1977 – Mar. 1, 1978. 14w-3T

LONGEST UNDEFEATED STREAK FROM START OF SEASON:
15 Games – **Edmonton Oilers**, 1984-85. 12w-3T
14 Games – Montreal Canadiens, 1943-44. 11w-3T

LONGEST HOME UNDEFEATED STREAK FROM START OF SEASON:
26 Games – **Philadelphia Flyers**, Oct. 11, 1979 – Feb. 3, 1980. 19w-7T

LONGEST ROAD UNDEFEATED STREAK FROM START OF SEASON:
15 Games – **Detroit Red Wings**, Oct. 18 – Dec. 20, 1951. 10w-5T

LONGEST UNDEFEATED STREAK, INCLUDING PLAYOFFS:
24 Games – **Montreal Canadiens**, Feb. 21 – Apr. 11, 1980.
15w-6T in regular season and 3w in playoffs.
21 Games – Philadelphia Flyers, Mar. 9 – May 4, 1975.
13w-1T in regular season and 7w in playoffs.
– Pittsburgh Penguins, Mar. 9 – Apr. 22, 1993.
17w-1T in regular season and 3w in playoffs.

LONGEST HOME UNDEFEATED STREAK, INCLUDING PLAYOFFS:
38 Games – **Montreal Canadiens**, Nov. 1, 1976 – Apr. 26, 1977.
28w-6T in regular season and 4w in playoffs.

LONGEST ROAD UNDEFEATED STREAK, INCLUDING PLAYOFFS:
13 Games – **Philadelphia Flyers**, Feb. 26 – Apr. 21, 1977. 6w-4T in
regular season and 3w in playoffs.
– **Montreal Canadiens**, Feb. 26 – Apr. 20, 1980. 6w-4T in
regular season and 3w in playoffs.
– **New York Islanders**, Mar. 16 – May 1, 1980. 3w-3T in regular
season and 7w in playoffs.

LOSING STREAKS

LONGEST LOSING STREAK, ONE SEASON:
17 Games – **Washington Capitals**, Feb. 18 – Mar. 26, 1975.
– **San Jose Sharks**, Jan. 4 – Feb. 12, 1993.
15 Games – Philadelphia Quakers, Nov. 29, 1930 – Jan. 8, 1931.

LONGEST HOME LOSING STREAK, ONE SEASON:
14 Games – **Pittsburgh Penguins**, Dec. 31, 2003 – Feb. 22, 2004.
11 Games – Boston Bruins, Dec. 8, 1924 – Feb. 17, 1925.
– Washington Capitals, Feb. 18 – Mar. 30, 1975.
– Ottawa Senators, Oct. 27 – Dec. 8, 1993.

LONGEST ROAD LOSING STREAK, ONE SEASON:
***38 Games** – **Ottawa Senators**, Oct. 10, 1992 – Apr. 3, 1993.
37 Games – Washington Capitals, Oct. 9, 1974 – Mar. 26, 1975.

LONGEST LOSING STREAK FROM START OF SEASON:
11 Games – **New York Rangers**, 1943-44.
7 Games – Montreal Canadiens, 1938-39.
– Chicago Blackhawks, 1947-48.
– Washington Capitals, 1983-84.
– Chicago Blackhawks, 1997-98.

LONGEST HOME LOSING STREAK FROM START OF SEASON:
8 Games – **Los Angeles Kings**, Oct. 13 – Nov. 6, 1971.

LONGEST ROAD LOSING STREAK FROM START OF SEASON:
***38 Games** – **Ottawa Senators**, Oct. 10, 1992 – Apr. 3, 1993.

WINLESS STREAKS

LONGEST WINLESS STREAK, ONE SEASON:
30 Games – **Winnipeg Jets**, Oct. 19 – Dec. 20, 1980. 23L-7T
27 Games – Kansas City Scouts, Feb. 12 – Apr. 4, 1976. 21L-6T
25 Games – Washington Capitals, Nov. 29, 1975 – Jan. 21, 1976. 22L-3T

LONGEST HOME WINLESS STREAK, ONE SEASON:
17 Games – **Ottawa Senators**, Oct. 28, 1995 – Jan. 27, 1996. 15L-2T
– **Atlanta Thrashers**, Jan. 19 – Mar. 29, 2000. 15L-2T
16 Games – Pittsburgh Penguins, Dec. 31, 2003 – Mar. 4, 2004. 15L-1T

LONGEST ROAD WINLESS STREAK, ONE SEASON:
***38 Games** – **Ottawa Senators**, Oct. 10, 1992 – Apr. 3, 1993. 38L
37 Games – Washington Capitals, Oct. 9, 1974 – Mar. 26, 1975. 37L

LONGEST WINLESS STREAK FROM START OF SEASON:
15 Games – **New York Rangers**, 1943-44. 14L-1T
11 Games – Pittsburgh Pirates, 1927-28. 8L-3T
– Minnesota North Stars, 1973-74. 5L-6T
– San Jose Sharks, 1995-96. 7L-4T

LONGEST HOME WINLESS STREAK FROM START OF SEASON:
11 Games – **Pittsburgh Penguins**, Oct. 8 – Nov. 19, 1983. 9L-2T

LONGEST ROAD WINLESS STREAK FROM START OF SEASON:
***38 Games** – **Ottawa Senators**, Oct. 10, 1992 – Apr. 3, 1993. 38L

NON-SHUTOUT STREAKS

LONGEST NON-SHUTOUT STREAK:
264 Games – **Calgary Flames**, Nov. 12, 1981 – Jan. 9, 1985.
261 Games – Los Angeles Kings, Mar. 15, 1986 – Oct. 22, 1989.
244 Games – Washington Capitals, Oct. 31, 1989 – Nov. 11, 1993.
236 Games – New York Rangers, Dec. 20, 1989 – Dec. 13, 1992.
230 Games – Quebec Nordiques, Feb. 10, 1980 – Jan. 12, 1983.

LONGEST NON-SHUTOUT STREAK, INCLUDING PLAYOFFS:
264 Games – **Los Angeles Kings**, Mar. 15, 1986 – Apr. 6, 1989.
(5 playoff games in 1987; 5 in 1988; 2 in 1989.)
262 Games – Chicago Blackhawks, Mar. 14, 1970 – Feb. 21, 1973.
(8 playoff games in 1970; 18 in 1971; 8 in 1972.)
251 Games – Quebec Nordiques, Feb. 10, 1980 – Jan. 12, 1983.
(5 playoff games in 1981; 16 in 1982.)
246 Games – Pittsburgh Penguins, Jan. 7, 1989 – Oct. 26, 1991.
(11 playoff games in 1989; 24 in 1991.)

* Does not include neutral site games

TEAM GOALS

Most Goals

MOST GOALS, ONE SEASON:
446 – Edmonton Oilers, 1983-84. 80GP
426 – Edmonton Oilers, 1985-86. 80GP
424 – Edmonton Oilers, 1982-83. 80GP
417 – Edmonton Oilers, 1981-82. 80GP
401 – Edmonton Oilers, 1984-85. 80GP

MOST GOALS, ONE TEAM, ONE GAME:
16 – Montreal Canadiens, Mar. 3, 1920, at Quebec. Montreal won 16-3.

MOST GOALS, BOTH TEAMS, ONE GAME:
21 – Montreal Canadiens (14), Toronto St. Patricks (7), Jan. 10, 1920, at Montreal.
– **Edmonton Oilers (12), Chicago Blackhawks (9)**, Dec. 11, 1985, at Chicago.
20 – Edmonton Oilers (12), Minnesota North Stars (8), Jan. 4, 1984, at Edmonton.
– Toronto Maple Leafs (11), Edmonton Oilers (9), Jan. 8, 1986, at Toronto.
19 – Montreal Wanderers (10), Toronto Arenas (9), Dec. 19, 1917, at Montreal.
– Montreal Canadiens (16), Quebec Bulldogs (3), Mar. 3, 1920, at Quebec.
– Montreal Canadiens (13), Hamilton Tigers (6), Feb. 26, 1921, at Montreal.
– Boston Bruins (10), New York Rangers (9), Mar. 4, 1944, at Boston.
– Detroit Red Wings (10), Boston Bruins (9), Mar. 16, 1944, at Detroit.
– Vancouver Canucks (10), Minnesota North Stars (9), Oct. 7, 1983, at Vancouver.

MOST GOALS, ONE TEAM, ONE PERIOD:
9 – Buffalo Sabres, Mar. 19, 1981, at Buffalo, second period during 14-4 win over Toronto.
8 – Detroit Red Wings, Jan. 23, 1944, at Detroit, third period during 15-0 win over NY Rangers.
– Boston Bruins, Mar. 16, 1969, at Boston, second period during 11-3 win over Toronto.
– New York Rangers, Nov. 21, 1971, at NY Rangers, third period during 12-1 win over California.
– Philadelphia Flyers, Mar. 31, 1973, at Philadelphia, second period during 10-2 win over NY Islanders.
– Buffalo Sabres, Dec. 21, 1975, at Buffalo, third period during 14-2 win over Washington.
– Minnesota North Stars, Nov. 11, 1981, at Minnesota, second period during 15-2 win over Winnipeg.
– Pittsburgh Penguins, Dec. 17, 1991, at Pittsburgh, second period during 10-2 win over San Jose.
– Washington Capitals, Feb. 3, 1999, at Washington, second period during 10-1 win over Tampa Bay.

MOST GOALS, BOTH TEAMS, ONE PERIOD:
12 – Buffalo Sabres (9), Toronto Maple Leafs (3), Mar. 19, 1981, at Buffalo, second period. Buffalo won 14-4.
– **Edmonton Oilers (6), Chicago Blackhawks (6)**, Dec. 11, 1985, at Chicago, second period. Edmonton won 12-9.
10 – New York Rangers (7), New York Americans (3), Mar. 16, 1939, at NY Americans, third period. NY Rangers won 11-5.
– Toronto Maple Leafs (6), Detroit Red Wings (4), Mar. 17, 1946, at Detroit, third period. Toronto won 11-7.
– Buffalo Sabres (6), Vancouver Canucks (4), Jan. 8, 1976, at Buffalo, third period. Buffalo won 8-5.
– Buffalo Sabres (5), Montreal Canadiens (5), Oct. 26, 1982, at Montreal, first period. Teams tied 7-7.
– Quebec Nordiques (6), Boston Bruins (4), Dec. 7, 1982, at Quebec, second period. Quebec won 10-5.
– Vancouver Canucks (6), Calgary Flames (4), Jan. 16, 1987, at Vancouver, first period. Vancouver won 9-5.
– Detroit Red Wings (7), Winnipeg Jets (3), Nov. 25, 1987, at Detroit, third period. Detroit won 10-8.
– Chicago Blackhawks (5), St. Louis Blues (5), Mar. 15, 1988, at St. Louis. Teams tied 7-7.

MOST CONSECUTIVE GOALS, ONE TEAM, ONE GAME:
15 – Detroit Red Wings, Jan. 23, 1944, at Detroit during 15-0 win over NY Rangers.

Fewest Goals

FEWEST GOALS, ONE SEASON:
33 – Chicago Blackhawks, 1928-29. 44GP
45 – Montreal Maroons, 1924-25. 30GP
46 – Pittsburgh Pirates, 1928-29. 44GP

FEWEST GOALS, ONE SEASON (MINIMUM 70-GAME SCHEDULE):
133 – Chicago Blackhawks, 1953-54. 70GP
147 – Toronto Maple Leafs, 1954-55. 70GP
– Boston Bruins, 1955-56. 70GP
150 – New York Rangers, 1954-55. 70GP

TEAM POWER-PLAY GOALS

MOST POWER-PLAY GOALS, ONE SEASON:
119 – Pittsburgh Penguins, 1988-89. 80GP
113 – Detroit Red Wings, 1992-93. 84GP
111 – New York Rangers, 1987-88. 80GP
110 – Pittsburgh Penguins, 1987-88. 80GP
– Winnipeg Jets, 1987-88. 80GP

TEAM SHORTHAND GOALS

MOST SHORTHAND GOALS, ONE SEASON:
36 – Edmonton Oilers, 1983-84. 80GP
28 – Edmonton Oilers, 1986-87. 80GP
27 – Edmonton Oilers, 1985-86. 80GP
– Edmonton Oilers, 1988-89. 80GP

TEAM GOALS-PER-GAME

HIGHEST GOALS-PER-GAME AVERAGE, ONE SEASON:
5.58 – Edmonton Oilers, 1983-84. 446G in 80GP.
5.38 – Montreal Canadiens, 1919-20. 129G in 24GP.
5.33 – Edmonton Oilers, 1985-86. 426G in 80GP.
5.30 – Edmonton Oilers, 1982-83. 424G in 80GP.
5.23 – Montreal Canadiens, 1917-18. 115G in 22GP.

LOWEST GOALS-PER-GAME AVERAGE, ONE SEASON:
0.75 – Chicago Blackhawks, 1928-29. 33G in 44GP.
1.05 – Pittsburgh Pirates, 1928-29. 46G in 44GP.
1.20 – New York Americans, 1928-29. 53G in 44GP.

TEAM ASSISTS

MOST ASSISTS, ONE SEASON:
737 – Edmonton Oilers, 1985-86. 80GP
736 – Edmonton Oilers, 1983-84. 80GP
706 – Edmonton Oilers, 1981-82. 80GP

FEWEST ASSISTS, ONE SEASON (Since 1926-27):
45 – New York Rangers, 1926-27. 44GP

FEWEST ASSISTS, ONE SEASON (MINIMUM 70-GAME SCHEDULE):
206 – Chicago Blackhawks, 1953-54. 70GP

TEAM TOTAL POINTS

MOST SCORING POINTS, ONE SEASON:
1,182 – Edmonton Oilers, 1983-84. (446G-736A) 80GP
1,163 – Edmonton Oilers, 1985-86. (426G-737A) 80GP
1,123 – Edmonton Oilers, 1981-82. (417G-706A) 80GP

MOST SCORING POINTS, ONE TEAM, ONE GAME:
40 – Buffalo Sabres, Dec. 21, 1975, at Buffalo. Buffalo defeated Washington 14-2, and had 26A.
39 – Minnesota North Stars, Nov. 11, 1981, at Minnesota. Minnesota defeated Winnipeg 15-2, and had 24A.
37 – Detroit Red Wings, Jan. 23, 1944, at Detroit. Detroit defeated NY Rangers 15-0, and had 22A.
– Toronto Maple Leafs, Mar. 16, 1957, at Toronto. Toronto defeated NY Rangers 14-1, and had 23A.
– Buffalo Sabres, Feb. 25, 1978, at Cleveland. Buffalo defeated Cleveland 13-3, and had 24A.
– Calgary Flames, Feb. 10, 1993, at Calgary. Calgary defeated San Jose 13-1, and had 24A.

MOST SCORING POINTS, BOTH TEAMS, ONE GAME:
62 – Edmonton Oilers, Chicago Blackhawks, Dec. 11, 1985, at Chicago. Edmonton won 12-9. Edmonton had 24A, Chicago, 17A.
53 – Quebec Nordiques, Washington Capitals, Feb. 22, 1981, at Washington. Quebec won 11-7. Quebec had 22A, Washington, 13A.
– Edmonton Oilers, Minnesota North Stars, Jan. 4, 1984, at Edmonton. Edmonton won 12-8. Edmonton had 20A, Minnesota, 13A.
– Minnesota North Stars, St. Louis Blues, Jan. 27, 1984, at St. Louis. Minnesota won 10-8. Minnesota had 19A, St. Louis, 16A.
– Toronto Maple Leafs, Edmonton Oilers, Jan. 8, 1986, at Toronto. Toronto won 11-9. Toronto had 17A, Edmonton, 16A.
52 – Montreal Maroons, New York Americans, Feb. 18, 1936, at NY Americans. Teams tied 8-8. NY Americans had 20A, Montreal, 16A. (3A allowed for each goal.)
– Vancouver Canucks, Minnesota North Stars, Oct. 7, 1983, at Vancouver. Vancouver won 10-9. Vancouver had 16A, Minnesota, 17A.

MOST SCORING POINTS, ONE TEAM, ONE PERIOD:
23 – New York Rangers, Nov. 21, 1971, at NY Rangers, third period during 12-1 win over California. NY Rangers had 8G, 15A.
– **Buffalo Sabres**, Dec. 21, 1975, at Buffalo, third period during 14-2 win over Washington. Buffalo had 8G, 15A.
– **Buffalo Sabres**, Mar. 19, 1981, at Buffalo, second period during 14-4 win over Toronto. Buffalo had 9G, 14A.
22 – Detroit Red Wings, Jan. 23, 1944, at Detroit, third period during 15-0 win over NY Rangers. Detroit had 8G, 14A.
– Boston Bruins, Mar. 16, 1969, at Boston, second period during 11-3 win over Toronto. Boston had 8G, 14A.
– Minnesota North Stars, Nov. 11, 1981, at Minnesota, second period during 15-2 win over Winnipeg. Minnesota had 8G, 14A.
– Pittsburgh Penguins, Dec. 17, 1991, at Pittsburgh, second period during 10-2 win over San Jose. Pittsburgh had 8G, 14A.
– Washington Capitals, Feb. 3, 1999, at Washington, second period during 10-1 win over Tampa Bay. Washington had 8G, 14A.

MOST SCORING POINTS, BOTH TEAMS, ONE PERIOD:
35 – Edmonton, Oilers, Chicago Blackhawks, Dec. 11, 1985, at Chicago, second period. Edmonton won 12-9. Edmonton had 6G, 12A; Chicago, 6G, 11A.
31 – Buffalo Sabres, Toronto Maple Leafs, Mar. 19, 1981, at Buffalo, second period. Buffalo won 14-4. Buffalo had 9G, 14A; Toronto, 3G, 5A.
29 – Winnipeg Jets, Detroit Red Wings, Nov. 25, 1987, at Detroit, third period. Detroit won 10-8. Detroit had 7G, 13A; Winnipeg, 3G, 6A.
– Chicago Blackhawks, St. Louis Blues, Mar. 15, 1988, at St. Louis, third period. Teams tied 7-7. St. Louis had 5G, 10A; Chicago, 5G, 9A.

FASTEST GOALS

FASTEST SIX GOALS, BOTH TEAMS:
3:00 – Quebec Nordiques, Washington Capitals, Feb. 22, 1981, at Washington. Scorers: Peter Stastny, Quebec, 18:51; Pierre Lacroix, Quebec, 19:57 (first period); Anton Stastny, Quebec, 0:34; Jacques Richard, Quebec, 1:07 and 1:37; Rick Green, Washington, 1:51 (second period). Quebec won 11-7.

3:15 – Montreal Canadiens, Toronto Maple Leafs, Jan. 4, 1944, at Montreal, first period. Scorers: Maurice Richard, Montreal, 14:10; Don Webster, Toronto, 15:13; Fern Majeau, Montreal, 15:41; Phil Watson, Montreal, 15:52; Lorne Carr, Toronto, 16:55; Butch Bouchard, Montreal, 17:25. Montreal won 6-3.

FASTEST FIVE GOALS, BOTH TEAMS:
1:24 – Chicago Blackhawks, Toronto Maple Leafs, Oct. 15, 1983, at Toronto, second period. Scorers: Gaston Gingras, Toronto, 16:49; Denis Savard, Chicago, 17:12; Steve Larmer, Chicago, 17:27; Denis Savard, Chicago, 17:42; John Anderson, Toronto, 18:13. Toronto won 10-8.

1:39 – Detroit Red Wings, Toronto Maple Leafs, Nov. 15, 1944, at Toronto, third period. Scorers: Ted Kennedy, Toronto, 10:36 and 10:55; Harold Jackson, Detroit, 11:48; Steve Wojciechowski, Detroit, 12:02; Don Grosso, Detroit, 12:15. Detroit won 8-4.

FASTEST FIVE GOALS, ONE TEAM:
2:07 – Pittsburgh Penguins, Nov. 22, 1972, at Pittsburgh, third period. Scorers: Bryan Hextall, Jr., 12:00; Jean Pronovost, 12:18; Al McDonough, 13:40; Ken Schinkel, 13:49; Ron Schock, 14:07. Pittsburgh defeated St. Louis 10-4.

2:37 – New York Islanders, Jan. 26, 1982, at NY Islanders, first period. Scorers: Duane Sutter, 1:31; John Tonelli, 2:30; Bryan Trottier, 2:46 and 3:31; Duane Sutter, 4:08. NY Islanders defeated Pittsburgh 9-2.

2:55 – Boston Bruins, Dec. 19, 1974, at Boston. Scorers: Bobby Schmautz, 19:13 (first period); Ken Hodge, 0:18; Phil Esposito, 0:43; Don Marcotte, 0:58; John Bucyk, 2:08 (second period). Boston defeated NY Rangers 11-3.

FASTEST FOUR GOALS, BOTH TEAMS:
0:53 – Chicago Blackhawks, Toronto Maple Leafs, Oct. 15, 1983, at Toronto, second period. Scorers: Gaston Gingras, Toronto, 16:49; Denis Savard, Chicago, 17:12; Steve Larmer, Chicago, 17:27; Denis Savard, Chicago, 17:42. Toronto won 10-8.

0:57 – Quebec Nordiques, Detroit Red Wings, Jan. 27, 1990, at Quebec, first period. Scorers: Paul Gillis, Quebec, 18:01; Claude Loiselle, Quebec, 18:12; Joe Sakic, Quebec, 18:27; Jimmy Carson, Detroit, 18:58. Detroit won 8-6.

1:01 – Colorado Rockies, New York Rangers, Jan. 15, 1980, at NY Rangers, first period. Scorers: Doug Sulliman, NY Rangers, 7:52; Eddie Johnstone, NY Rangers, 7:57; Warren Miller, NY Rangers, 8:20; Rob Ramage, Colorado, 8:53. Teams tied 6-6.

– Chicago Blackhawks, Toronto Maple Leafs, Oct. 15, 1983, at Toronto, second period. Scorers: Denis Savard, Chicago, 17:12; Steve Larmer, Chicago, 17:27; Denis Savard, Chicago, 17:42; John Anderson, Toronto, 18:13. Toronto won 10-8.

FASTEST FOUR GOALS, ONE TEAM:
1:20 – Boston Bruins, Jan. 21, 1945, at Boston, second period. Scorers: Bill Thoms, 6:34; Frank Mario, 7:08 and 7:27; Ken Smith, 7:54. Boston defeated NY Rangers 14-3.

FASTEST THREE GOALS, BOTH TEAMS:
0:15 – Minnesota North Stars, New York Rangers, Feb. 10, 1983, at Minnesota, second period. Scorers: Mark Pavelich, NY Rangers, 19:18; Ron Greschner, NY Rangers, 19:27; Willi Plett, Minnesota, 19:33. Minnesota won 7-5.

0:18 – Montreal Canadiens, New York Rangers, Dec. 12, 1963, at Montreal, first period. Scorers: Dave Balon, Montreal, 0:58; Gilles Tremblay, Montreal, 1:04; Camille Henry, NY Rangers, 1:16. Montreal won 6-4.

– California Golden Seals, Buffalo Sabres, Feb. 1, 1976, at California, third period. Scorers: Jim Moxey, California, 19:38; Wayne Merrick, California, 19:45; Danny Gare, Buffalo, 19:56. Buffalo won 9-5.

FASTEST THREE GOALS, ONE TEAM:
0:20 – Boston Bruins, Feb. 25, 1971, at Boston, third period. Scorers: John Bucyk, 4:50; Ed Westfall, 5:02; Ted Green, 5:10. Boston defeated Vancouver 8-3.

0:21 – Chicago Blackhawks, Mar. 23, 1952, at NY Rangers, third period. Bill Mosienko scored all three goals, at 6:09, 6:20 and 6:30. Chicago defeated NY Rangers 7-6.

– Washington Capitals, Nov. 23, 1990, at Washington, first period. Scorers: Michal Pivonka, 16:18; Stephen Leach, 16:29 and 16:39. Washington defeated Pittsburgh 7-3.

FASTEST THREE GOALS FROM START OF PERIOD, BOTH TEAMS:
1:05 – Hartford Whalers, Montreal Canadiens, Mar. 11, 1989, at Montreal, second period. Scorers: Kevin Dineen, Hartford, 0:11; Guy Carbonneau, Montreal, 0:36; Petr Svoboda, Montreal, 1:05. Montreal won 5-3.

FASTEST THREE GOALS FROM START OF PERIOD, ONE TEAM:
0:53 – Calgary Flames, Feb. 10, 1993, at Calgary, third period. Scorers: Gary Suter, 0:17; Chris Lindberg, 0:40; Ron Stern, 0:53. Calgary defeated San Jose 13-1.

FASTEST TWO GOALS, BOTH TEAMS:
0:02 – St. Louis Blues, Boston Bruins, Dec. 19, 1987, at Boston, third period. Scorers: Ken Linseman, Boston, 19:50; Doug Gilmour, St. Louis, 19:52. St. Louis won 7-5.

* **0:03 –** Chicago Blackhawks, Minnesota North Stars, Nov. 5, 1988, at Minnesota, third period. Scorers: Steve Thomas, Chicago, 6:03; Dave Gagner, Minnesota, 6:06. Teams tied 5-5.

* – Newspaper accounts of this game note that the clock was slow to start after the first goal was scored.

FASTEST TWO GOALS, ONE TEAM:
0:03 – Minnesota Wild, Jan. 21, 2004, at Minnesota, third period. Scorers: Jim Dowd, 19:44; Richard Park, 19:47. Minnesota defeated Chicago 4-2.

0:04 – Montreal Maroons, Jan. 3, 1931, at Montreal, third period. Nels Stewart scored both goals, at 8:24 and 8:28. Mtl. Maroons defeated Boston 5-3.

– Buffalo Sabres, Oct. 17, 1974, at Buffalo, third period. Scorers: Lee Fogolin, Jr., 14:55; Don Luce, 14:59. Buffalo defeated California 6-1.

– Toronto Maple Leafs, Dec. 29, 1988, at Quebec, third period. Scorers: Ed Olczyk, 5:24; Gary Leeman, 5:28. Toronto defeated Quebec 6-5.

– Calgary Flames, Oct. 17, 1989, at Quebec, third period. Scorers: Doug Gilmour, 19:45; Paul Ranheim, 19:49. Teams tied 8-8.

– NY Rangers, Oct. 9, 1991, at NY Rangers, third period. Scorers: Kris King, 19:45; James Patrick, 19:49. NY Rangers defeated NY Islanders 5-3.

– Winnipeg Jets, Dec. 15, 1995, at Winnipeg, second period. Deron Quint scored both goals, at 7:51 and 7:55. Winnipeg defeated Edmonton 9-4.

FASTEST TWO GOALS FROM START OF GAME, ONE TEAM:
0:24 – Edmonton Oilers, Mar. 28, 1982, at Los Angeles. Scorers: Mark Messier, 0:14; Dave Lumley, 0:24. Edmonton defeated Los Angeles 6-2.

0:27 – Boston Bruins, Feb. 14, 2003, at Florida. Mike Knuble scored both goals, at 0:10 and 0:27. Boston defeated Florida 6-5.

0:29 – Pittsburgh Penguins, Dec. 6, 1980, at Pittsburgh. Scorers: George Ferguson, 0:17; Greg Malone, 0:29. Pittsburgh defeated Chicago 6-4.

FASTEST TWO GOALS FROM START OF PERIOD, BOTH TEAMS:
0:14 – New York Rangers, Quebec Nordiques, Nov. 5, 1983, at Quebec, third period. Scorers: Andre Savard, Quebec, 0:08; Pierre Larouche, NY Rangers, 0:14. Teams tied 4-4.

0:25 – St. Louis Blues, Chicago Blackhawks, Feb. 2, 2006, at St. Louis, second period. Scorers: Peter Cajanek, St. Louis, 0:10; Tyler Arnason, Chicago, 0:25. St. Louis won 6-5.

0:28 – Boston Bruins, Montreal Canadiens, Oct. 11, 1989, at Montreal, third period. Scorers: Jim Wiemer, Boston 0:10; Tom Chorske, Montreal 0:28. Montreal won 4-2.

FASTEST TWO GOALS FROM START OF PERIOD, ONE TEAM:
0:21 – Chicago Blackhawks, Nov. 5, 1983, at Minnesota, second period. Scorers: Ken Yaremchuk, 0:12; Darryl Sutter, 0:21. Minnesota defeated Chicago 10-5.

0:24 – Edmonton Oilers, Mar. 28, 1982, at Los Angeles, first period. Scorers: Mark Messier, 0:14; Dave Lumley, 0:24. Edmonton defeated Los Angeles 6-2.

0:27 – Boston Bruins, Feb. 14, 2003, at Florida. Mike Knuble scored both goals, at 0:10 and 0:27. Boston defeated Florida 6-5.

50, 40, 30, 20-GOAL SCORERS

MOST 50-OR-MORE GOAL SCORERS, ONE SEASON:
3 – Edmonton Oilers, 1983-84. 80GP. Wayne Gretzky, 87; Glenn Anderson, 54; Jari Kurri, 52.
– **Edmonton Oilers**, 1985-86. 80GP. Jari Kurri, 68; Glenn Anderson, 54; Wayne Gretzky, 52.
2 – Boston Bruins, 1970-71. 78GP. Phil Esposito, 76; John Bucyk, 51.
– Boston Bruins, 1973-74. 78GP. Phil Esposito, 68; Ken Hodge, 50.
– Philadelphia Flyers, 1975-76. 80GP. Reggie Leach, 61; Bill Barber, 50.
– Pittsburgh Penguins, 1975-76. 80GP. Pierre Larouche, 53; Jean Pronovost, 52.
– Montreal Canadiens, 1976-77. 80GP. Steve Shutt, 60; Guy Lafleur, 56.
– Los Angeles Kings, 1979-80. 80GP. Charlie Simmer, 56; Marcel Dionne, 53.
– Montreal Canadiens, 1979-80. 80GP. Pierre Larouche, 50; Guy Lafleur, 50.
– Los Angeles Kings, 1980-81. 80GP. Marcel Dionne, 58; Charlie Simmer, 56.
– Edmonton Oilers, 1981-82. 80GP. Wayne Gretzky, 92; Mark Messier, 50.
– New York Islanders, 1981-82. 80GP. Mike Bossy, 64; Bryan Trottier, 50.
– Edmonton Oilers, 1984-85. 80GP. Wayne Gretzky, 73; Jari Kurri, 71.
– Washington Capitals, 1984-85. 80GP. Bob Carpenter, 53; Mike Gartner, 50.
– Edmonton Oilers, 1986-87. 80GP. Wayne Gretzky, 62; Jari Kurri, 54.
– Calgary Flames, 1987-88. 80GP. Joe Nieuwendyk, 51; Hakan Loob, 50.
– Los Angeles Kings, 1988-89. 80GP. Jimmy Carson, 55; Luc Robitaille, 53.
– Calgary Flames, 1988-89. 80GP. Joe Nieuwendyk, 51; Joe Mullen, 51.
– Los Angeles Kings, 1988-89. 80GP. Bernie Nicholls, 70; Wayne Gretzky, 54.
– Buffalo Sabres, 1992-93. 84GP. Alexander Mogilny, 76; Pat LaFontaine, 53.
– Pittsburgh Penguins, 1992-93. 84GP. Mario Lemieux, 69; Kevin Stevens, 55.
– St. Louis Blues, 1992-93. 84GP. Brett Hull, 54; Brendan Shanahan, 51.
– Detroit Red Wings, 1993-94. 84GP. Sergei Fedorov, 56; Ray Sheppard, 52.
– St. Louis Blues, 1993-94. 84GP. Brett Hull, 57; Brendan Shanahan, 52.
– Pittsburgh Penguins, 1995-96. 82GP. Mario Lemieux, 69; Jaromir Jagr, 62.

MOST 40-OR-MORE GOAL SCORERS, ONE SEASON:
4 – Edmonton Oilers, 1982-83. 80GP. Wayne Gretzky, 71; Glenn Anderson, 48; Mark Messier, 48; Jari Kurri, 45.
– **Edmonton Oilers**, 1983-84. 80GP. Wayne Gretzky, 87; Glenn Anderson, 54; Jari Kurri, 52; Paul Coffey, 40.
– **Edmonton Oilers**, 1984-85. 80GP. Wayne Gretzky, 73; Jari Kurri, 71; Mike Krushelnyski, 43; Glenn Anderson, 42.
– **Edmonton Oilers**, 1985-86. 80GP. Jari Kurri, 68; Glenn Anderson, 54; Wayne Gretzky, 52; Paul Coffey, 48.
– **Calgary Flames**, 1987-88. 80GP. Joe Nieuwendyk, 51; Hakan Loob, 50; Mike Bullard, 48; Joe Mullen, 44.
3 – Boston Bruins, 1970-71. 78GP. Phil Esposito, 76; John Bucyk, 51; Ken Hodge, 43.
– New York Rangers, 1971-72. 78GP. Vic Hadfield, 50; Jean Ratelle, 46; Rod Gilbert, 43.
– Buffalo Sabres, 1975-76. 80GP. Danny Gare, 50; Rick Martin, 49; Gilbert Perreault, 44.
– Montreal Canadiens, 1979-80. 80GP. Guy Lafleur, 50; Pierre Larouche, 50; Steve Shutt, 47.
– Buffalo Sabres, 1979-80. 80GP. Danny Gare, 56; Rick Martin, 45; Gilbert Perreault, 40.
– Los Angeles Kings, 1980-81. 80GP. Marcel Dionne, 58; Charlie Simmer, 56; Dave Taylor, 47.
– Los Angeles Kings, 1984-85. 80GP. Marcel Dionne, 46; Bernie Nicholls, 46; Dave Taylor, 41.
– New York Islanders, 1984-85. 80GP. Mike Bossy, 58; Brent Sutter, 42; John Tonelli, 42.

– Chicago Blackhawks, 1985-86. 80GP. Denis Savard, 47; Troy Murray, 45; Al Secord, 40.
– Chicago Blackhawks, 1987-88. 80GP. Denis Savard, 44; Rick Vaive, 43; Steve Larmer, 41.
– Edmonton Oilers, 1987-88. 80GP. Craig Simpson, 43; Jari Kurri, 43; Wayne Gretzky, 40.
– Los Angeles Kings, 1988-89. 80GP. Bernie Nicholls, 70; Wayne Gretzky, 54; Luc Robitaille, 46.
– Los Angeles Kings, 1990-91. 80GP. Luc Robitaille, 45; Tomas Sandstrom, 45; Wayne Gretzky, 41.
– Pittsburgh Penguins, 1991-92. 80GP. Kevin Stevens, 54; Mario Lemieux, 44; Joe Mullen, 42.
– Pittsburgh Penguins, 1992-93. 84GP. Mario Lemieux, 69; Kevin Stevens, 55; Rick Tocchet, 48.
– Calgary Flames, 1993-94. 84GP. Gary Roberts, 41; Robert Reichel, 40; Theoren Fleury, 40.
– Pittsburgh Penguins, 1995-96. 82GP. Mario Lemieux, 69; Jaromir Jagr, 62; Petr Nedved, 45.

MOST 30-OR-MORE GOAL SCORERS, ONE SEASON:

6 – Buffalo Sabres, 1974-75. 80GP. Rick Martin, 52; Rene Robert, 40; Gilbert Perreault, 39; Don Luce, 33; Rick Dudley, 31; Danny Gare, 31.
– **New York Islanders**, 1977-78. 80GP. Mike Bossy, 53; Bryan Trottier, 46; Clark Gillies, 35; Denis Potvin, 30; Bob Nystrom, 30; Bob Bourne, 30.
– **Winnipeg Jets**, 1984-85. 80GP. Dale Hawerchuk, 53; Paul MacLean, 41; Laurie Boschman, 32; Brian Mullen, 32; Doug Smail, 31; Thomas Steen, 30.
5 – Chicago Blackhawks, 1968-69. 76GP
– Boston Bruins, 1970-71. 78GP
– Montreal Canadiens, 1971-72. 78GP
– Philadelphia Flyers, 1972-73. 78GP
– Boston Bruins, 1973-74. 78GP
– Montreal Canadiens, 1974-75. 80GP
– Montreal Canadiens, 1975-76. 80GP
– Pittsburgh Penguins, 1975-76. 80GP
– New York Islanders, 1978-79. 80GP
– Detroit Red Wings, 1979-80. 80GP
– Philadelphia Flyers, 1979-80. 80GP
– New York Islanders, 1980-81. 80GP
– St. Louis Blues, 1980-81. 80GP
– Chicago Blackhawks, 1981-82. 80GP
– Edmonton Oilers, 1981-82. 80GP
– Montreal Canadiens, 1981-82. 80GP
– Quebec Nordiques, 1981-82. 80GP
– Washington Capitals, 1981-82. 80GP
– Edmonton Oilers, 1982-83. 80GP
– Edmonton Oilers, 1983-84. 80GP
– Edmonton Oilers, 1984-85. 80GP
– Los Angeles Kings, 1984-85. 80GP
– Edmonton Oilers, 1985-86. 80GP
– Edmonton Oilers, 1986-87. 80GP
– Edmonton Oilers, 1987-88. 80GP
– Edmonton Oilers, 1988-89. 80GP
– Detroit Red Wings, 1991-92. 80GP
– New York Rangers, 1991-92. 80GP
– Pittsburgh Penguins, 1991-92. 80GP
– Detroit Red Wings, 1992-93. 84GP
– Pittsburgh Penguins, 1992-93. 84GP

MOST 20-OR-MORE GOAL SCORERS, ONE SEASON:

11 – Boston Bruins, 1977-78. 80GP. Peter McNab, 41; Terry O'Reilly, 29; Bobby Schmautz, 27; Stan Jonathan, 27; Jean Ratelle, 25; Rick Middleton, 25; Wayne Cashman, 24; Gregg Sheppard, 23; Brad Park, 22; Don Marcotte, 20; Bob Miller, 20.
10 – Boston Bruins, 1970-71. 78GP
– Montreal Canadiens, 1974-75. 80GP
– St. Louis Blues, 1980-81. 80GP

100-POINT SCORERS

MOST 100 OR-MORE-POINT SCORERS, ONE SEASON:

4 – Boston Bruins, 1970-71. 78GP. Phil Esposito, 76G-76A-152PTS; Bobby Orr, 37G-102A-139PTS; John Bucyk, 51G-65A-116PTS; Ken Hodge, 43G-62A-105PTS.
– **Edmonton Oilers**, 1982-83. 80GP. Wayne Gretzky, 71G-125A-196PTS; Mark Messier, 48G-58A-106PTS; Glenn Anderson, 48G-56A-104PTS; Jari Kurri, 45G-59A-104PTS.
– **Edmonton Oilers**, 1983-84. 80GP. Wayne Gretzky, 87G-118A-205PTS; Paul Coffey, 40G-86A-126PTS; Jari Kurri, 52G-61A-113PTS; Mark Messier, 37G-64A-101PTS.
– **Edmonton Oilers**, 1985-86. 80GP. Wayne Gretzky, 52G-163A-215PTS; Paul Coffey, 48G-90A-138PTS; Jari Kurri, 68G-63A-131PTS; Glenn Anderson, 54G-48A-102PTS.
– **Pittsburgh Penguins**, 1992-93. 84GP. Mario Lemieux, 69G-91A-160PTS; Kevin Stevens, 55G-56A-111PTS; Rick Tocchet, 48G-61A-109PTS; Ron Francis, 24G-76A-100PTS.
3 – Boston Bruins, 1973-74. 78GP. Phil Esposito, 68G-77A-145PTS; Bobby Orr, 32G-90A-122PTS; Ken Hodge, 50G-55A-105PTS.
– New York Islanders, 1978-79. 80GP. Bryan Trottier, 47G-87A-134PTS; Mike Bossy, 69G-57A-126PTS; Denis Potvin, 31G-70A-101PTS.
– Los Angeles Kings, 1980-81. 80GP. Marcel Dionne, 58G-77A-135PTS; Dave Taylor, 47G-65A-112PTS; Charlie Simmer, 56G-49A-105PTS.
– Edmonton Oilers, 1984-85. 80GP. Wayne Gretzky, 73G-135A-208PTS; Jari Kurri, 71G-64A-135PTS; Paul Coffey, 37G-84A-121PTS.
– New York Islanders, 1984-85. 80GP. Mike Bossy, 58G-59A-117PTS; Brent Sutter, 42G-60A-102PTS; John Tonelli, 42G-58A-100PTS.
– Edmonton Oilers, 1986-87. 80GP. Wayne Gretzky, 62G-121A-183PTS; Jari Kurri, 54G-54A-108PTS; Mark Messier, 37G-70A-107PTS.
– Pittsburgh Penguins, 1988-89. 80GP. Mario Lemieux, 85G-114A-199PTS; Rob Brown, 49G-66A-115PTS; Paul Coffey, 30G-83A-113PTS.
– Pittsburgh Penguins, 1995-96. 82GP. Mario Lemieux, 69G-92A-161PTS; Jaromir Jagr, 62G-87A-149PTS; Ron Francis, 27G-92A-119PTS.

SHOTS ON GOAL

MOST SHOTS, BOTH TEAMS, ONE GAME:

141 – New York Americans, Pittsburgh Pirates, Dec. 26, 1925, at NY Americans. NY Americans won 3-1 with 73 shots; Pittsburgh had 68 shots.

MOST SHOTS, ONE TEAM, ONE GAME:

83 – Boston Bruins, Mar. 4, 1941, at Boston. Boston defeated Chicago 3-2.
73 – New York Americans, Dec. 26, 1925, at NY Americans. NY Americans defeated Pittsburgh 3-1.
– Boston Bruins, Mar. 21, 1991, at Boston. Boston tied Quebec 3-3.
72 – Boston Bruins, Dec. 10, 1970, at Boston. Boston defeated Buffalo 8-2.

MOST SHOTS, ONE TEAM, ONE PERIOD:

33 – Boston Bruins, Mar. 4, 1941, at Boston, second period. Boston defeated Chicago 3-2.

TEAM GOALS AGAINST

Fewest Goals Against

FEWEST GOALS AGAINST, ONE SEASON:

42 – Ottawa Senators, 1925-26. 36GP
43 – Montreal Canadiens, 1928-29. 44GP
48 – Montreal Canadiens, 1923-24. 24GP
– Montreal Canadiens, 1927-28. 44GP

FEWEST GOALS AGAINST, ONE SEASON (MINIMUM 70-GAME SCHEDULE):

131 – Toronto Maple Leafs, 1953-54. 70GP
– **Montreal Canadiens**, 1955-56. 70GP
132 – Detroit Red Wings, 1953-54. 70GP
133 – Detroit Red Wings, 1951-52. 70GP
– Detroit Red Wings, 1952-53. 70GP

LOWEST GOALS-AGAINST-PER-GAME AVERAGE, ONE SEASON:

0.98 – Montreal Canadiens, 1928-29. 43GA in 44GP.
1.09 – Montreal Canadiens, 1927-28. 48GA in 44GP.
1.17 – Ottawa Senators, 1925-26. 42GA in 36GP.

Most Goals Against

MOST GOALS AGAINST, ONE SEASON:

446 – Washington Capitals, 1974-75. 80GP
415 – Detroit Red Wings, 1985-86. 80GP
414 – San Jose Sharks, 1992-93. 84GP
407 – Quebec Nordiques, 1989-90. 80GP
403 – Hartford Whalers, 1982-83. 80GP

HIGHEST GOALS-AGAINST-PER-GAME AVERAGE, ONE SEASON:

7.38 – Quebec Bulldogs, 1919-20. 177GA in 24GP.
6.20 – New York Rangers, 1943-44. 310GA in 50GP.
5.58 – Washington Capitals, 1974-75. 446GA in 80GP.

MOST POWER-PLAY GOALS AGAINST, ONE SEASON:

122 – Chicago Blackhawks, 1988-89. 80GP
120 – Pittsburgh Penguins, 1987-88. 80GP
116 – Washington Capitals, 2005-06. 82GP
115 – New Jersey Devils, 1988-89. 80GP
– Ottawa Senators, 1992-93. 84GP
114 – Los Angeles Kings, 1992-93. 84GP

MOST SHORTHAND GOALS AGAINST, ONE SEASON:

22 – Pittsburgh Penguins, 1984-85. 80GP
– **Minnesota North Stars**, 1991-92. 80GP
– **Colorado Avalanche**, 1995-96. 82GP
21 – Calgary Flames, 1984-85. 80GP
– Pittsburgh Penguins, 1989-90. 80GP

SHUTOUTS

MOST SHUTOUTS, ONE SEASON:

22 – Montreal Canadiens, 1928-29. All by George Hainsworth. 44GP
16 – New York Americans, 1928-29. Roy Worters 13, Flat Walsh 3. 44GP
15 – Ottawa Senators, 1925-26. All by Alex Connell. 36GP
– Ottawa Senators, 1927-28. All by Alex Connell. 44GP
– Boston Bruins, 1927-28. All by Hal Winkler. 44GP
– Chicago Blackhawks, 1969-70. All by Tony Esposito. 76GP

MOST CONSECUTIVE SHUTOUTS, ONE SEASON:

6 – Ottawa Senators, Jan. 31 – Feb. 18, 1928. All by Alex Connell.

MOST CONSECUTIVE SHUTOUTS TO START SEASON:

5 – Toronto Maple Leafs, Nov. 13 – 22, 1930. Lorne Chabot 3, Benny Grant 2.

MOST GAMES SHUTOUT, ONE SEASON:

20 – Chicago Blackhawks, 1928-29. 44GP

MOST CONSECUTIVE GAMES SHUTOUT:

8 – Chicago Blackhawks, Feb. 7 – 28, 1929.

MOST CONSECUTIVE GAMES SHUTOUT TO START SEASON:

3 – Montreal Maroons, Nov. 11 – 18, 1930.

TEAM SHOOTOUT RECORDS

MOST SHOOTOUT GAMES, ONE SEASON:
20 – Phoenix, 2009-10 (14w, 6L)
19 – Edmonton, 2007-08 (15w, 4L)
– Boston, 2009-10 (10w, 9L)
18 – New Jersey, 2006-07 (10w, 8L)
– Los Angeles, 2009-10 (10w, 8L)

MOST SHOOTOUT GAMES, ALL-TIME:
77 – NY Rangers (46w, 31L)
76 – Edmonton (41w, 35L)
75 – Dallas (44w, 31L)

MOST SHOOTOUT WINS, ONE SEASON:
15 – Edmonton, 2007-08, 19GP
14 – Phoenix, 2009-10, 20GP
12 – Dallas, 2005-06, 13GP

MOST SHOOTOUT WINS, ALL-TIME:
46 – NY Rangers, 77GP
44 – Dallas, 75GP
42 – New Jersey, 67GP
42 – Pittsburgh, 69GP

MOST SHOOTOUT HOME WINS, ONE SEASON:
8 – Edmonton, 2007-08, 9GP
7 – NY Rangers, 2008-09, 9GP
– NY Islanders, 2009-10, 9GP
– Anaheim, 2007-08, 10GP
– Minnesota, 2006-07, 11GP

MOST SHOOTOUT HOME WINS, ALL-TIME:
22 – New Jersey, 35GP
21 – NY Rangers, 33GP
– Atlanta, 34GP
– NY Islanders, 25GP

MOST SHOOTOUT ROAD WINS, ONE SEASON:
8 – Phoenix, 2009-10, 12GP
– Calgary, 2010-11, 12GP
7 – NY Rangers, 2011-12, 7GP
– Dallas, 2005-06, 8GP
– Dallas, 2006-07, 9GP
– Edmonton, 2007-08, 10GP
– Boston, 2009-10, 10GP
– Pittsburgh, 2010-11, 10GP

MOST SHOOTOUT ROAD WINS, ALL-TIME:
26 – Dallas, 40GP
25 – Pittsburgh, 40GP
– NY Ranegrs, 44GP

MOST SHOOTOUT SHOTS TAKEN, ONE SEASON:
90 – Phoenix, 2009-10, 20GP
75 – Dallas, 2009-10, 17GP
74 – Los Angeles, 2009-10, 18GP

MOST SHOOTOUT SHOTS TAKEN, ALL-TIME:
290 – NY Rangers, 77GP
283 – Dallas, 75GP
276 – Edmonton, 76GP

MOST SHOOTOUT GOALS SCORED, ONE SEASON:
34 – Phoenix, 2009-10, 20GP
27 – Minnesota, 2006-07, 17GP
– Los Angeles, 2009-10, 18GP

MOST SHOOTOUT GOALS SCORED, ALL-TIME:
100 – Los Angeles, 68GP (262s)
– Dallas, 75GP (283s)
92 – NY Rangers, 77GP (290s)

BEST SHOOTOUT SCORING PERCENTAGE, ONE SEASON:
.583 – San Jose, 2006-07, 4GP (7G, 12s)
.571 – Dallas, 2005-06, 13GP (24G, 42s)
.517 – Atlanta, 2006-07, 11GP (15G, 29s)
– Pittsburgh, 2009-10, 10GP (15G, 29s)

BEST SHOOTOUT SCORING PERCENTAGE, ALL-TIME:
.391 – New Jersey, 72GP (88G, 225s)
.382 – Los Angeles, 68GP (100G, 262s)
.364 – NY Islanders, 65GP (88G, 242s)

FEWEST SHOOTOUT GOALS AGAINST, ONE SEASON:
2 – Colorado, 2010-11, 7GP (27SA)
3 – Los Angeles, 2005-06, 7GP (21SA)
– Tampa Bay, 2007-08, 3GP (9SA)
– Calgary, 2008-09, 5GP (14SA)

FEWEST SHOOTOUT GOALS AGAINST, ALL-TIME:
55 – Carolina, 47GP (150SA)
60 – Tampa Bay, 61GP (218SA)
61 – Nashville, 61GP (208SA)

BEST SHOOTOUT WINNING PERCENTAGE, ONE SEASON:
.923 – Dallas, 2005-06, 13GP (12w)
.875 – Atlanta, 2008-09, 8GP (7w)
.857 – Los Angeles, 2005-06, 7GP (6w)
– Colorado, 2010-11, 7GP (6w)

BEST SHOOTOUT WINNING PERCENTAGE, ALL-TIME:
.627 – New Jersey, 67GP (42w)
.617 – Dallas, 60GP (37w)
.609 – Pittsburgh, 69GP (42w)

TEAM PENALTIES

MOST PENALTY MINUTES, ONE SEASON:
2,713 – **Buffalo Sabres**, 1991-92. 80GP
2,670 – Pittsburgh Penguins, 1988-89. 80GP
2,663 – Chicago Blackhawks, 1991-92. 80GP
2,643 – Calgary Flames, 1991-92. 80GP
2,621 – Philadelphia Flyers, 1980-81. 80GP

MOST PENALTIES, BOTH TEAMS, ONE GAME:
85 – **Edmonton Oilers (44), Los Angeles Kings (41)**, Feb. 28, 1990, at Los Angeles. Edmonton received 26 minors, 7 majors, 6 10-minute misconducts, 4 game misconducts and 1 match penalty; Los Angeles received 26 minors, 9 majors, 3 10-minute misconducts and 3 game misconducts.

MOST PENALTY MINUTES, BOTH TEAMS, ONE GAME:
419 – **Ottawa Senators (206), Philadelphia Flyers (213)**, Mar. 5, 2004, at Philadelphia. Ottawa received 8 minors, 10 majors, 4 10-minute misconducts and 10 game misconducts. Philadelphia received 9 minors, 11 majors, 4 10-minute misconducts and 10 game misconducts.

MOST PENALTIES, ONE TEAM, ONE GAME:
44 – **Edmonton Oilers**, Feb. 28, 1990, at Los Angeles. Edmonton received 26 minors, 7 majors, 6 10-minute misconducts, 4 game misconducts and 1 match penalty.
42 – Minnesota North Stars, Feb. 26, 1981, at Boston. Minnesota received 18 minors, 13 majors, 4 10-minute misconducts and 7 game misconducts.
– Boston Bruins, Feb. 26, 1981, at Boston vs. Minnesota. Boston received 20 minors, 13 majors, 3 10-minute misconducts and 6 game misconducts.

MOST PENALTY MINUTES, ONE TEAM, ONE GAME:
213 – **Philadelphia Flyers**, Mar. 5, 2004, at Philadelphia. Philadelphia received 9 minors, 11 majors, 4 10-minute misconducts and 10 game misconducts.

MOST PENALTIES, BOTH TEAMS, ONE PERIOD:
67 – **Minnesota North Stars (34), Boston Bruins (33)**, Feb. 26, 1981, at Boston, first period. Minnesota received 15 minors, 8 majors, 4 10-minute misconducts and 7 game misconducts. Boston had 16 minors, 8 majors, 3 10-minute misconducts and 6 game misconducts.

MOST PENALTY MINUTES, BOTH TEAMS, ONE PERIOD:
409 – **Ottawa Senators (200), Philadelphia Flyers (209)**, Mar. 5, 2004, at Philadelphia, third period. Ottawa received 5 minors, 10 majors, 4 10-minute misconducts and 10 game misconducts. Philadelphia received 7 minors, 11 majors, 4 10-minute misconducts and 10 game misconducts.

MOST PENALTIES, ONE TEAM, ONE PERIOD:
34 – **Minnesota North Stars**, Feb. 26, 1981, at Boston, first period. Minnesota received 15 minors, 8 majors, 4 10-minute misconducts and 7 game misconducts.

MOST PENALTY MINUTES, ONE TEAM, ONE PERIOD:
209 – **Philadelphia Flyers**, Mar. 5, 2004, at Philadelphia vs. Ottawa, third period. Philadelphia received 7 minors, 11 majors, 4 10-minute misconducts and 10 game misconducts.
200 – Ottawa Senators, Mar. 5, 2004, at Philadelphia, third period. Ottawa received 5 minors, 10 majors, 4 10-minute misconducts and 10 game misconducts.

NHL Individual Scoring Records – History

Six individual scoring records stand as benchmarks in the history of the game: most goals, single-season and career; most assists, single-season and career; and most points, single-season and career. The evolution of these six records is traced here, beginning with 1917-18, the NHL's first season. New research has resulted in changes to scoring records in the NHL's first nine seasons.

MOST GOALS, ONE SEASON

44 —Joe Malone, Montreal, 1917-18.
    Scored goal #44 against Toronto's Harry Holmes on March 2, 1918 and finished the season with 44 goals.
50 —Maurice Richard, Montreal, 1944-45.
    Scored goal #45 against Toronto's Frank McCool on February 25, 1945 and finished the season with 50 goals.
50 —Bernie Geoffrion, Montreal, 1960-61.
    Scored goal #50 against Toronto's Cesare Maniago on March 16, 1961 and finished the season with 50 goals.
50 —Bobby Hull, Chicago, 1961-62.
    Scored goal #50 against NY Rangers' Gump Worsley on March 25, 1962 and finished the season with 50 goals.
54 —Bobby Hull, Chicago, 1965-66.
    Scored goal #51 against NY Rangers' Cesare Maniago on March 12, 1966 and finished the season with 54 goals.
58 —Bobby Hull, Chicago, 1968-69.
    Scored goal #55 against Boston's Gerry Cheevers on March 20, 1969 and finished the season with 58 goals.
76 —Phil Esposito, Boston, 1970-71.
    Scored goal #59 against Los Angeles' Denis DeJordy on March 11, 1971 and finished the season with 76 goals.
92 —Wayne Gretzky, Edmonton, 1981-82.
    Scored goal #77 against Buffalo's Don Edwards on February 24, 1982 and finished the season with 92 goals.

MOST ASSISTS, ONE SEASON

10 —Cy Denneny, Ottawa, 1917-18.
    —Reg Noble, Toronto, 1917-18.
    —Harry Cameron, Toronto, 1917-18.
    —Newsy Lalonde, Montreal, 1918-19.
15 —Frank Nighbor, Ottawa, 1919-20.
    —Jack Darragh, Ottawa, 1920-21.
17 —Harry Cameron, Toronto, 1921-22.
18 —Dick Irvin, Chicago, 1926-27.
    —Howie Morenz, Montreal, 1927-28.
36 —Frank Boucher, NY Rangers, 1929-30.
37 —Joe Primeau, Toronto, 1931-32.
45 —Bill Cowley, Boston, 1940-41.
    —Bill Cowley, Boston, 1942-43.
49 —Clint Smith, Chicago, 1943-44.
54 —Elmer Lach, Montreal, 1944-45.
55 —Ted Lindsay, Detroit, 1949-50.
56 —Bert Olmstead, Montreal, 1955-56.
58 —Jean Beliveau, Montreal, 1960-61.
    —Andy Bathgate, NY Rangers/Toronto, 1963-64.
59 —Stan Mikita, Chicago, 1964-65.
62 —Stan Mikita, Chicago, 1966-67.
77 —Phil Esposito, Boston, 1968-69.
87 —Bobby Orr, Boston, 1969-70.
102 —Bobby Orr, Boston, 1970-71.
109 —Wayne Gretzky, Edmonton, 1980-81.
120 —Wayne Gretzky, Edmonton, 1981-82.
125 —Wayne Gretzky, Edmonton, 1982-83.
135 —Wayne Gretzky, Edmonton, 1984-85.
163 —Wayne Gretzky, Edmonton, 1985-86.

MOST POINTS, ONE SEASON

48 —Joe Malone, Montreal, 1917-18.
49 —Joe Malone, Montreal, 1919-20.
51 —Howie Morenz, Montreal, 1927-28.
73 —Cooney Weiland, Boston, 1929-30.
    —Doug Bentley, Chicago, 1942-43.
82 —Herb Cain, Boston, 1943-44.
86 —Gordie Howe, Detroit, 1950-51.
95 —Gordie Howe, Detroit, 1952-53.
96 —Dickie Moore, Montreal, 1958-59.
97 —Bobby Hull, Chicago, 1965-66.
    —Stan Mikita, Chicago, 1966-67.
126 —Phil Esposito, Boston, 1968-69.
152 —Phil Esposito, Boston, 1970-71.
164 —Wayne Gretzky, Edmonton, 1980-81.
212 —Wayne Gretzky, Edmonton, 1981-82.
215 —Wayne Gretzky, Edmonton, 1985-86.

MOST REGULAR-SEASON GOALS, CAREER

44 —Joe Malone, Montreal.
    Malone led the NHL in goals in the league's first season with 44 goals in 20 games in 1917-18.
54 —Cy Denneny, Ottawa.
    Denneny passed Malone during the 1918-19 season, and led the NHL in goals with 54 after two seasons.
143 —Joe Malone, Montreal, Quebec Bulldogs, Hamilton.
    Malone passed Denneny during the 1919-20 season and finished his career with 143 goals.
248 —Cy Denneny, Ottawa, Boston.
    Denneny passed Malone with goal #144 during the 1922-23 season and finished his career with 248 goals.
271 —Howie Morenz, Montreal, Chicago, NY Rangers.
    Morenz passed Denneny with goal #249 during the 1933-34 season and finished his career with 271 goals.
324 —Nels Stewart, Montreal Maroons, Boston, NY Americans.
    Stewart passed Morenz with goal #272 during the 1936-37 season and finished his career with 324 goals.
544 —Maurice Richard, Montreal.
    Richard passed Stewart with goal #325 on Nov. 8, 1952 and finished his career with 544 goals.
801 —Gordie Howe, Detroit, Hartford.
    Howe passed Richard with goal #545 on Nov. 10, 1963 and finished his career with 801 goals.
894 —Wayne Gretzky, Edmonton, Los Angeles, St. Louis, NY Rangers.
    Gretzky passed Howe with goal #802 on March 23, 1994 and finished his career with 894 goals.

Future Bruins Hall of Famers Dit Clapper (#5) and Bill Cowley (#10) pose on the ice before the start of the 1945-46 season. Cowley's single-season assist record of 45 had been surpassed by that time, but a year-and-a-half later, he would become the NHL's all-time scoring leader. Cowley held that distinction for five years, from 1947 to 1952.

Phil Esposito congratulates Wayne Gretzky after scoring his 77th goal of the 1981-82 season in just his 64th game on February 24, 1982. Gretzky added two more goals that evening and would push the new single-season record to 92 by the end of the season.

MOST REGULAR-SEASON ASSISTS, CAREER

(minimum 100 assists)

100 —Frank Boucher, Ottawa, NY Rangers.
　　　In 1930-31, Boucher became the first NHL player to reach the 100-assist milestone.
263 —Frank Boucher, Ottawa, NY Rangers.
　　　Boucher retired as the NHL's career assist leader in 1938 with 253. He returned to the NHL in 1943-44 and remained the NHL's career assist leader until he was overtaken by Bill Cowley in 1943-44. He finished his career with 263 assists.
353 —Bill Cowley, St. Louis Eagles, Boston.
　　　Cowley passed Boucher with assist #264 in 1943-44. He retired as the NHL's career assist leader in 1947 with 353.
408 —Elmer Lach, Montreal.
　　　Lach passed Cowley with assist #354 in 1951-52. He retired as the NHL's career assist leader in 1954 with 408.
1,049 —Gordie Howe, Detroit, Hartford.
　　　Howe passed Lach with assist #409 in 1957-58. He retired as the NHL's career assist leader in 1980 with 1,049.
1,963 —Wayne Gretzky, Edmonton, Los Angeles, St. Louis, NY Rangers.
　　　Gretzky passed Howe with assist #1,050 in 1987-88. He retired as the NHL's current career assist leader with 1,963.

MOST REGULAR-SEASON POINTS, CAREER

(minimum 100 points)

100 —Joe Malone, Montreal, Quebec Bulldogs, Hamilton.
　　　In 1919-20, Malone became the first player in NHL history to record 100 points.
200 —Cy Denneny, Ottawa.
　　　In 1923-24, Denneny became the first player in NHL history to record 200 points.
300 —Cy Denneny, Ottawa.
　　　In 1926-27, Denneny became the first player in NHL history to record 300 points.
333 —Cy Denneny, Ottawa, Boston.
　　　Denneny retired as the NHL's career point-scoring leader in 1929 with 333 points.
472 —Howie Morenz, Montreal, Chicago, NY Rangers.
　　　Morenz passed Cy Denneny with point #334 in 1931-32. At the time his career ended in 1937, he was the NHL's career point- scoring leader with 472 points.
515 —Nels Stewart, Montreal Maroons, Boston, NY Americans.
　　　Stewart passed Morenz with point #473 in 1938-39. He retired as the NHL's career point-scoring leader in 1940 with 515 points.
528 —Syd Howe, Ottawa, Philadelphia Quakers, Toronto, St. Louis Eagles, Detroit.
　　　Howe passed Nels Stewart with point #516 on March 8, 1945. He retired as the NHL's career point-scoring leader in 1946 with 528 points.
548 —Bill Cowley, St. Louis Eagles, Boston.
　　　Cowley passed Syd Howe with point #529 on Feb. 12, 1947. He retired as the NHL's career point-scoring leader in 1947 with 548 points.
610 —Elmer Lach, Montreal.
　　　Lach passed Bill Cowley with point #549 on Feb. 23, 1952. He remained the NHL's career point-scoring leader until he was overtaken by Maurice Richard in 1953-54. He finished his career with 623 points.
946 —Maurice Richard, Montreal.
　　　Richard passed teammate Elmer Lach with point #611 on Dec. 12, 1953. He remained the NHL's career point-scoring leader until he was overtaken by Gordie Howe in 1959-60. He finished his career with 965 points.
1,850 —Gordie Howe, Detroit, Hartford.
　　　Howe passed Richard with point #947 on Jan. 16, 1960. He retired as the NHL's career point-scoring leader in 1980 with 1,850 points.
2,857 —Wayne Gretzky, Edmonton, Los Angeles, St. Louis, NY Rangers.
　　　Gretzky passed Howe with point #1,851 on Oct. 15, 1989. He retired as the NHL's current career points leader with 2,857.

Individual Records

Regular Season

SEASONS

MOST SEASONS:
26 – Gordie Howe, Detroit, 1946-47 – 1970-71; Hartford, 1979-80.
– Chris Chelios, Montreal, Chicago, Detroit, Atlanta 1983-84 – 2003-04, 2005-06 – 2009-10.
25 – Mark Messier, Edmonton, NY Rangers, Vancouver, 1979-80 – 2003-04.
24 – Alex Delvecchio, Detroit, 1950-51 – 1973-74.
 – Tim Horton, Toronto, NY Rangers, Pittsburgh, Buffalo, 1949-50, 1951-52 – 1973-74.
23 – John Bucyk, Detroit, Boston, 1955-56 – 1977-78.
 – Ron Francis, Hartford, Pittsburgh, Carolina, Toronto, 1981-82 – 2003-04.
 – Al MacInnis, Calgary, St. Louis, 1981-82 – 2003-04.
 – Dave Andreychuk, Buffalo, Toronto, New Jersey, Boston, Colorado, Tampa Bay, 1982-83 – 2003-04, 2005-06.

GAMES

MOST GAMES:
1,767 – Gordie Howe, Detroit, 1946-47 – 1970-71; Hartford, 1979-80.
1,756 – Mark Messier, Edmonton, NY Rangers, Vancouver, 1979-80 – 2003-04.
1,731 – Ron Francis, Hartford, Pittsburgh, Carolina, Toronto, 1981-82 – 2003-04.
1,652 – Mark Recchi, Pittsburgh, Philadelphia, Montreal, Carolina, Tampa Bay, Boston, 1988-89 – 2003-04, 2005-06 – 2010-11.
1,651 – Chris Chelios, Montreal, Chicago, Detroit, Atlanta, 1983-84 – 2003-04, 2005-06 – 2009-10.
1,639 – Dave Andreychuk, Buffalo, Toronto, New Jersey, Boston, Colorado, Tampa Bay, 1982-83 – 2003-04, 2005-06.
1,635 – Scott Stevens, Washington, St. Louis, New Jersey, 1982-83 – 2003-04.

MOST GAMES, INCLUDING PLAYOFFS:
1,992 – Mark Messier, Edmonton, NY Rangers, Vancouver, 1,756 regular-season games, 236 playoff games.
1,924 – Gordie Howe, Detroit, Hartford, 1,767 regular-season games, 157 playoff games.
1,917 – Chris Chelios, Montreal, Chicago, Detroit, Atlanta, 1,651 regular-season games, 266 playoff games.
1,902 – Ron Francis, Hartford, Pittsburgh, Carolina, Toronto, 1,731 regular-season games, 171 playoff games.
1,868 – Scott Stevens, Washington, St. Louis, New Jersey, 1,635 regular-season games, 233 playoff games.

MOST CONSECUTIVE GAMES:
964 – Doug Jarvis, Montreal, Washington, Hartford, Oct. 8, 1975 – Oct. 10, 1987.
914 – Garry Unger, Toronto, Detroit, St. Louis, Atlanta, Feb. 24, 1968 – Dec. 21, 1979.
884 – Steve Larmer, Chicago, Oct. 6, 1982 – Apr. 15, 1993.
776 – Craig Ramsay, Buffalo, Mar. 27, 1973 – Feb. 10, 1983.
630 – Andy Hebenton, NY Rangers, Boston, Oct. 7, 1955 – Mar. 22, 1964.

GOALS

MOST GOALS:
894 – Wayne Gretzky, Edmonton, Los Angeles, St. Louis, NY Rangers, in 20 seasons. 1,487GP
801 – Gordie Howe, Detroit, Hartford, in 26 seasons. 1,767GP
741 – Brett Hull, Calgary, St. Louis, Dallas, Detroit, Phoenix, in 19 seasons. 1,269GP
731 – Marcel Dionne, Detroit, Los Angeles, NY Rangers, in 18 seasons. 1,348GP
717 – Phil Esposito, Chicago, Boston, NY Rangers, in 18 seasons. 1,282GP

MOST GOALS, INCLUDING PLAYOFFS:
1,016 – Wayne Gretzky, Edmonton, Los Angeles, St. Louis, NY Rangers, 894G in 1,487 regular-season games, 122G in 208 playoff games.
869 – Gordie Howe, Detroit, Hartford, 801G in 1,767 regular-season games, 68G in 157 playoff games.
844 – Brett Hull, Calgary, St. Louis, Dallas, Detroit, Phoenix, 741G in 1,269 regular-season games, 103G in 202 playoff games.
803 – Mark Messier, Edmonton, NY Rangers, Vancouver, 694G in 1,756 regular-season games, 109G in 236 playoff games.
778 – Phil Esposito, Chicago, Boston, NY Rangers, 717G in 1,282 regular-season games, 61G in 130 playoff games.

MOST GOALS, ONE SEASON:
92 – Wayne Gretzky, Edmonton, 1981-82. 80GP – 80 game schedule.
87 – Wayne Gretzky, Edmonton, 1983-84. 74GP – 80 game schedule.
86 – Brett Hull, St. Louis, 1990-91. 78GP – 80 game schedule.
85 – Mario Lemieux, Pittsburgh, 1988-89. 76GP – 80 game schedule.
76 – Phil Esposito, Boston, 1970-71. 78GP – 78 game schedule.
 – Alexander Mogilny, Buffalo, 1992-93. 77GP – 84 game schedule.
 – Teemu Selanne, Winnipeg, 1992-93. 84GP – 84 game schedule.
73 – Wayne Gretzky, Edmonton, 1984-85. 80GP – 80 game schedule.
72 – Brett Hull, St. Louis, 1989-90. 80GP – 80 game schedule.
71 – Wayne Gretzky, Edmonton, 1982-83. 80GP – 80 game schedule.
 – Jari Kurri, Edmonton, 1984-85. 73GP – 80 game schedule.
70 – Mario Lemieux, Pittsburgh, 1987-88. 77GP – 80 game schedule.
 – Bernie Nicholls, Los Angeles, 1988-89. 79GP – 80 game schedule.
 – Brett Hull, St. Louis, 1991-92. 73GP – 80 game schedule.

MOST GOALS, ONE SEASON, INCLUDING PLAYOFFS:
100 – Wayne Gretzky, Edmonton, 1983-84, 87G in 74 regular-season games, 13G in 19 playoff games.
97 – Wayne Gretzky, Edmonton, 1981-82, 92G in 80 regular-season games, 5G in 5 playoff games.
 – Mario Lemieux, Pittsburgh, 1988-89, 85G in 76 regular-season games, 12G in 11 playoff games.
 – Brett Hull, St. Louis, 1990-91, 86G in 78 regular-season games, 11G in 13 playoff games.
90 – Wayne Gretzky, Edmonton, 1984-85, 73G in 80 regular-season games, 17G in 18 playoff games.
 – Jari Kurri, Edmonton, 1984-85, 71G in 80 regular-season games, 19G in 18 playoff games.
85 – Mike Bossy, NY Islanders, 1980-81, 68G in 79 regular-season games, 17G in 18 playoff games.
 – Brett Hull, St. Louis, 1989-90, 72G in 80 regular-season games, 13G in 12 playoff games.
83 – Wayne Gretzky, Edmonton, 1982-83, 71G in 73 regular-season games, 12G in 16 playoff games.
 – Alexander Mogilny, Buffalo, 1992-93, 76G in 77 regular-season games, 7G in 7 playoff games.

MOST GOALS, 50 GAMES FROM START OF SEASON:
61 – Wayne Gretzky, Edmonton, 1981-82. Oct. 7, 1981 – Jan. 22, 1982. (80-game schedule)
 – Wayne Gretzky, Edmonton, 1983-84. Oct. 5, 1983 – Jan. 25, 1984. (80-game schedule)
54 – Mario Lemieux, Pittsburgh, 1988-89. Oct. 7, 1988 – Jan. 31, 1989. (80-game schedule)
53 – Wayne Gretzky, Edmonton, 1984-85. Oct. 11, 1984 – Jan. 28, 1985. (80-game schedule)
52 – Brett Hull, St. Louis, 1990-91. Oct. 4, 1990 – Jan. 26, 1991. (80-game schedule)
50 – Maurice Richard, Montreal, 1944-45. Oct. 28, 1944 – Mar. 18, 1945. (50-game schedule)
 – Mike Bossy, NY Islanders, 1980-81. Oct. 11, 1980 – Jan. 24, 1981. (80-game schedule)
 – Brett Hull, St. Louis, 1991-92. Oct. 5, 1991 – Jan. 28, 1992. (80-game schedule)

MOST GOALS, ONE GAME:
7 – Joe Malone, Quebec, Jan. 31, 1920, at Quebec. Quebec 10, Toronto 6.
6 – Newsy Lalonde, Montreal, Jan. 10, 1920, at Montreal. Montreal 14, Toronto 7.
 – Joe Malone, Quebec, Mar. 10, 1920, at Quebec. Quebec 10, Ottawa 4.
 – Corb Denneny, Toronto, Jan. 26, 1921, at Toronto. Toronto 10, Hamilton 3.
 – Cy Denneny, Ottawa, Mar. 7, 1921, at Ottawa. Ottawa 12, Hamilton 5.
 – Syd Howe, Detroit, Feb. 3, 1944, at Detroit. Detroit 12, NY Rangers 2.
 – Red Berenson, St. Louis, Nov. 7, 1968, at Philadelphia. St. Louis 8, Philadelphia 0.
 – Darryl Sittler, Toronto, Feb. 7, 1976, at Toronto. Toronto 11, Boston 4.

Mark Recchi – who played 81 games during his 22nd season in 2010-11 and retired after helping Boston win the Stanley Cup – now ranks fourth all-time in games played. Recchi enjoyed his most productive season with 53 goals and 70 assists for Philadelphia back in 1992-93.

Detroit's Johan Franzen stuffs a loose puck past Robin Lehner of Ottawa for one of the five goals he scored in a game at Scotiabank Place on February 2, 2011. Franzen is one of only 16 players in NHL history to score five or more goals in a road game.

MOST GOALS, ONE ROAD GAME:
6 – **Red Berenson**, St. Louis, Nov. 7, 1968, at Philadelphia. St. Louis 8, Philadelphia 0.

5 – Joe Malone, Montreal, Dec. 19, 1917, at Ottawa. Montreal 7, Ottawa 4.
  – Red Green, Hamilton, Dec. 5, 1924, at Toronto. Hamilton 10, Toronto 3.
  – Babe Dye, Toronto, Dec. 22, 1924, at Boston. Toronto 10, Boston 1.
  – Punch Broadbent, Mtl. Maroons, Jan. 7, 1925, at Hamilton. Mtl. Maroons 6, Hamilton 2.
  – Don Murdoch, NY Rangers, Oct. 12, 1976, at Minnesota. NY Rangers 10, Minnesota 4.
  – Tim Young, Minnesota, Jan. 15, 1979, at NY Rangers. Minnesota 8, NY Rangers 1.
  – Willy Lindstrom, Winnipeg, Mar. 2, 1982, at Philadelphia. Winnipeg 7, Philadelphia 6.
  – Bengt Gustafsson, Washington, Jan. 8, 1984, at Philadelphia. Washington 7, Philadelphia 1.
  – Wayne Gretzky, Edmonton, Dec. 15, 1984, at St. Louis. Edmonton 8, St. Louis 2.
  – Dave Andreychuk, Buffalo, Feb. 6, 1986, at Boston. Buffalo 8, Boston 6.
  – Mats Sundin, Quebec, Mar. 5, 1992, at Hartford. Quebec 10, Hartford 4.
  – Mario Lemieux, Pittsburgh, Apr. 9, 1993, at NY Rangers. Pittsburgh 10, NY Rangers 4.
  – Mike Ricci, Quebec, Feb. 17, 1994, at San Jose. Quebec 8, San Jose 2.
  – Alex Zhamnov, Winnipeg, Apr. 1, 1995, at Los Angeles. Winnipeg 7, Los Angeles 7.
  – Johan Franzem, Detroit, Feb 2, 2011, at Ottawa. Detroit 7, Ottawa 5.

MOST GOALS, ONE PERIOD:
4 – **Busher Jackson**, Toronto, Nov. 20, 1934, at St. Louis, third period. Toronto 5, St. Louis 2.
  – **Max Bentley**, Chicago, Jan. 28, 1943, at Chicago, third period. Chicago 10, NY Rangers 1.
  – **Clint Smith**, Chicago, Mar. 4, 1945, at Chicago, third period. Chicago 6, Montreal 4.
  – **Red Berenson**, St. Louis, Nov. 7, 1968, at Philadelphia, second period. St. Louis 8, Philadelphia 0.
  – **Wayne Gretzky**, Edmonton, Feb. 18, 1981, at Edmonton, third period. Edmonton 9, St. Louis 2.
  – **Grant Mulvey**, Chicago, Feb. 3, 1982, at Chicago, first period. Chicago 9, St. Louis 5.
  – **Bryan Trottier**, NY Islanders, Feb. 13, 1982, at NY Islanders, second period. NY Islanders 8, Philadelphia 2.
  – **Al Secord**, Chicago, Jan. 7, 1987, at Chicago, second period. Chicago 6, Toronto 4.
  – **Joe Nieuwendyk**, Calgary, Jan. 11, 1989, at Calgary, second period. Calgary 8, Winnipeg 3.
  – **Peter Bondra**, Washington, Feb. 5, 1994, at Washington, first period. Washington 6, Tampa Bay 3.
  – **Mario Lemieux**, Pittsburgh, Jan. 26, 1997, at Montreal, third period. Pittsburgh 5, Montreal 2.

ASSISTS

MOST ASSISTS:
1,963 – **Wayne Gretzky,** Edmonton, Los Angeles, St. Louis, NY Rangers, in 20 seasons. 1,487GP

1,249 – Ron Francis, Hartford, Pittsburgh, Carolina, Toronto, in 23 seasons. 1,731GP

1,193 – Mark Messier, Edmonton, NY Rangers, Vancouver, in 25 seasons. 1,756GP

1,169 – Raymond Bourque, Boston, Colorado, in 22 seasons. 1,612GP

1,135 – Paul Coffey, Edmonton, Pittsburgh, Los Angeles, Detroit, Hartford, Philadelphia, Chicago, Carolina, Boston, in 21 seasons. 1,409GP

MOST ASSISTS, INCLUDING PLAYOFFS:
2,223 – **Wayne Gretzky**, Edmonton, Los Angeles, St. Louis, NY Rangers, 1,963A in 1,487 regular-season games, 260A in 208 playoff games.

1,379 – Mark Messier, Edmonton, NY Rangers, Vancouver, 1,193A in 1,756 regular-season games, 186A in 236 playoff games.

1,346 – Ron Francis, Hartford, Pittsburgh, Carolina, Toronto, 1,249A in 1,731 regular-season games, 97A in 171 playoff games.

1,308 – Raymond Bourque, Boston, Colorado, 1,169A in 1,612 regular-season games, 139A in 214 playoff games.

1,272 – Paul Coffey, Edmonton, Pittsburgh, Los Angeles, Detroit, Hartford, Philadelphia, Chicago, Carolina, Boston, 1,135A in 1,409 regular-season games, 137A in 194 playoff games.

MOST ASSISTS, ONE SEASON:
163 – **Wayne Gretzky**, Edmonton, 1985-86. 80GP – 80 game schedule.

135 – Wayne Gretzky, Edmonton, 1984-85. 80GP – 80 game schedule.

125 – Wayne Gretzky, Edmonton, 1982-83. 80GP – 80 game schedule.

122 – Wayne Gretzky, Los Angeles, 1990-91. 78GP – 80 game schedule.

121 – Wayne Gretzky, Edmonton, 1986-87. 79GP – 80 game schedule.

120 – Wayne Gretzky, Edmonton, 1981-82. 80GP – 80 game schedule.

118 – Wayne Gretzky, Edmonton, 1983-84. 74GP – 80 game schedule.

114 – Mario Lemieux, Pittsburgh, 1988-89. 76GP – 80 game schedule.
  – Wayne Gretzky, Los Angeles, 1988-89. 78GP – 80 game schedule.

109 – Wayne Gretzky, Edmonton, 1980-81. 80GP – 80 game schedule.
  – Wayne Gretzky, Edmonton, 1987-88. 64GP – 80 game schedule.

102 – Bobby Orr, Boston, 1970-71. 78GP – 78 game schedule.
  – Wayne Gretzky, Los Angeles, 1989-90. 73GP – 80 game schedule.

MOST ASSISTS, ONE SEASON, INCLUDING PLAYOFFS:
174 – **Wayne Gretzky**, Edmonton, 1985-86,
   163A in 80 regular-season games, 11A in 10 playoff games.
165 – Wayne Gretzky, Edmonton, 1984-85,
   135A in 80 regular-season games, 30A in 18 playoff games.
151 – Wayne Gretzky, Edmonton, 1982-83,
   125A in 80 regular-season games, 26A in 16 playoff games.
150 – Wayne Gretzky, Edmonton, 1986-87,
   121A in 79 regular-season games, 29A in 21 playoff games.
140 – Wayne Gretzky, Edmonton, 1983-84,
   118A in 74 regular-season games, 22A in 19 playoff games.
   – Wayne Gretzky, Edmonton, 1987-88,
   109A in 64 regular-season games, 31A in 19 playoff games.
133 – Wayne Gretzky, Los Angeles, 1990-91,
   122A in 78 regular-season games, 11A in 12 playoff games.
131 – Wayne Gretzky, Los Angeles, 1988-89,
   114A in 78 regular-season games, 17A in 11 playoff games.
127 – Wayne Gretzky, Edmonton, 1981-82,
   120A in 80 regular-season games, 7A in 5 playoff games.
.123 – Wayne Gretzky, Edmonton, 1980-81,
   109A in 80 regular-season games, 14A in 9 playoff games.
121 – Mario Lemieux, Pittsburgh, 1988-89,
   114A in 76 regular-season games, 7A in 11 playoff games.

MOST ASSISTS, ONE GAME:
7 – **Billy Taylor**, Detroit, Mar. 16, 1947, at Chicago. Detroit 10, Chicago 6.
   – **Wayne Gretzky**, Edmonton, Feb. 15, 1980, at Edmonton.
   Edmonton 8, Washington 2.
   – **Wayne Gretzky**, Edmonton, Dec. 11, 1985, at Chicago.
   Edmonton 12, Chicago 9.
   – **Wayne Gretzky**, Edmonton, Feb. 14, 1986, at Edmonton.
   Edmonton 8, Quebec 2.
6 – Six assists have been recorded in one game on 24 occasions since
   Elmer Lach of Montreal first accomplished the feat vs. Boston on
   Feb. 6, 1943. The most recent player is Eric Lindros of Philadelphia
   on Feb. 26, 1997 at Ottawa.

MOST ASSISTS, ONE ROAD GAME:
7 – **Billy Taylor**, Detroit, Mar. 16, 1947, at Chicago. Detroit 10, Chicago 6.
   – **Wayne Gretzky**, Edmonton, Dec. 11, 1985, at Chicago.
   Edmonton 12, Chicago 9.
6 – Bobby Orr, Boston, Jan. 1, 1973, at Vancouver. Boston 8, Vancouver 2.
   – Patrik Sundstrom, Vancouver, Feb. 29, 1984, at Pittsburgh.
   Vancouver 9, Pittsburgh 5.
   – Mario Lemieux, Pittsburgh, Dec. 5, 1992, at San Jose.
   Pittsburgh 9, San Jose 4.
   – Eric Lindros, Philadelphia, Feb. 26, 1997, at Ottawa.
   Philadelphia 8, Ottawa 5.

MOST ASSISTS, ONE PERIOD:
5 – **Dale Hawerchuk**, Winnipeg, Mar. 6, 1984, at Los Angeles,
   second period. Winnipeg 7, Los Angeles 3.
4 – Four assists have been recorded in one period on 69 occasions since
   Mickey Roach of Hamilton first accomplished the feat vs. Toronto
   on Feb. 23, 1921. The most recent player is Patrick Sharp of Chicago
   on Mar.14, 2011 vs. Washington.

POINTS

MOST POINTS:
2,857 – **Wayne Gretzky**, Edmonton, Los Angeles, St. Louis, NY Rangers,
   in 20 seasons. 1,487GP (894G-1,963A)
1,887 – Mark Messier, Edmonton, NY Rangers, Vancouver,
   in 25 seasons. 1,756GP (694G-1,193A)
1,850 – Gordie Howe, Detroit, Hartford, in 26 seasons. 1,767GP (801G-1,049A)
1,798 – Ron Francis, Hartford, Pittsburgh, Carolina, Toronto,
   in 23 seasons. 1,731GP (549G-1,249A)
1,771 – Marcel Dionne, Detroit, Los Angeles, NY Rangers,
   in 18 seasons. 1,348GP (731G-1,040A)

MOST POINTS, INCLUDING PLAYOFFS:
3,239 – **Wayne Gretzky**, Edmonton, Los Angeles, St. Louis, NY Rangers,
   2,857PTS in 1,487 regular-season games, 382PTS in 208 playoff games.
2,182 – Mark Messier, Edmonton, NY Rangers, Vancouver,
   1,887PTS in 1,756 regular-season games, 295PTS in 236 playoff games.
2,010 – Gordie Howe, Detroit, Hartford,
   1,850PTS in 1,767 regular-season games, 160PTS in 157 playoff games.
1,941 – Ron Francis, Hartford, Pittsburgh, Carolina, Toronto,
   1,798PTS in 1,731 regular-season games, 143PTS in 171 playoff games.
1,940 – Steve Yzerman, Detroit,
   1,755PTS in 1,514 regular-season games, 185PTS in 196 playoff games.

MOST POINTS, ONE SEASON:
215 – **Wayne Gretzky**, Edmonton, 1985-86. 80GP – 80 game schedule.
212 – Wayne Gretzky, Edmonton, 1981-82. 80GP – 80 game schedule.
208 – Wayne Gretzky, Edmonton, 1984-85. 80GP – 80 game schedule.
205 – Wayne Gretzky, Edmonton, 1983-84. 74GP – 80 game schedule.
199 – Mario Lemieux, Pittsburgh, 1988-89. 76GP – 80 game schedule.
196 – Wayne Gretzky, Edmonton, 1982-83. 80GP – 80 game schedule.
183 – Wayne Gretzky, Edmonton, 1986-87. 79GP – 80 game schedule.
168 – Mario Lemieux, Pittsburgh, 1987-88, 77GP – 80 game schedule.
   – Wayne Gretzky, Los Angeles, 1988-89. 78GP – 80 game schedule.
164 – Wayne Gretzky, Edmonton, 1980-81. 80GP – 80 game schedule.
163 – Wayne Gretzky, Los Angeles, 1990-91. 78GP – 80 game schedule.
161 – Mario Lemieux, Pittsburgh, 1995-96. 70GP – 82 game schedule.
160 – Mario Lemieux, Pittsburgh, 1992-93. 60GP – 84 game schedule.

MOST POINTS, ONE SEASON, INCLUDING PLAYOFFS:
255 – **Wayne Gretzky**, Edmonton, 1984-85,
   208PTS in 80 regular-season games, 47PTS in 18 playoff games.
240 – Wayne Gretzky, Edmonton, 1983-84,
   205PTS in 74 regular-season games, 35PTS in 19 playoff games.
234 – Wayne Gretzky, Edmonton, 1982-83,
   196PTS in 80 regular-season games, 38PTS in 16 playoff games.
   – Wayne Gretzky, Edmonton, 1985-86,
   215PTS in 80 regular-season games, 19PTS in 10 playoff games.
224 – Wayne Gretzky, Edmonton, 1981-82,
   212PTS in 80 regular-season games, 12PTS in 5 playoff games.
218 – Mario Lemieux, Pittsburgh, 1988-89,
   199PTS in 76 regular-season games, 19PTS in 11 playoff games.
217 – Wayne Gretzky, Edmonton, 1986-87,
   183PTS in 79 regular-season games, 34PTS in 21 playoff games.
192 – Wayne Gretzky, Edmonton, 1987-88,
   149PTS in 64 regular-season games, 43PTS in 19 playoff games.
190 – Wayne Gretzky, Los Angeles, 1988-89,
   168PTS in 78 regular-season games, 22PTS in 11 playoff games.
188 – Mario Lemieux, Pittsburgh, 1995-96,
   161PTS in 70 regular-season games, 27PTS in 18 playoff games.
185 – Wayne Gretzky, Edmonton, 1980-81,
   164PTS in 80 regular-season games, 21PTS in 9 playoff games.

MOST POINTS, ONE GAME:
10 – **Darryl Sittler**, Toronto, Feb. 7, 1976, at Toronto, 6G-4A.
   Toronto 11, Boston 4.
8 – Maurice Richard, Montreal, Dec. 28, 1944, at Montreal, 5G-3A.
   Montreal 9, Detroit 1.
   – Bert Olmstead, Montreal, Jan. 9, 1954, at Montreal, 4G-4A.
   Montreal 12, Chicago 1.
   – Tom Bladon, Philadelphia, Dec. 11, 1977, at Philadelphia, 4G-4A.
   Philadelphia 11, Cleveland 1.
   – Bryan Trottier, NY Islanders, Dec. 23, 1978, at NY Islanders, 5G-3A.
   NY Islanders 9, NY Rangers 4.
   – Peter Stastny, Quebec, Feb. 22, 1981, at Washington, 4G-4A.
   Quebec 11, Washington 7.
   – Anton Stastny, Quebec, Feb. 22, 1981, at Washington, 3G-5A.
   Quebec 11, Washington 7.
   – Wayne Gretzky, Edmonton, Nov. 19, 1983, at Edmonton, 3G-5A.
   Edmonton 13, New Jersey 4.
   – Wayne Gretzky, Edmonton, Jan. 4, 1984, at Edmonton, 4G-4A.
   Edmonton 12, Minnesota 8.
   – Paul Coffey, Edmonton, Mar. 14, 1986, at Edmonton, 2G-6A.
   Edmonton 12, Detroit 3.
   – Mario Lemieux, Pittsburgh, Oct. 15, 1988, at Pittsburgh, 2G-6A.
   Pittsburgh 9, St. Louis 2.
   – Bernie Nicholls, Los Angeles, Dec. 1, 1988, at Los Angeles, 2G-6A.
   Los Angeles 9, Toronto 3.
   – Mario Lemieux, Pittsburgh, Dec. 31, 1988, at Pittsburgh, 5G-3A.
   Pittsburgh 8, New Jersey 6.

MOST POINTS, ONE ROAD GAME:
8 – **Peter Stastny**, Quebec, Feb. 22, 1981, at Washington. 4G-4A.
   Quebec 11, Washington 7.
   – **Anton Stastny**, Quebec, Feb. 22, 1981, at Washington. 3G-5A.
   Quebec 11, Washington 7.
7 – Red Green, Hamilton, Dec. 5, 1924, at Toronto. 5G-2A.
   Hamilton 10, Toronto 3.
   – Billy Taylor, Detroit, Mar. 16, 1947, at Chicago. 7A. Detroit 10, Chicago 6.
   – Red Berenson, St. Louis, Nov. 7, 1968, at Philadelphia. 6G-1A.
   St. Louis 8, Philadelphia 0.
   – Gilbert Perreault, Buffalo, Feb. 1, 1976, at California. 2G-5A.
   Buffalo 9, California 5.
   – Peter Stastny, Quebec, Apr. 1, 1982, at Boston. 3G-4A. Quebec 8, Boston 5.
   – Wayne Gretzky, Edmonton, Nov. 6, 1983, at Winnipeg. 4G-3A.
   Edmonton 8, Winnipeg 5.
   – Patrik Sundstrom, Vancouver, Feb. 29, 1984, at Pittsburgh. 1G-6A.
   Vancouver 9, Pittsburgh 5.
   – Wayne Gretzky, Edmonton, Dec. 11, 1985, at Chicago. 7A.
   Edmonton 12, Chicago 9.
   – Cam Neely, Boston, Oct. 16, 1988, at Chicago. 3G-4A.
   Boston 10, Chicago 3.
   – Mario Lemieux, Pittsburgh, Jan. 21, 1989, at Edmonton. 2G-5A.
   Pittsburgh 7, Edmonton 4.
   – Dino Ciccarelli, Washington, Mar. 18, 1989, at Hartford. 4G-3A.
   Washington 8, Hartford 2.
   – Mats Sundin, Quebec, Mar. 5, 1992, at Hartford. 5G-2A.
   Quebec 10, Hartford 4.
   – Mario Lemieux, Pittsburgh, Dec. 5, 1992, at San Jose. 1G-6A.
   Pittsburgh 9, San Jose 4.
   – Eric Lindros, Philadelphia, Feb. 26, 1997, at Ottawa. 1G-6A.
   Philadelphia 8, Ottawa 5.
   – Daniel Alfredsson, Ottawa, Jan. 24, 2008, at Tampa Bay. 3G-4A.
   Ottawa 8, Tampa Bay 4.

MOST POINTS, ONE PERIOD:

6 – Bryan Trottier, NY Islanders, Dec. 23, 1978, at NY Islanders, second period. 3G–3A. NY Islanders 9, NY Rangers 4.
5 – Bill Cook, NY Rangers, Mar. 12, 1933, at NY Americans, third period. 3G–2A. NY Rangers 8, NY Americans 2.
  – Les Cunningham, Chicago, Jan. 28, 1940, at Chicago, third period. 2G–3A. Chicago 8, Montreal 1.
  – Max Bentley, Chicago, Jan. 28, 1943, at Chicago, third period. 4G–1A. Chicago 10, NY Rangers 1.
  – Leo Labine, Boston, Nov. 28, 1954, at Boston, second period. 3G–2A. Boston 6, Detroit 2.
  – Darryl Sittler, Toronto, Feb. 7, 1976, at Toronto, second period. 3G–2A. Toronto 11, Boston 4.
  – Grant Mulvey, Chicago, Feb. 3, 1982, at Chicago, first period. 4G–1A. Chicago 9, St. Louis 5.
  – Dale Hawerchuk, Winnipeg, Mar. 6, 1984, at Los Angeles, second period. 5A. Winnipeg 7, Los Angeles 3.
  – Jari Kurri, Edmonton, Oct. 26, 1984, at Edmonton, second period. 2G–3A. Edmonton 8, Los Angeles 2.
  – Pat Elynuik, Winnipeg, Jan. 20, 1989, at Winnipeg, second period. 2G–3A. Winnipeg 7, Pittsburgh 3.
  – Ray Ferraro, Hartford, Dec. 9, 1989, at Hartford, first period. 3G–2A. Hartford 7, New Jersey 3.
  – Stephane Richer, Montreal, Feb. 14, 1990, at Montreal, first period. 2G–3A. Montreal 10, Vancouver 1.
  – Cliff Ronning, Vancouver, Apr. 15, 1993, at Los Angeles, third period. 3G–2A. Vancouver 8, Los Angeles 6.
  – Peter Forsberg, Colorado, Mar. 3, 1999, at Florida, third period. 2G–3A. Colorado 7, Florida 5.

POWER-PLAY AND SHORTHAND GOALS

MOST POWER-PLAY GOALS, CAREER:

274 – Dave Andreychuk, Buffalo, Toronto, New Jersey, Boston, Colorado, Tampa Bay, in 23 seasons. 1,639GP
265 – Brett Hull, Calgary, St. Louis, Dallas, Detroit, Phoenix, in 19 seasons. 1,269GP
249 – Phil Esposito, Chicago, Boston, NY Rangers, in 18 seasons. 1,282GP

MOST POWER-PLAY GOALS, ONE SEASON:

34 – Tim Kerr, Philadelphia, 1985-86. 76GP – 80 game schedule.
32 – Dave Andreychuk, Buffalo, Toronto, 1992-93. 83GP – 84 game schedule.
31 – Joe Nieuwendyk, Calgary, 1987-88. 75GP – 80 game schedule.
  – Mario Lemieux, Pittsburgh, 1988-89. 76GP – 80 game schedule.
  – Mario Lemieux, Pittsburgh, 1995-96. 70GP – 82 game schedule.
29 – Michel Goulet, Quebec, 1987-88. 80GP – 80 game schedule.
  – Brett Hull, St. Louis, 1990-91. 78GP – 80 game schedule.
  – Brett Hull, St. Louis, 1992-93. 80GP – 84 game schedule.

MOST POWER-PLAY GOALS, ONE GAME

4 – Camille Henry, NY Rangers, Mar. 13, 1954, at Detroit. NY Rangers 5, Detroit 2.
  – Bernie Geoffrion, Montreal, Feb. 19, 1955, at Montreal. Montreal 10, NY Rangers 2.
  – Bryan Trottier, NY Islanders, Feb. 13, 1982, at NY Islanders. NY Islanders 8, Philadephia 2.
  – Chris Valentine, Washington, Feb. 27, 1982, at Washington. Washington 7, Hartford 1.
  – Dave Andreychuk, Buffalo, Mar. 19, 1992, at Los Angeles. Buffalo 8, Los Angeles 2.
  – Mario Lemieux, Pittsburgh, Mar. 20, 1993, at Pittsburgh. Pittsburgh 9, Philadephia 3.
  – Luc Robitaille, Los Angeles, Nov. 25, 1993, at Quebec. Quebec 8, Los Angeles 6.
  – Scott Mellanby, St. Louis, Mar. 6, 2003, at St. Louis. St. Louis 6, Phoenix 3.

MOST SHORTHAND GOALS, ONE SEASON:

13 – Mario Lemieux, Pittsburgh, 1988-89. 76GP – 80 game schedule.
12 – Wayne Gretzky, Edmonton, 1983-84. 74GP – 80 game schedule.
11 – Wayne Gretzky, Edmonton, 1984-85. 80GP – 80 game schedule.
10 – Marcel Dionne, Detroit, 1974-75. 80GP – 80 game schedule.
  – Mario Lemieux, Pittsburgh, 1987-88. 77GP – 80 game schedule.
  – Dirk Graham, Chicago, 1988-89. 80GP – 80 game schedule.

MOST SHORTHAND GOALS, ONE GAME:

3 – Theoren Fleury, Calgary, Mar. 9, 1991, at St. Louis. Calgary 8, St. Louis 4.

OVERTIME SCORING

MOST OVERTIME GOALS, CAREER:

15 – Mats Sundin, Quebec, Toronto.
  – Jaromir Jagr, Pittsburgh, Washington, NY Rangers.
  – Sergei Fedorov, Detroit, Anaheim, Columbus, Washington.
  – Patrik Elias, New Jersey.
13 – Steve Thomas, Toronto, Chicago, NY Islanders, New Jersey, Anaheim.
  – Olli Jokinen, Los Angeles, NY Islanders, Florida, NY Rangers.
  – Scott Niedermayer, New Jersey, Anaheim.
  – Ilya Kovalchuk, Atlanta, New Jersey.
12 – Nels Stewart, Mtl. Maroons, Boston, NY Americans.
  – Brett Hull, Calgary, St. Louis, Dallas, Detroit, Phoenix.
  – Brendan Shanahan, New Jersey, St. Louis, Hartford, Detroit, NY Rangers.

MOST OVERTIME ASSISTS, CAREER:

21 – Nicklas Lidstrom, Detroit.
18 – Mark Messier, Edmonton, NY Rangers, Vancouver.
  – Pavol Demitra, Ottawa, St. Louis, Los Angeles, Minnesota, Vancouver.
  – Tomas Kaberle, Toronto.
17 – Adam Oates, Detroit, St. Louis, Boston, Washington, Philadelphia, Anaheim.
  – Cory Stillman, Calgary, St. Louis, Tampa Bay, Carolina, Ottawa, Florida.
16 – Sergei Fedorov, Detroit, Anaheim, Columbus, Washington.
  – Patrik Elias, New Jersey.

MOST OVERTIME POINTS, CAREER:

31 – Sergei Fedorov, Detroit, Anaheim, Columbus, Washington. 15G–16A
  – Patrik Elias, New Jersey. 15G–16A
28 – Mats Sundin, Quebec, Toronto. 15G–13A
27 – Jaromir Jagr, Pittsburgh, Washington, NY Rangers. 15G–12A
  – Patrik Elias, New Jersey. 15G–12A
  – Pavol Demitra, Ottawa, St. Louis, Los Angeles, Minnesota, Vancouver. 9G–18A
26 – Mark Messier, Edmonton, NY Rangers, Vancouver. 8G–18A
  – Ilya Kovalchuk, Atlanta, New Jersey 13G–13A
25 – Tomas Kaberle, Toronto, Boston. 7G–18A
  – Nicklas Lidstrom, Detroit. 4G–21A

MOST OVERTIME GOALS, ONE SEASON:

4 – Howie Morenz, Montreal, 1929-30.
  – Frank Finnigan, Ottawa, 1929-30.
  – Johnny Gagnon, Montreal 1936-37.
  – Mats Sundin, Toronto, 1999-2000.
  – Scott Niedermayer, New Jersey, 2001-02.
  – Patrik Elias, New Jersey, 2003-04.
  – Markus Naslund, Vancouver, 2003-04.
  – Olli Jokinen, Florida, 2005-06.
  – Daniel Sedin, Vancouver, 2006-07.
  – Ilya Kovalchuk, New Jersey, 2010-11.

SHOOTOUT GOALS

MOST SHOOTOUT GOALS, ONE SEASON:

10 – Wojtek Wolski, Colorado, 2008-09, (12s)
  – Jussi Jokinen, Dallas, 2005-06, (13s)
  – Alex Tanguay, Calgary, 2010-11, (16s)
9 – Jarret Stoll, Los Angeles, 2010-11, (10s)

MOST SHOOTOUT GOALS, ALL-TIME:

28 – Jussi Jokinen, Dallas, Tampa Bay, Carolina, (60s)
27 – Vyacheslav Kozlov, Atlanta, (46s)
26 – Pavel Datsyuk, Detroit, (54s)
25 – Brad Richards, Tampa Bay, Dallas, (60s)

MOST SHOOTOUT SHOTS TAKEN, ONE SEASON:

18 – Radim Vrbata, Phoenix, 2009-10, (8G)
17 – Lauri Korpikoski, Phoenix, 2009-10, (7G)
  – Jack Johnson, Los Angeles, 2009-10, (6G)
  – Sam Gagner, Edmonton, 2007-08, (5G)
16 – Alex Tanguay, Calgary, 2010-11, (10G)
  – Anze Kopitar, Los Angeles, 2009-10, (8G)
  – Ales Hemsky, Edmonton, 2007-08, (6G)
  – Brad Richards, Dallas, 2009-10, (4G)

MOST SHOOTOUT SHOTS TAKEN, ALL-TIME:

60 – Jussi Jokinen, Dallas, Tampa Bay, Carolina, (28G)
  – Brad Richards, Tampa Bay, Dallas, (25G)
58 – Rick Nash, Columbus, (22G)
57 – Alex Ovechkin, Washington, (17G)

BEST SHOOTOUT SCORING PERCENTAGE, ONE SEASON: *(minimum 5 shots)*

.900 – Jarret Stoll, Los Angeles, 2010-11, (9G, 10s)
.857 – Petteri Nummelin, Minnesota, 2006-07, (6G, 7s)
.833 – Wojtek Wolski, Colorado, 2008-09, (10G, 12s)
  – Patrik Elias, New Jersey, 2007-08, (5G, 6s)
  – Thomas Vanek, Buffalo, 2010-11, (5G, 6s)
.800 – Sidney Crosby, Pittsburgh, 2009-10, (8G, 10s)
  – Patrick O'Sullivan, Los Angeles, 2007-08, (4G, 5s)
  – Kristian Huselius, Calgary, 2007-08, (4G, 5s)
  – Jeremy Roenick, San Jose, 2007-08, (4G, 5s)
  – Ray Whitney, Carolina, 2005-06, (4G, 5s)

BEST SHOOTOUT SCORING PERCENTAGE, CAREER: *(minimum 10 shots)*

.800 – Petteri Nummelin, Minnesota, (8G, 10s)
.593 – Frans Nielsen, NY Islanders, (16G, 27s)
.587 – Vyacheslav Kozlov, Atlanta, (27G, 46s)
.583 – Trevor Linden, Vancouver, (7G, 12s)

MOST GAME DECIDING SHOOTOUT GOALS, ONE SEASON:

6 – Adrian Aucoin, Phoenix, 2009-10, (9s)
5 – Miroslav Satan, NY Islanders, 2005-06, (10s)
  – Vyacheslav Kozlov, Atlanta, 2006-07, (11s)
  – Viktor Kozlov, New Jersey, 2005-06, (12s)
  – Phil Kessel, Boston, 2007-08, (13s)
  – Ales Kotalik, Buffalo, Edmonton, 2008-09, (13s)

MOST GAME DECIDING SHOOTOUT GOALS, CAREER:

13 – Sidney Crosby, Pittsburgh, (48s)
12 – Phil Kessel, Boston, Toronto, (43s)
11 – Erik Christensen, Pittsburgh, Atlanta, Anaheim, NY Rangers, (43s)
  – Ales Kotalik, Buffalo, Edmonton, NY Rangers, Calgary, (44s)
  – Vyacheslav Kozlov, Atlanta, (46s)
  – Brad Richards, Tampa Bay, Dallas, (60s)

SCORING BY A CENTER

MOST GOALS BY A CENTER, CAREER:
894 – Wayne Gretzky, Edmonton, Los Angeles, St. Louis, NY Rangers, in 20 seasons. 1,487GP
731 – Marcel Dionne, Detroit, Los Angeles, NY Rangers, in 18 seasons. 1,348GP
717 – Phil Esposito, Chicago, Boston, NY Rangers, in 18 seasons. 1,282GP
694 – Mark Messier, Edmonton, NY Rangers, Vancouver, in 25 seasons. 1,756GP
692 – Steve Yzerman, Detroit, in 22 seasons. 1,514GP

MOST GOALS BY A CENTER, ONE SEASON:
92 – Wayne Gretzky, Edmonton, 1981-82. 80GP – 80 game schedule.
87 – Wayne Gretzky, Edmonton, 1983-84. 74GP – 80 game schedule.
85 – Mario Lemieux, Pittsburgh, 1988-89. 76GP – 80 game schedule.
76 – Phil Esposito, Boston, 1970-71. 78GP – 78 game schedule.
73 – Wayne Gretzky, Edmonton, 1984-85. 80GP – 80 game schedule.

MOST ASSISTS BY A CENTER, CAREER:
1,963 – Wayne Gretzky, Edmonton, Los Angeles, St. Louis, NY Rangers, in 20 seasons. 1,487GP
1,249 – Ron Francis, Hartford, Pittsburgh, Carolina, Toronto, in 23 seasons. 1,731GP
1,193 – Mark Messier, Edmonton, NY Rangers, Vancouver, in 25 seasons. 1,756GP
1,079 – Adam Oates, Detroit, St. Louis, Boston, Washington, Philadelphia, Anaheim, Edmonton, in 19 seasons. 1,337GP
1,063 – Steve Yzerman, Detroit, in 22 seasons. 1,514GP

MOST ASSISTS BY A CENTER, ONE SEASON:
163 – Wayne Gretzky, Edmonton, 1985-86. 80GP – 80 game schedule.
135 – Wayne Gretzky, Edmonton, 1984-85. 80GP – 80 game schedule.
125 – Wayne Gretzky, Edmonton, 1982-83. 80GP – 80 game schedule.
122 – Wayne Gretzky, Los Angeles, 1990-91. 78GP – 80 game schedule.
121 – Wayne Gretzky, Edmonton, 1986-87. 79GP – 80 game schedule.

MOST POINTS BY A CENTER, CAREER:
2,857 – Wayne Gretzky, Edmonton, Los Angeles, St. Louis, NY Rangers, in 20 seasons. 1,487GP (894G-1,963A)
1,887 – Mark Messier, Edmonton, NY Rangers, Vancouver, in 25 seasons. 1,756GP (694G-1,193A)
1,798 – Ron Francis, Hartford, Pittsburgh, Carolina, Toronto, in 23 seasons. 1,731GP (549G-1,249A)
1,771 – Marcel Dionne, Detroit, Los Angeles, NY Rangers, in 18 seasons. 1,348GP (731G-1,040A)
1,755 – Steve Yzerman, Detroit, in 22 seasons. 1,514GP (692G-1,063A)

MOST POINTS BY A CENTER, ONE SEASON:
215 – Wayne Gretzky, Edmonton, 1985-86. 80GP – 80 game schedule.
212 – Wayne Gretzky, Edmonton, 1981-82. 80GP – 80 game schedule.
208 – Wayne Gretzky, Edmonton, 1984-85. 80GP – 80 game schedule.
205 – Wayne Gretzky, Edmonton, 1983-84. 74GP – 80 game schedule.
199 – Mario Lemieux, Pittsburgh, 1988-89. 76GP – 80 game schedule.

SCORING BY A LEFT WING

MOST GOALS BY A LEFT WING, CAREER:
668 – Luc Robitaille, Los Angeles, Pittsburgh, NY Rangers, Detroit, in 19 seasons. 1,431GP
656 – Brendan Shanahan, New Jersey, St. Louis, Hartford, Detroit, NY Rangers, in 21 seasons. 1,524GP
640 – Dave Andreychuk, Buffalo, Toronto, New Jersey, Boston, Colorado, Tampa Bay, in 23 seasons. 1,639GP
610 – Bobby Hull, Chicago, Winnipeg, Hartford, in 16 seasons. 1,063GP
556 – John Bucyk, Detroit, Boston, in 23 seasons. 1,540GP

MOST GOALS BY A LEFT WING, ONE SEASON:
65 – Alex Ovechkin, Washington, 2007-08. 82GP – 82 game schedule.
63 – Luc Robitaille, Los Angeles, 1992-93. 84GP – 84 game schedule.
60 – Steve Shutt, Montreal, 1976-77. 80GP – 80 game schedule.
58 – Bobby Hull, Chicago, 1968-69. 74GP – 76 game schedule.
57 – Michel Goulet, Quebec, 1982-83. 80GP – 80 game schedule.

MOST ASSISTS BY A LEFT WING, CAREER:
813 – John Bucyk, Detroit, Boston, in 23 seasons. 1,540GP
726 – Luc Robitaille, Los Angeles, Pittsburgh, NY Rangers, Detroit, in 19 seasons. 1,431GP
698 – Dave Andreychuk, Buffalo, Toronto, New Jersey, Boston, Colorado, Tampa Bay, in 23 seasons. 1,639GP
– Brendan Shanahan, New Jersey, St. Louis, Hartford, Detroit, NY Rangers, in 21 seasons. 1,524GP
604 – Michel Goulet, Quebec, Chicago, in 15 seasons. 1,089GP

MOST ASSISTS BY A LEFT WING, ONE SEASON:
70 – Joe Juneau, Boston, 1992-93. 84GP – 84 game schedule.
69 – Kevin Stevens, Pittsburgh, 1991-92. 80GP – 80 game schedule.
67 – Mats Naslund, Montreal, 1985-86. 80GP – 80 game schedule.
65 – John Bucyk, Boston, 1970-71. 78GP – 78 game schedule.
– Michel Goulet, Quebec, 1983-84. 75GP – 80 game schedule.
64 – Mark Messier, Edmonton, 1983-84. 73GP – 80 game schedule.

MOST POINTS BY A LEFT WING, CAREER:
1,394 – Luc Robitaille, Los Angeles, Pittsburgh, NY Rangers, Detroit, in 19 seasons. 1,431GP (668G-726A)
1,369 – John Bucyk, Detroit, Boston, in 23 seasons. 1,540GP (556G-813A)
1,354 – Brendan Shanahan, New Jersey, St. Louis, Hartford, Detroit, NY Rangers, in 21 seasons. 1,524GP (656G-698A)
1,338 – Dave Andreychuk, Buffalo, Toronto, New Jersey, Boston, Colorado, Tampa Bay, in 23 seasons. 1,639GP (640G-698A)
1,170 – Bobby Hull, Chicago, Winnipeg, Hartford, in 16 seasons. 1,063GP (610G-560A)

MOST POINTS BY A LEFT WING, ONE SEASON:
125 – Luc Robitaille, Los Angeles, 1992-93. 84GP – 84 game schedule.
123 – Kevin Stevens, Pittsburgh, 1991-92. 80GP – 80 game schedule.
121 – Michel Goulet, Quebec, 1983-84. 75GP – 80 game schedule.
116 – John Bucyk, Boston, 1970-71. 78GP – 78 game schedule.
112 – Bill Barber, Philadelphia, 1975-76. 80GP – 80 game schedule.
– Alex Ovechkin, Washington, 2007-08. 82GP – 82 game schedule.

SCORING BY A RIGHT WING

MOST GOALS BY A RIGHT WING, CAREER:
801 – Gordie Howe, Detroit, Hartford, in 26 seasons. 1,767GP
741 – Brett Hull, Calgary, St. Louis, Dallas, Detroit, Phoenix, in 19 seasons. 1,269GP
708 – Mike Gartner, Washington, Minnesota, NY Rangers, Toronto, Phoenix, in 19 seasons. 1,432GP
646 – Jaromir Jagr, Pittsburgh, Washington, NY Rangers, in 17 seasons. 1,273GP
637 – Teemu Selanne, Winnipeg, San Jose, Colorado, Anaheim, in 18 seasons. 1,259GP
608 – Dino Ciccarelli, Minnesota, Washington, Detroit, Tampa Bay, Florida, in 19 seasons. 1,232GP

MOST GOALS BY A RIGHT WING, ONE SEASON:
86 – Brett Hull, St. Louis, 1990-91. 78GP – 80 game schedule.
76 – Alexander Mogilny, Buffalo, 1992-93. 77GP – 84 game schedule.
– Teemu Selanne, Winnipeg, 1992-93. 84GP – 84 game schedule.
72 – Brett Hull, St. Louis, 1989-90. 80GP – 80 game schedule.
71 – Jari Kurri, Edmonton, 1984-85. 73GP – 80 game schedule.
70 – Brett Hull, St. Louis, 1991-92. 73GP – 80 game schedule.

MOST ASSISTS BY A RIGHT WING, CAREER:
1,049 – Gordie Howe, Detroit, Hartford, in 26 seasons. 1,767GP
956 – Mark Recchi, Pittsburgh, Philadelphia, Montreal, Carolina, Atlanta, Boston, in 22 seasons. 1,652GP
953 – Jaromir Jagr, Pittsburgh, Washington, NY Rangers, in 17 seasons. 1,273GP
797 – Jari Kurri, Edmonton, Los Angeles, NY Rangers, Anaheim, Colorado, in 17 seasons. 1,251GP
793 – Guy Lafleur, Montreal, NY Rangers, Quebec, in 17 seasons. 1,126GP

MOST ASSISTS BY A RIGHT WING, ONE SEASON:
87 – Jaromir Jagr, Pittsburgh, 1995-96. 82GP – 82 game schedule.
83 – Mike Bossy, NY Islanders, 1981-82. 80GP – 80 game schedule.
– Jaromir Jagr, Pittsburgh, 1998-99. 81GP – 82 game schedule.
80 – Guy Lafleur, Montreal, 1976-77. 80GP – 80 game schedule.
77 – Guy Lafleur, Montreal, 1978-79. 80GP – 80 game schedule.

Left winger Paul Kariya topped 100 points twice while playing in Anaheim, including a career high 50 goals and 58 assists in 1995-96. Kariya, Teemu Selanne and Corey Perry in 2010-11 are the only players in Ducks history to score 50 goals in a season.

MOST POINTS BY A RIGHT WING, CAREER:
1,850 – Gordie Howe, Detroit, Hartford, in 26 seasons. 1,767GP (801G–1,049A)
1,599 – Jaromir Jagr, Pittsburgh, Washington, NY Rangers,
    in 17 seasons. 1,273GP (646G–953A)
1,533 – Mark Recchi, Pittsburgh, Philadelphia, Montreal, Carolina, Atlanta,
    Boston, in 22 seasons. 1,652GP (577G–956A)
1,398 – Jari Kurri, Edmonton, Los Angeles, NY Rangers, Anaheim, Colorado,
    in 17 seasons. 1,251GP (601G–797A)
1,391 – Brett Hull, Calgary, St. Louis, Dallas, Detroit, Phoenix, in 19 seasons.
    1,269GP (741G–650A)

MOST POINTS BY A RIGHT WING, ONE SEASON:
149 – Jaromir Jagr, Pittsburgh, 1995-96. 82GP – 82 game schedule.
147 – Mike Bossy, NY Islanders, 1981-82. 80GP – 80 game schedule.
136 – Guy Lafleur, Montreal, 1976-77. 80GP – 80 game schedule.
135 – Jari Kurri, Edmonton, 1984-85. 73GP – 80 game schedule.
132 – Guy Lafleur, Montreal, 1977-78. 78GP – 80 game schedule.
   – Teemu Selanne, Winnipeg, 1992-93. 84GP – 84 game schedule.

SCORING BY A DEFENSEMAN

MOST GOALS BY A DEFENSEMAN, CAREER:
410 – Raymond Bourque, Boston, Colorado, in 22 seasons. 1,612GP
396 – Paul Coffey, Edmonton, Pittsburgh, Los Angeles, Detroit, Hartford,
    Philadelphia, Chicago, Carolina, Boston, in 21 seasons. 1,409GP
340 – Al MacInnis, Calgary, St. Louis, in 23 seasons. 1,416GP
338 – Phil Housley, Buffalo, Winnipeg, St. Louis, Calgary, New Jersey,
    Washington, Chicago, Toronto, in 21 seasons. 1,495GP
310 – Denis Potvin, NY Islanders, in 15 seasons. 1,060GP

MOST GOALS BY A DEFENSEMAN, ONE SEASON:
48 – Paul Coffey, Edmonton, 1985-86. 79GP – 80 game schedule.
46 – Bobby Orr, Boston, 1974-75. 80GP – 80 game schedule.
40 – Paul Coffey, Edmonton, 1983-84. 80GP – 80 game schedule.
39 – Doug Wilson, Chicago, 1981-82. 76GP – 80 game schedule.
37 – Bobby Orr, Boston, 1970-71. 78GP – 78 game schedule.
   – Bobby Orr, Boston, 1971-72. 76GP – 78 game schedule.
   – Paul Coffey, Edmonton, 1984-85. 80GP – 80 game schedule.

MOST GOALS BY A DEFENSEMAN, ONE GAME:
5 – Ian Turnbull, Toronto, Feb. 2, 1977, at Toronto. Toronto 9, Detroit 1.
4 – Harry Cameron, Toronto, Dec. 26, 1917, at Toronto. Toronto 7, Montreal 5.
   – Harry Cameron, Montreal, Mar. 3, 1920, at Quebec.
    Montreal 16, Quebec 3.
   – Sprague Cleghorn, Montreal, Jan. 14, 1922, at Montreal.
    Montreal 10, Hamilton 6.
   – John McKinnon, Pittsburgh, Nov. 19, 1929, at Pittsburgh.
    Pittsburgh 10, Toronto 5.
   – Hap Day, Toronto, Nov. 19, 1929, at Pittsburgh.
    Pittsburgh 10, Toronto 5.
   – Tom Bladon, Philadelphia, Dec. 11, 1977, at Philadelphia.
    Philadelphia 11, Cleveland 1.
   – Ian Turnbull, Los Angeles, Dec. 12, 1981, at Los Angeles.
    Los Angeles 7, Vancouver 5.
   – Paul Coffey, Edmonton, Oct. 26, 1984, at Calgary. Edmonton 6, Calgary 5.

MOST ASSISTS BY A DEFENSEMAN, CAREER:
1,169 – Raymond Bourque, Boston, Colorado, in 22 seasons. 1,612GP
1,135 – Paul Coffey, Edmonton, Pittsburgh, Los Angeles, Detroit, Hartford,
    Philadelphia, Chicago, Carolina, Boston, in 21 seasons. 1,409GP
  934 – Al MacInnis, Calgary, St. Louis, in 23 seasons. 1,416GP
  929 – Larry Murphy, Los Angeles, Washington, Minnesota,
    Pittsburgh, Toronto, Detroit, in 21 seasons. 1,615GP
  894 – Phil Housley, Buffalo, Winnipeg, St. Louis, Calgary, New Jersey,
    Washington, Chicago, Toronto, in 21 seasons. 1,495GP

MOST ASSISTS BY A DEFENSEMAN, ONE SEASON:
102 – Bobby Orr, Boston, 1970-71. 78GP – 78 game schedule.
 90 – Bobby Orr, Boston, 1973-74. 74GP – 78 game schedule.
   – Paul Coffey, Edmonton, 1985-86. 79GP – 80 game schedule.
 89 – Bobby Orr, Boston, 1974-75. 80GP – 80 game schedule.
 87 – Bobby Orr, Boston, 1969-70. 76GP – 78 game schedule.

MOST ASSISTS BY A DEFENSEMAN, ONE GAME:
6 – Babe Pratt, Toronto, Jan. 8, 1944, at Toronto. Toronto 12, Boston 3.
   – Pat Stapleton, Chicago, Mar. 30, 1969, at Chicago. Chicago 9, Detroit 5.
   – Bobby Orr, Boston, Jan. 1, 1973, at Vancouver. Boston 8, Vancouver 2.
   – Ron Stackhouse, Pittsburgh, Mar. 8, 1975, at Pittsburgh. Pittsburgh 8,
    Philadelphia 2.
   – Paul Coffey, Edmonton, Mar. 14, 1986, at Edmonton. Edmonton 12,
    Detroit 3.
   – Gary Suter, Calgary, Apr. 4, 1986, at Calgary. Calgary 9, Edmonton 3.

MOST POINTS BY A DEFENSEMAN, CAREER:
1,579 – Raymond Bourque, Boston, Colorado, in 22 seasons. 1,612GP
    (410G–1,169A)
1,531 – Paul Coffey, Edmonton, Pittsburgh, Los Angeles, Detroit, Hartford,
    Philadelphia, Chicago, Carolina, Boston, in 21 seasons. 1,409GP
    (396G–1,135A)
1,274 – Al MacInnis, Calgary, St. Louis, in 23 seasons. 1,416GP (340G–934A)
1,232 – Phil Housley, Buffalo, Winnipeg, St. Louis, Calgary, New Jersey,
    Washington, Chicago, Toronto, in 21 seasons. 1,495GP (338G–894A)
1,216 – Larry Murphy, Los Angeles, Washington, Minnesota,
    Pittsburgh, Toronto, Detroit, in 21 seasons. 1,615GP (287G–929A)

MOST POINTS BY A DEFENSEMAN, ONE SEASON:
139 – Bobby Orr, Boston, 1970-71. 78GP – 78 game schedule.
138 – Paul Coffey, Edmonton, 1985-86. 79GP – 80 game schedule.
135 – Bobby Orr, Boston, 1974-75. 80GP – 80 game schedule.
126 – Paul Coffey, Edmonton, 1983-84. 80GP – 80 game schedule.
122 – Bobby Orr, Boston, 1973-74. 74GP – 78 game schedule.

MOST POINTS BY A DEFENSEMAN, ONE GAME:
8 – Tom Bladon, Philadelphia, Dec. 11, 1977, at Philadelphia. 4G–4A.
    Philadelphia 11, Cleveland 1.
   – Paul Coffey, Edmonton, Mar. 14, 1986, at Edmonton. 2G–6A.
    Edmonton 12, Detroit 3.
7 – Bobby Orr, Boston, Nov. 15, 1973, at Boston. 3G–4A.
    Boston 10, NY Rangers 2.

SCORING BY A GOALTENDER

MOST POINTS BY A GOALTENDER, CAREER:
48 – Tom Barrasso, Buffalo, Pittsburgh, Ottawa, Carolina, Toronto, St. Louis,
    in 19 seasons. 777GP
46 – Grant Fuhr, Edmonton, Toronto, Buffalo, Los Angeles, St. Louis, Calgary,
    in 19 seasons. 868GP

MOST POINTS BY A GOALTENDER, ONE SEASON:
14 – Grant Fuhr, Edmonton, 1983-84. 45GP – 80 game schedule.
 9 – Curtis Joseph, St. Louis, 1991-92. 60GP – 80 game schedule.
 8 – Mike Palmateer, Washington, 1980-81. 49GP – 80 game schedule.
   – Grant Fuhr, Edmonton, 1987-88. 75GP – 80 game schedule.
   – Ron Hextall, Philadelphia, 1988-89. 64GP – 80 game schedule.
   – Tom Barrasso, Pittsburgh, 1992-93. 63GP – 84 game schedule.

MOST POINTS BY A GOALTENDER, ONE GAME:
3 – Jeff Reese, Calgary, Feb. 10, 1993, at Calgary. Calgary 13, San Jose 1.

Though he no longer ranks as the NHL's overall scoring leader, Gordie Howe still leads all right wingers in goals, assists and points. Howe became the first player in NHL history to score 600 goals on November 27, 1965.

SCORING BY A ROOKIE

MOST GOALS BY A ROOKIE, ONE SEASON:
  76 – Teemu Selanne, Winnipeg, 1992-93. 84GP – 84 game schedule.
  53 – Mike Bossy, NY Islanders, 1977-78. 73GP – 80 game schedule.
  52 – Alex Ovechkin, Washington, 2005-06. 81GP – 82 game schedule.
  51 – Joe Nieuwendyk, Calgary, 1987-88. 75GP – 80 game schedule.
  45 – Dale Hawerchuk, Winnipeg, 1981-82. 80GP – 80 game schedule.
    – Luc Robitaille, Los Angeles, 1986-87. 79GP – 80 game schedule.

MOST GOALS BY A PLAYER IN HIS FIRST NHL SEASON, ONE GAME:
  5 – Joe Malone, Montreal, three occasions, 1917-18.
    – **Harry Hyland**, Mtl. Wanderers, Dec. 19, 1917, at Montreal.
    Mtl Wanderers 10, Toronto 9.
    – **Mickey Roach**, Toronto, Mar. 6, 1920, at Toronto. Toronto 11, Quebec 2.
    – **Howie Meeker**, Toronto, Jan. 8, 1947, at Toronto. Toronto 10, Chicago 4.
    – **Don Murdoch**, NY Rangers, Oct. 12, 1976, at Minnesota.
    NY Rangers 10, Minnesota 4.

MOST GOALS BY A PLAYER IN HIS FIRST NHL GAME:
  5 – Joe Malone, Montreal, Dec. 19, 1917, at Ottawa. Montreal 7, Ottawa 4.
    – **Harry Hyland**, Mtl. Wanderers, Dec. 19, 1917, at Montreal.
    Mtl Wanderers 10, Toronto 9.
  3 – Alex Smart, Montreal, Jan. 14, 1943, at Montreal. Montreal 5, Chicago 1.
    – Real Cloutier, Quebec, Oct. 10, 1979, at Quebec. Atlanta 5, Quebec 3.
    – Fabian Brunnstrom, Dallas, Oct. 15, 2008, at Dallas.
    Dallas 6, Nashville 4.
    – Derek Stepan, NY Rangers, Oct. 9, 2010, at Buffalo.
    NY Rangers 6, Buffalo 3.

MOST ASSISTS BY A ROOKIE, ONE SEASON:
  70 – Peter Stastny, Quebec, 1980-81. 77GP – 80 game schedule.
    – **Joe Juneau**, Boston, 1992-93. 84GP – 84 game schedule.
  63 – Bryan Trottier, NY Islanders, 1975-76. 80GP – 80 game schedule.
    – Sidney Crosby, Pittsburgh, 2005–06. 81GP – 82 game schedule.
  62 – Sergei Makarov, Calgary, 1989-90. 80GP – 80 game schedule.
  60 – Larry Murphy, Los Angeles, 1980-81. 80GP – 80 game schedule.

MOST ASSISTS BY A PLAYER IN HIS FIRST NHL SEASON, ONE GAME:
  7 – Wayne Gretzky, Edmonton, Feb. 15, 1980, at Edmonton.
    Edmonton 8, Washington 2.
  6 – Gary Suter, Calgary, Apr. 4, 1986, at Calgary. Calgary 9, Edmonton 3.

MOST ASSISTS BY A PLAYER IN HIS FIRST NHL GAME:
  4 – Dutch Reibel, Detroit, Oct. 8, 1953, at Detroit. Detroit 4, NY Rangers 1.
    – **Roland Eriksson**, Minnesota, Oct. 6, 1976, at NY Rangers.
    NY Rangers 6, Minnesota 5.
  3 – Al Hill, Philadelphia, Feb. 14, 1977, at Philadelphia. Philadelphia 6,
    St. Louis 4.
    – Jarno Kultanen, Boston, Oct. 5, 2000, at Boston. Boston 4, Ottawa 4.
    – Stanislav Chistov, Anaheim, Oct. 10, 2002, at St. Louis. Anaheim 4,
    St. Louis 3.
    – Dominic Moore, NY Rangers, Nov. 1, 2003, at Montreal. NY Rangers 5,
    Montreal 1.

MOST POINTS BY A ROOKIE, ONE SEASON:
  132 – Teemu Selanne, Winnipeg, 1992-93. 84GP – 84 game schedule.
  109 – Peter Stastny, Quebec, 1980-81. 77GP – 80 game schedule.
  106 – Alex Ovechkin, Washington, 2005-06. 81GP – 82 game schedule.
  103 – Dale Hawerchuk, Winnipeg, 1981-82. 80GP – 80 game schedule.
  102 – Joe Juneau, Boston, 1992-93. 84GP – 84 game schedule.
    – Sidney Crosby, Pittsburgh, 2005–06. 81GP – 82 game schedule.
  100 – Mario Lemieux, Pittsburgh, 1984-85. 73GP – 80 game schedule.

MOST POINTS BY A PLAYER IN HIS FIRST NHL SEASON, ONE GAME:
  8 – Peter Stastny, Quebec, Feb. 22, 1981, at Washington. 4G-4A.
    Quebec 11, Washington 7.
    – **Anton Stastny**, Quebec, Feb. 22, 1981, at Washington. 3G-5A.
    Quebec 11, Washington 7.
  7 – Wayne Gretzky, Edmonton, Feb. 15, 1980, at Edmonton. 7A.
    Edmonton 8, Washington 2.
    – Sergei Makarov, Calgary, Feb. 25, 1990, at Calgary. 2G-5A.
    Calgary 10, Edmonton 4.
  6 – Wayne Gretzky, Edmonton, Mar. 29, 1980, at Toronto. 2G-4A.
    Edmonton 8, Toronto 5.
    – Gary Suter, Calgary, Apr. 4, 1986, at Calgary. 6A.
    Calgary 9, Edmonton 3.

MOST POINTS BY A PLAYER IN HIS FIRST NHL GAME:
  5 – Joe Malone, Montreal, Dec. 19, 1917, at Ottawa. 5G*.
    Montreal 7, Ottawa 4.
    – **Harry Hyland**, Mtl. Wanderers, Dec. 19, 1917, at Montreal. 5G*.
    Mtl Wanderers 10, Toronto 9.
    – **Al Hill**, Philadelphia, Feb. 14, 1977, at Philadelphia. 2G-3A.
    Philadelphia 6, St. Louis 4.
  4 – Alex Smart, Montreal, Jan. 14, 1943, at Montreal. 3G-1A.
    Montreal 5, Chicago 1.
    – Dutch Reibel, Detroit, Oct. 8, 1953, at Detroit. 4A.
    Detroit 4, NY Rangers 1.
    – Roland Eriksson, Minnesota, Oct. 6, 1976, at NY Rangers. 4A.
    NY Rangers 6, Minnesota 5.
    – Stanislav Chistov, Anaheim, Oct. 10, 2002, at St. Louis. 1G-3A.
    Anaheim 4, St. Louis 3.

  * – Official assists not awarded in 1917-18.

SCORING BY A ROOKIE DEFENSEMAN

MOST GOALS BY A ROOKIE DEFENSEMAN, ONE SEASON:
  23 – Brian Leetch, NY Rangers, 1988-89. 68GP – 80 game schedule.
  22 – Barry Beck, Colorado, 1977-78. 75GP – 80 game schedule.
  20 – Dion Phaneuf, Calgary, 2005-06. 82GP – 82 game schedule.

MOST ASSISTS BY A ROOKIE DEFENSEMAN, ONE SEASON:
  60 – Larry Murphy, Los Angeles, 1980-81. 80GP – 80 game schedule.
  55 – Chris Chelios, Montreal, 1984-85. 74GP – 80 game schedule.
  50 – Stefan Persson, NY Islanders, 1977-78. 66GP – 80 game schedule.
    – Gary Suter, Calgary, 1985-86. 80GP – 80 game schedule.
  49 – Nicklas Lidstrom, Detroit, 1991-92. 80GP – 80 game schedule.

MOST POINTS BY A ROOKIE DEFENSEMAN, ONE SEASON:
  76 – Larry Murphy, Los Angeles, 1980-81. 80GP – 80 game schedule.
  71 – Brian Leetch, NY Rangers, 1988-89. 68GP – 80 game schedule.
  68 – Gary Suter, Calgary, 1985-86. 80GP – 80 game schedule.
  66 – Phil Housley, Buffalo, 1982-83. 77GP – 80 game schedule.
  65 – Raymond Bourque, Boston, 1979-80. 80GP – 80 game schedule.

*Derek Stepan, seen showing off the three pucks and being congratulated at the New York Rangers bench after his second goal,
became just the fourth player since 1918 to score a hat trick in his very first NHL game on October 9, 2010.*

PER-GAME SCORING AVERAGES

HIGHEST GOALS-PER-GAME AVERAGE, CAREER
(AMONG PLAYERS WITH 200-OR-MORE GOALS):
.762 – **Mike Bossy**, NY Islanders, 1977-78 – 1986-87, with 573G in 752GP.
.756 – Cy Denneny, Ottawa, Boston, 1917-18 – 1928-29, with 248G in 328GP.
.754 – Mario Lemieux, Pittsburgh, 1984-85 – 1996-97, 2000-01 – 2003-04, 2005-06, with 690G in 915GP.
.742 – Babe Dye, Toronto, Hamilton, Chicago, NY Americans, 1919-20 – 1930-31, with 201G in 271GP.
.634 – Alex Ovechkin, Washington, 2005-06 – 2010-11, with 301G in 475GP.

HIGHEST GOALS-PER-GAME AVERAGE, ONE SEASON
(AMONG PLAYERS WITH 20-OR-MORE GOALS):
2.20 – **Joe Malone**, Montreal, 1917-18, with 44G in 20GP.
1.80 – Cy Denneny, Ottawa, 1917-18, with 36G in 20GP.
1.64 – Newsy Lalonde, Montreal, 1917-18, with 23G in 14GP.
1.63 – Joe Malone, Quebec, 1919-20, with 39G in 24GP.
1.61 – Newsy Lalonde, Montreal, 1919-20, with 37G in 23GP.

HIGHEST GOALS-PER-GAME AVERAGE, ONE SEASON
(AMONG PLAYERS WITH 50-OR-MORE GOALS):
1.18 – **Wayne Gretzky**, Edmonton, 1983-84, with 87G in 74GP.
1.15 – Wayne Gretzky, Edmonton, 1981-82, with 92G in 80GP.
– Mario Lemieux, Pittsburgh, 1992-93, with 69G in 60GP.
1.12 – Mario Lemieux, Pittsburgh, 1988-89, with 85G in 76GP.
1.10 – Brett Hull, St. Louis, 1990-91, with 86G in 78GP.
1.02 – Cam Neely, Boston, 1993-94, with 50G in 49GP.
1.00 – Maurice Richard, Montreal, 1944-45, with 50G in 50GP.

HIGHEST ASSISTS-PER-GAME AVERAGE, CAREER
(AMONG PLAYERS WITH 300-OR-MORE ASSISTS):
1.320 – **Wayne Gretzky**, Edmonton, Los Angeles, St. Louis, NY Rangers, 1979-80 – 1998-99, with 1,963A in 1,487GP.
1.129 – Mario Lemieux, Pittsburgh, 1984-85 – 1996-97, 2000-01 – 2003-04, 2005-06, with 1,033A in 915GP.
.982 – Bobby Orr, Boston, Chicago, 1966-67 – 1978-79, with 645A in 657GP.
.898 – Peter Forsberg, Quebec, Colorado, Philadelphia, Nashville, 1994-95 – 2000-01, 2002-03, 2003-04, 2005-06 – 2007-08, 2010-11 with 636A in 708GP.
.867 – Sidney Crosby, Pittsburgh, 2005-06 – 2010-11, with 357A in 412GP.

HIGHEST ASSISTS-PER-GAME AVERAGE, ONE SEASON
(AMONG PLAYERS WITH 35-OR-MORE ASSISTS):
2.04 – **Wayne Gretzky, Edmonton**, 1985-86, with 163A in 80GP.
1.70 – Wayne Gretzky, Edmonton, 1987-88, with 109A in 64GP.
1.69 – Wayne Gretzky, Edmonton, 1984-85, with 135A in 80GP.
1.59 – Wayne Gretzky, Edmonton, 1983-84, with 118A in 74GP.
1.56 – Wayne Gretzky, Edmonton, 1982-83, with 125A in 80GP.
– Wayne Gretzky, Los Angeles, 1990-91, with 122A in 78GP.
1.53 – Wayne Gretzky, Edmonton, 1986-87, with 121A in 79GP.
1.52 – Mario Lemieux, Pittsburgh, 1992-93, with 91A in 60GP.
1.50 – Wayne Gretzky, Edmonton, 1981-82, with 120A in 80GP.
– Mario Lemieux, Pittsburgh, 1988-89, with 114A in 76GP.

HIGHEST POINTS-PER-GAME AVERAGE, CAREER
(AMONG PLAYERS WITH 500-OR-MORE POINTS):
1.921 – **Wayne Gretzky**, Edmonton, Los Angeles, St. Louis, NY Rangers, 1979-80 – 1998-99, with 2,857PTS (894G-1,963A) in 1,487GP.
1.883 – Mario Lemieux, Pittsburgh, 1984-85 – 1996-97, 2000-01 – 2003-04, 2005-06, with 1,723PTS (690G-1,033A) in 915GP.
1.497 – Mike Bossy, NY Islanders, 1977-78 – 1986-87, with 1,126PTS (573G-553A) in 752GP.
1.393 – Bobby Orr, Boston, Chicago, 1966-67 – 1978-79, with 915PTS (270G-645A) in 657GP.
1.388 – Sidney Crosby, Pittsburgh, 2005-06 – 2010-11, with 572PTS (215G-357A) in 412GP.

HIGHEST POINTS-PER-GAME AVERAGE, ONE SEASON
(AMONG PLAYERS WITH 50-OR-MORE POINTS):
2.77 – **Wayne Gretzky**, Edmonton, 1983-84, with 205PTS in 74GP.
2.69 – Wayne Gretzky, Edmonton, 1985-86, with 215PTS in 80GP.
2.67 – Mario Lemieux, Pittsburgh, 1992-93, with 160PTS in 60GP.
2.65 – Wayne Gretzky, Edmonton, 1981-82, with 212PTS in 80GP.
2.62 – Mario Lemieux, Pittsburgh, 1988-89, with 199PTS in 76GP.
2.60 – Wayne Gretzky, Edmonton, 1984-85, with 208PTS in 80GP.
2.45 – Wayne Gretzky, Edmonton, 1982-83, with 196PTS in 80GP.
2.33 – Wayne Gretzky, Edmonton, 1987-88, with 149PTS in 64GP.
2.32 – Wayne Gretzky, Edmonton, 1986-87, with 183PTS in 79GP.
2.30 – Mario Lemieux, Pittsburgh, 1995-96, with 161PTS in 70GP.
2.18 – Mario Lemieux, Pittsburgh, 1987-88, with 168PTS in 77GP.
2.15 – Wayne Gretzky, Los Angeles, 1988-89, with 168PTS in 78GP.
2.09 – Wayne Gretzky, Los Angeles, 1990-91, with 163PTS in 78GP.
2.08 – Mario Lemieux, Pittsburgh, 1989-90, with 123PTS in 59GP.

SCORING PLATEAUS

MOST 20-OR-MORE GOAL SEASONS:
22 – **Gordie Howe**, Detroit, Hartford, in 26 seasons.
20 – Ron Francis, Hartford, Pittsburgh, Carolina, Toronto, in 23 seasons.
19 – Dave Andreychuk, Buffalo, Toronto, New Jersey, Boston, Colorado, Tampa Bay, in 23 seasons.
– Brendan Shanahan, New Jersey, St. Louis, Hartford, Detroit, NY Rangers, in 21 seasons.
17 – Marcel Dionne, Detroit, Los Angeles, NY Rangers, in 18 seasons.
– Mike Gartner, Washington, Minnesota, NY Rangers, Toronto, Phoenix, in 19 seasons.
– Wayne Gretzky, Edmonton, Los Angeles, St. Louis, NY Rangers, in 20 seasons.
– Mark Messier, Edmonton, NY Rangers, Vancouver, in 25 seasons.
– Brett Hull, Calgary, St. Louis, Dallas, Detroit, Phoenix, in 19 seasons.
– Joe Sakic, Quebec, Colorado, in 20 seasons.
– Mats Sundin, Quebec, Toronto, Vancouver, in 18 seasons.
– Jaromir Jagr, Pittsburgh, Washington, NY Rangers, in 17 seasons.

MOST CONSECUTIVE 20-OR-MORE GOAL SEASONS:
22 – **Gordie Howe**, Detroit, 1949-50 – 1970-71.
19 – Brendan Shanahan, New Jersey, St. Louis, Hartford, Detroit, NY Rangers, 1988-89 – 2007-08.
17 – Marcel Dionne, Detroit, Los Angeles, NY Rangers, 1971-72 – 1987-88.
– Brett Hull, Calgary, St. Louis, Dallas, Detroit, 1987-88 – 2003-04.
– Jaromir Jagr, Pittsburgh, Washington, NY Rangers, 1990-91 – 2007-08.
– Mats Sundin, Quebec, Toronto, 1990-91 – 2007-08.

Peter Forsberg, who abandoned a comeback attempt with Colorado after just two games in 2010-11, ranks fourth in NHL history in assists per game. With 885 points in just 708 career games, his 1.250 points-per-game average currently ranks him tenth all-time.

MOST 30-OR-MORE GOAL SEASONS:
17 – Mike Gartner, Washington, Minnesota, NY Rangers, Toronto, Phoenix, in 19 seasons.
15 – Jaromir Jagr, Pittsburgh, Washington, NY Rangers, in 17 seasons.
14 – Gordie Howe, Detroit, Hartford, in 26 seasons.
 – Marcel Dionne, Detroit, Los Angeles, NY Rangers, in 18 seasons.
 – Wayne Gretzky, Edmonton, Los Angeles, St. Louis, NY Rangers, in 20 seasons.
13 – Bobby Hull, Chicago, Winnipeg, Hartford, in 16 seasons.
 – Phil Esposito, Chicago, Boston, NY Rangers, in 18 seasons.
 – Brett Hull, Calgary, St. Louis, Dallas, Detroit, Phoenix, in 19 seasons.
 – Mats Sundin, Quebec, Toronto, Vancouver, in 18 seasons.

MOST CONSECUTIVE 30-OR-MORE GOAL SEASONS:
15 – Mike Gartner, Washington, Minnesota, NY Rangers, Toronto, 1979-80 – 1993-94.
 – **Jaromir Jagr**, Pittsburgh, Washington, NY Rangers, 1991-92 – 2006-07.
13 – Bobby Hull, Chicago, 1959-60 – 1971-72.
 – Phil Esposito, Boston, NY Rangers, 1967-68 – 1979-80.
 – Wayne Gretzky, Edmonton, Los Angeles, 1979-80 – 1991-92.

MOST 40-OR-MORE GOAL SEASONS:
12 – Wayne Gretzky, Edmonton, Los Angeles, St. Louis, NY Rangers, in 20 seasons.
10 – Marcel Dionne, Detroit, Los Angeles, NY Rangers, in 18 seasons.
 – Mario Lemieux, Pittsburgh, in 17 seasons.
 9 – Mike Bossy, NY Islanders, in 10 seasons.
 – Mike Gartner, Washington, Minnesota, NY Rangers, Toronto, Phoenix, in 19 seasons.

MOST CONSECUTIVE 40-OR-MORE GOAL SEASONS:
12 – Wayne Gretzky, Edmonton, Los Angeles, 1979-80 – 1990-91.
 9 – Mike Bossy, NY Islanders, 1977-78 – 1985-86.
 8 – Luc Robitaille, Los Angeles, 1986-87 – 1993-94.
 7 – Phil Esposito, Boston, 1968-69 – 1974-75.
 – Michel Goulet, Quebec, 1981-82 – 1987-88.
 – Jari Kurri, Edmonton, 1982-83 – 1988-89.

MOST 50-OR-MORE GOAL SEASONS:
9 – Mike Bossy, NY Islanders, in 10 seasons.
 – **Wayne Gretzky**, Edmonton, Los Angeles, St. Louis, NY Rangers, in 20 seasons.
 6 – Guy Lafleur, Montreal, NY Rangers, Quebec, in 17 seasons.
 – Marcel Dionne, Detroit, Los Angeles, NY Rangers, in 18 seasons.
 – Mario Lemieux, Pittsburgh, in 17 seasons.
 5 – Bobby Hull, Chicago, Winnipeg, Hartford, in 16 seasons.
 – Phil Esposito, Chicago, Boston, NY Rangers, in 18 seasons.
 – Brett Hull, Calgary, St. Louis, Dallas, Detroit, Phoenix, in 19 seasons.
 – Steve Yzerman, Detroit, in 22 seasons.
 – Pavel Bure, Vancouver, Florida, NY Rangers, in 12 seasons.

MOST CONSECUTIVE 50-OR-MORE GOAL SEASONS:
9 – Mike Bossy, NY Islanders, 1977-78 – 1985-86.
 8 – Wayne Gretzky, Edmonton, 1979-80 – 1986-87.
 6 – Guy Lafleur, Montreal, 1974-75 – 1979-80.
 5 – Phil Esposito, Boston, 1970-71 – 1974-75.
 – Marcel Dionne, Los Angeles, 1978-79 – 1982-83.
 – Brett Hull, St. Louis, 1989-90 – 1993-94.

MOST 60-OR-MORE GOAL SEASONS:
5 – Mike Bossy, NY Islanders, in 10 seasons.
 – **Wayne Gretzky**, Edmonton, Los Angeles, St. Louis, NY Rangers, in 20 seasons.
 4 – Phil Esposito, Chicago, Boston, NY Rangers, in 18 seasons.
 – Mario Lemieux, Pittsburgh, in 17 seasons.

MOST CONSECUTIVE 60-OR-MORE GOAL SEASONS:
4 – Wayne Gretzky, Edmonton, 1981-82 – 1984-85.
 3 – Mike Bossy, NY Islanders, 1980-81 – 1982-83.
 – Brett Hull, St. Louis, 1989-90 – 1991-92.
 2 – Phil Esposito, Boston, 1970-71 – 1971-72, 1973-74 – 1974-75.
 – Jari Kurri, Edmonton, 1984-85 – 1985-86.
 – Mario Lemieux, Pittsburgh, 1987-88 – 1988-89.
 – Steve Yzerman, Detroit, 1988-89 – 1989-90.
 – Pavel Bure, Vancouver, 1992-93 – 1993-94.

MOST 100-OR-MORE POINT SEASONS:
15 – Wayne Gretzky, Edmonton, Los Angeles, St. Louis, NY Rangers, in 20 seasons.
10 – Mario Lemieux, Pittsburgh, in 17 seasons.
 8 – Marcel Dionne, Detroit, Los Angeles, NY Rangers, in 18 seasons.
 7 – Mike Bossy, NY Islanders, in 10 seasons.
 – Peter Stastny, Quebec, New Jersey, St. Louis, in 15 seasons.

MOST CONSECUTIVE 100-OR-MORE POINT SEASONS:
13 – Wayne Gretzky, Edmonton, Los Angeles, 1979-80 – 1991-92.
 6 – Bobby Orr, Boston, 1969-70 – 1974-75.
 – Guy Lafleur, Montreal, 1974-75 – 1979-80.
 – Mike Bossy, NY Islanders, 1980-81 – 1985-86.
 – Peter Stastny, Quebec, 1980-81 – 1985-86.
 – Mario Lemieux, Pittsburgh, 1984-85 – 1989-90.
 – Steve Yzerman, Detroit, 1987-88 – 1992-93.

THREE-OR-MORE-GOAL GAMES

MOST THREE-OR-MORE GOAL GAMES, CAREER:
50 – Wayne Gretzky, Edmonton, Los Angeles, St. Louis, NY Rangers, in 20 seasons, 37 three-goal games, 9 four-goal games, 4 five-goal games.
40 – Mario Lemieux, Pittsburgh, in 17 seasons, 27 three-goal games, 10 four-goal games, 3 five-goal games.
39 – Mike Bossy, NY Islanders, in 10 seasons, 30 three-goal games, 9 four-goal games.
33 – Brett Hull, Calgary, St. Louis, Dallas, Detroit, Phoenix, in 19 seasons, 30 three-goal games, 3 four-goal games.
32 – Phil Esposito, Chicago, Boston, NY Rangers, in 18 seasons, 27 three-goal games, 5 four-goal games.

MOST THREE-OR-MORE GOAL GAMES, ONE SEASON:
10 – Wayne Gretzky, Edmonton, 1981-82. 6 three-goal games, 3 four-goal games, 1 five-goal game.
 – **Wayne Gretzky**, Edmonton, 1983-84. 6 three-goal games, 4 four-goal games.
 9 – Mike Bossy, NY Islanders, 1980-81. 6 three-goal games, 3 four-goal games.
 – Mario Lemieux, Pittsburgh, 1988-89. 7 three-goal games, 1 four-goal game, 1 five-goal game.
 8 – Brett Hull, St. Louis, 1991-92. 8 three-goal games.
 7 – Joe Malone, Montreal, 1917-18. 2 three-goal games, 2 four-goal games, 3 five-goal games.
 – Phil Esposito, Boston, 1970-71. 7 three-goal games.
 – Rick Martin, Buffalo, 1975-76. 6 three-goal games, 1 four-goal game.
 – Alexander Mogilny, Buffalo, 1992-93. 5 three-goal games, 2 four-goal games.

SCORING STREAKS

LONGEST CONSECUTIVE GOAL-SCORING STREAK:
16 Games – Punch Broadbent, Ottawa, 1921-22. 27G
14 Games – Joe Malone, Montreal, 1917-18. 35G
13 Games – Newsy Lalonde, Montreal, 1920-21. 24G
 – Charlie Simmer, Los Angeles, 1979-80. 17G
12 Games – Cy Denneny, Ottawa, 1917-18. 23G
 – Dave Lumley, Edmonton, 1981-82. 15G
 – Mario Lemieux, Pittsburgh, 1992-93. 18G

LONGEST CONSECUTIVE ASSIST-SCORING STREAK:
23 Games – Wayne Gretzky, Los Angeles, 1990-91. 48A
18 Games – Adam Oates, Boston, 1992-93. 28A
17 Games – Wayne Gretzky, Edmonton, 1983-84. 38A
 – Paul Coffey, Edmonton, 1985-86. 27A
 – Wayne Gretzky, Los Angeles, 1989-90. 35A
16 Games – Jaromir Jagr, Pittsburgh, 2000-01. 24A

LONGEST CONSECUTIVE POINT-SCORING STREAK:
51 Games – Wayne Gretzky, Edmonton, 1983-84. 61G-92A-153PTS
46 Games – Mario Lemieux, Pittsburgh, 1989-90. 39G-64A-103PTS
39 Games – Wayne Gretzky, Edmonton, 1985-86. 33G-75A-108PTS
30 Games – Wayne Gretzky, Edmonton, 1982-83. 24G-52A-76PTS
 – Mats Sundin, Quebec, 1992-93. 21G-25A-46PTS

LONGEST CONSECUTIVE POINT-SCORING STREAK FROM START OF SEASON:
51 Games – Wayne Gretzky, Edmonton, 1983-84. 61G-92A-153PTS. Streak ended by Los Angeles and goaltender Markus Mattsson on Jan. 28, 1984.

LONGEST CONSECUTIVE POINT-SCORING STREAK BY A DEFENSEMAN:
28 Games – Paul Coffey, Edmonton, 1985-86. 16G-39A-55PTS
19 Games – Raymond Bourque, Boston, 1987-88. 6G-21A-27PTS
17 Games – Raymond Bourque, Boston, 1984-85. 4G-24A-28PTS
 – Brian Leetch, NY Rangers, 1991-92. 5G-24A-29PTS
16 Games – Gary Suter, Calgary, 1987-88. 8G-17A-25PTS
15 Games – Bobby Orr, Boston, 1970-71. 10G-23A-33PTS
 – Bobby Orr, Boston, 1973-74. 8G-15A-23PTS
 – Steve Duchesne, Quebec, 1992-93. 4G-17A-21PTS
 – Chris Chelios, Chicago, 1995-96. 4G-16A-20PTS

LONGEST CONSECUTIVE POINT-SCORING STREAK BY A ROOKIE:
20 Games – Paul Stastny, Colorado, 2006-07. 11G-18A-29PTS
17 Games – Teemu Selanne, Winnipeg, 1992-93. 20G-14A-34PTS
16 Games – Peter Stastny, Quebec, 1980-81
15 Games – Jude Drouin, Minnesota North Stars, 1970-71

FASTEST GOALS AND ASSISTS

FASTEST GOAL FROM START OF A GAME:
0:05 – Doug Smail, Winnipeg, Dec. 20, 1981, at Winnipeg. Winnipeg 5, St. Louis 4.
 – **Bryan Trottier**, NY Islanders, Mar. 22, 1984, at Boston. NY Islanders 3, Boston 3.
 – **Alexander Mogilny**, Buffalo, Dec. 21, 1991, at Toronto. Buffalo 4, Toronto 1.
0:06 – Henry Boucha, Detroit, Jan. 28, 1973, at Montreal. Detroit 4, Montreal 2.
 – Jean Pronovost, Pittsburgh, Mar. 25, 1976, at St. Louis. St. Louis 5, Pittsburgh 2.
0:07 – Charlie Conacher, Toronto, Feb. 6, 1932, at Toronto. Toronto 6, Boston 0.
 – Danny Gare, Buffalo, Dec. 17, 1978, at Buffalo. Buffalo 6, Vancouver 3.
 – Tiger Williams, Los Angeles, Feb. 14, 1987, at Los Angeles. Los Angeles 5, Harford 2.
 – Evgeni Malkin, Pittsburgh, Jan. 5, 2011, at Pittsburgh. Pittsburgh 8, Tampa Bay 1.
0:08 – A goal has been scored at 0:08 of the first period on 15 occasions since Ron Martin of NY Americans accomplished the feat at home vs. Montreal Canadiens on, Dec. 4, 1932. Final score: NY Americans 4, Montreal 2. The most recent players to score at 0:08 are Alexander Semin and Alex Steen. Semin scored for Washington, Nov. 11, 2009 at Washington. (Final score: Washington 5, NY Islanders 4). Steen scored for St. Louis, Mar. 16, 2010 at St. Louis. Final score: Colorado 5, St. Louis 3.

FASTEST GOAL FROM START OF A PERIOD:
0:04 – Claude Provost, Montreal, Nov. 9, 1957, at Montreal,
second period. Montreal 4, Boston 2.
– Denis Savard, Chicago, Jan. 12, 1986, at Chicago,
third period. Chicago 4, Hartford 2.

FASTEST GOAL BY A PLAYER IN HIS FIRST NHL GAME:
0:15 – Gus Bodnar, Toronto, Oct. 30, 1943, at Toronto.
Toronto 5, NY Rangers 2.
0:18 – Danny Gare, Buffalo, Oct. 10, 1974, at Buffalo.
Buffalo 9, Boston 5.
0:20 – Alexander Mogilny, Buffalo, Oct. 5, 1989, at Buffalo.
Buffalo 4, Quebec 3.

FASTEST TWO GOALS FROM START OF A GAME:
0:27 – Mike Knuble, Boston, Feb. 14, 2003, at Florida.
0:10 and 0:27. Boston 6, Florida 5.

FASTEST TWO GOALS:
0:04 – Nels Stewart, Mtl. Maroons, Jan. 3, 1931, at Mtl. Maroons.
8:24 and 8:28, third period. Mtl. Maroons 5, Boston 3.
– Deron Quint, Winnipeg, Dec. 15, 1995, at Winnipeg.
7:51 and 7:55, second period. Winnipeg 9, Edmonton 4.
0:05 – Pete Mahovlich, Montreal, Dec. 20, 1971, at Montreal.
12:16 and 12:21, third period. Montreal 7, Chicago 1.
– Nathan Gerbe, Buffalo, January 21, 2011at Buffalo.
16:38 and 16:43, third period. NY Islanders 5, Buffalo 2.
0:06 – Jim Pappin, Chicago, Feb. 16, 1972, at Chicago.
2:57 and 3:03, third period. Chicago 3, Philadelphia 3.
– Ralph Backstrom, Los Angeles, Nov. 2, 1972, at Los Angeles.
8:30 and 8:36, third period. Los Angeles 5, Boston 2.
– Lanny McDonald, Calgary, Mar. 22, 1984, at Calgary.
16:23 and 16:29, first period. Detroit 6, Calgary 4.
– Sylvain Turgeon, Hartford, Mar. 28, 1987, at Hartford.
13:59 and 14:05, second period. Hartford 5, Pittsburgh 4.

FASTEST THREE GOALS:
0:21 – Bill Mosienko, Chicago, Mar. 23, 1952, at NY Rangers, against
goaltender Lorne Anderson. Mosienko scored at 6:09, 6:20 and 6:30 of
third period, all with both teams at full strength. Chicago 7, NY Rangers 6.
0:44 – Jean Béliveau, Montreal, Nov. 5, 1955, at Montreal, against goaltender
Terry Sawchuk. Béliveau scored at 0:42, 1:08 and 1:26 of second period,
all with Montreal holding a 6-4 man advantage. Montreal 4, Boston 2.

FASTEST THREE ASSISTS:
0:21 – Gus Bodnar, Chicago, Mar. 23, 1952, at NY Rangers, Bodnar assisted on
Bill Mosienko's three goals at 6:09, 6:20 and 6:30 of third period.
Chicago 7, NY Rangers 6.
0:44 – Bert Olmstead, Montreal, Nov. 5, 1955, at Montreal, Olmstead assisted on
Jean Béliveau's three goals at 0:42, 1:08 and 1:26 of second period.
Montreal 4, Boston 2.

SHOTS ON GOAL

MOST SHOTS ON GOAL, ONE SEASON:
550 – Phil Esposito, Boston, 1970-71. 78GP – 78 game schedule.
528 – Alex Ovechkin, Washington, 2008-09. 79GP – 82 game schedule.
446 – Alex Ovechkin, Washington, 2007-08. 82GP – 82 game schedule.
429 – Paul Kariya, Anaheim, 1998-99. 82GP – 82 game schedule.
426 – Phil Esposito, Boston, 1971-72. 76GP – 78 game schedule.

*One of the safest records in the NHL book is the 502 consecutive complete
games in goal Glenn Hall played with the Detroit Red Wings and Chicago
Blackhawks between the start of the 1955-56 season and the early days
of the 1962-63 campaign.*

PENALTIES

MOST PENALTY MINUTES, CAREER:
3,966 – Tiger Williams, Toronto, Vancouver, Detroit, Los Angeles, Hartford,
in 14 seasons. 962GP
3,565 – Dale Hunter, Quebec, Washington, Colorado, in 19 seasons. 1,407GP
3,515 – Tie Domi, Toronto, NY Rangers, Winnipeg, in 16 seasons. 1,020GP
3,381 – Marty McSorley, Pittsburgh, Edmonton, Los Angeles, NY Rangers, San Jose,
Boston, in 17 seasons. 961GP
3,300 – Bob Probert, Detroit, Chicago, in 17 seasons. 935GP

MOST PENALTY MINUTES, CAREER, INCLUDING PLAYOFFS:
4,421 – Tiger Williams, Toronto, Vancouver, Detroit, Los Angeles, Hartford,
3,966 in 962 regular-season games; 455 in 83 playoff games.
4,294 – Dale Hunter, Quebec, Washington, Colorado,
3,565 in 1,407 regular-season games; 729 in 186 playoff games.
3,755 – Marty McSorley, Pittsburgh, Edmonton, Los Angeles, NY Rangers, San Jose,
Boston, 3,381 in 961 regular-season games; 374 in 115 playoff games.
3,753 – Tie Domi, Toronto, NY Rangers, Winnipeg, 3,515 in 1,020 regular-season
games; 238 in 98 playoff games.
3,584 – Chris Nilan, Montreal, NY Rangers, Boston,
3,043 in 688 regular-season games; 541 in 111 playoff games.

MOST PENALTY MINUTES, ONE SEASON:
472 – Dave Schultz, Philadelphia, 1974-75.
409 – Paul Baxter, Pittsburgh, 1981-82.
408 – Mike Peluso, Chicago, 1991-92.
405 – Dave Schultz, Los Angeles, Pittsburgh, 1977-78.

MOST PENALTIES, ONE GAME:
10 – Chris Nilan, Boston, Mar. 31, 1991, at Boston vs. Hartford. 6 minors,
2 majors, 1 10-minute misconduct, 1 game misconduct.
9 – Jim Dorey, Toronto, Oct. 16, 1968, at Toronto vs. Pittsburgh. 4 minors,
2 majors, 2 10-minute misconducts, 1 game misconduct.
– Dave Schultz, Pittsburgh, Apr. 6, 1978, at Detroit. 5 minors, 2 majors,
2 10-minute misconducts.
– Randy Holt, Los Angeles, Mar. 11, 1979, at Philadelphia. 1 minor,
3 majors, 2 10-minute misconducts, 3 game misconducts.
– Russ Anderson, Pittsburgh, Jan. 19, 1980, at Pittsburgh vs. Edmonton.
3 minors, 3 majors, 3 game misconducts.
– Kim Clackson, Quebec, Mar. 8, 1981, at Quebec vs. Chicago. 4 minors,
3 majors, 2 game misconducts.
– Terry O'Reilly, Boston, Dec. 19, 1984, at Hartford. 5 minors, 3 majors,
1 game misconduct.
– Larry Playfair, Los Angeles, Dec. 9, 1986, at NY Islanders. 6 minors,
2 majors, 1 10-minute misconduct.
– Marty McSorley, Los Angeles, Apr. 14, 1992, at Vancouver. 5 minors,
2 majors, 1 10-minute misconduct, 1 game misconduct.
– Reed Low, St. Louis, Dec. 31, 2002, at Detroit. 4 minors,
1 major, 1 10-minute misconduct, 3 game misconducts.

MOST PENALTY MINUTES, ONE GAME:
67 – Randy Holt, Los Angeles, Mar. 11, 1979, at Philadelphia.
1 minor, 3 majors, 2 10-minute misconducts, 3 game misconducts.
57 – Brad Smith, Toronto, Nov. 15, 1986, at Toronto vs. Detroit.
1 minor, 3 majors, 2 10-minute misconducts, 2 game misconducts.
– Reed Low, St. Louis, Feb. 28, 2002, at St. Louis vs. Calgary.
1 minor, 3 majors, 1 10-minute misconduct, 3 game misconducts.

MOST PENALTIES, ONE PERIOD:
9 – Randy Holt, Los Angeles, Mar. 11, 1979, at Philadelphia, first period.
1 minor, 3 majors, 2 10-minute misconducts, 3 game misconducts.

MOST PENALTY MINUTES, ONE PERIOD:
67 – Randy Holt, Los Angeles, Mar. 11, 1979, at Philadelphia, first period.
1 minor, 3 majors, 2 10-minute misconducts, 3 game misconducts.

GOALTENDING

MOST GAMES APPEARED IN BY A GOALTENDER, CAREER:
1,132 – Martin Brodeur, New Jersey, 1991-92 – 2003-04, 2005-06 – 2010-11.
1,029 – Patrick Roy, Montreal, Colorado, 1984-85 – 2002-03.
971 – Terry Sawchuk, Detroit, Boston, Toronto, Los Angeles, NY Rangers,
1949-50 – 1969-70.
963 – Ed Belfour, Chicago, San Jose, Dallas, Toronto, Florida,
1988-89 – 2003-04, 2005-06, 2006-07.
943 – Curtis Joseph, St. Louis, Edmonton, Toronto, Detroit, Phoenix, Calgary,
1989-90 – 2003-04, 2005-06 – 2008-09.

MOST CONSECUTIVE COMPLETE GAMES BY A GOALTENDER:
502 – Glenn Hall, Detroit, Chicago. Played 502 games from beginning of
1955-56 season through first 12 games of 1962-63 season. In his 503rd
straight game, Nov. 7, 1962, at Chicago, Hall was removed from the
game against Boston with a back injury in the first period.

MOST GAMES APPEARED IN BY A GOALTENDER, ONE SEASON:
79 – Grant Fuhr, St. Louis, 1995-96.
78 – Martin Brodeur, New Jersey, 2006-07.
77 – Martin Brodeur, New Jersey, 1995-96.
– Bill Ranford, Edmonton, Boston, 1995-96.
– Arturs Irbe, Carolina, 2000-01.
– Marc Denis, Columbus, 2002-03.
– Evgeni Nabokov, San Jose, 2007-08.
– Martin Brodeur, New Jersey, 2007-08.
– Martin Brodeur, New Jersey, 2009-10.

MOST MINUTES PLAYED BY A GOALTENDER, CAREER:
66,637 – Martin Brodeur, New Jersey, 1991-92 – 2003-04, 2005-06 – 2010-11.
60,235 – Patrick Roy, Montreal, Colorado, 1984-85 – 2002-03.
57,194 – Terry Sawchuk, Detroit, Boston, Toronto, Los Angeles, NY Rangers,
1949-50 – 1969-70.

MOST MINUTES PLAYED BY A GOALTENDER, ONE SEASON:
 4,697 – Martin Brodeur, New Jersey, 2006-07.
 4,635 – Martin Brodeur, New Jersey, 2007-08.
 4,561 – Evgeni Nabokov, San Jose, 2007-08.
 4,555 – Martin Brodeur, New Jersey, 2003-04.
 4,511 – Marc Denis, Columbus, 2002-03.

MOST SHUTOUTS, CAREER:
 116 – Martin Brodeur, New Jersey, in 18 seasons.
   (1991-92, 1993-94 – 2003-04, 2005-06 – 2010-11)
 103 – Terry Sawchuk, Detroit, Boston, Toronto, Los Angeles, NY Rangers,
   in 21 seasons. (1949-50 – 1969-70)
  94 – George Hainsworth, Montreal, Toronto, in 11 seasons.
   (1926-27 – 1936-37)

MOST SHUTOUTS, ONE SEASON:
 22 – George Hainsworth, Montreal, 1928-29. 44GP
 15 – Alec Connell, Ottawa, 1925-26. 36GP
   – Alec Connell, Ottawa, 1927-28. 44GP
   – Hal Winkler, Boston, 1927-28. 44GP
   – Tony Esposito, Chicago, 1969-70. 63GP
 14 – George Hainsworth, Montreal, 1926-27. 44GP

LONGEST SHUTOUT SEQUENCE BY A GOALTENDER:
 461:29 – Alec Connell, Ottawa, 1927-28, six consecutive shutouts.
   (Forward passing not permitted in attacking zones in 1927-28.)
 343:05 – George Hainsworth, Montreal, 1928-29, four consecutive shutouts.
   (Forward passing not permitted in attacking zones in 1928-29.)
 332:01 – Brian Boucher, Phoenix, 2003-04, five consecutive shutouts.
 324:40 – Roy Worters, NY Americans, 1930-31, four consecutive shutouts.
 309:21 – Bill Durnan, Montreal, 1948-49, four consecutive shutouts.

MOST WINS BY A GOALTENDER, CAREER:
 625 – Martin Brodeur, New Jersey, in 18 seasons. 1,132 GP
 551 – Patrick Roy, Montreal, Colorado, in 19 seasons. 1,029GP
 484 – Ed Belfour, Chicago, San Jose, Dallas, Toronto, Florida,
   in 17 seasons. 963GP
 454 – Curtis Joseph, St. Louis, Edmonton, Toronto, Detroit, Phoenix,
   in 19 seasons. 943GP
 447 – Terry Sawchuk, Detroit, Boston, Toronto, Los Angeles, NY Rangers,
   in 21 seasons. 971GP

MOST WINS BY A GOALTENDER, ONE SEASON:
 48 – Martin Brodeur, New Jersey, 2006-07. 78GP
 47 – Bernie Parent, Philadelphia, 1973-74. 73GP
   – Roberto Luongo, Vancouver, 2006-07. 76GP
 46 – Evgeni Nabokov, San Jose, 2007-08. 77GP
 45 – Miikka Kiprusoff, Calgary, 2008-09. 76GP
   – Martin Brodeur, New Jersey, 2009-10. 77GP

LONGEST WINNING STREAK BY A GOALTENDER, ONE SEASON:
 17 – Gilles Gilbert, Boston, 1975-76.
 14 – Tiny Thompson, Boston, 1929-30.
   – Ross Brooks, Boston, 1973-74.
   – Don Beaupre, Minnesota, 1985-86.
   – Tom Barrasso, Pittsburgh, 1992-93.

LONGEST UNDEFEATED STREAK BY A GOALTENDER, ONE SEASON:
 32 Games – Gerry Cheevers, Boston, 1971-72. 24W-8T
 31 Games – Pete Peeters, Boston, 1982-83. 26W-5T
 27 Games – Pete Peeters, Philadelphia, 1979-80. 22W-5T

LONGEST UNDEFEATED STREAK BY A GOALTENDER IN HIS FIRST NHL SEASON:
 23 Games – Grant Fuhr, Edmonton, 1981-82. 15W-8T

LONGEST UNDEFEATED STREAK BY A GOALTENDER FROM START OF CAREER:
 16 Games – Patrick Lalime, Pittsburgh, 1996-97. 14W-2T

MOST 30-OR-MORE WIN SEASONS BY A GOALTENDER:
 13 – Patrick Roy, Montreal, Colorado, in 19 seasons.
   – Martin Brodeur, New Jersey, in 18 seasons.
  9 – Ed Belfour, Chicago, San Jose, Dallas, Toronto, Florida, in 17 seasons.
  8 – Tony Esposito, Montreal, Chicago, in 16 seasons.
  7 – Jacques Plante, Montreal, NY Rangers, St. Louis, Toronto, Boston,
   in 18 seasons.
   – Ken Dryden, Montreal, in 8 seasons.
   – Curtis Joseph, St. Louis, Edmonton, Toronto, Detroit, Phoenix, Calgary,
   in 19 seasons.
   – Dominik Hasek, Chicago, Buffalo, Detroit, Ottawa, in 16 seasons.

MOST CONSECUTIVE 30-OR-MORE WIN SEASONS BY A GOALTENDER:
 12 – Martin Brodeur, New Jersey, 1995-96 – 2003-04, 2005-06 – 2007-08.
  8 – Patrick Roy, Montreal, Colorado, 1995-96 – 2002-03.
  7 – Tony Esposito, Chicago, 1969-70 – 1975-76.
  6 – Jacques Plante, Montreal, 1954-55 – 1959-60.
   – Marty Turco, Dallas, 2002-03, 2003-04, 2005-06 – 2008-09.
   – Miikka Kiprusoff, 2005-06 – 2010-11.
   – Henrik Lundqvist, NY Rangers, 2005-06 – 2010-11.
   – Roberto Luongo, Florida, Vancouver, 2005-06 – 2010-11.
   – Ryan Miller, Buffalo, 2005-06 – 2010-11.

MOST 40-OR-MORE WIN SEASONS BY A GOALTENDER:
 8 – Martin Brodeur, New Jersey, in 18 seasons.
  3 – Terry Sawchuk, Detroit, Boston, Toronto, Los Angeles, NY Rangers,
   in 21 seasons.
   – Jacques Plante, Montreal, NY Rangers, St. Louis, Toronto, Boston,
   in 18 seasons.
   – Miikka Kiprusoff, San Jose, Calgary, in 10 seasons.
   – Evgeni Nabokov, San Jose, in 11 seasons.
  2 – Bernie Parent, Boston, Philadelphia, Toronto, in 13 seasons.
   – Ken Dryden, Montreal, in 8 seasons.
   – Ed Belfour, Chicago, San Jose, Dallas, Toronto, Florida, in 17 seasons.
   – Ryan Miller, Buffalo, in 8 seasons.

MOST CONSECUTIVE 40-OR-MORE WIN SEASONS BY A GOALTENDER:
 3 – Martin Brodeur, New Jersey, 2005-06 – 2007-08.
   – Evgeni Nabokov, San Jose, 2007-08 – 2009-10.
  2 – Terry Sawchuk, Detroit, 1950-51 – 1951-52.
   – Bernie Parent, Philadelphia, 1973-74 – 1974-75.
   – Ken Dryden, Montreal, 1975-76 – 1976-77.
   – Martin Brodeur, New Jersey, 1999-2000 – 2000-01.
   – Miikka Kiprusoff, Calgary, 2005-06 – 2006-07.

MOST LOSSES BY A GOALTENDER, CAREER:
 352 – Gump Worsley, NY Rangers, Montreal, Minnesota, in 21 seasons. 861GP
   – Curtis Joseph, St. Louis, Edmonton, Toronto, Detroit, Phoenix,
   in 19 seasons. 943GP
 351 – Gilles Meloche, Chicago, California, Cleveland, Minnesota, Pittsburgh,
   in 18 seasons. 788GP
 350 – Martin Brodeur, New Jersey in 18 seasons. 1,132GP.
 346 – John Vanbiesbrouck, NY Rangers, Florida, Philadelphia, NY Islanders,
   New Jersey, in 20 seasons. 882GP
 341 – Sean Burke, New Jersey, Hartford, Carolina, Vancouver, Philadelphia,
   Florida, Phoenix, Tampa Bay, Los Angeles, in 18 seasons. 820GP

MOST LOSSES BY A GOALTENDER, ONE SEASON:
 48 – Gary Smith, California, 1970-71. 71GP
 47 – Al Rollins, Chicago, 1953-54. 66GP
 46 – Peter Sidorkiewicz, Ottawa, 1992-93. 64GP

GOALTENDER SHOOTOUT RECORDS

MOST SHOOTOUT WINS, ONE SEASON:
 10 – Mathieu Garon, Edmonton, 2007-08, (10GP)
   – Jonathan Quick, Los Angelesm 2010-11, (10GP)
   – Ryan Miller, Buffalo, 2006-07, (14GP)
   – Martin Brodeur, New Jersey, 2006-07, (16GP)

MOST SHOOTOUT WINS, CAREER:
 37 – Henrik Lundqvist, NY Rangers, (61GP)
 35 – Martin Brodeur, New Jersey, (54GP)
 31 – Ryan Miller, Buffalo, (51GP)
 30 – Marty Turco, Dallas, (54GP)

MOST SHOOTOUT SHOTS AGAINST, ONE SEASON:
 62 – Ilya Bryzgalov, Phoenix, 2009-10, (17GA)
 60 – Martin Brodeur, New Jersey, 2006-07, (20GA)
 54 – Roberto Luongo, Vancouver, 2007-08, (15GA)
   – Jimmy Howard, Detroit, 2009-10, (17GA)

MOST SHOOTOUT SHOTS AGAINST, CAREER:
 237 – Henrik Lundqvist, NY Rangers, (55GA)
 202 – Marty Turco, Dallas, Chicago, (64GA)
 191 – Martin Brodeur, New Jersey, (54GA)
 181 – Roberto Luongo, Florida, Vancouver, (57GA)

BEST SHOOTOUT SAVE PERCENTAGE, ONE SEASON: *(minimum 20 shots)*
 .938 – Mathieu Garon, Edmonton, 2007-08, (32S, 2GA)
 .900 – Marc Denis, Tampa Bay, 2006-07, (20S, 2GA)
 .879 – Johan Holmqvist, Tampa Bay, 2006-07, (33S, 4GA)
 .850 – Kari Lehtonen, Atlanta, 2005-06, (20S, 3GA)

BEST SHOOTOUT SAVE PERCENTAGE, CAREER: *(minimum 40 shots)*
 .854 – Marc Denis, Columbus, Tampa Bay, Montreal, (41S, 6GA)
 .796 – Johan Hedberg, Dallas, Atlanta, (93S, 19GA)
 .788 – Brent Johnson, Washington, Pittsburgh, (52S, 11GA)
 .777 – Pekka Rinne, Nashville, (103S, 23GA)

Active NHL Players' Three-or-More-Goal Games

Regular Season

Teams named are the ones the players were with at the time of their multiple-scoring games. Players listed alphabetically.

Player	Team(s)	3-Goals	4-Goals	5-Goals
Alfredsson, Daniel	Ottawa	7	1	—
Antropov, Nik	Toronto	2	—	—
Arnott, Jason	Edm., N.J., Dal., Nsh.	8	—	—
Backes, David	St. Louis	1	—	—
Belanger, Eric	Los Angeles	1	—	—
Bergenheim, Sean	NY Islanders	1	—	—
Bergeron, Marc-Andre	Edmonton	1	—	—
Bergeron, Patrice	Boston	1	—	—
Bertuzzi, Todd	Vancouver	5	—	—
Blake, Jason	NYI, Tor.	6	—	—
Booth, David	Florida	2	—	—
Boulton, Eric	Atlanta	1	—	—
Bourque, Rene	Calgary	3	—	—
Boyes, Brad	Boston	1	—	—
Boyle, Dan	Tampa Bay	1	—	—
Briere, Danny	Buf., Phi.	4	—	—
Brown, Dustin	Los Angeles	2	—	—
Brunette, Andrew	Colorado	1	—	—
Brunnstrom, Fabian	Dallas	1	—	—
Burrows, Alexandre	Vancouver	3	—	—
Byfuglien, Dustin	Chicago	1	—	—
Callahan, Ryan	NY Rangers	1	—	—
Calvert, Matt	Columbus	1	—	—
Cammalleri, Michael	Cgy., Mtl.	4	—	—
Carcillo, Daniel	Phoenix	1	—	—
Carter, Jeff	Philadelphia	2	—	—
Chara, Zdeno	Boston	1	—	—
Cheechoo, Jonathan	San Jose	9	—	—
Clark, Chris	Washington	2	—	—
Cleary, Daniel	Detroit	1	—	—
Clowe, Ryane	San Jose	1	—	—
Cole, Erik	Car., Edm.	6	—	—
Comeau, Blake	NY Islanders	1	—	—
Corvo, Joe	Carolina	1	—	—
Crombeen, B.J.	St. Louis	1	—	—
Crosby, Sidney	Pittsburgh	7	—	—
Cullen, Matt	Carolina	1	—	—
Drury, Chris	Buf., NYR	2	—	—
Dumont, J.P.	Chi., Buf., Nsh.	4	—	—
Dupuis, Pascal	Pittsburgh	1	—	—
Dvorak, Radek	NYR, Fla.	2	1	—
Eaves, Patrick	Detroit	1	—	—
Elias, Patrik	New Jersey	7	1	—
Erat, Martin	Nashville	2	—	—
Eriksson, Loui	Dallas	2	—	—
Fiddler, Vernon	Phoenix	1	—	—
Filatov, Nikita	Columbus	1	—	—
Fisher, Mike	Ottawa	1	—	—
Fleischmann, Tomas	Colorado	1	—	—
Franzen, Johan	Detroit	—	—	1
Frolov, Alexander	Los Angeles	3	—	—
Gaborik, Marian	Min., NYR	11	1	1
Gagne, Simon	Philadelphia	3	—	—
Gagner, Sam	Edmonton	1	—	—
Geoffrion, Blake	Nashville	1	—	—
Gionta, Brian	New Jersey	1	—	—
Glencross, Curtis	Calgary	1	—	—
Gomez, Scott	New Jersey	2	—	—
Gonchar, Sergei	Washington	1	—	—
Grabner, Michael	Van., NYI	2	—	—
Grier, Mike	Edmonton	1	—	—
Hagman, Niklas	Dal., Tor.	2	—	—
Hall, Taylor	Edmonton	1	—	—
Handzus, Michal	St.L., L.A.	2	—	—
Hanzal, Martin	Phoenix	1	—	—
Hartnell, Scott	Nsh., Phi.	5	—	—
Havlat, Martin	Ottawa	3	1	—
Heatley, Dany	Atl., Ott., S.J.	8	1	—
Hecht, Jochen	Buffalo	1	—	—
Hejduk, Milan	Colorado	4	—	—
Higgins, Chris	Montreal	1	—	—
Holmstrom, Tomas	Detroit	3	—	—
Horcoff, Shawn	Edmonton	1	—	—
Horton, Nathan	Florida	2	—	—
Hossa, Marian	Ott., Atl.	6	1	—
Huselius, Kristian	Cgy., CBJ	2	—	—
Iginla, Jarome	Calgary	11	1	—
Jagr, Jaromir	Pit., NYR	13	1	—
Jokinen, Jussi	Dallas	—	1	—
Jokinen, Olli	Fla., Phx., Cgy.,	6	—	—
Jovanovski, Ed	Phoenix	1	—	—
Kaberle, Tomas	Toronto	1	—	—
Kelly, Chris	Ottawa	1	—	—
Kesler, Ryan	Vancouver	3	—	—
Kessel, Phil	Boston	2	—	—
Knuble, Mike	Philadelphia	1	—	—
Kobasew, Chuck	Cgy., Min.	2	—	—

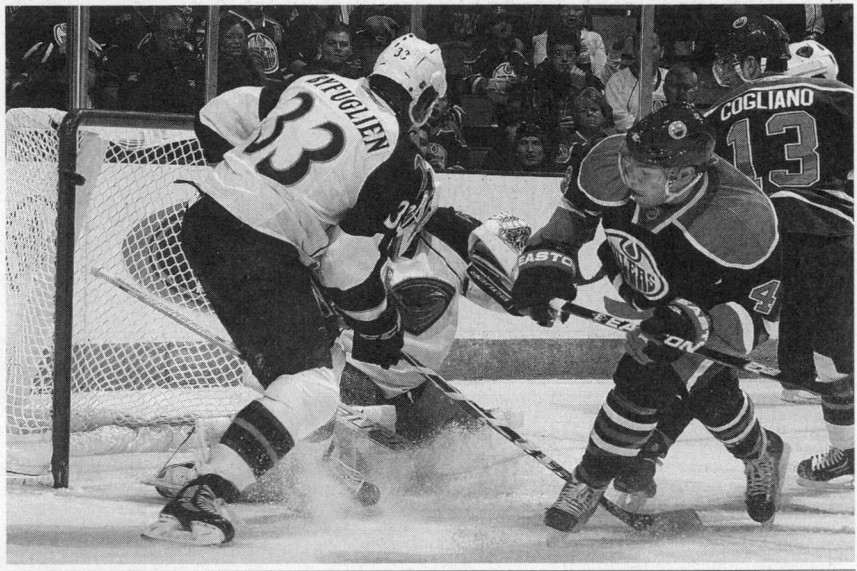

Edmonton rookie Taylor Hall just missed a fourth goal, bouncing this puck off the post during the game in which he scored his first career hat trick in a 5-3 win over Atlanta on February 19, 2011.

Player	Team(s)	3-Goals	4-Goals	5-Goals
Koivu, Saku	Montreal	1	—	—
Kopitar, Anze	Los Angeles	2	—	—
Kostitsyn, Andrei	Montreal	1	—	—
Kovalchuk, Ilya	Atlanta	10	1	—
Kovalev, Alex	NYR, Pit., Ott.	11	1	—
Krejci, David	Boston	1	—	—
Kunitz, Chris	Ana., Pit.	2	—	—
Ladd, Andrew	Chicago	1	—	—
Laich, Brooks	Washington	1	—	—
Langenbrunner, Jamie	New Jersey	1	—	—
Langkow, Daymond	Phx., Cgy.	3	—	—
Lapierre, Maxim	Montreal	1	—	—
Larose, Chad	Carolina	1	—	—
Latendresse, Guillaume	Minnesota	1	—	—
Lecavalier, Vincent	Tampa Bay	6	—	—
Legwand, David	Nashville	2	—	—
Leino, Ville	Philadelphia	1	—	—
Lidstrom, Nicklas	Detroit	1	—	—
Little, Bryan	Atlanta	1	—	—
Lombardi, Matthew	Calgary	1	—	—
Lucic, Milan	Boston	2	—	—
Lupul, Joffrey	Philadelphia	2	—	—
Madden, John	New Jersey	1	1	—
Malkin, Evgeni	Pittsburgh	6	—	—
Malone, Ryan	Pit., T.B.	3	—	—
Marleau, Patrick	San Jose	3	—	—
McClement, Jay	St. Louis	1	—	—
Michalek, Milan	Ottawa	1	—	—
Modano, Mike	Min., Dal.	6	1	—
Moreau, Ethan	Edmonton	1	—	—
Morrison, Brendan	Vancouver	1	—	—
Morrow, Brenden	Dallas	1	—	—
Moss, Dave	Calgary	1	—	—
Moulson, Matt	NY Islanders	2	—	—
Mueller, Peter	Phoenix	2	—	—
Nash, Rick	Columbus	5	—	—
Neal, James	Dallas	1	—	—
Nolan, Owen	Que., S.J., Cgy.	10	1	—
Ott, Steve	Dallas	1	—	—
Ovechkin, Alex	Washington	8	2	—
Parise, Zach	New Jersey	3	—	—
Parrish, Mark	Fla., NYI, Min., Dal.	5	1	—
Perron, David	St. Louis	1	—	—
Perry, Corey	Anaheim	3	—	—
Petersen, Toby	Pittsburgh	1	—	—
Pisani, Fernando	Edmonton	1	—	—
Plekanec, Thomas	Montreal	1	—	—
Pominville, Jason	Buffalo	2	—	—
Prospal, Vaclav	Ana., T.B.	2	—	—
Purcell, Teddy	Tampa Bay	1	—	—
Pyatt, Taylor	Buffalo	2	—	—
Raymond, Mason	Vancouver	2	—	—
Reinprecht, Steve	Col., Phx., Fla.	4	—	—
Ribeiro, Mike	Dallas	1	—	—
Richards, Mike	Philadelphia	2	—	—
Richardson, Brad	Los Angeles	1	—	—
Rolston, Brian	N.J., Min.	2	—	—

Player	Team(s)	3-Goals	4-Goals	5-Goals
Roy, Derek	Buffalo	4	—	—
Rupp, Mike	Pittsburgh	1	—	—
Ruutu, Tuomo	Carolina	1	—	—
Ryan, Bobby	Anaheim	3	—	—
Ryder, Michael	Montreal	2	—	—
St. Louis, Martin	Tampa Bay	4	—	—
Salo, Sami	Ottawa	1	—	—
Samsonov, Sergei	Boston	1	—	—
Samuelsson, Mikael	Vancouver	1	—	—
Savard, Marc	Cgy., Bos.	2	1	—
Sedin, Daniel	Vancouver	3	1	—
Sedin, Henrik	Vancouver	1	—	—
Selanne, Teemu	Wpg., Ana., S.J.	20	2	—
Semin, Alexander	Washington	7	—	—
Setoguchi, Devin	San Jose	1	—	—
Sharp, Patrick	Chicago	1	—	—
Sim, Jon	Florida	1	—	—
Sjostrom, Fredrik	Phoenix	1	—	—
Smyth, Ryan	Edmonton	5	—	—
Souray, Sheldon	Montreal	1	—	—
Spezza, Jason	Ottawa	3	—	—
Staal, Eric	Carolina	11	1	—
Staal, Jordan	Pittsburgh	2	—	—
Stafford, Drew	Buffalo	6	—	—
Stamkos, Steven	Tampa Bay	3	—	—
Stastny, Paul	Colorado	2	—	—
Steen, Alex	Toronto	1	—	—
Stempniak, Lee	Phoenix	1	—	—
Stepan, Derek	NY Rangers	1	—	—
Stewart, Anthony	Atlanta	1	—	—
Stewart, Chris	Colorado	2	—	—
Stillman, Cory	Cgy., St.L., Car.	4	—	—
Sturm, Marco	S.J., Bos.	2	—	—
Subban, P.K.	Montreal	1	—	—
Sullivan, Steve	Tor., Chi., Nsh.	6	1	—
Svatos, Marek	Colorado	1	—	—
Tambellini, Jeff	NY Islanders	1	—	—
Tanguay, Alex	Colorado	2	—	—
Tavares, John	NY Islanders	2	—	—
Thornton, Joe	Bos., S.J.	4	—	—
Toews, Jonathan	Chicago	2	—	—
Torres, Raffi	Vancouver	1	—	—
Umberger, R.J.	Phi., CBJ	2	—	—
Upshall, Scottie	Phoenix	1	—	—
Vanek, Thomas	Buffalo	6	1	—
van Riemsdyk, James	Philadelphia	1	—	—
Vermette, Antoine	Ottawa	1	—	—
Visnovsky, Lubomir	L.A., Ana.	2	—	—
Vrbata, Radim	Col., Car., Phx.	3	—	—
Weiss, Stephen	Florida	1	—	—
Wellwood, Kyle	Toronto	1	—	—
Wheeler, Blake	Boston	1	—	—
Whitney, Ray	CBJ, Car., Phx.	4	—	—
Williams, Jason	Detroit	1	—	—
Williams, Justin	Carolina	1	—	—
Zetterberg, Henrik	Detroit	3	—	—
Zubrus, Dainius	Mtl., N.J.	1	1	—

Top 100 All-Time Goal-Scoring Leaders

* active player

Player	Goals	Games	Goals per game	Seasons
1. **Wayne Gretzky**, Edm., L.A., St.L., NYR .	894	1487	.601	20
2. **Gordie Howe**, Det., Hfd.	801	1767	.453	26
3. **Brett Hull**, Cgy., St.L., Dal., Det., Phx. . .	741	1269	.584	20
4. **Marcel Dionne**, Det., L.A., NYR	731	1348	.542	18
5. **Phil Esposito**, Chi., Bos., NYR	717	1282	.559	18
6. **Mike Gartner**, Wsh., Min., NYR, Tor., Phx.	708	1432	.494	19
7. **Mark Messier**, Edm., NYR, Van.	694	1756	.395	25
8. **Steve Yzerman**, Det.	692	1514	.457	22
9. **Mario Lemieux**, Pit.	690	915	.754	18
10. **Luc Robitaille**, L.A., Pit., NYR, Det.	668	1431	.467	19
11. **Brendan Shanahan**, N.J., St.L., Hfd., Det., NYR	656	1524	.430	21
* 12. **Jaromir Jagr**, Pit., Wsh., NYR	646	1273	.507	17
13. **Dave Andreychuk**, Buf., Tor., N.J., Bos., Col., T.B.	640	1639	.390	23
* 14. **Teemu Selanne**, Wpg., Ana., S.J., Col. .	637	1259	.506	18
15. **Joe Sakic**, Que., Col.	625	1378	.454	20
16. **Bobby Hull**, Chi., Wpg., Hfd.	610	1063	.574	16
17. **Dino Ciccarelli**, Min., Wsh., Det., T.B., Fla.	608	1232	.494	19
18. **Jari Kurri**, Edm., L.A., NYR, Ana., Col. . .	601	1251	.480	17
19. **Mark Recchi**, Pit., Phi., Mtl., Car., Atl., T.B., Bos.	577	1652	.349	22
20. **Mike Bossy**, NYI	573	752	.762	10
21. **Joe Nieuwendyk**, Cgy., Dal., N.J., Tor., Fla.	564	1257	.449	20
22. **Mats Sundin**, Que., Tor., Van.	564	1346	.419	18
* 23. **Mike Modano**, Min., Dal., Det.	561	1499	.374	22
24. **Guy Lafleur**, Mtl., NYR, Que.	560	1126	.497	17
25. **John Bucyk**, Det., Bos.	556	1540	.361	23
26. **Ron Francis**, Hfd., Pit., Car., Tor.	549	1731	.317	23
27. **Michel Goulet**, Que., Chi.	548	1089	.503	15
28. **Maurice Richard**, Mtl.	544	978	.556	18
29. **Stan Mikita**, Chi.	541	1394	.388	22
30. **Keith Tkachuk**, Wpg., Phx., St.L., Atl. . .	538	1201	.448	18
31. **Frank Mahovlich**, Tor., Det., Mtl.	533	1181	.451	18
32. **Bryan Trottier**, NYI, Pit.	524	1279	.410	18
33. **Pat Verbeek**, N.J., Hfd., NYR, Dal., Det.	522	1424	.367	20
34. **Dale Hawerchuk**, Wpg., Buf., St.L., Phi.	518	1188	.436	16
35. **Pierre Turgeon**, Buf., NYI, Mtl., St.L., Dal., Col.	515	1294	.398	19
36. **Jeremy Roenick**, Chi., Phx., Phi., L.A., S.J.	513	1363	.376	20
37. **Gilbert Perreault**, Buf.	512	1191	.430	17
38. **Jean Beliveau**, Mtl.	507	1125	.451	20
39. **Peter Bondra**, Wsh., Ott., Atl., Chi.	503	1081	.465	16
40. **Joe Mullen**, St.L., Cgy., Pit., Bos.	502	1062	.473	17
41. **Lanny McDonald**, Tor., Col., Cgy.	500	1111	.450	16
42. **Glenn Anderson**, Edm., Tor., NYR, St.L.	498	1129	.441	16
43. **Jean Ratelle**, NYR, Bos.	491	1281	.383	21
44. **Norm Ullman**, Det., Tor.	490	1410	.348	20
45. **Brian Bellows**, Min., Mtl., T.B., Ana., Wsh.	485	1188	.408	17
46. **Darryl Sittler**, Tor., Phi., Det.	484	1096	.442	15
* 47. **Jarome Iginla**, Cgy.	484	1106	.438	15
48. **Sergei Fedorov**, Det., Ana., CBJ, Wsh. .	483	1248	.387	18
49. **Bernie Nicholls**, L.A., NYR, Edm., N.J., Chi., S.J.	475	1127	.421	18
50. **Alexander Mogilny**, Buf., Van., N.J., Tor.	473	990	.478	16
51. **Denis Savard**, Chi., Mtl., T.B.	473	1196	.395	17
52. **Pat LaFontaine**, NYI, Buf., NYR	468	865	.541	15
53. **Alex Delvecchio**, Det.	456	1549	.294	24
54. **Theoren Fleury**, Cgy., Col., NYR, Chi. . .	455	1084	.420	15
55. **Rod Brind'Amour**, St.L., Phi., Car.	452	1484	.305	21
56. **Peter Stastny**, Que., N.J., St.L.	450	977	.461	15
57. **Doug Gilmour**, St.L., Cgy., Tor., N.J., Chi., Buf., Mtl.	450	1474	.305	20
58. **Rick Middleton**, NYR, Bos.	448	1005	.446	14
59. **Rick Vaive**, Van., Tor., Chi., Buf.	441	876	.503	13
60. **Steve Larmer**, Chi., NYR	441	1006	.438	15
61. **Rick Tocchet**, Phi., Pit., L.A., Bos., Wsh., Phx.	440	1144	.385	18
62. **Gary Roberts**, Cgy., Car., Tor., Fla., Pit., T.B.	438	1224	.358	22
63. **Pavel Bure**, Van., Fla., NYR	437	702	.623	12
64. **Vincent Damphousse**, Tor., Edm., Mtl., S.J.	432	1378	.313	18
65. **Dave Taylor**, L.A.	431	1111	.388	17
66. **Bill Guerin**, N.J., Edm., Bos., Dal., St.L., S.J., NYI, Pit.	429	1263	.340	18
67. **Yvan Cournoyer**, Mtl.	428	968	.442	16
* 68. **Alex Kovalev**, NYR, Pit., Mtl., Ott.	428	1302	.329	18
69. **Brian Propp**, Phi., Bos., Min., Hfd.	425	1016	.418	15
70. **Steve Shutt**, Mtl., L.A.	424	930	.456	13

Jason Arnott (now a member of the St. Louis Blues) celebrates his 398th career goal on March 13, 2011. His final goal of the 2010-11 season on April 2 gave him 400 for his career.

Player	Goals	Games	Goals per game	Seasons
* 71. **Owen Nolan**, Que., Col., S.J., Tor., Phx., Cgy., Min.	422	1200	.352	18
72. **Stephane Richer**, Mtl., N.J., T.B., St.L., Pit.	421	1054	.399	17
73. **Steve Thomas**, Tor., Chi., NYI, N.J., Ana., Det.	421	1235	.341	20
74. **Bill Barber**, Phi.	420	903	.465	12
75. **Tony Amonte**, NYR, Chi., Phx., Phi., Cgy.	416	1174	.354	16
76. **Garry Unger**, Tor., Det., St.L., Atl., L.A., Edm.	413	1105	.374	16
77. **John MacLean**, N.J., S.J., NYR, Dal.	413	1194	.346	18
78. **Raymond Bourque**, Bos., Col.	410	1612	.254	22
79. **Ray Ferraro**, Hfd., NYI, NYR, L.A., Atl., St.L.	408	1258	.324	18
80. **John LeClair**, Mtl., Phi., Pit.	406	967	.420	16
81. **Rod Gilbert**, NYR	406	1065	.381	18
82. **John Ogrodnick**, Det., Que., NYR	402	928	.433	14
83. **Paul Kariya**, Ana., Col., Nsh., St.L.	402	989	.406	15
* 84. **Jason Arnott**, Edm., N.J., Dal., Nsh., Wsh.	400	1172	.341	17
85. **Dave Keon**, Tor., Hfd.	396	1296	.306	18
86. **Paul Coffey**, Edm., Pit., L.A., Det., Hfd., Phi., Chi., Car., Bos.	396	1409	.281	21
87. **Cam Neely**, Van., Bos.	395	726	.544	13
88. **Pierre Larouche**, Pit., Mtl., Hfd., NYR . .	395	812	.486	14
89. **Markus Naslund**, Pit., Van., NYR	395	1117	.354	15
90. **Tomas Sandstrom**, NYR, L.A., Pit., Det., Ana.	394	983	.401	15
91. **Bernie Geoffrion**, Mtl., NYR	393	883	.445	16
92. **Jean Pronovost**, Pit., Atl., Wsh.	391	998	.392	14
93. **Dean Prentice**, NYR, Bos., Det., Pit., Min.	391	1378	.284	22
* 94. **Daniel Alfredsson**, Ott.	389	1056	.368	15
* 95. **Marian Hossa**, Ott., Atl., Pit., Det., Chi.	388	897	.433	13
96. **Rick Martin**, Buf., L.A.	384	685	.561	11
97. **Reggie Leach**, Bos., Cal., Phi., Det.	381	934	.408	13
98. **Ted Lindsay**, Det., Chi.	379	1068	.355	17
99. **Claude Lemieux**, Mtl., N.J., Col., Phx., Dal., S.J.	379	1215	.312	21
100. **Butch Goring**, L.A., NYI, Bos.	375	1107	.339	16
101. **Trevor Linden**, Van., NYI, Mtl., Wsh. . . .	375	1382	.271	19

Top 100 Active Goal-Scoring Leaders

	Player	Goals	Games	Goals per game	Seasons
1.	**Jaromir Jagr**, Pit., Wsh., NYR	646	1273	.507	17
2.	**Teemu Selanne**, Wpg., Ana., S.J., Col.	637	1259	.506	18
3.	**Mike Modano**, Min., Dal., Det.	561	1499	.374	22
4.	**Jarome Iginla**, Cgy.	484	1106	.438	15
5.	**Alex Kovalev**, NYR, Pit., Mtl., Ott.	428	1302	.329	18
6.	**Owen Nolan**, Que., Col., S.J., Tor., Phx., Cgy., Min.	422	1200	.352	18
7.	**Jason Arnott**, Edm., N.J., Dal., Nsh., Wsh.	400	1172	.341	17
8.	**Daniel Alfredsson**, Ott.	389	1056	.368	15
9.	**Marian Hossa**, Ott., Atl., Pit., Det., Chi.	388	897	.433	13
10.	**Ilya Kovalchuk**, Atl., N.J.	369	702	.526	9
11.	**Milan Hejduk**, Col.	357	910	.392	12
12.	**Patrick Marleau**, S.J.	357	1035	.345	13
13.	**Ryan Smyth**, Edm., NYI, Col., L.A.	355	1069	.332	16
14.	**Vincent Lecavalier**, T.B.	351	934	.376	12
15.	**Ray Whitney**, S.J., Edm., Fla., CBJ, Det., Car., Phx.	341	1147	.297	19
16.	**Alexei Yashin**, Ott., NYI	337	850	.396	12
17.	**Patrik Elias**, N.J.	335	961	.349	15
18.	**Brian Rolston**, N.J., Col., Bos., Min.	335	1186	.282	16
19.	**Dany Heatley**, Atl., Ott., S.J.	325	669	.486	9
20.	**Joe Thornton**, Bos., S.J.	306	995	.308	13
21.	**Alex Ovechkin**, Wsh.	301	475	.634	6
22.	**Martin St. Louis**, Cgy., T.B.	298	854	.349	12
23.	**Shane Doan**, Wpg., Phx.	296	1119	.265	15
24.	**Todd Bertuzzi**, NYI, Van., Fla., Det., Ana., Cgy.	289	1022	.283	15
25.	**Marian Gaborik**, Min., NYR	283	640	.442	10
26.	**Cory Stillman**, Cgy., St.L., T.B., Car., Ott., Fla.	278	1025	.271	16
27.	**Simon Gagne**, Phi., T.B.	276	727	.380	11
28.	**Olli Jokinen**, L.A., NYI, Fla., Phx., Cgy., NYR	269	960	.280	13
29.	**Mike Knuble**, Det., NYR, Bos., Phi., Wsh.	268	968	.277	14
30.	**Steve Sullivan**, N.J., Tor., Chi., Nsh	266	890	.299	15
31.	**Danny Briere**, Phx., Buf., Phi.	264	743	.355	13
32.	**Rick Nash**, CBJ	259	592	.438	8
33.	**Daymond Langkow**, T.B., Phi., Phx., Cgy.	259	1017	.255	15
34.	**Andrew Brunette**, Wsh., Nsh., Atl., Min., Col.	256	1032	.248	15
35.	**Chris Drury**, Col., Cgy., Buf., NYR	255	892	.286	12
36.	**Nicklas Lidstrom**, Det.	253	1494	.169	19
37.	**Daniel Sedin**, Van.	249	787	.316	10
38.	**Marco Sturm**, S.J., Bos., L.A., Wsh.	239	890	.269	13
39.	**Jamie Langenbrunner**, Dal., N.J.	237	1035	.229	16
40.	**Sergei Samsonov**, Bos., Edm., Mtl., Chi., Car., Fla.	235	888	.265	13
41.	**Tomas Holmstrom**, Det.	232	952	.244	14
42.	**Henrik Zetterberg**, Det.	230	586	.392	8
43.	**Vinny Prospal**, Phi., Ott., Fla., T.B., Ana., NYR	227	978	.232	14
44.	**Eric Staal**, Car.	226	560	.404	7
45.	**Brenden Morrow**, Dal.	226	749	.302	11
46.	**Alex Tanguay**, Col., Cgy., Mtl., T.B.	225	818	.275	11
47.	**Saku Koivu**, Mtl., Ana.	225	938	.240	15
48.	**Pavel Datsyuk**, Det.	221	662	.334	9
49.	**Brad Richards**, T.B., Dal.	220	772	.285	10
50.	**Mark Parrish**, Fla., NYI, L.A., Min., Dal., T.B., Buf.	216	722	.299	12
51.	**Sidney Crosby**, Pit.	215	412	.522	6
52.	**Radek Dvorak**, Fla., NYR, Edm., St.L., Atl.	215	1118	.192	15
53.	**J.P. Dumont**, Chi., Buf., Nsh.	214	822	.260	12
54.	**Brian Gionta**, N.J., Mtl.	209	616	.339	9
55.	**Martin Havlat**, Ott., Chi., Min.	209	621	.337	10
56.	**Sergei Gonchar**, Wsh., Bos., Pit., Ott.	209	1058	.198	16
57.	**Marc Savard**, NYR, Cgy., Atl., Bos.	207	807	.257	13
58.	**Jason Blake**, L.A., NYI, Tor., Ana.	206	826	.249	12
59.	**Thomas Vanek**, Buf.	204	469	.435	6
60.	**Brendan Morrison**, N.J., Van., Ana., Dal., Wsh., Cgy.	196	895	.219	13
61.	**Jason Spezza**, Ott.	192	526	.365	8
62.	**Kristian Huselius**, Fla., Cgy., CBJ	190	660	.288	9
63.	**Dainius Zubrus**, Phi., Mtl., Wsh., Buf., N.J.	189	983	.192	14
64.	**Rob Niedermayer**, Fla., Cgy., Ana., N.J., Buf.	186	1153	.161	17
65.	**Scott Hartnell**, Nsh., Phi.	185	761	.243	10
66.	**Erik Cole**, Car., Edm.	184	620	.297	9
67.	**Jeff Carter**, Phi.	181	461	.393	6
68.	**Matt Cullen**, Ana., Fla., Car., NYR, Ott., Min.	181	958	.189	13
69.	**Michael Cammalleri**, L.A., Cgy., Mtl.	177	496	.357	8
70.	**Jochen Hecht**, St.L., Edm., Buf.	177	764	.232	12
71.	**Alexander Semin**, Wsh.	176	392	.449	6

Dany Heatley (now a member of the Minnesota Wild) reached the 300-goal plateau with his first goal of the 2010-11 season on October 16, 2010. San Jose's Joe Thornton scored his 300th on February 22, 2011.

	Player	Goals	Games	Goals per game	Seasons
72.	**Alex Frolov**, L.A., NYR	175	579	.302	8
73.	**Nik Antropov**, Tor., NYR, Atl.	172	679	.253	11
74.	**Mike Fisher**, Ott., Nsh.	172	702	.245	11
75.	**Michal Handzus**, St.L., Phx., Phi., Chi., L.A.	172	844	.204	12
76.	**Jonathan Cheechoo**, S.J., Ott.	170	501	.339	7
77.	**David Legwand**, Nsh.	169	768	.220	12
78.	**Corey Perry**, Ana.	168	450	.373	6
79.	**Nathan Horton**, Fla., Bos.	168	502	.335	7
80.	**Mike Comrie**, Edm., Phi., Phx., Ott., NYI, Pit.	168	589	.285	10
81.	**Scott Gomez**, N.J., NYR, Mtl.	167	864	.193	11
82.	**Andy McDonald**, Ana., St.L.	165	623	.265	10
83.	**Zach Parise**, N.J.	163	420	.388	6
84.	**Michael Ryder**, Mtl., Bos.	162	549	.295	7
85.	**John Madden**, N.J., Chi., Min.	162	867	.187	12
86.	**Mike Grier**, Edm., Wsh., Buf., S.J.	162	1060	.153	14
87.	**Patrick Sharp**, Phi., Chi.	160	493	.325	8
88.	**Ruslan Fedotenko**, Phi., T.B., NYI, Pit., NYR	160	743	.215	10
89.	**Evgeni Malkin**, Pit.	158	352	.449	5
90.	**Maxim Afinogenov**, Buf., Atl.	158	651	.243	10
91.	**Justin Williams**, Phi., Car., L.A.	157	625	.251	10
92.	**Henrik Sedin**, Van.	157	810	.194	10
93.	**Chris Pronger**, Hfd., St.L., Edm., Ana., Phi.	156	1154	.135	17
94.	**Mike Ribeiro**, Mtl., Dal.	155	663	.234	11
95.	**Roman Hamrlik**, T.B., Edm., NYI, Cgy., Mtl.	153	1311	.117	18
96.	**Brad Boyes**, S.J., Bos., St.L., Buf.	150	493	.304	7
97.	**Ryan Malone**, Pit., T.B.	148	492	.301	7
98.	**Radim Vrbata**, Col., Car., Chi., Phx., T.B.	148	601	.246	9
99.	**Ethan Moreau**, Chi., Edm., CBJ	146	900	.162	15
100.	**Jason Pominville**, Buf	145	459	.316	7

Top 100 All-Time Assist Leaders

* active player

	Player	Assists	Games	Assists per game	Seasons
1.	Wayne Gretzky, Edm., L.A., St.L., NYR .	1963	1487	1.320	20
2.	Ron Francis, Hfd., Pit., Car., Tor.	1249	1731	.722	23
3.	Mark Messier, Edm., NYR, Van.	1193	1756	.679	25
4.	Raymond Bourque, Bos., Col.	1169	1612	.725	22
5.	Paul Coffey, Edm., Pit., L.A., Det., Hfd., Phi., Chi., Car., Bos.	1135	1409	.806	21
6.	Adam Oates, Det., St.L., Bos., Wsh., Phi., Ana., Edm.	1079	1337	.807	19
7.	Steve Yzerman, Det.	1063	1514	.702	22
8.	Gordie Howe, Det., Hfd.	1049	1767	.594	26
9.	Marcel Dionne, Det., L.A., NYR	1040	1348	.772	18
10.	Mario Lemieux, Pit.	1033	915	1.129	18
11.	Joe Sakic, Que., Col.	1016	1378	.737	20
12.	Doug Gilmour, St.L., Cgy., Tor., N.J., Chi., Buf., Mtl.	964	1474	.654	20
13.	Mark Recchi, Pit., Phi., Mtl., Car., Atl., T.B., Bos.	956	1652	.579	22
* 14.	Jaromir Jagr, Pit., Wsh., NYR	953	1273	.749	17
15.	Al MacInnis, Cgy., St.L.	934	1416	.660	23
16.	Larry Murphy, L.A., Wsh., Min., Pit., Tor., Det.	929	1615	.575	21
17.	Stan Mikita, Chi.	926	1394	.664	22
18.	Bryan Trottier, NYI, Pit.	901	1279	.704	18
19.	Phil Housley, Buf., Wpg., St.L., Cgy., N.J., Wsh., Chi., Tor.	894	1495	.598	21
20.	Dale Hawerchuk, Wpg., Buf., St.L., Phi.	891	1188	.750	16
21.	Phil Esposito, Chi., Bos., NYR	873	1282	.681	18
22.	Denis Savard, Chi., Mtl., T.B.	865	1196	.723	17
* 23.	Nicklas Lidstrom, Det.	855	1494	.572	19
24.	Bobby Clarke, Phi.	852	1144	.745	15
25.	Alex Delvecchio, Det.	825	1549	.533	24
26.	Gilbert Perreault, Buf.	814	1191	.683	17
* 27.	Mike Modano, Min., Dal., Det.	813	1499	.542	22
28.	John Bucyk, Det., Bos.	813	1540	.528	23
29.	Pierre Turgeon, Buf., NYI, Mtl., St.L., Dal., Col.	812	1294	.628	19
30.	Jari Kurri, Edm., L.A., NYR, Ana., Col.	797	1251	.637	17
31.	Guy Lafleur, Mtl., NYR, Que.	793	1126	.704	17
32.	Peter Stastny, Que., N.J., St.L.	789	977	.808	15
33.	Mats Sundin, Que., Tor., Van.	785	1346	.583	18
34.	Brian Leetch, NYR, Tor., Bos.	781	1205	.648	18
35.	Jean Ratelle, NYR, Bos.	776	1281	.606	21
36.	Vincent Damphousse, Tor., Edm., Mtl., S.J.	773	1378	.561	18
37.	Chris Chelios, Mtl., Chi., Det., Atl.	763	1651	.462	26
38.	Bernie Federko, St.L., Det.	761	1000	.761	14
39.	Doug Weight, NYR, Edm., St.L., Car., Ana., NYI	755	1238	.610	20
40.	Larry Robinson, Mtl., L.A.	750	1384	.542	20
41.	Denis Potvin, NYI	742	1060	.700	15
42.	Norm Ullman, Det., Tor.	739	1410	.524	20
43.	Bernie Nicholls, L.A., NYR, Edm., N.J., Chi., S.J.	734	1127	.651	18
44.	Rod Brind'Amour, St.L., Phi., Car.	732	1484	.493	21
45.	Luc Robitaille, L.A., Pit., NYR, Det.	726	1431	.507	19
46.	Jean Beliveau, Mtl.	712	1125	.633	20
47.	Scott Stevens, Wsh., St.L., N.J.	712	1635	.435	22
* 48.	Teemu Selanne, Wpg., Ana., S.J., Col.	703	1259	.558	18
49.	Jeremy Roenick, Chi., Phx., Phi., L.A., S.J.	703	1363	.516	20
50.	Brendan Shanahan, N.J., St.L., Hfd., Det., NYR	698	1524	.458	21
51.	Dave Andreychuk, Buf., Tor., N.J., Bos., Col., T.B.	698	1639	.426	23
52.	Dale Hunter, Que., Wsh., Col.	697	1407	.495	19
53.	Sergei Fedorov, Det., Ana., CBJ, Wsh.	696	1248	.558	18
* 54.	Joe Thornton, Bos., S.J.	695	995	.698	13
55.	Henri Richard, Mtl.	688	1256	.548	20
56.	Brad Park, NYR, Bos., Det.	683	1113	.614	17
57.	Bobby Smith, Min., Mtl.	679	1077	.630	15
58.	Brett Hull, Cgy., St.L., Dal., Det., Phx.	650	1269	.512	20
59.	Bobby Orr, Bos., Chi.	645	657	.982	12
60.	Gary Suter, Cgy., Chi., S.J.	641	1145	.560	17
61.	Dave Taylor, L.A.	638	1111	.574	17
62.	Darryl Sittler, Tor., Phi., Det.	637	1096	.581	15
63.	Borje Salming, Tor., Det.	637	1148	.555	17
64.	Peter Forsberg, Que., Col., Phi., Nsh.	636	708	.898	14
* 65.	Daniel Alfredsson, Ott.	634	1056	.600	15
66.	Neal Broten, Min., Dal., N.J., L.A.	634	1099	.577	17
67.	Theoren Fleury, Cgy., Col., NYR, Chi.	633	1084	.584	15
68.	Mike Gartner, Wsh., Min., NYR, Tor., Phx.	627	1432	.438	19
69.	Andy Bathgate, NYR, Tor., Det., Pit.	624	1069	.584	17
70.	Sergei Zubov, NYR, Pit., Dal.	619	1068	.580	16
71.	Rod Gilbert, NYR	615	1065	.577	18
72.	Michel Goulet, Que., Chi.	604	1089	.555	15
73.	Kirk Muller, N.J., Mtl., NYI, Tor., Fla., Dal.	602	1349	.446	19

Teemu Selanne picked up his 700th career assist as part of a three goals, two assists night on March 28, 2011. Selanne was the first 40-year-old in NHL history to record a five-point game and the oldest player to score a goal on a penalty shot.

	Player	Assists	Games	Assists per game	Seasons
74.	Glenn Anderson, Edm., Tor., NYR, St.L.	601	1129	.532	16
* 75.	Alex Kovalev, NYR, Pit., Mtl., Ott.	596	1302	.458	18
76.	Dino Ciccarelli, Min., Wsh., Det., T.B., Fla.	592	1232	.481	19
77.	Doug Wilson, Chi., S.J.	590	1024	.576	16
78.	Dave Keon, Tor., Hfd.	590	1296	.455	18
79.	Paul Kariya, Ana., Col., Nsh., St.L.	587	989	.594	15
* 80.	Ray Whitney, S.J., Edm., Fla., CBJ, Det., Car., Phx.	585	1147	.510	19
81.	Dave Babych, Wpg., Hfd., Van., Phi., L.A.	581	1195	.486	19
82.	Brian Propp, Phi., Bos., Min., Hfd.	579	1016	.570	15
83.	Steve Larmer, Chi., NYR	571	1006	.568	15
84.	Frank Mahovlich, Tor., Det., Mtl.	570	1181	.483	18
85.	Scott Niedermayer, N.J., Ana.	568	1263	.450	18
86.	Craig Janney, Bos., St.L., S.J., Wpg., Phx., T.B., NYI	563	760	.741	12
87.	Cliff Ronning, St.L., Van., Phx., Nsh., L.A., Min., NYI	563	1137	.495	18
88.	Joe Nieuwendyk, Cgy., Dal., N.J., Tor., Fla.	562	1257	.447	20
89.	Joe Mullen, St.L., Cgy., Pit., Bos.	561	1062	.528	17
90.	Bobby Hull, Chi., Wpg., Hfd.	560	1063	.527	16
91.	Alexander Mogilny, Buf., Van., N.J., Tor.	559	990	.565	16
92.	Mike Bossy, NYI	553	752	.735	10
93.	Thomas Steen, Wpg.	553	950	.582	14
94.	Ken Linseman, Phi., Edm., Bos., Tor.	551	860	.641	14
95.	Tom Lysiak, Atl., Chi.	551	919	.600	13
96.	Pat LaFontaine, NYI, Buf., NYR.	545	865	.630	15
97.	Mark Howe, Hfd., Phi., Det.	545	929	.587	16
98.	Red Kelly, Det., Tor.	542	1316	.412	20
99.	Pat Verbeek, N.J., Hfd., NYR, Dal., Det.	541	1424	.380	20
100.	Rick Middleton, NYR, Bos.	540	1005	.537	14

Top 100 Active Assist Leaders

	Player	Assists	Games	Assists per game	Seasons
1.	**Jaromir Jagr**, Pit., Wsh., NYR	953	1273	.749	17
2.	**Nicklas Lidstrom**, Det.	855	1494	.572	19
3.	**Mike Modano**, Min., Dal., Det.	813	1499	.542	22
4.	**Teemu Selanne**, Wpg., Ana., S.J., Col.	703	1259	.558	18
5.	**Joe Thornton**, Bos., S.J.	695	995	.698	13
6.	**Daniel Alfredsson**, Ott.	634	1056	.600	15
7.	**Alex Kovalev**, NYR, Pit., Mtl., Ott.	596	1302	.458	18
8.	**Ray Whitney**, S.J., Edm., Fla., CBJ, Det., Car., Phx.	585	1147	.510	19
9.	**Chris Pronger**, Hfd., St.L., Edm., Ana., Phi.	530	1154	.459	17
10.	**Jarome Iginla**, Cgy.	522	1106	.472	15
11.	**Saku Koivu**, Mtl., Ana.	513	938	.547	15
12.	**Henrik Sedin**, Van.	509	810	.628	10
13.	**Scott Gomez**, N.J., NYR, Mtl.	508	864	.588	11
14.	**Jason Arnott**, Edm., N.J., Dal., Nsh., Wsh.	504	1172	.430	17
15.	**Sergei Gonchar**, Wsh., Bos., Pit., Ott.	502	1058	.474	16
16.	**Marc Savard**, NYR, Cgy., Atl., Bos.	499	807	.618	13
17.	**Brad Richards**, T.B., Dal.	496	772	.642	10
18.	**Patrik Elias**, N.J.	481	961	.501	15
19.	**Martin St. Louis**, Cgy., T.B.	480	854	.562	12
20.	**Roman Hamrlik**, T.B., Edm., NYI, Cgy., Mtl.	471	1311	.359	18
21.	**Owen Nolan**, Que., Col., S.J., Tor., Phx., Cgy., Min.	463	1200	.386	18
22.	**Alex Tanguay**, Col., Cgy., Mtl., T.B.	461	818	.564	11
23.	**Vinny Prospal**, Phi., Ott., Fla., T.B., Ana., NYR.	453	978	.463	14
24.	**Andrew Brunette**, Wsh., Nsh., Atl., Min., Col.	450	1032	.436	15
25.	**Cory Stillman**, Cgy., St.L., T.B., Car., Ott., Fla.	449	1025	.438	16
26.	**Tomas Kaberle**, Tor., Bos.	445	902	.493	12
27.	**Alexei Yashin**, Ott., NYI	444	850	.522	12
28.	**Vincent Lecavalier**, T.B.	442	934	.473	12
29.	**Shane Doan**, Wpg., Phx.	442	1119	.395	15
30.	**Marian Hossa**, Ott., Atl., Pit., Det., Chi.	439	897	.489	13
31.	**Pavel Datsyuk**, Det.	430	662	.650	9
32.	**Todd Bertuzzi**, NYI, Van., Fla., Det., Ana., Cgy.	424	1022	.415	15
33.	**Steve Sullivan**, N.J., Tor., Chi., Nsh.	416	890	.467	15
34.	**Patrick Marleau**, S.J.	409	1035	.395	13
35.	**Ryan Smyth**, Edm., NYI, Col., L.A.	405	1069	.379	16
36.	**Daniel Sedin**, Van.	402	787	.511	10
37.	**Brian Rolston**, N.J., Col., Bos., Min.	402	1186	.339	16
38.	**Jamie Langenbrunner**, Dal., N.J.	401	1035	.387	16
39.	**Milan Hejduk**, Col.	400	910	.440	12
40.	**Brendan Morrison**, N.J., Van., Ana., Dal., Wsh., Cgy.	394	895	.440	13
41.	**Daymond Langkow**, T.B., Phi., Phx., Cgy.	383	1017	.377	15
42.	**Bryan McCabe**, NYI, Van., Chi., Tor., Fla., NYR.	383	1135	.337	15
43.	**Dany Heatley**, Atl., Ott., S.J.	364	669	.544	9
44.	**Kimmo Timonen**, Nsh., Phi.	362	894	.405	12
45.	**Chris Drury**, Col., Cgy., Buf., NYR	360	892	.404	12
46.	**Sidney Crosby**, Pit.	357	412	.867	6
47.	**Olli Jokinen**, L.A., NYI, Fla., Phx., Cgy., NYR	353	960	.368	13
48.	**Ed Jovanovski**, Fla., Van., Phx.	348	1019	.342	15
49.	**Wade Redden**, Ott., NYR	344	994	.346	13
50.	**Mike Ribeiro**, Mtl., Dal.	342	663	.516	11
51.	**Dan Boyle**, Fla., T.B., S.J.	341	752	.453	12
52.	**Radek Dvorak**, Fla., NYR, Edm., St.L., Atl.	341	1118	.305	15
53.	**Jason Spezza**, Ott.	340	526	.646	8
54.	**Sergei Samsonov**, Bos., Edm., Mtl., Chi., Car., Fla.	336	888	.378	13
55.	**Ilya Kovalchuk**, Atl., N.J.	333	702	.474	9
56.	**Danny Briere**, Phx., Buf., Phi.	330	743	.444	13
57.	**Henrik Zetterberg**, Det.	325	586	.555	8
58.	**Matt Cullen**, Ana., Fla., Car., NYR, Ott., Min.	319	958	.333	13
59.	**Alex Ovechkin**, Wsh.	313	475	.659	6
60.	**Lubomir Visnovsky**, L.A., Edm., Ana.	312	703	.444	10
61.	**J.P. Dumont**, Chi., Buf., Nsh.	309	822	.376	12
62.	**Dainius Zubrus**, Phi., Mtl., Wsh., Buf., N.J.	306	983	.311	14
63.	**Martin Havlat**, Ott., Chi., Min.	303	621	.488	10
64.	**Derek Morris**, Cgy., Col., Phx., NYR, Bos.	300	946	.317	13
65.	**Ryan Getzlaf**, Ana.	289	430	.672	6
66.	**Marian Gaborik**, Min., NYR	288	640	.450	10
67.	**Simon Gagne**, Phi., T.B.	288	727	.396	11
68.	**Andrei Markov**, Mtl.	285	623	.457	10
69.	**Rob Niedermayer**, Fla., Cgy., Ana., N.J., Buf.	283	1153	.245	17
70.	**Zdeno Chara**, NYI, Ott., Bos.	282	928	.304	13

Second in assists among active NHL players, Nicklas Lidstrom became the first 40-year-old defenseman to get 60 points in a season in 2010-11 and became the oldest player to score his first career hat trick on February 15, 2011.

	Player	Assists	Games	Assists per game	Seasons
71.	**Ales Hemsky**, Edm.	281	490	.573	8
72.	**Andy McDonald**, Ana., St.L.	281	623	.451	10
73.	**David Legwand**, Nsh.	279	768	.363	12
74.	**Eric Staal**, Car.	278	560	.496	7
75.	**Tim Connolly**, NYI, Buf.	277	627	.442	11
76.	**Tomas Holmstrom**, Det.	274	952	.288	14
77.	**Jason Blake**, L.A., NYI, Tor., Ana.	268	826	.324	12
78.	**Adrian Aucoin**, Van., T.B., NYI, Chi., Cgy., Phx.	267	1008	.265	16
79.	**Brenden Morrow**, Dal.	265	749	.354	11
80.	**Jochen Hecht**, St.L., Edm., Buf.	264	764	.346	12
81.	**Pavel Kubina**, T.B., Tor., Atl.	264	901	.293	13
82.	**Jaroslav Spacek**, Fla., Chi., CBJ, Edm., Buf., Mtl.	263	834	.315	12
83.	**Michal Handzus**, St.L., Phx., Phi., Chi., L.A.	263	844	.312	12
84.	**Martin Erat**, Nsh.	262	616	.425	9
85.	**Kristian Huselius**, Fla., Cgy., CBJ	261	660	.395	9
86.	**Evgeni Malkin**, Pit.	260	352	.739	5
87.	**Shawn Horcoff**, Edm.	259	684	.379	10
88.	**Brian Campbell**, Buf., S.J., Chi.	258	626	.412	11
89.	**Tom Poti**, Edm., NYR, NYI, Wsh.	256	808	.317	12
90.	**Mike Knuble**, Det., NYR, Bos., Phi., Wsh.	254	968	.262	14
91.	**Mattias Ohlund**, Van., T.B.	250	909	.275	13
92.	**Justin Williams**, Phi., Car., L.A.	249	625	.398	10
93.	**Marco Sturm**, S.J., Bos., L.A., Wsh.	243	890	.273	13
94.	**Steve Reinprecht**, L.A., Col., Cgy., Phx., Fla.	242	663	.365	11
95.	**Todd White**, Chi., Phi., Ott., Min., Atl., NYR	240	653	.368	13
96.	**Nik Antropov**, Tor., NYR, Atl.	240	679	.353	11
97.	**Derek Roy**, Buf.	239	469	.510	7
98.	**Maxim Afinogenov**, Buf., Atl.	237	651	.364	10
99.	**Nicklas Backstrom**, Wsh.	236	323	.731	4
100.	**Rick Nash**, CBJ	229	592	.387	8

Top 100 All-Time Point Leaders

* active player

	Player	Points	Games	Points per game	Goals	Assists	Seasons
1.	**Wayne Gretzky**, Edm., L.A., St.L., NYR	**2857**	1487	1.921	894	1963	20
2.	**Mark Messier**, Edm., NYR, Van.	**1887**	1756	1.075	694	1193	25
3.	**Gordie Howe**, Det., Hfd.	**1850**	1767	1.047	801	1049	26
4.	**Ron Francis**, Hfd., Pit., Car., Tor.	**1798**	1731	1.039	549	1249	23
5.	**Marcel Dionne**, Det., L.A., NYR	**1771**	1348	1.314	731	1040	18
6.	**Steve Yzerman**, Det.	**1755**	1514	1.159	692	1063	22
7.	**Mario Lemieux**, Pit.	**1723**	915	1.883	690	1033	18
8.	**Joe Sakic**, Que., Col.	**1641**	1378	1.191	625	1016	20
* 9.	**Jaromir Jagr**, Pit., Wsh., NYR	**1599**	1273	1.256	646	953	17
10.	**Phil Esposito**, Chi., Bos., NYR	**1590**	1282	1.240	717	873	18
11.	**Raymond Bourque**, Bos., Col.	**1579**	1612	.980	410	1169	22
12.	**Mark Recchi**, Pit., Phi., Mtl., Car., Atl., T.B., Bos.	**1533**	1652	.928	577	956	22
13.	**Paul Coffey**, Edm., Pit., L.A., Det., Hfd., Phi., Chi., Car., Bos.	**1531**	1409	1.087	396	1135	21
14.	**Stan Mikita**, Chi.	**1467**	1394	1.052	541	926	22
15.	**Bryan Trottier**, NYI, Pit.	**1425**	1279	1.114	524	901	18
16.	**Adam Oates**, Det., St.L., Bos., Wsh., Phi., Ana., Edm.	**1420**	1337	1.062	341	1079	19
17.	**Doug Gilmour**, St.L., Cgy., Tor., N.J., Chi., Buf., Mtl.	**1414**	1474	.959	450	964	20
18.	**Dale Hawerchuk**, Wpg., Buf., St.L., Phi.	**1409**	1188	1.186	518	891	16
19.	**Jari Kurri**, Edm., L.A., NYR, Ana., Col.	**1398**	1251	1.118	601	797	17
20.	**Luc Robitaille**, L.A., Pit., NYR, Det.	**1394**	1431	.974	668	726	19
21.	**Brett Hull**, Cgy., St.L., Dal., Det., Phx.	**1391**	1269	1.096	741	650	20
* 22.	**Mike Modano**, Min., Dal., Det.	**1374**	1499	.917	561	813	22
23.	**John Bucyk**, Det., Bos.	**1369**	1540	.889	556	813	23
24.	**Brendan Shanahan**, N.J., St.L., Hfd., Det., NYR	**1354**	1524	.888	656	698	21
25.	**Guy Lafleur**, Mtl., NYR, Que.	**1353**	1126	1.202	560	793	17
26.	**Mats Sundin**, Que., Tor., Van.	**1349**	1346	1.002	564	785	18
* 27.	**Teemu Selanne**, Wpg., Ana., S.J., Col.	**1340**	1259	1.064	637	703	18
28.	**Denis Savard**, Chi., Mtl., T.B.	**1338**	1196	1.119	473	865	17
29.	**Dave Andreychuk**, Buf., Tor., N.J., Bos., Col., T.B.	**1338**	1639	.816	640	698	23
30.	**Mike Gartner**, Wsh., Min., NYR, Tor., Phx.	**1335**	1432	.932	708	627	19
31.	**Pierre Turgeon**, Buf., NYI, Mtl., St.L., Dal., Col.	**1327**	1294	1.026	515	812	19
32.	**Gilbert Perreault**, Buf.	**1326**	1191	1.113	512	814	17
33.	**Alex Delvecchio**, Det.	**1281**	1549	.827	456	825	24
34.	**Al MacInnis**, Cgy., St.L.	**1274**	1416	.900	340	934	23
35.	**Jean Ratelle**, NYR, Bos.	**1267**	1281	.989	491	776	21
36.	**Peter Stastny**, Que., N.J., St.L.	**1239**	977	1.268	450	789	15
37.	**Phil Housley**, Buf., Wpg., St.L., Cgy., N.J., Wsh., Chi., Tor., Pit.	**1232**	1495	.824	338	894	21
38.	**Norm Ullman**, Det., Tor.	**1229**	1410	.872	490	739	20
39.	**Jean Beliveau**, Mtl.	**1219**	1125	1.084	507	712	20
40.	**Jeremy Roenick**, Chi., Phx., Phi., L.A., S.J.	**1216**	1363	.892	513	703	20
41.	**Larry Murphy**, L.A., Wsh., Min., Pit., Tor., Det.	**1216**	1615	.753	287	929	21
42.	**Bobby Clarke**, Phi.	**1210**	1144	1.058	358	852	15
43.	**Bernie Nicholls**, L.A., NYR, Edm., N.J., Chi., S.J.	**1209**	1127	1.073	475	734	18
44.	**Vincent Damphousse**, Tor., Edm., Mtl., S.J.	**1205**	1378	.874	432	773	18
45.	**Dino Ciccarelli**, Min., Wsh., Det., T.B., Fla.	**1200**	1232	.974	608	592	19
46.	**Rod Brind'Amour**, St.L., Phi., Car.	**1184**	1484	.798	452	732	21
47.	**Sergei Fedorov**, Det., Ana., CBJ, Wsh.	**1179**	1248	.945	483	696	18
48.	**Bobby Hull**, Chi., Wpg., Hfd.	**1170**	1063	1.101	610	560	16
49.	**Michel Goulet**, Que., Chi.	**1152**	1089	1.058	548	604	15
50.	**Bernie Federko**, St.L., Det.	**1130**	1000	1.130	369	761	14
51.	**Mike Bossy**, NYI	**1126**	752	1.497	573	553	10
52.	**Joe Nieuwendyk**, Cgy., Dal., N.J., Tor., Fla.	**1126**	1257	.896	564	562	20
53.	**Darryl Sittler**, Tor., Phi., Det.	**1121**	1096	1.023	484	637	15
* 54.	**Nicklas Lidstrom**, Det.	**1108**	1494	.742	253	855	19
55.	**Frank Mahovlich**, Tor., Det., Mtl.	**1103**	1181	.934	533	570	18
56.	**Glenn Anderson**, Edm., Tor., NYR, St.L.	**1099**	1129	.973	498	601	16

Butch Goring spent the majority of his 16-year career with the Los Angeles Kings and the New York Islanders. He currently ranks 99th in NHL history in points and 100th all-time in goals scored.

	Player	Points	Games	Points per game	Goals	Assists	Seasons
57.	**Theoren Fleury**, Cgy., Col., NYR, Chi.	**1088**	1084	1.004	455	633	15
58.	**Dave Taylor**, L.A.	**1069**	1111	.962	431	638	17
59.	**Keith Tkachuk**, Wpg., Phx., St.L., Atl.	**1065**	1201	.887	538	527	18
60.	**Joe Mullen**, St.L., Cgy., Pit., Bos.	**1063**	1062	1.001	502	561	17
61.	**Pat Verbeek**, N.J., Hfd., NYR, Dal., Det.	**1063**	1424	.746	522	541	20
62.	**Denis Potvin**, NYI	**1052**	1060	.992	310	742	15
63.	**Henri Richard**, Mtl.	**1046**	1256	.833	358	688	20
64.	**Bobby Smith**, Min., Mtl.	**1036**	1077	.962	357	679	15
65.	**Doug Weight**, NYR, Edm., St.L., Car., Ana., NYI	**1033**	1238	.834	278	755	20
66.	**Alexander Mogilny**, Buf., Van., N.J., Tor.	**1032**	990	1.042	473	559	16
67.	**Brian Leetch**, NYR, Tor., Bos.	**1028**	1205	.853	247	781	18
* 68.	**Alex Kovalev**, NYR, Pit., Mtl., Ott.	**1024**	1302	.786	428	596	18
* 69.	**Daniel Alfredsson**, Ott.	**1023**	1056	.969	389	634	15
70.	**Brian Bellows**, Min., Mtl., T.B., Ana., Wsh.	**1022**	1188	.860	485	537	17
71.	**Rod Gilbert**, NYR	**1021**	1065	.959	406	615	18
72.	**Dale Hunter**, Que., Wsh., Col.	**1020**	1407	.725	323	697	19
73.	**Pat LaFontaine**, NYI, Buf., NYR	**1013**	865	1.171	468	545	15
74.	**Steve Larmer**, Chi., NYR	**1012**	1006	1.006	441	571	15
* 75.	**Jarome Iginla**, Cgy.	**1006**	1106	.910	484	522	15
76.	**Lanny McDonald**, Tor., Col., Cgy.	**1006**	1111	.905	500	506	16
77.	**Brian Propp**, Phi., Bos., Min., Hfd.	**1004**	1016	.988	425	579	15
* 78.	**Joe Thornton**, Bos., S.J.	**1001**	995	1.006	306	695	13
79.	**Paul Kariya**, Ana., Col., Nsh., St.L.	**989**	989	1.000	402	587	15
80.	**Rick Middleton**, NYR, Bos.	**988**	1005	.983	448	540	14
81.	**Dave Keon**, Tor., Hfd.	**986**	1296	.761	396	590	18
82.	**Andy Bathgate**, NYR, Tor., Det., Pit.	**973**	1069	.910	349	624	17
83.	**Maurice Richard**, Mtl.	**965**	978	.987	544	421	18
84.	**Kirk Muller**, N.J., Mtl., NYI, Tor., Fla., Dal.	**959**	1349	.711	357	602	19
85.	**Larry Robinson**, Mtl., L.A.	**958**	1384	.692	208	750	20
86.	**Rick Tocchet**, Phi., Pit., L.A., Bos., Wsh., Phx.	**952**	1144	.832	440	512	18
87.	**Chris Chelios**, Mtl., Chi., Det., Atl.	**948**	1651	.574	185	763	26
88.	**Steve Thomas**, Tor., Chi., NYI, N.J., Ana., Det.	**933**	1235	.755	421	512	20
* 89.	**Ray Whitney**, S.J., Edm., Fla., CBJ, Det., Car., Phx.	**926**	1147	.807	341	585	19
90.	**Neal Broten**, Min., Dal., N.J., L.A.	**923**	1099	.840	289	634	17
91.	**Bobby Orr**, Bos., Chi.	**915**	657	1.393	270	645	12
92.	**Gary Roberts**, Cgy., Car., Tor., Fla., Pit., T.B.	**910**	1224	.743	438	472	22
93.	**Scott Stevens**, Wsh., St.L., N.J.	**908**	1635	.555	196	712	22
* 94.	**Jason Arnott**, Edm., N.J., Dal., Nsh., Wsh.	**904**	1172	.771	400	504	16
95.	**Tony Amonte**, NYR, Chi., Phx., Phi., Cgy.	**900**	1174	.767	416	484	16
96.	**Ray Ferraro**, Hfd., NYI, NYR, L.A., Atl., St.L.	**898**	1258	.714	408	490	18
97.	**Brad Park**, NYR, Bos., Det.	**896**	1113	.805	213	683	17
98.	**Peter Bondra**, Wsh., Ott., Atl., Chi.	**892**	1081	.825	503	389	16
99.	**Butch Goring**, L.A., NYI, Bos.	**888**	1107	.802	375	513	16
100.	**Peter Forsberg**, Que., Col., Phi., Nsh.	**885**	708	1.250	249	636	14

Top 100 Active Points Leaders

Player	Points	Games	Points per game	Goals	Assists	Seasons
1. **Jaromir Jagr**, Pit., Wsh., NYR.	1599	1273	1.256	646	953	17
2. **Mike Modano**, Min., Dal., Det.	1374	1499	.917	561	813	22
3. **Teemu Selanne**, Wpg., Ana., S.J., Col.	1340	1259	1.064	637	703	18
4. **Nicklas Lidstrom**, Det.	1108	1494	.742	253	855	19
5. **Alex Kovalev**, NYR, Pit., Mtl., Ott.	1024	1302	.786	428	596	18
6. **Daniel Alfredsson**, Ott.	1023	1056	.969	389	634	15
7. **Jarome Iginla**, Cgy.	1006	1106	.910	484	522	15
8. **Joe Thornton**, Bos., S.J.	1001	995	1.006	306	695	13
9. **Ray Whitney**, S.J., Edm., Fla., CBJ, Det., Car., Phx.	926	1147	.807	341	585	19
10. **Jason Arnott**, Edm., N.J., Dal., Nsh., Wsh.	904	1172	.771	400	504	17
11. **Owen Nolan**, Que., Col., S.J., Tor., Phx., Cgy., Min.	885	1200	.738	422	463	18
12. **Marian Hossa**, Ott., Atl., Pit., Det., Chi.	827	897	.922	388	439	13
13. **Patrik Elias**, N.J.	816	961	.849	335	481	15
14. **Vincent Lecavalier**, T.B.	793	934	.849	351	442	12
15. **Alexei Yashin**, Ott., NYI	781	850	.919	337	444	12
16. **Martin St. Louis**, Cgy., T.B.	778	854	.911	298	480	12
17. **Patrick Marleau**, S.J.	766	1035	.740	357	409	13
18. **Ryan Smyth**, Edm., NYI, Col., L.A.	760	1069	.711	355	405	16
19. **Milan Hejduk**, Col.	757	910	.832	357	400	12
20. **Saku Koivu**, Mtl., Ana.	738	938	.787	225	513	15
21. **Shane Doan**, Wpg., Phx.	738	1119	.660	296	442	15
22. **Brian Rolston**, N.J., Col., Bos., Min.	737	1186	.621	335	402	16
23. **Cory Stillman**, Cgy., St.L., T.B., Car., Ott., Fla.	727	1025	.709	278	449	16
24. **Brad Richards**, T.B., Dal.	716	772	.927	220	496	10
25. **Todd Bertuzzi**, NYI, Van., Fla., Det., Ana., Cgy.	713	1022	.698	289	424	15
26. **Sergei Gonchar**, Wsh., Bos., Pit., Ott.	711	1058	.672	209	502	16
27. **Marc Savard**, NYR, Cgy., Atl., Bos.	706	807	.875	207	499	13
28. **Andrew Brunette**, Wsh., Nsh., Atl., Min., Col.	706	1032	.684	256	450	15
29. **Ilya Kovalchuk**, Atl., N.J.	702	702	1.000	369	333	9
30. **Dany Heatley**, Atl., Ott., S.J.	689	669	1.030	325	364	9
31. **Alex Tanguay**, Col., Cgy., Mtl., T.B.	686	818	.839	225	461	11
32. **Chris Pronger**, Hfd., St.L., Edm., Ana., Phi.	686	1154	.594	156	530	17
33. **Steve Sullivan**, N.J., Tor., Chi., Nsh.	682	890	.766	266	416	15
34. **Vinny Prospal**, Phi., Ott., Fla., T.B., Ana., NYR.	680	978	.695	227	453	14
35. **Scott Gomez**, N.J., NYR, Mtl.	675	864	.781	167	508	11
36. **Henrik Sedin**, Van.	666	810	.822	157	509	10
37. **Pavel Datsyuk**, Det.	651	662	.983	221	430	9
38. **Daniel Sedin**, Van.	651	787	.827	249	402	10
39. **Daymond Langkow**, T.B., Phi., Phx., Cgy.	642	1017	.631	259	383	15
40. **Jamie Langenbrunner**, Dal., N.J.	638	1035	.616	237	401	16
41. **Roman Hamrlik**, T.B., Edm., NYI, Cgy., Mtl.	624	1311	.476	153	471	18
42. **Olli Jokinen**, L.A., NYI, Fla., Phx., Cgy., NYR	622	960	.648	269	353	13
43. **Chris Drury**, Col., Cgy., Buf., NYR	615	892	.689	255	360	12
44. **Alex Ovechkin**, Wsh.	614	475	1.293	301	313	6
45. **Danny Briere**, Phx., Buf., Phi..	594	743	.799	264	330	12
46. **Brendan Morrison**, N.J., Van., Ana., Dal., Wsh., Cgy.	590	895	.659	196	394	13
47. **Sidney Crosby**, Pit.	572	412	1.388	215	357	6
48. **Marian Gaborik**, Min., NYR.	571	640	.892	283	288	10
49. **Sergei Samsonov**, Bos., Edm., Mtl., Chi., Car., Fla.	571	888	.643	235	336	13
50. **Simon Gagne**, Phi., T.B.	564	727	.776	276	288	11
51. **Radek Dvorak**, Fla., NYR, Edm., St.L., Atl.	556	1118	.497	215	341	15
52. **Henrik Zetterberg**, Det.	555	586	.947	230	325	8
53. **Jason Spezza**, Ott.	532	526	1.011	192	340	8
54. **Tomas Kaberle**, Tor., Bos.	529	902	.586	84	445	12
55. **Bryan McCabe**, NYI, Van., Chi., Tor., Fla., NYR	528	1135	.465	145	383	15
56. **J.P. Dumont**, Chi., Buf., Nsh.	523	822	.636	214	309	12
57. **Mike Knuble**, Det., NYR, Bos., Phi., Wsh.	522	968	.539	268	254	14
58. **Martin Havlat**, Ott., Chi., Min.	512	621	.824	209	303	10
59. **Tomas Holmstrom**, Det.	506	952	.532	232	274	14
60. **Eric Staal**, Car.	504	560	.900	226	278	7
61. **Matt Cullen**, Ana., Fla., Car., NYR, Ott., Min.	500	958	.522	181	319	13
62. **Mike Ribeiro**, Mtl., Dal.	497	663	.750	155	342	11
63. **Dainius Zubrus**, Phi., Mtl., Wsh., Buf., N.J.	495	983	.504	189	306	14
64. **Brenden Morrow**, Dal.	491	749	.656	226	265	11
65. **Rick Nash**, CBJ.	488	592	.824	259	229	8
66. **Marco Sturm**, S.J., Bos., L.A., Wsh.	482	890	.542	239	243	13
67. **Ed Jovanovski**, Fla., Van., Phx.	481	1019	.472	133	348	15
68. **Jason Blake**, L.A., NYI, Tor., Ana.	474	826	.574	206	268	12
69. **Rob Niedermayer**, Fla., Cgy., Ana., N.J., Buf.	469	1153	.407	186	283	17
70. **Kimmo Timonen**, Nsh., Phi.	464	894	.519	102	362	12
71. **Dan Boyle**, Fla., T.B., S.J.	457	752	.608	116	341	12
72. **Kristian Huselius**, Fla., Cgy., CBJ.	451	660	.683	190	261	9
73. **Wade Redden**, Ott., NYR.	450	994	.453	106	344	13
74. **David Legwand**, Nsh.	448	768	.583	169	279	12
75. **Andy McDonald**, Ana., St.L.	446	623	.716	165	281	10
76. **Jochen Hecht**, St.L., Edm., Buf.	441	764	.577	177	264	12
77. **Michal Handzus**, St.L., Phx., Phi., Chi., L.A.	435	844	.515	172	263	12
78. **Lubomir Visnovsky**, L.A., Edm., Ana.	423	703	.602	111	312	10
79. **Evgeni Malkin**, Pit.	418	352	1.188	158	260	5
80. **Ryan Getzlaf**, Ana.	415	430	.965	126	289	6
81. **Nik Antropov**, Tor., NYR, Atl.	412	679	.607	172	240	11
82. **Scott Hartnell**, Nsh., Phi.	407	761	.535	185	222	10
83. **Zdeno Chara**, NYI, Ott., Bos.	407	928	.439	125	282	13
84. **Justin Williams**, Phi., Car., L.A.	406	625	.650	157	249	10
85. **Brian Gionta**, N.J., Mtl.	404	616	.656	209	195	9
86. **Martin Erat**, Nsh.	402	616	.653	140	262	9
87. **Shawn Horcoff**, Edm.	401	684	.586	142	259	10
88. **Alex Frolov**, L.A., NYR	397	579	.686	175	222	8
89. **Ales Hemsky**, Edm.	395	490	.806	114	281	8
90. **Tim Connolly**, NYI, Buf.	395	627	.630	118	277	11
91. **Maxim Afinogenov**, Buf., Atl.	395	651	.607	158	237	10
92. **Erik Cole**, Car., Edm.	390	620	.629	184	206	9
93. **Mark Parrish**, Fla., NYI, L.A., Min., Dal., T.B., Buf.	387	722	.536	216	171	12
94. **Thomas Vanek**, Buf.	386	469	.823	204	182	6
95. **Adrian Aucoin**, Van., T.B., NYI, Chi., Cgy., Phx.	386	1008	.383	119	267	16
96. **Derek Morris**, Cgy., Col., Phx., NYR, Bos.	385	946	.407	85	300	13
97. **Michael Cammalleri**, L.A., Cgy., Mtl.	384	496	.774	177	207	8
98. **Derek Roy**, Buf.	383	469	.817	144	239	7
99. **Mike Grier**, Edm., Wsh., Buf., S.J.	383	1060	.361	162	221	14
100. **Steve Reinprecht**, L.A., Col., Cgy., Phx., Fla.	382	663	.576	140	242	11

San Jose's Joe Thornton joined Ottawa teammates Daniel Alfredsson and Alex Kovalev, as well as Calgary's Jarome Iginla, in reaching the 1,000-point plateau during the 2010-11 season.

Top 100 All-Time Games Played Leaders

* active player

Player	Games Played	Seasons
1. **Gordie Howe**, Det., Hfd.	1767	26
2. **Mark Messier**, Edm., NYR, Van.	1756	25
3. **Ron Francis**, Hfd., Pit., Car., Tor.	1731	23
4. **Mark Recchi**, Pit., Phi., Mtl., Car., Atl., T.B., Bos.	1652	22
5. **Chris Chelios**, Mtl., Chi., Det., Atl.	1651	26
6. **Dave Andreychuk**, Buf., Tor., N.J., Bos., Col., T.B.	1639	23
7. **Scott Stevens**, Wsh., St.L., N.J.	1635	22
8. **Larry Murphy**, L.A., Wsh., Min., Pit., Tor., Det.	1615	21
9. **Raymond Bourque**, Bos., Col.	1612	22
10. **Alex Delvecchio**, Det.	1549	24
11. **John Bucyk**, Det., Bos.	1540	23
12. **Brendan Shanahan**, N.J., St.L., Hfd., Det., NYR	1524	21
13. **Steve Yzerman**, Det.	1514	22
* 14. **Mike Modano**, Min., Dal., Det.	1499	22
15. **Phil Housley**, Buf., Wpg., St.L., Cgy., N.J., Wsh., Chi., Tor.	1495	21
* 16. **Nicklas Lidstrom**, Det.	1494	19
17. **Wayne Gretzky**, Edm., L.A., St.L., NYR	1487	20
18. **Rod Brind'Amour**, St.L., Phi., Car.	1484	21
19. **Doug Gilmour**, St.L., Cgy., Tor., N.J., Chi., Buf., Mtl.	1474	20
20. **Glen Wesley**, Bos., Hfd., Car., Tor.	1457	20
21. **Tim Horton**, Tor., NYR, Pit., Buf.	1446	24
22. **Mike Gartner**, Wsh., Min., NYR, Tor., Phx.	1432	19
23. **Luc Robitaille**, L.A., Pit., NYR, Det.	1431	19
24. **Scott Mellanby**, Phi., Edm., Fla., St.L., Atl.	1431	21
25. **Pat Verbeek**, N.J., Hfd., NYR, Dal., Det.	1424	20
26. **Luke Richardson**, Tor., Edm., Phi., CBJ, T.B., Ott.	1417	21
27. **Al MacInnis**, Cgy., St.L.	1416	23
28. **Harry Howell**, NYR, Oak., Cal., L.A.	1411	21
29. **Norm Ullman**, Det., Tor.	1410	20
30. **Paul Coffey**, Edm., Pit., L.A., Det., Hfd., Phi., Chi., Car., Bos.	1409	21
31. **Dale Hunter**, Que., Wsh., Col.	1407	19
32. **Stan Mikita**, Chi.	1394	22
33. **Doug Mohns**, Bos., Chi., Min., Atl., Wsh.	1390	22
34. **Larry Robinson**, Mtl., L.A.	1384	20
35. **Trevor Linden**, Van., NYI, Mtl., Wsh.	1382	19
36. **Vincent Damphousse**, Tor., Edm., Mtl., S.J.	1378	18
37. **Joe Sakic**, Que., Col.	1378	20
38. **Dean Prentice**, NYR, Bos., Det., Pit., Min.	1378	22
39. **Teppo Numminen**, Wpg., Phx., Dal., Buf.	1372	20
40. **Jeremy Roenick**, Chi., Phx., Phi., L.A., S.J.	1363	20
41. **Ron Stewart**, Tor., Bos., St.L., NYR, Van., NYI	1353	21
42. **Kirk Muller**, N.J., Mtl., NYI, Tor., Fla., Dal.	1349	19
43. **Marcel Dionne**, Det., L.A., NYR	1348	18
44. **Mats Sundin**, Que., Tor., Van.	1346	18
45. **Adam Oates**, Det., St.L., Bos., Wsh., Phi., Ana., Edm.	1337	19
46. **Guy Carbonneau**, Mtl., St.L., Dal.	1318	19
47. **Red Kelly**, Det., Tor.	1316	20
48. **Bobby Holik**, Hfd., N.J., NYR, Atl.	1314	18
* 49. **Roman Hamrlik**, T.B., Edm., NYI, Cgy., Mtl.	1311	18
* 50. **Alex Kovalev**, NYR, Pit., Mtl., Ott.	1302	18
51. **Dave Keon**, Tor., Hfd.	1296	18
52. **Pierre Turgeon**, Buf., NYI, Mtl., St.L., Dal., Col.	1294	19
53. **Darryl Sydor**, L.A., Dal., CBJ, T.B., Pit., St.L.	1291	18
54. **Mathieu Schneider**, Mtl., NYI, Tor., NYR, L.A., Det., Ana., Atl., Van., Phx.	1289	21
55. **Ken Daneyko**, N.J.	1283	20
56. **Phil Esposito**, Chi., Bos., NYR	1282	18
57. **Jean Ratelle**, NYR, Bos.	1281	21
58. **James Patrick**, NYR, Hfd., Cgy., Buf.	1280	21
59. **Bryan Trottier**, NYI, Pit.	1279	18
* 60. **Jaromir Jagr**, Pit., Wsh., NYR	1273	17
61. **Martin Gelinas**, Edm., Que., Van., Car., Cgy., Fla., Nsh.	1273	19
62. **Rob Blake**, L.A., Col., S.J.	1270	20
63. **Brett Hull**, Cgy., St.L., Dal., Det., Phx.	1269	20
64. **Bill Guerin**, N.J., Edm., Bos., Dal., St.L., S.J., NYI, Pit.	1263	18
65. **Scott Niedermayer**, N.J., Ana.	1263	18
* 66. **Teemu Selanne**, Wpg., Ana., S.J., Col.	1259	18
67. **Ray Ferraro**, Hfd., NYI, NYR, L.A., Atl., St.L.	1258	18
68. **Joe Nieuwendyk**, Cgy., Dal., N.J., Tor., Fla.	1257	20
69. **Craig Ludwig**, Mtl., NYI, Min., Dal.	1256	17
70. **Henri Richard**, Mtl.	1256	20
71. **Kevin Lowe**, Edm., NYR	1254	19
72. **Jari Kurri**, Edm., L.A., NYR, Ana., Col.	1251	17
73. **Sergei Fedorov**, Det., Ana., CBJ, Wsh.	1248	18
74. **Bill Gadsby**, Chi., NYR, Det.	1248	20
75. **Allan Stanley**, NYR, Chi., Bos., Tor., Phi.	1244	21
76. **Doug Weight**, NYR, Edm., St.L., Car., Ana., NYI	1238	20
77. **Steve Thomas**, Tor., Chi., NYI, N.J., Ana., Det.	1235	20
78. **Dino Ciccarelli**, Min., Wsh., Det., T.B., Fla.	1232	19
79. **Ed Westfall**, Bos., NYI	1226	18
80. **Gary Roberts**, Cgy., Car., Tor., Fla., Pit., T.B.	1224	22

Doug Weight, who announced his retirement and joined the Islanders coaching staff late in the 2010-11 season, ended his 20-year career with 1,238 games played to rank 76th in NHL history.

Player	Games Played	Seasons
81. **Brad McCrimmon**, Bos., Phi., Cgy., Det., Hfd., Phx.	1222	18
82. **Eric Nesterenko**, Tor., Chi.	1219	21
83. **Claude Lemieux**, Mtl., N.J., Col., Phx., Dal., S.J.	1215	21
84. **Marcel Pronovost**, Det., Tor.	1206	21
85. **Brian Leetch**, NYR, Tor., Bos.	1205	18
86. **Keith Tkachuk**, Wpg., Phx., St.L., Atl.	1201	18
* 87. **Owen Nolan**, Que., Col., S.J., Tor., Phx., Cgy., Min.	1200	18
88. **Denis Savard**, Chi., Mtl., T.B.	1196	17
89. **Todd Marchant**, NYR, Edm., CBJ, Ana.	1195	17
90. **Dave Babych**, Wpg., Hfd., Van., Phi., L.A.	1195	19
91. **John MacLean**, N.J., S.J., NYR, Dal.	1194	18
92. **Gilbert Perreault**, Buf.	1191	17
93. **Marc Bergevin**, Chi., NYI, Hfd., T.B., Det., St.L., Pit., Van.	1191	20
94. **Dale Hawerchuk**, Wpg., Buf., St.L., Phi.	1188	16
95. **Brian Bellows**, Min., Mtl., T.B., Ana., Wsh.	1188	17
96. **Kevin Dineen**, Hfd., Phi., Car., Ott., CBJ	1188	19
97. **George Armstrong**, Tor.	1187	21
* 98. **Brian Rolston**, N.J., Col., Bos., Min.	1186	16
99. **Kelly Buchberger**, Edm., Atl., L.A., Phx., Pit.	1182	18
100. **Vyacheslav Kozlov**, Det., Buf., Atl.	1182	18

Top 100 Active Games Played Leaders

Player	Games Played	Seasons
1. **Mike Modano**, Min., Dal., Det.	1499	22
2. **Nicklas Lidstrom**, Det.	1494	19
3. **Roman Hamrlik**, T.B., Edm., NYI, Cgy., Mtl.	1311	18
4. **Alex Kovalev**, NYR, Pit., Mtl., Ott.	1302	18
5. **Jaromir Jagr**, Pit., Wsh., NYR	1273	17
6. **Teemu Selanne**, Wpg., Ana., S.J., Col.	1259	18
7. **Owen Nolan**, Que., Col., S.J., Tor., Phx., Cgy., Min.	1200	18
8. **Brian Rolston**, N.J., Col., Bos., Min.	1186	16
9. **Sean O'Donnell**, L.A., Min., N.J., Bos., Phx., Ana., Phi.	1173	16
10. **Jason Arnott**, Edm., N.J., Dal., Nsh., Wsh.	1172	17
11. **Chris Pronger**, Hfd., St.L., Edm., Ana., Phi.	1154	17
12. **Rob Niedermayer**, Fla., Cgy., Ana., N.J., Buf.	1153	17
13. **Ray Whitney**, S.J., Edm., Fla., CBJ, Det., Car., Phx.	1147	19
14. **Bryan McCabe**, NYI, Van., Chi., Tor., Fla., NYR	1135	15
15. **Martin Brodeur**, N.J.	1132	18
16. **Shane Doan**, Wpg., Phx.	1119	15
17. **Radek Dvorak**, Fla., NYR, Edm., St.L., Atl.	1118	15
18. **Jarome Iginla**, Cgy.	1106	15
19. **Ryan Smyth**, Edm., NYI, Col., L.A.	1069	16
20. **Mike Grier**, Edm., Wsh., Buf., S.J.	1060	14
21. **Sergei Gonchar**, Wsh., Bos., Pit., Ott.	1058	16
22. **Daniel Alfredsson**, Ott.	1056	15
23. **Patrick Marleau**, S.J.	1035	13
24. **Jamie Langenbrunner**, Dal., N.J.	1035	16
25. **Andrew Brunette**, Wsh., Nsh., Atl., Min., Col.	1032	15
26. **Cory Stillman**, Cgy., St.L., T.B., Car., Ott., Fla.	1025	16
27. **Todd Bertuzzi**, NYI, Van., Fla., Det., Ana., Cgy.	1022	15
28. **Ed Jovanovski**, Fla., Van., Phx.	1019	15
29. **Daymond Langkow**, T.B., Phi., Phx., Cgy.	1017	15
30. **Adrian Aucoin**, Van., T.B., NYI, Chi., Cgy., Phx.	1008	16
31. **Joe Thornton**, Bos., S.J.	995	13
32. **Hal Gill**, Bos., Tor., Pit., Mtl.	994	13
33. **Wade Redden**, Ott., NYR	994	13
34. **Dainius Zubrus**, Phi., Mtl., Wsh., Buf., N.J.	983	14
35. **Vinny Prospal**, Phi., Ott., Fla., T.B., Ana., NYR	978	14
36. **Mike Knuble**, Det., NYR, Bos., Phi., Wsh.	968	14
37. **Patrik Elias**, N.J.	961	15
38. **Olli Jokinen**, L.A., NYI, Fla., Phx., Cgy., NYR	960	13
39. **Matt Cullen**, Ana., Fla., Car., NYR, Ott., Min.	958	13
40. **Tomas Holmstrom**, Det.	952	14
41. **Derek Morris**, Cgy., Col., Phx., NYR, Bos.	946	13
42. **Chris Phillips**, Ott.	945	13
43. **Saku Koivu**, Mtl., Ana.	938	15
44. **Steve Staios**, Bos., Van., Atl., Edm., Cgy.	936	15
45. **Vincent Lecavalier**, T.B.	934	12
46. **Zdeno Chara**, NYI, Ott., Bos.	928	13
47. **Craig Rivet**, Mtl., S.J., Buf., CBJ	923	16
48. **Ruslan Salei**, Ana., Fla., Col., Det.	917	14
49. **Milan Hejduk**, Col.	910	12
50. **Mattias Ohlund**, Van., T.B.	909	13
51. **Tomas Kaberle**, Tor., Bos.	902	12
52. **Pavel Kubina**, T.B., Tor., Atl.	901	13
53. **Ethan Moreau**, Chi., Edm., CBJ	900	15
54. **Marian Hossa**, Ott., Atl., Pit., Det., Chi.	897	13
55. **Brendan Morrison**, N.J., Van., Ana., Dal., Wsh., Cgy.	895	13
56. **Kimmo Timonen**, Nsh., Phi.	894	12
57. **Chris Drury**, Col., Cgy., Buf., NYR	892	12
58. **Marco Sturm**, S.J., Bos., L.A., Wsh.	890	13
59. **Steve Sullivan**, N.J., Tor., Chi., Nsh.	890	15
60. **Sergei Samsonov**, Bos., Edm., Mtl., Chi., Car., Fla.	888	13
61. **John Madden**, N.J., Chi., Min.	867	12
62. **Scott Gomez**, N.J., NYR, Mtl.	864	11
63. **Martin St. Louis**, Cgy., T.B.	854	12
64. **Alexei Yashin**, Ott., NYI	850	12
65. **Michal Handzus**, St.L., Phx., Phi., Chi., L.A.	844	12
66. **Jaroslav Spacek**, Fla., Chi., CBJ, Edm., Buf., Mtl.	834	12
67. **Karlis Skrastins**, Nsh., Col., Fla., Dal.	832	12
68. **Scott Hannan**, S.J., Col., Wsh.	830	12
69. **Robyn Regehr**, Cgy.	826	11
70. **Jason Blake**, L.A., NYI, Tor., Ana.	826	12
71. **Cory Sarich**, Buf., T.B., Cgy.	825	12
72. **J.P. Dumont**, Chi., Buf., Nsh.	822	12
73. **Alex Tanguay**, Col., Cgy., Mtl., T.B.	818	11
74. **Jamal Mayers**, St.L., Tor., Cgy., S.J.	815	13
75. **Jassen Cullimore**, Van., Mtl., T.B., Chi., Fla.	812	15
76. **Henrik Sedin**, Van.	810	10
77. **Tom Poti**, Edm., NYR, NYI, Wsh.	808	12
78. **Marc Savard**, NYR, Cgy., Atl., Bos.	807	13
79. **Matt Cooke**, Van., Wsh., Pit.	805	12
80. **Brad Stuart**, S.J., Bos., Cgy., L.A., Det.	795	11
81. **Jeff Halpern**, Wsh., Dal., T.B., L.A., Mtl.	792	11
82. **Daniel Sedin**, Van.	787	10
83. **Manny Malhotra**, NYR, Dal., CBJ, S.J., Van.	777	12
84. **Martin Skoula**, Col., Ana., Dal., Min., Pit., N.J.	776	10
85. **Brad Richards**, T.B., Dal.	772	10
86. **David Legwand**, Nsh.	768	12
87. **Jochen Hecht**, St.L., Edm., Buf.	764	12
88. **Scott Hartnell**, Nsh., Phi.	761	10
89. **Eric Brewer**, NYI, Edm., St.L., T.B.	758	12
90. **Dan Boyle**, Fla., T.B., S.J.	752	12
91. **Brenden Morrow**, Dal.	749	11
92. **Dan Cleary**, Chi., Edm., Phx., Det.	746	13
93. **Ruslan Fedotenko**, Phi., T.B., NYI, Pit., NYR	743	10
94. **Colin White**, N.J.	743	11
95. **Danny Briere**, Phx., Buf., Phi.	743	13
96. **Nikolai Khabibulin**, Phx., T.B., Chi., Edm.	743	15
97. **Toni Lydman**, Cgy., Buf., Ana.	738	10
98. **Paul Mara**, T.B., Phx., Bos., NYR, Mtl., Ana.	734	12
99. **Simon Gagne**, Phi., T.B.	727	11
100. **Stephane Robidas**, Mtl., Dal., Chi.	724	11

Ryan Smyth, who returns to Edmonton in 2011-12 after two seasons in Los Angeles, was one of 11 players to reach 1,000 games played during the 2010-11 season.

Goaltending Records

All-Time Shutout Leaders (Minimum 51 Shutouts)

Goaltender	Team	Shutouts	Games	Seasons
1. *Martin Brodeur (1991-2011)	New Jersey	**116**	1,132	18
2. Terry Sawchuk (1949-1970)	Detroit	85	734	14
	Boston	11	102	2
	Toronto	4	91	3
	Los Angeles	2	36	1
	NY Rangers	1	8	1
	Total	**103**	971	21
3. George Hainsworth (1926-1937)	Montreal	75	318	7½
	Toronto	19	147	3½
	Total	**94**	465	11
4. Glenn Hall (1952-1971)	Detroit	17	148	4
	Chicago	51	618	10
	St. Louis	16	140	4
	Total	**84**	906	18
5. Jacques Plante (1952-1973)	Montreal	58	556	11
	NY Rangers	5	98	2
	St. Louis	10	69	2
	Toronto	7	106	2¾
	Boston	2	8	¼
	Total	**82**	837	18
6. Alec Connell (1924-1937)	Ottawa	64	293	8
	Detroit	6	48	1
	NY Americans	0	1	1
	Mtl. Maroons	11	75	2
	Total	**81**	417	12
7. Tiny Thompson (1928-1940)	Boston	74	468	10¼
	Detroit	7	85	1¾
	Total	**81**	553	12
8. Dominik Hasek (1990-2008)	Chicago	1	25	2
	Buffalo	55	491	9
	Detroit	20	176	4
	Ottawa	5	43	1
	Total	**81**	735	16
9. Tony Esposito (1968-1984)	Montreal	2	13	1
	Chicago	74	873	15
	Total	**76**	886	16
10. Ed Belfour (1988-2007)	Chicago	30	415	7⅔
	San Jose	1	13	⅓
	Dallas	27	307	5
	Toronto	17	170	3
	Florida	1	58	1
	Total	**76**	963	17
11. Lorne Chabot (1926-1937)	NY Rangers	21	80	2
	Toronto	31	214	5
	Montreal	8	47	1
	Chicago	8	48	1
	Mtl. Maroons	2	16	1
	NY Americans	1	6	1
	Total	**71**	411	11
12. Harry Lumley (1943-1960)	Detroit	26	324	6½
	NY Rangers	0	1	½
	Chicago	5	134	2
	Toronto	34	267	4
	Boston	6	78	3
	Total	**71**	804	16
13. Roy Worters (1925-1937)	Pittsburgh Pirates	22	123	3
	NY Americans	45	360	9
	**Montreal	0	1	
	Total	**67**	484	12
14. Patrick Roy (1984-2003)	Montreal	29	551	11½
	Colorado	37	478	7½
	Total	**66**	1,029	19
15. Turk Broda (1936-1952)	Toronto	62	629	14
16. John Ross Roach (1921-1935)	Toronto	13	222	7
	NY Rangers	30	89	4
	Detroit	15	180	3
	Total	**58**	491	14
17. Clint Benedict (1917-1930)	Ottawa	19	158	7
	Mtl. Maroons	38	204	6
	Total	**57**	362	13
18. *Roberto Luongo (1999-2011)	NY Islanders	1	24	1
	Florida	26	317	5
	Vancouver	28	331	5
	Total	**55**	672	11
19. Bernie Parent (1965-1979)	Boston	1	57	2
	Philadelphia	50	486	9½
	Toronto	3	65	1½
	Total	**54**	608	13
20. Ed Giacomin (1965-1978)	NY Rangers	49	539	10¼
	Detroit	5	71	2¾
	Total	**54**	610	13
21. Dave Kerr (1930-1941)	Mtl. Maroons	11	101	3
	NY Americans	0	1	1
	NY Rangers	40	324	7
	Total	**51**	426	11
22. Rogie Vachon (1966-1982)	Montreal	13	206	5¼
	Los Angeles	32	389	6¾
	Detroit	4	109	2
	Boston	2	91	2
	Total	**51**	795	16
23. Curtis Joseph (1989-2009)	St. Louis	5	280	6
	Edmonton	14	177	3
	Toronto	17	270	5
	Detroit	7	92	2
	Phoenix	8	115	2
	Calgary	0	9	1
	Total	**51**	943	19

* Active goalie
** Played 1 game for Montreal in 1929-30.

Ten or More Shutouts, One Season

Number of Shutouts	Goaltender	Team	Season	Length of Schedule
22	George Hainsworth	Montreal	1928-29	44
15	Alec Connell	Ottawa	1925-26	36
	Alec Connell	Ottawa	1927-28	44
	Hal Winkler	Boston	1927-28	44
	Tony Esposito	Chicago	1969-70	76
14	George Hainsworth	Montreal	1926-27	44
13	Clint Benedict	Mtl. Maroons	1926-27	44
	Alec Connell	Ottawa	1926-27	44
	George Hainsworth	Montreal	1927-28	44
	John Ross Roach	NY Rangers	1928-29	44
	Roy Worters	NY Americans	1928-29	44
	Harry Lumley	Toronto	1953-54	70
	Dominik Hasek	Buffalo	1997-98	82
12	Tiny Thompson	Boston	1928-29	44
	Charlie Gardiner	Chicago	1930-31	44
	Terry Sawchuk	Detroit	1951-52	70
	Terry Sawchuk	Detroit	1953-54	70
	Terry Sawchuk	Detroit	1954-55	70
	Glenn Hall	Detroit	1955-56	70
	Bernie Parent	Philadelphia	1973-74	78
	Bernie Parent	Philadelphia	1974-75	80
	Martin Brodeur	New Jersey	2006-07	82
11	Lorne Chabot	NY Rangers	1927-28	44
	Hap Holmes	Detroit	1927-28	44
	Roy Worters	Pittsburgh Pirates	1927-28	44
	Clint Benedict	Mtl. Maroons	1928-29	44
	Joe Miller	Pittsburgh Pirates	1928-29	44
	Tiny Thompson	Boston	1932-33	48
	Terry Sawchuk	Detroit	1950-51	70
	Dominik Hasek	Buffalo	2000-01	82
	Martin Brodeur	New Jersey	2003-04	82
	Henrik Lundqvist	NY Rangers	**2010-11**	82
10	Lorne Chabot	NY Rangers	1926-27	44
	Lorne Chabot	Toronto	1928-29	44
	Dolly Dolson	Detroit	1928-29	44
	John Ross Roach	Detroit	1932-33	48
	Charlie Gardiner	Chicago	1933-34	48
	Tiny Thompson	Boston	1935-36	48
	Frank Brimsek	Boston	1938-39	48
	Bill Durnan	Montreal	1948-49	60
	Harry Lumley	Toronto	1952-53	70
	Gerry McNeil	Montreal	1952-53	70
	Tony Esposito	Chicago	1973-74	78
	Ken Dryden	Montreal	1976-77	80
	Martin Brodeur	New Jersey	1996-97	82
	Martin Brodeur	New Jersey	1997-98	82
	Byron Dafoe	Boston	1998-99	82
	Roman Cechmanek	Philadelphia	2000-01	82
	Ed Belfour	Toronto	2003-04	82
	Miikka Kiprusoff	Calgary	2005-06	82
	Henrik Lundqvist	NY Rangers	2007-08	82
	Steve Mason	Columbus	2008-09	82

All-Time Win Leaders

(Minimum 260 Wins)

	Goaltender	Wins	GP	Dec.	Losses	OT/Ties
1.	* Martin Brodeur	625	1132	1112	350	137
2.	Patrick Roy	551	1029	997	315	131
3.	Ed Belfour	484	963	929	320	125
4.	Curtis Joseph	454	943	902	352	96
5.	Terry Sawchuk	447	971	949	330	172
6.	Jacques Plante	437	837	829	247	145
7.	Tony Esposito	423	886	880	306	151
8.	Glenn Hall	407	906	896	326	163
9.	Grant Fuhr	403	868	812	295	114
10.	Chris Osgood	401	744	712	216	95
11.	Dominik Hasek	389	735	707	223	95
12.	Mike Vernon	385	781	750	273	92
13.	John Vanbiesbrouck	374	882	839	346	119
14.	Andy Moog	372	713	669	209	88
15.	Tom Barrasso	369	777	732	277	86
16.	Rogie Vachon	355	795	773	291	127
17.	Gump Worsley	335	861	837	352	150
18.	Harry Lumley	330	803	801	329	142
19.	Sean Burke	324	820	775	341	110
20.	* Nikolai Khabibulin	316	747	712	308	88
21.	* Roberto Luongo	308	672	652	279	75
22.	Billy Smith	305	680	643	233	105
23.	Olaf Kolzig	303	719	687	297	87
24.	Turk Broda	302	629	627	224	101
25.	Mike Richter	301	666	632	258	73
26.	Ron Hextall	296	608	579	214	69
27.	Mike Liut	294	664	639	271	74
28.	* Evgeni Nabokov	293	563	537	178	66
29.	Ed Giacomin	289	609	594	208	97
30.	Dan Bouchard	286	655	631	232	113
31.	Tiny Thompson	284	553	553	194	75
32.	* Miikka Kiprusoff	276	529	511	177	58
33.	* Marty Turco	273	538	504	165	66
34.	Bernie Parent	271	608	590	198	121
35.	Kelly Hrudey	271	677	624	265	88
36.	Gilles Meloche	270	788	752	351	131
37.	Don Beaupre	268	667	620	277	75
38.	Felix Potvin	266	635	611	260	85
39.	* Tomas Vokoun	262	632	605	267	76
40.	* Jose Theodore	260	550	547	232	55

* active player

Active Shutout Leaders

(Minimum 30 Shutouts)

	Goaltender	Teams	Shutouts	Games	Seasons
1.	Martin Brodeur	New Jersey	116	1,132	18
2.	Roberto Luongo	NYI, Fla., Van.	55	672	11
3.	Evgeni Nabokov	San Jose	50	563	10
4.	Tomas Vokoun	Mtl., Nsh., Fla.	44	632	13
5.	Nikolai Khabibulin	Wpg., Phx., T.B., Chi., Edm.	43	743	15
6.	Marty Turco	Dallas, Chicago	41	538	10
7.	Miikka Kiprusoff	San Jose, Calgary	40	529	10
8.	Henrik Lundqvist	NY Rangers	35	406	6
9.	Patrick Lalime	Pit., Ott., St.L., Chi., Buf.	35	444	12
10.	Jean-Sebastien Giguere	Hfd., Cgy., Ana., Tor.	34	525	13
11.	Jose Theodore	Mtl., Col., Wsh., Min.	30	580	14

All-Time Penalty-Minute Leaders

(Regular season. Minimum 2,900 minutes)

	Player, Teams	Penalty Mins.	Games	Mins. per game	Seasons
1.	**Tiger Williams**, Tor., Van., Det., L.A., Hfd.	3966	962	4.12	14
2.	**Dale Hunter**, Que., Wsh., Col.	3565	1407	2.53	19
3.	**Tie Domi**, Tor., NYR, Wpg.	3515	1020	3.45	16
4.	**Marty McSorley**, Pit., Edm., L.A., NYR, S.J., Bos.	3381	961	3.52	17
5.	**Bob Probert**, Det., Chi.	3300	935	3.53	16
6.	**Rob Ray**, Buf., Ott.	3207	900	3.56	15
7.	**Craig Berube**, Phi., Tor., Cgy., Wsh., NYI	3149	1054	2.99	17
8.	**Tim Hunter**, Cgy., Que., Van., S.J.	3146	815	3.86	16
9.	**Chris Nilan**, Mtl., NYR, Bos.	3043	688	4.42	13
10.	**Rick Tocchet**, Phi., Pit., L.A., Bos., Wsh., Phx.	2972	1144	2.60	18
11.	**Pat Verbeek**, N.J., Hfd., NYR, Dal., Det.	2905	1424	2.04	20

Goals-Against Average Leaders (Minimum 25 games played)

(Exceptions: Minimum 13 games played, 1994-95; minimum 26 games played, 1992-93 to 1993-94; minimum 15 games played, 1917-18 to 1925-26)

Season	Goaltender, Team	GP	Mins.	GA	SO	AVG.
2010-11	Tim Thomas, Boston	57	3,634	112	9	2.00
2009-10	Tuukka Rask, Boston	45	2,562	84	5	1.97
2008-09	Tim Thomas, Boston	54	3,259	114	5	2.10
2007-08	Chris Osgood, Detroit	43	2,409	84	4	2.09
2006-07	Niklas Backstrom, Minnesota	41	2,227	73	5	1.97
2005-06	Miikka Kiprusoff, Calgary	74	4,380	151	10	2.07
2003-04	Miikka Kiprusoff, Calgary	38	2,301	65	4	1.69
2002-03	Marty Turco, Dallas	55	3,203	92	7	1.72
2001-02	Patrick Roy, Colorado	63	3,773	122	9	1.94
2000-01	Marty Turco, Dallas	26	1,266	40	3	1.90
99-2000	Brian Boucher, Philadelphia	35	2,038	65	4	1.91
1998-99	Ron Tugnutt, Ottawa	43	2,508	75	3	1.79
1997-98	Ed Belfour, Dallas	61	3,581	112	9	1.88
1996-97	Martin Brodeur, New Jersey	67	3,838	120	10	1.88
1995-96	Ron Hextall, Philadelphia	53	3,102	112	4	2.17
1994-95	Dominik Hasek, Buffalo	41	2,416	85	5	2.11
1993-94	Dominik Hasek, Buffalo	58	3,358	109	7	1.95
1992-93	Felix Potvin, Toronto	48	2,781	116	2	2.50
1991-92	Patrick Roy, Montreal	67	3,935	155	5	2.36
1990-91	Ed Belfour, Chicago	74	4,127	170	4	2.47
1989-90	Mike Liut, Hartford, Washington	37	2,161	91	4	2.53
1988-89	Patrick Roy, Montreal	48	2,744	113	4	2.47
1987-88	Pete Peeters, Washington	35	1,896	88	2	2.78
1986-87	Brian Hayward, Montreal	37	2,178	102	1	2.81
1985-86	Bob Froese, Philadelphia	51	2,728	116	5	2.55
1984-85	Tom Barrasso, Buffalo	54	3,248	144	5	2.66
1983-84	Pat Riggin, Washington	41	2,299	102	4	2.66
1982-83	Pete Peeters, Boston	62	3,611	142	8	2.36
1981-82	Denis Herron, Montreal	27	1,547	68	3	2.64
1980-81	Richard Sevigny, Montreal	33	1,777	71	2	2.40
1979-80	Bob Sauve, Buffalo	32	1,880	74	4	2.36
1978-79	Ken Dryden, Montreal	47	2,814	108	5	2.30
1977-78	Ken Dryden, Montreal	52	3,071	105	5	2.05
1976-77	Michel Larocque, Montreal	26	1,525	53	4	2.09
1975-76	Ken Dryden, Montreal	62	3,580	121	8	2.03
1974-75	Bernie Parent, Philadelphia	68	4,041	137	12	2.03
1973-74	Bernie Parent, Philadelphia	73	4,314	136	12	1.89
1972-73	Ken Dryden, Montreal	54	3,165	119	6	2.26
1971-72	Tony Esposito, Chicago	48	2,780	82	9	1.77
1970-71	Jacques Plante, Toronto	40	2,329	73	4	1.88
1969-70	Ernie Wakely, St. Louis	30	1,651	58	4	2.11
1968-69	Jacques Plante, St. Louis	37	2,139	70	5	1.96
1967-68	Gump Worsley, Montreal	40	2,213	73	6	1.98
1966-67	Glenn Hall, Chicago	32	1,664	66	2	2.38
1965-66	Johnny Bower, Toronto	35	1,998	75	3	2.25
1964-65	Johnny Bower, Toronto	34	2,040	81	3	2.38
1963-64	Johnny Bower, Toronto	51	3,009	106	5	2.11
1962-63	Don Simmons, Toronto	28	1,680	69	1	2.46
1961-62	Jacques Plante, Montreal	70	4,200	166	4	2.37
1960-61	Charlie Hodge, Montreal	30	1,800	74	4	2.47
1959-60	Jacques Plante, Montreal	69	4,140	175	3	2.54
1958-59	Jacques Plante, Montreal	67	4,000	144	9	2.16
1957-58	Jacques Plante, Montreal	57	3,386	119	9	2.11
1956-57	Jacques Plante, Montreal	61	3,660	122	9	2.00
1955-56	Jacques Plante, Montreal	64	3,840	119	7	1.86
1954-55	Harry Lumley, Toronto	69	4,140	134	8	1.94
1953-54	Harry Lumley, Toronto	69	4,140	128	13	1.86
1952-53	Terry Sawchuk, Detroit	63	3,780	120	9	1.90
1951-52	Terry Sawchuk, Detroit	70	4,200	133	12	1.90
1950-51	Al Rollins, Toronto	40	2,367	70	5	1.77
1949-50	Bill Durnan, Montreal	64	3,840	141	8	2.20
1948-49	Bill Durnan, Montreal	60	3,600	126	10	2.10
1947-48	Turk Broda, Toronto	60	3,600	143	5	2.38
1946-47	Bill Durnan, Montreal	60	3,600	138	4	2.30
1945-46	Bill Durnan, Montreal	40	2,400	104	4	2.60
1944-45	Bill Durnan, Montreal	50	3,000	121	1	2.42
1943-44	Bill Durnan, Montreal	50	3,000	109	2	2.18
1942-43	Johnny Mowers, Detroit	50	3,010	124	6	2.47
1941-42	Frank Brimsek, Boston	47	2,930	115	3	2.35
1940-41	Turk Broda, Toronto	48	2,970	99	5	2.00
1939-40	Dave Kerr, NY Rangers	48	3,000	77	8	1.54
1938-39	Frank Brimsek, Boston	43	2,610	68	10	1.56
1937-38	Tiny Thompson, Boston	48	2,970	89	7	1.80
1936-37	Normie Smith, Detroit	48	2,980	102	6	2.05
1935-36	Tiny Thompson, Boston	48	2,930	82	10	1.68
1934-35	Lorne Chabot, Chicago	48	2,940	88	8	1.80
1933-34	Wilf Cude, Detroit, Montreal	30	1,920	47	5	1.47
1932-33	Tiny Thompson, Boston	48	3,000	88	11	1.76
1931-32	Charlie Gardiner, Chicago	48	2,989	92	4	1.85
1930-31	Roy Worters, NY Americans	44	2,760	74	8	1.61
1929-30	Tiny Thompson, Boston	44	2,680	98	3	2.19
1928-29	George Hainsworth, Montreal	44	2,800	43	22	0.92
1927-28	George Hainsworth, Montreal	44	2,730	48	13	1.05
1926-27	Clint Benedict, Mtl. Maroons	43	2,748	65	13	1.42
1925-26	Alec Connell, Ottawa	36	2,251	42	15	1.12
1924-25	Georges Vezina, Montreal	30	1,860	56	5	1.81
1923-24	Georges Vezina, Montreal	24	1,459	48	3	1.97
1922-23	Clint Benedict, Ottawa	24	1,478	54	4	2.18
1921-22	Clint Benedict, Ottawa	24	1,508	84	2	3.34
1920-21	Clint Benedict, Ottawa	24	1,457	75	2	3.09
1919-20	Clint Benedict, Ottawa	24	1,444	64	5	2.66
1918-19	Clint Benedict, Ottawa	18	1,113	53	2	2.86
1917-18	Georges Vezina, Montreal	21	1,282	84	1	3.93

All-Time Regular-Season NHL Coaching Register

Regular Season, 1917-2011

Coach	Team	Games Coached	Wins	Losses	O/T	Years	Cup Wins	Career
Abel, Sid	Chicago	140	39	79	22	2		
	Detroit	811	340	339	132	12		
	St. Louis	10	3	6	1	1		
	Kansas City	3	0	3	0	1		
	Totals	964	382	427	155	16		1952-76
Adams, Jack	Detroit	964	413	390	161	20	3	1927-47
Agnew, Gary	Columbus	5	0	4	1	1		2006-07
Allen, Keith	Philadelphia	150	51	67	32	2		1967-69
Allison, Dave	Ottawa	25	2	22	1	1		1995-96
Anderson, Jim	Washington	54	4	45	5	1		1974-75
Anderson, John	Atlanta	164	70	75	19	2		2008-10
Angotti, Lou	St. Louis	32	6	20	6	2		
	Pittsburgh	80	16	58	6	1		
	Totals	112	22	78	12	3		1973-84
Arbour, Al	St. Louis	107	42	40	25	3		
	NY Islanders	1500	740	537	223	20	4	
	Totals	1607	782	577	248	23	4	1970-08
Armstrong, George	Toronto	47	17	26	4	1		1988-89
Arniel, Scott	Columbus	82	34	35	13	1		2010-11
Babcock, Mike	Anaheim	164	69	62	33	3		
	Detroit	492	304	126	62	6	1	
	Totals	656	373	188	95	9	1	2002-11
Barber, Bill	Philadelphia	136	73	40	23	2		2000-02
Barkley, Doug	Detroit	77	20	46	11	3		1970-76
Beaulieu, Andre	Minnesota	32	6	23	3	1		1977-78
Belisle, Danny	Washington	96	28	51	17	2		1978-80
Berenson, Red	St. Louis	204	100	72	32	3		1979-82
Bergeron, Michel	Quebec	634	265	283	86	8		
	NY Rangers	158	73	67	18	2		
	Totals	792	338	350	104	10		1980-90
Berry, Bob	Los Angeles	240	107	94	39	3		
	Montreal	223	116	71	36	3		
	Pittsburgh	240	88	127	25	3		
	St. Louis	157	73	63	21	2		
	Totals	860	384	355	121	11		1978-94
Beverley, Nick	Toronto	17	9	6	2	1		1995-96
Blackburn, Don	Hartford	140	42	63	35	2		1979-81
Blair, Wren	Minnesota	147	48	65	34	3		1967-70
Blake, Toe	Montreal	914	500	255	159	13	8	1955-68
Boileau, Marc	Pittsburgh	151	66	61	24	3		1973-76
Boivin, Leo	St. Louis	97	28	53	16	2		1975-78
Boucher, Frank	NY Rangers	527	181	263	83	11	1	1939-54
Boucher, Georges	Mtl. Maroons	12	6	5	1	1		
	Ottawa	48	13	29	6	1		
	St. Louis	35	9	20	6	1		
	Boston	70	22	32	16	1		
	Totals	165	50	86	29	4		1930-50
Boucher, Guy	Tampa Bay	82	46	25	11	1		2010-11
Boudreau, Bruce	Washington	307	189	79	39	4		2007-11
Bowman, Scotty	St. Louis	238	110	83	45	4		
	Montreal	634	419	110	105	8	5	
	Buffalo	404	210	134	60	7		
	Pittsburgh	164	95	53	16	2	1	
	Detroit	701	410	193	98	9	3	
	Totals	2141	1244	573	324	30	9	1967-02
Bowness, Rick	Winnipeg	28	8	17	3	1		
	Boston	80	36	32	12	1		
	Ottawa	235	39	178	18	4		
	NY Islanders	100	38	50	12	2		
	Phoenix	20	2	12	6	2		
	Totals	463	123	289	51	10		1988-05
Brooks, Herb	NY Rangers	285	131	113	41	4		
	Minnesota	80	19	48	13	1		
	New Jersey	84	40	37	7	1		
	Pittsburgh	57	29	21	7	1		
	Totals	506	219	219	68	7		1981-00
Brophy, John	Toronto	193	64	111	18	3		1986-89
Burnett, George	Edmonton	35	12	20	3	1		1994-95
Burns, Charlie	Minnesota	86	22	50	14	2		1969-75
Burns, Pat	Montreal	320	174	104	42	4		
	Toronto	281	133	107	41	4		
	Boston	254	105	97	52	4		
	New Jersey	164	89	45	30	3	1	
	Totals	1019	501	353	165	15	1	1988-05
Bush, Eddie	Kansas City	32	1	23	8	1		1975-76
Bylsma, Dan	Pittsburgh	189	114	56	19	3	1	2008-11
Campbell, Colin	NY Rangers	269	118	108	43	4		1994-98
Capuano, Jack	NY Islanders	65	26	29	10	1		2010-11
Carbonneau, Guy	Montreal	230	124	83	23	3		2006-09
Carlyle, Randy	Anaheim	492	266	169	57	6	1	2005-11
Carpenter, Doug	New Jersey	290	100	166	24	4		
	Toronto	91	39	47	5	2		
	Totals	381	139	213	29	6		1984-91
Carroll, Dick	Toronto	40	18	22	0	2	1	1917-19
Carroll, Frank	Toronto	24	15	9	0	1		1920-21
Cashman, Wayne	Philadelphia	61	32	20	9	1		1997-98
Cassidy, Bruce	Washington	110	47	47	16	2		2002-04
Chambers, Dave	Quebec	98	19	64	15	2		1990-92
Chapman, Art	NY Americans	48	8	29	11	1		
	Brooklyn	48	16	29	3	1		
	Totals	96	24	58	14	2		1940-42
Charron, Guy	Calgary	16	6	7	3	1		
	Anaheim	49	14	26	9	1		
	Totals	65	20	33	12	2		1991-01
Cheevers, Gerry	Boston	376	204	126	46	5		1980-85
Cherry, Don	Boston	400	231	105	64	5		
	Colorado	80	19	48	13	1		
	Totals	480	250	153	77	6		1974-80
Clancy, King	Mtl. Maroons	18	6	11	1	1		
	Toronto	210	80	81	49	3		
	Totals	228	86	92	50	4		1937-56
Clapper, Dit	Boston	230	102	88	40	4		1945-49
Cleghorn, Odie	Pittsburgh	168	62	86	20	4		1925-29
Cleghorn, Sprague	Mtl. Maroons	48	19	22	7	1		1931-32
Clouston, Cory	Ottawa	198	95	83	20	3		2008-11
Colville, Neil	NY Rangers	93	26	41	26	2		1950-52
Conacher, Charlie	Chicago	162	56	84	22	3		1947-50
Conacher, Lionel	NY Americans	44	14	25	5	1		1929-30
Constantine, Kevin	San Jose	157	55	78	24	3		
	Pittsburgh	189	86	64	39	3		
	New Jersey	31	20	8	3	1		
	Totals	377	161	150	66	7		1993-02
Cook, Bill	NY Rangers	117	34	59	24	2		1951-53
Crawford, Marc	Quebec	48	30	13	5	1		
	Colorado	246	135	75	36	3	1	
	Vancouver	529	246	189	94	8		
	Los Angeles	164	59	84	21	2		
	Dallas	164	79	60	25	2		
	Totals	1151	549	421	181	16	1	1994-11
Creamer, Pierre	Pittsburgh	80	36	35	9	1		1987-88
Creighton, Fred	Atlanta	348	156	136	56	5		
	Boston	73	40	20	13	1		
	Totals	421	196	156	69	6		1974-80
Crisp, Terry	Calgary	240	144	63	33	3	1	
	Tampa Bay	391	142	204	45	6		
	Totals	631	286	267	78	9	1	1987-98
Crozier, Joe	Buffalo	192	77	80	35	3		
	Toronto	40	13	22	5	1		
	Totals	232	90	102	40	4		1971-81
Crozier, Roger	Washington	1	0	1	0	1		1981-82
Cunniff, John	Hartford	13	3	9	1	1		
	New Jersey	133	59	56	18	2		
	Totals	146	62	65	19	3		1982-91
Curry, Alex	Ottawa	36	24	8	4	1		1925-26
Dandurand, Leo	Montreal	163	78	76	9	6	1	1921-35
Day, Hap	Toronto	546	259	206	81	10	5	1940-50
Dea, Billy	Detroit	11	3	8	0	1		1981-82
DeBoer, Peter	Florida	246	103	107	36	3		2008-11
Delvecchio, Alex	Detroit	245	82	131	32	4		1973-77
Demers, Jacques	Quebec	80	25	44	11	1		
	St. Louis	240	106	106	28	3		
	Detroit	320	137	136	47	4		
	Montreal	220	107	86	27	4	1	
	Tampa Bay	147	34	96	17	2		
	Totals	1007	409	468	130	14	1	1979-99
Denneny, Cy	Boston	44	26	13	5	1	1	
	Ottawa	48	11	27	10	1		
	Totals	92	37	40	15	2	1	1928-33
Dineen, Bill	Philadelphia	140	60	60	20	2		1991-93
Dudley, Rick	Buffalo	188	85	72	31	3		
	Florida	40	13	15	12	1		
	Totals	228	98	87	43	4		1989-04
Duff, Dick	Toronto	2	0	2	0	1		1979-80
Dugal, Jules	Montreal	18	9	6	3	1		1938-39
Duncan, Art	Detroit	33	10	21	2	1		
	Toronto	47	21	16	10	2		
	Totals	80	31	37	12	3		1926-32
Dutton, Red	NY Americans	192	66	97	29	4		1936-40
Eddolls, Frank	Chicago	70	13	40	17	1		1954-55
Esposito, Phil	NY Rangers	45	24	21	0	2		1986-89
Evans, Jack	California	80	27	42	11	1		
	Cleveland	160	47	87	26	2		
	Hartford	374	163	174	37	5		
	Totals	614	237	303	74	8		1975-88
Fashoway, Gordie	Oakland	10	4	5	1	1		1967-68
Ferguson, John	NY Rangers	121	43	59	19	2		
	Winnipeg	14	7	6	1	1		
	Totals	135	50	65	20	3		1975-86
Filion, Maurice	Quebec	6	1	3	2	1		1980-81
Francis, Bob	Phoenix	390	165	144	81	5		1999-04
Francis, Emile	NY Rangers	654	342	209	103	10		
	St. Louis	124	46	64	14	3		
	Totals	778	388	273	117	13		1965-83
Fraser, Curt	Atlanta	279	64	169	46	4		1999-03
Fredrickson, Frank	Pittsburgh	44	5	36	3	1		1929-30
Ftorek, Robbie	Los Angeles	132	65	56	11	2		
	New Jersey	156	88	44	24	2		
	Boston	155	76	52	27	2		
	Totals	443	229	152	62	6		1987-03
Gadsby, Bill	Detroit	78	35	31	12	2		1968-70

Coach	Team	Games Coached	Wins	Losses	O/T	Years	Cup Wins	Career
Gainey, Bob	Minnesota	244	95	119	30	3		
	Dallas	171	70	71	30	3		
	Montreal	57	29	21	7	2		
	Totals	472	194	211	67	8		1990-09
Gallant, Gerard	Columbus	142	56	76	10	4		2003-07
Gardiner, Herb	Chicago	32	5	23	4	1		1928-29
Gardner, Jimmy	Hamilton	30	19	10	1	1		1924-25
Garvin, Ted	Detroit	11	2	8	1	1		1973-74
Geoffrion, Bernie	NY Rangers	43	22	18	3	1		
	Atlanta	208	77	92	39	3		
	Montreal	30	15	9	6	1		
	Totals	281	114	119	48	5		1968-80
Gerard, Eddie	Ottawa	22	9	13	0	1		
	Mtl. Maroons	294	129	122	43	7	1	
	NY Americans	92	34	40	18	2		
	St. Louis	13	2	11	0	1		
	Totals	421	174	186	61	11	1	1917-35
Gilbert, Greg	Calgary	121	42	56	23	3		2000-03
Gill, David	Ottawa	132	64	41	27	3	1	1926-29
Glover, Fred	Oakland	152	51	76	25	2		
	California	204	45	131	28	4		
	Los Angeles	68	18	42	8	1		
	Totals	424	114	249	61	6		1968-74
Goodfellow, Ebbie	Chicago	140	30	91	19	2		1950-52
Gordon, Jackie	Minnesota	289	116	123	50	5		1970-75
Gordon, Scott	NY Islanders	181	64	94	23	3		2008-11
Goring, Butch	Boston	93	42	38	13	2		
	NY Islanders	147	41	88	18	2		
	Totals	240	83	126	31	4		1985-01
Gorman, Tommy	NY Americans	80	31	33	16	2		
	Chicago	73	28	28	17	2	1	
	Mtl. Maroons	174	74	71	29	4	1	
	Totals	327	133	132	62	8	2	1925-38
Gottselig, Johnny	Chicago	187	62	105	20	4		1944-48
Goyette, Phil	NY Islanders	48	6	38	4	1		1972-73
Graham, Dirk	Chicago	59	16	35	8	1		1998-99
Granato, Tony	Colorado	215	104	78	33	3		2002-09
Green, Gary	Washington	157	50	78	29	3		1979-82
Green, Pete	Ottawa	150	94	52	4	6	3	1919-25
Green, Shorty	NY Americans	44	11	27	6	1		1927-28
Green, Ted	Edmonton	188	65	102	21	3		1991-94
Gretzky, Wayne	Phoenix	328	143	161	24	4		2005-09
Guidolin, Aldo	Colorado	59	12	39	8	1		1978-79
Guidolin, Bep	Boston	104	72	23	9	2		
	Kansas City	125	26	84	15	2		
	Totals	229	98	107	24	4		1972-76
Hanlon, Glen	Washington	239	78	122	39	5		2003-08
Harkness, Ned	Detroit	38	12	22	4	1		1970-71
Harris, Ted	Minnesota	179	48	104	27	3		1975-78
Hart, Cecil	Montreal	394	196	125	73	9	2	1926-39
Hartley, Bob	Colorado	359	193	108	58	5	1	
	Atlanta	291	136	118	37	6		
	Totals	650	329	226	95	10	1	1998-08
Hartsburg, Craig	Chicago	246	104	102	40	3		
	Anaheim	197	80	82	35	3		
	Ottawa	48	17	24	7	1		
	Totals	491	201	208	82	7		1995-09
Harvey, Doug	NY Rangers	70	26	32	12	1		1961-62
Hay, Don	Phoenix	82	38	37	7	1		
	Calgary	68	23	28	17	1		
	Totals	150	61	65	24	2		1996-01
Heffernan, Frank	Toronto	12	5	7	0	1		1919-20
Helmer, Rosie	NY Americans	48	16	25	7	1		1935-36
Henning, Lorne	Minnesota	158	68	72	18	2		
	NY Islanders	65	19	39	7	2		
	Totals	223	87	111	25	4		1985-01
Hitchcock, Ken	Dallas	503	277	154	72	7	1	
	Philadelphia	254	131	73	50	5		
	Columbus	284	125	123	36	4		
	Totals	1041	533	350	158	15	1	1995-10
Hlinka, Ivan	Pittsburgh	86	42	32	12	2		2000-02
Holmgren, Paul	Philadelphia	264	107	126	31	4		
	Hartford	161	54	93	14	4		
	Totals	425	161	219	45	8		1988-96
Howell, Harry	Minnesota	11	3	6	2	1		1978-79
Imlach, Punch	Toronto	770	370	275	125	12	4	
	Buffalo	119	32	62	25	2		
	Totals	889	402	337	150	14	4	1958-80
Ingarfield, Earl	NY Islanders	30	6	22	2	1		1972-73
Inglis, Bill	Buffalo	56	28	18	10	1		1978-79
Irvin, Dick	Chicago	126	45	62	19	3		
	Toronto	427	216	152	59	9	1	
	Montreal	896	431	313	152	15	3	
	Totals	1449	692	527	230	27	4	1928-56
Ivan, Tommy	Detroit	470	262	118	90	7	3	
	Chicago	103	26	56	21	2		
	Totals	573	288	174	111	9	3	1947-58
Iverson, Emil	Chicago	21	8	7	6	1		1932-33
Johnson, Bob	Calgary	400	193	155	52	5		
	Pittsburgh	80	41	33	6	1	1	
	Totals	480	234	188	58	6	1	1982-91
Johnson, Tom	Boston	208	142	43	23	3	1	1970-73
Johnston, Eddie	Chicago	80	34	27	19	1		
	Pittsburgh	516	232	224	60	7		
	Totals	596	266	251	79	8		1979-97

Coach	Team	Games Coached	Wins	Losses	O/T	Years	Cup Wins	Career
Johnston, Marshall	California	69	13	45	11	2		
	Colorado	56	15	32	9	1		
	Totals	125	28	77	20	3		1973-82
Julien, Claude	Montreal	159	72	62	25	4		
	New Jersey	79	47	24	8	1		
	Boston	328	179	103	55	4	1	
	Totals	566	298	189	88	9	1	2002-11
Kasper, Steve	Boston	164	66	78	20	2		1995-97
Keats, Duke	Detroit	11	2	7	2	1		1926-27
Keenan, Mike	Philadelphia	320	190	102	28	4		
	Chicago	320	153	126	41	4		
	NY Rangers	84	52	24	8	1	1	
	St. Louis	163	75	66	22	3		
	Vancouver	108	36	54	18	2		
	Boston	74	33	26	15	1		
	Florida	153	45	73	35	3		
	Calgary	164	88	60	16	2		
	Totals	1386	672	531	183	20	1	1984-09
Kehoe, Rick	Pittsburgh	160	55	81	22	2		2001-03
Kelly, Pat	Colorado	101	22	54	25	2		1977-79
Kelly, Red	Los Angeles	150	55	75	20	2		
	Pittsburgh	274	90	132	52	4		
	Toronto	318	133	123	62	4		
	Totals	742	278	330	134	10		1967-77
King, Dave	Calgary	216	109	76	31	3		
	Columbus	204	64	106	34	3		
	Totals	420	173	182	65	6		1992-03
Kingston, George	San Jose	164	28	129	7	2		1991-93
Kish, Larry	Hartford	49	12	32	5	1		1982-83
Kitchen, Mike	St. Louis	131	38	70	23	4		2003-07
Kromm, Bobby	Detroit	231	79	111	41	3		1977-80
Kurtenbach, Orland	Vancouver	125	36	62	27	2		1976-78
LaForge, Bill	Vancouver	20	4	14	2	1		1984-85
Lalonde, Newsy	Montreal	207	96	97	14	8		
	NY Americans	44	17	25	2	1		
	Ottawa	88	31	45	12	2		
	Totals	339	144	167	28	11		1917-35
Lamoriello, Lou	New Jersey	53	34	14	5	2		2005-07
Laperriere, Jacques	Montreal	1	0	1	0	1		1995-96
Lapointe, Ron	Quebec	89	33	50	6	2		1987-89
Laviolette, Peter	NY Islanders	164	77	62	25	2		
	Carolina	323	167	122	34	6	1	
	Philadelphia	139	75	47	17	2		
	Totals	626	319	231	76	10	1	2001-11
Laycoe, Hal	Los Angeles	24	5	18	1	1		
	Vancouver	156	44	96	16	2		
	Totals	180	49	114	17	3		1969-72
Lehman, Hugh	Chicago	21	3	17	1	1		1927-28
Lemaire, Jacques	Montreal	97	48	37	12	2		
	New Jersey	509	276	166	67	7	1	
	Minnesota	656	293	255	108	9		
	Totals	1262	617	458	187	18	1	1983-11
Lepine, Pit	Montreal	48	10	33	5	1		1939-40
LeSueur, Percy	Hamilton	10	3	7	0	1		1923-24
Lewis, Dave	Detroit *	169	100	42	27	4		
	Boston	82	35	41	6	1		
	Totals	251	135	83	33	5		1998-07

* Shared a record of 4-1-0 with co-coach Barry Smith in 1998-99

Coach	Team	Games Coached	Wins	Losses	O/T	Years	Cup Wins	Career
Ley, Rick	Hartford	160	69	71	20	2		
	Vancouver	124	47	50	27	2		
	Totals	284	116	121	47	4		1989-96
Lindsay, Ted	Detroit	29	5	21	3	2		1979-81
Long, Barry	Winnipeg	205	87	93	25	3		1983-86
Loughlin, Clem	Chicago	144	61	63	20	3		1934-37
Low, Ron	Edmonton	341	139	162	40	5		
	NY Rangers	164	69	81	14	2		
	Totals	505	208	243	54	7		1994-02
Lowe, Kevin	Edmonton	82	32	26	24	1		1999-00
Ludzik, Steve	Tampa Bay	121	31	67	23	2		1999-01
MacDonald, Parker	Minnesota	61	20	30	11	1		
	Los Angeles	42	13	24	5	1		
	Totals	103	33	54	16	2		1973-82
MacLean, Doug	Florida	187	83	71	33	3		
	Columbus	79	24	43	12	2		
	Totals	266	107	114	45	5		1995-04
MacLean, John	New Jersey	33	9	22	2	1		2010-11
MacMillan, Bill	Colorado	80	22	45	13	1		
	New Jersey	100	19	67	14	2		
	Totals	180	41	112	27	3		1980-84
MacNeil, Al	Montreal	55	31	15	9	1		
	Atlanta	80	35	32	13	1		
	Calgary	171	72	66	33	3		
	Totals	306	138	113	55	5	1	1970-03
MacTavish, Craig	Edmonton	656	301	252	103	9		2000-09
Magnuson, Keith	Chicago	132	49	57	26	2		1980-82
Mahoney, Bill	Minnesota	93	42	39	12	2		1983-85
Maloney, Dan	Toronto	160	45	100	15	2		
	Winnipeg	212	91	93	28	3		
	Totals	372	136	193	43	5		1984-89
Maloney, Phil	Vancouver	232	95	105	32	4		1973-77
Mantha, Sylvio	Montreal	48	11	26	11	1		1935-36
Marshall, Bert	Colorado	24	3	17	4	1		1981-82

Coach	Team	Games Coached	Wins	Losses	O/T	Years	Cup Wins	Career
Martin, Jacques	St. Louis	160	66	71	23	2		
	Ottawa	692	341	235	116	9		
	Florida	246	110	100	36	4		
	Montreal	164	83	63	18	2		
	Totals	1262	600	469	193	17		1986-11
Matheson, Godfrey	Chicago	2	0	2	0	1		1932-33
Maurice, Paul	Hartford	152	61	72	19	2		
	Carolina	743	315	306	122	10		
	Toronto	164	76	66	22	2		
	Totals	1059	452	444	163	14		1995-11
Maxner, Wayne	Detroit	129	34	68	27	2		1980-82
McCammon, Bob	Philadelphia	218	119	68	31	4		
	Vancouver	294	102	156	36	4		
	Totals	512	221	224	67	8		1978-91
McCreary, Bill	St. Louis	24	6	14	4	1		
	Vancouver	41	9	25	7	1		
	California	32	8	20	4	1		
	Totals	97	23	59	15	3		1971-75
McGuire, Pierre	Hartford	67	23	37	7	1		1993-94
McLellan, John	Toronto	310	126	139	45	4		1969-73
McLellan, Todd	San Jose	246	152	63	31	3		2008-11
McVie, Tom	Washington	204	49	122	33	3		
	Winnipeg	105	20	67	18	2		
	New Jersey	153	57	74	22	3		
	Totals	462	126	263	73	8		1975-92
Meeker, Howie	Toronto	70	21	34	15	1		1956-57
Melrose, Barry	Los Angeles	209	79	101	29	3		
	Tampa Bay	16	5	7	4	1		
	Totals	225	84	108	33	4		1992-09
Milbury, Mike	Boston	160	90	49	21	2		
	NY Islanders	191	56	111	24	4		
	Totals	351	146	160	45	6		1989-99
Molleken, Lorne	Chicago	47	18	19	10	2		1998-00
Muckler, John	Minnesota	35	6	23	6	1		
	Edmonton	160	75	65	20	2	1	
	Buffalo	268	125	109	34	4		
	NY Rangers	185	70	88	27	3		
	Totals	648	276	285	87	10	1	1968-00
Muldoon, Pete	Chicago	44	19	22	3	1		1926-27
Munro, Dunc	Mtl. Maroons	76	37	29	10	2		1929-31
Murdoch, Bob	Chicago	80	30	41	9	1		
	Winnipeg	160	63	75	22	2		
	Totals	240	93	116	31	3		1987-91
Murphy, Mike	Los Angeles	65	20	37	8	2		
	Toronto	164	60	87	17	2		
	Totals	229	80	124	25	4		1986-98
Murray, Andy	Los Angeles	480	215	176	89	7		
	St. Louis	258	118	102	38	4		
	Totals	738	333	278	127	11		1999-10
Murray, Bryan	Washington	672	343	246	83	9		
	Detroit	244	124	91	29	3		
	Florida	59	17	31	11	1		
	Anaheim	82	29	42	11	1		
	Ottawa	182	107	55	20	4		
	Totals	1239	620	465	154	18		1981-08
Murray, Terry	Washington	325	163	134	28	5		
	Philadelphia	212	118	64	30	3		
	Florida	200	79	79	42	3		
	Los Angeles	246	122	93	31	3		
	Totals	983	482	370	131	14		1989-11
Nanne, Lou	Minnesota	29	7	18	4	1		1977-78
Neale, Harry	Vancouver	407	142	189	76	6		
	Detroit	35	8	23	4	1		
	Totals	442	150	212	80	7		1978-86
Neilson, Roger	Toronto	160	75	62	23	2		
	Buffalo	80	39	20	21	1		
	Vancouver	133	51	61	21	3		
	Los Angeles	28	8	17	3	1		
	NY Rangers	280	141	104	35	4		
	Florida	132	53	56	23	2		
	Philadelphia	185	92	57	36	3		
	Ottawa	2	1	1	0	1		
	Totals	1000	460	378	162	16		1977-02
Noel, Claude	Columbus	24	10	8	6	1		2009-10
Nolan, Ted	Buffalo	164	73	72	19	2		
	NY Islanders	163	74	68	21	2		
	Totals	327	147	140	40	4		1995-08
Nykoluk, Mike	Toronto	280	89	144	47	4		1980-84
O'Connell, Mike	Boston	9	3	3	3	1		2002-03
O'Donoghue, George	Toronto	29	15	13	1	2	1	1921-23
Olczyk, Ed	Pittsburgh	113	31	64	18	3		2003-06
Oliver, Murray	Minnesota	37	18	12	7	1		1982-83
Olmstead, Bert	Oakland	64	11	37	16	1		1967-68
O'Reilly, Terry	Boston	227	115	86	26	3		1986-89
Paddock, John	Winnipeg	281	106	138	37	4		
	Ottawa	64	36	22	6	1		
	Totals	345	142	160	43	5		1991-08
Page, Pierre	Minnesota	160	63	77	20	2		
	Quebec	230	98	103	29	3		
	Calgary	164	66	78	20	2		
	Anaheim	82	26	43	13	1		
	Totals	636	253	301	82	8		1988-98
Park, Brad	Detroit	45	9	34	2	1		1985-86
Paterson, Rick	Tampa Bay	6	0	6	0	1		1997-98

Coach	Team	Games Coached	Wins	Losses	O/T	Years	Cup Wins	Career
Patrick, Craig	NY Rangers	95	37	45	13	2		
	Pittsburgh	74	29	36	9	2		
	Totals	169	66	81	22	4		1980-97
Patrick, Frank	Boston	96	48	36	12	2		1934-36
Patrick, Lester	NY Rangers	604	281	216	107	13	2	1926-39
Patrick, Lynn	NY Rangers	107	40	51	16	2		
	Boston	310	117	130	63	5		
	St. Louis	26	8	15	3	3		
	Totals	443	165	196	82	10		1948-76
Patrick, Muzz	NY Rangers	136	52	66	27	4		1953-63
Payne, Davis	St. Louis	124	61	48	15	2		2009-11
Perron, Jean	Montreal	240	126	84	30	3	1	
	Quebec	47	16	26	5	1		
	Totals	287	142	110	35	4	1	1985-89
Perry, Don	Los Angeles	168	52	85	31	3		1981-84
Pike, Alf	NY Rangers	123	36	66	21	2		1959-61
Pilous, Rudy	Chicago	387	162	151	74	6	1	1957-63
Plager, Barclay	St. Louis	178	49	96	33	4		1977-83
Plager, Bob	St. Louis	11	4	6	1	1		1992-93
Playfair, Jim	Calgary	82	43	29	10	1		2006-07
Pleau, Larry	Hartford	224	81	117	26	5		1980-89
Polano, Nick	Detroit	240	79	127	34	3		1982-85
Popein, Larry	NY Rangers	41	18	14	9	1		1973-74
Powers, Eddie	Toronto	66	31	32	3	2		1924-26
Primeau, Joe	Toronto	210	97	71	42	3	1	1950-53
Pronovost, Marcel	Buffalo	104	52	29	23	2		1977-79
Pulford, Bob	Los Angeles	396	178	150	68	5		
	Chicago	433	185	180	68	7		
	Totals	829	363	330	136	12		1972-00
Quenneville, Joel	St. Louis	593	307	191	95	8		
	Colorado	246	131	92	23	4		
	Chicago	242	141	73	28	3	1	
	Totals	1081	579	356	146	15	1	1996-11
Querrie, Charles	Toronto	72	29	38	5	3		1922-27
Quinn, Mike	Quebec	24	4	20	0	1		1919-20
Quinn, Pat	Philadelphia	262	141	73	48	4		
	Los Angeles	202	75	101	26	3		
	Vancouver	280	141	111	28	5		
	Toronto	574	300	196	78	8		
	Edmonton	82	27	47	8	1		
	Totals	1400	684	528	188	21		1978-10
Raeder, Cap	San Jose	1	1	0	0	1		2002-03
Ramsay, Craig	Buffalo	21	4	15	2	1		
	Philadelphia	28	12	12	4	1		
	Atlanta	82	34	36	12	1		
	Totals	131	50	63	18	3		1986-11
Randall, Ken	Hamilton	14	6	8	0	1		1923-24
Reay, Billy	Toronto	90	26	50	14	2		
	Chicago	1012	516	335	161	14		
	Totals	1102	542	385	175	16		1957-77
Regan, Larry	Los Angeles	88	27	47	14	2		1970-72
Renney, Tom	Vancouver	101	39	53	9	2		
	NY Rangers	327	164	117	46	6		
	Edmonton	82	25	45	12	1		
	Totals	510	228	215	67	9		1996-11
Richards, Todd	Minnesota	164	77	71	16	2		2009-11
Risebrough, Doug	Calgary	144	71	56	17	2		1990-92
Roberts, Jim	Buffalo	45	21	16	8	1		
	Hartford	80	26	41	13	1		
	St. Louis	9	3	3	3	1		
	Totals	134	50	60	24	3		1981-97
Robinson, Larry	Los Angeles	328	122	161	45	4		
	New Jersey	173	87	56	30	4	1	
	Totals	501	209	217	75	8	1	1995-06
Rodden, Mike	Toronto	2	0	2	0	1		1926-27
Romeril, Alex	Toronto	13	7	5	1	1		1926-27
Ross, Art	Mtl. Wanderers	6	1	5	0	1		
	Hamilton	24	6	18	0	1		
	Boston	728	361	277	90	16	1	
	Totals	758	368	300	90	18	1	1917-45
Ruel, Claude	Montreal	305	172	82	51	5	1	1968-81
Ruff, Lindy	Buffalo	1066	526	390	150	14		1997-11
Sacco, Joe	Colorado	164	73	74	17	2		2009-11
Sather, Glen	Edmonton	842	464	268	110	11	4	
	NY Rangers	90	33	39	18	2		
	Totals	932	497	307	128	13	4	1979-04
Sator, Ted	NY Rangers	99	41	48	10	2		
	Buffalo	207	96	89	22	3		
	Totals	306	137	137	32	4		1985-89
Savard, Andre	Quebec	24	10	13	1	1		1987-88
Savard, Denis	Chicago	147	65	66	16	3		2006-09
Schinkel, Ken	Pittsburgh	203	83	92	28	4		1972-77
Schmidt, Milt	Boston	726	245	360	121	11		
	Washington	44	5	34	5	2		
	Totals	770	250	394	126	13		1954-76
Schoenfeld, Jim	Buffalo	43	19	19	5	1		
	New Jersey	124	50	59	15	3		
	Washington	249	113	102	34	4		
	Phoenix	164	74	66	24	2		
	Totals	580	256	246	78	10		1985-99
Shaughnessy, Tom	Chicago	21	10	8	3	1		1929-30
Shaw, Brad	NY Islanders	40	18	18	4	1		2005-06

Coach	Team	Games Coached	Wins	Losses	O/T	Years	Cup Wins	Career
Shero, Fred	Philadelphia	554	308	151	95	7	2	
	NY Rangers	180	82	74	24	3		
	Totals	**734**	**390**	**225**	**119**	**10**	**2**	1971-81
Simpson, Joe	NY Americans	144	42	72	30	3		1932-35
Simpson, Terry	NY Islanders	187	81	82	24	3		
	Philadelphia	84	35	39	10	1		
	Winnipeg	97	43	47	7	2		
	Totals	**368**	**159**	**168**	**41**	**6**		1986-96
Sims, Al	San Jose	82	27	47	8	1		1996-97
Sinden, Harry	Boston	327	153	116	58	6	1	1966-85
Skinner, Jimmy	Detroit	247	123	78	46	4	1	1954-58
Smeaton, Cooper	Philadelphia	44	4	36	4	1		1930-31
Smith, Alf	Ottawa	18	12	6	0	1		1918-19
Smith, Barry	Detroit *	5	4	1	0	1		1998-99
	* Results Shared with co-coach Dave Lewis							
Smith, Floyd	Buffalo	241	143	62	36	4		
	Toronto	68	30	33	5	1		
	Totals	**309**	**173**	**95**	**41**	**5**		1971-80
Smith, Mike	Winnipeg	23	2	17	4	1		1980-81
Smith, Ron	NY Rangers	44	15	22	7	1		1992-93
Smythe, Conn	Toronto	134	57	57	20	4		1927-31
Sonmor, Glen	Minnesota	421	177	161	83	7		1978-87
Sproule, Harvey	Toronto	12	7	5	0	1		1919-20
Stanley, Barney	Chicago	23	4	17	2	1		1927-28
Stasiuk, Vic	Philadelphia	154	45	68	41	2		
	California	75	21	38	16	1		
	Vancouver	78	22	47	9	1		
	Totals	**307**	**88**	**153**	**66**	**4**		1969-73
Stevens, John	Philadelphia	263	120	109	34	4		2006-10
Stewart, Bill	NY Islanders	37	11	19	7	1		1998-99
Stewart, Bill	Chicago	69	22	35	12	2	1	1937-39
Stewart, Ron	NY Rangers	39	15	20	4	1		
	Los Angeles	80	31	34	15	1		
	Totals	**119**	**46**	**54**	**19**	**2**		1975-78
Stirling, Steve	NY Islanders	124	56	51	17	3		2003-06
Suhonen, Alpo	Chicago	82	29	41	12	1		2000-01
Sullivan, Mike	Boston	164	70	56	38	3		2003-06
Sullivan, Red	NY Rangers	196	58	103	35	4		
	Pittsburgh	150	47	79	24	2		
	Washington	18	2	16	0	1		
	Totals	**364**	**107**	**198**	**59**	**7**		1962-75
Sutherland, Bill	Winnipeg	32	7	22	3	2		1979-81
Sutter, Brent	New Jersey	164	97	56	11	2		
	Calgary	164	81	61	22	2		
	Totals	**328**	**178**	**117**	**33**	**4**		2007-11
Sutter, Brian	St. Louis	320	153	124	43	4		
	Boston	216	120	73	23	3		
	Calgary	246	87	117	42	3		
	Chicago	246	91	103	52	4		
	Totals	**1028**	**451**	**417**	**160**	**14**		1988-05
Sutter, Darryl	Chicago	216	110	80	26	3		
	San Jose	434	192	167	75	6		
	Calgary	210	107	73	30	4		
	Totals	**860**	**409**	**320**	**131**	**12**		1992-06
Sutter, Duane	Florida	72	22	35	15	2		2000-02
Talbot, Jean-Guy	St. Louis	120	52	53	15	2		
	NY Rangers	80	30	37	13	1		
	Totals	**200**	**82**	**90**	**28**	**3**		1972-78

Coach	Team	Games Coached	Wins	Losses	O/T	Years	Cup Wins	Career
Tessier, Orval	Chicago	213	99	93	21	3		1982-85
Therrien, Michel	Montreal	190	77	77	36	3		
	Pittsburgh	272	135	105	32	4		
	Totals	**462**	**212**	**182**	**68**	**7**		2000-09
Thompson, Paul	Chicago	272	104	127	41	7		1938-45
Thompson, Percy	Hamilton	48	13	35	0	2		1920-22
Tippett, Dave	Dallas	492	271	156	65	7		
	Phoenix	164	96	55	13	2		
	Totals	**656**	**367**	**211**	**78**	**9**		2002-11
Tobin, Bill	Chicago	71	29	29	13	2		1929-32
Tocchet, Rick	Tampa Bay	148	53	69	26	2		2008-10
Torchetti, John	Florida	27	10	12	5	1		
	Los Angeles	12	5	7	0	1		
	Totals	**39**	**15**	**19**	**5**	**2**		2003-06
Tortorella, John	NY Rangers	189	94	76	19	4		
	Tampa Bay	535	239	222	74	8	1	
	Totals	**724**	**333**	**298**	**93**	**12**	**1**	1999-11
Tremblay, Mario	Montreal	159	71	63	25	2		1995-97
Trottier, Bryan	NY Rangers	54	21	26	7	1		2002-03
Trotz, Barry	Nashville	984	455	398	131	13		1998-11
Ubriaco, Gene	Pittsburgh	106	50	47	9	2		1988-90
Vachon, Rogie	Los Angeles	10	4	3	3	3		1983-95
Vigneault, Alain	Montreal	266	109	118	39	4		
	Vancouver	410	236	133	41	5		
	Totals	**676**	**345**	**251**	**80**	**9**		1997-11
Waddell, Don	Atlanta	86	38	39	9	2		2002-08
Watson, Bryan	Edmonton	18	4	9	5	1		1980-81
Watson, Phil	NY Rangers	295	119	124	52	5		
	Boston	84	16	55	13	2		
	Totals	**379**	**135**	**179**	**65**	**7**		1955-63
Watt, Tom	Winnipeg	181	72	85	24	3		
	Vancouver	160	52	87	21	2		
	Toronto	149	52	80	17	2		
	Totals	**490**	**176**	**252**	**62**	**7**		1981-92
Webster, Tom	NY Rangers	18	5	9	4	1		
	Los Angeles	240	115	94	31	3		
	Totals	**258**	**120**	**103**	**35**	**4**		1986-92
Weiland, Cooney	Boston	96	58	20	18	2	1	1939-41
White, Bill	Chicago	46	16	24	6	1		1976-77
Wiley, Jim	San Jose	57	17	37	3	1		1995-96
Wilson, Johnny	Los Angeles	52	9	34	9	1		
	Detroit	145	67	56	22	2		
	Colorado	80	20	46	14	1		
	Pittsburgh	240	91	105	44	3		
	Totals	**517**	**187**	**241**	**89**	**7**		1969-80
Wilson, Larry	Detroit	36	3	29	4	1		1976-77
Wilson, Rick	Dallas	32	13	11	8	1		2001-02
Wilson, Ron	Anaheim	296	120	145	31	4		
	Washington	410	192	159	59	5		
	San Jose	385	206	122	57	6		
	Toronto	246	101	107	38	3		
	Totals	**1337**	**619**	**533**	**185**	**18**		1993-11
Yawney, Trent	Chicago	103	33	55	15	2		2005-07
Young, Garry	California	12	2	7	3	1		
	St. Louis	98	41	41	16	2		
	Totals	**110**	**43**	**48**	**19**	**3**		1972-76

Dan Bylsma (left) won the Jack Adams Award as coach of the year in 2010-11. Bylsma's Penguins overcame a total of 350 man-games lost due to injury to earn the second-most points (106) and victories (49) in franchise history. Alain Vigneault (center) won the Jack Adams in 2007 and led Vancouver to the Presidents' Trophy for the first time last season. Barry Trotz (right) earned his second straight nomination for coach of the year.

Year-by-Year Individual Regular-Season Leaders

Season	Goals	G	Assists	A	Points	Pts.	Penalty Minutes	PIM
1917-18	Joe Malone	44	Cy Denneny, Reg Noble, Harry Cameron	10	Joe Malone	48	Joe Hall	100
1918-19	Newsy Lalonde	22	Newsy Lalonde	10	Newsy Lalonde	32	Joe Hall	135
1919-20	Joe Malone	39	Frank Nighbor	15	Joe Malone	49	Cully Wilson	86
1920-21	Babe Dye	35	Jack Darragh	15	Newsy Lalonde	43	Bert Corbeau	86
1921-22	Punch Broadbent	32	Harry Cameron	17	Punch Broadbent	46	Sprague Cleghorn	63
1922-23	Babe Dye	26	Eddie Gerard	13	Babe Dye	37	Georges Boucher	58
1923-24	Cy Denneny	22	Georges Boucher	10	Cy Denneny	24	Reg Noble	79
1924-25	Babe Dye	38	Cy Denneny, Red Green	15	Babe Dye	46	Georges Boucher	95
1925-26	Nels Stewart	34	Frank Nighbor	13	Nels Stewart	42	Bert Corbeau	121
1926-27	Bill Cook	33	Dick Irvin	18	Bill Cook	37	Nels Stewart	133
1927-28	Howie Morenz	33	Howie Morenz	18	Howie Morenz	51	Eddie Shore	165
1928-29	Ace Bailey	22	Frank Boucher	16	Ace Bailey	32	Red Dutton	139
1929-30	Cooney Weiland	43	Frank Boucher	36	Cooney Weiland	73	Joe Lamb	119
1930-31	Charlie Conacher	31	Joe Primeau	32	Howie Morenz	51	Harvey Rockburn	118
1931-32	Charlie Conacher, Bill Cook	34	Joe Primeau	37	Busher Jackson	53	Red Dutton	107
1932-33	Bill Cook	28	Frank Boucher	28	Bill Cook	50	Red Horner	144
1933-34	Charlie Conacher	32	Joe Primeau	32	Charlie Conacher	52	Red Horner	126 *
1934-35	Charlie Conacher	36	Art Chapman	34	Charlie Conacher	57	Red Horner	125
1935-36	Charlie Conacher, Bill Thoms	23	Art Chapman	28	Sweeney Schriner	45	Red Horner	167
1936-37	Larry Aurie, Nels Stewart	23	Syl Apps	29	Sweeney Schriner	46	Red Horner	124
1937-38	Gordie Drillon	26	Syl Apps	29	Gordie Drillon	52	Art Coulter	90
1938-39	Roy Conacher	26	Bill Cowley	34	Toe Blake	47	Red Horner	85
1939-40	Bryan Hextall	24	Milt Schmidt	30	Milt Schmidt	52	Red Horner	87
1940-41	Bryan Hextall	26	Bill Cowley	45	Bill Cowley	62	Jimmy Orlando	99
1941-42	Lynn Patrick	32	Phil Watson	37	Bryan Hextall	56	Pat Egan	124
1942-43	Doug Bentley	33	Bill Cowley	45	Doug Bentley	73	Jimmy Orlando	89 *
1943-44	Doug Bentley	38	Clint Smith	49	Herb Cain	82	Mike McMahon	98
1944-45	Maurice Richard	50	Elmer Lach	54	Elmer Lach	80	Pat Egan	86
1945-46	Gaye Stewart	37	Elmer Lach	34	Max Bentley	61	Jack Stewart	73
1946-47	Maurice Richard	45	Billy Taylor	46	Max Bentley	72	Gus Mortson	133
1947-48	Ted Lindsay	33	Doug Bentley	37	Elmer Lach	61	Bill Barilko	147
1948-49	Sid Abel	28	Doug Bentley	43	Roy Conacher	68	Bill Ezinicki	145
1949-50	Maurice Richard	43	Ted Lindsay	55	Ted Lindsay	78	Bill Ezinicki	144
1950-51	Gordie Howe	43	Gordie Howe, Ted Kennedy	43	Gordie Howe	86	Gus Mortson	142
1951-52	Gordie Howe	47	Elmer Lach	50	Gordie Howe	86	Gus Kyle	127
1952-53	Gordie Howe	49	Gordie Howe	46	Gordie Howe	95	Maurice Richard	112
1953-54	Maurice Richard	37	Gordie Howe	48	Gordie Howe	81	Gus Mortson	132
1954-55	Maurice Richard, Bernie Geoffrion	38	Bert Olmstead	48	Bernie Geoffrion	75	Fern Flaman	150
1955-56	Jean Beliveau	47	Bert Olmstead	56	Jean Beliveau	88	Lou Fontinato	202
1956-57	Gordie Howe	44	Ted Lindsay	55	Gordie Howe	89	Gus Mortson	147
1957-58	Dickie Moore	36	Henri Richard	52	Dickie Moore	84	Lou Fontinato	152
1958-59	Jean Beliveau	45	Dickie Moore	55	Dickie Moore	96	Ted Lindsay	184
1959-60	Bobby Hull, Bronco Horvath	39	Don McKenney	49	Bobby Hull	81	Carl Brewer	150
1960-61	Bernie Geoffrion	50	Jean Beliveau	58	Bernie Geoffrion	95	Pierre Pilote	165
1961-62	Bobby Hull	50	Andy Bathgate	56	Bobby Hull, Andy Bathgate	84	Lou Fontinato	167
1962-63	Gordie Howe	38	Henri Richard	50	Gordie Howe	86	Howie Young	273
1963-64	Bobby Hull	43	Andy Bathgate	58	Stan Mikita	89	Vic Hadfield	151
1964-65	Norm Ullman	42	Stan Mikita	59	Stan Mikita	87	Carl Brewer	177
1965-66	Bobby Hull	54	Stan Mikita, Bobby Rousseau, Jean Beliveau	48	Bobby Hull	97	Reggie Fleming	166
1966-67	Bobby Hull	52	Stan Mikita	62	Stan Mikita	97	John Ferguson	177
1967-68	Bobby Hull	44	Phil Esposito	49	Stan Mikita	87	Barclay Plager	153
1968-69	Bobby Hull	58	Phil Esposito	77	Phil Esposito	126	Forbes Kennedy	219
1969-70	Phil Esposito	43	Bobby Orr	87	Bobby Orr	120	Keith Magnuson	213
1970-71	Phil Esposito	76	Bobby Orr	102	Phil Esposito	152	Keith Magnuson	291
1971-72	Phil Esposito	66	Bobby Orr	80	Phil Esposito	133	Bryan Watson	212
1972-73	Phil Esposito	55	Phil Esposito	75	Phil Esposito	130	Dave Schultz	259
1973-74	Phil Esposito	68	Bobby Orr	90	Phil Esposito	145	Dave Schultz	348
1974-75	Phil Esposito	61	Bobby Orr, Bobby Clarke	89	Bobby Orr	135	Dave Schultz	472
1975-76	Reggie Leach	61	Bobby Clarke	89	Guy Lafleur	125	Steve Durbano	370
1976-77	Steve Shutt	60	Guy Lafleur	80	Guy Lafleur	136	Tiger Williams	338
1977-78	Guy Lafleur	60	Bryan Trottier	77	Guy Lafleur	132	Dave Schultz	405
1978-79	Mike Bossy	69	Bryan Trottier	87	Bryan Trottier	134	Tiger Williams	298
1979-80	Charlie Simmer, Danny Gare, Blaine Stoughton	56	Wayne Gretzky	86	Marcel Dionne, Wayne Gretzky	137	Jimmy Mann	287
1980-81	Mike Bossy	68	Wayne Gretzky	109	Wayne Gretzky	164	Tiger Williams	343
1981-82	Wayne Gretzky	92	Wayne Gretzky	120	Wayne Gretzky	212	Paul Baxter	409
1982-83	Wayne Gretzky	71	Wayne Gretzky	125	Wayne Gretzky	196	Randy Holt	275
1983-84	Wayne Gretzky	87	Wayne Gretzky	118	Wayne Gretzky	205	Chris Nilan	338
1984-85	Wayne Gretzky	73	Wayne Gretzky	135	Wayne Gretzky	208	Chris Nilan	358
1985-86	Jari Kurri	68	Wayne Gretzky	163	Wayne Gretzky	215	Joe Kocur	377
1986-87	Wayne Gretzky	62	Wayne Gretzky	121	Wayne Gretzky	183	Tim Hunter	361
1987-88	Mario Lemieux	70	Wayne Gretzky	109	Mario Lemieux	168	Bob Probert	398
1988-89	Mario Lemieux	85	Mario Lemieux, Wayne Gretzky	114	Mario Lemieux	199	Tim Hunter	375
1989-90	Brett Hull	72	Wayne Gretzky	102	Wayne Gretzky	142	Basil McRae	351
1990-91	Brett Hull	86	Wayne Gretzky	122	Wayne Gretzky	163	Rob Ray	350
1991-92	Brett Hull	70	Wayne Gretzky	90	Mario Lemieux	131	Mike Peluso	408
1992-93	Teemu Selanne, Alexander Mogilny	76	Adam Oates	97	Mario Lemieux	160	Marty McSorley	399
1993-94	Pavel Bure	60	Wayne Gretzky	92	Wayne Gretzky	130	Tie Domi	347
1994-95	Peter Bondra	34	Ron Francis	48	Jaromir Jagr, Eric Lindros	70	Enrico Ciccone	225
1995-96	Mario Lemieux	69	Mario Lemieux, Ron Francis	92	Mario Lemieux	161	Matthew Barnaby	335
1996-97	Keith Tkachuk	52	Mario Lemieux, Wayne Gretzky	72	Mario Lemieux	122	Gino Odjick	371
1997-98	Teemu Selanne, Peter Bondra	52	Jaromir Jagr, Wayne Gretzky	67	Jaromir Jagr	102	Donald Brashear	372
1998-99	Teemu Selanne	47	Jaromir Jagr	83	Jaromir Jagr	127	Rob Ray	261
99-2000	Pavel Bure	58	Mark Recchi	63	Jaromir Jagr	96	Denny Lambert	219
2000-01	Pavel Bure	59	Jaromir Jagr, Adam Oates	69	Jaromir Jagr	121	Matthew Barnaby	265
2001-02	Jarome Iginla	52	Adam Oates	64	Jarome Iginla	96	Peter Worrell	354
2002-03	Milan Hejduk	50	Peter Forsberg	77	Peter Forsberg	106	Jody Shelley	249
2003-04	Rick Nash, Jarome Iginla, Ilya Kovalchuk	41	Scott Gomez, Martin St. Louis	56	Martin St. Louis	94	Sean Avery	261
2004-05	....	....	....	....	....	....	....	....
2005-06	Jonathan Cheechoo	56	Joe Thornton	96	Joe Thornton	125	Sean Avery	257
2006-07	Vincent Lecavalier	52	Joe Thornton	92	Sidney Crosby	120	Ben Eager	233
2007-08	Alex Ovechkin	65	Joe Thornton	67	Alex Ovechkin	112	Daniel Carcillo	324
2008-09	Alex Ovechkin	56	Evgeni Malkin	78	Evgeni Malkin	113	Daniel Carcillo	254
2009-10	Sidney Crosby, Steven Stamkos	51	Henrik Sedin	83	Henrik Sedin	112	Zenon Konopka	265
2010-11	Corey Perry	50	Henrik Sedin	75	Daniel Sedin	104	Zenon Konopka	307

* Match Misconduct penalty not included in total penalty minutes.
1946-47 was the first season that a Match penalty was automatically written into the player's total penalty minutes as 20 minutes.
Beginning in 1947-48 all penalties, Match, Game Misconduct, and Misconduct, are written as 10 minutes.

One Season Scoring Records

Goals-Per-Game Leaders, One Season

(Among players with 20 goals or more in one season)

Player	Team	Season	Games	Goals	Goals per game average
Joe Malone	Montreal	1917-18	20	44	2.20
Cy Denneny	Ottawa	1917-18	20	36	1.80
Newsy Lalonde	Montreal	1917-18	14	23	1.64
Joe Malone	Quebec	1919-20	24	39	1.63
Newsy Lalonde	Montreal	1919-20	23	37	1.61
Reg Noble	Toronto	1917-18	20	30	1.50
Babe Dye	Ham., Tor.	1920-21	24	35	1.46
Cy Denneny	Ottawa	1920-21	24	34	1.42
Joe Malone	Hamilton	1920-21	20	28	1.40
Newsy Lalonde	Montreal	1920-21	24	33	1.38
Punch Broadbent	Ottawa	1921-22	24	32	1.33
Babe Dye	Toronto	1924-25	29	38	1.31
Babe Dye	Toronto	1921-22	24	31	1.29
Newsy Lalonde	Montreal	1918-19	17	22	1.29
Odie Cleghorn	Montreal	1918-19	17	22	1.29
Cy Denneny	Ottawa	1921-22	22	27	1.23
Aurel Joliat	Montreal	1924-25	25	30	1.20
Wayne Gretzky	Edmonton	1983-84	74	87	1.18
Babe Dye	Toronto	1922-23	22	26	1.18
Wayne Gretzky	Edmonton	1981-82	80	92	1.15
Mario Lemieux	Pittsburgh	1992-93	60	69	1.15
Frank Nighbor	Ottawa	1919-20	23	26	1.13
Mario Lemieux	Pittsburgh	1988-89	76	85	1.12
Brett Hull	St. Louis	1990-91	78	86	1.10
Cam Neely	Boston	1993-94	49	50	1.02
Maurice Richard	Montreal	1944-45	50	50	1.00
Reg Noble	Toronto	1919-20	24	24	1.00
Corb Denneny	Toronto	1919-20	24	24	1.00
Joe Malone	Hamilton	1921-22	24	24	1.00
Billy Boucher	Montreal	1922-23	24	24	1.00
Cy Denneny	Ottawa	1923-24	22	22	1.00
Alexander Mogilny	Buffalo	1992-93	77	76	0.99
Mario Lemieux	Pittsburgh	1995-96	70	69	0.99
Cooney Weiland	Boston	1929-30	44	43	0.98
Phil Esposito	Boston	1970-71	78	76	0.97
Jari Kurri	Edmonton	1984-85	73	71	0.97

A six-time 50-goal scorer, Guy Lafleur could set up others too. He averaged an assist per game during the 80-game 1976-77 season and had 75 assists in 74 games played in 1979-80.

Assists-Per-Game Leaders, One Season

(Among players with 35 assists or more in one season)

Player	Team	Season	Games	Assists	Assists per game average
Wayne Gretzky	Edmonton	1985-86	80	163	2.04
Wayne Gretzky	Edmonton	1987-88	64	109	1.70
Wayne Gretzky	Edmonton	1984-85	80	135	1.69
Wayne Gretzky	Edmonton	1983-84	74	118	1.59
Wayne Gretzky	Edmonton	1982-83	80	125	1.56
Wayne Gretzky	Los Angeles	1990-91	78	122	1.56
Wayne Gretzky	Edmonton	1986-87	79	121	1.53
Mario Lemieux	Pittsburgh	1992-93	60	91	1.52
Wayne Gretzky	Edmonton	1981-82	80	120	1.50
Mario Lemieux	Pittsburgh	1988-89	76	114	1.50
Adam Oates	St. Louis	1990-91	61	90	1.48
Wayne Gretzky	Los Angeles	1988-89	78	114	1.46
Wayne Gretzky	Los Angeles	1989-90	73	102	1.40
Wayne Gretzky	Edmonton	1980-81	80	109	1.36
Mario Lemieux	Pittsburgh	1991-92	64	87	1.36
Mario Lemieux	Pittsburgh	1989-90	59	78	1.32
Bobby Orr	Boston	1970-71	78	102	1.31
Mario Lemieux	Pittsburgh	1995-96	70	92	1.31
Mario Lemieux	Pittsburgh	1987-88	77	98	1.27
Bobby Orr	Boston	1973-74	74	90	1.22
Wayne Gretzky	Los Angeles	1991-92	74	90	1.22
Joe Thornton	Bos., S.J.	2005-06	81	96	1.19
Ron Francis	Pittsburgh	1995-96	77	92	1.19
Mario Lemieux	Pittsburgh	1985-86	79	93	1.18
Bobby Clarke	Philadelphia	1975-76	76	89	1.17
Peter Stastny	Quebec	1981-82	80	93	1.16
Adam Oates	Boston	1992-93	84	97	1.15
Doug Gilmour	Toronto	1992-93	83	95	1.14
Wayne Gretzky	Los Angeles	1993-94	81	92	1.14
Paul Coffey	Edmonton	1985-86	79	90	1.14
Bobby Orr	Boston	1969-70	76	87	1.14
Bryan Trottier	NY Islanders	1978-79	76	87	1.14
Bobby Orr	Boston	1972-73	63	72	1.14
Bill Cowley	Boston	1943-44	36	41	1.14
Pat LaFontaine	Buffalo	1992-93	84	95	1.13
Steve Yzerman	Detroit	1988-89	80	90	1.13
Paul Coffey	Pittsburgh	1987-88	46	52	1.13
Joe Thornton	San Jose	2006-07	82	92	1.12
Bobby Orr	Boston	1974-75	80	89	1.11
Bobby Clarke	Philadelphia	1974-75	80	89	1.11
Paul Coffey	Pittsburgh	1988-89	75	83	1.11

Player	Team	Season	Games	Assists	Assists per game average
Wayne Gretzky	Los Angeles	1992-93	45	49	1.11
Denis Savard	Chicago	1982-83	78	86	1.10
Denis Savard	Chicago	1981-82	80	87	1.09
Denis Savard	Chicago	1987-88	80	87	1.09
Wayne Gretzky	Edmonton	1979-80	79	86	1.09
Ron Francis	Pittsburgh	1994-95	44	48	1.09
Paul Coffey	Edmonton	1983-84	80	86	1.08
Elmer Lach	Montreal	1944-45	50	54	1.08
Peter Stastny	Quebec	1985-86	76	81	1.07
Jaromir Jagr	Pittsburgh	1995-96	82	87	1.06
Mark Messier	Edmonton	1989-90	79	84	1.06
Sidney Crosby	Pittsburgh	2006-07	79	84	1.06
Peter Forsberg	Colorado	1995-96	82	86	1.05
Paul Coffey	Edmonton	1984-85	80	84	1.05
Marcel Dionne	Los Angeles	1979-80	80	84	1.05
Bobby Orr	Boston	1971-72	76	80	1.05
Mike Bossy	NY Islanders	1981-82	80	83	1.04
Adam Oates	Boston	1993-94	77	80	1.04
Phil Esposito	Boston	1968-69	74	77	1.04
Bryan Trottier	NY Islanders	1983-84	68	71	1.04
Jason Spezza	Ottawa	2005-06	68	71	1.04
Pete Mahovlich	Montreal	1974-75	80	82	1.03
Kent Nilsson	Calgary	1980-81	80	82	1.03
Peter Stastny	Quebec	1982-83	75	77	1.03
Peter Forsberg	Colorado	2002-03	75	77	1.03
Denis Savard	Chicago	1988-89	58	59	1.02
Jaromir Jagr	Pittsburgh	1998-99	81	83	1.02
Doug Gilmour	Toronto	1993-94	83	84	1.01
Henrik Sedin	Vancouver	2009-10	82	83	1.01
Bernie Nicholls	Los Angeles	1988-89	79	80	1.01
Guy Lafleur	Montreal	1979-80	74	75	1.01
Guy Lafleur	Montreal	1976-77	80	80	1.00
Marcel Dionne	Los Angeles	1984-85	80	80	1.00
Brian Leetch	NY Rangers	1991-92	80	80	1.00
Bryan Trottier	NY Islanders	1977-78	77	77	1.00
Mike Bossy	NY Islanders	1983-84	67	67	1.00
Jean Ratelle	NY Rangers	1971-72	63	63	1.00
Steve Yzerman	Detroit	1993-94	58	58	1.00
Ron Francis	Hartford	1985-86	53	53	1.00
Guy Chouinard	Calgary	1980-81	52	52	1.00
Elmer Lach	Montreal	1943-44	48	48	1.00

Points-Per-Game Leaders, One Season

(Among players with 50 points or more in one season)

Player	Team	Season	Games	Points	Points per game average	Player	Team	Season	Games	Points	Points per game average
Wayne Gretzky	Edmonton	1983-84	74	205	2.77	Denis Savard	Chicago	1987-88	80	131	1.64
Wayne Gretzky	Edmonton	1985-86	80	215	2.69	Wayne Gretzky	Los Angeles	1991-92	74	121	1.64
Mario Lemieux	Pittsburgh	1992-93	60	160	2.67	Steve Yzerman	Detroit	1992-93	84	137	1.63
Wayne Gretzky	Edmonton	1981-82	80	212	2.65	Marcel Dionne	Los Angeles	1978-79	80	130	1.63
Mario Lemieux	Pittsburgh	1988-89	76	199	2.62	Dale Hawerchuk	Winnipeg	1984-85	80	130	1.63
Wayne Gretzky	Edmonton	1984-85	80	208	2.60	Mark Messier	Edmonton	1989-90	79	129	1.63
Wayne Gretzky	Edmonton	1982-83	80	196	2.45	Bryan Trottier	NY Islanders	1983-84	68	111	1.63
Wayne Gretzky	Edmonton	1987-88	64	149	2.33	Pat LaFontaine	Buffalo	1991-92	57	93	1.63
Wayne Gretzky	Edmonton	1986-87	79	183	2.32	Charlie Simmer	Los Angeles	1980-81	65	105	1.62
Mario Lemieux	Pittsburgh	1995-96	70	161	2.30	Guy Lafleur	Montreal	1978-79	80	129	1.61
Mario Lemieux	Pittsburgh	1987-88	77	168	2.18	Bryan Trottier	NY Islanders	1981-82	80	129	1.61
Wayne Gretzky	Los Angeles	1988-89	78	168	2.15	Phil Esposito	Boston	1974-75	79	127	1.61
Wayne Gretzky	Los Angeles	1990-91	78	163	2.09	Steve Yzerman	Detroit	1989-90	79	127	1.61
Mario Lemieux	Pittsburgh	1989-90	59	123	2.08	Peter Stastny	Quebec	1985-86	76	122	1.61
Wayne Gretzky	Edmonton	1980-81	80	164	2.05	Mario Lemieux	Pittsburgh	1996-97	76	122	1.61
Mario Lemieux	Pittsburgh	1991-92	64	131	2.05	Michel Goulet	Quebec	1983-84	75	121	1.61
Bill Cowley	Boston	1943-44	36	71	1.97	Sidney Crosby	Pittsburgh	**2010-11**	41	66	1.61
Phil Esposito	Boston	1970-71	78	152	1.95	Wayne Gretzky	Los Angeles	1993-94	81	130	1.60
Wayne Gretzky	Los Angeles	1989-90	73	142	1.95	Bryan Trottier	NY Islanders	1977-78	77	123	1.60
Steve Yzerman	Detroit	1988-89	80	155	1.94	Bobby Orr	Boston	1972-73	63	101	1.60
Bernie Nicholls	Los Angeles	1988-89	79	150	1.90	Guy Chouinard	Calgary	1980-81	52	83	1.60
Adam Oates	St. Louis	1990-91	61	115	1.89	Elmer Lach	Montreal	1944-45	50	80	1.60
Phil Esposito	Boston	1973-74	78	145	1.86	Pierre Turgeon	NY Islanders	1992-93	83	132	1.59
Jari Kurri	Edmonton	1984-85	73	135	1.85	Steve Yzerman	Detroit	1987-88	64	102	1.59
Mike Bossy	NY Islanders	1981-82	80	147	1.84	Mike Bossy	NY Islanders	1978-79	80	126	1.58
Jaromir Jagr	Pittsburgh	1995-96	82	149	1.82	Paul Coffey	Edmonton	1983-84	80	126	1.58
Mario Lemieux	Pittsburgh	1985-86	79	141	1.78	Marcel Dionne	Los Angeles	1984-85	80	126	1.58
Bobby Orr	Boston	1970-71	78	139	1.78	Bobby Orr	Boston	1969-70	76	120	1.58
Jari Kurri	Edmonton	1983-84	64	113	1.77	Eric Lindros	Philadelphia	1995-96	73	115	1.58
Mario Lemieux	Pittsburgh	2000-01	43	76	1.77	Charlie Simmer	Los Angeles	1979-80	64	101	1.58
Pat LaFontaine	Buffalo	1992-93	84	148	1.76	Teemu Selanne	Winnipeg	1992-93	84	132	1.57
Bryan Trottier	NY Islanders	1978-79	76	134	1.76	Jaromir Jagr	Pittsburgh	1998-99	81	127	1.57
Mike Bossy	NY Islanders	1983-84	67	118	1.76	Bobby Clarke	Philadelphia	1975-76	76	119	1.57
Paul Coffey	Edmonton	1985-86	79	138	1.75	Guy Lafleur	Montreal	1975-76	80	125	1.56
Phil Esposito	Boston	1971-72	76	133	1.75	Dave Taylor	Los Angeles	1980-81	72	112	1.56
Peter Stastny	Quebec	1981-82	80	139	1.74	Denis Savard	Chicago	1982-83	78	121	1.55
Wayne Gretzky	Edmonton	1979-80	79	137	1.73	Ron Francis	Pittsburgh	1995-96	77	119	1.55
Jean Ratelle	NY Rangers	1971-72	63	109	1.73	Joe Thornton	Bos., S.J.	2005-06	81	125	1.54
Marcel Dionne	Los Angeles	1979-80	80	137	1.71	Mike Bossy	NY Islanders	1985-86	80	123	1.54
Herb Cain	Boston	1943-44	48	82	1.71	Kevin Stevens	Pittsburgh	1991-92	80	123	1.54
Guy Lafleur	Montreal	1976-77	80	136	1.70	Bobby Orr	Boston	1971-72	76	117	1.54
Dennis Maruk	Washington	1981-82	80	136	1.70	Mike Bossy	NY Islanders	1984-85	76	117	1.54
Phil Esposito	Boston	1968-69	74	126	1.70	Kevin Stevens	Pittsburgh	1992-93	72	111	1.54
Guy Lafleur	Montreal	1974-75	70	119	1.70	Doug Bentley	Chicago	1943-44	50	77	1.54
Mario Lemieux	Pittsburgh	1986-87	63	107	1.70	Doug Gilmour	Toronto	1992-93	83	127	1.53
Adam Oates	Boston	1992-93	84	142	1.69	Marcel Dionne	Los Angeles	1976-77	80	122	1.53
Bobby Orr	Boston	1974-75	80	135	1.69	Sidney Crosby	Pittsburgh	2006-07	79	120	1.52
Marcel Dionne	Los Angeles	1980-81	80	135	1.69	Jaromir Jagr	Pittsburgh	99-2000	63	96	1.52
Guy Lafleur	Montreal	1977-78	78	132	1.69	Eric Lindros	Philadelphia	1996-97	52	79	1.52
Guy Lafleur	Montreal	1979-80	74	125	1.69	Eric Lindros	Philadelphia	1994-95	46	70	1.52
Rob Brown	Pittsburgh	1988-89	68	115	1.69	Marcel Dionne	Detroit	1974-75	80	121	1.51
Jari Kurri	Edmonton	1985-86	78	131	1.68	Mike Bossy	NY Islanders	1980-81	79	119	1.51
Brett Hull	St. Louis	1990-91	78	131	1.68	Paul Coffey	Edmonton	1984-85	80	121	1.51
Phil Esposito	Boston	1972-73	78	130	1.67	Dale Hawerchuk	Winnipeg	1987-88	80	121	1.51
Cooney Weiland	Boston	1929-30	44	73	1.66	Paul Coffey	Pittsburgh	1988-89	75	113	1.51
Alexander Mogilny	Buffalo	1992-93	77	127	1.65	Alex Ovechkin	Washington	2009-10	72	109	1.51
Peter Stastny	Quebec	1982-83	75	124	1.65	Jaromir Jagr	Pittsburgh	1996-97	63	95	1.51
Bobby Orr	Boston	1973-74	74	122	1.65	Cam Neely	Boston	1993-94	49	74	1.51
Kent Nilsson	Calgary	1980-81	80	131	1.64						

Pittsburgh teammates Mario Lemieux and Jaromir Jagr finished 1-2 in the NHL scoring race in 1995-96. Lemieux had 161 points in 70 games played for a scoring average of 2.30 points per game while Jagr (who returns to the NHL with Philadelphia in 2011-12) had a career-high 149 points in 82 games for a 1.82 scoring average.

In his first full NHL season in 2010-11, Michael Grabner (left) scored 34 goals for the New York Islanders to rank among the all-time top goal-scoring rookies in NHL history. Jeff Skinner (right) jumped directly out of junior hockey as an 18-year-old and led all NHL rookies in scoring with 63 points on 31 goals and 32 assists.

Rookie Scoring Records

All-Time Top 50 Goal-Scoring Rookies

	Rookie	Team	Position	Season	GP	G	A	PTS
1.	* Teemu Selanne	Winnipeg	Right wing	1992-93	84	76	56	132
2.	* Mike Bossy	NY Islanders	Right wing	1977-78	73	53	38	91
3.	* Alex Ovechkin	Washington	Left wing	2005-06	81	52	54	106
4.	* Joe Nieuwendyk	Calgary	Center	1987-88	75	51	41	92
5.	* Dale Hawerchuk	Winnipeg	Center	1981-82	80	45	58	103
	* Luc Robitaille	Los Angeles	Left wing	1986-87	79	45	39	84
7.	Rick Martin	Buffalo	Left wing	1971-72	73	44	30	74
	Barry Pederson	Boston	Center	1981-82	80	44	48	92
9.	* Steve Larmer	Chicago	Right wing	1982-83	80	43	47	90
	* Mario Lemieux	Pittsburgh	Center	1984-85	73	43	57	100
11.	Eric Lindros	Philadelphia	Center	1992-93	61	41	34	75
12.	Darryl Sutter	Chicago	Left wing	1980-81	76	40	22	62
	Sylvain Turgeon	Hartford	Left wing	1983-84	76	40	32	72
	Warren Young	Pittsburgh	Left wing	1984-85	80	40	32	72
15.	* Eric Vail	Atlanta	Left wing	1974-75	72	39	21	60
	* Peter Stastny	Quebec	Center	1980-81	77	39	70	109
	Anton Stastny	Quebec	Left wing	1980-81	80	39	46	85
	Steve Yzerman	Detroit	Center	1983-84	80	39	48	87
	Sidney Crosby	Pittsburgh	Center	2005-06	81	39	63	102
20.	* Gilbert Perreault	Buffalo	Center	1970-71	78	38	34	72
	Neal Broten	Minnesota	Center	1981-82	73	38	60	98
	Ray Sheppard	Buffalo	Right wing	1987-88	74	38	27	65
	Mikael Renberg	Philadelphia	Left wing	1993-94	83	38	44	82
24.	Jorgen Pettersson	St. Louis	Left wing	1980-81	62	37	36	73
	Jimmy Carson	Los Angeles	Center	1986-87	80	37	42	79
26.	Mike Foligno	Detroit	Right wing	1979-80	80	36	35	71
	Paul MacLean	Winnipeg	Right wing	1981-82	74	36	25	61
	Mike Bullard	Pittsburgh	Center	1981-82	75	36	27	63
	Tony Granato	NY Rangers	Right wing	1988-89	78	36	27	63
30.	Marian Stastny	Quebec	Right wing	1981-82	74	35	54	89
	Brian Bellows	Minnesota	Right wing	1982-83	78	35	30	65
	Tony Amonte	NY Rangers	Right wing	1991-92	79	35	34	69
33.	Nels Stewart	Mtl. Maroons	Center	1925-26	36	34	8	42
	* Danny Grant	Minnesota	Left wing	1968-69	75	34	31	65
	Norm Ferguson	Oakland	Right wing	1968-69	76	34	20	54
	Brian Propp	Philadelphia	Left wing	1979-80	80	34	41	75
	Wendel Clark	Toronto	Left wing	1985-86	66	34	11	45
	* Pavel Bure	Vancouver	Right wing	1991-92	65	34	26	60
	Michael Grabner	NY Islanders	Right wing	2010-11	76	34	18	52
40.	* Willi Plett	Atlanta	Right wing	1976-77	64	33	23	56
	Dale McCourt	Detroit	Center	1977-78	76	33	39	72
	Steve Bozek	Los Angeles	Center	1981-82	71	33	23	56
	Ron Flockhart	Philadelphia	Center	1981-82	72	33	39	72
	Mark Pavelich	NY Rangers	Center	1981-82	79	33	43	76
	Jason Arnott	Edmonton	Center	1993-94	78	33	35	68
	* Evgeni Malkin	Pittsburgh	Center	2006-07	78	33	52	85
47.	Bill Mosienko	Chicago	Right wing	1943-44	50	32	38	70
	Michel Bergeron	Detroit	Right wing	1975-76	72	32	27	59
	* Bryan Trottier	NY Islanders	Center	1975-76	80	32	63	95
	Don Murdoch	NY Rangers	Right wing	1976-77	59	32	24	56
	Jari Kurri	Edmonton	Left wing	1980-81	75	32	43	75
	Bobby Carpenter	Washington	Center	1981-82	80	32	35	67
	Petr Klima	Detroit	Left wing	1985-86	74	32	24	56
	Kjell Dahlin	Montreal	Right wing	1985-86	77	32	39	71
	Darren Turcotte	NY Rangers	Right wing	1989-90	76	32	34	66
	Joe Juneau	Boston	Center	1992-93	84	32	70	102
	Marek Svatos	Colorado	Right wing	2005-06	61	32	18	50
	Logan Couture	San Jose	Center	2010-11	79	32	24	56

* Calder Trophy Winner

All-Time Top 50 Point-Scoring Rookies

	Rookie	Team	Position	Season	GP	G	A	PTS
1.	* Teemu Selanne	Winnipeg	Right wing	1992-93	84	76	56	132
2.	* Peter Stastny	Quebec	Center	1980-81	77	39	70	109
3.	* Alex Ovechkin	Washington	Left wing	2005-06	81	52	54	106
4.	* Dale Hawerchuk	Winnipeg	Center	1981-82	80	45	58	103
5.	Joe Juneau	Boston	Center	1992-93	84	32	70	102
	Sidney Crosby	Pittsburgh	Center	2005-06	81	39	63	102
7.	* Mario Lemieux	Pittsburgh	Center	1984-85	73	43	57	100
8.	Neal Broten	Minnesota	Center	1981-82	73	38	60	98
9.	* Bryan Trottier	NY Islanders	Center	1975-76	80	32	63	95
10.	Barry Pederson	Boston	Center	1981-82	80	44	48	92
	* Joe Nieuwendyk	Calgary	Center	1987-88	75	51	41	92
12.	* Mike Bossy	NY Islanders	Right wing	1977-78	73	53	38	91
13.	* Steve Larmer	Chicago	Right wing	1982-83	80	43	47	90
14.	Marian Stastny	Quebec	Right wing	1981-82	74	35	54	89
15.	Steve Yzerman	Detroit	Center	1983-84	80	39	48	87
16.	* Sergei Makarov	Calgary	Right wing	1989-90	80	24	62	86
17.	Anton Stastny	Quebec	Left wing	1980-81	80	39	46	85
18.	* Evgeni Malkin	Pittsburgh	Center	2006-07	78	33	52	85
19.	* Luc Robitaille	Los Angeles	Left wing	1986-87	79	45	39	84
20.	Mikael Renberg	Philadelphia	Left wing	1993-94	83	38	44	82
21.	Jimmy Carson	Los Angeles	Center	1986-87	80	37	42	79
	Sergei Fedorov	Detroit	Center	1990-91	77	31	48	79
	Alexei Yashin	Ottawa	Center	1993-94	83	30	49	79
24.	Paul Stastny	Colorado	Center	2006-07	82	28	50	78
25.	Marcel Dionne	Detroit	Center	1971-72	78	28	49	77
26.	Larry Murphy	Los Angeles	Defense	1980-81	80	16	60	76
	Mark Pavelich	NY Rangers	Center	1981-82	79	33	43	76
	Dave Poulin	Philadelphia	Center	1983-84	73	31	45	76
29.	Brian Propp	Philadelphia	Left wing	1979-80	80	34	41	75
	Jari Kurri	Edmonton	Left wing	1980-81	75	32	43	75
	Denis Savard	Chicago	Center	1980-81	76	28	47	75
	Mike Modano	Minnesota	Center	1989-90	80	29	46	75
	Eric Lindros	Philadelphia	Center	1992-93	61	41	34	75
34.	Rick Martin	Buffalo	Left wing	1971-72	73	44	30	74
	* Bobby Smith	Minnesota	Center	1978-79	80	30	44	74
36.	Jorgen Pettersson	St. Louis	Left wing	1980-81	62	37	36	73
37.	* Gilbert Perreault	Buffalo	Center	1970-71	78	38	34	72
	Dale McCourt	Detroit	Center	1977-78	76	33	39	72
	Ron Flockhart	Philadelphia	Center	1981-82	72	33	39	72
	Sylvain Turgeon	Hartford	Left wing	1983-84	76	40	32	72
	Carey Wilson	Calgary	Center	1984-85	74	24	48	72
	Warren Young	Pittsburgh	Left wing	1984-85	80	40	32	72
	Alex Zhamnov	Winnipeg	Center	1992-93	68	25	47	72
	* Patrick Kane	Chicago	Right wing	2007-08	82	21	51	72
45.	Mike Foligno	Detroit	Right wing	1979-80	80	36	35	71
	Dave Christian	Winnipeg	Center	1980-81	80	28	43	71
	Mats Naslund	Montreal	Left wing	1982-83	74	26	45	71
	Kjell Dahlin	Montreal	Right wing	1985-86	77	32	39	71
	* Brian Leetch	NY Rangers	Defense	1988-89	68	23	48	71
50.	Bill Mosienko	Chicago	Right wing	1943-44	50	32	38	70
	* Scott Gomez	New Jersey	Center	99-2000	82	19	51	70

* Calder Trophy Winner

50-Goal Seasons

Mickey Redmond

Guy Chouinard

Wayne Babych

Player	Team	Date of 50th Goal	Score			Goaltender	Player's Game No.	Team Game No.	Total Goals	Total Games	Age When First 50th Scored (Yrs. & Mos.)
Maurice Richard	Mtl.	Mar. 18/45	Mtl. 4	at	Bos. 2	Harvey Bennett	50	50	50	50	23.7
Bernie Geoffrion	Mtl.	Mar. 16/61	Tor. 2	at	Mtl. 5	Cesare Maniago	62	68	50	64	30.1
Bobby Hull	Chi.	Mar. 25/62	Chi. 1	at	NYR 4	Gump Worsley	70	70	50	70	23.2
Bobby Hull	Chi.	Mar. 2/66	Det. 4	at	Chi. 5	Hank Bassen	52	57	54	65	
Bobby Hull	Chi.	Mar. 18/67	Chi. 5	at	Tor. 9	Bruce Gamble	63	66	52	66	
Bobby Hull	Chi.	Mar. 5/69	NYR 4	at	Chi. 4	Ed Giacomin	64	66	58	74	
Phil Esposito	Bos.	Feb. 20/71	Bos. 4	at	L.A. 5	Denis DeJordy	58	58	76	78	29.0
John Bucyk	Bos.	Mar. 16/71	Bos. 11	at	Det. 4	Roy Edwards	69	69	51	78	35.10
Phil Esposito	Bos.	Feb. 20/72	Bos. 3	at	Chi. 1	Tony Esposito	60	60	66	76	
Bobby Hull	Chi.	Apr. 2/72	Det. 1	at	Chi. 6	Andy Brown	78	78	50	78	
Vic Hadfield	NYR	Apr. 2/72	Mtl. 6	at	NYR 5	Denis DeJordy	78	78	50	78	31.6
Phil Esposito	Bos.	Mar. 25/73	Buf. 1	at	Bos. 6	Roger Crozier	75	75	55	78	
Mickey Redmond	Det.	Mar. 27/73	Det. 8	at	Tor. 1	Ron Low	73	75	52	76	25.3
Rick MacLeish	Phi.	Apr. 1/73	Phi. 4	at	Pit. 5	Cam Newton	78	78	50	78	23.2
Phil Esposito	Bos.	Feb. 20/74	Bos. 5	at	Min. 5	Cesare Maniago	56	56	68	78	
Mickey Redmond	Det.	Mar. 23/74	NYR 3	at	Det. 5	Ed Giacomin	69	71	51	76	
Ken Hodge	Bos.	Apr. 6/74	Bos. 2	at	Mtl. 6	Michel Larocque	75	77	50	76	29.10
Rick Martin	Buf.	Apr. 7/74	St.L. 2	at	Buf. 5	Wayne Stephenson	78	78	52	78	22.9
Phil Esposito	Bos.	Feb. 8/75	Bos. 8	at	Det. 5	Jim Rutherford	54	54	61	79	
Guy Lafleur	Mtl.	Mar. 29/75	K.C. 1	at	Mtl. 4	Denis Herron	66	76	53	70	23.6
Danny Grant	Det.	Apr. 2/75	Wsh. 3	at	Det. 8	John Adams	78	78	50	80	29.2
Rick Martin	Buf.	Apr. 3/75	Bos. 2	at	Buf. 4	Ken Broderick	67	79	52	68	
Reggie Leach	Phi.	Mar. 14/76	Atl. 1	at	Phi. 6	Dan Bouchard	69	69	61	80	25.11
Jean Pronovost	Pit.	Mar. 24/76	Bos. 5	at	Pit. 5	Gilles Gilbert	74	74	52	80	30.3
Guy Lafleur	Mtl.	Mar. 27/76	K.C. 2	at	Mtl. 8	Denis Herron	76	76	56	80	
Bill Barber	Phi.	Apr. 3/76	Buf. 2	at	Phi. 5	Al Smith	79	79	50	80	23.9
Pierre Larouche	Pit.	Apr. 3/76	Wsh. 5	at	Pit. 4	Ron Low	75	79	53	76	20.5
Danny Gare	Buf.	Apr. 4/76	Tor. 2	at	Buf. 5	Gord McRae	79	80	50	79	21.11
Steve Shutt	Mtl.	Mar. 1/77	Mtl. 5	at	NYI 4	Glenn Resch	65	65	60	80	24.8
Guy Lafleur	Mtl.	Mar. 6/77	Mtl. 1	at	Buf. 4	Don Edwards	68	68	56	80	
Marcel Dionne	L.A.	Apr. 2/77	Min. 2	at	L.A. 7	Pete LoPresti	79	79	53	80	25.8
Guy Lafleur	Mtl.	Mar. 8/78	Wsh. 3	at	Mtl. 4	Jim Bedard	63	65	60	78	
Mike Bossy	NYI	Apr. 1/78	Wsh. 2	at	NYI 3	Bernie Wolfe	69	76	53	73	21.2
Mike Bossy	NYI	Feb. 24/79	Det. 1	at	NYI 3	Rogie Vachon	58	58	69	80	
Marcel Dionne	L.A.	Mar. 11/79	L.A. 3	at	Phi. 6	Wayne Stephenson	68	68	59	80	
Guy Lafleur	Mtl.	Mar. 31/79	Pit. 3	at	Mtl. 5	Denis Herron	76	76	52	80	
Guy Chouinard	Atl.	Apr. 6/79	NYR 2	at	Atl. 9	John Davidson	79	79	50	80	22.5
Marcel Dionne	L.A.	Mar. 12/80	L.A. 2	at	Pit. 4	Nick Ricci	70	70	53	80	
Mike Bossy	NYI	Mar. 16/80	NYI 6	at	Chi. 1	Tony Esposito	68	71	51	75	
Charlie Simmer	L.A.	Mar. 19/80	Det. 3	at	L.A. 4	Jim Rutherford	57	73	56	64	26.0
Pierre Larouche	Mtl.	Mar. 25/80	Chi. 4	at	Mtl. 8	Tony Esposito	72	75	50	73	
Danny Gare	Buf.	Mar. 27/80	Det. 1	at	Buf. 10	Jim Rutherford	71	75	56	76	
Blaine Stoughton	Hfd.	Mar. 28/80	Hfd. 4	at	Van. 4	Glen Hanlon	75	75	56	80	27.0
Guy Lafleur	Mtl.	Apr. 2/80	Mtl. 7	at	Det. 2	Rogie Vachon	72	78	50	74	
Wayne Gretzky	Edm.	Apr. 2/80	Min. 1	at	Edm. 1	Gary Edwards	78	79	51	79	19.2
Reggie Leach	Phi.	Apr. 3/80	Wsh. 2	at	Phi. 4	empty net	75	79	50	76	
Mike Bossy	NYI	Jan. 24/81	Que. 3	at	NYI 7	Ron Grahame	50	50	68	79	
Charlie Simmer	L.A.	Jan. 26/81	L.A. 7	at	Que. 5	Michel Dion	51	51	56	65	
Marcel Dionne	L.A.	Mar. 8/81	L.A. 4	at	Wpg. 1	Markus Mattsson	68	68	58	80	
Wayne Babych	St.L.	Mar. 12/81	St.L. 3	at	Mtl. 4	Richard Sevigny	70	68	54	78	22.9
Wayne Gretzky	Edm.	Mar. 15/81	Edm. 3	at	Cgy. 3	Pat Riggin	69	69	55	80	
Rick Kehoe	Pit.	Mar. 16/81	Pit. 7	at	Edm. 6	Eddie Mio	70	70	55	80	29.7
Jacques Richard	Que.	Mar. 29/81	Mtl. 0	at	Que. 4	Richard Sevigny	76	75	52	78	28.6
Dennis Maruk	Wsh.	Apr. 5/81	Det. 2	at	Wsh. 7	Larry Lozinski	80	80	50	80	25.3
Wayne Gretzky	Edm.	Dec. 30/81	Phi. 5	at	Edm. 7	empty net	39	39	92	80	
Dennis Maruk	Wsh.	Feb. 21/82	Wpg. 3	at	Wsh. 6	Doug Soetaert	61	61	60	80	
Mike Bossy	NYI	Mar. 4/82	Tor. 1	at	NYI 10	Michel Larocque	66	66	64	80	
Dino Ciccarelli	Min.	Mar. 8/82	St.L. 1	at	Min. 8	Mike Liut	67	68	55	76	22.1
Rick Vaive	Tor.	Mar. 24/82	St.L. 3	at	Tor. 4	Mike Liut	72	75	54	77	22.10
Blaine Stoughton	Hfd.	Mar. 28/82	Min. 5	at	Hfd. 2	Gilles Meloche	76	76	52	80	
Rick Middleton	Bos.	Mar. 28/82	Bos. 5	at	Buf. 9	Paul Harrison	72	77	51	75	28.11
Marcel Dionne	L.A.	Mar. 30/82	Cgy. 7	at	L.A. 5	Pat Riggin	75	77	50	78	
Mark Messier	Edm.	Mar. 31/82	L.A. 3	at	Edm. 7	Mario Lessard	78	79	50	78	21.3
Bryan Trottier	NYI	Apr. 3/82	Phi. 3	at	NYI 6	Pete Peeters	79	79	50	80	25.9
Lanny McDonald	Cgy.	Feb. 18/83	Cgy. 1	at	Buf. 5	Bob Sauve	60	60	66	80	30.0
Wayne Gretzky	Edm.	Feb. 19/83	Edm. 10	at	Pit. 7	Nick Ricci	60	60	71	80	
Michel Goulet	Que.	Mar. 5/83	Hfd. 3	at	Que. 10	Mike Veisor	67	67	57	80	22.11
Mike Bossy	NYI	Mar. 12/83	Wsh. 2	at	NYI 6	Al Jensen	70	71	60	79	
Marcel Dionne	L.A.	Mar. 17/83	Que. 3	at	L.A. 4	Dan Bouchard	71	71	56	80	
Al Secord	Chi.	Mar. 20/83	Tor. 3	at	Chi. 7	Mike Palmateer	73	73	54	80	25.0
Rick Vaive	Tor.	Mar. 30/83	Tor. 4	at	Det. 2	Gilles Gilbert	76	78	51	78	
Wayne Gretzky	Edm.	Jan. 7/84	Hfd. 3	at	Edm. 5	Greg Millen	42	42	87	74	
Michel Goulet	Que.	Mar. 8/84	Que. 8	at	Pit. 6	Denis Herron	63	69	56	75	
Rick Vaive	Tor.	Mar. 14/84	Min. 3	at	Tor. 3	Gilles Meloche	69	72	52	76	
Mike Bullard	Pit.	Mar. 14/84	Pit. 6	at	L.A. 7	Markus Mattsson	71	72	51	76	23.0
Jari Kurri	Edm.	Mar. 15/84	Edm. 2	at	Mtl. 3	Rick Wamsley	57	73	52	64	23.10
Glenn Anderson	Edm.	Mar. 21/84	Hfd. 3	at	Edm. 5	Greg Millen	76	76	54	80	23.6
Tim Kerr	Phi.	Mar. 22/84	Pit. 4	at	Phi. 13	Denis Herron	74	75	54	79	24.3

Player	Team	Date of 50th Goal	Score		Goaltender	Player's Game No.	Team Game No.	Total Goals	Total Games	Age When First 50th Scored (Yrs. & Mos.)
Mike Bossy	NYI	Mar. 31/84	NYI 3	at Wsh. 1	Pat Riggin	67	79	51	67	
Wayne Gretzky	Edm.	Jan. 26/85	Pit. 3	at Edm. 6	Denis Herron	49	49	73	80	
Jari Kurri	Edm.	Feb. 3/85	Hfd. 3	at Edm. 6	Greg Millen	50	53	71	73	
Mike Bossy	NYI	Mar. 5/85	Phi. 5	at NYI 4	Bob Froese	61	65	58	76	
Michel Goulet	Que.	Mar. 6/85	Buf. 3	at Que. 4	Tom Barrasso	62	73	55	69	
Tim Kerr	Phi.	Mar. 7/85	Wsh. 6	at Phi. 9	Pat Riggin	63	65	54	74	
John Ogrodnick	Det.	Mar. 13/85	Det. 6	at Edm. 7	Grant Fuhr	69	69	55	79	25.9
Bob Carpenter	Wsh.	Mar. 21/85	Wsh. 2	at Mtl. 3	Steve Penney	72	72	53	80	21.9
Dale Hawerchuk	Wpg.	Mar. 29/85	Chi. 5	at Wpg. 5	W. Skorodenski	77	77	53	80	21.11
Mike Gartner	Wsh.	Apr. 7/85	Pit. 3	at Wsh. 7	Brian Ford	80	80	50	80	25.5
Jari Kurri	Edm.	Mar. 4/86	Edm. 6	at Van. 2	Richard Brodeur	63	65	68	78	
Mike Bossy	NYI	Mar. 11/86	Cgy. 4	at NYI 8	Reggie Lemelin	67	67	61	80	
Glenn Anderson	Edm.	Mar. 14/86	Det. 3	at Edm. 12	Greg Stefan	63	71	54	72	
Michel Goulet	Que.	Mar. 17/86	Que. 8	at Mtl. 6	Patrick Roy	67	72	53	75	
Wayne Gretzky	Edm.	Mar. 18/86	Wpg. 2	at Edm. 6	Brian Hayward	72	72	52	80	
Tim Kerr	Phi.	Mar. 20/86	Pit. 1	at Phi. 5	Roberto Romano	68	72	58	76	
Wayne Gretzky	Edm.	Feb. 4/87	Edm. 6	at Min. 5	Don Beaupre	55	55	62	79	
Dino Ciccarelli	Min.	Mar. 7/87	Pit. 7	at Min. 3	Gilles Meloche	66	66	52	80	
Mario Lemieux	Pit.	Mar. 12/87	Que. 3	at Pit. 6	Mario Gosselin	53	70	54	63	21.5
Tim Kerr	Phi.	Mar. 17/87	NYR 1	at Phi. 4	J. Vanbiesbrouck	67	71	58	75	
Jari Kurri	Edm.	Mar. 17/87	N.J. 4	at Edm. 7	Craig Billington	69	70	54	79	
Mario Lemieux	Pit.	Feb. 2/88	Wsh. 2	at Pit. 3	Pete Peeters	51	54	70	77	
Steve Yzerman	Det.	Mar. 1/88	Buf. 0	at Det. 4	Tom Barrasso	64	64	50	64	22.10
Joe Nieuwendyk	Cgy.	Mar. 12/88	Buf. 4	at Cgy. 10	Tom Barrasso	66	70	51	75	21.5
Craig Simpson	Edm.	Mar. 15/88	Buf. 4	at Edm. 5	Jacques Cloutier	71	71	56	80	21.1
Jimmy Carson	L.A.	Mar. 26/88	Chi. 5	at L.A. 9	Darren Pang	77	77	55	88	19.8
Luc Robitaille	L.A.	Apr. 1/88	L.A. 6	at Cgy. 3	Mike Vernon	79	79	53	80	21.10
Hakan Loob	Cgy.	Apr. 3/88	Min. 1	at Cgy. 4	Don Beaupre	80	80	50	80	27.9
Stephane Richer	Mtl.	Apr. 3/88	Mtl. 4	at Buf. 4	Tom Barrasso	72	80	50	72	21.10
Mario Lemieux	Pit.	Jan. 20/89	Pit. 3	at Wpg. 7	Pokey Reddick	44	46	85	76	
Bernie Nicholls	L.A.	Jan. 28/89	Edm. 7	at L.A. 6	Grant Fuhr	51	51	70	79	27.7
Steve Yzerman	Det.	Feb. 5/89	Det. 6	at Wpg. 2	Pokey Reddick	55	55	65	80	
Wayne Gretzky	L.A.	Mar. 4/89	Phi. 2	at L.A. 6	Ron Hextall	66	67	54	78	
Joe Nieuwendyk	Cgy.	Mar. 21/89	NYI 1	at Cgy. 4	Mark Fitzpatrick	72	74	51	77	
Joe Mullen	Cgy.	Mar. 31/89	Wpg. 1	at Cgy. 4	Bob Essensa	78	79	51	79	32.1
Brett Hull	St.L.	Feb. 6/90	Tor. 4	at St.L. 6	Jeff Reese	54	54	72	80	25.6
Steve Yzerman	Det.	Feb. 24/90	Det. 3	at NYI 3	Glenn Healy	63	63	62	79	
Cam Neely	Bos.	Mar. 10/90	Bos. 3	at NYI 3	Mark Fitzpatrick	69	71	55	76	24.9
Brian Bellows	Min.	Mar. 22/90	Min. 5	at Det. 1	Tim Cheveldae	75	75	55	80	25.6
Pat LaFontaine	NYI	Mar. 24/90	NYI 5	at Edm. 5	Bill Ranford	71	77	54	74	25.1
Stephane Richer	Mtl.	Mar. 24/90	Mtl. 4	at Hfd. 7	Peter Sidorkiewicz	75	77	51	75	
Gary Leeman	Tor.	Mar. 28/90	NYI 6	at Tor. 3	Mark Fitzpatrick	78	78	51	80	26.1
Luc Robitaille	L.A.	Mar. 31/90	L.A. 3	at Van. 6	Kirk McLean	79	79	52	80	
Brett Hull	St.L.	Jan. 25/91	St.L. 9	at Det. 4	David Gagnon	49	49	86	78	
Cam Neely	Bos.	Mar. 26/91	Bos. 7	at Que. 4	empty net	67	78	51	69	
Theoren Fleury	Cgy.	Mar. 26/91	Van. 2	at Cgy. 7	Bob Mason	77	77	51	79	22.9
Steve Yzerman	Det.	Mar. 30/91	NYR 5	at Det. 6	Mike Richter	79	79	51	80	
Brett Hull	St.L.	Jan. 28/92	St.L. 3	at L.A. 3	Kelly Hrudey	50	50	70	73	
Jeremy Roenick	Chi.	Mar. 7/92	Chi. 2	at Bos. 1	Daniel Berthiaume	67	67	53	80	22.2
Kevin Stevens	Pit.	Mar. 24/92	Pit. 3	at Det. 4	Tim Cheveldae	74	74	54	80	26.11
Gary Roberts	Cgy.	Mar. 31/92	Edm. 2	at Cgy. 5	Bill Ranford	73	77	53	76	25.10
Alexander Mogilny	Buf.	Feb. 3/93	Hfd. 2	at Buf. 3	Sean Burke	46	53	76	77	23.11
Teemu Selanne	Wpg.	Feb. 28/93	Min. 6	at Wpg. 7	Darcy Wakaluk	63	63	76	84	22.6
Pavel Bure	Van.	Mar. 1/93	Van. 5	at Buf. 2*	Grant Fuhr	63	63	60	83	21.11
Steve Yzerman	Det.	Mar. 10/93	Det. 6	at Edm. 3	Bill Ranford	70	70	58	84	
Luc Robitaille	L.A.	Mar. 15/93	L.A. 4	at Buf. 2	Grant Fuhr	69	69	63	84	
Brett Hull	St.L.	Mar. 20/93	St.L. 2	at L.A. 3	Robb Stauber	73	73	54	80	
Mario Lemieux	Pit.	Mar. 21/93	Pit. 6	at Edm. 4**	Ron Tugnutt	48	72	69	60	
Kevin Stevens	Pit.	Mar. 21/93	Pit. 6	at Edm. 4**	Ron Tugnutt	62	72	55	72	
Dave Andreychuk	Tor.	Mar. 23/93	Tor. 5	at Wpg. 4	Bob Essensa	72	73	54	83	29.6
Pat LaFontaine	Buf.	Mar. 28/93	Ott. 1	at Buf. 3	Peter Sidorkiewicz	75	75	53	84	
Pierre Turgeon	NYI	Apr. 2/93	NYI 3	at NYR 2	Mike Richter	75	76	58	83	23.8
Mark Recchi	Phi.	Apr. 3/93	T.B. 2	at Phi. 6	J-C Bergeron	77	77	53	84	25.2
Brendan Shanahan	St.L.	Apr. 15/93	T.B. 5	at St.L. 6	Pat Jablonski	71	84	51	71	24.3
Jeremy Roenick	Chi.	Apr. 15/93	Tor. 2	at Chi. 3	Felix Potvin	84	84	50	84	
Cam Neely	Bos.	Mar. 7/94	Wsh. 3	at Bos. 6	Don Beaupre	44	66	50	49	
Sergei Fedorov	Det.	Mar. 15/94	Van. 2	at Det. 5	Kirk McLean	67	69	56	82	24.3
Pavel Bure	Van.	Mar. 23/94	Van. 6	at L.A. 3	empty net	65	73	60	76	
Adam Graves	NYR	Mar. 23/94	NYR 5	at Edm. 3	Bill Ranford	74	74	51	84	25.11
Dave Andreychuk	Tor.	Mar. 24/94	S.J. 2	at Tor. 1	Arturs Irbe	73	74	53	83	
Brett Hull	St.L.	Mar. 25/94	Dal. 3	at St.L. 5	Andy Moog	71	74	52	81	
Ray Sheppard	Det.	Mar. 29/94	Hfd. 2	at Det. 6	Sean Burke	74	76	52	82	27.10
Brendan Shanahan	St.L.	Apr. 12/94	St.L. 5	at Dal. 9	Andy Moog	80	83	52	81	
Mike Modano	Dal.	Apr. 12/94	St.L. 5	at Dal. 9	Curtis Joseph	75	83	50	76	23.11
Mario Lemieux	Pit.	Feb. 23/96	Hfd. 4	at Pit. 5	Sean Burke	50	59	69	70	
Jaromir Jagr	Pit.	Feb. 23/96	Hfd. 4	at Pit. 5	Sean Burke	59	59	62	82	24.0
Alexander Mogilny	Van.	Feb. 29/96	St.L. 2	at Van. 2	Grant Fuhr	60	63	55	79	
Peter Bondra	Wsh.	Apr. 3/96	Wsh. 5	at Buf. 1	Andrei Trefilov	62	77	52	67	28.1
Joe Sakic	Col.	Apr. 7/96	Col. 4	at Dal. 1	empty net	79	79	51	82	26.7
John LeClair	Phi.	Apr. 10/96	Phi. 5	at N.J. 1	Corey Schwab	80	80	51	82	26.7
Keith Tkachuk	Wpg.	Apr. 12/96	L.A. 3	at Wpg. 5	empty net	75	81	50	76	24.0
Paul Kariya	Ana.	Apr. 14/96	Wpg. 2	at Ana. 5	N. Khabibulin	82	82	50	82	21.5
Keith Tkachuk	Phx.	Apr. 6/97	Phx. 1	at Col. 2	Patrick Roy	78	79	52	81	
Teemu Selanne	Ana.	Apr. 9/97	L.A. 1	at Ana. 4	empty net	77	81	51	78	
Mario Lemieux	Pit.	Apr. 11/97	Pit. 2	at Fla. 4	J. Vanbiesbrouck	75	81	50	76	

Craig Simpson

Cam Neely

Pavel Bure

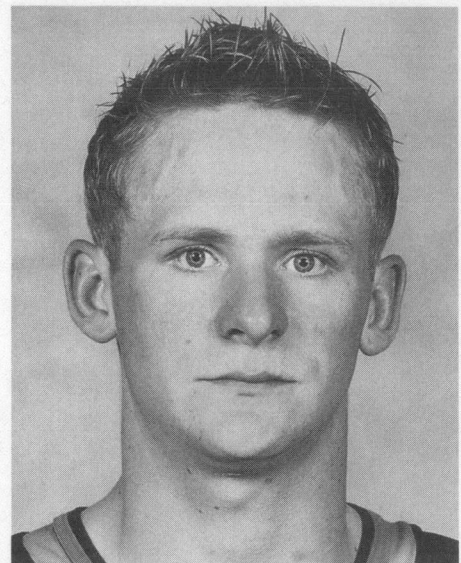

Corey Perry

Player	Team	Date of 50th Goal	Score		Goaltender	Player's Game No.	Team Game No.	Total Goals	Total Games	Age When First 50th Scored (Yrs. & Mos.)
John LeClair	Phi.	Apr. 13/97	N.J. 4	at Phi. 5	Mike Dunham	82	82	50	82	
Teemu Selanne	Ana.	Mar. 25/98	Ana. 3	at Chi. 2	Jeff Hackett	66	71	52	73	
John LeClair	Phi.	Apr. 13/98	Phi. 1	at Buf. 2	Dominik Hasek	79	79	51	82	
Pavel Bure	Van.	Apr. 17/98	Cgy. 4	at Van. 2	Dwayne Roloson	81	81	51	82	
Peter Bondra	Wsh.	Apr. 18/98	Wsh. 4	at Car. 3	Mike Fountain	75	80	52	76	
Pavel Bure	Fla.	Mar. 18/00	Fla. 4	at NYI 2	empty net	63	71	58	74	
Pavel Bure	Fla.	Mar. 16/01	Pit. 6	at Fla. 3	Johan Hedberg	72	72	59	82	
Joe Sakic	Col.	Apr. 4/01	Ana. 1	at Col. 1	J-S Giguere	80	80	54	82	
Jaromir Jagr	Pit.	Apr. 4/01	T.B. 2	at Pit. 4	Kevin Weekes	80	80	52	81	
Jarome Iginla	Cgy.	Apr. 7/02	Cgy. 2	at Chi. 3	Jocelyn Thibault	79	79	52	82	24.9
Milan Hejduk	Col.	Apr. 6/03	St. L. 2	at Col. 5	Brent Johnson	82	82	50	82	27.1
Jaromir Jagr	NYR	Mar. 24/06	NYR 2	at Fla. 3	Roberto Luongo	70	70	54	82	
Ilya Kovalchuk	Atl.	Apr. 6/06	Atl. 2	at T.B. 3	Sean Burke	72	76	52	78	22.11
Jonathan Cheechoo	S.J.	Apr. 10/06	S.J. 3	at Phx. 2	David LeNeveu	78	78	56	82	25.8
Alex Ovechkin	Wsh.	Apr. 13/06	Wsh. 3	at Atl. 5	Mike Dunham	78	79	52	81	20.6
Dany Heatley	Ott.	Apr. 18/06	Ott. 5	at NYR 1	Henrik Lundqvist	82	82	50	82	25.2
Vincent Lecavalier	T.B.	Mar. 30/07	T.B. 4	at Car. 2	Cam Ward	78	78	52	82	26.11
Dany Heatley	Ott.	Apr. 7/07	Ott. 6	at Bos. 3	Tim Thomas	82	82	50	82	
Alex Ovechkin	Wsh.	Mar. 3/08	Bos. 2	at Wsh. 10	Tim Thomas	67	67	65	82	
Ilya Kovalchuk	Atl.	Mar. 18/08	Atl. 2	at Phi. 3	Antero Niittymaki	72	75	52	79	
Jarome Iginla	Cgy.	Apr. 5/08	Cgy. 7	at Van. 1	Curtis Sanford	82	82	50	82	
Alex Ovechkin	Wsh.	Mar. 19/09	Wsh. 5	at T.B. 2	Mike McKenna	70	73	56	79	
Alex Ovechkin	Wsh.	Apr. 9/10	Atl. 2	at Wsh. 5	Ondrej Pavelec	71	81	50	72	
Steven Stamkos	T.B.	Apr. 10/10	Fla. 3	at T.B. 4	S. Clemmensen	81	81	51	82	20.2
Sidney Crosby	Pit.	Apr. 11/10	Pit. 6	at NYI 5	Dwayne Roloson	81	82	51	81	22.8
Corey Perry	Ana.	Apr. 6/11	S.J. 2	at Ana. 6	Antero Niittymaki	80	80	50	62	25.11

* neutral site game played at Hamilton; ** neutral site game played at Cleveland

100-Point Seasons

Bobby Orr

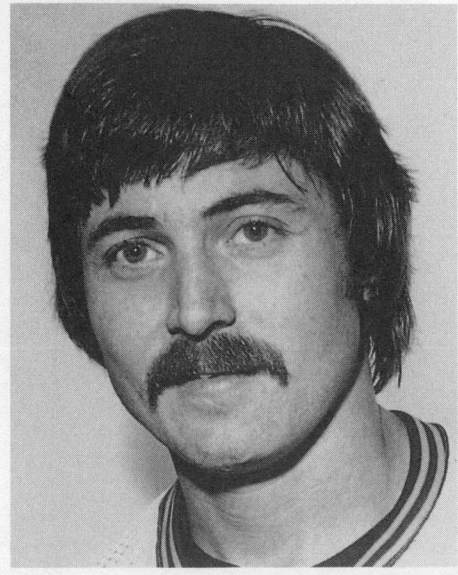

Rene Robert

Player	Team	Date of 100th Point	G or A	Score		Player's Game No.	Team Game No.	G - A PTS	Total Games	Age when first 100th point scored (Yrs. & Mos.)
Phil Esposito	Bos.	Mar. 2/69	(G)	Pit. 0	at Bos. 4	60	62	49-77 — 126	74	27.1
Bobby Hull	Chi.	Mar. 20/69	(G)	Chi. 5	at Bos. 5	71	71	58-49 — 107	76	30.2
Gordie Howe	Det.	Mar. 30/69	(G)	Det. 5	at Chi. 9	76	76	44-59 — 103	76	41.0
Bobby Orr	Bos.	Mar. 15/70	(G)	Det. 5	at Bos. 5	67	67	33-87 — 120	76	22.11
Phil Esposito	Bos.	Feb. 6/71	(A)	Buf. 3	at Bos. 4	51	51	76-76 — 152	78	
Bobby Orr	Bos.	Feb. 20/71	(A)	Bos. 4	at L.A. 5	58	58	37-102 — 139	78	
John Bucyk	Bos.	Mar. 13/71	(A)	Bos. 6	at Van. 3	68	68	51-65 — 116	78	35.10
Ken Hodge	Bos.	Mar. 21/71	(A)	Buf. 7	at Bos. 5	72	72	43-62 — 105	78	26.9
Jean Ratelle	NYR	Feb. 18/72	(A)	NYR 2	at Cal. 2	58	58	46-63 — 109	63	31.4
Phil Esposito	Bos.	Feb. 19/72	(A)	Bos. 6	at Min. 4	59	59	66-67 — 133	76	
Bobby Orr	Bos.	Mar. 2/72	(A)	Van. 3	at Bos. 7	64	64	37-80 — 117	76	
Vic Hadfield	NYR	Mar. 25/72	(A)	NYR 3	at Mtl. 3	74	74	50-56 — 106	78	31.5
Phil Esposito	Bos.	Mar. 3/73	(A)	Bos. 1	at Mtl. 5	64	64	55-75 — 130	78	
Bobby Clarke	Phi.	Mar. 29/73	(G)	Atl. 2	at Phi. 4	76	76	37-67 — 104	78	23.7
Bobby Orr	Bos.	Mar. 31/73	(G)	Bos. 3	at Tor. 7	62	77	29-72 — 101	63	
Rick MacLeish	Phi.	Apr. 1/73	(A)	Phi. 4	at Pit. 5	78	78	50-50 — 100	78	23.3
Phil Esposito	Bos.	Feb. 13/74	(A)	Bos. 9	at Cal. 6	53	53	68-77 — 145	78	
Bobby Orr	Bos.	Mar. 12/74	(A)	Buf. 0	at Bos. 4	62	66	32-90 — 122	74	
Ken Hodge	Bos.	Mar. 24/74	(A)	Mtl. 3	at Bos. 6	72	72	50-55 — 105	76	
Phil Esposito	Bos.	Feb. 8/75	(A)	Bos. 8	at Det. 5	54	54	61-66 — 127	79	
Bobby Orr	Bos.	Feb. 13/75	(A)	Bos. 1	at Buf. 3	57	57	46-89 — 135	80	
Guy Lafleur	Mtl.	Mar. 7/75	(G)	Wsh. 4	at Mtl. 8	56	66	53-66 — 119	70	24.6
Marcel Dionne	Det.	Mar. 9/75	(A)	Det. 5	at Phi. 8	67	67	47-74 — 121	80	23.7
Pete Mahovlich	Mtl.	Mar. 9/75	(G)	Mtl. 5	at NYR 3	67	67	35-82 — 117	80	29.5
Bobby Clarke	Phi.	Mar. 22/75	(A)	Min. 0	at Phi. 4	72	72	27-89 — 116	80	
Rene Robert	Buf.	Apr. 5/75	(A)	Buf. 4	at Tor. 2	74	80	40-60 — 100	74	26.4
Guy Lafleur	Mtl.	Mar. 10/76	(G)	Mtl. 5	at Chi. 1	69	69	56-69 — 125	80	
Bobby Clarke	Phi.	Mar. 11/76	(A)	Buf. 1	at Phi. 6	64	68	30-89 — 119	76	
Bill Barber	Phi.	Mar. 18/76	(A)	Van. 2	at Phi. 3	71	71	50-62 — 112	80	23.8
Gilbert Perreault	Buf.	Mar. 21/76	(A)	K.C. 1	at Buf. 3	73	73	44-69 — 113	80	25.4
Pierre Larouche	Pit.	Mar. 24/76	(G)	Bos. 5	at Pit. 5	70	74	53-58 — 111	76	20.4
Pete Mahovlich	Mtl.	Mar. 28/76	(A)	Mtl. 2	at Bos. 2	77	77	34-71 — 105	80	
Jean Ratelle	Bos.	Mar. 30/76	(G)	Buf. 4	at Bos. 4	77	77	36-69 — 105	80	
Jean Pronovost	Pit.	Apr. 3/76	(A)	Wsh. 5	at Pit. 4	79	79	52-52 — 104	80	30.4
Darryl Sittler	Tor.	Apr. 3/76	(A)	Bos. 4	at Tor. 2	78	79	41-59 — 100	79	25.7
Guy Lafleur	Mtl.	Feb. 26/77	(A)	Cle. 3	at Mtl. 5	63	63	56-80 — 136	80	
Marcel Dionne	L.A.	Mar. 5/77	(G)	Pit. 3	at L.A. 3	67	67	53-69 — 122	80	
Steve Shutt	Mtl.	Mar. 27/77	(A)	Mtl. 6	at Det. 0	77	77	60-45 — 105	80	24.9
Bryan Trottier	NYI	Feb. 25/78	(A)	Chi. 1	at NYI 7	59	60	46-77 — 123	77	21.7
Guy Lafleur	Mtl.	Feb. 28/78	(G)	Det. 3	at Mtl. 9	69	61	60-72 — 132	78	
Darryl Sittler	Tor.	Mar. 12/78	(A)	Tor. 7	at Pit. 1	67	67	45-72 — 117	80	

Player	Team	Date of 100th Point	G or A	Score			Player's Game No.	Team Game No.	G - A	PTS	Total Games	Age when first 100th point scored (Yrs. & Mos.)
Guy Lafleur	Mtl.	Feb. 27/79	(A)	Mtl. 3	at	NYI 7	61	61	52-77 —	129	80	
Bryan Trottier	NYI	Mar. 6/79	(A)	Buf. 3	at	NYI 2	59	63	47-87 —	134	76	
Marcel Dionne	L.A.	Mar. 8/79	(G)	L.A. 4	at	Buf. 6	66	66	59-71 —	130	80	
Mike Bossy	NYI	Mar. 11/79	(G)	NYI 4	at	Bos. 4	66	66	69-57 —	126	80	22.2
Bob MacMillan	Atl.	Mar. 15/79	(A)	Atl. 4	at	Phi. 5	68	69	37-71 —	108	79	26.6
Guy Chouinard	Atl.	Mar. 30/79	(G)	L.A. 3	at	Atl. 5	75	75	50-57 —	107	80	22.5
Denis Potvin	NYI	Apr. 8/79	(A)	NYI 5	at	NYR 2	73	80	31-70 —	101	73	25.5
Marcel Dionne	L.A.	Feb. 6/80	(A)	L.A. 3	at	Hfd. 7	53	53	53-84 —	137	80	
Guy Lafleur	Mtl.	Feb. 10/80	(A)	Mtl. 3	at	Bos. 2	55	55	50-75 —	125	74	
Wayne Gretzky	Edm.	Feb. 24/80	(A)	Bos. 4	at	Edm. 2	61	62	51-86 —	137	79	19.2
Bryan Trottier	NYI	Mar. 30/80	(A)	NYI 9	at	Que. 6	75	77	42-62 —	104	78	
Gilbert Perreault	Buf.	Apr. 1/80	(A)	Buf. 5	at	Atl. 2	77	77	40-66 —	106	80	
Mike Rogers	Hfd.	Apr. 4/80	(A)	Que. 2	at	Hfd. 9	79	79	44-61 —	105	80	25.5
Charlie Simmer	L.A.	Apr. 5/80	(G)	Van. 5	at	L.A. 3	64	80	56-45 —	101	64	26.0
Blaine Stoughton	Hfd.	Apr. 6/80	(A)	Det. 3	at	Hfd. 5	80	80	56-44 —	100	80	27.0
Wayne Gretzky	Edm.	Feb. 6/81	(G)	Wpg. 4	at	Edm. 10	53	53	55-109 —	164	80	
Marcel Dionne	L.A.	Feb. 12/81	(A)	L.A. 5	at	Chi. 5	58	58	58-77 —	135	80	
Charlie Simmer	L.A.	Feb. 14/81	(A)	Bos. 5	at	L.A. 4	59	59	56-49 —	105	65	
Kent Nilsson	Cgy.	Feb. 27/81	(G)	Hfd. 1	at	Cgy. 5	64	64	49-82 —	131	80	24.6
Mike Bossy	NYI	Mar. 3/81	(G)	Edm. 8	at	NYI 8	65	66	68-51 —	119	79	
Dave Taylor	L.A.	Mar. 14/81	(G)	Min. 4	at	L.A. 10	63	70	47-65 —	112	72	25.3
Mike Rogers	Hfd.	Mar. 22/81	(G)	Tor. 3	at	Hfd. 3	74	74	40-65 —	105	80	
Bernie Federko	St.L.	Mar. 28/81	(A)	Buf. 4	at	St.L. 7	74	76	31-73 —	104	78	24.10
Rick Middleton	Bos.	Mar. 28/81	(A)	Chi. 2	at	Bos. 5	76	76	44-59 —	103	80	27.4
Bryan Trottier	NYI	Mar. 29/81	(G)	NYI 5	at	Wsh. 4	69	76	31-72 —	103	73	
Jacques Richard	Que.	Mar. 29/81	(G)	Mtl. 0	at	Que. 4	75	76	52-51 —	103	78	28.6
Peter Stastny	Que.	Mar. 29/81	(A)	Mtl. 0	at	Que. 4	73	76	39-70 —	109	77	24.6
Wayne Gretzky	Edm.	Dec. 27/81	(G)	L.A. 3	at	Edm. 10	38	38	92-120 —	212	80	
Mike Bossy	NYI	Feb. 13/82	(A)	Phi. 2	at	NYI 8	55	55	64-83 —	147	80	
Peter Stastny	Que.	Feb. 16/82	(A)	Wpg. 3	at	Que. 7	60	60	46-93 —	139	80	
Dennis Maruk	Wsh.	Feb. 20/82	(G)	Wsh. 3	at	Min. 7	60	60	60-76 —	136	80	26.3
Bryan Trottier	NYI	Feb. 23/82	(G)	Chi. 1	at	NYI 5	61	61	50-79 —	129	80	
Denis Savard	Chi.	Feb. 27/82	(G)	Chi. 5	at	L.A. 3	64	64	32-87 —	119	80	21.1
Bobby Smith	Min.	Mar. 3/82	(A)	Det. 4	at	Min. 6	66	66	43-71 —	114	80	24.1
Marcel Dionne	L.A.	Mar. 6/82	(G)	L.A. 6	at	Hfd. 7	64	66	50-67 —	117	78	
Dave Taylor	L.A.	Mar. 20/82	(A)	Pit. 5	at	L.A. 7	71	72	39-67 —	106	78	
Dale Hawerchuk	Wpg.	Mar. 24/82	(A)	L.A. 3	at	Wpg. 5	74	74	45-58 —	103	80	18.11
Dino Ciccarelli	Min.	Mar. 27/82	(A)	Min. 6	at	Bos. 5	72	76	55-52 —	107	76	21.8
Glenn Anderson	Edm.	Mar. 28/82	(G)	Edm. 6	at	L.A. 2	78	78	38-67 —	105	80	21.7
Mike Rogers	NYR	Apr. 2/82	(G)	Pit. 7	at	NYR 5	79	79	38-65 —	103	80	
Wayne Gretzky	Edm.	Jan. 5/83	(A)	Edm. 8	at	Wpg. 3	42	42	71-125 —	196	80	
Mike Bossy	NYI	Mar. 3/83	(A)	Tor. 1	at	NYI 5	66	67	60-58 —	118	79	
Peter Stastny	Que.	Mar. 5/83	(A)	Hfd. 3	at	Que. 10	62	67	47-77 —	124	75	
Denis Savard	Chi.	Mar. 6/83	(G)	Mtl. 4	at	Chi. 5	65	67	35-86 —	121	78	
Mark Messier	Edm.	Mar. 23/83	(G)	Edm. 4	at	Wpg. 7	73	76	48-58 —	106	77	22.2
Barry Pederson	Bos.	Mar. 26/83	(A)	Hfd. 4	at	Bos. 7	73	76	46-61 —	107	77	22.0
Marcel Dionne	L.A.	Mar. 26/83	(A)	Edm. 9	at	L.A. 3	75	75	56-51 —	107	80	
Michel Goulet	Que.	Mar. 27/83	(A)	Que. 6	at	Buf. 6	77	77	57-48 —	105	80	22.11
Glenn Anderson	Edm.	Mar. 29/83	(A)	Edm. 7	at	Van. 4	70	78	48-56 —	104	72	
Jari Kurri	Edm.	Mar. 29/83	(A)	Edm. 7	at	Van. 4	78	78	45-59 —	104	80	22.10
Kent Nilsson	Cgy.	Mar. 29/83	(G)	L.A. 3	at	Cgy. 5	78	78	46-58 —	104	80	
Wayne Gretzky	Edm.	Dec. 18/83	(G)	Edm. 7	at	Wpg. 5	34	34	87-118 —	205	74	
Paul Coffey	Edm.	Mar. 4/84	(A)	Mtl. 1	at	Edm. 6	68	68	40-86 —	126	80	22.9
Michel Goulet	Que.	Mar. 4/84	(A)	Que. 1	at	Buf. 1	62	67	56-65 —	121	75	
Jari Kurri	Edm.	Mar. 7/84	(G)	Chi. 4	at	Edm. 7	53	69	52-61 —	113	64	
Peter Stastny	Que.	Mar. 8/84	(A)	Que. 8	at	Pit. 6	69	69	46-73 —	119	80	
Mike Bossy	NYI	Mar. 8/84	(G)	Tor. 5	at	NYI 9	56	68	51-67 —	118	67	
Barry Pederson	Bos.	Mar. 14/84	(A)	Bos. 4	at	Det. 2	71	71	39-77 —	116	80	
Bryan Trottier	NYI	Mar. 18/84	(A)	NYI 4	at	Hfd. 5	62	73	40-71 —	111	68	
Bernie Federko	St.L.	Mar. 20/84	(A)	Wpg. 3	at	St.L. 9	75	76	41-66 —	107	79	
Rick Middleton	Bos.	Mar. 27/84	(G)	Bos. 6	at	Que. 4	77	77	47-58 —	105	80	
Dale Hawerchuk	Wpg.	Mar. 27/84	(A)	Wpg. 3	at	L.A. 3	77	77	37-65 —	102	80	
Mark Messier	Edm.	Mar. 27/84	(G)	Edm. 9	at	Cgy. 2	72	79	37-64 —	101	73	
Wayne Gretzky	Edm.	Dec. 29/84	(A)	Det. 3	at	Edm. 6	35	35	73-135 —	208	80	
Jari Kurri	Edm.	Jan. 29/85	(G)	Edm. 4	at	Cgy. 2	48	51	71-64 —	135	73	
Mike Bossy	NYI	Feb. 23/85	(G)	Bos. 1	at	NYI 7	56	60	58-59 —	117	76	
Dale Hawerchuk	Wpg.	Feb. 25/85	(A)	Wpg. 12	at	NYR 5	64	64	53-77 —	130	80	
Marcel Dionne	L.A.	Mar. 5/85	(A)	Pit. 0	at	L.A. 6	66	66	46-80 —	126	80	
Brent Sutter	NYI	Mar. 12/85	(A)	NYI 6	at	St.L. 5	68	68	42-60 —	102	72	22.10
John Ogrodnick	Det.	Mar. 22/85	(A)	NYR 3	at	Det. 5	73	73	55-50 —	105	79	25.9
Paul Coffey	Edm.	Mar. 26/85	(G)	Edm. 7	at	NYI 5	74	74	37-84 —	121	80	
Denis Savard	Chi.	Mar. 29/85	(A)	Chi. 5	at	Wpg. 5	75	76	38-67 —	105	79	
Peter Stastny	Que.	Apr. 2/85	(A)	Bos. 4	at	Que. 6	74	77	32-68 —	100	75	
Bernie Federko	St.L.	Apr. 4/85	(A)	NYR 5	at	St.L. 4	74	78	30-73 —	103	76	
Paul MacLean	Wpg.	Apr. 6/85	(A)	Wpg. 6	at	Edm. 5	78	79	41-60 —	101	79	27.1
Bernie Nicholls	L.A.	Apr. 6/85	(A)	Van. 4	at	L.A. 4	80	80	46-54 —	100	80	22.9
John Tonelli	NYI	Apr. 6/85	(G)	N.J. 5	at	NYI 5	80	80	42-58 —	100	80	28.1
Mike Gartner	Wsh.	Apr. 7/85	(G)	Pit. 3	at	Wsh. 7	80	80	50-52 —	102	80	25.6
Mario Lemieux	Pit.	Apr. 7/85	(G)	Pit. 3	at	Wsh. 7	73	80	43-57 —	100	73	19.6
Wayne Gretzky	Edm.	Jan. 4/86	(A)	Hfd. 3	at	Edm. 4	39	39	52-163 —	215	80	
Mario Lemieux	Pit.	Feb. 15/86	(G)	Van. 4	at	Pit. 9	55	56	48-93 —	141	79	
Paul Coffey	Edm.	Feb. 19/86	(A)	Tor. 5	at	Edm. 9	59	60	48-90 —	138	79	
Peter Stastny	Que.	Mar. 1/86	(A)	Buf. 8	at	Que. 4	66	68	41-81 —	122	76	
Jari Kurri	Edm.	Mar. 2/86	(G)	Phi. 1	at	Edm. 2	62	64	68-63 —	131	78	

Wayne Gretzky

Dale Hawerchuk

Bernie Federko

Jimmy Carson

Adam Oates

Steve Yzerman

Player	Team	Date of 100th Point	G or A	Score			Player's Game No.	Team Game No.	G - A — PTS	Total Games	Age when first 100th point scored (Yrs. & Mos.)
Mike Bossy	NYI	Mar. 8/86	(G)	Wsh. 6	at	NYI 2	65	65	61-62 — 123	80	
Denis Savard	Chi.	Mar. 12/86	(A)	Buf. 7	at	Chi. 6	69	69	47-69 — 116	80	
Mats Naslund	Mtl.	Mar. 13/86	(A)	Mtl. 2	at	Bos. 3	70	70	43-67 — 110	80	26.4
Michel Goulet	Que.	Mar. 24/86	(A)	Que. 1	at	Min. 0	70	75	53-50 — 103	75	
Glenn Anderson	Edm.	Mar. 25/86	(G)	Edm. 7	at	Det. 2	66	74	54-48 — 102	72	
Neal Broten	Min.	Mar. 26/86	(A)	Min. 6	at	Tor. 1	76	76	29-76 — 105	80	26.4
Dale Hawerchuk	Wpg.	Mar. 31/86	(A)	Wpg. 5	at	L.A. 2	78	78	46-59 — 105	80	
Bernie Federko	St.L.	Apr. 5/86	(G)	Chi. 5	at	St.L. 7	79	79	34-68 — 102	80	
Wayne Gretzky	Edm.	Jan. 11/87	(A)	Cgy. 3	at	Edm. 5	42	42	62-121 — 183	79	
Jari Kurri	Edm.	Mar. 14/87	(A)	Buf. 3	at	Edm. 5	67	68	54-54 — 108	79	
Mario Lemieux	Pit.	Mar. 18/87	(A)	St.L. 4	at	Pit. 5	55	72	54-53 — 107	63	
Mark Messier	Edm.	Mar. 19/87	(A)	Edm. 4	at	Cgy. 5	71	71	37-70 — 107	77	
Dino Ciccarelli	Min.	Mar. 30/87	(A)	NYR 6	at	Min. 5	78	78	52-51 — 103	80	
Doug Gilmour	St.L.	Apr. 2/87	(A)	Buf. 3	at	St.L. 5	78	78	42-63 — 105	80	23.10
Dale Hawerchuk	Wpg.	Apr. 5/87	(A)	Wpg. 3	at	Cgy. 1	80	80	47-53 — 100	80	
Mario Lemieux	Pit.	Jan. 20/88	(G)	Pit. 8	at	Chi. 3	45	48	70-98 — 168	77	
Wayne Gretzky	Edm.	Feb. 11/88	(A)	Edm. 7	at	Van. 2	43	56	40-109 — 149	64	
Denis Savard	Chi.	Feb. 12/88	(A)	St.L. 3	at	Chi. 4	57	57	44-87 — 131	80	
Dale Hawerchuk	Wpg.	Feb. 23/88	(A)	Wpg. 4	at	Pit. 3	61	61	44-77 — 121	80	
Steve Yzerman	Det.	Feb. 27/88	(A)	Det. 4	at	Que. 5	63	63	50-52 — 102	64	22.10
Peter Stastny	Que.	Mar. 8/88	(A)	Hfd. 4	at	Que. 6	63	67	46-65 — 111	76	
Mark Messier	Edm.	Mar. 15/88	(A)	Buf. 4	at	Edm. 6	68	71	37-74 — 111	77	
Jimmy Carson	L.A.	Mar. 26/88	(A)	Chi. 5	at	L.A. 9	77	77	55-52 — 107	80	19.8
Hakan Loob	Cgy.	Mar. 26/88	(A)	Van. 1	at	Cgy. 6	76	76	50-56 — 106	80	27.9
Mike Bullard	Cgy.	Mar. 26/88	(A)	Van. 1	at	Cgy. 6	76	76	48-55 — 103	79	27.1
Michel Goulet	Que.	Mar. 27/88	(A)	Pit. 6	at	Que. 3	76	76	48-58 — 106	80	
Luc Robitaille	L.A.	Mar. 30/88	(G)	Cgy. 7	at	L.A. 9	78	78	53-58 — 111	80	22.1
Mario Lemieux	Pit.	Dec. 31/88	(A)	N.J. 6	at	Pit. 8	36	38	85-114 — 199	76	
Wayne Gretzky	L.A.	Jan. 21/89	(A)	L.A. 4	at	Hfd. 5	47	48	54-114 — 168	78	
Bernie Nicholls	L.A.	Jan. 21/89	(A)	L.A. 4	at	Hfd. 5	48	48	70-80 — 150	79	
Steve Yzerman	Det.	Jan. 27/89	(G)	Tor. 1	at	Det. 8	50	50	65-90 — 155	80	
Rob Brown	Pit.	Mar. 16/89	(A)	Pit. 2	at	N.J. 1	60	72	49-66 — 115	68	20.11
Paul Coffey	Pit.	Mar. 20/89	(A)	Pit. 2	at	Min. 7	69	74	30-83 — 113	75	
Joe Mullen	Cgy.	Mar. 23/89	(A)	L.A. 2	at	Cgy. 4	74	75	51-59 — 110	79	32.1
Jari Kurri	Edm.	Mar. 29/89	(A)	Edm. 5	at	Van. 2	75	79	44-58 — 102	76	
Jimmy Carson	Edm.	Apr. 2/89	(A)	Edm. 2	at	Cgy. 4	80	80	49-51 — 100	80	
Mario Lemieux	Pit.	Jan. 28/90	(G)	Pit. 2	at	Buf. 7	50	50	45-78 — 123	59	
Wayne Gretzky	L.A.	Jan. 30/90	(A)	N.J. 2	at	L.A. 5	51	51	40-102 — 142	73	
Steve Yzerman	Det.	Feb. 19/90	(A)	Mtl. 5	at	Det. 5	61	61	62-65 — 127	79	
Mark Messier	Edm.	Feb. 20/90	(A)	Edm. 4	at	Van. 2	62	62	45-84 — 129	79	
Brett Hull	St.L.	Mar. 3/90	(A)	NYI 4	at	St.L. 5	67	67	72-41 — 113	80	25.7
Bernie Nicholls	NYR	Mar. 12/90	(A)	L.A. 6	at	NYR 2	70	71	39-73 — 112	79	
Pierre Turgeon	Buf.	Mar. 25/90	(G)	N.J. 4	at	Buf. 3	76	76	40-66 — 106	80	20.7
Paul Coffey	Pit.	Mar. 25/90	(A)	Pit. 2	at	Hfd. 4	77	77	29-74 — 103	80	
Pat LaFontaine	NYI	Mar. 27/90	(G)	Cgy. 4	at	NYI 2	72	78	54-51 — 105	74	25.1
Adam Oates	St.L.	Mar. 29/90	(A)	Pit. 4	at	St.L. 5	79	79	23-79 — 102	80	27.7
Joe Sakic	Que.	Mar. 31/90	(G)	Hfd. 3	at	Que. 2	79	79	39-63 — 102	80	20.8
Ron Francis	Hfd.	Mar. 31/90	(G)	Hfd. 3	at	Que. 2	79	79	32-69 — 101	80	27.0
Luc Robitaille	L.A.	Apr. 1/90	(A)	L.A. 4	at	Cgy. 8	80	80	52-49 — 101	80	
Wayne Gretzky	L.A.	Jan. 30/91	(A)	N.J. 4	at	L.A. 2	50	51	41-122 — 163	78	
Brett Hull	St.L.	Feb. 23/91	(G)	Bos. 2	at	St.L. 9	60	62	86-45 — 131	78	
Mark Recchi	Pit.	Mar. 5/91	(G)	Van. 1	at	Pit. 4	66	67	40-73 — 113	78	23.1
Steve Yzerman	Det.	Mar. 10/91	(G)	Det. 4	at	St.L. 1	72	72	51-57 — 108	80	
John Cullen	Hfd.	Mar. 16/91	(G)	N.J. 2	at	Hfd. 6	71	71	39-71 — 110	78	26.7
Adam Oates	St.L.	Mar. 17/91	(A)	St.L. 4	at	Chi. 6	54	73	25-90 — 115	61	
Joe Sakic	Que.	Mar. 19/91	(A)	Edm. 7	at	Que. 6	74	74	48-61 — 109	80	
Steve Larmer	Chi.	Mar. 24/91	(A)	Min. 4	at	Chi. 5	76	76	44-57 — 101	80	29.9
Theoren Fleury	Cgy.	Mar. 26/91	(G)	Van. 2	at	Cgy. 7	77	77	51-53 — 104	79	22.9
Al MacInnis	Cgy.	Mar. 28/91	(A)	Edm. 4	at	Cgy. 4	78	78	28-75 — 103	78	27.8
Brett Hull	St.L.	Mar. 2/92	(G)	St.L. 5	at	Van. 3	66	66	70-39 — 109	73	
Wayne Gretzky	L.A.	Mar. 3/92	(A)	Phi. 1	at	L.A. 4	60	66	31-90 — 121	74	
Kevin Stevens	Pit.	Mar. 7/92	(A)	Pit. 3	at	L.A. 5	66	66	54-69 — 123	80	26.11
Mario Lemieux	Pit.	Mar. 10/92	(A)	Cgy. 2	at	Pit. 5	53	67	44-87 — 131	64	
Luc Robitaille	L.A.	Mar. 17/92	(A)	Wpg. 4	at	L.A. 5	73	73	44-63 — 107	80	
Mark Messier	NYR	Mar. 22/92	(A)	N.J. 3	at	NYR 6	74	75	35-72 — 107	79	
Jeremy Roenick	Chi.	Mar. 29/92	(A)	Tor. 1	at	Chi. 5	77	77	53-50 — 103	80	22.2
Steve Yzerman	Det.	Apr. 14/92	(G)	Det. 7	at	Min. 4	79	80	45-58 — 103	79	
Brian Leetch	NYR	Apr. 16/92	(G)	Pit. 1	at	NYR 7	80	80	22-80 — 102	80	24.1
Mario Lemieux	Pit.	Dec. 31/92	(G)	Tor. 3	at	Pit. 3	38	39	69-91 — 160	60	
Pat LaFontaine	Buf.	Feb. 10/93	(A)	Buf. 6	at	Wpg. 2	55	55	53-95 — 148	84	
Adam Oates	Bos.	Feb. 14/93	(A)	Bos. 3	at	T.B. 3	58	58	45-97 — 142	84	
Steve Yzerman	Det.	Feb. 24/93	(A)	Det. 7	at	Buf. 10	64	64	58-79 — 137	84	
Pierre Turgeon	NYI	Feb. 28/93	(G)	NYI 7	at	Hfd. 6	62	63	58-74 — 132	83	
Doug Gilmour	Tor.	Mar. 3/93	(A)	Min. 1	at	Tor. 3	64	64	32-95 — 127	83	
Alexander Mogilny	Buf.	Mar. 5/93	(A)	Hfd. 4	at	Buf. 2	58	65	76-51 — 127	77	24.1
Mark Recchi	Phi.	Mar. 7/93	(G)	Phi. 3	at	N.J. 7	66	66	53-70 — 123	84	
Teemu Selanne	Wpg.	Mar. 9/93	(A)	Wpg. 4	at	T.B. 2	68	68	76-56 — 132	84	22.7
Luc Robitaille	L.A.	Mar. 15/93	(A)	L.A. 4	at	Buf. 2	69	69	63-62 — 125	84	
Kevin Stevens	Pit.	Mar. 23/93	(A)	S.J. 2	at	Pit. 7	63	73	55-56 — 111	72	
Mats Sundin	Que.	Mar. 27/93	(G)	Phi. 3	at	Que. 5	71	75	47-67 — 114	80	22.1
Pavel Bure	Van.	Apr. 1/93	(G)	Van. 5	at	T.B. 3	77	77	60-50 — 110	83	22.0
Jeremy Roenick	Chi.	Apr. 4/93	(G)	St.L. 4	at	Chi. 5	79	79	50-57 — 107	84	
Craig Janney	St.L.	Apr. 4/93	(G)	St.L. 4	at	Chi. 5	79	79	24-82 — 106	84	25.7

Player	Team	Date of 100th Point	G or A	Score		Player's Game No.	Team Game No.	G - A PTS	Total Games	Age when first 100th point scored (Yrs. & Mos.)
Rick Tocchet	Pit.	Apr. 7/93	(G)	Mtl. 3	at Pit. 4	77	81	48-61 — 109	80	28.11
Joe Sakic	Que.	Apr. 8/93	(A)	Que. 2	at Bos. 6	75	81	48-57 — 105	78	
Ron Francis	Pit.	Apr. 9/93	(A)	Pit. 10	at NYR 4	82	82	24-76 — 100	84	
Brett Hull	St.L.	Apr. 11/93	(G)	Min. 1	at St.L. 5	78	82	54-47 — 101	80	
Theoren Fleury	Cgy.	Apr. 11/93	(G)	Cgy. 3	at Van. 6	82	82	34-66 — 100	83	
Joe Juneau	Bos.	Apr. 14/93	(A)	Bos. 4	at Ott. 2	84	84	32-70 — 102	84	25.3
Wayne Gretzky	L.A.	Feb. 14/94	(A)	Bos. 3	at L.A. 2	56	56	38-92 — 130	81	
Sergei Fedorov	Det.	Mar. 1/94	(A)	Cgy. 2	at Det. 5	63	63	56-64 — 120	82	24.2
Doug Gilmour	Tor.	Mar. 23/94	(A)	Tor. 1	at Fla. 1	74	74	27-84 — 111	83	
Adam Oates	Bos.	Mar. 26/94	(A)	Mtl. 3	at Bos. 6	68	75	32-80 — 112	77	
Mark Recchi	Phi.	Mar. 27/94	(A)	Ana. 3	at Phi. 2	76	76	40-67 — 107	84	
Pavel Bure	Van.	Mar. 28/94	(A)	Tor. 2	at Van. 3	68	76	60-47 — 107	76	
Jeremy Roenick	Chi.	Mar. 31/94	(G)	Chi. 3	at Wsh. 6	78	78	46-61 — 107	84	
Brendan Shanahan	St.L.	Apr. 12/94	(G)	St.L. 5	at Dal. 9	80	83	52-50 — 102	81	25.2
Mario Lemieux	Pit.	Jan. 16/96	(G)	Col. 5	at Pit. 2	38	44	69-92 — 161	70	
Jaromir Jagr	Pit.	Feb. 6/96	(G)	Bos. 5	at Pit. 6	52	52	62-87 — 149	82	23.11
Ron Francis	Pit.	Mar. 9/96	(A)	N.J. 4	at Pit. 3	61	66	27-92 — 119	77	
Peter Forsberg	Col.	Mar. 9/96	(A)	Col. 7	at Van. 5	68	68	30-86 — 116	82	22.7
Joe Sakic	Col.	Mar. 17/96	(A)	Edm. 1	at Col. 8	70	70	51-69 — 120	82	
Eric Lindros	Phi.	Mar. 25/96	(A)	Hfd. 0	at Phi. 3	65	73	47-68 — 115	73	23
Teemu Selanne	Ana.	Mar. 25/96	(A)	Ana. 1	at Det. 5	70	73	40-68 — 108	79	
Alexander Mogilny	Van.	Mar. 25/96	(A)	L.A. 1	at Van. 4	72	75	55-52 — 107	79	
Wayne Gretzky	St.L.	Mar. 28/96	(A)	N.J. 4	at St.L. 4	76	75	23-79 — 102	80	
Doug Weight	Edm.	Mar. 30/96	(G)	Tor. 4	at Edm. 3	76	76	25-79 — 104	82	25.3
Sergei Fedorov	Det.	Apr. 2/96	(A)	Det. 3	at S.J. 6	72	76	39-68 — 107	78	
Paul Kariya	Ana.	Apr. 7/96	(G)	Ana. 5	at S.J. 3	78	78	50-58 — 108	82	21.5
Mario Lemieux	Pit.	Mar. 8/97	(A)	Phi. 2	at Pit. 3	61	65	50-72 — 122	76	
Teemu Selanne	Ana.	Apr. 1/97	(A)	Chi. 3	at Ana. 3	74	78	51-58 — 109	78	
Jaromir Jagr	Pit.	Apr. 15/98	(G)	T.B. 1	at Pit. 5	76	80	35-67 — 102	77	
Jaromir Jagr	Pit.	Mar. 13/99	(G)	Phi. 0	at Pit. 4	65	65	44-83 — 127	81	
Teemu Selanne	Ana.	Apr. 5/99	(A)	Ana. 2	at Det. 3	69	76	47-60 — 107	75	
Paul Kariya	Ana.	Apr. 17/99	(G)	Ana. 3	at S.J. 3	82	82	39-62 — 101	82	
Jaromir Jagr	Pit.	Mar. 10/01	(G)	Cgy. 3	at Pit. 6	68	68	52-69 — 121	81	
Joe Sakic	Col.	Mar. 18/01	(G)	Min. 3	at Col. 4	72	72	54-64 — 118	82	
Markus Naslund	Van.	Mar. 27/03	(A)	Phx. 1	at Van. 5	78	78	48-56 — 104	82	29.8
Peter Forsberg	Col.	Mar. 31/03	(A)	S.J. 1	at Col. 3	72	79	29-77 — 106	79	
Joe Thornton	Bos.	Apr. 4/03	(A)	Buf. 5	at Bos. 8	77	82	36-65 — 101	77	23.9
Jaromir Jagr	NYR	Mar. 18/06	A	Tor. 2	at NYR 5	67	67	54-69 — 123	82	
Joe Thornton	S.J.	Mar. 21/06	A	S.J. 6	at St.L. 0	66	67	29-96 — 125	81	
Alex Ovechkin	Wsh.	Apr. 10/06	G	Wsh. 2	at Bos. 1	77	78	52-54 — 106	81	20.6
Dany Heatley	Ott.	Apr. 13/06	A	Fla. 5	at Ott. 4	80	80	50-53 — 103	82	25.2
Daniel Alfredsson	Ott.	Apr. 15/06	A	Fla. 5	at Ott. 4	76	81	43-60 — 103	77	33.4
Eric Staal	Car.	Apr. 15/06	A	Car. 2	at T.B. 3	81	81	45-55 — 100	82	21.5
Sidney Crosby	Pit.	Apr. 17/06	A	NYI 1	at Pit. 6	80	81	39-63 — 102	81	18.8
Sidney Crosby	Pit.	Mar. 10/07	G	NYR 2	at Pit. 3	65	68	36-84 — 120	79	
Joe Thornton	S.J.	Mar. 22/07	A	S.J. 5	at Atl. 1	75	75	22-92 — 114	82	
Vincent Lecavalier	T.B.	Mar. 24/07	A	Ott. 7	at T.B. 2	76	76	52-56 — 108	82	26.11
Dany Heatley	Ott.	Mar. 31/07	G	Ott. 5	at NYI 2	79	79	50-55 — 105	82	
Martin St. Louis	T.B.	Mar. 31/07	A	Wsh. 2	at T.B. 5	79	79	43-59 — 102	82	31.10
Marian Hossa	Atl.	Apr. 7/07	A	T.B. 2	at Atl. 3	82	82	43-57 — 100	82	28.3
Joe Sakic	Col.	Apr. 8/07	G	Cgy. 3	at Col. 6	82	82	36-64 — 100	82	
Alex Ovechkin	Wsh.	Mar. 18/08	A	Wsh. 4	at Nsh. 2	74	74	65-47 — 112	82	
Evgeni Malkin	Pit.	Mar. 22/08	G	N.J. 1	at Pit. 7	75	75	47-59 — 106	82	21.8
Evgeni Malkin	Pit.	Mar. 17/09	G	Atl. 2	at Pit. 6	72	72	35-78 — 113	82	
Alex Ovechkin	Wsh.	Mar. 27/09	G	T.B. 3	at Wsh. 5	73	76	56-54 — 110	79	
Sidney Crosby	Pit.	Apr. 7/09	G	Pit. 6	at T.B. 4	75	80	33-70 — 103	77	
Henrik Sedin	Van.	Mar. 27/10	A	Van. 2	at S.J. 4	75	75	29-83 — 112	82	29.7
Alex Ovechkin	Wsh.	Mar. 28/10	A	Cgy. 5	at Wsh. 3	65	75	50-59 — 109	72	
Sidney Crosby	Pit.	Apr. 6/10	A	Wsh. 6	at Pit. 3	78	79	51-58 — 109	81	
Nicklas Backstrom	Wsh.	Apr. 9/10	A	Atl. 2	at Wsh. 5	81	81	33-68 — 101	82	22.5
Daniel Sedin	Van.	Mar. 31/11	A	L.A. 1	at Van. 3	78	78	41-63 — 104	82	30.7

Alexander Mogilny

Henrik Sedin

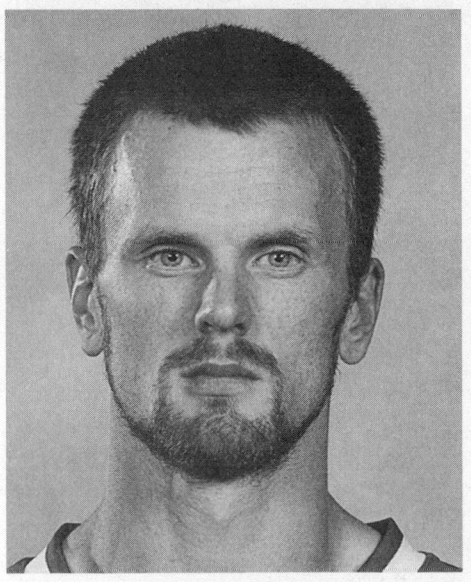

Daniel Sedin

Five-or-more-Goal Games

Player	Team	Date	Score			Opposing Goaltender
SEVEN GOALS						
Joe Malone	Quebec Bulldogs	Jan. 31/20	Tor. 6	at	Que. 10	Ivan Mitchell (4) empty net (1)
SIX GOALS						
Newsy Lalonde	Montreal	Jan. 10/20	Tor. 7	at	Mtl. 14	Ivan Mitchell (2) Howard Lockhart (4)
Joe Malone	Quebec Bulldogs	Mar. 10/20	Ott. 4	at	Que. 10	Clint Benedict
Corb Denneny	Toronto St. Pats	Jan. 26/21	Ham. 3	at	Tor. 10	Howard Lockhart
Cy Denneny	Ottawa Senators	Mar. 7/21	Ham. 5	at	Ott. 12	Howard Lockhart
Syd Howe	Detroit	Feb. 3/44	NYR 2	at	Det. 12	Ken McAuley
Red Berenson	St. Louis	Nov. 7/68	St.L. 8	at	Phi. 0	Doug Favell
Darryl Sittler	Toronto	Feb. 7/76	Bos. 4	at	Tor. 11	Dave Reece
FIVE GOALS						
Joe Malone	Montreal	Dec. 19/17	Mtl. 7	at	Ott. 4	Clint Benedict
Harry Hyland	Mtl. Wanderers	Dec. 19/17	Tor. 9	at	Mtl. W. 10	Art Brooks, Sammy Hebert
Joe Malone	Montreal	Jan. 12/18	Ott. 4	at	Mtl. 9	Clint Benedict
Joe Malone	Montreal	Feb. 2/18	Tor. 2	at	Mtl. 11	Hap Holmes
Mickey Roach	Toronto St. Pats	Mar. 6/20	Que. 2	at	Tor. 11	Howard Lockhart
Newsy Lalonde	Montreal	Feb. 16/21	Ham. 5	at	Mtl. 10	Howard Lockhart
Babe Dye	Toronto St. Pats	Dec. 16/22	Mtl. 2	at	Tor. 7	Georges Vezina
Red Green	Hamilton Tigers	Dec. 5/24	Ham. 10	at	Tor. 3	John Ross Roach
Babe Dye	Toronto St. Pats	Dec. 22/24	Tor. 10	at	Bos. 1	Hec Fowler
Punch Broadbent	Mtl. Maroons	Jan. 7/25	Mtl. 6	at	Ham. 2	Jake Forbes
Pit Lepine	Montreal	Dec. 14/29	Ott. 4	at	Mtl. 6	Alex Connell
Howie Morenz	Montreal	Mar. 18/30	NYA 3	at	Mtl. 8	Roy Worters
Charlie Conacher	Toronto	Jan. 19/32	NYA 3	at	Tor. 11	Roy Worters (3) Al Shields (2)
Ray Getliffe	Montreal	Feb. 6/43	Bos. 3	at	Mtl. 8	Frank Brimsek
Maurice Richard	Montreal	Dec. 28/44	Det. 1	at	Mtl. 9	Harry Lumley
Howie Meeker	Toronto	Jan. 8/47	Chi. 4	at	Tor. 10	Paul Bibeault
Bernie Geoffrion	Montreal	Feb. 19/55	NYR 2	at	Mtl. 10	Gump Worsley
Bobby Rousseau	Montreal	Feb. 1/64	Det. 3	at	Mtl. 9	Roger Crozier
Yvan Cournoyer	Montreal	Feb. 15/75	Chi. 3	at	Mtl. 12	Mike Veisor
Don Murdoch	NY Rangers	Oct. 12/76	NYR 10	at	Min. 4	Gary Smith
Ian Turnbull	Toronto	Feb. 2/77	Det. 1	at	Tor. 9	Ed Giacomin (2) Jim Rutherford (3)
Bryan Trottier	NY Islanders	Dec. 23/78	NYR 4	at	NYI 9	Wayne Thomas (4) John Davidson (1)
Tim Young	Minnesota	Jan. 15/79	Min. 8	at	NYR 1	Doug Soetaert (3) Wayne Thomas (2)
John Tonelli	NY Islanders	Jan. 6/81	Tor. 3	at	NYI 6	Jiri Crha (4) empty net (1)
Wayne Gretzky	Edmonton	Feb. 18/81	St.L. 2	at	Edm. 9	Mike Liut (3) Ed Staniowski (2)
Wayne Gretzky	Edmonton	Dec. 30/81	Phi. 5	at	Edm. 7	Pete Peeters (4) empty net (1)
Grant Mulvey	Chicago	Feb. 3/82	St.L. 5	at	Chi. 9	Mike Liut (4) Gary Edwards (1)
Bryan Trottier	NY Islanders	Feb. 13/82	Phi. 2	at	NYI 8	Pete Peeters
Willy Lindstrom	Winnipeg	Mar. 2/82	Wpg. 7	at	Phi. 6	Pete Peeters
Mark Pavelich	NY Rangers	Feb. 23/83	Hfd. 3	at	NYR 11	Greg Millen
Jari Kurri	Edmonton	Nov. 19/83	N.J. 4	at	Edm. 13	Glenn Resch (3) Ron Low (2)
Bengt Gustafsson	Washington	Jan. 8/84	Wsh. 7	at	Phi. 1	Pelle Lindbergh
Pat Hughes	Edmonton	Feb. 3/84	Cgy. 5	at	Edm. 10	Don Edwards (3) Reggie Lemelin (2)
Wayne Gretzky	Edmonton	Dec. 15/84	Edm. 8	at	St.L. 2	Rick Wamsley (4) Mike Liut(1)
Dave Andreychuk	Buffalo	Feb. 6/86	Buf. 8	at	Bos. 6	Pat Riggin (1) Doug Keans (4)
Wayne Gretzky	Edmonton	Dec. 6/87	Min. 4	at	Edm. 10	Don Beaupre (4) Kari Takko (1)
Mario Lemieux	Pittsburgh	Dec. 31/88	N.J. 6	at	Pit. 8	Bob Sauve (3) Chris Terreri (1) empty net (1)
Joe Nieuwendyk	Calgary	Jan. 11/89	Wpg. 3	at	Cgy. 8	Daniel Berthiaume Peter Sidorkiewicz (3)
Mats Sundin	Quebec	Mar. 5/92	Que. 10	at	Hfd. 4	Kay Whitmore (2) Corey Hirsch (2)
Mario Lemieux	Pittsburgh	Apr. 9/93	Pit. 10	at	NYR 4	Mike Richter (2)
Peter Bondra	Washington	Feb. 5/94	T.B. 3	at	Wsh. 6	Daren Puppa (4) Pat Jablonski (1)
Mike Ricci	Quebec	Feb. 17/94	Que. 8	at	S.J. 2	Arturs Irbe (3) Jimmy Waite (2)
Alex Zhamnov	Winnipeg	Apr. 1/95	Wpg. 7	at	L.A. 7	Kelly Hrudey (3) Grant Fuhr (2)
Mario Lemieux	Pittsburgh	Mar. 26/96	St.L. 4	at	Pit. 8	Grant Fuhr (1) Jon Casey (4)
Sergei Fedorov	Detroit	Dec. 26/96	Wsh. 4	at	Det. 5	Jim Carey
Marian Gaborik	Minnesota	Dec. 20/07	NYR 3	at	Min. 6	Henrik Lundqvist
Johan Franzen	Detroit	Feb. 2/11	Det. 7	at	Ott. 5	Robin Lehner (2) Brian Elliott (2) empty net (1)

Players' 500th Goals

Regular Season

Player	Team	Date	Game No.	Score			Opposing Goaltender	Total Goals	Total Games
Maurice Richard	Montreal	Oct. 19/57	863	Chi. 1	at	Mtl. 3	Glenn Hall	544	978
Gordie Howe	Detroit	Mar. 14/62	1,045	Det. 2	at	NYR 3	Gump Worsley	801	1,767
Bobby Hull	Chicago	Feb. 21/70	861	NYR. 2	at	Chi. 4	Ed Giacomin	610	1,063
Jean Béliveau	Montreal	Feb. 11/71	1,101	Min. 2	at	Mtl. 6	Gilles Gilbert	507	1,125
Frank Mahovlich	Montreal	Mar. 21/73	1,105	Van. 2	at	Mtl. 3	Dunc Wilson	533	1,181
Phil Esposito	Boston	Dec. 22/74	803	Det. 4	at	Bos. 5	Jim Rutherford	717	1,282
John Bucyk	Boston	Oct. 30/75	1,370	St.L. 2	at	Bos. 3	Yves Bélanger	556	1,540
Stan Mikita	Chicago	Feb. 27/77	1,221	Van. 4	at	Chi. 3	Cesare Maniago	541	1,394
Marcel Dionne	Los Angeles	Dec. 14/82	887	L.A. 2	at	Wsh. 7	Al Jensen	731	1,348
Guy Lafleur	Montreal	Dec. 20/83	918	Mtl. 6	at	N.J. 0	Glenn Resch	560	1,126
Mike Bossy	NY Islanders	Jan. 2/86	647	Bos. 5	at	NYI 7	empty net	573	752
Gilbert Perreault	Buffalo	Mar. 9/86	1,159	N.J. 3	at	Buf. 4	Alain Chevrier	512	1,191
Wayne Gretzky	Edmonton	Nov. 22/86	575	Van. 2	at	Edm. 5	empty net	894	1,487
Lanny McDonald	Calgary	Mar. 21/89	1,107	NYI 1	at	Cgy. 4	Mark Fitzpatrick	500	1,111
Bryan Trottier	NY Islanders	Feb. 13/90	1,104	Cgy. 4	at	NYI 2	Rick Wamsley	524	1,279
Mike Gartner	NY Rangers	Oct. 14/91	936	Wsh. 5	at	NYR 3	Mike Liut	708	1,432
Michel Goulet	Chicago	Feb. 16/92	951	Cgy. 5	at	Chi. 5	Jeff Reese	548	1,089
Jari Kurri	Los Angeles	Oct. 17/92	833	Bos. 6	at	L.A. 8	empty net	601	1,251
Dino Ciccarelli	Detroit	Jan. 8/94	946	Det. 6	at	L.A. 3	Kelly Hrudey	608	1,232
Mario Lemieux	Pittsburgh	Oct. 26/95	605	Pit. 7	at	NYI 5	Tommy Soderstrom	690	915
Mark Messier	NY Rangers	Nov. 6/95	1,141	Cgy. 2	at	NYR 4	Rick Tabaracci	694	1,756
Steve Yzerman	Detroit	Jan. 17/96	906	Col. 2	at	Det. 3	Patrick Roy	692	1,514
Dale Hawerchuk	St. Louis	Jan. 31/96	1,103	St.L. 4	at	Tor. 0	Felix Potvin	518	1,188
Brett Hull	St. Louis	Dec. 22/96	693	L.A. 4	at	St.L. 7	Stephane Fiset	741	1,269
Joe Mullen	Pittsburgh	Mar. 14/97	1,052	Pit. 3	at	Col. 6	Patrick Roy	502	1,062
Dave Andreychuk	New Jersey	May 15/97	1,070	Wsh. 2	at	N.J. 3	Bill Ranford	640	1,639
Luc Robitaille	Los Angeles	Jan. 7/99	928	Buf. 2	at	L.A. 4	Dwayne Roloson	668	1,431
Pat Verbeek	Detroit	Mar. 22/00	1,285	Cgy. 2	at	Det. 2	Fred Brathwaite	522	1,424
Ron Francis	Carolina	Jan. 2/02	1,533	Bos. 6	at	Car. 3	Byron Dafoe	549	1,731
Brendan Shanahan	Detroit	Mar. 23/02	1,100	Det. 2	at	Col. 0	Patrick Roy	656	1,524
Joe Sakic	Colorado	Dec. 11/02	1,044	Col. 1	at	Van. 3	Dan Cloutier	625	1,378
Joe Nieuwendyk	New Jersey	Jan. 17/03	1,094	N.J. 2	at	Car. 1	Kevin Weekes	564	1,257
Jaromir Jagr	Washington	Feb. 4/03	928	Wsh. 5	at	T.B. 1	John Grahame	646	1,273
Pierre Turgeon	Colorado	Nov. 8/05	1,229	S.J. 2	at	Col. 5	Vesa Toskala	515	1,294
Mats Sundin	Toronto	Oct. 14/06	1,162	Cgy. 4	at	Tor. 5	Miikka Kiprusoff	564	1,346
*Teemu Selanne	Anaheim	Nov. 22/06	982	Ana. 2	at	Col. 3	Jose Theodore	637	1,259
Peter Bondra	Chicago	Dec. 22/06	1,050	Tor. 1	at	Chi. 3	J.S. Aubin	503	1,081
Mark Recchi	Pittsburgh	Jan. 27/07	1,303	Pit. 4	at	Dal. 3	Marty Turco	577	1,652
*Mike Modano	Dallas	Mar. 13/07	1,225	Phi. 2	at	Dal. 3	Antero Niittymaki	561	1,499
Jeremy Roenick	San Jose	Nov. 10/07	1,267	Phx. 1	at	S.J. 4	Alex Auld	513	1,363
Keith Tkachuk	St. Louis	Apr. 6/08	1,055	St.L. 4	at	CBJ 1	empty net	538	1,201

*Active

Boston's John Bucyk became the seventh player in NHL history to score 500 goals on October 30, 1975. Bucyk beat Yves Belanger of the St. Louis Blues for the milestone goal.

Players' 1,000th Points

Regular Season

Player	Team	Date	Game No.	G or A	Score				Total Points G A PTS	Total Games
Gordie Howe	Detroit	Nov. 27/60	938	(A)	Tor. 0	at	Det. 2		801-1,049–1,850	1,767
Jean Béliveau	Montreal	Mar. 3/68	911	(G)	Mtl. 2	at	Det. 5		507-712–1,219	1,125
Alex Delvecchio	Detroit	Feb. 16/69	1,143	(A)	L.A. 3	at	Det. 6		456-825–1,281	1,549
Bobby Hull	Chicago	Dec. 13/70	909	(A)	Min. 2	at	Chi. 5		610-560–1,170	1,063
Norm Ullman	Toronto	Oct. 16/71	1,113	(A)	NYR 5	at	Tor. 3		490-739–1,229	1,410
Stan Mikita	Chicago	Oct. 15/72	924	(A)	St.L. 3	at	Chi. 1		541-926–1,467	1,394
John Bucyk	Boston	Nov. 9/72	1,144	(A)	Det. 3	at	Bos. 8		556-813–1,369	1,540
Frank Mahovlich	Montreal	Feb. 17/73	1,090	(A)	Phi. 7	at	Mtl. 6		533-570–1,103	1,181
Henri Richard	Montreal	Dec. 20/73	1,194	(A)	Mtl. 2	at	Buf. 2		358-688–1,046	1,256
Phil Esposito	Boston	Feb. 15/74	745	(A)	Bos. 4	at	Van. 2		717-873–1,590	1,282
Rod Gilbert	NY Rangers	Feb. 19/77	1,027	(G)	NYR 2	at	NYI 5		406-615–1,021	1,065
Jean Ratelle	Boston	Apr. 3/77	1,007	(A)	Tor. 4	at	Bos. 7		491-776–1,267	1,281
Marcel Dionne	Los Angeles	Jan. 7/81	740	(G)	L.A. 5	at	Hfd. 3		731-1,040–1,771	1,348
Guy Lafleur	Montreal	Mar. 4/81	720	(G)	Wpg. 3	at	Mtl. 9		560-793–1,353	1,126
Bobby Clarke	Philadelphia	Mar. 19/81	922	(G)	Bos. 3	at	Phi. 5		358-852–1,210	1,144
Gilbert Perreault	Buffalo	Apr. 3/82	871	(A)	Buf. 5	at	Mtl. 4		512-814–1,326	1,191
Darryl Sittler	Philadelphia	Jan. 20/83	927	(G)	Cgy. 2	at	Phi. 5		484-637–1,121	1,096
Wayne Gretzky	Edmonton	Dec. 19/84	424	(A)	L.A. 3	at	Edm. 7		894-1,963–2,875	1,487
Bryan Trottier	NY Islanders	Jan. 29/85	726	(G)	Min. 4	at	NYI 4		524-901–1,425	1,279
Mike Bossy	NY Islanders	Jan. 24/86	656	(G)	NYI 7	at	Wsh. 5		573-553–1,126	752
Denis Potvin	NY Islanders	Apr. 4/87	987	(G)	Buf. 6	at	NYI 6		310-742–1,052	1,060
Bernie Federko	St. Louis	Mar. 19/88	855	(A)	Hfd. 5	at	St.L. 3		369-761–1,130	1,000
Lanny McDonald	Calgary	Mar. 7/89	1,101	(G)	Wpg. 5	at	Cgy. 9		500-506–1,006	1,111
Peter Stastny	Quebec	Oct. 19/89	682	(G)	Que. 5	at	Chi. 3		450-789–1,239	977
Jari Kurri	Edmonton	Jan. 2/90	716	(A)	Edm. 6	at	St.L. 4		601-797–1,398	1,251
Denis Savard	Chicago	Mar. 11/90	727	(G)	St.L. 6	at	Chi. 4		473-865–1,338	1,196
Paul Coffey	Pittsburgh	Dec. 22/90	770	(A)	Pit. 4	at	NYI 3		396-1,135–1,531	1,409
Mark Messier	Edmonton	Jan. 13/91	822	(A)	Edm. 5	at	Phi. 3		694-1,193–1,887	1,756
Dave Taylor	Los Angeles	Feb. 5/91	930	(A)	L.A. 3	at	Phi. 2		431-638–1,069	1,111
Michel Goulet	Chicago	Feb. 23/91	878	(G)	Chi. 3	at	Min. 3		548-604–1,152	1,089
Dale Hawerchuk	Buffalo	Mar. 8/91	781	(G)	Chi. 5	at	Buf. 3		518-891–1,409	1,188
Bobby Smith	Minnesota	Nov. 30/91	986	(A)	Min. 4	at	Tor. 3		357-679–1,036	1,077
Mike Gartner	NY Rangers	Jan. 4/92	971	(G)	NYR 4	at	N.J. 6		708-627–1,335	1,432
Raymond Bourque	Boston	Feb. 29/92	933	(A)	Wsh. 5	at	Bos. 5		410-1,169–1,579	1,612
Mario Lemieux	Pittsburgh	Mar. 24/92	513	(A)	Pit. 3	at	Det. 4		690-1,033–1,723	915
Glenn Anderson	Toronto	Feb. 22/93	954	(G)	Tor. 8	at	Van. 1		498-601–1,099	1,129
Steve Yzerman	Detroit	Feb. 24/93	737	(A)	Det. 7	at	Buf. 10		692-1,063–1,755	1,514
Ron Francis	Pittsburgh	Oct. 28/93	893	(G)	Que. 7	at	Pit. 3		549-1,249–1,798	1,731
Bernie Nicholls	New Jersey	Feb. 13/94	858	(A)	N.J. 3	at	T.B. 3		475-734–1,209	1,127
Dino Ciccarelli	Detroit	Mar. 9/94	957	(G)	Det. 5	at	Cgy. 1		608-592–1,200	1,232
Brian Propp	Hartford	Mar. 19/94	1,008	(G)	Hfd. 5	at	Phi. 3		425-579–1,004	1,016
Joe Mullen	Pittsburgh	Feb. 7/95	935	(A)	Fla. 3	at	Pit. 7		502-561–1,063	1,062
Steve Larmer	NY Rangers	Mar. 8/95	983	(A)	N.J. 4	at	NYR 6		441-571–1,012	1,006
Doug Gilmour	Toronto	Dec. 23/95	935	(A)	Edm. 1	at	Tor. 6		450-964–1,414	1,474
Larry Murphy	Toronto	Mar. 27/96	1,228	(G)	Tor. 6	at	Van. 2		287-929–1,216	1,615
Dave Andreychuk	New Jersey	Apr. 7/96	998	(G)	NYR 2	at	N.J. 4		640-698–1,338	1,639
Adam Oates	Washington	Oct. 8/97	830	(G)	Wsh. 6	at	NYI 3		341-1,079–1,420	1,337
Phil Housley	Washington	Nov. 8/97	1,081	(A)	Edm. 1	at	Wsh. 2		338-894–1,232	1,495
Dale Hunter	Washington	Jan. 9/98	1,308	(G)	Phi. 1	at	Wsh. 4		323-697–1,020	1,407
Pat LaFontaine	NY Rangers	Jan. 22/98	847	(G)	Phi. 4	at	NYR 3		468-545–1,013	865
Luc Robitaille	Los Angeles	Jan. 29/98	882	(A)	Cgy. 3	at	L.A. 5		668-726–1,394	1,431
Al MacInnis	St. Louis	Apr. 7/98	1,056	(A)	St.L. 3	at	Det. 5		340-934–1,274	1,416
Brett Hull	Dallas	Nov. 14/98	815	(A)	Dal. 3	at	Bos. 1		741-650–1,391	1,269
Brian Bellows	Washington	Jan. 2/99	1,147	(A)	Tor. 2	at	Wsh. 5		485-537–1,022	1,188
Pierre Turgeon	St. Louis	Oct. 9/99	881	(G)	St.L. 4	at	Edm. 3		515-812–1,327	1,294
Joe Sakic	Colorado	Dec. 27/99	810	(A)	St.L. 1	at	Col. 5		625-1,016–1,641	1,378
Pat Verbeek	Detroit	Feb. 27/00	1,275	(A)	T.B. 1	at	Det. 3		522-541–1,063	1,424
V. Damphousse	San Jose	Oct. 14/00	1,090	(A)	Bos. 2	at	S.J. 5		432 773 1,205	1,378
*Jaromir Jagr	Pittsburgh	Dec. 30/00	763	(G)	Ott. 3	at	Pit. 5		646-953–1,599	1,273
Mark Recchi	Philadelphia	Mar. 13/01	920	(A)	St.L. 2	at	Phi. 5		577-956–1,533	1,652
Theoren Fleury	NY Rangers	Oct. 29/01	960	(A)	Dal. 2	at	NYR 4		455-633–1,088	1,084
B. Shanahan	Detroit	Jan. 12/02	1,073	(G)	Dal. 2	at	Det. 5		656-698–1,354	1,524
Jeremy Roenick	Philadelphia	Jan. 30/02	961	(A)	Phi. 1	at	Ott. 3		513-703–1,216	1,363
*Mike Modano	Dallas	Nov. 15/02	965	(A)	Col. 2	at	Dal. 4		561-813–1,374	1,499
Joe Nieuwendyk	New Jersey	Feb. 23/03	1,094	(A)	N.J. 4	at	Pit. 3		564-562–1,126	1,257
Mats Sundin	Toronto	Mar. 10/03	994	(A)	Tor. 3	at	Edm. 2		564-785–1,349	1,346
Sergei Fedorov	Anaheim	Feb. 14/04	965	(A)	Ana. 2	at	Van. 1		483-696–1,179	1,248
Alexander Mogilny	Toronto	Mar. 15/04	946	(G)	Tor. 6	at	Buf. 5		473-559–1,032	990
Brian Leetch	Boston	Oct. 18/05	1,151	(A)	Bos. 3	at	Mtl. 4		247-781–1,028	1,205
*Teemu Selanne	Anaheim	Jan. 30/06	928	(G)	L.A. 3	at	Ana. 4		637-703–1,340	1,259
Rod Brind'Amour	Carolina	Nov. 4/06	1,202	(G)	Car. 3	at	Ott. 2		452-732–1,184	1,484
Keith Tkachuk	St. Louis	Nov. 30/08	1,077	(G)	St.L. 4	at	Atl. 2		538-527–1,065	1,201
Doug Weight	NY Islanders	Jan. 2/09	1,167	(A)	NYI 4	at	Phx. 5		278-755–1,033	1,238
*Nicklas Lidstrom	Detroit	Oct. 15/09	1,336	(A)	L.A. 2	at	Det. 5		253-855–1,108	1,494
*Daniel Alfredsson	Ottawa	Oct. 22/10	1,009	(A)	Ott. 4	at	Buf. 2		389-634–1,023	1,056
*Alex Kovalev	Ottawa	Nov. 22/10	1,249	(G)	L.A. 2	at	Ott. 3		428-596–1,024	1,302
*Jarome Iginla	Calgary	Apr. 1/11	1,103	(G)	Cgy. 3	at	St.L. 2		484-522–1,006	1,106
*Joe Thornton	San Jose	Apr. 8/11	994	(G)	S.J. 3	at	Phx. 4		306-695–1,001	995

*Active

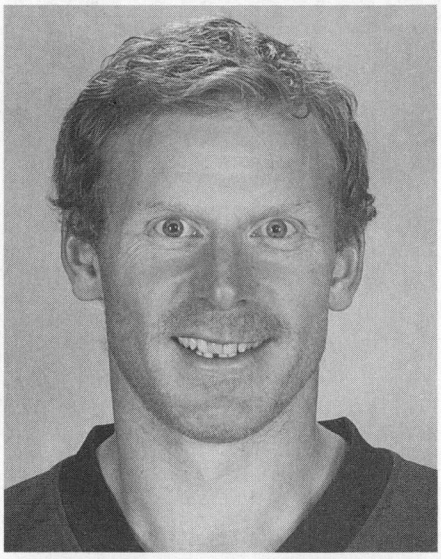

Ottawa teammates Daniel Alfredsson (top) and Alex Kovalev (middle) reached the 1,000-point plateau exactly one month apart early in the 2010-11 season. Calgary's Jarome Iginla (bottom) hit the milestone on April 1, 2011 and was followed a week later by San Jose's Joe Thornton.

Individual Awards

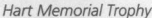

Hart Memorial Trophy

Art Ross Trophy

Calder Memorial Trophy

James Norris Memorial Trophy

HART MEMORIAL TROPHY

An annual award "to the player adjudged to be the most valuable to his team." Winner selected in a poll by the Professional Hockey Writers' Association in the 30 NHL cities at the end of the regular schedule.

History: The Hart Memorial Trophy was presented by the National Hockey League in 1960 after the original Hart Trophy was retired to the Hockey Hall of Fame. The original Hart Trophy was donated to the NHL in 1924 by Dr. David A. Hart, father of Cecil Hart, former manager-coach of the Montreal Canadiens.

2010-11 Winner: **Corey Perry, Anaheim Ducks**
Runners-up: **Daniel Sedin, Vancouver Canucks**
                   Martin St. Louis, Tampa Bay Lightning

Corey Perry, right winger with the Anaheim Ducks, became the first player in the history of the franchise to win the Hart Memorial Trophy. Perry received 67 first-place votes among the 126 ballots cast and accumulated 1,043 points to edge left winger Daniel Sedin of the Vancouver Canucks, whose twin brother Henrik won the Award in 2010. Daniel Sedin was the top selection on 51 ballots and earned 960 points. Tampa Bay's Martin St. Louis received a single first-place vote and 332 points. Goalies Pekka Rinne of Nashville, Tim Thomas of Boston, Carey Price of Montreal (with two), Marc-Andre Fleury of Pittsburgh and Roberto Luongo of Vancouver all received first-place votes with Rinne and Thomas finishing fourth and fifth in the overall voting with 175 and 171 points apiece. Vancouver's Ryan Kesler (69 points) was the only other player to receive a first-place vote but finished eight overall behind Chicago's Jonathan Toews (107 points) and Carey Price (90). Marc-Andre Fleury (57) and Vancouver's Henrik Sedin (57) rounded out the top ten.

Perry, who also won the Maurice Richard Trophy as NHL goal-scoring leader, finished with a late surge of 19 goals in his final 16 games that raised his season total to 50 and helped launch the Ducks from 11th place in the Western Conference to a season-ending fourth. The first-time Hart Trophy finalist shared the league lead in game-winning goals with Washington's Alex Ovechkin (11), tied for fifth place in power-play goals (14), shared fifth in shorthanded tallies (four) and led all players with 21 third-period goals. Twenty-five of his goals tied the score or put the Ducks ahead.

ART ROSS TROPHY

An annual award "to the player who leads the league in scoring points at the end of the regular season."

History: Arthur Howey Ross, former manager-coach of the Boston Bruins, presented the trophy to the National Hockey League in 1947. If two players finish the schedule with the same number of points, the trophy is awarded in the following manner: 1. Player with most goals. 2. Player with fewer games played. 3. Player scoring first goal of the season.

2010-11 Winner: **Daniel Sedin, Vancouver Canucks**
Runners-up: **Martin St. Louis, Tampa Bay Lightning**
                   Corey Perry, Anaheim Ducks

Left winger Daniel Sedin of the Vancouver Canucks received the Art Ross Trophy for the first time, keeping the award for leading the NHL in scoring in the family by finishing the season with a league-leading and career-high 104 points (41 goals, 63 assists). He was the only player in the NHL to top 100 points, finishing ahead of 2004 Art Ross Trophy winner Martin St. Louis of Tampa Bay (31 goals, 68 assists, 99 points) and Anaheim's Corey Perry (50-48-98). With twin brother Henrik claiming the award in 2009-10, this marks the first time in NHL history that brothers have won scoring titles in consecutive seasons. Daniel becomes the 10th player in the past 10 seasons to capture the Art Ross Trophy, joining Jaromir Jagr in 2001, Jarome Iginla in 2002, Peter Forsberg in 2003, Martin St. Louis in 2004, Joe Thornton in 2006, Sidney Crosby in 2007, Alex Ovechkin in 2008, Evgeni Malkin in 2009 and Henrik last season.

Daniel sparked the NHL's top-ranked power-play unit by tallying a league-leading 18 goals and 42 points with the man advantage. He also tied for second place among NHL forwards in plus-minus (+30).

CALDER MEMORIAL TROPHY

An annual award "to the player selected as the most proficient in his first year of competition in the National Hockey League." Winner selected in a poll by the Professional Hockey Writers' Association at the end of the regular schedule.

History: From 1936-37 until his death in 1943, Frank Calder, NHL President, bought a trophy each year to be given permanently to the outstanding rookie. After Calder's death, the NHL presented the Calder Memorial Trophy in his memory and the trophy is to be kept in perpetuity. To be eligible for the award, a player cannot have played more than 25 games in any single preceding season nor in six or more games in each of any two preceding seasons in any major professional league. Beginning in 1990-91, to be eligible for this award a player must not have attained his twenty-sixth birthday by September 15th of the season in which he is eligible.

2010-11 Winner: **Jeff Skinner, Carolina Hurricanes**
Runners-up: **Logan Couture, San Jose Sharks**
                   Michael Grabner, New York Islanders

Center Jeff Skinner of the Carolina Hurricanes won the Calder Memorial Trophy. Skinner received 71 of 127 first-place votes and 1,055 points to edge San Jose Sharks forward Logan Couture who was named first on 41 ballots and polled 908 points. The margin of victory was the smallest in Calder Trophy voting since St. Louis Blues defenseman Barret Jackman topped Detroit Red Wings forward Henrik Zetterberg 506-462 in 2003. Michael Grabner of the Islanders and goalie Corey Crawford of Chicago each received six first-place votes with Grabner garnering 497 points to Crawford's 336. John Carlson of Washington received the final three first-place votes and finished fifth in the standings with 188 points.

The Hurricanes reaped immediate dividends from their top pick in the 2010 Entry Draft as the 18-year-old Skinner, selected seventh overall last June, led all rookies in scoring as the NHL's youngest player. His performance over the first half of the season earned him a berth in the 2011 All-Star Game, played in front of a hometown crowd in Raleigh. He went on to lead all rookies in points (63), rank second in assists (32) and third in goals (31). Skinner netted his 30th goal of the season on April 6 against Detroit, becoming the seventh-youngest player in NHL history to reach the milestone (18 years, 325 days).

JAMES NORRIS MEMORIAL TROPHY

An annual award "to the defense player who demonstrates throughout the season the greatest all-round ability in the position." Winner selected in a poll by the Professional Hockey Writers' Association at the end of the regular schedule.

History: The James Norris Memorial Trophy was presented in 1953 by the four children of the late James Norris in memory of the former owner-president of the Detroit Red Wings.

2010-11 Winner: **Nicklas Lidstrom, Detroit Red Wings**
Runners-up: **Shea Weber, Nashville Predators**
                   Zdeno Chara, Boston Bruins

Nicklas Lidstrom of the Detroit Red Wings won the James Norris Memorial Trophy for the seventh time. The 41-year-old Vasteras, Sweden native is the third defenseman in NHL history with as many as seven Norris Trophy wins, joining Hockey Hall of Fame members Bobby Orr (eight) and Doug Harvey (seven). Lidstrom edged Shea Weber of the Nashville Predators 736-727 in the closest race for first place since 1996, when Chicago's Chris Chelios finished five points ahead of Boston's Raymond Bourque, 408-403. With Lidstrom, Weber and third-place finisher Zdeno Chara of the Boston Bruins (688 points) receiving similar first-place vote totals (Lidstrom 35, Weber 32, Chara 33) and the trio separated by just 48 points, this marks the tightest three-way race for the Norris Trophy since its introduction in 1954. Lubomir Visnovsky of Anaheim finished fourth in the balloting with 20 first-place votes and 573 points with Keith Yandle of Phoenix (five first-place vote, 312 points) finishing fifth. Pittsburgh's Kris Letang received two first-place votes and 144 points.

Lidstrom's 19th NHL season was one of his most productive, ranking second among NHL defensemen in scoring with 62 points (16 goals, 46 assists) in 82 games. He tied for fourth place among league defensemen in goals, was third in assists and tied for sixth in power-play goals (six). The Red Wings captain led the Central Division champions in ice time by averaging 23:28 per contest.

Vezina Trophy

Lady Byng Memorial Trophy

Frank J. Selke Trophy

Conn Smythe Trophy

VEZINA TROPHY

An annual award "to the goalkeeper adjudged to be the best at his position" as voted by the general managers of each of the 30 clubs.

History: Leo Dandurand, Louis Letourneau and Joe Cattarinich, former owners of the Montreal Canadiens, presented the trophy to the National Hockey League in 1926-27 in memory of Georges Vezina, outstanding goalkeeper of the Canadiens who collapsed during an NHL game on November 28, 1925, and died of tuberculosis a few months later. Before the 1981-82 season, the goalkeeper(s) of the team allowing the fewest number of goals during the regular season were awarded the Vezina Trophy.

2010-11 Winner: **Tim Thomas, Boston Bruins**
Runners-up: **Pekka Rinne, Nashville Predators**
       Roberto Luongo, Vancouver Canucks

Tim Thomas of the Boston Bruins captured the Vezina Trophy for the second time in the past three seasons. Thomas was named on 26 of 30 ballots, including 17 first-place selections, and collected 104 points, edging Pekka Rinne of the Nashville Predators (84 points). Rinne also earned votes on 26 ballots and received six first-place votes. Vancouver's Roberto Luongo received three first-place vote and 33 points while the Rangers' Henrik Lundqvist had three first-place votes and 23 points. Montreal's Carey Price received the final first-place vote and 10 points.

Thomas enjoyed a record-setting bounce-back season after undergoing offseason hip surgery. He won his first eight decisions, which broke a club record set by Tiny Thompson in 1937-38, and won his first nine road games - becoming the first NHL goaltender to do so since Chicago's Glenn Hall in 1965-66. The 2009 Vezina Trophy winner finished the season with a 35-11-9 record and .938 save percentage, eclipsing Dominik Hasek's .937 with Buffalo in 1998-99 as the best since the statistic was introduced in 1976-77. Thomas also led all goaltenders in goals-against average (2.00) and ranked second in shutouts (nine).

LADY BYNG MEMORIAL TROPHY

An annual award "to the player adjudged to have exhibited the best type of sportsmanship and gentlemanly conduct combined with a high standard of playing ability." Winner selected in a poll by the Professional Hockey Writers' Association at the end of the regular schedule.

History: Lady Byng, wife of Canada's Governor-General at the time, presented the Lady Byng Trophy in the 1924-25 season. After Frank Boucher of the New York Rangers won the award seven times in eight seasons, he was given the trophy to keep and Lady Byng donated another trophy in 1936. After Lady Byng's death in 1949, the National Hockey League presented a new trophy, changing the name to Lady Byng Memorial Trophy.

2010-11 Winner: **Martin St. Louis, Tampa Bay Lightning**
Runners-up: **Nicklas Lidstrom, Detroit Red Wings**
       Loui Eriksson, Dallas Stars

Tampa Bay Lightning right winger Martin St. Louis captured the Lady Byng Memorial Trophy for the second year in a row. St. Louis was a runaway winner for the second straight season, earning 70 first-place votes among the 127 cast and a total of 994 points. Detroit's Nicklas Lidstrom finished second in Lady Byng voting for the fifth time in his career, collecting 22 first-place votes and 464 points. Loui Eriksson of Dallas finished third with nine first-place votes and 347 points. Teemu Selanne of Anaheim also had nine first-place votes but only 163 points, finishing behind San Jose's Patrick Marleau (two first-place votes, 241 points) and Chicago's Jonathan Toews (two and 233).

St. Louis surged late in the season, tallying points in each of his last nine games and in 15 of his final 17 to finish second in NHL scoring with 99 points (31 goals, 68 assists). He tied a franchise record for assists in a season and posted the second-highest point total in his 12-year NHL career. St. Louis was assessed just 12 minutes in penalties, matching his career low.

FRANK J. SELKE TROPHY

An annual award "to the forward who best excels in the defensive aspects of the game." Winner selected in a poll by the Professional Hockey Writers' Association at the end of the regular schedule.

History: Presented to the National Hockey League in 1977 by the Board of Governors of the NHL in honor of Frank J. Selke, one of the great architects of Montreal and Toronto championship teams.

2010-11 Winner: **Ryan Kesler, Vancouver Canucks**
Runners-up: **Jonathan Toews, Chicago Blackhawks**
       Pavel Datsyuk, Detroit Red Wings

Vancouver Canucks center Ryan Kesler captured the Frank Selke Trophy for the first time after finishing second in the voting in 2010 and third in 2009. Kesler was a landslide winner, receiving 105 of the 127 first-place votes. He was named on 126 ballots and collected 1,179 points, ahead of second-place finisher Jonathan Toews of the Chicago Blackhawks who had five first-place votes and 476 points. Pavel Datsyuk of the Detroit Red Wings, attempting to become the first player since Montreal Canadiens right wing Bob Gainey to win the award for four consecutive seasons, finished third with four first-place votes and 348 points.

Kesler helped the Canucks record the lowest team goals-against average in the NHL (2.20) for the first time in franchise history. He ranked fourth among NHL forwards in blocked shots (80), appeared in all 82 games and averaged a career-high 20:30 in ice time to lead all Vancouver forwards. The speedy center ranked sixth in face-offs taken (1,496), winning a team-best and career-high 57.4 percent of them (859), dished out 124 hits; recorded a team-high 65 takeaways and posted a +24 rating while scoring 41 goals.

WILLIAM M. JENNINGS TROPHY

An annual award "to the goalkeeper(s) having played a minimum of 25 games for the team with the fewest goals scored against it." Winners selected on regular-season play.

History: The Jennings Trophy was presented in 1981-82 by the National Hockey League's Board of Governors to honor the late William M. Jennings, longtime governor and president of the New York Rangers and one of the great builders of hockey in the United States.

2010-11 Winners: **Roberto Luongo/Cory Schneider, Vancouver Canucks**
Runners-up: **Pekka Rinne, Nashville Predators**
       Tim Thomas/Tuukka Rask, Boston Bruins

Roberto Luongo captured the Jennings Trophy for the first time along with Cory Schneider as the Canucks allowed the fewest goals in the NHL (185) for the first time in franchise history. Luongo went 38-15-7 in 60 appearances, posting the best goals-against average in his 11-year NHL career (2.11) and his top save percentage since joining the Canucks in 2006-07 (.928). He tied for the NHL lead in victories, ranked second in goals-against average and fourth in save percentage. Schneider excelled in relief of Luongo in his first full NHL season. He posted a 16-4-2 record in 25 appearances, ranked third among NHL goaltenders in save percentage (.929) and was fourth in goals-against average (2.23).

CONN SMYTHE TROPHY

An annual award "to the most valuable player for his team in the playoffs." Winner selected by the Professional Hockey Writers' Association at the conclusion of the final game in the Stanley Cup Finals.

History: Presented by Maple Leaf Gardens Limited in 1964 to honor Conn Smythe, the former coach, manager, president and owner-governor of the Toronto Maple Leafs.

2010-11 Winner: **Tim Thomas, Boston Bruins**

Bruins goaltender Tim Thomas is the second American-born player to capture the Conn Smythe Trophy, joining New York Rangers defenseman Brian Leetch (1994). At age 37, Thomas is the oldest recipient of the NHL playoff MVP trophy. Thomas was the only goalie used by the Bruins during a playoff run that saw them become the first team in NHL history to win three seventh games en route to the Stanley Cup. Thomas had 16 wins and nine losses in 25 games and his 1.98 goals-against average and .940 save percentage led all playoff goaltenders. Thomas set new playoff records for most shots faced in one playoff year (849) and most saves (798).

William M. Jennings Trophy

Jack Adams Award

*Bill Masterton
Memorial Trophy*

Lester Patrick Trophy

JACK ADAMS AWARD

An annual award presented by the National Hockey League Broadcasters' Association to "the NHL coach adjudged to have contributed the most to his team's success." Winner selected by a poll among members of the NHL Broadcasters' Association at the end of the regular season.

History: The award was presented by the NHL Broadcasters' Association in 1974 to commemorate the late Jack Adams, coach and general manager of the Detroit Red Wings, whose lifetime dedication to hockey serves as an inspiration to all who aspire to further the game.

2010-11 Winner: **Dan Bylsma, Pittsburgh Penguins**
      Runners-up: Alain Vigneault, Vancouver Canucks
           Barry Trotz, Nashville Predators

Pittsburgh Penguins head coach Dan Bylsma captured the Jack Adams Award. Bylsma was named on 54 of 70 ballots, including 29 first-place votes, for 196 points. Alain Vigneault of the Vancouver Canucks finished in second place, garnering 19 first-place votes and 169 points. Nashville's Barry Trotz was third with eight first-place votes and 80 point. Guy Boucher of Tampa Bay (six), Jacques Lemaire of New Jersey (three), Bruce Boudreau of Washington (two), David Tippett of Phoenix (one) and Detroit's Mike Babcock (one) also received first-place votes.

Bylsma helped the Penguins (49-25-8) earned the second-most points (106) and victories (49) in franchise history, overcoming a total of 350 man-games lost due to injury in the process. Most notable were the prolonged absences of star centers Sidney Crosby and Evgeni Malkin, who missed most of Pittsburgh's final 35 games. During that stretch Pittsburgh went 20-11-4 for a .629 points percentage.

BILL MASTERTON MEMORIAL TROPHY

An annual award under the trusteeship of the Professional Hockey Writers' Association to "the National Hockey League player who best exemplifies the qualities of perseverance, sportsmanship and dedication to hockey." Winner selected by a poll among the 30 chapters of the PHWA at the end of the regular season. A $2,500 grant from the PHWA is awarded annually to the Bill Masterton Scholarship Fund, based in Bloomington, MN, in the name of the Masterton Trophy winner.

History: The trophy was presented by the NHL Writers' Association in 1968 to commemorate the late Bill Masterton, a player with the Minnesota North Stars, who exhibited to a high degree the qualities of perseverance, sportsmanship and dedication to hockey, and who died January 15, 1968.

2010-11 Winner: **Ian Laperriere, Philadelphia Flyers**
      Runners-up: Ray Emery, Anaheim Ducks
           Daymond Langkow, Calgary Flames

Ian Laperriere sustained a severe injury during the 2010 Stanley Cup playoffs when he blocked a shot with his face against New Jersey and suffered a concussion and fractured orbital bone. He returned a little more than a month later to finish the Flyers' playoff run that ended two games short of a championship. Laperriere attempted to return in training camp, but could not overcome his concussion-related symptoms and was on the long-term injury list all season. Nevertheless, he served the Flyers in several capacities, particularly as a mentor for young players in the organization.

LESTER PATRICK TROPHY

An annual award "for outstanding service to hockey in the United States." Eligible recipients are players, officials, coaches, executives and referees. Winners are selected by an award committee consisting of the commissioner of the NHL, an NHL governor, a representative of the New York Rangers, a member of the Hockey Hall of Fame builder's section, a member of the Hockey Hall of Fame player's section, a member of the U.S. Hockey Hall of Fame, a member of the NHL Broadcasters' Association and a member of the Professional Hockey Writers' Association. Each except the League Commissioner is rotated annually. The winner receives a miniature of the trophy.

History: Presented by the New York Rangers in 1966 to honor the late Lester Patrick, longtime general manager and coach of the New York Rangers, whose teams finished out of the playoffs only once in his first 16 years with the club.

2011 Winners: **Jeff Sauer**
             Tony Rossi
             Mark Johnson
             Bob Pulford

Jeff Sauer coached for 31 years in NCAA Division I hockey, winning 655 games (seventh all time) and two national championships, both with the University of Wisconsin (1983 and 1990). Born in Fort Atkinson, Wisconsin, he played high school hockey at Washington High School in St. Paul, Minnesota and collegiate hockey at Colorado College. He began his coaching career as an assistant to Bob Johnson at Colorado College and then followed him to Wisconsin. In 1971, Sauer left Madison to become the head coach at Colorado College, where he served for 11 years, compiling 166 wins, and twice being named WCHA Coach of the Year. Sauer became the head coach at the University of Wisconsin in 1982 and became the first coach to win a national championship in his inaugural season at a school. Over 20 years he became the "Dean of WCHA Coaches," racking up 489 wins and two national championships. Still involved as a coach, Sauer will lead the U.S. National Sled Hockey Team in 2011-12.

Tony Rossi was born in Illinois on April 9, 1941 and began his administrative career in his home state in the 1970s when he started a local hockey club for children. Rossi was elected to the USA Hockey Board of Directors in 1983 and was named a director of the Central District in 1989. In 1995, Rossi was named the USA Hockey Treasurer where he helped develop the USA Hockey Foundation to promote the growth of hockey in the United States. Rossi was elected USA Hockey Vice-President in 2003 and was elected to the International Ice Hockey Federation Council in 2008.

Mark Johnson was a star of the U.S. Miracle on Ice Olympic victory at Lake Placid in 1980 and the son of legendary coach "Badger Bob" Johnson. Born in Minneapolis on September 22, 1957 but raised in Madison, Wisconsin, Mark Johnson starred for his father at the University of Wisconsin, helping the school to the 1977 national championship during his freshman campaign. The first Badger ever to win WCHA Rookie of the Year honors, he went on to become the school's second all-time leading scorer with 256 points on a school-record 125 goals and 131 assists in just three seasons. After the Olympics, Johnson spent 11 years in the NHL with Pittsburgh, Minnesota North Stars, Hartford, St. Louis and New Jersey. He began his coaching career in the Colonial Hockey League in 1995-96 before returning to Wisconsin as an assistant coach from 1996 to 2002. Johnson has been head coach of the Wisconsin women's team since the 2002-03 season, winning four national championships and guiding the U.S. national women's team to a silver medal at the 2010 Vancouver Olympics.

Bob Pulford was born March 31, 1936 in Newton Robinson, Ontario north of Toronto. He played junior hockey with the Toronto Marlboros for three seasons from 1953 to 1956 and won the Memorial Cup twice before entering the NHL with the Maple Leafs in 1956-57. Pulford won the Stanley Cup four times with Toronto in the 1960s. He finished his career playing two seasons with the Los Angeles Kings before retiring to become coach of the team for the 1972-73 season. Pulford won the Jack Adams Award as coach of the year in 1975 after leading the Kings to a 105-point season that remains a franchise high. He became coach and general manager of the Chicago Blackhawks in 1977-78. He would remain in the Blackhawks' front office, several times taking on the job of coach and/or general manager again, until October of 2007 and is still an alternative governor for the team. Pulford was elected to the Hockey Hall of Fame in 1991.

King Clancy Memorial Trophy

Presidents' Trophy

Maurice "Rocket" Richard Trophy

Ted Lindsay Award

KING CLANCY MEMORIAL TROPHY

An annual award "to the player who best exemplifies leadership qualities on and off the ice and has made a noteworthy humanitarian contribution in his community."

History: The King Clancy Memorial Trophy was presented to the National Hockey League by the Board of Governors in 1988 to honor the late Frank "King" Clancy.

2010-11 Winner:　　Doug Weight, New York Islanders

New York Islanders center Doug Weight is the recipient of the King Clancy Memorial Trophy. Despite being injured for the majority of the season, Weight played a prominent role on the team and in the Long Island community.

When Weight went down with a back injury in November, he began working with teammates on ice at practices, sharpening the power play and other situational plays. After four months of rehab, team doctors still could not clear Weight to play and his season was deemed over. For the last two weeks of the regular season, Weight stepped behind the bench with the rest of the coaching staff to continue to lead the team.

The 19-year NHL veteran took his leadership role just as seriously in community events as he did in games and practices. His first philanthropic venture of the season was a live auction for the Islanders Children's Foundation in September, where he served as MC and host. The week before the season opener, Weight brought together the entire roster for the Isles' annual Children's Foundation Day at Adventureland, a Long Island amusement park where fans get a chance to meet the players. Weight also worked closely with teammates as the club fanned out to schools across Long Island for its annual School Day event. During the holiday season, he brought together over half of the team to purchase gifts for local children in need and he also visited local hospitals to hand-deliver the presents. Weight served as an ambassador for Charles Wang's Lighthouse International Tournament that brought youth hockey players from China, Finland and Japan to Nassau Coliseum.

Weight also was involved in the league-wide *Hockey for Huggies*, a campaign to assist those who struggle to provide diapers for their babies. He and his wife recorded the public service announcement that aired on Islanders television broadcasts and in-arena. He also kick-started the program by collecting donations from his teammates.

NHL GENERAL MANAGER OF THE YEAR AWARD

An annual award presented to recognize the work of the league's general managers, voting for this new award is conducted among the 30 club general managers and a panel of NHL executives, print and broadcast media at the conclusion of the regular season.

History: This award was first presented in 2010.

2010-11 Winner:　　Mike Gillis, Vancouver Canucks
Runners-up: Steve Yzerman, Tampa Bay Lightning
David Poile, Nashville Predators

Mike Gillis of the Vancouver Canucks is the winner of the NHL General Manager of the Year Award. Gillis received 14 first-place votes and a total of 96 points to finish ahead of first-year general manager Steve Yzerman of the Tampa Bay Lightning who had seven first-place votes and 61 points. David Poile of Nashville was third in voting with six first-place votes and 55 points. Other NHL general managers who received first-place votes were Bob Murray of Anaheim (four), Ray Shero of Pittsburgh (three), George McPhee of Washington (two), Peter Chiarelli of Boston (two), Stan Bowman of Chicago (one) and Detroit's Ken Holland (one).

Gillis built the Canucks into the NHL's top team in the 2010-11 regular season as they captured the Presidents' Trophy for the first time with a franchise-record 117 points (54-19-9) and claimed the Northwest Division title for the third time in his three years in Vancouver. Gillis strengthened the Canucks defensively over the offseason by adding blueliners Keith Ballard and Dan Hamhuis and shutdown center Manny Malhotra. Such was Vancouver's organizational depth that the club allowed the fewest goals in the NHL (185) despite suffering a rash of injuries that sidelined each of their top five defensemen. Gillis further bolstered team depth at the trade deadline with the acquisition of forwards Chris Higgins and Maxim Lapierre.

MAURICE "ROCKET" RICHARD TROPHY

An annual award "presented to the player finishing the regular season as the League's goal-scoring leader."

History: A gift to the NHL from the Montreal Canadiens in 1999, the Maurice "Rocket" Richard Trophy honors one of the game's greatest stars. During his 18-year career with the Canadiens from 1942-43 through 1959-60, Richard was the first player in NHL history to score 50 goals in a season and 500 in his career. He played on eight Stanley Cup champions and led the League in goal scoring five times.

2010-11 Winners:　　Corey Perry, Anaheim Ducks
Runners-up: Steven Stamkos, Tampa Bay Lightning
Jarome Iginla, Calgary Flames

Anaheim Ducks right winger Corey Perry won the Maurice Richard Trophy for the first time. Perry's late surge of 19 goals in his final 16 games raised his season total to 50 and helped launch the Ducks from 11th place in the Western Conference to a season-ending fourth. Perry became the third player in franchise history to reach the 50-goal mark, joining Paul Kariya in 1995-96 (50) and Teemu Selanne in 1996-97 and 1997-98 (51, 52). He shared the league lead in game-winning goals with Washington's Alex Ovechkin (11), tied for fifth place in power-play goals (14), shared fifth in shorthanded tallies (four) and led all players with 21 third period goals. Twenty-five of his goals tied the score or put the Ducks ahead. Perry was the NHL's only 50-goal scorer in 2010-11, finishing ahead of Tampa Bay's Steven Stamkos, who scored 45 goals, and Calgary's Jarome Iginla, who scored 43 times.

TED LINDSAY AWARD

The Ted Lindsay Award is presented annually to the "most outstanding player" in the NHL as voted by fellow members of the National Hockey League Players' Association. The winner receives $20,000, and the two finalists receive $10,000 each to donate to the grassroots hockey program of their choice, through the NHLPA's Goals & Dreams Fund.

History: On April 29, 2010, the Ted Lindsay Award was introduced to recognize Lindsay's pioneering efforts in the establishment of the NHL Players' Association. Carrying on the tradition established by the Lester B. Pearson Award, it remains the only award voted on by the players themselves. The award was originally created in 1971 in honor of the late Lester B. Pearson, former Prime Minister of Canada.

2010-11 Winner:　　Daniel Sedin, Vancouver Canucks
Runners-up: Corey Perry, Anaheim Ducks
Steven Stamkos, Tampa Bay Lightning

Daniel Sedin is just the second Canucks player to receive the "Most Outstanding Player" award as voted on by the players. He follows former teammate Markus Naslund (a fellow native of Ornskoldvik, Sweden) who received the honor in 2002-03, then known as the Lester B. Pearson Award. Sedin also becomes the first new recipient of the Ted Lindsay Award in three years as Alex Ovechkin received the "Most Outstanding Player" award in each of the last three seasons. His brother, Henrik, was a finalist for the Award last season.

Daniel had an exceptional 2010-11 campaign, one in which he appeared in all 82 games for the Canucks. He secured the Art Ross Trophy for most points in the regular season (104), tied for fourth in goals (41), and placed third in both assists (63) and game-winning goals (10), while also helping lead Vancouver to their first Presidents' Trophy in the regular season, prior to the team's run to the Stanley Cup Final.

MARK MESSIER NHL LEADERSHIP AWARD
presented by Bridgestone

An annual award presented "to the player who exemplifies great leadership qualitites to his team, on and off the ice during the regular season." Suggestions for nominees are solicited from fans, clubs and NHL personnel, but the selection of the three finalists and the ultimate winner is made by Mark Messier himself.

History: Presented by Bridgestone in honor of one of hockey's great leaders, this award was first handed out in 2007.

2010-11 Winner: **Zdeno Chara, Boston Bruins**
Runners-up: **Shane Doan, Phoenix Coyotes**
Nicklas Lidstrom, Detroit Red Wings

Boston Bruins captain Zdeno Chara is the recipient of the Mark Messier NHL Leadership Award. Since being named the 18th captain in franchise history to begin the 2006-07 season, Chara has led the Bruins' steady climb back to the NHL's elite level with two Northeast Division crowns in the last three years capped off with a Stanley Cup victory in 2011. Despite being among the NHL's top 10 in ice time in each of his five seasons as Bruins captain, he has missed a total of only 12 games. A Norris Trophy finalist for the fourth time this season, he won the award in 2008-09. A long-time supporter and contributor to Right to Play, the international program that uses sport to improve the lives of children from disadvantaged areas, Chara this past season also took over the Bruins' PJ Drive, which collects unused pajamas for local children in need. And he helped bring in unprecedented contributions to the Boston Bruins Cuts for a Cause - including the $1,500 a local restaurant owner bid to shave Chara's head.

PRESIDENTS' TROPHY

An annual award to the club finishing the regular-season with the best overall record.

History: Presented to the National Hockey League in 1985-86 by the NHL Board of Governors to recognize the team compiling the top regular-season record.

2010-11 Winner: **Vancouver Canucks**
Runners-up: **Washington Capitals**
Philadelphia Flyers

The Vancouver Canucks captured the Presidents' Trophy for the first time in franchise history, leading the NHL with 117 points by posting a record of 54-19-9. Both their 54 wins and 117 points set new club records. The Canucks led the NHL in both goals for (262) and goals against (185) and won the Northwest Division title for the third year in a row and the fourth time in the past six seasons. The Washington Capitals posted a record of 48-23-11 for 107 points and won the Southeast Division for the fourth year in a row. The Philadelphia Flyers won their first division title since 2003-04 with a record of 47-23-12 and 106 points. The Pittsburgh Penguins had 106 points and 49 wins, but the Flyers were ranked ahead of Pittsburgh because they had the greater number of games won, *excluding games won in the Shootout (NEW for 2010-11)*, with 44 to Pittsburgh's 39.

NHL FOUNDATION PLAYER AWARD

An annual award presented to "an NHL player who applies the core values of hockey – commitment, perseverance and teamwork – to enrich the lives of people in his community." In recognition of this dedication, the NHL Foundation annually awards $25,000 to a current player's charity.

History: NHL players have a long-standing tradition of supporting charities and other important causes in their communities. NHL member clubs are constant in their quest to help local schools, hospitals and charitable organizations. Clubs submit nominations for the NHL Foundation Player Award and the finalists are selected by a judging panel. This award was first presented in 1998.

2010-11 Winner: **Dustin Brown, Los Angeles Kings**
Runners-up: **Mike Green, Washington Capitals**
Daniel & Henrik Sedin, Vancouver Canucks

Los Angeles Kings forward Dustin Brown is the recipient of the 13th annual NHL Foundation Player Award. The NHL Foundation will present $25,000 to the *Dustin and Nicole Brown Charitable Fund*. Brown and his wife, Nicole, established the fund this past season to improve the quality of life for disadvantaged youth and their families in both Los Angeles and the Brown's hometown of Ithaca, New York.

The Kings' 26-year-old captain was a finalist for the NHL Foundation Player Award for the third consecutive season in recognition of his continued tireless involvement in countless community-benefiting endeavors. This season, Brown donated $50 for each of his 300 hits to contribute a total of $15,000 to Children's Hospital of Los Angeles' Newborn and Infant Critical Care Unit. In mid-December, through the *Make-A-Wish Foundation*, Brown hosted an unforgettable day behind the scenes at STAPLES Center and then the following night at the Kings-Wild game for Will McCloud, a six-year-old boy who was battling leukemia. Brown also again served as the team spokesman for the *Children's Cancer Research Fund*, an organization dedicated to providing support for clinical research in pediatric cancer, while improving the medical environment for all children. And he volunteered to be the spokesman for the Club's *Pancreatic Cancer Awareness Night*. In addition to adopting a local family over the holiday season as part of the Kings' *Adopt-a-Family* program, Brown and his wife independently adopted a large family with a child currently being treated at Children's Hospital of Los Angeles. He led extensive team participation in *Kings Community Corner*, a ticket-donation program that has enabled more than 15,000 Los Angeles youth and military members to experience Kings hockey live at STAPLES Center.

Through his budding engagement with social media, Brown (@DustinBrown23) has raised awareness for *Make My Day Monday*, which promotes committing random acts of kindness each Monday, and raised funds for Japanese earthquake relief, donating $1 for each of the 9,425 new followers he attracted on Twitter during a one-week period in March.

NATIONAL HOCKEY LEAGUE INDIVIDUAL AWARD WINNERS

CONN SMYTHE TROPHY

	Winner	
2011	Tim Thomas	Boston
2010	Jonathan Toews	Chicago
2009	Evgeni Malkin	Pittsburgh
2008	Henrik Zetterberg	Detroit
2007	Scott Niedermayer	Anaheim
2006	Cam Ward	Carolina
2005	....	
2004	Brad Richards	Tampa Bay
2003	Jean-Sebastien Giguere	Anaheim
2002	Nicklas Lidstrom	Detroit
2001	Patrick Roy	Colorado
2000	Scott Stevens	New Jersey
1999	Joe Nieuwendyk	Dallas
1998	Steve Yzerman	Detroit
1997	Mike Vernon	Detroit
1996	Joe Sakic	Colorado
1995	Claude Lemieux	New Jersey
1994	Brian Leetch	NY Rangers
1993	Patrick Roy	Montreal
1992	Mario Lemieux	Pittsburgh
1991	Mario Lemieux	Pittsburgh
1990	Bill Ranford	Edmonton
1989	Al MacInnis	Calgary
1988	Wayne Gretzky	Edmonton
1987	Ron Hextall	Philadelphia
1986	Patrick Roy	Montreal
1985	Wayne Gretzky	Edmonton
1984	Mark Messier	Edmonton
1983	Billy Smith	NY Islanders
1982	Mike Bossy	NY Islanders
1981	Butch Goring	NY Islanders
1980	Bryan Trottier	NY Islanders
1979	Bob Gainey	Montreal
1978	Larry Robinson	Montreal
1977	Guy Lafleur	Montreal
1976	Reggie Leach	Philadelphia
1975	Bernie Parent	Philadelphia
1974	Bernie Parent	Philadelphia
1973	Yvan Cournoyer	Montreal
1972	Bobby Orr	Boston
1971	Ken Dryden	Montreal
1970	Bobby Orr	Boston
1969	Serge Savard	Montreal
1968	Glenn Hall	St. Louis
1967	Dave Keon	Toronto
1966	Roger Crozier	Detroit
1965	Jean Beliveau	Montreal

FRANK J. SELKE TROPHY

	Winner		Runner-up
2011	Ryan Kesler, Van.		Jonathan Toews, Chi.
2010	Pavel Datsyuk, Det.		Ryan Kesler, Van.
2009	Pavel Datsyuk, Det.		Mike Richards, Phi.
2008	Pavel Datsyuk, Det.		John Madden, N.J.
2007	Rod Brind'Amour, Car.		Samuel Pahlsson, Ana.
2006	Rod Brind'Amour, Car.		Jere Lehtinen, Dal.
2005	....		....
2004	Kris Draper, Det.		John Madden, N.J.
2003	Jere Lehtinen, Dal.		John Madden, N.J.
2002	Michael Peca, NYI		Craig Conroy, Cgy.
2001	John Madden, N.J.		Joe Sakic, Col.
2000	Steve Yzerman, Det.		Michal Handzus, St.L.
1999	Jere Lehtinen, Dal.		Magnus Arvedson, Ott.
1998	Jere Lehtinen, Dal.		Michael Peca, Buf.
1997	Michael Peca, Buf.		Peter Forsberg, Col.
1996	Sergei Fedorov, Det.		Ron Francis, Pit.
1995	Ron Francis, Pit.		Esa Tikkanen, St.L.
1994	Sergei Fedorov, Det.		Doug Gilmour, Tor.
1993	Doug Gilmour, Tor.		Dave Poulin, Bos.
1992	Guy Carbonneau, Mtl.		Sergei Fedorov, Det.
1991	Dirk Graham, Chi.		Esa Tikkanen, Edm.
1990	Rick Meagher, St.L.		Guy Carbonneau, Mtl.
1989	Guy Carbonneau, Mtl.		Esa Tikkanen, Edm.
1988	Guy Carbonneau, Mtl.		Steve Kasper, Bos.
1987	Dave Poulin, Phi.		Guy Carbonneau, Mtl.
1986	Troy Murray, Chi.		Ron Sutter, Phi.
1985	Craig Ramsay, Buf.		Doug Jarvis, Wsh.
1984	Doug Jarvis, Wsh.		Bryan Trottier, NYI
1983	Bobby Clarke, Phi.		Jari Kurri, Edm.
1982	Steve Kasper, Bos.		Bob Gainey, Mtl.
1981	Bob Gainey, Mtl.		Craig Ramsay, Buf.
1980	Bob Gainey, Mtl.		Craig Ramsay, Buf.
1979	Bob Gainey, Mtl.		Don Marcotte, Bos.
1978	Bob Gainey, Mtl.		Craig Ramsay, Buf.

BILL MASTERTON MEMORIAL TROPHY

	Winner	
2011	Ian Laperriere	Philadelphia
2010	Jose Theodore	Washington
2009	Steve Sullivan	Nashville
2008	Jason Blake	Toronto
2007	Phil Kessel	Boston
2006	Teemu Selanne	Anaheim
2005	....	
2004	Bryan Berard	Chicago
2003	Steve Yzerman	Detroit
2002	Saku Koivu	Montreal
2001	Adam Graves	NY Rangers
2000	Ken Daneyko	New Jersey
1999	John Cullen	Tampa Bay
1998	Jamie McLennan	St. Louis
1997	Tony Granato	San Jose
1996	Gary Roberts	Calgary
1995	Pat LaFontaine	Buffalo
1994	Cam Neely	Boston
1993	Mario Lemieux	Pittsburgh
1992	Mark Fitzpatrick	NY Islanders
1991	Dave Taylor	Los Angeles
1990	Gord Kluzak	Boston
1989	Tim Kerr	Philadelphia
1988	Bob Bourne	Los Angeles
1987	Doug Jarvis	Hartford
1986	Charlie Simmer	Boston
1985	Anders Hedberg	NY Rangers
1984	Brad Park	Detroit
1983	Lanny McDonald	Calgary
1982	Glenn Resch	Colorado
1981	Blake Dunlop	St. Louis
1980	Al MacAdam	Minnesota
1979	Serge Savard	Montreal
1978	Butch Goring	Los Angeles
1977	Ed Westfall	NY Islanders
1976	Rod Gilbert	NY Rangers
1975	Don Luce	Buffalo
1974	Henri Richard	Montreal
1973	Lowell MacDonald	Pittsburgh
1972	Bobby Clarke	Philadelphia
1971	Jean Ratelle	NY Rangers
1970	Pit Martin	Chicago
1969	Ted Hampson	Oakland
1968	Claude Provost	Montreal

ART ROSS TROPHY

	Winner	Runner-up
2011	Daniel Sedin, Van.	Martin St. Louis, T.B.
2010	Henrik Sedin, Van.	Sidney Crosby, Pit.
2009	Evgeni Malkin, Pit.	Alex Ovechkin, Wsh.
2008	Alex Ovechkin, Wsh.	Evgeni Malkin, Pit.
2007	Sidney Crosby, Pit.	Joe Thornton, S.J.
2006	Joe Thornton, Bos., S.J.	Jaromir Jagr, NYR
2005	....	....
2004	Martin St. Louis, T.B.	Ilya Kovalchuk, Atl.
2003	Peter Forsberg, Col.	Markus Naslund, Van.
2002	Jarome Iginla, Cgy.	Markus Naslund, Van.
2001	Jaromir Jagr, Pit.	Joe Sakic, Col.
2000	Jaromir Jagr, Pit.	Pavel Bure, Fla.
1999	Jaromir Jagr, Pit.	Teemu Selanne, Ana.
1998	Jaromir Jagr, Pit.	Peter Forsberg, Col.
1997	Mario Lemieux, Pit.	Teemu Selanne, Ana.
1996	Mario Lemieux, Pit.	Jaromir Jagr, Pit.
1995	Jaromir Jagr, Pit.	Eric Lindros, Phi.
1994	Wayne Gretzky, L.A.	Sergei Fedorov, Det.
1993	Mario Lemieux, Pit.	Pat LaFontaine, Buf.
1992	Mario Lemieux, Pit.	Kevin Stevens, Pit.
1991	Wayne Gretzky, L.A.	Brett Hull, St.L.
1990	Wayne Gretzky, L.A.	Mark Messier, Edm.
1989	Mario Lemieux, Pit.	Wayne Gretzky, L.A.
1988	Mario Lemieux, Pit.	Wayne Gretzky, Edm.
1987	Wayne Gretzky, Edm.	Jari Kurri, Edm.
1986	Wayne Gretzky, Edm.	Mario Lemieux, Pit.
1985	Wayne Gretzky, Edm.	Jari Kurri, Edm.
1984	Wayne Gretzky, Edm.	Paul Coffey, Edm.
1983	Wayne Gretzky, Edm.	Peter Stastny, Que.
1982	Wayne Gretzky, Edm.	Mike Bossy, NYI
1981	Wayne Gretzky, Edm.	Marcel Dionne, L.A.
1980	Marcel Dionne, L.A.	Wayne Gretzky, Edm.
1979	Bryan Trottier, NYI	Marcel Dionne, L.A.
1978	Guy Lafleur, Mtl.	Bryan Trottier, NYI
1977	Guy Lafleur, Mtl.	Marcel Dionne, L.A.
1976	Guy Lafleur, Mtl.	Bobby Clarke, Phi.
1975	Bobby Orr, Bos.	Phil Esposito, Bos.
1974	Phil Esposito, Bos.	Bobby Orr, Bos.
1973	Phil Esposito, Bos.	Bobby Clarke, Phi.
1972	Phil Esposito, Bos.	Bobby Orr, Bos.
1971	Phil Esposito, Bos.	Bobby Orr, Bos.
1970	Bobby Orr, Bos.	Phil Esposito, Bos.
1969	Phil Esposito, Bos.	Bobby Hull, Chi.
1968	Stan Mikita, Chi.	Phil Esposito, Bos.
1967	Stan Mikita, Chi.	Bobby Hull, Chi.
1966	Bobby Hull, Chi.	Stan Mikita, Chi.
1965	Stan Mikita, Chi.	Norm Ullman, Det.
1964	Stan Mikita, Chi.	Bobby Hull, Chi.
1963	Gordie Howe, Det.	Andy Bathgate, NYR
1962	Bobby Hull, Chi.	Andy Bathgate, NYR
1961	Bernie Geoffrion, Mtl.	Jean Beliveau, Mtl.
1960	Bobby Hull, Chi.	Bronco Horvath, Bos.
1959	Dickie Moore, Mtl.	Jean Beliveau, Mtl.
1958	Dickie Moore, Mtl.	Henri Richard, Mtl.
1957	Gordie Howe, Det.	Ted Lindsay, Det.
1956	Jean Beliveau, Mtl.	Gordie Howe, Det.
1955	Bernie Geoffrion, Mtl.	Maurice Richard, Mtl.
1954	Gordie Howe, Det.	Maurice Richard, Mtl.
1953	Gordie Howe, Det.	Ted Lindsay, Det.
1952	Gordie Howe, Det.	Ted Lindsay, Det.
1951	Gordie Howe, Det.	Maurice Richard, Mtl.
1950	Ted Lindsay, Det.	Sid Abel, Det.
1949	Roy Conacher, Chi.	Doug Bentley, Chi.
1948*	Elmer Lach, Mtl.	Buddy O'Connor, NYR
1947	Max Bentley, Chi.	Maurice Richard, Mtl.
1946	Max Bentley, Chi.	Gaye Stewart, Tor.
1945	Elmer Lach, Mtl.	Maurice Richard, Mtl.
1944	Herb Cain, Bos.	Doug Bentley, Chi.
1943	Doug Bentley, Chi.	Bill Cowley, Bos.
1942	Bryan Hextall, NYR	Lynn Patrick, NYR
1941	Bill Cowley, Bos.	Bryan Hextall, NYR
1940	Milt Schmidt, Bos.	Woody Dumart, Bos.
1939	Toe Blake, Mtl.	Sweeney Schriner, NYA
1938	Gordie Drillon, Tor.	Syl Apps, Tor.
1937	Sweeney Schriner, NYA	Syl Apps, Tor.
1936	Sweeney Schriner, NYA	Marty Barry, Det.
1935	Charlie Conacher, Tor.	Syd Howe, St.L., Det.
1934	Charlie Conacher, Tor.	Joe Primeau, Tor
1933	Bill Cook, NYR	Busher Jackson, Tor.
1932	Busher Jackson, Tor.	Joe Primeau, Tor.
1931	Howie Morenz, Mtl.	Ebbie Goodfellow, Det.
1930	Cooney Weiland, Bos.	Frank Boucher, NYR
1929	Ace Bailey, Tor.	Nels Stewart, Mtl.M
1928	Howie Morenz, Mtl.	Aurel Joliat, Mtl.
1927	Bill Cook, NYR	Dick Irvin, Chi.
1926	Nels Stewart, Mtl.M.	Cy Denneny, Ott.
1925	Babe Dye, Tor.	Cy Denneny, Ott.
1924	Cy Denneny, Ott.	Billy Boucher, Mtl.
1923	Babe Dye, Tor.	Cy Denneny, Ott.
1922	Punch Broadbent, Ott.	Cy Denneny, Ott.
1921	Newsy Lalonde, Mtl.	Babe Dye, Ham., Tor.
1920	Joe Malone, Que.	Newsy Lalonde, Mtl.
1919	Newsy Lalonde, Mtl.	Odie Cleghorn, Mtl.
1918	Joe Malone, Mtl.	Cy Denneny, Ott.

* Trophy first awarded in 1948.
Scoring leaders listed from 1918 to 1947.

HART MEMORIAL TROPHY

	Winner	Runner-up
2011	Corey Perry, Ana.	Daniel Sedin, Van.
2010	Henrik Sedin, Van.	Alex Ovechkin, Wsh.
2009	Alex Ovechkin, Wsh.	Evgeni Malkin, Pit.
2008	Alex Ovechkin, Wsh.	Evgeni Malkin, Pit.
2007	Sidney Crosby, Pit.	Roberto Luongo, Van.
2006	Joe Thornton, Bos., S.J.	Jaromir Jagr, NYR
2005	....	....
2004	Martin St. Louis, T.B.	Jarome Iginla, Cgy.
2003	Peter Forsberg, Col.	Markus Naslund, Van.
2002	Jose Theodore, Mtl.	Jarome Iginla, Cgy.
2001	Joe Sakic, Col.	Mario Lemieux, Pit.
2000	Chris Pronger, St.L.	Jaromir Jagr, Pit.
1999	Jaromir Jagr, Pit.	Alexei Yashin, Ott.
1998	Dominik Hasek, Buf.	Jaromir Jagr, Pit.
1997	Dominik Hasek, Buf.	Paul Kariya, Ana.
1996	Mario Lemieux, Pit.	Mark Messier, NYR
1995	Eric Lindros, Phi.	Jaromir Jagr, Pit.
1994	Sergei Fedorov, Det.	Dominik Hasek, Buf.
1993	Mario Lemieux, Pit.	Doug Gilmour, Tor.
1992	Mark Messier, NYR	Patrick Roy, Mtl.
1991	Brett Hull, St.L.	Wayne Gretzky, L.A.
1990	Mark Messier, Edm.	Raymond Bourque, Bos.
1989	Wayne Gretzky, L.A.	Mario Lemieux, Pit.
1988	Mario Lemieux, Pit.	Grant Fuhr, Edm.
1987	Wayne Gretzky, Edm.	Raymond Bourque, Bos.
1986	Wayne Gretzky, Edm.	Mario Lemieux, Pit.
1985	Wayne Gretzky, Edm.	Dale Hawerchuk, Wpg.
1984	Wayne Gretzky, Edm.	Rod Langway, Wsh.
1983	Wayne Gretzky, Edm.	Pete Peeters, Bos.
1982	Wayne Gretzky, Edm.	Bryan Trottier, NYI
1981	Wayne Gretzky, Edm.	Mike Liut, St.L.
1980	Wayne Gretzky, Edm.	Marcel Dionne, L.A.
1979	Bryan Trottier, NYI	Guy Lafleur, Mtl
1978	Guy Lafleur, Mtl.	Bryan Trottier, NYI
1977	Guy Lafleur, Mtl.	Bobby Clarke, Phi.
1976	Bobby Clarke, Phi.	Denis Potvin, NYI
1975	Bobby Clarke, Phi.	Rogie Vachon, L.A.
1974	Phil Esposito, Bos.	Bernie Parent, Phi.
1973	Bobby Clarke, Phi.	Phil Esposito, Bos.
1972	Bobby Orr, Bos.	Ken Dryden, Mtl.
1971	Bobby Orr, Bos.	Phil Esposito, Bos.
1970	Bobby Orr, Bos.	Tony Esposito, Chi.
1969	Phil Esposito, Bos.	Jean Beliveau, Mtl.
1968	Stan Mikita, Chi.	Jean Beliveau, Mtl.
1967	Stan Mikita, Chi.	Ed Giacomin, NYR
1966	Bobby Hull, Chi.	Jean Beliveau, Mtl.
1965	Bobby Hull, Chi.	Norm Ullman, Det.
1964	Jean Beliveau, Mtl.	Bobby Hull, Chi.
1963	Gordie Howe, Det.	Stan Mikita, Chi.
1962	Jacques Plante, Mtl.	Doug Harvey, NYR
1961	Bernie Geoffrion, Mtl.	Johnny Bower, Tor.
1960	Gordie Howe, Det.	Bobby Hull, Chi.
1959	Andy Bathgate, NYR	Gordie Howe, Det.
1958	Gordie Howe, Det.	Andy Bathgate, NYR
1957	Gordie Howe, Det.	Jean Beliveau, Mtl.
1956	Jean Beliveau, Mtl.	Tod Sloan, Tor.
1955	Ted Kennedy, Tor.	Harry Lumley, Tor.
1954	Al Rollins, Chi.	Red Kelly, Det.
1953	Gordie Howe, Det.	Al Rollins, Chi.
1952	Gordie Howe, Det.	Elmer Lach, Mtl.
1951	Milt Schmidt, Bos.	Maurice Richard, Mtl.
1950	Chuck Rayner, NYR	Ted Kennedy, Tor.
1949	Sid Abel, Det.	Bill Durnan, Mtl.
1948	Buddy O'Connor, NYR	Frank Brimsek, Bos.
1947	Maurice Richard, Mtl.	Milt Schmidt, Bos.
1946	Max Bentley, Chi.	Gaye Stewart, Tor.
1945	Elmer Lach, Mtl.	Maurice Richard, Mtl.
1944	Babe Pratt, Tor.	Bill Cowley, Bos.
1943	Bill Cowley, Bos.	Doug Bentley, Chi.
1942	Tom Anderson, Bro.	Syl Apps, Tor.
1941	Bill Cowley, Bos.	Dit Clapper, Bos.
1940	Ebbie Goodfellow, Det.	Syl Apps, Tor.
1939	Toe Blake, Mtl.	Syl Apps, Tor.
1938	Eddie Shore, Bos.	Paul Thompson, Chi.
1937	Babe Siebert, Mtl.	Lionel Conacher, Mtl.M
1936	Eddie Shore, Bos.	Hooley Smith, Mtl.M
1935	Eddie Shore, Bos.	Charlie Conacher, Tor.
1934	Aurel Joliat, Mtl.	Lionel Conacher, Chi.
1933	Eddie Shore, Bos.	Bill Cook, NYR
1932	Howie Morenz, Mtl.	Ching Johnson, NYR
1931	Howie Morenz, Mtl.	Eddie Shore, Bos.
1930	Nels Stewart, Mtl.M.	Lionel Hitchman, Bos.
1929	Roy Worters, NYA	Ace Bailey, Tor.
1928	Howie Morenz, Mtl.	Roy Worters, Pit.
1927	Herb Gardiner, Mtl.	Bill Cook, NYR
1926	Nels Stewart, Mtl.M.	Sprague Cleghorn, Bos.
1925	Billy Burch, Ham.	Howie Morenz, Mtl.
1924	Frank Nighbor, Ott.	Sprague Cleghorn, Mtl.

WILLIAM M. JENNINGS TROPHY

	Winner	Runner-up
2011	Roberto Luongo, Van.	Pekka Rinne, Nsh.
	Cory Schneider, Van.	
2010	Martin Brodeur, N.J.	Tim Thomas, Bos.
		Tuukka Rask, Bos.
2009	Tim Thomas, Bos.	Niklas Backstrom, Min.
	Manny Fernandez, Bos.	
2008	Chris Osgood, Det.	Jean-Sebastien Giguere, Ana.
	Dominik Hasek, Det.	
2007	Niklas Backstrom, Min.	Dominik Hasek, Det.
	Manny Fernandez, Min.	
2006	Miikka Kiprusoff, Cgy.	Manny Legace, Det.
		Chris Osgood, Det.
2005	....	....
2004	Martin Brodeur, N.J.	Marty Turco, Dal.
2003	Martin Brodeur, N.J.	Marty Turco, Dal.
	Roman Cechmanek, Phi.	Ron Tugnutt, Dal.
	Robert Esche, Phi.	
2002	Patrick Roy, Col.	Tommy Salo, Edm.
2001	Dominik Hasek, Buf.	Ed Belfour, Dal.
		Marty Turco, Dal.
2000	Roman Turek, St.L.	John Vanbiesbrouck, Phi.
		Brian Boucher, Phi.
1999	Ed Belfour, Dal.	Dominik Hasek, Buf.
	Roman Turek, Dal.	
1998	Martin Brodeur, N.J.	Ed Belfour, Dal.
1997	Martin Brodeur, N.J.	Chris Osgood, Det.
	Mike Dunham, N.J.	Mike Vernon, Det.
1996	Chris Osgood, Det.	Martin Brodeur, N.J.
	Mike Vernon, Det.	
1995	Ed Belfour, Chi.	Mike Vernon, Det.
		Chris Osgood, Det.
1994	Dominik Hasek, Buf.	Martin Brodeur, N.J.
	Grant Fuhr, Buf.	Chris Terreri, N.J.
1993	Ed Belfour, Chi.	Felix Potvin, Tor.
		Grant Fuhr, Tor.
1992	Patrick Roy, Mtl.	Ed Belfour, Chi.
1991	Ed Belfour, Chi.	Patrick Roy, Mtl.
1990	Andy Moog, Bos.	Patrick Roy, Mtl.
	Reggie Lemelin, Bos.	Brian Hayward, Mtl.
1989	Patrick Roy, Mtl.	Mike Vernon, Cgy.
	Brian Hayward, Mtl.	Rick Wamsley, Cgy.
1988	Patrick Roy, Mtl.	Clint Malarchuk, Wsh.
	Brian Hayward, Mtl.	Pete Peeters, Wsh.
1987	Patrick Roy, Mtl.	Ron Hextall, Phi.
	Brian Hayward, Mtl.	
1986	Bob Froese, Phi.	Al Jensen, Wsh.
	Darren Jensen, Phi.	Pete Peeters, Wsh.
1985	Tom Barrasso, Buf.	Pat Riggin, Wsh.
	Bob Sauve, Buf.	
1984	Al Jensen, Wsh.	Tom Barrasso, Buf.
	Pat Riggin, Wsh.	Bob Sauve, Buf.
1983	Roland Melanson, NYI	Pete Peeters, Bos.
	Billy Smith, NYI	
1982	Rick Wamsley, Mtl.	Billy Smith, NYI
	Denis Herron, Mtl.	Roland Melanson, NYI

MAURICE "ROCKET" RICHARD TROPHY

	Winner	
2011	Corey Perry	Anaheim
2010	Sidney Crosby	Pittsburgh
	Steven Stamkos	Tampa Bay
2009	Alex Ovechkin	Washington
2008	Alex Ovechkin	Washington
2007	Vincent Lecavalier	Tampa Bay
2006	Jonathan Cheechoo	San Jose
2005	....	....
2004	Rick Nash	Columbus
	Jarome Iginla	Calgary
	Ilya Kovalchuk	Atlanta
2003	Milan Hejduk	Colorado
2002	Jarome Iginla	Calgary
2001	Pavel Bure	Florida
2000	Pavel Bure	Florida

MARK MESSIER NHL LEADERSHIP AWARD

	Winner	
2011	Zdeno Chara	Boston
2010	Sidney Crosby	Pittsburgh
2009	Jarome Iginla	Calgary
2008	Mats Sundin	Toronto
2007	Chris Chelios	Detroit

NHL GENERAL MANAGER OF THE YEAR AWARD

	Winner	
2011	Mike Gillis	Vancouver
2010	Don Maloney	Phoenix

LADY BYNG MEMORIAL TROPHY

	Winner	Runner-up
2011	Martin St. Louis, T.B.	Nicklas Lidstrom, Det.
2010	Martin St. Louis, T.B.	Brad Richards, Dal.
2009	Pavel Datsyuk, Det.	Martin St. Louis, T.B.
2008	Pavel Datsyuk, Det.	Martin St. Louis, T.B.
2007	Pavel Datsyuk, Det.	Martin St. Louis, T.B.
2006	Pavel Datsyuk, Det.	Brad Richards, T.B.
2005	....	....
2004	Brad Richards, T.B.	Daniel Alfredsson, Ott.
2003	Alexander Mogilny, Tor.	Nicklas Lidstrom, Det.
2002	Ron Francis, Car.	Joe Sakic, Col.
2001	Joe Sakic, Col.	Nicklas Lidstrom, Det.
2000	Pavol Demitra, St.L.	Nicklas Lidstrom, Det.
1999	Wayne Gretzky, NYR.	Nicklas Lidstrom, Det.
1998	Ron Francis, Pit.	Teemu Selanne, Ana.
1997	Paul Kariya, Ana.	Teemu Selanne, Ana.
1996	Paul Kariya, Ana.	Adam Oates, Bos.
1995	Ron Francis, Pit.	Adam Oates, Bos.
1994	Wayne Gretzky, L.A.	Adam Oates, Bos.
1993	Pierre Turgeon, NYI	Adam Oates, Bos.
1992	Wayne Gretzky, L.A.	Joe Sakic, Que.
1991	Wayne Gretzky, L.A.	Brett Hull, St.L.
1990	Brett Hull, St.L.	Wayne Gretzky, L.A.
1989	Joe Mullen, Cgy.	Wayne Gretzky, L.A.
1988	Mats Naslund, Mtl.	Wayne Gretzky, Edm.
1987	Joe Mullen, Cgy.	Wayne Gretzky, Edm.
1986	Mike Bossy, NYI	Jari Kurri, Edm.
1985	Jari Kurri, Edm.	Joe Mullen, St.L.
1984	Mike Bossy, NYI	Rick Middleton, Bos.
1983	Mike Bossy, NYI	Rick Middleton, Bos.
1982	Rick Middleton, Bos.	Mike Bossy, NYI
1981	Rick Kehoe, Pit.	Wayne Gretzky, Edm.
1980	Wayne Gretzky, Edm.	Marcel Dionne, L.A.
1979	Bob MacMillan, Atl.	Marcel Dionne, L.A.
1978	Butch Goring, L.A.	Peter McNab, Bos.
1977	Marcel Dionne, L.A.	Jean Ratelle, Bos.
1976	Jean Ratelle, NYR-Bos.	Jean Pronovost, Pit.
1975	Marcel Dionne, Det.	John Bucyk, Bos.
1974	John Bucyk, Bos.	Lowell MacDonald, Pit.
1973	Gilbert Perreault, Buf.	Jean Ratelle, NYR
1972	Jean Ratelle, NYR	John Bucyk, Bos.
1971	John Bucyk, Bos.	Dave Keon, Tor.
1970	Phil Goyette, St.L.	John Bucyk, Bos.
1969	Alex Delvecchio, Det.	Ted Hampson, Oak.
1968	Stan Mikita, Chi.	John Bucyk, Bos.
1967	Stan Mikita, Chi.	Dave Keon, Tor.
1966	Alex Delvecchio, Det.	Bobby Rousseau, Mtl.
1965	Bobby Hull, Chi.	Alex Delvecchio, Det.
1964	Kenny Wharram, Chi.	Dave Keon, Tor.
1963	Dave Keon, Tor.	Camille Henry, NYR
1962	Dave Keon, Tor.	Claude Provost, Mtl.
1961	Red Kelly, Tor.	Norm Ullman, Det.
1960	Don McKenney, Bos.	Andy Hebenton, NYR
1959	Alex Delvecchio, Det.	Andy Hebenton, NYR
1958	Camille Henry, NYR	Don Marshall, Mtl.
1957	Andy Hebenton, NYR	Dutch Reibel, Det.
1956	Dutch Reibel, Det.	Floyd Curry, Mtl.
1955	Sid Smith, Tor.	Danny Lewicki, NYR
1954	Red Kelly, Det.	Don Raleigh, NYR
1953	Red Kelly, Det.	Wally Hergesheimer, NYR
1952	Sid Smith, Tor.	Red Kelly, Det.
1951	Red Kelly, Det.	Woody Dumart, Bos.
1950	Edgar Laprade, NYR	Red Kelly, Det.
1949	Bill Quackenbush, Det.	Harry Watson, Tor.
1948	Buddy O'Connor, NYR	Syl Apps, Tor.
1947	Bobby Bauer, Bos.	Syl Apps, Tor.
1946	Toe Blake, Mtl.	Clint Smith, Chi.
1945	Bill Mosienko, Chi.	Syd Howe, Det.
1944	Clint Smith, Chi.	Herb Cain, Bos.
1943	Max Bentley, Chi.	Buddy O'Connor, Mtl.
1942	Syl Apps, Tor.	Gordie Drillon, Tor.
1941	Bobby Bauer, Bos.	Gordie Drillon, Tor.
1940	Bobby Bauer, Bos.	Clint Smith, NYR
1939	Clint Smith, NYR	Marty Barry, Det.
1938	Gordie Drillon, Tor.	Clint Smith, NYR
1937	Marty Barry, Det.	Gordie Drillon, Tor.
1936	Doc Romnes, Chi.	Sweeney Schriner, NYA
1935	Frank Boucher, NYR	Russ Blinco, Mtl.M
1934	Frank Boucher, NYR	Joe Primeau, Tor.
1933	Frank Boucher, NYR	Joe Primeau, Tor.
1932	Joe Primeau, Tor.	Frank Boucher, NYR
1931	Frank Boucher, NYR	Normie Himes, NYA
1930	Frank Boucher, NYR	Normie Himes, NYA
1929	Frank Boucher, NYR	Harold Darragh, Pit.
1928	Frank Boucher, NYR	George Hay, Det.
1927	Billy Burch, NYA	Dick Irvin, Chi.
1926	Frank Nighbor, Ott.	Billy Burch, NYA
1925	Frank Nighbor, Ott.	none

VEZINA TROPHY

	Winner	Runner-up
2011	Tim Thomas, Bos.	Pekka Rinne, Nsh.
2010	Ryan Miller, Buf.	Ilya Bryzgalov, Phx.
2009	Tim Thomas, Bos.	Steve Mason, CBJ
2008	Martin Brodeur, N.J.	Evgeni Nabokov, S.J.
2007	Martin Brodeur, N.J.	Roberto Luongo, Van.
2006	Miikka Kiprusoff, Cgy.	Martin Brodeur, N.J.
2005	....	....
2004	Martin Brodeur, N.J.	Miikka Kiprusoff, Cgy.
2003	Martin Brodeur, N.J.	Marty Turco, Dal.
2002	Jose Theodore, Mtl.	Patrick Roy, Col.
2001	Dominik Hasek, Buf.	Roman Cechmanek, Phi.
2000	Olaf Kolzig, Wsh.	Roman Turek, St.L.
1999	Dominik Hasek, Buf.	Curtis Joseph, Tor.
1998	Dominik Hasek, Buf.	Martin Brodeur, N.J.
1997	Dominik Hasek, Buf.	Martin Brodeur, N.J.
1996	Jim Carey, Wsh.	Chris Osgood, Det.
1995	Dominik Hasek, Buf.	Ed Belfour, Chi.
1994	Dominik Hasek, Buf.	John Vanbiesbrouck, Fla.
1993	Ed Belfour, Chi.	Tom Barrasso, Pit.
1992	Patrick Roy, Mtl.	Kirk McLean, Van.
1991	Ed Belfour, Chi.	Patrick Roy, Mtl.
1990	Patrick Roy, Mtl.	Daren Puppa, Buf.
1989	Patrick Roy, Mtl.	Mike Vernon, Cgy.
1988	Grant Fuhr, Edm.	Tom Barrasso, Buf.
1987	Ron Hextall, Phi.	Mike Liut, Hfd.
1986	John Vanbiesbrouck, NYR	Bob Froese, Phi.
1985	Pelle Lindbergh, Phi.	Tom Barrasso, Buf.
1984	Tom Barrasso, Buf.	Reggie Lemelin, Cgy.
1983	Pete Peeters, Bos.	Roland Melanson, NYI
1982	Billy Smith, NYI	Grant Fuhr, Edm.
1981	Richard Sevigny, Mtl.	Pete Peeters, Phi.
	Denis Herron, Mtl.	Rick St. Croix, Phi.
	Michel Larocque, Mtl.	
1980	Bob Sauve, Buf.	Gerry Cheevers, Bos.
	Don Edwards, Buf.	Gilles Gilbert, Bos.
1979	Ken Dryden, Mtl.	Glenn Resch, NYI
	Michel Larocque, Mtl.	Billy Smith, NYI
1978	Ken Dryden, Mtl.	Bernie Parent, Phi.
	Michel Larocque, Mtl.	Wayne Stephenson, Phi.
1977	Ken Dryden, Mtl.	Glenn Resch, NYI
	Michel Larocque, Mtl.	Billy Smith, NYI
1976	Ken Dryden, Mtl.	Glenn Resch, NYI
		Billy Smith, NYI
1975	Bernie Parent, Phi.	Rogie Vachon, L.A.
		Gary Edwards, L.A.
1974	Bernie Parent, Phi. (tie)	Gilles Gilbert, Bos.
	Tony Esposito, Chi. (tie)	
1973	Ken Dryden, Mtl.	Ed Giacomin, NYR
		Gilles Villemure, NYR
1972	Tony Esposito, Chi.	Cesare Maniago, Min.
	Gary Smith, Chi.	Gump Worsley, Min.
1971	Ed Giacomin, NYR	Tony Esposito, Chi.
	Gilles Villemure, NYR	
1970	Tony Esposito, Chi.	Jacques Plante, St.L.
		Ernie Wakely, St.L.
1969	Jacques Plante, St.L.	Ed Giacomin, NYR
	Glenn Hall, St.L.	
1968	Gump Worsley, Mtl.	Johnny Bower, Tor.
	Rogie Vachon, Mtl.	Bruce Gamble, Tor.
1967	Glenn Hall, Chi.	Charlie Hodge, Mtl.
	Denis DeJordy, Chi.	
1966	Gump Worsley, Mtl.	Glenn Hall, Chi.
	Charlie Hodge, Mtl.	
1965	Terry Sawchuk, Tor.	Roger Crozier, Det.
	Johnny Bower, Tor.	
1964	Charlie Hodge, Mtl.	Glenn Hall, Chi.
1963	Glenn Hall, Chi.	Johnny Bower, Tor.
		Don Simmons, Tor.
1962	Jacques Plante, Mtl.	Johnny Bower, Tor.
1961	Johnny Bower, Tor.	Glenn Hall, Chi.
1960	Jacques Plante, Mtl.	Glenn Hall, Chi.
1959	Jacques Plante, Mtl.	Johnny Bower, Tor.
		Ed Chadwick, Tor.
1958	Jacques Plante, Mtl.	Gump Worsley, NYR
		Marcel Paille, NYR
1957	Jacques Plante, Mtl.	Glenn Hall, Det.
1956	Jacques Plante, Mtl.	Glenn Hall, Det.
1955	Terry Sawchuk, Det.	Harry Lumley, Tor.
1954	Harry Lumley, Tor.	Terry Sawchuk, Det.
1953	Terry Sawchuk, Det.	Gerry McNeil, Mtl.
1952	Terry Sawchuk, Det.	Al Rollins, Tor.
1951	Al Rollins, Tor.	Terry Sawchuk, Det.
1950	Bill Durnan, Mtl.	Harry Lumley, Det.
1949	Bill Durnan, Mtl.	Harry Lumley, Det.
1948	Turk Broda, Tor.	Harry Lumley, Det.
1947	Bill Durnan, Mtl.	Turk Broda, Tor.
1946	Bill Durnan, Mtl.	Frank Brimsek, Bos.
1945	Bill Durnan, Mtl.	Frank McCool, Tor. (tie)
		Harry Lumley, Det. (tie)
1944	Bill Durnan, Mtl.	Paul Bibeault, Tor.
1943	Johnny Mowers, Det.	Turk Broda, Tor.
1942	Frank Brimsek, Bos.	Turk Broda, Tor.
1941	Turk Broda, Tor.	Frank Brimsek, Bos. (tie)
		Johnny Mowers, Det. (tie)
1940	Dave Kerr, NYR	Frank Brimsek, Bos.
1939	Frank Brimsek, Bos.	Dave Kerr, NYR
1938	Tiny Thompson, Bos.	Dave Kerr, NYR
1937	Normie Smith, Det.	Dave Kerr, NYR
1936	Tiny Thompson, Bos.	Mike Karakas, Chi.
1935	Lorne Chabot, Chi.	Alex Connell, Mtl.M
1934	Charlie Gardiner, Chi.	Wilf Cude, Det.
1933	Tiny Thompson, Bos.	John Ross Roach, Det.
1932	Charlie Gardiner, Chi.	Alex Connell, Det.
1931	Roy Worters, NYA	Charlie Gardiner, Chi.
1930	Tiny Thompson, Bos.	Charlie Gardiner, Chi.
1929	George Hainsworth, Mtl.	Tiny Thompson, Bos.
1928	George Hainsworth, Mtl.	Alex Connell, Ott.
1927	George Hainsworth, Mtl.	Clint Benedict, Mtl.M

CALDER MEMORIAL TROPHY

	Winner	Runner-up
2011	Jeff Skinner, Car.	Logan Couture, S.J.
2010	Tyler Myers, Buf.	Jimmy Howard, Det.
2009	Steve Mason, CBJ	Bobby Ryan, Ana.
2008	Patrick Kane, Chi.	Nicklas Backstrom, Wsh.
2007	Evgeni Malkin, Pit.	Paul Stastny, Col.
2006	Alex Ovechkin, Wsh.	Sidney Crosby, Pit.
2005	....	....
2004	Andrew Raycroft, Bos.	Michael Ryder, Mtl.
2003	Barret Jackman, St.L.	Henrik Zetterberg, Det.
2002	Dany Heatley, Atl.	Ilya Kovalchuk, Atl.
2001	Evgeni Nabokov, S.J.	Brad Richards, T.B.
2000	Scott Gomez, N.J.	Brad Stuart, S.J.
1999	Chris Drury, Col.	Marian Hossa, Ott.
1998	Sergei Samsonov, Bos.	Mattias Ohlund, Van.
1997	Bryan Berard, NYI	Jarome Iginla, Cgy.
1996	Daniel Alfredsson, Ott.	Eric Daze, Chi.
1995	Peter Forsberg, Que.	Jim Carey, Wsh.
1994	Martin Brodeur, N.J.	Jason Arnott, Edm.
1993	Teemu Selanne, Wpg.	Joe Juneau, Bos.
1992	Pavel Bure, Van.	Nicklas Lidstrom, Det
1991	Ed Belfour, Chi.	Sergei Fedorov, Det.
1990	Sergei Makarov, Cgy.	Mike Modano, Min.
1989	Brian Leetch, NYR	Trevor Linden, Van.
1988	Joe Nieuwendyk, Cgy.	Ray Sheppard, Buf.
1987	Luc Robitaille, L.A.	Ron Hextall, Phi.
1986	Gary Suter, Cgy.	Wendel Clark, Tor.
1985	Mario Lemieux, Pit.	Chris Chelios, Mtl.
1984	Tom Barrasso, Buf.	Steve Yzerman, Det.
1983	Steve Larmer, Chi.	Phil Housley, Buf.
1982	Dale Hawerchuk, Wpg.	Barry Pederson, Bos.
1981	Peter Stastny, Que.	Larry Murphy, L.A.
1980	Raymond Bourque, Bos.	Mike Foligno, Det.
1979	Bobby Smith, Min	Ryan Walter, Wsh.
1978	Mike Bossy, NYI	Barry Beck, Col.
1977	Willi Plett, Atl.	Don Murdoch, NYR
1976	Bryan Trottier, NYI	Glenn Resch, NYI
1975	Eric Vail, Atl.	Pierre Larouche, Pit.
1974	Denis Potvin, NYI	Tom Lysiak, Atl.
1973	Steve Vickers, NYR	Bill Barber, Phi.
1972	Ken Dryden, Mtl.	Rick Martin, Buf.
1971	Gilbert Perreault, Buf.	Jude Drouin, Min.
1970	Tony Esposito, Chi.	Bill Fairbairn, NYR
1969	Danny Grant, Min.	Norm Ferguson, Oak.
1968	Derek Sanderson, Bos.	Jacques Lemaire, Mtl.
1967	Bobby Orr, Bos.	Ed Van Impe, Chi.
1966	Brit Selby, Tor.	Bert Marshall, Det.
1965	Roger Crozier, Det.	Ron Ellis, Tor.
1964	Jacques Laperriere, Mtl.	John Ferguson, Mtl.
1963	Kent Douglas, Tor.	Doug Barkley, Det.
1962	Bobby Rousseau, Mtl.	Cliff Pennington, Bos.
1961	Dave Keon, Tor.	Bob Nevin, Tor.
1960	Bill Hay, Chi.	Murray Oliver, Det.
1959	Ralph Backstrom, Mtl.	Carl Brewer, Tor.
1958	Frank Mahovlich, Tor.	Bobby Hull, Chi.
1957	Larry Regan, Bos.	Ed Chadwick, Tor.
1956	Glenn Hall, Det.	Andy Hebenton, NYR
1955	Ed Litzenberger, Chi.	Don McKenney, Bos.
1954	Camille Henry, NYR	Dutch Reibel, Det.
1953	Gump Worsley, NYR	Gord Hannigan, Tor.
1952	Bernie Geoffrion, Mtl.	Hy Buller, NYR
1951	Terry Sawchuk, Det.	Al Rollins, Tor.
1950	Jack Gelineau, Bos.	Phil Maloney, Bos.
1949	Pentti Lund, NYR	Allan Stanley, NYR
1948	Jim McFadden, Det.	Pete Babando, Bos.
1947	Howie Meeker, Tor.	Jim Conacher, Det.
1946	Edgar Laprade, NYR	George Gee, Chi.
1945	Frank McCool, Tor.	Ken Smith, Bos.
1944	Gus Bodnar, Tor.	Bill Durnan, Mtl.
1943	Gaye Stewart, Tor.	Glen Harmon, Mtl.
1942	Grant Warwick, NYR	Buddy O'Connor, Mtl.
1941	John Quilty, Mtl.	Johnny Mowers, Det.
1940	Kilby MacDonald, NYR	Wally Stanowski, Tor.
1939	Frank Brimsek, Bos.	Roy Conacher, Bos.
1938	Cully Dahlstrom, Chi.	Murph Chamberlain, Tor.
1937	Syl Apps, Tor.	Gordie Drillon, Tor.
1936	Mike Karakas, Chi.	Bucko McDonald, Det.
1935	Sweeney Schriner, NYA	Bert Connelly, NYR
1934	Russ Blinco, Mtl.M.	none
1933	Carl Voss, Det.	none

KING CLANCY MEMORIAL TROPHY

	Winner	
2011	Doug Weight	NY Islanders
2010	Shane Doan	Phoenix
2009	Ethan Moreau	Edmonton
2008	Vincent Lecavalier	Tampa Bay
2007	Saku Koivu	Montreal
2006	Olaf Kolzig	Washington
2005	....	....
2004	Jarome Iginla	Calgary
2003	Brendan Shanahan	Detroit
2002	Ron Francis	Carolina
2001	Shjon Podein	Colorado
2000	Curtis Joseph	Toronto
1999	Rob Ray	Buffalo
1998	Kelly Chase	St. Louis
1997	Trevor Linden	Vancouver
1996	Kris King	Winnipeg
1995	Joe Nieuwendyk	Calgary
1994	Adam Graves	NY Rangers
1993	Dave Poulin	Boston
1992	Raymond Bourque	Boston
1991	Dave Taylor	Los Angeles
1990	Kevin Lowe	Edmonton
1989	Bryan Trottier	NY Islanders
1988	Lanny McDonald	Calgary

JAMES NORRIS MEMORIAL TROPHY

	Winner	Runner-up
2011	Nicklas Lidstrom, Det.	Shea Weber, Nsh.
2010	Duncan Keith, Chi.	Mike Green, Wsh.
2009	Zdeno Chara, Bos.	Mike Green, Wsh.
2008	Nicklas Lidstrom, Det.	Dion Phaneuf, Cgy.
2007	Nicklas Lidstrom, Det.	Scott Niedermayer, Ana.
2006	Nicklas Lidstrom, Det.	Scott Niedermayer, Ana.
2005	....	
2004	Scott Niedermayer, N.J.	Zdeno Chara, Ott.
2003	Nicklas Lidstrom, Det.	Al MacInnis, St.L.
2002	Nicklas Lidstrom, Det.	Chris Chelios, Det.
2001	Nicklas Lidstrom, Det.	Raymond Bourque, Col.
2000	Chris Pronger, St.L.	Nicklas Lidstrom, Det.
1999	Al MacInnis, St.L.	Nicklas Lidstrom, Det.
1998	Rob Blake, L.A.	Nicklas Lidstrom, Det.
1997	Brian Leetch, NYR	V. Konstantinov, Det.
1996	Chris Chelios, Chi.	Raymond Bourque, Bos.
1995	Paul Coffey, Det.	Chris Chelios, Chi.
1994	Raymond Bourque, Bos.	Scott Stevens, N.J.
1993	Chris Chelios, Chi.	Raymond Bourque, Bos.
1992	Brian Leetch, NYR	Raymond Bourque, Bos.
1991	Raymond Bourque, Bos.	Al MacInnis, Cgy.
1990	Raymond Bourque, Bos.	Al MacInnis, Cgy.
1989	Chris Chelios, Mtl	Paul Coffey, Pit.
1988	Raymond Bourque, Bos.	Scott Stevens, Wsh.
1987	Raymond Bourque, Bos.	Mark Howe, Phi.
1986	Paul Coffey, Edm.	Mark Howe, Phi.
1985	Paul Coffey, Edm.	Raymond Bourque, Bos.
1984	Rod Langway, Wsh.	Paul Coffey, Edm.
1983	Rod Langway, Wsh.	Mark Howe, Phi.
1982	Doug Wilson, Chi.	Raymond Bourque, Bos.
1981	Randy Carlyle, Pit.	Denis Potvin, NYI
1980	Larry Robinson, Mtl.	Borje Salming, Tor.
1979	Denis Potvin, NYI	Larry Robinson, Mtl.
1978	Denis Potvin, NYI	Brad Park, Bos.
1977	Larry Robinson, Mtl.	Borje Salming, Tor.
1976	Denis Potvin, NYI	Brad Park, NYR-Bos.
1975	Bobby Orr, Bos.	Denis Potvin, NYI
1974	Bobby Orr, Bos.	Brad Park, NYR
1973	Bobby Orr, Bos.	Guy Lapointe, Mtl.
1972	Bobby Orr, Bos.	Brad Park, NYR
1971	Bobby Orr, Bos.	Brad Park, NYR
1970	Bobby Orr, Bos.	Brad Park, NYR
1969	Bobby Orr, Bos.	Tim Horton, Tor.
1968	Bobby Orr, Bos.	J.C. Tremblay, Mtl
1967	Harry Howell, NYR	Pierre Pilote, Chi.
1966	Jacques Laperriere, Mtl.	Pierre Pilote, Chi.
1965	Pierre Pilote, Chi.	Jacques Laperriere, Mtl.
1964	Pierre Pilote, Chi.	Tim Horton, Tor.
1963	Pierre Pilote, Chi.	Carl Brewer, Tor.
1962	Doug Harvey, NYR	Pierre Pilote, Chi.
1961	Doug Harvey, Mtl.	Marcel Pronovost, Det.
1960	Doug Harvey, Mtl.	Allan Stanley, Tor.
1959	Tom Johnson, Mtl.	Bill Gadsby, NYR
1958	Doug Harvey, Mtl.	Bill Gadsby, NYR
1957	Doug Harvey, Mtl.	Red Kelly, Det.
1956	Doug Harvey, Mtl.	Bill Gadsby, NYR
1955	Doug Harvey, Mtl.	Red Kelly, Det.
1954	Red Kelly, Det.	Doug Harvey, Mtl.

JACK ADAMS AWARD

	Winner	Runner-up
2011	Dan Bylsma, Pit.	Alain Vigneault, Van.
2010	Dave Tippett, Phx.	Barry Trotz, Nsh.
2009	Claude Julien, Bos.	Andy Murray, St.L.
2008	Bruce Boudreau, Wsh.	Guy Carbonneau, Mtl.
2007	Alain Vigneault, Van.	Lindy Ruff, Buf.
2006	Lindy Ruff, Buf.	Peter Laviolette, Car.
2005	....	
2004	John Tortorella, T.B.	Ron Wilson, S.J.
2003	Jacques Lemaire, Min.	John Tortorella, T.B.
2002	Bob Francis, Phx.	Brian Sutter, Chi.
2001	Bill Barber, Phi.	Scotty Bowman, Det.
2000	Joel Quenneville, St.L.	Alain Vigneault, Mtl.
1999	Jacques Martin, Ott.	Pat Quinn, Tor.
1998	Pat Burns, Bos.	Larry Robinson, L.A.
1997	Ted Nolan, Buf.	Ken Hitchcock, Dal.
1996	Scotty Bowman, Det.	Doug MacLean, Fla.
1995	Marc Crawford, Que.	Scotty Bowman, Det.
1994	Jacques Lemaire, N.J.	Kevin Constantine, S.J.
1993	Pat Burns, Tor.	Brian Sutter, Bos.
1992	Pat Quinn, Van.	Roger Neilson, NYR
1991	Brian Sutter, St.L.	Tom Webster, L.A.
1990	Bob Murdoch, Wpg.	Mike Milbury, Bos.
1989	Pat Burns, Mtl.	Bob McCammon, Van.
1988	Jacques Demers, Det.	Terry Crisp, Cgy.
1987	Jacques Demers, Det.	Jack Evans, Hfd.
1986	Glen Sather, Edm.	Jacques Demers, St.L.
1985	Mike Keenan, Phi.	Barry Long, Wpg.
1984	Bryan Murray, Wsh.	Scotty Bowman, Buf.
1983	Orval Tessier, Chi.	
1982	Tom Watt, Wpg.	
1981	Red Berenson, St.L.	Bob Berry, L.A.
1980	Pat Quinn, Phi.	
1979	Al Arbour, NYI	Fred Shero, NYR
1978	Bobby Kromm, Det.	Don Cherry, Bos.
1977	Scotty Bowman, Mtl.	Tom McVie, Wsh.
1976	Don Cherry, Bos.	
1975	Bob Pulford, L.A.	
1974	Fred Shero, Phi.	

LESTER PATRICK TROPHY

	Winner	
2011	Jeff Sauer	Tony Rossi
	Mark Johnson	Bob Pulford
2010	Jerry York	Jack Parker
	Cam Neely	Dave Andrews
2009	Mark Messier	Jim Devellano
	Mike Richter	
2008	Brian Burke	Phil Housley
	Ted Lindsay	Bob Naegele, Jr.
2007	Brian Leetch	Cammi Granato
	Stan Fischler	John Halligan
2006	Red Berenson	Marcel Dionne
	Reed Larson	Glen Sonmor
	Steve Yzerman	
2005	....	
2004	John Davidson	Mike Emrick
	Ray Miron	
2003	Raymond Bourque	Ron DeGregorio
	Willie O'Ree	
2002	Herb Brooks	Larry Pleau
	1960 U.S. Olympic Team	
2001	Gary Bettman	Scotty Bowman
	David Poile	
2000	Mario Lemieux	Craig Patrick
	Lou Vairo	
1999	Harry Sinden	
	1998 U.S. Olympic Women's Team	
1998	Neal Broten	Peter Karmanos
	John Mayasich	Max McNab
1997	Bill Cleary	* Seymour H. Knox III
	Pat LaFontaine	
1996	George Gund	Ken Morrow
	Milt Schmidt	
1995	Bob Fleming	Brian Mullen
	Joe Mullen	
1994	Wayne Gretzky	Robert Ridder
1993	*Frank Boucher	* Mervyn "Red" Dutton
	Bruce McNall	Gil Stein
1992	Al Arbour	Art Berglund
	Lou Lamoriello	
1991	Rod Gilbert	Mike Ilitch
1990	Len Ceglarski	
1989	Dan Kelly	Lou Nanne
	*Lynn Patrick	Bud Poile
1988	Keith Allen	Fred Cusick
	Bob Johnson	
1987	*Hobey Baker	Frank Mathers
1986	John MacInnes	Jack Riley
1985	Jack Butterfield	Arthur M. Wirtz
1984	*Arthur Howey Ross	John A. Ziegler, Jr.
1983	Bill Torrey	
1982	Emile P. Francis	
1981	Charles M. Schulz	
1980	Bobby Clarke	Frederick A. Shero
	Edward M. Snider	1980 U.S. Olympic Team
1979	Bobby Orr	
1978	Phil Esposito	Tom Fitzgerald
	William T. Tutt	William W. Wirtz
1977	Murray A. Armstrong	John P. Bucyk
	John Mariucci	
1976	George A. Leader	Stanley Mikita
	Bruce A. Norris	
1975	William L. Chadwick	Donald M. Clark
	Thomas N. Ivan	
1974	*Weston W. Adams, Sr.	* Charles L. Crovat
	Alex Delvecchio	Murray Murdoch
1973	Walter L. Bush, Jr.	
1972	Clarence S. Campbell	John A. "Snooks" Kelly
	*James D. Norris	Ralph "Cooney" Weiland
1971	William M. Jennings	* Terrance G. Sawchuk
	*John B. Sollenberger	
1970	*James C. V. Hendy	Edward W. Shore
1969	Robert M. Hull	* Edward J. Jeremiah
1968	*Walter A. Brown	* Gen. John R. Kilpatrick
	Thomas F. Lockhart	
1967	*Charles F. Adams	Gordon Howe
	*James Norris, Sr.	
1966	J.J. "Jack" Adams	

* awarded posthumously

PRESIDENTS' TROPHY

	Winner	
2011	Vancouver Canucks	Washington Capitals
2010	Washington Capitals	San Jose Sharks
2009	San Jose Sharks	Boston Bruins
2008	Detroit Red Wings	San Jose Sharks
2007	Buffalo Sabres	Detroit Red Wings
2006	Detroit Red Wings	Ottawa Senators
2005	....	
2004	Detroit Red Wings	Tampa Bay Lightning
2003	Ottawa Senators	Dallas Stars
2002	Detroit Red Wings	Boston Bruins
2001	Colorado Avalanche	Detroit Red Wings
2000	St. Louis Blues	Detroit Red Wings
1999	Dallas Stars	New Jersey Devils
1998	Dallas Stars	New Jersey Devils
1997	Colorado Avalanche	Dallas Stars
1996	Detroit Red Wings	Colorado Avalanche
1995	Detroit Red Wings	Quebec Nordiques
1994	New York Rangers	New Jersey Devils
1993	Pittsburgh Penguins	Boston Bruins
1992	New York Rangers	Washington Capitals
1991	Chicago Blackhawks	St. Louis Blues
1990	Boston Bruins	Calgary Flames
1989	Calgary Flames	Montreal Canadiens
1988	Calgary Flames	Montreal Canadiens
1987	Edmonton Oilers	Philadelphia Flyers
1986	Edmonton Oilers	Philadelphia Flyers

TED LINDSAY AWARD

	Winner	
2011	Daniel Sedin	Vancouver
2010	Alex Ovechkin	Washington
2009	Alex Ovechkin	Washington
2008	Alex Ovechkin	Washington
2007	Sidney Crosby	Pittsburgh
2006	Jaromir Jagr	NY Rangers
2005	....	
2004	Martin St. Louis	Tampa Bay
2003	Markus Naslund	Vancouver
2002	Jarome Iginla	Calgary
2001	Joe Sakic	Colorado
2000	Jaromir Jagr	Pittsburgh
1999	Jaromir Jagr	Pittsburgh
1998	Dominik Hasek	Buffalo
1997	Dominik Hasek	Buffalo
1996	Mario Lemieux	Pittsburgh
1995	Eric Lindros	Philadelphia
1994	Sergei Fedorov	Detroit
1993	Mario Lemieux	Pittsburgh
1992	Mark Messier	NY Rangers
1991	Brett Hull	St. Louis
1990	Mark Messier	Edmonton
1989	Steve Yzerman	Detroit
1988	Mario Lemieux	Pittsburgh
1987	Wayne Gretzky	Edmonton
1986	Mario Lemieux	Pittsburgh
1985	Wayne Gretzky	Edmonton
1984	Wayne Gretzky	Edmonton
1983	Wayne Gretzky	Edmonton
1982	Wayne Gretzky	Edmonton
1981	Mike Liut	St. Louis
1980	Marcel Dionne	Los Angeles
1979	Marcel Dionne	Los Angeles
1978	Guy Lafleur	Montreal
1977	Guy Lafleur	Montreal
1976	Guy Lafleur	Montreal
1975	Bobby Orr	Boston
1974	Phil Esposito	Boston
1973	Bobby Clarke	Philadelphia
1972	Jean Ratelle	NY Rangers
1971	Phil Esposito	Boston

NHL LIFETIME ACHIEVEMENT AWARD

	Winner
2011	not awarded
2010	not awarded
2009	Jean Beliveau
2008	Gordie Howe

NHL FOUNDATION AWARD

	Winner	
2011	Dustin Brown	Los Angeles
2010	Ryan Miller	Buffalo
2009	Rick Nash	Columbus
2008	Trevor Linden	Vancouver
	Vincent Lecavalier	Tampa Bay
2007	Joe Sakic	Colorado
2006	Marty Turco	Dallas
2004	Jarome Iginla	Calgary
2003	Darren McCarty	Detroit
2002	Ron Francis	Carolina
2001	Olaf Kolzig	Washington
2000	Adam Graves	NY Rangers
1999	Rob Ray	Buffalo
1998	Kelly Chase	St. Louis

NHL Entry Draft

Draft Summary

Following is a summary of the players drafted from the Ontario Hockey League (OHL), Quebec Major Junior Hockey League (QMJHL), Western Hockey League (WHL), United States colleges, United States high schools, European leagues and other North American leagues since 1969. "Other" may include Canadian and U.S. Jr. A and Jr. B, minor professional leagues (AHL, IHL), midget and other teams playing in leagues not listed above.

Year	Total Picks	OHL Picks	%	QMJHL Picks	%	WHL Picks	%	College Picks	%	Hi School Picks	%	Int'l Picks	%	Other Picks	%
1969	84	36	42.9	11	13.1	20	23.8	7	8.3	-	-	1	1.2	9	10.7
1970	115	51	44.3	13	11.3	22	19.1	16	13.9	-	-	-	-	13	11.3
1971	117	41	35.0	13	11.1	28	23.9	22	18.8	-	-	-	-	13	11.1
1972	152	46	30.3	30	19.7	44	28.9	21	13.8	-	-	-	-	11	7.2
1973	168	56	33.3	24	14.3	49	29.2	25	14.9	-	-	-	-	14	8.3
1974	247	69	27.9	40	16.2	66	26.7	41	16.6	-	-	6	2.4	25	10.1
1975	217	55	25.3	28	12.9	57	26.3	59	27.2	-	-	6	2.8	12	5.5
1976	135	47	34.8	18	13.3	33	24.4	26	19.3	-	-	8	5.9	3	2.2
1977	185	42	22.7	40	21.6	44	23.8	49	26.5	-	-	5	2.7	5	2.7
1978	234	59	25.2	22	9.4	48	20.5	73	31.2	-	-	16	6.8	16	6.8
1979	126	48	38.1	19	15.1	37	29.4	15	11.9	-	-	6	4.8	1	0.8
1980	210	73	34.8	24	11.4	41	19.5	42	20.0	7	3.3	13	6.2	10	4.8
1981	211	59	28.0	28	13.3	37	17.5	21	10.0	17	8.1	32	15.2	17	8.1
1982	252	60	23.8	17	6.7	55	21.8	20	7.9	47	18.7	35	13.9	18	7.1
1983	242	57	23.6	24	9.9	41	16.9	14	5.8	35	14.5	34	14.0	37	15.3
1984	250	55	22.0	16	6.4	37	14.8	22	8.8	44	17.6	40	16.0	36	14.4
1985	252	59	23.4	15	6.0	48	19.0	20	7.9	48	19.0	31	12.3	31	12.3
1986	252	66	26.2	22	8.7	32	12.7	22	8.7	40	15.9	28	11.1	42	16.7
1987	252	32	12.7	17	6.7	36	14.3	40	15.9	69	27.4	38	15.1	20	7.9
1988	252	32	12.7	22	8.7	30	11.9	48	19.0	56	22.2	39	15.5	25	9.9
1989	252	39	15.5	16	6.3	44	17.5	48	19.0	47	18.7	38	15.1	20	7.9
1990	250	39	15.6	14	5.6	33	13.2	38	15.2	57	22.8	53	21.2	16	6.4
1991	264	43	16.3	25	9.5	40	15.2	43	16.3	37	14.0	55	20.8	21	8.0
1992	264	57	21.6	22	8.3	45	17.0	9	3.4	25	9.5	84	31.8	22	8.3
1993	286	60	21.0	23	8.0	44	15.4	17	5.9	33	11.5	78	27.3	31	10.8
1994	286	45	15.7	28	9.8	66	23.1	6	2.1	28	9.8	80	28.0	33	11.5
1995	234	54	23.1	35	15.0	55	23.5	5	2.1	2	0.9	69	29.5	14	6.0
1996	241	51	21.2	31	12.9	54	22.4	25	10.4	6	2.5	58	24.1	16	6.6
1997	246	52	21.1	19	7.7	63	25.6	26	10.6	4	1.6	63	25.6	19	7.7
1998	258	50	19.4	41	15.9	44	17.1	27	10.5	7	2.7	75	29.1	14	5.4
1999	272	52	19.1	20	7.4	40	14.7	36	13.2	9	3.3	94	34.6	21	7.7
2000	293	39	13.3	21	7.2	41	14.0	35	11.9	7	2.4	123	42.0	27	9.2
2001	289	41	14.2	26	9.0	45	15.6	24	8.3	8	2.8	119	41.2	26	9.0
2002	290	35	12.1	23	7.9	43	14.8	41	14.1	6	2.1	110	37.9	32	11.0
2003	292	44	15.1	38	13.0	41	14.0	23	7.9	10	3.4	93	31.8	43	14.7
2004	291	42	14.4	27	9.3	44	15.1	28	9.6	18	6.2	88	30.2	44	15.1
2005	230	43	18.7	23	10.0	43	18.7	13	5.6	18	7.8	50	21.7	40	17.4
2006	213	29	13.6	25	11.7	24	11.2	18	8.4	19	8.9	63	29.5	35	16.4
2007	211	35	16.6	25	11.8	37	17.5	8	3.8	14	6.6	36	17.0	56	56.5
2008	211	46	21.8	27	12.8	37	17.5	9	4.2	15	7.1	39	18.5	38	18.0
2009	210	45	21.4	23	11.0	31	14.8	7	3.3	19	9.0	41	19.5	44	21.0
2010	210	42	20.0	22	10.4	43	20.5	9	4.2	22	10.5	39	18.6	33	15.7
2011	210	46	21.9	22	10.4	33	15.7	11	5.2	18	8.6	48	22.9	32	15.2
Total	**2072**	**21.2**		**1019**	**10.4**	**1795**	**18.4**	**1109**	**11.4**	**792**	**8.1**	**1934**	**19.8**	**1035**	**10.6**

Total Players Drafted (1969-2011): 9,756

Easy as 1-2-3... Ryan Nugent-Hopkins from the Red Deer Rebels, selected first overall by Edmonton in the 2011 Entry Draft, is surrounded by #3 pick Jonathan Huberdeau from the Saint John Sea Dogs (Florida) and second choice Gabriel Landeskog from the Kitchener Rangers (Colorado).

History

Year	Location	Date	# Drafted
1963–1968	Montreal	—	122
1969	Queen Elizabeth Hotel, Montreal	June 12	84
1970	Queen Elizabeth Hotel, Montreal	June 11	115
1971	Queen Elizabeth Hotel, Montreal	June 10	117
1972	Queen Elizabeth Hotel, Montreal	June 8	152
1973	Mount Royal Hotel, Montreal	May 15	168
1974	NHL Montreal Office	May 28	247
1975	NHL Montreal Office	June 3	217
1976	NHL Montreal Office	June 1	135
1977	NHL Montreal Office	June 14	185
1978	Queen Elizabeth Hotel, Montreal	June 15	234
1979	Queen Elizabeth Hotel, Montreal	August 9	126
1980	Montreal Forum	June 11	210
1981	Montreal Forum	June 10	211
1982	Montreal Forum	June 9	252
1983	Montreal Forum	June 8	242
1984	Montreal Forum	June 9	250
1985	Toronto Convention Centre	June 15	252
1986	Montreal Forum	June 21	252
1987	Joe Louis Arena, Detroit	June 13	252
1988	Montreal Forum	June 11	252
1989	Met Sports Center, Minnesota	June 17	252
1990	B.C. Place, Vancouver	June 16	250
1991	Memorial Auditorium, Buffalo	June 22	264
1992	Montreal Forum	June 20	264
1993	Le Colisée, Quebec	June 26	286
1994	Hartford Civic Center	June 28-29	286
1995	Edmonton Coliseum	July 8	234
1996	Kiel Center, St. Louis	June 22	241
1997	Civic Arena, Pittsburgh	June 21	246
1998	Marine Midland Arena, Buffalo	June 27	258
1999	FleetCenter, Boston	June 26	272
2000	Saddledome, Calgary	June 24-25	293
2001	National Car Rental Center, Florida	June 23-24	289
2002	Air Canada Centre, Toronto	June 22-23	290
2003	Gaylord Entertainment Center, Nashville	June 21-22	292
2004	RBC Center, Carolina	June 26-27	291
2005	Sheraton Hotel and Towers, Ottawa	July 30	230
2006	General Motors Place, Vancouver	June 24	213
2007	Nationwide Arena, Columbus	June 22-23	211
2008	Scotiabank Place, Ottawa	June 20-21	211
2009	Bell Centre, Montreal	June 26-27	210
2010	STAPLES Center, Los Angeles	June 25-26	210
2011	Xcel Energy Center, Minnesota	June 24-25	210

First Selections

Year	Player	Pos	Team	Drafted From	Age
1963	Garry Monahan	LW	Montreal	St. Michael's Juveniles	16.7
1964	Claude Gauthier	RW	Detroit	Comite des jeunes (Rosemont)	16.9
1965	Andre Veilleux	RW	NY Rangers	Montreal Ranger Jr. B	17.5
1966	Barry Gibbs	D	Boston	Estevan Bruins	17.7
1967	Rick Pagnutti	D	Los Angeles	Garson Native Sons	20.6
1968	Michel Plasse	G	Montreal	Drummondville Rangers	20.0
1969	Rejean Houle	LW	Montreal	Montreal Jr. Canadiens	19.8
1970	Gilbert Perreault	C	Buffalo	Montreal Jr. Canadiens	19.7
1971	Guy Lafleur	RW	Montreal	Quebec Remparts	19.9
1972	Billy Harris	RW	NY Islanders	Toronto Marlboros	20.4
1973	Denis Potvin	D	NY Islanders	Ottawa 67's	19.7
1974	Greg Joly	D	Washington	Regina Pats	20.0
1975	Mel Bridgman	C	Philadelphia	Victoria Cougars	20.1
1976	Rick Green	D	Washington	London Knights	20.3
1977	Dale McCourt	C	Detroit	St. Catharines Fincups	20.4
1978	Bobby Smith	C	Minnesota	Ottawa 67's	20.4
1979	Rob Ramage	D	Colorado	London Knights	20.5
1980	Doug Wickenheiser	C	Montreal	Regina Pats	19.2
1981	Dale Hawerchuk	C	Winnipeg	Cornwall Royals	18.2
1982	Gord Kluzak	D	Boston	Nanaimo Islanders	18.3
1983	Brian Lawton	C	Minnesota	Mount St. Charles HS	18.11
1984	Mario Lemieux	C	Pittsburgh	Laval Voisins	18.8
1985	Wendel Clark	LW/D	Toronto	Saskatoon Blades	18.7
1986	Joe Murphy	C	Detroit	Michigan State Spartans	18.8
1987	Pierre Turgeon	C	Buffalo	Granby Bisons	17.10
1988	Mike Modano	C	Minnesota	Prince Albert Raiders	18.0
1989	Mats Sundin	RW	Quebec	Nacka (Sweden)	18.4
1990	Owen Nolan	RW	Quebec	Cornwall Royals	18.4
1991	Eric Lindros	C	Quebec	Oshawa Generals	18.3
1992	Roman Hamrlik	D	Tampa Bay	ZPS Zlin (Czech.)	18.2
1993	Alexandre Daigle	C	Ottawa	Victoriaville Tigres	18.5
1994	Ed Jovanovski	D	Florida	Windsor Spitfires	18.0
1995	Bryan Berard	D	Ottawa	Detroit Jr. Red Wings	18.4
1996	Chris Phillips	D	Ottawa	Prince Albert Raiders	18.3
1997	Joe Thornton	C	Boston	Sault Ste. Marie Greyhounds	17.11
1998	Vincent Lecavalier	C	Tampa Bay	Rimouski Oceanic	18.2
1999	Patrik Stefan	C	Atlanta	Long Beach Ice Dogs (IHL)	18.9
2000	Rick DiPietro	G	NY Islanders	Boston University Terriers	18.9
2001	Ilya Kovalchuk	LW	Atlanta	Spartak (Russia)	18.2
2002	Rick Nash	LW	Columbus	London Knights	18.0
2003	Marc-Andre Fleury	G	Pittsburgh	Cape Breton Screaming Eagles	18.0
2004	Alex Ovechkin	LW	Washington	Dynamo Moscow (Russia)	18.9
2005	Sidney Crosby	C	Pittsburgh	Rimouski Oceanic	17.11
2006	Erik Johnson	D	St. Louis	U.S. National U-18	18.3
2007	Patrick Kane	RW	Chicago	London Knights	18.7
2008	Steven Stamkos	C	Tampa Bay	Sarnia Sting	18.4
2009	John Tavares	C	NY Islanders	London Knights	18.9
2010	Taylor Hall	LW	Edmonton	Windsor Spitfires	18.7
2011	Ryan Nugent-Hopkins	C	Edmonton	Red Deer Rebels	18.2

Ontario Hockey League Draft Selections by Club

Total	Club	'11	'10	'09	'08	'07	'06	'05	'04	'03	'02	'01	'00	'99	'98	'97	'96	'95	'94	'93	'92	'91	'90	'89	'88	'87	'86	'85	'84	'83	'82	'81	'69 to '80
30	Barrie	2	2	2	2	—	1	—	1	1	3	6	3	4	2	—	—	—	—	—	—	—	—	—	—	—	—	—	—	—	—	—	—
67	Belleville	1	1	1	3	4	2	2	—	—	2	3	1	5	2	5	—	3	3	—	4	1	2	4	—	2	5	4	4	3	—	—	—
35	Brampton	—	2	2	3	—	4	4	2	4	3	3	6	2	—	—	—	—	—	—	—	—	—	—	—	—	—	—	—	—	—	—	—
28	Erie	—	2	3	1	5	—	2	—	2	2	3	2	1	3	—	—	—	—	—	—	—	—	—	—	—	—	—	—	—	—	—	—
78	Guelph	2	—	5	3	1	1	2	2	1	2	4	1	3	5	1	6	5	7	2	2	—	4	—	2	8	3	5	1	—	—	—	37
103	Kingston	—	2	2	2	—	4	2	—	1	1	2	—	4	1	4	4	3	2	5	3	2	2	—	1	1	4	3	3	1	2	5	37
147	Kitchener	3	1	1	2	4	—	4	2	1	4	1	1	—	5	3	2	4	2	4	1	3	5	7	1	2	3	6	4	8	5	5	53
149	London	2	2	3	1	3	1	3	6	4	2	2	2	1	4	8	1	4	1	1	4	3	1	3	3	6	2	3	1	7	3	5	54
19	Niagara/Mississauga	3	3	—	1	3	1	1	3	2	—	2	—	—	—	—	—	—	—	—	—	—	—	—	—	—	—	—	—	—	—	—	—
160	Oshawa	5	2	3	2	2	2	—	3	3	3	1	2	3	4	3	1	10	1	4	4	2	4	2	3	6	6	6	5	5	9	50	
142	Ottawa	2	4	1	2	1	1	2	3	2	—	3	2	6	2	5	2	1	1	4	6	5	5	—	1	2	3	3	2	2	9	4	56
39	Owen Sound	3	4	3	1	1	2	2	1	1	—	1	—	1	—	1	2	3	2	3	4	2	1	1	—	—	—	—	—	—	—	—	—
171	Peterborough	3	2	2	1	1	2	5	5	1	2	4	1	5	4	5	4	2	4	4	3	4	2	2	5	2	9	3	7	5	3	70	
67	Plymouth	4	3	2	2	3	2	3	3	3	3	6	2	2	4	3	6	2	7	2	2	—	—	—	—	—	—	—	—	—	—	—	—
75	Saginaw/North Bay	4	1	3	3	—	2	3	1	2	2	3	2	2	2	1	1	2	7	2	5	2	4	1	3	3	3	3	4	4	—	—	—
36	Sarnia	1	1	—	4	1	1	3	—	5	2	1	3	1	3	2	7	1	—	—	—	—	—	—	—	—	—	—	—	—	—	—	—
116	Sault Ste. Marie	4	2	1	2	3	—	1	3	1	1	1	1	1	1	4	3	4	3	7	2	1	3	2	1	7	5	4	6	1	8	28	
30	St. Michael's	3	3	4	4	—	—	4	5	1	5	1	—	—	—	—	—	—	—	—	—	—	—	—	—	—	—	—	—	—	—	—	—
116	Sudbury	3	1	2	1	2	4	—	1	1	2	—	5	5	3	1	2	2	10	2	8	2	1	—	1	3	5	2	—	4	2	39	
92	Windsor	1	4	5	4	2	2	3	2	2	2	2	2	2	1	5	1	4	3	—	3	—	1	2	5	—	7	3	2	2	3	5	12

Clubs no longer operating

Total	Club	'85	'84	'83	'82	'81	'69 to '80
27	Brantford	2	7	2	5	—	11
37	Cornwall						
62	Hamilton						43
20	Montreal						20
5	Newmarket						
72	Niagara Falls				6	6	29
52	St. Catharines						52
97	Toronto	2	1	4	6	2	69

(Cornwall: '94 5, '93 3, '92 3, '91 2, '90 3, '89 3, '88 2, '87 2, '86 3, '85 4, '84 7, '83 — · Hamilton: '91 2, '89 4, '88 4, '87 6, '86 3 · Newmarket: '95 2, '94 3 · Niagara Falls: '98 6, '97 2, '96 3, '95 4, '94 4, '93 4, '92 4)

Quebec Major Junior Hockey League Draft Selections by Club

Total	Club	'11	'10	'09	'08	'07	'06	'05	'04	'03	'02	'01	'00	'99	'98	'97	'96	'95	'94	'93	'92	'91	'90	'89	'88	'87	'86	'85	'84	'83	'82	'81	'69 to '80
10	Acadie-Bathurst	—	1	—	2	—	—	3	2	—	2	—	—	—	—	—	—	—	—	—	—	—	—	—	—	—	—	—	—	—	—	—	—
22	Baie-Comeau	1	—	1	2	1	3	—	3	2	1	3	2	—	3	—	—	—	—	—	—	—	—	—	—	—	—	—	—	—	—	—	—
17	Cape Breton	1	1	1	1	—	1	—	3	2	2	1	1	—	3	—	—	—	—	—	—	—	—	—	—	—	—	—	—	—	—	—	—
55	Chicoutimi	1	—	3	—	4	—	1	3	1	—	2	3	1	1	—	1	1	2	2	1	—	3	—	3	1	6	11					
59	Drummondville	2	—	3	—	2	2	1	1	—	1	1	—	2	2	3	4	1	2	2	4	—	1	4	2	2	2	1	—	—	14		
78	Gatineau/Hull	2	3	—	1	1	2	—	4	4	5	2	—	4	3	—	3	3	1	3	3	3	3	2	2	3	4	—	1	3	—	1	13
35	Halifax	2	3	—	—	2	3	1	3	6	—	3	2	—	3	3	1	3	—	—	—	—	—	—	—	—	—	—	—	—	—	—	—
80	Lewiston/Sher.	—	2	1	2	3	2	5	2	1	—	3	—	5	1	—	4	2	3	—	—	—	—	—	—	2	5	37					
23	Moncton	—	2	—	1	2	1	3	1	2	3	2	—	2	2	1	1	—	—	—	—	—	—	—	—	—	—	—	—	—	—	—	—
9	Montreal/St. John's	1	1	1	2	4	—	—	—	—	—	—	—	—	—	—	—	—	—	—	—	—	—	—	—	—	—	—	—	—	—	—	—
24	PEI/Mtl. Rocket	—	1	1	2	2	—	2	8	1	3	1	2	—	—	—	—	—	—	—	—	—	—	—	—	—	—	—	—	—	—	—	—
26	Quebec	—	1	1	3	2	2	1	3	1	3	—	3	4	—	—	—	—	—	—	—	—	—	—	—	—	—	—	—	—	—	—	—
32	Rimouski	—	2	2	2	—	2	3	4	—	4	2	2	5	—	—	—	—	—	—	—	—	—	—	—	—	—	—	—	—	—	—	—
19	Rouyn-Noranda	—	1	1	2	1	3	1	—	2	—	4	1	3	—	—	—	—	—	—	—	—	—	—	—	—	—	—	—	—	—	—	—
13	Saint John	5	2	2	1	2	1	—	—	—	—	—	—	—	—	—	—	—	—	—	—	—	—	—	—	—	—	—	—	—	—	—	—
85	Shawinigan	3	1	6	—	1	1	3	2	2	1	1	1	3	4	2	1	1	3	2	—	2	1	—	2	5	5	2	26				
27	Val-d'Or	3	1	—	2	—	—	2	1	1	2	2	3	—	2	4	2	1	—	—	—	—	—	—	—	—	—	—	—	—	—	—	—
38	Victoriaville	3	—	1	3	1	—	—	3	1	3	2	1	2	3	1	1	6	2	—	1	—	4	—	—	—	—	—	—	—	—	—	—

Clubs no longer operating

Total	Club	'97	'96	'95	'94	'93	'92	'91	'90	'89	'88	'87	'86	'85	'84	'83	'82	'81	'69 to '80
21	Beauport	3	3	7	3	1	3	1	—	—	—	—	—	—	—	—	—	—	—
45	Cornwall	—	—	—	—	—	—	—	—	—	—	—	—	—	—	—	5	—	40
30	Granby	1	3	2	5	1	—	2	—	2	—	4	2	2	3	1	2	—	—
54	Laval	3	1	2	4	5	2	1	4	3	3	1	3	5	—	2	1	2	12
12	Longueuil	—	—	—	—	3	2	—	1	2	1	2	1	—	—	—	—	—	—
32	Montreal Jrs.	—	—	—	—	—	—	—	—	—	—	—	—	—	3	—	29		
47	Quebec	—	—	—	—	—	—	—	—	—	3	2	2	1	2	37			
15	St. Hyacinthe	4	—	4	1	2	1	3	—	—	—	—	—	—	—	—	—	—	—
16	St. Jean	1	1	2	1	3	—	1	3	—	1	1	—	2	—	—	—	—	—
2	St. Jerome	—	—	—	—	—	—	—	—	—	—	—	—	—	—	—	—	—	2
28	Sorel	—	—	—	—	—	—	—	—	—	—	—	—	—	5	23			
47	Trois Rivieres	1	2	1	3	3	1	—	3	—	3	1	2	27					
27	Verdun	3	—	1	3	—	3	—	3	3	—	—	11						

2011 NHL Entry Draft Order of Selection

The first 14 picks of the 2011 Entry Draft were determined by the NHL's annual Draft Drawing, a weighted lottery system used to determine the order of selection.

The 14 teams that did not qualify for the 2011 Stanley Cup Playoffs, or clubs that acquired those clubs' 2011 first-round draft picks, participated in the drawing.

The club selected in the drawing may not move up more than four positions in the draft order, thus only the five clubs with the fewest regular-season points have the opportunity to select first overall. No club can move down more than one position as a result of the Draft Drawing. For 2011, the Edmonton Oilers won the right to the first overall pick.

In the first round of the 2011 Entry Draft, the order of selection was as follows:

a) The winner of the Draft Drawing followed by the remaining non-playoff teams, in inverse order of points. (Note that the original holder of each selection is listed followed by the club that acquired and used that selection in the first round of the 2011 Entry Draft.)

1. Edmonton
2. Colorado
3. Florida
4. New Jersey
5. NY Islanders
6. Ottawa
7. Winnipeg
8. CBJ – Phi.
9. Tor. – Bos.
10. Minnesota
11. St.L. – Col.
12. Carolina
13. Calgary
14. Dallas

b) Clubs eliminated in the first two rounds of the 2011 Stanley Cup Playoffs, regular-season division winners excluded, in inverse order of points;

15. NY Rangers
16. Buffalo
17. Montreal
18. Chicago
19. L.A. – Edm.
20. Phoenix
21. Nsh. – Ott.
22. Ana. – Tor.

c) Regular-season division winning clubs eliminated in the first two rounds of the 2011 Stanley Cup Playoffs, in inverse order of points;

23. Pittsburgh
24. Det. – Ott.
25. Phi. – Tor.
26. Wsh. – Chi.

d) Clubs eliminated in the 2011 Conference Finals, in inverse order of points;

27. Tampa Bay
28. S.J. – Min.

e) Loser of Stanley Cup Final
29. Vancouver

f) Stanley Cup champion
30. Boston – Anaheim

Because Edmonton Oilers were both the winner of the Draft Drawing and the Club with the fewest regular-season points, the order of selection in the second and subsequent rounds was identical to that used in the first round.

Montreal's P.K. Subban (top) was selected from the Belleville Bulls of the OHL 43rd overall in the second round in 2007. He played his first full NHL season in 2010-11. Boston's Brad Marchand helped the Bruins win the Stanley Cup as a rookie in 2011 after being the team's fourth choice (71st overall) from Moncton in the QMJHL in 2006.

Western Hockey League Draft Selections by Club

Total	Club	'11	'10	'09	'08	'07	'06	'05	'04	'03	'02	'01	'00	'99	'98	'97	'96	'95	'94	'93	'92	'91	'90	'89	'88	'87	'86	'85	'84	'83	'82	'81	'69 to '80
105	Brandon	1	2	2	2	1	1	2	–	3	4	2	–	–	4	5	2	6	5	2	1	1	1	–	3	3	1	2	3	1	2	2	41
40	Calgary	–	2	2	2	4	1	2	5	3	2	1	4	6	3	–	3	–	–	–	–	–	–	–	–	–	–	–	–	–	–	–	–
6	Chilliwack	–	3	1	–	2	–	–	–	–	–	–	–	–	–	–	–	–	–	–	–	–	–	–	–	–	–	–	–	–	–	–	–
6	Edmonton	4	1	1	–	–	–	–	–	–	–	–	–	–	–	–	–	–	–	–	–	–	–	–	–	–	–	–	–	–	–	–	–
13	Everett	–	3	2	1	3	4	–	–	–	–	–	–	–	–	–	–	–	–	–	–	–	–	–	–	–	–	–	–	–	–	–	–
110	Kamloops	–	2	2	–	1	1	2	5	2	5	2	4	4	1	3	4	5	9	2	3	6	4	5	1	3	4	4	4	4	2	–	16
39	Kelowna	1	1	3	4	2	–	2	4	4	1	1	1	2	2	7	4	–	–	–	–	–	–	–	–	–	–	–	–	–	–	–	–
21	Kootenay	1	3	1	–	1	1	3	2	1	3	2	1	2	–	–	–	–	–	–	–	–	–	–	–	–	–	–	–	–	–	–	–
92	Lethbridge	1	–	1	2	2	1	–	2	2	2	1	3	–	1	5	1	3	3	4	3	7	4	3	3	–	1	5	1	2	7	4	18
111	Medicine Hat	1	2	1	2	–	2	4	2	3	3	2	–	1	4	2	7	2	6	1	3	3	1	4	1	5	2	6	1	2	1	2	35
66	Moose Jaw	1	3	–	3	1	1	3	3	3	3	3	5	1	2	4	4	4	3	2	3	2	1	3	–	3	1	4	–	–	–	–	–
119	Portland	4	8	1	–	2	1	3	2	1	2	–	6	1	3	3	1	2	3	4	4	1	1	4	1	3	4	2	5	7	7	6	27
83	Prince Albert	2	–	1	–	–	–	2	4	2	1	4	2	3	3	5	3	4	3	5	2	6	4	3	3	1	6	6	2	2	4	–	–
28	Prince George	–	1	1	–	1	4	1	2	2	–	4	–	2	4	2	2	2	–	–	–	–	–	–	–	–	–	–	–	–	–	–	–
50	Red Deer	2	1	4	1	1	1	1	1	4	4	6	1	1	5	3	4	2	5	3	–	–	–	–	–	–	–	–	–	–	–	–	–
114	Regina	–	2	1	3	3	1	1	–	2	1	2	2	4	2	3	4	2	3	–	4	–	1	5	–	2	3	4	4	8	6	5	36
119	Saskatoon	4	4	3	3	3	–	4	1	–	–	4	1	4	2	2	2	2	4	2	3	2	2	3	4	4	5	1	3	5	5	3	34
97	Seattle	2	1	–	2	1	1	3	2	5	1	5	4	6	2	8	1	5	5	4	2	3	6	2	4	2	1	3	1	–	6	–	9
68	Spokane	3	–	2	3	3	1	4	1	–	3	3	2	1	1	4	5	4	4	4	7	5	1	2	3	1	–	–	–	–	–	1	–
68	Swift Current	3	–	1	4	2	2	1	2	2	4	1	3	1	2	2	1	4	4	5	1	1	2	2	2	5	–	–	–	–	–	–	11
56	Tri-City	1	2	–	2	–	–	2	4	1	3	2	2	1	4	1	6	6	2	2	5	3	3	4	–	–	–	–	–	–	–	–	–
20	Vancouver	2	2	1	3	4	1	3	2	1	1	–	–	–	–	–	–	–	–	–	–	–	–	–	–	–	–	–	–	–	–	–	–
Clubs no longer operating																																	
13	Billings	–	–	–	–	–	–	–	–	–	–	–	–	–	–	–	–	–	–	–	–	–	–	–	–	–	–	–	–	–	–	2	11
66	Calgary	–	–	–	–	–	–	–	–	–	–	–	–	–	–	–	–	–	–	–	–	–	–	–	–	–	2	3	3	3	4	5	46
38	Edmonton	–	–	–	–	–	–	–	–	–	–	–	–	–	–	4	–	–	–	–	–	–	–	–	–	–	–	–	–	–	–	–	34
12	Estevan	–	–	–	–	–	–	–	–	–	–	–	–	–	–	–	–	–	–	–	–	–	–	–	–	–	–	–	–	–	–	–	12
39	Flin Flon	–	–	–	–	–	–	–	–	–	–	–	–	–	–	–	–	–	–	–	–	–	–	–	–	–	–	–	–	–	–	–	39
11	Kelowna	–	–	–	–	–	–	–	–	–	–	–	–	–	–	–	–	–	–	–	–	–	–	–	–	–	–	5	4	2	–	–	–
6	Nanaimo	–	–	–	–	–	–	–	–	–	–	–	–	–	–	–	–	–	–	–	–	–	–	–	–	–	–	–	–	1	5	–	–
62	New Westm'r	–	–	–	–	–	–	–	–	–	–	–	–	–	–	–	–	–	–	–	–	–	–	–	1	2	1	1	2	–	–	–	55
12	Tacoma	–	–	–	–	–	–	–	–	–	–	–	–	–	–	–	–	2	5	2	3	–	–	–	–	–	–	–	–	–	–	–	–
2	Vancouver	–	–	–	–	–	–	–	–	–	–	–	–	–	–	–	–	–	–	–	–	–	–	–	–	–	–	–	–	–	–	–	2
79	Victoria	–	–	–	–	–	–	–	–	–	–	–	–	–	–	–	–	–	2	2	1	–	2	4	4	2	1	2	4	3	2	6	44
34	Winnipeg	–	–	–	–	–	–	–	–	–	–	–	–	–	–	–	–	–	–	–	–	–	–	–	–	–	–	–	–	1	4	1	28

U.S. College Hockey Draft Selections by School

Total	School	'11	'10	'09	'08	'07	'06	'05	'04	'03	'02	'01	'00	'99	'98	'97	'96	'95	'94	'93	'92	'91	'90	'89	'88	'87	'86	'85	'84	'83	'82	'81	'69 to '80
38	Boston College	–	–	–	1	–	1	1	1	1	3	2	3	–	3	3	2	–	–	–	–	–	–	2	–	2	1	–	–	–	1	1	10
56	Boston U.	3	–	1	1	–	1	–	1	–	3	2	1	3	2	1	1	1	–	1	1	2	2	1	3	2	2	1	1	–	–	1	18
28	Bowling Green	–	–	–	–	–	1	1	–	–	1	1	–	1	1	1	–	–	–	–	1	3	1	2	3	–	–	–	–	1	–	–	10
34	Clarkson	–	1	–	–	–	1	–	–	–	–	–	1	1	3	–	–	–	–	1	1	2	3	1	1	1	–	–	1	1	1	1	13
33	Colorado	–	–	–	–	1	–	1	–	2	1	1	2	1	3	–	–	1	–	–	–	–	2	–	1	–	1	–	3	–	–	–	13
34	Cornell	–	–	–	–	–	–	1	2	2	1	–	2	2	–	1	–	–	–	–	–	–	2	5	2	1	–	2	1	–	1	1	8
44	Denver	1	–	–	–	–	–	2	1	–	1	–	–	1	–	3	–	–	–	–	–	–	–	1	1	4	2	1	–	–	1	–	25
35	Harvard	–	1	–	–	–	–	1	–	–	3	2	2	1	2	1	3	–	1	2	–	–	–	2	1	1	–	2	–	1	1	–	8
25	Lake Superior	–	1	–	–	–	–	–	–	–	1	–	–	1	–	1	1	–	–	1	–	1	3	2	3	–	3	–	1	–	–	–	6
22	Maine	–	–	–	–	–	1	–	1	2	–	–	1	4	1	1	1	–	–	1	–	–	1	2	3	–	1	–	–	1	1	–	–
24	Miami U.	–	–	2	1	1	1	1	2	–	1	1	–	–	1	–	–	–	–	1	1	2	–	2	4	2	–	1	–	–	–	–	–
68	Michigan	–	1	–	–	1	2	1	3	2	3	2	1	2	3	1	3	–	1	1	2	4	5	3	2	1	–	1	1	–	–	–	22
49	Michigan State	–	1	–	–	–	1	–	2	1	4	–	2	2	1	1	1	–	1	1	1	4	5	4	4	1	1	–	2	–	2	–	7
46	Michigan Tech	–	–	–	–	–	–	–	–	–	–	1	–	–	–	–	1	–	2	1	–	2	1	2	1	1	2	2	2	–	1	–	27
69	Minnesota	–	–	1	–	1	1	1	–	2	3	–	3	3	1	2	3	2	–	–	–	–	–	1	1	1	2	–	–	1	1	1	38
31	New Hampshire	–	–	–	–	–	–	–	1	–	1	–	2	1	–	1	–	–	–	–	–	–	–	–	1	–	–	–	2	1	1	1	19
40	North Dakota	1	–	–	–	–	1	–	1	1	1	–	1	1	–	2	–	–	–	–	–	1	1	2	–	–	–	–	1	–	–	1	25
30	Northeastern	1	–	–	–	–	–	–	–	–	–	–	–	1	1	–	–	–	–	–	–	–	1	1	–	–	1	1	–	1	–	–	22
24	Northern Mich.	–	1	–	1	–	–	–	2	2	–	–	1	–	–	–	1	–	–	–	–	1	–	2	1	4	–	–	–	–	1	2	5
34	Notre Dame	1	1	–	–	1	1	–	2	–	2	1	1	2	–	2	1	–	–	–	–	–	–	–	–	–	–	–	–	–	–	–	19
21	Ohio State	–	–	–	–	–	–	1	–	1	2	2	–	1	–	1	1	–	–	1	1	1	1	–	2	2	–	–	1	–	–	–	3
36	Providence	–	–	–	–	–	2	–	–	1	1	–	2	–	2	1	–	–	–	–	–	–	1	–	–	–	1	1	–	2	1	4	17
27	RPI	1	–	–	1	–	–	–	–	–	–	1	2	2	–	1	–	–	–	–	1	3	–	–	2	2	–	1	–	1	1	2	6
23	St. Lawrence	–	–	–	–	–	–	–	–	–	1	–	–	1	–	1	1	–	–	1	–	2	1	1	1	1	1	1	1	–	3	–	6
20	Vermont	–	–	–	–	–	–	1	–	–	–	2	–	–	–	–	1	–	1	–	–	1	–	–	1	–	–	2	1	1	–	1	8
26	W. Michigan	1	–	1	–	–	1	–	–	–	1	–	–	–	1	1	–	–	–	2	–	4	1	1	1	1	2	–	2	2	–	–	4
47	Wisconsin	1	1	–	2	–	–	–	2	–	–	–	3	2	–	–	–	–	–	–	–	1	–	1	–	1	–	1	1	–	2	3	26
16	Yale	–	–	–	–	–	1	–	2	–	3	–	–	–	–	–	–	–	–	1	–	–	–	1	–	2	1	–	–	–	–	–	5

Colleges with fewer than 15 players selected: 14 - Brown; 13 - Colgate, Minn.-Duluth; 10 - Dartmouth, Princeton; 9 - Ferris State, Merrimack, St.Cloud State; 7 - Mass.-Lowell; 6 - Illinois-Chicago, St. Louis; 5 - Pennsylvania, Union College, Mass.-Amherst; 4 - Alaska-Anchorage, Nebraska-Omaha, Minnesota State (Mankato); 3 - Babson College, Alaska (Fairbanks); 1 - Air Force, American International College, Army, Bemidji State, Greenway, Hamilton, St. Anselm College, St. Thomas, Salem State, San Diego U., Wisconsin-River Falls.

U.S. High and Prep Schools Draft Selections by School (10 or more players drafted)

Total	School (State)	'11	'10	'09	'08	'07	'06	'05	'04	'03	'02	'01	'00	'99	'98	'97	'96	'95	'94	'93	'92	'91	'90	'89	'88	'87	'86	'85	'84	'83	'82	'80 to '81
15	Avon Old Farms (CT)	1	–	1	1	1	–	–	–	–	–	–	–	–	1	1	–	–	–	–	–	–	3	3	–	1	1	1	–	–	–	–
17	Belmont Hill (MA)	–	–	–	–	–	1	–	–	–	–	–	–	–	–	–	–	–	1	–	2	1	2	3	1	2	1	2	–	1	–	–
11	Canterbury (CT)	–	–	–	–	–	–	–	–	1	–	–	–	–	–	–	–	–	–	1	2	–	2	–	3	–	2	–	–	–	–	–
14	Catholic Memorial (MA)	–	–	–	–	–	–	–	2	–	–	–	–	–	1	–	–	–	2	1	2	–	–	2	1	1	–	2	–	–	–	–
12	Choate-Rosemary (CT)	1	–	–	1	–	–	–	–	–	–	–	1	–	–	–	–	–	–	–	1	1	1	–	3	2	–	1	–	–	–	–
12	Culver Mil. Acad. (IN)	–	–	–	–	–	–	–	–	–	–	–	–	–	–	–	–	–	–	2	2	1	2	2	1	2	–	–	–	–	–	–
22	Cushing Acad. (MA)	–	1	–	–	–	1	1	2	–	–	1	–	–	–	1	1	–	2	2	–	1	3	2	3	–	–	–	1	–	–	–
14	Deerfield (IL)	–	–	–	–	1	–	–	1	1	1	–	2	1	–	–	–	–	–	–	–	1	–	2	1	1	–	1	1	–	–	–
20	Edina (MN)	2	–	2	1	–	–	–	–	–	–	–	–	–	–	–	–	–	–	–	1	–	1	2	2	1	–	–	2	2	4	–
15	Hill-Murray (MN)	–	–	–	–	–	–	–	–	–	–	–	–	–	–	–	–	–	1	–	–	–	3	2	–	3	3	–	3	–	–	–
14	Hotchkiss (CT)	1	–	1	–	–	–	–	1	–	–	1	–	–	–	–	2	1	3	–	–	–	1	–	1	–	1	1	–	–	–	–
10	Lawrence Acad. (MA)	–	–	–	–	–	–	–	–	–	–	–	–	–	–	–	1	–	1	1	–	1	1	–	2	–	–	2	–	1	–	–
10	Matignon (MA)	–	–	–	–	–	–	–	–	–	–	–	–	–	–	–	–	–	–	–	–	1	–	–	–	3	–	–	3	–	1	2
13	Minnetonka (MN)	–	2	1	1	–	–	–	–	–	–	–	–	–	–	–	–	–	–	–	–	1	–	2	–	2	–	2	1	1	–	–
13	Mount St. Charles (RI)	–	–	–	–	–	–	–	–	–	–	–	–	–	–	–	–	–	–	–	–	–	1	1	3	1	2	–	1	3	–	1
20	Northwood Prep (NY)	–	–	–	1	–	–	–	1	–	–	–	1	–	–	–	–	–	1	1	–	–	3	1	1	3	2	2	–	1	2	–
12	Roseau (MN)	–	–	2	–	–	–	–	–	–	–	–	–	–	–	–	–	–	–	–	–	1	3	1	–	–	1	–	1	1	1	1
11	St. John's Prep (MA)	1	–	–	–	–	–	–	–	–	–	–	–	–	–	–	–	–	1	–	–	–	–	–	2	2	–	2	1	1	–	1
13	St. Sebastian's (MA)	–	–	–	–	–	1	–	–	4	1	1	–	–	1	–	–	–	1	2	2	–	–	–	–	–	–	–	–	–	–	–
16	Shattuck-St. Mary's (MN)	1	3	3	3	1	1	2	–	1	–	–	–	–	–	–	1	–	–	–	–	–	–	–	–	–	–	–	–	–	–	–
10	Thayer Acad. (MA)	–	–	–	–	–	–	2	1	–	–	–	–	2		–	–	–	–	–	2	–	–	–	2	–	1	–	–	–	–	–

U.S. College and High School Firsts

Joe Murphy played 779 games over 15 seasons with seven different teams in his NHL career.

1967 – First U.S. College Player Drafted • Michigan Tech center Al Karlander was selected 17th overall by the Detroit Red Wings.

1979 – First U.S. College First- Round Selection • Minnesota-born defenseman Mike Ramsey (currently an assistant coach with the Minnesota Wild) was selected 11th overall by the Buffalo Sabres.

1980 – First U.S. High School Player Drafted • Center Jay North of Bloomington-Jefferson H.S. was taken 62nd overall by the Buffalo Sabres in 1980.

1981 – First U.S. High School First- Round Selection • Center Bob Carpenter of St. John's prep school was selected third overall by Washington in 1981.

1983 – First U.S. High School Player Drafted First Overall • Minnesota North Stars selected left winger Brian Lawton from Mount St. Charles H.S. first overall in 1983.

1986 – First U.S. College Player Drafted First Overall • Detroit selected right winger Joe Murphy from Michigan State first overall in 1986.

2005 – Most U.S. College Players Selected in the First Round • The 2005 draft saw eight U.S. college players selected in the first round, the most in Entry Draft history. Seven were selected in the first round in 2003 and 1986, six in 2000, five in 2002, four in 2001 and three in each of the 1986 and 1999 Entry Drafts.

International

Ranked by total number of players drafted

Total	Country	'11	'10	'09	'08	'07	'06	'05	'04	'03	'02	'01	'00	'99	'98	'97	'96	'95	'94	'93	'92	'91	'90	'89	'88	'87	'86	'85	'84	'83	'82	'81	'69 to '80
535	Russia/CIS/USSR	6	4	6	9	7	16	11	24	32	33	36	44	29	22	16	17	27	35	31	45	25	14	18	11	2	1	2	1	5	3	–	3
532	Sweden	25	21	23	19	16	18	15	18	19	24	14	24	29	14	16	8	17	18	11	11	7	8	11	9	15	9	16	14	10	14	14	36
414	CzRep/Slovakia	5	1	3	2	4	11	15	24	20	21	28	20	20	17	14	21	18	15	17	9	21	8	5	11	6	8	13	9	13	4	–	3
337	Finland	10	7	8	6	4	13	8	14	12	26	29	19	17	12	11	7	12	8	9	8	6	9	3	7	6	10	4	10	9	5	12	16
49	Germany	–	3	1	1	4	2	1	1	4	1	7	1	–	–	3	1	1	3	2	1	–	–	2	1	–	1	2	1	–	–	2	2
46	Switzerland	1	1	–	1	1	3	–	4	5	4	5	7	3	2	3	1	–	1	2	–	1	–	–	–	–	–	–	–	–	–	–	1
9	Norway	1	–	–	1	–	–	–	–	–	–	1	–	–	–	–	–	1	–	–	–	1	2	–	2	–	–	–	–	–	–	–	–
5	Denmark	–	1	–	–	–	2	–	–	–	–	–	–	–	–	–	–	–	–	–	–	–	1	1	–	–	–	–	–	–	–	–	–
2	Japan	–	–	–	–	–	1	–	–	–	–	–	–	–	–	1	–	–	–	–	–	–	–	–	–	–	–	–	–	–	–	–	–
2	Poland	–	–	–	–	–	–	1	–	–	–	–	–	–	–	–	–	–	–	–	–	–	–	–	–	1	–	–	–	–	–	–	–
1	Hungary	–	–	–	–	–	–	–	–	1	–	–	–	–	–	–	–	–	–	–	–	–	–	–	–	–	–	–	–	–	–	–	–
1	Scotland	–	–	–	–	–	–	–	–	–	–	–	–	–	–	–	–	–	–	–	–	–	1	–	–	–	–	–	–	–	–	–	–
1	Belarus	–	1	–	–	–	–	–	–	–	–	–	–	–	–	–	–	–	–	–	–	–	–	–	–	–	–	–	–	–	–	–	–

Czech Republic and Slovakia

Total	Club	'11	'10	'09	'08	'07	'06	'05	'04	'03	'02	'01	'00	'99	'98	'97	'96	'95	'94	'93	'92	'91	'90	'89	'88	'87	'86	'85	'84	'83	'82	'81	'69 to '80
8	Brno	–	–	–	–	–	–	–	–	–	–	–	–	–	1	–	–	–	–	1	–	2	–	3	–	1	–	–	–	–	–	–	–
33	Ceske Budejovice	1	–	1	–	–	2	2	1	2	–	2	3	1	1	2	1	3	2	1	–	2	1	–	2	1	1	–	1	1	2	–	–
3	Havirov	–	–	–	–	–	–	–	2	–	1	–	–	–	–	–	–	–	–	–	–	–	–	–	–	–	–	–	–	–	–	–	–
28	Jihlava	–	–	–	–	–	–	–	1	–	–	–	2	2	1	1	2	3	1	1	3	–	1	3	4	2	–	–	–	–	–	–	–
4	Karlovy Vary	–	–	–	–	1	1	1	1	–	–	–	–	–	–	–	–	–	–	–	–	–	–	–	–	–	–	–	–	–	–	–	–
23	Kladno	–	–	–	3	1	1	1	–	1	1	2	–	2	–	2	1	–	2	1	–	1	–	1	–	1	–	1	1	2	–	–	–
16	Kosice	1	–	–	1	1	–	1	–	1	1	1	1	–	–	–	–	2	–	–	1	–	2	–	2	2	1	–	–	–	–	–	–
4	Liberec	–	–	–	1	1	–	2	–	–	–	–	–	–	–	–	–	–	–	–	–	–	–	–	–	–	–	–	–	–	–	–	–
34	Litvinov	–	–	–	–	3	2	–	1	1	2	2	4	2	3	1	2	2	–	1	–	1	–	1	–	2	1	3	–	–	–	–	–
6	Martin	–	–	–	1	–	1	1	–	–	–	2	–	–	–	1	–	–	–	–	–	–	–	–	–	–	–	–	–	–	–	–	–
7	Nitra	–	–	–	–	1	–	1	–	1	–	1	–	–	2	1	–	–	–	1	–	–	–	–	–	–	–	–	–	–	–	–	–
4	Olomouc	–	–	–	–	–	–	–	1	–	1	–	2	1	–	2	1	1	–	–	–	–	–	–	–	–	–	–	–	–	–	–	–
13	Pardubice	–	–	–	–	–	–	3	1	–	–	1	–	1	–	2	–	1	1	–	2	–	2	–	–	–	–	–	–	–	–	–	–
14	Plzen	–	–	1	–	–	–	–	2	1	1	–	1	–	1	1	–	3	–	1	1	–	1	–	–	–	–	–	–	–	–	–	–
3	Presov	–	–	–	–	–	1	–	1	–	–	–	–	–	1	–	–	–	1	–	–	–	–	–	–	–	–	–	–	–	–	–	–
29	Slavia Praha	1	–	–	1	–	1	1	2	2	5	3	2	5	4	–	1	–	–	1	–	–	–	–	–	–	–	–	–	–	–	–	–
22	Slovan Bratis.	–	–	–	–	–	–	3	1	–	2	2	1	1	–	3	–	–	1	–	–	–	1	1	1	–	–	2	–	2	–	–	2
29	Sparta Praha	1	–	–	–	1	2	4	1	2	1	–	1	1	–	1	1	–	1	1	2	1	2	1	1	1	–	1	–	–	–	–	–
31	Trencin	1	–	–	1	1	1	4	3	–	2	3	2	–	1	2	1	–	2	2	–	2	1	1	–	–	–	–	–	–	–	–	–
10	Trinec	–	–	1	1	–	1	1	–	1	1	1	1	2	–	–	–	–	–	–	–	–	–	–	–	–	–	–	–	–	–	–	–
19	Vitkovice	–	–	–	–	–	1	1	2	–	2	1	1	1	–	1	1	1	3	1	–	1	–	–	–	–	–	–	–	–	1	1	–
14	Vsetin	–	–	–	1	1	–	1	1	3	2	2	1	–	1	2	–	–	–	–	–	–	–	–	–	–	–	–	–	–	–	–	–
21	Zlin[1]	–	–	1	–	–	1	2	–	–	2	–	2	2	1	–	–	1	2	2	–	–	1	1	1	–	1	–	–	–	–	–	–
8	Zvolen	–	1	–	–	–	–	–	–	–	–	–	–	–	–	–	–	–	–	–	–	–	–	–	–	–	–	–	–	–	–	–	–

Former club names: [1]–Gottwaldov. Teams with two players selected: Ingstav Brno, IS Banska Bystrica, Dubnica, Michalovce, Partizan Liptovsky Mikulas, VTJ Pisek, Skalica, Spisska Nova Ves, Topolcany. Teams with one player selected: Banik Sokolov, KLH Chomutov, Havlickuv Brod, Ostrava, KC SKP Poprad, Povazska Bystrica, HK Trnava, KHM Zvolen, Slovak U20.

Finland

Total	Club	'11	'10	'09	'08	'07	'06	'05	'04	'03	'02	'01	'00	'99	'98	'97	'96	'95	'94	'93	'92	'91	'90	'89	'88	'87	'86	'85	'84	'83	'82	'81	'69 to '80
17	Assat	1	–	–	–	2	–	–	–	1	–	–	–	–	–	1	1	–	1	1	–	–	1	–	–	–	–	–	2	2	–	1	2
22	Blues Espoo	1	1	3	1	–	–	1	1	–	1	2	–	2	–	1	1	2	–	2	1	1	1	–	1	–	–	–	–	–	–	–	–
41	HIFK Helsinki	1	1	–	–	4	1	2	–	5	2	2	4	2	1	–	1	–	–	1	2	–	1	2	2	1	1	3	–	–	–	–	–
12	HPK	–	–	–	–	–	1	1	3	1	1	–	–	2	–	–	1	–	–	–	–	–	1	–	–	–	–	–	–	–	–	–	–
38	Ilves	1	2	1	1	–	3	3	–	2	4	3	1	2	–	2	–	1	1	1	–	1	–	2	2	–	2	3	–	–	–	–	–
40	Jokerit	3	1	–	2	–	1	2	6	4	3	3	1	1	–	3	–	2	1	1	1	–	1	–	–	–	1	2	–	–	–	–	–
13	JyP Jyvaskyla	1	–	1	–	–	–	2	1	–	2	1	–	2	–	1	–	–	–	–	–	–	–	–	–	–	–	–	–	–	–	–	–
13	KalPa	1	–	–	1	–	1	–	2	1	–	–	2	1	–	–	2	1	–	–	1	–	–	–	–	–	–	–	–	–	–	–	–
27	Karpat	1	1	1	–	2	2	3	3	3	–	1	1	–	–	1	–	–	2	2	–	1	–	1	–	–	–	–	–	–	–	–	1
3	Kiekoo-67	–	–	–	–	–	–	–	–	–	–	–	–	–	–	3	–	–	–	–	–	–	–	–	–	–	–	–	–	–	–	–	–
20	Lukko	–	–	–	1	1	–	1	1	3	1	2	–	–	–	1	–	1	–	1	–	1	–	1	2	–	3	–	–	–	–	–	–
9	Pelicans	–	–	–	1	–	1	–	–	–	–	–	–	2	–	–	1	–	1	1	1	–	–	–	–	–	–	–	–	–	–	–	–
7	SaiPa	–	–	1	1	–	1	1	1	–	–	–	–	–	–	–	–	–	–	–	–	–	–	–	–	–	1	–	–	–	–	–	–
25	Tappara	–	–	2	2	–	1	2	2	2	1	–	2	1	1	–	–	1	1	4	–	1	–	2	–	1	–	–	–	–	–	–	–
36	TPS Turku	–	–	–	–	–	1	1	3	3	3	1	3	2	3	–	–	–	1	1	–	1	1	–	6	1	–	–	–	–	–	–	–

Teams with two players selected: KooKoo Kouvola, Sapko Savonlinna, Sport Vaasa, TuTo.
Teams with one player selected: Ahmat Hyvinkaa, Hermes Kokkola, Junkkarit Kalajoki, GrIFK Kauniainen, LeKi, S-Kiekko Seinajoki, K-Vantaa.

Chosen 49th overall in 2003 from Kelowna in the WHL, Nashville's Shea Weber (top) was a first-time finalist for the Norris Trophy in 2011. Slovak Lubomir Visnovsky (right) was selected 118th overall in 2000. He led all NHL defensemen with 50 assists and 68 points in 2010-11.

Note: International draft selections played outside North America in their draft year.

European-born players drafted from the OHL, QMJHL, WHL, U.S. colleges or other North American leagues are not counted as International players.

For analysis by birthplace, see the following page.

Russia/CIS/USSR

Total	Club	'11	'10	'09	'08	'07	'06	'05	'04	'03	'02	'01	'00	'99	'98	'97	'96	'95	'94	'93	'92	'91	'90	'89	'88	'87	'86	'85	'84	'83	'82	'81	'69 to '80
6	Ak Bars Kazan	–	–	1	–	–	–	–	–	1	–	1	1	–	1	–	–	–	1	–	–	–	–	–	–	–	–	–	–	–	–	–	–
3	Ak Bars Kazan 2	–	–	–	–	–	–	–	–	1	–	1	1	–	1	–	–	–	1	–	–	–	–	–	–	–	–	–	–	–	–	–	–
9	Avangard Omsk	–	–	–	–	–	–	–	1	3	1	–	–	1	–	3	–	–	–	–	–	–	–	–	–	–	–	–	–	–	–	–	–
5	Avangard Omsk 2	–	–	–	–	–	1	1	3	–	–	–	–	–	–	–	–	–	–	–	–	–	–	–	–	–	–	–	–	–	–	–	–
5	CSK VVS Samara	–	–	–	–	–	–	1	1	–	1	1	–	1	–	–	–	–	–	–	–	–	–	–	–	–	–	–	–	–	–	–	–
65	CSKA Moscow	1	–	–	2	1	1	3	3	–	–	3	1	–	3	2	5	3	7	4	3	8	5	1	1	1	–	4	1	–	2		
14	CSKA Moscow 2	1	–	2	–	2	1	1	2	–	–	–	2	2	–	1	–	–	–	–	–	–	–	–	–	–	–	–	–	–	–		
46	Dynamo Moscow	–	–	–	–	–	1	1	2	–	2	2	1	1	7	1	2	10	7	4	3	2	–	–	–	–	–	–	–	–	–		
17	Dyn'o Moscow 2	–	1	–	–	–	–	–	4	–	3	3	–	3	2	1	–	–	–	–	–	–	–	–	–	–	–	–	–	–	–		
4	Dyn-Energ. Yekat.[1]	–	–	–	–	–	–	–	1	–	–	–	–	2	1	–	–	–	–	–	–	–	–	–	–	–	–	–	–	–	–		
16	Elektrostal	–	–	–	–	–	–	2	9	1	–	–	–	–	–	3	–	–	–	–	–	–	–	–	–	–	–	–	–	–	–		
11	HC CSKA	–	–	–	–	–	4	–	5	2	–	–	–	–	–	–	–	–	–	–	–	–	–	–	–	–	–	–	–	–	–		
3	Kristall Saratov	–	–	–	–	1	–	1	–	–	1	–	–	–	–	–	–	–	–	–	–	–	–	–	–	–	–	–	–	–	–		
33	Krylja Sovetov	–	–	–	1	1	2	–	1	1	2	1	1	2	1	1	2	3	5	1	3	4	2	1	1	–	–	–	–	–	–		
4	Krylja Sovetov 2	–	–	–	–	–	–	3	–	–	–	–	1	–	–	–	–	–	–	–	–	–	–	–	–	–	–	–	–	–	–		
19	Lada Togliatti	–	1	–	2	–	2	–	2	–	2	2	–	2	1	1	3	–	–	1	–	–	–	–	–	–	–	–	–	–	–		
6	Lada Togliatti 2	–	1	–	–	1	–	2	2	1	–	–	–	–	–	–	–	–	–	–	–	–	–	–	–	–	–	–	–	–	–		
23	Lokomotiv Yaro.[2]	1	–	–	–	–	4	2	1	1	3	1	1	5	1	–	2	1	–	–	–	–	–	–	–	–	–	–	–	–	–		
32	Lokomotiv Yaro.2	–	1	2	1	3	2	–	3	1	1	9	–	4	2	2	1	–	–	–	–	–	–	–	–	–	–	–	–	–	–		
7	Magnitogorsk	–	–	–	–	1	–	1	1	1	3	–	–	–	–	–	–	–	–	–	–	–	–	–	–	–	–	–	–	–	–		
7	Magnitogorsk 2	1	–	1	1	–	1	–	1	–	–	–	–	–	–	–	–	–	–	–	–	–	–	–	–	–	–	–	–	–	–		
6	Nizhnekamsk	–	–	–	–	–	1	–	2	2	–	–	1	–	–	–	–	–	–	–	–	–	–	–	–	–	–	–	–	–	–		
4	Nizhny Novgorod[3]	–	–	–	–	–	–	–	1	–	–	–	–	–	–	–	–	–	2	–	1	–	–	–	–	–	–	–	–	–	–		
9	Novokuznetsk	–	–	1	1	–	–	–	1	–	–	2	2	–	1	–	1	–	–	–	–	–	–	–	–	–	–	–	–	–	–		
9	Pardaugava Riga[4]	–	–	–	–	–	–	–	–	–	–	–	–	–	1	4	1	–	2	1	–	–	–	–	–	–	–	–	–	–	–		
5	Perm	–	–	–	–	–	1	1	1	–	–	–	1	–	–	–	–	–	–	–	–	–	1	–	–	–	–	–	–	–	–		
15	Severstal Cher.[5]	–	1	–	1	–	2	–	1	5	–	1	–	–	–	1	–	1	–	1	–	–	–	–	–	–	–	–	–	–	–		
4	Severstal Cher. 2	–	1	–	1	–	–	–	1	1	–	–	–	–	–	–	–	–	–	–	–	–	–	–	–	–	–	–	–	–	–		
12	SKA St. Pete.[6]	–	–	–	–	–	–	2	1	2	–	1	–	–	–	1	–	1	2	–	–	–	–	–	–	–	–	–	–	1	2		
11	Sokol Kiev	–	–	–	–	–	–	–	–	–	–	2	–	1	3	1	2	1	5	1	–	–	–	–	–	–	–	–	–	–	–		
22	Spartak Moscow	–	–	–	–	–	–	–	6	–	1	–	1	6	–	4	1	–	–	1	–	1	–	1	–	–	–	–	–	–	–		
9	THC Tver	–	–	–	–	–	–	3	3	–	1	2	–	–	–	–	–	–	–	–	–	–	–	–	–	–	–	–	–	–	–		
5	Tivali Minsk[7]	–	–	–	–	–	–	1	–	–	–	–	–	–	–	–	–	–	–	–	–	–	–	–	–	–	–	–	–	–	–		
22	Traktor Chelyabinsk	–	1	–	1	1	1	2	–	1	–	–	1	1	–	1	1	1	7	2	–	–	2	–	–	–	–	–	–	–	–		
9	Ufa	–	–	–	–	–	1	–	1	–	1	1	1	2	2	–	–	–	–	–	–	–	–	–	–	–	–	–	–	–	–		
9	Ust-Kamenogorsk	–	–	–	–	–	–	1	–	1	–	2	–	1	2	1	1	–	–	–	–	–	–	–	–	–	–	–	–	–	–		
14	Voskresensk	–	–	–	–	–	–	1	–	1	1	2	–	–	2	1	3	1	–	–	–	1	–	–	–	–	–	–	–	–	–		

Former club names: 1–Avtomobilist Yekaterinburg, 2–Torpedo Yaroslavl, 3–Torpedo Gorky, 4–Dynamo Riga,HC Riga, 5–Metallurg Cherepovets, 6–SKA Leningrad, 7–Dynamo Minsk.
Teams with two players selected: Dizelist Penza, Mechel Chelyabinsk, Metallurg Novokuznetsk 2, Salavat Yulayev Ufa 2, Spartak Moscow 2, Torpedo Nizhny Novgorod 2, Traktor Chelyabinsk 2, Yunost Minsk. **Teams with one player selected:** Amur Khabarovsk, Argus Moscow, Avangard Omsk, HC CSKA Moscow 2, Dynamo Khazov, Dynamo-81 Riga, Gazovik Tyumen, HK Gomel, Izohets St. Petersburg, Kapitan Stupino, Khimik Novopolotsk, Khimik Voskresensk 2, Metalurgs Liepaja, Mostovik Kurgan, Neftekhimik Nizhnekamsk 2, Neftyanik Almetjevsk, SKA St. Petersburg 2, Spartak St. Petersburg, Sibir Novosibirsk, Sibir Novosibirsk 2, Stalkers-Juniors, Torpedo Nizhny Novgorod 2, THC Tver, Vityaz Podolsk, Vityaz Podolsk 2.

Sweden

Total	Club	'11	'10	'09	'08	'07	'06	'05	'04	'03	'02	'01	'00	'99	'98	'97	'96	'95	'94	'93	'92	'91	'90	'89	'88	'87	'86	'85	'84	'83	'82	'81	'69 to '80
29	AIK Solna	1	4	–	–	–	–	–	–	1	1	–	3	1	1	–	1	–	1	1	1	–	4	–	1	3	2	3						
4	Almtuna	1	1	1	–	–	–	–	–	–	–	–	–	–	–	–	–	–	–	–	–	–	2	–	–								
9	Bjorkloven	–	–	1	–	2	1	–	–	–	–	–	–	–	–	–	–	1	–	1	–	1	–	1	2								
3	Boden	–	–	–	–	–	–	–	–	–	–	1	–	–	–	1	–	–	–	–	–	–	–	1									
37	Brynas Gavle	1	4	3	4	1	–	2	–	2	1	1	2	–	1	1	–	4	–	2	1	–	1	4									
47	Djurgarden	3	2	3	1	–	1	2	–	2	1	4	1	–	2	2	3	–	1	1	2	1	1	–	2	1	–	1	2	1	–	6		
3	Falun	–	–	–	–	–	–	–	–	–	–	–	–	–	–	–	–	–	–	–	–	1	–	1	1								
37	Farjestad	3	–	1	–	–	1	–	1	6	3	–	2	2	1	1	5	1	–	–	2	1	1	2	5								
53	Frolunda	3	1	3	4	5	3	3	4	2	3	4	2	1	–	1	1	3	–	1	1	1	1	1	2	–							
3	Grums	–	–	–	1	–	–	–	–	1	1	–	–	–	–	–	–	–	–	–	–	–	–	–	–								
10	Hammarby	–	–	–	–	–	–	3	–	1	–	1	–	–	–	–	–	–	1	–	1	–	–	–	2								
7	Huddinge	–	–	–	–	–	–	–	1	1	–	1	–	–	2	–	1	–	–	–	–	–	–	–	–								
28	HV 71	–	1	1	3	1	–	1	2	1	1	–	3	4	1	2	–	2	4	–	–	1	–	1	1								
32	Leksand	1	1	–	1	1	–	2	–	1	–	5	–	2	–	1	2	–	2	1	2	1	2	2	1	1	1						
9	Linkoping	3	–	1	1	1	1	1	–	–	–	–	–	–	–	–	–	–	–	–	–	–	–	–	–								
15	Lulea	–	–	1	–	3	–	1	–	–	2	1	–	1	–	–	–	–	1	–	1	1	1	–	1	–	1						
21	Malmo	2	–	1	1	1	1	1	4	1	–	3	–	–	1	–	–	1	–	2	–	–	–	–	–								
40	MODO	1	2	1	–	1	1	–	3	–	3	7	–	3	3	–	5	2	2	–	–	2	1	2	–	2							
8	Mora	1	1	–	–	–	–	–	–	1	1	1	–	–	–	–	–	–	2	–	–	–	–	–	–								
4	Morrum	–	–	–	–	–	–	–	–	1	1	–	–	–	–	–	1	–	1	–	–	–	–	–	–								
4	Nacka	–	–	–	–	–	–	–	–	–	–	1	–	–	3	–	–	–	–	–	–	–	–	–	–								
6	Orebro	–	–	–	–	–	–	–	1	1	1	–	–	–	1	–	–	–	–	2	–	–	–	–	–								
3	Pitea	–	–	–	–	–	–	1	–	–	–	–	–	1	–	–	–	1	–	–	–	–	–	–	–								
11	Rogle	1	–	–	1	1	–	–	–	–	–	1	–	1	2	2	–	–	–	–	–	–	–	–	–								
16	Skelleftea	1	2	3	–	1	–	–	–	1	–	–	–	–	1	–	–	1	–	1	–	1	2	1	2								
28	Sodertalje	1	2	–	1	2	3	1	2	1	2	–	–	–	1	–	1	1	1	–	2	–	2	2	1	1	1	1						
3	Stocksund	–	–	–	–	–	2	–	–	–	–	–	–	–	–	–	–	–	–	–	–	1	–	–	–								
3	Team Kiruna	–	–	–	–	–	–	–	–	–	–	–	–	–	–	1	–	–	–	–	–	1	–	–	1								
11	Timra	–	1	2	–	–	–	–	–	–	–	–	1	–	1	1	2	–	–	–	–	–	–	–	2	1							
4	Troja/Ljungby	–	–	–	–	–	1	–	–	1	–	1	–	–	–	1	–	–	–	–	–	–	–	–	–								
17	Vasteras	1	–	1	1	3	–	1	–	1	–	2	–	–	–	1	1	1	1	1	2	–	–	–	–								
3	Vita Hasten	–	–	1	–	–	1	–	–	–	–	–	–	–	–	–	–	–	–	–	–	–	–	–	1								

Teams with two players selected: Almtuna, Bofors, Ostersund, Skare, Skovde, Tingsryd. **Teams with one player selected:** Arboga, Arvika, Danderyd Hockey, Fagersta, Jamtland, Karskoga, Kumla, Skovde, Stocksund, S/G Hockey 83 Gavle, Sunne, Talje, Tunabro, Uppsala, Vallentuna, Vasby.

European Draft Firsts

1969 – First European (and Finn) • LW Tommi Salmelainen, 66th overall by St. Louis.

1974 – First Swede • C Per Alexandersson, 49th overall by Toronto. Four other Swedish-born players were selected that year, including defenseman Stefan Persson, 214th overall by the NY Islanders, who became the first European-trained player to be part of a Stanley Cup winner with the Islanders in 1980.

1975 – First Russian • C Viktor Khatulev, 160th overall by Philadelphia.

1976 – First European Taken in the First Round • Swedish D Bjorn Johansson, 5th overall by the California Seals.

1976 – First Swiss • C Jacques Soguel, 121st overall by St. Louis.

1978 – First Czechoslovak • LW Ladislav Svozil, 194th overall by Detroit.

1978 – First Germans • G Bernard Englbrecht, 196th overall by Atlanta and F Gerd Truntschka, 200th overall by St. Louis.

1989 – First European Taken First Overall • Swedish C Mats Sundin, 1st overall by Quebec in 1989.

2011 Entry Draft Analysis

BY BIRTHPLACE

Country of Origin

Country	Players Drafted
Canada	79
USA	64
Sweden	28
Finland	9
Czech Republic	8
Russia	8
Slovakia	4
Germany	2
Norway	2
Switzerland	2
Denmark	1
France	1
Lithuania	1
Ukraine	1
Total	**210**

Canadian-Born Players

Province	Players Drafted
Ontario	37
Alberta	11
Quebec	10
British Columbia	8
Saskatchewan	6
Manitoba	3
New Brunswick	2
Prince Edward Island	1
Nova Scotia	1
Total	**79**

U.S.-Born Players

State	Players Drafted
Minnesota	10
Illinois	9
New York	8
California	5
Connecticut	4
Pennsylvania	4
Massachusetts	3
Missouri	3
Texas	3
Arizona	2
Colorado	2
Florida	2
Michigan	2
Ohio	2
Wisconsin	2
Alaska	1
New Jersey	1
North Dakota	1
Total	**59**

BY BIRTH YEAR

Year	Players Drafted
1993	132
1992	55
1991	20
1990	3

BY POSITION

Position	Players Drafted
Defense	72
Center	62
Left Wing	32
Right Wing	25
Goaltender	19

Notes on 2011 First-Round Selections

1. EDMONTON • **RYAN NUGENT-HOPKINS** • C • A highly skilled player with very good on-ice awareness, Ryan Nugent-Hopkins was one of only three draft-eligible players to score 100 points in 2010-11. Nugent-Hopkins led the Western Hockey League with 75 assists and was fourth with 106 points. After going first overall in the WHL bantam draft in 2008, he was named rookie of the year in 2009-10. Nugent-Hopkins was an assistant captain with Canada's gold medal-winning team at the 2010 Under-18 Ivan Hlinka tournament.

2. COLORADO • **GABRIEL LANDESKOG** • LW • A player who competes hard at both ends of the ice, Gabriel Landeskog was captain of the Kitchener Rangers as a 17-year-old in 2010-11. Before coming to North America, Landeskog debuted in the Swedish Elite League in 2008-09 at 16 years and 90 days making him the youngest player in Djurgarden's history. He missed the 2011 World Junior Championship but has played at numerous international events.

3. FLORIDA • **JONATHAN HUBERDEAU** • C • With quick hands and great vision, Jonathan Huberdeau is an offensive force. After collecting just 35 points as a rookie in the Quebec Major Junior Hockey League, Huberdeau had 105 points in his second season of 2010-11. He was named MVP of both the QMJHL playoffs and the Memorial Cup when Saint John won the national junior championship in 2011. He was a member of Canada's gold medal team at the 2010 Ivan Hlinka event.

4. NEW JERSEY • **ADAM LARSSON** • D • A smart player with excellent speed and mobility, Adam Larsson in 2008 was just the third defenseman (after ex-NHLer Calle Johansson and current Tampa Bay blueliner Victor Hedman) to debut in the Swedish Elite League at age 16. Larsson represented Sweden at the 2010 and 2011 World Junior Championship, finishing as the team's highest scoring defender at the tournament in 2011 (1-3-4) and winning a bronze medal in 2010.

5. NY ISLANDERS • **RYAN STROME** • C • A creative playmaker with good hands who sees the ice well, Ryan Strome also battles hard in front of the net. Strome finished third in the Ontario Hockey League with 106 points (33-73-106) in 65 games in 2010-11 and his 1.63 points per game average ranked first among all the top producing OHL forwards. Strome was voted the Most Improved Player and the Best Playmaker in the 2011 OHL Eastern Conference Coaches Poll.

6. OTTAWA • **MIKA ZIBANEJAD** • C • A powerful skater with soft hands and good vision, Mika Zibanejad has a Finnish mother and Iranian father and speaks Swedish, Finnish and English. Zibanejad began the 2010-11 season with Djurgarden's junior team before getting the call up to the Swedish Elite League. He recorded five goals and nine points in six games at the 2010 Under-17 World Challenge.

7. WINNIPEG • **MARK SCHEIFELE** • C • A good playmaker who sees the ice well, Mark Scheifele led all Ontario Hockey League rookies with 53 assists in 2010-11. He had 11 of his 22 goals in the final 18 games of the season. Scheifele's breakout season continued at the 2011 Under-18 World Championship, leading all Canadian forwards with six goals and eight points in seven games.

8. PHILADELPHIA • **SEAN COUTURIER** • C • At 6'3" and 197 lbs., Sean Couturier is a big player who sees the ice well and has a strong work ethic. He was named the MVP of the Quebec Major Junior Hockey League after finishing the 2010-11 season fourth in scoring (36-60-96). Couturier led the QMJHL in scoring with 96 points in 2009-10. He was the youngest Canadian player at the 2011 World Junior tourney.

9. BOSTON • **DOUGIE HAMILTON** • D • A big, physical player (6'5", 193 lbs.) who uses his size well, Dougie Hamilton makes good decisions with the puck. Hamilton's father won a bronze medal in rowing at the 1984 Olympics and his mother won a World Championship gold in basketball. His older brother, Freddie, was selected 129th overall by San Jose in the 2010 NHL Entry Draft.

10. MINNESOTA • **JONAS BRODIN** • D • A mobile defenseman who handles the puck with confidence, Jonas Brodin (6'1", 166 lbs.) does not play a physical game but is effective in one-on-one situations. Brodin played with fellow Swedish prospect Oscar Klefbom on Farjestad, who won the Elite League title in 2010-11, as well as at the 2011 Under-18 World Championship where Sweden won a silver medal.

11. COLORADO • **DUNCAN SIEMENS** • D • A strong, smooth skater, Duncan Siemens is a skilled player who is good offensively and strong defensively. Siemens had a plus-minus rating of +40 to help the Saskatoon Blades to a first-place finish in the Eastern Conference of the Western Hockey League in 2010-11. He helped Canada win a gold medal at the 2010 Under-18 Ivan Hlinka tournament with a goal and two assists in five games.

12. CAROLINA • **RYAN MURPHY** • D • A gifted offensive defenseman who sees the ice very well, Ryan Murphy is outstanding on the power-play. He has excellent passing ability and a great shot. Murphy led Ontario Hockey League defensemen with 26 goals in 2010-11 and was second with 79 points. He led Canada and all defensemen with 13 points (4-9-13) in seven games and was named the top defenseman at the 2011 Under-18 World Championship.

13. CALGARY • **SVEN BAERTSCHI** • LW • A finesse player with very quick hands and great vision, Sven Baertschi is a deft puckhandler. Baertschi followed fellow Swiss native Nino Niederreiter to the Portland Winterhawks and led all Western Hockey League rookies with 85 points (34-51-85) in 2010-11. He also played for Switzerland at the 2011 World Junior Championship. Baertschi played in both the Swiss Elite Junior A League and the Swiss National League in 2009-10.

14. DALLAS • **JAMIESON OLEKSIAK** • D • At 6'7" and 241 lbs., Jamieson Oleksiak has soft hands for a big man and a good wrist shot from the blue line. As a young freshman at Northeastern University in 2010-11, he led the team with a plus-minus of +13. Born in Toronto to an American father, Oleksiak represented the United States at the 2009 Ivan Hlinka tournament and was the second-youngest player inviting to training camp for the 2011 U.S. World Junior team.

15. NY RANGERS • **JONATHAN MILLER** • C • A product of the United States National Team Development Program, Jonathan (J.T.) Miller is a skilled player with a solid work ethic. At the 2011 Under-18 World Championship, Miller led the U.S. with 13 points (4-9-13) and was named one of Team USA's top three players as the Americans won gold at the tournament for the third straight year.

16. BUFFALO • **JOEL ARMIA** • RW • A sniper with a heavy wrist shot that he gets off quickly, Joel Armia moves quickly for his size (6'3" and 192 lbs.) and has a knack for finding open spots on the ice. Playing in the Finnish elite league as a 17-year-old in 2010-11, Armia was the youngest player to represent his country at the 2011 World Junior Championship and was the team's top scorer with 13 points (4-9-13) at the 2011 Under-18 World Championship.

17. MONTREAL • **NATHAN BEAULIEU** • D • An offensive defenseman who is poised with the puck, Nathan Beaulieu is a good skater and good puck mover with a good shot. Beaulieu broke his own team record with a plus-minus rating of +44 for Saint John of the Quebec Major Junior Hockey League in 2010-11 and was named to the Memorial Cup all-star team after winning the national junior championship.

18. CHICAGO • **MARK McNEILL** • C • Solidly built at 6'1" and 211 pounds, Mark McNeill pays attention to details at both ends of the ice. His on-ice awareness is very good and he's a powerful skater with a great hockey sense. McNeill competed for Team Canada at the 2011 Under-18 World Championship and won a gold medal at the 2008 World Ball Hockey Championship in Slovakia.

19. EDMONTON • **OSCAR KLEFBOM** • D • At 6'3" and 204 lbs., Oscar Klefbom has the size to be an effective NHL defenseman. Klefbom saw limited action as a 17-year-old with league champion Farjestad in the Swedish Elite League in 2010-11 where he was a teammate of fellow prospect Jonas Brodin. He served as captain of Sweden's team at the 2011 Under-18 World Championship and won a silver medal.

20. PHOENIX • **CONNOR MURPHY** • D • The son of former NHLer Gord Murphy, Connor Murphy has been hampered by injuries during his two seasons with the United States National Team Development program but is considered an offensive defenseman with the size (6'3" and 190 lbs.) to play a physical game. Murphy led U.S. defensemen with three goals in six games to help the team win its third straight gold medal at the 2011 Under-18 World Championship.

21. OTTAWA • **STEFAN NOESEN** • RW • A smart and aggressive player who makes good decisions, Stefan Noesen backchecks hard and is very responsible defensively. Noesen was born in Texas but moved to Michigan to advance his hockey career. After playing sparingly for Plymouth in the Ontario Hockey League in 2009-10, he tied for the team lead in scoring with 77 points (33-44-77) in 2010-11.

22. TORONTO • **TYLER BIGGS** • RW • Big and strong at 6'2" and 205 lbs., Tyler Biggs skates well and is physical and tough. A member of the United States National Team Development Program, Biggs is a player with leadership qualities who was a unanimous choice as captain of his team. Biggs won gold at the Under-18 World Championship in 2010 and 2011 and at the 2009 World Junior A challenge. His father, Don Biggs, played 11 games in the NHL for the Flyers.

23. PITTSBURGH • **JOSEPH MORROW** • D • A physical defenseman who moves the puck well, Joseph Morrow was second among Western Hockey League defensemen in playoff scoring with 20 points (6-14-20) in 21 games in 2010-11. His father, Dave, was drafted by Vancouver in the 1977 Amateur Draft and played 10 games in the World Hockey Association. His brother, Josh, was drafted 203rd overall in 2002 by Nashville before a shoulder injury ended his career.

24. OTTAWA • **MATT PUEMPEL** • LW • A player who is not afraid to go to the net or play in traffic, Matt Puempel has produced back-to-back 30-goal seasons in the Ontario Hockey League despite a hip injury that cut short his 2010-11 campaign. Puempel is dangerous with the puck and has an excellent shot. He was both the OHL and Canadian Hockey League rookie of the year in 2009-10 and helped Canada win gold at the 2010 Under-18 Ivan Hlinka tournament.

25. TORONTO • **STUART PERCY** • D • A reliable defenseman who plays a smart game, Stuart Percy can be counted on in tough situations. He led all blueliners with four assists during the 2011 Memorial Cup and was named to the tournament all-star team. Percy plays with poise and makes good decisions in his own end. He was second among defensemen on the Mississauga St. Michael's Majors in playoff scoring with 12 points and had a plus-minus rating of +11.

26. CHICAGO • **PHILLIP DANAULT** • LW • A hard-working, two-way player, Phillip Danault has a passion for the game and excellent leadership qualities. He was named captain of the Victoriaville Tigres prior to the 2010-11 Quebec Major Junior Hockey League season after captaining teams throughout his minor hockey career. Danault helped Canada win gold at the 2010 Under-18 Ivan Hlinka tournament.

27. TAMPA BAY • **VLADISLAV NAMESTNIKOV** • C • A high-energy player who's aggressive in both ends of the ice, Vladislav Namestnikov has an excellent wrist shot that he can release with accuracy off the rush. In his first season in the Ontario Hockey League in 2010-11 Namestnikov led the London Knights with 30 goals. He represented Russia at the 2010 Under-18 World Championship. His father, Evgeny, played 17 games in the NHL and Slava Kozlov is his uncle.

28. MINNESOTA • **ZACH PHILLIPS** • C • A player with great vision who is strong on the puck, Zach Phillips is a gifted offensive player though not a great skater. Phillips improved by over 50 points to finish sixth in the Quebec Major Junior Hockey League in scoring (38-57-95) in 2010-11 and had 24 points (9-15-24) in the playoffs to help the Saint John Sea Dogs win the league title and then the Memorial Cup. Phillips had five points (1-4-5) in four games at the tournament.

29. VANCOUVER • **NICKLAS JENSEN** • LW/RW • Born to a Canadian father who played 16 seasons of pro hockey in Denmark, Nicklas Jensen has excellent puckhandling and playmaking abilities and an excellent wrist shot he gets off quickly. Jensen finished fifth in scoring (29-29-58) among rookies in the Ontario Hockey League in 2010-11 and helped Denmark win the 2011 Division I World Junior Championship.

30. ANAHEIM • **RICKARD RAKELL** • RW • A high-energy player with a good work ethic and hustle, Rickard Rakell works hard on the forecheck and the backcheck. He led all Plymouth Whalers rookies with 19 goals in 49 games in his first season in the Ontario Hockey League in 2010-11 and was the youngest player to compete for Sweden at the 2011 World Junior Championship.

1: Ryan Nugent-Hopkins
C – Edmonton

2: Gabriel Landeskog
LW – Colorado

3: Jonathan Huberdeau
C – Florida

4: Adam Larsson
D – New Jersey

5: Ryan Strome
C – NY Islanders

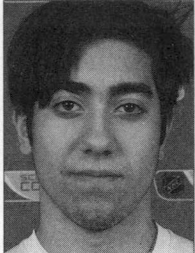

6: Mika Zibanejad
C – Ottawa

7: Mark Scheifele
C – Winnipeg

8: Sean Couturier
C – Philadelphia

9: Dougie Hamilton
D – Boston

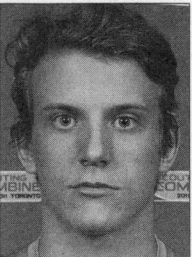

10: Jonas Brodin
D – Minnesota

Players selected first through tenth in the 2011 NHL Entry Draft.

2011 NHL ENTRY DRAFT

Pick	Claimed by		Amateur Club	Position

FIRST ROUND

1	EDM	Ryan Nugent-Hopkins	Red Deer	C
2	COL	Gabriel Landeskog	Kitchener	LW
3	FLA	Jonathan Huberdeau	Saint John	C
4	N.J.	Adam Larsson	Skelleftea	D
5	NYI	Ryan Strome	Niagara	C
6	OTT	Mika Zibanejad	Djurgarden	C
7	WPG	Mark Scheifele	Barrie	C
8	PHI	Sean Couturier	Drummondville	C
9	BOS	Dougie Hamilton	Niagara	D
10	MIN	Jonas Brodin	Farjestad	D
11	COL	Duncan Siemens	Saskatoon	D
12	CAR	Ryan Murphy	Kitchener	D
13	CGY	Sven Baertschi	Portland	LW
14	DAL	Jamieson Oleksiak	Northeastern	D
15	NYR	J.T. Miller	USA U-18	C
16	BUF	Joel Armia	Assat	RW
17	MTL	Nathan Beaulieu	Saint John	D
18	CHI	Mark McNeill	Prince Albert	C
19	EDM	Oscar Klefbom	Farjestad	D
20	PHX	Connor Murphy	USA U-18	D
21	OTT	Stefan Noesen	Plymouth	RW
22	TOR	Tyler Biggs	USA U-18	RW
23	PIT	Joe Morrow	Portland	D
24	OTT	Matt Puempel	Peterborough	LW
25	TOR	Stuart Percy	Mississauga St. Michael's	D
26	CHI	Phillip Danault	Victoriaville	LW
27	T.B.	Vladislav Namestnikov	London	C
28	MIN	Zack Phillips	Saint John	C
29	VAN	Nicklas Jensen	Oshawa	Lw/RW
30	ANA	Rickard Rakell	Plymouth	RW

SECOND ROUND

31	EDM	David Musil	Vancouver	D
32	STL	Ty Rattie	Portland	RW
33	FLA	Rocco Grimaldi	USA U-18	C
34	NYI	Scott Mayfield	Youngstown	D
35	DET	Tomas Jurco	Saint John	RW
36	CHI	Adam Clendening	Boston University	D
37	CBJ	Boone Jenner	Oshawa	C
38	NSH	Magnus Hellberg	Almtuna	G
39	ANA	John Gibson	USA U-18	G
40	BOS	Alexander Khokhlachev	Windsor	C/LW
41	STL	Dmitrij Jaskin	Slavia Praha	RW
42	CAR	Victor Rask	Leksand	C
43	CHI	Brandon Saad	Saginaw	LW
44	DAL	Brett Ritchie	Sarnia	RW
45	CGY	Markus Granlund	HIFK Jr.	C
46	STL	Joel Edmundson	Moose Jaw	D
47	S.J.	Matthew Nieto	Boston University	LW
48	DET	Xavier Ouellet	Montreal	D
49	L.A.	Christopher Gibson	Chicoutimi	G
50	NYI	Johan Sundstrom	Frolunda	C
51	PHX	Alexander Ruuttu	Jokerit Jr.	C
52	NSH	Miikka Salomaki	Karpat	RW
53	ANA	William Karlsson	Vasteras Jr.	C
54	PIT	Scott Harrington	London	D
55	DET	Ryan Sproul	Sault Ste. Marie	D
56	PHX	Lucas Lessio	Oshawa	LW
57	CGY	Tyler Wotherspoon	Portland	D
58	T.B.	Nikita Kucherov	CSKA 2	LW/RW
59	FLA	Rasmus Bengtsson	Rogle ANgleholm	D
60	MIN	Mario Lucia	Wayzata	LW
61	OTT	Shane Prince	Ottawa	C

THIRD ROUND

62	EDM	Samu Perhonen	JyP HT Jr.	G
63	NYI	Andrei Pedan	Guelph	D
64	FLA	Vincent Trocheck	Saginaw	C
65	ANA	Joseph Cramarossa	Mississauga St. Michael's	C
66	CBJ	T.J. Tynan	U. of Notre Dame	C
67	WPG	Adam Lowry	Swift Current	LW
68	PHI	Nick Cousins	Sault Ste. Marie	C
69	N.J.	forfeited		
70	CHI	Michael Paliotta	USA U-18	D
71	VAN	David Honzik	Victoriaville	G
72	NYR	Steven Fogarty	Edina High	C
73	CAR	Keegan Lowe	Edmonton	D
74	EDM	Travis Ewanyk	Edmonton	LW
75	N.J.	Blake Coleman	Indiana	C
76	FLA	Logan Shaw	Cape Breton	RW
77	BUF	Daniel Catenacci	Sault Ste. Marie	C
78	WPG	Brennan Serville	Stouffville	D
79	CHI	Klas Dahlbeck	Linkoping	D
80	L.A.	Andy Andreoff	Oshawa	C
81	BOS	Anthony Camara	Saginaw	LW
82	L.A.	Nick Shore	U. of Denver	C
83	ANA	Andy Welinski	Green Bay	D
84	PHX	Harrison Ruopp	Prince Albert	D
85	DET	Alan Quine	Peterborough	C
86	TOR	Josh Leivo	Sudbury	LW
87	FLA	Jonathan Racine	Shawinigan	D
88	STL	Jordan Binnington	Owen Sound	G
89	S.J.	Justin Sefton	Sudbury	D
90	VAN	Alexandre Grenier	Halifax	RW
91	FLA	Kyle Rau	Sioux Falls	C

FOURTH ROUND

92	EDM	Dillon Simpson	North Dakota	D
93	COL	Joachim Nermark	Linkoping Jr.	C
94	NSH	Josh Shalla	Saginaw	LW
95	NYI	Robbie Russo	USA U-18	D
96	OTT	Jean-Gabriel Pageau	Gatineau	C
97	MTL	Josiah Didier	Cedar Rapids	D
98	CBJ	Mike Reilly	Shattuck-St. Mary's	D
99	N.J.	Reid Boucher	USA U-18	C
100	TOR	Tom Nilsson	Mora Jr.	D
101	VAN	Joseph Labate	Holy Angels	C
102	STL	Yannick Veilleux	Shawinigan	LW
103	CAR	Gregory Hofmann	Ambri	C
104	CGY	John Gaudreau	Dubuque	LW
105	DAL	Emil Molin	Brynas Jr.	C
106	NYR	Michael St. Croix	Edmonton	C
107	BUF	Colin Jacobs	Seattle	C
108	MTL	Olivier Archambault	Val-d'Or	LW
109	CHI	Maxim Shalunov	Chelyabinsk 2	RW
110	L.A.	Michael Mersch	U. of Wisconsin	LW
111	PHX	Kale Kessy	Medicine Hat	LW
112	NSH	Garrett Noonan	Boston University	D
113	MTL	Magnus Nygren	Farjestad	D
114	EDM	Tobias Rieder	Kitchener	C
115	DET	Marek Tvrdon	Vancouver	RW
116	PHI	Colin Suellentrop	Oshawa	D
117	WSH	Steffen Soberg	Manglerud	G
118	PHI	Marcel Noebels	Seattle	LW
119	WPG	Zachary Yuen	Tri-City	D
120	VAN	Ludwig Blomstrand	Djurgarden Jr.	LW
121	BOS	Brian Ferlin	Indiana	RW

FIFTH ROUND

122	EDM	Martin Gernat	Kosice Jr.	D
123	COL	Garrett Meurs	Plymouth	C
124	FLA	Yaroslav Kosov	Magnitogorsk 2	Forward
125	NYI	John Persson	Red Deer	LW
126	OTT	Fredrik Claesson	Djurgarden	D
127	NYI	Brenden Kichton	Spokane	D
128	CBJ	Seth Ambroz	Omaha	RW
129	N.J.	Blake Pietila	USA U-18	LW
130	TOR	Tony Cameranesi	Wayzata	C
131	MIN	Nick Seeler	Eden Prairie	D
132	STL	Niklas Lundstrom	Aik Jr.	G
133	S.J.	Sean Kuraly	Indiana	C
134	NYR	Shane McColgan	Kelowna	RW
135	DAL	Troy Vance	Victoriaville	D
136	NYR	Samuel Noreau	Baie-Comeau	D
137	BUF	Alex Lepkowski	Barrie	D
138	MTL	Darren Dietz	Saskatoon	D
139	CHI	Andrew Shaw	Owen Sound	C
140	L.A.	Joel Lowry	Victoria	LW
141	PHX	Darian Dziurzynski	Saskatoon	LW
142	NSH	Simon Karlsson	Malmo Jr.	D
143	ANA	Max Friberg	Skovde	LW
144	PIT	Dominik Uher	Spokane	C
145	DET	Philippe Hudon	Choate-Rosemary	C/RW
146	DET	Mattias Backman	Linkoping Jr.	D
147	WSH	Patrick Koudys	RPI	D
148	T.B.	Nikita Nesterov	Chelyabinsk 2	D
149	WPG	Austen Brassard	Belleville	RW
150	VAN	Frank Corrado	Sudbury	D
151	BOS	Rob O'Gara	Milton Academy	D

SIXTH ROUND

152	TOR	David Broll	Sault Ste. Marie	LW
153	COL	Gabriel Beaupre	Val-d'Or	D
154	FLA	Eddie Wittchow	Burnsville	D
155	PHX	Andrew Fritsch	Owen Sound	RW
156	OTT	Darren Kramer	Spokane	C
157	WPG	Jason Kasdorf	Portage	G
158	CBJ	Lukas Sedlak	Ceske Budejovice Jr.	C
159	N.J.	Reece Scarlett	Swift Current	D
160	ANA	Josh Manson	Salmon Arm	D
161	MIN	Stephen Michalek	Loomis-Chaffee	G
162	STL	Ryan Tesink	Saint John	C
163	CAR	Matt Mahalak	Plymouth	G
164	CGY	Laurent Brossoit	Edmonton	G
165	DAL	Matej Stransky	Saskatoon	RW
166	S.J.	Daniil Sobchenko	Yaroslavl	C
167	BUF	Nathan Lieuwen	Kootenay	G
168	MTL	Daniel Pribyl	Sparta Jr.	C
169	CHI	Sam Jardine	Camrose	D
170	NSH	Chase Balisy	U. of Western Michigan	C
171	OTT	Max McCormick	Sioux City	LW
172	NYR	Peter Ceresnak	Trencin Jr.	D
173	TOR	Dennis Robertson	Brown U	D
174	PIT	Josh Archibald	Brainerd-High	Lw/RW
175	DET	Richard Nedomlel	Swift Current	D
176	PHI	Petr Placek	Hotchkiss School	RW
177	WSH	Travis Boyd	USA U-18	C
178	T.B.	Adam Wilcox	Green Bay	G
179	S.J.	Dylan Demelo	Mississauga St. Michael's	D
180	VAN	Pathrik Westerholm	Malmo	RW
181	BOS	Lars Volden	Blues Jr.	G

Pick	Claimed by	Amateur Club	Position

SEVENTH ROUND

182	EDM	Frans Tuohimaa	Jokerit Jr.	G
183	COL	Dillon Donnelly	Shawinigan	D
184	FLA	Iiro Pakarinen	Kalpa Kuopio	RW
185	NYI	Mitchell Theoret	Niagara	C
186	OTT	Jordan Fransoo	Brandon	D
187	WPG	Aaron Harstad	Green Bay	D
188	CBJ	Anton Forsberg	MODO Jr.	G
189	N.J.	Patrick Daly	Benilde-St.Margaret's	D
190	TOR	Garret Sparks	Guelph	G
191	MIN	Tyler Graovac	Ottawa	C
192	STL	Teemu Eronen	Jokerit	D
193	CAR	Brody Sutter	Lethbridge	C
194	S.J.	Colin Blackwell	St. John's Prep	C
195	DAL	Jyrki Jokipakka	Ilves Tampere	D
196	PHX	Zac Larraza	USA U-18	LW
197	BUF	Brad Navin	Waupaca	C
198	MTL	Colin Sullivan	Avon Old Farms	D
199	CHI	Alex Broadhurst	Green Bay	C
200	L.A.	Michael Schumacher	Frolunda Jr.	LW
201	T.B.	Matthew Peca	Pembroke	C
202	NSH	Brent Andrews	Halifax	LW
203	TOR	Max Everson	Edina High	D
204	OTT	Ryan Dzingel	Lincoln	C
205	DET	Alexei Marchenko	CSKA	D
206	PHI	Derek Mathers	Peterborough	RW
207	WSH	Garrett Haar	Fargo	D
208	T.B.	Ondrej Palat	Drummondville	LW
209	PIT	Scott Wilson	Georgetown	C/LW
210	VAN	Henrik Tommernes	Frolunda	D
211	CHI	Johan Mattsson	Sodertalje Jr.	G

First Two Rounds, 2010–2008

2010

FIRST ROUND

1	EDM	Taylor Hall	Windsor	LW
2	BOS	Tyler Seguin	Plymouth	C
3	FLA	Erik Gudbranson	Kingston	D
4	CBJ	Ryan Johansen	Portland	C
5	NYI	Nino Niederreiter	Portland	RW
6	T.B.	Brett Connolly	Prince George	RW
7	CAR	Jeff Skinner	Kitchener	C
8	ATL	Alexander Burmistrov	Barrie	C
9	MIN	Mikael Granlund	HIFK Helsinki	C/W
10	NYR	Dylan McIlrath	Moose Jaw	D
11	DAL	Jack Campbell	USA U-18	G
12	ANA	Cam Fowler	Windsor	D
13	PHX	Brandon Gormley	Moncton	D
14	STL	Jaden Schwartz	Tri-City	C
15	L.A.	Derek Forbort	USA U-18	D
16	STL	Vladimir Tarasenko	Novosibirsk	RW
17	COL	Joey Hishon	Owen Sound	C
18	NSH	Austin Watson	Peterborough	LW
19	FLA	Nick Bjugstad	Blaine	C
20	PIT	Beau Bennett	Penticton	RW
21	DET	Riley Sheahan	U. of Notre Dame	C
22	MTL	Jarred Tinordi	USA U-18	D
23	BUF	Mark Pysyk	Edmonton	D
24	CHI	Kevin Hayes	Nobles	RW
25	FLA	Quinton Howden	Moose Jaw	C
26	WSH	Evgeny Kuznetsov	Chelyabinsk	C
27	PHX	Mark Visentin	Niagara	G
28	S.J.	Charlie Coyle	South Shore	C/RW
29	ANA	Emerson Etem	Medicine Hat	RW
30	NYI	Brock Nelson	Warroad	C

SECOND ROUND

31	EDM	Tyler Pitlick	Minnesota State	C
32	BOS	Jared Knight	London	C
33	FLA	John McFarland	Sudbury	LW
34	CBJ	Dalton Smith	Ottawa	LW
35	CHI	Ludvig Rensfeldt	Brynas Jr.	LW
36	FLA	Alexander Petrovic	Red Deer	D
37	CAR	Justin Faulk	USA U-18	D
38	N.J.	Jonathon Merrill	USA U-18	D
39	MIN	Brett Bulmer	Kelowna	RW
40	NYR	Christian Thomas	Oshawa	RW
41	DAL	Patrik Nemeth	AIK-Jr.	D
42	ANA	Devante Smith-Pelly	Mississauga	RW
43	TOR	Brad Ross	Portland	LW
44	STL	Sebastian Wannstrom	Brynas Jr.	RW
45	BOS	Ryan Spooner	Peterborough	C
46	EDM	Martin Marincin	Slovakia U-20	D
47	L.A.	Tyler Toffoli	Ottawa	C
48	EDM	Curtis Hamilton	Saskatoon	LW
49	COL	Calvin Pickard	Seattle	G
50	FLA	Connor Brickley	Des Moines	C
51	DET	Calle Jarnkrok	Brynas	C
52	PHX	Philip Lane	Brampton	RW
53	CAR	Mark Alt	Cretin-Derham	D
54	CHI	Justin Holl	Minnetonka	D
55	CBJ	Petr Straka	Rimouski	RW
56	MIN	Johan Larsson	Brynas Jr.	LW
57	PHX	Oscar Lindberg	Skelleftea Jr.	C
58	CHI	Kent Simpson	Everett	G
59	MIN	Jason Zucker	USA U-18	LW
60	CHI	Stephen Johns	USA U-18	D

2009

FIRST ROUND

1	NYI	John Tavares	London	C
2	T.B.	Victor Hedman	MODO Ornskoldsvik	D
3	COL	Matt Duchene	Brampton	C
4	ATL	Evander Kane	Vancouver	C
5	L.A.	Brayden Schenn	Brandon	C
6	PHX	Oliver Ekman-Larsson	Leksand	D
7	TOR	Nazem Kadri	London	C
8	DAL	Scott Glennie	Brandon	RW
9	OTT	Jared Cowen	Spokane	D
10	EDM	Magnus Paajarvi-Svensson	Timra	LW
11	NSH	Ryan Ellis	Windsor	D
12	NYI	Calvin De Haan	Oshawa	D
13	BUF	Zack Kassian	Peterborough	RW
14	FLA	Dmitry Kulikov	Drummondville	D
15	ANA	Peter Holland	Guelph	C
16	MIN	Nick Leddy	Eden Prairie	D
17	STL	David Rundblad	Skelleftea	D
18	MTL	Louis Leblanc	Omaha	C
19	NYR	Chris Kreider	Andover	C
20	N.J.	Jacob Josefson	Djurgarden	C
21	CBJ	John Moore	Chicago Steel	D
22	VAN	Jordan Schroeder	U. of Minnesota	C
23	CGY	Tim Erixon	Skelleftea	D
24	WSH	Marcus Johansson	Farjestad	C
25	BOS	Jordan Caron	Rimouski	RW
26	ANA	Kyle Palmieri	USA U-18	C/RW
27	CAR	Philippe Paradis	Shawinigan	C
28	CHI	Dylan Olsen	Camrose	D
29	T.B.	Carter Ashton	Lethbridge	RW
30	PIT	Simon Despres	Saint John	D

SECOND ROUND

31	NYI	Mikko Koskinen	Blues	G
32	DET	Landon Ferraro	Red Deer	C
33	COL	Ryan O'Reilly	Erie	C
34	ATL	Carl Klingberg	Frolunda Jr.	LW
35	L.A.	Kyle Clifford	Barrie	LW
36	PHX	Chris Brown	USA U-18	C
37	ANA	Matt Clark	Brampton	D
38	DAL	Alex Chiasson	Des Moines	RW
39	OTT	Jakob Silfverberg	Brynas	LW
40	EDM	Anton Lander	Timra	C
41	NSH	Zach Budish	Edina High	RW
42	NSH	Charles-Olivier Roussel	Shawinigan	D
43	S.J.	William Wrenn	USA U-18	D
44	FLA	Drew Shore	USA U-18	C
45	ATL	Jeremy Morin	USA U-18	LW
46	OTT	Robin Lehner	Frolunda Jr.	G
47	NYR	Ethan Werek	Kingston	C
48	STL	Brett Ponich	Portland	D
49	COL	Stefan Elliott	Saskatoon	D
50	TOR	Kenny Ryan	USA U-18	RW
51	CAR	Brian Dumoulin	Jr. Monarchs	D
52	T.B.	Richard Panik	Trinec	RW
53	VAN	Anton Rodin	Brynas Jr.	RW
54	N.J.	Eric Gelinas	Lewiston	D
55	WSH	Dmitri Orlov	Novokuznetsk	D
56	CBJ	Kevin Lynch	USA U-18	C
57	S.J.	Taylor Doherty	Kingston	D
58	TOR	Jesse Blacker	Windsor	D
59	CHI	Brandon Pirri	Georgetown	C
60	DET	Tomas Tatar	Zvolen	C
61	PIT	Philip Samuelsson	Chicago Steel	D

The Bruins chose Tyler Seguin second overall behind Taylor Hall in the 2010 NHL Entry Draft. Seguin averaged 12:12 of playing time in 74 regular-season games as a rookie and gave Boston a burst of energy when he was inserted into the lineup during the Eastern Conference Final against Tampa Bay. He finished with seven points in 13 playoff games.

Pick	Claimed by	Amateur Club	Position	Pick	Claimed by	Amateur Club	Position	Pick	Claimed by	Amateur Club	Position

Defenseman Luke Schenn (left) jumped directly onto the Maple Leafs roster after Toronto chose him fifth overall in the 2008 Entry Draft. Brother Brayden Schenn (right) has been brought along more slowly since Los Angeles selected him fifth in 2009. The young center was traded to Philadelphia as part of the Mike Richards deal in the summer of 2011.

2008

FIRST ROUND

Pick		Claimed by	Amateur Club	Position
1	T.B.	Steven Stamkos	Sarnia	C
2	L.A.	Drew Doughty	Guelph	D
3	ATL	Zach Bogosian	Peterborough	D
4	STL	Alex Pietrangelo	Niagara	D
5	TOR	Luke Schenn	Kelowna	D
6	CBJ	Nikita Filatov	CSKA 2	LW
7	NSH	Colin Wilson	Boston University	C
8	PHX	Mikkel Boedker	Kitchener	LW
9	NYI	Joshua Bailey	Windsor	C
10	VAN	Cody Hodgson	Brampton	C
11	CHI	Kyle Beach	Everett	C
12	BUF	Tyler Myers	Kelowna	D
13	L.A.	Colten Teubert	Regina	D
14	CAR	Zach Boychuk	Lethbridge	C
15	OTT	Erik Karlsson	Frolunda Jr.	D
16	BOS	Joe Colborne	Camrose	C
17	ANA	Jake Gardiner	Minnetonka	D
18	NSH	Chet Pickard	Tri-City	G
19	PHI	Luca Sbisa	Lethbridge	D
20	NYR	Michael Del Zotto	Oshawa	D
21	WSH	Anton Gustafsson	Frolunda Jr.	C
22	EDM	Jordan Eberle	Regina	C
23	MIN	Tyler Cuma	Ottawa	D
24	N.J.	Mattias Tedenby	HV 71 Jonkoping	LW
25	CGY	Greg Nemisz	Windsor	C
26	BUF	Tyler Ennis	Medicine Hat	C
27	WSH	John Carlson	Indiana	D
28	PHX	Viktor Tikhonov	Cherepovets	W
29	ATL	Daultan Leveille	St. Catharines	C
30	DET	Thomas McCollum	Guelph	G

SECOND ROUND

Pick		Claimed by	Amateur Club	Position
31	FLA	Jacob Markstrom	Brynas Jr.	G
32	L.A.	Vjateslav Voinov	Chelyabinsk	D
33	STL	Philip McRae	London	C
34	STL	Jake Allen	St. John's	G
35	ANA	Nicolas Deschamps	Chicoutimi	C
36	NYI	Corey Trivino	Stouffville	C
37	CBJ	Cody Goloubef	U. of Wisconsin	D
38	NSH	Roman Josi	Bern	D
39	ANA	Eric O'Dell	Sudbury	C
40	NYI	Aaron Ness	Roseau High	D
41	VAN	Yann Sauve	Saint John	D
42	OTT	Patrick Wiercioch	Omaha	D
43	ANA	Justin Schultz	Westside	D
44	BUF	Luke Adam	St. John's	C
45	CAR	Zac Dalpe	Penticton	C/RW
46	FLA	Colby Robak	Brandon	D
47	BOS	Maxime Sauve	Val d'Or	C
48	CGY	Mitch Wahl	Spokane	C
49	PHX	Jared Staal	Sudbury	RW
50	COL	Cameron Gaunce	St. Michael's	D

Pick		Claimed by	Amateur Club	Position
51	NYR	Derek Stepan	Shattuck-St.Mary's	C
52	N.J.	Brandon Burlon	St. Michael's	D
53	NYI	Travis Hamonic	Moose Jaw	D
54	N.J.	Patrice Cormier	Rimouski	C
55	MIN	Marco Scandella	Val d'Or	D
56	MTL	Danny Kristo	USA U-18	RW
57	WSH	Eric Mestery	Tri-City	D
58	WSH	Dmitri Kugryshev	CSKA 2	RW
59	DAL	Tyler Beskorowany	Owen Sound	G
60	TOR	Jimmy Hayes	Lincoln	RW
61	COL	Peter Delmas	Lewiston	G

First Round and Other Notable Selections, 2007–1969

2007

FIRST ROUND

Pick		Claimed by	Amateur Club	Position
1	CHI	Patrick Kane	London	RW
2	PHI	James van Riemsdyk	USA U-18	LW
3	PHX	Kyle Turris	Burnaby	C
4	LA	Thomas Hickey	Seattle	D
5	WSH	Karl Alzner	Calgary	D
6	EDM	Sam Gagner	London	C/W
7	CBJ	Jakub Voracek	Halifax	RW
8	BOS	Zach Hamill	Everett	C
9	SJ	Logan Couture	Ottawa	C
10	FLA	Keaton Ellerby	Kamloops	D
11	CAR	Brandon Sutter	Red Deer	C/RW
12	MTL	Ryan McDonagh	Cretin-Derham	D
13	STL	Lars Eller	Frolunda Jr.	C
14	COL	Kevin Shattenkirk	USA U-18	D
15	EDM	Alex Plante	Calgary	D
16	MIN	Colton Gillies	Saskatoon	C
17	NYR	Alexei Cherepanov	Omsk	RW
18	STL	Ian Cole	USA U-18	D
19	ANA	Logan MacMillan	Halifax	C
20	PIT	Angelo Esposito	Quebec	C
21	EDM	Riley Nash	Salmon Arm	C
22	MTL	Max Pacioretty	Sioux City	LW
23	NSH	Jonathon Blum	Vancouver	D
24	CGY	Mikael Backlund	Vasteras	C
25	VAN	Patrick White	Tri-City	C
26	STL	David Perron	Lewiston	LW
27	DET	Brendan Smith	St. Michael's	D
28	SJ	Nicholas Petrecki	Omaha	D
29	OTT	Jim O'Brien	U. of Minnesota	C
30	PHX	Nick Ross	Regina	D

OTHER NOTABLE SELECTIONS

Pick		Claimed by	Amateur Club	Position
43	MTL	P.K. Subban	Belleville	D
55	COL	T.J. Galiardi	Dartmouth	W
61	LA	Wayne Simmonds	Owen Sound	RW
73	MTL	Yannick Weber	Kitchener	D
97	EDM	Linus Omark	Lulea	LW
117	NJ	Matt Halischuk	Kitchener	RW

2006

FIRST ROUND

Pick		Claimed by	Amateur Club	Position
1	STL	Erik Johnson	USA U-18	D
2	PIT	Jordan Staal	Peterborough	C
3	CHI	Jonathan Toews	U. of North Dakota	C
4	WSH	Nicklas Backstrom	Brynas Gavle	C
5	BOS	Phil Kessel	U. of Minnesota	C
6	CBJ	Derick Brassard	Drummondville	C
7	NYI	Kyle Okposo	Des Moines	RW
8	PHX	Peter Mueller	Everett	C
9	MIN	James Sheppard	Cape Breton	C
10	FLA	Michael Frolik	Kladno	C
11	L.A.	Jonathan Bernier	Lewiston	G
12	ATL	Bryan Little	Barrie	C
13	TOR	Jiri Tlusty	Kladno	C
14	VAN	Michael Grabner	Spokane	RW
15	T.B.	Riku Helenius	Ilves Tampere	G
16	S.J.	Ty Wishart	Prince George	D
17	L.A.	Trevor Lewis	Des Moines	C
18	COL	Chris Stewart	Kingston	RW
19	ANA	Mark Mitera	U. of Michigan	D
20	MTL	David Fischer	Apple Valley	D
21	NYR	Bobby Sanguinetti	Owen Sound	D
22	PHI	Claude Giroux	Gatineau	RW
23	WSH	Simeon Varlamov	Yaroslavl 2	G
24	BUF	Dennis Persson	Vasteras	D
25	STL	Patrik Berglund	Vasteras	C
26	CGY	Leland Irving	Everett	G
27	DAL	Ivan Vishnevskiy	Rouyn-Noranda	D
28	OTT	Nick Foligno	Sudbury	LW
29	PHX	Chris Summers	USA U-18	D
30	N.J.	Matthew Corrente	Saginaw	D

OTHER NOTABLE SELECTIONS

Pick		Claimed by	Amateur Club	Position
34	Wsh.	Michal Neuvirth	Sparta Jr.	G
39	Phi.	Andreas Nodl	Sioux Falls	RW
44	Tor.	Nikolai Kulemin	Magnitogorsk	W
50	Bos.	Milan Lucic	Vancouver	LW
54	NYR	Artem Anisimov	Yaroslavl	C
60	NYI	Jesse Joensuu	Assat	LW
69	CBJ	Steve Mason	London	G
128	Bos.	Andrew Bodnarchuk	Halifax	D
141	NYI	Kim Johansson	Malmo Jr.	D
161	Tor.	Viktor Stahlberg	Frolunda	LW

2005

FIRST ROUND

Pick	Claimed by	Player	Amateur Club	Position
1	PIT	Sidney Crosby	Rimouski	C
2	ANA	Bobby Ryan	Owen Sound	RW
3	CAR	Jack Johnson	USA U-18	D
4	MIN	Benoit Pouliot	Sudbury	LW
5	MTL	Carey Price	Tri-City	G
6	CBJ	Gilbert Brule	Vancouver	C
7	CHI	Jack Skille	USA U-18	RW
8	S.J.	Devin Setoguchi	Saskatoon	RW
9	OTT	Brian Lee	Moorhead	D
10	VAN	Luc Bourdon	Val d'Or	D
11	L.A.	Anze Kopitar	Sodertalje Jr.	C
12	NYR	Marc Staal	Sudbury	D
13	BUF	Marek Zagrapan	Chicoutimi	C
14	WSH	Sasha Pokulok	Cornell	D
15	NYI	Ryan O'Marra	Erie	C
16	ATL	Alex Bourret	Lewiston	RW
17	PHX	Martin Hanzal	Ceske Budejovice	C
18	NSH	Ryan Parent	Guelph	D
19	DET	Jakub Kindl	Kitchener	D
20	FLA	Kenndal McArdle	Moose Jaw	LW
21	TOR	Tuukka Rask	Ilves Jr.	G
22	BOS	Matt Lashoff	Kitchener	D
23	N.J.	Nicklas Bergfors	Sodertalje	RW
24	STL	T.J. Oshie	Warroad	C
25	EDM	Andrew Cogliano	St. Mike's Buzzers	C
26	CGY	Matt Pelech	Sarnia	D
27	WSH	Joe Finley	Sioux Falls	D
28	DAL	Matt Niskanen	Virginia	D
29	PHI	Steve Downie	Windsor	RW
30	T.B.	Vladimir Mihalik	Presov	D

OTHER NOTABLE SELECTIONS

Pick	Claimed by	Player	Amateur Club	Position
33	DAL	James Neal	Plymouth	LW
35	S.J.	Marc-Edouard Vlasic	Quebec	D
42	DET	Justin Abdelkader	Cedar Rapids	LW
44	COL	Paul Stastny	U. of Denver	C
45	MTL	Guillaume Latendresse	Drummondville	RW
51	VAN	Mason Raymond	Camrose	LW
62	PIT	Kris Letang	Val d'Or	D
72	L.A.	Jonathan Quick	Avon Old Farms	G
200	MTL	Sergei Kostitsyn	Gomel	LW

2004

FIRST ROUND

Pick	Claimed by	Player	Amateur Club	Position
1	WSH	Alex Ovechkin	Dynamo Moscow	LW
2	PIT	Evgeni Malkin	Magnitogorsk	C
3	CHI	Cam Barker	Medicine Hat	D
4	CAR	Andrew Ladd	Calgary	LW
5	PHX	Blake Wheeler	Breck	RW
6	NYR	Al Montoya	U. of Michigan	G
7	FLA	Rostislav Olesz	Vitkovice	C
8	CBJ	Alexandre Picard	Lewiston	LW
9	ANA	Ladislav Smid	Liberec	D
10	ATL	Boris Valabik	Kitchener	D
11	L.A.	Lauri Tukonen	Blues Espoo	RW
12	MIN	A.J. Thelen	Michigan State	D
13	BUF	Drew Stafford	U. of North Dakota	RW
14	EDM	Devan Dubnyk	Kamloops	G
15	NSH	Alexander Radulov	Tver	LW
16	NYI	Petteri Nokelainen	SaiPa	C
17	STL	Marek Schwarz	Sparta Praha	G
18	MTL	Kyle Chipchura	Prince Albert	C
19	NYR	Lauri Korpikoski	TPS Turku Jr.	LW
20	N.J.	Travis Zajac	Salmon Arm	C
21	COL	Wojtek Wolski	Brampton	LW
22	S.J.	Lukas Kaspar	Litvinov	RW
23	OTT	Andrej Meszaros	Trencin	D
24	CGY	Kris Chucko	Salmon Arm	LW
25	EDM	Rob Schremp	London	C
26	VAN	Cory Schneider	Phillips-Andover	G
27	WSH	Jeff Schultz	Calgary	D
28	DAL	Mark Fistric	Vancouver	D
29	WSH	Mike Green	Saskatoon	D
30	T.B.	Andy Rogers	Calgary	D

OTHER NOTABLE SELECTIONS

Pick	Claimed by	Player	Amateur Club	Position
32	CHI	Dave Bolland	London	C
53	FLA	David Booth	Michigan State	LW
60	NYR	Brandon Dubinsky	Portland	C
63	BOS	David Krejci	Kladno Jr.	C
91	VAN	Alexander Edler	Jamtland	D
97	DET	Johan Franzen	Linkoping	C
99	PIT	Tyler Kennedy	Sault Ste. Marie	C
127	NYR	Ryan Callahan	Guelph	RW
134	BOS	Kris Versteeg	Lethbridge	RW
150	MTL	Mikhail Grabovski	Nizhnekamsk	C
214	CHI	Troy Brouwer	Moose Jaw	RW
227	NYI	Chris Campoli	Erie	D
258	NSH	Pekka Rinne	Karpat	G
262	MTL	Mark Streit	Zurich	D

2003

FIRST ROUND

Pick	Claimed by	Player	Amateur Club	Position
1	PIT	Marc-Andre Fleury	Cape Breton	G
2	CAR	Eric Staal	Peterborough	C
3	FLA	Nathan Horton	Oshawa	C
4	CBJ	Nikolai Zherdev	CSKA Moscow	W
5	BUF	Thomas Vanek	U. of Minnesota	LW
6	S.J.	Milan Michalek	Budejovice	RW
7	NSH	Ryan Suter	USA U-18	D
8	ATL	Braydon Coburn	Portland	D
9	CGY	Dion Phaneuf	Red Deer	D
10	MTL	Andrei Kostitsyn	CSKA 2	RW
11	PHI	Jeff Carter	Sault Ste. Marie	C
12	NYR	Hugh Jessiman	Dartmouth	RW
13	L.A.	Dustin Brown	Guelph	RW
14	CHI	Brent Seabrook	Lethbridge	D
15	NYI	Robert Nilsson	Leksand	RW
16	S.J.	Steve Bernier	Moncton	RW
17	N.J.	Zach Parise	North Dakota	C
18	WSH	Eric Fehr	Brandon	RW
19	ANA	Ryan Getzlaf	Calgary	C
20	MIN	Brent Burns	Brampton	RW
21	BOS	Mark Stuart	Colorado College	D
22	EDM	Marc-Antoine Pouliot	Rimouski	C
23	VAN	Ryan Kesler	Ohio State	C
24	PHI	Mike Richards	Kitchener	C
25	FLA	Anthony Stewart	Kingston	C
26	L.A.	Brian Boyle	St. Sebastian's H.S.	C
27	L.A.	Jeff Tambellini	U. of Michigan	LW
28	ANA	Corey Perry	London	RW
29	OTT	Patrick Eaves	Boston College	RW
30	STL	Shawn Belle	Tri-City	D

OTHER NOTABLE SELECTIONS

Pick	Claimed by	Player	Amateur Club	Position
33	DAL	Loui Eriksson	Vastra Frolunda Jr	LW
45	BOS	Patrice Bergeron	Acadie-Bathurst	C
47	S.J.	Matt Carle	River City	D
49	NSH	Shea Weber	Kelowna	D
61	MTL	Maxim Lapierre	Montreal	C
62	ST.L.	David Backes	Lincoln	C
64	DET	Jimmy Howard	U. of Maine	G
73	PIT	Daniel Carcillo	Sarnia	LW
148	STL	Lee Stempniak	Dartmouth College	RW
205	S.J.	Joe Pavelski	Waterloo Jr. A	C
239	ATL	Tobias Enstrom	MODO Ornskolsvik	D
245	CHI	Dustin Byfuglien	Prince George	RW
271	MTL	Jaroslav Halak	Bratislava Jr.	G
291	OTT	Brian Elliott	Ajax	G

2002

FIRST ROUND

Pick	Claimed by	Player	Amateur Club	Position
1	CBJ	Rick Nash	London	LW
2	ATL	Kari Lehtonen	Jokerit	G
3	FLA	Jay Bouwmeester	Medicine Hat	D
4	PHI	Joni Pitkanen	Karpat	D
5	PIT	Ryan Whitney	Boston University	D
6	NSH	Scottie Upshall	Kamloops	RW
7	ANA	Joffrey Lupul	Medicine Hat	C
8	MIN	Pierre-Marc Bouchard	Chicoutimi	C
9	FLA	Petr Taticek	Sault Ste. Marie	C
10	CGY	Eric Nystrom	U. of Michigan	LW
11	BUF	Keith Ballard	U. of Minnesota	D
12	WSH	Steve Eminger	Kitchener	D
13	WSH	Alexander Semin	Chelyabinsk	LW
14	MTL	Christopher Higgins	Yale	C
15	EDM	Jesse Niinimaki	Ilves Tampere	C
16	OTT	Jakub Klepis	Portland	C
17	WSH	Boyd Gordon	Red Deer	RW
18	L.A.	Denis Grebeshkov	Yaroslavl	D
19	PHX	Jakub Koreis	Plzen	C
20	BUF	Dan Paille	Guelph	LW
21	CHI	Anton Babchuk	Elektrostal	D
22	NYI	Sean Bergenheim	Jokerit	C
23	PHX	Ben Eager	Oshawa	LW
24	TOR	Alexander Steen	Vastra Frolunda	C
25	CAR	Cam Ward	Red Deer	G
26	DAL	Martin Vagner	Hull	D
27	S.J.	Mike Morris	St. Sebastian's H.S.	RW
28	COL	Jonas Johansson	HV 71 Jonkoping Jr.	RW
29	BOS	Hannu Toivonen	HPK Jr.	G
30	ATL	Jim Slater	Michigan State	C

OTHER NOTABLE SELECTIONS

Pick	Claimed by	Player	Amateur Club	Position
36	EDM	Jarret Stoll	Kootenay	C
54	CHI	Duncan Keith	Michigan State	D
57	TOR	Matt Stajan	Belleville	C
58	DET	Jiri Hudler	Vsetin	C
90	CGY	Matthew Lomardi	Victoriaville	C
95	DET	Valtteri Filppula	Jokerit Jr.	C
183	TB	Paul Ranger	Oshawa	D
191	TOR	Ian White	Swift Current	D
234	PIT	Maxime Talbot	Hull	C
240	NYR	Petr Prucha	Pardubice	RW
241	BUF	Dennis Wideman	London	D
282	CHI	Adam Burish	Green Bay	RW
291	DET	Jonathan Ericsson	Hasten Jr.	D

2001

FIRST ROUND

Pick	Claimed by	Player	Amateur Club	Position
1	ATL	Ilya Kovalchuk	Spartak	LW
2	OTT	Jason Spezza	Windsor	C
3	T.B.	Alexander Svitov	Avangard Omsk	C
4	FLA	Stephen Weiss	Plymouth	C
5	ANA	Stanislav Chistov	Avangard Omsk	LW
6	MIN	Mikko Koivu	TPS Turku	C
7	MTL	Mike Komisarek	U. of Michigan	D
8	CBJ	Pascal Leclaire	Halifax	G
9	CHI	Tuomo Ruutu	Jokerit	C/LW
10	NYR	Dan Blackburn	Kootenay	G
11	PHX	Fredrik Sjostrom	Vastra Frolunda	RW
12	NSH	Dan Hamhuis	Prince George	D
13	EDM	Ales Hemsky	Hull	RW
14	CGY	Chuck Kobasew	Boston College	C
15	CAR	Igor Knyazev	Spartak	D
16	VAN	R.J. Umberger	Ohio State	C
17	TOR	Carlo Colaiacovo	Erie	D
18	L.A.	Jens Karlsson	Vastra Frolunda	RW
19	BOS	Shaone Morrisonn	Kamloops	D
20	S.J.	Marcel Goc	Schwenningen	C
21	PIT	Colby Armstrong	Red Deer	RW
22	BUF	Jiri Novotny	Budejovice	C
23	OTT	Tim Gleason	Windsor	D
24	FLA	Lukas Krajicek	Peterborough	D
25	MTL	Alexander Perezhogin	Avangard Omsk	C
26	DAL	Jason Bacashihua	Chicago Freeze	G
27	PHI	Jeff Woywitka	Red Deer	D
28	N.J.	Adrian Foster	Saskatoon	C
29	CHI	Adam Munro	Erie	G
30	L.A.	Dave Steckel	Ohio State	C

OTHER NOTABLE SELECTIONS

Pick	Claimed by	Player	Amateur Club	Position
32	BUF	Derek Roy	Kitchener	C
49	L.A.	Mike Cammalleri	U. of Michigan	C
55	BUF	Jason Pominville	Shawinigan	RW
71	MTL	Tomas Plekanec	Kladno	LW
95	PHI	Patrick Sharp	U. of Vermont	C
98	NSH	Jordin Tootoo	Brandon	RW
106	S.J.	Christoph Ehrhoff	Krefeld	D
134	TOR	Kyle Wellwood	Belleville	C
151	VAN	Kevin Bieksa	Bowling Green	D
172	PHI	Dennis Seidenberg	Mannheim	D
175	SJ	Ryan Clowe	Rimouski	RW
176	NSH	Marek Zidlicky	HIFK Helsinki	D
192	DAL	Jussi Jokinen	Karpat Jr.	F
193	OTT	Brooks Laich	Moose Jaw	C
214	L.A.	Cristobal Huet	Lugano	G
232	ANA	Martin Gerber	Langnau	G

2000

FIRST ROUND

Pick	Claimed by	Player	Amateur Club	Position
1	NYI	Rick DiPietro	Boston University	G
2	ATL	Dany Heatley	U. of Wisconsin	RW
3	MIN	Marian Gaborik	Dukla Trencin	RW
4	CBJ	Rostislav Klesla	Brampton	D
5	NYI	Raffi Torres	Brampton	LW
6	NSH	Scott Hartnell	Prince Albert	LW
7	BOS	Lars Jonsson	Leksand	D
8	T.B.	Nikita Alexeev	Erie	RW
9	CGY	Brent Krahn	Calgary	G
10	CHI	Mikhail Yakubov	Lada Togliatti	C
11	CHI	Pavel Vorobiev	Yaroslavl	RW
12	ANA	Alexei Smirnov	Tver	LW
13	MTL	Ron Hainsey	U. of Mass-Lowell	D
14	COL	Vaclav Nedorost	Budejovice	C
15	BUF	Artem Kryukov	Yaroslavl	C
16	MTL	Marcel Hossa	Portland	LW
17	EDM	Alexei Mikhnov	Yaroslavl	LW
18	PIT	Brooks Orpik	Boston College	D
19	PHX	Krys Kolanos	Boston College	C
20	L.A.	Alexander Frolov	Yaroslavl 2	LW
21	OTT	Anton Volchenkov	HK Moscow	D
22	N.J.	David Hale	Sioux City	D
23	VAN	Nathan Smith	Swift Current	C
24	TOR	Brad Boyes	Erie	C
25	DAL	Steve Ott	Windsor	C
26	WSH	Brian Sutherby	Moose Jaw	C
27	BOS	Martin Samuelsson	MoDo Ornskoldsvik	RW
28	PHI	Justin Williams	Plymouth	RW
29	DET	Niklas Kronwall	Djurgarden	D
30	STL	Jeff Taffe	U. of Minnesota	C

OTHER NOTABLE SELECTIONS

Pick	Claimed by	Player	Amateur Club	Position
33	MIN	Nick Schultz	Prince Albert	D
44	ANA	Ilya Bryzgalov	Lada Togliatti	G
46	CGY	Jarret Stoll	Kootenay	C
55	OTT	Antoine Vermette	Victoriaville	C
62	COL	Paul Martin	Elk River H.S.	D
95	NYR	Dominic Moore	Harvard	C
155	CGY	Travis Moen	Kelowna	LW
159	COL	John-Michael Liles	Michigan State	D
205	NYR	Henrik Lundqvist	Vastre Frolunda Jr.	G
215	BUF	Matthew Lombardi	Victoriaville	C
220	BUF	Paul Gaustad	Portland	C
224	DAL	Antti Miettinen	HPK Jr.	RW

1999

FIRST ROUND

Pick	Claimed by	Player	Amateur Club	Position
1	ATL	Patrik Stefan	Long Beach	C
2	VAN	Daniel Sedin	MoDo Ornskoldsvik	LW
3	VAN	Henrik Sedin	MoDo Ornskoldsvik	C
4	NYR	Pavel Brendl	Calgary	RW
5	NYI	Tim Connolly	Erie	C
6	NSH	Brian Finley	Barrie	G
7	WSH	Kris Beech	Calgary	C
8	NYI	Taylor Pyatt	Sudbury	LW
9	NYR	Jamie Lundmark	Moose Jaw	C
10	NYI	Branislav Mezei	Belleville	D
11	CGY	Oleg Saprykin	Seattle	LW
12	FLA	Denis Shvidki	Barrie	RW
13	EDM	Jani Rita	Jokerit	LW
14	S.J.	Jeff Jillson	U. of Michigan	D
15	PHX	Scott Kelman	Seattle	C
16	CAR	David Tanabe	U. of Wisconsin	D
17	STL	Barret Jackman	Regina	D
18	PIT	Konstantin Koltsov	Cherepovets	RW
19	PHX	Kirill Safronov	St. Petersburg	D
20	BUF	Barrett Heisten	U. of Maine	LW
21	BOS	Nick Boynton	Ottawa	D
22	PHI	Maxime Ouellet	Quebec	G
23	CHI	Steve McCarthy	Kootenay	D
24	TOR	Luca Cereda	Ambri	C
25	COL	Mikhail Kuleshov	Cherepovets	LW
26	OTT	Martin Havlat	Trinec	LW
27	N.J.	Ari Ahonen	JyP HT Jr.	G
28	NYI	Kristian Kudroc	Michalovce	D

OTHER NOTABLE SELECTIONS

Pick	Claimed by	Player	Amateur Club	Position
44	ANA	Jordan Leopold	U. of Minnesota	D
70	FLA	Niklas Hagman	HIFK Helsinki	LW
83	ANA	Niclas Havelid	Malmo	D
91	EDM	Mike Comrie	U. of Michigan	C
115	PIT	Ryan Malone	Omaha	LW
138	BUF	Ryan Miller	Soo	G
165	CHI	Michael Leighton	Windsor	G
191	NSH	Martin Erat	ZPS Zlin Jr.	LW
204	PIT	Tom Kostopolous	London	RW
210	DET	Henrik Zetterberg	Timra	LW
212	COL	Radim Vrbata	Hull	RW
222	L.A.	George Parros	Chicago Freeze	RW

1998

FIRST ROUND

Pick	Claimed by	Player	Amateur Club	Position
1	T.B.	Vincent Lecavalier	Rimouski	C
2	NSH	David Legwand	Plymouth	C
3	S.J.	Brad Stuart	Regina	D
4	VAN	Bryan Allen	Oshawa	D
5	ANA	Vitaly Vishnevski	Yaroslavl 2	D
6	CGY	Rico Fata	London	RW
7	NYR	Manny Malhotra	Guelph	C
8	CHI	Mark Bell	Ottawa	C
9	NYI	Mike Rupp	Erie	RW
10	TOR	Nik Antropov	Ust-Kamenogorsk	C
11	CAR	Jeff Heerema	Sarnia	RW
12	COL	Alex Tanguay	Halifax	LW
13	EDM	Michael Henrich	Barrie	RW
14	PHX	Patrick DesRochers	Sarnia	G
15	OTT	Mathieu Chouinard	Shawinigan	G
16	MTL	Eric Chouinard	Quebec	LW
17	COL	Martin Skoula	Barrie	D
18	BUF	Dmitri Kalinin	Chelyabinsk	D
19	COL	Robyn Regehr	Kamloops	D
20	COL	Scott Parker	Kelowna	RW
21	L.A.	Mathieu Biron	Shawinigan	D
22	PHI	Simon Gagne	Quebec	LW
23	PIT	Milan Kraft	Keramika Plzen Jr.	C
24	STL	Christian Backman	Vastra Frolunda Jr.	D
25	DET	Jiri Fischer	Hull	D
26	N.J.	Mike Van Ryn	U. of Michigan	D
27	N.J.	Scott Gomez	Tri-City	C

OTHER NOTABLE SELECTIONS

Pick	Claimed by	Player	Amateur Club	Position
29	S.J.	Jonathan Cheechoo	Belleville	RW
44	OTT	Mike Fisher	Sudbury	C
45	MTL	Mike Ribeiro	Rouyn-Noranda	C
64	T.B.	Brad Richards	Rimouski	C
68	VAN	Jarkko Ruutu	HIFK Helsinki	RW
71	CAR	Erik Cole	Clarkson	LW
75	MTL	Francois Beauchemin	Laval	D
82	NJ	Brian Gionta	Boston College	RW
87	TOR	Alexei Ponikarovsky	Dynamo 2	LW
99	EDM	Shawn Horcoff	Michigan State	C
117	FLA	Jaroslav Spacek	Farjestad	D
145	SJ	Mikael Samuelsson	Sodertalje	LW
161	OTT	Chris Neil	North Bay	RW
162	MTL	Andrei Markov	Khimik Voskresensk	D
164	BUF	Ales Kotalik	Ceske Budejovice Jr.	RW
168	PHI	Antero Niittymaki	TPS Turku Jr.	G
171	DET	Pavel Datsyuk	Yekateringburg	C
216	MTL	Michael Ryder	Hull	RW

1997

FIRST ROUND

Pick	Claimed by	Player	Amateur Club	Position
1	BOS	Joe Thornton	Sault Ste. Marie	C
2	S.J.	Patrick Marleau	Seattle	C
3	L.A.	Olli Jokinen	HIFK Helsinki	C
4	NYI	Roberto Luongo	Val-d'Or	G
5	NYI	Eric Brewer	Prince George	D
6	CGY	Daniel Tkaczuk	Barrie	C
7	T.B.	Paul Mara	Sudbury	D
8	BOS	Sergei Samsonov	Detroit	LW
9	WSH	Nick Boynton	Ottawa	D
10	VAN	Brad Ference	Spokane	D
11	MTL	Jason Ward	Erie	RW
12	OTT	Marian Hossa	Dukla Trencin	RW
13	CHI	Daniel Cleary	Belleville	RW
14	EDM	Michel Riesen	Biel-Bienne	RW
15	L.A.	Matt Zultek	Ottawa	LW
16	CHI	Ty Jones	Spokane	RW
17	PIT	Robert Dome	Las Vegas (IHL)	RW
18	ANA	Mikael Holmqvist	Djurgarden	C
19	NYR	Stefan Cherneski	Brandon	RW
20	FLA	Mike Brown	Red Deer	LW
21	BUF	Mika Noronen	Tappara Tampere	G
22	CAR	Nikos Tselios	Belleville	D
23	S.J.	Scott Hannan	Kelowna	D
24	N.J.	J-F Damphousse	Moncton	G
25	DAL	Brenden Morrow	Portland	LW
26	COL	Kevin Grimes	Kingston	D

OTHER NOTABLE SELECTIONS

Pick	Claimed by	Player	Amateur Club	Position
47	FLA	Kristian Huselius	Farjestad	LW
48	BUF	Henrik Tallinder	AIK Solna	D
69	BUF	Maxim Afinogenov	Dynamo Moscow	RW
78	COL	Ville Nieminen	Tappara Tampere	RW
83	L.A.	Joe Corvo	U. of Western Michigan	D
144	VAN	Matt Cooke	Windsor	C
156	BUF	Brian Campbell	Ottawa	D
177	STL	Ladislav Nagy	Dragon Presov	LW

1996

FIRST ROUND

Pick	Claimed by	Player	Amateur Club	Position
1	OTT	Chris Phillips	Prince Albert	D
2	S.J.	Andrei Zyuzin	Salavat Yulayev Ufa	D
3	NYI	J.P. Dumont	Val-d'Or	RW
4	WSH	Alexandre Volchkov	Barrie	C
5	DAL	Ric Jackman	Sault Ste. Marie	D
6	EDM	Boyd Devereaux	Kitchener	C
7	BUF	Erik Rasmussen	U. of Minnesota	LW/C
8	BOS	Johnathan Aitken	Medicine Hat	D
9	ANA	Ruslan Salei	Las Vegas (IHL)	D
10	N.J.	Lance Ward	Red Deer	D
11	PHX	Dan Focht	Tri-City	D
12	VAN	Josh Holden	Regina	C
13	CGY	Derek Morris	Regina	D
14	STL	Marty Reasoner	Boston College	C
15	PHI	Dainius Zubrus	Pembroke Jr. A	RW
16	T.B.	Mario Larocque	Hull	D
17	WSH	Jaroslav Svejkovsky	Tri-City	RW
18	MTL	Matt Higgins	Moose Jaw	C
19	EDM	Matthieu Descoteaux	Shawinigan	D
20	FLA	Marcus Nilson	Djurgarden	LW
21	S.J.	Marco Sturm	Landshut	LW
22	NYR	Jeff Brown	Sarnia	D
23	PIT	Craig Hillier	Ottawa	G
24	PHX	Daniel Briere	Drummondville	C
25	COL	Peter Ratchuk	Shattuck-St. Mary's	D
26	DET	Jesse Wallin	Red Deer	D

OTHER NOTABLE SELECTIONS

Pick	Claimed by	Player	Amateur Club	Position
35	ANA	Matt Cullen	St. Cloud State	C
49	N.J.	Colin White	Hull	D
56	NYI	Zdeno Chara	Dukla Trencin	D
59	EDM	Tom Poti	Cushing Academy	D
71	MTL	Arron Asham	Red Deer	RW
79	COL	Mark Parrish	St. Cloud State	RW
89	CGY	Toni Lydman	Reipas Lahti	D
96	L.A.	Eric Belanger	Beauport	C
102	S.J.	Matt Bradley	Kingston	RW
154	MTL	Brett Clark	U. of Maine	D
176	COL	Samuel Pahlsson	MoDo Ornskoldsvik	C
179	T.B.	Pavel Kubina	Vitkovice	D
199	N.J.	Willie Mitchell	Melfort Jr. A	D
204	TOR	Tomas Kaberle	Kladno	D
223	HFD	Craig Adams	Harvard	RW
239	OTT	Sami Salo	TPS Turku	D

1995

FIRST ROUND

Pick	Claimed by	Player	Amateur Club	Position
1	OTT	Bryan Berard	Detroit	D
2	NYI	Wade Redden	Brandon	D
3	L.A.	Aki Berg	Kiekko-67 Turku	D
4	ANA	Chad Kilger	Kingston	C
5	T.B.	Daymond Langkow	Tri-City	C
6	EDM	Steve Kelly	Prince Albert	C
7	WPG	Shane Doan	Kamloops	RW
8	MTL	Terry Ryan	Tri-City	LW
9	BOS	Kyle McLaren	Tacoma	D
10	FLA	Radek Dvorak	Ceske Budejovice	RW
11	DAL	Jarome Iginla	Kamloops	RW
12	S.J.	Teemu Riihijarvi	Kiekko-Espoo	LW
13	HFD	Jean-Sebastien Giguere	Halifax	G
14	BUF	Jay McKee	Niagara Falls	D
15	TOR	Jeff Ware	Oshawa	D
16	BUF	Martin Biron	Beauport	G
17	WSH	Brad Church	Prince Albert	LW
18	N.J.	Petr Sykora	Detroit	RW
19	CHI	Dmitri Nabokov	Krylja Sovetov	C/LW
20	CGY	Denis Gauthier	Drummondville	D
21	BOS	Sean Brown	Belleville	D
22	PHI	Brian Boucher	Tri-City	G
23	WSH	Miika Elomo	Kiekko-67 Turku	LW
24	PIT	Aleksey Morozov	Krylja Sovetov	RW
25	COL	Marc Denis	Chicoutimi	G
26	DET	Maxim Kuznetsov	Dynamo Moscow	D

OTHER NOTABLE SELECTIONS

Pick	Claimed by	Player	Amateur Club	Position
31	EDM	Georges Laraque	St-Jean	RW
49	STL	Jochen Hecht	Mannheim	C
67	WPG	Brad Isbister	Portland	LW
79	N.J.	Alyn McCauley	Ottawa	C
87	HFD	Sami Kapanen	HIFK Helsinki	RW
90	S.J.	Vesa Toskala	Ilves Tampere	G
91	NYR	Marc Savard	Oshawa	C
101	STL	Michal Handzus	Banska Bystrica	C
116	S.J.	Miikka Kiprusoff	TPS Turku Jr.	G
122	N.J.	Chris Mason	Prince George	G
129	COL	Brent Johnson	Owen Sound	G
144	VAN	Brent Sopel	Swift Current	D
164	MTL	Stephane Robidas	Shawinigan	D
166	FLA	Peter Worrell	Hull	LW
177	BOS	P.J. Axelsson	Vastra Frolunda	LW
192	FLA	Filip Kuba	Vitkovice Jr.	D

1994

FIRST ROUND

Pick	Claimed by	Player	Amateur Club	Position
1	FLA	Ed Jovanovski	Windsor	D
2	ANA	Oleg Tverdovsky	Krylja Sovetov	D
3	OTT	Radek Bonk	Las Vegas (IHL)	C
4	EDM	Jason Bonsignore	Niagara Falls	C
5	HFD	Jeff O'Neill	Guelph	RW
6	EDM	Ryan Smyth	Moose Jaw	LW
7	L.A.	Jamie Storr	Owen Sound	G
8	T.B.	Jason Wiemer	Portland	C
9	NYI	Brett Lindros	Kingston	RW
10	WSH	Nolan Baumgartner	Kamloops	D
11	S.J.	Jeff Friesen	Regina	LW
12	QUE	Wade Belak	Saskatoon	D/RW
13	VAN	Mattias Ohlund	Pitea	D
14	CHI	Ethan Moreau	Niagara Falls	LW
15	WSH	Alexander Kharlamov	CSKA Moscow	C
16	TOR	Eric Fichaud	Chictoutimi	G
17	BUF	Wayne Primeau	Owen Sound	C
18	MTL	Brad Brown	North Bay	D
19	CGY	Chris Dingman	Brandon	LW
20	DAL	Jason Botterill	U. of Michigan	LW
21	BOS	Evgeni Ryabchikov	Molot Perm	G
22	QUE	Jeffrey Kealty	Catholic Memorial H.S.	D
23	DET	Yan Golubovsky	Dynamo 2	D
24	PIT	Chris Wells	Seattle	C
25	N.J.	Vadim Sharifijanov	Salavat Yulayev Ufa	LW
26	NYR	Dan Cloutier	Sault Ste. Marie	G

OTHER NOTABLE SELECTIONS

Pick	Claimed by	Player	Amateur Club	Position
44	MTL	Jose Theodore	St-Jean	G
49	DET	Mathieu Dandenault	Sherbrooke	RW/D
50	PIT	Richard Park	Belleville	D
51	N.J.	Patrik Elias	Kladno	C
64	TOR	Fredrik Modin	Timra	LW
71	N.J.	Sheldon Souray	Tri-City	D
72	QUE	Chris Drury	Fairfield Prep	C
87	QUE	Milan Hejduk	Pardubice	RW
90	NYI	Brad Lukowich	Kamloops	D
124	DAL	Marty Turco	Cambridge Jr. A	G
133	OTT	Daniel Alfredsson	Vastra Frolunda	RW
151	BOS	Andre Roy	Chicoutimi	RW
217	QUE	Tim Thomas	U. of Vermont	G
218	PHI	Johan Hedberg	Leksand	G
219	S.J.	Evgeni Nabokov	Ust-Kamenogorsk	G
226	MTL	Tomas Vokoun	Kladno	G
233	N.J.	Steve Sullivan	Sault Ste. Marie	RW
249	WSH	Richard Zednik	Banska Bystricia	RW
257	DET	Tomas Holmstrom	Bodens IK	LW
286	NYR	Kim Johnsson	Malmo	D

1993

FIRST ROUND

Pick	Claimed by	Player	Amateur Club	Position
1	OTT	Alexandre Daigle	Victoriaville	C
2	HFD	Chris Pronger	Peterborough	D
3	T.B.	Chris Gratton	Kingston	C
4	ANA	Paul Kariya	U. of Maine	LW
5	FLA	Rob Niedermayer	Medicine Hat	C
6	S.J.	Viktor Kozlov	Dynamo Moscow	C

Pick	Claimed by	Amateur Club	Position
7 EDM	Jason Arnott	Oshawa	C
8 NYR	Niklas Sundstrom	MoDo Ornskoldsvik	RW
9 DAL	Todd Harvey	Detroit	RW/C
10 QUE	Jocelyn Thibault	Sherbrooke	G
11 WSH	Brendan Witt	Seattle	D
12 TOR	Kenny Jonsson	Rogle Angelholm	D
13 N.J.	Denis Pederson	Prince Albert	C/RW
14 QUE	Adam Deadmarsh	Portland	C
15 WPG	Mats Lindgren	Skelleftea	C/LW
16 EDM	Nick Stajduhar	London	D
17 WSH	Jason Allison	London	C
18 CGY	Jesper Mattsson	Malmo	C
19 TOR	Landon Wilson	Dubuque	RW
20 VAN	Mike Wilson	Sudbury	D
21 MTL	Saku Koivu	TPS Turku	C
22 DET	Anders Eriksson	MoDo Ornskoldsvik	D
23 NYI	Todd Bertuzzi	Guelph	RW
24 CHI	Eric Lecompte	Hull	LW
25 BOS	Kevyn Adams	Miami of Ohio	C
26 PIT	Stefan Bergkvist	Leksand	D

OTHER NOTABLE SELECTIONS

Pick	Claimed by	Amateur Club	Position
28 S.J.	Shean Donovan	Ottawa	RW
32 N.J.	Jay Pandolfo	Boston University	LW
35 DAL	Jamie Langenbrunner	Cloquet	C
39 NJ	Brendan Morrison	Spokane	D
40 NYI	Bryan McCabe	Spokane	D
41 FLA	Kevin Weekes	Owen Sound	G
71 PHI	Vinny Prospal	Ceske Budejovice	C
72 HFD	Marek Malik	Vitkovice	D

Pick	Claimed by	Amateur Club	Position
90 CHI	Eric Daze	Beauport	RW
111 EDM	Miroslav Satan	Dukla Trencin	LW
118 NYI	Tommy Salo	Vasteras	G
124 VAN	Scott Walker	Owen Sound	RW
151 MTL	Darcy Tucker	Kamloops	RW
164 NYR	Todd Marchant	Clarkson	C
174 WSH	Andrew Brunette	Owen Sound	LW
188 HFD	Manny Legace	Niagara Falls	G
207 BOS	Hal Gill	Nashoba H.S.	D
219 STL	Mike Grier	St. Sebastian's H.S.	RW
227 OTT	Pavol Demitra	Dukla Trencin	LW
250 LA	Kimmo Timonen	KalPa Kuopio	D

1992

FIRST ROUND

Pick	Claimed by	Amateur Club	Position
1 T.B.	Roman Hamrlik	ZPS Zlin	D
2 OTT	Alexei Yashin	Dynamo Moscow	C
3 S.J.	Mike Rathje	Medicine Hat	D
4 QUE	Todd Warriner	Windsor	LW
5 NYI	Darius Kasparaitis	Dynamo Moscow	D
6 CGY	Cory Stillman	Windsor	LW
7 PHI	Ryan Sittler	Nichols H.S.	LW
8 TOR	Brandon Convery	Sudbury	C
9 HFD	Robert Petrovicky	Dukla Trencin	C
10 S.J.	Andrei Nazarov	Dynamo Moscow	LW
11 BUF	David Cooper	Medicine Hat	D
12 CHI	Sergei Krivokrasov	CSKA Moscow	RW
13 EDM	Joe Hulbig	St. Sebastian's H.S.	LW
14 WSH	Sergei Gonchar	Traktor Chelyabinsk	D

Pick	Claimed by	Amateur Club	Position
15 PHI	Jason Bowen	Tri-City	D
16 BOS	Dmitri Kvartalnov	San Diego (IHL)	LW
17 WPG	Sergei Bautin	Dynamo Moscow	D
18 N.J.	Jason Smith	Regina	D
19 PIT	Martin Straka	Skoda Plzen	C
20 MTL	David Wilkie	Kamloops	D
21 VAN	Libor Polasek	Vitkovice	C
22 DET	Curtis Bowen	Ottawa	LW
23 TOR	Grant Marshall	Ottawa	RW
24 NYR	Peter Ferraro	Waterloo Jr. A	LW

OTHER NOTABLE SELECTIONS

Pick	Claimed by	Amateur Club	Position
32 WSH	Jim Carey	Catholic Memorial	G
33 MTL	Valeri Bure	Spokane	RW
38 STL	Igor Korolev	Dynamo Moscow	C
40 VAN	Michael Peca	Ottawa	C
42 N.J.	Sergei Brylin	CSKA Moscow	C
46 DET	Darren McCarty	Belleville	RW
48 NYR	Mattias Norstrom	AIK Solna	D
52 QUE	Manny Fernandez	Laval	G
65 EDM	Kirk Maltby	Owen Sound	RW
68 MTL	Craig Rivet	Kingston	D
88 MIN	Jere Lehtinen	Kiekko-Espoo	RW
117 VAN	Adrian Aucoin	Boston University	D
158 STL	Ian Laperriere	Drummondville	C/RW
186 N.J.	Stephane Yelle	Oshawa	C
204 WPG	Nikolai Khabibulin	CSKA Moscow	G
220 QUE	Anson Carter	Wexford Jr. A	C

1991

FIRST ROUND

Pick	Claimed by	Amateur Club	Position
1 QUE	Eric Lindros	Oshawa	C
2 S.J.	Pat Falloon	Spokane	RW
3 N.J.	Scott Niedermayer	Kamloops	D
4 NYI	Scott Lachance	Boston University	D
5 WPG	Aaron Ward	U. of Michigan	D
6 PHI	Peter Forsberg	MoDo Ornskoldsvik	C
7 VAN	Alek Stojanov	Hamilton	RW
8 MIN	Richard Matvichuk	Saskatoon	D
9 HFD	Patrick Poulin	St-Hyacinthe	C
10 DET	Martin Lapointe	Laval	RW
11 N.J.	Brian Rolston	Detroit Compuware Jr. A.	C/RW
12 EDM	Tyler Wright	Swift Current	C
13 BUF	Philippe Boucher	Granby	D
14 WSH	Pat Peake	Detroit	C
15 NYR	Alex Kovalev	Dynamo Moscow	RW
16 PIT	Markus Naslund	MoDo Ornskoldsvik	LW
17 MTL	Brent Bilodeau	Seattle	D
18 BOS	Glen Murray	Sudbury	RW
19 CGY	Niklas Sundblad	AIK Solna	RW
20 EDM	Martin Rucinsky	Litvinov	LW
21 WSH	Trevor Halverson	North Bay	LW
22 CHI	Dean McAmmond	Prince Albert	LW

OTHER NOTABLE SELECTIONS

Pick	Claimed by	Amateur Club	Position
23 S.J.	Ray Whitney	Spokane	LW
26 NYI	Ziggy Palffy	AC Nitra	RW
27 STL	Steve Staios	Niagara Falls	D
30 S.J.	Sandis Ozolinsh	Dynamo Riga	D
40 BOS	Jozef Stumpel	AC Nitra	C
47 TOR	Yanic Perreault	Trois-Rivieres	C
54 DET	Chris Osgood	Medicine Hat	G
58 WSH	Steve Konowalchuk	Portland	LW
59 HFD	Michael Nylander	Huddinge	C
76 DET	Mike Knuble	Kalamazoo Jr. A	RW
81 L.A.	Alexei Zhitnik	Sokol Kiev	D
106 BOS	Mariusz Czerkawski	GKS Tychy	RW
122 PHI	Dmitri Yushkevich	Yaroslavl	D
123 BUF	Sean O'Donnell	Sudbury	D
171 MTL	Brian Savage	Miami of Ohio	LW
203 WPG	Igor Ulanov	Khimik Voskresensk	D

1990

FIRST ROUND

Pick	Claimed by	Amateur Club	Position
1 QUE	Owen Nolan	Cornwall	RW
2 VAN	Petr Nedved	Seattle	C
3 DET	Keith Primeau	Niagara Falls	C
4 PHI	Mike Ricci	Peterborough	C
5 PIT	Jaromir Jagr	Kladno	RW
6 NYI	Scott Scissons	Saskatoon	C
7 L.A.	Darryl Sydor	Kamloops	D
8 MIN	Derian Hatcher	North Bay	D
9 WSH	John Slaney	Cornwall	D
10 TOR	Drake Berehowsky	Kingston	D
11 CGY	Trevor Kidd	Brandon	G
12 MTL	Turner Stevenson	Seattle	RW
13 NYR	Michael Stewart	Michigan State	D
14 BUF	Brad May	Niagara Falls	LW
15 HFD	Mark Greig	Lethbridge	RW
16 CHI	Karl Dykhuis	Hull	D
17 EDM	Scott Allison	Prince Albert	C
18 VAN	Shawn Antoski	North Bay	LW
19 WPG	Keith Tkachuk	Malden Catholic H.S.	LW
20 N.J.	Martin Brodeur	St-Hyacinthe	G
21 BOS	Bryan Smolinski	Michigan State	C

Anson Carter was the 220th pick in the 1992 Entry Draft. Selected by the Quebec Nordiques, he never played for that franchise but did wear the uniform of eight other teams during a 10-year career that saw him collect 202 goals and 219 assists in 674 games.

Pick	Claimed by		Amateur Club	Position

OTHER NOTABLE SELECTIONS

25	PHI	Chris Simon	Ottawa	LW
31	TOR	Felix Potvin	Chicoutimi	G
34	NYR	Doug Weight	Lake Superior State	C
36	HFD	Geoff Sanderson	Swift Current	LW
45	DET	Vyacheslav Kozlov	Khimik Voskresensk	RW
77	WPG	Alexei Zhamnov	Dynamo Moscow	C
85	NYR	Sergei Zubov	CSKA Moscow	D
113	MIN	Roman Turek	Plzen	G
123	MTL	Craig Conroy	Northwood Prep	C
133	L.A.	Robert Lang	CHZ Litvinov	C
156	WSH	Peter Bondra	Kosice	RW
158	QUE	Alexander Karpovtsev	VSZ Dynamo	D
177	WSH	Ken Klee	Bowling Green	D
244	NYR	Sergei Nemchinov	Krylja Sovetov	LW

1989

FIRST ROUND

1	QUE	Mats Sundin	Nacka	C
2	NYI	Dave Chyzowski	Kamloops	LW
3	TOR	Scott Thornton	Belleville	LW
4	WPG	Stu Barnes	Tri-City	C
5	N.J.	Bill Guerin	Springfield Jr. B.	RW
6	CHI	Adam Bennett	Sudbury	D
7	MIN	Doug Zmolek	John Marshall H.S.	D
8	VAN	Jason Herter	North Dakota	D
9	STL	Jason Marshall	Vernon Jr. A.	D
10	HFD	Bobby Holik	Dukla Jihlava	C
11	DET	Mike Sillinger	Regina	C
12	TOR	Rob Pearson	Belleville	RW
13	MTL	Lindsay Vallis	Seattle	D
14	BUF	Kevin Haller	Regina	D
15	EDM	Jason Soules	Niagara Falls	D
16	PIT	Jamie Heward	Regina	D
17	BOS	Shayne Stevenson	Kitchener	RW
18	N.J.	Jason Miller	Medicine Hat	LW
19	WSH	Olaf Kolzig	Tri-City	G
20	NYR	Steven Rice	Kitchener	RW
21	TOR	Steve Bancroft	Belleville	D

OTHER NOTABLE SELECTIONS

22	QUE	Adam Foote	Sault Ste. Marie	D
30	MTL	Patrice Brisebois	Laval	D
53	DET	Nicklas Lidstrom	Vasteras	D
62	WPG	Kris Draper	Canadian National	C
70	CGY	Robert Reichel	Litvinov	C
109	WPG	Dan Bylsma	Bowling Green	RW
74	DET	Sergei Fedorov	CSKA Moscow	C
113	VAN	Pavel Bure	CSKA Moscow	RW
116	DET	Dallas Drake	Northern Michigan	RW
183	BUF	Donald Audette	Laval	RW
191	NYI	Vladimir Malakhov	CSKA Moscow	D
196	MIN	Arturs Irbe	Dynamo Riga	G
221	DET	Vladimir Konstantinov	CSKA Moscow	D

1988

FIRST ROUND

1	MIN	Mike Modano	Prince Albert	C
2	VAN	Trevor Linden	Medicine Hat	RW
3	QUE	Curtis Leschyshyn	Saskatoon	D
4	PIT	Darrin Shannon	Windsor	LW
5	QUE	Daniel Dore	Drummondville	RW
6	TOR	Scott Pearson	Kingston	LW
7	L.A.	Martin Gelinas	Hull	LW
8	CHI	Jeremy Roenick	Thayer Academy	C
9	STL	Rod Brind'Amour	Notre Dame Jr. A	C
10	WPG	Teemu Selanne	Jokerit	RW
11	HFD	Chris Govedaris	Toronto	LW
12	N.J.	Corey Foster	Peterborough	D
13	BUF	Joel Savage	Victoria	RW
14	PHI	Claude Boivin	Drummondville	LW
15	WSH	Reggie Savage	Victoriaville	C
16	NYI	Kevin Cheveldayoff	Brandon	D
17	DET	Kory Kocur	Saskatoon	RW
18	BOS	Rob Cimetta	Toronto	W
19	EDM	Francois Leroux	St-Jean	D
20	MTL	Eric Charron	Trois-Rivieres	D
21	CGY	Jason Muzzatti	Michigan State	G

OTHER NOTABLE SELECTIONS

27	TOR	Tie Domi	Peterborough	RW
67	PIT	Mark Recchi	Kamloops	RW
68	NYR	Tony Amonte	Thayer Academy	RW
70	L.A.	Rob Blake	Bowling Green	D
76	BUF	Keith Carney	Mount St. Charles H.S.	D
81	BOS	Joe Juneau	RPI	C
89	BUF	Alexander Mogilny	CSKA Moscow	RW
97	BUF	Rob Ray	Cornwall	RW
129	QUE	Valeri Kamensky	CSKA Moscow	D
198	STL	Bret Hedican	North St. Paul H.S.	D
234	QUE	Claude Lapointe	Laval	LW/C

1987

FIRST ROUND

1	BUF	Pierre Turgeon	Granby	C
2	N.J.	Brendan Shanahan	London	LW
3	BOS	Glen Wesley	Portland	D
4	L.A.	Wayne McBean	Medicine Hat	D
5	PIT	Chris Joseph	Seattle	D
6	MIN	Dave Archibald	Portland	C/LW
7	TOR	Luke Richardson	Peterborough	D
8	CHI	Jimmy Waite	Chicoutimi	G
9	QUE	Bryan Fogarty	Kingston	D
10	NYR	Jay More	New Westminster	D
11	DET	Yves Racine	Longueuil	D
12	STL	Keith Osborne	North Bay	RW
13	NYI	Dean Chynoweth	Medicine Hat	D
14	BOS	Stephane Quintal	Granby	D
15	QUE	Joe Sakic	Swift Current	C
16	WPG	Bryan Marchment	Belleville	D
17	MTL	Andrew Cassels	Ottawa	C
18	HFD	Jody Hull	Peterborough	RW
19	CGY	Bryan Deasley	U. of Michigan	LW
20	PHI	Darren Rumble	Kitchener	D
21	EDM	Peter Soberlak	Swift Current	LW

OTHER NOTABLE SELECTIONS

33	MTL	John LeClair	Bellows Academy	LW
38	MTL	Eric Desjardins	Granby	D
44	MTL	Mathieu Schneider	Cornwall	D
71	TOR	Joe Sacco	Medford H.S.	RW
110	PIT	Shawn McEachern	Matignon H.S.	RW
114	QUE	Garth Snow	Mount St. Charles H.S.	G
118	NYI	Rob DiMaio	Medicine Hat	RW
149	N.J.	Jim Dowd	Brick H.S.	C
166	CGY	Theoren Fleury	Moose Jaw	RW

1986

FIRST ROUND

1	DET	Joe Murphy	Michigan State	RW
2	L.A.	Jimmy Carson	Verdun	C
3	N.J.	Neil Brady	Medicine Hat	C
4	PIT	Zarley Zalapski	Canadian National	D
5	BUF	Shawn Anderson	Canadian National	D
6	TOR	Vincent Damphousse	Laval	C
7	VAN	Dan Woodley	Portland	RW
8	WPG	Pat Elynuik	Prince Albert	RW
9	NYR	Brian Leetch	Avon Old Farms H.S.	D
10	STL	Jocelyn Lemieux	Laval	RW
11	HFD	Scott Young	Boston University	RW
12	MIN	Warren Babe	Lethbridge	LW
13	BOS	Craig Janney	Boston College	C
14	CHI	Everett Sanipass	Verdun	LW

15	MTL	Mark Pederson	Medicine Hat	LW
16	CGY	George Pelawa	Bemidji H.S.	RW
17	NYI	Tom Fitzgerald	Austin Prep	RW
18	QUE	Ken McRae	Sudbury	C
19	WSH	Jeff Greenlaw	Canadian National	LW
20	PHI	Kerry Huffman	Guelph	D
21	EDM	Kim Issel	Prince Albert	RW

OTHER NOTABLE SELECTIONS

22	DET	Adam Graves	Windsor	LW
29	WPG	Teppo Numminen	Tappara Tampere	D
67	PIT	Rob Brown	Kamloops	RW
72	NYR	Mark Janssens	Regina	C
81	QUE	Ron Tugnutt	Peterborough	G
85	DET	Johan Garpenlov	Nacka	LW
114	NYR	Darren Turcotte	North Bay	C
141	MTL	Lyle Odelein	Moose Jaw	D
143	NYI	Rich Pilon	Prince Albert AAA	D
202	BOS	Greg Hawgood	Kamloops	D

1985

FIRST ROUND

1	TOR	Wendel Clark	Saskatoon	LW/D
2	PIT	Craig Simpson	Michigan State	LW
3	N.J.	Craig Wolanin	Kitchener	D
4	VAN	Jim Sandlak	London	RW
5	HFD	Dana Murzyn	Calgary	D
6	NYI	Brad Dalgarno	Hamilton	RW
7	NYR	Ulf Dahlen	Ostersund	LW
8	DET	Brent Fedyk	Regina	LW
9	L.A.	Craig Duncanson	Sudbury	LW
10	L.A.	Dan Gratton	Oshawa	C
11	CHI	Dave Manson	Prince Albert	D
12	MTL	Jose Charbonneau	Drummondville	RW
13	NYI	Derek King	Sault Ste. Marie	LW
14	BUF	Calle Johansson	Vastra Frolunda	D
15	QUE	David Latta	Kitchener	LW
16	MTL	Tom Chorske	Minneapolis SW H.S.	LW
17	CGY	Chris Biotti	Belmont Hill H.S.	D
18	WPG	Ryan Stewart	Kamloops	C
19	WSH	Yvon Corriveau	Toronto	LW
20	EDM	Scott Metcalfe	Kingston	LW
21	PHI	Glen Seabrooke	Peterborough	C

OTHER NOTABLE SELECTIONS

24	N.J.	Sean Burke	Toronto	G
27	CGY	Joe Nieuwendyk	Cornell	C
28	NYR	Mike Richter	Northwood Prep	G
32	N.J.	Eric Weinrich	North Yarmouth Academy	D
35	BUF	Benoit Hogue	St-Jean	C
50	DET	Steve Chiasson	Guelph	D
52	BOS	Bill Ranford	New Westminster	G

Jimmy Mann was the first draft pick of the original Winnipeg Jets when they entered the NHL from the World Hockey Association in 1979. He played 72 games as a rookie in 1979-80 but would see only limited action over the rest of his eight-year career.

81	WPG	Fredrik Olausson	Farjestad	D
113	DET	Randy McKay	Michigan Tech	RW
157	BOS	Randy Burridge	Peterborough	LW
188	EDM	Kelly Buchberger	Moose Jaw	RW
189	PHI	Gord Murphy	Oshawa	D
214	VAN	Igor Larionov	CSKA Moscow	C
245	BUF	Ken Baumgartner	Prince Albert	D

1984

FIRST ROUND

1	PIT	Mario Lemieux	Laval	C
2	N.J.	Kirk Muller	Guelph	LW
3	CHI	Eddie Olczyk	Team USA	C
4	TOR	Al Iafrate	Belleville	D
5	MTL	Petr Svoboda	CHZ Litvinov	D
6	L.A.	Craig Redmond	U. of Denver	D
7	DET	Shawn Burr	Kitchener	LW/C
8	MTL	Shayne Corson	Brantford	LW
9	PIT	Doug Bodger	Kamloops	D
10	VAN	J.J. Daigneault	Longueuil	D
11	HFD	Sylvain Cote	Quebec	D
12	CGY	Gary Roberts	Ottawa	LW
13	MIN	David Quinn	Kent H.S.	D
14	NYR	Terry Carkner	Peterborough	D
15	QUE	Trevor Stienburg	Guelph	RW
16	PIT	Roger Belanger	Kingston	C
17	WSH	Kevin Hatcher	North Bay	D
18	BUF	Mikael Andersson	Vastra Frolunda	LW
19	BOS	Dave Pasin	Prince Albert	RW
20	NYI	Duncan MacPherson	Saskatoon	D
21	EDM	Selmar Odelein	Regina	D

OTHER NOTABLE SELECTIONS

25	TOR	Todd Gill	Windsor	D
27	PHI	Scott Mellanby	Henry Carr Jr. B.	RW
29	MTL	Stephane Richer	Granby	RW
36	QUE	Jeff Brown	Sudbury	D
51	MTL	Patrick Roy	Granby	G
107	N.J.	Kirk McLean	Oshawa	G
117	CGY	Brett Hull	Penticton Jr. A	RW
119	NYR	Kjell Samuelsson	Leksand	D
166	BOS	Don Sweeney	St. Paul's H.S.	D
171	L.A.	Luc Robitaille	Hull	LW
180	CGY	Gary Suter	U. of Wisconsin	D

1983

FIRST ROUND

1	MIN	Brian Lawton	Mount St. Charles H.S.	LW
2	HFD	Sylvain Turgeon	Hull	LW
3	NYI	Pat LaFontaine	Verdun	C
4	DET	Steve Yzerman	Peterborough	C
5	BUF	Tom Barrasso	Acton-Boxborough	G
6	N.J.	John MacLean	Oshawa	RW
7	TOR	Russ Courtnall	Victoria	RW
8	WPG	Andrew McBain	North Bay	RW
9	VAN	Cam Neely	Portland	RW
10	BUF	Normand Lacombe	New Hampshire	RW
11	BUF	Adam Creighton	Ottawa	C
12	NYR	Dave Gagner	Brantford	C
13	CGY	Dan Quinn	Belleville	C
14	WPG	Bobby Dollas	Laval	D
15	PIT	Bob Errey	Peterborough	LW
16	NYI	Gerald Diduck	Lethbridge	D
17	MTL	Alfie Turcotte	Portland	C
18	CHI	Bruce Cassidy	Ottawa	D
19	EDM	Jeff Beukeboom	Sault Ste. Marie	D
20	HFD	David Jensen	Lawrence Academy	C
21	BOS	Nevin Markwart	Regina	LW

OTHER NOTABLE SELECTIONS

26	MTL	Claude Lemieux	Trois-Rivieres	RW
27	MTL	Sergio Momesso	Shawinigan	LW
41	PHI	Peter Zezel	Toronto	C
82	EDM	Esa Tikkanen	HIFK Helsinki	LW
88	DET	Petr Klima	Dukla Jihlava	W
91	DET	Joe Kocur	Saskatoon	RW
112	L.A.	Kevin Stevens	Silver Lake H.S.	LW
125	PHI	Rick Tocchet	Sault Ste. Marie	RW
139	BUF	Christian Ruuttu	Assat Pori	C
150	N.J.	Viacheslav Fetisov	CSKA Moscow	D
207	CHI	Dominik Hasek	Pardubice	G
223	BUF	Uwe Krupp	Koln	D
241	CGY	Sergei Makarov	CSKA Moscow	RW

1982

FIRST ROUND

1	BOS	Gord Kluzak	Billings	D
2	MIN	Brian Bellows	Kitchener	LW
3	TOR	Gary Nylund	Portland	D
4	PHI	Ron Sutter	Lethbridge	C
5	WSH	Scott Stevens	Kitchener	D
6	BUF	Phil Housley	South St. Paul H.S.	D
7	CHI	Ken Yaremchuk	Portland	C
8	N.J.	Rocky Trottier	Nanaimo	RW
9	BUF	Paul Cyr	Victoria	LW
10	PIT	Rich Sutter	Lethbridge	RW
11	VAN	Michel Petit	Sherbrooke	D
12	WPG	Jim Kyte	Cornwall	D
13	QUE	David Shaw	Kitchener	D
14	HFD	Paul Lawless	Windsor	LW
15	NYR	Chris Kontos	Toronto	LW/C
16	BUF	Dave Andreychuk	Oshawa	LW
17	DET	Murray Craven	Medicine Hat	LW
18	N.J.	Ken Daneyko	Seattle	D
19	MTL	Alain Heroux	Chicoutimi	LW
20	EDM	Jim Playfair	Portland	D
21	NYI	Pat Flatley	U. of Wisconsin	RW

OTHER NOTABLE SELECTIONS

36	NYR	Tomas Sandstrom	Farjestad	RW
43	N.J.	Pat Verbeek	Sudbury	RW
45	TOR	Ken Wregget	Lethbridge	G
56	HFD	Kevin Dineen	U. of Denver	RW
67	HFD	Ulf Samuelsson	Leksand	D
75	WPG	Dave Ellett	Ottawa Jr. A	D
80	MIN	Bob Rouse	Nanaimo	D
88	HFD	Ray Ferraro	Penticton Jr. A	C
119	PHI	Ron Hextall	Brandon	G
120	NYR	Tony Granato	Northwood Prep	RW
134	STL	Doug Gilmour	Cornwall	C
140	PHI	Dave Brown	Saskatoon	RW

1981

FIRST ROUND

1	WPG	Dale Hawerchuk	Cornwall	C
2	L.A.	Doug Smith	Ottawa	C
3	WSH	Bob Carpenter	St. John's Prep	C
4	HFD	Ron Francis	Sault Ste. Marie	C
5	COL	Joe Cirella	Oshawa	D
6	TOR	Jim Benning	Portland	D
7	MTL	Mark Hunter	Brantford	RW
8	EDM	Grant Fuhr	Victoria	G
9	NYR	James Patrick	Prince Albert	D
10	VAN	Garth Butcher	Regina	D
11	QUE	Randy Moller	Lethbridge	D
12	CHI	Tony Tanti	Oshawa	RW
13	MIN	Ron Meighan	Niagara Falls	D
14	BOS	Normand Leveille	Chicoutimi	LW
15	CGY	Al MacInnis	Kitchener	D
16	PHI	Steve Smith	Sault Ste. Marie	D
17	BUF	Jiri Dudacek	Kladno	RW
18	MTL	Gilbert Delorme	Chicoutimi	D
19	MTL	Jan Ingman	Farjestad	LW
20	STL	Marty Ruff	Lethbridge	D
21	NYI	Paul Boutilier	Sherbrooke	D

OTHER NOTABLE SELECTIONS

22	WPG	Scott Arniel	Cornwall	LW
40	MTL	Chris Chelios	Moose Jaw	D
56	CGY	Mike Vernon	Calgary	G
72	NYR	John Vanbiesbrouck	Sault Ste. Marie	G
107	DET	Gerard Gallant	Sherbrooke	LW
108	COL	Bruce Driver	U. of Wisconsin	D
111	EDM	Steve Smith	London	D
145	MTL	Tom Kurvers	Minnesota-Duluth	D
152	WSH	Gaetan Duchesne	Quebec	LW

1980

FIRST ROUND

1	MTL	Doug Wickenheiser	Regina	C
2	WPG	Dave Babych	Portland	D
3	CHI	Denis Savard	Montreal	C
4	L.A.	Larry Murphy	Peterborough	D
5	WSH	Darren Veitch	Regina	D
6	EDM	Paul Coffey	Kitchener	D
7	VAN	Rick Lanz	Oshawa	D
8	HFD	Fred Arthur	Cornwall	D
9	PIT	Mike Bullard	Brantford	C
10	L.A.	Jim Fox	Ottawa	RW
11	DET	Mike Blaisdell	Regina	RW
12	STL	Rik Wilson	Kingston	D
13	CGY	Denis Cyr	Montreal	RW
14	NYR	Jim Malone	Toronto	C
15	CHI	Jerome Dupont	Toronto	D
16	MIN	Brad Palmer	Victoria	LW
17	NYI	Brent Sutter	Red Deer Jr. A	C
18	BOS	Barry Pederson	Victoria	C
19	COL	Paul Gagne	Windsor	LW
20	BUF	Steve Patrick	Brandon	RW
21	PHI	Mike Stothers	Kingston	D

OTHER NOTABLE SELECTIONS

37	MIN	Don Beaupre	Sudbury	G
38	NYI	Kelly Hrudey	Medicine Hat	G
57	CHI	Troy Murray	St. Albert Jr. A	C
61	MTL	Craig Ludwig	North Dakota	D
69	EDM	Jari Kurri	Jokerit	RW
73	L.A.	Bernie Nicholls	Kingston	C
80	NYI	Greg Gilbert	Toronto	LW
81	BOS	Steve Kasper	Verdun	C
106	COL	Aaron Broten	U. of Minnesota	LW/C
120	CHI	Steve Larmer	Niagara Falls	RW
124	MTL	Mike McPhee	RPI	LW
128	WPG	Brian Mullen	U.S. Jr. National	RW
132	EDM	Andy Moog	Billings	G
181	CGY	Hakan Loob	Farjestad	RW

1979

FIRST ROUND

1	COL	Rob Ramage	London	D
2	STL	Perry Turnbull	Portland	C
3	DET	Mike Foligno	Sudbury	RW
4	WSH	Mike Gartner	Niagara Falls	RW
5	VAN	Rick Vaive	Sherbrooke	RW
6	MIN	Craig Hartsburg	Sault Ste. Marie	D
7	CHI	Keith Brown	Portland	D
8	BOS	Raymond Bourque	Verdun	D
9	TOR	Laurie Boschman	Brandon	C
10	MIN	Tom McCarthy	Oshawa	LW
11	BUF	Mike Ramsey	U. of Minnesota	D
12	ATL	Paul Reinhart	Kitchener	D
13	NYR	Doug Sulliman	Kitchener	RW
14	PHI	Brian Propp	Brandon	LW
15	BOS	Brad McCrimmon	Brandon	D
16	L.A.	Jay Wells	Kingston	D
17	NYI	Duane Sutter	Lethbridge	RW
18	HFD	Ray Allison	Brandon	RW
19	WPG	Jimmy Mann	Sherbrooke	RW
20	QUE	Michel Goulet	Quebec	LW
21	EDM	Kevin Lowe	Quebec	D

OTHER NOTABLE SELECTIONS

32	BUF	Lindy Ruff	Lethbridge	D/LW
37	MTL	Mats Naslund	Brynas Gavle	LW
40	WPG	Dave Christian	North Dakota	RW
41	QUE	Dale Hunter	Sudbury	C
42	MIN	Neal Broten	U. of Minnesota	C
44	MTL	Guy Carbonneau	Chicoutimi	C
48	EDM	Mark Messier	St. Albert Jr. A	C
54	ATL	Tim Hunter	Seattle	RW
57	BOS	Keith Crowder	Peterborough	RW
58	MTL	Rick Wamsley	Brantford	G
66	DET	John Ogrodnick	New Westminster	LW
69	EDM	Glenn Anderson	U. of Denver	RW
75	ATL	Jim Peplinski	Toronto	RW
83	QUE	Anton Stastny	Slovan Bratislava	LW
89	VAN	Dirk Graham	Regina	RW/LW
103	WPG	Thomas Steen	Leksand	C
120	BOS	Mike Krushelnyski	Montreal	LW/C

1978

FIRST ROUND

1	MIN	Bobby Smith	Ottawa	C
2	WSH	Ryan Walter	Seattle	C/LW
3	STL	Wayne Babych	Portland	RW
4	VAN	Bill Derlago	Brandon	C
5	COL	Mike Gillis	Kingston	LW
6	PHI	Behn Wilson	Kingston	D
7	PHI	Ken Linseman	Kingston	C
8	MTL	Danny Geoffrion	Cornwall	RW
9	DET	Willie Huber	Hamilton	D
10	CHI	Tim Higgins	Ottawa	RW
11	ATL	Brad Marsh	London	D
12	DET	Brent Peterson	Portland	C
13	BUF	Larry Playfair	Portland	D
14	PHI	Danny Lucas	Sault Ste. Marie	RW
15	NYI	Steve Tambellini	Lethbridge	C
16	BOS	Al Secord	Hamilton	LW
17	MTL	Dave Hunter	Sudbury	LW
18	WSH	Tim Coulis	Hamilton	LW

OTHER NOTABLE SELECTIONS

19	MIN	Steve Payne	Ottawa	LW
21	TOR	Joel Quenneville	Windsor	D
22	VAN	Curt Fraser	Victoria	LW
26	NYR	Don Maloney	Kitchener	LW
32	BUF	Tony McKegney	Kingston	LW
40	VAN	Stan Smyl	New Westminster	RW
54	MIN	Curt Giles	Minnesota-Duluth	D
55	WSH	Bengt Gustafsson	Farjestad	RW
93	NYR	Tom Laidlaw	Northern Michigan	D
103	MTL	Keith Acton	Peterborough	C
109	STL	Paul MacLean	Hull	RW
153	BOS	Craig MacTavish	U. of Mass-Lowell	C
173	STL	Risto Siltanen	Ilves Tampere	D
179	CHI	Darryl Sutter	Lethbridge	LW
231	MTL	Chris Nilan	Northeastern	RW

1977

FIRST ROUND

1	DET	Dale McCourt	St. Catharines	C
2	COL	Barry Beck	New Westminster	D
3	WSH	Robert Picard	Montreal	D
4	VAN	Jere Gillis	Sherbrooke	LW
5	Cle.	Mike Crombeen	Kingston	RW
6	CHI	Doug Wilson	Ottawa	D
7	MIN	Brad Maxwell	New Westminster	D
8	NYR	Lucien DeBlois	Sorel	C
9	STL	Scott Campbell	London	D
10	MTL	Mark Napier	Toronto	RW
11	TOR	John Anderson	Toronto	RW
12	TOR	Trevor Johansen	Toronto	D
13	NYR	Ron Duguay	Sudbury	C/RW
14	BUF	Ric Seiling	St. Catharines	RW/C

15	NYI	Mike Bossy	Laval	RW
16	BOS	Dwight Foster	Kitchener	RW
17	PHI	Kevin McCarthy	Winnipeg	D
18	MTL	Norm Dupont	Montreal	LW

OTHER NOTABLE SELECTIONS

25	MIN	Dave Semenko	Brandon	LW
33	NYI	John Tonelli	Toronto	LW
36	MTL	Rod Langway	New Hampshire	D
40	VAN	Glen Hanlon	Brandon	G
54	MTL	Gordie Roberts	Victoria	D
66	PIT	Mark Johnson	U. of Wisconsin	C
102	PIT	Greg Millen	Peterborough	G
135	PHI	Pete Peeters	Medicine Hat	G
162	MTL	Craig Laughlin	Clarkson	RW

1976

FIRST ROUND

1	WSH	Rick Green	London	D
2	PIT	Blair Chapman	Saskatoon	RW
3	MIN	Glen Sharpley	Hull	C
4	DET	Fred Williams	Saskatoon	C
5	CAL	Bjorn Johansson	Orebro	D
6	NYR	Don Murdoch	Medicine Hat	RW
7	STL	Bernie Federko	Saskatoon	C
8	ATL	Dave Shand	Peterborough	D
9	CHI	Real Cloutier	Quebec	RW
10	ATL	Harold Phillipoff	New Westminster	LW
11	K.C.	Paul Gardner	Oshawa	C
12	MTL	Peter Lee	Ottawa	RW
13	MTL	Rod Schutt	Sudbury	LW
14	NYI	Alex McKendry	Sudbury	W
15	WSH	Greg Carroll	Medicine Hat	C
16	BOS	Clayton Pachal	New Westminster	C/LW
17	PHI	Mark Suzor	Kingston	D
18	MTL	Bruce Baker	Ottawa	RW

OTHER NOTABLE SELECTIONS

19	PIT	Greg Malone	Oshawa	C
20	STL	Brian Sutter	Lethbridge	LW
22	DET	Reed Larson	Minnesota-Duluth	D
30	TOR	Randy Carlyle	Sudbury	D
45	CHI	Thomas Gradin	MoDo Ornskoldsvik	C
47	PIT	Morris Lukowich	Medicine Hat	LW
56	STL	Mike Liut	Bowling Green	G
64	ATL	Kent Nilsson	Djurgarden	C
68	NYI	Ken Morrow	Bowling Green	D
133	MTL	Ron Wilson	St. Catharines	C

1975

FIRST ROUND

1	PHI	Mel Bridgman	Victoria	C
2	K.C.	Barry Dean	Medicine Hat	LW
3	CAL	Ralph Klassen	Saskatoon	C
4	MIN	Bryan Maxwell	Medicine Hat	D
5	DET	Rick Lapointe	Victoria	D
6	TOR	Don Ashby	Calgary	C
7	CHI	Greg Vaydik	Medicine Hat	C
8	ATL	Richard Mulhern	Sherbrooke	D
9	MTL	Robin Sadler	Edmonton	D
10	VAN	Rick Blight	Brandon	RW
11	NYI	Pat Price	Saskatoon	D
12	NYR	Wayne Dillon	Toronto	C
13	PIT	Gord Laxton	New Westminster	G
14	BOS	Doug Halward	Peterborough	D
15	MTL	Pierre Mondou	Montreal	C
16	L.A.	Tim Young	Ottawa	C

OTHER NOTABLE SELECTIONS

17	BUF	Bob Sauve	Laval	G
21	CAL	Dennis Maruk	London	C
22	MTL	Brian Engblom	U. of Wisconsin	D
24	TOR	Doug Jarvis	Peterborough	C
43	CHI	Mike O'Connell	Kingston	D
57	CAL	Greg Smith	Colorado College	D
80	ATL	Willi Plett	St. Catharines	RW
108	PHI	Paul Holmgren	U. of Minnesota	RW
210	L.A.	Dave Taylor	Clarkson	RW

1974

FIRST ROUND

1	WSH	Greg Joly	Regina	D
2	K.C.	Wilf Paiement	St. Catharines	RW
3	CAL	Rick Hampton	St. Catharines	LW/D
4	NYI	Clark Gillies	Regina	LW
5	MTL	Cam Connor	Flin Flon	RW
6	MIN	Doug Hicks	Flin Flon	D
7	MTL	Doug Risebrough	Kitchener	C
8	PIT	Pierre Larouche	Sorel	C
9	DET	Bill Lochead	Oshawa	LW
10	MTL	Rick Chartraw	Kitchener	D/RW
11	BUF	Lee Fogolin Jr.	Oshawa	D
12	MTL	Mario Tremblay	Montreal	RW
13	TOR	Jack Valiquette	Sault Ste. Marie	C
14	NYR	Dave Maloney	Kitchener	D
15	MTL	Gord McTavish	Sudbury	C
16	CHI	Grant Mulvey	Calgary	RW
17	CAL	Ron Chipperfield	Brandon	C
18	BOS	Don Larway	Swift Current	RW

OTHER NOTABLE SELECTIONS

22	NYI	Bryan Trottier	Swift Current	C
25	BOS	Mark Howe	Toronto	D
29	BUF	Danny Gare	Calgary	RW
31	TOR	Tiger Williams	Swift Current	LW
32	NYR	Ron Greschner	New Westminster	D
38	K.C.	Bob Bourne	Saskatoon	C
39	CAL	Charlie Simmer	Sault Ste. Marie	LW
52	CHI	Bob Murray	Cornwall	D
70	CHI	Terry Ruskowski	Swift Current	C
77	VAN	Mike Rogers	Calgary	C
85	TOR	Mike Palmateer	Toronto	G
125	PHI	Reggie Lemelin	Sherbrooke	G
199	MTL	Dave Lumley	New Hampshire	RW
214	NYI	Stefan Persson	Brynas Gavle	D

1973

FIRST ROUND

1	NYI	Denis Potvin	Ottawa	D
2	ATL	Tom Lysiak	Medicine Hat	C
3	VAN	Dennis Ververgaert	London	RW
4	TOR	Lanny McDonald	Medicine Hat	RW
5	STL	John Davidson	Calgary	G
6	BOS	Andre Savard	Quebec	C
7	PIT	Blaine Stoughton	Flin Flon	RW
8	MTL	Bob Gainey	Peterborough	LW
9	VAN	Bob Dailey	Toronto	D
10	TOR	Bob Neely	Peterborough	D
11	DET	Terry Richardson	New Westminster	G
12	BUF	Morris Titanic	Sudbury	LW
13	CHI	Darcy Rota	Edmonton	LW
14	NYR	Rick Middleton	Oshawa	RW
15	TOR	Ian Turnbull	Ottawa	D
16	ATL	Vic Mercredi	New Westminster	C

OTHER NOTABLE SELECTIONS

21	ATL	Eric Vail	Sudbury	LW
27	PIT	Colin Campbell	Peterborough	D
30	NYR	Pat Hickey	Hamilton	LW
33	NYI	Dave Lewis	Saskatoon	D
49	NYI	Andre St. Laurent	Montreal	C
85	ATL	Ken Houston	Chatham Jr. B	RW
130	CAL	Larry Patey	Braintree H.S.	C
134	PIT	Gord Lane	New Westminster	D
162	ATL	Greg Fox	U. of Michigan	D

1972

FIRST ROUND

1	NYI	Billy Harris	Toronto	RW
2	ATL	Jacques Richard	Quebec	LW
3	VAN	Don Lever	Niagara Falls	LW
4	MTL	Steve Shutt	Toronto	LW
5	BUF	Jim Schoenfeld	Niagara Falls	D
6	MTL	Michel Larocque	Ottawa	G
7	PHI	Bill Barber	Kitchener	LW
8	MTL	Dave Gardner	Toronto	C
9	STL	Wayne Merrick	Ottawa	C
10	NYR	Al Blanchard	Kitchener	LW
11	TOR	George Ferguson	Toronto	C
12	MIN	Jerry Byers	Kitchener	LW
13	CHI	Phil Russell	Edmonton	D
14	MTL	John Van Boxmeer	Guelph	D
15	NYR	Bob MacMillan	St. Catharines	RW
16	BOS	Mike Bloom	St. Catharines	LW

OTHER NOTABLE SELECTIONS

17	NYI	Lorne Henning	New Westminster	C
23	PHI	Tom Bladon	Edmonton	D
33	NYI	Bob Nystrom	Calgary	RW
39	PHI	Jimmy Watson	Calgary	D
55	PHI	Al MacAdam	U. of PEI	RW
85	BUF	Peter McNab	U. of Denver	C
97	NYI	Richard Brodeur	Cornwall	G
139	TOR	Pat Boutette	Minnesota-Duluth	C/RW
144	NYI	Garry Howatt	Flin Flon	LW

1971

FIRST ROUND

1	MTL	Guy Lafleur	Quebec	RW
2	DET	Marcel Dionne	St. Catharines	C
3	VAN	Jocelyn Guevremont	Montreal	D
4	STL	Gene Carr	Flin Flon	C
5	BUF	Rick Martin	Montreal	LW
6	BOS	Ron Jones	Edmonton	D
7	MTL	Chuck Arnason	Flin Flon	RW
8	PHI	Larry Wright	Regina	C
9	PHI	Pierre Plante	Drummondville	RW
10	NYR	Steve Vickers	Toronto	LW
11	MTL	Murray Wilson	Ottawa	LW
12	CHI	Dan Spring	Edmonton	C
13	NYR	Steve Durbano	Toronto	D
14	BOS	Terry O'Reilly	Oshawa	RW

OTHER NOTABLE SELECTIONS

17	VAN	Bobby Lalonde	Montreal	C
19	BUF	Craig Ramsay	Peterborough	LW
20	MTL	Larry Robinson	Kitchener	D
22	TOR	Rick Kehoe	Hamilton	RW
33	BUF	Bill Hajt	Saskatoon	D
48	L.A.	Neil Komadoski	Winnipeg	D
55	NYR	Jerry Butler	Hamilton	RW

1970

FIRST ROUND

1	BUF	Gilbert Perreault	Montreal	C
2	VAN	Dale Tallon	Toronto	D
3	BOS	Reggie Leach	Flin Flon	RW
4	BOS	Rick MacLeish	Peterborough	C
5	MTL	Ray Martyniuk	Flin Flon	G
6	MTL	Chuck Lefley	Canadian National	LW
7	PIT	Greg Polis	Estevan	LW
8	TOR	Darryl Sittler	London	C
9	BOS	Ron Plumb	Peterborough	D
10	CAL	Chris Oddleifson	Winnipeg	C
11	NYR	Norm Gratton	Montreal	LW
12	DET	Serge Lajeunesse	Montreal	D/RW
13	BOS	Bob Stewart	Oshawa	D
14	CHI	Dan Maloney	London	LW

OTHER NOTABLE SELECTIONS

18	PHI	Bill Clement	Ottawa	C
20	MIN	Fred Barrett	Toronto	D
22	TOR	Errol Thompson	Charlottetown Sr.	LW
25	NYR	Mike Murphy	Toronto	RW
27	BOS	Dan Bouchard	London	G
32	PHI	Bob Kelly	Oshawa	LW
40	DET	Yvon Lambert	Drummondville	LW
59	L.A.	Billy Smith	Cornwall	G
70	CHI	Gilles Meloche	Verdun	G
88	OAK	Terry Murray	Ottawa	D
103	TOR	Ron Low	Dauphin Jr. A	G

1969

FIRST ROUND

1	MTL	Rejean Houle	Montreal	W
2	MTL	Marc Tardif	Montreal	LW
3	BOS	Don Tannahill	Niagara Falls	LW
4	BOS	Frank Spring	Edmonton	RW
5	MIN	Dick Redmond	St. Catharines	D
6	PHI	Bob Currier	Cornwall	C
7	OAK	Tony Featherstone	Peterborough	RW
8	NYR	Andre Dupont	Montreal	D
9	TOR	Ernie Moser	Estevan	RW
10	DET	Jim Rutherford	Hamilton	G
11	BOS	Ivan Boldirev	Oshawa	C
12	NYR	Pierre Jarry	Ottawa	LW

OTHER NOTABLE SELECTIONS

13	CHI	J.P. Bordeleau	Montreal	RW
17	PHI	Bobby Clarke	Flin Flon	C
18	OAK	Ron Stackhouse	Peterborough	D
25	MIN	Gilles Gilbert	London	G
26	PIT	Michel Briere	Shawinigan	C
51	L.A.	Butch Goring	Dauphin Jr. A	C
52	PHI	Dave Schultz	Sorel	LW
55	TOR	Brian Spencer	Swift Current	LW
64	PHI	Don Saleski	Regina	RW

NHL All-Stars

Active Players' All-Star Selection Records

	Total	First Team Selections			Second Team Selections	
GOALTENDER						
Martin Brodeur	7	(3)	2002-03; 2003-04; 2006-07.	(4)	1996-97; 1997-98; 2005-06; 2007-08.	
Tim Thomas	2	(2)	2008-09; 2010-11.	(0)		
Roberto Luongo	2	(0)		(2)	2003-04; 2006-07.	
Miikka Kiprusoff	1	(1)	2005-06.	(0)		
Evgeni Nabokov	1	(1)	2007-08.	(0)		
Ryan Miller	1	(1)	2009-10.	(0)		
Chris Osgood	1	(0)		(1)	1995-96.	
Jose Theodore	1	(0)		(1)	2001-02.	
Marty Turco	1	(0)		(1)	2002-03.	
Steve Mason	1	(0)		(1)	2008-09.	
Ilya Bryzgalov	1	(0)		(1)	2009-10.	
Pekka Rinne	1	(0)		(1)	2010-11.	
DEFENSE						
Nicklas Lidstrom	12	(10)	1997-98; 1998-99; 99-2000; 2000-01; 2001-02; 2002-03; 2005-06; 2006-07; 2007-08; 2010-11.	(2)	2008-09; 2009-10.	
Zdeno Chara	5	(2)	2003-04; 2008-09.	(3)	2005-06; 2007-08; 2010-11.	
Chris Pronger	4	(1)	99-2000.	(3)	1997-98; 2003-04; 2006-07.	
Mike Green	2	(2)	2008-09; 2009-10.	(0)		
Sergei Gonchar	2	(0)		(2)	2001-02; 2002-03.	
Dan Boyle	2	(0)		(2)	2006-07; 2008-09.	
Dion Phaneuf	1	(1)	2007-08.	(0)		
Duncan Keith	1	(1)	2009-10.	(0)		
Shea Weber	1	(1)	2010-11.	(0)		
Bryan McCabe	1	(0)		(1)	2003-04.	
Brian Campbell	1	(0)		(1)	2007-08.	
Drew Doughty	1	(0)		(1)	2009-10.	
Lubomir Visnovsky	1	(0)		(1)	2010-11.	
CENTER						
Joe Thornton	3	(1)	2005-06.	(2)	2002-03; 2007-08.	
Evgeni Malkin	2	(2)	2007-08; 2008-09	(0)		
Henrik Sedin	2	(2)	2009-10; 2010-11.	(0)		
Sidney Crosby	2	(1)	2006-07.	(1)	2009-10.	
Mike Modano	1	(0)		(1)	99-2000.	
Eric Staal	1	(0)		(1)	2005-06.	
Vincent Lecavalier	1	(0)		(1)	2006-07.	
Pavel Datsyuk	1	(0)		(1)	2008-09.	
Steven Stamkos	1	(0)		(1)	2010-11.	
RIGHT WING						
Jaromir Jagr	8	(7)	1994-95; 1995-96; 1997-98 1998-99; 1999-00; 2000-01; 2005-06.	(1)	1996-97.	
Jarome Iginla	4	(3)	2001-02; 2007-08; 2008-09.	(1)	2003-04.	
Teemu Selanne	4	(2)	1992-93; 1996-97.	(2)	1997-98; 1998-99.	
Martin St. Louis	4	(1)	2003-04.	(3)	2006-07; 2009-10; 2010-11.	
Todd Bertuzzi	1	(1)	2002-03.	(0)		
Dany Heatley	1	(1)	2006-07.	(0)		
Patrick Kane	1	(1)	2009-10.	(0)		
Corey Perry	1	(1)	2010-11.	(0)		
Milan Hejduk	1	(0)		(1)	2002-03.	
Daniel Alfredsson	1	(0)		(1)	2005-06.	
Alex Kovalev	1	(0)		(1)	2007-08.	
Marian Hossa	1	(0)		(1)	2008-09.	
LEFT WING						
Alex Ovechkin	6	(5)	2005-06; 2006-07; 2007-08; 2008-09; 2009-10.	(1)	2010-11.	
Daniel Sedin	2	(1)	2010-11	(1)	2009-10.	
Patrik Elias	1	(1)	2000-01.	(0)		
Ilya Kovalchuk	1	(0)		(1)	2003-04.	
Dany Heatley	1	(0)		(1)	2005-06.	
Thomas Vanek	1	(0)		(1)	2006-07.	
Henrik Zetterberg	1	(0)		(1)	2007-08.	
Zach Parise	1	(0)		(1)	2008-09.	

Leading NHL All-Stars 1930-31 to 2010-11

Player	Pos.	Team(s)	Total Selections	First Team Selections	Second Team Selections	NHL Seasons
Gordie Howe	RW	Detroit	21	12	9	26
Raymond Bourque	D	Bos., Col.	19	13	6	22
Wayne Gretzky	C	Edm., L.A., NYR	15	8	7	20
Maurice Richard	RW	Montreal	14	8	6	18
Bobby Hull	LW	Chicago	12	10	2	16
* Nicklas Lidstrom	D	Detroit	12	10	2	19
Doug Harvey	D	Mtl., NYR	11	10	1	19
Glenn Hall	G	Det., Chi., St.L.	11	7	4	18
Jean Beliveau	C	Montreal	10	6	4	20
Earl Seibert	D	NYR, Chi.	10	4	6	15
Bobby Orr	D	Boston	9	8	1	12
Ted Lindsay	LW	Detroit	9	8	1	17
Mario Lemieux	C	Pittsburgh	9	5	4	17
Frank Mahovlich	LW	Tor., Det., Mtl.	9	3	6	18
Eddie Shore	D	Boston	8	7	1	14
* Jaromir Jagr	RW	Pit., NYR	8	7	1	17
Phil Esposito	C	Boston	8	6	2	18
Red Kelly	D	Detroit	8	6	2	20
Stan Mikita	C	Chicago	8	6	2	22
Mike Bossy	RW	NY Islanders	8	5	3	10
Pierre Pilote	D	Chicago	8	5	3	14
Luc Robitaille	LW	Los Angeles	8	5	3	19
Paul Coffey	D	Edm., Pit., Det.	8	4	4	21
Frank Brimsek	G	Boston	8	2	6	10
Denis Potvin	D	NY Islanders	7	5	2	15
Brad Park	D	NYR, Bos.	7	5	2	17
Chris Chelios	D	Mtl., Chi., Det.	7	5	2	25
Al MacInnis	D	Cgy., St.L.	7	4	3	23
Jacques Plante	G	Mtl., Tor.	7	3	4	18
Bill Gadsby	D	Chi., NYR, Det.	7	3	4	20
Terry Sawchuk	G	Detroit	7	3	4	21
* Martin Brodeur	G	New Jersey	7	3	4	18
Bill Durnan	G	Montreal	6	6	0	7
Dominik Hasek	G	Buffalo	6	6	0	15
Guy Lafleur	RW	Montreal	6	6	0	17
Ken Dryden	G	Montreal	6	5	1	8
Patrick Roy	G	Mtl., Col.	6	4	2	19
Dit Clapper	RW/D	Boston	6	3	3	20
Larry Robinson	D	Montreal	6	3	3	20
Tim Horton	D	Toronto	6	3	3	24
Borje Salming	D	Toronto	6	1	5	17
* Alex Ovechkin	LW	Washington	6	5	1	6
Bill Cowley	C	Boston	5	4	1	13
Busher Jackson	LW	Toronto	5	4	1	15
Mark Messier	LW/C	Edm., NYR	5	4	1	25
Charlie Conacher	RW	Toronto	5	3	2	12
Jack Stewart	D	Detroit	5	3	2	12
Toe Blake	LW	Montreal	5	3	2	14
Elmer Lach	C	Montreal	5	3	2	14
Bill Quackenbush	D	Det., Bos.	5	3	2	14
Michel Goulet	LW	Quebec	5	3	2	15
Paul Kariya	LW	Anaheim	5	3	2	15
Tony Esposito	G	Chicago	5	3	2	16
Ken Reardon	D	Montreal	5	2	3	7
Syl Apps	C	Toronto	5	2	3	10
Ed Giacomin	G	NY Rangers	5	2	3	13
* Zdeno Chara	D	Ott., Bos.	5	2	3	13
John LeClair	LW	Mtl., Phi.	5	2	3	16
Brian Leetch	D	NY Rangers	5	2	3	17
Jari Kurri	RW	Edmonton	5	2	3	17
Scott Stevens	D	Wsh., N.J.	5	2	3	21

* Active

Position Leaders in All-Star Selections

Position	Player	Total	First Team	Second Team	NHL Seasons	Career
GOALTENDER	Glenn Hall	11	7	4	18	1952-53 to 1970-71
	Frank Brimsek	8	2	6	10	1938-39 to 1949-50
	* Martin Brodeur	7	3	4	18	1991-92 to 2010-11
	Jacques Plante	7	3	4	18	1952-53 to 1972-73
	Terry Sawchuk	7	3	4	21	1949-50 to 1969-70
	Bill Durnan	6	6	0	7	1943-44 to 1949-50
	Dominik Hasek	6	6	0	15	1990-91 to 2007-08
	Ken Dryden	6	5	1	8	1970-71 to 1978-79
	Patrick Roy	6	4	2	19	1984-85 to 2002-03
DEFENSE	Raymond Bourque	19	13	6	22	1979-80 to 2000-01
	* Nicklas Lidstrom	12	10	2	19	1991-92 to 2010-11
	Doug Harvey	11	10	1	20	1947-48 to 1968-69
	Earl Seibert	10	4	6	15	1931-32 to 1945-46
	Bobby Orr	9	8	1	12	1966-67 to 1978-79
	Eddie Shore	8	7	1	14	1926-27 to 1939-40
	Red Kelly	8	6	2	20	1947-48 to 1966-67
	Pierre Pilote	8	5	3	14	1955-56 to 1968-69
	Paul Coffey	8	4	4	21	1980-81 to 2000-01
CENTER	Wayne Gretzky	15	8	7	20	1979-80 to 1998-99
	Jean Beliveau	10	6	4	20	1950-51 to 1970-71
	Mario Lemieux	9	5	4	18	1984-85 to 2005-06
	Phil Esposito	8	6	2	18	1963-64 to 1980-81
	Stan Mikita	8	6	2	22	1958-59 to 1979-80
RIGHT WING	Gordie Howe	21	12	9	26	1946-47 to 1979-80
	Maurice Richard	14	8	6	18	1942-43 to 1959-60
	* Jaromir Jagr	8	7	1	17	1990-91 to 2007-08
	Mike Bossy	8	5	3	10	1977-78 to 1986-87
	Guy Lafleur	6	6	0	17	1971-72 to 1990-91
LEFT WING	Bobby Hull	12	10	2	16	1957-58 to 1979-80
	Ted Lindsay	9	8	1	17	1944-45 to 1964-65
	Frank Mahovlich	9	3	6	18	1956-57 to 1973-74
	Luc Robitaille	8	5	3	19	1986-87 to 2005-06
	* Alex Ovechkin	6	5	1	6	2005-06 to 2010-11

* active player

All-Star Teams

1930-2011

Voting for the NHL All-Star Team is conducted among the representatives of the Professional Hockey Writers' Association at the end of the season.

Following is a list of the First and Second All-Star Teams since their inception in 1930-31.

2010-11

First Team	Pos	Second Team
Tim Thomas, Bos.	G	Pekka Rinne, Nsh.
Nicklas Lidstrom, Det.	D	Zdeno Chara, Bos.
Shea Weber, Nsh.	D	Lubomir Visnovsky, Ana.
Henrik Sedin, Van.	C	Steven Stamkos, T.B.
Corey Perry, Ana.	RW	Martin St. Louis, T.B.
Daniel Sedin, Van.	LW	Alex Ovechkin, Wsh.

2009-10

First Team	Pos	Second Team
Ryan Miller, Buf.	G	Ilya Bryzgalov, Phx.
Duncan Keith, Chi.	D	Drew Doughty, L.A..
Mike Green, Wsh.	D	Nicklas Lidstrom, Det.
Henrik Sedin, Van.	C	Sidney Crosby, Pit.
Patrick Kane, Chi.	RW	Martin St. Louis, T.B.
Alex Ovechkin, Wsh.	LW	Daniel Sedin, Van.

2008-09

First Team	Pos	Second Team
Tim Thomas, Bos.	G	Steve Mason, CBJ
Zdeno Chara, Bos	D	Nicklas Lidstrom, Det.
Mike Green, Wsh.	D	Dan Boyle, S.J.
Evgeni Malkin, Pit.	C	Pavel Datsyuk, Det.
Jarome Iginla, Cgy.	RW	Marian Hossa, Det.
Alex Ovechkin, Wsh.	LW	Zach Parise, N.J.

2007-08

First Team	Pos	Second Team
Evgeni Nabokov, S.J.	G	Martin Brodeur, N.J.
Nicklas Lidstrom, Det.	D	Brian Campbell, Buf., S.J.
Dion Phaneuf, Cgy.	D	Zdeno Chara, Bos.
Evgeni Malkin, Pit.	C	Joe Thornton, S.J.
Jarome Iginla, Cgy.	RW	Alex Kovalev, Mtl.
Alex Ovechkin, Wsh.	LW	Henrik Zetterberg, Det.

2006-07

First Team	Pos	Second Team
Martin Brodeur, N.J.	G	Roberto Luongo, Van.
Nicklas Lidstrom, Det.	D	Chris Pronger, Ana.
Scott Niedermayer, Ana.	D	Dan Boyle, T.B.
Sidney Crosby, Pit.	C	Vincent Lecavalier, T.B.
Dany Heatley, Ott.	RW	Martin St. Louis, T.B.
Alex Ovechkin, Wsh.	LW	Thomas Vanek, Buf.

2005-06

First Team	Pos	Second Team
Miikka Kiprusoff, Cgy.	G	Martin Brodeur, N.J.
Nicklas Lidstrom, Det.	D	Zdeno Chara, Ott.
Scott Niedermayer, Ana.	D	Sergei Zubov, Dal.
Joe Thornton, Bos., S.J.	C	Eric Staal, Car.
Jaromir Jagr, NYR	RW	Daniel Alfredsson, Ott.
Alex Ovechkin, Wsh.	LW	Dany Heatley, Ott.

2004-05

Season Cancelled

2003-04

First Team	Pos	Second Team
Martin Brodeur, N.J.	G	Roberto Luongo, Fla.
Scott Niedermayer, N.J.	D	Chris Pronger, St.L.
Zdeno Chara, Ott.	D	Bryan McCabe, Tor.
Joe Sakic, Col.	C	Mats Sundin, Tor.
Martin St. Louis, T.B.	RW	Jarome Iginla, Cgy.
Markus Naslund, Van.	LW	Ilya Kovalchuk, Atl.

2002-03

First Team	Pos	Second Team
Martin Brodeur, N.J.	G	Marty Turco, Dal.
Al MacInnis, St.L.	D	Sergei Gonchar, Wsh.
Nicklas Lidstrom, Det.	D	Derian Hatcher, Dal.
Peter Forsberg, Col.	C	Joe Thornton, Bos.
Todd Bertuzzi, Van.	RW	Milan Hejduk, Col.
Markus Naslund, Van.	LW	Paul Kariya, Ana.

2001-02

First Team	Pos	Second Team
Patrick Roy, Col.	G	Jose Theodore, Mtl.
Nicklas Lidstrom, Det.	D	Rob Blake, Col.
Chris Chelios, Det.	D	Sergei Gonchar, Wsh.
Joe Sakic, Col.	C	Mats Sundin, Tor.
Jarome Iginla, Cgy.	RW	Bill Guerin, Bos.
Markus Naslund, Van.	LW	Brendan Shanahan, Det.

2000-01

First Team	Pos	Second Team
Dominik Hasek, Buf.	G	Roman Cechmanek, Phi.
Nicklas Lidstrom, Det.	D	Rob Blake, L.A., Col.
Raymond Bourque, Col.	D	Scott Stevens, N.J.
Joe Sakic, Col.	C	Mario Lemieux, Pit.
Jaromir Jagr, Pit.	RW	Pavel Bure, Fla.
Patrik Elias, N.J.	LW	Luc Robitaille, L.A.

1999-2000

First Team	Pos	Second Team
Olaf Kolzig, Wsh.	G	Roman Turek, St.L.
Chris Pronger, St.L.	D	Rob Blake, L.A.
Nicklas Lidstrom, Det.	D	Eric Desjardins, Phi.
Steve Yzerman, Det.	C	Mike Modano, Dal.
Jaromir Jagr, Pit.	RW	Pavel Bure, Fla.
Brendan Shanahan, Det.	LW	Paul Kariya, Ana.

1998-99

First Team	Pos	Second Team
Dominik Hasek, Buf.	G	Byron Dafoe, Bos.
Al MacInnis, St.L.	D	Raymond Bourque, Bos.
Nicklas Lidstrom, Det.	D	Eric Desjardins, Phi.
Peter Forsberg, Col.	C	Alexei Yashin, Ott.
Jaromir Jagr, Pit.	RW	Teemu Selanne, Ana.
Paul Kariya, Ana.	LW	John LeClair, Phi.

1997-98

First Team	Pos	Second Team
Dominik Hasek, Buf.	G	Martin Brodeur, N.J.
Nicklas Lidstrom, Det.	D	Chris Pronger, St.L.
Rob Blake, L.A.	D	Scott Niedermayer, N.J.
Peter Forsberg, Col.	C	Wayne Gretzky, NYR
Jaromir Jagr, Pit.	RW	Teemu Selanne, Ana.
John LeClair, Phi.	LW	Keith Tkachuk, Phx.

1996-97

First Team	Pos	Second Team
Dominik Hasek, Buf.	G	Martin Brodeur, N.J.
Brian Leetch, NYR	D	Chris Chelios, Chi.
Sandis Ozolinsh, Col.	D	Scott Stevens, N.J.
Mario Lemieux, Pit.	C	Wayne Gretzky, NYR
Teemu Selanne, Ana.	RW	Jaromir Jagr, Pit.
Paul Kariya, Ana.	LW	John LeClair, Phi.

1995-96

First Team	Pos	Second Team
Jim Carey, Wsh.	G	Chris Osgood, Det.
Chris Chelios, Chi.	D	V. Konstantinov, Det.
Raymond Bourque, Bos.	D	Brian Leetch, NYR
Mario Lemieux, Pit.	C	Eric Lindros, Phi.
Jaromir Jagr, Pit.	RW	Alexander Mogilny, Van.
Paul Kariya, Ana.	LW	John LeClair, Phi.

1994-95

First Team	Pos	Second Team
Dominik Hasek, Buf.	G	Ed Belfour, Chi.
Paul Coffey, Det.	D	Raymond Bourque, Bos.
Chris Chelios, Chi.	D	Larry Murphy, Pit.
Eric Lindros, Phi.	C	Alexei Zhamnov, Wpg.
Jaromir Jagr, Pit.	RW	Theoren Fleury, Cgy.
John LeClair, Mtl., Phi.	LW	Keith Tkachuk, Wpg.

1993-94

First Team	Pos	Second Team
Dominik Hasek, Buf.	G	John Vanbiesbrouck, Fla.
Raymond Bourque, Bos.	D	Al MacInnis, Cgy.
Scott Stevens, N.J.	D	Brian Leetch, NYR
Sergei Fedorov, Det.	C	Wayne Gretzky, L.A.
Pavel Bure, Van.	RW	Cam Neely, Bos.
Brendan Shanahan, St.L.	LW	Adam Graves, NYR

1992-93

First Team	Pos	Second Team
Ed Belfour, Chi.	G	Tom Barrasso, Pit.
Chris Chelios, Chi.	D	Larry Murphy, Pit.
Raymond Bourque, Bos.	D	Al Iafrate, Wsh.
Mario Lemieux, Pit.	C	Pat LaFontaine, Buf.
Teemu Selanne, Wpg.	RW	Alexander Mogilny, Buf.
Luc Robitaille, L.A.	LW	Kevin Stevens, Pit.

1991-92

First Team	Pos	Second Team
Patrick Roy, Mtl.	G	Kirk McLean, Van.
Brian Leetch, NYR	D	Phil Housley, Wpg.
Raymond Bourque, Bos.	D	Scott Stevens, N.J.
Mark Messier, NYR	C	Mario Lemieux, Pit.
Brett Hull, St.L.	RW	Mark Recchi, Pit., Phi.
Kevin Stevens, Pit.	LW	Luc Robitaille, L.A.

1990-91

First Team	Pos	Second Team
Ed Belfour, Chi.	G	Patrick Roy, Mtl.
Raymond Bourque, Bos.	D	Chris Chelios, Chi.
Al MacInnis, Cgy.	D	Brian Leetch, NYR
Wayne Gretzky, L.A.	C	Adam Oates, St.L.
Brett Hull, St.L.	RW	Cam Neely, Bos.
Luc Robitaille, L.A.	LW	Kevin Stevens, Pit.

1989-90

First Team	Pos	Second Team
Patrick Roy, Mtl.	G	Daren Puppa, Buf.
Raymond Bourque, Bos.	D	Paul Coffey, Pit.
Al MacInnis, Cgy.	D	Doug Wilson, Chi.
Mark Messier, Edm.	C	Wayne Gretzky, L.A.
Brett Hull, St.L.	RW	Cam Neely, Bos.
Luc Robitaille, L.A.	LW	Brian Bellows, Min.

1988-89

First Team	Pos	Second Team
Patrick Roy, Mtl.	G	Mike Vernon, Cgy.
Chris Chelios, Mtl.	D	Al MacInnis, Cgy.
Paul Coffey, Pit.	D	Raymond Bourque, Bos.
Mario Lemieux, Pit.	C	Wayne Gretzky, L.A.
Joe Mullen, Cgy.	RW	Jari Kurri, Edm.
Luc Robitaille, L.A.	LW	Gerard Gallant, Det.

1987-88

First Team	Pos	Second Team
Grant Fuhr, Edm.	G	Patrick Roy, Mtl.
Raymond Bourque, Bos.	D	Gary Suter, Cgy.
Scott Stevens, Wsh.	D	Brad McCrimmon, Cgy.
Mario Lemieux, Pit.	C	Wayne Gretzky, Edm.
Hakan Loob, Cgy.	RW	Cam Neely, Bos.
Luc Robitaille, L.A.	LW	Michel Goulet, Que.

1986-87

First Team	Pos	Second Team
Ron Hextall, Phi.	G	Mike Liut, Hfd.
Raymond Bourque, Bos.	D	Larry Murphy, Wsh.
Mark Howe, Phi.	D	Al MacInnis, Cgy.
Wayne Gretzky, Edm.	C	Mario Lemieux, Pit.
Jari Kurri, Edm.	RW	Tim Kerr, Phi.
Michel Goulet, Que.	LW	Luc Robitaille, L.A.

1985-86

First Team	Pos	Second Team
John Vanbiesbrouck, NYR	G	Bob Froese, Phi.
Paul Coffey, Edm.	D	Larry Robinson, Mtl.
Mark Howe, Phi.	D	Raymond Bourque, Bos.
Wayne Gretzky, Edm.	C	Mario Lemieux, Pit.
Mike Bossy, NYI	RW	Jari Kurri, Edm.
Michel Goulet, Que.	LW	Mats Naslund, Mtl.

1984-85

First Team	Pos	Second Team
Pelle Lindbergh, Phi.	G	Tom Barrasso, Buf.
Paul Coffey, Edm.	D	Rod Langway, Wsh.
Raymond Bourque, Bos.	D	Doug Wilson, Chi.
Wayne Gretzky, Edm.	C	Dale Hawerchuk, Wpg.
Jari Kurri, Edm.	RW	Mike Bossy, NYI
John Ogrodnick, Det.	LW	John Tonelli, NYI

1983-84

First Team	Pos	Second Team
Tom Barrasso, Buf.	G	Pat Riggin, Wsh.
Rod Langway, Wsh.	D	Paul Coffey, Edm.
Raymond Bourque, Bos.	D	Denis Potvin, NYI
Wayne Gretzky, Edm.	C	Bryan Trottier, NYI
Mike Bossy, NYI	RW	Jari Kurri, Edm.
Michel Goulet, Que.	LW	Mark Messier, Edm.

1982-83

First Team	Pos	Second Team
Pete Peeters, Bos.	G	Roland Melanson, NYI
Mark Howe, Phi.	D	Raymond Bourque, Bos.
Rod Langway, Wsh.	D	Paul Coffey, Edm.
Wayne Gretzky, Edm.	C	Denis Savard, Chi.
Mike Bossy, NYI	RW	Lanny McDonald, Cgy.
Mark Messier, Edm.	LW	Michel Goulet, Que.

1981-82

First Team	Pos	Second Team
Billy Smith, NYI	G	Grant Fuhr, Edm.
Doug Wilson, Chi.	D	Paul Coffey, Edm.
Raymond Bourque, Bos.	D	Brian Engblom, Mtl.
Wayne Gretzky, Edm.	C	Bryan Trottier, NYI
Mike Bossy, NYI	RW	Rick Middleton, Bos.
Mark Messier, Edm.	LW	John Tonelli, NYI

1980-81

First Team	Pos	Second Team
Mike Liut, St.L.	G	Mario Lessard, L.A.
Denis Potvin, NYI	D	Larry Robinson, Mtl.
Randy Carlyle, Pit.	D	Raymond Bourque, Bos.
Wayne Gretzky, Edm.	C	Marcel Dionne, L.A.
Mike Bossy, NYI	RW	Dave Taylor, L.A.
Charlie Simmer, L.A.	LW	Bill Barber, Phi.

1979-80

First Team	Pos	Second Team
Tony Esposito, Chi.	G	Don Edwards, Buf.
Larry Robinson, Mtl.	D	Borje Salming, Tor.
Raymond Bourque, Bos.	D	Jim Schoenfeld, Buf.
Marcel Dionne, L.A.	C	Wayne Gretzky, Edm.
Guy Lafleur, Mtl.	RW	Danny Gare, Buf.
Charlie Simmer, L.A.	LW	Steve Shutt, Mtl.

1978-79

First Team	Pos	Second Team
Ken Dryden, Mtl.	G	Glenn Resch, NYI
Denis Potvin, NYI	D	Borje Salming, Tor.
Larry Robinson, Mtl.	D	Serge Savard, Mtl.
Bryan Trottier, NYI	C	Marcel Dionne, L.A.
Guy Lafleur, Mtl.	RW	Mike Bossy, NYI
Clark Gillies, NYI	LW	Bill Barber, Phi.

1977-78

First Team	Pos	Second Team
Ken Dryden, Mtl.	G	Don Edwards, Buf.
Denis Potvin, NYI	D	Larry Robinson, Mtl.
Brad Park, Bos.	D	Borje Salming, Tor.
Bryan Trottier, NYI	C	Darryl Sittler, Tor.
Guy Lafleur, Mtl.	RW	Mike Bossy, NYI
Clark Gillies, NYI	LW	Steve Shutt, Mtl.

1976-77

First Team	Pos	Second Team
Ken Dryden, Mtl.	G	Rogie Vachon, L.A.
Larry Robinson, Mtl.	D	Denis Potvin, NYI
Borje Salming, Tor.	D	Guy Lapointe, Mtl.
Marcel Dionne, L.A.	C	Gilbert Perreault, Buf.
Guy Lafleur, Mtl.	RW	Lanny McDonald, Tor.
Steve Shutt, Mtl.	LW	Rick Martin, Buf.

1975-76

First Team	Pos	Second Team
Ken Dryden, Mtl.	G	Glenn Resch, NYI
Denis Potvin, NYI	D	Borje Salming, Tor.
Brad Park, Bos.	D	Guy Lapointe, Mtl.
Bobby Clarke, Phi.	C	Gilbert Perreault, Buf.
Guy Lafleur, Mtl.	RW	Reggie Leach, Phi.
Bill Barber, Phi.	LW	Rick Martin, Buf.

1974-75

First Team	Pos	Second Team
Bernie Parent, Phi.	G	Rogie Vachon, L.A.
Bobby Orr, Bos.	D	Guy Lapointe, Mtl.
Denis Potvin, NYI	D	Borje Salming, Tor.
Bobby Clarke, Phi.	C	Phil Esposito, Bos.
Guy Lafleur, Mtl.	RW	René Robert, Buf.
Rick Martin, Buf.	LW	Steve Vickers, NYR

1973-74

First Team	Pos	Second Team
Bernie Parent, Phi.	G	Tony Esposito, Chi.
Bobby Orr, Bos.	D	Bill White, Chi.
Brad Park, NYR	D	Barry Ashbee, Phi.
Phil Esposito, Bos.	C	Bobby Clarke, Phi.
Ken Hodge, Bos.	RW	Mickey Redmond, Det.
Rick Martin, Buf.	LW	Wayne Cashman, Bos.

1972-73

First Team	Pos	Second Team
Ken Dryden, Mtl.	G	Tony Esposito, Chi.
Bobby Orr, Bos.	D	Brad Park, NYR
Guy Lapointe, Mtl.	D	Bill White, Chi.
Phil Esposito, Bos.	C	Bobby Clarke, Phi.
Mickey Redmond, Det.	RW	Yvan Cournoyer, Mtl.
Frank Mahovlich, Mtl.	LW	Dennis Hull, Chi.

1971-72

First Team	Pos	Second Team
Tony Esposito, Chi.	G	Ken Dryden, Mtl.
Bobby Orr, Bos.	D	Bill White, Chi.
Brad Park, NYR	D	Pat Stapleton, Chi.
Phil Esposito, Bos.	C	Jean Ratelle, NYR
Rod Gilbert, NYR	RW	Yvan Cournoyer, Mtl.
Bobby Hull, Chi.	LW	Vic Hadfield, NYR

1970-71

First Team	Pos	Second Team
Ed Giacomin, NYR	G	Jacques Plante, Tor.
Bobby Orr, Bos.	D	Brad Park, NYR
J.C. Tremblay, Mtl.	D	Pat Stapleton, Chi.
Phil Esposito, Bos.	C	Dave Keon, Tor.
Ken Hodge, Bos.	RW	Yvan Cournoyer, Mtl.
John Bucyk, Bos.	LW	Bobby Hull, Chi.

1969-70

First Team	Pos	Second Team
Tony Esposito, Chi.	G	Ed Giacomin, NYR
Bobby Orr, Bos.	D	Carl Brewer, Det.
Brad Park, NYR	D	Jacques Laperriere, Mtl.
Phil Esposito, Bos.	C	Stan Mikita, Chi.
Gordie Howe, Det.	RW	John McKenzie, Bos.
Bobby Hull, Chi.	LW	Frank Mahovlich, Det.

1968-69

First Team	Pos	Second Team
Glenn Hall, St.L.	G	Ed Giacomin, NYR
Bobby Orr, Bos.	D	Ted Green, Bos.
Tim Horton, Tor.	D	Ted Harris, Mtl.
Phil Esposito, Bos.	C	Jean Béliveau, Mtl.
Gordie Howe, Det.	RW	Yvan Cournoyer, Mtl.
Bobby Hull, Chi.	LW	Frank Mahovlich, Det.

1967-68

First Team	Pos	Second Team
Gump Worsley, Mtl.	G	Ed Giacomin, NYR
Bobby Orr, Bos.	D	J.C. Tremblay, Mtl.
Tim Horton, Tor.	D	Jim Neilson, Mtl.
Stan Mikita, Chi.	C	Phil Esposito, Bos.
Gordie Howe, Det.	RW	Rod Gilbert, NYR
Bobby Hull, Chi.	LW	John Bucyk, Bos.

1966-67

First Team	Pos	Second Team
Ed Giacomin, NYR	G	Glenn Hall, Chi.
Pierre Pilote, Chi.	D	Tim Horton, Tor.
Harry Howell, NYR	D	Bobby Orr, Bos.
Stan Mikita, Chi.	C	Norm Ullman, Det.
Kenny Wharram, Chi.	RW	Gordie Howe, Det.
Bobby Hull, Chi.	LW	Don Marshall, NYR

1965-66

First Team	Pos	Second Team
Glenn Hall, Chi.	G	Gump Worsley, Mtl.
Jacques Laperriere, Mtl.	D	Allan Stanley, Tor.
Pierre Pilote, Chi.	D	Pat Stapleton, Chi.
Stan Mikita, Chi.	C	Jean Béliveau, Mtl.
Gordie Howe, Det.	RW	Bobby Rousseau, Mtl.
Bobby Hull, Chi.	LW	Frank Mahovlich, Tor.

1964-65

First Team	Pos	Second Team
Roger Crozier, Det.	G	Charlie Hodge, Mtl.
Pierre Pilote, Chi.	D	Bill Gadsby, Det.
Jacques Laperriere, Mtl.	D	Carl Brewer, Tor.
Norm Ullman, Det.	C	Stan Mikita, Chi.
Claude Provost, Mtl.	RW	Gordie Howe, Det.
Bobby Hull, Chi.	LW	Frank Mahovlich, Tor.

1963-64

First Team	Pos	Second Team
Glenn Hall, Chi.	G	Charlie Hodge, Mtl.
Pierre Pilote, Chi.	D	Moose Vasko, Chi.
Tim Horton, Tor.	D	Jacques Laperriere, Mtl.
Stan Mikita, Chi.	C	Jean Béliveau, Mtl.
Kenny Wharram, Chi.	RW	Gordie Howe, Det.
Bobby Hull, Chi.	LW	Frank Mahovlich, Tor.

1962-63

First Team	Pos	Second Team
Glenn Hall, Chi.	G	Terry Sawchuk, Det.
Pierre Pilote, Chi.	D	Tim Horton, Tor.
Carl Brewer, Tor.	D	Moose Vasko, Chi.
Stan Mikita, Chi.	C	Henri Richard, Mtl.
Gordie Howe, Det.	RW	Andy Bathgate, NYR
Frank Mahovlich, Tor.	LW	Bobby Hull, Chi.

1961-62

First Team	Pos	Second Team
Jacques Plante, Mtl.	G	Glenn Hall, Chi.
Doug Harvey, NYR	D	Carl Brewer, Tor.
Jean-Guy Talbot, Mtl.	D	Pierre Pilote, Chi.
Stan Mikita, Chi.	C	Dave Keon, Tor.
Andy Bathgate, NYR	RW	Gordie Howe, Det.
Bobby Hull, Chi.	LW	Frank Mahovlich, Tor.

1960-61

First Team	Pos	Second Team
Johnny Bower, Tor.	G	Glenn Hall, Chi.
Doug Harvey, Mtl.	D	Allan Stanley, Tor.
Marcel Pronovost, Det.	D	Pierre Pilote, Chi.
Jean Béliveau, Mtl.	C	Henri Richard, Mtl.
Bernie Geoffrion, Mtl.	RW	Gordie Howe, Det.
Frank Mahovlich, Tor.	LW	Dickie Moore, Mtl.

1959-60

First Team	Pos	Second Team
Glenn Hall, Chi.	G	Jacques Plante, Mtl.
Doug Harvey, Mtl.	D	Allan Stanley, Tor.
Marcel Pronovost, Det.	D	Pierre Pilote, Chi.
Jean Béliveau, Mtl.	C	Bronco Horvath, Bos.
Gordie Howe, Det.	RW	Bernie Geoffrion, Mtl.
Bobby Hull, Chi.	LW	Dean Prentice, NYR

1958-59

First Team	Pos	Second Team
Jacques Plante, Mtl.	G	Terry Sawchuk, Det.
Tom Johnson, Mtl.	D	Marcel Pronovost, Det.
Bill Gadsby, NYR	D	Doug Harvey, Mtl.
Jean Béliveau, Mtl.	C	Henri Richard, Mtl.
Andy Bathgate, NYR	RW	Gordie Howe, Det.
Dickie Moore, Mtl.	LW	Alex Delvecchio, Det.

1957-58

First Team	Pos	Second Team
Glenn Hall, Chi.	G	Jacques Plante, Mtl.
Doug Harvey, Mtl.	D	Fern Flaman, Bos.
Bill Gadsby, NYR	D	Marcel Pronovost, Det.
Henri Richard, Mtl.	C	Jean Béliveau, Mtl.
Gordie Howe, Det.	RW	Andy Bathgate, NYR
Dickie Moore, Mtl.	LW	Camille Henry, NYR

1956-57

First Team		Second Team
Glenn Hall, Det.	G	Jacques Plante, Mtl.
Doug Harvey, Mtl.	D	Fern Flaman, Bos.
Red Kelly, Det.	D	Bill Gadsby, NYR
Jean Béliveau, Mtl.	C	Ed Litzenberger, Chi.
Gordie Howe, Det.	RW	Maurice Richard, Mtl.
Ted Lindsay, Det.	LW	Real Chevrefils, Bos.

1955-56

First Team		Second Team
Jacques Plante, Mtl.	G	Glenn Hall, Det.
Doug Harvey, Mtl.	D	Red Kelly, Det.
Bill Gadsby, NYR	D	Tom Johnson, Mtl.
Jean Béliveau, Mtl.	C	Tod Sloan, Tor.
Maurice Richard, Mtl.	RW	Gordie Howe, Det.
Ted Lindsay, Det.	LW	Bert Olmstead, Mtl.

1954-55

First Team		Second Team
Harry Lumley, Tor.	G	Terry Sawchuk, Det.
Doug Harvey, Mtl.	D	Bob Goldham, Det.
Red Kelly, Det.	D	Fern Flaman, Bos.
Jean Béliveau, Mtl.	C	Ken Mosdell, Mtl.
Maurice Richard, Mtl.	RW	Bernie Geoffrion, Mtl.
Sid Smith, Tor.	LW	Danny Lewicki, NYR

1953-54

First Team		Second Team
Harry Lumley, Tor.	G	Terry Sawchuk, Det.
Red Kelly, Det.	D	Bill Gadsby, Chi.
Doug Harvey, Mtl.	D	Tim Horton, Tor.
Ken Mosdell, Mtl.	C	Ted Kennedy, Tor.
Gordie Howe, Det.	RW	Maurice Richard, Mtl.
Ted Lindsay, Det.	LW	Ed Sandford, Bos.

1952-53

First Team		Second Team
Terry Sawchuk, Det.	G	Gerry McNeil, Mtl.
Red Kelly, Det.	D	Bill Quackenbush, Bos.
Doug Harvey, Mtl.	D	Bill Gadsby, Chi.
Fleming Mackell, Bos.	C	Alex Delvecchio, Det.
Gordie Howe, Det.	RW	Maurice Richard, Mtl.
Ted Lindsay, Det.	LW	Bert Olmstead, Mtl.

1951-52

First Team		Second Team
Terry Sawchuk, Det.	G	Jim Henry, Bos.
Red Kelly, Det.	D	Hy Buller, NYR
Doug Harvey, Mtl.	D	Jimmy Thomson, Tor.
Elmer Lach, Mtl.	C	Milt Schmidt, Bos.
Gordie Howe, Det.	RW	Maurice Richard, Mtl.
Ted Lindsay, Det.	LW	Sid Smith, Tor.

1950-51

First Team		Second Team
Terry Sawchuk, Det.	G	Chuck Rayner, NYR
Red Kelly, Det.	D	Jimmy Thomson, Tor.
Bill Quackenbush, Bos.	D	Leo Reise Jr., Det.
Milt Schmidt, Bos.	C	Sid Abel, Det.
		Ted Kennedy, Tor. (tied)
Gordie Howe, Det.	RW	Maurice Richard, Mtl.
Ted Lindsay, Det.	LW	Sid Smith, Tor.

1949-50

First Team		Second Team
Bill Durnan, Mtl.	G	Chuck Rayner, NYR
Gus Mortson, Tor.	D	Leo Reise Jr., Det.
Ken Reardon, Mtl.	D	Red Kelly, Det.
Sid Abel, Det.	C	Ted Kennedy, Tor.
Maurice Richard, Mtl.	RW	Gordie Howe, Det.
Ted Lindsay, Det.	LW	Tony Leswick, NYR

1948-49

First Team		Second Team
Bill Durnan, Mtl.	G	Chuck Rayner, NYR
Bill Quackenbush, Det.	D	Glen Harmon, Mtl.
Jack Stewart, Det.	D	Ken Reardon, Mtl.
Sid Abel, Det.	C	Doug Bentley, Chi.
Maurice Richard, Mtl.	RW	Gordie Howe, Det.
Roy Conacher, Chi.	LW	Ted Lindsay, Det.

1947-48

First Team		Second Team
Turk Broda, Tor.	G	Frank Brimsek, Bos.
Bill Quackenbush, Det.	D	Ken Reardon, Mtl.
Jack Stewart, Det.	D	Neil Colville, NYR
Elmer Lach, Mtl.	C	Buddy O'Connor, NYR
Maurice Richard, Mtl.	RW	Bud Poile, Chi.
Ted Lindsay, Det.	LW	Gaye Stewart, Chi.

1946-47

First Team		Second Team
Bill Durnan, Mtl.	G	Frank Brimsek, Bos.
Ken Reardon, Mtl.	D	Jack Stewart, Det.
Butch Bouchard, Mtl.	D	Bill Quackenbush, Det.
Milt Schmidt, Bos.	C	Max Bentley, Chi.
Maurice Richard, Mtl.	RW	Bobby Bauer, Bos.
Doug Bentley, Chi.	LW	Woody Dumart, Bos.

1945-46

First Team		Second Team
Bill Durnan, Mtl.	G	Frank Brimsek, Bos.
Jack Crawford, Bos.	D	Ken Reardon, Mtl.
Butch Bouchard, Mtl.	D	Jack Stewart, Det.
Max Bentley, Chi.	C	Elmer Lach, Mtl.
Maurice Richard, Mtl.	RW	Bill Mosienko, Chi.
Gaye Stewart, Tor.	LW	Toe Blake, Mtl.
Dick Irvin, Mtl.	Coach	Johnny Gottselig, Chi.

1944-45

First Team		Second Team
Bill Durnan, Mtl.	G	Mike Karakas, Chi.
Butch Bouchard, Mtl.	D	Glen Harmon, Mtl.
Flash Hollett, Det.	D	Babe Pratt, Tor.
Elmer Lach, Mtl.	C	Bill Cowley, Bos.
Maurice Richard, Mtl.	RW	Bill Mosienko, Chi.
Toe Blake, Mtl.	LW	Syd Howe, Det.
Dick Irvin, Mtl.	Coach	Jack Adams, Det.

1943-44

First Team		Second Team
Bill Durnan, Mtl.	G	Paul Bibeault, Tor.
Earl Seibert, Chi.	D	Butch Bouchard, Mtl.
Babe Pratt, Tor.	D	Dit Clapper, Bos.
Bill Cowley, Bos.	C	Elmer Lach, Mtl.
Lorne Carr, Tor.	RW	Maurice Richard, Mtl.
Doug Bentley, Chi.	LW	Herb Cain, Bos.
Dick Irvin, Mtl.	Coach	Hap Day, Tor.

1942-43

First Team		Second Team
Johnny Mowers, Det.	G	Frank Brimsek, Bos.
Earl Seibert, Chi.	D	Jack Crawford, Bos.
Jack Stewart, Det.	D	Flash Hollett, Det.
Bill Cowley, Bos.	C	Syl Apps, Tor.
Lorne Carr, Tor.	RW	Bryan Hextall, NYR
Doug Bentley, Chi.	LW	Lynn Patrick, NYR
Jack Adams, Det.	Coach	Art Ross, Bos.

1941-42

First Team		Second Team
Frank Brimsek, Bos.	G	Turk Broda, Tor.
Earl Seibert, Chi.	D	Pat Egan, Bro.
Tom Anderson, Bro.	D	Bucko McDonald, Tor.
Syl Apps, Tor.	C	Phil Watson, NYR
Bryan Hextall, NYR	RW	Gordie Drillon, Tor.
Lynn Patrick, NYR	LW	Sid Abel, Det.
Frank Boucher, NYR	Coach	Paul Thompson, Chi.

1940-41

First Team		Second Team
Turk Broda, Tor.	G	Frank Brimsek, Bos.
Dit Clapper, Bos.	D	Earl Seibert, Chi.
Wally Stanowski, Tor.	D	Ott Heller, NYR
Bill Cowley, Bos.	C	Syl Apps, Tor.
Bryan Hextall, NYR	RW	Bobby Bauer, Bos.
Sweeney Schriner, Tor.	LW	Woody Dumart, Bos.
Cooney Weiland, Bos.	Coach	Dick Irvin, Mtl.

1939-40

First Team		Second Team
Dave Kerr, NYR	G	Frank Brimsek, Bos.
Dit Clapper, Bos.	D	Art Coulter, NYR
Ebbie Goodfellow, Det.	D	Earl Seibert, Chi.
Milt Schmidt, Bos.	C	Neil Colville, NYR
Bryan Hextall, NYR	RW	Bobby Bauer, Bos.
Toe Blake, Mtl.	LW	Woody Dumart, Bos.
Paul Thompson, Chi.	Coach	Frank Boucher, NYR

1938-39

First Team		Second Team
Frank Brimsek, Bos.	G	Earl Robertson, NYA
Eddie Shore, Bos.	D	Earl Seibert, Chi.
Dit Clapper, Bos.	D	Art Coulter, NYR
Syl Apps, Tor.	C	Neil Colville, NYR
Gordie Drillon, Tor.	RW	Bobby Bauer, Bos.
Toe Blake, Mtl.	LW	Johnny Gottselig, Chi.
Art Ross, Bos.	Coach	Red Dutton, NYA

1937-38

First Team		Second Team
Tiny Thompson, Bos.	G	Dave Kerr, NYR
Eddie Shore, Bos.	D	Art Coulter, NYR
Babe Siebert, Mtl.	D	Earl Seibert, Chi.
Bill Cowley, Bos.	C	Syl Apps, Tor.
Cecil Dillon, NYR	RW	
Gordie Drillon, Tor. *(tied)*		
Paul Thompson, Chi.	LW	Toe Blake, Mtl.
Lester Patrick, NYR	Coach	Art Ross, Bos.

1936-37

First Team		Second Team
Normie Smith, Det.	G	Wilf Cude, Mtl.
Babe Siebert, Mtl.	D	Earl Seibert, Chi.
Ebbie Goodfellow, Det.	D	Lionel Conacher, Mtl. M.
Marty Barry, Det.	C	Art Chapman, NYA
Larry Aurie, Det.	RW	Cecil Dillon, NYR
Busher Jackson, Tor.	LW	Sweeney Schriner, NYA
Jack Adams, Det.	Coach	Cecil Hart, Mtl.

1935-36

First Team		Second Team
Tiny Thompson, Bos.	G	Wilf Cude, Mtl.
Eddie Shore, Bos.	D	Earl Seibert, Chi.
Babe Siebert, Bos.	D	Ebbie Goodfellow, Det.
Hooley Smith, Mtl. M.	C	Bill Thoms, Tor.
Charlie Conacher, Tor.	RW	Cecil Dillon, NYR
Sweeney Schriner, NYA	LW	Paul Thompson, Chi.
Lester Patrick, NYR	Coach	Tommy Gorman, Mtl. M.

1934-35

First Team		Second Team
Lorne Chabot, Chi.	G	Tiny Thompson, Bos.
Eddie Shore, Bos.	D	Cy Wentworth, Mtl. M.
Earl Seibert, NYR	D	Art Coulter, Chi.
Frank Boucher, NYR	C	Cooney Weiland, Det.
Charlie Conacher, Tor.	RW	Dit Clapper, Bos.
Busher Jackson, Tor.	LW	Aurel Joliat, Mtl.
Lester Patrick, NYR	Coach	Dick Irvin, Tor.

1933-34

First Team		Second Team
Charlie Gardiner, Chi.	G	Roy Worters, NYA
King Clancy, Tor.	D	Eddie Shore, Bos.
Lionel Conacher, Chi.	D	Ching Johnson, NYR
Frank Boucher, NYR	C	Joe Primeau, Tor.
Charlie Conacher, Tor.	RW	Bill Cook, NYR
Busher Jackson, Tor.	LW	Aurel Joliat, Mtl.
Lester Patrick, NYR	Coach	Dick Irvin, Tor.

1932-33

First Team		Second Team
John Ross Roach, Det.	G	Charlie Gardiner, Chi.
Eddie Shore, Bos.	D	King Clancy, Tor.
Ching Johnson, NYR	D	Lionel Conacher, Mtl. M.
Frank Boucher, NYR	C	Howie Morenz, Mtl.
Bill Cook, NYR	RW	Charlie Conacher, Tor.
Baldy Northcott, Mtl. M.	LW	Busher Jackson, Tor.
Lester Patrick, NYR	Coach	Dick Irvin, Tor.

1931-32

First Team		Second Team
Charlie Gardiner, Chi.	G	Roy Worters, NYA
Eddie Shore, Bos.	D	Sylvio Mantha, Mtl.
Ching Johnson, NYR	D	King Clancy, Tor.
Howie Morenz, Mtl.	C	Hooley Smith, Mtl. M.
Bill Cook, NYR	RW	Charlie Conacher, Tor.
Busher Jackson, Tor.	LW	Aurel Joliat, Mtl.
Lester Patrick, NYR	Coach	Dick Irvin, Tor.

1930-31

First Team		Second Team
Charlie Gardiner, Chi.	G	Tiny Thompson, Bos.
Eddie Shore, Bos.	D	Sylvio Mantha, Mtl.
King Clancy, Tor.	D	Ching Johnson, NYR
Howie Morenz, Mtl.	C	Frank Boucher, NYR
Bill Cook, NYR	RW	Dit Clapper, Bos.
Aurel Joliat, Mtl.	LW	Bun Cook, NYR
Lester Patrick, NYR	Coach	Dick Irvin, Chi.

NHL ALL-ROOKIE TEAM

Voting for the NHL All-Rookie Team is conducted among the representatives of the Professional Hockey Writers' Association at the end of the season. The rookie all-star team was first selected for the 1982-83 season.

	2010-11
Goal	Corey Crawford, Chicago
Defense	John Carlson, Washington
Defense	P.K. Subban, Montreal
Forward	Logan Couture, San Jose
Forward	Michael Grabner, NY Islanders
Forward	Jeff Skinner, Carolina

	2009-10
Goal	Jimmy Howard, Detroit
Defense	Tyler Myers, Buffalo
Defense	Michael Del Zotto, NY Rangers
Forward	John Tavares, NY Islanders
Forward	Matt Duchene, Colorado
Forward	Niclas Bergfors, N.J., Atl.

	2008-09
Goal	Steve Mason, Columbus
Defense	Drew Doughty, Los Angeles
Defense	Luke Schenn, Toronto
Forward	Patrik Berglund, St. Louis
Forward	Bobby Ryan, Anaheim
Forward	Kris Versteeg, Chicago

	2007-08
Goal	Carey Price, Montreal
Defense	Tobias Enstrom, Atlanta
Defense	Tom Gilbert, Edmonton
Forward	Nicklas Backstrom, Washington
Forward	Patrick Kane, Chicago
Forward	Jonathan Toews, Chicago

	2006-07
Goal	Mike Smith, Dallas
Defense	Matt Carle, San Jose
Defense	Marc-Edouard Vlasic, San Jose
Forward	Evgeni Malkin, Pittsburgh
Forward	Jordan Staal, Pittsburgh
Forward	Paul Stastny, Colorado

	2005-06
Goal	Henrik Lundqvist, NY Rangers
Defense	Andrej Meszaros, Ottawa
Defense	Dion Phaneuf, Calgary
Forward	Brad Boyes, Boston
Forward	Sidney Crosby, Pittsburgh
Forward	Alex Ovechkin, Washington

	2004-05
	Season Cancelled

	2003-04
Andrew Raycroft, Boston
John-Michael Liles, Colorado
Joni Pitkanen, Philadelphia
Trent Hunter, NY Islanders
Ryan Malone, Pittsburgh
Michael Ryder, Montreal

	2002-03
Sebastien Caron, Pittsburgh
Jay Bouwmeester, Florida
Barret Jackman, St. Louis
Tyler Arnason, Chicago
Rick Nash, Columbus
Henrik Zetterberg, Detroit

	2001-02
Dan Blackburn, NY Rangers
Nick Boynton, Boston
Rostislav Klesla, Columbus
Dany Heatley, Atlanta
Ilya Kovalchuk, Atlanta
Kristian Huselius, Florida

	2000-01
Evgeni Nabokov, San Jose
Lubomir Visnovsky, Los Angeles
Colin White, New Jersey
Martin Havlat, Ottawa
Brad Richards, Tampa Bay
Shane Willis, Carolina

	1999-2000
Brian Boucher, Philadelphia
Brian Rafalski, New Jersey
Brad Stuart, San Jose
Simon Gagne, Philadelphia
Scott Gomez, New Jersey
Michael York, NY Rangers

	1998-99
Jamie Storr, Los Angeles
Tom Poti, Edmonton
Sami Salo, Ottawa
Chris Drury, Colorado
Milan Hejduk, Colorado
Marian Hossa, Ottawa

	1997-98
Jamie Storr, Los Angeles
Mattias Ohlund, Vancouver
Derek Morris, Calgary
Sergei Samsonov, Boston
Patrick Elias, New Jersey
Mike Johnson, Toronto

	1996-97
Patrick Lalime, Pittsburgh
Bryan Berard, NY Islanders
Janne Niinimaa, Philadelphia
Jarome Iginla, Calgary
Jim Campbell, St. Louis
Sergei Berezin, Toronto

	1995-96
Corey Hirsch, Vancouver
Ed Jovanovski, Florida
Kyle McLaren, Boston
Daniel Alfredsson, Ottawa
Eric Daze, Chicago
Petr Sykora, New Jersey

	1994-95
Jim Carey, Washington
Chris Therien, Philadelphia
Kenny Jonsson, Toronto
Peter Forsberg, Quebec
Jeff Friesen, San Jose
Paul Kariya, Anaheim

	1993-94
Martin Brodeur, New Jersey
Chris Pronger, Hartford
Boris Mironov, Wpg./Edm.
Jason Arnott, Edmonton
Mikael Renberg, Philadelphia
Oleg Petrov, Montreal

	1992-93
Felix Potvin, Toronto
Vladimir Malakhov, NY Islanders
Scott Niedermayer, New Jersey
Eric Lindros, Philadelphia
Teemu Selanne, Winnipeg
Joe Juneau, Boston

	1991-92
Dominik Hasek, Chicago
Nicklas Lidstrom, Detroit
Vladimir Konstantinov, Detroit
Kevin Todd, New Jersey
Tony Amonte, NY Rangers
Gilbert Dionne, Montreal

	1990-91
Ed Belfour, Chicago
Eric Weinrich, New Jersey
Rob Blake, Los Angeles
Sergei Fedorov, Detroit
Ken Hodge, Boston
Jaromir Jagr, Pittsburgh

	1989-90
Bob Essensa, Winnipeg
Brad Shaw, Hartford
Geoff Smith, Edmonton
Mike Modano, Minnesota
Sergei Makarov, Calgary
Rod Brind'Amour, St. Louis

	1988-89
Peter Sidorkiewicz, Hartford
Brian Leetch, NY Rangers
Zarley Zalapski, Pittsburgh
Trevor Linden, Vancouver
Tony Granato, NY Rangers
David Volek, NY Islanders

	1987-88
Darren Pang, Chicago
Glen Wesley, Boston
Calle Johansson, Buffalo
Joe Nieuwendyk, Calgary
Ray Sheppard, Buffalo
Iain Duncan, Winnipeg

	1986-87
Ron Hextall, Philadelphia
Steve Duchesne, Los Angeles
Brian Benning, St. Louis
Jimmy Carson, Los Angeles
Jim Sandlak, Vancouver
Luc Robitaille, Los Angeles

	1985-86
Patrick Roy, Montreal
Gary Suter, Calgary
Dana Murzyn, Hartford
Mike Ridley, NY Rangers
Kjell Dahlin, Montreal
Wendel Clark, Toronto

	1984-85
Steve Penney, Montreal
Chris Chelios, Montreal
Bruce Bell, Quebec
Mario Lemieux, Pittsburgh
Tomas Sandstrom, NY Rangers
Warren Young, Pittsburgh

	1983-84
Tom Barrasso, Buffalo
Thomas Eriksson, Philadelphia
Jamie Macoun, Calgary
Steve Yzerman, Detroit
Hakan Loob, Calgary
Sylvain Turgeon, Hartford

	1982-83
Pelle Lindbergh, Philadelphia
Scott Stevens, Washington
Phil Housley, Buffalo
Dan Daoust, Mtl./Tor.
Steve Larmer, Chicago
Mats Naslund, Montreal

2011 All-Star Game Summary

JANUARY 30, 2011 at Carolina   Team Lidstrom 11, Team Staal 10

PLAYERS ON ICE: Team Lidstrom — Marc-Andre Fleury, Jonas Hiller, Tim Thomas, Duncan Keith, Keith Yandle, Nicklas Lidstrom, Shea Weber, Brent Burns, Matt Duchene, Anze Kopitar, Jonathan Toews, Loui Eriksson, Martin Havlat, Martin St. Louis, Dustin Byfuglien, Henrik Sedin, Danny Briere, Phil Kessel, Patrick Kane, Brad Richards, Steven Stamkos.

Team Staal — Cam Ward, Carey Price, Henrik Lundqvist, Alex Ovechkin, Corey Perry, Patrick Sharp, Eric Staal, Ryan Kesler, Marc Staal, Dan Boyle, Daniel Sedin, Patrik Elias, Paul Stastny, Claude Giroux, Zdeno Chara, David Backes, Mike Green, Jeff Skinner, Kris Letang, Rick Nash, Erik Karlsson.

SUMMARY
First Period
1.	Team Staal	Ovechkin	(Chara, Green)	0:50
2.	Team Staal	Stastny	(Sharp, Backes)	2:48
3.	Team Staal	Elias	(Stastny, Green)	3:20
4.	Team Staal	Giroux	(Sharp, Backes)	5:41
5.	Team Lidstrom	Kopitar	(Weber)	10:50
6.	Team Lidstrom	Byfuglien	(Kane, Keith)	13:17
7.	Team Lidstrom	Eriksson	(Toews)	16:07
8.	Team Lidstrom	Duchene	(Lidstrom, Weber)	16:30

PENALTIES: None

Second Period
9.	Team Staal	Sharp	(Giroux)	1:18
10.	Team Staal	Letang	(D. Sedin, Ovechkin)	6:10
11.	Team Lidstrom	Kopitar	(Eriksson, Havlat)	10:08
12.	Team Lidstrom	Stamkos	(St. Louis, Richards)	14:11
13.	Team Lidstrom	Briere	(H. Sedin, Weber)	15:31

PENALTIES: None

Third Period
14.	Team Staal	E. Staal	(Perry, Nash)	3:49
15.	Team Staal	Letang	(Elias, Skinner)	8:46
16.	Team Lidstrom	Briere	(H. Sedin, Weber)	9:57
17.	Team Lidstrom	Toews	(Eriksson, Havlat)	10:45
18.	Team Lidstrom	St. Louis	(Burns)	13:53
19.	Team Staal	Nash	(Perry, Chara)	15:11
20.	Team Lidstrom	Eriksson	(Toews, Havlat)	18:49 (en)
21.	Team Staal	E. Staal	(Boyle, Backes)	19:26

PENALTIES: None
Missed penalty shot – Duchene, Team Lidstrom 6:13

SHOTS ON GOAL BY:

Team Lidstrom	14	16	15	**45**
Team Staal	14	17	15	**46**

	Goaltenders:	**Time**	**SA**	**GA**	**ENG**	**Dec**
Team Lidstrom	Fleury	20:00	14	4	0	
Team Lidstrom	Hiller	20:00	17	2	0	
Team Lidstrom	Thomas	20:00	15	4	0	W
Team Staal	Ward	20:00	14	4	0	
Team Staal	Price	20:00	16	3	0	
Team Staal	Lundqvist	18:36	14	3	1	L

PP Conversions: Team Lidstrom 0/0; Team Staal 0/0.

Referees: Tom Kowal, Kevin Pollock
Linesmen: Don Henderson, Darren Gibbs
Attendance: 18,680

All-Star Game Results

Year	Venue	Score	Coaches	Attendance
2011	Carolina	Team Lidstrom 11, Team Staal 10	Joel Quenneville, Peter Laviolette	18,680
2009	Montreal	East 12, West 11	Claude Julien, Todd McLellan	21,273
2008	Atlanta	East 8, West 7	John Paddock, Mike Babcock	18,644
2007	Dallas	West 12, East 9	Lindy Ruff, Randy Carlyle	18,532
2004	Minnesota	East 6, West 4	Pat Quinn, Dave Lewis	19,434
2003	Florida	West 6, East 5	Marc Crawford, Jacques Martin	19,250
2002	Los Angeles	World 8, North America 5	Scotty Bowman, Pat Quinn	18,118
2001	Colorado	North America 14, World 12	Joel Quenneville, Jacques Martin	18,646
2000	Toronto	World 9, North America 4	Scotty Bowman, Pat Quinn	19,300
1999	Tampa Bay	North America 8, World 6	Lindy Ruff, Ken Hitchcock	19,758
1998	Vancouver	North America 8, World 7	Jacques Lemaire, Ken Hitchcock	18,422
1997	San Jose	East 11, West 7	Doug MacLean, Ken Hitchcock	17,422
1996	Boston	East 5, West 4	Doug MacLean, Scotty Bowman	17,565
1994	NY Rangers	East 9, West 8	Jacques Demers, Barry Melrose	18,200
1993	Montreal	Wales 16, Campbell 6	Scotty Bowman, Mike Keenan	17,137
1992	Philadelphia	Campbell 10, Wales 6	Bob Gainey, Scotty Bowman	17,380
1991	Chicago	Campbell 11, Wales 5	John Muckler, Mike Milbury	18,472
1990	Pittsburgh	Wales 12, Campbell 7	Pat Burns, Terry Crisp	16,236
1989	Edmonton	Campbell 9, Wales 5	Glen Sather, Terry O'Reilly	17,503
1988	St. Louis	Wales 6, Campbell 5 OT	Mike Keenan, Glen Sather	17,878
1986	Hartford	Wales 4, Campbell 3 OT	Mike Keenan, Glen Sather	15,100
1985	Calgary	Wales 6, Campbell 4	Al Arbour, Glen Sather	16,825
1984	New Jersey	Wales 7, Campbell 6	Al Arbour, Glen Sather	18,939
1983	NY Islanders	Campbell 9, Wales 3	Roger Neilson, Al Arbour	15,230
1982	Washington	Wales 4, Campbell 2	Al Arbour, Glen Sonmor	18,130
1981	Los Angeles	Campbell 4, Wales 1	Pat Quinn, Scotty Bowman	15,761
1980	Detroit	Wales 6, Campbell 3	Scotty Bowman, Al Arbour	21,002
1978	Buffalo	Wales 3, Campbell 2 OT	Scotty Bowman, Fred Shero	16,433
1977	Vancouver	Wales 4, Campbell 3	Scotty Bowman, Fred Shero	15,607
1976	Philadelphia	Wales 7, Campbell 5	Floyd Smith, Fred Shero	16,436
1975	Montreal	Wales 7, Campbell 1	Bep Guidolin, Fred Shero	16,080
1974	Chicago	West 6, East 4	Billy Reay, Scotty Bowman	16,426
1973	NY Rangers	East 5, West 4	Tom Johnson, Billy Reay	16,986
1972	Minnesota	East 3, West 2	Al MacNeil, Billy Reay	15,423
1971	Boston	West 2, East 1	Scotty Bowman, Harry Sinden	14,790
1970	St. Louis	East 4, West 1	Claude Ruel, Scotty Bowman	16,587
1969	Montreal	East 3, West 3	Toe Blake, Scotty Bowman	16,260
1968	Toronto	Toronto 4, All-Stars 3	Punch Imlach, Toe Blake	15,753
1967	Montreal	Montreal 3, All-Stars 0	Toe Blake, Sid Abel	14,284
1965	Montreal	All-Stars 5, Montreal 2	Billy Reay, Toe Blake	13,529
1964	Toronto	All-Stars 3, Toronto 2	Sid Abel, Punch Imlach	14,232
1963	Toronto	All-Stars 3, Toronto 3	Sid Abel, Punch Imlach	14,034
1962	Toronto	Toronto 4, All-Stars 1	Punch Imlach, Rudy Pilous	14,236
1961	Chicago	All-Stars 3, Chicago 1	Sid Abel, Rudy Pilous	14,534
1960	Montreal	All-Stars 2, Montreal 1	Punch Imlach, Toe Blake	13,949
1959	Montreal	Montreal 6, All-Stars 1	Toe Blake, Punch Imlach	13,818
1958	Montreal	Montreal 6, All-Stars 3	Toe Blake, Milt Schmidt	13,989
1957	Montreal	All-Stars 5, Montreal 3	Milt Schmidt, Toe Blake	13,003
1956	Montreal	All-Stars 1, Montreal 1	Jim Skinner, Toe Blake	13,095
1955	Detroit	Detroit 3, All-Stars 1	Jim Skinner, Dick Irvin	10,111
1954	Detroit	All-Stars 2, Detroit 2	King Clancy, Jim Skinner	10,689
1953	Montreal	All-Stars 3, Montreal 1	Lynn Patrick, Dick Irvin	14,153
1952	Detroit	1st Team 1, 2nd Team 1	Tommy Ivan, Dick Irvin	10,680
1951	Toronto	1st Team 2, 2nd Team 2	Joe Primeau, Dick Irvin	11,469
1950	Detroit	Detroit 7, All-Stars 1	Tommy Ivan, Lynn Patrick	9,166
1949	Toronto	All-Stars 3, Toronto 1	Tommy Ivan, Hap Day	13,541
1948	Chicago	All-Stars 3, Toronto 1	Tommy Ivan, Hap Day	12,794
1947	Toronto	All-Stars 4, Toronto 3	Dick Irvin, Hap Day	14,169

There was no All-Star contest during the calendar year of 1966 because the game was moved from the start of season to mid-season. In 1979, the Challenge Cup series between the Soviet Union and Team NHL replaced the All-Star Game. In 1987, Rendez-Vous '87, two games between the Soviet Union and Team NHL replaced the All-Star Game. In 1995 and 2005 the All-Star Game was not played due to a labour disruption affecting the NHL. In both 2006 and 2010 the All-Star Game was not played because of NHL players' participation in the Olympics.

NHL ALL-STAR GAME MVP

2011	Patrick Sharp, Chi.	1992	Brett Hull, St.L.	1975	Syl Apps Jr., Pit.
2009	Alex Kovalev, Mtl.	1991	Vincent Damphousse, Tor.	1974	Garry Unger, St.L.
2008	Eric Staal, Car.	1990	Mario Lemieux, Pit.	1973	Greg Polis, Pit.
2007	Danny Briere, Buf.	1989	Wayne Gretzky, L.A.	1972	Bobby Orr, Bos.
2004	Joe Sakic, Col..	1988	Mario Lemieux, Pit.	1971	Bobby Hull, Chi.
2003	Dany Heatley, Atl.	1986	Grant Fuhr, Edm.	1970	Bobby Hull, Chi.
2002	Eric Daze, Chi.	1985	Mario Lemieux, Pit.	1969	Frank Mahovlich, Det.
2001	Bill Guerin, Bos.	1984	Don Maloney, NYR	1968	Bruce Gamble, Tor.
2000	Pavel Bure, Fla.	1983	Wayne Gretzky, Edm.	1967	Henri Richard, Mtl.
1999	Wayne Gretzky, NYR	1982	Mike Bossy, NYI	1965	Gordie Howe, Det.
1998	Teemu Selanne, Ana.	1981	Mike Liut, St.L.	1964	Jean Beliveau, Mtl.
1997	Mark Recchi, Mtl.	1980	Reggie Leach, Phi.	1963	Frank Mahovlich, Tor.
1996	Raymond Bourque, Bos.	1978	Billy Smith, NYI	1962	Eddie Shack, Tor.
1994	Mike Richter, NYR	1977	Rick Martin, Buf.		
1993	Mike Gartner, NYR	1976	Pete Mahovlich, Mtl.		

All-Star Game Records 1947 through 2011

TEAM RECORDS

MOST GOALS, BOTH TEAMS, ONE GAME:
26 — North America 14, World 12, 2001 at Colorado
23 — East 12, West 11, 2009 at Montreal
22 — Wales 16, Campbell 6, 1993 at Montreal
21 — West 12, East 9, 2007 at Dallas
— Team Lidstrom 11, Team Staal 10, 2011 at Carolina
19 — Wales 12, Campbell 7, 1990 at Pittsburgh
18 — East 11, West 7, 1997 at San Jose

FEWEST GOALS, BOTH TEAMS, ONE GAME:
2 — First Team All-Stars 1, Second Team All-Stars 1, 1952 at Detroit
— NHL All-Stars 1, Montreal Canadiens 1, 1956 at Montreal
3 — NHL All-Stars 2, Montreal Canadiens 1, 1960 at Montreal
— Montreal Canadiens 3, NHL All-Stars 0, 1967 at Montreal
— West 2, East 1, 1971 at Boston

MOST GOALS, ONE TEAM, ONE GAME:
16 — Wales 16, Campbell 6, 1993 at Montreal
14 — North America 14, World 12, 2001 at Colorado
12 — Wales 12, Campbell 7, 1990 at Pittsburgh
— World 12, North America 14, 2001 at Colorado
— West 12, East 9, 2007 at Dallas
— East 12, West 11, 2009 at Montreal

FEWEST GOALS, ONE TEAM, ONE GAME:
0 — NHL All-Stars 0, Montreal Canadiens 3, 1967 at Montreal
1 — 17 times (1981, 1975, 1971, 1970, 1962, 1961, 1960, 1959, both teams 1956, 1955, 1953, both teams 1952, 1950, 1949, 1948)

MOST SHOTS, BOTH TEAMS, ONE GAME (SINCE 1955):
102 — 1994 at NY Rangers — East 9 (56 shots),
West 8 (46 shots)
2009 at Montreal — East 12 (48 shots)
— West 11 (54 shots)
98 — 2001 at Colorado — North America 14 (53 shots),
World 12 (45 shots)
91 — 2011 at Carolina — Team Lidstrom 11 (45 shots),
Team Staal 10 (46 shots)

FEWEST SHOTS, BOTH TEAMS, ONE GAME (SINCE 1955):
52 — 1978 at Buffalo — Campbell 2 (12 shots)
Wales 3 (40 shots)
53 — 1960 at Montreal — NHL All-Stars 2 (27 shots)
Montreal Canadiens 1 (26 shots)
55 — 1956 at Montreal — NHL All-Stars 1 (28 shots)
Montreal Canadiens 1 (27 shots)
— 1971 at Boston — West 2 (28 shots)
East 1 (27 shots)

MOST SHOTS, ONE TEAM, ONE GAME (SINCE 1955):
56 — 1994 at NY Rangers — East (9-8 vs. West)
54 — 2009 at Montreal — East (12-11 vs. West)
53 — 2001 at Colorado — North America (14-12 vs. World)
51 — 2008 at Atlanta — West (7-8 vs. East)

FEWEST SHOTS, ONE TEAM, ONE GAME (SINCE 1955):
12 — 1978 at Buffalo — Campbell (2-3 vs. Wales)
17 — 1970 at St. Louis — West (1-4 vs. East)
23 — 1961 at Chicago — Chicago Black Hawks (1-3 vs. NHL All-Stars)
24 — 1976 at Philadelphia — Campbell (5-7 vs. Wales)

MOST POWER-PLAY GOALS, BOTH TEAMS, ONE GAME (SINCE 1950):
3 — 1953 at Montreal — NHL All-Stars 3 (2 power-play goals),
Montreal Canadiens 1 (1 power-play goal)
— 1954 at Detroit — NHL All-Stars 2 (1 power-play goal)
Detroit Red Wings 2 (2 power-play goals)
— 1958 at Montreal — NHL All-Stars 3 (1 power-play goal)
Montreal Canadiens 6 (2 power-play goals)

FEWEST POWER-PLAY GOALS, BOTH TEAMS, ONE GAME (SINCE 1950):
0 — 26 times (1952, 1959, 1960, 1967, 1968, 1969, 1972, 1973, 1976, 1980, 1981, 1984, 1985, 1992, 1994, 1996, 1999, 2000, 2001, 2002, 2003, 2004, 2007, 2008, 2009, 2011)

FASTEST TWO GOALS, BOTH TEAMS, FROM START OF GAME:
0:37 — 1970 at St. Louis — Jacques Laperriere of East scored at 0:20 and Dean Prentice of West scored at 0:37. Final score: East 4, West 1.

1:20 — 2008 at Atlanta — Rick Nash of West scored at 0:12 and Eric Staal of East scored at 1:20. Final score: East 8, West 7.

2:15 — 1998 at Vancouver — Teemu Selanne scored at 0:53 and Jaromir Jagr scored at 2:15 for World. Final score: North America 8, World 7.

FASTEST TWO GOALS, BOTH TEAMS:
0:08 — 1997 at San Jose — Owen Nolan scored at 18:54 and 19:02 of second period for West. Final Score: East 11, West 7.

0:10 — 1976 at Philadelphia — Dennis Ververgaert scored at 4:33 and at 4:43 of third period for Campbell. Final score: Wales 7, Campbell 5.

0:13 — 1998 at Vancouver — Teemu Selanne scored at 4:00 of first period for World and John LeClair scored at 4:13 for North America. Final score: North America 8, World 7.

FASTEST THREE GOALS, BOTH TEAMS:
0:48 — 2007 at Dallas — Martin Havlat scored at 19:00 of third period for West; Sheldon Souray scored at 19:25 for East; Dion Phaneuf scored at 19:48 for West. Final score: West 12, East 9.

1:08 — 1993 at Montreal — all by Wales — Mike Gartner scored at 3:15 and at 3:37 of first period; Peter Bondra scored at 4:23. Final score: Wales 16, Campbell 6.

1:14 — 1994 at NY Rangers — Bob Kudelski scored at 9:46 of first period for East; Sergei Fedorov scored at 10:20 for West; Eric Lindros scored at 11:00 for East. Final score: East 9, West 8.

FASTEST FOUR GOALS, BOTH TEAMS:
2:24 — 1997 at San Jose — Brendan Shanahan scored at 16:38 of second period for West; Dale Hawerchuk scored at 17:28 for East; Owen Nolan scored at 18:54 and 19:02 for West. Final score: East 11, West 7.

2:49 — 2009 at Montreal — Evgeni Malkin scored at 7:45 of second period for East; Rick Nash scored at 8:27 for West; Milan Hejduk scored at 9:02 for West; Sheldon Souray scored at 10:34 for West.

2:52 — 2007 at Dallas — Rick Nash scored at 10:40 of second period for West; Martin Havlat scored at 11:34 for West; Yanic Perreault scored at 12:47 for West; Alex Ovechkin scored at 13:32 for East. Final score: West 12, East 9.

FASTEST TWO GOALS, ONE TEAM, FROM START OF GAME:
2:15 — 1998 at Vancouver — World — Teemu Selanne scored at 0:53 and Jaromir Jagr scored at 2:15. Final score: North America 8, World 7.

2:48 — 2011 at Carolina — Team Staal — Alex Ovechkin scored at 0:50 and Paul Stastny scored at 2:48. Final score: Team Lidstrom 11, Team Staal 10.

3:37 — 1993 at Montreal — Wales — Mike Gartner scored at 3:15 and at 3:37. Final score: Wales 16, Campbell 6.

FASTEST TWO GOALS, ONE TEAM:
0:08 — 1997 at San Jose — West — Owen Nolan scored at 18:54 and at 19:02 of second period. Final score: East 11, West 7.

0:10 — 1976 at Philadelphia — Campbell — Dennis Ververgaert scored at 4:33 and at 4:43 of third period. Final score: West 7, Campbell 5.

0:14 — 1989 at Edmonton — Campbell — Steve Yzerman and Gary Leeman scored at 17:21 and 17:35 of second period. Final score: Campbell 9, Wales 5.

FASTEST THREE GOALS, ONE TEAM:
1:08 — 1993 at Montreal — Wales — Mike Gartner scored at 3:15 and 3:37 of first period; Peter Bondra scored at 4:23. Final score: Wales 16, Campbell 6.

1:32 — 1980 at Detroit — Wales — Ron Stackhouse scored at 11:40 of third period; Craig Hartsburg scored at 12:40; Reed Larson scored at 13:12. Final score: Wales 6, Campbell 3.

1:39 — 2002 at Los Angeles — Markus Naslund scored at 18:17 of third period; Alex Zhamnov scored at 19:12; Sami Kapanen scored at 19:56. Final score: World 8, North America 5.

FASTEST FOUR GOALS, ONE TEAM:
2:57 — 2002 at Los Angeles — World — Sergei Fedorov scored at 16:59 of third period; Markus Naslund scored at 18:17; Alex Zhamnov scored at 19:12; Sami Kapanen scored at 19:56. Final score: World 8, North America 5.

4:17 — 2007 at Dallas — Brian Rolston scored at 8:30 of second period; Rick Nash scored at 10:40; Martin Havlat scored at 11:34; Yanic Perreault scored at 12:47. Final score: West 12, East 9.

4:19 — 1992 at Philadelphia — Campbell — Brian Bellows scored at 7:40 of second period; Jeremy Roenick scored at 8:13; Theoren Fleury scored at 11:06, Brett Hull scored at 11:59. Final score: Campbell 10, Wales 6.

MOST GOALS, BOTH TEAMS, ONE PERIOD:
10 — 1997 at San Jose — Second period — East (6), West (4). Final score: East 11, West 7.

— 2001 at Colorado — Second period — North America (6), World (4). Final score: North America 14, World 12.

— 2001 at Colorado — Third period — North America (5), World (5). Final score: North America 14, World 12.

— 2009 at Montreal — Second period — West (6), East (4). Final Score: East 12, West 11.

9 — 1990 at Pittsburgh — First period — Wales (7), Campbell (2). Final score: Wales 12, Campbell 7.

— 2007 at Dallas — Second period — West (6), East (3). Final score: West 12, East 9.

MOST GOALS, ONE TEAM, ONE PERIOD:
7 — 1990 at Pittsburgh — First period — Wales. Final score: Wales 12, Campbell 7.

6 — 1983 at NY Islanders — Third period — Campbell. Final score: Campbell 9, Wales 3.

— 1992 at Philadelphia — Second period — Campbell. Final score: Campbell 10, Wales 6.

— 1993 at Montreal — First period — Wales. Final score: Wales 16, Campbell 6.

— 1993 at Montreal — Second period — Wales. Final score: Wales 16, Campbell 6.

— 1997 at San Jose — Second period — East. Final score: East 11, West 7.

— 2001 at Colorado — Second period — North America. Final score: North America 14, World 12.

— 2007 at Dallas — Second period — West. Final score: West 12, East 9.

— 2009 at Montreal — Second period — West. Final score: East 12, West 11.

MOST SHOTS, BOTH TEAMS, ONE PERIOD:
42 — 2009 at Montreal — Second period — West (21), East (21). Final score: East 12, West 11.

39 — 1994 at NY Rangers — Second period — West (21), East (18). Final score: East 9, West 8.

— 2001 at Colorado — Third period — World (23), North America (16). Final score: North America 14, World 12.

36 — 1990 at Pittsburgh — Third period — Campbell (22), Wales (14). Final score: Wales 12, Campbell 7.

— 1994 at NY Rangers — First period — East (19), West (17). Final score: East 9, West 8.

— 2002 at Los Angeles — Third period — North America (20), World (16). Final score: World 8, North America 5.

MOST SHOTS, ONE TEAM, ONE PERIOD:
23 — 2001 at Colorado — Third period — World. Final score: North America 14, World 12.

22 — 1990 at Pittsburgh — Third period — Campbell. Final score: Wales 12, Campbell 7.

— 1991 at Chicago — Third period — Wales. Final score: Campbell 11, Wales 5.

— 1993 at Montreal — First period — Wales. Final score: Wales 16, Campbell 6.

FEWEST SHOTS, BOTH TEAMS, ONE PERIOD:
9 — 1971 at Boston — Third period — East (2), West (7). Final score: West 2, East 1.

— 1980 at Detroit — Second period — Campbell (4), Wales (5). Final score: Wales 6, Campbell 3.

13 — 1982 at Washington — Third period — Campbell (6), Wales (7). Final score: Wales 4, Campbell 2.

14 — 1978 at Buffalo — First period — Campbell (7), Wales (7). Final score: Wales 3, Campbell 2.

— 1986 at Hartford — First period — Campbell (6), Wales (8). Final score: Wales 4, Campbell 3.

FEWEST SHOTS, ONE TEAM, ONE PERIOD:
2 — 1971 at Boston — Third period — East. Final score: West 2, East 1.

— 1978 at Buffalo — Second period — Campbell. Final score: Wales 3, Campbell 2.

3 — 1978 at Buffalo — Third period — Campbell. Final score: Wales 3, Campbell 2.

4 — 1955 at Detroit — First period — NHL All-Stars. Final score: Detroit Red Wings 3, NHL All-Stars 1.

— 1980 at Detroit — Second period — Campbell. Final score: Wales 6, Campbell 3.

INDIVIDUAL RECORDS

Games

MOST GAMES PLAYED:
23 — **Gordie Howe,** 1948 through 1980
19 — Raymond Bourque, 1981 through 2001
18 — Wayne Gretzky, 1980 through 1999
15 — Frank Mahovlich, 1959 through 1974
— Mark Messier, 1982 through 2004

Goals

MOST GOALS, CAREER:
13 — **Wayne Gretzky** in 18GP
— **Mario Lemieux** in 10GP
10 — Gordie Howe in 23GP
9 — Teemu Selanne in 10GP
8 — Frank Mahovlich in 15GP
— Luc Robitaille in 8GP

MOST GOALS, ONE GAME:
4 — **Wayne Gretzky,** Campbell, 1983
— **Mario Lemieux,** Wales, 1990
— **Vince Damphousse,** Campbell, 1991
— **Mike Gartner,** Wales, 1993
— **Dany Heatley,** East, 2003
3 — Ted Lindsay, Detroit, 1950
— Mario Lemieux, Wales, 1988
— Pierre Turgeon, Wales, 1993
— Mark Recchi, East, 1997
— Owen Nolan, West, 1997
— Teemu Selanne, World, 1998
— Pavel Bure, World, 2000
— Bill Guerin, North America, 2001
— Joe Sakic, West, 2004
— Rick Nash, West, 2008

MOST GOALS, ONE PERIOD:
4 — **Wayne Gretzky,** Campbell, Third period, 1983
3 — Mario Lemieux, Wales, First period, 1990
— Vincent Damphousse, Campbell, Third period, 1991
— Mike Gartner, Wales, First period, 1993

Assists

MOST ASSISTS, CAREER:
16 — Joe Sakic in 12GP
14 — Mark Messier in 15GP
13 — Raymond Bourque in 19GP
12 — Adam Oates in 5GP
— Mats Sundin in 8GP
— Wayne Gretzky in 18GP

MOST ASSISTS, ONE GAME:
5 — Mats Naslund, Wales, 1988
4 — Raymond Bourque, Wales, 1985
— Adam Oates, Campbell, 1991
— Adam Oates, Wales, 1993
— Mark Recchi, Wales, 1993
— Pierre Turgeon, East, 1994
— Fredrik Modin, World, 2001
— Joe Sakic, West, 2007
— Danny Briere, East, 2007
— Marian Hossa, East, 2007
— Shea Weber, Team Lidstrom, 2011

MOST ASSISTS, ONE PERIOD:
4 — Adam Oates, Wales, First period, 1993
3 — Mark Messier, Campbell, Third period, 1983
3 — Marian Hossa, East, Third period, 2007

Points

MOST POINTS, CAREER:
25 — Wayne Gretzky (13G-12A in 18GP)
23 — Mario Lemieux (13G-10A in 10GP)
22 — Joe Sakic (6G-16A in 12GP)
20 — Mark Messier (6G-14A in 15GP)
19 — Gordie Howe (10G-9A in 23GP)

MOST POINTS, ONE GAME:
6 — Mario Lemieux, Wales, 1988 (3G-3A)
5 — Mats Naslund, Wales, 1988 (5A)
— Adam Oates, Campbell, 1991 (1G-4A)
— Mike Gartner, Wales, 1993 (4G-1A)
— Mark Recchi, Wales, 1993 (1G-4A)
— Pierre Turgeon, Wales, 1993 (3G-2A)
— Bill Guerin, North America, 2001 (3G-2A)
— Dany Heatley, East, 2003 (4G-1A)
— Danny Briere, East, 2007 (1G-4A)

MOST POINTS, ONE PERIOD:
4 — Wayne Gretzky, Campbell, Third period, 1983 (4G)
— Mike Gartner, Wales, First period, 1993 (3G-1A)
— Adam Oates, Wales, First period, 1993 (4A)
3 — Gordie Howe, NHL All-Stars, Second period, 1965 (1G-2A)
— Pete Mahovlich, Wales, First period, 1976 (1G-2A)
— Mark Messier, Campbell, Third period, 1983 (3A)
— Mario Lemieux, Wales, Second period, 1988 (1G-2A)
— Mario Lemieux, Wales, First period, 1990 (3G)
— Vince Damphousse, Campbell, Third period, 1991 (3G)
— Mark Recchi, Wales, Second period, 1993 (1G-2A)
— Tony Amonte, North America, Second period, 2001 (2G-1A)
— Daniel Alfredsson, East, Second period, 2004 (2G-1A)
— Marian Hossa, East, Third period, 2007 (3A)

Power-Play Goals

MOST POWER-PLAY GOALS, CAREER:
6 — Gordie Howe in 23GP
3 — Bobby Hull in 12GP
— Maurice Richard in 13GP

Fastest Goals

FASTEST GOAL FROM START OF GAME:
0:12 — Rick Nash, West, 2008
0:19 — Ted Lindsay, Detroit, 1950
0:20 — Jacques Laperriere, East, 1970
0:21 — Mario Lemieux, Wales, 1990
0:35 — Vincent Damphousse, North America, 2002

FASTEST GOAL FROM START OF A PERIOD:
0:12 — Rick Nash, West, 2008 (first period)
0:17 — Raymond Bourque, North America, 1999 (second period)
0:19 — Ted Lindsay, Detroit, 1950 (first period)
— Rick Tocchet, Wales, 1993 (second period)
0:20 — Jacques Laperriere, East, 1970 (first period)

FASTEST TWO GOALS, ONE PLAYER, FROM START OF GAME:
3:37 — Mike Gartner, Wales, 1993, at 3:15 and 3:37.
4:00 — Teemu Selanne, World, 1998, at 0:53 and 4:00
5:25 — Wally Hergesheimer, NHL All-Stars, 1953, at 4:06 and 5:25.

FASTEST TWO GOALS, ONE PLAYER, FROM START OF A PERIOD:
3:37 — Mike Gartner, Wales, 1993, at 3:15 and 3:37 of first period.
4:00 — Teemu Selanne, World, 1998, at 0:53 and 4:00 of first period.
4:43 — Dennis Ververgaert, Campbell, 1976, at 4:33 and 4:43 of third period.

FASTEST TWO GOALS, ONE PLAYER:
0:08 — Owen Nolan, West, 1997. Scored at 18:54 and 19:02 of second period.
0:10 — Dennis Ververgaert, Campbell, 1976. Scored at 4:33 and 4:43 of third period.
0:22 — Mike Gartner, Wales, 1993. Scored at 3:15 and 3:37 of first period.

Penalties

MOST PENALTY MINUTES:
25 — Gordie Howe in 23GP
21 — Gus Mortson in 9GP
16 — Harry Howell in 7GP

Goaltenders

MOST GAMES PLAYED:
13 — Glenn Hall from 1955 through 1969
11 — Terry Sawchuk from 1950 through 1968
— Patrick Roy from 1988 through 2003
9 — Martin Brodeur from 1996 through 2007
8 — Jacques Plante from 1956 through 1970

MOST MINUTES PLAYED:
540 — Glenn Hall in 13GP
467 — Terry Sawchuk in 11GP
370 — Jacques Plante in 8GP
250 — Patrick Roy in 11GP
209 — Turk Broda in 4GP

MOST GOALS AGAINST:
31 — Patrick Roy in 11GP
22 — Martin Brodeur in 9GP
— Glenn Hall in 13GP
21 — Mike Vernon in 5GP
19 — Terry Sawchuk in 11GP

BEST GOALS-AGAINST-AVERAGE AMONG THOSE WITH AT LEAST TWO GAMES PLAYED:
0.68 — Gilles Villemure in 3GP
1.49 — Gerry McNeil in 3GP
1.50 — Johnny Bower in 4GP
1.51 — Frank Brimsek in 3GP
1.64 — Gump Worsley in 4GP

The NHL introduced a new All-Star Format in 2011 in which the players themselves selected the teams from a pool of talent voted on by the fans and the league. Captains Nicklas Lidstrom and Eric Staal shake hands after Team Lidstrom rallied for an 11-10 victory over Team Staal.

Hockey Hall of Fame

(Year of induction is listed after each Honoured Members name)

Location: Brookfield Place, at the corner of Front and Yonge Streets in the heart of downtown Toronto. Easy access from all major highways running into Toronto. Close to TTC subway and Union Station.

Telephone: administration (416) 360-7735; information (416) 360-7765.

Public Hours of Operation: Open every day except Christmas Day, New Year's Day and Induction Day (November 14, 2011). Please call our information number (above) or visit our website (below) for times.

The Hockey Hall of Fame can be booked for private functions after hours.

Website address: www.hhof.com

History: The Hockey Hall of Fame was established in 1943. Members were first honoured in 1945. On August 26, 1961, the Hockey Hall of Fame opened its doors to the public in a building located on the grounds of the Canadian National Exhibition in Toronto. The Hockey Hall of Fame relocated to its current location and welcomed the hockey world on June 18, 1993.

Honour Roll: There are 366 Honoured Members in the Hockey Hall of Fame. 251 have been inducted as players including the first two women in 2010, 100 as builders and 15 as Referees/Linesmen. In addition, there are 86 media honourees.

Founding/Premiere Sponsors: Imperial Oil, International Ice Hockey Federation, National Hockey League, National Hockey League Players' Association, Panasonic Canada, Pepsi-Cola Canada, RBC Financial Group, The Toronto Sun, The Sports Network (TSN/RDS), Verizon.

Ed Belfour ranks third all-time in regular-season victories with 484 in an 18-year NHL career spent with Chicago, San Jose, Dallas, Toronto and Florida. He won the Vezina Trophy twice and the Stanley Cup with Dallas in 1999.

PLAYERS

* Abel, Sidney Gerald 1969
* Adams, John James "Jack" 1959
  Anderson, Glenn 2008
* Apps, Charles Joseph Sylvanus "Syl" 1961
  Armstrong, George Edward 1975
* Bailey, Irvine Wallace "Ace" 1975
* Bain, Donald H. "Dan" 1949
* Baker, Hobart "Hobey" 1945
  Barber, William Charles "Bill" 1990
* Barry, Martin J. "Marty" 1965
  Bathgate, Andrew James "Andy" 1978
* Bauer, Robert Theodore "Bobby" 1996
  Belfour, Ed 2011
  Béliveau, Jean Arthur 1972
* Benedict, Clinton S. 1965
* Bentley, Douglas Wagner 1964
* Bentley, Maxwell H. L. 1966
* Blake, Hector "Toe" 1966
  Boivin, Leo Joseph 1986
* Boon, Richard R. "Dickie" 1952
  Bossy, Michael 1991
  Bouchard, Emile Joseph "Butch" 1966
* Boucher, Frank 1958
* Boucher, Georges "Buck" 1960
  Bourque, Raymond 2004
  Bower, John William 1976
* Bowie, Russell 1947
* Brimsek, Francis Charles 1966
* Broadbent, Harry L. "Punch" 1962
* Broda, Walter Edward "Turk" 1967
  Bucyk, John Paul 1981
* Burch, Billy 1974
* Cameron, Harold Hugh "Harry" 1962
  Cheevers, Gerald Michael "Gerry" 1985
  Ciccarelli, Dino 2010
* Clancy, Francis Michael "King" 1958
* Clapper, Aubrey "Dit" 1947
  Clarke, Robert "Bobby" 1987
* Cleghorn, Sprague 1958
  Coffey, Paul 2004
* Colville, Neil MacNeil 1967
* Conacher, Charles W. 1961
* Conacher, Lionel Pretoria 1994
* Conacher, Roy Gordon 1998
* Connell, Alex 1958
* Cook, Fred "Bun" 1995
* Cook, William Osser 1952
* Coulter, Arthur Edmund 1974
  Cournoyer, Yvan Serge 1982
* Cowley, William Mailes 1968
* Crawford, Samuel Russell "Rusty" 1962
* Darragh, John Proctor "Jack" 1962

* Davidson, Allan M. "Scotty" 1950
* Day, Clarence Henry "Hap" 1961
  Delvecchio, Alex 1977
* Denneny, Cyril "Cy" 1959
  Dionne, Marcel 1992
* Drillon, Gordon Arthur 1975
* Drinkwater, Charles Graham 1950
  Dryden, Kenneth Wayne 1983
  Duff, Dick 2006
* Dumart, Woodrow "Woody" 1992
* Dunderdale, Thomas 1974
* Durnan, William Ronald 1964
* Dutton, Mervyn A. "Red" 1958
* Dye, Cecil Henry "Babe" 1970
  Esposito, Anthony James "Tony" 1988
  Esposito, Philip Anthony 1984
* Farrell, Arthur F. 1965
  Federko, Bernie 2002
  Fetisov, Viacheslav 2001
  Flaman, Ferdinand Charles "Fern" 1990
* Foyston, Frank 1958
  Francis, Ron 2007
* Fredrickson, Frank 1958
  Fuhr, Grant 2003
  Gadsby, William Alexander 1970
  Gainey, Bob 1992
* Gardiner, Charles Robert "Chuck" 1945
* Gardiner, Herbert Martin "Herb" 1958
* Gardner, James Henry "Jimmy" 1962
  Gartner, Michael Alfred 2001
* Geoffrion, Jos. A. Bernard "Boom Boom" 1972
* Gerard, Eddie 1945
  Giacomin, Edward "Eddie" 1987
  Gilbert, Rodrigue Gabriel "Rod" 1982
  Gillies, Clark 2002
  Gilmour, Doug 2011
* Gilmour, Hamilton Livingstone "Billy" 1962
* Goheen, Frank Xavier "Moose" 1952
* Goodfellow, Ebenezer R. "Ebbie" 1963
  Goulet, Michel 1998
  Granato, Cammi 2010
* Grant, Michael "Mike" 1950
* Green, Wilfred "Shorty" 1962
  Gretzky, Wayne Douglas 1999
* Griffis, Silas Seth "Si" 1950
* Hainsworth, George 1961
  Hall, Glenn Henry 1975
* Hall, Joseph Henry 1961
* Harvey, Douglas Norman 1973
  Hawerchuk, Dale Martin 2001
* Hay, George 1958

* Hern, William Milton "Riley" 1962
* Hextall, Bryan Aldwyn 1969
* Holmes, Harry "Hap" 1972
* Hooper, Charles Thomas "Tom" 1962
* Horner, George Reginald "Red" 1965
* Horton, Miles Gilbert "Tim" 1977
  Howe, Gordon 1972
  Howe, Mark 2011
* Howe, Sydney Harris 1965
  Howell, Henry Vernon "Harry" 1979
  Hull, Brett 2009
  Hull, Robert Marvin 1983
* Hutton, John Bower "Bouse" 1962
* Hyland, Harry M. 1962
* Irvin, James Dickenson "Dick" 1958
* Jackson, Harvey "Busher" 1971
  James, Angela 2010
* Johnson, Ernest "Moose" 1952
* Johnson, Ivan "Ching" 1958
* Johnson, Thomas Christian 1970
* Joliat, Aurel 1947
* Keats, Gordon "Duke" 1958
  Kelly, Leonard Patrick "Red" 1969
* Kennedy, Theodore Samuel "Teeder" 1966
  Keon, David Michael 1986
* Kharlamov, Valeri 2005
  Kurri, Jari 2001
  Lach, Elmer James 1966
  Lafleur, Guy Damien 1988
  LaFontaine, Pat 2003
* Lalonde, Edouard Charles "Newsy" 1950
  Langway, Rod Corry 2002
  Laperriere, Jacques 1987
  Lapointe, Guy 1993
  Laprade, Edgar 1993
  Larionov, Igor 2008
* Laviolette, Jean Baptiste "Jack" 1962
* Lehman, Hugh 1958
  Lemaire, Jacques Gerard 1984
  Lemieux, Mario 1997
* LeSueur, Percy 1961
  Leetch, Brian 2009
* Lewis, Herbert A. 1989
  Lindsay, Robert Blake Theodore "Ted" 1966
* Lumley, Harry 1980
  MacInnis, Al 2007
* MacKay, Duncan "Mickey" 1952
  Mahovlich, Frank William 1981
* Malone, Joseph "Joe" 1950
* Mantha, Sylvio 1960
* Marshall, John "Jack" 1965
* Maxwell, Fred G. "Steamer" 1962

  McDonald, Lanny 1992
* McGee, Frank 1945
* McGimsie, William George "Billy" 1962
* McNamara, George 1958
  Messier, Mark 2007
  Mikita, Stanley 1983
  Moore, Richard Winston "Dickie" 1974
* Moran, Patrick Joseph "Paddy" 1958
* Morenz, Howie 1945
* Mosienko, William "Billy" 1965
  Mullen, Joseph P. 2000
  Murphy, Larry 2004
  Neely, Cam 2005
  Nieuwendyk, Joe 2011
* Nighbor, Frank 1947
* Noble, Edward Reginald "Reg" 1962
* O'Connor, Herbert William "Buddy" 1988
* Oliver, Harry 1967
  Olmstead, Murray Bert "Bert" 1985
  Orr, Robert Gordon 1979
  Parent, Bernard Marcel 1984
  Park, Douglas Bradford "Brad" 1988
* Patrick, Joseph Lynn 1980
* Patrick, Lester 1947
  Perreault, Gilbert 1990
* Phillips, Tommy 1945
  Pilote, Joseph Albert Pierre Paul 1975
* Pitre, Didier "Pit" 1962
* Plante, Joseph Jacques Omer 1978
  Potvin, Denis 1991
* Pratt, Walter "Babe" 1966
* Primeau, A. Joseph 1963
  Pronovost, Joseph René Marcel 1978
  Pulford, Bob 1991
* Pulford, Harvey 1945
* Quackenbush, Hubert George "Bill" 1976
  Rankin, Frank 1961
  Ratelle, Joseph Gilbert Yvan Jean "Jean" 1985
* Rayner, Claude Earl "Chuck" 1973
* Reardon, Kenneth Joseph 1966
  Richard, Joseph Henri 1979
* Richard, Joseph Henri Maurice "Rocket" 1961
* Richardson, George Taylor 1950
* Roberts, Gordon 1971
  Robinson, Larry 1995
  Robitaille, Luc 2009
* Ross, Arthur Howey 1949
  Roy, Patrick 2006
* Russell, Blair 1965
* Russell, Ernest 1965

* Ruttan, J.D. "Jack" 1962
  Salming, Borje Anders 1996
  Savard, Denis Joseph 2000
  Savard, Serge 1986
* Sawchuk, Terrance Gordon "Terry" 1971
* Scanlan, Fred 1965
  Schmidt, Milton Conrad "Milt" 1961
* Schriner, David "Sweeney" 1962
* Seibert, Earl Walter 1963
* Seibert, Oliver Levi 1961
* Shore, Edward W. "Eddie" 1947
  Shutt, Stephen 1993
* Siebert, Albert C. "Babe" 1964
* Simpson, Harold Edward "Bullet Joe" 1962
  Sittler, Darryl Glen 1989
* Smith, Alfred E. 1962
* Smith, Clint 1991
* Smith, Reginald "Hooley" 1972
* Smith, Thomas James 1973
  Smith, William John "Billy" 1993
  Stanley, Allan Herbert 1981
* Stanley, Russell "Barney" 1962
  Stastny, Peter 1998
  Stevens, Scott 2007
* Stewart, John Sherratt "Black Jack" 1964
* Stewart, Nelson "Nels" 1952
* Stuart, Bruce 1961
* Stuart, Hod 1945
* Taylor, Frederick "Cyclone" (O.B.E.) 1947
* Thompson, Cecil R. "Tiny" 1959
  Tretiak, Vladislav 1989
* Trihey, Col. Harry J. 1950
  Trottier, Bryan 1997
  Ullman, Norman V. Alexander "Norm" 1982
* Vezina, Georges 1945
* Walker, John Phillip "Jack" 1960
* Walsh, Martin "Marty" 1962
* Watson, Harry E. 1962
* Watson, Harry 1994
* Weiland, Ralph "Cooney" 1971
* Westwick, Harry 1962
* Whitcroft, Fred 1962

* Wilson, Gordon Allan "Phat" 1962
* Worsley, Lorne John "Gump" 1980
* Worters, Roy 1969
  Yzerman, Steve 2009

BUILDERS

* Adams, Charles 1960
* Adams, Weston W. 1972
* Ahearn, Thomas Franklin "Frank" 1962
* Ahearne, John Francis "Bunny" 1977
* Allan, Sir Montagu (C.V.O.) 1945
  Allen, Keith 1992
  Arbour, Alger Joseph "Al" 1996
* Ballard, Harold Edwin 1977
* Bauer, Father David 1989
* Bickell, John Paris 1978
  Bowman, Scotty 1991
* Brooks, Herb 2006
* Brown, George V. 1961
* Brown, Walter A. 1962
* Buckland, Frank 1975
  Bush, Walter 2000
* Butterfield, Jack Arlington 1980
* Calder, Frank 1947
* Campbell, Angus D. 1964
* Campbell, Clarence Sutherland 1966
* Cattarinich, Joseph 1977
* Chynoweth, Ed 2008
  Costello, Murray 2005
* Dandurand, Joseph Viateur "Leo" 1963
  Devellano, Jim 2010
* Dilio, Francis Paul 1964
* Dudley, George S. 1958
* Dunn, James A. 1968
  Fletcher, Cliff 2004
  Francis, Emile 1982
* Gibson, Dr. John L. "Jack" 1976
* Gorman, Thomas Patrick "Tommy" 1963
  Gregory, Jim 2007
* Griffiths, Frank A. 1993
* Hanley, William 1986
* Hay, Charles 1974
* Hendy, James C. 1968

* Hewitt, Foster 1965
* Hewitt, William Abraham 1947
* Hotchkiss, Harley 2006
* Hume, Fred J. 1962
  Illitch, Mike 2003
* Imlach, George "Punch" 1984
* Ivan, Thomas N. 1974
* Jennings, William M. 1975
* Johnson, Bob 1992
* Juckes, Gordon W. 1979
* Kilpatrick, Gen. John Reed 1960
  Kilrea, Brian Blair 2003
* Knox, Seymour H. III 1993
  Lamoriello, Lou 2009
* Leader, George Alfred 1969
* LeBel, Robert 1970
* Lockhart, Thomas F. 1965
* Loicq, Paul 1961
* Mariucci, John 1985
* Mathers, Frank 1992
* McLaughlin, Major Frederic 1963
* Milford, John "Jake" 1984
* Molson, Hon. Hartland de Montarville 1973
  Morrison, Ian "Scotty" 1999
* Murray, Monsignor Athol 1998
* Neilson, Roger 2002
* Nelson, Francis 1947
* Norris, Bruce A. 1969
* Norris, Sr., James 1958
* Norris, James Dougan 1962
* Northey, William M. 1947
* O'Brien, John Ambrose 1962
  O'Neill, Brian 1994
* Page, Fred 1993
  Patrick, Craig 2001
* Patrick, Frank 1950
* Pickard, Allan W. 1958
* Pilous, Rudy 1985
* Poile, Norman "Bud" 1990
* Pollock, Samuel Patterson Smyth 1978
* Raymond, Sen. Donat 1958
* Robertson, John Ross 1947
* Robinson, Claude C. 1947
* Ross, Philip D. 1976
* Sabetzki, Dr. Gunther 1995
  Sather, Glen 1997

* Seaman, Daryl "Doc" 2010
* Selke, Frank J. 1960
  Sinden, Harry James 1983
* Smith, Frank D. 1962
* Smythe, Conn 1958
  Snider, Edward M. 1988
* Stanley of Preston, Lord (G.C.B.) 1945
* Sutherland, Cap. James T. 1947
* Tarasov, Anatoli V. 1974
  Torrey, Bill 1995
* Turner, Lloyd 1958
* Tutt, William Thayer 1978
* Voss, Carl Potter 1974
* Waghorne, Fred 1961
* Wirtz, Arthur Michael 1971
* Wirtz, William W. "Bill" 1976
  Ziegler, John A. Jr. 1987

REFEREES/LINESMEN

  Armstrong, Neil 1991
* Ashley, John George 1981
* Chadwick, William L. 1964
* D'Amico, John 1993
* Elliott, Chaucer 1961
* Hayes, George William 1988
* Hewitson, Robert W. 1963
* Ion, Fred J. "Mickey" 1961
  Pavelich, Matt 1987
* Rodden, Michael J. "Mike" 1962
  Scapinello, Ray 2008
* Smeaton, J. Cooper 1961
* Storey, Roy Alvin "Red" 1967
  Udvari, Frank Joseph 1973
  Van Hellemond, Andy 1999

Joe Nieuwendyk (left) scored 51 goals as a rookie with Calgary in 1987-88 and won the Stanley Cup in 1989. He would win it again in Dallas in 1999 and in New Jersey in 2003. Doug Gilmour (right) was a teammate on Calgary's 1989 Cup winner, but had his greatest statistical success with the Toronto Maple Leafs in the 1990s.

Foster Hewitt Memorial Award Winners

In recognition of members of the radio and television industry who made outstanding contributions to their profession and the game during their career in hockey broadcasting. Selected by the NHL Broadcasters' Association.

  Cole, Bob, Hockey Night in Canada 1996
* Cusick, Fred, Boston 1984
* Darling, Ted, Buffalo 1994
  Emrick, Mike, New Jersey, U.S. networks, 2008
  Davidson, John, MSG Network/HNIC 2009
* Gallivan, Danny, Montreal 1984
  Garneau, Richard, Montreal 1999
* Hart, Gene, Philadelphia 1997
* Hewitt, Bill, Hockey Night in Canada 2007
* Hewitt, Foster, Toronto 1984
  Irvin, Dick, Montreal 1988
  Kaiton, Chuck, Hartford/Carolina 2004
* Kelly, Dan, St. Louis 1989
  Lange, Mike, Pittsburgh 2001
* Lecavelier, René, Montreal 1984
  Lynch, Budd, Detroit 1985
  Maher, Peter, Calgary 2006
  Martyn, Bruce, Detroit 1991
  McDonald, Jiggs, Los Angeles, Atlanta, NY Islanders 1990
  McFarlane, Brian, Hockey Night in Canada 1995
* McKnight, Wes, Toronto 1986
  Meeker, Howie, Hockey Night in Canada 1998
  Messina, Sal, New York 2005
  Miller, Bob, Los Angeles 2000
* Pettit, Lloyd, Chicago 1986
  Phillips, Rod, Edmonton 2003
  Redmond, Mickey, Detroit 2011
  Robson, Jim, Vancouver 1992
  Shaver, Al, Minnesota 1993
* Smith, Doug, Montreal 1985
  Tremblay, Gilles, La Soirée du Hockey 2002
  Weber, Ron, Washington 2010
  Wilson, Bob, Boston 1987

* Deceased

Elmer Ferguson
Memorial Award Winners

In recognition of distinguished members of the newspaper profession whose words have brought honor to journalism and to hockey. Selected by the Professional Hockey Writers' Association.

* Barton, Charlie, Buffalo-Courier Express 1985
* Beauchamp, Jacques, Montreal Matin/Journal de Montréal 1984
* Brennan, Bill, Detroit News 1987
* Burchard, Jim, New York World Telegram 1984
* Burnett, Red, Toronto Star 1984
* Carroll, Dink, Montreal Gazette 1984
* Coleman, Jim, Southam Newspapers 1984
  Conway, Russ, Eagle-Tribune 1999
* Damata, Ted, Chicago Tribune 1984
  de Foy, Marc, Le Journal de Montreal/ ruefrontenac.com 2010
  Delano, Hugh, New York Post 1991
  Desjardins, Marcel, Montréal La Presse 1984
  Duhatschek, Eric, Calgary Herald/Globe and Mail 2001
* Dulmage, Jack, Windsor Star 1984
* Dunnell, Milt, Toronto Star 1984
  Dupont, Kevin Paul, Boston Globe 2002
  Elliott, Helene, Los Angeles Times 2005
  Farber, Michael, Montreal Gazette/Sports Illustrated 2003
  Fay, Dave, Washington Times 2007
* Ferguson, Elmer, Montreal Herald/Star 1984
* Fitzgerald, Tom, Boston Globe 1984
  Frayne, Trent, Toronto Telegram/Globe and Mail/Sun 1984
  Gatecliff, Jack, St. Catharines Standard 1995
* Gross, George, Toronto Telegram/Sun 1985
  Johnston, Dick, Buffalo News 1986
  Jones, Terry, Edmonton Sun 2011
* Kelley, Jim, Buffalo News 2004
* Laney, Al, New York Herald-Tribune 1984
* Larochelle, Claude, Le Soleil 1989
  L'Esperance, Zotique, Journal de Montréal/ le Petit Journal 1985
* MacLeod, Rex, Toronto Globe and Mail/Star 1987
  Matheson, Jim, Edmonton Journal 2000
* Mayer, Charles, Journal de Montréal/la Patrie 1985
* McKenzie, Ken, The Hockey News 1997
  Molinari, Dave, Pittsburgh Post-Gazette 2009
  Monahan, Leo, Boston Daily Record/Record-American/ Herald American 1986
  Moriarty, Tim, UPI/Newsday 1986
  Morrison, Scott, Toronto Sun/Rogers Sportsnet 2006
* Nichols, Joe, New York Times 1984
* O'Brien, Andy, Weekend Magazine 1985
  Orr, Frank, Toronto Star 1989
  Olan, Ben, New York Associated Press 1987
* O'Meara, Basil, Montreal Star 1984
  Pedneault, Yvon, La Presse/Journal de Montréal 1998
* Proudfoot, Jim, Toronto Star 1988
  Raymond, Bertrand, Journal de Montréal 1990
  Rosa, Fran, Boston Globe 1987
  Stevens, Neil, Canadian Press 2008
  Strachan, Al, Globe and Mail/Toronto Sun 1993
* Vipond, Jim, Toronto Globe and Mail 1984
  Walter, Lewis, Detroit Times 1984
* Young, Scott, Toronto Globe and Mail/Telegram 1988

United States Hockey Hall of Fame

On May 11, 2007, the U.S. Hockey Hall of Fame and USA Hockey came to a historic agreement that transferred rights to the selection process and induction event associated with the Hall, including the Wayne Gretzky International Award, to USA Hockey. As part of the agreement, the U.S. Hockey Hall of Fame Museum, located in Eveleth, Minn., formed a separate Board of Directors to govern the national shrine for American Hockey.

There are 148 enshrined members in the U.S. Hockey Hall of Fame (www.ushockeyhalloffame.com). New members are inducted annually and must have made a significant contribution to hockey in the United States during the course of their career. A special Wayne Gretzky International Award pays tribute to international individuals who have made major contributions to hockey in the USA.

The United States Hockey Hall of Fame Museum was opened on June 21, 1973. It is dedicated to honoring the sport of ice hockey in the United States by preserving those previous memories and legends of the game. It is located in Eveleth, Minn., 60 miles north of Duluth on Highway 53. The facility is open Memorial Day through Labor Day, Monday to Saturday, 9 a.m. to 5 p.m. and Sundays from 10 a.m. to 3 p.m. After Labor Day, it is open Friday through Sunday. Admission is $8.00 for adults, $7.00 for seniors and youths (13-17) and $6.00 for children (6-12). Children under 6 are free. For further information, call 800-443-7825 or 218-744-5167, or visit www.ushockeyhall.com.

INDIVIDUALS

* Abel, Clarence "Taffy" 1973
* Almquist, Oscar 1983
  Amonte, Tony 2009
* Baker, Hobart "Hobey" 1973
  Barrasso, Tom 2009
* Bartholome, Earl 1977
  Berglund, Art 2010
* Bessone, Amo 1992
* Bessone, Peter 1978
* Blake, Robert 1985
  Boucha, Henry 1995
* Brimsek, Frank 1973
* Brink, Milton "Curly" 2006
* Brooks, Herb 1990
  Broten, Aaron 2007
  Broten, Neal 2000
* Brown, George V. 1973
* Brown, Walter A. 1973
  Bush, Walter 1980
  Carpenter, Bobby 2007
  Cavanagh, Joe 1994
  Ceglarski, Len 1992
* Chadwick, William 1974
* Chaisson, Ray 1974
* Chase, John P. 1973
  Chelios, Chris 2011
  Christian, Dave 2001
  Christian, Roger 1989
* Christian, William "Bill" 1984
  Christiansen, Keith 2005
* Clark, Donald 1978
  Claypool, James 1995
  Cleary, Robert 1981
  Cleary, William 1976
* Conroy, Anthony 1975
  Coppo, Paul 2004
* Cunniff, John 2003
  Curran, Mike 1998
* Dahlstrom, Carl "Cully" 1973
* Desjardins, Victor 1974
* Desmond, Richard 1988
* Dill, Robert 1979
  Dougherty, Richard "Dick" 2003
  Emrick, Mike "Doc" 2011
* Everett, Doug 1974
  Ftorek, Robbie 1991
* Fullerton, James 1992
  Fusco, Mark 2002
  Fusco, Scott 2002
  Gambucci, Gary 2006
  Gambucci, Sergio 1996
* Garrison, John B. 1973
  Garrity, Jack 1986
* Gibson, J.C. "Doc" 1973
* Goheen, Frank "Moose" 1973
* Gordon, Malcolm K. 1973
  Granato, Cammi 2008

  Grant, Wally 1994
* Harding, Francis "Austie" 1975
* Harkness, Nevin D. "Ned" 1994
  Hatcher, Derian 2010
  Hatcher, Kevin 2010
* Heyliger, Victor 1974
* Holt, Jr. Charles E. 1997
  Housley, Phil 2004
  Howe, Mark 2003
  Hull, Brett 2008
* Iglehart, Stewart 1975
  Ikola, Willard 1990
  Ilitch, Mike 2004
* Jennings, William M. 1981
* Jeremiah, Edward J. 1973
* Johnson, Bob 1991
  Johnson, Mark 2004
  Johnson, Paul 2001
* Johnson, Virgil 1974
* Kahler, Nick 1980
* Karakas, Mike 1973
* Kelley, John "Snooks" 1974
  Kelley, John H. "Jack" 1993
  Kirrane, Jack 1987
  LaFontaine, Pat 2003
* Lane, Myles J. 1973
  Langevin, David R. 1993
  Langway, Rod 1999
  Larson, Reed 1996
  LeClair, John 2009
  Leetch, Brian 2008
* Linder, Joseph 1975
* Lockhart, Thomas F. 1973
* LoPresti, Sam L. 1973
  MacDonald, Lane 2005
* MacInnes, John 2007
* Mariucci, John 1973
* Marvin, Cal 1982
  Matchefts, John 1991
* Mather, Bruce 1998
  Mayasich, John 1976
  McCartan, Jack 1983
  Milbury, Mike 2006
* Moe, William 1974
  Morrow, Ken 1995
* Moseley, Fred 1975
  Mullen, Joe 1998
* Murray, Sr. Hugh "Muzz" 1987
  Nagobads, Dr. V. George 2010
  Nanne, Lou 1998
* Nelson, Hubert "Hub" 1978
* Nyrop, William D. 1997
* Olson, Eddie 1977
* Owen, Jr. George 1973
  Palazzari, Doug 2000
* Palmer, Winthrop 1973
  Paradise, Robert 1989

  Patrick, Craig 1996
  Pleau, Larry 2000
* Pleban, Jon "Connie" 1990
* Purpur, Clifford "Fido" 1974
  Ramsey, Mike 2001
  Richter, Mike 2008
* Ridder, Robert 1976
  Riley, Jack 1979
* Riley, Joe 2002
* Riley, William 1977
  Roberts, Gordie 1999
* Roberts, Moe 2005
  Roenick, Jeremy 2010
* Romnes, Elwin "Doc" 1973
* Rondeau, Richard 1985
* Ross, Larry 1988
* Schulz, Charles M. 1993
  Sheehy, Timothy K. 1997
  Snider, Ed 2011
* Stewart, William 1982
  Suter, Gary 2011
* Thompson, Clifford R. 1973
  Tkachuk, Keith 2011
  Trumble, Harold 1985
* Tutt, William Thayer 1973
  Vanbiesbrouck, John 2007
* Watson, Sid 1999
* Williams, Thomas 1981
  Williamson, Murray 2005
  Winsor, Alfred "Ralph" 1973
* Winters, Frank "Coddy" 1973
* Wirtz, William W. "Bill" 1984
  Woog, Doug 2002
* Wright, Lyle Z. 1973
* Yackel, Ken 1986
* Zamboni, Frank 2009

TEAMS

1960 Olympic Men's Team 2000
1980 Olympic Men's Team 2003
1998 Olympic Women's Team 2009

WAYNE GRETZKY INTERNATIONAL AWARD

Wayne Gretzky 1999
The Howe family 2000
Scotty Morrison 2001
Scotty Bowman 2002
Bobby Hull 2003
* Herb Brooks 2004
* Anatoli Tarasov 2008

* Deceased

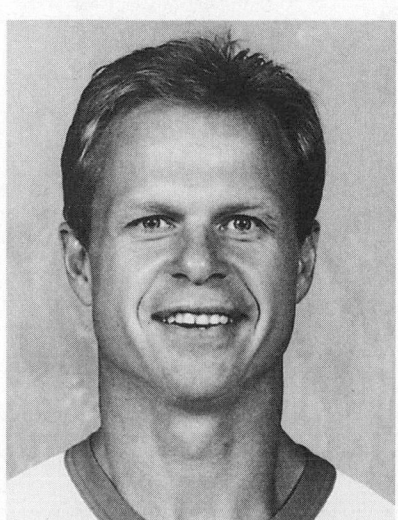

Mark Howe was elected to the United States Hockey Hall of Fame in 2003 and will join his father Gordie in the Hockey Hall of Fame in Toronto at the induction ceremony in 2011.

International Ice Hockey Federation Hall of Fame

The IIHF Hall of Fame was founded in 1997.

Candidates for election as Honoured Members in the player category shall be chosen on the basis of their playing ability, sportsmanship, character and their contribution to their team or teams and to the game of ice hockey in general.

Candidates for election as Honoured Members in the builder category shall be chosen on the basis of their coaching, managerial or executive ability, where applicable, their sportsmanship and character, and their contribution to their organization or organizations and to the game of ice hockey in general.

Candidates for election as Honoured Members in the referee or linesman category shall be chosen on the basis of their officiating ability, sportsmanship, character and their contribution to the game of ice hockey in general. The Paul Loicq Award, named for the longtime former IIHF president, is presented to honor a person for his service to the international hockey community.

Inductees' names are followed by their country and year of induction.

PLAYERS

Alexandrov, Veniamin, RUS, 2007
Balderis, Helmut, LAT, 1998
Ball, Rudi, GER, 2004
Bergqvist, Sven, SWE, 1999
Bjorn, Lars, SWE, 1998
Bobrov, Vsevolod, RUS, 1997
Bourbonnais, Roger, CAN, 1999
Bouzek, Vladimir, CzRep, 2007
Bozon, Phillippe, FRA 2008
Bubnik, Vlastimil, CzRep, 1997
Bye, Karyn, USA, 2011
Cattini, Ferdinand, SUI, 1998
Cattini, Hans, SUI, 1998
Cerny, Josef, CzRep, 2007
Christian, Bill, USA, 1998
Cleary, Bill, USA, 1997
Cosby, Gerry, USA, 1997
Craig, Jim, USA, 1999
Curran, Mike, USA, 1999
Davydov, Vitaly, RUS, 2004
Drobny, Jaroslav, CzRep, 1997
Dzurilla, Vladimir, SVK, 1998
Erhardt, Carl, G.B., 1998
Fetisov, Viacheslav, RUS, 2005
Firsov, Anatoli, RUS, 1998
Golonka, Josef, SVK, 1998
Granato, Cammi, USA 2008
Gretzky, Wayne, CAN, 2000
Gruth, Henryk, POL, 2006
Gustafsson, Bengt-Ake, SWE, 2003
Gut, Karel, CzRep, 1998
Heaney, Geraldine, CAN 2008
Hedberg, Anders, SWE, 1997
Hegen, Dieter, GER 2010
Hiti, Rudi, SLO, 2009
Hlinka, Ivan, CzRep, 2002
Holecek, Jiri, CzRep, 1998
Holik, Jiri, CzRep, 1999
Holmqvist, Leif, SWE, 1999
Huck, Fran, CAN, 1999
Irbe, Arturs, LAT 2010
Jaenecke, Gustav, GER, 1998
James, Angela, CAN 2008
Johnson, Mark, USA, 1999
Johnston, Marshall, CAN, 1998
Jonsson, Tomas, SWE, 2000
Jutila, Timo, FIN, 2003
Kasatonov, Alexei, RUS, 2009
Keinonen, Matti, FIN, 2002
Kharlamov, Valeri, RUS, 1998
Kiessling, Udo, GER, 2000
Kolliker, Jakob, SUI, 2007
Konovalenko, Viktor, RUS, 2007
Krutov, Vladimir, RUS 2010
Kuhnhackl, Erich, GER, 1997
Kurri, Jari, FIN, 2000
Kuzkin, Viktor, RUS, 2005
Lacarriere, Jacques, FRA, 1998
Larionov, Igor RUS 2008
Lemieux, Mario CAN 2008
Loktev, Konstantin, RUS, 2007
Loob, Hakan, SWE, 1998
Lundquist, Vic, CAN, 1997
Lundstrom, Tord, SWE, 2011

Machac, Oldrich, CzRep, 1999
MacKenzie, Barry, CAN, 1999
Makarov, Sergei, RUS, 2001
Malecek, Josef, CzRep, 2003
Maltsev, Alexander, RUS, 1999
Marjamaki, Pekka, FIN, 1998
Martin, Seth, CAN, 1997
Martinec, Vladimir, CzRep, 2001
Mayasich, John, USA, 1997
Mayorov, Boris, RUS, 1999
McCartan, Jack, USA, 1998
McLeod, Jackie, CAN, 1999
Mikhailov, Boris, RUS, 2000
Modry, Bohumil, CZE, 2011
Nanne, Lou, USA, 2004
Naslund, Mats, SWE, 2005
Nedomansky, Vaclav, CzRep, 1997
Nieminen-Valila, Riika, FIN, 2010
Nilsson, Kent, SWE, 2006
Nilsson, Nisse, SWE, 2002
O'Malley, Terry, CAN, 1998
Oksanen, Lasse, FIN, 1999
Pana, Eduard, ROU, 1998
Patton, Peter, G.B., 2002
Peltonen, Esa, FIN, 2007
Petrov, Vladimir, RUS, 2006
Pettersson, Ronald, SWE, 2004
Pospisil, Frantisek, CzRep, 1999
Puschnig, Josef, AUT, 1999
Ragulin, Alexander, RUS, 1997
Rampf, Hans, GER, 2001
Rundqvist, Thomas, SWE, 2007
Salming, Borje, SWE, 1998
Schloder, Alois, GER, 2005
Sinden, Harry, CAN, 1997
Sologubov, Nikolai, RUS, 2004
Starshinov, Vyacheslav, RUS, 2007
Stastny, Peter, SVK, 2000
Sterner, Ulf, SWE, 2001
Stoltz, Roland, SWE, 1999
Suchy, Jan, CzRep, 2009
Tikal, Frantisek, CzRep, 2004
Torriani, Bibi, SUI, 1997
Tretiak, Vladislav, RUS, 1997
Trojak, Ladislav, SVK, 2011
Tumba (Johansson), Sven, SWE, 1997
Tureanu, Doru, ROU, 2011
Valtonen, Jorma, FIN, 1999
Vasiliev, Valeri, RUS, 1998
Wahlsten, Vladimir, FIN, 2006
Watson, Harry, CAN, 1998
Yakushev, Alexander, RUS, 2003
Ylonen, Urpo, FIN, 1997
Zabrodsky, Vladimir, CzRep, 1997
Ziesche, Joachim, GER, 1999

BUILDERS

Ahearne, Bunny, G.B., 1997
Aljancic Sr., Ernest, SLO, 2002
Bauer, Father David, CAN, 1997
Berglund, Art USA 2008
Berglund, Curt, SWE, 2003
Bokac, Ludek, CzRep, 2007
Brooks, Herb, USA, 1999
Brown, Walter, USA, 1997
Buckna, Mike, CAN, 2004
Bush, Walter Jr. USA, 2009
Calcaterra, Enrico, ITA, 1999
Chernyshev, Arkady, RUS, 1999
Dimitriev, Igor, RUS, 2007
Dobida, Hans, AUT, 2007
Eklow, Rudolf, SWE, 1999
Fagerlund, Rickard SWE 2010
Grunander, Arne, SWE, 1997
Henschel, Heinz, GER, 2003
Hewitt, William, CAN, 1998
Holmes, Derek, CAN, 1999
Horsky, Ladislav, SVK, 2004
Hviid, Jorgen, DEN, 2005
Johannessen, Tore, NOR, 1999
Juckes, Gordon, CAN, 1997
Kawabuchi, Tsutomu, JPN, 2004
Khorozov, Anatoli, UKR, 2006
King, Dave, CAN, 2001
Kostka, Vladimir, CzRep, 1997
LeBel, Bob, CAN, 1997
Lindblad, Harry, FIN, 1999
Loicq, Paul, BEL, 1997
Luhti, Cesar W., SUI, 1998
Magnus, Louis, FRA, 1997
Numminen, Kalevi, FIN, 2011
Pasztor, Gyorgy, HUN, 2001
Renwick, Gordon, CAN, 2002
Ridder, Bob, USA, 1998
Riley, Jack, USA, 1998
Sabetzki, Dr. Gunther, GER, 1997
Starovoitov, Andrei, RUS, 1997
Starsi, Jan, SVK, 1999
Stromberg, Arne, SWE, 1998
Stubb, Goran, FIN, 2000
Subrt, Miroslav, CzRep, 2004
Tarasov, Anatoli, RUS, 1997
Tikhonov, Viktor, RUS, 1998
Tomita, Shoichi, JPN, 2006
Trumble, Hal, USA, 1999
Tsutsumi, Yoshiaki, JPN, 1999
Tutt, Thayer, USA, 2002
Unsinn, Xaver, GER, 1998
Wasservogel, Walter, AUT, 1997
Yurzinov, Vladimir, RUS, 2002

REFEREES

Adamec, Quido, CzRep, 2005
Dahlberg, Ove, SWE, 2004
Karandin, Yuri, RUS, 2004
Kompalla, Josef, GER, 2003
Schell, Laszlo, HUN, 2009
Wiitala, Unto, FIN, 2003

PAUL LOICQ AWARD

Montag, Wolf-Dieter, GER, 1998
Neumayer, Roman, GER, 1999
Kukushkin, Vsevolod, RUS, 2000
Kataoka, Isao, JPN, 2001
Marsh, Pat, G.B., 2002
Nagobads, George, USA, 2003
Kukulowicz, Aggie, CAN, 2004
Hrabcek, Rita, AUS, 2005
Tovland, Bo, SWE, 2006
Nadin, Bob, CAN, 2007
Okolicany, Juraj, SVK 2008
Griebel, Harald, GER, 2009
Vairo, Lou, USA 2010
Korolev, Yuri, RUS, 2011

CENTENNIAL ALL-STAR TEAM (1908-2008)

Goaltender: Vladislav Tretiak, RUS
Defenseman: Viacheslav Fetisov, RUS
Defenseman: Borje Salming, SWE
Winger: Valeri Kharlamov, RUS
Winger: Sergei Makarov, RUS
Center: Wayne Gretzky, CAN

TRIPLE GOLD CLUB

(Olympics, World Championship, Stanley Cup)
Tomas Jonsson, SWE
Mats Naslund, SWE
Hakan Loob, SWE
Valeri Kamensky, RUS
Alexei Gusarov, RUS
Peter Forsberg, SWE
Vyacheslav Fetisov, RUS
Igor Larionov, RUS
Alexander Mogilny, RUS
Vladimir Malakhov, RUS
Rob Blake, CAN
Joe Sakic, CAN
Brendan Shanahan, CAN
Scott Niedermayer, CAN
Jaromir Jagr, CzRep
Jiri Slegr, CzRep
Nicklas Lidstrom, SWE
Fredrik Modin, SWE
Chris Pronger, CAN
Niklas Kronwall, SWE
Henrik Zetterberg, SWE
Mikael Samuelsson, SWE
Eric Staal, CAN
Jonathan Toews, CAN
Mike Babcock (coach), CAN
Patrice Bergeron, CAN

Karyn Bye celebrates the American gold medal victory when women's hockey made its Olympic debut at the 1998 Nagano Games. Bye competed on the U.S. national women's team from 1992 to 2002.

2011 Stanley Cup Playoffs

Results

CONFERENCE QUARTER-FINALS
(Best-of-seven series)

Eastern Conference

Series 'A'
Wed. Apr. 13	(8) NY Rangers 1	at	(1) Washington 2	*
Fri. Apr. 15	NY Rangers 0	at	Washington 2	
Sun. Apr. 17	Washington 2	at	NY Rangers 3	
Wed. Apr. 20	Washington 4	at	NY Rangers 3	**
Sat. Apr. 23	NY Rangers 1	at	Washington 3	

   * Alexander Semin scored at 18:24 of overtime
   ** Jason Chimera scored at 32:36 of overtime
(Washington won series 4-1)

Series 'B'
Thu. Apr. 14	(7) Buffalo 1	at	(2) Philadelphia 0	
Sat. Apr. 16	Buffalo 4	at	Philadelphia 5	
Mon. Apr. 18	Philadelphia 4	at	Buffalo 2	
Wed. Apr. 20	Philadelphia 0	at	Buffalo 1	
Fri. Apr. 22	Buffalo 4	at	Philadelphia 3	*
Sun. Apr. 24	Philadelphia 5	at	Buffalo 4	**
Tue. Apr. 26	Buffalo 2	at	Philadelphia 5	

   * Tyler Ennis scored at 5:31 of overtime
   ** Ville Leino scored at 4:43 of overtime
(Philadelphia won series 4-3)

Series 'C'
Thu. Apr. 14	(6) Montreal 2	at	(3) Boston 0	
Sat. Apr. 16	Montreal 3	at	Boston 1	
Mon. Apr. 18	Boston 4	at	Montreal 2	
Thu. Apr. 21	Boston 5	at	Montreal 4	*
Sat. Apr. 23	Montreal 1	at	Boston 2	**
Tue. Apr. 26	Boston 1	at	Montreal 2	
Wed. Apr. 27	Montreal 3	at	Boston 4	***

   * Michael Ryder scored at 1:59 of overtime
   ** Nathan Horton scored at 29:03 of overtime
  *** Nathan Horton scored at 5:43 of overtime
(Boston won series 4-3)

Series 'D'
Wed. Apr. 13	(5) Tampa Bay 0	at	(4) Pittsburgh 3	
Fri. Apr. 15	Tampa Bay 5	at	Pittsburgh 1	
Mon. Apr. 18	Pittsburgh 3	at	Tampa Bay 2	
Wed. Apr. 20	Pittsburgh 3	at	Tampa Bay 2	*
Sat. Apr. 23	Tampa Bay 8	at	Pittsburgh 2	
Mon. Apr. 25	Pittsburgh 2	at	Tampa Bay 4	
Wed. Apr. 27	Tampa Bay 1	at	Pittsburgh 0	

   * James Neal scored at 23:38 of overtime
(Tampa Bay won series 4-3)

Western Conference

Series 'E'
Wed. Apr. 13	(8) Chicago 0	at	(1) Vancouver 2	
Fri. Apr. 15	Chicago 3	at	Vancouver 4	
Sun. Apr. 17	Vancouver 3	at	Chicago 2	
Tue. Apr. 19	Vancouver 2	at	Chicago 7	
Thu. Apr. 21	Chicago 5	at	Vancouver 0	
Sun. Apr. 24	Vancouver 3	at	Chicago 4	*
Tue. Apr. 26	Chicago 1	at	Vancouver 2	**

   * Ben Smith scored at 15:30 of overtime
   ** Alexandre Burrows scored at 5:22 of overtime
(Vancouver won series 4-3)

Series 'F'
Thu. Apr. 14	(7) Los Angeles 2	at	(2) San Jose 3	*
Sat. Apr. 16	Los Angeles 4	at	San Jose 0	
Tue. Apr. 19	San Jose 6	at	Los Angeles 5	**
Thu. Apr. 21	San Jose 6	at	Los Angeles 3	
Sat. Apr. 23	Los Angeles 3	at	San Jose 1	
Mon. Apr. 25	San Jose 4	at	Los Angeles 3	***

   * Joe Pavelski scored at 14:44 of overtime
   ** Devin Setoguchi scored at 3:09 of overtime
  *** Joe Thornton scored at 2:22 of overtime
(San Jose won series 4-2)

Series 'G'
Wed. Apr. 13	(6) Phoenix 2	at	(3) Detroit 4
Sat. Apr. 16	Phoenix 3	at	Detroit 4
Mon. Apr. 18	Detroit 4	at	Phoenix 2
Wed. Apr. 20	Detroit 6	at	Phoenix 3

(Detroit won series 4-0)

Series 'H'
Wed. Apr. 13	(5) Nashville 4	at	(4) Anaheim 1	
Fri. Apr. 15	Nashville 3	at	Anaheim 5	
Sun. Apr. 17	Anaheim 3	at	Nashville 4	
Wed. Apr. 20	Anaheim 6	at	Nashville 3	
Fri. Apr. 22	Nashville 4	at	Anaheim 3	*
Sun. Apr. 24	Anaheim 2	at	Nashville 4	

   * Jerred Smithson scored at 1:57 of overtime
(Nashville won series 4-2)

CONFERENCE SEMI-FINALS
(Best-of-seven series)

Eastern Conference

Series 'I'
Fri. Apr. 29	(5) Tampa Bay 4	at	(1) Washington 2	
Sun. May 1	Tampa Bay 3	at	Washington 2	*
Tue. May 3	Washington 3	at	Tampa Bay 4	
Wed. May 4	Washington 3	at	Tampa Bay 5	

   * Vincent Lecavalier scored at 6:19 of overtime
(Tampa Bay won series 4-0)

Series 'J'
Sat. Apr. 30	(3) Boston 7	at	(2) Philadelphia 3	
Mon. May 2	Boston 3	at	Philadelphia 2	*
Wed. May 4	Philadelphia 1	at	Boston 5	
Fri. May 6	Philadelphia 1	at	Boston 5	

   * David Krejci scored at 14:00 of overtime
(Boston won series 4-0)

Western Conference

Series 'K'
Thu. Apr. 28	(5) Nashville 0	at	(1) Vancouver 1	
Sat. Apr. 30	Nashville 2	at	Vancouver 1	*
Tue. May 3	Vancouver 3	at	Nashville 2	**
Thu. May 5	Vancouver 4	at	Nashville 2	
Sat. May 7	Nashville 4	at	Vancouver 3	
Mon. May 9	Vancouver 2	at	Nashville 1	

   * Matt Halischuk scored at 34:51 of overtime
   ** Ryan Kesler scored at 10:45 of overtime
(Vancouver won series 4-2)

Series 'L'
Fri. Apr. 29	(3) Detroit 1	at	(2) San Jose 2	*
Sun. May 1	Detroit 1	at	San Jose 2	
Wed. May 4	San Jose 4	at	Detroit 3	**
Fri. May 6	San Jose 3	at	Detroit 4	
Sun. May 8	Detroit 4	at	San Jose 3	
Tue. May 10	San Jose 1	at	Detroit 3	
Thu. May 12	Detroit 2	at	San Jose 3	

   * Benn Ferriero scored at 7:03 of overtime
   ** Devin Setoguchi scored at 9:21 of overtime
(San Jose won series 4-3)

CONFERENCE FINALS
(Best-of-seven series)

Eastern Conference

Series 'M'
Sat. May 14	(5) Tampa Bay 5	at	(3) Boston 2
Tue. May 17	Tampa Bay 5	at	Boston 6
Thu. May 19	Boston 2	at	Tampa Bay 0
Sat. May 21	Boston 3	at	Tampa Bay 5
Mon. May 23	Tampa Bay 1	at	Boston 3
Wed. May 25	Boston 4	at	Tampa Bay 5
Fri. May 27	Tampa Bay 0	at	Boston 1

(Boston won series 4-3)

Western Conference

Series 'N'
Sun. May 15	(2) San Jose 2	at	(1) Vancouver 3	
Wed. May 18	San Jose 3	at	Vancouver 7	
Fri. May 20	Vancouver 3	at	San Jose 4	
Sun. May 22	Vancouver 4	at	San Jose 2	
Tue. May 24	San Jose 2	at	Vancouver 3	*

   * Kevin Bieksa scored at 30:18 of overtime
(Vancouver won series 4-1)

STANLEY CUP FINAL
(Best-of-seven series)

Series 'O'
Wed. June 1	(3) Boston 0	at	(1) Vancouver 1	
Sat. June 4	Boston 2	at	Vancouver 3	*
Mon. June 6	Vancouver 1	at	Boston 8	
Wed. June 8	Vancouver 0	at	Boston 4	
Fri. June 10	Boston 0	at	Vancouver 1	
Mon. June 13	Vancouver 2	at	Boston 5	
Wed. June 15	Boston 4	at	Vancouver 0	

   * Alexandre Burrows scored at 0:11 of overtime
(Boston won series 4-3)

Team Playoff Records

	GP	W	L	GF	GA	%
Boston	25	16	9	81	53	.640
Vancouver	25	15	10	58	69	.600
Tampa Bay	18	11	7	59	45	.611
San Jose	18	9	9	51	58	.500
Detroit	11	7	4	36	28	.636
Nashville	12	6	6	33	34	.500
Washington	9	4	5	23	24	.444
Philadelphia	11	4	7	29	38	.364
Chicago	7	3	4	22	16	.429
Montreal	7	3	4	17	17	.429
Buffalo	7	3	4	18	22	.429
Pittsburgh	7	3	4	14	22	.429
Los Angeles	6	2	4	20	20	.333
Anaheim	6	2	4	20	22	.333
NY Rangers	5	1	4	8	13	.200
Phoenix	4	0	4	10	18	.000

Individual Leaders

Abbreviations: GP – games played; **G** – goals; **A** – assists; **PTS** – points; **+/–** – difference between Goals For (**GF**) scored when a player is on the ice with his team at even strength or shorthanded and Goals Against (**GA**) scored when the same player is on the ice with his team at even strength or on a power play; **PIM** – penalties in minutes; **PP** – power play goals; **SH** – shorthanded goals; **GW** – game-winning goals; **OT** – overtime goals; **S** – shots on goal; **%** – percentage of shots resulting in goals.

Playoff Scoring Leaders

Player	Team	GP	G	A	PTS	+/–	PIM	PP	SH	GW	OT	S	%
David Krejci	Boston	25	12	11	23	8	10	2	0	4	1	57	21.1
Henrik Sedin	Vancouver	25	3	19	22	-11	16	2	0	1	0	46	6.5
Martin St. Louis	Tampa Bay	18	10	10	20	-8	4	4	0	1	0	50	20.0
Daniel Sedin	Vancouver	25	9	11	20	-9	32	5	0	2	0	99	9.1
Patrice Bergeron	Boston	23	6	14	20	15	28	0	2	1	0	67	9.0
Brad Marchand*	Boston	25	11	8	19	12	40	0	1	1	0	61	18.0
Ryan Kesler	Vancouver	25	7	12	19	0	47	4	0	2	1	76	9.2
Vincent Lecavalier	Tampa Bay	18	6	13	19	6	16	3	0	3	1	56	10.7
Alexandre Burrows	Vancouver	25	9	8	17	0	34	1	1	2	2	62	14.5
Nathan Horton	Boston	21	8	9	17	11	35	1	0	3	2	52	15.4
Michael Ryder	Boston	25	8	9	17	8	8	2	0	2	1	44	18.2
Teddy Purcell	Tampa Bay	18	6	11	17	4	2	1	0	1	0	46	13.0
Joe Thornton	San Jose	18	3	14	17	-5	16	0	0	2	1	48	6.3
Dan Boyle	San Jose	18	4	12	16	-7	8	2	0	1	0	67	6.0
Ryane Clowe	San Jose	17	6	9	15	5	32	3	0	0	0	39	15.4
Pavel Datsyuk	Detroit	11	4	11	15	10	8	2	0	0	0	38	10.5
Logan Couture*	San Jose	18	7	7	14	2	2	1	0	0	0	64	10.9
Mark Recchi	Boston	25	5	9	14	7	8	2	0	1	0	40	12.5
Steve Downie	Tampa Bay	17	2	12	14	7	40	0	0	1	0	27	7.4

Playoff Defencemen Scoring Leaders

Player	Team	GP	G	A	PTS	+/–	PIM	PP	SH	GW	OT	S	%
Dan Boyle	San Jose	18	4	12	16	-7	8	2	0	1	0	67	6.0
Christian Ehrhoff	Vancouver	23	2	10	12	-13	16	1	0	0	0	50	4.0
Alexander Edler	Vancouver	25	2	9	11	-4	8	0	0	0	0	58	3.4
Dennis Seidenberg	Boston	25	1	10	11	12	31	0	0	0	0	63	1.6
Tomas Kaberle	Boston	25	0	11	11	8	4	0	0	0	0	33	0.0
Kevin Bieksa	Vancouver	25	5	5	10	6	51	1	0	1	1	47	10.6
Andrew Ference	Boston	25	4	6	10	10	37	1	0	1	0	38	10.5
Johnny Boychuk	Boston	25	3	6	9	12	12	0	0	1	0	51	5.9
Zdeno Chara	Boston	24	2	7	9	16	34	1	0	0	0	62	3.2
Ian White	San Jose	17	1	8	9	3	8	1	0	0	0	40	2.5
Nicklas Lidstrom	Detroit	11	4	4	8	8	4	2	0	0	0	26	15.4
Marc-Andre Gragnani*	Buffalo	7	1	6	7	0	4	1	0	0	0	9	11.1
Eric Brewer	Tampa Bay	18	1	6	7	-3	14	0	0	0	0	26	3.8
10 players tied with					6								

GOALTENDING LEADERS

Goals Against Average

Goaltender	Team	GP	Mins	GA	Avg.
Tim Thomas	Boston	25	1542	51	1.98
Carey Price	Montreal	7	455	16	2.11
Corey Crawford*	Chicago	7	435	16	2.21
Michal Neuvirth*	Washington	9	590	23	2.34
Jimmy Howard	Detroit	11	673	28	2.50
Dwayne Roloson	Tampa Bay	17	982	41	2.51
Marc-Andre Fleury	Pittsburgh	7	405	17	2.52
Roberto Luongo	Vancouver	25	1427	61	2.56
Pekka Rinne	Nashville	12	748	32	2.57
Ryan Miller	Buffalo	7	410	20	2.93

Wins

Goaltender	Team	GP	Mins	W	L
Tim Thomas	Boston	25	1542	16	9
Roberto Luongo	Vancouver	25	1427	15	10
Dwayne Roloson	Tampa Bay	17	982	10	6
Antti Niemi	San Jose	18	1044	8	9
Jimmy Howard	Detroit	11	673	7	4
Pekka Rinne	Nashville	12	748	6	6
Brian Boucher	Philadelphia	9	422	4	4
Michal Neuvirth*	Washington	9	590	4	5
Four goaltenders tied with				3	

Save Percentage

Goaltender	Team	GP	Mins	GA	SA	S%	W	L
Tim Thomas	Boston	25	1542	51	849	.940	16	9
Carey Price	Montreal	7	455	16	242	.934	3	4
Corey Crawford*	Chicago	7	435	16	218	.927	3	4
Dwayne Roloson	Tampa Bay	17	982	41	541	.924	10	6
Jimmy Howard	Detroit	11	673	28	364	.923	7	4
Ryan Miller	Buffalo	7	410	20	242	.917	3	4
Roberto Luongo	Vancouver	25	1427	61	711	.914	15	10
Michal Neuvirth*	Washington	9	590	23	261	.912	4	5
Pekka Rinne	Nashville	12	748	32	343	.907	6	6
Brian Boucher	Philadelphia	9	422	22	229	.904	4	4

Shutouts

Goaltender	Team	GP	Mins	SO	W	L
Roberto Luongo	Vancouver	25	1427	4	15	10
Tim Thomas	Boston	25	1542	4	16	9
Ryan Miller	Buffalo	7	410	2	3	4
Six goaltenders tied with				1		

* Rookie

Goals

Player	Team	GP	G
David Krejci	Boston	25	12
Brad Marchand*	Boston	25	11
Martin St. Louis	Tampa Bay	18	10
Sean Bergenheim	Tampa Bay	16	9
Daniel Sedin	Vancouver	25	9
Alexandre Burrows	Vancouver	25	9
Nathan Horton	Boston	21	8
Michael Ryder	Boston	25	8

Assists

Player	Team	GP	A
Henrik Sedin	Vancouver	25	19
Joe Thornton	San Jose	18	14
Patrice Bergeron	Boston	23	14
Vincent Lecavalier	Tampa Bay	18	13
Steve Downie	Tampa Bay	17	12
Dan Boyle	San Jose	18	12
Ryan Kesler	Vancouver	25	12

Power-play Goals

Player	Team	GP	PP
Daniel Sedin	Vancouver	25	5
Teemu Selanne	Anaheim	6	4
Thomas Vanek	Buffalo	7	4
Martin St. Louis	Tampa Bay	18	4
Ryan Kesler	Vancouver	25	4
Six players tied with			3

Game-winning Goals

Player	Team	GP	GW
David Krejci	Boston	25	4
Vincent Lecavalier	Tampa Bay	18	3
Nathan Horton	Boston	21	3
Chris Higgins	Vancouver	25	3
Brian Gionta	Montreal	7	2
Jason Chimera	Washington	9	2
Tomas Holmstrom	Detroit	11	2
Valtteri Filppula	Detroit	11	2
Joe Thornton	San Jose	18	2
Devin Setoguchi	San Jose	18	2
Michael Ryder	Boston	25	2
Daniel Sedin	Vancouver	25	2
Alexandre Burrows	Vancouver	25	2
Ryan Kesler	Vancouver	25	2
Rich Peverley	Boston	25	2

Shorthanded Goals

Player	Team	GP	SH
David Legwand	Nashville	12	2
Patrice Bergeron	Boston	23	2
Corey Perry	Anaheim	6	1
Tomas Plekanec	Montreal	7	1
Jonathan Toews	Chicago	7	1
Mattias Ohlund	Tampa Bay	18	1
Daniel Paille	Boston	25	1
Alexandre Burrows	Vancouver	25	1
Brad Marchand*	Boston	25	1

Overtime Goals

Player	Team	GP	OT
Devin Setoguchi	San Jose	18	2
Nathan Horton	Boston	21	2
Alexandre Burrows	Vancouver	25	2
16 players tied with			1

Shots

Player	Team	GP	S
Daniel Sedin	Vancouver	25	99
Ryan Kesler	Vancouver	25	76
James van Riemsdyk	Philadelphia	11	70
Dan Boyle	San Jose	18	67
Patrice Bergeron	Boston	23	67
Devin Setoguchi	San Jose	18	65
Logan Couture*	San Jose	18	64
Dennis Seidenberg	Boston	25	63
Zdeno Chara	Boston	24	62
Alexandre Burrows	Vancouver	25	62
Brad Marchand*	Boston	25	61

Plus/Minus

Player	Team	GP	+/–
Zdeno Chara	Boston	24	16
Patrice Bergeron	Boston	23	15
Dennis Seidenberg	Boston	25	12
Johnny Boychuk	Boston	25	12
Brad Marchand*	Boston	25	12
Nathan Horton	Boston	21	11
Chris Kelly	Boston	25	11
Milan Lucic	Boston	25	11
Pavel Datsyuk	Detroit	11	10
Andrew Ference	Boston	25	10

TEAMS' PLAYOFF HOME/ROAD RECORD

Team	HOME GP	W	L	GF	GA	Win %	ROAD GP	W	L	GF	GA	Win %
Boston	13	10	3	46	25	.769	12	6	6	35	28	.500
Vancouver	14	10	4	31	28	.714	11	5	6	27	41	.455
Tampa Bay	8	5	3	27	23	.625	10	6	4	32	22	.600
San Jose	9	5	4	20	24	.556	9	4	5	31	34	.444
Detroit	5	4	1	18	13	.800	6	3	3	18	15	.500
Nashville	6	2	4	16	20	.333	6	4	2	17	14	.667
Washington	5	3	2	11	9	.600	4	1	3	12	15	.250
Philadelphia	6	2	4	18	21	.333	5	2	3	11	17	.400
Chicago	3	2	1	13	8	.667	4	1	3	9	8	.250
Montreal	3	1	2	8	10	.333	4	2	2	9	7	.500
Buffalo	3	1	2	7	9	.333	4	2	2	11	13	.500
Pittsburgh	4	1	3	6	14	.250	3	2	1	8	8	.667
Los Angeles	3	0	3	11	16	.000	3	2	1	9	4	.667
Anaheim	3	1	2	9	11	.333	3	1	2	11	11	.333
NY Rangers	2	1	1	6	6	.500	3	0	3	2	7	.000
Phoenix	2	0	2	5	10	.000	2	0	2	5	8	.000
Totals	**89**	**48**	**41**	**252**	**247**	**.539**	**89**	**41**	**48**	**247**	**252**	**.461**

TEAM PENALTIES

Abbreviations: GP – games played; **PEN** – total penalty minutes, including bench penalties; **BMI** – total bench minor minutes; **AVG** – average penalty minutes/game arrived by dividing total penalty minutes by games played

Team	GP	PEN	BMI	AVG
Mtl.	7	54	4	7.7
Wsh.	9	84	4	9.3
Nsh.	12	121	0	10.1
Phx.	4	41	0	10.3
Chi.	7	76	0	10.9
Det.	11	125	0	11.4
T.B.	18	207	8	11.5
Pit.	7	82	0	11.7
NYR	5	62	4	12.4
L.A.	6	85	0	14.2
S.J.	18	276	6	15.3
Buf.	7	109	2	15.6
Phi.	11	173	4	15.7
Bos.	25	396	4	15.8
Van.	25	435	12	17.4
Ana.	6	109	0	18.2
Totals	**89**	**2435**	**48**	**27.4**

TEAMS' POWER-PLAY RECORD

Abbreviations: ADV-total advantages; **PPGF**-power play goals for; **%** arrived by dividing number of power-play goals by total advantages.

#	HOME Team	GP	ADV	PPGF	%	ROAD Team	GP	ADV	PPGF	%	OVERALL Team	GP	ADV	PPGF	%
1	Phx.	2	5	3	60.0	Ana.	3	10	4	40.0	Ana.	6	22	8	36.4
2	Ana.	3	12	4	33.3	L.A.	3	10	3	30.0	Phx.	4	18	6	33.3
3	Det.	5	22	6	27.3	S.J.	9	29	8	27.6	T.B.	18	67	17	25.4
4	T.B.	8	29	7	24.1	T.B.	10	38	10	26.3	Buf.	7	31	7	22.6
5	Chi.	3	17	4	23.5	Van.	11	50	13	26.0	Mtl.	7	27	6	22.2
6	Mtl.	3	14	3	21.4	Buf.	4	16	4	25.0	L.A.	6	24	5	20.8
7	Buf.	3	15	3	20.0	Phx.	2	13	3	23.1	Chi.	7	29	6	20.7
8	Bos.	13	48	8	16.7	Mtl.	4	13	3	23.1	Van.	25	93	19	20.4
9	Nsh.	6	25	4	16.0	Wsh.	4	15	3	20.0	S.J.	18	73	14	19.2
10	Phi.	6	33	5	15.2	Chi.	4	12	2	16.7	Det.	11	43	8	18.6
11	L.A.	3	14	2	14.3	Nsh.	6	23	3	13.0	Nsh.	12	48	7	14.6
12	Van.	14	43	6	14.0	Phi.	5	16	2	12.5	Wsh.	9	35	5	14.3
13	S.J.	9	44	6	13.6	Pit.	3	10	1	10.0	Phi.	11	49	7	14.3
14	Wsh.	5	20	2	10.0	Det.	6	21	2	9.5	Bos.	25	88	10	11.4
15	NYR	2	14	1	7.1	Bos.	12	40	2	5.0	NYR	5	20	1	5.0
16	Pit.	4	25	0	0.0	NYR	3	6	0	0.0	Pit.	7	35	1	2.9
	Totals	**89**	**380**	**64**	**16.8**		**89**	**322**	**63**	**19.6**		**89**	**702**	**127**	**18.1**

TEAMS' PENALTY KILLING RECORD

Abbreviations: TSH – Total times shorthanded; **PPGA** – power-play goals against; **%** arrived by dividing times shorthanded minus power-play goals against by times short.

#	HOME Team	GP	TSH	PPGA	%	ROAD Team	GP	TSH	PPGA	%	OVERALL Team	GP	TSH	PPGA	%
1	Mtl.	3	9	0	100.0	L.A.	3	11	0	100.0	Mtl.	7	21	0	100.0
2	Bos.	13	51	6	88.2	Mtl.	4	12	0	100.0	T.B.	18	78	6	92.3
3	Wsh.	5	15	2	86.7	T.B.	10	50	2	96.0	L.A.	6	23	2	91.3
4	NYR	2	7	1	85.7	Chi.	4	10	1	90.0	Wsh.	9	38	5	86.8
5	Phx.	2	7	1	85.7	Buf.	4	24	3	87.5	Buf.	7	35	5	85.7
6	T.B.	8	28	4	85.7	Wsh.	4	23	3	87.0	Bos.	25	96	15	84.4
7	Van.	14	43	7	83.7	Pit.	3	11	2	81.8	NYR	5	16	3	81.3
8	L.A.	3	12	2	83.3	Nsh.	6	20	4	80.0	Phi.	11	47	9	80.9
9	Phi.	6	23	4	82.6	Bos.	12	45	9	80.0	Van.	25	99	19	80.8
10	Buf.	3	11	2	81.8	Phi.	5	24	5	79.2	Ana.	6	27	6	77.8
11	Det.	5	23	5	78.3	Ana.	3	14	3	78.6	Chi.	7	18	4	77.8
12	Ana.	3	13	3	76.9	Van.	11	56	12	78.6	S.J.	18	76	18	76.3
13	S.J.	9	36	9	75.0	NYR	3	9	2	77.8	Det.	11	46	11	76.1
14	Chi.	3	8	3	62.5	S.J.	9	40	9	77.5	Phx.	4	15	4	73.3
15	Pit.	4	16	6	62.5	Det.	6	23	6	73.9	Pit.	7	27	8	70.4
16	Nsh.	6	20	8	60.0	Phx.	2	8	3	62.5	Nsh.	12	40	12	70.0
	Totals	**89**	**322**	**63**	**80.4**		**89**	**380**	**64**	**83.2**		**89**	**702**	**127**	**81.9**

SHORTHAND GOALS

GOALS FOR Team	GP	GF	GOALS AGAINST Team	GP	GA
Bos.	25	4	S.J.	18	0
Nsh.	12	2	Phi.	11	0
Ana.	6	1	Det.	11	0
Mtl.	7	1	Wsh.	9	0
Chi.	7	1	Buf.	7	0
T.B.	18	1	Mtl.	7	0
Van.	25	1	Chi.	7	0
Phx.	4	0	L.A.	6	0
NYR	5	0	Ana.	6	0
L.A.	6	0	NYR	5	0
Buf.	7	0	Phx.	4	0
Pit.	7	0	Bos.	25	1
Wsh.	9	0	T.B.	18	1
Phi.	11	0	Pit.	7	1
Det.	11	0	Nsh.	12	2
S.J.	18	0	Van.	25	6
Totals	**89**	**11**	**Totals**	**89**	**11**

Bruins captain Zdeno Chara had only two goals and seven assists in 24 playoff games but he lead all postseason performers with a plus-minus rating of +16. Chara's time on ice per game of 27:39 was more than any other player who made it past the second round.

Stanley Cup Record Book

History: The Stanley Cup, the oldest trophy competed for by professional athletes in North America, was donated by Frederick Arthur, Lord Stanley of Preston and son of the Earl of Derby, in 1893. Lord Stanley purchased the trophy for 10 guineas ($50 at that time) for presentation to the amateur hockey champions of Canada. Since 1906, when Canadian teams began to pay their players openly, the Stanley Cup has been the symbol of professional hockey supremacy. It has been competed for only by NHL teams since 1926-27 and has been under the exclusive control of the NHL since 1947.

Stanley Cup Standings

1918-2011

(ranked by Cup wins)

Teams	Cup Wins	Yrs.	Series	Wins	Losses	Games	Wins	Losses	Ties	Goals For	Goals Against	Winning %
Montreal[1,2]	24	79	145	89	55	709	410	291	8	2152	1799	.584
Toronto[3]	14	64	109	58	51	524	251	269	4	1350	1427	.483
Detroit	11	59	115	67	48	586	312	273	1	1677	1482	.533
Boston	6	66	113	53	60	568	275	287	6	1654	1647	.489
Edmonton	5	20	49	34	15	251	152	99	0	938	763	.606
Chicago	4	56	98	46	52	457	216	236	5	1313	1427	.478
NY Rangers	4	53	93	44	49	422	198	216	8	1175	1213	.479
NY Islanders	4	21	47	30	17	240	134	106	0	792	714	.558
Pittsburgh	3	26	51	28	23	277	150	127	0	850	826	.542
New Jersey[4]	3	21	40	22	18	230	122	108	0	629	564	.530
Philadelphia	2	35	75	42	33	403	209	194	0	1219	1187	.519
Colorado[5]	2	21	44	25	19	249	132	117	0	726	703	.530
Dallas[6]	1	29	56	28	28	307	154	153	0	897	910	.502
Calgary[7]	1	26	40	15	25	208	94	114	0	648	701	.452
Carolina[8]	1	13	22	10	12	127	59	68	0	323	368	.465
Anaheim	1	8	18	11	7	98	55	43	0	248	242	.561
Tampa Bay	1	6	12	7	5	69	37	32	0	181	185	.536
St. Louis	0	35	58	23	35	307	138	169	0	862	954	.450
Buffalo	0	29	50	21	29	256	124	132	0	763	765	.484
Los Angeles	0	25	36	11	25	182	69	113	0	549	694	.379
Vancouver	0	24	40	16	24	214	98	116	0	604	690	.458
Washington	0	22	34	12	22	191	86	105	0	573	583	.450
Phoenix[9]	0	18	20	2	18	103	32	71	0	273	387	.311
San Jose	0	13	24	11	13	140	67	73	0	348	411	.479
Ottawa[10]	0	12	20	8	12	109	51	58	0	254	265	.468
Nashville	0	6	7	1	6	40	14	26	0	93	113	.350
Florida	0	3	6	3	3	31	13	18	0	77	82	.419
Minnesota	0	3	5	2	3	29	11	18	0	64	72	.379
Winnipeg[11]	0	1	1	0	1	4	0	4	0	6	17	.000
Columbus	0	1	1	0	1	4	0	4	0	7	18	.000

1 Includes Stanley Cup championship won in 1916 prior to the formation of the NHL.
2 1919 final incomplete due to influenza epidemic.
3 Includes Stanley Cup championship won by Toronto Blueshirts in 1914 prior to the formation of the NHL.
4 Includes totals of Colorado Rockies 1976-82.
5 Includes totals of Quebec Nordiques 1979-95.
6 Includes totals of Minnesota North Stars 1967-93.
7 Includes totals of Atlanta Flames 1972-80.
8 Includes totals of Hartford Whalers 1979-97.
9 Includes totals of Winnipeg Jets 1979-96.
10 Modern Ottawa Senators franchise only, 1992 to date.
11 Includes totals of Atlanta Thrashers 1999-2011.

Stanley Cup Winners Prior to Formation of NHL in 1917

Season	Champions	Manager	Coach
1916-17	Seattle Metropolitans	Pete Muldoon	Pete Muldoon
1915-16	Montreal Canadiens	George Kennedy	George Kennedy
1914-15	Vancouver Millionaires	Frank Patrick	Frank Patrick
1913-14	Toronto Blueshirts	Jack Marshall	Scotty Davidson*
1912-13**	Quebec Bulldogs	M.J. Quinn	Joe Malone*
1911-12	Quebec Bulldogs	M.J. Quinn	Charley Nolan
1910-11	Ottawa Senators		Percy LeSueur
1909-10	Montreal Wanderers (Mar. 1910)	Dickie Boon	Pud Glass*
1909-10	Ottawa Senators (Jan. 1910)		Bruce Stuart*
1908-09	Ottawa Senators		Bruce Stuart*
1907-08	Montreal Wanderers	Dickie Boon	Cecil Blachford
1906-07	Montreal Wanderers (Mar. 25, 1907)	Dickie Boon	Cecil Blachford
1906-07	Kenora Thistles (Jan./Mar. 18, 1907)	F.A. Hudson	Tom Phillips*
1905-06	Montreal Wanderers (Mar. 1906)	Cecil Blachford*	
1905-06	Ottawa Silver Seven (Feb. 1906)		Alf Smith
1904-05	Ottawa Silver Seven		Alf Smith
1903-04	Ottawa Silver Seven		Alf Smith
1902-03	Ottawa Silver Seven (Mar. 1903)		Alf Smith
1902-03	Montreal A.A.A. (Feb. 1903)		C. McKerrow
1901-02	Montreal A.A.A. (Mar. 1902)		C. McKerrow
1901-02	Winnipeg Victorias (Jan. 1902)		
1900-01	Winnipeg Victorias		Dan Bain*
1899-1900	Montreal Shamrocks		Harry Trihey*
1898-99	Montreal Shamrocks (Mar. 1899)		Harry Trihey*
1898-99	Montreal Victorias (Feb. 1899)		Mike Grant*
1897-98	Montreal Victorias		Frank Richardson
1896-97	Montreal Victorias		Mike Grant*
1895-96	Montreal Victorias (Dec. 1896)		Mike Grant*
1895-96	Winnipeg Victorias (Feb. 1896)		Jack Armitage
1894-95	Montreal Victorias		Mike Grant*
1893-94	Montreal A.A.A.		
1892-93	Montreal A.A.A.		

* In the early years the teams were frequently run by the Captain. *Indicates Captain
** Victoria defeated Quebec in challenge series. No official recognition.

Stanley Cup Winners

Year	W-L-T in Finals	Winner	Coach	Finalist	Coach
2011	4-3	Boston	Claude Julien	Vancouver	Alain Vigneault
2010	4-2	Chicago	Joel Quenneville	Philadelphia	Peter Laviolette
2009	4-3	Pittsburgh	Dan Bylsma	Detroit	Mike Babcock
2008	4-2	Detroit	Mike Babcock	Pittsburgh	Michel Therrien
2007	4-1	Anaheim	Randy Carlyle	Ottawa	Bryan Murray
2006	4-3	Carolina	Peter Laviolette	Edmonton	Craig MacTavish
2005	....	....	....	....	....
2004	4-3	Tampa Bay	John Tortorella	Calgary	Darryl Sutter
2003	4-3	New Jersey	Pat Burns	Anaheim	Mike Babcock
2002	4-1	Detroit	Scotty Bowman	Carolina	Paul Maurice
2001	4-3	Colorado	Bob Hartley	New Jersey	Larry Robinson
2000	4-2	New Jersey	Larry Robinson	Dallas	Ken Hitchcock
1999	4-2	Dallas	Ken Hitchcock	Buffalo	Lindy Ruff
1998	4-0	Detroit	Scotty Bowman	Washington	Ron Wilson
1997	4-0	Detroit	Scotty Bowman	Philadelphia	Terry Murray
1996	4-0	Colorado	Marc Crawford	Florida	Doug MacLean
1995	4-0	New Jersey	Jacques Lemaire	Detroit	Scotty Bowman
1994	4-3	NY Rangers	Mike Keenan	Vancouver	Pat Quinn
1993	4-1	Montreal	Jacques Demers	Los Angeles	Barry Melrose
1992	4-0	Pittsburgh	Scotty Bowman	Chicago	Mike Keenan
1991	4-2	Pittsburgh	Bob Johnson	Minnesota	Bob Gainey
1990	4-1	Edmonton	John Muckler	Boston	Mike Milbury
1989	4-2	Calgary	Terry Crisp	Montreal	Pat Burns
1988	4-0	Edmonton	Glen Sather	Boston	Terry O'Reilly
1987	4-3	Edmonton	Glen Sather	Philadelphia	Mike Keenan
1986	4-1	Montreal	Jean Perron	Calgary	Bob Johnson
1985	4-1	Edmonton	Glen Sather	Philadelphia	Mike Keenan
1984	4-1	Edmonton	Glen Sather	NY Islanders	Al Arbour
1983	4-0	NY Islanders	Al Arbour	Edmonton	Glen Sather
1982	4-0	NY Islanders	Al Arbour	Vancouver	Roger Neilson
1981	4-1	NY Islanders	Al Arbour	Minnesota	Glen Sonmor
1980	4-2	NY Islanders	Al Arbour	Philadelphia	Pat Quinn
1979	4-1	Montreal	Scotty Bowman	NY Rangers	Fred Shero
1978	4-2	Montreal	Scotty Bowman	Boston	Don Cherry
1977	4-0	Montreal	Scotty Bowman	Boston	Don Cherry
1976	4-0	Montreal	Scotty Bowman	Philadelphia	Fred Shero
1975	4-2	Philadelphia	Fred Shero	Buffalo	Floyd Smith
1974	4-2	Philadelphia	Fred Shero	Boston	Bep Guidolin
1973	4-2	Montreal	Scotty Bowman	Chicago	Billy Reay
1972	4-2	Boston	Tom Johnson	NY Rangers	Emile Francis
1971	4-3	Montreal	Al MacNeil	Chicago	Billy Reay
1970	4-0	Boston	Harry Sinden	St. Louis	Scotty Bowman
1969	4-0	Montreal	Claude Ruel	St. Louis	Scotty Bowman
1968	4-0	Montreal	Toe Blake	St. Louis	Scotty Bowman
1967	4-2	Toronto	Punch Imlach	Montreal	Toe Blake
1966	4-2	Montreal	Toe Blake	Detroit	Sid Abel
1965	4-3	Montreal	Toe Blake	Chicago	Billy Reay
1964	4-3	Toronto	Punch Imlach	Detroit	Sid Abel
1963	4-1	Toronto	Punch Imlach	Detroit	Sid Abel
1962	4-2	Toronto	Punch Imlach	Chicago	Rudy Pilous
1961	4-2	Chicago	Rudy Pilous	Detroit	Sid Abel
1960	4-0	Montreal	Toe Blake	Toronto	Punch Imlach
1959	4-1	Montreal	Toe Blake	Toronto	Punch Imlach
1958	4-2	Montreal	Toe Blake	Boston	Milt Schmidt
1957	4-1	Montreal	Toe Blake	Boston	Milt Schmidt
1956	4-1	Montreal	Toe Blake	Detroit	Jimmy Skinner
1955	4-3	Detroit	Jimmy Skinner	Montreal	Dick Irvin
1954	4-3	Detroit	Tommy Ivan	Montreal	Dick Irvin
1953	4-1	Montreal	Dick Irvin	Boston	Lynn Patrick
1952	4-0	Detroit	Tommy Ivan	Montreal	Dick Irvin
1951	4-1	Toronto	Joe Primeau	Montreal	Dick Irvin
1950	4-3	Detroit	Tommy Ivan	NY Rangers	Lynn Patrick
1949	4-0	Toronto	Hap Day	Detroit	Tommy Ivan
1948	4-0	Toronto	Hap Day	Detroit	Tommy Ivan
1947	4-2	Toronto	Hap Day	Montreal	Dick Irvin
1946	4-1	Montreal	Dick Irvin	Boston	Dit Clapper
1945	4-3	Toronto	Hap Day	Detroit	Jack Adams
1944	4-0	Montreal	Dick Irvin	Chicago	Paul Thompson
1943	4-0	Detroit	Jack Adams	Boston	Art Ross
1942	4-3	Toronto	Hap Day	Detroit	Jack Adams
1941	4-0	Boston	Cooney Weiland	Detroit	Ebbie Goodfellow
1940	4-2	NY Rangers	Frank Boucher	Toronto	Dick Irvin
1939	4-1	Boston	Art Ross	Toronto	Dick Irvin
1938	3-1	Chicago	Bill Stewart	Toronto	Dick Irvin
1937	3-2	Detroit	Jack Adams	NY Rangers	Lester Patrick
1936	3-1	Detroit	Jack Adams	Toronto	Dick Irvin
1935	3-0	Mtl. Maroons	Tommy Gorman	Toronto	Dick Irvin
1934	3-1	Chicago	Tommy Gorman	Detroit	Herbie Lewis
1933	3-1	NY Rangers	Lester Patrick	Toronto	Dick Irvin
1932	3-0	Toronto	Dick Irvin	NY Rangers	Lester Patrick
1931	3-2	Montreal	Cecil Hart	Chicago	Dick Irvin
1930	2-0	Montreal	Cecil Hart	Boston	Art Ross
1929	2-0	Boston	Cy Denneny	NY Rangers	Lester Patrick
1928	3-2	NY Rangers	Lester Patrick	Mtl. Maroons	Eddie Gerard
1927	2-0-2	Ottawa	Dave Gill	Boston	Art Ross
		The National Hockey League assumed control of Stanley Cup competition after 1926			
1926	3-1	Mtl. Maroons	Eddie Gerard	Victoria	Lester Patrick
1925	3-1	Victoria	Lester Patrick	Montreal	Leo Dandurand
1924	2-0	Montreal	Leo Dandurand	Cgy. Tigers	Eddie Oatman
1923	2-0	Ottawa	Pete Green	Edm. Eskimos	Ken McKenzie
1922	3-2	Tor. St. Pats	George O'Donoghue	Van. Millionaires	Lloyd Cook/Frank Patrick
1921	3-2	Ottawa	Pete Green	Van. Millionaires	Lloyd Cook/Frank Patrick
1920	3-2	Ottawa	Pete Green	Seattle	Pete Muldoon
1919	2-2-1	No decision - series between Montreal and Seattle cancelled due to influenza epidemic			
1918	3-2	Tor. Arenas	Dick Carroll	Van. Millionaires	Frank Patrick

Championship Trophies

PRINCE OF WALES TROPHY

Beginning with the 1993-94 season, the club which advances to the Stanley Cup Finals as the winner of the Eastern Conference Championship is presented with the Prince of Wales Trophy.

History: His Royal Highness, the Prince of Wales, donated the trophy to the National Hockey League in 1925. It was originally awarded to the winner of the first game played in Madison Square Garden, December 15, 1925 (Montreal Canadiens 3 at NY Americans 1). It was then awarded to the NHL playoff champion in 1925-26 and 1926-27. From 1927-28 through 1937-38, the award was presented to the regular-season champion of the American Division of the NHL. (The team finishing first in the Canadian Division received the O'Brien Trophy during these years.) From 1938-39, when the NHL reverted to one section, to 1966-67, it was presented to the team winning the NHL regular-season championship. With expansion in 1967-68, it again became a divisional trophy, awarded to the regular-season champions of the East Division through to the end of the 1973-74 season. Beginning in 1974-75, it was awarded to the regular-season winner of the conference bearing the name of the trophy. From 1981-82 to 1992-93 the trophy was presented to the playoff champion in the Wales Conference. Since 1993-94, the trophy has been presented to the playoff champion in the Eastern Conference.

2010-11 Winner: Boston Bruins

The Boston Bruins won the Prince of Wales Trophy on May 27, 2011 after defeating the Tampa Bay Lightning 1-0 in game 7 of the Eastern Conference Finals. Before defeating the Lightning, Boston had series wins over the Montreal Canadiens and the Philadelphia Flyers.

Prince of Wales Trophy

Clarence S. Campbell Bowl

Stanley Cup

PRINCE OF WALES TROPHY WINNERS

2010-11	Boston	1980-81	Montreal	1951-52	Detroit
2009-10	Philadelphia	1979-80	Buffalo	1950-51	Detroit
2008-09	Pittsburgh	1978-79	Montreal	1949-50	Detroit
2007-08	Pittsburgh	1977-78	Montreal	1948-49	Detroit
2006-07	Ottawa	1976-77	Montreal	1947-48	Toronto
2005-06	Carolina	1975-76	Montreal	1946-47	Montreal
2003-04	Tampa Bay	1974-75	Buffalo	1945-46	Montreal
2002-03	New Jersey	1973-74	Boston	1944-45	Montreal
2001-02	Carolina	1972-73	Montreal	1943-44	Montreal
2000-01	New Jersey	1971-72	Boston	1942-43	Detroit
99-2000	New Jersey	1970-71	Boston	1941-42	NY Rangers
1998-99	Buffalo	1969-70	Chicago	1940-41	Boston
1997-98	Washington	1968-69	Montreal	1939-40	Boston
1996-97	Philadelphia	1967-68	Montreal	1938-39	Boston
1995-96	Florida	1966-67	Chicago	1937-38	Boston
1994-95	New Jersey	1965-66	Montreal	1936-37	Detroit
1993-94	NY Rangers	1964-65	Detroit	1935-36	Detroit
1992-93	Montreal	1963-64	Montreal	1934-35	Boston
1991-92	Pittsburgh	1962-63	Toronto	1933-34	Detroit
1990-91	Pittsburgh	1961-62	Montreal	1932-33	Boston
1989-90	Boston	1960-61	Montreal	1931-32	NY Rangers
1988-89	Montreal	1959-60	Montreal	1930-31	Boston
1987-88	Boston	1958-59	Montreal	1929-30	Boston
1986-87	Philadelphia	1957-58	Montreal	1928-29	Boston
1985-86	Montreal	1956-57	Detroit	1927-28	Boston
1984-85	Philadelphia	1955-56	Montreal	1926-27	Ottawa
1983-84	NY Islanders	1954-55	Detroit	1925-26	Mtl. Maroons
1982-83	NY Islanders	1953-54	Detroit	Dec. 15/25	Montreal
1981-82	NY Islanders	1952-53	Detroit	1923-24	Montreal*

* Engraved by Montreal Canadiens in 1925-26.

CLARENCE S. CAMPBELL BOWL

Beginning with the 1993-94 season, the club which advances to the Stanley Cup Finals as the winner of the Western Conference Championship is presented with the Clarence S. Campbell Bowl.

History: Presented by the member clubs in 1968 for perpetual competition by the National Hockey League in recognition of the services of Clarence S. Campbell, President of the NHL from 1946 to 1977. From 1967-68 through 1973-74, the trophy was awarded to the regular-season champions of the West Division. Beginning in 1974-75, it was awarded to the regular-season winner of the conference bearing the name of the trophy. From 1981-82 to 1992-93 the trophy was presented to the playoff champion in the Campbell Conference. Since 1993-94, the trophy has been presented to the playoff champion in the Western Conference. The trophy itself is a hallmark piece made of sterling silver and was crafted by a British silversmith in 1878.

2010-11 Winner: Vancouver Canucks

The Vancouver Canucks won the Clarence S. Campbell Bowl on May 24, 2011 after defeating the San Jose Sharks 3-2 in game 5 of the Western Conference Finals. Before defeating the Sharks, Vancouver had series wins over the Chicago Blackhawks and the Nashville Predators.

CLARENCE S. CAMPBELL BOWL WINNERS

2010-11	Vancouver	1994-95	Detroit	1979-80	Philadelphia
2009-10	Chicago	1993-94	Vancouver	1978-79	NY Islanders
2008-09	Detroit	1992-93	Los Angeles	1977-78	NY Islanders
2007-08	Detroit	1991-92	Chicago	1976-77	Philadelphia
2006-07	Anaheim	1990-91	Minnesota	1975-76	Philadelphia
2005-06	Edmonton	1989-90	Edmonton	1974-75	Philadelphia
2003-04	Calgary	1988-89	Calgary	1973-74	Philadelphia
2002-03	Anaheim	1987-88	Edmonton	1972-73	Chicago
2001-02	Detroit	1986-87	Edmonton	1971-72	Chicago
2000-01	Colorado	1985-86	Calgary	1970-71	Chicago
99-2000	Dallas	1984-85	Edmonton	1969-70	St. Louis
1998-99	Dallas	1983-84	Edmonton	1968-69	St. Louis
1997-98	Detroit	1982-83	Edmonton	1967-68	Philadelphia
1996-97	Detroit	1981-82	Vancouver		
1995-96	Colorado	1980-81	NY Islanders		

Stanley Cup Winners

Rosters and Final Series Scores

2010-11 — Boston Bruins — Zdeno Chara (Captain), Patrice Bergeron, Johnny Boychuk, Gregory Campbell, Andrew Ference, Nathan Horton, Tomas Kaberle, Chris Kelly, David Krejci, Milan Lucic, Brad Marchand, Adam McQuaid, Daniel Paille, Rich Peverley, Tuukka Rask, Mark Recchi, Michael Ryder, Marc Savard, Tyler Seguin, Dennis Seidenberg, Tim Thomas, Shawn Thornton, Jeremy and Margaret Jacobs, Charlie Jacobs, Louis Jacobs, Jerry Jacobs Jr. (Ownership), Cam Neely (President), Peter Chiarelli (General Manager), Jim Benning, Don Sweeney (Assistant General Managers), Claude Julien (Head Coach), Doug Jarvis, Geoff Ward, Doug Houda (Assistant Coaches), Bob Essensa (Goaltending Coach), Harry Sinden (Senior Advisor), John Bucyk (Team Road Service Coordinator), Scott Bradley (Director of Player Personnel), Wayne Smith (Director of Amateur Scouting), John Weisbrod (Director of Collegiate Scouting), Adam Creighton, Tom McVie (Scouts), Dale Hamilton-Powers (Director of Administration), Matt Chmura (Director of Communications), Ryan Nadeau (Manager of Hockey Administration), Don DelNegro (Athletic Trainer), John Whitesides (Strength and Conditioning Coach), Keith Robinson (Equipment Manager), Derek Repucci (Assistant Trainer and Massage Therapist), Jim "Beets" Johnson (Assistant Equipment Manager), Scott Waugh (Physical Therapist).

Scores: June 1, at Vancouver — Vancouver 1, Boston 0; June 4, at Vancouver — Vancouver 3, Boston 2; June 6, at Boston — Boston 8, Vancouver 1; June 8, at Boston — Boston 4, Vancouver 0; June 10, at Vancouver — Vancouver 1, Boston 0; June 13, at Boston — Boston 5, Vancouver 2; June 15, at Vancouver — Boston 4, Vancouver 0.

2009-10 — Chicago Blackhawks — Jonathan Toews (Captain), Dave Bolland, Nick Boynton, Troy Brouwer, Adam Burish, Dustin Byfuglien, Brian Campbell, Ben Eager, Colin Fraser, Jordan Hendry, Niklas Hjalmarsson, Marian Hossa, Cristobal Huet, Patrick Kane, Duncan Keith, Tomas Kopecky, Andrew Ladd, John Madden, Antti Niemi, Brent Seabrook, Patrick Sharp, Brent Sopel, Kris Versteeg, W. Rockwell Wirtz (Chairman), John McDonough (President), Jay Blunk (Senior VP, Business Operations), Stan Bowman (General Manager), Kevin Cheveldayoff (Assistant General Manager), Al MacIsaac (Senior Director, Hockey Administration/Assistant to the President), Scotty Bowman, Dale Tallon (Senior Advisors, Hockey Operations), Joel Quenneville (Head Coach), John Torchetti, Mike Haviland (Assistant Coaches), Stephane Waite (Goaltending Coach), Paul Goodman (Strength and Conditioning Coach), Brad Aldrich (Video Coach), Paul Vincent (Skating Coach), Marc Bergevin (Director, Player Personnel), Mark Bernard (G.M., Minor League Affiliations), Norm Maciver (Director, Player Development), Mark Kelley (Director, Amateur Scouting), Ron Anderson (Director, Player Recruitment), Michel Dumas (Chief Amateur Scout), Tony Ommen (Director Team Services), Dr. Michael Terry (Head Team Physician), Mike Gapski (Head Athletic Trainer), Troy Parchman (Equipment Manager), Pawel Prylinski (Massage Therapist), Jeff Thomas (Assistant Athletic Trainer), Clint Reif (Assistant Equipment Manager), Jim Heintzelman (Equipment Assistant).

Scores: May 29, at Chicago — Chicago 6, Philadelphia 5; May 31, at Chicago — Chicago 2, Philadelphia 1; June 2 at Philadelphia — Philadelphia 4, Chicago 3; June 4 at Philadelphia — Philadelphia 5, Chicago 3; June 6, at Chicago — Chicago 7, Philadelphia 4; June 9 at Philadelphia — Chicago 4, Philadelphia 3.

2008-09 — Pittsburgh Penguins — Sidney Crosby (Captain), Craig Adams, Philippe Boucher, Matt Cooke, Pascal Dupuis, Mark Eaton, Ruslan Fedotenko, Marc-Andre Fleury, Mathieu Garon, Hal Gill, Eric Godard, Alex Goligoski, Sergei Gonchar, Bill Guerin, Tyler Kennedy, Chris Kunitz, Kris Letang, Evgeni Malkin, Brooks Orpik, Miroslav Satan, Rob Scuderi, Jordan Staal, Petr Sykora, Maxime Talbot, Mike Zigomanis, Mario Lemieux (Co-owner/Chairman), Ron Burkle (Co-owner), Bill Kassling, Tom Grealish, Tony Liberati (Directors), Ken Sawyer (Chief Executive Officer), David Morehouse (President), Ray Shero (Executive Vice President amd General Manager), Chuck Fletcher (Assistant General Manager), Ed Johnston (Senior Advisor, Hockey Operations), Jason Botterill (Director of Hockey Administration), Dan Bylsma (Head Coach), Mike Yeo (Assistant Coach), Tom Fitzgerald (Director of Player Development), GIlles Meloche (Goaltending Coach), Mike Kadar (Strength and Conditioning Coach), Travis Ramsay (Video Coordinator), Chris Stewart (Head Athletic Trainer), Scott Adams (Assistant Athletic Trainer), Mark Mortland (Physical Therapist), Dana Heinze (Equipment Manager), Paul DeFazio, Danny Kroll (Assistant Equipment Managers), Frank Buonomo (Senior Director of Team Services and Communications), Tom McMillan (Vice President, Communications), Dan MacKinnon (Director of Professional Scouting), Jay Heinbuck (Director of Amateur Scouting).

Scores: May 30, at Detroit — Detroit 3, Pittsburgh 1; May 31 at Detroit — Detroit 3, Pittsburgh 1; June 2, at Pittsburgh — Pittsburgh 4, Detroit 2; June 4, at Pittsburgh — Pittsburgh 4, Detroit 2; June 6 at Detroit — Detroit 5, Pittsburgh 0; June 9, at Pittsburgh — Pittsburgh 2, Detroit 1; June 12, at Detroit — Pittsburgh 2, Detroit 1.

2007-08 — Detroit Red Wings — Nicklas Lidstrom (Captain), Chris Chelios, Daniel Cleary, Pavel Datsyuk, Aaron Downey, Dallas Drake, Kris Draper, Valtteri Filppula, Johan Franzen, Dominik Hasek, Darren Helm, Tomas Holmstrom, Jiri Hudler, Tomas Kopecky, Niklas Kronwall, Brett Lebda, Andreas Lilja, Kirk Maltby, Darren McCarty, Derek Meech, Chris Osgood, Brian Rafalski, Mikael Samuelsson, Brad Stuart, Henrik Zetterberg, Michael Ilitch (Owner/Governor), Marian Ilitch (Owner/Secretary-Treasurer), Christopher Ilitch (Vice President/Alternate Governor), Denise Ilitch, Ronald Ilitch, Michael Ilitch Jr., Lisa Ilitch Murray, Atanas Ilitch, Carole Ilitch. Jim Devellano (Senior Vice President/Alternate Governor), Ken Holland (General Manager/Alternate Governor), Steve Yzerman (Vice President/Alternate Governor), Jim Nill (Assistant General Manager), Ryan Martin (Director, Hockey Operations), Scotty Bowman (Consultant), Mike Babcock (Head Coach), Todd McLellan (Associate Coach), Paul MacLean (Assistant Coach), Jim Bedard (Goaltending Consultant), Jay Woodcroft (Video Coordinator), Mark Howe (Director, Pro Scouting), Joe McDonnell (Director, Amateur Scouting), Hakan Andersson (Director, Amateur Scouting Europe), Piet Van Zant (Athletic Trainer), Paul Boyer (Equipment Manager), Russ Baumann, Christopher Scoppetto (Assistant Athletic Trainers).

Scores: May 24, at Detroit — Detroit 4, Pittsburgh 0; May 26, at Detroit — Detroit 3, Pittsburgh 0; May 28, at Pittsburgh — Pittsburgh 3, Detroit 2; May 31, at Pittsburgh — Detroit 2, Pittsburgh 1; June 2, at Detroit — Pittsburgh 4, Detroit 3; June 4, at Pittsburgh — Detroit 3, Pittsburgh 2.

2006-07 — Anaheim Ducks — Scott Niedermayer (Captain), Rob Niedermayer, Chris Pronger, Teemu Selanne, Sean O'Donnell, Brad May, Todd Marchant, Jean-Sebastien Giguere, Andy McDonald, Samuel Pahlsson, Shawn Thornton, Ric Jackman, Joe DiPenta, Kent Huskins, Chris Kunitz, George Parros, Joe Motzko, Ilya Bryzgalov, Francois Beauchemin, Travis Moen, Ryan Carter, Drew Miller, Ryan Shannon, Dustin Penner, Ryan Getzlaf, Corey Perry; Henry Samueli, Susan Samueli (Owners), Michael Schulman (CEO), Brian Burke (Executive Vice President/General Manager), Tim Ryan (Executive Vice President/COO), Bob Wagner (Senior Vice President/Chief Marketing Officer), Bob Murray (Senior Vice President-Hockey Operations), David McNab (Assistant General Manager), Al Coates (Senior Advisor to GM), Randy Carlyle (Head Coach), Dave Farrish, Newell Brown (Assistant Coaches), Francois Allaire (Goaltending Consultant), Sean Skahan (Strength and Conditioning Coach), Joe Trotta (Video Coordinator), Tim Clark (Head Trainer), Mark O'Neill (Equipment Manager), John Allaway (Assistant Equipment Manager), James Partida (Massage Therapist), Rick Paterson (Director of Professional Scouting), Alain Chainey (Director of Amateur Scouting).

Scores: May 28, at Anaheim - Anaheim 3, Ottawa 2; May 30, at Anaheim - Anaheim 1, Ottawa 0; June 2, at Ottawa - Ottawa 5, Anaheim 3; June 4, at Ottawa - Anaheim 3, Ottawa 2; June 6, at Anaheim - Anaheim 6, Ottawa 2.

2005-06 — Carolina Hurricanes — Rod Brind'Amour (Captain), Glen Wesley, Cory Stillman, Kevyn Adams, Craig Adams, Anton Babchuk, Erik Cole, Mike Commodore, Matt Cullen, Martin Gerber, Bret Hedican, Andrew Hutchinson, Frantisek Kaberle, Andrew Ladd, Chad LaRose, Mark Recchi, Eric Staal, Oleg Tverdovsky, Josef Vasicek, Niclas Wallin, Aaron Ward, Cam Ward, Doug Weight, Ray Whitney, Justin Williams; Peter Karmanos Jr., Thomas Thewes (Owners), Jim Rutherford (President/General Manager), Jason Karmanos (Vice President/Assistant General Manager), Mike Amendola (Chief Financial Officer), Peter Laviolette (Head Coach), Kevin McCarthy, Jeff Daniels (Assistant Coaches), Greg Stefan (Goaltending Coach), Chris Huffine (Video Coordinator), Skip Cunningham, Wally Tatomir, Bob Gorman (Equipment Managers), Peter Friesen (Head Athletic Therapist/Strength and Conditioning Coach), Chris Stewart (Associate Athletic Trainer), Brian Tatum (Team Services Manager), Kelly Kirwin (Event Coordinator-Hockey Operations), Mike Sundheim (Director of Media Relations), Kyle Hanlin (Manager of Media Relations), Sheldon Ferguson (Director of Amateur Scouting), Marshall Johnston (Director of Professional Scouting), Claude Larose, Ron Smith (Professional Scouts), Bert Marshall, Tony MacDonald, Martin Madden (Amateur Scouts), Tom Rowe (Lowell (AHL) - Coach).

Scores: June 5, at Carolina - Carolina 5, Edmonton 4; June 7, at Carolina - Carolina 5, Edmonton 0; June 10, at Edmonton - Edmonton 2, Carolina 1; June 12, at Edmonton - Carolina 2, Edmonton 1; June 14, at Carolina - Edmonton 4, Carolina 3; June 17, at Edmonton - Edmonton 4, Carolina 0; June 19, at Carolina - Carolina 3, Edmonton 1.

2003-04 — Tampa Bay Lightning — Dave Andreychuk (Captain), Fredrik Modin, Vincent Lecavalier, Martin St. Louis, Brad Richards, Nikolai Khabibulin, Pavel Kubina, Dan Boyle, Ruslan Fedotenko, Darryl Sydor, Cory Sarich, Tim Taylor, Cory Stillman, Jassen Cullimore, John Grahame, Chris Dingman, Nolan Pratt, Brad Lukowich, Andre Roy, Dmitry Afanasenkov, Martin Cibak, Ben Clymer, Darren Rumble, Stan Neckar, Eric Perrin; William Davidson (Owner), Tom Wilson (Governor), Ron Campbell (President), Jay Feaster (General Manager), John Tortorella (Head Coach), Craig Ramsay (Associate Coach), Jeff Reese (Assistant Coach), Nigel Kirwan (Video Coach), Eric Lawson (Strength and Conditioning Coach), Tom Mulligan (Trainer), Adam Rambo (Assistant Trainer), Ray Thill (Equipment Manager), Dana Heinze, Jim Pickard (Assistant Equipment Managers), Mike Griebel (Massage Therapist), Bill Barber (Director of Player Personnel), Jake Goertzen (Head Scout), Phil Thibodeau (Director of Team Services), Ryan Belec (Assistant to the GM), Rick Paterson (Chief Pro Scout), Kari Kettunen, Glen Zacharias, Steve Baker, Dave Heitz, Yuri Yanchenkov, (Scouts), Bill Wickett (Senior Vice President - Communications), Sean Henry (Executive Vice President/COO).

Scores: May 25, at Tampa Bay - Calgary 4, Tampa Bay 1; May 27, at Tampa Bay - Tampa Bay 4, Calgary 1; May 29, at Calgary - Calgary 3, Tampa Bay 0; May 31, at Calgary - Tampa Bay 1, Calgary 0; June 3, at Tampa Bay - Calgary 3, Tampa Bay 2; June 5, at Calgary - Tampa Bay 3, Calgary 2; June 7, at Tampa Bay - Tampa Bay 2, Calgary 1.

2002-03 — New Jersey Devils — Tommy Albelin, Jiri Bicek, Martin Brodeur, Sergei Brylin, Ken Daneyko, Patrik Elias, Jeff Friesen, Brian Gionta, Scott Gomez, Jamie Langenbrunner, John Madden, Grant Marshall, Jim McKenzie, Scott Niedermayer, Joe Nieuwendyk, Jay Pandolfo, Brian Rafalski, Pascal Rheaume, Mike Rupp, Corey Schwab, Richard Smehlik, Scott Stevens (Captain), Turner Stevenson, Oleg Tverdovsky, Colin White; Raymond Chambers, Lewis Catz (Owners), Peter Simon (Chairman), Lou Lamoriello (CEO/President/General Manager), Pat Burns (Head Coach), Bob Carpenter, John MacLean (Assistant Coaches), Jacques Caron (Goaltending Coach), Larry Robinson (Special Assignment Coach), David Conte (Director - Scouting), Claude Carrier (Assistant Director - Scouting), Chris Lamoriello (Scout/Albany (AHL) - General Manager), Milt Fisher, Dan Labraaten, Marcel Pronovost (Scouts), Bob Hoffmeyer, Jan Ludvig (Pro Scouts), Dr. Barry Fisher (Orthopedist), Chris Modrzynski (Executive Vice President), Terry Farmer (Vice President - Ticket Operations), Vladimir Bure (Fitness Consultant), Taran Singleton (Hockey Operations), Bill Murray (Medical Trainer), Michael Vasalani (Strength and Conditioning Coordinator), Rick Matthews (Equipment Manager), Juergen Merz (Massage Therapist), Alex Abasto (Assistant Equipment Manager).

Scores: May 27, at New Jersey - New Jersey 3, Anaheim 0; May 29, at New Jersey - New Jersey 3, Anaheim 0; May 31, at Anaheim - Anaheim 3, New Jersey 2; June 2, at Anaheim - Anaheim 1, New Jersey 0; June 5, at New Jersey - New Jersey 6, Anaheim 3; June 7, at Anaheim - Anaheim 5, New Jersey 2; June 9, at New Jersey - New Jersey 3, Anaheim 0.

2001-02 — Detroit Red Wings — Steve Yzerman (Captain), Dominik Hasek, Manny Legace, Chris Chelios, Mathieu Dandenault, Steve Duchesne, Jiri Fischer, Nicklas Lidstrom, Fredrik Olausson, Jiri Slegr, Pavel Datsyuk, Boyd Devereaux, Kris Draper, Sergei Fedorov, Tomas Holmstrom, Brett Hull, Igor Larionov, Kirk Maltby, Darren McCarty, Luc Robitaille, Brendan Shanahan, Jason Williams; Michael Ilitch (Owner/Governor), Marian Ilitch (Owner/Secretary Treasurer), Christoper Ilitch (Vice President), Denise Ilitch (Alternate Governor), Ronald Ilitch, Michael Ilitch Jr., Lisa Ilitch Murray, Atanas Ilitch, Carole Ilitch, Jim Devellano (Senior Vice President), Ken Holland (General Manager), Jim Nill (Assistant General Manager), Scotty Bowman (Head Coach), Dave Lewis, Barry Smith (Associate Coaches), Jim Bedard (Goaltending Consultant), Joe Kocur (Video Coordinator), John Wharton (Athletic Trainer), Piet Van Zant (Assistant Athletic Trainer), Paul Boyer (Equipment Manager), Paul MacDonald (Senior Director of Finance), Nancy Beard (Executive Assistant), Dan Belisle, Mark Howe, Bob McCammon (Pro Scouts), Hakan Andersson (Director of European Scouting), Bruce Haralson, Mark Leach, Joe McDonnell, Glenn Merkosky (Scouts).

Scores: June 4, at Detroit - Carolina 3, Detroit 2; June 6, at Detroit - Detroit 3, Carolina 1; June 8, at Carolina - Detroit 3, Carolina 2; June 10, at Carolina - Detroit 3, Carolina 0; June 13, at Detroit - Detroit 3, Carolina 1.

2000-01 — Colorado Avalanche — David Aebischer, Rob Blake, Raymond Bourque, Greg de Vries, Chris Dingman, Chris Drury, Adam Foote, Peter Forsberg, Milan Hejduk, Dan Hinote, Jon Klemm, Eric Messier, Bryan Muir, Ville Nieminen, Scott Parker, Shjon Podein, Nolan Pratt, Dave Reid, Steve Reinprecht, Patrick Roy, Joe Sakic (Captain), Martin Skoula, Alex Tanguay, Stephane Yelle; E. Stanley Kroenke (Owner/Governor), Pierre Lacroix (President/ General Manager), Bob Hartley (Head Coach), Jacques Cloutier, Bryan Trottier (Assistant Coaches), Paul Fixter (Video Coach), Francois Giguere (Vice President - Hockey Operations), Brian MacDonald (Assistant General Manager), Michel Goulet (Vice President - Player Personnel), Jean Martineau (Vice President - Communications and Team Services), Pat Karns (Head Athletic Trainer), Matthew Sokolowski (Assistant Athletic Trainer), Wayne Flemming, Mark Miller (Equipment Managers), Dave Randolph (Assistant Equipment Manager), Paul Goldberg (Strength and Conditioning Coach), Gregorio Pradera (Massage Therapist), Brad Smith (Pro Scout), Jim Hammett (Chief Scout), Garth Joy, Steve Lyons, Joni Lehto, Orval Tessier (Scouts), Charlotte Grahame (Director of Hockey Administration).

Scores: May 26, at Colorado - Colorado 5, New Jersey 0; May 29, at Colorado - New Jersey 2, Colorado 1; May 31, at New Jersey - Colorado 3, New Jersey 1; June 2, at New Jersey - New Jersey 3, Colorado 2; June 4, at Colorado - New Jersey 4, Colorado 1; June 7, at New Jersey - Colorado 4, New Jersey 0; June 9, at Colorado - Colorado 3, New Jersey 1.

1999-2000 — New Jersey Devils — Jason Arnott, Brad Bombardir, Martin Brodeur, Steve Brule, Sergei Brylin, Ken Daneyko, Patrik Elias, Scott Gomez, Bobby Holik, Steve Kelly, Claude Lemieux, John Madden, Vladimir Malakhov, Randy McKay, Alexander Mogilny, Sergei Nemchinov, Scott Niedermayer, Krzysztof Oliwa, Jay Pandolfo, Brian Rafalski, Ken Sutton, Scott Stevens (Captain), Petr Sykora, Chris Terreri, Colin White; Dr. John J. McMullen (Owner/Chairman), Peter S. McMullen (Owner), Lou Lamoriello (President/General Manager), Larry Robinson (Head Coach), Viacheslav Fetisov (Assistant Coach), Jacques Caron (Goaltending Coach), Bob Carpenter (Assistant Coach), John Cuniff (Albany (AHL) - Coach), David Conte (Director of Scouting), Claude Carrier (Assistant Director of Scouting), Milt Fisher, Dan Labraaten, Marcel Pronovost (Scouts), Bob Hoffmeyer (Pro Scout), Dr. Barry Fisher (Orthopedist), Dennis Gendron (Albany (AHL) - Assistant Coach), Robbie Ftorek (Coach), Vladimir Bure (Consultant), Taran Singleton, Marie Carnevale, Callie Smith (Hockey Operations), Bill Murray (Medical Trainer), Michael Vasalani (Strength and Conditioning Coordinator), Dana McGuane (Equipment Manager), Juergen Merz (Massage Therapist), Harry Bricker, Lou Centanni Jr. (Assistant Equipment Managers).

Scores: May 30, at New Jersey - New Jersey 7, Dallas 3; June 1, at New Jersey - Dallas 2, New Jersey 1; June 3, at Dallas - New Jersey 2, Dallas 1; June 5, at Dallas - New Jersey 3, Dallas 1; June 8, at New Jersey - Dallas 1 - New Jersey 0; June 10, at Dallas, New Jersey 2 - Dallas 1.

1998-99 — Dallas Stars — Derian Hatcher (Captain), Mike Modano, Joe Nieuwendyk, Craig Ludwig, Sergei Zubov, Ed Belfour, Guy Carbonneau, Shawn Chambers, Benoit Hogue, Tony Hrkac, Brett Hull, Mike Keane, Jamie Langenbrunner, Jere Lehtinen, Grant Marshall, Richard Matvichuk, Derek Plante, Dave Reid, Brent Severyn, Jon Sim, Brian Skrudland, Blake Sloan, Darryl Sydor, Roman Turek, Pat Verbeek; Thomas Hicks (Chairman/Owner), Jim Lites (President), Bob Gainey (Vice President - Hockey Operations/General Manager), Doug Armstrong (Assistant General Manager), Craig Button (Director of Player Personnel), Ken Hitchcock (Head Coach), Doug Jarvis, Rick Wilson (Assistant Coaches), Rick McLaughlin (Vice President/Chief Financial Officer), Jeff Cogen (Vice President - Marketing and Promotion), Bill Strong (Vice President - Marketing and Broadcasting), Tim Bernhardt (Director of Amateur Scouting), Doug Overton (Director of Pro Scouting), Bob Gernander (Chief Scout), Stu MacGregor (Western Scout), Dave Suprenant (Medical Trainer), Dave Smith, Rich Matthews (Equipment Managers), J.J. McQueen (Strength and Conditioning Coach), Rick St. Croix (Goaltending Consultant), Dan Stuchal (Director of Team Services), Larry Kelly (Director of Public Relations).

Scores: June 8, at Dallas - Buffalo 3, Dallas 2; June 10, at Dallas - Dallas 4, Buffalo 2; June 12, at Buffalo - Dallas 2, Buffalo 1; June 15, at Buffalo - Buffalo 2, Dallas 1; June 17, at Dallas - Dallas 2, Buffalo 0; June 19, at Buffalo - Dallas 2, Buffalo 1.

1997-98 — Detroit Red Wings — Steve Yzerman (Captain), Doug Brown, Mathieu Dandenault, Kris Draper, Anders Eriksson, Sergei Fedorov, Viacheslav Fetisov, Brent Gilchrist, Kevin Hodson, Tomas Holmstrom, Mike Knuble, Joe Kocur, Vladimir Konstantinov, Vyacheslav Kozlov, Martin Lapointe, Igor Larionov, Nicklas Lidstrom, Jamie Macoun, Kirk Maltby, Darren McCarty, Dmitri Mironov, Larry Murphy, Chris Osgood, Bob Rouse, Brendan Shanahan, Aaron Ward; Mike Ilitch, (Owner/Chairman), Marian Ilitch (Owner), Atanas Ilitch, Christopher Ilitch (Vice Presidents), Denise Ilitch, Ronald Ilitch, Michael Ilitch Jr., Lisa Ilitch Murray, Carole Ilitch Trepeck, Jim Devellano (Senior Vice President), Ken Holland (General Manager), Don Waddell (Assistant General Manager), Scotty Bowman (Head Coach), Barry Smith, Dave Lewis (Associate Coaches), Jim Nill (Director of Player Development), Dan Belisle, Mark Howe (Pro Scouts), Jim Bedard (Goaltending Consultant), Hakan Andersson (Director of European Scouting), Mark Leach (USA Scout), Joe McDonnell (Eastern Scout), Bruce Haralson (Western Scout), John Wharton (Athletic Trainer), Paul Boyer (Equipment Manager), Tim Abbott (Assistant Equipment Manager), Bob Huddleston (Masseur), Sergei Mnatsakanov, Wally Crossman (Dressing Room Assistant).

Scores: June 9, at Detroit — Detroit 2, Washington 1; June 11, at Detroit — Detroit 5, Washington 4; June 13, at Washington — Detroit 2, Washington 1; June 16, at Washington — Detroit 4, Washington 1.

1996-97 — Detroit Red Wings — Steve Yzerman (Captain), Doug Brown, Mathieu Dandenault, Kris Draper, Sergei Fedorov, Viacheslav Fetisov, Kevin Hodson, Tomas Holmstrom, Joe Kocur, Vladimir Konstantinov, Vyacheslav Kozlov, Martin Lapointe, Igor Larionov, Nicklas Lidstrom, Kirk Maltby, Darren McCarty, Larry Murphy, Chris Osgood, Jamie Pushor, Bob Rouse, Tomas Sandstrom, Brendan Shanahan, Tim Taylor, Mike Vernon, Aaron Ward; Mike Ilitch (Owner/Chairman), Marian Ilitch (Owner), Atanas Ilitch, Christopher Ilitch (Vice Presidents), Denise Ilitch Lites, Ronald Ilitch, Michael Ilitch Jr., Lisa Ilitch Murray, Carole Ilitch Trepeck, Jim Devellano (Senior Vice President), Scotty Bowman (Head Coach/Director of Player Personnel), Ken Holland (Assistant General Manager), Barry Smith, Dave Lewis (Associate Coaches), Mike Krushelnyski (Assistant Coach), Jim Nill (Director of Player Development), Dan Belisle, Bruce Haralson, Mark Howe (Scouts), Hakan Andersson (Director of European Scouting), John Wharton (Athletic Trainer), Wally Crossman (Dressing Room Assistant), Mark Leach (Scout), Paul Boyer (Equipment Manager), Tim Abbott (Assistant Equipment Manager), Sergei Mnatsakanov (Masseur), Joe McDonnell (Scout).

Scores: May 31, at Philadelphia — Detroit 4, Philadelphia 2; June 3, at Philadelphia — Detroit 4, Philadelphia 2; June 5, at Detroit — Detroit 6, Philadelphia 1; June 7, at Detroit — Detroit 2, Philadelphia 1.

1995-96 — Colorado Avalanche — Rene Corbet, Adam Deadmarsh, Stephane Fiset, Adam Foote, Peter Forsberg, Alexei Gusarov, Dave Hannan, Valeri Kamensky, Mike Keane, Jon Klemm, Uwe Krupp, Sylvain Lefebvre, Claude Lemieux, Curtis Leschyshyn, Troy Murray, Sandis Ozolinsh, Mike Ricci, Patrick Roy, Warren Rychel, Joe Sakic (Captain), Chris Simon, Craig Wolanin, Stephane Yelle, Scott Young; Charlie Lyons (Chairman/CEO), Pierre Lacroix (Executive Vice President/General Manager), Marc Crawford (Head Coach), Joel Quenneville, Jacques Cloutier (Assistant Coaches), Francois Giguere (Assistant General Manager), Michel Goulet (Director of Player Personnel), Dave Draper (Chief Scout), Jean Martineau (Director of Public Relations), Pat Karns (Trainer), Matthew Sokolowski (Assistant Trainer), Rob McLean (Equipment Manager), Mike Kramer, Brock Gibbins (Assistant Equipment Managers), Skip Allen (Strength and Conditioning Coach), Paul Fixter (Video Coordinator), Leo Vyssokov (Massage Therapist).

Scores: June 4, at Colorado — Colorado 3, Florida 1; June 6, at Colorado — Colorado 8, Florida 1; June 8, at Florida — Colorado 3, Florida 2; June 10, at Florida — Colorado 1, Florida 0.

1994-95 — New Jersey Devils — Tommy Albelin, Martin Brodeur, Neal Broten, Sergei Brylin, Bob Carpenter, Shawn Chambers, Tom Chorske, Danton Cole, Ken Daneyko, Kevin Dean, Jim Dowd, Bruce Driver, Bill Guerin, Bobby Holik, Claude Lemieux, John MacLean, Chris McAlpine, Randy McKay, Scott Niedermayer, Mike Peluso, Stephane Richer, Brian Rolston, Scott Stevens (Captain), Chris Terreri, Valeri Zelepukin; Dr. John J. McMullen (Owner/Chairman), Peter S. McMullen (Owner), Lou Lamoriello (President/General Manager), Jacques Lemaire (Head Coach), Jacques Caron (Goaltender Coach), Dennis Gendron, Larry Robinson (Assistant Coaches), Robbie Ftorek (Albany (AHL) - Coach), Alex Abasto (Assistant Equipment Manager), Bob Huddleston (Massage Therapist), David Nichols (Equipment Manager), Ted Schuch (Medical Trainer), Michael Vasalani (Strength and Conditioning Coach), David Conte (Director of Scouting), Milt Fisher, Claude Carrier, Dan Labraaten, Marcel Pronovost (Scouts).

Scores: June 17, at Detroit — New Jersey 2, Detroit 1; June 20, at Detroit — New Jersey 4, Detroit 2; June 22, at New Jersey — New Jersey 5, Detroit 2; June 24, at New Jersey — New Jersey 5, Detroit 2.

1993-94 — New York Rangers — Mark Messier (Captain), Brian Leetch, Kevin Lowe, Adam Graves, Steve Larmer, Glenn Anderson, Jeff Beukeboom, Greg Gilbert, Glenn Healy, Mike Hudson, Alexander Karpovtsev, Joe Kocur, Alex Kovalev, Nick Kypreos, Doug Lidster, Stephane Matteau, Craig MacTavish, Sergei Nemchinov, Brian Noonan, Esa Tikkanen, Mike Richter, Jay Wells, Sergei Zubov, Ed Olczyk, Mike Hartman; Neil Smith (President/General Manager/Governor), Robert Gutkowski, Stanley Jaffe, Kenneth Munoz (Governors), Larry Pleau (Assistant General Manager), Mike Keenan (Head Coach), Colin Campbell (Associate Coach), Dick Todd (Assistant Coach), Matthew Loughren (Manager - Team Operations), Barry Watkins (Director - Communications), Christer Rockstrom, Tony Feltrin, Martin Madden, Herb Hammond, Darwin Bennett (Scouts), Dave Smith, Joe Murphy, Mike Folga, Bruce Lifrieri (Trainers).

Scores: May 31, at New York — Vancouver 3, NY Rangers 2; June 2, at New York — NY Rangers 3, Vancouver 1; June 4, at Vancouver — NY Rangers 5, Vancouver 1; June 7, at Vancouver — NY Rangers 4, Vancouver 2; June 9, at New York — Vancouver 6, at NY Rangers 3; June 11, at Vancouver — Vancouver 4, NY Rangers 1; June 14, at New York — NY Rangers 3, Vancouver 2.

1992-93 — Montreal Canadiens — Guy Carbonneau (Captain), Patrick Roy, Andre Racicot, Rob Ramage, Kirk Muller, Mike Keane, Kevin Haller, Paul DiPietro, John LeClair, Denis Savard, Benoit Brunet, Brian Bellows, Lyle Odelein, Vincent Damphousse, Gary Leeman, Mathieu Schneider, Eric Desjardins, Jesse Belanger, Ed Ronan, Mario Roberge, Donald Dufresne, Todd Ewen, Sean Hill, Patrice Brisebois, Gilbert Dionne, Stephan Lebeau, J.J. Daigneault; Ronald Corey (President), Serge Savard (Managing Director/Vice President - Hockey), Jacques Demers (Head Coach), Jacques Laperriere, Charles Thiffault (Assistant Coaches), Francois Allaire (Goaltending Instructor), Jean Béliveau (Senior Vice President - Corporate Affairs), Jacques Lemaire (Assistant to the Managing Director), André Boudrias (Assistant to the Managing Director/Director of Scouting), Gaeten Lefebvre (Athletic Trainer), John Shipman (Assistant to the Athletic Trainer), Eddy Palchak (Equipment Manager), Pierre Gervais, Robert Boulanger (Assistants to the Equipment Manager).

Scores: June 1, at Montreal — Los Angeles 4, Montreal 1; June 3, at Montreal — Montreal 3, Los Angeles 2; June 5, at Los Angeles — Montreal 4, Los Angeles 3; June 7, at Los Angeles — Montreal 3, Los Angeles 2; June 9, at Montreal — Montreal 4, Los Angeles 1.

1991-92 — Pittsburgh Penguins — Mario Lemieux (Captain), Ron Francis, Bryan Trottier, Kevin Stevens, Bob Errey, Phil Bourque, Troy Loney, Rick Tocchet, Joe Mullen, Jaromir Jagr, Jiri Hrdina, Shawn McEachern, Ulf Samuelsson, Kjell Samuelsson, Larry Murphy, Gordie Roberts, Jim Paek, Paul Stanton, Tom Barrasso, Ken Wregget, Jay Caufield, Jamie Leach, Wendell Young, Grant Jennings, Peter Taglianetti, Jock Callander, Dave Michayluk, Mike Needham, Jeff Chychrun, Ken Priestlay, Jeff Daniels; Morris Belzberg, Howard Baldwin, Thomas Ruta (Owners), Donn Patton (Executive Vice President/Chief Financial Officer), Paul Martha (Executive Vice President/General Counsel), Craig Patrick (Executive Vice President/General Manager), Bob Johnson (Head Coach), Scotty Bowman (Director of Player Development/Coach), Barry Smith, Rick Kehoe, Pierre McGuire, Gilles Meloche, Rick Paterson (Assistant Coaches), Steve Latin (Equipment Manager), Skip Thayer (Trainer), John Welday (Strength and Conditioning Coach), Greg Malone, Les Binkley, Charlie Hodge, John Gill, Ralph Cox (Scouts).

Scores: May 26, at Pittsburgh — Pittsburgh 5, Chicago 4; May 28, at Pittsburgh — Pittsburgh 3, Chicago 1; May 30, at Chicago — Pittsburgh 1, Chicago 0; June 1, at Chicago — Pittsburgh 6, Chicago 5.

1990-91 — Pittsburgh Penguins — Mario Lemieux (Captain), Paul Coffey, Randy Hillier, Bob Errey, Tom Barrasso, Phil Bourque, Jay Caufield, Ron Francis, Randy Gilhen, Jiri Hrdina, Jaromir Jagr, Grant Jennings, Troy Loney, Joe Mullen, Larry Murphy, Jim Paek, Frank Pietrangelo, Barry Pederson, Mark Recchi, Gordie Roberts, Ulf Samuelsson, Paul Stanton, Kevin Stevens, Peter Taglianetti, Bryan Trottier, Scott Young, Wendell Young; Edward J. DeBartolo Sr. (Owner), Marie D. DeBartolo York (President), Paul Martha (Vice President/General Counsel), Craig Patrick (General Manager), Scotty Bowman (Director of Player Development and Recruitment), Bob Johnson (Head Coach), Rick Kehoe, Rick Paterson, Barry Smith (Assistant Coaches), Gilles Meloche (Goaltending Coach/Scout), Steve Latin (Equipment Manager), Skip Thayer (Trainer), John Welday (Strength and Conditioning Coach), Greg Malone (Scout).

Scores: May 15, at Pittsburgh — Minnesota 5, Pittsburgh 4; May 17, at Pittsburgh — Pittsburgh 4, Minnesota 1; May 19, at Minnesota — Minnesota 3, Pittsburgh 1; May 21, at Minnesota — Pittsburgh 5, Minnesota 3; May 23, at Pittsburgh — Pittsburgh 6, Minnesota 4; May 25, at Minnesota — Pittsburgh 8, Minnesota 0.

1989-90 — Edmonton Oilers — Mark Messier (Captain), Jari Kurri, Kevin Lowe, Steve Smith, Jeff Beukeboom, Mark Lamb, Joe Murphy, Glenn Anderson, Adam Graves, Craig MacTavish, Kelly Buchberger, Craig Simpson, Martin Gelinas, Randy Gregg, Charlie Huddy, Geoff Smith, Reijo Ruotsalainen, Craig Muni, Bill Ranford, Dave Brown, Pokey Reddick, Petr Klima, Esa Tikkanen, Grant Fuhr; Peter Pocklington (Owner), Glen Sather (President/General Manager), John Muckler (Head Coach), Ted Green (Co-Coach), Ron Low (Assistant Coach), Bruce MacGregor (Assistant General Manager), Barry Fraser (Director of Player Personnel), Bill Tuele (Director of Public Relations), Werner Baum (Vice President), Dr. Gordon Cameron (Medical Chief of Staff), Dr. David Reid (Team Physician), Ken Lowe (Athletic Therapist), Barrie Stafford (Athletic Trainer), Stuart Poirier (Massage Therapist), Lyle Kulchisky (Assistant Trainer), John Blackwell (Cape Breton (AHL) - Director of Operations), Ace Bailey, Ed Chadwick, Lorne Davis, Harry Howell, Albert Reeves, Matti Vaisanen (Scouts).

Scores: May 15, at Boston — Edmonton 3, Boston 2; May 18, at Boston — Edmonton 7, Boston 2; May 20, at Edmonton — Boston 2, Edmonton 1; May 22, at Edmonton — Edmonton 5, Boston 1; May 24, at Boston — Edmonton 4, Boston 1.

1988-89 — Calgary Flames — Lanny McDonald (Co- Captain), Jim Peplinski (Co-Captain), Tim Hunter, Mike Vernon, Rick Wamsley, Al MacInnis, Brad McCrimmon, Dana Murzyn, Ric Nattress, Joe Mullen, Gary Roberts, Colin Patterson, Hakan Loob, Theoren Fleury, Jiri Hrdina, Gary Suter, Mark Hunter, Joe Nieuwendyk, Brian MacLellan, Joel Otto, Jamie Macoun, Doug Gilmour, Rob Ramage; Norman Green, Harley Hotchkiss, Norman Kwong, Sonia Scurfield, B.J. Seaman, D.K. Seaman (Owners), Cliff Fletcher (President/General Manager), Al MacNeil (Assistant General Manager), Al Coates (Assistant to the President), Terry Crisp (Head Coach), Doug Risebrough, Tom Watt (Assistant Coaches), Glenn Hall (Goaltending Consultant), Jim Murray (Trainer), Al Murray (Assistant Trainer), Bob Stewart (Equipment Manager).

Scores: May 14, at Calgary — Calgary 3, Montreal 2; May 17, at Calgary— Montreal 4, Calgary 2; May 19, at Montreal — Montreal 4, Calgary 3; May 21, at Montreal — Calgary 4, Montreal 2; May 23, at Calgary — Calgary 3, Montreal 2; May 25, at Montreal — Calgary 4, Montreal 2.

1987-88 — Edmonton Oilers — Wayne Gretzky (Captain), Keith Acton, Glenn Anderson, Jeff Beukeboom, Geoff Courtnall, Grant Fuhr, Randy Gregg, Dave Hannan, Charlie Huddy, Mike Krushelnyski, Jari Kurri, Normand Lacombe, Kevin Lowe, Craig MacTavish, Kevin McClelland, Marty McSorley, Mark Messier, Craig Muni, Bill Ranford, Craig Simpson, Steve Smith, Esa Tikkanen; Peter Pocklington (Owner), Glen Sather (General Manager/Coach), John Muckler (Co-Coach), Ted Green (Assistant Coach), Bruce MacGregor (Assistant General Manager), Barry Fraser (Director of Player Personnel), Bill Tuele (Director of Public Relations), Dr. Gordon Cameron (Team Doctor), Peter Millar (Athletic Therapist), Juergen Merz (Massage Therapist), Barrie Stafford (Trainer), Lyle Kulchisky (Assistant Trainer).

Scores: May 18, at Edmonton — Edmonton 2, Boston 1; May 20, at Edmonton — Edmonton 4, Boston 2; May 22, at Boston — Edmonton 6, Boston 3; May 24, at Boston — Boston 3, Edmonton 3 (suspended due to power failure); May 26, at Edmonton — Edmonton 6, Boston 3.

1986-87 — Edmonton Oilers — Wayne Gretzky (Captain), Glenn Anderson, Jeff Beukeboom, Kelly Buchberger, Paul Coffey, Grant Fuhr, Randy Gregg, Charlie Huddy, Dave Hunter, Mike Krushelnyski, Jari Kurri, Moe Lemay, Kevin Lowe, Craig MacTavish, Kevin McClelland, Marty McSorley, Mark Messier, Andy Moog, Craig Muni, Kent Nilsson, Jaroslav Pouzar, Reijo Ruotsalainen, Steve Smith, Esa Tikkanen; Peter Pocklington (Owner), Glen Sather (General Manager/Coach), Bruce MacGregor (Assistant General Manager), John Muckler (Co-Coach), Ted Green, Ron Low (Assistant Coaches), Barry Fraser (Director of Player Personnel), Garnet Bailey, Ed Chadwick, Lorne Davis, Matti Vaisanen (Scouts), Peter Millar (Athletic Therapist), Juergen Merz (Massage Therapist), Dr. Gordon Cameron (Team Doctor), Barrie Stafford (Trainer), Lyle Kulchisky (Assistant Trainer).
Scores: May 17, at Edmonton — Edmonton 4, Philadelphia 2; May 20, at Edmonton — Edmonton 3, Philadelphia 2; May 22, at Philadelphia — Philadelphia 5, Edmonton 3; May 24, at Philadelphia — Edmonton 4, Philadelphia 1; May 26, at Edmonton — Philadelphia 4, Edmonton 3; May 28, at Philadelphia — Philadelphia 3, Edmonton 2; May 31, at Edmonton — Edmonton 3, Philadelphia 1.

1985-86 — Montreal Canadiens — Bob Gainey (Captain), Doug Soetaert, Patrick Roy, Rick Green, David Maley, Ryan Walter, Serge Boisvert, Mario Tremblay, Bobby Smith, Craig Ludwig, Tom Kurvers, Kjell Dahlin, Larry Robinson, Guy Carbonneau, Chris Chelios, Petr Svoboda, Mats Naslund, Lucien DeBlois, Steve Rooney, Gaston Gingras, Mike Lalor, Chris Nilan, John Kordic, Claude Lemieux, Mike McPhee, Brian Skrudland, Stephane Richer; Ronald Corey (President), Serge Savard (General Manager), Jean Perron (Coach), Jacques Laperrière (Assistant Coach), Jean Béliveau, Francois-Xavier Seigneur, Fred Steer (Vice Presidents), Jacques Lemaire, André Boudrias (Assistant General Managers), Claude Ruel (Player Development), Yves Belanger (Athletic Therapist), Gaetan Lefebvre (Assistant Athletic Therapist), Eddy Palchak (Trainer), Sylvain Toupin (Assistant Trainer).
Scores: May 16, at Calgary — Calgary 5, Montreal 2; May 18, at Calgary — Montreal 3, Calgary 2; May 20, at Montreal — Montreal 5, Calgary 3; May 22, at Montreal — Montreal 1, Calgary 0; May 24, at Calgary — Montreal 4, Calgary 3.

1984-85 — Edmonton Oilers — Wayne Gretzky (Captain), Glenn Anderson, Billy Carroll, Paul Coffey, Lee Fogolin Jr., Grant Fuhr, Randy Gregg, Charlie Huddy, Pat Hughes, Dave Hunter, Don Jackson, Mike Krushelnyski, Jari Kurri, Willy Lindstrom, Kevin Lowe, Dave Lumley, Kevin McClelland, Larry Melnyk, Mark Messier, Andy Moog, Mark Napier, Jaroslav Pouzar, Dave Semenko, Esa Tikkanen; Peter Pocklington (Owner), Glen Sather (General Manager/Coach), Bruce MacGregor (Assistant General Manager), John Muckler, Ted Green (Assistant Coaches), Barry Fraser (Director of Player Personnel/Chief Scout), Garnet Bailey, Ed Chadwick, Lorne Davis, Matti Vaisanen (Scouts), Peter Millar (Athletic Therapist), Dr. Gordon Cameron (Team Doctor), Barrie Stafford (Trainer), Lyle Kulchisky (Assistant Trainer).
Scores: May 21, at Philadelphia — Philadelphia 4, Edmonton 1; May 23, at Philadelphia — Edmonton 3, Philadelphia 1; May 25, at Edmonton — Edmonton 4, Philadelphia 3; May 28, at Edmonton — Edmonton 5, Philadelphia 3; May 30, at Edmonton — Edmonton 8, Philadelphia 3.

1983-84 — Edmonton Oilers — Wayne Gretzky (Captain), Glenn Anderson, Paul Coffey, Pat Conacher, Lee Fogolin Jr., Grant Fuhr, Randy Gregg, Charlie Huddy, Pat Hughes, Dave Hunter, Don Jackson, Jari Kurri, Willy Lindstrom, Ken Linseman, Kevin Lowe, Dave Lumley, Kevin McClelland, Mark Messier, Andy Moog, Jaroslav Pouzar, Dave Semenko; Peter Pocklington (Owner), Glen Sather (General Manager/Coach), Bruce MacGregor (Assistant General Manager), John Muckler, Ted Green (Assistant Coaches), Barry Fraser (Director of Player Personnel/Chief Scout), Pete Millar (Athletic Therapist), Barrie Stafford (Trainer), Lyle Kulchisky (Assistant Trainer).
Scores: May 10, at New York — Edmonton 1, NY Islanders 0; May 12, at New York — NY Islanders 6, Edmonton 1; May 15, at Edmonton — Edmonton 7, NY Islanders 2; May 17, at Edmonton — Edmonton 7, NY Islanders 2; May 19, at Edmonton — Edmonton 5, NY Islanders 2.

1982-83 — New York Islanders — Denis Potvin (Captain), Mike Bossy, Bob Bourne, Paul Boutilier, Billy Carroll, Greg Gilbert, Clark Gillies, Butch Goring, Mats Hallin, Tomas Jonsson, Anders Kallur, Gord Lane, Dave Langevin, Mike McEwen, Roland Melanson, Wayne Merrick, Ken Morrow, Bob Nystrom, Stefan Persson, Billy Smith, Brent Sutter, Duane Sutter, John Tonelli, Bryan Trottier; Bill Torrey (President/General Manager), John Pickett Jr. (Chairman), Gerry Ehman (Assistant General Manager/Director of Scouting), Al Arbour (Coach), Lorne Henning (Assistant Coach), Ron Waske (Trainer), Jim Pickard (Assistant Trainer).
Scores: May 10, at Edmonton — NY Islanders 2, Edmonton 0; May 12, at Edmonton — NY Islanders 6, Edmonton 3; May 14, at New York — NY Islanders 5, Edmonton 1; May 17, at New York — NY Islanders 4, Edmonton 2

1981-82 — New York Islanders — Denis Potvin (Captain), Mike Bossy, Bob Bourne, Billy Carroll, Greg Gilbert, Clark Gillies, Butch Goring, Tomas Jonsson, Anders Kallur, Gord Lane, Dave Langevin, Hector Marini, Mike McEwen, Roland Melanson, Wayne Merrick, Ken Morrow, Bob Nystrom, Stefan Persson, Billy Smith, Brent Sutter, Duane Sutter, John Tonelli, Bryan Trottier; Bill Torrey (President/General Manager), John Pickett Jr. (Chairman), Jim Devellano (Assistant General Manager/Director of Scouting), Al Arbour (Coach), Lorne Henning (Assistant Coach), Gerry Ehman (Head Scout), Ron Waske (Trainer), Jim Pickard (Assistant Trainer).
Scores: May 8, at New York — NY Islanders 6, Vancouver 5; May 11, at New York — NY Islanders 6, Vancouver 4; May 13, at Vancouver — NY Islanders 3, Vancouver 0; May 16, at Vancouver — NY Islanders 3, Vancouver 1

1980-81 — New York Islanders — Denis Potvin (Captain), Mike Bossy, Bob Bourne, Billy Carroll, Clark Gillies, Butch Goring, Garry Howatt, Anders Kallur, Gord Lane, Dave Langevin, Bob Lorimer, Hector Marini, Mike McEwen, Roland Melanson, Wayne Merrick, Ken Morrow, Bob Nystrom, Stefan Persson, Jean Potvin, Billy Smith, Duane Sutter, John Tonelli, Bryan Trottier; Bill Torrey (President/General Manager), John Pickett Jr. (Chairman), Al Arbour (Coach), Lorne Henning (Player/Assistant Coach), Jim Devellano (Chief Scout), Gerry Ehman, Mario Saraceno, Harry Boyd (Scouts), Ron Waske (Trainer), Jim Pickard (Assistant Trainer).
Scores: May 12, at New York — NY Islanders 6, Minnesota 3; May 14, at New York — NY Islanders 6, Minnesota 3; May 17, at Minnesota — NY Islanders 7, Minnesota 5; May 19, at Minnesota— Minnesota 4, NY Islanders 2; May 21, at New York — NY Islanders 5, Minnesota 1.

1979-80 — New York Islanders — Denis Potvin (Captain), Mike Bossy, Bob Bourne, Clark Gillies, Butch Goring, Lorne Henning, Garry Howatt, Anders Kallur, Gord Lane, Dave Langevin, Bob Lorimer, Alex McKendry, Wayne Merrick, Ken Morrow, Bob Nystrom, Stefan Persson, Jean Potvin, Glenn Resch, Billy Smith, Duane Sutter, Steve Tambellini, John Tonelli, Bryan Trottier; Bill Torrey (President/General Manager), John Pickett Jr. (Chairman), Al Arbour (Coach), Billy MacMillan (Assistant Coach), Jim Devellano (Chief Scout), Gerry Ehman, Mario Saraceno, Harry Boyd (Scouts), Ron Waske (Trainer), Jim Pickard (Assistant Trainer).
Scores: May 13, at Philadelphia — NY Islanders 4, Philadelphia 3; May 15, at Philadelphia — Philadelphia 8, NY Islanders 3; May 17, at New York — NY Islanders 6, Philadelphia 2; May 19, at New York — NY Islanders 5, Philadelphia 2; May 22, at Philadelphia — Philadelphia 6, NY Islanders 3; May 24, at New York — NY Islanders 5, Philadelphia 4.

1978-79 — Montreal Canadiens — Yvan Cournoyer (Captain), Guy Lafleur, Ken Dryden, Rick Chartraw, Brian Engblom, Bob Gainey, Mario Tremblay, Guy Lapointe, Doug Risebrough, Réjean Houle, Pat Hughes, Michel Larocque, Doug Jarvis, Yvon Lambert, Pierre Larouche, Gilles Lupien, Rod Langway, Jacques Lemaire, Pierre Mondou, Larry Robinson, Mark Napier, Serge Savard, Steve Shutt, Cam Connor, Richard Sévigny; Jacques Courtois (President), Sam Pollock (Director), Irving Grundman (Vice President/Managing Director), Jean Beliveau (Vice President - Corporate Affairs), Scotty Bowman (Coach), Claude Ruel (Director of Player Development), Al MacNeil (Director of Player Personnel), Morgan McCammon (Director), Ron Caron (Director of Recruitment), Eddy Palchak (Trainer), Pierre Meilleur (Assistant Trainer).
Scores: May 13, at Montreal — NY Rangers 4, Montreal 1; May 15, at Montreal — Montreal 6, NY Rangers 2; May 17, at New York — Montreal 4, NY Rangers 1; May 19, at New York — Montreal 4, NY Rangers 3; May 21, at Montreal — Montreal 4, NY Rangers 1.

1977-78 — Montreal Canadiens — Yvan Cournoyer (Captain), Guy Lafleur, Ken Dryden, Michel Larocque, Rick Chartraw, Réjean Houle, Pierre Larouche, Brian Engblom, Yvon Lambert, Jacques Lemaire, Bob Gainey, Guy Lapointe, Doug Jarvis, Gilles Lupien, Pierre Mondou, Larry Robinson, Bill Nyrop, Murray Wilson, Serge Savard, Steve Shutt, Mario Tremblay, Pierre Bouchard, Doug Risebrough; Jacques Courtois (President), Sam Pollock (Vice President/General Manager), Jean Beliveau (Vice President/Director of Corporate Relations), Scotty Bowman (Coach), Peter Bronfman, Edward Bronfman (Directors), Al MacNeil (Director of Player Development), Eddy Palchak (Trainer), Pierre Meilleur (Assistant Trainer), Claude Ruel (Director of Player Development), Floyd Curry, Ron Caron (Assistant General Managers).
Scores: May 13, at Montreal — Montreal 4, Boston 1; May 16, at Montreal — Montreal 3, Boston 2; May 18, at Boston — Boston 4, Montreal 0; May 21, at Boston — Boston 4, Montreal 3; May 23, at Montreal — Montreal 4, Boston 1; May 25, at Boston — Montreal 4, Boston 1.

1976-77 — Montreal Canadiens — Yvan Cournoyer (Captain), Larry Robinson, Guy Lafleur, Pierre Bouchard, Rejean Houle, Yvon Lambert, Bob Gainey, Jacques Lemaire, Guy Lapointe, Ken Dryden, Rick Chartraw, Bill Nyrop, Michel Larocque, Pierre Mondou, Serge Savard, Steve Shutt, Mario Tremblay, Murray Wilson, Doug Jarvis, Mike Polich, Jimmy Roberts, Pete Mahovlich, Doug Risebrough, Jacques Courtois (President), Sam Pollock (Vice President/General Manager), Jean Beliveau (Vice President/Director of Corporate Relations), Scotty Bowman (Coach), Peter Bronfman, Edward Bronfman (Directors), Claude Ruel (Director of Player Development), Floyd Curry, Ron Caron (Assistant General Managers), Pierre Meilleur (Assistant Trainer), Eddy Palchak (Trainer).
Scores: May 7, at Montreal — Montreal 7, Boston 3; May 10, at Montreal — Montreal 3, Boston 0; May 12, at Boston — Montreal 4, Boston 2; May 14, at Boston — Montreal 2, Boston 1.

1975-76 — Montreal Canadiens — Yvan Cournoyer (Captain), Bob Gainey, Larry Robinson, Pierre Bouchard, Rick Chartraw, Ken Dryden, Pete Mahovlich, Guy Lafleur, Yvon Lambert, Michel Larocque, Serge Savard, Doug Jarvis, Jacques Lemaire, Guy Lapointe, Jimmy Roberts, Doug Risebrough, Steve Shutt, Murray Wilson, Mario Tremblay, Bill Nyrop; Jacques Courtois (President), Jean Beliveau (Vice President), Peter Bronfman (Chairman), Edward Bronfman (Director), Sam Pollock (Vice President/General Manager), Scotty Bowman (Coach), Eddy Palchak (Trainer), Pierre Meilleur (Assistant Trainer), Claude Ruel (Director of Player Development).
Scores: May 9, at Montreal — Montreal 4, Philadelphia 3; May 11, at Montreal — Montreal 2, Philadelphia 1; May 13, at Philadelphia — Montreal 3, Philadelphia 2; May 16, at Philadelphia — Montreal 5, Philadelphia 3.

1974-75 — Philadelphia Flyers — Bobby Clarke (Captain), Bernie Parent, Bobby Taylor, Wayne Stephenson, Ed Van Impe, Don Saleski, Tom Bladon, Larry Goodenough, Bill Barber, Gary Dornhoefer, Dave Schultz, Joe Watson, Ross Lonsberry, André Dupont, Terry Crisp, Orest Kindrachuk, Bill Clement, Bob Kelly, Rick MacLeish, Jimmy Watson, Reggie Leach, Ted Harris; Ed Snider (Chairman), Joe Scott (President), Eugene Dixon Jr. (Vice Chairman), Fred Shero (Coach), Keith Allen (Vice President/General Manager), Lou Scheinfeld (Vice President), Mike Nykoluk (Assistant Coach), Marcel Pelletier (Player Personnel Director), Barry Ashbee (Assistant Coach), Frank Lewis (Trainer), Jim McKenzie (Assistant Trainer).
Scores: May 15, at Philadelphia — Philadelphia 4, Buffalo 1; May 18, at Philadelphia — Philadelphia 2, Buffalo 1; May 20, at Buffalo — Buffalo 5, Philadelphia 4; May 22, at Buffalo — Buffalo 4, Philadelphia 2; May 25, at Philadelphia — Philadelphia 5, Buffalo 1; May 27, at Buffalo — Philadelphia 2, Buffalo 0.

1973-74 — Philadelphia Flyers — Bobby Clarke (Captain), Bernie Parent, Bobby Taylor, Bill Clement, Ross Lonsberry, Bill Barber, Orest Kindrachuk, Ed Van Impe, Don Saleski, Gary Dornhoefer, Barry Ashbee, Jimmy Watson, Dave Schultz, André Dupont, Bruce Cowick, Rick MacLeish, Terry Crisp, Bill Flett, Simon Nolet, Joe Watson, Bob Kelly, Tom Bladon; Ed Snider (Chairman), Joe Scott (President), Eugene Dixon Jr. (Vice Chairman), Fred Shero (Coach), Keith Allen (Vice President/General Manager), Mike Nykoluk (Assistant Coach), Marcel Pelletier (Player Personnel Director), Frank Lewis (Trainer), Jim McKenzie (Assistant Trainer).
Scores: May 7, at Boston — Boston 3, Philadelphia 2; May 9, at Boston — Philadelphia 3, Boston 2; May 12, at Philadelphia — Philadelphia 4, Boston 1; May 14, at Philadelphia — Philadelphia 4, Boston 2; May 16, at Boston — Boston 5, Philadelphia 1; May 19, at Philadelphia — Philadelphia 1, Boston 0.

1972-73 — Montreal Canadiens — Henri Richard (Captain), Jacques Laperrière, Ken Dryden, Yvan Cournoyer, Jacques Lemaire, Marc Tardif, Serge Savard, Pete Mahovlich, Guy Lapointe, Réjean Houle, Claude Larose, Pierre Bouchard, Frank Mahovlich, Jimmy Roberts, Chuck Lefley, Guy Lafleur, Bob Murdoch, Michel Plasse, Murray Wilson, Larry Robinson, Steve Shutt; Jacques Courtois (President), Jean Beliveau (Vice President), Peter Bronfman (Chairman), Sam Pollock (Vice President/General Manager), Edward Bronfman (Executive Director), Scotty Bowman (Coach), Bob Williams (Trainer).
Scores: April 29, at Montreal — Montreal 8, Chicago 3; May 1, at Montreal — Montreal 4, Chicago 1; May 3, at Chicago — Chicago 7, Montreal 4; May 6, at Chicago — Montreal 4, Chicago 0; May 8, at Montreal — Chicago 8, Montreal 7; May 10, at Chicago — Montreal 6, Chicago 4.

1971-72 — Boston Bruins — Bobby Orr, Gerry Cheevers, Eddie Johnston, Dallas Smith, Derek Sanderson, Carol Vadnais, Phil Esposito, Fred Stanfield, Don Awrey, Ted Green, Ken Hodge, John Bucyk, Wayne Cashman, John McKenzie, Ed Westfall, Mike Walton, Garnet Bailey, Don Marcotte; Weston Adams (Chairman), Weston Adams Jr. (President), Shelby Davis (Vice President), Charles Mulcahy (Junior Vice President/General Counsel), Eddie Powers (Vice President/Treasurer), Milt Schmidt (General Manager), Tom Johnson (Coach), Dan Canney (Trainer), John Forristall (Assistant Trainer).
Scores: April 30, at Boston — Boston 6, NY Rangers 5; May 2, at Boston — Boston 2, NY Rangers 1; May 4, at New York — NY Rangers 5, Boston 2; May 7, at New York — Boston 3, NY Rangers 2; May 9, at Boston — NY Rangers 3, Boston 2; May 11, at New York — Boston 3, NY Rangers 0.

1970-71 — Montreal Canadiens — Jean Béliveau (Captain), Pierre Bouchard, Yvan Cournoyer, John Ferguson, Jacques Laperrière, Terry Harper, Réjean Houle, Guy Lapointe, Claude Larose, Marc Tardif, Chuck Lefley, Jacques Lemaire, Frank Mahovlich, Henri Richard, Phil Roberto, Pete Mahovlich, Bob Murdoch, Serge Savard (37GP – injured), Bobby Sheehan, Leon Rochefort, J.C. Tremblay, Ken Dryden, Rogie Vachon; David Molson (President), William Molson, Peter Molson (Vice Presidents), Sam Pollock (Vice President/General Manager), Ron Caron (Assistant General Manager), Al MacNeil (Coach), Yves Belanger (Trainer), Phil Langlois, Eddie Palchak (Assistant Trainers).
Scores: May 4, at Chicago — Chicago 2, Montreal 1; May 6, at Chicago — Chicago 5, Montreal 3; May 9, at Montreal — Montreal 4, Chicago 2; May 11, at Montreal — Montreal 5, Chicago 2; May 13, at Chicago — Chicago 2, Montreal 0; May 16, at Montreal — Montreal 4, Chicago 3; May 18, at Chicago — Montreal 3, Chicago 2.

1969-70 — Boston Bruins — Don Awrey, John Bucyk, Garnet Bailey, Wayne Carleton, Wayne Cashman, Gary Doak, Phil Esposito, Ted Green, Ken Hodge, Bobby Orr, Don Marcotte, John McKenzie, Derek Sanderson, Dallas Smith, Rick Smith, Bill Speer, Fred Stanfield, Ed Westfall, Gerry Cheevers, Eddie Johnston, John Adams, Jim Lorentz, Ron Murphy, Bill Lesuk, Ivan Boldirev, Danny Schock; Weston Adams Sr. (Chairman), Weston Adams Jr. (President), Charles Mulcahy, Eddie Powers, Shelby Davis (Vice Presidents), Harry Sinden (Coach), Milt Schmidt (General Manager), Tom Johnson (Assistant General Manager), Dan Canney (Trainer), John Forristall (Assistant Trainer).
Scores: May 3, at St. Louis — Boston 6, St. Louis 1; May 5, at St. Louis — Boston 6, St. Louis 2; May 7, at Boston — Boston 4, St. Louis 1; May 10, at Boston — Boston 4, St. Louis 3.

1968-69 — Montreal Canadiens — Jean Béliveau (Captain), Ralph Backstrom, Jacques Lemaire, Dick Duff, Christian Bordeleau, Mickey Redmond, Yvan Cournoyer, Henri Richard, Bobby Rousseau, John Ferguson, Serge Savard, Terry Harper, Gilles Tremblay, Ted Harris, J.C. Tremblay, Larry Hillman, Jacques Laperrière, Claude Provost, Tony Esposito, Rogie Vachon, Gump Worsley; David Molson (President), William Molson, Peter Molson (Vice Presidents), Sam Pollock (Vice President/General Manager), Claude Ruel (Coach), Larry Aubut (Trainer), Eddie Palchak (Assistant Trainer).
Scores: April 27, at Montreal — Montreal 3, St. Louis 1; April 29, at Montreal — Montreal 3, St. Louis 1; May 1, at St. Louis — Montreal 4, St. Louis 0; May 4, at St. Louis — Montreal 2, St. Louis 1.

1967-68 — Montreal Canadiens — Jean Béliveau (Captain), Ralph Backstrom, Yvan Cournoyer, Dick Duff, John Ferguson, Danny Grant, Terry Harper, Ted Harris, Serge Savard, Jacques Laperrière, Claude Larose, Jacques Lemaire, Claude Provost, Mickey Redmond, Henri Richard, Bobby Rousseau, Gilles Tremblay, J.C. Tremblay, Carol Vadnais, Rogie Vachon, Ernie Wakely, Gump Worsley; Hartland Molson (Chairman), David Molson (President), Sam Pollock (Vice President/General Manager), Toe Blake (Coach), Larry Aubut (Trainer), Eddie Palchak (Assistant Trainer).
Scores: May 5, at St. Louis — Montreal 3, St. Louis 2; May 7, at St. Louis — Montreal 1, St. Louis 0; May 9, at Montreal — Montreal 4, St. Louis 3; May 11, at Montreal — Montreal 3, St. Louis 2.

1966-67 — Toronto Maple Leafs — George Armstrong (Captain), Bob Baun, Johnny Bower, Brian Conacher, Ron Ellis, Aut Erickson, Larry Hillman, Tim Horton, Red Kelly, Larry Jeffrey, Dave Keon, Frank Mahovlich, Milan Marcetta, Jim Pappin, Marcel Pronovost, Bob Pulford, Terry Sawchuk, Eddie Shack, Allan Stanley, Pete Stemkowski, Mike Walton; Stafford Smythe (President), Harold Ballard (Executive Vice President), John Bassett (Chairman), Punch Imlach (General Manager/Coach), King Clancy (Assistant Coach/Assistant General Manager), Bob Davidson (Chief Scout), John Anderson (Business Manager), Bob Haggert (Trainer), Tom Nayler (Assistant Trainer), Karl Elieff (Physiotherapist), Richard Smythe (Mascot).
Scores: April 20, at Montreal — Toronto 2, Montreal 6; April 22, at Montreal — Toronto 3, Montreal 0; April 25, at Toronto — Toronto 3, Montreal 2; April 27, at Toronto — Toronto 2, Montreal 6; April 29, at Montreal — Toronto 4, Montreal 1; May 2, at Toronto — Toronto 3, Montreal 1.

1965-66 — Montreal Canadiens — Jean Béliveau (Captain), Ralph Backstrom, Dave Balon, Yvan Cournoyer, Bobby Rousseau, Dick Duff, John Ferguson, Terry Harper, Ted Harris, Charlie Hodge, Jacques Laperrière, Claude Larose, Noel Price, Claude Provost, Henri Richard, Jimmy Roberts, Leon Rochefort, Jean-Guy Talbot, Gilles Tremblay, J.C. Tremblay, Gump Worsley; Hartland Molson (Chairman), David Molson (President), Sam Pollock (General Manager), Toe Blake (Coach), Andy Galley (Trainer), Larry Aubut (Assistant Trainer).
Scores: April 24, at Montreal — Detroit 3, Montreal 2; April 26, at Montreal — Detroit 5, Montreal 2; April 28, at Detroit — Montreal 4, Detroit 2; May 1, at Detroit — Montreal 2, Detroit 1; May 3, at Montreal — Montreal 5, Detroit 1; May 5, at Detroit — Montreal 3, Detroit 2.

1964-65 — Montreal Canadiens — Jean Béliveau (Captain), Ralph Backstrom, Dave Balon, Red Berenson, Yvan Cournoyer, Dick Duff, John Ferguson, Jean Gauthier, Charlie Hodge, Terry Harper, Ted Harris, Jacques Laperrière, Claude Larose, Garry Peters, Noel Picard, Claude Provost, Henri Richard, Jimmy Roberts, Bobby Rousseau, Jean-Guy Talbot, Gilles Tremblay, J.C. Tremblay, Ernie Wakely, Bryan Watson, Gump Worsley; Hartland Molson (Chairman), David Molson (President), Maurice Richard (Assistant to the President), Sam Pollock (General Manager), Toe Blake (Coach), Andy Galley (Trainer), Larry Aubut (Assistant Trainer).
Scores: April 17, at Montreal — Montreal 3, Chicago 2; April 20, at Montreal — Montreal 2, Chicago 0; April 22, at Chicago — Montreal 1, Chicago 3; April 25, at Chicago — Montreal 1, Chicago 5; April 7, at Montreal — Montreal 6, Chicago 0; April 29, at Chicago — Montreal 1, Chicago 2; May 1, at Montreal — Montreal 4, Chicago 0.

1963-64 — Toronto Maple Leafs — George Armstrong (Captain), Andy Bathgate, Bob Baun, Johnny Bower, Carl Brewer, Gerry Ehman, Billy Harris, Larry Hillman, Dave Keon, Tim Horton, Red Kelly, Frank Mahovlich, Don McKenney, Jim Pappin, Bob Pulford, Eddie Shack, Don Simmons, Allan Stanley, Ron Stewart, Al Arbour, Ed Litzenberger; Stafford Smythe (President), Harold Ballard (Executive Vice President), John Bassett (Chairman), Punch Imlach (Coach/General Manager), King Clancy (Assistant Coach/Assistant General Manager), Bob Haggert (Trainer), Tom Nayler (Assistant Trainer), Hugh Hoult (Stick Boy).
Scores April 11, at Toronto — Toronto 3, Detroit 2; April 14, at Toronto — Toronto 3, Detroit 4; April 16, at Detroit — Toronto 3, Detroit 4; April 18, at Detroit — Toronto 4, Detroit 2; April 21, at Toronto — Toronto 1, Detroit 2; April 23, at Detroit — Toronto 4, Detroit 3; April 25, at Toronto — Toronto 4, Detroit 0.

1962-63 — Toronto Maple Leafs — George Armstrong (Captain), Bob Baun, Johnny Bower, Carl Brewer, Kent Douglas, Dick Duff, Billy Harris, Larry Hillman, Tim Horton, Red Kelly, Dave Keon, Ed Litzenberger, John MacMillan, Frank Mahovlich, Bob Nevin, Bob Pulford, Eddie Shack, Don Simmons, Allan Stanley, Ron Stewart; Stafford Smythe (President), Harold Ballard (Executive Vice President), John Bassett (Chairman), Punch Imlach (Coach/General Manager), King Clancy (Assistant Coach/Assistant General Manager), Bob Haggert (Trainer), Tom Nayler (Assistant Trainer), Hugh Hoult (Stick Boy).
Scores: April 9, at Toronto — Toronto 4, Detroit 2; April 11, at Toronto — Toronto 4, Detroit 2; April 14, at Detroit — Toronto 2, Detroit 3; April 16, at Detroit — Toronto 4, Detroit 2; April 18, at Toronto — Toronto 3, Detroit 1.

1961-62 — Toronto Maple Leafs — George Armstrong (Captain), Al Arbour, Bob Baun, Johnny Bower, Carl Brewer, Dick Duff, Billy Harris, Larry Hillman, Dave Keon, Tim Horton, Red Kelly, Ed Litzenberger, John MacMillan, Frank Mahovlich, Bob Nevin, Bert Olmstead, Bob Pulford, Eddie Shack, Allan Stanley, Don Simmons, Ron Stewart; Stafford Smythe (President), Harold Ballard (Executive Vice President), John Bassett (Vice President), Conn Smythe (Chairman), Punch Imlach (Coach/General Manager), King Clancy (Assistant Coach), Bob Davidson (Chief Scout), Bob Haggert (Trainer), Tom Nayler (Assistant Trainer), Hugh Hoult (Stick Boy).
Scores: April 10, at Toronto — Toronto 4, Chicago 1; April 12, at Toronto — Toronto 3, Chicago 2; April 15, at Chicago — Toronto 0, Chicago 3; April 17, at Chicago — Toronto 1, Chicago 4; April 19, at Toronto —Toronto 8, Chicago 4; April 22, at Chicago — Toronto 2, Chicago 1.

1960-61 — Chicago Black Hawks — Ed Litzenberger (Captain), Al Arbour, Earl Balfour, Murray Balfour, Glenn Hall, Jack Evans, Roy Edwards, Denis DeJordy, Bill Hay, Wayne Hicks, Reggie Fleming, Wayne Hillman, Bobby Hull, Chico Maki, Ab McDonald, Moose Vasko, Stan Mikita, Ron Murphy, Eric Nesterenko, Pierre Pilote, Tod Sloan, Dollard St. Laurent, Kenny Wharram; Arthur Wirtz (President), Arthur Wirtz Jr. (Vice President), James Norris (Chairman), Tommy Ivan (General Manager), Rudy Pilous (Coach), Nick Garen, Walter Humeniuk (Trainers).
Scores: April 6, at Chicago — Chicago 3, Detroit 2; April 8, at Detroit — Detroit 3, Chicago 1; April 10, at Chicago — Chicago 3, Detroit 1; April 12, at Detroit — Detroit 2, Chicago 1; April 14, at Chicago — Chicago 6, Detroit 3; April 16, at Detroit — Chicago 5, Detroit 1.

1959-60 — Montreal Canadiens — Maurice Richard (Captain), Ralph Backstrom, Marcel Bonin, Jean Béliveau, Bernie Geoffrion, Phil Goyette, Doug Harvey, Bill Hicke, Charlie Hodge, Tom Johnson, Albert Langlois, Don Marshall, Dickie Moore, Ab McDonald, Jacques Plante, Henri Richard, André Pronovost, Claude Provost, Bob Turner, Jean-Guy Talbot; Senator Hartland Molson (President), Frank Selke (Managing Director), Ken Reardon (Vice President), Sam Pollock (Personnel Director), Toe Blake (Coach), Hector Dubois, Larry Aubut (Trainers).
Scores: April 7, at Montreal — Montreal 4, Toronto 2; April 9, at Montreal — Montreal 2, Toronto 1; April 12, at Toronto — Montreal 5, Toronto 2; April 14, at Toronto — Montreal 4, Toronto 0.

1958-59 — Montreal Canadiens — Maurice Richard (Captain), Ralph Backstrom, Marcel Bonin, Jean Béliveau, Ian Cushenan, Bernie Geoffrion, Charlie Hodge, Phil Goyette, Doug Harvey, Bill Hicke, Tom Johnson, Albert Langlois, Don Marshall, Ab McDonald, Dickie Moore, Jacques Plante, Ken Mosdell, André Pronovost, Claude Provost, Henri Richard, Jean-Guy Talbot, Bob Turner; Senator Hartland Molson (President), Frank Selke (Managing Director), Ken Reardon (Vice President), Sam Pollock (Personnel Director), Toe Blake (Coach), Hector Dubois, Larry Aubut (Trainers).
Scores: April 9, at Montreal — Montreal 5, Toronto 3; April 11, at Montreal — Montreal 3, Toronto 1; April 14, at Toronto — Toronto 3, Montreal 2; April 16, at Toronto — Montreal 3, Toronto 2; April 18, at Montreal — Montreal 5, Toronto 3.

1957-58 — Montreal Canadiens — Maurice Richard (Captain), Jean Béliveau, Marcel Bonin, Floyd Curry, Connie Broden, Bernie Geoffrion, Phil Goyette, Doug Harvey, Charlie Hodge, Tom Johnson, Albert Langlois, Don Marshall, Ab McDonald, Gerry McNeil, Dickie Moore, Bert Olmstead, Jacques Plante, André Pronovost, Henri Richard, Claude Provost, Dollard St. Laurent, Jean-Guy Talbot, Bob Turner; Senator Hartland Molson (President), Frank Selke (Managing Director), Ken Reardon (Vice President), Toe Blake (Coach), Hector Dubois, Larry Aubut (Trainers).
Scores: April 8, at Montreal —Montreal 2, Boston 1; April 10, at Montreal — Boston 5, Montreal 2; April 13, at Boston — Montreal 3, Boston 0; April 15, at Boston — Boston 3, Montreal 1; April 17, at Montreal — Montreal 3, Boston 2; April 20, at Boston — Montreal 5, Boston 3.

1956-57 — Montreal Canadiens — Maurice Richard (Captain), Jean Béliveau, Connie Broden, Floyd Curry, Bernie Geoffrion, Phil Goyette, Doug Harvey, Tom Johnson, Don Marshall, Gerry McNeil, Dickie Moore, Bert Olmstead, Jacques Plante, André Pronovost, Claude Provost, Henri Richard, Dollard St. Laurent, Jean-Guy Talbot, Bob Turner; William Northey (President), Donat Raymond (Chairman), Ken Reardon (Vice President), Frank Selke (Managing Director), Toe Blake (Coach), Hector Dubois, Larry Aubut (Trainers).
Scores: April 6, at Montreal — Montreal 5, Boston 1; April 9, at Montreal — Montreal 1, Boston 0; April 11, at Boston — Montreal 4, Boston 2; April 14, at Boston — Boston 2, Montreal 0; April 16, at Montreal — Montreal 5, Boston 1.

1955-56 — Montreal Canadiens — Butch Bouchard (Captain), Bob Turner, Jean Béliveau, Bert Olmstead, Floyd Curry, Bernie Geoffrion, Jacques Plante, Doug Harvey, Claude Provost, Charlie Hodge, Henri Richard, Tom Johnson, Maurice Richard, Jackie LeClair, Dollard St. Laurent, Don Marshall, Jean-Guy Talbot, Dickie Moore, Ken Mosdell; Donat Raymond (President), Frank Selke (Managing Director), D'Alton Coleman, William Northey (Vice Presidents), Ken Reardon (Assistant Manager), Toe Blake (Coach), Hector Dubois, Gaston Bettez (Trainers).
Scores: March 31, at Montreal — Montreal 6, Detroit 4; April 3, at Montreal — Montreal 5, Detroit 1; April 5, at Detroit — Detroit 3, Montreal 1; April 8, at Detroit — Montreal 3, Detroit 0; April 10, at Montreal — Montreal 3, Detroit 1.

1954-55 — Detroit Red Wings — Dutch Reibel, Terry Sawchuk, Jim Hay, Vic Stasiuk, Johnny Wilson, Gordie Howe, Red Kelly, Tony Leswick, Ted Lindsay (Captain), Marty Pavelich, Marcel Pronovost, Marcel Bonin, Alex Delvecchio, Bill Dineen, Bob Goldham, Benny Woit, Larry Hillman, Glen Skov; Bruce Norris (President), Marguerite Norris (President), Jack Adams (Manager), Jimmy Skinner (Coach), John Mitchell (Chief Scout), Fred Huber (Publicity Director), Carl Mattson, Lefty Wilson (Trainers).
Scores: April 3, at Detroit — Detroit 4, Montreal 2; April 5, at Detroit — Detroit 7, Montreal 1; April 7, at Montreal — Montreal 4, Detroit 2; April 9, at Montreal — Montreal 5, Detroit 3; April 10, at Detroit — Detroit 5, Montreal 1; April 12, at Montreal — Montreal 6, Detroit 3; April 14, at Detroit — Detroit 3, Montreal 1.

1953-54 — Detroit Red Wings — Marty Pavelich, Jimmy Peters, Marcel Pronovost, Metro Prystai, Dutch Reibel, Terry Sawchuk, Bob Goldham, Gordie Howe, Earl Johnson, Red Kelly, Tony Leswick, Ted Lindsay (Captain), Keith Allen, Al Arbour, Alex Delvecchio, Bill Dineen, Gilles Dube, Dave Gatherum, Glen Skov, Johnny Wilson, Benny Woit; Bruce Norris (Owner), Marguerite Norris (President), Jack Adams (Manager), Tommy Ivan (Coach), John Mitchell (Chief Scout), Fred Huber (Publicity Director), Carl Mattson, Lefty Wilson (Trainers), Wally Crossman (Assistant Trainer).
Scores: April 4, at Detroit — Detroit 3, Montreal 1; April 6, at Detroit — Montreal 3, Detroit 1; April 8, at Montreal — Detroit 5, Montreal 2; April 10, at Montreal — Detroit 2, Montreal 0; April 11, at Detroit — Montreal 1, Detroit 0; April 13, at Montreal — Montreal 4, Detroit 1; April 16, at Detroit — Detroit 2, Montreal 1.

1952-53 — Montreal Canadiens — Floyd Curry, Bernie Geoffrion, Bert Olmstead, Paul Meger, Dick Gamble, Dickie Moore, Tom Johnson, Bud MacPherson, Billy Reay, Ken Mosdell, Paul Masnick, John McCormack, Butch Bouchard (Captain), Maurice Richard, Elmer Lach, Gerry McNeil, Doug Harvey, Dollard St. Laurent, Jacques Plante, Lorne Davis, Calum MacKay, Eddie Mazur, Donat Raymond (President), Dalton Coleman (Director), William Northey (Special Advisor), Frank Selke (Manager), Dick Irvin (Coach), Hector Dubois, Gaston Bettez (Trainers).
Scores: April 9, at Montreal — Montreal 4, Boston 2; April 11, at Montreal — Boston 4, Montreal 1; April 12, at Boston — Montreal 3, Boston 0; April 14, at Boston — Montreal 7, Boston 3; April 16, at Montreal — Montreal 1, Boston 0.

1951-52 — Detroit Red Wings — Metro Prystai, Leo Reise Jr., Terry Sawchuk, Enio Sclisizzi, Glen Skov, Vic Stasiuk, Gordie Howe, Red Kelly, Tony Leswick, Ted Lindsay, Marty Pavelich, Marcel Pronovost, Sid Abel (Captain), Alex Delvecchio, Fred Glover, Bob Goldham, Glenn Hall, Benny Woit, Johnny Wilson, Larry Zeidel; James Norris (President), Bruce Norris (Owner), Jack Adams (Manager), Tommy Ivan (Coach), Fred Huber (Publicity Director), Carson Cooper (Scout), Carl Mattson, Lefty Wilson (Trainers), Wally Crossman (Assistant Trainer).
Scores: April 10, at Montreal — Detroit 3, Montreal 1; April 12, at Montreal — Detroit 2, Montreal 1; April 13, at Detroit — Detroit 3, Montreal 0; April 15, at Detroit — Detroit 3, Montreal 0.

1950-51 — Toronto Maple Leafs — Bill Barilko, Max Bentley, Hugh Bolton, Turk Broda, Fern Flaman, Cal Gardner, Bob Hassard, Bill Juzda, Ted Kennedy (Captain), Joe Klukay, Danny Lewicki, Fleming MacKell, Howie Meeker, Gus Mortson, John McCormack, Al Rollins, Tod Sloan, Sid Smith, Jimmy Thomson, Ray Timgren, Harry Watson; Joe Primeau (Coach), Bill MacBrien (Chairman), Conn Smythe (President/Manager), Hap Day (Assistant Manager), George McCullagh, J.Y. Murdoch (Vice Presidents), J.P. Bickell, Ed Bickle (Directors), Tim Daly (Trainer), Archie Campbell, Tommy Naylor (Assistant Trainers), Dr. Norman Delarue, Dr. James Murray, Dr. Horace MacIntyre (Club Doctors), Ed Fitkin (Publicity Director), Squib Walker (Chief Scout).
Scores: April 11, at Toronto — Toronto 3, Montreal 2; April 14, at Toronto — Montreal 3, Toronto 2; April 17, at Montreal — Toronto 2, Montreal 1; April 19, at Montreal — Toronto 3, Montreal 2; April 21, at Toronto — Toronto 3, Montreal 2.

1949-50 — Detroit Red Wings — Sid Abel (Captain), Pete Babando, Steve Black, Joe Carveth, Gerry Couture, Al Dewsbury, Lee Fogolin, George Gee, Gordie Howe, Red Kelly, Ted Lindsay, Harry Lumley, Clare Martin, Jim McFadden, Max McNab, Marty Pavelich, Jimmy Peters, Marcel Pronovost, Leo Reise Jr., Jack Stewart, Johnny Wilson, Larry Wilson, Doug McKay; James Norris (President), James Norris Jr. (Vice President), Arthur Wirtz (Secretary Treasurer), Jack Adams (Manager), Tommy Ivan (Coach), Fred Huber Jr. (Publicity Director), Carson Cooper (Head Scout), Carl Mattson (Trainer), Walter Humeniuk (Assistant Trainer).
Scores: April 11, at Detroit — Detroit 4, NY Rangers 1; April 13, at Toronto* — NY Rangers 3, Detroit 1; April 15, at Toronto* — Detroit 4, NY Rangers 0; April 18, at Detroit — NY Rangers 4, Detroit 3; April 20, at Detroit — NY Rangers 2, Detroit 1; April 22, at Detroit — Detroit 5, NY Rangers 4; April 23, at Detroit — Detroit 4, NY Rangers 3.
*Ice was unavailable in Madison Square Garden and NY Rangers elected to play second and third games on Toronto ice.

1948-49 — Toronto Maple Leafs — Bill Barilko, Max Bentley, Garth Boesch, Turk Broda, Bob Dawes, Bill Ezinicki, Cal Gardner, Bill Juzda, Ted Kennedy (Captain), Joe Klukay, Vic Lynn, Howie Meeker, Don Metz, Fleming MacKell, Gus Mortson, Sid Smith, Harry Taylor, Ray Timgren, Jimmy Thomson, Harry Watson; Hap Day (Coach), Bill MacBrien (Chairman), Conn Smythe (President/Manager), George McCullagh, J.Y. Murdoch (Vice Presidents), J.P. Bickell, Ed Bickle (Directors), Tim Daly (Trainer), Archie Campbell (Assistant Trainer), Dr. Norman Delarue, Dr. James Murray, Dr. Horace MacIntyre (Club Doctors), Ed Fitkin (Publicity Director), Squib Walker (Chief Scout), Kerry Day (Mascot).
Scores: April 8, at Detroit — Toronto 3, Detroit 2; April 10, at Detroit — Toronto 3, Detroit 1; April 13, at Toronto — Toronto 3, Detroit 1; April 16, at Toronto — Toronto 3, Detroit 1.

1947-48 — Toronto Maple Leafs — Syl Apps (Captain), Bill Barilko, Max Bentley, Garth Boesch, Turk Broda, Les Costello, Bill Ezinicki, Ted Kennedy, Joe Klukay, Vic Lynn, Howie Meeker, Nick Metz, Don Metz, Gus Mortson, Phil Samis, Sid Smith, Wally Stanowski, Jimmy Thomson, Harry Watson; Hap Day (Coach), Conn Smythe (Manager), Tim Daly (Trainer).
Scores: April 7, at Toronto — Toronto 5, Detroit 3; April 10, at Toronto — Toronto 4, Detroit 2; April 11, at Detroit — Toronto 2, Detroit 0; April 14, at Detroit — Toronto 7, Detroit 2.

1946-47 — Toronto Maple Leafs — Turk Broda, Garth Boesch, Gus Mortson, Jimmy Thomson, Wally Stanowski, Bill Barilko, Harry Watson, Bud Poile, Ted Kennedy, Syl Apps (Captain), Don Metz, Nick Metz, Bill Ezinicki, Vic Lynn, Howie Meeker, Gaye Stewart, Joe Klukay, Gus Bodnar, Bob Goldham; Conn Smythe (Manager), Hap Day (Coach), Tim Daly (Trainer).
Scores: April 8, at Montreal — Montreal 6, Toronto 0; April 10, at Montreal — Toronto 4, Montreal 0; April 12, at Toronto — Toronto 4, Montreal 2; April 15, at Toronto — Toronto 2, Montreal 1; April 17, at Montreal — Montreal 3, Toronto 1; April 19, at Toronto — Toronto 2, Montreal 1.

1945-46 — Montreal Canadiens — Elmer Lach, Toe Blake (Captain), Maurice Richard, Bob Fillion, Dutch Hiller, Murph Chamberlain, Ken Mosdell, Buddy O'Connor, Glen Harmon, Jimmy Peters, Butch Bouchard, Billy Reay, Ken Reardon, Leo Lamoureux, Frank Eddolls, Gerry Plamondon, Joe Benoit, Bill Durnan; Tommy Gorman (Manager), Dick Irvin (Coach), Ernie Cook (Trainer).
Scores: March 30, at Montreal — Montreal 4, Boston 3; April 2, at Montreal — Montreal 3, Boston 2; April 4, at Boston — Montreal 4, Boston 2; April 7, at Boston — Boston 3, Montreal 2; April 9, at Montreal — Montreal 6, Boston 3.

1944-45 — Toronto Maple Leafs — Don Metz, Frank McCool, Wally Stanowski, Reg Hamilton, Moe Morris, John McCreedy, Tom O'Neill, Ted Kennedy, Babe Pratt, Gus Bodnar, Art Jackson, Jack McLean, Mel Hill, Nick Metz, Bob Davidson (Captain), Sweeney Schriner, Lorne Carr, Pete Backor, Ross Johnstone; Conn Smythe (Manager), Frank Selke (Business Manager), Hap Day (Coach), Tim Daly (Trainer).
Scores: April 6, at Detroit — Toronto 1, Detroit 0; April 8, at Detroit — Toronto 2, Detroit 0; April 12, at Toronto — Toronto 1, Detroit 0; April 14, at Toronto — Detroit 5, Toronto 3; April 19, at Detroit — Detroit 2, Toronto 0; April 21, at Toronto — Detroit 1, Toronto 0; April 22, at Detroit — Toronto 2, Detroit 1.

1943-44 — Montreal Canadiens — Toe Blake (Captain), Maurice Richard, Elmer Lach, Ray Getliffe, Murph Chamberlain, Phil Watson, Butch Bouchard, Glen Harmon, Buddy O'Connor, Gerry Heffernan, Mike McMahon, Leo Lamoureux, Fern Majeau, Bob Fillion, Bill Durnan; Tommy Gorman (Manager), Dick Irvin (Coach), Ernie Cook (Trainer).
Scores: April 4, at Montreal — Montreal 5, Chicago 1; April 6, at Chicago — Montreal 3, Chicago 1; April 9, at Chicago — Montreal 3, Chicago 2; April 13, at Montreal — Montreal 5, Chicago 4.

1942-43 — Detroit Red Wings — Jack Stewart, Jimmy Orlando, Sid Abel (captain), Alex Motter, Harry Watson, Joe Carveth, Mud Bruneteau, Eddie Wares, Johnny Mowers, Cully Simon, Don Grosso, Carl Liscombe, Connie Brown, Syd Howe, Les Douglas, Harold Jackson, Joe Fisher, Adam Brown; Jack Adams (Manager), Ebbie Goodfellow (Playing Coach), Honey Walker (Trainer).
Scores: April 1, at Detroit — Detroit 6, Boston 2; April 4, at Detroit — Detroit 4, Boston 3; April 7, at Boston — Detroit 4, Boston 0; April 8, at Boston — Detroit 2, Boston 0.

1941-42 — Toronto Maple Leafs — Wally Stanowski, Syl Apps (Captain), Bob Goldham, Gordie Drillon, Hank Goldup, Ernie Dickens, Sweeney Schriner, Bucko McDonald, Bob Davidson, Nick Metz, Bingo Kampman, Don Metz, Gaye Stewart, Turk Broda, John McCreedy, Lorne Carr, Pete Langelle, Billy Taylor, Reg Hamilton; Conn Smythe (Manager), Hap Day (Coach), Frank Selke (Business Manager), Tim Daly (Trainer).
Scores: April 4, at Toronto — Detroit 3, Toronto 2; April 7, at Toronto — Detroit 4, Toronto 2; April 9, at Detroit — Detroit 5, Toronto 2; April 12, at Detroit — Toronto 4, Detroit 3; April 14, at Toronto — Toronto 9, Detroit 3; April 16, at Detroit — Toronto 3, Detroit 0; April 18, at Toronto — Toronto 3, Detroit 1.

1940-41 — Boston Bruins — Bill Cowley, Des Smith, Dit Clapper (Captain), Frank Brimsek, Flash Hollett, Jack Crawford, Bobby Bauer, Pat McReavy, Herb Cain, Mel Hill, Milt Schmidt, Woody Dumart, Roy Conacher, Terry Reardon, Art Jackson, Eddie Wiseman, Jack Shewchuck; Art Ross (Manager), Cooney Weiland (Coach), Win Green (Trainer).
Scores: April 6, at Boston — Detroit 2, Boston 3; April 8, at Boston — Detroit 1, Boston 2; April 10, at Detroit — Boston 4, Detroit 2; April 12, at Detroit — Boston 3, Detroit 1.

1939-40 — New York Rangers — Dave Kerr, Art Coulter (Captain), Ott Heller, Alex Shibicky, Mac Colville, Neil Colville, Phil Watson, Lynn Patrick, Clint Smith, Muzz Patrick, Babe Pratt, Bryan Hextall, Kilby MacDonald, Dutch Hiller, Alf Pike, Stan Smith; Lester Patrick (Manager), Frank Boucher (Coach), Harry Westerby (Trainer).
Scores: April 2, at New York — NY Rangers 2, Toronto 1; April 3, at New York — NY Rangers 6, Toronto 2; April 6, at Toronto — NY Rangers 1, Toronto 2; April 9, at Toronto — NY Rangers 0, Toronto 3; April 11, at Toronto — NY Rangers 2, Toronto 1; April 13, at Toronto — NY Rangers 3, Toronto 2.

1938-39 — Boston Bruins — Bobby Bauer, Mel Hill, Flash Hollett, Roy Conacher, Gord Pettinger, Charlie Sands, Milt Schmidt, Woody Dumart, Jack Crawford, Ray Getliffe, Frank Brimsek, Eddie Shore, Dit Clapper, Bill Cowley, Jack Portland, Red Hamill, Harry Frost, Cooney Weiland (Captain); Art Ross (Manager/Coach), Win Green (Trainer).
Scores: April 6, at Boston — Toronto 1, Boston 2; April 9, at Boston — Toronto 3, Boston 2; April 11, at Toronto — Toronto 1, Boston 3; April 13, at Toronto — Toronto 0, Boston 2; April 16, at Boston — Toronto 1, Boston 3.

1937-38 — Chicago Black Hawks — Art Wiebe, Carl Voss, Harold Jackson, Mike Karakas, Mush March, Jack Shill, Earl Seibert, Cully Dahlstrom, Alex Levinsky, Johnny Gottselig (Captain), Lou Trudel, Pete Palangio, Bill MacKenzie, Doc Romnes, Paul Thompson, Roger Jenkins, Alfie Moore, Bert Connelly, Virgil Johnson, Paul Goodman; Bill Stewart (Manager/Coach), Eddie Froelich (Trainer).
Scores: April 5, at Toronto — Chicago 3, Toronto 1; April 7, at Toronto — Chicago 1, Toronto 5; April 10, at Chicago — Chicago 2, Toronto 1; April 12, at Chicago — Chicago 4, Toronto 1.

1936-37 — Detroit Red Wings — Normie Smith, Pete Kelly, Larry Aurie, Herbie Lewis, Hec Kilrea, Mud Bruneteau, Syd Howe, Wally Kilrea, Jimmy Franks, Bucko McDonald, Gord Pettinger, Ebbie Goodfellow, John Gallagher, Ralph Bowman, John Sorrell, Marty Barry, Earl Robertson, John Sherf, Howie Mackie, Rolly Roulston, Doug Young (Captain); Jack Adams (Manager/Coach), Honey Walker (Trainer).
Scores: April 6, at New York — Detroit 1, NY Rangers 5; April 8, at Detroit — Detroit 4, NY Rangers 2; April 11, at Detroit — Detroit 0, NY Rangers 1; April 13, at Detroit — Detroit 1, NY Rangers 0; April 15, at Detroit — Detroit 3, NY Rangers 0.

1935-36 — Detroit Red Wings — John Sorrell, Syd Howe, Marty Barry, Herbie Lewis, Mud Bruneteau, Wally Kilrea, Hec Kilrea, Gord Pettinger, Bucko McDonald, Ralph Bowman, Pete Kelly, Doug Young (Captain), Ebbie Goodfellow, Normie Smith, Larry Aurie; Jack Adams (Manager/Coach), Honey Walker (Trainer).
Scores: April 5, at Detroit — Detroit 3, Toronto 1; April 7, at Detroit — Detroit 9, Toronto 4; April 9, at Toronto — Detroit 3, Toronto 4; April 11, at Toronto — Detroit 3, Toronto 2.

1934-35 — Montreal Maroons — Lionel Conacher, Cy Wentworth, Alec Connell, Toe Blake, Stewart Evans, Earl Robinson, Bill Miller, Dave Trottier, Jimmy Ward, Baldy Northcott, Hooley Smith (Captain), Russ Blinco, Al Shields, Sammy McManus, Gus Marker, Bob Gracie, Herb Cain, Dutch Gainor; Tommy Gorman (Manager/Coach), Bill O'Brien (Trainer).
Scores: April 4, at Toronto — Mtl. Maroons 3, Toronto 2; April 6, at Toronto — Mtl. Maroons 3, Toronto 1; April 9, at Montreal — Mtl. Maroons 4, Toronto 1.

1933-34 — Chicago Black Hawks — Clarence Abel, Rosie Couture, Lou Trudel, Lionel Conacher, Paul Thompson, Leroy Goldsworthy, Art Coulter, Roger Jenkins, Don McFadyen, Tom Cook, Doc Romnes, Mush March, Johnny Sheppard, Charlie Gardiner (Captain), Bill Kendall, Jack Leswick; Tommy Gorman (Manager/Coach), Eddie Froelich (Trainer).
Scores: April 3, at Detroit — Chicago 2, Detroit 1; April 5, at Detroit — Chicago 4, Detroit 1; April 8, at Chicago — Detroit 5, Chicago 2; April 10, at Chicago — Chicago 1, Detroit 0.

1932-33 — New York Rangers — Ching Johnson, Butch Keeling, Frank Boucher, Art Somers, Babe Siebert, Bun Cook, Andy Aitkenhead, Ott Heller, Oscar Asmundson, Gord Pettinger, Doug Brennan, Cecil Dillon, Bill Cook (Captain), Murray Murdoch, Earl Seibert; Lester Patrick (Manager/Coach), Harry Westerby (Trainer).
Scores: April 4, at New York — NY Rangers 5, Toronto 1; April 8, at Toronto — NY Rangers 3, Toronto 1; April 11, at Toronto — Toronto 3, NY Rangers 2; April 13, at Toronto — NY Rangers 1, Toronto 0.

1931-32 — Toronto Maple Leafs — Charlie Conacher, Busher Jackson, King Clancy, Andy Blair, Red Horner, Lorne Chabot, Alex Levinsky, Joe Primeau, Harold Darragh, Baldy Cotton, Frank Finnigan, Hap Day (Captain), Ace Bailey, Bob Gracie, Fred Robertson, Earl Miller; Conn Smythe (Manager), Dick Irvin (Coach), Tim Daly (Trainer).
Scores: April 5, at New York — Toronto 6, NY Rangers 4; April 7, at Boston* — Toronto 6, NY Rangers 2; April 9, at Toronto — Toronto 6, NY Rangers 4.

1930-31 — Montreal Canadiens — George Hainsworth, Wildor Larochelle, Marty Burke, Sylvio Mantha (Captain), Howie Morenz, Johnny Gagnon, Aurel Joliat, Armand Mondou, Pit Lepine, Albert Leduc, Georges Mantha, Art Lesieur, Nick Wasnie, Gus Rivers, Jean Pusie; Léo Dandurand (Manager), Cecil Hart (Coach), Ed Dufour (Trainer).
Scores: April 3, at Chicago — Montreal 2, Chicago 1; April 5, at Chicago — Chicago 2, Montreal 1; April 9, at Montreal — Chicago 3, Montreal 2; April 11, at Montreal — Montreal 4, Chicago 2; April 14, at Montreal — Montreal 2, Chicago 0.

1929-30 — Montreal Canadiens — George Hainsworth, Marty Burke, Sylvio Mantha (Captain), Howie Morenz, Bert McCaffrey, Aurel Joliat, Albert Leduc, Pit Lepine, Wildor Larochelle, Nick Wasnie, Gerry Carson, Armand Mondou, Georges Mantha, Gus Rivers; Léo Dandurand (Manager), Cecil Hart (Coach), Ed Dufour (Trainer).
Scores: April 1, at Boston — Montreal 3, Boston 0; April 3, at Montreal — Montreal 4, Boston 3.

1928-29 — Boston Bruins — Tiny Thompson, Eddie Shore, Lionel Hitchman (Captain), Percy Galbraith, Mickey MacKay, Red Green, Dutch Gainor, Harry Oliver, Eddie Rodden, Dit Clapper, Cooney Weiland, Lloyd Klein, Cy Denneny, Bill Carson, George Owen, Myles Lane; Art Ross (Manager/Coach), Win Green (Trainer).
Scores: March 28, at Boston — Boston 2, NY Rangers 0; March 29, at New York — Boston 2, NY Rangers 1.

1927-28 — New York Rangers — Lorne Chabot, Clarence Abel, Leo Bourgeault, Ching Johnson, Bill Cook (Captain), Bun Cook, Frank Boucher, Bill Boyd, Murray Murdoch, Paul Thompson, Alex Gray, Joe Miller, Patsy Callighen; Lester Patrick (Manager/Coach), Harry Westerby (Trainer).
Scores: April 5, at Montreal — Mtl. Maroons 2, NY Rangers 0; April 7, at Montreal — NY Rangers 2, Mtl. Maroons 1; April 10, at Montreal — Mtl. Maroons 2, NY Rangers 0; April 12, at Montreal — NY Rangers 1, Mtl. Maroons 0; April 14, at Montreal — NY Rangers 2, Mtl. Maroons 1.

1926-27 — Ottawa Senators — Alec Connell, King Clancy, Georges Boucher (Captain), Ed Gorman, Frank Finnigan, Alex Smith, Hec Kilrea, Hooley Smith, Cy Denneny, Frank Nighbor, Jack Adams, Milt Halliday; Dave Gill (Manager/Coach).
Scores: April 7, at Boston — Ottawa 0, Boston 0; April 9, at Boston — Ottawa 3, Boston 1; April 11, at Ottawa — Boston 1, Ottawa 1; April 13, at Ottawa — Ottawa 3, Boston 1.

1925-26 — Montreal Maroons — Clint Benedict, Reg Noble, Frank Carson, Dunc Munro (Captain), Nels Stewart, Punch Broadbent, Babe Siebert, Chuck Dinsmore, Merlyn Phillips, Hobie Kitchen, Sam Rothschild, Albert Holway, George Horne, Bernie Brophy; Eddie Gerard (Manager/Coach), Bill O'Brien (Trainer).
Scores: March 30, at Montreal — Mtl. Maroons 3, Victoria 0; April 1, at Montreal — Mtl. Maroons 3, Victoria 0; April 3, at Montreal — Victoria 3, Mtl. Maroons 2; April 6, at Montreal — Mtl. Maroons 2, Victoria 0.

The series in the spring of 1926 ended the annual playoffs between the champions of the East and the champions of the West. Since 1926-27 the annual playoffs in the National Hockey League have decided the Stanley Cup champions.

1924-25 — Victoria Cougars — Hap Holmes, Clem Loughlin (Captain), Gord Fraser, Frank Fredrickson, Jack Walker, Gizzy Hart, Harold Halderson, Frank Foyston, Wally Elmer, Harry Meeking, Jocko Anderson; Lester Patrick (Manager/Coach).
Scores: March 21, at Victoria — Victoria 5, Montreal 2; March 23, at Vancouver — Victoria 3, Montreal 1; March 27, at Victoria — Montreal 4, Victoria 2; March 30, at Victoria — Victoria 6, Montreal 1.

1923-24 — Montreal Canadiens — Georges Vezina, Sprague Cleghorn (Captain), Billy Coutu, Howie Morenz, Aurel Joliat, Billy Boucher, Odie Cleghorn, Sylvio Mantha, Bobby Boucher, Billy Bell, Billy Cameron, Joe Malone, Charles Fortier; Leo Dandurand (Manager/Coach).
Scores: March 22, at Montreal — Montreal 6, Cgy. Tigers 1; March 25, at Ottawa* — Montreal 3, Cgy. Tigers 0.

* Game transferred to Ottawa to benefit from artificial ice surface.

1922-23 — Ottawa Senators — Georges Boucher, Lionel Hitchman, Frank Nighbor, King Clancy, Harry Helman, Clint Benedict, Jack Darragh, Eddie Gerard (Captain), Cy Denneny, Punch Broadbent; Tommy Gorman (Manager), Pete Green (Coach), F. Dolan (Trainer).
Scores: March 29, at Vancouver — Ottawa 2, Edm. Eskimos 1; March 31, at Vancouver — Ottawa 1, Edm. Eskimos 0.

1921-22 — Toronto St. Patricks — Ted Stackhouse, Corb Denneny, Rod Smylie, Lloyd Andrews, John Ross Roach, Harry Cameron, Billy Stuart, Babe Dye, Ken Randall, Reg Noble (Captain), Eddie Gerard (borrowed for one game from Ottawa), Stan Jackson, Ivan Mitchell; Charlie Querrie (Manager), George O'Donoghue (Coach).
Scores: March 17, at Toronto — Van. Millionaires 4, Toronto 3; March 20, at Toronto — Toronto 2, Van. Millionaires 1; March 23, at Toronto — Van. Millionaires 3, Toronto 0; March 25, at Toronto — Toronto 6, Van. Millionaires 0; March 28, at Toronto — Toronto 5, Van. Millionaires 1.

Bruins' George Owen, Harry Oliver, Lloyd Klein, Eddie Shore, Mickey MacKay, Art Ross (coach), Lionel Hitchman and Tiny Thompson were all part of Boston's first Stanley Cup winner in 1929. Oliver, Shore, MacKay, Ross, Hitchman and Thompson were all future members of the Hockey Hall of Fame.

1920-21 — Ottawa Senators — Jack MacKell, Jack Darragh, Morley Bruce, Georges Boucher, Eddie Gerard (Captain), Clint Benedict, Sprague Cleghorn, Frank Nighbor, Punch Broadbent, Cy Denneny, Leth Graham; Tommy Gorman (Manager), Pete Green (Coach), F. Dolan (Trainer).
Scores: March 21, at Vancouver — Van. Millionaires 2, Ottawa 1; March 24, at Vancouver — Ottawa 4, Van. Millionaires 3; March 28, at Vancouver — Ottawa 3, Van. Millionaires 2; March 31, at Vancouver — Van. Millionaires 3, Ottawa 2; April 4, at Vancouver — Ottawa 2, Van. Millionaires 1.

1919-20 — Ottawa Senators — Jack MacKell, Jack Darragh, Morley Bruce, Horace Merrill, Georges Boucher, Eddie Gerard (Captain), Clint Benedict, Sprague Cleghorn, Frank Nighbor, Punch Broadbent, Cy Denneny, Tommy Gorman (Manager), Pete Green (Coach).
Scores: March 22, at Ottawa — Ottawa 3, Seattle 2; March 24, at Ottawa — Ottawa 3, Seattle 0; March 27, at Ottawa — Seattle 3, Ottawa 1; March 30, at Toronto* — Seattle 5, Ottawa 2; April 1, at Toronto* — Ottawa 6, Seattle 1.

* Games transferred to Toronto to benefit from artificial ice surface.

1918-19 — No decision, Series halted by Spanish influenza epidemic, illness of several players and death of Joe Hall of Montreal Canadiens from the flu. Five games had been played when the series was halted, each team having won two and tied one. Final scores are listed below.
Scores: March 19, at Seattle — Seattle 7, Montreal 0; March 22, at Seattle — Montreal 4, Seattle 2; March 24, at Seattle — Seattle 7, Montreal 2; March 26, at Seattle — Montreal 0, Seattle 0; March 30, at Seattle — Montreal 4, Seattle 3.

1917-18 — Toronto Arenas — Rusty Crawford, Harry Meeking, Ken Randall (Captain), Corb Denneny, Harry Cameron, Jack Adams, Alf Skinner, Harry Mummery, Hap Holmes, Reg Noble, Sammy Hebert, Jack Marks, Jack Coughlin; Charlie Querrie (Manager), Dick Carroll (Coach), Frank Carroll (Trainer).
Scores: March 20, at Toronto — Toronto 5, Van. Millionaires 3; March 23, at Toronto — Van. Millionaires 6, Toronto 4; March 26, at Toronto — Toronto 6, Van. Millionaires 3; March 28, at Toronto — Van. Millionaires 8, Toronto 1; March 30, at Toronto — Toronto 2, Van. Millionaires 1.

1916-17 — Seattle Metropolitans — Hap Holmes, Ed Carpenter, Cully Wilson, Jack Walker, Bernie Morris, Frank Foyston, Roy Rickey, Jim Riley, Bobby Rowe (Captain); Peter Muldoon (Manager).
Scores: March 17, at Seattle — Montreal 8, Seattle 4; March 20, at Seattle — Seattle 6, Montreal 1; March 23, at Seattle — Seattle 4, Montreal 1; March 26, at Seattle — Seattle 9, Montreal 1.

1915-16 — Montreal Canadiens — Georges Vezina, Bert Corbeau, Jack Laviolette, Newsy Lalonde, Louis Berlinquette, Goldie Prodger, Howard McNamara (Captain), Didier Pitre, Skene Ronan, Amos Arbour, Skinner Poulin, Jack Fournier; George Kennedy (Manager).
Scores: March 20, at Montreal — Portland 2, Montreal 0; March 22, at Montreal — Montreal 2, Portland 1; March 25, at Montreal — Montreal 6, Portland 3; March 28, at Montreal — Portland 6, Montreal 5; March 30, at Montreal — Montreal 2, Portland 1.

1914-15 — Vancouver Millionaires — Ken Mallen, Frank Nighbor, Cyclone Taylor, Hugh Lehman, Lloyd Cook, Mickey MacKay, Barney Stanley, Jim Seaborn, Si Griffis (Captain), Johnny Matz; Frank Patrick (Playing Manager).

Scores: March 22, at Vancouver — Van. Millionaires 6, Ottawa 2; March 24, at Vancouver — Van. Millionaires 8, Ottawa 3; March 26, at Vancouver — Van. Millionaires 12, Ottawa 3.

1913-14 — Toronto Blueshirts — Con Corbeau, Roy McGiffen, Jack Walker, George McNamara, Cully Wilson, Frank Foyston, Harry Cameron, Hap Holmes, Scotty Davidson (Captain), Harriston; Jack Marshall (Playing Manager), Frank Carroll, Dick Carroll (Trainers).
Scores: March 14, at Toronto — Toronto 5, Victoria 2; March 17, at Toronto — Toronto 6, Victoria 5; March 19, at Toronto — Toronto 2, Victoria 1.

Prior to 1914, teams could challenge the Stanley Cup champions for the title, thus there was more than one Championship Series played in most of the seasons between 1894 and 1913.

1912-13 — Quebec Bulldogs — Joe Malone (Captain), Joe Hall, Paddy Moran, Harry Mummery, Tommy Smith, Jack Marks, Rusty Crawford, Billy Creighton, Jeff Malone, Rocket Power; M.J. Quinn (Manager), D. Beland (Trainer).
Scores: March 8, at Quebec — Que. Bulldogs 14, Sydney 3; March 10, at Quebec — Que. Bulldogs 6, Sydney 2.

Victoria challenged Quebec but the Bulldogs refused to put the Stanley Cup in competition so the two teams played an exhibition series with Victoria winning two games to one by scores of 7-5, 3-6, 6-1. It was the first meeting between the Eastern champions and the Western champions. The following year, and until the Western Hockey League disbanded after the 1926 playoffs, the Cup went to the winner of the series between East and West.

1911-12 — Quebec Bulldogs — Goldie Prodger, Joe Hall, Walter Rooney, Paddy Moran, Jack Marks, Jack McDonald, Eddie Oatman, George Leonard, Joe Malone (Captain); Charley Nolan (Coach), M.J. Quinn (Manager), D. Beland (Trainer).
Scores: March 11, at Quebec — Que. Bulldogs 9, Moncton 3; March 13, at Quebec — Que. Bulldogs 8, Moncton 0.

1910-11 — Ottawa Senators — Hamby Shore, Percy LeSueur (Captain), Jack Darragh, Bruce Stuart, Marty Walsh, Bruce Ridpath, Fred Lake, Dubbie Kerr, Alex Currie, Horace Gaul.
Scores: March 13, at Ottawa — Ottawa 7, Galt 4; March 16, at Ottawa — Ottawa 13, Port Arthur 4.

1909-10 — (March) **— Montreal Wanderers —** Cecil Blachford, Moose Johnson, Ernie Russell, Riley Hern, Harry Hyland, Jack Marshall, Pud Glass (Captain), Jimmy Gardner; Dickie Boon (Manager).
Scores: March 12, at Montreal — Mtl. Wanderers 7, Berlin (Kitchener) 3.

By winning the 1910 NHA title, the Montreal Wanderers took possession of the Stanley Cup from Ottawa and accepted a challenge from Berlin, 1910 champions of the OPHL

1909-10 — (January) **— Ottawa Senators —** Dubbie Kerr, Fred Lake, Percy LeSueur, Ken Mallen, Bruce Ridpath, Gord Roberts, Hamby Shore, Bruce Stuart (Captain), Marty Walsh.

The Senators accepted two challenges as defending Cup champions. The first was against Galt in a 2-game, total-goals series, and the second was against Edmonton, also a 2-game, total-goals series.
Scores: January 5, at Ottawa — Ottawa 12, Galt 3; January 7, at Ottawa — Ottawa 3, Galt 1; January 18, at Ottawa — Ottawa 8, Edm. Eskimos 4; January 20, at Ottawa — Ottawa 13, Edm. Eskimos 7.

1908-09 — Ottawa Senators — Fred Lake, Percy LeSueur, Cyclone Taylor, Billy Gilmour, Dubbie Kerr, Edgar Dey, Marty Walsh, Bruce Stuart (Captain).

Ottawa, as champions of the Eastern Canada Hockey Association took over the Stanley Cup in 1909 and, although a challenge was accepted by the Cup trustees from Winnipeg Shamrocks, games could not be arranged because of the lateness of the season. No other challenges were made in 1909.

1907-08 — Montreal Wanderers — Riley Hern, Art Ross, Walter Smaill, Pud Glass, Bruce Stuart, Ernie Russell, Moose Johnson, Cecil Blachford (Captain), Tom Hooper, Larry Gilmour, Ernie Liffiton; Dickie Boon (Manager).
Scores: Wanderers accepted four challenges for the Cup: January 9, at Montreal — Mtl. Wanderers 9, Ott. Victorias 3; January 13, at Montreal — Mtl. Wanderers 13, Ott. Victorias 1; March 10, at Montreal — Mtl. Wanderers 11, Wpg. Maple Leafs 5; March 12, at Montreal — Mtl. Wanderers 9, Wpg. Maple Leafs 3; March 14, at Montreal — Mtl. Wanderers 6, Toronto (OPHL) 4. At start of following season, 1908-09, Wanderers were challenged by Edmonton. Results: December 28, at Montreal — Mtl. Wanderers 7, Edm. Eskimos 3; December 30, at Montreal — Edm. Eskimos 7, Mtl. Wanderers 6. Total goals: Mtl. Wanderers 13, Edm. Eskimos 10.

1906-07 — (March 25) **— Montreal Wanderers —** Billy Strachan, Riley Hern, Lester Patrick, Hod Stuart, Pud Glass, Ernie Russell, Cecil Blachford (Captain), Moose Johnson, Rod Kennedy, Jack Marshall; Dickie Boon (Manager).

1906-07 — (March 18) **— Kenora Thistles —** Eddie Giroux, Si Griffis, Tom Hooper, Fred Whitcroft, Alf Smith, Harry Westwick, Roxy Beaudro, Tommy Phillips (Captain), Russell Phillips.
Scores: March 16, at Winnipeg — Kenora 8, Brandon 6; March 18, at Winnipeg — Kenora 4, Brandon 1; March 23, at Winnipeg — Mtl. Wanderers 7, Kenora 2; March 25, at Winnipeg — Kenora 6, Mtl. Wanderers 5. Total goals: Mtl. Wanderers 12, Kenora 8.

1906-07 — (January) **— Kenora Thistles —** Eddie Giroux, Art Ross, Si Griffis, Tom Hooper, Billy McGimsie, Roxy Beaudro, Tommy Phillips (Captain), Joe Hall, Russell Phillips.
Scores: January 17, at Montreal — Kenora 4, Mtl. Wanderers 2; Jan. 21, at Montreal — Kenora 8, Mtl. Wanderers 6.

1906-07 — (December) **— Montreal Wanderers —** Riley Hern, Billy Strachan, Rod Kennedy, Lester Patrick, Pud Glass, Ernie Russell, Moose Johnson, Cecil Blachford (Captain), Dickie Boon (Manager).

1905-06 — (March) **— Montreal Wanderers —** Henri Menard, Billy Strachan, Rod Kennedy, Lester Patrick, Pud Glass, Ernie Russell, Moose Johnson, Cecil Blachford (Captain), Josh Arnold; Dickie Boon (Manager).
Scores: March 14, at Montreal — Mtl. Wanderers 9, Ottawa 1; March 17, at Ottawa — Ottawa 9, Mtl. Wanderers 3. Total goals: Mtl. Wanderers 12, Ottawa 10. Wanderers accepted a challenge from New Glasgow, N.S., prior to the start of the 1906-07 season. Results: December 27, at Montreal — Mtl. Wanderers 10, New Glasgow 3; December 29, at Montreal — Mtl. Wanderers 7, New Glasgow 2.

1905-06 — (February) **— Ottawa Silver Seven —** Harvey Pulford (Captain), Arthur Moore, Harry Westwick, Frank McGee, Alf Smith (Playing Coach), Billy Gilmour, Billy Hague, Harry Smith, Tommy Smith, Coo Dion, Jack Ebbs.
Scores: February 27, at Ottawa — Ottawa 16, Queen's University 7; February 28, at Ottawa — Ottawa 12, Queen's University 7; March 6, at Ottawa — Ottawa 6, Smiths Falls 5; March 8, at Ottawa — Ottawa 8, Smiths Falls 2.

1904-05 — Ottawa Silver Seven — Dave Finnie, Harvey Pulford (Captain), Arthur Moore, Harry Westwick, Frank McGee, Alf Smith (Playing Coach), Billy Gilmour, Frank White, Horace Gaul, Hamby Shore, Bones Allen.
Scores: January 13, at Ottawa — Ottawa 9, Dawson City 2; January 16, at Ottawa — Ottawa 23, Dawson City 2; March 7, at Ottawa — Rat Portage 9, Ottawa 3; March 9, at Ottawa — Ottawa 4, Rat Portage 2; March 11, at Ottawa — Ottawa 5, Rat Portage 4.

1903-04 — Ottawa Silver Seven — Suddy Gilmour, Arthur Moore, Frank McGee, Bouse Hutton, Billy Gilmour, Jim McGee, Harry Westwick, Harvey Pulford (Captain), Scott, Alf Smith (Playing Coach).
Scores: December 30, at Ottawa — Ottawa 9, Wpg. Rowing Club 1; January 1, at Ottawa — Wpg. Rowing Club 6, Ottawa 2; January 4, at Ottawa — Ottawa 2, Wpg. Rowing Club 0. February 23, at Ottawa — Ottawa 6, Tor. Marlboros 3; February 25, at Ottawa — Ottawa 11, Tor. Marlboros 2; March 2, at Montreal — Ottawa 5, Mtl. Wanderers 5. Following the tie game, a new two-game series was ordered to be played in Ottawa but the Wanderers refused unless the tie game was replayed in Montreal. When no settlement could be reached, the series was abandoned and Ottawa retained the Cup and accepted a two-game challenge from Brandon. Results: (both games at Ottawa), March 9, Ottawa 6, Brandon 3; March 11, Ottawa 9, Brandon 3.

1902-03 — (March) — Ottawa Silver Seven — Suddy Gilmour, Percy Sims, Bouse Hutton, Dave Gilmour, Billy Gilmour, Harry Westwick, Frank McGee, F.H. Wood, A.A. Fraser, Charles Spittal, Harvey Pulford (Captain), Arthur Moore; Alf Smith (Coach).
Scores: March 7, at Montreal — Ottawa 1, Mtl. Victorias 1; March 10, at Ottawa — Ottawa 8, Mtl. Victorias 0. Total goals: Ottawa 9, Mtl. Victorias 1; March 12, at Ottawa — Ottawa 6, Rat Portage 2; March 14, at Ottawa — Ottawa 4, Rat Portage 2.

1902-03 — (February) — Montreal AAA — Tom Hodge, Dickie Boon, Billy Nicholson, Tommy Phillips, Art Hooper, Billy Bellingham, Charles Liffiton, Jack Marshall, Jimmy Gardner, Cecil Blachford, George Smith.
Scores: January 29, at Montreal — Mtl. AAA 8, Wpg. Victorias 1; January 31, at Montreal — Wpg. Victorias 2, Mtl. AAA 2; February 2, at Montreal — Wpg. Victorias 4, Mtl. AAA 2; February 4, at Montreal — Mtl. AAA 5, Wpg. Victorias 1.

1901-02 — (March) — Montreal AAA — Tom Hodge, Dickie Boon, Billy Nicholson, Art Hooper, Billy Bellingham, Charles Liffiton, Jack Marshall, Roland Elliot, Jimmy Gardner.
Scores: March 13, at Winnipeg — Wpg. Victorias 1, Mtl. AAA 0; March 15, at Winnipeg — Mtl. AAA 5, Wpg. Victorias 0; March 17, at Winnipeg — Mtl. AAA 2, Wpg. Victorias 1.

1901-02 — (January) — Winnipeg Victorias — Burke Wood, Tony Gingras, Charles Johnstone, Rod Flett, Magnus Flett, Dan Bain (Captain), Fred Scanlon, F. Cadham, Art Brown.
Scores: January 21, at Winnipeg — Wpg. Victorias 5, Tor Wellingtons 3; January 23, at Winnipeg — Wpg. Victorias 5, Tor. Wellingtons 3.

1900-01 — Winnipeg Victorias — Burke Wood, Jack Marshall, Tony Gingras, Charles Johnstone, Rod Flett, Magnus Flett, Dan Bain (Captain), Art Brown, George Carruthers.
Scores: January 29, at Montreal — Wpg. Victorias 4, Mtl. Shamrocks 3; January 31, at Montreal — Wpg. Victorias 2, Mtl. Shamrocks 1.

1899-1900 — Montreal Shamrocks — oe McKenna, Frank Tansey, Frank Wall, Art Farrell, Fred Scanlon, Harry Trihey (Captain), Jack Brannen.
Scores: February 12, at Montreal — Mtl. Shamrocks 4, Wpg. Victorias 3; February 14, at Montreal — Wpg. Victorias 3, Mtl. Shamrocks 2; February 16, at Montreal — Mtl. Shamrocks 5, Wpg. Victorias 4; March 5, at Montreal — Mtl. Shamrocks 10, Halifax 2; March 7, at Montreal — Mtl. Shamrocks 11, Halifax 0.

1898-99 — (March) — Montreal Shamrocks — Joe McKenna, Frank Tansey, Frank Wall, Harry Trihey (Captain), Art Farrell, Fred Scanlon, Jack Brannen, John Dobby, Charles Hoerner.
Scores: March 14, at Montreal — Mtl. Shamrocks 6, Queen's University 2.

1898-99 — (February) — Montreal Victorias — Gordon Lewis, Mike Grant (Captain), Graham Drinkwater, Cam Davidson, Bob McDougall, Ernie McLea, Frank Richardson, Jack Ewing, Russell Bowie, Douglas Acer, Fred McRobie.
Scores: February 15, at Montreal — Mtl. Victorias 2, Wpg. Victorias 1; February 18, at Montreal — Mtl. Victorias 3, Wpg. Victorias 2.

1897-98 — Montreal Victorias — Gordon Lewis, Hartland McDougall, Mike Grant, Graham Drinkwater, Cam Davidson, Bob McDougall, Ernie McLea, Frank Richardson (Captain), Jack Ewing.

1896-97 — Montreal Victorias — Gordon Lewis, Harold Henderson, Mike Grant (Captain), Cam Davidson, Graham Drinkwater, Bob McDougall, Ernie McLea, Shirley Davidson, Hartland McDougall, Jack Ewing, Percy Molson, David Gillilan, McLellan.
Scores: December 27, at Montreal — Mtl. Victorias 15, Ott. Capitals 2.

1895-96 — (December) — Montreal Victorias — Harold Henderson, Mike Grant (Captain), Bob McDougall, Graham Drinkwater, Shirley Davidson, Hartland McDougall, Ernie McLea, Cam Davidson, David Gillilan, Stanley Willett, Gordon Lewis, W. Wallace.
Scores: December 30, at Winnipeg — Mtl. Victorias 6, Wpg. Victorias 5.

1895-96 — (February) — Winnipeg Victorias — Whitey Merritt, Rod Flett, Fred Higginbotham, Jack Armitage (Captain), Tote Campbell, Dan Bain, Charles Johnstone, Attie Howard.
Scores: February 14, at Montreal — Wpg. Victorias 2, Mtl. Victorias 0.

1894-95 — Montreal Victorias — Robert Jones, Harold Henderson, Mike Grant (Captain), Shirley Davidson, Hartland McDougall, Bob McDougall, Norman Rankin, Graham Drinkwater, Roland Elliot, William Pullan, Arthur Fenwick, A. McDougall.

1893-94 — Montreal AAA — Herb Collins, Allan Cameron, George James, Billy Barlow, Clare Mussen, Archie Hodgson, Haviland Routh, Alex Irving, James Stewart, E. O'Brien, Toad Wand, Alex Kingan.
Scores: March 17, at Mtl. Victorias — Mtl. AAA 3, Mtl. Victorias 2; March 22, at Montreal — Mtl. AAA 3, Ott. Capitals 1.

1892-93 — Montreal AAA — Tom Paton, James Stewart, Allan Cameron, Haviland Routh, Archie Hodgson, Billy Barlow, Alex Irving, Alex Kingan, G.S. Low.

All-Time NHL Playoff Formats

1917-18 — The regular-season was split into two halves. The winners of both halves faced each other in a two-game, total-goals series for the NHL championship and the right to meet the PCHA champion in the best-of-five Stanley Cup Finals.

1918-19 — Same as 1917-18, except that the Stanley Cup Finals was extended to a best-of-seven series.

1919-20 — Same as 1917-1918, except that Ottawa won both halves of the split regular-season schedule to earn an automatic berth into the best-of-five Stanley Cup Finals against the PCHA champions.

1921-22 — The top two teams at the conclusion of the regular-season faced each other in a two-game, total-goals series for the NHL championship. The NHL champion then moved on to play the winner of the PCHA-WCHL playoff series in the best-of-five Stanley Cup Finals.

1922-23 — The top two teams at the conclusion of the regular-season faced each other in a two-game, total-goals series for the NHL championship. The NHL champion then moved on to play the PCHA champion in the best-of-three Stanley Cup Semi-Finals, and the winner of the Semi-Finals played the WCHL champion, which had been given a bye, in the best-of-three Stanley Cup Finals.

1923-24 — The top two teams at the conclusion of the regular-season faced each other in a two-game, total-goals series for the NHL championship. The NHL champion then moved on to play the loser of the PCHA-WCHL playoff (the winner of the PCHA-WCHL playoff earned a bye into the Stanley Cup Finals) in the best-of-three Stanley Cup Semi-Finals. The winner of this series met the PCHA-WCHL playoff winner in the best-of-three Stanley Cup Finals.

1924-25 — The first place team (Hamilton) at the conclusion of the regular-season was supposed to play the winner of a two-game, total-goals series between the second (Toronto) and third (Montreal) place clubs. However, Hamilton refused to abide by this new format, demanding greater compensation than offered by the League. Thus, Toronto and Montreal played their two-game, total-goals series, and the winner (Montreal) earned the NHL title and then played the WCHL champion (Victoria) in the best-of-five Stanley Cup Finals.

1925-26 — The format which was intended for 1924-25 went into effect. The winner of the two-game, total-goals series between the second and third place teams squared off against the first place team in the two-game, total-goals NHL championship series. The NHL champion then moved on to play the WHL champion in the best-of-five Stanley Cup Finals.

After the 1925-26 season, the NHL was the only major professional hockey league still in existence and consequently took over sole control of the Stanley Cup competition.

1926-27 — The 10-team league was divided into two divisions — Canadian and American — of five teams apiece. In each division, the winner of the two-game, total-goals series between the second and third place teams faced the first place team in a two-game, total-goals series for the division title. The two division title winners then met in the best-of-five Stanley Cup Finals.

1928-29 — Both first place teams in the two divisions played each other in a best-of-five series. Both second place teams in the two divisions played each other in a two-game, total-goals series as did the two third place teams. The winners of these latter two series then played each other in a best-of-three series for the right to meet the winner of the series between the two first place clubs. This Stanley Cup Final was a best-of-three.

Series A: First in Canadian Division vs. first in American (best-of-five)
Series B: Second in Canadian Division vs. second in American (two-game, total-goals)
Series C: Third in Canadian Division vs. third in American (two-game, total-goals)
Series D: Winner of Series B vs. winner of Series C (best-of-three)
Series E: Winner of Series A vs. winner of Series D (best-of-three) for Stanley Cup

1931-32 — Same as 1928-29, except that Series D was changed to a two-game, total-goals format and Series E was changed to best-of-five.

1936-37 — Same as 1931-32, except that Series B, C, and D were each best-of-three.

1938-39 — With the NHL reduced to seven teams, the two-division system was replaced by one seven-team league. Based on final regular-season standings, the following playoff format was adopted:

Series A: First vs. Second (best-of-seven)
Series B: Third vs. Fourth (best-of-three)
Series C: Fifth vs. Sixth (best-of-three)
Series D: Winner of Series B vs. winner of Series C (best-of-three)
Series E: Winner of Series A vs. winner of Series D (best-of-seven)

1942-43 — With the NHL reduced to six teams (the "original six"), only the top four finishers qualified for playoff action. The best-of-seven Semi-Finals pitted Team #1 vs. Team #3 and Team #2 vs. Team #4. The winners of each Semi-Final series met in the best-of-seven Stanley Cup Finals.

1967-68 — When it doubled in size from 6 to 12 teams, the NHL once again was divided into two divisions — East and West — of six teams apiece. The top four clubs in each division qualified for the playoffs (all series were best-of-seven):

Series A: Team #1 (East) vs. Team #3 (East)
Series B: Team #2 (East) vs. Team #4 (East)
Series C: Team #1 (West) vs. Team #3 (West)
Series D: Team #2 (West) vs. Team #4 (West)
Series E: Winner of Series A vs. winner of Series B
Series F: Winner of Series C vs. winner of Series D
Series G: Winner of Series E vs. Winner of Series F

1970-71 — Same as 1967-68 except that Series E matched the winners of Series A and D, and Series F matched the winners of Series B and C.

1971-72 — Same as 1970-71, except that Series A and C matched Team #1 vs. Team #4, and Series B and D matched Team #2 vs. Team #3.

1974-75 — With the League now expanded to 18 teams in four divisions, a completely new playoff format was introduced. First, the #2 and #3 teams in each of the four divisions were pooled together in the Preliminary round. These eight (#2 and #3) clubs were ranked #1 to #8 based on regular-season record:

Series A: Team #1 vs. Team #8 (best-of-three)
Series B: Team #2 vs. Team #7 (best-of-three)
Series C: Team #3 vs. Team #6 (best-of-three)
Series D: Team #4 vs. Team #5 (best-of-three)
The winners of this Preliminary round then pooled together with the four division winners, which had received byes into this Quarter-Final round. These eight teams were again ranked #1 to #8 based on regular-season record:
Series E: Team #1 vs. Team #8 (best-of-seven)
Series F: Team #2 vs. Team #7 (best-of-seven)
Series G: Team #3 vs. Team #6 (best-of-seven)
Series H: Team #4 vs. Team #5 (best-of-seven)
The four Quarter-Finals winners, which moved on to the Semi-Finals, were then ranked #1 to #4 based on regular season record:
Series I: Team #1 vs. Team #4 (best-of-seven)
Series J: Team #2 vs. Team #3 (best-of-seven)
Series K: Winner of Series I vs. winner of Series J (best-of-seven)

1977-78 — Same as 1974-75, except that the Preliminary round consisted of the #2 teams in the four divisions and the next four teams based on regular-season record (not their standings within their divisions).

1979-80 — With the addition of four WHA franchises, the League expanded its playoff structure to include 16 of its 21 teams. The four first place teams in the four divisions automatically earned playoff berths. Among the 17 other clubs, the top 12, according to regular-season record, also earned berths. All 16 teams were then pooled together and ranked #1 to #16 based on regular-season record:

Series A: Team #1 vs. Team #16 (best-of-five)
Series B: Team #2 vs. Team #15 (best-of-five)
Series C: Team #3 vs. Team #14 (best-of-five)
Series D: Team #4 vs. Team #13 (best-of-five)
Series E: Team #5 vs. Team #12 (best-of-five)
Series F: Team #6 vs. Team #11 (best-of-five)
Series G: Team #7 vs. Team #10 (best-of-five)
Series H: Team #8 vs. Team # 9 (best-of-five)
The eight Preliminary round winners, ranked #1 to #8 based on regular-season record, moved on to the Quarter-Finals:
Series I: Team #1 vs. Team #8 (best-of-seven)
Series J: Team #2 vs. Team #7 (best-of-seven)
Series K: Team #3 vs. Team #6 (best-of-seven)
Series L: Team #4 vs. Team #5 (best-of-seven)
The four Quarter-Finals winners, ranked #1 to #4 based on regular-season record, moved on to the semi-finals:
Series M: Team #1 vs. Team #4 (best-of-seven)
Series N: Team #2 vs. Team #3 (best-of-seven)
Series O: Winner of Series M vs. winner of Series N (best-of-seven)

1981-82 — The first four teams in each division earned playoff berths. In each division, the first-place team opposed the fourth-place team and the second-place team opposed the third-place team in a best-of-five Division Semi-Final series (DSF). In each division, the two winners of the DSF met in a best-of-seven Division Final series (DF). The two DF winners in each conference met in a best-of-seven Conference Final series (CF). In the Prince of Wales Conference, the Adams Division winner opposed the Patrick Division winner; in the Clarence Campbell Conference, the Smythe Division winner opposed the Norris Division winner. The two CF winners met in a best-of-seven Stanley Cup Final (F) series.

1986-87 — Division Semi-Final series changed from best-of-five to best-of-seven.

1993-94 — The NHL's playoff draw is conference-based rather than division-based. At the conclusion of the regular season, the top eight teams in each of the Eastern and Western Conferences qualify for the playoffs. The teams that finish in first place in each of the League's divisions are seeded first and second in each conference's playoff draw and are assured of home ice advantage in the first two playoff rounds. The remaining teams are seeded based on their regular-season point totals. In each conference, the team seeded #1 plays #8; #2 vs. #7; #3 vs. #6; and #4 vs. #5. All series are best-of-seven with home ice rotating on a 2-2-1-1-1 basis, with the exception of matchups between Central and Pacific Division teams. These matchups will be played on a 2-3-2 basis to reduce travel. In a 2-3-2 series, the team with the most points will have its choice to start the series at home or on the road. The Eastern Conference champion will face the Western Conference champion in the Stanley Cup Final.

1994-95 — Same as 1993-94, except that in first, second or third-round playoff series involving Central and Pacific Division teams, the team with the better record has the choice of using either a 2-3-2 or a 2-2-1-1-1 format. When a 2-3-2 format is selected, the higher-ranked team also has the choice of playing games 1, 2, 6 and 7 at home or playing games 3, 4 and 5 at home. The format for the Stanley Cup Final remains 2-2-1-1-1.

1998-99 — The NHL's clubs are re-aligned into two conferences each consisting of three divisions. The number of teams qualifying for the Stanley Cup Playoffs remains unchanged at 16.

First-round playoff berths will be awarded to the first-place team in each division as well as to the next five best teams based on regular-season point totals in each conference. The three division winners in each conference will be seeded first through third, in order of points, for the playoffs and the next five best teams, in order of points, will be seeded fourth through eighth. In each conference, the team seeded #1 will play #8; #2 vs. #7; #3 vs. #6; and #4 vs. #5 in the quarterfinal round. Home ice in the Conference Quarter-Finals is granted to those teams seeded first through fourth in each conference.

In the Conference Semi-Finals and Conference Finals, teams will be re-seeded according to the same criteria as the Conference Quarter-Finals. Higher seeded teams will have home-ice advantage.

Home-ice advantage for the Stanley Cup Finals will be determined by points.

All series remain best-of-seven.

The Bruins were 10-3 at home during the Stanley Cup playoffs, including a perfect 3-0 during the Finals. They were 6-6 on the road, including their final victory in game seven in Vancouver.

Team Records

1918-2011

GAMES PLAYED

MOST GAMES PLAYED BY ALL TEAMS, ONE PLAYOFF YEAR:
92 — 1991. There were 51 DSF, 24 DF, 11 CF and 6 F games.
90 — 1994. There were 48 CQF, 23 CSF, 12 CF and 7 F games.
— 2002. There were 47 CQF, 25 CSF, 13 CF and 5 F games.

MOST GAMES PLAYED, ONE TEAM, ONE PLAYOFF YEAR:
26 — Philadelphia Flyers, 1987. Won DSF 4-2 vs. NY Rangers, DF 4-3 vs. NY Islanders, CF 4-2 vs. Montreal, and lost F 4-3 vs. Edmonton.
— **Calgary Flames,** 2004. Won DSF 4-3 vs. Vancouver, DF 4-2 vs. Detroit, CF 4-2 vs. San Jose, and lost F 4-3 vs. Tampa Bay.
25 — New Jersey Devils, 2001. Won CQF 4-2 vs. Carolina, CSF 4-3 vs. Toronto, CF 4-1 vs. Pittsburgh, and lost F 4-3 vs. Colorado.
— Carolina Hurricanes, 2006. Won CQF 4-2 vs. Montreal, CSF 4-1 vs. New Jersey, CF 4-3 vs. Buffalo, and F 4-3 vs. Edmonton
— Boston Bruins, 2011. Won CQF 4-3 vs. Montreal, CSF 4-0 vs. Philadelphia, CF 4-3 vs. Tampa Bay, and F 4-3 vs. Vancouver.
— Vancouver Canucks, 2011. Won CQF 4-3 vs. Chicago, CSF 4-2 vs. Nashville, CF 4-1 vs. San Jose, and lost F 4-3 vs. Boston.

PLAYOFF APPEARANCES

MOST STANLEY CUP CHAMPIONSHIPS (since 1893):
24 — Montreal Canadiens
(1916-24-30-31-44-46-53-56-57-58-59-60-65-66-68-69-71-73-76-77-78-79-86-93)
14 — Toronto Maple Leafs (1914-18-22-32-42-45-47-48-49-51-62-63-64-67)
11 — Detroit Red Wings (1936-37-43-50-52-54-55-97-98-2002-08)

MOST CONSECUTIVE STANLEY CUP CHAMPIONSHIPS:
5 — Montreal Canadiens (1956-57-58-59-60)
4 — Montreal Canadiens (1976-77-78-79)
— NY Islanders (1980-81-82-83)

MOST FINAL SERIES APPEARANCES:
32 — Montreal Canadiens in 94-year history.
24 — Detroit Red Wings in 85-year history.
21 — Toronto Maple Leafs in 94-year history.

MOST CONSECUTIVE FINAL SERIES APPEARANCES:
10 — Montreal Canadiens, (1951-60, inclusive)
5 — Montreal Canadiens, (1965-69, inclusive)
— NY Islanders, (1980-84, inclusive)

MOST YEARS IN PLAYOFFS:
79 — Montreal Canadiens in 94-year history.
66 — Boston Bruins in 87-year history.
64 — Toronto Maple Leafs in 94-year history.

MOST CONSECUTIVE PLAYOFF APPEARANCES:
29 — Boston Bruins (1968-96, inclusive)
28 — Chicago Blackhawks (1970-97, inclusive)
25 — St. Louis Blues (1980-2004, inclusive)
24 — Montreal Canadiens (1971-94, inclusive)
21 — Montreal Canadiens (1949-69, inclusive)

TEAM WINS

MOST HOME WINS, ONE TEAM, ONE PLAYOFF YEAR:
12 — New Jersey Devils, 2003 in 13 home games.
11 — Edmonton Oilers, 1988 in 11 home games.
— Detroit Red Wings, 2009 in 13 home games.
10 — Edmonton Oilers, 1985 in 10 home games.
— Montreal Canadiens, 1986 in 11 home games.
— Montreal Canadiens, 1993 in 11 home games.
— Carolina Hurricanes, 2006 in 14 home games.
— Anaheim Ducks, 2007 in 12 home games.
— Boston Bruins, 2011 in 13 home games.
— Vancouver Canucks, 2011 in 14 home games.

MOST HOME WINS, ALL TEAMS, ONE PLAYOFF YEAR:
57 — 1991. Of 92 games played, home teams won 57 (29 DSF, 17 DF, 8 CF and 3 in F).

MOST ROAD WINS, ONE TEAM, ONE PLAYOFF YEAR:
10 — New Jersey Devils, 1995. Won three at Boston in CQF; two at Pittsburgh in CSF; three at Philadelphia in CF; and two at Detroit in F.
— **New Jersey Devils,** 2000. Won two at Florida in CQF; two at Toronto in CSF; three at Philadelphia in CF; and three at Dallas in F.
— **Calgary Flames,** 2004. Won three at Vancouver in DSF; two at Detroit in DF; three at San Jose in CF; and two at Tampa Bay in F.
8 — NY Islanders, 1980. Won two at Los Angeles in PR; three at Boston in QF; two at Buffalo in SF; and one at Philadelphia in F.
— Philadelphia Flyers, 1987. Won two at NY Rangers in DSF; two at NY Islanders in DF; three at Montreal in CF; and one at Edmonton in F.
— Edmonton Oilers, 1990. Won one at Winnipeg in DF; two at Los Angeles in DF; two at Chicago in CF and three at Boston in F.
— Pittsburgh Penguins, 1992. Won two at Washington in DSF; two at NY Rangers in DF; two at Boston in CF; and two at Chicago in F.
— Vancouver Canucks, 1994. Won three at Calgary in CQF; two at Dallas in CSF; one at Toronto in CF; and two at NY Rangers in F.
— Colorado Avalanche, 1996. Won two at Vancouver in CQF; two at Chicago in CSF; two at Detroit in CF; and two at Florida in F.
— Detroit Red Wings, 1998. Won two at Phoenix in CQF; three at St. Louis in CSF; one at Dallas in CF; and two at Washington in F.
— Colorado Avalanche, 1999. Won three at San Jose in CQF; three at Detroit in CSF; and two at Dallas in CF.
— New Jersey Devils, 2001. Won two at Carolina in CQF; two at Toronto in CSF; two at Pittsburgh in CF; and two at Colorado in F.
— Detroit Red Wings, 2002. Won three at Vancouver in CQF; one at St. Louis in CSF; two at Colorado in CF; and two at Carolina in F.
— Chicago Blackhawks, 2010. Won two at Nashville in CQF; three at Vancouver in CSF; two at San Jose in CF; and one at Philadelphia in F.

MOST ROAD WINS, ALL TEAMS, ONE PLAYOFF YEAR:
46 — 1987. Of 87 games played, road teams won 46 (22 DSF, 14 DF, 8 CF and 2 in F).

MOST OVERTIME WINS, ONE TEAM, ONE PLAYOFF YEAR:
10 — Montreal Canadiens, 1993. Won two vs. Quebec in DSF; three vs. Buffalo in DF; two vs. NY Islanders in CF; and three vs. Los Angeles in F.
7 — Carolina Hurricanes, 2002. Won two vs. New Jersey in CQF; one vs. Montreal in CSF; three vs. Toronto in CF; and one vs. Detroit in F.
— Anaheim Mighty Ducks, 2003. Won two vs. Detroit in CQF; two vs. Dallas in CSF; one vs. Minnestoa in CF; and two vs. New Jersey in F.

MOST OVERTIME WINS AT HOME, ONE TEAM, ONE PLAYOFF YEAR:
4 — **St. Louis Blues, 1968.** Won one vs. Philadelphia in QF; three vs. Minnesota in SF.
— **Montreal Canadiens, 1993.** Won one vs. Quebec in DSF; one vs. Buffalo in DF, one vs. NY Islanders in CF; one vs. Los Angeles in F.

MOST OVERTIME WINS ON THE ROAD, ONE TEAM, ONE PLAYOFF YEAR:
6 — **Montreal Canadiens, 1993.** Won one vs. Quebec in DSF; two vs. Buffalo in DF; one vs. NY Islanders in CF; two vs. Los Angeles in F.

TEAM LOSSES

MOST LOSSES, ONE TEAM, ONE PLAYOFF YEAR:
11 — **Philadelphia Flyers, 1987.** Lost two vs. NY Rangers in DSF; three vs. NY Islanders in DF; two vs. Montreal in CF; four vs. Edmonton in F.
— **Calgary Flames, 2004.** Lost three vs. Vancouver in CQF; two vs. Detroit in CSF; two vs. San Jose in CF; four vs. Tampa Bay in F

MOST HOME LOSSES, ONE TEAM, ONE PLAYOFF YEAR:
7 — **Calgary Flames, 2004.** Lost two vs. Vancouver in CQF; one vs. Detroit in CSF; two vs. San Jose in CF; two vs. Tampa Bay in F.
6 — Philadelphia Flyers, 1987. Lost one vs. NY Rangers in DSF; two vs. NY Islanders in DF; two vs. Montreal in CF; one vs. Edmonton in F.
— Washington Capitals, 1998. Lost two vs. Boston in CF; two vs. Buffalo in CF; two vs. Detroit in F.
— Colorado Avalanche, 1999. Lost two vs. San Jose in CQF; two vs. Detroit in CSF; two vs. Dallas in CF.
— New Jersey Devils, 2001. Lost one vs. Carolina in CQF; two vs. Toronto in CSF; one vs. Pittsburgh in CF; two vs Colorado in F.
— Minnesota Wild, 2003. Lost two vs. Colorado in CQF; two vs. Vancouver in CSF; two vs. Anaheim in CF.

MOST ROAD LOSSES, ONE TEAM, ONE PLAYOFF YEAR:
7 — **New Jersey Devils, 2003.** Lost one at Boston in CQF; one at Tampa Bay in CSF; two at Ottawa in CF; three at Anaheim in F.
— **Philadelphia Flyers, 2010.** Lost one at New Jersey in CQF; two at Boston in CSF; one at Montreal in CF; three at Chicago in F.

MOST OVERTIME LOSSES, ONE TEAM, ONE PLAYOFF YEAR:
4 — **Montreal Canadiens, 1951.** Lost four vs. Toronto in F.
— **St. Louis Blues, 1968.** Lost one vs. Philadelphia in QF; one vs. Minnesota in SF; two vs. Montreal in F.
— **New York Rangers, 1979.** Lost one vs. Philadelphia in QF; two vs. NY Islanders in SF; one vs. Montreal in F.
— **Los Angeles Kings, 1991.** Lost one vs. Vancouver in DSF; three vs. Edmonton in DF.
— **Los Angeles Kings, 1993.** Lost one vs. Toronto in CF; three vs. Montreal in F.
— **New Jersey Devils, 1994.** Lost one vs. Buffalo in CQF; one vs. Boston in CSF; two vs. NY Rangers in CF.
— **Chicago Blackhawks, 1995.** Lost one vs. Toronto in CQF; three vs. Detroit in CF.
— **Philadelphia Flyers, 1996.** Lost two vs. Tampa Bay in CQF; two vs. Florida in CSF.
— **Dallas Stars, 1999.** Lost two vs. St. Louis in CSF; one vs. Colorado in CF; one vs. Buffalo in F.
— **Detroit Red Wings, 2002.** Lost one vs. Vancouver in CQF; two vs. Colorado in CF; one vs. Carolina in F.
— **New Jersey Devils, 2003.** Lost two vs. Ottawa in CF; two vs. Anaheim in F.

MOST OVERTIME LOSSES AT HOME, ONE TEAM, ONE PLAYOFF YEAR:
4 — **Detroit Red Wings, 2002.** Lost one vs. Vancouver in CQF; two vs. Colorado in CF; one vs. Carolina in F.

MOST OVERTIME LOSSES ON THE ROAD, ONE TEAM, ONE PLAYOFF YEAR:
3 — **Los Angeles Kings, 1991.** Lost one at Vancouver in DSF; two at Edmonton in DF.
— **Chicago Blackhawks, 1995.** Lost one at Toronto in CQF; two at Detroit in CF.
— **St. Louis Blues, 1996.** Lost two at Toronto in CQF; one at Detroit in CSF.
— **Dallas Stars, 1999.** Lost two at St. Louis in CSF; one at Colorado in CF.
— **New Jersey Devils, 2003.** Lost one at Ottawa in CF; two at Anaheim in F.

PLAYOFF WINNING STREAKS

LONGEST PLAYOFF WINNING STREAK:
14 — **Pittsburgh Penguins.** Streak started May 9, 1992 as Pittsburgh won the first of three straight games in DF vs. NY Rangers. Continued with four wins vs. Boston in 1992 CF and four wins vs. Chicago in 1992 F. Pittsburgh then won the first three games of 1993 DSF vs. New Jersey. New Jersey ended the streak April 25, 1993, at New Jersey with a 4-1 win vs. Pittsburgh in the fourth game of 1993 DSF.
12 — Edmonton Oilers. Streak started May 15, 1984 as Edmonton won the first of three straight games in F vs. NY Islanders. Continued with three wins vs. Los Angeles in 1985 DSF and four wins vs. Winnipeg in 1985 DF. Edmonton then won the first two games of 1985 CF vs. Chicago. Chicago ended the streak May 9, 1985, at Chicago with a 5-2 win vs. Edmonton in the third game of 1985 CF.

MOST CONSECUTIVE WINS, ONE TEAM, ONE PLAYOFF YEAR:
11 — **Chicago Blackhawks** in 1992. Chicago won last three games of DSF vs. St. Louis to win series 4-2, defeated Detroit 4-0 in DF and Edmonton 4-0 in CF.
— **Pittsburgh Penguins** in 1992. Pittsburgh won last three games of DF vs. NY Rangers to win series 4-2, defeated Boston 4-0 in CF and Chicago 4-0 in F.
— **Montreal Canadiens** in 1993. Montreal won last four games of DSF vs. Quebec to win series 4-2, defeated Buffalo 4-0 in DF and won first three games of CF vs. NY Islanders.

PLAYOFF LOSING STREAKS

LONGEST PLAYOFF LOSING STREAK:
16 — **Chicago Black Hawks.** Streak started April 20, 1975 at Chicago with a 6-2 loss in fourth game of QF vs. Buffalo, won by Buffalo 4-1. Continued with four consecutive losses vs. Montreal, in 1976 QF and two straight losses vs. NY Islanders in 1977 best-of-three PRE. Chicago then lost four games vs. Boston in 1978 QF and four games vs. NY Islanders in 1979 QF. Chicago ended the streak April 8, 1980, at Chicago with a 3-2 win vs. St. Louis in the opening game of 1980 PRE.
14 — Los Angeles Kings. Streak started June 3, 1993 at Montreal with a 3-2 loss in second game of F vs. Montreal, won by Montreal 4-1. Los Angeles failed to qualify for the playoffs for the next four years. Then Los Angeles lost four games vs. St. Louis in 1998 CQF; missed the 1999 playoffs and lost four games vs. Detroit in 2000 CQF. Los Angeles then lost the first two games of 2001 CQF vs. Detroit. Los Angeles ended the streak April 15, 2001, at Los Angeles with a 2-1 win vs. Detroit in the third game of 2001 CQF.

Patrick Roy stretches out to stop Wayne Gretzky during game four of the 1993 Stanley Cup Finals. Montreal's 3-2 win over Los Angeles that night marked the tenth overtime victory of the Canadiens' amazing playoff run.

MOST GOALS IN A SERIES, ONE TEAM

MOST GOALS, ONE TEAM, ONE PLAYOFF SERIES:
44 — **Edmonton Oilers** in 1985. Edmonton won best-of-seven CF 4-2, outscoring Chicago 44-25.
35 — Edmonton Oilers in 1983. Edmonton won best-of-seven DF 4-1, outscoring Calgary 35-13.
 — Calgary Flames in 1995. Calgary lost best-of-seven CQF 4-3, outscoring San Jose 35-26.

MOST GOALS, ONE TEAM, TWO-GAME SERIES:
11 — **Buffalo Sabres** in 1977. Buffalo won best-of-three PRE 2-0, outscoring Minnesota 11-3.
 — **Toronto Maple Leafs** in 1978. Toronto won best-of-three PRE 2-0, outscoring Los Angeles 11-3.

MOST GOALS, ONE TEAM, THREE-GAME SERIES:
23 — **Chicago Blackhawks** in 1985. Chicago won best-of-five DSF 3-0, outscoring Detroit 23-8.
20 — Minnesota North Stars in 1981. Minnesota won best-of-five PRE 3-0, outscoring Boston 20-13.
 — NY Islanders in 1981. NY Islanders won best-of-five PRE 3-0, outscoring Toronto 20-4.

MOST GOALS, ONE TEAM, FOUR-GAME SERIES:
28 — **Boston Bruins** in 1972. Boston won best-of-seven SF 4-0, outscoring St. Louis 28-8.

MOST GOALS, ONE TEAM, FIVE-GAME SERIES:
35 — **Edmonton Oilers** in 1983. Edmonton won best-of-seven DF 4-1, outscoring Calgary 35-13.
32 — Edmonton Oilers in 1987. Edmonton won best-of-seven DSF 4-1, outscoring Los Angeles 32-20.
30 — Calgary Flames in 1988. Calgary won best-of-seven DSF 4-1, outscoring Los Angeles 30-18.

MOST GOALS, ONE TEAM, SIX-GAME SERIES:
44 — **Edmonton Oilers** in 1985. Edmonton won best-of-seven CF 4-2, outscoring Chicago 44-25.
33 — Montreal Canadiens in 1973. Montreal won best-of-seven F 4-2, outscoring Chicago 33-23.
 — Chicago Blackhawks in 1985. Chicago won best-of-seven DF 4-2, outscoring Minnesota 33-29.
 — Los Angeles Kings in 1993. Los Angeles won best-of-seven DSF 4-2, outscoring Calgary 33-28.

MOST GOALS, ONE TEAM, SEVEN-GAME SERIES:
35 — **Calgary Flames** in 1995. Calgary lost best-of-seven CQF 4-3, outscoring San Jose 35-26.
33 — Philadelphia Flyers in 1976. Philadelphia won best-of-seven QF 4-3, outscoring Toronto 33-23.
 — Boston Bruins in 1983. Boston won best-of-seven DF 4-3, outscoring Buffalo 33-23.
 — Edmonton Oilers in 1984. Edmonton won best-of-seven DF 4-3, outscoring Calgary 33-27.

FEWEST GOALS IN A SERIES, ONE TEAM

FEWEST GOALS, ONE TEAM, TWO-GAME SERIES:
0 — **Toronto St. Patricks** in 1921. Toronto lost two-game, total-goals NHL F 7-0 vs. Ottawa.
 — **New York Americans** in 1929. NY Americans lost two-game, total-goals QF 1-0 vs. NY Rangers.
 — **New York Rangers** in 1931. NY Rangers lost two-game, total-goals SF 3-0 vs. Chicago.
 — **Chicago Black Hawks** in 1935. Chicago lost two-game, total-goals SF 1-0 vs. Mtl. Maroons.
 — **Montreal Maroons** in 1937. Mtl. Maroons lost best-of-three SF 2-0, outscored by NY Rangers 5-0.
 — **New York Americans** in 1939. NY Americans lost best-of-three QF 2-0, outscored by Toronto 5-0.

FEWEST GOALS, ONE TEAM, THREE-GAME SERIES:
1 — **Montreal Maroons** in 1936. Mtl. Maroons lost best-of-five SF 3-0, outscored by Detroit 6-1.

FEWEST GOALS, ONE TEAM, FOUR-GAME SERIES:
1 — **Minnesota Wild** in 2003. Minnesota lost best-of-seven CF 4-0, outscored by Anaheim 9-1.

FEWEST GOALS, ONE TEAM, FIVE-GAME SERIES:
2 — **Philadelphia Flyers** in 2002. Ottawa won best-of-seven CQF 4-1, while outscoring Philadelphia 11-2.

FEWEST GOALS, ONE TEAM, SIX-GAME SERIES:
5 — **Boston Bruins** in 1951. Toronto won best-of-seven SF 4-1 with 1 tie, outscoring Boston 17-5.

FEWEST GOALS, ONE TEAM, SEVEN-GAME SERIES:
9 — **Toronto Maple Leafs**, in 1945. Toronto won best-of- seven F 4-3; teams tied in scoring 9-9.
 — **Detroit Red Wings**, in 1945. Toronto won best-of-seven F 4-3; teams tied in scoring 9-9.

Theo Fleury collected seven goals and seven assists for Calgary during the highest-scoring seven-game series in NHL history between the Flames and the San Jose Sharks in the first round of the 1995 playoffs.

MOST GOALS IN A SERIES, BOTH TEAMS

MOST GOALS, BOTH TEAMS, ONE PLAYOFF SERIES:
69 — **Edmonton Oilers (44), Chicago Black Hawks (25)** in 1985. Edmonton won best-of-seven CF 4-2.
62 — Chicago Black Hawks (33), Minnesota North Stars (29) in 1985. Chicago won best-of-seven DF 4-2.
61 — Los Angeles Kings (33), Calgary Flames (28) in 1993. Los Angeles won best-of-seven DSF 4-2.
 — Calgary Flames (35), San Jose Sharks (26) in 1995. San Jose won best-of-seven CQF 4-3.

MOST GOALS, BOTH TEAMS, TWO-GAME SERIES:
17 — **Toronto St. Patricks (10), Montreal Canadiens (7)** in 1918. Toronto won two-game total-goals NHL F.
15 — Boston Bruins (10), Chicago Black Hawks (5) in 1927. Boston won two-game total-goals QF.
 — Pittsburgh Penguins (9), St. Louis Blues (6) in 1975. Pittsburgh won best-of-three PRE 2-0.

MOST GOALS, BOTH TEAMS, THREE-GAME SERIES:
33 — **Minnesota North Stars (20), Boston Bruins (13)** in 1981. Minnesota won best-of-five PRE 3-0.
31 — Chicago Black Hawks (23), Detroit Red Wings (8) in 1985. Chicago won best-of-five DSF 3-0.
28 — Toronto Maple Leafs (18), New York Rangers (10) in 1932. Toronto won best-of-five F 3-0.

MOST GOALS, BOTH TEAMS, FOUR-GAME SERIES:
36 — **Boston Bruins (28), St. Louis Blues (8)** in 1972. Boston won best-of-seven SF 4-0.
 — **Minnesota North Stars (18), Toronto Maple Leafs (18)** in 1983. Minnesota won best-of-seven DSF 3-1.
 — **Edmonton Oilers (25), Chicago Black Hawks (11)** in 1983. Edmonton won best-of-seven CF 4-0.
35 — New York Rangers (23), Los Angeles Kings (12) in 1981. NY Rangers won best-of-five PRE 3-1.

MOST GOALS, BOTH TEAMS, FIVE-GAME SERIES:
52 — **Edmonton Oilers (32), Los Angeles Kings (20)** in 1987. Edmonton won best-of-seven DSF 4-1.
50 — Los Angeles Kings (27), Edmonton Oilers (23) in 1982. Los Angeles won best-of-five DSF 3-2.
48 — Edmonton Oilers (35), Calgary Flames (13) in 1983. Edmonton won best-of-seven DF 4-1.
— Calgary Flames (30), Los Angeles Kings (18) in 1988. Calgary won best-of-seven DSF 4-1.

MOST GOALS, BOTH TEAMS, SIX-GAME SERIES:
69 — **Edmonton Oilers (44), Chicago Black Hawks (25)** in 1985. Edmonton won best-of-seven CF 4-2.
62 — Chicago Black Hawks (33), Minnesota North Stars (29) in 1985. Chicago won best-of-seven DF 4-2.
61 — Los Angeles Kings (33), Calgary Flames (28) in 1993. Los Angeles won best-of-seven DSF 4-2.

MOST GOALS, BOTH TEAMS, SEVEN-GAME SERIES:
61 — **Calgary Flames (35), San Jose Sharks (26)** in 1995. San Jose won best-of-seven CQF 4-3.
60 — Edmonton Oilers (33), Calgary Flames (27) in 1984. Edmonton won best-of-seven DF 4-3.

FEWEST GOALS IN A SERIES, BOTH TEAMS

FEWEST GOALS, BOTH TEAMS, TWO-GAME SERIES:
1 — **New York Rangers (1), New York Americans (0)** in 1929. NY Rangers won two-game total-goals QF.
— **Montreal Maroons (1), Chicago Black Hawks (0)** in 1935. Mtl. Maroons won two-game total-goals SF.

FEWEST GOALS, BOTH TEAMS, THREE-GAME SERIES:
7 — **Boston Bruins (5), Montreal Canadiens (2)** in 1929. Boston won best-of-five SF 3-0.
— **Detroit Red Wings (6), Montreal Maroons (1)** in 1936. Detroit won best-of-five SF 3-0.

FEWEST GOALS, BOTH TEAMS, FOUR-GAME SERIES:
9 — **Toronto Maple Leafs (7), Boston Bruins (2)** in 1935. Toronto won best-of-five SF 3-1.

FEWEST GOALS, BOTH TEAMS, FIVE-GAME SERIES:
11 — **Montreal Maroons (6), New York Rangers (5)** in 1928. NY Rangers won best-of-five F 3-2.

FEWEST GOALS, BOTH TEAMS, SIX-GAME SERIES:
16 — **Carolina Hurricanes (10), Toronto Maple Leafs (6)** in 2002. Carolina won best-of-seven CF 4-2.

FEWEST GOALS, BOTH TEAMS, SEVEN-GAME SERIES:
18 — **Toronto Maple Leafs (9), Detroit Red Wings (9)** in 1945. Toronto won best-of-seven F 4-3.

MOST GOALS IN A GAME OR PERIOD

MOST GOALS, ONE TEAM, ONE GAME:
13 — **Edmonton Oilers** April 9, 1987, vs. Los Angeles at Edmonton. Edmonton won 13-3.
12 — Los Angeles Kings, April 10, 1990, vs. Calgary at Los Angeles. Los Angeles won 12-4.
11 — Montreal Canadiens, March 30, 1944, vs. Toronto at Montreal. Montreal won 11-0.
— Edmonton Oilers, May 4, 1985, vs. Chicago at Edmonton. Edmonton won 11-2.

MOST GOALS, ONE TEAM, ONE PERIOD:
7 — **Montreal Canadiens,** March 30, 1944, vs. Toronto at Montreal, third period. Montreal won 11-0.

MOST GOALS, BOTH TEAMS, ONE GAME:
18 — **Los Angeles Kings (10), Edmonton Oilers (8)**, April 7, 1982, at Edmonton. Los Angeles won best-of-five DSF 3-2.
17 — Pittsburgh Penguins (10), Philadelphia Flyers (7), April 25, 1989, at Pittsburgh. Pittsburgh won best-of-seven DF 4-3.
16 — Edmonton Oilers (13), Los Angeles Kings (3), April 9, 1987, at Edmonton. Edmonton won best-of-seven DSF 4-1.
— Los Angeles Kings (12), Calgary Flames (4), April 10, 1990, at Los Angeles. Los Angeles won best-of-seven DF 4-2.

MOST GOALS, BOTH TEAMS, ONE PERIOD:
9 — **New York Rangers (6), Philadelphia Flyers (3)**, April 24, 1979, third period, at Philadelphia. NY Rangers won 8-3.
— **Los Angeles Kings (5), Calgary Flames (4)**, April 10, 1990, second period, at Los Angeles. Los Angeles won 12-4.
8 — Chicago Black Hawks (5), Montreal Canadiens (3), May 8, 1973, second period, at Montreal. Chicago won 8-7.
— Chicago Black Hawks (5), Edmonton Oilers (3), May 12, 1985, first period, at Chicago. Chicago won 8-6.
— Edmonton Oilers (6), Winnipeg Jets (2), April 6, 1988, third period, at Edmonton. Edmonton won 7-4.
— Hartford Whalers (5), Montreal Canadiens (3), April 10, 1988, third period, at Montreal. Hartford won 7-5.
— Vancouver Canucks (5), New York Rangers (3), June 9, 1994, third period, at NY Rangers. Vancouver won 6-3.
— Pittsburgh Penguins (5), Ottawa Senators (3), April 20, 2010, second period, at Ottawa. Pittsburgh won 7-4.

TEAM POWER-PLAY GOALS

MOST POWER-PLAY GOALS BY ALL TEAMS, ONE PLAYOFF YEAR:
199 — **1988** in 83 games.

MOST POWER-PLAY GOALS, ONE TEAM, ONE PLAYOFF YEAR:
35 — **Minnesota North Stars,** 1991 in 23 games.
32 — Edmonton Oilers, 1988 in 18 games.
31 — New York Islanders, 1981 in 18 games.

MOST POWER-PLAY GOALS, ONE TEAM, ONE SERIES:
15 — **New York Islanders** in 1980 F vs. Philadelphia. NY Islanders won series 4-2.
— **Minnesota North Stars** in 1991 DSF vs. Chicago. Minnesota won series 4-2.
13 — New York Islanders in 1981 QF vs. Edmonton. NY Islanders won series 4-2.
— Calgary Flames in 1986 CF vs. St. Louis. Calgary won series 4-3.
12 — Toronto Maple Leafs in 1976 QF vs. Philadelphia. Philadelphia won series 4-3.
— Quebec Nordiques in 1987 CQF vs. Hartford. Quebec won series 4-2.
— Colorado Avalanche in 1997 CQF vs. Chicago. Colorado won series 4-2.

MOST POWER-PLAY GOALS, BOTH TEAMS, ONE SERIES:
21 — **New York Islanders (15), Philadelphia Flyers (6)** in 1980 best-of-seven F won by NY Islanders 4-2.
— **New York Islanders (13), Edmonton Oilers (8)** in 1981 best-of-seven QF won by NY Islanders 4-2.
— **Philadelphia Flyers (11), Pittsburgh Penguins (10)** in 1989 best-of-seven DF won by Philadelphia 4-3.
— **Minnesota North Stars (15), Chicago Black Hawks (6)** in 1991 best-of-seven DSF won by Minnesota 4-2.
20 — Toronto Maple Leafs (12), Philadelphia Flyers (8) in 1976 best-of-seven QF won by Philadelphia 4-3.

MOST POWER-PLAY GOALS, ONE TEAM, ONE GAME:
6 — **Boston Bruins,** April 2, 1969, at Boston vs. Toronto. Boston won 10-0.

MOST POWER-PLAY GOALS, BOTH TEAMS, ONE GAME:
8 — **Minnesota North Stars (4), St. Louis Blues (4),** April 24, 1991, at Minnesota. Minnesota won 8-4.
7 — Minnesota North Stars (4), Edmonton Oilers (3), April 28, 1984, at Minnesota. Edmonton won 8-5.
— Philadelphia Flyers (4), New York Rangers (3), April 13, 1985, at NY Rangers. Philadelphia won 6-5.
— Chicago Black Hawks (5), Edmonton Oilers (2), May 14, 1985, at Edmonton. Edmonton won 10-5.
— Edmonton Oilers (5), Los Angeles Kings (2), April 9, 1987, at Edmonton. Edmonton won 13-3.
— Vancouver Canucks (4), Calgary Flames (3), April 9, 1989, at Vancouver. Vancouver won 5-3.

MOST POWER-PLAY GOALS, ONE TEAM, ONE PERIOD:
4 — **Toronto Maple Leafs,** March 26, 1936, second period vs. Boston at Toronto. Toronto won 8-3.
— **Minnesota North Stars,** April 28, 1984, second period vs. Edmonton at Minnesota. Edmonton won 8-5.
— **Boston Bruins,** April 11, 1991, third period vs. Hartford at Boston. Boston won 6-1.
— **Minnesota North Stars,** April 24, 1991, second period vs. St. Louis at Minnesota. Minnesota won 8-4.
— **St. Louis Blues,** April 27, 1998, third period at Los Angeles. St. Louis won 4-3.

MOST POWER-PLAY GOALS, BOTH TEAMS, ONE PERIOD:
5 — **Minnesota North Stars (4), Edmonton Oilers (1),** April 28, 1984, at Minnesota. Edmonton won 8-5.
— **Vancouver Canucks (3), Calgary Flames (2),** April 9, 1989, at Vancouver. Vancouver won 5-3.
— **Minnesota North Stars (4), St. Louis Blues (1),** April 24, 1991, at Minnesota. Minnesota won 8-4.

TEAM SHORTHAND GOALS

MOST SHORTHAND GOALS BY ALL TEAMS, ONE PLAYOFF YEAR:
33 — **1988,** in 83 games.

MOST SHORTHAND GOALS, ONE TEAM, ONE PLAYOFF YEAR:
10 — **Edmonton Oilers,** 1983, in 16 games.
9 — New York Islanders, 1981, in 19 games.
8 — Philadelphia Flyers, 1989, in 19 games.

MOST SHORTHAND GOALS, ONE TEAM, ONE SERIES:
6 — **Calgary Flames** in 1995 vs. San Jose in best-of-seven CQF won by San Jose 4-3.
— **Vancouver Canucks** in 1995 vs. St. Louis in best-of-seven CQF won by Vancouver 4-3.
5 — New York Rangers in 1979 vs. Philadelphia in best-of-seven QF won by NY Rangers 4-1.
— Edmonton Oilers in 1983 vs. Calgary in best-of-seven DF won by Edmonton 4-1.

MOST SHORTHAND GOALS, BOTH TEAMS, ONE SERIES:
7 — **Boston Bruins (4), New York Rangers (3),** in 1958 SF won by Boston 4-2.
— **Edmonton Oilers (5), Calgary Flames (2),** in 1983 DF won by Edmonton 4-1.
— **Vancouver Canucks (6), St. Louis Blues (1),** in 1995 CQF won by Vancouver 4-3.

MOST SHORTHAND GOALS, ONE TEAM, ONE GAME:
3 — **Boston Bruins,** April 11, 1981, at Minnesota North Stars. Minnesota won 6-3.
— **New York Islanders,** April 17, 1983, at NY Rangers. NY Rangers won 7-6.
— **Edmonton Oilers,** April 17, 1983, at Calgary Flames. Edmonton won 10-2.
— **Toronto Maple Leafs,** May 8, 1994, at San Jose Sharks. Toronto won 8-3.

MOST SHORTHAND GOALS, BOTH TEAMS, ONE GAME:

4 — **Boston Bruins (3), Minnesota North Stars (1),** April 11, 1981, at Minnesota. Minnesota won 6-3.
— **New York Islanders (3), New York Rangers (1),** April 17, 1983, at NY Rangers. NY Rangers won 7-6.
— **Toronto Maple Leafs (3), San Jose Sharks (1),** May 8, 1994, at San Jose. Toronto won 8-3.
3 — Toronto Maple Leafs (2), Detroit Red Wings (1), April 5, 1947, at Toronto. Toronto won 6-1.
— New York Rangers (2), Boston Bruins (1), April 1, 1958, at Boston. NY Rangers won 5-2.
— Minnesota North Stars (2), Philadelphia Flyers (1), May 4, 1980, at Minnesota. Philadelphia won 5-3.
— Winnipeg Jets (2), Edmonton Oilers (1), April 9, 1988, at Winnipeg. Winnipeg won 6-4.
— New York Islanders (2), New Jersey Devils (1), April 14, 1988, at New Jersey. New Jersey won 6-5.
— Montreal Canadiens (2), New Jersey Devils (1), April 17, 1997, at New Jersey. New Jersey won 5-2.
— Dallas Stars (2), San Jose Sharks (1), May 5, 2000, at San Jose. Dallas won 5-4.
— Detroit Red Wings (2), Calgary Flames (1), April 21, 2007, at Detroit. Detroit won 5-1.

MOST SHORTHAND GOALS, ONE TEAM, ONE PERIOD:

2 — **Toronto Maple Leafs,** April 5, 1947, first period vs. Detroit at Toronto. Toronto won 6-1.
— **Toronto Maple Leafs,** April 13, 1965, first period vs. Montreal at Toronto. Montreal won 4-3.
— **Boston Bruins,** April 20, 1969, first period vs. Montreal at Boston. Boston won 3-2.
— **Boston Bruins,** April 8, 1970, second period vs. NY Rangers at Boston. Boston won 8-2.
— **Boston Bruins,** April 30, 1972, first period vs. NY Rangers at Boston. Boston won 6-5.
— **Chicago Black Hawks,** May 3, 1973, first period vs. Montreal at Chicago. Chicago won 7-4.
— **Montreal Canadiens,** April 23, 1978, first period at Detroit. Montreal won 8-0.
— **New York Islanders,** April 8, 1980, second period vs. Los Angeles at NY Islanders. NY Islanders won 8-1.
— **Los Angeles Kings,** April 9, 1980, first period at NY Islanders. Los Angeles won 6-3.
— **Boston Bruins,** April 13, 1980, second period at Pittsburgh. Boston won 8-3.
— **Minnesota North Stars,** May 4, 1980, second period vs. Philadelphia at Minnesota. Philadelphia won 5-3.
— **Boston Bruins,** April 11, 1981, third period at Minnesota North Stars. Minnesota won 6-3.
— **New York Islanders,** May 12, 1981, first period vs. Minnesota North Stars at NY Islanders. NY Islanders won 6-3.
— **Montreal Canadiens,** April 7, 1982, third period vs. Quebec at Montreal. Montreal won 5-1.
— **Edmonton Oilers,** April 24, 1983, third period vs. Chicago at Edmonton. Edmonton won 8-4.
— **Winnipeg Jets,** April 14, 1985, second period at Calgary. Winnipeg won 5-3.
— **Boston Bruins,** April 6, 1988, first period vs. Buffalo at Boston. Boston won 7-3.
— **New York Islanders,** April 14, 1988, third period at New Jersey. New Jersey won 6-5.
— **Detroit Red Wings,** April 29, 1993, second period at Toronto. Detroit won 7-3.
— **Toronto Maple Leafs,** May 8, 1994, third period at San Jose. Toronto won 8-3.
— **Calgary Flames,** May 11, 1995, first period at San Jose. Calgary won 9-2.
— **Vancouver Canucks,** May 15, 1995, second period at St. Louis. Vancouver won 6-5.
— **Montreal Canadiens,** April 17, 1997, second period at New Jersey. New Jersey won 5-2.
— **Philadelphia Flyers,** April 26, 1997, first period vs. Pittsburgh at Philadelphia. Philadelphia won 6-3.
— **Phoenix Coyotes,** April 24, 1998, second period at Detroit. Phoenix won 7-4.
— **Buffalo Sabres,** April 27, 1998, second period vs. Philadelphia at Buffalo. Buffalo won 6-1.
— **San Jose Sharks,** April 30, 1999, third period at Colorado. San Jose won 7-3.
— **Detroit Red Wings,** April 27, 2002, second period at Vancouver. Detroit won 6-4.
— **Detroit Red Wings,** April 21, 2007, second period at Detroit. Detroit won 5-1.

Chicago's Michael Frolik scored the only penalty shot goal of the 2011 playoffs against Vancouver's Cory Schneider in game six of their first-round series.

MOST SHORTHAND GOALS, BOTH TEAMS, ONE PERIOD:

3 — **Toronto Maple Leafs (2), Detroit Red Wings (1),** April 5, 1947, first period at Toronto. Toronto won 6-1.
— **Toronto Maple Leafs (2), San Jose Sharks (1),** May 8, 1994, third period at San Jose. Toronto won 8-3.

FASTEST GOALS

FASTEST FIVE GOALS, BOTH TEAMS:

3:06 — **Minnesota North Stars, Chicago Black Hawks,** April 21, 1985, at Chicago. Keith Brown scored for Chicago at 1:12 of the second period; Ken Yaremchuk, Chicago, 1:27; Dino Ciccarelli, Minnesota, 2:48; Tony McKegney, Minnesota, 4:07; and Curt Fraser, Chicago, 4:18. Chicago won 6-2 and won best-of-seven DF 4-2.

3:20 — Minnesota North Stars, Philadelphia Flyers, April 29, 1980, at Philadelphia. Paul Shmyr scored for Minnesota at 13:20 of the first period; Steve Christoff, Minnesota, 13:59; Ken Linseman, Philadelphia, 14:54; Tom Gorence, Philadelphia, 15:36; and Ken Linseman, Philadelphia, 16:40. Minnesota won 6-5. Philadelphia won best-of-seven SF 4-1.

3:58 — Detroit Red Wings, Phoenix Coyotes, April 16, 2010, at Phoenix. Henrik Zetterberg scored for Detroit at 6:27 of the second period; Wojtek Wolski, Phoenix, 7:05; Pavel Datsyuk, Detroit, 8:20; Matthew Lombardi, Phoenix, 9:09; Valtteri Filppula, Detroit, 10:25. Detroit won 7-4 and won best-of-seven CQF 4-3.

FASTEST FIVE GOALS, ONE TEAM:

3:36 — **Montreal Canadiens,** March 30, 1944, at Montreal vs. Toronto. Toe Blake scored at 7:58 and 8:37 of the third period; Maurice Richard, 9:17; Ray Getliffe, 10:33; and Buddy O'Connor, 11:34. Canadiens won 11-0 and won best-of-seven SF 4-1.

FASTEST FOUR GOALS, BOTH TEAMS:

1:33 — **Toronto Maple Leafs, Philadelphia Flyers,** April 20, 1976, at Philadelphia. Don Saleski scored for Philadelphia at 10:04 of the second period; Bob Neely, Toronto, 10:42; Gary Dornhoefer, Philadelphia, 11:24; and Don Saleski, Philadelphia, 11:37. Philadelphia won 7-1 and won best-of-seven SF 4-3.

1:34 — Calgary Flames, Montreal Canadiens, May 20, 1986, at Montreal. Joel Otto scored for Calgary at 17:59 of the first period; Bobby Smith, Montreal, 18:25; Mats Naslund, Montreal, 19:17; and Bob Gainey, Montreal, 19:33. Montreal won 5-3 and won best-of-seven F 4-1.

1:38 — Boston Bruins, Philadelphia Flyers, April 26, 1977, at Philadelphia. Gregg Sheppard scored for Boston at 14:01 of the second period; Mike Milbury, Boston, 15:01; Gary Dornhoefer, Philadelphia, 15:16; and Jean Ratelle, Boston, 15:39. Boston won 5-4 and won best-of-seven SF 4-0.

FASTEST FOUR GOALS, ONE TEAM:

2:35 — **Montreal Canadiens,** March 30, 1944, at Montreal. Toe Blake scored at 7:58 and 8:37 of the third period; Maurice Richard, 9:17; and Ray Getliffe, 10:33. Montreal won 11-0 and won best-of-seven SF 4-1.

FASTEST THREE GOALS, BOTH TEAMS:

0:21 — **Chicago Black Hawks, Edmonton Oilers,** May 7, 1985, at Edmonton. Behn Wilson scored for Chicago at 19:22 of the third period; Jari Kurri, Edmonton, 19:36; and Glenn Anderson, Edmonton, 19:43. Edmonton won 7-3 and won best-of-seven CF 4-2.

0:27 — Phoenix Coyotes, Detroit Red Wings, April 24, 1998, at Detroit. Jeremy Roenick scored for Phoenix at 13:24 of the second period; Mathieu Dandenault, Detroit, 13:32; and Keith Tkachuk, Phoenix, 13:51. Phoenix won 7-4. Detroit won best-of-seven CQF 4-2.

0:30 — Pittsburgh Penguins, Chicago Blackhawks, June 1, 1992, at Chicago. Dirk Graham scored for Chicago at 6:21 of the first period; Kevin Stevens, Pittsburgh, 6:33; and Dirk Graham, Chicago, 6:51. Pittsburgh won 6-5 and won best-of-seven F 4-0.

FASTEST THREE GOALS, ONE TEAM:

0:23 — **Toronto Maple Leafs,** April 12, 1979, at Toronto vs. Atlanta Flames. Darryl Sittler scored at 4:04 and 4:16 of the first period; and Ron Ellis, 4:27. Toronto won 7-4 and won best-of-three PRE 2-0.

0:38 — New York Rangers, April 12, 1986, at NY Rangers vs. Philadelphia. Jim Weimer scored at 12:29 of the third period; Bob Brooke, 12:43; and Ron Greschner, 13:07. NY Rangers won 5-2 and won best-of-five DSF 3-2.

— Colorado Avalanche, April 18, 2001, at Vancouver. Peter Forsberg scored at 9:11 of the third period; Joe Sakic, 9:28; and Eric Messier, 9:49. Colorado won 5-1 and won best-of-seven CQF 4-0.

FASTEST TWO GOALS, BOTH TEAMS:

0:05 — **Pittsburgh Penguins, Buffalo Sabres,** April 14, 1979, at Buffalo. Gilbert Perreault scored for Buffalo at 12:59 of the first period; and Jim Hamilton, Pittsburgh, 13:04. Pittsburgh won 4-3 and won best-of-three PRE 2-1.

0:08 — St. Louis Blues, Minnesota North Stars, April 9, 1989, at Minnesota. Bernie Federko scored for St. Louis at 2:28 of the third period; and Perry Berezan, Minnesota, 2:36. Minnesota won 5-4. St. Louis won best-of-seven DSF 4-1.

— Phoenix Coyotes, Detroit Red Wings, April 24, 1998, at Detroit. Jeremy Roenick scored for Phoenix at 13:24 of the second period; and Mathieu Dandenault, Detroit, 13:32. Phoenix won 7-4. Detroit won best-of-seven CQF 4-2.

FASTEST TWO GOALS, ONE TEAM:

0:05 — **Detroit Red Wings,** April 11, 1965, at Detroit vs. Chicago. Norm Ullman scored at 17:35 and 17:40 of the second period. Detroit won 4-2. Chicago won best-of-seven SF 4-3.

Alexandre Burrows was named first star after scoring 11 seconds into overtime in game two of the Stanley Cup Finals. Burrows also scored in overtime in game seven of Vancouver's opening-round series against Chicago.

OVERTIME

SHORTEST OVERTIME:
0:09 — Montreal Canadiens, Calgary Flames, May 18, 1986, at Calgary. Montreal won 3-2 on Brian Skrudland's goal at 0:09 of the first overtime period. Montreal won best-of-seven F 4-1.
0:11 — New York Islanders, New York Rangers, April 11, 1975, at NY Rangers. NY Islanders won 4-3 on J.P. Parise's goal at 0:11 of the first overtime period. NY Islanders won best-of-three PRE 2-1.
— Vancouver Canucks, Boston Bruins, June 4, 2011, at Vancouver. Vancouver won 3-2 on Alexandre Burrows' goal at 0:11 of the first overtime period. Boston won best-of-seven F 4-3.

LONGEST OVERTIME:
116:30 — Detroit Red Wings, Montreal Maroons, March 24, 1936, at Montreal. Mtl. Maroons won 1-0 on Mud Bruneteau's goal at 16:30 of the sixth overtime period. Detroit won best-of-five SF 3-0.

MOST OVERTIME GAMES, ONE PLAYOFF YEAR:
28 — 1993. Of 85 games played, 28 went into overtime.
26 — 2001. Of 86 games played, 26 went into overtime.
22 — 2003. Of 89 games played, 22 went into overtime.
— 2011. Of 89 games played, 22 went into overtime.

FEWEST OVERTIME GAMES, ONE PLAYOFF YEAR:
0 — 1963. None of the 16 games went into overtime, the only year since 1926 that no overtime was required in any playoff series.

MOST OVERTIME GAMES, ONE SERIES:
5 — Toronto Maple Leafs, Montreal Canadiens in 1951. Toronto won best-of-seven F 4-1.
4 — Toronto Maple Leafs, Boston Bruins in 1933. Toronto won best-of-five SF 3-2.
— Boston Bruins, NY Rangers in 1939. Boston won best-of-seven SF 4-3.
— St. Louis Blues, Minnesota North Stars in 1968. St. Louis won best-of-seven SF 4-3.
— Dallas Stars, St. Louis Blues in 1999. Dallas won best-of-seven CSF 4-2.
— Dallas Stars, Edmonton Oilers in 2001. Dallas won best-of-seven CQF 4-2.
— Dallas Stars, San Jose Sharks in 2008. Dallas won best-of-seven CSF 4-2

TEAM HAT-TRICKS

MOST HAT-TRICKS, BY ALL TEAMS, ONE PLAYOFF YEAR:
12 — 1983 in 66 games.
— **1988** in 83 games.
11 — 1985 in 70 games.
— 1992 in 86 games.

MOST HAT-TRICKS, ONE TEAM, ONE PLAYOFF YEAR:
6 — Edmonton Oilers in 16 games, 1983.
— **Edmonton Oilers** in 18 games, 1985.

SHUTOUTS

MOST SHUTOUTS, ONE PLAYOFF YEAR, ALL TEAMS:
25 — 2002. Of 90 games played, Detroit had 6; Ottawa had 4; Carolina, Colorado, St. Louis and Toronto had 3 each; while Los Angeles, New Jersey and Philadelphia had 1 each.
23 — 2004. Of 89 games played, Tampa Bay and Calgary had 5 each; Toronto and San Jose had 3 each; while Boston, Colorado, Detroit, Montreal, Nashville, NY Islanders and Philadelphia had 1 each.
19 — 2001. Of 86 games played, Colorado and New Jersey had 4 each, Toronto had 3, Pittsburgh and Los Angeles had 2 each, while Buffalo, Washington, Detroit and San Jose had 1 each.

FEWEST SHUTOUTS, ONE PLAYOFF YEAR, ALL TEAMS:
0 — 1959. 18 games played.

MOST SHUTOUTS, BOTH TEAMS, ONE SERIES:
5 — Toronto Maple Leafs (3), Detroit Red Wings (2), in 1945. Toronto won best-of-seven F 4-3.
— **Toronto Maple Leafs (3), Detroit Red Wings (2),** in 1950. Detroit won best-of-seven SF 4-3.

TEAM PENALTIES

FEWEST PENALTIES, BOTH TEAMS, BEST-OF-SEVEN SERIES:
19 — Detroit Red Wings, Toronto Maple Leafs in 1945. Detroit received 10 minors, Toronto received 9 minors. Toronto won best-of-seven F 4-3.

FEWEST PENALTIES, ONE TEAM, BEST-OF-SEVEN SERIES:
9 — Toronto Maple Leafs in 1945 vs. Detroit. Toronto received 9 minors. Toronto won best-of-seven F 4-3.

MOST PENALTIES, BOTH TEAMS, ONE SERIES:
218 — New Jersey Devils, Washington Capitals in 1988. New Jersey received 97 minors, 11 majors, 9 misconducts and 1 match penalty. Washington received 80 minors, 11 majors, 8 misconducts and 1 match penalty. New Jersey won best-of-seven DF 4-3.

MOST PENALTY MINUTES, BOTH TEAMS, ONE SERIES:
654 — New Jersey Devils (349), Washington Capitals (305) in 1988. New Jersey won best-of-seven DF 4-3.

MOST PENALTIES, ONE TEAM, ONE SERIES:
118 — New Jersey Devils in 1988 vs. Washington. New Jersey received 97 minors, 11 majors, 9 misconducts and 1 match penalty. New Jersey won best-of-seven DF 4-3.

MOST PENALTY MINUTES, ONE TEAM, ONE SERIES:
349 — New Jersey Devils in 1988 vs. Washington. New Jersey won best-of-seven DF 4-3.

MOST PENALTIES, BOTH TEAMS, ONE GAME:
66 — Detroit Red Wings (33), St. Louis Blues (33), April 12, 1991, at St. Louis. St. Louis won 6-1.
63 — Minnesota North Stars (34), Chicago Blackhawks (29), April 6, 1990, at Chicago. Chicago won 5-3.
62 — New Jersey Devils (32), Washington Capitals (30), April 22, 1988, at New Jersey. New Jersey won 10-4.

MOST PENALTY MINUTES, BOTH TEAMS, ONE GAME:
298 — Detroit Red Wings (152), St. Louis Blues (146), April 12, 1991, at St. Louis. Detroit received 33 penalties; St. Louis received 33 penalties. St. Louis won 6-1.
267 — New York Rangers (142), Los Angeles Kings (125), April 9, 1981, at Los Angeles. NY Rangers received 31 penalties; Los Angeles received 28 penalties. Los Angeles won 5-4.

MOST PENALTIES, ONE TEAM, ONE GAME:
34 — Minnesota North Stars, April 6, 1990, at Chicago. Chicago won 5-3.
33 — Detroit Red Wings, April 12, 1991, at St. Louis. St. Louis won 6-1.
— St. Louis Blues, April 12, 1991, at St. Louis vs. Detroit. St. Louis won 6-1.

MOST PENALTY MINUTES, ONE TEAM, ONE GAME:
152 — Detroit Red Wings, April 12, 1991, at St. Louis. St. Louis won 6-1.
146 — St. Louis Blues, April 12, 1991, at St. Louis vs. Detroit. St. Louis won 6-1.
142 — New York Rangers, April 9, 1981, at Los Angeles. Los Angeles won 5-4.

MOST PENALTIES, BOTH TEAMS, ONE PERIOD:
43 — New York Rangers (24), Los Angeles Kings (19), April 9, 1981, first period at Los Angeles. Los Angeles won 5-4.

MOST PENALTY MINUTES, BOTH TEAMS, ONE PERIOD:
248 — New York Islanders (124), Boston Bruins (124), April 17, 1980, first period at Boston. NY Islanders won 5-4.

MOST PENALTIES, ONE TEAM, ONE PERIOD:
24 — New York Rangers, April 9, 1981, first period at Los Angeles. Los Angeles won 5-4.

MOST PENALTY MINUTES, ONE TEAM, ONE PERIOD:
125 — New York Rangers, April 9, 1981, first period at Los Angeles. Los Angeles won 5-4.

Individual Records

GAMES PLAYED

MOST YEARS IN PLAYOFFS:
24 — Chris Chelios, Montreal, Chicago, Detroit (1984-97 inclusive; 1999-2004 inclusive, 2006-2009 inclusive)
21 — Raymond Bourque, Boston, Colorado (1980-96 inclusive; 98-2001 inclusive)
20 — Gordie Howe, Detroit, Hartford
— Larry Robinson, Montreal, Los Angeles
— Larry Murphy, Los Angeles, Washington, Minnesota, Pittsburgh, Toronto, Detroit
— Scott Stevens, Washington, St. Louis, New Jersey
— Steve Yzerman, Detroit

MOST CONSECUTIVE YEARS IN PLAYOFFS:
20 — Larry Robinson, Montreal, Los Angeles (1973-92, inclusive).
19 — Brett Hull, Calgary, St. Louis, Dallas, Detroit (1986-2004, inclusive).
— Nicklas Lidstrom, Detroit (1992-2004 inclusive; 2006-2011 inclusive)
18 — Larry Murphy, Los Angeles, Washington, Minnesota, Pittsburgh, Toronto, Detroit (1984-2001, inclusive).
17 — Brad Park, NY Rangers, Boston, Detroit (1969-85, inclusive).
— Raymond Bourque, Boston (1980-96, inclusive).
— Kris Draper, Detroit (1994-2004 inclusive; 2006-2011 inclusive)

MOST PLAYOFF GAMES:
266 — Chris Chelios, Montreal, Chicago, Detroit
258 — Nicklas Lidstrom, Detroit
247 — Patrick Roy, Montreal, Colorado
236 — Mark Messier, Edmonton, NY Rangers
234 — Claude Lemieux, Montreal, New Jersey, Colorado, Phoenix, Dallas, San Jose

GOALS

MOST GOALS IN PLAYOFFS, CAREER:
122 — Wayne Gretzky, Edmonton, Los Angeles, St. Louis, NY Rangers
109 — Mark Messier, Edmonton, NY Rangers
106 — Jari Kurri, Edmonton, Los Angeles, NY Rangers, Anaheim
103 — Brett Hull, Calgary, St. Louis, Dallas, Detroit
93 — Glenn Anderson, Edmonton, Toronto, NY Rangers, St. Louis

MOST GOALS, ONE PLAYOFF YEAR:
19 — Reggie Leach, Philadelphia, 1976. 16 games.
— **Jari Kurri, Edmonton,** 1985. 18 games.
18 — Joe Sakic, Colorado, 1996. 22 games.
17 — Newsy Lalonde, Montreal, 1919. 10 games.
— Mike Bossy, NY Islanders, 1981. 18 games.
— Steve Payne, Minnesota, 1981. 19 games.
— Mike Bossy, NY Islanders, 1982. 19 games.
— Mike Bossy, NY Islanders, 1983. 19 games.
— Wayne Gretzky, Edmonton, 1985. 18 games.
— Kevin Stevens, Pittsburgh, 1991. 24 games.

MOST GOALS IN ONE SERIES (OTHER THAN FINAL):
12 — Jari Kurri, Edmonton, in 1985 CF, 6 games vs. Chicago.
11 — Newsy Lalonde, Montreal, in 1919 NHL F, 5 games vs. Ottawa.
10 — Tim Kerr, Philadelphia, in 1989 DF, 7 games vs. Pittsburgh.
9 — Reggie Leach, Philadelphia, in 1976 SF, 5 games vs. Boston.
— Bill Barber, Philadelphia, in 1980 SF, 5 games vs. Minnesota.
— Mike Bossy, NY Islanders, in 1983 CF, 6 games vs. Boston.
— Mario Lemieux, Pittsburgh, in 1989 DF, 7 games vs. Philadelphia.
— John Druce, Washington, in 1990 DF, 5 games vs. NY Rangers.
— Johan Franzen, Detroit, in 2008 CSF, 4 games vs. Colorado.

MOST GOALS IN FINAL SERIES (NHL PLAYERS ONLY):
9 — Babe Dye, Toronto, in 1922, 5 games vs. Van. Millionaires.
8 — Alf Skinner, Toronto, in 1918, 5 games vs. Van. Millionaires.
7 — Jean Beliveau, Montreal, in 1956, 5 games vs. Detroit.
— Mike Bossy, NY Islanders, in 1982, 4 games vs. Vancouver.
— Wayne Gretzky, Edmonton, in 1985, 5 games vs. Philadelphia.

MOST GOALS, ONE GAME:
5 — Newsy Lalonde, Montreal, March 1, 1919, at Montreal. Final score: Montreal 6, Ottawa 3.
— **Maurice Richard, Montreal,** March 23, 1944, at Montreal. Final score: Montreal 5, Toronto 1.
— **Darryl Sittler, Toronto,** April 22, 1976, at Toronto. Final score: Toronto 8, Philadelphia 5.
— **Reggie Leach, Philadelphia,** May 6, 1976, at Philadelphia. Final score: Philadelphia 6, Boston 3.
— **Mario Lemieux, Pittsburgh,** April 25, 1989, at Pittsburgh. Final score: Pittsburgh 10, Philadelphia 7.

MOST GOALS, ONE PERIOD:
4 — Tim Kerr, Philadelphia, April 13, 1985, at NY Rangers, second period. Final score: Philadelphia 6, NY Rangers 5.
— **Mario Lemieux, Pittsburgh,** April 25, 1989, at Pittsburgh vs. Philadelphia, first period. Final score: Pittsburgh 10, Philadelphia 7.

ASSISTS

MOST ASSISTS IN PLAYOFFS, CAREER:
260 — Wayne Gretzky, Edmonton, Los Angeles, St. Louis, NY Rangers
186 — Mark Messier, Edmonton, NY Rangers
139 — Raymond Bourque, Boston, Colorado
137 — Paul Coffey, Edmonton, Pittsburgh, Los Angeles, Detroit, Philadelphia, Carolina
129 — Nicklas Lidstrom, Detroit

MOST ASSISTS, ONE PLAYOFF YEAR:
31 — Wayne Gretzky, Edmonton, 1988. 19 games.
30 — Wayne Gretzky, Edmonton, 1985. 18 games.
29 — Wayne Gretzky, Edmonton, 1987. 21 games.
28 — Mario Lemieux, Pittsburgh, 1991. 23 games.
26 — Wayne Gretzky, Edmonton, 1983. 16 games.

MOST ASSISTS IN ONE SERIES (OTHER THAN FINAL):
14 — Rick Middleton, Boston, in 1983 DF, 7 games vs. Buffalo.
— **Wayne Gretzky, Edmonton,** in 1985 CF, 6 games vs. Chicago.
13 — Wayne Gretzky, Edmonton, in 1987 DSF, 5 games vs. Los Angeles.
— Doug Gilmour, Toronto, in 1994 CSF, 7 games vs. San Jose.
11 — Al MacInnis, Calgary, in 1984 DF, 7 games vs. Edmonton.
— Mark Messier, Edmonton, in 1988 DSF, 7 games vs. Los Angeles.
— Mike Ridley, Washington, in 1992 DSF, 7 games vs. Pittsburgh.
— Ron Francis, Pittsburgh, in 1995 CQF, 7 games vs. Washington.
— Henrik Sedin, Vancouver, in 2011 CF, 5 games vs. San Jose.

MOST ASSISTS IN FINAL SERIES:
10 — Wayne Gretzky, Edmonton, in 1988, 4 games plus suspended game vs. Boston.
9 — Jacques Lemaire, Montreal, in 1973, 6 games vs. Chicago.
— Wayne Gretzky, Edmonton, in 1987, 7 games vs. Philadelphia.
— Larry Murphy, Pittsburgh, in 1991, 6 games vs. Minnesota.
— Danny Briere, Philadelphia, in 2010, 6 games vs. Chicago.

MOST ASSISTS, ONE GAME:
6 — Mikko Leinonen, NY Rangers, April 8, 1982, at NY Rangers. Final score: NY Rangers 7, Philadelphia 3.
— **Wayne Gretzky, Edmonton,** April 9, 1987, at Edmonton. Final score: Edmonton 13, Los Angeles 3.
5 — Toe Blake, Montreal, March 23, 1944, at Montreal. Final score: Montreal 5, Toronto 1.
— Maurice Richard, Montreal, March 27, 1956, at Montreal. Final score: Montreal 7, NY Rangers 0.
— Bert Olmstead, Montreal, March 30, 1957, at Montreal. Final score: Montreal 8, NY Rangers 3.
— Don McKenney, Boston, April 5, 1958, at Boston. Final score: Boston 8, NY Rangers 2.
— Stan Mikita, Chicago, April 4, 1973, at Chicago. Final score: Chicago 7, St. Louis 1.
— Wayne Gretzky, Edmonton, April 8, 1981, at Montreal. Final score: Edmonton 6, Montreal 3.
— Paul Coffey, Edmonton, May 14, 1985, at Edmonton. Final score: Edmonton 10, Chicago 5.
— Doug Gilmour, St. Louis, April 15, 1986, at Minnesota. Final score: St. Louis 6, Minnesota 3.
— Risto Siltanen, Quebec, April 14, 1987, at Hartford. Final score: Quebec 7, Hartford 5.
— Patrik Sundstrom, New Jersey, April 22, 1988, at New Jersey. Final score: New Jersey 10, Washington 4.
— Geoff Courtnall, St. Louis, April 23, 1998, at St. Louis. Final score: St. Louis 8, Los Angeles 3.

MOST ASSISTS, ONE PERIOD:
3 — Three assists by one player in one period of a playoff game has been recorded on 84 occasions. Henrik Sedin of the Vancouver Canucks is the most recent to equal this mark with 3 assists in the second period at San Jose, May 22, 2011. Final score: Vancouver 4, San Jose 2.
— Wayne Gretzky has had 3 assists in one period 5 times; Raymond Bourque, 3 times; Toe Blake, Jean Beliveau, Doug Harvey and Bobby Orr, twice each. Joe Primeau of Toronto was the first player to be credited with 3 assists in one period of a playoff game; third period at Boston vs. NY Rangers, April 7, 1932. Final score: Toronto 6, NY Rangers 2.

POINTS

MOST POINTS IN PLAYOFFS, CAREER:
382 — Wayne Gretzky, Edmonton, Los Angeles, St. Louis, NY Rangers, 122G, 260A
295 — Mark Messier, Edmonton, NY Rangers, 109G, 186A
233 — Jari Kurri, Edmonton, Los Angeles, NY Rangers, Anaheim, 106G, 127A
214 — Glenn Anderson, Edmonton, Toronto, NY Rangers, St. Louis, 93G, 121A
196 — Paul Coffey, Edmonton, Pittsburgh, Los Angeles, Detroit, Philadelphia, Carolina, 59G, 137A

MOST POINTS, ONE PLAYOFF YEAR:
47 — Wayne Gretzky, Edmonton, in 1985. 17 goals, 30 assists in 18 games.
44 — Mario Lemieux, Pittsburgh, in 1991. 16 goals, 28 assists in 23 games.
43 — Wayne Gretzky, Edmonton, in 1988. 12 goals, 31 assists in 19 games.
40 — Wayne Gretzky, Los Angeles, in 1993. 15 goals, 25 assists in 24 games.
38 — Wayne Gretzky, Edmonton, in 1983. 12 goals, 26 assists in 16 games.

MOST POINTS IN ONE SERIES (OTHER THAN FINAL):
19 — Rick Middleton, Boston, in 1983 DF, 7 games vs. Buffalo. 5 goals, 14 assists.
18 — Wayne Gretzky, Edmonton, in 1985 CF, 6 games vs. Chicago. 4 goals, 14 assists.
17 — Mario Lemieux, Pittsburgh, in 1992 DSF, 6 games vs. Washington. 7 goals, 10 assists.
16 — Barry Pederson, Boston, in 1983 DF, 7 games vs. Buffalo. 7 goals, 9 assists.
— Doug Gilmour, Toronto, in 1994 CSF, 7 games vs. San Jose. 3 goals, 13 assists.
15 — Jari Kurri, Edmonton, in 1985 CF, 6 games vs. Chicago. 12 goals, 3 assists.
— Wayne Gretzky, Edmonton, in 1987 DSF, 5 games vs. Los Angeles. 2 goals, 13 assists.
— Tim Kerr, Philadelphia, in 1989 DF, 7 games vs. Pittsburgh. 10 goals, 5 assists.
— Mario Lemieux, Pittsburgh, in 1991 CF, 6 games vs. Boston. 6 goals, 9 assists.

MOST POINTS IN FINAL SERIES:
13 — Wayne Gretzky, Edmonton, in 1988, 4 games plus suspended game vs. Boston. 3 goals, 10 assists.
12 — Gordie Howe, Detroit, in 1955, 7 games vs. Montreal. 5 goals, 7 assists.
 — Yvan Cournoyer, Montreal, in 1973, 6 games vs. Chicago. 6 goals, 6 assists.
 — Jacques Lemaire, Montreal, in 1973, 6 games vs. Chicago. 3 goals, 9 assists.
 — Mario Lemieux, Pittsburgh, in 1991, 5 games vs. Minnesota. 5 goals, 7 assists.
 — Danny Briere, Philadelphia, in 2010, 6 games vs. Chicago. 3 goals, 9 assists.

MOST POINTS, ONE GAME:
8 — Patrik Sundstrom, New Jersey, April 22, 1988, at New Jersey in 10-4 win over Washington. Sundstrom had 3 goals, 5 assists.
 — **Mario Lemieux, Pittsburgh,** April 25, 1989, at Pittsburgh in 10-7 win over Philadelphia. Lemieux had 5 goals, 3 assists.
7 — Wayne Gretzky, Edmonton, April 17, 1983, at Calgary in 10-2 win. Gretzky had 4 goals, 3 assists.
 — Wayne Gretzky, Edmonton, April 25,1985, at Winnipeg in 8-3 win. Gretzky had 3 goals, 4 assists.
 — Wayne Gretzky, Edmonton, April 9, 1987, at Edmonton in 13-3 win over Los Angeles. Gretzky had 1 goal, 6 assists.
6 — Dickie Moore, Montreal, March 25, 1954, at Montreal in 8-1 win over Boston. Moore had 2 goals, 4 assists.
 — Phil Esposito, Boston, April 2, 1969, at Boston in 10-0 win over Toronto. Esposito had 4 goals, 2 assists.
 — Darryl Sittler, Toronto, April 22, 1976, at Toronto in 8-5 win over Philadelphia. Sittler had 5 goals, 1 assist.
 — Guy Lafleur, Montreal, April 11, 1977, at Montreal in 7-2 win over St. Louis. Lafleur had 3 goals, 3 assists.
 — Mikko Leinonen, NY Rangers, April 8, 1982, at NY Rangers in 7-3 win over Philadelphia. Leinonen had 6 assists.
 — Paul Coffey, Edmonton, May 14, 1985, at Edmonton in 10-5 win over Chicago. Coffey had 1 goal, 5 assists.
 — John Anderson, Hartford, April 12, 1986, at Hartford in 9-4 win over Quebec. Anderson had 2 goals, 4 assists.
 — Mario Lemieux, Pittsburgh, April 23, 1992, at Pittsburgh in 6-4 win over Washington. Lemieux had 3 goals, 3 assists.
 — Geoff Courtnall, St. Louis, April 23, 1998, at St. Louis in 8-3 win over Los Angeles. Courtnall had 1 goal, 5 assists.
 — Johan Franzen, Detroit, May 6, 2010, at Detroit in 7-1 win over San Jose. Franzen had 4 goals, 2 assists.

MOST POINTS, ONE PERIOD:
4 — Maurice Richard, Montreal, March 29, 1945, at Montreal, third period, in 10-3 win vs. Toronto. 3 goals, 1 assist.
 — **Dickie Moore,** Montreal, March 25, 1954, at Montreal, first period, in 8-1 win vs. Boston. 2 goals, 2 assists.
 — **Barry Pederson,** Boston, April 8, 1982, at Boston, second period, in 7-3 win vs. Buffalo. 3 goals, 1 assist.
 — **Peter McNab,** Boston, April 11, 1982, at Buffalo, second period, in 5-2 win vs. Buffalo. 1 goal, 3 assists.
 — **Tim Kerr,** Philadelphia, April 13, 1985, at NY Rangers, second period, in 6-5 win vs. NY Rangers. 4 goals.
 — **Ken Linseman,** Boston, April 14, 1985, at Boston, second period, in 7-6 win vs. Montreal. 2 goals, 2 assists.
 — **Wayne Gretzky,** Edmonton, April 12, 1987, at Los Angeles, third period, in 6-3 win vs. Los Angeles. 1 goal, 3 assists.
 — **Glenn Anderson,** Edmonton, April 6, 1988, at Edmonton, third period, in 7-4 win vs. Winnipeg. 3 goals, 1 assist.
 — **Mario Lemieux,** Pittsburgh, April 25, 1989, at Pittsburgh, first period, in 10-7 win vs. Philadelphia. 4 goals.
 — **Dave Gagner,** Minnesota North Stars, April 8, 1991, at Minnesota, first period, in 6-5 loss vs. Chicago. 2 goals, 2 assists.
 — **Mario Lemieux,** Pittsburgh, April 23, 1992, at Pittsburgh, second period, in 6-4 win vs. Washington. 2 goals, 2 assists.
 — **Alexander Mogilny,** New Jersey, April 28, 2001, at New Jersey, second period, in 6-5 win vs. Toronto. 1 goal, 3 assists.
 — **Brad Richards,** Dallas, April 27, 2008, at San Jose, third period, in 5-2 win vs. San Jose. 1 goal, 3 assists.
 — **Johan Franzen,** Detroit, May 6, 2010, at Detroit, first period, in 7-1 win over San Jose. 3 goals, 1 assist.
 — **Tyler Seguin,** Boston, May 17, 2011, at Boston, second period, in 6-5 win over Tampa Bay. 2 goals, 2 assists.

POWER-PLAY GOALS

MOST POWER-PLAY GOALS IN PLAYOFFS, CAREER:
38 — Brett Hull, St. Louis, Dallas, Detroit
35 — Mike Bossy, NY Islanders
34 — Dino Ciccarelli, Minnesota, Washington, Detroit
 — Wayne Gretzky, Edmonton, Los Angeles, St. Louis, NY Rangers
30 — Nicklas Lidstrom, Detroit

MOST POWER-PLAY GOALS, ONE PLAYOFF YEAR:
9 — Mike Bossy, NY Islanders, 1981. 18 games vs. Toronto, Edmonton, NY Rangers and Minnesota.
 — **Cam Neely, Boston,** 1991. 19 games vs. Hartford, Montreal and Pittsburgh.
8 — Tim Kerr, Philadelphia, 1989. 19 games.
 — John Druce, Washington, 1990. 15 games.
 — Brian Propp, Minnesota, 1991. 23 games.
 — Mario Lemieux, Pittsburgh, 1992. 15 games.

MOST POWER-PLAY GOALS, ONE PLAYOFF SERIES:
6 — Chris Kontos, Los Angeles, 1989 DSF vs. Edmonton, won by Los Angeles 4-3.
5 — Andy Bathgate, Detroit, 1966 SF vs. Chicago, won by Detroit 4-2.
 — Denis Potvin, NY Islanders, 1981 QF vs. Edmonton, won by NY Islanders 4-2.
 — Ken Houston, Calgary, 1981 QF vs. Philadelphia, won by Calgary 4-3.
 — Rick Vaive, Chicago, 1988 DSF vs. St. Louis, won by St. Louis 4-1.
 — Tim Kerr, Philadelphia, 1989 DF vs. Pittsburgh, won by Philadelphia 4-3.
 — Mario Lemieux, Pittsburgh, 1989 DF vs. Philadelphia, won by Philadelphia 4-3.
 — John Druce, Washington, 1990 DF vs. NY Rangers, won by Washington 4-1.
 — Pat LaFontaine, Buffalo, 1992 DSF vs. Boston, won by Boston 4-3.
 — Adam Graves, NY Rangers, 1996 CQF vs Montreal, won by NY Rangers 4-2.

MOST POWER-PLAY GOALS, ONE GAME:
3 — Syd Howe, Detroit, March 23, 1939, at Detroit vs. Montreal. Detroit won 7-3.
 — **Sid Smith, Toronto,** April 10, 1949, at Detroit. Toronto won 3-1.
 — **Phil Esposito, Boston,** April 2, 1969, at Boston vs. Toronto. Boston won 10-0.
 — **John Bucyk, Boston,** April 21, 1974, at Boston vs. Chicago. Boston won 8-6.
 — **Denis Potvin, NY Islanders,** April 17, 1981, at NY Islanders vs. Edmonton. NY Islanders won 6-3.
 — **Tim Kerr, Philadelphia,** April 13, 1985, at NY Rangers. Philadelphia won 6-5.
 — **Jari Kurri, Edmonton,** April 9, 1987, at Edmonton vs. Los Angeles. Edmonton won 13-3.
 — **Mark Johnson, New Jersey,** April 22, 1988, at New Jersey vs. Washington. New Jersey won 10-4.
 — **Dino Ciccarelli, Detroit,** April 29, 1993, at Toronto. Detroit won 7-3.
 — **Dino Ciccarelli, Detroit,** May 11, 1995, at Dallas. Detroit won 5-1.
 — **Valeri Kamensky, Colorado,** April 24, 1997, at Colorado vs. Chicago. Colorado won 7-0.
 — **Jonathan Toews, Chicago** May 7, 2010, at Vancouver. Chicago won 7-4.

MOST POWER-PLAY GOALS, ONE PERIOD:
3 — Tim Kerr, Philadelphia, April 13, 1985, at NY Rangers, second period in 6-5 win.
2 — Two power-play goals have been scored by one player in one period on 61 occasions. Charlie Conacher of Toronto was the first to score two power-play goals in one period, setting the mark with two power-play goals in the second period at Toronto vs. Boston, March 26, 1936. Final score: Toronto 8, Boston 3. Thomas Vanek of the Buffalo Sabres is the most recent to equal this mark with two power-play goals in the first period at Buffalo, April 24, 2011. Final score: Philadelphia 5, Buffalo 4.

SHORTHAND GOALS

MOST SHORTHAND GOALS IN PLAYOFFS, CAREER:
14 — Mark Messier, Edmonton, NY Rangers
11 — Wayne Gretzky, Edmonton, Los Angeles, St. Louis
10 — Jari Kurri, Edmonton, Los Angeles, NY Rangers
8 — Ed Westfall, Boston, NY Islanders
 — Hakan Loob, Calgary

MOST SHORTHAND GOALS, ONE PLAYOFF YEAR:
3 — Derek Sanderson, Boston, 1969. 1 vs. Toronto in QF, won by Boston 4-0; 2 vs. Montreal in SF, won by Montreal, 4-2.
 — **Bill Barber, Philadelphia,** 1980. All vs. Minnesota in SF, won by Philadelphia 4-1.
 — **Lorne Henning, NY Islanders,** 1980. 1 vs. Boston in QF, won by NY Islanders 4-1; 1 vs. Buffalo in SF, won by NY Islanders 4-2, 1 vs. Philadelphia in F, won by NY Islanders 4-2.
 — **Wayne Gretzky, Edmonton,** 1983. 2 vs. Winnipeg in DSF, won by Edmonton 3-0; 1 vs. Calgary in DF, won by Edmonton 4-1.
 — **Wayne Presley, Chicago,** 1989. All vs. Detroit in DSF, won by Chicago 4-2.
 — **Todd Marchant, Edmonton,** 1997. 1 vs. Dallas in CQF, won by Edmonton 4-3; 2 vs. Colorado in CSF, won by Colorado 4-1.

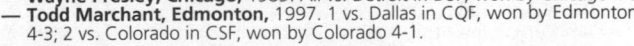

Patrice Bergeron took 497 face-offs for Boston during the playoffs and won an impressive 60.2 percent of them. He and Nashville's David Legwand were the only players with two shorthand goals during the playoffs. Both of Legwand's came in the Predators' second-round series with Vancouver.

MOST SHORTHAND GOALS, ONE PLAYOFF SERIES:

3 — **Bill Barber, Philadelphia,** 1980 SF vs. Minnesota, won by Philadelphia 4-1.
— **Wayne Presley, Chicago,** 1989 DSF vs. Detroit, won by Chicago 4-2.
2 — Mac Colville, NY Rangers, 1940 SF vs. Boston, won by NY Rangers 4-2.
— Jerry Toppazzini, Boston, 1958 SF vs. NY Rangers, won by Boston 4-2.
— Dave Keon, Toronto, 1963 F vs. Detroit, won by Toronto 4-1.
— Bob Pulford, Toronto, 1964 F vs. Detroit, won by Toronto 4-3.
— Serge Savard, Montreal, 1968 F vs. St. Louis, won by Montreal 4-0.
— Derek Sanderson, Boston, 1969 SF vs. Montreal, won by Montreal 4-2.
— Bryan Trottier, NY Islanders, 1980 PR vs. Los Angeles, won by NY Islanders 3-1.
— Bobby Lalonde, Boston, 1981 PR vs. Minnesota, won by Minnesota 3-0.
— Butch Goring, NY Islanders, 1981 SF vs. NY Rangers, won by NY Islanders 4-0.
— Wayne Gretzky, Edmonton, 1983 DSF vs. Winnipeg, won by Edmonton 3-0.
— Mark Messier, Edmonton, 1983 DF vs. Calgary, won by Edmonton 4-1.
— Jari Kurri, Edmonton, 1983 CF vs. Chicago, won by Edmonton 4-0.
— Wayne Gretzky, Edmonton, 1985 DF vs. Winnipeg, won by Edmonton 4-0.
— Kevin Lowe, Edmonton, 1987 F vs. Philadelphia, won by Edmonton 4-3.
— Bob Gould, Washington, 1988 DSF vs. Philadelphia, won by Washington 4-3.
— Dave Poulin, Philadelphia, 1989 DF vs. Pittsburgh, won by Philadelphia 4-3.
— Russ Courtnall, Montreal, 1991 DF vs. Boston, won by Boston 4-3.
— Sergei Fedorov, Detroit, 1992 DSF vs. Minnesota, won by Detroit 4-3.
— Mark Messier, NY Rangers, 1992 DSF vs. New Jersey, won by NY Rangers 4-3.
— Tom Fitzgerald, NY Islanders, 1993 DF vs. Pittsburgh, won by NY Islanders 4-3.
— Mark Osborne, Toronto, 1994 CSF vs. San Jose, won by Toronto 4-3.
— Tony Amonte, Chicago, 1997 CQF vs. Colorado, won by Colorado 4-2.
— Brian Rolston, New Jersey, 1997 CSF vs. Montreal, won by New Jersey 4-1.
— Rod Brind'Amour, Philadelphia, 1997 CQF vs. Pittsburgh, won by Philadelphia 4-1.
— Todd Marchant, Edmonton, 1997 CSF vs. Colorado, won by Colorado 4-1.
— Jeremy Roenick, Phoenix, 1998 CQF vs. Detroit, won by Detroit 4-2.
— Vincent Damphousse, San Jose, 1999 CQF vs. Colorado, won by Colorado 4-2.
— Dixon Ward, Buffalo, 1999 CF vs. Toronto, won by Buffalo 4-1.
— Curtis Brown, Buffalo, 2001 CSF vs. Pittsburgh, won by Pittsburgh 4-3.
— John Madden, New Jersey, 2006 CQF vs. NY Rangers, won by New Jersey 4-0.
— David Legwand, Nashville, 2011 CSF vs. Vancouver, won by Vancouver 4-2.

MOST SHORTHAND GOALS, ONE GAME:

2 — **Dave Keon, Toronto,** April 18, 1963, at Toronto, in 3-1 win vs. Detroit.
— **Bryan Trottier, NY Islanders,** April 8, 1980, at NY Islanders, in 8-1 win vs. Los Angeles.
— **Bobby Lalonde, Boston,** April 11, 1981, at Minnesota, in 6-3 loss vs. Minnesota.
— **Wayne Gretzky, Edmonton,** April 6, 1983, at Edmonton, in 6-3 win vs. Winnipeg.
— **Jari Kurri, Edmonton,** April 24, 1983, at Edmonton, in 8-3 win vs. Chicago.
— **Wayne Gretzky, Edmonton,** April 25, 1985, at Winnipeg, in 8-3 win by Edmonton.
— **Mark Messier, NY Rangers,** April 21, 1992, at NY Rangers, in 7-3 loss vs. New Jersey.
— **Tom Fitzgerald, NY Islanders,** May 8, 1993, at NY Islanders, in 6-5 win vs. Pittsburgh.
— **Rod Brind'Amour, Philadelphia,** April 26, 1997, at Philadelphia, in 6-3 win vs. Pittsburgh.
— **Jeremy Roenick, Phoenix,** April 24, 1998, at Detroit, in 7-4 win by Phoenix.
— **Vincent Damphousse, San Jose,** April 30, 1999, at Colorado, in 7-3 win by San Jose.
— **John Madden, New Jersey,** April 24, 2006, at New Jersey, in 4-1 win vs. NY Rangers.

MOST SHORTHAND GOALS, ONE PERIOD:

2 — **Bryan Trottier, NY Islanders,** April 8, 1980, second period, at NY Islanders, in 8-1 win vs. Los Angeles.
— **Bobby Lalonde, Boston,** April 11, 1981, third period, at Minnesota, in 6-3 loss vs. Minnesota.
— **Jari Kurri, Edmonton,** April 24, 1983, third period, at Edmonton, in 8-4 win vs. Chicago.
— **Rod Brind'Amour, Philadelphia,** April 26, 1997, first period, at Philadelphia, in 6-3 win vs. Pittsburgh.
— **Jeremy Roenick, Phoenix,** April 24, 1998, second period, at Detroit, in 7-4 win by Phoenix.
— **Vincent Damphousse, San Jose,** April 30, 1999, third period, at Colorado, in 7-3 win vs. Colorado.

GAME-WINNING GOALS

MOST GAME-WINNING GOALS IN PLAYOFFS, CAREER:

24 — **Wayne Gretzky, Edmonton, Los Angeles, St. Louis, NY Rangers**
— **Brett Hull, St. Louis, Dallas, Detroit**
19 — Claude Lemieux, Montreal, New Jersey, Colorado
— Joe Sakic, Colorado
18 — Maurice Richard, Montreal

MOST GAME-WINNING GOALS, ONE PLAYOFF YEAR:

7 — **Brad Richards, Tampa Bay,** 2004. 23 games.
6 — Joe Sakic, Colorado, 1996. 22 games.
— Joe Nieuwendyk, Dallas, 1999. 23 games.
5 — Mike Bossy, NY Islanders, 1983. 19 games.
— Jari Kurri, Edmonton, 1987. 21 games.
— Bobby Smith, Minnesota, 1991. 23 games.
— Mario Lemieux, Pittsburgh, 1992. 15 games.
— Fernando Pisani, Edmonton, 2006. 24 games.
— Johan Franzen, Detroit, 2008. 16 games.
— Dustin Byfuglien, Chicago, 2010. 22 games.

MOST GAME-WINNING GOALS, ONE PLAYOFF SERIES:

4 — **Mike Bossy, NY Islanders,** 1983 CF vs. Boston, won by NY Islanders 4-2.

OVERTIME GOALS

MOST OVERTIME GOALS IN PLAYOFFS, CAREER:

8 — **Joe Sakic, Colorado** (2 in 1996; 1 in 1998; 1 in 2001; 2 in 2004; 1 in 2006; 1 in 2008)
6 — Maurice Richard, Montreal
5 — Glenn Anderson, Edmonton, Toronto, St. Louis
4 — Bob Nystrom, NY Islanders
— Dale Hunter, Quebec, Washington
— Wayne Gretzky, Edmonton, Los Angeles
— Stephane Richer, Montreal, New Jersey
— Joe Murphy, Edmonton, Chicago
— Esa Tikkanen, Edmonton, NY Rangers
— Jaromir Jagr, Pittsburgh
— Kirk Muller, Montreal, Dallas
— Jeremy Roenick, Chicago, Philadelphia
— Chris Drury, Colorado, Buffalo
— Jamie Langenbrunner, Dallas, New Jersey

MOST OVERTIME GOALS, ONE PLAYOFF YEAR:

3 — **Mel Hill, Boston,** 1939. All vs. NY Rangers in best-of-seven SF, won by Boston 4-3.
— **Maurice Richard, Montreal,** 1951. 2 vs. Detroit in best-of-seven SF, won by Montreal 4-2; 1 vs. Toronto best-of-seven F, won by Toronto 4-1.

MOST OVERTIME GOALS, ONE PLAYOFF SERIES:

3 — **Mel Hill, Boston,** 1939, SF vs. NY Rangers, won by Boston 4-3. Hill scored at 59:25 of overtime March 21 for a 2-1 win; at 8:24 of overtime, March 23 for a 3-2 win; and at 48:00 of overtime, April 2 for a 2-1 win.

SCORING BY A DEFENSEMAN

MOST GOALS BY A DEFENSEMAN, ONE PLAYOFF YEAR:

12 — **Paul Coffey, Edmonton,** 1985. 18 games.
11 — Brian Leetch, NY Rangers, 1994. 23 games.
9 — Bobby Orr, Boston, 1970. 14 games.
— Brad Park, Boston, 1978. 15 games.
8 — Denis Potvin, NY Islanders, 1981. 18 games.
— Raymond Bourque, Boston, 1983. 17 games.
— Denis Potvin, NY Islanders, 1983. 20 games.
— Paul Coffey, Edmonton, 1984. 19 games.

MOST GOALS BY A DEFENSEMAN, ONE GAME:

3 — **Bobby Orr, Boston,** April 11, 1971, at Montreal. Final score: Boston 5, Montreal 2.
— **Dick Redmond, Chicago,** April 4, 1973, at Chicago. Final score: Chicago 7, St. Louis 1.
— **Denis Potvin, NY Islanders,** April 17, 1981, at NY Islanders. Final score: NY Islanders 6, Edmonton 3.
— **Paul Reinhart, Calgary,** April 14, 1983, at Edmonton. Final score: Edmonton 6, Calgary 3.
— **Doug Halward, Vancouver,** April 7, 1984, at Vancouver. Final score: Vancouver 7, Calgary 0.
— **Paul Reinhart, Calgary,** April 8, 1984, at Vancouver. Final score: Calgary 5, Vancouver 1.
— **Al Iafrate, Washington,** April 26, 1993, at Washington. Final score: Washington 6, NY Islanders 4.
— **Eric Desjardins, Montreal,** June 3, 1993, at Montreal. Final score: Montreal 3, Los Angeles 2.
— **Gary Suter, Chicago,** April 24, 1994, at Chicago. Final score: Chicago 4, Toronto 3.
— **Brian Leetch, NY Rangers,** May 22, 1995, at Philadelphia. Final score: Philadelphia 4, NY Rangers 3.
— **Andy Delmore, Philadelphia,** May 7, 2000, at Philadelphia. Final score: Philadelphia 6, Pittsburgh 3.

MOST ASSISTS BY A DEFENSEMAN, ONE PLAYOFF YEAR:

25 — **Paul Coffey, Edmonton,** 1985. 18 games.
24 — Al MacInnis, Calgary, 1989. 22 games.
23 — Brian Leetch, NY Rangers, 1994. 23 games.
19 — Bobby Orr, Boston, 1972. 15 games.
18 — Raymond Bourque, Boston, 1988. 23 games.
— Raymond Bourque, Boston, 1991. 19 games.
— Larry Murphy, Pittsburgh, 1991. 23 games.
— Chris Pronger, Philadelphia, 2010. 23 games.

MOST ASSISTS BY A DEFENSEMAN, ONE GAME:

5 — **Paul Coffey, Edmonton,** May 14, 1985, at Edmonton vs. Chicago. Edmonton won 10-5.
— **Risto Siltanen, Quebec,** April 14, 1987, at Hartford. Quebec won 7-5.

MOST POINTS BY A DEFENSEMAN, ONE PLAYOFF YEAR:

37 — **Paul Coffey, Edmonton,** 1985. 12 goals, 25 assists in 18 games.
34 — Brian Leetch, NY Rangers, 1994. 11 goals, 23 assists in 23 games.
31 — Al MacInnis, Calgary, 1989. 7 goals, 24 assists in 22 games.
25 — Denis Potvin, NY Islanders, 1981. 8 goals, 17 assists in 18 games.
— Raymond Bourque, Boston, 1991. 7 goals, 18 assists in 19 games.

MOST POINTS BY A DEFENSEMAN, ONE GAME:

6 — **Paul Coffey, Edmonton,** May 14, 1985, at Edmonton vs. Chicago. 1 goal, 5 assists. Edmonton won 10-5.
5 — Eddie Bush, Detroit, April 9, 1942, at Detroit vs. Toronto. 1 goal, 4 assists. Detroit won 5-2.
— Bob Dailey, Philadelphia, May 1, 1980, at Philadelphia vs. Minnesota. 1 goal, 4 assists. Philadelphia won 7-0.
— Denis Potvin, NY Islanders, April 17, 1981, at NY Islanders vs. Edmonton. 3 goals, 2 assists. NY Islanders won 6-3.
— Risto Siltanen, Quebec, April 14, 1987, at Hartford. 5 assists. Quebec won 7-5.

SCORING BY A ROOKIE

MOST GOALS BY A ROOKIE, ONE PLAYOFF YEAR:
14 — Dino Ciccarelli, Minnesota, 1981. 19 games.
11 — Jeremy Roenick, Chicago, 1990. 20 games.
— Brad Marchand, Boston, 2011. 25 games.
10 — Claude Lemieux, Montreal, 1986. 20 games.
9 — Pat Flatley, NY Islanders, 1984. 21 games

MOST ASSISTS BY A ROOKIE, ONE PLAYOFF YEAR:
14 — Ville Leino, Philadelphia, 2010. 19 games.
13 — Don Maloney, NY Rangers, 1979. 18 games.

MOST POINTS BY A ROOKIE, ONE PLAYOFF YEAR:
21 — Dino Ciccarelli, Minnesota, 1981. 14 goals, 7 assists in 19 games.
— **Ville Leino, Philadelphia,** 2010. 7 goals, 14 assists in 19 games.
20 — Don Maloney, NY Rangers, 1979. 7 goals, 13 assists in 18 games.

THREE-OR-MORE-GOAL GAMES

MOST THREE-OR-MORE-GOAL GAMES IN PLAYOFFS, CAREER:
10 — Wayne Gretzky, Edmonton, Los Angeles, NY Rangers. Eight three-goal games; two four-goal games.
7 — Maurice Richard, Montreal. Four three-goal games; two four-goal games; one five-goal game.
— Jari Kurri, Edmonton. Six three-goal games; one four-goal game.
6 — Dino Ciccarelli, Minnesota, Washington, Detroit. Five three-goal games; one four-goal game.
5 — Mike Bossy, NY Islanders. Four three-goal games; one four-goal game.

MOST THREE-OR-MORE-GOAL GAMES, ONE PLAYOFF YEAR:
4 — Jari Kurri, Edmonton, 1985. 1 four-goal game, 3 three-goal games.
3 — Mark Messier, Edmonton, 1983. 3 three-goal games.
— Mike Bossy, NY Islanders, 1983. 1 four-goal game, 2 three-goal games
2 — Newsy Lalonde, Montreal, 1919. 1 five-goal game, 1 four-goal game.
— Maurice Richard, Montreal, 1944. 1 five-goal game; 1 three-goal game.
— Doug Bentley, Chicago, 1944. 2 three-goal games.
— Norm Ullman, Detroit, 1964. 2 three-goal games.
— Phil Esposito, Boston, 1970. 2 three-goal games.
— Pit Martin, Chicago, 1973. 2 three-goal games.
— Rick MacLeish, Philadelphia, 1975. 2 three-goal games.
— Lanny McDonald, Toronto, 1977. 1 four-goal game; 1 three-goal game.
— Wayne Gretzky, Edmonton, 1981. 2 three-goal games.
— Wayne Gretzky, Edmonton, 1983. 2 four-goal games.
— Wayne Gretzky, Edmonton, 1985. 2 three-goal games.
— Petr Klima, Detroit, 1988. 2 three-goal games.
— Cam Neely, Boston, 1991. 2 three-goal games.
— Wayne Gretzky, NY Rangers, 1997. 2 three-goal games.
— Daniel Alfredsson, Ottawa, 1998. 2 three-goal games.
— Patrick Marleau, San Jose, 2004. 2 three-goal games.
— Johan Franzen, Detroit, 2008. 2 three-goal games.

MOST THREE-OR-MORE-GOAL GAMES, ONE PLAYOFF SERIES:
3 — Jari Kurri, Edmonton, 1985 CF vs. Chicago, won by Edmonton 4-2. Kurri scored 3 goals May 7 at Edmonton in 7-3 win, 3 goals May 14 at Edmonton in 10-5 win and 4 goals May 16 at Chicago in 8-2 win.
2 — Doug Bentley, Chicago, 1944 SF vs. Detroit, won by Chicago 4-1. Bentley scored 3 goals March 28 at Chicago in 7-1 win and 3 goals March 30 at Detroit in 5-2 win.
— Norm Ullman, Detroit, 1964 SF vs. Chicago, won by Detroit 4-3. Ullman scored 3 goals March 29 at Chicago in 5-4 win and 3 goals April 7 at Detroit in 7-2 win.
— Mark Messier, Edmonton, 1983 DF vs. Calgary, won by Edmonton 4-1. Messier scored 4 goals April 14 at Edmonton in 6-3 win and 3 goals April 17 at Calgary in 10-2 win.
— Mike Bossy, NY Islanders, 1983 CF vs. Boston, won by NY Islanders 4-2. Bossy scored 3 goals May 3 at NY Islanders in 8-3 win and 4 goals May 7 at New York in 8-4 win.
— Johan Franzen, Detroit, 2008 CSF vs. Colorado, won by Detroit 4-0. Franzen scored 3 goals Apr. 26 at Detroit in 5-1 win and 3 goals May 1 at Colorado in 8-2 win.

SCORING STREAKS

LONGEST CONSECUTIVE GOAL-SCORING STREAK, ONE PLAYOFF YEAR:
10 Games — Reggie Leach, Philadelphia, 1976. Streak started April 17 at Toronto and ended May 9 at Montreal. He scored one goal in each of eight games; two in one game; and five in another; a total of 15 goals.

LONGEST CONSECUTIVE POINT-SCORING STREAK, ONE PLAYOFF YEAR:
18 games — Bryan Trottier, NY Islanders, 1981. 11 goals, 18 assists, 29 points.
17 games — Wayne Gretzky, Edmonton, 1988. 12 goals, 29 assists, 41 points.
— Al MacInnis, Calgary, 1989. 7 goals, 19 assists, 26 points.

LONGEST CONSECUTIVE POINT-SCORING STREAK, MORE THAN ONE PLAYOFF YEAR:
27 games — Bryan Trottier, NY Islanders, 1980, 1981 and 1982. 7 games in 1980 (3 goals, 5 assists, 8 points), 18 games in 1981 (11 goals, 18 assists, 29 points), and two games in 1982 (2 goals, 3 assists, 5 points). Total points, 42.
19 games — Wayne Gretzky, Edmonton, Los Angeles, 1988 and 1989. 17 games in 1988 (12 goals, 29 assists, 41 points with Edmonton), 2 games in 1989 (1 goal, 2 assists, 3 points with Los Angeles). Total points, 44.
— Al MacInnis, Calgary, 1989 and 1990. 17 games in 1989 (7 goals, 19 assists, 26 points), and two games in 1990 (2 goals, 1 assist, 3 points). Total points, 29.

FASTEST GOALS

FASTEST GOAL FROM START OF GAME:
0:06 — Don Kozak, Los Angeles, April 17, 1977, at Los Angeles vs. Boston and goaltender Gerry Cheevers. Los Angeles won 7-4.
0:07 — Bob Gainey, Montreal, May 5, 1977, at NY Islanders vs. goaltender Chico Resch. Montreal won 2-1.
— Terry Murray, Philadelphia, April 12, 1981, at Quebec vs. goaltender Dan Bouchard. Quebec won 4-3 in overtime.

FASTEST GOAL FROM START OF PERIOD (OTHER THAN FIRST):
0:06 — Pelle Eklund, Philadelphia, April 25, 1989, at Pittsburgh vs. goaltender Tom Barrasso, second period. Pittsburgh won 10-7.
0:09 — Bill Collins, Minnesota, April 9, 1968, at Minnesota vs. Los Angeles and goaltender Wayne Rutledge, third period. Minnesota won 7-5.
— Dave Balon, Minnesota, April 25, 1968, at St. Louis vs. goaltender Glenn Hall, third period. Minnesota won 5-1.
— Murray Oliver, Minnesota, April 8, 1971, at St. Louis vs. goaltender Ernie Wakely, third period. St. Louis won 4-2.
— Clark Gillies, NY Islanders, April 15, 1977, at Buffalo vs. goaltender Don Edwards, third period. NY Islanders won 4-3.
— Eric Vail, Atlanta, April 11, 1978, at Atlanta vs. Detroit and goaltender Ron Low, third period. Detroit won 5-3.
— Stan Smyl, Vancouver, April 10, 1979, at Philadelphia vs. goaltender Wayne Stephenson, third period. Vancouver won 3-2.
— Wayne Gretzky, Edmonton, April 6, 1983, at Edmonton vs. Winnipeg and goaltender Brian Hayward, second period. Edmonton won 6-3.
— Mark Messier, Edmonton, April 16, 1984, at Calgary vs. goaltender Don Edwards, third period. Edmonton won 5-3.
— Brian Skrudland, Montreal, May 18, 1986, at Calgary vs. goaltender Mike Vernon, first overtime period. Montreal won 3-2.

FASTEST TWO GOALS:
0:05 — Norm Ullman, Detroit, April 11, 1965, at Detroit vs. Chicago and goaltender Glenn Hall. Ullman scored at 17:35 and 17:40 of second period. Detroit won 4-2.

FASTEST TWO GOALS FROM START OF A GAME:
1:08 — Dick Duff, Toronto, April 9, 1963, at Toronto vs. Detroit and goaltender Terry Sawchuk. Duff scored at 0:49 and 1:08. Toronto won 4-2.

FASTEST TWO GOALS FROM START OF A PERIOD:
0:35 — Pat LaFontaine, NY Islanders, May 19, 1984, at Edmonton vs. goaltender Andy Moog. LaFontaine scored at 0:13 and 0:35 of third period. Edmonton won 5-2.

PENALTIES

MOST PENALTY MINUTES IN PLAYOFFS, CAREER:
729 — Dale Hunter, Quebec, Washington, Colorado
541 — Chris Nilan, Montreal, NY Rangers, Boston
529 — Claude Lemieux, Montreal, New Jersey, Colorado, Phoenix, Dallas
471 — Rick Tocchet, Philadelphia, Pittsburgh, Boston, Phoenix
466 — Willi Plett, Atlanta, Calgary, Minnesota, Boston

MOST PENALTIES, ONE GAME:
8 — Forbes Kennedy, Toronto, April 2, 1969, at Boston. Kennedy was assessed 4 minors, 2 majors, 1 10-minute misconduct, 1 game misconduct. Boston won 10-0.
— **Kim Clackson, Pittsburgh,** April 14, 1980, at Boston. Clackson was assessed 5 minors, 2 majors, 1 10-minute misconduct. Boston won 6-2.

MOST PENALTY MINUTES, ONE GAME:
42 — Dave Schultz, Philadelphia, April 22, 1976, at Toronto. Schultz was assessed 1 minor, 2 majors, 1 10-minute misconduct and 2 game-misconducts. Toronto won 8-5.

MOST PENALTIES, ONE PERIOD AND MOST PENALTY MINUTES, ONE PERIOD:
6 Penalties; 39 Minutes — Ed Hospodar, NY Rangers, April 9, 1981, at Los Angeles, first period. Hospodar was assessed 2 minors, 1 major, 1 10-minute misconduct, 2 game misconducts. Los Angeles won 5-4.

GOALTENDING

MOST PLAYOFF GAMES APPEARED IN BY A GOALTENDER, CAREER:
247 — Patrick Roy, Montreal, Colorado
181 — Martin Brodeur, New Jersey
161 — Ed Belfour, Chicago, Dallas, Toronto
150 — Grant Fuhr, Edmonton, Buffalo, St. Louis
138 — Mike Vernon, Calgary, Detroit, San Jose, Florida

MOST MINUTES PLAYED BY A GOALTENDER, CAREER:
15,209 — Patrick Roy, Montreal, Colorado
11,248 — Martin Brodeur, New Jersey
9,945 — Ed Belfour, Chicago, Dallas, Toronto
8,834 — Grant Fuhr, Edmonton, Buffalo, St. Louis
8,214 — Mike Vernon, Calgary, Detroit, San Jose, Florida

MOST MINUTES PLAYED BY A GOALTENDER, ONE PLAYOFF YEAR:
1,655 — Miikka Kiprusoff, Calgary, 2004. 26 games.
1,544 — Kirk McLean, Vancouver, 1994. 24 games.
— Ed Belfour, Dallas, 1999. 23 games.
1,540 — Ron Hextall, Philadelphia, 1987. 26 games.
1,505 — Martin Brodeur, New Jersey, 2001. 25 games.

MOST SHUTOUTS IN PLAYOFFS, CAREER:
23 — Patrick Roy, Montreal, Colorado
— **Martin Brodeur, New Jersey**
16 — Curtis Joseph, St. Louis, Edmonton, Toronto, Detroit

MOST SHUTOUTS, ONE PLAYOFF YEAR:
7 — Martin Brodeur, New Jersey, 2003. 24 games.
6 — Dominik Hasek, Detroit, 2002. 23 games.
5 — Jean-Sebastien Giguere, Anaheim, 2003. 21 games.
— Nikolai Khabibulin, Tampa Bay, 2004. 23 games.
— Miikka Kiprusoff, Calgary, 2004. 26 games.

MOST SHUTOUTS, ONE PLAYOFF SERIES:
3 — Clint Benedict, Mtl. Maroons, 1926 F vs. Victoria. 4 games.
— **Dave Kerr, NY Rangers,** 1940 SF vs. Boston. 6 games.
— **Frank McCool, Toronto,** 1945 F vs. Detroit. 7 games.
— **Turk Broda, Toronto,** 1950 SF vs. Detroit. 7 games.
— **Felix Potvin, Toronto,** 1994 CQF vs. Chicago. 6 games.
— **Martin Brodeur, New Jersey,** 1995 CQF vs. Boston. 5 games.
— **Brent Johnson, St. Louis,** 2002 CQF vs. Chicago. 5 games.
— **Patrick Lalime, Ottawa,** 2002 CQF vs. Philadelphia. 5 games.
— **Jean-Sebastien Giguere, Anaheim,** 2003 CF vs. Minnesota. 4 games.
— **Martin Brodeur, New Jersey,** 2003 F vs. Anaheim. 7 games.
— **Ed Belfour, Toronto,** 2004 CQF vs. Ottawa. 7 games.
— **Nikolai Khabibulin, Tampa Bay,** 2004 CQF vs. NY Islanders. 5 games.
— **Marty Turco, Dallas,** 2007 CQF vs. Vancouver. 7 games.
— **Michael Leighton, Philadelphia,** 2010 CF vs. Montreal. 5 games.

MOST WINS BY A GOALTENDER, CAREER:
151 — Patrick Roy, Montreal, Colorado
99 — Martin Brodeur, New Jersey
92 — Grant Fuhr, Edmonton, Buffalo, St. Louis
88 — Billy Smith, NY Islanders
— Ed Belfour, Chicago, Dallas, Toronto

MOST WINS BY A GOALTENDER, ONE PLAYOFF YEAR:
16 — Sixteen wins by a goaltender in one playoff year has been recorded on 20 occasions. Tim Thomas of the Boston Bruins is the most recent to equal this mark, posting a record of 16 wins and 9 losses in 25 games in 2011. It was first accomplished by Grant Fuhr in 1988.

MOST CONSECUTIVE WINS BY A GOALTENDER, MORE THAN ONE PLAYOFF YEAR:
14 — Tom Barrasso, Pittsburgh, 1992, 1993; 3 wins vs. NY Rangers in 1992 DF, won by Pittsburgh 4-2; 4 wins vs. Boston in 1992 CF, won by Pittsburgh 4-0; 4 wins vs. Chicago in 1992 F, won by Pittsburgh 4-0; 3 wins vs. New Jersey in 1993 DSF, won by Pittsburgh 4-1.

MOST CONSECUTIVE WINS BY A GOALTENDER, ONE PLAYOFF YEAR:
11 — Ed Belfour, Chicago, 1992. 3 wins vs. St. Louis in DSF, won by Chicago 4-2; 4 wins vs. Detroit in DF, won by Chicago 4-0; and 4 wins vs. Edmonton in CF, won by Chicago 4-0.
— **Tom Barrasso, Pittsburgh,** 1992. 3 wins vs. NY Rangers in DF, won by Pittsburgh 4-2; 4 wins vs. Boston in CF, won by Pittsburgh 4-0; and 4 wins vs. Chicago in F, won by Pittsburgh 4-0.
— **Patrick Roy, Montreal,** 1993. 4 wins vs. Quebec in DSF, won by Montreal 4-2; 4 wins vs. Buffalo in DF, won by Montreal 4-0; and 3 wins vs. NY Islanders in CF, won by Montreal 4-1.

LONGEST SHUTOUT SEQUENCE:
270:08 — George Hainsworth, Montreal, 1930. Hainsworth's shutout streak began after Murray Murdoch scored a goal for the NY Rangers at 15:34 of the first period in the first game of a SF series on March 28, 1930. Hainsworth did not allow another goal in the final 113:18 of that game, won by Montreal 2-1 at 8:52 of the 4th overtime period. Hainsworth then shutout the NY Rangers in the next and final game of the series on March 30, 1930, won by Montreal 2-0. The streak continued with a 3-0 win over Boston in the opening game of the F series on April 1, 1930. His streak ended on April 3, 1930 when Boston's Eddie Shore scored at 16:50 of the second period in the second game of the F series.

MOST CONSECUTIVE SHUTOUTS:
3 — Clint Benedict, Mtl. Maroons, 1926. Benedict shut out Ottawa 1-0, March 27; he then shut out Victoria twice, 3-0, March 30; 3-0, April 1. Mtl. Maroons won NHL F vs. Ottawa 2 goals to 1 and won the best-of-five F vs. Victoria 3-1.
— **John Ross Roach, NY Rangers,** 1929. Roach shut out NY Americans twice, 0-0, March 19; 1-0, March 21; he then shut out Toronto 1-0, March 24. NY Rangers won QF vs. NY Americans 1 goal to 0 and won the best-of-three SF vs. Toronto 2-0.
— **Frank McCool, Toronto,** 1945. McCool shut out Detroit 1-0, April 6; 2-0, April 8; 1-0, April 12. Toronto won the best-of-seven F 4-3.
— **Brent Johnson, St. Louis,** 2002. Johnson shut out Chicago three times; 2-0, April 20; 4-0, April 21; 1-0, April 23. St. Louis won the best-of-seven CQF 4-1.
— **Patrick Lalime, Ottawa,** 2002. Lalime shut out Philadelphia three times; 3-0, April 20; 3-0, April 22; 3-0, April 24. Ottawa won the best-of-seven CQF 4-1.
— **Jean-Sebastien Giguere, Anaheim,** 2003. Giguere shut out Minnesota 1-0, May 10; 2-0, May 12; 4-0, May 14. Anaheim won the best-of-seven CF 4-0.

Early Playoff Records

1893-1918
Team Records

MOST GOALS, BOTH TEAMS, ONE GAME:
25 — Ottawa Silver Seven, Dawson City at Ottawa, Jan. 16, 1905. Ottawa 23, Dawson City 2. Ottawa won best-of-three series 2-0.

MOST GOALS, ONE TEAM, ONE GAME:
23 — Ottawa Silver Seven at Ottawa, Jan. 16, 1905. Ottawa defeated Dawson City 23-2.

MOST GOALS, BOTH TEAMS, BEST-OF-THREE SERIES:
42 — Ottawa Silver Seven, Queen's University at Ottawa, 1906. Ottawa defeated Queen's 16-7, Feb. 27, and 12-7, Feb. 28.

MOST GOALS, ONE TEAM, BEST-OF-THREE SERIES:
32 — Ottawa Silver Seven in 1905 at Ottawa. Defeated Dawson City 9-2, Jan. 13, and 23-2, Jan. 16.

MOST GOALS, BOTH TEAMS, BEST-OF-FIVE SERIES:
39 — Toronto Arenas, Vancouver Millionaires at Toronto, 1918. Toronto won 5-3, Mar. 20; 6-3, Mar. 26; 2-1, Mar. 30. Vancouver won 6-4, Mar. 23, and 8-1, Mar. 28. Toronto scored 18 goals; Vancouver 21.

MOST GOALS, ONE TEAM, BEST-OF-FIVE SERIES:
26 — Vancouver Millionaires in 1915 at Vancouver. Defeated Ottawa Senators 6-2, Mar. 22; 8-3, Mar. 24; and 12-3, Mar. 26.

Individual Records

MOST GOALS IN PLAYOFFS:
63 — Frank McGee, Ottawa Silver Seven, in 22 playoff games. Seven goals in four games, 1903; 21 goals in eight games, 1904; 18 goals in four games, 1905; 17 goals in six games, 1906.

MOST GOALS, ONE PLAYOFF SERIES:
15 — Frank McGee, Ottawa Silver Seven, in two games in 1905 at Ottawa. Scored one goal, Jan. 13, in 9-2 victory over Dawson City and 14 goals, Jan. 16, in 23-2 victory.

MOST GOALS, ONE PLAYOFF GAME:
14 — Frank McGee, Ottawa Silver Seven, at Ottawa, Jan. 16, 1905, in 23-2 victory over Dawson City.

FASTEST THREE GOALS:
40 Seconds — Marty Walsh, Ottawa Senators, at Ottawa, March 16, 1911, at 3:00, 3:10, and 3:40 of third period. Ottawa defeated Port Arthur 13-4.

All-Time Playoff Goal Leaders since 1918

(45 or more goals)

Player	Teams	Yrs.	GP	G
Wayne Gretzky	Edm., L.A., St.L., NYR	16	208	122
Mark Messier	Edm., NYR, Van.	17	236	109
Jari Kurri	Edm., L.A., NYR, Ana., Col.	15	200	106
Brett Hull	Cgy., St.L., Dal., Det., Phx.	19	202	103
Glenn Anderson	Edm., Tor., NYR, St.L.	15	225	93
Mike Bossy	NYI	10	129	85
Joe Sakic	Que., Col.	13	172	84
Maurice Richard	Mtl.	15	133	82
Claude Lemieux	Mtl., N.J., Col., Phx., Dal., S.J.	18	234	80
Jean Beliveau	Mtl.	17	162	79
* Jaromir Jagr	Pit., Wsh., NYR	15	169	77
Mario Lemieux	Pit.	8	107	76
Dino Ciccarelli	Min., Wsh., Det., T.B., Fla.	14	141	73
Esa Tikkanen	Edm., NYR, St.L., N.J., Van., Det.	13	186	72
Bryan Trottier	NYI, Pit.	17	221	71
Steve Yzerman	Det.	20	196	70
Gordie Howe	Det., Hfd.	20	157	68
Joe Nieuwendyk	Cgy., Dal., N.J., Tor., Fla.	16	158	66
Denis Savard	Chi., Mtl., T.B.	16	169	66
Yvan Cournoyer	Mtl.	12	147	64
Peter Forsberg	Que., Col., Phi., Nsh.	13	151	64
Brian Propp	Phi., Bos., Min., Hfd.	13	160	64
Bobby Smith	Min., Mtl.	13	184	64
Bobby Hull	Chi., Wpg., Hfd.	14	119	62
Phil Esposito	Chi., Bos., NYR	15	130	61
Jacques Lemaire	Mtl.	11	145	61
Mark Recchi	Pit., Phi., Mtl., Car., Atl., T.B., Bos.	14	189	61
Joe Mullen	St.L., Cgy., Pit., Bos.	15	143	60
Doug Gilmour	St.L., Cgy., Tor., N.J., Chi., Buf., Mtl.	17	182	60
Brendan Shanahan	N.J., St.L., Hfd., Det., NYR	19	184	60
Stan Mikita	Chi.	18	155	59
Paul Coffey	Edm., Pit., L.A., Det., Hfd., Phi., Chi., Car., Bos.	16	194	59
Guy Lafleur	Mtl., NYR, Que.	14	128	58
Bernie Geoffrion	Mtl., NYR	16	132	58
Luc Robitaille	L.A., Pit., NYR, Det.	15	159	58
* Mike Modano	Min., Dal., Det.	16	176	58
Cam Neely	Van., Bos.	9	93	57
Steve Larmer	Chi., NYR	13	140	56
Denis Potvin	NYI	14	185	56
Rick MacLeish	Phi., Hfd., Pit., Det.	11	114	54
Steve Thomas	Tor., Chi., NYI, N.J., Ana., Det.	16	174	54
* Nicklas Lidstrom	Det.	18	258	54
Bill Barber	Phi.	11	129	53
Stephane Richer	Mtl., N.J., T.B., St.L., Pit.	13	134	53
Jeremy Roenick	Chi., Phx., Phi., L.A., S.J.	17	154	53
* Patrick Marleau	S.J.	11	124	52
Rick Tocchet	Phi., Pit., L.A., Bos., Wsh., Phx.	13	145	52
Sergei Fedorov	Det., Ana., CBJ, Wsh.	15	183	52
Frank Mahovlich	Tor., Det., Mtl.	14	137	51
Brian Bellows	Min., Mtl., T.B., Ana., Wsh.	13	143	51
Rod Brind'Amour	St.L., Phi., Car.	12	159	51
Steve Shutt	Mtl., L.A.	12	99	50
* Henrik Zetterberg	Det.	7	104	49
Henri Richard	Mtl.	18	180	49
Reggie Leach	Bos., Cal., Phi., Det.	8	94	47
Ted Lindsay	Det., Chi.	16	133	47
* Chris Drury	Col., Cgy., Buf., NYR	9	135	47
Clark Gillies	NYI, Buf.	13	164	47
Kevin Stevens	Pit., Bos., L.A., NYR, Phi.	7	103	46
Dickie Moore	Mtl., Tor., St.L.	14	135	46
Ron Francis	Hfd., Pit., Car., Tor.	17	171	46
* Daniel Alfredsson	Ott.	11	107	45
Rick Middleton	NYR, Bos.	12	114	45
* Alex Kovalev	NYR, Pit., Mtl., Ott.	11	123	45
* Tomas Holmstrom	Det.	13	175	45

* Active

All-Time Playoff Assist Leaders since 1918

(65 or more assists)

Player	Teams	Yrs.	GP	A
Wayne Gretzky	Edm., L.A., St.L., NYR	16	208	260
Mark Messier	Edm., NYR, Van.	17	236	186
Raymond Bourque	Bos., Col.	21	214	139
Paul Coffey	Edm., Pit., L.A., Det., Hfd., Phi., Chi., Car., Bos.	16	194	137
* Nicklas Lidstrom	Det.	18	258	129
Doug Gilmour	St.L., Cgy., Tor., N.J., Chi., Buf., Mtl.	17	182	128
Jari Kurri	Edm., L.A., NYR, Ana., Col.	15	200	127
Sergei Fedorov	Det., Ana., CBJ, Wsh.	15	183	124
Al MacInnis	Cgy., St.L	19	177	121
Glenn Anderson	Edm., Tor., NYR, St.L.	15	225	121
Larry Robinson	Mtl., L.A.	20	227	116
Steve Yzerman	Det.	20	196	115
Larry Murphy	L.A., Wsh., Min., Pit., Tor., Det.	20	215	115
Adam Oates	Det., St.L., Bos., Wsh., Phi., Ana., Edm.	15	163	114
Bryan Trottier	NYI, Pit.	17	221	113
Chris Chelios	Mtl., Chi., Det., Atl.	24	266	113
Denis Savard	Chi., Mtl., T.B.	16	169	109
Denis Potvin	NYI	14	185	108
Peter Forsberg	Que., Col., Phi., Nsh.	13	151	107
* Jaromir Jagr	Pit., Wsh., NYR	15	169	104
Joe Sakic	Que., Col.	13	172	104
Jean Beliveau	Mtl.	17	162	97
Ron Francis	Hfd., Pit., Car., Tor.	17	171	97
Mario Lemieux	Pit.	8	107	96
Bobby Smith	Min., Mtl.	13	184	96
* Chris Pronger	Hfd., St.L., Edm., Ana., Phi.	14	173	95
Sergei Zubov	NYR, Pit., Dal.	13	164	93
Gordie Howe	Det., Hfd.	20	157	92
Scott Stevens	Wsh., St.L., N.J.	20	233	92
Stan Mikita	Chi.	18	155	91
Brad Park	NYR, Bos., Det.	17	161	90
* Mike Modano	Min., Dal., Det.	16	176	88
Brett Hull	Cgy., St.L., Dal., Det., Phx.	19	202	87
Craig Janney	Bos., St.L., S.J., Wpg., Phx., T.B., NYI	11	120	86
Mark Recchi	Pit., Phi., Mtl., Car., Atl., T.B., Bos.	14	189	86
Brian Propp	Phi., Bos., Min., Hfd.	13	160	84
Henri Richard	Mtl.	18	180	80
Jacques Lemaire	Mtl.	11	145	78
Claude Lemieux	Mtl., N.J., Col., Phx., Dal., S.J.	18	234	78
Ken Linseman	Phi., Edm., Bos., Tor.	11	113	77
Bobby Clarke	Phi.	13	136	77
* Patrik Elias	N.J.	12	138	77
Guy Lafleur	Mtl., NYR, Que.	14	128	76
Phil Esposito	Chi., Bos., NYR	15	130	76
Dale Hunter	Que., Wsh., Col.	18	186	76
Mike Bossy	NYI	10	129	75
Steve Larmer	Chi., NYR	13	140	75
John Tonelli	NYI, Cgy., L.A., Chi., Que.	13	172	75
Brendan Shanahan	N.J., St.L., Hfd., Det., NYR	19	184	74
Scott Niedermayer	N.J., Ana.	15	202	73
Peter Stastny	Que., N.J., St.L.	12	93	72
Bernie Nicholls	L.A., NYR, Edm., N.J., Chi., S.J.	13	118	72
Brian Bellows	Min., Mtl., T.B., Ana., Wsh.	13	143	71
Brian Rafalski	N.J., Det.	10	165	71
Gilbert Perreault	Buf.	11	90	70
* Scott Gomez	N.J., NYR, Mtl.	9	140	70
Geoff Courtnall	Bos., Edm., Wsh., St.L., Van.	15	156	70
Brian Leetch	NYR, Tor., Bos.	8	95	69
Dale Hawerchuk	Wpg., Buf., St.L., Phi.	15	97	69
Alex Delvecchio	Det.	14	121	69
Jeremy Roenick	Chi., Phx., Phi., L.A., S.J.	17	154	69
Luc Robitaille	L.A., Pit., NYR, Det.	15	159	69
Bobby Hull	Chi., Wpg., Hfd.	14	119	67
Sandis Ozolinsh	S.J., Col., Car., Fla., Ana., NYR	10	137	67
Frank Mahovlich	Tor., Det., Mtl.	14	137	67
Igor Larionov	Van., S.J., Det., Fla., N.J.	13	150	67
Bobby Orr	Bos., Chi.	8	74	66
Bernie Federko	St.L., Det.	11	91	66
Jean Ratelle	NYR, Bos.	15	123	66
Charlie Huddy	Edm., L.A., Buf., St.L	14	183	66
Trevor Linden	Van., NYI, Mtl., Wsh.	12	124	65

All-Time Playoff Point Leaders since 1918

(115 or more points)

Player	Teams	Yrs.	GP	G	A	Pts.
Wayne Gretzky	Edm., L.A., St.L., NYR	16	208	122	260	382
Mark Messier	Edm., NYR, Van.	17	236	109	186	295
Jari Kurri	Edm., L.A., NYR, Ana., Col.	15	200	106	127	233
Glenn Anderson	Edm., Tor., NYR, St.L.	15	225	93	121	214
Paul Coffey	Edm., Pit., L.A., Det., Hfd., Phi., Chi., Car., Bos.	16	194	59	137	196
Brett Hull	Cgy., St.L., Dal., Det., Phx.	19	202	103	87	190
Joe Sakic	Que., Col.	13	172	84	104	188
Doug Gilmour	St.L., Cgy., Tor., N.J., Chi., Buf., Mtl.	17	182	60	128	188
Steve Yzerman	Det.	20	196	70	115	185
Bryan Trottier	NYI, Pit.	17	221	71	113	184
* Nicklas Lidstrom	Det.	18	258	54	129	183
* Jaromir Jagr	Pit., Wsh., NYR	15	169	77	104	181
Raymond Bourque	Bos., Col.	21	214	41	139	180
Jean Beliveau	Mtl.	17	162	79	97	176
Sergei Fedorov	Det., Ana., CBJ, Wsh.	15	183	52	124	176
Denis Savard	Chi., Mtl., T.B.	16	169	66	109	175
Mario Lemieux	Pit.	8	107	76	96	172
Peter Forsberg	Que., Col., Phi., Nsh.	13	151	64	107	171
Denis Potvin	NYI	14	185	56	108	164
Mike Bossy	NYI	10	129	85	75	160
Gordie Howe	Det., Hfd.	20	157	68	92	160
Al MacInnis	Cgy., St.L	19	177	39	121	160
Bobby Smith	Min., Mtl.	13	184	64	96	160
Claude Lemieux	Mtl., N.J., Col., Phx., Dal., S.J.	18	234	80	78	158
Adam Oates	Det., St.L., Bos., Wsh., Phi., Ana., Edm.	15	163	42	114	156
Larry Murphy	L.A., Wsh., Min., Pit., Tor., Det.	20	215	37	115	152
Stan Mikita	Chi.	18	155	59	91	150
Brian Propp	Phi., Bos., Min., Hfd.	13	160	64	84	148
Mark Recchi	Pit., Phi., Mtl., Car., Atl., T.B., Bos.	14	189	61	86	147
* Mike Modano	Min., Dal., Det.	16	176	58	88	146
Larry Robinson	Mtl., L.A.	20	227	28	116	144
Chris Chelios	Mtl., Chi., Det., Atl.	24	266	31	113	144
Ron Francis	Hfd., Pit., Car., Tor.	17	171	46	97	143
Jacques Lemaire	Mtl.	11	145	61	78	139
Phil Esposito	Chi., Bos., NYR	15	130	61	76	137
Guy Lafleur	Mtl., NYR, Que.	14	128	58	76	134
Brendan Shanahan	N.J., St.L., Hfd., Det., NYR	19	184	60	74	134
Esa Tikkanen	Edm., NYR, St.L., N.J., Van., Fla., Wsh.	13	186	72	60	132
Steve Larmer	Chi., NYR	13	140	56	75	131
Bobby Hull	Chi., Wpg., Hfd.	14	119	62	67	129
Henri Richard	Mtl.	18	180	49	80	129
Yvan Cournoyer	Mtl.	12	147	64	63	127
Luc Robitaille	L.A., Pit., NYR, Det.	15	159	58	69	127
Maurice Richard	Mtl.	15	133	82	44	126
Brad Park	NYR, Bos., Det.	17	161	35	90	125
Brian Bellows	Min., Mtl., T.B., Ana., Phi., L.A., S.J.	13	143	51	71	122
Jeremy Roenick	Chi., Phx., Phi., L.A., S.J.	17	154	53	69	122
* Chris Pronger	Hfd., St.L., Edm., Ana., Phi.	14	173	26	95	121
Ken Linseman	Phi., Edm., Bos., Tor.	11	113	43	77	120
Bobby Clarke	Phi.	13	136	42	77	119
Bernie Geoffrion	Mtl., NYR	16	132	58	60	118
Frank Mahovlich	Tor., Det., Mtl.	14	137	51	67	118
Dino Ciccarelli	Min., Wsh., Det., T.B., Fla.	14	141	73	45	118
Dale Hunter	Que., Wsh., Col.	18	186	42	76	118
Scott Stevens	Wsh., St.L., N.J.	20	233	26	92	118
* Patrik Elias	N.J.	12	138	40	77	117
Sergei Zubov	NYR, Pit., Dal.	13	164	24	93	117
Joe Nieuwendyk	Cgy., Dal., N.J., Tor., Fla.	16	158	66	50	116
John Tonelli	NYI, Cgy., L.A., Chi., Que.	13	172	40	75	115

David Krejci led all 2011 playoff scorers with 12 goals and 23 points. His 12 goals were the most ever by a Czech player in one playoff year. Krejci scored three game-winning goals during Boston's four-game sweep of Philadelphia in the second round and four overall in the playoffs.

Leading Playoff Scorers, 1918–2011

Season	Player, Team	Games Played	Goals	Assists	Points	Season	Player, Team	Games Played	Goals	Assists	Points
2010-11	David Krejci, Boston	25	12	11	23	1960-61	Gordie Howe, Detroit	11	4	11	15
2009-10	Danny Briere, Philadelphia	23	12	18	30		Pierre Pilote, Chicago	12	3	12	15
2008-09	Evgeni Malkin, Pittsburgh	24	14	22	36	1959-60	Henri Richard, Montreal	8	3	9	12
2007-08	Henrik Zetterberg, Detroit	22	13	14	27		Bernie Geoffrion, Montreal	8	2	10	12
	Sidney Crosby, Pittsburgh	20	6	21	27	1958-59	Dickie Moore, Montreal	11	5	12	17
2006-07	Daniel Alfredsson, Ottawa	20	14	8	22	1957-58	Fleming MacKell, Boston	12	5	14	19
	Dany Heatley, Ottawa	20	7	15	22	1956-57	Bernie Geoffrion, Montreal	11	11	7	18
	Jason Spezza, Ottawa	20	7	15	22	1955-56	Jean Béliveau, Montreal	10	12	7	19
2005-06	Eric Staal, Carolina	25	9	19	28	1954-55	Gordie Howe, Detroit	11	9	11	20
2004-05	*Season Cancelled*					1953-54	Dickie Moore, Montreal	11	5	8	13
2003-04	Brad Richards, Tampa Bay	23	12	14	26	1952-53	Ed Sandford, Boston	11	8	3	11
2002-03	Jamie Langenbrunner, New Jersey	24	11	7	18	1951-52	Ted Lindsay, Detroit	8	5	2	7
	Scott Niedermayer, New Jersey	24	2	16	18		Floyd Curry, Montreal	11	4	3	7
2001-02	Peter Forsberg, Colorado	20	9	18	27		Metro Prystai, Detroit	8	2	5	7
2000-01	Joe Sakic, Colorado	21	13	13	26		Gordie Howe, Detroit	8	2	5	7
99-2000	Brett Hull, Dallas	23	11	13	24	1950-51	Maurice Richard, Montreal	11	9	4	13
1998-99	Peter Forsberg, Colorado	19	8	16	24		Max Bentley, Toronto	11	2	11	13
1997-98	Steve Yzerman, Detroit	22	6	18	24	1949-50	Pentti Lund, NY Rangers	12	6	5	11
1996-97	Eric Lindros, Philadelphia	19	12	14	26	1948-49	Gordie Howe, Detroit	11	8	3	11
1995-96	Joe Sakic, Colorado	22	18	16	34	1947-48	Ted Kennedy, Toronto	9	8	6	14
1994-95	Sergei Fedorov, Detroit	17	7	17	24	1946-47	Maurice Richard, Montreal	10	6	5	11
1993-94	Brian Leetch, NY Rangers	23	11	23	34	1945-46	Elmer Lach, Montreal	9	5	12	17
1992-93	Wayne Gretzky, Los Angeles	24	15	25	40	1944-45	Joe Carveth, Detroit	14	5	6	11
1991-92	Mario Lemieux, Pittsburgh	15	16	18	34	1943-44	Toe Blake, Montreal	9	7	11	18
1990-91	Mario Lemieux, Pittsburgh	23	16	28	44	1942-43	Carl Liscombe, Detroit	10	6	8	14
1989-90	Craig Simpson, Edmonton	22	16	15	31	1941-42	Don Grosso, Detroit	12	8	6	14
	Mark Messier, Edmonton	22	9	22	31		Syl Apps, Toronto	13	5	9	14
1988-89	Al MacInnis, Calgary	22	7	24	31	1940-41	Milt Schmidt, Boston	11	5	6	11
1987-88	Wayne Gretzky, Edmonton	19	12	31	43	1939-40	Phil Watson, NY Rangers	12	3	6	9
1986-87	Wayne Gretzky, Edmonton	21	5	29	34		Neil Colville, NY Rangers	12	2	7	9
1985-86	Doug Gilmour, St. Louis	19	9	12	21	1938-39	Bill Cowley, Boston	12	3	11	14
	Bernie Federko, St. Louis	19	7	14	21	1937-38	Johnny Gottselig, Chicago	10	5	3	8
1984-85	Wayne Gretzky, Edmonton	18	17	30	47		Gordie Drillon, Toronto	7	7	1	8
1983-84	Wayne Gretzky, Edmonton	19	13	22	35	1936-37	Marty Barry, Detroit	10	4	7	11
1982-83	Wayne Gretzky, Edmonton	16	12	26	38	1935-36	Frank Boll, Toronto	9	7	3	10
1981-82	Bryan Trottier, NY Islanders	19	6	23	29	1934-35	Baldy Northcott, Mtl. Maroons	7	4	1	5
1980-81	Mike Bossy, NY Islanders	18	17	18	35		Busher Jackson, Toronto	7	3	2	5
1979-80	Bryan Trottier, NY Islanders	21	12	17	29		Cy Wentworth, Mtl. Maroons	7	3	2	5
1978-79	Jacques Lemaire, Montreal	16	11	12	23		Charlie Conacher, Toronto	7	1	4	5
	Guy Lafleur, Montreal	16	10	13	23	1933-34	Larry Aurie, Detroit	9	3	7	10
1977-78	Guy Lafleur, Montreal	15	10	11	21	1932-33	Cecil Dillon, NY Rangers	8	8	2	10
	Larry Robinson, Montreal	15	4	17	21	1931-32	Frank Boucher, NY Rangers	7	3	6	9
1976-77	Guy Lafleur, Montreal	14	9	17	26	1930-31	Cooney Weiland, Boston	5	6	3	9
1975-76	Reggie Leach, Philadelphia	16	19	5	24	1929-30	Marty Barry, Boston	6	3	3	6
1974-75	Rick MacLeish, Philadelphia	17	11	9	20		Cooney Weiland, Boston	6	1	5	6
1973-74	Rick MacLeish, Philadelphia	17	13	9	22	1928-29	Andy Blair, Toronto	4	3	0	3
1972-73	Yvan Cournoyer, Montreal	17	15	10	25		Butch Keeling, NY Rangers	6	3	0	3
1971-72	Phil Esposito, Boston	15	9	15	24		Ace Bailey, Toronto	4	1	2	3
	Bobby Orr, Boston	15	5	19	24	1927-28	Frank Boucher, NY Rangers	9	7	3	10
1970-71	Frank Mahovlich, Montreal	20	14	13	27	1926-27	Harry Oliver, Boston	8	4	2	6
1969-70	Phil Esposito, Boston	14	13	14	27		Percy Galbraith, Boston	8	3	3	6
1968-69	Phil Esposito, Boston	10	8	10	18	1925-26	Nels Stewart, Mtl. Maroons	8	6	3	9
1967-68	Bill Goldsworthy, Minnesota	14	8	7	15	1924-25	Howie Morenz, Montreal	6	7	1	8
1966-67	Jim Pappin, Toronto	12	7	8	15	1923-24	Howie Morenz, Montreal	6	7	3	10
1965-66	Norm Ullman, Detroit	12	6	9	15	1922-23	Punch Broadbent, Ottawa	8	6	1	7
1964-65	Bobby Hull, Chicago	14	10	7	17	1921-22	Babe Dye, Toronto	7	11	1	12
1963-64	Gordie Howe, Detroit	14	9	10	19	1920-21	Cy Denneny, Ottawa	7	4	2	6
1962-63	Gordie Howe, Detroit	11	7	9	16	1919-20	Frank Nighbor, Ottawa	5	6	1	7
	Norm Ullman, Detroit	11	4	12	16		Jack Darragh, Ottawa	5	5	2	7
1961-62	Stan Mikita, Chicago	12	6	15	21	1918-19	Newsy Lalonde, Montreal	10	17	2	19
						1917-18	Alf Skinner, Toronto	7	8	3	11

Three-or-more-Goal Games, Playoffs 1918–2011

Player	Team	Date	City	Total Goals	Opposing Goaltender	Score
Wayne Gretzky (10)	Edm.	Apr. 11/81	Edm.	3	Richard Sevigny	Edm. 6 Mtl. 2
		Apr. 19/81	Edm.	3	Billy Smith	Edm. 5 NYI 2
		Apr. 6/83	Edm.	4	Brian Hayward	Edm. 6 Wpg. 3
		Apr. 17/83	Cgy.	4	Reggie Lemelin	Edm. 10 Cgy. 2
		Apr. 25/85	Wpg.	3	Brian Hayward (2) Marc Behrend (1)	Edm. 8 Wpg. 3
		May 25/85	Edm.	3	Pelle Lindbergh	Edm. 4 Phi. 3
		Apr. 24/86	Cgy.	3	Mike Vernon	Edm. 7 Cgy. 4
	L.A.	May 29/93	Tor.	3	Felix Potvin	L.A. 5 Tor. 4
	NYR	Apr. 23/97	NYR	3	John Vanbiesbrouck	NYR 3 Fla. 2
		May 18/97	Phi.	3	Garth Snow	NYR 5 Phi. 4
Maurice Richard (7)	Mtl.	Apr. 23/44	Mtl.	5	Paul Bibeault	Mtl. 5 Tor. 1
		Apr. 6/44	Chi.	3	Mike Karakas	Mtl. 3 Chi. 1
		Mar. 29/45	Mtl.	4	Frank McCool	Mtl. 10 Tor. 3
		Apr. 14/53	Bos.	3	Gord Henry	Mtl. 7 Bos. 3
		Mar. 20/56	Mtl.	3	Gump Worsley	Mtl. 7 NYR 1
		Apr. 6/57	Mtl.	3	Don Simmons	Mtl. 5 Bos. 1
		Apr. 1/58	Det.	3	Terry Sawchuk	Mtl. 4 Det. 3
Jari Kurri (7)	Edm.	Apr. 4/84	Edm.	3	Doug Soetaert (1) Mike Veisor (2)	Edm. 9 Wpg. 2
		Apr. 25/85	Wpg.	3	Brian Hayward (2) Marc Behrend (1)	Edm. 8 Wpg. 3
		May 7/85	Edm.	3	Murray Bannerman	Edm. 7 Chi. 3
		May 14/85	Edm.	3	Murray Bannerman	Edm. 10 Chi. 5
		May 16/85	Chi.	4	Murray Bannerman	Edm. 8 Chi. 2
		Apr. 9/87	Edm.	4	Rollie Melanson (2) Darren Eliot (2)	Edm. 13 L.A. 3
		May 18/90	Bos.	3	Andy Moog (2) Reggie Lemelin (1)	Edm. 7 Bos. 2
Dino Ciccarelli (6)	Min.	May 5/81	Min.	3	Pat Riggin	Min. 7 Cgy. 4
		Apr. 10/82	Min.	3	Murray Bannerman	Min. 7 Chi. 1
	Wsh.	Apr. 5/90	N.J.	3	Sean Burke	Wsh. 5 N.J. 4
		Apr. 25/92	Pit.	4	Tom Barrasso (1) Ken Wregget (3)	Wsh. 7 Pit. 2
	Det.	Apr. 29/93	Tor.	3	Felix Potvin (2) Daren Puppa (1)	Det. 7 Tor. 3
		May 11/95	Dal.	3	Andy Moog (2) Darcy Wakaluk (1)	Det. 5 Dal. 1
Mike Bossy (5)	NYI	Apr. 16/79	NYI	3	Tony Esposito	NYI 6 Chi. 2
		May 8/82	NYI	3	Richard Brodeur	NYI 6 Van. 5
		Apr. 10/83	Wsh.	3	Al Jensen	NYI 6 Wsh. 3
		May 3/83	NYI	3	Pete Peeters	NYI 8 Bos. 3
		May 7/83	NYI	4	Pete Peeters	NYI 8 Bos. 4
Phil Esposito (4)	Bos.	Apr. 2/69	Bos.	4	Bruce Gamble	Bos. 10 Tor. 0
		Apr. 8/70	Bos.	3	Ed Giacomin	Bos. 8 NYR 2
		Apr. 19/70	Chi.	3	Tony Esposito	Bos. 6 Chi. 3
		Apr. 8/75	Bos.	3	Tony Esposito (2) Michel Dumas (1)	Bos. 8 Chi. 2
Mark Messier (4)	Edm.	Apr. 14/83	Edm.	4	Reggie Lemelin	Edm. 6 Cgy. 3
		Apr. 17/83	Cgy.	3	Reggie Lemelin (1) Don Edwards (2)	Edm. 10 Cgy. 2
		Apr. 26/83	Edm.	3	Murray Bannerman	Edm. 8 Chi. 2
	NYR	May 25/94	N.J.	3	Martin Brodeur (2) ENG (1)	NYR 4 N.J. 2
Steve Yzerman (4)	Det.	Apr. 6/89	Det.	3	Alain Chevrier	Chi. 5 Det. 4
		Apr. 4/91	St.L.	3	Vincent Riendeau (2) Pat Jablonski (1)	Det. 6 St.L. 3
		May 8/96	St.L.	3	Jon Casey	St.L. 5 Det. 4
		Apr. 21/99	Det.	3	Guy Hebert (2) Pat Jablonski (1)	Det. 5 Ana. 3
Bernie Geoffrion (3)	Mtl.	Mar. 27/52	Mtl.	3	Jim Henry	Mtl. 4 Bos. 0
		Apr. 7/55	Mtl.	3	Terry Sawchuk	Mtl. 4 Det. 2
		Mar. 30/57	Mtl.	3	Gump Worsley	Mtl. 8 NYR 3
Norm Ullman (3)	Det.	Mar. 29/64	Chi.	3	Glenn Hall	Det. 5 Chi. 4
		Apr. 7/64	Det.	3	Glenn Hall (2) Denis DeJordy (1)	Det. 7 Chi. 2
		Apr. 11/65	Det.	3	Glenn Hall	Det. 4 Chi. 2
John Bucyk (3)	Bos.	May 3/70	St.L.	3	Jacques Plante (1) Ernie Wakely (2)	Bos. 6 St.L. 1
		Apr. 20/72	Bos.	3	Jacques Caron (1) Ernie Wakely (2)	Bos. 10 St.L. 2
		Apr. 21/74	Bos.	3	Tony Esposito	Bos. 8 Chi. 6
Rick MacLeish (3)	Phi.	Apr. 11/74	Phi.	3	Phil Myre	Phi. 5 Atl. 1
		Apr. 13/75	Phi.	3	Gord McRae	Phi. 6 Tor. 3
		May 13/75	Phi.	3	Glenn Resch	Phi. 4 NYI 1
Denis Savard (3)	Chi.	Apr. 19/82	Chi.	3	Mike Liut	Chi. 7 StL. 4
		Apr. 10/86	Chi.	4	Ken Wregget	Tor. 6 Chi. 4
		Apr. 9/88	St.L.	3	Greg Millen	Chi. 5 St.L. 3
Tim Kerr (3)	Phi.	Apr. 13/85	NYR	4	Glen Hanlon	Phi. 6 NYR 5
		Apr. 20/87	Phi.	3	Kelly Hrudey	Phi. 4 NYI 2
		Apr. 19/89	Pit.	3	Tom Barrasso	Phi. 4 Pit. 2
Cam Neely (3)	Bos.	Apr. 9/87	Mtl.	3	Patrick Roy	Mtl. 4 Bos. 3
		Apr. 5/91	Bos.	3	Peter Sidorkiewicz	Bos. 4 Hfd. 3
		Apr. 25/91	Bos.	3	Patrick Roy	Bos. 4 Mtl. 1
Petr Klima (3)	Det.	Apr. 7/88	Tor.	3	Allan Bester (2) Ken Wregget (1)	Det. 6 Tor. 2
		Apr. 21/88	St.L.	3	Greg Millen	Det. 6 St.L. 0
	Edm.	May 4/91	Edm.	3	Jon Casey	Edm. 7 Min. 2
Esa Tikkanen (3)	Edm.	May 22/88	Edm.	3	Reggie Lemelin	Edm. 6 Bos. 3
		Apr. 16/91	Cgy.	3	Mike Vernon	Edm. 5 Cgy. 4
		Apr. 26/92	L.A.	3	Kelly Hrudey (2) Tom Askey (1)	Edm. 5 L.A. 2
Mike Gartner (3)	NYR	Apr. 13/90	NYR	3	Mark Fitzpatrick (2) Glenn Healy (1)	NYR 6 NYI 5
		Apr. 27/92	NYR	3	Chris Terreri	NYR 8 N.J. 5
	Tor.	Apr. 25/96	Tor.	3	Jon Casey	Tor. 5 St.L. 4
Mario Lemieux (3)	Pit.	Apr. 25/89	Pit.	5	Ron Hextall	Pit. 10 Phi. 7
		Apr. 23/92	Pit.	3	Don Beaupre	Pit. 6 Wsh. 4
		May 11/96	Pit.	3	Mike Richter	Pit. 7 NYR 3
Patrick Marleau (3)	S.J.	Apr. 10/04	S.J.	3	Chris Osgood	S.J. 3 St.L. 1
		Apr. 22/04	S.J.	3	David Aebischer	S.J. 5 Col. 2
		Apr. 27/06	S.J.	3	Chris Mason	Nsh. 4 S.J. 5
Johan Franzen (3)	Det.	Apr. 26/08	Det.	3	Jose Theodore (2) Peter Budaj (1)	Det. 5 Col. 1
		May 1/08	Col.	3	Jose Theodore (1) Peter Budaj (2)	Det. 8 Col. 2
		May 6/10	Det.	4	Evgeni Nabokov (3) Thomas Greiss (1)	Det. 7 S.J. 1
Newsy Lalonde (2)	Mtl.	Mar. 1/19	Mtl.	5	Clint Benedict	Mtl. 6 Ott. 3
		Mar. 22/19	Sea.	4	Hap Holmes	Mtl. 4 Sea. 2
Howie Morenz (2)	Mtl.	Mar. 22/24	Mtl.	3	Charles Reid	Mtl. 6 Cgy.T. 1
		Mar. 27/25	Mtl.	3	Hap Holmes	Mtl. 4 Vic. 2
Doug Bentley (2)	Chi.	Mar. 28/44	Chi.	3	Connie Dion	Chi. 7 Det. 1
		Mar. 30/44	Chi.	3	Connie Dion	Chi. 5 Det. 2
Toe Blake (2)	Mtl.	Mar. 22/38	Mtl.	3	Mike Karakas	Mtl. 6 Chi. 4
		Mar. 26/46	Chi.	3	Mike Karakas	Mtl. 7 Chi. 2
Ted Kennedy (2)	Tor.	Apr. 14/45	Tor.	3	Harry Lumley	Det. 5 Tor. 3
		Apr. 27/48	Tor.	4	Frank Brimsek	Tor. 5 Bos. 3
F. St. Marseille (2)	St.L.	Apr. 28/70	St.L.	3	Al Smith	St.L. 5 Pit. 0
		Apr. 6/72	Min.	3	Cesare Maniago	Min. 6 St.L. 5
Bobby Hull (2)	Chi.	Apr. 7/63	Det.	3	Terry Sawchuk	Det. 7 Chi. 4
		Apr. 9/72	Pit.	3	Jim Rutherford	Chi. 6 Pit. 5
Pit Martin (2)	Chi.	Apr. 4/73	Chi.	3	Wayne Stephenson	Chi. 7 St.L. 1
		May 10/73	Chi.	3	Ken Dryden	Mtl. 6 Chi. 4
Yvan Cournoyer (2)	Mtl.	Apr. 5/73	Mtl.	3	Dave Dryden	Mtl. 7 Buf. 3
		Apr. 11/74	Mtl.	3	Ed Giacomin	Mtl. 4 NYR 1
Guy Lafleur (2)	Mtl.	May 1/75	Mtl.	3	Roger Crozier (1) Gerry Desjardins (2)	Mtl. 7 Buf. 0
		Apr. 11/77	Mtl.	3	Ed Staniowski	Mtl. 7 St.L. 2
Lanny McDonald (2)	Tor.	Apr. 9/77	Pit.	3	Denis Herron	Tor. 5 Pit. 2
		Apr. 17/77	Tor.	4	Wayne Stephenson	Phi. 6 Tor. 5
Bill Barber (2)	Phi.	May 4/80	Min.	4	Gilles Meloche	Phi. 5 Min. 3
		Apr. 9/81	Phi.	3	Dan Bouchard	Phi. 8 Que. 5
Bryan Trottier (2)	NYI	Apr. 8/80	NYI	3	Doug Keans	NYI 8 L.A. 1
		Apr. 9/81	NYI	3	Michel Larocque	NYI 5 Tor. 1
Butch Goring (2)	L.A.	Apr. 9/77	L.A.	3	Phil Myre	L.A. 4 Atl. 2
	NYI	May 17/81	Min.	3	Gilles Meloche	NYI 7 Min. 5
Paul Reinhart (2)	Cgy.	Apr. 14/83	Edm.	3	Andy Moog	Edm. 6 Cgy. 3
		Apr. 8/84	Van	3	Richard Brodeur	Cgy. 5 Van. 1
Brian Propp (2)	Phi.	Apr. 22/81	Phi.	3	Pat Riggin	Phi. 9 Cgy. 4
		Apr. 21/85	Phi.	3	Billy Smith	Phi. 5 NYI 2
Peter Stastny (2)	Que.	Apr. 5/83	Bos.	3	Pete Peeters	Bos. 4 Que. 3
		Apr. 11/87	Que.	3	Mike Liut (2) Steve Weeks (1)	Que. 5 Hfd. 1
Michel Goulet (2)	Que.	Apr. 23/85	Que.	3	Steve Penney	Que. 7 Mtl. 6
		Apr. 12/87	Que.	3	Mike Liut	Que. 4 Hfd. 1
Glenn Anderson (2)	Edm.	Apr. 26/83	Edm.	3	Murray Bannerman	Edm. 8 Chi. 2
		Apr. 6/88	Wpg.	3	Daniel Berthiaume	Edm. 7 Wpg. 4
Peter Zezel (2)	Phi.	Apr. 13/86	NYR	3	John Vanbiesbrouck	Phi. 7 NYR 4
	St.L.	Apr. 11/89	St.L.	3	Jon Casey (2) Kari Takko (1)	St.L. 6 Min. 1
Geoff Courtnall (2)	Van.	Apr. 4/91	L.A.	3	Kelly Hrudey	Van. 6 L.A. 5
		Apr. 30/92	Van.	3	Rick Tabaracci	Van. 5 Win. 0
Joe Sakic (2)	Que.	May 6/95	Que.	3	Mike Richter	Que. 5 NYR 4
	Col.	Apr. 25/96	Col.	3	Corey Hirsch	Col. 5 Van. 4
Daniel Alfredsson (2)	Ott.	Apr. 28/98	Ott.	3	Martin Brodeur	Ott. 4 N.J. 2
		May 11/98	Ott.	3	Olaf Kolzig	Ott. 4 Wsh. 3
Harry Meeking	Tor.	Mar. 11/18	Tor.	3	Georges Vezina	Tor. 7 Mtl. 3
Alf Skinner	Tor.	Mar. 23/18	Tor.	3	Hugh Lehman	Van.M. 6 Tor. 4
Joe Malone	Mtl.	Feb. 23/19	Mtl.	3	Clint Benedict	Mtl. 8 Ott. 4
Odie Cleghorn	Mtl.	Feb. 27/19	Ott.	3	Clint Benedict	Mtl. 5 Ott. 3
Jack Darragh	Ott.	Apr. 1/20	Tor.	3	Hap Holmes	Ott. 6 Sea. 1
George Boucher	Ott.	Mar. 10/21	Ott.	3	Jake Forbes	Ott. 5 Tor. 0
Babe Dye	Tor.	Mar. 28/22	Tor.	4	Hugh Lehman	Tor. 5 Van.M. 1
Percy Galbraith	Bos.	Mar. 31/27	Bos.	3	Hugh Lehman	Bos. 4 Chi. 4
Busher Jackson	Tor.	Apr. 5/32	NYR	3	John Ross Roach	Tor. 6 NYR 4
Frank Boucher	NYR	Apr. 9/32	Tor.	3	Lorne Chabot	Tor. 6 NYR 4
Charlie Conacher	Tor.	Mar. 26/36	Tor.	3	Tiny Thompson	Tor. 8 Bos. 3
Syd Howe	Det.	Mar. 23/39	Det.	3	Claude Bourque	Det. 7 Mtl. 3
Bryan Hextall	NYR	Mar. 3/40	NYR	3	Turk Broda	NYR 6 Tor. 2
Joe Benoit	Mtl.	Mar. 22/41	Mtl.	3	Sam LoPresti	Mtl. 4 Chi. 3
Syl Apps	Tor.	Mar. 25/41	Tor.	3	Frank Brimsek	Tor. 7 Bos. 2
Jack McGill	Bos.	Mar. 29/42	Bos.	3	Johnny Mowers	Bos. 4 Det. 3
Don Metz	Tor.	Apr. 14/42	Tor.	3	Johnny Mowers	Tor. 9 Det. 3
Mud Bruneteau	Det.	Apr. 1/43	Det.	3	Frank Brimsek	Det. 6 Bos. 2
Don Grosso	Det.	Apr. 7/43	Bos.	3	Frank Brimsek	Det. 4 Bos. 0
Carl Liscombe	Det.	Apr. 3/45	Bos.	4	Paul Bibeault	Det. 5 Bos. 3
Billy Reay	Mtl.	Apr. 1/47	Bos.	3	Frank Brimsek	Mtl. 5 Bos. 1

Three-or-more-Goal Games, Playoffs — *continued*

Player	Team	Date	City	Total Goals	Opposing Goaltender	Score	
Gerry Plamondon	Mtl.	Mar. 24/49	Det.	3	Harry Lumley	Mtl. 4	Det. 3
Sid Smith	Tor.	Apr. 10/49	Det.	3	Harry Lumley	Tor. 3	Det. 1
Pentti Lund	NYR	Apr. 2/50	NYR	3	Bill Durnan	NYR 4	Mtl. 1
Ted Lindsay	Det.	Apr. 5/55	Det.	4	Charlie Hodge (1) Jacques Plante (3)	Det. 7	Mtl. 1
Gordie Howe	Det.	Apr. 10/55	Det.	3	Jacques Plante	Det. 5	Mtl. 1
Phil Goyette	Mtl.	Mar. 25/58	Mtl.	3	Terry Sawchuk	Mtl. 8	Det. 1
Jerry Toppazzini	Bos.	Apr. 5/58	Bos.	3	Gump Worsley	Bos. 8	NYR 2
Bob Pulford	Tor.	Apr. 19/62	Tor.	3	Glenn Hall	Tor. 8	Chi. 4
Dave Keon	Tor.	Apr. 9/64	Mtl.	3	Charlie Hodge (2)	Tor. 3	Mtl. 1
Henri Richard	Mtl.	Apr. 20/67	Mtl.	3	Terry Sawchuk (2) Johnny Bower (1)	Mtl. 6	Tor. 2
Rosaire Paiement	Phi.	Apr. 13/68	Phi.	3	Glenn Hall (1) Seth Martin (2)	Phi. 6	St.L. 1
Jean Beliveau	Mtl.	Apr. 20/68	Mtl.	3	Denis DeJordy	Mtl. 4	Chi. 1
Red Berenson	St.L.	Apr. 15/69	St.L.	3	Gerry Desjardins	St.L. 4	L.A. 0
Ken Schinkel	Pit.	Apr. 11/70	Oak.	3	Gary Smith	Pit. 5	Oak. 2
Jim Pappin	Chi.	Apr. 11/71	Phi.	3	Bruce Gamble	Chi. 6	Phi. 2
Bobby Orr	Bos.	Apr. 11/71	Bos.	3	Ken Dryden	Bos. 5	Mtl. 2
Jacques Lemaire	Mtl.	Apr. 20/71	Mtl.	3	Gump Worsley	Mtl. 7	Min. 2
Vic Hadfield	NYR	Apr. 22/71	NYR	3	Tony Esposito	NYR 4	Chi. 1
Fred Stanfield	Bos.	Apr. 18/72	Bos.	3	Jacques Caron	Bos. 6	St.L. 1
Ken Hodge	Bos.	Apr. 30/72	Bos.	3	Ed Giacomin	Bos. 6	NYR 5
Dick Redmond	Chi.	Apr. 4/73	Chi.	3	Wayne Stephenson	Chi. 7	St.L. 1
Steve Vickers	NYR	Apr. 10/73	Bos.	3	Ross Brooks (2) Eddie Johnston (1)	NYR 6	Bos. 3
Tom Williams	L.A.	Apr. 14/74	L.A.	3	Mike Veisor	L.A. 5	Chi. 1
Marcel Dionne	L.A.	Apr. 15/76	L.A.	3	Gilles Gilbert	L.A. 6	Bos. 4
Don Saleski	Phi.	Apr. 20/76	Phi.	3	Wayne Thomas	Phi. 7	Tor. 1
Darryl Sittler	Tor.	Apr. 22/76	Tor.	5	Bernie Parent	Tor. 8	Phi. 5
Reggie Leach	Phi.	May 6/76	Phi.	5	Gilles Gilbert	Phi. 6	Bos. 3
Jim Lorentz	Buf.	Apr. 7/77	Min.	3	Pete LoPresti (2) Gary Smith (1)	Buf. 7	Min. 1
Bobby Schmautz	Bos.	Apr. 11/77	Bos.	3	Rogie Vachon	Bos. 8	L.A. 3
Billy Harris	NYI	Apr. 23/77	Mtl.	3	Ken Dryden	Mtl. 4	NYI 3
George Ferguson	Tor.	Apr. 11/78	Tor.	3	Rogie Vachon	Tor. 7	L.A. 3
Jean Ratelle	Bos.	May 3/79	Bos.	3	Ken Dryden	Bos. 4	Mtl. 3
Stan Jonathan	Bos.	May 8/79	Bos.	3	Ken Dryden	Bos. 5	Mtl. 2
Ron Duguay	NYR	Apr. 20/80	NYR	3	Pete Peeters	NYR 4	Phi. 2
Steve Shutt	Mtl.	Apr. 22/80	Mtl.	3	Gilles Meloche	Mtl. 6	Min. 2
Gilbert Perreault	Buf.	May 6/80	NYI	3	Billy Smith (2) ENG (1)	Buf. 7	NYI 4
Paul Holmgren	Phi.	May 15/80	Phi.	3	Billy Smith	Phi. 8	NYI 3
Steve Payne	Min.	Apr. 8/81	Bos.	3	Rogie Vachon	Min. 5	Bos. 4
Denis Potvin	NYI	Apr. 17/81	NYI	3	Andy Moog	NYI 6	Edm. 3
Barry Pederson	Bos.	Apr. 8/82	Bos.	3	Don Edwards	Bos. 7	Buf. 3
Duane Sutter	NYI	Apr. 15/83	NYI	3	Glen Hanlon	NYI 5	NYR 0
Doug Halward	Van.	Apr. 7/84	Van.	3	Reggie Lemelin (2) Don Edwards (1)	Van. 7	Cgy. 0
Jorgen Pettersson	St.L.	Apr. 8/84	Det.	3	Eddie Mio	St.L. 3	Det. 2
Clark Gillies	NYI	May 12/84	NYI	3	Grant Fuhr	NYI 6	Edm. 1
Ken Linseman	Bos.	Apr. 14/85	Bos.	3	Steve Penney	Bos. 7	Mtl. 6
Dave Andreychuk	Buf.	Apr. 14/85	Buf.	3	Dan Bouchard	Buf. 7	Que. 4
Greg Paslawski	St.L.	Apr. 15/86	Min.	3	Don Beaupre	St.L. 6	Min. 3
Doug Risebrough	Cgy.	May 4/86	Cgy.	3	Rick Wamsley	Cgy. 8	St.L. 2
Mike McPhee	Mtl.	Apr. 11/87	Bos.	3	Doug Keans	Mtl. 5	Bos. 4
John Ogrodnick	Que.	Apr. 14/87	Hfd.	3	Mike Liut	Que. 7	Hfd. 5
Pelle Eklund	Phi.	May 10/87	Mtl.	3	Patrick Roy (1) Brian Hayward (2)	Phi. 6	Mtl. 3
John Tucker	Buf.	Apr. 9/88	Bos.	4	Andy Moog	Buf. 6	Bos. 2
Tony Hrkac	St.L.	Apr. 10/88	St.L.	4	Darren Pang	St.L. 6	Chi. 5
Hakan Loob	Cgy.	Apr. 10/88	Cgy.	3	Glenn Healy	Cgy. 7	L.A. 3
Ed Olczyk	Tor.	Apr. 12/88	Tor.	3	Greg Stefan (2) Glen Hanlon (1)	Tor. 6	Det. 5
Aaron Broten	N.J.	Apr. 20/88	N.J.	3	Pete Peeters	N.J. 5	Wsh. 2
Mark Johnson	N.J.	Apr. 22/88	Wsh.	4	Pete Peeters	N.J. 10	Wsh. 4
Patrik Sundstrom	N.J.	Apr. 22/88	Wsh.	3	Pete Peeters (2) Clint Malarchuk (1)	N.J. 10	Wsh. 4
Bob Brooke	Min.	Apr. 5/89	St.L.	3	Greg Millen	St.L. 4	Min. 3
Chris Kontos	L.A.	Apr. 6/89	L.A.	3	Grant Fuhr	L.A. 5	Edm. 2
Wayne Presley	Chi.	Apr. 13/89	Chi.	3	Greg Stefan (1) Glen Hanlon (2)	Chi. 7	Det. 1
Tony Granato	L.A.	Apr. 10/90	L.A.	3	Mike Vernon (2) Rick Wamsley (2)	L.A. 12	Cgy. 4
Tomas Sandstrom	L.A.	Apr. 10/90	L.A.	3	Mike Vernon (1) Rick Wamsley (2)	L.A. 12	Cgy. 4
Dave Taylor	L.A.	Apr. 10/90	L.A.	3	Mike Vernon (1) Rick Wamsley (2)	L.A. 12	Cgy. 4
Bernie Nicholls	NYR	Apr. 19/90	NYR	3	Mike Liut	NYR 7	Wsh. 3
John Druce	Wsh.	Apr. 21/90	NYR	3	John Vanbiesbrouck	Wsh. 6	NYR 3
Adam Oates	St.L.	Apr. 12/91	St.L.	3	Tim Chevaldae	St.L. 6	Det. 1
Luc Robitaille	L.A.	Apr. 26/91	L.A.	3	Grant Fuhr	L.A. 5	Edm. 2
Ray Sheppard	Det.	Apr. 24/92	Min.	3	Jon Casey	Min. 5	Det. 2
Pavel Bure	Van.	Apr. 28/92	Wpg.	3	Rick Tabaracci	Van. 8	Wpg. 3
Joe Murphy	Edm.	May 6/92	Edm.	3	Kirk McLean	Edm. 5	Van. 2
Ron Francis	Pit.	May 9/92	Pit.	3	Mike Richter (2) John V'brouck (1)	Pit. 5	NYR. 4
Kevin Stevens	Pit.	May 21/92	Bos.	4	Andy Moog	Pit. 5	Bos. 2
Dirk Graham	Chi.	Jun. 1/92	Chi.	3	Tom Barrasso	Pit. 6	Chi. 5

Player	Team	Date	City	Total Goals	Opposing Goaltender	Score	
Brian Noonan	Chi.	Apr. 18/93	Chi.	3	Curtis Joseph	St.L. 4	Chi. 3
Dale Hunter	Wsh.	Apr. 20/93	Wsh.	3	Glenn Healy	NYI 5	Wsh. 4
Teemu Selanne	Wpg.	Apr. 23/93	Wpg.	3	Kirk McLean	Wpg. 5	Van. 4
Ray Ferraro	NYI	Apr. 26/93	Wsh.	4	Don Beaupre	Wsh. 6	NYI 4
Al Iafrate	Wsh.	Apr. 26/93	Wsh.	3	Glenn Healy (2) Mark Fitzpatrick (1)	Wsh. 6	NYI 4
Paul DiPietro	Mtl.	Apr. 28/93	Mtl.	3	Ron Hextall	Mtl. 6	Que. 2
Wendel Clark	Tor.	May 27/93	L.A.	3	Kelly Hrudey	L.A. 5	Tor. 4
Eric Desjardins	Mtl.	Jun. 3/93	Mtl.	3	Kelly Hrudey	Mtl. 3	L.A. 2
Tony Amonte	Chi.	Apr. 23/94	Chi.	3	Felix Potvin	Chi. 5	Tor. 4
Gary Suter	Chi.	Apr. 24/94	Chi.	3	Felix Potvin	Chi. 4	Tor. 3
Ulf Dahlen	S.J.	May 6/94	S.J.	3	Felix Potvin	S.J. 5	Tor. 2
Mike Sullivan	Cgy.	May 11/95	S.J.	3	Arturs Irbe (2) Wade Flaherty (1)	Cgy. 9	S.J. 2
Theoren Fleury	Cgy.	May 13/95	S.J.	4	Arturs Irbe (3) ENG (1)	Cgy. 6	S.J. 4
Brendan Shanahan	St.L.	May 13/95	Van.	3	Kirk McLean	St.L. 5	Van. 2
John LeClair	Phi.	May 21/95	Phi.	3	Mike Richter	Phi. 5	NYR 4
Brian Leetch	NYR	May 22/95	Phi.	3	Ron Hextall	Phi. 4	NYR 3
Trevor Linden	Van.	Apr. 25/96	Col.	3	Patrick Roy	Col. 5	Van. 4
Jaromir Jagr	Pit.	May 11/96	Pit.	3	Mike Richter	Pit. 7	NYR 3
Peter Forsberg	Col.	Jun. 6/96	Col.	3	John Vanbiesbrouck	Col. 8	Fla. 1
Valeri Zelepukin	N.J.	Apr. 22/97	Mtl.	3	Jocelyn Thibault	N.J. 6	Mtl. 4
Valeri Kamensky	Col.	Apr. 24/97	Col.	3	Jeff Hackett (2) Chris Terreri (1)	Col. 7	Chi. 0
Eric Lindros	Phi.	May 20/97	NYR	3	Mike Richter	Phi. 6	NYR 3
Matthew Barnaby	Buf.	May 10/98	Buf.	3	Andy Moog (2) ENG (1)	Buf. 6	Mtl. 3
Martin Straka	Pit.	Apr. 25/99	Pit.	3	Martin Brodeur	Pit. 4	N.J. 2
Martin Lapointe	Det.	Apr. 15/00	Det.	3	Stephane Fiset (2) Jamie Storr (1)	Det. 8	L.A. 5
Doug Weight	Edm.	Apr. 16/00	Edm.	3	Ed Belfour	Edm. 5	Dal. 2
Bill Guerin	Edm.	Apr. 18/00	Edm.	3	Ed Belfour	Dal. 4	Edm. 3
Scott Young	St.L.	Apr. 23/00	S.J.	3	Steve Shields	St.L. 6	S.J. 2
Andy Delmore	Phi.	May 7/00	Phi.	3	Ron Tugnutt (2) Peter Skudra (1)	Phi. 6	Pit. 3
Brett Hull	Det.	Apr. 27/02	Van.	3	Peter Skudra	Det. 6	Van. 4
Keith Tkachuk	St.L.	May 7/02	St.L.	3	Dominik Hasek	St.L. 6	Det. 1
Darren McCarty	Det.	May 18/02	Det.	3	Patrick Roy	Det. 5	Col. 3
Alexander Mogilny	Tor.	Apr. 9/03	Phi.	3	Roman Cechmanek (2) ENG (1)	Tor. 5	Phi. 3
Mike Sillinger	St.L.	May 12/04	St.L.	3	Evgeni Nabokov (2) ENG (1)	St.L. 4	S.J. 1
Keith Primeau	Phi.	May 2/04	Phi.	3	Ed Belfour (2) Trevor Kidd (1)	Phi. 7	Tor. 2
J.P. Dumont	Buf.	Apr. 24/06	Buf.	3	Antero Niittymaki (1) Robert Esche (2)	Phi. 2	Buf. 8
John Madden	N.J.	Apr. 24/06	N.J.	3	Kevin Weekes	NYR 1	N.J. 4
Jason Pominville	Buf.	Apr. 24/06	Buf.	3	Antero Niittymaki (2) Robert Esche (1)	Phi. 2	Buf. 8
Joffrey Lupul	Ana.	May 9/06	Col.	4	Jose Theodore	Ana. 4	Col. 3
Michael Nylander	NYR	Apr. 17/07	NYR	3	Kari Lehtonen	NYR 7	Atl. 0
Andy McDonald	Ana.	Apr. 25/07	Ana.	3	Dany Sabourin (1) Roberto Luongo (2)	Ana. 5	Van. 1
Pavel Datsyuk	Det.	May 12/08	Dal.	3	Marty Turco	Det. 5	Dal. 2
Alex Ovechkin	Wsh.	May 4/09	Wsh.	3	Marc-Andre Fleury	Wsh. 4	Pit. 3
Sidney Crosby	Pit.	May 4/09	Wsh.	3	Semyon Varlamov	Wsh. 4	Pit. 3
Patrick Kane	Chi.	May 11/09	Chi.	3	Roberto Luongo	Chi. 7	Van. 5
Evgeni Malkin	Pit.	May 21/09	Pit.	3	Cam Ward	Pit. 7	Car. 4
Henrik Zetterberg	Det.	Apr. 16/10	Phx.	3	Ilya Bryzgalov	Det. 7	Phx. 4
Andrei Kostitsyn	Mtl.	Apr. 17/10	Wsh.	3	Jose Theodore (1) Semyon Varlamov (2)	Wsh. 6	Mtl. 5
Nicklas Backstrom	Wsh.	Apr. 17/10	Wsh.	3	Jaroslav Halak	Wsh. 6	Mtl. 5
Dustin Byfuglien	Chi.	May 5/10	Van.	3	Roberto Luongo	Chi. 5	Van. 2
Jonathan Toews	Chi.	May 7/10	Van.	3	Roberto Luongo	Chi. 7	Van. 4
Devin Setoguchi	S.J.	May 4/11	Det.	3	Jimmy Howard	S.J. 4	Det. 3
David Krejci	Bos.	May 25/11	T.B.	3	Dwayne Roloson	T.B. 5	Bos. 4

Devin Setoguchi was one of only two players to score a hat trick in the 2011 playoffs and one of three (along with Nathan Horton and Alexandre Burrows) to score a pair of overtime goals.

Overtime Games since 1918

Abbreviations: Teams/Cities: — **Ana.** - Anaheim; **Atl.** - Atlanta; **Bos.** - Boston; **Buf.** - Buffalo; **Cgy.** - Calgary; **Cgy. T.** - Calgary Tigers (Western Canada Hockey League); **Car.** - Carolina; **Chi.** - Chicago; **Col.** - Colorado; **Dal.** - Dallas; **Det.** - Detroit; **Edm.** - Edmonton; **Edm. E.** - Edmonton Eskimos (WCHL); **Fla.** - Florida; **Hfd.** - Hartford; **L.A.** - Los Angeles; **Min.** - Minnesota; **Mtl.** - Montreal; **Mtl. M.** - Montreal Maroons; **Nsh.** - Nashville, **N.J.** - New Jersey; **NYA** - NY Americans; **NYI** - New York Islanders; **NYR** - New York Rangers; **Oak.** - Oakland; **Ott.** - Ottawa; **Phi.** - Philadelphia; **Phx.** - Phoenix; **Pit.** - Pittsburgh; **Que.** - Quebec; **St.L.** - St. Louis; **Sea.** - Seattle Metropolitans (Pacific Coast Hockey Association); **S.J.** - San Jose; **T.B.** - Tampa Bay; **Tor.** - Toronto; **Van.** - Vancouver; **Van. M.** - Vancouver Millionaires (PCHA); **Vic.** - Victoria Cougars (WCHL); **Wpg.** - Winnipeg; **Wsh.** - Washington.

SERIES — **CF** - conference final; **CQF** - conference quarter-final; **CSF** - conference semi-final; **DF** - division final; **DSF** - division semi-final; **F** - final; **PRE** - preliminary round; **QF** - quarter-final; **SF** - semi-final.

Date	City	Series	Score		Scorer	Overtime	Series Winner
Mar. 26/19	Sea.	F	Mtl. 0	Sea. 0	no scorer	20:00	....
Mar. 29/19	Sea.	F	Mtl. 4	Sea. 3	Jack McDonald	15:57	....
Mar. 20/22	Tor.	F	Tor. 2	Van. M. 1	Babe Dye	4:50	Tor.
Mar. 29/23	Van.	F	Ott. 2	Edm. E. 1	Cy Denneny	2:08	Ott.
Mar. 31/27	Mtl.	QF	Mtl. 1	Mtl. M. 0	Howie Morenz	12:05	Mtl.
Apr. 7/27	Bos.	F	Ott. 0	Bos. 0	no scorer	20:00	Ott.
Apr. 11/27	Ott.	F	Bos. 1	Ott. 1	no scorer	20:00	Ott.
Apr. 3/28	Mtl.	QF	Mtl. M. 1	Mtl. 0	Russell Oatman	8:20	Mtl. M.
Apr. 7/28	Mtl.	F	NYR 2	Mtl. M. 1	Frank Boucher	7:05	NYR
Mar. 21/29	NYR	QF	NYR 1	NYA 0	Butch Keeling	29:50	NYR
Mar. 26/29	Tor.	SF	NYR 2	Tor. 1	Frank Boucher	2:03	NYR
Mar. 20/30	Mtl.	SF	Bos. 2	Mtl. M. 1	Harry Oliver	45:35	Bos.
Mar. 25/30	Bos.	SF	Mtl. M. 1	Bos. 0	Archie Wilcox	26:27	Bos.
Mar. 26/30	Mtl.	QF	Chi. 2	Mtl. 2	Howie Morenz (Mtl.)	51:43	Mtl.
Mar. 28/30	Mtl.	SF	Mtl. 2	NYR 1	Gus Rivers	68:52	Mtl.
Mar. 24/31	Bos.	SF	Bos. 5	Mtl. 4	Cooney Weiland	18:56	Mtl.
Mar. 26/31	Chi.	QF	Chi. 2	Tor. 1	Stew Adams	19:20	Chi.
Mar. 28/31	Mtl.	SF	Mtl. 4	Bos. 3	Georges Mantha	5:10	Mtl.
Apr. 1/31	Mtl.	SF	Mtl. 3	Bos. 2	Wildor Larochelle	19:00	Mtl.
Apr. 5/31	Chi.	F	Chi. 2	Mtl. 1	Johnny Gottselig	24:50	Mtl.
Apr. 9/31	Mtl.	F	Chi. 3	Mtl. 2	Cy Wentworth	53:50	Mtl.
Mar. 26/32	Mtl.	SF	NYR 4	Mtl. 3	Fred Cook	59:32	NYR
Apr. 2/32	Tor.	SF	Tor. 3	Mtl. M. 2	Bob Gracie	17:59	Tor.
Mar. 25/33	Bos.	SF	Bos. 2	Tor. 1	Marty Barry	14:14	Tor.
Mar. 28/33	Bos.	SF	Tor. 1	Bos. 0	Busher Jackson	15:03	Tor.
Mar. 30/33	Tor.	SF	Bos. 2	Tor. 1	Eddie Shore	4:23	Tor.
Apr. 3/33	Tor.	SF	Tor. 1	Bos. 0	Ken Doraty	104:46	Tor.
Apr. 13/33	Tor.	F	NYR 1	Tor. 0	Bill Cook	7:33	NYR
Mar. 22/34	Tor.	SF	Det. 2	Tor. 1	Herbie Lewis	1:33	Det.
Mar. 25/34	Chi.	QF	Chi. 1	Mtl. 1	Mush March (Chi)	11:05	Chi.
Apr. 3/34	Det.	F	Chi. 2	Det. 1	Paul Thompson	21:10	Chi.
Apr. 10/34	Chi.	F	Chi. 1	Det. 0	Mush March	30:05	Chi.
Mar. 23/35	Bos.	SF	Bos. 1	Tor. 0	Dit Clapper	33:26	Tor.
Mar. 26/35	Chi.	QF	Mtl. M. 1	Chi. 0	Baldy Northcott	4:02	Mtl. M.
Mar. 30/35	Tor.	SF	Tor. 2	Bos. 1	Pep Kelly	1:36	Tor.
Apr. 4/35	Tor.	F	Mtl. M. 3	Tor. 2	Dave Trottier	5:28	Mtl. M.
Mar. 24/36	Mtl.	SF	Det. 1	Mtl. M. 0	Mud Bruneteau	116:30	Det.
Apr. 9/36	Tor.	F	Tor. 4	Det. 3	Buzz Boll	0:31	Det.
Mar. 25/37	NYR	QF	NYR 2	Tor. 1	Babe Pratt	13:05	NYR
Apr. 1/37	Mtl.	SF	Det. 2	Mtl. 1	Hec Kilrea	51:49	Det.
Mar. 22/38	NYR	QF	NYA 2	NYR 1	John Sorrell	21:25	NYA
Mar. 24/38	Tor.	SF	Tor. 1	Bos. 0	George Parsons	21:31	Tor.
Mar. 26/38	Mtl.	QF	Chi. 3	Mtl. 2	Paul Thompson	11:49	Chi.
Mar. 27/38	NYR	QF	NYA 3	NYR 2	Lorne Carr	60:40	NYA
Mar. 29/38	Bos.	SF	Tor. 3	Bos. 2	Gordie Drillon	10:04	Tor.
Mar. 31/38	Chi.	SF	Chi. 1	NYA 0	Cully Dahlstrom	33:01	Chi.
Mar. 21/39	NYR	SF	Bos. 2	NYR 1	Mel Hill	59:25	Bos.
Mar. 23/39	Bos.	SF	Bos. 3	NYR 2	Mel Hill	8:24	Bos.
Mar. 26/39	Det.	QF	Det. 1	Mtl. 0	Marty Barry	7:47	Det.
Mar. 30/39	Bos.	SF	NYR 2	Bos. 1	Clint Smith	17:19	Bos.
Apr. 1/39	Tor.	SF	Tor. 5	Det. 4	Gordie Drillon	5:42	Tor.
Apr. 2/39	Bos.	SF	Bos. 2	NYR 1	Mel Hill	48:00	Bos.
Apr. 9/39	Bos.	F	Tor. 3	Bos. 2	Doc Romnes	10:38	Bos.
Mar. 19/40	Det.	QF	Det. 2	NYA 1	Syd Howe	0:25	Det.
Mar. 19/40	Tor.	QF	Tor. 3	Chi. 2	Syl Apps	6:35	Tor.
Apr. 2/40	NYR	F	NYR 2	Tor. 1	Alf Pike	15:30	NYR
Apr. 11/40	Tor.	F	NYR 2	Tor. 1	Muzz Patrick	31:43	NYR
Apr. 13/40	Tor.	F	NYR 3	Tor. 2	Bryan Hextall	2:07	NYR
Mar. 20/41	Det.	QF	Det. 2	NYR 1	Syd Howe	12:01	Det.
Mar. 22/41	Mtl.	QF	Mtl. 4	Chi. 3	Charlie Sands	34:04	Chi.
Mar. 29/41	Bos.	SF	Tor. 2	Bos. 1	Pete Langelle	17:31	Bos.
Mar. 30/41	Chi.	SF	Det. 2	Chi. 1	Gus Giesebrecht	9:15	Det.
Mar. 22/42	Chi.	QF	Bos. 2	Chi. 1	Des Smith	6:51	Bos.
Mar. 21/43	Bos.	SF	Bos. 5	Mtl. 4	Don Gallinger	12:30	Bos.
Mar. 23/43	Det.	SF	Tor. 3	Det. 2	Jack McLean	70:18	Det.
Mar. 25/43	Mtl.	SF	Bos. 3	Mtl. 2	Busher Jackson	3:20	Bos.
Mar. 30/43	Tor.	SF	Det. 3	Tor. 2	Adam Brown	9:21	Det.
Mar. 30/43	Bos.	SF	Bos. 5	Mtl. 4	Ab DeMarco	3:41	Bos.
Apr. 13/44	Mtl.	F	Mtl. 5	Chi. 4	Toe Blake	9:12	Mtl.
Mar. 27/45	Tor.	SF	Tor. 4	Mtl. 3	Gus Bodnar	12:36	Tor.
Mar. 29/45	Det.	SF	Det. 3	Bos. 2	Mud Bruneteau	17:12	Det.
Apr. 21/45	Tor.	F	Det. 1	Tor. 0	Eddie Bruneteau	14:16	Tor.
Mar. 28/46	Bos.	SF	Bos. 4	Det. 3	Don Gallinger	9:51	Bos.
Mar. 30/46	Mtl.	F	Mtl. 4	Bos. 3	Maurice Richard	9:08	Mtl.
Apr. 2/46	Mtl.	F	Mtl. 3	Bos. 2	Jimmy Peters	16:55	Mtl.
Apr. 7/46	Bos.	F	Bos. 3	Mtl. 2	Terry Reardon	15:13	Mtl.
Mar. 26/47	Tor.	SF	Tor. 3	Det. 2	Howie Meeker	3:05	Tor.
Mar. 27/47	Mtl.	SF	Mtl. 2	Bos. 1	Ken Mosdell	5:38	Mtl.
Apr. 3/47	Mtl.	SF	Mtl. 4	Bos. 3	John Quilty	36:40	Mtl.
Apr. 15/47	Tor.	F	Tor. 2	Mtl. 1	Syl Apps	16:36	Tor.
Mar. 24/48	Tor.	SF	Tor. 5	Bos. 4	Nick Metz	17:03	Tor.
Mar. 22/49	Det.	SF	Det. 2	Mtl. 1	Max McNab	44:52	Det.
Mar. 24/49	Det.	SF	Mtl. 4	Det. 3	Gerry Plamondon	2:59	Det.
Mar. 26/49	Tor.	SF	Bos. 5	Tor. 4	Woody Dumart	16:14	Tor.
Apr. 8/49	Det.	F	Tor. 3	Det. 2	Joe Klukay	17:31	Tor.
Apr. 4/50	Tor.	SF	Det. 2	Tor. 1	Leo Reise Jr.	20:38	Det.
Apr. 4/50	Mtl.	SF	Mtl. 3	NYR 2	Elmer Lach	15:19	NYR
Apr. 9/50	Det.	SF	Det. 1	Tor. 0	Leo Reise Jr.	8:39	Det.
Apr. 18/50	Det.	F	NYR 4	Det. 3	Don Raleigh	8:34	Det.
Apr. 20/50	Det.	F	NYR 2	Det. 1	Don Raleigh	1:38	Det.
Apr. 23/50	Det.	F	Det. 4	NYR 3	Pete Babando	28:31	Det.
Mar. 27/51	Det.	SF	Mtl. 3	Det. 2	Maurice Richard	61:09	Mtl.
Mar. 29/51	Det.	SF	Mtl. 1	Det. 0	Maurice Richard	42:20	Mtl.
Mar. 31/51	Tor.	SF	Bos. 1	Tor. 1	no scorer	20:00	Tor.
Apr. 11/51	Tor.	F	Tor. 3	Mtl. 2	Sid Smith	5:51	Tor.
Apr. 14/51	Tor.	F	Mtl. 3	Tor. 2	Maurice Richard	2:55	Tor.
Apr. 17/51	Mtl.	F	Tor. 2	Mtl. 1	Ted Kennedy	4:47	Tor.
Apr. 19/51	Mtl.	F	Tor. 3	Mtl. 2	Harry Watson	5:15	Tor.
Apr. 21/51	Tor.	F	Tor. 3	Mtl. 2	Bill Barilko	2:53	Tor.
Apr. 6/52	Bos.	SF	Mtl. 3	Bos. 2	Paul Masnick	27:49	Mtl.
Mar. 29/53	Bos.	SF	Bos. 2	Det. 1	Jack McIntyre	12:29	Bos.
Mar. 29/53	Chi.	SF	Chi. 2	Mtl. 1	Al Dewsbury	5:18	Mtl.
Apr. 16/53	Mtl.	F	Mtl. 1	Bos. 0	Elmer Lach	1:22	Mtl.
Apr. 1/54	Det.	SF	Det. 4	Tor. 3	Ted Lindsay	21:01	Det.
Apr. 11/54	Det.	F	Mtl. 1	Det. 0	Ken Mosdell	5:45	Det.
Apr. 16/54	Det.	F	Det. 2	Mtl. 1	Tony Leswick	4:29	Det.
Mar. 29/55	Bos.	SF	Mtl. 4	Bos. 3	Don Marshall	3:05	Mtl.
Mar. 24/56	Tor.	SF	Det. 5	Tor. 4	Ted Lindsay	4:22	Det.
Mar. 28/57	NYR	SF	NYR 4	Mtl. 3	Andy Hebenton	13:38	Mtl.
Apr. 4/57	Mtl.	SF	Mtl. 4	NYR 3	Maurice Richard	1:11	Mtl.
Mar. 27/58	NYR	SF	Bos. 4	NYR 3	Jerry Toppazzini	4:46	Bos.
Mar. 30/58	Det.	SF	Mtl. 2	Det. 1	André Pronovost	11:52	Mtl.
Apr. 17/58	Mtl.	F	Mtl. 3	Bos. 2	Maurice Richard	5:45	Mtl.
Mar. 28/59	Tor.	SF	Tor. 3	Bos. 2	Gerry Ehman	5:02	Tor.
Mar. 31/59	Tor.	SF	Tor. 3	Bos. 2	Frank Mahovlich	11:21	Tor.
Apr. 14/59	Tor.	F	Tor. 3	Mtl. 2	Dick Duff	10:06	Mtl.
Mar. 26/60	Mtl.	SF	Mtl. 4	Chi. 3	Doug Harvey	8:38	Mtl.
Mar. 27/60	Det.	SF	Tor. 5	Det. 4	Frank Mahovlich	43:00	Tor.
Mar. 29/60	Det.	SF	Det. 2	Tor. 1	Gerry Melnyk	1:54	Tor.
Mar. 22/61	Tor.	SF	Tor. 3	Det. 2	George Armstrong	24:51	Det.
Mar. 26/61	Chi.	SF	Chi. 2	Mtl. 1	Murray Balfour	52:12	Chi.
Apr. 5/62	Tor.	SF	Tor. 3	NYR 2	Red Kelly	24:23	Tor.
Apr. 2/64	Det.	SF	Chi. 3	Det. 2	Murray Balfour	8:21	Det.
Apr. 14/64	Tor.	F	Det. 4	Tor. 3	Larry Jeffrey	7:52	Tor.
Apr. 23/64	Det.	F	Tor. 4	Det. 3	Bob Baun	1:43	Tor.
Apr. 6/65	Tor.	SF	Tor. 3	Mtl. 2	Dave Keon	4:17	Mtl.
Apr. 13/65	Tor.	SF	Mtl. 4	Tor. 3	Claude Provost	16:33	Mtl.
May 5/66	Det.	F	Mtl. 3	Det. 2	Henri Richard	2:20	Mtl.
Apr. 13/67	NYR	SF	Mtl. 2	NYR 1	John Ferguson	6:28	Mtl.
Apr. 25/67	Tor.	F	Tor. 3	Mtl. 2	Bob Pulford	28:26	Tor.
Apr. 10/68	St.L.	QF	St.L. 3	Phi. 2	Larry Keenan	24:10	St.L.
Apr. 16/68	St.L.	QF	Phi. 2	St.L. 1	Don Blackburn	31:18	St.L.
Apr. 16/68	Min.	QF	Min. 4	L.A. 3	Milan Marcetta	9:11	Min.
Apr. 22/68	Min.	SF	Min. 3	St.L. 2	Parker MacDonald	3:41	St.L.
Apr. 27/68	St.L.	SF	St.L. 4	Min. 3	Gary Sabourin	1:32	St.L.
Apr. 28/68	Mtl.	SF	Mtl. 4	Chi. 3	Jacques Lemaire	2:14	Mtl.
Apr. 29/68	St.L.	SF	St.L. 3	Min. 2	Bill McCreary	17:27	St.L.
May 3/68	St.L.	SF	St.L. 2	Min. 1	Ron Schock	22:50	St.L.
May 5/68	St.L.	F	Mtl. 3	St.L. 2	Jacques Lemaire	1:41	Mtl.
May 9/68	Mtl.	F	Mtl. 4	St.L. 3	Bobby Rousseau	1:13	Mtl.
Apr. 2/69	Oak.	QF	L.A. 5	Oak. 4	Ted Irvine	0:19	L.A.
Apr. 10/69	Mtl.	SF	Mtl. 3	Bos. 2	Ralph Backstrom	0:42	Mtl.
Apr. 13/69	Mtl.	SF	Mtl. 4	Bos. 3	Mickey Redmond	4:55	Mtl.
Apr. 24/69	Bos.	SF	Mtl. 2	Bos. 1	Jean Béliveau	31:28	Mtl.
Apr. 12/70	Oak.	QF	Pit. 3	Oak. 2	Michel Briere	8:28	Pit.
May 10/70	Bos.	F	Bos. 4	St.L. 3	Bobby Orr	0:40	Bos.
Apr. 15/71	Tor.	QF	NYR 2	Tor. 1	Bob Nevin	9:07	NYR
Apr. 18/71	Chi.	SF	NYR 2	Chi. 1	Pete Stemkowski	1:37	Chi.
Apr. 27/71	Chi.	SF	Chi. 3	NYR 2	Bobby Hull	6:35	Chi.
Apr. 29/71	NYR	SF	NYR 3	Chi. 2	Pete Stemkowski	41:29	Chi.
May 4/71	Chi.	F	Chi. 2	Mtl. 1	Jim Pappin	21:11	Mtl.
Apr. 6/72	Bos.	QF	Tor. 4	Bos. 3	Jim Harrison	2:58	Bos.
Apr. 6/72	Min.	QF	Min. 6	St.L. 5	Bill Goldsworthy	1:36	St.L.
Apr. 9/72	Pit.	QF	Chi. 6	Pit. 5	Pit Martin	0:12	Chi.
Apr. 16/72	Min.	QF	St.L. 2	Min. 1	Kevin O'Shea	10:07	St.L.
Apr. 1/73	Mtl.	QF	Buf. 3	Mtl. 2	René Robert	9:18	Mtl.
Apr. 10/73	Phi.	QF	Phi. 3	Min. 2	Gary Dornhoefer	8:35	Phi.
Apr. 14/73	Mtl.	SF	Phi. 5	Mtl. 4	Rick MacLeish	2:56	Mtl.
Apr. 17/73	Mtl.	SF	Mtl. 4	Phi. 3	Larry Robinson	6:45	Mtl.
Apr. 14/74	Tor.	QF	Bos. 4	Tor. 3	Ken Hodge	1:27	Bos.
Apr. 14/74	Atl.	QF	Phi. 4	Atl. 3	Dave Schultz	5:40	Phi.
Apr. 16/74	Mtl.	QF	NYR 3	Mtl. 2	Ron Harris	4:07	NYR
Apr. 23/74	Chi.	SF	Chi. 4	Bos. 3	Jim Pappin	3:48	Bos.
Apr. 28/74	NYR	SF	NYR 2	Phi. 1	Rod Gilbert	4:20	Phi.
May 9/74	Bos.	F	Phi. 3	Bos. 2	Bobby Clarke	12:01	Phi.
Apr. 8/75	L.A.	PRE	L.A. 3	Tor. 2	Mike Murphy	8:53	Tor.
Apr. 10/75	Tor.	PRE	Tor. 3	L.A. 2	Blaine Stoughton	10:19	Tor.
Apr. 10/75	Chi.	PRE	Chi. 4	Bos. 3	Ivan Boldirev	7:33	Chi.
Apr. 11/75	NYR	PRE	NYI 4	NYR 3	J.P. Parise	0:11	NYI
Apr. 17/75	Chi.	QF	Chi. 5	Buf. 4	Stan Mikita	2:31	Buf.
Apr. 19/75	Tor.	QF	Phi. 4	Tor. 3	André Dupont	1:45	Phi.
Apr. 22/75	Mtl.	QF	Mtl. 5	Van. 4	Guy Lafleur	17:06	Mtl.
Apr. 27/75	Buf.	SF	Buf. 6	Mtl. 5	Danny Gare	4:42	Buf.
May 1/75	Phi.	SF	Phi. 5	NYI 4	Bobby Clarke	2:56	Phi.
May 6/75	Buf.	SF	Buf. 5	Mtl. 4	René Robert	5:56	Buf.
May 7/75	NYI	SF	NYI 4	Phi. 3	Jude Drouin	1:53	Phi.
May 20/75	Buf.	F	Buf. 5	Phi. 4	René Robert	18:29	Phi.
Apr. 8/76	Buf.	PRE	Buf. 3	St.L. 2	Danny Gare	11:43	Buf.

Overtime Games since 1918 — *continued*

Date	City	Series	Score		Scorer	Overtime	Series Winner
Apr. 9/76	Buf.	PRE	Buf. 2	St.L. 1	Don Luce	14:27	Buf.
Apr. 13/76	Bos.	QF	L.A. 3	Bos. 2	Butch Goring	0:27	Bos.
Apr. 13/76	Buf.	QF	Buf. 3	NYI 2	Danny Gare	14:04	NYI
Apr. 22/76	L.A.	QF	L.A. 4	Bos. 3	Butch Goring	18:28	Bos.
Apr. 29/76	Phi.	SF	Phi. 2	Bos. 1	Reggie Leach	13:38	Phi.
Apr. 15/77	Tor.	QF	Phi. 4	Tor. 3	Rick MacLeish	2:55	Phi.
Apr. 17/77	Tor.	QF	Phi. 6	Tor. 5	Reggie Leach	19:10	Phi.
Apr. 24/77	Phi.	SF	Bos. 4	Phi. 3	Rick Middleton	2:57	Bos.
Apr. 26/77	Phi.	SF	Bos. 5	Phi. 4	Terry O'Reilly	30:07	Bos.
May 3/77	Mtl.	SF	NYI 4	Mtl. 3	Billy Harris	3:58	Mtl.
May 14/77	Bos.	F	Mtl. 2	Bos. 1	Jacques Lemaire	4:32	Mtl.
Apr. 11/78	Phi.	PRE	Phi. 3	Col. 2	Mel Bridgman	0:23	Phi.
Apr. 13/78	NYR	PRE	NYR 4	Buf. 3	Don Murdoch	1:37	Buf.
Apr. 19/78	Bos.	QF	Bos. 4	Chi. 3	Terry O'Reilly	1:50	Bos.
Apr. 19/78	NYI	QF	NYI 3	Tor. 2	Mike Bossy	2:50	Tor.
Apr. 21/78	Chi.	QF	Bos. 4	Chi. 3	Peter McNab	10:17	Bos.
Apr. 25/78	NYI	QF	NYI 2	Tor. 1	Bob Nystrom	8:02	Tor.
Apr. 29/78	NYI	QF	Tor. 2	NYI 1	Lanny McDonald	4:13	Tor.
May 2/78	Bos.	SF	Bos. 3	Phi. 2	Rick Middleton	1:43	Bos.
May 16/78	Mtl.	F	Mtl. 3	Bos. 2	Guy Lafleur	13:09	Mtl.
May 21/78	Bos.	F	Bos. 4	Mtl. 3	Bobby Schmautz	6:22	Mtl.
Apr. 12/79	L.A.	PRE	NYR 2	L.A. 1	Phil Esposito	6:11	NYR
Apr. 14/79	Buf.	PRE	Pit. 4	Buf. 3	George Ferguson	0:47	Pit.
Apr. 16/79	Phi.	QF	Phi. 3	NYR 2	Ken Linseman	0:44	NYR
Apr. 18/79	NYI	QF	NYI 1	Chi. 0	Mike Bossy	2:31	NYI
Apr. 21/79	Tor.	QF	Mtl. 4	Tor. 3	Cam Connor	25:25	Mtl.
Apr. 22/79	Tor.	QF	Mtl. 5	Tor. 4	Larry Robinson	4:14	Mtl.
Apr. 28/79	NYI	SF	NYI 4	NYR 3	Denis Potvin	8:02	NYR
May 3/79	NYR	SF	NYI 3	NYR 2	Bob Nystrom	3:40	NYR
May 3/79	Bos.	SF	Bos. 4	Mtl. 3	Jean Ratelle	3:46	Mtl.
May 10/79	Mtl.	SF	Mtl. 5	Bos. 4	Yvon Lambert	9:33	Mtl.
May 19/79	NYR	F	Mtl. 4	NYR 3	Serge Savard	7:25	Mtl.
Apr. 8/80	NYR	PRE	NYR 2	Atl. 1	Steve Vickers	0:33	NYR
Apr. 8/80	Phi.	PRE	Phi. 4	Edm. 3	Bobby Clarke	8:06	Phi.
Apr. 8/80	Chi.	PRE	Chi. 3	St.L. 2	Doug Lecuyer	12:34	Chi.
Apr. 11/80	Hfd.	PRE	Mtl. 4	Hfd. 3	Yvon Lambert	0:29	Mtl.
Apr. 11/80	Tor.	PRE	Min. 4	Tor. 3	Al MacAdam	0:32	Min.
Apr. 11/80	L.A.	PRE	NYI 4	L.A. 3	Ken Morrow	6:55	NYI
Apr. 11/80	Edm.	PRE	Phi. 3	Edm. 2	Ken Linseman	23:56	Phi.
Apr. 16/80	Bos.	QF	NYI 2	Bos. 1	Clark Gillies	1:02	NYI
Apr. 17/80	Bos.	QF	NYI 5	Bos. 4	Bob Bourne	1:24	NYI
Apr. 21/80	NYI	QF	Bos. 4	NYI 3	Terry O'Reilly	17:13	NYI
May 1/80	Buf.	SF	NYI 2	Buf. 1	Bob Nystrom	21:20	NYI
May 13/80	Phi.	F	NYI 4	Phi. 3	Denis Potvin	4:07	NYI
May 24/80	NYI	F	NYI 5	Phi. 4	Bob Nystrom	7:11	NYI
Apr. 8/81	Buf.	PRE	Buf. 3	Van. 2	Alan Haworth	5:00	Buf.
Apr. 8/81	Bos.	PRE	Min. 5	Bos. 4	Steve Payne	3:34	Min.
Apr. 11/81	Chi.	PRE	Cgy. 5	Chi. 4	Willi Plett	35:17	Cgy.
Apr. 12/81	Que.	PRE	Que. 4	Phi. 3	Dale Hunter	0:37	Phi.
Apr. 14/81	St.L.	PRE	St.L. 4	Pit. 3	Mike Crombeen	25:16	St.L.
Apr. 16/81	Buf.	QF	Min. 4	Buf. 3	Steve Payne	0:22	Min.
Apr. 20/81	Min.	QF	Buf. 5	Min. 4	Craig Ramsay	16:32	Min.
Apr. 20/81	Edm.	QF	NYI 5	Edm. 4	Ken Morrow	5:41	NYI
Apr. 7/82	Min.	DSF	Chi. 3	Min. 2	Greg Fox	3:34	Chi.
Apr. 8/82	Edm.	DSF	Edm. 3	L.A. 2	Wayne Gretzky	6:20	L.A.
Apr. 8/82	Van.	DSF	Van. 2	Cgy. 1	Tiger Williams	14:20	Van.
Apr. 10/82	Pit.	DSF	Pit. 2	NYI 1	Rick Kehoe	4:14	NYI
Apr. 10/82	L.A.	DSF	L.A. 6	Edm. 5	Daryl Evans	2:35	L.A.
Apr. 13/82	Mtl.	DSF	Que. 3	Mtl. 2	Dale Hunter	0:22	Que.
Apr. 13/82	NYI	DSF	NYI 4	Pit. 3	John Tonelli	6:19	NYI
Apr. 16/82	Van.	DF	L.A. 3	Van. 2	Steve Bozek	4:33	Van.
Apr. 18/82	Que.	DF	Que. 3	Bos. 2	Wilf Paiement	11:44	Que.
Apr. 18/82	NYR	DF	NYI 4	NYR 3	Bryan Trottier	3:00	NYI
Apr. 18/82	L.A.	DF	Van. 4	L.A. 3	Colin Campbell	1:23	Van.
Apr. 21/82	St.L.	DF	St.L. 3	Chi. 2	Bernie Federko	3:28	Chi.
Apr. 23/82	Que.	DF	Bos. 6	Que. 5	Peter McNab	10:54	Que.
Apr. 27/82	Chi.	CF	Van. 2	Chi. 1	Jim Nill	28:58	Van.
May 1/82	Que.	CF	NYI 5	Que. 4	Wayne Merrick	16:52	NYI
May 8/82	NYI	F	NYI 6	Van. 5	Mike Bossy	19:58	NYI
Apr. 5/83	Bos.	DSF	Bos. 4	Que. 3	Barry Pederson	1:46	Bos.
Apr. 6/83	Cgy.	DSF	Cgy. 4	Van. 3	Eddy Beers	12:27	Cgy.
Apr. 7/83	Min.	DSF	Min. 5	Tor. 4	Bobby Smith	5:03	Min.
Apr. 10/83	Tor.	DSF	Min. 5	Tor. 4	Dino Ciccarelli	8:05	Min.
Apr. 10/83	Van.	DSF	Cgy. 4	Van. 3	Greg Meredith	1:06	Cgy.
Apr. 18/83	Min.	DF	Chi. 4	Min. 3	Rich Preston	10:34	Chi.
Apr. 24/83	Bos.	DF	Bos. 3	Buf. 2	Brad Park	1:52	Bos.
Apr. 5/84	Edm.	DSF	Edm. 5	Wpg. 4	Randy Gregg	0:21	Edm.
Apr. 7/84	Det.	DSF	St.L. 4	Det. 3	Mark Reeds	37:07	St.L.
Apr. 8/84	Det.	DSF	St.L. 3	Det. 2	Jorgen Pettersson	2:42	St.L.
Apr. 10/84	NYI	DSF	NYI 3	NYR 2	Ken Morrow	8:56	NYI
Apr. 13/84	Min.	DF	St.L. 4	Min. 3	Doug Gilmour	16:16	Min.
Apr. 13/84	Edm.	DF	Cgy. 6	Edm. 5	Carey Wilson	3:42	Edm.
Apr. 13/84	NYI	DF	NYI 5	Wsh. 4	Anders Kallur	7:35	NYI
Apr. 16/84	Mtl.	DF	Que. 4	Mtl. 3	Bo Berglund	3:00	Mtl.
Apr. 20/84	Cgy.	DF	Cgy. 5	Edm. 4	Lanny McDonald	1:04	Edm.
Apr. 22/84	Min.	DF	Min. 4	St.L. 3	Steve Payne	6:00	Min.
Apr. 10/85	Phi.	DSF	Phi. 5	NYR 4	Mark Howe	8:01	Phi.
Apr. 10/85	Wsh.	DSF	Wsh. 4	NYI 3	Alan Haworth	2:28	NYI
Apr. 10/85	Edm.	DSF	Edm. 3	L.A. 2	Lee Fogolin	3:01	Edm.
Apr. 10/85	Wpg.	DSF	Wpg. 5	Cgy. 4	Brian Mullen	7:56	Wpg.
Apr. 11/85	Wsh.	DSF	Wsh. 2	NYI 1	Mike Gartner	21:23	NYI
Apr. 13/85	L.A.	DSF	Edm. 4	L.A. 3	Glenn Anderson	0:46	Edm.
Apr. 18/85	Mtl.	DF	Que. 2	Mtl. 1	Mark Kumpel	12:23	Que.
Apr. 23/85	Que.	DF	Que. 7	Mtl. 6	Dale Hunter	18:36	Que.

Date	City	Series	Score		Scorer	Overtime	Series Winner
Apr. 25/85	Min.	DF	Chi. 7	Min. 6	Darryl Sutter	21:57	Chi.
Apr. 28/85	Chi.	DF	Min. 5	Chi. 4	Dennis Maruk	1:14	Chi.
Apr. 30/85	Min.	DF	Chi. 6	Min. 5	Darryl Sutter	15:41	Chi.
May 2/85	Mtl.	DF	Que. 3	Mtl. 2	Peter Stastny	2:22	Que.
May 5/85	Que.	CF	Que. 2	Phi. 1	Peter Stastny	6:20	Phi.
Apr. 9/86	Que.	DSF	Hfd. 3	Que. 2	Sylvain Turgeon	2:36	Hfd.
Apr. 12/86	Wpg.	DSF	Cgy. 4	Wpg. 3	Lanny McDonald	8:25	Cgy.
Apr. 17/86	Wsh.	DF	NYR 4	Wsh. 3	Brian MacLellan	1:16	NYR
Apr. 20/86	Edm.	DF	Edm. 6	Cgy. 5	Glenn Anderson	1:04	Cgy.
Apr. 23/86	Hfd.	DF	Hfd. 2	Mtl. 1	Kevin Dineen	1:07	Mtl.
Apr. 23/86	NYR	DF	NYR 6	Wsh. 5	Bob Brooke	2:40	NYR
Apr. 26/86	St L.	DF	St L. 4	Tor. 3	Mark Reeds	7:11	St L.
Apr. 29/86	Mtl.	DF	Mtl. 2	Hfd. 1	Claude Lemieux	5:55	Mtl.
May 5/86	NYR	CF	Mtl. 4	NYR 3	Claude Lemieux	9:41	Mtl.
May 12/86	St L.	CF	St L. 6	Cgy. 5	Doug Wickenheiser	7:30	Cgy.
May 18/86	Cgy.	F	Mtl. 3	Cgy. 2	Brian Skrudland	0:09	Mtl.
Apr. 8/87	Hfd.	DSF	Hfd. 3	Que. 2	Paul MacDermid	2:20	Que.
Apr. 9/87	Mtl.	DSF	Mtl. 4	Bos. 3	Mats Naslund	2:38	Mtl.
Apr. 9/87	St.L.	DSF	Tor. 3	St.L. 2	Rick Lanz	10:17	Tor.
Apr. 11/87	Wpg.	DSF	Cgy. 3	Wpg. 2	Mike Bullard	3:53	Wpg.
Apr. 11/87	Chi.	DSF	Det. 4	Chi. 3	Shawn Burr	4:51	Det.
Apr. 16/87	Que.	DSF	Que. 5	Hfd. 4	Peter Stastny	6:05	Que.
Apr. 18/87	Wsh.	DSF	NYI 3	Wsh. 2	Pat LaFontaine	68:47	NYI
Apr. 21/87	Edm.	DF	Edm. 3	Wpg. 2	Glenn Anderson	0:36	Edm.
Apr. 26/87	Que.	DF	Mtl. 3	Que. 2	Mats Naslund	5:30	Mtl.
Apr. 27/87	Tor.	DF	Tor. 3	Det. 2	Mike Allison	9:31	Det.
May 4/87	Phi.	CF	Phi. 4	Mtl. 3	Ilkka Sinislao	9:11	Phi.
May 20/87	Edm.	F	Edm. 3	Phi. 2	Jari Kurri	6:50	Edm.
Apr. 6/88	NYI	DSF	NYI 4	N.J. 3	Pat LaFontaine	6:11	N.J.
Apr. 10/88	Phi.	DSF	Phi. 5	Wsh. 4	Murray Craven	1:18	Wsh.
Apr. 10/88	N.J.	DSF	NYI 5	N.J. 4	Brent Sutter	15:07	N.J.
Apr. 10/88	Buf.	DSF	Buf. 6	Bos. 5	John Tucker	5:32	Bos.
Apr. 12/88	Det.	DSF	Tor. 6	Det. 5	Ed Olczyk	0:34	Det.
Apr. 16/88	Wsh.	DSF	Wsh. 5	Phi. 4	Dale Hunter	5:57	Wsh.
Apr. 21/88	Cgy.	DF	Edm. 5	Cgy. 4	Wayne Gretzky	7:54	Edm.
May 4/88	Bos.	CF	N.J. 3	Bos. 2	Doug Brown	17:46	Bos.
May 9/88	Det.	CF	Edm. 4	Det. 3	Jari Kurri	11:02	Edm.
Apr. 5/89	St.L.	DSF	St.L. 4	Min. 3	Brett Hull	11:55	St.L.
Apr. 5/89	Cgy.	DSF	Van. 4	Cgy. 3	Paul Reinhart	2:47	Cgy.
Apr. 6/89	St.L.	DSF	St.L. 4	Min. 3	Rick Meagher	5:30	St.L.
Apr. 6/89	Det.	DSF	Chi. 5	Det. 4	Duane Sutter	14:36	Chi.
Apr. 8/89	Hfd.	DSF	Mtl. 5	Hfd. 4	Stephane Richer	5:01	Mtl.
Apr. 8/89	Phi.	DSF	Wsh. 4	Phi. 3	Kelly Miller	0:51	Phi.
Apr. 9/89	Hfd.	DSF	Mtl. 4	Hfd. 3	Russ Courtnall	15:12	Mtl.
Apr. 15/89	Cgy.	DSF	Cgy. 4	Van. 3	Joel Otto	19:21	Cgy.
Apr. 18/89	Cgy.	DF	Cgy. 4	L.A. 3	Doug Gilmour	7:47	Cgy.
Apr. 19/89	Mtl.	DF	Mtl. 3	Bos. 2	Bobby Smith	12:24	Mtl.
Apr. 20/89	St.L.	DF	St.L. 5	Chi. 4	Tony Hrkac	33:49	Chi.
Apr. 21/89	Phi.	DF	Pit. 4	Phi. 3	Phil Bourque	12:08	Phi.
May 8/89	Chi.	CF	Cgy. 2	Chi. 1	Al MacInnis	15:05	Cgy.
May 9/89	Mtl.	CF	Phi. 2	Mtl. 1	Dave Poulin	5:02	Mtl.
May 19/89	Mtl.	F	Mtl. 4	Cgy. 3	Ryan Walter	38:08	Cgy.
Apr. 5/90	N.J.	DSF	Wsh. 5	N.J. 4	Dino Ciccarelli	5:34	Wsh.
Apr. 6/90	Edm.	DSF	Edm. 3	Wpg. 2	Mark Lamb	4:21	Edm.
Apr. 8/90	Tor.	DSF	St.L. 6	Tor. 5	Sergio Momesso	6:04	St.L.
Apr. 8/90	L.A.	DSF	L.A. 2	Cgy. 1	Tony Granato	8:37	L.A.
Apr. 9/90	Mtl.	DSF	Mtl. 2	Buf. 1	Brian Skrudland	12:35	Mtl.
Apr. 9/90	NYI	DSF	NYI 4	NYR 3	Brent Sutter	20:59	NYR
Apr. 10/90	Wpg.	DSF	Wpg. 4	Edm. 3	Dave Ellett	21:08	Edm.
Apr. 14/90	L.A.	DSF	L.A. 4	Cgy. 3	Mike Krushelnyski	23:14	L.A.
Apr. 15/90	Hfd.	DSF	Hfd. 3	Bos. 2	Kevin Dineen	12:30	Bos.
Apr. 21/90	Bos.	DF	Bos. 5	Mtl. 4	Garry Galley	3:42	Bos.
Apr. 24/90	L.A.	DF	Edm. 6	L.A. 5	Joe Murphy	4:42	Edm.
Apr. 25/90	Wsh.	DF	Wsh. 4	NYR 3	Rod Langway	0:34	Wsh.
Apr. 27/90	NYR	DF	Wsh. 2	NYR 1	John Druce	6:48	Wsh.
May 15/90	Bos.	F	Edm. 3	Bos. 2	Petr Klima	55:13	Edm.
Apr. 4/91	Chi.	DSF	Min. 4	Chi. 3	Brian Propp	4:14	Min.
Apr. 5/91	Pit.	DSF	Pit. 5	N.J. 4	Jaromir Jagr	8:52	Pit.
Apr. 6/91	L.A.	DSF	L.A. 3	Van. 2	Wayne Gretzky	11:08	L.A.
Apr. 8/91	Van.	DSF	Van. 2	L.A. 1	Cliff Ronning	3:12	L.A.
Apr. 11/91	NYR	DSF	Wsh. 5	NYR 4	Dino Ciccarelli	6:44	Wsh.
Apr. 11/91	Mtl.	DSF	Mtl. 4	Buf. 3	Russ Courtnall	5:56	Mtl.
Apr. 14/91	Edm.	DSF	Cgy. 2	Edm. 1	Theoren Fleury	4:40	Edm.
Apr. 16/91	Cgy.	DSF	Edm. 5	Cgy. 4	Esa Tikkanen	6:58	Edm.
Apr. 18/91	L.A.	DF	L.A. 4	Edm. 3	Luc Robitaille	2:13	Edm.
Apr. 19/91	Bos.	DF	Mtl. 4	Bos. 3	Stephane Richer	0:27	Bos.
Apr. 19/91	Pit.	DF	Pit. 7	Wsh. 6	Kevin Stevens	8:10	Pit.
Apr. 20/91	L.A.	DF	Edm. 4	L.A. 3	Petr Klima	24:48	Edm.
Apr. 22/91	Edm.	DF	Edm. 4	L.A. 3	Esa Tikkanen	20:48	Edm.
Apr. 27/91	Mtl.	DF	Mtl. 3	Bos. 2	Shayne Corson	17:47	Bos.
Apr. 28/91	Edm.	DF	Edm. 4	L.A. 3	Craig MacTavish	16:57	Edm.
May 3/91	Bos.	CF	Bos. 5	Pit. 4	Vladimir Ruzicka	8:14	Pit.
Apr. 21/92	Bos.	DSF	Bos. 3	Buf. 2	Adam Oates	11:14	Bos.
Apr. 22/92	Min.	DSF	Det. 5	Min. 4	Yves Racine	1:15	Det.
Apr. 22/92	St.L.	DSF	St.L. 5	Chi. 4	Brett Hull	23:33	Chi.
Apr. 25/92	Buf.	DSF	Bos. 5	Buf. 4	Ted Donato	2:08	Bos.
Apr. 28/92	Min.	DSF	Det. 1	Min. 0	Sergei Fedorov	16:13	Det.
Apr. 29/92	Hfd.	DSF	Hfd. 2	Mtl. 1	Yvon Corriveau	0:24	Mtl.
May 1/92	Mtl.	DSF	Mtl. 3	Hfd. 2	Russ Courtnall	25:26	Mtl.
May 3/92	Van.	DF	Edm. 4	Van. 3	Joe Murphy	8:36	Edm.
May 5/92	Mtl.	DF	Bos. 3	Mtl. 2	Peter Douris	3:12	Bos.
May 7/92	Pit.	DF	NYR 6	Pit. 5	Kris King	1:29	Pit.
May 9/92	Pit.	DF	Pit. 5	NYR 4	Ron Francis	2:47	Pit.
May 17/92	Pit.	CF	Pit. 4	Bos. 3	Jaromir Jagr	9:44	Pit.

Overtime Games since 1918 — *continued*

Date	City	Series	Score		Scorer	Overtime	Series Winner
May 20/92	Edm.	CF	Chi. 4	Edm. 3	Jeremy Roenick	2:45	Chi.
Apr. 18/93	Bos.	DSF	Buf. 5	Bos. 4	Bob Sweeney	11:03	Buf.
Apr. 18/93	Que.	DSF	Que. 3	Mtl. 2	Scott Young	16:49	Mtl.
Apr. 20/93	Wsh.	DSF	NYI 5	Wsh. 4	Brian Mullen	34:50	NYI
Apr. 22/93	Mtl.	DSF	Mtl. 2	Que. 1	Vincent Damphousse	10:30	Mtl.
Apr. 22/93	Buf.	DSF	Buf. 4	Bos. 3	Yuri Khmylev	1:05	Buf.
Apr. 22/93	NYI	DSF	NYI 4	Wsh. 3	Ray Ferraro	4:46	NYI
Apr. 24/93	Buf.	DSF	Buf. 6	Bos. 5	Brad May	4:48	Buf.
Apr. 24/93	NYI	DSF	NYI 4	Wsh. 3	Ray Ferraro	25:40	NYI
Apr. 25/93	St.L.	DSF	St.L. 4	Chi. 3	Craig Janney	10:43	St.L.
Apr. 26/93	Que.	DSF	Mtl. 5	Que. 4	Kirk Muller	8:17	Mtl.
Apr. 27/93	Det.	DSF	Tor. 5	Det. 4	Mike Foligno	2:05	Tor.
Apr. 27/93	Van.	DSF	Wpg. 4	Van. 3	Teemu Selanne	6:18	Van.
Apr. 29/93	Wpg.	DSF	Van. 4	Wpg. 3	Greg Adams	4:30	Van.
May 1/93	Det.	DSF	Tor. 4	Det. 3	Nikolai Borschevsky	2:35	Tor.
May 3/93	Tor.	DF	Tor. 2	St.L. 1	Doug Gilmour	23:16	Tor.
May 4/93	Mtl.	DF	Mtl. 4	Buf. 3	Guy Carbonneau	2:50	Mtl.
May 5/93	Tor.	DF	St.L. 2	Tor. 1	Jeff Brown	23:03	Tor.
May 6/93	Buf.	DF	Mtl. 4	Buf. 3	Gilbert Dionne	8:28	Mtl.
May 8/93	Buf.	DF	Mtl. 4	Buf. 3	Kirk Muller	11:37	Mtl.
May 11/93	Van.	DF	L.A. 4	Van. 3	Gary Shuchuk	26:31	L.A.
May 14/93	Pit.	DF	NYI 4	Pit. 3	Dave Volek	5:16	NYI
May 18/93	Mtl.	CF	Mtl. 4	NYI 3	Stephan Lebeau	26:21	Mtl.
May 20/93	NYI	CF	Mtl. 2	NYI 1	Guy Carbonneau	12:34	Mtl.
May 25/93	Tor.	CF	Tor. 3	L.A. 2	Glenn Anderson	19:20	L.A.
May 27/93	L.A.	CF	L.A. 5	Tor. 4	Wayne Gretzky	1:41	L.A.
Jun. 3/93	Mtl.	F	Mtl. 3	L.A. 2	Eric Desjardins	0:51	Mtl.
Jun. 5/93	L.A.	F	Mtl. 4	L.A. 3	John LeClair	0:34	Mtl.
Jun. 7/93	L.A.	F	Mtl. 3	L.A. 2	John LeClair	14:37	Mtl.
Apr. 20/94	Tor.	CQF	Tor. 1	Chi. 0	Todd Gill	2:15	Tor.
Apr. 22/94	St.L.	CQF	Dal. 5	St.L. 4	Paul Cavallini	8:34	Dal.
Apr. 24/94	Chi.	CQF	Chi. 4	Tor. 3	Jeremy Roenick	1:23	Tor.
Apr. 25/94	Bos.	CQF	Mtl. 2	Bos. 1	Kirk Muller	17:18	Bos.
Apr. 26/94	Cgy.	CQF	Van. 2	Cgy. 1	Geoff Courtnall	7:15	Van.
Apr. 27/94	Buf.	CQF	Buf. 1	N.J. 0	Dave Hannan	65:43	N.J.
Apr. 28/94	Van.	CQF	Van. 3	Cgy. 2	Trevor Linden	16:43	Van.
Apr. 30/94	Cgy.	CQF	Van. 4	Cgy. 3	Pavel Bure	22:20	Van.
May 3/94	N.J.	CSF	Bos. 6	N.J. 5	Don Sweeney	9:08	N.J.
May 7/94	Bos.	CSF	N.J. 5	Bos. 4	Stephane Richer	14:19	N.J.
May 8/94	Van.	CSF	Van. 2	Dal. 1	Sergio Momesso	11:01	Van.
May 12/94	Tor.	CSF	Tor. 3	S.J. 2	Mike Gartner	8:53	Tor.
May 15/94	NYR	CF	N.J. 4	NYR 3	Stephane Richer	35:23	NYR
May 16/94	Tor.	CF	Tor. 3	Van. 2	Peter Zezel	16:55	Van.
May 19/94	N.J.	CF	NYR 3	N.J. 2	Stephane Matteau	26:13	NYR
May 24/94	Van.	CF	Van. 4	Tor. 3	Greg Adams	20:14	Van.
May 27/94	NYR	CF	NYR 2	N.J. 1	Stephane Matteau	24:24	NYR
May 31/94	NYR	F	Van. 3	NYR 2	Greg Adams	19:26	NYR
May 7/95	Phi.	CQF	Phi. 4	Buf. 3	Karl Dykhuis	10:06	Phi.
May 9/95	Cgy.	CQF	S.J. 5	Cgy. 4	Ulf Dahlen	12:21	S.J.
May 12/95	NYR	CQF	NYR 3	Que. 2	Steve Larmer	8:09	NYR
May 12/95	N.J.	CQF	N.J. 1	Bos. 0	Randy McKay	8:51	N.J.
May 14/95	Pit.	CQF	Pit. 6	Wsh. 5	Luc Robitaille	4:30	Pit.
May 15/95	St.L.	CQF	Van. 6	St.L. 5	Cliff Ronning	1:48	Van.
May 17/95	Tor.	CQF	Tor. 5	Chi. 4	Randy Wood	10:00	Chi.
May 19/95	Cgy.	CQF	S.J. 5	Cgy. 4	Ray Whitney	21:54	S.J.
May 21/95	Phi.	CSF	Phi. 5	NYR 4	Eric Desjardins	7:03	Phi.
May 21/95	Chi.	CSF	Chi. 2	Van. 1	Joe Murphy	9:04	Chi.
May 22/95	Phi.	CSF	Phi. 4	NYR 3	Kevin Haller	0:25	Phi.
May 25/95	Van.	CSF	Chi. 3	Van. 2	Chris Chelios	6:22	Chi.
May 26/95	N.J.	CSF	N.J. 2	Pit. 1	Neal Broten	18:36	N.J.
May 27/95	Van.	CSF	Chi. 4	Van. 3	Chris Chelios	5:35	Chi.
Jun. 1/95	Det.	CF	Det. 2	Chi. 1	Nicklas Lidstrom	1:01	Det.
Jun. 6/95	Chi.	CF	Det. 4	Chi. 3	Vladimir Konstantinov	29:25	Det.
Jun. 7/95	N.J.	CF	Phi. 3	N.J. 2	Eric Lindros	4:19	N.J.
Jun. 11/95	Det.	CF	Det. 2	Chi. 1	Vyacheslav Kozlov	22:25	Det.
Apr. 16/96	NYR	CQF	Mtl. 3	NYR 2	Vincent Damphousse	5:04	NYR
Apr. 18/96	Tor.	CQF	Tor. 5	St.L. 4	Mats Sundin	4:02	St.L.
Apr. 18/96	Phi.	CQF	T.B. 2	Phi. 1	Brian Bellows	9:05	Phi.
Apr. 21/96	St.L.	CQF	St.L. 3	Tor. 2	Glenn Anderson	1:24	St.L.
Apr. 21/96	T.B.	CQF	T.B. 5	Phi. 4	Alexander Selivanov	2:04	Phi.
Apr. 23/96	Cgy.	CQF	Chi. 2	Cgy. 1	Joe Murphy	50:02	Chi.
Apr. 24/96	Wsh.	CQF	Pit. 3	Wsh. 2	Petr Nedved	79:15	Pit.
Apr. 25/96	Col.	CQF	Col. 5	Van. 4	Joe Sakic	0:51	Col.
Apr. 25/96	Tor.	CQF	Tor. 5	St.L. 4	Mike Gartner	7:31	St.L.
May 2/96	Col.	CSF	Chi. 3	Col. 2	Jeremy Roenick	6:29	Col.
May 6/96	Chi.	CSF	Chi. 4	Col. 3	Sergei Krivokrasov	0:46	Col.
May 8/96	St.L.	CSF	St.L. 5	Det. 4	Igor Kravchuk	3:23	Det.
May 8/96	Chi.	CSF	Col. 3	Chi. 2	Joe Sakic	44:33	Col.
May 9/96	Fla.	CSF	Fla. 4	Phi. 3	Dave Lowry	4:06	Fla.
May 12/96	Phi.	CSF	Fla. 2	Phi. 1	Mike Hough	28:05	Fla.
May 13/96	Chi.	CSF	Col. 4	Chi. 3	Sandis Ozolinsh	25:18	Col.
May 16/96	Det.	CSF	Det. 1	St.L. 0	Steve Yzerman	21:15	Det.
May 19/96	Det.	CF	Col. 3	Det. 2	Mike Keane	17:31	Col.
Jun. 10/96	Fla.	F	Col. 1	Fla. 0	Uwe Krupp	44:31	Col.
Apr. 20/97	Chi.	CQF	Chi. 4	Col. 3	Sergei Krivokrasov	31:03	Col.
Apr. 20/97	Edm.	CQF	Edm. 4	Dal. 3	Kelly Buchberger	9:15	Edm.
Apr. 22/97	NYR	CQF	NYR 4	Fla. 3	Esa Tikkanen	16:29	NYR
Apr. 23/97	Ott.	CQF	Ott. 1	Buf. 0	Daniel Alfredsson	2:34	Buf.
Apr. 24/97	Mtl.	CQF	Mtl. 4	N.J. 3	Patrice Brisebois	47:37	N.J.
Apr. 25/97	Fla.	CQF	NYR 3	Fla. 2	Esa Tikkanen	12:02	NYR
Apr. 25/97	Dal.	CQF	Edm. 1	Dal. 0	Ryan Smyth	20:22	Edm.
Apr. 27/97	Phx.	CQF	Ana. 3	Phx. 2	Paul Kariya	7:29	Ana.
Apr. 29/97	Buf.	CQF	Buf. 3	Ott. 2	Derek Plante	5:24	Buf.
Apr. 29/97	Dal.	CQF	Edm. 4	Dal. 3	Todd Marchant	12:26	Edm.

Date	City	Series	Score		Scorer	Overtime	Series Winner
May 2/97	Det.	CSF	Det. 2	Ana. 1	Martin Lapointe	0:59	Det.
May 4/97	Det.	CSF	Det. 3	Ana. 2	Vyacheslav Kozlov	41:31	Det.
May 8/97	Ana.	CSF	Det. 3	Ana. 2	Brendan Shanahan	37:03	Det.
May 9/97	Phi.	CSF	Buf. 5	Phi. 4	Ed Ronan	6:24	Phi.
May 9/97	Edm.	CSF	Col. 3	Edm. 2	Claude Lemieux	8:35	Col.
May 11/97	N.J.	CSF	NYR 2	N.J. 1	Adam Graves	14:08	NYR
Apr. 22/98	N.J.	CQF	Ott. 2	N.J. 1	Bruce Gardiner	5:58	Ott.
Apr. 23/98	Pit.	CQF	Mtl. 3	Pit. 2	Benoit Brunet	18:43	Mtl.
Apr. 24/98	Wsh.	CQF	Bos. 4	Wsh. 3	Darren Van Impe	20:54	Wsh.
Apr. 26/98	Ott.	CQF	Ott. 2	N.J. 1	Alexei Yashin	2:47	Ott.
Apr. 26/98	Bos.	CQF	Wsh. 3	Bos. 2	Joe Juneau	26:31	Wsh.
Apr. 26/98	Edm.	CQF	Col. 5	Edm. 4	Joe Sakic	15:25	Edm.
Apr. 28/98	S.J.	CQF	S.J. 1	Dal. 0	Andrei Zyuzin	6:31	Dal.
May 1/98	Phi.	CQF	Buf. 3	Phi. 2	Michal Grosek	5:40	Buf.
May 2/98	S.J.	CQF	Dal. 3	S.J. 2	Mike Keane	3:43	Dal.
May 3/98	Bos.	CQF	Wsh. 3	Bos. 2	Brian Bellows	15:24	Wsh.
May 3/98	Buf.	CSF	Buf. 3	Mtl. 2	Geoff Sanderson	2:37	Buf.
May 11/98	Edm.	CSF	Dal. 1	Edm. 0	Benoit Hogue	13:07	Dal.
May 12/98	Mtl.	CSF	Buf. 5	Mtl. 4	Michael Peca	21:24	Buf.
May 12/98	St.L.	CSF	Det. 3	St.L. 2	Brendan Shanahan	31:12	Det.
May 25/98	Wsh.	CF	Wsh. 3	Buf. 2	Todd Krygier	3:01	Wsh.
May 28/98	Buf.	CF	Wsh. 4	Buf. 3	Peter Bondra	9:37	Wsh.
Jun. 3/98	Dal.	CF	Dal. 3	Det. 2	Jamie Langenbrunner	0:46	Det.
Jun. 4/98	Buf.	CF	Wsh. 3	Buf. 2	Joe Juneau	6:24	Wsh.
Jun. 11/98	Det.	F	Det. 5	Wsh. 4	Kris Draper	15:24	Det.
Apr. 23/99	Ott.	CQF	Buf. 3	Ott. 2	Miroslav Satan	30:35	Buf.
Apr. 24/99	Car.	CQF	Car. 3	Bos. 2	Ray Sheppard	17:05	Bos.
Apr. 24/99	Phx.	CQF	Phx. 4	St.L. 3	Shane Doan	8:58	St.L.
Apr. 26/99	S.J.	CQF	Col. 2	S.J. 1	Milan Hejduk	7:53	Col.
Apr. 27/99	Edm.	CQF	Dal. 3	Edm. 2	Joe Nieuwendyk	57:34	Dal.
Apr. 30/99	Tor.	CQF	Tor. 2	Phi. 1	Yanic Perreault	11:51	Tor.
Apr. 30/99	Car.	CQF	Bos. 4	Car. 3	Anson Carter	34:45	Bos.
Apr. 30/99	Phx.	CQF	St.L. 2	Phx. 1	Scott Young	5:43	St.L.
May 2/99	Pit.	CQF	Pit. 3	N.J. 2	Jaromir Jagr	8:59	Pit.
May 3/99	S.J.	CQF	Col. 3	S.J. 2	Milan Hejduk	13:12	Col.
May 4/99	Phx.	CQF	St.L. 1	Phx. 0	Pierre Turgeon	17:59	St.L.
May 7/99	Col.	CSF	Det. 3	Col. 2	Kirk Maltby	4:18	Col.
May 8/99	Dal.	CSF	Dal. 5	St.L. 4	Joe Nieuwendyk	8:22	Dal.
May 10/99	St.L.	CSF	St.L. 3	Dal. 2	Pavol Demitra	2:43	Dal.
May 12/99	St.L.	CSF	St.L. 3	Dal. 2	Pierre Turgeon	5:52	Dal.
May 13/99	Pit.	CSF	Tor. 3	Pit. 2	Sergei Berezin	2:18	Tor.
May 17/99	Pit.	CSF	Tor. 4	Pit. 3	Garry Valk	1:57	Tor.
May 17/99	St.L.	CSF	Dal. 2	St.L. 1	Mike Modano	2:21	Dal.
May 28/99	Col.	CF	Col. 3	Dal. 2	Chris Drury	19:29	Dal.
Jun. 8/99	Dal.	F	Buf. 3	Dal. 2	Jason Woolley	15:30	Dal.
Jun. 19/99	Buf.	F	Dal. 2	Buf. 1	Brett Hull	54:51	Dal.
Apr. 15/00	Pit.	CQF	Pit. 2	Wsh. 1	Jaromir Jagr	5:49	Pit.
Apr. 18/00	Buf.	CQF	Buf. 3	Phi. 2	Stu Barnes	4:42	Phi.
Apr. 22/00	Tor.	CQF	Tor. 2	Ott. 1	Steve Thomas	14:47	Tor.
May 2/00	Pit.	CSF	Phi. 4	Pit. 3	Andy Delmore	11:01	Phi.
May 3/00	Det.	CSF	Col. 3	Det. 2	Chris Drury	10:21	Col.
May 4/00	Pit.	CSF	Phi. 2	Pit. 1	Keith Primeau	92:01	Phi.
May 23/00	Dal.	CF	Dal. 3	Col. 2	Joe Nieuwendyk	12:10	Dal.
Jun. 8/00	N.J.	F	Dal. 1	N.J. 0	Mike Modano	46:21	N.J.
Jun. 10/00	Dal.	F	N.J. 2	Dal. 1	Jason Arnott	28:20	N.J.
Apr. 11/01	Dal.	CQF	Dal. 2	Edm. 1	Jamie Langenbrunner	2:08	Dal.
Apr. 13/01	Ott.	CQF	Tor. 1	Ott. 0	Mats Sundin	10:49	Tor.
Apr. 14/01	Phi.	CQF	Buf. 4	Phi. 3	Jay McKee	18:02	Buf.
Apr. 15/01	Edm.	CQF	Dal. 3	Edm. 2	Benoit Hogue	19:48	Dal.
Apr. 16/01	Tor.	CQF	Tor. 3	Ott. 2	Cory Cross	2:16	Tor.
Apr. 16/01	Van.	CQF	Col. 4	Van. 3	Peter Forsberg	2:50	Col.
Apr. 17/01	Buf.	CQF	Buf. 4	Phi. 3	Curtis Brown	6:13	Buf.
Apr. 17/01	Edm.	CQF	Edm. 2	Dal. 1	Mike Comrie	17:19	Dal.
Apr. 18/01	Car.	CQF	Car. 3	N.J. 2	Rod Brind'Amour	:46	N.J.
Apr. 18/01	Pit.	CQF	Wsh. 4	Pit. 3	Jeff Halpern	4:01	Pit.
Apr. 18/01	L.A.	CQF	L.A. 4	Det. 3	Eric Belanger	2:36	L.A.
Apr. 19/01	Dal.	CQF	Dal. 4	Edm. 3	Kirk Muller	8:01	Dal.
Apr. 19/01	St.L.	CQF	St.L. 3	S.J. 2	Bryce Salvador	9:54	St.L.
Apr. 23/01	Pit.	CQF	Pit. 4	Wsh. 3	Martin Straka	13:04	Pit.
Apr. 23/01	L.A.	CQF	L.A. 3	Det. 2	Adam Deadmarsh	4:48	L.A.
Apr. 26/01	Col.	CSF	L.A. 4	Col. 3	Jaroslav Modry	14:23	Col.
Apr. 28/01	N.J.	CSF	N.J. 6	Tor. 5	Randy McKay	5:31	N.J.
May 1/01	Tor.	CSF	N.J. 3	Tor. 2	Brian Rafalski	7:00	N.J.
May 1/01	St.L.	CSF	St.L. 3	Dal. 2	Cory Stillman	29:26	St.L.
May 5/01	Buf.	CSF	Buf. 3	Pit. 2	Stu Barnes	8:34	Pit.
May 6/01	L.A.	CSF	L.A. 1	Col. 0	Glen Murray	22:41	Col.
May 8/01	Pit.	CSF	Pit. 3	Buf. 2	Martin Straka	11:29	Pit.
May 10/01	Buf.	CSF	Pit. 3	Buf. 2	Darius Kasparaitis	13:01	Pit.
May 16/01	St.L.	CF	St.L. 4	Col. 3	Scott Young	30:27	Col.
May 18/01	St.L.	CF	Col. 4	St.L. 3	Stephane Yelle	4:23	Col.
May 21/01	Col.	CF	Col. 2	St.L. 1	Joe Sakic	:24	Col.
Apr. 17/02	Phi.	CQF	Phi. 1	Ott. 0	Ruslan Fedotenko	7:47	Ott.
Apr. 17/02	Det.	CQF	Van. 4	Det. 3	Henrik Sedin	13:59	Det.
Apr. 19/02	Car.	CQF	Car. 2	N.J. 1	Bates Battaglia	15:26	Car.
Apr. 24/02	Car.	CQF	Car. 3	N.J. 2	Josef Vasicek	8:16	Car.
Apr. 25/02	Col.	CQF	L.A. 1	Col. 0	Craig Johnson	2:19	Col.
Apr. 26/02	Phi.	CQF	Ott. 2	Phi. 1	Martin Havlat	7:33	Ott.
May 4/02	Tor.	CSF	Tor. 3	Ott. 2	Gary Roberts	44:30	Tor.
May 7/02	Mtl.	CSF	Mtl. 2	Car. 1	Donald Audette	2:26	Car.
May 9/02	Mtl.	CSF	Car. 4	Mtl. 3	Niclas Wallin	3:14	Car.
May 13/02	S.J.	CSF	Col. 2	S.J. 1	Peter Forsberg	2:47	Col.
May 19/02	Car.	CF	Car. 2	Tor. 1	Niclas Wallin	13:42	Car.
May 20/02	Det.	CF	Col. 4	Det. 3	Chris Drury	2:17	Det.

Overtime Games since 1918 *— continued*

Date	City	Series	Score		Scorer	Overtime	Series Winner
May 21/02	Tor.	CF	Car. 2	Tor. 1	Jeff O'Neill	6:01	Car.
May 22/02	Col.	CF	Det. 2	Col. 1	Fredrik Olausson	12:44	Det.
May 27/02	Det.	CF	Col. 2	Det. 1	Peter Forsberg	6:24	Det.
May 28/02	Tor.	CF	Car. 2	Tor. 1	Martin Gelinas	8:05	Car.
Jun. 4/02	Det.	F	Car. 3	Det. 2	Ron Francis	:58	Det.
Jun. 8/02	Car.	F	Det. 3	Car. 2	Igor Larionov	54:47	Det.
Apr. 10/03	Det.	CQF	Ana. 2	Det. 1	Paul Kariya	43:18	Ana.
Apr. 14/03	NYI	CQF	Ott. 3	NYI 2	Todd White	22:25	Ott.
Apr. 14/03	Tor.	CQF	Tor. 4	Phi. 3	Tomas Kaberle	27:20	Phi.
Apr. 15/03	Wsh.	CQF	T.B. 4	Wsh. 3	Vincent Lecavalier	2:29	T.B.
Apr. 16/03	Tor.	CQF	Phi. 3	Tor. 2	Mark Recchi	53:54	Phi.
Apr. 16/03	Ana.	CQF	Ana. 3	Det. 2	Steve Rucchin	6:53	Ana.
Apr. 20/03	Wsh.	CQF	T.B. 2	Wsh. 1	Martin St. Louis	44:03	T.B.
Apr. 21/03	Tor.	CQF	Tor. 2	Phi. 1	Travis Green	30:51	Phi.
Apr. 21/03	Min.	CQF	Min. 3	Col. 2	Richard Park	4:22	Min.
Apr. 22/03	Col.	CQF	Min. 3	Col. 2	Andrew Brunette	3:25	Min.
Apr. 24/03	Dal.	CSF	Ana. 4	Dal. 3	Petr Sykora	80:48	Ana.
Apr. 25/03	Van.	CSF	Van. 4	Min. 3	Trent Klatt	3:42	Min.
Apr. 26/03	N.J.	CSF	N.J. 3	T.B. 2	Jamie Langenbrunner	2:09	N.J.
Apr. 26/03	Dal.	CSF	Ana. 3	Dal. 2	Mike Leclerc	1:44	Ana.
Apr. 29/03	Phi.	CSF	Ott. 3	Phi. 2	Wade Redden	6:43	Ott.
May 2/03	Min.	CSF	Van. 3	Min. 2	Brent Sopel	15:52	Min.
May 2/03	N.J.	CSF	N.J. 2	T.B. 1	Grant Marshall	51:12	N.J.
May 10/03	Min.	CF	Ana. 1	Min. 0	Petr Sykora	28:06	Ana.
May 10/03	Ott.	CF	Ott. 3	N.J. 2	Shaun Van Allen	3:08	N.J.
May 21/03	N.J.	CF	Ott. 2	N.J. 1	Chris Phillips	15:51	N.J.
May 31/03	Ana.	F	Ana. 3	N.J. 2	Ruslan Salei	6:59	N.J.
Jun. 2/03	Ana.	F	Ana. 1	N.J. 0	Steve Thomas	0:39	N.J.
Apr. 8/04	S.J.	CQF	S.J. 1	St.L. 0	Niko Dimitrakos	9:16	S.J.
Apr. 9/04	Bos.	CQF	Bos. 2	Mtl. 1	Patrice Bergeron	1:26	Mtl.
Apr. 12/04	Dal.	CQF	Dal. 4	Col. 3	Steve Ott	2:11	Col.
Apr. 13/04	Mtl.	CQF	Bos. 4	Mtl. 3	Glen Murray	29:27	Mtl.
Apr. 14/04	Dal.	CQF	Col. 3	Dal. 2	Marek Svatos	25:21	Col.
Apr. 16/04	T.B.	CQF	T.B. 3	NYI 2	Martin St. Louis	4:07	T.B.
Apr. 17/04	Cgy.	CQF	Van. 5	Cgy. 4	Brendan Morrison	42:28	Cgy.
Apr. 18/04	Ott.	CQF	Ott. 2	Tor. 1	Mike Fisher	21:47	Tor.
Apr. 19/04	Van.	CQF	Cgy. 3	Van. 2	Martin Gelinas	1:25	Cgy.
Apr. 22/04	Det.	CSF	Cgy. 2	Det. 1	Marcus Nilson	2:39	Cgy.
Apr. 27/04	Mtl.	CSF	T.B. 4	Mtl 3	Brad Richards	1:05	T.B.
Apr. 28/04	Col	CSF	Col. 1	S.J. 0	Joe Sakic	5:15	S.J.
May 1/04	S.J.	CSF	Col. 2	S.J. 1	Joe Sakic	1:54	S.J.
May 3/04	Cgy	CSF	Cgy. 1	Det. 0	Martin Gelinas	19:13	Cgy.
May 4/04	Phi.	CSF	Phi. 3	Tor. 2	Jeremy Roenick	7:39	Phi.
May 9/04	S.J.	CF	Cgy. 4	S.J. 3	Steve Montador	18:43	Cgy.
May 20/04	Phi.	CF	Phi. 5	T.B. 4	Simon Gagne	18:18	T.B.
Jun. 3/04	T.B.	F	Cgy. 3	T.B. 2	Oleg Saprykin	14:40	T.B.
Jun. 5/04	Cgy.	F	T.B. 3	Cgy. 2	Martin St. Louis	20:33	T.B.
Apr. 21/06	Det.	CQF	Det. 3	Edm. 2	Kirk Maltby	22:39	Edm.
Apr. 21/06	Cgy.	CQF	Cgy. 2	Ana. 1	Darren McCarty	9:45	Ana.
Apr. 22/06	Buf.	CQF	Buf. 3	Phi. 2	Danny Briere	27:31	Buf.
Apr. 24/06	Car.	CQF	Mtl. 6	Car. 5	Michael Ryder	22:32	Car.
Apr. 24/06	Dal.	CQF	Col. 5	Dal. 4	Joe Sakic	4:36	Col.
Apr. 25/06	Edm.	CQF	Edm. 4	Det. 3	Jarret Stoll	28:44	Edm.
Apr. 26/06	Mtl.	CQF	Car. 2	Mtl. 1	Eric Staal	3:38	Car.
Apr. 26/06	Col.	CQF	Col. 4	Dal. 3	Alex Tanguay	1:09	Col.
Apr. 27/06	Ana.	CQF	Ana. 3	Cgy. 2	Sean O'Donnell	1:36	Ana.
Apr. 30/06	Dal.	CQF	Col. 3	Dal. 2	Andrew Brunette	13:55	Col.
May 2/06	Mtl.	CQF	Car. 2	Mtl. 1	Cory Stillman	1:19	Car.
May 5/06	Ott.	CSF	Buf. 7	Ott. 6	Chris Drury	0:18	Buf.
May 8/06	Car.	CSF	Car. 3	N.J. 2	Niclas Wallin	3:09	Car.
May 9/06	Col.	CSF	Ana. 4	Col. 3	Joffrey Lupul	16:30	Ana.
May 10/06	Buf.	CSF	Buf. 3	Ott. 2	J.P. Dumont	5:05	Buf.
May 10/06	Edm.	CSF	Edm. 3	S.J. 2	Shawn Horcoff	42:24	Edm.
May 13/06	Ott.	CSF	Buf. 3	Ott. 2	Jason Pominville	2:26	Buf.
May 28/06	Car.	CF	Car. 4	Buf. 3	Cory Stillman	8:46	Car.
May 30/06	Buf.	CF	Buf. 2	Car. 1	Danny Briere	4:22	Car.
June 14/06	Car.	F	Edm. 4	Car. 3	Fernando Pisani	3:31	Car.
Apr. 11/07	Nsh.	CQF	S.J. 5	Nsh. 4	Patrick Rissmiller	28:14	S.J.
Apr. 11/07	Van.	CQF	Van. 5	Dal. 4	Henrik Sedin	78:06	Van.
Apr. 15/07	Dal.	CQF	Van. 2	Dal. 1	Taylor Pyatt	7:47	Van.
Apr. 18/07	T.B.	CQF	N.J. 4	T.B. 3	Scott Gomez	12:54	N.J.
Apr. 19/07	Van.	CQF	Dal. 1	Van. 0	Brenden Morrow	6:22	Van.
Apr. 22/07	Cgy.	CQF	Det. 2	Cgy. 1	Johan Franzen	24:23	Det.
Apr. 27/07	Ana.	CSF	Van. 2	Ana. 1	Jeff Cowan	27:49	Ana.
Apr. 28/07	N.J.	CSF	N.J. 3	Ott. 2	Jamie Langenbrunner	21:55	Ott.
Apr. 29/07	NYR	CSF	NYR 2	Buf. 1	Michal Rozsival	36:43	Buf.
May 1/07	Van.	CSF	Ana. 3	Van. 2	Travis Moen	2:07	Ana.
May 2/07	S.J.	CSF	Det. 3	S.J. 2	Mathieu Schnieder	16:04	Det.
May 3/07	Ana.	CSF	Ana. 2	Van. 1	Scott Niedermayer	24:30	Ana.
May 4/07	Buf.	CSF	Buf. 2	NYR 1	Maxim Afinogenov	4:39	Buf.
May 12/07	Buf.	CF	Ott. 4	Buf. 3	Joe Corvo	24:58	Ott.
May 13/07	Det.	CF	Ana. 4	Det. 3	Scott Niedermayer	14:17	Ana.
May 19/07	Buf.	CF	Ott. 3	Buf. 2	Daniel Alfredsson	9:32	Ott.
May 20/07	Det.	CF	Ana. 2	Det. 1	Teemu Selanne	11:57	Ana.
Apr. 9/08	Min.	CQF	Col. 3	Min. 2	Joe Sakic	11:11	Col.
Apr. 11/08	Min.	CQF	Min. 3	Col. 2	Keith Carney	1:14	Col.
Apr. 12/08	Mtl.	CQF	Mtl. 3	Bos. 2	Alex Kovalev	2:30	Mtl.
Apr. 13/08	Mtl.	CQF	Bos. 2	Mtl.1	Marc Savard	9:25	Mtl.
Apr. 13/08	NYR	CQF	N.J. 4	NYR 3	John Madden	6:01	NYR
Apr. 14/08	Col.	CQF	Min. 3	Col. 2	Pierre-Marc Bouchard	11:58	Col.
Apr. 17/08	Phi.	CQF	Phi. 4	Wsh. 3	Mike Knuble	26:40	Phi.
Apr. 18/08	Det.	CQF	Det. 2	Nsh. 1	Johan Franzen	1:48	Det.
Apr. 22/08	Wsh.	CQF	Phi. 3	Wsh. 2	Joffrey Lupul	6:06	Phi.
Apr. 24/08	Mtl.	CSF	Mtl. 4	Phi. 3	Tom Kostopoulos	0:48	Phi.
Apr. 25/08	S.J.	CSF	Dal. 3	S.J. 2	Brenden Morrow	4:39	Dal.
Apr. 29/08	Dal.	CSF	Dal. 2	S.J. 1	Mattias Norstrom	4:37	Dal.
May 2/08	S.J.	CSF	S.J. 3	Dal. 2	Joe Pavelski	1:05	Dal.
May 4/08	Pit.	CSF	Pit. 3	NYR 2	Marian Hossa	7:10	Pit.
May 4/08	Dal.	CSF	Dal. 2	S.J. 1	Brenden Morrow	69:03	Dal.
June 2/08	Det.	F	Pit. 3	Det. 2	Petr Sykora	49:57	Det.
Apr. 16/09	Chi.	CQF	Chi. 3	Cgy. 2	Martin Havlat	0:12	Chi.
Apr. 17/09	Pit.	CQF	Pit. 3	Phi. 2	Bill Guerin	18:29	Pit.
Apr. 17/09	N.J.	CQF	Car. 2	N.J. 1	Tim Gleason	2:40	Car.
Apr. 19/09	Car.	CQF	N.J. 3	Car. 2	Travis Zajac	4:58	Car.
Apr. 21/09	St.L.	CQF	Van. 3	St.L. 2	Alex Burrows	19:41	Van.
Apr. 25/09	S.J.	CQF	S.J. 3	Ana. 2	Patrick Marleau	6:02	Ana.
May 3/09	Det.	CSF	Ana. 4	Det. 3	Todd Marchant	41:15	Det.
May 6/09	Pit.	CSF	Pit. 3	Wsh. 2	Kris Letang	11:23	Pit.
May 6/09	Car.	CSF	Car. 3	Bos. 2	Jussi Jokinen	2:48	Car.
May 7/09	Chi.	CSF	Chi. 2	Van. 1	Andrew Ladd	2:52	Chi.
May 9/09	Wsh.	CSF	Pit. 4	Wsh. 3	Evgeni Malkin	3:28	Pit.
May 11/09	Pit.	CSF	Wsh. 5	Pit. 4	David Steckel	6:22	Pit.
May 14/09	Bos.	CSF	Car. 3	Bos. 2	Scott Walker	18:46	Car.
May 19/09	Det.	CF	Det. 3	Chi. 2	Mikael Samuelsson	5:14	Det.
May 22/09	Chi.	CF	Chi. 4	Det. 3	Patrick Sharp	1:52	Det.
May 27/09	Det.	CF	Det. 2	Chi. 1	Darren Helm	3:58	Det.
Apr. 15/10	Wsh.	CQF	Mtl. 3	Wsh. 2	Tomas Plekanec	13:19	Mtl.
Apr. 15/10	Van.	CQF	Van. 3	L.A. 2	Mikael Samuelsson	8:52	Van.
Apr. 16/10	S.J.	CQF	S.J. 6	Col. 5	Devin Setoguchi	5:22	S.J.
Apr. 17/10	Wsh.	CQF	Wsh. 6	Mtl. 5	Nicklas Backstrom	0:31	Mtl.
Apr. 17/10	Van.	CQF	L.A. 3	Van. 2	Anze Kopitar	7:28	Van.
Apr. 18/10	Phi.	CQF	Phi. 3	N.J. 2	Daniel Carcillo	3:35	Phi.
Apr. 18/10	S.J.	CQF	Col. 1	S.J. 0	Ryan O'Reilly	0:51	S.J.
Apr. 20/10	Col.	CQF	S.J. 2	Col. 1	Joe Pavelski	10:24	S.J.
Apr. 21/10	Bos.	CQF	Bos. 3	Buf. 2	Miroslav Satan	27:41	Bos.
Apr. 22/10	Pit.	CQF	Ott. 4	Pit. 3	Matt Carkner	47:06	Pit.
Apr. 24/10	Chi.	CQF	Chi. 5	Nsh. 4	Marian Hossa	4:07	Chi.
Apr. 24/10	Ott.	CQF	Pit. 4	Ott. 3	Pascal Dupuis	9:56	Pit.
May 1/10	Bos.	CSF	Bos. 5	Phi. 4	Marc Savard	13:52	Phi.
May 4/10	Det.	CSF	S.J. 4	Det. 3	Patrick Marleau	7:07	S.J.
May 7/10	Phi.	CSF	Phi. 5	Bos. 4	Simon Gagne	14:40	Phi.
May 21/10	Chi.	CF	Chi. 3	S.J. 2	Dustin Byfuglien	12:24	Chi.
June 2/10	Phi.	F	Phi. 4	Chi. 3	Claude Giroux	5:59	Chi.
June 9/10	Phi.	F	Chi. 4	Phi. 3	Patrick Kane	4:06	Chi.
Apr. 13/11	Wsh.	CQF	Wsh. 2	NYR 1	Alexander Semin	18:24	Wsh.
Apr. 14/11	S.J.	CQF	S.J. 3	L.A. 2	Joe Pavelski	14:44	S.J.
Apr. 20/11	L.A.	CQF	S.J. 6	L.A. 5	Devin Setoguchi	3:09	S.J.
Apr. 20/11	NYR	CQF	Wsh. 4	NYR 3	Jason Chimera	32:36	Wsh.
Apr. 20/11	T.B.	CQF	Pit. 3	T.B. 2	James Neal	23:38	T.B.
Apr. 21/11	Mtl.	CQF	Bos. 5	Mtl. 4	Michael Ryder	1:59	Bos.
Apr. 22/11	Phi.	CQF	Buf. 4	Phi. 3	Tyler Ennis	5:31	Phi.
Apr. 22/11	Ana.	CQF	Nsh. 4	Ana. 3	Jerred Smithson	1:57	Nsh.
Apr. 23/11	Bos.	CQF	Bos. 2	Mtl. 1	Nathan Horton	29:03	Bos.
Apr. 24/11	Buf.	CQF	Phi. 5	Buf. 4	Ville Leino	4:43	Phi.
Apr. 24/11	Chi.	CQF	Chi. 4	Van. 3	Ben Smith	15:30	Van.
Apr. 25/11	L.A.	CQF	S.J. 4	L.A. 3	Joe Thornton	2:22	S.J.
Apr. 26/11	Van.	CQF	Van. 2	Chi. 3	Alexandre Burrows	5:22	Van.
Apr. 27/11	Bos.	CQF	Bos. 4	Mtl. 3	Nathan Horton	5:43	Bos.
Apr. 29/11	S.J.	CSF	S.J. 2	Det. 1	Benn Ferriero	7:03	S.J.
Apr. 30/11	Van.	CSF	Nsh. 2	Van. 1	Matt Halischuk	34:51	Van.
May 1/11	Wsh.	CSF	T.B. 3	Wsh. 2	Vincent Lecavalier	6:19	T.B.
May 2/11	Phi.	CSF	Bos. 3	Phi. 2	David Krejci	14:00	Bos.
May 3/11	Nsh.	CSF	Van. 3	Nsh. 2	Ryan Kesler	10:49	Van.
May 4/11	Det.	CSF	S.J. 4	Det. 3	Devin Setoguchi	9:21	S.J.
May 24/11	Van.	CF	Van. 3	S.J. 2	Kevin Bieksa	30:18	Van.
June 4/11	Van.	F	Van. 3	Bos. 2	Alexandre Burrows	0:11	Bos.

Ten Longest Overtime Games

Date	City	Series	Score		Scorer	Overtime	Series Winner
Mar. 24/36	Mtl.	SF	Det. 1	Mtl. M. 0	Mud Bruneteau	116:30	Det.
Apr. 3/33	Tor.	SF	Tor. 1	Bos. 0	Ken Doraty	104:46	Tor.
May 4/00	Pit.	CSF	Phi. 2	Pit. 1	Keith Primeau	92:01	Phi.
Apr. 24/03	Dal.	CSF	Ana. 4	Dal. 3	Petr Sykora	80:48	Ana.
Apr. 24/96	Wsh.	CQF	Pit. 3	Wsh. 2	Petr Nedved	79:15	Pit.
Apr. 11/07	Van.	CQF	Van. 5	Dal. 4	Henrik Sedin	78:06	Van.
Mar. 23/43	Det.	SF	Tor. 3	Det. 2	Jack McLean	70:18	Det.
May 4/08	Dal.	CSF	Dal. 2	S.J. 1	Brenden Morrow	69:03	Dal.
Mar. 28/30	Mtl.	SF	Mtl. 2	NYR 1	Gus Rivers	68:52	Mtl.
Apr. 18/87	Wsh.	DSF	NYI 3	Wsh. 2	Pat LaFontaine	68:47	NYI

Overtime Record of Current Teams

(Listed by number of OT games played)

Team	Overall				Home					Road				
	GP	W	L	T	GP	W	L	T	Last OT Game	GP	W	L	T	Last OT Game
Montreal	138	75	60	3	64	39	24	1	Apr. 21/11	74	36	36	2	Apr. 27/11
Boston	113	47	63	3	52	26	25	1	Apr. 27/11	61	21	38	2	Jun. 4/11
Toronto	106	54	51	1	68	36	31	1	May 4/04	38	18	20	0	Apr. 18/04
Detroit	91	39	52	0	55	20	35	0	May 4/11	36	19	17	0	Apr. 29/11
Chicago	73	37	34	2	36	22	13	1	Apr. 24/11	37	15	21	1	Apr. 26/11
Philadelphia	71	34	37	0	33	17	16	0	May 2/11	38	17	21	0	Apr. 24/11
NY Rangers	69	31	38	0	30	13	17	0	Apr. 20/11	39	18	21	0	Apr. 13/11
Dallas[1]	64	28	36	0	32	13	19	0	May 4/08	32	15	17	0	May 2/08
Colorado[2]	59	33	26	0	23	10	13	0	Apr. 20/10	36	23	13	0	Apr. 16/10
Buffalo	59	32	27	0	33	20	13	0	Apr. 24/11	26	12	14	0	Apr. 22/11
St. Louis	51	27	24	0	27	20	7	0	Apr. 21/09	24	7	17	0	Apr. 8/04
Vancouver	51	26	25	0	24	11	13	0	Jun. 4/11	27	15	12	0	May 3/11
Edmonton	42	24	18	0	23	13	10	0	May 10/06	19	11	8	0	Jun. 14/06
Washington	41	18	23	0	19	8	11	0	May 1/11	22	10	12	0	Apr. 20/11
Calgary[3]	41	17	24	0	19	6	13	0	Apr. 22/07	22	11	11	0	Apr. 16/09
NY Islanders	40	29	11	0	18	14	4	0	Apr. 14/03	22	15	7	0	Apr. 16/04
Los Angeles	40	18	22	0	21	11	10	0	Apr. 25/11	19	7	12	0	Apr. 14/11
New Jersey[4]	40	14	26	0	16	6	10	0	Apr. 17/09	24	8	16	0	Apr. 18/10
Pittsburgh	38	22	16	0	24	13	11	0	Apr. 22/10	14	9	5	0	Apr. 20/11
Carolina[5]	34	21	13	0	20	12	8	0	May 6/09	14	9	5	0	May 14/09
San Jose	32	15	17	0	15	7	8	0	Apr. 29/11	17	8	9	0	May 24/11
Ottawa	24	12	12	0	9	4	5	0	Apr. 24/10	15	8	7	0	Apr. 22/10
Anaheim	22	15	7	0	8	5	3	0	Apr. 22/11	14	10	4	0	May 3/09
Tampa Bay	14	8	6	0	5	2	3	0	Apr. 20/11	9	6	3	0	May 1/11
Phoenix[6]	12	5	7	0	8	3	5	0	May 4/99	4	2	2	0	Apr. 27/93
Minnesota	8	4	4	0	5	2	3	0	Apr. 11/08	3	2	1	0	Apr. 14/08
Nashville	6	2	4	0	2	0	2	0	May 3/11	4	2	2	0	Apr. 30/11
Florida	5	2	3	0	3	1	2	0	Apr. 25/97	2	1	1	0	Apr. 22/97
Columbus	0	0	0	0	0	0	0	0	....	0	0	0	0	....
Winnipeg[7]	0	0	0	0	0	0	0	0	....	0	0	0	0	....

[1] Totals include those of Minnesota North Stars 1967-93.
[2] Totals include those of Quebec 1979-95.
[3] Totals include those of Atlanta Flames 1972-80.
[4] Totals include those of Kansas City and Colorado Rockies 1974-82.
[5] Totals include those of Hartford 1979-97.
[6] Totals include those of Winnipeg 1979-96.
[7] Totals include those of Atlanta Thrashers 1999-2011.

Nathan Horton scored two overtime goals in Boston's first-round matchup with Montreal, including the series winner in game seven. He scored the series winner in regulation time in a 1-0 win over Tampa Bay in game seven of the Eastern Conference Final.

Penalty Shots in Stanley Cup Playoff Games

Date	Player, Team	Goaltender, Team	Scored	Final Score	Series
Mar. 25/37	Lionel Conacher, Mtl. Maroons	Tiny Thompson, Boston	No	Mtl. M. 0 at Bos. 4	QF
Apr. 15/37	Alex Shibicky, NY Rangers	Earl Robertson, Detroit	No	NYR 0 at Det. 3	F
Mar. 24/38	Mush March, Chicago	Wilf Cude, Montreal	No	Mtl. 0 at Chi. 4	QF
Mar. 29/38	Lorne Carr, NY Americans	Mike Karakas, Chicago	No	Chi. 1 at NYA 3	SF
Apr. 10/38	Art Wiebe, Chicago	Turk Broda, Toronto	No	Tor. 1 at Chi. 2	F
Mar. 24/42	Charlie Sands, Montreal	Johnny Mowers, Detroit	No	Det. 0 at Mtl. 5	QF
Apr. 13/44	Virgil Johnson, Chicago	Bill Durnan, Montreal	No	Chi. 4 at Mtl. 5*	F
Apr. 9/68	Wayne Connelly, Minnesota	Terry Sawchuk, Los Angeles	Yes	L.A. 5 at Min. 7	QF
Apr. 27/68	Jim Roberts, St. Louis	Cesare Maniago, Minnesota	No	St.L. 4 at Min. 3	SF
May 16/71	Frank Mahovlich, Montreal	Tony Esposito, Chicago	No	Chi. 3 at Mtl. 4	F
May 7/75	Bill Barber, Philadelphia	Glenn Resch, NY Islanders	No	Phi. 3 at NYI 4*	SF
Apr. 20/79	Mike Walton, Chicago	Glenn Resch, NY Islanders	No	NYI 4 at Chi. 0	QF
Apr. 9/81	Peter McNab, Boston	Don Beaupre, Minnesota	No	Min. 5 at Bos. 4*	PR
Apr. 17/81	Anders Hedberg, NY Rangers	Mike Liut, St. Louis	Yes	NYR 6 at St.L. 4	QF
Apr. 9/83	Denis Potvin, NY Islanders	Pat Riggin, Washington	No	NYI 6 at Wsh. 2	DSF
Apr. 28/84	Wayne Gretzky, Edmonton	Don Beaupre, Minnesota	Yes	Min. 8 at Min. 5	CF
May 1/84	Mats Naslund, Montreal	Billy Smith, NY Islanders	No	Mtl. 1 at NYI 3	CF
Apr. 14/85	Bob Carpenter, Washington	Billy Smith, NY Islanders	No	Wsh. 4 at NYI. 6	DF
Apr. 28/85	Ron Sutter, Philadelphia	Grant Fuhr, Edmonton	No	Phi. 3 at Edm. 5	F
May 30/85	Dave Poulin, Philadelphia	Grant Fuhr, Edmonton	No	Phi. 3 at Edm. 8	F
Apr. 9/88	John Tucker, Buffalo	Andy Moog, Boston	Yes	Bos. 2 at Buf. 6	DSF
Apr. 9/88	Petr Klima, Detroit	Allan Bester, Toronto	Yes	Det. 6 at Tor. 3	DSF
Apr. 8/89	Neal Broten, Minnesota	Greg Millen, St. Louis	Yes	St.L. 5 at Min. 3	DSF
Apr. 4/90	Al MacInnis, Calgary	Kelly Hrudey, Los Angeles	Yes	L.A. 5 at Cgy. 3	DSF
Apr. 5/90	Randy Wood, NY Islanders	Mike Richter, NY Rangers	No	NYI 1 at NYR 2	DSF
May 3/90	Kelly Miller, Washington	Andy Moog, Boston	No	Wsh. 3 at Bos. 5	CF
May 18/90	Petr Klima, Edmonton	Reggie Lemelin, Boston	No	Edm. 7 at Bos. 2	F
Apr. 6/91	Basil McRae, Minnesota	Ed Belfour, Chicago	Yes	Min. 2 at Chi. 5	DSF
Apr. 10/91	Steve Duchesne, Los Angeles	Kirk McLean, Vancouver	Yes	L.A. 6 at Van. 1	DSF
May 11/92	Jaromir Jagr, Pittsburgh	John Vanbiesbrouck, NYR	Yes	Pit. 3 at NYR 2	DF
May 13/92	Shawn McEachern, Pittsburgh	John Vanbiesbrouck, NYR	No	NYR 1 at Pit. 5	DF
June 7/94	Pavel Bure, Vancouver	Mike Richter, NYR	No	NYR 4 at Van. 1	F
May 9/95	Patrick Poulin, Chicago	Felix Potvin, Toronto	No	Tor. 3 at Chi. 0	CQF
May 10/95	Michal Pivonka, Washington	Tom Barrasso, Pittsburgh	No	Pit. 2 at Wsh. 6	CQF
Apr. 24/96	Joe Juneau, Washington	Ken Wregget, Pittsburgh	No	Pit. 3 at Wsh. 2**	CQF
May 11/97	Eric Lindros, Philadelphia	Steve Shields, Buffalo	Yes	Phi. 6 at Buf. 3	CSF
Apr. 23/98	Aleksey Morozov, Pittsburgh	Andy Moog, Montreal	No	Mtl. 3 at Pit. 2**	CQF

Date	Player, Team	Goaltender, Team	Scored	Final Score	Series
Apr. 22/99	Mats Sundin, Toronto	John Vanbiesbrouck, Phi.	No	Phi. 3 at Tor. 0	CQF
May 29/99	Mats Sundin, Toronto	Dominik Hasek, Buffalo	Yes	Tor. 2 at Buf. 5	CF
Apr. 16/00	Eric Desjardins, Philadelphia	Dominik Hasek, Buffalo	No	Phi. 2 at Buf. 0	CQF
Apr. 11/01	Mark Recchi, Philadelphia	Dominik Hasek, Buffalo	No	Buf. 2 at Phi. 1	CQF
May 2/01	Martin Straka, Pittsburgh	Dominik Hasek, Buffalo	No	Buf. 5 at Pit. 2	CSF
May 12/01	Joe Sakic, Colorado	Roman Turek, St. Louis	Yes	St.L. 1 at Col. 4	CF
Apr. 21/02	Todd Bertuzzi, Vancouver	Dominik Hasek, Detroit	No	Det. 3 at Van. 1	CQF
Apr. 24/02	Shawn Bates, NY Islanders	Curtis Joseph, Toronto	Yes	Tor. 3 at NYI 4	CQF
Apr. 26/02	Mike Johnson, Phoenix	Evgeni Nabokov, San Jose	Yes	Phx. 1 at S.J. 4	CQF
Apr. 15/03	Dainius Zubrus, Washington	Nikolai Khabibulin, Tampa Bay	No	T.B. 4 at Wsh. 3	CQF
Apr. 21/03	Robert Reichel, Toronto	Roman Cechmanek, Philadelphia	No	Phi. 1 at Tor. 2	CQF
Apr. 7/04	Steve Sullivan, Nashville	Manny Legace, Detroit	No	Nsh. 1 at Det. 3	CQF
Apr. 28/06	Derek Roy, Buffalo	Robert Esche, Philadelphia	No	Buf. 4 at Phi. 5	CQF
June 5/06	Chris Pronger, Edmonton***	Cam Ward, Carolina	No	Edm. 4 at Car. 5	F
Apr. 21/07	Daniel Cleary, Detroit	Miikka Kiprusoff, Calgary	Yes	Cgy. 1 at Det. 5	CQF
June 6/07	Antoine Vermette, Ottawa	J.S. Giguere, Anaheim	No	Ott. 2 at Ana. 6	F
Apr. 9/08	Ryan Smyth, Colorado	Niklas Backstrom, Minnesota	No	Col. 3 at Min. 2	CQF
Apr. 15/08	Mike Richards, Philadelphia	Cristobal Huet, Washington	Yes	Wsh. 3 at Phi. 6	CQF
Apr. 18/08	John Madden, New Jersey	Henrik Lundqvist, NY Rangers	No	NYR 5 at N.J. 3	CQF
Apr. 24/08	Andrei Kostitsyn, Montreal	Martin Biron, Philadelphia	No	Phi. 3 at Mtl. 4	CSF
Apr. 29/08	Niklas Hagman, Dallas	Evgeni Nabokov, San Jose	No	S.J. 1 at Dal. 2	CSF
May 1/08	Evgeni Malkin, Pittsburgh	Henrik Lundqvist, NY Rangers	No	Pit. 0 at NYR 3	CSF
Apr. 20/10	Martin Erat, Nashville	Antti Niemi, Chicago	Yes	Chi. 1 at Nsh. 4	CQF
May 4/10	Henrik Zetterberg, Detroit	Evgeni Nabokov, San Jose	No	S.J. 4 at Det. 3	CSF
May 8/10	Joe Pavelski, San Jose	Jimmy Howard, Detroit	No	S.J. 2 at Det. 1	CSF
May 12/10	Ville Leino, Philadelphia	Tuukka Rask, Boston	No	Phi. 2 at Bos. 1	CSF
Apr. 24/11	Michael Frolik, Chicago	Cory Schneider, Vancouver	Yes	Van. 3 at Chi. 4	CQF
Apr. 25/11	Chris Connor, Pittsburgh	Dwayne Roloson, Tampa Bay	No	Pit. 3 at T.B. 4	CQF
Apr. 26/11	Alexandre Burrows, Vancouver	Corey Crawford, Chicago	No	Chi. 1 at Van. 2	CQF

* Game was decided in overtime, but shot taken during regulation time.
** Shot taken in overtime.
*** First penalty shot scored in Stanley Cup Final history

All-Time Playoff NHL Coaching Register

Playoffs, 1917-2011

Coach	Team	Games Coached	Wins	Losses	T	Years	Cup Wins	Career
Abel, Sid	Chicago	7	3	4		1		
	Detroit	69	29	40		8		
	Totals	76	32	44		9		1952-76
Adams, Jack	Detroit	105	52	52	1	15	3	1927-47
Allen, Keith	Philadelphia	11	3	8		2		1967-69
Arbour, Al	St. Louis	11	4	7		1		
	NY Islanders	198	119	79		15	4	
	Totals	209	123	86		16	4	1970-08
Babcock, Mike	Anaheim	21	15	6		1		
	Detroit	92	55	37		6	1	
	Totals	113	70	43		7	1	2002-11
Barber, Bill	Philadelphia	11	3	8		2		2000-02
Berenson, Red	St. Louis	14	5	9		2		1979-82
Bergeron, Michel	Quebec	68	31	37		7		1980-90
Berry, Bob	Los Angeles	10	2	8		3		
	Montreal	8	2	6		2		
	St. Louis	15	7	8		2		
	Totals	33	11	22		7		1978-94
Beverley, Nick	Toronto	6	2	4		1		1995-96
Blackburn, Don	Hartford	3	0	3		1		1979-81
Blair, Wren	Minnesota	14	7	7		1		1967-70
Blake, Toe	Montreal	119	82	37		13	8	1955-68
Boileau, Marc	Pittsburgh	9	5	4		1		1973-76
Boivin, Leo	St. Louis	3	1	2		1		1975-78
Boucher, Frank	NY Rangers	27	13	14		4	1	1939-54
Boucher, Georges	Mtl. Maroons	2	0	2	0	1		1930-50
Boucher, Guy	Tampa Bay	18	11	7		1		2010-11
Boudreau, Bruce	Washington	37	17	20		4		2007-11
Bowman, Scotty	St. Louis	52	26	26		4		
	Montreal	98	70	28		8	5	
	Buffalo	36	18	18		5		
	Pittsburgh	33	23	10		2	1	
	Detroit	134	86	48		9	3	
	Totals	353	223	130		28	9	1967-02
Bowness, Rick	Boston	15	8	7		1		1988-05
Brooks, Herb	NY Rangers	24	12	12		3		
	New Jersey	5	1	4		1		
	Pittsburgh	11	6	5		1		
	Totals	40	19	21		5		1981-00
Brophy, John	Toronto	19	9	10		2		1986-89
Burns, Pat	Montreal	56	30	26		4		
	Toronto	46	23	23		3		
	Boston	18	8	10		2		
	New Jersey	29	17	12		2	1	
	Totals	149	78	71		11	1	1988-05
Burns, Charlie	Minnesota	6	2	4		1		1969-75
Bylsma, Dan	Pittsburgh	44	26	18		3	1	2008-11
Campbell, Colin	NY Rangers	36	18	18		3		1994-98
Carbonneau, Guy	Montreal	12	5	7		1		2006-09
Carlyle, Randy	Anaheim	62	36	26		5	1	2005-11
Carpenter, Doug	Toronto	5	1	4		1		1984-91
Carroll, Frank	Toronto	2	0	2	0	1		1920-21
Carroll, Dick	Toronto	2	1	1	0	1	1	1917-19
Cassidy, Bruce	Washington	6	2	4		1		2002-04
Cheevers, Gerry	Boston	34	15	19		4		1980-85
Cherry, Don	Boston	55	31	24		5		1974-80
Clancy, King	Toronto	14	2	12		3		1937-56
Clapper, Dit	Boston	25	8	17		4		1945-49
Cleghorn, Sprague	Mtl. Maroons	4	1	1	2	1		1931-32
Cleghorn, Odie	Pittsburgh	4	1	2	1	2		1925-29
Clouston, Cory	Ottawa	6	2	4		1		2008-11
Constantine, Kevin	San Jose	25	11	14		2		
	Pittsburgh	19	8	11		2		
	New Jersey	6	2	4		1		
	Totals	50	21	29		5		1993-02
Crawford, Marc	Quebec	6	2	4		1		
	Colorado	46	29	17		3	1	
	Vancouver	27	12	15		3		
	Totals	79	43	36		7	1	1994-11
Creighton, Fred	Atlanta	9	2	7		4		1974-80
Crisp, Terry	Calgary	37	22	15		3	1	
	Tampa Bay	6	2	4		1		
	Totals	43	24	19		4	1	1987-98
Crozier, Joe	Buffalo	6	2	4		1		1971-81
Cunniff, John	New Jersey	6	2	4		1		1982-91
Curry, Alex	Ottawa	2	0	1	1	1		1925-26
Dandurand, Leo	Montreal	8	5	3	0	4	1	1921-35
Day, Hap	Toronto	80	49	31		9	5	1940-50
Demers, Jacques	St. Louis	33	16	17		3		
	Detroit	38	20	18		3		
	Montreal	27	19	8		2	1	
	Totals	98	55	43		8	1	1979-99
Denneny, Cy	Boston	5	5	0	0	1	1	1928-33
Dudley, Rick	Buffalo	12	4	8		2		1989-04
Dugal, Jules	Montreal	3	1	2		1		1938-39
Duncan, Art	Toronto	2	0	1	1	1		1926-32
Dutton, Red	NY Americans	11	4	7		3		1936-40
Esposito, Phil	NY Rangers	10	2	8		2		1986-89
Evans, Jack	Hartford	16	8	8		2		1975-88
Ferguson, John	Winnipeg	3	0	3		1		1975-86
Francis, Bob	Phoenix	10	2	8		2		1999-04
Francis, Emile	NY Rangers	75	34	41		9		
	St. Louis	14	5	9		2		
	Totals	89	39	50		11		1965-83
Ftorek, Robbie	Los Angeles	16	5	11		2		
	New Jersey	7	3	4		1		
	Boston	6	2	4		1		
	Totals	29	10	19		4		1987-03
Gainey, Bob	Minnesota	30	17	13		2		
	Dallas	14	6	8		2		
	Montreal	10	2	8		2		
	Totals	54	25	29		6		1990-09
Geoffrion, Bernie	Atlanta	4	0	4		1		1968-80
Gerard, Eddie	Mtl. Maroons	21	8	8	5	5	1	1917-35
Gill, David	Ottawa	8	3	2	3	2	1	1926-29
Glover, Fred	Oakland	11	3	8		2		1968-74
Gordon, Jackie	Minnesota	25	11	14		3		1970-75
Goring, Butch	Boston	3	0	3		1		1985-01
Gorman, Tommy	NY Americans	2	0	1	1	1		
	Chicago	8	6	1	1	1	1	
	Mtl. Maroons	15	7	6	2	3	1	
	Totals	25	13	8	4	5	2	1925-38
Gottselig, Johnny	Chicago	4	0	4		1		1944-48
Granato, Tony	Colorado	18	9	9		2		2002-09
Green, Pete	Ottawa	8	3	4	1	4	3	1919-25
Green, Ted	Edmonton	16	8	8		1		1991-94
Guidolin, Bep	Boston	21	11	10		2		1972-76
Harris, Ted	Minnesota	2	0	2		1		1975-78
Hart, Cecil	Montreal	37	16	17	4	8	2	1926-39
Hartley, Bob	Colorado	80	49	31		4	1	
	Atlanta	4	0	4		1		
	Totals	84	49	35		5	1	1998-08
Hartsburg, Craig	Chicago	16	8	8		2		
	Anaheim	4	0	4		1		
	Totals	20	8	12		3		1995-09
Harvey, Doug	NY Rangers	6	2	4		1		1961-62
Hay, Don	Phoenix	7	3	4		1		1996-01
Helmer, Rosie	NY Americans	5	2	3	0	1		1935-36
Henning, Lorne	Minnesota	5	2	3		1		1985-01
Hitchcock, Ken	Dallas	80	47	33		5	1	
	Philadelphia	37	19	18		3		
	Columbus	4	0	4		1		
	Totals	121	66	55		9	1	1995-10
Hlinka, Ivan	Pittsburgh	18	9	9		1		2000-02
Holmgren, Paul	Philadelphia	19	10	9		1		1988-96
Imlach, Punch	Toronto	92	44	48		11	4	1958-80
Inglis, Bill	Buffalo	3	1	2		1		1978-79
Irvin, Dick	Chicago	9	5	3	1	1		
	Toronto	66	33	32	1	9	1	
	Montreal	115	62	53		14	3	
	Totals	190	100	88	2	24	4	1928-56
Ivan, Tommy	Detroit	67	36	31		7	3	1947-58
Johnson, Tom	Boston	22	15	7		2	1	1970-73
Johnson, Bob	Calgary	52	25	27		5		
	Pittsburgh	24	16	8		1	1	
	Totals	76	41	35		6	1	1982-91
Johnston, Eddie	Chicago	7	3	4		1		
	Pittsburgh	46	22	24		5		
	Totals	53	25	28		6		1979-97
Julien, Claude	Montreal	11	4	7		1		
	Boston	56	33	23		4	1	
	Totals	67	37	30		5	1	2002-11
Kasper, Steve	Boston	5	1	4		1		1995-97
Keenan, Mike	Philadelphia	57	32	25		4		
	Chicago	60	33	27		4		
	NY Rangers	23	16	7		1	1	
	St. Louis	20	10	10		2		
	Calgary	13	5	8		2		
	Totals	173	96	77		13	1	1984-09
Kelly, Red	Los Angeles	18	7	11		2		
	Pittsburgh	14	6	8		2		
	Toronto	30	11	19		4		
	Totals	62	24	38		8		1967-77
Kelly, Pat	Colorado	2	0	2		1		1977-79
King, Dave	Calgary	20	8	12		3		1992-03
Kromm, Bobby	Detroit	7	3	4		1		1977-80
Lalonde, Newsy	Montreal	11	5	4	2	4		
	Ottawa	2	0	1	1	1		
	Totals	13	5	5	3	5		1917-35
Lamoriello, Lou	New Jersey	20	10	10		2		2005-07
Laviolette, Peter	NY Islanders	12	4	8		2		
	Carolina	25	16	9		1	1	
	Philadelphia	34	18	16		2		
	Totals	71	38	33		5	1	2001-11
Lemaire, Jacques	Montreal	27	15	12		2		
	New Jersey	61	35	26		5	1	
	Minnesota	29	11	18		3		
	Totals	117	61	56		10	1	1983-11
Lewis, Dave	Detroit	16	6	10		2		1998-07
Ley, Rick	Hartford	13	5	8		2		
	Vancouver	11	4	7		1		
	Totals	24	9	15		3		1989-96
Long, Barry	Winnipeg	11	3	8		2		1983-86

Coach	Team	Games Coached	Wins	Losses	Ties	Years	Cup Wins	Career
Loughlin, Clem	**Chicago**	4	1	2	1	2		1934-37
Low, Ron	**Edmonton**	28	10	18		3		1994-02
Lowe, Kevin	**Edmonton**	5	1	4		1		1999-00
MacLean, Doug	**Florida**	27	13	14		2		1995-04
MacNeil, Al	Montreal	20	12	8		1	1	
	Atlanta	4	1	3		1		
	Calgary	19	9	10		2		
	Totals	43	22	21		4	1	1970-03
MacTavish, Craig	**Edmonton**	36	19	17		3		2000-09
Magnuson, Keith	**Chicago**	3	0	3		1		1980-82
Mahoney, Bill	**Minnesota**	16	7	9		1		1983-85
Maloney, Dan	Toronto	10	6	4		1		
	Winnipeg	15	5	10		2		
	Totals	25	11	14		3		1984-89
Maloney, Phil	**Vancouver**	7	1	6		2		1973-77
Martin, Jacques	St. Louis	16	7	9		2		
	Ottawa	69	31	38		8		
	Montreal	26	12	14		2		
	Totals	111	50	61		12		1986-11
Maurice, Paul	**Carolina**	53	25	37		4		1995-11
McCammon, Bob	Philadelphia	10	1	9		3		
	Vancouver	7	3	4		1		
	Totals	17	4	13		4		1978-91
McLellan, Todd	**San Jose**	39	19	20		3		2008-11
McLellan, John	**Toronto**	11	3	8		2		1969-73
McVie, Tom	**New Jersey**	14	6	8		2		1975-92
Melrose, Barry	**Los Angeles**	24	13	11		1		1992-09
Milbury, Mike	**Boston**	40	23	17		2		1989-99
Muckler, John	Edmonton	40	25	15		2	1	
	Buffalo	27	11	16		4		
	Totals	67	36	31		6	1	1968-00
Muldoon, Pete	**Chicago**	2	0	1	1	1		1926-27
Munro, Dunc	**Mtl. Maroons**	4	1	3	0	1		1929-31
Murdoch, Bob	Chicago	5	1	4		1		
	Winnipeg	7	3	4		1		
	Totals	12	4	8		2		1987-91
Murphy, Mike	**Los Angeles**	5	1	4		1		1986-98
Murray, Terry	Washington	39	18	21		4		
	Philadelphia	46	28	18		3		
	Florida	4	0	4		1		
	Los Angeles	68	6	4		2		
	Totals	157	52	47		10		1989-11
Murray, Bryan	Washington	53	24	29		7		
	Detroit	25	10	15		3		
	Ottawa	34	18	16		3		
	Totals	112	52	60		13		1981-08
Murray, Andy	Los Angeles	24	10	14		3		
	St. Louis	4	0	4		1		
	Totals	28	10	18		4		1999-10
Neale, Harry	**Vancouver**	14	3	11		4		1978-86
Neilson, Roger	Toronto	19	8	11		2		
	Buffalo	8	4	4		1		
	Vancouver	21	12	9		2		
	NY Rangers	29	13	16		3		
	Philadelphia	29	14	15		3		
	Totals	106	51	55		11		1977-02
Nolan, Ted	Buffalo	12	5	7		1		
	NY Islanders	5	1	4		1		
	Totals	17	6	11		2		1995-08
Nykoluk, Mike	**Toronto**	7	1	6		2		1980-84
O'Connell, Mike	**Boston**	5	1	4		1		2002-03
O'Donoghue, George	**Toronto**	2	1	0	1	1	1	1921-23
Oliver, Murray	**Minnesota**	9	4	5		1		1982-83
O'Reilly, Terry	**Boston ***	37	17	19	1	3		1986-89

* Playoff game May 24, 1988 suspended due to power failure. Score tied.

Coach	Team	Games Coached	Wins	Losses	Ties	Years	Cup Wins	Career
Paddock, John	**Winnipeg**	13	5	8		2		1991-08
Page, Pierre	Minnesota	12	4	8		2		
	Quebec	6	2	4		1		
	Calgary	4	0	4		1		
	Totals	22	6	16		4		1988-98
Patrick, Frank	**Boston**	6	2	4	0	2		1934-36
Patrick, Craig	NY Rangers	17	7	10		2		
	Pittsburgh	5	1	4		1		
	Totals	22	8	14		3		1980-97
Patrick, Lester	**NY Rangers**	65	32	26	7	12	2	1926-39
Patrick, Lynn	NY Rangers	12	7	5		1		
	Boston *	28	9	18	1	4		
	Totals	40	16	23	1	5		1948-76

* Playoff game March 31, 1951 suspended due to Toronto city curfew. Score tied.

Coach	Team	Games Coached	Wins	Losses	Ties	Years	Cup Wins	Career
Perron, Jean	**Montreal**	48	30	18		3	1	1985-89
Perry, Don	**Los Angeles**	10	4	6		1		1981-84
Pilous, Rudy	**Chicago**	41	19	22		5	1	1957-63
Plager, Barclay	**St. Louis**	4	1	3		1		1977-83
Playfair, Jim	**Calgary**	6	2	4		1		2006-07
Pleau, Larry	**Hartford**	10	2	8		2		1980-89
Polano, Nick	**Detroit**	7	1	6		2		1982-85
Powers, Eddie	**Toronto**	2	0	2	0	1		1924-26
Primeau, Joe	**Toronto ***	15	8	6	1	2	1	1950-53

* Playoff game March 31, 1951 suspended due to Toronto city curfew. Score tied.

Coach	Team	Games Coached	Wins	Losses	Ties	Years	Cup Wins	Career
Pronovost, Marcel	**Buffalo**	8	3	5		1		1977-79
Pulford, Bob	Los Angeles	26	10	16		4		
	Chicago	45	17	28		6		
	Totals	71	27	44		10		1972-00

Coach	Team	Games Coached	Wins	Losses	Ties	Years	Cup Wins	Career
Quenneville, Joel	St. Louis	68	34	34		7		
	Colorado	19	8	11		2		
	Chicago	46	28	18		3	1	
	Totals	133	70	63		12	1	1996-11
Quinn, Pat	Philadelphia	39	22	17		3		
	Los Angeles	3	0	3		1		
	Vancouver	61	31	30		5		
	Toronto	80	41	39		6		
	Totals	183	94	89		15		1978-10
Reay, Billy	**Chicago**	116	56	60		12		1957-77
Renney, Tom	**NY Rangers**	24	11	13		3		1996-11
Risebrough, Doug	**Calgary**	7	3	4		1		1990-92
Roberts, Jim	**Hartford**	7	3	4		1		1981-97
Robinson, Larry	Los Angeles	4	0	4		1		
	New Jersey	48	31	17		2	1	
	Totals	52	31	21		3	1	1995-06
Ross, Art	**Boston**	65	27	33	5	11	1	1917-45
Ruel, Claude	**Montreal**	27	18	9		3	1	1968-81
Ruff, Lindy	**Buffalo**	101	57	44		8		1997-11
Sacco, Joe	**Colorado**	6	2	4		1		2009-11
Sather, Glen	**Edmonton ***	127	89	37	1	10	4	1979-04

* Playoff game May 24, 1988 suspended due to power failure. Score tied.

Coach	Team	Games Coached	Wins	Losses	Ties	Years	Cup Wins	Career
Sator, Ted	NY Rangers	16	8	8		1		
	Buffalo	11	3	8		2		
	Totals	27	11	16		3		1985-89
Schinkel, Ken	**Pittsburgh**	6	2	4		2		1972-77
Schmidt, Milt	**Boston**	34	15	19		4		1954-76
Schoenfeld, Jim	New Jersey	20	11	9		1		
	Washington	24	10	14		3		
	Phoenix	13	5	8		2		
	Totals	57	26	31		6		1985-99
Shero, Fred	Philadelphia	83	48	35		6	2	
	NY Rangers	27	15	12		2		
	Totals	110	63	47		8	2	1971-81
Simpson, Terry	NY Islanders	20	9	11		2		
	Winnipeg	6	2	4		1		
	Totals	26	11	15		3		1986-96
Sinden, Harry	**Boston**	43	24	19		5	1	1966-85
Skinner, Jimmy	**Detroit**	26	14	12		3	1	1954-58
Smith, Floyd	**Buffalo**	32	16	16		3		1971-80
Smith, Alf	**Ottawa**	5	1	4	0	1		1918-19
Smythe, Conn	**Toronto**	4	2	2	0	1		1927-31
Sonmor, Glen	**Minnesota**	47	26	21		4		1978-87
Stasiuk, Vic	**Philadelphia**	4	0	4		1		1969-73
Stevens, John	**Philadelphia**	23	11	12		2		2006-10
Stewart, Ron	**Los Angeles**	2	0	2		1		1975-78
Stewart, Bill	**Chicago**	10	7	3		1	1	1937-39
Sutter, Brian	St. Louis	41	20	21		4		
	Boston	22	7	15		3		
	Chicago	5	1	4		1		
	Totals	68	28	40		8		1988-05
Sutter, Brent	**New Jersey**	12	4	8		2		2007-11
Sutter, Darryl	Chicago	26	11	15		3		
	San Jose	42	18	24		5		
	Calgary	33	18	15		2		
	Totals	101	47	54		10		1992-06
Talbot, Jean-Guy	St. Louis	5	1	4		1		
	NY Rangers	3	1	2		1		
	Totals	8	2	6		2		1972-78
Tessier, Orval	**Chicago**	18	9	9		2		1982-85
Therrien, Michel	Montreal	12	6	6		1		
	Pittsburgh	25	15	10		2		
	Totals	37	21	16		3		2000-09
Thompson, Paul	**Chicago**	19	7	12		4		1938-45
Tippett, Dave	Dallas	47	21	26		5		
	Phoenix	13	5	8		2		
	Totals	60	26	34		7		2002-11
Tobin, Bill	**Chicago**	4	1	2	1	2		1929-32
Tortorella, John	NY Rangers	12	4	8		2		
	Tampa Bay	45	24	21		4	1	
	Totals	57	28	29		6	1	1999-11
Tremblay, Mario	**Montreal**	11	3	8		2		1995-97
Trotz, Barry	**Nashville**	40	14	26		6		1998-11
Ubriaco, Gene	**Pittsburgh**	11	7	4		1		1988-90
Vigneault, Alain	Montreal	10	4	6		1		
	Vancouver	59	32	27		4		
	Totals	69	36	33		5		1997-11
Watson, Phil	**NY Rangers**	16	4	12		3		1955-63
Watt, Tom	Winnipeg	7	1	6		2		
	Vancouver	3	0	3		1		
	Totals	10	1	9		3		1981-92
Webster, Tom	**Los Angeles**	28	12	16		3		1986-92
Weiland, Cooney	**Boston**	17	10	7		2	1	1939-41
White, Bill	**Chicago**	2	0	2		1		1976-77
Wilson, Johnny	**Pittsburgh**	12	4	8		2		1969-80
Wilson, Ron	Anaheim	11	4	7		1		
	Washington	32	15	17		3		
	San Jose	52	28	24		4		
	Totals	95	47	48		8		1993-11
Young, Garry	**St. Louis**	2	0	2		1		1972-76

Key to Prospect, NHL Player and Goaltender Registers

Demographics: Position, shooting side (catching hand for goaltenders), height, weight, place and date of birth as well as draft information, if any, is located on this line.

Asterisks (*) indicates league leader in individual statistical categories.

Major and tier-II junior, NCAA, minor pro, European and NHL clubs form a permanent part of each player's data panel. If a player sees action with more than one club in any of the above categories, a separate line is included for each one.

Olympic Team statistics are also listed.

Players' NHL organization as of August 11, 2011. This includes players under contract, unsigned draft choices and other players on reserve lists. Free agents as of this date show a blank here.

The complete career data panels of players with NHL experience who announced their retirement before the start of the 2011-12 season are included in the Player Register and Goaltender Register.

These newly-retired players also show a blank here.

Each NHL club's minor-pro affiliates are listed on page 14.

Season	Club	League	GP	G	A	Pts	PIM	PP	SH	GW	S	%	+/-	TF	F%	Min	GP	G	A	Pts	PIM	PP	SH	GW	Min

CHARA, Zdeno — (CHAH-rah, z'DEHN-oh) — **BOS**

Defense. Shoots left. 6'9", 255 lbs. Born, Trencin, Czechoslovakia, March 18, 1977. NY Islanders' 3rd choice, 56th overall, in 1996 Entry Draft.

Season	Club	League	GP	G	A	Pts	PIM	PP	SH	GW	S	%	+/-	TF	F%	Min	GP	G	A	Pts	PIM	PP	SH	GW	Min
1994-95	Dukla Trencin U18	Svk-U18	30	22	22	44	13	....	....	....	....	....	....	....	....	....	....	....	....	....	....	....	....	....	....
	Dukla Trencin Jr.	Slovak-Jr.	2	0	0	0	0	....	....	....	....	....	....	....	....	....	....	....	....	....	....	....	....	....	....
1995-96	Dukla Trencin Jr.	Slovak-Jr.	22	1	13	14	80	....	....	....	....	....	....	....	....	....	....	....	....	....	....	....	....	....	....
	HK VTJ Piestany	Slovak-2	10	1	3	4	10	....	....	....	....	....	....	....	....	....	....	....	....	....	....	....	....	....	....
	Sparta Jr.	CzRep-Jr.	15	1	2	3	42	....	....	....	....	....	....	....	....	....	....	....	....	....	....	....	....	....	....
	HC Sparta Praha	CzRep	1	0	0	0	0	....	....	....	....	....	....	....	....	....	....	....	....	....	....	....	....	....	....
1996-97	Prince George	WHL	49	3	19	22	120	....	....	....	....	....	....	....	....	....	15	1	7	8	45	....	....	....	....
1997-98	**NY Islanders**	**NHL**	25	0	1	1	50	0	0	0	10	0.0	1	....	....	....	....	....	....	....	....	....	....	....	....
	Kentucky	AHL	48	4	9	13	125	....	....	....	....	....	....	....	....	....	1	0	0	0	4	....	....	....	....
1998-99	**NY Islanders**	**NHL**	59	2	6	8	83	0	1	0	56	3.6	-8	0	0.0	18:54	....	....	....	....	....	....	....	....	....
	Lowell	AHL	23	2	2	4	47	....	....	....	....	....	....	....	....	....	....	....	....	....	....	....	....	....	....
99-2000	NY Islanders	NHL	65	2	9	11	57	0	0	1	47	4.3	-27	0	0.0	22:52	....	....	....	....	....	....	....	....	....
2000-01	NY Islanders	NHL	82	2	7	9	157	0	1	0	83	2.4	-27	0	0.0	22:20	....	....	....	....	....	....	....	....	....
2001-02	Dukla Trencin	Slovakia	8	2	1	3	32	....	....	....	....	....	....	....	....	....	....	....	....	....	....	....	....	....	....
	Ottawa	NHL	75	10	13	23	156	4	1	2	105	9.5	30	0	0.0	22:16	10	0	1	1	2	0	0	0	26:07
2002-03	Ottawa	NHL	74	9	30	39	116	3	0	2	168	5.4	29	0	0.0	24:57	18	1	6	7	4	0	0	0	25:07
2003-04	Ottawa	NHL	79	16	25	41	147	7	0	3	185	8.6	33	0	0.0	24:38	7	1	1	2	8	0	0	0	24:38
2004-05	Farjestad	Sweden	33	10	15	25	132	....	....	....	....	....	....	....	....	....	13	3	5	8	82	....	....	....	....
2005-06	Ottawa	NHL	71	16	27	43	135	10	1	3	212	7.5	17	24	41.7	27:11	10	1	3	4	23	1	0	0	27:32
	Slovakia	Olympics	6	1	1	2	2	....	....	....	....	....	....	....	....	....	....	....	....	....	....	....	....	....	....
2006-07	Boston	NHL	80	11	32	43	100	9	0	3	204	5.4	-21	1	0.0	27:58	....	....	....	....	....	....	....	....	....
2007-08	Boston	NHL	77	17	34	51	114	9	1	0	207	8.2	14	0	0.0	26:50	7	1	1	2	1	1	0	0	25:52
2008-09	Boston	NHL	80	19	31	50	95	11	0	3	216	8.8	23	4	25.0	26:04	11	1	3	4	11	1	0	1	25:11
2009-10	Boston	NHL	80	7	37	44	87	4	0	1	242	2.9	19	2	50.0	25:22	13	2	6	8	0	0	0	1	28:08
	Slovakia	Olympics	7	0	3	3	6	....	....	....	....	....	....	....	....	....	....	....	....	....	....	....	....	....	....
2010-11♦	Boston	NHL	81	14	30	44	88	8	1	2	264	5.3	33	0	0.0	25:26	24	2	7	9	34	1	0	0	27:39
	NHL Totals		**928**	**125**	**282**	**407**	**1385**	**65**	**6**	**20**	**1999**	**6.3**		**31**	**38.7**	**24:42**	**100**	**9**	**27**	**36**	**144**	**4**	**0**	**2**	**26:29**

AHL All-Rookie Team (1998) • NHL First All-Star Team (2004, 2009) • NHL Second All-Star Team (2006, 2008, 2011) • James Norris Memorial Trophy (2009) • Mark Messier NHL Leadership Award (2011) • Played in NHL All-Star Game (2003, 2007, 2008, 2009, 2011)

Traded to **Ottawa** by **NY Islanders** with Bill Muckalt and NY Islanders' 1st round choice (Jason Spezza) in 2001 Entry Draft for Alexei Yashin, June 23, 2001. Signed as a free agent by **Farjestad** (Sweden), September 24, 2004. Signed as a free agent by **Boston**, July 1, 2006.

Diamond (♦) indicates member of Stanley Cup-winning team.

"Did not play" Indicates that a player did not participate in a professional, junior or college league for an entire season.

Birthplace reflects the world map at the time a player was born. The Czech Republic and Slovakia became independent on January 1, 1993. Previously, players were born in Czechoslovakia. The Russian Republic was established on January 1, 1992. Previously, players were born in the USSR. Germany was unified on October 3, 1990. Previously, players were born in either East or West Germany. Former Soviet Republics (Belarus Estonia, Kazakhstan, Latvia, Lithuania, Ukraine) achieved independence between August 20 and December 25, 1991.

Pronunciation of Player Names

United Press International phonetic style.

AY	long A as in mate
A	short A as in cat
AI	nasal A as on air
AH	short A as in father
AW	broad A as in talk
EE	long E as in meat
EH	short E as in get
UH	hollow E as in the
AY	French long E with acute accent as in Pathe
IH	middle E as in pretty
EW	EW dipthong as in few
IGH	long I as in time
EE	French long I as in machine
IH	short I as in pity
OH	long O as in note
AH	short O as in hot
AW	broad O as in fought
OI	OI dipthong as in noise
OO	long double OO as in fool
U	short double O as in foot
OW	OW dipthong as in how
EW	long U as in mule
OO	long U as in rule
U	middle U as in put
UH	short U as in shut or hurt
K	hard C as in cat
S	soft C as in cease
SH	soft CH as in machine
CH	hard CH or TCH as in catch
Z	hard S as in bells
S	soft S as in sun
G	hard G as in gang
J	soft G as in general
ZH	soft J as in French version of Joliet
KH	gutteral CH as in Scottish version of Loch

All trades, free agent signings and other transactions involving NHL clubs are listed here and are presented in chronological order. First draft selection for players who re-enter the NHL Entry Draft is noted here as well. Also listed are other special notes. These are highlighted with a bullet (•).

Dates for trades or free agent signings often differ depending upon source. Signings can be reported based on when contracts are filed with NHL Central Registry or on the date a club announces that it has made a trade or come to terms with a free agent.

All-Star Team selections and awards are listed below player's year-by-year data.

NHL All-Star Game appearances are listed above trade notes.

THIS **80**TH EDITION OF THE *NHL Official Guide & Record Book* includes additional statistical categories for forwards and defensemen in the National Hockey League. These categories are, from left to right in the sample panel above, power-play goals (PP), shorthand goals (SH), game-winning goals (GW), shots on goal (S), percentage of shots that score (%), plus-minus rating (+/–), total faceoffs taken (TF), faceoff winning percentage (F%), and average time-on-ice per game played (Min).

To integrate this data, the Player Register is split into two sections. The Prospect Register presents data on players who have yet to play in the NHL. The NHL Player Register, containing more information and a photo of each player, lists all active players who have appeared in an NHL regular-season or playoff game at any time.

Goaltenders, whether prospects or active NHLers, are included in one register. With the addition of the shootout to NHL regular-season play, the column formerly used to record tie games for goaltenders has been renamed "O/T." For NHL goaltenders beginning in 2005-06, it lists overtime losses and shootout losses; previous to 2005-06, it lists tie games.

Registers (with their starting page) are presented in the following order: Prospects (275), NHL Players (345), Goaltenders (583), Retired Players (610) and Retired Goaltenders (651).

League abbreviations, page 662. Late additions to the Registers, page 609.

Some information is unavailable at press time. Readers are encouraged to contribute. See page 5 for contact names and addresses.

2011-12 Prospect Register

Note: The 2011-12 Prospect Register lists forwards and defensemen only. Goaltenders are listed separately. The Prospect Register lists every player drafted in the 2011 Entry Draft, players on NHL Reserve Lists and other players who have not yet played in the NHL. Trades and roster changes are current as of August 12, 2011.

Abbreviations: GP – games played; **G** – goals; **A** – assists; **Pts** – points; **PIM** – penalties in minutes; ***** – league-leading total.

NHL Player Register begins on page 345.
Goaltender Register begins on page 583.
Retired Player Index begins on page 610.
Retired Goaltender Index begins on page 651.
League Abbreviations are listed on page 662.

ABELTSHAUSER, Konrad   (ah-behlts-HAHW-zuhr, KAWN-rad)   **S.J.**
Defense. Shoots left. 6'5", 215 lbs.   Born, Bad Tolz, Germany, September 2, 1992.
(San Jose's 6th choice, 163rd overall, in 2010 Entry Draft).

Season	Club	League	GP	G	A	Pts	PIM	GP	G	A	Pts	PIM
2007-08	EC Bad Tolz Jr.	Ger-Jr.	36	1	10	11	32	8	0	6	6	2
2008-09	EC Bad Tolz Jr.	Ger-Jr.	36	16	28	44	26	4	1	0	1	0
2009-10	Halifax	QMJHL	48	5	20	25	28	....				
2010-11	Halifax	QMJHL	58	8	19	27	47	4	3	0	3	0

ABNEY, Cameron   (AB-nee, KAM-ih-RUHN)   **EDM**
Right wing. Shoots right. 6'5", 205 lbs.   Born, Aldergrove, B.C., May 23, 1991.
(Edmonton's 4th choice, 82nd overall, in 2009 Entry Draft).

Season	Club	League	GP	G	A	Pts	PIM	GP	G	A	Pts	PIM
2007-08	North Delta Devils	PIJHL	42	12	14	26	110	5	1	0	1	27
	Everett Silvertips	WHL	4	0	0	0	0	....				
2008-09	Everett Silvertips	WHL	48	1	3	4	103	5	0	0	0	2
2009-10	Everett Silvertips	WHL	34	3	3	6	60	....				
	Edmonton	WHL	34	3	4	7	63	....				
2010-11	Edmonton	WHL	60	7	13	20	72	4	1	0	1	6

ACOLATSE, Sena   (ah-koh-LAWT-say, SEH-na)   **S.J.**
Defense. Shoots right. 5'11", 205 lbs.   Born, Hayward, CA, November 28, 1990.

Season	Club	League	GP	G	A	Pts	PIM	GP	G	A	Pts	PIM
2006-07	Seattle	WHL	45	0	4	4	61	11	0	0	0	8
2007-08	Seattle	WHL	71	7	24	31	107	12	1	2	3	12
2008-09	Seattle	WHL	70	7	14	21	143	5	1	1	2	0
2009-10	Seattle	WHL	39	13	9	22	35	....				
	Saskatoon Blades	WHL	30	3	10	13	25	7	1	1	2	17
2010-11	Saskatoon Blades	WHL	1	0	0	0	2	....				
	Prince George	WHL	66	15	48	63	128	4	3	4	7	4
	Worcester Sharks	AHL	1	0	0	0	0	....				

Signed as a free agent by **San Jose**, March 4, 2011.

ADAMS, Mark   (A-duhmz, MAHRK)   **BUF**
Defense. Shoots right. 6'1", 194 lbs.   Born, Boston, MA, May 23, 1991.
(Buffalo's 4th choice, 134th overall, in 2009 Entry Draft).

Season	Club	League	GP	G	A	Pts	PIM	GP	G	A	Pts	PIM
2007-08	Malden Cath.	High-MA	23	4	13	17	....					
2008-09	Malden Cath.	High-MA	23	6	23	29	....					
	Bos. Jr. Bruins	EJHL	32	5	10	15	18					
2009-10	Chicago Steel	USHL	53	4	10	14	85					
2010-11	Providence College	H-East	33	0	3	3	22					

AGOSTINO, Kenneth   (a-goh-STEE-noh, KEH-nehth)   **PIT**
Left wing. Shoots left. 5'11", 190 lbs.   Born, Morristown, NJ, April 30, 1992.
(Pittsburgh's 4th choice, 140th overall, in 2010 Entry Draft).

Season	Club	League	GP	G	A	Pts	PIM	GP	G	A	Pts	PIM
2007-08	Delbarton	High-NJ	....	24	48	72	....					
2008-09	Delbarton	High-NJ	....	....	....	74	....					
2009-10	Delbarton	High-NJ	27	50	33	83	40					
	USNTDP	U-18	2	0	0	0	2					
2010-11	Yale	ECAC	31	11	14	25	30					

AHNELOV, Jonas   (AH-neh-lawv, YOH-nuhs)   **PHX**
Defense. Shoots left. 6'2", 220 lbs.   Born, Huddinge, Sweden, December 11, 1987.
(Phoenix's 3rd choice, 88th overall, in 2006 Entry Draft).

Season	Club	League	GP	G	A	Pts	PIM	GP	G	A	Pts	PIM
2003-04	Huddinge IK U18	Swe-U18	6	0	3	3	8					
	Huddinge IK Jr.	Swe-Jr.	9	0	1	1	6					
2004-05	Huddinge IK U18	Swe-U18	2	0	0	0	2					
	Huddinge IK Jr.	Swe-Jr.	29	3	3	6	94	3	0	0	0	2
2005-06	Frolunda Jr.	Swe-Jr.	29	4	11	15	84	7	2	4	6	22
	Frolunda	Sweden	15	0	0	0	2					
2006-07	Frolunda Jr.	Swe-Jr.	9	4	5	9	22	8	2	3	5	8
	Frolunda	Sweden	46	1	3	4	20					
2007-08	Boras HC	Sweden-2	1	0	0	0	0					
	Frolunda	Sweden	51	3	4	7	30	6	0	0	0	0
2008-09	San Antonio	AHL	43	1	6	7	35	....				
2009-10	San Antonio	AHL	11	0	1	1	2	....				
2010-11	San Antonio	AHL	42	2	2	4	10	....				

AKESON, Jason   (AK-uh-suhn, JAY-suhn)   **PHI**
Right wing. Shoots right. 5'11", 183 lbs.   Born, Orleans, Ont., June 3, 1990.

Season	Club	League	GP	G	A	Pts	PIM	GP	G	A	Pts	PIM
2006-07	Cumberland	CJHL	54	17	36	53	40					
2007-08	Cumberland	CJHL	34	18	43	61	14					
	Kitchener Rangers	OHL	13	0	2	2	4	16	0	1	1	0
2008-09	Kitchener Rangers	OHL	56	20	44	64	16	....				
2009-10	Kitchener Rangers	OHL	65	24	56	80	24	20	8	11	19	14
2010-11	Kitchener Rangers	OHL	67	24	*84	*108	23	7	3	6	9	0

OHL Second All-Star Team (2011)
Signed as a free agent by **Philadelphia**, March 2, 2011.

ALEXANDROV, Viktor   (al-ehx-AN-drawv, VIHK-tohr)   **ST.L.**
Left wing. Shoots left. 5'11", 183 lbs.   Born, Ust-Kamenogorsk, USSR, December 28, 1985.
(St. Louis' 3rd choice, 83rd overall, in 2004 Entry Draft).

Season	Club	League	GP	G	A	Pts	PIM	GP	G	A	Pts	PIM
2001-02	Ust-Kamenogorsk	Russia-2	45	12	17	29	48	2	0	1	1	2
2002-03	Yaroslavl	Russia	2	0	0	0	2					
	Energiya Kemerovo	Russia-2	15	2	4	6	12					
	Novokuznetsk	Russia	11	0	0	0	4					
2003-04	Novokuznetsk	Russia	57	5	4	9	26	4	1	3	4	4
2004-05	Novokuznetsk	Russia	50	8	10	18	16	4	1	1	2	0
2005-06	SKA St. Petersburg	Russia	41	4	6	10	55					
	St. Petersburg 2	Russia-3	1	0	3	3	0					
2006-07	SKA St. Petersburg	Russia	19	1	10	11	18					
	St. Petersburg 2	Russia-3	5	2	7	9	12					
	MVD	Russia	20	2	6	8	8	2	0	2	2	2
2007-08	Novokuznetsk	Russia	55	20	24	44	26					
2008-09	Omsk	Rus-KHL	35	2	8	10	18	8	2	0	2	8
2009-10	Nizhny Novgorod	Rus-KHL	55	11	14	25	34					
2010-11	Chelyabinsk	Rus-KHL	14	3	2	5	4					
	Mechel	Russia-2	2	0	0	0	0					
	Barys Astana	Rus-KHL	11	1	1	2	10	4	0	0	0	2

ALEXANDROV, Yury   (al-ehx-AN-drawv, YOO-ree)   **BOS**
Defense. Shoots left. 6', 185 lbs.   Born, Cherepovets, USSR, June 24, 1988.
(Boston's 2nd choice, 37th overall, in 2006 Entry Draft).

Season	Club	League	GP	G	A	Pts	PIM	GP	G	A	Pts	PIM
2003-04	Cherepovets 2	Russia-3	32	0	2	2	10	4	0	0	0	0
2004-05	Cherepovets 2	Russia-3	STATISTICS NOT AVAILABLE									
2005-06	Cherepovets	Russia	37	1	0	1	18	2	0	0	0	2
2006-07	Cherepovets	Russia	45	1	1	2	38	5	0	0	0	8
2007-08	Cherepovets	Russia	45	5	4	9	32	8	0	0	0	8
2008-09	Cherepovets	Rus-KHL	26	3	5	8	40	....				
2009-10	Cherepovets	Rus-KHL	56	6	15	21	56	....				
	Cherepovets Jr.	Russia-Jr.						3	0	1	1	2
2010-11	Providence Bruins	AHL	66	6	13	19	44	....				

ALIU, Akim (ah-lee-OO, a-KEEM) WPG

Center. Shoots right. 6'4", 225 lbs. Born, Okene, Nigeria, April 24, 1989.
(Chicago's 3rd choice, 56th overall, in 2007 Entry Draft).

			Regular Season					Playoffs				
Season	Club	League	GP	G	A	Pts	PIM	GP	G	A	Pts	PIM
2004-05	Toronto Marlboros	GTHL	68	35	50	85	197	....	....	....	....	....
2005-06	Windsor Spitfires	OHL	18	3	4	7	25	....	....	....	....	....
	Sudbury Wolves	OHL	29	7	6	13	54	6	0	1	1	7
2006-07	Sudbury Wolves	OHL	53	20	22	42	104	21	1	5	6	50
2007-08	London Knights	OHL	60	28	33	61	133	5	2	1	3	15
	Rockford IceHogs	AHL	2	0	0	0	2	....	....	....	....	....
2008-09	London Knights	OHL	16	8	10	18	30	....	....	....	....	....
	Sudbury Wolves	OHL	29	10	16	26	61	6	2	1	3	14
	Rockford IceHogs	AHL	5	2	0	2	14	1	1	0	1	0
2009-10	Rockford IceHogs	AHL	48	11	6	17	69	....	....	....	....	....
	Toledo Walleye	ECHL	13	5	9	14	18	2	1	1	2	16
2010-11	Chicago Wolves	AHL	43	4	5	9	53	....	....	....	....	....
	Gwinnett	ECHL	16	12	8	20	22	....	....	....	....	....
	Peoria Rivermen	AHL	16	5	4	9	20	2	1	0	1	6

Traded to **Atlanta** by **Chicago** with Brent Sopel, Dustin Byfuglien and Ben Eager for Marty Reasoner, Joey Crabb, Jeremy Morin and New Jersey's 1st (previously acquired, Chicago selected Kevin Hayes) and 2nd (previously acquired, Chicago selected Justin Holl) round choices in 2010 Entry Draft, June 24, 2010. • Transferred to **Winnipeg** after **Atlanta** franchise relocated, June 21, 2011.

ALMQVIST, Adam (AHLM-kwihst, A-duhm) DET

Defense. Shoots left. 5'10", 169 lbs. Born, Jonkoping, Sweden, February 27, 1991.
(Detroit's 7th choice, 210th overall, in 2009 Entry Draft).

			Regular Season					Playoffs				
Season	Club	League	GP	G	A	Pts	PIM	GP	G	A	Pts	PIM
2006-07	HV 71 U18	Swe-U18	1	0	0	0	0	1	0	0	0	0
2007-08	HV 71 U18	Swe-U18	18	8	12	20	28	....	....	....	....	....
	HV 71 Jr.	Swe-Jr.	23	1	6	7	12	3	0	0	0	4
2008-09	HV 71 Jr.	Swe-Jr.	41	8	28	36	44	....	....	....	....	....
2009-10	HV 71 Jr.	Swe-Jr.	15	5	29	34	14	....	....	....	....	....
	HV 71 Jonkoping	Sweden	28	2	6	8	10	16	1	10	11	8
2010-11	HV 71 Jonkoping	Sweden	52	0	16	16	32	2	0	0	0	0
	HV 71 Jr.	Swe-Jr.	....	....	....	....	....	5	2	0	2	4

ALT, Mark (AHLT, MAHRK) CAR

Defense. Shoots right. 6'4", 201 lbs. Born, Kansas City, MO, October 18, 1991.
(Carolina's 3rd choice, 53rd overall, in 2010 Entry Draft).

			Regular Season					Playoffs				
Season	Club	League	GP	G	A	Pts	PIM	GP	G	A	Pts	PIM
2007-08	Cretin-Derham	High-MN	17	1	5	6	4	....	....	....	....	....
2008-09	Cretin-Derham	High-MN	26	11	16	27	10	....	....	....	....	....
2009-10	Cretin-Derham	High-MN	24	6	14	20	....	....	....	....	....	....
	Team Northeast	UMHSEL	24	13	9	22	....	....	....	....	....	....
2010-11	U. of Minnesota	WCHA	35	2	8	10	22	....	....	....	....	....

AMBROZ, Seth (AM-brohz, SEHTH) CBJ

Right wing. Shoots right. 6'2", 209 lbs. Born, New Prague, MN, April 3, 1993.
(Columbus' 4th choice, 128th overall, in 2011 Entry Draft).

			Regular Season					Playoffs				
Season	Club	League	GP	G	A	Pts	PIM	GP	G	A	Pts	PIM
2007-08	New Prague	High-MN	22	36	32	68	....	....	....	....	....	....
2008-09	Omaha Lancers	USHL	60	14	17	31	88	3	0	0	0	2
2009-10	Omaha Lancers	USHL	56	22	27	49	118	8	4	2	6	8
2010-11	Omaha Lancers	USHL	56	24	22	46	89	3	2	0	2	4

• Signed Letter of Intent to attend **University of Minnesota** (WCHA) in fall of 2011.

ANDERSON, Matt (AN-duhr-suhn, MAT) N.J.

Right wing. Shoots right. 5'11", 195 lbs. Born, West Islip, NY, October 31, 1982.

			Regular Season					Playoffs				
Season	Club	League	GP	G	A	Pts	PIM	GP	G	A	Pts	PIM
2002-03	Massachusetts	H-East	36	10	21	31	34	....	....	....	....	....
2003-04	Massachusetts	H-East	DID NOT PLAY – INJURED									
2004-05	Massachusetts	H-East	18	7	13	20	34	....	....	....	....	....
2005-06	Massachusetts	H-East	36	7	13	20	30	....	....	....	....	....
2006-07	Massachusetts	H-East	38	10	10	20	32	....	....	....	....	....
	Chicago Wolves	AHL	....	....	....	....	....	13	1	1	2	6
2007-08	Chicago Wolves	AHL	14	1	1	2	8	10	1	1	2	4
	Gwinnett	ECHL	37	14	14	28	28	8	3	2	5	0
2008-09	Chicago Wolves	AHL	66	13	18	31	32	....	....	....	....	....
2009-10	Chicago Wolves	AHL	63	16	29	45	18	14	0	12	12	4
2010-11	Albany Devils	AHL	76	23	32	55	49	....	....	....	....	....

• Missed entire 2003-04 due to shoulder injury. • Missed majority of 2004-05 due to broken ankle. Signed as a free agent by **Chicago** (AHL), March 30, 2007. Signed as a free agent by **Albany** (AHL), July 21, 2010.

ANDERSSON, Joakim (AN-duhr-suhn, YOH-ah-kihm) DET

Center. Shoots left. 6'2", 205 lbs. Born, Munkedal, Sweden, February 5, 1989.
(Detroit's 2nd choice, 88th overall, in 2007 Entry Draft).

			Regular Season					Playoffs				
Season	Club	League	GP	G	A	Pts	PIM	GP	G	A	Pts	PIM
2004-05	Munkedals BK	Sweden-5	STATISTICS NOT AVAILABLE									
2005-06	Frolunda U18	Swe-U18	1	0	0	0	0	2	0	1	1	0
	Frolunda Jr.	Swe-Jr.	35	9	11	20	10	7	2	5	7	4
2006-07	Frolunda U18	Swe-U18	2	1	2	3	2	6	3	2	5	28
	Frolunda Jr.	Swe-Jr.	41	20	26	46	60	8	0	7	7	4
	Frolunda	Sweden	1	0	0	0	0	....	....	....	....	....
2007-08	Boras HC	Sweden-2	33	6	17	23	26	....	....	....	....	....
	Frolunda Jr.	Swe-Jr.	6	8	2	10	30	5	6	3	9	4
	Frolunda	Sweden	9	1	0	1	2	4	1	1	2	0
2008-09	Boras HC	Sweden-2	4	2	2	4	2	....	....	....	....	....
	Frolunda	Sweden	49	6	6	12	22	11	0	0	0	4
	Grand Rapids	AHL	1	0	1	1	2	10	1	2	3	4
2009-10	Frolunda	Sweden	55	6	12	18	42	7	1	2	3	0
2010-11	Grand Rapids	AHL	79	7	15	22	30	....	....	....	....	....

ANDERSSON, Peter (AN-duhr-suhn, PEE-tuhr) VAN

Defense. Shoots left. 6'3", 194 lbs. Born, Kvidinge, Sweden, April 13, 1991.
(Vancouver's 5th choice, 143rd overall, in 2009 Entry Draft).

			Regular Season					Playoffs				
Season	Club	League	GP	G	A	Pts	PIM	GP	G	A	Pts	PIM
2007-08	Frolunda U18	Swe-U18	12	2	3	5	18	5	0	1	1	14
	Frolunda Jr.	Swe-Jr.	8	0	2	2	4	1	0	0	0	0
	Frolunda	Sweden	1	0	0	0	0	....	....	....	....	....
2008-09	Frolunda U18	Swe-U18	5	0	1	1	4	5	1	1	2	2
	Frolunda Jr.	Swe-Jr.	36	3	5	8	42	4	0	1	1	0
2009-10	Frolunda Jr.	Swe-Jr.	1	1	0	1	0	....	....	....	....	....
	Frolunda	Sweden	21	1	4	5	4	....	....	....	....	....
	Boras HC	Sweden-2	10	2	4	6	12	....	....	....	....	....
2010-11	Frolunda	Sweden	27	0	0	0	8	....	....	....	....	....
	Boras HC	Sweden-2	30	2	2	4	24	....	....	....	....	....
	Frolunda Jr.	Swe-Jr.	....	....	....	....	....	7	1	3	4	2

ANDREOFF, Andy (an-DRAY-awf, AN-dee) L.A.

Center. Shoots left. 6'1", 198 lbs. Born, Pickering, Ont., May 17, 1991.
(Los Angeles' 2nd choice, 80th overall, in 2011 Entry Draft).

			Regular Season					Playoffs				
Season	Club	League	GP	G	A	Pts	PIM	GP	G	A	Pts	PIM
2006-07	Ajax Pickering	Minor-ON	48	17	21	38	58	....	....	....	....	....
2007-08	Pickering Panthers	OPJHL	40	12	15	27	58	....	....	....	....	....
	Oshawa Generals	OHL	25	0	1	1	8	9	0	0	0	2
2008-09	Oshawa Generals	OHL	66	11	14	25	37	....	....	....	....	....
2009-10	Oshawa Generals	OHL	67	15	33	48	70	....	....	....	....	....
2010-11	Oshawa Generals	OHL	66	33	42	75	109	10	3	8	11	16

ANDREWS, Brent (AN-drooz, BREHNT) NSH

Left wing. Shoots left. 6'2", 200 lbs. Born, Hunter River, PEI, January 19, 1993.
(Nashville's 7th choice, 202nd overall, in 2011 Entry Draft).

			Regular Season					Playoffs				
Season	Club	League	GP	G	A	Pts	PIM	GP	G	A	Pts	PIM
2008-09	Cornwall Thunder	NBPEI	30	12	20	32	18	4	0	3	3	8
2009-10	Halifax	QMJHL	64	7	9	16	33	....	....	....	....	....
2010-11	Halifax	QMJHL	68	12	17	29	33	4	0	0	0	11

ANDRONOV, Sergei (an-DROH-nahv, SAIR-gay) ST.L.

Right wing. Shoots left. 6'2", 190 lbs. Born, Penza, USSR, July 19, 1989.
(St. Louis' 3rd choice, 78th overall, in 2009 Entry Draft).

			Regular Season					Playoffs				
Season	Club	League	GP	G	A	Pts	PIM	GP	G	A	Pts	PIM
2006-07	Lada Togliatti	Russia	3	0	0	0	2	....	....	....	....	....
2007-08	Lada Togliatti 2	Russia-3	16	10	2	12	16	8	7	2	9	0
	Lada Togliatti	Russia	38	2	5	7	2	4	1	0	1	6
2008-09	Lada Togliatti 2	Russia-3	7	5	2	7	6	3	0	2	2	32
	Lada Togliatti	Rus-KHL	47	9	5	14	22	5	0	1	1	8
2009-10	Lada Togliatti	Rus-KHL	33	5	9	14	20	....	....	....	....	....
	CSKA Moscow	Rus-KHL	19	5	3	8	6	3	0	0	0	0
2010-11	CSKA Moscow	Rus-KHL	53	5	2	7	14	....	....	....	....	....
	CSKA Jr.	Russia-Jr.	7	3	2	5	29	16	6	5	11	4

ANELOSKI, Bryce (a-nehl-AWZ-kee, BRIGHS) OTT

Defense. Shoots right. 6'2", 200 lbs. Born, Pekin, IL, April 27, 1990.
(Ottawa's 4th choice, 196th overall, in 2010 Entry Draft).

			Regular Season					Playoffs				
Season	Club	League	GP	G	A	Pts	PIM	GP	G	A	Pts	PIM
2007-08	Cedar Rapids	USHL	59	8	12	20	39	3	0	0	0	0
2008-09	Providence College	H-East	16	0	1	1	8	....	....	....	....	....
	Cedar Rapids	USHL	38	4	8	12	38	5	0	0	0	20
2009-10	Cedar Rapids	USHL	60	15	39	54	34	5	0	4	4	0
2010-11	Nebraska-Omaha	WCHA	39	2	17	19	14	....	....	....	....	....

USHL First All-Star Team (2010)

ANGELIDIS, Mike (AN-gehl-EE-dihs, MIGHK) T.B.

Left wing. Shoots left. 6'1", 210 lbs. Born, Woodbridge, Ont., June 27, 1985.

			Regular Season					Playoffs				
Season	Club	League	GP	G	A	Pts	PIM	GP	G	A	Pts	PIM
2002-03	Owen Sound	OHL	65	7	10	17	81	4	1	1	2	0
2003-04	Owen Sound	OHL	66	9	9	18	118	7	4	1	5	4
2004-05	Owen Sound	OHL	41	9	10	19	126	8	3	2	5	10
2005-06	Owen Sound	OHL	68	53	25	78	167	11	5	9	14	38
2006-07	Albany River Rats	AHL	27	4	5	9	44	4	0	0	0	10
	Florida Everblades	ECHL	24	10	8	18	54	....	....	....	....	....
2007-08	Albany River Rats	AHL	74	11	16	27	151	7	0	2	2	6
2008-09	Albany River Rats	AHL	67	15	10	25	142	....	....	....	....	....
2009-10	Albany River Rats	AHL	67	12	12	24	119	8	2	4	6	12
2010-11	Norfolk Admirals	AHL	80	20	18	38	169	3	0	0	0	2

OHL First All-Star Team (2006) • Canadian Major Junior Humanitarian Player of the Year (2006)

Signed as a free agent by **Carolina**, July 27, 2006. Signed as a free agent by **Tampa Bay**, August 3, 2010.

ANIKEYENKO, Vitali (ah-nih-KEH-ehn-koh, vih-TAL-ee) OTT

Defense. Shoots right. 6'3", 198 lbs. Born, Kiev, USSR, January 2, 1987.
(Ottawa's 2nd choice, 70th overall, in 2005 Entry Draft).

			Regular Season					Playoffs				
Season	Club	League	GP	G	A	Pts	PIM	GP	G	A	Pts	PIM
2003-04	Yaroslavl 2	Russia-3	40	2	9	11	68	....	....	....	....	....
2004-05	Yaroslavl 2	Russia-3	58	3	11	14	62	....	....	....	....	....
2005-06	Yaroslavl 2	Russia-3	19	3	5	8	20	....	....	....	....	....
	Yaroslavl	Russia	26	0	1	1	28	1	0	0	0	0
2006-07	Yaroslavl 2	Russia-3	15	1	6	7	59	....	....	....	....	....
	Yaroslavl	Russia	25	1	3	4	16	3	0	0	0	12
2007-08	Novokuznetsk	Russia	10	1	1	2	10	....	....	....	....	....
	Yaroslavl	Russia	40	4	9	13	48	16	0	0	0	20
2008-09	Yaroslavl	Rus-KHL	40	2	10	12	44	19	0	2	2	10
2009-10	Yaroslavl	Rus-KHL	52	7	11	18	50	9	1	0	1	8
2010-11	Yaroslavl	Rus-KHL	52	5	14	19	80	3	0	2	2	4

ANTHONY, Steven (AN-thuh-nee, STEE-vehn) **VAN**

Left wing. Shoots left. 6'2", 195 lbs. Born, Halifax, N.S., March 21, 1991.
(Vancouver's 7th choice, 187th overall, in 2009 Entry Draft).

			Regular Season					Playoffs				
Season	Club	League	GP	G	A	Pts	PIM	GP	G	A	Pts	PIM
2006-07	Dartmouth	NSMHL	35	33	31	64	78	9	8	16	24	10
2007-08	Saint John	QMJHL	55	6	8	14	38	10	1	1	2	2
2008-09	Saint John	QMJHL	67	19	29	48	47	4	1	2	3	4
2009-10	Saint John	QMJHL	61	18	23	41	28	5	0	0	0	6
2010-11	Saint John	QMJHL	61	23	37	60	23	14	5	7	12	12

ARCHAMBAULT, Olivier (AHR-sham-boh, oh-lih-VEE-ay) **MTL**

Left wing. Shoots left. 5'11", 176 lbs. Born, Le Gardeur, Que., February 16, 1993.
(Montreal's 7th choice, 108th overall, in 2011 Entry Draft).

			Regular Season					Playoffs				
Season	Club	League	GP	G	A	Pts	PIM	GP	G	A	Pts	PIM
2008-09	Esther-Blondin	QAAA	45	16	33	49	32	15	8	7	15	12
2009-10	Val-d'Or Foreurs	QMJHL	58	12	15	27	14	4	0	0	0	0
2010-11	Val-d'Or Foreurs	QMJHL	65	20	33	53	28	4	1	2	3	4

ARCHIBALD, Brandon (AHR-chih-bawld, BRAN-duhn) **CBJ**

Defense. Shoots right. 6'4", 205 lbs. Born, Port Huron, MI, March 31, 1992.
(Columbus' 4th choice, 94th overall, in 2010 Entry Draft).

			Regular Season					Playoffs				
Season	Club	League	GP	G	A	Pts	PIM	GP	G	A	Pts	PIM
2007-08	Det. Honeybaked	MWEHL	26	1	3	4	28	....	....	....	....	....
	Det. Honeybaked	Minor-MI	38	6	18	24	20	....	....	....	....	....
	Det. Honeybaked	Exhib.	7	1	1	2	8	....	....	....	....	....
2008-09	Sault Ste. Marie	OHL	61	0	8	8	45	....	....	....	....	....
2009-10	Sault Ste. Marie	OHL	68	5	28	33	81	5	1	1	2	6
2010-11	Sault Ste. Marie	OHL	37	2	17	19	40	....	....	....	....	....
	Saginaw Spirit	OHL	29	0	3	3	34	8	0	0	0	2

ARCHIBALD, Darren (ahr-CHIH-bawld, DAIR-ehn) **VAN**

Left wing. Shoots left. 6'3", 195 lbs. Born, Newmarket, Ont., February 9, 1990.

			Regular Season					Playoffs				
Season	Club	League	GP	G	A	Pts	PIM	GP	G	A	Pts	PIM
2007-08	Stouffville Spirit	OPJHL	49	21	27	48	46	15	9	9	18	35
2008-09	Barrie Colts	OHL	68	25	24	49	35	5	4	3	7	2
2009-10	Barrie Colts	OHL	57	26	33	59	62	16	5	5	10	16
2010-11	Barrie Colts	OHL	24	18	12	30	21	....	....	....	....	....
	Niagara Ice Dogs	OHL	37	23	13	36	30	14	10	4	14	6

Signed as a free agent by **Vancouver**, December 13, 2010.

ARCHIBALD, Josh (AHR-chih-bawld, JAWSH) **PIT**

Wing. Shoots right. 5'10", 161 lbs. Born, Regina, Sask., October 6, 1992.
(Pittsburgh's 4th choice, 174th overall, in 2011 Entry Draft).

			Regular Season					Playoffs				
Season	Club	League	GP	G	A	Pts	PIM	GP	G	A	Pts	PIM
2009-10	Brainerd	High-MN	25	20	30	50	72	2	2	5	7	2
2010-11	Team North	UMHSEL	21	8	7	15	49	3	0	2	2	6
	Brainerd	High-MN	25	27	46	73	40	2	3	2	5	0

• Signed Letter of Intent to attend **University of Nebraska-Omaha** (WCHA) in fall of 2011.

ARCOBELLO, Mark (ahr-koh-BEHL-oh, MAHRK) **EDM**

Right wing. Shoots right. 5'10", 185 lbs. Born, Milford, CT, August 12, 1988.

			Regular Season					Playoffs				
Season	Club	League	GP	G	A	Pts	PIM	GP	G	A	Pts	PIM
2006-07	Yale	ECAC	29	10	14	24	49	....	....	....	....	....
2007-08	Yale	ECAC	34	7	14	21	40	....	....	....	....	....
2008-09	Yale	ECAC	34	17	18	35	68	....	....	....	....	....
2009-10	Yale	ECAC	34	15	21	36	46	....	....	....	....	....
2010-11	Stockton Thunder	ECHL	33	7	13	20	10	....	....	....	....	....
	Oklahoma City	AHL	26	11	11	22	4	6	1	1	2	0

ECAC First All-Star Team (2009) • NCAA East Second All-American Team (2009)

Signed as a free agent by **Oklahoma City** (AHL), September, 2010. • Assigned to **Stckton** (ECHL) by **Oklahoma City** (AHL), October 12, 2010. Signed as a free agent by **Edmonton**, April 1, 2011.

ARMIA, Joel (ahr-MEE-uh, JOHL) **BUF**

Right wing. Shoots right. 6'3", 192 lbs. Born, Pori, Finland, May 31, 1993.
(Buffalo's 1st choice, 16th overall, in 2011 Entry Draft).

			Regular Season					Playoffs				
Season	Club	League	GP	G	A	Pts	PIM	GP	G	A	Pts	PIM
2008-09	Assat Pori U18	Fin-U18	8	3	1	4	2	....	....	....	....	....
2009-10	Assat Pori U18	Fin-U18	9	7	9	16	31	6	6	3	9	8
	Assat Pori Jr.	Fin-Jr.	27	15	6	21	32	5	1	1	2	0
2010-11	Suomi U20	Finland-2	4	0	3	3	6	....	....	....	....	....
	Assat Pori	Finland	48	18	11	29	24	5	2	0	2	4

ARMSTRONG, John (AHRM-strawng, JAWN)

Center. Shoots right. 6'2", 188 lbs. Born, Unionville, Ont., February 26, 1988.
(Calgary's 2nd choice, 87th overall, in 2006 Entry Draft).

			Regular Season					Playoffs				
Season	Club	League	GP	G	A	Pts	PIM	GP	G	A	Pts	PIM
2004-05	Plymouth Whalers	OHL	52	6	13	19	39	4	0	0	0	4
2005-06	Plymouth Whalers	OHL	65	14	23	37	75	13	4	7	11	18
2006-07	Plymouth Whalers	OHL	34	8	13	21	26	....	....	....	....	....
	Peterborough	OHL	27	11	13	24	34	....	....	....	....	....
2007-08	Peterborough	OHL	65	21	36	57	77	5	0	1	1	6
2008-09	Quad City Flames	AHL	68	5	15	20	72	....	....	....	....	....
2009-10	Abbotsford Heat	AHL	14	1	5	6	13	....	....	....	....	....
2010-11	Abbotsford Heat	AHL	78	9	8	17	91	....	....	....	....	....

• Missed majority of 2009-10 due to shoulder surgery and knee surgery.

ARNOLD, Bill (AHR-nohld, BIHL) **CGY**

Center. Shoots right. 6', 215 lbs. Born, Boston, MA, May 13, 1992.
(Calgary's 4th choice, 108th overall, in 2010 Entry Draft).

			Regular Season					Playoffs				
Season	Club	League	GP	G	A	Pts	PIM	GP	G	A	Pts	PIM
2008-09	Nobles	High-MA	29	28	27	55	....	....	....	....	....	....
	Bos. Little Bruins	Minor-MA	33	26	21	47	24	....	....	....	....	....
2009-10	USNTDP	USHL	26	8	15	23	20	....	....	....	....	....
	USNTDP	U-18	38	12	16	28	30	....	....	....	....	....
2010-11	Boston College	H-East	39	10	10	20	38	....	....	....	....	....

Hockey East All-Rookie Team (2011)

ARONSON, Taylor (AIR-uhn-suhn, TAY-luhr) **NSH**

Defense. Shoots right. 6'1", 205 lbs. Born, Placentia, CA, December 30, 1991.
(Nashville's 2nd choice, 78th overall, in 2010 Entry Draft).

			Regular Season					Playoffs				
Season	Club	League	GP	G	A	Pts	PIM	GP	G	A	Pts	PIM
2008-09	L.A. Jr. Kings	T1EHL	45	9	16	25	68	....	....	....	....	....
2009-10	Portland	WHL	71	5	25	30	65	11	2	7	9	13
2010-11	Portland	WHL	71	5	32	37	81	21	0	2	2	20

ASHTON, Carter (ASH-tuhn, KAHR-tuhr) **T.B.**

Right wing. Shoots left. 6'3", 215 lbs. Born, Winnipeg, Man., April 1, 1991.
(Tampa Bay's 2nd choice, 29th overall, in 2009 Entry Draft).

			Regular Season					Playoffs				
Season	Club	League	GP	G	A	Pts	PIM	GP	G	A	Pts	PIM
2006-07	Sask. Contacts	SMHL	41	28	38	66	99	....	....	....	....	....
	Lethbridge	WHL	2	0	0	0	0	....	....	....	....	....
2007-08	Lethbridge	WHL	40	5	4	9	21	19	0	1	1	12
2008-09	Lethbridge	WHL	70	30	20	50	93	11	1	2	3	15
2009-10	Lethbridge	WHL	28	13	13	26	52	....	....	....	....	....
	Regina Pats	WHL	37	11	14	25	57	....	....	....	....	....
	Norfolk Admirals	AHL	11	1	0	1	6	....	....	....	....	....
2010-11	Regina Pats	WHL	29	16	11	27	44	....	....	....	....	....
	Tri-City Americans	WHL	33	17	27	44	62	10	3	5	8	4
	Norfolk Admirals	AHL	....	....	....	....	....	2	0	0	0	0

ATKINSON, Cam (AT-kihn-suhn, KAM) **CBJ**

Right wing. Shoots right. 5'9", 165 lbs. Born, Riverside, CT, June 5, 1989.
(Columbus' 8th choice, 157th overall, in 2008 Entry Draft).

			Regular Season					Playoffs				
Season	Club	League	GP	G	A	Pts	PIM	GP	G	A	Pts	PIM
2005-06	Avon Old Farms	High-CT	25	15	20	35	16	....	....	....	....	....
2006-07	Avon Old Farms	High-CT	27	28	24	52	12	....	....	....	....	....
2007-08	Avon Old Farms	High-CT	28	26	37	63	10	....	....	....	....	....
2008-09	Boston College	H-East	36	7	12	19	28	....	....	....	....	....
2009-10	Boston College	H-East	42	*30	23	53	30	....	....	....	....	....
2010-11	Boston College	H-East	39	*31	21	*52	28	....	....	....	....	....
	Springfield Falcons	AHL	5	3	2	5	0	....	....	....	....	....

Hockey East Second All-Star Team (2010) • NCAA Championship All-Tournament Team (2010) • Hockey East First All-Star Team (2011) • NCAA East First All-American Team (2011)

ATYUSHOV, Vitali (a-tew-SHAWF, vih-TAL-ee) **OTT**

Defense. Shoots left. 6'1", 205 lbs. Born, Penza, USSR, July 4, 1979.
(Ottawa's 8th choice, 276th overall, in 2002 Entry Draft).

			Regular Season					Playoffs				
Season	Club	League	GP	G	A	Pts	PIM	GP	G	A	Pts	PIM
1997-98	Krylja Sovetov	Russia	4	0	0	0	2	....	....	....	....	....
1998-99	Dizelist Penza 2	Russia-4	2	1	1	2	2	....	....	....	....	....
	Dizelist Penza	Russia-2	22	0	0	0	22	....	....	....	....	....
	Krylja Sovetov	Russia	17	1	0	1	20	....	....	....	....	....
	Krylja Sovetov	Russia-Q	21	0	5	5	50	....	....	....	....	....
99-2000	Perm	Russia	38	4	0	4	50	3	0	0	0	12
2000-01	Perm	Russia	44	3	9	12	32	....	....	....	....	....
2001-02	Perm	Russia	51	4	8	12	66	....	....	....	....	....
2002-03	Ak Bars Kazan	Russia	33	0	9	9	12	2	0	0	0	0
2003-04	Magnitogorsk	Russia	56	5	9	14	26	14	2	3	5	6
2004-05	Magnitogorsk	Russia	58	6	18	24	42	5	2	0	2	0
2005-06	Magnitogorsk	Russia	51	7	12	19	64	11	2	0	2	4
2006-07	Magnitogorsk	Russia	54	7	20	27	46	15	3	9	12	10
2007-08	Magnitogorsk	Russia	56	10	33	43	32	10	1	4	5	2
2008-09	Magnitogorsk	Rus-KHL	55	8	27	35	34	12	1	6	7	8
2009-10	Magnitogorsk	Rus-KHL	49	5	17	22	45	10	1	3	4	6
2010-11	Magnitogorsk	Rus-KHL	46	6	14	20	36	20	0	7	7	16

AUBRY, Louis-Marc (AW-bree, LOO-ee-MAHRK) **DET**

Center. Shoots left. 6'4", 202 lbs. Born, Arthabaska, Que., November 11, 1991.
(Detroit's 3rd choice, 81st overall, in 2010 Entry Draft).

			Regular Season					Playoffs				
Season	Club	League	GP	G	A	Pts	PIM	GP	G	A	Pts	PIM
2007-08	Trois-Rivieres	QAAA	20	9	20	29	30	7	1	1	2	20
2008-09	Montreal	QMJHL	65	10	12	22	53	10	2	2	4	8
2009-10	Montreal	QMJHL	66	15	18	33	69	7	1	1	2	6
2010-11	Montreal	QMJHL	35	13	12	25	26	10	5	1	6	2

AVTSIN, Alexander (AV-tsihn, al-ehx-AN-duhr) **MTL**

Right wing. Shoots right. 6'2", 198 lbs. Born, Moscow, USSR, March 19, 1991.
(Montreal's 4th choice, 109th overall, in 2009 Entry Draft).

			Regular Season					Playoffs				
Season	Club	League	GP	G	A	Pts	PIM	GP	G	A	Pts	PIM
2008-09	Dyn'o Moscow 2	Russia-3	STATISTICS NOT AVAILABLE									
2009-10	Dynamo Moscow	Rus-KHL	30	3	6	9	10	....	....	....	....	....
	Dyn'o Moscow Jr.	Russia-Jr.	12	4	5	9	20	....	....	....	....	....
2010-11	Hamilton Bulldogs	AHL	58	5	15	20	22	4	0	2	2	2

AXELSSON, Dick (AHX-ehl-suhn, DIHK) **DET**

Wing. Shoots left. 6'2", 198 lbs. Born, Stockholm, Sweden, April 25, 1987.
(Detroit's 3rd choice, 62nd overall, in 2006 Entry Draft).

			Regular Season					Playoffs				
Season	Club	League	GP	G	A	Pts	PIM	GP	G	A	Pts	PIM
2003-04	Huddinge IK U18	Swe-U18	13	3	1	4	38	....	....	....	....	....
2004-05	Huddinge IK U18	Swe-U18	1	0	0	0	0	....	....	....	....	....
	Huddinge IK Jr.	Swe-Jr.	31	12	4	16	34	3	1	0	1	0
2005-06	Huddinge IK Jr.	Swe-Jr.	28	19	15	34	157	....	....	....	....	....
2006-07	Huddinge IK	Sweden-2	33	16	15	31	145	....	....	....	....	....
2007-08	Djurgarden	Sweden	47	12	13	25	44	5	1	0	1	2
2008-09	Djurgarden	Sweden	18	5	7	12	10	....	....	....	....	....
	Farjestad	Sweden	21	6	12	18	32	9	1	3	4	2
2009-10	Grand Rapids	AHL	17	2	3	5	6	....	....	....	....	....
	Farjestad	Sweden	15	6	4	10	24	7	1	2	3	6
2010-11	Farjestad	Sweden	47	15	15	30	126	14	4	6	10	24

AZEVEDO, Justin (a-zeh-VAY-doh, JUHS-tihn) L.A.

Center. Shoots right. 5'7", 175 lbs. Born, West Lorne, Ont., April 1, 1988.
(Los Angeles' 8th choice, 153rd overall, in 2008 Entry Draft).

			Regular Season					Playoffs				
Season	Club	League	GP	G	A	Pts	PIM	GP	G	A	Pts	PIM
2004-05	Kitchener Rangers	OHL	58	18	21	39	34	15	3	1	4	14
2005-06	Kitchener Rangers	OHL	60	29	40	69	80	5	0	3	3	12
2006-07	Kitchener Rangers	OHL	50	17	39	56	42	9	4	11	15	22
2007-08	Kitchener Rangers	OHL	67	43	*81	*124	69	20	10	*26	*36	33
2008-09	Manchester	AHL	49	12	24	36	31	....	....	....	....	....
2009-10	Manchester	AHL	46	14	13	27	31	16	3	6	9	12
2010-11	Manchester	AHL	79	18	35	53	71	7	3	7	10	10

OHL First All-Star Team (2008) • Memorial Cup All-Star Team (2008) • Ed Chynoweth Trophy (Memorial Cup - Leading Scorer) (2008) • Canadian Major Junior First All-Star Team (2008) • Canadian Major Junior Player of the Year (2008)

BACKMAN, Mattias (BAK-man, mah-TIGH-uhs) DET

Defense. Shoots left. 6'2", 169 lbs. Born, Linkoping, Sweden, October 3, 1992.
(Detroit's 7th choice, 146th overall, in 2011 Entry Draft).

			Regular Season					Playoffs				
Season	Club	League	GP	G	A	Pts	PIM	GP	G	A	Pts	PIM
2007-08	Linkopings HC U18	Swe-U18	21	0	2	2	14	....	....	....	....	....
2008-09	Linkopings HC U18	Swe-U18	30	5	8	13	16	1	0	1	1	0
	Linkopings HC Jr.	Swe-Jr.	2	0	0	0	2	....	....	....	....	....
2009-10	Linkopings HC U18	Swe-U18	2	2	1	3	4	3	0	0	0	2
	Linkopings HC	Sweden	5	0	0	0	2	....	....	....	....	....
	Linkopings HC Jr.	Swe-Jr.	33	4	5	9	38	6	1	0	1	10
	Linkopings HC	Sweden	5	0	0	0	2	....	....	....	....	....
2010-11	Linkopings HC Jr.	Swe-Jr.	27	2	18	20	34	3	0	2	2	4
	Linkopings HC	Sweden	6	0	0	0	4	....	....	....	....	....
	Mjolby HC	Sweden-3	2	1	2	3	2	....	....	....	....	....

BACKMAN, Sean (BAK-man, SHAWN) NYI

Right wing. Shoots right. 5'8", 165 lbs. Born, Cos Cob, CT, April 29, 1986.

			Regular Season					Playoffs				
Season	Club	League	GP	G	A	Pts	PIM	GP	G	A	Pts	PIM
2006-07	Yale	ECAC	29	18	13	31	38	....	....	....	....	....
2007-08	Yale	ECAC	32	18	9	27	16	....	....	....	....	....
2008-09	Yale	ECAC	32	20	13	33	44	....	....	....	....	....
2009-10	Yale	ECAC	29	21	14	35	12	....	....	....	....	....
2010-11	Texas Stars	AHL	67	7	16	23	20	6	0	0	0	6
	Idaho Steelheads	ECHL	5	2	2	4	4	....	....	....	....	....

ECAC Second All-Star Team (2009) • ECAC First All-Star Team (2010) • NCAA East Second All-American Team (2010)

Signed as a free agent by **Dallas**, March 30, 2010. Signed as a free agent by **NY Islanders**, August 8, 2011.

BAERTSCHI, Sven (BEHR-chee, SVEHN) CGY

Left wing. Shoots left. 5'10", 181 lbs. Born, Langenthal, Switzerland, October 5, 1992.
(Calgary's 1st choice, 13th overall, in 2011 Entry Draft).

			Regular Season					Playoffs				
Season	Club	League	GP	G	A	Pts	PIM	GP	G	A	Pts	PIM
2006-07	SC Langenthal U17	Swiss-U17	13	15	23	38	16	....	....	....	....	....
2007-08	SC Langenthal U17	Swiss-U17	17	16	22	38	22	....	....	....	....	....
	SC Langenthal Jr.	Swiss-Jr.	18	3	3	6	4	7	1	2	3	4
2008-09	SC Langenthal U17	Swiss-U17	3	4	4	8	0	....	....	....	....	....
	SC Langenthal Jr.	Swiss-Jr.	37	21	32	53	40	6	4	3	7	35
	SC Langenthal	Swiss-2	2	0	0	0	0	....	....	....	....	....
2009-10	SC Langenthal Jr.	Swiss-Jr.	2	3	0	3	2	....	....	....	....	....
	EV Zug Jr.	Swiss-Jr.	9	10	13	23	4	2	3	1	4	2
	SC Langenthal	Swiss-2	37	6	6	12	8	7	0	3	3	4
2010-11	Portland	WHL	66	34	51	85	74	21	10	17	27	16

BAIER, Paul (BAI-uhr, PAWL)

Defense. Shoots right. 6'3", 212 lbs. Born, Summit, NJ, February 2, 1985.
(Los Angeles' 2nd choice, 95th overall, in 2004 Entry Draft).

			Regular Season					Playoffs				
Season	Club	League	GP	G	A	Pts	PIM	GP	G	A	Pts	PIM
2002-03	Deerfield Academy	High-MA	25	2	15	17	24	....	....	....	....	....
2003-04	Deerfield Academy	High-MA	23	6	4	10	22	....	....	....	....	....
2004-05	Brown U.	ECAC	32	2	8	10	24	....	....	....	....	....
2005-06	Brown U.	ECAC	30	0	6	6	18	....	....	....	....	....
2006-07	Brown U.	ECAC	32	1	4	5	55	....	....	....	....	....
2007-08	Brown U.	ECAC	31	2	5	7	38	....	....	....	....	....
	Rochester	AHL	9	1	3	4	5	....	....	....	....	....
2008-09	Portland Pirates	AHL	62	3	8	11	67	3	0	0	0	6
2009-10	Binghamton	AHL	62	2	8	10	49	....	....	....	....	....
2010-11	Rochester	AHL	65	2	8	10	80	....	....	....	....	....

Signed as a free agent by **Rochester** (AHL), September 14, 2010.

BALAN, Stanislav (BAY-luhn, STAN-ihs-lahv) NSH

Center. Shoots left. 6'2", 161 lbs. Born, Hodonin, Czech., January 30, 1986.
(Nashville's 8th choice, 209th overall, in 2004 Entry Draft).

			Regular Season					Playoffs				
Season	Club	League	GP	G	A	Pts	PIM	GP	G	A	Pts	PIM
2001-02	HC Zlin Jr.	CzRep-Jr.	48	21	23	44	60	4	1	1	2	0
2002-03	HC Zlin Jr.	CzRep-Jr.	35	24	21	45	59	3	2	0	2	16
2003-04	HC Zlin Jr.	CzRep-Jr.	53	23	33	56	122	5	2	0	2	31
	HC Hame Zlin	CzRep	4	1	0	1	2	....	....	....	....	....
2004-05	SHK Hodonin	CzRep-3	5	3	2	5	20	....	....	....	....	....
	HC Zlin Jr.	CzRep-Jr.	37	10	13	23	131	2	0	0	0	2
2005-06	Portland	WHL	67	14	23	37	102	12	1	4	5	18
2006-07	HC Hame Zlin	CzRep	44	4	3	7	48	5	0	0	0	2
	Trebic	CzRep-2	7	3	2	5	12	....	....	....	....	....
2007-08	RI Okna Zlin	CzRep	57	4	6	10	54	....	....	....	....	....
2008-09	HC Dukla Jihlava	CzRep-2	5	4	3	7	4	....	....	....	....	....
	RI Okna Zlin	CzRep	46	5	3	8	61	4	0	0	0	2
2009-10	PSG Zlin	CzRep	52	5	11	16	85	6	0	2	2	4
2010-11	PSG Zlin	CzRep	50	8	8	16	30	4	0	3	3	4

BALDWIN, Gord (BAHLD-wihn, GOHRD)

Defense. Shoots left. 6'5", 199 lbs. Born, Winnipeg, Man., March 1, 1987.
(Calgary's 2nd choice, 69th overall, in 2005 Entry Draft).

			Regular Season					Playoffs				
Season	Club	League	GP	G	A	Pts	PIM	GP	G	A	Pts	PIM
2003-04	Wpg. Thrashers	MMHL	39	5	16	21	66	....	....	....	....	....
2004-05	Medicine Hat	WHL	66	3	8	11	73	....	....	....	....	....
2005-06	Medicine Hat	WHL	71	4	20	24	119	13	0	9	9	22
2006-07	Medicine Hat	WHL	53	7	19	26	70	23	2	6	8	32
2007-08	Quad City Flames	AHL	37	0	5	5	26	....	....	....	....	....
	Las Vegas	ECHL	12	0	1	1	9	....	....	....	....	....
2008-09	Quad City Flames	AHL	55	2	4	6	39	....	....	....	....	....
	Las Vegas	ECHL	3	0	1	1	23	....	....	....	....	....
2009-10	Abbotsford Heat	AHL	67	4	20	24	84	12	1	1	2	18
2010-11	Abbotsford Heat	AHL	75	2	11	13	58	....	....	....	....	....

Signed as a free agent by **Mlada Boleslav** (CzRep), July 25, 2011.

BALDWIN, Lee (BAHLD-wihn, LEE) NYR

Defense. Shoots left. 6'3", 200 lbs. Born, Victoria, B.C., April 26, 1988.

			Regular Season					Playoffs				
Season	Club	League	GP	G	A	Pts	PIM	GP	G	A	Pts	PIM
2006-07	Burnaby Express	BCHL	59	0	16	16	55	14	2	3	5	6
2007-08	Burnaby Express	BCHL	35	7	17	24	40	5	1	5	6	4
2008-09	Victoria Grizzlies	BCHL	56	13	41	54	79	14	2	6	8	10
2009-10	Hartford Wolf Pack	AHL	7	1	0	1	4	....	....	....	....	....
	Alaska-Anchorage	WCHA	32	1	9	10	51	....	....	....	....	....
2010-11	Connecticut Whale	AHL	21	0	0	0	17	....	....	....	....	....
	Greenville	ECHL	27	2	8	10	15	10	0	1	1	4

Signed as a free agent by **NY Rangers**, March 22, 2010.

BALISY, Chase (BAL-ih-see, CHAYS) NSH

Center. Shoots left. 5'11", 170 lbs. Born, Fullerton, CA, February 2, 1992.
(Nashville's 6th choice, 170th overall, in 2011 Entry Draft).

			Regular Season					Playoffs				
Season	Club	League	GP	G	A	Pts	PIM	GP	G	A	Pts	PIM
2007-08	Tor. Jr. Canadiens	GTHL	80	40	110	150	....	....	....	....	....	....
2008-09	USNTDP	NAHL	42	8	14	22	8	9	0	3	3	0
	USNTDP	U-17	16	4	10	14	6	....	....	....	....	....
2009-10	USNTDP	USHL	28	5	6	11	8	....	....	....	....	....
	USNTDP	U-18	35	4	10	14	6	....	....	....	....	....
2010-11	Western Mich.	CCHA	42	12	18	30	12	....	....	....	....	....

BANCKS, Carter (BANKS, KAHR-tuhr) CGY

Left wing. Shoots left. 5'11", 180 lbs. Born, Marysville, B.C., August 9, 1989.

			Regular Season					Playoffs				
Season	Club	League	GP	G	A	Pts	PIM	GP	G	A	Pts	PIM
2004-05	Kimberley	KIJHL	11	1	5	6	10	....	....	....	....	....
2005-06	Kimberley	KIJHL	50	24	49	73	57	13	5	7	12	6
	Lethbridge	WHL	2	0	0	0	0	6	0	0	0	4
2006-07	Lethbridge	WHL	67	11	20	31	64	....	....	....	....	....
2007-08	Lethbridge	WHL	70	15	30	45	56	19	6	4	10	19
2008-09	Lethbridge	WHL	53	13	34	47	68	3	0	0	0	4
2009-10	Lethbridge	WHL	70	19	36	55	96	....	....	....	....	....
	Abbotsford Heat	AHL	9	0	0	0	0	13	0	1	1	7
2010-11	Abbotsford Heat	AHL	29	5	14	19	16	....	....	....	....	....

• Missed majority of 2004-05 due to leg injury. Signed to a ATO (amateur tryout) contract by **Abbotsford** (AHL), March 18, 2010. Signed as a free agent by **Calgary**, July 1, 2011.

BARANOV, Konstantin (buh-RA-nawf, KAWN-stan-tihn) PHI

Right wing. Shoots left. 6'2", 185 lbs. Born, Omsk, USSR, January 11, 1982.
(Philadelphia's 3rd choice, 126th overall, in 2002 Entry Draft).

			Regular Season					Playoffs				
Season	Club	League	GP	G	A	Pts	PIM	GP	G	A	Pts	PIM
1998-99	Omsk 2	Russia-4	23	18	8	26	40	....	....	....	....	....
	Avangard Omsk	Russia	1	0	0	0	0	2	0	0	0	0
99-2000	Omsk 2	Russia-3	33	15	8	23	46	....	....	....	....	....
	Avangard Omsk	Russia	1	0	0	0	2	....	....	....	....	....
2000-01	Kristall Saratov	Russia-2	26	6	9	15	26	....	....	....	....	....
	Ufa	Russia	8	1	0	1	4	....	....	....	....	....
2001-02	Avangard Omsk	Russia	5	0	0	0	6	....	....	....	....	....
	Mechel	Russia	6	1	2	3	2	....	....	....	....	....
	Lada Togliatti	Russia	20	2	4	6	18	3	0	2	2	0
2002-03	Avangard Omsk	Russia	6	0	1	1	2	....	....	....	....	....
	Ufa	Russia	11	2	2	4	0	....	....	....	....	....
	CSKA Moscow	Russia	14	4	1	5	10	....	....	....	....	....
	Omsk 2	Russia-3	3	4	6	10	2	....	....	....	....	....
2003-04	Avangard Omsk	Russia	51	6	10	16	50	11	2	2	4	6
2004-05	Omsk 2	Russia-3	7	5	7	12	20	....	....	....	....	....
	Avangard Omsk	Russia	21	3	2	5	16	....	....	....	....	....
2005-06	Dynamo Moscow	Russia	19	0	5	5	10	....	....	....	....	....
	SKA St. Petersburg	Russia	12	1	2	3	18	3	0	0	0	2
2006-07	Amur Khabarovsk	Russia	7	0	1	1	16	....	....	....	....	....
	Novokuznetsk	Russia	21	2	2	4	28	3	3	1	4	0
2007-08	Avtomobilist	Russia-2	4	0	0	0	26	....	....	....	....	....
	Avtomobilist 2	Russia-3	6	3	2	5	10	....	....	....	....	....
	HK Dmitrov	Russia-2	33	5	14	19	56	2	1	0	1	0
2008-09	Gazovik Tyumen	Russia-2	31	5	11	16	50	....	....	....	....	....
	Kapitan Stupino	Russia-2	21	8	13	21	36	9	1	3	4	16
2009-10	HK Sarov	Russia-2	54	23	17	40	68	....	....	....	....	....
2010-11	HK Sarov	Russia-2	37	12	21	33	55	4	1	3	4	4

BARBERIO, Mark (bahr-BAIR-ee-oh, MAHRK) T.B.

Defense. Shoots left. 6'1", 197 lbs. Born, Montreal, Que., March 23, 1990.
(Tampa Bay's 5th choice, 152nd overall, in 2008 Entry Draft).

			Regular Season					Playoffs				
Season	Club	League	GP	G	A	Pts	PIM	GP	G	A	Pts	PIM
2005-06	Lac St-Louis Lions	QAAA	43	2	12	14	80	10	1	7	8	26
2006-07	Cape Breton	QMJHL	41	2	8	10	42	....	....	....	....	....
	Moncton Wildcats	QMJHL	19	1	6	7	21	7	0	2	2	8
2007-08	Moncton Wildcats	QMJHL	70	11	35	46	75	....	....	....	....	....
2008-09	Moncton Wildcats	QMJHL	66	15	30	45	42	10	0	4	4	8
2009-10	Moncton Wildcats	QMJHL	65	17	43	60	72	21	5	17	22	12
2010-11	Norfolk Admirals	AHL	68	9	22	31	28	6	1	0	1	4

QMJHL All-Rookie Team (2007) • QMJHL Second All-Star Team (2010)

BARRIBALL, Jay (BEHR-ih-bahl, JAY) ST.L.

Left wing. Shoots left. 5'9", 171 lbs. Born, Prior Lake, MN, May 27, 1987.
(San Jose's 6th choice, 203rd overall, in 2006 Entry Draft).

			Regular Season					Playoffs				
Season	Club	League	GP	G	A	Pts	PIM	GP	G	A	Pts	PIM
2004-05	Holy Angels	High-MN	30	32	49	81	....	....	....	....	....	....
2005-06	Holy Angels	High-MN	20	28	38	66	....	....	....	....	....	....
	Sioux Falls	USHL	13	5	7	12	2	5	2	1	3	0
2006-07	U. of Minnesota	WCHA	44	20	23	43	16	....	....	....	....	....
2007-08	U. of Minnesota	WCHA	41	6	15	21	34	....	....	....	....	....
2008-09	U. of Minnesota	WCHA	34	11	23	34	52	....	....	....	....	....
2009-10	U. of Minnesota	WCHA	5	2	2	4	10	....	....	....	....	....
2010-11	U. of Minnesota	WCHA	30	12	16	28	18	....	....	....	....	....
	Peoria Rivermen	AHL	6	0	1	1	4	1	0	0	0	0

Traded to **St. Louis** by **San Jose** with Ville Nieminen and New Jersey's 1st round choice (previously acquired, St. Louis selected David Perron) in 2007 Entry Draft for Bill Guerin, February 27, 2007.

BARRIE, Tyson (BAIR-ree, TIGH-suhn) COL

Defense. Shoots right. 5'10", 191 lbs. Born, Victoria, B.C., July 26, 1991.
(Colorado's 4th choice, 64th overall, in 2009 Entry Draft).

			Regular Season					Playoffs				
Season	Club	League	GP	G	A	Pts	PIM	GP	G	A	Pts	PIM
2006-07	Juan de Fuca	Minor-BC	72	43	87	130	....	....	....	....	....	....
	Kelowna Rockets	WHL	7	0	3	3	2	....	....	....	....	....
2007-08	Kelowna Rockets	WHL	64	9	34	43	32	7	1	3	4	0
2008-09	Kelowna Rockets	WHL	68	12	40	52	31	22	4	14	18	12
2009-10	Kelowna Rockets	WHL	63	19	53	72	31	12	3	8	11	6
2010-11	Kelowna Rockets	WHL	54	11	47	58	34	10	2	9	11	8

Canadian Major Junior All-Rookie Team (2008) • WHL West First All-Star Team (2010, 2011) • WHL Defenseman of the Year (2010) • Canadian Major Junior Second All-Star Team (2010)

BARTLEY, Victor (BAR-tlee, WAYD) NSH

Defense. Shoots right. 6', 203 lbs. Born, Maple Ridge, B.C., February 17, 1988.

			Regular Season					Playoffs				
Season	Club	League	GP	G	A	Pts	PIM	GP	G	A	Pts	PIM
2003-04	Kamloops Blazers	WHL	3	0	0	0	0	....	....	....	....	....
2004-05	Kamloops Blazers	WHL	68	4	6	10	58	5	0	3	3	4
2005-06	Kamloops Blazers	WHL	65	3	24	27	114	....	....	....	....	....
2006-07	Kamloops Blazers	WHL	67	4	39	43	104	4	0	2	2	8
2007-08	Kamloops Blazers	WHL	36	3	15	18	51	....	....	....	....	....
	Regina Pats	WHL	25	7	17	24	42	6	1	3	4	8
2008-09	Regina Pats	WHL	72	15	31	46	97	....	....	....	....	....
	Providence Bruins	AHL	10	0	0	0	6	....	....	....	....	....
2009-10	Bridgeport	AHL	8	2	0	2	6	....	....	....	....	....
	Utah Grizzlies	ECHL	21	2	11	13	21	....	....	....	....	....
2010-11	Rogle	Sweden-2	52	11	23	34	56	....	....	....	....	....

Signed as a free agent by **Rogle** (Sweden-2), May 26, 2010. Signed as a free agent by **Nashville**, May 24, 2011.

BASARABA, Joe (ba-za-RA-bah, JOH) FLA

Right wing. Shoots right. 6'2", 190 lbs. Born, Fort Frances, Ont., May 2, 1992.
(Florida's 7th choice, 69th overall, in 2010 Entry Draft).

			Regular Season					Playoffs				
Season	Club	League	GP	G	A	Pts	PIM	GP	G	A	Pts	PIM
2008-09	Shat.-St. Mary's	High-MN	54	20	24	44	54	....	....	....	....	....
2009-10	Shat.-St. Mary's	High-MN	52	24	22	46	39	....	....	....	....	....
2010-11	U. Minn-Duluth	WCHA	36	3	2	5	20	....	....	....	....	....

BASHKIROV, Ruslan (bash-KIHR-ahv, roos-LAHN) OTT

Left wing. Shoots left. 5'11", 193 lbs. Born, Moscow, USSR, March 7, 1989.
(Ottawa's 2nd choice, 60th overall, in 2007 Entry Draft).

			Regular Season					Playoffs				
Season	Club	League	GP	G	A	Pts	PIM	GP	G	A	Pts	PIM
2005-06	Spartak Moscow 2	Russia-3	35	16	9	25	44	....	....	....	....	....
2006-07	Quebec Remparts	QMJHL	64	30	37	67	117	5	1	3	4	6
2007-08	Mytischi	Russia	4	0	0	0	0	....	....	....	....	....
	Kristall Elektrostal	Russia-2	12	4	0	4	22	....	....	....	....	....
2008-09	Lada Togliatti	Rus-KHL	2	0	0	0	2	....	....	....	....	....
	Rys Podolsk	Russia-2	48	9	8	17	20	3	1	3	4	2
2009-10	Perm	Russia-2	37	10	8	18	12	10	2	3	5	4
2010-11	Perm	Russia-2	8	1	0	1	2	....	....	....	....	....
	HK Ryazan	Russia-2	28	8	10	18	18	3	0	0	0	12

BATHGATE, Andy (BATH-gayt, AHN-dee)

Center. Shoots left. 6', 175 lbs. Born, Brampton, Ont., February 26, 1991.
(Pittsburgh's 6th choice, 151st overall, in 2009 Entry Draft).

			Regular Season					Playoffs				
Season	Club	League	GP	G	A	Pts	PIM	GP	G	A	Pts	PIM
2007-08	Georgetown	OPJHL	40	14	30	44	24	10	1	6	7	10
	Belleville Bulls	OHL	5	0	1	1	2	5	0	0	0	0
2008-09	Belleville Bulls	OHL	44	4	12	16	10	....	....	....	....	....
2009-10	Belleville Bulls	OHL	59	13	27	40	16	....	....	....	....	....
2010-11	Belleville Bulls	OHL	64	25	35	60	36	4	0	0	0	0
	Wilkes-Barre	AHL	2	0	0	0	0	....	....	....	....	....

BEACH, Cody (BEECH, KOH-dee) ST.L.

Right wing. Shoots right. 6'6", 188 lbs. Born, Nanaimo, B.C., August 8, 1992.
(St. Louis' 6th choice, 134th overall, in 2010 Entry Draft).

			Regular Season					Playoffs				
Season	Club	League	GP	G	A	Pts	PIM	GP	G	A	Pts	PIM
2007-08	Okanagan Rockets	BCMML	37	8	17	25	68	6	1	3	4	16
2008-09	Calgary Hitmen	WHL	3	0	0	0	2	....	....	....	....	....
	Okanagan Rockets	BCMML	23	10	13	23	58	2	1	0	1	2
2009-10	Calgary Hitmen	WHL	51	3	11	14	157	19	1	7	8	34
2010-11	Calgary Hitmen	WHL	17	5	10	15	73	....	....	....	....	....
	Moose Jaw	WHL	40	6	28	34	163	....	....	....	....	....

BEACH, Kyle (BEECH, KIGH-uhl) CHI

Center. Shoots right. 6'3", 202 lbs. Born, Vancouver, B.C., January 13, 1990.
(Chicago's 1st choice, 11th overall, in 2008 Entry Draft).

			Regular Season					Playoffs				
Season	Club	League	GP	G	A	Pts	PIM	GP	G	A	Pts	PIM
2005-06	Okanagan Rockets	BCMML	25	23	18	41	220	....	....	....	....	....
	Everett Silvertips	WHL	4	2	1	3	4	9	1	3	4	31
2006-07	Everett Silvertips	WHL	65	29	32	61	196	11	5	6	11	19
2007-08	Everett Silvertips	WHL	60	27	33	60	222	4	0	0	0	4
2008-09	Everett Silvertips	WHL	30	9	21	30	106	....	....	....	....	....
	Lethbridge	WHL	24	15	18	33	59	10	1	1	2	31
	Rockford IceHogs	AHL	2	0	0	0	15	1	0	0	0	0
2009-10	Spokane Chiefs	WHL	68	*52	34	86	186	7	7	2	9	19
	Rockford IceHogs	AHL	4	0	0	0	0	4	3	0	3	6
2010-11	Rockford IceHogs	AHL	71	16	20	36	163	....	....	....	....	....

WHL Rookie of the Year (2007) • WHL West First All-Star Team (2010)

BEAUDOIN, Matt (boh-DWEH, MAT) PHX

Right wing. Shoots right. 5'11", 190 lbs. Born, Rock Forest, Que., April 6, 1984.

			Regular Season					Playoffs				
Season	Club	League	GP	G	A	Pts	PIM	GP	G	A	Pts	PIM
2003-04	Ohio State	CCHA	40	7	7	14	26	....	....	....	....	....
2004-05	Ohio State	CCHA	40	23	11	34	50	....	....	....	....	....
2005-06	Ohio State	CCHA	32	8	8	16	18	....	....	....	....	....
2006-07	Ohio State	CCHA	37	14	11	25	24	....	....	....	....	....
2007-08	Iowa Stars	AHL	3	0	0	0	0	....	....	....	....	....
	Rochester	AHL	1	0	0	0	0	....	....	....	....	....
	Hershey Bears	AHL	7	0	0	0	0	1	0	0	0	0
	Las Vegas	ECHL	1	0	1	1	0	....	....	....	....	....
	Dayton Bombers	ECHL	61	38	30	68	44	2	0	0	0	0
2008-09	San Antonio	AHL	1	0	1	1	2	....	....	....	....	....
	Milwaukee	AHL	2	0	0	0	0	....	....	....	....	....
	Houston Aeros	AHL	41	11	8	19	17	20	8	9	17	12
	Las Vegas	ECHL	15	10	6	16	10	....	....	....	....	....
2009-10	Texas Stars	AHL	72	19	25	44	22	22	4	3	7	4
2010-11	San Antonio	AHL	63	21	30	51	24	....	....	....	....	....

Signed as a free agent by **Phoenix**, July 3, 2010.

BEAULIEU, Nathan (BOl-loh, NAY-thun) MTL

Defense. Shoots left. 6'1", 179 lbs. Born, Strathroy, Ont., December 5, 1992.
(Montreal's 1st choice, 17th overall, in 2011 Entry Draft).

			Regular Season					Playoffs				
Season	Club	League	GP	G	A	Pts	PIM	GP	G	A	Pts	PIM
2007-08	Saint John Vito's	NBPEI	33	1	14	15	45	4	1	2	3	6
2008-09	Saint John	QMJHL	49	2	8	10	14	4	0	0	0	2
2009-10	Saint John	QMJHL	66	12	33	45	40	21	4	12	16	22
2010-11	Saint John	QMJHL	65	12	33	45	52	19	4	13	17	26

Memorial Cup All-Star Team (2011)

BEAUPRE, Gabriel (boh-PRAY, gay-BREE-ehl) COL

Defense. Shoots left. 6'2", 195 lbs. Born, Levis, Que., November 23, 1992.
(Colorado's 5th choice, 153rd overall, in 2011 Entry Draft).

			Regular Season					Playoffs				
Season	Club	League	GP	G	A	Pts	PIM	GP	G	A	Pts	PIM
2007-08	Levis	QAAA	45	2	6	8	52	3	0	0	0	6
2008-09	Val-d'Or Foreurs	QMJHL	52	0	3	3	48	....	....	....	....	....
2009-10	Val-d'Or Foreurs	QMJHL	56	2	5	7	94	6	1	1	2	8
2010-11	Val-d'Or Foreurs	QMJHL	66	3	15	18	73	4	0	1	1	4

BECK, Taylor (BEHK, TAY-luhr) NSH

Left wing. Shoots right. 6'2", 203 lbs. Born, St. Catharines, Ont., May 13, 1991.
(Nashville's 4th choice, 70th overall, in 2009 Entry Draft).

			Regular Season					Playoffs				
Season	Club	League	GP	G	A	Pts	PIM	GP	G	A	Pts	PIM
2006-07	Niag. Falls Thunder	Minor-ON	69	64	75	139	76	....	....	....	....	....
2007-08	Guelph Storm	OHL	56	7	14	21	43	7	0	0	0	4
2008-09	Guelph Storm	OHL	67	22	36	58	36	4	0	0	0	2
2009-10	Guelph Storm	OHL	61	39	54	93	54	5	3	3	6	2
2010-11	Guelph Storm	OHL	62	42	53	95	60	6	3	5	8	10
	Milwaukee	AHL	4	0	1	1	0	8	2	0	2	2

OHL Second All-Star Team (2010)

BELLEMORE, Brett (BEHL-mohr, BREHT) CAR

Defense. Shoots right. 6'4", 205 lbs. Born, Windsor, Ont., June 25, 1988.
(Carolina's 5th choice, 162nd overall, in 2007 Entry Draft).

			Regular Season					Playoffs				
Season	Club	League	GP	G	A	Pts	PIM	GP	G	A	Pts	PIM
2005-06	Plymouth Whalers	OHL	46	0	0	0	16	10	0	0	0	0
2006-07	Plymouth Whalers	OHL	50	0	12	12	50	20	0	5	5	28
2007-08	Plymouth Whalers	OHL	56	6	18	24	70	4	0	2	2	8
	Albany River Rats	AHL	4	0	0	0	6	5	0	0	0	6
2008-09	Plymouth Whalers	OHL	29	2	10	12	39	11	1	2	3	16
	Albany River Rats	AHL	6	0	0	0	4	....	....	....	....	....
2009-10	Albany River Rats	AHL	75	1	6	7	81	8	0	1	1	2
2010-11	Charlotte	AHL	71	2	8	10	74	16	1	1	2	12

BENGTSSON, Rasmus (BEHNG-tsuhn, RAZ-muhs) FLA

Defense. Shoots left. 6'2", 192 lbs. Born, Landskrona, Sweden, May 14, 1993.
(Florida's 3rd choice, 59th overall, in 2011 Entry Draft).

			Regular Season					Playoffs				
Season	Club	League	GP	G	A	Pts	PIM	GP	G	A	Pts	PIM
2008-09	Rogle U18	Swe-U18	23	1	6	7	6	....	....	....	....	....
2009-10	Rogle U18	Swe-U18	15	3	5	8	6	2	2	1	3	0
	Rogle Jr.	Swe-Jr.	42	3	20	23	14	2	1	1	2	0
2010-11	Rogle	Sweden-2	51	2	8	10	6	....	....	....	....	....
	Rogle Jr.	Swe-Jr.	17	1	3	4	8	3	1	1	2	0
	Rogle U18	Swe-U18	....	....	....	....	....	2	0	0	0	0

BENNETT, Beau (BEH-neht, BOH) PIT

Right wing. Shoots right. 6'1", 173 lbs. Born, Gardena, CA, November 27, 1991.
(Pittsburgh's 1st choice, 20th overall, in 2010 Entry Draft).

			Regular Season					Playoffs				
Season	Club	League	GP	G	A	Pts	PIM	GP	G	A	Pts	PIM
2008-09	L.A. Jr. Kings	T1EHL	46	25	33	58	10	....	....	....	....	....
2009-10	Penticton Vees	BCHL	56	41	79	*120	20	15	5	9	14	6
2010-11	U. of Denver	WCHA	37	9	16	25	18	....	....	....	....	....

BENNETT, Mac (BEHN-neht, MAK) MTL

Defense. Shoots left. 6', 170 lbs. Born, Warwick, RI, March 25, 1991.
(Montreal's 3rd choice, 79th overall, in 2009 Entry Draft).

			Regular Season					Playoffs				
Season	Club	League	GP	G	A	Pts	PIM	GP	G	A	Pts	PIM
2006-07	Hotchkiss School	High-CT	25	7	6	13	....	....	....	....	....	....
2007-08	Hotchkiss School	High-CT	25	6	9	15	....	....	....	....	....	....
2008-09	Neponset Valley	Minor-MA	16	5	19	24	....	....	....	....	....	....
	Hotchkiss School	High-CT	15	4	11	15	....	....	....	....	....	....
2009-10	Cedar Rapids	USHL	53	9	15	24	34	2	1	0	1	0
2010-11	U. of Michigan	CCHA	32	2	10	12	21	....	....	....	....	....

USHL All-Rookie Team (2010)

BERGER, Alain (bair-ZHAY, ah-LAYN) MTL

Right wing. Shoots right. 6'4", 208 lbs. Born, Burgsdorf, Switz., December 27, 1990.

			Regular Season					Playoffs				
Season	Club	League	GP	G	A	Pts	PIM	GP	G	A	Pts	PIM
2007-08	SC Bern	Swiss	1	0	0	0	0	....	....	....	....	....
	HC Neuchatel	Swiss-2	29	4	4	8	30	....	....	....	....	....
2008-09	SC Bern	Swiss	19	0	0	0	6	....	....	....	....	....
	HC Neuchatel	Swiss-2	22	9	9	18	32	....	....	....	....	....
2009-10	Oshawa Generals	OHL	44	19	14	33	56	....	....	....	....	....
2010-11	Oshawa Generals	OHL	65	29	23	52	86	10	5	3	8	14

Signed as a free agent by **Montreal**, April 8, 2011.

BERGIN, Mike (BUHR-gihn, MIGHK) DAL

Defense. Shoots left. 6'3", 200 lbs. Born, Kanata, Ont., June 30, 1988.
(Dallas' 5th choice, 209th overall, in 2008 Entry Draft).

			Regular Season					Playoffs				
Season	Club	League	GP	G	A	Pts	PIM	GP	G	A	Pts	PIM
2005-06	Smiths Falls Bears	CJHL	48	7	19	26	104	....	....	....	....	....
2006-07	Smiths Falls Bears	CJHL	53	10	35	45	114	11	2	7	9	18
2007-08	Smiths Falls Bears	CJHL	45	14	27	41	60	15	2	5	7	19
2008-09	RPI Engineers	ECAC	6	0	1	1	6	....	....	....	....	....
2009-10	RPI Engineers	ECAC	30	4	7	11	52	....	....	....	....	....
2010-11	RPI Engineers	ECAC	32	2	16	18	30	....	....	....	....	....

• Missed majority of 2008-09 due to shoulder injury vs. University of Massachusetts (Hockey East), October 21, 2008.

BERNHARDT, Justin (BAIRH-hahrdt, JUHS-tihn) PHX

Center. Shoots left. 6'1", 190 lbs. Born, Yorkton, Sask., February 25, 1985.

			Regular Season					Playoffs				
Season	Club	League	GP	G	A	Pts	PIM	GP	G	A	Pts	PIM
2003-04	Regina Pats	WHL	1	0	0	0	0	....	....	....	....	....
2004-05	Regina Pats	WHL	42	5	6	11	57	....	....	....	....	....
2005-06	Regina Pats	WHL	61	22	23	45	75	6	2	4	6	8
2006-07	Regina Pats	WHL	25	7	10	17	27	....	....	....	....	....
	Kelowna Rockets	WHL	40	8	12	20	45	....	....	....	....	....
2007-08	Kelowna Rockets	WHL	13	4	4	8	27	....	....	....	....	....
	Prince Albert	WHL	53	22	27	49	54	....	....	....	....	....
2008-09	Prince Albert	WHL	72	35	57	92	104	....	....	....	....	....
2009-10	San Antonio	AHL	14	1	2	3	15	....	....	....	....	....
	Las Vegas	ECHL	29	5	6	11	50	....	....	....	....	....
2010-11	Las Vegas	ECHL	47	6	19	25	29	5	0	2	2	14

Signed as a free agent by **Phoenix**, April 13, 2009.

BERRY, Alex (BAIR-ee, AL-ehx)

Right wing. Shoots right. 6'2", 218 lbs. Born, Danvers, MA, March 6, 1986.
(Toronto's 3rd choice, 153rd overall, in 2005 Entry Draft).

			Regular Season					Playoffs				
Season	Club	League	GP	G	A	Pts	PIM	GP	G	A	Pts	PIM
2003-04	Cushing	High-MA	31	19	16	35	50	....	....	....	....	....
2004-05	Bos. Jr. Bruins	EJHL	53	17	25	42	170	....	....	....	....	....
2005-06	Massachusetts	H-East	24	1	1	2	33	....	....	....	....	....
2006-07	Massachusetts	H-East	29	7	6	13	34	....	....	....	....	....
2007-08	Massachusetts	H-East	34	10	7	17	63	....	....	....	....	....
2008-09	Massachusetts	H-East	37	11	19	30	83	....	....	....	....	....
	Toronto Marlies	AHL	8	0	0	0	15	....	....	....	....	....
2009-10	Toronto Marlies	AHL	55	3	4	7	97	....	....	....	....	....
	Reading Royals	ECHL	5	0	5	5	2	16	2	4	6	4
2010-11	Norfolk Admirals	AHL	75	14	20	34	150	....	....	....	....	....

Traded to **Tampa Bay** by **Toronto** with Stefano Giliati for Matt Lashoff, August 27, 2010.

BERUBE, Jean-Sebastien (beh-ROO-bay, ZHAWN-seh-BAS-t'yehn) N.J.

Left wing. Shoots left. 6'4", 210 lbs. Born, Matane, Que., July 20, 1990.
(New Jersey's 9th choice, 205th overall, in 2008 Entry Draft).

			Regular Season					Playoffs				
Season	Club	League	GP	G	A	Pts	PIM	GP	G	A	Pts	PIM
2006-07	Rouyn-Noranda	QMJHL	40	3	7	10	22	16	0	0	0	4
2007-08	Rouyn-Noranda	QMJHL	64	12	12	24	118	17	1	3	4	16
2008-09	Rouyn-Noranda	QMJHL	64	15	11	26	143	6	0	1	1	10
2009-10	Rouyn-Noranda	QMJHL	64	24	21	45	130	11	1	1	2	10
	Lowell Devils	AHL	....	....	....	....	....	1	0	0	0	0
2010-11	Albany Devils	AHL	17	0	2	2	8	....	....	....	....	....
	Trenton Devils	ECHL	44	12	18	30	84	....	....	....	....	....

BEUKEBOOM, Brock (BOO-kuh-BOOM, BRAWK) ST.L.

Defense. Shoots right. 6'2", 197 lbs. Born, Greenwich, CT, April 1, 1992.
(Tampa Bay's 2nd choice, 63rd overall, in 2010 Entry Draft).

			Regular Season					Playoffs				
Season	Club	League	GP	G	A	Pts	PIM	GP	G	A	Pts	PIM
2007-08	Cent. Ont. Wolves	Minor-ON	40	15	30	45	50	....	....	....	....	....
2008-09	Sault Ste. Marie	OHL	55	2	9	11	26	....	....	....	....	....
2009-10	Sault Ste. Marie	OHL	66	7	19	26	64	1	0	0	0	0
2010-11	Sault Ste. Marie	OHL	44	1	7	8	54	....	....	....	....	....

Traded to **St. Louis** by **Tampa Bay** with Tampa Bay's 3rd round choice (Jordan Binnington) in 2011 Entr Draft for Eric Brewer, February 18, 2011.

BICKEL, Stu (BIH-kuhl, STEW) NYR

Defense. Shoots right. 6'4", 215 lbs. Born, Chanhassen, MN, October 2, 1986.

			Regular Season					Playoffs				
Season	Club	League	GP	G	A	Pts	PIM	GP	G	A	Pts	PIM
2004-05	Green Bay	USHL	13	0	0	0	20	....	....	....	....	....
2005-06	Green Bay	USHL	14	0	0	0	25	....	....	....	....	....
2006-07	Sioux Falls	USHL	57	2	11	13	*215	8	0	3	3	29
2007-08	U. of Minnesota	WCHA	45	1	6	7	*92	....	....	....	....	....
2008-09	Iowa Chops	AHL	21	0	1	1	51	....	....	....	....	....
2009-10	San Antonio	AHL	36	2	2	4	38	....	....	....	....	....
	Bakersfield	ECHL	24	1	12	13	50	9	0	2	2	14
2010-11	Syracuse Crunch	AHL	6	0	3	3	14	....	....	....	....	....
	Elmira Jackals	ECHL	1	0	0	0	0	....	....	....	....	....
	Connecticut Whale	AHL	54	2	7	9	135	6	0	1	1	6

Signed as a free agent by **Anaheim**, July 2, 2008. Traded to **NY Rangers** by **Anaheim** for Nigel Williams, November 23, 2010.

BIEGA, Alex (bee-AY-guh, AL-ehx) BUF

Defense. Shoots right. 5'11", 192 lbs. Born, Montreal, Que., April 4, 1988.
(Buffalo's 5th choice, 147th overall, in 2006 Entry Draft).

			Regular Season					Playoffs				
Season	Club	League	GP	G	A	Pts	PIM	GP	G	A	Pts	PIM
2004-05	Salisbury School	High-CT	27	9	22	31	45	....	....	....	....	....
2005-06	Salisbury School	High-CT	28	10	17	27	51	....	....	....	....	....
2006-07	Harvard Crimson	ECAC	33	6	12	18	36	....	....	....	....	....
2007-08	Harvard Crimson	ECAC	34	3	19	22	28	....	....	....	....	....
2008-09	Harvard Crimson	ECAC	31	4	16	20	46	....	....	....	....	....
2009-10	Harvard Crimson	ECAC	33	2	8	10	30	....	....	....	....	....
2010-11	Portland Pirates	AHL	61	3	15	18	52	12	1	1	2	6

ECAC All-Rookie Team (2007)

BIEGA, Danny (bee-AY-ga, DAN-ee) CAR

Defense. Shoots right. 6', 200 lbs. Born, Montreal, Que., September 29, 1991.
(Carolina's 4th choice, 67th overall, in 2010 Entry Draft).

			Regular Season					Playoffs				
Season	Club	League	GP	G	A	Pts	PIM	GP	G	A	Pts	PIM
2007-08	Salisbury School	High-CT	26	4	13	17	....	....	....	....	....	....
2008-09	Salisbury School	High-CT	29	8	14	22	....	....	....	....	....	....
2009-10	Harvard Crimson	ECAC	32	5	4	9	47	....	....	....	....	....
2010-11	Harvard Crimson	ECAC	34	11	19	30	34	....	....	....	....	....

BIGGS, Tyler (BIHGZ, TIGH-luhr) TOR

Right wing. Shoots right. 6'2", 205 lbs. Born, Binghamton, NY, April 30, 1993.
(Toronto's 1st choice, 22nd overall, in 2011 Entry Draft).

			Regular Season					Playoffs				
Season	Club	League	GP	G	A	Pts	PIM	GP	G	A	Pts	PIM
2008-09	Tor. Jr. Canadiens	GTHL	72	40	47	87	....	....	....	....	....	....
	Tor. Canadiens	ON-Jr.A	3	0	0	0	2	....	....	....	....	....
2009-10	USNTDP	USHL	24	6	5	11	54	....	....	....	....	....
	USNTDP	U-17	20	10	4	14	31	....	....	....	....	....
	USNTDP	U-18	9	0	0	0	6	....	....	....	....	....
2010-11	USNTDP	USHL	20	7	4	11	41	....	....	....	....	....
	USNTDP	U-18	35	12	8	20	120	....	....	....	....	....

• Signed Letter of Intent to attend **Miami University** (CCHA) in fall of 2011.

BIGOS, Kyle (BEE-gohs, KIGHL) EDM

Defense. Shoots right. 6'5", 230 lbs. Born, Upland, CA, May 12, 1989.
(Edmonton's 5th choice, 99th overall, in 2009 Entry Draft).

			Regular Season					Playoffs				
Season	Club	League	GP	G	A	Pts	PIM	GP	G	A	Pts	PIM
2006-07	Notre Dame	SMHL	39	12	24	36	165	....	....	....	....	....
	Notre Dame	SJHL	3	0	0	0	0	....	....	....	....	....
2007-08	Vernon Vipers	BCHL	58	2	15	17	152	10	0	2	2	28
2008-09	Vernon Vipers	BCHL	58	8	25	33	126	17	2	4	6	37
2009-10	Merrimack College	H-East	36	4	7	11	94	....	....	....	....	....
2010-11	Merrimack College	H-East	33	2	6	8	127	....	....	....	....	....

BIRCH, Braden (BUHRCH, BRAY-duhn) CHI

Defense. Shoots left. 6'4", 205 lbs. Born, Hamilton, Ont., September 25, 1989.
(Chicago's 6th choice, 179th overall, in 2008 Entry Draft).

			Regular Season					Playoffs				
Season	Club	League	GP	G	A	Pts	PIM	GP	G	A	Pts	PIM
2006-07	Stoney Creek	ON-Jr.B	43	10	11	21	86	....	....	....	....	....
2007-08	Nanaimo Clippers	BCHL	19	0	2	2	15	....	....	....	....	....
	Oakville Blades	OPJHL	13	1	4	5	6	19	0	2	2	4
2008-09	Oakville Blades	ON-Jr.A	35	7	18	25	46	27	4	6	10	20
2009-10	Cornell Big Red	ECAC	32	0	2	2	10	....	....	....	....	....
2010-11	Cornell Big Red	ECAC	30	2	6	8	46	....	....	....	....	....

BIRKHOLZ, Josh (BUHRK-hohlz, JAWSH) FLA

Right wing. Shoots right. 6'1", 182 lbs. Born, St. Louis Park, MN, March 28, 1991.
(Florida's 3rd choice, 67th overall, in 2009 Entry Draft).

			Regular Season					Playoffs				
Season	Club	League	GP	G	A	Pts	PIM	GP	G	A	Pts	PIM
2005-06	Blake Bears	High-MN	29	3	2	5	12	....	....	....	....	....
2006-07	Blake Bears	High-MN	21	11	8	19	20	....	....	....	....	....
2007-08	Blake Bears	High-MN	30	34	24	58	42	....	....	....	....	....
2008-09	Fargo Force	USHL	55	21	15	36	52	9	3	2	5	4
2009-10	U. of Minnesota	WCHA	36	5	1	6	20	....	....	....	....	....
2010-11	Everett Silvertips	WHL	68	18	11	29	64	4	0	2	2	2

BISHOP, Hunter (BIH-shuhp, HUHN-tuhr) MTL

Left wing. Shoots left. 6', 185 lbs. Born, Fairbanks, AK, September 5, 1987.

			Regular Season					Playoffs				
Season	Club	League	GP	G	A	Pts	PIM	GP	G	A	Pts	PIM
2003-04	Fairbanks Ice Dogs	NAHL	52	7	14	21	33	....	....	....	....	....
2004-05	Cedar Rapids	USHL	50	2	10	12	17	1	0	0	0	2
2005-06	Vernon Vipers	BCHL	56	25	29	54	39	....	....	....	....	....
2006-07	Vernon Vipers	BCHL	24	11	15	26	16	....	....	....	....	....
	North Dakota	WCHA	4	0	1	1	4	....	....	....	....	....
2007-08	Vernon Vipers	BCHL	60	57	40	97	45	....	....	....	....	....
2008-09	Ohio State	CCHA	42	14	17	31	18	....	....	....	....	....
2009-10	Ohio State	CCHA	33	15	12	27	22	....	....	....	....	....
	Hamilton Bulldogs	AHL	9	2	3	5	0	12	0	1	1	6
2010-11	Hamilton Bulldogs	AHL	34	4	4	8	10	....	....	....	....	....
	Wheeling Nailers	ECHL	9	2	3	5	4	....	....	....	....	....

Signed as a free agent by **Montreal**, March 18, 2010.

BITETTO, Anthony (bih-TEH-toh, AN-thuh-nee) NSH

Defense. Shoots left. 6'1", 210 lbs. Born, Island Park, NY, July 15, 1990.
(Nashville's 4th choice, 168th overall, in 2010 Entry Draft).

			Regular Season					Playoffs				
Season	Club	League	GP	G	A	Pts	PIM	GP	G	A	Pts	PIM
2007-08	NY Apple Core	EmJHL	12	4	10	14	32	....	....	....	....	....
	NY Apple Core	EJHL	17	2	6	8	28	....	....	....	....	....
2008-09	NY Apple Core	EJHL	30	2	9	11	50	....	....	....	....	....
	Indiana Ice	USHL	24	1	3	4	29	13	0	3	3	6
2009-10	Indiana Ice	USHL	58	11	29	40	99	9	2	2	4	19
2010-11	Northeastern	H-East	38	3	17	20	66	....	....	....	....	....

USHL Second All-Star Team (2010) • Hockey East All-Rookie Team (2011)

BJUGSTAD, Nick (BYOOG-stad, NIHK) FLA

Center. Shoots right. 6'4", 188 lbs. Born, Minneapolis, MN, July 17, 1992.
(Florida's 2nd choice, 19th overall, in 2010 Entry Draft).

			Regular Season					Playoffs				
Season	Club	League	GP	G	A	Pts	PIM	GP	G	A	Pts	PIM
2007-08	Blaine Bengals	High-MN	24	6	14	20	10	....	....	....	....	....
2008-09	Blaine Bengals	High-MN	25	26	25	51	20	....	....	....	....	....
2009-10	Team Northwest	UMHSEL	23	13	8	21	18	....	....	....	....	....
	Blaine Bengals	High-MN	30	35	34	69	26	....	....	....	....	....
	USNTDP	U-18	4	0	0	0	0	....	....	....	....	....
2010-11	U. of Minnesota	WCHA	29	8	12	20	51	....	....	....	....	....

BLACKER, Jesse (BLA-kuhr, JEH-see) TOR

Defense. Shoots right. 6'2", 190 lbs. Born, Toronto, Ont., April 19, 1991.
(Toronto's 3rd choice, 58th overall, in 2009 Entry Draft).

			Regular Season					Playoffs				
Season	Club	League	GP	G	A	Pts	PIM	GP	G	A	Pts	PIM
2006-07	Tor. Red Wings	GTHL	43	9	25	34	86	....	....	....	....	....
2007-08	Chatham Maroons	ON-Jr.B	8	1	2	3	25	....	....	....	....	....
	Windsor Spitfires	OHL	17	0	4	4	6	5	0	1	1	2
2008-09	Windsor Spitfires	OHL	67	4	17	21	54	20	0	4	4	18
2009-10	Windsor Spitfires	OHL	9	0	3	3	12	....	....	....	....	....
	Owen Sound	OHL	48	6	24	30	62	....	....	....	....	....
	Toronto Marlies	AHL	6	0	1	1	0	....	....	....	....	....
2010-11	Owen Sound	OHL	62	10	44	54	83	22	5	11	16	14

BLACKWELL, Colin (BLAK-wehl, KAWL-ihn) S.J.

Center. Shoots right. 5'8", 180 lbs. Born, Lawrence, MA, March 28, 1993.
(San Jose's 6th choice, 194th overall, in 2011 Entry Draft).

			Regular Season					Playoffs				
Season	Club	League	GP	G	A	Pts	PIM	GP	G	A	Pts	PIM
2007-08	St. John's Prep	High-MA	....	2	0	2	....	....	....	....	....	....
2008-09	St. John's Prep	High-MA	....	18	10	28	....	....	....	....	....	....
2009-10	St. John's Prep	High-MA	....	17	19	36	....	....	....	....	....	....
2010-11	St. John's Prep	High-MA	25	33	33	66	....	....	....	....	....	....

• Signed Letter of Intent to attend **Harvard University** (ECAC) in fall of 2011.

BLAIN, Jeremie (BLAYN, JAIR-uh-mee) EDM

Defense. Shoots right. 6'2", 189 lbs. Born, Le Moyne, Que., March 19, 1992.
(Edmonton's 6th choice, 91st overall, in 2010 Entry Draft).

			Regular Season					Playoffs				
Season	Club	League	GP	G	A	Pts	PIM	GP	G	A	Pts	PIM
2007-08	C.C. Lemoyne	QAAA	45	2	21	23	16	8	4	3	7	2
2008-09	Victoriaville Tigres	QMJHL	27	1	3	4	0	....	....	....	....	....
	Acadie-Bathurst	QMJHL	22	0	3	3	6	5	0	2	2	4
2009-10	Acadie-Bathurst	QMJHL	64	4	34	38	72	5	2	2	4	10
2010-11	Acadie-Bathurst	QMJHL	40	2	35	37	48	4	2	2	4	4

BLANCHARD, Nicolas (BLAN-shard, NIHK-oh-las) CAR

Center/Right wing. Shoots left. 6'3", 200 lbs. Born, Granby, Que., May 31, 1987.
(Carolina's 8th choice, 192nd overall, in 2005 Entry Draft).

			Regular Season					Playoffs				
Season	Club	League	GP	G	A	Pts	PIM	GP	G	A	Pts	PIM
2003-04	Antoine-Girouard	QAAA	42	24	28	52	28	13	9	6	15	4
2004-05	Chicoutimi	QMJHL	69	13	26	39	31	17	2	2	4	10
2005-06	Chicoutimi	QMJHL	60	15	29	44	51	9	1	2	3	4
2006-07	Chicoutimi	QMJHL	62	22	35	57	41	4	0	2	2	8
	Albany River Rats	AHL	7	1	2	3	2	5	0	0	0	2
2007-08	Albany River Rats	AHL	64	11	12	23	70	7	0	2	2	2
2008-09	Albany River Rats	AHL	55	7	12	19	132	....	....	....	....	....
2009-10	Albany River Rats	AHL	76	14	8	22	171	8	0	0	0	13
2010-11	Charlotte	AHL	72	8	10	18	101	16	2	3	5	16

BLIDSTRAND, Ricard (BLIHD-strahnd, REE-kahrd) PHI

Defense. Shoots left. 6'3", 202 lbs. Born, Stockholm, Sweden, April 20, 1992.
(Philadelphia's 5th choice, 206th overall, in 2010 Entry Draft).

			Regular Season					Playoffs				
Season	Club	League	GP	G	A	Pts	PIM	GP	G	A	Pts	PIM
2007-08	Djurgarden U18	Swe-U18	22	1	2	3	18	2	0	0	0	0
2008-09	Djurgarden U18	Swe-U18	17	1	8	9	26	....	....	....	....	....
	Djurgarden Jr.	Swe-Jr.	2	0	0	0	0	....	....	....	....	....
	Balsta HC	Sweden-3	2	0	1	1	0	....	....	....	....	....
	AIK IF Solna U18	Swe-U18	6	2	0	2	0	7	2	2	4	0
	AIK IF Solna Jr.	Swe-Jr.	5	0	0	0	2	....	....	....	....	....
2009-10	AIK IF Solna U18	Swe-U18	10	2	4	6	0	3	0	1	1	12
	AIK IF Solna Jr.	Swe-Jr.	33	2	6	8	4	....	....	....	....	....
2010-11	Regina Pats	WHL	70	3	14	17	26	....	....	....	....	....

BLOMQVIST, Anton (BLAWM-kvihst, AN-tawn) CBJ

Defense. Shoots left. 6'6", 204 lbs. Born, Kristianstad, Sweden, March 7, 1990.
(Columbus' 5th choice, 167th overall, in 2009 Entry Draft).

			Regular Season					Playoffs				
Season	Club	League	GP	G	A	Pts	PIM	GP	G	A	Pts	PIM
2005-06	Osby IK	Sweden-3	22	1	1	2	6	....	....	....	....	....
2006-07	Linkopings HC U18	Swe-U18	10	2	1	3	16	....	....	....	....	....
	Linkopings HC Jr.	Swe-Jr.	1	0	1	1	0	....	....	....	....	....
2007-08	Malmo U18	Swe-U18	20	2	2	4	57	2	0	0	0	2
	Malmo Jr.	Swe-Jr.	18	0	1	1	20	5	0	1	1	2
2008-09	Malmo Jr.	Swe-Jr.	31	2	14	16	73	....	....	....	....	....
	Malmo	Sweden-2	13	0	3	3	8	....	....	....	....	....
2009-10	Malmo	Sweden-2	49	3	2	5	55	5	0	0	0	10
	Malmo Jr.	Swe-Jr.	....	....	....	....	....	1	0	0	0	0
2010-11	Malmo	Sweden-2	27	0	1	1	14	....	....	....	....	....
	Springfield Falcons	AHL	5	0	1	1	21	....	....	....	....	....

BLOMSTRAND, Ludwig (BLAWM-strand, LUHD-wihg) VAN

Left wing. Shoots left. 6'1", 198 lbs. Born, Uppsala, Sweden, March 8, 1993.
(Vancouver's 5th choice, 120th overall, in 2011 Entry Draft).

			Regular Season					Playoffs				
Season	Club	League	GP	G	A	Pts	PIM	GP	G	A	Pts	PIM
2008-09	Almtuna U18	Swe-U18	10	3	0	3	8	....	....	....	....	....
	Gimo IF Hockey	Sweden-4	26	17	10	27	18	....	....	....	....	....
2009-10	Djurgarden U18	Swe-U18	35	9	19	28	24	5	0	2	2	0
2010-11	Djurgarden U18	Swe-U18	9	2	11	13	4	5	1	3	4	10
	Djurgarden Jr.	Swe-Jr.	35	3	4	7	14	3	0	0	0	2

BLOOD, Ben (BLUHD, BEHN) OTT

Defense. Shoots left. 6'3", 229 lbs. Born, Plymouth, MN, March 15, 1989.
(Ottawa's 4th choice, 120th overall, in 2007 Entry Draft).

			Regular Season					Playoffs				
Season	Club	League	GP	G	A	Pts	PIM	GP	G	A	Pts	PIM
2005-06	Shat.-St. Mary's	High-MN	73	3	22	25	32	....	....	....	....	....
2006-07	Shat.-St. Mary's	High-MN	63	11	25	36	144	....	....	....	....	....
2007-08	Des Moines	USHL	11	0	7	7	17	....	....	....	....	....
	Indiana Ice	USHL	46	10	6	16	83	4	1	2	3	14
2008-09	North Dakota	WCHA	31	0	1	1	12	....	....	....	....	....
2009-10	North Dakota	WCHA	43	5	9	14	96	....	....	....	....	....
2010-11	North Dakota	WCHA	44	2	10	12	48	....	....	....	....	....

BODROV, Denis (bawd-RAWV, DEH-nihs) PHI

Defense. Shoots left. 6', 185 lbs. Born, Togliatti, USSR, August 22, 1986.
(Philadelphia's 4th choice, 55th overall, in 2006 Entry Draft).

			Regular Season					Playoffs				
Season	Club	League	GP	G	A	Pts	PIM	GP	G	A	Pts	PIM
2002-03	Lada Togliatti 2	Russia-3	9	0	0	0	2	....	....	....	....	....
2003-04	Lada Togliatti 2	Russia-3	45	3	4	7	58	....	....	....	....	....
2004-05	CSK VVS Samara	Russia-2	33	1	6	7	57	....	....	....	....	....
2005-06	Lada Togliatti	Russia	35	2	2	4	42	8	0	0	0	8
2006-07	Lada Togliatti	Russia	49	1	5	6	70	3	0	1	1	6
2007-08	Lada Togliatti 2	Russia-3	8	3	4	7	38	....	....	....	....	....
	Lada Togliatti	Russia	46	2	9	11	74	4	1	0	1	2
2008-09	Lada Togliatti	Rus-KHL	24	1	5	6	20	....	....	....	....	....
	Mytischi	Rus-KHL	21	1	4	5	24	4	0	1	1	0
2009-10	Mytischi	Rus-KHL	12	1	0	1	6	....	....	....	....	....
	Adirondack	AHL	17	1	3	4	6	....	....	....	....	....
2010-11	Spartak Moscow	Rus-KHL	45	3	8	11	46	4	0	2	2	4

Traded to **Mytischi** (Russia-KHL) by **Togliatti** (Russia-KHL) for Mikhail Glukov, November 22, 2008. Signed as a free agent by **Spartak Moscow** (Russia-KHL), July 12, 2010.

BOLLIG, Brandon (BOH-lihg, BRAN-duhn) CHI

Left wing. Shoots left. 6'3", 215 lbs. Born, St. Charles, MO, January 31, 1987.

			Regular Season					Playoffs				
Season	Club	League	GP	G	A	Pts	PIM	GP	G	A	Pts	PIM
2005-06	Lincoln Stars	USHL	58	8	8	16	175	9	1	2	3	12
2006-07	Lincoln Stars	USHL	57	14	12	26	207	4	0	2	2	2
2007-08	Lincoln Stars	USHL	58	15	16	31	211	8	2	4	6	40
2008-09	St. Lawrence	ECAC	36	6	7	13	51	....	....	....	....	....
2009-10	St. Lawrence	ECAC	42	7	18	25	83	....	....	....	....	....
	Rockford IceHogs	AHL	3	1	1	2	7	....	....	....	....	....
2010-11	Rockford IceHogs	AHL	55	4	0	4	115	....	....	....	....	....

Signed as a free agent by **Chicago**, April 3, 2010.

BONNEAU, Jimmy (BAW-noh, JIHM-mee)

Left wing. Shoots left. 6'3", 214 lbs. Born, Baie-Comeau, Que., March 22, 1985.
(Montreal's 10th choice, 241st overall, in 2003 Entry Draft).

			Regular Season					Playoffs				
Season	Club	League	GP	G	A	Pts	PIM	GP	G	A	Pts	PIM
2000-01	Jonquiere Elites	QAAA	1	0	0	0	0	....	....	....	....	....
2001-02	Jonquiere Elites	QAAA	40	5	10	15	55	3	1	1	2	2
2002-03	Montreal Rocket	QMJHL	65	1	5	6	261	7	0	0	0	12
2003-04	P.E.I. Rocket	QMJHL	70	7	12	19	263	11	1	0	1	12
2004-05	P.E.I. Rocket	QMJHL	70	11	11	22	234	....	....	....	....	....
2005-06	Long Beach	ECHL	65	1	5	6	137	....	....	....	....	....
2006-07	Hamilton Bulldogs	AHL	9	0	0	0	59	....	....	....	....	....
	Cincinnati	ECHL	46	2	5	7	89	10	0	0	0	23
2007-08	Hamilton Bulldogs	AHL	6	1	0	1	5	....	....	....	....	....
	Cincinnati	ECHL	18	0	4	4	61	3	0	0	0	0
2008-09	Portland Pirates	AHL	46	0	6	6	122	....	....	....	....	....
2009-10	Rochester	AHL	57	4	2	6	187	....	....	....	....	....
2010-11	Hamilton Bulldogs	AHL	77	1	2	3	180	15	1	2	3	16

Signed as a free agent by **Buffalo**, August 13, 2008. Signed as a free agent by **Hamilton** (AHL), July 2, 2010.

BORDELEAU, Patrick (BOHR-duh-loh, PAT-rihk) COL

Left wing. Shoots left. 6'5", 195 lbs. Born, Montreal, Que., March 23, 1986.
(Minnesota's 6th choice, 114th overall, in 2004 Entry Draft).

			Regular Season					Playoffs				
Season	Club	League	GP	G	A	Pts	PIM	GP	G	A	Pts	PIM
2002-03	Gatineau Intrepide	QAAA	39	8	13	21	50	....	....	....	....	....
2003-04	Val-d'Or Foreurs	QMJHL	68	7	11	18	97	7	1	1	2	8
2004-05	Val-d'Or Foreurs	QMJHL	63	14	24	38	51	....	....	....	....	....
2005-06	Val-d'Or Foreurs	QMJHL	67	23	33	56	87	5	1	0	1	7
2006-07	Drummondville	QMJHL	3	0	2	2	6	....	....	....	....	....
	Acadie-Bathurst	QMJHL	17	7	12	19	26	....	....	....	....	....
2007-08	Charlotte	ECHL	10	1	2	3	11	....	....	....	....	....
	Wheeling Nailers	ECHL	3	0	1	1	0	....	....	....	....	....
	Pensacola	ECHL	38	7	11	18	60	....	....	....	....	....
2008-09	Augusta Lynx	ECHL	18	4	6	10	57	....	....	....	....	....
	Albany River Rats	AHL	6	0	2	2	21	....	....	....	....	....
	Florida Everblades	ECHL	29	4	9	13	81	....	....	....	....	....
	Springfield Falcons	AHL	4	0	0	0	4	....	....	....	....	....
	Lake Erie Monsters	AHL	3	0	1	1	17	....	....	....	....	....
	Milwaukee	AHL	2	0	0	0	0	....	....	....	....	....
2009-10	Lake Erie Monsters	AHL	60	1	2	3	106	....	....	....	....	....
2010-11	Lake Erie Monsters	AHL	72	2	10	12	125	7	0	0	0	6

Signed to a PTO (professional tryout) contract by **Albany** (AHL), December 5, 2008. Signed to a PTO (professional tryout) contract by **Springfield** (AHL), January 5, 2009. Signed to a PTO (professional tryout) contract by **Lake Erie** (AHL), March 31, 2009. Signed to a PTO (professional tryout) contract by **Milwaukee** (AHL), April 6, 2009. Signed as a free agent by **Colorado**, July 1, 2011.

BORDSON, Rob (BOHRD-suhn, RAWB)

Center. Shoots left. 6'2", 190 lbs. Born, Duluth, MN, June 9, 1988.

			Regular Season					Playoffs				
Season	Club	League	GP	G	A	Pts	PIM	GP	G	A	Pts	PIM
2006-07	Cedar Rapids	USHL	47	6	29	35	26	5	0	1	1	0
2007-08	U. Minn-Duluth	WCHA	27	1	6	7	6	....	....	....	....	....
2008-09	U. Minn-Duluth	WCHA	15	0	0	0	6	....	....	....	....	....
2009-10	U. Minn-Duluth	WCHA	40	12	28	40	18	....	....	....	....	....
2010-11	Syracuse Crunch	AHL	15	1	2	3	4	....	....	....	....	....
	Adirondack	AHL	61	7	14	21	28	....	....	....	....	....

Signed as a free agent by **Anaheim**, March 23, 2010. Traded to **Philadelphia** by **Anaheim** with Danny Syvret for Patrick Maroon and David Laliberte, November 21, 2010. Traded to **Los Angeles** by **Philadelphia** with Mike Richards for Brayden Schenn, Wayne Simmonds and Los Angeles' 2nd round choice in 2012 Entry Draft, June 23, 2011.

BOROWIECKI, Mark (boh-roh-WIH-kee, MAHRK) OTT

Defense. Shoots left. 6'1", 205 lbs. Born, Ottawa, Ont., July 12, 1989.
(Ottawa's 6th choice, 139th overall, in 2008 Entry Draft).

			Regular Season					Playoffs				
Season	Club	League	GP	G	A	Pts	PIM	GP	G	A	Pts	PIM
2006-07	Smiths Falls Bears	CJHL	53	3	25	28	85	6	0	0	0	10
2007-08	Smiths Falls Bears	CJHL	46	2	24	26	80	15	1	10	11	22
2008-09	Clarkson Knights	ECAC	33	1	1	2	24	....	....	....	....	....
2009-10	Clarkson Knights	ECAC	35	8	11	19	55	....	....	....	....	....
2010-11	Clarkson Knights	ECAC	31	3	8	11	67	....	....	....	....	....
	Binghamton	AHL	9	0	0	0	6	21	0	2	2	8

BORTUZZO, Robert (bohr-TOOZ-oh, RAW-buhrt) PIT

Defense. Shoots right. 6'3", 196 lbs. Born, Thunder Bay, Ont., March 18, 1989.
(Pittsburgh's 3rd choice, 78th overall, in 2007 Entry Draft).

			Regular Season					Playoffs				
Season	Club	League	GP	G	A	Pts	PIM	GP	G	A	Pts	PIM
2005-06	F-Wm. North Stars	SIJHL	40	4	18	22	....	....	....	....	....	....
2006-07	Kitchener Rangers	OHL	63	2	12	14	67	9	1	2	3	8
2007-08	Kitchener Rangers	OHL	52	3	15	18	61	18	0	8	8	14
2008-09	Kitchener Rangers	OHL	23	1	16	17	24	....	....	....	....	....
2009-10	Wilkes-Barre	AHL	75	2	10	12	109	4	0	0	0	0
2010-11	Wilkes-Barre	AHL	79	4	22	26	111	12	0	1	1	6

BOUCHARD, Francois (BOO-shahrd, frahn-SWUH) WSH

Right wing. Shoots left. 6'1", 195 lbs. Born, Sherbrooke, Que., April 26, 1988.
(Washington's 4th choice, 35th overall, in 2006 Entry Draft).

			Regular Season					Playoffs				
Season	Club	League	GP	G	A	Pts	PIM	GP	G	A	Pts	PIM
2004-05	Baie-Comeau	QMJHL	54	11	13	24	13	6	1	1	2	2
2005-06	Baie-Comeau	QMJHL	69	33	69	102	66	4	1	0	1	6
2006-07	Baie-Comeau	QMJHL	68	45	*80	*125	72	11	7	11	18	4
2007-08	Baie-Comeau	QMJHL	68	36	56	92	70	5	1	1	2	6
	Hershey Bears	AHL	4	1	0	1	2	1	0	0	0	2
2008-09	Hershey Bears	AHL	64	15	20	35	34	11	1	2	3	8
2009-10	Hershey Bears	AHL	77	21	31	52	55	21	5	5	10	28
2010-11	Hershey Bears	AHL	74	12	12	24	30	6	1	0	1	0

QMJHL Second All-Star Team (2007)

BOUCHER, Reid (BOO-shay, REED) N.J.

Center. Shoots left. 5'11", 190 lbs. Born, Lansing, MI, September 8, 1993.
(New Jersey's 4th choice, 99th overall, in 2011 Entry Draft).

			Regular Season					Playoffs				
Season	Club	League	GP	G	A	Pts	PIM	GP	G	A	Pts	PIM
2008-09	Lansing Capitals	Minor-MI	64	79	41	120	119	....	....	....	....	....
2009-10	USNTDP	USHL	24	10	4	14	22	....	....	....	....	....
	USNTDP	U-17	17	7	9	16	16	....	....	....	....	....
	USNTDP	U-18	1	0	0	0	0	....	....	....	....	....
2010-11	USNTDP	USHL	24	14	6	20	13	....	....	....	....	....
	USNTDP	U-18	35	12	8	20	120	....	....	....	....	....

BOURDON, Marc-Andre (boor-DOHN, MAHRK-AHN-dray) PHI

Defense. Shoots left. 6', 206 lbs. Born, St-Hyacinthe, Que., September 17, 1989.
(Philadelphia's 2nd choice, 67th overall, in 2008 Entry Draft).

			Regular Season					Playoffs				
Season	Club	League	GP	G	A	Pts	PIM	GP	G	A	Pts	PIM
2006-07	Rouyn-Noranda	QMJHL	63	2	26	28	80	16	0	4	4	21
2007-08	Rouyn-Noranda	QMJHL	69	12	47	59	114	17	2	16	18	25
2008-09	Rouyn-Noranda	QMJHL	37	11	27	38	89	....	....	....	....	....
	Rimouski Oceanic	QMJHL	17	7	15	22	23	13	1	12	13	25
2009-10	Adirondack	AHL	61	2	17	19	53	....	....	....	....	....
2010-11	Adirondack	AHL	46	1	9	10	84	....	....	....	....	....
	Greenville	ECHL	5	0	2	2	14	10	0	3	3	16

QMJHL First All-Star Team (2008, 2009) • Canadian Major Junior Second All-Star Team (2008)

BOURNIVAL, Michael (boor-nee-VAHL, MIGH-kuhl) MTL

Left wing. Shoots left. 6', 187 lbs. Born, Shawinigan, Que., May 31, 1992.
(Colorado's 3rd choice, 71st overall, in 2010 Entry Draft).

			Regular Season					Playoffs				
Season	Club	League	GP	G	A	Pts	PIM	GP	G	A	Pts	PIM
2007-08	Trois-Rivieres	QAAA	52	33	23	56	66	7	3	3	6	10
2008-09	Shawinigan	QMJHL	46	11	11	22	29	21	1	3	4	12
2009-10	Shawinigan	QMJHL	58	24	38	62	37	6	2	2	4	6
2010-11	Shawinigan	QMJHL	56	28	36	64	28	12	5	8	13	10

Traded to **Montreal** by **Colorado** for Ryan O'Byrne, November 11, 2010.

BOURQUE, Gabriel (BOHRK, gah-BREE-ehl) NSH

Left wing. Shoots left. 5'10", 192 lbs. Born, Rimouski, Que., September 23, 1990.
(Nashville's 9th choice, 132nd overall, in 2009 Entry Draft).

			Regular Season					Playoffs				
Season	Club	League	GP	G	A	Pts	PIM	GP	G	A	Pts	PIM
2006-07	Ecole Notre Dame	QAAA	43	15	35	50	115	13	8	16	24	14
2007-08	Baie-Comeau	QMJHL	65	10	18	28	38	5	0	0	0	0
2008-09	Baie-Comeau	QMJHL	60	22	39	61	82	5	0	2	2	16
2009-10	Baie-Comeau	QMJHL	30	13	25	38	61	....	....	....	....	....
	Moncton Wildcats	QMJHL	25	3	11	14	37	21	19	10	29	18
2010-11	Milwaukee	AHL	78	18	18	36	19	13	7	6	13	4

BOURQUE, Ryan (BOHRK, RIGH-uhn) NYR

Center. Shoots left. 5'9", 164 lbs. Born, Boxford, MA, January 3, 1991.
(NY Rangers' 3rd choice, 80th overall, in 2009 Entry Draft).

			Regular Season					Playoffs				
Season	Club	League	GP	G	A	Pts	PIM	GP	G	A	Pts	PIM
2006-07	Cushing	High-MA	29	19	31	50	....	....	....	....	....	....
2007-08	USNTDP	NAHL	34	11	9	20	14	....	....	....	....	....
	USNTDP	U-17	7	4	3	7	10	....	....	....	....	....
	USNTDP	U-18	27	4	12	16	18	....	....	....	....	....
2008-09	USNTDP	NAHL	14	7	9	16	10	....	....	....	....	....
	USNTDP	U-18	43	14	24	38	48	....	....	....	....	....
2009-10	Quebec Remparts	QMJHL	44	19	24	43	20	9	3	7	10	6
2010-11	Quebec Remparts	QMJHL	49	26	33	59	22	18	5	11	16	8

BOYCHUK, Riley (BOY-chuhk, RIGH-lee) BUF

Left wing. Shoots left. 6'5", 220 lbs. Born, Vancouver, B.C., February 20, 1991.
(Buffalo's 9th choice, 208th overall, in 2010 Entry Draft).

			Regular Season					Playoffs				
Season	Club	League	GP	G	A	Pts	PIM	GP	G	A	Pts	PIM
2006-07	Fraser Valley	BCMML	29	18	18	36	72	....	....	....	....	....
2007-08	Portland	WHL	5	0	1	1	0	....	....	....	....	....
2008-09	Portland	WHL	62	7	10	17	86	....	....	....	....	....
2009-10	Portland	WHL	66	14	16	30	157	13	2	1	3	24
2010-11	Portland	WHL	60	18	17	35	148	21	4	8	12	*50

• Missed majority of 2007-08 due to surgeries on both hips.

BOYD, R.J. (BOID, AHR-JAY) FLA

Defense. Shoots left. 6'2", 175 lbs. Born, Sarasota, FL, February 7, 1991.
(Florida's 13th choice, 183rd overall, in 2010 Entry Draft).

			Regular Season					Playoffs				
Season	Club	League	GP	G	A	Pts	PIM	GP	G	A	Pts	PIM
2007-08	Cushing	High-MA	35	0	3	3	....	....	....	....	....	....
2008-09	Cushing	High-MA	35	2	11	13	35	....	....	....	....	....
2009-10	Cushing	High-MA	31	4	18	22	....	....	....	....	....	....
2010-11	Sacred Heart	AH	15	1	3	4	16	....	....	....	....	....
	Chicago Steel	USHL	33	2	0	2	42	....	....	....	....	....

BOYD, Travis (BOID, TRA-vihs) WSH

Center. Shoots right. 5'11", 185 lbs. Born, Edina, MN, September 14, 1993.
(Washington's 3rd choice, 177th overall, in 2011 Entry Draft).

			Regular Season					Playoffs				
Season	Club	League	GP	G	A	Pts	PIM	GP	G	A	Pts	PIM
2008-09	Hopkins Royals	High-MN	26	26	25	51	....	....	....	....	....	....
2009-10	USNTDP	USHL	35	8	10	18	18	....	....	....	....	....
	USNTDP	U-17	17	2	4	6	4	....	....	....	....	....
	USNTDP	U-18	1	0	0	0	0	....	....	....	....	....
2010-11	USNTDP	USHL	24	5	13	18	10	....	....	....	....	....
	USNTDP	U-18	36	8	12	20	6	....	....	....	....	....

• Signed Letter of Intent to attend **University of Minnesota** (WCHA).

BRASSARD, Austen (BRA-sahrd, AWS-tuhn) WPG

Right wing. Shoots right. 6'2", 188 lbs. Born, Windsor, Ont., January 14, 1993.
(Winnipeg's 5th choice, 149th overall, in 2011 Entry Draft).

			Regular Season					Playoffs				
Season	Club	League	GP	G	A	Pts	PIM	GP	G	A	Pts	PIM
2008-09	Wind. Jr. Spitfires	Minor-ON	69	55	66	121	111	....	....	....	....	....
2009-10	Windsor Spitfires	OHL	37	4	8	12	36	....	....	....	....	....
	Belleville Bulls	OHL	26	6	11	17	9	....	....	....	....	....
2010-11	Belleville Bulls	OHL	67	19	15	34	78	4	1	0	1	4

BREEN, Christopher (BREEN, KRIHS-toh-fuhr) CGY

Defense. Shoots left. 6'7", 224 lbs. Born, Uxbridge, Ont., June 29, 1989.

			Regular Season					Playoffs				
Season	Club	League	GP	G	A	Pts	PIM	GP	G	A	Pts	PIM
2005-06	Mississauga	OPJHL	33	1	6	7	10	....	....	....	....	....
	Saginaw Spirit	OHL	25	0	0	0	10	....	....	....	....	....
2006-07	Saginaw Spirit	OHL	39	1	2	3	32	2	0	0	0	2
2007-08	Saginaw Spirit	OHL	55	0	6	6	67	4	0	1	1	0
2008-09	Saginaw Spirit	OHL	6	0	1	1	9	....	....	....	....	....
	Erie Otters	OHL	59	0	12	12	31	5	0	1	1	7
2009-10	Erie Otters	OHL	12	0	2	2	11	....	....	....	....	....
	Peterborough	OHL	53	4	8	12	36	4	1	0	1	5
	Abbotsford Heat	AHL	1	0	1	1	4	....	....	....	....	....
2010-11	Abbotsford Heat	AHL	73	4	7	11	47	....	....	....	....	....

Signed to an ATO (amateur tryout) contract by **Abbotsford** (AHL), March 30, 2010. Signed as a free agent by **Calgary**, May 28, 2010.

BRENNAN, Mike (BREH-nan, MIGHK)

Defense. Shoots right. 6', 205 lbs. Born, Smithtown, NY, January 24, 1986.

			Regular Season					Playoffs				
Season	Club	League	GP	G	A	Pts	PIM	GP	G	A	Pts	PIM
2002-03	USNTDP	U-17	18	2	4	6	8	....	....	....	....	....
	USNTDP	NAHL	44	1	2	3	89	....	....	....	....	....
2003-04	USNTDP	U-17	43	2	5	7	58	....	....	....	....	....
	USNTDP	NAHL	11	2	3	5	19	....	....	....	....	....
2004-05	Boston College	H-East	40	2	6	8	46	....	....	....	....	....
2005-06	Boston College	H-East	42	2	10	12	95	....	....	....	....	....
2006-07	Boston College	H-East	42	0	11	11	89	....	....	....	....	....
2007-08	Boston College	H-East	44	3	5	8	52	....	....	....	....	....
2008-09	Rockford IceHogs	AHL	64	0	6	6	77	2	0	0	0	2
2009-10	Rockford IceHogs	AHL	72	3	6	9	113	3	0	0	0	0
2010-11	Toronto Marlies	AHL	72	3	7	10	110	....	....	....	....	....

NCAA Championship All-Tournament Team (2008)

Signed as a free agent by **Chicago**, April 16, 2008. Signed as a free agent by **Toronto**, September 25, 2010.

BRENNAN, T.J. (BREH-nan, TEE-JAY) BUF

Defense. Shoots left. 6'1", 214 lbs. Born, Willingboro, NJ, April 3, 1989.
(Buffalo's 1st choice, 31st overall, in 2007 Entry Draft).

			Regular Season					Playoffs				
Season	Club	League	GP	G	A	Pts	PIM	GP	G	A	Pts	PIM
2005-06	Phi. Little Flyers	AtJHL	42	9	23	32	....	....	....	....	....	....
2006-07	Saint John	QMJHL	68	16	25	41	79	4	1	1	2	4
2007-08	St. John's	QMJHL	65	16	25	41	92	6	2	4	6	12
2008-09	Montreal	QMJHL	59	5	29	34	63	10	4	8	12	34
2009-10	Portland Pirates	AHL	65	6	17	23	64	4	0	1	1	2
2010-11	Portland Pirates	AHL	72	15	24	39	49	4	0	1	1	6

BRENNER, Tyler (BREH-nuhr, TIGH-luhr) TOR

Right wing. Shoots right. 6'2", 200 lbs. Born, Linwood, Ont., April 5, 1988.

			Regular Season					Playoffs				
Season	Club	League	GP	G	A	Pts	PIM	GP	G	A	Pts	PIM
2008-09	RIT Tigers	AH	38	14	21	35	35	....	....	....	....	....
2009-10	RIT Tigers	AH	33	15	11	26	24	....	....	....	....	....
2010-11	RIT Tigers	AH	37	26	15	41	39	....	....	....	....	....
	Toronto Marlies	AHL	8	2	4	6	2	....	....	....	....	....

Signed as a free agent by **Toronto**, March 21, 2011.

BRICKLEY, Connor (BRIH-klee, KAW-nuhr) FLA

Center. Shoots left. 6', 190 lbs. Born, Malden, MA, February 25, 1992.
(Florida's 6th choice, 50th overall, in 2010 Entry Draft).

			Regular Season					Playoffs				
Season	Club	League	GP	G	A	Pts	PIM	GP	G	A	Pts	PIM
2008-09	Belmont Hill	High-MA	30	17	18	35	60	....	....	....	....	....
2009-10	Des Moines	USHL	52	22	21	43	68	....	....	....	....	....
	USNTDP	U-18	14	2	5	7	6	....	....	....	....	....
2010-11	U. of Vermont	H-East	35	4	9	13	33	....	....	....	....	....

BRITTAIN, Josh (BRIH-tehn, JAWSH) ANA

Left wing. Shoots left. 6'5", 226 lbs. Born, Milton, Ont., January 3, 1990.
(Anaheim's 5th choice, 71st overall, in 2008 Entry Draft).

			Regular Season					Playoffs				
Season	Club	League	GP	G	A	Pts	PIM	GP	G	A	Pts	PIM
2005-06	Tor. Jr. Canadiens	GTHL	33	19	21	40	47	....	....	....	....	....
2006-07	Kingston	OHL	54	5	12	17	38	2	0	0	0	0
2007-08	Kingston	OHL	68	28	23	51	106	....	....	....	....	....
2008-09	Kingston	OHL	27	17	7	24	31	....	....	....	....	....
	Barrie Colts	OHL	41	15	13	28	65	5	1	2	3	4
2009-10	Barrie Colts	OHL	12	3	5	8	29	....	....	....	....	....
	Plymouth Whalers	OHL	56	12	12	24	101	9	1	0	1	5
2010-11	Syracuse Crunch	AHL	13	0	1	1	48	....	....	....	....	....
	Elmira Jackals	ECHL	38	3	8	11	92	4	1	0	1	2

BROADHURST, Alex (BRAWD-hurst, AL-ehx) CHI

Center. Shoots left. 5'10", 150 lbs. Born, Orland Park, IL, March 7, 1993.
(Chicago's 10th choice, 199th overall, in 2011 Entry Draft).

			Regular Season					Playoffs				
Season	Club	League	GP	G	A	Pts	PIM	GP	G	A	Pts	PIM
2006-07	Chicago Mission	MWEHL	31	20	29	49	10	....	....	....	....	....
2007-08	Chicago Fury	MWEHL	31	4	4	8	6	....	....	....	....	....
2008-09	Team Illinois	T1EHL	31	8	18	26	22	....	....	....	....	....
2009-10	Chicago Mission	T1EHL	48	16	29	45	26	....	....	....	....	....
2010-11	Green Bay	USHL	55	13	20	33	22	11	3	6	9	4

• Signed Letter of Intent to attend **University of Nebraska-Omaha** (WCHA).

BRODA, Joel (BROH-da, JOHL) MIN

Center. Shoots left. 6', 209 lbs. Born, Yorkton, Sask., November 24, 1989.
(Washington's 6th choice, 144th overall, in 2008 Entry Draft).

			Regular Season					Playoffs				
Season	Club	League	GP	G	A	Pts	PIM	GP	G	A	Pts	PIM
2004-05	Beardy's	SMHL	44	13	13	26	28	....	....	....	....	....
	Tri-City Americans	WHL	2	0	0	0	0	....	....	....	....	....
2005-06	Tri-City Americans	WHL	51	3	1	4	10	5	0	0	0	0
2006-07	Tri-City Americans	WHL	71	16	28	44	62	6	2	0	2	0
2007-08	Tri-City Americans	WHL	3	2	1	3	2	....	....	....	....	....
	Moose Jaw	WHL	70	28	22	50	72	6	1	1	2	0
2008-09	Moose Jaw	WHL	39	*36	12	48	45	....	....	....	....	....
	Calgary Hitmen	WHL	28	*17	22	39	19	18	11	13	24	8
2009-10	Calgary Hitmen	WHL	66	39	34	73	65	23	*13	4	17	16
2010-11	Houston Aeros	AHL	22	5	2	7	16	....	....	....	....	....
	Bakersfield	ECHL	32	17	13	30	39	4	0	1	1	0

WHL East Second All-Star Team (2009)

Signed as a free agent by **Minnesota**, July 14, 2010.

BRODEUR, Mathieu (broh-DUHR, MA-tyew) PHX

Defense. Shoots left. 6'5", 230 lbs. Born, Laval, Que., June 21, 1990.
(Phoenix's 5th choice, 76th overall, in 2008 Entry Draft).

			Regular Season					Playoffs				
Season	Club	League	GP	G	A	Pts	PIM	GP	G	A	Pts	PIM
2006-07	Laurentides	QAAA	44	5	7	12	58	15	2	4	6	18
2007-08	Cape Breton	QMJHL	69	1	6	7	27	11	0	0	0	6
2008-09	Cape Breton	QMJHL	61	3	12	15	15	11	1	3	4	4
2009-10	Cape Breton	QMJHL	65	4	25	29	31	5	0	0	0	9
	San Antonio	AHL	2	0	1	1	0	....	....	....	....	....
2010-11	San Antonio	AHL	4	0	0	0	2	....	....	....	....	....
	Las Vegas	ECHL	52	0	1	1	43	....	....	....	....	....

BRODIN, Daniel (broh-DEEN, DAN-yehl) TOR

Left wing. Shoots right. 6'1", 172 lbs. Born, Tyreso, Sweden, February 9, 1990.
(Toronto's 6th choice, 146th overall, in 2010 Entry Draft).

			Regular Season					Playoffs				
Season	Club	League	GP	G	A	Pts	PIM	GP	G	A	Pts	PIM
2006-07	Almtuna U18	Swe-U18	....	14	7	21	36	....	....	....	....	....
	Almtuna Jr.	Swe-Jr.	24	3	3	6	16	2	0	0	0	0
2007-08	Djurgarden U18	Swe-U18	35	9	16	25	30	4	0	0	0	0
	Djurgarden Jr.	Swe-Jr.	2	0	0	0	0	....	....	....	....	....
2008-09	Djurgarden Jr.	Swe-Jr.	41	11	12	23	90	6	1	1	2	8
	Djurgarden	Sweden	1	0	0	0	0	....	....	....	....	....
2009-10	Djurgarden Jr.	Swe-Jr.	20	5	2	7	12	....	....	....	....	....
	Djurgarden	Sweden	30	2	3	5	26	16	0	0	0	2
2010-11	Djurgarden	Sweden	51	4	9	13	61	7	2	0	2	6

BRODIN, Jonas (BROH-deen, YOH-nuhs) MIN

Defense. Shoots left. 6'1", 166 lbs. Born, Karlstad, Sweden, July 12, 1993.
(Minnesota's 1st choice, 10th overall, in 2011 Entry Draft).

			Regular Season					Playoffs				
Season	Club	League	GP	G	A	Pts	PIM	GP	G	A	Pts	PIM
2008-09	Farjestad U18	Swe-U18	22	3	8	11	10	4	1	1	2	4
2009-10	Farjestad	Sweden	3	0	0	0	2	....	....	....	....	....
	Skare BK Jr.	Swe-Jr.	2	0	1	1	2	....	....	....	....	....
	Skare BK	Sweden-3	21	1	6	7	10	....	....	....	....	....
	Farjestad U18	Swe-U18	19	6	11	17	6	7	3	8	11	8
2010-11	Farjestad U18	Swe-U18	2	0	1	1	2	....	....	....	....	....
	Farjestad	Sweden	42	0	4	4	12	14	2	0	2	2

BROLL, David (BROHL, DAY-vihd) TOR

Left wing. Shoots left. 6'2", 225 lbs. Born, Mississauga, Ont., January 4, 1993.
(Toronto's 6th choice, 152nd overall, in 2011 Entry Draft).

			Regular Season					Playoffs				
Season	Club	League	GP	G	A	Pts	PIM	GP	G	A	Pts	PIM
2008-09	Tor. Young Nats	GTHL	73	31	26	57	....	....	....	....	....	....
2009-10	Erie Otters	OHL	64	9	9	18	42	4	0	0	0	2
2010-11	Erie Otters	OHL	41	8	14	22	51	....	....	....	....	....
	Sault Ste. Marie	OHL	24	5	7	12	34	....	....	....	....	....

BROWN, Chris (BROWN, KRIHS) PHX

Center. Shoots right. 6'2", 191 lbs. Born, Flower Mound, TX, February 3, 1991.
(Phoenix's 2nd choice, 36th overall, in 2009 Entry Draft).

			Regular Season					Playoffs				
Season	Club	League	GP	G	A	Pts	PIM	GP	G	A	Pts	PIM
2007-08	USNTDP	NAHL	43	8	6	14	66	3	0	0	0	0
	USNTDP	U-17	17	5	1	6	8	....	....	....	....	....
2008-09	USNTDP	NAHL	15	6	2	8	37	....	....	....	....	....
	USNTDP	U-18	47	14	16	30	83	....	....	....	....	....
2009-10	U. of Michigan	CCHA	45	13	15	28	58	....	....	....	....	....
2010-11	U. of Michigan	CCHA	42	9	14	23	59	....	....	....	....	....

CCHA All-Rookie Team (2010)

BROWN, Tyler (BROWN, TIGH-luhr) PHI

Center. Shoots left. 6'2", 184 lbs. Born, Wasaga Beach, Ont., February 7, 1991.

			Regular Season					Playoffs				
Season	Club	League	GP	G	A	Pts	PIM	GP	G	A	Pts	PIM
2007-08	Plymouth Whalers	OHL	38	1	5	6	13	3	0	1	1	2
2008-09	Plymouth Whalers	OHL	49	8	13	21	18	11	1	2	3	0
2009-10	Plymouth Whalers	OHL	66	14	25	39	28	9	2	1	3	2
2010-11	Plymouth Whalers	OHL	67	25	34	59	44	11	3	11	14	8

Signed as a free agent by **Philadelphia**, March 2, 2011.

BRUESS, Trevor (BRIHS, TREH-vuhr)

Right wing. Shoots right. 6', 205 lbs. Born, Minneapolis, MN, January 6, 1986.

			Regular Season					Playoffs				
Season	Club	League	GP	G	A	Pts	PIM	GP	G	A	Pts	PIM
2004-05	Fargo-Moorhead	NAHL	51	11	17	28	72	....	....	....	....	....
2005-06	Lincoln Stars	USHL	56	10	17	27	108	9	1	0	1	8
2006-07	Minnesota State	WCHA	37	3	11	14	102	....	....	....	....	....
2007-08	Minnesota State	WCHA	38	9	21	30	54	....	....	....	....	....
2008-09	Minnesota State	WCHA	35	12	5	17	117	....	....	....	....	....
2009-10	Hershey Bears	AHL	14	1	1	2	15	....	....	....	....	....
	South Carolina	ECHL	46	8	17	25	74	5	1	0	1	10
2010-11	Hershey Bears	AHL	36	0	5	5	76	....	....	....	....	....

Signed as a free agent by **Washington**, March 20, 2009.

BUDISH, Zach (BOO-dihsh, ZAK) NSH

Right wing. Shoots right. 6'3", 221 lbs. Born, Edina, MN, May 9, 1991.
(Nashville's 2nd choice, 41st overall, in 2009 Entry Draft).

			Regular Season					Playoffs				
Season	Club	League	GP	G	A	Pts	PIM	GP	G	A	Pts	PIM
2006-07	Edina Hornets	High-MN	31	22	25	47	....	....	....	....	....	....
2007-08	Edina Hornets	High-MN	30	26	37	63	....	....	....	....	....	....
2008-09	Team Southwest	UMHSEL	15	14	13	27	12	....	....	....	....	....
	Edina Hornets	High-MN	DID NOT PLAY – INJURED									
2009-10	U. of Minnesota	WCHA	39	7	10	17	45	....	....	....	....	....
2010-11	U. of Minnesota	WCHA	7	2	4	6	2	....	....	....	....	....

• Missed 2008-09 (High-MN) due to knee injury in football.

BULMER, Brett (BUHL-muhr, BREHT) MIN

Right wing. Shoots right. 6'3", 186 lbs. Born, Prince George, B.C., April 26, 1992.
(Minnesota's 2nd choice, 39th overall, in 2010 Entry Draft).

			Regular Season					Playoffs				
Season	Club	League	GP	G	A	Pts	PIM	GP	G	A	Pts	PIM
2007-08	Cariboo Cougars	BCMML	40	20	19	39	40	6	2	7	9	4
2008-09	Cariboo Cougars	BCMML	36	28	35	63	56	5	4	2	6	8
	Kelowna Rockets	WHL	3	0	0	0	2	....	....	....	....	....
2009-10	Kelowna Rockets	WHL	65	13	27	40	95	12	3	2	5	6
2010-11	Kelowna Rockets	WHL	57	18	31	49	109	10	4	2	6	4
	Houston Aeros	AHL	....	....	....	....	....	8	0	0	0	6

BUMAGIN, Alexander (buh-MAH-gihn, al-EHX-AN-duhr) EDM

Wing. Shoots left. 6', 180 lbs. Born, Togliatti, USSR, March 1, 1987.
(Edmonton's 5th choice, 170th overall, in 2006 Entry Draft).

			Regular Season					Playoffs				
Season	Club	League	GP	G	A	Pts	PIM	GP	G	A	Pts	PIM
2002-03	Lada Togliatti 2	Russia-3	9	4	1	5	2	....	....	....	....	....
2003-04	Lada Togliatti 2	Russia-3	22	4	9	13	12	4	0	1	1	4
2004-05	Lada Togliatti 2	Russia-3	STATISTICS NOT AVAILABLE									
	Lada Togliatti	Russia	7	2	0	2	2	....	....	....	....	....
2005-06	Lada Togliatti	Russia	40	9	12	21	28	8	0	3	3	4
2006-07	Lada Togliatti	Russia	41	2	3	5	18	3	0	0	0	0
2007-08	Mytischi	Russia	31	8	7	15	37	5	0	0	0	0
2008-09	Mytischi	Rus-KHL	40	4	7	11	20	6	2	1	3	0
2009-10	Nizhnekamsk	Rus-KHL	51	8	13	21	28	3	0	0	0	0
2010-11	Nizhnekamsk	Rus-KHL	4	1	2	3	4	....	....	....	....	....
	Novokuznetsk	Rus-KHL	39	6	5	11	24	....	....	....	....	....

BURAVCHIKOV, Vyacheslav (burh-AV-chih-kawf,V'YATCH-ih-slav) BUF

Defense. Shoots left. 6'1", 189 lbs. Born, Moscow, USSR, May 22, 1987.
(Buffalo's 7th choice, 191st overall, in 2005 Entry Draft).

			Regular Season					Playoffs				
Season	Club	League	GP	G	A	Pts	PIM	GP	G	A	Pts	PIM
2003-04	Krylja Sovetov 2	Russia-3	STATISTICS NOT AVAILABLE									
2004-05	Krylja Sovetov 2	Russia-3	15	5	6	11	22	....	....	....	....	....
	Krylja Sovetov	Russia-2	26	4	1	5	14	3	0	0	0	2
2005-06	Mytischi	Russia	43	1	2	3	24	9	1	0	1	4
2006-07	Ak Bars Kazan	Russia	35	0	3	3	20	....	....	....	....	....
2007-08	Ak Bars Kazan	Russia	46	1	0	1	12	10	1	0	1	4
2008-09	Ak Bars Kazan	Rus-KHL	44	4	6	10	14	18	0	1	1	16
2009-10	Ak Bars Kazan	Rus-KHL	35	3	3	6	26	6	0	1	1	0
2010-11	Ak Bars Kazan	Rus-KHL	21	2	0	2	8	....	....	....	....	....
	CSKA Moscow	Rus-KHL	17	0	3	3	2	....	....	....	....	....

BURKE, Greg (BUHRK, GREHG) WSH

Left wing. Shoots left. 6'1", 185 lbs. Born, Portsmouth, NH, May 16, 1990.
(Washington's 7th choice, 174th overall, in 2008 Entry Draft).

			Regular Season					Playoffs				
Season	Club	League	GP	G	A	Pts	PIM	GP	G	A	Pts	PIM
2006-07	N.H. Jr. Monarchs	EJHL	34	6	12	18	22	....	....	....	....	....
2007-08	N.H. Jr. Monarchs	EJHL	40	21	25	46	46	6	5	4	9	6
2008-09	Cedar Rapids	USHL	8	2	0	2	8	....	....	....	....	....
2009-10	New Hampshire	H-East	32	2	8	10	18	....	....	....	....	....
2010-11	New Hampshire	H-East	18	2	1	3	12	....	....	....	....	....

• Missed majority of 2008-09 due to shoulder injury.

BURLON, Brandon (BUHR-lohn, BRAN-duhn) N.J.

Defense. Shoots left. 6', 190 lbs. Born, Nobleton, Ont., March 5, 1990.
(New Jersey's 2nd choice, 52nd overall, in 2008 Entry Draft).

			Regular Season					Playoffs				
Season	Club	League	GP	G	A	Pts	PIM	GP	G	A	Pts	PIM
2005-06	Vaughan Kings	GTHL	55	19	29	48	38	....	....	....	....	....
2006-07	St. Michael's	OPJHL	45	4	19	23	46	4	0	1	1	4
2007-08	St. Michael's	OPJHL	32	7	17	24	41	10	2	4	6	8
2008-09	U. of Michigan	CCHA	33	5	10	15	14	....	....	....	....	....
2009-10	U. of Michigan	CCHA	45	3	11	14	24	....	....	....	....	....
2010-11	U. of Michigan	CCHA	38	5	13	18	28	....	....	....	....	....

CCHA All-Rookie Team (2009)

BUT, Anton (BOOT, AN-tawn) T.B.

Left wing. Shoots left. 6'1", 201 lbs. Born, Kharkov, USSR, July 3, 1980.
(New Jersey's 7th choice, 119th overall, in 1998 Entry Draft).

			Regular Season					Playoffs				
Season	Club	League	GP	G	A	Pts	PIM	GP	G	A	Pts	PIM
1995-96	Yaroslavl 2	CIS-2	60	30	12	42	10	....	....	....	....	....
1996-97	Yaroslavl 2	Russia-3	70	30	20	50	20	....	....	....	....	....
1997-98	Yaroslavl 2	Russia-2	48	12	5	17	28	....	....	....	....	....
1998-99	Yaroslavl 2	Russia-3	22	12	8	20	59	....	....	....	....	....
	Torpedo Yaroslavl	Russia	5	0	0	0	0	....	....	....	....	....
99-2000	Yaroslavl 2	Russia-3	1	0	0	0	2	....	....	....	....	....
	Torpedo Yaroslavl	Russia	26	2	5	7	16	8	2	1	3	0
2000-01	Yaroslavl	Russia	42	14	6	20	14	11	1	3	4	8
2001-02	Yaroslavl	Russia	48	14	11	25	14	6	0	1	1	2
2002-03	Yaroslavl	Russia	44	16	13	29	16	9	1	2	3	6
2003-04	Yaroslavl	Russia	51	11	10	21	24	3	0	0	0	0
2004-05	Yaroslavl	Russia	60	12	22	34	58	8	3	3	6	0
2005-06	Yaroslavl	Russia	49	16	21	37	26	11	2	1	3	2
2006-07	SKA St. Petersburg	Russia	52	13	13	26	61	2	0	1	1	2
2007-08	SKA St. Petersburg	Russia	57	15	13	28	40	9	4	1	5	6
2008-09	CSKA Moscow	Rus-KHL	55	12	21	33	36	8	2	1	3	2
2009-10	SKA St. Petersburg	Rus-KHL	56	19	9	28	30	4	0	0	0	2
2010-11	SKA St. Petersburg	Rus-KHL	53	12	24	36	28	11	3	2	5	2

• Rights traded to **Tampa Bay** by **New Jersey** with Josef Boumedienne and Sascha Goc for Andrei Zyuzin, November 9, 2001.

BUTTON, Ryan (BUH-tuhn, RIGH-uhn) BOS

Defense. Shoots left. 6'1", 190 lbs. Born, Edmonton, Alta., March 26, 1991.
(Boston's 2nd choice, 86th overall, in 2009 Entry Draft).

			Regular Season					Playoffs				
Season	Club	League	GP	G	A	Pts	PIM	GP	G	A	Pts	PIM
2006-07	Edmonton CAC	AMHL	28	2	6	8	74	....	....	....	....	....
2007-08	Prince Albert	WHL	58	0	8	8	30	....	....	....	....	....
2008-09	Prince Albert	WHL	70	5	32	37	43	....	....	....	....	....
2009-10	Prince Albert	WHL	67	6	27	33	46	....	....	....	....	....
2010-11	Prince Albert	WHL	44	3	20	23	31	....	....	....	....	....
	Seattle	WHL	25	2	10	12	18	....	....	....	....	....
	Providence Bruins	AHL	7	0	1	1	2	....	....	....	....	....

CALLA, Brady (KAL-luh, BRAY-dee)

Right wing. Shoots right. 6', 190 lbs. Born, North Vancouver, B.C., March 14, 1988.
(Florida's 2nd choice, 73rd overall, in 2006 Entry Draft).

			Regular Season					Playoffs				
Season	Club	League	GP	G	A	Pts	PIM	GP	G	A	Pts	PIM
2004-05	Everett Silvertips	WHL	68	11	10	21	38	11	1	1	2	0
2005-06	Everett Silvertips	WHL	66	8	25	33	52	11	1	2	3	4
2006-07	Everett Silvertips	WHL	29	3	6	9	23	....	....	....	....	....
	Moose Jaw	WHL	39	12	20	32	19	....	....	....	....	....
2007-08	Moose Jaw	WHL	14	2	8	10	10	....	....	....	....	....
	Kamloops Blazers	WHL	52	10	20	30	52	4	0	2	2	4
	Rochester	AHL	6	2	2	4	2	....	....	....	....	....
2008-09	Kamloops Blazers	WHL	19	5	8	13	31	....	....	....	....	....
	Spokane Chiefs	WHL	31	11	14	25	27	12	1	3	4	6
	Rochester	AHL	8	0	1	1	9	....	....	....	....	....
2009-10	Rochester	AHL	33	1	5	6	14	....	....	....	....	....
	Florida Everblades	ECHL	16	2	2	4	23	....	....	....	....	....
2010-11	Rochester	AHL	17	2	2	4	0	....	....	....	....	....
	Cincinnati	ECHL	35	7	16	23	30	4	0	1	1	4

CALLAHAN, Mitchell (kal-AH-han, MIH-chuhl) DET

Right wing. Shoots right. 5'11", 175 lbs. Born, Whittier, CA, August 17, 1991.
(Detroit's 6th choice, 180th overall, in 2009 Entry Draft).

			Regular Season					Playoffs				
Season	Club	League	GP	G	A	Pts	PIM	GP	G	A	Pts	PIM
2007-08	L.A. Jr. Kings	Minor-CA	52	32	37	69	62	....	....	....	....	....
2008-09	Kelowna Rockets	WHL	70	14	13	27	188	22	1	3	4	43
2009-10	Kelowna Rockets	WHL	72	20	27	47	165	12	2	4	6	10
2010-11	Kelowna Rockets	WHL	62	23	31	54	87	10	5	4	9	17

CAMARA, Anthony (kuh-MAR-uh, an-THUH-nee) BOS

Left wing. Shoots left. 6', 194 lbs. Born, Toronto, Ont., September 4, 1993.
(Boston's 3rd choice, 81st overall, in 2011 Entry Draft).

			Regular Season					Playoffs				
Season	Club	League	GP	G	A	Pts	PIM	GP	G	A	Pts	PIM
2008-09	Miss. Senators	GTHL	50	31	25	56	94	....	....	....	....	....
2009-10	Saginaw Spirit	OHL	65	6	6	12	96	6	1	1	2	5
2010-11	Saginaw Spirit	OHL	64	8	9	17	132	12	0	1	1	25

CAMERANESI, Tony (kam-uhr-ihn-AY-zee, TOH-nee) TOR

Center. Shoots right. 5'9", 162 lbs. Born, Maple Grove, MN, August 12, 1993.
(Toronto's 5th choice, 130th overall, in 2011 Entry Draft).

			Regular Season					Playoffs				
Season	Club	League	GP	G	A	Pts	PIM	GP	G	A	Pts	PIM
2009-10	Wayzata	High-MN	25	16	29	45	6	2	2	1	3	0
2010-11	Team Northwest	UMHSEL	21	16	17	33	18	3	2	4	6	2
	Wayzata	High-MN	25	15	39	54	26	3	2	7	9	4

• Signed Letter of Intent to attend **University of Minnesota-Duluth** (WCHA) in fall of 2012.

CAMERON, Bryan (KAM-ruhn, BRIGH-uhn) CGY

Right wing. Shoots right. 5'11", 186 lbs. Born, Brampton, Ont., February 25, 1989.
(Los Angeles' 4th choice, 82nd overall, in 2007 Entry Draft).

			Regular Season					Playoffs				
Season	Club	League	GP	G	A	Pts	PIM	GP	G	A	Pts	PIM
2004-05	Toronto Marlboros	GTHL	75	73	47	120	76	....	....	....	....	....
	Milton Icehawks	OPJHL	2	0	0	0	0	....	....	....	....	....
2005-06	Belleville Bulls	OHL	64	20	9	29	46	6	1	2	3	6
2006-07	Belleville Bulls	OHL	60	33	25	58	50	15	4	8	12	15
2007-08	Belleville Bulls	OHL	68	41	37	78	56	21	4	9	13	10
2008-09	Belleville Bulls	OHL	64	37	44	81	51	17	7	7	14	18
2009-10	Barrie Colts	OHL	62	*53	25	78	68	17	11	9	20	16
2010-11	Abbotsford Heat	AHL	60	6	9	15	41	....	....	....	....	....
	Victoria	ECHL	7	3	3	6	2	....	....	....	....	....

OHL All-Rookie Team (2006) • OHL First All-Star Team (2009, 2010)

Signed as a free agent by **Calgary**, April 30, 2010.

CAMPBELL, Andrew (KAM-buhl, AN-droo) L.A.

Defense. Shoots left. 6'4", 207 lbs. Born, Caledonia, Ont., February 4, 1988.
(Los Angeles' 5th choice, 74th overall, in 2008 Entry Draft).

			Regular Season					Playoffs				
Season	Club	League	GP	G	A	Pts	PIM	GP	G	A	Pts	PIM
2005-06	Sault Ste. Marie	OHL	31	1	3	4	23	3	0	0	0	4
2006-07	Sault Ste. Marie	OHL	63	4	14	18	75	13	0	1	1	6
2007-08	Sault Ste. Marie	OHL	68	13	22	35	64	14	2	3	5	13
2008-09	Manchester	AHL	72	3	5	8	72	....	....	....	....	....
2009-10	Manchester	AHL	74	2	9	11	68	16	1	4	5	6
2010-11	Manchester	AHL	76	1	11	12	68	7	0	0	0	0

CAMPBELL, Max (KAM-behl, MAX) NYR

Center. Shoots left. 6'1", 185 lbs. Born, Strathroy, Ont., December 21, 1988.
(NY Rangers' 3rd choice, 138th overall, in 2007 Entry Draft).

			Regular Season					Playoffs				
Season	Club	League	GP	G	A	Pts	PIM	GP	G	A	Pts	PIM
2005-06	Strathroy Rockets	ON-Jr.B	48	17	18	35	10	12	4	10	14	2
2006-07	Strathroy Rockets	ON-Jr.B	46	46	49	95	84	18	11	9	20	4
2007-08	Western Mich.	CCHA	38	6	16	22	10	....	....	....	....	....
2008-09	Western Mich.	CCHA	40	16	15	31	44	....	....	....	....	....
2009-10	Western Mich.	CCHA	34	6	13	19	43	....	....	....	....	....
2010-11	Western Mich.	CCHA	42	18	17	35	16	....	....	....	....	....

CAMPER, Carter (KAM-puhr, KAR-tuhr) BOS

Right wing. Shoots right. 5'9", 173 lbs. Born, Rocky River, OH, July 6, 1988.

			Regular Season					Playoffs				
Season	Club	League	GP	G	A	Pts	PIM	GP	G	A	Pts	PIM
2004-05	Cleveland Barons	NAHL	54	14	23	37	12	....	....	....	....	....
2005-06	Cleveland Barons	NAHL	57	31	51	82	26	....	....	....	....	....
2006-07	Lincoln Stars	USHL	56	23	48	71	40	4	1	1	2	2
2007-08	Miami U.	CCHA	33	15	26	41	20	....	....	....	....	....
2008-09	Miami U.	CCHA	40	20	22	42	24	....	....	....	....	....
2009-10	Miami U.	CCHA	44	15	28	43	14	....	....	....	....	....
2010-11	Miami U.	CCHA	39	19	38	57	27	....	....	....	....	....
	Providence Bruins	AHL	3	1	1	2	2	....	....	....	....	....

CCHA All-Rookie Team (2008) • CCHA First All-Star Team (2009) • NCAA West Second All-American Team (2009, 2011)

Signed as a free agent by **Boston**, April 7, 2011.

CANNONE, Pat (ka-NOHN, PAT) OTT

Right wing. Shoots right. 5'11", 204 lbs. Born, Bayport, NY, August 9, 1986.

			Regular Season					Playoffs				
Season	Club	League	GP	G	A	Pts	PIM	GP	G	A	Pts	PIM
2006-07	Cedar Rapids	USHL	59	18	37	55	46	6	1	7	8	6
2007-08	Miami U.	CCHA	42	6	24	30	20	....	....	....	....	....
2008-09	Miami U.	CCHA	41	11	24	35	16	....	....	....	....	....
2009-10	Miami U.	CCHA	44	14	17	31	22	....	....	....	....	....
2010-11	Miami U.	CCHA	39	14	23	37	25	....	....	....	....	....
	Binghamton	AHL	2	1	1	2	2	....	....	....	....	....

Signed as a free agent by **Ottawa**, April 8, 2011.

CANTIN, Marc (KAN-tihn, MAHRK) BOS

Defense. Shoots left. 6'1", 201 lbs. Born, Peterborough, Ont., March 27, 1990.

			Regular Season					Playoffs				
Season	Club	League	GP	G	A	Pts	PIM	GP	G	A	Pts	PIM
2006-07	Lindsay Muskies	OPJHL	40	2	14	16	60	2	0	0	0	2
	Belleville Bulls	OHL	9	0	1	1	12	6	0	0	0	2
2007-08	Belleville Bulls	OHL	60	2	6	8	33	13	0	1	1	9
2008-09	Belleville Bulls	OHL	62	1	14	15	51	17	0	2	2	26
2009-10	Belleville Bulls	OHL	33	1	7	8	63	....	....	....	....	....
	Windsor Spitfires	OHL	24	2	5	7	41	19	3	3	6	21
	Windsor Spitfires	M-Cup	....	....	....	....	....	4	1	1	2	2
2010-11	St. Michael's	OHL	61	10	31	41	78	20	0	6	6	18

OHL Second All-Star Team (2011) • George Parsons Trophy (Memorial Cup - Most Sportsmanlike Player) (2011)

Signed as a free agent by **Boston**, March 23, 2011.

CAPORUSSO, Louie (kap-oh-ROO-soh, LOO-ee) OTT

Center/Left wing. Shoots left. 5'10", 198 lbs. Born, Toronto, Ont., June 21, 1989.
(Ottawa's 3rd choice, 90th overall, in 2007 Entry Draft).

			Regular Season					Playoffs				
Season	Club	League	GP	G	A	Pts	PIM	GP	G	A	Pts	PIM
2004-05	Tor. Red Wings	GTHL	53	38	28	66	28	....	....	....	....	....
2005-06	St. Michael's	OPJHL	48	29	44	73	44	25	8	10	18	16
2006-07	St. Michael's	OPJHL	37	23	27	50	45	20	14	19	33	14
2007-08	U. of Michigan	CCHA	33	12	9	21	18	....	....	....	....	....
2008-09	U. of Michigan	CCHA	41	*24	25	49	30	....	....	....	....	....
2009-10	U. of Michigan	CCHA	45	*21	22	43	26	....	....	....	....	....
2010-11	U. of Michigan	CCHA	41	11	20	31	22	....	....	....	....	....

CCHA First All-Star Team (2009) • NCAA West First All-American Team (2009)

CAREY, Paul (KAIR-ee, PAWL) COL

Center. Shoots left. 6', 175 lbs. Born, Boston, MA, September 24, 1988.
(Colorado's 7th choice, 135th overall, in 2007 Entry Draft).

			Regular Season					Playoffs				
Season	Club	League	GP	G	A	Pts	PIM	GP	G	A	Pts	PIM
2005-06	Salisbury School	High-CT	27	14	11	25	18	....	....	....	....	....
2006-07	Salisbury School	High-CT	24	16	11	27	16	....	....	....	....	....
2007-08	Indiana Ice	USHL	60	34	32	66	32	4	1	2	3	2
2008-09	Boston College	H-East	24	5	4	9	8	....	....	....	....	....
2009-10	Boston College	H-East	41	9	12	21	29	....	....	....	....	....
2010-11	Boston College	H-East	38	13	13	26	18	....	....	....	....	....

USHL All-Rookie Team (2008) • USHL Second All-Star Team (2008)

CARMAN, Mike (KAR-mahn, MIGHK) COL

Center. Shoots left. 6', 180 lbs. Born, Augusta, GA, April 14, 1988.
(Colorado's 4th choice, 81st overall, in 2006 Entry Draft).

			Regular Season					Playoffs				
Season	Club	League	GP	G	A	Pts	PIM	GP	G	A	Pts	PIM
2003-04	Holy Angels	High-MN	29	19	40	59	....	....	....	....	....	....
2004-05	USNTDP	U-17	14	2	9	11	40	....	....	....	....	....
	USNTDP	NAHL	39	12	15	27	38	10	2	4	6	10
2005-06	USNTDP	U-18	43	15	23	38	78	....	....	....	....	....
	USNTDP	NAHL	17	6	10	16	24	....	....	....	....	....
2006-07	U. of Minnesota	WCHA	41	9	11	20	55	....	....	....	....	....
2007-08	U. of Minnesota	WCHA	23	4	7	11	28	....	....	....	....	....
2008-09	U. of Minnesota	WCHA	32	8	9	17	32	....	....	....	....	....
2009-10	U. of Minnesota	WCHA	39	8	10	18	39	....	....	....	....	....
	Lake Erie Monsters	AHL	10	2	0	2	10	....	....	....	....	....
2010-11	Lake Erie Monsters	AHL	69	9	8	17	59	7	0	1	1	2

CARON, Josh (kah-ROHN, JAWSH) MIN

Defense. Shoots right. 6'2", 215 lbs. Born, Campbell River, B.C., February 10, 1991.

			Regular Season					Playoffs				
Season	Club	League	GP	G	A	Pts	PIM	GP	G	A	Pts	PIM
2007-08	Kamloops Storm	KIJHL	47	1	4	5	86	21	0	0	0	53
	Merritt	BCHL	5	0	0	0	0					
2008-09	Kamloops Storm	KIJHL	29	4	8	12	182	....	....	....	....	....
	Kamloops Blazers	WHL	21	0	1	1	50	4	0	0	0	9
2009-10	Kamloops Blazers	WHL	60	1	5	6	190	4	0	1	1	10
2010-11	Kamloops Blazers	WHL	27	1	1	2	47					

Signed as a free agent by **Minnesota**, September 23, 2010.

CARRICK, Sam (KAIR-ihk, SAM) TOR

Center. Shoots right. 6', 188 lbs. Born, Markham, Ont., February 4, 1992.
(Toronto's 5th choice, 144th overall, in 2010 Entry Draft).

			Regular Season					Playoffs				
Season	Club	League	GP	G	A	Pts	PIM	GP	G	A	Pts	PIM
2007-08	Tor. Red Wings	GTHL	55	40	30	70	130	....	....	....	....	....
2008-09	Brampton	OHL	61	10	11	21	47	21	1	0	1	16
2009-10	Brampton	OHL	66	21	21	42	96	8	2	2	4	8
2010-11	Brampton	OHL	59	16	23	39	74	4	0	1	1	4

CARRIER, Samuel (kair-ee-AIR, SAM-yoo-ehl) WSH

Defense. Shoots right. 6', 186 lbs. Born, Laval, Que., April 28, 1992.
(Washington's 5th choice, 176th overall, in 2010 Entry Draft).

			Regular Season					Playoffs				
Season	Club	League	GP	G	A	Pts	PIM	GP	G	A	Pts	PIM
2007-08	Antoine-Girouard	QAAA	45	8	25	33	64	15	7	4	11	14
2008-09	Quebec Remparts	QMJHL	56	4	5	9	49	3	1	0	1	4
2009-10	Lewiston	QMJHL	66	10	32	42	65	4	1	0	1	14
2010-11	Lewiston	QMJHL	61	11	39	50	72	15	2	14	16	12

CARUSO, Michael (kah-ROO-soh, MIGH-kuhl) FLA

Defense. Shoots left. 6'2", 191 lbs. Born, Mississauga, Ont., July 5, 1988.
(Florida's 3rd choice, 103rd overall, in 2006 Entry Draft).

			Regular Season					Playoffs				
Season	Club	League	GP	G	A	Pts	PIM	GP	G	A	Pts	PIM
2004-05	Guelph Storm	OHL	56	0	3	3	31	4	0	0	0	2
2005-06	Guelph Storm	OHL	66	1	15	16	85	15	1	2	3	24
2006-07	Guelph Storm	OHL	64	4	16	20	119	4	0	0	0	8
2007-08	Guelph Storm	OHL	62	10	24	34	103	10	2	6	8	22
2008-09	Rochester	AHL	73	1	9	10	66	....	....	....	....	....
2009-10	Rochester	AHL	67	1	10	11	42	....	....	....	....	....
2010-11	Rochester	AHL	75	5	4	9	77	....	....	....	....	....

CATENACCI, Daniel (ka-tehn-A-chee, DAN-yehl) BUF

Center. Shoots left. 5'9", 190 lbs. Born, Newmarket, Ont., March 9, 1993.
(Buffalo's 2nd choice, 77th overall, in 2011 Entry Draft).

			Regular Season					Playoffs				
Season	Club	League	GP	G	A	Pts	PIM	GP	G	A	Pts	PIM
2008-09	York Simcoe	Minor-ON	39	42	45	87	152	....	....	....	....	....
	Villanova Knights	ON-Jr.A	1	1	0	1	2	....	....	....	....	....
2009-10	Sault Ste. Marie	OHL	65	10	20	30	68	5	1	1	2	6
2010-11	Sault Ste. Marie	OHL	67	26	45	71	117	....	....	....	....	....

CAYER, Julien (KAY-uhr, JOO-lee-ehn) DET

Center. Shoots left. 6'4", 186 lbs. Born, Longueuil, Que., July 6, 1989.
(Detroit's 4th choice, 151st overall, in 2008 Entry Draft).

			Regular Season					Playoffs				
Season	Club	League	GP	G	A	Pts	PIM	GP	G	A	Pts	PIM
2005-06	C.C. Lemoyne	QAAA	42	11	21	32	46	8	1	2	3	14
2006-07	St-Jerome	QJHL	45	6	23	29	84	10	1	3	4	2
2007-08	Northwood	High-NY	42	24	32	56	56	....	....	....	....	....
2008-09	Clarkson Knights	ECAC	29	4	6	10	30	....	....	....	....	....
2009-10	Clarkson Knights	ECAC	22	2	3	5	18	....	....	....	....	....
2010-11	Clarkson Knights	ECAC	23	3	5	8	22	....	....	....	....	....

CEHLIN, Patrick (seh-LIHN, PAHT-rihk) NSH

Right wing. Shoots right. 5'11", 170 lbs. Born, Huddinge, Sweden, July 27, 1991.
(Nashville's 3rd choice, 126th overall, in 2010 Entry Draft).

			Regular Season					Playoffs				
Season	Club	League	GP	G	A	Pts	PIM	GP	G	A	Pts	PIM
2006-07	Djurgarden U18	Swe-U18	27	10	18	28	49	3	1	2	3	0
2007-08	Djurgarden U18	Swe-U18	12	7	16	23	10	8	0	5	5	12
	Djurgarden Jr.	Swe-Jr.	22	5	3	8	8	4	0	1	1	4
2008-09	Djurgarden U18	Swe-U18	4	5	2	7	0	1	0	0	0	2
	Djurgarden Jr.	Swe-Jr.	36	10	25	35	110	6	1	2	3	6
	Djurgarden	Sweden	2	0	0	0	0	....	....	....	....	....
2009-10	Djurgarden Jr.	Swe-Jr.	9	3	3	6	4	....	....	....	....	....
	Djurgarden	Sweden	54	5	6	11	10	16	0	2	2	2
2010-11	Djurgarden	Sweden	48	4	12	16	14	7	1	0	1	2
	Djurgarden Jr.	Swe-Jr.	....	....	....	....	....	5	4	2	6	0

CERESNAK, Peter (CHUHR-ehsh-nak, PEE-tuhr) NYR

Defense. Shoots right. 6'3", 209 lbs. Born, Trencin, Slovakia, January 26, 1993.
(NY Rangers' 6th choice, 172nd overall, in 2011 Entry Draft).

			Regular Season					Playoffs				
Season	Club	League	GP	G	A	Pts	PIM	GP	G	A	Pts	PIM
2007-08	Dukla Trencin U18	Svk-U18	10	0	2	2	10	....	....	....	....	....
2008-09	Dukla Trencin U18	Svk-U18	28	1	2	3	10	....	....	....	....	....
	Dukla Trencin Jr.	Slovak-Jr.	15	1	1	2	0	8	0	0	0	0
2009-10	Dukla Trencin U18	Svk-U18	2	1	2	3	0	....	....	....	....	....
	Dukla Trencin Jr.	Slovak-Jr.	40	4	17	21	30	7	0	1	1	8
2010-11	Slovakia U20	Slovakia	25	1	3	4	16	....	....	....	....	....
	Dukla Trencin Jr.	Slovak-Jr.	8	0	3	3	4	11	0	3	3	37
	Dukla Trencin	Slovakia	7	0	0	0	0	....	....	....	....	....
	Dukla Trencin U18	Svk-U18	....	....	....	....	....	3	2	2	4	4

CHAMPAGNE, Joel (sham-PAYN, JOHL)

Center. Shoots left. 6'4", 214 lbs. Born, Chateauguay, Que., January 24, 1990.
(Toronto's 5th choice, 129th overall, in 2008 Entry Draft).

			Regular Season					Playoffs				
Season	Club	League	GP	G	A	Pts	PIM	GP	G	A	Pts	PIM
2005-06	Chateauguay	QAAA	42	9	29	38	22	19	7	10	17	20
2006-07	Chicoutimi	QMJHL	62	6	16	22	51	4	0	0	0	6
2007-08	Chicoutimi	QMJHL	70	18	22	40	45	6	1	1	2	6
2008-09	Chicoutimi	QMJHL	28	10	11	21	34	....	....	....	....	....
	P.E.I. Rocket	QMJHL	24	14	26	40	18	3	0	1	1	4
2009-10	P.E.I. Rocket	QMJHL	36	18	25	43	32	....	....	....	....	....
	Victoriaville Tigres	QMJHL	29	20	16	36	15	16	7	6	13	16
2010-11	Quebec Remparts	QMJHL	68	24	58	82	47	18	11	9	20	16

Signed as a free agent by **Milwaukee** (AHL), May 31, 2011.

CHAPPELL, Chris (CHA-puhl, KRIHS) NYR

Left wing. Shoots left. 6'4", 212 lbs. Born, Pickering, Ont., March 21, 1988.

			Regular Season					Playoffs				
Season	Club	League	GP	G	A	Pts	PIM	GP	G	A	Pts	PIM
2003-04	Pickering Panthers	OPJHL	10	2	2	4	2	....	....	....	....	....
2004-05	Pickering Panthers	OPJHL	49	8	27	35	11	....	....	....	....	....
2005-06	Saginaw Spirit	OHL	60	8	12	20	53	4	0	0	0	2
2006-07	Saginaw Spirit	OHL	66	10	14	24	47	6	0	1	1	6
2007-08	Saginaw Spirit	OHL	54	14	20	34	55	4	2	1	3	4
2008-09	Saginaw Spirit	OHL	68	38	38	76	88	8	2	6	8	8
2009-10	Hartford Wolf Pack	AHL	6	0	0	0	5	....	....	....	....	....
	Charlotte	ECHL	11	1	3	4	2	....	....	....	....	....
2010-11	Connecticut Whale	AHL	5	0	0	0	0	....	....	....	....	....
	Greenville	ECHL	53	9	12	21	38	8	0	1	1	21

Signed as a free agent by **NY Rangers**, July 2, 2009.

CHAPUT, Michael (sha-PUT, MIGH-kuhl) CBJ

Center. Shoots left. 6'2", 189 lbs. Born, Ile Bizard, Que., April 9, 1992.
(Philadelphia's 1st choice, 89th overall, in 2010 Entry Draft).

			Regular Season					Playoffs				
Season	Club	League	GP	G	A	Pts	PIM	GP	G	A	Pts	PIM
2007-08	Lac St-Louis Royals	Minor-QU	STATISTICS NOT AVAILABLE									
	Lac St-Louis Lions	QAAA	4	0	0	0	0	....	....	....	....	....
2008-09	Lewiston	QMJHL	29	3	7	10	34	....	....	....	....	....
2009-10	Lewiston	QMJHL	68	28	27	55	60	4	0	1	1	2
2010-11	Lewiston	QMJHL	62	25	34	59	97	13	7	13	20	11

• Missed majority of 2008-09 due to recurring shoulder injury. Traded to **Columbus** **Philadelphia** with Greg Moore for Tom Sestito, February 28, 2011.

CHAPUT, Stefan (sha-PEW, STEH-fan) BOS

Center. Shoots left. 6', 190 lbs. Born, Montreal, Que., March 11, 1988.
(Carolina's 4th choice, 153rd overall, in 2006 Entry Draft).

			Regular Season					Playoffs				
Season	Club	League	GP	G	A	Pts	PIM	GP	G	A	Pts	PIM
2003-04	West Island Lions	QAAA	29	7	12	19	32	7	1	3	4	4
2004-05	West Island Lions	QAAA	39	29	25	54	86	5	2	2	4	16
	Lewiston	QMJHL	8	2	3	5	2	8	1	0	1	2
2005-06	Lewiston	QMJHL	69	19	29	48	44	6	0	1	1	4
2006-07	Lewiston	QMJHL	57	17	29	46	43	17	6	5	11	20
2007-08	Lewiston	QMJHL	62	33	36	69	56	6	2	1	3	12
	Albany River Rats	AHL	1	0	0	0	0	....	....	....	....	....
2008-09	Albany River Rats	AHL	15	4	7	11	10	....	....	....	....	....
2009-10	Albany River Rats	AHL	75	10	28	38	18	2	0	1	1	2
2010-11	Charlotte	AHL	20	0	3	3	9	....	....	....	....	....
	Syracuse Crunch	AHL	27	3	4	7	6	....	....	....	....	....
	Providence Bruins	AHL	15	3	4	7	4	....	....	....	....	....

Traded to **Anaheim** by **Carolina** with Matt Kennedy for Ryan Carter, November 23, 2010.
Traded to **Boston** by **Anaheim** with David Laliberte for Brian McGrattan and Sean Zimmerman, February 27, 2011.

CHIAROT, Ben (CHAIR-awt, BEHN) WPG

Defense. Shoots left. 6'3", 224 lbs. Born, Hamilton, Ont., May 9, 1991.
(Atlanta's 5th choice, 120th overall, in 2009 Entry Draft).

			Regular Season					Playoffs				
Season	Club	League	GP	G	A	Pts	PIM	GP	G	A	Pts	PIM
2006-07	Mississauga Reps	GTHL	60	21	42	63	166	....	....	....	....	....
2007-08	Guelph Storm	OHL	31	0	0	0	14	....	....	....	....	....
2008-09	Guelph Storm	OHL	67	2	10	12	111	4	0	3	3	8
2009-10	Guelph Storm	OHL	41	4	9	13	106	....	....	....	....	....
	Sudbury Wolves	OHL	26	4	4	8	61	4	1	1	2	6
	Chicago Wolves	AHL	1	0	0	0	4	....	....	....	....	....
2010-11	Sudbury Wolves	OHL	25	5	8	13	62	....	....	....	....	....
	Saginaw Spirit	OHL	39	5	19	24	51	12	1	4	5	21

CHIASSON, Alex (CHAY-sahn, Al-ehx) DAL

Right wing. Shoots right. 6'4", 187 lbs. Born, Montreal, Que., October 1, 1990.
(Dallas' 2nd choice, 38th overall, in 2009 Entry Draft).

			Regular Season					Playoffs				
Season	Club	League	GP	G	A	Pts	PIM	GP	G	A	Pts	PIM
2007-08	Northwood	High-NY	45	35	46	81	....	....	....	....	....	....
2008-09	Des Moines	USHL	56	17	33	50	101	....	....	....	....	....
2009-10	Boston University	H-East	35	7	12	19	44	....	....	....	....	....
2010-11	Boston University	H-East	35	14	20	34	75	....	....	....	....	....

CHOUINARD, Joel (SHWEE-nahrd, JOHL) COL

Defense. Shoots left. 6'1", 186 lbs. Born, Longueuil, Que., April 8, 1990.
(Colorado's 5th choice, 167th overall, in 2008 Entry Draft).

			Regular Season					Playoffs				
Season	Club	League	GP	G	A	Pts	PIM	GP	G	A	Pts	PIM
2005-06	Magog	QAAA	44	4	14	18	70	13	1	5	6	6
2006-07	Magog	QAAA	33	8	30	38	88	....	....	....	....	....
	Victoriaville Tigres	QMJHL	23	3	3	6	20	6	0	1	1	0
2007-08	Victoriaville Tigres	QMJHL	69	7	28	35	95	6	2	0	2	4
2008-09	Victoriaville Tigres	QMJHL	64	12	23	35	65	4	0	1	1	6
2009-10	Victoriaville Tigres	QMJHL	65	23	45	68	56	16	3	10	13	6
2010-11	Lake Erie Monsters	AHL	35	8	9	17	14	2	0	0	0	0

QMJHL First All-Star Team (2010)

CHUDINOV, Maxim (choo-DEE-nawf, max-EEM) BOS

Defense. Shoots right. 5'11", 187 lbs. Born, Cherepovets, USSR, March 25, 1990.
(Boston's 7th choice, 195th overall, in 2010 Entry Draft).

			Regular Season					Playoffs				
Season	Club	League	GP	G	A	Pts	PIM	GP	G	A	Pts	PIM
2006-07	Cherepovets	Russia	2	0	0	0	0	3	0	0	0	2
2007-08	Cherepovets 2	Russia-3	STATISTICS NOT AVAILABLE									
	Cherepovets	Russia	18	0	0	0	10	1	0	0	0	0
2008-09	Cherepovets	Rus-KHL	26	0	0	0	14	....	....	....	....	....
2009-10	Cherepovets Jr.	Russia-Jr.	4	1	0	1	12	2	0	1	1	4
	Cherepovets	Rus-KHL	47	6	8	14	30	....	....	....	....	....
2010-11	Cherepovets	Rus-KHL	52	8	15	23	30	6	0	2	2	4
	Cherepovets Jr.	Russia-Jr.	....	....	....	....	....	5	2	2	4	8

CICHY, Michael (KEE-chee, MIGH-kuhl) MTL

Center. Shoots left. 5'11", 187 lbs. Born, New Britain, CT, July 8, 1990.
(Montreal's 7th choice, 199th overall, in 2009 Entry Draft).

			Regular Season					Playoffs				
Season	Club	League	GP	G	A	Pts	PIM	GP	G	A	Pts	PIM
2006-07	USNTDP	NAHL	32	2	8	10	35	....	....	....	....	....
	USNTDP	U-17	7	4	1	5	4	....	....	....	....	....
2007-08	Tri-City Storm	USHL	59	16	29	45	45	....	....	....	....	....
2008-09	Tri-City Storm	USHL	26	*10	19	29	11	....	....	....	....	....
	Indiana Ice	USHL	30	*24	23	47	12	13	6	*19	*25	6
2009-10	North Dakota	WCHA	23	2	2	4	6	....	....	....	....	....
2010-11	North Dakota	WCHA	25	3	4	7	6	....	....	....	....	....

USHL First All-Star Team (2009)

CISSE, Yasin (SIH-say, YA-sihn) WPG

Right wing. Shoots right. 6'3", 210 lbs. Born, Westmount, Que., March 11, 1992.
(Atlanta's 5th choice, 150th overall, in 2010 Entry Draft).

			Regular Season					Playoffs				
Season	Club	League	GP	G	A	Pts	PIM	GP	G	A	Pts	PIM
2007-08	Lac St-Louis Lions	QAAA	44	20	38	58	66	13	6	10	16	28
2008-09	Des Moines	USHL	31	2	6	8	46	....	....	....	....	....
2009-10	Des Moines	USHL	18	13	6	19	16	....	....	....	....	....
2010-11	Boston University	H-East	1	0	0	0	0	....	....	....	....	....

• Missed majority of 2009-10 due to ankle injury. • Missed majority of 2010-11 due to injury vs. Wisconsin (WCHA), October 8. 20110.

CIZIKAS, Casey (sih-ZEE-kuhs, KAY-see) NYI

Center. Shoots left. 5'10", 193 lbs. Born, Toronto, Ont., February 27, 1991.
(NY Islanders' 5th choice, 92nd overall, in 2009 Entry Draft).

			Regular Season					Playoffs				
Season	Club	League	GP	G	A	Pts	PIM	GP	G	A	Pts	PIM
2006-07	Mississauga Reps	GTHL	77	46	60	106	88	....	....	....	....	....
2007-08	St. Michael's	OHL	62	18	23	41	41	4	1	2	3	6
2008-09	St. Michael's	OHL	55	16	20	36	39	11	5	4	9	11
2009-10	St. Michael's	OHL	68	25	37	62	77	16	7	7	14	16
2010-11	St. Michael's	OHL	52	29	35	64	40	16	5	14	19	14

CLACKSON, Matt (KLAK-suhn, MA-thyew)

Left wing. Shoots right. 6', 196 lbs. Born, Saskatoon, Sask., April 26, 1985.
(Philadelphia's 6th choice, 215th overall, in 2005 Entry Draft).

			Regular Season					Playoffs				
Season	Club	League	GP	G	A	Pts	PIM	GP	G	A	Pts	PIM
2002-03	Pittsburgh Hornets	MWEHL	64	22	22	44	169	....	....	....	....	....
2003-04	Chicago Steel	USHL	42	5	4	9	108	5	0	1	1	8
2004-05	Chicago Steel	USHL	56	10	15	25	270	....	....	....	....	....
2005-06	Western Mich.	CCHA	34	1	1	2	52	....	....	....	....	....
2006-07	Western Mich.	CCHA	36	0	8	8	80	....	....	....	....	....
2007-08	Western Mich.	CCHA	35	3	3	6	87	....	....	....	....	....
	Philadelphia	AHL	2	0	0	0	19	....	....	....	....	....
2008-09	Philadelphia	AHL	80	3	6	9	263	4	0	0	0	4
2009-10	Adirondack	AHL	60	2	4	6	174	....	....	....	....	....
2010-11	Adirondack	AHL	62	1	2	3	118	....	....	....	....	....

Traded to **Phoenix** by **Philadelphia** with Pittsburgh's 3rd round choice in (previously acquired, Phoenix selected Harrison Ruopp) in 2011 Entry Draft and future considerations for Ilya Bryzgalov, June 7, 2011.

CLAESSON, Fredrik (KLA-suhn, FREH-drihk) OTT

Defense. Shoots left. 6'1", 196 lbs. Born, Stockholm, Sweden, November 24, 1992.
(Ottawa's 6th choice, 126th overall, in 2011 Entry Draft).

			Regular Season					Playoffs				
Season	Club	League	GP	G	A	Pts	PIM	GP	G	A	Pts	PIM
2007-08	Hammarby U18	Swe-U18	15	1	2	3	29	....	....	....	....	....
	Hammarby	Sweden-2	2	0	0	0	2	....	....	....	....	....
2008-09	Djurgarden U18	Swe-U18	28	9	8	17	4	....	....	....	....	....
	Djurgarden Jr.	Swe-Jr.	7	0	0	0	0	....	....	....	....	....
2009-10	Djurgarden U18	Swe-U18	3	1	1	2	0	5	0	3	3	6
	Djurgarden Jr.	Swe-Jr.	22	0	4	4	18	....	....	....	....	....
2010-11	Djurgarden Jr.	Swe-Jr.	18	2	3	5	6	5	0	1	1	0
	Djurgarden	Sweden	35	2	0	2	6	7	0	1	1	0

CLARK, Jason (KLARK, JAY-suhn) NYI

Center/Left wing. Shoots left. 6'2", 180 lbs. Born, Eden Prairie, MN, February 27, 1992.
(NY Islanders' 4th choice, 82nd overall, in 2010 Entry Draft).

			Regular Season					Playoffs				
Season	Club	League	GP	G	A	Pts	PIM	GP	G	A	Pts	PIM
2008-09	Shat.-St. Mary's	High-MN	52	18	26	44	68	....	....	....	....	....
2009-10	Shat.-St. Mary's	High-MN	54	23	23	46	80	....	....	....	....	....
2010-11	U. of Wisconsin	WCHA	14	0	1	1	6	....	....	....	....	....

CLARK, Mat (KLAHRK, MAT) ANA

Defense. Shoots right. 6'3", 221 lbs. Born, Wheat Ridge, CO, October 17, 1990.
(Anaheim's 3rd choice, 37th overall, in 2009 Entry Draft).

			Regular Season					Playoffs				
Season	Club	League	GP	G	A	Pts	PIM	GP	G	A	Pts	PIM
2006-07	Brampton Capitals	OPJHL	47	2	7	9	50	8	1	1	2	19
2007-08	Brampton Capitals	OPJHL	46	6	11	17	64	8	1	4	5	45
2008-09	Brampton	OHL	63	3	20	23	91	21	0	5	5	37
2009-10	Brampton	OHL	66	7	16	23	88	7	2	4	6	9
	Manitoba Moose	AHL	1	0	0	0	0	6	0	0	0	2
2010-11	Syracuse Crunch	AHL	80	2	14	16	128	....	....	....	....	....

CLENDENING, Adam (klehn-DEHN-ihng, A-duhm) CHI

Defense. Shoots right. 5'11", 187 lbs. Born, Niagara Falls, NY, October 26, 1992.
(Chicago's 3rd choice, 36th overall, in 2011 Entry Draft).

			Regular Season					Playoffs				
Season	Club	League	GP	G	A	Pts	PIM	GP	G	A	Pts	PIM
2007-08	Toronto Marlboros	GTHL	60	8	42	50	116	....	....	....	....	....
2008-09	USNTDP	NAHL	34	0	9	9	38	....	....	....	....	....
	USNTDP	U-17	15	1	5	6	18	....	....	....	....	....
	USNTDP	U-18	13	1	5	6	14	....	....	....	....	....
2009-10	USNTDP	USHL	26	4	13	17	44	....	....	....	....	....
	USNTDP	U-18	39	10	22	32	76	....	....	....	....	....
2010-11	Boston University	H-East	39	5	21	26	80	....	....	....	....	....

Hockey East All-Rookie Team (2011)

COETZEE, Willie (KOHT-zee, WIHL-ee) DET

Right wing. Shoots right. 5'10", 185 lbs. Born, Maple Ridge, B.C., November 7, 1990.

			Regular Season					Playoffs				
Season	Club	League	GP	G	A	Pts	PIM	GP	G	A	Pts	PIM
2007-08	Cowichan Valley	BCHL	33	5	11	16	19	....	....	....	....	....
	Red Deer Rebels	WHL	23	2	0	2	14	....	....	....	....	....
2008-09	Red Deer Rebels	WHL	72	18	24	42	42	....	....	....	....	....
2009-10	Red Deer Rebels	WHL	72	29	52	81	32	4	1	0	1	0
	Grand Rapids	AHL	2	0	0	0	0	....	....	....	....	....
2010-11	Grand Rapids	AHL	25	0	5	5	8	....	....	....	....	....
	Toledo Walleye	ECHL	36	9	11	20	4	....	....	....	....	....

Signed as a free agent by **Detroit**, September 18, 2009.

COHEN, Zach (KOHN, ZAK) COL

Left wing. Shoots left. 6'3", 208 lbs. Born, Schaumburg, IL, February 6, 1987.

			Regular Season					Playoffs				
Season	Club	League	GP	G	A	Pts	PIM	GP	G	A	Pts	PIM
2004-05	Tri-City Storm	USHL	48	8	10	18	32	....	....	....	....	....
2005-06	Tri-City Storm	USHL	60	18	15	33	46	....	....	....	....	....
2006-07	Boston University	H-East	33	1	2	3	8	....	....	....	....	....
2007-08	Boston University	H-East	18	2	4	6	8	....	....	....	....	....
2008-09	Boston University	H-East	41	13	5	18	22	....	....	....	....	....
2009-10	Boston University	H-East	38	15	10	25	30	....	....	....	....	....
	Lake Erie Monsters	AHL	10	1	3	4	4	....	....	....	....	....
2010-11	Lake Erie Monsters	AHL	63	2	8	10	35	2	0	0	0	0

Signed as a free agent by **Colorado**, March 23, 2010.

COLEMAN, Blake (KOHL-man, BLAYK) N.J.

Center. Shoots left. 5'11", 205 lbs. Born, Plano, TX, November 28, 1991.
(New Jersey's 3rd choice, 75th overall, in 2011 Entry Draft).

			Regular Season					Playoffs				
Season	Club	League	GP	G	A	Pts	PIM	GP	G	A	Pts	PIM
2009-10	Tri-City Storm	USHL	22	2	10	12	32	....	....	....	....	....
	Indiana Ice	USHL	36	8	8	16	24	9	0	2	2	13
2010-11	Indiana Ice	USHL	59	34	*58	*92	72	5	2	2	4	10

USHL First All-Star Team (2011) • USHL Player of the Year (2011)
• Signed Letter of Intent to attend **Miami University** (CCHA) in fall of 2011.

COLLINS, Sean (KAW-lihnz, SHAWN) CBJ

Center. Shoots left. 6'1", 199 lbs. Born, Saskatoon, Sask., December 29, 1988.
(Columbus' 9th choice, 187th overall, in 2008 Entry Draft).

			Regular Season					Playoffs				
Season	Club	League	GP	G	A	Pts	PIM	GP	G	A	Pts	PIM
2006-07	Waywayseecappo	MJHL	70	20	69	89	34	....	....	....	....	....
2007-08	Waywayseecappo	MJHL	60	51	64	115	34	7	9	4	13	10
2008-09	Cornell Big Red	ECAC	33	3	3	6	16	....	....	....	....	....
2009-10	Cornell Big Red	ECAC	34	7	3	10	12	....	....	....	....	....
2010-11	Cornell Big Red	ECAC	34	7	8	15	20	....	....	....	....	....

COMRIE, Adam (KAWM-ree, A-duhm) FLA

Defense. Shoots left. 6'4", 205 lbs. Born, Kanata, Ont., July 31, 1990.
(Florida's 3rd choice, 80th overall, in 2008 Entry Draft).

			Regular Season					Playoffs				
Season	Club	League	GP	G	A	Pts	PIM	GP	G	A	Pts	PIM
2006-07	Ohio	USHL	19	6	4	10	28	....	....	....	....	....
	Omaha Lancers	USHL	38	1	6	7	27	5	0	0	0	4
2007-08	Saginaw Spirit	OHL	58	10	18	28	90	4	0	0	0	4
2008-09	Saginaw Spirit	OHL	52	9	21	30	70	8	0	2	2	8
2009-10	Guelph Storm	OHL	68	14	26	40	79	5	1	2	3	4
2010-11	Rochester	AHL	44	0	5	5	18	....	....	....	....	....
	Cincinnati	ECHL	13	4	4	8	18	2	1	0	1	2

CONBOY, Andrew (KAWN-boi, AN-droo) MTL

Left wing. Shoots left. 6'4", 199 lbs. Born, Burnsville, MN, May 16, 1988.
(Montreal's 7th choice, 142nd overall, in 2007 Entry Draft).

			Regular Season					Playoffs				
Season	Club	League	GP	G	A	Pts	PIM	GP	G	A	Pts	PIM
2005-06	Wichita Falls	NAHL	51	7	8	15	158	5	0	2	2	2
2006-07	Omaha Lancers	USHL	56	25	25	50	105	....	....	....	....	....
2007-08	Omaha Lancers	USHL	58	17	21	38	188	14	*9	1	10	24
2008-09	Michigan State	CCHA	21	3	2	5	76	....	....	....	....	....
	Hamilton Bulldogs	AHL	15	0	1	1	6	1	0	0	0	2
2009-10	Hamilton Bulldogs	AHL	68	8	5	13	73	19	1	2	3	28
2010-11	Hamilton Bulldogs	AHL	64	13	10	23	116	20	1	3	4	41

CONDON, Nathan (KOHN-duhn, NAY-thun) COL

Center. Shoots left. 6', 180 lbs. Born, Wausau, WI, May 29, 1990.
(Colorado's 7th choice, 200th overall, in 2008 Entry Draft).

			Regular Season					Playoffs				
Season	Club	League	GP	G	A	Pts	PIM	GP	G	A	Pts	PIM
2004-05	Wausau West	High-WI	22	1	4	5	4	....	....	....	....	....
2005-06	Wausau West	High-WI	22	21	22	43	6	....	....	....	....	....
	Team Wisconsin	UMHSEL	24	16	13	29	10	....	....	....	....	....
2006-07	Wausau West	High-WI	21	21	27	48	10	....	....	....	....	....
	Team Wisconsin	UMHSEL	23	14	9	23	6	....	....	....	....	....
2007-08	Wausau West	High-WI	23	33	26	59	10	....	....	....	....	....
	Team Wisconsin	UMHSEL	24	20	25	45	6	....	....	....	....	....
2008-09	Fargo Force	USHL	58	11	18	29	20	10	1	5	6	2
2009-10	Fargo Force	USHL	60	23	28	51	20	13	3	2	5	6
2010-11	U. of Minnesota	WCHA	35	8	9	17	14	....	....	....	....	....

CONNAUTON, Kevin (kuh-NAW-tuhn, KEH-vihn) VAN

Defense. Shoots left. 6'1", 196 lbs. Born, Edmonton, Alta., February 23, 1990.
(Vancouver's 3rd choice, 83rd overall, in 2009 Entry Draft).

			Regular Season					Playoffs				
Season	Club	League	GP	G	A	Pts	PIM	GP	G	A	Pts	PIM
2007-08	Spruce Grove	AJHL	56	13	32	45	59	15	5	0	5	18
2008-09	Western Mich.	CCHA	40	7	11	18	44	....	....	....	....	....
2009-10	Vancouver Giants	WHL	69	24	48	72	107	16	3	10	13	21
2010-11	Manitoba Moose	AHL	73	11	12	23	51	6	1	0	1	0

WHL West First All-Star Team (2010) • Canadian Major Junior All-Rookie Team (2010)

CONNELLY, Brian (KAW-nuh-lee, BRIGH-uhn) CHI

Defense. Shoots left. 5'10", 167 lbs. Born, Bloomington, MN, June 10, 1986.

			Regular Season					Playoffs				
Season	Club	League	GP	G	A	Pts	PIM	GP	G	A	Pts	PIM
2004-05	Bloomington-Jeff.	High-MN	....	18	45	63	....	....	....	....	....	....
	Tri-City Storm	USHL	20	0	3	3	12	9	0	1	1	2
2005-06	Tri-City Storm	USHL	54	3	9	12	16	5	1	0	1	0
2006-07	Colorado College	WCHA	35	2	15	17	22	....	....	....	....	....
2007-08	Colorado College	WCHA	41	3	16	19	32	....	....	....	....	....
2008-09	Colorado College	WCHA	38	3	24	27	46	....	....	....	....	....
	Rockford IceHogs	AHL	9	1	2	3	6	3	0	0	0	2
2009-10	Rockford IceHogs	AHL	78	4	31	35	28	4	0	3	3	2
2010-11	Rockford IceHogs	AHL	80	11	41	52	39	....	....	....	....	....

Signed to an ATO (amateur tryout) contract by **Chicago**, March 23, 2009.

CONNOLLY, Brett (KAW-nuh-lee, BREHT) T.B.

Right wing. Shoots right. 6'2", 198 lbs. Born, Prince George, B.C., May 2, 1992.
(Tampa Bay's 1st choice, 6th overall, in 2010 Entry Draft).

			Regular Season					Playoffs				
Season	Club	League	GP	G	A	Pts	PIM	GP	G	A	Pts	PIM
2007-08	Cariboo Cougars	BCMML	38	16	16	32	80	6	4	1	5	10
	Prince George	WHL	4	0	0	0	0	....	....	....	....	....
2008-09	Prince George	WHL	65	30	30	60	38	4	0	2	2	6
2009-10	Prince George	WHL	16	10	9	19	8	....	....	....	....	....
2010-11	Prince George	WHL	59	46	27	73	26	1	0	0	0	0

WHL Rookie of the Year (2009) • Canadian Major Junior All-Rookie Team (2009) • Canadian Major Junior Rookie of the Year (2009)

• Missed majority of 2009-10 due to pre-season hip injury..

CONNOLLY, Mike (KAW-nuhl-lee, MIGHK) S.J.

Left wing. Shoots left. 5'9", 180 lbs. Born, Calgary, Alta., July 3, 1989.

			Regular Season					Playoffs				
Season	Club	League	GP	G	A	Pts	PIM	GP	G	A	Pts	PIM
2006-07	Camrose Kodiaks	AJHL	47	18	30	48	79	17	7	13	20	28
2007-08	Camrose Kodiaks	AJHL	37	25	41	66	39	12	3	5	8	38
2008-09	U. Minn-Duluth	WCHA	43	13	29	42	53	....	....	....	....	....
2009-10	U. Minn-Duluth	WCHA	38	14	26	40	24	....	....	....	....	....
2010-11	U. Minn-Duluth	WCHA	42	28	26	54	59	....	....	....	....	....

Signed as a free agent by **San Jose**, April 15, 2011.

CORNET, Philippe (kohr-NAY, fih-LEEP) EDM

Left wing. Shoots left. 6', 196 lbs. Born, Val-Senneville, Que., March 28, 1990.
(Edmonton's 3rd choice, 133rd overall, in 2008 Entry Draft).

			Regular Season					Playoffs				
Season	Club	League	GP	G	A	Pts	PIM	GP	G	A	Pts	PIM
2006-07	Rimouski Oceanic	QMJHL	46	7	14	21	8	....	....	....	....	....
2007-08	Rimouski Oceanic	QMJHL	61	23	26	49	24	9	3	3	6	6
2008-09	Rimouski Oceanic	QMJHL	63	29	48	77	34	13	4	11	15	14
2009-10	Rouyn-Noranda	QMJHL	65	28	49	77	32	11	5	6	11	6
2010-11	Oklahoma City	AHL	60	7	16	23	8	....	....	....	....	....

CORRADO, Frank (koh-RA-doh, FRANK) VAN

Defense. Shoots right. 6', 190 lbs. Born, Woodbridge, Ont., March 26, 1993.
(Vancouver's 6th choice, 150th overall, in 2011 Entry Draft).

			Regular Season					Playoffs				
Season	Club	League	GP	G	A	Pts	PIM	GP	G	A	Pts	PIM
2008-09	Vaughan Kings	GTHL	62	15	33	48	136	....	....	....	....	....
2009-10	Sudbury Wolves	OHL	63	1	8	9	46	4	0	1	1	0
2010-11	Sudbury Wolves	OHL	67	4	26	30	94	8	1	4	5	8

COSTELLO, Jeff (kaw-STEHL-oh, JEHF) OTT

Left wing. Shoots left. 6', 190 lbs. Born, Milwaukee, WI, November 20, 1990.
(Ottawa's 6th choice, 146th overall, in 2009 Entry Draft).

			Regular Season					Playoffs				
Season	Club	League	GP	G	A	Pts	PIM	GP	G	A	Pts	PIM
2005-06	Catholic Memorial	High-WI	....	13	16	29	....	....	....	....	....	....
2006-07	Catholic Memorial	High-WI	....	34	20	54	....	....	....	....	....	....
2007-08	Catholic Memorial	High-WI	22	31	17	48	60	....	....	....	....	....
	Team Wisconsin	UMHSEL	....	18	18	36	....	....	....	....	....	....
2008-09	Cedar Rapids	USHL	54	24	9	33	73	5	0	2	2	0
2009-10	Cedar Rapids	USHL	54	29	19	48	149	5	2	3	5	8
2010-11	U. of Notre Dame	CCHA	44	12	6	18	56	....	....	....	....	....

COUSINS, Nick (KUH-zihnz, NIHK) PHI

Center. Shoots left. 5'10", 169 lbs. Born, Belleville, Ont., July 20, 1993.
(Philadelphia's 2nd choice, 68th overall, in 2011 Entry Draft).

			Regular Season					Playoffs				
Season	Club	League	GP	G	A	Pts	PIM	GP	G	A	Pts	PIM
2008-09	Quinte Red Devils	Minor-ON	71	72	67	139	....	....	....	....	....	....
	Trenton Hercs	ON-Jr.A	5	0	1	1	2	....	....	....	....	....
2009-10	Sault Ste. Marie	OHL	67	11	21	32	34	5	0	1	1	2
2010-11	Sault Ste. Marie	OHL	68	29	39	68	56	....	....	....	....	....

COUTURIER, Sean (koo-TOO-ree-ay, SHAWN) PHI

Center. Shoots left. 6'3", 197 lbs. Born, Phoenix, AZ, December 7, 1992.
(Philadelphia's 1st choice, 8th overall, in 2011 Entry Draft).

			Regular Season					Playoffs				
Season	Club	League	GP	G	A	Pts	PIM	GP	G	A	Pts	PIM
2007-08	Notre Dame	SMHL	40	19	37	56	32	10	3	8	11	10
2008-09	Drummondville	QMJHL	58	9	22	31	14	19	1	7	8	8
2009-10	Drummondville	QMJHL	68	41	55	*96	47	14	10	8	18	18
2010-11	Drummondville	QMJHL	58	36	60	96	36	10	6	5	11	14

QMJHL Second All-Star Team (2010) • QMJHL First All-Star Team (2011) • QMJHL Player of the Year (2011)

COWICK, Corey (KOW-ihk, KOH-ree) OTT

Left wing. Shoots left. 6'3", 208 lbs. Born, Gloucester, Ont., August 1, 1989.
(Ottawa's 7th choice, 160th overall, in 2009 Entry Draft).

			Regular Season					Playoffs				
Season	Club	League	GP	G	A	Pts	PIM	GP	G	A	Pts	PIM
2006-07	Oshawa Generals	OHL	67	4	4	8	54	9	0	0	0	2
2007-08	Oshawa Generals	OHL	63	11	14	25	79	15	1	1	2	22
2008-09	Ottawa 67's	OHL	68	34	26	60	48	7	7	2	9	14
2009-10	Ottawa 67's	OHL	27	15	6	21	33	12	9	3	12	27
2010-11	Binghamton	AHL	30	1	3	4	20	....	....	....	....	....
	Elmira Jackals	ECHL	31	5	9	14	76	....	....	....	....	....

• Missed majority of 2009-10 due to pre-season shoulder injury at Kingston (OHL), August 30, 2009.

COYLE, Charlie (KOYL, CHAR-lee) MIN

Center/Right wing. Shoots right. 6'2", 205 lbs. Born, E. Weymouth, MA, March 2, 1992.
(San Jose's 1st choice, 28th overall, in 2010 Entry Draft).

			Regular Season					Playoffs				
Season	Club	League	GP	G	A	Pts	PIM	GP	G	A	Pts	PIM
2007-08	Thayer Academy	High-MA	....	14	23	37	....	....	....	....	....	....
2008-09	Thayer Academy	High-MA	26	20	28	48	4	....	....	....	....	....
2009-10	South Shore	EJHL	42	21	42	63	50	....	....	....	....	....
	USNTDP	U-18	4	1	0	1	2	....	....	....	....	....
2010-11	Boston University	H-East	37	7	19	26	34	....	....	....	....	....

Hockey East All-Rookie Team (2011) • Hockey East Rookie of the Year (2011)

Traded to **Minnesota** by **San Jose** with Devin Setoguchi and San Jose's 1st round choice (Zack Phillips) in 2011 Entry Draft for Brent Burns and Minnesota's 2nd round choice in 2012 Entry Draft, June 24, 2011.

COYLE, Jace (KOYL, JAYS) DAL

Defense. Shoots right. 5'11", 180 lbs. Born, Cranbrook, B.C., May 24, 1990.

			Regular Season					Playoffs				
Season	Club	League	GP	G	A	Pts	PIM	GP	G	A	Pts	PIM
2007-08	Spokane Chiefs	WHL	52	1	8	9	23	....	....	....	....	....
2008-09	Medicine Hat	WHL	72	8	16	24	74	11	1	2	3	6
2009-10	Medicine Hat	WHL	68	10	36	46	64	12	3	1	4	14
2010-11	Medicine Hat	WHL	49	6	22	28	42	15	3	12	15	12

Signed as a free agent by **Dallas**, July 1, 2010.

CRAMAROSSA, Joseph (kra-ma-ROH-sa, JOH-sehf) ANA

Center. Shoots left. 6', 190 lbs. Born, Toronto, Ont., October 26, 1992.
(Anaheim's 4th choice, 65th overall, in 2011 Entry Draft).

			Regular Season					Playoffs				
Season	Club	League	GP	G	A	Pts	PIM	GP	G	A	Pts	PIM
2007-08	Markham Majors	GTHL	70	31	37	68	64	....	....	....	....	....
2008-09	Markham Waxers	ON-Jr.A	38	7	3	10	14	12	1	2	3	0
2009-10	St. Michael's	OHL	64	6	10	16	60	14	0	2	2	11
2010-11	St. Michael's	OHL	59	12	20	32	101	14	2	2	4	6

CRANE, Chris (KRAYN, KRIHS-tuh-fuhr) S.J.

Right wing. Shoots right. 6'1", 185 lbs. Born, Virginia Beach, VA, December 2, 1991.
(San Jose's 8th choice, 200th overall, in 2010 Entry Draft).

			Regular Season					Playoffs				
Season	Club	League	GP	G	A	Pts	PIM	GP	G	A	Pts	PIM
2008-09	Green Bay	USHL	48	10	9	19	120	5	2	1	3	2
2009-10	Green Bay	USHL	52	15	14	29	107	12	2	3	5	27
2010-11	Ohio State	CCHA	37	4	6	10	37	....	....	....	....	....

CRAWFORD, Nick (KRAW-fuhrd, NIHK) **BUF**

Defense. Shoots left. 6'1", 191 lbs. Born, Brampton, Ont., February 23, 1990.
(Buffalo's 8th choice, 164th overall, in 2008 Entry Draft).

			Regular Season					Playoffs				
Season	Club	League	GP	G	A	Pts	PIM	GP	G	A	Pts	PIM
2006-07	Saginaw Spirit	OHL	63	1	7	8	32	5	0	1	1	0
2007-08	Saginaw Spirit	OHL	68	4	16	20	58	4	1	1	2	2
2008-09	Saginaw Spirit	OHL	65	7	35	42	41	8	1	4	5	4
2009-10	Saginaw Spirit	OHL	19	4	17	21	4	....	....	....	....	....
	Barrie Colts	OHL	49	7	42	49	20	17	0	12	12	4
2010-11	Portland Pirates	AHL	76	7	24	31	27	12	0	2	2	4

OHL First All-Star Team (2010) • Canadian Major Junior Second All-Star Team (2010)

CRESCENZI, Andrew (kruh-SEHN-zee, AN-droo) **TOR**

Center. Shoots left. 6'5", 208 lbs. Born, Thornhill, Ont., July 29, 1992.

			Regular Season					Playoffs				
Season	Club	League	GP	G	A	Pts	PIM	GP	G	A	Pts	PIM
2008-09	Villanova Knights	ON-Jr.A	45	6	17	23	40	....	....	....	....	....
2009-10	Kitchener Rangers	OHL	68	8	4	12	42	20	1	2	3	11
2010-11	Kitchener Rangers	OHL	55	12	11	23	74	7	1	1	2	6
	Toronto Marlies	AHL	2	0	1	1	0	....	....	....	....	....

Signed as a free agent by **Toronto**, September 24, 2010.

CROSS, Tommy (KRAWS, TAW-mee) **BOS**

Defense. Shoots left. 6'3", 195 lbs. Born, Hartford, CT, September 12, 1989.
(Boston's 2nd choice, 35th overall, in 2007 Entry Draft).

			Regular Season					Playoffs				
Season	Club	League	GP	G	A	Pts	PIM	GP	G	A	Pts	PIM
2004-05	Simsbury	High-CT	23	5	40	45	18	....	....	....	....	....
2005-06	Simsbury	High-CT	22	15	35	50	....	....	....	....	....	....
2006-07	Westminster	High-CT	25	8	12	20	20	....	....	....	....	....
	USNTDP	NAHL	2	0	2	2	0	....	....	....	....	....
	USNTDP	U-18	11	0	1	1	8	....	....	....	....	....
2007-08	Westminster	High-CT	25	9	12	21	....	....	....	....	....	....
	Ohio	USHL	9	0	4	4	8	....	....	....	....	....
2008-09	Boston College	H-East	24	0	8	8	24	....	....	....	....	....
2009-10	Boston College	H-East	38	5	5	10	36	....	....	....	....	....
2010-11	Boston College	H-East	28	7	11	18	45	....	....	....	....	....

CULEK, Jakub (TSOO-lehk, YA-koob) **OTT**

Left wing. Shoots left. 6'3", 180 lbs. Born, Klatovy, Czechoslovakia, September 7, 1992.
(Ottawa's 1st choice, 76th overall, in 2010 Entry Draft).

			Regular Season					Playoffs				
Season	Club	League	GP	G	A	Pts	PIM	GP	G	A	Pts	PIM
2006-07	HC Kladno U17	CzR-U17	5	1	0	1	0	....	....	....	....	....
2007-08	HC Plzen U17	CzR-U17	44	12	22	34	76	8	1	4	5	10
2008-09	HC Plzen U17	CzR-U17	29	15	16	31	98	1	0	0	0	0
	HC Plzen Jr.	CzRep-Jr.	12	3	2	5	10	5	3	0	3	0
2009-10	Rimouski Oceanic	QMJHL	63	13	34	47	54	12	6	3	9	4
2010-11	Rimouski Oceanic	QMJHL	55	7	15	22	37	5	0	2	2	2

CUMA, Tyler (KOO-ma, TIGH-luhr) **MIN**

Defense. Shoots left. 6'2", 196 lbs. Born, Toronto, Ont., January 19, 1990.
(Minnesota's 1st choice, 23rd overall, in 2008 Entry Draft).

			Regular Season					Playoffs				
Season	Club	League	GP	G	A	Pts	PIM	GP	G	A	Pts	PIM
2005-06	Mississauga Reps	GTHL	40	15	20	35	52	....	....	....	....	....
2006-07	Ottawa 67's	OHL	63	3	16	19	55	5	0	2	2	6
2007-08	Ottawa 67's	OHL	59	4	28	32	69	4	1	1	2	2
2008-09	Ottawa 67's	OHL	21	1	8	9	27	....	....	....	....	....
2009-10	Ottawa 67's	OHL	52	5	17	22	73	12	0	5	5	20
2010-11	Houston Aeros	AHL	31	1	3	4	15	....	....	....	....	....

• Missed majority of 2008-09 due to knee injury in Team Canada Jr. training camp, December 12, 2008.

CUNDARI, Mark (kuhn-DAHR-ee, MAHRK) **ST.L.**

Defense. Shoots left. 5'9", 200 lbs. Born, Woodbridge, Ont., April 23, 1990.

			Regular Season					Playoffs				
Season	Club	League	GP	G	A	Pts	PIM	GP	G	A	Pts	PIM
2005-06	Vaughan Kings	GTHL	STATISTICS NOT AVAILABLE									
	Vaughan Vipers	OPJHL	2	0	0	0	0	....	....	....	....	....
2006-07	Windsor Spitfires	OHL	62	6	16	22	130	....	....	....	....	....
2007-08	Windsor Spitfires	OHL	63	6	17	23	141	3	0	0	0	10
2008-09	Windsor Spitfires	OHL	60	10	22	32	143	20	1	8	9	38
2009-10	Windsor Spitfires	OHL	63	8	46	54	139	19	3	15	18	42
2010-11	Peoria Rivermen	AHL	69	10	20	30	106	3	0	1	1	4

Signed as a free agent by **St. Louis**, September 24, 2008.

CUNNING, Cam (KUH-nihng, KAM)

Left wing. Shoots left. 6', 197 lbs. Born, Powell River, B.C., June 4, 1985.
(Calgary's 8th choice, 240th overall, in 2003 Entry Draft).

			Regular Season					Playoffs				
Season	Club	League	GP	G	A	Pts	PIM	GP	G	A	Pts	PIM
2002-03	Kamloops Blazers	WHL	71	7	13	20	54	6	1	0	1	2
2003-04	Kamloops Blazers	WHL	65	14	13	27	62	5	1	1	2	10
2004-05	Kamloops Blazers	WHL	39	14	8	22	63	....	....	....	....	....
	Vancouver Giants	WHL	30	3	7	10	19	6	1	3	4	14
2005-06	Red Deer Rebels	WHL	40	19	13	32	52	....	....	....	....	....
	Omaha	AHL	30	2	4	6	24	....	....	....	....	....
2006-07	Omaha	AHL	60	12	5	17	45	6	0	2	2	2
2007-08	Quad City Flames	AHL	68	11	4	15	80	....	....	....	....	....
2008-09	Quad City Flames	AHL	63	7	14	21	38	....	....	....	....	....
2009-10	Abbotsford Heat	AHL	69	19	19	38	64	13	1	2	3	6
2010-11	Abbotsford Heat	AHL	52	14	8	22	46	....	....	....	....	....

CUNNINGHAM, Craig (KUN-ihng-ham, KRAYG) **BOS**

Left wing. Shoots right. 5'10", 181 lbs. Born, Trail, B.C., September 13, 1990.
(Boston's 4th choice, 97th overall, in 2010 Entry Draft).

			Regular Season					Playoffs				
Season	Club	League	GP	G	A	Pts	PIM	GP	G	A	Pts	PIM
2005-06	Beaver Valley	KIJHL	47	19	25	44	22	16	4	5	9	29
2006-07	Vancouver Giants	WHL	48	0	5	5	38	15	0	1	1	15
2007-08	Vancouver Giants	WHL	67	11	14	25	72	10	1	2	3	6
2008-09	Vancouver Giants	WHL	72	28	22	50	62	17	5	9	14	12
2009-10	Vancouver Giants	WHL	72	37	60	97	44	16	12	12	24	12
2010-11	Vancouver Giants	WHL	36	10	35	45	31	....	....	....	....	....
	Portland	WHL	35	17	25	42	25	21	7	14	21	12

WHL West First All-Star Team (2010)

CZARNIK, Robert (CHAHR-nihk, RAW-buhrt) **L.A.**

Right wing. Shoots right. 6', 185 lbs. Born, Detroit, MI, January 25, 1990.
(Los Angeles' 4th choice, 63rd overall, in 2008 Entry Draft).

			Regular Season					Playoffs				
Season	Club	League	GP	G	A	Pts	PIM	GP	G	A	Pts	PIM
2005-06	Det. Honeybaked	MWEHL	....	53	78	131	....	....	....	....	....	....
2006-07	USNTDP	U-17	19	10	2	12	22	....	....	....	....	....
	USNTDP	NAHL	46	7	10	17	46	....	....	....	....	....
2007-08	USNTDP	U-18	43	15	18	33	30	....	....	....	....	....
	USNTDP	NAHL	14	4	2	6	12	....	....	....	....	....
2008-09	U. of Michigan	CCHA	39	5	11	16	32	....	....	....	....	....
2009-10	U. of Michigan	CCHA	12	3	3	6	4	....	....	....	....	....
2010-11	Plymouth Whalers	OHL	61	33	44	77	46	11	4	5	9	6

CZERWONKA, Drew (chuhr-WAWN-kuh, DROO) **EDM**

Left wing. Shoots left. 6'2", 197 lbs. Born, Wolseley, Sask., July 1, 1992.
(Edmonton's 9th choice, 166th overall, in 2010 Entry Draft).

			Regular Season					Playoffs				
Season	Club	League	GP	G	A	Pts	PIM	GP	G	A	Pts	PIM
2007-08	Reg. Pat Cdns.	SMHL	42	18	10	28	113	5	2	0	2	44
	Kootenay Ice	WHL	2	0	0	0	0	....	....	....	....	....
2008-09	Kootenay Ice	WHL	55	16	2	18	83	4	0	0	0	5
2009-10	Kootenay Ice	WHL	54	4	9	13	106	6	1	2	3	9
2010-11	Kootenay Ice	WHL	68	14	29	43	78	13	2	3	5	4

D'AGOSTINO, Nicholas (DA-goh-STEE-noh, NIHK-oh-las) **PIT**

Defense. Shoots left. 6'2", 181 lbs. Born, Mississauga, Ont., June 24, 1990.
(Pittsburgh's 4th choice, 210th overall, in 2008 Entry Draft).

			Regular Season					Playoffs				
Season	Club	League	GP	G	A	Pts	PIM	GP	G	A	Pts	PIM
2006-07	Tor. Young Nats	GTHL	30	5	21	26	....	5	0	4	4	....
	Young Nats	Exhib.	8	1	5	6	....	....	....	....	....	....
2007-08	St. Michael's	OPJHL	46	5	18	23	22	12	0	3	3	8
2008-09	St. Michael's	ON-Jr.A	43	9	24	33	34	6	2	3	5	8
2009-10	Cornell Big Red	ECAC	32	4	14	18	6	....	....	....	....	....
2010-11	Cornell Big Red	ECAC	32	7	10	17	20	....	....	....	....	....

DAHLBECK, Klas (DAHL-behk, KLAHS) **CHI**

Defense. Shoots left. 6'2", 194 lbs. Born, Katrineholm, Sweden, July 6, 1991.
(Chicago's 6th choice, 79th overall, in 2011 Entry Draft).

			Regular Season					Playoffs				
Season	Club	League	GP	G	A	Pts	PIM	GP	G	A	Pts	PIM
2007-08	Vaxjo U18	Swe-U18	16	7	10	17	4	....	....	....	....	....
	Vaxjo Jr.	Swe-Jr.	22	3	4	7	14	....	....	....	....	....
2008-09	Vaxjo U18	Swe-U18	14	4	5	9	6	....	....	....	....	....
	Vaxjo Jr.	Swe-Jr.	15	4	6	10	8	....	....	....	....	....
2009-10	Linkopings HC Jr.	Swe-Jr.	39	4	7	11	8	6	1	1	2	4
	Mjolby HC	Sweden-3	2	0	0	0	0	....	....	....	....	....
	Linkopings HC	Sweden	6	0	0	0	0	3	0	0	0	0
2010-11	Linkopings HC	Sweden	47	0	8	8	12	7	0	0	0	0

DAHLSTROM, Andreas (DAHL-stuhm, an–DRAY-uhs) **ANA**

Center. Shoots left. 5'11", 176 lbs. Born, Huddinge, Sweden, June 22, 1991.
(Anaheim's 6th choice, 161st overall, in 2010 Entry Draft).

			Regular Season					Playoffs				
Season	Club	League	GP	G	A	Pts	PIM	GP	G	A	Pts	PIM
2007-08	AIK IF Solna U18	Swe-U18	25	6	10	16	16	....	....	....	....	....
	AIK IF Solna Jr.	Swe-Jr.	9	1	2	3	8	....	....	....	....	....
2008-09	AIK IF Solna U18	Swe-U18	11	6	9	15	33	7	2	11	13	31
	AIK IF Solna Jr.	Swe-Jr.	28	5	5	10	67	....	....	....	....	....
	AIK IF Solna	Sweden-2	4	0	0	0	0	....	....	....	....	....
2009-10	AIK IF Solna Jr.	Swe-Jr.	5	4	6	10	2	....	....	....	....	....
	AIK IF Solna	Sweden-2	6	1	2	3	4	....	....	....	....	....
2010-11	AIK IF Solna Jr.	Swe-Jr.	18	4	6	10	6	....	....	....	....	....

DALY, Patrick (DAY-lee, PAT-rihk) **N.J.**

Defense. Shoots left. 6', 180 lbs. Born, Minneapolis, MN, June 9, 1992.
(New Jersey's 7th choice, 189th overall, in 2011 Entry Draft).

			Regular Season					Playoffs				
Season	Club	League	GP	G	A	Pts	PIM	GP	G	A	Pts	PIM
2009-10	Benilde	High-MN	8	1	11	12	2	2	0	0	0	6
2010-11	Team Southeast	UMHSEL	19	3	8	11	16	3	0	4	4	0
	Benilde	High-MN	25	3	34	37	14	2	0	3	3	2

• Signed Letter of Intent to attend **University of Wisconsin** (WCHA) in fall of 2011.

D'AMIGO, Jerry (dah-MEE-goh, JAIR-ree) **TOR**

Right wing. Shoots left. 5'11", 213 lbs. Born, Binghamton, NY, February 19, 1991.
(Toronto's 6th choice, 158th overall, in 2009 Entry Draft).

			Regular Season					Playoffs				
Season	Club	League	GP	G	A	Pts	PIM	GP	G	A	Pts	PIM
2007-08	USNTDP	NAHL	44	5	12	17	59	3	1	1	2	6
	USNTDP	U-17	17	5	4	9	10	....	....	....	....	....
2008-09	USNTDP	NAHL	11	8	6	14	4	....	....	....	....	....
	USNTDP	U-18	42	15	27	42	57	....	....	....	....	....
2009-10	RPI Engineers	ECAC	35	10	24	34	37	....	....	....	....	....
2010-11	Toronto Marlies	AHL	43	5	10	15	23	....	....	....	....	....
	Kitchener Rangers	OHL	21	12	16	28	12	7	6	3	9	0

ECAC All-Rookie Team (2010) • ECAC Rookie of the Year (2010)

• Loaned to **Kitchener** (OHL) by **Toronto** (Toronto-AHL), February 3, 2011.

DANAULT, Phillip (duh-NOH, FIHL-ihp) **CHI**

Left wing. Shoots left. 6', 181 lbs. Born, Victoriaville, Que., February 24, 1993.
(Chicago's 2nd choice, 26th overall, in 2011 Entry Draft).

			Regular Season					Playoffs				
Season	Club	League	GP	G	A	Pts	PIM	GP	G	A	Pts	PIM
2008-09	Trois-Rivieres	QAAA	44	8	19	27	39	19	4	11	15	8
2009-10	Victoriaville Tigres	QMJHL	61	10	18	28	54	16	0	1	1	8
2010-11	Victoriaville Tigres	QMJHL	64	23	44	67	59	9	5	10	15	6

DANIELS, Drew (DA-nyehlz, DROO) S.J.

Right wing. Shoots right. 6'1", 190 lbs. Born, Suffern, NY, June 7, 1989.
(San Jose's 7th choice, 194th overall, in 2008 Entry Draft).

			Regular Season					Playoffs				
Season	Club	League	GP	G	A	Pts	PIM	GP	G	A	Pts	PIM
2006-07	Kent Prep School	High-CT	....	12	22	34	....	....	....	....	....	....
2007-08	Kent Prep School	High-CT	25	12	35	47	14	....	....	....	....	....
2008-09	Sioux City	USHL	53	9	19	28	24	....	....	....	....	....
2009-10	Northeastern	H-East	32	4	4	8	4	....	....	....	....	....
2010-11	Northeastern	H-East	38	3	6	9	18	....	....	....	....	....

DANIELS, Justin (DA-nyehlz, JUHS-tihn) S.J.

Center. Shoots right. 6'1", 175 lbs. Born, Suffern, NY, June 7, 1989.
(San Jose's 1st choice, 62nd overall, in 2008 Entry Draft).

			Regular Season					Playoffs				
Season	Club	League	GP	G	A	Pts	PIM	GP	G	A	Pts	PIM
2006-07	Kent Prep School	High-CT	....	14	32	46	....	....	....	....	....	....
2007-08	Kent Prep School	High-CT	25	17	37	54	10	....	....	....	....	....
2008-09	Sioux City	USHL	56	9	28	37	17	....	....	....	....	....
2009-10	Northeastern	H-East	32	8	7	15	10	....	....	....	....	....
2010-11	Northeastern	H-East	28	0	6	6	8	....	....	....	....	....

DANIS-PEPIN, Simon (da-NEE-peh-PEHN, see-MOHN) CHI

Defense. Shoots right. 6'6", 229 lbs. Born, Gatineau, Que., April 11, 1988.
(Chicago's 3rd choice, 61st overall, in 2006 Entry Draft).

			Regular Season					Playoffs				
Season	Club	League	GP	G	A	Pts	PIM	GP	G	A	Pts	PIM
2003-04	Gatineau Intrepide	QAAA	33	2	14	16	20	2	0	0	0	0
2004-05	Gatineau Intrepide	QAAA	39	6	31	37	64	14	6	7	13	25
2005-06	N.H. Jr. Monarchs	EJHL	2	0	0	0	0	....	....	....	....	....
	U. of Maine	H-East	23	0	5	5	14	....	....	....	....	....
2006-07	U. of Maine	H-East	40	2	4	6	18	....	....	....	....	....
2007-08	U. of Maine	H-East	34	4	8	12	20	....	....	....	....	....
2008-09	U. of Maine	H-East	36	0	13	13	29	....	....	....	....	....
2009-10	Rockford IceHogs	AHL	38	1	7	8	10	....	....	....	....	....
	Toledo Walleye	ECHL	13	1	9	10	13	4	1	3	4	0
2010-11	Rockford IceHogs	AHL	23	1	3	4	20	....	....	....	....	....
	Toledo Walleye	ECHL	33	3	9	12	35	....	....	....	....	....

DAOUST, Jean-Michel (DAH-oo, ZHAWN-MEE-shehl)

Right wing. Shoots right. 5'7", 154 lbs. Born, Valleyfield, Que., November 24, 1983.

			Regular Season					Playoffs				
Season	Club	League	GP	G	A	Pts	PIM	GP	G	A	Pts	PIM
2000-01	Hull Olympiques	QMJHL	68	23	27	50	84	5	0	0	0	8
2001-02	Hull Olympiques	QMJHL	72	16	20	36	91	10	2	1	3	11
2002-03	Hull Olympiques	QMJHL	72	34	60	94	104	20	12	25	37	28
2003-04	Gatineau	QMJHL	60	31	65	96	82	15	7	15	22	16
2005-06	Danbury Trashers	UHL	70	30	35	65	73	18	7	4	11	8
2006-07	Cincinnati	ECHL	71	32	30	62	63	10	3	5	8	8
2007-08	Cincinnati	ECHL	36	27	24	51	54	17	6	12	18	14
	Rockford IceHogs	AHL	1	0	0	0	0	....	....	....	....	....
	Wilkes-Barre	AHL	37	5	13	18	4	2	0	0	0	0
2008-09	Wilkes-Barre	AHL	58	10	18	28	24	12	5	4	9	12
2009-10	Houston Aeros	AHL	78	21	34	55	38	....	....	....	....	....
2010-11	Houston Aeros	AHL	72	12	18	30	39	11	4	1	5	2

Signed as a free agent by **Houston** (AHL), October 13, 2009. Signed as a free agent by **Minnesota**, May 13, 2010.

DASILVA, Dan (duh-SIHL-vah, DAN)

Right wing. Shoots right. 6'1", 195 lbs. Born, Saskatoon, Sask., April 30, 1985.

			Regular Season					Playoffs				
Season	Club	League	GP	G	A	Pts	PIM	GP	G	A	Pts	PIM
2002-03	Portland	WHL	64	9	13	22	81	7	0	4	4	16
2003-04	Portland	WHL	65	36	20	56	120	5	0	1	1	6
2004-05	Portland	WHL	71	31	42	73	127	5	1	1	2	6
2005-06	Lowell	AHL	25	3	2	5	27	....	....	....	....	....
	San Diego Gulls	ECHL	4	5	3	8	2	....	....	....	....	....
2006-07	Albany River Rats	AHL	43	11	8	19	33	....	....	....	....	....
	Arizona Sundogs	CHL	14	9	13	22	10	....	....	....	....	....
2007-08	Lake Erie Monsters	AHL	54	9	14	23	50	....	....	....	....	....
2008-09	Worcester Sharks	AHL	26	6	7	13	27	12	3	7	10	6
	Phoenix	ECHL	36	9	12	21	40	....	....	....	....	....
2009-10	Worcester Sharks	AHL	72	21	32	53	65	11	2	6	8	8
2010-11	Worcester Sharks	AHL	80	16	25	41	68	....	....	....	....	....

Signed as a free agent by **Colorado**, October 11, 2005.

DAVIDSON, Brandon (DAY-vihn-suhn, BRAN-duhn) EDM

Defense. Shoots left. 6'2", 194 lbs. Born, Lethbridge, Alta., August 21, 1991.
(Edmonton's 8th choice, 162nd overall, in 2010 Entry Draft).

			Regular Season					Playoffs				
Season	Club	League	GP	G	A	Pts	PIM	GP	G	A	Pts	PIM
2008-09	Lethbridge	AMHL	31	7	14	21	52	7	2	5	7	14
2009-10	Regina Pats	WHL	59	1	33	34	37	....	....	....	....	....
2010-11	Regina Pats	WHL	72	8	43	51	71	....	....	....	....	....
	Oklahoma City	AHL	1	0	0	0	0	1	0	0	0	0

DAY, Brian (DAY, BRIGH-uhn) NYI

Right wing. Shoots right. 6', 195 lbs. Born, Boston, MA, August 4, 1988.
(NY Islanders' 11th choice, 171st overall, in 2006 Entry Draft).

			Regular Season					Playoffs				
Season	Club	League	GP	G	A	Pts	PIM	GP	G	A	Pts	PIM
2003-04	Gov. Dummer	High-MA	25	8	15	23	....	....	....	....	....	....
2004-05	Gov. Dummer	High-MA	25	11	13	24	30	....	....	....	....	....
2005-06	Gov. Dummer	High-MA	28	9	13	22	34	....	....	....	....	....
2006-07	Gov. Academy	High-MA	27	20	18	38	....	....	....	....	....	....
2007-08	Colgate	ECAC	41	9	13	22	53	....	....	....	....	....
2008-09	Colgate	ECAC	34	14	13	27	26	....	....	....	....	....
2009-10	Colgate	ECAC	34	21	15	36	26	....	....	....	....	....
2010-11	Colgate	ECAC	40	10	15	25	56	....	....	....	....	....
	Bridgeport	AHL	10	2	3	5	7	....	....	....	....	....

DE HAAN, Calvin (DUH HAWN, CAL-vihn) NYI

Defense. Shoots left. 6'1", 189 lbs. Born, Ottawa, Ont., May 9, 1991.
(NY Islanders' 2nd choice, 12th overall, in 2009 Entry Draft).

			Regular Season					Playoffs				
Season	Club	League	GP	G	A	Pts	PIM	GP	G	A	Pts	PIM
2006-07	Ott. Valley Titans	Minor-ON	32	4	22	26	20	....	....	....	....	....
2007-08	Kemptville 73's	CJHL	58	3	39	42	14	....	....	....	....	....
2008-09	Oshawa Generals	OHL	68	8	55	63	40	....	....	....	....	....
2009-10	Oshawa Generals	OHL	34	5	19	24	14	....	....	....	....	....
2010-11	Oshawa Generals	OHL	55	6	42	48	48	10	1	11	12	6

DEE, Robby (DEE, RAW-bee) EDM

Center/Wing. Shoots left. 6'2", 185 lbs. Born, Minneapolis, MN, April 9, 1987.
(Edmonton's 4th choice, 86th overall, in 2005 Entry Draft).

			Regular Season					Playoffs				
Season	Club	League	GP	G	A	Pts	PIM	GP	G	A	Pts	PIM
2004-05	Breck Mustangs	High-MN	28	49	38	87	14	....	....	....	....	....
2005-06	Omaha Lancers	USHL	32	6	6	12	20	3	1	0	1	2
2006-07	Omaha Lancers	USHL	34	11	14	25	60	....	....	....	....	....
2007-08	U. of Maine	H-East	24	1	2	3	18	....	....	....	....	....
2008-09	U. of Maine	H-East	33	6	5	11	24	....	....	....	....	....
2009-10	U. of Maine	H-East	33	13	12	25	32	....	....	....	....	....
2010-11	U. of Maine	H-East	36	13	22	35	43	....	....	....	....	....

de GRAY, John (DIH-gray, JAWN)

Defense. Shoots left. 6'4", 204 lbs. Born, Richmond Hill, Ont., March 14, 1988.
(Anaheim's 3rd choice, 83rd overall, in 2006 Entry Draft).

			Regular Season					Playoffs				
Season	Club	League	GP	G	A	Pts	PIM	GP	G	A	Pts	PIM
2003-04	Rich. Hill Stars	Minor-ON	76	5	35	40	107	....	....	....	....	....
2004-05	Brampton	OHL	52	2	8	10	51	6	0	0	0	2
2005-06	Brampton	OHL	68	0	10	10	103	11	0	0	0	8
2006-07	Brampton	OHL	65	4	13	17	75	4	1	0	1	10
2007-08	Brampton	OHL	67	4	13	17	140	5	0	0	0	12
	Portland Pirates	AHL	6	0	0	0	0	3	0	0	0	0
2008-09	Iowa Chops	AHL	62	2	5	7	67	....	....	....	....	....
2009-10	Bakersfield	ECHL	29	5	6	11	28	....	....	....	....	....
	Rochester	AHL	41	1	5	6	31	2	0	0	0	2
2010-11	Syracuse Crunch	AHL	34	0	5	5	15	....	....	....	....	....
	Elmira Jackals	ECHL	23	2	7	9	32	....	....	....	....	....

• Loaned to **Rochester** (AHL) by **Anaheim** (Bakersfield-ECHL), December 30, 2009.

DELISLE, Dan (deh-LIGH-uhl, DAN) CHI

Center/Left wing. Shoots left. 6'4", 222 lbs. Born, Minneapolis, MN, September 24, 1990.
(Chicago's 3rd choice, 89th overall, in 2009 Entry Draft).

			Regular Season					Playoffs				
Season	Club	League	GP	G	A	Pts	PIM	GP	G	A	Pts	PIM
2006-07	Totino-Grace	High-MN	....	21	26	47	....	....	....	....	....	....
2007-08	Totino-Grace	High-MN	27	25	31	56	26	....	....	....	....	....
2008-09	Totino-Grace	High-MN	27	32	24	56	16	....	....	....	....	....
	Team Northeast	UMHSEL	24	12	11	23	....	....	....	....	....	....
2009-10	U. Minn-Duluth	WCHA	25	0	1	1	24	....	....	....	....	....
2010-11	U. Minn-Duluth	WCHA	31	4	2	6	12	....	....	....	....	....

DELISLE, Steven (deh-LIH-uhl, STEE-vehn) CBJ

Defense. Shoots right. 6'6", 233 lbs. Born, Levise, Que., July 30, 1990.
(Columbus' 3rd choice, 107th overall, in 2008 Entry Draft).

			Regular Season					Playoffs				
Season	Club	League	GP	G	A	Pts	PIM	GP	G	A	Pts	PIM
2006-07	Gatineau	QMJHL	56	1	11	12	47	5	0	0	0	0
2007-08	Gatineau	QMJHL	70	6	23	29	82	19	0	10	10	16
2008-09	Gatineau	QMJHL	63	5	25	30	94	10	2	3	5	15
2009-10	Gatineau	QMJHL	39	4	19	23	61	....	....	....	....	....
	Rouyn-Noranda	QMJHL	25	1	5	6	16	11	1	3	4	12
2010-11	Fort Wayne	CHL	6	0	0	0	2	....	....	....	....	....

• Missed majority of 2010-11 due to shoulder injury.

DEMELO, Dylan (dih-MEH-loh, DIH-luhn) S.J.

Defense. Shoots right. 6', 195 lbs. Born, London, Ont., May 1, 1993.
(San Jose's 5th choice, 179th overall, in 2011 Entry Draft).

			Regular Season					Playoffs				
Season	Club	League	GP	G	A	Pts	PIM	GP	G	A	Pts	PIM
2008-09	Lon. Jr. Knights	Minor-ON	74	11	34	45	46	....	....	....	....	....
2009-10	Mississauga	ON-Jr.A	36	9	20	29	24	....	....	....	....	....
	St. Michael's	OHL	20	0	1	1	12	....	....	....	....	....
2010-11	St. Michael's	OHL	67	3	24	27	70	20	1	4	5	15

DENISOV, Denis (den-NEES-ahf, deh-NEES) BUF

Left wing. Shoots left. 6', 183 lbs. Born, Kalinin, USSR, December 31, 1981.
(Buffalo's 4th choice, 149th overall, in 2000 Entry Draft).

			Regular Season					Playoffs				
Season	Club	League	GP	G	A	Pts	PIM	GP	G	A	Pts	PIM
1997-98	HK CSKA Moscow	Russia	7	0	0	0	4	....	....	....	....	....
1998-99	HK CSKA Moscow	Russia-2	42	1	6	7	16	....	....	....	....	....
99-2000	HK Moscow	Russia-2	39	1	8	9	16	....	....	....	....	....
2000-01	HK Moscow	Russia-2	41	0	3	3	6	....	....	....	....	....
2001-02	Krylja Sovetov	Russia	47	3	4	7	37	....	....	....	....	....
	Krylja Sovetov 2	Russia-3	3	0	1	1	18	....	....	....	....	....
2002-03	Ufa	Russia	50	2	8	10	12	3	0	1	1	0
2003-04	Ak Bars Kazan	Russia	51	4	11	15	34	7	0	0	0	4
2004-05	Ak Bars Kazan	Russia	57	4	7	11	30	4	0	0	0	2
2005-06	Ak Bars Kazan	Russia	22	0	2	2	51	2	0	0	0	4
2006-07	Avangard Omsk	Russia	52	2	10	12	32	9	1	2	3	4
2007-08	Avangard Omsk	Russia	51	7	12	19	34	4	0	2	2	4
2008-09	Dynamo Moscow	Rus-KHL	56	7	15	22	95	10	2	2	4	10
2009-10	Dynamo Moscow	Rus-KHL	54	8	12	20	69	4	1	0	1	4
2010-11	SKA St. Petersburg	Rus-KHL	48	4	12	16	42	11	3	3	6	8

DERLYUK, Roman (duhr-LYUHK, ROH-muhn) FLA

Defense. Shoots left. 6'3", 198 lbs. Born, Leningrad, USSR, October 27, 1986.
(Florida's 7th choice, 164th overall, in 2005 Entry Draft).

			Regular Season					Playoffs				
Season	**Club**	**League**	**GP**	**G**	**A**	**Pts**	**PIM**	**GP**	**G**	**A**	**Pts**	**PIM**
2003-04	Lokom. St. Pete.	Russia-3	STATISTICS NOT AVAILABLE									
2004-05	Spartak St. Pet.	Russia-2	51	0	3	3	74	....	....	....	....	....
2005-06	SKA St. Petersburg	Russia	32	0	3	3	63	2	1	0	1	0
	St. Petersburg 2	Russia-3	2	0	1	1	0	....	....	....	....	....
2006-07	SKA St. Petersburg	Russia	6	0	1	1	4	....	....	....	....	....
	St. Petersburg 2	Russia-3	6	1	4	5	6	....	....	....	....	....
	THK Tver	Russia-3	2	0	2	2	0	....	....	....	....	....
	MVD	Russia	19	0	3	3	14	1	0	0	0	0
2007-08	MVD 2	Russia-3	24	1	5	6	36	....	....	....	....	....
	MVD	Russia	26	3	3	6	26	3	0	0	0	2
2008-09	MVD	Rus-KHL	54	3	8	11	50	....	....	....	....	....
2009-10	MVD	Rus-KHL	25	2	7	9	34	15	1	3	4	16
2010-11	Dynamo Moscow	Rus-KHL	44	5	9	14	18	6	0	2	2	8

DESCHAMPS, Nicolas (day-SHAWMP, NIHK-oh-las) ANA

Center. Shoots left. 6'1", 207 lbs. Born, Lasalle, Que., January 6, 1990.
(Anaheim's 2nd choice, 35th overall, in 2008 Entry Draft).

			Regular Season					Playoffs				
Season	**Club**	**League**	**GP**	**G**	**A**	**Pts**	**PIM**	**GP**	**G**	**A**	**Pts**	**PIM**
2005-06	C.C. Lemoyne	QAAA	23	5	4	9	14	8	0	0	0	12
2006-07	C.C. Lemoyne	QAAA	35	20	28	48	60	10	4	7	11	22
2007-08	Chicoutimi	QMJHL	70	24	43	67	63	6	2	3	5	6
2008-09	Chicoutimi	QMJHL	65	24	41	65	40	4	3	1	4	12
	Iowa Chops	AHL	2	0	1	1	0	....	....	....	....	....
2009-10	Chicoutimi	QMJHL	31	18	26	*44	20	....	....	....	....	....
	Moncton Wildcats	QMJHL	33	21	31	*52	20	15	5	9	14	10
2010-11	Syracuse Crunch	AHL	80	15	31	46	26	....	....	....	....	....

QMJHL All-Rookie Team (2008) • Canadian Major Junior All-Rookie Team (2008) • QMJHL Second All-Star Team (2010)

DESLAURIERS, Nicolas (duh-LOHR-ree-AY, NIH-koh-las) L.A.

Defense. Shoots left. 6', 205 lbs. Born, LaSalle, Que., February 22, 1991.
(Los Angeles' 3rd choice, 84th overall, in 2009 Entry Draft).

			Regular Season					Playoffs				
Season	**Club**	**League**	**GP**	**G**	**A**	**Pts**	**PIM**	**GP**	**G**	**A**	**Pts**	**PIM**
2006-07	Chateauguay	QAAA	43	2	10	12	28	3	1	0	1	4
2007-08	Rouyn-Noranda	QMJHL	42	2	7	9	38	4	0	0	0	0
2008-09	Rouyn-Noranda	QMJHL	68	11	19	30	80	6	2	2	4	8
2009-10	Rouyn-Noranda	QMJHL	65	9	36	45	72	11	2	6	8	2
2010-11	Gatineau	QMJHL	48	13	30	43	53	24	5	15	20	19

DESPRES, Simon (duh-PRAY, see-MOHN) PIT

Defense. Shoots left. 6'4", 225 lbs. Born, Laval, Que., July 27, 1991.
(Pittsburgh's 1st choice, 30th overall, in 2009 Entry Draft).

			Regular Season					Playoffs				
Season	**Club**	**League**	**GP**	**G**	**A**	**Pts**	**PIM**	**GP**	**G**	**A**	**Pts**	**PIM**
2006-07	Laval-Bourassa	QAAA	42	8	31	39	36	5	0	2	2	8
2007-08	Saint John	QMJHL	64	1	13	14	30	14	0	4	4	18
2008-09	Saint John	QMJHL	66	2	30	32	74	4	0	4	4	2
2009-10	Saint John	QMJHL	63	9	38	47	87	21	2	17	19	18
2010-11	Saint John	QMJHL	47	13	28	41	54	19	4	8	12	16

QMJHL All-Rookie Team (2008) • QMJHL First All-Star Team (2011) • QMJHL Defenseman of the Year (2011)

DEVANE, Jamie (deh-VAYN, JAY-mee) TOR

Left wing. Shoots left. 6'5", 220 lbs. Born, Mississauga, Ont., February 20, 1991.
(Toronto's 4th choice, 68th overall, in 2009 Entry Draft).

			Regular Season					Playoffs				
Season	**Club**	**League**	**GP**	**G**	**A**	**Pts**	**PIM**	**GP**	**G**	**A**	**Pts**	**PIM**
2007-08	Vaughan Kings	GTHL	15	4	11	15	24	....	....	....	....	....
	Vaughan Vipers	OPJHL	19	2	0	2	17	1	0	0	0	0
2008-09	Plymouth Whalers	OHL	64	5	12	17	92	11	0	0	0	17
2009-10	Plymouth Whalers	OHL	51	6	8	14	84	9	0	1	1	12
	Toronto Marlies	AHL	2	0	0	0	4	....	....	....	....	....
2010-11	Plymouth Whalers	OHL	63	18	20	38	131	10	2	3	5	19

DIAZ, Raphael (DEE-az, ra-FIGH-ehl) MTL

Defense. Shoots right. 5'11", 194 lbs. Born, Baar, Switz., January 9, 1986.

			Regular Season					Playoffs				
Season	**Club**	**League**	**GP**	**G**	**A**	**Pts**	**PIM**	**GP**	**G**	**A**	**Pts**	**PIM**
2001-02	EV Zug Jr.	Swiss-Jr.	4	0	1	1	0	....	....	....	....	....
2002-03	EV Zug Jr.	Swiss-Jr.	30	7	10	17	32	7	1	1	2	12
2003-04	EV Zug Jr.	Swiss-Jr.	15	6	5	11	22	....	....	....	....	....
	EV Zug	Swiss	38	2	1	3	16	5	0	0	0	2
2004-05	EV Zug	Swiss	41	1	4	5	12	9	0	0	0	4
2005-06	EV Zug	Swiss	35	5	2	7	34	7	0	0	0	4
2006-07	EV Zug	Swiss	44	2	4	6	22	12	0	1	1	6
2007-08	EV Zug	Swiss	50	3	11	14	44	7	0	0	0	4
2008-09	EV Zug	Swiss	50	4	9	13	36	10	1	1	2	4
2009-10	EV Zug	Swiss	49	4	27	31	22	13	1	5	6	10
	Switzerland	Olympics	....	....	....	....	....	5	0	0	0	4
2010-11	EV Zug	Swiss	45	12	27	39	26	10	2	4	6	4

Signed as a free agent by **Montreal**, May 13, 2011.

DIDIER, Josiah (DIH-dee-ay, joh-SIGH-uh) MTL

Defense. Shoots right. 6'2", 199 lbs. Born, Littleton, CO, April 8, 1993.
(Montreal's 2nd choice, 97th overall, in 2011 Entry Draft).

			Regular Season					Playoffs				
Season	**Club**	**League**	**GP**	**G**	**A**	**Pts**	**PIM**	**GP**	**G**	**A**	**Pts**	**PIM**
2009-10	Colorado T-birds	Minor-CO	19	3	15	18	12	....	....	....	....	....
	Colorado T-birds	Exhib.	9	5	2	7	12	....	....	....	....	....
2010-11	Cedar Rapids	USHL	58	8	13	21	81	8	0	2	2	7

• Signed Letter of Intent to attend **University of Denver** (WCHA) in fall of 2011.

DIDIOMETE, Devin (dih-dee-OH-meht, DEH-vihn)

Left wing. Shoots left. 5'11", 195 lbs. Born, Stratford, Ont., May 9, 1988.
(Calgary's 7th choice, 187th overall, in 2006 Entry Draft).

			Regular Season					Playoffs				
Season	**Club**	**League**	**GP**	**G**	**A**	**Pts**	**PIM**	**GP**	**G**	**A**	**Pts**	**PIM**
2004-05	Sudbury Wolves	OHL	58	7	8	15	113	11	0	1	1	11
2005-06	Sudbury Wolves	OHL	60	15	21	36	202	10	0	4	4	26
2006-07	Sudbury Wolves	OHL	62	21	19	40	205	21	6	6	12	62
2007-08	Sarnia Sting	OHL	56	23	33	56	216	9	1	2	3	*40
2008-09	Hartford Wolf Pack	AHL	73	4	5	9	239	4	0	0	0	6
2009-10	Hartford Wolf Pack	AHL	34	0	2	2	119	....	....	....	....	....
	Charlotte	ECHL	15	2	2	4	128	....	....	....	....	....
2010-11	Connecticut Whale	AHL	63	6	4	10	303	....	....	....	....	....

Signed as a free agent by **NY Rangers**, October 20, 2008.

DIDOMENICO, Chris (dee-DOH-mehn-ih-koh,KRIHS) CHI

Center. Shoots right. 5'11", 165 lbs. Born, Toronto, Ont., February 20, 1989.
(Toronto's 5th choice, 164th overall, in 2007 Entry Draft).

			Regular Season					Playoffs				
Season	**Club**	**League**	**GP**	**G**	**A**	**Pts**	**PIM**	**GP**	**G**	**A**	**Pts**	**PIM**
2005-06	North York	GTHL	36	28	35	63	....	....	....	....	....	....
	North York	OPJHL	2	2	0	2	0	....	....	....	....	....
2006-07	Saint John	QMJHL	70	25	50	75	60	....	....	....	....	....
2007-08	Saint John	QMJHL	70	39	56	95	103	14	8	11	19	20
2008-09	Saint John	QMJHL	26	11	23	34	34	....	....	....	....	....
	Drummondville	QMJHL	25	8	17	25	28	15	4	*31	35	24
2009-10	Drummondville	QMJHL	12	7	15	22	10	14	7	14	21	18
2010-11	Rockford IceHogs	AHL	25	0	4	4	6	....	....	....	....	....
	Toledo Walleye	ECHL	37	9	16	25	31	....	....	....	....	....

QMJHL All-Rookie Team (2007)

• Missed majority of 2009-10 due to leg injury in playoff game vs. Shawinigan (QMJHL), May 5, 2009. Traded to **Chicago** by **Toronto** with Viktor Stalberg and Phillipe Paradis for Kris Versteeg and Bill Sweatt, June 30, 2010.

DIETRICH, Robert (DEET-rihkh, RAW-buhrt) NSH

Defense. Shoots right. 5'10", 178 lbs. Born, Ordzhonikidze, USSR, July 25, 1986.
(Nashville's 8th choice, 174th overall, in 2007 Entry Draft).

			Regular Season					Playoffs				
Season	**Club**	**League**	**GP**	**G**	**A**	**Pts**	**PIM**	**GP**	**G**	**A**	**Pts**	**PIM**
2001-02	Kaufbeuren Jr.	Ger-Jr.	9	1	2	3	2	....	....	....	....	....
2002-03	Mannheim Jr.	Ger-Jr.	33	4	13	17	39	3	0	1	1	4
2003-04	EC Peiting	German-3	42	5	9	24	83	....	....	....	....	....
2004-05	ETC Crimmitschau	German-2	45	3	14	17	34	10	0	0	0	6
2005-06	Straubing Tigers	German-2	46	5	3	8	55	15	0	1	1	8
	Dusseldorf	Germany	4	0	0	0	2	....	....	....	....	....
2006-07	Dusseldorf	Germany	52	3	19	22	28	9	2	4	6	22
2007-08	Dusseldorf	Germany	9	1	1	2	12	13	1	2	3	4
2008-09	Milwaukee	AHL	63	4	15	19	32	11	1	7	8	2
2009-10	Milwaukee	AHL	79	6	37	43	28	2	0	1	1	2
2010-11	Adler Mannheim	Germany	42	3	15	18	69	6	0	2	2	8

Signed as a free agent by **Mannheim** (Germany), June 8, 2010.

DIETZ, Darren (DEETZ, DAIR-uhn) MTL

Defense. Shoots right. 6'1", 193 lbs. Born, Medicine Hat, Alta., July 17, 1993.
(Montreal's 4th choice, 138th overall, in 2011 Entry Draft).

			Regular Season					Playoffs				
Season	**Club**	**League**	**GP**	**G**	**A**	**Pts**	**PIM**	**GP**	**G**	**A**	**Pts**	**PIM**
2008-09	Medicine Hat	AMHL	34	0	4	4	62	....	....	....	....	....
2009-10	Lethbridge	AMHL	33	9	15	24	105	5	4	3	7	14
	Saskatoon Blades	WHL	8	1	1	2	4	3	0	0	0	2
2010-11	Saskatoon Blades	WHL	68	8	19	27	66	10	1	4	5	15

DILLON, Brenden (DIHL-uhn, BREHN-duhn) DAL

Defense. Shoots left. 6'3", 209 lbs. Born, Surrey, B.C., November 13, 1990.

			Regular Season					Playoffs				
Season	**Club**	**League**	**GP**	**G**	**A**	**Pts**	**PIM**	**GP**	**G**	**A**	**Pts**	**PIM**
2007-08	Seattle	WHL	71	1	10	11	54	12	0	2	2	21
2008-09	Seattle	WHL	70	0	10	10	68	5	0	1	1	6
2009-10	Seattle	WHL	67	2	12	14	101	....	....	....	....	....
2010-11	Seattle	WHL	72	8	51	59	139	....	....	....	....	....
	Texas Stars	AHL	10	0	0	0	8	6	0	2	2	7

Signed as a free agent by **Dallas**, March 1, 2011.

DIXON, Stephen (DIHX-uhn, STEE-vehn) ANA

Center. Shoots left. 5'11", 188 lbs. Born, Halifax, N.S., September 7, 1985.
(Pittsburgh's 9th choice, 229th overall, in 2003 Entry Draft).

			Regular Season					Playoffs				
Season	**Club**	**League**	**GP**	**G**	**A**	**Pts**	**PIM**	**GP**	**G**	**A**	**Pts**	**PIM**
2001-02	Cape Breton	QMJHL	64	16	15	31	12	16	3	5	8	12
2002-03	Cape Breton	QMJHL	72	28	42	70	58	4	0	0	0	6
2003-04	Cape Breton	QMJHL	55	22	50	72	33	5	1	0	1	0
2004-05	Cape Breton	QMJHL	45	17	34	51	40	....	....	....	....	....
2005-06	Wilkes-Barre	AHL	80	12	17	29	45	11	0	1	1	4
2006-07	Wilkes-Barre	AHL	80	17	24	41	43	11	2	3	5	6
2007-08	Portland Pirates	AHL	80	17	28	45	43	18	6	4	10	10
2008-09	Brynas IF Gavle	Sweden	53	8	19	27	32	4	0	0	0	2
2009-10	Brynas IF Gavle	Sweden	53	20	15	35	55	5	0	0	0	2
2010-11	Amur Khabarovsk	Rus-KHL	47	7	10	17	8	....	....	....	....	....

Traded to **Anaheim** by **Pittsburgh** for Tim Brent, June 23, 2007.

DOBRYSHKIN, Yuri (doh-BRIHSH-kihn, YOO-ree) WPG

Right wing. Shoots right. 6', 189 lbs. Born, Penza, USSR, July 19, 1979.
(Atlanta's 7th choice, 159th overall, in 1999 Entry Draft).

			Regular Season					Playoffs				
Season	Club	League	GP	G	A	Pts	PIM	GP	G	A	Pts	PIM
1996-97	Krylja Sovetov 2	Russia-3	35	13	5	18	42	....	....	....	....	....
	Krylja Sovetov	Russia	2	0	0	0	0	2	0	0	0	0
1997-98	Krylja Sovetov 2	Russia-3	26	12	5	17	68	....	....	....	....	....
	Krylja Sovetov	Russia	22	4	0	4	12	....	....	....	....	....
1998-99	Krylja Sovetov	Russia	50	11	5	16	86	....	....	....	....	....
99-2000	Ak Bars Kazan	Russia	27	6	9	15	24	17	2	0	2	10
2000-01	Ak Bars Kazan	Russia	40	10	5	15	32	4	2	0	2	2
2001-02	Ak Bars Kazan	Russia	38	9	8	17	22	11	0	2	2	6
2002-03	Cherepovets	Russia	49	19	7	26	82	12	5	2	7	12
2003-04	Cherepovets	Russia	53	11	7	18	75	....	....	....	....	....
2004-05	Magnitogorsk	Russia	54	14	6	20	42	2	0	0	0	0
2005-06	Magnitogorsk	Russia	15	3	1	4	22	8	0	0	0	0
	Magnitogorsk 2	Russia-3	2	3	1	4	2	....	....	....	....	....
2006-07	CSKA Moscow	Russia	50	5	10	15	65	12	3	0	3	12
2007-08	Nizhny Novgorod	Russia	48	15	6	21	60	....	....	....	....	....
2008-09	Nizhny Novgorod	Rus-KHL	19	2	1	3	12	....	....	....	....	....
	Mytischi	Rus-KHL	8	1	0	1	2	2	0	0	0	0
2009-10	MVD	Rus-KHL	33	13	5	18	12	9	1	0	1	4
2010-11	Dynamo Moscow	Rus-KHL	18	2	2	4	16	....	....	....	....	....

DODGE, Nick (DAWGE, NIHK)

Right wing. Shoots right. 5'10", 185 lbs. Born, Oakville, Ont., May 1, 1986.
(Carolina's 5th choice, 183rd overall, in 2006 Entry Draft).

			Regular Season					Playoffs				
Season	Club	League	GP	G	A	Pts	PIM	GP	G	A	Pts	PIM
2004-05	Clarkson Knights	ECAC	37	6	12	18	42	....	....	....	....	....
2005-06	Clarkson Knights	ECAC	38	16	25	41	72	....	....	....	....	....
2006-07	Clarkson Knights	ECAC	36	18	21	39	32	....	....	....	....	....
2007-08	Clarkson Knights	ECAC	39	12	14	26	26	....	....	....	....	....
2008-09	Albany River Rats	AHL	80	13	26	39	34	....	....	....	....	....
2009-10	Albany River Rats	AHL	80	16	20	36	30	8	4	1	5	6
2010-11	Charlotte	AHL	57	5	8	13	18	16	4	2	6	8

ECAC First All-Star Team (2007) • NCAA East Second All-American Team (2007)

DOHERTY, Taylor (DOHR-eh-tee, TAY-luhr) S.J.

Defense. Shoots right. 6'7", 230 lbs. Born, Cambridge, Ont., March 2, 1991.
(San Jose's 2nd choice, 57th overall, in 2009 Entry Draft).

			Regular Season					Playoffs				
Season	Club	League	GP	G	A	Pts	PIM	GP	G	A	Pts	PIM
2006-07	Cambridge Hawks	Minor-ON	70	10	37	47	169	....	....	....	....	....
2007-08	Kingston	OHL	64	6	14	20	118	....	....	....	....	....
2008-09	Kingston	OHL	68	2	18	20	140	....	....	....	....	....
2009-10	Kingston	OHL	63	16	28	44	114	5	1	4	5	0
2010-11	Kingston	OHL	68	14	39	53	86	5	0	3	3	12
	Worcester Sharks	AHL	3	0	0	0	0	....	....	....	....	....

DONNELLY, Dillon (DAWN-ah-lee, DIH-luhn) COL

Defense. Shoots left. 6'2", 193 lbs. Born, Buffalo, NY, September 7, 1993.
(Colorado's 6th choice, 183rd overall, in 2011 Entry Draft).

			Regular Season					Playoffs				
Season	Club	League	GP	G	A	Pts	PIM	GP	G	A	Pts	PIM
2008-09	Lac St-Louis Lions	QAAA	43	4	9	13	124	5	0	0	0	28
2009-10	Moncton Wildcats	QMJHL	26	0	1	1	39	....	....	....	....	....
	Montreal	QMJHL	25	0	2	2	60	6	0	0	0	0
2010-11	Shawinigan	QMJHL	63	1	7	8	153	9	0	1	1	12

DONOVAN, Matt (DAWN-uh-vuhn, MAT) NYI

Defense. Shoots left. 6', 195 lbs. Born, Edmond, OK, May 9, 1990.
(NY Islanders' 8th choice, 96th overall, in 2008 Entry Draft).

			Regular Season					Playoffs				
Season	Club	League	GP	G	A	Pts	PIM	GP	G	A	Pts	PIM
2006-07	Dallas Stars AAA	NTHL	....	22	46	68	54	....	....	....	....	....
2007-08	Cedar Rapids	USHL	59	12	18	30	41	3	0	1	1	4
2008-09	Cedar Rapids	USHL	57	19	32	51	43	5	0	4	4	2
2009-10	U. of Denver	WCHA	36	7	14	21	50	....	....	....	....	....
2010-11	U. of Denver	WCHA	42	9	23	32	64	....	....	....	....	....
	Bridgeport	AHL	6	1	4	5	10	....	....	....	....	....

USHL All-Rookie Team (2008) • USHL First All-Star Team (2009) • WCHA All-Rookie Team (2010) • WCHA Second All-Star Team (2011)

DONSKOI, Joonas (DAWN-skoy, YOH-nuhs) FLA

Right wing. Shoots right. 6', 180 lbs. Born, Raahe, Finland, April 13, 1992.
(Florida's 10th choice, 99th overall, in 2010 Entry Draft).

			Regular Season					Playoffs				
Season	Club	League	GP	G	A	Pts	PIM	GP	G	A	Pts	PIM
2007-08	Karpat Oulu U18	Fin-U18	30	18	20	38	26	5	3	4	7	0
2008-09	Karpat Oulu U18	Fin-U18	4	2	5	7	0	6	6	7	13	0
	Karpat Oulu Jr.	Fin-Jr.	32	7	17	24	12	....	....	....	....	....
2009-10	Suomi U20	Finland-2	4	1	0	1	0	....	....	....	....	....
	Karpat Oulu Jr.	Fin-Jr.	18	14	15	29	2	12	5	10	15	4
	Karpat Oulu	Finland	18	2	2	4	4	....	....	....	....	....
	Karpat Oulu U18	Fin-U18	....	....	....	....	....	1	1	1	2	0
2010-11	Suomi U20	Finland-2	2	1	0	1	0	....	....	....	....	....
	Karpat Oulu	Finland	52	16	11	27	10	3	1	0	1	0

DOWD, Nic (DOWD, NIHK) L.A.

Center. Shoots right. 6'1", 175 lbs. Born, Huntsville, AL, May 27, 1990.
(Los Angeles' 10th choice, 198th overall, in 2009 Entry Draft).

			Regular Season					Playoffs				
Season	Club	League	GP	G	A	Pts	PIM	GP	G	A	Pts	PIM
2007-08	Culver Academy	High-IN	45	15	31	46	38	....	....	....	....	....
2008-09	Wenatchee Wild	NAHL	43	16	33	49	71	13	8	*14	*22	34
2009-10	Indiana Ice	USHL	46	16	23	39	48	9	2	4	6	2
2010-11	St. Cloud State	WCHA	36	5	13	18	34	....	....	....	....	....

DROZDETSKY, Alexander (drawz-DEHT-skee, al-EHX-AN-duhr) PHI

Right wing. Shoots left. 6', 180 lbs. Born, Moscow, USSR, November 10, 1981.
(Philadelphia's 2nd choice, 94th overall, in 2000 Entry Draft).

			Regular Season					Playoffs				
Season	Club	League	GP	G	A	Pts	PIM	GP	G	A	Pts	PIM
1997-98	St. Petersburg 2	Russia-3	19	0	1	1	0	....	....	....	....	....
1998-99	St. Petersburg 2	Russia-4	24	5	3	8	12	....	....	....	....	....
99-2000	St. Petersburg 2	Russia-3	4	4	1	5	2	....	....	....	....	....
	SKA St. Petersburg	Russia	32	2	0	2	10	4	0	0	0	0
2000-01	SKA St. Petersburg	Russia	42	6	7	13	74	....	....	....	....	....
2001-02	CSKA Moscow	Russia	49	11	6	17	26	....	....	....	....	....
2002-03	CSKA Moscow	Russia	46	14	13	27	30	....	....	....	....	....
2003-04	Ak Bars Kazan	Russia	57	16	15	31	62	1	0	0	0	2
2004-05	Ak Bars Kazan	Russia	32	3	4	7	28	....	....	....	....	....
	Ak Bars Kazan 2	Russia-3	....	10	8	18	....	....	....	....	....	....
	Nizhnekamsk	Russia	7	5	1	6	4	....	....	....	....	....
2005-06	Avangard Omsk	Russia	30	6	6	12	26	....	....	....	....	....
	SKA St. Petersburg	Russia	16	4	10	14	6	3	0	0	0	0
2006-07	SKA St. Petersburg	Russia	45	11	15	26	66	3	0	2	2	0
2007-08	St. Petersburg 2	Russia-3	12	9	9	18	6	....	....	....	....	....
	Spartak Moscow	Russia	32	11	6	17	40	5	4	3	7	2
2008-09	Spartak Moscow	Rus-KHL	47	14	13	27	38	6	1	3	4	2
2009-10	Cherepovets	Rus-KHL	11	1	0	1	4	....	....	....	....	....
	Nizhnekamsk	Rus-KHL	26	4	7	11	14	9	0	1	1	4
2010-11	Nizhnekamsk	Rus-KHL	6	0	0	0	4	....	....	....	....	....

DUMONT, Gabriel (doo-MAWNT, gah-BREE-ehl) MTL

Center. Shoots right. 5'9", 170 lbs. Born, Ville Degelis, Que., October 6, 1990.
(Montreal's 5th choice, 139th overall, in 2009 Entry Draft).

			Regular Season					Playoffs				
Season	Club	League	GP	G	A	Pts	PIM	GP	G	A	Pts	PIM
2006-07	Ecole Notre Dame	QAAA	39	30	42	72	127	13	11	12	23	20
	Drummondville	QMJHL	8	1	1	2	6	6	0	2	2	0
2007-08	Drummondville	QMJHL	59	11	14	25	103	....	....	....	....	....
2008-09	Drummondville	QMJHL	51	28	21	49	63	19	6	13	19	32
2009-10	Drummondville	QMJHL	62	*51	42	93	127	14	*11	10	21	19
	Hamilton Bulldogs	AHL	....	....	....	....	....	11	2	0	2	12
2010-11	Hamilton Bulldogs	AHL	64	5	13	18	79	20	6	3	9	6

QMJHL First All-Star Team (2010) • Canadian Major Junior Second All-Star Team (2010)

DUMOULIN, Brian (DOO-moh-lihn, BRIGH-uhn) CAR

Defense. Shoots left. 6'3", 205 lbs. Born, Biddeford, ME, September 6, 1991.
(Carolina's 2nd choice, 51st overall, in 2009 Entry Draft).

			Regular Season					Playoffs				
Season	Club	League	GP	G	A	Pts	PIM	GP	G	A	Pts	PIM
2007-08	Biddeford Tigers	High-ME	24	13	48	61	10	....	....	....	....	....
2008-09	N.H. Jr. Monarchs	EJHL	41	7	23	30	30	7	0	3	3	2
2009-10	Boston College	H-East	42	1	21	22	16	....	....	....	....	....
2010-11	Boston College	H-East	37	3	30	33	6	....	....	....	....	....

NCAA Championship All-Tournament Team (2010) • Hockey East First All-Star Team (2011) • NCAA East First All-American Team (2011)

DUROCHER, Corey (doo-ROH-shay, KOH-ree) FLA

Left wing. Shoots left. 6'3", 183 lbs. Born, Ottawa, Ont., May 30, 1992.
(Florida's 12th choice, 153rd overall, in 2010 Entry Draft).

			Regular Season					Playoffs				
Season	Club	League	GP	G	A	Pts	PIM	GP	G	A	Pts	PIM
2007-08	Ott. Jr. Senators	Minor-ON	53	18	22	40	12	....	....	....	....	....
2008-09	Gloucester	CJHL	60	7	20	27	16	4	0	2	2	0
2009-10	Kingston	OHL	66	15	11	26	31	7	2	0	2	4
2010-11	Kingston	OHL	63	14	23	37	26	5	0	1	1	2

DZINGEL, Ryan (ZIHN-guhl, RIGH-uhn) OTT

Center. Shoots left. 5'11", 180 lbs. Born, Wheaton, IL, March 9, 1992.
(Ottawa's 10th choice, 204th overall, in 2011 Entry Draft).

			Regular Season					Playoffs				
Season	Club	League	GP	G	A	Pts	PIM	GP	G	A	Pts	PIM
2006-07	Chicago Mission	MWEHL	31	12	8	20	26	....	....	....	....	....
2007-08	Team Illinois	MWEHL	31	6	14	20	20	....	....	....	....	....
2008-09	Team Illinois	T1EHL	31	18	15	33	30	....	....	....	....	....
2009-10	Team Illinois	T1EHL	31	19	27	46	28	....	....	....	....	....
2010-11	Lincoln Stars	USHL	54	23	44	67	8	2	1	0	1	2

• Signed Letter of Intent to attend **Ohio State** (CCHA).

DZIURZYNSKI, Darian (z'yuhr-ZIHN-skee, dair-EE-uhn) PHX

Left wing. Shoots left. 6'1", 208 lbs. Born, Prince Albert, Sask., March 30, 1991.
(Phoenix's 6th choice, 141st overall, in 2011 Entry Draft).

			Regular Season					Playoffs				
Season	Club	League	GP	G	A	Pts	PIM	GP	G	A	Pts	PIM
2007-08	Lloydminster	AMHL	26	20	15	35	98	....	....	....	....	....
	Saskatoon Blades	WHL	33	3	1	4	18	....	....	....	....	....
	Lloydminster	AJHL	2	0	0	0	0	....	....	....	....	....
2008-09	Saskatoon Blades	WHL	64	10	15	25	96	7	0	1	1	6
2009-10	Saskatoon Blades	WHL	70	14	15	29	156	7	3	6	9	9
2010-11	Saskatoon Blades	WHL	72	35	22	57	125	10	3	3	6	18

DZIURZYNSKI, David (z'yuhr-IHN-skee, DAY-vihd) OTT

Center. Shoots left. 6'3", 214 lbs. Born, Lloydminster, Alta., October 6, 1989.

			Regular Season					Playoffs				
Season	Club	League	GP	G	A	Pts	PIM	GP	G	A	Pts	PIM
2007-08	Lloydminster	AJHL	52	8	12	20	82	3	0	0	0	4
2008-09	Lloydminster	AJHL	54	12	25	37	185	4	0	1	1	2
2009-10	Alberni Valley	BCHL	57	21	53	74	79	13	9	10	19	8
2010-11	Binghamton	AHL	75	6	14	20	57	14	0	3	3	4

Signed as a free agent by **Ottawa**, April 6, 2010.

EAKIN, Cody (EE-kihn, KOH-dee) **WSH**

Center. Shoots left. 6', 189 lbs. Born, Winnipeg, Man., May 24, 1991.
(Washington's 3rd choice, 85th overall, in 2009 Entry Draft).

			Regular Season					Playoffs				
Season	Club	League	GP	G	A	Pts	PIM	GP	G	A	Pts	PIM
2006-07	Winnipeg Wild	MMHL	38	29	35	64	62	7	5	4	9	10
	Swift Current	WHL	3	0	0	0	0	....	....	....	....	....
2007-08	Swift Current	WHL	55	11	6	17	52	12	3	4	7	6
2008-09	Swift Current	WHL	54	24	24	48	42	7	3	0	3	10
2009-10	Swift Current	WHL	70	47	44	91	71	4	1	1	2	2
	Hershey Bears	AHL	4	2	0	2	2	5	0	0	0	2
2010-11	Swift Current	WHL	30	18	21	39	24	....	....	....	....	....
	Kootenay Ice	WHL	26	18	26	44	19	19	11	16	27	14

WHL East Second All-Star Team (2010, 2011)

EDMUNDSON, Joel (EHD-muhnd-suhn, JOHL) **ST.L.**

Defense. Shoots left. 6'5", 190 lbs. Born, Brandon, MB, June 28, 1993.
(St. Louis' 3rd choice, 46th overall, in 2011 Entry Draft).

			Regular Season					Playoffs				
Season	Club	League	GP	G	A	Pts	PIM	GP	G	A	Pts	PIM
2008-09	Brandon	MMHL	41	5	18	23	58	6	2	4	6	4
2009-10	Brandon	MMHL	44	10	25	35	54	7	0	5	5	10
2010-11	Moose Jaw	WHL	71	2	18	20	95	6	0	0	0	2

EHRHARDT, Travis (AIR-hahrt, TRA-vihs) **DET**

Defense. Shoots left. 5'11", 204 lbs. Born, Calgary, Alta., April 12, 1989.

			Regular Season					Playoffs				
Season	Club	League	GP	G	A	Pts	PIM	GP	G	A	Pts	PIM
2004-05	Cgy. North Stars	AMHL	11	0	0	0	0	....	....	....	....	....
	Moose Jaw	WHL	2	0	1	1	2	....	....	....	....	....
2005-06	Moose Jaw	WHL	45	1	10	11	37	18	0	2	2	18
2006-07	Moose Jaw	WHL	69	0	29	29	83	....	....	....	....	....
2007-08	Moose Jaw	WHL	18	3	9	12	27	....	....	....	....	....
	Portland	WHL	54	7	22	29	53	....	....	....	....	....
2008-09	Portland	WHL	68	9	28	37	109	....	....	....	....	....
	Manitoba Moose	AHL	3	0	0	0	0	....	....	....	....	....
2009-10	Grand Rapids	AHL	42	0	5	5	38	....	....	....	....	....
	Toledo Walleye	ECHL	3	1	1	2	0	....	....	....	....	....
2010-11	Grand Rapids	AHL	52	4	11	15	36	....	....	....	....	....

Signed as a free agent by **Detroit**, July 7, 2009.

EKHOLM, Mattias (EHK-hohlm, ma-TEE-uhs) **NSH**

Defense. Shoots left. 6'4", 204 lbs. Born, Borlange, Sweden, May 24, 1990.
(Nashville's 7th choice, 102nd overall, in 2009 Entry Draft).

			Regular Season					Playoffs				
Season	Club	League	GP	G	A	Pts	PIM	GP	G	A	Pts	PIM
2006-07	Mora IK U18	Swe-U18	5	2	2	4	6	....	....	....	....	....
	Mora IK Jr.	Swe-Jr.	36	0	4	4	28	2	0	0	0	0
2007-08	Mora IK U18	Swe-U18	9	4	5	9	12	....	....	....	....	....
	Mora IK Jr.	Swe-Jr.	37	5	7	12	54	....	....	....	....	....
	Mora IK	Sweden	1	0	0	0	0	....	....	....	....	....
	Mora IK	Sweden-Q	6	0	0	0	2	....	....	....	....	....
2008-09	Mora IK Jr.	Swe-Jr.	21	3	5	8	32	....	....	....	....	....
	Mora IK	Sweden-2	38	2	11	13	12	3	0	0	0	4
2009-10	Mora IK	Sweden-2	41	1	21	22	54	2	0	0	0	6
2010-11	Brynas IF Gavle	Sweden	55	10	23	33	38	5	0	4	4	10

ELLINGTON, Taylor (EHL-ihng-tuhn, TAY-luhr) **VAN**

Defense. Shoots left. 6', 200 lbs. Born, Victoria, B.C., October 31, 1988.
(Vancouver's 2nd choice, 33rd overall, in 2007 Entry Draft).

			Regular Season					Playoffs				
Season	Club	League	GP	G	A	Pts	PIM	GP	G	A	Pts	PIM
2004-05	Everett Silvertips	WHL	47	0	0	0	48	8	0	1	1	4
2005-06	Everett Silvertips	WHL	63	0	7	7	62	15	1	2	3	16
2006-07	Everett Silvertips	WHL	60	5	8	13	65	6	1	0	1	2
2007-08	Everett Silvertips	WHL	48	3	11	14	66	4	0	0	0	0
2008-09	Everett Silvertips	WHL	69	6	26	32	130	5	0	5	5	6
	Manitoba Moose	AHL	1	1	0	1	0	....	....	....	....	....
2009-10	Manitoba Moose	AHL	19	1	3	4	9	....	....	....	....	....
	Victoria	ECHL	48	3	11	14	49	....	....	....	....	....
2010-11	Victoria	ECHL	14	0	3	3	18	....	....	....	....	....

ELLIOTT, Stefan (ehl-LEE-awt, STEH-fan) **COL**

Defense. Shoots right. 6'1", 192 lbs. Born, Vancouver, B.C., January 30, 1991.
(Colorado's 3rd choice, 49th overall, in 2009 Entry Draft).

			Regular Season					Playoffs				
Season	Club	League	GP	G	A	Pts	PIM	GP	G	A	Pts	PIM
2006-07	Van. NW Giants	BCMML	36	12	19	31	18	....	....	....	....	....
	Saskatoon Blades	WHL	1	0	0	0	0	....	....	....	....	....
2007-08	Saskatoon Blades	WHL	67	9	31	40	17	....	....	....	....	....
2008-09	Saskatoon Blades	WHL	71	16	39	55	26	7	1	3	4	4
2009-10	Saskatoon Blades	WHL	72	26	39	65	24	10	3	5	8	4
2010-11	Saskatoon Blades	WHL	71	31	50	81	14	10	3	5	8	0
	Lake Erie Monsters	AHL	....	....	....	....	....	5	0	2	2	0

Canadian Major Junior Scholastic Player of the Year (2009) • WHL East First All-Star Team (2011)

ELLIS, Morgan (EHL-ihs, MOHR-guhn) **MTL**

Defense. Shoots right. 6'2", 198 lbs. Born, Summerside, P.E.I., April 30, 1992.
(Montreal's 3rd choice, 117th overall, in 2010 Entry Draft).

			Regular Season					Playoffs				
Season	Club	League	GP	G	A	Pts	PIM	GP	G	A	Pts	PIM
2007-08	Charlottetown	NBPEI	33	3	4	7	28	7	0	2	2	10
	Charlottetown	Exhib.	16	2	6	8	16	....	....	....	....	....
2008-09	Cape Breton	QMJHL	52	0	6	6	45	10	0	1	1	4
2009-10	Cape Breton	QMJHL	60	4	25	29	56	5	1	0	1	10
2010-11	Cape Breton	QMJHL	65	8	28	36	65	4	0	0	0	8

ELLIS, Ryan (EHL-ihs, RIGH-uhn) **NSH**

Defense. Shoots right. 5'10", 179 lbs. Born, Hamilton, Ont., January 3, 1991.
(Nashville's 1st choice, 11th overall, in 2009 Entry Draft).

			Regular Season					Playoffs				
Season	Club	League	GP	G	A	Pts	PIM	GP	G	A	Pts	PIM
2006-07	Cambridge Hawks	Minor-ON	75	37	56	93	151	....	....	....	....	....
2007-08	Windsor Spitfires	OHL	63	15	48	63	51	5	2	3	5	2
2008-09	Windsor Spitfires	OHL	57	22	*67	89	57	20	8	*23	31	20
2009-10	Windsor Spitfires	OHL	48	12	49	61	38	19	3	*30	33	14
2010-11	Windsor Spitfires	OHL	58	24	77	101	61	18	6	13	19	12
	Milwaukee	AHL	....	....	....	....	....	7	1	1	2	2

Canadian Major Junior All-Rookie Team (2008) • OHL First All-Star Team (2009, 2011) • Canadian Major Junior First All-Star Team (2009) • Memorial Cup All-Star Team (2009, 2010) • OHL Second All-Star Team (2010) • Canadian Major Junior Defenseman of the Year (2011) • Canadian Major Junior Player of the Year (2011)

ELSNER, David (EHLZ-nuhr, DAY-vihd) **NSH**

Left wing. Shoots right. 6', 184 lbs. Born, Landshut, Germany, March 22, 1992.
(Nashville's 5th choice, 194th overall, in 2010 Entry Draft).

			Regular Season					Playoffs				
Season	Club	League	GP	G	A	Pts	PIM	GP	G	A	Pts	PIM
2007-08	EV Landshut Jr.	Ger-Jr.	36	11	8	19	16	3	1	0	1	4
2008-09	EV Landshut Jr.	Ger-Jr.	36	17	18	35	46	9	2	8	10	10
2009-10	EV Landshut Jr.	Ger-Jr.	17	10	7	17	63	5	2	4	6	12
	Landshut Cann.	German-2	29	6	3	9	6	6	0	0	0	16
2010-11	ERC Ingolstadt	Germany	3	1	0	1	0	....	....	....	....	....
	Landshut Cann.	German-2	31	4	1	5	65	6	0	1	1	6
	EV Landshut Jr.	Ger-Jr.	6	2	4	6	6	9	5	4	9	2

• Loaned to **Ingolstadt** (Germany) by **Landshut** (German-2) for start of 2010-11 season.

ERIXON, Sebastian (AIR-ihk-suhn, seh-BAZ-tee-ehn) **VAN**

Defense. Shoots left. 5'10", 183 lbs. Born, Sundsvalll, Sweden, September 12, 1989.

			Regular Season					Playoffs				
Season	Club	League	GP	G	A	Pts	PIM	GP	G	A	Pts	PIM
2004-05	Timra IK Jr.	Swe-Jr.	2	0	0	0	0	....	....	....	....	....
2005-06	Timra IK Jr.	Swe-Jr.	14	3	2	5	16	....	....	....	....	....
2006-07	Timra IK Jr.	Swe-Jr.	4	3	0	3	6	....	....	....	....	....
	Timra IK	Sweden	2	0	0	0	0	....	....	....	....	....
2007-08	Timra IK	Sweden	27	0	0	0	2	....	....	....	....	....
	Sundsvall	Sweden-2	23	2	3	5	7	....	....	....	....	....
2009-10	Timra IK	Sweden	46	4	3	7	14	....	....	....	....	....
2010-11	Timra IK	Sweden	44	5	15	20	20	....	....	....	....	....

Signed as a free agent by **Vancouver**, April 20, 2011.

ERIXON, Tim (AIR-ihx-uhn, TIHM) **NYR**

Defense. Shoots left. 6'2", 190 lbs. Born, Port Chester, NY, February 24, 1991.
(Calgary's 1st choice, 23rd overall, in 2009 Entry Draft).

			Regular Season					Playoffs				
Season	Club	League	GP	G	A	Pts	PIM	GP	G	A	Pts	PIM
2005-06	Skelleftea U18	Swe-U18	9	0	2	2	4	....	....	....	....	....
2006-07	Skelleftea U18	Swe-U18	8	2	2	4	20	....	....	....	....	....
	Skelleftea Jr.	Swe-Jr.	8	0	2	2	2	2	0	0	0	4
2007-08	Skelleftea U18	Swe-U18	4	0	1	1	10	....	....	....	....	....
	Skelleftea Jr.	Swe-Jr.	28	3	11	14	78	1	0	1	1	4
	Skelleftea AIK HK	Sweden	2	0	0	0	0	....	....	....	....	....
2008-09	Skelleftea AIK U18	Swe-U18	1	0	2	2	10	5	1	5	6	14
	Skelleftea AIK Jr.	Swe-Jr.	9	2	12	14	10	5	1	2	3	4
	Malmo	Sweden-2	3	0	2	2	0	....	....	....	....	....
	Skelleftea AIK	Sweden	45	2	5	7	12	9	0	0	0	4
2009-10	Skelleftea AIK	Sweden	45	7	6	13	44	12	1	0	1	8
2010-11	Skelleftea AIK	Sweden	48	5	19	24	40	18	3	5	8	12

Traded to **NY Rangers** by **Calgary** with Calgary's 5th round choice (Shane McColgan) in 2011 Entry Draft for Roman Horak, NY Rangers' 2nd round choice (Markus Granlund) in 2011 Entry Draft and Pittsburgh's 2nd round choice (previously acquired, Calgary selected Tyler Wotherspoon) in 2011 Entry Draft, June 1, 2011.

ERONEN, Teemu (AIR-roh-nehn, TEE-moo) **ST.L.**

Defense. Shoots left. 5'11", 180 lbs. Born, Vantaa, Finland, November 22, 1990.
(St. Louis' 8th choice, 192nd overall, in 2011 Entry Draft).

			Regular Season					Playoffs				
Season	Club	League	GP	G	A	Pts	PIM	GP	G	A	Pts	PIM
2006-07	Jokerit U18	Fin-U18	33	7	19	26	42	3	1	1	2	0
2007-08	Jokerit U18	Fin-U18	25	4	22	26	43	3	0	4	4	2
	Jokerit Helsinki Jr.	Fin-Jr.	16	3	0	3	14	4	0	1	1	6
2008-09	Suomi U20	Finland-2	2	0	0	0	2	....	....	....	....	....
	Jokerit Helsinki Jr.	Fin-Jr.	41	5	22	27	18	4	0	1	1	2
	Jokerit Helsinki	Finland	1	0	0	0	0	....	....	....	....	....
2009-10	Suomi U20	Finland-2	2	0	1	1	0	....	....	....	....	....
	Jokerit Helsinki Jr.	Fin-Jr.	11	0	14	14	8	....	....	....	....	....
	Jokerit Helsinki	Finland	33	1	11	12	18	2	0	2	2	0
2010-11	Jokerit Helsinki	Finland	48	2	11	13	24	7	1	2	3	6

ERSTAD, Travis (UHR-stad, TRA-vihs) **ST.L.**

Center/Right wing. Shoots right. 6'4", 199 lbs. Born, Madison, WI, November 9, 1988.
(St. Louis' 8th choice, 100th overall, in 2007 Entry Draft).

			Regular Season					Playoffs				
Season	Club	League	GP	G	A	Pts	PIM	GP	G	A	Pts	PIM
2005-06	Stevens Point High	High-WI	STATISTICS NOT AVAILABLE									
2006-07	Stevens Point High	High-WI	24	31	33	64	....	....	....	....	....	....
	Lincoln Stars	USHL	8	0	0	0	4	3	1	0	1	0
2007-08	Lincoln Stars	USHL	52	9	10	19	104	8	1	2	3	8
2008-09	Wisc-Stevens Pt.	NCHA	26	10	7	17	56	....	....	....	....	....
2009-10	Wisc-Stevens Pt.	NCHA	23	5	10	15	....	....	....	....	....	....
2010-11	Wisc-Stevens Pt.	NCHA	DID NOT PLAY – INJURED									

• Missed entire 2010-11 due to back surgery.

ESPOSITO, Angelo (EHS-poh-ZEE-toh, AN-jul-loh) FLA

Center. Shoots left. 6'2", 190 lbs. Born, Montreal, Que., February 20, 1989.
(Pittsburgh's 1st choice, 20th overall, in 2007 Entry Draft).

			Regular Season					Playoffs				
Season	Club	League	GP	G	A	Pts	PIM	GP	G	A	Pts	PIM
2004-05	Shat.-St. Mary's	High-MN	68	31	35	66	47	....	....	....	....	....
2005-06	Quebec Remparts	QMJHL	57	39	59	98	45	23	6	5	11	4
2006-07	Quebec Remparts	QMJHL	60	27	52	79	63	5	4	3	7	2
2007-08	Quebec Remparts	QMJHL	56	30	39	69	69	11	4	6	10	6
	Chicago Wolves	AHL	1	0	0	0	0	....	....	....	....	....
2008-09	Montreal	QMJHL	35	24	18	42	25	....	....	....	....	....
2009-10	Chicago Wolves	AHL	12	0	4	4	2	....	....	....	....	....
2010-11	Chicago Wolves	AHL	57	3	10	13	35	....	....	....	....	....

QMJHL All-Rookie Team (2006) • QMJHL Offensive Rookie of the Year (2006)

Traded to **Atlanta** by **Pittsburgh** with Colby Armstrong, Erik Christensen and Pittsburgh's 1st round choice (Daultan Leveille) in 2008 Entry Draft for Marian Hossa and Pascal Dupuis, February 26, 2008. • Missed majority of 2009-10 due to knee injury vs. Texas (AHL), November 22, 2009. • Transferred to **Winnipeg** after **Atlanta** franchise relocated, June 21, 2011. Traded to **Florida** by **Winnipeg** for Kenndal McArdle, July 9, 2011.

ETEM, Emerson (EE-tehm, EHM-ur-suhn) ANA

Right wing. Shoots left. 6'1", 197 lbs. Born, Long Beach, CA, June 16, 1992.
(Anaheim's 2nd choice, 29th overall, in 2010 Entry Draft).

			Regular Season					Playoffs				
Season	Club	League	GP	G	A	Pts	PIM	GP	G	A	Pts	PIM
2007-08	Shat.-St. Mary's	High-MN	58	13	15	28	20	....	....	....	....	....
2008-09	USNTDP	NAHL	40	19	14	33	16	9	4	4	8	4
	USNTDP	U-17	13	6	7	13	0	....	....	....	....	....
2009-10	Medicine Hat	WHL	72	37	28	65	26	12	7	3	10	0
2010-11	Medicine Hat	WHL	65	45	35	80	24	15	10	11	21	7

EVERSON, Max (EHV-uhr-suhn, MAX) TOR

Defense. Shoots left. 6'1", 185 lbs. Born, Edina, MN, February 22, 1993.
(Toronto's 9th choice, 203rd overall, in 2011 Entry Draft).

			Regular Season					Playoffs				
Season	Club	League	GP	G	A	Pts	PIM	GP	G	A	Pts	PIM
2009-10	Edina Hornets	High-MN	21	2	8	10	10	6	1	1	2	2
2010-11	Team Southwest	UMHSEL	7	1	4	5	0	2	0	0	0	0
	Edina Hornets	High-MN	22	4	17	21	20	6	0	4	4	4
	USNTDP	USHL	5	1	1	2	2	....	....	....	....	....
	USNTDP	U-18	12	0	1	1	10	....	....	....	....	....

• Signed Letter of Intent to attend **Harvard University** (ECAC) in fall of 2011.

EWANYK, Travis (ee-WAHN-ihk, TRA-vihs) EDM

Left wing. Shoots left. 6'1", 176 lbs. Born, North Vancouver, B.C., March 29, 1993.
(Edmonton's 5th choice, 74th overall, in 2011 Entry Draft).

			Regular Season					Playoffs				
Season	Club	League	GP	G	A	Pts	PIM	GP	G	A	Pts	PIM
2007-08	St. Albert Sabres	AMBHL	30	12	19	31	66	2	0	1	1	2
2008-09	St. Albert Raiders	AMHL	33	7	12	19	14	2	0	0	0	4
	Edmonton	WHL	2	0	0	0	0	3	0	0	0	0
2009-10	Edmonton	WHL	42	1	4	5	45	....	....	....	....	....
2010-11	Edmonton	WHL	72	16	11	27	126	4	0	0	0	13

EZHOV, Denis (YEHZH-awf, DEH-nihs) BUF

Defense. Shoots left. 5'11", 200 lbs. Born, Togliatti, USSR, February 28, 1985.
(Buffalo's 5th choice, 114th overall, in 2003 Entry Draft).

			Regular Season					Playoffs				
Season	Club	League	GP	G	A	Pts	PIM	GP	G	A	Pts	PIM
99-2000	Lada Togliatti 2	Russia-3	4	0	0	0	4	....	....	....	....	....
2000-01	Lada Togliatti 2	Russia-3	STATISTICS NOT AVAILABLE									
2001-02	Lada Togliatti 2	Russia-3	4	2	4	6	6	....	....	....	....	....
	Lada Togliatti	Russia	15	0	0	0	6	....	....	....	....	....
2002-03	Lada Togliatti 2	Russia-3	15	2	7	9	4	....	....	....	....	....
	CSK VVS Samara	Russia-2	9	0	1	1	8	....	....	....	....	....
2003-04	Novokuznetsk	Russia	19	0	1	1	2	3	0	0	0	0
	CSKA Moscow 2	Russia-3	4	1	2	3	2	....	....	....	....	....
2004-05	Novokuznetsk	Russia	28	0	0	0	16	4	0	0	0	2
2005-06	Mytischi	Russia	24	1	0	1	10	....	....	....	....	....
	Kristall Elektrostal	Russia-3	STATISTICS NOT AVAILABLE									
2006-07	Chelyabinsk	Russia	54	2	6	8	73	....	....	....	....	....
2007-08	Chelyabinsk	Russia	57	4	9	13	64	3	0	0	0	10
2008-09	Omsk	Rus-KHL	55	2	8	10	58	8	1	0	1	2
2009-10	Omsk	Rus-KHL	31	0	4	4	58	....	....	....	....	....
2010-11	Chelyabinsk	Rus-KHL	44	2	2	4	40	....	....	....	....	....

FAIRCHILD, Cade (FAIR-chighld, KAYD) ST.L.

Defense. Shoots left. 5'11", 190 lbs. Born, Duluth, MN, January 15, 1989.
(St. Louis' 7th choice, 96th overall, in 2007 Entry Draft).

			Regular Season					Playoffs				
Season	Club	League	GP	G	A	Pts	PIM	GP	G	A	Pts	PIM
2004-05	Duluth East	High-MN	29	10	32	42	....	....	....	....	....	....
2005-06	USNTDP	U-17	18	2	7	9	4	....	....	....	....	....
	USNTDP	NAHL	36	8	9	17	10	2	0	0	0	0
2006-07	USNTDP	U-18	36	3	16	19	34	....	....	....	....	....
	USNTDP	NAHL	13	1	6	7	16	....	....	....	....	....
2007-08	U. of Minnesota	WCHA	40	2	13	15	22	....	....	....	....	....
2008-09	U. of Minnesota	WCHA	35	9	24	33	52	....	....	....	....	....
2009-10	U. of Minnesota	WCHA	39	4	17	21	36	....	....	....	....	....
2010-11	U. of Minnesota	WCHA	35	6	18	24	12	....	....	....	....	....

WCHA All-Rookie Team (2008)

FALLSTROM, Alexander (FAHL-struhm, al-ehx-AN-duhr) BOS

Right wing. Shoots right. 6'2", 192 lbs. Born, Goteborg, Sweden, September 15, 1990.
(Minnesota's 4th choice, 116th overall, in 2009 Entry Draft).

			Regular Season					Playoffs				
Season	Club	League	GP	G	A	Pts	PIM	GP	G	A	Pts	PIM
2005-06	Djurgarden U18	Swe-U18	11	1	2	3	2	....	....	....	....	....
2006-07	Djurgarden U18	Swe-U18	33	22	15	37	52	3	2	1	3	2
	Djurgarden Jr.	Swe-Jr.	2	0	0	0	0	1	0	0	0	0
2007-08	Shat.-St. Mary's	High-MN	62	20	27	47	56	....	....	....	....	....
2008-09	Shat.-St. Mary's	High-MN	52	40	47	87	52	....	....	....	....	....
2009-10	Harvard Crimson	ECAC	32	4	8	12	23	....	....	....	....	....
2010-11	Harvard Crimson	ECAC	22	7	5	12	17	....	....	....	....	....

Traded to **Boston** by **Minnesota** with Craig Weller and Minnesota's 2nd round choice (Alexander Khokhlachev) in 2011 Entry Draft for Chuck Kobasew, October 18, 2009.

FASTH, Jesper (FAHST, YEHS-puhr) NYR

Right wing. Shoots right. 5'11", 165 lbs. Born, Nassjo, Sweden, December 2, 1991.
(NY Rangers' 5th choice, 157th overall, in 2010 Entry Draft).

			Regular Season					Playoffs				
Season	Club	League	GP	G	A	Pts	PIM	GP	G	A	Pts	PIM
2007-08	HV 71 U18	Swe-U18	30	15	11	26	14	....	....	....	....	....
	HV 71 Jr.	Swe-Jr.	3	0	0	0	2	....	....	....	....	....
2008-09	HV 71 U18	Swe-U18	3	2	2	4	2	....	....	....	....	....
	HV 71 Jr.	Swe-Jr.	37	7	7	14	16	7	2	1	3	6
2009-10	HV 71 Jr.	Swe-Jr.	37	23	26	49	10	3	0	2	2	0
	HV 71 Jonkoping	Sweden	2	0	0	0	0	....	....	....	....	....
2010-11	HV 71 Jonkoping	Sweden	36	7	9	16	6	3	0	0	0	0
	HV 71 Jr.	Swe-Jr.	6	3	7	10	4	3	2	2	4	2

FAULK, Justin (FAWLK, JUHS-tihn) CAR

Defense. Shoots right. 6', 205 lbs. Born, South St. Paul, MN, March 20, 1992.
(Carolina's 2nd choice, 37th overall, in 2010 Entry Draft).

			Regular Season					Playoffs				
Season	Club	League	GP	G	A	Pts	PIM	GP	G	A	Pts	PIM
2007-08	South St. Paul	High-MN	26	6	15	21	32	....	....	....	....	....
2008-09	USNTDP	NAHL	38	3	9	12	20	9	3	3	6	6
	USNTDP	U-17	17	7	9	16	35	....	....	....	....	....
	USNTDP	U-18	1	0	0	0	0	....	....	....	....	....
2009-10	USNTDP	USHL	21	9	3	12	46	....	....	....	....	....
	USNTDP	U-18	39	12	9	21	20	....	....	....	....	....
2010-11	U. Minn-Duluth	WCHA	39	8	25	33	47	....	....	....	....	....
	Charlotte	AHL	....	....	....	....	....	13	0	2	2	2

WCHA All-Rookie Team (2011)

FAUST, Joe (FOWST, JOH) N.J.

Defense. Shoots right. 6', 195 lbs. Born, Edina, MN, November 15, 1991.
(New Jersey's 3rd choice, 114th overall, in 2010 Entry Draft).

			Regular Season					Playoffs				
Season	Club	League	GP	G	A	Pts	PIM	GP	G	A	Pts	PIM
2007-08	Bloomington-Jeff.	High-MN	28	4	14	18	10	....	....	....	....	....
2008-09	Bloomington-Jeff.	High-MN	28	14	26	40	12	....	....	....	....	....
2009-10	Team Southeast	UMHSEL	24	3	6	9	....	....	....	....	....	....
	Bloomington-Jeff.	High-MN	25	12	28	40	18	3	2	4	6	2
2010-11	U. of Wisconsin	WCHA	20	1	1	2	8	....	....	....	....	....

FEDUN, Taylor (fuh-DOON, TAY-luhr) EDM

Defense. Shoots right. 6'1", 210 lbs. Born, Edmonton, Alta., June 4, 1988.

			Regular Season					Playoffs				
Season	Club	League	GP	G	A	Pts	PIM	GP	G	A	Pts	PIM
2004-05	Ft. Saskatchewan	AJHL	1	0	1	1	0	....	....	....	....	....
2005-06	Ft. Saskatchewan	AJHL	60	13	18	31	72	3	1	1	2	4
2006-07	Spruce Grove	AJHL	50	10	33	43	103	10	3	5	8	31
2007-08	Princeton	ECAC	32	4	10	14	32	....	....	....	....	....
2008-09	Princeton	ECAC	35	3	12	15	50	....	....	....	....	....
2009-10	Princeton	ECAC	31	3	14	17	34	....	....	....	....	....
2010-11	Princeton	ECAC	29	10	12	22	38	....	....	....	....	....

Signed as a free agent by **Edmonton**, March 8, 2011.

FERLAND, Michael (FAIR-land, MIGH-kuhl) CGY

Left wing. Shoots left. 6'2", 208 lbs. Born, Swan River, Man., April 20, 1992.
(Calgary's 5th choice, 133rd overall, in 2010 Entry Draft).

			Regular Season					Playoffs				
Season	Club	League	GP	G	A	Pts	PIM	GP	G	A	Pts	PIM
2007-08	Brandon	MMHL	40	12	8	20	20	6	3	2	5	4
2008-09	Brandon	MMHL	44	45	40	85	52	6	4	5	9	8
2009-10	Brandon	WHL	61	9	19	28	85	15	3	1	4	8
2010-11	Brandon	WHL	56	23	33	56	110	6	4	2	6	4

FERLIN, Brian (FUHR-lihn, BRIGH-uhn) BOS

Right wing. Shoots right. 6'2", 201 lbs. Born, Jacksonville, FL, June 3, 1992.
(Boston's 4th choice, 121st overall, in 2011 Entry Draft).

			Regular Season					Playoffs				
Season	Club	League	GP	G	A	Pts	PIM	GP	G	A	Pts	PIM
2009-10	Indiana Ice	USHL	57	6	10	16	36	8	1	2	3	2
2010-11	Indiana Ice	USHL	55	25	48	73	26	5	1	4	5	4

• Signed Letter of Intent to attend **Cornell University** (ECAC).

FERRARO, Landon (fuh-RAHR-oh, LAN-duhn) DET

Center. Shoots right. 6', 170 lbs. Born, Trail, B.C., August 8, 1991.
(Detroit's 1st choice, 32nd overall, in 2009 Entry Draft).

			Regular Season					Playoffs				
Season	Club	League	GP	G	A	Pts	PIM	GP	G	A	Pts	PIM
2006-07	Van. NW Giants	BCMML	25	21	13	34	77	....	....	....	....	....
	Red Deer Rebels	WHL	4	0	0	0	0	1	0	0	0	0
2007-08	Red Deer Rebels	WHL	54	13	11	24	65	....	....	....	....	....
2008-09	Red Deer Rebels	WHL	68	37	18	55	99	....	....	....	....	....
2009-10	Red Deer Rebels	WHL	53	16	30	46	55	3	0	0	0	2
	Grand Rapids	AHL	2	0	0	0	0	....	....	....	....	....
2010-11	Everett Silvertips	WHL	41	10	17	27	51	4	0	3	3	13

FERRIERO, Cody (fair-ee-AIR-oh, KOH-dee) S.J.

Center. Shoots right. 5'11", 200 lbs. Born, Boston, MA, December 19, 1991.
(San Jose's 3rd choice, 127th overall, in 2010 Entry Draft).

			Regular Season					Playoffs				
Season	Club	League	GP	G	A	Pts	PIM	GP	G	A	Pts	PIM
2006-07	Gov. Academy	High-MA	27	6	3	9	26	....	....	....	....	....
2007-08	Gov. Academy	High-MA	25	13	9	22	26	....	....	....	....	....
2008-09	Gov. Academy	High-MA	27	10	10	20	87	....	....	....	....	....
2009-10	Gov. Academy	High-MA	27	21	19	40	112	....	....	....	....	....
2010-11	Northeastern	H-East	34	4	3	7	38	....	....	....	....	....

FIENHAGE, Corey
(fihn-AW-gee, KOH-ree)   **BUF**

Defense. Shoots right. 6'2", 215 lbs.   Born, Topeka, KS, May 4, 1990.
(Buffalo's 4th choice, 81st overall, in 2008 Entry Draft).

			Regular Season					Playoffs			
Season	Club	League	GP	G	A	Pts	PIM	GP	G	A Pts	PIM
2005-06	Eastview High	High-MN	25	1	6	7	32	....	....	....	....
2006-07	Eastview High	High-MN	20	4	11	15	....	....	....	....	....
	Team Southeast	UMWEHL	11	4	4	8	....	....	....	....	....
2007-08	Eastview High	High-MN	26	6	10	16	87	....	....	....	....
	Team Southeast	UMWEHL	12	2	4	6	....	....	....	....	....
	Indiana Ice	USHL	12	1	2	3	12	2	0	0 0	0
2008-09	North Dakota	WCHA	9	0	1	1	28	....	....	....	....
2009-10	North Dakota	WCHA	30	0	2	2	28	....	....	....	....
2010-11	Kamloops Blazers	WHL	70	4	10	14	96	....	....	....	....
	Portland Pirates	AHL	4	0	0	0	6	6	0	0 0	4

FIGREN, Robin
(FIH-grehn, RAW-bihn)

Wing. Shoots right. 5'11", 188 lbs.   Born, Stockholm, Sweden, March 7, 1988.
(NY Islanders' 3rd choice, 70th overall, in 2006 Entry Draft).

			Regular Season					Playoffs			
Season	Club	League	GP	G	A	Pts	PIM	GP	G	A Pts	PIM
2003-04	Hammarby U18	Swe-U18	11	5	5	10	22	....	....	....	....
2004-05	Frolunda U18	Swe-U18	12	13	8	21	94	7	4	4 8	10
	Frolunda Jr.	Swe-Jr.	4	1	2	3	0	....	....	....	....
2005-06	Frolunda Jr.	Swe-Jr.	38	10	18	28	72	7	4	2 6	6
	Frolunda	Sweden	2	0	0	0	0	....	....	....	....
	Frolunda U18	Swe-U18	1	1	0	1	2	2	2	0 2	0
2006-07	Calgary Hitmen	WHL	62	10	17	27	54	18	4	4 8	18
2007-08	Edmonton	WHL	35	18	13	31	46	....	....	....	....
2008-09	Djurgarden	Sweden	49	3	6	9	28	....	....	....	....
	Bridgeport	AHL	3	0	1	1	2	....	....	....	....
2009-10	Bridgeport	AHL	62	3	4	7	24	4	1	1 2	6
2010-11	Bridgeport	AHL	76	14	16	30	39	....	....	....	....

FILPPULA, Ilari
(FIHL-poo-luh)

Left wing. Shoots left. 5'11", 189 lbs.   Born, Vantaa, Finland, November 5, 1981.

			Regular Season					Playoffs			
Season	Club	League	GP	G	A	Pts	PIM	GP	G	A Pts	PIM
1996-97	Kiekko-Vantaa Jr.	Fin-Jr.	1	0	2	2	0	....	....	....	....
1997-98	K-Vantaa U18	Fin-U18	21	10	17	27	12	....	....	....	....
	Kiekko-Vantaa Jr.	Fin-Jr.	1	1	1	2	0	....	....	....	....
1998-99	Kiekko-Vantaa Jr.	Fin-Jr.	19	7	5	12	4	....	....	....	....
99-2000	K-Vantaa U18	Fin-U18	4	2	1	3	0	....	....	....	....
	Kiekko-Vantaa Jr.	Fin-Jr.	28	12	44	56	39	....	....	....	....
	Kiekko-Vantaa	Finland-3	2	0	0	0	0	....	....	....	....
2000-01	Jokerit Helsinki Jr.	Fin-Jr.	38	18	40	58	16	2	1	0 1	0
2001-02	Kiekko-Vantaa	Finland-2	44	13	22	35	20	5	4	2 6	2
2002-03	Kiekko-Vantaa	Finland-2	41	19	28	47	14	12	0	7 7	4
	Jokerit Helsinki	Finland	1	0	0	0	0	....	....	....	....
2003-04	JYP Jyvaskyla	Finland	47	3	6	9	12	1	0	0 0	0
2004-05	JYP Jyvaskyla	Finland	55	8	10	18	10	3	1	0 1	0
2005-06	Jokerit Helsinki	Finland	56	9	16	25	14	....	....	....	....
2006-07	JYP Jyvaskyla	Finland	54	15	26	41	36	....	....	....	....
2007-08	JYP Jyvaskyla	Finland	56	7	15	22	20	6	0	1 1	0
2008-09	TPS Turku	Finland	48	6	17	23	47	8	0	3 3	6
2009-10	TPS Turku	Finland	58	12	37	49	24	15	2	*12 14	6
2010-11	Grand Rapids	AHL	76	20	44	64	24	....	....	....	....

Signed as a free agent by **Detroit**, June 16, 2010.

FLEMMING, Brett
(FLEH-mihng, BREHT)   **WSH**

Defense. Shoots right. 5'11", 184 lbs.   Born, Regina, Sask., February 26, 1991.
(Washington's 5th choice, 145th overall, in 2009 Entry Draft).

			Regular Season					Playoffs			
Season	Club	League	GP	G	A	Pts	PIM	GP	G	A Pts	PIM
2006-07	Burlington Eagles	Minor-ON	67	15	36	51	130	....	....	....	....
2007-08	St. Michael's	OHL	47	1	9	10	30	4	0	0 0	6
2008-09	St. Michael's	OHL	64	3	25	28	89	10	1	3 4	2
2009-10	St. Michael's	OHL	68	1	23	24	90	16	0	5 5	10
2010-11	St. Michael's	OHL	68	4	39	43	79	20	1	12 13	28

FLICK, Rob
(FLIHK, RAWB)   **CHI**

Center. Shoots left. 6'2", 208 lbs.   Born, London, Ont., March 28, 1991.
(Chicago's 7th choice, 120th overall, in 2010 Entry Draft).

			Regular Season					Playoffs			
Season	Club	League	GP	G	A	Pts	PIM	GP	G	A Pts	PIM
2007-08	Lon. Jr. Knights	Minor-ON	57	32	29	61	160	....	....	....	....
	London Nationals	ON-Jr.B	8	0	1	1	25	....	....	....	....
2008-09	St. Michael's	OHL	48	4	4	8	69	10	1	1 2	14
2009-10	St. Michael's	OHL	65	15	19	34	157	16	2	2 4	*44
2010-11	St. Michael's	OHL	68	27	30	57	167	20	8	8 16	34

FLOREK, Justin
(FLOHR-ehk, JUHS-tihn)   **BOS**

Left wing. Shoots left. 6'4", 194 lbs.   Born, Marquette, MI, May 18, 1990.
(Boston's 5th choice, 135th overall, in 2010 Entry Draft).

			Regular Season					Playoffs			
Season	Club	League	GP	G	A	Pts	PIM	GP	G	A Pts	PIM
2006-07	USNTDP	NAHL	47	11	10	21	40	6	3	0 3	4
	USNTDP	U-17	13	6	1	7	8	....	....	....	....
2007-08	USNTDP	NAHL	13	3	3	6	8	....	....	....	....
	USNTDP	U-17	1	0	0	0	2	....	....	....	....
	USNTDP	U-18	41	5	5	10	20	....	....	....	....
2008-09	Northern Mich.	CCHA	40	9	8	17	6	....	....	....	....
2009-10	Northern Mich.	CCHA	41	12	23	35	22	....	....	....	....
2010-11	Northern Mich.	CCHA	39	13	15	28	14	....	....	....	....

FLYNN, Ryan
(FLIHN, RIGH-uhn)   **NSH**

Right wing. Shoots right. 6'3", 210 lbs.   Born, St. Paul, MN, March 22, 1988.
(Nashville's 4th choice, 176th overall, in 2006 Entry Draft).

			Regular Season					Playoffs			
Season	Club	League	GP	G	A	Pts	PIM	GP	G	A Pts	PIM
2003-04	Centennial	High-MN	30	29	39	68	....	....	....	....	....
2004-05	USNTDP	U-17	14	4	5	9	12	....	....	....	....
	USNTDP	NAHL	41	11	8	19	31	9	2	4 6	7
2005-06	USNTDP	U-18	42	10	12	22	57	....	....	....	....
	USNTDP	NAHL	17	6	5	11	20	....	....	....	....
2006-07	U. of Minnesota	WCHA	43	5	8	13	58	....	....	....	....
2007-08	U. of Minnesota	WCHA	38	4	11	15	51	....	....	....	....
2008-09	U. of Minnesota	WCHA	37	6	13	19	62	....	....	....	....
2009-10	U. of Minnesota	WCHA	38	2	8	10	36	....	....	....	....
	Milwaukee	AHL	2	0	0	0	0	1	0	0 0	0
2010-11	Milwaukee	AHL	65	6	6	12	41	9	0	0 0	4

FOGARTY, Steven
(FOH-guhr-tee, STEE-vehn)   **NYR**

Center. Shoots right. 6'2", 194 lbs.   Born, Chambersburg, PA, April 19, 1993.
(NY Rangers' 2nd choice, 72nd overall, in 2011 Entry Draft).

			Regular Season					Playoffs			
Season	Club	League	GP	G	A	Pts	PIM	GP	G	A Pts	PIM
2009-10	Edina Hornets	High-MN	25	18	12	30	4	6	3	7 10	2
2010-11	Team Southwest	UMHSEL	19	10	4	14	10	3	2	5 7	4
	Edina Hornets	High-MN	24	23	17	40	12	6	2	7 9	10
	Chicago Steel	USHL	6	2	0	2	2	....	....	....	....

• Signed Letter of Intent to attend **University of Notre Dame** (CCHA) in fall of 2012.

FOLIGNO, Marcus
(foh-LEE-noh, MAHR-kuhs)   **BUF**

Left wing. Shoots left. 6'3", 227 lbs.   Born, Buffalo, NY, August 10, 1991.
(Buffalo's 3rd choice, 104th overall, in 2009 Entry Draft).

			Regular Season					Playoffs			
Season	Club	League	GP	G	A	Pts	PIM	GP	G	A Pts	PIM
2006-07	Sud. Nickel Cap's	Minor-ON	30	21	15	36	70	....	....	....	....
2007-08	Sudbury Wolves	OHL	66	5	6	11	38	....	....	....	....
2008-09	Sudbury Wolves	OHL	65	12	18	30	96	6	1	2 3	9
2009-10	Sudbury Wolves	OHL	67	14	25	39	156	4	1	1 2	6
2010-11	Sudbury Wolves	OHL	47	23	36	59	92	8	2	1 3	24

OHL Second All-Star Team (2011)

FONTAINE, Justin
(fawn-TAYN, JUHS-tihn)   **MIN**

Right wing. Shoots right. 5'10", 175 lbs.   Born, Bonnyville, Alta., November 6, 1987.

			Regular Season					Playoffs			
Season	Club	League	GP	G	A	Pts	PIM	GP	G	A Pts	PIM
2004-05	Bonnyville Pontiacs	AJHL	12	1	4	5	12	....	....	....	....
2005-06	Bonnyville Pontiacs	AJHL	50	26	55	81	36	9	1	6 7	4
2006-07	Bonnyville Pontiacs	AJHL	52	30	41	71	60	5	3	5 8	10
2007-08	U. Minn-Duluth	WCHA	35	4	8	12	8	....	....	....	....
2008-09	U. Minn-Duluth	WCHA	43	15	33	48	18	....	....	....	....
2009-10	U. Minn-Duluth	WCHA	39	21	25	46	22	....	....	....	....
2010-11	U. Minn-Duluth	WCHA	42	22	36	58	42	....	....	....	....

WCHA Second All-Star Team (2010, 2011)
Signed as a free agent by **Minnesota**, April 19, 2011.

FORBORT, Derek
(FOHR-bohrt, DAIR-ihk)   **L.A.**

Defense. Shoots left. 6'5", 198 lbs.   Born, Duluth, MN, March 4, 1992.
(Los Angeles' 1st choice, 15th overall, in 2010 Entry Draft).

			Regular Season					Playoffs			
Season	Club	League	GP	G	A	Pts	PIM	GP	G	A Pts	PIM
2008-09	Duluth East	High-MN	25	7	21	28	....	....	....	....	....
	USNTDP	NAHL	2	0	1	1	6	....	....	....	....
	USNTDP	U-17	7	1	4	5	4	....	....	....	....
2009-10	USNTDP	USHL	26	4	10	14	26	....	....	....	....
	USNTDP	U-18	39	1	13	14	20	....	....	....	....
2010-11	North Dakota	WCHA	38	0	15	15	26	....	....	....	....

FORD, Matthew
(FOHRD, MA-thew)   **WSH**

Right wing. Shoots right. 6'1", 207 lbs.   Born, West Hills, CA, October 9, 1984.
(Chicago's 16th choice, 256th overall, in 2004 Entry Draft).

			Regular Season					Playoffs			
Season	Club	League	GP	G	A	Pts	PIM	GP	G	A Pts	PIM
2003-04	Sioux Falls	USHL	60	*37	31	68	60	....	....	....	....
2004-05	U. of Wisconsin	WCHA	21	5	5	10	18	....	....	....	....
2005-06	U. of Wisconsin	WCHA	31	5	2	7	14	....	....	....	....
2006-07	U. of Wisconsin	WCHA	39	7	6	13	38	....	....	....	....
2007-08	U. of Wisconsin	WCHA	33	4	5	9	30	....	....	....	....
2008-09	Hartford Wolf Pack	AHL	25	1	2	3	10	....	....	....	....
	Lake Erie Monsters	AHL	5	0	0	0	2	....	....	....	....
	Charlotte	ECHL	28	21	17	38	25	6	2	3 5	21
2009-10	Lake Erie Monsters	AHL	45	13	14	27	28	....	....	....	....
	Charlotte	ECHL	3	0	2	2	6	....	....	....	....
2010-11	Lake Erie Monsters	AHL	76	26	16	42	46	7	3	1 4	8

USHL Rookie of the Year (2004)

FORNEY, Michael
(FOHR-NEE, MIGH-kuhl)   **WPG**

Right wing. Shoots right. 6'2", 200 lbs.   Born, Thief River Falls, MN, May 14, 1988.
(Atlanta's 3rd choice, 80th overall, in 2006 Entry Draft).

			Regular Season					Playoffs			
Season	Club	League	GP	G	A	Pts	PIM	GP	G	A Pts	PIM
2002-03	Thief River Falls	High-MN	28	4	10	14	....	....	....	....	....
2003-04	Thief River Falls	High-MN	24	14	22	36	....	....	....	....	....
2004-05	Thief River Falls	High-MN	28	34	33	67	....	....	....	....	....
2005-06	Thief River Falls	High-MN	21	23	37	60	28	....	....	....	....
	Des Moines	USHL	3	0	0	0	0	....	....	....	....
2006-07	North Dakota	WCHA	16	0	2	2	10	....	....	....	....
2007-08	North Dakota	WCHA	3	0	0	0	2	....	....	....	....
2008-09	Green Bay	USHL	59	26	34	60	53	7	3	7 10	2
2009-10	Chicago Wolves	AHL	3	0	0	0	0	....	....	....	....
	Gwinnett	ECHL	63	11	15	26	66	....	....	....	....
2010-11	Chicago Wolves	AHL	9	0	2	2	0	....	....	....	....
	Gwinnett	ECHL	66	21	45	66	79	....	....	....	....

FORTIER, Olivier (FOHR-t'yay, OH-lihv-ee-ay) MTL

Center. Shoots left. 5'11", 181 lbs. Born, Quebec City, Que., May 2, 1989.
(Montreal's 4th choice, 65th overall, in 2007 Entry Draft).

			Regular Season					Playoffs				
Season	**Club**	**League**	**GP**	**G**	**A**	**Pts**	**PIM**	**GP**	**G**	**A**	**Pts**	**PIM**
2004-05	Sem. St-Francois	QAAA	31	7	17	24	8	4	2	1	3	4
2005-06	Drummondville	QMJHL	13	2	2	4	14	....	....	....	....	....
	Rimouski Oceanic	QMJHL	27	4	8	12	16	....	....	....	....	....
2006-07	Rimouski Oceanic	QMJHL	69	28	36	64	28	....	....	....	....	....
2007-08	Rimouski Oceanic	QMJHL	67	23	23	46	37	3	1	0	1	4
2008-09	Rimouski Oceanic	QMJHL	29	8	27	35	12	13	4	5	9	12
2009-10	Hamilton Bulldogs	AHL	1	0	0	0	0	10	1	0	1	0
2010-11	Hamilton Bulldogs	AHL	68	9	11	20	20	1	1	0	1	0

• Missed majority of 2008-09 due to knee injury at Baie-Comeau (QMJHL), October 31, 2008. • Missed majority of 2009-10 due to shoulder injury.

FOSS, Jeff (FAWS, JEHF)

Defense. Shoots right. 6'2", 205 lbs. Born, Fargo, ND, December 12, 1988.
(Nashville's 5th choice, 166th overall, in 2008 Entry Draft).

			Regular Season					Playoffs				
Season	**Club**	**League**	**GP**	**G**	**A**	**Pts**	**PIM**	**GP**	**G**	**A**	**Pts**	**PIM**
2004-05	Moorhead Spuds	High-MN	22	1	4	5	6	....	....	....	....	....
2005-06	Moorhead Spuds	High-MN	26	4	17	21	16	....	....	....	....	....
	Team Great Plains	UMWEHL	11	4	9	13	....	....	....	....	....	....
2006-07	Moorhead Spuds	High-MN	26	15	31	46	28	....	....	....	....	....
	Team Great Plains	UMWEHL	12	3	13	16	....	....	....	....	....	....
	Sioux Falls	USHL	11	0	1	1	10	4	0	1	1	2
2007-08	RPI Engineers	ECAC	38	1	3	4	28	....	....	....	....	....
2008-09	RPI Engineers	ECAC	39	2	9	11	58	....	....	....	....	....
2009-10	RPI Engineers	ECAC	39	2	7	9	32	....	....	....	....	....
2010-11	RPI Engineers	ECAC	38	3	11	14	48	....	....	....	....	....
	Milwaukee	AHL	5	0	1	1	10	....	....	....	....	....

FOUCAULT, Kris (foo-KOH, KRIHS) MIN

Left wing. Shoots left. 6'1", 202 lbs. Born, Calgary, Alta., December 12, 1990.
(Minnesota's 3rd choice, 103rd overall, in 2009 Entry Draft).

			Regular Season					Playoffs				
Season	**Club**	**League**	**GP**	**G**	**A**	**Pts**	**PIM**	**GP**	**G**	**A**	**Pts**	**PIM**
2006-07	Calgary Buffaloes	AMHL	35	7	6	13	46	....	....	....	....	....
	Swift Current	WHL	3	0	0	0	0	....	....	....	....	....
2007-08	Kootenay Ice	WHL	33	0	3	3	12	8	2	1	3	2
2008-09	Kootenay Ice	WHL	4	0	1	1	4	....	....	....	....	....
	Canmore Eagles	AJHL	32	18	23	41	84	....	....	....	....	....
	Calgary Hitmen	WHL	22	9	7	16	12	18	11	5	16	10
2009-10	Calgary Hitmen	WHL	68	22	21	43	31	23	9	7	16	21
2010-11	Calgary Hitmen	WHL	65	25	23	48	60	....	....	....	....	....
	Houston Aeros	AHL	1	0	0	0	0	....	....	....	....	....

FOURNIER, Gleason (FOHR-nyay, GLEE-suhn) DET

Defense. Shoots left. 6', 184 lbs. Born, Rimouski, Que., September 8, 1991.
(Detroit's 4th choice, 90th overall, in 2009 Entry Draft).

			Regular Season					Playoffs				
Season	**Club**	**League**	**GP**	**G**	**A**	**Pts**	**PIM**	**GP**	**G**	**A**	**Pts**	**PIM**
2006-07	Ecole Notre Dame	QAAA	44	3	17	20	32	13	0	2	2	30
2007-08	Rimouski Oceanic	QMJHL	56	3	8	11	26	3	0	0	0	0
2008-09	Rimouski Oceanic	QMJHL	66	3	25	28	64	4	0	0	0	0
2009-10	Rimouski Oceanic	QMJHL	58	13	37	50	76	12	2	10	12	10
2010-11	Rimouski Oceanic	QMJHL	57	12	32	44	58	4	1	1	2	12

FRANSOO, Jordan (FRAN-soo, JOHR-duhn) OTT

Defense. Shoots right. 6'2", 180 lbs. Born, North Battleford, Sask., April 25, 1993.
(Ottawa's 9th choice, 186th overall, in 2011 Entry Draft).

			Regular Season					Playoffs				
Season	**Club**	**League**	**GP**	**G**	**A**	**Pts**	**PIM**	**GP**	**G**	**A**	**Pts**	**PIM**
2008-09	Battleford Stars	SMHL	28	1	4	5	32	....	....	....	....	....
2009-10	Sask. Contacts	SMHL	42	11	20	31	56	11	1	3	4	21
	Brandon	WHL	....	....	....	....	....	4	0	0	0	0
2010-11	Brandon	WHL	63	6	12	18	72	6	0	1	1	6

FRANSSON, Johan (FRAN-suhn, YOH-han) L.A.

Defense. Shoots left. 6'1", 192 lbs. Born, Kalix, Sweden, February 18, 1985.
(Dallas' 2nd choice, 34th overall, in 2004 Entry Draft).

			Regular Season					Playoffs				
Season	**Club**	**League**	**GP**	**G**	**A**	**Pts**	**PIM**	**GP**	**G**	**A**	**Pts**	**PIM**
2000-01	Kalix HF	Sweden-3	19	0	6	6	8	....	....	....	....	....
2001-02	Lulea HF U18	Swe-U18	5	2	0	2	0	....	....	....	....	....
	Lulea HF Jr.	Swe-Jr.	29	4	4	8	28	5	0	1	1	8
2002-03	Lulea HF Jr.	Swe-Jr.	24	2	4	6	67	....	....	....	....	....
	Lulea HF U18	Swe-U18	2	0	0	0	2	....	....	....	....	....
	Lulea HF	Sweden	3	0	0	0	0	....	....	....	....	....
2003-04	Lulea HF Jr.	Swe-Jr.	5	0	2	2	10	....	....	....	....	....
	Lulea HF	Sweden	44	3	3	6	28	2	0	0	0	4
2004-05	Lulea HF Jr.	Swe-Jr.	1	1	1	2	0	7	1	2	3	4
	Lulea HF	Sweden	43	1	6	7	30	3	0	0	0	0
2005-06	Lulea HF	Sweden	50	3	5	8	74	6	1	1	2	6
2006-07	Frolunda	Sweden	35	0	6	6	18	....	....	....	....	....
	Assat Pori	Finland	6	0	1	1	2	....	....	....	....	....
	Linkopings HC	Sweden	8	0	0	0	4	15	0	0	0	2
2007-08	Linkopings HC	Sweden	48	5	9	14	24	16	0	5	5	16
2008-09	Linkopings HC	Sweden	40	3	7	10	24	....	....	....	....	....
	HC Lugano	Swiss	7	2	3	5	2	4	2	0	2	0
2009-10	Lulea HF	Sweden	54	11	19	30	26	....	....	....	....	....
2010-11	SKA St. Petersburg	Rus-KHL	38	6	10	16	22	11	0	2	2	2

• Rights traded to **Los Angeles** by **Dallas** with Jaroslav Modry, Dallas' 2nd (Oscar Moller) and 3rd (Bryan Cameron) round choices in 2007 Entry Draft and Dallas' 1st round choice (later traded to Phoenix - Phoenix selected Viktor Tikhonov) in 2008 Entry Draft for Mattias Norstrom, Konstantin Pushkarev and Los Angeles' 3rd (Sergei Korostin) and 4th (later traded to Columbus - Columbus selected Maxim Mayorov) round choices in 2007 Entry Draft, February 27, 2007. • Loaned to **St. Petersburg** (Russia-KHL) by **Los Angeles**, October 13, 2010.

FRASER, Matt (FRAY-zuhr, MAT) DAL

Left wing. Shoots left. 6'2", 218 lbs. Born, Red Deer, Alta., May 20, 1990.

			Regular Season					Playoffs				
Season	**Club**	**League**	**GP**	**G**	**A**	**Pts**	**PIM**	**GP**	**G**	**A**	**Pts**	**PIM**
2005-06	Red Deer Chiefs	Minor-AB	33	31	23	54	62	....	....	....	....	....
	Red Deer	AMHL	1	0	1	1	0	....	....	....	....	....
2006-07	Red Deer	AMHL	23	8	17	25	47	10	1	6	7	4
	Red Deer Rebels	WHL	3	0	0	0	2	1	0	0	0	0
2007-08	Red Deer Rebels	WHL	5	0	0	0	2	....	....	....	....	....
	Kootenay Ice	WHL	63	9	11	20	48	8	1	1	2	0
2008-09	Kootenay Ice	WHL	63	10	14	24	123	4	0	2	2	12
2009-10	Kootenay Ice	WHL	65	32	24	56	117	6	1	1	2	12
	Peoria Rivermen	AHL	2	0	0	0	0	....	....	....	....	....
2010-11	Kootenay Ice	WHL	66	36	38	74	115	19	*17	10	27	18

Signed as a free agent by **Dallas**, November 18, 2010.

FRIBERG, Max (FREE-buhrg, MAX) ANA

Right wing. Shoots right. 5'10", 195 lbs. Born, Skovde, Sweden, November 20, 1992.
(Anaheim's 6th choice, 143rd overall, in 2011 Entry Draft).

			Regular Season					Playoffs				
Season	**Club**	**League**	**GP**	**G**	**A**	**Pts**	**PIM**	**GP**	**G**	**A**	**Pts**	**PIM**
2007-08	Skovde IK U18	Swe-U18	24	6	3	9	44	....	....	....	....	....
	Skovde IK Jr.	Swe-Jr.	12	1	2	3	0	....	....	....	....	....
2008-09	Skovde IK U18	Swe-U18	10	14	18	32	4	....	....	....	....	....
	Skovde IK Jr.	Swe-Jr.	17	13	7	20	18	....	....	....	....	....
	Skovde IK	Sweden-3	24	1	3	4	2	....	....	....	....	....
2009-10	Skovde IK U18	Swe-U18	5	5	6	11	2	....	....	....	....	....
	Skovde IK Jr.	Swe-Jr.	1	0	3	3	0	....	....	....	....	....
	Skovde IK	Sweden-3	36	12	18	30	22	....	....	....	....	....
2010-11	Skovde IK Jr.	Swe-Jr.	2	1	3	4	2	....	....	....	....	....
	Skovde IK	Sweden-3	34	13	27	40	6	....	....	....	....	....

FRIESEN, Alex (FREE-zuhn, Al-ehx) VAN

Center. Shoots left. 5'10", 186 lbs. Born, Niagara-on-the-Lake, Ont., January 30, 1991.
(Vancouver's 3rd choice, 172nd overall, in 2010 Entry Draft).

			Regular Season					Playoffs				
Season	**Club**	**League**	**GP**	**G**	**A**	**Pts**	**PIM**	**GP**	**G**	**A**	**Pts**	**PIM**
2006-07	Niag. Falls Thunder	Minor-ON	69	45	67	112	66	....	....	....	....	....
2007-08	Niagara Ice Dogs	OHL	46	5	9	14	26	10	0	2	2	6
2008-09	Niagara Ice Dogs	OHL	64	11	22	33	94	12	3	7	10	25
2009-10	Niagara Ice Dogs	OHL	60	23	37	60	94	5	1	6	7	8
2010-11	Niagara Ice Dogs	OHL	60	26	40	66	61	14	2	8	10	19

FRITSCH, Andrew (FRIHTCH, AN-droo) PHX

Right wing. Shoots right. 6', 187 lbs. Born, Brantford, Ont., March 24, 1993.
(Phoenix's 7th choice, 155th overall, in 2011 Entry Draft).

			Regular Season					Playoffs				
Season	**Club**	**League**	**GP**	**G**	**A**	**Pts**	**PIM**	**GP**	**G**	**A**	**Pts**	**PIM**
2008-09	Brantford 99s	Minor-ON	59	33	38	71	12	....	....	....	....	....
2009-10	Niagara Ice Dogs	OHL	62	11	7	18	13	5	1	0	1	0
2010-11	Niagara Ice Dogs	OHL	2	1	0	1	0	....	....	....	....	....
	Owen Sound	OHL	58	27	35	62	18	7	0	2	2	2

FROESE, Byron (FRAYZ, BIGH-ruhn) CHI

Center. Shoots right. 6'1", 180 lbs. Born, Winkler, Man., March 12, 1991.
(Chicago's 4th choice, 119th overall, in 2009 Entry Draft).

			Regular Season					Playoffs				
Season	**Club**	**League**	**GP**	**G**	**A**	**Pts**	**PIM**	**GP**	**G**	**A**	**Pts**	**PIM**
2007-08	Pembina Valley	MMHL	23	14	20	34	8	11	7	7	14	8
2008-09	Everett Silvertips	WHL	72	19	38	57	30	5	0	3	3	4
2009-10	Everett Silvertips	WHL	70	29	32	61	37	7	3	2	5	0
2010-11	Red Deer Rebels	WHL	70	43	38	81	37	9	5	2	7	4

GABRIEL, Oliver (gah-BREE-ehl, AWL-ih-vuhr) CBJ

Left wing. Shoots left. 6'2", 193 lbs. Born, Edmonton, Alta., May 13, 1991.

			Regular Season					Playoffs				
Season	**Club**	**League**	**GP**	**G**	**A**	**Pts**	**PIM**	**GP**	**G**	**A**	**Pts**	**PIM**
2006-07	CAC United Cycle	Minor-AB	31	11	17	28	71	....	....	....	....	....
2007-08	CAC B & P	Minor-AB	STATISTICS NOT AVAILABLE									
	Gregg Distributors	AMHL	1	1	0	1	0	....	....	....	....	....
2008-09	Portland	WHL	50	6	5	11	32	....	....	....	....	....
2009-10	Portland	WHL	41	10	14	24	28	13	2	4	6	9
2010-11	Portland	WHL	41	11	21	32	36	....	....	....	....	....

Signed as a free agent by **Columbus**, October 7, 2010.

GAEDE, Max (GAYD, MAX) S.J.

Right wing. Shoots right. 6'2", 190 lbs. Born, Maryland, MN, March 27, 1992.
(San Jose's 2nd choice, 88th overall, in 2010 Entry Draft).

			Regular Season					Playoffs				
Season	**Club**	**League**	**GP**	**G**	**A**	**Pts**	**PIM**	**GP**	**G**	**A**	**Pts**	**PIM**
2007-08	Woodbury	High-MN	26	5	11	16	2	....	....	....	....	....
2008-09	Woodbury	High-MN	27	16	28	44	66	....	....	....	....	....
2009-10	Team Southeast	UMHSEL	23	5	6	11	....	....	....	....	....	....
	Woodbury	High-MN	25	19	17	36	36	3	3	0	3	0
2010-11	Sioux City	USHL	54	10	18	28	57	3	0	0	0	2

• Signed Letter of Intent to attend **Minnesota State University** (WCHA) in fall of 2011.

GALIEV, Stanislav (gah-LEE-ehv, stan-ihs-LAHV) WSH

Right wing. Shoots right. 6'1", 188 lbs. Born, Moscow, Russia, January 17, 1992.
(Washington's 2nd choice, 86th overall, in 2010 Entry Draft).

			Regular Season					Playoffs				
Season	**Club**	**League**	**GP**	**G**	**A**	**Pts**	**PIM**	**GP**	**G**	**A**	**Pts**	**PIM**
2008-09	Indiana Ice	USHL	60	29	35	64	46	13	5	4	9	8
2009-10	Saint John	QMJHL	67	15	45	60	38	21	8	11	19	14
2010-11	Saint John	QMJHL	64	37	28	65	40	19	10	17	27	12

QMJHL All-Rookie Team (2010)

GALLACHER, Benjamin (gal-lah-CHUR, BEHN-jah-mihn) FLA

Defense. Shoots left. 5'11", 183 lbs. Born, Calgary, Alta., September 11, 1992.
(Florida's 9th choice, 93rd overall, in 2010 Entry Draft).

			Regular Season					Playoffs				
Season	**Club**	**League**	**GP**	**G**	**A**	**Pts**	**PIM**	**GP**	**G**	**A**	**Pts**	**PIM**
2008 09	Camrose Kodiaks	AJHL	43	4	6	10	58	9	0	1	1	4
2009-10	Camrose Kodiaks	AJHL	34	3	19	22	61	11	1	1	2	43
2010-11	Camrose Kodiaks	AJHL	37	5	22	27	119	18	3	5	8	52

• Signed Letter of Intent to attend **Ohio State University** (CCHA) in fall of 2011.

GALLAGHER, Brendan (gal-lah-GUR, BREHN-duhn) MTL

Right wing. Shoots right. 5'8", 170 lbs. Born, Edmonton, Alta., May 6, 1992.
(Montreal's 4th choice, 147th overall, in 2010 Entry Draft).

			Regular Season					Playoffs				
Season	Club	League	GP	G	A	Pts	PIM	GP	G	A	Pts	PIM
2007-08	Greater Van.	BCMML	39	23	33	56	66	2	0	1	1	0
2008-09	Vancouver Giants	WHL	52	10	21	31	61	16	1	2	3	10
2009-10	Vancouver Giants	WHL	72	41	40	81	111	16	11	10	21	14
2010-11	Vancouver Giants	WHL	66	44	47	91	108	4	2	0	2	16

WHL West First All-Star Team (2011)

GARBUTT, Ryan (GAHR-buht, RIGH-uhn) DAL

Center. Shoots left. 6'1", 185 lbs. Born, Winnipeg, Man., August 12, 1985.

			Regular Season					Playoffs				
Season	Club	League	GP	G	A	Pts	PIM	GP	G	A	Pts	PIM
2003-04	Wpg. South Blues	MJHL	60	23	25	48	143	....	....	....	....	....
2004-05	Wpg. South Blues	MJHL	63	47	34	81	303	....	....	....	....	....
2005-06	Brown U.	ECAC	28	2	4	6	61	....	....	....	....	....
2006-07	Brown U.	ECAC	29	9	4	13	30	....	....	....	....	....
2007-08	Brown U.	ECAC	29	12	11	23	56	....	....	....	....	....
2008-09	Brown U.	ECAC	30	6	10	16	56	....	....	....	....	....
2009-10	Corpus Christi	CHL	64	22	28	50	204	1	0	0	0	2
2010-11	Chicago Wolves	AHL	65	19	18	37	118	....	....	....	....	....
	Gwinnett	ECHL	10	10	7	17	24	....	....	....	....	....

Signed as a free agent by **Dallas**, July 1, 2011.

GARDINER, Jake (GAHR-dih-nuhr, JAYK) TOR

Defense. Shoots left. 6'2", 184 lbs. Born, Deephaven, MN, July 4, 1990.
(Anaheim's 1st choice, 17th overall, in 2008 Entry Draft).

			Regular Season					Playoffs				
Season	Club	League	GP	G	A	Pts	PIM	GP	G	A	Pts	PIM
2005-06	Minnetonka High	High-MN	21	2	14	16	6	....	....	....	....	....
2006-07	Minnetonka High	High-MN	19	10	22	32	20	....	....	....	....	....
	Team Southwest	UMWEHL	11	4	3	7	....	....	....	....	....	....
2007-08	Minnetonka High	High-MN	24	20	28	48	14	....	....	....	....	....
	Team Southwest	UMWEHL	11	8	7	15	....	....	....	....	....	....
2008-09	U. of Wisconsin	WCHA	39	3	18	21	16	....	....	....	....	....
2009-10	U. of Wisconsin	WCHA	41	6	7	13	20	....	....	....	....	....
2010-11	U. of Wisconsin	WCHA	41	10	31	41	24	....	....	....	....	....
	Toronto Marlies	AHL	10	0	3	3	4	....	....	....	....	....

WCHA All-Rookie Team (2009) • WCHA Second All-Star Team (2011) • NCAA West Second All-American Team (2011)

Traded to **Toronto** by **Anaheim** with Joffrey Lupul for Francois Beauchemin, February 9, 2011.

GARDINER, Max (GAR-dih-nuhr, MAX) ST.L.

Center. Shoots left. 6'3", 176 lbs. Born, Edina, MN, May 7, 1992.
(St. Louis' 4th choice, 74th overall, in 2010 Entry Draft).

			Regular Season					Playoffs				
Season	Club	League	GP	G	A	Pts	PIM	GP	G	A	Pts	PIM
2007-08	Minnetonka High	High-MN	27	9	12	21	16	....	....	....	....	....
2008-09	Minnetonka High	High-MN	28	15	28	43	8	....	....	....	....	....
2009-10	Team Southwest	UMHSEL	22	6	6	12	....	....	....	....	....	....
	Minnetonka High	High-MN	17	17	26	43	14	6	5	6	11	0
2010-11	U. of Minnesota	WCHA	17	1	2	3	24	....	....	....	....	....

GAUDREAU, John (GAW-droh, JAWN) CGY

Left wing. Shoots left. 5'6", 137 lbs. Born, Salem, NJ, August 13, 1993.
(Calgary's 4th choice, 104th overall, in 2011 Entry Draft).

			Regular Season					Playoffs				
Season	Club	League	GP	G	A	Pts	PIM	GP	G	A	Pts	PIM
2009-10	Team Comcast	T1EHL	48	29	29	58	16	....	....	....	....	....
2010-11	Dubuque	USHL	60	36	36	72	36	11	5	6	11	6

USHL Second All-Star Team (2011) • USHL Rookie of the Year (2011)

GAUTHIER-LEDUC, Jerome (GOH-t'yay-leh-DOOK, Jah-ROHM) BUF

Defense. Shoots right. 6'1", 188 lbs. Born, Quebec City, Que., July 30, 1992.
(Buffalo's 2nd choice, 68th overall, in 2010 Entry Draft).

			Regular Season					Playoffs				
Season	Club	League	GP	G	A	Pts	PIM	GP	G	A	Pts	PIM
2007-08	Sem. St-Francois	QAAA	43	10	12	22	10	17	2	6	8	26
2008-09	Rouyn-Noranda	QMJHL	52	1	16	17	8	6	0	2	2	5
2009-10	Rouyn-Noranda	QMJHL	68	20	26	46	16	11	2	4	6	2
2010-11	Rimouski Oceanic	QMJHL	61	18	38	56	26	5	1	2	3	6

GAZDIC, Luke (GAZ-dihk, LEWK) DAL

Left wing. Shoots left. 6'3", 228 lbs. Born, Toronto, Ont., July 25, 1989.
(Dallas' 8th choice, 172nd overall, in 2007 Entry Draft).

			Regular Season					Playoffs				
Season	Club	League	GP	G	A	Pts	PIM	GP	G	A	Pts	PIM
2004-05	North York	GTHL	38	13	16	29	24	....	....	....	....	....
2005-06	Wexford Raiders	OPJHL	47	17	16	33	105	....	....	....	....	....
2006-07	Erie Otters	OHL	58	5	8	13	136	....	....	....	....	....
2007-08	Erie Otters	OHL	67	17	12	29	144	....	....	....	....	....
2008-09	Erie Otters	OHL	63	20	10	30	127	5	0	0	0	9
	Idaho Steelheads	ECHL	2	1	0	1	14	2	0	0	0	0
2009-10	Texas Stars	AHL	49	3	1	4	155	....	....	....	....	....
	Idaho Steelheads	ECHL	4	1	1	2	10	....	....	....	....	....
2010-11	Texas Stars	AHL	72	9	8	17	110	5	0	0	0	2

GEDIG, Curtis (GEH-dihg, KUHR-tihs) N.J.

Defense. Shoots left. 6'2", 190 lbs. Born, Penticton, B.C., September 14, 1991.
(New Jersey's 7th choice, 204th overall, in 2009 Entry Draft).

			Regular Season					Playoffs				
Season	Club	League	GP	G	A	Pts	PIM	GP	G	A	Pts	PIM
2007-08	Okanagan Rockets	BCMML	40	4	14	18	36	....	....	....	....	....
	Princeton Posse	KIJHL	9	0	2	2	4	1	0	0	0	0
2008-09	Merritt	BCHL	16	2	4	6	2	....	....	....	....	....
	Cowichan Valley	BCHL	30	2	10	12	16	10	0	3	3	2
2009-10	Cowichan Valley	BCHL	23	6	3	9	14	....	....	....	....	....
	Vernon Vipers	BCHL	30	5	7	12	6	19	1	5	6	10
2010-11	Ohio State	CCHA	34	0	12	12	6	....	....	....	....	....

GELINAS, Eric (ZHEHL-ih-nuh, AIR-ihk) N.J.

Defense. Shoots left. 6'4", 195 lbs. Born, Vanier, Ont., May 8, 1991.
(New Jersey's 2nd choice, 54th overall, in 2009 Entry Draft).

			Regular Season					Playoffs				
Season	Club	League	GP	G	A	Pts	PIM	GP	G	A	Pts	PIM
2006-07	C.C. Lemoyne	QAAA	44	5	14	19	50	10	1	4	5	14
2007-08	Lewiston	QMJHL	54	3	16	19	34	5	0	0	0	2
2008-09	Lewiston	QMJHL	67	10	29	39	80	4	0	1	1	12
2009-10	Lewiston	QMJHL	33	3	16	19	33	....	....	....	....	....
	Chicoutimi	QMJHL	28	3	9	12	26	6	1	4	5	6
2010-11	Chicoutimi	QMJHL	35	9	15	24	41	....	....	....	....	....
	Saint John	QMJHL	27	3	17	20	26	19	5	8	13	25

GENEROUS, Matt (GEHN-uhr-uhs, MAT)

Defense. Shoots right. 6'3", 208 lbs. Born, Methuen, MA, May 4, 1985.
(Buffalo's 8th choice, 208th overall, in 2005 Entry Draft).

			Regular Season					Playoffs				
Season	Club	League	GP	G	A	Pts	PIM	GP	G	A	Pts	PIM
2003-04	N.E. Jr. Falcons	EJHL	43	6	9	15	134	....	....	....	....	....
2004-05	N.E. Jr. Falcons	EJHL	49	8	16	24	105	....	....	....	....	....
2005-06	St. Lawrence	ECAC	34	4	11	15	34	....	....	....	....	....
2006-07	St. Lawrence	ECAC	37	3	6	9	34	....	....	....	....	....
2007-08	St. Lawrence	ECAC	33	3	12	15	31	....	....	....	....	....
2008-09	St. Lawrence	ECAC	35	8	9	17	34	....	....	....	....	....
	Portland Pirates	AHL	4	1	0	1	13	4	0	0	0	0
2009-10	Portland Pirates	AHL	61	2	11	13	74	....	....	....	....	....
2010-11	Reading Royals	ECHL	22	1	4	5	20	....	....	....	....	....
	Lake Erie Monsters	AHL	40	1	4	5	63	7	0	0	0	2

ECAC All-Rookie Team (2006)

Signed as a free agent by **Reading** (ECHL), October 1, 2010. Signed to a PTO (professional tryout) contract by **Lake Erie** (AHL), December 14, 2010.

GENOWAY, Chay (GEHN-oh-way, CHAY) MIN

Defense. Shoots left. 5'9", 177 lbs. Born, Swan River, Man., December 20, 1986.

			Regular Season					Playoffs				
Season	Club	League	GP	G	A	Pts	PIM	GP	G	A	Pts	PIM
2005-06	Vernon Vipers	BCHL	56	17	32	49	71	10	0	8	8	9
2006-07	North Dakota	WCHA	43	5	14	19	42	....	....	....	....	....
2007-08	North Dakota	WCHA	38	8	21	29	46	....	....	....	....	....
2008-09	North Dakota	WCHA	42	3	29	32	46	....	....	....	....	....
2009-10	North Dakota	WCHA	9	4	6	10	6	....	....	....	....	....
2010-11	North Dakota	WCHA	36	6	31	37	26	....	....	....	....	....

WCHA First All-Star Team (2009, 2011) • NCAA West Second All-American Team (2009) • NCAA West First All-American Team (2011)

• Missed majority of 2009-10 due to concussion vs. St. Cloud State (WCHA), November 13, 2009. Signed as a free agent by **Minnesota**, April 12, 2011.

GERNAT, Martin (GAIR-naht, MAR-tihn) EDM

Defense. Shoots left. 6'5", 187 lbs. Born, Presov, Slovakia, April 11, 1993.
(Edmonton's 8th choice, 122nd overall, in 2011 Entry Draft).

			Regular Season					Playoffs				
Season	Club	League	GP	G	A	Pts	PIM	GP	G	A	Pts	PIM
2008-09	P.H.K. Presov U18	Svk-U18	41	6	28	34	36	....	....	....	....	....
2009-10	HC Kosice U18	Svk-U18	36	4	21	25	20	5	0	3	3	2
	HC Kosice Jr.	Slovak-Jr.	....	....	....	....	....	2	0	0	0	2
2010-11	HC Kosice U18	Svk-U18	8	3	4	7	22	1	0	0	0	2
	HC Kosice Jr.	Slovak-Jr.	28	3	15	18	20	12	3	3	6	10

GIBBONS, Brian (GIH-buhnz, BRIGH-uhn) PIT

Center. Shoots left. 5'8", 165 lbs. Born, Braintree, MA, February 26, 1988.

			Regular Season					Playoffs				
Season	Club	League	GP	G	A	Pts	PIM	GP	G	A	Pts	PIM
2006-07	Salisbury School	High-CT	25	8	19	27	....	....	....	....	....	....
2007-08	Boston College	H-East	43	13	22	35	32	....	....	....	....	....
2008-09	Boston College	H-East	36	9	19	28	52	....	....	....	....	....
2009-10	Boston College	H-East	42	16	34	50	78	....	....	....	....	....
2010-11	Boston College	H-East	39	18	*33	51	79	....	....	....	....	....

Hockey East First All-Star Team (2010) • Hockey East Second All-Star Team (2011)

Signed as a free agent by **Pittsburgh**, April 4, 2011.

GILBERT, David (zhihl-BAIR, DAY-vihd) CHI

Center. Shoots left. 6'2", 185 lbs. Born, Chateauguay, Que., February 9, 1991.
(Chicago's 8th choice, 209th overall, in 2009 Entry Draft).

			Regular Season					Playoffs				
Season	Club	League	GP	G	A	Pts	PIM	GP	G	A	Pts	PIM
2006-07	Antoine-Girouard	QAAA	44	19	26	45	10	4	2	1	3	2
2007-08	Antoine-Girouard	QAAA	29	29	24	53	54	....	....	....	....	....
	Quebec Remparts	QMJHL	28	7	7	14	12	11	1	0	1	2
2008-09	Quebec Remparts	QMJHL	67	11	32	43	24	17	6	2	8	11
2009-10	Quebec Remparts	QMJHL	31	6	12	18	15	....	....	....	....	....
	Acadie-Bathurst	QMJHL	31	18	12	30	22	5	5	2	7	6
	Rockford IceHogs	AHL	1	0	1	1	0	....	....	....	....	....
2010-11	Acadie-Bathurst	QMJHL	52	28	23	51	39	4	2	1	3	0
	Rockford IceHogs	AHL	5	2	1	3	2	....	....	....	....	....

GILIATI, Stefano (jihl-ee-A-tee, steh-FA-noh)

Left wing. Shoots left. 5'11", 198 lbs. Born, Montreal, Que., October 7, 1987.

			Regular Season					Playoffs				
Season	Club	League	GP	G	A	Pts	PIM	GP	G	A	Pts	PIM
2004-05	Shawinigan	QMJHL	54	9	5	14	23	3	0	0	0	2
2005-06	Lewiston	QMJHL	70	21	28	49	72	6	2	0	2	6
2006-07	Lewiston	QMJHL	68	24	33	57	73	17	4	11	15	22
2007-08	Lewiston	QMJHL	65	40	47	87	103	6	1	3	4	10
	Toronto Marlies	AHL	1	0	0	0	0	....	....	....	....	....
2008-09	Toronto Marlies	AHL	53	6	9	15	16	....	....	....	....	....
2009-10	Toronto Marlies	AHL	25	3	6	9	8	....	....	....	....	....
	Reading Royals	ECHL	46	23	32	55	76	13	4	4	8	18
2010-11	Norfolk Admirals	AHL	69	7	14	21	39	6	1	0	1	0

QMJHL First All-Star Team (2008)

Signed as a free agent by **Toronto**, April 3, 2008. Traded to **Tampa Bay** by **Toronto** with Alex Berry for Matt Lashoff, August 27, 2010.

GIMAYEV, Sergei (gih-MIGH-ehv, SAIR-gay) OTT

Defense. Shoots left. 6'1", 183 lbs. Born, Moscow, USSR, February 16, 1984.
(Ottawa's 6th choice, 166th overall, in 2003 Entry Draft).

			Regular Season					Playoffs				
Season	Club	League	GP	G	A	Pts	PIM	GP	G	A	Pts	PIM
2001-02	CSKA Moscow 2	Russia-3	36	0	10	10	50	....	....	....	....	....
2002-03	Cherepovets	Russia	11	0	0	0	4	....	....	....	....	....
2003-04	Cherepovets	Russia	50	1	3	4	32	....	....	....	....	....
2004-05	Cherepovets	Russia	5	0	1	1	2	....	....	....	....	....
	Sibir Novosibirsk	Russia	31	1	6	7	34	....	....	....	....	....
2005-06	Dynamo Moscow	Russia	46	1	3	4	36	2	0	0	0	0
2006-07	Dynamo Moscow	Russia	23	0	2	2	28	2	0	0	0	6
2007-08	Cherepovets	Russia	39	1	0	1	30	8	1	1	2	4
2008-09	Barys Astana	Rus-KHL	45	0	2	2	79	....	....	....	....	....
2009-10	Barys Astana	Rus-KHL	54	6	6	12	73	3	0	0	0	8
2010-11	Barys Astana	Rus-KHL	52	5	3	8	44	4	0	0	0	4

GLASS, Andrew (GLAS, AN-droo) WSH

Left wing. Shoots left. 5'11", 180 lbs. Born, Wrentham, MA, July 14, 1989.
(Washington's 10th choice, 199th overall, in 2007 Entry Draft).

			Regular Season					Playoffs				
Season	Club	League	GP	G	A	Pts	PIM	GP	G	A	Pts	PIM
2003-04	Bos. Little Bruins	Minor-MA	61	15	23	38	2	....	....	....	....	....
2004-05	Bos. Little Bruins	Minor-MA	33	5	13	18	15	....	....	....	....	....
	Nobles	High-MA	29	7	15	22	6	....	....	....	....	....
2005-06	Bos. Little Bruins	Minor-MA	19	9	11	20	17	....	....	....	....	....
	Nobles	High-MA	29	15	24	39	8	....	....	....	....	....
2006-07	Bos. Little Bruins	Minor-MA	12	7	8	15	4	....	....	....	....	....
	Nobles	High-MA	18	7	10	17	6	....	....	....	....	....
2007-08	Nobles	High-MA	29	27	23	50	....	....	....	....	....	....
2008-09	Boston University	H-East	15	2	1	3	2	....	....	....	....	....
2009-10	Boston University	H-East	24	1	1	2	14	....	....	....	....	....
2010-11	Boston University	H-East	15	2	3	5	6	....	....	....	....	....

GLASSER, Matthew (GLAS-uhr, MA-thew) EDM

Left wing. Shoots left. 5'10", 175 lbs. Born, Saskatoon, Sask., January 11, 1987.
(Edmonton's 8th choice, 220th overall, in 2005 Entry Draft).

			Regular Season					Playoffs				
Season	Club	League	GP	G	A	Pts	PIM	GP	G	A	Pts	PIM
2003-04	Fort McMurray	AJHL	55	13	12	25	24	....	....	....	....	....
2004-05	Fort McMurray	AJHL	62	25	24	49	14	....	....	....	....	....
2005-06	Fort McMurray	AJHL	58	15	20	35	36	17	5	2	7	38
2006-07	U. of Denver	WCHA	12	0	0	0	2	....	....	....	....	....
2007-08	U. of Denver	WCHA	40	6	2	8	20	....	....	....	....	....
2008-09	U. of Denver	WCHA	40	4	3	7	18	....	....	....	....	....
2009-10	U. of Denver	WCHA	41	3	3	6	20	....	....	....	....	....
2010-11	Colorado Eagles	CHL	60	6	15	21	18	22	2	3	5	2

GLAZACHEV, Konstantin (GLAH-zuh-chehv, KAWN-stan-tihn) NSH

Left wing. Shoots right. 6', 186 lbs. Born, Arkhangelsk, USSR, February 18, 1985.
(Nashville's 2nd choice, 35th overall, in 2003 Entry Draft).

			Regular Season					Playoffs				
Season	Club	League	GP	G	A	Pts	PIM	GP	G	A	Pts	PIM
2001-02	Yaroslavl 2	Russia-3	7	5	6	11	6	....	....	....	....	....
2002-03	Yaroslavl 2	Russia-3	STATISTICS NOT AVAILABLE									
	Yaroslavl	Russia	13	3	4	7	4	4	0	0	0	0
2003-04	Yaroslavl 2	Russia-3	9	6	5	11	8	....	....	....	....	....
	Yaroslavl	Russia	35	4	3	7	4	2	0	0	0	0
2004-05	Sibir Novosibirsk	Russia	24	4	9	13	6	....	....	....	....	....
	Yaroslavl	Russia	9	0	3	3	2	....	....	....	....	....
	Yaroslavl 2	Russia-3	20	17	9	26	14	....	....	....	....	....
2005-06	Yaroslavl	Russia	29	7	4	11	8	9	0	2	2	0
2006-07	Yaroslavl	Russia	14	4	1	5	10	....	....	....	....	....
	Yaroslavl 2	Russia-3	4	2	5	7	0	....	....	....	....	....
	Amur Khabarovsk	Russia	22	4	7	11	14	....	....	....	....	....
2007-08	Novokuznetsk	Russia	50	7	9	16	10	....	....	....	....	....
2008-09	Barys Astana	Rus-KHL	56	28	24	52	30	3	3	0	3	2
2009-10	Barys Astana	Rus-KHL	42	16	17	33	18	2	0	0	0	0
2010-11	Dynamo Minsk	Rus-KHL	52	12	23	35	28	7	2	4	6	2

GLEASON, Joe (GLEE-suhn, JOH) CHI

Defense. Shoots right. 5'9", 171 lbs. Born, Edina, MN, March 30, 1990.
(Chicago's 7th choice, 192nd overall, in 2008 Entry Draft).

			Regular Season					Playoffs				
Season	Club	League	GP	G	A	Pts	PIM	GP	G	A	Pts	PIM
2006-07	Edina Hornets	High-MN	21	10	23	33	....	....	....	....	....	....
	Team Southwest	UMWEHL	11	4	6	10	....	....	....	....	....	....
2007-08	Edina Hornets	High-MN	23	9	33	42	....	....	....	....	....	....
	Team Southwest	UMWEHL	12	6	14	20	....	....	....	....	....	....
2008-09	Des Moines	USHL	59	5	16	21	40	....	....	....	....	....
2009-10	North Dakota	WCHA	39	0	9	9	31	....	....	....	....	....
2010-11	North Dakota	WCHA	22	1	3	4	19	....	....	....	....	....

GLENNIE, Scott (GLEH-nee, SKAWT) DAL

Right wing. Shoots right. 6'1", 180 lbs. Born, Winnipeg, Man., February 22, 1991.
(Dallas' 1st choice, 8th overall, in 2009 Entry Draft).

			Regular Season					Playoffs				
Season	Club	League	GP	G	A	Pts	PIM	GP	G	A	Pts	PIM
2006-07	Winnipeg Wild	MMHL	38	31	37	68	64	7	3	3	6	16
2007-08	Brandon	WHL	61	26	32	58	50	6	1	0	1	7
2008-09	Brandon	WHL	55	28	42	70	25	12	3	15	18	11
2009-10	Brandon	WHL	66	32	57	89	50	15	3	7	10	14
2010-11	Brandon	WHL	70	35	56	91	58	6	3	7	10	6
	Texas Stars	AHL	4	0	0	0	2	6	1	0	1	2

GLUKHOV, Alexei (GLUH-khawv, al-EHX-ay) T.B.

Right wing. Shoots left. 6'3", 213 lbs. Born, Voskresensk, USSR, April 5, 1984.
(Tampa Bay's 12th choice, 286th overall, in 2002 Entry Draft).

			Regular Season					Playoffs				
Season	Club	League	GP	G	A	Pts	PIM	GP	G	A	Pts	PIM
99-2000	Voskresensk 2	Russia-3	10	2	2	4	2	....	....	....	....	....
2000-01	Voskresensk	Russia-2	9	0	1	1	6	....	....	....	....	....
2001-02	Voskresensk 2	Russia-3	34	8	22	30	54	....	....	....	....	....
	Voskresensk	Russia-2	4	0	0	0	0	....	....	....	....	....
2002-03	Voskresensk	Russia-2	38	4	4	8	30	....	....	....	....	....
2003-04	Voskresensk	Russia	28	0	0	0	12	....	....	....	....	....
2004-05	Kristall Elektrostal	Russia-2	16	2	2	4	20	....	....	....	....	....
	Voskresensk	Russia	9	0	0	0	6	....	....	....	....	....
	Victoria	ECHL	32	5	12	17	12	....	....	....	....	....
	Springfield Falcons	AHL	3	0	1	1	6	....	....	....	....	....
2005-06	Mytischi	Russia	45	2	14	16	70	9	2	1	3	10
2006-07	Cherepovets	Russia	52	2	14	16	97	5	0	0	0	4
2007-08	Cherepovets	Russia	57	7	13	20	86	8	2	0	2	12
2008-09	Mytischi	Rus-KHL	43	10	10	20	28	7	1	1	2	4
2009-10	Mytischi	Rus-KHL	51	5	12	17	34	4	0	0	0	0
2010-11	Mytischi	Rus-KHL	54	5	12	17	34	24	2	5	7	12

Signed to PTO (professional tryout) contract by **Springfield** (AHL), April 14, 2005.

GOGGIN, Mark (GAW-gihn, MAHRK) BOS

Center. Shoots left. 5'11", 177 lbs. Born, Chicago, IL, July 29, 1990.
(Boston's 6th choice, 197th overall, in 2008 Entry Draft).

			Regular Season					Playoffs				
Season	Club	League	GP	G	A	Pts	PIM	GP	G	A	Pts	PIM
2006-07	Choate-Rosemary	High-CT	....	15	20	35	....	....	....	....	....	....
2007-08	Choate-Rosemary	High-CT	21	15	21	36	10	....	....	....	....	....
	USNTDP	U-17	3	1	1	2	0	....	....	....	....	....
	USNTDP	NAHL	5	1	1	2	2	....	....	....	....	....
2008-09	Choate-Rosemary	High-CT	25	14	20	34	....	....	....	....	....	....
	Chicago Steel	USHL	17	5	4	9	10	....	....	....	....	....
2009-10	Dartmouth	ECAC	21	4	2	6	10	....	....	....	....	....
2010-11			DID NOT PLAY – INJURED									

GOGOL, Curt (GOH-guhl, KUHRT) S.J.

Left wing. Shoots left. 6', 185 lbs. Born, Calgary, Alta., September 21, 1991.

			Regular Season					Playoffs				
Season	Club	League	GP	G	A	Pts	PIM	GP	G	A	Pts	PIM
2007-08	Calgary Flames	AMHL	31	10	4	14	96	....	....	....	....	....
	Kelowna Rockets	WHL	1	0	0	0	0	....	....	....	....	....
2008-09	Kelowna Rockets	WHL	63	1	4	5	144	22	1	0	1	30
2009-10	Kelowna Rockets	WHL	35	0	6	6	120	....	....	....	....	....
	Saskatoon Blades	WHL	8	1	0	1	29	10	1	3	4	23
2010-11	Saskatoon Blades	WHL	15	1	1	2	59	....	....	....	....	....
	Chilliwack Bruins	WHL	47	4	8	12	142	5	0	1	1	6

Signed as a free agent by **San Jose**, September 20, 2010.

GOGULLA, Philip (GOH-goo-lah, FIHL-ihp) BUF

Right wing. Shoots left. 6'2", 182 lbs. Born, Dusseldorf, West Germany, July 31, 1987.
(Buffalo's 2nd choice, 48th overall, in 2005 Entry Draft).

			Regular Season					Playoffs				
Season	Club	League	GP	G	A	Pts	PIM	GP	G	A	Pts	PIM
2002-03	Krefelder EV Jr.	Ger-Jr.	32	11	23	34	42	2	0	0	0	2
2003-04	Krefelder EV Jr.	Ger-Jr.	35	35	44	79	22	2	0	2	2	27
2004-05	Essen	German-2	3	0	0	0	0	....	....	....	....	....
	Koln Jr.	Ger-Jr.	7	4	5	9	18	....	....	....	....	....
	Kolner Haie	Germany	47	1	1	2	14	7	0	0	0	2
2005-06	Kolner Haie	Germany	48	7	15	22	49	9	3	2	5	40
2006-07	Kolner Haie	Germany	44	8	13	21	26	7	0	0	0	8
2007-08	Kolner Haie	Germany	51	11	33	44	30	14	3	9	12	6
2008-09	Kolner Haie	Germany	48	17	21	38	58	....	....	....	....	....
2009-10	Portland Pirates	AHL	76	15	20	35	27	3	0	0	0	0
2010-11	Kolner Haie	Germany	52	13	33	46	50	5	2	2	4	0

GOLOUBEF, Cody (GOH-luh-behf, KOH-dee) CBJ

Defense. Shoots right. 6', 195 lbs. Born, Mississauga, Ont., November 30, 1989.
(Columbus' 2nd choice, 37th overall, in 2008 Entry Draft).

			Regular Season					Playoffs				
Season	Club	League	GP	G	A	Pts	PIM	GP	G	A	Pts	PIM
2003-04	Toronto Marlboros	GTHL	89	10	27	37	44	....	....	....	....	....
2004-05	Toronto Marlboros	GTHL	69	14	47	61	56	....	....	....	....	....
2005-06	Milton Icehawks	OPJHL	42	9	29	38	38	7	1	3	4	10
2006-07	Oakville Blades	OPJHL	9	5	5	10	46	10	2	10	12	18
2007-08	U. of Wisconsin	WCHA	40	4	6	10	36	....	....	....	....	....
2008-09	U. of Wisconsin	WCHA	36	5	8	13	38	....	....	....	....	....
2009-10	U. of Wisconsin	WCHA	42	3	11	14	64	....	....	....	....	....
2010-11	Springfield Falcons	AHL	50	5	12	17	42	....	....	....	....	....

• Missed majority of 2006-07 due to various injuries.

GONCHAROV, Maxim (gohn-CHAR-ahv, mahx-EEM) PHX

Defense. Shoots right. 6'4", 208 lbs. Born, Moscow, USSR, June 15, 1989.
(Phoenix's 6th choice, 123rd overall, in 2007 Entry Draft).

			Regular Season					Playoffs				
Season	Club	League	GP	G	A	Pts	PIM	GP	G	A	Pts	PIM
2005-06	CSKA Moscow 2	Russia-3	STATISTICS NOT AVAILABLE									
2006-07	CSKA Moscow 2	Russia-3	STATISTICS NOT AVAILABLE									
	CSKA Moscow	Russia	18	0	0	0	10	5	0	0	0	2
2007-08	CSKA Moscow	Russia	47	3	2	5	38	6	0	2	2	0
	CSKA Moscow 2	Russia-3	4	0	2	2	35	3	0	0	0	8
2008-09	CSKA Moscow	Rus-KHL	47	7	8	15	50	7	0	0	0	4
2009-10	CSKA Moscow	Rus-KHL	51	4	13	17	52	3	1	0	1	2
2010-11	San Antonio	AHL	61	6	9	15	65	....	....	....	....	....

GORMLEY, Brandon (GOHRM-lee, BRAN-duhn) PHX

Defense. Shoots left. 6'2", 190 lbs. Born, Charlottetown, P.E.I., February 18, 1992.
(Phoenix's 1st choice, 13th overall, in 2010 Entry Draft).

			Regular Season					Playoffs				
Season	Club	League	GP	G	A	Pts	PIM	GP	G	A	Pts	PIM
2007-08	Notre Dame	SMHL	42	23	33	56	63	9	1	6	7	18
2008-09	Moncton Wildcats	QMJHL	62	7	20	27	34	10	1	3	4	6
2009-10	Moncton Wildcats	QMJHL	58	9	34	43	54	21	2	15	17	10
2010-11	Moncton Wildcats	QMJHL	47	13	35	48	42	5	0	1	1	6
	San Antonio	AHL	4	1	0	1	0	....	....	....	....	....

QMJHL All-Rookie Team (2009) • QMJHL Second All-Star Team (2010, 2011)

GOTOVETS, Kirill (goh-TOH-vets, kih-RIHL) T.B.

Defense. Shoots left. 5'11", 203 lbs. Born, Minsk, USSR, June 25, 1991.
(Tampa Bay's 7th choice, 183rd overall, in 2009 Entry Draft).

			Regular Season					Playoffs				
Season	Club	League	GP	G	A	Pts	PIM	GP	G	A	Pts	PIM
2007-08	Yunior Minsk	Belarus-2	45	2	8	10	54	....	....	....	....	....
2008-09	Shat.-St. Mary's	High-MN	54	7	25	32	70	....	....	....	....	....
2009-10	Shat.-St. Mary's	High-MN	44	8	19	27	73	....	....	....	....	....
2010-11	Cornell Big Red	ECAC	34	1	6	7	32	....	....	....	....	....

GOULET, Alain (goo-LAY, AL-eh) BOS

Defense. Shoots right. 6'2", 186 lbs. Born, Kapuskasing, Ont., September 22, 1988.
(Boston's 4th choice, 159th overall, in 2007 Entry Draft).

			Regular Season					Playoffs				
Season	Club	League	GP	G	A	Pts	PIM	GP	G	A	Pts	PIM
2005-06	Ottawa Jr. Sens	CJHL	41	6	14	20	22	....	....	....	....	....
2006-07	Aurora Tigers	OPJHL	43	10	32	42	34	25	5	16	21	32
2007-08	Nebraska-Omaha	CCHA	37	6	8	14	14	....	....	....	....	....
2008-09	Nebraska-Omaha	CCHA	17	2	3	5	21	....	....	....	....	....
	Gatineau	QMJHL	32	16	19	35	10	10	0	10	10	18
2009-10	Providence Bruins	AHL	71	3	15	18	28	....	....	....	....	....
2010-11	Providence Bruins	AHL	16	2	6	8	10	....	....	....	....	....
	Reading Royals	ECHL	43	4	14	18	29	6	0	1	1	2

GRANBERG, Petter (GRAN-buhrg, PEH-tuhr) TOR

Defense. Shoots right. 6'3", 205 lbs. Born, Gallivare, Sweden, August 27, 1992.
(Toronto's 4th choice, 116th overall, in 2010 Entry Draft).

			Regular Season					Playoffs				
Season	Club	League	GP	G	A	Pts	PIM	GP	G	A	Pts	PIM
2007-08	Skelleftea U18	Swe-U18	28	1	3	4	4	....	....	....	....	....
2008-09	Skelleftea AIK U18	Swe-U18	32	0	8	8	20	8	0	0	0	4
	Skelleftea AIK Jr.	Swe-Jr.	4	0	0	0	0	2	0	0	0	6
2009-10	Skelleftea AIK U18	Swe-U18	6	0	1	1	2	3	0	3	3	4
	Skelleftea AIK Jr.	Swe-Jr.	40	2	7	9	39	4	1	0	1	4
	Skelleftea AIK	Sweden	1	0	0	0	0	....	....	....	....	....
2010-11	Skelleftea AIK Jr.	Swe-Jr.	34	2	6	8	16	5	0	1	1	0
	Pitea HC	Sweden-3	1	0	0	0	0	....	....	....	....	....
	Skelleftea AIK	Sweden	23	0	1	1	6	11	0	1	1	2

GRANLUND, Markus (GRAN-luhnd, mahr-KUHS) CGY

Center. Shoots left. 5'11", 166 lbs. Born, Oulu, Finland, April 16, 1993.
(Calgary's 2nd choice, 45th overall, in 2011 Entry Draft).

			Regular Season					Playoffs				
Season	Club	League	GP	G	A	Pts	PIM	GP	G	A	Pts	PIM
2008-09	Karpat Oulu U18	Fin-U18	4	1	3	4	0	....	....	....	....	....
2009-10	HIFK Helsinki U18	Fin-U18	11	9	20	29	6	....	....	....	....	....
	HIFK Helsinki Jr.	Fin-Jr.	37	17	25	42	38	14	2	11	13	18
2010-11	Suomi U20	Finland-2	6	3	3	6	6	....	....	....	....	....
	HIFK Helsinki	Finland	2	0	0	0	0	....	....	....	....	....
	HIFK Helsinki Jr.	Fin-Jr.	40	20	32	52	49	5	4	5	9	6

GRANLUND, Mikael (GRAHN-lund, mih-kigh-EHL) MIN

Center. Shoots left. 5'10", 180 lbs. Born, Oulu, Finland, February 26, 1992.
(Minnesota's 1st choice, 9th overall, in 2010 Entry Draft).

			Regular Season					Playoffs				
Season	Club	League	GP	G	A	Pts	PIM	GP	G	A	Pts	PIM
2007-08	Karpat Oulu U18	Fin-U18	31	22	27	49	20	5	3	5	8	0
2008-09	Suomi U20	Finland-2	6	4	3	7	0	....	....	....	....	....
	Karpat Oulu Jr.	Fin-Jr.	38	22	44	66	45	....	....	....	....	....
	Karpat Oulu	Finland	2	0	0	0	0	....	....	....	....	....
	Karpat Oulu U18	Fin-U18	....	....	....	....	....	3	2	4	6	2
2009-10	Suomi U20	Finland-2	1	0	0	0	0	....	....	....	....	....
	HIFK Helsinki	Finland	43	13	27	40	2	6	1	5	6	0
2010-11	HIFK Helsinki	Finland	39	8	28	36	14	15	5	*11	*16	4

GRANT, Alex (GRANT, AL-ehx) PIT

Defense. Shoots right. 6'2", 185 lbs. Born, Antigonish, N.S., January 20, 1989.
(Pittsburgh's 6th choice, 118th overall, in 2007 Entry Draft).

			Regular Season					Playoffs				
Season	Club	League	GP	G	A	Pts	PIM	GP	G	A	Pts	PIM
2004-05	Antigonish	MJrHL	50	7	9	16	36	3	1	1	2	2
2005-06	Saint John	QMJHL	47	4	9	13	58	....	....	....	....	....
2006-07	Saint John	QMJHL	68	12	20	32	108	....	....	....	....	....
2007-08	Saint John	QMJHL	70	15	33	48	96	14	3	11	14	12
2008-09	Saint John	QMJHL	37	9	22	31	51	....	....	....	....	....
	Shawinigan	QMJHL	23	4	15	19	11	21	4	5	9	18
2009-10	Wilkes-Barre	AHL	14	3	2	5	28	2	0	0	0	0
	Wheeling Nailers	ECHL	40	7	20	27	36	....	....	....	....	....
2010-11	Wilkes-Barre	AHL	4	0	0	0	0	....	....	....	....	....
	Wheeling Nailers	ECHL	14	3	2	5	6	17	2	0	2	13

• Missed majority of 2010-11 due to wrist injury.

GRANT, Derek (GRANT, DAIR-ihk) OTT

Center. Shoots left. 6'3", 197 lbs. Born, Abbotsford, B.C., April 20, 1990.
(Ottawa's 5th choice, 119th overall, in 2008 Entry Draft).

			Regular Season					Playoffs				
Season	Club	League	GP	G	A	Pts	PIM	GP	G	A	Pts	PIM
2006-07	Abbotsford Pilots	PIJHL	47	31	20	51	42	11	6	5	11	20
2007-08	Langley Chiefs	BCHL	57	24	39	63	44	12	5	5	10	15
2008-09	Langley Chiefs	BCHL	35	25	35	60	22	4	2	1	3	2
2009-10	Michigan State	CCHA	38	12	18	30	10	....	....	....	....	....
2010-11	Michigan State	CCHA	38	8	25	33	44	....	....	....	....	....
	Binghamton	AHL	14	1	5	6	0	7	1	1	2	2

GRANT, Tommy (GRANT, TAW-mee) NYR

Left wing. Shoots left. 6'2", 195 lbs. Born, North Vancouver, B.C., August 29, 1986.

			Regular Season					Playoffs				
Season	Club	League	GP	G	A	Pts	PIM	GP	G	A	Pts	PIM
2004-05	Victoria Salsa	BCHL	51	11	8	19	47	5	1	1	2	6
2005-06	Victoria Salsa	BCHL	50	6	10	16	54	16	5	9	14	32
2006-07	Quesnel	BCHL	11	6	6	12	26	....	....	....	....	....
	Westside Warriors	BCHL	45	30	33	63	103	6	2	2	4	12
2007-08	Alaska-Anchorage	WCHA	31	5	2	7	26	....	....	....	....	....
2008-09	Alaska-Anchorage	WCHA	32	15	10	25	54	....	....	....	....	....
2009-10	Alaska-Anchorage	WCHA	34	9	17	26	42	....	....	....	....	....
2010-11	Alaska-Anchorage	WCHA	37	16	16	32	57	....	....	....	....	....
	Connecticut Whale	AHL	7	0	3	3	2	6	1	1	2	6

Signed as a free agent by **NY Rangers**, March 29, 2011.

GRANTHAM, Ryley (GRAN-thum, RIGH-lee) CGY

Center. Shoots left. 6'3", 207 lbs. Born, Hanna, Alta., January 7, 1988.
(Calgary's 6th choice, 168th overall, in 2008 Entry Draft).

			Regular Season					Playoffs				
Season	Club	League	GP	G	A	Pts	PIM	GP	G	A	Pts	PIM
2005-06	Brooks Bandits	AJHL	43	6	3	9	98	13	2	0	2	16
2006-07	Brooks Bandits	AJHL	....	3	11	14	....	....	....	....	....	....
	Moose Jaw	WHL	33	1	1	2	50	....	....	....	....	....
2007-08	Moose Jaw	WHL	66	10	9	19	163	6	0	0	0	8
2008-09	Moose Jaw	WHL	38	8	5	13	132	....	....	....	....	....
	Kelowna Rockets	WHL	29	4	12	16	61	22	4	1	5	16
2009-10	Abbotsford Heat	AHL	67	1	3	4	163	....	....	....	....	....
2010-11	Abbotsford Heat	AHL	22	0	3	3	39	....	....	....	....	....
	Utah Grizzlies	ECHL	14	4	1	5	49	....	....	....	....	....

GRAOVAC, Tyler (GRAW-vak, TIGH-luhr) MIN

Center. Shoots left. 6'3", 179 lbs. Born, Brampton, Ont., April 27, 1993.
(Minnesota's 6th choice, 191st overall, in 2011 Entry Draft).

			Regular Season					Playoffs				
Season	Club	League	GP	G	A	Pts	PIM	GP	G	A	Pts	PIM
2008-09	Mississauga Reps	GTHL	26	13	18	31	12	....	....	....	....	....
2009-10	Ottawa 67's	OHL	52	2	7	9	17	12	0	0	0	2
2010-11	Ottawa 67's	OHL	66	10	11	21	10	....	....	....	....	....

GRAVEL, Kevin (gra-VEHL, KEH-vihn) L.A.

Defense. Shoots left. 6'4", 185 lbs. Born, Kingsford, MI, March 6, 1992.
(Los Angeles' 4th choice, 148th overall, in 2010 Entry Draft).

			Regular Season					Playoffs				
Season	Club	League	GP	G	A	Pts	PIM	GP	G	A	Pts	PIM
2008-09	Marquette	NAHL	58	3	11	14	29	....	....	....	....	....
	USNTDP	U-17	3	0	1	1	4	....	....	....	....	....
2009-10	Sioux City	USHL	53	3	3	6	36	....	....	....	....	....
2010-11	St. Cloud State	WCHA	36	1	5	6	4	....	....	....	....	....

GREENOP, Richard (GREEN-awp, RIH-chuhrd) TOR

Center. Shoots right. 6'4", 246 lbs. Born, Bowmanville, Ont., February 24, 1989.
(Chicago's 7th choice, 156th overall, in 2007 Entry Draft).

			Regular Season					Playoffs				
Season	Club	League	GP	G	A	Pts	PIM	GP	G	A	Pts	PIM
2005-06	Oshawa	OPJHL	47	10	4	14	97	4	0	0	0	21
2006-07	Windsor Spitfires	OHL	48	3	9	12	149	....	....	....	....	....
2007-08	Windsor Spitfires	OHL	60	2	3	5	194	5	0	0	0	2
2008-09	Windsor Spitfires	OHL	60	4	4	8	156	15	0	0	0	28
2009-10	Toronto Marlies	AHL	42	2	3	5	136	....	....	....	....	....
2010-11	Toronto Marlies	AHL	11	0	3	3	28	....	....	....	....	....
	Reading Royals	ECHL	19	1	2	3	24	....	....	....	....	....

Signed as a free agent by **Toronto**, July 6, 2009.

GREGOIRE, Jason (GREHG-wahr, JAY-suhn) WPG

Left wing. Shoots left. 6'1", 196 lbs. Born, Winnipeg, Man., February 24, 1989.
(NY Islanders' 2nd choice, 76th overall, in 2007 Entry Draft).

			Regular Season					Playoffs				
Season	Club	League	GP	G	A	Pts	PIM	GP	G	A	Pts	PIM
2005-06	Wpg. South Blues	MJHL	57	22	28	50	46	14	12	11	23	....
2006-07	Lincoln Stars	USHL	32	16	20	36	10	4	4	0	4	2
2007-08	Lincoln Stars	USHL	54	*37	32	69	41	8	3	9	*12	6
2008-09	North Dakota	WCHA	42	12	17	29	28	....	....	....	....	....
2009-10	North Dakota	WCHA	43	20	17	37	10	....	....	....	....	....
2010-11	North Dakota	WCHA	35	25	18	43	8	....	....	....	....	....

USHL First All-Star Team (2008) • USHL Player of the Year (2008)

Signed as a free agent by **Winnipeg**, July 7, 2011.

GRENIER, Alexandre (GREHN-yay, al-ehx-AHN-druh) VAN

Right wing. Shoots right. 6'5", 200 lbs. Born, Laval, Que., May 9, 1991.
(Vancouver's 3rd choice, 90th overall, in 2011 Entry Draft).

			Regular Season					Playoffs				
Season	Club	League	GP	G	A	Pts	PIM	GP	G	A	Pts	PIM
2009-10	St-Jerome	QJHL	51	26	28	54	63	7	1	3	4	2
2010-11	St-Jerome	QJHL	33	25	35	60	34	....	....	....	....	....
	Quebec Remparts	QMJHL	31	9	15	24	6	15	8	8	16	4

GRIMALDI, Rocco (grih-MAL-dee, RAW-koh) FLA

Center. Shoots right. 5'6", 160 lbs. Born, Anaheim, CA, February 8, 1993.
(Florida's 2nd choice, 33rd overall, in 2011 Entry Draft).

			Regular Season					Playoffs				
Season	Club	League	GP	G	A	Pts	PIM	GP	G	A	Pts	PIM
2008-09	Little Caesars	T1EHL	32	11	9	20	22	7	1	5	6	0
	Little Caesars	Exhib.	19	19	15	34	....	....	....	....	....	....
2009-10	USNTDP	USHL	32	11	9	20	22	....	....	....	....	....
	USNTDP	U-17	16	7	18	25	20	....	....	....	....	....
	USNTDP	U-18	14	3	15	18	12	....	....	....	....	....
2010-11	USNTDP	USHL	23	12	13	25	18	....	....	....	....	....
	USNTDP	U-18	35	27	21	48	47	....	....	....	....	....

• Signed Letter of Intent to attend **University of North Dakota** (WCHA).

GROULX, Danny (GROO, DA-nee)
Defense. Shoots left. 6', 205 lbs. Born, LaSalle, Que., June 23, 1981.

			Regular Season					Playoffs			
Season	Club	League	GP	G	A	Pts	PIM	GP	G	A	Pts	PIM
1996-97	Charles-Lemoyne	QAAA	40	2	26	28	...	15	3	15	18	...
1997-98	Val-d'Or Foreurs	QMJHL	63	4	16	20	61	19	1	4	5	18
1998-99	Val-d'Or Foreurs	QMJHL	36	3	26	29	55	...	...	...	...	...
	Acadie-Bathurst	QMJHL	36	2	15	17	51	18	0	2	2	6
99-2000	Victoriaville Tigres	QMJHL	66	12	55	67	131	6	0	4	4	14
2000-01	Victoriaville Tigres	QMJHL	72	16	71	87	164	13	2	19	21	46
2001-02	Victoriaville Tigres	QMJHL	68	29	83	112	165	22	9	*30	39	68
2002-03	Grand Rapids	AHL	71	3	7	10	52	7	0	1	1	7
2003-04	Grand Rapids	AHL	79	8	13	21	93	3	0	0	0	0
2004-05	Grand Rapids	AHL	53	1	11	12	90	...	...	...	...	...
	Manitoba Moose	AHL	16	2	6	8	16	13	1	3	4	14
2005-06	Kassel Huskies	Germany	51	2	11	13	93	5	0	1	1	6
2006-07	Hamilton Bulldogs	AHL	58	0	16	16	62	22	6	6	12	14
2007-08	Manitoba Moose	AHL	58	4	20	24	32	6	2	1	3	12
2008-09	Rockford IceHogs	AHL	80	6	34	40	58	4	0	2	2	2
2009-10	Worcester Sharks	AHL	80	14	52	66	80	10	1	6	7	6
2010-11	Nizhny Novgorod	Rus-KHL	38	2	23	25	50	...	...	...	...	...

QMJHL First All-Star Team (2001, 2002) • Canadian Major Junior First All-Star Team (2002) • Memorial Cup All-Star Team (2002) • Stafford Smythe Memorial Trophy (Memorial Cup MVP) (2002) • AHL First All-Star Team (2010) • Eddie Shore Award (AHL – Outstanding Defenseman) (2010)
Signed as a free agent by **Detroit**, August 12, 2002. • Loaned to **Manitoba** (AHL) by **Detroit** (Grand Rapids-AHL) for cash, March 15, 2005. Signed as a free agent by **Kassel** (Germany), August 25, 2005. Signed as a free agent by **San Jose**, July 16, 2009. Signed as a free agent by **Novgorod** ((Russia-KHL), July 1, 2010.

GRYBA, Eric (GREE-buh, AIR-ihk) OTT
Defense. Shoots right. 6'3", 214 lbs. Born, Saskatoon, Sask., April 14, 1988.
(Ottawa's 2nd choice, 68th overall, in 2006 Entry Draft).

			Regular Season					Playoffs			
Season	Club	League	GP	G	A	Pts	PIM	GP	G	A	Pts	PIM
2003-04	Sask. Contacts	SMHL	39	1	10	11	89	10	4	8	12	20
2004-05	Sask. Contacts	SMHL	32	11	29	40	83	11	5	7	12	22
2005-06	Green Bay	USHL	56	3	12	15	*205	3	1	1	2	27
2006-07	Boston University	H-East	38	1	3	4	76	...	...	...	...	...
2007-08	Boston University	H-East	32	1	1	2	54	...	...	...	...	...
2008-09	Boston University	H-East	45	0	6	6	106	...	...	...	...	...
2009-10	Boston University	H-East	38	4	6	10	*118	...	...	...	...	...
	Binghamton	AHL	6	1	0	1	2	...	...	...	...	...
2010-11	Binghamton	AHL	66	3	4	7	133	10	0	1	1	26

GUDAS, Radko (GOO-duhs, RAHD-koh) T.B.
Defense. Shoots right. 6', 210 lbs. Born, Prague, Czechoslovakia, June 5, 1990.
(Tampa Bay's 3rd choice, 66th overall, in 2010 Entry Draft).

			Regular Season					Playoffs			
Season	Club	League	GP	G	A	Pts	PIM	GP	G	A	Pts	PIM
2004-05	HC Kladno U17	CzR-U17	46	1	5	6	70	7	0	0	0	10
2005-06	HC Kladno U17	CzR-U17	46	12	14	26	178	5	1	2	3	8
2006-07	HC Kladno U17	CzR-U17	16	6	7	13	34	7	4	1	5	14
	HC KEB Kladno Jr.	CzRep-Jr.	15	0	1	1	18	1	0	0	0	0
	Beroun	CzRep-2	9	0	1	1	6	...	...	...	...	...
2007-08	Beroun	CzRep-2	43	1	5	6	90	...	...	...	...	...
	Kladno	CzRep						1	0	0	0	0
2008-09	HC KEB Kladno Jr.	CzRep-Jr.	2	0	1	1	0	...	...	...	...	...
	Beroun	CzRep-2	32	1	6	7	110	...	...	...	...	...
	Kladno	CzRep	14	0	1	1	10	...	...	...	...	...
2009-10	Everett Silvertips	WHL	65	7	30	37	151	3	0	2	2	4
2010-11	Norfolk Admirals	AHL	76	4	13	17	165	6	0	0	0	7

WHL West Second All-Star Team (2010)

GUDBRANSON, Erik (guhd-BRAN-suhn, AIR-ihk) FLA
Defense. Shoots right. 6'4", 206 lbs. Born, Ottawa, Ont., January 7, 1992.
(Florida's 1st choice, 3rd overall, in 2010 Entry Draft).

			Regular Season					Playoffs			
Season	Club	League	GP	G	A	Pts	PIM	GP	G	A	Pts	PIM
2007-08	Ottawa Jr. 67's	Minor-ON	70	15	40	55	118	...	...	...	...	...
2008-09	Kingston	OHL	63	3	19	22	69	...	...	...	...	...
2009-10	Kingston	OHL	41	2	21	23	68	7	1	2	3	6
2010-11	Kingston	OHL	44	12	22	34	105	5	1	3	4	10

GUPTILL, Alexander (GUP-tihl, al-ehx-AN-duhr) DAL
Left wing. Shoots left. 6'3", 185 lbs. Born, Burlington, Ont., March 5, 1992.
(Dallas' 3rd choice, 77th overall, in 2010 Entry Draft).

			Regular Season					Playoffs			
Season	Club	League	GP	G	A	Pts	PIM	GP	G	A	Pts	PIM
2008-09	Brampton Capitals	ON-Jr.A	49	30	34	64	28	3	0	1	1	0
2009-10	Brampton Capitals	ON-Jr.A	10	6	5	11	24	...	...	...	...	...
	Orangeville	ON-Jr.A	19	13	13	26	26	2	1	0	1	2
2010-11	Waterloo	USHL	43	13	12	25	53	2	0	0	0	0

• Signed Letter of Intent to attend **University of Michigan** (CCHA) in fall of 2011.

GYSBERS, Simon (GIGHZ-buhrz, SIGH-muhn) TOR
Defense. Shoots right. 6'4", 200 lbs. Born, Richmond Hill, Ont., May 7, 1987.

			Regular Season					Playoffs			
Season	Club	League	GP	G	A	Pts	PIM	GP	G	A	Pts	PIM
2004-05	Stouffville Spirit	OPJHL	46	11	23	34	32	...	...	...	...	...
2005-06	Stouffville Spirit	OPJHL	46	8	24	32	94	31	1	9	10	40
2006-07	Lake Superior	CCHA	41	4	9	13	45	...	...	...	...	...
2007-08	Lake Superior	CCHA	37	6	13	19	46	...	...	...	...	...
2008-09	Lake Superior	CCHA	39	3	18	21	28	...	...	...	...	...
2009-10	Lake Superior	CCHA	38	6	9	15	46	...	...	...	...	...
	Toronto Marlies	AHL	14	0	1	1	2	...	...	...	...	...
2010-11	Toronto Marlies	AHL	60	7	25	32	32	...	...	...	...	...

Signed to an ATO (amateur tryout) contact by **Toronto** (AHL), March 11, 2010.

HAAR, Garrett (HAHR, GAIR-eht) WSH
Defense. Shoots left. 5'11", 190 lbs. Born, Huntington Beach, CA, August 16, 1993.
(Washington's 4th choice, 207th overall, in 2011 Entry Draft).

			Regular Season					Playoffs			
Season	Club	League	GP	G	A	Pts	PIM	GP	G	A	Pts	PIM
2008-09	L.A. Selects	Minor-CA	STATISTICS NOT AVAILABLE									
2009-10	Russell Stover	T1EHL	42	4	34	38	28	...	...	...	...	...
2010-11	Fargo Force	USHL	51	7	16	23	38	5	1	2	3	2

Signed Athletic Aid Offer with **Western Michigan** (CCHA) for the fall of 2011.

HADDAD, Joey (HA-DAD, JOH-ee)
Left wing. Shoots left. 6'2", 195 lbs. Born, Sydney, N.S., December 10, 1988.

			Regular Season					Playoffs			
Season	Club	League	GP	G	A	Pts	PIM	GP	G	A	Pts	PIM
2005-06	P.E.I. Rocket	QMJHL	48	3	12	15	73	1	0	0	0	0
2006-07	P.E.I. Rocket	QMJHL	68	9	12	21	78	5	0	0	0	6
2007-08	Cape Breton	QMJHL	70	31	31	62	103	11	7	5	12	12
2008-09	Cape Breton	QMJHL	50	30	25	55	91	11	8	4	12	32
2009-10	Wilkes-Barre	AHL	29	1	5	6	24	...	...	...	...	...
	Wheeling Nailers	ECHL	34	7	13	20	52	...	...	...	...	...
2010-11	Wilkes-Barre	AHL	16	1	3	4	15	...	...	...	...	...
	Wheeling Nailers	ECHL	50	21	22	43	93	17	7	7	14	38

Signed as a free agent by **Pittsburgh**, October 10, 2008.

HAGEL, Kyle (HAY-guhl, KIGHL) ST.L.
Defense. Shoots left. 6', 205 lbs. Born, Hamilton, Ont., January 21, 1985.

			Regular Season					Playoffs			
Season	Club	League	GP	G	A	Pts	PIM	GP	G	A	Pts	PIM
2002-03	Hamilton	OPJHL	48	4	13	17	119	...	...	...	...	...
2003-04	Hamilton	OPJHL	39	4	13	17	51	...	...	...	...	...
2004-05	Princeton	ECAC	26	0	2	2	12	...	...	...	...	...
2005-06	Princeton	ECAC	30	6	5	11	6	...	...	...	...	...
2006-07	Princeton	ECAC	29	4	2	6	32	...	...	...	...	...
2007-08	Princeton	ECAC	32	2	3	5	30	...	...	...	...	...
2008-09	Fresno Falcons	ECHL	23	5	3	8	97	...	...	...	...	...
	Reading Royals	ECHL	15	2	3	5	46	...	...	...	...	...
	Rochester	AHL	3	0	0	0	5	...	...	...	...	...
2009-10	Las Vegas	ECHL	42	7	8	15	77	5	3	1	4	9
	Rockford IceHogs	AHL	9	0	0	0	36	...	...	...	...	...
2010-11	Rockford IceHogs	AHL	77	5	8	13	245	...	...	...	...	...

Signed as a free agent by **St. Louis**, May 9, 2011.

HAGELIN, Carl (HAG-eh-lihn, KARL) NYR
Left wing. Shoots left. 5'11", 176 lbs. Born, Sodertalje, Sweden, August 23, 1988.
(NY Rangers' 4th choice, 168th overall, in 2007 Entry Draft).

			Regular Season					Playoffs			
Season	Club	League	GP	G	A	Pts	PIM	GP	G	A	Pts	PIM
2004-05	Sodertalje SK U18	Swe-U18	14	10	7	17	16	2	0	2	2	0
2005-06	Sodertalje SK U18	Swe-U18	7	4	8	12	2	...	...	...	...	...
	Sodertalje SK Jr.	Swe-Jr.	41	20	20	40	42	4	1	2	3	22
2006-07	Sodertalje SK Jr.	Swe-Jr.	40	24	31	55	42	3	1	5	6	20
2007-08	U. of Michigan	CCHA	41	11	11	22	28	...	...	...	...	...
2008-09	U. of Michigan	CCHA	41	13	18	31	32	...	...	...	...	...
2009-10	U. of Michigan	CCHA	45	19	*31	*50	34	...	...	...	...	...
2010-11	U. of Michigan	CCHA	44	18	31	49	39	...	...	...	...	...
	Connecticut Whale	AHL	...	...	...	...	...	5	1	1	2	4

NCAA West Second All-American Team (2011)

HAKANPAA, Jani (HAHK-an-pah, YAH-nee) ST.L.
Defense. Shoots right. 6'4", 211 lbs. Born, Kirkkonummi, Finland, March 31, 1992.
(St. Louis' 5th choice, 104th overall, in 2010 Entry Draft).

			Regular Season					Playoffs			
Season	Club	League	GP	G	A	Pts	PIM	GP	G	A	Pts	PIM
2007-08	K-Vantaa U18	Fin-U18	2	0	1	1	2	2	0	0	0	0
2008-09	K-Vantaa U18	Fin-U18	10	3	4	7	14	...	...	...	...	...
2009-10	K-Vantaa U18	Fin-U18	32	3	16	19	69	6	0	2	2	6
2010-11	Suomi U20	Finland-2	8	1	2	3	31	...	...	...	...	...
	Blues Espoo Jr.	Fin-Jr.	36	3	20	23	61	12	3	2	5	10

HAMBURG, Anthony (HAM-buhrg, AN-thuh-nee) MIN
Center. Shoots right. 6'1", 185 lbs. Born, Houston, TX, August 30, 1991.
(Minnesota's 8th choice, 193rd overall, in 2009 Entry Draft).

			Regular Season					Playoffs			
Season	Club	League	GP	G	A	Pts	PIM	GP	G	A	Pts	PIM
2007-08	Dallas Stars AAA	Exhib.	65	20	57	77	68	...	...	...	...	...
2008-09	Dallas Stars AAA	T1EHL	46	16	38	54	38	...	...	...	...	...
	Dallas Stars AAA	Exhib.	24	13	32	45	38	...	...	...	...	...
2009-10	Omaha Lancers	USHL	54	5	17	22	35	3	0	0	0	2
2010-11	Colgate	ECAC	7	0	3	3	4	...	...	...	...	...
	Omaha Lancers	USHL	31	6	15	21	15	3	1	1	2	0

HAMILTON, Curtis (HAM-ihl-tuhn, KUHR-tihs) EDM
Left wing. Shoots left. 6'3", 206 lbs. Born, Tacoma, WA, December 4, 1991.
(Edmonton's 4th choice, 48th overall, in 2010 Entry Draft).

			Regular Season					Playoffs			
Season	Club	League	GP	G	A	Pts	PIM	GP	G	A	Pts	PIM
2006-07	Okanagan Rockets	BCMML	37	26	27	53	68	...	...	...	...	...
	Saskatoon Blades	WHL	2	0	0	0	0	...	...	...	...	...
2007-08	Saskatoon Blades	WHL	68	14	13	27	43	...	...	...	...	...
2008-09	Saskatoon Blades	WHL	58	20	28	48	24	7	1	1	2	2
2009-10	Saskatoon Blades	WHL	26	7	9	16	6	5	2	1	3	6
2010-11	Saskatoon Blades	WHL	62	26	56	82	22	10	4	7	11	4

HAMILTON, Dougie (HAM-ihl-tuhn, DUH-gee) BOS
Defense. Shoots right. 6'5", 193 lbs. Born, Toronto, Ont., June 17, 1993.
(Boston's 1st choice, 9th overall, in 2011 Entry Draft).

			Regular Season					Playoffs			
Season	Club	League	GP	G	A	Pts	PIM	GP	G	A	Pts	PIM
2008-09	St. Cath. Falcons	Minor-ON	67	20	33	53	26	...	...	...	...	...
2009-10	Niagara Ice Dogs	OHL	64	3	13	16	36	5	0	1	1	4
2010-11	Niagara Ice Dogs	OHL	67	12	46	58	77	14	4	12	16	16

OHL Second All-Star Team (2011) • Canadian Major Junior Scholastic Player of the Year (2011)

HAMILTON, Freddie (HAM-ihl-tuhn, FREH-dee) S.J.
Center. Shoots right. 6'1", 190 lbs. Born, Toronto, Ont., January 1, 1992.
(San Jose's 4th choice, 129th overall, in 2010 Entry Draft).

			Regular Season					Playoffs			
Season	Club	League	GP	G	A	Pts	PIM	GP	G	A	Pts	PIM
2007-08	Toronto Marlboros	GTHL	51	39	42	81	4	...	...	...	...	...
2008-09	Niagara Ice Dogs	OHL	65	10	18	28	8	12	2	2	4	4
2009-10	Niagara Ice Dogs	OHL	64	25	30	55	12	5	1	1	2	6
2010-11	Niagara Ice Dogs	OHL	68	38	45	83	20	14	4	10	14	4

HAMILTON, Ryan (HAM-ihl-tuhn, RIGH-uhn) TOR

Left wing. Shoots left. 6'2", 230 lbs. Born, Oshawa, Ont., April 15, 1985.

			Regular Season					Playoffs				
Season	Club	League	GP	G	A	Pts	PIM	GP	G	A	Pts	PIM
2002-03	Couchiching	OPJHL	11	5	8	13	2	....	....	....	....	....
	Peterborough Bees	OPJHL	27	3	10	13	43	....	....	....	....	....
	Trenton Sting	OPJHL	17	3	8	11	24	....	....	....	....	....
	Barrie Colts	OHL	24	3	2	5	10	6	1	0	1	0
2003-04	Kingston	OPJHL	14	1	5	6	23	....	....	....	....	....
	Barrie Colts	OHL	46	17	10	27	21	7	0	1	1	8
2004-05	Barrie Colts	OHL	37	13	11	24	6	6	2	0	2	2
2005-06	Barrie Colts	OHL	63	46	26	72	58	14	8	9	17	11
	Houston Aeros	AHL	....	....	....	....	....	1	0	0	0	0
2006-07	Houston Aeros	AHL	62	7	9	16	36	....	....	....	....	....
2007-08	Houston Aeros	AHL	72	20	19	39	38	2	1	0	1	0
2008-09	Houston Aeros	AHL	29	8	4	12	24	....	....	....	....	....
	Toronto Marlies	AHL	36	7	6	13	33	6	1	2	3	4
2009-10	Toronto Marlies	AHL	47	16	9	25	37	....	....	....	....	....
2010-11	Toronto Marlies	AHL	45	16	13	29	21	....	....	....	....	....

Signed as a free agent by **Minnesota**, July 5, 2006. Traded to **Toronto** by **Minnesota** for Robbie Earl, January 21, 2009.

HAMILTON, Wacey (HAM-ihl-tuhn, WAY-see) OTT

Center. Shoots left. 5'11", 173 lbs. Born, Calgary, Alta., September 10, 1990.

			Regular Season					Playoffs				
Season	Club	League	GP	G	A	Pts	PIM	GP	G	A	Pts	PIM
2006-07	Camrose Kodiaks	AJHL	49	11	6	17	38	5	1	1	2	8
2007-08	Medicine Hat	WHL	63	13	19	32	95	5	1	0	1	6
2008-09	Medicine Hat	WHL	37	4	13	17	64	11	1	3	4	24
2009-10	Medicine Hat	WHL	67	24	47	71	100	12	3	5	8	23
2010-11	Medicine Hat	WHL	67	20	53	73	113	15	4	8	12	20

Signed as a free agent by **Ottawa**, March 8, 2011.

HANNAY, Sawyer (HA-NAY, SOY-yuhr) VAN

Defense. Shoots right. 6'4", 196 lbs. Born, Moncton, N.B., September 6, 1992.
(Vancouver's 5th choice, 205th overall, in 2010 Entry Draft).

			Regular Season					Playoffs				
Season	Club	League	GP	G	A	Pts	PIM	GP	G	A	Pts	PIM
2007-08	Moncton Flyers	NBPEI	35	2	1	3	50	8	0	0	0	12
2008-09	Moncton Flyers	NBPEI	34	5	17	22	74	8	2	4	6	36
2009-10	Halifax	QMJHL	54	1	5	6	158	....	....	....	....	....
2010-11	Halifax	QMJHL	58	0	7	7	164	4	0	1	1	13

HANOWSKI, Ben (ha-NOW-skee, BEHN) PIT

Wing. Shoots left. 6'2", 198 lbs. Born, Little Falls, MN, October 18, 1990.
(Pittsburgh's 3rd choice, 63rd overall, in 2009 Entry Draft).

			Regular Season					Playoffs				
Season	Club	League	GP	G	A	Pts	PIM	GP	G	A	Pts	PIM
2005-06	Little Falls Flyers	High-MN	31	35	29	64	....	....	....	....	....	....
2006-07	Little Falls Flyers	High-MN	29	40	71	111	....	....	....	....	....	....
2007-08	Little Falls Flyers	High-MN	26	48	47	95	....	....	....	....	....	....
	Team North	UMHSEL	....	17	16	33	....	....	....	....	....	....
2008-09	Little Falls Flyers	High-MN	31	73	62	135	16	....	....	....	....	....
	Team North	UMHSEL	19	14	8	22	....	....	....	....	....	....
2009-10	St. Cloud State	WCHA	43	9	10	19	19	....	....	....	....	....
2010-11	St. Cloud State	WCHA	37	13	7	20	18	....	....	....	....	....

HANSEN, Jake (HAHN-suhn, JAYK) CBJ

Wing. Shoots right. 6'2", 189 lbs. Born, St.Paul, MN, August 21, 1989.
(Columbus' 4th choice, 68th overall, in 2007 Entry Draft).

			Regular Season					Playoffs				
Season	Club	League	GP	G	A	Pts	PIM	GP	G	A	Pts	PIM
2005-06	White Bear Lake	High-MN		STATISTICS NOT AVAILABLE								
2006-07	White Bear Lake	High-MN	25	28	43	71	....	....	....	....	....	....
	Sioux Falls	USHL	15	4	4	8	14	7	0	2	2	6
2007-08	Sioux Falls	USHL	60	31	27	58	57	3	1	0	1	0
2008-09	U. of Minnesota	WCHA	33	2	5	7	38	....	....	....	....	....
2009-10	U. of Minnesota	WCHA	38	7	5	12	20	....	....	....	....	....
2010-11	U. of Minnesota	WCHA	35	11	9	20	49	....	....	....	....	....

USHL Second All-Star Team (2008)

HARPER, Shane (HAHR-puhr, SHAYN) PHI

Right wing. Shoots right. 5'11", 193 lbs. Born, Valencia, CA, February 1, 1989.

			Regular Season					Playoffs				
Season	Club	League	GP	G	A	Pts	PIM	GP	G	A	Pts	PIM
2005-06	Everett Silvertips	WHL	62	6	4	10	8	5	1	0	1	0
2006-07	Everett Silvertips	WHL	58	3	12	15	23	8	1	2	3	0
2007-08	Everett Silvertips	WHL	71	17	26	43	18	4	0	2	2	0
2008-09	Everett Silvertips	WHL	72	32	34	66	10	5	0	4	4	0
2009-10	Everett Silvertips	WHL	72	42	38	80	38	7	6	4	10	6
	Adirondack	AHL	5	1	0	1	2	....	....	....	....	....
2010-11	Adirondack	AHL	20	1	2	3	4	....	....	....	....	....
	Greenville	ECHL	48	22	23	45	20	11	4	6	10	2

WHL West Second All-Star Team (2010)

Signed as a free agent by **Philadelphia**, March 4, 2010.

HARRINGTON, Scott (HAIR-ihng-tuhn, SKAWT) PIT

Defense. Shoots left. 6'1", 200 lbs. Born, Kingston, Ont., March 10, 1993.
(Pittsburgh's 2nd choice, 54th overall, in 2011 Entry Draft).

			Regular Season					Playoffs				
Season	Club	League	GP	G	A	Pts	PIM	GP	G	A	Pts	PIM
2008-09	King. Jr. Front.	Minor-ON	66	19	48	67	46	....	....	....	....	....
	Kingston	ON-Jr.A	2	1	0	1	2	18	1	6	7	6
2009-10	London Knights	OHL	55	1	13	14	20	12	0	2	2	4
2010-11	London Knights	OHL	67	6	16	22	51	6	0	1	1	0

OHL All-Rookie Team (2010)

HARSTAD, Aaron (HAHR-stad, AIR-uhn) WPG

Defense. Shoots left. 6'2", 199 lbs. Born, Stevens Point, WI, April 27, 1992.
(Winnipeg's 7th choice, 187th overall, in 2011 Entry Draft).

			Regular Season					Playoffs				
Season	Club	League	GP	G	A	Pts	PIM	GP	G	A	Pts	PIM
2008-09	Green Bay	USHL	10	0	0	0	2	5	0	0	0	6
2009-10	Green Bay	USHL	47	2	6	8	61	11	0	3	3	9
2010-11	Green Bay	USHL	51	7	14	21	73	11	2	2	4	26

• Signed Letter of Intent to attend **Colorado College** (WCHA).

HAULA, Erik (HOW-la, AIR-ihk) MIN

Left wing. Shoots left. 5'11", 170 lbs. Born, Pori, Finland, March 23, 1991.
(Minnesota's 7th choice, 182nd overall, in 2009 Entry Draft).

			Regular Season					Playoffs				
Season	Club	League	GP	G	A	Pts	PIM	GP	G	A	Pts	PIM
2006-07	Assat Pori U18	Fin-U18	29	19	24	43	24	6	1	3	4	4
2007-08	Assat Pori U18	Fin-U18	3	1	1	2	0	2	4	2	6	14
	Assat Pori Jr.	Fin-Jr.	40	7	15	22	26	12	2	0	2	4
2008-09	Shat.-St. Mary's	High-MN	53	26	58	84	46	....	....	....	....	....
2009-10	Omaha Lancers	USHL	56	28	44	72	59	8	2	9	11	2
2010-11	U. of Minnesota	WCHA	34	6	18	24	22	....	....	....	....	....

USHL All-Rookie Team (2010) • USHL Second All-Star Team (2010)

HAUSWIRTH, Jake (HAWZ-wuhrth, JAYK) FLA

Centre. Shoots left. 6'5", 209 lbs. Born, Merrill, WI, February 16, 1988.

			Regular Season					Playoffs				
Season	Club	League	GP	G	A	Pts	PIM	GP	G	A	Pts	PIM
2006-07	Marquette	NAHL	55	21	19	40	74	....	....	....	....	....
2007-08	Omaha Lancers	USHL	57	13	10	23	36	13	2	4	6	10
2008-09	Omaha Lancers	USHL	58	28	24	52	22	3	1	0	1	0
2009-10	South Carolina	ECHL	62	17	27	44	24	2	0	1	1	0
2010-11	South Carolina	ECHL	37	10	4	14	8	....	....	....	....	....
	Cincinnati	ECHL	12	2	2	4	8	....	....	....	....	....

Signed as a free agent by **Washington**, May 26, 2009. Traded to **Florida** by **Washington** with Washington's 3rd round choice (Jonathan Racine) in 2011 Entry Draft for Dennis Wideman, February 28, 2011.

HAYES, Jimmy (HAYZ, JIH-mee) CHI

Right wing. Shoots right. 6'5", 210 lbs. Born, Boston, MA, November 21, 1989.
(Toronto's 2nd choice, 60th overall, in 2008 Entry Draft).

			Regular Season					Playoffs				
Season	Club	League	GP	G	A	Pts	PIM	GP	G	A	Pts	PIM
2006-07	USNTDP	U-17	42	17	14	31	37	....	....	....	....	....
	USNTDP	NAHL	14	6	8	14	4	....	....	....	....	....
2007-08	USNTDP	U-18	18	2	5	7	6	....	....	....	....	....
	USNTDP	NAHL	19	2	8	10	6	....	....	....	....	....
	Lincoln Stars	USHL	21	4	11	15	18	8	4	5	9	8
2008-09	Boston College	H-East	36	8	5	13	22	....	....	....	....	....
2009-10	Boston College	H-East	42	13	22	35	14	....	....	....	....	....
2010-11	Boston College	H-East	39	21	12	33	24	....	....	....	....	....
	Rockford IceHogs	AHL	7	0	0	0	2	....	....	....	....	....

Traded to **Chicago** by **Toronto** for Calgary's 2nd round choice (previously acquired, Toronto selected Brad Ross) in 2010 Entry Draft, June 25, 2010.

HAYES, Kevin (HAYZ, KEH-vihn) CHI

Right wing. Shoots left. 6'2", 201 lbs. Born, Boston, MA, May 8, 1992.
(Chicago's 1st choice, 24th overall, in 2010 Entry Draft).

			Regular Season					Playoffs				
Season	Club	League	GP	G	A	Pts	PIM	GP	G	A	Pts	PIM
2007-08	Nobles	High-MA	29	8	5	13	2	....	....	....	....	....
2008-09	Nobles	High-MA	23	28	27	55	15	....	....	....	....	....
2009-10	Cape Cod Whalers	Minor-MA	25	21	30	51	....	....	....	....	....	....
	Nobles	High-MA	29	25	44	69	8	....	....	....	....	....
	USNTDP	U-18	2	2	0	2	0	....	....	....	....	....
2010-11	Boston College	H-East	31	4	10	14	8	....	....	....	....	....

HAZEN, Jonathan (HAY-zuhn, JAWN-ah-thuhn) FLA

Right wing. Shoots right. 6', 168 lbs. Born, Val Belair, Que., June 18, 1990.

			Regular Season					Playoffs				
Season	Club	League	GP	G	A	Pts	PIM	GP	G	A	Pts	PIM
2007-08	Val-d'Or Foreurs	QMJHL	65	21	19	40	25	4	2	1	3	0
2008-09	Val-d'Or Foreurs	QMJHL	62	20	25	45	26	....	....	....	....	....
2009-10	Val-d'Or Foreurs	QMJHL	53	24	35	59	59	6	2	1	3	2
2010-11	Val-d'Or Foreurs	QMJHL	62	41	42	83	29	1	0	0	0	5

Signed as a free agent by **Florida**, March 19, 2011.

HEED, Tim (HEH-ehd, TIHM) ANA

Defense. Shoots right. 6', 170 lbs. Born, Gothenburg, Sweden, January 27, 1991.
(Anaheim's 5th choice, 132nd overall, in 2010 Entry Draft).

			Regular Season					Playoffs				
Season	Club	League	GP	G	A	Pts	PIM	GP	G	A	Pts	PIM
2007-08	Sodertalje SK U18	Swe-U18	36	4	23	27	34	2	0	0	0	4
	Sodertalje SK Jr.	Swe-Jr.	2	0	0	0	0	....	....	....	....	....
2008-09	Sodertalje SK U18	Swe-U18	14	7	10	17	10	3	3	2	5	2
	Sodertalje SK Jr.	Swe-Jr.	32	1	7	8	10	2	0	1	1	0
2009-10	Sodertalje SK Jr.	Swe-Jr.	32	8	29	37	20	....	....	....	....	....
	Sodertalje SK	Sweden	27	1	9	10	2	....	....	....	....	....
	Sodertalje SK	Sweden-Q	10	0	4	4	0	....	....	....	....	....
2010-11	Sodertalje SK Jr.	Swe-Jr.	2	0	2	2	2	....	....	....	....	....
	Vaxjo Lakers HC	Sweden-2	29	3	20	23	8	....	....	....	....	....
	Sodertalje SK	Sweden	12	1	0	1	0	....	....	....	....	....
	Sodertalje SK	Sweden-Q	10	0	4	4	4	....	....	....	....	....

HEGARTY, Ryan (HEH-gahr-tee, RIGH-uhn) ANA

Defense. Shoots left. 6', 201 lbs. Born, Stoneham, MA, May 16, 1990.
(Anaheim's 8th choice, 113th overall, in 2008 Entry Draft).

			Regular Season					Playoffs				
Season	Club	League	GP	G	A	Pts	PIM	GP	G	A	Pts	PIM
2006-07	USNTDP	U-17	15	1	2	3	10	....	....	....	....	....
	USNTDP	NAHL	43	1	2	3	54	6	0	0	0	4
2007-08	USNTDP	U-18	41	5	8	13	38	....	....	....	....	....
	USNTDP	NAHL	14	2	8	10	18	....	....	....	....	....
2008-09	U. of Maine	H-East	24	0	3	3	22	....	....	....	....	....
2009-10	U. of Maine	H-East	33	1	7	8	36	....	....	....	....	....
2010-11	U. of Maine	H-East	26	1	3	4	14	....	....	....	....	....

HELGESON, Seth (HEHL-guh-suhn, SEHTH) N.J.

Defense. Shoots left. 6'4", 215 lbs. Born, Faribault, MN, October 8, 1990.
(New Jersey's 4th choice, 114th overall, in 2009 Entry Draft).

			Regular Season					Playoffs				
Season	Club	League	GP	G	A	Pts	PIM	GP	G	A	Pts	PIM
2006-07	Faribault Falcons	High-MN	27	19	17	36	....	....	....	....	....	....
2007-08	Sioux City	USHL	58	3	8	11	41	4	0	1	1	2
2008-09	Sioux City	USHL	58	4	12	16	64	....	....	....	....	....
2009-10	U. of Minnesota	WCHA	31	1	0	1	24	....	....	....	....	....
2010-11	U. of Minnesota	WCHA	36	1	6	7	66	....	....	....	....	....

HENDERSON, Kevin (HEHN-duhr-SOHN, KEH-vihn)

Left wing. Shoots left. 6'3", 210 lbs. Born, Toronto, Ont., December 3, 1986.

			Regular Season					Playoffs				
Season	Club	League	GP	G	A	Pts	PIM	GP	G	A	Pts	PIM
2003-04	Pickering Panthers	OPJHL	47	11	23	34	44	....	....	....	....	....
2004-05	Kitchener Rangers	OHL	47	5	8	13	46	15	0	3	3	8
	Tor. T-Birds	OPJHL	11	5	9	14	33	....	....	....	....	....
2005-06	Kitchener Rangers	OHL	63	6	11	17	66	2	1	0	1	0
2006-07	Kitchener Rangers	OHL	56	33	15	48	69	9	4	6	10	13
2007-08	New Brunswick	AUAA	27	5	10	15	22	....	....	....	....	....
2008-09	New Brunswick	AUAA	28	19	31	50	28	....	....	....	....	....
2009-10	Worcester Sharks	AHL	64	2	13	15	45	11	0	1	1	4
2010-11	Worcester Sharks	AHL	73	8	13	21	45	....	....	....	....	....

Signed as a free agent by **San Jose**, April 22, 2009.

HENLEY, Cedrick (HEHN-lee, SEH-drihk) **BUF**

Left wing. Shoots left. 6'4", 206 lbs. Born, Val D'Or, Que., January 10, 1992.
(Buffalo's 7th choice, 173rd overall, in 2010 Entry Draft).

			Regular Season					Playoffs				
Season	Club	League	GP	G	A	Pts	PIM	GP	G	A	Pts	PIM
2007-08	Filon De Malartic	Minor-QU	STATISTICS NOT AVAILABLE									
	Amos Forestiers	QAAA	14	6	12	18	12	....	....	....	....	....
2008-09	Val-d'Or Foreurs	QMJHL	61	7	12	19	26	....	....	....	....	....
2009-10	Val-d'Or Foreurs	QMJHL	44	5	7	12	43	6	0	0	0	6
2010-11	Val-d'Or Foreurs	QMJHL	22	5	12	17	26	4	0	0	0	6

HENRY, Jordan (HEHN-ree, JOHR-duhn) **CGY**

Defense. Shoots right. 6'2", 200 lbs. Born, Milo, Alta., February 11, 1986.

			Regular Season					Playoffs				
Season	Club	League	GP	G	A	Pts	PIM	GP	G	A	Pts	PIM
2003-04	Moose Jaw	WHL	61	0	4	4	82	10	0	0	0	6
2004-05	Moose Jaw	WHL	68	2	12	14	137	5	2	0	2	26
2005-06	Moose Jaw	WHL	40	1	12	13	104	....	....	....	....	....
	Red Deer Rebels	WHL	29	2	8	10	51	....	....	....	....	....
2006-07	Red Deer Rebels	WHL	72	7	25	32	162	7	0	4	4	26
2007-08	Rochester	AHL	49	3	5	8	73	....	....	....	....	....
	Florida Everblades	ECHL	20	2	2	4	14	....	....	....	....	....
2008-09	Rochester	AHL	69	4	12	16	111	....	....	....	....	....
2009-10	Rochester	AHL	76	13	18	31	104	7	4	0	4	23
2010-11	Dynamo Minsk	Rus-KHL	36	1	1	2	53	6	1	1	2	33

Signed as a free agent by **Florida**, October 8, 2007. Signed as a free agent by **Minsk** (Russia-KHL), July 25, 2010. Traded to **Calgary** by **Florida** for Keith Seabrook, July 9, 2011.

HERBERT, Caleb (HUHR-buhrt, KAY-lehb) **WSH**

Center. Shoots right. 5'10", 180 lbs. Born, St. Paul, MN, October 12, 1991.
(Washington's 4th choice, 142nd overall, in 2010 Entry Draft).

			Regular Season					Playoffs				
Season	Club	League	GP	G	A	Pts	PIM	GP	G	A	Pts	PIM
2007-08	Bloomington-Jeff.	High-MN	6	4	3	7	6	....	....	....	....	....
2008-09	Bloomington-Jeff.	High-MN	27	29	24	53	36	....	....	....	....	....
2009-10	Team Southeast	UMHSEL	24	14	8	22	....	....	....	....	....	....
	Bloomington-Jeff.	High-MN	25	26	28	54	42	3	4	4	8	2
2010-11	Sioux City	USHL	51	23	27	50	61	3	0	0	0	4

• Signed Letter of Intent to attend **University of Minnesota-Duluth** (WCHA) in fall of 2011.

HEXTALL, Brett (HEHX-tahl, BREHT) **PHX**

Center. Shoots right. 5'10", 186 lbs. Born, Philadelphia, PA, April 2, 1988.
(Phoenix's 7th choice, 159th overall, in 2008 Entry Draft).

			Regular Season					Playoffs				
Season	Club	League	GP	G	A	Pts	PIM	GP	G	A	Pts	PIM
2006-07	Penticton Vees	BCHL	59	18	27	45	156	11	2	2	4	8
2007-08	Penticton Vees	BCHL	54	24	48	72	52	15	*12	3	15	12
2008-09	North Dakota	WCHA	42	12	24	36	91	....	....	....	....	....
2009-10	North Dakota	WCHA	34	14	12	26	88	....	....	....	....	....
2010-11	North Dakota	WCHA	39	13	16	29	63	....	....	....	....	....

HICKEY, Thomas (HIH-kee, TAW-muhs) **L.A.**

Defense. Shoots left. 5'11", 184 lbs. Born, Calgary, Alta., February 8, 1989.
(Los Angeles' 1st choice, 4th overall, in 2007 Entry Draft).

			Regular Season					Playoffs				
Season	Club	League	GP	G	A	Pts	PIM	GP	G	A	Pts	PIM
2003-04	Cgy. Royals	CBHL	32	13	25	38	51	....	....	....	....	....
2004-05	Calgary Royals	AMHL	33	9	13	22	36	....	....	....	....	....
	Seattle	WHL	5	2	1	3	6	....	....	....	....	....
2005-06	Seattle	WHL	69	1	27	28	53	7	1	3	4	10
2006-07	Seattle	WHL	68	9	41	50	70	11	3	4	7	4
2007-08	Seattle	WHL	63	11	34	45	49	9	1	9	10	4
2008-09	Seattle	WHL	57	16	35	51	30	5	2	1	3	4
	Manchester	AHL	7	1	6	7	2	....	....	....	....	....
2009-10	Manchester	AHL	19	1	5	6	12	4	0	3	3	0
2010-11	Manchester	AHL	77	6	18	24	38	7	0	2	2	0

WHL West Second All-Star Team (2007) • WHL West First All-Star Team (2008, 2009)
• Missed majority of 2009-10 due to recurring shoulder injury and follow-up surgery.

HISEY, Rob (HIGH-zee, RAWB)

Center. Shoots left. 5'9", 172 lbs. Born, Oakville, Ont., September 24, 1984.

			Regular Season					Playoffs				
Season	Club	League	GP	G	A	Pts	PIM	GP	G	A	Pts	PIM
2001-02	Sault Ste. Marie	OHL	68	20	33	53	33	6	0	0	0	6
2002-03	Sault Ste. Marie	OHL	23	9	16	25	10	....	....	....	....	....
	Erie Otters	OHL	50	19	30	49	46	....	....	....	....	....
2003-04	Erie Otters	OHL	63	38	58	96	63	8	2	3	5	8
	Port Huron	UHL	....	....	....	....	....	6	3	6	9	4
2004-05	Erie Otters	OHL	25	8	26	34	41	....	....	....	....	....
	Barrie Colts	OHL	41	21	31	52	40	6	2	8	10	6
	Reading Royals	ECHL	....	....	....	....	....	7	2	2	4	2
2005-06	Assat Pori	Finland	46	12	13	25	101	14	4	2	6	40
2006-07	Hannover Scorp.	Germany	51	12	17	29	54	6	0	1	1	8
2007-08	EC Graz	Austria	22	3	13	16	36	....	....	....	....	....
	Assat Pori	Finland	14	2	4	6	16	....	....	....	....	....
	Mora IK	Sweden	12	6	4	10	10	....	....	....	....	....
2008-09	Hannover Ind.	German-3	34	19	39	58	137	7	10	8	18	8
2009-10	Tulsa Oilers	CHL	24	19	22	41	27	....	....	....	....	....
	Springfield Falcons	AHL	37	11	14	25	29	....	....	....	....	....
2010-11	Bridgeport	AHL	59	16	32	48	42	....	....	....	....	....

Signed as a free agent by **Tulsa** (CHL), October 12, 2009. Signed as a free agent by **Springfield** (AHL), December 28, 2009. Signed as a free agent by **NY Islanders**, August 18, 2010.

HISHON, Joey (HIHS-hawn, JOH-ee) **COL**

Center. Shoots left. 5'10", 175 lbs. Born, Stratford, Ont., October 20, 1991.
(Colorado's 1st choice, 17th overall, in 2010 Entry Draft).

			Regular Season					Playoffs				
Season	Club	League	GP	G	A	Pts	PIM	GP	G	A	Pts	PIM
2006-07	Stratford Warriors	Minor-ON	50	44	42	86	114	....	....	....	....	....
2007-08	Owen Sound	OHL	63	20	27	47	38	....	....	....	....	....
2008-09	Owen Sound	OHL	65	37	44	81	34	4	4	3	7	6
2009-10	Owen Sound	OHL	36	16	24	40	26	....	....	....	....	....
2010-11	Owen Sound	OHL	50	37	50	87	64	22	5	*19	*24	32

OHL First All-Star Team (2011)

HOBBS, Danny (HAWBZ, DA-nee) **NYR**

Center/Right wing. Shoots left. 5'11", 192 lbs. Born, Shawville, Ont., June 21, 1989.
(NY Rangers' 6th choice, 198th overall, in 2007 Entry Draft).

			Regular Season					Playoffs				
Season	Club	League	GP	G	A	Pts	PIM	GP	G	A	Pts	PIM
2005-06	Stanstead	QJHL	46	58	32	90	15	....	....	....	....	....
2006-07	Ohio	USHL	60	10	11	21	36	4	0	2	2	2
2007-08	Ohio	USHL	54	15	16	31	22	....	....	....	....	....
2008-09	Massachusetts	H-East	24	1	1	2	20	....	....	....	....	....
2009-10	Massachusetts	H-East	33	3	6	9	12	....	....	....	....	....
2010-11	Massachusetts	H-East	31	12	16	28	20	....	....	....	....	....

HOEFFEL, Mike (HOH-fuhl, MIGHK) **N.J.**

Left wing. Shoots left. 6'3", 205 lbs. Born, North Oaks, MN, April 9, 1989.
(New Jersey's 1st choice, 57th overall, in 2007 Entry Draft).

			Regular Season					Playoffs				
Season	Club	League	GP	G	A	Pts	PIM	GP	G	A	Pts	PIM
2004-05	Hill-Murray	High-MN	26	24	19	43	10	....	....	....	....	....
2005-06	Hill-Murray	High-MN	30	27	46	73	20	....	....	....	....	....
2006-07	USNTDP	U-18	33	10	2	12	18	....	....	....	....	....
	USNTDP	NAHL	11	6	5	11	10	....	....	....	....	....
2007-08	U. of Minnesota	WCHA	45	9	10	19	22	....	....	....	....	....
2008-09	U. of Minnesota	WCHA	35	12	8	20	38	....	....	....	....	....
2009-10	U. of Minnesota	WCHA	34	14	10	24	22	....	....	....	....	....
2010-11	U. of Minnesota	WCHA	35	13	11	24	24	....	....	....	....	....
	Albany Devils	AHL	10	2	0	2	6	....	....	....	....	....

HOEFFLIN, Mirko (HOHF-lihn, MIHR-koh) **CHI**

Center. Shoots left. 6', 174 lbs. Born, Freiburg, Germany, June 18, 1992.
(Chicago's 8th choice, 151st overall, in 2010 Entry Draft).

			Regular Season					Playoffs				
Season	Club	League	GP	G	A	Pts	PIM	GP	G	A	Pts	PIM
2007-08	Heil./Mann. Jr.	Ger-Jr.	34	8	7	15	28	8	0	2	2	4
2008-09	Heil./Mann. Jr.	Ger-Jr.	36	14	30	44	26	8	6	8	14	0
2009-10	Heil./Mann. Jr.	Ger-Jr.	24	32	35	67	20	8	5	9	14	2
	Heilbronner Falken	German-2	18	0	3	3	0	5	0	0	0	2
2010-11	Quebec Remparts	QMJHL	54	14	31	45	16	15	4	10	14	12

HOFFMAN, Mike (HAWF-muhn, MIGHK) **OTT**

Center/Left wing. Shoots left. 6', 175 lbs. Born, Kitchener, Ont., November 24, 1989.
(Ottawa's 5th choice, 130th overall, in 2009 Entry Draft).

			Regular Season					Playoffs				
Season	Club	League	GP	G	A	Pts	PIM	GP	G	A	Pts	PIM
2006-07	Kitchener	ON-Jr.B	47	28	29	57	70	6	3	5	8	6
	Kitchener Rangers	OHL	2	0	0	0	2	4	0	0	0	0
2007-08	Gatineau	QMJHL	19	5	7	12	16	....	....	....	....	....
	Drummondville	QMJHL	43	19	17	36	77	....	....	....	....	....
2008-09	Drummondville	QMJHL	62	52	42	94	86	19	21	13	34	26
2009-10	Saint John	QMJHL	56	46	39	85	38	21	11	13	24	23
2010-11	Binghamton	AHL	74	7	18	25	16	19	1	8	9	16
	Elmira Jackals	ECHL	4	0	3	3	0	....	....	....	....	....

QMJHL First All-Star Team (2009, 2010) • QMJHL Player of the Year (2010) • Canadian Major Junior Second All-Star Team (2010)

HOFMANN, Gregory (HAWF-man, GREH-goh-ree) **CAR**

Center. Shoots left. 6', 178 lbs. Born, Tramelan, Switzerland, November 13, 1992.
(Carolina's 4th choice, 103rd overall, in 2011 Entry Draft).

			Regular Season					Playoffs				
Season	Club	League	GP	G	A	Pts	PIM	GP	G	A	Pts	PIM
2006-07	Chaux-de-Fonds Jr.	Swiss-Jr.	2	0	0	0	0	....	....	....	....	....
2007-08	HC Luzern U17	Swiss-U17	6	2	5	7	14	....	....	....	....	....
	Ambri U17	Swiss-U17	22	14	11	25	64	5	4	3	7	20
	Ambri Jr.	Swiss-Jr.	11	4	1	5	6	8	0	0	0	2
2008-09	Ambri U17	Swiss-U17	20	9	16	25	42	....	....	....	....	....
	Ambri Jr.	Swiss-Jr.	22	10	7	17	26	2	0	0	0	2
2009-10	Ambri Jr.	Swiss-Jr.	34	25	30	55	20	3	1	2	3	6
	HC Ambri-Piotta	Swiss	1	0	0	0	0	1	0	0	0	0
2010-11	Ambri Jr.	Swiss-Jr.	2	2	0	2	2	....	....	....	....	....
	HC Ambri-Piotta	Swiss	41	3	9	12	2	12	0	2	2	2
	HC Ambri-Piotta	Swiss-Q	....	....	....	....	....	5	1	2	3	2

HOLL, Justin (HOHL, JUHS-tihn) **CHI**

Defense. Shoots right. 6'2", 170 lbs. Born, Edina, MN, January 30, 1992.
(Chicago's 3rd choice, 54th overall, in 2010 Entry Draft).

			Regular Season					Playoffs				
Season	Club	League	GP	G	A	Pts	PIM	GP	G	A	Pts	PIM
2007-08	Minnetonka High	High-MN	24	0	1	1	0	....	....	....	....	....
2008-09	Minnetonka High	High-MN	28	1	6	7	4	....	....	....	....	....
2009-10	Team Southwest	UMHSEL	STATISTICS NOT AVAILABLE									
	Minnetonka High	High-MN	25	17	14	31	8	6	3	3	6	0
2010-11	U. of Minnesota	WCHA	25	1	6	7	12	....	....	....	....	....

HOLLAND, Patrick (HAW-luhnd, PAT-rihk) **CGY**

Right wing. Shoots right. 6', 175 lbs. Born, Lethbridge, Alta., January 7, 1992.
(Calgary's 6th choice, 193rd overall, in 2010 Entry Draft).

			Regular Season					Playoffs				
Season	Club	League	GP	G	A	Pts	PIM	GP	G	A	Pts	PIM
2007-08	Leth. Hurricanes	Minor-AB	32	33	21	54	34	....	....	....	....	....
2008-09	Lethbridge	AMHL	34	17	28	45	20	7	5	11	16	2
	Lethbridge	Exhib.	6	5	3	8	0	....	....	....	....	....
	Tri-City Americans	WHL	1	0	0	0	0	....	....	....	....	....
2009-10	Tri-City Americans	WHL	59	16	20	36	14	22	3	7	10	10
2010-11	Tri-City Americans	WHL	71	22	40	62	24	10	4	4	8	2

HOLLAND, Peter (HAW-luhnd, PEE-tuhr) ANA

Center. Shoots left. 6'2", 195 lbs. Born, Toronto, Ont., January 14, 1991.
(Anaheim's 1st choice, 15th overall, in 2009 Entry Draft).

			Regular Season					Playoffs				
Season	Club	League	GP	G	A	Pts	PIM	GP	G	A	Pts	PIM
2006-07	Brampton	Minor-ON	60	59	60	119	107	....	....	....	....	....
2007-08	Guelph Storm	OHL	62	8	15	23	31	10	0	1	1	4
2008-09	Guelph Storm	OHL	68	28	39	67	42	4	4	0	4	2
2009-10	Guelph Storm	OHL	59	30	50	80	40	5	3	5	8	12
2010-11	Guelph Storm	OHL	67	37	51	88	57	6	3	6	9	4
	Syracuse Crunch	AHL	3	3	3	6	0	....	....	....	....	....

HOLLOWAY, Bud (HAHL-OH-way, BUHD) L.A.

Center. Shoots right. 6'1", 201 lbs. Born, Wapella, Sask., March 1, 1988.
(Los Angeles' 5th choice, 86th overall, in 2006 Entry Draft).

			Regular Season					Playoffs				
Season	Club	League	GP	G	A	Pts	PIM	GP	G	A	Pts	PIM
2003-04	Yorkton Harvest	SMHL	43	15	21	36	22	....	....	....	....	....
	Seattle	WHL	2	0	0	0	0	....	....	....	....	....
2004-05	Seattle	WHL	67	4	11	15	27	12	0	1	1	0
2005-06	Seattle	WHL	72	21	13	34	18	7	3	2	5	4
2006-07	Seattle	WHL	71	27	38	65	50	11	3	3	6	8
2007-08	Seattle	WHL	70	43	40	83	55	12	5	5	10	4
2008-09	Manchester	AHL	38	7	5	12	6	....	....	....	....	....
	Ontario Reign	ECHL	23	14	8	22	8	7	5	9	14	8
2009-10	Manchester	AHL	75	19	28	47	26	16	7	7	14	9
2010-11	Manchester	AHL	78	28	33	61	58	7	4	7	11	10

Signed as a free aget by **Skelleftea** (Sweden), July 25, 2011.

HOLZAPFEL, Riley (HOHL-za-fehl, RIGH-lee) WPG

Center. Shoots left. 6'2", 190 lbs. Born, Regina, Sask., August 18, 1988.
(Atlanta's 2nd choice, 43rd overall, in 2006 Entry Draft).

			Regular Season					Playoffs				
Season	Club	League	GP	G	A	Pts	PIM	GP	G	A	Pts	PIM
2004-05	Moose Jaw	WHL	63	15	13	28	32	5	1	2	3	8
2005-06	Moose Jaw	WHL	64	19	38	57	46	22	7	9	16	20
2006-07	Moose Jaw	WHL	72	39	43	82	94	....	....	....	....	....
2007-08	Moose Jaw	WHL	49	18	23	41	43	6	3	5	8	12
	Chicago Wolves	AHL	1	0	0	0	0	....	....	....	....	....
2008-09	Chicago Wolves	AHL	73	13	19	32	38	....	....	....	....	....
2009-10	Chicago Wolves	AHL	60	7	16	23	30	14	0	3	3	6
2010-11	Chicago Wolves	AHL	68	12	15	27	20	....	....	....	....	....

WHL East First All-Star Team (2007)

• Transferred to **Winnipeg** after **Atlanta** franchise relocated, June 21, 2011.

HORAK, Roman (HOH-rak, ROH-muhn) CGY

Center. Shoots left. 6', 170 lbs. Born, Ceske Budejovice, Czech., May 21, 1991.
(NY Rangers' 4th choice, 127th overall, in 2009 Entry Draft).

			Regular Season					Playoffs				
Season	Club	League	GP	G	A	Pts	PIM	GP	G	A	Pts	PIM
2004-05	C. Budejovice U17	CzR-U17	2	0	0	0	0	....	....	....	....	....
2005-06	C. Budejovice U17	CzR-U17	34	5	3	8	10	3	0	0	0	4
2006-07	C. Budejovice U17	CzR-U17	24	22	16	38	38	2	1	0	1	4
	C. Budejovice Jr.	CzRep-Jr.	16	1	4	5	6	1	0	0	0	0
2007-08	C. Budejovice U17	CzR-U17	2	3	2	5	0	....	....	....	....	....
	C. Budejovice Jr.	CzRep-Jr.	34	17	11	28	14	3	0	1	1	0
	C. Budejovice	CzRep	1	0	0	0	0	....	....	....	....	....
2008-09	C. Budejovice Jr.	CzRep-Jr.	31	16	17	33	14	2	0	0	0	0
	C. Budejovice	CzRep	17	1	0	1	0	....	....	....	....	....
2009-10	Chilliwack Bruins	WHL	66	21	26	47	39	6	2	4	6	4
2010-11	Chilliwack Bruins	WHL	64	26	52	78	60	5	1	2	3	0

Traded to **Calgary** by **NY Rangers** with NY Rangers' 2nd round choice (Markus Granlund) in 2011 Entry Draft and Pittsburgh's 2nd round choice (previously acquired, Calgary selected Tyler Wotherspoon) in 2011 Entry Draft for Tim Erixon and Calgary's 5th round choice (Shane McColgan) in 2011 Entry Draft, June 1, 2011.

HOSTETTER, Tyler (HAWS-the-tuhr, TIGH-luhr) PHI

Defense. Shoots right. 5'11", 200 lbs. Born, Lititz, PA, January 30, 1991.

			Regular Season					Playoffs				
Season	Club	League	GP	G	A	Pts	PIM	GP	G	A	Pts	PIM
2007-08	Erie Otters	OHL	57	1	10	11	31	....	....	....	....	....
2008-09	Erie Otters	OHL	61	6	17	23	49	5	1	1	2	2
2009-10	Erie Otters	OHL	59	2	24	26	37	4	0	1	1	2
2010-11	Erie Otters	OHL	36	6	17	23	17	7	2	2	4	2
	Adirondack	AHL	3	0	0	0	0	....	....	....	....	....

Signed as a free agent by **Philadelphia**, September 21, 2009.

HOUSE, Tanner (HOWS, TA-nuhr) EDM

Center. Shoots right. 6'1", 195 lbs. Born, Cochrane, Alta., April 27, 1986.

			Regular Season					Playoffs				
Season	Club	League	GP	G	A	Pts	PIM	GP	G	A	Pts	PIM
2002-03	Canmore Eagles	AJHL	2	0	0	0	0	....	....	....	....	....
2003-04	Canmore Eagles	AJHL	58	13	19	32	48	....	....	....	....	....
2004-05	Canmore Eagles	AJHL	58	11	18	29	119	....	....	....	....	....
2005-06	Penticton Vees	BCHL	52	14	17	31	36	15	5	4	9	11
2006-07	Penticton Vees	BCHL	58	14	55	69	69	13	4	6	10	12
2007-08	U. of Maine	H-East	29	1	10	11	12	....	....	....	....	....
2008-09	U. of Maine	H-East	39	10	14	24	24	....	....	....	....	....
2009-10	U. of Maine	H-East	35	18	21	39	29	....	....	....	....	....
2010-11	U. of Maine	H-East	35	10	25	35	56	....	....	....	....	....
	Oklahoma City	AHL	6	1	4	5	0	1	0	0	0	0

Signed as a free agent by **Edmonton**, March 19, 2011.

HOWDEN, Quinton (HOW-duhn, KWIHN-tuhn) FLA

Center. Shoots left. 6'3", 183 lbs. Born, Winnipeg, Man., January 21, 1992.
(Florida's 3rd choice, 25th overall, in 2010 Entry Draft).

			Regular Season					Playoffs				
Season	Club	League	GP	G	A	Pts	PIM	GP	G	A	Pts	PIM
2007-08	Eastman Selects	MMHL	37	23	27	50	36	....	....	....	....	....
	Moose Jaw	WHL	5	0	0	0	0	....	....	....	....	....
2008-09	Moose Jaw	WHL	62	13	17	30	22	....	....	....	....	....
2009-10	Moose Jaw	WHL	65	28	37	65	44	2	0	2	2	2
2010-11	Moose Jaw	WHL	60	40	39	79	43	6	5	2	7	2

WHL East Second All-Star Team (2011)

HOWSE, Ryan (HOWS, RIGH-uhn) CGY

Left wing. Shoots left. 5'11", 195 lbs. Born, Prince George, B.C., July 6, 1991.
(Calgary's 2nd choice, 74th overall, in 2009 Entry Draft).

			Regular Season					Playoffs				
Season	Club	League	GP	G	A	Pts	PIM	GP	G	A	Pts	PIM
2006-07	Cariboo Cougars	BCMML	30	21	16	37	40	....	....	....	....	....
	Chilliwack Bruins	WHL	5	1	0	1	2	1	0	0	0	0
2007-08	Chilliwack Bruins	WHL	54	10	7	17	12	4	1	1	2	2
2008-09	Chilliwack Bruins	WHL	61	31	13	44	12	....	....	....	....	....
2009-10	Chilliwack Bruins	WHL	72	47	25	72	27	6	5	1	6	2
2010-11	Chilliwack Bruins	WHL	70	51	32	83	40	5	1	0	1	2

WHL West Second All-Star Team (2011)

HROMAS, Karel (huh-ROM-mahs, KAH-rehl) CHI

Left wing. Shoots left. 6'2", 189 lbs. Born, Beroun, Czech., January 27, 1986.
(Chicago's 8th choice, 123rd overall, in 2004 Entry Draft).

			Regular Season					Playoffs				
Season	Club	League	GP	G	A	Pts	PIM	GP	G	A	Pts	PIM
2000-01	Sparta U17	CzR-U17	34	4	18	22	6	....	....	....	....	....
2001-02	Sparta U17	CzR-U17	39	19	15	34	55	6	3	2	5	6
2002-03	Sparta U17	CzR-U17	1	3	1	4	0	....	....	....	....	....
	Sparta Jr.	CzRep-Jr.	32	6	7	13	14	3	0	1	1	4
2003-04	Sparta Jr.	CzRep-Jr.	21	10	10	20	16	....	....	....	....	....
	HC Sparta Praha	CzRep	13	0	0	0	0	2	0	0	0	0
2004-05	Everett Silvertips	WHL	65	18	11	29	22	11	2	2	4	4
2005-06	Everett Silvertips	WHL	52	11	11	22	14	14	2	0	2	10
2006-07	HC Sparta Praha	CzRep	48	1	0	1	20	11	1	0	1	0
2007-08	HC Sparta Praha	CzRep	52	0	1	1	42	4	0	0	0	0
2008-09	HC Sparta Praha	CzRep	52	2	4	6	64	11	0	3	3	20
2009-10	HC Sparta Praha	CzRep	48	2	12	14	75	7	0	1	1	10
2010-11	HC Sparta Praha	CzRep	64	8	5	13	38	....	....	....	....	....

HUBERDEAU, Jonathan (hoo-BAIR-doh, JAWN-ah-thuhn) FLA

Center. Shoots left. 6'1", 171 lbs. Born, Saint-Jerome, Que., June 4, 1993.
(Florida's 1st choice, 3rd overall, in 2011 Entry Draft).

			Regular Season					Playoffs				
Season	Club	League	GP	G	A	Pts	PIM	GP	G	A	Pts	PIM
2008-09	Saint-Eustache	QAAA	43	20	30	50	60	8	2	7	9	18
2009-10	Saint John	QMJHL	61	15	20	35	43	21	11	7	18	22
2010-11	Saint John	QMJHL	67	43	62	105	88	19	*16	14	30	16

QMJHL First All-Star Team (2011) • Memorial Cup All-Star Team (2011)

HUDON, Philippe (hoo-DAWN, fihl-EEP) DET

Center/Right wing. Shoots right. 6', 197 lbs. Born, Montreal, Que., April 15, 1993.
(Detroit's 6th choice, 145th overall, in 2011 Entry Draft).

			Regular Season					Playoffs				
Season	Club	League	GP	G	A	Pts	PIM	GP	G	A	Pts	PIM
2008-09	Choate-Rosemary	High-CT	24	8	12	20	....	....	....	....	....	....
2009-10	Choate-Rosemary	High-CT	20	9	11	20	....	....	....	....	....	....
2010-11	Choate-Rosemary	High-CT	22	10	10	20	44	....	....	....	....	....

• Signed Letter of Intent to attend **Cornell University** (ECAC) in fall of 2011.

HUTCHINGS, Alex (HUH-chihngz, Al-ehx) T.B.

Left wing. Shoots right. 5'10", 178 lbs. Born, Burlington, Ont., November 7, 1990.
(Tampa Bay's 4th choice, 93rd overall, in 2009 Entry Draft).

			Regular Season					Playoffs				
Season	Club	League	GP	G	A	Pts	PIM	GP	G	A	Pts	PIM
2006-07	Barrie Colts	OHL	30	1	4	5	24	....	....	....	....	....
2007-08	Barrie Colts	OHL	68	29	25	54	48	9	0	5	5	18
2008-09	Barrie Colts	OHL	63	34	34	68	60	5	3	4	7	6
2009-10	Barrie Colts	OHL	68	47	34	81	58	13	2	8	10	12
2010-11	Norfolk Admirals	AHL	1	0	0	0	0	1	0	0	0	2
	Florida Everblades	ECHL	51	13	13	26	41	4	1	2	3	6

HYMAN, Zach (HIGH-muhn, ZAK) FLA

Center. Shoots right. 6'2", 195 lbs. Born, Toronto, Ont., June 9, 1992.
(Florida's 11th choice, 123rd overall, in 2010 Entry Draft).

			Regular Season					Playoffs				
Season	Club	League	GP	G	A	Pts	PIM	GP	G	A	Pts	PIM
2008-09	Hamilton	ON-Jr.A	49	13	24	37	24	5	2	2	4	4
2009-10	Hamilton	ON-Jr.A	49	35	40	75	30	11	7	9	16	4
2010-11	Hamilton	ON-Jr.A	43	42	60	102	24	7	3	5	8	6

CJHL Player of the Year (2011)

• Signed Letter of Intent to attend **Princeton University** (ECAC) in fall of 2011.

ILLO, Radoslav (IHL-oh, RAD-oh-slav) ANA

Center. Shoots left. 6', 178 lbs. Born, Povazska Bystrica, Czech., January 21, 1990.
(Anaheim's 6th choice, 136th overall, in 2009 Entry Draft).

			Regular Season					Playoffs				
Season	Club	League	GP	G	A	Pts	PIM	GP	G	A	Pts	PIM
2005-06	P. Bystrica U18	Svk-U18	4	1	1	2	2	....	....	....	....	....
2006-07	Bratislava U18	Svk-U18	26	9	14	23	12	....	....	....	....	....
2007-08	Hampton Roads	MJHL	....	48	38	86	....	....	....	....	....	....
2008-09	Tri-City Storm	USHL	47	21	12	33	37	....	....	....	....	....
2009-10	Tri-City Storm	USHL	50	24	19	43	56	1	1	0	1	0
2010-11	Bemidji State	WCHA	37	4	2	6	20	....	....	....	....	....

IRWIN, Matt (UHR-wihn, MAT) S.J.

Defense. Shoots left. 6'2", 210 lbs. Born, Brentwood Bay, B.C., November 29, 1987.

			Regular Season					Playoffs				
Season	Club	League	GP	G	A	Pts	PIM	GP	G	A	Pts	PIM
2004-05	Nanaimo Clippers	BCHL	3	0	0	0	2	....	....	....	....	....
2005-06	Nanaimo Clippers	BCHL	56	3	6	9	41	....	....	....	....	....
2006-07	Nanaimo Clippers	BCHL	60	22	27	49	67	....	....	....	....	....
2007-08	Nanaimo Clippers	BCHL	59	16	37	53	40	....	....	....	....	....
2008-09	Massachusetts	H-East	31	7	11	18	8	....	....	....	....	....
2009-10	Massachusetts	H-East	36	7	17	24	16	....	....	....	....	....
	Worcester Sharks	AHL	3	0	0	0	2	1	0	0	0	0
2010-11	Worcester Sharks	AHL	72	10	21	31	43	....	....	....	....	....

Signed as a free agent by **San Jose**, March 23, 2010.

ISACKSON, Christian (IGH-zak-suhn, KRIHS-ch'yehn) BUF

Right wing. Shoots right. 5'11", 188 lbs. Born, Pine City, MN, January 20, 1992.
(Buffalo's 8th choice, 203rd overall, in 2010 Entry Draft).

			Regular Season					Playoffs				
Season	Club	League	GP	G	A	Pts	PIM	GP	G	A	Pts	PIM
2006-07	Saint Thomas	High-MN	31	6	12	18	....	....	....	....	....	....
2007-08	Saint Thomas	High-MN	31	22	34	56	....	....	....	....	....	....
2008-09	Saint Thomas	High-MN	27	18	39	57	....	....	....	....	....	....
2009-10	Team Southeast	UMHSEL	24	11	11	22	....	....	....	....	....	....
	Saint Thomas	High-MN	25	24	33	57	26	3	1	2	3	0
2010-11	Sioux Falls	USHL	58	17	27	44	31	10	3	5	8	8

• Signed Letter of Intent to attend **University of Minnesota** (WCHA) in fall of 2011.

JACOBS, Colin (JAY-kuhbz, KAWL-ihn) BUF

Center. Shoots right. 6'1", 202 lbs. Born, Coppell, TX, January 20, 1993.
(Buffalo's 3rd choice, 107th overall, in 2011 Entry Draft).

			Regular Season					Playoffs				
Season	Club	League	GP	G	A	Pts	PIM	GP	G	A	Pts	PIM
2007-08	Dallas Ice Jets	Minor-TX	51	61	50	111	88	....	....	....	....	....
2008-09	Dallas Stars U16	Minor-TX	50	36	36	72	147	....	....	....	....	....
	Seattle	WHL	2	0	0	0	0	4	2	1	3	0
2009-10	Seattle	WHL	72	13	13	26	119	....	....	....	....	....
2010-11	Seattle	WHL	68	22	22	44	69	....	....	....	....	....

JANOSIK, Adam (YA-noh-shihk, A-duhm) T.B.

Defense. Shoots left. 6', 179 lbs. Born, Spisska Nova Ves, SVK, September 7, 1992.
(Tampa Bay's 4th choice, 72nd overall, in 2010 Entry Draft).

			Regular Season					Playoffs				
Season	Club	League	GP	G	A	Pts	PIM	GP	G	A	Pts	PIM
2006-07	HC Liberec U17	CzR-U17	12	0	0	0	12	....	....	....	....	....
2007-08	HC Liberec U17	CzR-U17	42	4	15	19	38	4	1	0	1	2
2008-09	HC Liberec U17	CzR-U17	20	7	19	26	39	7	2	6	8	2
	HC Liberec Jr.	CzRep-Jr.	22	1	8	9	12	....	....	....	....	....
2009-10	Gatineau	QMJHL	63	9	26	35	45	10	5	2	7	4
2010-11	Gatineau	QMJHL	60	7	25	32	37	24	5	4	9	12

JARDINE, Sam (jar-DEEN, SAM) CHI

Defense. Shoots left. 6'1", 190 lbs. Born, Lacombe, Alta., August 12, 1993.
(Chicago's 9th choice, 169th overall, in 2011 Entry Draft).

			Regular Season					Playoffs				
Season	Club	League	GP	G	A	Pts	PIM	GP	G	A	Pts	PIM
2008-09	Red Deer Chiefs	Minor-AB	32	6	21	27	36	....	....	....	....	....
	Red Deer	AMHL	4	0	1	1	0	....	....	....	....	....
2009-10	Red Deer	AMHL	34	9	15	24	18	....	....	....	....	....
	Camrose Kodiaks	AJHL	3	0	0	0	2	....	....	....	....	....
2010-11	Camrose Kodiaks	AJHL	50	6	16	22	56	23	4	7	11	24

• Signed Letter of Intent to attend **Ohio State** (CCHA) in fall of 2012.

JARNKROK, Calle (YAHRN-krohk, KAHL-leh) DET

Center. Shoots right. 5'11", 165 lbs. Born, Gavle, Sweden, September 25, 1991.
(Detroit's 2nd choice, 51st overall, in 2010 Entry Draft).

			Regular Season					Playoffs				
Season	Club	League	GP	G	A	Pts	PIM	GP	G	A	Pts	PIM
2007-08	Brynas U18	Swe-U18	13	4	4	8	4	5	0	1	1	0
	Brynas IF Gavle Jr.	Swe-Jr.	2	0	0	0	2	....	....	....	....	....
2008-09	Brynas U18	Swe-U18	7	5	7	12	12	2	0	1	1	2
	Brynas IF Gavle Jr.	Swe-Jr.	41	8	18	26	37	7	4	3	7	2
2009-10	Brynas IF Gavle Jr.	Swe-Jr.	19	11	20	31	30	2	0	1	1	0
	Brynas IF Gavle	Sweden	33	4	6	10	2	5	1	1	2	0
2010-11	Brynas IF Gavle	Sweden	49	11	16	27	4	3	3	0	3	2

JASKIN, Dmitrij (YASH-kihn, dih-MEE-tree) ST.L.

Right wing. Shoots left. 6'2", 196 lbs. Born, Omsk, Russia, March 23, 1993.
(St. Louis' 2nd choice, 41st overall, in 2011 Entry Draft).

			Regular Season					Playoffs				
Season	Club	League	GP	G	A	Pts	PIM	GP	G	A	Pts	PIM
2006-07	HC Vsetin U17	CzR-U17	4	1	0	1	0	....	....	....	....	....
2007-08	HC Vsetin U17	CzR-U17	40	15	25	40	72	2	2	0	2	6
2008-09	Slavia U17	CzR-U17	46	28	19	47	34	9	6	2	8	8
2009-10	Slavia U18	CzR-U18	12	15	12	27	36	2	1	3	4	4
	HC Slavia Praha Jr.	CzRep-Jr.	40	13	10	23	67	7	2	5	7	26
2010-11	HC Slavia Praha Jr.	CzRep-Jr.	1	0	0	0	0	2	2	3	5	2
	HC Slavia Praha	CzRep	33	3	7	10	16	17	2	1	3	31

JENKS, A.J. (JEHKS, AY-JAY) FLA

Left wing. Shoots left. 6'2", 206 lbs. Born, Detroit, MI, June 27, 1990.
(Florida's 4th choice, 100th overall, in 2008 Entry Draft).

			Regular Season					Playoffs				
Season	Club	League	GP	G	A	Pts	PIM	GP	G	A	Pts	PIM
2004-05	Det. Compuware	MWEHL	28	7	12	19	54	....	....	....	....	....
2005-06	Det. Honeybaked	MWEHL	21	7	10	17	23	....	....	....	....	....
2006-07	Plymouth Whalers	OHL	68	9	14	23	50	20	0	1	1	8
2007-08	Plymouth Whalers	OHL	68	26	29	55	94	4	1	0	1	4
2008-09	Plymouth Whalers	OHL	61	21	31	52	78	11	1	2	3	18
2009-10	Plymouth Whalers	OHL	52	23	40	63	58	9	4	8	12	14
2010-11	Rochester	AHL	63	8	13	21	48	....	....	....	....	....

JENNER, Boone (JEH-nuhr, BOON) CBJ

Center. Shoots left. 6'2", 196 lbs. Born, Dorchester, Ont., June 15, 1993.
(Columbus' 1st choice, 37th overall, in 2011 Entry Draft).

			Regular Season					Playoffs				
Season	Club	League	GP	G	A	Pts	PIM	GP	G	A	Pts	PIM
2008-09	Elgin-Mid. Chiefs	Minor-ON	54	49	54	103	72	....	....	....	....	....
	St. Thomas Stars	ON-Jr.B	4	0	0	0	16	....	....	....	....	....
2009-10	Oshawa Generals	OHL	65	19	30	49	91	....	....	....	....	....
2010-11	Oshawa Generals	OHL	63	25	41	66	57	10	7	5	12	14

OHL All-Rookie Team (2010)

JENSEN, Nick (JEHN-suhn, NIHK) DET

Defense. Shoots right. 6'1", 187 lbs. Born, St. Paul, MN, September 21, 1990.
(Detroit's 5th choice, 150th overall, in 2009 Entry Draft).

			Regular Season					Playoffs				
Season	Club	League	GP	G	A	Pts	PIM	GP	G	A	Pts	PIM
2006-07	Rogers Royals	High-MN	21	20	17	37	....	....	....	....	....	....
2007-08	Rogers Royals	High-MN	14	14	13	27	....	....	....	....	....	....
2008-09	Green Bay	USHL	52	5	17	22	27	7	0	1	1	2
2009-10	Green Bay	USHL	53	6	21	27	35	12	2	6	8	6
2010-11	St. Cloud State	WCHA	38	5	18	23	18	....	....	....	....	....

JENSEN, Nicklas (YEHN-suhn, NIHK-luhs) VAN

Left wing. Shoots left. 6'2", 202 lbs. Born, Herning, Denmark, March 6, 1993.
(Vancouver's 1st choice, 29th overall, in 2011 Entry Draft).

			Regular Season					Playoffs				
Season	Club	League	GP	G	A	Pts	PIM	GP	G	A	Pts	PIM
2008-09	Herning IK Jr.	Den-Jr.	28	28	15	43	30	....	....	....	....	....
	Herning IK II	Den-2	4	3	0	3	0	....	....	....	....	....
2009-10	Herning Blue Fox	Denmark	34	12	14	26	28	10	6	4	10	8
2010-11	Oshawa Generals	OHL	61	29	29	58	42	10	7	4	11	2

JOBKE, Colton (JAWB-kee, KOHL-tuhn) MIN

Defense. Shoots left. 6', 175 lbs. Born, Vancouver, B.C., April 20, 1992.

			Regular Season					Playoffs				
Season	Club	League	GP	G	A	Pts	PIM	GP	G	A	Pts	PIM
2007-08	Greater Van.	BCMML	38	4	10	14	24	....	....	....	....	....
2008-09	Penticton Vees	BCHL	46	3	8	11	11	....	....	....	....	....
2009-10	Kelowna Rockets	WHL	69	0	8	8	71	12	0	4	4	14
2010-11	Kelowna Rockets	WHL	51	1	9	10	84	9	0	0	0	7

Signed as a free agent by **Minnesota**, September 23, 2010.

JOHANSEN, Ryan (joh-HAN-suhn, RIGH-uhn) CBJ

Center. Shoots right. 6'3", 202 lbs. Born, Port Moody, B.C., July 31, 1992.
(Columbus' 1st choice, 4th overall, in 2010 Entry Draft).

			Regular Season					Playoffs				
Season	Club	League	GP	G	A	Pts	PIM	GP	G	A	Pts	PIM
2007-08	Van. NE Chiefs	BCMML	41	18	30	48	26	....	....	....	....	....
2008-09	Penticton Vees	BCHL	47	5	12	17	21	10	4	3	7	2
2009-10	Portland	WHL	71	25	44	69	53	13	6	12	18	18
2010-11	Portland	WHL	63	40	52	92	64	21	13	15	*28	6

WHL West First All-Star Team (2011)

JOHNS, Stephen (JAWNZ, STEE-vehn) CHI

Defense. Shoots right. 6'3", 215 lbs. Born, Ellwood City, PA, April 18, 1992.
(Chicago's 5th choice, 60th overall, in 2010 Entry Draft).

			Regular Season					Playoffs				
Season	Club	League	GP	G	A	Pts	PIM	GP	G	A	Pts	PIM
2007-08	Pittsburgh Hornets	MWEHL	26	4	7	11	24	....	....	....	....	....
	Pittsburgh Hornets	Minor-PA	50	12	22	34	46	....	....	....	....	....
2008-09	USNTDP	NAHL	31	3	5	8	30	....	....	....	....	....
	USNTDP	U-17	16	2	6	8	20	....	....	....	....	....
2009-10	USNTDP	USHL	23	1	7	8	29	....	....	....	....	....
	USNTDP	U-18	39	2	9	11	38	....	....	....	....	....
2010-11	U. of Notre Dame	CCHA	44	2	11	13	*98	....	....	....	....	....

JOHNSON, Jamie (JAHN-suhn, JAY-mee) DET

Center. Shoots right. 5'10", 185 lbs. Born, Port Franks, Ont., January 23, 1982.

			Regular Season					Playoffs				
Season	Club	League	GP	G	A	Pts	PIM	GP	G	A	Pts	PIM
99-2000	Sarnia Sting	OHL	61	6	14	20	24	7	0	2	2	2
2000-01	Sarnia Sting	OHL	9	0	5	5	7	....	....	....	....	....
	Oshawa Generals	OHL	56	8	38	46	14	....	....	....	....	....
2001-02	Oshawa Generals	OHL	68	17	61	78	46	5	2	4	6	2
2002-03	Oshawa Generals	OHL	68	24	76	100	34	13	1	13	14	16
2003-04	Louisiana	ECHL	71	12	45	57	46	9	3	6	9	4
2004-05	Augusta Lynx	ECHL	72	22	58	80	26	....	....	....	....	....
2005-06	Augusta Lynx	ECHL	7	2	4	6	6	....	....	....	....	....
	Iowa Stars	AHL	68	9	28	37	24	7	0	4	4	21
2006-07	Augusta Lynx	ECHL	31	14	30	44	26	....	....	....	....	....
	Iowa Stars	AHL	8	1	3	4	2	....	....	....	....	....
	Bridgeport	AHL	34	5	11	16	18	....	....	....	....	....
2007-08	Albany River Rats	AHL	79	21	37	58	28	7	0	2	2	0
2008-09	TPS Turku	Finland	42	8	20	28	24	6	0	3	3	2
2009-10	Rochester	AHL	80	27	44	71	24	7	2	4	6	5
2010-11	Grand Rapids	AHL	78	12	26	38	32	....	....	....	....	....

Signed as a free agent by **Turku** (Finland), May 27. 2008. Signed as a free agent by **Florida**, July 15, 2009. Signed as a free agent by **Detroit**, July 6, 2010.

JOHNSON, Patrick (JAWN-suhn, PAT-rihk) MTL

Left wing. Shoots left. 5'9", 155 lbs. Born, Madison, WI, April 21, 1989.
(Montreal's 5th choice, 206th overall, in 2008 Entry Draft).

			Regular Season					Playoffs				
Season	Club	League	GP	G	A	Pts	PIM	GP	G	A	Pts	PIM
2006-07	Lincoln Stars	USHL	49	11	16	27	50	4	1	0	1	14
2007-08	U. of Wisconsin	WCHA	40	8	13	21	36	....	....	....	....	....
2008-09	U. of Wisconsin	WCHA	35	3	4	7	44	....	....	....	....	....
2009-10	U. of Wisconsin	WCHA	37	3	4	7	14	....	....	....	....	....
2010-11	U. of Wisconsin	WCHA	41	8	11	19	46	....	....	....	....	....

JOHNSON, Tyler (JAWN-suhn, TIGH-luhr) T.B.

Center. Shoots right. 5'8", 174 lbs. Born, Spokane, WA, July 29, 1990.

			Regular Season					Playoffs				
Season	Club	League	GP	G	A	Pts	PIM	GP	G	A	Pts	PIM
2007-08	Spokane Chiefs	WHL	69	13	22	35	34	21	5	3	8	24
	Spokane Chiefs	M-Cup	....	....	....	....	....	4	0	0	0	2
2008-09	Spokane Chiefs	WHL	62	26	35	61	52	12	5	3	8	8
2009-10	Spokane Chiefs	WHL	64	36	35	71	32	7	3	5	8	0
2010-11	Spokane Chiefs	WHL	71	*53	62	115	48	14	7	7	14	9

Signed as a free agent by **Tampa Bay**, March 7, 2011.

JOKINEN, Justin (YOH-kihn-ihn, JUHS-tihn) **BUF**

Right wing. Shoots right. 6'3", 185 lbs. Born, Cloquet, MN, November 25, 1989.
(Buffalo's 5th choice, 101st overall, in 2008 Entry Draft).

			Regular Season					Playoffs				
Season	Club	League	GP	G	A	Pts	PIM	GP	G	A	Pts	PIM
2005-06	Cloquet	High-MN	....	7	11	18	....	....	....	....	....	....
2006-07	Cloquet	High-MN	....	26	25	51	18	....	....	....	....	....
	Team North	UMWEHL	11	6	5	11	....	....	....	....	....	....
2007-08	Cloquet	High-MN	30	22	21	43	....	....	....	....	....	....
	Team North	UMWEHL	12	5	13	18	....	....	....	....	....	....
2008-09	Minnesota State	WCHA	24	3	2	5	6	....	....	....	....	....
2009-10	Minnesota State	WCHA	24	3	1	4	14	....	....	....	....	....
2010-11	Minnesota State	WCHA	38	9	8	17	24	....	....	....	....	....

JOKIPAKKA, Jyrki (yoh-kih-PA-ka, YUHR-kee) **DAL**

Defense. Shoots left. 6'3", 191 lbs. Born, Tampere, Finland, August 20, 1991.
(Dallas' 6th choice, 195th overall, in 2011 Entry Draft).

			Regular Season					Playoffs				
Season	Club	League	GP	G	A	Pts	PIM	GP	G	A	Pts	PIM
2007-08	Ilves Tampere U17	Fin-U17	24	6	15	21	26	2	1	1	2	0
2008-09	Ilves Tampere U18	Fin-U18	33	4	7	11	12	....	....	....	....	....
	Ilves Tampere Jr.	Fin-Jr.	4	0	0	0	2	....	....	....	....	....
2009-10	Ilves Tampere Jr.	Fin-Jr.	38	3	12	15	77	5	1	0	1	2
2010-11	Suomi U20	Finland-2	6	0	3	3	2	....	....	....	....	....
	Ilves Tampere Jr.	Fin-Jr.	3	0	0	0	6	2	0	0	0	2
	LeKi Lempaala	Finland-2	1	0	0	0	0	....	....	....	....	....
	Ilves Tampere	Finland	48	1	8	9	18	5	0	0	0	2

JONES, Kellen (JOHNZ, KEHL-ehn) **EDM**

Forward. Shoots left. 5'9", 164 lbs. Born, Montrose, B.C., August 16, 1990.
(Edmonton's 11th choice, 202nd overall, in 2010 Entry Draft).

			Regular Season					Playoffs				
Season	Club	League	GP	G	A	Pts	PIM	GP	G	A	Pts	PIM
2006-07	Beaver Valley	KIJHL	50	32	35	67	48	13	8	4	12	6
	Vernon Vipers	BCHL	2	0	1	1	0	16	3	5	8	8
2007-08	Vernon Vipers	BCHL	60	12	55	67	30	10	7	4	11	8
2008-09	Vernon Vipers	BCHL	51	15	37	52	16	17	6	12	18	8
2009-10	Vernon Vipers	BCHL	41	12	41	53	18	19	5	14	19	14
2010-11	Quinnipiac	ECAC	38	8	14	22	33	....	....	....	....	....

JORDAN, Michal (JOHR-duhn, MEE-khuhl) **CAR**

Defense. Shoots left. 6'1", 186 lbs. Born, Zlin, Czech., July 17, 1990.
(Carolina's 3rd choice, 105th overall, in 2008 Entry Draft).

			Regular Season					Playoffs				
Season	Club	League	GP	G	A	Pts	PIM	GP	G	A	Pts	PIM
2005-06	HC Zlin U17	CzR-U17	43	7	15	22	12	5	0	1	1	2
2006-07	HC Zlin U17	CzR-U17	1	0	0	0	4	....	....	....	....	....
	HC Zlin Jr.	CzRep-Jr.	40	7	11	18	20	12	1	5	6	12
2007-08	Windsor Spitfires	OHL	22	1	5	6	12	....	....	....	....	....
	Plymouth Whalers	OHL	39	5	17	22	32	4	0	3	3	6
2008-09	Plymouth Whalers	OHL	58	12	30	42	39	11	0	3	3	12
2009-10	Plymouth Whalers	OHL	41	13	19	32	18	9	0	5	5	8
2010-11	Charlotte	AHL	67	4	14	18	35	16	0	2	2	0

JORG, Mauro (YOHRG, MAHW-roh) **N.J.**

Left wing. Shoots left. 6', 200 lbs. Born, Chur, Switzerland, April 29, 1990.
(New Jersey's 5th choice, 204th overall, in 2010 Entry Draft).

			Regular Season					Playoffs				
Season	Club	League	GP	G	A	Pts	PIM	GP	G	A	Pts	PIM
2006-07	HC Lugano Jr.	Swiss-Jr.	4	2	3	5	6	....	....	....	....	....
	EHC Arosa	Swiss-3	7	4	1	5	8	1	0	0	0	2
	EHC Chur	Swiss-2	20	1	1	2	0	....	....	....	....	....
2007-08	Switzerland U20	Swiss-2	1	0	0	0	0	....	....	....	....	....
	EHC Chur Jr.	Swiss-Jr.	4	4	1	5	18	....	....	....	....	....
	EHC Chur	Swiss-2	40	11	9	20	33	....	....	....	....	....
	HC Lugano Jr.	Swiss-Jr.	8	5	2	7	12	....	....	....	....	....
	HC Lugano	Swiss	....	....	....	....	....	1	0	0	0	0
2008-09	HC Lugano	Swiss	47	3	3	6	6	7	0	0	0	0
	Switzerland U20	Swiss-2	5	1	0	1	0	....	....	....	....	....
	HC Ceresio Lugano	Swiss-3	1	0	0	0	0	....	....	....	....	....
	HC Lugano Jr.	Swiss-Jr.	3	0	3	3	0	2	0	3	3	4
2009-10	HC Lugano	Swiss	44	1	7	8	14	4	0	0	0	0
	HC Lugano Jr.	Swiss-Jr.	1	0	0	0	0	....	....	....	....	....
	EHC Visp	Swiss-2	....	....	....	....	....	7	0	1	1	0
2010-11	HC Lugano	Swiss	50	3	9	12	26	4	0	0	0	2

JOSI, Roman (YAW-see, ROH-man) **NSH**

Defense. Shoots left. 6'2", 198 lbs. Born, Bern, Switzerland, June 1, 1990.
(Nashville's 3rd choice, 38th overall, in 2008 Entry Draft).

			Regular Season					Playoffs				
Season	Club	League	GP	G	A	Pts	PIM	GP	G	A	Pts	PIM
2005-06	SC Bern Future Jr.	Swiss-Jr.	5	0	0	0	0	....	....	....	....	....
2006-07	SC Bern Future Jr.	Swiss-Jr.	33	14	16	30	28	14	1	3	4	2
	Switzerland U20	Swiss-2	5	1	1	2	2	....	....	....	....	....
	SC Bern	Swiss	3	0	1	1	0	....	....	....	....	....
2007-08	Switzerland U20	Swiss-2	2	0	1	1	0	....	....	....	....	....
	HC Neuchatel	Swiss-2	3	2	0	2	4	....	....	....	....	....
	SC Bern	Swiss	35	2	6	8	10	6	0	0	0	0
2008-09	SC Bern	Swiss	42	7	17	24	16	6	0	0	0	2
2009-10	SC Bern	Swiss	26	9	12	21	12	15	6	7	13	8
2010-11	Milwaukee	AHL	69	6	34	40	22	13	1	6	7	8

JOUDREY, Andrew (JOO-dree, AN-droo) **CBJ**

Center. Shoots left. 5'11", 185 lbs. Born, Halifax, N.S., July 15, 1984.
(Washington's 5th choice, 249th overall, in 2003 Entry Draft).

			Regular Season					Playoffs				
Season	Club	League	GP	G	A	Pts	PIM	GP	G	A	Pts	PIM
2000-01	Dartmouth	NSMHL	82	51	70	121	....	....	....	....	....	....
2001-02	Notre Dame	SJHL	57	24	38	62	14	....	....	....	....	....
2002-03	Notre Dame	SJHL	53	27	51	78	16	....	....	....	....	....
2003-04	U. of Wisconsin	WCHA	42	7	15	22	2	....	....	....	....	....
2004-05	U. of Wisconsin	WCHA	41	7	17	24	18	....	....	....	....	....
2005-06	U. of Wisconsin	WCHA	37	8	10	18	14	....	....	....	....	....
2006-07	U. of Wisconsin	WCHA	40	9	20	29	18	....	....	....	....	....
	Hershey Bears	AHL	5	2	1	3	0	10	0	2	2	0
2007-08	Hershey Bears	AHL	61	11	14	25	22	5	0	1	1	0
2008-09	Hershey Bears	AHL	69	7	20	27	22	22	1	3	4	6
2009-10	Hershey Bears	AHL	78	15	19	34	11	21	1	2	3	4
2010-11	Hershey Bears	AHL	66	7	7	14	20	6	0	1	1	0

Signed as a free agent by **Columbus**, July 1, 2011.

JURCO, Tomas (YUHR-koh, TAW-mahsh) **DET**

Right wing. Shoots left. 6'1", 191 lbs. Born, Kosice, Czechoslovakia, December 28, 1992.
(Detroit's 1st choice, 35th overall, in 2011 Entry Draft).

			Regular Season					Playoffs				
Season	Club	League	GP	G	A	Pts	PIM	GP	G	A	Pts	PIM
2007-08	HC Kosice U18	Svk-U18	57	28	24	52	30	....	....	....	....	....
2008-09	HC Kosice U18	Svk-U18	5	8	5	13	2	....	....	....	....	....
	HC Kosice Jr.	Slovak-Jr.	48	19	30	49	20	3	5	0	5	0
2009-10	Saint John	QMJHL	64	26	25	51	24	21	7	10	17	8
2010-11	Saint John	QMJHL	60	31	25	56	17	19	6	12	18	8

KABANOV, Kirill (kuh-BAH-nawf, kih-RIHL) **NYI**

Left wing. Shoots right. 6'2", 176 lbs. Born, Moscow, Russia, July 16, 1992.
(NY Islanders' 3rd choice, 65th overall, in 2010 Entry Draft).

			Regular Season					Playoffs				
Season	Club	League	GP	G	A	Pts	PIM	GP	G	A	Pts	PIM
2008-09	Spartak Moscow	Rus-KHL	6	0	0	0	2	5	0	0	0	0
	Spartak Moscow 2	Russia-3	STATISTICS NOT AVAILABLE									
2009-10	Moncton Wildcats	QMJHL	22	10	13	23	34	1	0	0	0	2
2010-11	Moncton Wildcats	QMJHL	2	0	0	0	6	....	....	....	....	....
	Lewiston	QMJHL	37	11	17	28	38	15	8	12	20	18

KARLSSON, Mattias (KARL-suhn, mat-TEE-uhs) **OTT**

Defense. Shoots left. 6'2", 192 lbs. Born, Stora, Sweden, April 15, 1985.
(Ottawa's 4th choice, 135th overall, in 2003 Entry Draft).

			Regular Season					Playoffs				
Season	Club	League	GP	G	A	Pts	PIM	GP	G	A	Pts	PIM
2001-02	Brynas U18	Swe-U18	5	2	1	3	6	....	....	....	....	....
	Brynas IF Gavle Jr.	Swe-Jr.	13	0	1	1	12	....	....	....	....	....
2002-03	Brynas IF Gavle Jr.	Swe-Jr.	27	11	6	17	93	2	0	0	0	4
	Brynas IF Gavle	Sweden	3	0	0	0	0	....	....	....	....	....
	Brynas IF Gavle	Sweden-Q	3	0	0	0	0	....	....	....	....	....
2003-04	Brynas IF Gavle Jr.	Swe-Jr.	20	5	8	13	67	5	0	4	4	10
	Brynas IF Gavle	Sweden	39	0	0	0	6	....	....	....	....	....
2004-05	Brynas IF Gavle Jr.	Swe-Jr.	13	3	5	8	40	....	....	....	....	....
	Almtuna	Sweden-2	22	0	2	2	18	....	....	....	....	....
	Brynas IF Gavle	Sweden	9	0	0	0	2	....	....	....	....	....
	Brynas IF Gavle	Sweden-Q	1	0	0	0	0	....	....	....	....	....
2005-06	Almtuna Jr.	Swe-Jr.	2	0	1	1	4	....	....	....	....	....
	Almtuna	Sweden-2	32	3	4	7	40	....	....	....	....	....
2006-07	Bofors	Sweden-2	44	11	21	32	34	....	....	....	....	....
2007-08	Binghamton	AHL	2	0	0	0	0	....	....	....	....	....
	Farjestad	Sweden	13	2	2	4	4	12	1	3	4	20
2008-09	Binghamton	AHL	73	9	42	51	40	....	....	....	....	....
2009-10	Timra IK	Sweden	37	5	10	15	38	5	1	0	1	29
2010-11	Timra IK	Sweden	54	6	9	15	24	....	....	....	....	....

AHL All-Rookie Team (2009)

KARLSSON, Simon (KARL-suhn, SIGH-muhn) **NSH**

Defense. Shoots right. 6'2", 178 lbs. Born, Karlskrona, Sweden, July 23, 1993.
(Nashville's 5th choice, 142nd overall, in 2011 Entry Draft).

			Regular Season					Playoffs				
Season	Club	League	GP	G	A	Pts	PIM	GP	G	A	Pts	PIM
2008-09	Karlskrona HK U18	Swe-U18	14	3	7	10	34	....	....	....	....	....
	Karlskrona HK Jr.	Swe-Jr.	12	1	1	2	26	....	....	....	....	....
2009-10	Malmo U18	Swe-U18	30	1	2	3	28	....	....	....	....	....
	Malmo Jr.	Swe-Jr.	3	1	0	1	0	....	....	....	....	....
2010-11	Malmo U18	Swe-U18	19	10	12	22	32	....	....	....	....	....
	Malmo Jr.	Swe-Jr.	32	3	10	13	34	5	0	0	0	2
	Malmo	Sweden-2	4	0	0	0	0	....	....	....	....	....

KARLSSON, William (KARL-suhn, WIHL-yuhm) **ANA**

Center. Shoots left. 6', 163 lbs. Born, Marsta, Sweden, January 8, 1993.
(Anaheim's 3rd choice, 53rd overall, in 2011 Entry Draft).

			Regular Season					Playoffs				
Season	Club	League	GP	G	A	Pts	PIM	GP	G	A	Pts	PIM
2007-08	Arlanda U18	Swe-U18	5	2	7	9	4	....	....	....	....	....
2008-09	Arlanda U18	Swe-U18	33	10	18	28	16	....	....	....	....	....
2009-10	Vasteras U18	Swe-U18	39	23	21	44	62	....	....	....	....	....
	Vasteras Jr.	Swe-Jr.	6	0	1	1	2	2	0	1	1	0
2010-11	Vasteras U18	Swe-U18	11	5	9	14	10	6	7	8	15	2
	Vasteras Jr.	Swe-Jr.	38	20	34	54	45	....	....	....	....	....
	VIK Vasteras HK	Sweden-2	14	1	3	4	2	....	....	....	....	....

KASSIAN, Zack (KA-see-uhn, ZAK) **BUF**

Right wing. Shoots right. 6'3", 228 lbs. Born, Windsor, Ont., January 24, 1991.
(Buffalo's 1st choice, 13th overall, in 2009 Entry Draft).

			Regular Season					Playoffs				
Season	Club	League	GP	G	A	Pts	PIM	GP	G	A	Pts	PIM
2006-07	Wind. Jr. Spitfires	Minor-ON	57	32	48	80	136	....	....	....	....	....
	Leamington Flyers	ON-Jr.B	2	0	0	0	6	....	....	....	....	....
2007-08	Peterborough	OHL	58	9	12	21	74	5	1	0	1	2
2008-09	Peterborough	OHL	61	24	39	63	136	4	0	2	2	8
2009-10	Peterborough	OHL	33	8	19	27	58	....	....	....	....	....
	Windsor Spitfires	OHL	5	4	0	4	23	19	7	9	16	38
2010-11	Windsor Spitfires	OHL	56	26	51	77	67	16	6	10	16	37
	Portland Pirates	AHL	....	....	....	....	....	3	0	0	0	2

KAUNISTO, Ray (kow-NEES-tow, RAY) **L.A.**

Left wing. Shoots left. 6'3", 185 lbs. Born, Sault Ste. Marie, MI, February 7, 1987.

			Regular Season					Playoffs				
Season	Club	League	GP	G	A	Pts	PIM	GP	G	A	Pts	PIM
2003-04	Soo Indians	NAHL	4	1	1	2	6	....	....	....	....	....
2004-05	Soo	NAHL	55	20	20	40	72	....	....	....	....	....
2005-06	Cedar Rapids	USHL	53	5	14	19	78	....	....	....	....	....
2006-07	Northern Mich.	CCHA	41	3	0	3	30	....	....	....	....	....
2007-08	Northern Mich.	CCHA	40	8	5	13	44	....	....	....	....	....
2008-09	Northern Mich.	CCHA	40	7	7	14	56	....	....	....	....	....
2009-10	Northern Mich.	CCHA	40	18	14	32	78	....	....	....	....	....
2010-11	Manchester	AHL	57	8	6	14	50	7	2	1	3	4

Signed as a free agent by **Los Angeles**, March 31, 2010.

KAZIONOV, Denis (ka-zee-OH-nahv, DEH-nihs) T.B.

Left wing. Shoots left. 6'3", 187 lbs. Born, Perm, USSR, December 8, 1987.
(Tampa Bay's 4th choice, 198th overall, in 2006 Entry Draft).

			Regular Season					Playoffs				
Season	Club	League	GP	G	A	Pts	PIM	GP	G	A	Pts	PIM
2003-04	CSKA Moscow 2	Russia-3	2	0	1	1	2	....	....	....	....	....
2004-05	Dyn'o Moscow 2	Russia-3	STATISTICS NOT AVAILABLE									
2005-06	MVD	Russia	26	0	0	0	12	3	0	0	0	0
	HK MVD-THK Tver	Russia-3	31	6	13	19	34	....	....	....	....	....
2006-07	THK Tver	Russia-3	13	23	15	38	42	....	....	....	....	....
	MVD	Russia	24	2	0	2	8	2	0	0	0	2
2007-08	Novokuznetsk	Russia	8	0	0	0	8	....	....	....	....	....
	Avangard Omsk 2	Russia-3	13	10	6	16	16	....	....	....	....	....
	Avangard Omsk	Russia	18	0	0	0	4	3	0	0	0	6
2008-09	Amur Khabarovsk	Rus-KHL	6	0	0	0	6	....	....	....	....	....
	Trebic	CzRep-2	2	0	1	1	2	....	....	....	....	....
	BK Mlada Boleslav	CzRep	33	4	6	10	99	....	....	....	....	....
	BK Mlada Boleslav	CzRep-Q	....	....	....	....	....	2	0	0	0	0
2009-10	Avtomobilist	Rus-KHL	51	5	4	9	20	4	0	0	0	6
2010-11	Novokuznetsk	Rus-KHL	4	0	1	1	29	....	....	....	....	....
	Chelyabinsk	Rus-KHL	3	0	0	0	0	....	....	....	....	....
	Izhstal Izhevsk	Russia-2	33	8	7	15	48	....	....	....	....	....

KAZIONOV, Dmitri (ka-zee-OH-nahv, dih-MEE-tree) T.B.

Center. Shoots left. 6'3", 185 lbs. Born, Moscow, USSR, May 13, 1984.
(Tampa Bay's 2nd choice, 100th overall, in 2002 Entry Draft).

			Regular Season					Playoffs				
Season	Club	League	GP	G	A	Pts	PIM	GP	G	A	Pts	PIM
99-2000	Dyn'o Moscow 2	Russia-3	2	1	0	1	0	....	....	....	....	....
2000-01	THK Tver	Russia-2	33	1	1	2	6	....	....	....	....	....
2001-02	HK CSKA Moscow	Russia-2	2	0	1	1	0	....	....	....	....	....
	HK CSKA 2	Russia-3	10	1	0	1	4	....	....	....	....	....
	Lada Togliatti	Russia	3	0	0	0	0	....	....	....	....	....
	Lada Togliatti 2	Russia-3	16	10	9	19	0	....	....	....	....	....
2002-03	Lada Togliatti	Russia	5	0	1	1	4	....	....	....	....	....
	Lada Togliatti 2	Russia-3	34	14	13	27	26	....	....	....	....	....
2003-04	Lada Togliatti 2	Russia-3	5	3	2	5	0	4	0	0	0	0
	Lada Togliatti	Russia	47	5	5	10	34	5	0	0	0	4
2004-05	Lada Togliatti	Russia	46	3	7	10	32	2	0	0	0	0
	Lada Togliatti 2	Russia-3	2	1	0	1	4	....	....	....	....	....
2005-06	Lada Togliatti	Russia	13	0	3	3	18	....	....	....	....	....
	Dynamo Moscow	Russia	27	2	2	4	24	4	1	0	1	6
2006-07	Ak Bars Kazan	Russia	48	10	11	21	34	13	2	3	5	4
2007-08	Ak Bars Kazan	Russia	56	7	13	20	46	10	0	3	3	16
2008-09	Ak Bars Kazan	Rus-KHL	55	10	11	21	30	21	2	6	8	12
2009-10	Ak Bars Kazan	Rus-KHL	52	18	9	27	18	22	3	5	8	12
2010-11	Ak Bars Kazan	Rus-KHL	44	2	5	7	32	5	0	0	0	4

KEARNS, Bracken (KUHNRZ, BRAK-en) FLA

Center. Shoots right. 6', 195 lbs. Born, Vancouver, B.C., May 12, 1981.

			Regular Season					Playoffs				
Season	Club	League	GP	G	A	Pts	PIM	GP	G	A	Pts	PIM
2001-02	U. of Calgary	CWUAA	26	0	8	8	2	....	....	....	....	....
2002-03	U. of Calgary	CWUAA	29	8	9	17	14	....	....	....	....	....
2003-04	U. of Calgary	CWUAA	38	11	12	23	22	....	....	....	....	....
2004-05	U. of Calgary	CWUAA	43	12	23	35	18	....	....	....	....	....
2005-06	Cleveland Barons	AHL	1	0	1	1	0	....	....	....	....	....
	Toledo Storm	ECHL	71	33	36	69	66	13	7	6	13	6
2006-07	Milwaukee	AHL	79	11	15	26	59	4	0	0	0	8
2007-08	Norfolk Admirals	AHL	53	9	16	25	40	....	....	....	....	....
	Reading Royals	ECHL	17	5	13	18	17	....	....	....	....	....
2008-09	Norfolk Admirals	AHL	53	12	10	22	63	....	....	....	....	....
2009-10	Rockford IceHogs	AHL	80	15	36	51	99	4	0	2	2	2
2010-11	San Antonio	AHL	72	20	23	43	104	....	....	....	....	....

Signed as a free agent by **Phoenix**, July 27, 2010. Signed as a free agent by **Florida**, July 14, 2011.

KELLER, Justin (KEHL-uhr, JUHS-tihn)

Left wing. Shoots left. 5'11", 185 lbs. Born, Nelson, B.C., March 4, 1986.
(Tampa Bay's 8th choice, 245th overall, in 2004 Entry Draft).

			Regular Season					Playoffs				
Season	Club	League	GP	G	A	Pts	PIM	GP	G	A	Pts	PIM
2002-03	Penticton Panthers	BCHL	32	17	11	28	17	....	....	....	....	....
2003-04	Kelowna Rockets	WHL	72	25	21	46	44	17	4	5	9	18
2004-05	Kelowna Rockets	WHL	72	31	22	53	103	23	12	10	22	44
2005-06	Kelowna Rockets	WHL	72	*51	37	88	82	12	3	6	9	14
2006-07	Springfield Falcons	AHL	60	13	11	24	26	....	....	....	....	....
2007-08	Norfolk Admirals	AHL	70	15	22	37	45	....	....	....	....	....
2008-09	Norfolk Admirals	AHL	58	18	19	37	52	....	....	....	....	....
	Augusta Lynx	ECHL	4	4	1	5	2	....	....	....	....	....
2009-10	Norfolk Admirals	AHL	68	17	7	24	45	....	....	....	....	....
2010-11	EHC Linz	Austria	34	21	12	33	24	5	1	0	1	6

WHL West First All-Star Team (2006)

KELLY, Dan (KEHL-lee, DAN) N.J.

Defense. Shoots left. 6'1", 200 lbs. Born, Morrisonville, NY, May 17, 1989.

			Regular Season					Playoffs				
Season	Club	League	GP	G	A	Pts	PIM	GP	G	A	Pts	PIM
2005-06	Kitchener Rangers	OHL	9	0	3	3	8	....	....	....	....	....
2006-07	Kitchener Rangers	OHL	59	0	19	19	79	9	1	1	2	10
2007-08	Kitchener Rangers	OHL	65	1	17	18	61	8	0	2	2	4
2008-09	Kitchener Rangers	OHL	44	4	11	15	30	....	....	....	....	....
2009-10	Kitchener Rangers	OHL	58	6	21	27	99	20	4	9	13	23
2010-11	Albany Devils	AHL	61	2	5	7	71	....	....	....	....	....

Signed as a free agent by **New Jersey**, May 19, 2010.

KENNEDY, Matt (KEH-nuh-dee, MAT) ANA

Right wing. Shoots right. 6'2", 202 lbs. Born, Richmond Hill, Ont., March 4, 1989.
(Carolina's 4th choice, 131st overall, in 2009 Entry Draft).

			Regular Season					Playoffs				
Season	Club	League	GP	G	A	Pts	PIM	GP	G	A	Pts	PIM
2005-06	Seguin Bruins	OPJHL	47	11	16	27	71	6	0	0	0	8
	Guelph Storm	OHL	13	1	0	1	31	13	0	2	2	8
2006-07	Guelph Storm	OHL	63	10	12	22	78	4	1	1	2	10
2007-08	Guelph Storm	OHL	45	17	4	21	99	10	3	1	4	25
2008-09	Guelph Storm	OHL	67	33	40	73	95	4	3	2	5	0
	Syracuse Crunch	AHL	4	1	0	1	2	....	....	....	....	....
2009-10	Guelph Storm	OHL	14	10	6	16	15	....	....	....	....	....
	Barrie Colts	OHL	29	8	10	18	18	17	9	6	15	11
2010-11	Charlotte	AHL	8	0	1	1	6	....	....	....	....	....
	Syracuse Crunch	AHL	57	4	9	13	67	....	....	....	....	....

Traded to **Anaheim** by **Carolina** with Stefan Chaput for Ryan Carter, November 23, 2010.

KESSEL, Blake (KEH-suhl, BLAYK)

Defense. Shoots right. 6'2", 205 lbs. Born, Madison, WI, April 13, 1989.
(NY Islanders' 4th choice, 166th overall, in 2007 Entry Draft).

			Regular Season					Playoffs				
Season	Club	League	GP	G	A	Pts	PIM	GP	G	A	Pts	PIM
2005-06	Madison Capitols	MAHL	62	33	47	80	....	....	....	....	....	....
2006-07	Waterloo	USHL	59	11	27	38	38	9	1	5	6	8
2007-08	Waterloo	USHL	59	19	38	57	26	11	1	*10	11	12
2008-09	New Hampshire	H-East	37	6	7	13	24	....	....	....	....	....
2009-10	New Hampshire	H-East	38	10	28	38	28	....	....	....	....	....
2010-11	New Hampshire	H-East	39	5	22	27	32	....	....	....	....	....

USHL All-Rookie Team (2007) • USHL Defenseman of the Year (2008) • USHL First All-Star Team (2008) • Hockey East First All-Star Team (2010, 2011) • NCAA East Second All-American Team (2010) • NCAA East First All-American Team (2011)

KESSY, Kale (KEH-see, KAYL) PHX

Left wing. Shoots left. 6'3", 184 lbs. Born, Shaunavon, Sask., December 4, 1992.
(Phoenix's 5th choice, 111th overall, in 2011 Entry Draft).

			Regular Season					Playoffs				
Season	Club	League	GP	G	A	Pts	PIM	GP	G	A	Pts	PIM
2008-09	Medicine Hat	AMHL	33	17	12	29	42	....	....	....	....	....
	Medicine Hat	WHL	9	0	0	0	2	....	....	....	....	....
2009-10	Medicine Hat	WHL	70	11	18	29	123	12	1	3	4	10
2010-11	Medicine Hat	WHL	65	10	14	24	129	14	3	3	6	37

KHOKHLACHEV, Alexander (khohkh-luh-CHAWV, al-ehx-AHN-duhr) BOS

Center. Shoots left. 5'10", 183 lbs. Born, Moscow, Russia, September 9, 1993.
(Boston's 2nd choice, 40th overall, in 2011 Entry Draft).

			Regular Season					Playoffs				
Season	Club	League	GP	G	A	Pts	PIM	GP	G	A	Pts	PIM
2009-10	Spartak Jr.	Russia-Jr.	51	15	25	40	22	....	....	....	....	....
2010-11	Windsor Spitfires	OHL	67	34	42	76	28	18	9	11	20	8

KHOMUTOV, Ivan (khoh-moo-TAWF, ee-VAHN) N.J.

Center. Shoots left. 6'3", 220 lbs. Born, Saratov, USSR, March 11, 1985.
(New Jersey's 3rd choice, 93rd overall, in 2003 Entry Draft).

			Regular Season					Playoffs				
Season	Club	League	GP	G	A	Pts	PIM	GP	G	A	Pts	PIM
2001-02	HK CSKA 2	Russia-3	30	11	8	19	14	....	....	....	....	....
2002-03	Elektrostal	Russia-2	20	1	1	2	8	....	....	....	....	....
2003-04	London Knights	OHL	40	9	12	21	25	15	3	1	4	7
2004-05	Albany River Rats	AHL	66	6	11	17	30	....	....	....	....	....
2005-06	Albany River Rats	AHL	60	9	20	29	44	....	....	....	....	....
2006-07	Lowell Devils	AHL	3	1	1	2	2	....	....	....	....	....
	Trenton Titans	ECHL	5	0	1	1	2	....	....	....	....	....
2007-08	Lowell Devils	AHL	72	13	19	32	53	....	....	....	....	....
2008-09	CSKA Moscow	Rus-KHL	47	9	7	16	32	7	1	0	1	4
2009-10	Avtomobilist	Rus-KHL	17	0	5	5	14	....	....	....	....	....
2010-11	Kristall Saratov	Russia-2	41	3	12	15	24	7	0	1	1	16

KICHTON, Brenden (KIHCH-tuhn, BREHN-duhn) NYI

Defense. Shoots right. 5'10", 175 lbs. Born, Edmonton, Alta., June 18, 1992.
(NY Islanders' 7th choice, 127th overall, in 2011 Entry Draft).

			Regular Season					Playoffs				
Season	Club	League	GP	G	A	Pts	PIM	GP	G	A	Pts	PIM
2007-08	St. Albert	AMHL	35	10	16	26	14	1	0	0	0	2
2008-09	Spokane Chiefs	WHL	57	1	8	9	12	8	0	0	0	0
2009-10	Spokane Chiefs	WHL	70	4	15	19	21	7	0	0	0	4
2010-11	Spokane Chiefs	WHL	64	23	58	81	31	17	1	10	11	2

WHL West Second All-Star Team (2011)

KILLORN, Alexander (KIHL-ohrn, al-ehx-AN-duhr) T.B.

Center. Shoots left. 6'1", 203 lbs. Born, Halifax, N.S., September 14, 1989.
(Tampa Bay's 3rd choice, 77th overall, in 2007 Entry Draft).

			Regular Season					Playoffs				
Season	Club	League	GP	G	A	Pts	PIM	GP	G	A	Pts	PIM
2005-06	Lac St-Louis Lions	QAAA	43	18	34	52	94	10	9	6	15	8
2006-07	Deerfield Academy	High-MA	25	18	14	32	....	....	....	....	....	....
2007-08	Deerfield Academy	High-MA	24	28	27	55	....	....	....	....	....	....
2008-09	Harvard Crimson	ECAC	30	6	8	14	46	....	....	....	....	....
2009-10	Harvard Crimson	ECAC	32	9	11	20	26	....	....	....	....	....
2010-11	Harvard Crimson	ECAC	34	15	14	29	36	....	....	....	....	....

KING, Tristan (KIHNG, TRIHS-tuhn) DAL

Center. Shoots right. 6', 183 lbs. Born, Elk River, MN, November 7, 1990.

			Regular Season					Playoffs				
Season	Club	League	GP	G	A	Pts	PIM	GP	G	A	Pts	PIM
2006-07	Portland	WHL	64	6	9	15	26	....	....	....	....	....
2007-08	Portland	WHL	69	9	16	25	39	....	....	....	....	....
2008-09	Medicine Hat	WHL	47	14	22	36	33	2	0	0	0	0
2009-10	Medicine Hat	WHL	70	21	44	65	65	12	3	3	6	12
2010-11	Texas Stars	AHL	11	2	2	4	6	....	....	....	....	....
	Idaho Steelheads	ECHL	24	3	10	13	13	6	2	1	3	0

Signed as a free agent by **Dallas**, September 18, 2009.

KISHEL, Scott (KIH-shuhl, SKAWT) MTL

Defense. Shoots left. 5'11", 170 lbs. Born, Virginia, MN, April 21, 1989.
(Montreal's 9th choice, 192nd overall, in 2007 Entry Draft).

			Regular Season					Playoffs				
Season	Club	League	GP	G	A	Pts	PIM	GP	G	A	Pts	PIM
2004-05	Virginia Blue Devils	High-MN	....	4	9	13	....	....	....	....	....	....
2005-06	Virginia Blue Devils	High-MN	5	25	30	....		....	....	....	....	....
2006-07	Virginia Blue Devils	High-MN	24	14	34	48	....	....	....	....	....	....
2007-08	Sioux Falls	USHL	57	3	11	14	34	3	0	0	0	0
2008-09	U. Minn-Duluth	WCHA	12	0	2	2	2	....	....	....	....	....
2009-10	U. Minn-Duluth	WCHA	28	0	8	8	14	....	....	....	....	....
2010-11	U. Minn-Duluth	WCHA	7	0	1	1	4	....	....	....	....	....

KITSYN, Maxim (KIHT-sihn, max-EEM) L.A.

Left wing. Shoots right. 6'2", 183 lbs. Born, Novokuznetsk, USSR, December 24, 1991.
(Los Angeles' 5th choice, 158th overall, in 2010 Entry Draft).

			Regular Season					Playoffs				
Season	Club	League	GP	G	A	Pts	PIM	GP	G	A	Pts	PIM
2007-08	Novokuznetsk 2	Russia-3	4	1	0	1	0	....	....	....	....	....
2008-09	Novokuznetsk 2	Russia-3	STATISTICS NOT AVAILABLE									
	Novokuznetsk	Rus-KHL	31	5	2	7	26	....	....	....	....	....
2009-10	Novokuznetsk Jr.	Russia-Jr.	11	6	12	18	26	17	9	12	21	42
	Novokuznetsk	Rus-KHL	21	1	1	2	12	....	....	....	....	....
2010-11	Novokuznetsk Jr.	Russia-Jr.	3	1	1	2	2	....	....	....	....	....
	Novokuznetsk	Rus-KHL	18	3	4	7	8	....	....	....	....	....
	St. Michael's	OHL	32	9	17	26	24	20	10	9	19	14

KIVISTO, Tommi (K'VIHS-toh, TAW-mee) CAR

Defense. Shoots left. 6'1", 195 lbs. Born, Vantaa, Finland, June 7, 1991.
(Carolina's 6th choice, 208th overall, in 2009 Entry Draft).

			Regular Season					Playoffs				
Season	Club	League	GP	G	A	Pts	PIM	GP	G	A	Pts	PIM
2006-07	Jokerit U18	Fin-U18	24	0	2	2	10	....	....	....	....	....
2007-08	Jokerit U18	Fin-U18	26	6	10	16	50	4	0	3	3	4
	Jokerit Helsinki Jr.	Fin-Jr.	9	2	0	2	4	4	0	3	3	2
2008-09	Red Deer Rebels	WHL	65	1	21	22	49	....	....	....	....	....
2009-10	Suomi U20	Finland-2	2	0	0	0	2	....	....	....	....	....
	Jokerit Helsinki	Finland	22	0	2	2	12	3	0	0	0	0
	Kiekko-Vantaa	Finland-2	2	0	0	0	2	....	....	....	....	....
	Jokerit Helsinki Jr.	Fin-Jr.	18	2	5	7	58	2	0	0	0	0
2010-11	Suomi U20	Finland-2	4	0	1	1	0	....	....	....	....	....
	Jokerit Helsinki Jr.	Fin-Jr.	5	0	6	6	8	....	....	....	....	....
	Kiekko-Vantaa	Finland-2	5	1	2	3	0	....	....	....	....	....
	Jokerit Helsinki	Finland	38	0	5	5	22	7	0	0	0	16

KLASSEN, Sam (klah-SIHN, SAM) NYR

Defense. Shoots left. 6'2", 202 lbs. Born, Watrous, Sask., January 1, 1989.

			Regular Season					Playoffs				
Season	Club	League	GP	G	A	Pts	PIM	GP	G	A	Pts	PIM
2006-07	Humboldt Broncos	SJHL	32	2	9	11	74	....	....	....	....	....
	Saskatoon Blades	WHL	39	1	5	6	52	....	....	....	....	....
2007-08	Saskatoon Blades	WHL	71	1	24	25	103	....	....	....	....	....
2008-09	Saskatoon Blades	WHL	72	2	18	20	92	7	0	1	1	10
2009-10	Saskatoon Blades	WHL	67	3	27	30	98	10	0	2	2	8
2010-11	Greenville	ECHL	66	3	14	17	80	11	2	3	5	8
	Connecticut Whale	AHL	3	0	0	0	4	....	....	....	....	....

Signed as a free agent by **NY Rangers**, July 27, 2009.

KLEFBOM, Oscar (KLEHF-bawm, AWS-kuhr) EDM

Defense. Shoots left. 6'3", 204 lbs. Born, Karlstad, Sweden, July 20, 1993.
(Edmonton's 2nd choice, 19th overall, in 2011 Entry Draft).

			Regular Season					Playoffs				
Season	Club	League	GP	G	A	Pts	PIM	GP	G	A	Pts	PIM
2008-09	Farjestad U18	Swe-U18	15	2	2	4	4	4	0	1	1	2
2009-10	Farjestad U18	Swe-U18	31	10	18	28	37	6	0	0	0	0
	IFK Munkfors	Sweden-3	3	0	1	1	0	....	....	....	....	....
	Skare BK	Sweden-3	2	0	0	0	2	....	....	....	....	....
2010-11	Farjestad U18	Swe-U18	8	3	3	6	2	....	....	....	....	....
	Skare BK	Sweden-3	12	0	1	1	0	....	....	....	....	....
	Farjestad	Sweden	23	1	1	2	2	....	....	....	....	....

KLINGBERG, John (KLIHNG-buhrg, JAWN) DAL

Defense. Shoots right. 6', 158 lbs. Born, Lerum, Sweden, August 14, 1992.
(Dallas' 5th choice, 131st overall, in 2010 Entry Draft).

			Regular Season					Playoffs				
Season	Club	League	GP	G	A	Pts	PIM	GP	G	A	Pts	PIM
2008-09	Frolunda U18	Swe-U18	30	3	12	15	12	3	0	0	0	0
2009-10	Frolunda U18	Swe-U18	20	3	13	16	22	7	2	9	11	10
	Frolunda Jr.	Swe-Jr.	27	0	5	5	32	5	1	0	1	6
2010-11	Frolunda	Sweden	26	0	5	5	10	....	....	....	....	....
	Boras HC	Sweden-2	7	1	0	1	2	....	....	....	....	....
	Frolunda Jr.	Swe-Jr.	13	3	14	17	29	7	1	10	11	6

KLUBERTANZ, Kyle (KLOO-buhr-tanz, KIGHL) MTL

Defense. Shoots right. 6'1", 178 lbs. Born, Madison, WI, September 23, 1985.
(Anaheim's 3rd choice, 74th overall, in 2004 Entry Draft).

			Regular Season					Playoffs				
Season	Club	League	GP	G	A	Pts	PIM	GP	G	A	Pts	PIM
2002-03	Green Bay	USHL	60	8	26	34	74	....	....	....	....	....
2003-04	Green Bay	USHL	57	6	21	27	124	....	....	....	....	....
2004-05	U. of Wisconsin	WCHA	41	3	15	18	64	....	....	....	....	....
2005-06	U. of Wisconsin	WCHA	43	4	17	21	44	....	....	....	....	....
2006-07	U. of Wisconsin	WCHA	34	1	12	13	46	....	....	....	....	....
2007-08	U. of Wisconsin	WCHA	40	4	16	20	52	....	....	....	....	....
	Portland Pirates	AHL	5	0	0	0	2	1	0	0	0	0
2008-09	TPS Turku	Finland	51	5	7	12	62	8	3	0	3	20
2009-10	Djurgarden	Sweden	55	12	19	31	32	16	3	2	5	18
2010-11	Hamilton Bulldogs	AHL	76	10	22	32	46	20	0	10	10	22

WCHA All-Rookie Team (2005)

Signed as a free agent by **Montreal**, May 27, 2010.

KNACKSTEDT, Jordan (NAK-stehd, JOHR-dahn)

Right wing. Shoots right. 6'2", 195 lbs. Born, Saskatoon, Sask., September 28, 1988.
(Boston's 6th choice, 189th overall, in 2007 Entry Draft).

			Regular Season					Playoffs				
Season	Club	League	GP	G	A	Pts	PIM	GP	G	A	Pts	PIM
2003-04	Beardy's	SMHL	44	22	19	41	20	4	2	1	3	0
2004-05	Red Deer Rebels	WHL	52	1	2	3	34	7	0	0	0	2
2005-06	Red Deer Rebels	WHL	72	12	28	40	36	....	....	....	....	....
2006-07	Red Deer Rebels	WHL	33	10	7	17	54	....	....	....	....	....
	Moose Jaw	WHL	39	13	26	39	44	....	....	....	....	....
2007-08	Moose Jaw	WHL	72	31	54	85	116	6	1	1	2	8
	Providence Bruins	AHL	5	2	0	2	2	4	1	0	1	0
2008-09	Providence Bruins	AHL	71	10	16	26	55	16	3	1	4	11
2009-10	Providence Bruins	AHL	67	14	24	38	30	....	....	....	....	....
2010-11	Providence Bruins	AHL	22	7	5	12	12	....	....	....	....	....
	Rochester	AHL	44	5	9	14	26	....	....	....	....	....

Traded to **Florida** by **Boston** with Jeff LoVecchio for Sean Zimmerman and future considerations, December 9, 2010.

KNIGHT, Corban (NIGHT, KOHR-buhn) FLA

Center. Shoots right. 6'1", 180 lbs. Born, Oliver, B.C., September 10, 1990.
(Florida's 5th choice, 135th overall, in 2009 Entry Draft).

			Regular Season					Playoffs				
Season	Club	League	GP	G	A	Pts	PIM	GP	G	A	Pts	PIM
2006-07	UFA Bisons	AMHL	36	6	18	24	44	8	2	4	6	16
2007-08	UFA Bisons	AMHL	36	29	36	65	64	6	5	4	9	10
	Okotoks Oilers	AJHL	4	1	0	1	0	7	0	0	0	0
2008-09	Okotoks Oilers	AJHL	61	34	38	72	55	9	10	2	12	12
2009-10	North Dakota	WCHA	37	6	7	13	35	....	....	....	....	....
2010-11	North Dakota	WCHA	44	14	30	44	34	....	....	....	....	....

KNIGHT, Jared (NIGHT, JAIR-uhd) BOS

Center. Shoots right. 5'11", 202 lbs. Born, Battle Creek, MI, January 16, 1992.
(Boston's 2nd choice, 32nd overall, in 2010 Entry Draft).

			Regular Season					Playoffs				
Season	Club	League	GP	G	A	Pts	PIM	GP	G	A	Pts	PIM
2007-08	Det. Compuware	MWEHL	22	8	21	29	21	....	....	....	....	....
	Det. Compuware	Exhib.	5	1	2	3	8	....	....	....	....	....
2008-09	London Knights	OHL	67	15	15	30	60	14	3	0	3	2
2009-10	London Knights	OHL	63	36	21	57	39	12	10	7	17	12
2010-11	London Knights	OHL	68	25	45	70	39	6	4	2	6	2
	Providence Bruins	AHL	3	0	2	2	2	....	....	....	....	....

KNODEL, Eric (NOH-dehl, AIR-ihk) TOR

Defense. Shoots left. 6'6", 216 lbs. Born, West Chesteer, PA, June 8, 1990.
(Toronto's 5th choice, 128th overall, in 2009 Entry Draft).

			Regular Season					Playoffs				
Season	Club	League	GP	G	A	Pts	PIM	GP	G	A	Pts	PIM
2007-08	Phi. Jr. Flyers	AYHL	16	5	6	11	6	....	....	....	....	....
	Phi. Jr. Flyers	Exhib.	35	11	17	28	30	....	....	....	....	....
2008-09	Phi. Jr. Flyers	AYHL	16	2	13	15	12	....	....	....	....	....
	Phi. Jr. Flyers	Exhib.	35	11	19	30	18	....	....	....	....	....
2009-10	Des Moines	USHL	50	3	17	20	37	....	....	....	....	....
2010-11	New Hampshire	H-East	DID NOT PLAY – FRESHMAN									

KOLOMATIS, David (koh-loh-MA-tihs, DAY-vihd) L.A.

Defense. Shoots right. 5'11", 195 lbs. Born, Livingston, NJ, February 25, 1989.
(Los Angeles' 6th choice, 126th overall, in 2009 Entry Draft).

			Regular Season					Playoffs				
Season	Club	League	GP	G	A	Pts	PIM	GP	G	A	Pts	PIM
2005-06	USNTDP	NAHL	16	1	0	1	4	....	....	....	....	....
	USNTDP	U-17	3	0	0	0	2	....	....	....	....	....
2006-07	Owen Sound	OHL	67	4	16	20	54	4	0	0	0	0
2007-08	Owen Sound	OHL	68	9	36	45	68	....	....	....	....	....
2008-09	Owen Sound	OHL	63	18	28	46	52	4	2	2	4	0
	Providence Bruins	AHL	4	0	0	0	0	16	0	1	1	2
2009-10	Manchester	AHL	76	8	21	29	30	15	0	1	1	2
2010-11	Manchester	AHL	70	8	20	28	58	7	2	2	4	2

KOLOSOV, Sergei (KOH-leh-sawf, SAIR-gay)

Defense. Shoots left. 6'4", 217 lbs. Born, Novopolotsk, USSR, May 22, 1986.
(Detroit's 3rd choice, 151st overall, in 2004 Entry Draft).

			Regular Season					Playoffs				
Season	Club	League	GP	G	A	Pts	PIM	GP	G	A	Pts	PIM
2003-04	Dynamo Minsk	Belarus	STATISTICS NOT AVAILABLE									
2004-05	Dynamo Minsk	BelOpen	37	2	6	8	24	....	....	....	....	....
	Yunost-Minsk	BelOpen	1	0	0	0	2	9	0	0	0	4
2005-06	Cedar Rapids	USHL	50	2	8	10	66	8	0	0	0	10
2006-07	Cedar Rapids	USHL	51	1	10	11	79	5	0	0	0	4
2007-08	Dynamo Minsk	Belarus	55	5	9	14	83	....	....	....	....	....
2008-09	Grand Rapids	AHL	70	4	7	11	36	10	0	0	0	9
2009-10	Grand Rapids	AHL	66	2	6	8	29	....	....	....	....	....
	Belarus	Olympics	4	0	0	0	0	....	....	....	....	....
2010-11	Grand Rapids	AHL	56	0	1	1	48	....	....	....	....	....

KOPER, Levko (KOE-puhr, LEHV-koh)

Left wing. Shoots left. 6', 190 lbs. Born, Edmonton, Alta., October 5, 1990.
(Atlanta's 8th choice, 185th overall, in 2009 Entry Draft).

			Regular Season					Playoffs				
Season	Club	League	GP	G	A	Pts	PIM	GP	G	A	Pts	PIM
2005-06	SSAC Bulldogs	Minor-AB	36	39	50	89	34	....	....	....	....	....
	SSAC Athletics	AMHL	1	0	1	1	0	....	....	....	....	....
2006-07	Spokane Chiefs	WHL	50	3	2	5	14	5	0	0	0	0
2007-08	Spokane Chiefs	WHL	69	12	14	26	45	21	4	5	9	14
2008-09	Spokane Chiefs	WHL	71	23	36	59	57	12	3	7	10	6
2009-10	Spokane Chiefs	WHL	68	27	27	54	51	7	2	3	5	13
2010-11	Spokane Chiefs	WHL	72	32	50	82	67	17	9	7	16	21

KORNEEV, Konstantin (kor-NEE-ehv, KAWN-stan-tihn) MTL

Defense. Shoots right. 5'11", 176 lbs. Born, Moscow, USSR, June 5, 1984.
(Montreal's 6th choice, 275th overall, in 2002 Entry Draft).

			Regular Season					Playoffs				
Season	Club	League	GP	G	A	Pts	PIM	GP	G	A	Pts	PIM
99-2000	Krylja Sovetov 2	Russia-3	1	0	0	0	0	....	....	....	....	....
2000-01	Russia Jr.	Exhib.	12	0	4	4	10	....	....	....	....	....
2001-02	Krylja Sovetov 2	Russia-3	26	9	19	28	44	....	....	....	....	....
	Krylja Sovetov	Russia	4	0	2	2	0	2	0	0	0	2
2002-03	Krylja Sovetov	Russia	49	2	8	10	28	....	....	....	....	....
2003-04	Ak Bars Kazan	Russia	55	1	4	5	8	8	0	1	1	2
2004-05	Ak Bars Kazan 2	Russia-3	....	6	16	22		....	....	....	....	....
	Ak Bars Kazan	Russia	35	0	4	4	10	1	0	0	0	0
2005-06	Ak Bars Kazan	Russia	30	1	3	4	14	4	0	0	0	0
2006-07	CSKA Moscow	Russia	54	8	14	22	40	12	2	4	6	6
2007-08	CSKA Moscow	Russia	57	6	18	24	52	6	0	1	1	0
2008-09	CSKA Moscow	Rus-KHL	54	6	18	24	46	8	1	0	1	6
2009-10	CSKA Moscow	Rus-KHL	55	7	22	29	28	3	0	2	2	0
	Russia	Olympics	4	0	0	0	4	....	....	....	....	....
2010-11	CSKA Moscow	Rus-KHL	35	7	14	21	34	....	....	....	....	....
	Ak Bars Kazan	Rus-KHL	17	1	5	6	4	9	0	4	4	4

KOSOV, Yaroslav (KAW-sawf, YAHR-oh-slahv) FLA

Center. Shoots left. 6'3", 220 lbs. Born, Magnitogorsk, Russia, July 5, 1993.
(Florida's 8th choice, 124th overall, in 2011 Entry Draft).

			Regular Season					Playoffs				
Season	Club	League	GP	G	A	Pts	PIM	GP	G	A	Pts	PIM
2010-11	Magnitogorsk Jr.	Russia-Jr.	42	11	10	21	22	17	6	1	7	0

KOSTKA, Mike (KOHST-kuh, MIGHK)

Defense. Shoots right. 6'1", 210 lbs. Born, Ajax, Ont., November 28, 1985.

			Regular Season					Playoffs				
Season	Club	League	GP	G	A	Pts	PIM	GP	G	A	Pts	PIM
2001-02	Ajax Axemen	OPJHL	19	1	4	5	8	....	....	....	....	....
2002-03	Ajax Axemen	OPJHL	39	4	11	15	32	....	....	....	....	....
2003-04	Aurora Tigers	OPJHL	42	9	27	36	4	....	....	....	....	....
2004-05	Massachusetts	H-East	32	1	5	6	14	....	....	....	....	....
2005-06	Massachusetts	H-East	36	2	6	8	20	....	....	....	....	....
2006-07	Massachusetts	H-East	39	3	15	18	20	....	....	....	....	....
2007-08	Massachusetts	H-East	36	9	12	21	20	....	....	....	....	....
	Rochester	AHL	1	0	0	0	2	....	....	....	....	....
2008-09	Portland Pirates	AHL	80	4	26	30	33	4	1	0	1	6
2009-10	Portland Pirates	AHL	76	2	25	27	37	4	0	0	0	0
2010-11	Rochester	AHL	80	16	38	54	46	....	....	....	....	....

Hockey East Second All-Star Team (2008)

Signed as a free agent by **Buffalo**, March 25, 2008. Signed as a free agent by **Rochester** (AHL), August 25, 2010.

KOUDYS, Patrick (KOO-dihs, PAT-rihk) WSH

Defense. Shoots left. 6'3", 198 lbs. Born, Hamilton, Ont., November 15, 1992.
(Washington's 2nd choice, 147th overall, in 2011 Entry Draft).

			Regular Season					Playoffs				
Season	Club	League	GP	G	A	Pts	PIM	GP	G	A	Pts	PIM
2008-09	Welland Tigers	Minor-ON	52	1	11	12	48	....	....	....	....	....
2009-10	Burlington	ON-Jr.A	50	5	28	33	42	12	0	1	1	16
2010-11	RPI Engineers	ECAC	31	1	2	3	14	....	....	....	....	....

KOZEK, Andrew (KOH-zehk, AN-droo) WPG

Left wing. Shoots left. 5'11", 205 lbs. Born, Sicamous, B.C., May 26, 1986.
(Atlanta's 4th choice, 53rd overall, in 2005 Entry Draft).

			Regular Season					Playoffs				
Season	Club	League	GP	G	A	Pts	PIM	GP	G	A	Pts	PIM
2003-04	Surrey Eagles	BCHL	58	19	22	41	67	....	....	....	....	....
2004-05	Surrey Eagles	BCHL	60	48	49	97	81	....	....	....	....	....
2005-06	North Dakota	WCHA	46	7	6	13	22	....	....	....	....	....
2006-07	North Dakota	WCHA	41	5	6	11	12	....	....	....	....	....
2007-08	North Dakota	WCHA	42	18	3	21	18	....	....	....	....	....
2008-09	North Dakota	WCHA	38	8	12	20	40	....	....	....	....	....
	Chicago Wolves	AHL	5	2	0	2	2	....	....	....	....	....
2009-10	Chicago Wolves	AHL	69	12	10	22	36	7	0	1	1	0
2010-11	Chicago Wolves	AHL	57	7	5	12	43	....	....	....	....	....
	Hershey Bears	AHL	14	4	4	8	2	6	1	1	2	7

KOZUN, Brandon (KOH-zuhn, BRAN-duhn) L.A.

Right wing. Shoots right. 5'8", 156 lbs. Born, Los Angeles, CA, March 8, 1990.
(Los Angeles' 8th choice, 179th overall, in 2009 Entry Draft).

			Regular Season					Playoffs				
Season	Club	League	GP	G	A	Pts	PIM	GP	G	A	Pts	PIM
2006-07	Calgary Royals	AJHL	39	20	22	42	38	4	2	1	3	2
	Calgary Hitmen	WHL	11	1	1	2	4	....	....	....	....	....
2007-08	Calgary Hitmen	WHL	69	19	34	53	46	16	4	14	18	6
2008-09	Calgary Hitmen	WHL	72	40	68	108	58	18	7	12	19	8
2009-10	Calgary Hitmen	WHL	65	32	*75	*107	50	23	8	*22	*30	12
2010-11	Manchester	AHL	73	23	25	48	48	7	1	3	4	2

WHL East First All-Star Team (2009, 2010) • Canadian Major Junior First All-Star Team (2010)

KRAMER, Darren (KRAY-muhr, DAIR-uhn) OTT

Center. Shoots left. 6'1", 206 lbs. Born, Peace River, Alta., November 19, 1991.
(Ottawa's 7th choice, 156th overall, in 2011 Entry Draft).

			Regular Season					Playoffs				
Season	Club	League	GP	G	A	Pts	PIM	GP	G	A	Pts	PIM
2007-08	Peace River Royals	Minor-AB	30	26	22	48	58	9	9	8	17	18
	Peace River	NWJHL	1	0	0	0	0	....	....	....	....	....
2008-09	Grande Prairie	AJHL	38	4	0	4	220	14	1	0	1	45
2009-10	Grande Prairie	AJHL	58	19	11	30	*311	9	2	2	4	23
2010-11	Grande Prairie	AJHL	10	4	1	5	28	....	....	....	....	....
	Spokane Chiefs	WHL	68	7	7	14	*306	17	5	3	8	21

KREIDER, Chris (KRIGH-duhr, KRIHS) NYR

Center. Shoots left. 6'3", 217 lbs. Born, Boxford, MA, April 30, 1991.
(NY Rangers' 1st choice, 19th overall, in 2009 Entry Draft).

			Regular Season					Playoffs				
Season	Club	League	GP	G	A	Pts	PIM	GP	G	A	Pts	PIM
2005-06	Masconomet	High-MA	19	5	10	15	....	....	....	....	....	....
2006-07	Masconomet	High-MA	20	28	13	41	....	....	....	....	....	....
2007-08	Andover	High-MA	24	26	15	41	....	....	....	....	....	....
2008-09	Andover	High-MA	26	33	23	56	10	....	....	....	....	....
	Valley Jr. Warriors	Minor-MA	5	4	2	6	....	....	....	....	....	....
2009-10	Boston College	H-East	38	15	8	23	26	....	....	....	....	....
2010-11	Boston College	H-East	32	11	13	24	37	....	....	....	....	....

Hockey East All-Rookie Team (2010)

KRISTO, Danny (KRIHS-toh, DAN-ee) MTL

Right wing. Shoots right. 5'11", 172 lbs. Born, Edina, MN, June 18, 1990.
(Montreal's 1st choice, 56th overall, in 2008 Entry Draft).

			Regular Season					Playoffs				
Season	Club	League	GP	G	A	Pts	PIM	GP	G	A	Pts	PIM
2006-07	USNTDP	U-17	14	4	5	9	0	....	....	....	....	....
	USNTDP	NAHL	39	8	10	18	34	6	0	1	1	2
2007-08	USNTDP	U-18	43	18	14	32	18	....	....	....	....	....
	USNTDP	NAHL	14	4	4	8	6	....	....	....	....	....
2008-09	Omaha Lancers	USHL	50	22	35	57	18	3	3	0	3	2
2009-10	North Dakota	WCHA	41	15	21	36	8	....	....	....	....	....
2010-11	North Dakota	WCHA	34	8	20	28	18	....	....	....	....	....

WCHA All-Rookie Team (2010) • WCHA Rookie of the Year (2010)

KRUEGER, Justin (KROO-guhr, JUHS-tihn) CAR

Defense. Shoots right. 6'2", 205 lbs. Born, Dusseldorf, West Germany, October 6, 1986.
(Carolina's 6th choice, 213th overall, in 2006 Entry Draft).

			Regular Season					Playoffs				
Season	Club	League	GP	G	A	Pts	PIM	GP	G	A	Pts	PIM
2002-03	HC Davos Jr.	Swiss-Jr.	12	0	0	0	4	2	0	0	0	0
2003-04	HC Davos Jr.	Swiss-Jr.	33	2	0	2	14	....	....	....	....	....
2004-05	HC Davos Jr.	Swiss-Jr.	38	5	12	17	76	4	1	2	3	2
2005-06	Penticton Vees	BCHL	55	7	15	22	25	....	....	....	....	....
2006-07	Cornell Big Red	ECAC	31	1	5	6	24	....	....	....	....	....
2007-08	Cornell Big Red	ECAC	35	4	5	9	33	....	....	....	....	....
2008-09	Cornell Big Red	ECAC	35	1	4	5	24	....	....	....	....	....
2009-10	Cornell Big Red	ECAC	34	1	11	12	22	....	....	....	....	....
2010-11	SC Bern	Swiss	50	1	10	11	61	11	0	2	2	8

Signed as a free agent by **Bern** (Swiss), May 26, 2010.

KRUPP, Bjorn (KROOP, B'YOHRN) MIN

Defense. Shoots right. 6'3", 200 lbs. Born, Manhattan Beach, CA, March 6, 1991.

			Regular Season					Playoffs				
Season	Club	League	GP	G	A	Pts	PIM	GP	G	A	Pts	PIM
2007-08	USNTDP	NAHL	43	0	3	3	40	....	....	....	....	....
2008-09	Belleville Bulls	OHL	57	1	3	4	22	17	0	0	0	9
2009-10	Belleville Bulls	OHL	67	0	11	11	53	....	....	....	....	....
2010-11	Belleville Bulls	OHL	61	1	10	11	54	4	0	0	0	2

Signed as a free agent by **Minnesota**, September 18, 2009.

KRYSANOV, Anton (KREE-sa-nahf, AN-tawn) PHX

Center. Shoots left. 6'3", 198 lbs. Born, Togliatti, USSR, March 25, 1987.
(Phoenix's 4th choice, 148th overall, in 2005 Entry Draft).

			Regular Season					Playoffs				
Season	Club	League	GP	G	A	Pts	PIM	GP	G	A	Pts	PIM
2002-03	Lada Togliatti 2	Russia-3	9	1	3	4	2	....	....	....	....	....
2003-04	Lada Togliatti 2	Russia-3	18	2	3	5	2	....	....	....	....	....
2004-05	Lada Togliatti 2	Russia-3	34	13	13	26	32	....	....	....	....	....
	Lada Togliatti	Russia	15	1	0	1	2	....	....	....	....	....
2005-06	Lada Togliatti	Russia	46	3	3	6	24	8	0	0	0	2
2006-07	Lada Togliatti	Russia	48	1	15	16	14	3	0	0	0	4
2007-08	Lada Togliatti 2	Russia-3	2	2	1	3	2	....	....	....	....	....
	Lada Togliatti	Russia	54	9	11	20	22	4	0	1	1	0
2008-09	Lada Togliatti	Rus-KHL	46	8	10	18	14	5	0	3	3	4
2009-10	Dynamo Moscow	Rus-KHL	41	8	6	14	14	2	0	0	0	2
2010-11	Nizhnekamsk	Rus-KHL	33	4	9	13	12	5	1	0	1	2

KRYUKOV, Artem (KREE-oo-kahf, AHR-tehm) BUF

Center. Shoots left. 6'3", 180 lbs. Born, Novosibirsk, USSR, March 5, 1982.
(Buffalo's 1st choice, 15th overall, in 2000 Entry Draft).

			Regular Season					Playoffs				
Season	Club	League	GP	G	A	Pts	PIM	GP	G	A	Pts	PIM
1997-98	Torpedo Yaroslavl	Russia	7	0	0	0	2	....	....	....	....	....
1998-99	Yaroslavl 2	Russia-3	20	2	2	4	6	....	....	....	....	....
99-2000	Yaroslavl 2	Russia-3	14	1	1	2	12	....	....	....	....	....
	Torpedo Yaroslavl	Russia	3	0	0	0	4	....	....	....	....	....
2000-01	Yaroslavl 2	Russia-3	6	0	0	0	2	11	0	0	0	8
	SKA St. Petersburg	Russia	14	0	2	2	14	....	....	....	....	....
2001-02	Yaroslavl	Russia	15	1	3	4	10	6	1	0	1	8
2002-03	Sibir Novosibirsk	Russia	9	0	0	0	27	....	....	....	....	....
2003-04	Yaroslavl 2	Russia-3	30	5	4	9	26	....	....	....	....	....
	Yaroslavl	Russia	4	0	2	2	0	....	....	....	....	....
2004-05	Yaroslavl	Russia	60	8	9	17	44	7	1	0	1	4
2005-06	Yaroslavl	Russia	33	1	2	3	42	1	0	0	0	0
	Yaroslavl 2	Russia-3	6	3	3	6	18	....	....	....	....	....
2006-07	Vityaz Chekhov	Russia	12	0	0	0	20	....	....	....	....	....
	Yaroslavl 2	Russia-3	13	4	10	14	10	....	....	....	....	....
	Yaroslavl	Russia	19	1	3	4	20	....	....	....	....	....
2007-08	SKA St. Petersburg	Russia	51	7	8	15	54	9	0	2	2	8
2008-09	SKA St. Petersburg	Rus-KHL	50	8	3	11	48	....	....	....	....	....
2009-10		DID NOT PLAY – INJURED										
2010-11	VMF	Russia-2	2	0	0	0	4	....	....	....	....	....
	SKA St. Petersburg	Rus-KHL	25	1	4	5	14	4	0	0	0	0

• Missed 2009-10 due to knee injury in pre-season.

KUCHEROV, Nikita (KOO-chuhr-awv, nih-KEE-tuh) T.B.

Left wing. Shoots left. 5'11", 171 lbs. Born, Maikop, Russia, June 17, 1993.
(Tampa Bay's 2nd choice, 58th overall, in 2011 Entry Draft).

			Regular Season					Playoffs				
Season	Club	League	GP	G	A	Pts	PIM	GP	G	A	Pts	PIM
2009-10	CSKA Jr.	Russia-Jr.	53	29	25	54	40	5	0	2	2	2
2010-11	CSKA Jr.	Russia-Jr.	41	27	31	58	81	10	5	8	13	16
	CSKA Moscow	Rus-KHL	8	0	2	2	0	....	....	....	....	....

KUGRYSHEV, Dmitry (koo-GRIH-shev, dih-MEE-tree) WSH

Right wing. Shoots right. 5'11", 183 lbs. Born, Balakovo, USSR, January 18, 1990.
(Washington's 4th choice, 58th overall, in 2008 Entry Draft).

			Regular Season					Playoffs				
Season	Club	League	GP	G	A	Pts	PIM	GP	G	A	Pts	PIM
2005-06	CSKA Moscow 2	Russia-3	STATISTICS NOT AVAILABLE									
2006-07	CSKA Moscow 2	Russia-3	STATISTICS NOT AVAILABLE									
2007-08	CSKA Moscow 2	Russia-3	29	25	25	50	60	7	5	6	11	6
2008-09	Quebec Remparts	QMJHL	57	34	40	74	38	17	6	14	20	24
2009-10	Quebec Remparts	QMJHL	66	29	58	87	52	9	4	6	10	8
2010-11	Hershey Bears	AHL	64	6	8	14	10	....	....	....	....	....
	South Carolina	ECHL	3	0	1	1	2	....	....	....	....	....

QMJHL All-Rookie Team (2009) • Canadian Major Junior All-Rookie Team (2009)

KUHNHACKL, Tom (koon-HAH-kuhl, TAWM) PIT

Center. Shoots left. 6'2", 183 lbs. Born, Landshut, Germany, January 21, 1992.
(Pittsburgh's 3rd choice, 110th overall, in 2010 Entry Draft).

			Regular Season					Playoffs				
Season	Club	League	GP	G	A	Pts	PIM	GP	G	A	Pts	PIM
2007-08	EV Landshut Jr.	Ger-Jr.	30	21	20	41	102	3	1	0	1	2
2008-09	EV Landshut Jr.	Ger-Jr.	6	4	3	7	31	7	5	5	10	27
	Landshut Cann.	German-2	42	11	10	21	34	6	1	0	1	6
2009-10	EV Landshut Jr.	Ger-Jr.	2	1	3	4	0	3	4	4	8	12
	Landshut Cann.	German-2	38	12	9	21	38	6	0	0	0	2
	Augsburg	Germany	4	0	0	0	0	....	....	....	....	....
2010-11	Windsor Spitfires	OHL	63	39	29	68	47	18	11	12	23	10

KULYASH, Denis (kuh-L'YASH, DEH-nihs) NSH

Defense. Shoots left. 6'3", 199 lbs. Born, Omsk, USSR, May 31, 1983.
(Nashville's 9th choice, 243rd overall, in 2004 Entry Draft).

			Regular Season					Playoffs				
Season	Club	League	GP	G	A	Pts	PIM	GP	G	A	Pts	PIM
2003-04	CSK VVS Samara 2	Russia-3	STATISTICS NOT AVAILABLE									
	CSKA Moscow	Russia	10	1	0	1	8	....	....	....	....	....
2004-05	CSKA Moscow	Russia	59	8	10	18	58	....	....	....	....	....
2005-06	Dynamo Moscow	Russia	44	12	5	17	117	4	0	2	2	6
2006-07	Dynamo Moscow	Russia	48	3	9	12	58	2	0	0	0	2
2007-08	CSKA Moscow	Russia	53	9	13	22	79	6	1	1	2	34
2008-09	CSKA Moscow	Rus-KHL	56	16	10	26	62	8	2	1	3	20
2009-10	CSKA Moscow	Rus-KHL	35	11	10	21	34	....	....	....	....	....
	Omsk	Rus-KHL	6	1	1	2	6	3	0	0	0	4
2010-11	Omsk	Rus-KHL	48	11	15	26	45	14	3	3	6	12

KUNDRATEK, Tomas (kuhn-DRAT-ehk, TAW-mahsh) NYR

Defense. Shoots right. 6'2", 201 lbs. Born, Prerov, Czech., December 26, 1989.
(NY Rangers' 4th choice, 90th overall, in 2008 Entry Draft).

			Regular Season					Playoffs				
Season	Club	League	GP	G	A	Pts	PIM	GP	G	A	Pts	PIM
2003-04	HC Prerov U17	CzR-U17	6	0	0	0	0	....	....	....	....	....
2004-05	HC Prerov U17	CzR-U17	38	2	7	9	26	4	0	1	1	4
2005-06	HC Trinec U17	CzR-U17	39	5	13	18	96	2	0	1	1	10
	HC Trinec Jr.	CzRep-Jr.	12	1	1	2	16	7	1	1	2	4
2006-07	HC Trinec Jr.	CzRep-Jr.	33	4	13	17	93	3	1	1	2	10
	HC Ocelari Trinec	CzRep	22	0	1	1	4	4	0	0	0	6
2007-08	HC Trinec Jr.	CzRep-Jr.	14	3	6	9	28	....	....	....	....	....
	Prostejov	CzRep-2	15	1	0	1	10	....	....	....	....	....
	HC Havirov	CzRep-2	2	0	0	0	2	....	....	....	....	....
	HC Ocelari Trinec	CzRep	14	0	1	1	10	7	0	2	2	8
2008-09	Medicine Hat	WHL	51	4	19	23	63	11	0	6	6	12
	Hartford Wolf Pack	AHL	....	....	....	....	....	1	0	0	0	0
2009-10	Medicine Hat	WHL	65	2	33	35	62	12	1	5	6	23
2010-11	Connecticut Whale	AHL	70	2	10	12	42	6	0	2	2	2

KURALY, Sean (KUH-ra-lee, SHAWN) S.J.

Center. Shoots left. 6'2", 190 lbs. Born, Lewiston, NY, January 20, 1993.
(San Jose's 3rd choice, 133rd overall, in 2011 Entry Draft).

			Regular Season					Playoffs				
Season	Club	League	GP	G	A	Pts	PIM	GP	G	A	Pts	PIM
2009-10	Ohio Blue Jackets	T1EHL	37	19	30	49	24	....	....	....	....	....
	Indiana Ice	USHL	5	1	2	3	0	....	....	....	....	....
2010-11	Indiana Ice	USHL	51	8	21	29	45	5	1	1	2	4

• Signed Letter of Intent to attend **Miami University** (CCHA) in fall of 2012.

KUZNETSOV, Evgeny (kooz-neht-SAWF, ehv-GEH-nee) WSH

Center. Shoots left. 6', 172 lbs. Born, Chelyabinsk, Russia, May 19, 1992.
(Washington's 1st choice, 26th overall, in 2010 Entry Draft).

			Regular Season					Playoffs				
Season	Club	League	GP	G	A	Pts	PIM	GP	G	A	Pts	PIM
2007-08	Chelyabinsk 2	Russia-3	2	0	0	0	0	....	....	....	....	....
2008-09	Chelyabinsk 2	Russia-3	22	5	11	16	40	....	....	....	....	....
2009-10	Chelyabinsk Jr.	Russia-Jr.	9	4	12	16	8	2	1	2	3	4
	Chelyabinsk	Rus-KHL	35	2	6	8	10	4	1	0	1	0
2010-11	Chelyabinsk	Rus-KHL	44	17	15	32	30	....	....	....	....	....
	Chelyabinsk Jr.	Russia-Jr.	8	10	5	15	4	5	0	2	2	10

KVETON, David (KVEH-tuhn, DAY-vihd) NYR

Right wing. Shoots left. 6', 199 lbs. Born, Novy Jicin, Czech., January 3, 1988.
(NY Rangers' 4th choice, 104th overall, in 2006 Entry Draft).

			Regular Season					Playoffs				
Season	Club	League	GP	G	A	Pts	PIM	GP	G	A	Pts	PIM
2003-04	HC Vsetin U17	CzR-U17	14	9	11	20	35	....	....	....	....	....
	HC Vsetin Jr.	CzRep-Jr.	41	12	11	23	14	5	2	3	5	2
	TJ Novy Jicin	CzRep-3	1	0	1	1	0	....	....	....	....	....
	HC Vsetin	CzRep	1	0	0	0	0	....	....	....	....	....
2004-05	HC Vsetin U17	CzR-U17	1	1	0	1	0	....	....	....	....	....
	HC Vsetin Jr.	CzRep-Jr.	36	21	27	48	66	8	6	5	11	4
	TJ Novy Jicin	CzRep-3	7	0	1	1	6	....	....	....	....	....
	HC Vsetin	CzRep	6	1	0	1	0	....	....	....	....	....
2005-06	HC Vsetin Jr.	CzRep-Jr.	1	1	1	2	0	1	0	1	1	0
	HC Sareza Ostrava	CzRep-2	7	2	1	3	2	....	....	....	....	....
	HC Vsetin	CzRep	45	6	4	10	18	....	....	....	....	....
	TJ Novy Jicin	CzRep-3	....	....	....	....	....	5	5	0	5	18
	HC Vsetin	CzRep-Q	....	....	....	....	....	3	1	1	2	2
2006-07	Gatineau	QMJHL	31	5	27	32	17	5	0	0	0	4
	HC Vsetin	CzRep	19	2	0	2	8	....	....	....	....	....
2007-08	HC Ocelari Trinec	CzRep	28	10	5	15	10	....	....	....	....	....
2008-09	HC Ocelari Trinec	CzRep	46	22	22	44	20	5	3	2	5	16
2009-10	HC Ocelari Trinec	CzRep	52	18	17	35	59	5	1	1	2	24
2010-11	HC Ocelari Trinec	CzRep	52	14	18	32	26	18	7	12	19	8

KYTNAR, Milan (KIHT-nahr, MEE-lan) EDM

Center. Shoots left. 6', 190 lbs. Born, Topolcany, Czech., May 19, 1989.
(Edmonton's 5th choice, 127th overall, in 2007 Entry Draft).

			Regular Season					Playoffs				
Season	Club	League	GP	G	A	Pts	PIM	GP	G	A	Pts	PIM
2003-04	Topolcany U18	Svk-U18	42	17	22	39	90	....	....	....	....	....
2004-05	Topolcany U18	Svk-U18	53	36	65	101	105	....	....	....	....	....
	Topolcany Jr.	Slovak-Jr.	10	2	2	4	8	....	....	....	....	....
2005-06	HK Trnava U18	Svk-U18	30	18	23	41	106	....	....	....	....	....
	HK Trnava Jr.	Slovak-Jr.	12	1	2	3	20	....	....	....	....	....
	Topolcany U18	Svk-U18	8	4	4	8	4	....	....	....	....	....
	Topolcany Jr.	Slovak-Jr.	6	6	4	10	8	....	....	....	....	....
2006-07	HC Topolcany U18	Svk-U18	53	37	54	91	84	....	....	....	....	....
	HC Topolcany	Slovak-2	22	4	7	11	53	5	1	1	2	4
2007-08	Kelowna Rockets	WHL	62	9	13	22	66	7	0	0	0	4
2008-09	Saskatoon Blades	WHL	65	27	37	64	89	7	3	1	4	14
2009-10	Saskatoon Blades	WHL	3	0	1	1	2	....	....	....	....	....
	Vancouver Giants	WHL	42	14	25	39	40	16	3	12	15	23
2010-11	Oklahoma City	AHL	78	13	16	29	35	1	0	0	0	0

LABATE, Joseph (luh-BA-tay, JOH-sehf) VAN

Center. Shoots left. 6'4", 190 lbs. Born, Burnsville, MN, April 16, 1993.
(Vancouver's 4th choice, 101st overall, in 2011 Entry Draft).

			Regular Season					Playoffs				
Season	Club	League	GP	G	A	Pts	PIM	GP	G	A	Pts	PIM
2009-10	Holy Angels	High-MN	25	29	29	58	26	2	0	1	1	2
2010-11	Team Southeast	UMHSEL	5	2	6	8	2	3	4	2	6	0
	Holy Angels	High-MN	25	27	22	49	42	1	2	1	3	0

• Signed Letter of Intent to attend **University of Wisconsin** (WCHA) in fall of 2011.

LABRIE, Hubert (la-BREE, hew-BAIR) DAL

Defense. Shoots left. 5'11", 190 lbs. Born, Victoriaville, Que., July 12, 1991.

			Regular Season					Playoffs				
Season	Club	League	GP	G	A	Pts	PIM	GP	G	A	Pts	PIM
2007-08	Gatineau	QMJHL	61	2	15	17	79	19	1	3	4	26
2008-09	Gatineau	QMJHL	55	1	3	4	82	5	0	0	0	14
2009-10	Gatineau	QMJHL	67	4	16	20	99	11	3	4	7	20
2010-11	Gatineau	QMJHL	9	3	4	7	8	24	4	8	12	30

Signed as a free agent by **Dallas**, September 18, 2009.

LABRIE, Pierre-Cedric (la-BREE, pee-AIR-SEH-DRIHK)

Left wing. Shoots right. 6'2", 212 lbs. Born, Baie Comeau, Que., December 6, 1986.

			Regular Season					Playoffs				
Season	Club	League	GP	G	A	Pts	PIM	GP	G	A	Pts	PIM
2003-04	Coaticook	QJHL	46	13	12	25	96	....	....	....	....	....
	Quebec Remparts	QMJHL	1	0	0	0	0	....	....	....	....	....
2004-05	Coaticook	QJHL	15	3	4	7	59	....	....	....	....	....
2005-06	Restigouche Tigers	MJrHL	54	43	43	86	153	....	....	....	....	....
	Baie-Comeau	QMJHL	....	....	....	....	....	4	2	2	4	6
2006-07	Baie-Comeau	QMJHL	68	35	28	63	113	11	8	6	14	35
2007-08	Manitoba Moose	AHL	67	7	11	18	108	3	0	0	0	2
2008-09	Manitoba Moose	AHL	63	6	9	15	79	14	0	1	1	37
2009-10	Manitoba Moose	AHL	45	5	1	6	69	....	....	....	....	....
	Peoria Rivermen	AHL	16	0	1	1	16	....	....	....	....	....
2010-11	Norfolk Admirals	AHL	64	7	19	26	148	6	0	1	1	4

Signed as a free agent by **Vancouver**, July 3, 2007. Traded to **St. Louis** by **Vancouver** for Yan Stastny, March 3, 2010. Signed as a free agent by **Norfolk** (AHL), December 8, 2010.

LAGACE, Jacob (LEH-gah-see, JAY-kawb) BUF

Left wing. Shoots left. 5'11", 199 lbs. Born, Beloeil, Que., January 9, 1990.
(Buffalo's 7th choice, 134th overall, in 2008 Entry Draft).

			Regular Season					Playoffs				
Season	Club	League	GP	G	A	Pts	PIM	GP	G	A	Pts	PIM
2005-06	C.A.-Girouord	QAAA	38	10	11	21	....	8	0	2	2	4
2006-07	C.A.-Girouord	QAAA	44	24	29	53	46	4	1	4	5	2
2007-08	Chicoutimi	QMJHL	67	23	39	62	40	6	3	2	5	7
2008-09	Chicoutimi	QMJHL	64	32	37	69	52	4	1	2	3	4
2009-10	Chicoutimi	QMJHL	35	30	23	53	20	....	....	....	....	....
	Cape Breton	QMJHL	25	5	15	20	32	5	0	3	3	4
	Portland Pirates	AHL	....	....	....	....	....	1	0	0	0	0
2010-11	Portland Pirates	AHL	58	10	13	23	34	3	0	0	0	0
	Greenville	ECHL	13	0	6	6	0	....	....	....	....	....

QMJHL All-Rookie Team (2008)

LAJUNEN, Jani (LA-joo-nehn, YAH-nee) NSH

Center. Shoots left. 6'1", 190 lbs. Born, Helsinki, Finland, June 16, 1990.
(Nashville's 6th choice, 201st overall, in 2008 Entry Draft).

			Regular Season					Playoffs				
Season	Club	League	GP	G	A	Pts	PIM	GP	G	A	Pts	PIM
2005-06	K-Vantaa U18	Fin-U18	2	0	0	0	0	....	....	....	....	....
2006-07	Blues Espoo U18	Fin-U18	28	5	12	17	20	6	1	1	2	4
2007-08	Blues Espoo U18	Fin-U18	1	1	0	1	2	4	2	2	4	0
	Blues Espoo Jr.	Fin-Jr.	25	4	10	14	14	3	0	0	0	0
	Blues Espoo	Finland	1	0	0	0	0	....	....	....	....	....
2008-09	Suomi U20	Finland-2	2	2	2	4	0	....	....	....	....	....
	Blues Espoo Jr.	Fin-Jr.	25	16	10	26	24	8	2	1	3	12
	Blues Espoo	Finland	25	1	1	2	4	2	0	0	0	0
2009-10	Blues Espoo Jr.	Fin-Jr.	4	1	1	2	0	....	....	....	....	....
	Suomi U20	Finland-2	2	0	0	0	0	....	....	....	....	....
	Blues Espoo	Finland	46	6	9	15	34	3	0	0	0	2
2010-11	Blues Espoo	Finland	60	10	12	22	46	18	3	4	7	12

LALONDE, Shawn (la-LAWND, SHAWN) CHI

Defense. Shoots right. 6'1", 192 lbs. Born, Ottawa, Ont., March 10, 1990.
(Chicago's 2nd choice, 68th overall, in 2008 Entry Draft).

			Regular Season					Playoffs				
Season	Club	League	GP	G	A	Pts	PIM	GP	G	A	Pts	PIM
2005-06	Cumberland	Minor-ON	60	18	36	54	98	....	....	....	....	....
2006-07	Belleville Bulls	OHL	58	6	20	26	71	13	1	1	2	6
2007-08	Belleville Bulls	OHL	66	9	22	31	67	21	2	7	9	25
2008-09	Belleville Bulls	OHL	66	19	34	53	73	17	3	9	12	36
2009-10	Belleville Bulls	OHL	58	13	43	56	87	....	....	....	....	....
	Rockford IceHogs	AHL	8	1	1	2	11	3	0	0	0	2
2010-11	Rockford IceHogs	AHL	73	5	27	32	76	....	....	....	....	....

LANDER, Anton (LAN-duhr, AN-tawn) **EDM**

Center. Shoots left. 6', 194 lbs. Born, Sundsvall, Sweden, April 24, 1991.
(Edmonton's 2nd choice, 40th overall, in 2009 Entry Draft).

			Regular Season					Playoffs				
Season	Club	League	GP	G	A	Pts	PIM	GP	G	A	Pts	PIM
2005-06	Timra IK U18	Swe-U18	14	1	6	7	14	....	....	....	....	....
2006-07	Timra IK U18	Swe-U18	12	6	10	16	14	2	1	2	3	0
	Timra IK Jr.	Swe-Jr.	10	2	1	3	10	....	....	....	....	....
2007-08	Timra IK U18	Swe-U18	4	6	4	10	8	....	....	....	....	....
	Timra IK Jr.	Swe-Jr.	18	5	14	19	39	....	....	....	....	....
	Timra IK	Sweden	32	1	2	3	4	10	0	0	0	0
2008-09	Timra IK Jr.	Swe-Jr.	8	5	1	6	8	....	....	....	....	....
	Timra IK	Sweden	47	4	6	10	12	7	0	0	0	4
2009-10	Timra IK	Sweden	49	7	9	16	14	5	0	2	2	2
2010-11	Timra IK	Sweden	49	11	15	26	38	....	....	....	....	....
	Timra IK Jr.	Swe-Jr.	....	....	....	....	....	2	1	2	3	0

LANDESKOG, Gabriel (LAND-ehs-kawg, GAY-bree-ehl) **COL**

Left wing. Shoots left. 6'1", 204 lbs. Born, Stockholm, Sweden, November 23, 1992.
(Colorado's 1st choice, 2nd overall, in 2011 Entry Draft).

			Regular Season					Playoffs				
Season	Club	League	GP	G	A	Pts	PIM	GP	G	A	Pts	PIM
2007-08	Djurgarden U18	Swe-U18	23	12	10	22	4	2	0	0	0	0
	Djurgarden Jr.	Swe-Jr.	1	0	0	0	0	....	....	....	....	....
2008-09	Djurgarden U18	Swe-U18	8	5	7	12	41	2	0	0	0	0
	Djurgarden Jr.	Swe-Jr.	31	7	14	21	63	6	1	0	1	8
	Djurgarden	Sweden	3	0	1	1	2	....	....	....	....	....
2009-10	Kitchener Rangers	OHL	61	24	22	46	51	20	8	15	23	18
2010-11	Kitchener Rangers	OHL	53	36	30	66	61	7	6	4	10	4

OHL All-Rookie Team (2010)

LANDRY, Charles (LAN-dree, CHAR-uhlz) **T.B.**

Defense. Shoots right. 6', 196 lbs. Born, Napierville, Que., June 3, 1991.

			Regular Season					Playoffs				
Season	Club	League	GP	G	A	Pts	PIM	GP	G	A	Pts	PIM
2007-08	Drummondville	QMJHL	61	5	8	13	47	....	....	....	....	....
2008-09	Drummondville	QMJHL	48	0	13	13	41	19	2	2	4	8
2009-10	Drummondville	QMJHL	68	6	24	30	41	14	3	2	5	10
2010-11	Montreal	QMJHL	57	11	29	40	30	10	1	3	4	12
	Norfolk Admirals	AHL	....	....	....	....	....	1	0	0	0	0

Signed as a free agent by **Tampa Bay**, September 15, 2010.

LANE, Philip (LAYN, FIHL-ihp) **PHX**

Right wing. Shoots right. 6'3", 195 lbs. Born, Rochester, NY, May 29, 1992.
(Phoenix's 3rd choice, 52nd overall, in 2010 Entry Draft).

			Regular Season					Playoffs				
Season	Club	League	GP	G	A	Pts	PIM	GP	G	A	Pts	PIM
2008-09	Buffalo Jr. Sabres	ON-Jr.A	45	18	24	42	72	5	0	0	0	6
2009-10	Brampton	OHL	64	18	14	32	52	11	3	0	3	14
2010-11	Brampton	OHL	54	17	17	34	113	4	0	1	1	2

LANE, Tanner (LAYN, TA-nuhr) **WPG**

Center. Shoots left. 6'2", 175 lbs. Born, Detroit Lakes, MN, August 13, 1992.
(Atlanta's 7th choice, 160th overall, in 2010 Entry Draft).

			Regular Season					Playoffs				
Season	Club	League	GP	G	A	Pts	PIM	GP	G	A	Pts	PIM
2007-08	Detroit Lakes	High-MN	26	24	20	44	28	....	....	....	....	....
2008-09	Detroit Lakes	High-MN	26	26	26	52	50	....	....	....	....	....
2009-10	Team Great Plains	UMHSEL	21	8	7	15	....	....	....	....	....	....
	Detroit Lakes	High-MN	25	49	41	*90	62	1	0	0	0	2
2010-11	Fargo Force	USHL	57	4	9	13	48	5	0	0	0	0

• Signed Letter of Intent to attend **University of Nebraska-Omaha** (WCHA).

LAPOINT, Derrick (luh-POYNT, DAIR-ihk) **FLA**

Defense. Shoots left. 6'3", 175 lbs. Born, Eau Claire, MA, May 13, 1988.
(Florida's 4th choice, 116th overall, in 2006 Entry Draft).

			Regular Season					Playoffs				
Season	Club	League	GP	G	A	Pts	PIM	GP	G	A	Pts	PIM
2004-05	Eau Claire North	High-WI	23	9	28	37	14	....	....	....	....	....
2005-06	Eau Claire North	High-WI	23	6	26	32	34	....	....	....	....	....
2006-07	Green Bay	USHL	59	13	36	49	48	4	0	2	2	2
2007-08	North Dakota	WCHA	31	2	5	7	34	....	....	....	....	....
2008-09	North Dakota	WCHA	32	1	4	5	12	....	....	....	....	....
2009-10	North Dakota	WCHA	43	2	20	22	16	....	....	....	....	....
2010-11	North Dakota	WCHA	43	2	8	10	8	....	....	....	....	....

USHL All-Rookie Team (2007) • USHL First All-Star Team (2007)

LARKIN, Thomas (LAHR-kihn, TAW-muhs) **CBJ**

Defense. Shoots right. 6'5", 223 lbs. Born, London, England, December 31, 1990.
(Columbus' 4th choice, 137th overall, in 2009 Entry Draft).

			Regular Season					Playoffs				
Season	Club	League	GP	G	A	Pts	PIM	GP	G	A	Pts	PIM
2006-07	Exeter	High-NH	28	1	7	8	5	....	....	....	....	....
2007-08	Exeter	High-NH	29	6	15	21	18	....	....	....	....	....
2008-09	Exeter	High-NH	35	14	38	52	30	....	....	....	....	....
	Bos. Little Bruins	Minor-MA	18	1	1	2	10	....	....	....	....	....
2009-10	Colgate	ECAC	33	3	16	19	32	....	....	....	....	....
2010-11	Colgate	ECAC	41	5	6	11	41	....	....	....	....	....

LARRAZA, Zac (Luh-RAZ-uh, ZAK) **PHX**

Left wing. Shoots left. 6'2", 194 lbs. Born, Scottsdale, AZ, February 25, 1993.
(Phoenix's 8th choice, 196th overall, in 2011 Entry Draft).

			Regular Season					Playoffs				
Season	Club	League	GP	G	A	Pts	PIM	GP	G	A	Pts	PIM
2008-09	P.F. Changs	T1EHL	26	11	8	19	8	....	....	....	....	....
2009-10	USNTDP	USHL	30	6	5	11	26	....	....	....	....	....
	USNTDP	U-17	20	2	4	6	32	....	....	....	....	....
	USNTDP	U-18	1	0	1	1	0	....	....	....	....	....
2010-11	USNTDP	USHL	24	6	3	9	16	....	....	....	....	....
	USNTDP	U-18	33	3	6	9	10	....	....	....	....	....

• Signed Letter of Intent to attend **University of Denver** (WCHA).

LARSON, Nicholas (LAHR-suhn, NIHK-oh-las) **CGY**

Left wing. Shoots left. 6'1", 175 lbs. Born, St.Paul, MN, November 14, 1989.
(Calgary's 4th choice, 108th overall, in 2008 Entry Draft).

			Regular Season					Playoffs				
Season	Club	League	GP	G	A	Pts	PIM	GP	G	A	Pts	PIM
2006-07	Saint Thomas	High-MN	25	20	30	50	....	....	....	....	....	....
	Team Southeast	UMWEHL	11	5	6	11	....	....	....	....	....	....
2007-08	Waterloo	USHL	57	19	19	38	66	9	3	2	5	31
2008-09	Waterloo	USHL	51	19	17	36	144	3	0	0	0	4
2009-10	U. of Notre Dame	CCHA	35	6	5	11	47	....	....	....	....	....
2010-11	U. of Notre Dame	CCHA	43	10	9	19	42	....	....	....	....	....

LARSON, Nick (LAR-suhn, NIHK) **WSH**

Center. Shoots right. 6'1", 186 lbs. Born, Stillwater, MN, January 16, 1989.
(Washington's 9th choice, 185th overall, in 2007 Entry Draft).

			Regular Season					Playoffs				
Season	Club	League	GP	G	A	Pts	PIM	GP	G	A	Pts	PIM
2004-05	Hill-Murray	High-MN	26	9	15	24	6	....	....	....	....	....
2005-06	Hill-Murray	High-MN	....	41	38	79	....	....	....	....	....	....
2006-07	Hill-Murray	High-MN	29	31	30	61	16	....	....	....	....	....
	Omaha Lancers	USHL	10	3	2	5	6	....	....	....	....	....
2007-08			DID NOT PLAY – INJURED									
2008-09	U. of Minnesota	WCHA	13	1	1	2	2	....	....	....	....	....
2009-10	U. of Minnesota	WCHA	33	4	4	8	10	....	....	....	....	....
2010-11	U. of Minnesota	WCHA	30	5	6	11	8	....	....	....	....	....

• Missed 2007-08 and start of 2008-09 due to back injury.

LARSSON, Adam (LARH-suhn, A-duhm) **N.J.**

Defense. Shoots right. 6'3", 210 lbs. Born, Skelleftea, Sweden, November 12, 1992.
(New Jersey's 1st choice, 4th overall, in 2011 Entry Draft).

			Regular Season					Playoffs				
Season	Club	League	GP	G	A	Pts	PIM	GP	G	A	Pts	PIM
2007-08	Skelleftea U18	Swe-U18	24	5	15	20	30	....	....	....	....	....
	Skelleftea Jr.	Swe-Jr.	3	0	5	5	6	....	....	....	....	....
2008-09	Skelleftea AIK U18	Swe-U18	7	3	8	11	6	8	0	6	6	6
	Skelleftea AIK Jr.	Swe-Jr.	26	2	7	9	28	5	0	4	4	2
	Skelleftea AIK	Sweden	1	0	0	0	0	....	....	....	....	....
2009-10	Skelleftea AIK Jr.	Swe-Jr.	1	1	0	1	2	....	....	....	....	....
	Skelleftea AIK	Sweden	49	4	13	17	18	11	0	1	1	31
2010-11	Skelleftea AIK	Sweden	37	1	8	9	41	17	0	4	4	12

LARSSON, Johan (LAHR-suhn, YOH-han) **MIN**

Left wing. Shoots left. 5'10", 200 lbs. Born, Lau, Sweden, July 25, 1992.
(Minnesota's 3rd choice, 56th overall, in 2010 Entry Draft).

			Regular Season					Playoffs				
Season	Club	League	GP	G	A	Pts	PIM	GP	G	A	Pts	PIM
2005-06	Sudrets HC Hemse	Sweden-4	2	0	2	2	2	....	....	....	....	....
2006-07	Sudrets HC Hemse	Sweden-4	29	13	7	20	40	....	....	....	....	....
2007-08	Sudrets HC Hemse	Sweden-4	25	11	11	22	71	....	....	....	....	....
2008-09	Brynas U18	Swe-U18	11	6	4	10	76	3	0	3	3	2
	Brynas IF Gavle Jr.	Swe-Jr.	33	4	5	9	55	5	0	0	0	2
2009-10	Brynas U18	Swe-U18	4	1	1	2	2	4	4	4	8	6
	Brynas IF Gavle Jr.	Swe-Jr.	40	15	19	34	80	5	1	1	2	2
2010-11	Brynas IF Gavle	Sweden	43	4	4	8	18	5	0	2	2	4
	Brynas IF Gavle Jr.	Swe-Jr.	10	6	9	15	8	1	0	0	0	0

LASHOFF, Brian (LASH-awf, BRIGH-uhn) **DET**

Defense. Shoots left. 6'3", 208 lbs. Born, Albany, NY, July 16, 1990.

			Regular Season					Playoffs				
Season	Club	League	GP	G	A	Pts	PIM	GP	G	A	Pts	PIM
2006-07	Barrie Colts	OHL	47	2	10	12	20	5	0	1	1	2
2007-08	Barrie Colts	OHL	50	5	15	20	44	8	0	1	1	4
2008-09	Barrie Colts	OHL	25	1	12	13	19	....	....	....	....	....
	Kingston	OHL	35	6	13	19	32	....	....	....	....	....
	Grand Rapids	AHL	6	1	4	5	0	8	1	4	5	2
2009-10	Kingston	OHL	58	6	21	27	71	7	0	0	0	12
	Grand Rapids	AHL	6	0	2	2	2	....	....	....	....	....
2010-11	Grand Rapids	AHL	37	0	3	3	25	....	....	....	....	....
	Toledo Walleye	ECHL	3	0	1	1	0	....	....	....	....	....

Signed as a free agent by **Detroit**, October 1, 2008.

LATTA, Michael (LA-tuh, MIGH-kuhl) **NSH**

Center. Shoots right. 6', 209 lbs. Born, Kitchener, Ont., May 25, 1991.
(Nashville's 5th choice, 72nd overall, in 2009 Entry Draft).

			Regular Season					Playoffs				
Season	Club	League	GP	G	A	Pts	PIM	GP	G	A	Pts	PIM
2006-07	Waterloo Wolves	Minor-ON	73	52	66	118	213	....	....	....	....	....
2007-08	Ottawa 67's	OHL	50	14	14	28	78	4	0	1	1	2
2008-09	Ottawa 67's	OHL	23	8	13	21	32	....	....	....	....	....
	Guelph Storm	OHL	42	14	22	36	60	4	0	2	2	12
2009-10	Guelph Storm	OHL	58	33	40	73	157	5	2	7	9	14
	Milwaukee	AHL	....	....	....	....	....	1	0	0	0	0
2010-11	Guelph Storm	OHL	68	34	55	89	158	6	5	5	10	11
	Milwaukee	AHL	4	0	1	1	2	7	0	0	0	12

LAURIDSEN, Oliver (LAWR-ihd-suhn, AW-lih-vuhr) **PHI**

Defense. Shoots left. 6'6", 220 lbs. Born, Gentofte, Denmark, March 24, 1989.
(Philadelphia's 6th choice, 196th overall, in 2009 Entry Draft).

			Regular Season					Playoffs				
Season	Club	League	GP	G	A	Pts	PIM	GP	G	A	Pts	PIM
2004-05	IC Gentofte Jr.	Den-Jr.	24	4	12	16	22	....	....	....	....	....
	IC Gentofte	Den-2	8	0	1	1	0	....	....	....	....	....
2005-06	Rogle Jr.	Swe-Jr.	28	1	1	2	32	....	....	....	....	....
2006-07	Linkopings HC Jr.	Swe-Jr.	34	0	2	2	95	5	0	0	0	8
2007-08	Linkopings HC U18	Swe-U18	2	1	3	4	0	....	....	....	....	....
	Tranas AIF	Sweden-3	1	0	0	0	0	....	....	....	....	....
	Linkopings HC Jr.	Swe-Jr.	35	5	6	11	159	1	0	1	1	0
2008-09	St. Cloud State	WCHA	28	0	1	1	38	....	....	....	....	....
2009-10	St. Cloud State	WCHA	43	6	6	12	54	....	....	....	....	....
2010-11	St. Cloud State	WCHA	37	1	8	9	51	....	....	....	....	....
	Adirondack	AHL	2	0	0	0	30	....	....	....	....	....

LAVIN, Joe (LA-vihn, JOH) CHI

Defense. Shoots left. 6'1", 199 lbs. Born, Worcester, MA, July 17, 1989.
(Chicago's 6th choice, 126th overall, in 2007 Entry Draft).

			Regular Season					Playoffs				
Season	Club	League	GP	G	A	Pts	PIM	GP	G	A	Pts	PIM
2004-05	Boston Jr. Bruins	EmJHL	64	11	44	55	....	....	....	....	....	....
2005-06	USNTDP	U-17	19	2	1	3	30	....	....	....	....	....
	USNTDP	NAHL	37	8	10	18	16	12	3	2	5	4
2006-07	USNTDP	U-18	23	1	0	1	18	....	....	....	....	....
	USNTDP	NAHL	18	1	8	9	22	6	0	2	2	4
2007-08	Providence College	H-East	36	0	8	8	26	....	....	....	....	....
2008-09	Providence College	H-East	12	0	1	1	10	....	....	....	....	....
	Omaha Lancers	USHL	33	7	15	22	28	3	0	4	4	8
2009-10	Omaha Lancers	USHL	24	5	12	17	16	....	....	....	....	....
2010-11	U. of Notre Dame	CCHA	44	6	11	17	22	....	....	....	....	....
	Rockford IceHogs	AHL	2	0	1	1	4	....	....	....	....	....

LAWSON, Kyle (LAW-suhn, KIGHL) CAR

Defense. Shoots right. 5'11", 205 lbs. Born, Southfield, MI, January 11, 1987.
(Carolina's 9th choice, 198th overall, in 2005 Entry Draft).

			Regular Season					Playoffs				
Season	Club	League	GP	G	A	Pts	PIM	GP	G	A	Pts	PIM
2003-04	Det. Honeybaked	MWEHL	61	17	41	58	68	....	....	....	....	....
	Texarkana Bandits	NAHL	....	....	....	....	....	3	0	1	1	0
2004-05	USNTDP	U-18	23	2	12	14	6	....	....	....	....	....
	USNTDP	NAHL	8	1	3	4	0	....	....	....	....	....
2005-06	Tri-City Storm	USHL	49	9	13	22	40	1	0	0	0	0
2006-07	U. of Notre Dame	CCHA	38	4	15	19	14	....	....	....	....	....
2007-08	U. of Notre Dame	CCHA	45	5	21	26	36	....	....	....	....	....
2008-09	U. of Notre Dame	CCHA	40	4	19	23	44	....	....	....	....	....
2009-10	U. of Notre Dame	CCHA	38	4	18	22	44	....	....	....	....	....
	Albany River Rats	AHL	10	0	1	1	0	....	....	....	....	....
2010-11	Charlotte	AHL	18	0	0	0	4	....	....	....	....	....
	Florida Everblades	ECHL	51	0	12	12	54	4	0	0	0	2

CCHA All-Rookie Team (2007) • NCAA Championship All-Tournament Team (2008) • CCHA Second All-Star Team (2009)

LEACH, Joey (LEECH, JOH-ee) CGY

Defense. Shoots left. 6'4", 194 lbs. Born, Wadena, Sask., January 29, 1992.
(Calgary's 2nd choice, 73rd overall, in 2010 Entry Draft).

			Regular Season					Playoffs				
Season	Club	League	GP	G	A	Pts	PIM	GP	G	A	Pts	PIM
2007-08	Tisdale Trojans	SMHL	42	1	13	14	30	9	1	1	2	2
	Tisdale Trojans	Exhib.	3	1	2	3	0	....	....	....	....	....
2008-09	Tisdale Trojans	SMHL	42	3	26	29	99	6	1	0	1	8
	Kootenay Ice	WHL	12	1	0	1	4	3	0	0	0	0
2009-10	Kootenay Ice	WHL	70	3	23	26	77	6	1	0	1	16
2010-11	Kootenay Ice	WHL	56	5	25	30	78	19	0	6	6	14

LEBLANC, Louis (luh-BLAWNK, LOU-ee) MTL

Center. Shoots right. 6', 180 lbs. Born, Pointe-Claire, Que., January 26, 1991.
(Montreal's 1st choice, 18th overall, in 2009 Entry Draft).

			Regular Season					Playoffs				
Season	Club	League	GP	G	A	Pts	PIM	GP	G	A	Pts	PIM
2006-07	Lac St-Louis Lions	QAAA	40	31	18	49	72	22	14	7	21	10
2007-08	Lac St-Louis Lions	QAAA	43	54	37	91	152	14	8	14	22	76
2008-09	Omaha Lancers	USHL	60	28	31	59	78	3	2	1	3	2
2009-10	Harvard Crimson	ECAC	31	11	12	23	50	....	....	....	....	....
2010-11	Montreal	QMJHL	51	26	32	58	100	10	6	3	9	16

USHL All-Rookie Team (2009) • USHL Rookie of the Year (2009) • ECAC All-Rookie Team (2010)

LEBLANC, Peter (luh-BLAHNK, PEE-tuhr) CHI

Center. Shoots left. 5'10", 175 lbs. Born, Hamilton, Ont., February 3, 1988.
(Chicago's 9th choice, 186th overall, in 2006 Entry Draft).

			Regular Season					Playoffs				
Season	Club	League	GP	G	A	Pts	PIM	GP	G	A	Pts	PIM
2004-05	Hamilton	OPJHL	49	14	22	36	....	....	....	....	....	....
2005-06	Hamilton	OPJHL	21	10	12	22	25	14	8	8	16	8
2006-07	New Hampshire	H-East	39	1	4	5	4	....	....	....	....	....
2007-08	New Hampshire	H-East	37	5	10	15	37	....	....	....	....	....
2008-09	New Hampshire	H-East	38	14	16	30	8	....	....	....	....	....
2009-10	New Hampshire	H-East	39	14	21	35	24	....	....	....	....	....
2010-11	Rockford IceHogs	AHL	57	12	18	30	12	....	....	....	....	....
	Toledo Walleye	ECHL	22	8	14	22	6	....	....	....	....	....

OPJHL Rookie of the Year (2005)

• Missed majority of 2005-06 due to mononucleosis. Signed as a free agent by **Rockford** (AHL), July 29, 2010.

LEE, Anders (LEE, AN-duhrz) NYI

Center. Shoots left. 6'2", 216 lbs. Born, St.Paul, MN, July 3, 1990.
(NY Islanders' 7th choice, 152nd overall, in 2009 Entry Draft).

			Regular Season					Playoffs				
Season	Club	League	GP	G	A	Pts	PIM	GP	G	A	Pts	PIM
2006-07	Saint Thomas	High-MN	31	24	17	41	....	....	....	....	....	....
2007-08	Edina Hornets	High-MN	31	32	22	54	....	....	....	....	....	....
2008-09	Edina Hornets	High-MN	31	25	59	84	30	....	....	....	....	....
	Team Southwest	UMHSEL	18	12	17	29	....	....	....	....	....	....
2009-10	Green Bay	USHL	59	35	31	66	54	12	*10	*12	*22	13
2010-11	U. of Notre Dame	CCHA	44	24	20	44	16	....	....	....	....	....

USHL All-Rookie Team (2010) • USHL First All-Star Team (2010) • USHL Rookie of the Year (2010)

LEE, Chris (LEE, KRIHS)

Defense. Shoots left. 6', 185 lbs. Born, MacTier, Ont., October 3, 1980.

			Regular Season					Playoffs				
Season	Club	League	GP	G	A	Pts	PIM	GP	G	A	Pts	PIM
2004-05	Florida Everblades	ECHL	68	5	22	27	16	15	2	9	11	6
2005-06	Florida Everblades	ECHL	52	10	27	37	56	8	2	1	3	4
2006-07	Albany River Rats	AHL	3	0	1	1	4	....	....	....	....	....
	Bridgeport	AHL	1	0	0	0	0	....	....	....	....	....
	Omaha	AHL	32	4	13	17	16	6	3	0	3	6
	Florida Everblades	ECHL	37	6	19	25	22	9	3	1	4	0
2007-08	Iowa Stars	AHL	68	7	21	28	42	....	....	....	....	....
2008-09	Bridgeport	AHL	66	6	24	30	36	5	0	3	3	2
2009-10	Wilkes-Barre	AHL	79	9	30	39	30	4	0	1	1	0
2010-11	Kolner Haie	Germany	43	6	15	21	34	5	2	1	3	16

Signed as a free agent by **NY Islanders**, July 3, 2008. Signed as a free agent by **Pittsburgh**, July 5, 2009. Signed as a free agent by **Koln** (Germany), August 3, 2010.

LEE, John (LEE, JAWN) FLA

Defense. Shoots right. 6'2", 173 lbs. Born, Fargo, ND, January 16, 1989.
(Florida's 5th choice, 131st overall, in 2007 Entry Draft).

			Regular Season					Playoffs				
Season	Club	League	GP	G	A	Pts	PIM	GP	G	A	Pts	PIM
2004-05	Moorhead Spuds	High-MN	3	0	1	1	0	....	....	....	....	....
2005-06	Moorhead Spuds	High-MN	26	6	21	27	50	....	....	....	....	....
2006-07	Moorhead Spuds	High-MN	26	6	33	39	62	....	....	....	....	....
	Waterloo	USHL	27	2	7	9	56	9	0	3	3	4
2007-08	Waterloo	USHL	59	1	11	12	106	11	0	4	4	24
2008-09	U. of Denver	WCHA	39	0	5	5	38	....	....	....	....	....
2009-10	U. of Denver	WCHA	41	2	10	12	55	....	....	....	....	....
2010-11	U. of Denver	WCHA	39	3	9	12	32	....	....	....	....	....

LEFEBVRE, Philippe (luh-FAYV, fihl-EEP) MTL

Left wing. Shoots left. 5'11", 175 lbs. Born, Trois-Rivieres, Que., February 28, 1991.

			Regular Season					Playoffs				
Season	Club	League	GP	G	A	Pts	PIM	GP	G	A	Pts	PIM
2006-07	Trois-Rivieres	QAAA	43	25	23	48	56	8	3	6	9	6
2007-08	Drummondville	QMJHL	62	10	15	25	16	....	....	....	....	....
2008-09	Drummondville	QMJHL	68	21	27	48	38	19	3	5	8	2
2009-10	Drummondville	QMJHL	66	26	29	55	38	14	2	4	6	9
2010-11	Montreal	QMJHL	60	19	27	46	38	10	3	5	8	0

Signed as a free agent by **Montreal**, September 15, 2009.

LEGAULT, Maxime (luh-GOH, max-EEM)

Right wing. Shoots right. 6'2", 195 lbs. Born, Ste. Agathe, Que., March 28, 1989.
(Buffalo's 6th choice, 194th overall, in 2009 Entry Draft).

			Regular Season					Playoffs				
Season	Club	League	GP	G	A	Pts	PIM	GP	G	A	Pts	PIM
2005-06	Laval-Laurentides	QAAA	36	13	15	28	138	4	2	1	3	21
2006-07	Shawinigan	QMJHL	55	7	12	19	98	4	0	0	0	4
2007-08	Shawinigan	QMJHL	31	6	4	10	61	....	....	....	....	....
2008-09	Shawinigan	QMJHL	63	28	16	44	66	21	10	3	13	23
2009-10	Shawinigan	QMJHL	22	10	10	20	29	....	....	....	....	....
	Cape Breton	QMJHL	21	7	12	19	25	5	1	0	1	4
	Portland Pirates	AHL	5	0	0	0	4	....	....	....	....	....
2010-11	Portland Pirates	AHL	67	12	12	24	83	9	1	1	2	8

LEGEIN, Stefan (LEE-gihn, STEH-fan) PHI

Right wing. Shoots right. 5'9", 170 lbs. Born, Oakville, Ont., November 24, 1988.
(Columbus' 2nd choice, 37th overall, in 2007 Entry Draft).

			Regular Season					Playoffs				
Season	Club	League	GP	G	A	Pts	PIM	GP	G	A	Pts	PIM
2003-04	Tor. Red Wings	GTHL	33	19	14	33	63	....	....	....	....	....
2004-05	Milton Icehawks	OPJHL	26	7	12	19	18	....	....	....	....	....
	Mississauga	OHL	49	3	5	8	37	5	0	1	1	0
2005-06	Mississauga	OHL	59	7	9	16	101	....	....	....	....	....
2006-07	Mississauga	OHL	64	43	32	75	115	5	3	2	5	0
2007-08	Niagara Ice Dogs	OHL	30	24	13	37	80	10	7	11	18	28
	Syracuse Crunch	AHL	....	....	....	....	....	2	0	0	0	0
2008-09	Syracuse Crunch	AHL	26	1	0	1	4	....	....	....	....	....
2009-10	Syracuse Crunch	AHL	6	2	1	3	0	....	....	....	....	....
	Adirondack	AHL	71	24	10	34	48	....	....	....	....	....
2010-11	Adirondack	AHL	41	5	12	17	24	....	....	....	....	....
	Greenville	ECHL	2	0	0	0	2	....	....	....	....	....

OHL Second All-Star Team (2008)

Traded to **Philadelphia** by **Columbus** for Michael Ratchuk, October 20, 2009.

LEHTERA, Jori (LEH-tuhr-a, YOHR-ee) ST.L.

Center. Shoots left. 6'2", 191 lbs. Born, Helsinki, Finland, December 23, 1987.
(St. Louis' 4th choice, 65th overall, in 2008 Entry Draft).

			Regular Season					Playoffs				
Season	Club	League	GP	G	A	Pts	PIM	GP	G	A	Pts	PIM
2003-04	Jokerit U18	Fin-U18	19	0	6	6	2	5	3	1	4	0
2004-05	Jokerit U18	Fin-U18	30	13	37	50	24	7	6	5	11	2
2005-06	Suomi U20	Finland-2	2	0	0	0	0	....	....	....	....	....
	Jokerit Helsinki Jr.	Fin-Jr.	39	14	33	47	16	4	1	4	5	0
2006-07	Suomi U20	Finland-2	10	4	7	11	10	....	....	....	....	....
	Jokerit Helsinki Jr.	Fin-Jr.	24	18	48	66	20	5	1	7	8	2
	Jokerit Helsinki	Finland	28	6	6	12	14	....	....	....	....	....
2007-08	Tappara Tampere	Finland	54	13	29	42	32	11	4	2	6	8
2008-09	Tappara Tampere	Finland	58	9	38	47	34	3	4	5	9	4
	Peoria Rivermen	AHL	7	0	1	1	2	7	1	1	2	10
2009-10	Tappara Tampere	Finland	57	19	*50	*69	58	9	1	9	10	8
2010-11	Yaroslavl	Rus-KHL	53	16	21	37	38	18	0	3	3	14

LEHTIVUORI, Joonas (leh-tee-VWOO-aw-ree, YOH-nuhs) PHI

Defense. Shoots left. 5'11", 167 lbs. Born, Tampere, Finland, July 19, 1988.
(Philadelphia's 6th choice, 101st overall, in 2006 Entry Draft).

			Regular Season					Playoffs				
Season	Club	League	GP	G	A	Pts	PIM	GP	G	A	Pts	PIM
2004-05	Ilves Tampere U18	Fin-U18	25	5	11	16	12	5	1	1	2	8
2005-06	Ilves Tampere U18	Fin-U18	2	0	1	1	0	6	1	4	5	4
	Ilves Tampere Jr.	Fin-Jr.	39	9	16	25	22	3	0	0	0	4
	Ilves Tampere	Finland	1	0	0	0	0	....	....	....	....	....
2006-07	Ilves Tampere Jr.	Fin-Jr.	15	3	8	11	51	5	0	1	1	2
	Suomi U20	Finland-2	2	0	0	0	0	....	....	....	....	....
	Ilves Tampere	Finland	40	0	0	0	18	4	0	0	0	0
2007-08	Suomi U20	Finland-2	2	0	1	1	2	....	....	....	....	....
	Ilves Tampere	Finland	48	8	13	21	10	9	1	1	2	2
2008-09	Ilves Tampere	Finland	44	4	8	12	16	3	0	0	0	0
2009-10	Adirondack	AHL	66	5	18	23	18	....	....	....	....	....
2010-11	Adirondack	AHL	32	2	7	9	24	....	....	....	....	....
	KalPa Kuopio	Finland	19	0	2	2	14	4	0	1	1	2

• Loaned to **KalPa** (Finland) by **Philadelphia** (Adirondack-AHL), January 15, 2011.

LEIVO, Josh (LEE-voh, JAWSH) TOR

Left wing. Shoots right. 6'2", 180 lbs. Born, Innisfil, Ont., May 26, 1993.
(Toronto's 3rd choice, 86th overall, in 2011 Entry Draft).

			Regular Season					Playoffs				
Season	Club	League	GP	G	A	Pts	PIM	GP	G	A	Pts	PIM
2008-09	Barrie Colts	Minor-ON	71	31	35	66	65	....	....	....	....	....
2009-10	Barrie Colts	Minor-ON	52	27	41	68	59	....	....	....	....	....
2010-11	Sudbury Wolves	OHL	64	13	17	30	37	8	6	7	13	4

LEPKOWSKI, Alex (lep-KAWZ-kee, AL-ehx) **BUF**

Defense. Shoots left. 6'4", 202 lbs. Born, Buffalo, NY, April 8, 1993.
(Buffalo's 4th choice, 137th overall, in 2011 Entry Draft).

			Regular Season					Playoffs				
Season	Club	League	GP	G	A	Pts	PIM	GP	G	A	Pts	PIM
2008-09	St. Francis	High-NY	40	6	20	26	....	....	....	....	....	....
2009-10	Saginaw Spirit	OHL	53	0	1	1	39	3	0	0	0	0
2010-11	Saginaw Spirit	OHL	24	0	3	3	33	....	....	....	....	....
	Barrie Colts	OHL	15	0	3	3	42	....	....	....	....	....

LERG, Bryan (LEHRG, BRIGH-uhn)

Center. Shoots left. 5'10", 175 lbs. Born, Livonia, MI, January 20, 1986.

			Regular Season					Playoffs				
Season	Club	League	GP	G	A	Pts	PIM	GP	G	A	Pts	PIM
2002-03	USNTDP	U-17	19	11	6	17	5	....	....	....	....	....
	USNTDP	NAHL	46	10	12	22	32	....	....	....	....	....
2003-04	USNTDP	U-18	46	22	25	47	....	....	....	....	....	....
	USNTDP	NAHL	11	5	7	12	10	....	....	....	....	....
2004-05	Michigan State	CCHA	41	10	5	15	14	....	....	....	....	....
2005-06	Michigan State	CCHA	45	15	23	38	26	....	....	....	....	....
2006-07	Michigan State	CCHA	41	23	13	36	21	....	....	....	....	....
2007-08	Michigan State	CCHA	42	20	19	39	18	....	....	....	....	....
	Springfield Falcons	AHL	4	0	2	2	2	....	....	....	....	....
2008-09	Springfield Falcons	AHL	42	9	8	17	24	....	....	....	....	....
	Stockton Thunder	ECHL	7	2	8	10	4	....	....	....	....	....
2009-10	Springfield Falcons	AHL	36	4	3	7	11	....	....	....	....	....
2010-11	Geneve	Swiss	1	0	0	0	0	....	....	....	....	....
	Wilkes-Barre	AHL	65	15	17	32	21	9	1	2	3	4

Signed as a free agent by **Edmonton**, April 2, 2008. Signed as a free agent by **Geneve** (Swiss), September 3, 2010. Signed as a free agent by **Wilkes-Barre** (AHL), December 8, 2010.

LESSIO, Lucas (LEH-see-oh, LOO-kuhs) **PHX**

Left wing. Shoots left. 6'1", 200 lbs. Born, Maple, Ont., January 23, 1993.
(Phoenix's 3rd choice, 56th overall, in 2011 Entry Draft).

			Regular Season					Playoffs				
Season	Club	League	GP	G	A	Pts	PIM	GP	G	A	Pts	PIM
2008-09	Toronto Marlboros	GTHL	72	53	60	113	126	....	....	....	....	....
2009-10	St. Michael's	ON-Jr.A	41	30	42	72	87	5	0	3	3	10
2010-11	Oshawa Generals	OHL	66	27	27	54	66	10	5	4	9	6

LEVEILLE, Daultan (leh-VAY-yay, DAWL-tuhn) **WPG**

Center. Shoots left. 6', 175 lbs. Born, St. Catharines, Ont., August 10, 1990.
(Atlanta's 2nd choice, 29th overall, in 2008 Entry Draft).

			Regular Season					Playoffs				
Season	Club	League	GP	G	A	Pts	PIM	GP	G	A	Pts	PIM
2005-06	St. Cath. Falcons	Minor-ON	46	25	31	56	32	....	....	....	....	....
2006-07	St. Catharines	ON-Jr.B	48	19	26	45	30	....	....	....	....	....
2007-08	St. Catharines	ON-Jr.B	45	29	27	56	38	16	*14	16	30	14
2008-09	Michigan State	CCHA	38	9	8	17	12	....	....	....	....	....
2009-10	Michigan State	CCHA	38	6	19	25	16	....	....	....	....	....
2010-11	Michigan State	CCHA	34	8	10	18	18	....	....	....	....	....

LEVI, Austin (LEH-vee, AW-stuhn) **CAR**

Defense. Shoots left. 6'3", 192 lbs. Born, Columbus, OH, February 16, 1992.
(Carolina's 5th choice, 85th overall, in 2010 Entry Draft).

			Regular Season					Playoffs				
Season	Club	League	GP	G	A	Pts	PIM	GP	G	A	Pts	PIM
2007-08	Det. Compuware	MWEHL	22	0	5	5	33	....	....	....	....	....
2008-09	Plymouth Whalers	OHL	12	0	2	2	4	5	0	0	0	5
2009-10	Plymouth Whalers	OHL	68	3	9	12	116	9	0	0	0	8
2010-11	Plymouth Whalers	OHL	66	6	19	25	87	11	1	4	5	8

LIND, Kevin (LIHND, KEH-vihn) **ANA**

Defense. Shoots left. 6'3", 218 lbs. Born, Homer Glen, IL, March 31, 1992.
(Anaheim's 7th choice, 177th overall, in 2010 Entry Draft).

			Regular Season					Playoffs				
Season	Club	League	GP	G	A	Pts	PIM	GP	G	A	Pts	PIM
2008-09	Chicago Mission	T1EHL	25	3	0	3	16	....	....	....	....	....
	Chicago Steel	USHL	50	2	3	5	45	....	....	....	....	....
2009-10	Chicago Steel	USHL	55	6	10	16	76	....	....	....	....	....
2010-11	U. of Notre Dame	CCHA	32	1	10	11	24	....	....	....	....	....

LINDBERG, Oscar (LIHND-buhrg, AWS-kuhr) **NYR**

Center. Shoots left. 6', 187 lbs. Born, Skelleftea, Sweden, October 29, 1991.
(Phoenix's 4th choice, 57th overall, in 2010 Entry Draft).

			Regular Season					Playoffs				
Season	Club	League	GP	G	A	Pts	PIM	GP	G	A	Pts	PIM
2007-08	Skelleftea U18	Swe-U18	31	19	29	48	36	....	....	....	....	....
	Skelleftea Jr.	Swe-Jr.	1	0	0	0	2	2	0	1	1	0
2008-09	Skelleftea AIK U18	Swe-U18	6	8	10	18	14	7	4	5	9	8
	Skelleftea AIK Jr.	Swe-Jr.	38	14	19	33	54	5	0	1	1	4
2009-10	Skelleftea AIK Jr.	Swe-Jr.	30	14	23	37	44	1	1	1	2	12
	Skelleftea AIK	Sweden	36	1	1	2	35	10	2	0	2	2
2010-11	Skelleftea AIK Jr.	Swe-Jr.	9	8	4	12	8	....	....	....	....	....
	Skelleftea AIK	Sweden	41	5	9	14	31	18	3	4	7	4

Traded to **NY Rangers** by **Phoenix** for Ethan Werek, May 8, 2011.

LINDSTROM, Mattias (LIHND-struhm, ma-TEE-uhs) **CAR**

Left wing. Shoots left. 6'4", 205 lbs. Born, Lulea, Sweden, March 21, 1991.
(Carolina's 3rd choice, 88th overall, in 2009 Entry Draft).

			Regular Season					Playoffs				
Season	Club	League	GP	G	A	Pts	PIM	GP	G	A	Pts	PIM
2007-08	Skelleftea U18	Swe-U18	3	1	0	1	0	....	....	....	....	....
	Skelleftea Jr.	Swe-Jr.	21	5	1	6	40	....	....	....	....	....
2008-09	Skelleftea AIK U18	Swe-U18	2	0	0	0	6	5	0	1	1	10
	Skelleftea AIK Jr.	Swe-Jr.	31	8	5	13	46	5	2	0	2	0
	Skelleftea AIK	Sweden	7	1	0	1	0	7	1	0	1	0
2009-10	Skelleftea AIK Jr.	Swe-Jr.	1	0	0	0	0	....	....	....	....	....
2010-11	Skelleftea AIK Jr.	Swe-Jr.	28	3	8	11	38	5	0	2	2	4
	Bodens HF	Sweden-3	2	0	0	0	2	....	....	....	....	....
	Skelleftea AIK	Sweden	11	0	0	0	8	9	0	0	0	0

• Missed majority of 2009-10 due to knee injury.

LITVINENKO, Alexei (liht-vihn-EHN-koh, al-EHX-ay) **PHX**

Defense. Shoots left. 6'4", 220 lbs. Born, Ust-Kamenogorsk, USSR, March 7, 1980.
(Phoenix's 9th choice, 262nd overall, in 1999 Entry Draft).

			Regular Season					Playoffs				
Season	Club	League	GP	G	A	Pts	PIM	GP	G	A	Pts	PIM
1997-98	Ust-Kam'gorsk 2	Russia-3	12	0	0	0	8	....	....	....	....	....
	Ust-Kamenogorsk	Russia-2	2	0	0	0	0	....	....	....	....	....
1998-99	Ust-Kam'gorsk 2	Russia-4	31	3	4	7	52	....	....	....	....	....
	Ust-Kam'gorsk 2	Russia-4	16	0	4	4	14	....	....	....	....	....
99-2000	Dynamo Moscow	Russia	7	0	0	0	4	....	....	....	....	....
2000-01	Dynamo Moscow	Russia	6	0	0	0	0	....	....	....	....	....
	Yekaterinburg	Russia	26	0	0	0	42	....	....	....	....	....
2001-02	Magnitogorsk	Russia	20	0	3	3	29	9	1	1	2	20
2002-03	Magnitogorsk	Russia	21	0	2	2	28	....	....	....	....	....
2003-04	Magnitogorsk	Russia	7	0	0	0	8	....	....	....	....	....
	Magnitogorsk 2	Russia-3	6	3	5	8	31	....	....	....	....	....
2004-05	Magnitogorsk 2	Russia-3	15	2	7	9	24	....	....	....	....	....
	Magnitogorsk	Russia	3	0	0	0	2	....	....	....	....	....
	St. Petersburg 2	Russia-3	2	1	1	2	4	....	....	....	....	....
	SKA St. Petersburg	Russia	24	0	0	0	34	....	....	....	....	....
2005-06	Spartak Moscow	Russia	50	4	4	8	54	3	1	0	1	0
	Spartak Moscow 2	Russia-3	1	0	0	0	0	....	....	....	....	....
2006-07	Magnitogorsk	Russia	18	2	3	5	28	....	....	....	....	....
2007-08	Magnitogorsk 2	Russia-3	18	7	6	13	24	....	....	....	....	....
	Spartak Moscow	Russia	9	0	0	0	18	....	....	....	....	....
2008-09	Vityaz Chekhov	Rus-KHL	30	0	3	3	88	....	....	....	....	....
2009-10	Vityaz Chekhov	Rus-KHL	51	6	4	10	181	....	....	....	....	....
2010-11	Barys Astana	Rus-KHL	9	0	1	1	24	....	....	....	....	....
	Barys Astana 2	Kazakhstan	2	0	1	1	0	1	0	0	0	4

LIVINGSTON, James (LIH-vihng-stuhn, JAYMZ) **S.J.**

Right wing. Shoots right. 6'1", 210 lbs. Born, Halifax, N.S., March 8, 1990.
(St. Louis' 5th choice, 70th overall, in 2008 Entry Draft).

			Regular Season					Playoffs				
Season	Club	League	GP	G	A	Pts	PIM	GP	G	A	Pts	PIM
2005-06	York Simcoe	Minor-ON	51	25	32	57	....	....	....	....	....	....
2006-07	Sault Ste. Marie	OHL	60	2	5	7	95	13	1	0	1	15
2007-08	Sault Ste. Marie	OHL	68	21	23	44	135	14	2	3	5	14
2008-09	Sault Ste. Marie	OHL	66	20	17	37	98	....	....	....	....	....
2009-10	Sault Ste. Marie	OHL	36	14	12	26	47	....	....	....	....	....
	Plymouth Whalers	OHL	24	3	6	9	57	9	1	1	2	6
2010-11	Plymouth Whalers	OHL	62	22	27	49	52	11	4	1	5	8

Signed as a free agent by **San Jose**, March 11, 2011.

LONG, Colin (LAWNG, KAW-lihn) **PHX**

Center. Shoots right. 5'11", 187 lbs. Born, Santa Ana, CA, June 19, 1989.
(Phoenix's 6th choice, 99th overall, in 2008 Entry Draft).

			Regular Season					Playoffs				
Season	Club	League	GP	G	A	Pts	PIM	GP	G	A	Pts	PIM
2005-06	Kelowna Rockets	WHL	20	1	3	4	6	3	0	0	0	0
2006-07	Kelowna Rockets	WHL	69	11	17	28	38	....	....	....	....	....
2007-08	Kelowna Rockets	WHL	72	31	69	100	41	7	2	10	12	6
2008-09	Kelowna Rockets	WHL	68	33	58	91	28	22	4	12	16	16
2009-10	San Antonio	AHL	29	2	2	4	10	....	....	....	....	....
2010-11	San Antonio	AHL	5	0	0	0	0	....	....	....	....	....
	Las Vegas	ECHL	50	16	21	37	12	5	0	2	2	4

WHL West First All-Star Team (2008) • WHL West Second All-Star Team (2009)
• Missed majority of 2009-10 due to various injuries.

LOPRIENO, Joe (loh-PRE-eh-noh, JOH)

Defense. Shoots right. 6'3", 225 lbs. Born, Bloomingdale, IL, October 8, 1986.

			Regular Season					Playoffs				
Season	Club	League	GP	G	A	Pts	PIM	GP	G	A	Pts	PIM
2004-05	Chicago Steel	USHL	50	0	3	3	78	1	0	0	0	6
2005-06	Chicago Steel	USHL	45	3	10	13	73	....	....	....	....	....
2006-07	Merrimack College	H-East	32	1	3	4	66	....	....	....	....	....
2007-08	Merrimack College	H-East	34	2	3	5	74	....	....	....	....	....
2008-09	Merrimack College	H-East	22	2	2	4	50	....	....	....	....	....
2009-10	Worcester Sharks	AHL	46	0	4	4	52	....	....	....	....	....
2010-11	Worcester Sharks	AHL	52	3	1	4	61	....	....	....	....	....

Signed as a free agent by **San Jose**, March 30, 2009.

LORENZ, Sean (lohr-EHNZ, SHAWN) **MIN**

Defense. Shoots right. 6'1", 191 lbs. Born, Littleton, CO, March 10, 1990.
(Minnesota's 3rd choice, 115th overall, in 2008 Entry Draft).

			Regular Season					Playoffs				
Season	Club	League	GP	G	A	Pts	PIM	GP	G	A	Pts	PIM
2006-07	USNTDP	U-17	6	6	9	15	28	....	....	....	....	....
	USNTDP	NAHL	45	1	7	8	26	6	0	0	0	2
2007-08	USNTDP	U-18	50	0	8	8	28	....	....	....	....	....
	USNTDP	NAHL	14	2	1	3	4	....	....	....	....	....
2008-09	U. of Notre Dame	CCHA	40	0	3	3	18	....	....	....	....	....
2009-10	U. of Notre Dame	CCHA	34	2	1	3	14	....	....	....	....	....
2010-11	U. of Notre Dame	CCHA	44	4	11	15	36	....	....	....	....	....

LoVECCHIO, Jeff (LOH-veh-kee-oh, JEHF)

Left wing. Shoots left. 6'2", 195 lbs. Born, Arlington Heights, IL, August 26, 1985.

			Regular Season					Playoffs				
Season	Club	League	GP	G	A	Pts	PIM	GP	G	A	Pts	PIM
2003-04	River City Lancers	USHL	58	16	13	29	29	3	0	1	1	2
2004-05	Omaha Lancers	USHL	57	17	27	44	82	5	1	0	1	0
2005-06	Western Mich.	CCHA	40	7	11	18	46	....	....	....	....	....
2006-07	Western Mich.	CCHA	37	19	15	34	24	....	....	....	....	....
2007-08	Western Mich.	CCHA	36	9	12	21	28	....	....	....	....	....
	Providence Bruins	AHL	14	3	2	5	6	6	0	1	1	2
2008-09			DID NOT PLAY – INJURED									
2009-10	Providence Bruins	AHL	65	15	9	24	32	....	....	....	....	....
2010-11	Providence Bruins	AHL	22	0	3	3	9	....	....	....	....	....
	Rochester	AHL	51	8	8	16	25	....	....	....	....	....

Signed as a free agent by **Boston**, March 18, 2008. • Missed 2008-09 due to concussion. Traded to **Florida** by **Boston** with Jordan Knackstedt for Sean Zimmerman and future considerations, December 9, 2010.

LOWE, Keegan (LOH, KEE-guhn) **CAR**

Defense. Shoots left. 6'2", 189 lbs. Born, Greenwich, CT, March 29, 1993.
(Carolina's 3rd choice, 73rd overall, in 2011 Entry Draft).

			Regular Season					Playoffs				
Season	Club	League	GP	G	A	Pts	PIM	GP	G	A	Pts	PIM
2008-09	Shattuck U-16	High-MN	55	7	26	33	77	....	....	....	....	....
2009-10	Edmonton	WHL	69	2	12	14	60	....	....	....	....	....
2010-11	Edmonton	WHL	71	2	22	24	123	4	1	0	1	4

LOWRY, Adam (LOW-ree, A-duhm) **WPG**

Left wing. Shoots left. 6'4", 187 lbs. Born, Calgary, Alta., March 29, 1993.
(Winnipeg's 2nd choice, 67th overall, in 2011 Entry Draft).

			Regular Season					Playoffs				
Season	Club	League	GP	G	A	Pts	PIM	GP	G	A	Pts	PIM
2007-08	Calgary Bisons	AMBHL	33	27	21	48	56	12	4	6	10	10
	Cgy. Blackhawks	Minor-AB	1	0	1	1	0	....	....	....	....	....
2008-09	Calgary Rangers	Minor-AB	29	29	25	54	51	....	....	....	....	....
2009-10	Swift Current	WHL	61	15	19	34	57	3	0	1	1	6
2010-11	Swift Current	WHL	66	18	27	45	84	....	....	....	....	....

LOWRY, Joel (LOW-ree, JOHL) **L.A.**

Left wing. Shoots left. 6'1", 180 lbs. Born, St.Louis, MO, November 15, 1991.
(Los Angeles' 5th choice, 140th overall, in 2011 Entry Draft).

			Regular Season					Playoffs				
Season	Club	League	GP	G	A	Pts	PIM	GP	G	A	Pts	PIM
2008-09	Calgary Buffaloes	AMHL	32	14	16	30	32	15	5	6	11	20
	Okotoks Oilers	AJHL	3	0	0	0	0	....	....	....	....	....
2009-10	Victoria Grizzlies	BCHL	57	15	29	44	55	6	1	4	5	2
2010-11	Victoria Grizzlies	BCHL	42	24	43	67	35	12	5	12	17	6

• Signed Letter of Intent to attend **Cornell University** (ECAC) in fall of 2011.

LUCIA, Mario (LOO-chee-a, MAR-ee-oh) **MIN**

Left wing. Shoots left. 6'2", 187 lbs. Born, Fairbanks, AK, August 25, 1993.
(Minnesota's 3rd choice, 60th overall, in 2011 Entry Draft).

			Regular Season					Playoffs				
Season	Club	League	GP	G	A	Pts	PIM	GP	G	A	Pts	PIM
2009-10	Wayzata	High-MN	25	15	25	40	6	2	0	2	2	0
2010-11	Team Northwest	UMHSEL	10	6	6	12	4	1	0	0	0	0
	Wayzata	High-MN	24	25	22	47	14	3	5	2	7	2
	USNTDP	USHL	6	3	0	3	0	....	....	....	....	....
	USNTDP	U-18	9	1	1	2	0	....	....	....	....	....

LUCIA, Tony (loo-CHEE-ah, TOH-nee) **S.J.**

Left wing. Shoots left. 6', 190 lbs. Born, Wayzata, MN, August 23, 1987.
(San Jose's 8th choice, 193rd overall, in 2005 Entry Draft).

			Regular Season					Playoffs				
Season	Club	League	GP	G	A	Pts	PIM	GP	G	A	Pts	PIM
2003-04	Wayzata	High-MN	31	13	22	35	....	....	....	....	....	....
2004-05	Wayzata	High-MN	24	27	36	63	32	....	....	....	....	....
	Omaha Lancers	USHL	11	1	0	1	0	....	....	....	....	....
2005-06	Omaha Lancers	USHL	56	12	23	35	25	5	0	0	0	2
2006-07	U. of Minnesota	WCHA	43	7	12	19	28	....	....	....	....	....
2007-08	U. of Minnesota	WCHA	44	7	11	18	41	....	....	....	....	....
2008-09	U. of Minnesota	WCHA	34	9	8	17	43	....	....	....	....	....
2009-10	U. of Minnesota	WCHA	39	11	17	28	22	....	....	....	....	....
	Worcester Sharks	AHL	4	1	0	1	0	1	0	0	0	0
2010-11	Worcester Sharks	AHL	2	0	0	0	0	....	....	....	....	....

• Missed majority of 2010-11 due to concussion.

LUCIANI, Anthony (loo-chee-AN-ee, AN-thun-ee) **FLA**

Right wing. Shoots right. 5'8", 185 lbs. Born, Maple, Ont., May 13, 1990.

			Regular Season					Playoffs				
Season	Club	League	GP	G	A	Pts	PIM	GP	G	A	Pts	PIM
2005-06	Don Mills Flyers	GTHL	STATISTICS NOT AVAILABLE									
	Wexford Raiders	OPJHL	2	0	0	0	2	....	....	....	....	....
2006-07	Huntsville	OPJHL	42	6	8	14	35	5	0	0	0	0
2007-08	Georgetown	OPJHL	13	7	7	14	19	7	1	3	4	17
2008-09	Erie Otters	OHL	59	6	8	14	84	4	0	1	1	5
2009-10	Erie Otters	OHL	68	38	30	68	67	3	2	1	3	7
2010-11	Erie Otters	OHL	54	29	49	78	30	7	7	3	10	12
	Rochester	AHL	3	2	1	3	2	....	....	....	....	....

Signed as a free agent by **Florida**, April 7, 2011.

LUDWIG, Trevor (LUHD-wihg, TREH-vuhr)

Defense. Shoots left. 6', 205 lbs. Born, Rhinelander, WI, May 24, 1985.
(Dallas' 7th choice, 183rd overall, in 2004 Entry Draft).

			Regular Season					Playoffs				
Season	Club	League	GP	G	A	Pts	PIM	GP	G	A	Pts	PIM
2002-03	Texas Tornado	NAHL	55	4	5	9	39	....	....	....	....	....
2003-04	Texas Tornado	NAHL	54	5	25	30	50	....	....	....	....	....
2004-05	Providence College	H-East	33	1	6	7	36	....	....	....	....	....
2005-06	Providence College	H-East	27	0	2	2	6	....	....	....	....	....
2006-07	Providence College	H-East	26	0	2	2	37	....	....	....	....	....
2007-08	Providence College	H-East	29	1	3	4	28	....	....	....	....	....
	Iowa Stars	AHL	7	0	3	3	12	....	....	....	....	....
2008-09	Manitoba Moose	AHL	16	0	0	0	18	....	....	....	....	....
	Idaho Steelheads	ECHL	35	2	8	10	41	4	0	0	0	13
2009-10	Texas Stars	AHL	47	3	5	8	62	19	0	1	1	18
	Idaho Steelheads	ECHL	14	1	5	6	24	....	....	....	....	....
2010-11	Texas Stars	AHL	64	1	6	7	58	....	....	....	....	....

NAHL All-Rookie Team (2003) • NAHL First All-Star Team (2004)

LUUKKO, Nick (LOO-koh, NIHK) **PHI**

Defense. Shoots right. 6'2", 180 lbs. Born, West Chester, PA, November 29, 1991.
(Philadelphia's 4th choice, 179th overall, in 2010 Entry Draft).

			Regular Season					Playoffs				
Season	Club	League	GP	G	A	Pts	PIM	GP	G	A	Pts	PIM
2008-09	Team Comcast	AYHL	3	0	1	1	2	....	....	....	....	....
	The Gunnery	High-CT	34	4	11	15	....	....	....	....	....	....
2009-10	The Gunnery	High-CT	....	3	22	25	....	....	....	....	....	....
2010-11	Dubuque	USHL	45	7	10	17	20	11	1	4	5	2

• Signed Letter of Intent to attend **University of Vermont** (Hockey-East) in fall of 2011.

LYAMIN, Kirill (L'YAH-mihn, kih-RIHL) **OTT**

Defense. Shoots left. 6'2", 211 lbs. Born, Moscow, USSR, January 13, 1986.
(Ottawa's 2nd choice, 58th overall, in 2004 Entry Draft).

			Regular Season					Playoffs				
Season	Club	League	GP	G	A	Pts	PIM	GP	G	A	Pts	PIM
2001-02	Moscow 18	Exhib.	5	0	3	3	4	....	....	....	....	....
2002-03	CSKA Moscow 2	Russia-3	5	0	0	0	10	....	....	....	....	....
	Moscow 18	Exhib.	5	0	0	0	6	....	....	....	....	....
2003-04	CSKA Moscow 2	Russia-3	STATISTICS NOT AVAILABLE									
	CSKA Moscow	Russia	28	0	3	3	12	....	....	....	....	....
2004-05	CSKA Moscow 2	Russia-3	STATISTICS NOT AVAILABLE									
2005-06	CSKA Moscow	Russia	25	0	1	1	28	2	0	0	0	0
2006-07	CSKA Moscow	Russia	47	1	7	8	48	12	1	0	1	8
2007-08	Mytischi	Russia	40	1	6	7	77	3	0	0	0	0
2008-09	Spartak Moscow	Rus-KHL	54	1	7	8	82	6	0	0	0	4
2009-10	Spartak Moscow	Rus-KHL	48	3	9	12	52	9	0	1	1	8
2010-11	Cherepovets	Rus-KHL	49	3	9	12	66	6	1	2	3	8

LYNCH, Kevin (LIHNCH, KEH-vihn) **CBJ**

Center. Shoots right. 6'1", 204 lbs. Born, Grosse Pointe, MI, April 23, 1991.
(Columbus' 2nd choice, 56th overall, in 2009 Entry Draft).

			Regular Season					Playoffs				
Season	Club	League	GP	G	A	Pts	PIM	GP	G	A	Pts	PIM
2006-07	Det. Honeybaked	MWEHL	28	14	14	28	16	....	....	....	....	....
	Det. Honeybaked	Exhib.	24	22	10	32	....	....	....	....	....	....
2007-08	USNTDP	NAHL	43	11	4	15	24	3	2	0	2	2
	USNTDP	U-17	17	6	2	8	18	....	....	....	....	....
2008-09	USNTDP	NAHL	16	8	7	15	14	....	....	....	....	....
	USNTDP	U-18	47	16	17	33	40	....	....	....	....	....
2009-10	U. of Michigan	CCHA	45	6	10	16	44	....	....	....	....	....
2010-11	U. of Michigan	CCHA	44	11	5	16	36	....	....	....	....	....

LYUBUSHIN, Mikhail (l'yoo-BOOSH-ihn, mih-kigh-EHL) **L.A.**

Defense. Shoots left. 6'1", 216 lbs. Born, Moscow, USSR, July 24, 1983.
(Los Angeles' 9th choice, 215th overall, in 2002 Entry Draft).

			Regular Season					Playoffs				
Season	Club	League	GP	G	A	Pts	PIM	GP	G	A	Pts	PIM
99-2000	Vityaz Podolsk 2	Russia-3	24	2	2	4	69	....	....	....	....	....
2000-01	Krylja Sovetov	Russia-2	2	0	1	1	0	1	0	0	0	0
2001-02	Krylja Sovetov 2	Russia-3	20	3	6	9	24	....	....	....	....	....
	THK Tver	Russia-2	22	1	0	1	18	....	....	....	....	....
	Krylja Sovetov	Russia	13	0	1	1	14	3	0	0	0	0
2002-03	Krylja Sovetov	Russia	49	0	6	6	26	....	....	....	....	....
2003-04	Dynamo Moscow	Russia	38	1	2	3	18	2	0	0	0	2
2004-05	Voskresensk	Russia	21	1	2	3	16	....	....	....	....	....
	Vityaz Chekhov	Russia-2	8	0	2	2	6	14	1	0	1	8
2005-06	Cherepovets	Russia	23	1	4	5	10	....	....	....	....	....
	Avangard Omsk	Russia	26	0	1	1	20	8	0	0	0	4
2006-07	Avangard Omsk	Russia	21	0	1	1	16	3	0	0	0	2
	Avangard Omsk 2	Russia-3	2	0	1	1	4	....	....	....	....	....
2007-08	Avangard Omsk	Russia	42	1	3	4	28	4	0	0	0	2
2008-09	Omsk	Rus-KHL	4	0	1	1	4	....	....	....	....	....
	Nizhny Novgorod	Rus-KHL	25	0	2	2	32	2	0	0	0	2
2009-10	Nizhny Novgorod	Rus-KHL	14	1	0	1	8	....	....	....	....	....
2010-11	Magnitogorsk	Rus-KHL	25	0	1	1	12	11	0	1	1	4

MacAULAY, Stephen (muh-KAWL-ee, STEE-vehn) **ST.L.**

Left wing. Shoots left. 6'2", 185 lbs. Born, Halifax, N.S., April 20, 1992.
(St. Louis' 7th choice, 164th overall, in 2010 Entry Draft).

			Regular Season					Playoffs				
Season	Club	League	GP	G	A	Pts	PIM	GP	G	A	Pts	PIM
2007-08	Cole Harbour	NSMHL	34	7	15	22	34	14	8	6	14	....
2008-09	Saint John	QMJHL	47	2	4	6	8	2	0	0	0	0
2009-10	Saint John	QMJHL	56	8	13	21	39	21	2	8	10	10
2010-11	Saint John	QMJHL	58	15	16	31	36	19	6	4	10	25

MacDERMID, Lane (MAK-duhr-mihd, LAYN) **BOS**

Left wing. Shoots left. 6'3", 205 lbs. Born, Hartford, CT, August 25, 1989.
(Boston's 3rd choice, 112th overall, in 2009 Entry Draft).

			Regular Season					Playoffs				
Season	Club	League	GP	G	A	Pts	PIM	GP	G	A	Pts	PIM
2005-06	Owen Sound	ON-Jr.B	48	1	7	8	....	....	....	....	....	....
2006-07	Owen Sound	OHL	57	2	5	7	115	4	1	0	1	2
2007-08	Owen Sound	OHL	66	13	11	24	190	....	....	....	....	....
2008-09	Owen Sound	OHL	26	8	6	14	85	....	....	....	....	....
	Windsor Spitfires	OHL	38	7	14	21	112	20	4	5	9	38
2009-10	Providence Bruins	AHL	65	2	3	5	155	....	....	....	....	....
2010-11	Providence Bruins	AHL	78	7	12	19	158	....	....	....	....	....

MACEK, Brooks (MA-chehk, BRUKS) **DET**

Center. Shoots right. 5'11", 175 lbs. Born, Winnipeg, Man., May 15, 1992.
(Detroit's 6th choice, 171st overall, in 2010 Entry Draft).

			Regular Season					Playoffs				
Season	Club	League	GP	G	A	Pts	PIM	GP	G	A	Pts	PIM
2007-08	Notre Dame	SMHL	44	32	30	62	37	10	10	6	16	10
	Notre Dame	Exhib.	1	0	1	1	0	....	....	....	....	....
2008-09	Tri-City Americans	WHL	60	8	16	24	24	11	3	0	3	0
2009-10	Tri-City Americans	WHL	72	21	52	73	26	21	6	11	17	17
2010-11	Tri-City Americans	WHL	38	8	16	24	26	....	....	....	....	....
	Calgary Hitmen	WHL	25	5	12	17	10	....	....	....	....	....

MACENAUER, Maxime (MAY-sehn-owr, mahx-EEM) **ANA**

Center. Shoots left. 6', 205 lbs. Born, Laval, Que., January 4, 1989.
(Anaheim's 3rd choice, 63rd overall, in 2007 Entry Draft).

			Regular Season					Playoffs				
Season	Club	League	GP	G	A	Pts	PIM	GP	G	A	Pts	PIM
2004-05	Ecole Montpetit	QAAA	37	17	22	39	56	3	0	0	0	0
2005-06	Rimouski Oceanic	QMJHL	41	8	14	22	30	....	....	....	....	....
2006-07	Rouyn-Noranda	QMJHL	14	1	3	4	10	....	....	....	....	....
2007-08	Rouyn-Noranda	QMJHL	67	23	37	60	53	17	6	10	16	8
2008-09	Rouyn-Noranda	QMJHL	35	15	9	24	34	....	....	....	....	....
	Shawinigan	QMJHL	19	7	9	16	18	21	5	9	14	20
2009-10	Bakersfield	ECHL	45	5	16	21	49	6	1	0	1	0
2010-11	Syracuse Crunch	AHL	79	13	19	32	65	....	....	....	....	....

MacINTYRE, Cam (MAK-ihn-tighr, KAM) **S.J.**

Right wing. Shoots right. 6'1", 225 lbs. Born, Sooke, B.C., October 3, 1985.

			Regular Season					Playoffs				
Season	**Club**	**League**	**GP**	**G**	**A**	**Pts**	**PIM**	**GP**	**G**	**A**	**Pts**	**PIM**
2006-07	Princeton	ECAC	32	9	4	13	34	....	....	....	....	....
2007-08	Princeton	ECAC	31	13	18	31	35	....	....	....	....	....
2008-09	Princeton	ECAC	15	1	5	6	4	....	....	....	....	....
2009-10	Princeton	ECAC	10	6	4	10	8	....	....	....	....	....
2010-11	Worcester Sharks	AHL	42	4	4	8	32	....	....	....	....	....

Signed as a free agent by **San Jose**, April 5, 2010.

MACKENZIE, Drew (muh-KEHN-zee , DROO) **BUF**

Defense. Shoots left. 6'2", 200 lbs. Born, Stamford, CT, December 17, 1988.
(Buffalo's 8th choice, 209th overall, in 2007 Entry Draft).

			Regular Season					Playoffs				
Season	**Club**	**League**	**GP**	**G**	**A**	**Pts**	**PIM**	**GP**	**G**	**A**	**Pts**	**PIM**
2004-05	Taft Rhinos	High-CT	....	0	1	1	....	....	....	....	....	....
2005-06	Taft Rhinos	High-CT	....	0	11	11	....	....	....	....	....	....
2006-07	Taft Rhinos	High-CT	24	3	10	13	10	....	....	....	....	....
2007-08	Waterloo	USHL	57	4	14	18	103	11	0	6	6	4
2008-09	U. of Vermont	H-East	31	1	9	10	14	....	....	....	....	....
2010-11	U. of Vermont	H-East	34	5	12	17	16	....	....	....	....	....

MacKENZIE, Matt (muh-KEHN-zee, MAT) **BUF**

Defense. Shoots right. 6'1", 194 lbs. Born, New Westminster, B.C., October 15, 1991.
(Buffalo's 4th choice, 83rd overall, in 2010 Entry Draft).

			Regular Season					Playoffs				
Season	**Club**	**League**	**GP**	**G**	**A**	**Pts**	**PIM**	**GP**	**G**	**A**	**Pts**	**PIM**
2006-07	Van. NW Giants	BCMML	40	5	11	16	64	....	....	....	....	....
2007-08	Calgary Hitmen	WHL	39	2	6	8	8	6	1	2	3	2
2008-09	Calgary Hitmen	WHL	49	3	9	12	24	16	0	2	2	4
2009-10	Calgary Hitmen	WHL	64	6	34	40	62	23	6	10	16	31
2010-11	Calgary Hitmen	WHL	40	2	21	23	50	....	....	....	....	....
	Tri-City Americans	WHL	33	5	10	15	36	10	1	4	5	6

MacLEOD, Isaac (muh-KLOWD, IGH-zihk) **S.J.**

Defense. Shoots left. 6'4", 205 lbs. Born, Nelson, B.C., February 22, 1992.
(San Jose's 5th choice, 136th overall, in 2010 Entry Draft).

			Regular Season					Playoffs				
Season	**Club**	**League**	**GP**	**G**	**A**	**Pts**	**PIM**	**GP**	**G**	**A**	**Pts**	**PIM**
2008-09	Nelson Leafs	KIJHL	45	3	16	19	68	13	3	2	5	48
	Penticton Vees	BCHL	3	0	1	1	0	....	....	....	....	....
2009-10	Penticton Vees	BCHL	56	0	23	23	51	14	0	1	1	6
2010-11	Boston College	H-East	22	0	3	3	10	....	....	....	....	....

MacMILLAN, Logan (muhk-MIHL-uhn , LOH-guhn) **CGY**

Center. Shoots left. 6'1", 172 lbs. Born, Charlottetown, P.E.I., July 5, 1989.
(Anaheim's 1st choice, 19th overall, in 2007 Entry Draft).

			Regular Season					Playoffs				
Season	**Club**	**League**	**GP**	**G**	**A**	**Pts**	**PIM**	**GP**	**G**	**A**	**Pts**	**PIM**
2004-05	Notre Dame	SJHL	41	9	19	28	27	....	....	....	....	....
2005-06	Halifax	QMJHL	62	9	9	18	31	11	1	0	1	0
2006-07	Halifax	QMJHL	68	20	35	55	82	12	9	11	20	6
2007-08	Halifax	QMJHL	46	15	26	41	77	15	3	10	13	20
2008-09	Halifax	QMJHL	15	4	6	10	27	....	....	....	....	....
	Rimouski Oceanic	QMJHL	28	5	16	21	37	13	3	3	6	20
2009-10	Abbotsford Heat	AHL	7	0	0	0	7	....	....	....	....	....
	Bakersfield	ECHL	30	2	4	6	20	....	....	....	....	....
2010-11	Abbotsford Heat	AHL	55	5	6	11	32	....	....	....	....	....

Traded to **Calgary** by **Anaheim** with future considerations for Jason Jaffray and future considerations, June 30, 2010.

MacMILLAN, Mark (muhk-MIHL-uhn, MAHRK) **MTL**

Forward. Shoots left. 6', 150 lbs. Born, Penticton, B.C., January 23, 1992.
(Montreal's 2nd choice, 113th overall, in 2010 Entry Draft).

			Regular Season					Playoffs				
Season	**Club**	**League**	**GP**	**G**	**A**	**Pts**	**PIM**	**GP**	**G**	**A**	**Pts**	**PIM**
2008-09	Okanagan Prep	Minor-BC	50	16	21	37	34	....	....	....	....	....
2009-10	Alberni Valley	BCHL	59	26	54	80	44	13	5	9	14	16
2010-11	Penticton Vees	BCHL	40	21	36	57	43	3	0	5	5	6

• Signed Letter of Intent to attend **University of North Dakota** (WCHA) in fall of 2011.

MacWILLIAM, Andrew (MAK-WIHL-yuhm, AN-droo) **TOR**

Defense. Shoots left. 6'2", 220 lbs. Born, Calgary, Alta., March 25, 1990.
(Toronto's 8th choice, 188th overall, in 2008 Entry Draft).

			Regular Season					Playoffs				
Season	**Club**	**League**	**GP**	**G**	**A**	**Pts**	**PIM**	**GP**	**G**	**A**	**Pts**	**PIM**
2006-07	Calgary Royals	AMHL	35	5	13	18	125	....	....	....	....	....
	Camrose Kodiaks	AJHL	2	0	0	0	0	1	0	0	0	0
2007-08	Camrose Kodiaks	AJHL	54	0	13	13	130	18	0	5	5	49
2008-09	Camrose Kodiaks	AJHL	57	8	21	29	220	11	0	4	4	39
2009-10	North Dakota	WCHA	43	0	3	3	87	....	....	....	....	....
2010-11	North Dakota	WCHA	37	0	8	8	49	....	....	....	....	....

MADAISKY, Austin (muh-DAY-skee, AW-stuhn) **CBJ**

Defense. Shoots right. 6'2", 199 lbs. Born, Surrey, B.C., January 30, 1992.
(Columbus' 6th choice, 124th overall, in 2010 Entry Draft).

			Regular Season					Playoffs				
Season	**Club**	**League**	**GP**	**G**	**A**	**Pts**	**PIM**	**GP**	**G**	**A**	**Pts**	**PIM**
2007-08	Valley West Hawks	BCMML	35	6	23	29	38	....	....	....	....	....
2008-09	Calgary Hitmen	WHL	48	2	7	9	16	2	0	0	0	2
2009-10	Calgary Hitmen	WHL	39	5	13	18	46	....	....	....	....	....
	Kamloops Blazers	WHL	26	2	7	9	28	4	3	3	6	6
2010-11	Kamloops Blazers	WHL	55	7	20	27	104	....	....	....	....	....

MAKAROV, Igor (MAK-ah-rahv, EE-gohr) **CHI**

Right wing. Shoots right. 6'1", 195 lbs. Born, Moscow, USSR, September 19, 1987.
(Chicago's 2nd choice, 33rd overall, in 2006 Entry Draft).

			Regular Season					Playoffs				
Season	**Club**	**League**	**GP**	**G**	**A**	**Pts**	**PIM**	**GP**	**G**	**A**	**Pts**	**PIM**
2003-04	Krylja Sovetov 2	Russia-3	1	0	0	0	0	....	....	....	....	....
2004-05	Krylja Sovetov 2	Russia-3	38	13	15	28	44	....	....	....	....	....
	Krylja Sovetov	Russia-2	6	2	2	4	4	1	0	0	0	0
2005-06	Krylja Sovetov	Russia-2	35	9	7	16	20	17	3	4	7	20
2006-07	SKA St. Petersburg	Russia	49	7	2	9	47	3	1	0	1	2
2007-08	St. Petersburg 2	Russia-3	3	1	3	4	2	2	1	2	3	2
	SKA St. Petersburg	Russia	50	4	11	15	26	9	2	1	3	35
2008-09	SKA St. Petersburg	Rus-KHL	42	9	8	17	61	3	1	0	1	2
2009-10	SKA St. Petersburg	Rus-KHL	26	4	2	6	28	....	....	....	....	....
	Dynamo Moscow	Rus-KHL	25	1	2	3	33	4	0	0	0	0
2010-11	Rockford IceHogs	AHL	68	11	13	24	49	....	....	....	....	....

MALONE, Brad (MA-lohn, BRAD) **COL**

Center/Left wing. Shoots left. 6'2", 207 lbs. Born, Miramichi, N.B., May 20, 1989.
(Colorado's 5th choice, 105th overall, in 2007 Entry Draft).

			Regular Season					Playoffs				
Season	**Club**	**League**	**GP**	**G**	**A**	**Pts**	**PIM**	**GP**	**G**	**A**	**Pts**	**PIM**
2005-06	Cushing	High-MA		STATISTICS NOT AVAILABLE								
2006-07	Sioux Falls	USHL	57	14	19	33	134	8	3	1	4	24
2007-08	North Dakota	WCHA	34	1	2	3	44	....	....	....	....	....
2008-09	North Dakota	WCHA	41	5	12	17	75	....	....	....	....	....
2009-10	North Dakota	WCHA	43	11	14	25	*102	....	....	....	....	....
2010-11	North Dakota	WCHA	43	16	24	40	*108	....	....	....	....	....
	Lake Erie Monsters	AHL	....	....	....	....	....	3	0	1	1	2

MANNING, Brandon (MAN-nihng, BRAN-duhn) **PHI**

Defense. Shoots left. 6'1", 195 lbs. Born, Prince George, B.C., June 4, 1990.

			Regular Season					Playoffs				
Season	**Club**	**League**	**GP**	**G**	**A**	**Pts**	**PIM**	**GP**	**G**	**A**	**Pts**	**PIM**
2007-08	Prince George	BCHL	58	7	19	26	107	4	0	3	3	6
	Chilliwack Bruins	WHL	6	0	0	0	8	4	0	0	0	4
2008-09	Chilliwack Bruins	WHL	72	11	18	29	140	....	....	....	....	....
2009-10	Chilliwack Bruins	WHL	69	13	41	54	138	6	0	6	6	10
2010-11	Chilliwack Bruins	WHL	53	21	32	53	129	5	1	0	1	8

Signed as a free agent by **Philadelphia**, November 23, 2010.

MANSON, Josh (MAN-suhn, JAWSH) **ANA**

Defense. Shoots right. 6'3", 205 lbs. Born, Prince Albert, Sask., October 7, 1991.
(Anaheim's 7th choice, 160th overall, in 2011 Entry Draft).

			Regular Season					Playoffs				
Season	**Club**	**League**	**GP**	**G**	**A**	**Pts**	**PIM**	**GP**	**G**	**A**	**Pts**	**PIM**
2008-09	Prince Albert	SMHL	40	19	16	35	64	3	1	0	1	4
2009-10	Salmon Arm	BCHL	54	10	14	24	75	6	1	0	1	15
2010-11	Salmon Arm	BCHL	57	12	35	47	80	14	2	7	9	15

• Signed Letter of Intent to attend **Quinnipac University** (ECAC) in fall of 2012.

MARCHENKO, Alexei (MAHR-chehn-koh, al-EHX-ay) **DET**

Defense. Shoots right. 6'2", 183 lbs. Born, Moscow, Russia, January 2, 1992.
(Detroit's 9th choice, 205th overall, in 2011 Entry Draft).

			Regular Season					Playoffs				
Season	**Club**	**League**	**GP**	**G**	**A**	**Pts**	**PIM**	**GP**	**G**	**A**	**Pts**	**PIM**
2009-10	CSKA Jr.	Russia-Jr.	43	11	23	34	59	2	0	0	0	4
	CSKA Moscow	Rus-KHL	10	0	0	0	0	....	....	....	....	....
2010-11	CSKA Jr.	Russia-Jr.	36	5	33	38	28	15	3	8	11	31
	CSKA Moscow	Rus-KHL	22	0	2	2	4	....	....	....	....	....

MARCINKO, Tomas (mahr-TSIHN-koh, TAW-mahsh) **NYI**

Center. Shoots right. 6'4", 216 lbs. Born, Poprad, Czech., April 11, 1988.
(NY Islanders' 6th choice, 115th overall, in 2006 Entry Draft).

			Regular Season					Playoffs				
Season	**Club**	**League**	**GP**	**G**	**A**	**Pts**	**PIM**	**GP**	**G**	**A**	**Pts**	**PIM**
2003-04	HC Kosice U18	Svk-U18	42	19	23	42	60	2	0	0	0	4
	HC Kosice Jr.	Slovak-Jr.	7	0	2	2	4	3	0	1	1	0
2004-05	HC Kosice Jr.	Slovak-Jr.	38	11	18	29	28	8	1	2	3	6
	HC Kosice	Slovakia	6	0	0	0	0	....	....	....	....	....
	HC Kosice	Slovakia	6	0	0	0	0	....	....	....	....	....
2005-06	HC Kosice Jr.	Slovak-Jr.	35	26	21	47	50	3	1	0	1	4
	HKm Humenne	Slovak-2	9	3	5	8	10	....	....	....	....	....
	HC Kosice	Slovakia	18	2	0	2	2	5	0	0	0	0
2006-07	Barrie Colts	OHL	56	19	21	40	56	8	0	1	1	8
2007-08	Barrie Colts	OHL	48	19	26	45	54	9	4	3	7	14
2008-09	Bridgeport	AHL	58	4	7	11	30	4	0	0	0	0
2009-10	Bridgeport	AHL	54	4	2	6	27	5	0	1	1	2
2010-11	Bridgeport	AHL	66	4	7	11	56	....	....	....	....	....

MARCOU, James (mar-KOO, JAYMZ) **S.J.**

Right wing. Shoots right. 5'8", 165 lbs. Born, Huntington, NY, February 19, 1988.

			Regular Season					Playoffs				
Season	**Club**	**League**	**GP**	**G**	**A**	**Pts**	**PIM**	**GP**	**G**	**A**	**Pts**	**PIM**
2004-05	USNTDP	NAHL	6	0	2	2	0	....	....	....	....	....
2005-06	Waterloo	USHL	51	18	14	32	26	....	....	....	....	....
2006-07	Waterloo	USHL	58	24	47	71	60	9	6	6	12	4
2007-08	Massachusetts	H-East	36	8	24	32	20	....	....	....	....	....
2008-09	Massachusetts	H-East	39	15	32	47	34	....	....	....	....	....
2009-10	Massachusetts	H-East	36	11	40	51	36	....	....	....	....	....
	Worcester Sharks	AHL	4	1	2	3	0	1	0	0	0	0
2010-11	Worcester Sharks	AHL	41	4	15	19	18	....	....	....	....	....

USHL Second All-Star Team (2007) • Hockey East All-Rookie Team (2008) • Hockey East First All-Star Team (2009) • NCAA East Second All-American Team (2009) • Hockey East Second All-Star Team (2010)

Signed as a free agent by **San Jose**, March 23, 2010.

MAREK, Jan (MAIR-ehk, YAHN) L.A.

Center. Shoots right. 5'10", 185 lbs. Born, Jindrichuv Hradec, Czech., December 31, 1979.
(NY Rangers' 10th choice, 243rd overall, in 2003 Entry Draft).

			Regular Season					Playoffs				
Season	Club	League	GP	G	A	Pts	PIM	GP	G	A	Pts	PIM
1998-99	Trinec	CzRep	32	2	2	4	2	6	0	0	0	0
99-2000	HC Trinec Jr.	CzRep-Jr.	6	5	5	10	10	1	0	0	0	0
	HC Slezan Opava	CzRep-2	3	0	1	1	4	....	....	....	....	....
	Jind. Hradec	CzRep-2	4	0	3	3	10	....	....	....	....	....
	HC Ocelari Trinec	CzRep	32	1	5	6	4	2	0	0	0	0
2000-01	HC Ocelari Trinec	CzRep	38	7	4	11	2	....	....	....	....	....
2001-02	HC Ocelari Trinec	CzRep	52	13	27	40	44	6	1	3	4	6
2002-03	HC Ocelari Trinec	CzRep	51	*32	30	62	42	12	6	4	10	22
2003-04	HC Sparta Praha	CzRep	50	21	30	51	62	11	4	9	13	26
2004-05	HC Sparta Praha	CzRep	38	7	21	28	26	5	2	2	4	2
2005-06	HC Sparta Praha	CzRep	48	22	32	*54	66	17	4	4	8	24
2006-07	Magnitogorsk	Russia	47	17	30	47	70	15	7	10	17	10
2007-08	Magnitogorsk	Russia	49	16	32	48	40	11	4	3	7	2
2008-09	Magnitogorsk	Rus-KHL	53	*38	37	75	62	12	6	4	10	26
2009-10	Magnitogorsk	Rus-KHL	35	7	13	20	14	10	3	1	4	4
2010-11	CSKA Moscow	Rus-KHL	46	14	24	38	46	....	....	....	....	....
	Mytischi	Rus-KHL	5	2	0	2	8	20	7	10	17	10

Traded to **Los Angeles** by **NY Rangers** with Jason Ward, Marc-Andre Cliche and NY Rangers' 3rd round choice (later traded to Buffalo - Buffalo selected Corey Fienhage) in 2008 Entry Draft for Sean Avery and John Seymour, February 5, 2007.

MARINCIN, Martin (mah-RIHN-chihn, MAHR-tihn) EDM

Defense. Shoots left. 6'5", 196 lbs. Born, Kosice, Czechoslovakia, February 18, 1992.
(Edmonton's 3rd choice, 46th overall, in 2010 Entry Draft).

			Regular Season					Playoffs				
Season	Club	League	GP	G	A	Pts	PIM	GP	G	A	Pts	PIM
2006-07	HC Kosice U18	Svk-U18	16	0	3	3	6	....	....	....	....	....
2007-08	HC Kosice U18	Svk-U18	59	3	29	32	36	....	....	....	....	....
2008-09	HC Kosice U18	Svk-U18	5	4	4	8	35	....	....	....	....	....
	HC Kosice Jr.	Slovak-Jr.	46	11	15	26	50	3	0	0	0	0
2009-10	Slovakia U20	Slovakia	35	2	4	6	71	....	....	....	....	....
	HC Kosice Jr.	Slovak-Jr.	....	....	....	....	....	2	0	0	0	0
2010-11	Prince George	WHL	67	14	42	56	65	4	1	4	5	6
	Oklahoma City	AHL	1	0	0	0	2	....	....	....	....	....

MAROON, Patrick (ma-ROON, PAT-rihk) ANA

Left wing. Shoots left. 6'4", 225 lbs. Born, St Louis, MO, April 23, 1988.
(Philadelphia's 6th choice, 161st overall, in 2007 Entry Draft).

			Regular Season					Playoffs				
Season	Club	League	GP	G	A	Pts	PIM	GP	G	A	Pts	PIM
2005-06	Texarkana Bandits	NAHL	57	23	37	60	61	8	3	1	4	22
2006-07	St. Louis Bandits	NAHL	57	40	55	*95	152	12	*10	*13	*23	12
2007-08	London Knights	OHL	64	35	55	90	57	5	0	1	1	10
	Philadelphia	AHL	1	0	0	0	0	....	....	....	....	....
2008-09	Philadelphia	AHL	80	23	31	54	62	4	1	2	3	13
2009-10	Adirondack	AHL	67	11	33	44	125	....	....	....	....	....
2010-11	Adirondack	AHL	9	5	3	8	30	....	....	....	....	....
	Syracuse Crunch	AHL	57	21	27	48	68	....	....	....	....	....

Traded to **Anaheim** by **Philadelphia** with David Laliberte for Danny Syvret and Rob Bordson, November 21, 2010.

MARQUARDT, Matt (MAR-kwart, MAT)

Left wing. Shoots left. 6'3", 220 lbs. Born, North Bay, Ont., July 19, 1987.
(Columbus' 10th choice, 194th overall, in 2006 Entry Draft).

			Regular Season					Playoffs				
Season	Club	League	GP	G	A	Pts	PIM	GP	G	A	Pts	PIM
2003-04	Huntsville Wildcats	OPJHL	STATISTICS NOT AVAILABLE									
	Brockville Braves	CJHL	11	1	2	3	17	....	....	....	....	....
2004-05	Brockville Braves	CJHL	55	19	22	41	78	7	2	1	3	8
2005-06	Moncton Wildcats	QMJHL	68	16	9	25	69	20	5	3	8	12
2006-07	Moncton Wildcats	QMJHL	67	41	29	70	68	7	1	3	4	14
2007-08	Moncton Wildcats	QMJHL	35	20	13	33	38	....	....	....	....	....
	Baie-Comeau	QMJHL	33	23	13	36	33	5	1	1	2	6
2008-09	Providence Bruins	AHL	71	9	13	22	45	9	1	1	2	2
2009-10	Providence Bruins	AHL	42	1	9	10	21	....	....	....	....	....
	Reading Royals	ECHL	9	1	2	3	14	....	....	....	....	....
	Springfield Falcons	AHL	4	0	0	0	4	....	....	....	....	....
	Stockton Thunder	ECHL	7	1	1	2	4	15	6	4	10	15
2010-11	Oklahoma City	AHL	63	5	7	12	20	....	....	....	....	....

CJHL Rookie of the Year (2005)

Traded to **Boston** by **Columbus** for Jonathon Sigalet, May 27, 2008. Traded to **Edmonton** by **Boston** for Cody Wild, March 2, 2010.

MARSHALL, Ben (MAR-shuhl, BEHN) DET

Defense. Shoots left. 5'9", 160 lbs. Born, St. Paul, MN, August 30, 1992.
(Detroit's 7th choice, 201st overall, in 2010 Entry Draft).

			Regular Season					Playoffs				
Season	Club	League	GP	G	A	Pts	PIM	GP	G	A	Pts	PIM
2007-08	Mahtomedi	High-MN	6	3	0	3	....	....	....	....	....	....
2008-09	Mahtomedi	High-MN	29	21	29	50	30	....	....	....	....	....
2009-10	Team Northeast	UMHSEL	16	1	3	4	....	....	....	....	....	....
	Minnetonka High	High-MN	23	18	30	48	40	6	2	10	12	10
2010-11	Omaha Lancers	USHL	56	11	21	32	34	3	0	1	1	0

USHL Second All-Star Team (2011)

• Signed Letter of Intent to attend **University of Minnesota** (WCHA) in fall of 2011.

MARSHALL, Kevin (MAR-shuhl, KEH-vihn) PHI

Defense. Shoots left. 6'1", 191 lbs. Born, Boucherville, Que., March 10, 1989.
(Philadelphia's 2nd choice, 41st overall, in 2007 Entry Draft).

			Regular Season					Playoffs				
Season	Club	League	GP	G	A	Pts	PIM	GP	G	A	Pts	PIM
2004-05	C.C. Lemoyne	QAAA	39	2	9	11	88	5	0	1	1	16
2005-06	Lewiston	QMJHL	60	1	10	11	112	6	0	1	1	14
2006-07	Lewiston	QMJHL	70	5	27	32	141	17	0	7	7	38
2007-08	Lewiston	QMJHL	66	11	24	35	143	6	1	1	2	12
2008-09	Quebec Remparts	QMJHL	61	9	29	38	125	17	1	10	11	32
2009-10	Adirondack	AHL	75	2	7	9	80	....	....	....	....	....
2010-11	Adirondack	AHL	78	3	11	14	120	....	....	....	....	....

QMJHL Second All-Star Team (2008)

MARSHALL, Matt (MAR-shuhl, MAT) T.B.

Center/Right wing. Shoots right. 6'1", 202 lbs. Born, Boston, MA, August 30, 1988.
(Tampa Bay's 5th choice, 150th overall, in 2007 Entry Draft).

			Regular Season					Playoffs				
Season	Club	League	GP	G	A	Pts	PIM	GP	G	A	Pts	PIM
2005-06	Hingham	High-MA	STATISTICS NOT AVAILABLE									
2006-07	Nobles	High-MA	27	14	10	24	6	....	....	....	....	....
2007-08	Nobles	High-MA	29	25	26	51	....	....	....	....	....	....
2008-09	U. of Vermont	H-East	24	1	3	4	12	....	....	....	....	....
2009-10	U. of Vermont	H-East	33	1	4	5	16	....	....	....	....	....
2010-11	U. of Vermont	H-East	27	3	2	5	4	....	....	....	....	....

MARTINDALE, Ryan (MAHR-tihn-dayl, RIGH-uhn) EDM

Center. Shoots left. 6'3", 190 lbs. Born, Oshawa, Ont., October 27, 1991.
(Edmonton's 5th choice, 61st overall, in 2010 Entry Draft).

			Regular Season					Playoffs				
Season	Club	League	GP	G	A	Pts	PIM	GP	G	A	Pts	PIM
2006-07	Whitby Wildcats	Minor-ON	79	65	67	132	....	....	....	....	....	....
2007-08	Ottawa 67's	OHL	64	9	8	17	18	4	0	0	0	2
2008-09	Ottawa 67's	OHL	53	23	24	47	14	7	2	1	3	7
2009-10	Ottawa 67's	OHL	61	19	41	60	37	12	4	5	9	6
2010-11	Ottawa 67's	OHL	65	34	49	83	30	4	3	2	5	2

MASSE, Dany (ma-SAY, DA-nee) MTL

Left wing. Shoots left. 5'10", 177 lbs. Born, La Pocatiere, Que., May 12, 1988.

			Regular Season					Playoffs				
Season	Club	League	GP	G	A	Pts	PIM	GP	G	A	Pts	PIM
2004-05	Val-d'Or Foreurs	QMJHL	58	2	8	10	43	....	....	....	....	....
2005-06	Val-d'Or Foreurs	QMJHL	67	9	20	29	64	5	0	0	0	0
2006-07	Acadie-Bathurst	QMJHL	69	26	30	56	84	12	1	6	7	12
2007-08	Acadie-Bathurst	QMJHL	70	29	50	79	38	12	1	6	7	14
2008-09	Drummondville	QMJHL	68	44	66	110	52	19	15	20	35	18
2009-10	Hamilton Bulldogs	AHL	25	3	2	5	6	9	0	1	1	0
2010-11	Hamilton Bulldogs	AHL	36	3	6	9	18	20	0	2	2	6
	Wheeling Nailers	ECHL	29	1	8	9	12	....	....	....	....	....

QMJHL First All-Star Team (2009)

Signed as a free agent by **Montreal**, April 15, 2009. • Reassigned to **Wheeling** (ECHL) by **Montreal** (Hamilton-AHL), October 25, 2010.

MATHERS, Derek (MA-thurz, DAIR-ihk) PHI

Right wing. Shoots right. 6'3", 226 lbs. Born, Strathroy, Ont., August 4, 1993.
(Philadelphia's 6th choice, 206th overall, in 2011 Entry Draft).

			Regular Season					Playoffs				
Season	Club	League	GP	G	A	Pts	PIM	GP	G	A	Pts	PIM
2008-09	Elgin-Mid. Chiefs	Minor-ON	30	2	5	7	60	....	....	....	....	....
2009-10	Strathroy Rockets	ON-Jr.B	43	2	5	7	53	5	0	3	3	4
2010-11	Peterborough	OHL	55	1	4	5	*171	....	....	....	....	....

MATSON, Taylor (MAT-suhn, TAY-luhr) VAN

Center. Shoots right. 5'10", 165 lbs. Born, Mound, MN, September 16, 1988.
(Vancouver's 5th choice, 176th overall, in 2007 Entry Draft).

			Regular Season					Playoffs				
Season	Club	League	GP	G	A	Pts	PIM	GP	G	A	Pts	PIM
2005-06	Holy Angels	High-MN	27	30	40	70	28	....	....	....	....	....
2006-07	Holy Angels	High-MN	11	16	15	31	16	....	....	....	....	....
	Des Moines	USHL	10	1	2	3	6	6	0	1	1	10
2007-08	Des Moines	USHL	55	13	24	37	38	....	....	....	....	....
2008-09	U. of Minnesota	WCHA	13	1	0	1	2	....	....	....	....	....
2009-10	U. of Minnesota	WCHA	19	2	3	5	6	....	....	....	....	....
2010-11	U. of Minnesota	WCHA	33	10	3	13	16	....	....	....	....	....

MATTSON, Nick (MAT-suhn, NIHK) CHI

Defense. Shoots left. 6'1", 189 lbs. Born, Salem, OR, October 25, 1991.
(Chicago's 9th choice, 180th overall, in 2010 Entry Draft).

			Regular Season					Playoffs				
Season	Club	League	GP	G	A	Pts	PIM	GP	G	A	Pts	PIM
2006-07	Chaska Hawks	High-MN	41	5	15	20	....	....	....	....	....	....
2007-08	USNTDP	NAHL	43	1	10	11	16	3	0	0	0	0
	USNTDP	U-17	17	0	9	9	....	....	....	....	....	....
2008-09	USNTDP	NAHL	16	1	5	6	4	....	....	....	....	....
	USNTDP	U-18	47	3	14	17	4	....	....	....	....	....
2009-10	Indiana Ice	USHL	51	5	14	19	14	9	0	6	6	2
2010-11	Indiana Ice	USHL	57	6	30	36	12	5	0	2	2	0

USHL First All-Star Team (2011)

• Signed Letter of Intent to attend **University of North Dakota** (WCHA) in fall of 2011.

MAYFIELD, Scott (MAY-feeld, SKAWT) NYI

Defense. Shoots right. 6'4", 203 lbs. Born, St. Louis, MO, October 14, 1992.
(NY Islanders' 2nd choice, 34th overall, in 2011 Entry Draft).

			Regular Season					Playoffs				
Season	Club	League	GP	G	A	Pts	PIM	GP	G	A	Pts	PIM
2008-09	St.L. AAA Blues	Minor-MO	62	10	20	30	84	....	....	....	....	....
2009-10	Youngstown	USHL	59	10	12	22	145	....	....	....	....	....
2010-11	Youngstown	USHL	52	7	9	16	159	....	....	....	....	....

• Signed Letter of Intent to attend **University of Denver** (WCHA).

McCAULEY, Dennis (muh-KAW-lee, DEH-nihs) BUF

Left wing. Shoots left. 6'3", 225 lbs. Born, Billerica, MA, August 15, 1985.

			Regular Season					Playoffs				
Season	Club	League	GP	G	A	Pts	PIM	GP	G	A	Pts	PIM
2003-04	Sioux City	USHL	58	12	9	21	176	7	1	0	1	26
2004-05	Sioux City	USHL	54	18	21	39	236	12	2	3	5	46
2005-06	Northeastern	H-East	32	7	7	14	57	....	....	....	....	....
2006-07	Northeastern	H-East	33	5	9	14	90	....	....	....	....	....
2007-08	Northeastern	H-East	28	4	2	6	70	....	....	....	....	....
2008-09	Northeastern	H-East	36	6	5	11	49	....	....	....	....	....
2009-10	Worcester Sharks	AHL	45	10	4	14	84	8	0	2	2	2
2010-11	Portland Pirates	AHL	73	12	21	33	114	4	1	1	2	6

Signed as a free agent by **Buffalo**, July 30, 2010.

MCCOLGAN, Shane (mih-KOHL-guhn, SHAYN) NYR

Right wing. Shoots right. 5'8", 165 lbs. Born, Torrance, CA, January 1, 1993.
(NY Rangers' 4th choice, 134th overall, in 2011 Entry Draft).

			Regular Season					Playoffs				
Season	Club	League	GP	G	A	Pts	PIM	GP	G	A	Pts	PIM
2008-09	L.A. Jr. Kings	T1EHL	44	14	35	49	52	....	....	....	....	....
	Kelowna Rockets	WHL	4	1	2	3	4	4	0	0	0	0
2009-10	Kelowna Rockets	WHL	71	25	44	69	45	12	1	3	4	22
2010-11	Kelowna Rockets	WHL	67	21	45	66	62	10	8	11	19	8

MCCORMICK, Max (muh-KOHR-mihk, MAX) OTT

Left wing. Shoots left. 5'11", 178 lbs. Born, De Pere, WI, May 1, 1992.
(Ottawa's 8th choice, 171st overall, in 2011 Entry Draft).

			Regular Season					Playoffs				
Season	Club	League	GP	G	A	Pts	PIM	GP	G	A	Pts	PIM
2007-08	Notre Dame	High-WI	16	19	20	39	....	....	....	....	....	....
2008-09	Team Wisconsin	UMHSEL	STATISTICS NOT AVAILABLE									
	Notre Dame	High-WI	18	19	38	57	....	....	....	....	....	....
2009-10	Team Wisconsin	UMHSEL	24	....	....	24	....	....	....	....	....	....
	Notre Dame	High-WI	29	38	37	75	74	....	....	....	....	....
2010-11	Sioux City	USHL	55	21	21	42	102	3	1	2	3	4

• Signed Letter of Intent to attend **Ohio State University** (CCHA).

McFARLAND, John (muhk-FAHR-luhnd, JAWN) FLA

Left wing. Shoots right. 6'1", 205 lbs. Born, Richmond Hill, Ont., April 2, 1992.
(Florida's 4th choice, 33rd overall, in 2010 Entry Draft).

			Regular Season					Playoffs				
Season	Club	League	GP	G	A	Pts	PIM	GP	G	A	Pts	PIM
2007-08	Tor. Jr. Canadiens	GTHL	76	96	69	165	176	....	....	....	....	....
2008-09	Sudbury Wolves	OHL	58	21	31	52	36	6	1	3	4	2
2009-10	Sudbury Wolves	OHL	64	20	30	50	70	4	3	0	3	2
2010-11	Sudbury Wolves	OHL	12	6	4	10	13	....	....	....	....	....
	Saginaw Spirit	OHL	37	19	9	28	33	12	5	4	9	6

McFAULL, Kendall (muhk-FAWL, KEN-duhl) WPG

Defense. Shoots left. 6'2", 185 lbs. Born, Rosetown, Sask., April 10, 1992.
(Atlanta's 6th choice, 155th overall, in 2010 Entry Draft).

			Regular Season					Playoffs				
Season	Club	League	GP	G	A	Pts	PIM	GP	G	A	Pts	PIM
2008-09	Sask. Contacts	SMHL	42	4	14	18	73	10	1	5	6	21
	Sask. Contacts	Exhib.	8	2	4	6	21	....	....	....	....	....
2009-10	Moose Jaw	WHL	62	4	6	10	70	7	0	1	1	10
2010-11	Moose Jaw	WHL	69	1	6	7	78	6	0	1	1	12

McGINN, Tye (muhk-GIHN, TIGH) PHI

Left wing. Shoots left. 6'3", 207 lbs. Born, Fergus, Ont., July 29, 1990.
(Philadelphia's 2nd choice, 119th overall, in 2010 Entry Draft).

			Regular Season					Playoffs				
Season	Club	League	GP	G	A	Pts	PIM	GP	G	A	Pts	PIM
2006-07	Waterloo Wolves	Minor-ON	62	41	55	96	42	....	....	....	....	....
2007-08	Ottawa 67's	OHL	59	3	8	11	25	4	0	0	0	2
2008-09	Listowel Cyclones	ON-Jr.B	14	10	18	28	10	....	....	....	....	....
	Gatineau	QMJHL	48	8	22	30	25	10	7	6	13	19
2009-10	Gatineau	QMJHL	50	27	35	62	50	10	2	5	7	12
2010-11	Gatineau	QMJHL	42	31	33	64	39	14	5	8	13	17

McILRATH, Dylan (MAK-ihl-rayth, DIH-luhn) NYR

Defense. Shoots right. 6'5", 215 lbs. Born, Winnipeg, Man., April 20, 1992.
(NY Rangers' 1st choice, 10th overall, in 2010 Entry Draft).

			Regular Season					Playoffs				
Season	Club	League	GP	G	A	Pts	PIM	GP	G	A	Pts	PIM
2007-08	Winnipeg Warriors	Minor-MB	34	5	17	22	68	....	....	....	....	....
2008-09	Moose Jaw	WHL	53	1	3	4	102	....	....	....	....	....
2009-10	Moose Jaw	WHL	65	7	17	24	169	7	0	1	1	21
2010-11	Moose Jaw	WHL	62	5	18	23	153	6	0	0	0	15
	Connecticut Whale	AHL	2	0	0	0	7	....	....	....	....	....

McINTYRE, David (MAK-ihn-tigh-uhr, DAY-vihd) MIN

Center. Shoots left. 6', 190 lbs. Born, Oakville, Ont., February 4, 1987.
(Dallas' 4th choice, 138th overall, in 2006 Entry Draft).

			Regular Season					Playoffs				
Season	Club	League	GP	G	A	Pts	PIM	GP	G	A	Pts	PIM
2004-05	Newmarket	OPJHL	46	17	14	31	33	16	8	7	15	20
2005-06	Newmarket	OPJHL	46	42	50	92	143	11	4	8	12	42
2006-07	Colgate	ECAC	40	9	8	17	75	....	....	....	....	....
2007-08	Colgate	ECAC	39	15	17	32	38	....	....	....	....	....
2008-09	Colgate	ECAC	37	21	22	43	54	....	....	....	....	....
2009-10	Colgate	ECAC	35	11	28	39	60	....	....	....	....	....
	Lowell Devils	AHL	12	3	2	5	8	5	1	1	2	0
2010-11	Albany Devils	AHL	78	12	18	30	51	....	....	....	....	....

ECAC First All-Star Team (2009) • NCAA East First All-American Team (2009) • ECAC Second All-Star Team (2010)

Traded to **Anaheim** by **Dallas** with Dallas' 6th round choice (Andreas Dahlstrom) in 2010 Entry Draft for Brian Sutherby, December 14, 2008. Traded to **New Jersey** by **Anaheim** for Sheldon Brookbank, February 3, 2009. Traded to **Minnesota** by **New Jersey** for Maxim Noreau, June 16, 2011.

McKEGG, Greg (Muhk-ehg, GREHG) TOR

Center. Shoots left. 6', 195 lbs. Born, St.Thomas, Ont., June 17, 1992.
(Toronto's 2nd choice, 62nd overall, in 2010 Entry Draft).

			Regular Season					Playoffs				
Season	Club	League	GP	G	A	Pts	PIM	GP	G	A	Pts	PIM
2007-08	Elgin-Mid. Chiefs	Minor-ON	64	73	53	126	....	....	....	....	....	....
	St. Thomas Stars	ON-Jr.B	3	4	1	5	2	....	....	....	....	....
2008-09	Erie Otters	OHL	64	8	10	18	22	5	2	1	3	4
2009-10	Erie Otters	OHL	67	37	48	85	32	4	2	1	3	0
2010-11	Erie Otters	OHL	66	49	43	92	35	7	4	1	5	12
	Toronto Marlies	AHL	2	1	0	1	0	....	....	....	....	....

McKELVIE, Zach (muh-KEHL-vee, ZAK) BOS

Defense. Shoots . 6'2", 200 lbs. Born, St. Paul, MN, February 22, 1985.

			Regular Season					Playoffs				
Season	Club	League	GP	G	A	Pts	PIM	GP	G	A	Pts	PIM
2004-05	Bozeman IceDogs	NAHL	53	0	6	6	108	....	....	....	....	....
2005-06	Army	AH	32	2	8	10	64	....	....	....	....	....
2006-07	Army	AH	34	3	9	12	48	....	....	....	....	....
2007-08	Army	AH	35	4	13	17	48	....	....	....	....	....
2008-09	Army	AH	33	5	12	17	48	....	....	....	....	....
2009-10	Army	AH	MILITARY SERVICE									
2010-11	Army	AH	MILITARY SERVICE									

Signed as a free agent by **Boston**, July 13, 2009. • Did not play in 2009-10 and 2010-11 fulfilling his U.S. military service requirements as per his enrollment at West Point.

McKENZIE, Curtis (muh-KEHN-zee, KUHR-tihs) DAL

Left wing. Shoots left. 6'2", 192 lbs. Born, Golden, B.C., February 22, 1991.
(Dallas' 5th choice, 159th overall, in 2009 Entry Draft).

			Regular Season					Playoffs				
Season	Club	League	GP	G	A	Pts	PIM	GP	G	A	Pts	PIM
2007-08	Penticton Vees	BCHL	49	3	7	10	81	7	0	1	1	9
2008-09	Penticton Vees	BCHL	53	30	34	64	90	10	3	7	10	81
2009-10	Miami U.	CCHA	42	6	21	27	88	....	....	....	....	....
2010-11	Miami U.	CCHA	37	7	5	12	57	....	....	....	....	....

McNABB, Brayden (muhk-NAB, BRAY-duhn) BUF

Defense. Shoots left. 6'5", 212 lbs. Born, Saskatoon, Sask., January 21, 1991.
(Buffalo's 2nd choice, 66th overall, in 2009 Entry Draft).

			Regular Season					Playoffs				
Season	Club	League	GP	G	A	Pts	PIM	GP	G	A	Pts	PIM
2006-07	Notre Dame	SMHL	41	5	13	18	72	....	....	....	....	....
	Kootenay Ice	WHL	3	0	0	0	0	....	....	....	....	....
2007-08	Kootenay Ice	WHL	65	2	9	11	63	10	0	1	1	10
2008-09	Kootenay Ice	WHL	67	10	26	36	140	4	0	5	5	2
2009-10	Kootenay Ice	WHL	64	17	40	57	121	6	0	4	4	18
2010-11	Kootenay Ice	WHL	59	21	51	72	95	19	3	*24	27	37

WHL East First All-Star Team (2010, 2011)

McNALLY, Patrick (muhk-NAL-ee, PAT-rihk) VAN

Defense. Shoots left. 6'2", 180 lbs. Born, Glen Head, NY, December 4, 1991.
(Vancouver's 1st choice, 115th overall, in 2010 Entry Draft).

			Regular Season					Playoffs				
Season	Club	League	GP	G	A	Pts	PIM	GP	G	A	Pts	PIM
2008-09	Suffolk PAL S.S.	MtJHL	52	25	41	66	72	....	....	....	....	....
2009-10	Milton Academy	High-MA	28	14	21	35	....	....	....	....	....	....
2010-11	Milton Academy	High-MA	STATISTICS NOT AVAILABLE									

• Signed Letter of Intent to attend **Harvard University** (ECAC) in fall of 2011.

McNAUGHT, Randy (muhk-NAWT, RAN-dee) NYR

Right wing. Shoots right. 6'4", 217 lbs. Born, Nanaimo, B.C., August 5, 1990.
(NY Rangers' 6th choice, 190th overall, in 2010 Entry Draft).

			Regular Season					Playoffs				
Season	Club	League	GP	G	A	Pts	PIM	GP	G	A	Pts	PIM
2006-07	Nanaimo Clippers	BCHL	39	3	4	7	59	2	0	0	0	4
2007-08	Nanaimo Clippers	BCHL	25	2	3	5	54	....	....	....	....	....
	Chilliwack Bruins	WHL	30	3	1	4	53	4	0	0	0	2
2008-09	Chilliwack Bruins	WHL	51	5	4	9	78	....	....	....	....	....
2009-10	Chilliwack Bruins	WHL	6	0	0	0	32	....	....	....	....	....
	Saskatoon Blades	WHL	59	6	6	12	131	5	0	0	0	11
2010-11	Vancouver Giants	WHL	8	1	1	2	27	....	....	....	....	....

McNEELY, Tyler (muhk-NEE-lee, TIGH-luhr) NYI

Left wing. Shoots left. 5'10", 165 lbs. Born, Burnaby, B.C., April 8, 1987.

			Regular Season					Playoffs				
Season	Club	League	GP	G	A	Pts	PIM	GP	G	A	Pts	PIM
2003-04	Surrey Eagles	BCHL	3	0	0	0	2	2	0	0	0	5
2004-05	Coquitlam Express	BCHL	46	12	19	31	79	6	2	3	5	2
2005-06	Burnaby Express	BCHL	60	30	50	80	93	20	13	24	37	16
2006-07	Burnaby Express	BCHL	52	32	72	104	85	9	5	14	19	11
2007-08	Northeastern	H-East	37	11	12	23	36	....	....	....	....	....
2008-09	Northeastern	H-East	34	8	12	20	71	....	....	....	....	....
2009-10	Northeastern	H-East	33	12	16	28	42	....	....	....	....	....
2010-11	Northeastern	H-East	38	13	21	34	52	....	....	....	....	....
	Bridgeport	AHL	10	5	6	11	4	....	....	....	....	....

Signed to a ATO (amateur tryout) contract by **Bridgeport** (AHL), March 24, 2011. Signed as a free agent by **NY Islanders**, April 20, 2011.

McNEILL, Mark (muhk-NEEL, MAHRK) CHI

Center. Shoots right. 6'1", 211 lbs. Born, Langley, B.C., February 22, 1993.
(Chicago's 1st choice, 18th overall, in 2011 Entry Draft).

			Regular Season					Playoffs				
Season	Club	League	GP	G	A	Pts	PIM	GP	G	A	Pts	PIM
2008-09	SSAC Athletics	AMHL	33	21	18	39	38	4	2	0	2	2
	Prince Albert	WHL	4	0	0	0	0	....	....	....	....	....
2009-10	Prince Albert	WHL	68	9	15	24	27	....	....	....	....	....
2010-11	Prince Albert	WHL	70	32	49	81	53	6	2	3	5	2

McNEILL, Patrick (muhk-NEEL, PAT-rihk) WSH

Defense. Shoots left. 6', 198 lbs. Born, Strathroy, Ont., March 17, 1987.
(Washington's 4th choice, 118th overall, in 2005 Entry Draft).

			Regular Season					Playoffs				
Season	Club	League	GP	G	A	Pts	PIM	GP	G	A	Pts	PIM
2002-03	Strathroy Rockets	ON-Jr.B	45	6	13	19	53	....	....	....	....	....
2003-04	Saginaw Spirit	OHL	57	3	11	14	28	....	....	....	....	....
2004-05	Saginaw Spirit	OHL	66	7	26	33	31	....	....	....	....	....
2005-06	Saginaw Spirit	OHL	68	21	56	77	64	4	1	3	4	6
2006-07	Saginaw Spirit	OHL	58	22	36	58	49	6	3	2	5	6
2007-08	Hershey Bears	AHL	48	1	13	14	16	2	0	0	0	0
	South Carolina	ECHL	19	5	11	16	16	5	0	2	2	4
2008-09	Hershey Bears	AHL	46	3	15	18	20	10	0	3	3	4
2009-10	Hershey Bears	AHL	62	8	27	35	36	11	3	3	6	2
2010-11	Hershey Bears	AHL	51	7	20	27	30	6	1	2	3	4

OHL Second All-Star Team (2006)

McNEILL, Reid   (muhk-NEEL, REED)   PIT

Defense. Shoots left. 6'4", 201 lbs.   Born, London, Ont., April 29, 1992.
(Pittsburgh's 6th choice, 170th overall, in 2010 Entry Draft).

			Regular Season						Playoffs			
Season	Club	League	GP	G	A	Pts	PIM	GP	G	A	Pts	PIM
2008-09	Lambeth Lancers	ON-Jr.D	16	0	4	4	12	....	....	....	....	....
	Lucas High School	High-ON		STATISTICS NOT AVAILABLE								
2009-10	London Nationals	ON-Jr.B	20	0	7	7	6	....	....	....	....	....
	London Knights	OHL	53	2	3	5	32	12	0	1	1	0
2010-11	London Knights	OHL	62	2	4	6	70	6	0	0	0	4

McNICOLL, Cedric   (mihk-NIH-kohl, SEH-DRIHK)   CAR

Center. Shoots left. 5'10", 180 lbs.   Born, Longueuil, Que., August 28, 1988.

			Regular Season						Playoffs			
Season	Club	League	GP	G	A	Pts	PIM	GP	G	A	Pts	PIM
2004-05	C.C. Lemoyne	QAAA	41	20	24	44	30	4	2	2	4	21
	Shawinigan	QMJHL	1	0	1	1	0	1	0	0	0	0
2005-06	Shawinigan	QMJHL	67	13	17	30	34	10	1	7	8	2
2006-07	Shawinigan	QMJHL	47	16	30	46	14	4	4	1	5	0
2007-08	Shawinigan	QMJHL	69	43	40	83	20	5	0	8	8	6
2008-09	Shawinigan	QMJHL	65	38	66	104	22	21	16	17	33	6
2009-10	Lake Erie Monsters	AHL	45	5	8	13	10	....	....	....	....	....
	Charlotte	ECHL	3	1	3	4	0	....	....	....	....	....
	Albany River Rats	AHL	7	2	0	2	0	....	....	....	....	....
	Florida Everblades	ECHL	5	1	3	4	0	6	0	2	2	0
2010-11	Charlotte	AHL	15	6	8	14	2	....	....	....	....	....
	Florida Everblades	ECHL	29	7	17	24	8	....	....	....	....	....

QMJHL First All-Star Team (2009) • Canadian Major Junior Second All-Star Team (2009) • Canadian Major Junior Sportsman of the Year (2008, 2009)

Signed as a free agent by **Colorado**, March 6, 2009. Traded to **Carolina** by **Colorado** with Colorado's 6th round choice (Tyler Stahl) in 2010 Entry Draft for Stephane Yelle and Harrison Reed, March 3, 2010.

McPHERSON, Corbin   (muhk-FUHR-suhn, KOHR-bihn)   N.J.

Defense. Shoots right. 6'4", 215 lbs.   Born, Folsom, CA, September 7, 1988.
(New Jersey's 3rd choice, 87th overall, in 2007 Entry Draft).

			Regular Season						Playoffs			
Season	Club	League	GP	G	A	Pts	PIM	GP	G	A	Pts	PIM
2005-06	San Jose Jr. Sharks	Minor-CA	59	5	16	21	45	....	....	....	....	....
2006-07	Cowichan Valley	BCHL	44	4	10	14	63	18	1	3	4	14
2007-08	Cowichan Valley	BCHL	55	3	14	17	84	....	....	....	....	....
2008-09	Colgate	ECAC	37	0	5	5	50	....	....	....	....	....
2009-10	Colgate	ECAC	35	2	6	8	20	....	....	....	....	....
2010-11	Colgate	ECAC	41	4	6	10	36	....	....	....	....	....

MECKLER, David   (MEHK-luhr, DAY-vihd)   L.A.

Center. Shoots right. 5'11", 204 lbs.   Born, Highland Park, IL, July 9, 1987.
(Los Angeles' 7th choice, 134th overall, in 2006 Entry Draft).

			Regular Season						Playoffs			
Season	Club	League	GP	G	A	Pts	PIM	GP	G	A	Pts	PIM
2004-05	Waterloo	USHL	60	30	15	45	32	5	3	2	5	2
2005-06	Yale	ECAC	31	7	3	10	28	....	....	....	....	....
2006-07	London Knights	OHL	67	38	35	73	53	16	*15	7	22	20
2007-08	Manchester	AHL	76	23	13	36	24	4	1	1	2	2
2008-09	Manchester	AHL	74	14	15	29	28	....	....	....	....	....
2009-10	Manchester	AHL	73	11	9	20	22	14	1	0	1	2
2010-11	Manchester	AHL	75	16	17	33	28	7	2	0	2	0

MEDVEC, Kyle   (MEHD-vek, KIGHL)   MIN

Defense. Shoots left. 6'5", 191 lbs.   Born, Westminster, CO, June 16, 1988.
(Minnesota's 4th choice, 102nd overall, in 2006 Entry Draft).

			Regular Season						Playoffs			
Season	Club	League	GP	G	A	Pts	PIM	GP	G	A	Pts	PIM
2003-04	Apple Valley	High-MN	27	1	12	13	30	....	....	....	....	....
2004-05	Apple Valley	High-MN	23	4	16	20	18	....	....	....	....	....
2005-06	Apple Valley	High-MN	28	13	22	35	44	....	....	....	....	....
	Sioux City	USHL	3	0	0	0	0	....	....	....	....	....
2006-07	Sioux City	USHL	57	4	14	18	83	7	0	0	0	4
2007-08	U. of Vermont	H-East	30	1	4	5	18	....	....	....	....	....
2008-09	U. of Vermont	H-East	39	2	10	12	40	....	....	....	....	....
2009-10	U. of Vermont	H-East	39	5	10	15	50	....	....	....	....	....
2010-11	U. of Vermont	H-East	29	2	4	6	28	....	....	....	....	....

MEGALINSKY, Dmitri   (meh-gahl-IHN-skee, dih-MEE-tree)   OTT

Defense. Shoots left. 6'2", 212 lbs.   Born, Perm, USSR, April 15, 1985.
(Ottawa's 7th choice, 186th overall, in 2005 Entry Draft).

			Regular Season						Playoffs			
Season	Club	League	GP	G	A	Pts	PIM	GP	G	A	Pts	PIM
2003-04	HK Voronezh	Russia-2	42	4	8	12	159	....	....	....	....	....
	Yaroslavl	Russia	1	0	0	0	0	....	....	....	....	....
	Yaroslavl 2	Russia-3	11	0	4	4	16	....	....	....	....	....
2004-05	Yaroslavl	Russia	1	0	0	0	2	....	....	....	....	....
	Yaroslavl 2	Russia-3	30	6	12	18	82	....	....	....	....	....
2005-06	Yaroslavl 2	Russia-3	12	4	10	14	6	....	....	....	....	....
	Yaroslavl	Russia	20	0	1	1	8	8	0	0	0	6
2006-07	Khimik	Russia-2	33	4	7	11	34	7	0	1	1	16
2007-08	Vityaz Chekhov	Russia	25	2	7	9	20	....	....	....	....	....
2008-09	Vityaz Chekhov	Rus-KHL	52	2	5	7	72	....	....	....	....	....
2009-10	Vityaz Chekhov	Rus-KHL	52	4	16	20	98	....	....	....	....	....
2010-11	Vityaz Chekhov	Rus-KHL	27	0	3	3	18	....	....	....	....	....

MEGAN, Wade   (MEE-guhn, WAYD)   FLA

Center. Shoots left. 6'1", 185 lbs.   Born, Canton, NY, July 22, 1990.
(Florida's 6th choice, 138th overall, in 2009 Entry Draft).

			Regular Season						Playoffs			
Season	Club	League	GP	G	A	Pts	PIM	GP	G	A	Pts	PIM
2007-08	Kent Prep School	High-CT	34	24	29	53	....	....	....	....	....	....
2008-09	Kent Prep School	High-CT	32	27	36	63	18	....	....	....	....	....
	Neponset Valley	Minor-MA	16	8	8	16		....	....	....	....	....
2009-10	Boston University	H-East	35	5	7	12	22	....	....	....	....	....
2010-11	Boston University	H-East	39	8	5	13	32	....	....	....	....	....

MELCHIORI, Julian   (mehl-KEE-awr-ee, JOO-lee-ehn)   WPG

Defense. Shoots left. 6'4", 210 lbs.   Born, Richmond Hill, Ont., December 6, 1991.
(Atlanta's 2nd choice, 87th overall, in 2010 Entry Draft).

			Regular Season						Playoffs			
Season	Club	League	GP	G	A	Pts	PIM	GP	G	A	Pts	PIM
2007-08	Toronto Marlboros	GTHL	43	2	13	15	36	....	....	....	....	....
2008-09	Newmarket	ON-Jr.A	48	2	20	22	34	9	1	2	3	14
2009-10	Newmarket	ON-Jr.A	39	7	16	23	16	20	2	9	11	10
2010-11	Kitchener Rangers	OHL	63	1	18	19	55	3	0	0	0	0

MELYAKOV, Igor   (mehl-yuh-KAHF, EE-gohr)   L.A.

Left wing. Shoots left. 5'10", 200 lbs.   Born, Lipetsk, USSR, December 23, 1976.
(Los Angeles' 6th choice, 137th overall, in 1995 Entry Draft).

			Regular Season						Playoffs			
Season	Club	League	GP	G	A	Pts	PIM	GP	G	A	Pts	PIM
1993-94	Torpedo Yaroslavl	CIS	39	4	3	7	10	4	0	0	0	0
1994-95	Torpedo Yaroslavl	CIS	50	6	8	14	34	4	0	1	1	0
1995-96	Torpedo Yaroslavl	CIS	39	5	1	6	6	3	0	0	0	2
1996-97	Torpedo Yaroslavl	Russia	8	0	0	0	0	....	....	....	....	....
	Nizhny Novgorod	Russia	12	2	3	5	10	....	....	....	....	....
1997-98	Nizhny Novgorod	Russia	13	3	3	6	6	....	....	....	....	....
1998-99	Nizhny Novgorod	Russia-2	36	13	17	30	14	....	....	....	....	....
99-2000	Nizhny Novgorod	Russia	34	1	8	9	10	5	1	0	1	4
2000-01	Nizhny Novgorod	Russia	24	2	3	5	10	....	....	....	....	....
2001-02	HK Lipetsk	Russia-2	68	16	37	53	94	....	....	....	....	....
2002-03	Voskresensk	Russia-2	48	9	22	31	16	....	....	....	....	....
2003-04	Nizhny Novgorod	Russia	45	5	10	15	18	....	....	....	....	....
	Nizh. Novgorod 2	Russia-3	4	1	6	7	4	....	....	....	....	....
2004-05	Nizhny Novgorod	Russia-2	52	14	30	44	32	11	2	4	6	18
2005-06	Magnitogorsk	Russia	25	7	8	15	10	3	0	0	0	2
2006-07	Novokuznetsk	Russia	22	0	1	1	8	....	....	....	....	....
	Nizhny Novgorod	Russia-2	16	2	6	8	10	12	2	5	7	6
2007-08	Nizhny Novgorod	Russia	8	1	0	1	6	....	....	....	....	....
	Zauralje Kurgan	Russia-2	24	2	11	13	38	....	....	....	....	....
2008-09	Zauralje Kurgan	Russia-2	46	3	22	25	32	....	....	....	....	....
2009-10	Titan Klin	Russia-2	54	10	25	35	30	13	2	2	4	6
2010-11	Titan Klin	Russia-3	42	7	15	22	26	....	....	....	....	....

MERRILL, Jonathon   (MAIR-ihl, JAWN-ah-thuhn)   N.J.

Defense. Shoots left. 6'3", 210 lbs.   Born, Oklahoma City, OK, February 3, 1992.
(New Jersey's 1st choice, 38th overall, in 2010 Entry Draft).

			Regular Season						Playoffs			
Season	Club	League	GP	G	A	Pts	PIM	GP	G	A	Pts	PIM
2007-08	Det. Caesars	MWEHL	25	2	9	11	26	....	....	....	....	....
	Little Caesars	Minor-MI	....	7	21	28	....	....	....	....	....	....
2008-09	USNTDP	NAHL	26	2	2	4	14	....	....	....	....	....
	USNTDP	U-17	8	0	1	1	6	....	....	....	....	....
	USNTDP	U-18	9	1	2	3	4	....	....	....	....	....
2009-10	USNTDP	USHL	22	1	8	9	12	....	....	....	....	....
	USNTDP	U-18	34	4	19	23	6	....	....	....	....	....
2010-11	U. of Michigan	CCHA	42	7	18	25	16	....	....	....	....	....

CCHA All-Rookie Team (2011)

MERSCH, Michael   (MUHRSH, MIGH-kuhl)   L.A.

Left wing. Shoots left. 6'2", 198 lbs.   Born, Park Ridge, IL, October 2, 1992.
(Los Angeles' 4th choice, 110th overall, in 2011 Entry Draft).

			Regular Season						Playoffs			
Season	Club	League	GP	G	A	Pts	PIM	GP	G	A	Pts	PIM
2007-08	Team Illinois	MWEHL	31	13	16	29	46	....	....	....	....	....
	Team Illinois	Exhib.	....	22	24	46	29	....	....	....	....	....
2008-09	USNTDP	NAHL	42	15	13	28	50	9	5	2	7	4
	USNTDP	U-17	14	7	4	11	4	....	....	....	....	....
2009-10	USNTDP	USHL	26	4	4	8	22	....	....	....	....	....
	USNTDP	U-18	23	0	6	6	8	....	....	....	....	....
2010-11	U. of Wisconsin	WCHA	41	8	11	19	32	....	....	....	....	....

MEURS, Garrett   (MEWRZ, GAIR-eht)   COL

Center. Shoots right. 5'11", 169 lbs.   Born, Wingham, Ont., January 12, 1993.
(Colorado's 4th choice, 123rd overall, in 2011 Entry Draft).

			Regular Season						Playoffs			
Season	Club	League	GP	G	A	Pts	PIM	GP	G	A	Pts	PIM
2008-09	Huron-Perth	Minor-ON	67	52	43	95	67	....	....	....	....	....
2009-10	Plymouth Whalers	OHL	62	16	18	34	22	9	1	2	3	0
2010-11	Plymouth Whalers	OHL	68	10	31	41	61	11	1	2	3	8

MEYERS, Josh   (MIGH-uhrs, JAWSH)

Defense. Shoots right. 6'2", 180 lbs.   Born, Alexandria, MN, December 7, 1985.
(Los Angeles' 7th choice, 206th overall, in 2005 Entry Draft).

			Regular Season						Playoffs			
Season	Club	League	GP	G	A	Pts	PIM	GP	G	A	Pts	PIM
2003-04	Minnesota Blizzard	NAHL	27	2	12	14		....	....	....	....	....
2004-05	Sioux City	USHL	57	8	24	32	92	13	1	9	10	18
2005-06	U. Minn-Duluth	WCHA	27	3	7	10	20	....	....	....	....	....
2006-07	U. Minn-Duluth	WCHA	37	11	13	24	30	....	....	....	....	....
2007-08	U. Minn-Duluth	WCHA	36	6	8	14	72	....	....	....	....	....
2008-09	U. Minn-Duluth	WCHA	43	10	18	28	42	....	....	....	....	....
2009-10	Abbotsford Heat	AHL	54	3	15	18	28	11	1	0	1	13
	Utah Grizzlies	ECHL	12	0	3	3	2	....	....	....	....	....
2010-11	Abbotsford Heat	AHL	49	3	8	11	39	....	....	....	....	....
	Utah Grizzlies	ECHL	2	0	1	1	2	....	....	....	....	....

Signed as a free agent by **Abbotsford** (AHL), October 2, 2009.

MICFLIKIER, Jacob (mihk-FLIH-kuhr, JAY-kuhb) WSH

Left wing. Shoots left. 5'8", 180 lbs. Born, Winnipeg, Man., July 11, 1984.

			Regular Season					Playoffs				
Season	Club	League	GP	G	A	Pts	PIM	GP	G	A	Pts	PIM
2001-02	Sioux Falls	USHL	61	24	20	44	30	3	0	0	0	6
2002-03	Sioux Falls	USHL	59	31	36	67	26	....	....	....	....	....
2003-04	New Hampshire	H-East	39	11	15	26	24	....	....	....	....	....
2004-05	New Hampshire	H-East	42	20	24	44	44	....	....	....	....	....
2005-06	New Hampshire	H-East	37	16	26	42	52	....	....	....	....	....
2006-07	New Hampshire	H-East	36	11	27	38	37	....	....	....	....	....
	Springfield Falcons	AHL	9	3	1	4	4	....	....	....	....	....
2007-08	Springfield Falcons	AHL	8	1	4	5	0	....	....	....	....	....
	Stockton Thunder	ECHL	29	10	27	37	29	6	4	9	13	10
2008-09	Rochester	AHL	39	4	12	16	12	....	....	....	....	....
	Florida Everblades	ECHL	10	10	14	24	21	6	2	2	4	8
2009-10	Albany River Rats	AHL	59	18	22	40	30	7	1	1	2	2
	Florida Everblades	ECHL	16	9	23	32	15	....	....	....	....	....
2010-11	Charlotte	AHL	78	29	32	61	80	14	0	3	3	6

Signed as a free agent by **Washington**, July 14, 2011.

MIELE, Andy (MEE-lee, AN-dee) PHX

Left wing. Shoots left. 5'9", 180 lbs. Born, Grosse Pointe Woods, MI, April 15, 1988.

			Regular Season					Playoffs				
Season	Club	League	GP	G	A	Pts	PIM	GP	G	A	Pts	PIM
2005-06	Cedar Rapids	USHL	52	10	17	27	41	8	0	4	4	4
2006-07	Cedar Rapids	USHL	13	7	8	15	15	....	....	....	....	....
	Chicago Steel	USHL	45	13	29	42	70	4	2	4	6	14
2007-08	Chicago Steel	USHL	29	30	11	41	78	....	....	....	....	....
	Miami U.	CCHA	18	6	8	14	4	....	....	....	....	....
2008-09	Miami U.	CCHA	41	15	16	31	34	....	....	....	....	....
2009-10	Miami U.	CCHA	43	15	29	44	61	....	....	....	....	....
2010-11	Miami U.	CCHA	39	24	*47	*71	35	....	....	....	....	....

CCHA Second All-Star Team (2010) • CCHA Player of the Year (2011) • NCAA West First All-American Team (2011) • Hobey Baker Memorial Award (Top U.S. Collegiate Player) (2011)

Signed as a free agent by **Phoenix**, April 2, 2011.

MIKUS, Juraj (MEE-kuhsh, YUHR-ay) TOR

Defense. Shoots left. 6'4", 210 lbs. Born, Trencin, Czech., November 30, 1988.
(Toronto's 4th choice, 134th overall, in 2007 Entry Draft).

			Regular Season					Playoffs				
Season	Club	League	GP	G	A	Pts	PIM	GP	G	A	Pts	PIM
2004-05	Piestany U18	Svk-U18	2	1	2	3	2	....	....	....	....	....
	Dukla Trencin U18	Svk-U18	39	2	7	9	20	5	0	0	0	0
2005-06	Piestany Jr.	Slovak-Jr.	6	0	4	4	2	....	....	....	....	....
	Dukla Trencin Jr.	Slovak-Jr.	17	1	4	5	2	....	....	....	....	....
	Dukla Trencin U18	Svk-U18	40	3	18	21	36	7	1	5	6	12
2006-07	Dukla Trencin Jr.	Slovak-Jr.	42	9	15	24	72	7	2	1	3	10
	P. Bystrica	Slovak-2	7	0	3	3	2	1	0	0	0	0
	Dukla Trencin	Slovakia	22	0	0	0	2	7	0	0	0	0
2007-08	HK VSR SR 20	Slovakia	21	1	4	5	30	....	....	....	....	....
	Dukla Trencin	Slovakia	14	0	3	3	4	14	0	1	1	2
2008-09	HC Dukla Senica	Slovak-2	9	1	1	2	4	1	0	0	0	0
	Dukla Trencin	Slovakia	51	2	1	3	18	4	2	0	2	0
	Dukla Trencin Jr.	Slovak-Jr.	....	....	....	....	....	2	0	0	0	2
2009-10	Toronto Marlies	AHL	68	5	18	23	38	....	....	....	....	....
2010-11	Toronto Marlies	AHL	56	4	12	16	14	....	....	....	....	....

MILLER, J.T. (MIHL-luhr, JAY-TEE) NYR

Center. Shoots left. 6'1", 189 lbs. Born, East Palestine, OH, March 14, 1993.
(NY Rangers' 1st choice, 15th overall, in 2011 Entry Draft).

			Regular Season					Playoffs				
Season	Club	League	GP	G	A	Pts	PIM	GP	G	A	Pts	PIM
2008-09	Pittsburgh Hornets	T1EHL	45	21	21	42	76	....	....	....	....	....
2009-10	USNTDP	USHL	29	5	7	12	32	....	....	....	....	....
	USNTDP	U-17	17	10	9	19	47	....	....	....	....	....
	USNTDP	U-18	1	0	0	0	0	....	....	....	....	....
2010-11	USNTDP	USHL	21	3	12	15	48	....	....	....	....	....
	USNTDP	U-18	35	12	23	35	38	....	....	....	....	....

MIRNOV, Igor (mihr-NAWF, EE-gohr) OTT

Left wing. Shoots left. 6', 187 lbs. Born, Chita, USSR, September 19, 1984.
(Ottawa's 2nd choice, 67th overall, in 2003 Entry Draft).

			Regular Season					Playoffs				
Season	Club	League	GP	G	A	Pts	PIM	GP	G	A	Pts	PIM
2001-02	Dyn'o Moscow 2	Russia-3	30	33	17	50	34	....	....	....	....	....
	Dynamo Moscow	Russia	6	0	0	0	0	....	....	....	....	....
2002-03	Dynamo Moscow	Russia	50	3	7	10	49	5	0	0	0	2
2003-04	Dynamo Moscow	Russia	53	11	10	21	26	3	0	0	0	2
2004-05	Dynamo Moscow	Russia	55	13	13	26	50	9	2	4	6	0
2005-06	Dynamo Moscow	Russia	32	8	10	18	36	4	0	2	2	4
2006-07	Dynamo Moscow	Russia	49	21	25	46	54	3	2	1	3	4
2007-08	Dynamo Moscow	Russia	24	3	3	6	16	....	....	....	....	....
	Magnitogorsk	Russia	23	9	6	15	20	13	3	1	4	4
2008-09	Magnitogorsk	Rus-KHL	39	11	8	19	24	11	2	7	9	8
2009-10	Mytischi	Rus-KHL	20	2	4	6	0	....	....	....	....	....
	MVD	Rus-KHL	10	1	3	4	4	....	....	....	....	....
	Sibir Novosibirsk	Rus-KHL	12	7	5	12	8	....	....	....	....	....
2010-11	Sibir Novosibirsk	Rus-KHL	53	16	25	41	30	4	0	2	2	2

MISKOVIC, Zach (MIHS-koh-vihch, ZAK) WSH

Defense. Shoots right. 6'1", 190 lbs. Born, River Forest, IL, May 8, 1985.

			Regular Season					Playoffs				
Season	Club	League	GP	G	A	Pts	PIM	GP	G	A	Pts	PIM
2002-03	Cedar Rapids	USHL	60	2	6	8	91	7	0	0	0	12
2003-04	Cedar Rapids	USHL	60	6	15	21	139	4	1	1	2	2
2004-05	Cedar Rapids	USHL	60	4	16	20	149	8	1	0	1	14
2005-06	St. Lawrence	ECAC	40	1	15	16	30	....	....	....	....	....
2006-07	St. Lawrence	ECAC	39	2	10	12	48	....	....	....	....	....
2007-08	St. Lawrence	ECAC	37	8	12	20	36	....	....	....	....	....
2008-09	St. Lawrence	ECAC	38	16	9	25	32	....	....	....	....	....
2009-10	Hershey Bears	AHL	59	6	20	26	25	6	1	1	2	0
2010-11	Hershey Bears	AHL	58	7	9	16	58	5	0	0	0	8

ECAC First All-Star Team (2009) • NCAA East First All-American Team (2009)

Signed as a free agent by **Washington**, March 25, 2009.

MITCHELL, Dale (MIH-chuhl, DAYL) TOR

Right wing. Shoots right. 5'9", 200 lbs. Born, Etobicoke, Ont., April 9, 1989.
(Toronto's 1st choice, 74th overall, in 2007 Entry Draft).

			Regular Season					Playoffs				
Season	Club	League	GP	G	A	Pts	PIM	GP	G	A	Pts	PIM
2005-06	Oshawa Generals	OHL	65	20	23	43	63	....	....	....	....	....
2006-07	Oshawa Generals	OHL	67	43	37	80	81	9	1	4	5	12
2007-08	Oshawa Generals	OHL	63	24	36	60	79	15	10	6	16	23
	Toronto Marlies	AHL	....	....	....	....	....	2	0	1	1	2
2008-09	Windsor Spitfires	OHL	66	33	35	68	87	20	14	15	29	24
2009-10	Windsor Spitfires	OHL	32	16	27	43	44	19	7	10	17	16
	Toronto Marlies	AHL	9	2	1	3	2	....	....	....	....	....
2010-11	Toronto Marlies	AHL	49	5	8	13	29	....	....	....	....	....
	Reading Royals	ECHL	5	2	2	4	14	2	0	0	0	0

MITCHELL, Garrett (MIH-chuhl, GAIR-reht) WSH

Right wing. Shoots right. 5'10", 180 lbs. Born, Regina, Sask., September 2, 1991.
(Washington's 6th choice, 175th overall, in 2009 Entry Draft).

			Regular Season					Playoffs				
Season	Club	League	GP	G	A	Pts	PIM	GP	G	A	Pts	PIM
2006-07	Reg. Pat Cdns.	SMHL	42	14	11	25	140	....	....	....	....	....
	Regina Pats	WHL	4	0	1	1	2	....	....	....	....	....
2007-08	Regina Pats	WHL	62	8	5	13	73	6	1	0	1	6
2008-09	Regina Pats	WHL	71	10	5	15	140	....	....	....	....	....
2009-10	Regina Pats	WHL	57	15	16	31	110	....	....	....	....	....
	Hershey Bears	AHL	1	0	0	0	0	....	....	....	....	....
2010-11	Regina Pats	WHL	70	18	34	52	140	....	....	....	....	....
	Hershey Bears	AHL	2	0	0	0	5	....	....	....	....	....

MITERA, Mark (MIH-tair-a, MAHRK) MTL

Defense. Shoots left. 6'3", 213 lbs. Born, Royal Oak, MI, October 22, 1987.
(Anaheim's 1st choice, 19th overall, in 2006 Entry Draft).

			Regular Season					Playoffs				
Season	Club	League	GP	G	A	Pts	PIM	GP	G	A	Pts	PIM
2003-04	USNTDP	U-17	16	2	6	8	22	....	....	....	....	....
	USNTDP	NAHL	43	2	13	15	69	7	0	2	2	10
2004-05	USNTDP	U-18	45	5	10	15	91	....	....	....	....	....
	USNTDP	NAHL	16	2	6	8	32	....	....	....	....	....
2005-06	U. of Michigan	CCHA	39	0	10	10	59	....	....	....	....	....
2006-07	U. of Michigan	CCHA	41	1	17	18	52	....	....	....	....	....
2007-08	U. of Michigan	CCHA	43	2	21	23	60	....	....	....	....	....
2008-09	U. of Michigan	CCHA	8	1	2	3	4	....	....	....	....	....
	Iowa Chops	AHL	5	0	2	2	2	....	....	....	....	....
2009-10	San Antonio	AHL	5	0	0	0	6	....	....	....	....	....
	Abbotsford Heat	AHL	27	0	3	3	12	13	0	2	2	9
	Bakersfield	ECHL	36	3	11	14	62	....	....	....	....	....
2010-11	Syracuse Crunch	AHL	71	6	16	22	50	....	....	....	....	....

CCHA Second All-Star Team (2008)

Traded to **Montreal** by **Anaheim** for Mathieu Carle, July 15, 2011.

MOFFATT, Luke (MAW-fuht, LEWK) COL

Center. Shoots right. 6'1", 187 lbs. Born, Scottsdale, AZ, June 11, 1992.
(Colorado's 8th choice, 197th overall, in 2010 Entry Draft).

			Regular Season					Playoffs				
Season	Club	League	GP	G	A	Pts	PIM	GP	G	A	Pts	PIM
2007-08	Det. Compuware	MWEHL	30	37	19	56	....	....	....	....	....	....
	Det. Compuware	Minor-MI	5	4	1	5	4	....	....	....	....	....
2008-09	USNTDP	NAHL	42	17	10	27	30	9	0	3	3	4
	USNTDP	U-17	16	4	7	11	2	....	....	....	....	....
2009-10	USNTDP	USHL	28	5	10	15	22	....	....	....	....	....
	USNTDP	U-18	37	13	9	22	14	....	....	....	....	....
2010-11	U. of Michigan	CCHA	36	5	8	13	12	....	....	....	....	....

MOFFIE, Lee (MAW-fee, LEE) S.J.

Defense. Shoots left. 6'1", 205 lbs. Born, Wallingford, CT, August 29, 1990.
(San Jose's 7th choice, 188th overall, in 2010 Entry Draft).

			Regular Season					Playoffs				
Season	Club	League	GP	G	A	Pts	PIM	GP	G	A	Pts	PIM
2008-09	Waterloo	USHL	55	9	35	44	97	3	0	0	0	6
2009-10	U. of Michigan	CCHA	29	4	8	12	27	....	....	....	....	....
2010-11	U. of Michigan	CCHA	32	8	9	17	16	....	....	....	....	....

MOLIN, Emil (moh-LEEN, eh-MIHL) DAL

Right wing. Shoots left. 6', 170 lbs. Born, Gavle, Sweden, February 3, 1993.
(Dallas' 3rd choice, 105th overall, in 2011 Entry Draft).

			Regular Season					Playoffs				
Season	Club	League	GP	G	A	Pts	PIM	GP	G	A	Pts	PIM
2009-10	Brynas U18	Swe-U18	38	22	35	57	24	4	2	6	8	0
2010-11	Brynas U18	Swe-U18	36	31	50	81	60	5	3	5	8	0
	Brynas IF Gavle Jr.	Swe-Jr.	9	0	1	1	2	1	0	0	0	0

MONTGOMERY, Kevin (mawnt-GUHM-uhr-ee, KEH-vihn) EDM

Defense. Shoots left. 6'1", 185 lbs. Born, Rochester, NY, April 4, 1988.
(Colorado's 5th choice, 110th overall, in 2006 Entry Draft).

			Regular Season					Playoffs				
Season	Club	League	GP	G	A	Pts	PIM	GP	G	A	Pts	PIM
2003-04	Syracuse Jr. Stars	EmJHL	62	7	28	35	....	....	....	....	....	....
2004-05	USNTDP	U-17	8	1	4	5	4	....	....	....	....	....
	USNTDP	NAHL	38	4	12	16	46	9	1	3	4	6
2005-06	USNTDP	U-18	42	2	10	12	61	....	....	....	....	....
	USNTDP	NAHL	17	4	6	10	15	....	....	....	....	....
2006-07	Ohio State	CCHA	17	1	4	5	18	....	....	....	....	....
	London Knights	OHL	31	1	16	17	50	9	0	0	0	6
2007-08	London Knights	OHL	63	9	34	43	95	5	0	1	1	4
	Lake Erie Monsters	AHL	5	0	0	0	2	....	....	....	....	....
2008-09	London Knights	OHL	46	2	34	36	41	14	0	4	4	6
	Lake Erie Monsters	AHL	5	0	1	1	2	....	....	....	....	....
2009-10	Lake Erie Monsters	AHL	65	1	6	7	37	....	....	....	....	....
2010-11	Lake Erie Monsters	AHL	51	2	17	19	34	....	....	....	....	....
	Oklahoma City	AHL	16	2	5	7	12	2	0	0	0	2

Traded to **Edmonton** by **Colorado** for Shawn Belle, February 28, 2011.

MORROW, Joe (MOH-row, JOH) PIT

Defense. Shoots left. 6', 199 lbs. Born, Edmonton, Alta., December 9, 1992.
(Pittsburgh's 1st choice, 23rd overall, in 2011 Entry Draft).

			Regular Season					Playoffs				
Season	Club	League	GP	G	A	Pts	PIM	GP	G	A	Pts	PIM
2006-07	Strathcona	AMBHL	32	16	16	32	75	4	2	3	5	8
2007-08	Sherwood Park	Minor-AB	24	7	11	18	57	....	....	....	....	....
	Portland	WHL	1	0	0	0	0	....	....	....	....	....
2008-09	Portland	WHL	41	0	7	7	26	....	....	....	....	....
2009-10	Portland	WHL	63	7	24	31	59	13	0	2	2	6
2010-11	Portland	WHL	60	9	40	49	67	21	6	14	20	27

MULLEN, Patrick (MUHL-uhn, PA-trihk) L.A.

Defense. Shoots right. 5'11", 180 lbs. Born, Pittsburgh, PA, May 6, 1986.

			Regular Season					Playoffs				
Season	Club	League	GP	G	A	Pts	PIM	GP	G	A	Pts	PIM
2004-05	Sioux City	USHL	60	14	23	37	8	....	....	....	....	....
2005-06	U. of Denver	WCHA	37	7	10	17	24	....	....	....	....	....
2006-07	U. of Denver	WCHA	37	5	12	17	20	....	....	....	....	....
2007-08	U. of Denver	WCHA	40	4	18	22	65	....	....	....	....	....
2008-09	U. of Denver	WCHA	38	4	21	25	39	....	....	....	....	....
2009-10	Manchester	AHL	44	4	6	10	16	2	0	0	0	2
	Ontario Reign	ECHL	1	0	0	0	0	....	....	....	....	....
2010-11	Manchester	AHL	67	3	17	20	32	7	0	1	1	4

Signed as a free agent by **Los Angeles**, April 3, 2009.

MULLIN, Jimmy (MUH-lihn, JIHM-ee) T.B.

Right wing. Shoots right. 5'10", 157 lbs. Born, Philadelphia, PA, February 24, 1992.
(Tampa Bay's 6th choice, 118th overall, in 2010 Entry Draft).

			Regular Season					Playoffs				
Season	Club	League	GP	G	A	Pts	PIM	GP	G	A	Pts	PIM
2006-07	Shattuck Bantam	High-MN	67	24	34	58	24	....	....	....	....	....
2007-08	Shattuck U-16	High-MN	52	20	29	49	32	....	....	....	....	....
2008-09	Shattuck U-16	High-MN	56	62	44	106	38	....	....	....	....	....
2009-10	Shat.-St. Mary's	High-MN	55	32	40	72	26	....	....	....	....	....
2010-11	Fargo Force	USHL	52	23	37	60	26	5	0	0	0	0

USHL First All-Star Team (2011)

• Signed Letter of Intent to attend **Miami University** (CCHA) in fall of 2011.

MURPHY, Connor (MUHR-fee, KAW-nuhr) PHX

Defense. Shoots right. 6'3", 190 lbs. Born, Boston, MA, March 26, 1993.
(Phoenix's 1st choice, 20th overall, in 2011 Entry Draft).

			Regular Season					Playoffs				
Season	Club	League	GP	G	A	Pts	PIM	GP	G	A	Pts	PIM
2008-09	Ohio Blue Jackets	Ind.	35	7	11	18	....	....	....	....	....	....
2009-10	USNTDP	USHL	2	0	0	0	2	....	....	....	....	....
	USNTDP	U-17	6	1	0	1	2	....	....	....	....	....
2010-11	USNTDP	USHL	9	3	1	4	6	....	....	....	....	....
	USNTDP	U-18	13	3	3	6	0	....	....	....	....	....

• Missed majority of 2009-10 and 2010-11 due to a recurring back injury.

MURPHY, Ryan (MUHR-fee, RIGH-uhn) CAR

Defense. Shoots right. 5'11", 176 lbs. Born, Aurora, Ont., March 31, 1993.
(Carolina's 1st choice, 12th overall, in 2011 Entry Draft).

			Regular Season					Playoffs				
Season	Club	League	GP	G	A	Pts	PIM	GP	G	A	Pts	PIM
2008-09	York Simcoe	Minor-ON	73	30	65	95	52	....	....	....	....	....
	Villanova Knights	ON-Jr.A	4	4	2	6	0	....	....	....	....	....
2009-10	Kitchener Rangers	OHL	62	6	33	39	22	20	5	12	17	16
2010-11	Kitchener Rangers	OHL	63	26	53	79	36	7	2	9	11	8

OHL All-Rookie Team (2010) • OHL First All-Star Team (2011)

MUSIL, David (moo-SIHL, DAY-vihd) EDM

Defense. Shoots left. 6'3", 196 lbs. Born, Calgary, AB, Alta., April 9, 1993.
(Edmonton's 3rd choice, 31st overall, in 2011 Entry Draft).

			Regular Season					Playoffs				
Season	Club	League	GP	G	A	Pts	PIM	GP	G	A	Pts	PIM
2005-06	Jihlava U17	CzR-U17	5	0	0	0	0	....	....	....	....	....
2006-07	Jihlava U17	CzR-U17	36	7	23	30	42	....	....	....	....	....
	Trebic U17	CzR-U17	14	1	3	4	26	....	....	....	....	....
2007-08	Jihlava U17	CzR-U17	42	8	27	35	98	3	0	1	1	6
	Jihlava Jr.	CzRep-Jr.	9	0	5	5	6	....	....	....	....	....
2008-09	Jihlava U17	CzR-U17	9	3	3	6	46	....	....	....	....	....
	Jihlava Jr.	CzRep-Jr.	27	9	12	21	46	8	3	3	6	10
	HC Dukla Jihlava	CzRep-2	14	0	1	1	4	4	0	0	0	4
2009-10	Vancouver Giants	WHL	71	7	25	32	67	16	2	2	4	8
2010-11	Vancouver Giants	WHL	62	6	19	25	83	4	0	1	1	2

NAGY, Kory (NAH-gee, KOHR-ee) N.J.

Left wing. Shoots left. 5'11", 195 lbs. Born, London, Ont., October 12, 1989.
(New Jersey's 6th choice, 142nd overall, in 2008 Entry Draft).

			Regular Season					Playoffs				
Season	Club	League	GP	G	A	Pts	PIM	GP	G	A	Pts	PIM
2005-06	Lindsay Muskies	OPJHL	47	11	12	23	14	4	0	0	0	0
	Oshawa Generals	OHL	16	0	1	1	8	....	....	....	....	....
2006-07	Oshawa Generals	OHL	64	0	5	5	18	9	0	0	0	4
2007-08	Oshawa Generals	OHL	57	5	12	17	47	15	6	3	9	4
2008-09	Oshawa Generals	OHL	63	17	38	55	83	....	....	....	....	....
2009-10	Lowell Devils	AHL	31	2	4	6	10	2	0	0	0	2
	Trenton Devils	ECHL	33	4	9	13	27	....	....	....	....	....
2010-11	Albany Devils	AHL	13	0	1	1	8	....	....	....	....	....
	Trenton Devils	ECHL	57	9	13	22	23	....	....	....	....	....

NAMESTNIKOV, Vladislav (nah-MEHST-nih-kawv, vla-dih-SLAHV) T.B.

Center. Shoots left. 5'11", 173 lbs. Born, Zhukovsky, Russia, November 22, 1992.
(Tampa Bay's 1st choice, 27th overall, in 2011 Entry Draft).

			Regular Season					Playoffs				
Season	Club	League	GP	G	A	Pts	PIM	GP	G	A	Pts	PIM
2009-10	Khimik	Russia-2	33	12	9	21	18	2	1	0	1	2
2010-11	London Knights	OHL	68	30	39	69	49	6	1	4	5	6

NASH, Riley (NASH, RIGH-lee) CAR

Center. Shoots right. 6'1", 191 lbs. Born, Consort, Alta., May 9, 1989.
(Edmonton's 3rd choice, 21st overall, in 2007 Entry Draft).

			Regular Season					Playoffs				
Season	Club	League	GP	G	A	Pts	PIM	GP	G	A	Pts	PIM
2005-06	Thompson Blazers	BCMML	31	29	31	60	100	....	....	....	....	....
	Salmon Arm	BCHL	1	0	0	0	0	5	1	2	3	0
2006-07	Salmon Arm	BCHL	55	38	46	84	87	11	4	7	11	31
2007-08	Cornell Big Red	ECAC	36	12	20	32	28	....	....	....	....	....
2008-09	Cornell Big Red	ECAC	36	13	22	35	34	....	....	....	....	....
2009-10	Cornell Big Red	ECAC	30	12	23	35	39	....	....	....	....	....
2010-11	Charlotte	AHL	79	14	18	32	26	16	1	3	4	16

ECAC All-Rookie Team (2008) • ECAC Rookie of the Year (2008) • ECAC First All-Star Team (2009)

Traded to **Carolina** by **Edmonton** for Ottawa's 2nd round choice (previously acquired, Edmonton selected Martin Marincin) in 2010 Entry Draft, June 25, 2010.

NATTINEN, Joonas (NA-tih-nuhn, YOH-nuhs) MTL

Center. Shoots right. 6'2", 183 lbs. Born, Jamsa, Finland, January 3, 1991.
(Montreal's 2nd choice, 65th overall, in 2009 Entry Draft).

			Regular Season					Playoffs				
Season	Club	League	GP	G	A	Pts	PIM	GP	G	A	Pts	PIM
2006-07	JyP Jyvaskyla U18	Fin-U18	30	10	25	35	22	8	5	7	12	0
2007-08	JyP Jyvaskyla U18	Fin-U18	34	14	34	48	22	2	0	0	0	0
	JyP Jyvaskyla Jr.	Fin-Jr.	8	0	2	2	2	3	0	2	2	2
2008-09	Suomi U20	Finland-2	5	2	2	4	0	....	....	....	....	....
	Blues Espoo Jr.	Fin-Jr.	30	9	29	38	6	10	3	10	13	4
	Blues Espoo	Finland	14	0	0	0	4	....	....	....	....	....
2009-10	Blues Espoo	Finland	23	0	3	3	4	1	0	0	0	0
	Suomi U20	Finland-2	7	0	8	8	6	....	....	....	....	....
	Hokki Kajaani	Finland-2	10	2	2	4	4	....	....	....	....	....
	Blues Espoo Jr.	Fin-Jr.	11	7	6	13	2	....	....	....	....	....
2010-11	Suomi U20	Finland-2	2	0	0	0	0	....	....	....	....	....
	Blues Espoo Jr.	Fin-Jr.	2	0	2	2	0	....	....	....	....	....
	Blues Espoo	Finland	11	0	0	0	6	....	....	....	....	....
	HPK Hameenlinna	Finland	10	0	2	2	6	1	0	1	1	0

NAVIN, Brad (NA-vihn, BRAD) BUF

Center. Shoots left. 6'2", 190 lbs. Born, Waupaca, WI, June 5, 1992.
(Buffalo's 6th choice, 197th overall, in 2011 Entry Draft).

			Regular Season					Playoffs				
Season	Club	League	GP	G	A	Pts	PIM	GP	G	A	Pts	PIM
2007-08	Waupaca Comets	High-WI	16	20	17	37	....	....	....	....	....	....
2008-09	Waupaca Comets	High-WI	16	25	18	43	....	....	....	....	....	....
2009-10	Waupaca Comets	High-WI	23	53	39	92	57	....	....	....	....	....
2010-11	Waupaca Comets	High-WI	14	29	23	52	40	....	....	....	....	....

• Signed Letter of Intent to attend **University of Wisconsin** (WCHA) in fall of 2011.

NEAL, Michael (NEEL, MIGH-kuhl) DAL

Left wing. Shoots left. 6'3", 205 lbs. Born, Whitby, Ont., April 3, 1989.
(Dallas' 7th choice, 149th overall, in 2007 Entry Draft).

			Regular Season					Playoffs				
Season	Club	League	GP	G	A	Pts	PIM	GP	G	A	Pts	PIM
2004-05	Whitby Wildcats	Minor-ON	52	20	29	49	67	....	....	....	....	....
2005-06	Belleville Bulls	OHL	46	1	3	4	6	....	....	....	....	....
2006-07	Belleville Bulls	OHL	52	4	4	8	25	15	0	1	1	6
2007-08	Belleville Bulls	OHL	....	....	....	....	....	7	0	0	0	2
2008-09	Belleville Bulls	OHL	3	0	0	0	0	....	....	....	....	....
	Sarnia Sting	OHL	63	9	12	21	48	5	0	1	1	4
2009-10	Texas Stars	AHL	6	0	0	0	2	....	....	....	....	....
	Idaho Steelheads	ECHL	57	5	10	15	33	5	0	1	1	0
2010-11	Texas Stars	AHL	16	3	0	3	12	....	....	....	....	....
	Idaho Steelheads	ECHL	46	6	9	15	10	8	0	0	0	4

• Missed majority of 2007-08 due to knee injury.

NEDOMLEL, Richard (NEHD-oh-muh-lehl, rih-CHUHRD) DET

Defense. Shoots left. 6'4", 204 lbs. Born, Prague, Czech Republic, July 1, 1993.
(Detroit's 8th choice, 175th overall, in 2011 Entry Draft).

			Regular Season					Playoffs				
Season	Club	League	GP	G	A	Pts	PIM	GP	G	A	Pts	PIM
2008-09	Chomutov U17	CzR-U17	17	0	3	3	47	....	....	....	....	....
	Slavia U17	CzR-U17	25	0	4	4	18	9	1	1	2	4
2009-10	Slavia U18	CzR-U18	44	9	10	19	221	4	1	0	1	54
2010-11	Swift Current	WHL	66	0	10	10	107	....	....	....	....	....

NELSON, Brock (NEHL-suhn, BRAWK) NYI

Center. Shoots left. 6'3", 205 lbs. Born, Minneapolis, MN, October 15, 1991.
(NY Islanders' 2nd choice, 30th overall, in 2010 Entry Draft).

			Regular Season					Playoffs				
Season	Club	League	GP	G	A	Pts	PIM	GP	G	A	Pts	PIM
2007-08	Warroad Warriors	High-MN	31	14	9	23	....	....	....	....	....	....
2008-09	Warroad Warriors	High-MN	31	45	36	81	....	....	....	....	....	....
2009-10	Team Great Plains	UMHSEL	24	5	10	15	....	....	....	....	....	....
	Warroad Warriors	High-MN	25	39	34	73	38	6	14	8	22	8
2010-11	North Dakota	WCHA	42	8	13	21	27	....	....	....	....	....

NELSON, Levi (NELH-suhn, LEE-vigh)

Center. Shoots left. 5'11", 167 lbs. Born, Calgary, Alta., April 28, 1988.
(Boston's 6th choice, 158th overall, in 2006 Entry Draft).

			Regular Season					Playoffs				
Season	Club	League	GP	G	A	Pts	PIM	GP	G	A	Pts	PIM
2004-05	Cgy. North Stars	AMHL	35	15	13	28	70	....	....	....	....	....
	Swift Current	WHL	2	1	0	1	0	....	....	....	....	....
2005-06	Swift Current	WHL	63	21	17	38	63	4	0	0	0	4
2006-07	Swift Current	WHL	66	18	34	52	125	6	4	3	7	4
	Providence Bruins	AHL	1	0	0	0	2	4	1	0	1	2
2007-08	Swift Current	WHL	67	25	36	61	152	12	7	8	15	16
2008-09	Providence Bruins	AHL	59	2	5	7	37	5	1	1	2	2
	Reading Royals	ECHL	8	2	1	3	28	....	....	....	....	....
2009-10	Providence Bruins	AHL	44	8	5	13	29	....	....	....	....	....
2010-11	Providence Bruins	AHL	14	4	3	7	19	....	....	....	....	....
	Norfolk Admirals	AHL	20	3	1	4	7	5	0	0	0	2

Traded to **Tampa Bay** by **Boston** for Juraj Simek, December 9, 2010.

NEMETH, Patrik (NEH-meht, PAHT-rihk) DAL

Defense. Shoots left. 6'3", 201 lbs. Born, Stockholm, Sweden, February 8, 1992.
(Dallas' 2nd choice, 41st overall, in 2010 Entry Draft).

			Regular Season					Playoffs				
Season	Club	League	GP	G	A	Pts	PIM	GP	G	A	Pts	PIM
2007-08	Hammarby U18	Swe-U18	13	1	3	4	12	....	....	....	....	....
2008-09	AIK IF Solna U18	Swe-U18	27	3	10	13	123	4	1	0	1	29
	AIK IF Solna Jr.	Swe-Jr.	19	0	0	0	43	....	....	....	....	....
	AIK IF Solna	Sweden-2	1	0	1	1	0	....	....	....	....	....
2009-10	AIK IF Solna U18	Swe-U18	3	0	1	1	4	1	0	1	1	0
	AIK IF Solna Jr.	Swe-Jr.	38	1	19	20	120	5	1	2	3	10
	AIK IF Solna	Sweden-2	19	0	3	3	8	....	....	....	....	....
2010-11	AIK IF Solna	Sweden	38	1	6	7	18	7	0	0	0	2

NEPRYAYEV, Ivan (neh-pree-YIGH-ehv, IGH-vuhn) WSH

Center. Shoots left. 6'1", 180 lbs. Born, Yaroslavl, USSR, February 4, 1982.
(Washington's 5th choice, 163rd overall, in 2000 Entry Draft).

			Regular Season					Playoffs				
Season	Club	League	GP	G	A	Pts	PIM	GP	G	A	Pts	PIM
1997-98	Torpedo Yaroslavl	Russia	6	0	0	0	0	....	....	....	....	....
1998-99	Yaroslavl 2	Russia-3	15	1	0	1	0	....	....	....	....	....
99-2000	Yaroslavl 2	Russia-3	40	8	14	22	....	....	....	....	....	....
2000-01	Yaroslavl	Russia	10	0	0	0	2	....	....	....	....	....
2001-02	Yaroslavl 2	Russia-3	2	1	0	1	18	....	....	....	....	....
	Yaroslavl	Russia	36	3	8	11	28	....	....	....	....	....
2002-03	Yaroslavl	Russia	26	3	6	9	12	6	1	0	1	0
2003-04	Yaroslavl 2	Russia-3	13	5	10	15	12	....	....	....	....	....
2004-05	Yaroslavl	Russia	56	10	10	20	73	9	1	0	1	16
2005-06	Yaroslavl	Russia	43	7	16	23	70	11	0	0	0	8
	Russia	Olympics	2	0	0	0	2	....	....	....	....	....
2006-07	Yaroslavl	Russia	52	17	9	26	66	7	0	4	4	2
2007-08	Yaroslavl	Russia	56	9	17	26	84	15	3	6	9	41
2008-09	Dynamo Moscow	Rus-KHL	52	14	13	27	48	12	0	4	4	10
2009-10	Dynamo Moscow	Rus-KHL	44	4	9	13	46	4	0	0	0	4
2010-11	Mytischi	Rus-KHL	54	5	10	15	50	24	4	3	7	49

NERMARK, Joachim (N'YAIR-mahrk, yoh-A-kheem) COL

Center. Shoots left. 6', 185 lbs. Born, Sunne, Sweden, May 12, 1993.
(Colorado's 3rd choice, 93rd overall, in 2011 Entry Draft).

			Regular Season					Playoffs				
Season	Club	League	GP	G	A	Pts	PIM	GP	G	A	Pts	PIM
2007-08	Sunne IK U18	Swe-U18	17	9	5	14	4	....	....	....	....	....
	Sunne IK Jr.	Swe-Jr.	1	0	0	0	0	....	....	....	....	....
2008-09	Sunne IK U18	Swe-U18	19	8	14	22	8	1	0	0	0	0
	Sunne IK Jr.	Swe-Jr.	15	4	4	8	4	....	....	....	....	....
	Sunne IK	Sweden-3	16	3	2	5	0	....	....	....	....	....
2009-10	Leksands IF U18	Swe-U18	14	8	4	12	6	4	2	4	6	0
	Leksands IF Jr.	Swe-Jr.	35	6	7	13	2	5	1	1	2	0
2010-11	Linkopings HC U18	Swe-U18	4	1	3	4	0	5	2	4	6	2
	Linkopings HC Jr.	Swe-Jr.	37	8	18	26	16	3	0	0	0	0
	Linkopings HC	Sweden	12	0	1	1	2	....	....	....	....	....

NESS, Aaron (NEHS, AIR-uhn) NYI

Defense. Shoots left. 5'10", 170 lbs. Born, Bemidji, MN, May 18, 1990.
(NY Islanders' 3rd choice, 40th overall, in 2008 Entry Draft).

			Regular Season					Playoffs				
Season	Club	League	GP	G	A	Pts	PIM	GP	G	A	Pts	PIM
2005-06	Roseau Rams	High-MN	30	3	18	21	8	....	....	....	....	....
2006-07	Roseau Rams	High-MN	31	13	38	51	12	....	....	....	....	....
	Team Great Plains	UMWEHL	11	0	8	8	....	....	....	....	....	....
2007-08	Roseau Rams	High-MN	31	28	44	72	16	....	....	....	....	....
	Team Great Plains	UMWEHL	11	2	11	13	....	....	....	....	....	....
2008-09	U. of Minnesota	WCHA	37	2	15	17	16	....	....	....	....	....
2009-10	U. of Minnesota	WCHA	39	2	10	12	24	....	....	....	....	....
2010-11	U. of Minnesota	WCHA	35	2	12	14	41	....	....	....	....	....
	Bridgeport	AHL	13	1	3	4	4	....	....	....	....	....

NESTEROV, Nikita (NEHS-tehr-awf, nih-KEE-tuh) T.B.

Defense. Shoots left. 6', 183 lbs. Born, Chelyabinsk, Russia, March 28, 1993.
(Tampa Bay's 3rd choice, 148th overall, in 2011 Entry Draft).

			Regular Season					Playoffs				
Season	Club	League	GP	G	A	Pts	PIM	GP	G	A	Pts	PIM
2009-10	Chelyabinsk Jr.	Russia-Jr.	9	5	2	7	8	4	0	0	0	6
2010-11	Chelyabinsk Jr.	Russia-Jr.	46	5	14	19	72	5	0	0	0	6

NESTRASIL, Andrej (NEHS-tra-shihl, ahn-DRAY) DET

Right wing. Shoots left. 6'3", 206 lbs. Born, Prague, Czechoslovakia, February 22, 1991.
(Detroit's 3rd choice, 75th overall, in 2009 Entry Draft).

			Regular Season					Playoffs				
Season	Club	League	GP	G	A	Pts	PIM	GP	G	A	Pts	PIM
2004-05	Slavia U17	CzR-U17	3	0	1	1	2	....	....	....	....	....
2005-06	Slavia U17	CzR-U17	41	6	12	18	18	....	....	....	....	....
2006-07	Slavia U17	CzR-U17	43	24	37	61	75	5	2	2	4	6
2007-08	Slavia U17	CzR-U17	....	....	....	....	....	2	1	0	1	2
	HC Slavia Praha Jr.	CzRep-Jr.	40	12	16	28	58	5	1	2	3	4
2008-09	Victoriaville Tigres	QMJHL	66	22	35	57	67	4	2	1	3	10
2009-10	Victoriaville Tigres	QMJHL	50	16	35	51	40	16	2	4	6	10
2010-11	P.E.I. Rocket	QMJHL	58	19	51	70	40	5	1	5	6	2

NEWTON, Jake (NOO-tuhn, JAYK) ANA

Defense. Shoots left. 6'2", 218 lbs. Born, San Jacinto, CA, September 22, 1988.

			Regular Season					Playoffs				
Season	Club	League	GP	G	A	Pts	PIM	GP	G	A	Pts	PIM
2006-07	Texas Tornado	NAHL	61	12	15	27	35	....	....	....	....	....
2007-08	Lincoln Stars	USHL	56	11	14	25	22	8	3	3	6	4
2008-09	Lincoln Stars	USHL	59	10	28	38	22	7	2	2	4	0
2009-10	Northeastern	H-East	34	9	13	22	10	....	....	....	....	....
2010-11	Syracuse Crunch	AHL	48	2	7	9	6	....	....	....	....	....

Hockey East All-Rookie Team (2010)

Signed as a free agent by **Anaheim**, March 17, 2010.

NICASTRO, Max (nih-KAS-troh, MAX) DET

Defense. Shoots right. 6'2", 189 lbs. Born, Thousand Oaks, CA, March 2, 1990.
(Detroit's 2nd choice, 91st overall, in 2008 Entry Draft).

			Regular Season					Playoffs				
Season	Club	League	GP	G	A	Pts	PIM	GP	G	A	Pts	PIM
2006-07	L.A. Jr. Kings	Minor-CA	48	17	19	36	44	....	....	....	....	....
2007-08	Chicago Steel	USHL	58	6	14	20	78	7	1	2	3	12
2008-09	Chicago Steel	USHL	57	9	22	31	84	....	....	....	....	....
2009-10	Boston University	H-East	37	3	12	15	26	....	....	....	....	....
2010-11	Boston University	H-East	38	5	4	9	59	....	....	....	....	....

Hockey East All-Rookie Team (2010)

NICHOLLS, Josh (NIH-kuhls, JAWSH) TOR

Right wing. Shoots right. 6'2", 186 lbs. Born, Tsawwassen, B.C., April 27, 1992.
(Toronto's 7th choice, 182nd overall, in 2010 Entry Draft).

			Regular Season					Playoffs				
Season	Club	League	GP	G	A	Pts	PIM	GP	G	A	Pts	PIM
2007-08	Greater Van.	BCMML	39	18	30	48	68	2	0	0	0	20
2008-09	Saskatoon Blades	WHL	63	9	16	25	37	7	2	0	2	4
2009-10	Saskatoon Blades	WHL	71	18	30	48	55	10	0	5	5	6
2010-11	Saskatoon Blades	WHL	71	34	53	87	47	10	4	2	6	6

NIEMI, Jyri (nee-YEH-mee, YEW-ree) NYR

Defense. Shoots left. 6'3", 203 lbs. Born, Hameenkyro, Finland, June 15, 1990.
(NY Islanders' 6th choice, 72nd overall, in 2008 Entry Draft).

			Regular Season					Playoffs				
Season	Club	League	GP	G	A	Pts	PIM	GP	G	A	Pts	PIM
2006-07	HPK U18	Fin-U18	1	0	1	1	4	....	....	....	....	....
	HPK Jr.	Fin-Jr.	40	7	5	12	82	....	....	....	....	....
2007-08	Saskatoon Blades	WHL	49	14	20	34	57	....	....	....	....	....
2008-09	Saskatoon Blades	WHL	60	7	25	32	74	6	1	6	7	10
2009-10	Saskatoon Blades	WHL	50	8	21	29	67	10	2	0	2	26
2010-11	Connecticut Whale	AHL	46	3	6	9	22	....	....	....	....	....

Traded to **NY Rangers** by **NY Islanders** for NY Rangers' 6th round choice (later traded to Atlanta – Atlanta selected Tanner Lane) in 2010 Entry Draft, May 25, 2010.

NIETO, Matthew (NEE-eh-toh, MA-thew) S.J.

Left wing. Shoots left. 5'11", 177 lbs. Born, Long Beach, CA, November 5, 1992.
(San Jose's 1st choice, 47th overall, in 2011 Entry Draft).

			Regular Season					Playoffs				
Season	Club	League	GP	G	A	Pts	PIM	GP	G	A	Pts	PIM
2007-08	Salisbury School	High-CT	23	8	10	18	....	....	....	....	....	....
2008-09	USNTDP	NAHL	38	11	24	35	14	....	....	....	....	....
	USNTDP	U-17	14	9	9	18	8	....	....	....	....	....
	USNTDP	U-18	13	6	8	14	14	....	....	....	....	....
2009-10	USNTDP	USHL	24	15	14	29	19	....	....	....	....	....
	USNTDP	U-18	30	13	12	25	12	....	....	....	....	....
2010-11	Boston University	H-East	39	10	13	23	16	....	....	....	....	....

NIGRO, Anthony (NIGH-groh, AN-thuh-nee) ST.L.

Center. Shoots left. 5'11", 180 lbs. Born, Vaughan, Ont., January 11, 1990.
(St. Louis' 9th choice, 155th overall, in 2008 Entry Draft).

			Regular Season					Playoffs				
Season	Club	League	GP	G	A	Pts	PIM	GP	G	A	Pts	PIM
2006-07	Guelph Storm	OHL	56	4	13	17	26	4	0	0	0	2
2007-08	Guelph Storm	OHL	67	24	24	48	65	10	2	3	5	7
2008-09	Guelph Storm	OHL	25	7	11	18	31	....	....	....	....	....
	Ottawa 67's	OHL	42	23	28	51	28	7	4	4	8	4
2009-10	Ottawa 67's	OHL	61	16	46	62	49	12	6	7	13	12
2010-11	Peoria Rivermen	AHL	54	9	6	15	22	4	0	0	0	4

NIKULIN, Ilja (nih-KOO-lihn, IHL-yah) WPG

Defense. Shoots left. 6'3", 211 lbs. Born, Moscow, USSR, March 12, 1982.
(Atlanta's 2nd choice, 31st overall, in 2000 Entry Draft).

			Regular Season					Playoffs				
Season	Club	League	GP	G	A	Pts	PIM	GP	G	A	Pts	PIM
1998-99	Dyn'o Moscow 2	Russia-3	23	0	2	2	18	....	....	....	....	....
99-2000	Dyn'o Moscow 2	Russia-3	4	2	1	3	10	....	....	....	....	....
	THK Tver	Russia-2	39	3	6	9	84	....	....	....	....	....
2000-01	Dynamo Moscow	Russia	44	0	4	4	61	....	....	....	....	....
2001-02	Dyn'o Moscow 2	Russia-3	2	0	1	1	2	....	....	....	....	....
	Dynamo Moscow	Russia	47	2	1	3	44	3	0	0	0	0
2002-03	Dynamo Moscow	Russia	40	1	4	5	46	5	0	1	1	4
2003-04	Dynamo Moscow	Russia	54	1	5	6	56	3	0	0	0	2
2004-05	Dynamo Moscow	Russia	50	1	9	10	65	10	0	3	3	8
2005-06	Ak Bars Kazan	Russia	49	9	9	18	48	13	4	0	4	36
2006-07	Ak Bars Kazan	Russia	51	11	14	25	99	16	4	5	9	18
2007-08	Ak Bars Kazan	Russia	57	3	15	18	95	10	1	3	4	14
2008-09	Ak Bars Kazan	Rus-KHL	53	7	26	33	72	17	2	8	10	22
2009-10	Ak Bars Kazan	Rus-KHL	49	6	27	33	86	22	5	6	11	14
	Russia	Olympics	4	0	1	1	2	....	....	....	....	....
2010-11	Ak Bars Kazan	Rus-KHL	49	6	35	41	56	9	1	3	4	10

NILL, Trevor (NIHL, TREH-vuhr) ST.L.

Center. Shoots right. 6'3", 195 lbs. Born, Detroit, MI, April 11, 1989.
(St. Louis' 10th choice, 190th overall, in 2007 Entry Draft).

			Regular Season					Playoffs				
Season	Club	League	GP	G	A	Pts	PIM	GP	G	A	Pts	PIM
2004-05	Det. Compuware	MWEHL	25	10	8	18	8	4	2	1	3	0
2005-06	Det. Compuware	MWEHL	21	4	9	13	20	4	1	0	1	2
2006-07	Det. Compuware	MWEHL	24	6	10	16	23	6	2	4	6	2
2007-08	Penticton Vees	BCHL	53	5	6	11	16	11	0	2	2	0
2008-09	Michigan State	CCHA	34	1	2	3	6	....	....	....	....	....
2009-10	Michigan State	CCHA	26	2	7	9	12	....	....	....	....	....
2010-11	Michigan State	CCHA	29	1	2	3	10	....	....	....	....	....

NILSSON, Tom (NIHL-suhn, TAWM) TOR

Defense. Shoots right. 6', 176 lbs. Born, Tyreso, Sweden, August 19, 1993.
(Toronto's 4th choice, 100th overall, in 2011 Entry Draft).

			Regular Season					Playoffs				
Season	Club	League	GP	G	A	Pts	PIM	GP	G	A	Pts	PIM
2009-10	Mora IK U18	Swe-U18	35	11	9	20	30	....	....	....	....	....
	Mora IK Jr.	Swe-Jr.	3	0	0	0	0	....	....	....	....	....
2010-11	Mora IK U18	Swe-U18	11	1	7	8	10	1	0	0	0	12
	Mora IK Jr.	Swe-Jr.	37	2	6	8	26	....	....	....	....	....
	Mora IK	Sweden-2	16	0	1	1	12	....	....	....	....	....

NOEBELS, Marcel (N'YOH-behlz, MAHR-sehl) PHI

Left wing. Shoots left. 6'3", 200 lbs. Born, Tönisvorst, Germany, March 14, 1992.
(Philadelphia's 4th choice, 118th overall, in 2011 Entry Draft).

			Regular Season					Playoffs				
Season	Club	League	GP	G	A	Pts	PIM	GP	G	A	Pts	PIM
2007-08	Heil./Mann. Jr.	Ger-Jr.	36	13	18	31	22	8	4	6	10	4
2008-09	Heil./Mann. Jr.	Ger-Jr.	36	23	27	50	26	7	6	11	17	6
2009-10	Krefelder EV Jr.	Ger-Jr.	25	17	36	53	52	5	3	3	6	31
	Krefeld Pinguine	Germany	33	1	2	3	29	....	....	....	....	....
2010-11	Seattle	WHL	66	28	26	54	23	....	....	....	....	....

NOESEN, Stefan (NAY-sehn, STEH-fan) OTT

Right wing. Shoots right. 6'1", 194 lbs. Born, Plano, TX, February 12, 1993.
(Ottawa's 2nd choice, 21st overall, in 2011 Entry Draft).

			Regular Season					Playoffs				
Season	Club	League	GP	G	A	Pts	PIM	GP	G	A	Pts	PIM
2006-07	Dallas Ice Jets	Minor-TX	52	78	60	138	78	....	....	....	....	....
2007-08	Det. Compuware	MWEHL	31	31	14	45	54	....	....	....	....	....
	Det. Compuware	Exhib.	4	3	2	5	4	....	....	....	....	....
2008-09	Det. Compuware	T1EHL	28	14	9	23	67	5	4	5	9	0
	Det. Compuware	Exhib.	20	6	10	16	....	....	....	....	....	....
2009-10	Plymouth Whalers	OHL	33	3	5	8	4	....	....	....	....	....
2010-11	Plymouth Whalers	OHL	68	33	44	77	80	11	6	5	11	16

NOLAN, Jordan (NOH-luhn, JOHR-dahn) L.A.

Center. Shoots left. 6'3", 217 lbs. Born, St. Catharines, Ont., June 23, 1989.
(Los Angeles' 9th choice, 186th overall, in 2009 Entry Draft).

			Regular Season					Playoffs				
Season	Club	League	GP	G	A	Pts	PIM	GP	G	A	Pts	PIM
2005-06	Erie Otters	OHL	33	3	4	7	20	....	....	....	....	....
2006-07	Windsor Spitfires	OHL	60	11	16	27	100	....	....	....	....	....
2007-08	Windsor Spitfires	OHL	62	13	14	27	69	5	3	0	3	2
2008-09	Sault Ste. Marie	OHL	64	16	27	43	158	....	....	....	....	....
2009-10	Sault Ste. Marie	OHL	49	23	25	48	88	5	1	1	2	4
	Ontario Reign	ECHL	3	1	1	2	4	....	....	....	....	....
2010-11	Manchester	AHL	75	5	12	17	115	7	0	2	2	4

NOONAN, Garrett (NOO-nuhn, GAIR-eht) NSH

Defense. Shoots left. 6', 205 lbs. Born, Norfolk, MA, January 28, 1991.
(Nashville's 4th choice, 112th overall, in 2011 Entry Draft).

			Regular Season					Playoffs				
Season	Club	League	GP	G	A	Pts	PIM	GP	G	A	Pts	PIM
2008-09	Catholic Memorial	High-MA	30	12	22	34	....	....	....	....	....	....
2009-10	Vernon Vipers	BCHL	58	2	16	18	60	19	3	3	6	16
2010-11	Boston University	H-East	38	4	11	15	89	....	....	....	....	....

NORDSTROM, Joakim (NOHRD-stuhm, YOH-a-kihm) CHI

Center. Shoots left. 6'1", 160 lbs. Born, Tyreso, Sweden, February 25, 1992.
(Chicago's 6th choice, 90th overall, in 2010 Entry Draft).

			Regular Season					Playoffs				
Season	Club	League	GP	G	A	Pts	PIM	GP	G	A	Pts	PIM
2008-09	AIK IF Solna U18	Swe-U18	35	8	16	24	32	7	2	2	4	2
	AIK IF Solna Jr.	Swe-Jr.	4	2	0	2	2	....	....	....	....	....
2009-10	AIK IF Solna U18	Swe-U18	2	1	1	2	0	3	1	2	3	4
	AIK IF Solna Jr.	Swe-Jr.	28	6	9	15	53	....	....	....	....	....
	AIK IF Solna	Sweden-2	2	0	0	0	0	....	....	....	....	....
2010-11	AIK IF Solna Jr.	Swe-Jr.	25	9	11	20	36	....	....	....	....	....
	Almtuna	Sweden-2	12	0	1	1	4	....	....	....	....	....
	AIK IF Solna	Sweden	11	0	1	1	0	1	0	0	0	0

NOREAU, Samuel (noh-ROH, SAM-ew-l) NYR

Defense. Shoots right. 6'5", 206 lbs. Born, Montreal, Que., January 31, 1993.
(NY Rangers' 5th choice, 136th overall, in 2011 Entry Draft).

			Regular Season					Playoffs				
Season	Club	League	GP	G	A	Pts	PIM	GP	G	A	Pts	PIM
2008-09	Lac St-Louis Tigres	Minor-QU	33	5	20	25	8	....	....	....	....	....
2009-10	Baie-Comeau	QMJHL	34	1	3	4	17	....	....	....	....	....
2010-11	Baie-Comeau	QMJHL	67	5	5	10	141	....	....	....	....	....

NUGENT-HOPKINS, Ryan (NOO-jehnt-HAWP-kihnz, RIGH-uhn) EDM

Center. Shoots left. 6', 171 lbs. Born, Burnaby, B.C., April 12, 1993.
(Edmonton's 1st choice, 1st overall, in 2011 Entry Draft).

			Regular Season					Playoffs				
Season	Club	League	GP	G	A	Pts	PIM	GP	G	A	Pts	PIM
2006-07	Burnaby W.C.	Minor-BC	65	43	43	86	34	....	....	....	....	....
2007-08	Burnaby W.C.	Minor-BC	66	119	95	214	84	....	....	....	....	....
2008-09	Van. NW Giants	BCMML	36	*40	*47	*87	78	5	*5	*5	*10	4
	Red Deer Rebels	WHL	5	2	4	6	0	....	....	....	....	....
2009-10	Red Deer Rebels	WHL	67	24	41	65	28	4	0	2	2	0
2010-11	Red Deer Rebels	WHL	69	31	*75	106	51	9	4	7	11	6

WHL Rookie of the Year (2010) • Canadian Major Junior All-Rookie Team (2010) • WHL East First All-Star Team (2011)

NYGREN, Magnus (NEW-grihn, MAG-nuhs) MTL

Defense. Shoots right. 6'1", 191 lbs. Born, Karlstad, Sweden, June 7, 1990.
(Montreal's 3rd choice, 113th overall, in 2011 Entry Draft).

			Regular Season					Playoffs				
Season	Club	League	GP	G	A	Pts	PIM	GP	G	A	Pts	PIM
2006-07	Farjestad U18	Swe-U18	7	0	4	4	4	8	1	2	3	6
2007-08	Farjestad U18	Swe-U18	31	9	19	28	61	8	2	6	8	12
2008-09	Skare Jr.	Swe-Jr.	2	2	3	5	0	....	....	....	....	....
	Skare BK Karlstad	Sweden-3	41	7	21	28	32	3	1	0	1	2
2009-10	Skare BK	Sweden-3	24	9	18	27	10	....	....	....	....	....
	Farjestad	Sweden	9	0	0	0	4	....	....	....	....	....
	Mora IK	Sweden-2	21	2	5	7	10	2	0	1	1	2
2010-11	Bofors	Sweden-2	35	5	6	11	10	....	....	....	....	....
	Farjestad	Sweden	22	4	11	15	4	14	3	7	10	6

NYQUIST, Gustav (NEW-kwihst, GUHS-tav) DET

Right wing. Shoots left. 5'10", 169 lbs. Born, Halmstad, Sweden, September 1, 1989.
(Detroit's 3rd choice, 121st overall, in 2008 Entry Draft).

			Regular Season					Playoffs				
Season	Club	League	GP	G	A	Pts	PIM	GP	G	A	Pts	PIM
2005-06	Malmo U18	Swe-U18	14	9	3	12	10	6	1	3	4	0
2006-07	Malmo Jr.	Swe-Jr.	42	21	23	44	57	4	2	2	4	6
2007-08	Malmo Jr.	Swe-Jr.	24	11	20	31	20	7	5	5	10	6
2008-09	U. of Maine	H-East	38	13	19	32	28	....	....	....	....	....
2009-10	U. of Maine	H-East	39	19	*42	*61	20	....	....	....	....	....
2010-11	U. of Maine	H-East	36	18	*33	51	20	....	....	....	....	....
	Grand Rapids	AHL	8	1	3	4	2	....	....	....	....	....

Hockey East All-Rookie Team (2009) • Hockey East First All-Star Team (2010, 2011) • NCAA East First All-American Team (2010) • NCAA East Second All-American Team (2011)

O'DELL, Eric (OH-DEHL, AIR-ihk) WPG

Center. Shoots right. 6'1", 181 lbs. Born, Ottawa, Ont., June 21, 1990.
(Anaheim's 3rd choice, 39th overall, in 2008 Entry Draft).

			Regular Season					Playoffs				
Season	Club	League	GP	G	A	Pts	PIM	GP	G	A	Pts	PIM
2006-07	Ottawa West	ON-Jr.B	40	28	20	48	45	....	....	....	....	....
	Ottawa Jr. Sens	CJHL	2	1	0	1	0	....	....	....	....	....
2007-08	Cumberland	CJHL	34	23	33	56	12	....	....	....	....	....
	Sudbury Wolves	OHL	26	14	18	32	19	....	....	....	....	....
2008-09	Sudbury Wolves	OHL	65	33	30	63	55	6	0	4	4	4
2009-10	Sudbury Wolves	OHL	68	33	35	68	63	4	0	2	2	7
	Chicago Wolves	AHL	3	0	0	0	0	....	....	....	....	....
2010-11	Sudbury Wolves	OHL	39	20	24	44	34	8	7	5	12	15

Traded to **Atlanta** by **Anaheim** for Erik Christensen, March 4, 2009.

O'DONNELL, Brendan (OH'DAW-nuhl, BREHN-duhn) T.B.

Center. Shoots left. 6', 185 lbs. Born, Flin Flon, Man., June 25, 1992.
(Tampa Bay's 7th choice, 156th overall, in 2010 Entry Draft).

			Regular Season					Playoffs				
Season	Club	League	GP	G	A	Pts	PIM	GP	G	A	Pts	PIM
2008-09	Winnipeg Wild	MMHL	38	....	....	83	....	10	....	....	20	....
2009-10	Wpg. South Blues	MJHL	53	29	32	61	55	4	2	1	3	4
2010-11	Penticton Vees	BCHL	58	29	43	72	28	6	1	5	6	9

• Signed Letter of Intent to attend **University of North Dakota** (WCHA) in fall of 2011.

O'GARA, Rob (OH-GAR-uh, RAWB) BOS

Defense. Shoots left. 6'3", 185 lbs. Born, Massapequa, NY, July 6, 1993.
(Boston's 5th choice, 151st overall, in 2011 Entry Draft).

			Regular Season					Playoffs				
Season	Club	League	GP	G	A	Pts	PIM	GP	G	A	Pts	PIM
2007-08	Long Island	AYHL	27	1	6	7	22	....	....	....	....	....
2008-09	Long Island	AYHL	17	1	4	5	16	....	....	....	....	....
2009-10	Long Island	AYHL	33	8	17	25	48	....	....	....	....	....
2010-11	Milton Academy	High-MA	30	2	7	9	22	....	....	....	....	....

• Signed Letter of Intent to attend **Yale University** (ECAC) in fall of 2011.

OLDEN, Sondre (OHL-duhn, SAWN-dreh) TOR

Center. Shoots left. 6'4", 176 lbs. Born, Oslo, Norway, August 29, 1992.
(Toronto's 3rd choice, 79th overall, in 2010 Entry Draft).

			Regular Season					Playoffs				
Season	Club	League	GP	G	A	Pts	PIM	GP	G	A	Pts	PIM
2007-08	Manglerud Jr.	Norway-Jr.	19	20	18	38	12	3	0	2	2	4
2008-09	Manglerud U17	Nor-U17	1	2	3	5	0	4	8	6	14	33
	Manglerud Jr.	Norway-Jr.	19	32	35	67	18	7	5	9	14	16
	Manglerud	Norway-2	29	11	19	30	6	....	....	....	....	....
2009-10	MODO U18	Swe-U18	24	21	18	39	22	5	1	0	1	6
	MODO Jr.	Swe-Jr.	32	7	20	27	22	....	....	....	....	....
2010-11	MODO	Sweden	3	0	0	0	0	....	....	....	....	....
	MODO Jr.	Swe-Jr.	33	7	15	22	18	6	2	4	6	2

OLEKSIAK, Jamieson (oh-LEHK-see-ak, JAY-mih-suhn) DAL

Defense. Shoots left. 6'7", 241 lbs. Born, Toronto, Ont., December 21, 1992.
(Dallas' 1st choice, 14th overall, in 2011 Entry Draft).

			Regular Season					Playoffs				
Season	Club	League	GP	G	A	Pts	PIM	GP	G	A	Pts	PIM
2007-08	Tor. Young Nats	GTHL	51	1	10	11	46	....	....	....	....	....
2008-09	Little Caesars	T1EHL	30	3	7	10	31	....	....	....	....	....
	Chicago Steel	USHL	29	0	4	4	47	....	....	....	....	....
2009-10	Chicago Steel	USHL	29	0	10	10	43	....	....	....	....	....
	Sioux Falls	USHL	24	2	2	4	32	3	0	1	1	2
2010-11	Northeastern	H-East	38	4	9	13	57	....	....	....	....	....

OLIMB, Mathis (OH-lihmb, MA-this)

Center. Shoots left. 5'10", 176 lbs. Born, Oslo, Norway, February 1, 1986.

			Regular Season					Playoffs				
Season	Club	League	GP	G	A	Pts	PIM	GP	G	A	Pts	PIM
2001-02	Valerenga Jr.	Norway-Jr.	1	0	0	0	0	....	....	....	....	....
2002-03	Valerenga U18	Nor-U18	....	....	....	....	....	3	2	4	6	0
	Valerenga Jr.	Norway-Jr.	29	15	22	37	16	5	1	4	5	0
	Valerengen IF Oslo	Norway	10	4	3	7	4	....	....	....	....	....
2003-04	Valerenga Jr.	Norway-Jr.	2	4	8	12	2	....	....	....	....	....
	Valerengen IF Oslo	Norway	3	0	0	0	0	....	....	....	....	....
	Manglerud	Norway	29	5	7	12	16	....	....	....	....	....
2004-05	London Knights	OHL	10	0	2	2	4	....	....	....	....	....
	Sarnia Sting	OHL	47	8	23	31	12	....	....	....	....	....
2005-06	Valerengen IF Oslo	Norway	39	11	14	25	46	13	4	3	7	8
2006-07	Valerengen IF Oslo	Norway	42	19	44	63	59	15	3	7	10	4
2007-08	Augsburg	Germany	54	14	25	39	71	....	....	....	....	....
2008-09	Augsburg	Germany	43	13	28	41	14	....	....	....	....	....
2009-10	Frolunda	Sweden	55	9	25	34	20	7	1	3	4	4
2010-11	Rockford IceHogs	AHL	60	10	22	32	22	....	....	....	....	....

Signed as a free agent by **Chicago**, June 17, 2010.

OLIVER, Nick (aw-LIH-vuhr, NIHK) NSH

Center/Left wing. Shoots left. 6'1", 194 lbs. Born, Grand Forks, ND, May 4, 1991.
(Nashville's 8th choice, 110th overall, in 2009 Entry Draft).

			Regular Season					Playoffs				
Season	Club	League	GP	G	A	Pts	PIM	GP	G	A	Pts	PIM
2006-07	Roseau Rams	High-MN	31	12	14	26	51	....	....	....	....	....
2007-08	Roseau Rams	High-MN	30	17	25	42	45	....	....	....	....	....
2008-09	Roseau Rams	High-MN	11	5	11	16	8	....	....	....	....	....
	Fargo Force	USHL	12	1	1	2	11	1	0	0	0	0
2009-10	Fargo Force	USHL	53	5	13	18	95	13	1	1	2	4
2010-11	Fargo Force	USHL	56	7	10	17	64	5	0	0	0	6

• Signed Letter of Intent to attend **St. Cloud State University** (WCHA) in fall of 2011.

OLSEN, Dylan (OHL-suhn, DIH-luhn) CHI

Defense. Shoots left. 6'2", 206 lbs. Born, Salt Lake City, UT, January 3, 1991.
(Chicago's 1st choice, 28th overall, in 2009 Entry Draft).

			Regular Season					Playoffs				
Season	Club	League	GP	G	A	Pts	PIM	GP	G	A	Pts	PIM
2006-07	Calgary Blazers	SAMHL	53	19	41	60	119	....	....	....	....	....
	Camrose Kodiaks	AJHL	2	1	0	1	0	....	....	....	....	....
2007-08	Camrose Kodiaks	AJHL	49	8	16	24	45	16	1	5	6	6
2008-09	Camrose Kodiaks	AJHL	53	10	19	29	123	10	1	6	7	12
2009-10	U. Minn-Duluth	WCHA	36	1	10	11	49	....	....	....	....	....
2010-11	U. Minn-Duluth	WCHA	17	1	12	13	8	....	....	....	....	....
	Rockford IceHogs	AHL	42	0	4	4	10	....	....	....	....	....

OLSON, Drew (OHL-suhn, DROO) CBJ

Defense. Shoots left. 6', 215 lbs. Born, Brainerd, MN, April 4, 1990.
(Columbus' 4th choice, 118th overall, in 2008 Entry Draft).

			Regular Season					Playoffs				
Season	Club	League	GP	G	A	Pts	PIM	GP	G	A	Pts	PIM
2006-07	Brainerd	High-MN	STATISTICS NOT AVAILABLE									
	Team North	UMWEHL	11	2	4	6	....	....	....	....	....	....
2007-08	Brainerd	High-MN	27	20	16	36	....	....	....	....	....	....
	Team North	UMWEHL	11	3	4	7	....	....	....	....	....	....
2008-09	Omaha Lancers	USHL	39	2	6	8	43	....	....	....	....	....
2009-10	U. Minn-Duluth	WCHA	34	0	2	2	12	....	....	....	....	....
2010-11	U. Minn-Duluth	WCHA	34	1	3	4	18	....	....	....	....	....

O'NEILL, Will (oh-NEEL, WIHL) WPG

Defense. Shoots left. 6', 193 lbs. Born, Boston, MA, April 28, 1988.
(Atlanta's 8th choice, 210th overall, in 2006 Entry Draft).

			Regular Season					Playoffs				
Season	Club	League	GP	G	A	Pts	PIM	GP	G	A	Pts	PIM
2004-05	Tabor	High-MA	....	1	16	17	....	....	....	....	....	....
2005-06	Tabor	High-MA	28	5	25	30	38	....	....	....	....	....
2006-07	Omaha Lancers	USHL	57	4	9	13	73	5	0	0	0	8
2007-08	Omaha Lancers	USHL	58	5	19	24	95	14	1	6	7	38
2008-09	U. of Maine	H-East	34	4	12	16	82	....	....	....	....	....
2009-10	U. of Maine	H-East	39	8	23	31	69	....	....	....	....	....
2010-11	U. of Maine	H-East	28	4	17	21	44	....	....	....	....	....

ORLOV, Dmitri (ohr-LAWF, dih-MEE-tree) WSH

Defense. Shoots left. 6', 197 lbs. Born, Novokuznetsk, USSR, July 23, 1991.
(Washington's 2nd choice, 55th overall, in 2009 Entry Draft).

			Regular Season					Playoffs				
Season	Club	League	GP	G	A	Pts	PIM	GP	G	A	Pts	PIM
2007-08	Novokuznetsk	Russia	6	0	0	0	0	....	....	....	....	....
2008-09	Novokuznetsk 2	Russia-3	STATISTICS NOT AVAILABLE									
	Novokuznetsk	Rus-KHL	16	1	0	1	4	....	....	....	....	....
2009-10	Novokuznetsk	Rus-KHL	41	4	3	7	49	....	....	....	....	....
	Novokuznetsk Jr.	Russia-Jr.	7	7	6	13	6	17	9	10	19	26
2010-11	Novokuznetsk	Rus-KHL	45	2	11	13	43	....	....	....	....	....
	Novokuznetsk Jr.	Russia-Jr.	1	0	0	0	0	....	....	....	....	....
	Hershey Bears	AHL	19	2	7	9	12	6	0	1	1	4

OSLUND, Nick (OZ-luhnd, NIHK) DET

Right wing. Shoots right. 6'3", 195 lbs. Born, Burnsville, MN, November 15, 1987.
(Detroit's 6th choice, 191st overall, in 2006 Entry Draft).

			Regular Season					Playoffs				
Season	Club	League	GP	G	A	Pts	PIM	GP	G	A	Pts	PIM
2004-05	Burnsville Blaze	High-MN	27	29	18	47	28	....	....	....	....	....
2005-06	Burnsville Blaze	High-MN	26	22	30	52	30	....	....	....	....	....
2006-07	Tri-City Storm	USHL	56	7	14	21	24	9	0	1	1	0
2007-08	St. Cloud State	WCHA	38	4	1	5	27	....	....	....	....	....
2008-09	St. Cloud State	WCHA	35	4	3	7	26	....	....	....	....	....
2009-10	St. Cloud State	WCHA	43	4	5	9	24	....	....	....	....	....
2010-11	St. Cloud State	WCHA	30	3	1	4	10	....	....	....	....	....

OSTRCIL, Radim (AWS-tuhr-chihl, RA-dihm) BOS

Defense. Shoots left. 5'11", 194 lbs. Born, Vsetin, Czech., January 15, 1989.
(Boston's 5th choice, 169th overall, in 2007 Entry Draft).

			Regular Season					Playoffs				
Season	Club	League	GP	G	A	Pts	PIM	GP	G	A	Pts	PIM
2002-03	HC Vsetin U17	CzR-U17	33	1	2	3	8	11	1	1	2	2
2003-04	HC Vsetin U17	CzR-U17	43	0	12	12	44	2	0	0	0	0
2004-05	HC Vsetin U17	CzR-U17	31	8	15	23	85	3	1	3	4	4
	HC Vsetin Jr.	CzRep-Jr.	19	0	3	3	14	3	0	0	0	2
2005-06	HC Vsetin U17	CzR-U17	1	1	1	2	0	3	2	2	4	0
	HC Vsetin Jr.	CzRep-Jr.	41	6	8	14	50	5	1	1	2	6
	Hr. Kralove	CzRep-2	1	0	0	0	0	1	0	0	0	0
	HC Vsetin	CzRep	3	0	0	0	6	....	....	....	....	....
2006-07	HC Vsetin Jr.	CzRep-Jr.	25	8	13	21	69	8	4	4	8	6
	HC Vsetin	CzRep	37	1	1	2	20	....	....	....	....	....
2007-08	Ottawa 67's	OHL	59	0	13	13	69	4	0	0	0	2
2008-09	HC Olomouc Jr.	CzRep-Jr.	5	3	2	5	10	....	....	....	....	....
	HC Olomouc	CzRep-2	38	1	3	4	18	5	0	0	0	4
2009-10	HC Kometa Brno	CzRep	2	0	0	0	2	3	0	0	0	0
	Trebic	CzRep-2	41	1	12	13	38	11	2	5	7	12
2010-11	HC Kometa Brno	CzRep	19	0	5	5	16	....	....	....	....	....
	Trebic	CzRep-2	42	4	17	21	38	4	0	2	2	0

OUELLET, Xavier (OO-leht, ehx-AV-ee-ay) DET

Defense. Shoots left. 6', 179 lbs. Born, Bayonne, France, July 29, 1993.
(Detroit's 2nd choice, 48th overall, in 2011 Entry Draft).

			Regular Season					Playoffs				
Season	Club	League	GP	G	A	Pts	PIM	GP	G	A	Pts	PIM
2008-09	Esther-Blondin	QAAA	41	2	9	11	49	14	1	3	4	24
2009-10	Montreal	QMJHL	43	2	14	16	22	7	0	3	3	12
2010-11	Montreal	QMJHL	67	8	35	43	44	10	0	8	8	6

QMJHL All-Rookie Team (2010)

OWENS, Jordan (OH-wehns , JOHR-dahn)

Left wing. Shoots left. 6', 193 lbs. Born, Toronto, Ont., May 1, 1986.

			Regular Season					Playoffs				
Season	Club	League	GP	G	A	Pts	PIM	GP	G	A	Pts	PIM
2004-05	Mississauga	OHL	66	11	14	25	45	5	0	0	0	2
2005-06	Mississauga	OHL	66	26	28	54	47	....	....	....	....	....
2006-07	Mississauga	OHL	60	32	42	74	51	5	1	2	3	6
	Hartford Wolf Pack	AHL	2	0	0	0	0	6	0	0	0	9
2007-08	Hartford Wolf Pack	AHL	41	7	7	14	44	5	0	0	0	0
	Charlotte	ECHL	20	3	10	13	28	2	0	0	0	0
2008-09	Hartford Wolf Pack	AHL	67	12	25	37	66	6	1	2	3	0
2009-10	Hartford Wolf Pack	AHL	50	6	13	19	53	....	....	....	....	....
	Grand Rapids	AHL	17	1	4	5	22	....	....	....	....	....
2010-11	Grand Rapids	AHL	60	6	14	20	101	....	....	....	....	....

Signed as a free agent by **Hartford** (AHL), June 12, 2007. Signed as a free agent by **NY Rangers**, May 5, 2009. Traded to **Detroit** by **NY Rangers** for Kris Newbury, March 3, 2010.

OWUYA, Sebastian (oh-WUH-yuh, seh-BAS-t'yehn) WPG

Defense. Shoots left. 6'3", 195 lbs. Born, Stockholm, Sweden, October 8, 1991.
(Atlanta's 8th choice, 169th overall, in 2010 Entry Draft).

			Regular Season					Playoffs				
Season	Club	League	GP	G	A	Pts	PIM	GP	G	A	Pts	PIM
2006-07	Djurgarden U18	Swe-U18	1	0	0	0	0	....	....	....	....	....
2007-08	Timra IK U18	Swe-U18	36	3	6	9	50	....	....	....	....	....
2008-09	Timra IK U18	Swe-U18	31	0	9	9	54	1	0	1	1	14
	Timra IK Jr.	Swe-Jr.	4	0	1	1	4	....	....	....	....	....
2009-10	Timra IK Jr.	Swe-Jr.	42	4	15	19	120	....	....	....	....	....
	Timra IK	Sweden	11	0	0	0	0	....	....	....	....	....
2010-11	Medicine Hat	WHL	66	0	10	10	69	14	1	5	6	18

PACAN, David (PAY-cuhn, DAY-vihd) FLA

Center. Shoots right. 6'3", 187 lbs. Born, Ottawa, Ont., March 31, 1991.
(Chicago's 6th choice, 177th overall, in 2009 Entry Draft).

			Regular Season					Playoffs				
Season	Club	League	GP	G	A	Pts	PIM	GP	G	A	Pts	PIM
2007-08	Cumberland	CJHL	60	12	22	34	30	6	3	7	10	6
2008-09	Cumberland	CJHL	58	22	38	60	78	6	2	6	8	6
2009-10	U. of Vermont	H-East	39	7	7	14	22	....	....	....	....	....
2010-11	Niagara Ice Dogs	OHL	65	20	42	62	39	14	5	4	9	8

Traded to **Florida** by **Chicago** with Jack Skille and Hugh Jessiman for Michael Frolik and Alexander Salak, February 9, 2011.

PAGEAU, Jean-Gabriel (pah-ZHOH, ZHAWN-ga-BREE-ehl) OTT

Center. Shoots right. 5'9", 165 lbs. Born, Ottawa, Ont., November 11, 1992.
(Ottawa's 5th choice, 96th overall, in 2011 Entry Draft).

			Regular Season					Playoffs				
Season	Club	League	GP	G	A	Pts	PIM	GP	G	A	Pts	PIM
2008-09	Gatineau Intrepide	QAAA	37	15	16	31	6	....	....	....	....	....
2009-10	Gatineau	QMJHL	62	16	15	31	20	4	1	0	1	0
2010-11	Gatineau	QMJHL	67	32	47	79	22	24	13	16	29	20

PAKARINEN, Iiro (pa-ka-REE-nehn, YEE-roh) FLA

Right wing. Shoots right. 6'1", 198 lbs. Born, Suonenjoki, Finland, August 25, 1991.
(Florida's 10th choice, 184th overall, in 2011 Entry Draft).

			Regular Season					Playoffs				
Season	Club	League	GP	G	A	Pts	PIM	GP	G	A	Pts	PIM
2006-07	KalPa Kuopio U18	Fin-U18	2	1	1	2	0	....	....	....	....	....
2007-08	KalPa Kuopio U18	Fin-U18	20	14	14	28	59	2	0	0	0	4
	KalPa Kuopio Jr.	Fin-Jr.	1	0	0	0	0	....	....	....	....	....
2008-09	KalPa Kuopio Jr.	Fin-Jr.	37	11	10	21	44	5	1	0	1	2
2009-10	Suomi U20	Finland-2	6	1	2	3	6	....	....	....	....	....
	KalPa Kuopio Jr.	Fin-Jr.	11	8	4	12	10	....	....	....	....	....
	KalPa Kuopio	Finland	38	3	5	8	37	12	3	0	3	8
2010-11	Suomi U20	Finland-2	3	0	0	0	0	....	....	....	....	....
	KalPa Kuopio Jr.	Fin-Jr.	4	3	2	5	6	....	....	....	....	....
	KalPa Kuopio	Finland	47	7	3	10	34	7	1	0	1	37

PALAT, Ondrej (PAL-at, AWN-dray) T.B.

Left wing. Shoots left. 5'11", 157 lbs. Born, Frydek-Mistek, Czechoslovakia, March 28, 1991.
(Tampa Bay's 6th choice, 208th overall, in 2011 Entry Draft).

			Regular Season					Playoffs				
Season	Club	League	GP	G	A	Pts	PIM	GP	G	A	Pts	PIM
2005-06	HC Vitkovice U17	CzR-U17	22	2	7	9	4	1	0	0	0	0
2006-07	HC Vitkovice U17	CzR-U17	33	32	24	56	18	9	3	6	9	4
	HC Vitkovice Jr.	CzRep-Jr.	13	5	2	7	12	3	0	0	0	0
2007-08	HC Vitkovice U17	CzR-U17	4	2	3	5	0	2	1	1	2	2
	HC Vitkovice Jr.	CzRep-Jr.	42	19	18	37	28	2	1	0	1	2
2008-09	HC Vitkovice Jr.	CzRep-Jr.	42	23	33	56	14	10	8	6	14	12
2009-10	Drummondville	QMJHL	59	17	23	40	24	7	1	1	2	0
2010-11	Drummondville	QMJHL	61	39	57	96	24	10	4	7	11	6

PALIN, Brett (PAY-lihn, BREHT)

Defense. Shoots right. 6'1", 200 lbs. Born, Nanaimo, B.C., June 23, 1984.

			Regular Season					Playoffs				
Season	Club	League	GP	G	A	Pts	PIM	GP	G	A	Pts	PIM
2000-01	Kelowna Rockets	WHL	39	0	0	0	25	....	....	....	....	....
2001-02	Kelowna Rockets	WHL	70	0	1	1	88	15	0	0	0	4
2002-03	Kelowna Rockets	WHL	71	1	17	18	118	19	0	4	4	12
2003-04	Kelowna Rockets	WHL	72	1	16	17	106	17	0	5	5	24
2004-05	Kelowna Rockets	WHL	72	4	21	25	71	24	4	6	10	52
2005-06	Omaha	AHL	64	0	5	5	46	....	....	....	....	....
2006-07	Omaha	AHL	78	1	9	10	71	6	1	0	1	0
2007-08	Quad City Flames	AHL	67	0	10	10	68	....	....	....	....	....
2008-09	Quad City Flames	AHL	57	5	10	15	40	....	....	....	....	....
2009-10	Abbotsford Heat	AHL	21	0	3	3	17	2	0	0	0	2
2010-11	Milwaukee	AHL	80	4	14	18	70	13	0	1	1	4

Signed as a free agent by **Calgary**, August 5, 2005. • Missed majority of 2009-10 due to concussion. Signed as a free agent by **Nashville**, July 9, 2010.

PALIOTTA, Michael (pal-ee-AW-tuh, MIGH-kuhl) CHI

Defense. Shoots right. 6'3", 198 lbs. Born, Westport, CT, April 6, 1993.
(Chicago's 5th choice, 70th overall, in 2011 Entry Draft).

			Regular Season					Playoffs				
Season	Club	League	GP	G	A	Pts	PIM	GP	G	A	Pts	PIM
2008-09	Choate-Rosemary	High-CT	24	1	14	15	....	....	....	....	....	....
2009-10	USNTDP	USHL	32	1	6	7	43	....	....	....	....	....
	USNTDP	U-17	18	1	6	7	10	....	....	....	....	....
2010-11	USNTDP	USHL	24	0	5	5	35	....	....	....	....	....
	USNTDP	U-18	36	1	9	10	42	....	....	....	....	....

• Signed Letter of Intent to attend **University of Vermont** (Hockey East).

PALMER, Jarod (PAHL-muhr, JAIR-uhd) MIN

Right wing. Shoots right. 6', 200 lbs. Born, Fridley, MN, February 10, 1986.

			Regular Season					Playoffs				
Season	Club	League	GP	G	A	Pts	PIM	GP	G	A	Pts	PIM
2004-05	Tri-City Storm	USHL	52	15	26	41	67	9	1	0	1	14
2005-06	Tri-City Storm	USHL	58	15	37	52	91	5	1	1	2	9
2006-07	Miami U.	CCHA	42	11	19	30	26	....	....	....	....	....
2007-08	Miami U.	CCHA	42	10	25	35	32	....	....	....	....	....
2008-09	Miami U.	CCHA	41	8	19	27	34	....	....	....	....	....
2009-10	Miami U.	CCHA	44	18	27	45	40	....	....	....	....	....
2010-11	Houston Aeros	AHL	65	9	19	28	64	24	3	2	5	7

CCHA First All-Star Team (2010)

Signed as a free agent by **Minnesota**, April 26, 2010.

PANIK, Richard (PAH-nihk, RIH-chuhrd) T.B.

Right wing. Shoots left. 6'1", 211 lbs. Born, Martin, Czechoslovakia, February 7, 1991.
(Tampa Bay's 3rd choice, 52nd overall, in 2009 Entry Draft).

			Regular Season					Playoffs				
Season	Club	League	GP	G	A	Pts	PIM	GP	G	A	Pts	PIM
2005-06	MHC Martin U18	Svk-U18	40	11	13	24	20	4	4	2	6	4
2006-07	HC Trinec U17	CzR-U17	12	10	6	16	48	3	1	4	5	8
	HC Trinec Jr.	CzRep-Jr.	27	16	9	25	30	4	1	4	5	6
2007-08	HC Trinec Jr.	CzRep-Jr.	39	35	27	62	70	8	8	4	12	52
	HC Ocelari Trinec	CzRep	6	0	0	0	0	....	....	....	....	....
2008-09	HC Trinec Jr.	CzRep-Jr.	16	10	9	19	36	8	6	1	7	41
	HC Havirov	CzRep-2	3	2	1	3	0	....	....	....	....	....
	HC Ocelari Trinec	CzRep	15	1	1	2	4	4	0	0	0	0
2009-10	Windsor Spitfires	OHL	33	9	9	18	19	....	....	....	....	....
	Belleville Bulls	OHL	27	12	11	23	36	....	....	....	....	....
	Norfolk Admirals	AHL	5	0	1	1	0	....	....	....	....	....
2010-11	Belleville Bulls	OHL	27	14	17	31	33	....	....	....	....	....
	Guelph Storm	OHL	24	13	12	25	42	6	1	2	3	10

PAQUETTE, Danick (pa-KETT, DA-nihk) WSH

Right wing. Shoots right. 6'1", 210 lbs. Born, Montreal, Que., July 17, 1990.
(Atlanta's 3rd choice, 64th overall, in 2008 Entry Draft).

			Regular Season					Playoffs				
Season	Club	League	GP	G	A	Pts	PIM	GP	G	A	Pts	PIM
2005-06	Ecole Montpetit	QAAA	36	17	16	33	191	3	0	1	1	6
2006-07	Lewiston	QMJHL	63	4	14	18	112	14	0	0	0	18
2007-08	Lewiston	QMJHL	63	29	13	42	213	5	1	2	3	30
2008-09	Lewiston	QMJHL	61	25	25	50	230	2	1	2	3	25
	Chicago Wolves	AHL	4	0	0	0	12	....	....	....	....	....
2009-10	Quebec Remparts	QMJHL	64	36	29	65	136	5	1	3	4	21
2010-11	Gwinnett	ECHL	59	13	7	20	179	....	....	....	....	....

• Transferred to **Winnipeg** after **Atlanta** franchise relocated, June 21, 2011. Traded to **Washington** by **Winnipeg** with Winnipeg's 4th round choice in 2012 Entry Draft for Eric Fehr, July 8, 2011.

PARADIS, Philippe (PAIR-a-dee, fihl-EEP) CHI

Center. Shoots left. 6'2", 212 lbs. Born, Dolbeau, Que., January 2, 1991.
(Carolina's 1st choice, 27th overall, in 2009 Entry Draft).

			Regular Season					Playoffs				
Season	Club	League	GP	G	A	Pts	PIM	GP	G	A	Pts	PIM
2006-07	Jonquiere Elites	QAAA	38	5	12	17	76	3	1	1	2	6
2007-08	Shawinigan	QMJHL	45	11	12	23	44	3	0	0	0	0
2008-09	Shawinigan	QMJHL	66	19	31	50	74	21	6	6	12	20
2009-10	Shawinigan	QMJHL	63	24	20	44	104	6	2	1	3	4
	Toronto Marlies	AHL	4	0	2	2	0	....	....	....	....	....
2010-11	P.E.I. Rocket	QMJHL	59	23	30	53	85	5	1	1	2	8
	Rockford IceHogs	AHL	4	1	0	1	2	....	....	....	....	....

Traded to **Toronto** by **Carolina** for Jiri Tlusty, December 3, 2009. Traded to **Chicago** by **Toronto** with Viktor Stalberg and Chris Didomenico for Kris Versteeg and Bill Sweatt, June 30, 2010.

PARE, Francis (pa-RAY, FRAN-sihs) DET

Right wing. Shoots right. 5'10", 195 lbs. Born, Lemoyne, Que., June 30, 1987.

			Regular Season					Playoffs				
Season	Club	League	GP	G	A	Pts	PIM	GP	G	A	Pts	PIM
2003-04	Shawinigan	QMJHL	5	2	0	2	2	....	....	....	....	....
2004-05	Shawinigan	QMJHL	70	24	23	47	52	4	0	3	3	4
2005-06	Shawinigan	QMJHL	50	26	48	74	66	5	1	3	4	4
2006-07	Shawinigan	QMJHL	68	29	44	73	37	4	1	1	2	8
2007-08	Chicoutimi	QMJHL	69	54	48	102	54	6	5	3	8	4
2008-09	Grand Rapids	AHL	63	24	24	48	14	10	2	2	4	2
2009-10	Grand Rapids	AHL	77	16	23	39	20	....	....	....	....	....
2010-11	Grand Rapids	AHL	80	24	30	54	49	....	....	....	....	....

QMJHL First All-Star Team (2008) • Canadian Major Junior Second All-Star Team (2008)

Signed as a free agent by **Grand Rapids** (AHL), June 13, 2008. Signed as a free agent by **Detroit**, April 7, 2009.

PARKES, Trevor (PAHRKS, TREH-vuhr) DET

Right wing. Shoots right. 6'2", 185 lbs. Born, Fort Erie, Ont., May 13, 1991.

			Regular Season					Playoffs				
Season	Club	League	GP	G	A	Pts	PIM	GP	G	A	Pts	PIM
2008-09	Fort Erie Meteors	ON-Jr.B	52	23	20	43	34	5	0	1	1	2
2009-10	Montreal	QMJHL	66	27	20	47	34	....	....	....	....	....
2010-11	Montreal	QMJHL	60	33	29	62	32	10	6	2	8	12

Signed as a free agent by **Detroit**, September 23, 2010.

PARKS, Michael (PARKS, MIGH-kuhl) PHI

Right wing. Shoots right. 5'11", 188 lbs. Born, O'Fallon, MO, February 15, 1992.
(Philadelphia's 3rd choice, 149th overall, in 2010 Entry Draft).

			Regular Season					Playoffs				
Season	Club	League	GP	G	A	Pts	PIM	GP	G	A	Pts	PIM
2008-09	St. Louis Selects	Exhib.	46	38	47	85	26	....	....	....	....	....
2009-10	Cedar Rapids	USHL	51	11	11	22	57	5	0	1	1	0
2010-11	Cedar Rapids	USHL	56	25	17	42	42	8	3	1	4	6

• Signed Letter of Intent to attend **University of Notre Dame** (CCHA) in fall of 2011.

PARLETT, Blake (pahr-LET, BLAYK) NYR

Defense. Shoots right. 6'1", 205 lbs. Born, Bracebridge, Ont., May 13, 1989.

			Regular Season					Playoffs				
Season	Club	League	GP	G	A	Pts	PIM	GP	G	A	Pts	PIM
2004-05	Huntsville	OPJHL	48	4	12	16	56	....	....	....	....	....
2005-06	Barrie Colts	OHL	38	0	2	2	39	14	0	2	2	6
2006-07	Barrie Colts	OHL	36	1	5	6	47	....	....	....	....	....
	Windsor Spitfires	OHL	30	5	10	15	30	....	....	....	....	....
2007-08	Windsor Spitfires	OHL	33	3	3	6	10	....	....	....	....	....
	St. Michael's	OHL	28	0	7	7	53	4	0	0	0	8
2008-09	St. Michael's	OHL	68	8	26	34	74	10	0	2	2	13
2009-10	St. Michael's	OHL	68	11	35	46	108	16	1	4	5	18
2010-11	Connecticut Whale	AHL	24	2	10	12	17	6	1	2	3	2
	Greenville	ECHL	46	7	25	32	40	2	0	1	1	2

Signed as a free agent by **Connecticut** (AHL), July 28, 2010. • Assigned to **Greenville** (ECHL) by **Connecticut** (AHL), October 6, 2010. Signed as a free agent by **NY Rangers**, June 2, 2011.

PARSHIN, Denis (PAHR-shihn, DEH-nihs) COL

Right wing. Shoots left. 5'10", 165 lbs. Born, Rybinsk, USSR, February 1, 1986.
(Colorado's 3rd choice, 72nd overall, in 2004 Entry Draft).

			Regular Season					Playoffs				
Season	Club	League	GP	G	A	Pts	PIM	GP	G	A	Pts	PIM
2002-03	CSKA Moscow 2	Russia-3	4	1	0	1	2	....	....	....	....	....
2003-04	CSKA Moscow	Russia	27	2	4	6	4	....	....	....	....	....
	CSKA Moscow 2	Russia-3	STATISTICS NOT AVAILABLE									
2004-05	CSKA Moscow	Russia	42	3	4	7	18	....	....	....	....	....
2005-06	CSKA Moscow 2	Russia-3	STATISTICS NOT AVAILABLE									
	CSKA Moscow	Russia	37	2	8	10	22	6	0	2	2	2
2006-07	CSKA Moscow	Russia	54	18	14	32	24	12	2	2	4	8
2007-08	CSKA Moscow	Russia	56	12	23	35	46	6	1	0	1	0
2008-09	CSKA Moscow	Rus-KHL	48	13	14	27	34	8	1	0	1	6
2009-10	CSKA Moscow	Rus-KHL	56	21	22	43	28	3	0	1	1	6
2010-11	CSKA Moscow	Rus-KHL	49	16	17	33	32	....	....	....	....	....

PASHNIN, Mikhail (pahsh-NIHN, mih-KHIGH-eel) NYR

Defense. Shoots left. 6'1", 191 lbs. Born, Chelyabinsk, USSR, May 11, 1989.
(NY Rangers' 7th choice, 200th overall, in 2009 Entry Draft).

			Regular Season					Playoffs				
Season	Club	League	GP	G	A	Pts	PIM	GP	G	A	Pts	PIM
2005-06	Mechel 2	Russia-3	25	0	5	5	30	....	....	....	....	....
2006-07	Mechel 2	Russia-3	12	1	3	4	26	....	....	....	....	....
	Mechel	Russia-2	41	0	2	2	40	4	0	0	0	8
2007-08	Mechel 2	Russia-3	8	4	1	5	12	....	....	....	....	....
	Mechel	Russia-2	49	2	5	7	58	....	....	....	....	....
2008-09	Mechel 2	Russia-3	3	0	1	1	4	....	....	....	....	....
	Mechel	Russia-2	35	2	4	6	40	7	0	2	2	8
2009-10	CSKA Moscow	Rus-KHL	44	1	4	5	52	1	0	0	0	0
	CSKA Jr.	Russia-Jr.	4	0	3	3	2	4	1	1	2	20
2010-11	CSKA Moscow	Rus-KHL	42	2	2	4	38	....	....	....	....	....
	CSKA Jr.	Russia-Jr.	10	2	2	4	14	16	1	4	5	60

PATERYN, Greg (PA-tuhr-ihn, GREHG) MTL

Defense. Shoots right. 6'2", 212 lbs. Born, Sterling Heights, MI, June 20, 1990.
(Toronto's 4th choice, 128th overall, in 2008 Entry Draft).

			Regular Season					Playoffs				
Season	Club	League	GP	G	A	Pts	PIM	GP	G	A	Pts	PIM
2004-05	Brother Rice	High-MI	29	2	8	10	42	....	....	....	....	....
2005-06	Brother Rice	High-MI	24	0	8	8	34	....	....	....	....	....
2006-07	Brother Rice	High-MI	27	9	19	28	44	....	....	....	....	....
2007-08	Ohio	USHL	60	3	24	27	145	....	....	....	....	....
2008-09	U. of Michigan	CCHA	28	0	5	5	32	....	....	....	....	....
2009-10	U. of Michigan	CCHA	33	1	5	6	18	....	....	....	....	....
2010-11	U. of Michigan	CCHA	40	3	14	17	28	....	....	....	....	....

Traded to **Montreal** by **Toronto** with Toronto's 2nd round choice (later traded to Chicago, later traded back to Toronto, later traded to Boston - Boston selected Jared Knight) in 2010 Entry Draft for Mikhail Grabovski, July 3, 2008.

PATTERSON, Gaelan (PA-tuhr-suhn, GAY-luhn) CGY

Center. Shoots left. 6', 204 lbs. Born, La Ronge, Sask., August 22, 1990.
(Calgary's 6th choice, 201st overall, in 2009 Entry Draft).

			Regular Season					Playoffs				
Season	Club	League	GP	G	A	Pts	PIM	GP	G	A	Pts	PIM
2005-06	Beardy's	SMHL	38	7	10	17	16	....	....	....	....	....
2006-07	Saskatoon Blades	WHL	53	3	1	4	24	....	....	....	....	....
2007-08	Saskatoon Blades	WHL	51	4	6	10	38	....	....	....	....	....
2008-09	Saskatoon Blades	WHL	71	22	35	57	41	7	1	1	2	2
2009-10	Saskatoon Blades	WHL	71	26	33	59	31	10	4	6	10	6
	Abbotsford Heat	AHL	....	....	....	....	....	3	1	0	1	0
2010-11	Abbotsford Heat	AHL	61	7	14	21	15	....	....	....	....	....

PECA, Matthew (PEH-kuh, MA-thew) T.B.

Center. Shoots left. 5'9", 166 lbs. Born, Petawawa, Ont., April 27, 1993.
(Tampa Bay's 5th choice, 201st overall, in 2011 Entry Draft).

			Regular Season					Playoffs				
Season	Club	League	GP	G	A	Pts	PIM	GP	G	A	Pts	PIM
2008-09	Ott. Valley Titans	Minor-ON	23	10	17	27	12	6	2	3	5	2
	Ottawa Valley	Exhib.	12	7	13	20	6	....	....	....	....	....
2009-10	Pembroke	CJHL	60	21	26	47	10	15	3	3	6	6
2010-11	Pembroke	CJHL	50	26	46	72	14	14	11	10	21	6

• Signed Letter of Intent to attend **Quinnipiac University** (ECAC) in fall of 2011.

PEDAN, Andrey (peh-DAHN, AWN-dray) NYI

Defense. Shoots left. 6'4", 201 lbs. Born, Kaunas, Lithuania, July 3, 1993.
(NY Islanders' 4th choice, 63rd overall, in 2011 Entry Draft).

			Regular Season					Playoffs				
Season	Club	League	GP	G	A	Pts	PIM	GP	G	A	Pts	PIM
2009-10	Dyn.Moscow U18	Rus-U18	3	2	1	3	12	....	....	....	....	....
2010-11	Guelph Storm	OHL	51	2	10	12	89	6	0	8	8	8

PELECH, Michael (PEH-lehch, MIGH-kuhl)

Center/Left wing. Shoots left. 6'3", 209 lbs. Born, Toronto, Ont., October 6, 1989.
(Los Angeles' 7th choice, 156th overall, in 2009 Entry Draft).

			Regular Season					Playoffs				
Season	Club	League	GP	G	A	Pts	PIM	GP	G	A	Pts	PIM
2004-05	St. Mike's B's	OPJHL	47	12	25	37	22	23	1	7	8	20
2005-06	Kitchener Rangers	OHL	48	3	6	9	32	2	0	0	0	0
2006-07	St. Michael's	OHL	65	12	35	47	54	....	....	....	....	....
2007-08	St. Michael's	OHL	68	17	32	49	72	4	1	1	2	6
2008-09	St. Michael's	OHL	68	19	46	65	121	11	4	9	13	23
2009-10	Ontario Reign	ECHL	72	10	25	35	133	....	....	....	....	....
2010-11	Ontario Reign	ECHL	63	9	19	28	127	....	....	....	....	....
	Manchester	AHL	5	0	0	0	6	....	....	....	....	....

PELSS, Kristians (PEHLSH, KRIHS-tyehns) EDM

Left wing. Shoots left. 5'11", 175 lbs. Born, Preili, Latvia, September 9, 1992.
(Edmonton's 10th choice, 181st overall, in 2010 Entry Draft).

			Regular Season					Playoffs				
Season	Club	League	GP	G	A	Pts	PIM	GP	G	A	Pts	PIM
2007-08	Daugavpils U18	LatviaU18	27	33	21	54	26	....	....	....	....	....
2008-09	Daugavpils Jr.	Latvia-Jr.	8	3	9	12	16	....	....	....	....	....
	Latgale 2	Latvia	22	9	11	20	24	....	....	....	....	....
	Latgale	Belarus	31	3	4	7	14	....	....	....	....	....
2009-10	Dyn. Jr. Riga	Belarus	46	6	3	9	28	....	....	....	....	....
2010-11	Edmonton	WHL	63	14	19	33	31	4	0	2	2	6

PELTZ, Brad (PEHLTZ, BRAD) OTT

Left wing. Shoots right. 6', 172 lbs. Born, New York, NY, October 2, 1989.
(Ottawa's 8th choice, 190th overall, in 2009 Entry Draft).

			Regular Season					Playoffs				
Season	Club	League	GP	G	A	Pts	PIM	GP	G	A	Pts	PIM
2005-06	Avon Old Farms	High-CT	19	2	0	2	6	....	....	....	....	....
2006-07	Avon Old Farms	High-CT	26	8	7	15	8	....	....	....	....	....
2007-08	Avon Old Farms	High-CT	27	12	19	31	12	....	....	....	....	....
2008-09	Avon Old Farms	High-CT		DID NOT PLAY – INJURED								
2009-10	Bos. Jr. Bruins	EJHL	45	19	15	34	28	3	2	0	2	0
2010-11	Yale	ECAC		DID NOT PLAY – FRESHMAN								

PELUSO, Anthony (puh-LOO-soh, AN-toh-nee) ST.L.

Defense. Shoots right. 6'3", 235 lbs. Born, North York, Ont., April 18, 1989.
(St. Louis' 9th choice, 160th overall, in 2007 Entry Draft).

			Regular Season					Playoffs				
Season	Club	League	GP	G	A	Pts	PIM	GP	G	A	Pts	PIM
2004-05	Rich. Hill Stars	Minor-ON	30	22	20	42	80	....	....	....	....	....
2005-06	Erie Otters	OHL	68	5	3	8	66	....	....	....	....	....
2006-07	Erie Otters	OHL	52	7	3	10	176	....	....	....	....	....
2007-08	Erie Otters	OHL	21	3	3	6	41	....	....	....	....	....
	Sault Ste. Marie	OHL	42	4	11	15	83	14	2	1	3	12
2008-09	Sault Ste. Marie	OHL	36	9	6	15	68	....	....	....	....	....
	Brampton	OHL	27	11	11	22	57	21	8	7	15	29
2009-10	Peoria Rivermen	AHL	22	1	1	2	57	....	....	....	....	....
	Alaska Aces	ECHL	27	4	7	11	48	4	1	0	1	6
2010-11	Peoria Rivermen	AHL	62	5	2	7	102	4	1	0	1	0

PERCY, Stuart (PUHR-see, STEW-uhrt) TOR

Defense. Shoots left. 6'1", 187 lbs. Born, Oakville, Ont., May 18, 1993.
(Toronto's 2nd choice, 25th overall, in 2011 Entry Draft).

			Regular Season					Playoffs				
Season	Club	League	GP	G	A	Pts	PIM	GP	G	A	Pts	PIM
2008-09	Toronto Marlboros	GTHL	79	13	44	57	42	....	....	....	....	....
2009-10	St. Michael's	OHL	52	3	15	18	40	16	0	1	1	12
2010-11	St. Michael's	OHL	64	4	30	34	50	20	2	10	12	14

Memorial Cup All-Star Team (2011)

PERKOVICH, Nathan (puhr-KOH-vihch, NAY-thuhn) N.J.

Right wing. Shoots right. 6'5", 215 lbs. Born, Canton, MI, October 15, 1985.
(New Jersey's 6th choice, 250th overall, in 2004 Entry Draft).

			Regular Season					Playoffs				
Season	Club	League	GP	G	A	Pts	PIM	GP	G	A	Pts	PIM
2003-04	Cedar Rapids	USHL	35	1	7	8	23	4	1	0	1	0
2004-05	Chicago Steel	USHL	37	6	2	8	55	7	2	2	4	4
2005-06	Chicago Steel	USHL	56	28	24	52	121	....	....	....	....	....
2006-07	Lake Superior	CCHA	42	15	7	22	59	....	....	....	....	....
2007-08	Lake Superior	CCHA	36	17	8	25	52	....	....	....	....	....
2008-09	Lake Superior	CCHA	35	12	12	24	68	....	....	....	....	....
	Trenton Devils	ECHL	....	....	....	....	....	6	1	3	4	4
2009-10	Lowell Devils	AHL	68	19	14	33	81	5	0	1	1	0
2010-11	Albany Devils	AHL	40	8	9	17	59	....	....	....	....	....

PERLINI, Brett (PUHR-lee-nee, BREHT) ANA

Right wing. Shoots right. 6'2", 200 lbs. Born, Sault Ste. Marie, Ont., June 14, 1990.
(Anaheim's 8th choice, 192nd overall, in 2010 Entry Draft).

			Regular Season					Playoffs				
Season	Club	League	GP	G	A	Pts	PIM	GP	G	A	Pts	PIM
2006-07	Soo Thunderbirds	NOJHL	48	38	19	57	20	12	6	6	12	6
2007-08	Ohio	USHL	19	1	4	5	0	....	....	....	....	....
	Soo Thunderbirds	NOJHL	16	16	16	32	12	6	4	3	7	6
2008-09	Michigan State	CCHA	26	2	1	3	4	....	....	....	....	....
2009-10	Michigan State	CCHA	20	7	5	12	10	....	....	....	....	....
2010-11	Michigan State	CCHA	38	18	12	30	12	....	....	....	....	....

PERSSON, Dennis (PAIR-suhn, DEH-nihs) BUF

Defense. Shoots left. 6'1", 192 lbs. Born, Nykoping, Sweden, June 2, 1988.
(Buffalo's 1st choice, 24th overall, in 2006 Entry Draft).

			Regular Season					Playoffs				
Season	Club	League	GP	G	A	Pts	PIM	GP	G	A	Pts	PIM
2004-05	Vasteras U18	Swe-U18	3	0	1	1	2	4	0	1	1	0
	Vasteras Jr.	Swe-Jr.	27	3	3	6	24	....	....	....	....	....
2005-06	Vasteras Jr.	Swe-Jr.	28	11	15	26	22	....	....	....	....	....
	VIK Vasteras HK	Sweden-2	19	0	2	2	6	....	....	....	....	....
2006-07	Djurgarden	Sweden	9	0	0	0	2	....	....	....	....	....
	Almtuna	Sweden-2	3	0	0	0	2	....	....	....	....	....
	Nykoping	Sweden-2	29	4	4	8	38	....	....	....	....	....
	Djurgarden Jr.	Swe-Jr.	11	1	3	4	8	5	2	3	5	2
2007-08	Djurgarden Jr.	Swe-Jr.	4	0	0	0	10	....	....	....	....	....
	Djurgarden	Sweden	21	0	1	1	6	....	....	....	....	....
	Nykoping	Sweden-2	21	1	3	4	14	....	....	....	....	....
2008-09	Timra IK	Sweden	46	1	5	6	24	7	0	0	0	0
	Timra IK Jr.	Swe-Jr.	1	0	0	0	0	....	....	....	....	....
	Portland Pirates	AHL	8	0	2	2	6	3	0	0	0	0
2009-10	Portland Pirates	AHL	60	1	6	7	16	....	....	....	....	....
2010-11	Portland Pirates	AHL	64	4	13	17	18	11	0	4	4	0

PERSSON, John (PAIR-suhn, JAWN) NYI

Left wing. Shoots left. 6'2", 199 lbs. Born, Ostersund, Sweden, May 18, 1992.
(NY Islanders' 6th choice, 125th overall, in 2011 Entry Draft).

			Regular Season					Playoffs				
Season	Club	League	GP	G	A	Pts	PIM	GP	G	A	Pts	PIM
2008-09	Mora IK U18	Swe-U18	24	18	12	30	6	....	....	....	....	....
	Mora IK Jr.	Swe-Jr.	12	4	2	6	12	....	....	....	....	....
2009-10	Red Deer Rebels	WHL	62	7	4	11	12	2	0	0	0	2
2010-11	Red Deer Rebels	WHL	68	33	28	61	34	9	2	3	5	4

PERVYSHIN, Andrei (pair-VIHSH-ihn, AWN-dray) ST.L.

Defense. Shoots left. 5'8", 165 lbs. Born, Arkhangelsk, USSR, February 2, 1985.
(St. Louis' 11th choice, 253rd overall, in 2003 Entry Draft).

			Regular Season					Playoffs				
Season	Club	League	GP	G	A	Pts	PIM	GP	G	A	Pts	PIM
2003-04	Spartak Moscow	Russia-2	59	3	6	9	14	13	0	1	1	4
2004-05	Ak Bars Kazan	Russia	52	0	3	3	10	2	0	0	0	0
	Ak Bars Kazan 2	Russia-3	....	0	1	1	....	....	....	....	....	....
2005-06	Ak Bars Kazan	Russia	48	3	7	10	22	13	0	3	3	14
2006-07	Ak Bars Kazan	Russia	45	5	8	13	71	12	2	3	5	8
2007-08	Ak Bars Kazan	Russia	55	7	8	15	40	10	1	1	2	2
2008-09	Ak Bars Kazan	Rus-KHL	54	6	21	27	28	21	1	9	10	10
2009-10	Ak Bars Kazan	Rus-KHL	53	5	15	20	26	17	0	2	2	6
2010-11	Omsk	Rus-KHL	52	5	19	24	28	14	2	3	5	10

PESTUNOV, Dmitri (pehs-too-NAWF, dih-MEE-tree) PHX

Center. Shoots left. 5'9", 196 lbs. Born, Ust-Kamenogorsk, USSR, January 22, 1985.
(Phoenix's 2nd choice, 80th overall, in 2003 Entry Draft).

			Regular Season					Playoffs				
Season	Club	League	GP	G	A	Pts	PIM	GP	G	A	Pts	PIM
2002-03	Magnitogorsk	Russia	32	4	0	4	0	....	....	....	....	....
2003-04	Magnitogorsk	Russia	51	6	7	13	40	14	0	3	3	25
	Magnitogorsk 2	Russia-3	6	3	15	18	2	3	0	2	2	4
2004-05	Magnitogorsk	Russia	37	4	4	8	46	....	....	....	....	....
	Spartak Moscow	Russia	12	1	1	2	14	....	....	....	....	....
2005-06	Magnitogorsk	Russia	48	6	13	19	58	4	0	1	1	0
2006-07	Magnitogorsk	Russia	53	5	18	23	26	11	0	0	0	8
2007-08	Spartak Moscow	Russia	51	8	17	25	56	5	0	0	0	16
2008-09	Omsk	Rus-KHL	56	7	34	41	58	9	0	3	3	16
2009-10	Omsk	Rus-KHL	48	5	18	23	30	2	0	0	0	0
2010-11	Chelyabinsk	Rus-KHL	43	6	11	17	46	....	....	....	....	....
	Dynamo Moscow	Rus-KHL	10	3	2	5	4	6	1	1	2	2

Signed as a free agent by **Spartak Moscow** (Russia), February 16, 2005. Signed as a free agent by **Omsk** (Russia-KHL), May 16, 2008. Signed as a free agent by **Chelyabinsk** (Russia-KHL), July 15, 2010. Signed as a free agent by **Dynamo Moscow** (Russia-KHL), January 18, 2011.

PETERSEN, Nick (PEE-tuhr-suhn, NIHK) PIT

Right wing. Shoots right. 6'2", 186 lbs. Born, Wakefield, Que., May 27, 1989.
(Pittsburgh's 4th choice, 121st overall, in 2009 Entry Draft).

			Regular Season					Playoffs				
Season	Club	League	GP	G	A	Pts	PIM	GP	G	A	Pts	PIM
2006-07	Georgetown Prep.	High-MD	....	28	14	42	....	....	....	....	....	....
	Wsh. Jr. Nationals	AtJHL	40	24	34	58	40	....	....	....	....	....
2007-08	Shawinigan	QMJHL	51	11	18	29	38	5	5	1	6	8
2008-09	Shawinigan	QMJHL	68	37	53	90	42	21	10	12	22	22
2009-10	Saint John	QMJHL	59	39	40	79	55	21	7	*21	28	14
2010-11	Wilkes-Barre	AHL	23	5	9	14	4	11	2	0	2	6
	Wheeling Nailers	ECHL	40	24	33	57	30	....	....	....	....	....

PETERSSON, Andre (PEH-tuhr-suhn, AHN-dray) OTT

Right wing. Shoots right. 5'9", 172 lbs. Born, Olofstrom, Sweden, September 11, 1990.
(Ottawa's 4th choice, 109th overall, in 2008 Entry Draft).

			Regular Season					Playoffs				
Season	Club	League	GP	G	A	Pts	PIM	GP	G	A	Pts	PIM
2005-06	Tingsryds AIF U18	Swe-U18	9	5	3	8	0	....	....	....	....	....
2006-07	HV 71 U18	Swe-U18	10	14	10	24	6	2	1	2	3	0
	HV 71 Jr.	Swe-Jr.	6	1	1	2	8	....	....	....	....	....
2007-08	HV 71 U18	Swe-U18	4	4	5	9	4	....	....	....	....	....
	HV 71 Jr.	Swe-Jr.	36	16	22	38	34	3	0	0	0	2
2008-09	HV 71 Jonkoping	Sweden	10	0	1	1	0	....	....	....	....	....
	HV 71 Jr.	Swe-Jr.	36	24	31	55	28	7	7	4	11	8
2009-10	Boras HC	Sweden-2	1	1	0	1	0	....	....	....	....	....
	HV 71 Jonkoping	Sweden	37	10	5	15	14	6	0	1	1	2
2010-11	HV 71 Jonkoping	Sweden	31	8	4	12	18	....	....	....	....	....

PETRECKI, Nicholas (peh-TREH-kee, NIH-koh-las) S.J.

Defense. Shoots left. 6'3", 230 lbs. Born, Schenectady, NY, July 11, 1989.
(San Jose's 2nd choice, 28th overall, in 2007 Entry Draft).

			Regular Season					Playoffs				
Season	Club	League	GP	G	A	Pts	PIM	GP	G	A	Pts	PIM
2004-05	Capital District	EmJHL	53	5	18	23	159	....	....	....	....	....
2005-06	Omaha Lancers	USHL	53	0	3	3	110	5	0	0	0	0
2006-07	Omaha Lancers	USHL	54	11	14	25	177	5	0	0	0	10
2007-08	Boston College	H-East	42	5	7	12	*102	....	....	....	....	....
2008-09	Boston College	H-East	35	0	7	7	*161	....	....	....	....	....
2009-10	Worcester Sharks	AHL	65	2	12	14	106	....	....	....	....	....
2010-11	Worcester Sharks	AHL	67	3	11	14	129	....	....	....	....	....

USHL Second All-Star Team (2007)

PETRELL, Lennart (peh-TREHL, LEH-nahrt) EDM

Center. Shoots left. 6'3", 220 lbs. Born, Helsinki, Finland, April 13, 1984.
(Columbus' 8th choice, 190th overall, in 2004 Entry Draft).

			Regular Season					Playoffs				
Season	Club	League	GP	G	A	Pts	PIM	GP	G	A	Pts	PIM
2000-01	K-Kissat Jr.	Fin-Jr.	4	3	2	5	0	....	....	....	....	....
	K-Kissat	Finland-4	1	0	0	0	0	....	....	....	....	....
2001-02	HIFK Helsinki U18	Fin-U18	18	10	8	18	12	8	2	0	2	2
	HIFK Helsinki Jr.	Fin-Jr.	5	0	0	0	0	....	....	....	....	....
2002-03	HIFK Helsinki Jr.	Fin-Jr.	28	2	2	4	35	7	3	1	4	29
2003-04	Suomi U20	Finland-2	7	1	0	1	0	....	....	....	....	....
	HIFK Helsinki Jr.	Fin-Jr.	33	11	17	28	28	10	6	7	13	2
	HIFK Helsinki	Finland	8	0	0	0	2	1	0	0	0	0
2004-05	HIFK Helsinki Jr.	Fin-Jr.	12	5	5	10	10	2	0	1	1	0
	HIFK Helsinki	Finland	35	3	2	5	35	4	0	1	1	2
2005-06	HIFK Helsinki	Finland	51	12	8	20	88	10	1	2	3	20
2006-07	HIFK Helsinki	Finland	53	19	11	30	74	5	0	0	0	2
2007-08	HIFK Helsinki	Finland	48	10	17	27	34	7	1	1	2	2
2008-09	HIFK Helsinki	Finland	43	7	13	20	85	2	0	0	0	2
2009-10	HIFK Helsinki	Finland	56	12	12	24	61	6	1	0	1	2
2010-11	HIFK Helsinki	Finland	56	13	22	35	34	13	7	5	12	8

Signed as a free agent by **Edmonton**, June 15, 2011.

PETROV, Kirill (peh-TRAWF, kih-RIHL) NYI

Right wing. Shoots left. 6'3", 198 lbs. Born, Kazan, USSR, April 13, 1990.
(NY Islanders' 7th choice, 73rd overall, in 2008 Entry Draft).

			Regular Season					Playoffs				
Season	Club	League	GP	G	A	Pts	PIM	GP	G	A	Pts	PIM
2005-06	Ak Bars Kazan 2	Russia-3	STATISTICS NOT AVAILABLE									
2006-07	Ak Bars Kazan 2	Russia-3	STATISTICS NOT AVAILABLE									
	Ak Bars Kazan	Russia	9	1	1	2	8	3	0	0	0	2
2007-08	Ak Bars Kazan	Russia	47	4	6	10	54	8	1	1	2	0
2008-09	Ak Bars Kazan 2	Russia-3	9	4	10	14	26	....	....	....	....	....
	Ak Bars Kazan	Rus-KHL	6	1	0	1	2	....	....	....	....	....
2009-10	Ak Bars Kazan	Rus-KHL	8	0	0	0	4	3	0	1	1	0
	Bars Kazan Jr.	Russia-Jr.	4	2	1	3	4	....	....	....	....	....
	Almetjevsk	Russia-2	22	7	13	20	48	13	12	7	19	24
2010-11	Ak Bars Kazan	Rus-KHL	2	0	0	0	0	....	....	....	....	....
	Bars Kazan Jr.	Russia-Jr.	3	1	1	2	4	....	....	....	....	....
	Khanty-Mansiisk	Rus-KHL	47	8	11	19	20	6	2	2	4	8

PETROVIC, Alex (peh-TROH-vihch, AL-ehx) FLA

Defense. Shoots right. 6'4", 193 lbs. Born, Edmonton, Alta., March 3, 1992.
(Florida's 5th choice, 36th overall, in 2010 Entry Draft).

			Regular Season					Playoffs				
Season	Club	League	GP	G	A	Pts	PIM	GP	G	A	Pts	PIM
2007-08	Edm. MLAC	AMHL	31	3	8	11	80	....	....	....	....	....
	Red Deer Rebels	WHL	10	1	0	1	2	....	....	....	....	....
2008-09	Red Deer Rebels	WHL	66	1	12	13	70	....	....	....	....	....
2009-10	Red Deer Rebels	WHL	57	8	19	27	87	4	0	0	0	4
2010-11	Red Deer Rebels	WHL	69	7	50	57	140	9	0	6	6	23

WHL East Second All-Star Team (2011)

PHILLIPS, Paul (FIHL-ihps, PAWL) CHI

Defense. Shoots left. 6'1", 195 lbs. Born, Darien, IL, July 16, 1991.
(Chicago's 7th choice, 195th overall, in 2009 Entry Draft).

			Regular Season					Playoffs				
Season	Club	League	GP	G	A	Pts	PIM	GP	G	A	Pts	PIM
2006-07	Chicago Fury	MWEHL	26	7	5	12	40	....	....	....	....	....
2007-08	Cedar Rapids	USHL	43	1	2	3	25	3	0	0	0	4
2008-09	Cedar Rapids	USHL	60	8	25	33	56	5	0	0	0	6
2009-10	U. of Denver	WCHA	31	0	4	4	16	....	....	....	....	....
2010-11	U. of Denver	WCHA	38	0	4	4	22	....	....	....	....	....

PHILLIPS, Zack (FIHL-ihps, ZAK) MIN

Center. Shoots right. 6', 175 lbs. Born, Fredericton, NB, October 28, 1992.
(Minnesota's 2nd choice, 28th overall, in 2011 Entry Draft).

			Regular Season					Playoffs				
Season	Club	League	GP	G	A	Pts	PIM	GP	G	A	Pts	PIM
2008-09	Lawrence	High-MA	30	19	29	48	....	....	....	....	....	....
2009-10	Saint John	QMJHL	65	16	28	44	31	21	2	4	6	4
2010-11	Saint John	QMJHL	67	38	57	95	16	17	9	15	24	8

PICHE, Sebastien (PEE-shay, suh-BAS-tee-yehn) DET

Defense. Shoots left. 6', 198 lbs. Born, Lasarre, Que., February 4, 1988.

			Regular Season					Playoffs				
Season	Club	League	GP	G	A	Pts	PIM	GP	G	A	Pts	PIM
2004-05	Rouyn-Noranda	QMJHL	2	0	0	0	2	....	....	....	....	....
	Lewiston	QMJHL	24	0	3	3	33	8	0	1	1	18
2005-06	Lewiston	QMJHL	65	1	14	15	83	6	0	1	1	12
2006-07	Lewiston	QMJHL	62	4	23	27	122	10	3	3	6	8
2007-08	Shawinigan	QMJHL	18	1	11	12	21	....	....	....	....	....
	Rouyn-Noranda	QMJHL	32	1	27	28	44	17	4	19	23	*39
2008-09	Rimouski Oceanic	QMJHL	62	23	49	72	69	12	2	4	6	14
2009-10	Grand Rapids	AHL	9	0	0	0	4	....	....	....	....	....
	Toledo Walleye	ECHL	46	5	23	28	67	4	0	2	2	4
2010-11	Grand Rapids	AHL	11	0	2	2	13	....	....	....	....	....
	Toledo Walleye	ECHL	48	12	21	33	52	....	....	....	....	....

QMJHL Second All-Star Team (2009)

Signed as a free agent by **Detroit**, April 12, 2009.

PIERRO-ZABOTEL, Casey (PEE-air-oh-ZA-boh-tuhl, KAY-see) PIT

Center. Shoots left. 6'1", 205 lbs. Born, Ashcroft, B.C., November 8, 1988.
(Pittsburgh's 4th choice, 80th overall, in 2007 Entry Draft).

			Regular Season					Playoffs				
Season	Club	League	GP	G	A	Pts	PIM	GP	G	A	Pts	PIM
2004-05	Merritt	BCHL	58	6	6	12	19	5	0	0	0	0
2005-06	Merritt	BCHL	60	20	35	55	29	9	9	4	13	10
2006-07	Merritt	BCHL	55	51	65	116	42	7	8	3	11	13
2007-08	Vancouver Giants	WHL	49	19	29	48	8	10	2	4	6	4
2008-09	Vancouver Giants	WHL	72	36	*79	*115	52	17	4	13	17	16
2009-10	Wilkes-Barre	AHL	9	0	1	1	0	....	....	....	....	....
	Wheeling Nailers	ECHL	49	12	29	41	26	....	....	....	....	....
2010-11	Wheeling Nailers	ECHL	42	14	20	34	42	....	....	....	....	....
	Cincinnati	ECHL	25	4	16	20	8	4	0	0	0	0

WHL West First All-Star Team (2009) • Canadian Major Junior Second All-Star Team (2009)

PIETILA, Blake (pee-EH-tihl-a, BLAYK) N.J.

Left wing. Shoots left. 5'11", 190 lbs. Born, Milford, MI, February 20, 1993.
(New Jersey's 5th choice, 129th overall, in 2011 Entry Draft).

			Regular Season					Playoffs				
Season	Club	League	GP	G	A	Pts	PIM	GP	G	A	Pts	PIM
2008-09	Det. Compuware	T1EHL	31	8	11	19	8	5	1	5	6	0
2009-10	USNTDP	USHL	28	5	3	8	27	....	....	....	....	....
	USNTDP	U-17	18	1	6	7	10	....	....	....	....	....
	USNTDP	U-18	1	0	0	0	0	....	....	....	....	....
2010-11	USNTDP	USHL	24	4	5	9	20	....	....	....	....	....
	USNTDP	U-18	13	10	4	14	33	....	....	....	....	....

• Signed Letter of Intent to attend **Michigan Tech University** (WCHA).

PINIZZOTTO, Steve (pih-nih-ZAW-toh, STEEV) VAN

Center. Shoots right. 6'1", 200 lbs. Born, Mississauga, Ont., April 26, 1984.

			Regular Season					Playoffs				
Season	Club	League	GP	G	A	Pts	PIM	GP	G	A	Pts	PIM
2001-02	Oakville Blades	OPJHL	34	10	16	26	40	....	....	....	....	....
2002-03	Oakville Blades	OPJHL	44	16	24	40	152	2	0	0	0	2
2003-04	Oakville Blades	OPJHL	39	17	34	51	177	....	....	....	....	....
2004-05	Oakville Blades	OPJHL	48	33	62	95	86	....	....	....	....	....
2005-06	RIT Tigers	NCAA	20	7	6	13	32	....	....	....	....	....
2006-07	RIT Tigers	AH	34	13	31	44	76	....	....	....	....	....
	Hershey Bears	AHL	5	0	0	0	4	....	....	....	....	....
2007-08	Hershey Bears	AHL	23	0	4	4	12	5	0	0	0	13
	South Carolina	ECHL	40	15	17	32	58	10	1	2	3	34
2008-09	Hershey Bears	AHL	45	4	7	11	61	21	3	2	5	28
	South Carolina	ECHL	11	4	6	10	19	....	....	....	....	....
2009-10	Hershey Bears	AHL	69	13	28	41	124	21	5	3	8	33
2010-11	Hershey Bears	AHL	68	17	25	42	178	6	2	2	4	6

Signed as a free agent by **Washington**, March 16, 2007. Signed as a free agent by **Vancouver**, July 3, 2011.

PISTILLI, Matthew (pihs-TIHL-lee, MATH-yew) CAR

Right wing. Shoots right. 6'2", 219 lbs. Born, Montreal, Que., October 17, 1988.

			Regular Season					Playoffs				
Season	Club	League	GP	G	A	Pts	PIM	GP	G	A	Pts	PIM
2004-05	Trois-Rivieres	QAAA	41	20	28	48	34	....	....	....	....	....
	Shawinigan	QMJHL	2	1	1	2	6	....	....	....	....	....
2005-06	Shawinigan	QMJHL	34	5	5	10	20	....	....	....	....	....
	Gatineau	QMJHL	32	10	13	23	16	17	2	2	4	8
2006-07	Gatineau	QMJHL	65	22	29	51	44	5	1	1	2	2
2007-08	Gatineau	QMJHL	63	37	56	93	51	19	11	17	28	14
2008-09	Shawinigan	QMJHL	63	45	41	86	37	21	13	7	20	4
2009-10	Albany River Rats	AHL	41	5	3	8	10	....	....	....	....	....
	Florida Everblades	ECHL	11	2	2	4	4	8	3	6	9	2
2010-11	Charlotte	AHL	50	8	11	19	15	5	0	1	1	0
	Florida Everblades	ECHL	27	15	16	31	12	....	....	....	....	....

Canadian Major Junior Humanitarian Player of the Year (2009)

Signed as a free agent by **Carolina**, May 20, 2009.

PITHER, Luke (PIH-tuhr, LEWK) PHI

Center. Shoots left. 6', 186 lbs. Born, Burketon, Ont., April 26, 1989.

			Regular Season					Playoffs				
Season	Club	League	GP	G	A	Pts	PIM	GP	G	A	Pts	PIM
2004-05	Bowmanville	OPJHL	2	1	0	1	0	....	....	....	....	....
2005-06	Kingston	OHL	68	4	9	13	26	6	0	1	1	2
2006-07	Kingston	OHL	5	1	0	1	2	....	....	....	....	....
	Guelph Storm	OHL	52	15	13	28	22	4	1	0	1	2
2007-08	Guelph Storm	OHL	51	13	29	42	31	10	0	2	2	0
2008-09	Guelph Storm	OHL	41	16	14	30	22	....	....	....	....	....
	Belleville Bulls	OHL	23	19	23	42	10	17	6	13	19	6
2009-10	Barrie Colts	OHL	67	36	58	94	44	17	9	11	20	4
2010-11	Adirondack	AHL	67	9	11	20	19	....	....	....	....	....

Signed as a free agent by **Philadelphia**, March 4, 2010.

PITLICK, Tyler (PIHT-lihk, TIGH-luhr) EDM

Center. Shoots right. 6'2", 195 lbs. Born, Minneapolis, MN, November 1, 1991.
(Edmonton's 2nd choice, 31st overall, in 2010 Entry Draft).

			Regular Season					Playoffs				
Season	Club	League	GP	G	A	Pts	PIM	GP	G	A	Pts	PIM
2007-08	Centennial	High-MN	....	25	34	59	....	....	....	....	....	....
2008-09	Centennial	High-MN	25	31	33	64	....	....	....	....	....	....
2009-10	Minnesota State	WCHA	38	11	8	19	27	....	....	....	....	....
2010-11	Medicine Hat	WHL	56	27	35	62	31	....	....	....	....	....

PLACEK, Petr (PLAH-chehk, PEH-tuhr) PHI

Right wing. Shoots right. 6'4", 210 lbs. Born, Slany, Czech., December 28, 1992.
(Philadelphia's 5th choice, 176th overall, in 2011 Entry Draft).

			Regular Season					Playoffs				
Season	Club	League	GP	G	A	Pts	PIM	GP	G	A	Pts	PIM
2006-07	HC Kladno U17	CzR-U17	3	1	0	1	4	....	....	....	....	....
2007-08	HC Kladno U17	CzR-U17	46	10	12	22	10	3	0	1	1	0
2008-09	Hotchkiss School	High-CT	21	7	8	15	....	....	....	....	....	....
2009-10	Hotchkiss School	High-CT	22	16	16	32	....	....	....	....	....	....
2010-11	Junior Bobcats	Indep.	STATISTICS NOT AVAILABLE									
	Hotchkiss School	High-CT	8	7	6	13	10	....	....	....	....	....

• Missed majority of 2008-09 due to knee and ankle injuries. • Signed Letter of Intent to attend **Harvard University** (ECAC) in fall of 2011. • Missed majority of 2010-11 due to knee surgery.

POLASEK, Adam (poh-LAH-shehk, A-duhm) VAN

Defense. Shoots left. 6'3", 200 lbs. Born, Ostrava, Czechoslovakia, July 12, 1991.
(Vancouver's 2nd choice, 145th overall, in 2010 Entry Draft).

			Regular Season					Playoffs				
Season	Club	League	GP	G	A	Pts	PIM	GP	G	A	Pts	PIM
2005-06	HC Vitkovice U17	CzR-U17	17	1	0	1	2	....	....	....	....	....
2006-07	HC Vitkovice U17	CzR-U17	43	6	13	19	83	9	0	1	1	12
	HC Vitkovice Jr.	CzRep-Jr.	1	0	0	0	2	....	....	....	....	....
2007-08	HC Vitkovice U17	CzR-U17	18	3	2	5	50	2	0	0	0	0
	HC Vitkovice Jr.	CzRep-Jr.	23	0	3	3	16	2	0	1	1	0
2008-09	HC Vitkovice Jr.	CzRep-Jr.	38	7	13	20	68	9	0	9	9	18
2009-10	P.E.I. Rocket	QMJHL	66	13	28	41	91	5	0	0	0	2
2010-11	P.E.I. Rocket	QMJHL	61	7	32	39	59	5	0	0	0	8

QMJHL All-Rookie Team (2010) • Canadian Major Junior All-Rookie Team (2010)

PONICH, Brett (PAW-nihch, BREHT) ST.L.

Defense. Shoots left. 6'7", 225 lbs. Born, Edmonton, Alta., February 22, 1991.
(St. Louis' 2nd choice, 48th overall, in 2009 Entry Draft).

			Regular Season					Playoffs				
Season	Club	League	GP	G	A	Pts	PIM	GP	G	A	Pts	PIM
2006-07	Leduc Oil Kings	AMHL	35	1	10	11	64	13	1	6	7	24
	Portland	WHL	2	0	0	0	0	....	....	....	....	....
2007-08	Portland	WHL	64	0	3	3	63	....	....	....	....	....
2008-09	Portland	WHL	72	1	17	18	117	....	....	....	....	....
2009-10	Portland	WHL	66	1	13	14	87	13	1	2	3	13
2010-11	Portland	WHL	45	0	12	12	60	....	....	....	....	....

POPE, Matt (POHP, MAT)

Right wing. Shoots right. 6'1", 185 lbs. Born, Langley, B.C., August 5, 1984.

			Regular Season					Playoffs				
Season	Club	League	GP	G	A	Pts	PIM	GP	G	A	Pts	PIM
2003-04	Langley Hornets	BCHL	60	27	44	71	92	....	....	....	....	....
2004-05	Bemidji State	CHA	37	7	7	14	28	....	....	....	....	....
2005-06	Bemidji State	CHA	37	7	14	21	44	....	....	....	....	....
2006-07	Bemidji State	CHA	33	5	8	13	14	....	....	....	....	....
2007-08	Bemidji State	CHA	36	14	9	23	40	....	....	....	....	....
2008-09	Binghamton	AHL	4	2	1	3	4	....	....	....	....	....
	Manitoba Moose	AHL	8	2	3	5	6	12	3	3	6	2
	Bakersfield	ECHL	54	30	33	63	72	....	....	....	....	....
2009-10	Manitoba Moose	AHL	40	3	5	8	23	2	0	1	1	10
	Bakersfield	ECHL	6	4	4	8	2	....	....	....	....	....
2010-11	San Antonio	AHL	55	4	7	11	35	....	....	....	....	....

Signed as a free agent by **Vancouver**, July 2, 2009. Signed to a PTO (professional tryout) contract by **San Antonio** (AHL), October 10, 2010.

POPOV, Andrei (PAH-pawv, AWN-dray) PHI

Right wing. Shoots left. 6', 187 lbs. Born, Chelyabinsk, USSR, July 15, 1988.
(Philadelphia's 10th choice, 205th overall, in 2006 Entry Draft).

			Regular Season					Playoffs				
Season	Club	League	GP	G	A	Pts	PIM	GP	G	A	Pts	PIM
2003-04	Chelyabinsk 2	Russia-3	6	3	0	3	4	....	....	....	....	....
2004-05	Chelyabinsk 2	Russia-3	17	7	1	8	4	....	....	....	....	....
2005-06	Chelyabinsk 2	Russia-3	2	1	4	5	0	....	....	....	....	....
	Chelyabinsk	Russia-2	37	8	8	16	26	5	2	0	2	2
2006-07	Chelyabinsk 2	Russia-3	2	1	1	2	0	....	....	....	....	....
	Chelyabinsk	Russia	44	2	10	12	36	....	....	....	....	....
2007-08	Chelyabinsk 2	Russia-3	6	4	3	7	4	....	....	....	....	....
	Chelyabinsk	Russia	33	5	2	7	12	2	0	0	0	4
2008-09	Chelyabinsk	Rus-KHL	54	4	5	9	38	3	0	0	0	0
2009-10	Chelyabinsk	Rus-KHL	50	15	11	26	24	4	0	1	1	2
	Chelyabinsk Jr.	Russia-Jr.	5	6	6	12	4	9	5	9	14	8
2010-11	Chelyabinsk	Rus-KHL	54	10	13	23	30	....	....	....	....	....

PRIBYL, Daniel (PRIH-buhl, DAN-yehl) MTL

Center. Shoots right. 6'3", 189 lbs. Born, Pisek, Czechoslovakia, December 18, 1992.
(Montreal's 5th choice, 168th overall, in 2011 Entry Draft).

			Regular Season					Playoffs				
Season	Club	League	GP	G	A	Pts	PIM	GP	G	A	Pts	PIM
2008-09	IHC Pisek U17	CzR-U17	44	30	17	47	88	....	....	....	....	....
2009-10	Sparta U18	CzR-U18	38	19	18	37	30	3	2	1	3	0
	Sparta Jr.	CzRep-Jr.	7	1	1	2	10	1	0	0	0	0
2010-11	Sparta Jr.	CzRep-Jr.	41	27	31	58	22	4	4	1	5	2
	Beroun	CzRep-2	1	0	0	0	0	....	....	....	....	....
	HC Sparta Praha	CzRep	7	2	1	3	0	....	....	....	....	....

PRICE, Jeremy (PRIGHS, JAIR-eh-mee) VAN

Defense. Shoots right. 6'1", 190 lbs. Born, Milton, Ont., September 26, 1990.
(Vancouver's 4th choice, 113th overall, in 2009 Entry Draft).

			Regular Season					Playoffs				
Season	Club	League	GP	G	A	Pts	PIM	GP	G	A	Pts	PIM
2006-07	Milton Icehawks	OPJHL	37	1	6	7	51	5	2	1	3	9
2007-08	Milton Icehawks	OPJHL	44	10	22	32	28	10	0	6	6	4
2008-09	Nepean Raiders	CJHL	55	12	29	41	50	14	2	4	6	14
2009-10	Colgate	ECAC	35	6	8	14	32	....	....	....	....	....
2010-11	Colgate	ECAC	42	5	14	19	28	....	....	....	....	....

PRINCE, Shane (PRIHNS, SHAYN) OTT

Center. Shoots left. 5'11", 183 lbs. Born, Rochester, NY, November 16, 1992.
(Ottawa's 4th choice, 61st overall, in 2011 Entry Draft).

			Regular Season					Playoffs				
Season	Club	League	GP	G	A	Pts	PIM	GP	G	A	Pts	PIM
2007-08	Maksymum	EmJHL	34	15	31	46	10	....	....	....	....	....
	Maksymum	Exhib.	10	3	4	7	4	....	....	....	....	....
	Syracuse Stars	EJHL	11	3	3	6	4	2	0	0	0	0
2008-09	Kitchener Rangers	OHL	63	3	9	12	34	....	....	....	....	....
2009-10	Kitchener Rangers	OHL	39	8	9	17	32	....	....	....	....	....
	Ottawa 67's	OHL	26	7	6	13	13	12	2	2	4	4
2010-11	Ottawa 67's	OHL	59	25	63	88	18	3	1	0	1	0

PROUT, Dalton (PROWT, DAHL-tuhn) CBJ

Defense. Shoots right. 6'3", 223 lbs. Born, LaSalle, Ont., March 13, 1990.
(Columbus' 7th choice, 154th overall, in 2010 Entry Draft).

			Regular Season					Playoffs				
Season	Club	League	GP	G	A	Pts	PIM	GP	G	A	Pts	PIM
2005-06	Wind. Jr. Spitfires	Minor-ON	58	11	19	30	78	....	....	....	....	....
2006-07	Sarnia Sting	OHL	49	1	2	3	36	4	0	0	0	0
2007-08	Sarnia Sting	OHL	32	0	2	2	43	....	....	....	....	....
	Barrie Colts	OHL	25	0	3	3	39	8	0	2	2	16
2008-09	Barrie Colts	OHL	65	0	6	6	98	5	0	1	1	10
2009-10	Barrie Colts	OHL	63	7	14	21	121	17	1	6	7	20
2010-11	Barrie Colts	OHL	23	7	14	21	55	....	....	....	....	....
	Saginaw Spirit	OHL	29	2	8	10	44	12	2	0	2	27

PRYOR, Nick (PRIGH-uhr, NIHK) ANA

Defense. Shoots left. 5'11", 184 lbs. Born, St. Paul, MN, September 9, 1990.
(Anaheim's 10th choice, 208th overall, in 2008 Entry Draft).

			Regular Season					Playoffs				
Season	Club	League	GP	G	A	Pts	PIM	GP	G	A	Pts	PIM
2006-07	USNTDP	U-17	7	2	3	5	2	....	....	....	....	....
	USNTDP	NAHL	37	1	3	4	10	4	1	0	1	0
2007-08	USNTDP	U-18	41	3	9	12	6	....	....	....	....	....
	USNTDP	NAHL	12	0	2	2	6	....	....	....	....	....
2008-09	Des Moines	USHL	31	6	12	18	26	....	....	....	....	....
	Waterloo	USHL	12	1	5	6	10	....	....	....	....	....
2009-10	U. of Maine	H-East	6	0	0	0	2	....	....	....	....	....
2010-11	U. of Maine	H-East	5	0	2	2	0	....	....	....	....	....

• Missed majority of 2009-10 and 2010-11 due to various injuries.

PUEMPEL, Matt (PUHM-puhl, MAT) OTT

Left wing. Shoots left. 6'1", 202 lbs. Born, Windsor, Ont., January 24, 1993.
(Ottawa's 3rd choice, 24th overall, in 2011 Entry Draft).

			Regular Season					Playoffs				
Season	Club	League	GP	G	A	Pts	PIM	GP	G	A	Pts	PIM
2008-09	Sun County	Minor-ON	76	88	56	144	....	....	....	....	....	....
	Leamington Flyers	ON-Jr.B	1	2	0	2	0	....	....	....	....	....
2009-10	Peterborough	OHL	59	33	31	64	43	4	1	1	2	6
2010-11	Peterborough	OHL	55	34	35	69	49	....	....	....	....	....

OHL All-Rookie Team (2010) • OHL Rookie of the Year (2010) • Canadian Major Junior All-Rookie Team (2010) • Canadian Major Junior Rookie of the Year (2010)

PULKKINEN, Teemu (PUHL-kih-nuhn, TEE-moo) DET

Left wing. Shoots right. 5'11", 183 lbs. Born, Vantaa, Finland, January 2, 1992.
(Detroit's 4th choice, 111th overall, in 2010 Entry Draft).

			Regular Season					Playoffs				
Season	Club	League	GP	G	A	Pts	PIM	GP	G	A	Pts	PIM
2007-08	Jokerit U18	Fin-U18	32	36	24	60	8	6	11	6	17	6
2008-09	Suomi U20	Finland-2	1	0	0	0	0	....	....	....	....	....
	Jokerit U18	Fin-U18	9	16	19	35	4	....	....	....	....	....
	Jokerit Helsinki Jr.	Fin Jr.	24	15	13	28	12	....	....	....	....	....
	Jokerit Helsinki	Finland	3	0	0	0	6	....	....	....	....	....
2009-10	Jokerit Helsinki Jr.	Fin-Jr.	17	20	21	41	41	4	3	3	6	0
	Jokerit Helsinki	Finland	12	1	2	3	6	....	....	....	....	....
2010-11	Suomi U20	Finland-2	1	1	0	1	0	....	....	....	....	....
	Jokerit Helsinki	Finland	55	18	36	54	32	3	0	1	1	0

PUUSTINEN, Juuso (POOS-tih-nehn, YUH-soh) NSH

Right wing. Shoots right. 6'2", 187 lbs. Born, Kuopio, Finland, April 5, 1988.
(Calgary's 5th choice, 149th overall, in 2006 Entry Draft).

			Regular Season					Playoffs				
Season	Club	League	GP	G	A	Pts	PIM	GP	G	A	Pts	PIM
2004-05	KalPa Kuopio U18	Fin-U18	26	14	15	29	81	6	1	2	3	4
	KalPa Kuopio Jr.	Fin-Jr.	1	0	0	0	0	....	....	....	....	....
2005-06	KalPa Kuopio U18	Fin-U18	7	8	7	15	18	1	0	0	0	2
	KalPa Kuopio Jr.	Fin-Jr.	29	9	5	14	46	5	0	0	0	0
2006-07	Suomi U20	Finland-2	2	0	1	1	2	....	....	....	....	....
	Kamloops Blazers	WHL	64	32	39	71	52	4	0	3	3	4
2007-08	Kamloops Blazers	WHL	60	27	26	53	26	4	1	1	2	2
2008-09	Blues Espoo	Finland	53	13	20	33	14	14	1	1	2	4
2009-10	Blues Espoo	Finland	54	8	13	21	64	2	0	1	1	0
2010-11	HPK Hameenlinna	Finland	59	26	12	38	46	2	1	0	1	4

Signed as a free agent by **Nashville**, June 16, 2011.

PYETT, Logan (PIGH-eht, LOH-guhn) DET

Defense. Shoots right. 5'10", 195 lbs. Born, Regina, Sask., May 26, 1988.
(Detroit's 7th choice, 212th overall, in 2006 Entry Draft).

			Regular Season					Playoffs				
Season	Club	League	GP	G	A	Pts	PIM	GP	G	A	Pts	PIM
2002-03	Balgonie	SSMHL	35	27	46	73	40	....	....	....	....	....
2003-04	Reg. Pat Cdns.	SMHL	44	18	27	45	34	....	....	....	....	....
	Regina Pats	WHL	2	0	1	1	0	3	0	0	0	0
2004-05	Regina Pats	WHL	67	5	19	24	67	....	....	....	....	....
2005-06	Regina Pats	WHL	71	10	35	45	89	6	1	6	7	12
2006-07	Regina Pats	WHL	71	14	48	62	84	10	3	6	9	4
2007-08	Regina Pats	WHL	62	20	34	54	54	6	1	3	4	0
2008-09	Grand Rapids	AHL	61	3	11	14	12	1	0	0	0	0
2009-10	Grand Rapids	AHL	80	9	21	30	41	....	....	....	....	....
2010-11	Grand Rapids	AHL	74	9	13	22	38	....	....	....	....	....

WHL East First All-Star Team (2008) • Canadian Major Junior Second All-Star Team (2008)

PYSYK, Mark (PIH-zihk, MAHRK) BUF

Defense. Shoots right. 6'1", 186 lbs. Born, Edmonton, Alta., January 11, 1992.
(Buffalo's 1st choice, 23rd overall, in 2010 Entry Draft).

			Regular Season					Playoffs				
Season	Club	League	GP	G	A	Pts	PIM	GP	G	A	Pts	PIM
2007-08	Sherwood Park	AMHL	34	10	10	20	60	2	1	0	1	16
	Edmonton	WHL	14	1	2	3	8	....	....	....	....	....
2008-09	Edmonton	WHL	61	5	15	20	27	4	0	0	0	2
2009-10	Edmonton	WHL	48	7	17	24	47	....	....	....	....	....
2010-11	Edmonton	WHL	63	6	34	40	88	4	0	0	0	6

QUAILER, Steve (KWAY-luhr, STEEV) MTL

Left wing. Shoots left. 6'3", 184 lbs. Born, Arvada, CO, August 5, 1989.
(Montreal's 2nd choice, 86th overall, in 2008 Entry Draft).

			Regular Season					Playoffs				
Season	Club	League	GP	G	A	Pts	PIM	GP	G	A	Pts	PIM
2006-07	Rocky Mountain	Minor-CO	53	14	23	37	25	....	....	....	....	....
2007-08	Sioux City	USHL	60	19	30	49	55	4	1	2	3	4
2008-09	Northeastern	H-East	41	10	15	25	12	....	....	....	....	....
2009-10	Northeastern	H-East	DID NOT PLAY – INJURED									
2010-11	Northeastern	H-East	38	3	10	13	39	....	....	....	....	....

USHL All-Rookie Team (2008) • Hockey East All-Rookie Team (2009)

• Missed 2009-10 due to knee injury in pre-season vs. St. Thomas University (MIAC), October 3, 2009.

QUINE, Alan (KWIH-nee, AL-uhn) DET

Center. Shoots left. 5'11", 184 lbs. Born, Belleville, Ont., February 25, 1993.
(Detroit's 4th choice, 85th overall, in 2011 Entry Draft).

			Regular Season					Playoffs				
Season	Club	League	GP	G	A	Pts	PIM	GP	G	A	Pts	PIM
2008-09	Tor. Jr. Canadiens	GTHL	35	26	26	52	8	....	....	....	....	....
	Tor. Canadiens	ON-Jr.A	2	1	1	2	0	....	....	....	....	....
2009-10	Kingston	OHL	64	11	17	28	8	7	1	2	3	0
2010-11	Kingston	OHL	17	4	7	11	2	....	....	....	....	....
	Peterborough	OHL	52	22	20	42	6	....	....	....	....	....

RACINE, Jonathan (RAY-seen, JAWN-ah-thuhn) FLA

Defense. Shoots left. 6'1", 183 lbs. Born, Montreal, Que., May 28, 1993.
(Florida's 6th choice, 87th overall, in 2011 Entry Draft).

			Regular Season					Playoffs				
Season	Club	League	GP	G	A	Pts	PIM	GP	G	A	Pts	PIM
2008-09	Saint-Eustache	QAAA	45	5	7	12	74	8	0	2	2	12
2009-10	Shawinigan	QMJHL	55	0	4	4	43	6	0	0	0	0
2010-11	Shawinigan	QMJHL	68	2	5	7	86	12	0	1	1	22

RAEDEKE, Brent (RAD-kee, BREHNT) DET

Left wing. Shoots left. 6', 200 lbs. Born, Regina, Sask., May 29, 1990.

			Regular Season					Playoffs				
Season	Club	League	GP	G	A	Pts	PIM	GP	G	A	Pts	PIM
2005-06	Regina Pat Cdns.	SAHA	41	7	7	14	36	2	0	0	0	0
2006-07	Regina Pat Cdns.	SAHA	40	16	20	36	74	1	1	0	1	0
2007-08	Edmonton	WHL	72	15	16	31	62	....	....	....	....	....
2008-09	Edmonton	WHL	70	19	36	55	80	4	1	1	2	6
	Grand Rapids	AHL	2	0	0	0	0	....	....	....	....	....
2009-10	Edmonton	WHL	39	16	15	31	60	....	....	....	....	....
	Brandon	WHL	33	7	18	25	35	15	5	7	12	16
2010-11	Grand Rapids	AHL	67	8	5	13	17	....	....	....	....	....

Signed as a free agent by **Detroit**, October 1, 2008.

RAI, Prab (RIGH, PRAB) VAN

Center. Shoots left. 5'11", 191 lbs. Born, Surrey, B.C., November 22, 1989.
(Vancouver's 3rd choice, 131st overall, in 2008 Entry Draft).

			Regular Season					Playoffs				
Season	Club	League	GP	G	A	Pts	PIM	GP	G	A	Pts	PIM
2006-07	Prince George	WHL	24	2	3	5	12	....	....	....	....	....
	Seattle	WHL	38	5	14	19	18	8	1	4	5	0
2007-08	Seattle	WHL	72	20	45	65	21	11	2	4	6	4
2008-09	Seattle	WHL	61	25	40	65	29	5	1	1	2	0
2009-10	Seattle	WHL	67	41	28	69	20	....	....	....	....	....
2010-11	Manitoba Moose	AHL	DID NOT PLAY – INJURED									

WHL West Second All-Star Team (2010)

RAJALA, Toni (ray-YAH-lah, TOH-nee) EDM

Left wing. Shoots left. 5'10", 163 lbs. Born, Parkano, Finland, March 29, 1991.
(Edmonton's 6th choice, 101st overall, in 2009 Entry Draft).

			Regular Season					Playoffs				
Season	Club	League	GP	G	A	Pts	PIM	GP	G	A	Pts	PIM
2006-07	Ilves Tampere U18	Fin-U18	30	18	26	44	32	3	2	1	3	4
	Ilves Tampere Jr.	Fin-Jr.	1	0	0	0	0	....	....	....	....	....
2007-08	Ilves Tampere U18	Fin-U18	13	10	15	25	18	....	....	....	....	....
	Ilves Tampere Jr.	Fin-Jr.	33	13	22	35	10	5	1	3	4	8
2008-09	Suomi U20	Finland-2	4	1	2	3	2	....	....	....	....	....
	Ilves Tampere Jr.	Fin-Jr.	31	14	17	31	18	....	....	....	....	....
	Ilves Tampere	Finland	21	2	3	5	0	3	0	0	0	2
2009-10	Brandon	WHL	60	26	37	63	24	15	4	3	7	8
2010-11	Suomi U20	Finland-2	2	0	1	1	0	....	....	....	....	....
	LeKi Lempaala	Finland-2	2	0	1	1	0	....	....	....	....	....
	Ilves Tampere	Finland	44	9	13	22	4	6	4	0	4	0

George Parsons Trophy (Memorial Cup - Most Sportsmanlike Player) (2010)

RAKELL, Rickard (ra-KEHL, REE-kahrd) ANA

Right wing. Shoots right. 6', 199 lbs. Born, Sundbyberg, Sweden, May 5, 1993.
(Anaheim's 1st choice, 30th overall, in 2011 Entry Draft).

			Regular Season					Playoffs				
Season	Club	League	GP	G	A	Pts	PIM	GP	G	A	Pts	PIM
2007-08	Spanga Hockey	Sweden-4	24	4	3	7	12	....	....	....	....	....
2008-09	AIK IF Solna U18	Swe-U18	16	2	3	5	22	....	....	....	....	....
2009-10	AIK IF Solna U18	Swe-U18	30	25	16	41	18	3	2	2	4	0
	AIK IF Solna Jr.	Swe-Jr.	8	3	1	4	2	2	1	0	1	0
2010-11	Plymouth Whalers	OHL	49	20	25	45	12	1	0	0	0	0

RALLO, Greg (RA-loh, GREHG) FLA

Center. Shoots right. 6', 195 lbs. Born, Gurnee, IL, August 26, 1981.

			Regular Season					Playoffs				
Season	Club	League	GP	G	A	Pts	PIM	GP	G	A	Pts	PIM
2002-03	Ferris State	CCHA	41	15	14	29	46	....	....	....	....	....
2003-04	Ferris State	CCHA	38	7	11	18	42	....	....	....	....	....
2004-05	Ferris State	CCHA	33	7	15	22	22	....	....	....	....	....
2005-06	Ferris State	CCHA	40	17	22	39	30	....	....	....	....	....
	Idaho Steelheads	ECHL	7	2	2	4	2	7	2	1	3	4
2006-07	Idaho Steelheads	ECHL	37	13	18	31	43	14	8	3	11	12
	Iowa Stars	AHL	28	3	2	5	25	2	1	0	1	2
2007-08	Idaho Steelheads	ECHL	39	17	19	36	47	....	....	....	....	....
	Albany River Rats	AHL	5	0	0	0	0	....	....	....	....	....
	Rockford IceHogs	AHL	2	0	0	0	0	....	....	....	....	....
	Manitoba Moose	AHL	13	4	5	9	2	3	0	0	0	9
2008-09	Manitoba Moose	AHL	55	4	5	9	17	20	2	2	4	9
2009-10	Texas Stars	AHL	69	19	25	44	25	24	3	7	10	0
2010-11	Texas Stars	AHL	78	26	28	54	46	6	1	1	2	8

Signed as a free agent by **Florida**, July 2, 2011.

RAMAGE, John (RAM-ihj, JAWN) CGY

Defense. Shoots right. 6', 201 lbs. Born, Mississauga, Ont., February 7, 1991.
(Calgary's 3rd choice, 103rd overall, in 2010 Entry Draft).

			Regular Season					Playoffs				
Season	Club	League	GP	G	A	Pts	PIM	GP	G	A	Pts	PIM
2007-08	St. Louis Bandits	NAHL	45	4	5	9	75	11	0	2	2	2
	USNTDP	U-17	3	0	0	0	0	....	....	....	....	....
2008-09	USNTDP	NAHL	14	1	4	5	12	....	....	....	....	....
	USNTDP	U-18	40	1	4	5	32	....	....	....	....	....
2009-10	U. of Wisconsin	WCHA	41	2	10	12	51	....	....	....	....	....
2010-11	U. of Wisconsin	WCHA	37	1	10	11	59	....	....	....	....	....

RANDELL, Tyler (RAN-duhl, TIGH-luhr) BOS

Right wing. Shoots right. 6'1", 197 lbs. Born, Scarborough, Ont., June 15, 1991.
(Boston's 4th choice, 176th overall, in 2009 Entry Draft).

			Regular Season					Playoffs				
Season	Club	League	GP	G	A	Pts	PIM	GP	G	A	Pts	PIM
2006-07	Brampton	Minor-ON	63	53	38	91	81	....	....	....	....	....
2007-08	Belleville Bulls	OHL	62	5	6	11	24	19	0	0	0	0
2008-09	Belleville Bulls	OHL	36	10	5	15	60	....	....	....	....	....
	Kitchener Rangers	OHL	37	14	8	22	39	....	....	....	....	....
2009-10	Kitchener Rangers	OHL	47	9	12	21	88	20	1	4	5	19
2010-11	Kitchener Rangers	OHL	68	20	12	32	160	7	0	0	0	7

RANFORD, Brendan (RAN-fohrd, BREHN-duhn) PHI

Left wing. Shoots left. 5'10", 186 lbs. Born, Edmonton, Alta., May 3, 1992.
(Philadelphia's 6th choice, 209th overall, in 2010 Entry Draft).

			Regular Season					Playoffs				
Season	Club	League	GP	G	A	Pts	PIM	GP	G	A	Pts	PIM
2007-08	Gregg Distributors	AMHL	35	*33	46	*79	58	12	10	5	15	6
	Kamloops Blazers	WHL	3	0	0	0	0	....	....	....	....	....
2008-09	Kamloops Blazers	WHL	66	13	14	27	46	4	0	3	3	2
2009-10	Kamloops Blazers	WHL	72	29	36	65	83	4	2	3	5	4
2010-11	Kamloops Blazers	WHL	68	33	53	86	68	....	....	....	....	....

WHL West Second All-Star Team (2011)

RASK, Joonas (RASK, YOH-nuhs) NSH

Center. Shoots right. 5'11", 176 lbs. Born, Savonlinna, Finland, March 24, 1990.
(Nashville's 6th choice, 198th overall, in 2010 Entry Draft).

			Regular Season					Playoffs				
Season	Club	League	GP	G	A	Pts	PIM	GP	G	A	Pts	PIM
2005-06	SaPKo Jr.	Fin-Jr.	2	3	1	4	0	....	....	....	....	....
2006-07	Ilves Tampere U18	Fin-U18	32	17	23	40	46	....	....	....	....	....
	Ilves Tampere Jr.	Fin-Jr.	1	0	0	0	0	....	....	....	....	....
2007-08	Ilves Tampere U18	Fin-U18	6	3	9	12	22	....	....	....	....	....
	Ilves Tampere Jr.	Fin-Jr.	32	11	18	29	34	5	1	3	4	2
2008-09	Suomi U20	Finland-2	8	0	6	6	0	....	....	....	....	....
	Ilves Tampere Jr.	Fin-Jr.	25	8	11	19	8	....	....	....	....	....
	LeKi Lempaala	Finland-2	1	1	2	3	2	....	....	....	....	....
	Ilves Tampere	Finland	24	1	0	1	8	3	0	1	1	0
2009-10	Ilves Tampere	Finland	43	10	9	19	32	....	....	....	....	....
	Suomi U20	Finland-2	1	0	0	0	0	....	....	....	....	....
	Ilves Tampere Jr.	Fin-Jr.	2	0	0	0	2	4	2	2	4	0
	Ilves Tampere	Finland-Q	....	....	....	....	....	5	3	0	3	0
2010-11	Ilves Tampere	Finland	60	14	13	27	18	5	1	1	2	2

RASK, Victor (RASK, VIHK-tohr) CAR

Center. Shoots left. 6'2", 194 lbs. Born, Leksand, Sweden, March 1, 1993.
(Carolina's 2nd choice, 42nd overall, in 2011 Entry Draft).

			Regular Season					Playoffs				
Season	Club	League	GP	G	A	Pts	PIM	GP	G	A	Pts	PIM
2007-08	Leksands IF U18	Swe-U18	8	0	2	2	2	2	0	0	0	0
2008-09	Leksands IF U18	Swe-U18	26	9	6	15	8	....	....	....	....	....
2009-10	Leksands IF U18	Swe-U18	10	6	3	9	4	4	4	3	7	2
	Leksands IF Jr.	Swe-Jr.	39	22	19	41	35	5	3	2	5	2
	Leksands IF	Sweden-2	8	0	0	0	0	....	....	....	....	....
2010-11	Leksands IF U18	Swe-U18	4	4	4	8	0	6	3	2	5	6
	Leksands IF Jr.	Swe-Jr.	13	3	9	12	2	....	....	....	....	....
	Leksands IF	Sweden-2	37	5	6	11	8	....	....	....	....	....

RATCHUK, Michael (RAT-chuhk, MIGH-kuhl)

Defense. Shoots left. 5'10", 175 lbs. Born, Buffalo, NY, February 20, 1988.
(Philadelphia's 3rd choice, 42nd overall, in 2006 Entry Draft).

			Regular Season					Playoffs				
Season	Club	League	GP	G	A	Pts	PIM	GP	G	A	Pts	PIM
2004-05	USNTDP	U-17	15	1	4	5	16	....	....	....	....	....
	USNTDP	NAHL	33	3	6	9	14	10	1	1	2	2
2005-06	USNTDP	U-18	39	8	14	22	52	....	....	....	....	....
	USNTDP	NAHL	16	4	4	8	4	....	....	....	....	....
2006-07	Michigan State	CCHA	40	4	8	12	28	....	....	....	....	....
2007-08	Michigan State	CCHA	42	6	19	25	48	....	....	....	....	....
	Philadelphia	AHL	3	1	2	3	2	5	0	1	1	0
2008-09	Philadelphia	AHL	77	5	12	17	44	4	0	1	1	2
2009-10	Adirondack	AHL	5	0	1	1	2	....	....	....	....	....
	Syracuse Crunch	AHL	35	3	7	10	10	....	....	....	....	....
2010-11	Springfield Falcons	AHL	15	1	0	1	6	....	....	....	....	....
	Fort Wayne	CHL	22	1	12	13	8	8	2	1	3	0

Traded to **Columbus** by **Philadelphia** for Stefan Legein, October 20, 2009.

RATTIE, Ty (RA-tee, TIGH) ST.L.

Right wing. Shoots right. 5'11", 165 lbs. Born, Calgary, Alta., February 5, 1993.
(St. Louis' 1st choice, 32nd overall, in 2011 Entry Draft).

			Regular Season					Playoffs				
Season	Club	League	GP	G	A	Pts	PIM	GP	G	A	Pts	PIM
2007-08	Airdrie Xtreme	AMBHL	33	*75	56	*131	24	10	12	*11	*23	16
2008-09	UFA Bisons	AMHL	34	29	25	54	12	3	1	4	5	2
	Portland	WHL	10	1	0	1	0	....	....	....	....	....
	Brooks Bandits	AJHL	2	0	0	0	0	2	0	1	1	0
2009-10	Portland	WHL	61	17	20	37	38	13	2	2	4	12
2010-11	Portland	WHL	67	28	51	79	55	21	9	13	22	22

RAU, Chad (ROW, CHAD) MIN

Center. Shoots right. 5'11", 186 lbs. Born, Eden Prairie, MN, January 18, 1987.
(Toronto's 6th choice, 228th overall, in 2005 Entry Draft).

			Regular Season					Playoffs				
Season	Club	League	GP	G	A	Pts	PIM	GP	G	A	Pts	PIM
2004-05	Des Moines	USHL	57	31	40	71	32	....	....	....	....	....
2005-06	Colorado College	WCHA	42	13	17	30	8	....	....	....	....	....
2006-07	Colorado College	WCHA	39	14	17	31	4	....	....	....	....	....
2007-08	Colorado College	WCHA	40	*28	14	42	8	....	....	....	....	....
2008-09	Colorado College	WCHA	38	18	19	37	6	....	....	....	....	....
2009-10	Houston Aeros	AHL	79	19	19	38	7	....	....	....	....	....
2010-11	Houston Aeros	AHL	60	13	27	40	12	24	6	3	9	2

USHL All-Rookie Team (2005) • USHL First All-Star Team (2005) • USHL Rookie of the Year (2005) • WCHA First All-Star Team (2008, 2009) • NCAA West Second All-American Team (2008, 2009)

Signed as a free agent by **Houston** (AHL), October 6, 2009. Signed as a free agent by **Minnesota**, May 17, 2010.

RAU, Kyle (ROW, KIGHL) FLA

Center. Shoots left. 5'8", 163 lbs. Born, Hoffman Estates, IL, October 24, 1992.
(Florida's 7th choice, 91st overall, in 2011 Entry Draft).

			Regular Season					Playoffs				
Season	Club	League	GP	G	A	Pts	PIM	GP	G	A	Pts	PIM
2009-10	Eden Prairie Eagles	High-MN	25	38	39	77	12	3	2	2	4	0
2010-11	Team Southwest	UMHSEL	19	16	7	23	14	3	0	0	0	0
	Eden Prairie Eagles	High-MN	25	33	36	69	16	6	8	4	12	2
	Sioux Falls	USHL	11	4	6	10	15	10	*7	5	*12	4

• Signed Letter of Intent to attend **University of Minnesota** (WCHA) in fall of 2011.

READ, Matt (REED, MAT) PHI

Right wing. Shoots right. 5'10", 185 lbs. Born, Ilderton, Ont., June 14, 1986.

			Regular Season					Playoffs				
Season	Club	League	GP	G	A	Pts	PIM	GP	G	A	Pts	PIM
2005-06	Milton Icehawks	OPJHL	48	34	34	68	52	11	6	13	19	6
2006-07	Des Moines	USHL	58	28	34	62	110	8	2	0	2	6
2007-08	Bemidji State	CHA	36	9	18	27	37	....	....	....	....	....
2008-09	Bemidji State	CHA	37	15	25	40	50	....	....	....	....	....
2009-10	Bemidji State	CHA	37	19	22	41	32	....	....	....	....	....
2010-11	Bemidji State	WCHA	37	22	13	35	34	....	....	....	....	....
	Adirondack	AHL	11	7	6	13	6	....	....	....	....	....

CHA All-Rookie Team (2008) • CHA Rookie of the Year (2008) • CHA First All-Star Team (2009) • NCAA West Second All-American Team (2010)

Signed as a free agent by **Philadelphia**, March 24, 2011.

REDMOND, Zach (REHD-muhnd, ZAK) WPG

Defense. Shoots right. 6'2", 197 lbs. Born, Traverse City, MI, July 26, 1988.
(Atlanta's 7th choice, 184th overall, in 2008 Entry Draft).

			Regular Season					Playoffs				
Season	Club	League	GP	G	A	Pts	PIM	GP	G	A	Pts	PIM
2005-06	Sioux Falls	USHL	48	4	7	11	57	11	1	2	3	4
2006-07	Sioux Falls	USHL	60	8	31	39	37	8	3	7	10	8
2007-08	Ferris State	CCHA	37	6	13	19	33	....	....	....	....	....
2008-09	Ferris State	CCHA	38	3	21	24	48	....	....	....	....	....
2009-10	Ferris State	CCHA	40	6	21	27	46	....	....	....	....	....
2010-11	Ferris State	CCHA	26	7	13	20	20	....	....	....	....	....
	Chicago Wolves	AHL	3	0	0	0	4	....	....	....	....	....

CCHA Second All-Star Team (2010) • NCAA West Second All-American Team (2011)

REED, Harrison (REED, HAIR-rih-suhn)

Center/Right wing. Shoots right. 6'1", 185 lbs. Born, Newmarket, Ont., January 18, 1988.
(Carolina's 2nd choice, 93rd overall, in 2006 Entry Draft).

			Regular Season					Playoffs				
Season	Club	League	GP	G	A	Pts	PIM	GP	G	A	Pts	PIM
2004-05	Petrolia Jets	ON-Jr.B	43	11	18	29	43	....	....	....	....	....
	London Knights	OHL	6	0	0	0	0	4	0	1	1	0
2005-06	Sarnia Sting	OHL	68	26	24	50	50	....	....	....	....	....
2006-07	Sarnia Sting	OHL	67	29	52	81	30	4	0	4	4	8
2007-08	Sarnia Sting	OHL	28	6	12	18	20	....	....	....	....	....
	Guelph Storm	OHL	41	8	21	29	20	10	3	2	5	12
2008-09	Albany River Rats	AHL	70	5	4	9	22	....	....	....	....	....
	Florida Everblades	ECHL	1	1	1	2	0	....	....	....	....	....
2009-10	Albany River Rats	AHL	49	1	5	6	10	....	....	....	....	....
	Florida Everblades	ECHL	9	8	5	13	9	....	....	....	....	....
	Lake Erie Monsters	AHL	17	0	1	1	19	....	....	....	....	....
2010-11	Tulsa Oilers	CHL	28	13	17	30	12	....	....	....	....	....
	Lake Erie Monsters	AHL	38	3	0	3	8	4	0	0	0	0

Traded to **Colorado** by **Carolina** with Stephane Yelle for Cedric Lalonde-McNicoll and Colorado's 6th round choice (Tyler Stahl) in 2010 Entry Draft, March 3, 2010. • Reassigned to **Tulsa** (CHL) by **Colorado** (Lake Erie-AHL), October 12, 2010.

REGNER, Brent (REHG-nuhr, BREHNT) CBJ

Defense. Shoots right. 5'11", 189 lbs. Born, Westlock, Alta., May 17, 1989.
(Columbus' 7th choice, 137th overall, in 2008 Entry Draft).

			Regular Season					Playoffs				
Season	Club	League	GP	G	A	Pts	PIM	GP	G	A	Pts	PIM
2004-05	Ft. Saskatchewan	AMHL	36	2	13	15	24	....	....	....	....	....
2005-06	Ft. Saskatchewan	AMHL	36	9	25	34	30	14	1	7	8	2
	Vancouver Giants	WHL	1	0	0	0	0	....	....	....	....	....
2006-07	Vancouver Giants	WHL	64	1	5	6	19	22	0	6	6	10
2007-08	Vancouver Giants	WHL	72	8	39	47	45	10	0	10	10	10
2008-09	Vancouver Giants	WHL	70	15	52	67	42	17	2	11	13	6
2009-10	Syracuse Crunch	AHL	50	4	16	20	22	....	....	....	....	....
2010-11	Springfield Falcons	AHL	56	6	13	19	17	....	....	....	....	....

WHL West Second All-Star Team (2009)

REID, Brodie (REED, BROH-dee) S.J.

Right wing. Shoots right. 6'1", 195 lbs. Born, Delta, B.C., August 25, 1989.

			Regular Season					Playoffs				
Season	Club	League	GP	G	A	Pts	PIM	GP	G	A	Pts	PIM
2005-06	Surrey Eagles	BCHL	7	1	0	1	0	....	....	....	....	....
2006-07	Surrey Eagles	BCHL	50	4	6	10	17	4	0	0	0	0
2007-08	Burnaby Express	BCHL	60	52	35	87	37	5	3	4	7	9
2008-09	Burnaby Express	BCHL	9	4	7	11	15	....	....	....	....	....
	Penticton Vees	BCHL	31	13	15	28	10	10	1	5	6	2
2009-10	Lincoln Stars	USHL	46	16	20	36	46	....	....	....	....	....
2010-11	Northeastern	H-East	37	11	17	28	18	....	....	....	....	....

Hockey East All-Rookie Team (2011)

Signed as a free agent by **San Jose**, April 15, 2011.

REID, Cameron (REED, KAM-uhr-UHN) NSH

Center. Shoots left. 6'2", 198 lbs. Born, Delta, B.C., August 25, 1991.
(Nashville's 10th choice, 192nd overall, in 2009 Entry Draft).

			Regular Season					Playoffs				
Season	Club	League	GP	G	A	Pts	PIM	GP	G	A	Pts	PIM
2007-08	Victoria Grizzlies	BCHL	55	10	16	26	25	11	2	3	5	4
2008-09	Victoria Grizzlies	BCHL	41	6	17	23	32	....	....	....	....	....
	Westside Warriors	BCHL	17	6	11	17	10	8	4	3	7	0
2009-10	Westside Warriors	BCHL	54	27	45	72	70	11	2	6	8	16
2010-11	St. Cloud State	WCHA	37	8	21	29	27	....	....	....	....	....

REILLY, Mike (RIGH-lee, MIGHK) CBJ

Defense. Shoots left. 6', 161 lbs. Born, Chicago, IL, July 13, 1993.
(Columbus' 3rd choice, 98th overall, in 2011 Entry Draft).

			Regular Season					Playoffs				
Season	Club	League	GP	G	A	Pts	PIM	GP	G	A	Pts	PIM
2009-10	Holy Angels	High-MN	24	4	29	33	19	2	3	2	5	0
2010-11	Shat.-St. Mary's	High-MN	54	14	34	48	30	....	....	....	....	....

REINHART, Max (RIGHN-hart, MAX) CGY

Center. Shoots left. 6', 182 lbs. Born, West Vancouver, B.C., February 4, 1992.
(Calgary's 1st choice, 64th overall, in 2010 Entry Draft).

			Regular Season					Playoffs				
Season	Club	League	GP	G	A	Pts	PIM	GP	G	A	Pts	PIM
2008-09	Kootenay Ice	WHL	62	11	16	27	21	4	1	0	1	2
2009-10	Kootenay Ice	WHL	72	21	30	51	38	6	1	1	2	6
2010-11	Kootenay Ice	WHL	71	34	45	79	41	19	15	12	27	12

RENSFELDT, Ludvig (REHNS-fehldt, LOOD-vihg) CHI

Left wing. Shoots left. 6'3", 192 lbs. Born, Gavle, Sweden, January 29, 1992.
(Chicago's 2nd choice, 35th overall, in 2010 Entry Draft).

			Regular Season					Playoffs				
Season	Club	League	GP	G	A	Pts	PIM	GP	G	A	Pts	PIM
2007-08	Brynas U18	Swe-U18	5	1	2	3	0	....	....	....	....	....
2008-09	Brynas U18	Swe-U18	31	13	23	36	14	3	0	1	1	0
	Brynas IF Gavle Jr.	Swe-Jr.	2	0	0	0	2	1	0	0	0	0
2009-10	Brynas U18	Swe-U18	6	5	7	12	16	4	3	5	8	0
	Brynas IF Gavle Jr.	Swe-Jr.	39	21	29	50	37	5	3	0	3	0
2010-11	Brynas IF Gavle Jr.	Swe-Jr.	26	17	19	36	12	1	0	0	0	0
	Bofors	Sweden-2	11	5	2	7	4	....	....	....	....	....
	Brynas IF Gavle	Sweden	16	0	1	1	0	5	0	0	0	2

RHEAULT, Jon (RAY-oh, JAWN) CGY

Right wing. Shoots right. 5'11", 200 lbs. Born, Arlington, TX, August 1, 1986.
(Philadelphia's 8th choice, 145th overall, in 2006 Entry Draft).

			Regular Season					Playoffs				
Season	Club	League	GP	G	A	Pts	PIM	GP	G	A	Pts	PIM
2003-04	N.H. Jr. Monarchs	EJHL	....	49	46	*95	....	....	....	....	....	....
2004-05	Providence College	H-East	36	11	8	19	36	....	....	....	....	....
2005-06	Providence College	H-East	35	16	14	30	29	....	....	....	....	....
2006-07	Providence College	H-East	35	12	13	25	38	....	....	....	....	....
2007-08	Providence College	H-East	36	17	14	31	23	....	....	....	....	....
2008-09	Ontario Reign	ECHL	51	19	22	41	56	7	4	4	8	4
	Manchester	AHL	24	2	3	5	12	....	....	....	....	....
2009-10	Ontario Reign	ECHL	30	19	16	35	24	....	....	....	....	....
	Providence Bruins	AHL	4	0	0	0	4	....	....	....	....	....
	Manchester	AHL	35	3	3	6	14	....	....	....	....	....
	Abbotsford Heat	AHL	5	3	2	5	0	13	6	2	8	2
2010-11	Abbotsford Heat	AHL	79	12	22	34	46	....	....	....	....	....

Signed as a free agent by **Ontario** (ECHL), August 29, 2008. Signed to a PTO (professional tryout) contract by **Manchester** (AHL), December 13, 2008. Signed as a free agent by **Ontario** (ECHL), July 21, 2009. Signed to a PTO (professional tryout) contract by **Providence** (AHL), November 13, 2009. Signed to a PTO (professional tryout) contract by **Manchester** (AHL), December 1, 2009. Signed to a PTO (professional tryout) contract by **Abbotsford** (AHL), March 29, 2010. Signed as a free agent by **Abbotsford** (AHL), June 16, 2010. Signed as a free agent by **Calgary**, July 27, 2011.

RIEDER, Tobias (REE-duhr, TOH-bee-uhs) EDM

Center. Shoots left. 5'10", 180 lbs. Born, Landshut, Germany, January 10, 1993.
(Edmonton's 7th choice, 114th overall, in 2011 Entry Draft).

			Regular Season					Playoffs				
Season	Club	League	GP	G	A	Pts	PIM	GP	G	A	Pts	PIM
2008-09	EV Landshut Jr.	Ger-Jr.	36	27	24	51	18	9	6	8	14	10
2009-10	EV Landshut Jr.	Ger-Jr.	5	6	3	9	25	4	5	1	6	2
	Landshut Cann.	German-2	45	10	13	23	28	6	0	0	0	0
2010-11	Kitchener Rangers	OHL	65	23	26	49	35	7	0	2	2	4

RIENDEAU, Yannick (ree-EHN-doh, YAH-nihk) BOS

Right wing. Shoots left. 5'11", 180 lbs. Born, Boucherville, Que., June 18, 1988.

			Regular Season					Playoffs				
Season	Club	League	GP	G	A	Pts	PIM	GP	G	A	Pts	PIM
2004-05	Rouyn-Noranda	QMJHL	58	10	15	25	22	6	0	1	1	0
2005-06	Rouyn-Noranda	QMJHL	67	27	38	65	40	5	0	2	2	6
2006-07	Rouyn-Noranda	QMJHL	67	32	40	72	38	10	9	5	14	6
2007-08	HC Chamonix	France	24	11	11	22	87	5	7	7	14	20
	Rouyn-Noranda	QMJHL	42	23	26	49	18	17	8	13	21	14
2008-09	Drummondville	QMJHL	64	*58	*68	*126	31	19	*29	23	*52	16
	Drummondville	M-Cup	....	....	....	....	....	4	2	6	8	2
2009-10	Providence Bruins	AHL	22	1	4	5	6	....	....	....	....	....
	Reading Royals	ECHL	6	3	2	5	0	5	3	2	5	0
2010-11	Providence Bruins	AHL	6	0	0	0	2	....	....	....	....	....
	Reading Royals	ECHL	54	18	25	43	24	8	5	3	8	2

QMJHL First All-Star Team (2009) • Canadian Major Junior First All-Star Team (2009)

Signed as a free agent by **Boston**, April 2, 2009.

RISSANEN, Rasmus (RIH-sa-nehn, RAS-mus) CAR

Defense. Shoots left. 6'2", 202 lbs. Born, Kuopio, Finland, July 13, 1991.
(Carolina's 5th choice, 178th overall, in 2009 Entry Draft).

			Regular Season					Playoffs				
Season	Club	League	GP	G	A	Pts	PIM	GP	G	A	Pts	PIM
2006-07	KalPa Kuopio U18	Fin-U18	9	1	1	2	28	3	0	1	1	8
2007-08	KalPa Kuopio U18	Fin-U18	29	7	9	16	99	2	0	0	0	8
	KalPa Kuopio Jr.	Fin-Jr.	5	0	0	0	10	....	....	....	....	....
2008-09	KalPa Kuopio Jr.	Fin-Jr.	29	1	8	9	56	4	0	1	1	6
2009-10	Everett Silvertips	WHL	71	4	11	15	103	7	0	1	1	8
2010-11	Everett Silvertips	WHL	68	1	11	12	89	4	2	0	2	8
	Charlotte	AHL	1	0	0	0	0	....	....	....	....	....

RITCHIE, Brett (RIH-chee, BREHT) DAL

Right wing. Shoots right. 6'3", 209 lbs. Born, Orangeville, Ont., July 1, 1993.
(Dallas' 2nd choice, 44th overall, in 2011 Entry Draft).

			Regular Season					Playoffs				
Season	Club	League	GP	G	A	Pts	PIM	GP	G	A	Pts	PIM
2008-09	Toronto Marlboros	GTHL	71	36	33	69	67	....	....	....	....	....
2009-10	Sarnia Sting	OHL	65	13	16	29	35	....	....	....	....	....
2010-11	Sarnia Sting	OHL	49	21	20	41	47	....	....	....	....	....

ROBAK, Colby (ROH-bak, KOHL-bee) FLA

Defense. Shoots left. 6'3", 194 lbs. Born, Dauphin, Man., April 24, 1990.
(Florida's 2nd choice, 46th overall, in 2008 Entry Draft).

			Regular Season					Playoffs				
Season	Club	League	GP	G	A	Pts	PIM	GP	G	A	Pts	PIM
2005-06	Parkland Rangers	MMHL	40	14	20	34	14	....	....	....	....	....
2006-07	Brandon	WHL	39	2	3	5	12	1	0	0	0	0
2007-08	Brandon	WHL	71	6	24	30	25	6	0	2	2	8
2008-09	Brandon	WHL	65	13	29	42	41	12	6	8	14	4
2009-10	Brandon	WHL	71	16	50	66	9	15	3	9	12	2
2010-11	Rochester	AHL	76	7	17	24	22	....	....	....	....	....

WHL East Second All-Star Team (2010)

ROBERTSON, Dennis (RAW-buhrt-suhn, DEH-nihs) TOR

Defense. Shoots left. 6', 195 lbs. Born, Fort St. John, B.C., May 24, 1991.
(Toronto's 7th choice, 173rd overall, in 2011 Entry Draft).

			Regular Season					Playoffs				
Season	Club	League	GP	G	A	Pts	PIM	GP	G	A	Pts	PIM
2006-07	Okanagan Prep	Minor-BC	62	15	15	30	78	....	....	....	....	....
2007-08	Summerland Sting	KIJHL	50	9	18	27	66	4	2	1	3	12
2008-09	Langley Chiefs	BCHL	55	1	11	12	64	4	0	1	1	4
2009-10	Langley Chiefs	BCHL	53	9	25	34	83	10	2	2	4	14
2010-11	Brown U.	ECAC	30	6	11	17	48	....	....	....	....	....

RODIN, Anton (ROH-dihn, AN-tawn) VAN

Right wing. Shoots left. 5'11", 174 lbs. Born, Stockholm, Sweden, November 21, 1990.
(Vancouver's 2nd choice, 53rd overall, in 2009 Entry Draft).

			Regular Season					Playoffs				
Season	Club	League	GP	G	A	Pts	PIM	GP	G	A	Pts	PIM
2006-07	Brynas U18	Swe-U18	14	7	4	11	4	3	0	0	0	2
	Brynas IF Gavle Jr.	Swe-Jr.	1	0	0	0	0	....	....	....	....	....
2007-08	Brynas U18	Swe-U18	6	2	7	9	8	5	2	5	7	0
	Brynas IF Gavle Jr.	Swe-Jr.	35	8	11	19	36	7	1	0	1	0
2008-09	Brynas IF Gavle Jr.	Swe-Jr.	37	29	26	55	34	7	2	10	12	4
	IK Oskarshamn	Sweden-2	6	0	0	0	2	....	....	....	....	....
2009-10	Brynas IF Gavle Jr.	Swe-Jr.	4	0	3	3	4	3	0	3	3	0
	Brynas IF Gavle	Sweden	36	1	4	5	8	5	1	0	1	4
	Mora IK	Sweden-2	8	2	2	4	0	....	....	....	....	....
2010-11	Brynas IF Gavle	Sweden	53	7	19	26	16	5	1	1	2	0

RODWELL, Derek (RAWD-wehl, DAIR-ihk) N.J.

Left wing. Shoots right. 6'2", 190 lbs. Born, Taber, Alta., July 8, 1990.
(New Jersey's 5th choice, 144th overall, in 2009 Entry Draft).

			Regular Season					Playoffs				
Season	Club	League	GP	G	A	Pts	PIM	GP	G	A	Pts	PIM
2007-08	Okotoks Oilers	AJHL	62	9	10	19	69	9	0	3	3	6
2008-09	Okotoks Oilers	AJHL	41	17	12	29	69	9	1	2	3	6
2009-10	Okotoks Oilers	AJHL	55	18	35	53	38	11	6	3	9	20
2010-11	North Dakota	WCHA	39	5	4	9	20	....	....	....	....	....

ROE, Garrett (ROH, GAIR-eht) L.A.

Left wing. Shoots left. 5'8", 162 lbs. Born, Vienna, VA, February 22, 1988.
(Los Angeles' 9th choice, 183rd overall, in 2008 Entry Draft).

			Regular Season					Playoffs				
Season	Club	League	GP	G	A	Pts	PIM	GP	G	A	Pts	PIM
2004-05	Indiana Ice	USHL	49	6	15	21	62	3	0	3	3	4
2005-06	Indiana Ice	USHL	49	21	32	53	93	2	3	0	3	0
2006-07	Indiana Ice	USHL	57	24	39	63	143	6	3	10	13	8
2007-08	St. Cloud State	WCHA	39	18	27	45	55	....	....	....	....	....
2008-09	St. Cloud State	WCHA	38	17	31	48	72	....	....	....	....	....
2009-10	St. Cloud State	WCHA	41	20	29	49	65	....	....	....	....	....
2010-11	St. Cloud State	WCHA	38	10	26	36	48	....	....	....	....	....

WCHA All-Rookie Team (2008)

ROGALSKI, Joe (roh-GAL-skee, JOH) PIT

Defense. Shoots right. 6'2", 185 lbs. Born, Buffalo, NY, November 29, 1991.
(Pittsburgh's 5th choice, 152nd overall, in 2010 Entry Draft).

			Regular Season					Playoffs				
Season	Club	League	GP	G	A	Pts	PIM	GP	G	A	Pts	PIM
2006-07	Buffalo Saints	Minor-NY	54	11	30	41	62	....	....	....	....	....
2007-08	Sarnia Sting	OHL	53	0	5	5	33	9	0	0	0	2
2008-09	Sarnia Sting	OHL	68	2	11	13	40	5	0	0	0	4
2009-10	Sarnia Sting	OHL	66	6	23	29	75	....	....	....	....	....
2010-11	Sarnia Sting	OHL	63	7	25	32	44	....	....	....	....	....

ROMAN, Ondrej (ROH-mahn, AWN-dray) DAL

Center. Shoots left. 6', 173 lbs. Born, Ostrava, Czech., April 8, 1989.
(Dallas' 6th choice, 136th overall, in 2007 Entry Draft).

			Regular Season					Playoffs				
Season	Club	League	GP	G	A	Pts	PIM	GP	G	A	Pts	PIM
2002-03	HC Ostrava U17	CzR-U17	6	1	1	2	0	....	....	....	....	....
2003-04	HC Ostrava U17	CzR-U17	55	38	27	65	61	....	....	....	....	....
2004-05	HC Ostrava U17	CzR-U17	8	8	16	24	22	....	....	....	....	....
	HC Ostrava Jr.	CzRep-Jr.	7	2	2	4	6	....	....	....	....	....
	HC Vitkovice U17	CzR-U17	2	0	3	3	2	....	....	....	....	....
	HC Vitkovice Jr.	CzRep-Jr.	30	8	3	11	12	....	....	....	....	....
2005-06	HC Vitkovice U17	CzR-U17	....	....	....	....	....	4	1	8	9	0
	HC Vitkovice Jr.	CzRep-Jr.	46	17	27	44	42	5	0	3	3	4
	HC Vitkovice Steel	CzRep	1	0	0	0	0	....	....	....	....	....
2006-07	Spokane Chiefs	WHL	70	4	44	48	42	6	1	4	5	0
2007-08	Spokane Chiefs	WHL	72	15	46	61	28	21	9	11	20	6
2008-09	HC Vitkovice Jr.	CzRep-Jr.	4	1	3	4	0	....	....	....	....	....
	HC Vitkovice Steel	CzRep	26	3	6	9	2	....	....	....	....	....
	Spokane Chiefs	WHL	32	10	22	32	19	12	1	4	5	10
2009-10	HC Vitkovice Jr.	CzRep-Jr.	10	9	17	26	8	....	....	....	....	....
	HC Vitkovice Steel	CzRep	26	1	2	3	6	....	....	....	....	....
	Havirov	CzRep-2	11	1	6	7	16	....	....	....	....	....
2010-11	Texas Stars	AHL	72	8	14	22	32	2	0	1	1	0

ROMANO, Tony (roh-MAHN-oh, TOH-nee) NYI

Center. Shoots right. 5'10", 177 lbs. Born, Smithtown, NY, January 5, 1988.
(New Jersey's 7th choice, 178th overall, in 2006 Entry Draft).

			Regular Season					Playoffs				
Season	Club	League	GP	G	A	Pts	PIM	GP	G	A	Pts	PIM
2004-05	New York Bobcats	AtJHL	....	47	54	101	....	....	....	....	....	....
2005-06	New York Bobcats	AtJHL	40	*50	52	*102	38	....	....	....	....	....
2006-07	Cornell Big Red	ECAC	29	9	10	19	18	....	....	....	....	....
2007-08	London Knights	OHL	66	12	10	22	40	4	1	0	1	0
2008-09	Peterborough	OHL	65	36	33	69	86	2	2	1	3	4
2009-10	Bridgeport	AHL	21	1	1	2	12	....	....	....	....	....
	Utah Grizzlies	ECHL	34	9	15	24	35	....	....	....	....	....
	Toledo Walleye	ECHL	12	6	6	12	19	4	1	0	1	4
2010-11	Bridgeport	AHL	67	7	12	19	56	....	....	....	....	....

Traded to **NY Islanders** by **New Jersey** for Ben Walter and future considerations, June 30, 2009.

ROSS, Brad (RAWS, BRAD) TOR

Left wing. Shoots left. 6'1", 175 lbs. Born, Lethbridge, Alta., May 28, 1992.
(Toronto's 1st choice, 43rd overall, in 2010 Entry Draft).

			Regular Season					Playoffs				
Season	Club	League	GP	G	A	Pts	PIM	GP	G	A	Pts	PIM
2007-08	Lethbridge	AMHL	35	10	14	24	82	6	6	5	11	22
	Portland	WHL	3	0	0	0	0	....	....	....	....	....
2008-09	Portland	WHL	61	9	17	26	119	....	....	....	....	....
2009-10	Portland	WHL	71	27	41	68	*203	13	2	7	9	36
2010-11	Portland	WHL	67	31	38	69	171	16	4	2	6	33

ROSS, Nick (RAWS, NIHK) PHX

Defense. Shoots left. 6'1", 196 lbs. Born, Edmonton, Alta., February 10, 1989.
(Phoenix's 2nd choice, 30th overall, in 2007 Entry Draft).

			Regular Season					Playoffs				
Season	Club	League	GP	G	A	Pts	PIM	GP	G	A	Pts	PIM
2004-05	Lethbridge	AMHL	33	8	20	28	123	....	....	....	....	....
	Regina Pats	WHL	10	0	1	1	2	....	....	....	....	....
2005-06	Regina Pats	WHL	62	7	16	23	38	6	0	1	1	2
2006-07	Regina Pats	WHL	70	7	24	31	87	10	1	5	6	14
2007-08	Regina Pats	WHL	41	3	25	28	60	....	....	....	....	....
	Kamloops Blazers	WHL	31	5	14	19	55	4	0	2	2	10
	San Antonio	AHL	4	1	0	1	0	....	....	....	....	....
2008-09	Kamloops Blazers	WHL	40	4	18	22	51	....	....	....	....	....
	Vancouver Giants	WHL	34	7	14	21	32	17	1	8	9	14
2009-10	San Antonio	AHL	47	0	2	2	19	....	....	....	....	....
	Las Vegas	ECHL	7	0	1	1	2	....	....	....	....	....
2010-11	San Antonio	AHL	29	0	6	6	16	....	....	....	....	....
	Las Vegas	ECHL	21	2	9	11	8	....	....	....	....	....

ROUSSEL, Charles-Olivier (roo-SEHL, CHAR-uhlz-OH-lihv-ee-ay) NSH

Defense. Shoots right. 6'1", 201 lbs. Born, St. Eustache, Que., September 13, 1991.
(Nashville's 3rd choice, 42nd overall, in 2009 Entry Draft).

			Regular Season					Playoffs				
Season	Club	League	GP	G	A	Pts	PIM	GP	G	A	Pts	PIM
2006-07	Laurentides	QAAA	44	8	24	32	90	15	2	9	11	24
2007-08	Shawinigan	QMJHL	50	3	13	16	28	5	1	2	3	2
2008-09	Shawinigan	QMJHL	68	11	33	44	77	21	5	13	18	14
2009-10	Shawinigan	QMJHL	64	15	36	51	70	6	0	1	1	4
2010-11	Montreal	QMJHL	59	5	25	30	46	10	1	3	4	10

QMJHL Second All-Star Team (2009)

ROWE, Andrew (ROH, AN-droo) PHI

Left wing. Shoots left. 6'2", 185 lbs. Born, Muskegon, MI, January 22, 1988.

			Regular Season					Playoffs				
Season	Club	League	GP	G	A	Pts	PIM	GP	G	A	Pts	PIM
2005-06	Sioux City	USHL	50	8	8	16	30	....	....	....	....	....
2006-07	Sioux City	USHL	60	19	15	34	28	7	2	1	3	0
2007-08	Michigan State	CCHA	21	3	4	7	8	....	....	....	....	....
2008-09	Michigan State	CCHA	35	6	8	14	14	....	....	....	....	....
2009-10	Michigan State	CCHA	38	17	11	28	38	....	....	....	....	....
2010-11	Adirondack	AHL	55	7	5	12	20	....	....	....	....	....
	Greenville	ECHL	10	6	2	8	2	11	3	3	6	2

Signed as a free agent by **Philadelphia**, May 6, 2010.

RUDENKO, Konstantin (roo-DEHN-koh, KAWN-stan-tihn) PHI

Left wing. Shoots right. 5'11", 180 lbs. Born, Ust-Kamenogorsk, USSR, July 23, 1981.
(Philadelphia's 3rd choice, 160th overall, in 1999 Entry Draft).

			Regular Season					Playoffs				
Season	Club	League	GP	G	A	Pts	PIM	GP	G	A	Pts	PIM
1997-98	Omsk 2	Russia-3	22	7	8	15	4	....	....	....	....	....
1998-99	Cherepovets	Russia	28	15	9	24	67	....	....	....	....	....
	Cherepovets 2	Russia-3	3	0	1	1	4	....	....	....	....	....
99-2000	St. Petersburg 2	Russia-3	7	2	4	6	2	....	....	....	....	....
	SKA St. Petersburg	Russia	19	1	1	2	10	1	0	0	0	0
2000-01	Yaroslavl	Russia	18	2	3	5	28	9	2	1	3	8
2001-02	Yaroslavl 2	Russia-3	2	1	1	2	2	....	....	....	....	....
	Yaroslavl	Russia	8	0	2	2	12	1	0	0	0	0
2002-03	Yaroslavl	Russia	20	3	4	7	20	2	0	0	0	0
2003-04	Yaroslavl 2	Russia-3	4	4	2	6	4	....	....	....	....	....
	Yaroslavl	Russia	43	10	12	22	18	3	0	0	0	0
2004-05	Yaroslavl 2	Russia-3	20	13	14	27	42	....	....	....	....	....
	Yaroslavl	Russia	21	1	0	1	8	2	0	0	0	0
2005-06	Yaroslavl	Russia	49	11	17	28	55	11	1	2	3	0
2006-07	Yaroslavl	Russia	35	11	8	19	30	7	2	2	4	6
2007-08	Yaroslavl	Russia	46	6	16	22	28	7	0	1	1	8
2008-09	Yaroslavl	Rus-KHL	48	10	18	28	26	19	4	8	12	24
2009-10	Yaroslavl	Rus-KHL	31	3	7	10	4	17	5	6	11	24
2010-11	Yaroslavl	Rus-KHL	31	7	11	18	24	11	0	4	4	0

RUFENACH, Bryan (RUHF-ehn-ak, BRIGH-uhn) DET

Defense. Shoots left. 6', 192 lbs. Born, Cameron, Ont., April 15, 1989.
(Detroit's 5th choice, 208th overall, in 2007 Entry Draft).

			Regular Season					Playoffs				
Season	Club	League	GP	G	A	Pts	PIM	GP	G	A	Pts	PIM
2005-06	Lindsay Muskies	OPJHL	48	11	15	26	50	4	1	1	2	6
2006-07	Lindsay Muskies	OPJHL	31	11	21	32	28	5	1	2	3	8
2007-08	Clarkson Knights	ECAC	35	3	3	6	12	....	....	....	....	....
2008-09	Clarkson Knights	ECAC	34	9	9	18	32	....	....	....	....	....
2009-10	Clarkson Knights	ECAC	34	5	15	20	49	....	....	....	....	....
2010-11	Clarkson Knights	ECAC	33	4	7	11	14	....	....	....	....	....
	Toledo Walleye	ECHL	6	1	1	2	4	....	....	....	....	....

RUNDBLAD, David (RUHND-blahd, DAY-vihd) **OTT**

Defense. Shoots right. 6'2", 190 lbs. Born, Lycksele, Sweden, October 8, 1990.
(St. Louis' 1st choice, 17th overall, in 2009 Entry Draft).

			Regular Season					Playoffs				
Season	Club	League	GP	G	A	Pts	PIM	GP	G	A	Pts	PIM
2004-05	Lycksele SK	Sweden-4	1	0	0	0	0	....	....	....	....	....
2005-06	Lycksele SK	Sweden-4	11	5	2	7	2	....	....	....	....	....
2006-07	Skelleftea U18	Swe-U18	4	1	1	2	0	....	....	....	....	....
	Skelleftea Jr.	Swe-Jr.	14	3	4	7	12	2	0	0	0	2
2007-08	Skelleftea U18	Swe-U18	4	3	2	5	29	....	....	....	....	....
	Skelleftea Jr.	Swe-Jr.	35	11	15	26	44	2	1	3	4	6
	Skelleftea AIK HK	Sweden	6	0	0	0	2	....	....	....	....	....
2008-09	Skelleftea AIK Jr.	Swe-Jr.	10	8	7	15	2	....	....	....	....	....
	Skelleftea AIK	Sweden	45	0	10	10	8	10	1	1	2	2
2009-10	Skelleftea AIK Jr.	Swe-Jr.	3	2	2	4	4	....	....	....	....	....
	Skelleftea AIK	Sweden	47	1	12	13	14	12	0	1	1	2
2010-11	Skelleftea AIK	Sweden	55	11	*39	50	14	18	3	7	10	20

Traded to **Ottawa** by **St. Louis** for Ottawa's 1st round choice (Vladimir Tarasenko) in 2010 Entry Draft, June 25, 2010.

RUOPP, Harrison (ROO-awp, HAIR-ih-suhn) **PHX**

Defense. Shoots right. 6'2", 198 lbs. Born, Zehner, Sask., March 17, 1993.
(Phoenix's 4th choice, 84th overall, in 2011 Entry Draft).

			Regular Season					Playoffs				
Season	Club	League	GP	G	A	Pts	PIM	GP	G	A	Pts	PIM
2007-08	Balgonie	Minor-SK	26	9	11	20	37	7	0	3	3	4
2008-09	Reg. Pat Cdns.	SMHL	36	0	1	1	46	5	0	1	1	4
2009-10	Prince Albert	WHL	33	0	0	0	38	....	....	....	....	....
2010-11	Prince Albert	WHL	54	0	9	9	98	6	0	0	0	9

RUSSELL, Ryan (RUH-sehl, RIGH-uhn) **CBJ**

Center. Shoots left. 5'10", 180 lbs. Born, Caroline, Alta., May 2, 1987.
(NY Rangers' 9th choice, 211th overall, in 2005 Entry Draft).

			Regular Season					Playoffs				
Season	Club	League	GP	G	A	Pts	PIM	GP	G	A	Pts	PIM
2003-04	Kootenay Ice	WHL	67	3	9	12	27	4	0	0	0	0
2004-05	Kootenay Ice	WHL	66	32	21	53	18	16	6	7	13	12
2005-06	Kootenay Ice	WHL	72	33	42	75	30	6	3	5	8	2
2006-07	Kootenay Ice	WHL	58	30	46	76	40	7	3	6	9	2
2007-08	Hamilton Bulldogs	AHL	25	2	1	3	4	....	....	....	....	....
	Cincinnati	ECHL	12	6	4	10	4	15	3	4	7	0
2008-09	Hamilton Bulldogs	AHL	79	20	19	39	24	6	1	3	4	2
2009-10	Hamilton Bulldogs	AHL	74	19	18	37	8	19	7	5	12	0
2010-11	Hamilton Bulldogs	AHL	65	10	11	21	48	20	7	2	9	0

Traded to **Montreal** by **NY Rangers** for Montreal's 7th round choice (David Skokan) in 2007 Entry Draft, May 31, 2007. Traded to **Columbus** by **Montreal** for Michael Blunden, July 7, 2011.

RUSSO, Robbie (ROO-soh, RAW-bee) **NYI**

Defense. Shoots right. 5'11", 186 lbs. Born, Westmount, IL, February 15, 1993.
(NY Islanders' 5th choice, 95th overall, in 2011 Entry Draft).

			Regular Season					Playoffs				
Season	Club	League	GP	G	A	Pts	PIM	GP	G	A	Pts	PIM
2008-09	Chicago Mission	T1EHL	46	5	17	22	10	....	....	....	....	....
	Chicago Mission	Exhib.	....	5	3	8	10	....	....	....	....	....
2009-10	USNTDP	USHL	34	3	17	20	36	....	....	....	....	....
	USNTDP	U-17	18	4	7	11	22	....	....	....	....	....
2010-11	USNTDP	USHL	24	0	6	6	11	....	....	....	....	....
	USNTDP	U-18	36	4	20	24	16	....	....	....	....	....

• Signed Letter of Intent to attend **University of Notre Dame** (CCHA).

RUST, Bryan (RUHST, BRIGH-uhn) **PIT**

Right wing. Shoots right. 6', 191 lbs. Born, Pontiac, MI, May 11, 1992.
(Pittsburgh's 2nd choice, 80th overall, in 2010 Entry Draft).

			Regular Season					Playoffs				
Season	Club	League	GP	G	A	Pts	PIM	GP	G	A	Pts	PIM
2007-08	Det. Honeybaked	MWEHL	31	17	28	45	6	....	....	....	....	....
	Det. Honeybaked	Minor-MI	37	27	20	47	....	....	....	....	....	....
2008-09	USNTDP	NAHL	42	6	9	15	18	9	0	2	2	4
	USNTDP	U-17	16	3	2	5	4	....	....	....	....	....
2009-10	USNTDP	USHL	27	10	13	23	6	....	....	....	....	....
	USNTDP	U-17	1	0	0	0	0	....	....	....	....	....
	USNTDP	U-18	38	16	13	29	18	....	....	....	....	....
2010-11	U. of Notre Dame	CCHA	40	6	13	19	4	....	....	....	....	....

RUST, Matt (RUHST, MAT) **CBJ**

Center. Shoots left. 5'10", 192 lbs. Born, Bloomfield Hills, MI, March 23, 1989.
(Florida's 4th choice, 101st overall, in 2007 Entry Draft).

			Regular Season					Playoffs				
Season	Club	League	GP	G	A	Pts	PIM	GP	G	A	Pts	PIM
2004-05	Det. Honeybaked	MWEHL	50	16	24	40	....	....	....	....	....	....
2005-06	USNTDP	U-17	20	5	5	10	22	....	....	....	....	....
	USNTDP	NAHL	36	9	8	17	36	12	2	0	2	0
2006-07	USNTDP	U-18	36	3	16	19	34	....	....	....	....	....
	USNTDP	NAHL	15	9	6	15	31	....	....	....	....	....
2007-08	U. of Michigan	CCHA	38	12	11	23	69	....	....	....	....	....
2008-09	U. of Michigan	CCHA	37	11	11	22	39	....	....	....	....	....
2009-10	U. of Michigan	CCHA	45	13	27	40	24	....	....	....	....	....
2010-11	U. of Michigan	CCHA	44	5	21	26	41	....	....	....	....	....

Traded to **Columbus** by **Florida** for Mathieu Roy, March 3, 2010.

RUTH, Theo (ROOTH, THEE-oh) **CBJ**

Defense. Shoots right. 6'1", 210 lbs. Born, Naperville, IL, February 14, 1989.
(Washington's 3rd choice, 46th overall, in 2007 Entry Draft).

			Regular Season					Playoffs				
Season	Club	League	GP	G	A	Pts	PIM	GP	G	A	Pts	PIM
2004-05	Chicago Mission	MAHL	46	8	8	16	....	....	....	....	....	....
2005-06	USNTDP	U-17	18	2	3	5	22	....	....	....	....	....
	USNTDP	NAHL	36	1	2	3	33	12	0	2	2	8
2006-07	USNTDP	U-18	39	2	6	8	52	....	....	....	....	....
	USNTDP	NAHL	9	3	6	9	14	....	....	....	....	....
2007-08	U. of Notre Dame	CCHA	42	2	3	5	36	....	....	....	....	....
2008-09	U. of Notre Dame	CCHA	36	2	5	7	42	....	....	....	....	....
2009-10	U. of Notre Dame	CCHA	22	0	5	5	52	....	....	....	....	....
2010-11	Springfield Falcons	AHL	52	1	5	6	21	....	....	....	....	....

Traded to **Columbus** by **Washington** for Sergei Fedorov, February 26, 2008.

RUTKOWSKI, Troy (ruht-KOW-skee, TROI) **COL**

Defense. Shoots right. 6'2", 195 lbs. Born, Edmonton, Alta., April 29, 1992.
(Colorado's 6th choice, 137th overall, in 2010 Entry Draft).

			Regular Season					Playoffs				
Season	Club	League	GP	G	A	Pts	PIM	GP	G	A	Pts	PIM
2007-08	SSAC Athletics	AMHL	36	6	16	22	28	....	....	....	....	....
2008-09	Portland	WHL	64	6	9	15	34	....	....	....	....	....
2009-10	Portland	WHL	71	12	31	43	70	13	4	3	7	8
2010-11	Portland	WHL	72	10	37	47	65	21	4	9	13	16

RUUTTU, Alexander (ROO-too, al-ehx-AHN-duhr) **PHX**

Center. Shoots right. 6'1", 185 lbs. Born, Chicago, IL, IL, December 9, 1992.
(Phoenix's 2nd choice, 51st overall, in 2011 Entry Draft).

			Regular Season					Playoffs				
Season	Club	League	GP	G	A	Pts	PIM	GP	G	A	Pts	PIM
2009-10	Jokerit U18	Fin-U18	31	11	18	29	34	4	3	0	3	0
2010-11	Suomi U20	Finland-2	2	1	1	2	0	....	....	....	....	....
	Jokerit Helsinki	Finland	1	0	0	0	0	....	....	....	....	....
	Jokerit Helsinki Jr.	Fin-Jr.	41	18	13	31	14	6	1	1	2	6

RUZICKA, Vladimir (roo-ZHEECH-kuh, vla-DIH-meer) **PHX**

Center. Shoots left. 6'1", 196 lbs. Born, Most, Czech., February 17, 1989.
(Phoenix's 5th choice, 103rd overall, in 2007 Entry Draft).

			Regular Season					Playoffs				
Season	Club	League	GP	G	A	Pts	PIM	GP	G	A	Pts	PIM
2002-03	Slavia U17	CzR-U17	20	1	5	6	2	1	0	0	0	0
2003-04	Slavia U17	CzR-U17	51	18	35	53	24	7	5	8	13	4
2004-05	Slavia U17	CzR-U17	38	22	39	61	38	6	4	4	8	10
2005-06	Slavia U17	CzR-U17	3	3	6	9	22	6	5	7	12	14
	HC Slavia Praha Jr.	CzRep-Jr.	37	15	26	41	42	1	0	1	1	0
	HC Slavia Praha	CzRep	13	1	1	2	4	....	....	....	....	....
2006-07	HC Slavia Praha Jr.	CzRep-Jr.	37	24	34	58	54	4	1	2	3	4
	HC Slavia Praha	CzRep	3	0	0	0	0	....	....	....	....	....
2007-08	HC Slavia Praha Jr.	CzRep-Jr.	1	0	0	0	4	1	0	0	0	2
	HC Slavia Praha	CzRep	42	7	8	15	18	19	1	0	1	4
2008-09	HC Slavia Praha	CzRep	36	5	6	11	14	14	2	1	3	6
2009-10	Havl. Brod	CzRep-2	3	1	2	3	0	....	....	....	....	....
	HC Slavia Praha	CzRep	47	6	10	16	22	15	3	1	4	4
2010-11	HC Slavia Praha	CzRep	32	8	7	15	16	....	....	....	....	....

RYAN, Ben (RIGH-uhn, BEHN) **NSH**

Center. Shoots right. 5'11", 193 lbs. Born, Detroit, MI, October 16, 1988.
(Nashville's 5th choice, 114th overall, in 2007 Entry Draft).

			Regular Season					Playoffs				
Season	Club	League	GP	G	A	Pts	PIM	GP	G	A	Pts	PIM
2005-06	Des Moines	USHL	60	14	23	37	38	11	4	1	5	4
2006-07	Des Moines	USHL	59	22	42	64	66	8	3	5	8	8
2007-08	U. of Notre Dame	CCHA	47	10	16	26	22	....	....	....	....	....
2008-09	U. of Notre Dame	CCHA	39	12	15	27	30	....	....	....	....	....
2009-10	U. of Notre Dame	CCHA	29	7	12	19	24	....	....	....	....	....
2010-11	U. of Notre Dame	CCHA	44	6	19	25	37	....	....	....	....	....
	Milwaukee	AHL	2	0	1	1	0	6	0	0	0	2

RYAN, Kenny (RIGH-uhn, KEHN-nee) **TOR**

Right wing. Shoots right. 6', 210 lbs. Born, Franklin Village, MI, July 10, 1991.
(Toronto's 2nd choice, 50th overall, in 2009 Entry Draft).

			Regular Season					Playoffs				
Season	Club	League	GP	G	A	Pts	PIM	GP	G	A	Pts	PIM
2006-07	Det. Honeybaked	MWEHL	31	16	17	33	34	....	....	....	....	....
	Det. Honeybaked	Exhib.	34	17	24	41	....	....	....	....	....	....
2007-08	USNTDP	NAHL	36	10	8	18	53	....	....	....	....	....
	USNTDP	U-17	13	0	5	5	12	....	....	....	....	....
2008-09	USNTDP	NAHL	16	4	9	13	12	....	....	....	....	....
	USNTDP	U-18	46	23	13	36	38	....	....	....	....	....
2009-10	Windsor Spitfires	OHL	52	14	21	35	33	19	3	2	5	14
2010-11	Windsor Spitfires	OHL	63	21	37	58	42	18	4	8	12	25

SAAD, Brandon (SAHD, BRAN-duhn) **CHI**

Left wing. Shoots left. 6'1", 203 lbs. Born, Pittsburgh, PA, October 27, 1992.
(Chicago's 4th choice, 43rd overall, in 2011 Entry Draft).

			Regular Season					Playoffs				
Season	Club	League	GP	G	A	Pts	PIM	GP	G	A	Pts	PIM
2007-08	Pittsburgh Hornets	MWEHL	26	11	19	30	16	....	....	....	....	....
2008-09	Mahoning Valley	NAHL	47	29	18	47	48	7	5	1	6	10
	USNTDP	U-17	7	6	5	11	2	....	....	....	....	....
2009-10	USNTDP	USHL	24	12	14	26	18	....	....	....	....	....
	USNTDP	U-18	39	17	15	32	16	....	....	....	....	....
2010-11	Saginaw Spirit	OHL	59	27	28	55	47	12	3	9	12	10

SACCHETTI, Nico (SA-sheh-tee, NEE-koh) **DAL**

Center. Shoots right. 5'11", 189 lbs. Born, Virginia, MN, August 21, 1989.
(Dallas' 1st choice, 50th overall, in 2007 Entry Draft).

			Regular Season					Playoffs				
Season	Club	League	GP	G	A	Pts	PIM	GP	G	A	Pts	PIM
2004-05	Virginia Blue Devils	High-MN	29	25	29	54	....	....	....	....	....	....
2005-06	Virginia Blue Devils	High-MN	27	29	45	74	....	....	....	....	....	....
2006-07	Virginia Blue Devils	High-MN	25	38	52	90	22	....	....	....	....	....
2007-08	Omaha Lancers	USHL	56	10	14	24	51	14	1	2	3	10
2008-09	U. of Minnesota	WCHA	36	4	3	7	43	....	....	....	....	....
2009-10	U. of Minnesota	WCHA	38	4	11	15	12	....	....	....	....	....
2010-11	U. of Minnesota	WCHA	30	3	4	7	20	....	....	....	....	....

ST. CROIX, Michael (SAYNT KR'WAH, MIGH-kuhl) **NYR**

Center. Shoots right. 5'10", 177 lbs. Born, Winnipeg, MB, April 10, 1993.
(NY Rangers' 3rd choice, 106th overall, in 2011 Entry Draft).

			Regular Season					Playoffs				
Season	Club	League	GP	G	A	Pts	PIM	GP	G	A	Pts	PIM
2008-09	Winnipeg Wild	MMHL	41	*56	47	*103	10	9	8	12	20	4
	Edmonton	WHL	2	1	1	2	0	....	....	....	....	....
2009-10	Edmonton	WHL	66	18	28	46	30	....	....	....	....	....
2010-11	Edmonton	WHL	68	27	48	75	48	4	1	0	1	9

ST. DENIS, Frederic (SAINT-deh-nee, FREHD-uhr-ihk) **MTL**

Defense. Shoots left. 5'11", 192 lbs. Born, Greenfield Park, Que., January 23, 1986.

			Regular Season					Playoffs				
Season	Club	League	GP	G	A	Pts	PIM	GP	G	A	Pts	PIM
2001-02	C.C. Lemoyne	QAAA	42	4	6	10	4	....	....	....	....	....
2002-03	C.C. Lemoyne	QAAA	31	8	15	23	6	....	....	....	....	....
	Drummondville	QMJHL	14	0	0	0	0	....	....	....	....	....
2003-04	Drummondville	QMJHL	67	7	10	17	30	5	0	1	1	2
2004-05	Drummondville	QMJHL	70	11	22	33	36	6	2	3	5	0
2005-06	Drummondville	QMJHL	69	17	50	67	74	....	....	....	....	....
2006-07	Drummondville	QMJHL	65	9	29	38	59	12	1	7	8	8
2007-08	U. Quebec T-R	OUAA	28	4	14	18	4	....	....	....	....	....
2008-09	Hamilton Bulldogs	AHL	7	1	1	2	6	....	....	....	....	....
	Cincinnati	ECHL	41	1	22	23	22	15	0	5	5	14
2009-10	Hamilton Bulldogs	AHL	59	3	14	17	38	19	0	1	1	20
2010-11	Hamilton Bulldogs	AHL	76	5	18	23	34	20	1	9	10	12

QMJHL Second All-Star Team (2006)

Signed as a free agent by **Hamilton** (AHL), September 27, 2008. Signed as a free agent by **Montreal**, July 1, 2010.

SALOMAKI, Miikka (sa-loh-MYA-kee, MEEKA) **NSH**

Right wing. Shoots left. 5'11", 198 lbs. Born, Raahe, Finland, March 9, 1993.
(Nashville's 2nd choice, 52nd overall, in 2011 Entry Draft).

			Regular Season					Playoffs				
Season	Club	League	GP	G	A	Pts	PIM	GP	G	A	Pts	PIM
2008-09	Laser HT U18	Fin-U18	23	13	30	43	71	....	....	....	....	....
2009-10	Karpat Oulu U18	Fin-U18	3	4	2	6	4	....	....	....	....	....
	Karpat Oulu Jr.	Fin-Jr.	37	18	25	43	93	....	....	....	....	....
2010-11	Suomi U20	Finland-2	3	1	1	2	27	....	....	....	....	....
	Karpat Oulu	Finland	40	4	6	10	53	3	0	1	1	27
	Karpat Oulu U18	Fin-U18	....	....	....	....	....	2	0	1	1	2

SAMUELSSON, Philip (SAM-yuhl-suhn, FIHL-ihp) **PIT**

Defense. Shoots left. 6'3", 198 lbs. Born, Leksand, Sweden, July 26, 1991.
(Pittsburgh's 2nd choice, 61st overall, in 2009 Entry Draft).

			Regular Season					Playoffs				
Season	Club	League	GP	G	A	Pts	PIM	GP	G	A	Pts	PIM
2006-07	P.F. Chang's	Minor-AZ	54	9	31	40	70	....	....	....	....	....
2007-08	P.F. Chang's	Minor-AZ	41	8	25	33	48	....	....	....	....	....
2008-09	Chicago Steel	USHL	54	0	22	22	60	....	....	....	....	....
	USNTDP	U-18	4	0	0	0	6	....	....	....	....	....
2010-11	Boston College	H-East	39	4	12	16	72	....	....	....	....	....

SAMUELS-THOMAS, Jordan (SAM-yewlz-TAW-muhs, JOHR-dahn) **WPG**

Left wing. Shoots left. 6'3", 198 lbs. Born, Hartford, CT, May 28, 1990.
(Atlanta's 9th choice, 203rd overall, in 2009 Entry Draft).

			Regular Season					Playoffs				
Season	Club	League	GP	G	A	Pts	PIM	GP	G	A	Pts	PIM
2006-07	Hartford	AtJHL	43	21	37	58	44	....	....	....	....	....
2007-08	Waterloo	USHL	56	8	3	11	65	11	0	2	2	10
2008-09	Waterloo	USHL	59	32	22	54	59	3	2	1	3	2
2009-10	Bowling Green	CCHA	35	11	14	25	30	....	....	....	....	....
2010-11	Bowling Green	CCHA	36	9	12	21	46	....	....	....	....	....

SANTORELLI, Mark (san-toh-REHL-ee, MAHRK) **NSH**

Center. Shoots right. 6'1", 188 lbs. Born, Edmonton, Alta., August 6, 1988.
(Nashville's 6th choice, 119th overall, in 2007 Entry Draft).

			Regular Season					Playoffs				
Season	Club	League	GP	G	A	Pts	PIM	GP	G	A	Pts	PIM
2003-04	Abbotsford Pilots	PIJHL	40	12	19	31	33	....	....	....	....	....
	Chilliwack Chiefs	BCHL	1	0	1	1	0	....	....	....	....	....
2004-05	Salmon Arm	BCHL	59	9	16	25	10	11	2	3	5	6
2005-06	Salmon Arm	BCHL	20	2	10	12	11	....	....	....	....	....
	Burnaby Express	BCHL	39	15	28	43	16	20	2	14	16	14
2006-07	Chilliwack Bruins	WHL	72	29	53	82	46	5	2	3	5	2
2007-08	Chilliwack Bruins	WHL	72	27	*74	*101	40	4	1	4	5	4
	Milwaukee	AHL	1	0	0	0	0	2	0	0	0	0
2008-09	Milwaukee	AHL	53	1	6	7	8	....	....	....	....	....
	Cincinnati	ECHL	6	1	2	3	0	15	1	6	7	0
2009-10	Milwaukee	AHL	68	11	13	24	6	6	1	2	3	0
2010-11	Milwaukee	AHL	64	8	13	21	26	8	0	2	2	0

WHL West Second All-Star Team (2008)

SAPONARI, Vinny (sa-pawn-AIR-ee, VIH-nee) **WPG**

Right wing. Shoots right. 6', 179 lbs. Born, Powder Springs, GA, February 15, 1990.
(Atlanta's 4th choice, 94th overall, in 2008 Entry Draft).

			Regular Season					Playoffs				
Season	Club	League	GP	G	A	Pts	PIM	GP	G	A	Pts	PIM
2006-07	USNTDP	U-17	4	11	6	17	....	....	....	....	....	....
	USNTDP	U-18	21	4	3	7	6	....	....	....	....	....
	USNTDP	NAHL	35	9	10	19	43	....	....	....	....	....
2007-08	USNTDP	U-18	42	12	16	28	42	....	....	....	....	....
	USNTDP	NAHL	15	1	7	8	0	....	....	....	....	....
2008-09	Boston University	H-East	44	8	9	17	39	....	....	....	....	....
2009-10	Boston University	H-East	38	12	18	30	32	....	....	....	....	....
2010-11	Dubuque	USHL	56	18	46	64	35	11	5	4	9	6

USHL Second All-Star Team (2011)

SAUVE, Max (soh-VAY, max) **BOS**

Center. Shoots left. 6', 170 lbs. Born, Tours, France, January 30, 1990.
(Boston's 2nd choice, 47th overall, in 2008 Entry Draft).

			Regular Season					Playoffs				
Season	Club	League	GP	G	A	Pts	PIM	GP	G	A	Pts	PIM
2005-06	Laval-Laurentides	QAAA	41	16	30	46	54	5	1	3	4	2
2006-07	Quebec Remparts	QMJHL	60	10	6	16	24	2	0	0	0	2
2007-08	Quebec Remparts	QMJHL	38	12	20	32	22	....	....	....	....	....
	Val-d'Or Foreurs	QMJHL	32	14	19	33	8	4	2	3	5	2
2008-09	Val-d'Or Foreurs	QMJHL	64	27	49	76	43	....	....	....	....	....
2009-10	Val-d'Or Foreurs	QMJHL	25	13	22	35	26	6	5	2	7	2
	Providence Bruins	AHL	6	2	0	2	2	....	....	....	....	....
2010-11	Providence Bruins	AHL	61	21	17	38	36	....	....	....	....	....

SAVARD, David (suh-VAHRD, DAY-vihd) **CBJ**

Defense. Shoots right. 6'2", 214 lbs. Born, St. Hyacinthe, Que., October 22, 1990.
(Columbus' 3rd choice, 94th overall, in 2009 Entry Draft).

			Regular Season					Playoffs				
Season	Club	League	GP	G	A	Pts	PIM	GP	G	A	Pts	PIM
2006-07	Sem. St-Francois	QAAA	44	10	16	26	52	18	1	12	13	10
2007-08	Baie-Comeau	QMJHL	35	1	6	7	22	....	....	....	....	....
	Moncton Wildcats	QMJHL	32	0	5	5	18	....	....	....	....	....
2008-09	Moncton Wildcats	QMJHL	68	9	35	44	33	10	5	5	10	10
2009-10	Moncton Wildcats	QMJHL	64	13	*64	77	36	21	1	14	15	8
2010-11	Springfield Falcons	AHL	72	11	32	43	18	....	....	....	....	....

QMJHL First All-Star Team (2010) • Canadian Major Junior First All-Star Team (2010) • Canadian Major Junior Defenseman of the Year (2010)

SCARLETT, Reece (SKAR-leht, REES) **N.J.**

Defense. Shoots right. 6'1", 170 lbs. Born, Edmonton, Alta., March 31, 1993.
(New Jersey's 6th choice, 159th overall, in 2011 Entry Draft).

			Regular Season					Playoffs				
Season	Club	League	GP	G	A	Pts	PIM	GP	G	A	Pts	PIM
2007-08	Sherwood Park	AMBHL	33	14	16	30	48	12	4	5	9	26
	Sherwood Park	Minor-AB	3	1	0	1	4	....	....	....	....	....
2008-09	Sherwood Park	AMHL	34	4	13	17	60	11	2	6	8	4
	Swift Current	WHL	1	0	0	0	0	....	....	....	....	....
2009-10	Swift Current	WHL	65	1	9	10	49	4	0	2	2	4
2010-11	Swift Current	WHL	72	6	18	24	59	....	....	....	....	....

SCHAUS, Nick (SHAWS, NIHK)

Defense. Shoots right. 5'11", 200 lbs. Born, Orchard Park, NY, July 3, 1986.

			Regular Season					Playoffs				
Season	Club	League	GP	G	A	Pts	PIM	GP	G	A	Pts	PIM
2002-03	River City Lancers	USHL	60	4	9	13	60	11	0	0	0	10
2003-04	River City Lancers	USHL	57	1	12	13	144	3	0	0	0	6
2004-05	Omaha Lancers	USHL	58	1	21	22	141	5	0	0	0	8
2005-06	Omaha Lancers	USHL	60	9	44	53	80	5	0	2	2	6
2006-07	U. Mass-Lowell	H-East	36	1	13	14	56	....	....	....	....	....
2007-08	U. Mass-Lowell	H-East	37	0	6	6	83	....	....	....	....	....
2008-09	U. Mass-Lowell	H-East	38	5	17	22	65	....	....	....	....	....
2009-10	U. Mass-Lowell	H-East	37	4	19	23	16	....	....	....	....	....
	Worcester Sharks	AHL	4	0	3	3	2	11	0	3	3	14
2010-11	Worcester Sharks	AHL	77	4	15	19	46	....	....	....	....	....

Signed as a free agent by **San Jose**, March 22, 2010.

SCHEIFELE, Mark (SHIHF-lee, MAHRK) **WPG**

Center. Shoots right. 6'2", 184 lbs. Born, Kitchener, Ont., March 15, 1993.
(Winnipeg's 1st choice, 7th overall, in 2011 Entry Draft).

			Regular Season					Playoffs				
Season	Club	League	GP	G	A	Pts	PIM	GP	G	A	Pts	PIM
2008-09	Kit. Jr. Rangers	Minor-ON	31	20	19	39	16	....	....	....	....	....
	Kit. Jr. Rangers	Exhib.	18	20	20	40	14	....	....	....	....	....
2009-10	Kitchener	ON-Jr.B	51	18	37	55	20	5	0	3	3	6
2010-11	Barrie Colts	OHL	66	22	53	75	35	....	....	....	....	....

SCHEMITSCH, Geoffrey (SHEHM-ihtsch, JEHF-ree) **T.B.**

Defense. Shoots right. 6'2", 185 lbs. Born, Toronto, Ont., April 1, 1992.
(Tampa Bay's 5th choice, 96th overall, in 2010 Entry Draft).

			Regular Season					Playoffs				
Season	Club	League	GP	G	A	Pts	PIM	GP	G	A	Pts	PIM
2008-09	Mississauga Reps	GTHL	33	9	22	31	20	....	....	....	....	....
2009-10	Owen Sound	OHL	62	4	36	40	24	....	....	....	....	....
2010-11	Owen Sound	OHL	45	1	19	20	14	20	1	10	11	2

SCHIESTEL, Drew (SHIGHS-tuhl, DROO) **BUF**

Defense. Shoots right. 6'1", 197 lbs. Born, Hamilton, Ont., March 9, 1989.
(Buffalo's 2nd choice, 59th overall, in 2007 Entry Draft).

			Regular Season					Playoffs				
Season	Club	League	GP	G	A	Pts	PIM	GP	G	A	Pts	PIM
2004-05	Hamilton Reps	Minor-ON	68	21	27	46	....	....	....	....	....	....
2005-06	Mississauga	OHL	40	1	4	5	42	....	....	....	....	....
2006-07	Mississauga	OHL	66	6	15	21	40	5	0	6	6	2
2007-08	Niagara Ice Dogs	OHL	68	8	29	37	40	10	1	6	7	10
2008-09	Niagara Ice Dogs	OHL	63	10	38	48	75	12	2	6	8	14
2009-10	Portland Pirates	AHL	52	1	11	12	19	4	0	0	0	0
2010-11	Portland Pirates	AHL	45	5	18	23	32	....	....	....	....	....

SCHIRA, Craig (SHIH-rah, KRAYG) **OTT**

Defense. Shoots right. 6', 196 lbs. Born, Spiritwood, Sask., April 21, 1988.

			Regular Season					Playoffs				
Season	Club	League	GP	G	A	Pts	PIM	GP	G	A	Pts	PIM
2003-04	Saskatoon Blazers	SMHL	39	2	10	12	20	....	....	....	....	....
	Regina Pats	WHL	2	0	0	0	2	....	....	....	....	....
2004-05	Regina Pats	WHL	60	1	7	8	25	....	....	....	....	....
2005-06	Regina Pats	WHL	71	5	28	33	72	6	1	1	2	2
2006-07	Regina Pats	WHL	71	3	23	26	74	10	0	0	0	4
2007-08	Regina Pats	WHL	2	0	1	1	0	....	....	....	....	....
	Vancouver Giants	WHL	63	8	22	30	58	10	0	1	1	0
2008-09	Vancouver Giants	WHL	71	16	43	59	46	17	2	4	6	4
2009-10	Binghamton	AHL	68	8	13	21	27	....	....	....	....	....
2010-11	Binghamton	AHL	67	3	10	13	18	7	0	1	1	0

Signed as a free agent by **Ottawa**, March 9, 2009.

SCHNEIDER, Stefan (SHNIGH-duhr, STEH-fan) **VAN**

Center. Shoots right. 6'4", 199 lbs. Born, Vernon, B.C., December 13, 1989.

			Regular Season					Playoffs				
Season	Club	League	GP	G	A	Pts	PIM	GP	G	A	Pts	PIM
2006-07	Beaver Valley	KIJHL	57	9	23	32	40	....	....	....	....	....
2007-08	Vancouver Giants	WHL	36	0	4	4	36	4	0	0	0	0
2008-09	Vancouver Giants	WHL	67	11	5	16	45	....	....	....	....	....
2009-10	Portland	WHL	72	12	11	23	43	13	3	2	5	10
2010-11	Manitoba Moose	AHL	47	2	2	4	9	3	0	0	0	0

Signed as a free agent by **Vancouver**, March 29, 2010.

SCHOFIELD, Rick (SKOH-feeld, RIHK) ANA

Center. Shoots left. 6'2", 198 lbs. Born, Pickering, Ont., April 23, 1987.

			Regular Season					Playoffs				
Season	Club	League	GP	G	A	Pts	PIM	GP	G	A	Pts	PIM
2003-04	Pickering Panthers	OPJHL	40	14	10	24	14	....	....	....	....	....
2004-05	Pickering Panthers	OPJHL	3	1	2	3	0	....	....	....	....	....
2005-06	Pickering Panthers	OPJHL	47	20	24	44	22	....	....	....	....	....
2006-07	Pickering Panthers	OPJHL	48	36	34	70	42	....	....	....	....	....
2007-08	Lake Superior	CCHA	33	10	10	20	16	....	....	....	....	....
2008-09	Lake Superior	CCHA	36	9	12	21	37	....	....	....	....	....
2009-10	Lake Superior	CCHA	36	15	13	28	41	....	....	....	....	....
2010-11	Lake Superior	CCHA	39	17	18	35	22	....	....	....	....	....
	Syracuse Crunch	AHL	11	3	4	7	2	....	....	....	....	....

Signed as a free agent by **Anaheim**, March 21, 2011.

SCHROEDER, Jordan (SHRAY-duhr, JOHR-dahn) VAN

Center. Shoots right. 5'8", 175 lbs. Born, Prior Lake, MN, September 29, 1990.
(Vancouver's 1st choice, 22nd overall, in 2009 Entry Draft).

			Regular Season					Playoffs				
Season	Club	League	GP	G	A	Pts	PIM	GP	G	A	Pts	PIM
2005-06	Saint Thomas	High-MN	31	27	35	62	....	....	....	....	....	....
	Team Southeast	UMHSEL	....	7	14	21		....	....	....	....	....
2006-07	USNTDP	NAHL	31	12	11	23	10	....	....	....	....	....
	USNTDP	U-17	8	2	8	10	2	....	....	....	....	....
	USNTDP	U-18	17	6	13	19	4	....	....	....	....	....
2007-08	USNTDP	NAHL	14	1	8	9	4	....	....	....	....	....
	USNTDP	U-18	41	21	23	44	12	....	....	....	....	....
2008-09	U. of Minnesota	WCHA	35	13	32	45	29	....	....	....	....	....
2009-10	U. of Minnesota	WCHA	37	9	19	28	14	....	....	....	....	....
	Manitoba Moose	AHL	11	4	5	9	0	6	3	3	6	4
2010-11	Manitoba Moose	AHL	61	10	18	28	10	14	1	5	6	2

WCHA All-Rookie Team (2009) • WCHA Second All-Star Team (2009) • WCHA Rookie of the Year (2009)

SCHULTZ, Ian (SHUHLTZ, EE-an) MTL

Right wing. Shoots right. 6'1", 179 lbs. Born, Calgary, Alta., February 4, 1990.
(St. Louis' 6th choice, 87th overall, in 2008 Entry Draft).

			Regular Season					Playoffs				
Season	Club	League	GP	G	A	Pts	PIM	GP	G	A	Pts	PIM
2006-07	Calgary Buffaloes	AMHL	32	13	25	38	92	7	2	7	9	26
	Calgary Hitmen	WHL	1	1	0	1	0	....	....	....	....	....
2007-08	Calgary Hitmen	WHL	67	15	15	30	128	16	2	7	9	19
2008-09	Calgary Hitmen	WHL	58	15	26	41	127	18	5	7	12	24
2009-10	Calgary Hitmen	WHL	70	24	31	55	150	23	8	7	15	26
2010-11	Hamilton Bulldogs	AHL	45	3	1	4	49	15	2	0	2	15

Traded to **Montreal** by **St. Louis** with Lars Eller for Jaroslav Halak, June 17, 2010.

SCHULTZ, Justin (SHUHLTZ, JUHS-tihn) ANA

Defense. Shoots right. 6'1", 183 lbs. Born, Kelowna, B.C., July 6, 1990.
(Anaheim's 4th choice, 43rd overall, in 2008 Entry Draft).

			Regular Season					Playoffs				
Season	Club	League	GP	G	A	Pts	PIM	GP	G	A	Pts	PIM
2006-07	Westside Warriors	Minor-BC	....	29	29	58	29	....	....	....	....	....
2007-08	Westside Warriors	BCHL	57	9	31	40	28	11	3	5	8	4
2008-09	Westside Warriors	BCHL	49	15	35	50	29	6	1	2	3	2
2009-10	U. of Wisconsin	WCHA	43	6	16	22	12	....	....	....	....	....
2010-11	U. of Wisconsin	WCHA	41	18	29	47	28	....	....	....	....	....

WCHA All-Rookie Team (2010) • WCHA First All-Star Team (2011) • NCAA West First All-American Team (2011)

SCHUMACHER, Michael (SHOO-mah-kuhr, MIGH-kuhl) L.A.

Right wing. Shoots left. 6'3", 198 lbs. Born, Stenungsund, Sweden, August 25, 1993.
(Los Angeles' 6th choice, 200th overall, in 2011 Entry Draft).

			Regular Season					Playoffs				
Season	Club	League	GP	G	A	Pts	PIM	GP	G	A	Pts	PIM
2007-08	Stenungsund U18	Swe-U18	3	2	1	3	....	....	....	....	....	....
2008-09	Stenungsund U18	Swe-U18	STATISTICS NOT AVAILABLE									
2009-10	Frolunda U18	Swe-U18	38	21	8	29	14	8	6	2	8	20
	Frolunda Jr.	Swe-Jr.	1	0	0	0	0	....	....	....	....	....
2010-11	Frolunda U18	Swe-U18	25	18	14	32	18	5	1	3	4	12
	Frolunda Jr.	Swe-Jr.	22	4	3	7	28	....	....	....	....	....

SCHWARTZ, Jaden (SHWOHRTZ, JAY-duhn) ST.L.

Center. Shoots left. 5'10", 180 lbs. Born, Melfort, Sask., June 25, 1992.
(St. Louis' 1st choice, 14th overall, in 2010 Entry Draft).

			Regular Season					Playoffs				
Season	Club	League	GP	G	A	Pts	PIM	GP	G	A	Pts	PIM
2008-09	Notre Dame	SJHL	46	34	42	76	15	....	....	....	....	....
2009-10	Tri-City Storm	USHL	60	33	50	*83	18	3	3	0	3	0
2010-11	Colorado College	WCHA	30	17	30	47	22	....	....	....	....	....

USHL First All-Star Team (2010) • WCHA All-Rookie Team (2011)

SCOTT, Greg (SKAWT, GREHG) TOR

Right wing. Shoots right. 6', 193 lbs. Born, Victoria, B.C., June 3, 1988.

			Regular Season					Playoffs				
Season	Club	League	GP	G	A	Pts	PIM	GP	G	A	Pts	PIM
2004-05	Peninsula Panthers	VIJHL	48	34	40	74	65	....	....	....	....	....
	Victoria Salsa	BCHL	7	1	1	2	0	....	....	....	....	....
2005-06	Seattle	WHL	69	8	14	22	37	7	1	3	4	4
2006-07	Seattle	WHL	72	18	14	32	62	11	0	2	2	2
2007-08	Seattle	WHL	72	38	37	75	56	12	5	4	9	9
2008-09	Seattle	WHL	65	32	44	76	39	5	0	6	6	2
2009-10	Toronto Marlies	AHL	71	10	22	32	28	....	....	....	....	....
	Reading Royals	ECHL	5	1	1	2	2	13	1	9	10	0
2010-11	Toronto Marlies	AHL	55	10	21	31	30	....	....	....	....	....

Signed as a free agent by **Toronto**, July 3, 2008.

SDAO, Michael (S'DAY-oh, MIGH-kuhl) OTT

Defense. Shoots left. 6'4", 207 lbs. Born, Bloomington, MN, July 3, 1989.
(Ottawa's 9th choice, 191st overall, in 2009 Entry Draft).

			Regular Season					Playoffs				
Season	Club	League	GP	G	A	Pts	PIM	GP	G	A	Pts	PIM
2005-06	Culver Academy	High-IN	40	1	6	7	38	....	....	....	....	....
2006-07	Culver Academy	High-IN	43	1	6	7	85	....	....	....	....	....
2007-08	Lincoln Stars	USHL	53	3	6	9	178	8	0	1	1	20
2008-09	Lincoln Stars	USHL	51	3	7	10	162	7	0	0	0	*33
2009-10	Princeton	ECAC	30	5	4	9	48	....	....	....	....	....
2010-11	Princeton	ECAC	27	3	7	10	65	....	....	....	....	....

SEABROOK, Keith (SEE-bruk, KEETH) FLA

Defense. Shoots right. 6', 198 lbs. Born, Delta, B.C., August 2, 1988.
(Washington's 5th choice, 52nd overall, in 2006 Entry Draft).

			Regular Season					Playoffs				
Season	Club	League	GP	G	A	Pts	PIM	GP	G	A	Pts	PIM
2004-05	Coquitlam Express	BCHL	58	8	20	28	70	....	....	....	....	....
2005-06	Burnaby Express	BCHL	57	10	24	34	81	....	....	....	....	....
2006-07	U. of Denver	WCHA	37	2	11	13	24	....	....	....	....	....
2007-08	Calgary Hitmen	WHL	59	4	13	17	47	14	0	5	5	13
2008-09	Calgary Hitmen	WHL	64	15	40	55	58	18	4	11	15	26
2009-10	Abbotsford Heat	AHL	78	10	18	28	53	12	2	1	3	30
2010-11	Abbotsford Heat	AHL	48	4	16	20	18	....	....	....	....	....
	Manitoba Moose	AHL	15	1	2	3	8	10	2	1	3	0

• Left **University of Denver** (WCHA) and signed with **Calgary** (WHL), July 30, 2007. Traded to **Calgary** by **Washington** for future considerations, July 17, 2009. Traded to **Florida** by **Calgary** for Jordan Henry, July 9, 2011.

SEDLAK, Lukas (SEHD-lak, LOO-kuhsh) CBJ

Center. Shoots left. 6', 198 lbs. Born, Ceske Budejovice, Czech Republic, February 25, 1993.
(Columbus' 5th choice, 158th overall, in 2011 Entry Draft).

			Regular Season					Playoffs				
Season	Club	League	GP	G	A	Pts	PIM	GP	G	A	Pts	PIM
2007-08	C. Budejovice U17	CzR-U17	6	0	2	2	4	2	0	0	0	2
2008-09	C. Budejovice U17	CzR-U17	44	12	17	29	14	4	0	0	0	4
2009-10	C. Budejovice U18	CzR-U18	37	29	27	56	76	4	5	1	6	39
	C. Budejovice Jr.	CzRep-Jr.	11	4	8	12	4	....	....	....	....	....
2010-11	C. Budejovice Jr.	CzRep-Jr.	47	14	13	27	65	....	....	....	....	....
	C. Budejovice U18	CzR-U18	....	....	....	....	....	1	0	1	1	0

SEDOV, Pavel (se-DAHF, PAH-vehl) T.B.

Right wing. Shoots left. 6'3", 200 lbs. Born, Voskresensk, USSR, January 12, 1982.
(Tampa Bay's 5th choice, 161st overall, in 2000 Entry Draft).

			Regular Season					Playoffs				
Season	Club	League	GP	G	A	Pts	PIM	GP	G	A	Pts	PIM
99-2000	Voskresensk	Russia-2	10	0	0	0	2	....	....	....	....	....
	Voskresensk 2	Russia-3	21	5	5	10	26	....	....	....	....	....
2000-01	Voskresensk	Russia-2	38	2	1	3	10	....	....	....	....	....
2001-02	Voskresensk 2	Russia-3	12	4	1	5	0	....	....	....	....	....
	Voskresensk	Russia-2	18	3	1	4	0	....	....	....	....	....
2002-03	Voskresensk	Russia-2	25	1	5	6	6	....	....	....	....	....
	Voskresensk 2	Russia-3	7	2	4	6	4	....	....	....	....	....
2003-04	THK Tver	Russia-2	26	2	6	8	6	....	....	....	....	....
	Voskresensk	Russia	10	1	0	1	2	....	....	....	....	....
	Voskresensk 2	Russia-3	STATISTICS NOT AVAILABLE									
2004-05	HK Tver	Russia-3	STATISTICS NOT AVAILABLE									
	HK Dmitrov	Russia-3	STATISTICS NOT AVAILABLE									
	HK Ryazan	Russia-4	STATISTICS NOT AVAILABLE									
2005-06			DID NOT PLAY									
2006-07	HK Ryazan	Russia-3	70	24	29	53	16	....	....	....	....	....
2007-08	HK Ryazan	Russia-2	50	6	10	16	14	....	....	....	....	....
2008-09	HK Ryazan	Russia-2	63	13	13	26	18	8	3	4	7	2
2009-10	HK Ryazan	Russia-2	44	14	8	22	14	8	0	1	1	4
2010-11	HK Ryazan	Russia-2	52	11	7	18	14	3	0	0	0	0

SEELER, Nick (SEE-luhr, NIHK) MIN

Defense. Shoots left. 6'1", 185 lbs. Born, Eden Prairie, MN, June 3, 1993.
(Minnesota's 4th choice, 131st overall, in 2011 Entry Draft).

			Regular Season					Playoffs				
Season	Club	League	GP	G	A	Pts	PIM	GP	G	A	Pts	PIM
2009-10	Eden Prairie Eagles	High-MN	25	3	14	17	12	3	1	3	4	0
2010-11	Team Southwest	UMHSEL	21	3	7	10	32	3	0	3	3	16
	Eden Prairie Eagles	High-MN	22	7	27	34	38	6	2	7	9	10

• Signed Letter of Intent to attend **University of Nebraska-Omaha** (WCHA) in fall of 2012.

SEFTON, Justin (SEHF-tuhn, JUHS-tihn) S.J.

Defense. Shoots right. 6'3", 215 lbs. Born, Thunder Bay, Ont., April 14, 1993.
(San Jose's 2nd choice, 89th overall, in 2011 Entry Draft).

			Regular Season					Playoffs				
Season	Club	League	GP	G	A	Pts	PIM	GP	G	A	Pts	PIM
2008-09	Notre Dame	SMHL	40	19	15	34	133	8	2	6	8	64
2009-10	Sudbury Wolves	OHL	65	1	6	7	83	4	0	0	0	6
2010-11	Sudbury Wolves	OHL	66	5	6	11	124	8	0	1	1	4

SELLECK, Eric (SEHL-ehk, AIR-ihk) FLA

Left wing. Shoots left. 6'2", 208 lbs. Born, Spencerville, Ont., October 20, 1987.

			Regular Season					Playoffs				
Season	Club	League	GP	G	A	Pts	PIM	GP	G	A	Pts	PIM
2006-07	Pembroke	CJHL	53	23	24	47	137	15	4	8	12	29
2007-08	Pembroke	CJHL	49	43	38	81	120	14	8	21	29	28
2008-09	Oswego State	NCAA-3	26	13	13	26	45	....	....	....	....	....
2009-10	Oswego State	NCAA-3	28	21	33	54	48	....	....	....	....	....
2010-11	Rochester	AHL	67	5	11	16	214	....	....	....	....	....

SUNYAC (NCAA-3) Rookie of the Year (2009) • SUNYAC (NCAA-3) Player of the Year (2010) • NCAA-3 East All-American Team (2010)

Signed as a free agent by **Florida**, April 21, 2010.

SEMIN, Dmitri (SEH-min, dih-MEE-tree) **ST.L.**

Center. Shoots left. 5'10", 185 lbs. Born, Moscow, USSR, August 14, 1983.
(St. Louis' 4th choice, 159th overall, in 2001 Entry Draft).

			Regular Season					Playoffs				
Season	Club	League	GP	G	A	Pts	PIM	GP	G	A	Pts	PIM
99-2000	Spartak Moscow 2	Russia-3	27	9	10	19	10	....	....	....	....	....
	Spartak Moscow	Russia-2	1	0	0	0	0	....	....	....	....	....
2000-01	Spartak Moscow	Russia-2	21	6	3	9	4	11	2	3	5	4
2001-02	Spartak Moscow 2	Russia-3	4	5	0	5	4	....	....	....	....	....
	Spartak Moscow	Russia	44	2	6	8	14	....	....	....	....	....
2002-03	Spartak Moscow	Russia	51	9	13	22	30	....	....	....	....	....
2003-04	Spartak Moscow	Russia-2	60	15	23	38	34	13	2	2	4	2
2004-05	Spartak Moscow	Russia	53	7	7	14	34	....	....	....	....	....
2005-06	Spartak Moscow	Russia	51	12	14	26	38	3	0	1	1	0
2006-07	Yaroslavl	Russia	41	13	13	26	30	7	3	2	5	2
2007-08	Yaroslavl	Russia	54	9	14	23	46	16	1	2	3	10
2008-09	Yaroslavl	Rus-KHL	53	7	13	20	28	16	4	5	9	33
2009-10	Mytischi	Rus-KHL	55	5	21	26	46	4	1	0	1	4
2010-11	Omsk	Rus-KHL	54	9	8	17	42	14	2	5	7	8

SERVILLE, Brennan (SUHR-vihl, BREH-nuhn) **WPG**

Defense. Shoots right. 6'3", 184 lbs. Born, Scarborough, Ont., June 2, 1993.
(Winnipeg's 3rd choice, 78th overall, in 2011 Entry Draft).

			Regular Season					Playoffs				
Season	Club	League	GP	G	A	Pts	PIM	GP	G	A	Pts	PIM
2008-09	Ajax Pickering	Minor-ON	56	4	15	19	28	....	....	....	....	....
2009-10	Stouffville Spirit	ON-Jr.A	43	3	12	15	26	4	1	2	3	0
2010-11	Stouffville Spirit	ON-Jr.A	36	3	27	30	29	19	2	10	12	20

• Signed Letter of Intent to attend **University of Michigan** (CCHA).

SEVERYN, C.J. (SEH-vuhr-ihn, SEE-JAY) **CGY**

Left wing. Shoots left. 6', 185 lbs. Born, Beaver, PA, June 2, 1989.
(Calgary's 5th choice, 186th overall, in 2007 Entry Draft).

			Regular Season					Playoffs				
Season	Club	League	GP	G	A	Pts	PIM	GP	G	A	Pts	PIM
2004-05	Pittsburgh Hornets	MWEHL	65	27	44	71	....	....	....	....	....	....
2005-06	USNTDP	U-17	19	2	3	5	40	....	....	....	....	....
	USNTDP	NAHL	32	2	13	15	77	12	1	0	1	12
2006-07	USNTDP	U-18	42	8	8	16	32	....	....	....	....	....
	USNTDP	NAHL	15	0	3	3	22	....	....	....	....	....
2007-08	Ohio State	CCHA	32	0	2	2	20	....	....	....	....	....
2008-09	Ohio State	CCHA	33	9	3	12	24	....	....	....	....	....
2009-10	Ohio State	CCHA	38	9	6	15	40	....	....	....	....	....
2010-11	Ohio State	CCHA	37	7	5	12	53	....	....	....	....	....

SEXTON, Ben (SEHKS-tuhn, BEHN) **BOS**

Center. Shoots right. 6', 194 lbs. Born, Ottawa, Ont., June 6, 1991.
(Boston's 5th choice, 206th overall, in 2009 Entry Draft).

			Regular Season					Playoffs				
Season	Club	League	GP	G	A	Pts	PIM	GP	G	A	Pts	PIM
2007-08	Nepean Raiders	CJHL	48	15	15	30	71	6	1	5	6	4
2008-09	Nepean Raiders	CJHL	38	14	21	35	54	11	3	9	12	22
2009-10	Penticton Vees	BCHL	50	13	29	42	83	5	1	2	3	4
2010-11	Clarkson Knights	ECAC	12	5	3	8	12	....	....	....	....	....

• Missed majority of 2010-11 due to injury vs. Colgate (ECAC), November 5, 2010.

SGARBOSSA, Michael (s'gahr-BOH-suh, MIGH-kuhl) **S.J.**

Center. Shoots left. 5'11", 170 lbs. Born, Campbellville, Ont., July 25, 1992.

			Regular Season					Playoffs				
Season	Club	League	GP	G	A	Pts	PIM	GP	G	A	Pts	PIM
2008-09	Barrie Colts	OHL	67	10	33	43	43	5	3	3	6	10
2009-10	Barrie Colts	OHL	19	7	13	20	14	....	....	....	....	....
	Saginaw Spirit	OHL	48	13	19	32	49	6	0	2	2	4
2010-11	Saginaw Spirit	OHL	26	7	13	20	24	....	....	....	....	....
	Sudbury Wolves	OHL	37	29	33	62	53	8	5	9	14	16

Signed as a free agent by **San Jose**, September 20, 2010.

SHAFIGULIN, Grigory (sha-fih-GOO-lihn, grih-GOH-ree) **NSH**

Center. Shoots left. 6'2", 185 lbs. Born, Chelyabinsk, USSR, January 13, 1985.
(Nashville's 8th choice, 98th overall, in 2003 Entry Draft).

			Regular Season					Playoffs				
Season	Club	League	GP	G	A	Pts	PIM	GP	G	A	Pts	PIM
2000-01	Chelyabinsk 2	Russia-3	6	3	2	5	8	....	....	....	....	....
2001-02	Yaroslavl 2	Russia-3	19	2	2	4	12	....	....	....	....	....
2002-03	Yaroslavl 2	Russia-3	33	18	12	30	46	7	0	4	4	31
	Yaroslavl	Russia	11	0	1	1	4	8	0	0	0	4
2003-04	Yaroslavl 2	Russia-3	11	3	8	11	22	....	....	....	....	....
	Yaroslavl	Russia	29	3	0	3	4	2	0	0	0	0
2004-05	Yaroslavl 2	Russia-3	1	0	2	2	0	....	....	....	....	....
	Yaroslavl	Russia	46	5	6	11	49	9	0	0	0	10
2005-06	Yaroslavl	Russia	32	3	6	9	20	3	0	0	0	6
	Yaroslavl 2	Russia-3	7	1	3	4	18	....	....	....	....	....
2006-07	Yaroslavl	Russia	54	5	16	21	46	7	3	0	3	14
2007-08	Ak Bars Kazan	Russia	39	5	5	10	112	8	1	0	1	4
2008-09	Ak Bars Kazan	Rus-KHL	28	4	5	9	18	....	....	....	....	....
	Vityaz Chekhov	Rus-KHL	14	3	5	8	6	....	....	....	....	....
2009-10	Nizhny Novgorod	Rus-KHL	40	5	12	17	62	....	....	....	....	....
2010-11	Dynamo Moscow	Rus-KHL	20	1	5	6	16	....	....	....	....	....

SHALLA, Josh (SHAL-uh, JAWSH) **NSH**

Left wing. Shoots left. 6'1", 202 lbs. Born, Whitby, Ont., September 25, 1991.
(Nashville's 3rd choice, 94th overall, in 2011 Entry Draft).

			Regular Season					Playoffs				
Season	Club	League	GP	G	A	Pts	PIM	GP	G	A	Pts	PIM
2006-07	Whitby Wildcats	Minor-ON	80	56	60	116	....	....	....	....	....	....
2007-08	Bowmanville	OPJHL	49	26	11	37	20	7	5	2	7	6
	Brampton	OHL	6	0	0	0	0	....	....	....	....	....
2008-09	Brampton	OHL	37	11	4	15	12	....	....	....	....	....
	Guelph Storm	OHL	24	3	2	5	16	4	0	0	0	4
2009-10	Saginaw Spirit	OHL	68	32	33	65	62	6	0	0	1	1	2
2010-11	Saginaw Spirit	OHL	68	47	25	72	62	12	8	7	15	8

SHALUNOV, Maxim (shal-oo-NAWV, max-EEM) **CHI**

Right wing. Shoots left. 6'3", 185 lbs. Born, Chelyabinsk, Russia, January 31, 1993.
(Chicago's 7th choice, 109th overall, in 2011 Entry Draft).

			Regular Season					Playoffs				
Season	Club	League	GP	G	A	Pts	PIM	GP	G	A	Pts	PIM
2009-10	Chelyabinsk Jr.	Russia-Jr.	3	2	3	5	12	4	6	1	7	6
2010-11	Chelyabinsk Jr.	Russia-Jr.	39	22	14	36	30	5	1	6	7	2
	Chelyabinsk	Rus-KHL	6	0	1	1	0	....	....	....	....	....

SHATTOCK, Tyler (SHA-tuhk, TIGH-luhr) **ST.L.**

Right wing. Shoots right. 6'2", 205 lbs. Born, Vernon, B.C., February 10, 1990.
(St. Louis' 4th choice, 108th overall, in 2009 Entry Draft).

			Regular Season					Playoffs				
Season	Club	League	GP	G	A	Pts	PIM	GP	G	A	Pts	PIM
2005-06	Thompson Blazers	BCMML	STATISTICS NOT AVAILABLE									
	Kamloops Blazers	WHL	2	0	1	1	2	....	....	....	....	....
2006-07	Kamloops Blazers	WHL	58	7	9	16	51	4	0	0	0	0
2007-08	Kamloops Blazers	WHL	48	9	14	23	45	4	1	1	2	4
2008-09	Kamloops Blazers	WHL	68	30	39	69	82	4	0	1	1	6
2009-10	Kamloops Blazers	WHL	42	22	28	50	65	....	....	....	....	....
	Calgary Hitmen	WHL	30	8	20	28	26	21	5	12	17	24
2010-11	Peoria Rivermen	AHL	67	3	12	15	60	4	0	0	0	4

SHAW, Andrew (SHAW, AN-droo) **CHI**

Center. Shoots right. 5'11", 180 lbs. Born, Belleville, Ont., July 20, 1991.
(Chicago's 8th choice, 139th overall, in 2011 Entry Draft).

			Regular Season					Playoffs				
Season	Club	League	GP	G	A	Pts	PIM	GP	G	A	Pts	PIM
2006-07	Quinte Red Devils	Minor-ON	32	24	27	51	88	3	1	2	3	....
	Quinte Red Devils	Exhib.	18	14	18	32	....	....	....	....	....	....
2007-08	Quinte Red Devils	Minor-ON	STATISTICS NOT AVAILABLE									
2008-09	Niagara Ice Dogs	OHL	56	8	9	17	97	12	2	1	3	22
2009-10	Niagara Ice Dogs	OHL	68	11	25	36	129	5	0	0	0	4
2010-11	Owen Sound	OHL	66	22	32	54	135	20	10	7	17	*53

Memorial Cup All-Star Team (2011)

SHAW, Logan (SHAW, LOH-guhn) **FLA**

Right wing. Shoots right. 6'3", 193 lbs. Born, Glace Bay, N.S., October 5, 1992.
(Florida's 5th choice, 76th overall, in 2011 Entry Draft).

			Regular Season					Playoffs				
Season	Club	League	GP	G	A	Pts	PIM	GP	G	A	Pts	PIM
2007-08	Cape Breton	NSMHL	34	17	22	39	55	10	3	9	12	8
	Cape Breton	Exhib.	2	1	0	1	0	....	....	....	....	....
2008-09	Cape Breton	QMJHL	49	5	3	8	22	8	0	0	0	0
2009-10	Cape Breton	QMJHL	67	9	15	24	31	5	0	0	0	4
2010-11	Cape Breton	QMJHL	68	26	20	46	37	4	0	1	1	4

SHEAHAN, Riley (SHEE-huhn, RIGH-lee) **DET**

Center. Shoots left. 6'2", 202 lbs. Born, St. Catharines, Ont., December 7, 1991.
(Detroit's 1st choice, 21st overall, in 2010 Entry Draft).

			Regular Season					Playoffs				
Season	Club	League	GP	G	A	Pts	PIM	GP	G	A	Pts	PIM
2007-08	St. Catharines	ON-Jr.B	45	22	39	61	39	16	5	10	15	14
2008-09	St. Catharines	ON-Jr.B	40	27	46	73	55	11	8	5	13	30
2009-10	U. of Notre Dame	CCHA	37	6	11	17	22	....	....	....	....	....
2010-11	U. of Notre Dame	CCHA	40	5	17	22	28	....	....	....	....	....

SHEFER, Andrei (SHEH-fuhr, AWN-dray) **L.A.**

Left wing. Shoots left. 6'1", 194 lbs. Born, Yekaterinburg, USSR, July 26, 1981.
(Los Angeles' 1st choice, 43rd overall, in 1999 Entry Draft).

			Regular Season					Playoffs				
Season	Club	League	GP	G	A	Pts	PIM	GP	G	A	Pts	PIM
1997-98	Yekaterinburg 2	Russia-3	16	3	3	6	18	....	....	....	....	....
1998-99	Cherepovets 3	Russia-4	6	2	2	4	18	....	....	....	....	....
	Cherepovets 2	Russia-3	21	6	5	11	20	....	....	....	....	....
	Cherepovets	Russia	8	1	0	1	4	....	....	....	....	....
99-2000	Halifax	QMJHL	72	34	42	76	30	10	0	5	5	4
2000-01	SKA St. Petersburg	Russia	11	6	1	7	4	....	....	....	....	....
	Cherepovets	Russia	20	1	1	2	10	6	1	0	1	0
2001-02	Cherepovets 2	Russia-3	3	1	2	3	2	....	....	....	....	....
	Cherepovets	Russia	8	0	0	0	6	....	....	....	....	....
	SKA St. Petersburg	Russia	28	4	4	8	10	....	....	....	....	....
2002-03	Cherepovets	Russia	37	2	4	6	10	10	0	0	0	0
	Cherepovets 2	Russia-3	3	1	2	3	2	....	....	....	....	....
2003-04	Cherepovets	Russia	55	4	6	10	46	....	....	....	....	....
2004-05	Cherepovets	Russia	46	1	11	12	18	....	....	....	....	....
2005-06	Cherepovets	Russia	45	2	1	3	32	4	0	1	1	0
2006-07	CSKA Moscow	Russia	45	7	7	14	48	2	0	0	0	2
2007-08	CSKA Moscow	Russia	53	3	14	17	34	6	1	1	2	0
2008-09	Cherepovets	Rus-KHL	37	3	5	8	16	....	....	....	....	....
2009-10	Cherepovets	Rus-KHL	51	5	12	17	26	....	....	....	....	....
2010-11	Cherepovets	Rus-KHL	38	3	12	15	28	6	1	0	1	2

SHIELDS, David (SHEELDZ, DAY-vihd) **ST.L.**

Defense. Shoots right. 6'3", 215 lbs. Born, Buffalo, NY, January 27, 1991.
(St. Louis' 5th choice, 168th overall, in 2009 Entry Draft).

			Regular Season					Playoffs				
Season	Club	League	GP	G	A	Pts	PIM	GP	G	A	Pts	PIM
2006-07	Maksymum	Minor-NY	37	4	16	20	60	....	....	....	....	....
2007-08	Erie Otters	OHL	60	1	3	4	31	....	....	....	....	....
2008-09	Erie Otters	OHL	61	1	16	17	28	5	0	0	0	5
2009-10	Erie Otters	OHL	68	7	12	19	42	4	0	0	0	12
2010-11	Erie Otters	OHL	61	6	21	27	48	7	1	4	5	4

SHIPLEY, Steven (SHIHP-lee, STEE-vehn) **BUF**

Center. Shoots left. 6'2", 214 lbs. Born, London, Ont., April 22, 1992.
(Buffalo's 5th choice, 98th overall, in 2010 Entry Draft).

			Regular Season					Playoffs				
Season	Club	League	GP	G	A	Pts	PIM	GP	G	A	Pts	PIM
2007-08	Elgin-Mid. Chiefs	Minor-ON	65	53	51	104	....	....	....	....	....	....
2008-09	Owen Sound	OHL	63	16	23	39	19	4	0	0	0	0
2009-10	Owen Sound	OHL	68	23	40	63	32	....	....	....	....	....
2010-11	Niagara Ice Dogs	OHL	65	18	32	50	29	14	1	6	7	8

SHORE, Drew (SHOHR, DROO) FLA

Center. Shoots right. 6'3", 190 lbs. Born, Denver, CO, January 29, 1991.
(Florida's 2nd choice, 44th overall, in 2009 Entry Draft).

			Regular Season					Playoffs				
Season	Club	League	GP	G	A	Pts	PIM	GP	G	A	Pts	PIM
2006-07	Det. Honeybaked	MWEHL	31	9	25	34	20	....	....	....	....	....
	Det. Honeybaked	Exhib.	34	17	23	40	....	....	....	....	....	....
2007-08	USNTDP	NAHL	35	9	16	25	12	3	0	1	1	0
	USNTDP	U-17	16	4	8	12	6	....	....	....	....	....
2008-09	USNTDP	NAHL	15	7	7	14	16	....	....	....	....	....
	USNTDP	U-18	47	10	25	35	30	....	....	....	....	....
2009-10	U. of Denver	WCHA	41	5	14	19	18	....	....	....	....	....
2010-11	U. of Denver	WCHA	40	23	23	46	38	....	....	....	....	....

WCHA Second All-Star Team (2011)

SHORE, Nick (SHOHR, NIHK) L.A.

Center. Shoots right. 6', 184 lbs. Born, Denver, CO, September 26, 1992.
(Los Angeles' 3rd choice, 82nd overall, in 2011 Entry Draft).

			Regular Season					Playoffs				
Season	Club	League	GP	G	A	Pts	PIM	GP	G	A	Pts	PIM
2007-08	Colorado T-birds	Minor-CO	....	64	71	135	....	....	....	....	....	....
2008-09	USNTDP	NAHL	42	10	11	21	30	9	2	2	4	6
	USNTDP	U-17	16	7	6	13	18	....	....	....	....	....
2009-10	USNTDP	USHL	26	6	14	20	10	....	....	....	....	....
	USNTDP	U-18	39	13	24	37	30	....	....	....	....	....
2010-11	U. of Denver	WCHA	33	7	11	18	37	....	....	....	....	....

SHUGG, Justin (SHUHG, JUHS-tihn) CAR

Left wing. Shoots right. 5'11", 194 lbs. Born, Niagara Falls, Ont., December 24, 1991.
(Carolina's 6th choice, 105th overall, in 2010 Entry Draft).

			Regular Season					Playoffs				
Season	Club	League	GP	G	A	Pts	PIM	GP	G	A	Pts	PIM
2006-07	Niag. Falls Thunder	Minor-ON	70	65	46	111	42	....	....	....	....	....
2007-08	Oshawa Generals	OHL	38	4	10	14	10	....	....	....	....	....
	Windsor Spitfires	OHL	23	0	3	3	2	3	0	0	0	0
2008-09	Windsor Spitfires	OHL	68	17	16	33	48	20	5	4	9	16
2009-10	Windsor Spitfires	OHL	67	39	40	79	43	18	5	10	15	10
2010-11	St. Michael's	OHL	66	41	45	86	43	20	10	9	19	14

SIEMENS, Duncan (SEE-muhns, DUHN-kuhn) COL

Defense. Shoots left. 6'3", 196 lbs. Born, Edmonton, Alta., September 7, 1993.
(Colorado's 2nd choice, 11th overall, in 2011 Entry Draft).

			Regular Season					Playoffs				
Season	Club	League	GP	G	A	Pts	PIM	GP	G	A	Pts	PIM
2007-08	Sherwood Park	AMBHL	32	14	22	36	54	12	5	7	12	32
2008-09	Sherwood Park	AMHL	34	5	13	18	68	11	2	6	8	24
	Saskatoon Blades	WHL	2	0	1	1	2	....	....	....	....	....
2009-10	Saskatoon Blades	WHL	57	3	17	20	89	7	0	0	0	11
2010-11	Saskatoon Blades	WHL	72	5	38	43	121	10	1	3	4	15

WHL East Second All-Star Team (2011)

SILAS, Stephen (SIGH-luhs, STEE-vehn) COL

Defense. Shoots left. 6', 205 lbs. Born, Brampton, Ont., June 26, 1992.
(Colorado's 4th choice, 95th overall, in 2010 Entry Draft).

			Regular Season					Playoffs				
Season	Club	League	GP	G	A	Pts	PIM	GP	G	A	Pts	PIM
2007-08	Halton Hurricanes	Minor-ON	73	25	52	77	69	....	....	....	....	....
2008-09	Belleville Bulls	OHL	63	3	14	17	18	17	0	0	0	10
2009-10	Belleville Bulls	OHL	66	4	45	49	61	....	....	....	....	....
2010-11	Belleville Bulls	OHL	68	2	34	36	52	4	0	0	0	2

SILFVERBERG, Jakob (SIHL-vuhr-buhrg, YA-kuhb) OTT

Left wing. Shoots right. 6'2", 195 lbs. Born, Gavle, Sweden, October 13, 1990.
(Ottawa's 2nd choice, 39th overall, in 2009 Entry Draft).

			Regular Season					Playoffs				
Season	Club	League	GP	G	A	Pts	PIM	GP	G	A	Pts	PIM
2005-06	Brynas U18	Swe-U18	8	0	0	0	0	....	....	....	....	....
2006-07	Brynas U18	Swe-U18	14	3	8	11	6	3	0	0	0	0
	Brynas IF Gavle Jr.	Swe-Jr.	6	1	3	4	0	....	....	....	....	....
2007-08	Brynas U18	Swe-U18	5	5	3	8	2	5	3	4	7	2
	Brynas IF Gavle Jr.	Swe-Jr.	30	8	12	20	8	7	3	0	3	2
2008-09	Brynas IF Gavle Jr.	Swe-Jr.	30	14	24	38	6	....	....	....	....	....
	Brynas IF Gavle	Sweden	16	3	1	4	2	4	0	0	0	2
2009-10	Brynas IF Gavle Jr.	Swe-Jr.	1	1	1	2	0	3	3	2	5	0
	Brynas IF Gavle	Sweden	48	8	8	16	4	5	1	1	2	2
2010-11	Brynas IF Gavle	Sweden	53	18	16	34	16	5	0	4	4	2

SILL, Zach (SIHL, ZAK) PIT

Center. Shoots left. 6', 200 lbs. Born, Truro, N.S., May 4, 1988.

			Regular Season					Playoffs				
Season	Club	League	GP	G	A	Pts	PIM	GP	G	A	Pts	PIM
2006-07	U. of Maine	H-East	6	1	1	2	2	....	....	....	....	....
2007-08	Moncton Wildcats	QMJHL	66	18	8	26	95	....	....	....	....	....
2008-09	Moncton Wildcats	QMJHL	58	9	15	24	78	10	4	1	5	10
2009-10	Moncton Wildcats	QMJHL	54	5	6	11	48	4	0	0	0	2
	Wheeling Nailers	ECHL	6	1	2	3	15	....	....	....	....	....
2010-11	Wilkes-Barre	AHL	80	11	19	30	85	12	1	2	3	6

Signed as a free agent by **Pittsburgh**, May 16, 2011.

SIMEK, Juraj (SEE-mehk, YUHR-ay)

Left wing. Shoots left. 6', 202 lbs. Born, Presov, Czech., September 29, 1987.
(Vancouver's 4th choice, 167th overall, in 2006 Entry Draft).

			Regular Season					Playoffs				
Season	Club	League	GP	G	A	Pts	PIM	GP	G	A	Pts	PIM
2002-03	SC Bern Jr.	Swiss-Jr.	2	1	0	1	0	2	0	0	0	0
2003-04	Kloten Flyers Jr.	Swiss-Jr.	36	8	6	14	28	....	....	....	....	....
2004-05	Kloten Flyers Jr.	Swiss-Jr.	39	17	13	30	62	9	2	3	5	10
	Kloten Flyers	Swiss	18	0	0	0	0	....	....	....	....	....
2005-06	Kloten Flyers Jr.	Swiss-Jr.	45	24	44	68	202	....	....	....	....	....
	Kloten Flyers	Swiss	8	0	1	1	4	....	....	....	....	....
	EHC Biel-Bienne	Swiss-2	3	0	0	0	2	....	....	....	....	....
2006-07	Brandon	WHL	58	28	29	57	41	9	1	5	6	6
2007-08	Manitoba Moose	AHL	66	7	10	17	30	1	1	0	1	0
2008-09	Norfolk Admirals	AHL	63	9	13	22	49	....	....	....	....	....
2009-10	Norfolk Admirals	AHL	75	21	15	36	31	....	....	....	....	....
2010-11	Norfolk Admirals	AHL	21	3	6	9	0	....	....	....	....	....
	Providence Bruins	AHL	11	0	0	0	6	....	....	....	....	....
	Geneve	Swiss	2	0	0	0	0	5	1	0	1	2

Traded to **Tampa Bay** by **Vancouver** with Lukas Krajicek for Shane O'Brien and Michel Ouellet, October 6, 2008. Signed as a free agent by **Riga** (Russia-KHL), June 22, 2010. Traded to **Boston** by **Tampa Bay** for Levi Nelson, December 9, 2010. Signed as a free agent by **Geneve** (Swiss), January 26, 2011.

SIMPSON, Dillon (SIHMP-suhn, DIH-luhn) EDM

Defense. Shoots left. 6'1", 192 lbs. Born, Edmonton, Alta., February 10, 1993.
(Edmonton's 6th choice, 92nd overall, in 2011 Entry Draft).

			Regular Season					Playoffs				
Season	Club	League	GP	G	A	Pts	PIM	GP	G	A	Pts	PIM
2007-08	Southgate	AMBHL	33	7	31	38	32	4	4	2	6	2
2008-09	SSAC Athletics	AMHL	34	3	12	15	8	4	0	0	0	0
	Spruce Grove	AJHL	1	0	0	0	0	1	0	0	0	2
2009-10	Spruce Grove	AJHL	58	12	29	41	19	16	0	6	6	6
2010-11	North Dakota	WCHA	30	2	8	10	8	....	....	....	....	....

SINDEL, Jakub (SHIHN-dehl, YA-kuhb) CHI

Center. Shoots right. 6', 172 lbs. Born, Jihlava, Czech., January 24, 1986.
(Chicago's 5th choice, 54th overall, in 2004 Entry Draft).

			Regular Season					Playoffs				
Season	Club	League	GP	G	A	Pts	PIM	GP	G	A	Pts	PIM
99-2000	Slavia U17	CzR-U17	32	10	6	16	6	....	....	....	....	....
2000-01	Slavia U17	CzR-U17	26	12	15	27	2	6	1	0	1	0
2001-02	Slavia U17	CzR-U17	34	32	14	46	34	2	0	1	1	2
	HC Slavia Praha Jr.	CzRep-Jr.	14	7	4	11	10	....	....	....	....	....
2002-03	HC Slavia Praha Jr.	CzRep-Jr.	35	12	11	23	39	2	0	1	1	0
2003-04	HC Sparta Praha	CzRep	34	5	1	6	14	13	1	1	2	2
	Sparta Jr.	CzRep-Jr.	13	8	14	22	4	....	....	....	....	....
	HC Dukla Jihlava	CzRep-2	1	0	0	0	0	....	....	....	....	....
2004-05	Sparta Jr.	CzRep-Jr.	9	5	16	21	16	....	....	....	....	....
	HC Sparta Praha	CzRep	10	0	2	2	0	....	....	....	....	....
	Trebic	CzRep-2	5	0	0	0	0	....	....	....	....	....
	Brandon	WHL	35	16	13	29	12	24	7	4	11	22
2005-06	HC Sparta Praha	CzRep	12	1	1	2	6	....	....	....	....	....
	Plzen	CzRep	31	11	8	19	18	....	....	....	....	....
2006-07	Plzen	CzRep	50	16	10	26	30	....	....	....	....	....
	BK Mlada Boleslav	CzRep-2	4	1	0	1	4	8	5	5	10	20
2007-08	Plzen	CzRep	45	19	4	23	16	4	0	2	2	4
	BK Mlada Boleslav	CzRep-2	....	....	....	....	....	11	5	2	7	8
2008-09	Plzen	CzRep	22	4	4	8	12	....	....	....	....	....
	Pelicans Lahti	Finland	23	7	8	15	12	8	2	2	4	8
2009-10	HC Kometa Brno	CzRep	56	16	10	26	44	....	....	....	....	....
2010-11	Pelicans Lahti	Finland	59	15	18	33	16	....	....	....	....	....
	Pelicans Lahti	Finland-Q	....	....	....	....	....	4	3	1	4	0

SISLO, Mike (SIHS-loh, MIGHK) N.J.

Right wing. Shoots right. 5'11", 190 lbs. Born, Superior, WI, January 20, 1988.

			Regular Season					Playoffs				
Season	Club	League	GP	G	A	Pts	PIM	GP	G	A	Pts	PIM
2005-06	Green Bay	USHL	57	3	3	6	36	3	0	0	0	5
2006-07	Green Bay	USHL	60	23	26	49	28	4	3	1	4	2
2007-08	New Hampshire	H-East	38	3	5	8	12	....	....	....	....	....
2008-09	New Hampshire	H-East	38	19	12	31	12	....	....	....	....	....
2009-10	New Hampshire	H-East	39	14	15	29	20	....	....	....	....	....
2010-11	New Hampshire	H-East	39	15	*33	48	38	....	....	....	....	....
	Albany Devils	AHL	3	0	0	0	0	....	....	....	....	....

Signed as a free agent by **New Jersey**, April 5, 2011.

SJOGREN, Mattias (SHOH-grehn, ma-TEE-uhs) WSH

Center. Shoots left. 6'2", 214 lbs. Born, Landskrona, Sweden, November 27, 1987.

			Regular Season					Playoffs				
Season	Club	League	GP	G	A	Pts	PIM	GP	G	A	Pts	PIM
2003-04	Rogle U18	Swe-U18	13	10	3	13	12	....	....	....	....	....
	Rogle Jr.	Swe-Jr.	5	0	0	0	0	....	....	....	....	....
2004-05	Rogle U18	Swe-U18	3	0	1	1	16	....	....	....	....	....
	Rogle Jr.	Swe-Jr.	34	6	6	12	26	....	....	....	....	....
	Rogle	Sweden-2	1	0	0	0	0	....	....	....	....	....
2005-06	Rogle Jr.	Swe-Jr.	20	5	6	11	61	....	....	....	....	....
	Rogle	Sweden-2	50	1	5	6	10	....	....	....	....	....
2006-07	Rogle Jr.	Swe-Jr.	7	3	3	6	18	....	....	....	....	....
	Rogle	Sweden-2	55	0	3	3	38	....	....	....	....	....
2007-08	Rogle	Sweden-2	55	8	12	20	46	....	....	....	....	....
2008-09	Rogle	Sweden	43	6	7	13	16	....	....	....	....	....
	Rogle	Sweden-Q	10	4	2	6	10	....	....	....	....	....
2009-10	Rogle	Sweden	54	11	11	22	20	....	....	....	....	....
	Rogle	Sweden-Q	10	4	5	9	4	....	....	....	....	....
2010-11	Farjestad	Sweden	51	7	17	24	44	13	1	8	9	4

Signed as a free agent by **Washington**, June 1, 2011.

SKACHKOV, Evgeny (skatch-KAWF, yehv-GEH-nee) ST.L.

Left wing. Shoots right. 6', 194 lbs. Born, Penza, USSR, July 14, 1984.
(St. Louis' 10th choice, 221st overall, in 2003 Entry Draft).

			Regular Season					Playoffs				
Season	Club	League	GP	G	A	Pts	PIM	GP	G	A	Pts	PIM
2000-01	Dizelist Penza	Russia-2	9	0	0	0	0	....	....	....	....	....
2001-02	Kapitan Stupino	Russia-3		STATISTICS NOT AVAILABLE								
2002-03	Stupino	Russia-3		STATISTICS NOT AVAILABLE								
	Kapitan Stupino	EEHL	34	4	4	8	2	....	....	....	....	....
2003-04	CSKA Moscow	Russia	1	0	0	0	2	....	....	....	....	....
	CSKA Moscow 2	Russia-3		DID NOT PLAY – INJURED								
2004-05	Spartak Moscow	Russia	9	0	2	2	0	....	....	....	....	....
2005-06	Spartak Moscow 2	Russia-3	55	25	31	56	98	....	....	....	....	....
	Spartak Moscow	Russia	2	0	0	0	6	....	....	....	....	....
2006-07	Chelyabinsk	Russia	52	13	9	22	52	....	....	....	....	....
2007-08	Chelyabinsk	Russia	53	14	13	27	58	3	1	0	1	6
2008-09	Chelyabinsk	Rus-KHL	54	14	18	32	56	3	0	0	0	14
2009-10	Chelyabinsk	Rus-KHL	51	22	14	36	143	....	....	....	....	....
2010-11	Ak Bars Kazan	Rus-KHL	21	7	5	12	14	....	....	....	....	....

SKOKAN, David (SKOH-kahn, DAY-vihd) NYR

Center. Shoots left. 6', 185 lbs. Born, Poprad, Czech., December 6, 1988.
(NY Rangers' 5th choice, 193rd overall, in 2007 Entry Draft).

			Regular Season					Playoffs				
Season	Club	League	GP	G	A	Pts	PIM	GP	G	A	Pts	PIM
2003-04	Poprad U18	Svk-U18	38	17	28	45	110	6	1	5	6	37
	HK SKP Poprad Jr.	Slovak-Jr.	7	2	0	2	7	....	....	....	....	....
2004-05	Poprad U18	Svk-U18	4	4	6	10	37	....	....	....	....	....
	HK SKP Poprad Jr.	Slovak-Jr.	24	5	19	24	52	....	....	....	....	....
	HK SKP Poprad	Slovakia	8	0	0	0	6	2	0	0	0	25
2005-06	Rimouski Oceanic	QMJHL	53	6	15	21	143	....	....	....	....	....
2006-07	Rimouski Oceanic	QMJHL	52	14	21	35	62	....	....	....	....	....
2007-08	Rimouski Oceanic	QMJHL	53	19	21	40	92	8	0	5	5	10
2008-09	HK Poprad	Slovakia	33	9	9	18	115	....	....	....	....	....
	HK Poprad	Slovak-Q	1	0	0	0	25	....	....	....	....	....
2009-10	Bratislava	Slovakia	32	11	4	15	70	15	3	3	6	14
2010-11	Bratislava	Slovakia	56	13	9	22	78	7	1	2	3	8

SLANEY, Robert (SLAY-nee, RAW-buhrt) NSH

Left wing. Shoots left. 6'2", 203 lbs. Born, Upper Island Cove, Nfld., October 13, 1988.

			Regular Season					Playoffs				
Season	Club	League	GP	G	A	Pts	PIM	GP	G	A	Pts	PIM
2005-06	Cape Breton	QMJHL	54	3	4	7	21	7	0	3	3	4
2006-07	Cape Breton	QMJHL	58	13	12	25	67	15	5	5	10	8
2007-08	Cape Breton	QMJHL	64	26	29	55	63	11	6	3	9	10
2008-09	Cape Breton	QMJHL	63	36	45	81	78	7	5	4	9	18
2009-10	Toronto Marlies	AHL	34	0	6	6	15	....	....	....	....	....
	Reading Royals	ECHL	22	1	10	11	22	....	....	....	....	....
2010-11	Toronto Marlies	AHL	9	0	1	1	2	....	....	....	....	....
	Reading Royals	ECHL	61	7	17	24	34	4	1	3	4	0

Canadian Major Junior Scholastic Player of the Year (2008)

Signed as a free agent by **Toronto**, April 14, 2009. Traded to **Nashville** by **Toronto** with Brett Lebda and future considerations for Cody Franson, Matthew Lombardi and future considerations, July 3, 2011.

SMITH, Austin (SMIHTH, AUZ-tihn) DAL

Right wing. Shoots right. 5'11", 160 lbs. Born, Dallas, TX, November 7, 1988.
(Dallas' 4th choice, 128th overall, in 2007 Entry Draft).

			Regular Season					Playoffs				
Season	Club	League	GP	G	A	Pts	PIM	GP	G	A	Pts	PIM
2003-04	Dallas Jesuit Prep	High-TX		STATISTICS NOT AVAILABLE								
2004-05	Dallas Jesuit Prep	High-TX		STATISTICS NOT AVAILABLE								
	Alliance Bulldogs	NTHL	53	29	46	75	24	....	....	....	....	....
2005-06	The Gunnery	High-CT	31	23	20	43	22	....	....	....	....	....
2006-07	The Gunnery	High-CT	30	25	38	63	36	....	....	....	....	....
2007-08	Penticton Vees	BCHL	60	32	35	67	42	15	11	11	22	12
2008-09	Colgate	ECAC	37	17	14	31	24	....	....	....	....	....
2009-10	Colgate	ECAC	36	16	25	41	20	....	....	....	....	....
2010-11	Colgate	ECAC	41	10	21	31	36	....	....	....	....	....

SMITH, Brendan (SMIHTH, BREHN-duhn) DET

Defense. Shoots left. 6'2", 195 lbs. Born, Toronto, Ont., February 8, 1989.
(Detroit's 1st choice, 27th overall, in 2007 Entry Draft).

			Regular Season					Playoffs				
Season	Club	League	GP	G	A	Pts	PIM	GP	G	A	Pts	PIM
2004-05	Toronto Marlboros	GTHL	66	22	63	85	120	....	....	....	....	....
2005-06	St. Michael's	OPJHL	39	5	21	26	55	17	1	5	6	44
2006-07	St. Michael's	OPJHL	39	12	24	36	90	16	6	14	20	30
2007-08	U. of Wisconsin	WCHA	22	2	10	12	26	....	....	....	....	....
2008-09	U. of Wisconsin	WCHA	31	9	14	23	75	....	....	....	....	....
2009-10	U. of Wisconsin	WCHA	42	15	37	52	76	....	....	....	....	....
2010-11	Grand Rapids	AHL	63	12	20	32	124	....	....	....	....	....

WCHA First All-Star Team (2010) • NCAA West First All-American Team (2010) • NCAA Championship All-Tournament Team (2010) • AHL All-Rookie Team (2011)

SMITH, Craig (SMIHTH, KRAYG) NSH

Center. Shoots right. 6'1", 197 lbs. Born, Madison, WI, September 5, 1989.
(Nashville's 6th choice, 98th overall, in 2009 Entry Draft).

			Regular Season					Playoffs				
Season	Club	League	GP	G	A	Pts	PIM	GP	G	A	Pts	PIM
2004-05	Madison Lancers	High-WI	20	16	24	40	....	....	....	....	....	....
2005-06	Madison Lancers	High-WI	20	35	26	61	....	....	....	....	....	....
2006-07	Waterloo	USHL	45	8	10	18	28	4	0	1	1	8
2007-08	Waterloo	USHL	58	13	10	23	90	11	2	3	5	8
2008-09	Waterloo	USHL	54	28	48	76	108	3	1	3	4	26
2009-10	U. of Wisconsin	WCHA	41	8	25	33	72	....	....	....	....	....
2010-11	U. of Wisconsin	WCHA	41	19	24	43	87	....	....	....	....	....

USHL First All-Star Team (2009) • WCHA All-Rookie Team (2010)

SMITH, Dalton (SMIHTH, DAHL-tuhn) CBJ

Left wing. Shoots left. 6'2", 206 lbs. Born, Markham, Ont., June 30, 1992.
(Columbus' 2nd choice, 34th overall, in 2010 Entry Draft).

			Regular Season					Playoffs				
Season	Club	League	GP	G	A	Pts	PIM	GP	G	A	Pts	PIM
2007-08	Osh. Generals	Minor-ON	62	22	38	60	192	....	....	....	....	....
2008-09	Whitby Fury	ON-Jr.A	40	10	13	23	109	4	2	1	3	12
	Ottawa 67's	OHL	17	2	5	7	8	7	0	0	0	0
2009-10	Ottawa 67's	OHL	62	21	23	44	129	12	3	3	6	27
2010-11	Ottawa 67's	OHL	64	12	17	29	124	4	2	2	4	12

SMITH, Reilly (SMIHTH, RIGH-lee) DAL

Right wing. Shoots left. 6'1", 175 lbs. Born, Toronto, Ont., April 1, 1991.
(Dallas' 3rd choice, 69th overall, in 2009 Entry Draft).

			Regular Season					Playoffs				
Season	Club	League	GP	G	A	Pts	PIM	GP	G	A	Pts	PIM
2007-08	Tor. Young Nats	GTHL	70	80	77	157	56	....	....	....	....	....
	St. Michael's	OPJHL	13	2	7	9	22	1	0	0	0	2
2008-09	St. Michael's	ON-Jr.A	49	27	48	75	44	6	9	6	15	10
2009-10	Miami U.	CCHA	44	8	12	20	24	....	....	....	....	....
2010-11	Miami U.	CCHA	38	28	26	54	18	....	....	....	....	....

SMITH-PELLY, Devante (SMITH-PEH-lee, deh-VAHN-tay) ANA

Right wing. Shoots right. 6', 215 lbs. Born, Scarborough, Ont., June 14, 1992.
(Anaheim's 3rd choice, 42nd overall, in 2010 Entry Draft).

			Regular Season					Playoffs				
Season	Club	League	GP	G	A	Pts	PIM	GP	G	A	Pts	PIM
2007-08	Tor. Jr. Canadiens	GTHL	85	38	39	77	159	....	....	....	....	....
2008-09	St. Michael's	OHL	57	13	12	25	24	11	2	3	5	4
2009-10	St. Michael's	OHL	60	29	33	62	35	16	8	6	14	20
2010-11	St. Michael's	OHL	67	36	30	66	50	20	*15	6	21	16

Memorial Cup All-Star Team (2011)

SMOLYANINOV, Vitali (smoh-LEE-ya-NEE-nohv, vih-TAL-ee) T.B.

Left wing. Shoots left. 6'3", 205 lbs. Born, Nizhnekamsk, USSR, August 5, 1983.
(Tampa Bay's 12th choice, 261st overall, in 2001 Entry Draft).

			Regular Season					Playoffs				
Season	Club	League	GP	G	A	Pts	PIM	GP	G	A	Pts	PIM
1998-99	Nizhnekamsk 2	Russia-4	12	1	0	1	0	....	....	....	....	....
99-2000	Nizhnekamsk 2	Russia-3	54	7	7	14	28	....	....	....	....	....
2000-01	Nizhnekamsk 2	Russia-3		STATISTICS NOT AVAILABLE								
2001-02	Nizhnekamsk	Russia	1	0	0	0	0	....	....	....	....	....
2002-03	HK Voronezh	Russia-2	14	1	1	2	12	....	....	....	....	....
2003-04	Karaganda	Kazakh.	9	2	3	5	0	....	....	....	....	....
	Karaganda	Russia-2	19	0	1	1	32	....	....	....	....	....
2004-05	Karaganda	Kazakh.	7	5	3	8	2	....	....	....	....	....
	Karaganda	Russia-2	20	1	5	6	10	....	....	....	....	....
2005-06	Irtysh Pavlodar	Kazakh.	14	8	6	14	12	....	....	....	....	....
	Irtysh Pavlodar	Russia-3		STATISTICS NOT AVAILABLE								
2006-07	Barys Astana	Russia-3	42	8	19	27	36	....	....	....	....	....
	Barys Astana	Kazakh.	22	10	6	16	52	....	....	....	....	....
2007-08	Barys Astana	Russia-2	51	18	21	39	54	7	1	1	2	2
2008-09	Barys Astana	Rus-KHL	14	1	2	3	10	....	....	....	....	....
	Khanty-Mansiisk	Russia-2	2	0	1	1	2	....	....	....	....	....
	Gazovik Tyumen	Russia-2	20	7	7	14	12	8	3	0	3	6
2009-10	Gazovik Tyumen	Russia-2	36	5	18	23	24	7	3	1	4	2
2010-11	Rubin Tyumen	Russia-2	35	9	7	16	40	12	2	2	4	20

SNEEP, Carl (SNEEP, KAHRL) PIT

Defense. Shoots right. 6'4", 210 lbs. Born, St. Louis Park, MN, November 5, 1987.
(Pittsburgh's 2nd choice, 32nd overall, in 2006 Entry Draft).

			Regular Season					Playoffs				
Season	Club	League	GP	G	A	Pts	PIM	GP	G	A	Pts	PIM
2004-05	Brainerd	High-MN	26	20	21	41	25	....	....	....	....	....
2005-06	Brainerd	High-MN	26	14	23	37	34	....	....	....	....	....
	Lincoln Stars	USHL	13	1	3	4	9	9	0	1	1	6
2006-07	Boston College	H-East	38	1	9	10	8	....	....	....	....	....
2007-08	Boston College	H-East	44	3	12	15	15	....	....	....	....	....
2008-09	Boston College	H-East	33	2	9	11	26	....	....	....	....	....
2009-10	Boston College	H-East	42	11	17	28	26	....	....	....	....	....
2010-11	Wilkes-Barre	AHL	61	4	13	17	39	2	0	0	0	0

SOBCHENKO, Daniil (SAWB-chehn-koh, DAN-ihl) S.J.

Center. Shoots left. 6'2", 215 lbs. Born, Kiev, USSR, April 13, 1991.
(San Jose's 4th choice, 166th overall, in 2011 Entry Draft).

			Regular Season					Playoffs				
Season	Club	League	GP	G	A	Pts	PIM	GP	G	A	Pts	PIM
2007-08	Yaroslavl 2	Russia-3	14	6	4	10	2	8	0	3	3	0
2008-09	Yaroslavl 2	Russia-3	66	44	43	87	53	4	0	2	2	2
2009-10	Loko Yaroslavl Jr.	Russia-Jr.	6	0	4	4	4	....	....	....	....	....
	Yaroslavl	Rus-KHL	35	5	1	6	6	6	0	0	0	2
2010-11	Loko Yaroslavl Jr.	Russia-Jr.	14	10	10	20	8	....	....	....	....	....
	Yaroslavl	Rus-KHL	16	1	1	2	4	11	0	1	1	16

SODERBERG, Carl (SOH-dehr-buhrg, KAHRL) BOS

Center. Shoots left. 6'3", 198 lbs. Born, Malmo, Sweden, October 12, 1985.
(St. Louis' 2nd choice, 49th overall, in 2004 Entry Draft).

			Regular Season					Playoffs				
Season	Club	League	GP	G	A	Pts	PIM	GP	G	A	Pts	PIM
2000-01	Skane	Exhib.	8	1	2	3	2	....	....	....	....	....
	Malmo U18	Swe-U18	3	1	1	2	0	....	....	....	....	....
2001-02	Malmo U18	Swe-U18	13	9	20	29	18	....	....	....	....	....
	Malmo Jr.	Swe-Jr.	4	0	2	2	2	7	0	2	2	4
2002-03	Malmo U18	Swe-U18	4	6	3	9	25	....	....	....	....	....
	Malmo Jr.	Swe-Jr.	28	17	18	35	22	6	2	4	6	8
2003-04	Malmo	Sweden	24	1	1	2	8	....	....	....	....	....
	Malmo U18	Swe-U18	27	23	25	48	30	6	1	2	3	10
	Malmo	Sweden-Q	8	1	1	2	4	....	....	....	....	....
2004-05	Morrums GoIS IK	Sweden-2	14	5	6	11	8	....	....	....	....	....
	Malmo Jr.	Swe-Jr.	12	13	6	19	43	3	2	1	3	12
	Malmo	Sweden	38	0	5	5	8	....	....	....	....	....
	Malmo	Sweden-Q	7	0	0	0	0	....	....	....	....	....
2005-06	Malmo	Sweden-2	49	20	27	47	47	....	....	....	....	....
2006-07	Malmo	Sweden	31	12	18	30	14	....	....	....	....	....
2007-08	Malmo	Sweden-2	42	22	36	58	18	....	....	....	....	....
2008-09	Malmo	Sweden-2	45	18	41	59	26	....	....	....	....	....
2009-10	Malmo	Sweden-2	51	20	31	51	53	5	0	1	1	0
2010-11	Malmo	Sweden-2	52	12	34	46	18	....	....	....	....	....

Traded to **Boston** by **St. Louis** for Hannu Toivonen, July 23, 2007.

SOIN, Sergei (SOY-ihn, SAIR-gay) NSH

Center/Left wing. Shoots left. 6', 185 lbs. Born, Moscow, USSR, March 31, 1982.
(Colorado's 3rd choice, 50th overall, in 2000 Entry Draft).

			Regular Season					Playoffs				
Season	Club	League	GP	G	A	Pts	PIM	GP	G	A	Pts	PIM
1997-98	Krylja Sovetov 2	Russia-3	2	0	0	0	0	....	....	....	....	....
1998-99	Krylja Sovetov	Russia	34	1	4	5	12	....	....	....	....	....
99-2000	Krylja Sovetov 2	Russia-3	8	2	3	5	12	....	....	....	....	....
	Krylja Sovetov	Russia-2	32	8	8	16	28	14	0	2	2	6
2000-01	Krylja Sovetov 2	Russia-3	8	2	3	5	12	....	....	....	....	....
	Krylja Sovetov	Russia-2	19	6	3	9	8	11	2	2	4	2
2001-02	Krylja Sovetov 2	Russia-3	5	2	6	8	20	....	....	....	....	....
	Krylja Sovetov	Russia	41	5	7	12	8	....	....	....	....	....
2002-03	Krylja Sovetov	Russia	49	8	6	14	40	....	....	....	....	....
2003-04	CSKA Moscow	Russia	49	1	6	7	32	....	....	....	....	....
2004-05	CSKA Moscow	Russia	19	3	3	6	10	....	....	....	....	....
2005-06	Cherepovets	Russia	48	5	12	17	36	4	1	1	2	0
2006-07	Cherepovets	Russia	52	12	12	24	78	5	2	1	3	0
2007-08	Cherepovets	Russia	52	9	11	20	22	7	1	1	2	4
2008-09	Cherepovets	Rus-KHL	51	7	19	26	38	....	....	....	....	....
2009-10	Cherepovets	Rus-KHL	52	7	13	20	30	....	....	....	....	....
2010-11	Cherepovets	Rus-KHL	54	4	10	14	26	6	1	0	1	0

Traded to **Nashville** by **Colorado** for Tomas Slovak, June 21, 2003.

SOL, Cody (SAWL, KOH-dee) WPG

Defense. Shoots left. 6'5", 242 lbs. Born, Woodstock, Ont., February 11, 1991.
(Atlanta's 6th choice, 125th overall, in 2009 Entry Draft).

			Regular Season					Playoffs				
Season	Club	League	GP	G	A	Pts	PIM	GP	G	A	Pts	PIM
2007-08	St. Mary's Lincolns	ON-Jr.B	20	2	2	4	30	....	....	....	....	....
	Saginaw Spirit	OHL	12	0	0	0	4	1	0	0	0	0
2008-09	Saginaw Spirit	OHL	66	1	6	7	128	8	0	2	2	14
2009-10	Saginaw Spirit	OHL	55	7	8	15	151	6	0	0	0	8
	Chicago Wolves	AHL	1	0	0	0	0	....	....	....	....	....
2010-11	Kitchener Rangers	OHL	60	4	12	16	114	7	0	3	3	10

SOLAREV, Ilja (SOH-luh-rehv, IHL-yuh) T.B.

Left wing. Shoots left. 6'3", 176 lbs. Born, Perm, USSR, August 2, 1982.
(Tampa Bay's 13th choice, 281st overall, in 2001 Entry Draft).

			Regular Season					Playoffs				
Season	Club	League	GP	G	A	Pts	PIM	GP	G	A	Pts	PIM
1997-98	Perm 2	Russia-3	4	1	0	1	0	....	....	....	....	....
1998-99	Perm 2	Russia-4	20	2	6	8	10	....	....	....	....	....
99-2000	Perm 2	Russia-3	35	3	2	5	24	....	....	....	....	....
2000-01	Perm 2	Russia-3	STATISTICS NOT AVAILABLE									
	Perm	Russia	5	0	1	1	0	....	....	....	....	....
2001-02	Leninogorsk	Russia-2	31	3	5	8	20	....	....	....	....	....
	HK Tambov	Russia-3	2	0	0	0	0	....	....	....	....	....
2002-03	Perm 2	Russia-3	STATISTICS NOT AVAILABLE									
	HK Brest	Belarus	STATISTICS NOT AVAILABLE									
2003-04	Motor Barnaul	Russia-2	34	6	6	12	20	1	0	0	0	0
2004-05	Energiya Kemerovo	Russia-2	36	3	2	5	28	....	....	....	....	....
2005-06	HK Lipetsk	Russia-2	49	4	6	10	30	3	0	0	0	0
2006-07	Satpayev	Russia-2	44	17	16	33	24	....	....	....	....	....
	Satpayev	Kazakh.	21	7	2	9	12	....	....	....	....	....
2007-08	Satpayev	Russia-2	29	10	10	20	24	....	....	....	....	....
	Barys Astana	Russia-2	22	4	9	13	26	7	2	1	3	6
2008-09	Barys Astana	Rus-KHL	46	8	7	15	24	....	....	....	....	....
2009-10	Barys Astana	Rus-KHL	37	5	4	9	20	3	0	1	1	4
2010-11	Barys Astana	Rus-KHL	4	1	1	2	2	4	0	0	0	2
	Barys Astana 2	Kazakhstan	40	19	30	49	22	15	3	2	5	14

SONNE, Brett (SOHNE, BREHT) ST.L.

Center/Left wing. Shoots left. 6', 201 lbs. Born, Chilliwack, B.C., March 16, 1989.
(St. Louis' 6th choice, 85th overall, in 2007 Entry Draft).

			Regular Season					Playoffs				
Season	Club	League	GP	G	A	Pts	PIM	GP	G	A	Pts	PIM
2004-05	Port Coquitlam	PIJHL	47	21	34	55	125	....	....	....	....	....
	Calgary Hitmen	WHL	6	0	0	0	2	....	....	....	....	....
2005-06	Calgary Hitmen	WHL	64	12	9	21	38	13	1	2	3	8
2006-07	Calgary Hitmen	WHL	71	21	9	30	65	18	5	1	6	22
2007-08	Calgary Hitmen	WHL	29	8	12	20	12	16	3	1	4	14
2008-09	Calgary Hitmen	WHL	62	48	52	100	58	14	7	9	16	18
2009-10	Peoria Rivermen	AHL	77	11	13	24	33	....	....	....	....	....
2010-11	Peoria Rivermen	AHL	62	5	4	9	45	4	0	0	0	2

WHL East First All-Star Team (2009) • WHL Player of the Year (2009) • Canadian Major Junior Second All-Star Team (2009)

SORENSEN, Marcus (SOHR-ehn-suhn, MAHR-kuhs) OTT

Right wing. Shoots left. 5'11", 162 lbs. Born, Sodertalje, Sweden, April 7, 1992.
(Ottawa's 2nd choice, 106th overall, in 2010 Entry Draft).

			Regular Season					Playoffs				
Season	Club	League	GP	G	A	Pts	PIM	GP	G	A	Pts	PIM
2008-09	Sodertalje SK U18	Swe-U18	32	16	12	28	92	4	2	3	5	6
2009-10	Sodertalje SK U18	Swe-U18	15	15	27	42	61	2	1	1	2	2
	Sodertalje SK Jr.	Swe-Jr.	27	7	10	17	54	....	....	....	....	....
2010-11	Djurgarden	Sweden	8	1	1	2	0	....	....	....	....	....
	Djurgarden Jr.	Swe-Jr.	31	14	22	36	53	4	3	0	3	2

SORYAL, Justin (SOHR-yahl, JUHS-tihn) CAR

Left wing. Shoots left. 6'3", 211 lbs. Born, Newmarket, Ont., June 29, 2007.

			Regular Season					Playoffs				
Season	Club	League	GP	G	A	Pts	PIM	GP	G	A	Pts	PIM
2003-04	Aurora Tigers	OPJHL	3	0	0	0	2	....	....	....	....	....
2004-05	Peterborough	OHL	29	0	1	1	54	14	0	1	1	21
2005-06	Peterborough	OHL	53	3	3	6	136	17	0	1	1	16
2006-07	Peterborough	OHL	60	26	27	53	125	....	....	....	....	....
2007-08	Peterborough	OHL	59	17	22	39	140	5	2	0	2	8
2008-09	Hartford Wolf Pack	AHL	43	3	7	10	114	....	....	....	....	....
2009-10	Hartford Wolf Pack	AHL	67	5	4	9	159	....	....	....	....	....
2010-11	Connecticut Whale	AHL	79	3	3	6	220	1	0	0	0	0

Signed as a free agent by **NY Rangers**, March 12, 2008. Signed as a free agent by **Carolina**, July 2, 2011.

SOVA, Joe (SOH-vah, JOH) N.J.

Defense. Shoots left. 6'3", 205 lbs. Born, Berwyn, IL, May 8, 1988.

			Regular Season					Playoffs				
Season	Club	League	GP	G	A	Pts	PIM	GP	G	A	Pts	PIM
2005-06	Waterloo	USHL	40	2	5	7	40	....	....	....	....	....
2006-07	Sioux City	USHL	58	4	19	23	86	7	1	0	1	16
2007-08	Omaha Lancers	USHL	59	7	11	18	98	14	1	2	3	40
2008-09	Alaska	CCHA	39	3	7	10	42	....	....	....	....	....
2009-10	Alaska	CCHA	39	6	18	24	30	....	....	....	....	....
2010-11	Alaska	CCHA	37	4	20	24	60	....	....	....	....	....
	Albany Devils	AHL	11	1	3	4	2	....	....	....	....	....

Signed as a free agent by **New Jersey**, March 19, 2011.

SPINA, David (SPEE-nuh, DAY-vihd)

Left wing. Shoots left. 5'10", 190 lbs. Born, Mesa, AZ, June 5, 1983.

			Regular Season					Playoffs				
Season	Club	League	GP	G	A	Pts	PIM	GP	G	A	Pts	PIM
99-2000	Texas Tornado	NAHL	54	15	26	41	31	....	....	....	....	....
2000-01	USNTDP	USHL	23	3	7	10	28	....	....	....	....	....
2001-02	Boston College	H-East	36	13	13	26	39	....	....	....	....	....
2002-03	Boston College	H-East	37	17	20	37	34	....	....	....	....	....
2003-04	Boston College	H-East	25	6	6	12	20	....	....	....	....	....
2004-05	Boston College	H-East	40	13	15	28	42	....	....	....	....	....
	Utah Grizzlies	AHL	9	0	0	0	2	....	....	....	....	....
2005-06	Springfield Falcons	AHL	54	11	13	24	36	....	....	....	....	....
	South Carolina	ECHL	11	7	0	7	6	....	....	....	....	....
2006-07	Springfield Falcons	AHL	73	15	20	35	80	....	....	....	....	....
	Johnstown Chiefs	ECHL	6	4	2	6	4	....	....	....	....	....
2007-08	San Antonio	AHL	76	21	29	50	35	7	3	0	3	2
2008-09	San Antonio	AHL	63	16	38	54	55	....	....	....	....	....
2009-10	San Antonio	AHL	26	6	11	17	29	....	....	....	....	....
2010-11	Peoria Rivermen	AHL	74	11	27	38	42	4	0	1	1	0

Signed as a free agent by **Phoenix**, July 2, 2008. • Missed majority of 2009-10 due to chest injury in pre-season game. Signed as a free agent by **St. Louis**, August 30, 2010.

SPOONER, Ryan (SPOO-nuhr, RIGH-uhn) BOS

Center. Shoots left. 5'10", 175 lbs. Born, Ottawa, Ont., January 30, 1992.
(Boston's 3rd choice, 45th overall, in 2010 Entry Draft).

			Regular Season					Playoffs				
Season	Club	League	GP	G	A	Pts	PIM	GP	G	A	Pts	PIM
2007-08	Ott. Jr. Senators	Minor-ON	53	52	45	97	16	....	....	....	....	....
2008-09	Peterborough	OHL	62	30	28	58	8	4	0	1	1	0
2009-10	Peterborough	OHL	47	19	35	54	12	3	0	1	1	2
2010-11	Peterborough	OHL	14	10	9	19	2	....	....	....	....	....
	Kingston	OHL	50	25	37	62	6	5	4	2	6	2
	Providence Bruins	AHL	3	2	1	3	0	....	....	....	....	....

SPROUL, Ryan (SPROHL, RIGH-uhn) DET

Defense. Shoots right. 6'3", 185 lbs. Born, Mississauga, Ont., January 13, 1993.
(Detroit's 3rd choice, 55th overall, in 2011 Entry Draft).

			Regular Season					Playoffs				
Season	Club	League	GP	G	A	Pts	PIM	GP	G	A	Pts	PIM
2008-09	Vaughan Kings	GTHL	31	2	7	9	14	....	....	....	....	....
2009-10	Bramalea Blues	ON-Jr.A	6	0	1	1	6	....	....	....	....	....
	Vaughan Vipers	ON-Jr.A	8	1	1	2	0	2	0	0	0	0
2010-11	Vaughan Vipers	ON-Jr.A	3	1	2	3	4	....	....	....	....	....
	Sault Ste. Marie	OHL	61	14	19	33	36	....	....	....	....	....

STAAL, Jared (STAWL, JAIR-uhd) CAR

Right wing. Shoots right. 6'4", 210 lbs. Born, Thunder Bay, Ont., August 21, 1990.
(Phoenix's 3rd choice, 49th overall, in 2008 Entry Draft).

			Regular Season					Playoffs				
Season	Club	League	GP	G	A	Pts	PIM	GP	G	A	Pts	PIM
2005-06	Thunder Bay Kings	Minor-ON	64	24	25	49	72	....	....	....	....	....
2006-07	Sudbury Wolves	OHL	63	2	1	3	18	21	1	0	1	2
2007-08	Sudbury Wolves	OHL	60	21	28	49	44	....	....	....	....	....
2008-09	Sudbury Wolves	OHL	67	19	33	52	38	6	0	1	1	2
	San Antonio	AHL	5	0	0	0	0	....	....	....	....	....
2009-10	Sudbury Wolves	OHL	59	12	37	49	57	3	0	0	0	4
	San Antonio	AHL	5	0	1	1	2	....	....	....	....	....
2010-11	Charlotte	AHL	13	1	1	2	2	....	....	....	....	....
	Florida Everblades	ECHL	33	6	5	11	6	....	....	....	....	....

Traded to **Carolina** by **Phoenix** for Nashville's 5th round choice (previously acquired, Phoenix selected Louis Domingue) in 2010 Entry Draft, May 13, 2010.

STAHL, Tyler (STAHL, TIGH-luhr) CAR

Defense. Shoots right. 6'1", 196 lbs. Born, Drumheller, Alta., January 29, 1992.
(Carolina's 7th choice, 167th overall, in 2010 Entry Draft).

			Regular Season					Playoffs				
Season	Club	League	GP	G	A	Pts	PIM	GP	G	A	Pts	PIM
2007-08	Caronport	Minor-SK	36	6	11	17	104	....	....	....	....	....
	Chilliwack Bruins	WHL	1	0	0	0	0	....	....	....	....	....
2008-09	Drumheller	AJHL	1	0	0	0	2	....	....	....	....	....
	Caronport	Minor-SK	35	23	21	44	182	....	....	....	....	....
2009-10	Chilliwack Bruins	WHL	59	0	6	6	146	6	0	0	0	18
2010-11	Chilliwack Bruins	WHL	67	1	9	10	182	3	0	0	0	11

STANTON, Ryan (STAN-tuhn, RIGH-uhn) CHI

Defense. Shoots left. 6'2", 205 lbs. Born, St. Albert, Alta., July 20, 1989.

			Regular Season					Playoffs				
Season	Club	League	GP	G	A	Pts	PIM	GP	G	A	Pts	PIM
2005-06	Moose Jaw	WHL	2	0	0	0	2	....	....	....	....	....
2006-07	Moose Jaw	WHL	54	0	8	8	75	....	....	....	....	....
2007-08	Moose Jaw	WHL	58	4	16	20	68	6	0	0	0	2
2008-09	Moose Jaw	WHL	69	5	29	34	111	....	....	....	....	....
2009-10	Moose Jaw	WHL	59	10	30	40	81	7	0	6	6	4
	Rockford IceHogs	AHL	2	0	1	1	0	2	0	0	0	0
2010-11	Rockford IceHogs	AHL	73	3	14	17	76	....	....	....	....	....

Signed as a free agent by **Chicago**, March 12, 2010.

STASYUK, Denis (stah-S'YUHK, DEH-nihs) **FLA**

Center. Shoots left. 6'1", 165 lbs. Born, Novokuznetsk, USSR, September 2, 1985.
(Florida's 9th choice, 171st overall, in 2003 Entry Draft).

			Regular Season					Playoffs				
Season	**Club**	**League**	**GP**	**G**	**A**	**Pts**	**PIM**	**GP**	**G**	**A**	**Pts**	**PIM**
2002-03	Novokuznetsk 2	Russia-3	STATISTICS NOT AVAILABLE									
	Novokuznetsk	Russia	11	1	0	1	0	....	....	....	....	....
2003-04	Novokuznetsk	Russia	5	0	0	0	0	....	....	....	....	....
	Novokuznetsk 2	Russia-3	STATISTICS NOT AVAILABLE									
2004-05	Amur Khabarovsk	Russia-2	44	11	10	21	12	10	1	2	3	6
2005-06	Novokuznetsk	Russia	41	7	2	9	18	3	0	0	0	0
2006-07	Novokuznetsk	Russia	26	0	1	1	16	3	0	0	0	0
2007-08	Novokuznetsk	Russia	33	4	2	6	14	....	....	....	....	....
2008-09	Novokuznetsk	Rus-KHL	44	2	8	10	12	....	....	....	....	....
2009-10	Novokuznetsk	Rus-KHL	55	8	5	13	12	....	....	....	....	....
2010-11	Novokuznetsk	Rus-KHL	24	1	0	1	12	....	....	....	....	....
	Yermak Angarsk	Russia-2	28	12	6	18	10	8	1	2	3	25

STEFANOVICH, Mikhail (steh-fan-AWV-ihch, mih-kigh-EHL) **DAL**

Centre. Shoots right. 6'2", 202 lbs. Born, Minsk, USSR, November 27, 1989.
(Toronto's 3rd choice, 98th overall, in 2008 Entry Draft).

			Regular Season					Playoffs				
Season	**Club**	**League**	**GP**	**G**	**A**	**Pts**	**PIM**	**GP**	**G**	**A**	**Pts**	**PIM**
2004-05	Dynamo Minsk 2	Belarus-2	19	3	7	10	8	....	....	....	....	....
	HK Gomel 2	Belarus-2	14	3	0	3	6	....	....	....	....	....
2005-06	HK Gomel 2	Belarus-2	37	18	12	30	64	....	....	....	....	....
2006-07	HK Gomel 2	Belarus-2	3	3	1	4	4	....	....	....	....	....
	HK Gomel	Belarus	41	16	9	25	43	5	1	0	1	2
2007-08	HK Gomel	Belarus	1	0	0	0	0	....	....	....	....	....
	Quebec Remparts	QMJHL	62	32	34	66	32	11	4	4	8	10
2008-09	Quebec Remparts	QMJHL	56	49	27	76	17	17	11	5	16	6
2009-10	Quebec Remparts	QMJHL	53	25	43	68	24	8	3	9	12	10
2010-11	Toronto Marlies	AHL	2	0	0	0	0	....	....	....	....	....
	Reading Royals	ECHL	4	3	2	5	2	....	....	....	....	....
	Dynamo Minsk	Rus-KHL	21	1	0	1	4	4	1	1	2	0

• Loaned to **Minsk** (Russia-KHL) by **Toronto** (Toronto-AHL), November 28, 2010. Traded to **Dallas** by **Toronto** for Fabian Brunnstrom, January 13, 2011.

STEFISHEN, Taylor (STEH-fih-shehn, TAY-luhr) **WSH**

Left wing. Shoots right. 5'11", 191 lbs. Born, North Vancouver, B.C., August 15, 1990.
(Nashville's 4th choice, 136th overall, in 2008 Entry Draft).

			Regular Season					Playoffs				
Season	**Club**	**League**	**GP**	**G**	**A**	**Pts**	**PIM**	**GP**	**G**	**A**	**Pts**	**PIM**
2006-07	Langley Chiefs	BCHL	59	25	31	56	73	7	5	1	6	8
2007-08	Langley Chiefs	BCHL	57	33	48	81	71	12	6	10	16	19
2008-09	Ohio State	CCHA	15	3	5	8	2	....	....	....	....	....
2009-10	Ohio State	CCHA	27	5	8	13	12	....	....	....	....	....
2010-11	Prince George	WHL	68	24	43	67	72	4	2	2	4	2

Traded to **Washington** by **Nashville** for future considerations, June 2, 2011.

STEJSKAL, Joe (STAY-kuhl, JOH) **MTL**

Defense. Shoots right. 6'3", 211 lbs. Born, Grand Rapids, MN, April 30, 1988.
(Montreal's 6th choice, 133rd overall, in 2007 Entry Draft).

			Regular Season					Playoffs				
Season	**Club**	**League**	**GP**	**G**	**A**	**Pts**	**PIM**	**GP**	**G**	**A**	**Pts**	**PIM**
2003-04	Grand Rapids	High-MN	....	1	7	8	....	....	....	....	....	....
2004-05	Grand Rapids	High-MN	....	2	8	10	....	....	....	....	....	....
2005-06	Grand Rapids	High-MN	....	7	18	25	....	....	....	....	....	....
2006-07	Grand Rapids	High-MN	24	11	17	28	42	....	....	....	....	....
2007-08	Dartmouth	ECAC	32	1	4	5	46	....	....	....	....	....
2008-09	Dartmouth	ECAC	29	7	5	12	53	....	....	....	....	....
2009-10	Dartmouth	ECAC	32	3	7	10	26	....	....	....	....	....
2010-11	Dartmouth	ECAC	33	3	2	5	37	....	....	....	....	....
	Hamilton Bulldogs	AHL	7	0	0	0	0	5	1	0	1	2

STEPHENSON, Logan (STEE-vehn-suhn, LOH-guhn) **PHX**

Defense. Shoots left. 6'3", 210 lbs. Born, Saskatoon, Sask., February 19, 1986.
(Phoenix's 2nd choice, 35th overall, in 2004 Entry Draft).

			Regular Season					Playoffs				
Season	**Club**	**League**	**GP**	**G**	**A**	**Pts**	**PIM**	**GP**	**G**	**A**	**Pts**	**PIM**
2001-02	Notre Dame	SMHL	37	4	2	6	74	....	....	....	....	....
	Tri-City Americans	WHL	....	....	....	....	....	3	0	0	0	0
2002-03	Tri-City Americans	WHL	50	0	6	6	121	....	....	....	....	....
2003-04	Tri-City Americans	WHL	69	3	8	11	112	11	1	1	2	10
2004-05	Tri-City Americans	WHL	59	6	9	15	86	5	0	0	0	2
2005-06	Tri-City Americans	WHL	71	10	43	53	162	5	1	0	1	18
2006-07	San Antonio	AHL	73	3	5	8	90	....	....	....	....	....
2007-08	San Antonio	AHL	74	1	7	8	94	7	0	1	1	6
2008-09	San Antonio	AHL	19	1	1	2	40	....	....	....	....	....
	Iowa Chops	AHL	25	0	2	2	21	....	....	....	....	....
	Rockford IceHogs	AHL	16	1	2	3	31	4	0	0	0	14
2009-10	Adirondack	AHL	62	1	7	8	140	....	....	....	....	....
2010-11	Adirondack	AHL	43	2	3	5	46	....	....	....	....	....

WHL West Second All-Star Team (2006)

Traded to **Anaheim** by **Phoenix** for Joakim Lindstrom, December 3, 2008. Traded to **Chicago** by **Anaheim** with Samuel Pahlsson and future considerations for James Wisniewski and Petri Kontiola, March 4, 2009. Signed as a free agent by **Adirondack** (AHL), October 2, 2009. Signed as a free agent by **Jesenice** (Austria), July 21, 2011.

STEVENSON, Dustin (STEE-vehn-suhn, DUHS-tihn) **WSH**

Defense. Shoots left. 6'5", 220 lbs. Born, Gull Lake, Sask., August 12, 1989.

			Regular Season					Playoffs				
Season	**Club**	**League**	**GP**	**G**	**A**	**Pts**	**PIM**	**GP**	**G**	**A**	**Pts**	**PIM**
2007-08	La Ronge	SJHL	53	2	11	13	63	6	0	2	2	2
2008-09	La Ronge	SJHL	53	15	24	39	124	....	....	....	....	....
2009-10	La Ronge	SJHL	56	11	36	47	134	....	....	....	....	....
2010-11	South Carolina	ECHL	63	3	9	12	44	....	....	....	....	....

Signed as a free agent by **Washington**, April 5, 2010.

STOESZ, Myles (STOHZ, MIGH-uhlz)

Left wing. Shoots right. 6'2", 210 lbs. Born, Steinbach, Man., February 15, 1987.
(Atlanta's 8th choice, 207th overall, in 2005 Entry Draft).

			Regular Season					Playoffs				
Season	**Club**	**League**	**GP**	**G**	**A**	**Pts**	**PIM**	**GP**	**G**	**A**	**Pts**	**PIM**
2003-04	Spokane Chiefs	WHL	43	1	1	2	133	....	....	....	....	....
2004-05	Spokane Chiefs	WHL	67	1	8	9	238	....	....	....	....	....
2005-06	Spokane Chiefs	WHL	56	0	2	2	260	....	....	....	....	....
2006-07	Chilliwack Bruins	WHL	40	3	2	5	135	....	....	....	....	....
	Regina Pats	WHL	29	4	2	6	89	9	0	0	0	21
2007-08	Gwinnett	ECHL	64	4	2	6	*291	1	0	0	0	0
2008-09	Gwinnett	ECHL	43	4	3	7	158	....	....	....	....	....
	Trenton Devils	ECHL	10	0	0	0	30	3	0	0	0	9
2009-10	Lowell Devils	AHL	35	1	1	2	148	....	....	....	....	....
	Trenton Devils	ECHL	19	4	2	6	97	....	....	....	....	....
2010-11	Albany Devils	AHL	7	0	0	0	30	....	....	....	....	....
	Trenton Devils	ECHL	37	1	3	4	165	....	....	....	....	....

Traded to **New Jersey** by **Atlanta** with Niclas Havelid for Anssi Salmela, March 1, 2009.

STONE, Mark (STOHN, MAHRK) **OTT**

Right wing. Shoots right. 6'3", 202 lbs. Born, Winnipeg, Man., May 13, 1992.
(Ottawa's 3rd choice, 178th overall, in 2010 Entry Draft).

			Regular Season					Playoffs				
Season	**Club**	**League**	**GP**	**G**	**A**	**Pts**	**PIM**	**GP**	**G**	**A**	**Pts**	**PIM**
2007-08	Wpg. Thrashers	MMHL	40	22	31	53	28	9	7	7	14	2
2008-09	Brandon	WHL	56	17	22	39	27	12	1	3	4	4
2009-10	Brandon	WHL	39	11	17	28	25	15	1	3	4	4
2010-11	Brandon	WHL	71	37	69	106	28	6	1	9	10	4

WHL East First All-Star Team (2011)

STONE, Michael (STOHN, MIGH-kuhl) **PHX**

Defense. Shoots right. 6'4", 207 lbs. Born, Winnipeg, Man., June 7, 1990.
(Phoenix's 4th choice, 69th overall, in 2008 Entry Draft).

			Regular Season					Playoffs				
Season	**Club**	**League**	**GP**	**G**	**A**	**Pts**	**PIM**	**GP**	**G**	**A**	**Pts**	**PIM**
2005-06	Wpg. Thrashers	MMHL	40	14	18	32	14	....	....	....	....	....
2006-07	Calgary Hitmen	WHL	55	2	18	20	32	17	0	3	3	14
2007-08	Calgary Hitmen	WHL	71	10	25	35	28	14	3	4	7	10
2008-09	Calgary Hitmen	WHL	69	19	42	61	87	18	2	11	13	16
2009-10	Calgary Hitmen	WHL	69	21	44	65	91	23	5	15	20	26
2010-11	San Antonio	AHL	70	2	11	13	27	....	....	....	....	....

WHL East Second All-Star Team (2009) • WHL East First All-Star Team (2010)

STOYKEWYCH, Peter (STOY-kuh-wihch, PEE-tuhr) **WPG**

Defense. Shoots left. 6'2", 190 lbs. Born, Winnipeg, Man., July 14, 1992.
(Atlanta's 9th choice, 199th overall, in 2010 Entry Draft).

			Regular Season					Playoffs				
Season	**Club**	**League**	**GP**	**G**	**A**	**Pts**	**PIM**	**GP**	**G**	**A**	**Pts**	**PIM**
2007-08	Winnipeg Wild	MMHL	39	1	21	22	22	....	....	....	....	....
2008-09	Wpg. South Blues	MJHL	28	2	7	9	....	....	....	....	....	....
2009-10	Wpg. South Blues	MJHL	56	6	25	31	63	4	1	0	1	16
2010-11	Des Moines	USHL	58	5	10	15	77	....	....	....	....	....

• Signed Letter of Intent to attend **Colorado College** (WCHA) in fall of 2011.

STRAKA, Petr (STRAH-kuh, PEH-tuhr) **CBJ**

Right wing. Shoots left. 6'1", 191 lbs. Born, Plzen, Czechoslovakia, June 15, 1992.
(Columbus' 3rd choice, 55th overall, in 2010 Entry Draft).

			Regular Season					Playoffs				
Season	**Club**	**League**	**GP**	**G**	**A**	**Pts**	**PIM**	**GP**	**G**	**A**	**Pts**	**PIM**
2006-07	HC Plzen U17	CzR-U17	22	5	6	11	14	7	0	0	0	0
2007-08	HC Plzen U17	CzR-U17	46	40	34	74	42	8	5	9	14	4
2008-09	HC Plzen U17	CzR-U17	1	1	2	3	4	1	0	2	2	2
	HC Plzen Jr.	CzRep-Jr.	27	13	10	23	6	5	3	1	4	2
2009-10	Rimouski Oceanic	QMJHL	62	28	36	64	54	12	5	9	14	10
2010-11	Rimouski Oceanic	QMJHL	41	10	15	25	33	5	2	2	4	0

QMJHL All-Rookie Team (2010) • Canadian Major Junior All-Rookie Team (2010)

STRANSKY, Matej (STRAHN-skee, MAH-tay) **DAL**

Right wing. Shoots right. 6'3", 193 lbs. Born, Ostrava, Czech Republic, July 11, 1993.
(Dallas' 5th choice, 165th overall, in 2011 Entry Draft).

			Regular Season					Playoffs				
Season	**Club**	**League**	**GP**	**G**	**A**	**Pts**	**PIM**	**GP**	**G**	**A**	**Pts**	**PIM**
2006-07	HC Vitkovice U17	CzR-U17	1	0	0	0	0	....	....	....	....	....
2007-08	HC Vitkovice U17	CzR-U17	43	5	14	19	22	3	1	1	2	2
2008-09	HC Vitkovice U17	CzR-U17	46	40	23	63	68	7	5	5	10	6
2009-10	HC Vitkovice U18	CzR-U18	43	17	33	50	112	2	1	2	3	4
	HC Vitkovice Jr.	CzRep-Jr.	11	2	1	3	4	....	....	....	....	....
2010-11	Saskatoon Blades	WHL	71	14	12	26	53	10	3	6	9	8

STROME, Ryan (STROHM, RIGH-uhn) **NYI**

Center. Shoots right. 6', 177 lbs. Born, Mississauga, Ont., July 11, 1993.
(NY Islanders' 1st choice, 5th overall, in 2011 Entry Draft).

			Regular Season					Playoffs				
Season	**Club**	**League**	**GP**	**G**	**A**	**Pts**	**PIM**	**GP**	**G**	**A**	**Pts**	**PIM**
2008-09	Toronto Marlboros	GTHL	76	41	63	104	86	....	....	....	....	....
2009-10	Barrie Colts	OHL	34	5	9	14	35	....	....	....	....	....
	Niagara Ice Dogs	OHL	27	3	10	13	26	5	0	3	3	0
2010-11	Niagara Ice Dogs	OHL	65	33	73	106	82	14	6	6	12	19

OHL Second All-Star Team (2011)

SUELLENTROP, Colin (SUHL-ehn-trawp, KAWL-ihn) **PHI**

Defense. Shoots right. 6'1", 190 lbs. Born, Plantation, FL, June 10, 1993.
(Philadelphia's 3rd choice, 116th overall, in 2011 Entry Draft).

			Regular Season					Playoffs				
Season	**Club**	**League**	**GP**	**G**	**A**	**Pts**	**PIM**	**GP**	**G**	**A**	**Pts**	**PIM**
2009-10	Oshawa Generals	OHL	54	1	5	6	74	....	....	....	....	....
2010-11	Oshawa Generals	OHL	59	0	14	14	70	10	0	2	2	6

SULLIVAN, Colin (SUHL-ih-vuhn, KAWL-ihn) **MTL**

Defense. Shoots right. 6'1", 196 lbs. Born, Milford, CT, March 26, 1993.
(Montreal's 6th choice, 198th overall, in 2011 Entry Draft).

			Regular Season					Playoffs				
Season	**Club**	**League**	**GP**	**G**	**A**	**Pts**	**PIM**	**GP**	**G**	**A**	**Pts**	**PIM**
2009-10	Avon Old Farms	High-CT	29	1	8	9	16	....	....	....	....	....
2010-11	Avon Old Farms	High-CT	27	3	12	15	14	....	....	....	....	....

• Signed Letter of Intent to attend **Yale University** (ECAC) in fall of 2011.

SULLIVAN, Sean (SUHL-ih-vuhn, SHAWN) **S.J.**

Defense. Shoots left. 6', 190 lbs. Born, Boston, MA, March 29, 1984.
(Phoenix's 7th choice, 272nd overall, in 2003 Entry Draft).

			Regular Season					Playoffs				
Season	**Club**	**League**	**GP**	**G**	**A**	**Pts**	**PIM**	**GP**	**G**	**A**	**Pts**	**PIM**
2001-02	St. Sebastian's	High-MA	31	3	11	14	4	....	....	....	....	....
2002-03	St. Sebastian's	High-MA	41	9	30	39	59	....	....	....	....	....
2003-04	Boston University	H-East	36	2	5	7	14	....	....	....	....	....
2004-05	Boston University	H-East	41	1	3	4	10	....	....	....	....	....
2005-06	Boston University	H-East	40	3	14	17	32	....	....	....	....	....
2006-07	Boston University	H-East	38	3	12	15	12	....	....	....	....	....
	San Antonio	AHL	7	0	0	0	0	....	....	....	....	....
2007-08	San Antonio	AHL	34	0	8	8	13	1	0	0	0	4
	Arizona Sundogs	CHL	22	9	16	25	19	....	....	....	....	....
2008-09	San Antonio	AHL	65	9	23	32	24	....	....	....	....	....
2009-10	San Antonio	AHL	77	12	37	49	32	....	....	....	....	....
2010-11	Worcester Sharks	AHL	73	12	23	35	46	....	....	....	....	....

NCAA East Second All-American Team (2007)

Signed as a free agent by **San Jose**, July 15, 2010.

SUNDHER, Kevin (SUHND-hurh, KEH-vihn) **BUF**

Center. Shoots left. 5'11", 184 lbs. Born, Surrey, B.C., January 18, 1992.
(Buffalo's 3rd choice, 75th overall, in 2010 Entry Draft).

			Regular Season					Playoffs				
Season	**Club**	**League**	**GP**	**G**	**A**	**Pts**	**PIM**	**GP**	**G**	**A**	**Pts**	**PIM**
2007-08	Valley West Hawks	BCMML	40	20	34	54	86	....	....	....	....	....
	Chilliwack Bruins	WHL	6	0	1	1	2	....	....	....	....	....
2008-09	Chilliwack Bruins	WHL	67	19	20	39	68	....	....	....	....	....
2009-10	Chilliwack Bruins	WHL	72	25	36	61	101	6	3	2	5	4
2010-11	Chilliwack Bruins	WHL	70	24	52	76	93	5	3	4	7	6

SUNDSTROM, Johan (SOOND-struhm, YOH-han) **NYI**

Center. Shoots right. 6'2", 196 lbs. Born, Gothenburg, Sweden, September 21, 1992.
(NY Islanders' 3rd choice, 50th overall, in 2011 Entry Draft).

			Regular Season					Playoffs				
Season	**Club**	**League**	**GP**	**G**	**A**	**Pts**	**PIM**	**GP**	**G**	**A**	**Pts**	**PIM**
2008-09	Frolunda U18	Swe-U18	22	6	7	13	4	7	0	2	2	0
2009-10	Frolunda U18	Swe-U18	5	6	4	10	6	1	0	0	0	0
	Frolunda Jr.	Swe-Jr.	37	13	17	30	14	1	0	0	0	0
	Frolunda	Sweden	1	0	0	0	0	....	....	....	....	....
2010-11	Frolunda Jr.	Swe-Jr.	15	10	9	19	4	7	8	7	15	2
	Boras HC	Sweden-2	1	0	0	0	0	....	....	....	....	....
	Frolunda	Sweden	41	1	0	1	10	....	....	....	....	....

SUTCH, Gregg (SUHCH, GREHG) **BUF**

Right wing. Shoots right. 6'2", 200 lbs. Born, Scarborough, Ont., February 9, 1992.
(Buffalo's 6th choice, 143rd overall, in 2010 Entry Draft).

			Regular Season					Playoffs				
Season	**Club**	**League**	**GP**	**G**	**A**	**Pts**	**PIM**	**GP**	**G**	**A**	**Pts**	**PIM**
2007-08	York Simcoe	Minor-ON	69	52	29	81	74	....	....	....	....	....
2008-09	Sarnia Sting	OHL	60	7	8	15	53	5	0	1	1	2
2009-10	St. Michael's	OHL	43	3	5	8	55	16	4	1	5	10
2010-11	St. Michael's	OHL	53	8	20	28	79	9	0	0	0	4

SUTTER, Brody (SUH-tuhr, BROH-dee) **CAR**

Center. Shoots right. 6'5", 203 lbs. Born, Viking, Alta., September 26, 1991.
(Carolina's 6th choice, 193rd overall, in 2011 Entry Draft).

			Regular Season					Playoffs				
Season	**Club**	**League**	**GP**	**G**	**A**	**Pts**	**PIM**	**GP**	**G**	**A**	**Pts**	**PIM**
2007-08	Calgary Buffaloes	AMHL	32	8	11	19	24	12	4	6	10	4
2008-09	Saskatoon Blades	WHL	18	0	2	2	4	....	....	....	....	....
	Lethbridge	WHL	30	4	3	7	7	10	0	0	0	2
2009-10	Lethbridge	WHL	72	5	9	14	42	....	....	....	....	....
2010-11	Lethbridge	WHL	46	18	24	42	35	....	....	....	....	....

SWEATT, Bill (SWEHT, BIHL) **VAN**

Left wing. Shoots left. 6', 190 lbs. Born, Elburn, IL, September 21, 1988.
(Chicago's 2nd choice, 38th overall, in 2007 Entry Draft).

			Regular Season					Playoffs				
Season	**Club**	**League**	**GP**	**G**	**A**	**Pts**	**PIM**	**GP**	**G**	**A**	**Pts**	**PIM**
2003-04	Team Illinois	MWEHL	74	33	37	70		....	....	....	....	....
2004-05	USNTDP	U-17	11	5	10	15	54	....	....	....	....	....
	USNTDP	NAHL	41	7	9	16	12	10	4	3	7	6
2005-06	USNTDP	U-18	42	19	11	30	24	....	....	....	....	....
	USNTDP	NAHL	17	10	15	25	4	....	....	....	....	....
2006-07	Colorado College	WCHA	30	9	17	26	18	....	....	....	....	....
2007-08	Colorado College	WCHA	37	10	17	27	38	....	....	....	....	....
2008-09	Colorado College	WCHA	37	12	11	23	28	....	....	....	....	....
2009-10	Colorado College	WCHA	39	15	18	33	18	....	....	....	....	....
2010-11	Manitoba Moose	AHL	80	19	27	46	28	14	1	5	6	2

Traded to **Toronto** by **Chicago** with Kris Versteeg for Viktor Stalberg, Chris Didomenico and Phillipe Paradis, June 30, 2010. Signed as a free agent by **Vancouver**, August 19, 2010.

SWEETLAND, Andrew (SWEET-land, AN-droo)

Left wing. Shoots left. 6'2", 204 lbs. Born, Bonavista, Nfld., October 21, 1986.

			Regular Season					Playoffs				
Season	**Club**	**League**	**GP**	**G**	**A**	**Pts**	**PIM**	**GP**	**G**	**A**	**Pts**	**PIM**
2004-05	Couchiching	OPJHL	42	34	24	58	8	....	....	....	....	....
2005-06	Couchiching	OPJHL	30	18	15	33	6	....	....	....	....	....
2006-07	Amherst Ramblers	MJAHL	54	56	61	117	20	6	3	8	11	0
2007-08	U. of Maine	H-East	28	8	9	17	2	....	....	....	....	....
2008-09	Rochester	AHL	48	1	2	3	12	....	....	....	....	....
	Florida Everblades	ECHL	23	10	13	23	8	11	2	4	6	2
2009-10	Rochester	AHL	51	5	8	13	10	....	....	....	....	....
2010-11	Elmira Jackals	ECHL	38	21	7	28	10	....	....	....	....	....
	Binghamton	AHL	14	4	3	7	2	....	....	....	....	....

Signed as a free agent by **Florida**, March 31, 2008. Signed as a free agent by **Elmira** (ECHL), September 10, 2010. Signed to a PTO (professional tryout) contract by **Binghamton** (AHL), January 16, 2011.

SWIFT, Michael (SWIHFT, MIGH-kuhl)

Center. Shoots left. 5'8", 175 lbs. Born, Peterborough, Ont., March 26, 1987.

			Regular Season					Playoffs				
Season	**Club**	**League**	**GP**	**G**	**A**	**Pts**	**PIM**	**GP**	**G**	**A**	**Pts**	**PIM**
2003-04	Mississauga	OHL	9	2	2	4	6	....	....	....	....	....
2004-05	Mississauga	OHL	67	15	17	32	46	5	0	0	0	4
2005-06	Mississauga	OHL	65	22	32	54	46	....	....	....	....	....
2006-07	Mississauga	OHL	67	34	59	93	76	5	0	1	1	6
	Laredo Bucks	CHL	....	....	....	....	....	12	1	3	4	8
2007-08	Niagara Ice Dogs	OHL	68	38	62	100	130	10	9	9	18	22
2008-09	Lowell Devils	AHL	52	12	15	27	50	....	....	....	....	....
2009-10	Lowell Devils	AHL	76	24	31	55	71	4	0	1	1	4
2010-11	Albany Devils	AHL	48	16	12	28	48	....	....	....	....	....
	Worcester Sharks	AHL	18	1	6	7	28	....	....	....	....	....

Signed as a free agent by **New Jersey**, April 19, 2008. Traded to **San Jose** by **New Jersey** with Patrick Davis for Jay Leach and Steven Zalewski, February 9, 2011.

SZWARZ, Jordan (SWAWRZ, JOHR-dahn) **PHX**

Right wing. Shoots right. 6', 189 lbs. Born, Burlington, Ont., May 14, 1991.
(Phoenix's 4th choice, 97th overall, in 2009 Entry Draft).

			Regular Season					Playoffs				
Season	**Club**	**League**	**GP**	**G**	**A**	**Pts**	**PIM**	**GP**	**G**	**A**	**Pts**	**PIM**
2006-07	Burlington Eagles	Minor-ON	66	56	54	110	88	....	....	....	....	....
2007-08	Saginaw Spirit	OHL	65	12	21	33	56	4	0	0	0	2
2008-09	Saginaw Spirit	OHL	67	17	34	51	76	8	1	5	6	10
2009-10	Saginaw Spirit	OHL	65	26	28	54	82	6	1	2	3	0
	San Antonio	AHL	1	0	0	0	0	....	....	....	....	....
2010-11	Saginaw Spirit	OHL	65	27	39	66	90	12	4	9	13	8

SZYDLOWSKI, Shawn (sihd-LOW-skee, SHAWN) **BUF**

Right wing. Shoots right. 6', 206 lbs. Born, St. Clair Shores, MI, August 5, 1990.

			Regular Season					Playoffs				
Season	**Club**	**League**	**GP**	**G**	**A**	**Pts**	**PIM**	**GP**	**G**	**A**	**Pts**	**PIM**
2007-08	Erie Otters	OHL	66	9	16	25	57	....	....	....	....	....
2008-09	Erie Otters	OHL	61	23	23	46	80	5	3	0	3	14
2009-10	Erie Otters	OHL	65	21	27	48	90	4	1	4	5	2
2010-11	Erie Otters	OHL	66	41	37	78	79	7	2	5	7	14
	Portland Pirates	AHL	2	0	0	0	0	....	....	....	....	....

Signed as a free agent by **Buffalo**, April 8, 2011.

TALBOT, Julian (TAL-buht, JOO-lee-uhn)

Center. Shoots left. 6', 185 lbs. Born, Wahnapitae, Ont., March 24, 1985.

			Regular Season					Playoffs				
Season	**Club**	**League**	**GP**	**G**	**A**	**Pts**	**PIM**	**GP**	**G**	**A**	**Pts**	**PIM**
2002-03	Ottawa 67's	OHL	62	10	18	28	13	23	1	7	8	2
2003-04	Ottawa 67's	OHL	68	18	31	49	56	7	1	4	5	6
2004-05	Ottawa 67's	OHL	68	25	41	66	50	21	8	12	20	31
2005-06	Ottawa 67's	OHL	65	30	47	77	70	3	1	2	3	8
2006-07	Providence Bruins	AHL	7	1	2	3	0	....	....	....	....	....
	Alaska Aces	ECHL	66	20	33	53	54	15	9	11	20	8
2007-08	Peoria Rivermen	AHL	78	24	26	50	53	....	....	....	....	....
2008-09	Peoria Rivermen	AHL	65	20	23	43	43	7	0	1	1	4
2009-10	Peoria Rivermen	AHL	76	17	15	32	34	....	....	....	....	....
2010-11	Lake Erie Monsters	AHL	77	13	32	45	41	7	1	1	2	2

Signed as a free agent by **St. Louis**, March 19, 2008. Traded to **Colorado** by **St. Louis** for T.J. Hensick, June 17, 2010.

TARASENKO, Vladimir (ta-rah-SEHN-koh, vla-DIH-meer) **ST.L.**

Right wing. Shoots left. 5'11", 202 lbs. Born, Yaroslavl, USSR, December 13, 1991.
(St. Louis' 2nd choice, 16th overall, in 2010 Entry Draft).

			Regular Season					Playoffs				
Season	**Club**	**League**	**GP**	**G**	**A**	**Pts**	**PIM**	**GP**	**G**	**A**	**Pts**	**PIM**
2007-08	Sibir Novosibirsk 2	Russia-3	17	6	4	10	2	....	....	....	....	....
2008-09	Sibir Novosibirsk 2	Russia-3	STATISTICS NOT AVAILABLE									
	Sibir Novosibirsk	Rus-KHL	38	7	3	10	2	....	....	....	....	....
2009-10	Novosibirsk Jr.	Russia-Jr.	1	1	0	1	0	....	....	....	....	....
	Sibir Novosibirsk	Rus-KHL	42	13	11	24	18	....	....	....	....	....
2010-11	Sibir Novosibirsk	Rus-KHL	42	9	10	19	8	3	0	0	0	0
	Novosibirsk Jr.	Russia-Jr.	3	2	2	4	2	....	....	....	....	....

TARDIF, Jamie (tahr-DIHF, JAY-mee) **BOS**

Right wing. Shoots right. 6', 205 lbs. Born, Welland, Ont., January 23, 1985.
(Calgary's 4th choice, 112th overall, in 2003 Entry Draft).

			Regular Season					Playoffs				
Season	**Club**	**League**	**GP**	**G**	**A**	**Pts**	**PIM**	**GP**	**G**	**A**	**Pts**	**PIM**
2001-02	Peterborough	OHL	64	22	22	44	30	6	0	1	1	2
2002-03	Peterborough	OHL	68	31	29	60	32	7	3	4	7	0
2003-04	Peterborough	OHL	64	25	28	53	56	....	....	....	....	....
2004-05	Peterborough	OHL	66	37	27	64	84	14	8	3	11	14
2005-06	Peterborough	OHL	62	40	29	69	108	19	6	6	12	18
2006-07	Toledo Storm	ECHL	34	10	20	30	37	....	....	....	....	....
	Manitoba Moose	AHL	1	0	0	0	0	....	....	....	....	....
	Iowa Stars	AHL	2	0	0	0	0	....	....	....	....	....
	Grand Rapids	AHL	27	9	6	15	18	2	0	0	0	0
2007-08	Grand Rapids	AHL	80	17	17	34	90	....	....	....	....	....
2008-09	Grand Rapids	AHL	55	9	9	18	43	10	2	0	2	8
2009-10	Grand Rapids	AHL	77	16	17	33	90	....	....	....	....	....
2010-11	Grand Rapids	AHL	77	27	27	54	81	....	....	....	....	....

Signed as a free agent by **Toledo** (ECHL), October 5, 2006. Signed as a free agent by **Manitoba** (AHL), December 2, 2006. Signed as a free agent by **Iowa** (AHL), December 28, 2006. • Assigned to **Grand Rapids** (AHL), January 26, 2007. Signed as a free agent by **Detroit** July 26, 2007. Signed as a free agent by **Boston**, July 5, 2011.

TARDY, Maxwell (TAHR-dee, MAX-wehl) **ST.L.**

Center. Shoots right. 6', 181 lbs. Born, Duluth, MN, October 27, 1990.
(St. Louis' 6th choice, 202nd overall, in 2009 Entry Draft).

			Regular Season					Playoffs				
Season	**Club**	**League**	**GP**	**G**	**A**	**Pts**	**PIM**	**GP**	**G**	**A**	**Pts**	**PIM**
2007-08	Duluth East	High-MN	9	1	3	4	8	....	....	....	....	....
2008-09	Duluth East	High-MN	30	35	25	60	24	....	....	....	....	....
	Team North	UMHSEL	24	19	20	39						
2009-10	Tri-City Storm	USHL	52	12	24	36	34	3	0	1	1	4
2010-11	U. Minn-Duluth	WCHA	26	1	2	3	14	....	....	....	....	....

TATARINOV, Alexander (ta-TAHR-ee-nahf, al-ehx-AN-duhr) PHX

Right wing. Shoots left. 5'11", 180 lbs. Born, Sverdlovsk, USSR, April 14, 1982.
(Phoenix's 2nd choice, 53rd overall, in 2000 Entry Draft).

			Regular Season					Playoffs				
Season	Club	League	GP	G	A	Pts	PIM	GP	G	A	Pts	PIM
1998-99	Yaroslavl 2	Russia-3	32	11	10	21	89					
	Spartak Moscow	Russia	3	0	0	0	0					
99-2000	Yaroslavl 2	Russia-3	35	12	12	24	36					
2000-01	Kristall Saratov	Russia-2	24	3	3	6	8					
	Yaroslavl	Russia	2	0	1	1	0	1	0	0	0	0
2001-02	Yaroslavl	Russia	21	4	3	7	8					
	Amur Khabarovsk	Russia	11	0	0	0	0					
	Yaroslavl 2	Russia-3	5	5	2	7	12					
2002-03	Perm	Russia	31	6	5	11	16					
2003-04	Spartak Moscow	Russia-2	43	8	11	19	14	9	2	5	7	2
2004-05	Mechel 2	Russia-3	1	0	0	0	0					
	Mechel	Russia-2	44	7	17	24	32	7	0	1	1	0
2005-06	Khimik	Russia-2	19	1	3	4	10					
	Novokuznetsk	Russia	16	1	2	3	12	3	1	0	1	2
2006-07	Novokuznetsk	Russia	49	6	7	13	38	3	0	0	0	2
2007-08	Novokuznetsk	Russia	30	1	1	2	22					
	Novokuznetsk 2	Russia-3	2	0	1	1	0					
2008-09	Novokuznetsk	Rus-KHL	48	5	5	10	42					
2009-10	Novokuznetsk	Rus-KHL	54	6	6	12	16					
2010-11	Avtomobilist	Rus-KHL	38	3	5	8	37					

TELEGIN, Ivan (tuh-LEH-gihn, ih-VUHN) WPG

Left wing. Shoots left. 6'4", 199 lbs. Born, Novokuznetsk, Russia, February 28, 1992.
(Atlanta's 3rd choice, 101st overall, in 2010 Entry Draft).

			Regular Season					Playoffs				
Season	Club	League	GP	G	A	Pts	PIM	GP	G	A	Pts	PIM
2008-09	Novokuznetsk 2	Russia-3	STATISTICS NOT AVAILABLE									
2009-10	Saginaw Spirit	OHL	51	26	18	44	20	6	1	1	2	6
2010-11	Saginaw Spirit	OHL	59	20	41	61	35	12	2	8	10	8

TERRY, Chris (TAIR-ee, KRIHS) CAR

Left wing. Shoots left. 5'10", 190 lbs. Born, Brampton, Ont., April 7, 1989.
(Carolina's 4th choice, 132nd overall, in 2007 Entry Draft).

			Regular Season					Playoffs				
Season	Club	League	GP	G	A	Pts	PIM	GP	G	A	Pts	PIM
2003-04	Markham	GTHL	66	39	50	89	....					
2004-05	Markham	GTHL	60	42	53	95	113	9	0	9	9	14
2005-06	Plymouth Whalers	OHL	64	9	19	28	72	11	3	2	5	4
2006-07	Plymouth Whalers	OHL	68	22	44	66	98	20	8	10	18	21
2007-08	Plymouth Whalers	OHL	68	44	57	101	107	4	4	3	7	6
	Albany River Rats	AHL	1	0	0	0	0					
2008-09	Plymouth Whalers	OHL	53	39	55	94	75	11	7	9	16	18
2009-10	Albany River Rats	AHL	80	17	30	47	47	8	2	4	6	0
2010-11	Charlotte	AHL	80	34	30	64	52	16	6	3	9	14

TESINK, Ryan (TEH-sihnk, RIGH-uhn) ST.L.

Center. Shoots left. 6', 153 lbs. Born, Saint John, N.B., May 21, 1993.
(St. Louis' 7th choice, 162nd overall, in 2011 Entry Draft).

			Regular Season					Playoffs				
Season	Club	League	GP	G	A	Pts	PIM	GP	G	A	Pts	PIM
2008-09	Holderness School	High-NH	28	4	13	17	....					
2009-10	Woodstock	MJrHL	44	10	19	29	96	14	4	6	10	12
2010-11	Saint John	QMJHL	59	8	27	35	38	19	3	2	5	10

TESTWUIDE, Mike (TEHST-wud, MIGHK) PHI

Right wing. Shoots right. 6'3", 210 lbs. Born, Vail, CO, February 5, 1987.

			Regular Season					Playoffs				
Season	Club	League	GP	G	A	Pts	PIM	GP	G	A	Pts	PIM
2004-05	Waterloo	USHL	46	2	8	10	43	4	0	1	1	4
2005-06	Waterloo	USHL	54	18	13	31	88					
2006-07	Colorado College	WCHA	29	8	2	10	25					
2007-08	Colorado College	WCHA	33	11	10	21	31					
2008-09	Colorado College	WCHA	36	4	5	9	20					
2009-10	Colorado College	WCHA	36	21	10	31	26					
2010-11	Adirondack	AHL	76	18	21	39	62					

Signed as a free agent by **Philadelphia**, March 19, 2010.

TEUBERT, Colten (TEW-buhrt, KOHL-tuhn) EDM

Defense. Shoots right. 6'4", 195 lbs. Born, White Rock, B.C., March 8, 1990.
(Los Angeles' 2nd choice, 13th overall, in 2008 Entry Draft).

			Regular Season					Playoffs				
Season	Club	League	GP	G	A	Pts	PIM	GP	G	A	Pts	PIM
2005-06	South West Hawks	Minor-BC	29	8	12	20	122					
	Regina Pats	WHL	14	0	2	2	16	6	0	1	1	4
2006-07	Regina Pats	WHL	63	3	8	11	91	10	0	1	1	13
2007-08	Regina Pats	WHL	66	7	16	23	135	6	1	4	5	6
2008-09	Regina Pats	WHL	60	12	25	37	136					
	Ontario Reign	ECHL	8	0	1	1	10	6	0	1	1	19
2009-10	Regina Pats	WHL	60	10	30	40	115					
	Ontario Reign	ECHL	10	1	2	3	10					
2010-11	Manchester	AHL	39	2	8	10	57					
	Oklahoma City	AHL	20	2	5	7	26	2	0	0	0	0

Traded to **Edmonton** by **Los Angeles** with Los Angeles' 1st round choice (Oscar Klefborn) in 2011 Entry Draft and future considerations for Dustin Penner, February 28, 2011.

THANG, Ryan (THAYNG, RIGH-uhn) NSH

Left wing. Shoots right. 6', 194 lbs. Born, Chicago, IL, May 11, 1987.
(Nashville's 4th choice, 81st overall, in 2007 Entry Draft).

			Regular Season					Playoffs				
Season	Club	League	GP	G	A	Pts	PIM	GP	G	A	Pts	PIM
2004-05	Sioux Falls	USHL	58	9	22	31	45					
2005-06	Sioux Falls	USHL	32	8	14	22	52					
	Omaha Lancers	USHL	25	15	15	30	26	5	2	1	3	2
2006-07	U. of Notre Dame	CCHA	42	20	21	41	22					
2007-08	U. of Notre Dame	CCHA	47	18	14	32	48					
2008-09	U. of Notre Dame	CCHA	33	10	9	19	36					
2009-10	U. of Notre Dame	CCHA	37	9	14	23	55					
	Milwaukee	AHL	12	3	3	6	4	7	1	3	4	2
2010-11	Milwaukee	AHL	78	14	27	41	32	13	5	8	13	10

CCHA All-Rookie Team (2007)

THEORET, Mitchell (THAIR-ay, MIH-chuhl) NYI

Center. Shoots left. 6'1", 210 lbs. Born, Montreal, Que., June 8, 1993.
(NY Islanders' 8th choice, 185th overall, in 2011 Entry Draft).

			Regular Season					Playoffs				
Season	Club	League	GP	G	A	Pts	PIM	GP	G	A	Pts	PIM
2008-09	Kit. Jr. Rangers	Minor-ON	49	20	22	42	30					
2009-10	Niagara Ice Dogs	OHL	53	2	6	8	41	5	0	1	1	9
2010-11	Niagara Ice Dogs	OHL	66	9	11	20	52	14	2	1	3	2

THERIAU, Alex (TAIR-ee-oh, Al-ehx) DAL

Defense. Shoots left. 6'2", 193 lbs. Born, Duncan, B.C., February 14, 1992.
(Dallas' 4th choice, 109th overall, in 2010 Entry Draft).

			Regular Season					Playoffs				
Season	Club	League	GP	G	A	Pts	PIM	GP	G	A	Pts	PIM
2007-08	Valley West Hawks	BCMML	37	7	22	29	77					
	Lethbridge	WHL	4	0	0	0	2					
2008-09	Lethbridge	WHL	29	0	4	4	17					
	Everett Silvertips	WHL	26	1	0	1	11	1	0	0	0	0
2009-10	Everett Silvertips	WHL	70	4	20	24	68	7	0	2	2	4
2010-11	Everett Silvertips	WHL	37	0	7	7	27					
	Medicine Hat	WHL	15	1	8	9	4	14	1	5	6	10

THOMAS, Christian (TAW-mas, KRIHS-ch'yehn) NYR

Right wing. Shoots right. 5'9", 170 lbs. Born, Toronto, Ont., May 26, 1992.
(NY Rangers' 2nd choice, 40th overall, in 2010 Entry Draft).

			Regular Season					Playoffs				
Season	Club	League	GP	G	A	Pts	PIM	GP	G	A	Pts	PIM
2007-08	Toronto Marlboros	GTHL	52	32	34	66	36					
2008-09	London Knights	OHL	32	4	7	11	4					
	Oshawa Generals	OHL	27	4	10	14	10					
2009-10	Oshawa Generals	OHL	64	41	25	66	27					
2010-11	Oshawa Generals	OHL	66	54	45	99	38	10	9	10	19	4

THOMPSON, Paul (TAWM-suhn, PAWL) PIT

Right wing. Shoots right. 6', 210 lbs. Born, Melrose, MA, November 30, 1988.

			Regular Season					Playoffs				
Season	Club	League	GP	G	A	Pts	PIM	GP	G	A	Pts	PIM
2005-06	N.H. Jr. Monarchs	EJHL	38	13	17	30	20					
2006-07	N.H. Jr. Monarchs	EJHL	44	45	38	83	56					
2007-08	New Hampshire	H-East	35	6	6	12	22					
2008-09	New Hampshire	H-East	27	4	5	9	22					
2009-10	New Hampshire	H-East	39	19	20	39	24					
2010-11	New Hampshire	H-East	39	28	24	*52	30					
	Wilkes-Barre	AHL	6	1	2	3	2	4	0	1	1	2

Hockey East First All-Star Team (2011) • NCAA East First All-American Team (2011) • Hockey East Player of the Year (2011)

Signed as a free agent by **Pittsburgh**, March 28, 2011.

TINORDI, Jarred (tih-NOHR-dee, JAIR-uhd) MTL

Defense. Shoots left. 6'7", 212 lbs. Born, Burnsville, MN, February 20, 1992.
(Montreal's 1st choice, 22nd overall, in 2010 Entry Draft).

			Regular Season					Playoffs				
Season	Club	League	GP	G	A	Pts	PIM	GP	G	A	Pts	PIM
2008-09	USNTDP	NAHL	42	2	13	15	53	9	1	0	1	6
	USNTDP	U-17	16	3	1	4	12					
	USNTDP	U-18	1	0	1	1	0					
2009-10	USNTDP	USHL	26	4	5	9	68					
	USNTDP	U-18	39	2	6	8	37					
2010-11	London Knights	OHL	63	1	13	14	140	6	0	0	0	17

TOCHKIN, Kellan (TAWCH-kihn, KEHL-uhn) VAN

Right wing. Shoots right. 5'9", 167 lbs. Born, Abbotsford, B.C., February 15, 1991.

			Regular Season					Playoffs				
Season	Club	League	GP	G	A	Pts	PIM	GP	G	A	Pts	PIM
2006-07	Fraser Valley	BCMML	37	34	34	68	48					
	Everett Silvertips	WHL	3	0	0	0	2					
2007-08	Ridge Meadow	PIJHL	32	24	35	59	56	10	3	8	11	2
	Langley Chiefs	BCHL	1	0	1	1	0					
2008-09	Everett Silvertips	WHL	72	20	54	74	37	2	1	0	1	2
2009-10	Everett Silvertips	WHL	72	28	40	68	64	7	1	1	2	11
2010-11	Everett Silvertips	WHL	38	17	19	36	30					
	Medicine Hat	WHL	32	12	16	28	38	15	5	7	12	20

Signed as a free agent by **Vancouver**, July 27, 2009.

TOFFOLI, Tyler (TAW-foh-lee, TIGH-luhr) L.A.

Center. Shoots right. 6'1", 181 lbs. Born, Scarborough, Ont., April 24, 1992.
(Los Angeles' 2nd choice, 47th overall, in 2010 Entry Draft).

			Regular Season					Playoffs				
Season	Club	League	GP	G	A	Pts	PIM	GP	G	A	Pts	PIM
2007-08	Tor. Jr. Canadiens	GTHL	83	68	106	174	72					
2008-09	Ottawa 67's	OHL	54	17	29	46	16	7	2	6	8	4
2009-10	Ottawa 67's	OHL	65	37	42	79	54	12	7	6	13	10
2010-11	Ottawa 67's	OHL	68	*57	51	*108	33	4	3	5	8	4
	Manchester	AHL	1	1	0	1	0	5	1	0	1	6

OHL First All-Star Team (2011)

TOMMERNES, Henrik (TOHM-uhr-nehs, HEHN-rihk) VAN

Defense. Shoots left. 6'1", 176 lbs. Born, Karlstad, Sweden, August 28, 1990.
(Vancouver's 8th choice, 210th overall, in 2011 Entry Draft).

			Regular Season					Playoffs				
Season	Club	League	GP	G	A	Pts	PIM	GP	G	A	Pts	PIM
2006-07	Farjestad U18	Swe-U18	14	3	6	9	32	8	3	4	7	4
2007-08	Farjestad U18	Swe-U18	22	4	16	20	10	8	0	3	3	10
2008-09	Frolunda Jr.	Swe-Jr.	40	10	22	32	52	5	2	6	8	8
	Frolunda	Sweden	11	0	0	0	0					
2009-10	Frolunda Jr.	Swe-Jr.	4	1	1	2	4					
	Boras HC	Sweden-2	23	5	9	14	43					
	Frolunda	Sweden	27	0	3	3	10	7	0	1	1	2
2010-11	Frolunda	Sweden	47	3	17	20	24					

TOUSIGNANT, Mathieu (TOO-saynt, ma-t'yoo) DAL

Center. Shoots left. 6', 182 lbs. Born, St-Etienne De Lauzon, Que., November 21, 1989.

			Regular Season					Playoffs				
Season	Club	League	GP	G	A	Pts	PIM	GP	G	A	Pts	PIM
2004-05	Magog	QAAA	8	2	1	3	0	....	....	....	....	....
2005-06	Magog	QAAA	43	22	36	58	50	13	6	9	15	26
	Baie-Comeau	QMJHL	1	0	1	1	2	....	....	....	....	....
2006-07	Baie-Comeau	QMJHL	70	8	25	33	93	9	2	2	4	9
2007-08	Baie-Comeau	QMJHL	36	14	20	34	68	....	....	....	....	....
	P.E.I. Rocket	QMJHL	27	8	14	22	61	4	2	4	6	14
2008-09	P.E.I. Rocket	QMJHL	35	14	24	38	72	....	....	....	....	....
	Chicoutimi	QMJHL	33	15	24	39	73	4	1	1	2	11
2009-10	Texas Stars	AHL	45	4	3	7	62	....	....	....	....	....
	Idaho Steelheads	ECHL	20	6	11	17	53	13	1	2	3	27
2010-11	Texas Stars	AHL	78	10	13	23	120	5	1	0	1	0

Signed as a free agent by **Dallas**, March 24, 2010.

TREMBLAY, Hunter (TRAHM-blay, HUN-tuhr) EDM

Left wing. Shoots left. 5'11", 200 lbs. Born, Timmins, Ont., January 15, 1986.

			Regular Season					Playoffs				
Season	Club	League	GP	G	A	Pts	PIM	GP	G	A	Pts	PIM
2002-03	Barrie Colts	OHL	56	6	13	19	22	6	1	0	1	2
2003-04	Barrie Colts	OHL	67	13	14	27	34	11	1	3	4	2
2004-05	Barrie Colts	OHL	62	30	32	62	23	6	2	4	6	4
2005-06	Barrie Colts	OHL	68	31	46	77	72	14	4	8	12	18
2006-07	Barrie Colts	OHL	64	35	54	89	54	8	5	3	8	6
2007-08	New Brunswick	AUAA	26	16	34	50	14	....	....	....	....	....
2008-09	New Brunswick	AUAA	28	14	36	50	26	....	....	....	....	....
2009-10	New Brunswick	AUAA	27	25	32	57	12	....	....	....	....	....
2010-11	New Brunswick	AUAA	27	22	22	44	38	....	....	....	....	....
	Oklahoma City	AHL	3	0	0	0	0	5	1	0	1	2

Signed as a free agent by **Edmonton**, March 31, 2011.

TREMBLAY, Nick (TRAWM-blay, NIHK-oh-las) BOS

Center. Shoots left. 5'11", 190 lbs. Born, Ottawa, Ont., April 5, 1988.
(Boston's 5th choice, 173rd overall, in 2008 Entry Draft).

			Regular Season					Playoffs				
Season	Club	League	GP	G	A	Pts	PIM	GP	G	A	Pts	PIM
2005-06	Champlain College	QJHL	48	13	22	35	36	9	1	1	2	8
2006-07	Champlain College	QJHL	53	26	26	52	58	7	1	2	3	2
2007-08	Smiths Falls Bears	CJHL	57	*51	59	*110	12	9	5	8	13	10
2008-09	Clarkson Knights	ECAC	36	4	7	11	22	....	....	....	....	....
2009-10	Clarkson Knights	ECAC	37	3	17	20	12	....	....	....	....	....
2010-11	Clarkson Knights	ECAC	33	9	12	21	18	....	....	....	....	....

TREVELYAN, T.J. (truh-VEHL-yuhn, TEE-JAY)

Left wing. Shoots left. 5'9", 185 lbs. Born, Mississauga, Ont., March 6, 1984.

			Regular Season					Playoffs				
Season	Club	League	GP	G	A	Pts	PIM	GP	G	A	Pts	PIM
2002-03	St. Lawrence	ECAC	34	10	12	22	38	....	....	....	....	....
2003-04	St. Lawrence	ECAC	38	*23	16	39	62	....	....	....	....	....
2004-05	St. Lawrence	ECAC	38	*25	20	45	61	....	....	....	....	....
2005-06	St. Lawrence	ECAC	40	20	28	*48	43	....	....	....	....	....
2006-07	Providence Bruins	AHL	60	28	24	52	41	13	3	6	9	12
	Long Beach	ECHL	15	9	8	17	16	....	....	....	....	....
2007-08	Providence Bruins	AHL	72	18	20	38	23	10	5	3	8	6
2008-09	Iowa Chops	AHL	76	23	24	47	18	....	....	....	....	....
2009-10	Worcester Sharks	AHL	63	28	16	44	16	8	4	2	6	2
2010-11	Worcester Sharks	AHL	73	19	21	40	31	....	....	....	....	....

ECAC First All-Star Team (2005, 2006) • ECAC Player of the Year (2006) • NCAA East First All-American Team (2006)

Signed as a free agent by **Boston**, August 17, 2006. Signed as a free agent by **San Jose**, September 9, 2009.

TRIVINO, Corey (trih-VEE-noh, KOH-ree) NYI

Center. Shoots left. 6'1", 170 lbs. Born, Etobicoke, Ont., January 12, 1990.
(NY Islanders' 2nd choice, 36th overall, in 2008 Entry Draft).

			Regular Season					Playoffs				
Season	Club	League	GP	G	A	Pts	PIM	GP	G	A	Pts	PIM
2005-06	Toronto Marlboros	GTHL	30	17	22	39	4	....	....	....	....	....
2006-07	Stouffville Spirit	OPJHL	49	24	34	58	24	9	1	6	7	16
2007-08	Stouffville Spirit	OPJHL	39	19	50	69	22	15	5	17	22	10
2008-09	Boston University	H-East	32	6	7	13	14	....	....	....	....	....
2009-10	Boston University	H-East	28	4	11	15	2	....	....	....	....	....
2010-11	Boston University	H-East	37	8	20	28	23	....	....	....	....	....

TROCHECK, Vincent (TROH-chehk, VOHN-sihnt) FLA

Center. Shoots right. 5'10", 178 lbs. Born, Pittsburgh, PA, July 11, 1993.
(Florida's 4th choice, 64th overall, in 2011 Entry Draft).

			Regular Season					Playoffs				
Season	Club	League	GP	G	A	Pts	PIM	GP	G	A	Pts	PIM
2008-09	Little Caesars	T1EHL	44	27	19	46	32	7	1	4	5	0
2009-10	Saginaw Spirit	OHL	68	15	28	43	56	6	2	2	4	2
2010-11	Saginaw Spirit	OHL	68	26	36	62	60	12	6	5	11	4

TROPP, Corey (TROHP, KOHR-ee) BUF

Right wing. Shoots right. 6', 195 lbs. Born, Grosse Pointe, MI, July 25, 1989.
(Buffalo's 3rd choice, 89th overall, in 2007 Entry Draft).

			Regular Season					Playoffs				
Season	Club	League	GP	G	A	Pts	PIM	GP	G	A	Pts	PIM
2005-06	Sioux Falls	USHL	46	7	8	15	21	14	2	3	5	8
2006-07	Sioux Falls	USHL	54	26	36	62	76	8	4	9	*13	0
2007-08	Michigan State	CCHA	42	6	11	17	16	....	....	....	....	....
2008-09	Michigan State	CCHA	21	3	8	11	45	....	....	....	....	....
2009-10	Michigan State	CCHA	37	20	22	42	50	....	....	....	....	....
2010-11	Portland Pirates	AHL	76	10	30	40	113	12	2	5	7	12

CCHA Second All-Star Team (2010)

TROTMAN, Zach (TRAWT-muhn, ZAK) BOS

Defense. Shoots right. 6'3", 195 lbs. Born, Novi, MI, August 26, 1990.
(Boston's 8th choice, 210th overall, in 2010 Entry Draft).

			Regular Season					Playoffs				
Season	Club	League	GP	G	A	Pts	PIM	GP	G	A	Pts	PIM
2008-09	Wichita Falls	NAHL	47	2	4	6	79	5	0	1	1	8
2009-10	Lake Superior	CCHA	36	2	6	8	18	....	....	....	....	....
2010-11	Lake Superior	CCHA	38	6	14	20	12	....	....	....	....	....

TRUKHNO, Viacheslav (trookh-NOH, V'YTACH-ih-slav)

Left wing. Shoots left. 6'1", 197 lbs. Born, Khimki, USSR, February 22, 1987.
(Edmonton's 6th choice, 120th overall, in 2005 Entry Draft).

			Regular Season					Playoffs				
Season	Club	League	GP	G	A	Pts	PIM	GP	G	A	Pts	PIM
2002-03	Rungstead IK	Den-2	1	2	3	5	0	....	....	....	....	....
	Rungstead	Denmark	27	7	4	11	8	12	0	1	1	8
2003-04	Rungstead	Denmark	35	12	11	23	18	7	0	0	0	8
2004-05	P.E.I. Rocket	QMJHL	64	25	34	59	57	....	....	....	....	....
2005-06	P.E.I. Rocket	QMJHL	60	28	68	96	81	3	2	2	4	0
2006-07	Gatineau	QMJHL	60	25	77	102	67	5	0	6	6	19
2007-08	Springfield Falcons	AHL	64	14	21	35	44	....	....	....	....	....
2008-09	Springfield Falcons	AHL	56	7	19	26	35	....	....	....	....	....
2009-10	Springfield Falcons	AHL	73	12	14	26	57	....	....	....	....	....
2010-11	Bakersfield	ECHL	51	12	40	52	73	4	0	2	2	2
	Peoria Rivermen	AHL	3	1	1	2	2	....	....	....	....	....

QMJHL All-Rookie Team (2005) • Canadian Major Junior All-Rookie Team (2005) • QMJHL First All-Star Team (2007)

Signed to a PTO (professional tryout) contract by **Peoria** (AHL), February 8, 2011.

TRUNEV, Maxim (troo-NAWF, max-EEM) MTL

Right wing. Shoots right. 5'11", 174 lbs. Born, Kirovo-Chepetsk, USSR, September 7, 1990.
(Montreal's 4th choice, 138th overall, in 2008 Entry Draft).

			Regular Season					Playoffs				
Season	Club	League	GP	G	A	Pts	PIM	GP	G	A	Pts	PIM
2005-06	Cherepovets 2	Russia-3		STATISTICS NOT AVAILABLE								
2006-07	Cherepovets 2	Russia-3		STATISTICS NOT AVAILABLE								
2007-08	Cherepovets 2	Russia-3		STATISTICS NOT AVAILABLE								
	Cherepovets	Russia	1	0	0	0	0	....	....	....	....	....
2008-09	Cherepovets	Rus-KHL	32	4	1	5	8	....	....	....	....	....
2009-10	Cherepovets	Rus-KHL	30	3	1	4	12	....	....	....	....	....
	Cherepovets Jr.	Russia-Jr.	14	10	14	24	58	3	1	0	1	2
2010-11	Cherepovets	Rus-KHL	39	1	6	7	20	6	0	0	0	2
	Cherepovets Jr.	Russia-Jr.	9	3	4	7	80	3	0	1	1	8

TURNBULL, Joshua (TUHRN-buhl, JAWSH-oo-uh) L.A.

Center. Shoots right. 5'10", 185 lbs. Born, Hayward, WI, July 12, 1988.
(Los Angeles' 8th choice, 137th overall, in 2007 Entry Draft).

			Regular Season					Playoffs				
Season	Club	League	GP	G	A	Pts	PIM	GP	G	A	Pts	PIM
2005-06	Duluth East	High-MN		STATISTICS NOT AVAILABLE								
2006-07	Waterloo	USHL	60	25	29	54	66	9	3	1	4	12
2007-08	U. of Wisconsin	WCHA	37	4	7	11	44	....	....	....	....	....
2008-09	U. of Wisconsin	WCHA	24	4	2	6	26	....	....	....	....	....
2009-10	U. of Wisconsin	WCHA	12	2	0	2	10	....	....	....	....	....
2010-11	U. of Wisconsin	WCHA	38	13	7	20	28	....	....	....	....	....

USHL All-Rookie Team (2007)

TURNBULL, Travis (TUHRN-buhl, TRA-vihs) BUF

Center. Shoots right. 6', 197 lbs. Born, Chesterfield, MO, July 7, 1986.

			Regular Season					Playoffs				
Season	Club	League	GP	G	A	Pts	PIM	GP	G	A	Pts	PIM
2003-04	Sioux City	USHL	56	7	12	19	73	7	0	0	0	9
2004-05	Sioux City	USHL	44	17	21	38	103	13	4	2	6	61
2005-06	U. of Michigan	CCHA	41	9	9	18	67	....	....	....	....	....
2006-07	U. of Michigan	CCHA	41	8	9	17	54	....	....	....	....	....
2007-08	U. of Michigan	CCHA	43	15	12	27	48	....	....	....	....	....
2008-09	U. of Michigan	CCHA	41	8	20	28	74	....	....	....	....	....
	Portland Pirates	AHL	3	0	0	0	5	5	0	0	0	4
2009-10	Portland Pirates	AHL	57	9	9	18	98	4	0	0	0	2
2010-11	Portland Pirates	AHL	20	5	4	9	28	10	1	1	2	2

Signed as a free agent by **Buffalo**, April 6, 2009.

TVRDON, Marek (T'VAIR-doin, MAIR-ehk) DET

Right wing. Shoots left. 6'2", 210 lbs. Born, Nitra, Slovakia, January 31, 1993.
(Detroit's 5th choice, 115th overall, in 2011 Entry Draft).

			Regular Season					Playoffs				
Season	Club	League	GP	G	A	Pts	PIM	GP	G	A	Pts	PIM
2007-08	HK Ardo Nitra U18	Svk-U18	20	5	4	9	10	....	....	....	....	....
2008-09	HK Nitra U18	Svk-U18	58	50	33	83	113	....	....	....	....	....
	HK Nitra Jr.	Slovak-Jr.	....	....	....	....	....	1	0	0	0	0
2009-10	HK Nitra	Slovakia	6	0	0	0	2	1	0	0	0	0
	HK Nitra Jr.	Slovak-Jr.	45	25	31	56	90	....	....	....	....	....
	HK Nitra	Slovakia	6	0	0	0	2	1	0	0	0	0
2010-11	Vancouver Giants	WHL	12	6	5	11	14	....	....	....	....	....

TYNAN, T.J. (TIGH-nuhn, TAW-muhs) CBJ

Center. Shoots right. 5'8", 165 lbs. Born, Orland Park, IL, February 25, 1992.
(Columbus' 2nd choice, 66th overall, in 2011 Entry Draft).

			Regular Season					Playoffs				
Season	Club	League	GP	G	A	Pts	PIM	GP	G	A	Pts	PIM
2009-10	Des Moines	USHL	60	17	*55	72	55	....	....	....	....	....
2010-11	U. of Notre Dame	CCHA	44	23	31	54	36	....	....	....	....	....

USHL All-Rookie Team (2010)

TYRVAINEN, Antti (TUHR-va-nihn, AHN-tee) EDM

Left wing. Shoots left. 5'11", 200 lbs. Born, Seinajoki, Finland, April 3, 1989.

			Regular Season					Playoffs				
Season	Club	League	GP	G	A	Pts	PIM	GP	G	A	Pts	PIM
2006-07	Pelicans Lahti Jr.	Fin-Jr.	19	1	4	5	51	....	....	....	....	....
2007-08	Pelicans Lahti Jr.	Fin-Jr.	41	5	13	18	56	....	....	....	....	....
2008-09	Pelicans Lahti Jr.	Fin-Jr.	27	9	9	18	104	....	....	....	....	....
	HeKi Heinola	Finland-2	3	0	0	0	25	....	....	....	....	....
	Pelicans Lahti	Finland	5	0	0	0	0	1	0	0	0	0
2009-10	Pelicans Lahti	Finland	32	8	3	11	85	....	....	....	....	....
2010-11	Pelicans Lahti	Finland	52	14	9	23	186	....	....	....	....	....
	Pelicans Lahti	Finland-Q	....	....	....	....	....	4	3	2	5	24

Signed as a free agent by **Edmonton**, June 15, 2011.

UHER, Dominik (OO-hair, DOHM-ih-NIHK) PIT

Center. Shoots left. 6', 195 lbs. Born, Frydek-Mistek, Czechoslovakia, December 31, 1992.
(Pittsburgh's 3rd choice, 144th overall, in 2011 Entry Draft).

			Regular Season					Playoffs				
Season	Club	League	GP	G	A	Pts	PIM	GP	G	A	Pts	PIM
2006-07	HC Trinec U17	CzR-U17	6	1	1	2	2	3	1	0	1	0
2007-08	HC Trinec U17	CzR-U17	44	5	11	16	44	5	1	0	1	4
2008-09	HC Trinec U17	CzR-U17	38	19	27	46	46	9	5	6	11	6
	HC Trinec Jr.	CzRep-Jr.	2	0	1	1	2	....	....	....	....	....
2009-10	Spokane Chiefs	WHL	53	4	12	16	45	6	0	0	0	2
2010-11	Spokane Chiefs	WHL	65	21	39	60	60	17	2	9	11	18

ULLSTROM, David (UHL-struhm, DAY-vihd) NYI

Center. Shoots left. 6'2", 194 lbs. Born, Jonkoping, Sweden, April 22, 1989.
(NY Islanders' 9th choice, 102nd overall, in 2008 Entry Draft).

			Regular Season					Playoffs				
Season	Club	League	GP	G	A	Pts	PIM	GP	G	A	Pts	PIM
2005-06	HV 71 U18	Swe-U18	13	5	8	13	14	5	4	1	5	14
	HV 71 Jr.	Swe-Jr.	1	0	0	0	0	....	....	....	....	....
2006-07	HV 71 U18	Swe-U18	1	0	0	0	2	5	2	6	8	10
	HV 71 Jr.	Swe-Jr.	39	16	14	30	30	4	0	2	2	0
2007-08	HV 71 Jr.	Swe-Jr.	40	27	27	54	86	3	2	2	4	0
	HV 71 Jonkoping	Sweden	7	0	0	0	0	....	....	....	....	....
2008-09	HV 71 Jr.	Swe-Jr.	2	0	0	0	0	....	....	....	....	....
	Boras HC	Sweden-2	15	9	7	16	22	....	....	....	....	....
	HV 71 Jonkoping	Sweden	19	1	3	4	6	14	1	0	1	4
2009-10	HV 71 Jonkoping	Sweden	47	5	11	16	27	16	2	0	2	0
	HV 71 Jr.	Swe-Jr.	1	1	0	1	2	....	....	....	....	....
2010-11	Bridgeport	AHL	67	17	24	41	36	....	....	....	....	....

UTKIN, Dmitri (OOT-kihn, dih-MEE-tree) BOS

Left wing. Shoots left. 6', 170 lbs. Born, Yaroslavl, USSR, June 10, 1984.
(Boston's 5th choice, 228th overall, in 2002 Entry Draft).

			Regular Season					Playoffs				
Season	Club	League	GP	G	A	Pts	PIM	GP	G	A	Pts	PIM
2000-01	Yaroslavl 2	Russia-3	49	12	1	13	10	....	....	....	....	....
2001-02	Yaroslavl 2	Russia-3	32	15	7	22	33	....	....	....	....	....
2002-03	Yaroslavl	Russia	4	0	1	1	0	....	....	....	....	....
2003-04	Spartak Moscow	Russia-2	57	10	10	20	8	13	3	3	6	2
2004-05	Keramin Minsk	BelOpen	8	2	0	2	31	....	....	....	....	....
	HK Brest	BelOpen	20	4	12	16	4	....	....	....	....	....
	HK Riga 2000	BelOpen	....	....	....	....	....	3	0	0	0	0
	HK Riga 2000	Latvia	....	....	....	....	....	6	3	2	5	0
2005-06	Spartak Moscow	Russia	33	3	1	4	4	2	0	0	0	0
	Spartak Moscow 2	Russia-3	10	5	2	7	8	....	....	....	....	....
2006-07	Chelyabinsk	Russia	50	6	8	14	20	....	....	....	....	....
2007-08	Chelyabinsk 2	Russia-3	16	4	3	7	2	....	....	....	....	....
	Chelyabinsk	Russia	5	1	0	1	2	....	....	....	....	....
	Avtomobilist	Russia-2	11	2	0	2	0	6	1	0	1	0
2008-09	Mechel	Russia-2	40	13	8	21	40	....	....	....	....	....
	Khanty-Mansiisk	Russia-2	8	4	3	7	0	16	2	7	9	4
2009-10	Khanty-Mansiisk	Russia-2	22	3	5	8	4	....	....	....	....	....
	Toros Neftekamsk	Russia-2	18	2	1	3	0	13	3	3	6	2
2010-11	Nizhny Tagil	Russia-2	54	10	18	28	12	4	0	2	2	0

VAIVE, Justin (VIGHV, JUHS-tihn) ANA

Left wing. Shoots left. 6'5", 226 lbs. Born, Buffalo, NY, July 8, 1989.
(Anaheim's 4th choice, 92nd overall, in 2007 Entry Draft).

			Regular Season					Playoffs				
Season	Club	League	GP	G	A	Pts	PIM	GP	G	A	Pts	PIM
2004-05	Toronto Marlboros	GTHL	72	38	64	102	....	....	....	....	....	....
2005-06	USNTDP	U-17	13	3	5	8	18	....	....	....	....	....
	USNTDP	NAHL	24	4	8	12	34	5	1	1	2	6
2006-07	USNTDP	U-18	43	7	8	15	49	....	....	....	....	....
	USNTDP	NAHL	15	4	1	5	22	....	....	....	....	....
2007-08	Miami U.	CCHA	41	3	7	10	65	....	....	....	....	....
2008-09	Miami U.	CCHA	37	6	6	12	44	....	....	....	....	....
2009-10	Miami U.	CCHA	43	5	3	8	51	....	....	....	....	....
2010-11	Miami U.	CCHA	39	9	7	16	48	....	....	....	....	....

VALENTENKO, Pavel (val-ehn-TEHN-koh, PAH-vehl) NYR

Defense. Shoots left. 6'2", 225 lbs. Born, Nizhnekamsk, USSR, October 20, 1987.
(Montreal's 5th choice, 139th overall, in 2006 Entry Draft).

			Regular Season					Playoffs				
Season	Club	League	GP	G	A	Pts	PIM	GP	G	A	Pts	PIM
2002-03	Lada Togliatti 2	Russia-3	6	0	0	0	4	....	....	....	....	....
2003-04	Nizhnekamsk 2	Russia-3	26	0	1	1	28	....	....	....	....	....
2004-05	Nizhnekamsk 2	Russia-3	STATISTICS NOT AVAILABLE									
2005-06	Nizhnekamsk 2	Russia-3	STATISTICS NOT AVAILABLE									
	Nizhnekamsk	Russia	2	0	0	0	2	....	....	....	....	....
2006-07	Nizhnekamsk	Russia	50	0	2	2	62	4	0	0	0	2
2007-08	Hamilton Bulldogs	AHL	57	1	15	16	58	....	....	....	....	....
2008-09	Hamilton Bulldogs	AHL	4	0	2	2	2	....	....	....	....	....
	Dynamo Moscow	Rus-KHL	8	0	1	1	8	1	0	0	0	2
2009-10	Dynamo Moscow	Rus-KHL	7	0	0	0	2	....	....	....	....	....
2010-11	Connecticut Whale	AHL	79	5	12	17	38	6	0	0	0	12

• Missed majority of 2008-09 for personal reasons. Signed as a free agent by **Dynamo Moscow** (Russia-KHL), October 31, 2008. Traded to **NY Rangers** by **Montreal** with Chris Higgins and Ryan McDonagh for Scott Gomez, Tom Pyatt and Michael Busto, June 30, 2009.

VANCE, Troy (VANS, TROI) DAL

Defense. Shoots right. 6'6", 200 lbs. Born, Goshen, NY, August 2, 1993.
(Dallas' 4th choice, 135th overall, in 2011 Entry Draft).

			Regular Season					Playoffs				
Season	Club	League	GP	G	A	Pts	PIM	GP	G	A	Pts	PIM
2010-11	Phi. Revolution	EmJHL	9	1	9	10	10	....	....	....	....	....
	Phi. Revolution	EJHL	18	1	2	3	33	....	....	....	....	....
	Victoriaville Tigres	QMJHL	23	1	3	4	21	9	1	3	4	4

VARONE, Phil (vah-ROHN, FIHL)

Center. Shoots left. 5'10", 180 lbs. Born, Vaughan, Ont., December 4, 1990.
(San Jose's 3rd choice, 147th overall, in 2009 Entry Draft).

			Regular Season					Playoffs				
Season	Club	League	GP	G	A	Pts	PIM	GP	G	A	Pts	PIM
2005-06	Vaughan M.M.	GTHL	49	34	29	63	....	....	....	....	....	....
	Vaughan Midgets	GTHL	4	6	1	7	2	....	....	....	....	....
2006-07	Kitchener	ON-Jr.B	20	10	11	21	21	....	....	....	....	....
	Kitchener Rangers	OHL	13	1	3	4	2	....	....	....	....	....
2007-08	Kitchener Rangers	OHL	35	5	20	25	12	....	....	....	....	....
	London Knights	OHL	31	10	26	36	14	5	1	1	2	7
2008-09	London Knights	OHL	58	19	33	52	32	14	10	9	19	19
2009-10	London Knights	OHL	31	9	22	31	17	....	....	....	....	....
2010-11	London Knights	OHL	4	1	0	1	2	....	....	....	....	....
	Erie Otters	OHL	55	33	48	81	30	7	3	10	13	4

VATANEN, Sami (VAH-ta-nehn, SA-mee) ANA

Defense. Shoots right. 5'9", 163 lbs. Born, Jyvaskyla, Finland, June 3, 1991.
(Anaheim's 5th choice, 106th overall, in 2009 Entry Draft).

			Regular Season					Playoffs				
Season	Club	League	GP	G	A	Pts	PIM	GP	G	A	Pts	PIM
2006-07	JyP Jyvaskyla U18	Fin-U18	....	....	....	....	....	7	1	0	1	2
2007-08	JyP Jyvaskyla U18	Fin-U18	35	9	29	38	30	1	0	0	0	0
	JyP Jyvaskyla Jr.	Fin-Jr.	....	....	....	....	....	2	0	0	0	0
2008-09	JyP Jyvaskyla U18	Fin-U18	2	0	0	0	0	1	1	1	2	14
	Suomi U20	Finland-2	2	0	0	0	2	....	....	....	....	....
	D Team Jyvaskyla	Finland-2	5	1	1	2	8	....	....	....	....	....
	JyP Jyvaskyla Jr.	Fin-Jr.	20	3	7	10	22	....	....	....	....	....
2009-10	Suomi U20	Finland-2	1	0	0	0	2	....	....	....	....	....
	JYP Jyvaskyla	Finland	55	7	23	30	44	14	3	4	7	6
2010-11	Suomi U20	Finland-2	1	0	0	0	0	....	....	....	....	....
	JYP Jyvaskyla	Finland	52	11	20	31	30	3	1	1	2	0

VEILLEUX, Keven (VAY-oo, KEH-vihn) PIT

Center. Shoots right. 6'5", 218 lbs. Born, Saint-René, Que., June 27, 1989.
(Pittsburgh's 2nd choice, 51st overall, in 2007 Entry Draft).

			Regular Season					Playoffs				
Season	Club	League	GP	G	A	Pts	PIM	GP	G	A	Pts	PIM
2004-05	Levis	QAAA	11	1	0	1	0	2	0	1	1	0
2005-06	Levis	QAAA	26	12	23	35	53	....	....	....	....	....
	Victoriaville Tigres	QMJHL	33	2	13	15	4	5	0	1	1	2
2006-07	Victoriaville Tigres	QMJHL	70	20	35	55	53	6	1	5	6	4
2007-08	Victoriaville Tigres	QMJHL	42	10	32	42	54	....	....	....	....	....
	Rimouski Oceanic	QMJHL	19	7	15	22	22	9	3	4	7	2
2008-09	Rimouski Oceanic	QMJHL	29	15	33	48	47	13	7	12	19	31
2009-10	Wilkes-Barre	AHL	9	2	1	3	12	....	....	....	....	....
2010-11	Wilkes-Barre	AHL	66	12	24	36	122	11	2	2	4	12

• Missed majority of 2009-10 due to shoulder injury.

VEILLEUX, Yannick (VAY-oo, YA-nihk) ST.L.

Left wing. Shoots left. 6'2", 190 lbs. Born, Saint-Hippolyte, Que., February 22, 1993.
(St. Louis' 5th choice, 102nd overall, in 2011 Entry Draft).

			Regular Season					Playoffs				
Season	Club	League	GP	G	A	Pts	PIM	GP	G	A	Pts	PIM
2008-09	Saint-Eustache	QAAA	43	21	13	34	44	5	1	4	5	23
2009-10	Shawinigan	QMJHL	55	3	6	9	17	6	0	0	0	6
2010-11	Shawinigan	QMJHL	68	19	29	48	40	12	2	5	7	14

VELISCHEK, Alex (VEHL-ih-shehk, Al-ehx) PIT

Defense. Shoots left. 6', 200 lbs. Born, Quebec City, Que., December 17, 1990.
(Pittsburgh's 5th choice, 123rd overall, in 2009 Entry Draft).

			Regular Season					Playoffs				
Season	Club	League	GP	G	A	Pts	PIM	GP	G	A	Pts	PIM
2005-06	Delbarton	High-NJ	26	8	14	22	18	....	....	....	....	....
2006-07	Delbarton	High-NJ	24	12	14	26	26	....	....	....	....	....
2007-08	Delbarton	High-NJ	27	9	14	23	36	....	....	....	....	....
2008-09	Delbarton	High-NJ	30	16	35	51	42	....	....	....	....	....
2009-10	Providence College	H-East	34	1	11	12	44	....	....	....	....	....
2010-11	Providence College	H-East	9	1	1	2	2	....	....	....	....	....
	Sioux City	USHL	33	2	8	10	42	3	1	0	1	2

VEY, Linden (VAY, LIHN-duhn) L.A.

Center. Shoots right. 6', 181 lbs. Born, Wakaw, Sask., July 17, 1991.
(Los Angeles' 5th choice, 96th overall, in 2009 Entry Draft).

			Regular Season					Playoffs				
Season	Club	League	GP	G	A	Pts	PIM	GP	G	A	Pts	PIM
2006-07	Beardy's	SMHL	44	28	44	72	26	....	....	....	....	....
	Medicine Hat	WHL	2	0	0	0	2	....	....	....	....	....
2007-08	Medicine Hat	WHL	48	8	9	17	21	5	0	1	1	2
2008-09	Medicine Hat	WHL	71	24	48	72	20	11	2	5	7	2
2009-10	Medicine Hat	WHL	72	24	51	75	34	12	2	6	8	8
2010-11	Medicine Hat	WHL	69	46	70	*116	36	15	12	13	25	8

WHL East First All-Star Team (2011)

VIEDENSKY, Marek (vee-ehd-EHN-skee, MAR-ehk) S.J.

Center. Shoots right. 6'3", 208 lbs. Born, Handlova, Czechoslovakia, August 18, 1990.
(San Jose's 4th choice, 189th overall, in 2009 Entry Draft).

			Regular Season					Playoffs				
Season	Club	League	GP	G	A	Pts	PIM	GP	G	A	Pts	PIM
2004-05	Prievidza U18	Svk-U18	10	2	1	3	2	....	....	....	....	....
2005-06	Prievidza U18	Svk-U18	31	18	18	36	18	....	....	....	....	....
2006-07	Dukla Trencin U18	Svk-U18	12	6	12	18	6	....	....	....	....	....
	Dukla Trencin Jr.	Slovak-Jr.	30	5	3	8	8	7	1	1	2	16
2007-08	Dukla Trencin U18	Svk-U18	2	0	1	1	0	....	....	....	....	....
	Dukla Trencin Jr.	Slovak-Jr.	33	11	15	26	24	7	1	1	2	6
2008-09	Prince George	WHL	59	16	24	40	34	4	2	0	2	2
2009-10	Prince George	WHL	31	4	21	25	37	....	....	....	....	....
	Saskatoon Blades	WHL	30	16	18	34	27	10	7	3	10	0
2010-11	Saskatoon Blades	WHL	63	36	52	88	52	10	1	5	6	4

VISHNYAKOV, Albert (vihsh-nyeh-KAWF, al-BAIRT) T.B.

Left wing. Shoots right. 6'1", 178 lbs. Born, Almyetevsk, USSR, December 30, 1983.
(Tampa Bay's 9th choice, 273rd overall, in 2003 Entry Draft).

			Regular Season					Playoffs				
Season	Club	League	GP	G	A	Pts	PIM	GP	G	A	Pts	PIM
99-2000	Almetjevsk 2	Russia-3	41	11	5	16	68	....	....	....	....	....
2000-01	Almetjevsk	Russia-2	29	0	0	0	2	....	....	....	....	....
2001-02	Ak Bars Kazan	Russia	9	0	1	1	2	....	....	....	....	....
	Nizhny Novgorod	Russia	6	1	0	1	0	....	....	....	....	....
	Nizh. Novgorod 2	Russia-3	4	2	2	4	10	....	....	....	....	....
2002-03	Ak Bars Kazan	Russia	47	7	6	13	47	5	1	0	1	0
2003-04	Nizhnekamsk	Russia	10	2	3	5	10	....	....	....	....	....
	Ak Bars Kazan 2	Russia-3	STATISTICS NOT AVAILABLE									
	Ak Bars Kazan	Russia	10	1	1	2	8	....	....	....	....	....
2004-05	Dynamo Moscow	Russia	28	1	2	3	10	....	....	....	....	....
2005-06	Dynamo Moscow	Russia	48	9	3	12	78	3	0	0	0	0
2006-07	Dynamo Moscow	Russia	33	9	6	15	36	1	0	0	0	0
2007-08	Spartak Moscow	Russia	8	2	0	2	14	....	....	....	....	....
	Novokuznetsk	Russia	19	1	7	8	12	....	....	....	....	....
2008-09	Novokuznetsk	Rus-KHL	50	6	9	15	28	....	....	....	....	....
2009-10	Novokuznetsk	Rus-KHL	52	11	9	20	42	....	....	....	....	....
2010-11	Novokuznetsk	Rus-KHL	6	0	1	1	2	....	....	....	....	....
	Nizhnekamsk	Rus-KHL	9	0	0	0	8	....	....	....	....	....
	Perm	Russia-2	10	1	3	4	26	....	....	....	....	....

VOGELHUBER, Trent (VOH-guhl-hew-buhr, TREHNT) CBJ

Right wing. Shoots right. 6'2", 185 lbs. Born, Cleveland, OH, July 13, 1988.
(Columbus' 7th choice, 211th overall, in 2007 Entry Draft).

			Regular Season					Playoffs				
Season	Club	League	GP	G	A	Pts	PIM	GP	G	A	Pts	PIM
2004-05	Ohio AAA	Ind.	67	32	30	62	77	....	....	....	....	....
2005-06	Ohio AAA	GLHL	44	27	52	79	28	....	....	....	....	....
2006-07	St. Louis Bandits	NAHL	31	10	16	26	24	....	....	....	....	....
2007-08	Des Moines	USHL	2	0	1	1	0	....	....	....	....	....
2008-09	Miami U.	CCHA	29	2	2	4	22	....	....	....	....	....
2009-10	Miami U.	CCHA	42	8	4	12	30	....	....	....	....	....
2010-11	Miami U.	CCHA	39	7	14	21	16	....	....	....	....	....

• Missed majority of 2007-08 due to knee injury.

VOROSHNIN, Pavel (vo-rohsh-NIHN, PAH-vehl) BUF

Defense. Shoots left. 6'2", 183 lbs. Born, Chelyabinsk, USSR, March 23, 1984.
(Buffalo's 7th choice, 172nd overall, in 2003 Entry Draft).

			Regular Season					Playoffs				
Season	Club	League	GP	G	A	Pts	PIM	GP	G	A	Pts	PIM
2001-02	Chelyabinsk	Russia-2	32	0	2	2	10	....	....	....	....	....
2002-03	Mississauga	OHL	68	9	27	36	81	1	0	0	0	2
2003-04	Mississauga	OHL	18	0	4	4	6	....	....	....	....	....
	Owen Sound	OHL	40	3	18	21	36	7	0	2	2	4
2004-05	Metallurg Serov	Russia-2	34	0	1	1	12	....	....	....	....	....
2005-06	Lada Togliatti	Russia	33	0	1	1	18	8	0	1	1	0
2006-07	Lada Togliatti	Russia	3	0	0	0	2	....	....	....	....	....
	Mytischi	Russia	9	0	1	1	0	....	....	....	....	....
2007-08	Mytischi	Russia	18	0	0	0	12	....	....	....	....	....
2008-09	Khimik	Rus-KHL	41	1	5	6	28	....	....	....	....	....
2009-10	Gazovik Tyumen	Russia-2	19	0	2	2	16	....	....	....	....	....
	Khanty-Mansiisk	Russia-2	2	0	0	0	4	....	....	....	....	....
	Mechel 2	Russia-3	2	0	3	3	0	....	....	....	....	....
	Mechel	Russia-2	4	0	0	0	0	8	1	0	1	6
2010-11	Krylja Sovetov	Russia-2	5	1	0	1	4	....	....	....	....	....

VOYNOV, Viatcheslav (VOY-nawf, v'ya-cheh-SLAV) L.A.

Defense. Shoots right. 5'11", 193 lbs. Born, Chelyabinsk, USSR, January 15, 1990.
(Los Angeles' 3rd choice, 32nd overall, in 2008 Entry Draft).

			Regular Season					Playoffs				
Season	Club	League	GP	G	A	Pts	PIM	GP	G	A	Pts	PIM
2005-06	Chelyabinsk 2	Russia-3	2	0	0	0	0	....	....	....	....	....
2006-07	Chelyabinsk	Russia	31	0	0	0	12	....	....	....	....	....
2007-08	Chelyabinsk 2	Russia-3	2	1	0	1	0	....	....	....	....	....
	Chelyabinsk	Russia	36	1	3	4	20	2	0	0	0	0
2008-09	Manchester	AHL	61	8	15	23	46	....	....	....	....	....
2009-10	Manchester	AHL	79	10	19	29	43	9	1	3	4	0
2010-11	Manchester	AHL	76	15	36	51	36	7	2	3	5	6

AHL Second All-Star Team (2011)

WAGNER, Chris (WAG-nuhr, KRIHS) ANA

Right wing. Shoots right. 6', 194 lbs. Born, Wellesley, MA, May 27, 1991.
(Anaheim's 4th choice, 122nd overall, in 2010 Entry Draft).

			Regular Season					Playoffs				
Season	Club	League	GP	G	A	Pts	PIM	GP	G	A	Pts	PIM
2008-09	South Shore	EJHL	38	20	14	34	72	2	2	0	2	0
2009-10	South Shore	EJHL	44	34	49	*83	70	4	3	6	9	8
2010-11	Colgate	ECAC	41	9	10	19	26	....	....	....	....	....

WAHL, Mitch (WAWL, MIHTCH) CGY

Center. Shoots right. 6', 175 lbs. Born, Long Beach, CA, January 22, 1990.
(Calgary's 2nd choice, 48th overall, in 2008 Entry Draft).

			Regular Season					Playoffs				
Season	Club	League	GP	G	A	Pts	PIM	GP	G	A	Pts	PIM
2005-06	L.A. Jr. Kings	Minor-CA	64	40	50	90	95	....	....	....	....	....
	Spokane Chiefs	WHL	2	0	0	0	0	....	....	....	....	....
2006-07	Spokane Chiefs	WHL	69	16	32	48	50	4	0	1	1	5
2007-08	Spokane Chiefs	WHL	67	20	53	73	63	21	6	8	14	20
2008-09	Spokane Chiefs	WHL	63	32	35	67	78	12	2	11	13	6
2009-10	Spokane Chiefs	WHL	72	30	66	96	96	7	4	5	9	8
	Abbotsford Heat	AHL	4	1	3	4	0	12	2	4	6	4
2010-11	Abbotsford Heat	AHL	17	1	4	5	8	....	....	....	....	....

Memorial Cup All-Star Team (2008) • WHL West First All-Star Team (2010)

WALKER, Luke (WAW-kuhr, LEWK) COL

Right wing. Shoots right. 6'1", 174 lbs. Born, New Haven, CT, February 19, 1990.
(Colorado's 7th choice, 139th overall, in 2010 Entry Draft).

			Regular Season					Playoffs				
Season	Club	League	GP	G	A	Pts	PIM	GP	G	A	Pts	PIM
2006-07	Okanagan Prep	Minor-BC	52	50	42	92	87	....	....	....	....	....
2007-08	Portland	WHL	70	9	12	21	84	....	....	....	....	....
2008-09	Portland	WHL	71	29	23	52	84	....	....	....	....	....
2009-10	Portland	WHL	61	27	30	57	103	13	6	4	10	17
2010-11	Lake Erie Monsters	AHL	75	10	8	18	40	5	1	1	2	0

WALSH, Dustin (WAWLSH, DUHS-tihn) MTL

Center. Shoots left. 6'3", 190 lbs. Born, Shannonville, Ont., March 20, 1991.
(Montreal's 6th choice, 169th overall, in 2009 Entry Draft).

			Regular Season					Playoffs				
Season	Club	League	GP	G	A	Pts	PIM	GP	G	A	Pts	PIM
2007-08	Trenton Hercs	OPJHL	22	11	7	18	10	....	....	....	....	....
2008-09	Trenton Hercs	ON-Jr.A	32	22	20	42	20	....	....	....	....	....
	Kingston	ON-Jr.A	12	10	11	21	8	25	13	11	24	10
2009-10	Dartmouth	ECAC	22	8	2	10	6	....	....	....	....	....
2010-11	Dartmouth	ECAC	34	10	10	20	8	....	....	....	....	....

WANNSTROM, Sebastian (VAN-strohm, seh-BAS-t'yehn) ST.L.

Right wing. Shoots right. 6'1", 180 lbs. Born, Gavle, Sweden, March 3, 1991.
(St. Louis' 3rd choice, 44th overall, in 2010 Entry Draft).

			Regular Season					Playoffs				
Season	Club	League	GP	G	A	Pts	PIM	GP	G	A	Pts	PIM
2006-07	Brynas U18	Swe-U18	11	0	4	4	4	3	0	0	0	4
2007-08	Brynas U18	Swe-U18	5	0	1	1	4	5	1	3	4	2
	Brynas IF Gavle Jr.	Swe-Jr.	15	0	4	4	8	....	....	....	....	....
2008-09	Brynas U18	Swe-U18	9	6	12	18	12	2	0	3	3	0
	Brynas IF Gavle Jr.	Swe-Jr.	32	11	9	20	4	6	0	0	0	0
2009-10	Brynas IF Gavle Jr.	Swe-Jr.	35	30	27	57	55	5	2	3	5	0
	Brynas IF Gavle	Sweden	18	0	0	0	2	1	0	0	0	0
2010-11	Brynas IF Gavle Jr.	Swe-Jr.	7	5	4	9	0	1	0	0	0	10
	Leksands IF	Sweden-2	2	0	0	0	0	....	....	....	....	....
	Brynas IF Gavle	Sweden	45	0	2	2	6	5	0	0	0	0

WARSOFSKY, David (wawr-SAWF-skee, DAY-vihd) BOS

Defense. Shoots left. 5'8", 160 lbs. Born, Marshfield, MA, May 30, 1990.
(St. Louis' 7th choice, 95th overall, in 2008 Entry Draft).

			Regular Season					Playoffs				
Season	Club	League	GP	G	A	Pts	PIM	GP	G	A	Pts	PIM
2005-06	Cushing	High-MA	....	8	26	34	....	....	....	....	....	....
2006-07	Cushing	High-MA	29	15	34	49	55	....	....	....	....	....
2007-08	USNTDP	U-18	41	5	29	34	26	....	....	....	....	....
	USNTDP	NAHL	15	4	2	6	8	....	....	....	....	....
2008-09	Boston University	H-East	45	3	20	23	28	....	....	....	....	....
2009-10	Boston University	H-East	34	12	11	23	48	....	....	....	....	....
2010-11	Boston University	H-East	34	7	15	22	46	....	....	....	....	....
	Providence Bruins	AHL	10	0	3	3	6	....	....	....	....	....

Hockey East Second All-Star Team (2011)

Traded to **Boston** by **St. Louis** for Vladimir Sobotka, June 26, 2010.

WATKINS, Matt (WAHT-kihns, MAT) PHX

Right wing. Shoots left. 5'10", 180 lbs. Born, Aylesbury, Sask., November 22, 1986.
(Dallas' 6th choice, 160th overall, in 2005 Entry Draft).

			Regular Season					Playoffs				
Season	Club	League	GP	G	A	Pts	PIM	GP	G	A	Pts	PIM
2003-04	Tisdale Trojans	SMHL	44	34	37	71	52	....	....	....	....	....
2004-05	Vernon Vipers	BCHL	60	36	38	74	53	....	....	....	....	....
2005-06	North Dakota	WCHA	46	5	4	9	45	....	....	....	....	....
2006-07	North Dakota	WCHA	38	6	11	17	31	....	....	....	....	....
2007-08	North Dakota	WCHA	43	8	10	18	34	....	....	....	....	....
2008-09	North Dakota	WCHA	41	7	7	14	40	....	....	....	....	....
2009-10	San Antonio	AHL	51	12	10	22	17	....	....	....	....	....
	Las Vegas	ECHL	14	4	7	11	12	....	....	....	....	....
2010-11	San Antonio	AHL	64	15	20	35	45	....	....	....	....	....

Signed as a free agent by **Phoenix**, September 30, 2009.

WATSON, Austin (WAWT-suhn, AW-stuhn) NSH

Left wing. Shoots right. 6'4", 193 lbs. Born, Ann Arbor, MI, January 13, 1992.
(Nashville's 1st choice, 18th overall, in 2010 Entry Draft).

			Regular Season					Playoffs				
Season	Club	League	GP	G	A	Pts	PIM	GP	G	A	Pts	PIM
2007-08	Det. Compuware	Minor-MI	....	45	104	149	....	....	....	....	....	....
2008-09	Windsor Spitfires	OHL	63	10	19	29	41	20	0	3	3	15
2009-10	Windsor Spitfires	OHL	42	11	23	34	14	....	....	....	....	....
	Peterborough	OHL	10	9	11	20	8	4	2	0	2	2
2010-11	Peterborough	OHL	68	34	34	68	54	....	....	....	....	....
	Milwaukee	AHL	5	0	0	0	0	3	0	0	0	0

WATSON, Ryan (WAWT-suhn , RIGH-uhn) FLA

Left wing. Shoots left. 6'1", 175 lbs. Born, Cambridge, Ont., March 1, 1988.
(Florida's 7th choice, 191st overall, in 2007 Entry Draft).

			Regular Season					Playoffs				
Season	Club	League	GP	G	A	Pts	PIM	GP	G	A	Pts	PIM
2005-06	Cambridge	ON-Jr.B	46	7	19	26	58	16	5	5	10	14
2006-07	Cambridge	ON-Jr.B	37	27	29	56	55	9	2	7	9	18
2007-08	Western Mich.	CCHA	34	4	4	8	16	....	....	....	....	....
2008-09	Western Mich.	CCHA	35	4	2	6	22	....	....	....	....	....
2009-10	Western Mich.	CCHA	20	2	0	2	10	....	....	....	....	....
2010-11	Western Mich.	CCHA	41	6	8	14	35	....	....	....	....	....

WATT, J.D. (WAHT , JAY-DEE)

Right wing. Shoots right. 6'1", 198 lbs. Born, Calgary, Alta., May 25, 1987.
(Calgary's 4th choice, 111th overall, in 2005 Entry Draft).

			Regular Season					Playoffs				
Season	Club	League	GP	G	A	Pts	PIM	GP	G	A	Pts	PIM
2003-04	Drumheller	AJHL	59	20	17	37	245	....	....	....	....	....
	Vancouver Giants	WHL	3	1	0	1	0	10	0	3	3	14
2004-05	Vancouver Giants	WHL	66	6	7	13	213	....	....	....	....	....
2005-06	Vancouver Giants	WHL	58	8	29	37	199	18	4	3	7	42
2006-07	Vancouver Giants	WHL	70	34	19	53	182	21	2	3	5	72
2007-08	Red Deer Rebels	WHL	29	7	8	15	87	....	....	....	....	....
	Regina Pats	WHL	29	6	16	22	82	6	2	6	8	19
2008-09	Quad City Flames	AHL	42	0	2	2	146	....	....	....	....	....
	Las Vegas	ECHL	18	5	9	14	51	16	3	4	7	70
2009-10	Abbotsford Heat	AHL	70	8	5	13	267	2	0	0	0	9
	Utah Grizzlies	ECHL	1	0	0	0	5	....	....	....	....	....
2010-11	Abbotsford Heat	AHL	27	1	3	4	73	....	....	....	....	....
	San Antonio	AHL	10	1	1	2	13	....	....	....	....	....

Signed to a PTO (professional tryout) contract by **San Antonio** (AHL), January 9, 2011.

WEAL, Jordan (WEEL, JOHR-dahn) **L.A.**

Center. Shoots right. 5'9", 165 lbs. Born, North Vancouver, B.C., April 15, 1992.
(Los Angeles' 3rd choice, 70th overall, in 2010 Entry Draft).

			Regular Season					Playoffs				
Season	Club	League	GP	G	A	Pts	PIM	GP	G	A	Pts	PIM
2007-08	Van. NW Giants	BCMML	40	*39	*61	*100	44	2	0	2	2	2
	Regina Pats	WHL	3	0	1	1	0	4	0	0	0	0
2008-09	Regina Pats	WHL	65	16	54	70	26	....	....	....	....	....
2009-10	Regina Pats	WHL	72	35	67	102	54	....	....	....	....	....
2010-11	Regina Pats	WHL	72	43	53	96	70	....	....	....	....	....
	Manchester	AHL	7	0	1	1	0	....	....	....	....	....

WEBER, Will (WEH-buhr, WIHL) **CBJ**

Defense. Shoots left. 6'4", 219 lbs. Born, Gaylord, MI, October 28, 1988.
(Columbus' 3rd choice, 53rd overall, in 2007 Entry Draft).

			Regular Season					Playoffs				
Season	Club	League	GP	G	A	Pts	PIM	GP	G	A	Pts	PIM
2003-04	Gaylord	High-MI	STATISTICS NOT AVAILABLE									
2004-05	Gaylord	High-MI	STATISTICS NOT AVAILABLE									
2005-06	Gaylord	High-MI	STATISTICS NOT AVAILABLE									
2006-07	Gaylord	High-MI	25	18	20	38	104	....	....	....	....	....
2007-08	Chicago Steel	USHL	46	8	10	18	137	....	....	....	....	....
2008-09	Miami U.	CCHA	38	3	2	5	75	....	....	....	....	....
2009-10	Miami U.	CCHA	43	1	9	10	62	....	....	....	....	....
2010-11	Miami U.	CCHA	33	1	10	11	57	....	....	....	....	....

WELINSKI, Andy (wehl-IHN-skee, AN-dee) **ANA**

Defense. Shoots right. 6'1", 188 lbs. Born, Duluth, MN, April 27, 1993.
(Anaheim's 5th choice, 83rd overall, in 2011 Entry Draft).

			Regular Season					Playoffs				
Season	Club	League	GP	G	A	Pts	PIM	GP	G	A	Pts	PIM
2009-10	Duluth East	High-MN	19	3	12	15	16	6	2	7	9	2
2010-11	Green Bay	USHL	51	6	8	14	14	11	2	0	2	4

• Signed Letter of Intent to attend **University of Minnesota-Duluth** (WCHA) in fall of 2011.

WELLER, Justin (WEHL-uhr, JUHS-tihn) **PHX**

Defense. Shoots right. 6'3", 208 lbs. Born, Daysland, Alta., July 26, 1991.
(Phoenix's 5th choice, 105th overall, in 2009 Entry Draft).

			Regular Season					Playoffs				
Season	Club	League	GP	G	A	Pts	PIM	GP	G	A	Pts	PIM
2006-07	Sherwood Park	AMHL	35	0	8	8	46	9	3	2	5	10
2007-08	Red Deer Rebels	WHL	49	0	3	3	40	....	....	....	....	....
2008-09	Red Deer Rebels	WHL	32	0	4	4	30	....	....	....	....	....
2009-10	Red Deer Rebels	WHL	71	2	7	9	88	4	0	1	1	16
2010-11	Red Deer Rebels	WHL	68	4	13	17	104	9	2	1	3	10

WELLER, Shawn (WEHL-uhr, SHAWN)

Left wing. Shoots left. 6'2", 205 lbs. Born, Glens Falls, NY, July 8, 1986.
(Ottawa's 3rd choice, 77th overall, in 2004 Entry Draft).

			Regular Season					Playoffs				
Season	Club	League	GP	G	A	Pts	PIM	GP	G	A	Pts	PIM
2001-02	South Glen Falls	High-NY	25	32	21	53	....	....	....	....	....	....
2002-03	Capital District	EJHL	STATISTICS NOT AVAILABLE									
2003-04	Capital District	EJHL	37	18	25	43	110	3	3	3	6	6
	Capital District	Exhib.	30	16	19	35	78	....	....	....	....	....
2004-05	Clarkson Knights	ECAC	33	3	11	14	72	....	....	....	....	....
2005-06	Clarkson Knights	ECAC	37	14	10	24	*103	....	....	....	....	....
2006-07	Clarkson Knights	ECAC	39	19	21	40	62	....	....	....	....	....
	Binghamton	AHL	5	0	0	0	4	....	....	....	....	....
2007-08	Binghamton	AHL	59	8	8	16	40	....	....	....	....	....
	Elmira Jackals	ECHL	10	4	5	9	11	....	....	....	....	....
2008-09	Binghamton	AHL	70	4	5	9	57	....	....	....	....	....
	Elmira Jackals	ECHL	4	1	1	2	2	....	....	....	....	....
2009-10	Abbotsford Heat	AHL	31	8	4	12	19	3	1	1	2	14
	Bakersfield	ECHL	42	18	28	46	55	....	....	....	....	....
2010-11	Manitoba Moose	AHL	67	12	11	23	50	10	0	0	0	4

Traded to **Anaheim** by **Ottawa** for Jason Bailey, September 4, 2009. Signed as a free agent by **Manitoba** (AHL), July 26, 2010.

WEREK, Ethan (WAIR-ehk, EE-thuhn) **PHX**

Center. Shoots left. 6'2", 200 lbs. Born, Markham, Ont., June 7, 1991.
(NY Rangers' 2nd choice, 47th overall, in 2009 Entry Draft).

			Regular Season					Playoffs				
Season	Club	League	GP	G	A	Pts	PIM	GP	G	A	Pts	PIM
2006-07	Toronto Marlboros	GTHL	55	59	69	128	72	....	....	....	....	....
2007-08	Stouffville Spirit	OPJHL	37	29	41	70	76	15	6	13	19	44
2008-09	Kingston	OHL	66	32	32	64	83	....	....	....	....	....
2009-10	Kingston	OHL	57	30	34	64	68	6	3	2	5	9
2010-11	Kingston	OHL	47	24	28	52	51	3	0	3	3	12

Traded to **Phoenix** by **NY Rangers** for Oscar Lindberg, May 8, 2011.

WESTERHOLM, Pathrik (VEHST-uhr-hohlm, PAT-rihk) **VAN**

Center. Shoots left. 6', 187 lbs. Born, Karlskrona, Sweden, January 6, 1992.
(Vancouver's 7th choice, 180th overall, in 2011 Entry Draft).

			Regular Season					Playoffs				
Season	Club	League	GP	G	A	Pts	PIM	GP	G	A	Pts	PIM
2007-08	Karlskrona HK U18	Swe-U18	16	36	11	47	10	....	....	....	....	....
	Karlskrona HK Jr.	Swe-Jr.	11	14	10	24	6	....	....	....	....	....
2008-09	Malmo U18	Swe-U18	23	20	24	44	10	4	1	1	2	10
	Malmo Jr.	Swe-Jr.	21	7	5	12	6	....	....	....	....	....
2009-10	Malmo U18	Swe-U18	3	5	5	10	0	....	....	....	....	....
	Malmo Jr.	Swe-Jr.	39	22	24	46	18	3	2	2	4	4
	Malmo	Sweden-2	1	0	0	0	0	....	....	....	....	....
2010-11	Malmo Jr.	Swe-Jr.	26	32	25	57	8	5	2	4	6	2
	Malmo	Sweden-2	34	8	13	21	8	....	....	....	....	....

WESTIN, John (WEHS-tihn, JAWN) **MTL**

Left wing. Shoots left. 6', 183 lbs. Born, Kramfors, Sweden, May 19, 1992.
(Montreal's 5th choice, 207th overall, in 2010 Entry Draft).

			Regular Season					Playoffs				
Season	Club	League	GP	G	A	Pts	PIM	GP	G	A	Pts	PIM
2007-08	Kramfors U18	Swe-U18	21	24	17	41	40	....	....	....	....	....
2008-09	MODO U18	Swe-U18	30	7	14	21	40	5	6	2	8	33
	MODO Jr.	Swe-Jr.	5	0	2	2	2	2	0	0	0	0
2009-10	MODO U18	Swe-U18	13	8	7	15	12	1	1	0	1	0
	MODO Jr.	Swe-Jr.	31	16	10	26	18	3	1	1	2	0
2010-11	MODO	Sweden	1	0	0	0	0	....	....	....	....	....
	MODO Jr.	Swe-Jr.	11	6	1	7	8	6	1	2	3	0

WEY, Patrick (WAY, PAT-rihk) **WSH**

Defense. Shoots right. 6'3", 203 lbs. Born, Pittsburgh, PA, March 21, 1991.
(Washington's 4th choice, 115th overall, in 2009 Entry Draft).

			Regular Season					Playoffs				
Season	Club	League	GP	G	A	Pts	PIM	GP	G	A	Pts	PIM
2006-07	Pittsburgh Hornets	MWEHL	18	0	5	5	14	....	....	....	....	....
2007-08	Waterloo	USHL	35	1	5	6	30	8	1	0	1	2
2008-09	Waterloo	USHL	58	7	27	34	75	3	0	0	0	0
2009-10	Boston College	H-East	27	0	5	5	24	....	....	....	....	....
2010-11	Boston College	H-East	37	1	7	8	45	....	....	....	....	....

WHITMORE, Derek (WHIHT-mohr, DAIR-ihk) **BUF**

Left wing. Shoots left. 5'11", 185 lbs. Born, Rochester, NY, December 17, 1984.

			Regular Season					Playoffs				
Season	Club	League	GP	G	A	Pts	PIM	GP	G	A	Pts	PIM
2002-03	Waterloo	USHL	58	15	13	28	51	6	1	0	1	0
2003-04	Waterloo	USHL	10	2	0	2	6	....	....	....	....	....
	Lincoln Stars	USHL	45	19	23	42	22	....	....	....	....	....
2004-05	Bowling Green	CCHA	33	11	6	17	14	....	....	....	....	....
2005-06	Bowling Green	CCHA	34	13	6	19	17	....	....	....	....	....
2006-07	Bowling Green	CCHA	38	19	10	29	20	....	....	....	....	....
2007-08	Bowling Green	CCHA	38	27	10	37	33	....	....	....	....	....
	Rochester	AHL	8	1	0	1	2	....	....	....	....	....
2008-09	Portland Pirates	AHL	77	11	11	22	17	5	1	1	2	2
2009-10	Portland Pirates	AHL	78	18	16	34	24	4	2	1	3	0
2010-11	Portland Pirates	AHL	80	27	20	47	20	12	4	4	8	4

CCHA Second All-Star Team (2008)

Signed as a free agent by **Buffalo**, March 26, 2008.

WIDEMAN, Chris (WIGHD-muhn, KRIHS) **OTT**

Defense. Shoots right. 5'10", 181 lbs. Born, St. Louis, MO, January 7, 1990.
(Ottawa's 4th choice, 100th overall, in 2009 Entry Draft).

			Regular Season					Playoffs				
Season	Club	League	GP	G	A	Pts	PIM	GP	G	A	Pts	PIM
2006-07	St.L. AAA Blues	Minor-MO	62	9	21	30	122	....	....	....	....	....
	St. Louis Bandits	NAHL	1	0	0	0	0	7	0	1	1	4
2007-08	Cedar Rapids	USHL	53	2	12	14	51	1	0	0	0	0
2008-09	Miami U.	CCHA	39	0	26	26	56	....	....	....	....	....
2009-10	Miami U.	CCHA	44	5	17	22	63	....	....	....	....	....
2010-11	Miami U.	CCHA	39	3	20	23	32	....	....	....	....	....

CCHA All-Rookie Team (2009)

WILLIAMS, Nigel (WIHL-yuhms, NIGH-juhl)

Defense. Shoots left. 6'5", 237 lbs. Born, Aurora, IL, April 18, 1988.
(Colorado's 2nd choice, 51st overall, in 2006 Entry Draft).

			Regular Season					Playoffs				
Season	Club	League	GP	G	A	Pts	PIM	GP	G	A	Pts	PIM
2004-05	Team Illinois	MWEHL	60	14	18	32	....	....	....	....	....	....
	USNTDP	U-17	3	2	1	3	4	....	....	....	....	....
2005-06	USNTDP	U-18	40	3	6	9	40	....	....	....	....	....
	USNTDP	NAHL	19	3	4	7	23	....	....	....	....	....
2006-07	U. of Wisconsin	WCHA	1	0	0	0	2	....	....	....	....	....
	Saginaw Spirit	OHL	46	17	19	36	92	6	2	1	3	10
2007-08	Saginaw Spirit	OHL	29	5	19	24	60	....	....	....	....	....
	Belleville Bulls	OHL	38	10	12	22	40	21	7	11	18	20
2008-09	Lake Erie Monsters	AHL	70	7	14	21	55	....	....	....	....	....
2009-10	Hartford Wolf Pack	AHL	56	4	16	20	50	....	....	....	....	....
2010-11	Connecticut Whale	AHL	12	0	1	1	2	....	....	....	....	....
	Syracuse Crunch	AHL	28	0	3	3	9	....	....	....	....	....

Traded to **NY Rangers** by **Colorado** for Brian Fahey, July 16, 2009. Traded to **Anaheim** by **NY Rangers** for Stu Bickel, November 23, 2010.

WILSON, Garrett (WIHL-suhn, GAIR-reht) **FLA**

Left wing. Shoots left. 6'3", 206 lbs. Born, Barrie, Ont., March 16, 1991.
(Florida's 4th choice, 107th overall, in 2009 Entry Draft).

			Regular Season					Playoffs				
Season	Club	League	GP	G	A	Pts	PIM	GP	G	A	Pts	PIM
2007-08	Tecumseh Chiefs	ON-Jr.B	46	11	26	37	40	14	13	8	21	22
	Windsor Spitfires	OHL	7	1	0	1	2	3	0	0	0	0
2008-09	Owen Sound	OHL	53	17	18	35	44	4	1	3	4	7
2009-10	Owen Sound	OHL	65	36	26	62	80	....	....	....	....	....
2010-11	Owen Sound	OHL	66	40	46	86	114	22	11	10	21	28

OHL First All-Star Team (2011)

WILSON, Jason (WIHL-suhn, JAY-suhn) **NYR**

Left wing. Shoots left. 6'3", 208 lbs. Born, Toronto, Ont., April 15, 1990.
(NY Rangers' 4th choice, 130th overall, in 2010 Entry Draft).

			Regular Season					Playoffs				
Season	Club	League	GP	G	A	Pts	PIM	GP	G	A	Pts	PIM
2007-08	Tor. Canadiens	OPJHL	37	7	10	17	69	11	1	1	2	4
2008-09	London Knights	OHL	52	12	5	17	104	14	0	2	2	8
2009-10	Owen Sound	OHL	46	17	18	35	101	....	....	....	....	....
2010-11	Niagara Ice Dogs	OHL	64	18	25	43	94	14	5	7	12	19

WILSON, Kelsey (WIHL-suhn, KEHL-see)

Left wing. Shoots left. 6'1", 214 lbs. Born, Sault Ste. Marie, Ont., January 22, 1986.

			Regular Season					Playoffs				
Season	Club	League	GP	G	A	Pts	PIM	GP	G	A	Pts	PIM
2003-04	Sarnia Sting	OHL	62	5	11	16	106	5	0	0	0	4
2004-05	Sarnia Sting	OHL	37	0	3	3	118	....	....	....	....	....
	Guelph Storm	OHL	23	7	4	11	78	4	0	0	0	9
2005-06	Guelph Storm	OHL	67	38	31	69	196	15	12	6	18	33
2006-07	Milwaukee	AHL	74	9	10	19	215	4	0	0	0	6
2007-08	Milwaukee	AHL	66	8	11	19	179	6	1	0	1	22
2008-09	Milwaukee	AHL	80	15	17	32	160	10	1	2	3	20
2009-10	Salzburg	Austria	64	19	24	43	265	....	....	....	....	....
2010-11	Milwaukee	AHL	74	10	12	22	145	9	1	7	8	11

Signed as a free agent by **Nashville**, October 6, 2006.

WILSON, Scott (WIHL-suhn, SKAWT) PIT

Center/Left wing. Shoots left. 5'11", 166 lbs. Born, Oakville, Ont., April 24, 1992.
(Pittsburgh's 5th choice, 209th overall, in 2011 Entry Draft).

			Regular Season					Playoffs				
Season	Club	League	GP	G	A	Pts	PIM	GP	G	A	Pts	PIM
2008-09	Oakville Rangers	Minor-ON	STATISTICS NOT AVAILABLE									
	Georgetown	ON-Jr.A	6	0	1	1	2	1	0	0	0	0
2009-10	Georgetown	ON-Jr.A	56	24	43	67	28	11	9	8	17	2
2010-11	Georgetown	ON-Jr.A	42	20	41	61	59	4	1	2	3	8

• Signed Letter of Intent to attend **University of Massachusetts-Lowell** (Hockey East) in fall of 2011.

WINKLER, Scott (WIHNK-luhr, SKAWT) DAL

Center. Shoots right. 6'2", 195 lbs. Born, Asker, Norway, February 22, 1990.
(Dallas' 2nd choice, 89th overall, in 2008 Entry Draft).

			Regular Season					Playoffs				
Season	Club	League	GP	G	A	Pts	PIM	GP	G	A	Pts	PIM
2005-06	Frisk Asker IF/NTG	Norway-Jr.	3	1	0	1	0	....	....	....	....	....
2006-07	Frisk Asker IF/NTG	Norway-Jr.	26	34	30	64	20	8	5	3	8	2
	Asker 2	Norway-2	25	6	6	12	2	....	....	....	....	....
2007-08	Russell Stover	Minor-MO	70	40	52	92	36	....	....	....	....	....
2008-09	Cedar Rapids	USHL	55	10	26	36	35	5	0	2	2	0
2009-10	Colorado College	WCHA	21	1	1	2	4	....	....	....	....	....
2010-11	Colorado College	WCHA	26	3	6	9	4	....	....	....	....	....

WITKOWSKI, Luke (wiht-KOW-skee, LEWK) T.B.

Defense. Shoots right. 6'2", 200 lbs. Born, Holland, MI, April 14, 1990.
(Tampa Bay's 6th choice, 160th overall, in 2008 Entry Draft).

			Regular Season					Playoffs				
Season	Club	League	GP	G	A	Pts	PIM	GP	G	A	Pts	PIM
2006-07	Team nXi Majors	Minor-MI	59	18	22	40	172	....	....	....	....	....
2007-08	Ohio	USHL	58	3	10	13	139	....	....	....	....	....
2008-09	Fargo Force	USHL	55	6	16	22	118	10	2	1	3	29
2009-10	Western Mich.	CCHA	32	2	4	6	67	....	....	....	....	....
2010-11	Western Mich.	CCHA	42	1	8	9	56	....	....	....	....	....

WITTCHOW, Eddie (WIHT-chow, EH-dee) FLA

Defense. Shoots left. 6'3", 189 lbs. Born, Burnsville, MN, October 31, 1992.
(Florida's 9th choice, 154th overall, in 2011 Entry Draft).

			Regular Season					Playoffs				
Season	Club	League	GP	G	A	Pts	PIM	GP	G	A	Pts	PIM
2009-10	Burnsville Blaze	High-MN	25	2	5	7	20	2	0	1	1	0
2010-11	Burnsville Blaze	High-MN	25	9	14	23	28	3	2	1	3	2

WOHLBERG, David (WOHL-buhrg, DAY-vihd) N.J.

Center. Shoots left. 6'1", 190 lbs. Born, Southfield, MI, July 18, 1990.
(New Jersey's 7th choice, 172nd overall, in 2008 Entry Draft).

			Regular Season					Playoffs				
Season	Club	League	GP	G	A	Pts	PIM	GP	G	A	Pts	PIM
2006-07	USNTDP	U-17	12	2	6	8	42	....	....	....	....	....
	USNTDP	NAHL	45	10	10	20	99	6	1	4	5	22
2007-08	USNTDP	U-18	37	9	7	16	48	....	....	....	....	....
	USNTDP	NAHL	22	10	5	15	27	....	....	....	....	....
2008-09	U. of Michigan	CCHA	40	15	15	30	51	....	....	....	....	....
2009-10	U. of Michigan	CCHA	44	10	17	27	76	....	....	....	....	....
2010-11	U. of Michigan	CCHA	37	15	6	21	42	....	....	....	....	....

CCHA All-Rookie Team (2009) • CCHA Rookie of the Year (2009)

WOTHERSPOON, Tyler (WUH-thuhr-spoon, TIGH-luhr) CGY

Defense. Shoots left. 6'1", 196 lbs. Born, Burnaby, B.C., March 12, 1993.
(Calgary's 3rd choice, 57th overall, in 2011 Entry Draft).

			Regular Season					Playoffs				
Season	Club	League	GP	G	A	Pts	PIM	GP	G	A	Pts	PIM
2008-09	Valley West Hawks	BCMML	37	11	13	24	85	....	....	....	....	....
	Portland	WHL	4	0	0	0	0	....	....	....	....	....
2009-10	Portland	WHL	43	1	4	5	21	2	0	0	0	0
2010-11	Portland	WHL	64	2	10	12	73	20	3	1	4	10

WRENN, William (REHN, WILL-yuhm) S.J.

Defense. Shoots right. 6'1", 205 lbs. Born, Anchorage, AK, March 16, 1991.
(San Jose's 1st choice, 43rd overall, in 2009 Entry Draft).

			Regular Season					Playoffs				
Season	Club	League	GP	G	A	Pts	PIM	GP	G	A	Pts	PIM
2007-08	USNTDP	NAHL	43	0	5	5	36	3	0	0	0	15
	USNTDP	U-17	17	0	2	2	14	....	....	....	....	....
2008-09	USNTDP	NAHL	13	1	4	5	37	....	....	....	....	....
	USNTDP	U-18	47	5	7	12	46	....	....	....	....	....
2009-10	U. of Denver	WCHA	23	0	7	7	36	....	....	....	....	....
2010-11	U. of Denver	WCHA	18	0	1	1	2	....	....	....	....	....
	Portland	WHL	29	2	11	13	17	21	1	4	5	10

YACHMENEV, Denis (YATCH-muh-nehv, DEH-nihs) FLA

Left wing. Shoots left. 6'1", 185 lbs. Born, Chelyabinsk, USSR, June 4, 1984.
(Florida's 9th choice, 200th overall, in 2002 Entry Draft).

			Regular Season					Playoffs				
Season	Club	League	GP	G	A	Pts	PIM	GP	G	A	Pts	PIM
2000-01	Chelyabinsk 2	Russia-3	36	40	27	67	....	....	....	....	....	....
2001-02	North Bay	OHL	65	17	12	29	32	5	2	0	2	0
2002-03	Saginaw Spirit	OHL	68	17	28	45	69	....	....	....	....	....
2003-04	Amur Khabarovsk	Russia	25	0	1	1	4	....	....	....	....	....
	Omsk 2	Russia-3	13	12	4	16	10	....	....	....	....	....
2004-05	Amur Khabarovsk	Russia-2	42	7	14	21	28	13	3	1	4	8
2005-06	Amur Khabarovsk	Russia-2	46	9	14	23	43	11	2	3	5	6
2006-07	Sibir Novosibirsk 2	Russia-3	6	0	3	3	8	....	....	....	....	....
	Sibir Novosibirsk	Russia	16	0	0	0	8	1	0	0	0	0
2007-08	Chelyabinsk	Russia	40	2	7	9	22	2	0	0	0	0
2008-09	Chelyabinsk	Rus-KHL	8	0	0	0	2	....	....	....	....	....
	Chelyabinsk 2	Russia-3	49	29	20	49	48	....	....	....	....	....
2009-10	Gazovik Tyumen	Russia-2	40	11	5	16	12	7	0	4	4	6
2010-11	Rubin Tyumen	Russia-2	55	13	12	25	30	15	3	3	6	8

YEMELIN, Alexei (yeh-MUH-lehn, al-EHX-ay) MTL

Defense. Shoots left. 6'2", 223 lbs. Born, Togliatti, USSR, April 25, 1986.
(Montreal's 2nd choice, 84th overall, in 2004 Entry Draft).

			Regular Season					Playoffs				
Season	Club	League	GP	G	A	Pts	PIM	GP	G	A	Pts	PIM
2002-03	Lada Togliatti 2	Russia-3	31	1	1	2	20	....	....	....	....	....
2003-04	Lada Togliatti 2	Russia-3	2	0	0	0	10	....	....	....	....	....
	CSK VVS Samara	Russia-2	52	2	4	6	180	1	0	0	0	18
2004-05	Lada Togliatti	Russia	12	0	1	1	24	2	0	0	0	2
2005-06	Lada Togliatti	Russia	44	6	6	12	131	6	0	1	1	*47
2006-07	Lada Togliatti	Russia	43	2	5	7	74	3	0	0	0	4
2007-08	Ak Bars Kazan	Russia	56	0	5	5	123	10	0	1	1	10
2008-09	Ak Bars Kazan	Rus-KHL	51	0	3	3	58	7	1	0	1	20
2009-10	Ak Bars Kazan	Rus-KHL	46	1	6	7	50	22	5	8	13	24
2010-11	Ak Bars Kazan	Rus-KHL	52	11	16	27	92	9	0	0	0	4

YOGAN, Andrew (YOH-guhn, An-DROO) NYR

Center/Left wing. Shoots left. 6'3", 200 lbs. Born, Coral Springs, FL, December 4, 1991.
(NY Rangers' 3rd choice, 100th overall, in 2010 Entry Draft).

			Regular Season					Playoffs				
Season	Club	League	GP	G	A	Pts	PIM	GP	G	A	Pts	PIM
2006-07	Fla. Jr. Panthers	Minor-FL	52	45	36	81	34	....	....	....	....	....
2007-08	Windsor Spitfires	OHL	50	5	2	7	32	5	0	0	0	6
2008-09	Windsor Spitfires	OHL	16	5	3	8	24	....	....	....	....	....
	Erie Otters	OHL	35	17	17	34	32	....	....	....	....	....
2009-10	Erie Otters	OHL	63	25	30	55	97	....	....	....	....	....
2010-11	Erie Otters	OHL	10	3	1	4	6	3	0	2	2	4
	Connecticut Whale	AHL	2	2	1	3	0	....	....	....	....	....

YOUNG, Gus (YUHNG, GUHS) COL

Defense. Shoots left. 6'2", 190 lbs. Born, Dedham, MA, July 10, 1991.
(Colorado's 7th choice, 184th overall, in 2009 Entry Draft).

			Regular Season					Playoffs				
Season	Club	League	GP	G	A	Pts	PIM	GP	G	A	Pts	PIM
2006-07	Nobles	High-MA	31	3	10	13	14	....	....	....	....	....
2007-08	Bos. Little Bruins	Minor-MA	11	0	6	6	....	....	....	....	....	....
	Nobles	High MA	29	6	9	15	....	....	....	....	....	....
2008-09	Cape Cod Whalers	Minor-MA	14	3	11	14	....	....	....	....	....	....
	Nobles	High-MA	29	5	29	34	16	....	....	....	....	....
2009-10	Cape Cod Whalers	Minor-MA	33	13	27	40	....	....	....	....	....	....
	Nobles	High-MA	29	12	26	38	10	....	....	....	....	....
2010-11	Yale	ECAC	5	0	1	1	4	....	....	....	....	....

YOUNG, Harry (YUHNG, HAIR-ee) N.J.

Defense. Shoots left. 6'4", 215 lbs. Born, Windsor, Ont., November 12, 1989.
(New Jersey's 8th choice, 202nd overall, in 2008 Entry Draft).

			Regular Season					Playoffs				
Season	Club	League	GP	G	A	Pts	PIM	GP	G	A	Pts	PIM
2005-06	Guelph Storm	OHL	44	0	4	4	20	....	....	....	....	....
2006-07	Guelph Storm	OHL	7	0	2	2	11	....	....	....	....	....
	Windsor Spitfires	OHL	47	0	3	3	72	....	....	....	....	....
2007-08	Windsor Spitfires	OHL	68	2	12	14	155	5	0	1	1	8
2008-09	Windsor Spitfires	OHL	46	8	4	12	138	20	1	4	5	*41
2009-10	Windsor Spitfires	OHL	65	9	11	20	153	19	0	1	1	24
2010-11	Albany Devils	AHL	52	1	4	5	142	....	....	....	....	....
	Trenton Devils	ECHL	3	0	1	1	12	....	....	....	....	....

YUEN, Zachary (YEW-ehn, ZA-kuh-ree) WPG

Defense. Shoots left. 6', 196 lbs. Born, Vancouver, B.C., March 3, 1993.
(Winnipeg's 4th choice, 119th overall, in 2011 Entry Draft).

			Regular Season					Playoffs				
Season	Club	League	GP	G	A	Pts	PIM	GP	G	A	Pts	PIM
2008-09	Greater Van.	BCMML	35	6	13	19	60	6	0	3	3	2
	Tri-City Americans	WHL	4	0	0	0	0	7	1	0	1	2
2009-10	Tri-City Americans	WHL	42	1	3	4	19	22	1	1	2	12
2010-11	Tri-City Americans	WHL	72	8	24	32	65	10	0	3	3	12

YUNKOV, Mikhail (yuhn-KAWF, mih-kigh-EHL) WSH

Center. Shoots left. 6', 180 lbs. Born, Voskresensk, USSR, February 16, 1986.
(Washington's 5th choice, 62nd overall, in 2004 Entry Draft).

			Regular Season					Playoffs				
Season	Club	League	GP	G	A	Pts	PIM	GP	G	A	Pts	PIM
2001-02	Krylja Sovetov 2	Russia-3	4	0	1	1	0	....	....	....	....	....
2002-03	Krylja Sovetov 2	Russia-3	3	0	1	1	0	....	....	....	....	....
	Krylja Sovetov	Russia	7	1	0	1	2	....	....	....	....	....
2003-04	Krylja Sovetov	Russia-2	38	5	10	15	12	4	0	1	1	0
	Krylja Sovetov 2	Russia-3	STATISTICS NOT AVAILABLE									
2004-05	Krylja Sovetov 2	Russia-3	1	0	0	0	0	....	....	....	....	....
	Krylja Sovetov	Russia-2	38	9	14	23	22	3	0	1	1	4
2005-06	Ak Bars Kazan	Russia	33	3	4	7	35	11	0	1	1	6
2006-07	Ak Bars Kazan	Russia	47	3	6	9	12	16	1	2	3	8
2007-08	Spartak Moscow	Russia	57	4	6	10	20	5	1	0	1	6
2008-09	Spartak Moscow	Rus-KHL	54	7	14	21	30	6	0	2	2	6
2009-10	Ak Bars Kazan	Rus-KHL	32	0	3	3	12	4	0	1	1	2
2010-11	Spartak Moscow	Rus-KHL	47	6	7	13	22	4	0	3	3	4

ZAGRAPAN, Marek (ZAG-rah-pahn, MAIR-ehk) BUF

Center. Shoots left. 6'1", 195 lbs. Born, Presov, Czech., December 6, 1986.
(Buffalo's 1st choice, 13th overall, in 2005 Entry Draft).

			Regular Season					Playoffs				
Season	Club	League	GP	G	A	Pts	PIM	GP	G	A	Pts	PIM
2001-02	HC Zlin U17	CzR-U17	48	23	14	37	24	6	1	0	1	2
2002-03	HC Zlin U17	CzR-U17	15	18	16	34	14	3	1	0	1	6
	HC Zlin Jr.	CzRep-Jr.	25	9	13	22	10	....	....	....	....	....
	HC Hame Zlin	CzRep	13	1	1	2	10	....	....	....	....	....
2003-04	HC Zlin Jr.	CzRep-Jr.	42	23	12	35	40	7	1	3	4	4
	HC Hame Zlin	CzRep	5	0	0	0	0	....	....	....	....	....
	HC Kometa Brno	CzRep-2	5	0	1	1	0	....	....	....	....	....
2004-05	Chicoutimi	QMJHL	59	32	50	82	50	17	11	6	17	28
2005-06	Chicoutimi	QMJHL	59	35	52	87	63	8	4	6	10	4
2006-07	Rochester	AHL	71	17	21	38	39	6	1	0	1	2
2007-08	Rochester	AHL	76	18	22	40	66	....	....	....	....	....
2008-09	Portland Pirates	AHL	80	21	28	49	44	5	2	1	3	2
2009-10	Cherepovets	Rus-KHL	51	10	6	16	40	....	....	....	....	....
2010-11	Khanty-Mansiisk	Rus-KHL	18	3	2	5	6	....	....	....	....	....
	HC Ocelari Trinec	CzRep	18	3	2	5	2	9	0	3	3	2

Signed as a free agent by **Cherepovets** (Russia-KHL), May 29, 2009. Signed as a free agent by **Khanty-Mansiisk** (Russia-KHL), June 22, 2010. Signed as a free agent by **Trinec** (Russia-KHL), December 26, 2010.

ZAJAC, Darcy (ZAY-jak, DAHR-see) **N.J.**
Right wing. Shoots right. 6'3", 200 lbs. Born, Winnipeg, Man., September 23, 1986.

Season	Club	League	GP	G	A	Pts	PIM	GP	G	A	Pts	PIM
						Regular Season					Playoffs	
2004-05	Salmon Arm	BCHL	60	12	21	33	75	....	....	....	....	....
2005-06	Salmon Arm	BCHL	57	37	43	80	76	....	....	....	....	....
2006-07	North Dakota	WCHA	41	8	2	10	18	....	....	....	....	....
2007-08	North Dakota	WCHA	41	3	5	8	46	....	....	....	....	....
2008-09	North Dakota	WCHA	43	5	12	17	32	....	....	....	....	....
2009-10	North Dakota	WCHA	41	8	11	19	49	....	....	....	....	....
	Adirondack	AHL	2	0	0	0	4	....	....	....	....	....
2010-11	Albany Devils	AHL	40	4	5	9	60	....	....	....	....	....
	Trenton Devils	ECHL	32	6	17	23	35	....	....	....	....	....

Signed as a free agent by **Adirondack** (AHL), April 8, 2010. Signed as a free agent by **Albany** (AHL), June 26, 2010.

ZELISKA, Lukas (zeh-LIHS-kah, LOO-kahsh) **NYR**
Center. Shoots right. 5'11", 176 lbs. Born, Martin, Czech., January 8, 1988.
(NY Rangers' 7th choice, 204th overall, in 2006 Entry Draft).

Season	Club	League	GP	G	A	Pts	PIM	GP	G	A	Pts	PIM
						Regular Season					Playoffs	
2003-04	HC Trinec U17	CzR-U17	48	39	41	80	166	5	2	2	4	4
	HC Trinec Jr.	CzRep-Jr.	7	1	1	2	2	....	....	....	....	....
2004-05	HC Trinec U17	CzR-U17	11	7	11	18	40	....	....	....	....	....
	HC Trinec Jr.	CzRep-Jr.	13	1	2	3	6	....	....	....	....	....
2005-06	HC Trinec Jr.	CzRep-Jr.	29	8	3	11	81	7	4	1	5	22
	HC Ocelari Trinec	CzRep	1	0	0	0	0	....	....	....	....	....
2006-07	Prince Albert	WHL	61	4	25	29	77	5	1	4	5	4
2007-08	Prostejov	CzRep-2	2	0	0	0	0	....	....	....	....	....
	HC Trinec Jr.	CzRep-Jr.	38	23	29	52	236	7	2	4	6	10
2008-09	HC Ocelari Trinec	CzRep	14	0	0	0	0	....	....	....	....	....
	HC Havirov	CzRep-2	32	10	5	15	52	4	0	1	1	6
2009-10	Havirov	CzRep-2	28	4	5	9	26	....	....	....	....	....
	MHC Martin	Slovakia	13	1	0	1	2	12	0	0	0	0
	MHK Dolny Kubin	Slovak-2	1	1	1	2	0	....	....	....	....	....
2010-11	MHC Martin	Slovakia	37	0	10	10	22	....	....	....	....	....
	MHK Dolny Kubin	Slovak-2	17	8	10	18	22	....	....	....	....	....

ZIBANEJAD, Mika (zih-BAN-ih-jad, MEEKA) **OTT**
Center. Shoots right. 6'2", 200 lbs. Born, Huddinge, Sweden, April 18, 1993.
(Ottawa's 1st choice, 6th overall, in 2011 Entry Draft).

Season	Club	League	GP	G	A	Pts	PIM	GP	G	A	Pts	PIM
						Regular Season					Playoffs	
2008-09	AIK IF Solna U18	Swe-U18	11	2	2	4	2	....	....	....	....	....
2009-10	Djurgarden U18	Swe-U18	28	14	22	36	18	5	5	4	9	4
	Djurgarden Jr.	Swe-Jr.	14	2	2	4	4	....	....	....	....	....
2010-11	Djurgarden U18	Swe-U18	2	3	2	5	2	....	....	....	....	....
	Djurgarden Jr.	Swe-Jr.	27	12	9	21	12	3	1	2	3	0
	Djurgarden	Sweden	26	5	4	9	2	7	1	1	2	2

ZIMMERMAN, Sean (ZIH-mehr-man, SHAWN) **ANA**
Defense. Shoots right. 6'3", 205 lbs. Born, Denver, CO, May 24, 1987.
(New Jersey's 6th choice, 170th overall, in 2005 Entry Draft).

Season	Club	League	GP	G	A	Pts	PIM	GP	G	A	Pts	PIM
						Regular Season					Playoffs	
2002-03	Spokane Braves	KIJHL	45	3	5	8	70	....	....	....	....	....
2003-04	Spokane Chiefs	WHL	67	4	4	8	16	4	0	0	0	0
2004-05	Spokane Chiefs	WHL	71	2	14	16	36	....	....	....	....	....
2005-06	Spokane Chiefs	WHL	72	2	19	21	44	....	....	....	....	....
	Albany River Rats	AHL	6	0	0	0	4	....	....	....	....	....
2006-07	Spokane Chiefs	WHL	60	2	12	14	69	6	0	2	2	2
	Lowell Devils	AHL	1	0	0	0	2	....	....	....	....	....
2007-08	Lowell Devils	AHL	66	0	6	6	47	....	....	....	....	....
	Trenton Devils	ECHL	8	0	1	1	10	....	....	....	....	....
2008-09	San Antonio	AHL	36	2	0	2	30	....	....	....	....	....
	Arizona Sundogs	CHL	20	0	3	3	20	....	....	....	....	....
2009-10	San Antonio	AHL	72	2	7	9	105	....	....	....	....	....
2010-11	Rochester	AHL	7	0	0	0	0	....	....	....	....	....
	Providence Bruins	AHL	23	0	4	4	23	....	....	....	....	....
	Syracuse Crunch	AHL	21	0	3	3	24	....	....	....	....	....

Traded to **Phoenix** by **New Jersey** for Kevin Cormier, September 12, 2008. Traded to **Vancouver** by **Phoenix** with Phoenix's 6th round choice (Alex Friesen) in 2010 Entry Draft for Mathieu Schneider, March 3, 2010. Traded to **Florida** by **Vancouver** for Nathan Paetsch, October 7, 2010. Traded to **Boston** by **Florida** with future considerations for Jeff LoVecchio and Jordan Knackstedt, December 9, 2010. Traded to **Anaheim** by **Boston** with Brian McGrattan for David Laliberte and Stefan Chaput, February 27, 2011.

ZOLNIERCZYK, Harry (ZOHL-nuhr-chuhk, HAIR-ee) **PHI**
Left wing. Shoots left. 5'11", 180 lbs. Born, Toronto, Ont., September 1, 1987.

Season	Club	League	GP	G	A	Pts	PIM	GP	G	A	Pts	PIM
						Regular Season					Playoffs	
2005-06	Alberni Valley	BCHL	53	9	13	22	40	6	1	3	4	10
2006-07	Alberni Valley	BCHL	47	20	18	38	85	6	3	2	5	10
2007-08	Brown U.	ECAC	16	0	3	3	2	....	....	....	....	....
2008-09	Brown U.	ECAC	31	1	1	2	30	....	....	....	....	....
2009-10	Brown U.	ECAC	37	13	20	33	78	....	....	....	....	....
2010-11	Brown U.	ECAC	30	16	15	31	*128	....	....	....	....	....
	Adirondack	AHL	16	3	2	5	37	....	....	....	....	....

Signed as a free agent by **Philadelphia**, March 8, 2011.

ZUCKER, Jason (ZOO-kuhr, JAY-suhn) **MIN**
Left wing. Shoots left. 5'11", 174 lbs. Born, Las Vegas, NV, January 16, 1992.
(Minnesota's 4th choice, 59th overall, in 2010 Entry Draft).

Season	Club	League	GP	G	A	Pts	PIM	GP	G	A	Pts	PIM
						Regular Season					Playoffs	
2007-08	Det. Compuware	MWEHL	30	17	21	38	30	....	....	....	....	....
	Det. Compuware	Minor-MI	42	29	35	64		....	....	....	....	....
2008-09	USNTDP	NAHL	36	11	4	15	55	....	....	....	....	....
	USNTDP	U-17	12	8	6	14		....	....	....	....	....
	USNTDP	U-18	16	2	6	8	8	....	....	....	....	....
2009-10	USNTDP	USHL	22	11	7	18	23	....	....	....	....	....
	USNTDP	U-18	38	18	17	35	24	....	....	....	....	....
2010-11	U. of Denver	WCHA	40	23	22	45	59	....	....	....	....	....

WCHA All-Rookie Team (2011) • WCHA Second All-Star Team (2011) • WCHA Rookie of the Year (2011)

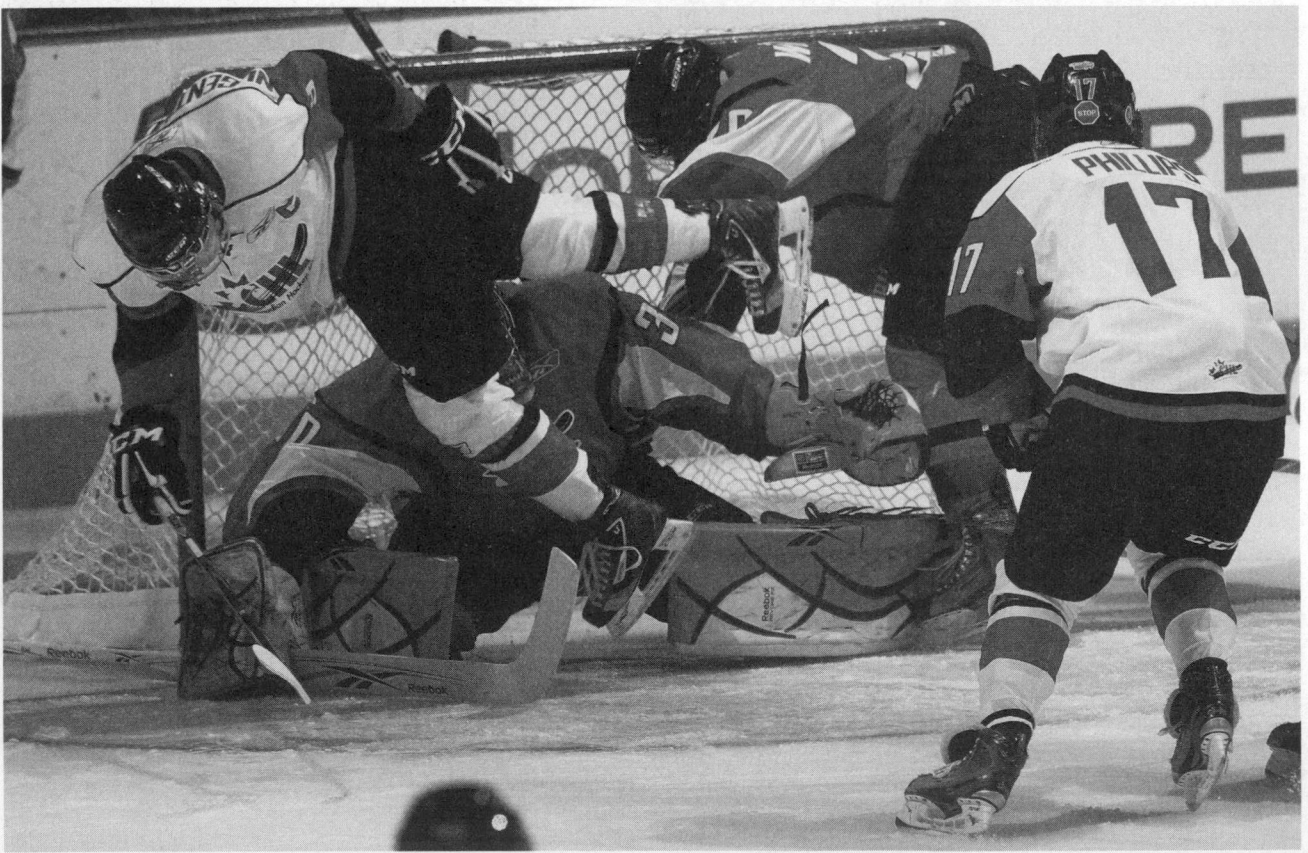

Captain Ryan Nugent-Hopkins of Team Cherry goes airborne in front of goalie David Honzik after a hit from Team Orr's Tyler Wotherspoon at the 2011 NHL Top Prospects Game. Nugent-Hopkins (first overall to Edmonton) and Zack Phillips (#17, 28th overall to Minnesota) were both selected in the first round of the 2011 Entry Draft. Wotherspoon was chosen 57th by Calgary. Honzik went 71st to Vancouver.

2011-12 NHL Player Register

Note: The 2011-12 NHL Player Register lists forwards and defensemen only. Goaltenders are listed separately. The NHL Player Register lists every active skater who played in the NHL in 2010-11 plus additional players with NHL experience. Trades and roster changes are current as of August 12, 2011.

Abbreviations: GP – games played; **G** – goals; **A** – assists; **Pts** – points; **PIM** – penalties in minutes; **PP** – power-play goals; **SH** – shorthanded goals; **GW** – game-winning goals; **S** – shots; **%** – shooting percentage; **+/–** – plus/minus; **TF** – total faceoffs taken; **F%** – faceoff winning percentage; **Min** – average time on ice per game; ***** – league-leading total
♦ – member of Stanley Cup-winning team.

Prospect Register begins on page 275.
Goaltender Register begins on page 583.
Retired Player Index begins on page 610.
Retired Goaltender Index begins on page 651.
League abbreviations are listed on page 662.

ABDELKADER, Justin

(abdehl-KAY-duhr, JUHS-tihn) **DET**

Left wing. Shoots left. 6'1", 212 lbs. Born, Muskegon, MI, February 25, 1987. Detroit's 2nd choice, 42nd overall, in 2005 Entry Draft.

			Regular Season														Playoffs								
Season	Club	League	GP	G	A	Pts	PIM	PP	SH	GW	S	%	+/-	TF	F%	Min	GP	G	A	Pts	PIM	PP	SH	GW	Min
2003-04	Muskegon M.S.	High-MI	28	37	43	80	....	....	....	....	....	....	....	....	....	....	....	....	....	....	....	....	....	....	....
2004-05	Cedar Rapids	USHL	60	27	25	52	86	....	....	....	....	....	....	....	....	....	11	0	4	4	8	....	....	....	....
2005-06	Michigan State	CCHA	44	10	12	22	83	....	....	....	....	....	....	....	....	....	....	....	....	....	....	....	....	....	....
2006-07	Michigan State	CCHA	38	15	18	33	91	....	....	....	....	....	....	....	....	....	....	....	....	....	....	....	....	....	....
2007-08	Michigan State	CCHA	42	19	21	40	107	....	....	....	....	....	....	....	....	....	....	....	....	....	....	....	....	....	....
	Detroit	**NHL**	**2**	**0**	**0**	**0**	**2**	**0**	**0**	**0**	**6**	**0.0**	**0**	**12**	**41.7**	**12:13**	....	....	....	....	....	....	....	....	....
2008-09	**Detroit**	**NHL**	**2**	**0**	**0**	**0**	**0**	**0**	**0**	**0**	**2**	**0.0**	**0**	**7**	**57.1**	**9:18**	**10**	**2**	**1**	**3**	**0**	**0**	**0**	**0**	**6:58**
	Grand Rapids	AHL	76	24	28	52	102	....	....	....	....	....	....	....	....	....	10	6	2	8	23	....	....	....	....
2009-10	**Detroit**	**NHL**	**50**	**3**	**3**	**6**	**35**	**0**	**0**	**0**	**79**	**3.8**	**–11**	**318**	**46.5**	**10:35**	**11**	**1**	**1**	**2**	***36**	**0**	**0**	**0**	**7:30**
	Grand Rapids	AHL	33	11	13	24	86	....	....	....	....	....	....	....	....	....	....	....	....	....	....	....	....	....	....
2010-11	**Detroit**	**NHL**	**74**	**7**	**12**	**19**	**61**	**0**	**0**	**1**	**129**	**5.4**	**15**	**430**	**52.8**	**12:18**	**11**	**0**	**0**	**0**	**22**	**0**	**0**	**0**	**13:27**
	NHL Totals		**128**	**10**	**15**	**25**	**98**	**0**	**0**	**1**	**216**	**4.6**		**767**	**50.1**	**11:35**	**32**	**3**	**2**	**5**	**58**	**0**	**0**	**0**	**9:23**

NCAA Championship All-Tournament Team (2007) • NCAA Championship Tournament MVP (2007) • AHL All-Rookie Team (2009)

ADAM, Luke

(A-duhm, LEWK) **BUF**

Center. Shoots left. 6'2", 216 lbs. Born, St. John's, Nfld., June 18, 1990. Buffalo's 3rd choice, 44th overall, in 2008 Entry Draft.

Season	Club	League	GP	G	A	Pts	PIM	PP	SH	GW	S	%	+/-	TF	F%	Min	GP	G	A	Pts	PIM	PP	SH	GW	Min
2006-07	St. John's	QMJHL	63	6	9	15	51	....	....	....	....	....	....	....	....	....	4	0	2	2	4	....	....	....	....
2007-08	St. John's	QMJHL	70	36	30	66	72	....	....	....	....	....	....	....	....	....	6	3	5	8	8	....	....	....	....
2008-09	Montreal	QMJHL	47	22	27	49	59	....	....	....	....	....	....	....	....	....	....	....	....	....	....	....	....	....	....
2009-10	Cape Breton	QMJHL	56	49	41	90	75	....	....	....	....	....	....	....	....	....	5	3	1	4	2	....	....	....	....
	Portland Pirates	AHL	....	....	....	....	....	....	....	....	....	....	....	....	....	....	3	0	2	2	0	....	....	....	....
2010-11	**Buffalo**	**NHL**	**19**	**3**	**1**	**4**	**12**	**0**	**0**	**1**	**31**	**9.7**	**–6**	**119**	**34.5**	**11:13**	....	....	....	....	....	....	....	....	....
	Portland Pirates	AHL	57	29	33	62	46	....	....	....	....	....	....	....	....	....	12	4	3	7	14	....	....	....	....
	NHL Totals		**19**	**3**	**1**	**4**	**12**	**0**	**0**	**1**	**31**	**9.7**		**119**	**34.5**	**11:13**	....	....	....	....	....	....	....	....	....

QMJHL First All-Star Team (2010) • AHL All-Rookie Team (2011) • Dudley "Red" Garrett Memorial Award (AHL – Rookie of the Year) (2011)

ADAMS, Craig

(A-duhmz, KRAYG) **PIT**

Right wing. Shoots right. 6', 197 lbs. Born, Seria, Brunei, April 26, 1977. Hartford's 9th choice, 223rd overall, in 1996 Entry Draft.

Season	Club	League	GP	G	A	Pts	PIM	PP	SH	GW	S	%	+/-	TF	F%	Min	GP	G	A	Pts	PIM	PP	SH	GW	Min
1995-96	Harvard Crimson	ECAC	34	8	9	17	56	....	....	....	....	....	....	....	....	....	....	....	....	....	....	....	....	....	....
1996-97	Harvard Crimson	ECAC	32	6	4	10	36	....	....	....	....	....	....	....	....	....	....	....	....	....	....	....	....	....	....
1997-98	Harvard Crimson	ECAC	12	6	6	12	12	....	....	....	....	....	....	....	....	....	....	....	....	....	....	....	....	....	....
1998-99	Harvard Crimson	ECAC	31	9	14	23	53	....	....	....	....	....	....	....	....	....	....	....	....	....	....	....	....	....	....
99-2000	Cincinnati	IHL	73	12	12	24	124	....	....	....	....	....	....	....	....	....	8	0	1	1	14	....	....	....	....
2000-01	**Carolina**	**NHL**	**44**	**1**	**0**	**1**	**20**	**0**	**0**	**0**	**15**	**6.7**	**–7**	**4**	**25.0**	**4:30**	**3**	**0**	**0**	**0**	**0**	**0**	**0**	**0**	**3:45**
	Cincinnati	IHL	4	0	1	1	9	....	....	....	....	....	....	....	....	....	1	0	0	0	2	....	....	....	....
2001-02	**Carolina**	**NHL**	**33**	**0**	**1**	**1**	**38**	**0**	**0**	**0**	**17**	**0.0**	**2**	**9**	**33.3**	**5:54**	**1**	**0**	**0**	**0**	**0**	**0**	**0**	**0**	**7:41**
	Lowell	AHL	22	5	4	9	51	....	....	....	....	....	....	....	....	....	....	....	....	....	....	....	....	....	....
2002-03	**Carolina**	**NHL**	**81**	**6**	**12**	**18**	**71**	**1**	**0**	**1**	**107**	**5.6**	**–11**	**20**	**35.0**	**12:12**	....	....	....	....	....	....	....	....	....
2003-04	**Carolina**	**NHL**	**80**	**7**	**10**	**17**	**69**	**0**	**1**	**0**	**110**	**6.4**	**–5**	**20**	**45.0**	**13:41**	....	....	....	....	....	....	....	....	....
2004-05	HC Milano	Italy	30	15	14	29	57	....	....	....	....	....	....	....	....	....	15	4	7	11	26	....	....	....	....
2005-06♦	**Carolina**	**NHL**	**67**	**10**	**11**	**21**	**51**	**1**	**1**	**2**	**68**	**14.7**	**1**	**13**	**53.9**	**12:18**	**25**	**0**	**0**	**0**	**10**	**0**	**0**	**0**	**8:16**
	Lowell	AHL	13	4	3	7	20	....	....	....	....	....	....	....	....	....	....	....	....	....	....	....	....	....	....
2006-07	**Carolina**	**NHL**	**82**	**7**	**7**	**14**	**54**	**0**	**1**	**1**	**71**	**9.9**	**–9**	**36**	**30.6**	**10:04**	....	....	....	....	....	....	....	....	....
2007-08	**Carolina**	**NHL**	**40**	**2**	**3**	**5**	**34**	**0**	**0**	**0**	**31**	**6.5**	**–8**	**11**	**27.3**	**9:48**	....	....	....	....	....	....	....	....	....
	Chicago	**NHL**	**35**	**2**	**4**	**6**	**24**	**0**	**1**	**1**	**32**	**6.3**	**–8**	**30**	**53.3**	**11:56**	....	....	....	....	....	....	....	....	....
2008-09	**Chicago**	**NHL**	**36**	**2**	**4**	**6**	**22**	**1**	**0**	**0**	**38**	**5.3**	**–3**	**16**	**37.5**	**8:43**	....	....	....	....	....	....	....	....	....
	♦ **Pittsburgh**	**NHL**	**9**	**0**	**1**	**1**	**0**	**0**	**0**	**0**	**9**	**0.0**	**0**	**5**	**40.0**	**8:34**	**24**	**3**	**2**	**5**	**16**	**0**	**0**	**0**	**9:45**
2009-10	**Pittsburgh**	**NHL**	**82**	**0**	**10**	**10**	**72**	**0**	**0**	**0**	**84**	**0.0**	**–5**	**562**	**43.8**	**11:06**	**13**	**2**	**1**	**3**	**15**	**0**	**0**	**1**	**10:38**
2010-11	**Pittsburgh**	**NHL**	**80**	**4**	**11**	**15**	**76**	**0**	**2**	**1**	**90**	**4.4**	**–5**	**465**	**41.7**	**12:11**	**7**	**1**	**0**	**1**	**2**	**0**	**0**	**0**	**13:06**
	NHL Totals		**669**	**41**	**74**	**115**	**531**	**3**	**6**	**6**	**672**	**6.1**		**1191**	**42.4**	**10:47**	**73**	**6**	**3**	**9**	**43**	**0**	**0**	**1**	**9:26**

• Rights transferred to **Carolina** after **Hartford** franchise relocated, June 25, 1997. • Missed majority of 1997-98 due to shoulder injury vs. University of Wisconsin (WCHA), December 27, 1997. Signed as a free agent by **Milano**, (Italy), July 28, 2004. Signed as a free agent by **Anaheim**, August 25, 2005. Traded to **Carolina** by **Anaheim** for Bruno St. Jacques, October 3, 2005. Traded to **Chicago** by **Carolina** for future considerations, January 17, 2008. Claimed on waivers by **Pittsburgh** from **Chicago**, March 4, 2009.

AFINOGENOV, Maxim

(ah-fihn-ah-GEHN-ahf, max-IHM)

Right wing. Shoots left. 6', 190 lbs. Born, Moscow, USSR, September 4, 1979. Buffalo's 3rd choice, 69th overall, in 1997 Entry Draft.

Season	Club	League	GP	G	A	Pts	PIM	PP	SH	GW	S	%	+/-	TF	F%	Min	GP	G	A	Pts	PIM	PP	SH	GW	Min
1996-97	Dynamo Moscow	Russia	29	6	5	11	10	....	....	....	....	....	....	....	....	....	4	0	2	2	0	....	....	....	....
	Dynamo Moscow	EuroHL	3	0	0	0	0	....	....	....	....	....	....	....	....	....	3	1	0	1	4	....	....	....	....
1997-98	Dynamo Moscow	Russia	35	10	5	15	53	....	....	....	....	....	....	....	....	....	....	....	....	....	....	....	....	....	....
	Dynamo Moscow	EuroHL	6	3	1	4	27	....	....	....	....	....	....	....	....	....	....	....	....	....	....	....	....	....	....
1998-99	Dynamo Moscow	Russia	38	8	13	21	24	....	....	....	....	....	....	....	....	....	16	*10	6	*16	14	....	....	....	....
	Dynamo Moscow	EuroHL	5	3	5	8	29	....	....	....	....	....	....	....	....	....	4	2	1	3	27	....	....	....	....

Season	Club	League	GP	G	A	Pts	PIM	PP	SH	GW	S	%	+/-	TF	F%	Min	GP	G	A	Pts	PIM	PP	SH	GW	Min
			Regular Season														Playoffs								
99-2000	Buffalo	NHL	65	16	18	34	41	2	0	2	128	12.5	–4	0	0.0	13:09	5	0	1	1	2	0	0	0	12:53
	Rochester	AHL	15	6	12	18	8	....	....	....	....	....	....	....	....	....	8	3	1	4	4	....	....	....	....
2000-01	Buffalo	NHL	78	14	22	36	40	3	0	5	190	7.4	1	2	0.0	14:32	11	2	3	5	4	0	0	0	10:56
2001-02	Buffalo	NHL	81	21	19	40	69	3	1	0	234	9.0	–9	1	100.0	15:22	....	....	....	....	....	....	....	....	....
	Russia	Olympics	6	2	2	4	4	....	....	....	....	....	....	....	....	....	....	....	....	....	....	....	....	....	....
2002-03	Buffalo	NHL	35	5	6	11	21	2	0	2	77	6.5	–12	4	50.0	13:24	....	....	....	....	....	....	....	....	....
2003-04	Buffalo	NHL	73	17	14	31	57	3	0	4	148	11.5	–4	9	22.2	13:46	....	....	....	....	....	....	....	....	....
2004-05	Dynamo Moscow	Russia	36	13	14	27	91	....	....	....	....	....	....	....	....	....	10	4	4	8	8	....	....	....	....
2005-06	Buffalo	NHL	77	22	51	73	84	11	0	3	241	9.1	6	17	17.7	16:20	18	3	5	8	10	0	0	0	16:53
	Russia	Olympics	8	0	1	1	10	....	....	....	....	....	....	....	....	....	....	....	....	....	....	....	....	....	....
2006-07	Buffalo	NHL	56	23	38	61	66	7	0	3	151	15.2	19	3	66.7	17:03	15	5	4	9	6	3	0	2	15:24
2007-08	Buffalo	NHL	56	10	18	28	42	1	0	1	114	8.8	–16	5	20.0	16:03	....	....	....	....	....	....	....	....	....
2008-09	Buffalo	NHL	48	6	14	20	20	0	0	0	93	6.5	–7	3	0.0	12:36	....	....	....	....	....	....	....	....	....
2009-10	Atlanta	NHL	82	24	37	61	46	6	0	3	181	13.3	–17	3	33.3	17:24	....	....	....	....	....	....	....	....	....
	Russia	Olympics	4	1	1	2	0	....	....	....	....	....	....	....	....	....	....	....	....	....	....	....	....	....	....
2010-11	St. Petersburg	Rus-KHL	51	13	20	33	50	....	....	....	....	....	....	....	....	....	11	4	1	5	10	....	....	....	....
	NHL Totals		651	158	237	395	486	38	1	23	1557	10.1		47	25.5	15:08	49	10	13	23	22	3	0	2	14:41

• Missed majority of 2002-03 due to concussion prior to training camp, August, 2002. Signed as a free agent by **Dynamo Moscow** (Russia), June 19, 2004. Signed as a free agent by **Atlanta**, September 29, 2009. Signed as a free agent by **St. Petersburg** (Russia-KHL), August 6, 2010.

ALBERTS, Andrew

(AL-buhrts, AN-droo) **VAN**

Defense. Shoots left. 6'5", 209 lbs. Born, Minneapolis, MN, June 30, 1981. Boston's 5th choice, 179th overall, in 2001 Entry Draft.

Season	Club	League	GP	G	A	Pts	PIM	PP	SH	GW	S	%	+/-	TF	F%	Min	GP	G	A	Pts	PIM	PP	SH	GW	Min
1998-99	Benilde	High-MN	26	10	25	35	....	....	....	....	....	....	....	....	....	....	....	....	....	....	....	....	....	....	....
99-2000	Waterloo	USHL	49	2	2	4	55	....	....	....	....	....	....	....	....	....	4	0	0	0	12	....	....	....	....
2000-01	Waterloo	USHL	54	4	10	14	128	....	....	....	....	....	....	....	....	....	....	....	....	....	....	....	....	....	....
2001-02	Boston College	H-East	38	2	10	12	52	....	....	....	....	....	....	....	....	....	....	....	....	....	....	....	....	....	....
2002-03	Boston College	H-East	39	6	16	22	60	....	....	....	....	....	....	....	....	....	....	....	....	....	....	....	....	....	....
2003-04	Boston College	H-East	42	4	12	16	64	....	....	....	....	....	....	....	....	....	....	....	....	....	....	....	....	....	....
2004-05	Boston College	H-East	30	4	12	16	67	....	....	....	....	....	....	....	....	....	....	....	....	....	....	....	....	....	....
	Providence Bruins	AHL	8	0	0	0	16	....	....	....	....	....	....	....	....	....	16	1	4	5	40	....	....	....	....
2005-06	Boston	NHL	73	1	6	7	68	0	1	0	30	3.3	3	2	50.0	12:50	....	....	....	....	....	....	....	....	....
	Providence Bruins	AHL	6	0	1	1	7	....	....	....	....	....	....	....	....	....	....	....	....	....	....	....	....	....	....
2006-07	Boston	NHL	76	0	10	10	124	0	0	0	41	0.0	–15	1	0.0	19:40	....	....	....	....	....	....	....	....	....
2007-08	Boston	NHL	35	0	2	2	39	0	0	0	25	0.0	4	2	50.0	20:37	2	0	0	0	0	0	0	0	11:07
2008-09	Philadelphia	NHL	79	1	12	13	61	0	0	0	46	2.2	6	0	0.0	15:48	6	0	1	1	10	0	0	0	13:40
2009-10	Carolina	NHL	62	2	8	10	74	0	0	0	38	5.3	7	0	0.0	15:04	....	....	....	....	....	....	....	....	....
	Vancouver	NHL	14	1	1	2	13	0	0	0	12	8.3	–1	1	0.0	16:45	10	0	1	1	27	0	0	0	12:27
2010-11	Vancouver	NHL	42	1	6	7	41	0	0	0	21	4.8	0	0	0.0	15:10	9	0	0	0	6	0	0	0	12:48
	NHL Totals		381	6	45	51	420	0	1	0	213	2.8		6	33.3	16:17	27	0	2	2	43	0	0	0	12:44

Hockey East Second All-Star Team (2004) • NCAA East First All-American Team (2004, 2005) • Hockey East First All-Star Team (2005)

• Missed majority of 2007-08 due to post-concussion syndrome. Traded to **Philadelphia** by **Boston** for Ned Lukacevic and Philadelphia's 4th round choice (Lane MacDermid) in 2009 Entry Draft, October 14, 2008. Signed as a free agent by **Carolina**, July 15, 2009. Traded to **Vancouver** by **Carolina** for Vancouver's 3rd round choice (Austin Levi) in 2010 Entry Draft, March 3, 2010.

ALFREDSSON, Daniel

(AHL-frehd-suhn, DAN-yehl) **OTT**

Right wing. Shoots right. 5'11", 200 lbs. Born, Gothenburg, Sweden, December 11, 1972. Ottawa's 5th choice, 133rd overall, in 1994 Entry Draft.

Season	Club	League	GP	G	A	Pts	PIM	PP	SH	GW	S	%	+/-	TF	F%	Min	GP	G	A	Pts	PIM	PP	SH	GW	Min
1990-91	Molndal Hockey	Sweden-2	3	0	0	0	2	....	....	....	....	....	....	....	....	....	8	4	4	8	4	....	....	....	....
1991-92	Molndal	Sweden-2	32	12	8	20	43	....	....	....	....	....	....	....	....	....	....	....	....	....	....	....	....	....	....
1992-93	V.Frolunda	Sweden	20	1	5	6	8	....	....	....	....	....	....	....	....	....	....	....	....	....	....	....	....	....	....
1993-94	V.Frolunda	Sweden	39	20	10	30	18	....	....	....	....	....	....	....	....	....	4	1	1	2	....	....	....	....	....
1994-95	V.Frolunda	Sweden	22	7	11	18	22	....	....	....	....	....	....	....	....	....	....	....	....	....	....	....	....	....	....
1995-96	Ottawa	NHL	82	26	35	61	28	8	2	3	212	12.3	–18	....	....	....	....	....	....	....	....	....	....	....	....
1996-97	Ottawa	NHL	76	24	47	71	30	11	1	1	247	9.7	5	....	....	....	7	5	2	7	6	3	0	2	....
1997-98	Ottawa	NHL	55	17	28	45	18	7	0	7	149	11.4	7	....	....	....	11	7	2	9	20	2	1	1	....
	Sweden	Olympics	4	2	3	5	2	....	....	....	....	....	....	....	....	....	....	....	....	....	....	....	....	....	....
1998-99	Ottawa	NHL	58	11	22	33	14	3	0	5	163	6.7	8	7	57.1	17:22	4	1	2	3	4	1	0	0	22:23
99-2000	Ottawa	NHL	57	21	38	59	28	4	2	0	164	12.8	11	3	66.7	18:45	6	1	3	4	2	1	0	0	20:22
2000-01	Ottawa	NHL	68	24	46	70	30	10	0	3	206	11.7	11	8	50.0	18:47	4	1	0	1	2	0	0	0	21:20
2001-02	Ottawa	NHL	78	37	34	71	45	9	1	4	243	15.2	3	30	30.0	20:19	12	7	6	13	4	3	0	3	21:43
	Sweden	Olympics	4	1	4	5	2	....	....	....	....	....	....	....	....	....	....	....	....	....	....	....	....	....	....
2002-03	Ottawa	NHL	78	27	51	78	42	9	0	6	240	11.3	15	40	40.0	19:32	18	4	4	8	12	4	0	1	18:00
2003-04	Ottawa	NHL	77	32	48	80	24	9	0	5	230	13.9	12	33	24.2	19:24	7	1	2	3	2	0	0	0	20:03
2004-05	Frolunda	Sweden	15	8	9	17	10	....	....	....	....	....	....	....	....	....	14	*12	6	*18	8	....	....	....	....
2005-06	Ottawa	NHL	77	43	60	103	50	16	5	8	249	17.3	29	44	20.5	21:41	10	2	8	10	4	1	0	0	21:10
	Sweden	Olympics	8	5	5	10	4	....	....	....	....	....	....	....	....	....	....	....	....	....	....	....	....	....	....
2006-07	Ottawa	NHL	77	29	58	87	42	7	2	7	240	12.1	42	43	34.9	21:35	20	*14	8	*22	10	*6	1	*4	23:20
2007-08	Ottawa	NHL	70	40	49	89	34	9	*7	5	217	18.4	15	39	53.9	22:17	2	0	0	0	0	0	0	0	19:20
2008-09	Ottawa	NHL	79	24	50	74	24	8	1	3	204	11.8	7	17	23.5	20:53	....	....	....	....	....	....	....	....	....
2009-10	Ottawa	NHL	70	20	51	71	22	4	1	5	168	11.9	8	40	35.0	19:40	6	2	6	8	2	0	0	0	22:54
	Sweden	Olympics	4	3	0	3	0	....	....	....	....	....	....	....	....	....	....	....	....	....	....	....	....	....	....
2010-11	Ottawa	NHL	54	14	17	31	18	7	0	1	96	14.6	–19	12	16.7	19:17	....	....	....	....	....	....	....	....	....
	NHL Totals		1056	389	634	1023	449	121	22	63	3028	12.8		316	34.2	20:04	107	45	43	88	68	21	2	11	21:05

NHL All-Rookie Team (1996) • Calder Memorial Trophy (1996) • NHL Second All-Star Team (2006)

Played in NHL All-Star Game (1996, 1997, 1998, 2004, 2008)

Signed as a free agent by **Frolunda** (Sweden), November 10, 2004.

ALLEN, Bryan

(AHL-lehn, BRIGH-uhn) **CAR**

Defense. Shoots left. 6'5", 226 lbs. Born, Kingston, Ont., August 21, 1980. Vancouver's 1st choice, 4th overall, in 1998 Entry Draft.

Season	Club	League	GP	G	A	Pts	PIM	PP	SH	GW	S	%	+/-	TF	F%	Min	GP	G	A	Pts	PIM	PP	SH	GW	Min
1995-96	Ernestown Jets	ON-Jr.C	36	1	16	17	71	....	....	....	....	....	....	....	....	....	....	....	....	....	....	....	....	....	....
1996-97	Oshawa Generals	OHL	60	2	4	6	76	....	....	....	....	....	....	....	....	....	18	1	3	4	26	....	....	....	....
1997-98	Oshawa Generals	OHL	48	6	13	19	126	....	....	....	....	....	....	....	....	....	5	0	5	5	18	....	....	....	....
1998-99	Oshawa Generals	OHL	37	7	15	22	77	....	....	....	....	....	....	....	....	....	15	0	3	3	26	....	....	....	....
99-2000	Oshawa Generals	OHL	3	0	2	2	12	....	....	....	....	....	....	....	....	....	3	0	0	0	13	....	....	....	....
	Syracuse Crunch	AHL	9	1	1	2	11	....	....	....	....	....	....	....	....	....	2	0	0	0	2	....	....	....	....
2000-01	Vancouver	NHL	6	0	0	0	0	0	0	0	2	0.0	0	0	0.0	9:20	2	0	0	0	2	0	0	0	13:47
	Kansas City	IHL	75	5	20	25	99	....	....	....	....	....	....	....	....	....	....	....	....	....	....	....	....	....	....
2001-02	Vancouver	NHL	11	0	0	0	6	0	0	0	4	0.0	1	0	0.0	10:47	....	....	....	....	....	....	....	....	....
	Manitoba Moose	AHL	68	7	18	25	121	....	....	....	....	....	....	....	....	....	5	0	1	1	8	....	....	....	....
2002-03	Vancouver	NHL	48	5	3	8	73	0	0	1	43	11.6	8	0	0.0	12:56	1	0	0	0	2	0	0	0	10:35
	Manitoba Moose	AHL	7	0	1	1	4	....	....	....	....	....	....	....	....	....	....	....	....	....	....	....	....	....	....
2003-04	Vancouver	NHL	74	2	5	7	94	0	0	0	70	2.9	–10	0	0.0	16:51	4	0	0	0	2	0	0	0	14:37
2004-05	Voskresensk	Russia	19	0	3	3	34	....	....	....	....	....	....	....	....	....	....	....	....	....	....	....	....	....	....
2005-06	Vancouver	NHL	77	7	10	17	115	1	0	0	88	8.0	4	0	0.0	20:27	....	....	....	....	....	....	....	....	....
2006-07	Florida	NHL	82	4	21	25	112	0	0	0	99	4.0	7	1	0.0	21:36	....	....	....	....	....	....	....	....	....
2007-08	Florida	NHL	73	2	14	16	67	0	0	0	67	3.0	5	0	0.0	21:17	....	....	....	....	....	....	....	....	....
2008-09	Florida	NHL	2	0	1	1	0	0	0	0	5	0.0	2	0	0.0	27:11	....	....	....	....	....	....	....	....	....
2009-10	Florida	NHL	74	4	9	13	99	0	1	2	78	5.1	–8	0	0.0	19:10	....	....	....	....	....	....	....	....	....
2010-11	Florida	NHL	53	4	8	12	63	0	0	1	50	8.0	–5	0	0.0	19:13	....	....	....	....	....	....	....	....	....
	Carolina	NHL	19	0	5	5	19	0	0	0	8	0.0	4	0	0.0	15:51	....	....	....	....	....	....	....	....	....
	NHL Totals		519	28	76	104	648	1	1	4	514	5.4		1	0.0	18:45	7	0	0	0	6	0	0	0	13:48

OHL First All-Star Team (1999)

• Missed majority of 1999-2000 due to knee injury in training camp, September 21, 1999. Signed as a free agent by **Voskresensk** (Russia), December 20, 2004. Traded to **Florida** by **Vancouver** with Todd Bertuzzi and Alex Auld for Roberto Luongo, Lukas Krajicek and Florida's 6th round choice (Sergei Shirokov) in 2006 Entry Draft, June 23, 2006. • Missed majority of 2008-09 due to off-season arthroscopic knee surgery and follow-up cartilage surgery, October 27, 2008. Traded to **Carolina** by **Florida** for Sergei Samsonov, February 28, 2011.

ALMOND, Cody
(al-MUHND, KOH-dee) **MIN**

Center. Shoots left. 6'2", 217 lbs. Born, Calgary, Alta., July 24, 1989. Minnesota's 3rd choice, 140th overall, in 2007 Entry Draft.

Season	Club	League	GP	G	A	Pts	PIM	PP	SH	GW	S	%	+/-	TF	F%	Min	Playoffs GP	G	A	Pts	PIM	PP	SH	GW	Min
2004-05	Cgy. Stampeders	SAMHL	30	28	15	43	108	....	....	....	....	....	....	....	....	....	....	....	....	....	....	....	....	....	....
2005-06	Kelowna Rockets	WHL	23	2	1	3	7	....	....	....	....	....	....	....	....	....	8	0	0	0	0	....	....	....	....
2006-07	Kelowna Rockets	WHL	68	15	28	43	72	....	....	....	....	....	....	....	....	....	....	....	....	....	....	....	....	....	....
2007-08	Kelowna Rockets	WHL	69	22	34	56	114	....	....	....	....	....	....	....	....	....	7	1	2	3	2	....	....	....	....
2008-09	Kelowna Rockets	WHL	70	33	33	66	105	....	....	....	....	....	....	....	....	....	22	10	17	27	*51	....	....	....	....
2009-10	**Minnesota**	**NHL**	**7**	**1**	**0**	**1**	**9**	**0**	**0**	**0**	**6**	**16.7**	**–3**	**30**	**60.0**	**7:45**	....	....	....	....	....	....	....	....	....
	Houston Aeros	AHL	48	7	11	18	77	....	....	....	....	....	....	....	....	....	....	....	....	....	....	....	....	....	....
2010-11	**Minnesota**	**NHL**	**8**	**0**	**0**	**0**	**2**	**0**	**0**	**0**	**3**	**0.0**	**0**	**32**	**40.6**	**7:02**	....	....	....	....	....	....	....	....	....
	Houston Aeros	AHL	65	15	19	34	124	....	....	....	....	....	....	....	....	....	22	0	6	6	20	....	....	....	....
	NHL Totals		**15**	**1**	**0**	**1**	**11**	**0**	**0**	**0**	**9**	**11.1**		**62**	**50.0**	**7:22**	....	....	....	....	....	....	....	....	....

ALZNER, Karl
(ALZ-nuhr, KARL) **WSH**

Defense. Shoots left. 6'3", 206 lbs. Born, Burnaby, B.C., September 24, 1988. Washington's 1st choice, 5th overall, in 2007 Entry Draft.

Season	Club	League	GP	G	A	Pts	PIM	PP	SH	GW	S	%	+/-	TF	F%	Min	Playoffs GP	G	A	Pts	PIM	PP	SH	GW	Min
2002-03	Burnaby W.C.	Minor-BC	64	17	31	48	24	....	....	....	....	....	....	....	....	....	....	....	....	....	....	....	....	....	....
2003-04	Richmond	PIJHL	41	3	9	12	8	....	....	....	....	....	....	....	....	....	13	0	2	2	0	....	....	....	....
	Calgary Hitmen	WHL	1	0	0	0	0	....	....	....	....	....	....	....	....	....	....	....	....	....	....	....	....	....	....
2004-05	Calgary Hitmen	WHL	66	0	10	10	19	....	....	....	....	....	....	....	....	....	12	0	3	3	9	....	....	....	....
2005-06	Calgary Hitmen	WHL	70	4	20	24	28	....	....	....	....	....	....	....	....	....	13	1	3	4	4	....	....	....	....
2006-07	Calgary Hitmen	WHL	63	8	39	47	32	....	....	....	....	....	....	....	....	....	18	1	12	13	4	....	....	....	....
2007-08	Calgary Hitmen	WHL	60	7	29	36	15	....	....	....	....	....	....	....	....	....	16	6	2	8	4	....	....	....	....
2008-09	**Washington**	**NHL**	**30**	**1**	**4**	**5**	**2**	**0**	**0**	**0**	**31**	**3.2**	**–1**	**0**	**0.0**	**19:25**	....	....	....	....	....	....	....	....	....
	Hershey Bears	AHL	48	4	16	20	10	....	....	....	....	....	....	....	....	....	10	0	2	2	2	....	....	....	....
2009-10	**Washington**	**NHL**	**21**	**0**	**5**	**5**	**8**	**0**	**0**	**0**	**16**	**0.0**	**–2**	**0**	**0.0**	**16:24**	**1**	**0**	**0**	**0**	**0**	**0**	**0**	**0**	**15:09**
	Hershey Bears	AHL	56	3	18	21	10	....	....	....	....	....	....	....	....	....	20	3	7	10	4	....	....	....	....
2010-11	**Washington**	**NHL**	**82**	**2**	**10**	**12**	**24**	**0**	**0**	**0**	**64**	**3.1**	**14**	**0**	**0.0**	**20:01**	**9**	**0**	**1**	**1**	**0**	**0**	**0**	**0**	**22:44**
	NHL Totals		**133**	**3**	**19**	**22**	**34**	**0**	**0**	**0**	**111**	**2.7**		**0**	**0.0**	**19:19**	**10**	**0**	**1**	**1**	**0**	**0**	**0**	**0**	**21:59**

WHL East Second All-Star Team (2007) • Canadian Major Junior Second All-Star Team (2007) • WHL East First All-Star Team (2008) • WHL Defenseman of the Year (2008) • WHL Player of the Year (2008) • Canadian Major Junior First All-Star Team (2008) • Canadian Major Junior Defenseman of the Year (2008)

ANDERSSON, Jonas
(AN-duhr-suhn, YOH-nuhs)

Right wing. Shoots left. 6'3", 204 lbs. Born, Stockholm, Sweden, February 24, 1981. Nashville's 2nd choice, 33rd overall, in 1999 Entry Draft.

Season	Club	League	GP	G	A	Pts	PIM	PP	SH	GW	S	%	+/-	TF	F%	Min	Playoffs GP	G	A	Pts	PIM	PP	SH	GW	Min
1997-98	AIK Solna Jr.	Swe-Jr.	33	14	16	30	32	....	....	....	....	....	....	....	....	....	....	....	....	....	....	....	....	....	....
1998-99	AIK Solna Jr.	Swe-Jr.	16	3	7	10	18	....	....	....	....	....	....	....	....	....	....	....	....	....	....	....	....	....	....
99-2000	North Bay	OHL	67	31	36	67	27	....	....	....	....	....	....	....	....	....	6	2	2	4	2	....	....	....	....
	Milwaukee	IHL	2	1	0	1	0	....	....	....	....	....	....	....	....	....	2	0	0	0	2	....	....	....	....
2000-01	Milwaukee	IHL	52	6	7	13	44	....	....	....	....	....	....	....	....	....	5	0	0	0	2	....	....	....	....
2001-02	**Nashville**	**NHL**	**5**	**0**	**0**	**0**	**2**	**0**	**0**	**0**	**4**	**0.0**	**–2**	**0**	**0.0**	**9:06**	....	....	....	....	....	....	....	....	....
	Milwaukee	AHL	71	13	17	30	19	....	....	....	....	....	....	....	....	....	....	....	....	....	....	....	....	....	....
2002-03	Milwaukee	AHL	49	7	4	11	12	....	....	....	....	....	....	....	....	....	5	0	1	1	4	....	....	....	....
2003-04			DID NOT PLAY – INJURED																						
2004-05	Sodertalje SK	Sweden	34	0	4	4	8	....	....	....	....	....	....	....	....	....	....	....	....	....	....	....	....	....	....
	Brynas IF Gavle	Sweden	7	2	0	2	2	....	....	....	....	....	....	....	....	....	....	....	....	....	....	....	....	....	....
2005-06	Ilves Tampere	Finland	48	8	10	18	26	....	....	....	....	....	....	....	....	....	4	2	0	2	0	....	....	....	....
2006-07	HPK Hameenlinna	Finland	23	6	7	13	20	....	....	....	....	....	....	....	....	....	9	0	1	1	8	....	....	....	....
2007-08	HPK Hameenlinna	Finland	42	11	13	24	42	....	....	....	....	....	....	....	....	....	....	....	....	....	....	....	....	....	....
	Karpat Oulu	Finland	13	1	7	8	4	....	....	....	....	....	....	....	....	....	10	3	7	10	4	....	....	....	....
2008-09	Karpat Oulu	Finland	55	24	33	57	54	....	....	....	....	....	....	....	....	....	15	6	4	10	10	....	....	....	....
2009-10	Dynamo Minsk	Rus-KHL	30	7	13	20	12	....	....	....	....	....	....	....	....	....	....	....	....	....	....	....	....	....	....
2010-11	**Vancouver**	**NHL**	**4**	**0**	**0**	**0**	**0**	**0**	**0**	**0**	**1**	**0.0**	**1**	**0**	**0.0**	**6:03**	....	....	....	....	....	....	....	....	....
	Manitoba Moose	AHL	20	5	6	11	16	....	....	....	....	....	....	....	....	....	....	....	....	....	....	....	....	....	....
	Ak Bars Kazan	Rus-KHL	7	1	3	4	0	....	....	....	....	....	....	....	....	....	3	0	0	0	0	....	....	....	....
	NHL Totals		**9**	**0**	**0**	**0**	**2**	**0**	**0**	**0**	**5**	**0.0**		**0**	**0.0**	**7:45**	....	....	....	....	....	....	....	....	....

• Missed entire 2003-04 due to wrist injury in training camp, September 30, 2003. Signed as a free agent by **Sodertalje** (Sweden), April 28, 2004. Signed as a free agent by **Gavle** (Sweden), January 22, 2005. Signed as a free agent by **Ilves Tampere** (Finland), August 22, 2005. Signed as a free agent by **Hameenlinna** (Finland), April 23, 2006. Signed as a free agent by **Oulu** (Finland), January 23, 2008. Signed as a free agent by **Minsk** (Russia-KHL), April 16, 2009. Signed as a free agent by **Nashville**, July 1, 2010. Traded to **Vancouver** by **Nashville** with Ryan Parent for Shane O'Brien and Dan Gendur, October 5, 2010. Signed as a free agent by **Kazan** (Russia-KHL), January 21, 2011.

ANISIMOV, Artem
(a-NEE-see-mawv, AHR-tehm) **NYR**

Center. Shoots left. 6'4", 197 lbs. Born, Yaroslavl, USSR, May 24, 1988. NY Rangers' 2nd choice, 54th overall, in 2006 Entry Draft.

Season	Club	League	GP	G	A	Pts	PIM	PP	SH	GW	S	%	+/-	TF	F%	Min	Playoffs GP	G	A	Pts	PIM	PP	SH	GW	Min
2004-05	Yaroslavl 2	Russia-3	24	3	5	8	10	....	....	....	....	....	....	....	....	....	....	....	....	....	....	....	....	....	....
2005-06	Yaroslavl	Russia	10	0	1	1	4	....	....	....	....	....	....	....	....	....	....	....	....	....	....	....	....	....	....
	Yaroslavl 2	Russia-3	32	15	12	27	28	....	....	....	....	....	....	....	....	....	....	....	....	....	....	....	....	....	....
2006-07	Yaroslavl 2	Russia-3	2	2	0	2	0	....	....	....	....	....	....	....	....	....	....	....	....	....	....	....	....	....	....
	Yaroslavl	Russia	39	2	8	10	26	....	....	....	....	....	....	....	....	....	7	3	2	5	4	....	....	....	....
2007-08	Hartford	AHL	74	16	27	43	30	....	....	....	....	....	....	....	....	....	5	1	0	1	2	....	....	....	....
2008-09	**NY Rangers**	**NHL**	**1**	**0**	**0**	**0**	**0**	**0**	**0**	**0**	**1**	**0.0**	**0**	**5**	**40.0**	**9:27**	**1**	**0**	**0**	**0**	**0**	**0**	**0**	**0**	**5:35**
	Hartford	AHL	80	37	44	81	50	....	....	....	....	....	....	....	....	....	6	2	0	2	0	....	....	....	....
2009-10	**NY Rangers**	**NHL**	**82**	**12**	**16**	**28**	**32**	**1**	**0**	**2**	**124**	**9.7**	**–2**	**690**	**44.9**	**12:54**	....	....	....	....	....	....	....	....	....
2010-11	**NY Rangers**	**NHL**	**82**	**18**	**26**	**44**	**20**	**3**	**0**	**2**	**190**	**9.5**	**3**	**688**	**44.5**	**16:12**	**5**	**1**	**0**	**1**	**0**	**0**	**0**	**0**	**15:10**
	NHL Totals		**165**	**30**	**42**	**72**	**52**	**4**	**0**	**4**	**315**	**9.5**		**1383**	**44.7**	**14:31**	**6**	**1**	**0**	**1**	**0**	**0**	**0**	**0**	**13:34**

ANTROPOV, Nik
(an-TROH-pahv, NIHK) **WPG**

Center. Shoots left. 6'6", 245 lbs. Born, Ust-Kamenogorsk, USSR, February 18, 1980. Toronto's 1st choice, 10th overall, in 1998 Entry Draft.

Season	Club	League	GP	G	A	Pts	PIM	PP	SH	GW	S	%	+/-	TF	F%	Min	Playoffs GP	G	A	Pts	PIM	PP	SH	GW	Min
1996-97	Ust-Kamenogorsk	Russia-2	8	2	1	3	6	....	....	....	....	....	....	....	....	....	....	....	....	....	....	....	....	....	....
1997-98	Ust-Kamenogorsk	Russia-2	42	15	24	39	62	....	....	....	....	....	....	....	....	....	....	....	....	....	....	....	....	....	....
1998-99	Dynamo Moscow	Russia	30	5	9	14	30	....	....	....	....	....	....	....	....	....	11	0	1	1	4	....	....	....	....
99-2000	**Toronto**	**NHL**	**66**	**12**	**18**	**30**	**41**	**0**	**0**	**2**	**89**	**13.5**	**14**	**501**	**46.3**	**12:48**	**3**	**0**	**0**	**0**	**4**	**0**	**0**	**0**	**10:14**
	St. John's	AHL	2	0	0	0	4	....	....	....	....	....	....	....	....	....	....	....	....	....	....	....	....	....	....
2000-01	**Toronto**	**NHL**	**52**	**6**	**11**	**17**	**30**	**0**	**0**	**1**	**71**	**8.5**	**5**	**431**	**44.3**	**10:02**	**9**	**2**	**1**	**3**	**12**	**1**	**0**	**1**	**11:04**
2001-02	**Toronto**	**NHL**	**11**	**1**	**1**	**2**	**4**	**0**	**0**	**0**	**12**	**8.3**	**–1**	**31**	**38.7**	**8:57**	....	....	....	....	....	....	....	....	....
	St. John's	AHL	34	11	24	35	47	....	....	....	....	....	....	....	....	....	....	....	....	....	....	....	....	....	....
2002-03	**Toronto**	**NHL**	**72**	**16**	**29**	**45**	**124**	**2**	**1**	**6**	**102**	**15.7**	**11**	**621**	**40.1**	**15:00**	**3**	**0**	**0**	**0**	**0**	**0**	**0**	**0**	**19:17**
2003-04	**Toronto**	**NHL**	**62**	**13**	**18**	**31**	**62**	**1**	**1**	**2**	**89**	**14.6**	**7**	**309**	**40.8**	**15:18**	**13**	**0**	**2**	**2**	**18**	**0**	**0**	**0**	**15:56**
2004-05	Ak Bars Kazan	Russia	10	2	3	5	6	....	....	....	....	....	....	....	....	....	....	....	....	....	....	....	....	....	....
	Yaroslavl	Russia	26	4	15	19	44	....	....	....	....	....	....	....	....	....	9	3	4	7	18	....	....	....	....
2005-06	**Toronto**	**NHL**	**57**	**12**	**19**	**31**	**56**	**2**	**1**	**0**	**113**	**10.6**	**13**	**172**	**34.3**	**15:34**	....	....	....	....	....	....	....	....	....
	Kazakhstan	Olympics	5	1	0	1	4	....	....	....	....	....	....	....	....	....	....	....	....	....	....	....	....	....	....
2006-07	**Toronto**	**NHL**	**54**	**18**	**15**	**33**	**44**	**4**	**0**	**4**	**125**	**14.4**	**8**	**34**	**35.3**	**16:36**	....	....	....	....	....	....	....	....	....
2007-08	**Toronto**	**NHL**	**72**	**26**	**30**	**56**	**92**	**12**	**0**	**5**	**165**	**15.8**	**10**	**271**	**42.1**	**20:07**	....	....	....	....	....	....	....	....	....
2008-09	**Toronto**	**NHL**	**63**	**21**	**25**	**46**	**24**	**6**	**0**	**2**	**171**	**12.3**	**–13**	**195**	**41.0**	**17:13**	....	....	....	....	....	....	....	....	....
	NY Rangers	**NHL**	**18**	**7**	**6**	**13**	**6**	**2**	**0**	**2**	**53**	**13.2**	**–1**	**4**	**0.0**	**17:05**	**7**	**2**	**1**	**3**	**6**	**1**	**0**	**0**	**16:42**
2009-10	**Atlanta**	**NHL**	**76**	**24**	**43**	**67**	**44**	**8**	**0**	**4**	**126**	**19.0**	**13**	**1108**	**43.4**	**18:14**	....	....	....	....	....	....	....	....	....
2010-11	**Atlanta**	**NHL**	**76**	**16**	**25**	**41**	**42**	**5**	**0**	**2**	**105**	**15.2**	**–17**	**534**	**48.7**	**15:39**	....	....	....	....	....	....	....	....	....
	NHL Totals		**679**	**172**	**240**	**412**	**569**	**42**	**3**	**30**	**1221**	**14.1**		**4211**	**43.1**	**15:45**	**35**	**4**	**4**	**8**	**40**	**2**	**0**	**1**	**14:38**

Signed as a free agent by **Kazan** (Russia), October 27, 2004. Signed as a free agent by **Yaroslavl** (Russia), December 20, 2004. Traded to **NY Rangers** by **Toronto** for NY Ranger's 2nd round choice (Kenny Ryan) in 2009 Entry Draft, March 4, 2009. Signed as a free agent by **Atlanta**, July 2, 2009. • Transferred to **Winnipeg** after **Atlanta** franchise relocated, June 21, 2011.

ARMSTRONG, Colby
(AHRM-strawng, KOHL-bee) **TOR**

Right wing. Shoots right. 6'2", 195 lbs. Born, Lloydminster, Sask., November 23, 1982. Pittsburgh's 1st choice, 21st overall, in 2001 Entry Draft.

			Regular Season														Playoffs								
Season	Club	League	GP	G	A	Pts	PIM	PP	SH	GW	S	%	+/-	TF	F%	Min	GP	G	A	Pts	PIM	PP	SH	GW	Min
1998-99	Sask. Contacts	SMHL	33	21	19	40	103	....	....	....	....	....	....	....	....	....	....	....	....	....	....	....	....	....	....
	Red Deer Rebels	WHL	1	0	1	1	0	....	....	....	....	....	....	....	....	....	....	....	....	....	....	....	....	....	....
99-2000	Red Deer Rebels	WHL	68	13	25	38	122	....	....	....	....	....	....	....	....	....	2	0	1	1	11	....	....	....	....
2000-01	Red Deer Rebels	WHL	72	36	42	78	156	....	....	....	....	....	....	....	....	....	21	6	6	12	39	....	....	....	....
2001-02	Red Deer Rebels	WHL	64	27	41	68	115	....	....	....	....	....	....	....	....	....	23	6	10	16	32	....	....	....	....
2002-03	Wilkes-Barre	AHL	73	7	11	18	76	....	....	....	....	....	....	....	....	....	3	0	0	0	4	....	....	....	....
2003-04	Wilkes-Barre	AHL	67	10	17	27	71	....	....	....	....	....	....	....	....	....	24	3	1	4	45	....	....	....	....
2004-05	Wilkes-Barre	AHL	80	18	37	55	89	....	....	....	....	....	....	....	....	....	10	4	2	6	14	....	....	....	....
2005-06	**Pittsburgh**	**NHL**	**47**	**16**	**24**	**40**	**58**	**7**	**2**	**3**	**86**	**18.6**	**15**	**44**	**27.3**	**19:04**	....	....	....	....	....	....	....	....	....
	Wilkes-Barre	AHL	31	11	18	29	44	....	....	....	....	....	....	....	....	....	....	....	....	....	....	....	....	....	....
2006-07	**Pittsburgh**	**NHL**	**80**	**12**	**22**	**34**	**67**	**1**	**1**	**3**	**145**	**8.3**	**2**	**13**	**15.4**	**16:50**	**5**	**0**	**1**	**1**	**11**	**0**	**0**	**0**	**15:18**
2007-08	**Pittsburgh**	**NHL**	**54**	**9**	**15**	**24**	**50**	**0**	**0**	**2**	**84**	**10.7**	**6**	**12**	**25.0**	**15:24**	....	....	....	....	....	....	....	....	....
	Atlanta	**NHL**	**18**	**4**	**7**	**11**	**6**	**1**	**0**	**1**	**29**	**13.8**	**–2**	**3**	**0.0**	**18:02**	....	....	....	....	....	....	....	....	....
2008-09	**Atlanta**	**NHL**	**82**	**22**	**18**	**40**	**75**	**3**	**0**	**2**	**141**	**15.6**	**5**	**28**	**28.6**	**15:09**	....	....	....	....	....	....	....	....	....
2009-10	**Atlanta**	**NHL**	**79**	**15**	**14**	**29**	**61**	**0**	**1**	**1**	**101**	**14.9**	**6**	**20**	**50.0**	**14:48**	....	....	....	....	....	....	....	....	....
2010-11	**Toronto**	**NHL**	**50**	**8**	**15**	**23**	**38**	**0**	**0**	**0**	**69**	**11.6**	**–1**	**8**	**37.5**	**16:07**	....	....	....	....	....	....	....	....	....
	NHL Totals		**410**	**86**	**115**	**201**	**355**	**12**	**4**	**12**	**655**	**13.1**		**128**	**29.7**	**16:08**	**5**	**0**	**1**	**1**	**11**	**0**	**0**	**0**	**15:18**

Traded to **Atlanta** by **Pittsburgh** with Erik Christensen, Angelo Esposito and Pittsburgh's 1st round choice (Daultan Leveille) in 2008 Entry Draft for Marian Hossa and Pascal Dupuis, February 26, 2008. Signed as a free agent by **Toronto**, July 1, 2010.

ARMSTRONG, Riley
(AHRM-strawng, RIGH-lee)

Right wing. Shoots right. 5'11", 185 lbs. Born, Saskatoon, Sask., November 8, 1984.

Season	Club	League	GP	G	A	Pts	PIM	PP	SH	GW	S	%	+/-	TF	F%	Min	GP	G	A	Pts	PIM	PP	SH	GW	Min
2001-02	Yorkton Terriers	SMHL	42	43	34	77	....	....	....	....	....	....	....	....	....	....	....	....	....	....	....	....	....	....	....
2002-03	Kootenay Ice	WHL	65	6	10	16	69	....	....	....	....	....	....	....	....	....	10	0	1	1	14	....	....	....	....
2003-04	Everett Silvertips	WHL	69	18	26	44	119	....	....	....	....	....	....	....	....	....	21	5	4	9	46	....	....	....	....
2004-05	Cleveland Barons	AHL	70	8	11	19	117	....	....	....	....	....	....	....	....	....	....	....	....	....	....	....	....	....	....
2005-06	Cleveland Barons	AHL	64	4	5	9	67	....	....	....	....	....	....	....	....	....	....	....	....	....	....	....	....	....	....
2006-07	Worcester Sharks	AHL	73	19	17	36	108	....	....	....	....	....	....	....	....	....	6	0	1	1	12	....	....	....	....
2007-08	Worcester Sharks	AHL	64	15	19	34	91	....	....	....	....	....	....	....	....	....	....	....	....	....	....	....	....	....	....
2008-09	**San Jose**	**NHL**	**2**	**0**	**0**	**0**	**2**	**0**	**0**	**0**	**1**	**0.0**	**–1**	**0**	**0.0**	**7:26**	....	....	....	....	....	....	....	....	....
	Worcester Sharks	AHL	71	25	17	42	101	....	....	....	....	....	....	....	....	....	12	3	10	13	46	....	....	....	....
2009-10	Abbotsford Heat	AHL	38	11	8	19	55	....	....	....	....	....	....	....	....	....	....	....	....	....	....	....	....	....	....
	Grand Rapids	AHL	17	3	2	5	14	....	....	....	....	....	....	....	....	....	....	....	....	....	....	....	....	....	....
2010-11	Utah Grizzlies	ECHL	2	0	2	2	4	....	....	....	....	....	....	....	....	....	....	....	....	....	....	....	....	....	....
	Augsburg	Germany	17	5	3	8	40	....	....	....	....	....	....	....	....	....	....	....	....	....	....	....	....	....	....
	Barys Astana	Rus-KHL	9	1	0	1	16	....	....	....	....	....	....	....	....	....	....	....	....	....	....	....	....	....	....
	NHL Totals		**2**	**0**	**0**	**0**	**2**	**0**	**0**	**0**	**1**	**0.0**		**0**	**0.0**	**7:26**	....	....	....	....	....	....	....	....	....

Signed as a free agent by **San Jose**, September 15, 2004. Signed as a free agent by **Calgary**, July 2, 2009. Traded to **Detroit** by **Calgary** for Andy Delmore, March 3, 2010. Signed as a free agent by **Utah** (ECHL), November 6, 2010. Signed as a free agent by **Astana** (Russia-KHL), November 22, 2010. Signed as a free agent by **Augsburg** (Germany), December 29, 2010.

ARNIEL, Jamie
(ahr-NEEL, JAY-mee) **BOS**

Center. Shoots right. 5'11", 183 lbs. Born, Kingston, Ont., November 16, 1989. Boston's 4th choice, 97th overall, in 2008 Entry Draft.

Season	Club	League	GP	G	A	Pts	PIM	PP	SH	GW	S	%	+/-	TF	F%	Min	GP	G	A	Pts	PIM	PP	SH	GW	Min
2005-06	Guelph Storm	OHL	61	11	8	19	30	....	....	....	....	....	....	....	....	....	15	2	0	2	4	....	....	....	....
2006-07	Guelph Storm	OHL	68	31	31	62	51	....	....	....	....	....	....	....	....	....	4	2	2	4	0	....	....	....	....
2007-08	Guelph Storm	OHL	20	9	4	13	16	....	....	....	....	....	....	....	....	....	....	....	....	....	....	....	....	....	....
	Sarnia Sting	OHL	40	18	16	34	22	....	....	....	....	....	....	....	....	....	9	2	2	4	6	....	....	....	....
2008-09	Sarnia Sting	OHL	63	32	36	68	28	....	....	....	....	....	....	....	....	....	5	1	2	3	4	....	....	....	....
	Providence Bruins	AHL	....	....	....	....	....	....	....	....	....	....	....	....	....	....	8	1	0	1	0	....	....	....	....
2009-10	Providence Bruins	AHL	67	12	16	28	16	....	....	....	....	....	....	....	....	....	....	....	....	....	....	....	....	....	....
2010-11	**Boston**	**NHL**	**1**	**0**	**0**	**0**	**0**	**0**	**0**	**0**	**3**	**0.0**	**–1**	**0**	**0.0**	**12:26**	....	....	....	....	....	....	....	....	....
	Providence Bruins	AHL	78	23	27	50	26	....	....	....	....	....	....	....	....	....	....	....	....	....	....	....	....	....	....
	NHL Totals		**1**	**0**	**0**	**0**	**0**	**0**	**0**	**0**	**3**	**0.0**		**0**	**0.0**	**12:26**	....	....	....	....	....	....	....	....	....

ARNOTT, Jason
(AHR-nawt, JAY-suhn) **ST.L.**

Center. Shoots right. 6'5", 220 lbs. Born, Collingwood, Ont., October 11, 1974. Edmonton's 1st choice, 7th overall, in 1993 Entry Draft.

Season	Club	League	GP	G	A	Pts	PIM	PP	SH	GW	S	%	+/-	TF	F%	Min	GP	G	A	Pts	PIM	PP	SH	GW	Min
1989-90	Stayner Siskins	ON-Jr.C	34	21	31	52	12	....	....	....	....	....	....	....	....	....	....	....	....	....	....	....	....	....	....
1990-91	Lindsay Bears	ON-Jr.B	42	17	44	61	10	....	....	....	....	....	....	....	....	....	8	9	8	17	6	....	....	....	....
1991-92	Oshawa Generals	OHL	57	9	15	24	12	....	....	....	....	....	....	....	....	....	....	....	....	....	....	....	....	....	....
1992-93	Oshawa Generals	OHL	56	41	57	98	74	....	....	....	....	....	....	....	....	....	13	9	9	18	20	....	....	....	....
1993-94	**Edmonton**	**NHL**	**78**	**33**	**35**	**68**	**104**	**10**	**0**	**4**	**194**	**17.0**	**1**	....	....	....	....	....	....	....	....	....	....	....	....
1994-95	**Edmonton**	**NHL**	**42**	**15**	**22**	**37**	**128**	**7**	**0**	**1**	**156**	**9.6**	**–14**	....	....	....	....	....	....	....	....	....	....	....	....
1995-96	**Edmonton**	**NHL**	**64**	**28**	**31**	**59**	**87**	**8**	**0**	**5**	**244**	**11.5**	**–6**	....	....	....	....	....	....	....	....	....	....	....	....
1996-97	**Edmonton**	**NHL**	**67**	**19**	**38**	**57**	**92**	**10**	**1**	**2**	**248**	**7.7**	**–21**	....	....	....	**12**	**3**	**6**	**9**	**18**	**1**	**0**	**0**	....
1997-98	**Edmonton**	**NHL**	**35**	**5**	**13**	**18**	**78**	**1**	**0**	**0**	**100**	**5.0**	**–16**	....	....	....	....	....	....	....	....	....	....	....	....
	New Jersey	**NHL**	**35**	**5**	**10**	**15**	**21**	**3**	**0**	**2**	**99**	**5.1**	**–8**	....	....	....	**5**	**0**	**2**	**2**	**0**	**0**	**0**	**0**	....
1998-99	**New Jersey**	**NHL**	**74**	**27**	**27**	**54**	**79**	**8**	**0**	**3**	**200**	**13.5**	**10**	**872**	**49.3**	**15:24**	**7**	**2**	**2**	**4**	**4**	**1**	**0**	**0**	**16:48**
99-2000♦	**New Jersey**	**NHL**	**76**	**22**	**34**	**56**	**51**	**7**	**0**	**4**	**244**	**9.0**	**22**	**1172**	**46.9**	**17:05**	**23**	**8**	**12**	**20**	**18**	**3**	**0**	**1**	**16:29**
2000-01	**New Jersey**	**NHL**	**54**	**21**	**34**	**55**	**75**	**8**	**0**	**3**	**138**	**15.2**	**23**	**760**	**49.6**	**16:12**	**23**	**8**	**7**	**15**	**16**	***5**	**0**	**0**	**15:49**
2001-02	**New Jersey**	**NHL**	**63**	**22**	**19**	**41**	**59**	**8**	**0**	**1**	**169**	**13.0**	**3**	**934**	**47.8**	**17:13**	....	....	....	....	....	....	....	....	....
	Dallas	**NHL**	**10**	**3**	**1**	**4**	**6**	**2**	**0**	**2**	**28**	**10.7**	**–1**	**77**	**52.0**	**18:13**	....	....	....	....	....	....	....	....	....
2002-03	**Dallas**	**NHL**	**72**	**23**	**24**	**47**	**51**	**7**	**0**	**6**	**169**	**13.6**	**9**	**1130**	**53.3**	**16:12**	**11**	**3**	**2**	**5**	**6**	**1**	**0**	**0**	**15:35**
2003-04	**Dallas**	**NHL**	**73**	**21**	**36**	**57**	**66**	**5**	**0**	**5**	**143**	**14.7**	**23**	**1203**	**53.0**	**17:00**	**5**	**1**	**1**	**2**	**2**	**1**	**0**	**0**	**17:23**
2004-05				DID NOT PLAY																					
2005-06	**Dallas**	**NHL**	**81**	**32**	**44**	**76**	**102**	**11**	**1**	**5**	**167**	**19.2**	**13**	**1306**	**51.2**	**17:12**	**5**	**0**	**3**	**3**	**4**	**0**	**0**	**0**	**20:04**
2006-07	**Nashville**	**NHL**	**68**	**27**	**27**	**54**	**48**	**12**	**0**	**6**	**190**	**14.2**	**15**	**1145**	**50.6**	**17:59**	**5**	**2**	**1**	**3**	**2**	**1**	**0**	**0**	**19:17**
2007-08	**Nashville**	**NHL**	**79**	**28**	**44**	**72**	**54**	**13**	**0**	**3**	**248**	**11.3**	**19**	**1260**	**48.7**	**18:59**	**4**	**1**	**0**	**1**	**4**	**0**	**0**	**1**	**18:29**
2008-09	**Nashville**	**NHL**	**65**	**33**	**24**	**57**	**49**	**9**	**0**	**5**	**196**	**16.8**	**2**	**1037**	**50.6**	**18:55**	....	....	....	....	....	....	....	....	....
2009-10	**Nashville**	**NHL**	**63**	**19**	**27**	**46**	**26**	**6**	**0**	**3**	**216**	**8.8**	**0**	**1077**	**48.8**	**18:42**	**6**	**2**	**0**	**2**	**0**	**1**	**0**	**0**	**17:51**
2010-11	**New Jersey**	**NHL**	**62**	**13**	**11**	**24**	**32**	**2**	**0**	**0**	**139**	**9.4**	**–9**	**750**	**51.3**	**15:27**	....	....	....	....	....	....	....	....	....
	Washington	**NHL**	**11**	**4**	**3**	**7**	**8**	**2**	**0**	**1**	**30**	**13.3**	**3**	**144**	**44.4**	**15:53**	**9**	**1**	**5**	**6**	**2**	**1**	**0**	**0**	**16:02**
	NHL Totals		**1172**	**400**	**504**	**904**	**1216**	**139**	**2**	**61**	**3318**	**12.1**		**12867**	**50.1**	**17:12**	**115**	**31**	**41**	**72**	**76**	**15**	**0**	**2**	**16:45**

NHL All-Rookie Team (1994)

Played in NHL All-Star Game (1997, 2008)

Traded to **New Jersey** by **Edmonton** with Bryan Muir for Valeri Zelepukin and Bill Guerin, January 4, 1998. Traded to **Dallas** by **New Jersey** with Randy McKay and New Jersey's 1st round choice (later traded to Columbus, later traded to Buffalo – Buffalo selected Daniel Paille) in 2002 Entry Draft for Joe Nieuwendyk and Jamie Langenbrunner, March 19, 2002. Signed as a free agent by **Nashville**, July 2, 2006. Traded to **New Jersey** by **Nashville** for Matt Halischuk and New Jersey's 2nd round choice (Magnus Hellberg) in 2011 Entry Draft, June 19, 2010. Traded to **Washington** by **New Jersey** for David Steckel and Washington's 2nd round choice in 2012 Entry Draft, February 28, 2011. Signed as a free agent by **St. Louis**, July 6, 2011.

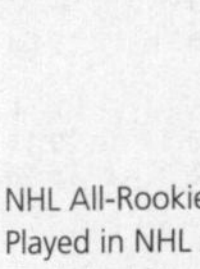

ARSENE, Dean
(ahr-SEH-nee, DEEN) **PHX**

Defense. Shoots left. 6'2", 195 lbs. Born, Abbotsford, B.C., July 20, 1980.

Season	Club	League	GP	G	A	Pts	PIM	PP	SH	GW	S	%	+/-	TF	F%	Min	GP	G	A	Pts	PIM	PP	SH	GW	Min
1996-97	Regina Pats	WHL	62	0	8	8	53	....	....	....	....	....	....	....	....	....	3	0	0	0	2	....	....	....	....
1997-98	Regina Pats	WHL	31	2	7	9	47	....	....	....	....	....	....	....	....	....	....	....	....	....	....	....	....	....	....
	Edmonton Ice	WHL	43	0	12	12	90	....	....	....	....	....	....	....	....	....	....	....	....	....	....	....	....	....	....
1998-99	Kootenay Ice	WHL	68	1	4	5	111	....	....	....	....	....	....	....	....	....	4	0	0	0	4	....	....	....	....
99-2000	Kootenay Ice	WHL	66	4	7	11	150	....	....	....	....	....	....	....	....	....	21	1	2	3	59	....	....	....	....
2000-01	Kootenay Ice	WHL	68	1	10	11	178	....	....	....	....	....	....	....	....	....	11	0	1	1	34	....	....	....	....
2001-02	Charlotte	ECHL	63	3	10	13	101	....	....	....	....	....	....	....	....	....	5	0	2	2	16	....	....	....	....
2002-03	Hartford	AHL	50	1	3	4	94	....	....	....	....	....	....	....	....	....	....	....	....	....	....	....	....	....	....
2003-04	Hershey Bears	AHL	22	0	2	2	44	....	....	....	....	....	....	....	....	....	....	....	....	....	....	....	....	....	....
	Reading Royals	ECHL	46	0	6	6	118	....	....	....	....	....	....	....	....	....	15	1	5	6	34	....	....	....	....

			Regular Season														Playoffs								
Season	Club	League	GP	G	A	Pts	PIM	PP	SH	GW	S	%	+/-	TF	F%	Min	GP	G	A	Pts	PIM	PP	SH	GW	Min
2004-05	Hershey Bears	AHL	56	1	5	6	140	....	....	....	....	....	....	....	....	....	....	....	....	....	....	....	....	....	....
2005-06	Hershey Bears	AHL	68	2	5	7	181	....	....	....	....	....	....	....	....	....	21	0	1	1	29	....	....	....	....
2006-07	Hershey Bears	AHL	61	3	12	15	187	....	....	....	....	....	....	....	....	....	6	0	2	2	8	....	....	....	....
2007-08	Hershey Bears	AHL	14	0	2	2	23	....	....	....	....	....	....	....	....	....	....	....	....	....	....	....	....	....	....
2008-09	Hershey Bears	AHL	46	1	10	11	99	....	....	....	....	....	....	....	....	....	22	0	2	2	14	....	....	....	....
2009-10	**Edmonton**	**NHL**	**13**	**0**	**0**	**0**	**41**	**0**	**0**	**0**	**4**	**0.0**	**–3**	**0**	**0.0**	**12:57**	....	....	....	....	....	....	....	....	....
	Springfield	AHL	56	2	9	11	100	....	....	....	....	....	....	....	....	....	....	....	....	....	....	....	....	....	....
2010-11	Peoria Rivermen	AHL	77	1	10	11	137	....	....	....	....	....	....	....	....	....	4	0	0	0	6	....	....	....	....
	NHL Totals		**13**	**0**	**0**	**0**	**41**	**0**	**0**	**0**	**4**	**0.0**		**0**	**0.0**	**12:57**	....	....	....	....	....	....	....	....	....

Signed as a free agent by **Washington**, July 26, 2006. Signed as a free agent by **Edmonton**, July 16, 2009. Signed as a free agent by **St. Louis**, August 11, 2010. Signed as a free agent by **Phoenix**, July 6, 2011.

ARTYUKHIN, Evgeny

(ahr-TYEW-khin, ehv-GEH-nee)

Right wing. Shoots left. 6'4", 255 lbs. Born, Moscow, USSR, April 4, 1983. Tampa Bay's 4th choice, 94th overall, in 2001 Entry Draft.

99-2000	Vityaz Podolsk 2	Russia-3	26	9	8	17	46	....	....	....	....	....	....	....	....	....	....	....	....	....	....	....	....	....	....
	Vityaz Podolsk	Russia-2	3	0	0	0	2	....	....	....	....	....	....	....	....	....	....	....	....	....	....	....	....	....	....
2000-01	Vityaz Podolsk	Russia	24	0	1	1	14	....	....	....	....	....	....	....	....	....	....	....	....	....	....	....	....	....	....
2001-02	Vityaz Podolsk 2	Russia-3	4	3	1	4	6	....	....	....	....	....	....	....	....	....	....	....	....	....	....	....	....	....	....
	Vityaz Podolsk	Russia-2	49	15	7	22	94	....	....	....	....	....	....	....	....	....	12	0	1	1	18	....	....	....	....
2002-03	Moncton Wildcats	QMJHL	53	13	27	40	204	....	....	....	....	....	....	....	....	....	6	1	2	3	29	....	....	....	....
2003-04	Hershey Bears	AHL	36	3	3	6	111	....	....	....	....	....	....	....	....	....	....	....	....	....	....	....	....	....	....
	Pensacola	ECHL	6	1	0	1	14	....	....	....	....	....	....	....	....	....	....	....	....	....	....	....	....	....	....
2004-05	Springfield	AHL	62	9	19	28	142	....	....	....	....	....	....	....	....	....	....	....	....	....	....	....	....	....	....
2005-06	**Tampa Bay**	**NHL**	**72**	**4**	**13**	**17**	**90**	**1**	**0**	**0**	**79**	**5.1**	**–4**	**0**	**0.0**	**8:43**	**5**	**1**	**0**	**1**	**6**	**0**	**0**	**0**	**8:14**
	Springfield	AHL	4	2	1	3	4	....	....	....	....	....	....	....	....	....	....	....	....	....	....	....	....	....	....
2006-07	Yaroslavl	Russia	44	5	8	13	183	....	....	....	....	....	....	....	....	....	1	0	0	0	0	....	....	....	....
2007-08	Avangard Omsk	Russia	19	3	2	5	40	....	....	....	....	....	....	....	....	....	....	....	....	....	....	....	....	....	....
	CSKA Moscow	Russia	23	3	5	8	99	....	....	....	....	....	....	....	....	....	6	4	0	4	6	....	....	....	....
2008-09	**Tampa Bay**	**NHL**	**73**	**6**	**10**	**16**	**151**	**1**	**0**	**0**	**100**	**6.0**	**1**	**2**	**0.0**	**10:40**	....	....	....	....	....	....	....	....	....
2009-10	**Anaheim**	**NHL**	**37**	**4**	**5**	**9**	**41**	**0**	**0**	**0**	**21**	**19.0**	**0**	**1**	**0.0**	**9:04**	....	....	....	....	....	....	....	....	....
	Atlanta	**NHL**	**17**	**5**	**2**	**7**	**31**	**0**	**0**	**0**	**21**	**23.8**	**–4**	**1**	**100.0**	**8:39**	....	....	....	....	....	....	....	....	....
2010-11	St. Petersburg	Rus-KHL	26	4	5	9	115	....	....	....	....	....	....	....	....	....	11	2	1	3	6	....	....	....	....
	NHL Totals		**199**	**19**	**30**	**49**	**313**	**2**	**0**	**0**	**221**	**8.6**		**4**	**25.0**	**9:30**	**5**	**1**	**0**	**1**	**6**	**0**	**0**	**0**	**8:14**

Signed as a free agent by **Yaroslavl** (Russia), August 5, 2006. Signede as a free agent by **Omsk** (Russia), July 26, 2007. • Transferred to **CSKA Moscow** (Russia) from **Omsk** (Russia), October 24 2007. Traded to **Anaheim** by **Tampa Bay** for Drew Miller and Anaheim's 3rd round choice (Adam Janosik) in 2010 Entry Draft, August 13, 2009. Traded to **Atlanta** by **Anaheim** for Nathan Oystrick and future considerations, March 1, 2010. Signed as a free agent by **St. Petersburg** (Russia-KHL), November 2, 2010.

ASHAM, Arron

(ASH-uhm, AIR-ruhn) **PIT**

Right wing. Shoots right. 5'11", 205 lbs. Born, Portage La Prairie, Man., April 13, 1978. Montreal's 3rd choice, 71st overall, in 1996 Entry Draft.

1993-94	Portage	MAHA	21	18	19	37	82	....	....	....	....	....	....	....	....	....	....	....	....	....	....	....	....	....	....
1994-95	Red Deer Rebels	WHL	62	11	16	27	126	....	....	....	....	....	....	....	....	....	....	....	....	....	....	....	....	....	....
1995-96	Red Deer Rebels	WHL	70	32	45	77	174	....	....	....	....	....	....	....	....	....	10	6	3	9	20	....	....	....	....
1996-97	Red Deer Rebels	WHL	67	45	51	96	149	....	....	....	....	....	....	....	....	....	16	12	14	26	36	....	....	....	....
1997-98	Red Deer Rebels	WHL	67	43	49	92	153	....	....	....	....	....	....	....	....	....	5	0	2	2	8	....	....	....	....
	Fredericton	AHL	2	1	1	2	0	....	....	....	....	....	....	....	....	....	2	0	1	1	0	....	....	....	....
1998-99	**Montreal**	**NHL**	**7**	**0**	**0**	**0**	**0**	**0**	**0**	**0**	**5**	**0.0**	**–4**	**0**	**0.0**	**7:27**	....	....	....	....	....	....	....	....	....
	Fredericton	AHL	60	16	18	34	118	....	....	....	....	....	....	....	....	....	13	8	6	14	11	....	....	....	....
99-2000	**Montreal**	**NHL**	**33**	**4**	**2**	**6**	**24**	**0**	**1**	**1**	**29**	**13.8**	**–7**	**1**	**0.0**	**10:14**	....	....	....	....	....	....	....	....	....
	Quebec Citadelles	AHL	13	4	5	9	32	....	....	....	....	....	....	....	....	....	2	0	0	0	2	....	....	....	....
2000-01	**Montreal**	**NHL**	**46**	**2**	**3**	**5**	**59**	**0**	**0**	**0**	**32**	**6.3**	**–9**	**3**	**100.0**	**8:28**	....	....	....	....	....	....	....	....	....
	Quebec Citadelles	AHL	15	7	9	16	51	....	....	....	....	....	....	....	....	....	7	1	2	3	2	....	....	....	....
2001-02	**Montreal**	**NHL**	**35**	**5**	**4**	**9**	**55**	**0**	**0**	**0**	**30**	**16.7**	**7**	**4**	**25.0**	**8:13**	**3**	**0**	**1**	**1**	**0**	**0**	**0**	**0**	**5:39**
	Quebec Citadelles	AHL	24	9	14	23	35	....	....	....	....	....	....	....	....	....	....	....	....	....	....	....	....	....	....
2002-03	**NY Islanders**	**NHL**	**78**	**15**	**19**	**34**	**57**	**4**	**0**	**1**	**114**	**13.2**	**1**	**17**	**41.2**	**12:13**	**5**	**0**	**0**	**0**	**16**	**0**	**0**	**0**	**15:09**
2003-04	**NY Islanders**	**NHL**	**79**	**12**	**12**	**24**	**92**	**1**	**0**	**0**	**108**	**11.1**	**–12**	**23**	**34.8**	**13:13**	**5**	**0**	**1**	**1**	**4**	**0**	**0**	**0**	**8:44**
2004-05	EHC Visp	Swiss-2	5	2	4	6	6	....	....	....	....	....	....	....	....	....	4	1	1	2	8	....	....	....	....
2005-06	**NY Islanders**	**NHL**	**63**	**9**	**15**	**24**	**103**	**2**	**1**	**0**	**99**	**9.1**	**–5**	**63**	**41.3**	**13:33**	....	....	....	....	....	....	....	....	....
2006-07	**NY Islanders**	**NHL**	**80**	**11**	**12**	**23**	**63**	**0**	**0**	**2**	**85**	**12.9**	**3**	**10**	**60.0**	**9:20**	**5**	**1**	**0**	**1**	**0**	**0**	**0**	**0**	**10:08**
2007-08	**New Jersey**	**NHL**	**77**	**6**	**4**	**10**	**84**	**0**	**0**	**2**	**68**	**8.8**	**–6**	**3**	**0.0**	**8:33**	**5**	**0**	**1**	**1**	**2**	**0**	**0**	**0**	**5:04**
2008-09	**Philadelphia**	**NHL**	**78**	**8**	**12**	**20**	**155**	**0**	**0**	**1**	**74**	**10.8**	**0**	**15**	**46.7**	**8:45**	**6**	**1**	**1**	**2**	**6**	**0**	**0**	**1**	**7:55**
2009-10	**Philadelphia**	**NHL**	**72**	**10**	**14**	**24**	**126**	**0**	**0**	**2**	**91**	**11.0**	**–2**	**13**	**15.4**	**10:04**	**23**	**4**	**3**	**7**	**10**	**0**	**0**	**0**	**11:14**
2010-11	**Pittsburgh**	**NHL**	**44**	**5**	**6**	**11**	**46**	**0**	**0**	**0**	**60**	**8.3**	**0**	**9**	**33.3**	**9:33**	**7**	**3**	**1**	**4**	**2**	**0**	**0**	**0**	**10:00**
	NHL Totals		**692**	**87**	**103**	**190**	**864**	**7**	**2**	**9**	**795**	**10.9**		**161**	**39.1**	**10:20**	**59**	**9**	**8**	**17**	**40**	**0**	**0**	**1**	**9:58**

Traded to **NY Islanders** by **Montreal** with Montreal's 5th round choice (Marcus Paulsson) in 2002 Entry Draft for Mariusz Czerkawski, June 22, 2002. Signed as a free agent by **Visp** (Swiss-2), January 19, 2005. Signed as a free agent by **New Jersey**, August 7, 2007. Signed as a free agent by **Philadelphia**, July 7, 2008. Signed as a free agent by **Pittsburgh**, August 20, 2010.

AUCOIN, Adrian

(oh-KOIN, AY-dree-uhn) **PHX**

Defense. Shoots right. 6'2", 217 lbs. Born, Ottawa, Ont., July 3, 1973. Vancouver's 7th choice, 117th overall, in 1992 Entry Draft.

1989-90	Nepean Raiders	CJHL	54	2	14	16	95	....	....	....	....	....	....	....	....	....	4	0	1	1	....	....	....	....	....
1990-91	Nepean Raiders	CJHL	56	17	33	50	125	....	....	....	....	....	....	....	....	....	....	....	....	....	....	....	....	....	....
1991-92	Boston University	H-East	32	2	10	12	60	....	....	....	....	....	....	....	....	....	....	....	....	....	....	....	....	....	....
1992-93	Canada	Nat-Tm	42	8	10	18	71	....	....	....	....	....	....	....	....	....	....	....	....	....	....	....	....	....	....
1993-94	Canada	Nat-Tm	59	5	12	17	80	....	....	....	....	....	....	....	....	....	....	....	....	....	....	....	....	....	....
	Canada	Olympics	4	0	0	0	2	....	....	....	....	....	....	....	....	....	....	....	....	....	....	....	....	....	....
	Hamilton	AHL	13	1	2	3	19	....	....	....	....	....	....	....	....	....	4	0	2	2	6	....	....	....	....
1994-95	Syracuse Crunch	AHL	71	13	18	31	52	....	....	....	....	....	....	....	....	....	....	....	....	....	....	....	....	....	....
	Vancouver	**NHL**	**1**	**1**	**0**	**1**	**0**	**0**	**0**	**0**	**2**	**50.0**	**1**	....	....	....	**4**	**1**	**0**	**1**	**0**	**1**	**0**	**0**	....
1995-96	**Vancouver**	**NHL**	**49**	**4**	**14**	**18**	**34**	**2**	**0**	**0**	**85**	**4.7**	**8**	....	....	....	**6**	**0**	**0**	**0**	**2**	**0**	**0**	**0**	....
	Syracuse Crunch	AHL	29	5	13	18	47	....	....	....	....	....	....	....	....	....	....	....	....	....	....	....	....	....	....
1996-97	**Vancouver**	**NHL**	**70**	**5**	**16**	**21**	**63**	**1**	**0**	**0**	**116**	**4.3**	**0**	....	....	....	....	....	....	....	....	....	....	....	....
1997-98	**Vancouver**	**NHL**	**35**	**3**	**3**	**6**	**21**	**1**	**0**	**1**	**44**	**6.8**	**–4**	....	....	....	....	....	....	....	....	....	....	....	....
1998-99	**Vancouver**	**NHL**	**82**	**23**	**11**	**34**	**77**	**18**	**2**	**3**	**174**	**13.2**	**–14**	**1**	**100.0**	**23:52**	....	....	....	....	....	....	....	....	....
99-2000	**Vancouver**	**NHL**	**57**	**10**	**14**	**24**	**30**	**4**	**0**	**1**	**126**	**7.9**	**7**	**0**	**0.0**	**23:06**	....	....	....	....	....	....	....	....	....
2000-01	**Vancouver**	**NHL**	**47**	**3**	**13**	**16**	**20**	**1**	**0**	**0**	**99**	**3.0**	**13**	**0**	**0.0**	**18:21**	....	....	....	....	....	....	....	....	....
	Tampa Bay	**NHL**	**26**	**1**	**11**	**12**	**25**	**1**	**0**	**0**	**60**	**1.7**	**–8**	**0**	**0.0**	**23:34**	....	....	....	....	....	....	....	....	....
2001-02	**NY Islanders**	**NHL**	**81**	**12**	**22**	**34**	**62**	**7**	**0**	**1**	**232**	**5.2**	**23**	**0**	**0.0**	**28:54**	**7**	**2**	**5**	**7**	**4**	**2**	**0**	**0**	**32:19**
2002-03	**NY Islanders**	**NHL**	**73**	**8**	**27**	**35**	**70**	**5**	**0**	**1**	**175**	**4.6**	**–5**	**0**	**0.0**	**29:01**	**5**	**1**	**2**	**3**	**4**	**0**	**0**	**0**	**31:43**
2003-04	**NY Islanders**	**NHL**	**81**	**13**	**31**	**44**	**54**	**4**	**0**	**2**	**213**	**6.1**	**29**	**0**	**0.0**	**26:38**	**5**	**0**	**0**	**0**	**6**	**0**	**0**	**0**	**28:21**
2004-05	MODO	Sweden	14	2	4	6	32	....	....	....	....	....	....	....	....	....	6	1	0	1	16	....	....	....	....
2005-06	**Chicago**	**NHL**	**33**	**1**	**5**	**6**	**38**	**1**	**0**	**0**	**59**	**1.7**	**–13**	**0**	**0.0**	**22:58**	....	....	....	....	....	....	....	....	....
2006-07	**Chicago**	**NHL**	**59**	**4**	**12**	**16**	**50**	**2**	**0**	**3**	**96**	**4.2**	**–22**	**0**	**0.0**	**20:50**	....	....	....	....	....	....	....	....	....
2007-08	**Calgary**	**NHL**	**76**	**10**	**25**	**35**	**37**	**5**	**0**	**1**	**121**	**8.3**	**13**	**0**	**0.0**	**20:58**	**7**	**0**	**3**	**3**	**4**	**0**	**0**	**0**	**18:13**
2008-09	**Calgary**	**NHL**	**81**	**10**	**24**	**34**	**46**	**3**	**0**	**3**	**126**	**7.9**	**–8**	**0**	**0.0**	**22:18**	**6**	**2**	**1**	**3**	**2**	**0**	**0**	**0**	**21:10**
2009-10	**Phoenix**	**NHL**	**82**	**8**	**20**	**28**	**56**	**1**	**0**	**2**	**144**	**5.6**	**2**	**1**	**100.0**	**22:33**	**7**	**0**	**2**	**2**	**10**	**0**	**0**	**0**	**21:16**
2010-11	**Phoenix**	**NHL**	**75**	**3**	**19**	**22**	**52**	**0**	**0**	**0**	**99**	**3.0**	**18**	**1**	**100.0**	**21:40**	**4**	**0**	**0**	**0**	**2**	**0**	**0**	**0**	**19:17**
	NHL Totals		**1008**	**119**	**267**	**386**	**735**	**56**	**2**	**18**	**1971**	**6.0**		**3**	**100.0**	**23:43**	**51**	**6**	**13**	**19**	**34**	**3**	**0**	**0**	**24:34**

Played in NHL All-Star Game (2004)

• Missed majority of 1997-98 due to ankle (October 4, 1997 vs. Anaheim) and groin (November 1, 1997 vs. Pittsburgh) injuries. Traded to **Tampa Bay** by **Vancouver** with Vancouver's 2nd round choice (Alexander Polushin) in 2001 Entry Draft for Dan Cloutier, February 7, 2001. Traded to **NY Islanders** by **Tampa Bay** with Alexander Kharitonov for Mathieu Biron and NY Islanders' 2nd round choice (later traded to Washington, later traded to Vancouver – Vancouver selected Denis Grot) in 2002 Entry Draft, June 22, 2001. Signed as a free agent by **MODO** (Sweden), December 21, 2004. Signed as a free agent by **Chicago**, August 2, 2005. Traded to **Calgary** by **Chicago** with Chicago's 7th round choice (C.J. Severyn) in 2007 Entry Draft for Andrei Zyuzin and Steve Marr, June 22, 2007. Signed as a free agent by **Phoenix**, July 2, 2009.

			Regular Season														Playoffs								
Season	Club	League	GP	G	A	Pts	PIM	PP	SH	GW	S	%	+/-	TF	F%	Min	GP	G	A	Pts	PIM	PP	SH	GW	Min

AUCOIN, Keith

(oh-KOIN, KEETH) **WSH**

Center. Shoots right. 5'9", 162 lbs. Born, Waltham, MA, November 6, 1978.

Season	Club	League	GP	G	A	Pts	PIM	PP	SH	GW	S	%	+/-	TF	F%	Min	GP	G	A	Pts	PIM	PP	SH	GW	Min
1997-98	Norwich U.	ECAC-3	26	19	14	33	....	....	....	....	....	....	....	....	....	....	....	....	....	....	....	....	....	....	....
1998-99	Norwich U.	ECAC-3	31	33	39	72	....	....	....	....	....	....	....	....	....	....	....	....	....	....	....	....	....	....	....
99-2000	Norwich U.	ECAC-3	31	36	41	77	14	....	....	....	....	....	....	....	....	....	....	....	....	....	....	....	....	....	....
2000-01	Norwich U.	ECAC-3	28	26	30	56	26	....	....	....	....	....	....	....	....	....	....	....	....	....	....	....	....	....	....
2001-02	Lowell	AHL	30	6	10	16	8	....	....	....	....	....	....	....	....	....	....	....	....	....	....	....	....	....	....
	Florida Everblades	ECHL	1	0	2	2	0	....	....	....	....	....	....	....	....	....	....	....	....	....	....	....	....	....	....
	BC Icemen	UHL	44	23	35	58	42	....	....	....	....	....	....	....	....	....	10	3	5	8	4	....	....	....	....
2002-03	Providence Bruins	AHL	78	25	49	74	71	....	....	....	....	....	....	....	....	....	4	0	1	1	6	....	....	....	....
2003-04	Cincinnati	AHL	80	18	30	48	64	....	....	....	....	....	....	....	....	....	9	0	3	3	4	....	....	....	....
2004-05	Memphis	CHL	5	4	5	9	10	....	....	....	....	....	....	....	....	....	....	....	....	....	....	....	....	....	....
	Providence Bruins	AHL	72	21	45	66	49	....	....	....	....	....	....	....	....	....	17	4	*14	18	18	....	....	....	....
2005-06	**Carolina**	**NHL**	**7**	**0**	**1**	**1**	**4**	**0**	**0**	**0**	**3**	**0.0**	**–4**	**4**	**100.0**	**5:19**	....	....	....	....	....	....	....	....	....
	Lowell	AHL	72	29	56	85	68	....	....	....	....	....	....	....	....	....	....	....	....	....	....	....	....	....	....
2006-07	**Carolina**	**NHL**	**8**	**0**	**1**	**1**	**0**	**0**	**0**	**0**	**6**	**0.0**	**1**	**29**	**65.5**	**6:17**	....	....	....	....	....	....	....	....	....
	Albany River Rats	AHL	65	27	72	99	108	....	....	....	....	....	....	....	....	....	5	1	3	4	7	....	....	....	....
2007-08	**Carolina**	**NHL**	**38**	**5**	**8**	**13**	**10**	**0**	**0**	**0**	**65**	**7.7**	**3**	**327**	**37.9**	**13:28**	....	....	....	....	....	....	....	....	....
	Albany River Rats	AHL	38	8	37	45	38	....	....	....	....	....	....	....	....	....	....	....	....	....	....	....	....	....	....
2008-09	**Washington**	**NHL**	**12**	**2**	**4**	**6**	**4**	**1**	**0**	**0**	**15**	**13.3**	**5**	**83**	**39.8**	**10:19**	....	....	....	....	....	....	....	....	....
	Hershey Bears	AHL	70	25	*71	96	73	....	....	....	....	....	....	....	....	....	21	5	*18	23	16	....	....	....	....
2009-10	**Washington**	**NHL**	**9**	**1**	**4**	**5**	**0**	**0**	**0**	**0**	**4**	**25.0**	**–2**	**56**	**55.4**	**8:48**	....	....	....	....	....	....	....	....	....
	Hershey Bears	AHL	72	35	*71	*106	49	....	....	....	....	....	....	....	....	....	21	2	*23	25	2	....	....	....	....
2010-11	**Washington**	**NHL**	**1**	**0**	**0**	**0**	**0**	**0**	**0**	**0**	**0**	**0.0**	**0**	**3**	**33.3**	**11:47**	....	....	....	....	....	....	....	....	....
	Hershey Bears	AHL	53	18	54	72	49	....	....	....	....	....	....	....	....	....	6	2	6	8	2	....	....	....	....
	NHL Totals		**75**	**8**	**18**	**26**	**18**	**1**	**0**	**0**	**93**	**8.6**	....	**502**	**42.2**	**10:51**	....	....	....	....	....	....	....	....	....

ECAC-3 First All-Star Team (2000, 2001) • ECAC-3 Player of the Year (2000, 2001) • AHL Second All-Star Team (2006, 2007, 2011) • AHL First All-Star Team (2009, 2010) • John B. Sollenberger Trophy (AHL – Leading Scorer) (2010) • Les Cunningham Award (AHL – MVP) (2010)

Signed as a free agent by **Lowell** (AHL), June 19, 2001. Signed as a free agent by **Providence** (AHL), August 2, 2002. Signed as a free agent by **Anaheim**, August 29, 2003. Signed to a PTO (professional tryout) contract by **Providence** (AHL), November 4, 2004, Signed as a free agent by **Providence** (AHL), December 9, 2004. Signed as a free agent by **Carolina**, August 4, 2005. Signed as a free agent by **Washington**, July 3, 2008.

AULIE, Keith

(AW-lee, KEETH) **TOR**

Defense. Shoots left. 6'5", 217 lbs. Born, Rouleau, Sask., June 11, 1989. Calgary's 3rd choice, 116th overall, in 2007 Entry Draft.

Season	Club	League	GP	G	A	Pts	PIM	PP	SH	GW	S	%	+/-	TF	F%	Min	GP	G	A	Pts	PIM	PP	SH	GW	Min
2004-05	Notre Dame	SJHL	38	2	7	9	53	....	....	....	....	....	....	....	....	....	....	....	....	....	....	....	....	....	....
2005-06	Brandon	WHL	38	0	2	2	32	....	....	....	....	....	....	....	....	....	4	0	0	0	4	....	....	....	....
2006-07	Brandon	WHL	66	1	8	9	82	....	....	....	....	....	....	....	....	....	11	0	2	2	14	....	....	....	....
2007-08	Brandon	WHL	72	5	12	17	81	....	....	....	....	....	....	....	....	....	6	0	3	3	11	....	....	....	....
2008-09	Brandon	WHL	58	6	27	33	83	....	....	....	....	....	....	....	....	....	12	2	7	9	12	....	....	....	....
2009-10	Abbotsford Heat	AHL	43	2	4	6	32	....	....	....	....	....	....	....	....	....	....	....	....	....	....	....	....	....	....
	Toronto Marlies	AHL	5	0	0	0	6	....	....	....	....	....	....	....	....	....	....	....	....	....	....	....	....	....	....
2010-11	**Toronto**	**NHL**	**40**	**2**	**0**	**2**	**32**	**0**	**0**	**0**	**32**	**6.3**	**–1**	**0**	**0.0**	**19:08**	....	....	....	....	....	....	....	....	....
	Toronto Marlies	AHL	36	3	6	9	61	....	....	....	....	....	....	....	....	....	....	....	....	....	....	....	....	....	....
	NHL Totals		**40**	**2**	**0**	**2**	**32**	**0**	**0**	**0**	**32**	**6.3**		**0**	**0.0**	**19:08**	....	....	....	....	....	....	....	....	....

WHL East First All-Star Team (2009)

Traded to **Toronto** by **Calgary** with Dion Phaneuf and Fredrik Sjostrom for Matt Stajan, Niklas Hagman, Jamal Mayers and Ian White, January 31, 2010.

AVERY, Sean

(AY-vuhr-ee, SHAWN) **NYR**

Center. Shoots left. 5'10", 195 lbs. Born, Pickering, Ont., April 10, 1980.

Season	Club	League	GP	G	A	Pts	PIM	PP	SH	GW	S	%	+/-	TF	F%	Min	GP	G	A	Pts	PIM	PP	SH	GW	Min
1995-96	Markham	Minor-ON	70	34	81	115	180	....	....	....	....	....	....	....	....	....	....	....	....	....	....	....	....	....	....
	Markham Waxers	ON-Jr.A	1	0	0	0	4	....	....	....	....	....	....	....	....	....	....	....	....	....	....	....	....	....	....
1996-97	Owen Sound	OHL	58	10	21	31	86	....	....	....	....	....	....	....	....	....	4	1	0	1	4	....	....	....	....
1997-98	Owen Sound	OHL	47	13	41	54	105	....	....	....	....	....	....	....	....	....	....	....	....	....	....	....	....	....	....
1998-99	Owen Sound	OHL	28	22	23	45	70	....	....	....	....	....	....	....	....	....	....	....	....	....	....	....	....	....	....
	Kingston	OHL	33	14	25	39	88	....	....	....	....	....	....	....	....	....	5	1	3	4	13	....	....	....	....
99-2000	Kingston	OHL	55	28	56	84	215	....	....	....	....	....	....	....	....	....	5	2	2	4	26	....	....	....	....
2000-01	Cincinnati	AHL	58	8	15	23	304	....	....	....	....	....	....	....	....	....	4	1	0	1	19	....	....	....	....
2001-02	**Detroit**	**NHL**	**36**	**2**	**2**	**4**	**68**	**0**	**0**	**1**	**30**	**6.7**	**1**	**299**	**51.8**	**7:51**	....	....	....	....	....	....	....	....	....
	Cincinnati	AHL	36	14	7	21	106	....	....	....	....	....	....	....	....	....	....	....	....	....	....	....	....	....	....
2002-03	**Detroit**	**NHL**	**39**	**5**	**6**	**11**	**120**	**0**	**0**	**2**	**40**	**12.5**	**7**	**224**	**58.0**	**7:03**	....	....	....	....	....	....	....	....	....
	Grand Rapids	AHL	15	6	6	12	82	....	....	....	....	....	....	....	....	....	....	....	....	....	....	....	....	....	....
	Los Angeles	**NHL**	**12**	**1**	**3**	**4**	**33**	**0**	**0**	**0**	**19**	**5.3**	**0**	**49**	**46.9**	**13:50**	....	....	....	....	....	....	....	....	....
	Manchester	AHL	....	....	....	....	....	....	....	....	....	....	....	....	....	....	3	2	1	3	8	....	....	....	....
2003-04	**Los Angeles**	**NHL**	**76**	**9**	**19**	**28**	***261**	**0**	**0**	**2**	**125**	**7.2**	**2**	**124**	**54.8**	**11:41**	....	....	....	....	....	....	....	....	....
2004-05	Pelicans Lahti	Finland	2	3	0	3	26	....	....	....	....	....	....	....	....	....	....	....	....	....	....	....	....	....	....
	Motor City	UHL	16	15	11	26	149	....	....	....	....	....	....	....	....	....	....	....	....	....	....	....	....	....	....
2005-06	**Los Angeles**	**NHL**	**75**	**15**	**24**	**39**	***257**	**1**	**3**	**1**	**189**	**7.9**	**–5**	**226**	**44.3**	**13:37**	....	....	....	....	....	....	....	....	....
2006-07	**Los Angeles**	**NHL**	**55**	**10**	**18**	**28**	**116**	**1**	**1**	**2**	**160**	**6.3**	**–10**	**180**	**47.2**	**16:52**	....	....	....	....	....	....	....	....	....
	NY Rangers	**NHL**	**29**	**8**	**12**	**20**	**58**	**1**	**0**	**0**	**89**	**9.0**	**11**	**110**	**52.7**	**17:49**	**10**	**1**	**4**	**5**	**27**	**0**	**0**	**0**	**19:27**
2007-08	**NY Rangers**	**NHL**	**57**	**15**	**18**	**33**	**154**	**2**	**0**	**4**	**125**	**12.0**	**6**	**28**	**39.3**	**15:50**	**8**	**4**	**3**	**7**	**6**	**1**	**0**	**1**	**14:14**
2008-09	**Dallas**	**NHL**	**23**	**3**	**7**	**10**	**77**	**0**	**0**	**0**	**49**	**6.1**	**2**	**12**	**41.7**	**14:59**	....	....	....	....	....	....	....	....	....
	Hartford	AHL	8	2	1	3	8	....	....	....	....	....	....	....	....	....	....	....	....	....	....	....	....	....	....
	NY Rangers	**NHL**	**18**	**5**	**7**	**12**	**34**	**2**	**0**	**0**	**50**	**10.0**	**4**	**6**	**66.7**	**16:44**	**6**	**0**	**2**	**2**	**24**	**0**	**0**	**0**	**17:38**
2009-10	**NY Rangers**	**NHL**	**69**	**11**	**20**	**31**	**160**	**3**	**0**	**1**	**139**	**7.9**	**0**	**14**	**28.6**	**13:23**	....	....	....	....	....	....	....	....	....
2010-11	**NY Rangers**	**NHL**	**76**	**3**	**21**	**24**	**174**	**0**	**0**	**1**	**137**	**2.2**	**–4**	**24**	**62.5**	**11:14**	**4**	**0**	**1**	**1**	**12**	**0**	**0**	**0**	**12:22**
	NHL Totals		**565**	**87**	**157**	**244**	**1512**	**10**	**4**	**14**	**1152**	**7.6**		**1296**	**50.8**	**13:06**	**28**	**5**	**10**	**15**	**69**	**1**	**0**	**1**	**16:34**

Signed as a free agent by **Detroit**, September 21, 1999. Traded to **Los Angeles** by **Detroit** with Maxim Kuznetsov, Detroit's 1st round choice (Jeff Tambellini) in 2003 Entry Draft and Detroit's 2nd round choice (later traded to Boston – Boston selected Martins Karsums) in 2004 Entry Draft for Mathieu Schneider, March 11, 2003. Signed as a free agent by **Lahti** (Finland), November 24, 2004. Signed as a free agent by **Motor City** (UHL), February 11, 2005. Traded to **NY Rangers** by **Los Angeles** with John Seymour for Jason Ward, Jan Marek, Marc-Andre Cliche and NY Rangers' 3rd round choice (later traded to Buffalo - Buffalo selected Corey Fienhage) in 2008 Entry Draft, February 5, 2007. Signed as a free agent by **Dallas**, July 2, 2008. Claimed on waivers by **NY Rangers** from **Dallas**, March 3, 2009.

BABCHUK, Anton

(bab-CHUHK, AN-tawn) **CGY**

Defense. Shoots right. 6'5", 212 lbs. Born, Kiev, USSR, May 6, 1984. Chicago's 1st choice, 21st overall, in 2002 Entry Draft.

Season	Club	League	GP	G	A	Pts	PIM	PP	SH	GW	S	%	+/-	TF	F%	Min	GP	G	A	Pts	PIM	PP	SH	GW	Min
99-2000	Elektrostal 2	Russia-3	6	0	0	0	8	....	....	....	....	....	....	....	....	....	....	....	....	....	....	....	....	....	....
	Elektrostal 2	Russia-3	18	0	1	1	18	....	....	....	....	....	....	....	....	....	....	....	....	....	....	....	....	....	....
2000-01	Elektrostal	Russia-2	7	0	0	0	12	....	....	....	....	....	....	....	....	....	....	....	....	....	....	....	....	....	....
	Russia 17	Nat-Tm	15	1	3	4	12	....	....	....	....	....	....	....	....	....	....	....	....	....	....	....	....	....	....
2001-02	Elektrostal	Russia-2	40	7	8	15	90	....	....	....	....	....	....	....	....	....	....	....	....	....	....	....	....	....	....
	Elektrostal 2	Russia-3	3	0	0	0	8	....	....	....	....	....	....	....	....	....	....	....	....	....	....	....	....	....	....
2002-03	Ak Bars Kazan	Russia	10	0	0	0	4	....	....	....	....	....	....	....	....	....	....	....	....	....	....	....	....	....	....
	St. Petersburg	Russia	20	3	0	3	10	....	....	....	....	....	....	....	....	....	....	....	....	....	....	....	....	....	....
	Spartak St. Pet.	Russia-2	1	1	0	1	0	....	....	....	....	....	....	....	....	....	....	....	....	....	....	....	....	....	....
2003-04	**Chicago**	**NHL**	**5**	**0**	**2**	**2**	**2**	**0**	**0**	**0**	**11**	**0.0**	**–1**	**0**	**0.0**	**12:43**	....	....	....	....	....	....	....	....	....
	Norfolk Admirals	AHL	73	8	14	22	89	....	....	....	....	....	....	....	....	....	8	0	2	2	6	....	....	....	....
2004-05	Norfolk Admirals	AHL	66	8	16	24	88	....	....	....	....	....	....	....	....	....	2	0	0	0	2	....	....	....	....
2005-06	**Chicago**	**NHL**	**17**	**2**	**3**	**5**	**16**	**1**	**0**	**0**	**24**	**8.3**	**–5**	**0**	**0.0**	**16:38**	....	....	....	....	....	....	....	....	....
	Norfolk Admirals	AHL	24	5	7	12	22	....	....	....	....	....	....	....	....	....	....	....	....	....	....	....	....	....	....
	♦ **Carolina**	**NHL**	**22**	**3**	**2**	**5**	**6**	**2**	**0**	**0**	**32**	**9.4**	**–2**	**0**	**0.0**	**13:22**	....	....	....	....	....	....	....	....	....
	Lowell	AHL	5	1	3	4	0	....	....	....	....	....	....	....	....	....	....	....	....	....	....	....	....	....	....
2006-07	**Carolina**	**NHL**	**52**	**2**	**12**	**14**	**30**	**0**	**0**	**2**	**63**	**3.2**	**–6**	**0**	**0.0**	**17:26**	....	....	....	....	....	....	....	....	....
	Albany River Rats	AHL	9	1	6	7	2	....	....	....	....	....	....	....	....	....	....	....	....	....	....	....	....	....	....
2007-08	Avangard Omsk	Russia	57	9	17	26	30	....	....	....	....	....	....	....	....	....	4	1	1	2	6	....	....	....	....
2008-09	**Carolina**	**NHL**	**72**	**16**	**19**	**35**	**16**	**9**	**0**	**4**	**127**	**12.6**	**13**	**0**	**0.0**	**18:04**	**13**	**0**	**1**	**1**	**10**	**0**	**0**	**0**	**16:03**
2009-10	Omsk	Rus-KHL	49	9	13	22	36	....	....	....	....	....	....	....	....	....	2	0	0	0	0	....	....	....	....

			Regular Season														Playoffs								
Season	Club	League	GP	G	A	Pts	PIM	PP	SH	GW	S	%	+/-	TF	F%	Min	GP	G	A	Pts	PIM	PP	SH	GW	Min
2010-11	**Carolina**	**NHL**	**17**	**3**	**5**	**8**	**12**	**1**	**0**	**1**	**45**	**6.7**	**–4**	**0**	**0.0**	**19:07**									
	Calgary	**NHL**	**65**	**8**	**19**	**27**	**20**	**5**	**1**	**1**	**87**	**9.2**	**18**	**0**	**0.0**	**15:37**									
	NHL Totals		**250**	**34**	**62**	**96**	**102**	**18**	**1**	**8**	**389**	**8.7**		**0**	**0.0**	**16:45**	**13**	**0**	**1**	**1**	**10**	**0**	**0**	**0**	**16:03**

Traded to **Carolina** by **Chicago** for Danny Richmond and Columbus' 4th round choice (previously acquired, later traded to Toronto - Toronto selected James Reimer) in 2006 Entry Draft, January 20, 2006. Signed as a free agent by **Omsk** (Russia-KHL), September 20, 2009. Traded to **Calgary** by **Carolina** with Tom Kostopoulos for Ian White and Brett Sutter, November 17, 2010.

BACKES, David
(BA-kuhs, DAY-vihd) **ST.L.**

Center. Shoots right. 6'3", 225 lbs. Born, Blaine, MN, May 1, 1984. St. Louis' 2nd choice, 62nd overall, in 2003 Entry Draft.

Season	Club	League	GP	G	A	Pts	PIM	PP	SH	GW	S	%	+/-	TF	F%	Min	GP	G	A	Pts	PIM	PP	SH	GW	Min
99-2000	Spring Lake Park	High-MN	24	17	20	37																			
2000-01	Spring Lake Park	High-MN	24	29	46	75																			
2001-02	Chicago Steel	USHL	25	31	36	67											2	1	1	2					
	Lincoln Stars	USHL	30	11	10	21	54										3	0	0	0	2				
2002-03	Lincoln Stars	USHL	57	28	41	69	126										7	4	1	5	17				
2003-04	Minnesota State	WCHA	39	16	21	37	66																		
2004-05	Minnesota State	WCHA	38	17	23	40	55																		
2005-06	Minnesota State	WCHA	38	13	29	42	91																		
	Peoria Rivermen	AHL	12	5	5	10	10										3	1	1	2	8				
2006-07	**St. Louis**	**NHL**	**49**	**10**	**13**	**23**	**37**	**2**	**0**	**2**	**89**	**11.2**	**6**	**26**	**46.2**	**13:25**									
	Peoria Rivermen	AHL	31	10	3	13	47																		
2007-08	**St. Louis**	**NHL**	**72**	**13**	**18**	**31**	**99**	**3**	**0**	**2**	**129**	**10.1**	**–11**	**67**	**44.8**	**14:41**									
2008-09	**St. Louis**	**NHL**	**82**	**31**	**23**	**54**	**165**	**6**	**2**	**1**	**208**	**14.9**	**–3**	**477**	**44.4**	**17:41**	**4**	**1**	**2**	**3**	**10**	**0**	**0**	**0**	**22:56**
2009-10	**St. Louis**	**NHL**	**79**	**17**	**31**	**48**	**106**	**5**	**0**	**3**	**163**	**10.4**	**–4**	**1065**	**47.3**	**18:18**									
	United States	Olympics	6	1	2	3	2																		
2010-11	**St. Louis**	**NHL**	**82**	**31**	**31**	**62**	**93**	**5**	**0**	**2**	**211**	**14.7**	**32**	**1138**	**44.5**	**19:42**									
	NHL Totals		**364**	**102**	**116**	**218**	**500**	**21**	**2**	**10**	**800**	**12.8**		**2773**	**45.6**	**17:06**	**4**	**1**	**2**	**3**	**10**	**0**	**0**	**0**	**22:56**

USHL First All-Star Team (2003) • WCHA All-Rookie Team (2004) • WCHA Second All-Star Team (2006) • NCAA West Second All-American Team (2006)
Played in NHL All-Star Game (2011)

BACKLUND, Mikael
(BAHK-luhnd, mih-KIGH-ehl) **CGY**

Center. Shoots left. 6', 196 lbs. Born, Vasteras, Sweden, March 17, 1989. Calgary's 1st choice, 24th overall, in 2007 Entry Draft.

Season	Club	League	GP	G	A	Pts	PIM	PP	SH	GW	S	%	+/-	TF	F%	Min	GP	G	A	Pts	PIM	PP	SH	GW	Min
2004-05	Vasteras U18	Swe-U18	14	5	6	11	14										4	2	1	3	2				
2005 06	Vasteras Jr.	Swe-Jr.	25	15	16	31	30																		
	VIK Vasteras HK	Sweden-2	12	2	2	4	14																		
2006-07	Vasteras U18	Swe-U18	2	2	1	3	2										1	0	0	0	10				
	Vasteras Jr.	Swe-Jr.	7	5	4	9	8										5	1	0	1	4				
	VIK Vasteras HK	Sweden-2	18	1	2	3	14																		
2007-08	Vasteras Jr.	Swe-Jr.	9	7	6	13	20																		
	VIK Vasteras HK	Sweden-2	46	11	4	15	28										5	4	3	7	0				
2008-09	Vasteras Jr.	Swe-Jr.	2	3	2	5	0																		
	VIK Vasteras HK	Sweden-2	17	4	4	8	39																		
	Calgary	**NHL**	**1**	**0**	**0**	**0**	**0**	**0**	**0**	**0**	**1**	**0.0**	**0**	**7**	**28.6**	**10:44**									
	Kelowna Rockets	WHL	28	12	18	30	26										19	*13	10	23	26				
2009-10	**Calgary**	**NHL**	**23**	**1**	**9**	**10**	**6**	**0**	**0**	**0**	**47**	**2.1**	**5**	**191**	**53.4**	**12:36**									
	Abbotsford Heat	AHL	54	15	17	32	26										13	1	8	9	14				
2010-11	**Calgary**	**NHL**	**73**	**10**	**15**	**25**	**18**	**2**	**0**	**1**	**144**	**6.9**	**4**	**664**	**48.0**	**12:05**									
	Abbotsford Heat	AHL	1	0	0	0	0																		
	NHL Totals		**97**	**11**	**24**	**35**	**24**	**2**	**0**	**1**	**192**	**5.7**		**862**	**49.1**	**12:11**									

• Assigned to **Vasteras** (Sweden-2) by **Calgary**, October 4, 2008.

BACKSTROM, Nicklas
(BAK-struhm, NIHK-luhs) **WSH**

Center. Shoots left. 6'1", 210 lbs. Born, Gavle, Sweden, November 23, 1987. Washington's 1st choice, 4th overall, in 2006 Entry Draft.

Season	Club	League	GP	G	A	Pts	PIM	PP	SH	GW	S	%	+/-	TF	F%	Min	GP	G	A	Pts	PIM	PP	SH	GW	Min
2001-02	Brynas U18	Swe-U18	2	0	0	0	0																		
2002-03	Brynas U18	Swe-U18	STATISTICS NOT AVAILABLE																						
2003-04	Brynas U18	Swe-U18	6	9	5	14	4										3	0	3	3	0				
	Brynas IF Gavle Jr.	Swe-Jr.	21	2	6	8	2										5	0	0	0	4				
2004-05	Brynas IF Gavle Jr.	Swe-Jr.	29	17	17	34	24																		
	Brynas IF Gavle	Sweden	19	0	0	0	2																		
2005-06	Brynas IF Gavle	Sweden	46	10	16	26	30										4	1	0	1	2				
	Brynas IF Gavle Jr.	Swe-Jr.															1	0	0	0	2				
2006-07	Brynas IF Gavle	Sweden	45	12	28	40	46										7	3	3	6	6				
2007-08	**Washington**	**NHL**	**82**	**14**	**55**	**69**	**24**	**3**	**0**	**4**	**153**	**9.2**	**13**	**874**	**46.3**	**19:00**	**7**	**4**	**2**	**6**	**2**	**3**	**0**	**0**	**20:26**
2008-09	**Washington**	**NHL**	**82**	**22**	**66**	**88**	**46**	**14**	**0**	**1**	**174**	**12.6**	**16**	**1171**	**48.7**	**19:57**	**14**	**3**	**12**	**15**	**8**	**2**	**0**	**0**	**21:40**
2009-10	**Washington**	**NHL**	**82**	**33**	**68**	**101**	**50**	**11**	**0**	**4**	**222**	**14.9**	**37**	**1336**	**49.9**	**20:27**	**7**	**5**	**4**	**9**	**4**	**0**	**0**	**1**	**21:03**
	Sweden	Olympics	4	1	5	6	0																		
2010-11	**Washington**	**NHL**	**77**	**18**	**47**	**65**	**40**	**4**	**1**	**2**	**202**	**8.9**	**24**	**1315**	**52.5**	**20:36**	**9**	**0**	**2**	**2**	**4**	**0**	**0**	**0**	**23:18**
	NHL Totals		**323**	**87**	**236**	**323**	**160**	**32**	**1**	**11**	**751**	**11.6**		**4696**	**49.7**	**19:59**	**37**	**12**	**20**	**32**	**18**	**5**	**0**	**1**	**21:43**

NHL All-Rookie Team (2008)

BAGNALL, Drew
(BAG-nuhl, DROO) **MIN**

Defense. Shoots left. 6'3", 220 lbs. Born, Oakbank, Man., October 26, 1983. Dallas' 9th choice, 195th overall, in 2003 Entry Draft.

Season	Club	League	GP	G	A	Pts	PIM	PP	SH	GW	S	%	+/-	TF	F%	Min	GP	G	A	Pts	PIM	PP	SH	GW	Min
2000-01	Battlefords	SJHL	58	7	20	27	205																		
2001-02	Battlefords	SJHL	60	16	23	39	247																		
2002-03	Battlefords	SJHL	55	17	46	63	248										4	0	1	1	4				
2003-04	St. Lawrence	ECAC	40	5	13	18	61																		
2004-05	St. Lawrence	ECAC	37	7	12	19	68																		
2005-06	St. Lawrence	ECAC	24	1	9	10	32																		
2006-07	St. Lawrence	ECAC	39	6	19	25	74																		
2007-08	Manchester	AHL	54	1	11	12	115										4	0	0	0	4				
	Reading Royals	ECHL	10	1	2	3	32																		
2008-09	Manchester	AHL	79	0	6	6	150																		
2009-10	Manchester	AHL	58	2	10	12	113										16	0	3	3	21				
2010-11	**Minnesota**	**NHL**	**2**	**0**	**0**	**0**	**4**	**0**	**0**	**0**	**1**	**0.0**	**–2**	**0**	**0.0**	**13:00**									
	Houston Aeros	AHL	72	0	2	2	112										24	1	1	2	22				
	NHL Totals		**2**	**0**	**0**	**0**	**4**	**0**	**0**	**0**	**1**	**0.0**		**0**	**0.0**	**13:00**									

Traded to **Florida** by **Dallas** with Dallas' 2nd round compensatory choice (later traded to Phoenix - Phoenix selected Enver Lisin) in 2004 Entry Draft for Valeri Bure, March 8, 2004. Signed as a free agent by **Los Angeles**, August 23, 2007. Signed as a free agent by **Minnesota**, July 2, 2010.

BAILEY, Josh
(BAY-lee, JAWSH) **NYI**

Center. Shoots left. 6'1", 201 lbs. Born, Bowmanville, Ont., October 2, 1989. NY Islanders' 1st choice, 9th overall, in 2008 Entry Draft.

Season	Club	League	GP	G	A	Pts	PIM	PP	SH	GW	S	%	+/-	TF	F%	Min	GP	G	A	Pts	PIM	PP	SH	GW	Min
2004-05	Clarington	Minor-ON	69	53	59	112	38																		
2005-06	Owen Sound	OHL	55	7	19	26	8										11	0	0	0	0				
2006-07	Owen Sound	OHL	27	11	15	26	8																		
	Windsor Spitfires	OHL	42	11	24	35	16																		
2007-08	Windsor Spitfires	OHL	67	29	67	96	32										5	1	5	6	2				
2008-09	**NY Islanders**	**NHL**	**68**	**7**	**18**	**25**	**16**	**3**	**0**	**0**	**74**	**9.5**	**–14**	**807**	**41.1**	**15:29**									
2009-10	**NY Islanders**	**NHL**	**73**	**16**	**19**	**35**	**18**	**3**	**1**	**2**	**112**	**14.3**	**5**	**426**	**40.1**	**15:09**									
2010-11	**NY Islanders**	**NHL**	**70**	**11**	**17**	**28**	**37**	**5**	**0**	**2**	**102**	**10.8**	**–13**	**615**	**44.4**	**17:50**									
	Bridgeport	AHL	11	6	11	17	4																		
	NHL Totals		**211**	**34**	**54**	**88**	**71**	**11**	**1**	**4**	**288**	**11.8**		**1848**	**42.0**	**16:09**									

BALLARD, Keith (BAL-uhrd, KEETH) VAN

Defense. Shoots left. 5'11", 208 lbs. Born, Baudette, MN, November 26, 1982. Buffalo's 1st choice, 11th overall, in 2002 Entry Draft.

			Regular Season														Playoffs								
Season	Club	League	GP	G	A	Pts	PIM	PP	SH	GW	S	%	+/-	TF	F%	Min	GP	G	A	Pts	PIM	PP	SH	GW	Min
99-2000	USNTDP	U-18	6	1	1	2	4	....	....	....	....	....	....	....	....	....	....	....	....	....	....	....	....	....	....
	USNTDP	USHL	58	12	21	33	119	....	....	....	....	....	....	....	....	....	....	....	....	....	....	....	....	....	....
2000-01	Omaha Lancers	USHL	56	22	29	51	168	....	....	....	....	....	....	....	....	....	10	1	6	7	8	....	....	....	....
2001-02	U. of Minnesota	WCHA	41	10	13	23	42	....	....	....	....	....	....	....	....	....	....	....	....	....	....	....	....	....	....
2002-03	U. of Minnesota	WCHA	41	12	29	41	78	....	....	....	....	....	....	....	....	....	....	....	....	....	....	....	....	....	....
2003-04	U. of Minnesota	WCHA	37	11	25	36	83	....	....	....	....	....	....	....	....	....	....	....	....	....	....	....	....	....	....
2004-05	Utah Grizzlies	AHL	60	2	18	20	88	....	....	....	....	....	....	....	....	....	....	....	....	....	....	....	....	....	....
2005-06	**Phoenix**	**NHL**	**82**	**8**	**31**	**39**	**99**	**1**	**3**	**1**	**102**	**7.8**	**-18**	**0**	**0.0**	**19:59**	....	....	....	....	....	....	....	....	....
2006-07	**Phoenix**	**NHL**	**69**	**5**	**22**	**27**	**59**	**2**	**0**	**0**	**79**	**6.3**	**-7**	**0**	**0.0**	**22:00**	....	....	....	....	....	....	....	....	....
2007-08	**Phoenix**	**NHL**	**82**	**6**	**15**	**21**	**85**	**2**	**1**	**1**	**105**	**5.7**	**7**	**0**	**0.0**	**21:16**	....	....	....	....	....	....	....	....	....
2008-09	**Florida**	**NHL**	**82**	**6**	**28**	**34**	**72**	**1**	**0**	**1**	**106**	**5.7**	**14**	**1**	**0.0**	**22:23**	....	....	....	....	....	....	....	....	....
2009-10	**Florida**	**NHL**	**82**	**8**	**20**	**28**	**88**	**1**	**0**	**1**	**90**	**8.9**	**-7**	**0**	**0.0**	**22:24**	....	....	....	....	....	....	....	....	....
2010-11	**Vancouver**	**NHL**	**65**	**2**	**5**	**7**	**53**	**0**	**0**	**0**	**53**	**3.8**	**10**	**0**	**0.0**	**15:54**	**10**	**0**	**0**	**0**	**6**	**0**	**0**	**0**	**14:14**
	NHL Totals		**462**	**35**	**121**	**156**	**456**	**7**	**4**	**4**	**535**	**6.5**		**1**	**0.0**	**20:48**	**10**	**0**	**0**	**0**	**6**	**0**	**0**	**0**	**14:14**

USHL First All-Star Team (2001) • WCHA All-Rookie Team (2002) • WCHA First All-Star Team (2003, 2004) • NCAA West First All-American Team (2004)

Traded to **Colorado** by **Buffalo** for Steve Reinprecht, July 3, 2003. Traded to **Phoenix** by **Colorado** with Derek Morris for Ossi Vaananen, Chris Gratton and Phoenix's 2nd round choice (Paul Stastny) in 2005 Entry Draft, March 9, 2004. Traded to **Florida** by **Phoenix** with Nick Boynton and Ottawa's 2nd round choice (previously acquired, later traded back to Phoenix - Phoenix selected Jared Staal) in 2008 Entry Draft for Olli Jokinen, June 20, 2008. Traded to **Vancouver** by **Florida** with Victor Oreskovich for Steve Bernier, Michael Grabner and Vancouver's 1st round choice (Quinton Howden) in 2010 Entry Draft, June 25, 2010.

BARANKA, Ivan (ba-RAN-kuh, IGH-vuhn) NYR

Defense. Shoots left. 6'3", 205 lbs. Born, Ilava, Czech., May 19, 1985. NY Rangers' 2nd choice, 50th overall, in 2003 Entry Draft.

Season	Club	League	GP	G	A	Pts	PIM	PP	SH	GW	S	%	+/-	TF	F%	Min	GP	G	A	Pts	PIM	PP	SH	GW	Min
2002-03	Dubnica Jr.	Slovak-Jr.	27	1	7	8	44	....	....	....	....	....	....	....	....	....	....	....	....	....	....	....	....	....	....
	Dubnica	Slovak-2	2	0	0	0	0	....	....	....	....	....	....	....	....	....	....	....	....	....	....	....	....	....	....
2003-04	Everett Silvertips	WHL	58	3	12	15	69	....	....	....	....	....	....	....	....	....	20	3	5	8	26	....	....	....	....
2004-05	Everett Silvertips	WHL	64	7	16	23	64	....	....	....	....	....	....	....	....	....	11	3	1	4	6	....	....	....	....
	Hartford	AHL	....	....	....	....	....	....	....	....	....	....	....	....	....	....	1	0	0	0	0	....	....	....	....
2005-06	Hartford	AHL	59	5	16	21	87	....	....	....	....	....	....	....	....	....	....	....	....	....	....	....	....	....	....
2006-07	Hartford	AHL	54	3	20	23	50	....	....	....	....	....	....	....	....	....	....	....	....	....	....	....	....	....	....
2007-08	**NY Rangers**	**NHL**	**1**	**0**	**1**	**1**	**0**	**0**	**0**	**0**	**1**	**0.0**	**1**	**0**	**0.0**	**12:44**	....	....	....	....	....	....	....	....	....
	Hartford	AHL	61	5	21	26	53	....	....	....	....	....	....	....	....	....	5	0	2	2	2	....	....	....	....
2008-09	Spartak Moscow	Rus-KHL	47	2	8	10	50	....	....	....	....	....	....	....	....	....	6	1	2	3	6	....	....	....	....
2009-10	Spartak Moscow	Rus-KHL	55	10	22	32	56	....	....	....	....	....	....	....	....	....	10	2	2	4	12	....	....	....	....
	Slovakia	Olympics	7	1	0	1	0	....	....	....	....	....	....	....	....	....	....	....	....	....	....	....	....	....	....
2010-11	Spartak Moscow	Rus-KHL	50	8	9	17	48	....	....	....	....	....	....	....	....	....	3	1	2	3	4	....	....	....	....
	NHL Totals		**1**	**0**	**1**	**1**	**0**	**0**	**0**	**0**	**1**	**0.0**		**0**	**0.0**	**12:44**	....	....	....	....	....	....	....	....	....

Signed as a free agent by **Spartak Moscow** (Russia-KHL), May 13, 2008.

BARCH, Krys (BAHRCH, KRIHS) DAL

Right wing. Shoots left. 6'1", 209 lbs. Born, Hamilton, Ont., March 26, 1980. Washington's 3rd choice, 106th overall, in 1998 Entry Draft.

Season	Club	League	GP	G	A	Pts	PIM	PP	SH	GW	S	%	+/-	TF	F%	Min	GP	G	A	Pts	PIM	PP	SH	GW	Min
1995-96	Georgetown	OPJHL	41	6	8	14	10	....	....	....	....	....	....	....	....	....	....	....	....	....	....	....	....	....	....
1996-97	Georgetown	OPJHL	51	18	26	44	58	....	....	....	....	....	....	....	....	....	....	....	....	....	....	....	....	....	....
1997-98	London Knights	OHL	65	9	27	36	62	....	....	....	....	....	....	....	....	....	16	4	3	7	16	....	....	....	....
1998-99	London Knights	OHL	66	18	20	38	66	....	....	....	....	....	....	....	....	....	25	9	17	26	15	....	....	....	....
99-2000	London Knights	OHL	56	23	26	49	78	....	....	....	....	....	....	....	....	....	....	....	....	....	....	....	....	....	....
	Portland Pirates	AHL	....	....	....	....	....	....	....	....	....	....	....	....	....	....	4	0	2	2	2	....	....	....	....
2000-01	Portland Pirates	AHL	76	10	15	25	91	....	....	....	....	....	....	....	....	....	2	0	0	0	0	....	....	....	....
2001-02	Portland Pirates	AHL	29	3	8	11	28	....	....	....	....	....	....	....	....	....	....	....	....	....	....	....	....	....	....
	Richmond	ECHL	25	6	4	10	43	....	....	....	....	....	....	....	....	....	....	....	....	....	....	....	....	....	....
2002-03	Portland Pirates	AHL	36	1	7	8	49	....	....	....	....	....	....	....	....	....	....	....	....	....	....	....	....	....	....
2003-04			DID NOT PLAY																						
2004-05	Norfolk Admirals	AHL	9	1	0	1	37	....	....	....	....	....	....	....	....	....	....	....	....	....	....	....	....	....	....
	Greenville	ECHL	55	11	19	30	154	....	....	....	....	....	....	....	....	....	3	0	0	0	36	....	....	....	....
2005-06	Iowa Stars	AHL	43	7	6	13	129	....	....	....	....	....	....	....	....	....	7	0	1	1	37	....	....	....	....
	Greenville	ECHL	14	10	4	14	75	....	....	....	....	....	....	....	....	....	....	....	....	....	....	....	....	....	....
2006-07	**Dallas**	**NHL**	**26**	**3**	**2**	**5**	**107**	**0**	**0**	**2**	**12**	**25.0**	**2**	**1**	**0.0**	**5:38**	....	....	....	....	....	....	....	....	....
	Iowa Stars	AHL	31	3	5	8	110	....	....	....	....	....	....	....	....	....	....	....	....	....	....	....	....	....	....
2007-08	**Dallas**	**NHL**	**48**	**1**	**2**	**3**	**105**	**0**	**0**	**0**	**23**	**4.3**	**-3**	**2**	**0.0**	**6:30**	**3**	**0**	**0**	**0**	**2**	**0**	**0**	**0**	**2:21**
2008-09	**Dallas**	**NHL**	**72**	**4**	**5**	**9**	**133**	**0**	**0**	**1**	**27**	**14.8**	**1**	**7**	**28.6**	**6:27**	....	....	....	....	....	....	....	....	....
2009-10	**Dallas**	**NHL**	**63**	**0**	**6**	**6**	**130**	**0**	**0**	**0**	**29**	**0.0**	**0**	**3**	**0.0**	**7:03**	....	....	....	....	....	....	....	....	....
2010-11	**Dallas**	**NHL**	**44**	**2**	**1**	**3**	**80**	**0**	**0**	**0**	**16**	**12.5**	**-7**	**4**	**50.0**	**5:13**	....	....	....	....	....	....	....	....	....
	NHL Totals		**253**	**10**	**16**	**26**	**555**	**0**	**0**	**3**	**107**	**9.3**		**17**	**23.5**	**6:19**	**3**	**0**	**0**	**0**	**2**	**0**	**0**	**0**	**2:21**

Signed as a free agent by **Dallas**, July 18, 2006.

BARKER, Cam (BAR-kuhr, KAM) EDM

Defense. Shoots left. 6'3", 215 lbs. Born, Winnipeg, Man., April 4, 1986. Chicago's 1st choice, 3rd overall, in 2004 Entry Draft.

Season	Club	League	GP	G	A	Pts	PIM	PP	SH	GW	S	%	+/-	TF	F%	Min	GP	G	A	Pts	PIM	PP	SH	GW	Min
2001-02	Cornwall Colts	CJHL	72	6	23	29	132	....	....	....	....	....	....	....	....	....	....	....	....	....	....	....	....	....	....
	Medicine Hat	WHL	3	0	1	1	0	....	....	....	....	....	....	....	....	....	....	....	....	....	....	....	....	....	....
2002-03	Medicine Hat	WHL	64	10	37	47	79	....	....	....	....	....	....	....	....	....	11	3	4	7	17	....	....	....	....
2003-04	Medicine Hat	WHL	69	21	44	65	105	....	....	....	....	....	....	....	....	....	20	3	9	12	18	....	....	....	....
2004-05	Medicine Hat	WHL	52	15	33	48	99	....	....	....	....	....	....	....	....	....	12	3	3	6	16	....	....	....	....
2005-06	**Chicago**	**NHL**	**1**	**0**	**0**	**0**	**0**	**0**	**0**	**0**	**1**	**0.0**	**0**	**0**	**0.0**	**11:02**	....	....	....	....	....	....	....	....	....
	Medicine Hat	WHL	26	5	13	18	63	....	....	....	....	....	....	....	....	....	13	4	8	12	*59	....	....	....	....
2006-07	**Chicago**	**NHL**	**35**	**1**	**7**	**8**	**44**	**1**	**0**	**0**	**38**	**2.6**	**-12**	**0**	**0.0**	**19:19**	....	....	....	....	....	....	....	....	....
	Norfolk Admirals	AHL	34	5	10	15	53	....	....	....	....	....	....	....	....	....	6	1	3	4	13	....	....	....	....
2007-08	**Chicago**	**NHL**	**45**	**6**	**12**	**18**	**52**	**2**	**0**	**0**	**42**	**14.3**	**-3**	**0**	**0.0**	**17:12**	....	....	....	....	....	....	....	....	....
	Rockford IceHogs	AHL	29	8	11	19	67	....	....	....	....	....	....	....	....	....	....	....	....	....	....	....	....	....	....
2008-09	**Chicago**	**NHL**	**68**	**6**	**34**	**40**	**65**	**5**	**0**	**1**	**101**	**5.9**	**-6**	**1**	**0.0**	**18:20**	**17**	**3**	**6**	**9**	**2**	**0**	**0**	**0**	**16:39**
	Rockford IceHogs	AHL	7	3	2	5	6	....	....	....	....	....	....	....	....	....	....	....	....	....	....	....	....	....	....
2009-10	**Chicago**	**NHL**	**51**	**4**	**10**	**14**	**58**	**3**	**0**	**1**	**74**	**5.4**	**7**	**0**	**0.0**	**13:06**	....	....	....	....	....	....	....	....	....
	Minnesota	**NHL**	**19**	**1**	**6**	**7**	**10**	**1**	**0**	**0**	**31**	**3.2**	**-2**	**0**	**0.0**	**22:02**	....	....	....	....	....	....	....	....	....
2010-11	**Minnesota**	**NHL**	**52**	**1**	**4**	**5**	**34**	**0**	**0**	**1**	**44**	**2.3**	**-10**	**0**	**0.0**	**16:24**	....	....	....	....	....	....	....	....	....
	NHL Totals		**271**	**19**	**73**	**92**	**263**	**12**	**0**	**3**	**331**	**5.7**		**1**	**0.0**	**17:09**	**17**	**3**	**6**	**9**	**2**	**0**	**0**	**0**	**16:39**

Traded to **Minnesota** by **Chicago** for Kim Johnsson and Nick Leddy, February 12, 2010. Signed as a free agent by **Edmonton**, July 1, 2011.

BARTKOWSKI, Matt (bahrt-KOW-skee, MATT) BOS

Defense. Shoots left. 6'1", 196 lbs. Born, Pittsburgh, PA, June 4, 1988. Florida's 5th choice, 190th overall, in 2008 Entry Draft.

Season	Club	League	GP	G	A	Pts	PIM	PP	SH	GW	S	%	+/-	TF	F%	Min	GP	G	A	Pts	PIM	PP	SH	GW	Min
2006-07	Lincoln Stars	USHL	57	3	6	9	95	....	....	....	....	....	....	....	....	....	3	0	0	0	2	....	....	....	....
2007-08	Lincoln Stars	USHL	60	4	37	41	135	....	....	....	....	....	....	....	....	....	8	1	4	5	10	....	....	....	....
2008-09	Ohio State	CCHA	41	5	15	20	46	....	....	....	....	....	....	....	....	....	....	....	....	....	....	....	....	....	....
2009-10	Ohio State	CCHA	39	6	12	18	*99	....	....	....	....	....	....	....	....	....	....	....	....	....	....	....	....	....	....
2010-11	**Boston**	**NHL**	**6**	**0**	**0**	**0**	**4**	**0**	**0**	**0**	**2**	**0.0**	**-1**	**0**	**0.0**	**9:10**	....	....	....	....	....	....	....	....	....
	Providence Bruins	AHL	69	5	18	23	42	....	....	....	....	....	....	....	....	....	....	....	....	....	....	....	....	....	....
	NHL Totals		**6**	**0**	**0**	**0**	**4**	**0**	**0**	**0**	**2**	**0.0**		**0**	**0.0**	**9:10**	....	....	....	....	....	....	....	....	....

CCHA All-Rookie Team (2009) • USHL First All-Star Team (2008)

Traded to **Boston** by **Florida** with Dennis Seidenberg for Byron Bitz, Craig Weller and Tampa Bay's 2nd round choice (previously acquired, Florida selected Alexander Petrovic) in 2010 Entry Draft, March 3, 2010.

BARTULIS, Oskars

(bahr-TEW-lihs, AWZ-kahrz) **PHI**

Defense. Shoots left. 6'2", 184 lbs. Born, Ogre, Latvia, January 21, 1987. Philadelphia's 2nd choice, 91st overall, in 2005 Entry Draft.

			Regular Season														Playoffs								
Season	Club	League	GP	G	A	Pts	PIM	PP	SH	GW	S	%	+/-	TF	F%	Min	GP	G	A	Pts	PIM	PP	SH	GW	Min
2001-02	Prizma '83 Riga	EEHL-B	3	1	0	1	2	....	....	....	....	....	....	....	....	....	....	....	....	....	....	....	....	....	....
	Prizma '83 Riga	Latvia	6	0	1	1	2	....	....	....	....	....	....	....	....	....	....	....	....	....	....	....	....	....	....
2002-03	Prizma '83 Riga	EEHL-B	12	5	5	10	12	....	....	....	....	....	....	....	....	....	....	....	....	....	....	....	....	....	....
	Vilki Riga	Latvia	....	0	1	1	12	....	....	....	....	....	....	....	....	....	....	....	....	....	....	....	....	....	....
2003-04	CSKA Moscow 2	Russia-3	65	3	9	12	....	....	....	....	....	....	....	....	....	....	....	....	....	....	....	....	....	....	....
2004-05	Moncton Wildcats	QMJHL	62	5	19	24	55	....	....	....	....	....	....	....	....	....	12	1	1	2	16	....	....	....	....
2005-06	Moncton Wildcats	QMJHL	54	6	25	31	84	....	....	....	....	....	....	....	....	....	21	1	9	10	22	....	....	....	....
2006-07	Cape Breton	QMJHL	55	13	35	48	52	....	....	....	....	....	....	....	....	....	16	3	9	12	24	....	....	....	....
2007-08	Philadelphia	AHL	57	1	20	21	42	....	....	....	....	....	....	....	....	....	....	....	....	....	....	....	....	....	....
2008-09	Philadelphia	AHL	80	2	11	13	59	....	....	....	....	....	....	....	....	....	4	0	0	0	4	....	....	....	....
2009-10	**Philadelphia**	**NHL**	**53**	**1**	**8**	**9**	**28**	**0**	**0**	**0**	**26**	**3.8**	**–12**	**0**	**0.0**	**13:59**	**7**	**0**	**0**	**0**	**4**	**0**	**0**	**0**	**6:44**
	Adirondack	AHL	12	2	2	4	14	....	....	....	....	....	....	....	....	....	....	....	....	....	....	....	....	....	....
	Latvia	Olympics	4	0	0	0	2	....	....	....	....	....	....	....	....	....	....	....	....	....	....	....	....	....	....
2010-11	**Philadelphia**	**NHL**	**13**	**0**	**0**	**0**	**4**	**0**	**0**	**0**	**7**	**0.0**	**–4**	**0**	**0.0**	**13:01**	....	....	....	....	....	....	....	....	....
	Adirondack	AHL	4	0	1	1	2	....	....	....	....	....	....	....	....	....	....	....	....	....	....	....	....	....	....
	NHL Totals		**66**	**1**	**8**	**9**	**32**	**0**	**0**	**0**	**33**	**3.0**		**0**	**0.0**	**13:48**	**7**	**0**	**0**	**0**	**4**	**0**	**0**	**0**	**6:44**

QMJHL All-Rookie Team (2005) • Canadian Major Junior All-Rookie Team (2005) • QMJHL Second All-Star Team (2007)

• Missed majority of 2010-11 due to shoulder injury and as a healthy reserve .

BASS, Cody

(BAS, KOH-dee) **CBJ**

Center. Shoots right. 6'1", 204 lbs. Born, Owen Sound, Ont., January 7, 1987. Ottawa's 3rd choice, 95th overall, in 2005 Entry Draft.

Season	Club	League	GP	G	A	Pts	PIM	PP	SH	GW	S	%	+/-	TF	F%	Min	GP	G	A	Pts	PIM	PP	SH	GW	Min
2003-04	Mississauga	OHL	61	3	7	10	30	....	....	....	....	....	....	....	....	....	24	2	3	5	21	....	....	....	....
2004-05	Mississauga	OHL	66	11	17	28	103	....	....	....	....	....	....	....	....	....	5	1	1	2	8	....	....	....	....
2005-06	Mississauga	OHL	67	16	25	41	152	....	....	....	....	....	....	....	....	....	....	....	....	....	....	....	....	....	....
	Binghamton	AHL	9	1	0	1	2	....	....	....	....	....	....	....	....	....	....	....	....	....	....	....	....	....	....
2006-07	Mississauga	OHL	23	5	11	16	37	....	....	....	....	....	....	....	....	....	....	....	....	....	....	....	....	....	....
	Saginaw Spirit	OHL	30	5	24	29	49	....	....	....	....	....	....	....	....	....	6	1	2	3	10	....	....	....	....
	Binghamton	AHL	5	0	2	2	9	....	....	....	....	....	....	....	....	....	....	....	....	....	....	....	....	....	....
2007-08	**Ottawa**	**NHL**	**21**	**2**	**2**	**4**	**19**	**0**	**1**	**1**	**12**	**16.7**	**–1**	**73**	**43.8**	**5:19**	**4**	**1**	**0**	**1**	**6**	**0**	**0**	**0**	**8:21**
	Binghamton	AHL	24	3	5	8	44	....	....	....	....	....	....	....	....	....	....	....	....	....	....	....	....	....	....
2008-09	**Ottawa**	**NHL**	**12**	**0**	**0**	**0**	**15**	**0**	**0**	**0**	**5**	**0.0**	**–2**	**50**	**42.0**	**5:41**	....	....	....	....	....	....	....	....	....
	Binghamton	AHL	18	1	1	2	41	....	....	....	....	....	....	....	....	....	....	....	....	....	....	....	....	....	....
2009-10	Binghamton	AHL	57	5	6	11	109	....	....	....	....	....	....	....	....	....	....	....	....	....	....	....	....	....	....
2010-11	**Ottawa**	**NHL**	**1**	**0**	**0**	**0**	**0**	**0**	**0**	**0**	**0**	**0.0**	**0**	**0**	**0.0**	**7:09**	....	....	....	....	....	....	....	....	....
	Binghamton	AHL	58	6	9	15	111	....	....	....	....	....	....	....	....	....	18	2	2	4	24	....	....	....	....
	NHL Totals		**34**	**2**	**2**	**4**	**34**	**0**	**1**	**1**	**17**	**11.8**		**123**	**43.1**	**5:30**	**4**	**1**	**0**	**1**	**6**	**0**	**0**	**0**	**8:21**

Yanick Dupre Memorial Award (AHL - Outstanding Humanitarian Contribution) (2011)

• Missed remainder of 2008-09 due to shoulder injury in game at Calgary, December 27, 2008. Signed as a free agent by **Columbus**. July 13, 2011.

BAUMGARTNER, Nolan

(BAWM-gahrt-nuhr, NOH-luhn) **VAN**

Defense. Shoots right. 6'2", 195 lbs. Born, Calgary, Alta., March 23, 1976. Washington's 1st choice, 10th overall, in 1994 Entry Draft.

Season	Club	League	GP	G	A	Pts	PIM	PP	SH	GW	S	%	+/-	TF	F%	Min	GP	G	A	Pts	PIM	PP	SH	GW	Min
1991-92	Calgary Flames	AMHL	39	11	29	40	40	....	....	....	....	....	....	....	....	....	....	....	....	....	....	....	....	....	....
1992-93	Kamloops Blazers	WHL	43	0	5	5	30	....	....	....	....	....	....	....	....	....	11	1	1	2	0	....	....	....	....
1993-94	Kamloops Blazers	WHL	69	13	42	55	109	....	....	....	....	....	....	....	....	....	19	3	14	17	33	....	....	....	....
1994-95	Kamloops Blazers	WHL	62	8	36	44	71	....	....	....	....	....	....	....	....	....	21	4	13	17	16	....	....	....	....
1995-96	Kamloops Blazers	WHL	28	13	15	28	45	....	....	....	....	....	....	....	....	....	16	1	9	10	26	....	....	....	....
	Washington	**NHL**	**1**	**0**	**0**	**0**	**0**	**0**	**0**	**0**	**0**	**0.0**	**–1**	....	....	....	**1**	**0**	**0**	**0**	**10**	**0**	**0**	**0**	
1996-97	Portland Pirates	AHL	8	2	2	4	4	....	....	....	....	....	....	....	....	....	....	....	....	....	....	....	....	....	....
1997-98	**Washington**	**NHL**	**4**	**0**	**1**	**1**	**0**	**0**	**0**	**0**	**4**	**0.0**	**0**	....	....	....	....	....	....	....	....	....	....	....	....
	Portland Pirates	AHL	70	2	24	26	70	....	....	....	....	....	....	....	....	....	10	1	4	5	10	....	....	....	....
1998-99	**Washington**	**NHL**	**5**	**0**	**0**	**0**	**0**	**0**	**0**	**0**	**1**	**0.0**	**–3**	**0**	**0.0**	**8:41**	....	....	....	....	....	....	....	....	....
	Portland Pirates	AHL	38	5	14	19	62	....	....	....	....	....	....	....	....	....	....	....	....	....	....	....	....	....	....
99-2000	**Washington**	**NHL**	**8**	**0**	**1**	**1**	**2**	**0**	**0**	**0**	**6**	**0.0**	**1**	**0**	**0.0**	**10:31**	....	....	....	....	....	....	....	....	....
	Portland Pirates	AHL	71	5	18	23	56	....	....	....	....	....	....	....	....	....	4	1	2	3	10	....	....	....	....
2000-01	**Chicago**	**NHL**	**8**	**0**	**0**	**0**	**6**	**0**	**0**	**0**	**7**	**0.0**	**–4**	**2**	**50.0**	**12:40**	....	....	....	....	....	....	....	....	....
	Norfolk Admirals	AHL	63	5	28	33	75	....	....	....	....	....	....	....	....	....	9	2	3	5	11	....	....	....	....
2001-02	Norfolk Admirals	AHL	76	10	24	34	72	....	....	....	....	....	....	....	....	....	4	0	1	1	2	....	....	....	....
2002-03	**Vancouver**	**NHL**	**8**	**1**	**2**	**3**	**4**	**1**	**0**	**0**	**7**	**14.3**	**4**	**0**	**0.0**	**11:36**	**2**	**0**	**0**	**0**	**0**	**0**	**0**	**0**	**11:07**
	Manitoba Moose	AHL	59	8	31	39	82	....	....	....	....	....	....	....	....	....	1	0	0	0	4	....	....	....	....
2003-04	**Pittsburgh**	**NHL**	**5**	**0**	**0**	**0**	**2**	**0**	**0**	**0**	**6**	**0.0**	**–7**	**0**	**0.0**	**19:20**	....	....	....	....	....	....	....	....	....
	Vancouver	**NHL**	**9**	**0**	**3**	**3**	**2**	**0**	**0**	**0**	**9**	**0.0**	**3**	**0**	**0.0**	**11:52**	....	....	....	....	....	....	....	....	....
	Manitoba Moose	AHL	55	6	21	27	101	....	....	....	....	....	....	....	....	....	....	....	....	....	....	....	....	....	....
2004-05	Manitoba Moose	AHL	78	9	30	39	51	....	....	....	....	....	....	....	....	....	14	0	4	4	10	....	....	....	....
2005-06	**Vancouver**	**NHL**	**70**	**5**	**29**	**34**	**30**	**4**	**1**	**1**	**73**	**6.8**	**11**	**1**	**0.0**	**16:29**	....	....	....	....	....	....	....	....	....
2006-07	**Philadelphia**	**NHL**	**6**	**0**	**1**	**1**	**21**	**0**	**0**	**0**	**4**	**0.0**	**0**	**0**	**0.0**	**15:00**	....	....	....	....	....	....	....	....	....
	Philadelphia	AHL	51	6	20	26	46	....	....	....	....	....	....	....	....	....	....	....	....	....	....	....	....	....	....
	Dallas	**NHL**	**7**	**0**	**2**	**2**	**0**	**0**	**0**	**0**	**4**	**0.0**	**0**	**0**	**0.0**	**12:14**	....	....	....	....	....	....	....	....	....
2007-08	Iowa Stars	AHL	56	5	13	18	47	....	....	....	....	....	....	....	....	....	....	....	....	....	....	....	....	....	....
	Manitoba Moose	AHL	18	0	6	6	10	....	....	....	....	....	....	....	....	....	3	0	1	1	4	....	....	....	....
2008-09	Manitoba Moose	AHL	72	11	22	33	50	....	....	....	....	....	....	....	....	....	22	0	5	5	22	....	....	....	....
2009-10	**Vancouver**	**NHL**	**12**	**1**	**1**	**2**	**2**	**0**	**0**	**0**	**12**	**8.3**	**7**	**0**	**0.0**	**14:12**	**1**	**0**	**0**	**0**	**0**	**0**	**0**	**0**	**9:27**
	Manitoba Moose	AHL	37	3	9	12	22	....	....	....	....	....	....	....	....	....	....	....	....	....	....	....	....	....	....
2010-11	Manitoba Moose	AHL	66	4	25	29	36	....	....	....	....	....	....	....	....	....	14	0	3	3	10	....	....	....	....
	NHL Totals		**143**	**7**	**40**	**47**	**69**	**5**	**1**	**1**	**133**	**5.3**		**3**	**33.3**	**14:41**	**4**	**0**	**0**	**0**	**10**	**0**	**0**	**0**	**10:33**

Memorial Cup Tournement All-Star Team (1994, 1995) • WHL West First All-Star Team (1995, 1996) • Canadian Major Junior First All-Star Team (1995) • Canadian Major Junior Defenseman of the Year (1995)

Traded to **Chicago** by **Washington** for Remi Royer, July 20, 2000. Signed as a free agent by **Vancouver**, July 11, 2002. Claimed by **Pittsburgh** from **Vancouver** in Waiver Draft, October 3, 2003. Claimed on waivers by **Vancouver** from **Pittsburgh**, November 1, 2003. Signed as a free agent by **Philadelphia**, July 1, 2006. Claimed on waivers by **Dallas** from **Philadelphia**, February 24, 2007. Signed as a free agent by **Vancouver**, July 2, 2008.

BAYDA, Ryan

(BAY-duh, RIGH-uhn)

Left wing. Shoots left. 5'11", 185 lbs. Born, Saskatoon, Sask., December 9, 1980. Carolina's 2nd choice, 80th overall, in 2000 Entry Draft.

Season	Club	League	GP	G	A	Pts	PIM	PP	SH	GW	S	%	+/-	TF	F%	Min	GP	G	A	Pts	PIM	PP	SH	GW	Min
1995-96	Saskatoon Flyers	SMHL	60	85	74	159	85	....	....	....	....	....	....	....	....	....	....	....	....	....	....	....	....	....	....
1996-97	Sask. Contacts	SMHL	44	22	23	45	18	....	....	....	....	....	....	....	....	....	....	....	....	....	....	....	....	....	....
1997-98	Sask. Contacts	SMHL	41	29	49	78	103	....	....	....	....	....	....	....	....	....	....	....	....	....	....	....	....	....	....
1998-99	Vernon Vipers	BCHL	45	24	58	82	15	....	....	....	....	....	....	....	....	....	....	....	....	....	....	....	....	....	....
99-2000	North Dakota	WCHA	44	17	23	40	30	....	....	....	....	....	....	....	....	....	....	....	....	....	....	....	....	....	....
2000-01	North Dakota	WCHA	46	25	34	59	48	....	....	....	....	....	....	....	....	....	....	....	....	....	....	....	....	....	....
2001-02	North Dakota	WCHA	37	19	28	47	52	....	....	....	....	....	....	....	....	....	....	....	....	....	....	....	....	....	....
	Lowell	AHL	3	1	1	2	0	....	....	....	....	....	....	....	....	....	5	3	0	3	0	....	....	....	....
2002-03	**Carolina**	**NHL**	**25**	**4**	**10**	**14**	**16**	**0**	**0**	**1**	**49**	**8.2**	**–5**	**2**	**100.0**	**17:15**	....	....	....	....	....	....	....	....	....
	Lowell	AHL	53	11	32	43	32	....	....	....	....	....	....	....	....	....	....	....	....	....	....	....	....	....	....
2003-04	**Carolina**	**NHL**	**44**	**3**	**3**	**6**	**22**	**0**	**0**	**1**	**65**	**4.6**	**–14**	**4**	**0.0**	**10:57**	....	....	....	....	....	....	....	....	....
	Lowell	AHL	34	7	15	22	28	....	....	....	....	....	....	....	....	....	....	....	....	....	....	....	....	....	....
2004-05	Lowell	AHL	80	13	27	40	91	....	....	....	....	....	....	....	....	....	9	3	3	6	4	....	....	....	....
2005-06	Manitoba Moose	AHL	59	13	25	38	52	....	....	....	....	....	....	....	....	....	13	1	6	7	27	....	....	....	....
2006-07	**Carolina**	**NHL**	**9**	**1**	**1**	**2**	**2**	**0**	**0**	**0**	**10**	**10.0**	**–1**	**0**	**0.0**	**8:41**	....	....	....	....	....	....	....	....	....
	Albany River Rats	AHL	55	29	25	54	66	....	....	....	....	....	....	....	....	....	5	3	2	5	4	....	....	....	....
2007-08	**Carolina**	**NHL**	**31**	**3**	**3**	**6**	**28**	**0**	**0**	**0**	**58**	**5.2**	**–2**	**2**	**0.0**	**12:36**	....	....	....	....	....	....	....	....	....
	Albany River Rats	AHL	21	7	10	17	6	....	....	....	....	....	....	....	....	....	....	....	....	....	....	....	....	....	....
2008-09	**Carolina**	**NHL**	**70**	**5**	**7**	**12**	**26**	**0**	**0**	**0**	**62**	**8.1**	**2**	**18**	**44.4**	**10:27**	**15**	**2**	**2**	**4**	**18**	**0**	**0**	**0**	**6:21**

			Regular Season														Playoffs								
Season	Club	League	GP	G	A	Pts	PIM	PP	SH	GW	S	%	+/-	TF	F%	Min	GP	G	A	Pts	PIM	PP	SH	GW	Min
2009-10	Wilkes-Barre	AHL	21	8	3	11	14	....	....	....	....	....	....	....	....	....	....	....	....	....	....	....	....	....	....
2010-11	Nurnberg	Germany	52	17	24	41	70	....	....	....	....	....	....	....	....	....	2	0	1	1	0	....	....	....	....
	NHL Totals		**179**	**16**	**24**	**40**	**94**	**0**	**0**	**2**	**244**	**6.6**		**26**	**38.5**	**11:48**	**15**	**2**	**2**	**4**	**18**	**0**	**0**	**0**	**6:21**

BCHL Rookie of the Year (1999) • WCHA All-Rookie Team (2000) • WCHA Second All-Star Team (2001, 2002)

• Missed majority of 2009-10 due to knee injury at Hershey, November 13, 2009. Signed as a free agent by **Nurnberg** (Germany), July 18, 2010.

BEAGLE, Jay

(BEE-guhl, JAY) **WSH**

Right wing. Shoots right. 6'3", 204 lbs. Born, Calgary, Alta., October 16, 1985.

Season	Club	League	GP	G	A	Pts	PIM	PP	SH	GW	S	%	+/-	TF	F%	Min	GP	G	A	Pts	PIM	PP	SH	GW	Min
2003-04	Calgary Royals	AJHL	58	10	27	37	100	....	....	....	....	....	....	....	....	....	....	....	....	....	....	....	....	....	....
2004-05	Calgary Royals	AJHL	64	28	42	70	114	....	....	....	....	....	....	....	....	....	....	....	....	....	....	....	....	....	....
2005-06	Alaska Anchorage	WCHA	31	4	6	10	40	....	....	....	....	....	....	....	....	....	....	....	....	....	....	....	....	....	....
2006-07	Alaska Anchorage	WCHA	36	10	10	20	93	....	....	....	....	....	....	....	....	....	....	....	....	....	....	....	....	....	....
	Idaho Steelheads	ECHL	8	2	8	10	4	....	....	....	....	....	....	....	....	....	18	1	2	3	22	....	....	....	....
2007-08	Hershey Bears	AHL	64	19	18	37	41	....	....	....	....	....	....	....	....	....	5	0	1	1	2	....	....	....	....
2008-09	**Washington**	**NHL**	**3**	**0**	**0**	**0**	**2**	**0**	**0**	**0**	**5**	**0.0**	**–3**	**13**	**38.5**	**7:36**	**4**	**0**	**0**	**0**	**0**	**0**	**0**	**0**	**3:33**
	Hershey Bears	AHL	47	4	5	9	37	....	....	....	....	....	....	....	....	....	18	1	3	4	16	....	....	....	....
2009-10	**Washington**	**NHL**	**7**	**1**	**1**	**2**	**2**	**0**	**0**	**0**	**10**	**10.0**	**–1**	**31**	**54.8**	**9:16**	....	....	....	....	....	....	....	....	....
	Hershey Bears	AHL	66	16	19	35	25	....	....	....	....	....	....	....	....	....	21	2	6	8	0	....	....	....	....
2010-11	**Washington**	**NHL**	**31**	**2**	**1**	**3**	**8**	**0**	**0**	**2**	**27**	**7.4**	**–2**	**105**	**55.2**	**10:30**	....	....	....	....	....	....	....	....	....
	Hershey Bears	AHL	34	8	6	14	26	....	....	....	....	....	....	....	....	....	....	....	....	....	....	....	....	....	....
	NHL Totals		**41**	**3**	**2**	**5**	**12**	**0**	**0**	**2**	**42**	**7.1**		**149**	**53.7**	**10:05**	**4**	**0**	**0**	**0**	**0**	**0**	**0**	**0**	**3:33**

Signed as a free agent by **Washington**, March 26, 2008.

BEAUCHEMIN, Francois

(boh-sheh-MEH, frahn-SWUH) **ANA**

Defense. Shoots left. 6', 207 lbs. Born, Sorel, Que., June 4, 1980. Montreal's 3rd choice, 75th overall, in 1998 Entry Draft.

Season	Club	League	GP	G	A	Pts	PIM	PP	SH	GW	S	%	+/-	TF	F%	Min	GP	G	A	Pts	PIM	PP	SH	GW	Min
1995-96	Richelieu Riverains	QAAA	40	9	23	32	59	....	....	....	....	....	....	....	....	....	....	....	....	....	....	....	....	....	....
1996-97	Laval Titan	QMJHL	66	7	20	27	112	....	....	....	....	....	....	....	....	....	3	0	0	0	2	....	....	....	....
1997-98	Laval Titan	QMJHL	70	12	35	47	132	....	....	....	....	....	....	....	....	....	16	1	3	4	23	....	....	....	....
1998-99	Acadie-Bathurst	QMJHL	31	4	17	21	53	....	....	....	....	....	....	....	....	....	23	2	16	18	55	....	....	....	....
99-2000	Acadie-Bathurst	QMJHL	38	11	36	47	64	....	....	....	....	....	....	....	....	....	....	....	....	....	....	....	....	....	....
	Moncton Wildcats	QMJHL	33	8	31	39	35	....	....	....	....	....	....	....	....	....	16	2	11	13	14	....	....	....	....
2000-01	Quebec Citadelles	AHL	56	3	6	9	44	....	....	....	....	....	....	....	....	....	....	....	....	....	....	....	....	....	....
2001-02	Quebec Citadelles	AHL	56	8	11	19	88	....	....	....	....	....	....	....	....	....	....	....	....	....	....	....	....	....	....
	Mississippi	ECHL	7	1	3	4	2	....	....	....	....	....	....	....	....	....	3	0	1	1	0	....	....	....	....
2002-03	**Montreal**	**NHL**	**1**	**0**	**0**	**0**	**0**	**0**	**0**	**0**	**1**	**0.0**	**–1**	**0**	**0.0**	**17:11**	....	....	....	....	....	....	....	....	....
	Hamilton	AHL	75	7	21	28	92	....	....	....	....	....	....	....	....	....	23	1	9	10	16	....	....	....	....
2003-04	Hamilton	AHL	77	9	27	36	57	....	....	....	....	....	....	....	....	....	10	2	4	6	18	....	....	....	....
2004-05	Syracuse Crunch	AHL	72	3	27	30	55	....	....	....	....	....	....	....	....	....	....	....	....	....	....	....	....	....	....
2005-06	**Columbus**	**NHL**	**11**	**0**	**2**	**2**	**11**	**0**	**0**	**0**	**16**	**0.0**	**–6**	**0**	**0.0**	**17:16**	....	....	....	....	....	....	....	....	....
	Anaheim	**NHL**	**61**	**8**	**26**	**34**	**41**	**4**	**0**	**3**	**121**	**6.6**	**8**	**1**	**0.0**	**24:14**	**16**	**3**	**6**	**9**	**11**	**3**	**0**	**0**	**27:26**
2006-07♦	**Anaheim**	**NHL**	**71**	**7**	**21**	**28**	**49**	**2**	**0**	**0**	**128**	**5.5**	**7**	**1**	**0.0**	**25:28**	**20**	**4**	**4**	**8**	**16**	**4**	**0**	**0**	**30:33**
2007-08	**Anaheim**	**NHL**	**82**	**2**	**19**	**21**	**59**	**0**	**0**	**2**	**144**	**1.4**	**–9**	**1**	**0.0**	**25:32**	**6**	**0**	**0**	**0**	**26**	**0**	**0**	**0**	**21:02**
2008-09	**Anaheim**	**NHL**	**20**	**4**	**1**	**5**	**12**	**0**	**0**	**2**	**45**	**8.9**	**–3**	**0**	**0.0**	**24:54**	**13**	**1**	**0**	**1**	**15**	**0**	**0**	**0**	**21:25**
2009-10	**Toronto**	**NHL**	**82**	**5**	**21**	**26**	**33**	**4**	**0**	**1**	**170**	**2.9**	**–13**	**4**	**75.0**	**25:28**	....	....	....	....	....	....	....	....	....
2010-11	**Toronto**	**NHL**	**54**	**2**	**10**	**12**	**16**	**0**	**0**	**0**	**76**	**2.6**	**–4**	**0**	**0.0**	**23:45**	....	....	....	....	....	....	....	....	....
	Anaheim	**NHL**	**27**	**3**	**2**	**5**	**16**	**1**	**0**	**0**	**30**	**10.0**	**–4**	**1**	**0.0**	**21:42**	**6**	**0**	**2**	**2**	**2**	**0**	**0**	**0**	**23:32**
	NHL Totals		**409**	**31**	**102**	**133**	**237**	**11**	**0**	**8**	**731**	**4.2**		**8**	**37.5**	**24:33**	**61**	**8**	**12**	**20**	**70**	**7**	**0**	**0**	**26:10**

QMJHL All-Rookie Team (1997) • QMJHL Second All-Star Team (2000)

Claimed on waivers by **Columbus** from **Montreal**, September 15, 2004. Traded to **Anaheim** by **Columbus** with Tyler Wright for Sergei Fedorov and Anaheim's 5th round choice (Maxime Frechette) in 2006 Entry Draft, November 15, 2005. • Missed remainder of 2008-09 regular due to knee injury vs. Nashville, November 14, 2008. Signed as a free agent by **Toronto**, July 6, 2009. Traded to **Anaheim** by **Toronto** for Joffrey Lupul and Jake Gardiner, February 9, 2011.

BEGIN, Steve

(bay-ZHIN, STEEV)

Center. Shoots left. 6', 192 lbs. Born, Trois-Rivieres, Que., June 14, 1978. Calgary's 3rd choice, 40th overall, in 1996 Entry Draft.

Season	Club	League	GP	G	A	Pts	PIM	PP	SH	GW	S	%	+/-	TF	F%	Min	GP	G	A	Pts	PIM	PP	SH	GW	Min
1993-94	Cap-d-Madelaine	QAAA	8	0	1	1	6	....	....	....	....	....	....	....	....	....	2	0	0	0	0	....	....	....	....
1994-95	Cap-d-Madelaine	QAAA	35	9	15	24	48	....	....	....	....	....	....	....	....	....	3	0	0	0	2	....	....	....	....
1995-96	Val-d'Or Foreurs	QMJHL	64	13	23	36	218	....	....	....	....	....	....	....	....	....	13	1	3	4	33	....	....	....	....
1996-97	Val-d'Or Foreurs	QMJHL	58	13	33	46	207	....	....	....	....	....	....	....	....	....	10	0	3	3	8	....	....	....	....
	Saint John Flames	AHL	....	....	....	....	....	....	....	....	....	....	....	....	....	....	4	0	2	2	6	....	....	....	....
1997-98	**Calgary**	**NHL**	**5**	**0**	**0**	**0**	**23**	**0**	**0**	**0**	**2**	**0.0**	**0**	....	....	....	....	....	....	....	....	....	....	....	....
	Val-d'Or Foreurs	QMJHL	35	18	17	35	73	....	....	....	....	....	....	....	....	....	15	2	12	14	34	....	....	....	....
1998-99	Saint John Flames	AHL	73	11	9	20	156	....	....	....	....	....	....	....	....	....	7	2	0	2	18	....	....	....	....
99-2000	**Calgary**	**NHL**	**13**	**1**	**1**	**2**	**18**	**0**	**0**	**0**	**3**	**33.3**	**–3**	**19**	**47.4**	**7:13**	....	....	....	....	....	....	....	....	....
	Saint John Flames	AHL	47	13	12	25	99	....	....	....	....	....	....	....	....	....	....	....	....	....	....	....	....	....	....
2000-01	**Calgary**	**NHL**	**4**	**0**	**0**	**0**	**21**	**0**	**0**	**0**	**3**	**0.0**	**0**	**0**	**0.0**	**6:04**	....	....	....	....	....	....	....	....	....
	Saint John Flames	AHL	58	14	14	28	109	....	....	....	....	....	....	....	....	....	19	10	7	17	18	....	....	....	....
2001-02	**Calgary**	**NHL**	**51**	**7**	**5**	**12**	**79**	**1**	**0**	**0**	**65**	**10.8**	**–3**	**129**	**53.5**	**9:25**	....	....	....	....	....	....	....	....	....
2002-03	**Calgary**	**NHL**	**50**	**3**	**1**	**4**	**51**	**0**	**0**	**1**	**59**	**5.1**	**–7**	**50**	**60.0**	**9:13**	....	....	....	....	....	....	....	....	....
2003-04	**Montreal**	**NHL**	**52**	**10**	**5**	**15**	**41**	**0**	**1**	**1**	**91**	**11.0**	**6**	**436**	**48.6**	**12:32**	**9**	**0**	**1**	**1**	**10**	**0**	**0**	**0**	**12:26**
2004-05	Hamilton	AHL	21	10	3	13	20	....	....	....	....	....	....	....	....	....	4	0	2	2	8	....	....	....	....
2005-06	**Montreal**	**NHL**	**76**	**11**	**12**	**23**	**113**	**1**	**2**	**2**	**134**	**8.2**	**9**	**573**	**50.1**	**14:19**	**2**	**0**	**0**	**0**	**2**	**0**	**0**	**0**	**13:42**
2006-07	**Montreal**	**NHL**	**52**	**5**	**5**	**10**	**46**	**0**	**0**	**0**	**64**	**7.8**	**–6**	**159**	**49.7**	**11:55**	....	....	....	....	....	....	....	....	....
2007-08	**Montreal**	**NHL**	**44**	**3**	**5**	**8**	**48**	**0**	**0**	**0**	**67**	**4.5**	**0**	**69**	**34.8**	**11:38**	**12**	**0**	**3**	**3**	**8**	**0**	**0**	**0**	**12:45**
2008-09	**Montreal**	**NHL**	**42**	**6**	**4**	**10**	**27**	**0**	**0**	**1**	**65**	**9.2**	**–5**	**78**	**53.9**	**10:51**	....	....	....	....	....	....	....	....	....
	Dallas	**NHL**	**20**	**1**	**1**	**2**	**15**	**0**	**0**	**0**	**25**	**4.0**	**–1**	**55**	**41.8**	**10:26**	....	....	....	....	....	....	....	....	....
2009-10	**Boston**	**NHL**	**77**	**5**	**9**	**14**	**53**	**0**	**1**	**2**	**110**	**4.5**	**–7**	**694**	**53.5**	**12:50**	**13**	**1**	**0**	**1**	**10**	**0**	**0**	**0**	**11:57**
2010-11	**Nashville**	**NHL**	**2**	**0**	**0**	**0**	**4**	**0**	**0**	**0**	**2**	**0.0**	**–2**	**0**	**0.0**	**9:48**	....	....	....	....	....	....	....	....	....
	Milwaukee	AHL	36	3	3	6	30	....	....	....	....	....	....	....	....	....	13	3	4	7	12	....	....	....	....
	NHL Totals		**488**	**52**	**48**	**100**	**539**	**2**	**4**	**7**	**690**	**7.5**		**2262**	**50.7**	**11:36**	**36**	**1**	**4**	**5**	**30**	**0**	**0**	**0**	**12:26**

Jack A. Butterfield Trophy (AHL – Playoff MVP) (2001)

Traded to **Buffalo** by **Calgary** with Chris Drury for Steve Reinprecht and Rhett Warrener, July 3, 2003. Claimed by **Montreal** from **Buffalo** in Waiver Draft, October 3, 2003. Traded to **Dallas** by **Montreal** for Doug Janik, February 26, 2009. Signed as a free agent by **Boston**, July 1, 2009. Signed as a free agent by **Nashville**, October 20, 2010. • Missed majority of 2010-11 due to various injuries.

BELAK, Wade

(BEE-lak, WAYD)

Right wing. Shoots right. 6'5", 222 lbs. Born, Saskatoon, Sask., July 3, 1976. Quebec's 1st choice, 12th overall, in 1994 Entry Draft.

Season	Club	League	GP	G	A	Pts	PIM	PP	SH	GW	S	%	+/-	TF	F%	Min	GP	G	A	Pts	PIM	PP	SH	GW	Min
1991-92	North Battleford	SMBHL	57	6	20	26	186	....	....	....	....	....	....	....	....	....	....	....	....	....	....	....	....	....	....
1992-93	North Battleford	SJHL	50	5	15	20	146	....	....	....	....	....	....	....	....	....	....	....	....	....	....	....	....	....	....
	Saskatoon Blades	WHL	7	0	0	0	23	....	....	....	....	....	....	....	....	....	7	0	0	0	0	....	....	....	....
1993-94	Saskatoon Blades	WHL	69	4	13	17	226	....	....	....	....	....	....	....	....	....	16	2	2	4	43	....	....	....	....
1994-95	Saskatoon Blades	WHL	72	4	14	18	290	....	....	....	....	....	....	....	....	....	9	0	0	0	36	....	....	....	....
	Cornwall Aces	AHL	....	....	....	....	....	....	....	....	....	....	....	....	....	....	11	1	2	3	40	....	....	....	....
1995-96	Saskatoon Blades	WHL	63	3	15	18	207	....	....	....	....	....	....	....	....	....	4	0	0	0	9	....	....	....	....
	Cornwall Aces	AHL	5	0	0	0	18	....	....	....	....	....	....	....	....	....	2	0	0	0	2	....	....	....	....
1996-97	**Colorado**	**NHL**	**5**	**0**	**0**	**0**	**11**	**0**	**0**	**0**	**1**	**0.0**	**–1**	....	....	....	....	....	....	....	....	....	....	....	....
	Hershey Bears	AHL	65	1	7	8	320	....	....	....	....	....	....	....	....	....	16	0	1	1	61	....	....	....	....
1997-98	**Colorado**	**NHL**	**8**	**1**	**1**	**2**	**27**	**0**	**0**	**1**	**2**	**50.0**	**–3**	....	....	....	....	....	....	....	....	....	....	....	....
	Hershey Bears	AHL	11	0	0	0	30	....	....	....	....	....	....	....	....	....	....	....	....	....	....	....	....	....	....
1998-99	**Colorado**	**NHL**	**22**	**0**	**0**	**0**	**71**	**0**	**0**	**0**	**5**	**0.0**	**–2**	**0**	**0.0**	**6:48**	....	....	....	....	....	....	....	....	....
	Hershey Bears	AHL	17	0	1	1	49	....	....	....	....	....	....	....	....	....	....	....	....	....	....	....	....	....	....
	Calgary	**NHL**	**9**	**0**	**1**	**1**	**23**	**0**	**0**	**0**	**2**	**0.0**	**3**	**0**	**0.0**	**10:46**	....	....	....	....	....	....	....	....	....
	Saint John Flames	AHL	12	0	2	2	43	....	....	....	....	....	....	....	....	....	6	0	1	1	23	....	....	....	....
99-2000	**Calgary**	**NHL**	**40**	**0**	**2**	**2**	**122**	**0**	**0**	**0**	**11**	**0.0**	**–4**	**1**	**0.0**	**7:33**	....	....	....	....	....	....	....	....	....
2000-01	**Calgary**	**NHL**	**23**	**0**	**0**	**0**	**79**	**0**	**0**	**0**	**8**	**0.0**	**–2**	**0**	**0.0**	**6:54**	....	....	....	....	....	....	....	....	....
	Toronto	**NHL**	**16**	**1**	**1**	**2**	**31**	**0**	**0**	**0**	**8**	**12.5**	**–4**	**0**	**0.0**	**13:38**	....	....	....	....	....	....	....	....	....
2001-02	**Toronto**	**NHL**	**63**	**1**	**3**	**4**	**142**	**0**	**0**	**0**	**47**	**2.1**	**2**	**0**	**0.0**	**9:14**	**16**	**1**	**0**	**1**	**18**	**0**	**0**	**0**	**7:28**
2002-03	**Toronto**	**NHL**	**55**	**3**	**6**	**9**	**196**	**0**	**0**	**0**	**33**	**9.1**	**–2**	**0**	**0.0**	**10:50**	**2**	**0**	**0**	**0**	**4**	**0**	**0**	**0**	**8:22**

			Regular Season														Playoffs								
Season	Club	League	GP	G	A	Pts	PIM	PP	SH	GW	S	%	+/-	TF	F%	Min	GP	G	A	Pts	PIM	PP	SH	GW	Min
2003-04	Toronto	NHL	34	1	1	2	109	0	0	0	15	6.7	0	0	0.0	7:00	4	0	0	0	14	0	0	0	9:59
2004-05	Coventry Blaze	Britain	20	3	5	8	109	....	....	....	....	....	....	....	....	....	8	1	1	2	16	....	....	....	....
2005-06	Toronto	NHL	55	0	3	3	109	0	0	0	16	0.0	–13	0	0.0	9:59	....	....	....	....	....	....	....	....	....
2006-07	Toronto	NHL	65	0	3	3	110	0	0	0	16	0.0	–8	0	0.0	5:02	....	....	....	....	....	....	....	....	....
2007-08	Toronto	NHL	30	1	0	1	66	0	0	0	13	7.7	–2	1	0.0	4:02	....	....	....	....	....	....	....	....	....
	Florida	NHL	17	0	0	0	12	0	0	0	4	0.0	0	0	0.0	4:09	....	....	....	....	....	....	....	....	....
2008-09	Florida	NHL	15	0	0	0	25	0	0	0	4	0.0	0	0	0.0	4:25	....	....	....	....	....	....	....	....	....
	Nashville	NHL	38	0	2	2	54	0	0	0	15	0.0	–1	0	0.0	5:35	....	....	....	....	....	....	....	....	....
2009-10	Nashville	NHL	39	0	2	2	58	0	0	0	8	0.0	0	0	0.0	4:21	....	....	....	....	....	....	....	....	....
2010-11	Nashville	NHL	15	0	0	0	18	0	0	0	4	0.0	–1	0	0.0	3:47	....	....	....	....	....	....	....	....	....
	NHL Totals		**549**	**8**	**25**	**33**	**1263**	**0**	**0**	**1**	**212**	**3.8**		**2**	**0.0**	**7:18**	**22**	**1**	**0**	**1**	**36**	**0**	**0**	**0**	**8:00**

• Rights transferred to **Colorado** after **Quebec** franchise relocated, June 21, 1995. Traded to **Calgary** by **Colorado** with Rene Corbet, Robyn Regehr and Colorado's 2nd round compensatory choice (Jarret Stoll) in 2000 Entry Draft for Theoren Fleury and Chris Dingman, February 28, 1999. • Missed majority of 1999-2000 and 2000-01 due to shoulder injury vs. Colorado, February 10, 2000. Claimed on waivers by **Toronto** from **Calgary**, February 16, 2001. • Missed majority of 2003-04 due to abdomen (November 20, 2003 vs. Edmonton) and knee (January 6, 2004 vs. Nashville) injuries. Signed as a free agent by **Coventry** (Britain), November 8, 2004. Traded to **Florida** by **Toronto** for Florida's 5th round choice (Jerome Flaake) in 2008 Entry Draft, February 26, 2008. Traded to **Nashville** by **Florida** for Nick Tarnasky, November 27, 2008. • Missed majority of 2010-11 as a healthy reserve.

BELANGER, Eric

(buh-LAWN-zhay, AIR-ihk) **EDM**

Center. Shoots left. 5'11", 185 lbs. Born, Sherbrooke, Que., December 16, 1977. Los Angeles' 5th choice, 96th overall, in 1996 Entry Draft.

Season	Club	League	GP	G	A	Pts	PIM	PP	SH	GW	S	%	+/-	TF	F%	Min	GP	G	A	Pts	PIM	PP	SH	GW	Min
1993-94	Magog	QAAA	32	19	24	43	24	....	....	....	....	....	....	....	....	....	13	5	6	11	36	....	....	....	....
1994-95	Beauport	QMJHL	71	12	28	40	24	....	....	....	....	....	....	....	....	....	18	5	9	14	25	....	....	....	....
1995-96	Beauport	QMJHL	59	35	48	83	18	....	....	....	....	....	....	....	....	....	20	13	14	27	6	....	....	....	....
1996-97	Beauport	QMJHL	33	16	37	53	32	....	....	....	....	....	....	....	....	....	....	....	....	....	....	....	....	....	....
	Rimouski Oceanic	QMJHL	29	23	41	64	34	....	....	....	....	....	....	....	....	....	4	2	3	5	10	....	....	....	....
1997-98	Fredericton	AHL	56	17	34	51	28	....	....	....	....	....	....	....	....	....	4	2	1	3	2	....	....	....	....
1998-99	Springfield	AHL	33	8	18	26	10	....	....	....	....	....	....	....	....	....	3	0	1	1	2	....	....	....	....
	Long Beach	IHL	1	0	0	0	0	....	....	....	....	....	....	....	....	....	....	....	....	....	....	....	....	....	....
99-2000	Lowell	AHL	65	15	25	40	20	....	....	....	....	....	....	....	....	....	7	3	3	6	2	....	....	....	....
2000-01	Los Angeles	NHL	62	9	12	21	16	1	2	1	80	11.3	14	849	56.4	13:25	13	1	4	5	2	0	0	1	13:47
	Lowell	AHL	13	8	10	18	4	....	....	....	....	....	....	....	....	....	....	....	....	....	....	....	....	....	....
2001-02	Los Angeles	NHL	53	8	16	24	21	2	1	1	67	11.9	2	882	57.7	14:33	7	0	0	0	4	0	0	0	12:57
2002-03	Los Angeles	NHL	62	16	19	35	26	0	3	1	114	14.0	–5	1143	51.8	17:42	....	....	....	....	....	....	....	....	....
2003-04	Los Angeles	NHL	81	13	20	33	44	0	1	2	132	9.8	–16	1418	53.7	17:01	....	....	....	....	....	....	....	....	....
2004-05	HC Forst Bolzano	Italy	12	13	10	23	20	....	....	....	....	....	....	....	....	....	9	3	7	10	33	....	....	....	....
2005-06	Los Angeles	NHL	65	17	20	37	62	5	0	1	119	14.3	–5	1179	49.0	17:33	....	....	....	....	....	....	....	....	....
2006-07	Carolina	NHL	56	8	12	20	14	3	0	1	100	8.0	–2	689	53.4	14:51	....	....	....	....	....	....	....	....	....
	Atlanta	NHL	24	9	6	15	12	1	0	0	49	18.4	0	517	52.6	19:29	4	1	0	1	12	1	0	0	16:47
2007-08	Minnesota	NHL	75	13	24	37	30	7	1	3	115	11.3	–6	1195	49.1	17:13	6	0	0	0	4	0	0	0	18:34
2008-09	Minnesota	NHL	79	13	23	36	26	4	0	4	147	8.8	–5	1205	52.0	17:50	....	....	....	....	....	....	....	....	....
2009-10	Minnesota	NHL	60	13	22	35	28	3	0	3	120	10.8	–1	722	57.6	15:45	....	....	....	....	....	....	....	....	....
	Washington	NHL	17	2	4	6	4	0	0	0	31	6.5	3	202	52.0	14:40	7	0	1	1	4	0	0	0	14:05
2010-11	Phoenix	NHL	82	13	27	40	36	1	1	2	127	10.2	11	1297	55.3	17:21	4	0	0	0	2	0	0	0	15:57
	NHL Totals		**716**	**134**	**205**	**339**	**319**	**27**	**9**	**19**	**1201**	**11.2**		**11298**	**53.2**	**16:32**	**41**	**2**	**5**	**7**	**28**	**1**	**0**	**1**	**14:54**

Signed as a free agent by **Bolzano** (Italy), December 22, 2004. Traded to **Carolina** by **Los Angeles** with Tim Gleason for Oleg Tverdovsky and Jack Johnson, September 29, 2006. Traded to **Nashville** by **Carolina** for Josef Vasicek, February 9, 2007. Traded to **Atlanta** by **Nashville** for Vitaly Vishnevski, February 10, 2007. Signed as a free agent by **Minnesota**, July 3, 2007. Traded to **Washington** by **Minnesota** for Washington's 2nd round choice (Johan Larsson) in 2010 Entry Draft, March 3, 2010. Signed as a free agent by **Phoenix**, September 14, 2010. Signed as a free agent by **Edmonton**, July 1, 2011.

BELESKEY, Matt

(beh-LEH-skee, MAT) **ANA**

Left wing. Shoots left. 6', 198 lbs. Born, Windsor, Ont., June 7, 1988. Anaheim's 4th choice, 112th overall, in 2006 Entry Draft.

Season	Club	League	GP	G	A	Pts	PIM	PP	SH	GW	S	%	+/-	TF	F%	Min	GP	G	A	Pts	PIM	PP	SH	GW	Min
2004-05	Belleville Bulls	OHL	68	10	13	23	118	....	....	....	....	....	....	....	....	....	5	0	0	0	18	....	....	....	....
2005-06	Belleville Bulls	OHL	61	20	20	40	119	....	....	....	....	....	....	....	....	....	6	1	2	3	10	....	....	....	....
2006-07	Belleville Bulls	OHL	66	27	41	68	124	....	....	....	....	....	....	....	....	....	15	4	10	14	18	....	....	....	....
2007-08	Belleville Bulls	OHL	62	41	49	90	106	....	....	....	....	....	....	....	....	....	21	12	21	33	23	....	....	....	....
2008-09	Anaheim	NHL	2	0	0	0	0	0	0	0	0	0.0	0	2	0.0	11:10	....	....	....	....	....	....	....	....	....
	Iowa Chops	AHL	58	11	24	35	58	....	....	....	....	....	....	....	....	....	....	....	....	....	....	....	....	....	....
2009-10	Anaheim	NHL	60	11	7	18	35	0	0	3	123	8.9	–10	20	40.0	13:59	....	....	....	....	....	....	....	....	....
	San Antonio	AHL	12	1	4	5	19	....	....	....	....	....	....	....	....	....	....	....	....	....	....	....	....	....	....
	Toronto Marlies	AHL	3	1	1	2	2	....	....	....	....	....	....	....	....	....	....	....	....	....	....	....	....	....	....
2010-11	Anaheim	NHL	35	3	7	10	36	0	0	0	58	5.2	–10	8	37.5	12:59	6	1	0	1	4	0	0	0	11:14
	Syracuse Crunch	AHL	27	11	13	24	39	....	....	....	....	....	....	....	....	....	....	....	....	....	....	....	....	....	....
	NHL Totals		**97**	**14**	**14**	**28**	**71**	**0**	**0**	**3**	**181**	**7.7**		**30**	**36.7**	**13:34**	**6**	**1**	**0**	**1**	**4**	**0**	**0**	**0**	**11:15**

BELL, Brendan

(BEHL, BREHN-duhn) **NYR**

Defense. Shoots left. 6'2", 211 lbs. Born, Ottawa, Ont., March 31, 1983. Toronto's 3rd choice, 65th overall, in 2001 Entry Draft.

Season	Club	League	GP	G	A	Pts	PIM	PP	SH	GW	S	%	+/-	TF	F%	Min	GP	G	A	Pts	PIM	PP	SH	GW	Min
1998-99	Ott. Jr. Senators	CJHL	54	7	20	27	46	....	....	....	....	....	....	....	....	....	....	....	....	....	....	....	....	....	....
99-2000	Ottawa 67's	OHL	48	1	32	33	34	....	....	....	....	....	....	....	....	....	5	0	1	1	4	....	....	....	....
2000-01	Ottawa 67's	OHL	68	7	32	39	59	....	....	....	....	....	....	....	....	....	20	1	11	12	22	....	....	....	....
2001-02	Ottawa 67's	OHL	67	10	36	46	56	....	....	....	....	....	....	....	....	....	13	2	5	7	25	....	....	....	....
2002-03	Ottawa 67's	OHL	55	14	39	53	46	....	....	....	....	....	....	....	....	....	23	8	19	27	25	....	....	....	....
2003-04	St. John's	AHL	74	7	18	25	72	....	....	....	....	....	....	....	....	....	....	....	....	....	....	....	....	....	....
2004-05	St. John's	AHL	75	6	25	31	57	....	....	....	....	....	....	....	....	....	5	0	1	1	2	....	....	....	....
2005-06	Toronto	NHL	1	0	0	0	0	0	0	0	2	0.0	0	0	0.0	14:00	....	....	....	....	....	....	....	....	....
	Toronto Marlies	AHL	70	6	37	43	99	....	....	....	....	....	....	....	....	....	5	0	4	4	10	....	....	....	....
2006-07	Toronto	NHL	31	1	4	5	19	1	0	0	29	3.4	–3	1	0.0	12:08	....	....	....	....	....	....	....	....	....
	Phoenix	NHL	14	0	2	2	8	0	0	0	18	0.0	–8	0	0.0	17:07	....	....	....	....	....	....	....	....	....
2007-08	Phoenix	NHL	2	0	0	0	0	0	0	0	0	0.0	–2	0	0.0	14:49	....	....	....	....	....	....	....	....	....
	San Antonio	AHL	69	7	24	31	80	....	....	....	....	....	....	....	....	....	7	2	5	7	10	....	....	....	....
2008-09	Ottawa	NHL	53	6	15	21	24	5	0	1	76	7.9	–5	0	0.0	17:44	....	....	....	....	....	....	....	....	....
	Binghamton	AHL	15	6	9	15	12	....	....	....	....	....	....	....	....	....	....	....	....	....	....	....	....	....	....
2009-10	Peoria Rivermen	AHL	22	4	13	17	26	....	....	....	....	....	....	....	....	....	....	....	....	....	....	....	....	....	....
	Syracuse Crunch	AHL	49	10	25	35	30	....	....	....	....	....	....	....	....	....	....	....	....	....	....	....	....	....	....
2010-11	Omsk	Rus-KHL	1	0	2	2	0	....	....	....	....	....	....	....	....	....	....	....	....	....	....	....	....	....	....
	EHC Biel-Bienne	Swiss	29	2	9	11	14	....	....	....	....	....	....	....	....	....	6	0	4	4	10	....	....	....	....
	NHL Totals		**101**	**7**	**21**	**28**	**51**	**6**	**0**	**1**	**125**	**5.6**		**1**	**0.0**	**15:50**	....	....	....	....	....	....	....	....	....

OHL First All-Star Team (2003) • Canadian Major Junior First All-Star Team (2003) • Canadian Major Junior Defenseman of the Year (2003)

Traded to **Phoenix** by **Toronto** with Toronto's 2nd round choice (later traded to Nashville - Nashville selected Roman Josi) in 2008 Entry Draft for Yanic Perreault and Phoenix's 5th round choice (Joel Champagne) in 2008 Entry Draft, February 27, 2007. Signed as a free agent by **Ottawa**, July 11, 2008. Signed as a free agent by **St. Louis**, July 31, 2009. Traded to **Columbus** by **St. Louis** with Tomas Kana for Pascal Pelletier, December 8, 2009. Signed as a free agent by **Omsk** (Russia-KHL), May 20, 2010. Signed as a free agent by **NY Rangers**, August 9, 2011.

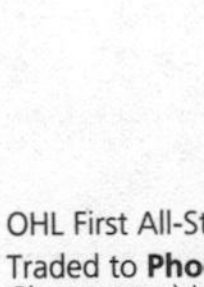

BELL, Mark

(BEHL, MAHRK) **ANA**

Center. Shoots left. 6'3", 220 lbs. Born, St. Pauls, Ont., August 5, 1980. Chicago's 1st choice, 8th overall, in 1998 Entry Draft.

Season	Club	League	GP	G	A	Pts	PIM	PP	SH	GW	S	%	+/-	TF	F%	Min	GP	G	A	Pts	PIM	PP	SH	GW	Min
1995-96	Stratford Cullitons	ON-Jr.B	47	8	15	23	32	....	....	....	....	....	....	....	....	....	....	....	....	....	....	....	....	....	....
1996-97	Ottawa 67's	OHL	65	8	12	20	40	....	....	....	....	....	....	....	....	....	24	4	7	11	13	....	....	....	....
1997-98	Ottawa 67's	OHL	55	34	26	60	87	....	....	....	....	....	....	....	....	....	13	6	5	11	14	....	....	....	....
1998-99	Ottawa 67's	OHL	44	29	26	55	69	....	....	....	....	....	....	....	....	....	9	6	5	11	8	....	....	....	....
99-2000	Ottawa 67's	OHL	48	34	38	72	95	....	....	....	....	....	....	....	....	....	2	0	1	1	0	....	....	....	....
2000-01	Chicago	NHL	13	0	1	1	4	0	0	0	14	0.0	0	141	48.9	12:00	....	....	....	....	....	....	....	....	....
	Norfolk Admirals	AHL	61	15	27	42	126	....	....	....	....	....	....	....	....	....	9	4	3	7	10	....	....	....	....
2001-02	Chicago	NHL	80	12	16	28	124	1	0	1	120	10.0	–6	47	42.6	12:39	5	0	0	0	8	0	0	0	9:18
2002-03	Chicago	NHL	82	14	15	29	113	0	2	0	127	11.0	0	377	52.5	14:04	....	....	....	....	....	....	....	....	....
2003-04	Chicago	NHL	82	21	24	45	106	2	0	1	202	10.4	–14	387	48.3	17:37	....	....	....	....	....	....	....	....	....
2004-05	Trondheim IK	Norway	25	10	17	27	87	....	....	....	....	....	....	....	....	....	11	6	6	12	44	....	....	....	....
2005-06	Chicago	NHL	82	25	23	48	107	11	1	1	227	11.0	–14	1034	48.5	17:37	....	....	....	....	....	....	....	....	....
2006-07	San Jose	NHL	71	11	10	21	83	3	0	2	116	9.5	–9	108	48.2	12:57	4	0	0	0	2	0	0	0	10:16
2007-08	Toronto	NHL	35	4	6	10	60	0	0	0	42	9.5	–2	179	41.3	9:45	....	....	....	....	....	....	....	....	....

			Regular Season														Playoffs								
Season	Club	League	GP	G	A	Pts	PIM	PP	SH	GW	S	%	+/-	TF	F%	Min	GP	G	A	Pts	PIM	PP	SH	GW	Min
2008-09	Toronto Marlies	AHL	56	12	15	27	34	....	....	....	....	....	....	....	....	....	....	....	....	....	....	....	....	....	....
	Hartford	AHL	18	6	8	14	31	....	....	....	....	....	....	....	....	....	5	1	0	1	4	....	....	....	....
2009-10	Kloten Flyers	Swiss	39	13	14	27	69	....	....	....	....	....	....	....	....	....	10	1	4	5	29	....	....	....	....
2010-11	Kloten Flyers	Swiss	41	16	10	26	58	....	....	....	....	....	....	....	....	....	18	6	3	9	*60	....	....	....	....
	NHL Totals		**445**	**87**	**95**	**182**	**597**	**17**	**3**	**5**	**848**	**10.3**		**2273**	**48.4**	**14:33**	**9**	**0**	**0**	**0**	**10**	**0**	**0**	**0**	**9:44**

Signed as a free agent by **Trondheim** (Norway), November 6, 2004. Traded to **San Jose** by **Chicago** for Tom Preissing and Josh Hennessy, July 10, 2006. Traded to **Toronto** by **San Jose** with Vesa Toskala for Toronto's 1st (later traded to St. Louis – St. Louis selected Lars Eller) and 2nd (later traded to St. Louis – St. Louis selected Aaron Palushaj) round choices in 2007 Entry Draft and Toronto's 4th round choice (later traded to Nashville – Nashville selected Craig Smith) in 2009 Entry Draft, June 22, 2007. • Suspended by NHL for 15 games for substance abuse violations. • Missed majority of 2007-08 due to facial injury at Pittsburgh, January 3, 2008. Claimed on waivers by **NY Rangers** from **Toronto**, February 25, 2009. Signed as a free agent by **Kloten** (Swiss), October 6, 2009. Signed as a free agent by **Anaheim**, July 20, 2011.

BELLE, Shawn

(BEHL, SHAWN)

Defense. Shoots left. 6'1", 235 lbs. Born, Edmonton, Alta., January 3, 1985. St. Louis' 1st choice, 30th overall, in 2003 Entry Draft.

Season	Club	League	GP	G	A	Pts	PIM	PP	SH	GW	S	%	+/-	TF	F%	Min	GP	G	A	Pts	PIM	PP	SH	GW	Min
99-2000	K of C Squires	AMBHL	34	7	20	27	36	....	....	....	....	....	....	....	....	....	....	....	....	....	....	....	....	....	....
2000-01	K of C Squires	AMBHL	39	18	30	48	69	....	....	....	....	....	....	....	....	....	....	....	....	....	....	....	....	....	....
	Regina Pats	WHL	4	0	3	3	0	....	....	....	....	....	....	....	....	....	....	....	....	....	....	....	....	....	....
	Tri-City	WHL	2	0	1	1	0	....	....	....	....	....	....	....	....	....	....	....	....	....	....	....	....	....	....
2001-02	Tri-City	WHL	64	1	17	18	51	....	....	....	....	....	....	....	....	....	5	2	1	3	2	....	....	....	....
2002-03	Tri-City	WHL	66	7	14	21	77	....	....	....	....	....	....	....	....	....	....	....	....	....	....	....	....	....	....
2003-04	Tri-City	WHL	55	9	20	29	68	....	....	....	....	....	....	....	....	....	11	3	5	8	15	....	....	....	....
2004-05	Tri-City	WHL	62	13	32	45	76	....	....	....	....	....	....	....	....	....	5	1	1	2	6	....	....	....	....
2005-06	Iowa Stars	AHL	45	1	2	3	63	....	....	....	....	....	....	....	....	....	....	....	....	....	....	....	....	....	....
	Houston Aeros	AHL	16	1	1	2	18	....	....	....	....	....	....	....	....	....	8	1	0	1	4	....	....	....	....
2006-07	**Minnesota**	**NHL**	**9**	**0**	**1**	**1**	**0**	**0**	**0**	**0**	**3**	**0.0**	**4**	**0**	**0.0**	**9:56**	....	....	....	....	....	....	....	....	....
	Houston Aeros	AHL	57	4	14	18	73	....	....	....	....	....	....	....	....	....	....	....	....	....	....	....	....	....	....
2007-08	Houston Aeros	AHL	63	1	2	3	74	....	....	....	....	....	....	....	....	....	3	0	0	0	2	....	....	....	....
2008-09	Hamilton	AHL	60	3	10	13	93	....	....	....	....	....	....	....	....	....	6	1	0	1	16	....	....	....	....
2009-10	**Montreal**	**NHL**	**2**	**0**	**0**	**0**	**0**	**0**	**0**	**0**	**1**	**0.0**	**–2**	**0**	**0.0**	**10:38**	....	....	....	....	....	....	....	....	....
	Hamilton	AHL	70	3	16	19	69	....	....	....	....	....	....	....	....	....	19	1	6	7	20	....	....	....	....
2010-11	**Edmonton**	**NHL**	**5**	**0**	**0**	**0**	**0**	**0**	**0**	**0**	**7**	**0.0**	**–2**	**0**	**0.0**	**16:26**	....	....	....	....	....	....	....	....	....
	Oklahoma City	AHL	39	3	17	20	61	....	....	....	....	....	....	....	....	....	....	....	....	....	....	....	....	....	....
	Colorado	**NHL**	**4**	**0**	**0**	**0**	**2**	**0**	**0**	**0**	**1**	**0.0**	**1**	**0**	**0.0**	**18:02**	....	....	....	....	....	....	....	....	....
	Lake Erie	AHL	12	3	3	6	8	....	....	....	....	....	....	....	....	....	7	0	3	3	8	....	....	....	....
	NHL Totals		**20**	**0**	**1**	**1**	**2**	**0**	**0**	**0**	**12**	**0.0**		**0**	**0.0**	**13:15**	....	....	....	....	....	....	....	....	....

• Rights traded to **Dallas** by **St. Louis** for Jason Bacashihua, June 25, 2004. Traded to **Minnesota** by **Dallas** with Martin Skoula for Willie Mitchell and Minnesota's 2nd round choice (Nico Sacchetti) in 2007 Entry Draft, March 9, 2006. Traded to **Montreal** by **Minnesota** for Cory Locke, July 11, 2008. Signed as a free agent by **Edmonton**, July 13, 2010. Traded to **Colorado** by **Edmonton** for Kevin Montgomery, February 28, 2011.

BENN, Jamie

(BEHN, JAY-mee) **DAL**

Left wing. Shoots left. 6'2", 208 lbs. Born, Victoria, B.C., July 18, 1989. Dallas' 5th choice, 129th overall, in 2007 Entry Draft.

Season	Club	League	GP	G	A	Pts	PIM	PP	SH	GW	S	%	+/-	TF	F%	Min	GP	G	A	Pts	PIM	PP	SH	GW	Min
2004-05	Peninsula Eagles	Minor-BC	STATISTICS NOT AVAILABLE																						
	Peninsula	VIJHL	4	1	2	3	2	....	....	....	....	....	....	....	....	....	2	0	0	0	0	....	....	....	....
2005-06	Peninsula	VIJHL	38	31	24	55	92	....	....	....	....	....	....	....	....	....	7	5	7	10	20	....	....	....	....
2006-07	Victoria Grizzlies	BCHL	53	42	23	65	78	....	....	....	....	....	....	....	....	....	11	5	4	9	12	....	....	....	....
2007-08	Kelowna Rockets	WHL	51	33	32	65	68	....	....	....	....	....	....	....	....	....	7	3	8	11	4	....	....	....	....
2008-09	Kelowna Rockets	WHL	56	46	36	82	71	....	....	....	....	....	....	....	....	....	19	*13	*20	*33	18	....	....	....	....
2009-10	**Dallas**	**NHL**	**82**	**22**	**19**	**41**	**45**	**2**	**0**	**3**	**182**	**12.1**	**–1**	**236**	**46.2**	**14:42**	....	....	....	....	....	....	....	....	....
	Texas Stars	AHL	....	....	....	....	....	....	....	....	....	....	....	....	....	....	24	*14	12	26	22	....	....	....	....
2010-11	**Dallas**	**NHL**	**69**	**22**	**34**	**56**	**52**	**6**	**4**	**3**	**177**	**12.4**	**–5**	**195**	**43.1**	**18:01**	....	....	....	....	....	....	....	....	....
	NHL Totals		**151**	**44**	**53**	**97**	**97**	**8**	**4**	**6**	**359**	**12.3**		**431**	**44.8**	**16:13**	....	....	....	....	....	....	....	....	....

WHL West First All-Star Team (2009)

BENOIT, Andre

(behn-WAH, AWN-dray)

Defense. Shoots left. 5'11", 186 lbs. Born, St. Albert, Ont., January 6, 1984.

Season	Club	League	GP	G	A	Pts	PIM	PP	SH	GW	S	%	+/-	TF	F%	Min	GP	G	A	Pts	PIM	PP	SH	GW	Min
2000-01	Kitchener Rangers	OHL	65	16	19	35	37	....	....	....	....	....	....	....	....	....	....	....	....	....	....	....	....	....	....
2001-02	Kitchener Rangers	OHL	62	13	32	45	77	....	....	....	....	....	....	....	....	....	4	1	0	1	8	....	....	....	....
2002-03	Kitchener Rangers	OHL	65	22	45	67	77	....	....	....	....	....	....	....	....	....	21	1	16	17	16	....	....	....	....
2003-04	Kitchener Rangers	OHL	65	24	51	75	67	....	....	....	....	....	....	....	....	....	5	1	1	2	6	....	....	....	....
2004-05	Kitchener Rangers	OHL	67	24	53	77	72	....	....	....	....	....	....	....	....	....	15	5	13	18	6	....	....	....	....
2005-06	Hamilton	AHL	70	7	19	26	60	....	....	....	....	....	....	....	....	....	....	....	....	....	....	....	....	....	....
2006-07	Hamilton	AHL	64	10	21	31	41	....	....	....	....	....	....	....	....	....	22	2	11	13	22	....	....	....	....
2007-08	Tappara Tampere	Finland	54	12	26	38	96	....	....	....	....	....	....	....	....	....	11	2	3	5	10	....	....	....	....
2008-09	Sodertalje SK	Sweden	54	4	16	20	34	....	....	....	....	....	....	....	....	....	....	....	....	....	....	....	....	....	....
	Sodertalje SK	Sweden-Q	10	0	2	2	10	....	....	....	....	....	....	....	....	....	....	....	....	....	....	....	....	....	....
2009-10	Hamilton	AHL	78	6	30	36	63	....	....	....	....	....	....	....	....	....	19	3	11	14	8	....	....	....	....
2010-11	**Ottawa**	**NHL**	**8**	**0**	**1**	**1**	**6**	**0**	**0**	**0**	**17**	**0.0**	**–1**	**0**	**0.0**	**16:50**	....	....	....	....	....	....	....	....	....
	Binghamton	AHL	73	11	44	55	53	....	....	....	....	....	....	....	....	....	23	3	*15	18	14	....	....	....	....
	NHL Totals		**8**	**0**	**1**	**1**	**6**	**0**	**0**	**0**	**17**	**0.0**		**0**	**0.0**	**16:50**	....	....	....	....	....	....	....	....	....

AHL Second All-Star Team (2011)

Signed as a free agent by **Montreal**, January 9, 2006. Signed as a free agent by **Tappara Tampere** (Finland), June 21, 2007. Signed as a free agent by **Montreal**, May 13, 2009. Signed as a free agent by **Ottawa**, August 6, 2010.

BENTIVOGLIO, Sean

(behn-tih-VOHG-lee-oh, SHAWN)

Left wing. Shoots left. 5'10", 190 lbs. Born, Thorold, Ont., October 16, 1985.

Season	Club	League	GP	G	A	Pts	PIM	PP	SH	GW	S	%	+/-	TF	F%	Min	GP	G	A	Pts	PIM	PP	SH	GW	Min
2003-04	Niagara University	CHA	39	2	19	21	14	....	....	....	....	....	....	....	....	....	....	....	....	....	....	....	....	....	....
2004-05	Niagara University	CHA	36	9	18	27	20	....	....	....	....	....	....	....	....	....	....	....	....	....	....	....	....	....	....
2005-06	Niagara University	CHA	33	16	22	38	55	....	....	....	....	....	....	....	....	....	....	....	....	....	....	....	....	....	....
2006-07	Niagara University	CHA	37	16	30	46	53	....	....	....	....	....	....	....	....	....	....	....	....	....	....	....	....	....	....
	Providence Bruins	AHL	15	3	11	14	8	....	....	....	....	....	....	....	....	....	13	3	6	9	14	....	....	....	....
2007-08	Bridgeport	AHL	68	9	23	32	28	....	....	....	....	....	....	....	....	....	....	....	....	....	....	....	....	....	....
2008-09	**NY Islanders**	**NHL**	**1**	**0**	**0**	**0**	**2**	**0**	**0**	**0**	**2**	**0.0**	**0**	**1**	**0.0**	**11:31**	....	....	....	....	....	....	....	....	....
	Bridgeport	AHL	78	13	19	32	47	....	....	....	....	....	....	....	....	....	4	1	1	2	4	....	....	....	....
2009-10	Bridgeport	AHL	80	19	26	45	64	....	....	....	....	....	....	....	....	....	5	1	1	2	12	....	....	....	....
2010-11	Augsburg	Germany	40	5	16	21	54	....	....	....	....	....	....	....	....	....	....	....	....	....	....	....	....	....	....
	NHL Totals		**1**	**0**	**0**	**0**	**2**	**0**	**0**	**0**	**2**	**0.0**		**1**	**0.0**	**11:31**	....	....	....	....	....	....	....	....	....

Signed as a free agent by **NY Islanders**, May 19, 2007. Signed as a free agent by **Augsburg** (Germany), July 22, 2010.

BERGENHEIM, Sean

(BUHR-gehn-highm, SHAWN) **FLA**

Left wing. Shoots left. 5'11", 200 lbs. Born, Helsinki, Finland, February 8, 1984. NY Islanders' 1st choice, 22nd overall, in 2002 Entry Draft.

Season	Club	League	GP	G	A	Pts	PIM	PP	SH	GW	S	%	+/-	TF	F%	Min	GP	G	A	Pts	PIM	PP	SH	GW	Min
99-2000	Jokerit U18	Fin-U18	30	22	11	33	34	....	....	....	....	....	....	....	....	....	3	1	0	1	0	....	....	....	....
	Jokerit U18	Fin-U18	17	10	8	18	14	....	....	....	....	....	....	....	....	....	3	1	0	1	2	....	....	....	....
2000-01	Jokerit U18	Fin-U18	1	1	0	1	4	....	....	....	....	....	....	....	....	....	6	9	5	14	8	....	....	....	....
	Jokerit Helsinki Jr.	Fin-Jr.	18	6	4	10	26	....	....	....	....	....	....	....	....	....	2	0	0	0	4	....	....	....	....
2001-02	Jokerit U18	Fin-U18	....	....	....	....	....	....	....	....	....	....	....	....	....	....	5	6	2	8	18	....	....	....	....
	Jokerit Helsinki Jr.	Fin-Jr.	23	11	19	30	36	....	....	....	....	....	....	....	....	....	1	0	0	0	2	....	....	....	....
	Kiekko-Vantaa	Finland-2	4	0	0	0	52	....	....	....	....	....	....	....	....	....	....	....	....	....	....	....	....	....	....
	Jokerit Helsinki	Finland	28	2	2	4	4	....	....	....	....	....	....	....	....	....	....	....	....	....	....	....	....	....	....
2002-03	Jokerit Helsinki Jr.	Fin-Jr.	2	3	0	3	2	....	....	....	....	....	....	....	....	....	....	....	....	....	....	....	....	....	....
	Jokerit Helsinki	Finland	38	3	3	6	4	....	....	....	....	....	....	....	....	....	2	0	0	0	0	....	....	....	....
2003-04	**NY Islanders**	**NHL**	**18**	**1**	**1**	**2**	**4**	**0**	**1**	**0**	**12**	**8.3**	**–4**	**2**	**50.0**	**8:55**	....	....	....	....	....	....	....	....	....
	Jokerit Helsinki	Finland	20	2	2	4	18	....	....	....	....	....	....	....	....	....	3	1	1	2	0	....	....	....	....
	Bridgeport	AHL	....	....	....	....	....	....	....	....	....	....	....	....	....	....	7	2	3	5	10	....	....	....	....
2004-05	Bridgeport	AHL	61	15	14	29	69	....	....	....	....	....	....	....	....	....	....	....	....	....	....	....	....	....	....

			Regular Season														Playoffs								
Season	Club	League	GP	G	A	Pts	PIM	PP	SH	GW	S	%	+/-	TF	F%	Min	GP	G	A	Pts	PIM	PP	SH	GW	Min
2005-06	**NY Islanders**	**NHL**	**28**	**4**	**5**	**9**	**20**	**0**	**0**	**1**	**63**	**6.3**	**–11**	**14**	**28.6**	**13:17**	....	....	....	....	....	....	....	....	....
	Bridgeport	AHL	55	25	22	47	112	....	....	....	....	....	....	....	....	....	7	0	2	2	24	....	....	....	....
2006-07	Yaroslavl	Russia	9	1	4	5	26	....	....	....	....	....	....	....	....	....	....	....	....	....	....	....	....	....	....
	Frolunda	Sweden	36	16	17	33	80	....	....	....	....	....	....	....	....	....	....	....	....	....	....	....	....	....	....
2007-08	**NY Islanders**	**NHL**	**78**	**10**	**12**	**22**	**62**	**1**	**0**	**1**	**155**	**6.5**	**–3**	**15**	**60.0**	**11:15**	....	....	....	....	....	....	....	....	....
2008-09	**NY Islanders**	**NHL**	**59**	**15**	**9**	**24**	**64**	**0**	**4**	**5**	**152**	**9.9**	**–2**	**22**	**40.9**	**14:15**	....	....	....	....	....	....	....	....	....
2009-10	**NY Islanders**	**NHL**	**63**	**10**	**13**	**23**	**45**	**0**	**2**	**0**	**133**	**7.5**	**1**	**17**	**29.4**	**14:04**	....	....	....	....	....	....	....	....	....
2010-11	**Tampa Bay**	**NHL**	**80**	**14**	**15**	**29**	**56**	**2**	**0**	**1**	**182**	**7.7**	**0**	**51**	**49.0**	**13:59**	**16**	**9**	**2**	**11**	**8**	**0**	**0**	**1**	**14:09**
	NHL Totals		**326**	**54**	**55**	**109**	**251**	**3**	**7**	**8**	**697**	**7.7**		**121**	**43.8**	**13:03**	**16**	**9**	**2**	**11**	**8**	**0**	**0**	**1**	**14:10**

Signed as a free agent by **Yaroslavl** (Russia), August 5, 2006. Signed as a free agent by **Frolunda** (Sweden), November 3, 2006. Signed as a free agent by **Tampa Bay**, August 17, 2010. Signed as a free agent by **Florida**, July 1, 2011.

BERGERON, Marc-Andre

(BAIR-zhur-uhn, MAHRK-AWN-dray) **T.B.**

Defense. Shoots left. 5'9", 198 lbs. Born, St-Louis-de-France, Que., October 13, 1980.

Season	Club	League	GP	G	A	Pts	PIM	PP	SH	GW	S	%	+/-	TF	F%	Min	GP	G	A	Pts	PIM	PP	SH	GW	Min
1996-97	Cap-d-Madeleine	QAAA	4	0	1	1	0	....	....	....	....	....	....	....	....	....	2	0	0	0	0	....	....	....	....
1997-98	Baie-Comeau	QMJHL	40	6	14	20	48	....	....	....	....	....	....	....	....	....	....	....	....	....	....	....	....	....	....
1998-99	Baie-Comeau	QMJHL	47	9	14	23	57	....	....	....	....	....	....	....	....	....	....	....	....	....	....	....	....	....	....
	Shawinigan	QMJHL	23	5	7	12	66	....	....	....	....	....	....	....	....	....	5	2	2	4	24	....	....	....	....
99-2000	Shawinigan	QMJHL	70	24	50	74	173	....	....	....	....	....	....	....	....	....	13	4	7	11	45	....	....	....	....
2000-01	Shawinigan	QMJHL	69	42	59	101	185	....	....	....	....	....	....	....	....	....	10	4	11	15	24	....	....	....	....
2001-02	Hamilton	AHL	50	2	13	15	61	....	....	....	....	....	....	....	....	....	9	1	4	5	8	....	....	....	....
2002-03	**Edmonton**	**NHL**	**5**	**1**	**1**	**2**	**9**	**0**	**0**	**0**	**5**	**20.0**	**2**	**0**	**0.0**	**16:30**	**1**	**0**	**1**	**1**	**0**	**0**	**0**	**0**	**19:20**
	Hamilton	AHL	66	8	31	39	73	....	....	....	....	....	....	....	....	....	20	0	7	7	25	....	....	....	....
2003-04	**Edmonton**	**NHL**	**54**	**9**	**17**	**26**	**26**	**3**	**0**	**0**	**105**	**8.6**	**13**	**0**	**0.0**	**17:39**	....	....	....	....	....	....	....	....	....
	Toronto	AHL	17	4	3	7	23	....	....	....	....	....	....	....	....	....	....	....	....	....	....	....	....	....	....
2004-05	Brynas IF Gavle	Sweden	10	3	2	5	72	....	....	....	....	....	....	....	....	....	....	....	....	....	....	....	....	....	....
	Brynas IF Gavle	Sweden-Q	9	1	2	3	8	....	....	....	....	....	....	....	....	....	....	....	....	....	....	....	....	....	....
2005-06	**Edmonton**	**NHL**	**75**	**15**	**20**	**35**	**38**	**8**	**0**	**1**	**144**	**10.4**	**3**	**0**	**0.0**	**21:14**	**18**	**2**	**1**	**3**	**14**	**2**	**0**	**0**	**14:56**
2006-07	**Edmonton**	**NHL**	**55**	**8**	**17**	**25**	**28**	**6**	**0**	**3**	**111**	**7.2**	**–9**	**0**	**0.0**	**17:27**	....	....	....	....	....	....	....	....	....
	NY Islanders	**NHL**	**23**	**6**	**15**	**21**	**10**	**4**	**0**	**1**	**55**	**10.9**	**5**	**0**	**0.0**	**23:07**	**5**	**1**	**1**	**2**	**6**	**1**	**0**	**1**	**27:21**
2007-08	**NY Islanders**	**NHL**	**46**	**9**	**9**	**18**	**16**	**8**	**0**	**1**	**96**	**9.4**	**–14**	**0**	**0.0**	**18:17**	....	....	....	....	....	....	....	....	....
	Anaheim	**NHL**	**9**	**0**	**1**	**1**	**4**	**0**	**0**	**0**	**12**	**0.0**	**–2**	**0**	**0.0**	**12:50**	....	....	....	....	....	....	....	....	....
2008-09	**Minnesota**	**NHL**	**72**	**14**	**18**	**32**	**30**	**7**	**0**	**3**	**140**	**10.0**	**5**	**0**	**0.0**	**16:54**	....	....	....	....	....	....	....	....	....
2009-10	**Montreal**	**NHL**	**60**	**13**	**21**	**34**	**16**	**7**	**0**	**4**	**123**	**10.6**	**–7**	**0**	**0.0**	**15:04**	**19**	**2**	**4**	**6**	**10**	**2**	**0**	**0**	**16:27**
	Hamilton	AHL	3	0	6	6	0	....	....	....	....	....	....	....	....	....	....	....	....	....	....	....	....	....	....
2010-11	**Tampa Bay**	**NHL**	**23**	**2**	**6**	**8**	**8**	**0**	**0**	**1**	**37**	**5.4**	**–10**	**0**	**0.0**	**14:19**	**14**	**2**	**1**	**3**	**9**	**2**	**0**	**1**	**12:58**
	Norfolk Admirals	AHL	13	2	6	8	6	....	....	....	....	....	....	....	....	....	....	....	....	....	....	....	....	....	....
	NHL Totals		**422**	**77**	**125**	**202**	**185**	**43**	**0**	**14**	**828**	**9.3**		**0**	**0.0**	**17:50**	**57**	**7**	**8**	**15**	**39**	**7**	**0**	**2**	**16:07**

QMJHL First All-Star Team (2001) • Canadian Major Junior First All-Star Team (2001) • Canadian Major Junior Defenseman of the Year (2001) • AHL Second All-Star Team (2003)

Signed as a free agent by **Edmonton**, July 20, 2001. Signed as a free agent by **Gavle** (Sweden), January 23, 2005. Traded to **NY Islanders** by **Edmonton** with Edmonton's 3rd round choice (later traded back to Edmonton, later traded to Anaheim, later traded back to NY Islanders - NY Islanders selected Kirill Petrov) in 2008 Entry Draft for Denis Grebeshkov, February 18, 2007. Traded to **Anaheim** by **NY Islanders** for Edmonton's 3rd round choice (previously acquired, NY Islanders selected Kirill Petrov) in 2008 Entry Draft, February 26, 2008. Traded to **Minnesota** by **Anaheim** for Minnesota's 3rd round choice (Brandon McMillan) in 2008 Entry Draft, June 10, 2008. Signed as a free agent by **Montreal**, October 6, 2009. Signed as a free agent by **Tampa Bay**, January 4, 2011.

BERGERON, Patrice

(BUHR-zhuhr-uhn, pa-TREES) **BOS**

Center. Shoots right. 6'2", 194 lbs. Born, Ancienne-Lorette, Que., July 24, 1985. Boston's 2nd choice, 45th overall, in 2003 Entry Draft.

Season	Club	League	GP	G	A	Pts	PIM	PP	SH	GW	S	%	+/-	TF	F%	Min	GP	G	A	Pts	PIM	PP	SH	GW	Min
2000-01	Ste-Foy	QAAA	5	1	2	3	0	....	....	....	....	....	....	....	....	....	....	....	....	....	....	....	....	....	....
2001-02	St-Francois	QAAA	38	25	37	62	18	....	....	....	....	....	....	....	....	....	8	6	4	10	10	....	....	....	....
	Acadie-Bathurst	QMJHL	4	0	1	1	0	....	....	....	....	....	....	....	....	....	....	....	....	....	....	....	....	....	....
2002-03	Acadie-Bathurst	QMJHL	70	23	50	73	62	....	....	....	....	....	....	....	....	....	11	6	9	15	6	....	....	....	....
2003-04	**Boston**	**NHL**	**71**	**16**	**23**	**39**	**22**	**7**	**0**	**2**	**133**	**12.0**	**5**	**699**	**49.4**	**16:21**	**7**	**1**	**3**	**4**	**0**	**0**	**0**	**1**	**17:13**
2004-05	Providence Bruins	AHL	68	21	40	61	59	....	....	....	....	....	....	....	....	....	16	5	7	12	4	....	....	....	....
2005-06	**Boston**	**NHL**	**81**	**31**	**42**	**73**	**22**	**12**	**1**	**6**	**310**	**10.0**	**3**	**1447**	**54.7**	**20:36**	....	....	....	....	....	....	....	....	....
2006-07	**Boston**	**NHL**	**77**	**22**	**48**	**70**	**26**	**14**	**0**	**6**	**224**	**9.8**	**–28**	**1560**	**51.2**	**20:49**	....	....	....	....	....	....	....	....	....
2007-08	**Boston**	**NHL**	**10**	**3**	**4**	**7**	**2**	**2**	**0**	**0**	**24**	**12.5**	**2**	**175**	**50.3**	**18:10**	....	....	....	....	....	....	....	....	....
2008-09	**Boston**	**NHL**	**64**	**8**	**31**	**39**	**16**	**1**	**1**	**1**	**155**	**5.2**	**2**	**1025**	**54.5**	**17:59**	**11**	**0**	**5**	**5**	**11**	**0**	**0**	**0**	**17:56**
2009-10	**Boston**	**NHL**	**73**	**19**	**33**	**52**	**28**	**0**	**1**	**4**	**184**	**10.3**	**6**	**1342**	**58.0**	**18:54**	**13**	**4**	**7**	**11**	**2**	**0**	**0**	**1**	**20:23**
	Canada	Olympics	7	0	1	1	2	....	....	....	....	....	....	....	....	....	....	....	....	....	....	....	....	....	....
2010-11♦	**Boston**	**NHL**	**80**	**22**	**35**	**57**	**26**	**3**	**2**	**4**	**211**	**10.4**	**20**	**1439**	**56.6**	**17:53**	**23**	**6**	**14**	**20**	**28**	**0**	***2**	**1**	**18:42**
	NHL Totals		**456**	**121**	**216**	**337**	**142**	**39**	**5**	**23**	**1241**	**9.8**		**7687**	**54.3**	**18:48**	**54**	**11**	**29**	**40**	**41**	**0**	**2**	**3**	**18:45**

QAAA Second All-Star Team (2002)

• Missed majority of 2007-08 due to concussion vs. Philadelphia, October 27, 2007.

BERGFORS, Niclas

(BUHRG-fohrs, NIHK-luhs) **NSH**

Right wing. Shoots right. 6', 200 lbs. Born, Sodertalje, Sweden, March 7, 1987. New Jersey's 1st choice, 23rd overall, in 2005 Entry Draft.

Season	Club	League	GP	G	A	Pts	PIM	PP	SH	GW	S	%	+/-	TF	F%	Min	GP	G	A	Pts	PIM	PP	SH	GW	Min
2002-03	Sodertalje SK U18	Swe-U18	4	4	4	8	0	....	....	....	....	....	....	....	....	....	....	....	....	....	....	....	....	....	....
	Sodertalje SK Jr.	Swe-Jr.	13	1	5	6	4	....	....	....	....	....	....	....	....	....	....	....	....	....	....	....	....	....	....
2003-04	Sodertalje SK U18	Swe-U18	5	14	4	18	4	....	....	....	....	....	....	....	....	....	2	0	1	1	6	....	....	....	....
	Sodertalje SK Jr.	Swe-Jr.	31	13	17	30	22	....	....	....	....	....	....	....	....	....	2	1	1	2	0	....	....	....	....
2004-05	Sodertalje SK Jr.	Swe-Jr.	21	18	16	34	25	....	....	....	....	....	....	....	....	....	3	0	3	3	4	....	....	....	....
	Sodertalje SK	Sweden	25	1	0	1	2	....	....	....	....	....	....	....	....	....	2	0	0	0	0	....	....	....	....
2005-06	Albany River Rats	AHL	65	17	23	40	10	....	....	....	....	....	....	....	....	....	....	....	....	....	....	....	....	....	....
2006-07	Lowell Devils	AHL	60	13	19	32	8	....	....	....	....	....	....	....	....	....	....	....	....	....	....	....	....	....	....
2007-08	**New Jersey**	**NHL**	**1**	**0**	**0**	**0**	**0**	**0**	**0**	**0**	**3**	**0.0**	**–1**	**1**	**0.0**	**11:17**	....	....	....	....	....	....	....	....	....
	Lowell Devils	AHL	66	12	15	27	22	....	....	....	....	....	....	....	....	....	....	....	....	....	....	....	....	....	....
2008-09	**New Jersey**	**NHL**	**8**	**1**	**0**	**1**	**0**	**0**	**0**	**0**	**6**	**16.7**	**–1**	**0**	**0.0**	**5:48**	....	....	....	....	....	....	....	....	....
	Lowell Devils	AHL	66	22	29	51	14	....	....	....	....	....	....	....	....	....	....	....	....	....	....	....	....	....	....
2009-10	**New Jersey**	**NHL**	**54**	**13**	**14**	**27**	**10**	**8**	**0**	**4**	**134**	**9.7**	**–7**	**7**	**71.4**	**14:53**	....	....	....	....	....	....	....	....	....
	Atlanta	**NHL**	**27**	**8**	**9**	**17**	**0**	**1**	**0**	**2**	**83**	**9.6**	**–3**	**12**	**33.3**	**16:30**	....	....	....	....	....	....	....	....	....
2010-11	**Atlanta**	**NHL**	**52**	**11**	**18**	**29**	**6**	**3**	**0**	**1**	**99**	**11.1**	**–11**	**3**	**66.7**	**14:09**	....	....	....	....	....	....	....	....	....
	Florida	**NHL**	**20**	**1**	**6**	**7**	**2**	**0**	**0**	**0**	**53**	**1.9**	**2**	**6**	**33.3**	**16:19**	....	....	....	....	....	....	....	....	....
	NHL Totals		**162**	**34**	**47**	**81**	**18**	**12**	**0**	**7**	**378**	**9.0**		**29**	**44.8**	**14:37**	....	....	....	....	....	....	....	....	....

NHL All-Rookie Team (2010)

Traded to **Atlanta** by **New Jersey** with Johnny Oduya, Patrice Cormier and New Jersey's 1st (later traded to Chicago – Chicago selected Kevin Hayes) and 2nd (later traded to Chicago – Chicago selected Justin Holl) round choices in 2010 Entry Draft for Ilya Kovalchuk, Anssi Salmela and Atlanta's 2nd round choice (Jonathon Merrill) in 2010 Entry Draft, February 4, 2010. Traded to **Florida** by **Atlanta** with Patrick Rissmiller for Radek Dvorak and Carolina's 5th round choice (previously acquired, later traded to San Jose – San Jose selected Sean Kuraly) in 2011 Entry Draft, February 27, 2011. Signed as a free agent by **Nashville**, July 3, 2011.

BERGLUND, Patrik

(BUHRG-luhnd, PAT-rihk) **ST.L.**

Center. Shoots left. 6'4", 218 lbs. Born, Vasteras, Sweden, June 2, 1988. St. Louis' 2nd choice, 25th overall, in 2006 Entry Draft.

Season	Club	League	GP	G	A	Pts	PIM	PP	SH	GW	S	%	+/-	TF	F%	Min	GP	G	A	Pts	PIM	PP	SH	GW	Min
2002-03	Vasteras U18	Swe-U18	1	0	1	1	0	....	....	....	....	....	....	....	....	....	....	....	....	....	....	....	....	....	....
2003-04	Vasteras U18	Swe-U18	10	4	1	5	18	....	....	....	....	....	....	....	....	....	....	....	....	....	....	....	....	....	....
2004-05	Vasteras U18	Swe-U18	5	2	1	3	4	....	....	....	....	....	....	....	....	....	3	0	1	1	6	....	....	....	....
	Vasteras Jr.	Swe-Jr.	25	5	5	10	14	....	....	....	....	....	....	....	....	....	....	....	....	....	....	....	....	....	....
2005-06	Vasteras Jr.	Swe-Jr.	27	17	12	29	38	....	....	....	....	....	....	....	....	....	....	....	....	....	....	....	....	....	....
	VIK Vasteras HK	Sweden-2	21	3	1	4	4	....	....	....	....	....	....	....	....	....	....	....	....	....	....	....	....	....	....
2006-07	VIK Vasteras HK	Sweden-2	35	21	27	48	30	....	....	....	....	....	....	....	....	....	1	0	0	0	2	....	....	....	....
	Vasteras Jr.	Swe-Jr.	....	....	....	....	....	....	....	....	....	....	....	....	....	....	5	4	5	9	6	....	....	....	....
2007-08	VIK Vasteras HK	Sweden-2	46	22	32	54	26	....	....	....	....	....	....	....	....	....	5	1	2	3	6	....	....	....	....
2008-09	**St. Louis**	**NHL**	**76**	**21**	**26**	**47**	**16**	**7**	**0**	**1**	**143**	**14.7**	**19**	**540**	**39.8**	**14:43**	**4**	**0**	**0**	**0**	**2**	**0**	**0**	**0**	**10:11**
2009-10	**St. Louis**	**NHL**	**71**	**13**	**13**	**26**	**16**	**6**	**0**	**4**	**129**	**10.1**	**–5**	**504**	**43.7**	**13:30**	....	....	....	....	....	....	....	....	....
2010-11	**St. Louis**	**NHL**	**81**	**22**	**30**	**52**	**26**	**8**	**0**	**1**	**175**	**12.6**	**–3**	**974**	**46.2**	**17:11**	....	....	....	....	....	....	....	....	....
	NHL Totals		**228**	**56**	**69**	**125**	**58**	**21**	**0**	**6**	**447**	**12.5**		**2018**	**43.9**	**15:13**	**4**	**0**	**0**	**0**	**2**	**0**	**0**	**0**	**10:11**

NHL All-Rookie Team (2009)

BERNIER, Steve

(BAIRN-yay, STEEV)

Right wing. Shoots right. 6'2", 216 lbs. Born, Quebec City, Que., March 31, 1985. San Jose's 2nd choice, 16th overall, in 2003 Entry Draft.

			Regular Season														Playoffs								
Season	Club	League	GP	G	A	Pts	PIM	PP	SH	GW	S	%	+/-	TF	F%	Min	GP	G	A	Pts	PIM	PP	SH	GW	Min
1998-99	Quebec AA Aces	QAHA	28	33	23	56	24	....	....	....	....	....	....	....	....	....	....	....	....	....	....	....	....	....	....
99-2000	Quebec AA Aces	QAHA	26	12	23	35	42	....	....	....	....	....	....	....	....	....	....	....	....	....	....	....	....	....	....
2000-01	Ste-Foy	QAAA	39	17	35	52	48	....	....	....	....	....	....	....	....	....	16	9	17	26	8	....	....	....	....
2001-02	Moncton Wildcats	QMJHL	66	31	28	59	51	....	....	....	....	....	....	....	....	....	....	....	....	....	....	....	....	....	....
2002-03	Moncton Wildcats	QMJHL	71	49	52	101	90	....	....	....	....	....	....	....	....	....	2	1	0	1	2	....	....	....	....
2003-04	Moncton Wildcats	QMJHL	66	36	46	82	80	....	....	....	....	....	....	....	....	....	20	7	10	17	17	....	....	....	....
2004-05	Moncton Wildcats	QMJHL	68	35	36	71	114	....	....	....	....	....	....	....	....	....	12	6	13	19	22	....	....	....	....
2005-06	**San Jose**	**NHL**	**39**	**14**	**13**	**27**	**35**	**2**	**1**	**1**	**75**	**18.7**	**4**	**8**	**62.5**	**14:08**	**11**	**1**	**5**	**6**	**8**	**1**	**0**	**1**	**15:17**
	Cleveland Barons	AHL	49	20	23	43	33	....	....	....	....	....	....	....	....	....	....	....	....	....	....	....	....	....	....
2006-07	**San Jose**	**NHL**	**62**	**15**	**16**	**31**	**29**	**6**	**0**	**4**	**104**	**14.4**	**5**	**18**	**27.8**	**13:35**	**11**	**0**	**1**	**1**	**2**	**0**	**0**	**0**	**10:39**
	Worcester Sharks	AHL	10	3	4	7	2	....	....	....	....	....	....	....	....	....	....	....	....	....	....	....	....	....	....
2007-08	**San Jose**	**NHL**	**59**	**13**	**10**	**23**	**62**	**4**	**0**	**0**	**96**	**13.5**	**–2**	**10**	**50.0**	**13:07**	....	....	....	....	....	....	....	....	....
	Buffalo	**NHL**	**17**	**3**	**6**	**9**	**2**	**0**	**0**	**0**	**35**	**8.6**	**1**	**5**	**20.0**	**14:06**	....	....	....	....	....	....	....	....	....
2008-09	**Vancouver**	**NHL**	**81**	**15**	**17**	**32**	**27**	**2**	**0**	**4**	**137**	**10.9**	**4**	**21**	**23.8**	**13:50**	**10**	**2**	**2**	**4**	**7**	**2**	**0**	**2**	**15:00**
2009-10	**Vancouver**	**NHL**	**59**	**11**	**11**	**22**	**21**	**3**	**0**	**0**	**95**	**11.6**	**0**	**34**	**20.6**	**14:10**	**12**	**4**	**1**	**5**	**0**	**2**	**0**	**0**	**9:59**
2010-11	**Florida**	**NHL**	**68**	**5**	**10**	**15**	**21**	**3**	**0**	**0**	**97**	**5.2**	**–14**	**17**	**23.5**	**13:02**	....	....	....	....	....	....	....	....	....
	NHL Totals		**385**	**76**	**83**	**159**	**197**	**20**	**1**	**9**	**639**	**11.9**		**113**	**28.3**	**13:38**	**44**	**7**	**9**	**16**	**17**	**5**	**0**	**3**	**12:37**

QMJHL All-Rookie Team (2002) • QMJHL Second All-Star Team (2003, 2004) • Canadian Major Junior Second All-Star Team (2003)

Traded to **Buffalo** by **San Jose** with San Jose's 1st round choice (Tyler Ennis) in 2008 Entry Draft for Brian Campbell and Buffalo's 7th round choice (Drew Daniels) in 2008 Entry Draft, February 26, 2008. Traded to **Vancouver** by **Buffalo** for Los Angeles' 3rd round choice (previously acquired, Buffalo selected Brayden McNabb) in 2009 Entry Draft and Vancouver's 2nd round choice (later traded to Columbus – Columbus selected Petr Straka) in 2010 Entry Draft, July 4, 2008. Traded to **Florida** by **Vancouver** with Michael Grabner and Vancouver's 1st round choice (Quinton Howden) in 2010 Entry Draft for Keith Ballard and Victor Oreskovich, June 25, 2010.

BERTUZZI, Todd

(buhr-TOO-zee, TAWD) **DET**

Right wing. Shoots left. 6'3", 225 lbs. Born, Sudbury, Ont., February 2, 1975. NY Islanders' 1st choice, 23rd overall, in 1993 Entry Draft.

			Regular Season														Playoffs								
Season	Club	League	GP	G	A	Pts	PIM	PP	SH	GW	S	%	+/-	TF	F%	Min	GP	G	A	Pts	PIM	PP	SH	GW	Min
1990-91	Sudbury Legion	NOHA	48	25	46	71	247	....	....	....	....	....	....	....	....	....	....	....	....	....	....	....	....	....	....
	Sudbury Cubs	NOJHA	3	3	2	5	10	....	....	....	....	....	....	....	....	....	....	....	....	....	....	....	....	....	....
1991-92	Guelph Storm	OHL	47	7	14	21	145	....	....	....	....	....	....	....	....	....	....	....	....	....	....	....	....	....	....
1992-93	Guelph Storm	OHL	59	27	32	59	164	....	....	....	....	....	....	....	....	....	5	2	2	4	6	....	....	....	....
1993-94	Guelph Storm	OHL	61	28	54	82	165	....	....	....	....	....	....	....	....	....	9	2	6	8	30	....	....	....	....
1994-95	Guelph Storm	OHL	62	54	65	119	58	....	....	....	....	....	....	....	....	....	14	*15	18	33	41	....	....	....	....
1995-96	**NY Islanders**	**NHL**	**76**	**18**	**21**	**39**	**83**	**4**	**0**	**2**	**127**	**14.2**	**–14**	....	....	....	....	....	....	....	....	....	....	....	....
1996-97	**NY Islanders**	**NHL**	**64**	**10**	**13**	**23**	**68**	**3**	**0**	**1**	**79**	**12.7**	**–3**	....	....	....	....	....	....	....	....	....	....	....	....
	Utah Grizzlies	IHL	13	5	5	10	16	....	....	....	....	....	....	....	....	....	....	....	....	....	....	....	....	....	....
1997-98	**NY Islanders**	**NHL**	**52**	**7**	**11**	**18**	**58**	**1**	**0**	**1**	**63**	**11.1**	**–19**	....	....	....	....	....	....	....	....	....	....	....	....
	Vancouver	**NHL**	**22**	**6**	**9**	**15**	**63**	**1**	**1**	**1**	**39**	**15.4**	**2**	....	....	....	....	....	....	....	....	....	....	....	....
1998-99	**Vancouver**	**NHL**	**32**	**8**	**8**	**16**	**44**	**1**	**0**	**3**	**72**	**11.1**	**–6**	**191**	**43.5**	**18:28**	....	....	....	....	....	....	....	....	....
99-2000	**Vancouver**	**NHL**	**80**	**25**	**25**	**50**	**126**	**4**	**0**	**2**	**173**	**14.5**	**–2**	**476**	**46.6**	**15:24**	....	....	....	....	....	....	....	....	....
2000-01	**Vancouver**	**NHL**	**79**	**25**	**30**	**55**	**93**	**14**	**0**	**3**	**203**	**12.3**	**–18**	**84**	**45.2**	**17:13**	**4**	**2**	**2**	**4**	**8**	**0**	**0**	**0**	**19:01**
2001-02	**Vancouver**	**NHL**	**72**	**36**	**49**	**85**	**110**	**14**	**0**	**3**	**203**	**17.7**	**21**	**151**	**49.0**	**19:40**	**6**	**2**	**2**	**4**	**14**	**1**	**0**	**0**	**21:50**
2002-03	**Vancouver**	**NHL**	**82**	**46**	**51**	**97**	**144**	***25**	**0**	**7**	**243**	**18.9**	**2**	**208**	**47.1**	**20:34**	**14**	**2**	**4**	**6**	***60**	**0**	**0**	**0**	**21:05**
2003-04	**Vancouver**	**NHL**	**69**	**17**	**43**	**60**	**122**	**8**	**0**	**2**	**156**	**10.9**	**21**	**111**	**45.1**	**21:00**	....	....	....	....	....	....	....	....	....
2004-05			DID NOT PLAY – SUSPENDED																						
2005-06	**Vancouver**	**NHL**	**82**	**25**	**46**	**71**	**120**	**12**	**0**	**3**	**200**	**12.5**	**–17**	**363**	**43.8**	**19:08**	....	....	....	....	....	....	....	....	....
	Canada	Olympics	6	0	3	3	6	....	....	....	....	....	....	....	....	....	....	....	....	....	....	....	....	....	....
2006-07	**Florida**	**NHL**	**7**	**1**	**6**	**7**	**13**	**1**	**0**	**0**	**8**	**12.5**	**–4**	**0**	**0.0**	**16:32**	....	....	....	....	....	....	....	....	....
	Detroit	**NHL**	**8**	**2**	**2**	**4**	**6**	**0**	**0**	**0**	**15**	**13.3**	**3**	**2**	**50.0**	**15:32**	**16**	**3**	**4**	**7**	**15**	**1**	**0**	**0**	**14:25**
2007-08	**Anaheim**	**NHL**	**68**	**14**	**26**	**40**	**97**	**4**	**0**	**2**	**121**	**11.6**	**8**	**110**	**45.5**	**16:27**	**6**	**0**	**2**	**2**	**14**	**0**	**0**	**0**	**14:15**
2008-09	**Calgary**	**NHL**	**66**	**15**	**29**	**44**	**74**	**6**	**0**	**4**	**127**	**11.8**	**–13**	**45**	**46.7**	**18:36**	**6**	**1**	**1**	**2**	**8**	**0**	**0**	**0**	**17:25**
2009-10	**Detroit**	**NHL**	**82**	**18**	**26**	**44**	**80**	**4**	**0**	**4**	**216**	**8.3**	**–7**	**23**	**47.8**	**16:46**	**12**	**2**	**9**	**11**	**12**	**1**	**0**	**0**	**17:08**
2010-11	**Detroit**	**NHL**	**81**	**16**	**29**	**45**	**71**	**2**	**0**	**2**	**138**	**11.6**	**–7**	**40**	**45.0**	**15:57**	**11**	**2**	**4**	**6**	**15**	**0**	**0**	**0**	**13:42**
	NHL Totals		**1022**	**289**	**424**	**713**	**1372**	**104**	**1**	**40**	**2183**	**13.2**		**1804**	**45.7**	**18:01**	**75**	**14**	**28**	**42**	**146**	**3**	**0**	**0**	**17:03**

OHL Second All-Star Team (1995) • NHL First All-Star Team (2003)

Played in NHL All-Star Game (2003, 2004)

Traded to **Vancouver** by **NY Islanders** with Bryan McCabe and NY Islanders' 3rd round choice (Jarkko Ruutu) in 1998 Entry Draft for Trevor Linden, February 6, 1998. • Missed majority of 1998-99 due to leg injury vs. Washington, November 1, 1998. • Suspended indefinitely by NHL for deliberate injury to Steve Moore in game vs. Colorado, March 8, 2004. • Reinstated by NHL on August 8, 2005. Traded to **Florida** by **Vancouver** with Bryan Allen and Alex Auld for Roberto Luongo, Lukas Krajicek and Florida's 6th round choice (Sergei Shirokov) in 2006 Entry Draft, June 23, 2006. Traded to **Detroit** by **Florida** for Shawn Matthias and Detroit's 2nd round choice (later traded to Nashville - Nashville selected Nick Spaling) in 2007 Entry Draft, February 27, 2007. • Missed majority of 2006-07 due to recurring back injury. Signed as a free agent by **Anaheim**, July 2, 2007. Signed as a free agent by **Calgary**, July 7, 2008. Signed as a free agent by **Detroit**, August 18, 2009.

BETTS, Blair

(BEHTS, BLAIR) **PHI**

Center. Shoots left. 6'3", 210 lbs. Born, Edmonton, Alta., February 16, 1980. Calgary's 2nd choice, 33rd overall, in 1998 Entry Draft.

			Regular Season														Playoffs								
Season	Club	League	GP	G	A	Pts	PIM	PP	SH	GW	S	%	+/-	TF	F%	Min	GP	G	A	Pts	PIM	PP	SH	GW	Min
1995-96	Sherwood Park	AMHL	34	22	19	41	69	....	....	....	....	....	....	....	....	....	....	....	....	....	....	....	....	....	....
1996-97	Prince George	WHL	58	12	18	30	12	....	....	....	....	....	....	....	....	....	15	2	2	4	6	....	....	....	....
1997-98	Prince George	WHL	71	35	41	76	38	....	....	....	....	....	....	....	....	....	11	4	6	10	8	....	....	....	....
1998-99	Prince George	WHL	42	20	22	42	39	....	....	....	....	....	....	....	....	....	7	3	2	5	8	....	....	....	....
99-2000	Prince George	WHL	44	24	35	59	38	....	....	....	....	....	....	....	....	....	13	11	11	22	6	....	....	....	....
2000-01	Saint John Flames	AHL	75	13	15	28	28	....	....	....	....	....	....	....	....	....	19	2	3	5	4	....	....	....	....
2001-02	**Calgary**	**NHL**	**6**	**1**	**0**	**1**	**2**	**0**	**0**	**1**	**4**	**25.0**	**–1**	**39**	**48.7**	**7:05**	....	....	....	....	....	....	....	....	....
	Saint John Flames	AHL	67	20	29	49	10	....	....	....	....	....	....	....	....	....	....	....	....	....	....	....	....	....	....
2002-03	**Calgary**	**NHL**	**9**	**1**	**3**	**4**	**0**	**0**	**0**	**0**	**16**	**6.3**	**3**	**71**	**53.5**	**11:33**	....	....	....	....	....	....	....	....	....
	Saint John Flames	AHL	19	6	7	13	6	....	....	....	....	....	....	....	....	....	....	....	....	....	....	....	....	....	....
2003-04	**Calgary**	**NHL**	**20**	**1**	**2**	**3**	**10**	**1**	**0**	**1**	**21**	**4.8**	**–1**	**248**	**54.0**	**12:46**	....	....	....	....	....	....	....	....	....
2004-05	Hartford	AHL	16	5	4	9	4	....	....	....	....	....	....	....	....	....	....	....	....	....	....	....	....	....	....
2005-06	**NY Rangers**	**NHL**	**66**	**8**	**2**	**10**	**24**	**0**	**1**	**0**	**94**	**8.5**	**–10**	**817**	**53.4**	**12:55**	**4**	**1**	**1**	**2**	**2**	**0**	**0**	**0**	**16:12**
2006-07	**NY Rangers**	**NHL**	**82**	**9**	**4**	**13**	**24**	**1**	**1**	**0**	**120**	**7.5**	**–4**	**1186**	**52.3**	**14:02**	**10**	**0**	**0**	**0**	**4**	**0**	**0**	**0**	**11:15**
2007-08	**NY Rangers**	**NHL**	**75**	**2**	**5**	**7**	**20**	**0**	**0**	**0**	**85**	**2.4**	**–4**	**771**	**50.3**	**11:52**	**8**	**0**	**0**	**0**	**2**	**0**	**0**	**0**	**7:16**
2008-09	**NY Rangers**	**NHL**	**81**	**6**	**4**	**10**	**16**	**0**	**2**	**1**	**83**	**7.2**	**–5**	**884**	**49.3**	**10:37**	**6**	**0**	**0**	**0**	**0**	**0**	**0**	**0**	**9:08**
2009-10	**Philadelphia**	**NHL**	**63**	**8**	**10**	**18**	**14**	**1**	**1**	**2**	**63**	**12.7**	**7**	**855**	**50.9**	**12:37**	**23**	**1**	**1**	**2**	**4**	**0**	**0**	**0**	**11:19**
2010-11	**Philadelphia**	**NHL**	**75**	**5**	**7**	**12**	**8**	**0**	**1**	**2**	**51**	**9.8**	**–3**	**817**	**50.3**	**10:27**	**11**	**0**	**0**	**0**	**0**	**0**	**0**	**0**	**11:51**
	NHL Totals		**477**	**41**	**37**	**78**	**118**	**3**	**6**	**7**	**537**	**7.6**		**5688**	**51.3**	**12:01**	**62**	**2**	**2**	**4**	**12**	**0**	**0**	**0**	**10:59**

• Missed majority of 2002-03 due to shoulder injury in training camp, September 27, 2002. • Missed majority of 2003-04 due to shoulder injuries vs. Chicago (November 22, 2003) and Colorado (December 31, 2003). Traded to **NY Rangers** by **Calgary** with Jamie McLennan and Greg Moore for Chris Simon and NY Rangers' 7th round choice (Matt Schneider) in 2004 Entry Draft, March 6, 2004. Signed as a free agent by **Philadelphia**, October 1, 2009.

BICKELL, Bryan

(BIH-kuhl, BRIGH-uhn) **CHI**

Left wing. Shoots left. 6'4", 223 lbs. Born, Bowmanville, Ont., March 9, 1986. Chicago's 3rd choice, 41st overall, in 2004 Entry Draft.

			Regular Season														Playoffs								
Season	Club	League	GP	G	A	Pts	PIM	PP	SH	GW	S	%	+/-	TF	F%	Min	GP	G	A	Pts	PIM	PP	SH	GW	Min
2000-01	Tor. Red Wings	GTHL	68	24	26	50	20	....	....	....	....	....	....	....	....	....	5	3	1	4	4	....	....	....	....
2001-02	Tor. Red Wings	GTHL	65	31	41	72	76	....	....	....	....	....	....	....	....	....	2	2	2	4	0	....	....	....	....
2002-03	Ottawa 67's	OHL	50	7	10	17	4	....	....	....	....	....	....	....	....	....	20	5	3	8	12	....	....	....	....
2003-04	Ottawa 67's	OHL	59	20	16	36	76	....	....	....	....	....	....	....	....	....	7	3	0	3	11	....	....	....	....
2004-05	Ottawa 67's	OHL	66	22	32	54	95	....	....	....	....	....	....	....	....	....	21	5	12	17	32	....	....	....	....
2005-06	Ottawa 67's	OHL	41	28	22	50	41	....	....	....	....	....	....	....	....	....	....	....	....	....	....	....	....	....	....
	Windsor Spitfires	OHL	26	17	16	33	19	....	....	....	....	....	....	....	....	....	7	5	5	10	10	....	....	....	....
2006-07	**Chicago**	**NHL**	**3**	**2**	**0**	**2**	**0**	**0**	**0**	**0**	**10**	**20.0**	**1**	**0**	**0.0**	**11:49**	....	....	....	....	....	....	....	....	....
	Norfolk Admirals	AHL	48	10	15	25	66	....	....	....	....	....	....	....	....	....	2	0	0	0	0	....	....	....	....
2007-08	**Chicago**	**NHL**	**4**	**0**	**0**	**0**	**2**	**0**	**0**	**0**	**3**	**0.0**	**–1**	**0**	**0.0**	**9:08**	....	....	....	....	....	....	....	....	....
	Rockford IceHogs	AHL	73	19	20	39	52	....	....	....	....	....	....	....	....	....	12	2	3	5	11	....	....	....	....
2008-09	Rockford IceHogs	AHL	42	6	8	14	60	....	....	....	....	....	....	....	....	....	4	0	2	2	4	....	....	....	....
2009-10	**Chicago**	**NHL**	**16**	**3**	**1**	**4**	**5**	**0**	**0**	**1**	**20**	**15.0**	**4**	**2**	**0.0**	**9:36**	**4**	**0**	**1**	**1**	**2**	**0**	**0**	**0**	**13:14**
	Rockford IceHogs	AHL	65	16	15	31	58	....	....	....	....	....	....	....	....	....	....	....	....	....	....	....	....	....	....
2010-11	**Chicago**	**NHL**	**78**	**17**	**20**	**37**	**40**	**2**	**0**	**2**	**130**	**13.1**	**6**	**12**	**25.0**	**13:50**	**5**	**2**	**2**	**4**	**0**	**0**	**0**	**0**	**13:05**
	NHL Totals		**101**	**22**	**21**	**43**	**47**	**2**	**0**	**3**	**163**	**13.5**		**14**	**21.4**	**12:55**	**9**	**2**	**3**	**5**	**2**	**0**	**0**	**0**	**13:09**

			Regular Season														Playoffs								
Season	Club	League	GP	G	A	Pts	PIM	PP	SH	GW	S	%	+/-	TF	F%	Min	GP	G	A	Pts	PIM	PP	SH	GW	Min

BIEKSA, Kevin (BEE-ehks-ah, KEH-vihn) **VAN**

Defense. Shoots right. 6', 198 lbs. Born, Grimsby, Ont., June 16, 1981. Vancouver's 4th choice, 151st overall, in 2001 Entry Draft.

Season	Club	League	GP	G	A	Pts	PIM	PP	SH	GW	S	%	+/-	TF	F%	Min	GP	G	A	Pts	PIM	PP	SH	GW	Min
1997-98	Stoney Creek	ON-Jr.B	STATISTICS NOT AVAILABLE																						
	Burlington	OPJHL	27	0	3	3	10	....	....	....	....	....	....				....	....	....	....	....	....	....	....
1998-99	Burlington	OPJHL	49	8	29	37	83	....	....	....	....	....	....				....	....	....	....	....	....	....	....
99-2000	Burlington	OPJHL	49	6	27	33	139	....	....	....	....	....	....				....	....	....	....	....	....	....	....
2000-01	Bowling Green	CCHA	35	4	9	13	90	....	....	....	....	....	....				....	....	....	....	....	....	....	....
2001-02	Bowling Green	CCHA	40	5	10	15	68	....	....	....	....	....	....				....	....	....	....	....	....	....	....
2002-03	Bowling Green	CCHA	34	8	17	25	92	....	....	....	....	....	....				....	....	....	....	....	....	....	....
2003-04	Bowling Green	CCHA	38	7	15	22	66	....	....	....	....	....	....				....	....	....	....	....	....	....	....
	Manitoba Moose	AHL	4	0	2	2	2	....	....	....	....	....	....				....	....	....	....	....	....	....	....
2004-05	Manitoba Moose	AHL	80	12	27	39	192	....	....	....	....	....	....				14	1	1	2	52	....	....	....	....
2005-06	**Vancouver**	**NHL**	39	0	6	6	77	0	0	0	38	0.0	−1	0	0.0	16:06	13	0	10	10	38	....	....	....	....
	Manitoba Moose	AHL	23	3	17	20	71	....	....	....	....	....	....				....	....	....	....	....	....	....	....
2006-07	**Vancouver**	**NHL**	81	12	30	42	134	6	0	2	203	5.9	1	0	0.0	24:16	9	0	0	0	20	0	0	0	28:01
2007-08	**Vancouver**	**NHL**	34	2	10	12	90	1	0	1	64	3.1	−11	0	0.0	23:24	....	....	....	....	....	....	....	....
	Manitoba Moose	AHL	1	0	1	1	2	....	....	....	....	....	....				....	....	....	....	....	....	....	....
2008-09	**Vancouver**	**NHL**	72	11	32	43	97	5	0	2	153	7.2	−4	0	0.0	23:29	10	0	5	5	14	0	0	0	24:08
2009-10	**Vancouver**	**NHL**	55	3	19	22	85	1	0	0	95	3.2	−5	0	0.0	21:49	12	3	5	8	14	1	0	1	22:37
2010-11	**Vancouver**	**NHL**	66	6	16	22	73	1	0	2	105	5.7	32	0	0.0	22:28	25	5	5	10	51	1	0	1	25:40
	NHL Totals		347	34	113	147	556	14	0	7	658	5.2		0	0.0	22:23	56	8	15	23	99	2	0	2	25:07

AHL All-Rookie Team (2005)

BISSONNETTE, Paul (bih-sawn-EHT, PAWL) **PHX**

Left wing. Shoots left. 6'3", 220 lbs. Born, Welland, Ont., March 11, 1985. Pittsburgh's 5th choice, 121st overall, in 2003 Entry Draft.

Season	Club	League	GP	G	A	Pts	PIM	PP	SH	GW	S	%	+/-	TF	F%	Min	GP	G	A	Pts	PIM	PP	SH	GW	Min
2001-02	North Bay	OHL	57	3	3	6	21	....	....	....	....	....	....				5	0	0	0	2	....	....	....	....
2002-03	Saginaw Spirit	OHL	67	7	16	23	57	....	....	....	....	....	....				....	....	....	....	....	....	....	....
2003-04	Saginaw Spirit	OHL	67	5	14	19	96	....	....	....	....	....	....				....	....	....	....	....	....	....	....
2004-05	Saginaw Spirit	OHL	28	1	6	7	46	....	....	....	....	....	....				8	1	3	4	2	....	....	....	....
	Owen Sound	OHL	35	2	11	13	46	....	....	....	....	....	....				11	0	1	1	4	....	....	....	....
2005-06	Wilkes-Barre	AHL	55	1	5	6	60	....	....	....	....	....	....				....	....	....	....	....	....	....	....
	Wheeling Nailers	ECHL	14	3	7	10	4	....	....	....	....	....	....				....	....	....	....	....	....	....	....
2006-07	Wilkes-Barre	AHL	3	0	0	0	6	....	....	....	....	....	....				....	....	....	....	....	....	....	....
	Wheeling Nailers	ECHL	65	10	32	42	115	....	....	....	....	....	....				7	0	0	0	11	....	....	....	....
2007-08	Wilkes-Barre	AHL	46	3	5	8	145	....	....	....	....	....	....				....	....	....	....	....	....	....	....
	Wheeling Nailers	ECHL	22	3	14	17	43	....	....	....	....	....	....				....	....	....	....	....	....	....	....
2008-09	**Pittsburgh**	**NHL**	15	0	1	1	22	0	0	0	4	0.0	−1	0	0.0	3:31	....	....	....	....	....	....	....	....
	Wilkes-Barre	AHL	57	9	7	16	176	....	....	....	....	....	....				8	0	2	2	9	....	....	....	....
2009-10	**Phoenix**	**NHL**	41	3	2	5	117	0	0	1	25	12.0	−2	0	0.0	5:52	....	....	....	....	....	....	....	....
2010-11	**Phoenix**	**NHL**	48	1	0	1	71	0	0	0	18	5.6	6	3	66.7	5:15	1	0	0	0	0	0	0	0	4:05
	NHL Totals		104	4	3	7	210	0	0	1	47	8.5		3	66.7	5:15	1	0	0	0	0	0	0	0	4:05

Claimed on waivers by **Phoenix** from **Pittsburgh**, September 30, 2009.

BITZ, Byron (BIHTZ, BIGH-ruhn) **VAN**

Right wing. Shoots right. 6'5", 215 lbs. Born, Saskatoon, Sask., July 21, 1984. Boston's 4th choice, 107th overall, in 2003 Entry Draft.

Season	Club	League	GP	G	A	Pts	PIM	PP	SH	GW	S	%	+/-	TF	F%	Min	GP	G	A	Pts	PIM	PP	SH	GW	Min
2000-01	Saskatoon	SMHL	40	17	35	52	....	....	....	....	....	....	....				....	....	....	....	....	....	....	....
2001-02	Sask. Contacts	SMHL	41	25	48	73	69	....	....	....	....	....	....				11	12	10	22	9	....	....	....	....
2002-03	Nanaimo Clippers	BCHL	58	27	46	73	59	....	....	....	....	....	....				....	....	....	....	....	....	....	....
2003-04	Cornell Big Red	ECAC	31	5	16	21	36	....	....	....	....	....	....				....	....	....	....	....	....	....	....
2004-05	Cornell Big Red	ECAC	29	5	10	15	20	....	....	....	....	....	....				....	....	....	....	....	....	....	....
2005-06	Cornell Big Red	ECAC	35	10	18	28	52	....	....	....	....	....	....				....	....	....	....	....	....	....	....
2006-07	Cornell Big Red	ECAC	29	8	16	24	49	....	....	....	....	....	....				....	....	....	....	....	....	....	....
2007-08	Providence Bruins	AHL	61	13	14	27	70	....	....	....	....	....	....				10	1	1	2	6	....	....	....	....
2008-09	**Boston**	**NHL**	35	4	3	7	18	0	0	0	31	12.9	0	50	42.0	10:22	5	1	1	2	2	0	0	0	11:27
	Providence Bruins	AHL	37	3	7	10	68	....	....	....	....	....	....				....	....	....	....	....	....	....	....
2009-10	**Boston**	**NHL**	45	4	5	9	31	0	0	2	51	7.8	−9	17	41.2	10:57	....	....	....	....	....	....	....	....
	Florida	**NHL**	7	1	1	2	2	0	0	0	7	14.3	1	1	0.0	11:37	....	....	....	....	....	....	....	....
2010-11			DID NOT PLAY – INJURED																						
	NHL Totals		87	9	9	18	51	0	0	2	89	10.1		68	41.2	10:46	5	1	1	2	2	0	0	0	11:27

Traded to **Florida** by **Boston** with Craig Weller and Tampa Bay's 2nd round choice (previously acquired, Florida selected Alexander Petrovic) in 2010 Entry Draft for Dennis Seidenberg and Matt Bartkowski, March 3, 2010. • Missed 2010-11 due to hernia surgery. Signed as a free agent by **Vancouver**, July 26, 2011.

BLAKE, Jason (BLAYK, JAY-suhn) **ANA**

Left wing. Shoots left. 5'10", 190 lbs. Born, Moorhead, MN, September 2, 1973.

Season	Club	League	GP	G	A	Pts	PIM	PP	SH	GW	S	%	+/-	TF	F%	Min	GP	G	A	Pts	PIM	PP	SH	GW	Min
1991-92	Moorhead Spuds	High-MN	25	30	30	60	....	....	....	....	....	....	....				....	....	....	....	....	....	....	....
1992-93	Waterloo	USHL	45	24	27	51	107	....	....	....	....	....	....				....	....	....	....	....	....	....	....
1993-94	Waterloo	USHL	47	50	50	100	76	....	....	....	....	....	....				....	....	....	....	....	....	....	....
1994-95	Ferris State	CCHA	36	16	16	32	46	....	....	....	....	....	....				....	....	....	....	....	....	....	....
1995-96	North Dakota	WCHA	DID NOT PLAY – TRANSFERRED COLLEGES																						
1996-97	North Dakota	WCHA	43	19	32	51	44	....	....	....	....	....	....				....	....	....	....	....	....	....	....
1997-98	North Dakota	WCHA	38	24	27	51	62	....	....	....	....	....	....				....	....	....	....	....	....	....	....
1998-99	North Dakota	WCHA	38	*28	*41	*69	49	....	....	....	....	....	....				....	....	....	....	....	....	....	....
	Los Angeles	**NHL**	1	1	0	1	0	0	0	0	5	20.0	1	14	35.7	17:13	....	....	....	....	....	....	....	....
	Orlando	IHL	5	3	5	8	6	....	....	....	....	....	....				13	3	4	7	20	....	....	....	....
99-2000	**Los Angeles**	**NHL**	64	5	18	23	26	0	0	1	131	3.8	4	269	43.9	11:17	3	0	0	0	0	0	0	0	9:35
	Long Beach	IHL	7	3	6	9	2	....	....	....	....	....	....				....	....	....	....	....	....	....	....
2000-01	**Los Angeles**	**NHL**	17	1	3	4	10	0	0	0	27	3.7	−8	13	61.5	10:03	....	....	....	....	....	....	....	....
	Lowell	AHL	2	0	1	1	2	....	....	....	....	....	....				....	....	....	....	....	....	....	....
	NY Islanders	**NHL**	30	4	8	12	24	1	1	0	73	5.5	−12	118	44.1	15:43	....	....	....	....	....	....	....	....
2001-02	**NY Islanders**	**NHL**	82	8	10	18	36	0	0	1	136	5.9	−11	23	43.5	12:54	7	0	1	1	13	0	0	0	12:13
2002-03	**NY Islanders**	**NHL**	81	25	30	55	58	3	1	4	253	9.9	16	22	18.2	17:38	5	0	1	1	2	0	0	0	19:39
2003-04	**NY Islanders**	**NHL**	75	22	25	47	56	1	4	3	243	9.1	11	70	41.4	18:49	4	2	0	2	2	0	0	0	18:09
2004-05	HC Lugano	Swiss	7	2	2	4	4	....	....	....	....	....	....				....	....	....	....	....	....	....	....
2005-06	**NY Islanders**	**NHL**	76	28	29	57	60	12	2	2	304	9.2	4	152	42.8	18:47	....	....	....	....	....	....	....	....
	United States	Olympics	6	0	0	0	2	....	....	....	....	....	....				....	....	....	....	....	....	....	....
2006-07	**NY Islanders**	**NHL**	82	40	29	69	34	14	0	7	305	13.1	1	117	57.3	18:09	5	1	2	3	2	0	0	0	17:04
2007-08	**Toronto**	**NHL**	82	15	37	52	28	2	0	0	332	4.5	−4	28	50.0	17:49	....	....	....	....	....	....	....	....
2008-09	**Toronto**	**NHL**	78	25	38	63	40	5	1	5	302	8.3	−2	77	46.8	18:21	....	....	....	....	....	....	....	....
2009-10	**Toronto**	**NHL**	56	10	16	26	26	2	0	2	170	5.9	−4	53	35.9	15:50	....	....	....	....	....	....	....	....
	Anaheim	**NHL**	26	6	9	15	10	4	0	0	69	8.7	−6	28	42.9	16:02	6	3	1	4	0	2	0	0	13:45
2010-11	**Anaheim**	**NHL**	76	16	16	32	41	4	0	1	187	8.6	−5	5	20.0	14:46	6	3	0	3	0	0	0	0	15:06
	NHL Totals		826	206	268	449		47	9	28	2537	8.1		989	44.5	16:21	30	6	5	11	19	2	0	0	15:06

USHL Player of the Year (1994) • WCHA First All-Star Team (1997, 1998, 1999) • NCAA West Second All-American Team (1998) • WCHA Player of the Year (1999) • NCAA West First All-American Team (1999) • Bill Masterton Memorial Trophy (2008)
Played in NHL All-Star Game (2007)

Signed as a free agent by **Los Angeles**, April 20, 1999. Traded to **NY Islanders** by **Los Angeles** for NY Islanders' 5th round choice (Joel Andresen) in 2002 Entry Draft, January 3, 2001. Signed as a free agent by **Lugano** (Swiss), December 1, 2004. Signed as a free agent by **Toronto**, July 1, 2007. Traded to **Anaheim** by **Toronto** with Vesa Toskala for Jean-Sebastien Giguere, January 31, 2010.

BLIZNAK, Mario

(BLIZH-nak, MAHR-ee-oh)

Center. Shoots left. 6', 185 lbs. Born, Trencin, Czech., March 6, 1987. Vancouver's 6th choice, 205th overall, in 2005 Entry Draft.

Season	Club	League	Regular Season GP	G	A	Pts	PIM	PP	SH	GW	S	%	+/-	TF	F%	Min	Playoffs GP	G	A	Pts	PIM	PP	SH	GW	Min
2003-04	Dubnica U18	Svk-U18	46	25	26	51	62	....	....	....	....	....	....	....	....	....	....	....	....	....	....	....	....	....	....
	Dubnica Jr.	Slovak-Jr.	2	1	0	1	2	....	....	....	....	....	....	....	....	....	....	....	....	....	....	....	....	....	....
2004-05	Dubnica U18	Svk-U18	14	5	8	13	45	....	....	....	....	....	....	....	....	....	....	....	....	....	....	....	....	....	....
	Dubnica Jr.	Slovak-Jr.	36	22	17	39	38	....	....	....	....	....	....	....	....	....	....	....	....	....	....	....	....	....	....
	Dubnica	Slovakia	19	0	0	0	14	....	....	....	....	....	....	....	....	....	....	....	....	....	....	....	....	....	....
2005-06	Vancouver Giants	WHL	69	9	12	21	29	....	....	....	....	....	....	....	....	....	18	4	1	5	14	....	....	....	....
2006-07	Vancouver Giants	WHL	47	8	14	22	20	....	....	....	....	....	....	....	....	....	22	6	6	12	14	....	....	....	....
2007-08	Vancouver Giants	WHL	67	19	32	51	36	....	....	....	....	....	....	....	....	....	10	3	5	8	2	....	....	....	....
2008-09	Manitoba Moose	AHL	64	7	9	16	24	....	....	....	....	....	....	....	....	....	21	3	2	5	8	....	....	....	....
2009-10	**Vancouver**	**NHL**	**2**	**0**	**0**	**0**	**0**	**0**	**0**	**0**	**1**	**0.0**	**–2**	**14**	**64.3**	**8:31**	....	....	....	....	....	....	....	....	....
	Manitoba Moose	AHL	76	13	15	28	40	....	....	....	....	....	....	....	....	....	6	2	1	3	2	....	....	....	....
2010-11	**Vancouver**	**NHL**	**4**	**1**	**0**	**1**	**0**	**0**	**0**	**0**	**1**	**100.0**	**1**	**21**	**33.3**	**6:37**	....	....	....	....	....	....	....	....	....
	Manitoba Moose	AHL	74	11	16	27	22	....	....	....	....	....	....	....	....	....	14	1	1	2	8	....	....	....	....
	NHL Totals		**6**	**1**	**0**	**1**	**0**	**0**	**0**	**0**	**2**	**50.0**		**35**	**45.7**	**7:15**	....	....	....	....	....	....	....	....	....

BLUM, Jonathon

(BLUHM, JAWN-ah-thuhn) **NSH**

Defense. Shoots right. 6'1", 190 lbs. Born, Long Beach, CA, January 30, 1989. Nashville's 1st choice, 23rd overall, in 2007 Entry Draft.

Season	Club	League	GP	G	A	Pts	PIM	PP	SH	GW	S	%	+/-	TF	F%	Min	GP	G	A	Pts	PIM	PP	SH	GW	Min
2004-05	California Wave	Minor-CA	55	15	50	65	65	....	....	....	....	....	....	....	....	....	....	....	....	....	....	....	....	....	....
2005-06	Vancouver Giants	WHL	61	7	17	24	25	....	....	....	....	....	....	....	....	....	18	1	7	8	16	....	....	....	....
2006-07	Vancouver Giants	WHL	72	8	43	51	48	....	....	....	....	....	....	....	....	....	22	3	6	9	8	....	....	....	....
2007-08	Vancouver Giants	WHL	64	18	45	63	44	....	....	....	....	....	....	....	....	....	10	3	4	7	10	....	....	....	....
2008-09	Vancouver Giants	WHL	51	16	50	66	30	....	....	....	....	....	....	....	....	....	17	7	11	18	6	....	....	....	....
	Milwaukee	AHL	....	....	....	....	....	....	....	....	....	....	....	....	....	....	5	0	0	0	0	....	....	....	....
2009-10	Milwaukee	AHL	80	11	30	41	32	....	....	....	....	....	....	....	....	....	7	1	7	8	0	....	....	....	....
2010-11	**Nashville**	**NHL**	**23**	**3**	**5**	**8**	**8**	**1**	**0**	**1**	**18**	**16.7**	**8**	**0**	**0.0**	**17:45**	**12**	**0**	**2**	**2**	**0**	**0**	**0**	**0**	**18:51**
	Milwaukee	AHL	54	7	27	34	20	....	....	....	....	....	....	....	....	....	1	0	0	0	0	....	....	....	....
	NHL Totals		**23**	**3**	**5**	**8**	**8**	**1**	**0**	**1**	**18**	**16.7**		**0**	**0.0**	**17:45**	**12**	**0**	**2**	**2**	**0**	**0**	**0**	**0**	**18:51**

WHL West Second All-Star Team (2008) • WHL West First All-Star Team (2009) • WHL Defenseman of the Year (2009) • Canadian Major Junior First All-Star Team (2009) • Canadian Major Junior Defenseman of the Year (2009)

BLUNDEN, Michael

(BLUHN-dehn, MIGH-kuhl) **MTL**

Right wing. Shoots right. 6'4", 211 lbs. Born, Toronto, Ont., December 15, 1986. Chicago's 2nd choice, 43rd overall, in 2005 Entry Draft.

Season	Club	League	GP	G	A	Pts	PIM	PP	SH	GW	S	%	+/-	TF	F%	Min	GP	G	A	Pts	PIM	PP	SH	GW	Min
2002-03	Erie Otters	OHL	63	10	7	17	55	....	....	....	....	....	....	....	....	....	....	....	....	....	....	....	....	....	....
2003-04	Erie Otters	OHL	52	22	17	39	53	....	....	....	....	....	....	....	....	....	3	0	0	0	0	....	....	....	....
2004-05	Erie Otters	OHL	61	22	19	41	75	....	....	....	....	....	....	....	....	....	2	0	0	0	2	....	....	....	....
2005-06	Erie Otters	OHL	60	46	38	84	63	....	....	....	....	....	....	....	....	....	....	....	....	....	....	....	....	....	....
	Norfolk Admirals	AHL	11	1	5	6	2	....	....	....	....	....	....	....	....	....	1	0	0	0	0	....	....	....	....
2006-07	**Chicago**	**NHL**	**9**	**0**	**0**	**0**	**10**	**0**	**0**	**0**	**10**	**0.0**	**–5**	**1**	**0.0**	**11:23**	....	....	....	....	....	....	....	....	....
	Norfolk Admirals	AHL	17	4	5	9	15	....	....	....	....	....	....	....	....	....	....	....	....	....	....	....	....	....	....
2007-08	**Chicago**	**NHL**	**1**	**0**	**0**	**0**	**0**	**0**	**0**	**0**	**1**	**0.0**	**–1**	**0**	**0.0**	**7:51**	....	....	....	....	....	....	....	....	....
	Rockford IceHogs	AHL	74	16	21	37	83	....	....	....	....	....	....	....	....	....	12	1	3	4	35	....	....	....	....
2008-09	Rockford IceHogs	AHL	37	3	7	10	42	....	....	....	....	....	....	....	....	....	....	....	....	....	....	....	....	....	....
	Syracuse Crunch	AHL	39	9	12	21	68	....	....	....	....	....	....	....	....	....	....	....	....	....	....	....	....	....	....
2009-10	Syracuse Crunch	AHL	25	7	9	16	43	....	....	....	....	....	....	....	....	....	....	....	....	....	....	....	....	....	....
	Columbus	**NHL**	**40**	**2**	**2**	**4**	**59**	**0**	**0**	**0**	**40**	**5.0**	**3**	**90**	**32.2**	**8:07**	....	....	....	....	....	....	....	....	....
2010-11	**Columbus**	**NHL**	**1**	**0**	**0**	**0**	**0**	**0**	**0**	**0**	**2**	**0.0**	**–1**	**10**	**50.0**	**10:31**	....	....	....	....	....	....	....	....	....
	Springfield	AHL	37	12	9	21	41	....	....	....	....	....	....	....	....	....	....	....	....	....	....	....	....	....	....
	NHL Totals		**51**	**2**	**2**	**4**	**69**	**0**	**0**	**0**	**53**	**3.8**		**101**	**33.7**	**8:44**	....	....	....	....	....	....	....	....	....

• Missed majority of 2006-07 due to shoulder injury sufffered during game vs. Hershey (AHL), December 10, 2006. Traded to **Columbus** by **Chicago** for Adam Pineault, January 10, 2008. • Missed majority of 2010-11 due to shoulder injury. Traded to **Montreal** by **Columbus** for Ryan Russell, July 7, 2011.

BOCHENSKI, Brandon

(boh-CHEHN-skee, BRAN-duhn)

Right wing. Shoots right. 6'1", 187 lbs. Born, Blaine, MN, April 4, 1982. Ottawa's 9th choice, 223rd overall, in 2001 Entry Draft.

Season	Club	League	GP	G	A	Pts	PIM	PP	SH	GW	S	%	+/-	TF	F%	Min	GP	G	A	Pts	PIM	PP	SH	GW	Min
99-2000	Blaine Bengals	High-MN	28	32	30	62	....	....	....	....	....	....	....	....	....	....	....	....	....	....	....	....	....	....	....
2000-01	Lincoln Stars	USHL	55	*47	33	80	22	....	....	....	....	....	....	....	....	....	11	5	7	12	4	....	....	....	....
2001-02	North Dakota	WCHA	36	17	15	32	36	....	....	....	....	....	....	....	....	....	....	....	....	....	....	....	....	....	....
2002-03	North Dakota	WCHA	43	35	27	62	42	....	....	....	....	....	....	....	....	....	....	....	....	....	....	....	....	....	....
2003-04	North Dakota	WCHA	41	27	33	60	40	....	....	....	....	....	....	....	....	....	....	....	....	....	....	....	....	....	....
2004-05	Binghamton	AHL	75	34	36	70	16	....	....	....	....	....	....	....	....	....	6	1	0	1	2	....	....	....	....
2005-06	**Ottawa**	**NHL**	**20**	**6**	**7**	**13**	**14**	**2**	**0**	**0**	**39**	**15.4**	**7**	**4**	**50.0**	**12:17**	....	....	....	....	....	....	....	....	....
	Binghamton	AHL	33	22	24	46	36	....	....	....	....	....	....	....	....	....	....	....	....	....	....	....	....	....	....
	Chicago	**NHL**	**20**	**2**	**2**	**4**	**8**	**0**	**0**	**0**	**23**	**8.7**	**–9**	**8**	**37.5**	**8:53**	....	....	....	....	....	....	....	....	....
	Norfolk Admirals	AHL	....	....	....	....	....	....	....	....	....	....	....	....	....	....	3	1	1	2	0	....	....	....	....
2006-07	**Chicago**	**NHL**	**10**	**2**	**0**	**2**	**2**	**0**	**0**	**0**	**20**	**10.0**	**–2**	**1**	**0.0**	**9:59**	....	....	....	....	....	....	....	....	....
	Norfolk Admirals	AHL	35	33	33	66	31	....	....	....	....	....	....	....	....	....	....	....	....	....	....	....	....	....	....
	Boston	**NHL**	**31**	**11**	**11**	**22**	**14**	**3**	**0**	**2**	**72**	**15.3**	**3**	**4**	**25.0**	**14:59**	....	....	....	....	....	....	....	....	....
2007-08	**Boston**	**NHL**	**20**	**0**	**6**	**6**	**6**	**0**	**0**	**0**	**30**	**0.0**	**2**	**6**	**33.3**	**12:48**	....	....	....	....	....	....	....	....	....
	Providence Bruins	AHL	2	1	0	1	0	....	....	....	....	....	....	....	....	....	....	....	....	....	....	....	....	....	....
	Anaheim	**NHL**	**12**	**2**	**2**	**4**	**6**	**1**	**0**	**0**	**17**	**11.8**	**2**	**1**	**0.0**	**12:28**	....	....	....	....	....	....	....	....	....
	Nashville	**NHL**	**8**	**1**	**2**	**3**	**0**	**0**	**0**	**0**	**9**	**11.1**	**2**	**0**	**0.0**	**9:01**	**3**	**0**	**0**	**0**	**0**	**0**	**0**	**0**	**6:36**
2008-09	**Tampa Bay**	**NHL**	**7**	**0**	**1**	**1**	**2**	**0**	**0**	**0**	**11**	**0.0**	**–3**	**0**	**0.0**	**10:47**	....	....	....	....	....	....	....	....	....
	Norfolk Admirals	AHL	69	27	26	53	48	....	....	....	....	....	....	....	....	....	....	....	....	....	....	....	....	....	....
2009-10	**Tampa Bay**	**NHL**	**28**	**4**	**9**	**13**	**2**	**1**	**0**	**0**	**43**	**9.3**	**–1**	**5**	**40.0**	**12:16**	....	....	....	....	....	....	....	....	....
	Norfolk Admirals	AHL	42	21	19	40	16	....	....	....	....	....	....	....	....	....	....	....	....	....	....	....	....	....	....
2010-11	Barys Astana	Rus-KHL	40	22	23	45	36	....	....	....	....	....	....	....	....	....	4	0	1	1	2	....	....	....	....
	NHL Totals		**156**	**28**	**40**	**68**	**54**	**7**	**0**	**2**	**264**	**10.6**		**29**	**34.5**	**12:05**	**3**	**0**	**0**	**0**	**0**	**0**	**0**	**0**	**6:36**

USHL First All-Star Team (2001) • USHL Rookie of the Year (2001) • WCHA All-Rookie Team (2002) • WCHA Rookie of the Year (2002) • WCHA Second All-Star Team (2003) • WCHA First All-Star Team (2004) • NCAA West First All-American Team (2004) • AHL All-Rookie Team (2005)

Traded to **Chicago** by **Ottawa** with Ottawa's 2nd round choice (Simon Danis-Pepin) in 2006 Entry Draft for Tyler Arnason, March 9, 2006. Traded to **Boston** by **Chicago** for Kris Versteeg and future considerations, February 3, 2007. Traded to **Anaheim** by **Boston** for Shane Hnidy and Anaheim's 6th round choice (Nicholas Tremblay) in 2008 Entry Draft, January 2, 2008. Traded to **Nashville** by **Anaheim** for future considerations, February 26, 2008. Signed as a free agent by **Tampa Bay**, July 8, 2008. Signed as a free agent by **Astana** (Russia-KHL), May 7, 2010.

BODIE, Troy

(BOH-dee, TROI)

Right wing. Shoots right. 6'4", 196 lbs. Born, Portage La Prairie, Man., January 25, 1985. Edmonton's 12th choice, 278th overall, in 2003 Entry Draft.

Season	Club	League	GP	G	A	Pts	PIM	PP	SH	GW	S	%	+/-	TF	F%	Min	GP	G	A	Pts	PIM	PP	SH	GW	Min
2001-02	Central Plains	MMMHL	40	22	21	43	10	....	....	....	....	....	....	....	....	....	....	....	....	....	....	....	....	....	....
2002-03	Kelowna Rockets	WHL	35	4	4	8	36	....	....	....	....	....	....	....	....	....	11	1	1	2	2	....	....	....	....
2003-04	Kelowna Rockets	WHL	71	8	12	20	112	....	....	....	....	....	....	....	....	....	17	7	3	10	6	....	....	....	....
2004-05	Kelowna Rockets	WHL	72	24	24	48	96	....	....	....	....	....	....	....	....	....	24	4	13	17	26	....	....	....	....
2005-06	Kelowna Rockets	WHL	72	28	25	53	117	....	....	....	....	....	....	....	....	....	12	5	4	9	8	....	....	....	....
2006-07	Hamilton	AHL	20	0	1	1	29	....	....	....	....	....	....	....	....	....	....	....	....	....	....	....	....	....	....
	Stockton Thunder	ECHL	46	21	17	38	80	....	....	....	....	....	....	....	....	....	6	0	2	2	6	....	....	....	....
2007-08	Springfield	AHL	62	9	6	15	108	....	....	....	....	....	....	....	....	....	....	....	....	....	....	....	....	....	....
2008-09	**Anaheim**	**NHL**	**4**	**0**	**0**	**0**	**0**	**0**	**0**	**0**	**5**	**0.0**	**0**	**2**	**50.0**	**8:09**	....	....	....	....	....	....	....	....	....
	Iowa Chops	AHL	71	15	12	27	105	....	....	....	....	....	....	....	....	....	....	....	....	....	....	....	....	....	....
2009-10	**Anaheim**	**NHL**	**44**	**5**	**2**	**7**	**80**	**0**	**1**	**1**	**58**	**8.6**	**–8**	**1**	**0.0**	**11:15**	....	....	....	....	....	....	....	....	....
	San Antonio	AHL	16	2	1	3	43	....	....	....	....	....	....	....	....	....	....	....	....	....	....	....	....	....	....
	Toronto Marlies	AHL	16	6	4	10	13	....	....	....	....	....	....	....	....	....	....	....	....	....	....	....	....	....	....
2010-11	**Anaheim**	**NHL**	**9**	**0**	**1**	**1**	**7**	**0**	**0**	**0**	**5**	**0.0**	**–3**	**0**	**0.0**	**9:43**	....	....	....	....	....	....	....	....	....
	Carolina	**NHL**	**50**	**1**	**2**	**3**	**54**	**0**	**0**	**0**	**39**	**2.6**	**–4**	**1**	**0.0**	**6:19**	....	....	....	....	....	....	....	....	....
	NHL Totals		**107**	**6**	**5**	**11**	**141**	**0**	**1**	**1**	**107**	**5.6**		**4**	**25.0**	**8:42**	....	....	....	....	....	....	....	....	....

Signed as a free agent by **Anaheim**, July 22, 2008. Claimed on waivers by **Carolina** from **Anaheim**, November 16, 2010.

BODNARCHUK, Andrew

(BAWD-nahr-chuhk, AN-droo) **BOS**

Defense. Shoots left. 5'11", 172 lbs. Born, Drumheller, Alta., July 11, 1988. Boston's 5th choice, 128th overall, in 2006 Entry Draft.

Season	Club	League	GP	G	A	Pts	PIM	PP	SH	GW	S	%	+/-	TF	F%	Min	Playoffs GP	G	A	Pts	PIM	PP	SH	GW	Min
2003-04	Dartmouth	NSMHL	58	16	23	39	81	....	....	....	....	....	....	....	....	....	....	....	....	....	....	....	....	....	....
2004-05	St. Paul's School	High-NH	36	3	15	18	....	....	....	....	....	....	....	....	....	....	....	....	....	....	....	....	....	....	....
2005-06	Halifax	QMJHL	68	6	17	23	136	....	....	....	....	....	....	....	....	....	11	0	2	2	22	....	....	....	....
2006-07	Halifax	QMJHL	63	16	41	57	96	....	....	....	....	....	....	....	....	....	12	1	10	11	25	....	....	....	....
	Providence Bruins	AHL	....	....	....	....	....	....	....	....	....	....	....	....	....	....	1	0	0	0	0	....	....	....	....
2007-08	Halifax	QMJHL	65	10	33	43	89	....	....	....	....	....	....	....	....	....	14	0	9	9	16	....	....	....	....
2008-09	Providence Bruins	AHL	62	1	8	9	33	....	....	....	....	....	....	....	....	....	15	0	2	2	22	....	....	....	....
2009-10	**Boston**	**NHL**	**5**	**0**	**0**	**0**	**2**	**0**	**0**	**0**	**0**	**0.0**	**–2**	**0**	**0.0**	**7:19**	....	....	....	....	....	....	....	....	....
	Providence Bruins	AHL	70	5	10	15	51	....	....	....	....	....	....	....	....	....	....	....	....	....	....	....	....	....	....
2010-11	Providence Bruins	AHL	75	1	15	16	91	....	....	....	....	....	....	....	....	....	....	....	....	....	....	....	....	....	....
	NHL Totals		**5**	**0**	**0**	**0**	**2**	**0**	**0**	**0**	**0**	**0.0**		**0**	**0.0**	**7:19**	....	....	....	....	....	....	....	....	....

QMJHL All-Rookie Team (2006)

BOEDKER, Mikkel

(BAWD-kuhr, MIH-kehl) **PHX**

Right wing. Shoots left. 5'11", 202 lbs. Born, Brondby, Denmark, December 16, 1989. Phoenix's 1st choice, 8th overall, in 2008 Entry Draft.

Season	Club	League	GP	G	A	Pts	PIM	PP	SH	GW	S	%	+/-	TF	F%	Min	Playoffs GP	G	A	Pts	PIM	PP	SH	GW	Min
2004-05	Rodovre IK	Den-2	1	0	1	1	0	....	....	....	....	....	....	....	....	....	....	....	....	....	....	....	....	....	....
2005-06	Frolunda U18	Swe-U18	5	2	0	2	0	....	....	....	....	....	....	....	....	....	2	0	1	1	0	....	....	....	....
	Frolunda Jr.	Swe-Jr.	37	9	8	17	22	....	....	....	....	....	....	....	....	....	2	1	2	3	0	....	....	....	....
2006-07	Frolunda U18	Swe-U18	3	3	2	5	2	....	....	....	....	....	....	....	....	....	6	5	4	9	2	....	....	....	....
	Frolunda Jr.	Swe-Jr.	39	19	30	49	14	....	....	....	....	....	....	....	....	....	8	6	5	11	6	....	....	....	....
	Frolunda	Sweden	2	0	0	0	0	....	....	....	....	....	....	....	....	....	....	....	....	....	....	....	....	....	....
2007-08	Kitchener Rangers	OHL	62	29	44	73	14	....	....	....	....	....	....	....	....	....	20	9	*26	35	2	....	....	....	....
2008-09	**Phoenix**	**NHL**	**78**	**11**	**17**	**28**	**18**	**2**	**0**	**3**	**116**	**9.5**	**–6**	**8**	**12.5**	**15:32**	....	....	....	....	....	....	....	....	....
2009-10	**Phoenix**	**NHL**	**14**	**1**	**2**	**3**	**0**	**0**	**0**	**0**	**7**	**14.3**	**2**	**0**	**0.0**	**8:43**	....	....	....	....	....	....	....	....	....
	San Antonio	AHL	64	11	27	38	4	....	....	....	....	....	....	....	....	....	....	....	....	....	....	....	....	....	....
2010-11	**Phoenix**	**NHL**	**34**	**4**	**10**	**14**	**8**	**0**	**0**	**0**	**39**	**10.3**	**11**	**5**	**60.0**	**10:54**	**4**	**0**	**1**	**1**	**2**	**0**	**0**	**0**	**8:58**
	San Antonio	AHL	36	12	22	34	8	....	....	....	....	....	....	....	....	....	....	....	....	....	....	....	....	....	....
	NHL Totals		**126**	**16**	**29**	**45**	**26**	**2**	**0**	**3**	**162**	**9.9**		**13**	**30.8**	**13:32**	**4**	**0**	**1**	**1**	**2**	**0**	**0**	**0**	**8:58**

BOGOSIAN, Zach

(buh-GOH-zhuhn, ZAK) **WPG**

Defense. Shoots right. 6'3", 215 lbs. Born, Massena, NY, July 15, 1990. Atlanta's 1st choice, 3rd overall, in 2008 Entry Draft.

Season	Club	League	GP	G	A	Pts	PIM	PP	SH	GW	S	%	+/-	TF	F%	Min	Playoffs GP	G	A	Pts	PIM	PP	SH	GW	Min
2005-06	Cushing	High-MA	36	1	16	17	....	....	....	....	....	....	....	....	....	....	....	....	....	....	....	....	....	....	....
2006-07	Peterborough	OHL	67	7	26	33	63	....	....	....	....	....	....	....	....	....	....	....	....	....	....	....	....	....	....
2007-08	Peterborough	OHL	60	11	50	61	72	....	....	....	....	....	....	....	....	....	5	0	3	3	8	....	....	....	....
2008-09	**Atlanta**	**NHL**	**47**	**9**	**10**	**19**	**47**	**2**	**1**	**1**	**90**	**10.0**	**11**	**0**	**0.0**	**18:06**	....	....	....	....	....	....	....	....	....
	Chicago Wolves	AHL	5	1	0	1	0	....	....	....	....	....	....	....	....	....	....	....	....	....	....	....	....	....	....
2009-10	**Atlanta**	**NHL**	**81**	**10**	**13**	**23**	**61**	**3**	**1**	**0**	**155**	**6.5**	**–18**	**0**	**0.0**	**21:25**	....	....	....	....	....	....	....	....	....
2010-11	**Atlanta**	**NHL**	**71**	**5**	**12**	**17**	**29**	**0**	**0**	**1**	**155**	**3.2**	**–27**	**0**	**0.0**	**22:24**	....	....	....	....	....	....	....	....	....
	NHL Totals		**199**	**24**	**35**	**59**	**137**	**5**	**2**	**2**	**400**	**6.0**		**0**	**0.0**	**20:59**	....	....	....	....	....	....	....	....	....

OHL First All-Star Team (2008)
- Transferred to **Winnipeg** after **Atlanta** franchise relocated, June 21, 2011.

BOLDUC, Alexandre

(bohl-DUHK, ahl-ehx-AHN-druh) **PHX**

Center. Shoots left. 6'3", 200 lbs. Born, Montreal, Que., June 26, 1985. St. Louis' 6th choice, 127th overall, in 2003 Entry Draft.

Season	Club	League	GP	G	A	Pts	PIM	PP	SH	GW	S	%	+/-	TF	F%	Min	Playoffs GP	G	A	Pts	PIM	PP	SH	GW	Min
2000-01	Notre Dame	SMHL	61	17	35	52	....	....	....	....	....	....	....	....	....	....	....	....	....	....	....	....	....	....	....
2001-02	Rouyn-Noranda	QMJHL	64	6	14	20	69	....	....	....	....	....	....	....	....	....	4	1	1	2	4	....	....	....	....
2002-03	Rouyn-Noranda	QMJHL	66	14	29	43	131	....	....	....	....	....	....	....	....	....	4	0	2	2	2	....	....	....	....
2003-04	Rouyn-Noranda	QMJHL	65	23	35	58	115	....	....	....	....	....	....	....	....	....	11	3	4	7	18	....	....	....	....
2004-05	Rouyn-Noranda	QMJHL	33	7	10	17	46	....	....	....	....	....	....	....	....	....	....	....	....	....	....	....	....	....	....
	Shawinigan	QMJHL	29	7	11	18	14	....	....	....	....	....	....	....	....	....	3	0	0	0	0	....	....	....	....
2005-06	Manitoba Moose	AHL	29	3	7	10	35	....	....	....	....	....	....	....	....	....	....	....	....	....	....	....	....	....	....
	Bakersfield	ECHL	24	10	6	16	56	....	....	....	....	....	....	....	....	....	11	4	4	8	28	....	....	....	....
2006-07	Manitoba Moose	AHL	32	4	5	9	35	....	....	....	....	....	....	....	....	....	5	0	0	0	8	....	....	....	....
	Bakersfield	ECHL	16	7	17	24	42	....	....	....	....	....	....	....	....	....	6	2	4	6	9	....	....	....	....
2007-08	Manitoba Moose	AHL	70	18	19	37	93	....	....	....	....	....	....	....	....	....	6	1	0	1	6	....	....	....	....
2008-09	**Vancouver**	**NHL**	**7**	**0**	**1**	**1**	**4**	**0**	**0**	**0**	**7**	**0.0**	**1**	**13**	**38.5**	**7:20**	....	....	....	....	....	....	....	....	....
	Manitoba Moose	AHL	63	12	21	33	116	....	....	....	....	....	....	....	....	....	13	5	4	9	14	....	....	....	....
2009-10	**Vancouver**	**NHL**	**15**	**0**	**0**	**0**	**13**	**0**	**0**	**0**	**14**	**0.0**	**–3**	**87**	**54.0**	**9:58**	....	....	....	....	....	....	....	....	....
	Manitoba Moose	AHL	13	2	1	3	20	....	....	....	....	....	....	....	....	....	....	....	....	....	....	....	....	....	....
2010-11	**Vancouver**	**NHL**	**24**	**2**	**2**	**4**	**21**	**0**	**0**	**1**	**21**	**9.5**	**1**	**97**	**45.4**	**7:26**	**3**	**0**	**0**	**0**	**0**	**0**	**0**	**0**	**3:38**
	Manitoba Moose	AHL	26	6	9	15	28	....	....	....	....	....	....	....	....	....	14	4	0	4	20	....	....	....	....
	NHL Totals		**46**	**2**	**3**	**5**	**38**	**0**	**0**	**1**	**42**	**4.8**		**197**	**48.7**	**8:15**	**3**	**0**	**0**	**0**	**0**	**0**	**0**	**0**	**3:39**

Signed as a free agent by **Vancouver**, July 2, 2008. • Missed majority of 2009-10 due to shoulder injury. Signed as a free agent by **Phoenix**, July 2, 2011.

BOLL, Jared

(BOWL, JAIR-ehd) **CBJ**

Right wing. Shoots right. 6'2", 214 lbs. Born, Charlotte, NC, May 13, 1986. Columbus' 4th choice, 101st overall, in 2005 Entry Draft.

Season	Club	League	GP	G	A	Pts	PIM	PP	SH	GW	S	%	+/-	TF	F%	Min	Playoffs GP	G	A	Pts	PIM	PP	SH	GW	Min
2003-04	Lincoln Stars	USHL	57	6	8	14	*176	....	....	....	....	....	....	....	....	....	....	....	....	....	....	....	....	....	....
2004-05	Lincoln Stars	USHL	59	23	24	47	*294	....	....	....	....	....	....	....	....	....	4	1	3	4	25	....	....	....	....
2005-06	Plymouth Whalers	OHL	65	19	22	41	205	....	....	....	....	....	....	....	....	....	13	2	4	6	21	....	....	....	....
2006-07	Plymouth Whalers	OHL	66	28	27	55	198	....	....	....	....	....	....	....	....	....	20	6	4	10	*66	....	....	....	....
2007-08	**Columbus**	**NHL**	**75**	**5**	**5**	**10**	**226**	**0**	**0**	**3**	**63**	**7.9**	**–4**	**6**	**33.3**	**8:01**	....	....	....	....	....	....	....	....	....
2008-09	**Columbus**	**NHL**	**75**	**4**	**10**	**14**	**180**	**1**	**0**	**0**	**73**	**5.5**	**–6**	**4**	**0.0**	**8:54**	**1**	**0**	**0**	**0**	**0**	**0**	**0**	**0**	**5:17**
2009-10	**Columbus**	**NHL**	**68**	**4**	**3**	**7**	**149**	**0**	**0**	**0**	**56**	**7.1**	**–8**	**3**	**0.0**	**7:12**	....	....	....	....	....	....	....	....	....
2010-11	**Columbus**	**NHL**	**73**	**7**	**5**	**12**	**182**	**0**	**0**	**2**	**66**	**10.6**	**–2**	**6**	**0.0**	**7:40**	....	....	....	....	....	....	....	....	....
	NHL Totals		**291**	**20**	**23**	**43**	**737**	**1**	**0**	**5**	**258**	**7.8**		**19**	**10.5**	**7:58**	**1**	**0**	**0**	**0**	**0**	**0**	**0**	**0**	**5:17**

BOLLAND, Dave

(BOHL-uhnd, DAYV) **CHI**

Center. Shoots right. 6', 181 lbs. Born, Toronto, Ont., June 5, 1986. Chicago's 2nd choice, 32nd overall, in 2004 Entry Draft.

Season	Club	League	GP	G	A	Pts	PIM	PP	SH	GW	S	%	+/-	TF	F%	Min	Playoffs GP	G	A	Pts	PIM	PP	SH	GW	Min
2000-01	Tor. Red Wings	GTHL	95	79	67	146	....	....	....	....	....	....	....	....	....	....	....	....	....	....	....	....	....	....	....
2001-02	Tor. Red Wings	GTHL	36	35	35	70	40	....	....	....	....	....	....	....	....	....	....	....	....	....	....	....	....	....	....
2002-03	London Knights	OHL	64	7	10	17	21	....	....	....	....	....	....	....	....	....	14	2	1	3	2	....	....	....	....
2003-04	London Knights	OHL	65	37	30	67	58	....	....	....	....	....	....	....	....	....	15	3	10	13	18	....	....	....	....
2004-05	London Knights	OHL	66	34	51	85	97	....	....	....	....	....	....	....	....	....	18	11	14	25	30	....	....	....	....
2005-06	London Knights	OHL	59	*57	73	130	104	....	....	....	....	....	....	....	....	....	15	*15	9	24	41	....	....	....	....
2006-07	**Chicago**	**NHL**	**1**	**0**	**0**	**0**	**0**	**0**	**0**	**0**	**1**	**0.0**	**–1**	**11**	**36.4**	**11:17**	....	....	....	....	....	....	....	....	....
	Norfolk Admirals	AHL	65	17	32	49	53	....	....	....	....	....	....	....	....	....	6	0	4	4	17	....	....	....	....
2007-08	**Chicago**	**NHL**	**39**	**4**	**13**	**17**	**28**	**0**	**0**	**0**	**49**	**8.2**	**6**	**385**	**46.5**	**13:43**	....	....	....	....	....	....	....	....	....
	Rockford IceHogs	AHL	16	6	4	10	22	....	....	....	....	....	....	....	....	....	7	0	0	0	8	....	....	....	....
2008-09	**Chicago**	**NHL**	**81**	**19**	**28**	**47**	**52**	**2**	**2**	**4**	**111**	**17.1**	**19**	**1177**	**44.4**	**16:27**	**17**	**4**	**8**	**12**	**24**	**1**	**1**	**1**	**18:43**
2009-10 ♦	**Chicago**	**NHL**	**39**	**6**	**10**	**16**	**28**	**1**	**0**	**0**	**52**	**11.5**	**5**	**555**	**49.4**	**17:22**	**22**	**8**	**8**	**16**	**30**	**2**	**2**	**1**	**18:40**
2010-11	**Chicago**	**NHL**	**61**	**15**	**22**	**37**	**34**	**4**	**0**	**1**	**102**	**14.7**	**11**	**1008**	**45.1**	**17:39**	**4**	**2**	**4**	**6**	**4**	**0**	**0**	**0**	**19:58**
	NHL Totals		**221**	**44**	**73**	**117**	**142**	**7**	**2**	**5**	**315**	**14.0**		**3136**	**45.7**	**16:26**	**43**	**14**	**20**	**34**	**58**	**3**	**3**	**2**	**18:48**

OHL First All-Star Team (2006) • Canadian Major Junior First All-Star Team (2006)
- Missed majority of 2009-10 due to back injury.

BONINO, Nick

(boh-NEE-noh, NIHK) **ANA**

Center. Shoots left. 6'1", 186 lbs. Born, Hartford, CT, April 20, 1988. San Jose's 6th choice, 173rd overall, in 2007 Entry Draft.

Season	Club	League	Regular Season GP	G	A	Pts	PIM	PP	SH	GW	S	%	+/-	TF	F%	Min	Playoffs GP	G	A	Pts	PIM	PP	SH	GW	Min
2003-04	Farmington	High-CT	24	44	23	67	10	....	....	....	....	....	....	....	....	....	....	....	....	....	....	....	....	....	....
2004-05	Farmington	High-CT	24	68	23	91	12	....	....	....	....	....	....	....	....	....	....	....	....	....	....	....	....	....	....
2005-06	Avon Old Farms	High-CT	25	26	30	56	10	....	....	....	....	....	....	....	....	....	....	....	....	....	....	....	....	....	....
2006-07	Avon Old Farms	High-CT	26	24	42	66	14	....	....	....	....	....	....	....	....	....	....	....	....	....	....	....	....	....	....
2007-08	Boston University	H-East	39	16	13	29	10	....	....	....	....	....	....	....	....	....	....	....	....	....	....	....	....	....	....
2008-09	Boston University	H-East	44	18	32	50	30	....	....	....	....	....	....	....	....	....	....	....	....	....	....	....	....	....	....
2009-10	Boston University	H-East	33	11	27	38	12	....	....	....	....	....	....	....	....	....	....	....	....	....	....	....	....	....	....
	Anaheim	NHL	9	1	1	2	6	1	0	0	14	7.1	0	78	43.6	14:13	....	....	....	....	....	....	....	....	....
2010-11	Anaheim	NHL	26	0	0	0	4	0	0	0	23	0.0	–3	166	47.0	9:48	4	0	0	0	2	0	0	0	11:36
	Syracuse Crunch	AHL	50	12	33	45	32	....	....	....	....	....	....	....	....	....	....	....	....	....	....	....	....	....	....
	NHL Totals		35	1	1	2	10	1	0	0	37	2.7		244	45.9	10:57	4	0	0	0	2	0	0	0	11:37

NCAA Championship All-Tournament Team (2009)

Traded to **Anaheim** by **San Jose** with Timo Pielmeier and future considerations for Travis Moen and Kent Huskins, March 4, 2009.

BOOGAARD, Derek

(BOO-gard, DAIR-ihk)

Left wing. Shoots right. 6'7", 265 lbs. Born, Saskatoon, Sask., June 23, 1982. Minnesota's 6th choice, 202nd overall, in 2001 Entry Draft.

Season	Club	League	GP	G	A	Pts	PIM	PP	SH	GW	S	%	+/-	TF	F%	Min	GP	G	A	Pts	PIM	PP	SH	GW	Min
1998-99	Regina Caps	SJHL	35	2	3	5	166	....	....	....	....	....	....	....	....	....	....	....	....	....	....	....	....	....	....
99-2000	Regina Pats	WHL	5	0	0	0	17	....	....	....	....	....	....	....	....	....	....	....	....	....	....	....	....	....	....
	Prince George	WHL	33	0	0	0	149	....	....	....	....	....	....	....	....	....	....	....	....	....	....	....	....	....	....
2000-01	Prince George	WHL	61	1	8	9	245	....	....	....	....	....	....	....	....	....	6	1	0	1	31	....	....	....	....
2001-02	Prince George	WHL	2	0	0	0	16	....	....	....	....	....	....	....	....	....	....	....	....	....	....	....	....	....	....
	Medicine Hat	WHL	46	1	8	9	178	....	....	....	....	....	....	....	....	....	....	....	....	....	....	....	....	....	....
2002-03	Medicine Hat	WHL	27	1	2	3	65	....	....	....	....	....	....	....	....	....	....	....	....	....	....	....	....	....	....
	Louisiana	ECHL	33	1	2	3	240	....	....	....	....	....	....	....	....	....	2	0	0	0	0	....	....	....	....
2003-04	Houston Aeros	AHL	53	0	4	4	207	....	....	....	....	....	....	....	....	....	2	0	1	1	16	....	....	....	....
2004-05	Houston Aeros	AHL	56	1	4	5	259	....	....	....	....	....	....	....	....	....	5	0	0	0	38	....	....	....	....
2005-06	Minnesota	NHL	65	2	4	6	158	0	0	1	15	13.3	2	0	0.0	5:23	....	....	....	....	....	....	....	....	....
2006-07	Minnesota	NHL	48	0	1	1	120	0	0	0	11	0.0	0	0	0.0	4:38	4	0	1	1	20	0	0	0	5:59
2007-08	Minnesota	NHL	34	0	0	0	74	0	0	0	6	0.0	–5	0	0.0	3:56	6	0	0	0	24	0	0	0	4:48
2008-09	Minnesota	NHL	51	0	3	3	87	0	0	0	13	0.0	3	0	0.0	5:00	....	....	....	....	....	....	....	....	....
2009-10	Minnesota	NHL	57	0	4	4	105	0	0	0	26	0.0	–12	0	0.0	6:09	....	....	....	....	....	....	....	....	....
2010-11	NY Rangers	NHL	22	1	1	2	45	0	0	0	4	25.0	0	0	0.0	4:33	....	....	....	....	....	....	....	....	....
	NHL Totals		277	3	13	16	589	0	0	1	75	4.0		0	0.0	5:06	10	0	1	1	44	0	0	0	5:16

Signed as a free agent by **NY Rangers**, July 1, 2010. • Missed remainder of 2010-11 due to head and shoulder injuries at Ottawa, December 9, 2010. • Passed away on May 13, 2011.

BOOTH, David

(BOOTH, DAY-vihd) **FLA**

Left wing. Shoots left. 6', 212 lbs. Born, Detroit, MI, November 24, 1984. Florida's 3rd choice, 53rd overall, in 2004 Entry Draft.

Season	Club	League	GP	G	A	Pts	PIM	PP	SH	GW	S	%	+/-	TF	F%	Min	GP	G	A	Pts	PIM	PP	SH	GW	Min
2000-01	Det. Compuware	NAHL	42	17	13	30	44	....	....	....	....	....	....	....	....	....	2	1	0	1	2	....	....	....	....
2001-02	USNTDP	U-18	40	12	6	18	17	....	....	....	....	....	....	....	....	....	....	....	....	....	....	....	....	....	....
	USNTDP	USHL	12	4	3	7	6	....	....	....	....	....	....	....	....	....	....	....	....	....	....	....	....	....	....
	USNTDP	NAHL	6	1	3	4	18	....	....	....	....	....	....	....	....	....	....	....	....	....	....	....	....	....	....
2002-03	Michigan State	CCHA	39	17	19	36	53	....	....	....	....	....	....	....	....	....	....	....	....	....	....	....	....	....	....
2003-04	Michigan State	CCHA	30	8	10	18	30	....	....	....	....	....	....	....	....	....	....	....	....	....	....	....	....	....	....
2004-05	Michigan State	CCHA	29	7	9	16	30	....	....	....	....	....	....	....	....	....	....	....	....	....	....	....	....	....	....
2005-06	Michigan State	CCHA	37	13	22	35	50	....	....	....	....	....	....	....	....	....	....	....	....	....	....	....	....	....	....
2006-07	Florida	NHL	48	3	7	10	12	0	0	1	86	3.5	0	11	36.4	9:34	....	....	....	....	....	....	....	....	....
	Rochester	AHL	25	7	7	14	26	....	....	....	....	....	....	....	....	....	6	0	2	2	4	....	....	....	....
2007-08	Florida	NHL	73	22	18	40	26	1	0	6	228	9.6	13	38	34.2	16:10	....	....	....	....	....	....	....	....	....
2008-09	Florida	NHL	72	31	29	60	38	11	0	5	246	12.6	10	17	41.2	17:05	....	....	....	....	....	....	....	....	....
2009-10	Florida	NHL	28	8	8	16	23	0	0	1	95	8.4	–3	10	20.0	18:08	....	....	....	....	....	....	....	....	....
2010-11	Florida	NHL	82	23	17	40	26	8	0	3	280	8.2	–31	48	50.0	18:54	....	....	....	....	....	....	....	....	....
	NHL Totals		303	87	79	166	125	20	0	16	935	9.3		124	40.3	16:16	....	....	....	....	....	....	....	....	....

CCHA All-Rookie Team (2003)

• Missed majority of 2009-10 due to concussion at Philadelphia, October 24, 2009.

BORER, Casey

(BOHR-uhr, KAY-see)

Defense. Shoots left. 6'2", 205 lbs. Born, Minneapolis, MN, July 28, 1985. Carolina's 3rd choice, 69th overall, in 2004 Entry Draft.

Season	Club	League	GP	G	A	Pts	PIM	PP	SH	GW	S	%	+/-	TF	F%	Min	GP	G	A	Pts	PIM	PP	SH	GW	Min
2002-03	USNTDP	U-18	46	2	2	4	36	....	....	....	....	....	....	....	....	....	....	....	....	....	....	....	....	....	....
	USNTDP	NAHL	10	1	2	3	10	....	....	....	....	....	....	....	....	....	....	....	....	....	....	....	....	....	....
2003-04	St. Cloud State	WCHA	31	0	8	8	18	....	....	....	....	....	....	....	....	....	....	....	....	....	....	....	....	....	....
2004-05	St. Cloud State	WCHA	35	0	11	11	40	....	....	....	....	....	....	....	....	....	....	....	....	....	....	....	....	....	....
2005-06	St. Cloud State	WCHA	42	3	8	11	24	....	....	....	....	....	....	....	....	....	....	....	....	....	....	....	....	....	....
2006-07	St. Cloud State	WCHA	40	2	9	11	30	....	....	....	....	....	....	....	....	....	....	....	....	....	....	....	....	....	....
	Albany River Rats	AHL	1	0	0	0	0	....	....	....	....	....	....	....	....	....	....	....	....	....	....	....	....	....	....
2007-08	Carolina	NHL	11	1	2	3	4	0	0	0	5	20.0	–3	0	0.0	15:17	....	....	....	....	....	....	....	....	....
	Albany River Rats	AHL	61	6	13	19	58	....	....	....	....	....	....	....	....	....	....	....	....	....	....	....	....	....	....
2008-09	Carolina	NHL	3	0	0	0	5	0	0	0	0	0.0	0	0	0.0	11:05	....	....	....	....	....	....	....	....	....
	Albany River Rats	AHL	51	4	6	10	26	....	....	....	....	....	....	....	....	....	....	....	....	....	....	....	....	....	....
2009-10	Carolina	NHL	2	0	0	0	0	0	0	0	0	0.0	–1	0	0.0	10:46	....	....	....	....	....	....	....	....	....
	Albany River Rats	AHL	30	1	8	9	13	....	....	....	....	....	....	....	....	....	6	0	1	1	0	....	....	....	....
2010-11	Charlotte	AHL	67	2	12	14	26	....	....	....	....	....	....	....	....	....	15	1	2	3	12	....	....	....	....
	NHL Totals		16	1	2	3	9	0	0	0	5	20.0		0	0.0	13:56	....	....	....	....	....	....	....	....	....

Fred T. Hunt Memorial Award (AHL – Sportsmanship) (2010)

• Missed majority of 2009-10 due to neck injury.

BOUCHARD, Pierre-Marc

(BOO-shahrd, PEE-air- MAHRK) **MIN**

Center. Shoots left. 5'10", 178 lbs. Born, Sherbrooke, Que., April 27, 1984. Minnesota's 1st choice, 8th overall, in 2002 Entry Draft.

Season	Club	League	GP	G	A	Pts	PIM	PP	SH	GW	S	%	+/-	TF	F%	Min	GP	G	A	Pts	PIM	PP	SH	GW	Min
1998-99	Mtl.-Bourassa	QAHA	28	23	41	64	....	....	....	....	....	....	....	....	....	....	....	....	....	....	....	....	....	....	....
99-2000	Charles-Lemoyne	QAAA	42	28	*45	*74	20	....	....	....	....	....	....	....	....	....	9	4	8	12	6	....	....	....	....
2000-01	Chicoutimi	QMJHL	67	38	57	95	20	....	....	....	....	....	....	....	....	....	6	5	8	13	0	....	....	....	....
2001-02	Chicoutimi	QMJHL	69	46	*94	*140	54	....	....	....	....	....	....	....	....	....	4	2	3	5	4	....	....	....	....
2002-03	Minnesota	NHL	50	7	13	20	18	5	0	1	53	13.2	1	474	40.7	13:16	5	0	1	1	2	0	0	0	13:15
2003-04	Minnesota	NHL	61	4	18	22	22	2	0	0	60	6.7	–7	60	50.0	14:00	....	....	....	....	....	....	....	....	....
2004-05	Houston Aeros	AHL	67	12	42	54	46	....	....	....	....	....	....	....	....	....	5	0	1	1	0	....	....	....	....
2005-06	Minnesota	NHL	80	17	42	59	28	7	0	3	118	14.4	3	15	46.7	15:15	....	....	....	....	....	....	....	....	....
2006-07	Minnesota	NHL	82	20	37	57	14	5	0	3	173	11.6	13	18	33.3	15:59	5	1	1	2	0	0	0	0	14:48
2007-08	Minnesota	NHL	81	13	50	63	34	6	0	4	129	10.1	11	10	40.0	16:51	6	2	2	4	2	1	0	1	17:47
2008-09	Minnesota	NHL	71	16	30	46	20	2	0	1	142	11.3	–5	19	57.9	16:59	....	....	....	....	....	....	....	....	....
2009-10	Minnesota	NHL	1	0	0	0	2	0	0	0	0	0.0	0	3	33.3	10:44	....	....	....	....	....	....	....	....	....
2010-11	Minnesota	NHL	59	12	26	38	14	0	0	2	98	12.2	–3	43	39.5	15:43	....	....	....	....	....	....	....	....	....
	NHL Totals		485	89	216	305	152	27	0	14	773	11.5		642	41.9	15:35	16	3	4	7	4	1	0	1	15:26

QMJHL Rookie of the Year (2001) • QMJHL First All-Star Team (2002) • Canadian Major Junior First All-Star Team (2002) • Canadian Major Junior Player of the Year (2002)

• Missed majority of 2009-10 due to post-concussion syndrome.

BOUILLON, Francis

(BOO-liawn, FRAN-sihs) **NSH**

Defense. Shoots left. 5'8", 198 lbs. Born, New York, NY, October 17, 1975.

			Regular Season														Playoffs								
Season	Club	League	GP	G	A	Pts	PIM	PP	SH	GW	S	%	+/-	TF	F%	Min	GP	G	A	Pts	PIM	PP	SH	GW	Min
1991-92	Mtl-Bourassa	QAAA	42	2	5	7	28										9	1	0	1	6				
1992-93	Laval Titan	QMJHL	45	0	6	6	45																		
1993-94	Laval Titan	QMJHL	68	3	14	17	131										19	2	9	11	48				
1994-95	Laval Titan	QMJHL	72	8	25	33	115										20	3	11	14	21				
1995-96	Granby	QMJHL	68	11	35	46	156										21	2	12	14	30				
1996-97	Wheeling Nailers	ECHL	69	10	32	42	77										3	0	2	2	10				
1997-98	Quebec Rafales	IHL	71	8	27	35	76																		
1998-99	Fredericton	AHL	79	19	36	55	174										5	2	1	3	0				
99-2000	**Montreal**	**NHL**	**74**	**3**	**13**	**16**	**38**	**2**	**0**	**1**	**76**	**3.9**	**–7**	**1**	**0.0**	**15:52**									
2000-01	**Montreal**	**NHL**	**29**	**0**	**6**	**6**	**26**	**0**	**0**	**0**	**24**	**0.0**	**3**	**0**	**0.0**	**13:24**									
	Quebec Citadelles	AHL	4	0	0	0	0																		
2001-02	**Montreal**	**NHL**	**28**	**0**	**5**	**5**	**33**	**0**	**0**	**0**	**24**	**0.0**	**–5**	**0**	**0.0**	**18:47**									
	Quebec Citadelles	AHL	38	8	14	22	30																		
2002-03	**Nashville**	**NHL**	**4**	**0**	**0**	**0**	**2**	**0**	**0**	**0**	**0**	**0.0**	**–1**	**0**	**0.0**	**12:52**									
	Montreal	**NHL**	**20**	**3**	**1**	**4**	**2**	**0**	**1**	**0**	**30**	**10.0**	**–1**	**0**	**0.0**	**20:24**									
	Hamilton	AHL	29	1	12	13	31																		
2003-04	**Montreal**	**NHL**	**73**	**2**	**16**	**18**	**70**	**0**	**0**	**0**	**86**	**2.3**	**1**	**0**	**0.0**	**19:39**	**11**	**0**	**0**	**0**	**7**	**0**	**0**	**0**	**18:00**
2004-05	Leksands IF	Sweden-2	31	10	21	31	46																		
2005-06	**Montreal**	**NHL**	**67**	**3**	**19**	**22**	**34**	**3**	**0**	**1**	**75**	**4.0**	**–6**	**0**	**0.0**	**20:47**	**6**	**1**	**2**	**3**	**10**	**1**	**0**	**0**	**22:24**
2006-07	**Montreal**	**NHL**	**62**	**3**	**11**	**14**	**52**	**1**	**0**	**1**	**56**	**5.4**	**–10**	**0**	**0.0**	**18:19**									
2007-08	**Montreal**	**NHL**	**74**	**2**	**6**	**8**	**61**	**0**	**0**	**0**	**60**	**3.3**	**9**	**0**	**0.0**	**17:22**	**7**	**1**	**2**	**3**	**4**	**0**	**0**	**0**	**15:55**
2008-09	**Montreal**	**NHL**	**54**	**5**	**4**	**9**	**53**	**0**	**0**	**1**	**51**	**9.8**	**–7**	**0**	**0.0**	**16:30**	**1**	**0**	**0**	**0**	**0**	**0**	**0**	**0**	**1:46**
2009-10	**Nashville**	**NHL**	**81**	**3**	**8**	**11**	**50**	**1**	**0**	**1**	**86**	**3.5**	**5**	**0**	**0.0**	**19:18**	**6**	**0**	**0**	**0**	**6**	**0**	**0**	**0**	**19:37**
2010-11	**Nashville**	**NHL**	**44**	**1**	**9**	**10**	**27**	**0**	**0**	**0**	**47**	**2.1**	**–3**	**0**	**0.0**	**20:14**									
	NHL Totals		**610**	**25**	**98**	**123**	**448**	**7**	**1**	**5**	**615**	**4.1**		**1**	**0.0**	**18:16**	**31**	**2**	**4**	**6**	**27**	**1**	**0**	**0**	**18:10**

Signed as a free agent by **Montreal**, August 18, 1998. • Missed majority of 2000-01 due to ankle injury vs. Calgary, December 31, 2000. Claimed by **Nashville** from **Montreal** in Waiver Draft, October 4, 2002. Claimed on waivers by **Montreal** from **Nashville**, October 25, 2002. Signed as a free agent by **Leksands** (Sweden-2), November 15, 2004. Signed as a free agent by **Nashville**, September 30, 2009.

BOULERICE, Jesse

(BOO-luhr-ighs, JEH-see)

Right wing. Shoots right. 6'2", 215 lbs. Born, Plattsburgh, NY, August 10, 1978. Philadelphia's 4th choice, 133rd overall, in 1996 Entry Draft.

Season	Club	League	GP	G	A	Pts	PIM	PP	SH	GW	S	%	+/-	TF	F%	Min	GP	G	A	Pts	PIM	PP	SH	GW	Min
1994-95	Hawkesbury	CJHL	46	1	8	9	160																		
1995-96	Detroit	OHL	64	2	5	7	150										16	0	0	0	12				
1996-97	Detroit	OHL	33	10	14	24	209																		
1997-98	Plymouth Whalers	OHL	53	20	23	43	170										13	2	4	6	35				
1998-99	Philadelphia	AHL	24	1	2	3	82																		
	New Orleans	ECHL	12	0	1	1	38																		
99-2000	Philadelphia	AHL	40	3	4	7	85										4	0	2	2	4				
	Trenton Titans	ECHL	25	8	8	16	90																		
2000-01	Philadelphia	AHL	60	3	4	7	256										10	1	1	2	28				
2001-02	**Philadelphia**	**NHL**	**3**	**0**	**0**	**0**	**5**	**0**	**0**	**0**	**1**	**0.0**	**–1**	**0**	**0.0**	**4:18**									
	Philadelphia	AHL	41	2	5	7	204																		
	Lowell	AHL	15	2	4	6	80										5	0	2	2	6				
2002-03	**Carolina**	**NHL**	**48**	**2**	**1**	**3**	**108**	**0**	**0**	**0**	**12**	**16.7**	**–2**	**0**	**0.0**	**3:54**									
2003-04	**Carolina**	**NHL**	**76**	**6**	**1**	**7**	**127**	**0**	**0**	**0**	**46**	**13.0**	**–5**	**0**	**0.0**	**6:32**									
2004-05			DID NOT PLAY																						
2005-06	**Carolina**	**NHL**	**26**	**0**	**0**	**0**	**51**	**0**	**0**	**0**	**3**	**0.0**	**–3**	**0**	**0.0**	**2:30**									
	St. Louis	**NHL**	**12**	**0**	**0**	**0**	**13**	**0**	**0**	**0**	**2**	**0.0**	**–4**	**0**	**0.0**	**2:39**									
2006-07	Albany River Rats	AHL	16	4	3	7	36																		
2007-08	**Philadelphia**	**NHL**	**5**	**0**	**0**	**0**	**29**	**0**	**0**	**0**	**1**	**0.0**	**–2**	**0**	**0.0**	**3:52**									
	Philadelphia	AHL	36	2	4	6	101										7	0	0	0	2				
2008-09	Lake Erie	AHL	41	4	3	7	97																		
	Edmonton	**NHL**	**2**	**0**	**0**	**0**	**0**	**0**	**0**	**0**	**0**	**0.0**	**0**	**0**	**0.0**	**3:43**									
2009-10	Wilkes-Barre	AHL	54	4	3	7	124										4	0	0	0	6				
2010-11	Wilkes-Barre	AHL	67	4	7	11	147										7	0	0	0	11				
	NHL Totals		**172**	**8**	**2**	**10**	**333**	**0**	**0**	**0**	**65**	**12.3**		**0**	**0.0**	**4:46**									

Traded to **Carolina** by **Philadelphia** for Greg Koehler, February 13, 2002. Traded to **St. Louis** by **Carolina** with Mike Zigomanis, the rights to Magnus Kahnberg, Carolina's 1st round choice (later traded to New Jersey - New Jersey selected Matthew Corrente) in 2006 Entry Draft, Toronto's 4th round choice (previously acquired, St. Louis selected Reto Berra) in 2006 Entry Draft and Chicago's 4th round choice (previously acquired, St. Louis selected Cade Fairchild) in 2007 Entry Draft for Doug Weight and Erkki Rajamaki, January 30, 2006. Signed as a free agent by **Carolina**, August 2, 2006. Signed as a free agent by **Philadelphia**, October 3, 2007. Signed to a PTO (professional tryout) contract by **Lake Erie** (AHL), October 8, 2008. Signed as a free agent by **Colorado**, November 8, 2008. Claimed on waivers by **Edmonton** from **Colorado**, November 11, 2008. Signed to a PTO (professional tryout) contract by **Wilkes-Barre/Scranton** (AHL), September 10, 2009.. Signed as a free agent by **Wilkes-Barre/Scranton** (AHL), October 3, 2009.

BOULTON, Eric

(BOHL-tuhn, AIR-ihk) **N.J.**

Left wing. Shoots left. 6'1", 225 lbs. Born, Halifax, N.S., August 17, 1976. NY Rangers' 12th choice, 234th overall, in 1994 Entry Draft.

Season	Club	League	GP	G	A	Pts	PIM	PP	SH	GW	S	%	+/-	TF	F%	Min	GP	G	A	Pts	PIM	PP	SH	GW	Min
1992-93	Cole Harbour	MJrHL	44	12	15	27	212																		
1993-94	Oshawa Generals	OHL	45	4	3	7	149										5	0	0	0	16				
1994-95	Oshawa Generals	OHL	27	7	5	12	125																		
	Sarnia Sting	OHL	24	3	7	10	134										4	0	1	1	10				
1995-96	Sarnia Sting	OHL	66	14	29	43	243										9	0	3	3	29				
1996-97	Binghamton	AHL	23	2	3	5	67										3	0	0	0	4				
	Charlotte	ECHL	44	14	11	25	325										3	0	1	1	6				
1997-98	Charlotte	ECHL	53	11	16	27	202										4	1	0	1	0				
	Fort Wayne	IHL	8	0	2	2	42																		
1998-99	Kentucky	AHL	34	3	3	6	154										10	0	1	1	36				
	Florida Everblades	ECHL	26	9	13	22	143																		
	Houston Aeros	IHL	7	1	0	1	41																		
99-2000	Rochester	AHL	76	2	2	4	276										18	2	1	3	53				
2000-01	**Buffalo**	**NHL**	**35**	**1**	**2**	**3**	**94**	**0**	**0**	**0**	**20**	**5.0**	**–1**	**2**	**0.0**	**5:42**									
2001-02	**Buffalo**	**NHL**	**35**	**2**	**3**	**5**	**129**	**0**	**0**	**1**	**21**	**9.5**	**–1**	**0**	**0.0**	**6:08**									
2002-03	**Buffalo**	**NHL**	**58**	**1**	**5**	**6**	**178**	**0**	**0**	**0**	**33**	**3.0**	**1**	**6**	**33.3**	**6:35**									
2003-04	**Buffalo**	**NHL**	**44**	**1**	**2**	**3**	**110**	**0**	**0**	**0**	**20**	**5.0**	**–2**	**1**	**0.0**	**4:52**									
2004-05	Columbia Inferno	ECHL	48	23	16	39	124										4	2	3	5	8				
2005-06	**Atlanta**	**NHL**	**51**	**4**	**5**	**9**	**87**	**0**	**0**	**0**	**28**	**14.3**	**–4**	**2**	**50.0**	**4:54**									
2006-07	**Atlanta**	**NHL**	**45**	**3**	**4**	**7**	**49**	**0**	**0**	**0**	**42**	**7.1**	**2**	**2**	**50.0**	**6:16**	**4**	**0**	**0**	**0**	**24**	**0**	**0**	**0**	**5:04**
2007-08	**Atlanta**	**NHL**	**74**	**4**	**5**	**9**	**127**	**0**	**0**	**0**	**64**	**6.3**	**–10**	**4**	**25.0**	**7:27**									
2008-09	**Atlanta**	**NHL**	**76**	**3**	**10**	**13**	**176**	**0**	**0**	**0**	**71**	**4.2**	**–3**	**4**	**25.0**	**7:33**									
2009-10	**Atlanta**	**NHL**	**62**	**2**	**6**	**8**	**113**	**1**	**0**	**0**	**39**	**5.1**	**–1**	**4**	**50.0**	**6:51**									
2010-11	**Atlanta**	**NHL**	**69**	**6**	**4**	**10**	**87**	**0**	**0**	**1**	**51**	**11.8**	**1**	**3**	**0.0**	**8:57**									
	NHL Totals		**549**	**27**	**46**	**73**	**1150**	**1**	**0**	**2**	**389**	**6.9**		**28**	**28.6**	**6:45**	**4**	**0**	**0**	**0**	**24**	**0**	**0**	**0**	**5:04**

Signed as a free agent by **Buffalo**, September 14, 1999. Signed as a free agent by **Columbia** (ECHL), November 24, 2004. Signed as a free agent by **Atlanta**, August 8, 2005. • Transferred to **Winnipeg** after **Atlanta** franchise relocated, June 21, 2011. Signed as a free agent by **New Jersey**, July 15, 2011.

BOUMA, Lance

(BOW-ma, LANTZ) **CGY**

Center. Shoots left. 6'1", 210 lbs. Born, Provost, Alta., March 25, 1990. Calgary's 3rd choice, 78th overall, in 2008 Entry Draft.

Season	Club	League	GP	G	A	Pts	PIM	PP	SH	GW	S	%	+/-	TF	F%	Min	GP	G	A	Pts	PIM	PP	SH	GW	Min
2005-06	Wainwright	RAMHL	37	21	29	50	....																		
	Vancouver Giants	WHL	5	1	3	4	0																		
2006-07	Vancouver Giants	WHL	49	3	5	8	31										22	3	3	6	12				
2007-08	Vancouver Giants	WHL	71	12	23	35	93										10	0	1	1	8				
2008-09	Vancouver Giants	WHL	48	9	16	25	116										17	7	5	12	30				
2009-10	Vancouver Giants	WHL	57	14	29	43	134										16	4	13	17	*47				
	Abbotsford Heat	AHL	....	....	....	....	....										5	1	0	1	2				
2010-11	**Calgary**	**NHL**	**16**	**0**	**1**	**1**	**2**	**0**	**0**	**0**	**9**	**0.0**	**–1**	**3**	**0.0**	**5:52**									
	Abbotsford Heat	AHL	61	12	8	20	53																		
	NHL Totals		**16**	**0**	**1**	**1**	**2**	**0**	**0**	**0**	**9**	**0.0**		**3**	**0.0**	**5:52**									

							Regular Season										Playoffs							
Season	Club	League	GP	G	A	Pts	PIM	PP	SH	GW	S	%	+/-	TF	F%	Min	GP	G	A	Pts	PIM	PP	SH	GW	Min

BOURQUE, Chris (BOHRK, KRIHS) WSH

Center. Shoots left. 5'8", 180 lbs.   Born, Boston, MA, January 29, 1986. Washington's 4th choice, 33rd overall, in 2004 Entry Draft.

Season	Club	League	GP	G	A	Pts	PIM	PP	SH	GW	S	%	+/-	TF	F%	Min	GP	G	A	Pts	PIM	PP	SH	GW	Min
2002-03	Cushing	High-MA	28	31	26	57	49	....	....	....	....	....	....	....	....	....	....	....	....	....	....	....	....	....	....
2003-04	Cushing	High-MA	31	37	53	90	96	....	....	....	....	....	....	....	....	....	....	....	....	....	....	....	....	....	....
2004-05	Boston University	H-East	35	10	13	23	50	....	....	....	....	....	....	....	....	....	....	....	....	....	....	....	....	....	....
	Portland Pirates	AHL	6	1	1	2	2	....	....	....	....	....	....	....	....	....	....	....	....	....	....	....	....	....	....
2005-06	Hershey Bears	AHL	52	8	28	36	40										1	0	0	0	0				
2006-07	Hershey Bears	AHL	76	25	33	58	49										19	2	6	8	18				
2007-08	**Washington**	**NHL**	**4**	**0**	**0**	**0**	**2**	0	0	0	4	0.0	0	1	0.0	8:42	....	....	....	....	....				
	Hershey Bears	AHL	73	28	35	63	56										5	1	3	4	8				
2008-09	**Washington**	**NHL**	**8**	**1**	**0**	**1**	**0**	0	0	0	11	9.1	0	0	0.0	9:46	....	....	....	....	....				
	Hershey Bears	AHL	69	21	52	73	57										22	5	16	21	30				
2009-10	**Pittsburgh**	**NHL**	**20**	**0**	**3**	**3**	**10**	0	0	0	20	0.0	–4	0	0.0	9:35	....	....	....	....	....				
	Washington	**NHL**	**1**	**0**	**0**	**0**	**0**	0	0	0	1	0.0	–2	0	0.0	9:37	....	....	....	....	....				
	Hershey Bears	AHL	49	22	48	70	26										21	7	20	*27	10				
2010-11	Mytischi	Rus-KHL	8	1	0	1	0										....	....	....	....	....				
	HC Lugano	Swiss	39	14	19	33	24										2	1	4	5	0				
	NHL Totals		**33**	**1**	**3**	**4**	**12**	**0**	**0**	**0**	**36**	**2.8**		**1**	**0.0**	**9:31**	....	....	....	....	....				

Hockey East All-Rookie Team (2005) • Jack A. Butterfield Trophy (AHL – Playoff MVP) (2010)
Claimed on waivers by **Pittsburgh** from **Washington**, September 30, 2009. Claimed on waivers by **Washington** from **Pittsburgh**, December 5, 2009. Signed as a free agent by **Mytischi** (Russia-KHL), June 23, 2010. Signed as a free agent by **Lugano** (Swiss), October 4, 2010.

BOURQUE, Rene (BOHRK, reh-NAY) CGY

Left wing. Shoots left. 6'2", 213 lbs.   Born, Lac La Biche, Alta., December 10, 1981.

Season	Club	League	GP	G	A	Pts	PIM	PP	SH	GW	S	%	+/-	TF	F%	Min	GP	G	A	Pts	PIM	PP	SH	GW	Min
2000-01	U. of Wisconsin	WCHA	32	10	5	15	18	....	....	....	....	....	....	....	....	....	....	....	....	....	....				
2001-02	U. of Wisconsin	WCHA	38	12	7	19	26	....	....	....	....	....	....	....	....	....	....	....	....	....	....				
2002-03	U. of Wisconsin	WCHA	40	19	8	27	54	....	....	....	....	....	....	....	....	....	....	....	....	....	....				
2003-04	U. of Wisconsin	WCHA	42	16	20	36	74	....	....	....	....	....	....	....	....	....	....	....	....	....	....				
2004-05	Norfolk Admirals	AHL	78	33	27	60	105										6	1	0	1	8				
2005-06	**Chicago**	**NHL**	**77**	**16**	**18**	**34**	**56**	4	0	2	180	8.9	3	11	36.4	15:20	....	....	....	....	....				
2006-07	**Chicago**	**NHL**	**44**	**7**	**10**	**17**	**38**	2	1	1	82	8.5	–4	9	22.2	16:01	....	....	....	....	....				
	Norfolk Admirals	AHL	1	0	0	0	0										....	....	....	....	....				
2007-08	**Chicago**	**NHL**	**62**	**10**	**14**	**24**	**42**	0	5	2	103	9.7	6	8	25.0	15:16	....	....	....	....	....				
2008-09	**Calgary**	**NHL**	**58**	**21**	**19**	**40**	**70**	0	1	2	149	14.1	18	18	50.0	16:05	5	1	0	1	22	0	0	0	17:06
2009-10	**Calgary**	**NHL**	**73**	**27**	**31**	**58**	**88**	6	4	5	215	12.6	7	25	32.0	18:19	....	....	....	....	....				
2010-11	**Calgary**	**NHL**	**80**	**27**	**23**	**50**	**42**	6	1	6	218	12.4	–17	24	29.2	17:45	....	....	....	....	....				
	NHL Totals		**394**	**108**	**115**	**223**	**336**	**18**	**12**	**16**	**947**	**11.4**		**95**	**33.7**	**16:33**	**5**	**1**	**0**	**1**	**22**	**0**	**0**	**0**	**17:06**

AHL All-Rookie Team (2005) • Dudley "Red" Garrett Memorial Trophy (AHL - Top Rookie) (2005)
Signed as a free agent by **Chicago**, July 29, 2004. Traded to **Calgary** by **Chicago** for Calgary's 2nd round choice (later traded to Toronto – Toronto selected Brad Ross) in 2010 Entry Draft, July 1, 2008.

BOUWMEESTER, Jay (BOW-mee-stuhr, JAY) CGY

Defense. Shoots left. 6'4", 215 lbs.   Born, Edmonton, Alta., September 27, 1983. Florida's 1st choice, 3rd overall, in 2002 Entry Draft.

Season	Club	League	GP	G	A	Pts	PIM	PP	SH	GW	S	%	+/-	TF	F%	Min	GP	G	A	Pts	PIM	PP	SH	GW	Min
1998-99	Edmonton SSAC	AMHL	32	14	29	43	36	....	....	....	....	....	....	....	....	....	....	....	....	....	....				
	Medicine Hat	WHL	8	2	1	3	2	....	....	....	....	....	....	....	....	....	....	....	....	....	....				
99-2000	Medicine Hat	WHL	64	13	21	34	26	....	....	....	....	....	....	....	....	....	....	....	....	....	....				
2000-01	Medicine Hat	WHL	61	14	39	53	44	....	....	....	....	....	....	....	....	....	....	....	....	....	....				
2001-02	Medicine Hat	WHL	61	11	50	61	42	....	....	....	....	....	....	....	....	....	....	....	....	....	....				
2002-03	**Florida**	**NHL**	**82**	**4**	**12**	**16**	**14**	2	0	0	110	3.6	–29	0	0.0	20:09	....	....	....	....	....				
2003-04	**Florida**	**NHL**	**61**	**2**	**18**	**20**	**30**	0	0	0	85	2.4	–15	0	0.0	23:02	....	....	....	....	....				
	San Antonio	AHL	2	0	1	1	2										....	....	....	....	....				
2004-05	San Antonio	AHL	64	4	13	17	50										....	....	....	....	....				
	Chicago Wolves	AHL	18	6	3	9	12										18	0	0	0	14				
2005-06	**Florida**	**NHL**	**82**	**5**	**41**	**46**	**79**	0	0	0	189	2.6	1	1	0.0	25:29	....	....	....	....	....				
	Canada	Olympics	6	0	0	0	0										....	....	....	....	....				
2006-07	**Florida**	**NHL**	**82**	**12**	**30**	**42**	**66**	3	0	3	174	6.9	23	0	0.0	26:09	....	....	....	....	....				
2007-08	**Florida**	**NHL**	**82**	**15**	**22**	**37**	**72**	4	0	0	182	8.2	–5	0	0.0	27:28	....	....	....	....	....				
2008-09	**Florida**	**NHL**	**82**	**15**	**27**	**42**	**68**	9	0	2	182	8.2	–2	0	0.0	26:59	....	....	....	....	....				
2009-10	**Calgary**	**NHL**	**82**	**3**	**26**	**29**	**48**	1	0	0	130	2.3	–4	0	0.0	25:55	....	....	....	....	....				
2010-11	**Calgary**	**NHL**	**82**	**4**	**20**	**24**	**44**	1	0	1	121	3.3	–2	0	0.0	25:59	....	....	....	....	....				
	NHL Totals		**635**	**60**	**196**	**256**	**421**	**20**	**0**	**6**	**1173**	**5.1**		**1**	**0.0**	**25:13**	....	....	....	....	....				

WHL East First All-Star Team (2002) • NHL All-Rookie Team (2003)
Played in NHL All-Star Game (2007, 2009)
• Loaned to **Chicago** (AHL) by **Florida** (San Antonio-AHL) for cash, March 8, 2005. Traded to **Calgary** by **Florida** for Jordan Leopold and Phoenix's 3rd round choice (previously acquired, Florida selected Josh Birkholz) in 2009 Entry Draft, June 27, 2009.

BOWMAN, Drayson (BOH-muhn, DRAY-suhn) CAR

Center/Left wing. Shoots left. 6'1", 190 lbs.   Born, Grand Rapids, MI, March 8, 1989. Carolina's 2nd choice, 72nd overall, in 2007 Entry Draft.

Season	Club	League	GP	G	A	Pts	PIM	PP	SH	GW	S	%	+/-	TF	F%	Min	GP	G	A	Pts	PIM	PP	SH	GW	Min
2004-05	Kimberley	KIJHL	47	29	30	59	108	....	....	....	....	....	....	....	....	....	....	....	....	....	....				
	Spokane Chiefs	WHL	4	0	0	0	0	....	....	....	....	....	....	....	....	....	....	....	....	....	....				
2005-06	Spokane Chiefs	WHL	72	17	17	34	51	....	....	....	....	....	....	....	....	....	....	....	....	....	....				
2006-07	Spokane Chiefs	WHL	61	24	19	43	55										6	2	5	7	4				
2007-08	Spokane Chiefs	WHL	66	42	40	82	62										21	11	9	20	8				
2008-09	Spokane Chiefs	WHL	62	47	36	83	107										12	8	5	13	8				
2009-10	**Carolina**	**NHL**	**9**	**2**	**0**	**2**	**4**	1	0	0	17	11.8	–1	0	0.0	12:01	....	....	....	....	....				
	Albany River Rats	AHL	56	17	15	32	29										8	3	6	9	12				
2010-11	**Carolina**	**NHL**	**23**	**0**	**1**	**1**	**12**	0	0	0	28	0.0	0	0	0.0	9:49	....	....	....	....	....				
	Charlotte	AHL	51	12	18	30	53										15	2	6	8	6				
	NHL Totals		**32**	**2**	**1**	**3**	**16**	**1**	**0**	**0**	**45**	**4.4**		**0**	**0.0**	**10:26**	....	....	....	....	....				

WHL West Second All-Star Team (2008, 2009) • Memorial Cup All-Star Team (2008)

BOYCE, Darryl (BOIS, DAIR-uhl) TOR

Center. Shoots left. 6', 200 lbs.   Born, Summerside, P.E.I., July 7, 1984.

Season	Club	League	GP	G	A	Pts	PIM	PP	SH	GW	S	%	+/-	TF	F%	Min	GP	G	A	Pts	PIM	PP	SH	GW	Min
2001-02	St. Michael's	OHL	67	10	11	21	71	....	....	....	....	....	....	....	....	....	15	2	5	7	46				
2002-03	St. Michael's	OHL	64	16	21	37	119	....	....	....	....	....	....	....	....	....	19	1	3	4	28				
2003-04	St. Michael's	OHL	64	13	24	37	110	....	....	....	....	....	....	....	....	....	18	1	3	4	23				
2004-05	St. Michael's	OHL	67	15	35	50	152	....	....	....	....	....	....	....	....	....	10	2	5	7	28				
2005-06	New Brunswick	AUAA	28	15	17	32	50	....	....	....	....	....	....	....	....	....	....	....	....	....	....				
2006-07	New Brunswick	AUAA	25	14	19	33	63	....	....	....	....	....	....	....	....	....	....	....	....	....	....				
2007-08	Toronto Marlies	AHL	41	8	16	24	71										....	....	....	....	....				
	Toronto	**NHL**	**1**	**0**	**0**	**0**	**0**	0	0	0	0	0.0	0	2100.0		3:20	....	....	....	....	....				
2008-09	Toronto Marlies	AHL	73	12	18	30	131										6	2	0	2	27				
2009-10	Toronto Marlies	AHL	20	2	9	11	48										....	....	....	....	....				
2010-11	**Toronto**	**NHL**	**46**	**5**	**8**	**13**	**33**	0	0	1	27	18.5	8	457	46.4	11:23	....	....	....	....	....				
	Toronto Marlies	AHL	35	6	10	16	48										....	....	....	....	....				
	NHL Totals		**47**	**5**	**8**	**13**	**33**	**0**	**0**	**1**	**27**	**18.5**		**459**	**46.6**	**11:13**	....	....	....	....	....				

Signed as a free agent by **Toronto** (AHL), April, 2007. Signed as a free agent by **Toronto**, January 1, 2008. • Missed majority of 2009-10 due to various injuries.

BOYCHUK, Johnny
(BOY-chuhk, JAW-nee) **BOS**

Defense. Shoots right. 6'2", 225 lbs. Born, Edmonton, Alta., January 19, 1984. Colorado's 2nd choice, 61st overall, in 2002 Entry Draft.

Season	Club	League	GP	G	A	Pts	PIM	PP	SH	GW	S	%	+/-	TF	F%	Min	GP	G	A	Pts	PIM	PP	SH	GW	Min
			Regular Season														Playoffs								
1998-99	Edm. Cycle	AMBHL	36	8	20	28	59	....	....	....	....	....	....	....	....	....	....	....	....	....	....	....	....	....	....
99-2000	Edm. Cycle	AMHL	35	6	17	23	59	....	....	....	....	....	....	....	....	....	....	....	....	....	....	....	....	....	....
	Calgary Hitmen	WHL	1	0	0	0	0	....	....	....	....	....	....	....	....	....	....	....	....	....	....	....	....	....	....
2000-01	Calgary Hitmen	WHL	66	4	8	12	61	....	....	....	....	....	....	....	....	....	12	1	1	2	17	....	....	....	....
2001-02	Calgary Hitmen	WHL	70	8	32	40	85	....	....	....	....	....	....	....	....	....	7	1	1	2	6	....	....	....	....
2002-03	Calgary Hitmen	WHL	40	8	18	26	58	....	....	....	....	....	....	....	....	....	....	....	....	....	....	....	....	....	....
	Moose Jaw	WHL	27	5	17	22	32	....	....	....	....	....	....	....	....	....	13	2	6	8	29	....	....	....	....
2003-04	Moose Jaw	WHL	62	13	20	33	71	....	....	....	....	....	....	....	....	....	10	1	9	10	9	....	....	....	....
2004-05	Hershey Bears	AHL	80	3	12	15	69	....	....	....	....	....	....	....	....	....	....	....	....	....	....	....	....	....	....
2005-06	Lowell	AHL	74	6	26	32	73	....	....	....	....	....	....	....	....	....	....	....	....	....	....	....	....	....	....
2006-07	Albany River Rats	AHL	80	10	18	28	125	....	....	....	....	....	....	....	....	....	5	1	1	2	4	....	....	....	....
2007-08	**Colorado**	**NHL**	**4**	**0**	**0**	**0**	**0**	**0**	**0**	**0**	**3**	**0.0**	**1**	**1**	**0.0**	**8:57**	....	....	....	....	....	....	....	....	....
	Lake Erie	AHL	60	8	18	26	63	....	....	....	....	....	....	....	....	....	....	....	....	....	....	....	....	....	....
2008-09	**Boston**	**NHL**	**1**	**0**	**0**	**0**	**0**	**0**	**0**	**0**	**0**	**0.0**	**0**	**0**	**0.0**	**14:48**	....	....	....	....	....	....	....	....	....
	Providence Bruins	AHL	78	20	46	66	61	....	....	....	....	....	....	....	....	....	16	3	5	8	19	....	....	....	....
2009-10	**Boston**	**NHL**	**51**	**5**	**10**	**15**	**43**	**0**	**0**	**0**	**96**	**5.2**	**10**	**0**	**0.0**	**17:39**	**13**	**2**	**4**	**6**	**6**	**1**	**0**	**0**	**26:10**
	Providence Bruins	AHL	2	1	0	1	0	....	....	....	....	....	....	....	....	....	....	....	....	....	....	....	....	....	....
2010-11 ♦	**Boston**	**NHL**	**69**	**3**	**13**	**16**	**45**	**1**	**0**	**1**	**154**	**1.9**	**15**	**0**	**0.0**	**20:30**	**25**	**3**	**6**	**9**	**12**	**0**	**0**	**1**	**20:38**
	NHL Totals		**125**	**8**	**23**	**31**	**88**	**1**	**0**	**1**	**253**	**3.2**		**1**	**0.0**	**18:56**	**38**	**5**	**10**	**15**	**18**	**1**	**0**	**1**	**22:32**

AHL First All-Star Team (2009) • Eddie Shore Award (AHL – Outstanding Defenseman) (2009)

Traded to **Boston** by **Colorado** for Matt Hendricks, June 24, 2008.

BOYCHUK, Zach
(BOY-chuhk, ZAK) **CAR**

Center. Shoots left. 5'10", 185 lbs. Born, Airdrie, Alta., October 4, 1989. Carolina's 1st choice, 14th overall, in 2008 Entry Draft.

Season	Club	League	GP	G	A	Pts	PIM	PP	SH	GW	S	%	+/-	TF	F%	Min	GP	G	A	Pts	PIM	PP	SH	GW	Min
2004-05	UFA Bisons	AMHL	36	13	14	27	18	....	....	....	....	....	....	....	....	....	16	10	5	15	....	....	....	....	....
2005-06	Lethbridge	WHL	64	18	33	51	30	....	....	....	....	....	....	....	....	....	6	0	5	5	2	....	....	....	....
2006-07	Lethbridge	WHL	69	31	60	91	52	....	....	....	....	....	....	....	....	....	....	....	....	....	....	....	....	....	....
2007-08	Lethbridge	WHL	61	33	39	72	80	....	....	....	....	....	....	....	....	....	18	*13	8	21	6	....	....	....	....
2008-09	**Carolina**	**NHL**	**2**	**0**	**0**	**0**	**0**	**0**	**0**	**0**	**0**	**0.0**	**0**	**1**	**0.0**	**12:03**	....	....	....	....	....	....	....	....	....
	Lethbridge	WHL	43	28	29	57	22	....	....	....	....	....	....	....	....	....	11	7	6	13	12	....	....	....	....
	Albany River Rats	AHL	2	0	1	1	2	....	....	....	....	....	....	....	....	....	....	....	....	....	....	....	....	....	....
2009-10	**Carolina**	**NHL**	**31**	**3**	**6**	**9**	**2**	**0**	**0**	**0**	**37**	**8.1**	**1**	**9**	**55.6**	**10:45**	....	....	....	....	....	....	....	....	....
	Albany River Rats	AHL	52	15	21	36	24	....	....	....	....	....	....	....	....	....	8	2	3	5	4	....	....	....	....
2010-11	**Carolina**	**NHL**	**23**	**4**	**3**	**7**	**4**	**1**	**0**	**1**	**44**	**9.1**	**–2**	**5**	**20.0**	**10:43**	....	....	....	....	....	....	....	....	....
	Charlotte	AHL	60	22	43	65	48	....	....	....	....	....	....	....	....	....	16	3	6	9	14	....	....	....	....
	NHL Totals		**56**	**7**	**9**	**16**	**6**	**1**	**0**	**1**	**81**	**8.6**		**15**	**40.0**	**10:47**	....	....	....	....	....	....	....	....	....

WHL East Second All-Star Team (2007, 2008)

BOYD, Dustin
(BOID, DUHS-tihn)

Center. Shoots left. 6', 187 lbs. Born, Winnipeg, Man., July 16, 1986. Calgary's 3rd choice, 98th overall, in 2004 Entry Draft.

Season	Club	League	GP	G	A	Pts	PIM	PP	SH	GW	S	%	+/-	TF	F%	Min	GP	G	A	Pts	PIM	PP	SH	GW	Min
2001-02	Wpg. Warriors	MMMHL	40	50	57	107	16	....	....	....	....	....	....	....	....	....	....	....	....	....	....	....	....	....	....
2002-03	Moose Jaw	WHL	63	11	17	28	15	....	....	....	....	....	....	....	....	....	13	0	3	3	2	....	....	....	....
2003-04	Moose Jaw	WHL	72	18	20	38	40	....	....	....	....	....	....	....	....	....	10	2	2	4	8	....	....	....	....
2004-05	Moose Jaw	WHL	66	26	35	61	57	....	....	....	....	....	....	....	....	....	5	1	2	3	2	....	....	....	....
2005-06	Moose Jaw	WHL	64	48	42	90	34	....	....	....	....	....	....	....	....	....	22	7	11	18	10	....	....	....	....
2006-07	**Calgary**	**NHL**	**13**	**2**	**2**	**4**	**4**	**0**	**0**	**1**	**8**	**25.0**	**5**	**16**	**50.0**	**10:09**	....	....	....	....	....	....	....	....	....
	Omaha	AHL	66	27	33	60	34	....	....	....	....	....	....	....	....	....	6	1	1	2	0	....	....	....	....
2007-08	**Calgary**	**NHL**	**48**	**7**	**5**	**12**	**6**	**0**	**0**	**1**	**46**	**15.2**	**–11**	**129**	**50.4**	**9:49**	....	....	....	....	....	....	....	....	....
	Quad City Flames	AHL	18	2	7	9	4	....	....	....	....	....	....	....	....	....	....	....	....	....	....	....	....	....	....
2008-09	**Calgary**	**NHL**	**71**	**11**	**11**	**22**	**10**	**1**	**1**	**3**	**74**	**14.9**	**–11**	**477**	**45.5**	**12:52**	**5**	**1**	**0**	**1**	**0**	**0**	**0**	**0**	**9:52**
	Quad City Flames	AHL	5	2	0	2	2	....	....	....	....	....	....	....	....	....	....	....	....	....	....	....	....	....	....
2009-10	**Calgary**	**NHL**	**60**	**8**	**11**	**19**	**15**	**0**	**0**	**2**	**80**	**10.0**	**5**	**368**	**49.7**	**12:14**	....	....	....	....	....	....	....	....	....
	Nashville	**NHL**	**18**	**3**	**2**	**5**	**4**	**0**	**0**	**1**	**32**	**9.4**	**1**	**105**	**58.1**	**12:11**	**4**	**0**	**0**	**0**	**0**	**0**	**0**	**0**	**7:03**
2010-11	**Montreal**	**NHL**	**10**	**1**	**0**	**1**	**2**	**0**	**0**	**0**	**8**	**12.5**	**–6**	**55**	**41.8**	**9:50**	....	....	....	....	....	....	....	....	....
	Hamilton	AHL	47	20	9	29	22	....	....	....	....	....	....	....	....	....	20	5	11	16	10	....	....	....	....
	NHL Totals		**220**	**32**	**31**	**63**	**41**	**1**	**1**	**8**	**248**	**12.9**		**1150**	**48.4**	**11:41**	**9**	**1**	**0**	**1**	**0**	**0**	**0**	**0**	**8:37**

WHL East First All-Star Team (2006)

Traded to **Nashville** by **Calgary** for Nashville's 4th round choice (Bill Arnold) in 2010 Entry Draft, March 3, 2010. Traded to **Montreal** by **Nashville** with Dan Ellis and future considerations for Sergei Kostitsyn and future considerations, June 29, 2010. Signed as a free agent by **Astana** (Russia-KHL), May 31, 2011.

BOYES, Brad
(BOIZ, BRAD) **BUF**

Right wing. Shoots right. 6', 204 lbs. Born, Mississauga, Ont., April 17, 1982. Toronto's 1st choice, 24th overall, in 2000 Entry Draft.

Season	Club	League	GP	G	A	Pts	PIM	PP	SH	GW	S	%	+/-	TF	F%	Min	GP	G	A	Pts	PIM	PP	SH	GW	Min
1997-98	Mississauga Reps	MTHL	44	27	50	77	....	....	....	....	....	....	....	....	....	....	....	....	....	....	....	....	....	....	....
1998-99	Erie Otters	OHL	59	24	36	60	30	....	....	....	....	....	....	....	....	....	5	1	2	3	10	....	....	....	....
99-2000	Erie Otters	OHL	68	36	46	82	38	....	....	....	....	....	....	....	....	....	13	6	8	14	10	....	....	....	....
2000-01	Erie Otters	OHL	59	45	45	90	42	....	....	....	....	....	....	....	....	....	15	10	13	23	8	....	....	....	....
2001-02	Erie Otters	OHL	47	36	41	77	42	....	....	....	....	....	....	....	....	....	21	22	*19	41	27	....	....	....	....
2002-03	St. John's	AHL	65	23	28	51	45	....	....	....	....	....	....	....	....	....	....	....	....	....	....	....	....	....	....
	Cleveland Barons	AHL	15	7	6	13	21	....	....	....	....	....	....	....	....	....	....	....	....	....	....	....	....	....	....
2003-04	**San Jose**	**NHL**	**1**	**0**	**0**	**0**	**2**	**0**	**0**	**0**	**0**	**0.0**	**–2**	**0**	**0.0**	**13:03**	....	....	....	....	....	....	....	....	....
	Cleveland Barons	AHL	61	25	35	60	38	....	....	....	....	....	....	....	....	....	....	....	....	....	....	....	....	....	....
	Providence Bruins	AHL	17	6	6	12	13	....	....	....	....	....	....	....	....	....	2	1	0	1	0	....	....	....	....
2004-05	Providence Bruins	AHL	80	33	42	75	58	....	....	....	....	....	....	....	....	....	16	8	7	15	23	....	....	....	....
2005-06	**Boston**	**NHL**	**82**	**26**	**43**	**69**	**30**	**8**	**0**	**3**	**203**	**12.8**	**11**	**265**	**53.6**	**15:46**	....	....	....	....	....	....	....	....	....
2006-07	**Boston**	**NHL**	**62**	**13**	**21**	**34**	**25**	**1**	**1**	**1**	**139**	**9.4**	**–17**	**220**	**44.1**	**16:04**	....	....	....	....	....	....	....	....	....
	St. Louis	**NHL**	**19**	**4**	**8**	**12**	**4**	**0**	**0**	**1**	**43**	**9.3**	**0**	**93**	**58.1**	**17:25**	....	....	....	....	....	....	....	....	....
2007-08	**St. Louis**	**NHL**	**82**	**43**	**22**	**65**	**20**	**11**	**0**	**9**	**207**	**20.8**	**1**	**236**	**44.5**	**17:57**	....	....	....	....	....	....	....	....	....
2008-09	**St. Louis**	**NHL**	**82**	**33**	**39**	**72**	**26**	**16**	**0**	**11**	**220**	**15.0**	**–20**	**315**	**49.2**	**19:08**	**4**	**2**	**1**	**3**	**0**	**1**	**0**	**0**	**21:34**
2009-10	**St. Louis**	**NHL**	**82**	**14**	**28**	**42**	**26**	**2**	**0**	**3**	**197**	**7.1**	**1**	**311**	**44.4**	**16:47**	....	....	....	....	....	....	....	....	....
2010-11	**St. Louis**	**NHL**	**62**	**12**	**29**	**41**	**30**	**4**	**0**	**2**	**132**	**9.1**	**11**	**135**	**41.5**	**17:10**	....	....	....	....	....	....	....	....	....
	Buffalo	**NHL**	**21**	**5**	**9**	**14**	**6**	**2**	**0**	**1**	**46**	**10.9**	**2**	**185**	**43.2**	**16:28**	**7**	**1**	**0**	**1**	**0**	**1**	**0**	**0**	**14:23**
	NHL Totals		**493**	**150**	**199**	**349**	**169**	**44**	**1**	**31**	**1187**	**12.6**		**1760**	**47.0**	**17:10**	**11**	**3**	**1**	**4**	**0**	**2**	**0**	**0**	**17:00**

Canadian Major Junior Scholastic Player of the Year (2000) • OHL Second All-Star Team (2001) • OHL First All-Star Team (2002) • Canadian Major Junior Second All-Star Team (2002) • Canadian Major Junior Sportsman of the Year (2002) • AHL All-Rookie Team (2003) • AHL Second All-Star Team (2004) • NHL All-Rookie Team (2006)

Traded to **San Jose** by **Toronto** with Alyn McCauley and Toronto's 1st round choice (later traded to Boston – Boston selected Mark Stuart) in 2003 Entry Draft for Owen Nolan, March 5, 2003. Traded to **Boston** by **San Jose** for Jeff Jillson, March 9, 2004. Traded to **St. Louis** by **Boston** for Dennis Wideman, February 27, 2007. Traded to **Buffalo** by **St. Louis** for Buffalo's 2nd round choice (Joel Edmundson) in 2011 Entry Draft, February 27, 2011.

BOYLE, Brian
(BOIL, BRIGH-uhn) **NYR**

Center. Shoots left. 6'7", 244 lbs. Born, Hingham, MA, December 18, 1984. Los Angeles' 2nd choice, 26th overall, in 2003 Entry Draft.

Season	Club	League	GP	G	A	Pts	PIM	PP	SH	GW	S	%	+/-	TF	F%	Min	GP	G	A	Pts	PIM	PP	SH	GW	Min
2000-01	St. Sebastian's	High-MA	25	20	19	39	23	....	....	....	....	....	....	....	....	....	....	....	....	....	....	....	....	....	....
2001-02	St. Sebastian's	High-MA	28	21	26	47	22	....	....	....	....	....	....	....	....	....	....	....	....	....	....	....	....	....	....
2002-03	St. Sebastian's	High-MA	31	32	31	62	46	....	....	....	....	....	....	....	....	....	....	....	....	....	....	....	....	....	....
2003-04	Boston College	H-East	35	5	3	8	36	....	....	....	....	....	....	....	....	....	....	....	....	....	....	....	....	....	....
2004-05	Boston College	H-East	40	19	8	27	64	....	....	....	....	....	....	....	....	....	....	....	....	....	....	....	....	....	....
2005-06	Boston College	H-East	42	22	*30	52	90	....	....	....	....	....	....	....	....	....	....	....	....	....	....	....	....	....	....
2006-07	Boston College	H-East	42	19	*34	*53	*104	....	....	....	....	....	....	....	....	....	....	....	....	....	....	....	....	....	....
	Manchester	AHL	2	0	0	0	2	....	....	....	....	....	....	....	....	....	16	3	5	8	13	....	....	....	....
2007-08	**Los Angeles**	**NHL**	**8**	**4**	**1**	**5**	**4**	**0**	**0**	**0**	**19**	**21.1**	**4**	**80**	**46.3**	**13:38**	....	....	....	....	....	....	....	....	....
	Manchester	AHL	70	31	31	62	87	....	....	....	....	....	....	....	....	....	....	....	....	....	....	....	....	....	....
2008-09	**Los Angeles**	**NHL**	**28**	**4**	**1**	**5**	**42**	**0**	**0**	**1**	**36**	**11.1**	**–9**	**225**	**45.3**	**10:08**	....	....	....	....	....	....	....	....	....
	Manchester	AHL	42	10	11	21	73	....	....	....	....	....	....	....	....	....	....	....	....	....	....	....	....	....	....

			Regular Season														Playoffs								
Season	Club	League	GP	G	A	Pts	PIM	PP	SH	GW	S	%	+/-	TF	F%	Min	GP	G	A	Pts	PIM	PP	SH	GW	Min
2009-10	NY Rangers	NHL	71	4	2	6	47	0	0	1	73	5.5	–6	323	38.7	8:25	....	....	....	....	....	....	....	....	....
2010-11	NY Rangers	NHL	82	21	14	35	74	4	1	2	218	9.6	2	1101	48.5	15:44	5	0	0	0	6	0	0	0	21:30
	NHL Totals		189	33	18	51	167	4	1	4	346	9.5		1729	46.2	12:04	5	0	0	0	6	0	0	0	21:30

Hockey East First All-Star Team (2006, 2007) • NCAA East Second All-American Team (2006) • NCAA East First All-American Team (2007) • NCAA Championship All-Tournament Team (2007) • AHL All-Rookie Team (2008)

Traded to **NY Rangers** by **Los Angeles** for NY Rangers' 3rd round choice (Jordan Weal) in 2010 Entry Draft, June 27, 2009.

BOYLE, Dan

(BOIL, DAN) **S.J.**

Defense. Shoots right. 5'11", 190 lbs. Born, Ottawa, Ont., July 12, 1976.

Season	Club	League	GP	G	A	Pts	PIM	PP	SH	GW	S	%	+/-	TF	F%	Min	GP	G	A	Pts	PIM	PP	SH	GW	Min
1992-93	Gloucester	CJHL	55	22	51	73	60	....	....	....	....	....	....	....	....	....	....	....	....	....	....	....	....	....	....
1993-94	Gloucester	CJHL	53	27	54	81	155	....	....	....	....	....	....	....	....	....	....	....	....	....	....	....	....	....	....
1994-95	Miami U.	CCHA	35	8	18	26	24	....	....	....	....	....	....	....	....	....	....	....	....	....	....	....	....	....	....
1995-96	Miami U.	CCHA	36	7	20	27	70	....	....	....	....	....	....	....	....	....	....	....	....	....	....	....	....	....	....
1996-97	Miami U.	CCHA	40	11	43	54	52	....	....	....	....	....	....	....	....	....	....	....	....	....	....	....	....	....	....
1997-98	Miami U.	CCHA	37	14	26	40	58	....	....	....	....	....	....	....	....	....	....	....	....	....	....	....	....	....	....
1998-99	Florida	NHL	22	3	5	8	6	1	0	1	31	9.7	0	1	100.0	18:50	....	....	....	....	....	....	....	....	....
	Kentucky	AHL	53	8	34	42	87	....	....	....	....	....	....	....	....	....	12	3	5	8	16	....	....	....	....
99-2000	Florida	NHL	13	0	3	3	4	0	0	0	9	0.0	–2	0	0.0	16:57	....	....	....	....	....	....	....	....	....
	Louisville Panthers	AHL	58	14	38	52	75	....	....	....	....	....	....	....	....	....	4	0	2	2	8	....	....	....	....
2000-01	Florida	NHL	69	4	18	22	28	1	0	0	83	4.8	–14	0	0.0	16:56	....	....	....	....	....	....	....	....	....
	Louisville Panthers	AHL	6	0	5	5	12	....	....	....	....	....	....	....	....	....	....	....	....	....	....	....	....	....	....
2001-02	Florida	NHL	25	3	3	6	12	1	0	0	31	9.7	–1	2	50.0	15:40	....	....	....	....	....	....	....	....	....
	Tampa Bay	NHL	41	5	15	20	27	2	0	1	68	7.4	–15	0	0.0	22:28	....	....	....	....	....	....	....	....	....
2002-03	Tampa Bay	NHL	77	13	40	53	44	8	0	1	136	9.6	9	2	0.0	24:31	11	0	7	7	6	0	0	0	27:45
2003-04 ♦	Tampa Bay	NHL	78	9	30	39	60	3	0	2	137	6.6	23	0	0.0	22:46	23	2	8	10	16	1	0	0	21:27
2004-05	Djurgarden	Sweden	32	9	9	18	47	....	....	....	....	....	....	....	....	....	12	2	3	5	26	....	....	....	....
2005-06	Tampa Bay	NHL	79	15	38	53	38	6	0	4	153	9.8	–8	1	0.0	23:26	5	1	3	4	6	0	0	0	25:54
	Canada	Olympics	DID NOT PLAY																						
2006-07	Tampa Bay	NHL	82	20	43	63	62	10	1	4	203	9.9	–5	1	0.0	27:03	6	0	1	1	2	0	0	0	28:03
2007-08	Tampa Bay	NHL	37	4	21	25	57	2	0	1	74	5.4	–29	0	0.0	27:24	....	....	....	....	....	....	....	....	....
2008-09	San Jose	NHL	77	16	41	57	52	8	0	4	213	7.5	6	1	0.0	24:46	6	2	2	4	8	1	0	0	23:17
2009-10	San Jose	NHL	76	15	43	58	70	6	0	3	180	8.3	6	3	0.0	26:13	15	2	12	14	8	1	0	0	27:11
	Canada	Olympics	7	1	5	6	2	....	....	....	....	....	....	....	....	....	....	....	....	....	....	....	....	....	....
2010-11	San Jose	NHL	76	9	41	50	67	4	0	2	199	4.5	2	2	0.0	26:14	18	4	12	16	8	2	0	1	26:10
	NHL Totals		752	116	341	457	527	52	1	23	1517	7.6		13	15.4	23:37	84	11	45	56	54	5	0	1	25:11

CCHA First All-Star Team (1997, 1998) • NCAA West First All-American Team (1997, 1998) • AHL All-Rookie Team (1999) • AHL Second All-Star Team (1999, 2000) • NHL Second All-Star Team (2007, 2009)

Played in NHL All-Star Game (2009, 2011)

Signed as a free agent by **Florida**, March 30, 1998. Traded to **Tampa Bay** by **Florida** for Tampa Bay's 5th round choice (Martin Tuma) in 2003 Entry Draft, January 7, 2002. Signed as a free agent by **Djurgarden** (Sweden), November 14, 2004. • Missed majority of 2007-08 due to off-ice wrist injury, September 22, 2007 and follow-up surgery, November 6, 2007. Traded to **San Jose** by **Tampa Bay** with Brad Lukowich for Matt Carle, Ty Wishart, San Jose's 1st round choice (later traded to Ottawa, later traded to NY Islanders, later traded to Columbus, later traded to Anahaim - Anaheim selected Kyle Palmieri) in 2009 Entry Draft and San Jose's 4th round choice (James Mullin) in 2010 Entry Draft, July 4, 2008.

BOYNTON, Nick

(BOIN-tuhn, NIHK)

Defense. Shoots right. 6'1", 218 lbs. Born, Nobleton, Ont., January 14, 1979. Boston's 1st choice, 21st overall, in 1999 Entry Draft.

Season	Club	League	GP	G	A	Pts	PIM	PP	SH	GW	S	%	+/-	TF	F%	Min	GP	G	A	Pts	PIM	PP	SH	GW	Min
1993-94	Caledon	ON-Jr.A	4	0	1	1	0	....	....	....	....	....	....	....	....	....	....	....	....	....	....	....	....	....	....
1994-95	Caledon	ON-Jr.A	44	10	35	45	139	....	....	....	....	....	....	....	....	....	....	....	....	....	....	....	....	....	....
1995-96	Ottawa 67's	OHL	64	10	14	24	90	....	....	....	....	....	....	....	....	....	4	0	3	3	10	....	....	....	....
1996-97	Ottawa 67's	OHL	63	13	51	64	143	....	....	....	....	....	....	....	....	....	24	4	*24	28	38	....	....	....	....
1997-98	Ottawa 67's	OHL	40	7	31	38	94	....	....	....	....	....	....	....	....	....	13	0	4	4	24	....	....	....	....
1998-99	Ottawa 67's	OHL	51	11	48	59	83	....	....	....	....	....	....	....	....	....	9	1	9	10	18	....	....	....	....
99-2000	Boston	NHL	5	0	0	0	0	0	0	0	6	0.0	–5	0	0.0	21:21	....	....	....	....	....	....	....	....	....
	Providence Bruins	AHL	53	5	14	19	66	....	....	....	....	....	....	....	....	....	12	1	0	1	6	....	....	....	....
2000-01	Boston	NHL	1	0	0	0	0	0	0	0	1	0.0	–1	0	0.0	14:27	....	....	....	....	....	....	....	....	....
	Providence Bruins	AHL	78	6	27	33	105	....	....	....	....	....	....	....	....	....	17	0	2	2	35	....	....	....	....
2001-02	Boston	NHL	80	4	14	18	107	0	0	1	136	2.9	18	0	0.0	18:30	6	1	2	3	8	0	0	0	21:30
2002-03	Boston	NHL	78	7	17	24	99	0	1	2	160	4.4	8	1	0.0	22:41	5	0	1	1	4	0	0	0	23:22
2003-04	Boston	NHL	81	6	24	30	98	1	1	1	178	3.4	17	0	0.0	22:32	7	0	2	2	2	0	0	0	24:44
2004-05	Nottingham	Britain	9	1	3	4	4	....	....	....	....	....	....	....	....	....	6	1	2	3	22	....	....	....	....
2005-06	Boston	NHL	54	5	7	12	93	1	1	0	89	5.6	–7	1	100.0	20:39	....	....	....	....	....	....	....	....	....
2006-07	Phoenix	NHL	59	2	9	11	138	1	0	0	53	3.8	–13	1	0.0	16:48	....	....	....	....	....	....	....	....	....
2007-08	Phoenix	NHL	79	3	9	12	125	0	1	0	94	3.2	–9	0	0.0	17:01	....	....	....	....	....	....	....	....	....
2008-09	Florida	NHL	68	5	16	21	91	0	0	1	104	4.8	7	0	0.0	16:36	....	....	....	....	....	....	....	....	....
2009-10	Anaheim	NHL	42	1	6	7	59	1	0	0	39	2.6	1	0	0.0	16:45	....	....	....	....	....	....	....	....	....
	Manitoba Moose	AHL	9	0	4	4	4	....	....	....	....	....	....	....	....	....	....	....	....	....	....	....	....	....	....
♦	Chicago	NHL	7	0	1	1	12	0	0	0	11	0.0	4	0	0.0	15:56	3	0	0	0	2	0	0	0	8:23
	Rockford IceHogs	AHL	6	0	1	1	18	....	....	....	....	....	....	....	....	....	....	....	....	....	....	....	....	....	....
2010-11	Chicago	NHL	41	1	7	8	36	0	0	0	42	2.4	2	0	0.0	15:43	....	....	....	....	....	....	....	....	....
	Philadelphia	NHL	10	0	0	0	4	0	0	0	1	0.0	–3	0	0.0	10:15	....	....	....	....	....	....	....	....	....
	NHL Totals		605	34	110	144	862	4	4	5	914	3.7		3	33.3	18:44	21	1	5	6	16	0	0	0	21:09

• Re-entered NHL Entry Draft. Originally Washington's 1st choice, 9th overall, in 1997 Entry Draft.

OHL All-Rookie Team (1996) • Memorial Cup All-Star Team (1999) • Stafford Smythe Memorial Trophy (Memorial Cup - MVP) (1999) • NHL All-Rookie Team (2002)

Played in NHL All-Star Game (2004)

Signed as a free agent by **Nottingham** (Britain), January 26, 2005. Traded to **Phoenix** by **Boston** with Boston's 4th round choice (later traded to Toronto – Toronto selected Matt Frattin) in 2007 Entry Draft for Paul Mara and Phoenix's 3rd round choice (later traded to Anaheim - Anaheim selected Maxime Macenauer) in 2007 Entry Draft, June 26, 2006. Traded to **Florida** by **Phoenix** with Keith Ballard and Ottawa's 2nd round choice (previously acquired, later traded back to Phoenix – Phoenix selected Jared Staal) in 2008 Entry Draft for Olli Jokinen, June 20, 2008. Signed as a free agent by **Anaheim**, July 9, 2009. Traded to **Chicago** by **Anaheim** for future considerations, March 2, 2010. Claimed on waivers by **Philadelphia** from **Chicago**, February 26, 2011.

BOZAK, Tyler

(BOH-zak, TIGH-luhr) **TOR**

Center. Shoots right. 6'1", 195 lbs. Born, Regina, Sask., March 19, 1986.

Season	Club	League	GP	G	A	Pts	PIM	PP	SH	GW	S	%	+/-	TF	F%	Min	GP	G	A	Pts	PIM	PP	SH	GW	Min
2003-04	Reg. Pat Cdns.	SMHL	42	17	19	36	40	....	....	....	....	....	....	....	....	....	....	....	....	....	....	....	....	....	....
2004-05	Victoria Salsa	BCHL	55	15	16	31	24	....	....	....	....	....	....	....	....	....	5	0	2	2	2	....	....	....	....
2005-06	Victoria Salsa	BCHL	56	31	38	69	26	....	....	....	....	....	....	....	....	....	16	8	8	16	14	....	....	....	....
2006-07	Victoria Grizzlies	BCHL	59	45	83	128	45	....	....	....	....	....	....	....	....	....	....	....	....	....	....	....	....	....	....
2007-08	U. of Denver	WCHA	41	18	16	34	22	....	....	....	....	....	....	....	....	....	....	....	....	....	....	....	....	....	....
2008-09	U. of Denver	WCHA	19	8	15	23	10	....	....	....	....	....	....	....	....	....	....	....	....	....	....	....	....	....	....
2009-10	Toronto	NHL	37	8	19	27	6	2	0	1	51	15.7	–5	648	55.3	19:14	....	....	....	....	....	....	....	....	....
	Toronto Marlies	AHL	32	4	16	20	6	....	....	....	....	....	....	....	....	....	....	....	....	....	....	....	....	....	....
2010-11	Toronto	NHL	82	15	17	32	14	6	1	4	120	12.5	–29	1441	54.6	19:17	....	....	....	....	....	....	....	....	....
	NHL Totals		119	23	36	59	20	8	1	5	171	13.5		2089	54.8	19:16	....	....	....	....	....	....	....	....	....

WCHA All-Rookie Team (2008)

Signed as a free agent by **Toronto**, April 3, 2009.

BRADLEY, Matt

(BRAD-lee, MAT) **FLA**

Right wing. Shoots right. 6'3", 201 lbs. Born, Stittsville, Ont., June 13, 1978. San Jose's 4th choice, 102nd overall, in 1996 Entry Draft.

Season	Club	League	GP	G	A	Pts	PIM	PP	SH	GW	S	%	+/-	TF	F%	Min	GP	G	A	Pts	PIM	PP	SH	GW	Min
1994-95	Cumberland	CJHL	49	13	20	33	18																		
1995-96	Kingston	OHL	55	10	14	24	17	....	....	....	....	....	....	....	....	....	6	0	1	1	6	....	....	....	....
1996-97	Kingston	OHL	65	24	24	48	41	....	....	....	....	....	....	....	....	....	5	0	4	4	2	....	....	....	....
	Kentucky	AHL	1	0	1	1	0	....	....	....	....	....	....	....	....	....	....	....	....	....	....	....	....	....	....
1997-98	Kingston	OHL	55	33	50	83	24	....	....	....	....	....	....	....	....	....	8	3	4	7	7	....	....	....	....
1998-99	Kentucky	AHL	79	23	20	43	57	....	....	....	....	....	....	....	....	....	10	1	4	5	4	....	....	....	....
99-2000	Kentucky	AHL	80	22	19	41	81	....	....	....	....	....	....	....	....	....	9	6	3	9	9	....	....	....	....
2000-01	San Jose	NHL	21	1	1	2	19	0	0	0	16	6.3	0	0	0.0	6:58	....	....	....	....	....	....	....	....	....
	Kentucky	AHL	22	5	8	13	16	....	....	....	....	....	....	....	....	....	1	1	0	1	5	....	....	....	....
2001-02	San Jose	NHL	54	9	13	22	43	0	0	2	63	14.3	22	2	0.0	8:27	10	0	0	0	0	0	0	0	5:16

			Regular Season														Playoffs								
Season	Club	League	GP	G	A	Pts	PIM	PP	SH	GW	S	%	+/-	TF	F%	Min	GP	G	A	Pts	PIM	PP	SH	GW	Min
2002-03	**San Jose**	**NHL**	**46**	**2**	**3**	**5**	**37**	**0**	**0**	**0**	**21**	**9.5**	**–1**	**1**	**0.0**	**7:54**	....	....	....	....	....	....	....	....	....
2003-04	**Pittsburgh**	**NHL**	**82**	**7**	**9**	**16**	**65**	**0**	**0**	**1**	**85**	**8.2**	**–27**	**29**	**41.4**	**12:48**	....	....	....	....	....	....	....	....	....
2004-05	Dornbirn	Austria-2	6	5	2	7	18	....	....	....	....	....	....	....	....	....	....	....	....	....	....	....	....	....	....
2005-06	**Washington**	**NHL**	**74**	**7**	**12**	**19**	**72**	**0**	**0**	**1**	**87**	**8.0**	**–8**	**25**	**52.0**	**12:36**	....	....	....	....	....	....	....	....	....
2006-07	**Washington**	**NHL**	**57**	**4**	**9**	**13**	**47**	**0**	**0**	**0**	**77**	**5.2**	**–5**	**20**	**45.0**	**11:55**	....	....	....	....	....	....	....	....	....
2007-08	**Washington**	**NHL**	**77**	**7**	**11**	**18**	**74**	**1**	**1**	**2**	**111**	**6.3**	**1**	**32**	**43.8**	**10:00**	**7**	**0**	**2**	**2**	**2**	**0**	**0**	**0**	**11:40**
2008-09	**Washington**	**NHL**	**81**	**5**	**6**	**11**	**59**	**0**	**0**	**1**	**98**	**5.1**	**–1**	**24**	**41.7**	**10:37**	**14**	**2**	**4**	**6**	**0**	**0**	**1**	**1**	**12:45**
2009-10	**Washington**	**NHL**	**77**	**10**	**14**	**24**	**47**	**0**	**1**	**5**	**98**	**10.2**	**6**	**28**	**39.3**	**11:02**	**7**	**1**	**2**	**3**	**2**	**0**	**0**	**0**	**10:36**
2010-11	**Washington**	**NHL**	**61**	**4**	**7**	**11**	**68**	**0**	**0**	**0**	**58**	**6.9**	**–3**	**11**	**36.4**	**10:29**	**9**	**0**	**0**	**0**	**4**	**0**	**0**	**0**	**8:48**
	NHL Totals		**630**	**56**	**85**	**141**	**531**	**1**	**2**	**12**	**714**	**7.8**		**172**	**42.4**	**10:42**	**47**	**3**	**8**	**11**	**8**	**0**	**1**	**1**	**9:55**

Traded to **Pittsburgh** by **San Jose** for Wayne Primeau, March 11, 2003. Signed as a free agent by **Dornbirn** (Austria-2), November 14, 2004. Signed as a free agent by **Washington**, August 18, 2005. Signed as a free agent by **Florida**, July 2, 2011.

BRASSARD, Derick

(bruh-SAHRD, DAIR-ihk) **CBJ**

Center. Shoots left. 6'1", 199 lbs. Born, Hull, Que., September 22, 1987. Columbus' 1st choice, 6th overall, in 2006 Entry Draft.

Season	Club	League	GP	G	A	Pts	PIM	PP	SH	GW	S	%	+/-	TF	F%	Min	GP	G	A	Pts	PIM	PP	SH	GW	Min
2003-04	Drummondville	QMJHL	10	0	1	1	0	....	....	....	....	....	....	....	....	....	7	0	0	0	0	....	....	....	....
2004-05	Drummondville	QMJHL	69	25	51	76	25	....	....	....	....	....	....	....	....	....	6	1	5	6	6	....	....	....	....
2005-06	Drummondville	QMJHL	58	44	72	116	92	....	....	....	....	....	....	....	....	....	7	5	4	9	10	....	....	....	....
2006-07	Drummondville	QMJHL	14	6	19	25	24	....	....	....	....	....	....	....	....	....	12	9	15	24	12	....	....	....	....
2007-08	**Columbus**	**NHL**	**17**	**1**	**1**	**2**	**6**	**0**	**0**	**0**	**13**	**7.7**	**–4**	**80**	**42.5**	**9:03**	....	....	....	....	....	....	....	....	....
	Syracuse Crunch	AHL	42	15	36	51	51	....	....	....	....	....	....	....	....	....	13	4	9	13	10	....	....	....	....
2008-09	**Columbus**	**NHL**	**31**	**10**	**15**	**25**	**17**	**3**	**0**	**1**	**59**	**16.9**	**12**	**332**	**48.5**	**14:25**	....	....	....	....	....	....	....	....	....
2009-10	**Columbus**	**NHL**	**79**	**9**	**27**	**36**	**48**	**4**	**0**	**0**	**125**	**7.2**	**–17**	**503**	**41.8**	**14:57**	....	....	....	....	....	....	....	....	....
2010-11	**Columbus**	**NHL**	**74**	**17**	**30**	**47**	**55**	**6**	**0**	**3**	**183**	**9.3**	**–11**	**888**	**46.6**	**17:02**	....	....	....	....	....	....	....	....	....
	NHL Totals		**201**	**37**	**73**	**110**	**126**	**13**	**0**	**4**	**380**	**9.7**		**1803**	**45.4**	**15:08**	....	....	....	....	....	....	....	....	....

QMJHL First All-Star Team (2006) • Canadian Major Junior Second All-Star Team (2006)

• Missed majority of 2006-07 due to recurring shoulder injury. • Missed majority of 2008-09 due to shoulder injury at Dallas, December 18, 2008.

BRAUN, Justin

(BRAWN, JUHS-tihn) **S.J.**

Defense. Shoots right. 6'1", 205 lbs. Born, St. Paul, MN, February 10, 1987. San Jose's 7th choice, 201st overall, in 2007 Entry Draft.

Season	Club	League	GP	G	A	Pts	PIM	PP	SH	GW	S	%	+/-	TF	F%	Min	GP	G	A	Pts	PIM	PP	SH	GW	Min
2004-05	White Bear Lake	High-MN	STATISTICS NOT AVAILABLE																						
	Green Bay	USHL	10	0	0	0	2	....	....	....	....	....	....	....	....	....	....	....	....	....	....	....	....	....	....
2005-06	Green Bay	USHL	59	2	11	13	69	....	....	....	....	....	....	....	....	....	3	0	0	0	2	....	....	....	....
2006-07	Massachusetts	H-East	39	4	10	14	20	....	....	....	....	....	....	....	....	....	....	....	....	....	....	....	....	....	....
2007-08	Massachusetts	H-East	36	4	16	20	20	....	....	....	....	....	....	....	....	....	....	....	....	....	....	....	....	....	....
2008-09	Massachusetts	H-East	39	7	16	23	50	....	....	....	....	....	....	....	....	....	....	....	....	....	....	....	....	....	....
2009-10	Massachusetts	H-East	36	8	23	31	30	....	....	....	....	....	....	....	....	....	....	....	....	....	....	....	....	....	....
	Worcester Sharks	AHL	3	0	3	3	0	....	....	....	....	....	....	....	....	....	11	0	3	3	4	....	....	....	....
2010-11	**San Jose**	**NHL**	**28**	**2**	**9**	**11**	**2**	**2**	**0**	**0**	**44**	**4.5**	**–1**	**0**	**0.0**	**16:30**	**1**	**0**	**0**	**0**	**0**	**0**	**0**	**0**	**15:32**
	Worcester Sharks	AHL	34	5	18	23	8	....	....	....	....	....	....	....	....	....	....	....	....	....	....	....	....	....	....
	NHL Totals		**28**	**2**	**9**	**11**	**2**	**2**	**0**	**0**	**44**	**4.5**		**0**	**0.0**	**16:30**	**1**	**0**	**0**	**0**	**0**	**0**	**0**	**0**	**15:32**

Hockey East All-Rookie Team (2007) • Hockey East Second All-Star Team (2009) • Hockey East First All-Star Team (2010) • NCAA East Second All-American Team (2010)

BRENT, Tim

(BREHNT, TIHM) **CAR**

Center. Shoots right. 6', 188 lbs. Born, Cambridge, Ont., March 10, 1984. Anaheim's 3rd choice, 75th overall, in 2004 Entry Draft.

Season	Club	League	GP	G	A	Pts	PIM	PP	SH	GW	S	%	+/-	TF	F%	Min	GP	G	A	Pts	PIM	PP	SH	GW	Min
99-2000	Cambridge	ON-Jr.B	40	19	16	35	42	....	....	....	....	....	....	....	....	....	....	....	....	....	....	....	....	....	....
2000-01	St. Michael's	OHL	64	9	19	28	31	....	....	....	....	....	....	....	....	....	18	2	8	10	6	....	....	....	....
2001-02	St. Michael's	OHL	61	19	40	59	52	....	....	....	....	....	....	....	....	....	14	7	12	19	20	....	....	....	....
2002 03	St. Michael's	OHL	60	24	42	66	74	....	....	....	....	....	....	....	....	....	19	7	17	24	14	....	....	....	....
2003-04	St. Michael's	OHL	53	26	41	67	105	....	....	....	....	....	....	....	....	....	18	4	13	17	24	....	....	....	....
2004-05	Cincinnati	AHL	46	5	13	18	42	....	....	....	....	....	....	....	....	....	12	0	1	1	6	....	....	....	....
2005-06	Portland Pirates	AHL	37	15	9	24	32	....	....	....	....	....	....	....	....	....	15	4	4	8	16	....	....	....	....
2006-07	**Anaheim**	**NHL**	**15**	**1**	**0**	**1**	**6**	**0**	**0**	**0**	**14**	**7.1**	**–5**	**86**	**48.8**	**6:55**	....	....	....	....	....	....	....	....	....
	Portland Pirates	AHL	48	16	14	30	40	....	....	....	....	....	....	....	....	....	....	....	....	....	....	....	....	....	....
2007-08	**Pittsburgh**	**NHL**	**1**	**0**	**0**	**0**	**0**	**0**	**0**	**0**	**0**	**0.0**	**–1**	**5**	**60.0**	**4:34**	....	....	....	....	....	....	....	....	....
	Wilkes-Barre	AHL	74	18	43	61	79	....	....	....	....	....	....	....	....	....	23	*12	15	27	10	....	....	....	....
2008-09	**Chicago**	**NHL**	**2**	**0**	**0**	**0**	**2**	**0**	**0**	**0**	**0**	**0.0**	**0**	**10**	**50.0**	**8:21**	....	....	....	....	....	....	....	....	....
	Rockford IceHogs	AHL	64	20	42	62	59	....	....	....	....	....	....	....	....	....	4	0	1	1	2	....	....	....	....
2009-10	**Toronto**	**NHL**	**1**	**0**	**0**	**0**	**0**	**0**	**0**	**0**	**3**	**0.0**	**0**	**8**	**50.0**	**13:21**	....	....	....	....	....	....	....	....	....
	Toronto Marlies	AHL	33	13	15	28	19	....	....	....	....	....	....	....	....	....	....	....	....	....	....	....	....	....	....
2010-11	**Toronto**	**NHL**	**79**	**8**	**12**	**20**	**33**	**0**	**1**	**1**	**60**	**13.3**	**–4**	**788**	**52.0**	**11:39**	....	....	....	....	....	....	....	....	....
	NHL Totals		**98**	**9**	**12**	**21**	**41**	**0**	**1**	**1**	**77**	**11.7**		**897**	**51.7**	**10:48**	....	....	....	....	....	....	....	....	....

• Re-entered NHL Entry Draft. Originally Anaheim's 2nd choice, 37th overall, in 2002 Entry Draft.

Traded to **Pittsburgh** by **Anaheim** for Stephen Dixon, June 23, 2007. Traded to **Chicago** by **Pittsburgh** for Danny Richmond, July 17, 2008. Signed as a free agent by **Toronto**, July 6, 2009. • Missed majority of 2009-10 due to recurring chest injury. Signed as a free agent by **Carolina**, July 1, 2011.

BREWER, Eric

(BREW-uhr, AIR-ihk) **T.B.**

Defense. Shoots left. 6'3", 220 lbs. Born, Vernon, B.C., April 17, 1979. NY Islanders' 2nd choice, 5th overall, in 1997 Entry Draft.

Season	Club	League	GP	G	A	Pts	PIM	PP	SH	GW	S	%	+/-	TF	F%	Min	GP	G	A	Pts	PIM	PP	SH	GW	Min
1994-95	Kamloops	Minor-BC	40	19	19	38	62	....	....	....	....	....	....	....	....	....	....	....	....	....	....	....	....	....	....
1995-96	Prince George	WHL	63	4	10	14	25	....	....	....	....	....	....	....	....	....	....	....	....	....	....	....	....	....	....
1996-97	Prince George	WHL	71	5	24	29	81	....	....	....	....	....	....	....	....	....	15	2	4	6	16	....	....	....	....
1997-98	Prince George	WHL	34	5	28	33	45	....	....	....	....	....	....	....	....	....	11	4	2	6	19	....	....	....	....
1998-99	**NY Islanders**	**NHL**	**63**	**5**	**6**	**11**	**32**	**2**	**0**	**0**	**63**	**7.9**	**–14**	**0**	**0.0**	**15:28**	....	....	....	....	....	....	....	....	....
99-2000	**NY Islanders**	**NHL**	**26**	**0**	**2**	**2**	**20**	**0**	**0**	**0**	**30**	**0.0**	**–11**	**0**	**0.0**	**18:33**	....	....	....	....	....	....	....	....	....
	Lowell	AHL	25	2	2	4	26	....	....	....	....	....	....	....	....	....	7	0	0	0	0	....	....	....	....
2000-01	**Edmonton**	**NHL**	**77**	**7**	**14**	**21**	**53**	**2**	**0**	**2**	**91**	**7.7**	**15**	**0**	**0.0**	**18:31**	**6**	**1**	**5**	**6**	**2**	**1**	**0**	**0**	**28:12**
2001-02	**Edmonton**	**NHL**	**81**	**7**	**18**	**25**	**45**	**6**	**0**	**2**	**165**	**4.2**	**–5**	**0**	**0.0**	**23:56**	....	....	....	....	....	....	....	....	....
	Canada	Olympics	6	2	0	2	0	....	....	....	....	....	....	....	....	....	....	....	....	....	....	....	....	....	....
2002-03	**Edmonton**	**NHL**	**80**	**8**	**21**	**29**	**45**	**1**	**0**	**1**	**147**	**5.4**	**–11**	**1**	**100.0**	**24:56**	**6**	**1**	**3**	**4**	**6**	**0**	**0**	**0**	**25:31**
2003-04	**Edmonton**	**NHL**	**77**	**7**	**18**	**25**	**67**	**3**	**0**	**1**	**135**	**5.2**	**–6**	**0**	**0.0**	**24:40**	....	....	....	....	....	....	....	....	....
2004-05			DID NOT PLAY																						
2005-06	**St. Louis**	**NHL**	**32**	**6**	**3**	**9**	**45**	**1**	**0**	**1**	**64**	**9.4**	**–17**	**0**	**0.0**	**23:28**	....	....	....	....	....	....	....	....	....
2006-07	**St. Louis**	**NHL**	**82**	**6**	**23**	**29**	**69**	**2**	**0**	**1**	**111**	**5.4**	**–10**	**0**	**0.0**	**24:32**	....	....	....	....	....	....	....	....	....
2007-08	**St. Louis**	**NHL**	**77**	**1**	**21**	**22**	**91**	**0**	**0**	**0**	**101**	**1.0**	**–18**	**0**	**0.0**	**24:38**	....	....	....	....	....	....	....	....	....
2008-09	**St. Louis**	**NHL**	**28**	**1**	**5**	**6**	**24**	**1**	**0**	**0**	**49**	**2.0**	**–14**	**0**	**0.0**	**25:07**	....	....	....	....	....	....	....	....	....
2009-10	**St. Louis**	**NHL**	**59**	**8**	**7**	**15**	**46**	**0**	**0**	**0**	**84**	**9.5**	**–17**	**0**	**0.0**	**21:27**	....	....	....	....	....	....	....	....	....
2010-11	**St. Louis**	**NHL**	**54**	**8**	**6**	**14**	**57**	**0**	**0**	**1**	**86**	**9.3**	**1**	**0**	**0.0**	**22:14**	....	....	....	....	....	....	....	....	....
	Tampa Bay	**NHL**	**22**	**1**	**1**	**2**	**24**	**0**	**0**	**0**	**24**	**4.2**	**5**	**0**	**0.0**	**21:34**	**18**	**1**	**6**	**7**	**14**	**0**	**0**	**0**	**25:36**
	NHL Totals		**758**	**65**	**145**	**210**	**618**	**18**	**0**	**9**	**1150**	**5.7**		**1**	**100.0**	**22:27**	**30**	**3**	**14**	**17**	**22**	**1**	**0**	**0**	**26:07**

WHL West Second All-Star Team (1998)

Played in NHL All-Star Game (2003)

Traded to **Edmonton** by **NY Islanders** with Josh Green and NY Islanders' 2nd round choice (Brad Winchester) in 2000 Entry Draft for Roman Hamrlik, June 24, 2000. Traded to **St. Louis** by **Edmonton** with Doug Lynch and Jeff Woywitka for Chris Pronger, August 2, 2005. • Missed majority of 2005-06 due to shoulder injuries at Columbus (November 16, 2005) and Atlanta (January 13, 2006). • Missed majority of 2008-09 due to back injury at Los Angeles, December 11, 2008. Traded to **Tampa Bay** by **St. Louis** for Brock Beukeboom and Tampa Bay's 3rd round choice (Jordan Binnington) in 2011 Entry Draft, February 18, 2011.

BRIERE, Danny

(bree-AIR, DA-nee) **PHI**

Center. Shoots right. 5'10", 179 lbs. Born, Gatineau, Que., October 6, 1977. Phoenix's 2nd choice, 24th overall, in 1996 Entry Draft.

Season	Club	League	GP	G	A	Pts	PIM	PP	SH	GW	S	%	+/-	TF	F%	Min	GP	G	A	Pts	PIM	PP	SH	GW	Min
			Regular Season														Playoffs								
1992-93	Abitibi Regents	QAAA	42	24	30	54	28	....	....	....	....	....	....	....	....	....	3	0	3	3	8	....	....	....	....
1993-94	Gatineau	QAAA	44	56	47	103	56	....	....	....	....	....	....	....	....	....	....	....	....	....	....	....	....	....	....
1994-95	Drummondville	QMJHL	72	51	72	123	54	....	....	....	....	....	....	....	....	....	4	2	3	5	2	....	....	....	....
1995-96	Drummondville	QMJHL	67	*67	*96	*163	84	....	....	....	....	....	....	....	....	....	6	6	12	18	8	....	....	....	....
1996-97	Drummondville	QMJHL	59	52	78	130	86	....	....	....	....	....	....	....	....	....	8	7	7	14	14	....	....	....	....
1997-98	Phoenix	NHL	5	1	0	1	2	0	0	0	4	25.0	1	....	....	....	....	....	....	....	....	....	....	....	....
	Springfield	AHL	68	36	56	92	42	....	....	....	....	....	....	....	....	....	4	1	2	3	4	....	....	....	....
1998-99	Phoenix	NHL	64	8	14	22	30	2	0	2	90	8.9	–3	484	47.5	11:13	....	....	....	....	....	....	....	....	....
	Las Vegas	IHL	1	1	1	2	0	....	....	....	....	....	....	....	....	....	....	....	....	....	....	....	....	....	....
	Springfield	AHL	13	2	6	8	20	....	....	....	....	....	....	....	....	....	3	0	1	1	2	....	....	....	....
99-2000	Phoenix	NHL	13	1	1	2	0	0	0	0	9	11.1	0	65	49.2	7:41	1	0	0	0	0	0	0	0	6:16
	Springfield	AHL	58	29	42	71	56	....	....	....	....	....	....	....	....	....	....	....	....	....	....	....	....	....	....
2000-01	Phoenix	NHL	30	11	4	15	12	9	0	1	43	25.6	–2	210	50.0	10:50	....	....	....	....	....	....	....	....	....
	Springfield	AHL	30	21	25	46	30	....	....	....	....	....	....	....	....	....	....	....	....	....	....	....	....	....	....
2001-02	Phoenix	NHL	78	32	28	60	52	12	0	5	149	21.5	6	951	51.8	15:44	5	2	1	3	2	1	0	1	16:25
2002-03	Phoenix	NHL	68	17	29	46	50	4	0	3	142	12.0	–21	1108	52.5	17:02	....	....	....	....	....	....	....	....	....
	Buffalo	NHL	14	7	5	12	12	5	0	1	39	17.9	1	206	50.0	17:49	....	....	....	....	....	....	....	....	....
2003-04	Buffalo	NHL	82	28	37	65	70	11	0	3	194	14.4	–7	1066	47.1	18:20	....	....	....	....	....	....	....	....	....
2004-05	SC Bern	Swiss	36	16	29	45	26	....	....	....	....	....	....	....	....	....	11	1	6	7	2	....	....	....	....
2005-06	Buffalo	NHL	48	25	33	58	48	11	0	4	147	17.0	3	517	50.7	19:04	18	8	11	19	12	3	0	2	18:48
2006-07	Buffalo	NHL	81	32	63	95	89	9	0	6	234	13.7	17	1089	49.6	19:19	16	3	12	15	16	2	0	1	20:53
2007-08	Philadelphia	NHL	79	31	41	72	68	14	0	3	182	17.0	–22	1250	50.5	18:52	17	9	7	16	20	*6	0	3	18:26
2008-09	Philadelphia	NHL	29	11	14	25	26	4	0	0	54	20.4	–1	147	46.3	15:39	6	1	3	4	8	1	0	0	16:41
2009-10	Philadelphia	NHL	75	26	27	53	71	8	0	1	193	13.5	–2	120	44.2	16:35	23	12	18	*30	18	4	0	4	19:37
2010-11	Philadelphia	NHL	77	34	34	68	87	6	0	6	246	13.8	20	820	48.2	18:19	11	7	2	9	14	2	0	1	19:56
	NHL Totals		**743**	**264**	**330**	**594**	**617**	**95**	**0**	**35**	**1726**	**15.3**		**8033**	**49.7**	**16:45**	**97**	**42**	**54**	**96**	**90**	**19**	**0**	**12**	**19:01**

QMJHL All-Rookie Team (1995) • QMJHL Offensive Rookie of the Year (1995) • QMJHL Second All-Star Team (1996, 1997) • AHL All-Rookie Team (1998) • AHL First All-Star Team (1998) • Dudley "Red" Garrett Memorial Award (AHL – Rookie of the Year) (1998)

Played in NHL All-Star Game (2007, 2011)

Traded to **Buffalo** by **Phoenix** with Phoenix's 3rd round choice (Andrej Sekera) in 2004 Entry Draft for Chris Gratton and Buffalo's 4th round choice (later traded to Edmonton – Edmonton selected Liam Reddox) in 2004 Entry Draft, March 10, 2003. Signed as a free agent by **Bern** (Swiss), September 28, 2004. Signed as a free agent by **Philadelphia**, July 1, 2007. • Missed majority of 2008-09 due to abdominal surgery (October 25, 2008) and groin surgery (January 22, 2009).

BRINE, David

(BRIGHN, DAY-vihd)

Center. Shoots left. 6'1", 201 lbs. Born, Truro, N.S., January 6, 1985.

Season	Club	League	GP	G	A	Pts	PIM	PP	SH	GW	S	%	+/-	TF	F%	Min	GP	G	A	Pts	PIM	PP	SH	GW	Min
2002-03	Truro Bearcats	MJrHL	52	21	32	53	29	....	....	....	....	....	....	....	....	....	....	....	....	....	....	....	....	....	....
2003-04	Halifax	QMJHL	70	22	25	47	20	....	....	....	....	....	....	....	....	....	....	....	....	....	....	....	....	....	....
2004-05	Halifax	QMJHL	67	14	37	51	36	....	....	....	....	....	....	....	....	....	13	6	7	13	8	....	....	....	....
2005-06	Halifax	QMJHL	70	34	66	100	80	....	....	....	....	....	....	....	....	....	11	1	5	6	23	....	....	....	....
	Manitoba Moose	AHL	....	....	....	....	....	....	....	....	....	....	....	....	....	....	9	0	1	1	2	....	....	....	....
2006-07	Rochester	AHL	22	4	4	8	4	....	....	....	....	....	....	....	....	....	....	....	....	....	....	....	....	....	....
	Florida Everblades	ECHL	52	9	21	30	22	....	....	....	....	....	....	....	....	....	15	6	4	10	22	....	....	....	....
2007-08	Florida	NHL	9	0	1	1	4	0	0	0	3	0.0	–1	44	38.6	6:02	....	....	....	....	....	....	....	....	....
	Rochester	AHL	66	9	11	20	26	....	....	....	....	....	....	....	....	....	....	....	....	....	....	....	....	....	....
2008-09	Rochester	AHL	79	8	23	31	35	....	....	....	....	....	....	....	....	....	....	....	....	....	....	....	....	....	....
2009-10	Rochester	AHL	69	14	18	32	14	....	....	....	....	....	....	....	....	....	7	0	1	1	2	....	....	....	....
2010-11	San Antonio	AHL	67	2	12	14	27	....	....	....	....	....	....	....	....	....	....	....	....	....	....	....	....	....	....
	NHL Totals		**9**	**0**	**1**	**1**	**4**	**0**	**0**	**0**	**3**	**0.0**		**44**	**38.6**	**6:02**	....	....	....	....	....	....	....	....	....

Signed as a free agent by **Florida**, September 14, 2006. Signed as a free agent by **San Antonio** (AHL), September 9, 2010.

BRODIE, T.J.

(BROH-dee, TEE-JAY) **CGY**

Defense. Shoots left. 6'1", 182 lbs. Born, Chatham, Ont., June 7, 1990. Calgary's 5th choice, 114th overall, in 2008 Entry Draft.

Season	Club	League	GP	G	A	Pts	PIM	PP	SH	GW	S	%	+/-	TF	F%	Min	GP	G	A	Pts	PIM	PP	SH	GW	Min
2006-07	Leamington Flyers	ON-Jr.B	43	8	38	46	104	....	....	....	....	....	....	....	....	....	5	1	2	3	12	....	....	....	....
	Saginaw Spirit	OHL	20	0	4	4	23	....	....	....	....	....	....	....	....	....	3	0	1	1	2	....	....	....	....
2007-08	Saginaw Spirit	OHL	68	4	26	30	73	....	....	....	....	....	....	....	....	....	4	0	3	3	2	....	....	....	....
2008-09	Saginaw Spirit	OHL	63	12	38	50	67	....	....	....	....	....	....	....	....	....	8	3	6	9	8	....	....	....	....
2009-10	Saginaw Spirit	OHL	19	4	19	23	20	....	....	....	....	....	....	....	....	....	....	....	....	....	....	....	....	....	....
	Barrie Colts	OHL	46	3	30	33	38	....	....	....	....	....	....	....	....	....	17	1	14	15	14	....	....	....	....
2010-11	Calgary	NHL	3	0	0	0	2	0	0	0	1	0.0	–3	0	0.0	16:00	....	....	....	....	....	....	....	....	....
	Abbotsford Heat	AHL	68	5	29	34	32	....	....	....	....	....	....	....	....	....	....	....	....	....	....	....	....	....	....
	NHL Totals		**3**	**0**	**0**	**0**	**2**	**0**	**0**	**0**	**1**	**0.0**		**0**	**0.0**	**16:00**	....	....	....	....	....	....	....	....	....

BRODZIAK, Kyle

(brohd-ZEE-ak, KIGHL) **MIN**

Center. Shoots right. 6'2", 209 lbs. Born, St. Paul, Alta., May 25, 1984. Edmonton's 9th choice, 214th overall, in 2003 Entry Draft.

Season	Club	League	GP	G	A	Pts	PIM	PP	SH	GW	S	%	+/-	TF	F%	Min	GP	G	A	Pts	PIM	PP	SH	GW	Min
99-2000	Ft. Saskatchewan	AMBHL	36	23	33	56	57	....	....	....	....	....	....	....	....	....	....	....	....	....	....	....	....	....	....
	Moose Jaw	WHL	2	0	0	0	0	....	....	....	....	....	....	....	....	....	....	....	....	....	....	....	....	....	....
2000-01	Moose Jaw	WHL	57	2	8	10	47	....	....	....	....	....	....	....	....	....	3	0	0	0	0	....	....	....	....
2001-02	Moose Jaw	WHL	72	8	12	20	56	....	....	....	....	....	....	....	....	....	12	0	3	3	11	....	....	....	....
2002-03	Moose Jaw	WHL	72	32	30	62	84	....	....	....	....	....	....	....	....	....	13	5	3	8	16	....	....	....	....
2003-04	Moose Jaw	WHL	70	39	54	93	58	....	....	....	....	....	....	....	....	....	10	5	4	9	10	....	....	....	....
2004-05	Edmonton	AHL	56	6	26	32	49	....	....	....	....	....	....	....	....	....	....	....	....	....	....	....	....	....	....
2005-06	Edmonton	NHL	10	0	0	0	4	0	0	0	7	0.0	–4	75	52.0	11:02	....	....	....	....	....	....	....	....	....
	Iowa Stars	AHL	55	12	19	31	41	....	....	....	....	....	....	....	....	....	7	1	3	4	2	....	....	....	....
2006-07	Edmonton	NHL	6	1	0	1	2	0	0	0	11	9.1	0	48	52.1	17:08	....	....	....	....	....	....	....	....	....
	Wilkes-Barre	AHL	62	24	32	56	44	....	....	....	....	....	....	....	....	....	11	1	5	6	14	....	....	....	....
2007-08	Edmonton	NHL	80	14	17	31	33	0	1	3	125	11.2	–6	297	51.5	12:55	....	....	....	....	....	....	....	....	....
2008-09	Edmonton	NHL	79	11	16	27	21	1	1	3	99	11.1	4	947	51.6	12:43	....	....	....	....	....	....	....	....	....
2009-10	Minnesota	NHL	82	9	23	32	22	0	0	3	140	6.4	–3	1001	48.4	15:20	....	....	....	....	....	....	....	....	....
2010-11	Minnesota	NHL	80	16	21	37	56	2	1	1	126	12.7	–4	1088	48.9	15:47	....	....	....	....	....	....	....	....	....
	NHL Totals		**337**	**51**	**77**	**128**	**138**	**3**	**3**	**10**	**508**	**10.0**		**3456**	**49.8**	**14:09**	....	....	....	....	....	....	....	....	....

WHL East First All-Star Team (2004) • Canadian Major Junior Second All-Star Team (2004)

Traded to **Minnesota** by **Edmonton** with Edmonton's 6th round choice (Darcy Kuemper) in 2009 Entry Draft for Dallas's 4th round choice (previously acquired, Edmonton selected Kyle Bigos) in 2009 Entry Draft and Minnesota's 5th round choice (Olivier Roy) in 2009 Entry Draft, June 27, 2009.

BROOKBANK, Sheldon

(BRUK-bank, SHEHL-duhn) **ANA**

Defense. Shoots right. 6'1", 202 lbs. Born, Lanigan, Sask., October 3, 1980.

Season	Club	League	GP	G	A	Pts	PIM	PP	SH	GW	S	%	+/-	TF	F%	Min	GP	G	A	Pts	PIM	PP	SH	GW	Min
2000-01	Humboldt	SJHL	59	14	35	49	281	....	....	....	....	....	....	....	....	....	....	....	....	....	....	....	....	....	....
2001-02	Grand Rapids	AHL	6	0	1	1	24	....	....	....	....	....	....	....	....	....	....	....	....	....	....	....	....	....	....
	Mississippi	ECHL	62	8	21	29	137	....	....	....	....	....	....	....	....	....	10	1	4	5	27	....	....	....	....
2002-03	Grand Rapids	AHL	69	2	11	13	136	....	....	....	....	....	....	....	....	....	15	1	3	4	28	....	....	....	....
2003-04	Cincinnati	AHL	74	2	9	11	216	....	....	....	....	....	....	....	....	....	9	0	2	2	20	....	....	....	....
2004-05	Cincinnati	AHL	60	1	11	12	181	....	....	....	....	....	....	....	....	....	11	0	0	0	40	....	....	....	....
2005-06	Milwaukee	AHL	73	9	26	35	232	....	....	....	....	....	....	....	....	....	21	1	8	9	49	....	....	....	....
2006-07	Nashville	NHL	3	0	1	1	12	0	0	0	3	0.0	0	0	0.0	8:16	....	....	....	....	....	....	....	....	....
	Milwaukee	AHL	78	15	38	53	176	....	....	....	....	....	....	....	....	....	4	0	0	0	6	....	....	....	....
2007-08	New Jersey	NHL	44	0	8	8	63	0	0	0	43	0.0	0	0	0.0	15:08	....	....	....	....	....	....	....	....	....
	Lowell Devils	AHL	1	0	0	0	5	....	....	....	....	....	....	....	....	....	....	....	....	....	....	....	....	....	....
2008-09	New Jersey	NHL	15	0	0	0	25	0	0	0	6	0.0	1	0	0.0	8:51	....	....	....	....	....	....	....	....	....
	Anaheim	NHL	29	1	3	4	51	0	0	0	24	4.2	3	0	0.0	13:50	13	0	0	0	18	0	0	0	11:13

Season	Club	League	GP	G	A	Pts	PIM	PP	SH	GW	S	%	+/-	TF	F%	Min	GP	G	A	Pts	PIM	PP	SH	GW	Min
			Regular Season														Playoffs								
2009-10	**Anaheim**	**NHL**	**66**	**0**	**9**	**9**	**114**	**0**	**0**	**0**	**60**	**0.0**	**10**	**0**	**0.0**	**14:58**	....	....	....	....	....	....	....	....	....
2010-11	**Anaheim**	**NHL**	**40**	**0**	**0**	**0**	**63**	**0**	**0**	**0**	**29**	**0.0**	**–8**	**0**	**0.0**	**13:20**	**4**	**0**	**0**	**0**	**14**	**0**	**0**	**0**	**14:35**
	NHL Totals		**197**	**1**	**21**	**22**	**328**	**0**	**0**	**0**	**165**	**0.6**		**0**	**0.0**	**13:56**	**17**	**0**	**0**	**0**	**32**	**0**	**0**	**0**	**12:00**

AHL First All-Star Team (2007) • Eddie Shore Award (AHL - Outstanding Defenseman) (2007)

Signed as a free agent by **Anaheim**, July 21, 2003. Signed as a free agent by **Nashville**, August 4, 2005. Signed as a free agent by **Columbus**, July 1, 2007. Claimed on waivers by **New Jersey** from **Columbus**, October 2, 2007. Traded to **Anaheim** by **New Jersey** for David McIntyre, February 3, 2009.

BROOKBANK, Wade

(BRUK-bank, WAYD)

Defense. Shoots left. 6'4", 225 lbs. Born, Lanigan, Sask., September 29, 1977.

Season	Club	League	GP	G	A	Pts	PIM	PP	SH	GW	S	%	+/-	TF	F%	Min	GP	G	A	Pts	PIM	PP	SH	GW	Min
1997-98	Melville	SJHL	58	8	21	29	330	....	....	....	....	....	....	....	....	....	....	....	....	....	....	....	....	....	....
	Anchorage Aces	WCHL	7	0	0	0	46	....	....	....	....	....	....	....	....	....	4	0	0	0	20	....	....	....	....
1998-99	Anchorage Aces	WCHL	56	0	4	4	337	....	....	....	....	....	....	....	....	....	....	....	....	....	....	....	....	....	....
99-2000	Oklahoma City	CHL	68	3	9	12	354	....	....	....	....	....	....	....	....	....	7	1	1	2	29	....	....	....	....
2000-01	Orlando	IHL	29	0	1	1	122	....	....	....	....	....	....	....	....	....	4	0	0	0	6	....	....	....	....
	Oklahoma City	CHL	46	1	13	14	267	....	....	....	....	....	....	....	....	....	5	0	0	0	24	....	....	....	....
2001-02	Grand Rapids	AHL	73	1	6	7	337	....	....	....	....	....	....	....	....	....	3	0	1	1	14	....	....	....	....
2002-03	Binghamton	AHL	8	0	0	0	28	....	....	....	....	....	....	....	....	....	....	....	....	....	....	....	....	....	....
2003-04	**Nashville**	**NHL**	**9**	**0**	**0**	**0**	**38**	**0**	**0**	**0**	**1**	**0.0**	**–4**	**0**	**0.0**	**3:28**	....	....	....	....	....	....	....	....	....
	Milwaukee	AHL	6	0	0	0	6	....	....	....	....	....	....	....	....	....	....	....	....	....	....	....	....	....	....
	Binghamton	AHL	4	0	0	0	31	....	....	....	....	....	....	....	....	....	....	....	....	....	....	....	....	....	....
	Vancouver	**NHL**	**20**	**2**	**0**	**2**	**95**	**0**	**0**	**1**	**6**	**33.3**	**3**	**0**	**0.0**	**3:50**	....	....	....	....	....	....	....	....	....
	Manitoba Moose	AHL	4	0	0	0	12	....	....	....	....	....	....	....	....	....	....	....	....	....	....	....	....	....	....
2004-05	Manitoba Moose	AHL	68	0	10	10	285	....	....	....	....	....	....	....	....	....	9	0	0	0	10	....	....	....	....
2005-06	**Vancouver**	**NHL**	**32**	**1**	**2**	**3**	**81**	**0**	**0**	**0**	**10**	**10.0**	**3**	**0**	**0.0**	**4:56**	....	....	....	....	....	....	....	....	....
2006-07	**Boston**	**NHL**	**7**	**1**	**0**	**1**	**15**	**0**	**0**	**0**	**1**	**100.0**	**–1**	**1**	**0.0**	**4:25**	....	....	....	....	....	....	....	....	....
	Providence Bruins	AHL	4	0	0	0	15	....	....	....	....	....	....	....	....	....	....	....	....	....	....	....	....	....	....
	Wilkes-Barre	AHL	39	1	0	1	116	....	....	....	....	....	....	....	....	....	5	0	0	0	6	....	....	....	....
2007-08	**Carolina**	**NHL**	**32**	**1**	**1**	**2**	**76**	**0**	**0**	**0**	**12**	**8.3**	**4**	**4**	**25.0**	**3:48**	....	....	....	....	....	....	....	....	....
	Albany River Rats	AHL	25	0	2	2	28	....	....	....	....	....	....	....	....	....	....	....	....	....	....	....	....	....	....
2008-09	**Carolina**	**NHL**	**27**	**1**	**0**	**1**	**40**	**0**	**0**	**0**	**8**	**12.5**	**0**	**0**	**0.0**	**2:30**	....	....	....	....	....	....	....	....	....
	Norfolk Admirals	AHL	24	0	1	1	46	....	....	....	....	....	....	....	....	....	....	....	....	....	....	....	....	....	....
2009-10	Wilkes-Barre	AHL	68	3	4	7	168	....	....	....	....	....	....	....	....	....	4	0	0	0	6	....	....	....	....
2010-11	Rockford IceHogs	AHL	56	2	0	2	143	....	....	....	....	....	....	....	....	....	....	....	....	....	....	....	....	....	....
	NHL Totals		**127**	**6**	**3**	**9**	**345**	**0**	**0**	**1**	**38**	**15.8**		**5**	**20.0**	**3:50**	....	....	....	....	....	....	....	....	....

Signed as a free agent by **Orlando** (IHL), September 1, 2000. Signed as a free agent by **Ottawa**, July 27, 2001. • Missed majority of 2002-03 due to knee injury vs. Wilkes-Barre (AHL), November 2, 2002. Claimed by **Nashville** from **Ottawa** in Waiver Draft, October 3, 2003. Traded to **Vancouver** by **Nashville** for future considerations, December 17, 2003. Claimed on waivers by **Ottawa** from **Vancouver**, December 19, 2003. Traded to **Florida** by **Ottawa** for future considerations, December 29, 2003. Claimed on waivers by **Vancouver** from **Florida**, January 3, 2004. • Missed majority of 2005-06 due to two concussions. Signed as a free agent by **Boston**, July 21, 2006. Traded to **Pittsburgh** by **Boston** for future considerations, December 19, 2006. Signed as a free agent by **Carolina**, July 1, 2007. Traded to **Tampa Bay** by **Carolina** with Josef Melichar and future considerations for Jussi Jokinen, February 7, 2009. Signed as a free agent by **Pittsburgh**, July 31, 2009. Signed as a free agent by **Rockford** (AHL), July 21, 2010.

BROPHEY, Evan

(BROH-fee, EH-vuhn) **COL**

Center. Shoots left. 6'2", 199 lbs. Born, Kitchener, Ont., December 3, 1986. Chicago's 4th choice, 68th overall, in 2005 Entry Draft.

Season	Club	League	GP	G	A	Pts	PIM	PP	SH	GW	S	%	+/-	TF	F%	Min	GP	G	A	Pts	PIM	PP	SH	GW	Min
2002-03	Barrie Colts	OHL	61	12	14	26	36	....	....	....	....	....	....	....	....	....	6	0	0	0	2	....	....	....	....
2003-04	Barrie Colts	OHL	67	14	11	25	63	....	....	....	....	....	....	....	....	....	12	4	3	7	4	....	....	....	....
2004-05	Barrie Colts	OHL	10	3	7	10	13	....	....	....	....	....	....	....	....	....	....	....	....	....	....	....	....	....	....
	Belleville Bulls	OHL	53	25	36	61	42	....	....	....	....	....	....	....	....	....	5	2	1	3	2	....	....	....	....
2005-06	Belleville Bulls	OHL	22	9	17	26	39	....	....	....	....	....	....	....	....	....	....	....	....	....	....	....	....	....	....
	Plymouth Whalers	OHL	40	10	25	35	42	....	....	....	....	....	....	....	....	....	13	4	7	11	18	....	....	....	....
2006-07	Plymouth Whalers	OHL	68	36	71	107	91	....	....	....	....	....	....	....	....	....	20	9	14	23	26	....	....	....	....
2007-08	Rockford IceHogs	AHL	74	4	15	19	64	....	....	....	....	....	....	....	....	....	1	0	0	0	0	....	....	....	....
2008-09	Rockford IceHogs	AHL	79	16	23	39	65	....	....	....	....	....	....	....	....	....	4	1	0	1	0	....	....	....	....
2009-10	Rockford IceHogs	AHL	79	14	17	31	39	....	....	....	....	....	....	....	....	....	4	0	0	0	2	....	....	....	....
2010-11	**Chicago**	**NHL**	**1**	**0**	**0**	**0**	**0**	**0**	**0**	**0**	**1**	**0.0**	**0**	**5**	**80.0**	**7:09**	....	....	....	....	....	....	....	....	....
	Rockford IceHogs	AHL	67	10	9	19	65	....	....	....	....	....	....	....	....	....	....	....	....	....	....	....	....	....	....
	NHL Totals		**1**	**0**	**0**	**0**	**0**	**0**	**0**	**0**	**1**	**0.0**		**5**	**80.0**	**7:09**	....	....	....	....	....	....	....	....	....

Signed as a free agent by **Colorado**, July 8, 2011.

BROUWER, Troy

(BROW-uhr, TROI) **WSH**

Right wing. Shoots right. 6'2", 214 lbs. Born, Vancouver, B.C., August 17, 1985. Chicago's 13th choice, 214th overall, in 2004 Entry Draft.

Season	Club	League	GP	G	A	Pts	PIM	PP	SH	GW	S	%	+/-	TF	F%	Min	GP	G	A	Pts	PIM	PP	SH	GW	Min
2001-02	Moose Jaw	WHL	13	0	0	0	7	....	....	....	....	....	....	....	....	....	....	....	....	....	....	....	....	....	....
2002-03	Moose Jaw	WHL	59	9	12	21	54	....	....	....	....	....	....	....	....	....	13	1	2	3	14	....	....	....	....
2003-04	Moose Jaw	WHL	72	23	26	49	111	....	....	....	....	....	....	....	....	....	10	3	0	3	12	....	....	....	....
2004-05	Moose Jaw	WHL	71	22	25	47	132	....	....	....	....	....	....	....	....	....	5	1	2	3	8	....	....	....	....
2005-06	Moose Jaw	WHL	72	49	53	*102	122	....	....	....	....	....	....	....	....	....	17	10	4	14	34	....	....	....	....
2006-07	**Chicago**	**NHL**	**10**	**0**	**0**	**0**	**7**	**0**	**0**	**0**	**7**	**0.0**	**–7**	**0**	**0.0**	**9:55**	....	....	....	....	....	....	....	....	....
	Norfolk Admirals	AHL	66	41	38	79	70	....	....	....	....	....	....	....	....	....	6	1	0	1	4	....	....	....	....
2007-08	**Chicago**	**NHL**	**2**	**0**	**1**	**1**	**0**	**0**	**0**	**0**	**0**	**0.0**	**1**	**0**	**0.0**	**11:56**	....	....	....	....	....	....	....	....	....
	Rockford IceHogs	AHL	75	35	19	54	154	....	....	....	....	....	....	....	....	....	12	5	4	9	16	....	....	....	....
2008-09	**Chicago**	**NHL**	**69**	**10**	**16**	**26**	**50**	**4**	**1**	**0**	**126**	**7.9**	**7**	**20**	**45.0**	**15:05**	**17**	**0**	**2**	**2**	**12**	**0**	**0**	**0**	**11:51**
	Rockford IceHogs	AHL	5	2	6	8	20	....	....	....	....	....	....	....	....	....	....	....	....	....	....	....	....	....	....
2009-10 ♦	**Chicago**	**NHL**	**78**	**22**	**18**	**40**	**66**	**7**	**1**	**7**	**116**	**19.0**	**9**	**9**	**55.6**	**16:22**	**19**	**4**	**4**	**8**	**8**	**0**	**0**	**0**	**11:01**
2010-11	**Chicago**	**NHL**	**79**	**17**	**19**	**36**	**38**	**7**	**0**	**5**	**122**	**13.9**	**–2**	**25**	**48.0**	**15:06**	**7**	**0**	**0**	**0**	**11**	**0**	**0**	**0**	**14:25**
	NHL Totals		**238**	**49**	**54**	**103**	**161**	**18**	**2**	**12**	**371**	**13.2**		**54**	**48.1**	**15:16**	**43**	**4**	**6**	**10**	**31**	**0**	**0**	**0**	**11:54**

WHL East First All-Star Team (2006) • Canadian Major Junior Second All-Star Team (2006) • AHL All-Rookie Team (2007) • AHL Second All-Star Team (2007)

Traded to **Washington** by **Chicago** for Washington's 1st round choice (Phillip Danault) in 2011 Entry Draft, June 24, 2011.

BROWN, Dustin

(BROWN, DUHS-tihn) **L.A.**

Left wing. Shoots right. 6', 209 lbs. Born, Ithaca, NY, November 4, 1984. Los Angeles' 1st choice, 13th overall, in 2003 Entry Draft.

Season	Club	League	GP	G	A	Pts	PIM	PP	SH	GW	S	%	+/-	TF	F%	Min	GP	G	A	Pts	PIM	PP	SH	GW	Min
1998-99	Ithaca	High-NY	18	4	13	17	....	....	....	....	....	....	....	....	....	....	....	....	....	....	....	....	....	....	....
99-2000	Ithaca	High-NY	24	33	21	53	....	....	....	....	....	....	....	....	....	....	....	....	....	....	....	....	....	....	....
2000-01	Guelph Storm	OHL	53	23	22	45	45	....	....	....	....	....	....	....	....	....	4	0	0	0	10	....	....	....	....
2001-02	Guelph Storm	OHL	63	41	32	73	56	....	....	....	....	....	....	....	....	....	9	8	5	13	14	....	....	....	....
2002-03	Guelph Storm	OHL	58	34	42	76	89	....	....	....	....	....	....	....	....	....	11	7	8	15	6	....	....	....	....
2003-04	**Los Angeles**	**NHL**	**31**	**1**	**4**	**5**	**16**	**0**	**0**	**0**	**40**	**2.5**	**0**	**1**	**0.0**	**10:29**	....	....	....	....	....	....	....	....	....
2004-05	Manchester	AHL	79	29	45	74	96	....	....	....	....	....	....	....	....	....	6	5	2	7	10	....	....	....	....
2005-06	**Los Angeles**	**NHL**	**79**	**14**	**14**	**28**	**80**	**6**	**0**	**2**	**159**	**8.8**	**–10**	**15**	**66.7**	**13:59**	....	....	....	....	....	....	....	....	....
2006-07	**Los Angeles**	**NHL**	**81**	**17**	**29**	**46**	**54**	**13**	**0**	**1**	**195**	**8.7**	**–21**	**77**	**49.4**	**18:43**	....	....	....	....	....	....	....	....	....
2007-08	**Los Angeles**	**NHL**	**78**	**33**	**27**	**60**	**55**	**12**	**2**	**4**	**219**	**15.1**	**–13**	**40**	**50.0**	**20:18**	....	....	....	....	....	....	....	....	....
2008-09	**Los Angeles**	**NHL**	**80**	**24**	**29**	**53**	**64**	**7**	**0**	**6**	**292**	**8.2**	**–15**	**54**	**46.3**	**19:24**	....	....	....	....	....	....	....	....	....
2009-10	**Los Angeles**	**NHL**	**82**	**24**	**32**	**56**	**41**	**7**	**0**	**3**	**248**	**9.7**	**–6**	**39**	**43.6**	**19:15**	**6**	**1**	**4**	**5**	**6**	**1**	**0**	**0**	**18:53**
	United States	Olympics	6	0	0	0	0	....	....	....	....	....	....	....	....	....	....	....	....	....	....	....	....	....	....
2010-11	**Los Angeles**	**NHL**	**82**	**28**	**29**	**57**	**67**	**7**	**0**	**2**	**228**	**12.3**	**17**	**37**	**48.7**	**19:22**	**6**	**1**	**1**	**2**	**6**	**1**	**0**	**0**	**20:00**
	NHL Totals		**513**	**141**	**164**	**305**	**377**	**52**	**2**	**18**	**1381**	**10.2**		**263**	**48.7**	**18:02**	**12**	**2**	**5**	**7**	**12**	**2**	**0**	**0**	**19:27**

OHL All-Rookie Team (2001) • Canadian Major Junior Scholastic Player of the Year (2003) • NHL Foundation Award (2011)

Played in NHL All-Star Game (2009)

• Missed majority of 2003-04 due to ankle injury vs. Chicago, November 29, 2003.

			Regular Season															Playoffs							
Season	Club	League	GP	G	A	Pts	PIM	PP	SH	GW	S	%	+/-	TF	F%	Min	GP	G	A	Pts	PIM	PP	SH	GW	Min

BROWN, Mike — (BROWN, MIGHK) — TOR

Right wing. Shoots right. 5'11", 205 lbs. Born, Chicago, IL, June 24, 1985. Vancouver's 4th choice, 159th overall, in 2004 Entry Draft.

Season	Club	League	GP	G	A	Pts	PIM	PP	SH	GW	S	%	+/-	TF	F%	Min	GP	G	A	Pts	PIM	PP	SH	GW	Min
2000-01	Chicago Chill	USAHA	66	27	23	50	....																		
2001-02	USNTDP	U-17	17	6	4	10	13																		
	USNTDP	NAHL	46	5	11	16	56																		
2002-03	USNTDP	U-18	34	5	3	8	16																		
	USNTDP	NAHL	9	0	3	3	29																		
2003-04	U. of Michigan	CCHA	42	8	5	13	51																		
2004-05	U. of Michigan	CCHA	35	3	5	8	95																		
2005-06	Manitoba Moose	AHL	73	7	8	15	139										13	1	2	3	17				
2006-07	Manitoba Moose	AHL	62	3	0	3	194										13	1	2	2	16				
2007-08	**Vancouver**	**NHL**	19	1	0	1	55	0	0	0	9	11.1	-2	0	0.0	6:19									
	Manitoba Moose	AHL	54	10	3	13	201										6	2	0	2	11				
2008-09	**Vancouver**	**NHL**	20	0	1	1	85	0	0	0	6	0.0	-5	2	0.0	5:29									
	Anaheim	**NHL**	28	2	1	3	60	0	0	2	38	5.3	-2	4	0.0	10:02	13	0	2	2	25	0	0	0	8:28
2009-10	**Anaheim**	**NHL**	75	6	1	7	106	0	1	2	82	7.3	1	7	0.0	8:21									
2010-11	**Toronto**	**NHL**	50	3	5	8	69	1	0	0	59	5.1	1	15	26.7	10:06									
	NHL Totals		192	12	8	20	375	1	1	4	194	6.2		28	14.3	8:33	13	0	2	2	25	0	0	0	8:28

Traded to **Anaheim** by **Vancouver** for Nathan McIver, February 4, 2009. Traded to **Toronto** by **Anaheim** for Toronto's 5th round choice (Chris Wagner) in 2010 Entry Draft, June 25, 2010.

BRULE, Gilbert — (broo-LAY, zhihl-BAIR) — EDM

Center. Shoots right. 5'11", 186 lbs. Born, Edmonton, Alta., January 1, 1987. Columbus' 1st choice, 6th overall, in 2005 Entry Draft.

Season	Club	League	GP	G	A	Pts	PIM	PP	SH	GW	S	%	+/-	TF	F%	Min	GP	G	A	Pts	PIM	PP	SH	GW	Min
2002-03	Quesnel	BCHL	48	32	25	57	71																		
	Vancouver Giants	WHL	1	0	0	0	0										4	1	0	1	0				
2003-04	Vancouver Giants	WHL	67	25	35	60	100										11	4	5	9	10				
2004-05	Vancouver Giants	WHL	70	39	48	87	169										6	1	3	4	8				
2005-06	**Columbus**	**NHL**	7	2	2	4	0	0	0	0	11	18.2	-2	60	43.3	13:11									
	Vancouver Giants	WHL	27	23	15	38	40										18	*16	14	*30	44				
2006-07	**Columbus**	**NHL**	78	9	10	19	28	3	0	0	98	9.2	-21	268	45.9	10:39									
2007-08	**Columbus**	**NHL**	61	1	8	9	24	0	0	1	74	1.4	-4	78	51.3	9:54									
	Syracuse Crunch	AHL	16	5	5	10	44										13	2	3	5	16				
2008-09	**Edmonton**	**NHL**	11	2	1	3	12	0	0	0	13	15.4	-3	5	80.0	9:52									
	Springfield	AHL	39	13	11	24	58																		
2009-10	**Edmonton**	**NHL**	65	17	20	37	38	2	0	3	121	14.0	0	274	52.6	14:14									
2010-11	**Edmonton**	**NHL**	41	7	2	9	41	1	0	0	72	9.7	-7	199	53.3	13:48									
	NHL Totals		263	38	43	81	143	6	0	6	389	9.8		884	50.1	11:53									

WHL West First All-Star Team (2005) • Canadian Major Junior Second All-Star Team (2005) • Canadian Major Junior Scholastic Player of the Year (2005) • WHL West Second All-Star Team (2006) • Memorial Cup All-Star Team (2006) • Ed Chynoweth Trophy (Memorial Cup - Leading Scorer) (2006)
• Missed majority of 2005-06 due to sternum (October 7, 2005 vs. Calgary) and leg (November 30, 2005 at Minnesota) injuries. Traded to **Edmonton** by **Columbus** for Raffi Torres, July 1, 2008.

BRUNETTE, Andrew — (broo-NEHT, AN-droo) — CHI

Left wing. Shoots left. 6'1", 210 lbs. Born, Sudbury, Ont., August 24, 1973. Washington's 6th choice, 174th overall, in 1993 Entry Draft.

Season	Club	League	GP	G	A	Pts	PIM	PP	SH	GW	S	%	+/-	TF	F%	Min	GP	G	A	Pts	PIM	PP	SH	GW	Min
1989-90	Rayside-Balfour	NOHA	32	38	*65	*103	....																		
	Rayside-Balfour	NOJHA	4	1	1	2	0																		
1990-91	Owen Sound	OHL	63	15	20	35	15																		
1991-92	Owen Sound	OHL	66	51	47	98	42																		
1992-93	Owen Sound	OHL	66	*62	*100	*162	91										5	5	0	5	8				
1993-94	Portland Pirates	AHL	23	9	11	20	10										8	8	6	14	16				
	Providence Bruins	AHL	3	0	0	0	0										2	0	1	1	0				
	Hampton Roads	ECHL	20	12	18	30	32										7	7	6	13	18				
1994-95	Portland Pirates	AHL	79	30	50	80	53										7	3	3	6	10				
1995-96	**Washington**	**NHL**	11	3	3	6	0	0	0	1	16	18.8	5				6	1	3	4	0	0	0	0	0
	Portland Pirates	AHL	69	28	66	94	125										20	11	18	29	15				
1996-97	**Washington**	**NHL**	23	4	7	11	12	2	0	0	23	17.4	-3												
	Portland Pirates	AHL	50	22	51	73	48										5	1	2	3	0				
1997-98	**Washington**	**NHL**	28	11	12	23	12	4	0	2	42	26.2	2												
	Portland Pirates	AHL	43	21	46	67	64										10	1	11	12	...				
1998-99	**Nashville**	**NHL**	77	11	20	31	26	7	0	1	65	16.9	-10	8	50.0	13:13									
99-2000	**Atlanta**	**NHL**	81	23	27	50	30	9	0	0	107	21.5	-32	8	25.0	15:42									
2000-01	**Atlanta**	**NHL**	77	15	44	59	26	6	0	4	104	14.4	-5	11	54.6	16:58									
2001-02	**Minnesota**	**NHL**	81	21	48	69	18	10	0	2	106	19.8	-4	111	58.6	16:02									
2002-03	**Minnesota**	**NHL**	82	18	28	46	30	9	0	0	97	18.6	-10	59	44.1	14:29	18	7	6	13	4	4	0	1	15:00
2003-04	**Minnesota**	**NHL**	82	15	34	49	12	7	0	3	90	16.7	3	49	46.9	15:32									
2004-05		DID NOT PLAY																						
2005-06	**Colorado**	**NHL**	82	24	39	63	48	11	0	2	129	18.6	9	18	33.3	15:01	9	3	6	9	8	1	0	1	17:47
2006-07	**Colorado**	**NHL**	82	27	56	83	36	9	0	2	173	15.6	-8	8	62.5	17:31									
2007-08	**Colorado**	**NHL**	82	19	40	59	14	7	0	2	125	15.2	5	8	37.5	15:33	10	5	3	8	2	3	0	0	17:02
2008-09	**Minnesota**	**NHL**	80	22	28	50	18	9	0	3	118	18.6	5	9	22.2	16:57									
2009-10	**Minnesota**	**NHL**	82	25	36	61	12	12	0	3	129	19.4	-5	10	50.0	17:02									
2010-11	**Minnesota**	**NHL**	82	18	28	46	16	6	0	3	114	15.7	-7	18	38.9	16:48									
	NHL Totals		1032	256	450	706	310	110	0	32	1441	17.8		317	48.6	15:54	43	16	18	34	14	8	0	2	16:13

OHL First All-Star Team (1993) • Canadian Major Junior Second All-Star Team (1993) • AHL Second All-Star Team (1995)
Claimed by **Nashville** from **Washington** in Expansion Draft, June 26, 1998. Traded to **Atlanta** by **Nashville** for Atlanta's 5th round choice (Matt Hendricks) in 2000 Entry Draft, June 21, 1999. Signed as a free agent by **Minnesota**, July 17, 2001. Signed as a free agent by **Colorado**, August 6, 2005. Signed as a free agent by **Minnesota**, July 1, 2008. Signed as a free agent by **Chicago**, July 1, 2011.

BRUNNSTROM, Fabian — {BRUHN-struhm, FAY-bee-yehn}

Left wing. Shoots left. 6'1", 206 lbs. Born, Jonstorp, Sweden, February 6, 1985.

Season	Club	League	GP	G	A	Pts	PIM	PP	SH	GW	S	%	+/-	TF	F%	Min	GP	G	A	Pts	PIM	PP	SH	GW	Min
2002-03	Jonstorps IF	Sweden-3	STATISTICS NOT AVAILABLE																						
2003-04	Helsingborgs HC	Sweden-4	..	6	7	13	....																		
2004-05	Helsingborgs HC	Sweden-4	..	18	11	29	....																		
2005-06	Jonstorps IF	Sweden-3	38	21	23	44	8																		
	Rogle	Sweden-2	3	0	0	0	2																		
2006-07	Boras HC	Sweden-2	49	38	41	79	32										2	1	3	4	0				
2007-08	Farjestad	Sweden	54	9	28	37	16										12	1	0	1	6				
2008-09	**Dallas**	**NHL**	55	17	12	29	8	4	0	5	81	21.0	-8	0	0.0	11:37									
	Manitoba Moose	AHL	1	0	0	0	0																		
2009-10	**Dallas**	**NHL**	44	2	9	11	10	0	0	0	38	5.3	-3	3	33.3	10:40									
	Texas Stars	AHL	8	1	4	5	2																		
2010-11	Texas Stars	AHL	37	11	10	21	16																		
	Toronto Marlies	AHL	35	4	10	14	4																		
	NHL Totals		99	19	21	40	18	4	0	5	119	16.0		3	33.3	11:12									

Signed as a free agent by **Dallas**, May 8, 2008. Traded to **Toronto** by **Dallas** for Mikhail Stefanovich, January 13, 2011.

BURISH, Adam — (BUHR-ish, A-duhm) — DAL

Right wing. Shoots right. 6', 190 lbs. Born, Madison, WI, January 6, 1983. Chicago's 9th choice, 282nd overall, in 2002 Entry Draft.

Season	Club	League	GP	G	A	Pts	PIM	PP	SH	GW	S	%	+/-	TF	F%	Min	GP	G	A	Pts	PIM	PP	SH	GW	Min
2000-01	Edgewood	High-WI	22	25	30	55	22																		
2001-02	Green Bay	USHL	61	24	33	57	122										1	0	0	0	0				
2002-03	U. of Wisconsin	WCHA	19	0	6	6	32																		
2003-04	U. of Wisconsin	WCHA	43	6	13	19	63																		
2004-05	U. of Wisconsin	WCHA	41	13	7	20	41																		
2005-06	U. of Wisconsin	WCHA	42	9	24	33	67																		
2006-07	**Chicago**	**NHL**	9	0	0	0					12	0.0	-4	6	50.0	11:08									
	Norfolk Admirals	AHL	64	11	10	21	146										6	1	1	2	4				
2007-08	**Chicago**	**NHL**	81	4	4	8	214	0	1	1	69	5.8	-13	264	42.1	11:45									
2008-09	**Chicago**	**NHL**	66	6	3	9	93	0	0	2	83	7.2	3	124	39.5	9:12	17	3	2	5	30	0	0	1	11:02

			Regular Season														Playoffs								
Season	Club	League	GP	G	A	Pts	PIM	PP	SH	GW	S	%	+/-	TF	F%	Min	GP	G	A	Pts	PIM	PP	SH	GW	Min
2009-10 ♦	Chicago	NHL	13	1	3	4	14	0	0	0	9	11.1	2	21	33.3	8:46	15	0	0	0	2	0	0	0	5:35
2010-11	Dallas	NHL	63	8	6	14	91	0	0	1	89	9.0	2	477	53.5	14:21	....	....	....	....	....	....	....	....	....
	NHL Totals		232	19	16	35	414	0	1	4	262	7.3		892	47.6	11:32	32	3	2	5	32	0	0	1	8:29

NCAA Championship All-Tournament Team (2006)

• Missed majority of 2009-10 due to knee injury, in pre-season at Minnesota, September 20, 2009. Signed as a free agent by **Dallas**, July 1, 2010.

BURMISTROV, Alexander

(buhr-MIHS-trawf, al-ehx-AN-duhr) **WPG**

Center. Shoots left. 6'1", 180 lbs. Born, Kazan, USSR, October 21, 1991. Atlanta's 1st choice, 8th overall, in 2010 Entry Draft.

Season	Club	League	GP	G	A	Pts	PIM	PP	SH	GW	S	%	+/-	TF	F%	Min	GP	G	A	Pts	PIM	PP	SH	GW	Min
2008-09	Ak Bars Kazan 2	Russia-3	34	25	25	50	54	....	....	....	....	....	....	....	....	....	....	....	....	....	....	....	....	....	....
	Ak Bars Kazan	Rus-KHL	1	0	0	0	0	....	....	....	....	....	....	....	....	....	....	....	....	....	....	....	....	....	....
2009-10	Barrie Colts	OHL	62	22	43	65	49	....	....	....	....	....	....	....	....	....	17	8	8	16	22	....	....	....	....
2010-11	**Atlanta**	**NHL**	**74**	**6**	**14**	**20**	**27**	**0**	**0**	**2**	**92**	**6.5**	**–12**	**696**	**41.5**	**13:13**	....	....	....	....	....	....	....	....	....
	NHL Totals		**74**	**6**	**14**	**20**	**27**	**0**	**0**	**2**	**92**	**6.5**		**696**	**41.5**	**13:13**	....	....	....	....	....	....	....	....	....

• Transferred to **Winnipeg** after **Atlanta** franchise relocated, June 21, 2011.

BURNS, Brent

(BUHRNZ, BREHNT) **S.J.**

Defense. Shoots right. 6'5", 219 lbs. Born, Ajax, Ont., March 9, 1985. Minnesota's 1st choice, 20th overall, in 2003 Entry Draft.

Season	Club	League	GP	G	A	Pts	PIM	PP	SH	GW	S	%	+/-	TF	F%	Min	GP	G	A	Pts	PIM	PP	SH	GW	Min
2001-02	Couchiching	OPJHL	46	4	7	11	16	....	....	....	....	....	....	....	....	....	....	....	....	....	....	....	....	....	....
2002-03	Brampton	OHL	68	15	25	40	14	....	....	....	....	....	....	....	....	....	11	5	6	11	6	....	....	....	....
2003-04	**Minnesota**	**NHL**	**36**	**1**	**5**	**6**	**12**	**0**	**0**	**0**	**34**	**2.9**	**–10**	**7**	**28.6**	**13:29**	....	....	....	....	....	....	....	....	....
	Houston Aeros	AHL	1	0	1	1	2	....	....	....	....	....	....	....	....	....	....	....	....	....	....	....	....	....	....
2004-05	Houston Aeros	AHL	73	11	16	27	57	....	....	....	....	....	....	....	....	....	5	0	0	0	4	....	....	....	....
2005-06	**Minnesota**	**NHL**	**72**	**4**	**12**	**16**	**32**	**1**	**0**	**1**	**73**	**5.5**	**–7**	**11**	**54.6**	**14:07**	....	....	....	....	....	....	....	....	....
2006-07	**Minnesota**	**NHL**	**77**	**7**	**18**	**25**	**26**	**3**	**0**	**3**	**108**	**6.5**	**16**	**4**	**25.0**	**15:48**	**5**	**0**	**1**	**1**	**14**	**0**	**0**	**0**	**18:59**
2007-08	**Minnesota**	**NHL**	**82**	**15**	**28**	**43**	**80**	**8**	**0**	**4**	**158**	**9.5**	**12**	**1**	**100.0**	**23:06**	**6**	**0**	**2**	**2**	**6**	**0**	**0**	**0**	**27:35**
2008-09	**Minnesota**	**NHL**	**59**	**8**	**19**	**27**	**45**	**4**	**0**	**2**	**147**	**5.4**	**–7**	**5**	**60.0**	**22:25**	....	....	....	....	....	....	....	....	....
2009-10	**Minnesota**	**NHL**	**47**	**3**	**17**	**20**	**32**	**2**	**0**	**0**	**104**	**2.9**	**–15**	**0**	**0.0**	**22:22**	....	....	....	....	....	....	....	....	....
2010-11	**Minnesota**	**NHL**	**80**	**17**	**29**	**46**	**98**	**8**	**0**	**3**	**170**	**10.0**	**–10**	**2**	**50.0**	**25:03**	....	....	....	....	....	....	....	....	....
	NHL Totals		**453**	**55**	**128**	**183**	**325**	**26**	**0**	**13**	**794**	**6.9**		**30**	**46.7**	**19:51**	**11**	**0**	**3**	**3**	**20**	**0**	**0**	**0**	**23:40**

Played in NHL All-Star Game (2011)

• Missed majority of 2003-04 season on assignment to Team Canada and as a healthy reserve. • Missed majority of 2009-10 due to concussion vs. Phoenix, November 18, 2009. Traded to **San Jose** by **Minnesota** with Minnesota's 2nd round choice in 2012 Entry Draft for Devin Setoguchi, Charlie Coyle and San Jose's 1st round choice (Zack Phillips) in 2011 Entry Draft, June 24, 2011.

BURROWS, Alexandre

(BUHR-ohz, al-ehx-AHN-druh) **VAN**

Left wing. Shoots left. 6'1", 199 lbs. Born, Pincourt, Que., April 11, 1981.

Season	Club	League	GP	G	A	Pts	PIM	PP	SH	GW	S	%	+/-	TF	F%	Min	GP	G	A	Pts	PIM	PP	SH	GW	Min
2000-01	Shawinigan	QMJHL	63	16	14	30	105	....	....	....	....	....	....	....	....	....	10	2	1	3	8	....	....	....	....
2001-02	Shawinigan	QMJHL	64	35	35	70	184	....	....	....	....	....	....	....	....	....	12	9	11	20	34	....	....	....	....
2002-03	Greenville	ECHL	53	9	17	26	201	....	....	....	....	....	....	....	....	....	....	....	....	....	....	....	....	....	....
	Baton Rouge	ECHL	13	4	2	6	64	....	....	....	....	....	....	....	....	....	....	....	....	....	....	....	....	....	....
2003-04	Manitoba Moose	AHL	2	0	0	0	0	....	....	....	....	....	....	....	....	....	....	....	....	....	....	....	....	....	....
	Columbia Inferno	ECHL	64	29	44	73	194	....	....	....	....	....	....	....	....	....	4	2	0	2	28	....	....	....	....
2004-05	Manitoba Moose	AHL	72	9	17	26	107	....	....	....	....	....	....	....	....	....	14	0	3	3	37	....	....	....	....
	Columbia Inferno	ECHL	4	5	1	6	4	....	....	....	....	....	....	....	....	....	....	....	....	....	....	....	....	....	....
2005-06	**Vancouver**	**NHL**	**43**	**7**	**5**	**12**	**61**	**0**	**1**	**1**	**49**	**14.3**	**5**	**19**	**47.4**	**10:24**	....	....	....	....	....	....	....	....	....
	Manitoba Moose	AHL	33	12	18	30	57	....	....	....	....	....	....	....	....	....	13	6	7	13	27	....	....	....	....
2006-07	**Vancouver**	**NHL**	**81**	**3**	**6**	**9**	**93**	**0**	**0**	**1**	**70**	**4.3**	**–7**	**16**	**43.8**	**11:26**	**11**	**1**	**0**	**1**	**14**	**0**	**0**	**0**	**10:34**
2007-08	**Vancouver**	**NHL**	**82**	**12**	**19**	**31**	**179**	**1**	**3**	**3**	**126**	**9.5**	**11**	**37**	**35.1**	**15:06**	....	....	....	....	....	....	....	....	....
2008-09	**Vancouver**	**NHL**	**82**	**28**	**23**	**51**	**150**	**0**	**4**	**3**	**175**	**16.0**	**23**	**80**	**46.3**	**16:51**	**10**	**3**	**1**	**4**	**20**	**0**	**0**	**1**	**18:48**
2009-10	**Vancouver**	**NHL**	**82**	**35**	**32**	**67**	**121**	**4**	**5**	**3**	**209**	**16.7**	**34**	**34**	**41.2**	**17:52**	**12**	**3**	**3**	**6**	**22**	**0**	**0**	**0**	**18:51**
2010-11	**Vancouver**	**NHL**	**72**	**26**	**22**	**48**	**77**	**1**	**1**	**4**	**152**	**17.1**	**26**	**14**	**42.9**	**17:02**	**25**	**9**	**8**	**17**	**34**	**1**	**1**	**2**	**20:40**
	NHL Totals		**442**	**111**	**107**	**218**	**681**	**6**	**14**	**15**	**781**	**14.2**		**200**	**43.0**	**15:07**	**58**	**16**	**12**	**28**	**90**	**1**	**1**	**3**	**18:03**

Signed as a free agent by **Manitoba** (AHL), October 21, 2003. Signed as a free agent by **Vancouver**, November 8, 2005.

BUTLER, Bobby

(BUHT-luhr, BAW-bee) **OTT**

Right wing. Shoots right. 6', 185 lbs. Born, Marlborough, MA, April 26, 1987.

Season	Club	League	GP	G	A	Pts	PIM	PP	SH	GW	S	%	+/-	TF	F%	Min	GP	G	A	Pts	PIM	PP	SH	GW	Min
2002-03	Bos. Little Bruins	Minor-MA	35	21	27	48	12	....	....	....	....	....	....	....	....	....	....	....	....	....	....	....	....	....	....
	Bos. Jr. Bruins	EJHL	13	1	3	4	0	....	....	....	....	....	....	....	....	....	....	....	....	....	....	....	....	....	....
2003-04	Bos. Jr. Bruins	EJHL	59	15	18	33	28	....	....	....	....	....	....	....	....	....	....	....	....	....	....	....	....	....	....
2004-05	Bos. Jr. Bruins	EJHL	56	19	20	39	20	....	....	....	....	....	....	....	....	....	....	....	....	....	....	....	....	....	....
2005-06	Bos. Jr. Bruins	EJHL	61	28	30	58	48	....	....	....	....	....	....	....	....	....	....	....	....	....	....	....	....	....	....
2006-07	New Hampshire	H-East	38	9	3	12	12	....	....	....	....	....	....	....	....	....	....	....	....	....	....	....	....	....	....
2007-08	New Hampshire	H-East	38	14	12	26	20	....	....	....	....	....	....	....	....	....	....	....	....	....	....	....	....	....	....
2008-09	New Hampshire	H-East	38	9	21	30	36	....	....	....	....	....	....	....	....	....	....	....	....	....	....	....	....	....	....
2009-10	New Hampshire	H-East	39	29	24	53	20	....	....	....	....	....	....	....	....	....	....	....	....	....	....	....	....	....	....
	Ottawa	**NHL**	**2**	**0**	**0**	**0**	**0**	**0**	**0**	**0**	**2**	**0.0**	**–1**	**0**	**0.0**	**8:21**	....	....	....	....	....	....	....	....	....
2010-11	**Ottawa**	**NHL**	**36**	**10**	**11**	**21**	**10**	**1**	**0**	**3**	**73**	**13.7**	**–16**	**2**	**0.0**	**15:26**	....	....	....	....	....	....	....	....	....
	Binghamton	AHL	47	22	11	33	35	....	....	....	....	....	....	....	....	....	23	13	4	17	6	....	....	....	....
	NHL Totals		**38**	**10**	**11**	**21**	**10**	**1**	**0**	**3**	**75**	**13.3**		**2**	**0.0**	**15:03**	....	....	....	....	....	....	....	....	....

Hockey East First All-Star Team (2010) • Hockey East Player of the Year (2010) • NCAA East First All-American Team (2010)

Signed as a free agent by **Ottawa**, March 29, 2010.

BUTLER, Chris

(BUHT-luhr, KRIHS) **CGY**

Defense. Shoots left. 6'1", 200 lbs. Born, St. Louis, MO, October 27, 1986. Buffalo's 4th choice, 96th overall, in 2005 Entry Draft.

Season	Club	League	GP	G	A	Pts	PIM	PP	SH	GW	S	%	+/-	TF	F%	Min	GP	G	A	Pts	PIM	PP	SH	GW	Min
2003-04	Sioux City	USHL	55	3	6	9	37	....	....	....	....	....	....	....	....	....	7	0	1	1	6	....	....	....	....
2004-05	Sioux City	USHL	60	6	22	28	90	....	....	....	....	....	....	....	....	....	13	1	6	7	10	....	....	....	....
2005-06	U. of Denver	WCHA	35	7	15	22	28	....	....	....	....	....	....	....	....	....	....	....	....	....	....	....	....	....	....
2006-07	U. of Denver	WCHA	39	10	17	27	42	....	....	....	....	....	....	....	....	....	....	....	....	....	....	....	....	....	....
2007-08	U. of Denver	WCHA	41	3	14	17	38	....	....	....	....	....	....	....	....	....	....	....	....	....	....	....	....	....	....
2008-09	**Buffalo**	**NHL**	**47**	**2**	**4**	**6**	**18**	**0**	**0**	**1**	**36**	**5.6**	**11**	**0**	**0.0**	**16:43**	....	....	....	....	....	....	....	....	....
	Portland Pirates	AHL	27	2	10	12	14	....	....	....	....	....	....	....	....	....	4	0	0	0	0	....	....	....	....
2009-10	**Buffalo**	**NHL**	**59**	**1**	**20**	**21**	**22**	**0**	**0**	**0**	**61**	**1.6**	**–15**	**0**	**0.0**	**20:01**	....	....	....	....	....	....	....	....	....
2010-11	**Buffalo**	**NHL**	**49**	**2**	**7**	**9**	**26**	**0**	**0**	**0**	**52**	**3.8**	**8**	**0**	**0.0**	**18:10**	**7**	**0**	**1**	**1**	**10**	**0**	**0**	**0**	**22:59**
	NHL Totals		**155**	**5**	**31**	**36**	**66**	**0**	**0**	**1**	**149**	**3.4**		**0**	**0.0**	**18:26**	**7**	**0**	**1**	**1**	**10**	**0**	**0**	**0**	**23:00**

USHL First All-Star Team (2005) • WCHA All-Rookie Team (2006) • WCHA Second All-Star Team (2008) • NCAA West Second All-American Team (2008)

Traded to **Calgary** by **Buffalo** with Paul Byron for Robyn Regehr, Ales Kotalok and Calgary's 2nd round choice in 2012 Entry Draft, June 25, 2011.

BYERS, Dane

(BIGH-uhrs, DAYN) **CBJ**

Left wing. Shoots left. 6'3", 204 lbs. Born, Nipawin, Sask., February 21, 1986. NY Rangers' 4th choice, 48th overall, in 2004 Entry Draft.

Season	Club	League	GP	G	A	Pts	PIM	PP	SH	GW	S	%	+/-	TF	F%	Min	GP	G	A	Pts	PIM	PP	SH	GW	Min
2002-03	Prince Albert	WHL	49	8	6	14	46	....	....	....	....	....	....	....	....	....	....	....	....	....	....	....	....	....	....
2003-04	Prince Albert	WHL	51	9	8	17	134	....	....	....	....	....	....	....	....	....	6	1	2	3	17	....	....	....	....
2004-05	Prince Albert	WHL	65	11	9	20	181	....	....	....	....	....	....	....	....	....	17	4	6	10	18	....	....	....	....
2005-06	Prince Albert	WHL	71	21	27	48	157	....	....	....	....	....	....	....	....	....	....	....	....	....	....	....	....	....	....
	Hartford	AHL	5	0	2	2	6	....	....	....	....	....	....	....	....	....	....	....	....	....	....	....	....	....	....
2006-07	Hartford	AHL	78	17	30	47	213	....	....	....	....	....	....	....	....	....	7	2	0	2	16	....	....	....	....
2007-08	**NY Rangers**	**NHL**	**1**	**0**	**0**	**0**	**0**	**0**	**0**	**0**	**0**	**0.0**	**–1**	**0**	**0.0**	**5:05**	....	....	....	....	....	....	....	....	....
	Hartford	AHL	73	23	23	46	184	....	....	....	....	....	....	....	....	....	5	2	1	3	2	....	....	....	....
2008-09	Hartford	AHL	9	4	3	7	18	....	....	....	....	....	....	....	....	....	6	3	1	4	7	....	....	....	....
2009-10	**NY Rangers**	**NHL**	**5**	**1**	**0**	**1**	**31**	**0**	**0**	**0**	**3**	**33.3**	**1**	**0**	**0.0**	**6:21**	....	....	....	....	....	....	....	....	....
	Hartford	AHL	74	25	27	52	100	....	....	....	....	....	....	....	....	....	....	....	....	....	....	....	....	....	....

			Regular Season														Playoffs								
Season	Club	League	GP	G	A	Pts	PIM	PP	SH	GW	S	%	+/-	TF	F%	Min	GP	G	A	Pts	PIM	PP	SH	GW	Min
2010-11	Connecticut	AHL	16	3	6	9	25	....	....	....	....	....	....	....	....	....	....	....	....	....	....	....	....	....	....
	Springfield	AHL	48	9	16	25	95	....	....	....	....	....	....	....	....	....	....	....	....	....	....	....	....	....	....
	San Antonio	AHL	21	3	9	12	41	....	....	....	....	....	....	....	....	....	....	....	....	....	....	....	....	....	....
	NHL Totals		6	1	0	1	31	0	0	0	3	33.3		0	0.0	6:09	....	....	....	....	....	....	....	....	....

• Missed majority of 2008-09 due to knee injury vs. Worcester (AHL), October 31, 2008. Traded to **Columbus** by **NY Rangers** for Chad Kolarik, November 11, 2010. Traded to **Phoenix** by **Columbus** with Rostislav Klesla for Scottie Upshall and Sami Lepisto, February 28, 2011. Signed as a free agent by **Columbus**. July 11, 2011.

BYFUGLIEN, Dustin

(BUHF-lihn, DUHS-tihn) **WPG**

Defense. Shoots right. 6'5", 265 lbs. Born, Minneapolis, MN, March 27, 1985. Chicago's 8th choice, 245th overall, in 2003 Entry Draft.

2001-02	Chicago Mission	MAHL	52	32	30	62	40	....	....	....	....	....	....	....	....	....	....	....	....	....	....	....	....	....	....
	Brandon	WHL	3	0	0	0	0	....	....	....	....	....	....	....	....	....	....	....	....	....	....	....	....	....	....
2002-03	Brandon	WHL	8	1	1	2	4	....	....	....	....	....	....	....	....	....	....	....	....	....	....	....	....	....	....
	Prince George	WHL	48	9	28	37	74	....	....	....	....	....	....	....	....	....	5	1	3	4	12	....	....	....	....
2003-04	Prince George	WHL	66	16	29	45	137	....	....	....	....	....	....	....	....	....	....	....	....	....	....	....	....	....	....
2004-05	Prince George	WHL	64	22	36	58	184	....	....	....	....	....	....	....	....	....	....	....	....	....	....	....	....	....	....
2005-06	**Chicago**	**NHL**	**25**	**3**	**2**	**5**	**24**	**0**	**0**	**1**	**45**	**6.7**	**-6**	**0**	**0.0**	**17:19**	....	....	....	....	....	....	....	....	....
	Norfolk Admirals	AHL	53	8	15	23	75	....	....	....	....	....	....	....	....	....	4	1	2	3	4	....	....	....	....
2006-07	**Chicago**	**NHL**	**9**	**1**	**2**	**3**	**10**	**0**	**0**	**0**	**18**	**5.6**	**-2**	**0**	**0.0**	**17:18**	....	....	....	....	....	....	....	....	....
	Norfolk Admirals	AHL	63	16	28	44	146	....	....	....	....	....	....	....	....	....	6	0	2	2	18	....	....	....	....
2007-08	**Chicago**	**NHL**	**67**	**19**	**17**	**36**	**59**	**7**	**0**	**4**	**163**	**11.7**	**-7**	**1**	**0.0**	**17:02**	....	....	....	....	....	....	....	....	....
	Rockford IceHogs	AHL	8	2	5	7	25	....	....	....	....	....	....	....	....	....	....	....	....	....	....	....	....	....	....
2008-09	**Chicago**	**NHL**	**77**	**15**	**16**	**31**	**81**	**3**	**0**	**4**	**202**	**7.4**	**7**	**11**	**18.2**	**14:52**	**17**	**3**	**6**	**9**	**26**	**1**	**0**	**0**	**17:11**
2009-10♦	**Chicago**	**NHL**	**82**	**17**	**17**	**34**	**94**	**6**	**0**	**3**	**211**	**8.1**	**-7**	**2**	**50.0**	**16:25**	**22**	**11**	**5**	**16**	**20**	**5**	**0**	**5**	**16:16**
2010-11	**Atlanta**	**NHL**	**81**	**20**	**33**	**53**	**93**	**8**	**0**	**6**	**347**	**5.8**	**-2**	**0**	**0.0**	**23:18**	....	....	....	....	....	....	....	....	....
	NHL Totals		**341**	**75**	**87**	**162**	**361**	**24**	**0**	**18**	**986**	**7.6**		**14**	**21.4**	**17:55**	**39**	**14**	**11**	**25**	**46**	**6**	**0**	**5**	**16:40**

AHL Second All-Star Team (2007)

Played in NHL All-Star Game (2011)

Traded to **Atlanta** by **Chicago** with Brent Sopel, Ben Eager and Akim Aliu for Marty Reasoner, Joey Crabb, Jeremy Morin and New Jersey's 1st (previously acquired, Chicago selected Kevin Hayes) and 2nd (previously acquired, Chicago selected Justin Holl) round choices in 2010 Entry Draft, June 24, 2010. • Transferred to **Winnipeg** after **Atlanta** franchise relocated, June 21, 2011.

BYRON, Paul

(BIGH-ruhn, PAWL) **CGY**

Center. Shoots left. 5'9", 144 lbs. Born, Ottawa, Ont., April 27, 1989. Buffalo's 6th choice, 179th overall, in 2007 Entry Draft.

2005-06	Ottawa West	ON-Jr.B	33	20	23	43	33	....	....	....	....	....	....	....	....	....	7	3	8	11	4	....	....	....	....
2006-07	Gatineau	QMJHL	68	21	23	44	46	....	....	....	....	....	....	....	....	....	5	5	1	6	2	....	....	....	....
2007-08	Gatineau	QMJHL	52	37	31	68	25	....	....	....	....	....	....	....	....	....	19	*21	11	32	12	....	....	....	....
2008-09	Gatineau	QMJHL	64	33	66	99	32	....	....	....	....	....	....	....	....	....	10	2	14	16	4	....	....	....	....
2009-10	Portland Pirates	AHL	57	14	19	33	59	....	....	....	....	....	....	....	....	....	4	0	0	0	0	....	....	....	....
2010-11	**Buffalo**	**NHL**	**8**	**1**	**1**	**2**	**2**	**0**	**0**	**0**	**5**	**20.0**	**0**	**71**	**40.9**	**10:57**	....	....	....	....	....	....	....	....	....
	Portland Pirates	AHL	67	26	27	53	52	....	....	....	....	....	....	....	....	....	12	2	5	7	6	....	....	....	....
	NHL Totals		**8**	**1**	**1**	**2**	**2**	**0**	**0**	**0**	**5**	**20.0**		**71**	**40.8**	**10:57**	....	....	....	....	....	....	....	....	....

QMJHL Second All-Star Team (2009)

Traded to **Calgary** by **Buffalo** with Chris Butler for Robyn Regehr, Ales Kotalik and Calgary's 2nd round choice in 2012 Entry Draft, June 25, 2011.

CALLAHAN, Joe

(kal-AH-han, JOH)

Defense. Shoots right. 6'3", 210 lbs. Born, Brockton, MA, December 20, 1982. Phoenix's 4th choice, 70th overall, in 2002 Entry Draft.

2001-02	Yale	ECAC	31	3	8	11	20	....	....	....	....	....	....	....	....	....	....	....	....	....	....	....	....	....	....
2002-03	Yale	ECAC	32	2	11	13	38	....	....	....	....	....	....	....	....	....	....	....	....	....	....	....	....	....	....
2003-04	Yale	ECAC	31	6	14	20	38	....	....	....	....	....	....	....	....	....	....	....	....	....	....	....	....	....	....
	Springfield	AHL	13	0	4	4	12	....	....	....	....	....	....	....	....	....	....	....	....	....	....	....	....	....	....
2004-05	Utah Grizzlies	AHL	75	4	7	11	66	....	....	....	....	....	....	....	....	....	....	....	....	....	....	....	....	....	....
2005-06	San Antonio	AHL	80	1	5	6	88	....	....	....	....	....	....	....	....	....	....	....	....	....	....	....	....	....	....
2006-07	San Antonio	AHL	78	1	13	14	65	....	....	....	....	....	....	....	....	....	....	....	....	....	....	....	....	....	....
2007-08	Portland Pirates	AHL	65	1	23	24	59	....	....	....	....	....	....	....	....	....	18	1	11	12	25	....	....	....	....
2008-09	**NY Islanders**	**NHL**	**18**	**0**	**2**	**2**	**4**	**0**	**0**	**0**	**6**	**0.0**	**5**	**1**	**0.0**	**15:00**	....	....	....	....	....	....	....	....	....
	Bridgeport	AHL	56	4	9	13	38	....	....	....	....	....	....	....	....	....	5	1	2	3	4	....	....	....	....
2009-10	**San Jose**	**NHL**	**1**	**0**	**1**	**1**	**0**	**0**	**0**	**0**	**0**	**0.0**	**1**	**0**	**0.0**	**9:34**	....	....	....	....	....	....	....	....	....
	Worcester Sharks	AHL	35	4	11	15	19	....	....	....	....	....	....	....	....	....	2	0	0	0	2	....	....	....	....
2010-11	**Florida**	**NHL**	**27**	**0**	**1**	**1**	**12**	**0**	**0**	**0**	**21**	**0.0**	**-1**	**0**	**0.0**	**15:53**	....	....	....	....	....	....	....	....	....
	Rochester	AHL	48	4	9	13	12	....	....	....	....	....	....	....	....	....	....	....	....	....	....	....	....	....	....
	NHL Totals		**46**	**0**	**4**	**4**	**16**	**0**	**0**	**0**	**27**	**0.0**		**1**	**0.0**	**15:24**	....	....	....	....	....	....	....	....	....

Signed as a free agent by **Anaheim**, July 12, 2007. Signed as a free agent by **NY Islanders**, July 8, 2008. Signed as a free agent by **San Jose**, July 16, 2009. • Missed majority of 2009-10 due to upper body injury, February 11, 2010. Signed as a free agent by **Florida**, August 3, 2010.

CALLAHAN, Ryan

(kal-AH-han, RIGH-uhn) **NYR**

Right wing. Shoots right. 5'10", 190 lbs. Born, Rochester, NY, March 21, 1985. NY Rangers' 9th choice, 127th overall, in 2004 Entry Draft.

2002-03	Guelph Storm	OHL	59	14	17	31	47	....	....	....	....	....	....	....	....	....	11	0	3	3	2	....	....	....	....
2003-04	Guelph Storm	OHL	68	36	32	68	86	....	....	....	....	....	....	....	....	....	22	*13	8	21	20	....	....	....	....
2004-05	Guelph Storm	OHL	60	28	26	54	108	....	....	....	....	....	....	....	....	....	4	1	1	2	6	....	....	....	....
2005-06	Guelph Storm	OHL	62	52	32	84	126	....	....	....	....	....	....	....	....	....	13	7	17	24	20	....	....	....	....
2006-07	**NY Rangers**	**NHL**	**14**	**4**	**2**	**6**	**9**	**0**	**0**	**1**	**40**	**10.0**	**5**	**3**	**66.7**	**10:31**	**10**	**2**	**1**	**3**	**6**	**1**	**0**	**0**	**12:19**
	Hartford	AHL	60	35	20	55	74	....	....	....	....	....	....	....	....	....	....	....	....	....	....	....	....	....	....
2007-08	**NY Rangers**	**NHL**	**52**	**8**	**5**	**13**	**31**	**0**	**1**	**1**	**92**	**8.7**	**7**	**5**	**20.0**	**12:22**	**10**	**2**	**2**	**4**	**10**	**0**	**1**	**1**	**15:55**
	Hartford	AHL	11	7	8	15	27	....	....	....	....	....	....	....	....	....	....	....	....	....	....	....	....	....	....
2008-09	**NY Rangers**	**NHL**	**81**	**22**	**18**	**40**	**45**	**2**	**1**	**1**	**237**	**9.3**	**7**	**10**	**70.0**	**17:04**	**7**	**2**	**0**	**2**	**4**	**1**	**0**	**1**	**19:44**
2009-10	**NY Rangers**	**NHL**	**77**	**19**	**18**	**37**	**48**	**9**	**0**	**3**	**204**	**9.3**	**-12**	**35**	**48.6**	**19:24**	....	....	....	....	....	....	....	....	....
	United States	Olympics	6	0	1	1	2	....	....	....	....	....	....	....	....	....	....	....	....	....	....	....	....	....	....
2010-11	**NY Rangers**	**NHL**	**60**	**23**	**25**	**48**	**46**	**10**	**0**	**5**	**179**	**12.8**	**-7**	**17**	**11.8**	**19:54**	....	....	....	....	....	....	....	....	....
	NHL Totals		**284**	**76**	**68**	**144**	**179**	**21**	**2**	**11**	**752**	**10.1**		**70**	**41.4**	**17:07**	**27**	**6**	**3**	**9**	**20**	**2**	**1**	**2**	**15:34**

OHL Second All-Star Team (2006) • AHL All-Rookie Team (2007)

CALVERT, Matt

(KAL-vuhrt, MAT) **CBJ**

Left wing. Shoots left. 5'11", 189 lbs. Born, Brandon, Man., December 24, 1989. Columbus' 5th choice, 127th overall, in 2008 Entry Draft.

2005-06	Brandon	MMHL	38	24	30	54	48	....	....	....	....	....	....	....	....	....	6	3	6	9	18	....	....	....	....
2006-07	Brandon	MMHL	30	28	55	83	46	....	....	....	....	....	....	....	....	....	16	5	13	18	16	....	....	....	....
	Winkler Flyers	MJHL	1	0	0	0	15	....	....	....	....	....	....	....	....	....	....	....	....	....	....	....	....	....	....
2007-08	Brandon	WHL	72	24	40	64	53	....	....	....	....	....	....	....	....	....	6	1	2	3	2	....	....	....	....
2008-09	Brandon	WHL	58	28	39	67	58	....	....	....	....	....	....	....	....	....	12	9	8	17	22	....	....	....	....
2009-10	Brandon	WHL	68	47	52	99	70	....	....	....	....	....	....	....	....	....	15	9	7	16	15	....	....	....	....
2010-11	**Columbus**	**NHL**	**42**	**11**	**9**	**20**	**12**	**3**	**0**	**1**	**50**	**22.0**	**3**	**9**	**33.3**	**11:06**	....	....	....	....	....	....	....	....	....
	Springfield	AHL	38	13	12	25	12	....	....	....	....	....	....	....	....	....	....	....	....	....	....	....	....	....	....
	NHL Totals		**42**	**11**	**9**	**20**	**12**	**3**	**0**	**1**	**50**	**22.0**		**9**	**33.3**	**11:06**	....	....	....	....	....	....	....	....	....

WHL East Second All-Star Team (2010) • Memorial Cup All-Star Team (2010)

CAMMALLERI, Michael

(kam-UH-LAIR-ee, MIGH-kuhl) **MTL**

Center. Shoots left. 5'9", 182 lbs. Born, Richmond Hill, Ont., June 8, 1982. Los Angeles' 3rd choice, 49th overall, in 2001 Entry Draft.

1997-98	Bramalea Blues	OPJHL	46	36	52	88	30	....	....	....	....	....	....	....	....	....	....	....	....	....	....	....	....	....	....
1998-99	Bramalea Blues	OPJHL	41	31	72	103	51	....	....	....	....	....	....	....	....	....	....	....	....	....	....	....	....	....	....
99-2000	U. of Michigan	CCHA	39	13	13	26	32	....	....	....	....	....	....	....	....	....	....	....	....	....	....	....	....	....	....
2000-01	U. of Michigan	CCHA	42	*29	32	61	24	....	....	....	....	....	....	....	....	....	....	....	....	....	....	....	....	....	....
2001-02	U. of Michigan	CCHA	29	23	21	44	28	....	....	....	....	....	....	....	....	....	....	....	....	....	....	....	....	....	....
2002-03	**Los Angeles**	**NHL**	**28**	**5**	**3**	**8**	**22**	**2**	**0**	**2**	**40**	**12.5**	**-4**	**253**	**51.4**	**14:05**	....	....	....	....	....	....	....	....	....
	Manchester	AHL	13	5	15	20	12	....	....	....	....	....	....	....	....	....	....	....	....	....	....	....	....	....	....

			Regular Season														Playoffs								
Season	Club	League	GP	G	A	Pts	PIM	PP	SH	GW	S	%	+/-	TF	F%	Min	GP	G	A	Pts	PIM	PP	SH	GW	Min
2003-04	**Los Angeles**	**NHL**	**31**	**9**	**6**	**15**	**20**	**2**	**0**	**2**	**53**	**17.0**	**1**	**280**	**53.6**	**13:18**	....	....	....	....	....	....	....	....	....
	Manchester	AHL	41	20	19	39	28	....	....	....	....	....	....	....	....	....	1	0	1	1	0	....	....	....	....
2004-05	Manchester	AHL	79	*46	63	109	60	....	....	....	....	....	....	....	....	....	6	1	5	6	0	....	....	....	....
2005-06	**Los Angeles**	**NHL**	**80**	**26**	**29**	**55**	**50**	**15**	**0**	**4**	**206**	**12.6**	**–14**	**578**	**53.5**	**16:45**	....	....	....	....	....	....	....	....	....
2006-07	**Los Angeles**	**NHL**	**81**	**34**	**46**	**80**	**48**	**16**	**0**	**5**	**299**	**11.4**	**5**	**301**	**54.2**	**18:03**	....	....	....	....	....	....	....	....	....
2007-08	**Los Angeles**	**NHL**	**63**	**19**	**28**	**47**	**30**	**10**	**0**	**1**	**210**	**9.0**	**–16**	**380**	**54.2**	**18:35**	....	....	....	....	....	....	....	....	....
2008-09	**Calgary**	**NHL**	**81**	**39**	**43**	**82**	**44**	**19**	**0**	**6**	**255**	**15.3**	**–2**	**368**	**60.3**	**17:33**	**6**	**1**	**2**	**3**	**2**	**0**	**0**	**0**	**18:02**
2009-10	**Montreal**	**NHL**	**65**	**26**	**24**	**50**	**16**	**4**	**0**	**4**	**218**	**11.9**	**7**	**51**	**51.0**	**19:31**	**19**	***13**	**6**	**19**	**6**	**4**	**0**	**3**	**20:40**
2010-11	**Montreal**	**NHL**	**67**	**19**	**28**	**47**	**33**	**7**	**0**	**2**	**193**	**9.8**	**2**	**74**	**44.6**	**18:29**	**7**	**3**	**7**	**10**	**0**	**1**	**0**	**0**	**23:35**
	NHL Totals		**496**	**177**	**207**	**384**	**263**	**75**	**0**	**26**	**1474**	**12.0**		**2285**	**54.2**	**17:33**	**32**	**17**	**15**	**32**	**8**	**5**	**0**	**3**	**20:49**

CCHA First All-Star Team (2001) • NCAA West Second All-American Team (2001) • CCHA Second All-Star Team (2002) • NCAA West First All-American Team (2002) • AHL Second All-Star Team (2005) • Willie Marshall Award (AHL - Top Goal-scorer) (2005)

• Missed majority of 2002-03 due to concussion vs. San Jose, January 28, 2003. Traded to **Calgary** by **Los Angeles** with Calgary's 2nd round choice (previously acquired, Calgary selected Mitch Wahl) in 2008 Entry Draft for Calgary's 1st round choice (later traded to Anaheim – Anaheim selected Jake Gardiner) in 2008 Entry Draft and Calgary's 2nd round choice (later traded to Carolina – Carolina selected Brian Dumoulin) in 2009 Entry Draft, June 20, 2008. Signed as a free agent by **Montreal**, July 1, 2009.

CAMPANALE, Matt

(kam-pan-AL-ay, MAT)

Defense. Shoots left. 5'11", 200 lbs. Born, Chester Springs, PA, February 14, 1988.

Season	Club	League	GP	G	A	Pts	PIM	PP	SH	GW	S	%	+/-	TF	F%	Min	GP	G	A	Pts	PIM	PP	SH	GW	Min
2007-08	New Hampshire	H-East	6	0	0	0	0	....	....	....	....	....	....	....	....	....	....	....	....	....	....	....	....	....	....
2008-09	New Hampshire	H-East	22	0	1	1	6	....	....	....	....	....	....	....	....	....	....	....	....	....	....	....	....	....	....
2009-10	New Hampshire	H-East	39	3	9	12	10	....	....	....	....	....	....	....	....	....	....	....	....	....	....	....	....	....	....
2010-11	New Hampshire	H-East	39	0	11	11	16	....	....	....	....	....	....	....	....	....	....	....	....	....	....	....	....	....	....
	Bridgeport	AHL	5	0	0	0	0	....	....	....	....	....	....	....	....	....	....	....	....	....	....	....	....	....	....
	NY Islanders	**NHL**	**1**	**0**	**0**	**0**	**2**	**0**	**0**	**0**	**0**	**0.0**	**0**	**0**	**0.0**	**8:21**	....	....	....	....	....	....	....	....	....
	NHL Totals		**1**	**0**	**0**	**0**	**2**	**0**	**0**	**0**	**0**	**0.0**		**0**	**0.0**	**8:21**	....	....	....	....	....	....	....	....	....

Signed to a ATO (amateur tryout) contract by **Bridgeport** (AHL), March 30, 2011. Signed to a ATO (amateur tryout) contract by **NY Islanders**, April 5, 2011.

CAMPBELL, Brian

(KAM-behl, BRIGH-uhn) **FLA**

Defense. Shoots left. 6', 189 lbs. Born, Strathroy, Ont., May 23, 1979. Buffalo's 7th choice, 156th overall, in 1997 Entry Draft.

Season	Club	League	GP	G	A	Pts	PIM	PP	SH	GW	S	%	+/-	TF	F%	Min	GP	G	A	Pts	PIM	PP	SH	GW	Min
1994-95	Petrolia Oil Barons	OHA-B	49	11	27	38	43	....	....	....	....	....	....	....	....	....	....	....	....	....	....	....	....	....	....
1995-96	Ottawa 67's	OHL	66	5	22	27	23	....	....	....	....	....	....	....	....	....	4	0	1	1	2	....	....	....	....
1996-97	Ottawa 67's	OHL	66	7	36	43	12	....	....	....	....	....	....	....	....	....	24	2	11	13	8	....	....	....	....
1997-98	Ottawa 67's	OHL	66	14	39	53	31	....	....	....	....	....	....	....	....	....	13	1	14	15	0	....	....	....	....
1998-99	Ottawa 67's	OHL	62	12	75	87	27	....	....	....	....	....	....	....	....	....	9	2	10	12	6	....	....	....	....
	Rochester	AHL	....	....	....	....	....	....	....	....	....	....	....	....	....	....	2	0	0	0	0	....	....	....	....
99-2000	**Buffalo**	**NHL**	**12**	**1**	**4**	**5**	**4**	**0**	**0**	**0**	**10**	**10.0**	**–2**	**0**	**0.0**	**15:48**	....	....	....	....	....	....	....	....	....
	Rochester	AHL	67	2	24	26	22	....	....	....	....	....	....	....	....	....	21	0	3	3	0	....	....	....	....
2000-01	**Buffalo**	**NHL**	**8**	**0**	**0**	**0**	**2**	**0**	**0**	**0**	**7**	**0.0**	**–2**	**0**	**0.0**	**15:40**	....	....	....	....	....	....	....	....	....
	Rochester	AHL	65	7	25	32	24	....	....	....	....	....	....	....	....	....	4	0	1	1	0	....	....	....	....
2001-02	**Buffalo**	**NHL**	**29**	**3**	**3**	**6**	**12**	**0**	**0**	**0**	**30**	**10.0**	**0**	**1**	**0.0**	**15:18**	....	....	....	....	....	....	....	....	....
	Rochester	AHL	45	2	35	37	13	....	....	....	....	....	....	....	....	....	....	....	....	....	....	....	....	....	....
2002-03	**Buffalo**	**NHL**	**65**	**2**	**17**	**19**	**20**	**0**	**0**	**1**	**90**	**2.2**	**–8**	**1**	**0.0**	**18:40**	....	....	....	....	....	....	....	....	....
2003-04	**Buffalo**	**NHL**	**53**	**3**	**8**	**11**	**12**	**0**	**0**	**0**	**45**	**6.7**	**–8**	**0**	**0.0**	**16:02**	....	....	....	....	....	....	....	....	....
2004-05	Jokerit Helsinki	Finland	44	12	13	25	12	....	....	....	....	....	....	....	....	....	12	3	4	7	6	....	....	....	....
2005-06	**Buffalo**	**NHL**	**79**	**12**	**32**	**44**	**16**	**5**	**0**	**5**	**105**	**11.4**	**–14**	**0**	**0.0**	**17:43**	**18**	**0**	**6**	**6**	**12**	**0**	**0**	**0**	**20:29**
2006-07	**Buffalo**	**NHL**	**82**	**6**	**42**	**48**	**35**	**1**	**0**	**1**	**92**	**6.5**	**28**	**0**	**0.0**	**21:53**	**16**	**3**	**4**	**7**	**14**	**2**	**0**	**0**	**21:39**
2007-08	**Buffalo**	**NHL**	**63**	**5**	**38**	**43**	**12**	**3**	**0**	**0**	**102**	**4.9**	**–1**	**0**	**0.0**	**25:06**	....	....	....	....	....	....	....	....	....
	San Jose	**NHL**	**20**	**3**	**16**	**19**	**8**	**2**	**0**	**0**	**40**	**7.5**	**9**	**0**	**0.0**	**25:07**	**13**	**1**	**6**	**7**	**4**	**0**	**0**	**0**	**29:19**
2008-09	**Chicago**	**NHL**	**82**	**7**	**45**	**52**	**22**	**4**	**0**	**1**	**108**	**6.5**	**5**	**0**	**0.0**	**22:34**	**17**	**2**	**8**	**10**	**0**	**2**	**0**	**0**	**20:29**
2009-10 ♦	**Chicago**	**NHL**	**68**	**7**	**31**	**38**	**18**	**3**	**0**	**2**	**131**	**5.3**	**18**	**0**	**0.0**	**23:13**	**19**	**1**	**4**	**5**	**2**	**0**	**0**	**0**	**19:35**
2010-11	**Chicago**	**NHL**	**65**	**5**	**22**	**27**	**6**	**2**	**0**	**1**	**84**	**6.0**	**28**	**0**	**0.0**	**22:59**	**7**	**1**	**2**	**3**	**6**	**0**	**0**	**0**	**26:26**
	NHL Totals		**626**	**54**	**258**	**312**	**167**	**20**	**0**	**11**	**844**	**6.4**		**2**	**0.0**	**20:48**	**90**	**8**	**30**	**38**	**38**	**4**	**0**	**0**	**22:14**

OHL First All-Star Team (1999) • OHL MVP (1999) • Canadian Major Junior First All-Star Team (1999) • Canadian Major Junior Player of the Year (1999) • George Parsons Trophy (Memorial Cup - Most Sportsmanlike Player) (1999) • NHL Second All-Star Team (2008)

Played in NHL All-Star Game (2007, 2008, 2009)

Signed as a free agent by **Jokerit Helsinki** (Finland), October 19, 2004. Traded to **San Jose** by **Buffalo** with Buffalo's 7th round choice (Drew Daniels) in 2008 Entry Draft for Steve Bernier and San Jose's 1st round choice (Tyler Ennis) in 2008 Entry Draft, February 26, 2008. Signed as a free agent by **Chicago**, July 1, 2008. Traded to **Florida** by **Chicago** for Rostislav Olesz, June 25, 2011.

CAMPBELL, Gregory

(KAM-behl, GREH-goh-ree) **BOS**

Left wing. Shoots left. 6', 197 lbs. Born, London, Ont., December 17, 1983. Florida's 4th choice, 67th overall, in 2002 Entry Draft.

Season	Club	League	GP	G	A	Pts	PIM	PP	SH	GW	S	%	+/-	TF	F%	Min	GP	G	A	Pts	PIM	PP	SH	GW	Min
1998-99	Aylmer Aces	ON-Jr.B	49	5	9	14	44	....	....	....	....	....	....	....	....	....	....	....	....	....	....	....	....	....	....
99-2000	St. Thomas Stars	ON-Jr.B	51	12	8	20	51	....	....	....	....	....	....	....	....	....	....	....	....	....	....	....	....	....	....
2000-01	Plymouth Whalers	OHL	65	2	12	14	40	....	....	....	....	....	....	....	....	....	10	0	0	0	7	....	....	....	....
2001-02	Plymouth Whalers	OHL	65	17	36	53	105	....	....	....	....	....	....	....	....	....	6	0	2	2	13	....	....	....	....
2002-03	Kitchener Rangers	OHL	55	23	33	56	116	....	....	....	....	....	....	....	....	....	21	15	4	19	34	....	....	....	....
2003-04	**Florida**	**NHL**	**2**	**0**	**0**	**0**	**5**	**0**	**0**	**0**	**0**	**0.0**	**–1**	**1**	**0.0**	**9:09**	....	....	....	....	....	....	....	....	....
	San Antonio	AHL	76	13	16	29	73	....	....	....	....	....	....	....	....	....	....	....	....	....	....	....	....	....	....
2004-05	San Antonio	AHL	70	12	16	28	113	....	....	....	....	....	....	....	....	....	....	....	....	....	....	....	....	....	....
2005-06	**Florida**	**NHL**	**64**	**3**	**6**	**9**	**40**	**0**	**0**	**0**	**59**	**5.1**	**–11**	**38**	**34.2**	**8:38**	....	....	....	....	....	....	....	....	....
	Rochester	AHL	11	3	3	6	30	....	....	....	....	....	....	....	....	....	....	....	....	....	....	....	....	....	....
2006-07	**Florida**	**NHL**	**79**	**6**	**3**	**9**	**66**	**0**	**1**	**0**	**103**	**5.8**	**–10**	**588**	**45.2**	**10:34**	....	....	....	....	....	....	....	....	....
2007-08	**Florida**	**NHL**	**81**	**5**	**13**	**18**	**72**	**0**	**2**	**1**	**113**	**4.4**	**–12**	**460**	**51.1**	**12:27**	....	....	....	....	....	....	....	....	....
2008-09	**Florida**	**NHL**	**77**	**13**	**19**	**32**	**76**	**1**	**0**	**1**	**135**	**9.6**	**0**	**1018**	**50.0**	**16:47**	....	....	....	....	....	....	....	....	....
2009-10	**Florida**	**NHL**	**60**	**2**	**15**	**17**	**53**	**0**	**0**	**1**	**84**	**2.4**	**–5**	**341**	**46.3**	**15:24**	....	....	....	....	....	....	....	....	....
2010-11 ♦	**Boston**	**NHL**	**80**	**13**	**16**	**29**	**93**	**1**	**1**	**1**	**98**	**13.3**	**11**	**832**	**51.7**	**13:26**	**25**	**1**	**3**	**4**	**4**	**0**	**0**	**0**	**10:59**
	NHL Totals		**443**	**42**	**72**	**114**	**405**	**2**	**4**	**4**	**592**	**7.1**		**3278**	**49.1**	**12:53**	**25**	**1**	**3**	**4**	**4**	**0**	**0**	**0**	**11:00**

Memorial Cup All-Star Team (2003) • George Parsons Trophy (Memorial Cup - Most Sportsmanlike Player) (2003) • Ed Chynoweth Trophy (Memorial Cup - Leading Scorer) (2003)

Traded to **Boston** by **Florida** with Nathan Horton for Dennis Wideman, Boston's 1st round choice (later traded to Los Angeles – Los Angeles selected Derek Forbert) in 2010 Entry Draft and Boston's 3rd round choice (Kyle Rau) in 2011 Entry Draft, June 22, 2010.

CAMPOLI, Chris

(kam-POH-lee, KRIHS)

Defense. Shoots left. 6', 200 lbs. Born, North York, Ont., July 9, 1984. NY Islanders' 8th choice, 227th overall, in 2004 Entry Draft.

Season	Club	League	GP	G	A	Pts	PIM	PP	SH	GW	S	%	+/-	TF	F%	Min	GP	G	A	Pts	PIM	PP	SH	GW	Min
2000-01	Erie Otters	OHL	52	1	9	10	47	....	....	....	....	....	....	....	....	....	15	0	0	0	4	....	....	....	....
2001-02	Erie Otters	OHL	68	2	24	26	117	....	....	....	....	....	....	....	....	....	20	0	5	5	18	....	....	....	....
2002-03	Erie Otters	OHL	60	8	40	48	82	....	....	....	....	....	....	....	....	....	....	....	....	....	....	....	....	....	....
2003-04	Erie Otters	OHL	67	20	46	66	66	....	....	....	....	....	....	....	....	....	8	0	6	6	16	....	....	....	....
2004-05	Bridgeport	AHL	79	15	34	49	78	....	....	....	....	....	....	....	....	....	....	....	....	....	....	....	....	....	....
2005-06	**NY Islanders**	**NHL**	**80**	**9**	**25**	**34**	**46**	**2**	**0**	**2**	**123**	**7.3**	**–16**	**0**	**0.0**	**18:32**	....	....	....	....	....	....	....	....	....
2006-07	**NY Islanders**	**NHL**	**51**	**1**	**13**	**14**	**23**	**0**	**0**	**0**	**41**	**2.4**	**–3**	**0**	**0.0**	**14:50**	**5**	**1**	**1**	**2**	**2**	**0**	**0**	**0**	**13:30**
	Bridgeport	AHL	15	3	3	6	8	....	....	....	....	....	....	....	....	....	....	....	....	....	....	....	....	....	....
2007-08	**NY Islanders**	**NHL**	**46**	**4**	**14**	**18**	**16**	**2**	**1**	**0**	**68**	**5.9**	**–1**	**0**	**0.0**	**19:09**	....	....	....	....	....	....	....	....	....
2008-09	**NY Islanders**	**NHL**	**51**	**6**	**11**	**17**	**43**	**0**	**1**	**2**	**53**	**11.3**	**–20**	**0**	**0.0**	**19:50**	....	....	....	....	....	....	....	....	....
	Ottawa	**NHL**	**25**	**5**	**8**	**13**	**12**	**2**	**0**	**2**	**38**	**13.2**	**4**	**0**	**0.0**	**18:58**	....	....	....	....	....	....	....	....	....
2009-10	**Ottawa**	**NHL**	**67**	**4**	**14**	**18**	**16**	**1**	**0**	**1**	**71**	**5.6**	**–3**	**1**	**0.0**	**17:51**	**6**	**0**	**2**	**2**	**4**	**0**	**0**	**0**	**19:48**
2010-11	**Ottawa**	**NHL**	**58**	**3**	**11**	**14**	**34**	**0**	**0**	**0**	**59**	**5.1**	**–3**	**0**	**0.0**	**18:49**	....	....	....	....	....	....	....	....	....
	Chicago	**NHL**	**19**	**1**	**6**	**7**	**2**	**1**	**0**	**1**	**25**	**4.0**	**3**	**0**	**0.0**	**20:08**	**7**	**0**	**1**	**1**	**2**	**0**	**0**	**0**	**18:56**
	NHL Totals		**397**	**33**	**102**	**135**	**192**	**8**	**2**	**8**	**478**	**6.9**		**1**	**0.0**	**18:20**	**18**	**1**	**4**	**5**	**8**	**0**	**0**	**0**	**17:43**

OHL Humanitarian Player of the Year (2004) • Canadian Major Junior Humanitarian Player of the Year (2004) • AHL All-Rookie Team (2005)

Traded to **Ottawa** by **NY Islanders** with Mike Comrie for Dean McAmmond and San Jose's 1st round choice (previously acquired, later traded to Columbus, later traded to Anahaim – Anaheim selected Kyle Palmieri) in 2009 Entry Draft, February 20, 2009. Traded to **Chicago** by **Ottawa** with future considerations for Ryan Potulny and Chicago's 2nd round choice (later traded to Detroit – Detroit selected Xavier Ouellet) in 2011 Entry Draft, February 28, 2011.

CAPUTI, Luca

(ka-POO-tee, LOO-ka) **TOR**

Left wing. Shoots left. 6'3", 200 lbs. Born, Toronto, Ont., October 1, 1988. Pittsburgh's 5th choice, 111th overall, in 2007 Entry Draft.

Season	Club	League	Regular Season GP	G	A	Pts	PIM	PP	SH	GW	S	%	+/-	TF	F%	Min	Playoffs GP	G	A	Pts	PIM	PP	SH	GW	Min
2003-04	Tor. Jr. Canadiens	GTHL	53	52	55	107	127																			
2004-05	Mississauga	OHL	48	5	1	6	25																			
2005-06	Mississauga	OHL	32	3	0	3	43																			
2006-07	Mississauga	OHL	68	27	38	65	66										5	2	1	3	0				
2007-08	Niagara Ice Dogs	OHL	66	51	60	111	107										10	8	9	17	14				
	Wilkes-Barre	AHL															19	4	4	8	8				
2008-09	**Pittsburgh**	**NHL**	**5**	**1**	**0**	**1**	**4**	**0**	**0**	**0**	**7**	**14.3**	**–1**	**0**	**0.0**	**10:16**									
	Wilkes-Barre	AHL	66	18	27	45	45										12	3	5	8	10				
	Wheeling Nailers	ECHL	3	2	1	3	0																		
2009-10	**Pittsburgh**	**NHL**	**4**	**1**	**1**	**2**	**2**	**0**	**0**	**0**	**4**	**25.0**	**–1**	**0**	**0.0**	**11:46**									
	Wilkes-Barre	AHL	54	23	24	47	61																		
	Toronto	**NHL**	**19**	**1**	**5**	**6**	**10**	**0**	**0**	**0**	**32**	**3.1**	**0**	**23**	**43.5**	**14:38**									
2010-11	**Toronto**	**NHL**	**7**	**0**	**0**	**0**	**4**	**0**	**0**	**0**	**8**	**0.0**	**–2**	**6**	**33.3**	**11:04**									
	Toronto Marlies	AHL	13	1	4	5	30																		
	NHL Totals		**35**	**3**	**6**	**9**	**20**	**0**	**0**	**0**	**51**	**5.9**		**29**	**41.4**	**12:58**									

OHL Second All-Star Team (2008)

Traded to **Toronto** by **Pittsburgh** with Martin Skoula for Alexei Ponikarovsky, March 2, 2010. • Missed majority of 2010-11 due to sports hernia surgery.

CARCILLO, Daniel

(KAR-sihl-oh, DAN-yuhl) **CHI**

Left wing. Shoots left. 6', 205 lbs. Born, King City, Ont., January 28, 1985. Pittsburgh's 4th choice, 73rd overall, in 2003 Entry Draft.

Season	Club	League	GP	G	A	Pts	PIM	PP	SH	GW	S	%	+/-	TF	F%	Min	GP	G	A	Pts	PIM	PP	SH	GW	Min
2001-02	Milton Merchants	ON-Jr.B	47	15	16	31	162																		
2002-03	Sarnia Sting	OHL	68	29	37	66	157										6	0	4	4	14				
2003-04	Sarnia Sting	OHL	61	30	29	59	148										4	1	2	3	12				
2004-05	Sarnia Sting	OHL	12	2	7	9	40																		
	Mississauga	OHL	20	8	10	18	75										5	3	1	4	18				
2005-06	Wilkes-Barre	AHL	51	11	13	24	311										11	1	0	1	47				
	Wheeling Nailers	ECHL	6	3	2	5	32																		
2006-07	Wilkes-Barre	AHL	52	21	9	30	183																		
	Phoenix	**NHL**	**18**	**4**	**3**	**7**	**74**	**3**	**0**	**0**	**32**	**12.5**	**–7**	**0**	**0.0**	**14:56**									
2007-08	**Phoenix**	**NHL**	**57**	**13**	**11**	**24**	***324**	**3**	**0**	**1**	**106**	**12.3**	**1**	**5**	**80.0**	**12:43**									
	San Antonio	AHL	5	2	1	3	16																		
2008-09	**Phoenix**	**NHL**	**54**	**3**	**7**	**10**	***174**	**2**	**0**	**0**	**95**	**3.2**	**–13**	**18**	**55.6**	**11:59**									
	Philadelphia	**NHL**	**20**	**0**	**4**	**4**	***80**	**0**	**0**	**0**	**35**	**0.0**	**–2**	**2**	**100.0**	**10:16**	**5**	**1**	**1**	**2**	**5**	**0**	**0**	**0**	**8:11**
2009-10	**Philadelphia**	**NHL**	**76**	**12**	**10**	**22**	**207**	**1**	**0**	**1**	**105**	**11.4**	**5**	**3**	**33.3**	**11:15**	**17**	**2**	**4**	**6**	**34**	**0**	**0**	**1**	**10:32**
2010-11	**Philadelphia**	**NHL**	**57**	**4**	**2**	**6**	**127**	**0**	**0**	**2**	**56**	**7.1**	**–14**	**2**	**50.0**	**7:46**	**11**	**2**	**1**	**3**	**30**	**0**	**0**	**0**	**8:25**
	NHL Totals		**282**	**36**	**37**	**73**	**986**	**9**	**0**	**4**	**429**	**8.4**		**30**	**60.0**	**11:09**	**33**	**5**	**6**	**11**	**69**	**0**	**0**	**1**	**9:28**

Traded to **Phoenix** by **Pittsburgh** with Pittsburgh's 3rd round choice (later traded to NY Rangers - NY Rangers selected Tomas Kundratek) in 2008 Entry Draft for Georges Laraque, February 27, 2007. Traded to **Philadelphia** by **Phoenix** for Scottie Upshall and Philadelphia's 2nd round choice (Lucas Lessio) in 2011 Entry Draft, March 4, 2009. Signed as a free agent by **Chicago**, July 1, 2011.

CARKNER, Matt

(KARK-nehr, MAT) **OTT**

Defense. Shoots right. 6'4", 238 lbs. Born, Winchester, Ont., November 3, 1980. Montreal's 2nd choice, 58th overall, in 1999 Entry Draft.

Season	Club	League	GP	G	A	Pts	PIM	PP	SH	GW	S	%	+/-	TF	F%	Min	GP	G	A	Pts	PIM	PP	SH	GW	Min
1996-97	Winchester	ON-Jr.B	29	1	18	19																			
1997-98	Peterborough	OHL	57	0	6	6	121										4	0	0	0	2				
1998-99	Peterborough	OHL	60	2	16	18	173										5	0	0	0	20				
99-2000	Peterborough	OHL	62	3	13	16	177										5	0	1	1	6				
2000-01	Peterborough	OHL	53	8	8	16	128										7	0	3	3	25				
2001-02	Cleveland Barons	AHL	74	0	3	3	335																		
2002-03	Cleveland Barons	AHL	39	1	4	5	104																		
2003-04	Cleveland Barons	AHL	60	2	11	13	115										9	0	3	3	39				
2004-05	Cleveland Barons	AHL	73	0	10	10	192																		
2005-06	**San Jose**	**NHL**	**1**	**0**	**1**	**1**	**2**	**0**	**0**	**0**	**0**	**0.0**	**0**	**0**	**0.0**	**6:01**									
	Cleveland Barons	AHL	69	10	21	31	202																		
2006-07	Wilkes-Barre	AHL	75	6	24	30	167										8	1	0	1	19				
2007-08	Binghamton	AHL	67	10	15	25	218																		
2008-09	**Ottawa**	**NHL**	**1**	**0**	**0**	**0**	**0**	**0**	**0**	**0**	**0**	**0.0**	**0**	**0**	**0.0**	**4:08**									
	Binghamton	AHL	67	3	18	21	210																		
2009-10	**Ottawa**	**NHL**	**81**	**2**	**9**	**11**	**190**	**0**	**0**	**0**	**87**	**2.3**	**0**	**0**	**0.0**	**16:55**	**6**	**1**	**0**	**1**	**12**	**0**	**0**	**1**	**18:38**
2010-11	**Ottawa**	**NHL**	**50**	**1**	**6**	**7**	**136**	**0**	**0**	**0**	**40**	**2.5**	**0**	**0**	**0.0**	**14:53**									
	NHL Totals		**133**	**3**	**16**	**19**	**328**	**0**	**0**	**0**	**127**	**2.4**		**0**	**0.0**	**15:58**	**6**	**1**	**0**	**1**	**12**	**0**	**0**	**1**	**18:38**

Yanick Dupre Memorial Award (AHL - Outstanding Humanitarian Contribution) (2007)

Signed as a free agent by **San Jose**, June 6, 2001. • Missed majority of 2002-03 due to knee injury vs. Utah (AHL), January 4, 2003. Signed as a free agent by **Pittsburgh**, July 23, 2006. Signed as a free agent by **Ottawa**, July 3, 2007.

CARLE, Mathieu

(KAHRL, MA-tyew) **ANA**

Defense. Shoots right. 6', 200 lbs. Born, Gatineau, Que., September 30, 1987. Montreal's 3rd choice, 53rd overall, in 2006 Entry Draft.

Season	Club	League	GP	G	A	Pts	PIM	PP	SH	GW	S	%	+/-	TF	F%	Min	GP	G	A	Pts	PIM	PP	SH	GW	Min
2003-04	Acadie-Bathurst	QMJHL	59	11	12	23	57																		
2004-05	Acadie-Bathurst	QMJHL	69	4	29	33	53																		
2005-06	Acadie-Bathurst	QMJHL	67	18	51	69	122										17	1	14	15	29				
2006-07	Acadie-Bathurst	QMJHL	38	12	39	51	52																		
	Rouyn-Noranda	QMJHL	25	4	15	19	27										16	6	10	16	16				
2007-08	Hamilton	AHL	64	7	17	24	43																		
2008-09	Hamilton	AHL	59	7	22	29	43										6	0	2	2	4				
2009-10	**Montreal**	**NHL**	**3**	**0**	**0**	**0**	**4**	**0**	**0**	**0**	**2**	**0.0**	**1**	**0**	**0.0**	**14:28**									
	Hamilton	AHL	31	5	10	15	26										1	0	0	0	0				
2010-11	Hamilton	AHL	68	11	18	29	44										19	3	9	12	8				
	NHL Totals		**3**	**0**	**0**	**0**	**4**	**0**	**0**	**0**	**2**	**0.0**		**0**	**0.0**	**14:28**									

QMJHL All-Rookie Team (2004)

• Missed majority of 2009-10 due to concussion in pre-season vs. Chicago, September 24, 2009. Traded to **Anaheim** by **Montreal** for Mark Mitera, July 15, 2011.

CARLE, Matt

(KAHRL, MAT) **PHI**

Defense. Shoots left. 6', 205 lbs. Born, Anchorage, AK, September 25, 1984. San Jose's 4th choice, 47th overall, in 2003 Entry Draft.

Season	Club	League	GP	G	A	Pts	PIM	PP	SH	GW	S	%	+/-	TF	F%	Min	GP	G	A	Pts	PIM	PP	SH	GW	Min
99-2000	Alaska All-Stars	AASHA	42	14	28	42																			
2000-01	USNTDP	U-17	13	0	1	1																			
	USNTDP	NAHL	55	1	4	5	33																		
2001-02	USNTDP	U-18	45	3	13	16	30																		
	USNTDP	NAHL	7	1	2	3	0																		
	USNTDP	USHL	12	0	0	0	21																		
2002-03	River City Lancers	USHL	59	12	30	42	98										11	2	2	4	20				
2003-04	U. of Denver	WCHA	30	5	20	25	33																		
2004-05	U. of Denver	WCHA	43	13	31	44	68																		
2005-06	U. of Denver	WCHA	39	11	*42	53	58																		
	San Jose	**NHL**	**12**	**3**	**3**	**6**	**14**	**2**	**0**	**1**	**11**	**27.3**	**–2**	**0**	**0.0**	**16:07**	**11**	**0**	**3**	**3**	**4**	**0**	**0**	**0**	**15:17**
2006-07	**San Jose**	**NHL**	**77**	**11**	**31**	**42**	**30**	**8**	**0**	**1**	**111**	**9.9**	**9**	**1**	**0.0**	**18:08**	**11**	**2**	**3**	**5**	**0**	**1**	**0**	**1**	**14:51**
	Worcester Sharks	AHL	3	0	2	2	0																		
2007-08	**San Jose**	**NHL**	**62**	**2**	**13**	**15**	**26**	**2**	**0**	**1**	**63**	**3.2**	**–8**	**1**	**100.0**	**16:33**	**11**	**0**	**1**	**1**	**4**	**0**	**0**	**0**	**13:56**
2008-09	**Tampa Bay**	**NHL**	**12**	**1**	**1**	**2**	**6**	**0**	**0**	**0**	**13**	**7.7**	**1**	**0**	**0.0**	**21:58**									
	Philadelphia	**NHL**	**64**	**4**	**20**	**24**	**16**	**0**	**0**	**2**	**72**	**5.6**	**2**	**0**	**0.0**	**21:17**	**6**	**0**	**3**	**3**	**4**	**0**	**0**	**0**	**22:15**

			Regular Season														Playoffs								
Season	Club	League	GP	G	A	Pts	PIM	PP	SH	GW	S	%	+/-	TF	F%	Min	GP	G	A	Pts	PIM	PP	SH	GW	Min
2009-10	**Philadelphia**	**NHL**	**80**	**6**	**29**	**35**	**16**	**2**	**0**	**1**	**137**	**4.4**	**19**	**0**	**0.0**	**23:23**	**23**	**1**	**12**	**13**	**8**	**0**	**0**	**0**	**25:54**
2010-11	**Philadelphia**	**NHL**	**82**	**1**	**39**	**40**	**23**	**0**	**0**	**0**	**117**	**0.9**	**30**	**0**	**0.0**	**21:59**	**11**	**0**	**4**	**4**	**2**	**0**	**0**	**0**	**23:24**
	NHL Totals		**389**	**28**	**136**	**164**	**131**	**14**	**0**	**6**	**524**	**5.3**		**2**	**50.0**	**20:21**	**73**	**3**	**26**	**29**	**22**	**1**	**0**	**1**	**20:09**

USHL First All-Star Team (2003) • USHL Defenseman of the Year (2003) • WCHA All-Rookie Team (2004) • WCHA First All-Star Team (2005, 2006) • NCAA West First All-American Team (2005, 2006) • NCAA Championship All-Tournament Team (2005) • WCHA Player of the Year (2006) • Hobey Baker Memorial Award (Top U.S. Collegiate Player) (2006) • NHL All-Rookie Team (2007)

Traded to **Tampa Bay** by **San Jose** with Ty Wishart, San Jose's 1st round choice (later traded to Ottawa, later traded to NY Islanders, later traded to Columbus, later traded to Anahaim – Anaheim selected Kyle Palmieri) in 2009 Entry Draft and San Jose's 4th round choice (James Mullin) in 2010 Entry Draft for Dan Boyle and Brad Lukowich, July 4, 2008. Traded to **Philadelphia** by **Tampa Bay** with San Jose's 3rd round choice (previously acquired, Philadelphia selected Simon Bertilsson) in 2009 Entry Draft for Steve Eminger, Steve Downie and Tampa Bay's 4th round choice (previously acquired, Tampa Bay selected Alex Hutchings) in 2009 Entry Draft, November 7, 2008.

CARLSON, John

(KAHRL-suhn, JAWN) **WSH**

Defense. Shoots right. 6'3", 208 lbs. Born, Natick, MA, January 10, 1990. Washington's 2nd choice, 27th overall, in 2008 Entry Draft.

Season	Club	League	GP	G	A	Pts	PIM	PP	SH	GW	S	%	+/-	TF	F%	Min	GP	G	A	Pts	PIM	PP	SH	GW	Min
2005-06	N.J. Rockets	AtJHL	38	2	10	12	42	....	....	....	....	....	....	....	....	....	....	....	....	....	....	....	....	....	....
2006-07	N.J. Rockets	AtJHL	44	12	38	50	96	....	....	....	....	....	....	....	....	....	....	....	....	....	....	....	....	....	....
	Indiana Ice	USHL	2	0	0	0	6	....	....	....	....	....	....	....	....	....	....	....	....	....	....	....	....	....	....
2007-08	Indiana Ice	USHL	59	12	31	43	72	....	....	....	....	....	....	....	....	....	4	1	0	1	0	....	....	....	....
2008-09	London Knights	OHL	59	16	60	76	65	....	....	....	....	....	....	....	....	....	14	7	15	22	16	....	....	....	....
	Hershey Bears	AHL	....	....	....	....	....	....	....	....	....	....	....	....	....	....	16	2	1	3	0	....	....	....	....
2009-10	**Washington**	**NHL**	**22**	**1**	**5**	**6**	**8**	**0**	**0**	**0**	**21**	**4.8**	**11**	**0**	**0.0**	**15:15**	**7**	**1**	**3**	**4**	**0**	**0**	**0**	**0**	**20:14**
	Hershey Bears	AHL	48	4	35	39	26	....	....	....	....	....	....	....	....	....	13	2	4	6	8	....	....	....	....
2010-11	**Washington**	**NHL**	**82**	**7**	**30**	**37**	**44**	**1**	**0**	**3**	**144**	**4.9**	**21**	**0**	**0.0**	**22:39**	**9**	**2**	**1**	**3**	**4**	**0**	**0**	**0**	**24:23**
	NHL Totals		**104**	**8**	**35**	**43**	**52**	**1**	**0**	**3**	**165**	**4.8**		**0**	**0.0**	**21:05**	**16**	**3**	**4**	**7**	**4**	**0**	**0**	**0**	**22:35**

USHL All-Rookie Team (2008) • USHL Second All-Star Team (2008) • OHL Second All-Star Team (2009) • Canadian Major Junior All-Rookie Team (2009) • AHL All-Rookie Team (2010) • NHL All-Rookie Team (2011)

CARON, Jordan

(kuh-RAWN, JOHR-dihn) **BOS**

Right wing. Shoots left. 6'2", 202 lbs. Born, Sayabec, Que., November 2, 1990. Boston's 1st choice, 25th overall, in 2009 Entry Draft.

Season	Club	League	GP	G	A	Pts	PIM	PP	SH	GW	S	%	+/-	TF	F%	Min	GP	G	A	Pts	PIM	PP	SH	GW	Min
2005-06	Notre Dame	SMHL	35	8	16	24	32	....	....	....	....	....	....	....	....	....	....	....	....	....	....	....	....	....	....
2006-07	Rimouski Oceanic	QMJHL	59	18	22	40	41	....	....	....	....	....	....	....	....	....	....	....	....	....	....	....	....	....	....
2007-08	Rimouski Oceanic	QMJHL	46	20	23	43	42	....	....	....	....	....	....	....	....	....	9	3	1	4	18	....	....	....	....
2008-09	Rimouski Oceanic	QMJHL	56	36	31	67	66	....	....	....	....	....	....	....	....	....	13	6	5	11	16	....	....	....	....
2009-10	Rimouski Oceanic	QMJHL	20	9	11	20	8	....	....	....	....	....	....	....	....	....	....	....	....	....	....	....	....	....	....
	Rouyn-Noranda	QMJHL	23	17	16	33	16	....	....	....	....	....	....	....	....	....	11	7	11	18	15	....	....	....	....
2010-11	**Boston**	**NHL**	**23**	**3**	**4**	**7**	**6**	**0**	**0**	**1**	**27**	**11.1**	**3**	**7**	**14.3**	**12:40**	....	....	....	....	....	....	....	....	....
	Providence Bruins	AHL	47	12	16	28	16	....	....	....	....	....	....	....	....	....	....	....	....	....	....	....	....	....	....
	NHL Totals		**23**	**3**	**4**	**7**	**6**	**0**	**0**	**1**	**27**	**11.1**		**7**	**14.3**	**12:40**	....	....	....	....	....	....	....	....	....

CARSON, Brett

(KAR-suhn, BREHT) **CGY**

Defense. Shoots right. 6'4", 220 lbs. Born, Regina, Sask., November 29, 1985. Carolina's 4th choice, 109th overall, in 2004 Entry Draft.

Season	Club	League	GP	G	A	Pts	PIM	PP	SH	GW	S	%	+/-	TF	F%	Min	GP	G	A	Pts	PIM	PP	SH	GW	Min
99-2000	Pipestone Valley	SSMHL	8	0	0	0	0	....	....	....	....	....	....	....	....	....	....	....	....	....	....	....	....	....	....
2000-01	Pipestone Valley	SSMHL	31	5	17	22	20	....	....	....	....	....	....	....	....	....	....	....	....	....	....	....	....	....	....
2001-02	Yorkton Terriers	SMHL	41	16	37	53	32	....	....	....	....	....	....	....	....	....	....	....	....	....	....	....	....	....	....
	Moose Jaw	WHL	6	0	0	0	0	....	....	....	....	....	....	....	....	....	12	2	0	2	0	....	....	....	....
2002-03	Moose Jaw	WHL	28	1	4	5	28	....	....	....	....	....	....	....	....	....	....	....	....	....	....	....	....	....	....
	Calgary Hitmen	WHL	30	3	6	9	4	....	....	....	....	....	....	....	....	....	5	2	1	3	0	....	....	....	....
2003-04	Calgary Hitmen	WHL	71	5	27	32	49	....	....	....	....	....	....	....	....	....	7	0	0	0	6	....	....	....	....
2004-05	Calgary Hitmen	WHL	61	8	16	24	61	....	....	....	....	....	....	....	....	....	8	2	2	4	8	....	....	....	....
2005-06	Calgary Hitmen	WHL	72	11	29	40	62	....	....	....	....	....	....	....	....	....	13	1	6	7	20	....	....	....	....
2006-07	Albany River Rats	AHL	63	2	16	18	26	....	....	....	....	....	....	....	....	....	5	0	2	2	0	....	....	....	....
	Florida Everblades	ECHL	3	1	1	2	0	....	....	....	....	....	....	....	....	....	....	....	....	....	....	....	....	....	....
2007-08	Albany River Rats	AHL	77	2	22	24	32	....	....	....	....	....	....	....	....	....	7	1	3	4	11	....	....	....	....
2008-09	**Carolina**	**NHL**	**5**	**0**	**0**	**0**	**4**	**0**	**0**	**0**	**2**	**0.0**	**–3**	**0**	**0.0**	**15:44**	....	....	....	....	....	....	....	....	....
	Albany River Rats	AHL	69	6	29	35	34	....	....	....	....	....	....	....	....	....	....	....	....	....	....	....	....	....	....
2009-10	**Carolina**	**NHL**	**54**	**2**	**10**	**12**	**12**	**0**	**0**	**0**	**42**	**4.8**	**5**	**0**	**0.0**	**17:22**	....	....	....	....	....	....	....	....	....
	Albany River Rats	AHL	14	3	8	11	0	....	....	....	....	....	....	....	....	....	....	....	....	....	....	....	....	....	....
2010-11	**Carolina**	**NHL**	**13**	**0**	**0**	**0**	**4**	**0**	**0**	**0**	**8**	**0.0**	**7**	**0**	**0.0**	**10:50**	....	....	....	....	....	....	....	....	....
	Charlotte	AHL	38	4	16	20	14	....	....	....	....	....	....	....	....	....	....	....	....	....	....	....	....	....	....
	Calgary	**NHL**	**6**	**0**	**0**	**0**	**0**	**0**	**0**	**0**	**4**	**0.0**	**2**	**0**	**0.0**	**12:46**	....	....	....	....	....	....	....	....	....
	NHL Totals		**78**	**2**	**10**	**12**	**20**	**0**	**0**	**0**	**56**	**3.6**		**0**	**0.0**	**15:49**	....	....	....	....	....	....	....	....	....

WHL East First All-Star Team (2006)

Claimed on waivers by **Calgary** from **Carolina**, February 28, 2011.

CARTER, Jeff

(KAHR-tuhr, JEHF) **CBJ**

Center. Shoots right. 6'3", 200 lbs. Born, London, Ont., January 1, 1985. Philadelphia's 1st choice, 11th overall, in 2003 Entry Draft.

Season	Club	League	GP	G	A	Pts	PIM	PP	SH	GW	S	%	+/-	TF	F%	Min	GP	G	A	Pts	PIM	PP	SH	GW	Min
2000-01	Strathroy Rockets	ON-Jr.B	49	27	20	47	10	....	....	....	....	....	....	....	....	....	....	....	....	....	....	....	....	....	....
2001-02	Sault Ste. Marie	OHL	63	18	17	35	12	....	....	....	....	....	....	....	....	....	4	0	0	0	2	....	....	....	....
2002-03	Sault Ste. Marie	OHL	61	35	36	71	55	....	....	....	....	....	....	....	....	....	4	0	2	2	2	....	....	....	....
2003-04	Sault Ste. Marie	OHL	57	36	30	66	26	....	....	....	....	....	....	....	....	....	....	....	....	....	....	....	....	....	....
	Philadelphia	AHL	....	....	....	....	....	....	....	....	....	....	....	....	....	....	12	4	1	5	0	....	....	....	....
2004-05	Sault Ste. Marie	OHL	55	34	40	74	40	....	....	....	....	....	....	....	....	....	7	5	5	10	6	....	....	....	....
	Philadelphia	AHL	3	0	1	1	4	....	....	....	....	....	....	....	....	....	21	12	11	23	12	....	....	....	....
2005-06	**Philadelphia**	**NHL**	**81**	**23**	**19**	**42**	**40**	**6**	**2**	**7**	**189**	**12.2**	**10**	**683**	**48.2**	**12:04**	**6**	**0**	**0**	**0**	**10**	**0**	**0**	**0**	**13:04**
2006-07	**Philadelphia**	**NHL**	**62**	**14**	**23**	**37**	**48**	**3**	**2**	**1**	**215**	**6.5**	**–17**	**1062**	**45.4**	**19:00**	....	....	....	....	....	....	....	....	....
2007-08	**Philadelphia**	**NHL**	**82**	**29**	**24**	**53**	**55**	**7**	**2**	**5**	**260**	**11.2**	**6**	**1378**	**47.7**	**18:51**	**17**	**6**	**5**	**11**	**12**	**3**	**0**	**1**	**20:08**
2008-09	**Philadelphia**	**NHL**	**82**	**46**	**38**	**84**	**68**	**13**	**4**	***12**	**342**	**13.5**	**23**	**1725**	**48.3**	**20:57**	**6**	**1**	**0**	**1**	**8**	**0**	**0**	**0**	**20:21**
2009-10	**Philadelphia**	**NHL**	**74**	**33**	**28**	**61**	**38**	**11**	**2**	**6**	**319**	**10.3**	**2**	**1314**	**52.4**	**19:18**	**12**	**5**	**2**	**7**	**2**	**2**	**0**	**1**	**17:57**
2010-11	**Philadelphia**	**NHL**	**80**	**36**	**30**	**66**	**39**	**8**	**0**	**7**	**335**	**10.7**	**27**	**605**	**54.7**	**18:15**	**6**	**1**	**1**	**2**	**2**	**1**	**0**	**0**	**15:15**
	NHL Totals		**461**	**181**	**162**	**343**	**288**	**48**	**12**	**38**	**1660**	**10.9**		**6767**	**49.1**	**18:01**	**47**	**13**	**8**	**21**	**34**	**6**	**0**	**2**	**18:04**

OHL Second All-Star Team (2004) • OHL First All-Star Team (2005) • Canadian Major Junior Sportsman of the Year (2005) • Canadian Major Junior First All-Star Team (2005)

Played in NHL All-Star Game (2009)

Traded to **Columbus** by **Philadelphia** for Jakub Voracek and Columbus's 1st (Sean Couturier) and 3rd (Nick Cousins) round choices in 2011 Entry Draft, June 23, 2011.

CARTER, Ryan

(KAHR-tuhr, RIGH-uhn) **FLA**

Center. Shoots left. 6'2", 200 lbs. Born, White Bear Lake, MN, August 3, 1983.

Season	Club	League	GP	G	A	Pts	PIM	PP	SH	GW	S	%	+/-	TF	F%	Min	GP	G	A	Pts	PIM	PP	SH	GW	Min
2002-03	Green Bay	USHL	55	19	17	36	94	....	....	....	....	....	....	....	....	....	....	....	....	....	....	....	....	....	....
2003-04	Green Bay	USHL	59	22	23	45	131	....	....	....	....	....	....	....	....	....	....	....	....	....	....	....	....	....	....
2004-05	Minnesota State	WCHA	37	15	8	23	44	....	....	....	....	....	....	....	....	....	....	....	....	....	....	....	....	....	....
2005-06	Minnesota State	WCHA	39	19	16	35	71	....	....	....	....	....	....	....	....	....	....	....	....	....	....	....	....	....	....
2006-07	Portland Pirates	AHL	76	16	20	36	85	....	....	....	....	....	....	....	....	....	....	....	....	....	....	....	....	....	....
	♦ Anaheim	**NHL**	....	....	....	....	....	....	....	....	....	....	....	....	....	....	**4**	**0**	**0**	**0**	**0**	**0**	**0**	**0**	**3:12**
2007-08	**Anaheim**	**NHL**	**34**	**4**	**4**	**8**	**36**	**0**	**0**	**1**	**56**	**7.1**	**–2**	**299**	**61.5**	**10:29**	**6**	**0**	**0**	**0**	**6**	**0**	**0**	**0**	**11:03**
	Portland Pirates	AHL	13	3	2	5	38	....	....	....	....	....	....	....	....	....	....	....	....	....	....	....	....	....	....
2008-09	**Anaheim**	**NHL**	**48**	**3**	**6**	**9**	**52**	**0**	**0**	**1**	**40**	**7.5**	**3**	**304**	**48.0**	**9:06**	**10**	**2**	**3**	**5**	**0**	**1**	**0**	**0**	**12:14**
2009-10	**Anaheim**	**NHL**	**38**	**4**	**5**	**9**	**31**	**0**	**0**	**1**	**38**	**10.5**	**0**	**221**	**52.5**	**9:51**	....	....	....	....	....	....	....	....	....
2010-11	**Anaheim**	**NHL**	**18**	**1**	**2**	**3**	**22**	**0**	**0**	**0**	**23**	**4.3**	**–4**	**171**	**50.3**	**10:44**	....	....	....	....	....	....	....	....	....
	Carolina	**NHL**	**32**	**0**	**3**	**3**	**22**	**0**	**0**	**0**	**26**	**0.0**	**0**	**208**	**50.5**	**8:18**	....	....	....	....	....	....	....	....	....
	Florida	**NHL**	**12**	**2**	**1**	**3**	**22**	**0**	**0**	**0**	**14**	**14.3**	**3**	**99**	**51.5**	**13:30**	....	....	....	....	....	....	....	....	....
	NHL Totals		**182**	**14**	**21**	**35**	**185**	**0**	**0**	**3**	**197**	**7.1**		**1302**	**52.8**	**9:50**	**20**	**2**	**3**	**5**	**6**	**1**	**0**	**0**	**10:04**

Signed as a free agent by **Anaheim**, July 12, 2006. • Missed majority of 2009-10 due to foot injury in pre-game skate at Columbus, November 13, 2009. Traded to **Carolina** by **Anaheim** for Stefan Chaput and Matt Kennedy, November 23, 2010. Traded to **Florida** by **Carolina** with Carolina's 5th round choice (later traded to Atlanta, later traded to San Jose – San Jose selected Sean Kuraly) in 2011 Entry Draft for Cory Stillman, February 24, 2011.

CHARA, Zdeno

(CHAH-rah, z'DEHN-oh) **BOS**

Defense. Shoots left. 6'9", 255 lbs. Born, Trencin, Czechoslovakia, March 18, 1977. NY Islanders' 3rd choice, 56th overall, in 1996 Entry Draft.

Season	Club	League	GP	G	A	Pts	PIM	PP	SH	GW	S	%	+/-	TF	F%	Min	GP	G	A	Pts	PIM	PP	SH	GW	Min
			Regular Season														Playoffs								
1994-95	Dukla Trencin U18	Svk-U18	30	22	22	44	113	....	....	....	....	....	....	....	....	....	....	....	....	....	....	....	....	....	....
	Dukla Trencin Jr.	Slovak-Jr.	2	0	0	0	0	....	....	....	....	....	....	....	....	....	....	....	....	....	....	....	....	....	....
1995-96	Dukla Trencin Jr.	Slovak-Jr.	22	1	13	14	80	....	....	....	....	....	....	....	....	....	....	....	....	....	....	....	....	....	....
	HK VTJ Piestany	Slovak-2	10	1	3	4	10	....	....	....	....	....	....	....	....	....	....	....	....	....	....	....	....	....	....
	Sparta Jr.	CzRep-Jr.	15	1	2	3	42	....	....	....	....	....	....	....	....	....	....	....	....	....	....	....	....	....	....
	HC Sparta Praha	CzRep	1	0	0	0	0	....	....	....	....	....	....	....	....	....	....	....	....	....	....	....	....	....	....
1996-97	Prince George	WHL	49	3	19	22	120	....	....	....	....	....	....	....	....	....	15	1	7	8	45	....	....	....	....
1997-98	**NY Islanders**	**NHL**	**25**	**0**	**1**	**1**	**50**	**0**	**0**	**0**	**10**	**0.0**	**1**	....	....	....	....	....	....	....	....	....	....	....	....
	Kentucky	AHL	48	4	9	13	125	....	....	....	....	....	....	....	....	....	1	0	0	0	4	....	....	....	....
1998-99	**NY Islanders**	**NHL**	**59**	**2**	**6**	**8**	**83**	**0**	**1**	**0**	**56**	**3.6**	**−8**	**0**	**0.0**	**18:54**	....	....	....	....	....	....	....	....	....
	Lowell	AHL	23	2	2	4	47	....	....	....	....	....	....	....	....	....	....	....	....	....	....	....	....	....	....
99-2000	**NY Islanders**	**NHL**	**65**	**2**	**9**	**11**	**57**	**0**	**0**	**1**	**47**	**4.3**	**−27**	**0**	**0.0**	**22:52**	....	....	....	....	....	....	....	....	....
2000-01	**NY Islanders**	**NHL**	**82**	**2**	**7**	**9**	**157**	**0**	**1**	**0**	**83**	**2.4**	**−27**	**0**	**0.0**	**22:20**	....	....	....	....	....	....	....	....	....
2001-02	Dukla Trencin	Slovakia	8	2	2	4	32	....	....	....	....	....	....	....	....	....	....	....	....	....	....	....	....	....	....
	Ottawa	**NHL**	**75**	**10**	**13**	**23**	**156**	**4**	**1**	**2**	**105**	**9.5**	**30**	**0**	**0.0**	**22:16**	**10**	**0**	**1**	**1**	**12**	**0**	**0**	**0**	**26:07**
2002-03	**Ottawa**	**NHL**	**74**	**9**	**30**	**39**	**116**	**3**	**0**	**2**	**168**	**5.4**	**29**	**0**	**0.0**	**24:57**	**18**	**1**	**6**	**7**	**14**	**0**	**0**	**0**	**25:07**
2003-04	**Ottawa**	**NHL**	**79**	**16**	**25**	**41**	**147**	**7**	**0**	**3**	**185**	**8.6**	**33**	**0**	**0.0**	**24:38**	**7**	**1**	**1**	**2**	**8**	**0**	**0**	**0**	**24:38**
2004-05	Farjestad	Sweden	33	10	15	25	132	....	....	....	....	....	....	....	....	....	13	3	5	8	82	....	....	....	....
2005-06	**Ottawa**	**NHL**	**71**	**16**	**27**	**43**	**135**	**10**	**1**	**3**	**212**	**7.5**	**17**	**24**	**41.7**	**27:11**	**10**	**1**	**3**	**4**	**23**	**1**	**0**	**0**	**27:32**
	Slovakia	Olympics	6	1	1	2	2	....	....	....	....	....	....	....	....	....	....	....	....	....	....	....	....	....	....
2006-07	**Boston**	**NHL**	**80**	**11**	**32**	**43**	**100**	**9**	**0**	**3**	**204**	**5.4**	**−21**	**1**	**0.0**	**27:58**	....	....	....	....	....	....	....	....	....
2007-08	**Boston**	**NHL**	**77**	**17**	**34**	**51**	**114**	**9**	**1**	**0**	**207**	**8.2**	**14**	**0**	**0.0**	**26:50**	**7**	**1**	**1**	**2**	**12**	**1**	**0**	**0**	**25:52**
2008-09	**Boston**	**NHL**	**80**	**19**	**31**	**50**	**95**	**11**	**0**	**3**	**216**	**8.8**	**23**	**4**	**25.0**	**26:04**	**11**	**1**	**3**	**4**	**12**	**1**	**0**	**1**	**25:11**
2009-10	**Boston**	**NHL**	**80**	**7**	**37**	**44**	**87**	**4**	**0**	**1**	**242**	**2.9**	**19**	**2**	**50.0**	**25:22**	**13**	**2**	**5**	**7**	**29**	**0**	**0**	**1**	**28:08**
	Slovakia	Olympics	7	0	3	3	6	....	....	....	....	....	....	....	....	....	....	....	....	....	....	....	....	....	....
2010-11♦	**Boston**	**NHL**	**81**	**14**	**30**	**44**	**88**	**8**	**1**	**2**	**264**	**5.3**	***33**	**0**	**0.0**	**25:26**	**24**	**2**	**7**	**9**	**34**	**1**	**0**	**0**	**27:39**
	NHL Totals		**928**	**125**	**282**	**407**	**1385**	**65**	**6**	**20**	**1999**	**6.3**		**31**	**38.7**	**24:42**	**100**	**9**	**27**	**36**	**144**	**4**	**0**	**2**	**26:29**

AHL All-Rookie Team (1998) • NHL First All-Star Team (2004, 2009) • NHL Second All-Star Team (2006, 2008, 2011) • James Norris Memorial Trophy (2009) • Mark Messier NHL Leadership Award (2011)

Played in NHL All-Star Game (2003, 2007, 2008, 2009, 2011)

Traded to **Ottawa** by **NY Islanders** with Bill Muckalt and NY Islanders' 1st round choice (Jason Spezza) in 2001 Entry Draft for Alexei Yashin, June 23, 2001. Signed as a free agent by **Farjestad** (Sweden), September 24, 2004. Signed as a free agent by **Boston**, July 1, 2006.

CHEECHOO, Jonathan

(CHEE-choo, JAWN-ah-thuhn) **ST.L.**

Right wing. Shoots right. 6'1", 200 lbs. Born, Moose Factory, Ont., July 15, 1980. San Jose's 2nd choice, 29th overall, in 1998 Entry Draft.

1996-97	Kitchener	ON-Jr.B	43	35	41	76	33	....	....	....	....	....	....	....	....	....	....	....	....	....	....	....	....	....	....
1997-98	Belleville Bulls	OHL	64	31	45	76	62	....	....	....	....	....	....	....	....	....	10	4	2	6	10	....	....	....	....
1998-99	Belleville Bulls	OHL	63	35	47	82	74	....	....	....	....	....	....	....	....	....	21	15	15	30	27	....	....	....	....
99-2000	Belleville Bulls	OHL	66	45	46	91	102	....	....	....	....	....	....	....	....	....	16	5	12	17	16	....	....	....	....
2000-01	Kentucky	AHL	75	32	34	66	63	....	....	....	....	....	....	....	....	....	3	0	0	0	0	....	....	....	....
2001-02	Cleveland Barons	AHL	53	21	25	46	54	....	....	....	....	....	....	....	....	....	....	....	....	....	....	....	....	....	....
2002-03	**San Jose**	**NHL**	**66**	**9**	**7**	**16**	**39**	**0**	**0**	**3**	**94**	**9.6**	**−5**	**8**	**37.5**	**10:43**	....	....	....	....	....	....	....	....	....
	Cleveland Barons	AHL	9	3	4	7	16	....	....	....	....	....	....	....	....	....	....	....	....	....	....	....	....	....	....
2003-04	**San Jose**	**NHL**	**81**	**28**	**19**	**47**	**33**	**8**	**0**	**9**	**175**	**16.0**	**5**	**7**	**14.3**	**16:12**	**17**	**4**	**6**	**10**	**10**	**1**	**0**	**0**	**17:37**
2004-05	HV 71 Jonkoping	Sweden	20	5	0	5	10	....	....	....	....	....	....	....	....	....	....	....	....	....	....	....	....	....	....
2005-06	**San Jose**	**NHL**	**82**	***56**	**37**	**93**	**58**	**24**	**2**	***11**	**317**	**17.7**	**23**	**20**	**20.0**	**19:57**	**11**	**4**	**5**	**9**	**8**	**1**	**0**	**1**	**24:00**
2006-07	**San Jose**	**NHL**	**76**	**37**	**32**	**69**	**69**	**15**	**0**	**5**	**250**	**14.8**	**11**	**32**	**31.3**	**17:34**	**11**	**3**	**3**	**6**	**6**	**1**	**0**	**1**	**16:25**
2007-08	**San Jose**	**NHL**	**69**	**23**	**14**	**37**	**46**	**10**	**0**	**4**	**220**	**10.5**	**11**	**20**	**20.0**	**16:36**	**13**	**4**	**4**	**8**	**4**	**0**	**0**	**1**	**18:21**
2008-09	**San Jose**	**NHL**	**66**	**12**	**17**	**29**	**59**	**5**	**1**	**4**	**152**	**7.9**	**−3**	**4**	**25.0**	**15:19**	**6**	**1**	**1**	**2**	**4**	**0**	**0**	**0**	**10:10**
2009-10	**Ottawa**	**NHL**	**61**	**5**	**9**	**14**	**20**	**0**	**0**	**0**	**117**	**4.3**	**−13**	**10**	**40.0**	**11:57**	**1**	**0**	**0**	**0**	**0**	**0**	**0**	**0**	**7:13**
	Binghamton	AHL	25	8	6	14	37	....	....	....	....	....	....	....	....	....	....	....	....	....	....	....	....	....	....
2010-11	Worcester Sharks	AHL	55	18	29	47	14	....	....	....	....	....	....	....	....	....	....	....	....	....	....	....	....	....	....
	NHL Totals		**501**	**170**	**135**	**305**	**324**	**62**	**3**	**36**	**1325**	**12.8**		**101**	**26.7**	**15:43**	**59**	**16**	**19**	**35**	**32**	**3**	**0**	**3**	**17:49**

OHL All-Rookie Team (1998) • AHL All-Rookie Team (2001) • Maurice "Rocket" Richard Trophy (2006)

Played in NHL All-Star Game (2007)

Signed as a free agent by **Jonkoping** (Sweden), December 21, 2004. Traded to **Ottawa** by **San Jose** with Milan Michalek and San Jose's 2nd round choice (later traded to NY Islanders, later traded to Chicago - Chicago selected Kent Simpson) in 2010 Entry Draft for Dany Heatley and Ottawa's 5th round choice (Isaac MacLeod) in 2010 Entry Draft, September 12, 2009. Signed to a PTO (professional tryout) contract by **Worcester** (AHL), October 6, 2010. Signed as a free agent by **St. Louis**, July 13, 2011.

CHIMERA, Jason

(shih-MAIR-uh, JAY-suhn) **WSH**

Left wing. Shoots left. 6'2", 216 lbs. Born, Edmonton, Alta., May 2, 1979. Edmonton's 5th choice, 121st overall, in 1997 Entry Draft.

1994-95	Edmonton Pats	AMHL	33	27	31	58	42	....	....	....	....	....	....	....	....	....	....	....	....	....	....	....	....	....	....
1995-96	Edmonton Pats	AMHL	34	23	24	47	44	....	....	....	....	....	....	....	....	....	....	....	....	....	....	....	....	....	....
1996-97	Medicine Hat	WHL	71	16	23	39	54	....	....	....	....	....	....	....	....	....	4	0	1	1	4	....	....	....	....
1997-98	Medicine Hat	WHL	72	34	32	66	93	....	....	....	....	....	....	....	....	....	....	....	....	....	....	....	....	....	....
	Hamilton	AHL	4	0	0	0	8	....	....	....	....	....	....	....	....	....	....	....	....	....	....	....	....	....	....
1998-99	Medicine Hat	WHL	37	18	22	40	84	....	....	....	....	....	....	....	....	....	....	....	....	....	....	....	....	....	....
	Brandon	WHL	21	14	12	26	32	....	....	....	....	....	....	....	....	....	5	4	1	5	8	....	....	....	....
99-2000	Hamilton	AHL	78	15	13	28	77	....	....	....	....	....	....	....	....	....	10	0	2	2	12	....	....	....	....
2000-01	**Edmonton**	**NHL**	**1**	**0**	**0**	**0**	**0**	**0**	**0**	**0**	**0**	**0.0**	**0**	**0**	**0.0**	**6:58**	....	....	....	....	....	....	....	....	....
	Hamilton	AHL	78	29	25	54	93	....	....	....	....	....	....	....	....	....	....	....	....	....	....	....	....	....	....
2001-02	**Edmonton**	**NHL**	**3**	**1**	**0**	**1**	**0**	**0**	**0**	**0**	**3**	**33.3**	**−3**	**0**	**0.0**	**12:44**	....	....	....	....	....	....	....	....	....
	Hamilton	AHL	77	26	51	77	158	....	....	....	....	....	....	....	....	....	15	4	6	10	10	....	....	....	....
2002-03	**Edmonton**	**NHL**	**66**	**14**	**9**	**23**	**36**	**0**	**1**	**4**	**90**	**15.6**	**−2**	**11**	**54.6**	**10:46**	**2**	**0**	**2**	**2**	**0**	**0**	**0**	**0**	**10:55**
2003-04	**Edmonton**	**NHL**	**60**	**4**	**8**	**12**	**57**	**0**	**0**	**1**	**79**	**5.1**	**−1**	**22**	**31.8**	**10:07**	....	....	....	....	....	....	....	....	....
2004-05	AS Varese Hockey	Italy	15	7	3	10	34	....	....	....	....	....	....	....	....	....	5	2	1	3	31	....	....	....	....
2005-06	**Columbus**	**NHL**	**80**	**17**	**13**	**30**	**95**	**1**	**1**	**5**	**127**	**13.4**	**−10**	**16**	**50.0**	**12:41**	....	....	....	....	....	....	....	....	....
2006-07	**Columbus**	**NHL**	**82**	**15**	**21**	**36**	**91**	**2**	**2**	**2**	**151**	**9.9**	**2**	**38**	**36.8**	**15:22**	....	....	....	....	....	....	....	....	....
2007-08	**Columbus**	**NHL**	**81**	**14**	**17**	**31**	**98**	**1**	**1**	**3**	**198**	**7.1**	**−5**	**35**	**45.7**	**17:30**	....	....	....	....	....	....	....	....	....
2008-09	**Columbus**	**NHL**	**49**	**8**	**14**	**22**	**41**	**1**	**0**	**1**	**115**	**7.0**	**8**	**42**	**42.9**	**16:15**	**4**	**0**	**1**	**1**	**2**	**0**	**0**	**0**	**13:21**
2009-10	**Columbus**	**NHL**	**39**	**8**	**9**	**17**	**47**	**1**	**0**	**1**	**92**	**8.7**	**−7**	**23**	**65.2**	**14:47**	....	....	....	....	....	....	....	....	....
	Washington	**NHL**	**39**	**7**	**10**	**17**	**51**	**0**	**0**	**0**	**68**	**10.3**	**6**	**17**	**41.2**	**12:36**	**7**	**1**	**2**	**3**	**2**	**0**	**0**	**1**	**11:46**
2010-11	**Washington**	**NHL**	**81**	**10**	**16**	**26**	**64**	**2**	**0**	**1**	**162**	**6.2**	**−10**	**39**	**51.3**	**13:15**	**9**	**2**	**2**	**4**	**2**	**0**	**0**	**2**	**12:53**
	NHL Totals		**581**	**98**	**117**	**215**	**580**	**8**	**5**	**18**	**1085**	**9.0**		**243**	**45.7**	**13:45**	**22**	**3**	**7**	**10**	**6**	**0**	**0**	**3**	**12:26**

AHL First All-Star Team (2002)

Traded to **Phoenix** by **Edmonton** with Edmonton's 3rd round choice (later traded to Carolina, later traded to NY Rangers – NY Rangers selected Billy Ryan) in 2004 Entry Draft for New Jersey's 2nd round choice (previously acquired, Edmonton selected Geoff Paukovich) in 2004 Entry Draft and Buffalo's 4th round choice (previously acquired, Edmonton selected Liam Reddox) in 2004 Entry Draft, June 26, 2004. Signed as a free agent by **Varese** (Italy), December 15, 2004. Traded to **Columbus** by **Phoenix** with Cale Hulse and Mike Rupp for Geoff Sanderson and Tim Jackman, October 8, 2005. Traded to **Washington** by **Columbus** for Chris Clark and Milan Jurcina, December 28, 2009.

CHIPCHURA, Kyle

(chip-CHUHR-a, KIGHL) **PHX**

Center. Shoots left. 6'2", 206 lbs. Born, Westlock, Alta., February 19, 1986. Montreal's 1st choice, 18th overall, in 2004 Entry Draft.

2000-01	Spruce Grove	AMBHL	36	26	34	60	48	....	....	....	....	....	....	....	....	....	....	....	....	....	....	....	....	....	....
2001-02	Ft. Saskatchewan	AMHL	33	15	36	51	78	....	....	....	....	....	....	....	....	....	17	16	20	36	....	....	....	....	....
	Prince Albert	WHL	2	0	0	0	0	....	....	....	....	....	....	....	....	....	....	....	....	....	....	....	....	....	....
2002-03	Prince Albert	WHL	63	9	21	30	89	....	....	....	....	....	....	....	....	....	....	....	....	....	....	....	....	....	....
2003-04	Prince Albert	WHL	64	15	33	48	118	....	....	....	....	....	....	....	....	....	6	2	4	6	12	....	....	....	....
2004-05	Prince Albert	WHL	28	14	18	32	32	....	....	....	....	....	....	....	....	....	14	4	7	11	25	....	....	....	....
2005-06	Prince Albert	WHL	59	21	34	55	81	....	....	....	....	....	....	....	....	....	....	....	....	....	....	....	....	....	....
	Hamilton	AHL	8	1	2	3	6	....	....	....	....	....	....	....	....	....	....	....	....	....	....	....	....	....	....
2006-07	Hamilton	AHL	80	12	27	39	56	....	....	....	....	....	....	....	....	....	22	6	7	13	20	....	....	....	....
2007-08	**Montreal**	**NHL**	**36**	**4**	**7**	**11**	**10**	**0**	**0**	**0**	**36**	**11.1**	**−1**	**317**	**43.9**	**11:22**	....	....	....	....	....	....	....	....	....
	Hamilton	AHL	39	10	11	21	27	....	....	....	....	....	....	....	....	....	....	....	....	....	....	....	....	....	....
2008-09	**Montreal**	**NHL**	**13**	**0**	**3**	**3**	**5**	**0**	**0**	**0**	**5**	**0.0**	**−6**	**107**	**43.9**	**10:18**	....	....	....	....	....	....	....	....	....
	Hamilton	AHL	51	14	21	35	65	....	....	....	....	....	....	....	....	....	6	3	0	3	2	....	....	....	....

Season	Club	League	GP	G	A	Pts	PIM	PP	SH	GW	S	%	+/-	TF	F%	Min	GP	G	A	Pts	PIM	PP	SH	GW	Min
			Regular Season														Playoffs								
2009-10	**Montreal**	**NHL**	**19**	**0**	**0**	**0**	**16**	**0**	**0**	**0**	**11**	**0.0**	**–10**	**106**	**53.8**	**8:38**	....	....	....	....	....	....	....	....	....
	Anaheim	**NHL**	**55**	**6**	**6**	**12**	**56**	**0**	**1**	**1**	**43**	**14.0**	**–2**	**670**	**47.9**	**12:29**	....	....	....	....	....	....	....	....	....
2010-11	**Anaheim**	**NHL**	**40**	**0**	**2**	**2**	**32**	**0**	**0**	**0**	**23**	**0.0**	**1**	**283**	**46.6**	**8:00**	....	....	....	....	....	....	....	....	....
	NHL Totals		**163**	**10**	**18**	**28**	**119**	**0**	**1**	**1**	**118**	**8.5**		**1483**	**46.9**	**10:31**	....	....	....	....	....	....	....	....	....

WHL East Second All-Star Team (2006)

Traded to **Anaheim** by **Montreal** for Anaheim's 4th round choice (Magnus Nygren) in 2011 Entry Draft, December 1, 2009. • Missed majority of 2010-11 due to concussion at San Jose, October 30, 2010, and as a healthy reserve. Signed as a free agent by **Phoenix**, July 19, 2011.

CHORNEY, Taylor

(CHOHR-nee, TAY-luhr) **EDM**

Defense. Shoots left. 6', 193 lbs. Born, Thunder Bay, Ont., April 27, 1987. Edmonton's 2nd choice, 36th overall, in 2005 Entry Draft.

Season	Club	League	GP	G	A	Pts	PIM	PP	SH	GW	S	%	+/-	TF	F%	Min	GP	G	A	Pts	PIM	PP	SH	GW	Min
2003-04	Shat.-St. Mary's	High-MN	74	12	44	56	58	....	....	....	....	....	....	....	....	....	....	....	....	....	....	....	....	....	....
2004-05	Shat.-St. Mary's	High-MN	50	4	30	34	52	....	....	....	....	....	....	....	....	....	....	....	....	....	....	....	....	....	....
2005-06	North Dakota	WCHA	44	3	15	18	54	....	....	....	....	....	....	....	....	....	....	....	....	....	....	....	....	....	....
2006-07	North Dakota	WCHA	39	8	23	31	48	....	....	....	....	....	....	....	....	....	....	....	....	....	....	....	....	....	....
2007-08	North Dakota	WCHA	43	3	21	24	24	....	....	....	....	....	....	....	....	....	....	....	....	....	....	....	....	....	....
2008-09	**Edmonton**	**NHL**	**2**	**0**	**0**	**0**	**0**	**0**	**0**	**0**	**0**	**0.0**	**–4**	**0**	**0.0**	**15:43**	....	....	....	....	....	....	....	....	....
	Springfield	AHL	68	5	16	21	22	....	....	....	....	....	....	....	....	....	....	....	....	....	....	....	....	....	....
2009-10	**Edmonton**	**NHL**	**42**	**0**	**3**	**3**	**12**	**0**	**0**	**0**	**35**	**0.0**	**–21**	**0**	**0.0**	**17:24**	....	....	....	....	....	....	....	....	....
	Springfield	AHL	32	4	9	13	14	....	....	....	....	....	....	....	....	....	....	....	....	....	....	....	....	....	....
2010-11	**Edmonton**	**NHL**	**12**	**1**	**3**	**4**	**4**	**1**	**0**	**1**	**13**	**7.7**	**–5**	**0**	**0.0**	**15:59**	....	....	....	....	....	....	....	....	....
	Oklahoma City	AHL	46	3	13	16	22	....	....	....	....	....	....	....	....	....	....	....	....	....	....	....	....	....	....
	NHL Totals		**56**	**1**	**6**	**7**	**16**	**1**	**0**	**1**	**48**	**2.1**		**0**	**0.0**	**17:02**	....	....	....	....	....	....	....	....	....

WCHA Second All-Star Team (2007) • NCAA West Second All-American Team (2007) • WCHA First All-Star Team (2008)

CHRISTENSEN, Erik

(KRIHS-tehn-suhn, AIR-ihk) **NYR**

Center. Shoots left. 6'1", 200 lbs. Born, Edmonton, Alta., December 17, 1983. Pittsburgh's 3rd choice, 69th overall, in 2002 Entry Draft.

Season	Club	League	GP	G	A	Pts	PIM	PP	SH	GW	S	%	+/-	TF	F%	Min	GP	G	A	Pts	PIM	PP	SH	GW	Min
1998-99	Leduc Oil Kings	AMBHL	36	34	42	76	70	....	....	....	....	....	....	....	....	....	....	....	....	....	....	....	....	....	....
99-2000	Kamloops Blazers	WHL	66	9	5	14	39	....	....	....	....	....	....	....	....	....	4	0	0	0	2	....	....	....	....
2000-01	Kamloops Blazers	WHL	72	21	23	44	36	....	....	....	....	....	....	....	....	....	4	1	1	2	0	....	....	....	....
2001-02	Kamloops Blazers	WHL	70	22	36	58	68	....	....	....	....	....	....	....	....	....	4	0	0	0	4	....	....	....	....
2002-03	Kamloops Blazers	WHL	67	*54	54	*108	60	....	....	....	....	....	....	....	....	....	6	1	7	8	14	....	....	....	....
2003-04	Kamloops Blazers	WHL	29	10	14	24	40	....	....	....	....	....	....	....	....	....	....	....	....	....	....	....	....	....	....
	Brandon	WHL	34	17	21	38	20	....	....	....	....	....	....	....	....	....	11	8	4	12	8	....	....	....	....
2004-05	Wilkes-Barre	AHL	77	14	13	27	33	....	....	....	....	....	....	....	....	....	11	1	6	7	4	....	....	....	....
2005-06	**Pittsburgh**	**NHL**	**33**	**6**	**7**	**13**	**34**	**2**	**0**	**0**	**85**	**7.1**	**–3**	**381**	**53.0**	**14:17**	....	....	....	....	....	....	....	....	....
	Wilkes-Barre	AHL	48	24	22	46	50	....	....	....	....	....	....	....	....	....	11	2	2	4	2	....	....	....	....
2006-07	**Pittsburgh**	**NHL**	**61**	**18**	**15**	**33**	**26**	**6**	**0**	**1**	**133**	**13.5**	**–3**	**240**	**56.3**	**11:38**	**4**	**0**	**0**	**0**	**6**	**0**	**0**	**0**	**8:15**
	Wilkes-Barre	AHL	16	12	12	24	8	....	....	....	....	....	....	....	....	....	....	....	....	....	....	....	....	....	....
2007-08	**Pittsburgh**	**NHL**	**49**	**9**	**11**	**20**	**28**	**2**	**0**	**0**	**109**	**8.3**	**–3**	**314**	**58.6**	**12:37**	....	....	....	....	....	....	....	....	....
	Atlanta	**NHL**	**10**	**2**	**2**	**4**	**2**	**0**	**0**	**0**	**23**	**8.7**	**–7**	**160**	**58.1**	**16:57**	....	....	....	....	....	....	....	....	....
2008-09	**Atlanta**	**NHL**	**47**	**5**	**14**	**19**	**14**	**1**	**0**	**0**	**90**	**5.6**	**–7**	**427**	**54.6**	**14:16**	....	....	....	....	....	....	....	....	....
	Anaheim	**NHL**	**17**	**2**	**7**	**9**	**6**	**1**	**0**	**0**	**32**	**6.3**	**–2**	**70**	**62.9**	**11:55**	**8**	**0**	**2**	**2**	**0**	**0**	**0**	**0**	**10:37**
2009-10	**Anaheim**	**NHL**	**9**	**0**	**0**	**0**	**2**	**0**	**0**	**0**	**9**	**0.0**	**–3**	**51**	**41.2**	**11:27**	....	....	....	....	....	....	....	....	....
	Manitoba Moose	AHL	6	2	0	2	0	....	....	....	....	....	....	....	....	....	....	....	....	....	....	....	....	....	....
	NY Rangers	**NHL**	**49**	**8**	**18**	**26**	**24**	**1**	**0**	**1**	**77**	**10.4**	**14**	**623**	**49.4**	**15:28**	....	....	....	....	....	....	....	....	....
2010-11	**NY Rangers**	**NHL**	**63**	**11**	**16**	**27**	**18**	**4**	**0**	**1**	**86**	**12.8**	**3**	**639**	**49.5**	**12:46**	**5**	**1**	**0**	**1**	**2**	**1**	**0**	**0**	**13:04**
	NHL Totals		**338**	**61**	**90**	**151**	**154**	**17**	**0**	**3**	**644**	**9.5**		**2905**	**52.9**	**13:20**	**17**	**1**	**2**	**3**	**8**	**1**	**0**	**0**	**10:47**

WHL West First All-Star Team (2003) • Canadian Major Junior Second All-Star Team (2003)

Traded to **Atlanta** by **Pittsburgh** with Colby Armstrong, Angelo Esposito and Pittsburgh's 1st round choice (Daultan Leveille) in 2008 Entry Draft for Marian Hossa and Pascal Dupuis, February 26, 2008. Traded to **Anaheim** by **Atlanta** for Eric O'Dell, March 4, 2009. Claimed on waivers by **NY Rangers** from **Anaheim**, December 2, 2009.

CHUCKO, Kris

(CHUH-koh, KRIHS)

Left wing. Shoots right. 6'2", 190 lbs. Born, Burnaby, B.C., March 13, 1986. Calgary's 1st choice, 24th overall, in 2004 Entry Draft.

Season	Club	League	GP	G	A	Pts	PIM	PP	SH	GW	S	%	+/-	TF	F%	Min	GP	G	A	Pts	PIM	PP	SH	GW	Min
2002-03	Salmon Arm	BCHL	59	14	19	33	80	....	....	....	....	....	....	....	....	....	11	5	3	8	12	....	....	....	....
2003-04	Salmon Arm	BCHL	53	32	55	87	161	....	....	....	....	....	....	....	....	....	14	10	9	19	36	....	....	....	....
2004-05	U. of Minnesota	WCHA	44	10	11	21	61	....	....	....	....	....	....	....	....	....	....	....	....	....	....	....	....	....	....
2005-06	U. of Minnesota	WCHA	33	4	9	13	40	....	....	....	....	....	....	....	....	....	....	....	....	....	....	....	....	....	....
2006-07	Omaha	AHL	80	14	14	28	72	....	....	....	....	....	....	....	....	....	6	0	0	0	2	....	....	....	....
2007-08	Quad City Flames	AHL	80	15	15	30	38	....	....	....	....	....	....	....	....	....	....	....	....	....	....	....	....	....	....
2008-09	**Calgary**	**NHL**	**2**	**0**	**0**	**0**	**2**	**0**	**0**	**0**	**0**	**0.0**	**0**	**1**	**0.0**	**7:02**	....	....	....	....	....	....	....	....	....
	Quad City Flames	AHL	74	28	23	51	59	....	....	....	....	....	....	....	....	....	....	....	....	....	....	....	....	....	....
2009-10	Abbotsford Heat	AHL	41	9	9	18	56	....	....	....	....	....	....	....	....	....	....	....	....	....	....	....	....	....	....
2010-11	Abbotsford Heat	AHL	2	0	0	0	2	....	....	....	....	....	....	....	....	....	....	....	....	....	....	....	....	....	....
	NHL Totals		**2**	**0**	**0**	**0**	**2**	**0**	**0**	**0**	**0**	**0.0**		**1**	**0.0**	**7:02**	....	....	....	....	....	....	....	....	....

• Missed majority of 2010-11 due to post-concussion syndrome.

CLARK, Brett

(KLAHRK, BREHT) **T.B.**

Defense. Shoots left. 6', 194 lbs. Born, Wapella, Sask., December 23, 1976. Montreal's 7th choice, 154th overall, in 1996 Entry Draft.

Season	Club	League	GP	G	A	Pts	PIM	PP	SH	GW	S	%	+/-	TF	F%	Min	GP	G	A	Pts	PIM	PP	SH	GW	Min
1994-95	Melville	SJHL	62	19	32	51	77	....	....	....	....	....	....	....	....	....	....	....	....	....	....	....	....	....	....
1995-96	U. of Maine	H-East	39	7	31	38	22	....	....	....	....	....	....	....	....	....	....	....	....	....	....	....	....	....	....
1996-97	Canada	Nat-Tm	57	6	21	27	52	....	....	....	....	....	....	....	....	....	....	....	....	....	....	....	....	....	....
1997-98	**Montreal**	**NHL**	**41**	**1**	**0**	**1**	**20**	**0**	**0**	**0**	**26**	**3.8**	**–3**	....	....	....	....	....	....	....	....	....	....	....	....
	Fredericton	AHL	20	0	6	6	6	....	....	....	....	....	....	....	....	....	4	0	1	1	17	....	....	....	....
1998-99	**Montreal**	**NHL**	**61**	**2**	**2**	**4**	**16**	**0**	**0**	**0**	**36**	**5.6**	**–3**	**0**	**0.0**	**13:11**	....	....	....	....	....	....	....	....	....
	Fredericton	AHL	3	1	0	1	0	....	....	....	....	....	....	....	....	....	....	....	....	....	....	....	....	....	....
99-2000	**Atlanta**	**NHL**	**14**	**0**	**1**	**1**	**4**	**0**	**0**	**0**	**13**	**0.0**	**–12**	**0**	**0.0**	**16:51**	....	....	....	....	....	....	....	....	....
	Orlando	IHL	63	9	17	26	31	....	....	....	....	....	....	....	....	....	6	0	1	1	0	....	....	....	....
2000-01	**Atlanta**	**NHL**	**28**	**1**	**2**	**3**	**14**	**0**	**0**	**0**	**35**	**2.9**	**–12**	**0**	**0.0**	**18:02**	....	....	....	....	....	....	....	....	....
	Orlando	IHL	43	2	9	11	32	....	....	....	....	....	....	....	....	....	15	1	6	7	2	....	....	....	....
2001-02	**Atlanta**	**NHL**	**2**	**0**	**0**	**0**	**0**	**0**	**0**	**0**	**0**	**0.0**	**–3**	**1**	**100.0**	**15:32**	....	....	....	....	....	....	....	....	....
	Chicago Wolves	AHL	42	3	17	20	18	....	....	....	....	....	....	....	....	....	....	....	....	....	....	....	....	....	....
	Hershey Bears	AHL	32	7	9	16	12	....	....	....	....	....	....	....	....	....	8	0	2	2	6	....	....	....	....
2002-03	Hershey Bears	AHL	80	8	27	35	26	....	....	....	....	....	....	....	....	....	5	0	4	4	4	....	....	....	....
2003-04	**Colorado**	**NHL**	**12**	**1**	**1**	**2**	**6**	**0**	**0**	**0**	**14**	**7.1**	**3**	**0**	**0.0**	**10:26**	....	....	....	....	....	....	....	....	....
	Hershey Bears	AHL	64	11	21	32	37	....	....	....	....	....	....	....	....	....	....	....	....	....	....	....	....	....	....
2004-05	Hershey Bears	AHL	67	7	37	44	54	....	....	....	....	....	....	....	....	....	....	....	....	....	....	....	....	....	....
2005-06	**Colorado**	**NHL**	**80**	**9**	**27**	**36**	**56**	**4**	**0**	**1**	**148**	**6.1**	**3**	**1**	**0.0**	**19:39**	**9**	**2**	**2**	**4**	**2**	**0**	**1**	**0**	**24:17**
2006-07	**Colorado**	**NHL**	**82**	**10**	**29**	**39**	**50**	**4**	**0**	**1**	**140**	**7.1**	**5**	**1**	**100.0**	**23:41**	....	....	....	....	....	....	....	....	....
2007-08	**Colorado**	**NHL**	**57**	**5**	**16**	**21**	**33**	**1**	**0**	**0**	**87**	**5.7**	**5**	**0**	**0.0**	**23:09**	....	....	....	....	....	....	....	....	....
2008-09	**Colorado**	**NHL**	**76**	**2**	**10**	**12**	**32**	**0**	**0**	**1**	**97**	**2.1**	**–16**	**0**	**0.0**	**22:20**	....	....	....	....	....	....	....	....	....
2009-10	**Colorado**	**NHL**	**64**	**3**	**17**	**20**	**28**	**2**	**0**	**1**	**75**	**4.0**	**6**	**0**	**0.0**	**19:08**	**1**	**0**	**0**	**0**	**0**	**0**	**0**	**0**	**17:55**
2010-11	**Tampa Bay**	**NHL**	**82**	**9**	**22**	**31**	**14**	**6**	**0**	**1**	**87**	**10.3**	**2**	**0**	**0.0**	**18:53**	**18**	**1**	**2**	**3**	**8**	**0**	**0**	**0**	**17:35**
	NHL Totals		**599**	**43**	**127**	**170**	**273**	**17**	**0**	**5**	**758**	**5.7**		**3**	**66.7**	**19:43**	**28**	**3**	**4**	**7**	**10**	**0**	**1**	**0**	**19:45**

Claimed by **Atlanta** from **Montreal** in Expansion Draft, June 25, 1999. Traded to **Colorado** by **Atlanta** for Frederic Cassivi, January 24, 2002. Signed as a free agent by **Tampa Bay**, July 5, 2010.

CLARK, Chris

(KLAHRK, KRIHS)

Right wing. Shoots right. 6', 191 lbs. Born, South Windsor, CT, March 8, 1976. Calgary's 3rd choice, 77th overall, in 1994 Entry Draft.

Season	Club	League	GP	G	A	Pts	PIM	PP	SH	GW	S	%	+/-	TF	F%	Min	GP	G	A	Pts	PIM	PP	SH	GW	Min
1990-91	South Windsor	High-CT	23	16	15	31	24	....	....	....	....	....	....	....	....	....	....	....	....	....	....	....	....	....	....
1991-92	Spring. Olympics	NEJHL	49	21	29	50	56	....	....	....	....	....	....	....	....	....	....	....	....	....	....	....	....	....	....
1992-93	Spring. Olympics	NEJHL	43	17	60	77	120	....	....	....	....	....	....	....	....	....	....	....	....	....	....	....	....	....	....
1993-94	Spring. Olympics	NEJHL	35	31	26	57	185	....	....	....	....	....	....	....	....	....	....	....	....	....	....	....	....	....	....
1994-95	Clarkson Knights	ECAC	32	12	11	23	92	....	....	....	....	....	....	....	....	....	....	....	....	....	....	....	....	....	....
1995-96	Clarkson Knights	ECAC	38	10	8	18	108	....	....	....	....	....	....	....	....	....	....	....	....	....	....	....	....	....	....
1996-97	Clarkson Knights	ECAC	37	23	25	48	*86	....	....	....	....	....	....	....	....	....	....	....	....	....	....	....	....	....	....

			Regular Season														Playoffs								
Season	Club	League	GP	G	A	Pts	PIM	PP	SH	GW	S	%	+/-	TF	F%	Min	GP	G	A	Pts	PIM	PP	SH	GW	Min
1997-98	Clarkson Knights	ECAC	35	18	21	39	*106	....	....	....	....	....	....	....	....	....	....	....	....	....	....	....	....	....	....
1998-99	Saint John Flames	AHL	73	13	27	40	123	....	....	....	....	....	....	....	....	....	7	2	4	6	15	....	....	....	....
99-2000	**Calgary**	**NHL**	**22**	**0**	**1**	**1**	**14**	**0**	**0**	**0**	**17**	**0.0**	**–3**	**0**	**0.0**	**9:02**	....	....	....	....	....	....	....	....	....
	Saint John Flames	AHL	48	16	17	33	134	....	....	....	....	....	....	....	....	....	....	....	....	....	....	....	....	....	....
2000-01	**Calgary**	**NHL**	**29**	**5**	**1**	**6**	**38**	**1**	**0**	**0**	**43**	**11.6**	**0**	**3**	**33.3**	**11:56**	....	....	....	....	....	....	....	....	....
	Saint John Flames	AHL	48	18	17	35	131	....	....	....	....	....	....	....	....	....	18	4	10	14	49	....	....	....	....
2001-02	**Calgary**	**NHL**	**64**	**10**	**7**	**17**	**79**	**2**	**1**	**4**	**109**	**9.2**	**–12**	**21**	**33.3**	**13:57**	....	....	....	....	....	....	....	....	....
2002-03	**Calgary**	**NHL**	**81**	**10**	**12**	**22**	**126**	**2**	**0**	**2**	**156**	**6.4**	**–11**	**40**	**32.5**	**14:24**	....	....	....	....	....	....	....	....	....
2003-04	**Calgary**	**NHL**	**82**	**10**	**15**	**25**	**106**	**4**	**0**	**2**	**137**	**7.3**	**–3**	**97**	**36.1**	**14:05**	**26**	**3**	**3**	**6**	**30**	**1**	**0**	**0**	**14:34**
2004-05	SC Bern	Swiss	3	0	0	0	6	....	....	....	....	....	....	....	....	....	....	....	....	....	....	....	....	....	....
	Storhamar	Norway	15	10	4	14	86	....	....	....	....	....	....	....	....	....	7	4	4	8	14	....	....	....	....
2005-06	**Washington**	**NHL**	**78**	**20**	**19**	**39**	**110**	**1**	**3**	**0**	**144**	**13.9**	**9**	**209**	**49.3**	**15:24**	....	....	....	....	....	....	....	....	....
2006-07	**Washington**	**NHL**	**74**	**30**	**24**	**54**	**66**	**9**	**4**	**2**	**164**	**18.3**	**–10**	**118**	**50.9**	**18:25**	....	....	....	....	....	....	....	....	....
2007-08	**Washington**	**NHL**	**18**	**5**	**4**	**9**	**43**	**1**	**0**	**1**	**29**	**17.2**	**0**	**13**	**46.2**	**16:54**	....	....	....	....	....	....	....	....	....
2008-09	**Washington**	**NHL**	**32**	**1**	**5**	**6**	**32**	**0**	**0**	**0**	**36**	**2.8**	**–3**	**6**	**50.0**	**11:34**	**8**	**1**	**0**	**1**	**8**	**0**	**0**	**0**	**6:32**
2009-10	**Washington**	**NHL**	**38**	**4**	**11**	**15**	**27**	**0**	**0**	**1**	**59**	**6.8**	**–4**	**10**	**30.0**	**11:39**	....	....	....	....	....	....	....	....	....
	Columbus	**NHL**	**36**	**3**	**2**	**5**	**21**	**0**	**0**	**0**	**46**	**6.5**	**–8**	**10**	**40.0**	**12:06**	....	....	....	....	....	....	....	....	....
2010-11	**Columbus**	**NHL**	**53**	**5**	**10**	**15**	**38**	**2**	**0**	**0**	**83**	**6.0**	**–3**	**16**	**18.8**	**14:39**	....	....	....	....	....	....	....	....	....
	NHL Totals		**607**	**103**	**111**	**214**	**700**	**22**	**8**	**12**	**1023**	**10.1**		**543**	**43.8**	**14:15**	**34**	**4**	**3**	**7**	**38**	**1**	**0**	**0**	**12:41**

ECAC Second All-Star Team (1998)

Signed as a free agent by **Bern** (Swiss), October 3, 2004. Signed as a free agent by **Storhamar** (Norway), December 29, 2004. Traded to **Washington** by **Calgary** with Calgary's 7th round choice (Andrew Glass) in 2007 Entry Draft for Washington's 7th round choice (Devin Didiomete) in 2006 Entry Draft and Washington's 6th round choice (later traded to Colorado - Colorado selected Jens Hellgren) in 2007 Entry Draft, August 4, 2005. • Missed majority of 2007-08 due to recurring groin injury. • Missed majority of 2008-09 due to wrist surgery, February 4, 2009. Traded to **Columbus** by **Washington** with Milan Jurcina for Jason Chimera, December 28, 2009.

CLARKSON, David
(KLAHRK-suhn, DAYV-ihd) **N.J.**

Right wing. Shoots right. 6'1", 200 lbs. Born, Toronto, Ont., March 31, 1984.

Season	Club	League	GP	G	A	Pts	PIM	PP	SH	GW	S	%	+/-	TF	F%	Min	GP	G	A	Pts	PIM	PP	SH	GW	Min
2001-02	Belleville Bulls	OHL	22	2	7	9	34	....	....	....	....	....	....	....	....	....	8	1	1	2	6	....	....	....	....
2002-03	Belleville Bulls	OHL	3	0	0	0	11	....	....	....	....	....	....	....	....	....	....	....	....	....	....	....	....	....	....
	Kitchener Rangers	OHL	54	17	11	28	122	....	....	....	....	....	....	....	....	....	21	4	3	7	23	....	....	....	....
2003-04	Kitchener Rangers	OHL	55	22	17	39	173	....	....	....	....	....	....	....	....	....	....	....	....	....	....	....	....	....	....
2004-05	Kitchener Rangers	OHL	51	33	21	54	145	....	....	....	....	....	....	....	....	....	15	6	2	8	40	....	....	....	....
2005-06	Albany River Rats	AHL	56	13	21	34	233	....	....	....	....	....	....	....	....	....	....	....	....	....	....	....	....	....	....
2006-07	**New Jersey**	**NHL**	**7**	**3**	**1**	**4**	**6**	**2**	**0**	**1**	**18**	**16.7**	**–1**	**1**	**0.0**	**17:02**	**3**	**0**	**0**	**0**	**2**	**0**	**0**	**0**	**6:42**
	Lowell Devils	AHL	67	20	18	38	150	....	....	....	....	....	....	....	....	....	....	....	....	....	....	....	....	....	....
2007-08	**New Jersey**	**NHL**	**81**	**9**	**13**	**22**	**183**	**0**	**0**	**1**	**151**	**6.0**	**1**	**15**	**40.0**	**12:02**	**5**	**0**	**0**	**0**	**4**	**0**	**0**	**0**	**12:20**
2008-09	**New Jersey**	**NHL**	**82**	**17**	**15**	**32**	**164**	**4**	**0**	**3**	**158**	**10.8**	**–1**	**7**	**28.6**	**12:03**	**7**	**2**	**0**	**2**	**19**	**1**	**0**	**1**	**8:32**
2009-10	**New Jersey**	**NHL**	**46**	**11**	**13**	**24**	**85**	**3**	**0**	**2**	**106**	**10.4**	**3**	**20**	**30.0**	**14:27**	**5**	**0**	**0**	**0**	**22**	**0**	**0**	**0**	**12:28**
2010-11	**New Jersey**	**NHL**	**82**	**12**	**6**	**18**	**116**	**1**	**0**	**1**	**192**	**6.3**	**–20**	**45**	**42.2**	**13:37**	....	....	....	....	....	....	....	....	....
	NHL Totals		**298**	**52**	**48**	**100**	**554**	**10**	**0**	**8**	**625**	**8.3**		**88**	**37.5**	**12:58**	**20**	**2**	**0**	**2**	**47**	**1**	**0**	**1**	**10:11**

Signed as a free agent by **New Jersey**, August 12, 2005.

CLEARY, Dan
(KLIH-ree, DAN) **DET**

Right wing. Shoots left. 6', 205 lbs. Born, Carbonear, Nfld., December 18, 1978. Chicago's 1st choice, 13th overall, in 1997 Entry Draft.

Season	Club	League	GP	G	A	Pts	PIM	PP	SH	GW	S	%	+/-	TF	F%	Min	GP	G	A	Pts	PIM	PP	SH	GW	Min
1993-94	Kingston	ON-Jr.A	41	18	28	46	33	....	....	....	....	....	....	....	....	....	2	0	1	1	0	....	....	....	....
1994-95	Belleville Bulls	OHL	62	26	55	81	62	....	....	....	....	....	....	....	....	....	16	7	10	17	23	....	....	....	....
1995-96	Belleville Bulls	OHL	64	53	62	115	74	....	....	....	....	....	....	....	....	....	14	10	17	27	40	....	....	....	....
1996-97	Belleville Bulls	OHL	64	32	48	80	88	....	....	....	....	....	....	....	....	....	6	3	4	7	6	....	....	....	....
1997-98	**Chicago**	**NHL**	**6**	**0**	**0**	**0**	**0**	**0**	**0**	**0**	**4**	**0.0**	**–2**	....	....	....	....	....	....	....	....	....	....	....	....
	Belleville Bulls	OHL	30	16	31	47	14	....	....	....	....	....	....	....	....	....	10	6	*17	*23	10	....	....	....	....
	Indianapolis Ice	IHL	4	2	1	3	6	....	....	....	....	....	....	....	....	....	....	....	....	....	....	....	....	....	....
1998-99	**Chicago**	**NHL**	**35**	**4**	**5**	**9**	**24**	**0**	**0**	**0**	**49**	**8.2**	**–1**	**13**	**46.2**	**14:21**	....	....	....	....	....	....	....	....	....
	Portland Pirates	AHL	30	9	17	26	74	....	....	....	....	....	....	....	....	....	....	....	....	....	....	....	....	....	....
	Hamilton	AHL	9	0	1	1	7	....	....	....	....	....	....	....	....	....	3	0	0	0	0	....	....	....	....
99-2000	**Edmonton**	**NHL**	**17**	**3**	**2**	**5**	**8**	**0**	**0**	**1**	**18**	**16.7**	**–1**	**1**	**100.0**	**9:44**	**4**	**0**	**1**	**1**	**2**	**0**	**0**	**0**	**8:40**
	Hamilton	AHL	58	22	52	74	108	....	....	....	....	....	....	....	....	....	5	2	3	5	18	....	....	....	....
2000-01	**Edmonton**	**NHL**	**81**	**14**	**21**	**35**	**37**	**2**	**0**	**2**	**107**	**13.1**	**5**	**13**	**23.1**	**12:58**	**6**	**1**	**1**	**2**	**8**	**1**	**0**	**0**	**14:09**
2001-02	**Edmonton**	**NHL**	**65**	**10**	**19**	**29**	**51**	**2**	**1**	**1**	**75**	**13.3**	**–1**	**5**	**60.0**	**12:43**	....	....	....	....	....	....	....	....	....
2002-03	**Edmonton**	**NHL**	**57**	**4**	**13**	**17**	**31**	**0**	**0**	**1**	**89**	**4.5**	**5**	**5**	**40.0**	**11:58**	....	....	....	....	....	....	....	....	....
2003-04	**Phoenix**	**NHL**	**68**	**6**	**11**	**17**	**42**	**0**	**3**	**0**	**83**	**7.2**	**–8**	**51**	**39.2**	**13:12**	....	....	....	....	....	....	....	....	....
2004-05	Mora IK	Sweden	47	11	26	37	138	....	....	....	....	....	....	....	....	....	....	....	....	....	....	....	....	....	....
2005-06	**Detroit**	**NHL**	**77**	**3**	**12**	**15**	**40**	**0**	**0**	**1**	**106**	**2.8**	**5**	**286**	**45.8**	**10:30**	**6**	**0**	**1**	**1**	**6**	**0**	**0**	**0**	**10:44**
2006-07	**Detroit**	**NHL**	**71**	**20**	**20**	**40**	**24**	**6**	**2**	**5**	**135**	**14.8**	**6**	**411**	**51.1**	**15:28**	**18**	**4**	**8**	**12**	**30**	**1**	***2**	**0**	**16:28**
2007-08♦	**Detroit**	**NHL**	**63**	**20**	**22**	**42**	**33**	**5**	**0**	**3**	**177**	**11.3**	**21**	**110**	**50.9**	**17:23**	**22**	**2**	**1**	**3**	**4**	**0**	**1**	**0**	**17:50**
2008-09	**Detroit**	**NHL**	**74**	**14**	**26**	**40**	**46**	**3**	**0**	**3**	**163**	**8.6**	**0**	**121**	**55.4**	**16:56**	**23**	**9**	**6**	**15**	**12**	**0**	**0**	***3**	**16:55**
2009-10	**Detroit**	**NHL**	**64**	**15**	**19**	**34**	**29**	**2**	**0**	**2**	**140**	**10.7**	**–3**	**119**	**49.6**	**17:14**	**12**	**2**	**0**	**2**	**4**	**0**	**0**	**0**	**14:47**
2010-11	**Detroit**	**NHL**	**68**	**26**	**20**	**46**	**20**	**5**	**0**	**8**	**192**	**13.5**	**–1**	**91**	**38.5**	**16:38**	**11**	**2**	**4**	**6**	**6**	**0**	**0**	**1**	**17:09**
	NHL Totals		**746**	**139**	**190**	**329**	**385**	**25**	**6**	**27**	**1338**	**10.4**		**1226**	**48.4**	**14:21**	**102**	**20**	**22**	**42**	**72**	**2**	**3**	**4**	**15:57**

OHL All-Rookie Team (1995) • OHL First All-Star Team (1996, 1997) • AHL Second All-Star Team (2000)

Traded to **Edmonton** by **Chicago** with Chad Kilger, Ethan Moreau and Christian Laflamme for Boris Mironov, Dean McAmmond and Jonas Elofsson, March 20, 1999. Signed as a free agent by **Phoenix**, July 15, 2003. Signed as a free agent by **Mora** (Sweden), September 6, 2004. Signed as a free agent by **Detroit**, October 4, 2005.

CLICHE, Marc-Andre
(KLEESH, MAHRK-AWN-dray) **L.A.**

Center. Shoots right. 6', 200 lbs. Born, Rouyn-Noranda, Que., March 23, 1987. NY Rangers' 3rd choice, 56th overall, in 2005 Entry Draft.

Season	Club	League	GP	G	A	Pts	PIM	PP	SH	GW	S	%	+/-	TF	F%	Min	GP	G	A	Pts	PIM	PP	SH	GW	Min
2003-04	Lewiston	QMJHL	52	8	10	18	17	....	....	....	....	....	....	....	....	....	7	1	2	3	0	....	....	....	....
2004-05	Lewiston	QMJHL	19	4	4	8	8	....	....	....	....	....	....	....	....	....	....	....	....	....	....	....	....	....	....
2005-06	Lewiston	QMJHL	66	37	45	82	60	....	....	....	....	....	....	....	....	....	6	2	2	4	0	....	....	....	....
2006-07	Lewiston	QMJHL	52	24	30	54	42	....	....	....	....	....	....	....	....	....	16	6	16	22	10	....	....	....	....
2007-08	Manchester	AHL	52	11	10	21	25	....	....	....	....	....	....	....	....	....	4	0	1	1	2	....	....	....	....
2008-09	Manchester	AHL	31	5	4	9	19	....	....	....	....	....	....	....	....	....	....	....	....	....	....	....	....	....	....
2009-10	**Los Angeles**	**NHL**	**1**	**0**	**0**	**0**	**0**	**0**	**0**	**0**	**0**	**0.0**	**1**	**6**	**66.7**	**7:23**	....	....	....	....	....	....	....	....	....
	Manchester	AHL	66	11	14	25	45	....	....	....	....	....	....	....	....	....	12	1	1	2	8	....	....	....	....
2010-11	Manchester	AHL	63	14	21	35	35	....	....	....	....	....	....	....	....	....	....	....	....	....	....	....	....	....	....
	NHL Totals		**1**	**0**	**0**	**0**	**0**	**0**	**0**	**0**	**0**	**0.0**		**6**	**66.7**	**7:23**	....	....	....	....	....	....	....	....	....

• Missed majority of 2004-05 due to recurring shoulder injury. Traded to **Los Angeles** by **NY Rangers** with Jason Ward, Jan Marek and NY Rangers' 3rd round choice (later traded to Buffalo - Buffalo selected Corey Fienhage) in 2008 Entry Draft for Sean Avery and John Seymour, February 5, 2007. • Missed majority of 2008-09 due to shoulder injury in training camp.

CLIFFORD, Kyle
(KLIHF-fuhrd, KIGHL) **L.A.**

Left wing. Shoots left. 6'2", 207 lbs. Born, Ayr, Ont., January 13, 1991. Los Angeles' 2nd choice, 35th overall, in 2009 Entry Draft.

Season	Club	League	GP	G	A	Pts	PIM	PP	SH	GW	S	%	+/-	TF	F%	Min	GP	G	A	Pts	PIM	PP	SH	GW	Min
2006-07	Cambridge	Minor-ON	70	31	49	80	119	....	....	....	....	....	....	....	....	....	....	....	....	....	....	....	....	....	....
2007-08	Barrie Colts	OHL	66	1	14	15	83	....	....	....	....	....	....	....	....	....	9	0	1	1	4	....	....	....	....
2008-09	Barrie Colts	OHL	60	16	12	28	133	....	....	....	....	....	....	....	....	....	5	0	0	0	13	....	....	....	....
2009-10	Barrie Colts	OHL	58	28	29	57	111	....	....	....	....	....	....	....	....	....	17	5	9	14	28	....	....	....	....
	Manchester	AHL	....	....	....	....	....	....	....	....	....	....	....	....	....	....	7	0	2	2	12	....	....	....	....
2010-11	**Los Angeles**	**NHL**	**76**	**7**	**7**	**14**	**141**	**0**	**0**	**0**	**69**	**10.1**	**–10**	**15**	**53.3**	**9:30**	**6**	**3**	**2**	**5**	**7**	**0**	**0**	**1**	**13:17**
	NHL Totals		**76**	**7**	**7**	**14**	**141**	**0**	**0**	**0**	**69**	**10.1**		**15**	**53.3**	**9:30**	**6**	**3**	**2**	**5**	**7**	**0**	**0**	**1**	**13:18**

CLITSOME, Grant
(KLIHT-suhm, GRANT) **CBJ**

Defense. Shoots left. 6', 208 lbs. Born, Gloucester, Ont., April 14, 1985. Columbus' 12th choice, 271st overall, in 2004 Entry Draft.

Season	Club	League	GP	G	A	Pts	PIM	PP	SH	GW	S	%	+/-	TF	F%	Min	GP	G	A	Pts	PIM	PP	SH	GW	Min
			Regular Season														Playoffs								
2003-04	Nepean Raiders	CJHL	55	13	26	39	67	....	....	....	....	....	....	....	....	....	17	1	10	11	6	....	....	....	....
2004-05	Clarkson Knights	ECAC	39	2	11	13	36	....	....	....	....	....	....	....	....	....	....	....	....	....	....	....	....	....	....
2005-06	Clarkson Knights	ECAC	34	2	17	19	20	....	....	....	....	....	....	....	....	....	....	....	....	....	....	....	....	....	....
2006-07	Clarkson Knights	ECAC	38	7	12	19	38	....	....	....	....	....	....	....	....	....	....	....	....	....	....	....	....	....	....
2007-08	Clarkson Knights	ECAC	39	5	17	22	28	....	....	....	....	....	....	....	....	....	....	....	....	....	....	....	....	....	....
	Syracuse Crunch	AHL	....	....	....	....	....	....	....	....	....	....	....	....	....	....	1	0	0	0	0	....	....	....	....
2008-09	Syracuse Crunch	AHL	73	4	15	19	74	....	....	....	....	....	....	....	....	....	....	....	....	....	....	....	....	....	....
2009-10	**Columbus**	**NHL**	**11**	**1**	**2**	**3**	**6**	**0**	**0**	**0**	**7**	**14.3**	**0**	**0**	**0.0**	**14:44**	....	....	....	....	....	....	....	....	....
	Syracuse Crunch	AHL	64	5	15	20	42	....	....	....	....	....	....	....	....	....	....	....	....	....	....	....	....	....	....
2010-11	**Columbus**	**NHL**	**31**	**4**	**15**	**19**	**16**	**2**	**0**	**0**	**50**	**8.0**	**2**	**0**	**0.0**	**21:16**	....	....	....	....	....	....	....	....	....
	Springfield	AHL	32	5	10	15	22	....	....	....	....	....	....	....	....	....	....	....	....	....	....	....	....	....	....
	NHL Totals		**42**	**5**	**17**	**22**	**22**	**2**	**0**	**0**	**57**	**8.8**		**0**	**0.0**	**19:34**	....	....	....	....	....	....	....	....	....

ECAC First All-Star Team (2008) • NCAA East Second All-American Team (2008)

CLOWE, Ryane
(KLOH, RIGH-uhn) **S.J.**

Right wing. Shoots left. 6'2", 225 lbs. Born, St. John's, Nfld., September 30, 1982. San Jose's 5th choice, 175th overall, in 2001 Entry Draft.

Season	Club	League	GP	G	A	Pts	PIM	PP	SH	GW	S	%	+/-	TF	F%	Min	GP	G	A	Pts	PIM	PP	SH	GW	Min
2000-01	Rimouski Oceanic	QMJHL	32	15	10	25	43	....	....	....	....	....	....	....	....	....	11	8	1	9	12	....	....	....	....
2001-02	Rimouski Oceanic	QMJHL	53	28	45	73	120	....	....	....	....	....	....	....	....	....	7	1	6	7	2	....	....	....	....
2002-03	Rimouski Oceanic	QMJHL	17	8	19	27	44	....	....	....	....	....	....	....	....	....	....	....	....	....	....	....	....	....	....
	Montreal Rocket	QMJHL	43	18	30	48	60	....	....	....	....	....	....	....	....	....	7	3	7	10	6	....	....	....	....
2003-04	Cleveland Barons	AHL	72	11	29	40	97	....	....	....	....	....	....	....	....	....	8	3	1	4	9	....	....	....	....
2004-05	Cleveland Barons	AHL	74	27	35	62	101	....	....	....	....	....	....	....	....	....	....	....	....	....	....	....	....	....	....
2005-06	**San Jose**	**NHL**	**18**	**0**	**2**	**2**	**9**	**0**	**0**	**0**	**14**	**0.0**	**-2**	**2**	**0.0**	**9:40**	**1**	**0**	**0**	**0**	**0**	**0**	**0**	**0**	**5:06**
	Cleveland Barons	AHL	35	13	21	34	35	....	....	....	....	....	....	....	....	....	....	....	....	....	....	....	....	....	....
2006-07	**San Jose**	**NHL**	**58**	**16**	**18**	**34**	**78**	**4**	**0**	**3**	**93**	**17.2**	**4**	**5**	**60.0**	**13:11**	**11**	**4**	**2**	**6**	**17**	**0**	**0**	**1**	**15:19**
2007-08	**San Jose**	**NHL**	**15**	**3**	**5**	**8**	**22**	**2**	**0**	**0**	**22**	**13.6**	**-1**	**14**	**35.7**	**14:17**	**13**	**5**	**4**	**9**	**12**	**2**	**0**	**0**	**19:00**
2008-09	**San Jose**	**NHL**	**71**	**22**	**30**	**52**	**51**	**11**	**0**	**1**	**161**	**13.7**	**8**	**120**	**40.8**	**17:47**	**6**	**1**	**1**	**2**	**8**	**0**	**0**	**0**	**18:22**
2009-10	**San Jose**	**NHL**	**82**	**19**	**38**	**57**	**131**	**2**	**0**	**2**	**189**	**10.1**	**0**	**73**	**48.0**	**17:10**	**15**	**2**	**8**	**10**	**28**	**0**	**0**	**0**	**20:11**
2010-11	**San Jose**	**NHL**	**75**	**24**	**38**	**62**	**100**	**5**	**0**	**2**	**185**	**13.0**	**13**	**41**	**41.5**	**17:58**	**17**	**6**	**9**	**15**	**32**	**3**	**0**	**0**	**19:27**
	NHL Totals		**319**	**84**	**131**	**215**	**391**	**24**	**0**	**8**	**664**	**12.7**		**255**	**42.7**	**16:12**	**63**	**18**	**24**	**42**	**97**	**5**	**0**	**1**	**18:29**

• Missed majority of 2007-08 due to knee injury at Columbus, October 27, 2007.

CLUNE, Rich
(KLOON, RITCH) **L.A.**

Left wing. Shoots left. 5'10", 199 lbs. Born, Toronto, Ont., April 25, 1987. Dallas' 3rd choice, 71st overall, in 2005 Entry Draft.

Season	Club	League	GP	G	A	Pts	PIM	PP	SH	GW	S	%	+/-	TF	F%	Min	GP	G	A	Pts	PIM	PP	SH	GW	Min
2003-04	Sarnia Sting	OHL	58	3	13	16	72	....	....	....	....	....	....	....	....	....	5	0	1	1	0	....	....	....	....
2004-05	Sarnia Sting	OHL	68	21	13	34	103	....	....	....	....	....	....	....	....	....	....	....	....	....	....	....	....	....	....
2005-06	Sarnia Sting	OHL	61	20	32	52	126	....	....	....	....	....	....	....	....	....	....	....	....	....	....	....	....	....	....
2006-07	Barrie Colts	OHL	67	32	46	78	151	....	....	....	....	....	....	....	....	....	8	3	4	7	8	....	....	....	....
	Iowa Stars	AHL	1	0	0	0	2	....	....	....	....	....	....	....	....	....	....	....	....	....	....	....	....	....	....
2007-08	Iowa Stars	AHL	38	3	5	8	137	....	....	....	....	....	....	....	....	....	....	....	....	....	....	....	....	....	....
	Idaho Steelheads	ECHL	19	1	9	10	41	....	....	....	....	....	....	....	....	....	....	....	....	....	....	....	....	....	....
2008-09	Manchester	AHL	35	3	6	9	87	....	....	....	....	....	....	....	....	....	....	....	....	....	....	....	....	....	....
2009-10	**Los Angeles**	**NHL**	**14**	**0**	**2**	**2**	**26**	**0**	**0**	**0**	**7**	**0.0**	**1**	**5**	**40.0**	**7:17**	**4**	**0**	**0**	**0**	**5**	**0**	**0**	**0**	**5:12**
	Manchester	AHL	44	4	10	14	126	....	....	....	....	....	....	....	....	....	....	....	....	....	....	....	....	....	....
2010-11	Manchester	AHL	66	8	14	22	222	....	....	....	....	....	....	....	....	....	7	0	3	3	6	....	....	....	....
	NHL Totals		**14**	**0**	**2**	**2**	**26**	**0**	**0**	**0**	**7**	**0.0**		**5**	**40.0**	**7:17**	**4**	**0**	**0**	**0**	**5**	**0**	**0**	**0**	**5:12**

Traded to **Los Angeles** by **Dallas** for Lauri Tukonen, July 21, 2008.

CLUTTERBUCK, Cal
(KLUH-tuhr-buhck, KAL) **MIN**

Right wing. Shoots right. 5'11", 213 lbs. Born, Welland, Ont., November 18, 1987. Minnesota's 3rd choice, 72nd overall, in 2006 Entry Draft.

Season	Club	League	GP	G	A	Pts	PIM	PP	SH	GW	S	%	+/-	TF	F%	Min	GP	G	A	Pts	PIM	PP	SH	GW	Min
2004-05	St. Michael's	OHL	38	10	6	16	55	....	....	....	....	....	....	....	....	....	....	....	....	....	....	....	....	....	....
	Oshawa Generals	OHL	27	9	9	18	42	....	....	....	....	....	....	....	....	....	....	....	....	....	....	....	....	....	....
2005-06	Oshawa Generals	OHL	66	35	33	68	139	....	....	....	....	....	....	....	....	....	....	....	....	....	....	....	....	....	....
2006-07	Oshawa Generals	OHL	65	35	54	89	153	....	....	....	....	....	....	....	....	....	9	8	5	13	21	....	....	....	....
2007-08	**Minnesota**	**NHL**	**2**	**0**	**0**	**0**	**0**	**0**	**0**	**0**	**0**	**0.0**	**0**	**1**	**100.0**	**7:05**	....	....	....	....	....	....	....	....	....
	Houston Aeros	AHL	73	11	13	24	97	....	....	....	....	....	....	....	....	....	5	0	0	0	14	....	....	....	....
2008-09	**Minnesota**	**NHL**	**78**	**11**	**7**	**18**	**76**	**1**	**0**	**1**	**136**	**8.1**	**-5**	**17**	**11.8**	**13:00**	....	....	....	....	....	....	....	....	....
	Houston Aeros	AHL	2	0	0	0	0	....	....	....	....	....	....	....	....	....	....	....	....	....	....	....	....	....	....
2009-10	**Minnesota**	**NHL**	**74**	**13**	**8**	**21**	**52**	**1**	**2**	**1**	**136**	**9.6**	**-8**	**10**	**30.0**	**14:17**	....	....	....	....	....	....	....	....	....
2010-11	**Minnesota**	**NHL**	**76**	**19**	**15**	**34**	**79**	**4**	**0**	**3**	**191**	**9.9**	**-5**	**11**	**27.3**	**15:51**	....	....	....	....	....	....	....	....	....
	NHL Totals		**230**	**43**	**30**	**73**	**207**	**6**	**2**	**5**	**463**	**9.3**		**39**	**23.1**	**14:18**	....	....	....	....	....	....	....	....	....

COBURN, Braydon
(KOH-buhrn, BRAY-duhn) **PHI**

Defense. Shoots left. 6'5", 220 lbs. Born, Calgary, Alta., February 27, 1985. Atlanta's 1st choice, 8th overall, in 2003 Entry Draft.

Season	Club	League	GP	G	A	Pts	PIM	PP	SH	GW	S	%	+/-	TF	F%	Min	GP	G	A	Pts	PIM	PP	SH	GW	Min
2000-01	Notre Dame	SMHL	32	3	19	22	70	....	....	....	....	....	....	....	....	....	....	....	....	....	....	....	....	....	....
	Portland	WHL	2	0	1	1	0	....	....	....	....	....	....	....	....	....	14	0	4	4	2	....	....	....	....
2001-02	Portland	WHL	68	4	33	37	100	....	....	....	....	....	....	....	....	....	7	1	1	2	9	....	....	....	....
2002-03	Portland	WHL	53	3	16	19	147	....	....	....	....	....	....	....	....	....	7	0	1	1	8	....	....	....	....
2003-04	Portland	WHL	55	10	20	30	92	....	....	....	....	....	....	....	....	....	5	0	1	1	10	....	....	....	....
2004-05	Portland	WHL	60	12	32	44	144	....	....	....	....	....	....	....	....	....	7	1	5	6	6	....	....	....	....
	Chicago Wolves	AHL	3	0	1	1	5	....	....	....	....	....	....	....	....	....	18	0	1	1	36	....	....	....	....
2005-06	**Atlanta**	**NHL**	**9**	**0**	**1**	**1**	**4**	**0**	**0**	**0**	**4**	**0.0**	**-2**	**0**	**0.0**	**7:43**	....	....	....	....	....	....	....	....	....
	Chicago Wolves	AHL	73	6	20	26	134	....	....	....	....	....	....	....	....	....	....	....	....	....	....	....	....	....	....
2006-07	**Atlanta**	**NHL**	**29**	**0**	**4**	**4**	**30**	**0**	**0**	**0**	**21**	**0.0**	**1**	**0**	**0.0**	**11:41**	....	....	....	....	....	....	....	....	....
	Chicago Wolves	AHL	15	1	10	11	36	....	....	....	....	....	....	....	....	....	....	....	....	....	....	....	....	....	....
	Philadelphia	**NHL**	**20**	**3**	**4**	**7**	**16**	**1**	**0**	**0**	**33**	**9.1**	**-2**	**0**	**0.0**	**20:58**	....	....	....	....	....	....	....	....	....
2007-08	**Philadelphia**	**NHL**	**78**	**9**	**27**	**36**	**74**	**5**	**0**	**2**	**113**	**8.0**	**17**	**0**	**0.0**	**21:14**	**14**	**0**	**6**	**6**	**14**	**0**	**0**	**0**	**22:25**
2008-09	**Philadelphia**	**NHL**	**80**	**7**	**21**	**28**	**97**	**3**	**0**	**0**	**130**	**5.4**	**7**	**0**	**0.0**	**24:37**	**6**	**0**	**3**	**3**	**7**	**0**	**0**	**0**	**26:29**
2009-10	**Philadelphia**	**NHL**	**81**	**5**	**14**	**19**	**54**	**1**	**0**	**0**	**122**	**4.1**	**-6**	**0**	**0.0**	**21:08**	**23**	**1**	**3**	**4**	**22**	**1**	**0**	**1**	**25:09**
2010-11	**Philadelphia**	**NHL**	**82**	**2**	**14**	**16**	**53**	**0**	**0**	**0**	**114**	**1.8**	**15**	**0**	**0.0**	**21:04**	**11**	**1**	**2**	**3**	**6**	**0**	**0**	**0**	**24:07**
	NHL Totals		**379**	**26**	**85**	**111**	**328**	**10**	**0**	**2**	**537**	**4.8**		**0**	**0.0**	**20:50**	**54**	**2**	**14**	**16**	**49**	**1**	**0**	**1**	**24:23**

WHL Rookie of the Year (2002) • WHL West First All-Star Team (2004, 2005) • Canadian Major Junior Second All-Star Team (2005)
Traded to **Philadelphia** by **Atlanta** for Alexei Zhitnik, February 24, 2007.

COGLIANO, Andrew
(kawg-lee-A-noh, AN-droo) **ANA**

Center. Shoots left. 5'10", 188 lbs. Born, Toronto, Ont., June 14, 1987. Edmonton's 1st choice, 25th overall, in 2005 Entry Draft.

Season	Club	League	GP	G	A	Pts	PIM	PP	SH	GW	S	%	+/-	TF	F%	Min	GP	G	A	Pts	PIM	PP	SH	GW	Min
2002-03	Vaughan Kings	GTHL	58	39	54	93	122	....	....	....	....	....	....	....	....	....	....	....	....	....	....	....	....	....	....
2003-04	St. Mike's B's	OPJHL	36	26	47	73	14	....	....	....	....	....	....	....	....	....	24	11	20	31	12	....	....	....	....
2004-05	St. Mike's B's	OPJHL	49	36	*66	*102	33	....	....	....	....	....	....	....	....	....	25	*22	*24	*46	20	....	....	....	....
2005-06	U. of Michigan	CCHA	39	12	16	28	38	....	....	....	....	....	....	....	....	....	....	....	....	....	....	....	....	....	....
2006-07	U. of Michigan	CCHA	38	24	26	50	12	....	....	....	....	....	....	....	....	....	....	....	....	....	....	....	....	....	....
2007-08	**Edmonton**	**NHL**	**82**	**18**	**27**	**45**	**20**	**1**	**2**	**5**	**98**	**18.4**	**1**	**542**	**39.5**	**13:40**	....	....	....	....	....	....	....	....	....
2008-09	**Edmonton**	**NHL**	**82**	**18**	**20**	**38**	**22**	**4**	**0**	**4**	**116**	**15.5**	**-6**	**702**	**37.2**	**14:24**	....	....	....	....	....	....	....	....	....
2009-10	**Edmonton**	**NHL**	**82**	**10**	**18**	**28**	**31**	**1**	**0**	**1**	**139**	**7.2**	**-5**	**379**	**43.0**	**14:11**	....	....	....	....	....	....	....	....	....
2010-11	**Edmonton**	**NHL**	**82**	**11**	**24**	**35**	**64**	**0**	**1**	**3**	**129**	**8.5**	**-12**	**1108**	**41.6**	**17:15**	....	....	....	....	....	....	....	....	....
	NHL Totals		**328**	**57**	**89**	**146**	**137**	**6**	**3**	**13**	**482**	**11.8**		**2731**	**40.2**	**14:52**	....	....	....	....	....	....	....	....	....

CCHA All-Rookie Team (2006)
Traded to **Anaheim** by **Edmonton** for Anaheim's 2nd round choice in 2013 Entry Draft, July 12, 2011.

COHEN, Colby

(KOH-uhn, KOHL-bee) **BOS**

Defense. Shoots right. 6'2", 200 lbs. Born, Villanova, PA, April 25, 1989. Colorado's 2nd choice, 45th overall, in 2007 Entry Draft.

			Regular Season														Playoffs								
Season	Club	League	GP	G	A	Pts	PIM	PP	SH	GW	S	%	+/-	TF	F%	Min	GP	G	A	Pts	PIM	PP	SH	GW	Min
2004-05	Syracuse Stars	EmJHL	50	13	30	41	....	....	....	....	....	....	....	....	....	....	....	....	....	....	....	....	....	....	....
2005-06	USNTDP	U-17	18	2	3	5	22	....	....	....	....	....	....	....	....	....	....	....	....	....	....	....	....	....	....
	USNTDP	NAHL	37	5	9	14	33	....	....	....	....	....	....	....	....	....	10	1	1	2	0	....	....	....	....
2006-07	Lincoln Stars	USHL	53	13	47	60	110	....	....	....	....	....	....	....	....	....	4	0	0	0	2	....	....	....	....
	USNTDP	NAHL	4	1	3	4	0	....	....	....	....	....	....	....	....	....	....	....	....	....	....	....	....	....	....
2007-08	Boston University	H-East	39	3	13	16	34	....	....	....	....	....	....	....	....	....	....	....	....	....	....	....	....	....	....
2008-09	Boston University	H-East	43	8	24	32	65	....	....	....	....	....	....	....	....	....	....	....	....	....	....	....	....	....	....
2009-10	Boston University	H-East	36	14	16	30	82	....	....	....	....	....	....	....	....	....	....	....	....	....	....	....	....	....	....
	Lake Erie	AHL	3	0	1	1	9	....	....	....	....	....	....	....	....	....	....	....	....	....	....	....	....	....	....
2010-11	**Colorado**	**NHL**	**3**	**0**	**0**	**0**	**4**	**0**	**0**	**0**	**2**	**0.0**	**–1**	**0**	**0.0**	**17:44**	....	....	....	....	....	....	....	....	....
	Lake Erie	AHL	14	1	0	1	12	....	....	....	....	....	....	....	....	....	....	....	....	....	....	....	....	....	....
	Providence Bruins	AHL	46	1	11	12	46	....	....	....	....	....	....	....	....	....	....	....	....	....	....	....	....	....	....
	NHL Totals		**3**	**0**	**0**	**0**	**4**	**0**	**0**	**0**	**2**	**0.0**		**0**	**0.0**	**17:44**	....	....	....	....	....	....	....	....	....

USHL Second All-Star Team (2007) • NCAA Championship All-Tournament Team (2009) • NCAA Championship Tournament MVP (2009) • Hockey East First All-Star Team (2010) • NCAA East First All-American Team (2010)

Traded to **Boston** by **Colorado** for Matt Hunwick, November 29, 2010.

COLAIACOVO, Carlo

(koh-lee-A-KOH-voh, KAHR-loh) **ST.L.**

Defense. Shoots left. 6'1", 205 lbs. Born, Toronto, Ont., January 27, 1983. Toronto's 1st choice, 17th overall, in 2001 Entry Draft.

1998-99	Mississauga Reps	GTHL	44	10	12	23	28	....	....	....	....	....	....	....	....	....	....	....	....	....	....	....	....	....	....
99-2000	Erie Otters	OHL	52	4	18	22	12	....	....	....	....	....	....	....	....	....	13	2	4	6	9	....	....	....	....
2000-01	Erie Otters	OHL	62	12	27	39	59	....	....	....	....	....	....	....	....	....	14	4	7	11	16	....	....	....	....
2001-02	Erie Otters	OHL	60	13	27	40	49	....	....	....	....	....	....	....	....	....	21	7	10	17	20	....	....	....	....
2002-03	**Toronto**	**NHL**	**2**	**0**	**1**	**1**	**0**	**0**	**0**	**0**	**1**	**0.0**	**0**	**0**	**0.0**	**13:43**	....	....	....	....	....	....	....	....	....
	Erie Otters	OHL	35	14	21	35	12	....	....	....	....	....	....	....	....	....	....	....	....	....	....	....	....	....	....
2003-04	**Toronto**	**NHL**	**2**	**0**	**1**	**1**	**2**	**0**	**0**	**0**	**0**	**0.0**	**1**	**0**	**0.0**	**13:56**	....	....	....	....	....	....	....	....	....
	St. John's	AHL	62	6	25	31	50	....	....	....	....	....	....	....	....	....	....	....	....	....	....	....	....	....	....
2004-05	St. John's	AHL	49	4	20	24	59	....	....	....	....	....	....	....	....	....	5	0	1	1	2	....	....	....	....
2005-06	**Toronto**	**NHL**	**21**	**2**	**5**	**7**	**17**	**1**	**0**	**0**	**21**	**9.5**	**0**	**1**	**0.0**	**15:26**	....	....	....	....	....	....	....	....	....
	Toronto Marlies	AHL	14	5	6	11	14	....	....	....	....	....	....	....	....	....	....	....	....	....	....	....	....	....	....
2006-07	**Toronto**	**NHL**	**48**	**8**	**9**	**17**	**22**	**0**	**0**	**1**	**60**	**13.3**	**5**	**0**	**0.0**	**17:57**	....	....	....	....	....	....	....	....	....
	Toronto Marlies	AHL	5	1	5	6	4	....	....	....	....	....	....	....	....	....	....	....	....	....	....	....	....	....	....
2007-08	**Toronto**	**NHL**	**28**	**2**	**4**	**6**	**10**	**0**	**0**	**1**	**30**	**6.7**	**–4**	**0**	**0.0**	**17:26**	....	....	....	....	....	....	....	....	....
	Toronto Marlies	AHL	2	0	0	0	0	....	....	....	....	....	....	....	....	....	....	....	....	....	....	....	....	....	....
2008-09	**Toronto**	**NHL**	**10**	**0**	**1**	**1**	**6**	**0**	**0**	**0**	**9**	**0.0**	**–2**	**0**	**0.0**	**16:52**	....	....	....	....	....	....	....	....	....
	St. Louis	**NHL**	**63**	**3**	**26**	**29**	**29**	**0**	**0**	**0**	**78**	**3.8**	**2**	**0**	**0.0**	**18:29**	**4**	**0**	**0**	**0**	**2**	**0**	**0**	**0**	**22:19**
2009-10	**St. Louis**	**NHL**	**67**	**7**	**25**	**32**	**60**	**4**	**1**	**1**	**74**	**9.5**	**8**	**1**	**100.0**	**17:18**	....	....	....	....	....	....	....	....	....
2010-11	**St. Louis**	**NHL**	**65**	**6**	**20**	**26**	**23**	**1**	**0**	**1**	**81**	**7.4**	**–4**	**0**	**0.0**	**18:08**	....	....	....	....	....	....	....	....	....
	NHL Totals		**306**	**28**	**92**	**120**	**169**	**6**	**1**	**4**	**354**	**7.9**		**2**	**50.0**	**17:39**	**4**	**0**	**0**	**0**	**2**	**0**	**0**	**0**	**22:19**

OHL Second All-Star Team (2002, 2003)

• Missed remainder of 2005-06 due to concussion at Ottawa, January 23, 2006. • Missed majority of 2007-08 due to recurring knee injury. Traded to **St. Louis** by **Toronto** with Alex Steen for Lee Stempniak, November 24, 2008.

COLBORNE, Joe

(KOHL-bohrn, JOH) **TOR**

Center. Shoots left. 6'5", 213 lbs. Born, Calgary, Alta., January 30, 1990. Boston's 1st choice, 16th overall, in 2008 Entry Draft.

2004-05	Calgary Titans	Minor-AB	44	13	13	26	28	....	....	....	....	....	....	....	....	....	....	....	....	....	....	....	....	....	....
2005-06	Notre Dame	SMHL	48	13	14	27	26	....	....	....	....	....	....	....	....	....	....	....	....	....	....	....	....	....	....
2006-07	Camrose Kodiaks	AJHL	53	20	28	48	44	....	....	....	....	....	....	....	....	....	16	5	1	6	10	....	....	....	....
2007-08	Camrose Kodiaks	AJHL	55	33	*57	90	48	....	....	....	....	....	....	....	....	....	18	8	8	*16	26	....	....	....	....
2008-09	U. of Denver	WCHA	40	10	21	31	24	....	....	....	....	....	....	....	....	....	....	....	....	....	....	....	....	....	....
2009-10	U. of Denver	WCHA	39	22	19	41	30	....	....	....	....	....	....	....	....	....	....	....	....	....	....	....	....	....	....
	Providence Bruins	AHL	6	0	2	2	2	....	....	....	....	....	....	....	....	....	....	....	....	....	....	....	....	....	....
2010-11	Providence Bruins	AHL	55	12	14	26	35	....	....	....	....	....	....	....	....	....	....	....	....	....	....	....	....	....	....
	Toronto	**NHL**	**1**	**0**	**1**	**1**	**0**	**0**	**0**	**0**	**1**	**0.0**	**1**	**9**	**33.3**	**18:41**	....	....	....	....	....	....	....	....	....
	Toronto Marlies	AHL	20	8	8	16	8	....	....	....	....	....	....	....	....	....	....	....	....	....	....	....	....	....	....
	NHL Totals		**1**	**0**	**1**	**1**	**0**	**0**	**0**	**0**	**1**	**0.0**		**9**	**33.3**	**18:41**	....	....	....	....	....	....	....	....	....

WCHA All-Rookie Team (2009)

Traded to **Toronto** by **Boston** with Boston's 1st round choice (later traded to Anaheim - Anaheim selected Rickard Rakell) in 2011 Entry Draft and Boston's 2nd round choice (later traded to Colorado) in 2012 Entry Draft for Tomas Kaberle, February 18, 2011.

COLE, Erik

(KOHL, AIR-ihk) **MTL**

Left wing. Shoots left. 6'2", 205 lbs. Born, Oswego, NY, November 6, 1978. Carolina's 3rd choice, 71st overall, in 1998 Entry Draft.

1995-96	Oswego	High-NY	40	49	41	90	....	....	....	....	....	....	....	....	....	....	....	....	....	....	....	....	....	....	....
1996-97	Des Moines	USHL	48	30	34	64	140	....	....	....	....	....	....	....	....	....	5	2	0	2	6	....	....	....	....
1997-98	Clarkson Knights	ECAC	34	11	20	31	55	....	....	....	....	....	....	....	....	....	....	....	....	....	....	....	....	....	....
1998-99	Clarkson Knights	ECAC	36	*22	20	42	50	....	....	....	....	....	....	....	....	....	....	....	....	....	....	....	....	....	....
99-2000	Clarkson Knights	ECAC	33	19	11	30	46	....	....	....	....	....	....	....	....	....	....	....	....	....	....	....	....	....	....
	Cincinnati	IHL	9	4	3	7	2	....	....	....	....	....	....	....	....	....	7	1	1	2	2	....	....	....	....
2000-01	Cincinnati	IHL	69	23	20	43	28	....	....	....	....	....	....	....	....	....	5	1	0	1	2	....	....	....	....
2001-02	**Carolina**	**NHL**	**81**	**16**	**24**	**40**	**35**	**3**	**0**	**2**	**159**	**10.1**	**–10**	**17**	**47.1**	**16:04**	**23**	**6**	**3**	**9**	**30**	**1**	**0**	**1**	**18:27**
2002-03	**Carolina**	**NHL**	**53**	**14**	**13**	**27**	**72**	**6**	**2**	**3**	**125**	**11.2**	**1**	**56**	**39.3**	**17:08**	....	....	....	....	....	....	....	....	....
2003-04	**Carolina**	**NHL**	**80**	**18**	**24**	**42**	**93**	**2**	**2**	**3**	**172**	**10.5**	**–4**	**15**	**46.7**	**18:06**	....	....	....	....	....	....	....	....	....
2004-05	Eisbaren Berlin	Germany	39	6	21	27	76	....	....	....	....	....	....	....	....	....	8	5	1	6	37	....	....	....	....
2005-06♦	**Carolina**	**NHL**	**60**	**30**	**29**	**59**	**54**	**3**	**3**	**8**	**164**	**18.3**	**19**	**19**	**36.8**	**19:18**	**2**	**0**	**0**	**0**	**0**	**0**	**0**	**0**	**15:29**
	United States	Olympics	6	1	2	3	0	....	....	....	....	....	....	....	....	....	....	....	....	....	....	....	....	....	....
2006-07	**Carolina**	**NHL**	**71**	**29**	**32**	**61**	**76**	**9**	**0**	**4**	**166**	**17.5**	**2**	**27**	**40.7**	**18:01**	....	....	....	....	....	....	....	....	....
2007-08	**Carolina**	**NHL**	**73**	**22**	**29**	**51**	**76**	**10**	**0**	**4**	**216**	**10.2**	**5**	**38**	**23.7**	**19:22**	....	....	....	....	....	....	....	....	....
2008-09	**Edmonton**	**NHL**	**63**	**16**	**11**	**27**	**63**	**5**	**0**	**1**	**145**	**11.0**	**–3**	**48**	**39.6**	**17:05**	....	....	....	....	....	....	....	....	....
	Carolina	**NHL**	**17**	**2**	**13**	**15**	**10**	**0**	**0**	**0**	**33**	**6.1**	**3**	**1**	**100.0**	**19:36**	**18**	**0**	**5**	**5**	**22**	**0**	**0**	**0**	**17:17**
2009-10	**Carolina**	**NHL**	**40**	**11**	**5**	**16**	**29**	**2**	**0**	**1**	**81**	**13.6**	**–9**	**15**	**26.7**	**16:23**	....	....	....	....	....	....	....	....	....
2010-11	**Carolina**	**NHL**	**82**	**26**	**26**	**52**	**49**	**3**	**1**	**9**	**201**	**12.9**	**–1**	**34**	**20.6**	**18:27**	....	....	....	....	....	....	....	....	....
	NHL Totals		**620**	**184**	**206**	**390**	**557**	**43**	**8**	**35**	**1462**	**12.6**		**270**	**35.2**	**17:53**	**43**	**6**	**8**	**14**	**52**	**1**	**0**	**1**	**17:50**

USHL Second All-Star Team (1997) • ECAC Rookie of the Year (1998) (co-winner - Willie Mitchell) • ECAC First All-Star Team (1999) • NCAA East Second All-American Team (1999) • ECAC Second All-Star Team (2000)

Signed as a free agent by **Berlin** (Germany), October 24, 2004. Traded to **Edmonton** by **Carolina** for Joni Pitkanen, July 1, 2008. Traded to **Carolina** by **Edmonton** with Edmonton's 5th round choice (Matt Kennedy) in 2009 Entry Draft for Patrick O'Sullivan and Carolina's 2nd round choice (later traded to Buffalo, later traded to Toronto – Toronto selected Jesse Blacker) in 2009 Entry Draft, March 4, 2009. • Missed majority of 2009-10 due to leg and upper body injuries. Signed as a free agent by **Montreal**, July 1, 2011.

COLE, Ian

(KOHL, EE-an) **ST.L.**

Defense. Shoots left. 6'1", 221 lbs. Born, Ann Arbour, MI, February 21, 1989. St. Louis' 2nd choice, 18th overall, in 2007 Entry Draft.

2004-05	Det. Victory Honda	MWEHL	60	15	25	40	....	....	....	....	....	....	....	....	....	....	....	....	....	....	....	....	....	....	....
2005-06	USNTDP	U-17	18	2	1	3	14	....	....	....	....	....	....	....	....	....	....	....	....	....	....	....	....	....	....
	USNTDP	NAHL	40	2	8	10	75	....	....	....	....	....	....	....	....	....	12	0	3	3	14	....	....	....	....
2006-07	USNTDP	U-18	42	6	11	17	36	....	....	....	....	....	....	....	....	....	....	....	....	....	....	....	....	....	....
	USNTDP	NAHL	16	2	7	9	28	....	....	....	....	....	....	....	....	....	....	....	....	....	....	....	....	....	....
2007-08	U. of Notre Dame	CCHA	43	8	12	20	40	....	....	....	....	....	....	....	....	....	....	....	....	....	....	....	....	....	....
2008-09	U. of Notre Dame	CCHA	38	6	20	26	58	....	....	....	....	....	....	....	....	....	....	....	....	....	....	....	....	....	....
2009-10	U. of Notre Dame	CCHA	30	3	16	19	55	....	....	....	....	....	....	....	....	....	....	....	....	....	....	....	....	....	....
	Peoria Rivermen	AHL	9	1	4	5	4	....	....	....	....	....	....	....	....	....	....	....	....	....	....	....	....	....	....

Season	Club	League	GP	G	A	Pts	PIM	PP	SH	GW	S	%	+/-	TF	F%	Min	GP	G	A	Pts	PIM	PP	SH	GW	Min
			Regular Season														Playoffs								
2010-11	St. Louis	NHL	26	1	3	4	35	0	0	0	22	4.5	6	0	0.0	17:36	....	....	....	....	....	....	....	....	....
	Peoria Rivermen	AHL	44	5	10	15	63	....	....	....	....	....	....	....	....	....	....	....	....	....	....	....	....	....	....
	NHL Totals		26	1	3	4	35	0	0	0	22	4.5		0	0.0	17:36	....	....	....	....	....	....	....	....	....

CCHA First All-Star Team (2009) • NCAA West First All-American Team (2009)

COLLINS, Sean (KAW-lihnz, SHAWN) WSH

Defense. Shoots right. 6'1", 207 lbs. Born, Troy, MI, October 30, 1983.

Season	Club	League	GP	G	A	Pts	PIM	PP	SH	GW	S	%	+/-	TF	F%	Min	GP	G	A	Pts	PIM	PP	SH	GW	Min
2002-03	Sioux City	USHL	59	6	22	28	89	....	....	....	....	....	....	....	....	....	4	0	1	1	2	....	....	....	....
2003-04	Ohio State	CCHA	41	3	12	15	57	....	....	....	....	....	....	....	....	....	....	....	....	....	....	....	....	....	....
2004-05	Ohio State	CCHA	40	9	17	26	40	....	....	....	....	....	....	....	....	....	....	....	....	....	....	....	....	....	....
2005-06	Ohio State	CCHA	39	7	11	18	63	....	....	....	....	....	....	....	....	....	....	....	....	....	....	....	....	....	....
2006-07	Ohio State	CCHA	37	9	19	28	50	....	....	....	....	....	....	....	....	....	....	....	....	....	....	....	....	....	....
	Hershey Bears	AHL	3	0	0	0	2	....	....	....	....	....	....	....	....	....	....	....	....	....	....	....	....	....	....
2007-08	Hershey Bears	AHL	12	0	0	0	11	....	....	....	....	....	....	....	....	....	....	....	....	....	....	....	....	....	....
	South Carolina	ECHL	31	1	13	14	16	....	....	....	....	....	....	....	....	....	20	1	8	9	24	....	....	....	....
2008-09	Washington	NHL	15	1	1	2	12	0	0	0	14	7.1	1	0	0.0	14:32	....	....	....	....	....	....	....	....	....
	Hershey Bears	AHL	39	1	7	8	38	....	....	....	....	....	....	....	....	....	6	0	2	2	2	....	....	....	....
2009-10	Hershey Bears	AHL	63	1	17	18	55	....	....	....	....	....	....	....	....	....	15	1	2	3	16	....	....	....	....
2010-11	Washington	NHL	4	1	0	1	0	0	0	1	4	25.0	2	0	0.0	14:44	1	0	0	0	0	0	0	0	6:10
	Hershey Bears	AHL	73	4	16	20	78	....	....	....	....	....	....	....	....	....	....	....	....	....	....	....	....	....	....
	NHL Totals		19	2	1	3	12	0	0	1	18	11.1		0	0.0	14:35	1	0	0	0	0	0	0	0	6:10

Signed as a free agent by **Washington**, March 19, 2007.

COLLITON, Jeremy (KAW-lih-tuhn, JAIR-eh-mee) NYI

Center. Shoots right. 6'2", 195 lbs. Born, Blackie, Alta., January 13, 1985. NY Islanders' 4th choice, 58th overall, in 2003 Entry Draft.

Season	Club	League	GP	G	A	Pts	PIM	PP	SH	GW	S	%	+/-	TF	F%	Min	GP	G	A	Pts	PIM	PP	SH	GW	Min
99-2000	Airdrie Express	AMHL	33	16	25	41	28	....	....	....	....	....	....	....	....	....	....	....	....	....	....	....	....	....	....
2000-01	Crowsnest Pass	AJHL	63	18	30	48	98	....	....	....	....	....	....	....	....	....	....	....	....	....	....	....	....	....	....
2001-02	Prince Albert	WHL	68	11	21	32	53	....	....	....	....	....	....	....	....	....	....	....	....	....	....	....	....	....	....
2002-03	Prince Albert	WHL	58	20	28	48	76	....	....	....	....	....	....	....	....	....	....	....	....	....	....	....	....	....	....
2003-04	Prince Albert	WHL	62	24	26	50	73	....	....	....	....	....	....	....	....	....	6	5	5	10	8	....	....	....	....
2004-05	Prince Albert	WHL	41	16	30	46	25	....	....	....	....	....	....	....	....	....	17	3	4	7	21	....	....	....	....
2005-06	NY Islanders	NHL	19	1	1	2	6	0	0	0	9	11.1	2	76	40.8	6:18	....	....	....	....	....	....	....	....	....
	Bridgeport	AHL	66	20	32	52	44	....	....	....	....	....	....	....	....	....	6	0	1	1	2	....	....	....	....
2006-07	NY Islanders	NHL	1	0	0	0	0	0	0	0	0	0.0	-1	0	0.0	4:40	....	....	....	....	....	....	....	....	....
	Bridgeport	AHL	45	10	12	22	32	....	....	....	....	....	....	....	....	....	....	....	....	....	....	....	....	....	....
2007-08	NY Islanders	NHL	16	0	0	0	8	0	0	0	16	0.0	-4	104	51.9	8:46	....	....	....	....	....	....	....	....	....
	Bridgeport	AHL	65	9	11	20	44	....	....	....	....	....	....	....	....	....	....	....	....	....	....	....	....	....	....
2008-09	NY Islanders	NHL	6	0	1	1	2	0	0	0	4	0.0	-2	70	64.3	11:03	....	....	....	....	....	....	....	....	....
	Bridgeport	AHL	56	8	28	36	36	....	....	....	....	....	....	....	....	....	2	0	1	1	0	....	....	....	....
2009-10	Rogle	Sweden	46	11	10	21	24	....	....	....	....	....	....	....	....	....	....	....	....	....	....	....	....	....	....
	Rogle	Sweden-Q	10	3	3	6	8	....	....	....	....	....	....	....	....	....	....	....	....	....	....	....	....	....	....
2010-11	NY Islanders	NHL	15	2	1	3	10	2	0	0	7	28.6	-7	84	61.9	11:53	....	....	....	....	....	....	....	....	....
	Bridgeport	AHL	53	18	27	45	57	....	....	....	....	....	....	....	....	....	....	....	....	....	....	....	....	....	....
	NHL Totals		57	3	3	6	26	2	0	0	36	8.3		334	54.5	8:56	....	....	....	....	....	....	....	....	....

Signed as a free agent by **Rogle** (Sweden), June 19, 2009. Signed as a free agent by **NY Islanders**, November 30, 2010.

COMEAU, Blake (KOH-moh, BLAYK) NYI

Right wing. Shoots right. 6', 198 lbs. Born, Meadow Lake, Sask., February 18, 1986. NY Islanders' 2nd choice, 47th overall, in 2004 Entry Draft.

Season	Club	League	GP	G	A	Pts	PIM	PP	SH	GW	S	%	+/-	TF	F%	Min	GP	G	A	Pts	PIM	PP	SH	GW	Min
2001-02	Sask. Contacts	SMHL	42	27	33	60	72	....	....	....	....	....	....	....	....	....	....	....	....	....	....	....	....	....	....
	Kelowna Rockets	WHL	3	0	0	0	4	....	....	....	....	....	....	....	....	....	....	....	....	....	....	....	....	....	....
2002-03	Kelowna Rockets	WHL	54	5	18	23	77	....	....	....	....	....	....	....	....	....	19	2	1	3	20	....	....	....	....
2003-04	Kelowna Rockets	WHL	71	10	23	33	123	....	....	....	....	....	....	....	....	....	17	4	2	6	23	....	....	....	....
2004-05	Kelowna Rockets	WHL	65	24	23	47	108	....	....	....	....	....	....	....	....	....	24	6	12	18	34	....	....	....	....
2005-06	Kelowna Rockets	WHL	60	21	53	74	85	....	....	....	....	....	....	....	....	....	12	4	9	13	22	....	....	....	....
	Bridgeport	AHL	....	....	....	....	....	....	....	....	....	....	....	....	....	....	7	0	3	3	0	....	....	....	....
2006-07	NY Islanders	NHL	3	0	0	0	0	0	0	0	1	0.0	0	0	0.0	9:25	....	....	....	....	....	....	....	....	....
	Bridgeport	AHL	61	12	31	43	46	....	....	....	....	....	....	....	....	....	....	....	....	....	....	....	....	....	....
2007-08	NY Islanders	NHL	51	8	7	15	22	1	0	1	67	11.9	1	27	29.6	11:40	....	....	....	....	....	....	....	....	....
	Bridgeport	AHL	31	4	15	19	30	....	....	....	....	....	....	....	....	....	....	....	....	....	....	....	....	....	....
2008-09	NY Islanders	NHL	53	7	18	25	32	2	0	0	78	9.0	-17	45	31.1	16:17	....	....	....	....	....	....	....	....	....
	Bridgeport	AHL	19	4	15	19	22	....	....	....	....	....	....	....	....	....	2	0	0	0	0	....	....	....	....
2009-10	NY Islanders	NHL	61	17	18	35	40	0	1	2	133	12.8	-2	21	47.6	15:25	....	....	....	....	....	....	....	....	....
2010-11	NY Islanders	NHL	77	24	22	46	43	5	1	3	182	13.2	-17	112	31.3	18:41	....	....	....	....	....	....	....	....	....
	NHL Totals		245	56	65	121	137	8	2	6	461	12.1		205	32.7	15:47	....	....	....	....	....	....	....	....	....

WHL West First All-Star Team (2006)

COMMODORE, Mike (KAWM-uh-dohr, MIGHK) DET

Defense. Shoots right. 6'4", 233 lbs. Born, Fort Saskatchewan, Alta., November 7, 1979. New Jersey's 2nd choice, 42nd overall, in 1999 Entry Draft.

Season	Club	League	GP	G	A	Pts	PIM	PP	SH	GW	S	%	+/-	TF	F%	Min	GP	G	A	Pts	PIM	PP	SH	GW	Min
1996-97	Ft. Saskatchewan	AJHL	51	3	8	11	244	....	....	....	....	....	....	....	....	....	....	....	....	....	....	....	....	....	....
1997-98	North Dakota	WCHA	29	0	5	5	74	....	....	....	....	....	....	....	....	....	....	....	....	....	....	....	....	....	....
1998-99	North Dakota	WCHA	39	5	8	13	154	....	....	....	....	....	....	....	....	....	....	....	....	....	....	....	....	....	....
99-2000	North Dakota	WCHA	38	5	7	12	*154	....	....	....	....	....	....	....	....	....	....	....	....	....	....	....	....	....	....
2000-01	New Jersey	NHL	20	1	4	5	14	0	0	0	11	9.1	5	0	0.0	12:46	....	....	....	....	....	....	....	....	....
	Albany River Rats	AHL	41	2	5	7	59	....	....	....	....	....	....	....	....	....	....	....	....	....	....	....	....	....	....
2001-02	New Jersey	NHL	37	0	1	1	30	0	0	0	22	0.0	-12	0	0.0	12:37	....	....	....	....	....	....	....	....	....
	Albany River Rats	AHL	14	0	3	3	31	....	....	....	....	....	....	....	....	....	....	....	....	....	....	....	....	....	....
2002-03	Cincinnati	AHL	61	2	9	11	210	....	....	....	....	....	....	....	....	....	....	....	....	....	....	....	....	....	....
	Calgary	NHL	6	0	1	1	19	0	0	0	5	0.0	2	0	0.0	11:35	....	....	....	....	....	....	....	....	....
	Saint John Flames	AHL	7	0	3	3	18	....	....	....	....	....	....	....	....	....	....	....	....	....	....	....	....	....	....
2003-04	Calgary	NHL	12	0	0	0	25	0	0	0	10	0.0	-4	0	0.0	15:17	20	0	2	2	19	0	0	0	11:34
	Lowell	AHL	37	5	11	16	75	....	....	....	....	....	....	....	....	....	....	....	....	....	....	....	....	....	....
2004-05	Lowell	AHL	73	6	29	35	175	....	....	....	....	....	....	....	....	....	11	1	2	3	18	....	....	....	....
2005-06♦	Carolina	NHL	72	3	10	13	138	0	0	2	72	4.2	12	1	0.0	15:30	25	2	2	4	33	0	1	0	19:27
2006-07	Carolina	NHL	82	7	22	29	113	0	2	1	136	5.1	0	0	0.0	19:54	....	....	....	....	....	....	....	....	....
2007-08	Carolina	NHL	41	3	9	12	74	0	0	0	67	4.5	2	0	0.0	19:16	....	....	....	....	....	....	....	....	....
	Ottawa	NHL	26	0	2	2	26	0	0	0	30	0.0	-9	0	0.0	16:33	4	0	2	2	0	0	0	0	20:14
2008-09	Columbus	NHL	81	5	19	24	100	0	0	0	103	4.9	11	3	66.7	22:54	4	0	0	0	18	0	0	0	21:32
2009-10	Columbus	NHL	57	2	9	11	62	0	0	1	54	3.7	-9	0	0.0	19:00	....	....	....	....	....	....	....	....	....
2010-11	Columbus	NHL	20	2	4	6	44	0	0	2	32	6.3	-8	1	0.0	18:34	....	....	....	....	....	....	....	....	....
	Springfield	AHL	11	0	2	2	20	....	....	....	....	....	....	....	....	....	....	....	....	....	....	....	....	....	....
	NHL Totals		454	23	81	104	645	0	2	6	542	4.2		5	40.0	18:10	53	2	6	8	70	0	1	0	16:42

NCAA Championship All-Tournament Team (2000)

Traded to **Anaheim** by **New Jersey** with Petr Sykora, Jean-Francois Damphousse and Igor Pohanka for Jeff Friesen, Oleg Tverdovsky and Maxim Balmochnykh, July 6, 2002. Traded to **Calgary** by **Anaheim** with Jean-Francois Damphousse for Rob Niedermayer, March 11, 2003. Traded to **Carolina** by **Calgary** for Atlanta's 3rd round choice (previously acquired, Calgary selected Gord Baldwin) in 2005 Entry Draft, July 29, 2005. Traded to **Ottawa** by **Carolina** with Cory Stillman for Joe Corvo and Patrick Eaves, February 11, 2008. Signed as a free agent by **Columbus**, July 1, 2008. • Missed majority of 2010-11 due to hand injury and as a healthy reserve. Signed as a free agent by **Detroit**, July 1, 2011.

COMRIE, Mike

(KAWM-ree, MIGHK)

Center. Shoots left. 5'10", 185 lbs. Born, Edmonton, Alta., September 11, 1980. Edmonton's 5th choice, 91st overall, in 1999 Entry Draft.

			Regular Season														Playoffs								
Season	Club	League	GP	G	A	Pts	PIM	PP	SH	GW	S	%	+/-	TF	F%	Min	GP	G	A	Pts	PIM	PP	SH	GW	Min
1995-96	Edmonton SSAC	AMHL	33	51	52	103	....	....	....	....	....	....	....	....	....	....	....	....	....	....	....	....	....	....	....
1996-97	St. Albert Saints	AJHL	63	37	41	78	44	....	....	....	....	....	....	....	....	....	....	....	....	....	....	....	....	....	....
1997-98	St. Albert Saints	AJHL	58	*60	*78	*138	134	....	....	....	....	....	....	....	....	....	19	*24	*24	*48	51	....	....	....	....
1998-99	U. of Michigan	CCHA	42	19	25	44	38	....	....	....	....	....	....	....	....	....	....	....	....	....	....	....	....	....	....
99-2000	U. of Michigan	CCHA	40	24	35	59	95	....	....	....	....	....	....	....	....	....	....	....	....	....	....	....	....	....	....
2000-01	Kootenay Ice	WHL	37	39	40	79	79	....	....	....	....	....	....	....	....	....	....	....	....	....	....	....	....	....	....
	Edmonton	**NHL**	**41**	**8**	**14**	**22**	**14**	**3**	**0**	**1**	**62**	**12.9**	**6**	**372**	**43.3**	**11:23**	**6**	**1**	**2**	**3**	**0**	**1**	**0**	**1**	**15:00**
2001-02	**Edmonton**	**NHL**	**82**	**33**	**27**	**60**	**45**	**8**	**0**	**5**	**170**	**19.4**	**16**	**1198**	**47.3**	**17:32**	....	....	....	....	....	....	....	....	....
2002-03	**Edmonton**	**NHL**	**69**	**20**	**31**	**51**	**90**	**8**	**0**	**6**	**170**	**11.8**	**–18**	**1069**	**47.1**	**17:51**	**6**	**1**	**0**	**1**	**10**	**0**	**0**	**0**	**13:07**
2003-04	**Philadelphia**	**NHL**	**21**	**4**	**5**	**9**	**12**	**0**	**0**	**1**	**36**	**11.1**	**2**	**165**	**50.9**	**12:51**	....	....	....	....	....	....	....	....	....
	Phoenix	**NHL**	**28**	**8**	**7**	**15**	**16**	**1**	**1**	**1**	**65**	**12.3**	**–8**	**304**	**50.3**	**17:50**	....	....	....	....	....	....	....	....	....
2004-05	Farjestad	Sweden	10	1	6	7	10	....	....	....	....	....	....	....	....	....	....	....	....	....	....	....	....	....	....
2005-06	**Phoenix**	**NHL**	**80**	**30**	**30**	**60**	**55**	**10**	**0**	**4**	**190**	**15.8**	**2**	**781**	**52.8**	**16:01**	....	....	....	....	....	....	....	....	....
2006-07	**Phoenix**	**NHL**	**24**	**7**	**13**	**20**	**20**	**4**	**0**	**1**	**38**	**18.4**	**1**	**210**	**48.6**	**16:36**	....	....	....	....	....	....	....	....	....
	Ottawa	**NHL**	**41**	**13**	**12**	**25**	**24**	**3**	**0**	**2**	**87**	**14.9**	**–1**	**244**	**50.0**	**14:27**	**20**	**2**	**4**	**6**	**17**	**0**	**0**	**0**	**12:41**
2007-08	**NY Islanders**	**NHL**	**76**	**21**	**28**	**49**	**87**	**4**	**0**	**3**	**194**	**10.8**	**–21**	**1227**	**46.0**	**19:11**	....	....	....	....	....	....	....	....	....
2008-09	**NY Islanders**	**NHL**	**41**	**7**	**13**	**20**	**26**	**2**	**0**	**0**	**80**	**8.8**	**–8**	**390**	**41.3**	**16:28**	....	....	....	....	....	....	....	....	....
	Ottawa	**NHL**	**22**	**3**	**4**	**7**	**6**	**0**	**0**	**1**	**41**	**7.3**	**–7**	**27**	**37.0**	**14:17**	....	....	....	....	....	....	....	....	....
2009-10	**Edmonton**	**NHL**	**43**	**13**	**8**	**21**	**30**	**5**	**0**	**0**	**97**	**13.4**	**–9**	**47**	**53.2**	**14:14**	....	....	....	....	....	....	....	....	....
2010-11	**Pittsburgh**	**NHL**	**21**	**1**	**5**	**6**	**18**	**0**	**0**	**0**	**25**	**4.0**	**–4**	**40**	**37.5**	**11:49**	....	....	....	....	....	....	....	....	....
	NHL Totals		**589**	**168**	**197**	**365**	**443**	**48**	**1**	**25**	**1255**	**13.4**		**6074**	**47.4**	**16:06**	**32**	**4**	**6**	**10**	**27**	**1**	**0**	**1**	**13:12**

CCHA All-Rookie Team (1999) • CCHA First All-Star Team (1999) • CCHA Rookie of the Year (1999) • CCHA First All-Star Team (2000) • NCAA West Second All-American Team (2000)

• Left **University of Michigan** (CCHA) and signed as a free agent by **Kootenay** (WHL), August 23, 2000. • Left **Kootenay** (WHL) and signed with **Edmonton**, December 30, 2000. Traded to **Philadelphia** by **Edmonton** for Jeff Woywitka, Philadelphia's 1st round choice (Rob Schremp) in 2004 Entry Draft and Philadelphia's 3rd round choice (Danny Syvret) in 2005 Entry Draft, December 16, 2003. Traded to **Phoenix** by **Philadelphia** for Sean Burke, Branko Radivojevic and Ben Eager, February 9, 2004. Signed as a free agent by **Farjestad** (Sweden), October 30, 2004. Traded to **Ottawa** by **Phoenix** for Alexei Kaigorodov, January 3, 2007. Signed as a free agent by **NY Islanders**, July 5, 2007. Traded to **Ottawa** by **NY Islanders** with Chris Campoli for Dean McAmmond and San Jose's 1st round choice (previously acquired, later traded to Columbus, later traded to Anaheim – Anaheim selected Kyle Palmieri) in 2009 Entry Draft, February 20, 2009. Signed as a free agent by **Edmonton**, September 10, 2009. Signed as a free agent by **Pittsburgh**, September 3, 2010. • Missed majority of 2010-11 due to hip injury vs. Montreal, October 9, 2010

CONBOY, Tim

(KAWN-boi, TIHM) **OTT**

Defense. Shoots right. 6'2", 210 lbs. Born, Farmington, MN, March 22, 1982. San Jose's 6th choice, 217th overall, in 2002 Entry Draft.

99-2000	Brainerd	High-MN	22	20	26	46	....	....	....	....	....	....	....	....	....	....	....	....	....	....	....	....	....	....	....
2000-01	Rochester	USHL	51	5	9	14	256	....	....	....	....	....	....	....	....	....	....	....	....	....	....	....	....	....	....
2001-02	Rochester	USHL	14	1	6	7	65	....	....	....	....	....	....	....	....	....	....	....	....	....	....	....	....	....	....
	Topeka	USHL	29	4	15	19	128	....	....	....	....	....	....	....	....	....	....	....	....	....	....	....	....	....	....
2002-03	St. Cloud State	WCHA	31	3	12	15	48	....	....	....	....	....	....	....	....	....	....	....	....	....	....	....	....	....	....
2003-04	St. Cloud State	WCHA	32	5	5	10	68	....	....	....	....	....	....	....	....	....	....	....	....	....	....	....	....	....	....
	Cleveland Barons	AHL	....	....	....	....	....	....	....	....	....	....	....	....	....	....	3	0	3	3	4	....	....	....	....
2004-05	Cleveland Barons	AHL	61	4	11	15	134	....	....	....	....	....	....	....	....	....	....	....	....	....	....	....	....	....	....
2005-06	Cleveland Barons	AHL	78	6	14	20	124	....	....	....	....	....	....	....	....	....	....	....	....	....	....	....	....	....	....
2006-07	Albany River Rats	AHL	75	3	7	10	163	....	....	....	....	....	....	....	....	....	5	0	1	1	6	....	....	....	....
2007-08	**Carolina**	**NHL**	**19**	**0**	**5**	**5**	**60**	**0**	**0**	**0**	**16**	**0.0**	**1**	**0**	**0.0**	**6:58**	....	....	....	....	....	....	....	....	....
	Albany River Rats	AHL	52	2	2	4	191	....	....	....	....	....	....	....	....	....	1	0	0	0	21	....	....	....	....
2008-09	**Carolina**	**NHL**	**28**	**0**	**1**	**1**	**37**	**0**	**0**	**0**	**13**	**0.0**	**–1**	**0**	**0.0**	**5:21**	**3**	**0**	**0**	**0**	**9**	**0**	**0**	**0**	**4:22**
	Albany River Rats	AHL	39	1	5	6	127	....	....	....	....	....	....	....	....	....	....	....	....	....	....	....	....	....	....
2009-10	**Carolina**	**NHL**	**12**	**0**	**0**	**0**	**24**	**0**	**0**	**0**	**5**	**0.0**	**–5**	**0**	**0.0**	**4:18**	....	....	....	....	....	....	....	....	....
	Albany River Rats	AHL	37	0	3	3	87	....	....	....	....	....	....	....	....	....	8	0	1	1	18	....	....	....	....
2010-11	Portland Pirates	AHL	70	0	12	12	233	....	....	....	....	....	....	....	....	....	12	1	1	2	10	....	....	....	....
	NHL Totals		**59**	**0**	**6**	**6**	**121**	**0**	**0**	**0**	**34**	**0.0**		**0**	**0.0**	**5:40**	**3**	**0**	**0**	**0**	**9**	**0**	**0**	**0**	**4:22**

Signed as a free agent by **Carolina**, July 21, 2006. Signed as a free agent by **Buffalo**, July 16, 2010. Signed as a free agent by **Ottawa**, July 11, 2011.

CONDRA, Erik

(KAWN-druh, AIR-ihk) **OTT**

Right wing. Shoots right. 6', 188 lbs. Born, Trenton, MI, August 6, 1986. Ottawa's 7th choice, 211th overall, in 2006 Entry Draft.

2004-05	Lincoln Stars	USHL	60	30	30	60	56	....	....	....	....	....	....	....	....	....	4	0	2	2	4	....	....	....	....
2005-06	U. of Notre Dame	CCHA	36	6	28	34	32	....	....	....	....	....	....	....	....	....	....	....	....	....	....	....	....	....	....
2006-07	U. of Notre Dame	CCHA	42	14	34	48	18	....	....	....	....	....	....	....	....	....	....	....	....	....	....	....	....	....	....
2007-08	U. of Notre Dame	CCHA	41	15	23	38	26	....	....	....	....	....	....	....	....	....	....	....	....	....	....	....	....	....	....
2008-09	U. of Notre Dame	CCHA	40	13	25	38	34	....	....	....	....	....	....	....	....	....	....	....	....	....	....	....	....	....	....
2009-10	Binghamton	AHL	80	11	27	38	61	....	....	....	....	....	....	....	....	....	....	....	....	....	....	....	....	....	....
2010-11	**Ottawa**	**NHL**	**26**	**6**	**5**	**11**	**12**	**1**	**0**	**2**	**48**	**12.5**	**–1**	**4**	**50.0**	**15:52**	....	....	....	....	....	....	....	....	....
	Binghamton	AHL	55	17	30	47	28	....	....	....	....	....	....	....	....	....	23	5	12	17	8	....	....	....	....
	NHL Totals		**26**	**6**	**5**	**11**	**12**	**1**	**0**	**2**	**48**	**12.5**		**4**	**50.0**	**15:52**	....	....	....	....	....	....	....	....	....

CCHA All-Rookie Team (2006) • CCHA Second All-Star Team (2009) • NCAA West Second All-American Team (2009)

CONNER, Chris

(KAWN-uhr, KRIHS) **DET**

Right wing. Shoots left. 5'8", 180 lbs. Born, Westland, MI, December 23, 1983.

2002-03	Michigan Tech	WCHA	38	13	24	37	8	....	....	....	....	....	....	....	....	....	....	....	....	....	....	....	....	....	....
2003-04	Michigan Tech	WCHA	38	25	14	39	12	....	....	....	....	....	....	....	....	....	....	....	....	....	....	....	....	....	....
2004-05	Michigan Tech	WCHA	37	14	10	24	6	....	....	....	....	....	....	....	....	....	....	....	....	....	....	....	....	....	....
2005-06	Michigan Tech	WCHA	38	17	12	29	18	....	....	....	....	....	....	....	....	....	....	....	....	....	....	....	....	....	....
	Iowa Stars	AHL	15	2	3	5	0	....	....	....	....	....	....	....	....	....	7	1	1	2	2	....	....	....	....
2006-07	**Dallas**	**NHL**	**11**	**1**	**2**	**3**	**4**	**0**	**0**	**0**	**18**	**5.6**	**–3**	**1**	**100.0**	**11:15**	....	....	....	....	....	....	....	....	....
	Iowa Stars	AHL	48	19	18	37	24	....	....	....	....	....	....	....	....	....	12	2	5	7	2	....	....	....	....
2007-08	**Dallas**	**NHL**	**22**	**3**	**2**	**5**	**6**	**0**	**0**	**0**	**27**	**11.1**	**0**	**1**	**100.0**	**12:00**	**1**	**0**	**0**	**0**	**0**	**0**	**0**	**0**	**4:17**
	Iowa Stars	AHL	55	13	26	39	17	....	....	....	....	....	....	....	....	....	....	....	....	....	....	....	....	....	....
2008-09	**Dallas**	**NHL**	**38**	**3**	**10**	**13**	**10**	**0**	**0**	**1**	**34**	**8.8**	**–5**	**1**	**0.0**	**10:56**	....	....	....	....	....	....	....	....	....
	Peoria Rivermen	AHL	30	16	12	28	10	....	....	....	....	....	....	....	....	....	....	....	....	....	....	....	....	....	....
2009-10	**Pittsburgh**	**NHL**	**8**	**2**	**1**	**3**	**0**	**0**	**0**	**1**	**11**	**18.2**	**–1**	**1**	**0.0**	**9:36**	**1**	**0**	**0**	**0**	**0**	**0**	**0**	**0**	**11:03**
	Wilkes-Barre	AHL	59	19	37	56	21	....	....	....	....	....	....	....	....	....	4	2	2	4	2	....	....	....	....
2010-11	**Pittsburgh**	**NHL**	**60**	**7**	**9**	**16**	**10**	**0**	**0**	**3**	**91**	**7.7**	**5**	**4**	**25.0**	**11:49**	**7**	**1**	**0**	**1**	**0**	**0**	**0**	**0**	**12:22**
	Wilkes-Barre	AHL	11	3	6	9	2	....	....	....	....	....	....	....	....	....	....	....	....	....	....	....	....	....	....
	NHL Totals		**139**	**16**	**24**	**40**	**30**	**0**	**0**	**5**	**181**	**8.8**		**8**	**37.5**	**11:26**	**9**	**1**	**0**	**1**	**0**	**0**	**0**	**0**	**11:20**

WCHA Second All-Star Team (2004)

Signed as a free agent by **Dallas**, July 13, 2006. Signed as a free agent by **Pittsburgh**, July 5. 2009. Signed as a free agent by **Detroit**, July 5, 2011.

CONNOLLY, Tim

(KAW-nuhl-lee, TIHM) **TOR**

Center. Shoots right. 6'1", 190 lbs. Born, Syracuse, NY, May 7, 1981. NY Islanders' 1st choice, 5th overall, in 1999 Entry Draft.

1996-97	Syracuse	ON-Jr.A	50	42	62	104	34	....	....	....	....	....	....	....	....	....	....	....	....	....	....	....	....	....	....
1997-98	Erie Otters	OHL	59	30	32	62	32	....	....	....	....	....	....	....	....	....	7	1	6	7	6	....	....	....	....
1998-99	Erie Otters	OHL	46	34	34	68	50	....	....	....	....	....	....	....	....	....	....	....	....	....	....	....	....	....	....
99-2000	**NY Islanders**	**NHL**	**81**	**14**	**20**	**34**	**44**	**2**	**1**	**1**	**114**	**12.3**	**–25**	**786**	**36.3**	**16:18**	....	....	....	....	....	....	....	....	....
2000-01	**NY Islanders**	**NHL**	**82**	**10**	**31**	**41**	**42**	**5**	**0**	**0**	**171**	**5.8**	**–14**	**989**	**41.7**	**20:02**	....	....	....	....	....	....	....	....	....
2001-02	**Buffalo**	**NHL**	**82**	**10**	**35**	**45**	**34**	**3**	**0**	**3**	**126**	**7.9**	**4**	**1074**	**39.6**	**16:58**	....	....	....	....	....	....	....	....	....
2002-03	**Buffalo**	**NHL**	**80**	**12**	**13**	**25**	**32**	**6**	**0**	**2**	**159**	**7.5**	**–28**	**845**	**42.8**	**16:00**	....	....	....	....	....	....	....	....	....
2003-04	**Buffalo**	**NHL**	DID NOT PLAY – INJURED																						
2004-05	Langnau	Swiss	16	7	3	10	14	....	....	....	....	....	....	....	....	....	....	....	....	....	....	....	....	....	....
2005-06	**Buffalo**	**NHL**	**63**	**16**	**39**	**55**	**28**	**7**	**0**	**3**	**99**	**16.2**	**5**	**844**	**42.5**	**18:00**	**8**	**5**	**6**	**11**	**0**	**1**	**1**	**1**	**17:29**
2006-07	**Buffalo**	**NHL**	**2**	**1**	**0**	**1**	**2**	**0**	**0**	**0**	**2**	**50.0**	**1**	**13**	**53.9**	**13:07**	**16**	**0**	**9**	**9**	**4**	**0**	**0**	**0**	**16:56**
2007-08	**Buffalo**	**NHL**	**48**	**7**	**33**	**40**	**8**	**3**	**1**	**3**	**111**	**6.3**	**4**	**463**	**48.0**	**18:41**	....	....	....	....	....	....	....	....	....
2008-09	**Buffalo**	**NHL**	**48**	**18**	**29**	**47**	**22**	**5**	**1**	**5**	**126**	**14.3**	**12**	**544**	**42.1**	**19:07**	....	....	....	....	....	....	....	....	....

			Regular Season														Playoffs								
Season	Club	League	GP	G	A	Pts	PIM	PP	SH	GW	S	%	+/-	TF	F%	Min	GP	G	A	Pts	PIM	PP	SH	GW	Min
2009-10	**Buffalo**	**NHL**	**73**	**17**	**48**	**65**	**28**	**7**	**1**	**5**	**206**	**8.3**	**10**	**764**	**46.9**	**18:37**	**6**	**0**	**1**	**1**	**2**	**0**	**0**	**0**	**17:49**
2010-11	**Buffalo**	**NHL**	**68**	**13**	**29**	**42**	**20**	**6**	**0**	**3**	**151**	**8.6**	**–10**	**969**	**45.9**	**16:55**	**6**	**0**	**2**	**2**	**2**	**0**	**0**	**0**	**19:04**
	NHL Totals		**627**	**118**	**277**	**395**	**260**	**44**	**4**	**25**	**1265**	**9.3**		**7291**	**42.6**	**17:44**	**36**	**5**	**18**	**23**	**8**	**1**	**1**	**1**	**17:34**

Traded to **Buffalo** by **NY Islanders** with Taylor Pyatt for Michael Peca, June 24, 2001. • Missed entire 2003-04 due to concussion in pre-season vs. Chicago, October 2, 2003. Signed as a free agent by **Langnau** (Swiss), October 10, 2004. • Missed majority of 2006-07 due to concussion in playoff game vs. Ottawa, May 8, 2006. Signed as a free agent by **Toronto**, July 2, 2011.

CONROY, Craig

(KAWN-roi, KRAYG)

Center. Shoots right. 6'2", 193 lbs. Born, Potsdam, NY, September 4, 1971. Montreal's 7th choice, 123rd overall, in 1990 Entry Draft.

1989-90	Northwood	High-NY	31	33	43	76	....	....	....	....	....	....	....	....	....	....	....	....	....	....	....	....	....	....	....
1990-91	Clarkson Knights	ECAC	40	8	21	29	24	....	....	....	....	....	....	....	....	....	....	....	....	....	....	....	....	....	....
1991-92	Clarkson Knights	ECAC	31	19	17	36	36	....	....	....	....	....	....	....	....	....	....	....	....	....	....	....	....	....	....
1992-93	Clarkson Knights	ECAC	35	10	23	33	26	....	....	....	....	....	....	....	....	....	....	....	....	....	....	....	....	....	....
1993-94	Clarkson Knights	ECAC	34	26	*40	*66	46	....	....	....	....	....	....	....	....	....	....	....	....	....	....	....	....	....	....
1994-95	Fredericton	AHL	55	26	18	44	29	....	....	....	....	....	....	....	....	....	11	7	3	10	6	....	....	....	....
	Montreal	**NHL**	**6**	**1**	**0**	**1**	**0**	**0**	**0**	**0**	**4**	**25.0**	**–1**	....	....	....	....	....	....	....	....	....	....	....	....
1995-96	**Montreal**	**NHL**	**7**	**0**	**0**	**0**	**2**	**0**	**0**	**0**	**1**	**0.0**	**–4**	....	....	....	....	....	....	....	....	....	....	....	....
	Fredericton	AHL	67	31	38	69	65	....	....	....	....	....	....	....	....	....	10	5	7	12	6	....	....	....	....
1996-97	Fredericton	AHL	9	10	6	16	10	....	....	....	....	....	....	....	....	....	....	....	....	....	....	....	....	....	....
	St. Louis	**NHL**	**61**	**6**	**11**	**17**	**43**	**0**	**0**	**1**	**74**	**8.1**	**0**	....	....	....	**6**	**0**	**0**	**0**	**8**	**0**	**0**	**0**	....
	Worcester IceCats	AHL	5	5	6	11	2	....	....	....	....	....	....	....	....	....	....	....	....	....	....	....	....	....	....
1997-98	**St. Louis**	**NHL**	**81**	**14**	**29**	**43**	**46**	**0**	**3**	**1**	**118**	**11.9**	**20**	....	....	....	**10**	**1**	**2**	**3**	**8**	**0**	**0**	**1**	....
1998-99	**St. Louis**	**NHL**	**69**	**14**	**25**	**39**	**38**	**0**	**1**	**1**	**134**	**10.4**	**14**	**1190**	**54.6**	**16:39**	**13**	**2**	**1**	**3**	**6**	**0**	**0**	**0**	**15:09**
99-2000	**St. Louis**	**NHL**	**79**	**12**	**15**	**27**	**36**	**1**	**2**	**3**	**98**	**12.2**	**5**	**1339**	**53.6**	**14:48**	**7**	**0**	**2**	**2**	**2**	**0**	**0**	**0**	**13:13**
2000-01	**St. Louis**	**NHL**	**69**	**11**	**14**	**25**	**46**	**0**	**3**	**2**	**101**	**10.9**	**2**	**729**	**55.1**	**14:01**	....	....	....	....	....	....	....	....	....
	Calgary	**NHL**	**14**	**3**	**4**	**7**	**14**	**0**	**1**	**0**	**32**	**9.4**	**0**	**264**	**52.7**	**18:08**	....	....	....	....	....	....	....	....	....
2001-02	**Calgary**	**NHL**	**81**	**27**	**48**	**75**	**32**	**7**	**2**	**4**	**146**	**18.5**	**24**	**1654**	**54.3**	**20:56**	....	....	....	....	....	....	....	....	....
2002-03	**Calgary**	**NHL**	**79**	**22**	**37**	**59**	**36**	**5**	**0**	**2**	**143**	**15.4**	**–4**	**1579**	**57.0**	**19:47**	....	....	....	....	....	....	....	....	....
2003-04	**Calgary**	**NHL**	**63**	**8**	**39**	**47**	**44**	**2**	**0**	**0**	**112**	**7.1**	**13**	**1402**	**53.9**	**19:13**	**26**	**6**	**11**	**17**	**12**	**2**	**0**	**1**	**20:23**
2004-05			DID NOT PLAY																						
2005-06	**Los Angeles**	**NHL**	**78**	**22**	**44**	**66**	**78**	**5**	**3**	**3**	**154**	**14.3**	**13**	**1429**	**51.2**	**19:13**	....	....	....	....	....	....	....	....	....
	United States	Olympics	6	1	4	5	2	....	....	....	....	....	....	....	....	....	....	....	....	....	....	....	....	....	....
2006-07	**Los Angeles**	**NHL**	**52**	**5**	**11**	**16**	**38**	**4**	**0**	**2**	**73**	**6.8**	**–13**	**802**	**51.5**	**15:29**	....	....	....	....	....	....	....	....	....
	Calgary	**NHL**	**28**	**8**	**13**	**21**	**18**	**0**	**1**	**0**	**39**	**20.5**	**10**	**443**	**50.3**	**16:00**	**6**	**1**	**1**	**2**	**8**	**0**	**0**	**0**	**15:33**
2007-08	**Calgary**	**NHL**	**79**	**12**	**22**	**34**	**71**	**1**	**0**	**4**	**116**	**10.3**	**6**	**1411**	**51.5**	**17:09**	**7**	**0**	**2**	**2**	**8**	**0**	**0**	**0**	**16:43**
2008-09	**Calgary**	**NHL**	**82**	**12**	**36**	**48**	**28**	**0**	**1**	**1**	**104**	**11.5**	**20**	**1382**	**52.8**	**15:22**	**6**	**0**	**1**	**1**	**0**	**0**	**0**	**0**	**12:35**
2009-10	**Calgary**	**NHL**	**63**	**3**	**12**	**15**	**25**	**0**	**0**	**1**	**52**	**5.8**	**–6**	**879**	**51.5**	**13:34**	....	....	....	....	....	....	....	....	....
2010-11	**Calgary**	**NHL**	**18**	**2**	**0**	**2**	**8**	**0**	**0**	**1**	**11**	**18.2**	**–1**	**189**	**53.4**	**9:18**	....	....	....	....	....	....	....	....	....
	NHL Totals		**1009**	**182**	**360**	**542**	**603**	**25**	**17**	**26**	**1512**	**12.0**		**14692**	**53.4**	**16:52**	**81**	**10**	**20**	**30**	**52**	**2**	**0**	**2**	**17:00**

ECAC First All-Star Team (1994) • NCAA East First All-American Team (1994) • NCAA Final Four All-Tournament Team (1994)

Traded to **St. Louis** by **Montreal** with Pierre Turgeon and Rory Fitzpatrick for Murray Baron, Shayne Corson and St. Louis' 5th round choice (Gennady Razin) in 1997 Entry Draft, October 29, 1996. Traded to **Calgary** by **St. Louis** with St. Louis' 7th round choice (David Moss) in 2001 Entry Draft for Cory Stillman, March 13, 2001. Signed as a free agent by **Los Angeles**, July 6, 2004. Traded to **Calgary** by **Los Angeles** for Jamie Lundmark, Calgary's 4th round choice (Dwight King) in 2007 Entry Draft and Calgary's 2nd round choice (later traded back to Calgary – Calgary selected Mitch Wahl) in 2008 Entry Draft, January 29, 2007. • Officially announced his retirement, February 4, 2011.

COOKE, Matt

(KUK, MAT) **PIT**

Center. Shoots left. 5'11", 205 lbs. Born, Belleville, Ont., September 7, 1978. Vancouver's 8th choice, 144th overall, in 1997 Entry Draft.

1994-95	Wellington Dukes	ON-Jr.A	46	9	23	32	62	....	....	....	....	....	....	....	....	....	....	....	....	....	....	....	....	....	....
1995-96	Windsor Spitfires	OHL	61	8	11	19	102	....	....	....	....	....	....	....	....	....	7	1	3	4	6	....	....	....	....
1996-97	Windsor Spitfires	OHL	65	45	50	95	146	....	....	....	....	....	....	....	....	....	5	5	5	10	10	....	....	....	....
1997-98	Windsor Spitfires	OHL	23	14	19	33	50	....	....	....	....	....	....	....	....	....	....	....	....	....	....	....	....	....	....
	Kingston	OHL	25	8	13	21	49	....	....	....	....	....	....	....	....	....	12	8	8	16	20	....	....	....	....
1998-99	**Vancouver**	**NHL**	**30**	**0**	**2**	**2**	**27**	**0**	**0**	**0**	**22**	**0.0**	**–12**	**189**	**40.2**	**8:07**	....	....	....	....	....	....	....	....	....
	Syracuse Crunch	AHL	37	15	18	33	119	....	....	....	....	....	....	....	....	....	....	....	....	....	....	....	....	....	....
99-2000	**Vancouver**	**NHL**	**51**	**5**	**7**	**12**	**39**	**0**	**1**	**1**	**58**	**8.6**	**3**	**71**	**39.4**	**11:48**	....	....	....	....	....	....	....	....	....
	Syracuse Crunch	AHL	18	5	8	13	27	....	....	....	....	....	....	....	....	....	....	....	....	....	....	....	....	....	....
2000-01	**Vancouver**	**NHL**	**81**	**14**	**13**	**27**	**94**	**0**	**2**	**0**	**121**	**11.6**	**5**	**321**	**43.0**	**14:35**	**4**	**0**	**0**	**0**	**4**	**0**	**0**	**0**	**12:04**
2001-02	**Vancouver**	**NHL**	**82**	**13**	**20**	**33**	**111**	**1**	**0**	**2**	**103**	**12.6**	**4**	**28**	**32.1**	**14:03**	**6**	**3**	**2**	**5**	**0**	**1**	**0**	**0**	**15:09**
2002-03	**Vancouver**	**NHL**	**82**	**15**	**27**	**42**	**82**	**1**	**4**	**0**	**118**	**12.7**	**21**	**31**	**35.5**	**13:24**	**14**	**2**	**1**	**3**	**12**	**0**	**0**	**0**	**14:07**
2003-04	**Vancouver**	**NHL**	**53**	**11**	**12**	**23**	**73**	**1**	**1**	**4**	**79**	**13.9**	**5**	**34**	**52.9**	**14:06**	**7**	**3**	**1**	**4**	**12**	**0**	**0**	**1**	**18:23**
2004-05			DID NOT PLAY																						
2005-06	**Vancouver**	**NHL**	**45**	**8**	**10**	**18**	**71**	**0**	**0**	**2**	**67**	**11.9**	**–8**	**25**	**24.0**	**13:57**	....	....	....	....	....	....	....	....	....
2006-07	**Vancouver**	**NHL**	**81**	**10**	**20**	**30**	**64**	**1**	**0**	**3**	**133**	**7.5**	**0**	**19**	**47.4**	**15:37**	**1**	**0**	**0**	**0**	**2**	**0**	**0**	**0**	**9:51**
2007-08	**Vancouver**	**NHL**	**61**	**7**	**9**	**16**	**64**	**0**	**0**	**1**	**68**	**10.3**	**–4**	**26**	**42.3**	**13:24**	....	....	....	....	....	....	....	....	....
	Washington	**NHL**	**17**	**3**	**4**	**7**	**27**	**0**	**1**	**0**	**18**	**16.7**	**5**	**2**	**50.0**	**12:19**	**7**	**0**	**0**	**0**	**4**	**0**	**0**	**0**	**13:55**
2008-09 ♦	**Pittsburgh**	**NHL**	**76**	**13**	**18**	**31**	**101**	**0**	**0**	**1**	**86**	**15.1**	**0**	**19**	**36.8**	**14:13**	**24**	**1**	**6**	**7**	**22**	**0**	**0**	**0**	**15:09**
2009-10	**Pittsburgh**	**NHL**	**79**	**15**	**15**	**30**	**106**	**2**	**0**	**1**	**105**	**14.3**	**17**	**24**	**54.2**	**14:47**	**13**	**4**	**2**	**6**	**22**	**0**	**0**	**0**	**15:11**
2010-11	**Pittsburgh**	**NHL**	**67**	**12**	**18**	**30**	**129**	**0**	**3**	**2**	**95**	**12.6**	**14**	**29**	**27.6**	**15:38**	....	....	....	....	....	....	....	....	....
	NHL Totals		**805**	**126**	**175**	**301**	**988**	**6**	**12**	**17**	**1073**	**11.7**		**818**	**41.0**	**13:58**	**76**	**13**	**12**	**25**	**78**	**1**	**0**	**1**	**14:55**

Traded to **Washington** by **Vancouver** for Matt Pettinger, February 26, 2008. Signed as a free agent by **Pittsburgh**, July 6, 2008.

CORMIER, Patrice

(KOHR-mee-ay, pa-TREEZ) **WPG**

Center. Shoots left. 6'2", 215 lbs. Born, Moncton, N.B., June 14, 1990. New Jersey's 3rd choice, 54th overall, in 2008 Entry Draft.

2006-07	Rimouski Oceanic	QMJHL	53	11	10	21	73	....	....	....	....	....	....	....	....	....	....	....	....	....	....	....	....	....	....
2007-08	Rimouski Oceanic	QMJHL	51	18	23	41	84	....	....	....	....	....	....	....	....	....	9	4	5	9	10	....	....	....	....
2008-09	Rimouski Oceanic	QMJHL	54	23	28	51	118	....	....	....	....	....	....	....	....	....	13	4	6	10	30	....	....	....	....
2009-10	Rimouski Oceanic	QMJHL	28	11	15	26	57	....	....	....	....	....	....	....	....	....	....	....	....	....	....	....	....	....	....
	Rouyn-Noranda	QMJHL	3	0	5	5	7	....	....	....	....	....	....	....	....	....	....	....	....	....	....	....	....	....	....
	Chicago Wolves	AHL	....	....	....	....	....	....	....	....	....	....	....	....	....	....	9	0	0	0	8	....	....	....	....
2010-11	**Atlanta**	**NHL**	**21**	**1**	**1**	**2**	**4**	**0**	**0**	**0**	**27**	**3.7**	**–5**	**67**	**58.2**	**9:39**	....	....	....	....	....	....	....	....	....
	Chicago Wolves	AHL	11	2	3	5	14	....	....	....	....	....	....	....	....	....	....	....	....	....	....	....	....	....	....
	NHL Totals		**21**	**1**	**1**	**2**	**4**	**0**	**0**	**0**	**27**	**3.7**		**67**	**58.2**	**9:39**	....	....	....	....	....	....	....	....	....

Traded to **Atlanta** by **New Jersey** with Johnny Oduya, Niclas Bergfors and New Jersey's 1st (later traded to Chicago - Chicago selected Kevin Hayes) and 2nd (later traded to Chicago - Chicago selected Justin Holl) round choices in 2010 Entry Draft for Ilya Kovalchuk, Anssi Salmela and Atlanta's 2nd round choice (Jonathon Merrill) in 2010 Entry Draft, February 4, 2010. • Missed majority of 2010-11 due to foot injury in training camp and upper body injury at Phoenix, February 17, 2011. • Transferred to **Winnipeg** after **Atlanta** franchise relocated, June 21, 2011.

CORRENTE, Matthew

(kohr-REHN-tay, MA-thew) **N.J.**

Defense. Shoots right. 6', 205 lbs. Born, Mississauga, Ont., March 17, 1988. New Jersey's 1st choice, 30th overall, in 2006 Entry Draft.

2004-05	Saginaw Spirit	OHL	62	6	9	15	89	....	....	....	....	....	....	....	....	....	....	....	....	....	....	....	....	....	....
2005-06	Saginaw Spirit	OHL	61	6	24	30	172	....	....	....	....	....	....	....	....	....	4	1	1	2	8	....	....	....	....
2006-07	Saginaw Spirit	OHL	29	2	13	15	67	....	....	....	....	....	....	....	....	....	....	....	....	....	....	....	....	....	....
	Mississauga	OHL	14	1	10	11	27	....	....	....	....	....	....	....	....	....	5	0	1	1	8	....	....	....	....
2007-08	Niagara Ice Dogs	OHL	21	2	13	15	64	....	....	....	....	....	....	....	....	....	10	0	5	5	33	....	....	....	....
2008-09	Lowell Devils	AHL	67	6	12	18	161	....	....	....	....	....	....	....	....	....	....	....	....	....	....	....	....	....	....
2009-10	**New Jersey**	**NHL**	**12**	**0**	**0**	**0**	**24**	**0**	**0**	**0**	**6**	**0.0**	**0**	**0**	**0.0**	**8:51**	**2**	**0**	**0**	**0**	**2**	**0**	**0**	**0**	**5:51**
	Lowell Devils	AHL	43	5	15	20	74	....	....	....	....	....	....	....	....	....	....	....	....	....	....	....	....	....	....
2010-11	**New Jersey**	**NHL**	**22**	**0**	**6**	**6**	**44**	**0**	**0**	**0**	**21**	**0.0**	**–5**	**0**	**0.0**	**13:36**	....	....	....	....	....	....	....	....	....
	Albany Devils	AHL	3	0	1	1	10	....	....	....	....	....	....	....	....	....	....	....	....	....	....	....	....	....	....
	NHL Totals		**34**	**0**	**6**	**6**	**68**	**0**	**0**	**0**	**27**	**0.0**		**0**	**0.0**	**11:56**	**2**	**0**	**0**	**0**	**2**	**0**	**0**	**0**	**5:51**

• Missed majority of 2010-11 due to shoulder injury at Tampa Bay, January 14, 2011.

CORVO, Joe

(KOHR-voh, JOH) **BOS**

Defense. Shoots right. 6'1", 210 lbs. Born, Oak Park, IL, June 20, 1977. Los Angeles' 4th choice, 83rd overall, in 1997 Entry Draft.

			Regular Season														Playoffs								
Season	Club	League	GP	G	A	Pts	PIM	PP	SH	GW	S	%	+/-	TF	F%	Min	GP	G	A	Pts	PIM	PP	SH	GW	Min
1995-96	Western Mich.	CCHA	41	5	25	30	38	....	....	....	....	....	....	....	....	....	....	....	....	....	....	....	....	....	....
1996-97	Western Mich.	CCHA	32	12	21	33	85	....	....	....	....	....	....	....	....	....	....	....	....	....	....	....	....	....	....
1997-98	Western Mich.	CCHA	32	5	12	17	93	....	....	....	....	....	....	....	....	....	....	....	....	....	....	....	....	....	....
1998-99	Springfield	AHL	50	5	15	20	32	....	....	....	....	....	....	....	....	....	....	....	....	....	....	....	....	....	....
	Hampton Roads	ECHL	5	0	0	0	15	....	....	....	....	....	....	....	....	....	4	0	1	1	0	....	....	....	....
99-2000			DID NOT PLAY																						
2000-01	Lowell	AHL	77	10	23	33	31	....	....	....	....	....	....	....	....	....	4	3	1	4	0	....	....	....	....
2001-02	Manchester	AHL	80	13	37	50	30	....	....	....	....	....	....	....	....	....	5	0	5	5	0	....	....	....	....
2002-03	**Los Angeles**	**NHL**	**50**	**5**	**7**	**12**	**14**	**2**	**0**	**0**	**84**	**6.0**	**2**	**0**	**0.0**	**18:37**	....	....	....	....	....	....	....	....	....
	Manchester	AHL	26	8	18	26	8	....	....	....	....	....	....	....	....	....	3	0	0	0	0	....	....	....	....
2003-04	**Los Angeles**	**NHL**	**72**	**8**	**17**	**25**	**36**	**0**	**0**	**3**	**150**	**5.3**	**7**	**1**	**0.0**	**21:09**	....	....	....	....	....	....	....	....	....
2004-05	Chicago Wolves	AHL	23	7	7	14	14	....	....	....	....	....	....	....	....	....	18	4	5	9	12	....	....	....	....
2005-06	**Los Angeles**	**NHL**	**81**	**14**	**26**	**40**	**38**	**7**	**0**	**3**	**190**	**7.4**	**16**	**0**	**0.0**	**19:59**	....	....	....	....	....	....	....	....	....
2006-07	**Ottawa**	**NHL**	**76**	**8**	**29**	**37**	**42**	**3**	**0**	**2**	**160**	**5.0**	**8**	**0**	**0.0**	**18:04**	**20**	**2**	**7**	**9**	**6**	**1**	**0**	**1**	**17:18**
2007-08	**Ottawa**	**NHL**	**51**	**6**	**21**	**27**	**18**	**1**	**0**	**1**	**111**	**5.4**	**13**	**0**	**0.0**	**17:41**	....	....	....	....	....	....	....	....	....
	Carolina	**NHL**	**23**	**7**	**14**	**21**	**8**	**5**	**0**	**2**	**56**	**12.5**	**4**	**0**	**0.0**	**20:46**	....	....	....	....	....	....	....	....	....
2008-09	**Carolina**	**NHL**	**81**	**14**	**24**	**38**	**18**	**8**	**1**	**6**	**213**	**6.6**	**–1**	**0**	**0.0**	**24:19**	**18**	**2**	**5**	**7**	**4**	**1**	**0**	**1**	**25:27**
2009-10	**Carolina**	**NHL**	**34**	**4**	**8**	**12**	**10**	**4**	**0**	**0**	**76**	**5.3**	**–6**	**0**	**0.0**	**25:13**	....	....	....	....	....	....	....	....	....
	Washington	**NHL**	**18**	**2**	**4**	**6**	**2**	**1**	**0**	**0**	**23**	**8.7**	**–4**	**0**	**0.0**	**19:41**	**7**	**1**	**1**	**2**	**4**	**0**	**0**	**0**	**16:53**
2010-11	**Carolina**	**NHL**	**82**	**11**	**29**	**40**	**18**	**5**	**1**	**1**	**191**	**5.8**	**–14**	**1**	**0.0**	**24:47**	....	....	....	....	....	....	....	....	....
	NHL Totals		**568**	**79**	**179**	**258**	**204**	**36**	**2**	**18**	**1254**	**6.3**		**2**	**0.0**	**21:12**	**45**	**5**	**13**	**18**	**14**	**2**	**0**	**2**	**20:30**

CCHA All-Rookie Team (1996) • CCHA Second All-Star Team (1997)

• Missed 1999-2000 after failing to come to contract terms with **Los Angeles.** Signed as a free agent by **Chicago** (AHL), February 24, 2005. Signed as a free agent by **Ottawa**, July 1, 2006. Traded to **Carolina** by **Ottawa** with Patrick Eaves for Cory Stillman and Mike Commodore, February 11, 2008. • Missed majority of 2009-10 due to leg injury vs. Washington, November 30, 2009. Traded to **Washington** by **Carolina** for Brian Pothier, Oskar Osala and Washington's 2nd round choice (later traded to NY Rangers, later traded to Calgary – Calgary selected Tyler Wotherspoon) in 2011 Entry Draft, March 3, 2010. Signed as a free agent by **Carolina**, July 7, 2010. Traded to **Boston** by **Carolina** for Boston's 4th round choice in 2012 Entry Draft, July 5, 2011.

COUTURE, Logan

(koh-TYOOR, LOH-guhn) **S.J.**

Center. Shoots left. 6'1", 195 lbs. Born, Guelph, Ont., March 28, 1989. San Jose's 1st choice, 9th overall, in 2007 Entry Draft.

Season	Club	League	GP	G	A	Pts	PIM	PP	SH	GW	S	%	+/-	TF	F%	Min	GP	G	A	Pts	PIM	PP	SH	GW	Min
2004-05	St. Thomas Stars	ON-Jr.B	48	24	22	46	....	....	....	....	....	....	....	....	....	....	....	....	....	....	....	....	....	....	....
2005-06	Ottawa 67's	OHL	65	25	39	64	52	....	....	....	....	....	....	....	....	....	6	3	4	7	0	....	....	....	....
2006-07	Ottawa 67's	OHL	54	26	52	78	24	....	....	....	....	....	....	....	....	....	5	1	7	8	4	....	....	....	....
2007-08	Ottawa 67's	OHL	51	21	37	58	37	....	....	....	....	....	....	....	....	....	4	2	1	3	0	....	....	....	....
2008-09	Ottawa 67's	OHL	62	39	48	87	46	....	....	....	....	....	....	....	....	....	7	3	7	10	6	....	....	....	....
	Worcester Sharks	AHL	4	0	0	0	7	....	....	....	....	....	....	....	....	....	12	2	1	3	11	....	....	....	....
2009-10	**San Jose**	**NHL**	**25**	**5**	**4**	**9**	**6**	**1**	**0**	**1**	**42**	**11.9**	**4**	**143**	**52.5**	**10:16**	**15**	**4**	**0**	**4**	**4**	**0**	**0**	**1**	**11:23**
	Worcester Sharks	AHL	42	20	33	53	12	....	....	....	....	....	....	....	....	....	....	....	....	....	....	....	....	....	....
2010-11	**San Jose**	**NHL**	**79**	**32**	**24**	**56**	**41**	**10**	**0**	**8**	**253**	**12.6**	**18**	**888**	**53.4**	**17:49**	**18**	**7**	**7**	**14**	**2**	**1**	**0**	**0**	**19:23**
	NHL Totals		**104**	**37**	**28**	**65**	**47**	**11**	**0**	**9**	**295**	**12.5**		**1031**	**53.2**	**16:00**	**33**	**11**	**7**	**18**	**6**	**1**	**0**	**1**	**15:45**

AHL All-Rookie Team (2010) • NHL All-Rookie Team (2011)

COWAN, Jeff

(KOW-an, JEHF)

Left wing. Shoots left. 6'2", 205 lbs. Born, Scarborough, Ont., September 27, 1976.

Season	Club	League	GP	G	A	Pts	PIM	PP	SH	GW	S	%	+/-	TF	F%	Min	GP	G	A	Pts	PIM	PP	SH	GW	Min
1992-93	Guelph	ON-Jr.B	45	8	8	16	22	....	....	....	....	....	....	....	....	....	....	....	....	....	....	....	....	....	....
1993-94	Guelph	ON-Jr.B	43	30	26	56	96	....	....	....	....	....	....	....	....	....	....	....	....	....	....	....	....	....	....
	Guelph Storm	OHL	17	1	0	1	5	....	....	....	....	....	....	....	....	....	....	....	....	....	....	....	....	....	....
1994-95	Guelph Storm	OHL	51	10	7	17	14	....	....	....	....	....	....	....	....	....	14	1	1	2	0	....	....	....	....
1995-96	Barrie Colts	OHL	66	38	14	52	29	....	....	....	....	....	....	....	....	....	5	1	2	3	6	....	....	....	....
1996-97	Saint John Flames	AHL	22	5	5	10	8	....	....	....	....	....	....	....	....	....	....	....	....	....	....	....	....	....	....
	Roanoke Express	ECHL	47	21	13	34	42	....	....	....	....	....	....	....	....	....	....	....	....	....	....	....	....	....	....
1997-98	Saint John Flames	AHL	69	15	13	28	23	....	....	....	....	....	....	....	....	....	13	4	1	5	14	....	....	....	....
1998-99	Saint John Flames	AHL	71	7	12	19	117	....	....	....	....	....	....	....	....	....	4	0	1	1	10	....	....	....	....
99-2000	**Calgary**	**NHL**	**13**	**4**	**1**	**5**	**16**	**0**	**0**	**0**	**26**	**15.4**	**2**	**0**	**0.0**	**10:22**	....	....	....	....	....	....	....	....	....
	Saint John Flames	AHL	47	15	10	25	77	....	....	....	....	....	....	....	....	....	....	....	....	....	....	....	....	....	....
2000-01	**Calgary**	**NHL**	**51**	**9**	**4**	**13**	**74**	**2**	**0**	**1**	**48**	**18.8**	**–8**	**5**	**20.0**	**9:06**	....	....	....	....	....	....	....	....	....
2001-02	**Calgary**	**NHL**	**19**	**1**	**0**	**1**	**40**	**0**	**0**	**1**	**13**	**7.7**	**–3**	**2**	**50.0**	**7:44**	....	....	....	....	....	....	....	....	....
	Atlanta	**NHL**	**38**	**4**	**1**	**5**	**50**	**0**	**0**	**1**	**51**	**7.8**	**–11**	**5**	**20.0**	**12:27**	....	....	....	....	....	....	....	....	....
2002-03	**Atlanta**	**NHL**	**66**	**3**	**5**	**8**	**115**	**0**	**0**	**0**	**52**	**5.8**	**–15**	**10**	**30.0**	**8:24**	....	....	....	....	....	....	....	....	....
2003-04	**Atlanta**	**NHL**	**58**	**9**	**15**	**24**	**68**	**1**	**0**	**1**	**74**	**12.2**	**2**	**9**	**22.2**	**10:04**	....	....	....	....	....	....	....	....	....
	Los Angeles	**NHL**	**13**	**2**	**1**	**3**	**24**	**1**	**0**	**0**	**15**	**13.3**	**–1**	**2**	**50.0**	**11:43**	....	....	....	....	....	....	....	....	....
2004-05			DID NOT PLAY																						
2005-06	**Los Angeles**	**NHL**	**46**	**8**	**1**	**9**	**73**	**0**	**0**	**0**	**53**	**15.1**	**–8**	**4**	**25.0**	**8:26**	....	....	....	....	....	....	....	....	....
2006-07	**Los Angeles**	**NHL**	**21**	**0**	**2**	**2**	**32**	**0**	**0**	**0**	**28**	**0.0**	**–1**	**1**	**0.0**	**7:37**	....	....	....	....	....	....	....	....	....
	Vancouver	**NHL**	**42**	**7**	**3**	**10**	**93**	**0**	**1**	**0**	**46**	**15.2**	**4**	**0**	**0.0**	**8:15**	**10**	**2**	**0**	**2**	**22**	**0**	**0**	**1**	**11:38**
2007-08	**Vancouver**	**NHL**	**46**	**0**	**1**	**1**	**110**	**0**	**0**	**0**	**35**	**0.0**	**–5**	**1**	**0.0**	**8:45**	....	....	....	....	....	....	....	....	....
2008-09	Peoria Rivermen	AHL	71	5	10	15	94	....	....	....	....	....	....	....	....	....	7	1	1	2	0	....	....	....	....
2009-10	Portland Pirates	AHL	62	18	13	31	57	....	....	....	....	....	....	....	....	....	4	0	0	0	0	....	....	....	....
2010-11	Toronto Marlies	AHL	47	8	8	16	23	....	....	....	....	....	....	....	....	....	....	....	....	....	....	....	....	....	....
	NHL Totals		**413**	**47**	**34**	**81**	**695**	**4**	**1**	**4**	**441**	**10.7**		**39**	**25.6**	**9:13**	**10**	**2**	**0**	**2**	**22**	**0**	**0**	**1**	**11:38**

Signed as a free agent by **Calgary**, October 2, 1995. Traded to **Atlanta** by **Calgary** with the rights to Kurtis Foster for Petr Buzek and Atlanta's 6th round choice (Adam Pardy) in 2004 Entry Draft, December 18, 2001. Traded to **Los Angeles** by **Atlanta** for Kip Brennan, March 9, 2004. Claimed on waivers by **Vancouver** from **Los Angeles**, December 30, 2006. Signed as a free agent by **Buffalo**, August 20, 2009. Signed to a PTO (professional tryout) contract by **Toronto** (AHL), December 14, 2010.

COWEN, Jared

(KOW-ehn, JAIR-ehd) **OTT**

Defense. Shoots left. 6'5", 226 lbs. Born, Saskatoon, Sask., January 25, 1991. Ottawa's 1st choice, 9th overall, in 2009 Entry Draft.

Season	Club	League	GP	G	A	Pts	PIM	PP	SH	GW	S	%	+/-	TF	F%	Min	GP	G	A	Pts	PIM	PP	SH	GW	Min
2006-07	Sask. Contacts	SMHL	41	6	22	28	103	....	....	....	....	....	....	....	....	....	....	....	....	....	....	....	....	....	....
	Spokane Chiefs	WHL	6	0	2	2	2	....	....	....	....	....	....	....	....	....	6	0	1	1	6	....	....	....	....
2007-08	Spokane Chiefs	WHL	68	4	14	18	62	....	....	....	....	....	....	....	....	....	21	1	3	4	17	....	....	....	....
2008-09	Spokane Chiefs	WHL	48	7	14	21	45	....	....	....	....	....	....	....	....	....	....	....	....	....	....	....	....	....	....
2009-10	Spokane Chiefs	WHL	59	8	22	30	74	....	....	....	....	....	....	....	....	....	7	1	1	2	8	....	....	....	....
	Ottawa	**NHL**	**1**	**0**	**0**	**0**	**2**	**0**	**0**	**0**	**0**	**0.0**	**0**	**0**	**0.0**	**6:46**	....	....	....	....	....	....	....	....	....
2010-11	Spokane Chiefs	WHL	58	18	30	48	91	....	....	....	....	....	....	....	....	....	17	2	12	14	16	....	....	....	....
	Binghamton	AHL	....	....	....	....	....	....	....	....	....	....	....	....	....	....	10	0	4	4	0	....	....	....	....
	NHL Totals		**1**	**0**	**0**	**0**	**2**	**0**	**0**	**0**	**0**	**0.0**		**0**	**0.0**	**6:46**	....	....	....	....	....	....	....	....	....

WHL West Second All-Star Team (2010) • WHL West First All-Star Team (2011)

CRABB, Joey

(KRAB, JOH-ee) **TOR**

Right wing. Shoots right. 6'1", 190 lbs. Born, Anchorage, AK, April 3, 1983. NY Rangers' 7th choice, 226th overall, in 2002 Entry Draft.

Season	Club	League	GP	G	A	Pts	PIM	PP	SH	GW	S	%	+/-	TF	F%	Min	GP	G	A	Pts	PIM	PP	SH	GW	Min
99-2000	USNTDP	NAHL	55	13	10	23	69	....	....	....	....	....	....	....	....	....	3	1	0	1	4	....	....	....	....
2000-01	USNTDP	U-18	39	10	10	20	22	....	....	....	....	....	....	....	....	....	....	....	....	....	....	....	....	....	....
	USNTDP	USHL	21	2	3	5	18	....	....	....	....	....	....	....	....	....	....	....	....	....	....	....	....	....	....
2001-02	Green Bay	USHL	61	15	27	42	94	....	....	....	....	....	....	....	....	....	7	4	8	12	21	....	....	....	....
2002-03	Colorado College	WCHA	35	4	4	8	40	....	....	....	....	....	....	....	....	....	....	....	....	....	....	....	....	....	....
2003-04	Colorado College	WCHA	39	15	12	27	20	....	....	....	....	....	....	....	....	....	....	....	....	....	....	....	....	....	....
2004-05	Colorado College	WCHA	43	16	16	32	44	....	....	....	....	....	....	....	....	....	....	....	....	....	....	....	....	....	....
2005-06	Colorado College	WCHA	42	18	25	43	45	....	....	....	....	....	....	....	....	....	....	....	....	....	....	....	....	....	....
2006-07	Chicago Wolves	AHL	63	7	15	22	25	....	....	....	....	....	....	....	....	....	6	0	0	0	0	....	....	....	....
2007-08	Chicago Wolves	AHL	72	9	26	35	78	....	....	....	....	....	....	....	....	....	24	1	4	5	20	....	....	....	....
2008-09	**Atlanta**	**NHL**	**29**	**4**	**5**	**9**	**28**	**0**	**1**	**1**	**33**	**12.1**	**–2**	**33**	**39.4**	**12:13**	....	....	....	....	....	....	....	....	....
	Chicago Wolves	AHL	42	15	14	29	62	....	....	....	....	....	....	....	....	....	....	....	....	....	....	....	....	....	....
2009-10	Chicago Wolves	AHL	79	24	29	53	59	....	....	....	....	....	....	....	....	....	14	6	5	11	12	....	....	....	....

			Regular Season														Playoffs								
Season	Club	League	GP	G	A	Pts	PIM	PP	SH	GW	S	%	+/-	TF	F%	Min	GP	G	A	Pts	PIM	PP	SH	GW	Min
2010-11	**Toronto**	**NHL**	**48**	**3**	**12**	**15**	**24**	**0**	**1**	**2**	**51**	**5.9**	**–1**	**22**	**22.7**	**12:59**	....	....	....	....	....	....	....	....	....
	Toronto Marlies	AHL	34	11	7	18	31	....	....	....	....	....	....	....	....	....	....	....	....	....	....	....	....	....	....
	NHL Totals		**77**	**7**	**17**	**24**	**52**	**0**	**2**	**3**	**84**	**8.3**		**55**	**32.7**	**12:41**	....	....	....	....	....	....	....	....	....

Signed as a free agent by **Atlanta**, August 31, 2006. Traded to **Chicago** by **Atlanta** with Marty Reasoner, Jeremy Morin and New Jersey's 1st (previously acquired, Chicago selected Kevin Hayes) and 2nd (previously acquired, Chicago selected Justin Holl) round choices in 2010 Entry Draft for Brent Sopel, Dustin Byfuglien, Ben Eager and Akim Aliu, June 24, 2010. Signed as a free agent by **Toronto**, July 15, 2010.

CRACKNELL, Adam (krak-NEHL, A-duhm) ST.L.

Right wing. Shoots right. 6'2", 216 lbs. Born, Prince Albert, Sask., July 15, 1985. Calgary's 10th choice, 279th overall, in 2004 Entry Draft.

Season	Club	League	GP	G	A	Pts	PIM	PP	SH	GW	S	%	+/-	TF	F%	Min	GP	G	A	Pts	PIM	PP	SH	GW	Min
2002-03	Kootenay Ice	WHL	67	7	4	11	37	....	....	....	....	....	....	....	....	....	11	0	0	0	2	....	....	....	....
2003-04	Kootenay Ice	WHL	72	26	35	61	63	....	....	....	....	....	....	....	....	....	4	1	1	2	2	....	....	....	....
2004-05	Kootenay Ice	WHL	72	19	29	48	65	....	....	....	....	....	....	....	....	....	16	8	8	16	6	....	....	....	....
2005-06	Kootenay Ice	WHL	72	42	51	93	85	....	....	....	....	....	....	....	....	....	6	1	4	5	6	....	....	....	....
	Omaha	AHL	6	1	2	3	2	....	....	....	....	....	....	....	....	....	....	....	....	....	....	....	....	....	....
2006-07	Las Vegas	ECHL	31	8	14	22	35	....	....	....	....	....	....	....	....	....	8	3	3	6	6	....	....	....	....
2007-08	Quad City Flames	AHL	4	1	0	1	0	....	....	....	....	....	....	....	....	....	....	....	....	....	....	....	....	....	....
	Las Vegas	ECHL	61	29	30	59	47	....	....	....	....	....	....	....	....	....	21	9	13	22	4	....	....	....	....
2008-09	Quad City Flames	AHL	79	10	16	26	36	....	....	....	....	....	....	....	....	....	....	....	....	....	....	....	....	....	....
2009-10	Peoria Rivermen	AHL	76	17	21	38	40	....	....	....	....	....	....	....	....	....	....	....	....	....	....	....	....	....	....
2010-11	**St. Louis**	**NHL**	**24**	**3**	**4**	**7**	**8**	**0**	**0**	**0**	**26**	**11.5**	**1**	**118**	**39.0**	**8:55**	....	....	....	....	....	....	....	....	....
	Peoria Rivermen	AHL	61	6	19	25	54	....	....	....	....	....	....	....	....	....	4	2	0	2	0	....	....	....	....
	NHL Totals		**24**	**3**	**4**	**7**	**8**	**0**	**0**	**0**	**26**	**11.5**		**118**	**39.0**	**8:55**	....	....	....	....	....	....	....	....	....

WHL West Second All-Star Team (2006)

Signed as a free agent by **St. Louis**, July 23, 2009.

CRAIG, Ryan (KRAIG, RIGH-uhn) PIT

Center. Shoots left. 6'1", 215 lbs. Born, Abbotsford, B.C., January 6, 1982. Tampa Bay's 10th choice, 255th overall, in 2002 Entry Draft.

Season	Club	League	GP	G	A	Pts	PIM	PP	SH	GW	S	%	+/-	TF	F%	Min	GP	G	A	Pts	PIM	PP	SH	GW	Min
1997-98	Abbotsford	Minor-BC	80	118	120	238	110	....	....	....	....	....	....	....	....	....	....	....	....	....	....	....	....	....	....
	Brandon	WHL	1	0	0	0	0	....	....	....	....	....	....	....	....	....	....	....	....	....	....	....	....	....	....
1998-99	Brandon	WHL	54	11	12	23	46	....	....	....	....	....	....	....	....	....	5	0	0	0	4	....	....	....	....
99-2000	Brandon	WHL	65	17	19	36	40	....	....	....	....	....	....	....	....	....	....	....	....	....	....	....	....	....	....
2000-01	Brandon	WHL	70	38	33	71	49	....	....	....	....	....	....	....	....	....	6	3	0	3	7	....	....	....	....
2001-02	Brandon	WHL	52	29	35	64	52	....	....	....	....	....	....	....	....	....	19	11	10	21	13	....	....	....	....
2002-03	Brandon	WHL	60	42	32	74	69	....	....	....	....	....	....	....	....	....	17	5	8	13	29	....	....	....	....
2003-04	Hershey Bears	AHL	61	4	8	12	24	....	....	....	....	....	....	....	....	....	....	....	....	....	....	....	....	....	....
	Pensacola	ECHL	5	3	5	8	0	....	....	....	....	....	....	....	....	....	2	0	1	1	0	....	....	....	....
2004-05	Springfield	AHL	80	27	14	41	50	....	....	....	....	....	....	....	....	....	....	....	....	....	....	....	....	....	....
2005-06	**Tampa Bay**	**NHL**	**48**	**15**	**13**	**28**	**6**	**6**	**0**	**0**	**81**	**18.5**	**–4**	**95**	**46.3**	**15:21**	**5**	**0**	**0**	**0**	**10**	**0**	**0**	**0**	**12:59**
	Springfield	AHL	28	12	10	22	14	....	....	....	....	....	....	....	....	....	....	....	....	....	....	....	....	....	....
2006-07	**Tampa Bay**	**NHL**	**72**	**14**	**13**	**27**	**55**	**4**	**0**	**2**	**130**	**10.8**	**–11**	**110**	**40.0**	**15:20**	**6**	**0**	**0**	**0**	**12**	**0**	**0**	**0**	**7:02**
2007-08	**Tampa Bay**	**NHL**	**7**	**1**	**1**	**2**	**0**	**1**	**0**	**0**	**8**	**12.5**	**–1**	**1**	**100.0**	**13:04**	....	....	....	....	....	....	....	....	....
	Norfolk Admirals	AHL	2	1	2	3	2	....	....	....	....	....	....	....	....	....	....	....	....	....	....	....	....	....	....
2008-09	**Tampa Bay**	**NHL**	**54**	**2**	**4**	**6**	**60**	**0**	**0**	**0**	**64**	**3.1**	**–7**	**222**	**49.6**	**10:16**	....	....	....	....	....	....	....	....	....
2009-10	**Tampa Bay**	**NHL**	**3**	**0**	**0**	**0**	**5**	**0**	**0**	**0**	**5**	**0.0**	**0**	**1**	**0.0**	**9:47**	....	....	....	....	....	....	....	....	....
	Norfolk Admirals	AHL	73	23	22	45	64	....	....	....	....	....	....	....	....	....	....	....	....	....	....	....	....	....	....
2010-11	**Pittsburgh**	**NHL**	**6**	**0**	**0**	**0**	**22**	**0**	**0**	**0**	**7**	**0.0**	**–3**	**5**	**60.0**	**9:49**	....	....	....	....	....	....	....	....	....
	Wilkes-Barre	AHL	71	19	29	48	84	....	....	....	....	....	....	....	....	....	12	3	4	7	12	....	....	....	....
	NHL Totals		**190**	**32**	**31**	**63**	**148**	**11**	**0**	**2**	**295**	**10.8**		**434**	**46.5**	**13:33**	**11**	**0**	**0**	**0**	**22**	**0**	**0**	**0**	**9:44**

WHL East First All-Star Team (2003) • Canadian Major Junior Humanitarian Player of the Year (2003)

• Missed majority of 2007-08 due to back and knee injuries. Signed as a free agent by **Pittsburgh**, July 2, 2010.

CROMBEEN, B.J. (KRAWM-been, BEE-JAY) ST.L.

Right wing. Shoots right. 6'2", 214 lbs. Born, Denver, CO, July 10, 1985. Dallas' 3rd choice, 54th overall, in 2003 Entry Draft.

Season	Club	League	GP	G	A	Pts	PIM	PP	SH	GW	S	%	+/-	TF	F%	Min	GP	G	A	Pts	PIM	PP	SH	GW	Min
2000-01	Newmarket	OPJHL	35	14	14	28	63	....	....	....	....	....	....	....	....	....	....	....	....	....	....	....	....	....	....
2001-02	Barrie Colts	OHL	60	12	13	25	118	....	....	....	....	....	....	....	....	....	20	1	1	2	31	....	....	....	....
2002-03	Barrie Colts	OHL	63	22	24	46	133	....	....	....	....	....	....	....	....	....	6	1	0	1	8	....	....	....	....
2003-04	Barrie Colts	OHL	62	21	29	50	154	....	....	....	....	....	....	....	....	....	12	5	7	12	35	....	....	....	....
2004-05	Barrie Colts	OHL	63	31	18	49	111	....	....	....	....	....	....	....	....	....	6	2	4	6	35	....	....	....	....
2005-06	Iowa Stars	AHL	52	5	7	12	97	....	....	....	....	....	....	....	....	....	5	1	0	1	9	....	....	....	....
	Idaho Steelheads	ECHL	8	5	3	8	5	....	....	....	....	....	....	....	....	....	....	....	....	....	....	....	....	....	....
2006-07	Assat Pori	Finland	55	13	9	22	152	....	....	....	....	....	....	....	....	....	....	....	....	....	....	....	....	....	....
	Idaho Steelheads	ECHL	13	7	4	11	43	....	....	....	....	....	....	....	....	....	22	5	5	10	45	....	....	....	....
2007-08	**Dallas**	**NHL**	**8**	**0**	**2**	**2**	**39**	**0**	**0**	**0**	**9**	**0.0**	**1**	**1**	**0.0**	**6:38**	**5**	**0**	**0**	**0**	**0**	**0**	**0**	**0**	**4:16**
	Iowa Stars	AHL	65	14	14	28	158	....	....	....	....	....	....	....	....	....	....	....	....	....	....	....	....	....	....
2008-09	**Dallas**	**NHL**	**15**	**1**	**4**	**5**	**26**	**0**	**0**	**0**	**12**	**8.3**	**–1**	**0**	**0.0**	**8:14**	....	....	....	....	....	....	....	....	....
	St. Louis	**NHL**	**66**	**11**	**6**	**17**	**122**	**0**	**1**	**3**	**112**	**9.8**	**–8**	**7**	**42.9**	**13:45**	**4**	**0**	**0**	**0**	**12**	**0**	**0**	**0**	**9:46**
2009-10	**St. Louis**	**NHL**	**79**	**7**	**8**	**15**	**168**	**0**	**1**	**1**	**120**	**5.8**	**–5**	**51**	**35.3**	**13:05**	....	....	....	....	....	....	....	....	....
2010-11	**St. Louis**	**NHL**	**80**	**7**	**7**	**14**	**154**	**0**	**1**	**0**	**113**	**6.2**	**–18**	**64**	**29.7**	**12:48**	....	....	....	....	....	....	....	....	....
	NHL Totals		**248**	**26**	**27**	**53**	**509**	**0**	**3**	**4**	**366**	**7.1**		**123**	**32.5**	**12:40**	**9**	**0**	**0**	**0**	**12**	**0**	**0**	**0**	**6:43**

Signed as a free agent by **Pori** (Finland), August 2, 2006. Claimed on waivers by **St. Louis** from **Dallas**, November 18, 2008.

CROSBY, Sidney (KRAWZ-bee, SIHD-nee) PIT

Center. Shoots left. 5'11", 200 lbs. Born, Cole Harbour, N.S., August 7, 1987. Pittsburgh's 1st choice, 1st overall, in 2005 Entry Draft.

Season	Club	League	GP	G	A	Pts	PIM	PP	SH	GW	S	%	+/-	TF	F%	Min	GP	G	A	Pts	PIM	PP	SH	GW	Min
2001-02	Dartmouth	NSMHL	74	95	98	193	114	....	....	....	....	....	....	....	....	....	....	....	....	....	....	....	....	....	....
2002-03	Shat.-St. Mary's	High-MN	57	72	90	162	....	....	....	....	....	....	....	....	....	....	....	....	....	....	....	....	....	....	....
2003-04	Rimouski Oceanic	QMJHL	59	54	*81	*135	74	....	....	....	....	....	....	....	....	....	9	7	9	16	10	....	....	....	....
2004-05	Rimouski Oceanic	QMJHL	62	*66	*102	*168	84	....	....	....	....	....	....	....	....	....	13	*14	*17	*31	16	....	....	....	....
2005-06	**Pittsburgh**	**NHL**	**81**	**39**	**63**	**102**	**110**	**16**	**0**	**5**	**278**	**14.0**	**–1**	**1174**	**45.5**	**20:08**	....	....	....	....	....	....	....	....	....
2006-07	**Pittsburgh**	**NHL**	**79**	**36**	**84**	***120**	**60**	**13**	**0**	**4**	**250**	**14.4**	**10**	**1686**	**49.8**	**20:46**	**5**	**3**	**2**	**5**	**4**	**1**	**0**	**1**	**21:40**
2007-08	**Pittsburgh**	**NHL**	**53**	**24**	**48**	**72**	**39**	**6**	**0**	**4**	**173**	**13.9**	**18**	**1103**	**51.4**	**20:51**	**20**	**6**	***21**	***27**	**12**	**2**	**0**	**1**	**20:42**
2008-09♦	**Pittsburgh**	**NHL**	**77**	**33**	**70**	**103**	**76**	**7**	**0**	**3**	**238**	**13.9**	**3**	**1615**	**51.3**	**21:57**	**24**	***15**	**16**	**31**	**14**	**5**	**0**	**2**	**20:49**
2009-10	**Pittsburgh**	**NHL**	**81**	***51**	**58**	**109**	**71**	**13**	**2**	**6**	**298**	**17.1**	**15**	**1791**	**55.9**	**21:57**	**13**	**6**	**13**	**19**	**6**	**1**	**0**	**1**	**23:32**
	Canada	Olympics	7	4	3	7	4	....	....	....	....	....	....	....	....	....	....	....	....	....	....	....	....	....	....
2010-11	**Pittsburgh**	**NHL**	**41**	**32**	**34**	**66**	**31**	**10**	**1**	**3**	**161**	**19.9**	**20**	**981**	**55.7**	**21:55**	....	....	....	....	....	....	....	....	....
	NHL Totals		**412**	**215**	**357**	**572**	**387**	**65**	**3**	**25**	**1398**	**15.4**		**8350**	**51.7**	**21:13**	**62**	**30**	**52**	**82**	**36**	**9**	**0**	**5**	**21:25**

QMJHL All-Rookie Team (2004) • QMJHL First All-Star Team (2004, 2005) • QMJHL Player of the Year (2004, 2005) • Canadian Major Junior First All-Star Team (2004, 2005) • Canadian Major Junior Rookie of the Year (2004) • Canadian Major Junior Player of the Year (2004, 2005) • Memorial Cup All-Star Team (2005) • Ed Chynoweth Trophy (Memorial Cup - Leading Scorer) (2005) • NHL All-Rookie Team (2006) • NHL First All-Star Team (2007) • Art Ross Trophy (2007) • Lester B. Pearson Award (2007) • Hart Memorial Trophy (2007) • NHL Second All-Star Team (2010) • Mark Messier NHL Leadership Award (2010) • Maurice "Rocket" Richard Trophy (2010) (tied with Steven Stamkos)

Played in NHL All-Star Game (2007)

• Missed majority of 2010-11 due to post-concussion syndrome.

CULLEN, Mark (KUH-lehn, MAHRK) FLA

Center. Shoots left. 5'11", 182 lbs. Born, Moorhead, MN, October 28, 1978.

Season	Club	League	GP	G	A	Pts	PIM	PP	SH	GW	S	%	+/-	TF	F%	Min	GP	G	A	Pts	PIM	PP	SH	GW	Min
1996-97	Fargo High	High-ND	30	20	45	65		....	....	....	....	....	....	....	....	....	....	....	....	....	....	....	....	....	....
1997-98	Fargo-Moorhead	USHL	30	17	37	54	16	....	....	....	....	....	....	....	....	....	4	3	0	3	25	....	....	....	....
1998-99	Colorado College	WCHA	42	8	25	33	22	....	....	....	....	....	....	....	....	....	....	....	....	....	....	....	....	....	....
99-2000	Colorado College	WCHA	37	11	20	31	22	....	....	....	....	....	....	....	....	....	....	....	....	....	....	....	....	....	....
2000-01	Colorado College	WCHA	31	20	33	53	26	....	....	....	....	....	....	....	....	....	....	....	....	....	....	....	....	....	....
2001-02	Colorado College	WCHA	43	14	36	50	14	....	....	....	....	....	....	....	....	....	....	....	....	....	....	....	....	....	....
2002-03	Houston Aeros	AHL	72	22	25	47	20	....	....	....	....	....	....	....	....	....	15	3	7	10	4	....	....	....	....
2003-04	Houston Aeros	AHL	53	10	28	38	28	....	....	....	....	....	....	....	....	....	2	0	0	0	0	....	....	....	....
2004-05	Houston Aeros	AHL	64	10	24	34	26	....	....	....	....	....	....	....	....	....	5	1	1	2	0	....	....	....	....

			Regular Season														Playoffs								
Season	Club	League	GP	G	A	Pts	PIM	PP	SH	GW	S	%	+/-	TF	F%	Min	GP	G	A	Pts	PIM	PP	SH	GW	Min
2005-06	Chicago	NHL	29	7	9	16	2	0	0	0	45	15.6	7	281	48.8	13:15									
	Norfolk Admirals	AHL	54	29	39	68	48										4	2	2	4	0				
2006-07	Philadelphia	NHL	3	0	0	0	0	0	0	0	4	0.0	–3	14	50.0	6:15									
	Philadelphia	AHL	56	16	36	52	34																		
2007-08	Grand Rapids	AHL	59	16	31	47	61																		
2008-09	Manitoba Moose	AHL	56	14	25	39	22										20	4	9	13	0				
2009-10	Rockford IceHogs	AHL	62	21	32	53	16										4	0	2	2	2				
2010-11	Rochester	AHL	28	5	9	14	6																		
	NHL Totals		32	7	9	16	2	0	0	0	49	14.3		295	48.8	12:36									

USHL All-Rookie Team (1998) • USHL Rookie of the Year (1998) • WCHA First All-Star Team (2001, 2002) • NCAA West Second All-American Team (2001) • Fred Hunt Memorial Trophy (AHL - Sportsmanship) (2006)

Signed as a free agent by **Minnesota**, April 8, 2002. Signed as a free agent by **Chicago**, August 4, 2005. Signed as a free agent by **Philadelphia**, July 5, 2006. Signed as a free agent by **Detroit**, July 16, 2007. Signed as a free agent by **Vancouver**, July 4, 2008. Signed as a free agent by **Chicago**, July 13, 2009. Signed as a free agent by **Florida**, July 24, 2010.

CULLEN, Matt

(KUH-lehn, MAT) **MIN**

Center. Shoots left. 6'1", 196 lbs. Born, Virginia, MN, November 2, 1976. Anaheim's 2nd choice, 35th overall, in 1996 Entry Draft.

Season	Club	League	GP	G	A	Pts	PIM	PP	SH	GW	S	%	+/-	TF	F%	Min	GP	G	A	Pts	PIM	PP	SH	GW	Min
1993-94	Moorhead Spuds	High-MN	STATISTICS NOT AVAILABLE																						
1994-95	Moorhead Spuds	High-MN	28	47	42	89	78																		
1995-96	St. Cloud State	WCHA	39	12	29	41	28																		
1996-97	St. Cloud State	WCHA	36	15	30	45	70																		
	Baltimore Bandits	AHL	6	3	3	6	7										3	0	2	2	0				
1997-98	Anaheim	NHL	61	6	21	27	23	2	0	0	75	8.0	–4												
	Cincinnati	AHL	18	15	12	27	2																		
1998-99	Anaheim	NHL	75	11	14	25	47	5	1	1	112	9.8	–12	1047	47.7	15:31	4	0	0	0	0	0	0	0	15:30
	Cincinnati	AHL	3	1	2	3	8																		
99-2000	Anaheim	NHL	80	13	26	39	24	1	0	1	137	9.5	5	1247	44.6	16:54									
2000-01	Anaheim	NHL	82	10	30	40	38	4	0	1	159	6.3	–23	1478	48.0	18:15									
2001-02	Anaheim	NHL	79	18	30	48	24	3	1	4	164	11.0	–1	1283	51.4	17:01									
2002-03	Anaheim	NHL	50	7	14	21	12	1	0	1	77	9.1	–4	271	50.6	14:18									
	Florida	NHL	30	6	6	12	22	2	1	1	54	11.1	–4	423	47.3	14:43									
2003-04	Florida	NHL	56	6	13	19	24	1	0	2	75	8.0	–2	735	50.6	14:12									
2004-05	SG Cortina	Italy	36	*27	33	60	64										18	8	14	22	32				
2005-06 ♦	Carolina	NHL	78	25	24	49	40	8	0	5	214	11.7	4	583	52.1	16:26	25	4	14	18	12	2	0	1	15:37
2006-07	NY Rangers	NHL	80	16	25	41	52	2	3	2	217	7.4	0	1134	54.6	17:10	10	1	3	4	6	0	0	1	16:55
2007-08	Carolina	NHL	59	13	36	49	32	8	0	1	137	9.5	2	649	56.1	16:52									
2008-09	Carolina	NHL	69	22	21	43	20	4	2	2	139	15.8	11	884	51.7	16:48	18	3	3	6	14	0	1	0	16:41
2009-10	Carolina	NHL	60	12	28	40	26	1	2	1	137	8.8	0	898	49.1	19:02									
	Ottawa	NHL	21	4	4	8	8	1	0	1	58	6.9	–7	223	58.7	17:59	6	3	5	8	0	2	0	0	23:14
2010-11	Minnesota	NHL	78	12	27	39	34	5	4	2	150	8.0	–14	843	56.1	18:02									
	NHL Totals		958	181	319	500	426	48	14	25	1905	9.5		11698	50.6	16:46	63	11	25	36	32	4	1	2	16:51

WCHA Second All-Star Team (1997)

Traded to **Florida** by **Anaheim** with Pavel Trnka and Anaheim's 4th round choice (James Pemberton) in 2003 Entry Draft for Sandis Ozolinsh and Lance Ward, January 30, 2003. Signed as a free agent by **Carolina**, August 5, 2004. Signed as a free agent by **Cortina** (Italy), September 18, 2004. Signed as a free agent by **NY Rangers**, July 1, 2006. Traded to **Carolina** by **NY Rangers** for Andrew Hutchinson, Joe Barnes and Carolina's 3rd round choice (Evgeny Grachev) in 2008 Entry Draft, July 17, 2007. Traded to **Ottawa** by **Carolina** for Alexandre Picard and Ottawa's 2nd round choice (later traded to Edmonton – Edmonton selected Martin Marincin) in 2010 Entry Draft, February 12, 2010. Signed as a free agent by **Minnesota**, July 1, 2010.

CULLIMORE, Jassen

(KUHL-ih-mohr, JAY-suhn)

Defense. Shoots left. 6'5", 235 lbs. Born, Simcoe, Ont., December 4, 1972. Vancouver's 2nd choice, 29th overall, in 1991 Entry Draft.

Season	Club	League	GP	G	A	Pts	PIM	PP	SH	GW	S	%	+/-	TF	F%	Min	GP	G	A	Pts	PIM	PP	SH	GW	Min
1986-87	Caledonia	ON-Jr.C	18	2	0	2	9																		
1987-88	Simcoe Rams	ON-Jr.C	35	11	14	25	92																		
1988-89	Peterborough	ON-Jr.B	29	11	17	28	88																		
	Peterborough	OHL	20	2	1	3	6																		
1989-90	Peterborough	OHL	59	2	6	8	61										11	0	2	2	8				
1990-91	Peterborough	OHL	62	8	16	24	74										4	1	0	1	7				
1991-92	Peterborough	OHL	54	9	37	46	65										10	3	6	9	8				
1992-93	Hamilton	AHL	56	5	7	12	60																		
1993-94	Hamilton	AHL	71	8	20	28	86										3	0	1	1	2				
1994-95	Syracuse Crunch	AHL	33	2	7	9	66																		
	Vancouver	NHL	34	1	2	3	39	0	0	0	30	3.3	–2				11	0	0	0	12	0	0	0	
1995-96	Vancouver	NHL	27	1	1	2	21	0	0	1	12	8.3	4												
1996-97	Vancouver	NHL	3	0	0	0	2	0	0	0	2	0.0	–2												
	Montreal	NHL	49	2	6	8	42	0	1	1	52	3.8	4				2	0	0	0	2	0	0	0	
1997-98	Montreal	NHL	3	0	0	0	4	0	0	0	1	0.0	0												
	Fredericton	AHL	5	1	0	1	8																		
	Tampa Bay	NHL	25	1	2	3	22	1	0	0	17	5.9	–4												
1998-99	Tampa Bay	NHL	78	5	12	17	81	1	1	1	73	6.8	–22	0	0.0	20:14									
99-2000	Providence Bruins	AHL	16	5	10	15	31																		
	Tampa Bay	NHL	46	1	1	2	66	0	0	0	23	4.3	–12	2	0.0	15:38									
2000-01	Tampa Bay	NHL	74	1	6	7	80	0	0	0	56	1.8	–6	0	0.0	19:43									
2001-02	Tampa Bay	NHL	78	4	9	13	58	0	0	1	84	4.8	–1	0	0.0	20:07									
2002-03	Tampa Bay	NHL	28	1	3	4	31	0	0	0	23	4.3	3	0	0.0	18:25	11	1	1	2	4	0	0	0	22:11
2003-04 ♦	Tampa Bay	NHL	79	2	5	7	58	0	0	1	78	2.6	8	0	0.0	19:02	11	0	2	2	6	0	0	0	15:15
2004-05			DID NOT PLAY																						
2005-06	Chicago	NHL	54	1	6	7	53	1	0	1	23	4.3	–24	0	0.0	16:58									
2006-07	Chicago	NHL	65	1	6	7	64	0	0	0	17	5.9	–6	0	0.0	16:17									
2007-08	Florida	NHL	65	3	10	13	38	0	0	1	55	5.5	21	1	100.0	18:04									
	Rochester	AHL	3	0	1	1	4																		
2008-09	Florida	NHL	68	2	8	10	37	0	0	0	52	3.8	–10	0	0.0	16:48									
2009-10	Rockford IceHogs	AHL	59	2	6	8	52																		
2010-11	Chicago	NHL	36	0	8	8	8	0	0	0	22	0.0	4	0	0.0	12:38									
	Rockford IceHogs	AHL	41	2	7	9	26																		
	NHL Totals		812	26	85	111	704	3	2	7	620	4.2		3	33.3	18:01	35	1	3	4	24	0	0	0	18:43

OHL Second All-Star Team (1992)

Traded to **Montreal** by **Vancouver** for Donald Brashear, November 13, 1996. Claimed on waivers by **Tampa Bay** from **Montreal**, January 22, 1998. • Loaned to **Providence** (AHL) by **Tampa Bay**, October 1, 1999. • Missed majority of 2002-03 due to elbow injury vs. Vancouver, November 29, 2002. Signed as a free agent by **Chicago**, July 22, 2004. Traded to **Montreal** by **Chicago** with Tony Salmelainen for Sergei Samsonov, June 16, 2007. Signed as a free agent by **Florida**, October 26, 2007. Signed to a PTO (professional tryout) contract by **Rockford** (AHL), October 22, 2009. Signed as a free agent by **Chicago**, February 17, 2010. Signed as a free agent by **Iserlohn** (Germany), July 25, 2011.

CUMISKEY, Kyle

(kuh-MIHS-kee, KIGHL) **COL**

Defense. Shoots left. 5'10", 185 lbs. Born, Abbotsford, B.C., December 2, 1986. Colorado's 9th choice, 222nd overall, in 2005 Entry Draft.

Season	Club	League	GP	G	A	Pts	PIM	PP	SH	GW	S	%	+/-	TF	F%	Min	GP	G	A	Pts	PIM	PP	SH	GW	Min
2002-03	Penticton	BCHL	59	10	11	21	36																		
2003-04	Kelowna Rockets	WHL	54	2	7	9	20										17	0	0	0	0				
2004-05	Kelowna Rockets	WHL	72	4	36	40	47										24	0	13	13	12				
2005-06	Kelowna Rockets	WHL	51	6	24	30	52										12	0	6	6	8				
2006-07	Colorado	NHL	9	1	1	2	2	0	0	0	8	12.5	0	0	0.0	13:28									
	Albany River Rats	AHL	63	7	26	33	32										5	0	2	2	6				
2007-08	Colorado	NHL	38	0	5	5	16	0	0	0	19	0.0	–3	0	0.0	12:08									
	Lake Erie	AHL	5	1	1	2	4																		
2008-09	Colorado	NHL	6	0	0	0	0	0	0	0	2	0.0	–2	0	0.0	8:32									
	Lake Erie	AHL	28	5	12	17	16																		
2009-10	Colorado	NHL	61	7	13	20	20	2	0	1	74	9.5	0	0	0.0	19:48	6	1	1	2	2	0	0	0	22:37
2010-11	Colorado	NHL	18	1	7	8	10	0	0	0	21	4.8	–3	0	0.0	19:40									
	NHL Totals		132	9	26	35	48	2	0	1	124	7.3		0	0.0	16:38	6	1	1	2	2	0	0	0	22:37

• Missed majority of 2010-11 due to post-concussion syndrome.

					Regular Season														Playoffs							
Season	Club	League	GP	G	A	Pts	PIM	PP	SH	GW	S	%	+/-	TF	F%	Min	GP	G	A	Pts	PIM	PP	SH	GW	Min

DA COSTA, Stephane   (DA-KAWS-tuh, steh-FAN)   **OTT**

Center. Shoots right. 5'11", 183 lbs.   Born, Paris, France, July 11, 1989.

Season	Club	League	GP	G	A	Pts	PIM	PP	SH	GW	S	%	+/-	TF	F%	Min	GP	G	A	Pts	PIM	PP	SH	GW	Min
2006-07	Texas Tornado	NAHL	50	23	17	40	31	....	....	....	....	....	....			....	10	4	3	7	6	....	....	....	....
2007-08	Sioux City	USHL	51	12	25	37	22	....	....	....	....	....	....			....	4	1	2	3	8	....	....	....	....
2008-09	Sioux City	USHL	48	31	36	67	23	....	....	....	....	....	....			....	....	....	....	....	....	....	....	....	....
2009-10	Merrimack	H-East	34	16	29	45	41	....	....	....	....	....	....			....	....	....	....	....	....	....	....	....	....
2010-11	Merrimack	H-East	33	14	31	45	42	....	....	....	....	....	....			....	....	....	....	....	....	....	....	....	....
	Ottawa	NHL	4	0	0	0	0	0	0	0	9	0.0	-1	21	28.6	11:25	....	....	....	....	....	....	....	....	....
	NHL Totals		**4**	**0**	**0**	**0**	**0**	**0**	**0**	**0**	**9**	**0.0**		**21**	**28.6**	**11:25**	....	....	....	....	....	....	....	....	....

Hockey East All-Rookie Team (2010) • Hockey East Second All-Star Team (2010, 2011) • Hockey East Rookie of the Year (2010) • NCAA Rookie of the Year (2010) • NCAA East Second All-American Team (2011)

Signed as a free agent by **Ottawa**. March 31, 2011.

DADONOV, Evgeny   (do-DON-nauv, ehv-GEH-nee)   **FLA**

Right wing. Shoots left. 5'10", 178 lbs.   Born, Chelyabinsk, USSR, March 12, 1989. Florida's 3rd choice, 71st overall, in 2007 Entry Draft.

Season	Club	League	GP	G	A	Pts	PIM	PP	SH	GW	S	%	+/-	TF	F%	Min	GP	G	A	Pts	PIM	PP	SH	GW	Min
2005-06	Chelyabinsk 2	Russia-3	12	1	4	5	2	....	....	....	....	....	....			....	1	0	0	0	0	....	....	....	....
	Chelyabinsk	Russia-2	....	....	....	....	....	....	....	....	....	....	....			....	....	....	....	....	....	....	....	....	....
2006-07	Chelyabinsk 2	Russia-3	4	2	0	2	14	....	....	....	....	....	....			....	....	....	....	....	....	....	....	....	....
	Chelyabinsk	Russia	24	1	1	2	8	....	....	....	....	....	....			....	....	....	....	....	....	....	....	....	....
2007-08	Chelyabinsk 2	Russia-3	12	4	7	11	32	....	....	....	....	....	....			....	2	0	0	0	0	....	....	....	....
	Chelyabinsk	Russia	43	7	13	20	20	....	....	....	....	....	....			....	3	0	0	0	2	....	....	....	....
2008-09	Chelyabinsk	Rus-KHL	40	11	4	15	8	....	....	....	....	....	....			....	....	....	....	....	....	....	....	....	....
2009-10	Florida	NHL	4	0	0	0	0	0	0	0	4	0.0	-1	0	0.0	13:14	....	....	....	....	....	....	....	....	....
	Rochester	AHL	76	17	23	40	36	....	....	....	....	....	....			....	7	0	1	1	0	....	....	....	....
2010-11	Florida	NHL	36	8	9	17	14	1	0	0	60	13.3	0	5	20.0	14:15	....	....	....	....	....	....	....	....	....
	Rochester	AHL	24	8	8	16	4	....	....	....	....	....	....			....	....	....	....	....	....	....	....	....	....
	NHL Totals		**40**	**8**	**9**	**17**	**14**	**1**	**0**	**0**	**64**	**12.5**		**5**	**20.0**	**14:09**	....	....	....	....	....	....	....	....	....

D'AGOSTINI, Matt   (DAG-uh-stee-noh, MAT)   **ST.L.**

Right wing. Shoots right. 6', 200 lbs.   Born, Sault Ste. Marie, Ont., October 23, 1986. Montreal's 5th choice, 190th overall, in 2005 Entry Draft.

Season	Club	League	GP	G	A	Pts	PIM	PP	SH	GW	S	%	+/-	TF	F%	Min	GP	G	A	Pts	PIM	PP	SH	GW	Min
2003-04	Soo North Stars	GNML	36	36	23	59	41	....	....	....	....	....	....			....	4	0	2	2	8	....	....	....	....
2004-05	Guelph Storm	OHL	59	24	22	46	29	....	....	....	....	....	....			....	15	8	20	28	16	....	....	....	....
2005-06	Guelph Storm	OHL	66	25	54	79	81	....	....	....	....	....	....			....	22	4	9	13	18	....	....	....	....
2006-07	Hamilton	AHL	63	21	28	49	33	....	....	....	....	....	....			....	....	....	....	....	....	....	....	....	....
2007-08	Montreal	NHL	1	0	0	0	2	0	0	0	0	0.0	0	0	0.0	8:49	....	....	....	....	....	....	....	....	....
	Hamilton	AHL	76	23	30	53	38	....	....	....	....	....	....			....	....	....	....	....	....	....	....	....	....
2008-09	Montreal	NHL	53	12	9	21	16	3	0	1	116	10.3	-17	9	33.3	13:25	3	0	0	0	0	0	0	0	11:49
	Hamilton	AHL	20	14	11	25	16	....	....	....	....	....	....			....	....	....	....	....	....	....	....	....	....
2009-10	Montreal	NHL	40	2	2	4	26	0	0	0	48	4.2	-12	3	66.7	9:53	....	....	....	....	....	....	....	....	....
	Hamilton	AHL	3	0	1	1	2	....	....	....	....	....	....			....	....	....	....	....	....	....	....	....	....
	St. Louis	NHL	7	0	0	0	2	0	0	0	6	0.0	-3	7	71.4	9:13	....	....	....	....	....	....	....	....	....
2010-11	St. Louis	NHL	82	21	25	46	40	6	0	5	163	12.9	8	55	38.2	14:46	....	....	....	....	....	....	....	....	....
	NHL Totals		**183**	**35**	**36**	**71**	**86**	**9**	**0**	**6**	**333**	**10.5**		**74**	**41.9**	**13:04**	**3**	**0**	**0**	**0**	**0**	**0**	**0**	**0**	**11:49**

Traded to **St. Louis** by **Montreal** for Aaron Palushaj, March 2, 2010.

DALEY, Trevor   (DAY-lee, TREH-vuhr)   **DAL**

Defense. Shoots left. 5'11", 205 lbs.   Born, Toronto, Ont., October 9, 1983. Dallas' 5th choice, 43rd overall, in 2002 Entry Draft.

Season	Club	League	GP	G	A	Pts	PIM	PP	SH	GW	S	%	+/-	TF	F%	Min	GP	G	A	Pts	PIM	PP	SH	GW	Min
1998-99	Vaughan Vipers	OPJHL	44	10	36	46	79	....	....	....	....	....	....			....	....	....	....	....	....	....	....	....	....
99-2000	Sault Ste. Marie	OHL	54	16	30	46	77	....	....	....	....	....	....			....	15	3	7	10	12	....	....	....	....
2000-01	Sault Ste. Marie	OHL	58	14	27	41	105	....	....	....	....	....	....			....	6	2	2	4	4	....	....	....	....
2001-02	Sault Ste. Marie	OHL	47	9	39	48	38	....	....	....	....	....	....			....	1	0	0	0	2	....	....	....	....
2002-03	Sault Ste. Marie	OHL	57	20	33	53	128	....	....	....	....	....	....			....	....	....	....	....	....	....	....	....	....
2003-04	Dallas	NHL	27	1	5	6	14	1	0	0	34	2.9	-6	0	0.0	16:02	1	0	0	0	0	0	0	0	10:21
	Utah Grizzlies	AHL	40	8	6	14	76	....	....	....	....	....	....			....	4	0	1	1	2	....	....	....	....
2004-05	Hamilton	AHL	78	7	27	34	109	....	....	....	....	....	....			....	3	0	0	0	0	0	0	0	11:30
2005-06	Dallas	NHL	81	3	11	14	87	0	0	1	91	3.3	2	0	0.0	18:40	3	0	0	0	0	0	0	0	11:30
2006-07	Dallas	NHL	74	4	8	12	63	0	0	0	68	5.9	2	0	0.0	19:23	7	1	0	1	4	0	0	0	22:26
2007-08	Dallas	NHL	82	5	19	24	85	0	0	1	87	5.7	-1	1100.0		19:48	18	1	0	1	20	0	0	0	18:52
2008-09	Dallas	NHL	75	7	18	25	73	0	0	2	104	6.7	2	1	0.0	22:00	....	....	....	....	....	....	....	....	....
2009-10	Dallas	NHL	77	6	16	22	25	2	0	2	107	5.6	3	0	0.0	22:11	....	....	....	....	....	....	....	....	....
2010-11	Dallas	NHL	82	8	19	27	34	2	0	1	131	6.1	7	0	0.0	22:29	....	....	....	....	....	....	....	....	....
	NHL Totals		**498**	**34**	**96**	**130**	**381**	**5**	**0**	**8**	**622**	**5.5**		**2**	**50.0**	**20:30**	**29**	**2**	**0**	**2**	**24**	**0**	**0**	**0**	**18:40**

DALPE, Zac   (DAL-pee, ZAK)   **CAR**

Right wing. Shoots right. 6'1", 195 lbs.   Born, Paris, Ont., November 1, 1989. Carolina's 2nd choice, 45th overall, in 2008 Entry Draft.

Season	Club	League	GP	G	A	Pts	PIM	PP	SH	GW	S	%	+/-	TF	F%	Min	GP	G	A	Pts	PIM	PP	SH	GW	Min
2006-07	Stratford Cullitons	ON-Jr.B	52	30	43	73	68	....	....	....	....	....	....			....	15	8	9	17	4	....	....	....	....
2007-08	Penticton Vees	BCHL	46	27	36	63	14	....	....	....	....	....	....			....	....	....	....	....	....	....	....	....	....
2008-09	Ohio State	CCHA	37	13	12	25	25	....	....	....	....	....	....			....	....	....	....	....	....	....	....	....	....
2009-10	Ohio State	CCHA	39	*21	24	45	19	....	....	....	....	....	....			....	8	3	3	6	0	....	....	....	....
	Albany River Rats	AHL	9	6	2	8	0	....	....	....	....	....	....			....	....	....	....	....	....	....	....	....	....
2010-11	Carolina	NHL	15	3	1	4	0	0	0	1	16	18.8	0	26	26.9	7:56	....	....	....	....	....	....	....	....	....
	Charlotte	AHL	61	23	34	57	21	....	....	....	....	....	....			....	16	6	7	13	6	....	....	....	....
	NHL Totals		**15**	**3**	**1**	**4**	**0**	**0**	**0**	**1**	**16**	**18.8**		**26**	**26.9**	**7:56**	....	....	....	....	....	....	....	....	....

CCHA All-Rookie Team (2009) • CCHA First All-Star Team (2010) • NCAA West Second All-American Team (2010) • AHL All-Rookie Team (2011)

DARCHE, Mathieu   (DAHRSH, MA-thew)   **MTL**

Left wing. Shoots left. 6'1", 215 lbs.   Born, St. Laurent, Que., November 26, 1976.

Season	Club	League	GP	G	A	Pts	PIM	PP	SH	GW	S	%	+/-	TF	F%	Min	GP	G	A	Pts	PIM	PP	SH	GW	Min
1995-96	Choate-Rosemary	High-CT			STATISTICS NOT AVAILABLE																				
1996-97	McGill Redmen	OUAA	23	1	2	3	27	....	....	....	....	....	....			....	....	....	....	....	....	....	....	....	....
1997-98	McGill Redmen	OUAA	40	28	17	45	69	....	....	....	....	....	....			....	....	....	....	....	....	....	....	....	....
1998-99	McGill Redmen	OUAA	32	16	24	40	60	....	....	....	....	....	....			....	....	....	....	....	....	....	....	....	....
99-2000	McGill Redmen	OUAA	33	31	41	*72	38	....	....	....	....	....	....			....	5	2	8	10	16	....	....	....	....
2000-01	Columbus	NHL	9	0	0	0	0	0	0	0	9	0.0	-4	1	0.0	10:07	....	....	....	....	....	....	....	....	....
	Syracuse Crunch	AHL	66	16	24	40	21	....	....	....	....	....	....			....	5	0	1	1	4	....	....	....	....
2001-02	Columbus	NHL	14	1	1	2	6	0	0	0	15	6.7	-5	3	33.3	9:49	....	....	....	....	....	....	....	....	....
	Syracuse Crunch	AHL	63	22	23	45	26	....	....	....	....	....	....			....	10	2	5	7	2	....	....	....	....
2002-03	Columbus	NHL	1	0	0	0	0	0	0	0	0	0.0	-1	0	0.0	6:57	....	....	....	....	....	....	....	....	....
	Syracuse Crunch	AHL	76	32	32	64	38	....	....	....	....	....	....			....	22	6	8	14	8	....	....	....	....
2003-04	Nashville	NHL	2	0	0	0	0	0	0	0	1	0.0	-1	0	0.0	6:39	....	....	....	....	....	....	....	....	....
	Milwaukee	AHL	76	28	31	59	41	....	....	....	....	....	....			....	5	1	3	4	4	....	....	....	....
2005-06	Fuchse Duisburg	Germany	52	12	13	25	88	....	....	....	....	....	....			....	....	....	....	....	....	....	....	....	....
2006-07	San Jose	NHL	2	0	0	0	0	0	0	0	3	0.0	0	0	0.0	9:13	....	....	....	....	....	....	....	....	....
	Worcester Sharks	AHL	76	35	45	80	72	....	....	....	....	....	....			....	5	2	2	4	2	....	....	....	....
2007-08	Tampa Bay	NHL	73	7	15	22	20	1	1	0	120	5.8	-14	89	48.3	14:26	....	....	....	....	....	....	....	....	....
	Norfolk Admirals	AHL	4	3	7	10	2	....	....	....	....	....	....			....	....	....	....	....	....	....	....	....	....
2008-09	Portland Pirates	AHL	80	31	35	66	37	....	....	....	....	....	....			....	0	0	0	4	....	....	....	....	....

			Regular Season														Playoffs								
Season	Club	League	GP	G	A	Pts	PIM	PP	SH	GW	S	%	+/-	TF	F%	Min	GP	G	A	Pts	PIM	PP	SH	GW	Min
2009-10	**Montreal**	**NHL**	29	5	5	10	4	0	0	3	43	11.6	2	5	60.0	10:51	11	0	1	1	2	0	0	0	6:14
	Hamilton	AHL	32	16	9	25	4	....	....	....	....	....	....	....	....	....	....	....	....	....	....	....	....	....	....
2010-11	**Montreal**	**NHL**	59	12	14	26	10	2	0	1	90	13.3	7	21	33.3	11:16	7	1	1	2	0	1	0	1	15:42
	NHL Totals		189	25	35	60	40	3	1	4	281	8.9		119	45.4	12:10	18	1	2	3	2	1	0	1	9:55

OUAA East Second All-Star Team (1998) • OUAA East First All-Star Team (1999) • OUAA First All-Star Team (2000) • CIAU All-Canadian Team (2000)

Signed as a free agent by **Columbus**, May 16, 2000. Signed as a free agent by **Nashville**, September 10, 2003. Signed as a free agent by **Colorado**, July 26, 2004. Signed as a free agent by **San Jose**, July 10, 2006. Signed as a free agent by **Tampa Bay**, July 2, 2007. Signed as a free agent by **Buffalo**, July 24, 2008. Signed as a free agent by **Montreal**, July 2, 2009.

DATSYUK, Pavel

(daht-SOOK, PAH-vehl) **DET**

Center. Shoots left. 5'11", 194 lbs. Born, Sverdlovsk, USSR, July 20, 1978. Detroit's 8th choice, 171st overall, in 1998 Entry Draft.

1996-97	Yekaterinburg 2	Russia-3	18	2	2	4	4	....	....	....	....	....	....	....	....	....	....	....	....	....	....	....	....	....	....
	Yekaterinburg	Russia	36	12	10	22	12	....	....	....	....	....	....	....	....	....	....	....	....	....	....	....	....	....	....
1997-98	Yekaterinburg	Russia	24	3	5	8	4	....	....	....	....	....	....	....	....	....	....	....	....	....	....	....	....	....	....
	Yekaterinburg 2	Russia-3	22	7	8	15	4	....	....	....	....	....	....	....	....	....	....	....	....	....	....	....	....	....	....
1998-99	Yekaterinburg 2	Russia-4	10	14	14	28	4	....	....	....	....	....	....	....	....	....	....	....	....	....	....	....	....	....	....
	Yekaterinburg	Russia-2	35	21	23	44	14	....	....	....	....	....	....	....	....	....	9	3	7	10	10	....	....	....	....
99-2000	Yekaterinburg	Russia	15	1	3	4	4	....	....	....	....	....	....	....	....	....	....	....	....	....	....	....	....	....	....
2000-01	Ak Bars Kazan	Russia	42	9	18	27	10	....	....	....	....	....	....	....	....	....	4	0	1	1	2	....	....	....	....
2001-02♦	**Detroit**	**NHL**	70	11	24	35	4	2	0	1	79	13.9	4	794	47.7	13:39	21	3	3	6	2	1	0	1	10:40
	Russia	Olympics	6	1	2	3	0	....	....	....	....	....	....	....	....	....	....	....	....	....	....	....	....	....	....
2002-03	**Detroit**	**NHL**	64	12	39	51	16	1	0	1	82	14.6	20	778	48.2	15:28	4	0	0	0	0	0	0	0	18:48
2003-04	**Detroit**	**NHL**	75	30	38	68	35	8	1	4	136	22.1	−2	1314	54.0	18:16	12	0	6	6	2	0	0	0	17:23
2004-05	Dynamo Moscow	Russia	47	15	17	32	16	....	....	....	....	....	....	....	....	....	10	*6	3	9	4	....	....	....	....
2005-06	**Detroit**	**NHL**	75	28	59	87	22	11	0	4	145	19.3	26	1059	53.1	17:53	5	0	3	3	0	0	0	0	20:05
	Russia	Olympics	8	1	7	8	10	....	....	....	....	....	....	....	....	....	....	....	....	....	....	....	....	....	....
2006-07	**Detroit**	**NHL**	79	27	60	87	20	5	2	5	207	13.0	36	845	56.2	19:57	18	8	8	16	8	4	0	2	22:03
2007-08♦	**Detroit**	**NHL**	82	31	66	97	20	10	1	6	264	11.7	*41	833	54.4	21:23	22	10	13	23	6	4	0	1	21:40
2008-09	**Detroit**	**NHL**	81	32	65	97	22	11	1	3	248	12.9	34	1135	56.0	19:13	16	1	8	9	9	1	0	0	20:05
2009-10	**Detroit**	**NHL**	80	27	43	70	18	9	0	3	203	13.3	17	1070	55.1	20:21	12	6	7	13	8	1	0	1	18:49
	Russia	Olympics	4	1	2	3	2	....	....	....	....	....	....	....	....	....	....	....	....	....	....	....	....	....	....
2010-11	**Detroit**	**NHL**	56	23	36	59	15	6	1	5	137	16.8	11	785	54.7	19:19	11	4	11	15	8	2	0	0	21:09
	NHL Totals		662	221	430	651	172	63	6	32	1501	14.7		8613	53.5	18:31	121	32	59	91	43	13	0	5	18:42

Lady Byng Memorial Trophy (2006, 2007, 2008, 2009) • Frank J. Selke Trophy (2008, 2009, 2010) • NHL Second All-Star Team (2009)

Played in NHL All-Star Game (2004, 2008)

• Spent majority of 1999-2000 season on **Kazan** (Russia) reserve squad. Signed as a free agent by **Dynamo Moscow** (Russia), June 19, 2004.

DAUGAVINS, Kaspars

(DAH-gah-vihnsh, KAS-purz) **OTT**

Left wing. Shoots left. 6'1", 204 lbs. Born, Riga, Latvia, May 18, 1988. Ottawa's 3rd choice, 91st overall, in 2006 Entry Draft.

2003-04	HK Riga 2000	EEHL	2	0	1	1	0	....	....	....	....	....	....	....	....	....	....	....	....	....	....	....	....	....	....
	Prizma/Riga 86	Latvia	14	6	6	12	10	....	....	....	....	....	....	....	....	....	2	1	1	2	4	....	....	....	....
2004-05	CSKA Moscow 2	Russia-3	STATISTICS NOT AVAILABLE																						
2005-06	HK Riga 2000	Latvia	....	4	6	10	16	....	....	....	....	....	....	....	....	....	....	....	....	....	....	....	....	....	....
	HK Riga 2000	BelOpen	45	4	11	15	16	....	....	....	....	....	....	....	....	....	....	....	....	....	....	....	....	....	....
2006-07	St. Michael's	OHL	61	18	42	60	64	....	....	....	....	....	....	....	....	....	....	....	....	....	....	....	....	....	....
	Binghamton	AHL	11	2	0	2	9	....	....	....	....	....	....	....	....	....	....	....	....	....	....	....	....	....	....
2007-08	St. Michael's	OHL	62	40	34	74	42	....	....	....	....	....	....	....	....	....	4	2	1	3	4	....	....	....	....
	Binghamton	AHL	3	0	1	1	0	....	....	....	....	....	....	....	....	....	....	....	....	....	....	....	....	....	....
2008-09	Binghamton	AHL	23	2	1	3	9	....	....	....	....	....	....	....	....	....	....	....	....	....	....	....	....	....	....
	St. Michael's	OHL	30	11	17	28	35	....	....	....	....	....	....	....	....	....	11	2	7	9	14	....	....	....	....
2009-10	**Ottawa**	**NHL**	1	0	0	0	0	0	0	0	2	0.0	0	0	0.0	8:26	....	....	....	....	....	....	....	....	....
	Binghamton	AHL	72	21	25	46	16	....	....	....	....	....	....	....	....	....	....	....	....	....	....	....	....	....	....
	Latvia	Olympics	4	0	0	0	2	....	....	....	....	....	....	....	....	....	....	....	....	....	....	....	....	....	....
2010-11	Binghamton	AHL	73	19	35	54	34	....	....	....	....	....	....	....	....	....	23	10	10	20	8	....	....	....	....
	NHL Totals		1	0	0	0	0	0	0	0	2	0.0		0	0.0	8:26	....	....	....	....	....	....	....	....	....

OHL All-Rookie Team (2007)

Signed as a free agent by **Dynamo Riga** (Russia-KHL), July 20, 2011.

DAVIS, Patrick

(DAY-vihs, PAT-rihk)

Right wing. Shoots right. 6'2", 195 lbs. Born, Sterling, MI, December 28, 1986. New Jersey's 4th choice, 99th overall, in 2005 Entry Draft.

2002-03	Detroit Belle Tire	MWEHL	STATISTICS NOT AVAILABLE																						
	Sioux City	USHL	16	3	2	5	8	....	....	....	....	....	....	....	....	....	1	0	0	0	2	....	....	....	....
2003-04	Kitchener Rangers	OHL	27	8	10	18	21	....	....	....	....	....	....	....	....	....	....	....	....	....	....	....	....	....	....
2004-05	Kitchener Rangers	OHL	59	20	30	50	41	....	....	....	....	....	....	....	....	....	14	3	4	7	20	....	....	....	....
2005-06	Kitchener Rangers	OHL	22	13	4	17	30	....	....	....	....	....	....	....	....	....	....	....	....	....	....	....	....	....	....
	Windsor Spitfires	OHL	38	22	29	51	64	....	....	....	....	....	....	....	....	....	7	2	6	8	12	....	....	....	....
	Albany River Rats	AHL	3	0	0	0	2	....	....	....	....	....	....	....	....	....	....	....	....	....	....	....	....	....	....
2006-07	Lowell Devils	AHL	41	5	13	18	26	....	....	....	....	....	....	....	....	....	....	....	....	....	....	....	....	....	....
2007-08	Lowell Devils	AHL	60	7	12	19	58	....	....	....	....	....	....	....	....	....	....	....	....	....	....	....	....	....	....
2008-09	**New Jersey**	**NHL**	1	0	0	0	0	0	0	0	0	0.0	0	0	0.0	4:30	....	....	....	....	....	....	....	....	....
	Lowell Devils	AHL	74	13	17	30	45	....	....	....	....	....	....	....	....	....	....	....	....	....	....	....	....	....	....
2009-10	**New Jersey**	**NHL**	8	1	0	1	0	0	0	0	8	12.5	−2	6	66.7	12:37	....	....	....	....	....	....	....	....	....
	Lowell Devils	AHL	73	15	20	35	39	....	....	....	....	....	....	....	....	....	5	2	0	2	2	....	....	....	....
2010-11	Albany Devils	AHL	40	3	10	13	22	....	....	....	....	....	....	....	....	....	....	....	....	....	....	....	....	....	....
	Worcester Sharks	AHL	26	4	4	8	2	....	....	....	....	....	....	....	....	....	....	....	....	....	....	....	....	....	....
	NHL Totals		9	1	0	1	0	0	0	0	8	12.5		6	66.7	11:42	....	....	....	....	....	....	....	....	....

Traded to **San Jose** by **New Jersey** with Michael Swift for Jay Leach and Steven Zalewski, February 9, 2011.

DAVISON, Rob

(DAY-vihs-ohn, RAWB)

Defense. Shoots left. 6'3", 220 lbs. Born, St. Catharines, Ont., May 1, 1980. San Jose's 4th choice, 98th overall, in 1998 Entry Draft.

1996-97	St. Mike's B's	OPJHL	45	2	6	8	93	....	....	....	....	....	....	....	....	....	6	0	0	0	9	....	....	....	....
1997-98	North Bay	OHL	59	0	11	11	200	....	....	....	....	....	....	....	....	....	....	....	....	....	....	....	....	....	....
1998-99	North Bay	OHL	59	2	17	19	150	....	....	....	....	....	....	....	....	....	4	0	1	1	12	....	....	....	....
99-2000	North Bay	OHL	67	4	6	10	194	....	....	....	....	....	....	....	....	....	6	0	1	1	8	....	....	....	....
2000-01	Kentucky	AHL	72	0	4	4	230	....	....	....	....	....	....	....	....	....	3	0	0	0	0	....	....	....	....
2001-02	Cleveland Barons	AHL	70	1	3	4	206	....	....	....	....	....	....	....	....	....	....	....	....	....	....	....	....	....	....
2002-03	**San Jose**	**NHL**	15	1	2	3	22	0	0	0	15	6.7	4	0	0.0	17:53	....	....	....	....	....	....	....	....	....
	Cleveland Barons	AHL	42	1	3	4	82	....	....	....	....	....	....	....	....	....	....	....	....	....	....	....	....	....	....
2003-04	**San Jose**	**NHL**	55	0	3	3	92	0	0	0	33	0.0	−3	0	0.0	14:22	5	0	2	2	4	0	0	0	9:01
2004-05	Cardiff Devils	Britain	24	2	3	5	114	....	....	....	....	....	....	....	....	....	8	0	1	1	12	....	....	....	....
2005-06	**San Jose**	**NHL**	69	1	5	6	76	0	0	0	36	2.8	6	0	0.0	13:50	1	0	0	0	0	0	0	0	8:00
2006-07	**San Jose**	**NHL**	22	0	2	2	27	0	0	0	14	0.0	−2	0	0.0	9:19	....	....	....	....	....	....	....	....	....
2007-08	**San Jose**	**NHL**	15	0	0	0	21	0	0	0	10	0.0	−3	0	0.0	7:47	....	....	....	....	....	....	....	....	....
	NY Islanders	**NHL**	19	1	1	2	32	0	1	0	22	4.5	−3	0	0.0	18:40	....	....	....	....	....	....	....	....	....
2008-09	**Vancouver**	**NHL**	23	0	2	2	51	0	0	0	15	0.0	−4	0	0.0	10:05	....	....	....	....	....	....	....	....	....
2009-10	**New Jersey**	**NHL**	1	0	0	0	0	0	0	0	0	0.0	0	0	0.0	3:59	....	....	....	....	....	....	....	....	....
	Lowell Devils	AHL	70	4	13	17	182	....	....	....	....	....	....	....	....	....	5	0	1	1	12	....	....	....	....
2010-11	Albany Devils	AHL	63	4	14	18	151	....	....	....	....	....	....	....	....	....	....	....	....	....	....	....	....	....	....
	NHL Totals		219	3	15	18	321	0	1	0	145	2.1		0	0.0	13:22	6	0	2	2	4	0	0	0	8:51

Signed as a free agent by **Cardiff** (Britain), October 5, 2004. Traded to **NY Islanders** by **San Jose** for NY Islanders' 7th round choice (Jason Demers) in 2008 Entry Draft, February 26, 2008. Signed as a free agent by **Vancouver**, July 10, 2008. • Missed majority of 2006-07, 2007-08 and 2008-09 due to various injuries and as a healthy reserve. Signed as a free agent by **New Jersey**, July 31, 2009.

DAWES, Nigel

(DAWZ, NIGH-juhl)

Left wing. Shoots left. 5'9", 200 lbs. Born, Winnipeg, Man., February 9, 1985. NY Rangers' 5th choice, 149th overall, in 2003 Entry Draft.

			Regular Season														Playoffs								
Season	Club	League	GP	G	A	Pts	PIM	PP	SH	GW	S	%	+/-	TF	F%	Min	GP	G	A	Pts	PIM	PP	SH	GW	Min
2000-01	Wpg. Warriors	MMMHL	36	55	41	96	74	....	....	....	....	....	....	....	....	....	....	....	....	....	....	....	....	....	....
2001-02	Kootenay Ice	WHL	54	15	19	34	14	....	....	....	....	....	....	....	....	....	22	9	6	15	8	....	....	....	....
2002-03	Kootenay Ice	WHL	72	47	45	92	54	....	....	....	....	....	....	....	....	....	11	4	8	12	6	....	....	....	....
2003-04	Kootenay Ice	WHL	56	47	23	70	31	....	....	....	....	....	....	....	....	....	4	1	2	3	10	....	....	....	....
	Hartford	AHL	4	0	0	0	0	....	....	....	....	....	....	....	....	....	....	....	....	....	....	....	....	....	....
2004-05	Kootenay Ice	WHL	63	50	26	76	30	....	....	....	....	....	....	....	....	....	12	5	10	15	5	....	....	....	....
2005-06	Hartford	AHL	77	35	31	66	21	....	....	....	....	....	....	....	....	....	13	6	6	12	9	....	....	....	....
2006-07	**NY Rangers**	**NHL**	**8**	**1**	**0**	**1**	**0**	**0**	**0**	**0**	**7**	**14.3**	**-4**	**1**	**0.0**	**6:44**	**1**	**0**	**0**	**0**	**0**	**0**	**0**	**0**	**9:02**
	Hartford	AHL	65	27	33	60	29	....	....	....	....	....	....	....	....	....	7	5	6	11	9	....	....	....	....
2007-08	**NY Rangers**	**NHL**	**61**	**14**	**15**	**29**	**10**	**3**	**0**	**4**	**121**	**11.6**	**11**	**2**	**50.0**	**12:59**	**10**	**2**	**2**	**4**	**0**	**0**	**0**	**0**	**12:31**
	Hartford	AHL	20	14	20	34	2	....	....	....	....	....	....	....	....	....	....	....	....	....	....	....	....	....	....
2008-09	**NY Rangers**	**NHL**	**52**	**10**	**9**	**19**	**15**	**3**	**0**	**4**	**96**	**10.4**	**-2**	**0**	**0.0**	**13:03**	....	....	....	....	....	....	....	....	....
	Phoenix	**NHL**	**12**	**0**	**2**	**2**	**0**	**0**	**0**	**0**	**19**	**0.0**	**-4**	**0**	**0.0**	**14:09**	....	....	....	....	....	....	....	....	....
2009-10	**Calgary**	**NHL**	**66**	**14**	**18**	**32**	**18**	**4**	**0**	**2**	**96**	**14.6**	**1**	**1**	**0.0**	**14:32**	....	....	....	....	....	....	....	....	....
2010-11	**Atlanta**	**NHL**	**9**	**0**	**1**	**1**	**0**	**0**	**0**	**0**	**9**	**0.0**	**-6**	**0**	**0.0**	**11:11**	....	....	....	....	....	....	....	....	....
	Chicago Wolves	AHL	47	27	17	44	17	....	....	....	....	....	....	....	....	....	....	....	....	....	....	....	....	....	....
	Montreal	**NHL**	**4**	**0**	**0**	**0**	**0**	**0**	**0**	**0**	**3**	**0.0**	**0**	**0**	**0.0**	**6:44**	....	....	....	....	....	....	....	....	....
	Hamilton	AHL	19	14	14	28	7	....	....	....	....	....	....	....	....	....	20	*14	8	22	8	....	....	....	....
	NHL Totals		**212**	**39**	**45**	**84**	**43**	**10**	**0**	**10**	**351**	**11.1**		**4**	**25.0**	**13:07**	**11**	**2**	**2**	**4**	**0**	**0**	**0**	**0**	**12:12**

WHL West Second All-Star Team (2003) • WHL West First All-Star Team (2004, 2005) • AHL Second All-Star Team (2011)

Traded to **Phoenix** by **NY Rangers** with Dmitri Kalinin and Petr Prucha for Derek Morris, March 4, 2009. Claimed on waivers by **Calgary**, July 15, 2009. Signed as a free agent by **Atlanta**, September 13, 2010. Traded to **Montreal** by **Atlanta** with Brent Sopel for Ben Maxwell and Montreal's 4th round choice (later traded back to Montreal - Montreal selected Olivier Archambault) in 2011 Entry Draft, February 24, 2011. Signed as a free agent by **Astana** (Russia-KHL), May 31, 2011.

DEL ZOTTO, Michael

(DEHL ZAW-toh, MIGH-kuhl) **NYR**

Defense. Shoots left. 6', 193 lbs. Born, Stouffville, Ont., June 24, 1990. NY Rangers' 1st choice, 20th overall, in 2008 Entry Draft.

Season	Club	League	GP	G	A	Pts	PIM	PP	SH	GW	S	%	+/-	TF	F%	Min	GP	G	A	Pts	PIM	PP	SH	GW	Min
2005-06	Markham Waxers	Minor-ON	73	30	90	120	90	....	....	....	....	....	....	....	....	....	....	....	....	....	....	....	....	....	....
2006-07	Oshawa Generals	OHL	64	10	47	57	78	....	....	....	....	....	....	....	....	....	9	3	9	12	14	....	....	....	....
2007-08	Oshawa Generals	OHL	64	16	47	63	82	....	....	....	....	....	....	....	....	....	15	2	6	8	38	....	....	....	....
2008-09	Oshawa Generals	OHL	34	7	26	33	48	....	....	....	....	....	....	....	....	....	....	....	....	....	....	....	....	....	....
	London Knights	OHL	28	6	24	30	30	....	....	....	....	....	....	....	....	....	14	3	16	19	18	....	....	....	....
2009-10	**NY Rangers**	**NHL**	**80**	**9**	**28**	**37**	**32**	**4**	**0**	**1**	**81**	**11.1**	**-20**	**0**	**0.0**	**18:58**	....	....	....	....	....	....	....	....	....
2010-11	**NY Rangers**	**NHL**	**47**	**2**	**9**	**11**	**20**	**2**	**0**	**0**	**58**	**3.4**	**-5**	**0**	**0.0**	**19:29**	....	....	....	....	....	....	....	....	....
	Connecticut	AHL	11	0	7	7	8	....	....	....	....	....	....	....	....	....	....	....	....	....	....	....	....	....	....
	NHL Totals		**127**	**11**	**37**	**48**	**52**	**6**	**0**	**1**	**139**	**7.9**		**0**	**0.0**	**19:10**	....	....	....	....	....	....	....	....	....

NHL All-Rookie Team (2010)

DELLA ROVERE, Stefan

(DEHL-ah ROH-vair, STEH-fan) **ST.L.**

Left wing. Shoots left. 5'11", 200 lbs. Born, Richmond Hill, Ont., February 25, 1990. Washington's 8th choice, 204th overall, in 2008 Entry Draft.

Season	Club	League	GP	G	A	Pts	PIM	PP	SH	GW	S	%	+/-	TF	F%	Min	GP	G	A	Pts	PIM	PP	SH	GW	Min
2005-06	Tor. Jr. Canadiens	GTHL	47	25	31	56	69	....	....	....	....	....	....	....	....	....	....	....	....	....	....	....	....	....	....
2006-07	Barrie Colts	OHL	48	7	7	14	37	....	....	....	....	....	....	....	....	....	6	0	0	0	0	....	....	....	....
2007-08	Barrie Colts	OHL	68	13	19	32	171	....	....	....	....	....	....	....	....	....	9	1	2	3	16	....	....	....	....
2008-09	Barrie Colts	OHL	57	27	24	51	146	....	....	....	....	....	....	....	....	....	5	2	2	4	19	....	....	....	....
	South Carolina	ECHL	2	0	1	1	6	....	....	....	....	....	....	....	....	....	....	....	....	....	....	....	....	....	....
2009-10	Barrie Colts	OHL	57	18	23	41	125	....	....	....	....	....	....	....	....	....	17	8	1	9	29	....	....	....	....
	Hershey Bears	AHL	....	....	....	....	....	....	....	....	....	....	....	....	....	....	2	0	0	0	0	....	....	....	....
2010-11	**St. Louis**	**NHL**	**7**	**0**	**0**	**0**	**11**	**0**	**0**	**0**	**4**	**0.0**	**0**	**4**	**75.0**	**6:05**	....	....	....	....	....	....	....	....	....
	Peoria Rivermen	AHL	66	8	8	16	110	....	....	....	....	....	....	....	....	....	1	0	0	0	0	....	....	....	....
	NHL Totals		**7**	**0**	**0**	**0**	**11**	**0**	**0**	**0**	**4**	**0.0**		**4**	**75.0**	**6:05**	....	....	....	....	....	....	....	....	....

Traded to **St. Louis** by **Washington** for D.J. King, July 28, 2010.

DEMERS, Jason

(duh-MAIRZ, JAY-suhn) **S.J.**

Defense. Shoots right. 6'1", 195 lbs. Born, Dorval, Que., June 9, 1988. San Jose's 6th choice, 186th overall, in 2008 Entry Draft.

Season	Club	League	GP	G	A	Pts	PIM	PP	SH	GW	S	%	+/-	TF	F%	Min	GP	G	A	Pts	PIM	PP	SH	GW	Min
2004-05	Moncton Wildcats	QMJHL	25	0	1	1	10	....	....	....	....	....	....	....	....	....	....	....	....	....	....	....	....	....	....
2005-06	Moncton Wildcats	QMJHL	21	1	3	4	15	....	....	....	....	....	....	....	....	....	....	....	....	....	....	....	....	....	....
	Victoriaville Tigres	QMJHL	33	2	13	15	58	....	....	....	....	....	....	....	....	....	5	0	2	2	10	....	....	....	....
2006-07	Victoriaville Tigres	QMJHL	69	5	19	24	98	....	....	....	....	....	....	....	....	....	6	0	0	0	2	....	....	....	....
2007-08	Victoriaville Tigres	QMJHL	67	9	55	64	91	....	....	....	....	....	....	....	....	....	6	1	5	6	6	....	....	....	....
2008-09	Worcester Sharks	AHL	78	2	31	33	54	....	....	....	....	....	....	....	....	....	12	0	4	4	6	....	....	....	....
2009-10	**San Jose**	**NHL**	**51**	**4**	**17**	**21**	**21**	**3**	**0**	**1**	**52**	**7.7**	**5**	**0**	**0.0**	**15:26**	**15**	**1**	**4**	**5**	**8**	**1**	**0**	**0**	**11:10**
	Worcester Sharks	AHL	25	4	13	17	24	....	....	....	....	....	....	....	....	....	....	....	....	....	....	....	....	....	....
2010-11	**San Jose**	**NHL**	**75**	**2**	**22**	**24**	**28**	**0**	**0**	**0**	**105**	**1.9**	**19**	**0**	**0.0**	**19:30**	**13**	**2**	**1**	**3**	**8**	**0**	**0**	**0**	**19:56**
	NHL Totals		**126**	**6**	**39**	**45**	**49**	**3**	**0**	**1**	**157**	**3.8**		**0**	**0.0**	**17:51**	**28**	**3**	**5**	**8**	**16**	**1**	**0**	**0**	**15:15**

DESBIENS, Guillaume

(deh-BYEHN, GEE-OHM) **CGY**

Right wing. Shoots right. 6'3", 216 lbs. Born, Alma, Que., April 20, 1985. Atlanta's 3rd choice, 116th overall, in 2003 Entry Draft.

Season	Club	League	GP	G	A	Pts	PIM	PP	SH	GW	S	%	+/-	TF	F%	Min	GP	G	A	Pts	PIM	PP	SH	GW	Min
2001-02	Rouyn-Noranda	QMJHL	65	14	10	24	115	....	....	....	....	....	....	....	....	....	4	1	1	2	9	....	....	....	....
2002-03	Rouyn-Noranda	QMJHL	64	15	18	33	233	....	....	....	....	....	....	....	....	....	4	0	0	0	4	....	....	....	....
2003-04	Rouyn-Noranda	QMJHL	58	20	21	41	199	....	....	....	....	....	....	....	....	....	11	2	2	4	24	....	....	....	....
2004-05	Rouyn-Noranda	QMJHL	56	27	16	43	206	....	....	....	....	....	....	....	....	....	10	1	4	5	25	....	....	....	....
2005-06	Chicago Wolves	AHL	3	0	0	0	7	....	....	....	....	....	....	....	....	....	....	....	....	....	....	....	....	....	....
	Gwinnett	ECHL	65	33	27	60	187	....	....	....	....	....	....	....	....	....	17	10	6	16	38	....	....	....	....
2006-07	Chicago Wolves	AHL	54	3	6	9	118	....	....	....	....	....	....	....	....	....	6	0	1	1	2	....	....	....	....
2007-08	Chicago Wolves	AHL	23	2	1	3	30	....	....	....	....	....	....	....	....	....	1	0	1	1	0	....	....	....	....
	Gwinnett	ECHL	10	2	5	7	46	....	....	....	....	....	....	....	....	....	8	3	6	9	10	....	....	....	....
2008-09	Manitoba Moose	AHL	78	21	26	47	158	....	....	....	....	....	....	....	....	....	22	4	8	12	18	....	....	....	....
2009-10	**Vancouver**	**NHL**	**1**	**0**	**0**	**0**	**2**	**0**	**0**	**0**	**0**	**0.0**	**0**	**0**	**0.0**	**9:25**	....	....	....	....	....	....	....	....	....
	Manitoba Moose	AHL	67	19	15	34	144	....	....	....	....	....	....	....	....	....	6	3	6	9	17	....	....	....	....
2010-11	**Vancouver**	**NHL**	**12**	**0**	**0**	**0**	**10**	**0**	**0**	**0**	**4**	**0.0**	**-3**	**1**	**100.0**	**7:21**	....	....	....	....	....	....	....	....	....
	Manitoba Moose	AHL	53	11	16	27	104	....	....	....	....	....	....	....	....	....	13	1	3	4	31	....	....	....	....
	NHL Totals		**13**	**0**	**0**	**0**	**12**	**0**	**0**	**0**	**4**	**0.0**		**1**	**100.0**	**7:31**	....	....	....	....	....	....	....	....	....

Signed as a free agent by **Manitoba** (AHL), December 15, 2008. Signed as a free agent by **Vancouver**, July 22, 2009. Signed as a free agent by **Calgary**, July 4, 2011.

DESJARDINS, Andrew

(deh-ZHAHR-dai, AN-droo) **S.J.**

Center. Shoots right. 6'1", 200 lbs. Born, Lively, Ont., July 27, 1986.

Season	Club	League	GP	G	A	Pts	PIM	PP	SH	GW	S	%	+/-	TF	F%	Min	GP	G	A	Pts	PIM	PP	SH	GW	Min
2003-04	Sault Ste. Marie	OHL	55	3	6	9	41	....	....	....	....	....	....	....	....	....	....	....	....	....	....	....	....	....	....
2004-05	Sault Ste. Marie	OHL	68	17	17	34	49	....	....	....	....	....	....	....	....	....	7	0	0	0	2	....	....	....	....
2005-06	Sault Ste. Marie	OHL	6	12	16	28	78	....	....	....	....	....	....	....	....	....	4	2	3	5	10	....	....	....	....
2006-07	Sault Ste. Marie	OHL	65	16	26	42	96	....	....	....	....	....	....	....	....	....	13	2	5	7	18	....	....	....	....
2007-08	Laredo Bucks	CHL	64	22	37	59	112	....	....	....	....	....	....	....	....	....	11	2	4	6	21	....	....	....	....
2008-09	Phoenix	ECHL	5	2	0	2	6	....	....	....	....	....	....	....	....	....	....	....	....	....	....	....	....	....	....
	Worcester Sharks	AHL	74	8	14	22	99	....	....	....	....	....	....	....	....	....	12	4	2	6	13	....	....	....	....
2009-10	Worcester Sharks	AHL	80	19	27	46	126	....	....	....	....	....	....	....	....	....	11	2	2	4	32	....	....	....	....
2010-11	**San Jose**	**NHL**	**17**	**1**	**2**	**3**	**4**	**0**	**0**	**0**	**12**	**8.3**	**-1**	**56**	**55.4**	**7:08**	**3**	**1**	**0**	**1**	**4**	**0**	**0**	**0**	**6:48**
	Worcester Sharks	AHL	58	12	17	29	69	....	....	....	....	....	....	....	....	....	....	....	....	....	....	....	....	....	....
	NHL Totals		**17**	**1**	**2**	**3**	**4**	**0**	**0**	**0**	**12**	**8.3**		**56**	**55.4**	**7:08**	**3**	**1**	**0**	**1**	**4**	**0**	**0**	**0**	**6:48**

Signed as a free agent by **Worcester** (AHL), October, 2008. Signed as a free agent by **San Jose**, June 26, 2010.

DESHARNAIS, David

(day-hahr-NAY, DAY-vihd) **MTL**

Center. Shoots left. 5'7", 177 lbs. Born, Laurier-Station, Que., September 14, 1986.

			Regular Season														Playoffs								
Season	Club	League	GP	G	A	Pts	PIM	PP	SH	GW	S	%	+/-	TF	F%	Min	GP	G	A	Pts	PIM	PP	SH	GW	Min
2003-04	Chicoutimi	QMJHL	70	23	28	51	12										18	4	7	11	8				
2004-05	Chicoutimi	QMJHL	68	32	65	97	39										17	5	10	15	8				
2005-06	Chicoutimi	QMJHL	63	33	85	118	44										9	2	9	11	4				
2006-07	Chicoutimi	QMJHL	61	38	70	108	32										4	1	5	6	2				
	Bridgeport	AHL	7	1	1	2	4																		
2007-08	Hamilton	AHL	4	0	1	1	6																		
	Cincinnati	ECHL	68	29	*77	*106	18										22	9	*24	*33	18				
2008-09	Hamilton	AHL	77	24	34	58	20										6	1	3	4	4				
2009-10	**Montreal**	**NHL**	**6**	**0**	**1**	**1**	**0**	**0**	**0**	**0**	**2**	**0.0**	**-1**	**28**	**57.1**	**8:27**									
	Hamilton	AHL	60	27	51	78	34										19	10	13	23	16				
2010-11	**Montreal**	**NHL**	**43**	**8**	**14**	**22**	**12**	**4**	**0**	**0**	**55**	**14.5**	**-3**	**445**	**49.7**	**12:52**	**5**	**0**	**1**	**1**	**2**	**0**	**0**	**0**	**11:03**
	Hamilton	AHL	35	10	35	45	24																		
	NHL Totals		**49**	**8**	**15**	**23**	**12**	**4**	**0**	**0**	**57**	**14.0**		**473**	**50.1**	**12:20**	**5**	**0**	**1**	**1**	**2**	**0**	**0**	**0**	**11:04**

ECHL Rookie of the Year (2008) • ECHL Leading Scorer (2008) • ECHL MVP (2008)
Signed as a free agent by **Montreal**, November 5, 2008.

DEVEAUX, Andre

(de-VOH, AWN-dray)

Center. Shoots right. 6'3", 220 lbs. Born, Welland, Ont., February 23, 1984. Montreal's 4th choice, 182nd overall, in 2002 Entry Draft.

Season	Club	League	GP	G	A	Pts	PIM	PP	SH	GW	S	%	+/-	TF	F%	Min	GP	G	A	Pts	PIM	PP	SH	GW	Min
2000-01	Belleville Bulls	OHL	58	3	6	9	65										10	3	6	9	6				
2001-02	Belleville Bulls	OHL	64	8	13	21	89										11	1	2	3	30				
2002-03	Belleville Bulls	OHL	34	6	12	18	93																		
	Owen Sound	OHL	29	9	10	19	33										4	2	2	4	6				
2003-04	Owen Sound	OHL	64	16	30	46	151										7	3	3	6	21				
2004-05	Springfield	AHL	73	4	8	12	210																		
2005-06	Springfield	AHL	59	6	5	11	135																		
	Johnstown Chiefs	ECHL	11	4	7	11	36										5	1	1	2	2				
2006-07	Springfield	AHL	8	1	2	3	8																		
	Johnstown Chiefs	ECHL	21	6	8	14	51																		
	Chicago Wolves	AHL	28	4	4	8	105										14	3	2	5	48				
2007-08	Chicago Wolves	AHL	66	7	11	18	232										24	0	2	2	67				
2008-09	**Toronto**	**NHL**	**21**	**0**	**1**	**1**	**75**	**0**	**0**	**0**	**15**	**0.0**	**-3**	**7**	**28.6**	**7:14**									
	Toronto Marlies	AHL	38	14	11	25	114										6	0	3	3	14				
2009-10	**Toronto**	**NHL**	**1**	**0**	**0**	**0**	**0**	**0**	**0**	**0**	**1**	**0.0**	**-1**	**1**	**100.0**	**6:09**									
	Toronto Marlies	AHL	72	16	25	41	216																		
2010-11	Chicago Wolves	AHL	73	23	23	46	194																		
	NHL Totals		**22**	**0**	**1**	**1**	**75**	**0**	**0**	**0**	**16**	**0.0**		**8**	**37.5**	**7:11**									

Signed as a free agent by **Tampa Bay**, September 15, 2004. Traded to **Atlanta** by **Tampa Bay** with Andy Delmore for and Stephen Baby and Kyle Wanvig, February 1, 2007. Signed as a free agent by **Toronto**, July 21, 2008. Signed as a free agent by **Chicago** (AHL), August 25, 2010.

DIBENEDETTO, Justin

(dih-behn-ih-DEH-toh, JUHS-tihn) **NYI**

Center. Shoots left. 6', 188 lbs. Born, Etobicoke, Ont., August 25, 1988. NY Islanders' 13th choice, 175th overall, in 2008 Entry Draft.

Season	Club	League	GP	G	A	Pts	PIM	PP	SH	GW	S	%	+/-	TF	F%	Min	GP	G	A	Pts	PIM	PP	SH	GW	Min
2004-05	St. Michael's	OHL	64	3	6	9	37										9	0	0	0	0				
2005-06	St. Michael's	OHL	61	17	13	30	58										4	1	0	1	11				
2006-07	Sarnia Sting	OHL	58	28	35	63	46										4	2	1	3	4				
2007-08	Sarnia Sting	OHL	58	39	54	93	61										9	3	7	10	12				
2008-09	Sarnia Sting	OHL	62	45	48	93	85										5	0	3	3	12				
	Bridgeport	AHL															3	1	0	1	4				
2009-10	Bridgeport	AHL	67	6	8	14	62																		
2010-11	**NY Islanders**	**NHL**	**8**	**0**	**1**	**1**	**2**	**0**	**0**	**0**	**6**	**0.0**	**-2**	**0**	**0.0**	**9:04**									
	Bridgeport	AHL	51	19	11	30	45																		
	NHL Totals		**8**	**0**	**1**	**1**	**2**	**0**	**0**	**0**	**6**	**0.0**		**0**	**0.0**	**9:04**									

OHL Second All-Star Team (2009)

DiPENTA, Joe

(DIH-pehn-tah, JOH)

Defense. Shoots left. 6'2", 199 lbs. Born, Barrie, Ont., February 25, 1979. Florida's 2nd choice, 61st overall, in 1998 Entry Draft.

Season	Club	League	GP	G	A	Pts	PIM	PP	SH	GW	S	%	+/-	TF	F%	Min	GP	G	A	Pts	PIM	PP	SH	GW	Min
1996-97	Smiths Falls Bears	CJHL	54	13	22	35	92																		
1997-98	Boston University	H-East	38	2	16	18	50																		
1998-99	Boston University	H-East	36	2	15	17	72																		
99-2000	Halifax	QMJHL	63	13	43	56	83										10	3	4	7	26				
2000-01	Philadelphia	AHL	71	3	5	8	65										10	1	2	3	15				
2001-02	Philadelphia	AHL	61	2	4	6	71																		
	Chicago Wolves	AHL	15	0	2	2	15										25	1	3	4	22				
2002-03	**Atlanta**	**NHL**	**3**	**1**	**1**	**2**	**0**	**0**	**0**	**0**	**2**	**50.0**	**3**	**0**	**0.0**	**15:47**									
	Chicago Wolves	AHL	76	2	17	19	107										9	0	1	1	7				
2003-04	Chicago Wolves	AHL	73	0	6	6	105										10	1	0	1	13				
2004-05	Manitoba Moose	AHL	73	2	10	12	48										14	0	5	5	2				
2005-06	**Anaheim**	**NHL**	**72**	**2**	**6**	**8**	**46**	**0**	**0**	**0**	**27**	**7.4**	**8**	**0**	**0.0**	**13:31**	**16**	**0**	**0**	**0**	**13**	**0**	**0**	**0**	**11:34**
2006-07♦	**Anaheim**	**NHL**	**76**	**2**	**6**	**8**	**48**	**0**	**0**	**1**	**33**	**6.1**	**1**	**1**	**0.0**	**12:09**	**16**	**0**	**0**	**0**	**4**	**0**	**0**	**0**	**8:12**
2007-08	**Anaheim**	**NHL**	**23**	**1**	**4**	**5**	**16**	**0**	**0**	**0**	**5**	**20.0**	**3**	**0**	**0.0**	**10:39**									
2008-09	Frolunda	Sweden	47	1	5	6	71										11	0	1	1	12				
2009-10	Portland Pirates	AHL	65	2	5	7	83										4	0	0	0	4				
2010-11	Syracuse Crunch	AHL	70	1	3	4	62																		
	NHL Totals		**174**	**6**	**17**	**23**	**110**	**0**	**0**	**1**	**67**	**9.0**		**1**	**0.0**	**12:35**	**32**	**0**	**0**	**0**	**17**	**0**	**0**	**0**	**9:53**

• Left **Boston University** (Hockey East) and signed with **Halifax** (QMJHL), May 2, 1999. Signed as a free agent by **Philadelphia**, July 12, 2000. Traded to **Atlanta** by **Philadelphia** for Jarrod Skalde, March 5, 2002. Signed as a free agent by **Vancouver**, August 19, 2004. Signed as a free agent by **Anaheim**, August 11, 2005. • Missed majority of 2007-08 as a healthy reserve. Signed as a free agent by **Frolunda** (Sweden), July 15, 2008. Signed as a free agent by **Buffalo**, July 11, 2009. Signed as a free agent by **Syracuse** (AHL), August 26, 2010.

DiSALVATORE, Jon

(dih-SAL-vuh-tohr, JAWN) **MIN**

Right wing. Shoots right. 6'1", 200 lbs. Born, Bangor, ME, March 30, 1981. San Jose's 2nd choice, 104th overall, in 2000 Entry Draft.

Season	Club	League	GP	G	A	Pts	PIM	PP	SH	GW	S	%	+/-	TF	F%	Min	GP	G	A	Pts	PIM	PP	SH	GW	Min
1997-98	N.E. Jr. Coyotes	EJHL	38	24	41	65																			
1998-99	N.E. Jr. Coyotes	EJHL	48	44	76	*120	38																		
99-2000	Providence	H-East	38	15	12	27	12																		
2000-01	Providence	H-East	36	9	16	25	29																		
2001-02	Providence	H-East	38	16	26	42	6																		
2002-03	Providence	H-East	36	19	29	48	12																		
2003-04	Cleveland Barons	AHL	74	22	24	46	30										8	1	1	2	2				
2004-05	Worcester IceCats	AHL	79	22	23	45	42																		
2005-06	**St. Louis**	**NHL**	**5**	**0**	**0**	**0**	**2**	**0**	**0**	**0**	**3**	**0.0**	**-1**	**0**	**0.0**	**8:27**									
	Peoria Rivermen	AHL	72	22	45	67	42										4	0	0	0	0				
2006-07	Peoria Rivermen	AHL	76	21	39	60	50																		
2007-08	San Antonio	AHL	66	22	24	46	46										7	2	1	3	9				
2008-09	Lowell Devils	AHL	76	20	33	53	32																		
2009-10	Houston Aeros	AHL	79	21	31	52	28																		
2010-11	Houston Aeros	AHL	80	28	33	61	57										24	7	5	12	12				
	NHL Totals		**5**	**0**	**0**	**0**	**2**	**0**	**0**	**0**	**3**	**0.0**		**0**	**0.0**	**8:27**									

Signed as a free agent by **St. Louis**, June 30, 2004. Signed as a free agent by **Phoenix**, July 9, 2007. Signed as a free agent by **New Jersey**, July 17, 2008. Signed as a free agent by **Minnesota**, July 17, 2009.

Season	Club	League	GP	G	A	Pts	PIM	PP	SH	GW	S	%	+/-	TF	F%	Min	GP	G	A	Pts	PIM	PP	SH	GW	Min
			Regular Season														Playoffs								

DOAN, Shane
(DOHN, SHAYN) **PHX**

Right wing. Shoots right. 6'1", 230 lbs. Born, Halkirk, Alta., October 10, 1976. Winnipeg's 1st choice, 7th overall, in 1995 Entry Draft.

Season	Club	League	GP	G	A	Pts	PIM	PP	SH	GW	S	%	+/-	TF	F%	Min	GP	G	A	Pts	PIM	PP	SH	GW	Min
1991-92	Killam Selects	AAHA	56	80	84	164	74	....	....	....	....	....	....	....	....	....	....	....	....	....	....	....	....	....	....
1992-93	Kamloops Blazers	WHL	51	7	12	19	65	....	....	....	....	....	....	....	....	....	13	0	1	1	8	....	....	....	....
1993-94	Kamloops Blazers	WHL	52	24	24	48	88	....	....	....	....	....	....	....	....	....	....	....	....	....	....	....	....	....	....
1994-95	Kamloops Blazers	WHL	71	37	57	94	106	....	....	....	....	....	....	....	....	....	21	6	10	16	16	....	....	....	....
1995-96	**Winnipeg**	**NHL**	**74**	**7**	**10**	**17**	**101**	**1**	**0**	**3**	**106**	**6.6**	**-9**	....	....	....	**6**	**0**	**0**	**0**	**6**	**0**	**0**	**0**	....
1996-97	**Phoenix**	**NHL**	**63**	**4**	**8**	**12**	**49**	**0**	**0**	**0**	**100**	**4.0**	**-3**	....	....	....	**4**	**0**	**0**	**0**	**2**	**0**	**0**	**0**	....
1997-98	**Phoenix**	**NHL**	**33**	**5**	**6**	**11**	**35**	**0**	**0**	**3**	**42**	**11.9**	**-3**	....	....	....	**6**	**1**	**0**	**1**	**6**	**0**	**0**	**0**	....
	Springfield	AHL	39	21	21	42	64	....	....	....	....	....	....	....	....	....	....	....	....	....	....	....	....	....	....
1998-99	**Phoenix**	**NHL**	**79**	**6**	**16**	**22**	**54**	**0**	**0**	**0**	**156**	**3.8**	**-5**	**6**	**16.7**	**12:42**	**7**	**2**	**2**	**4**	**6**	**0**	**0**	**2**	**17:58**
99-2000	**Phoenix**	**NHL**	**81**	**26**	**25**	**51**	**66**	**1**	**1**	**4**	**221**	**11.8**	**6**	**25**	**36.0**	**16:51**	**4**	**1**	**2**	**3**	**8**	**1**	**0**	**0**	**18:11**
2000-01	**Phoenix**	**NHL**	**76**	**26**	**37**	**63**	**89**	**6**	**1**	**6**	**220**	**11.8**	**0**	**15**	**40.0**	**19:32**	....	....	....	....	....	....	....	....	....
2001-02	**Phoenix**	**NHL**	**81**	**20**	**29**	**49**	**61**	**6**	**0**	**2**	**205**	**9.8**	**11**	**52**	**44.2**	**18:10**	**5**	**2**	**2**	**4**	**6**	**0**	**0**	**0**	**17:21**
2002-03	**Phoenix**	**NHL**	**82**	**21**	**37**	**58**	**86**	**7**	**0**	**2**	**225**	**9.3**	**3**	**623**	**39.8**	**18:47**	....	....	....	....	....	....	....	....	....
2003-04	**Phoenix**	**NHL**	**79**	**27**	**41**	**68**	**47**	**9**	**2**	**1**	**254**	**10.6**	**-11**	**55**	**40.0**	**21:46**	....	....	....	....	....	....	....	....	....
2004-05			DID NOT PLAY																						
2005-06	**Phoenix**	**NHL**	**82**	**30**	**36**	**66**	**123**	**17**	**0**	**7**	**254**	**11.8**	**-9**	**126**	**43.7**	**19:08**	....	....	....	....	....	....	....	....	....
	Canada	Olympics	6	2	1	3	2	....	....	....	....	....	....	....	....	....	....	....	....	....	....	....	....	....	....
2006-07	**Phoenix**	**NHL**	**73**	**27**	**28**	**55**	**73**	**11**	**0**	**7**	**209**	**12.9**	**-14**	**174**	**39.1**	**20:27**	....	....	....	....	....	....	....	....	....
2007-08	**Phoenix**	**NHL**	**80**	**28**	**50**	**78**	**59**	**9**	**2**	**5**	**243**	**11.5**	**4**	**187**	**41.2**	**20:46**	....	....	....	....	....	....	....	....	....
2008-09	**Phoenix**	**NHL**	**82**	**31**	**42**	**73**	**72**	**10**	**0**	**4**	**230**	**13.5**	**5**	**362**	**44.2**	**20:15**	....	....	....	....	....	....	....	....	....
2009-10	**Phoenix**	**NHL**	**82**	**18**	**37**	**55**	**41**	**5**	**0**	**4**	**234**	**7.7**	**3**	**153**	**45.8**	**19:10**	**3**	**1**	**1**	**2**	**4**	**0**	**0**	**0**	**13:22**
2010-11	**Phoenix**	**NHL**	**72**	**20**	**40**	**60**	**67**	**11**	**0**	**6**	**221**	**9.0**	**5**	**159**	**45.9**	**19:17**	**4**	**3**	**2**	**5**	**6**	**2**	**0**	**0**	**21:42**
	NHL Totals		**1119**	**296**	**442**	**738**	**1023**	**93**	**6**	**54**	**2920**	**10.1**		**1937**	**41.9**	**18:53**	**39**	**10**	**9**	**19**	**44**	**3**	**0**	**2**	**17:55**

Memorial Cup All-Star Team (1995) • Stafford Smythe Memorial Trophy (Memorial Cup - MVP) (1995) • King Clancy Memorial Trophy (2010)

Played in NHL All-Star Game (2004, 2009)

• Transferred to **Phoenix** after **Winnipeg** franchise relocated, July 1, 1996.

DOELL, Kevin
(DOH-ehl, KEH-vihn)

Center. Shoots left. 5'11", 190 lbs. Born, Saskatoon, Sask., July 15, 1979.

Season	Club	League	GP	G	A	Pts	PIM	PP	SH	GW	S	%	+/-	TF	F%	Min	GP	G	A	Pts	PIM	PP	SH	GW	Min
99-2000	U. of Denver	WCHA	40	8	15	23	18	....	....	....	....	....	....	....	....	....	....	....	....	....	....	....	....	....	....
2000-01	U. of Denver	WCHA	36	9	10	19	26	....	....	....	....	....	....	....	....	....	....	....	....	....	....	....	....	....	....
2001-02	U. of Denver	WCHA	41	20	23	43	28	....	....	....	....	....	....	....	....	....	....	....	....	....	....	....	....	....	....
2002-03	U. of Denver	WCHA	41	25	26	51	34	....	....	....	....	....	....	....	....	....	....	....	....	....	....	....	....	....	....
2003-04	Chicago Wolves	AHL	8	1	1	2	6	....	....	....	....	....	....	....	....	....	1	0	0	0	0	....	....	....	....
	Gwinnett	ECHL	63	33	41	74	88	....	....	....	....	....	....	....	....	....	13	1	6	7	12	....	....	....	....
2004-05	Chicago Wolves	AHL	45	4	8	12	69	....	....	....	....	....	....	....	....	....	....	....	....	....	....	....	....	....	....
	Gwinnett	ECHL	11	6	9	15	14	....	....	....	....	....	....	....	....	....	8	2	1	3	14	....	....	....	....
2005-06	Chicago Wolves	AHL	78	17	34	51	72	....	....	....	....	....	....	....	....	....	....	....	....	....	....	....	....	....	....
2006-07	Chicago Wolves	AHL	80	14	19	33	107	....	....	....	....	....	....	....	....	....	15	2	4	6	14	....	....	....	....
2007-08	**Atlanta**	**NHL**	**8**	**0**	**1**	**1**	**4**	**0**	**0**	**0**	**6**	**0.0**	**-2**	**53**	**47.2**	**9:40**	....	....	....	....	....	....	....	....	....
	Chicago Wolves	AHL	68	16	17	33	75	....	....	....	....	....	....	....	....	....	24	4	5	9	41	....	....	....	....
2008-09	Leksands IF	Sweden-2	37	22	27	49	105	....	....	....	....	....	....	....	....	....	....	....	....	....	....	....	....	....	....
2009-10	Chicago Wolves	AHL	79	16	21	37	69	....	....	....	....	....	....	....	....	....	9	3	0	3	2	....	....	....	....
2010-11	Tappara Tampere	Finland	58	18	20	38	105	....	....	....	....	....	....	....	....	....	....	....	....	....	....	....	....	....	....
	NHL Totals		**8**	**0**	**1**	**1**	**4**	**0**	**0**	**0**	**6**	**0.0**		**53**	**47.2**	**9:40**	....	....	....	....	....	....	....	....	....

ECHL All-Rookie Team (2004) • ECHL Rookie of the Year (2004)

Signed as a free agent by **Atlanta**, June 30, 2004. Signed as a free agent by **Leksands** (Sweden-2), July 31, 2008. Signed as a free agent by **Chicago** (AHL), July 29, 2009. Signed as a free agent by **Tappara Tampere** (Finland), September 13, 2010.

DOORNBOSCH, Jamie
(DOHRN-bawsh, JAY-mee)

Defense. Shoots left. 6'2", 190 lbs. Born, Richmond Hill, Ont., February 1, 1990.

Season	Club	League	GP	G	A	Pts	PIM	PP	SH	GW	S	%	+/-	TF	F%	Min	GP	G	A	Pts	PIM	PP	SH	GW	Min
2006-07	Markham Waxers	OPJHL	1	0	0	0	0	....	....	....	....	....	....	....	....	....	....	....	....	....	....	....	....	....	....
	Peterborough	OHL	4	0	0	0	0	....	....	....	....	....	....	....	....	....	....	....	....	....	....	....	....	....	....
2007-08	Peterborough	OHL	60	2	10	12	53	....	....	....	....	....	....	....	....	....	5	0	1	1	2	....	....	....	....
2008-09	Peterborough	OHL	64	8	29	37	60	....	....	....	....	....	....	....	....	....	4	0	0	0	2	....	....	....	....
2009-10	Peterborough	OHL	68	12	38	50	52	....	....	....	....	....	....	....	....	....	4	0	1	1	6	....	....	....	....
2010-11	Kitchener Rangers	OHL	68	19	29	48	44	....	....	....	....	....	....	....	....	....	7	1	1	2	8	....	....	....	....
	NY Islanders	**NHL**	**1**	**0**	**0**	**0**	**0**	**0**	**0**	**0**	**1**	**0.0**	**-1**	**0**	**0.0**	**5:21**	....	....	....	....	....	....	....	....	....
	NHL Totals		**1**	**0**	**0**	**0**	**0**	**0**	**0**	**0**	**1**	**0.0**		**0**	**0.0**	**5:21**	....	....	....	....	....	....	....	....	....

Signed to a ATO (amateur tryout) contract by **NY Islanders**, April 8, 2011.

DORSETT, Derek
(DOHRS-iht, DAIR-ihk) **CBJ**

Right wing. Shoots right. 6', 190 lbs. Born, Kindersley, Sask., December 20, 1986. Columbus' 9th choice, 189th overall, in 2006 Entry Draft.

Season	Club	League	GP	G	A	Pts	PIM	PP	SH	GW	S	%	+/-	TF	F%	Min	GP	G	A	Pts	PIM	PP	SH	GW	Min
2004-05	Medicine Hat	WHL	51	5	11	16	108	....	....	....	....	....	....	....	....	....	13	5	1	6	35	....	....	....	....
2005-06	Medicine Hat	WHL	68	25	23	48	*279	....	....	....	....	....	....	....	....	....	13	8	4	12	53	....	....	....	....
2006-07	Medicine Hat	WHL	61	19	45	64	206	....	....	....	....	....	....	....	....	....	17	8	8	16	56	....	....	....	....
2007-08	Syracuse Crunch	AHL	64	10	8	18	289	....	....	....	....	....	....	....	....	....	12	0	1	1	56	....	....	....	....
2008-09	**Columbus**	**NHL**	**52**	**4**	**1**	**5**	**150**	**0**	**0**	**1**	**59**	**6.8**	**-1**	**9**	**44.4**	**8:53**	**3**	**0**	**0**	**0**	**2**	**0**	**0**	**0**	**9:11**
	Syracuse Crunch	AHL	7	1	5	6	35	....	....	....	....	....	....	....	....	....	....	....	....	....	....	....	....	....	....
2009-10	**Columbus**	**NHL**	**51**	**4**	**10**	**14**	**105**	**0**	**0**	**0**	**57**	**7.0**	**6**	**33**	**27.3**	**10:53**	....	....	....	....	....	....	....	....	....
2010-11	**Columbus**	**NHL**	**76**	**4**	**13**	**17**	**184**	**0**	**0**	**0**	**112**	**3.6**	**-15**	**51**	**37.3**	**13:12**	....	....	....	....	....	....	....	....	....
	NHL Totals		**179**	**12**	**24**	**36**	**439**	**0**	**0**	**1**	**228**	**5.3**		**93**	**34.4**	**11:18**	**3**	**0**	**0**	**0**	**2**	**0**	**0**	**0**	**9:11**

DOUGHTY, Drew
(DOW-tee, DROO) **L.A.**

Defense. Shoots right. 6', 212 lbs. Born, London, Ont., December 8, 1989. Los Angeles' 1st choice, 2nd overall, in 2008 Entry Draft.

Season	Club	League	GP	G	A	Pts	PIM	PP	SH	GW	S	%	+/-	TF	F%	Min	GP	G	A	Pts	PIM	PP	SH	GW	Min
2004-05	Lon. Jr. Knights	Minor-ON	55	19	30	49	31	....	....	....	....	....	....	....	....	....	....	....	....	....	....	....	....	....	....
2005-06	Guelph Storm	OHL	65	5	28	33	40	....	....	....	....	....	....	....	....	....	14	0	13	13	18	....	....	....	....
2006-07	Guelph Storm	OHL	67	21	53	74	76	....	....	....	....	....	....	....	....	....	4	2	3	5	8	....	....	....	....
2007-08	Guelph Storm	OHL	58	13	37	50	68	....	....	....	....	....	....	....	....	....	10	3	6	9	14	....	....	....	....
2008-09	**Los Angeles**	**NHL**	**81**	**6**	**21**	**27**	**56**	**3**	**0**	**1**	**126**	**4.8**	**-17**	**0**	**0.0**	**23:50**	....	....	....	....	....	....	....	....	....
2009-10	**Los Angeles**	**NHL**	**82**	**16**	**43**	**59**	**54**	**9**	**0**	**5**	**142**	**11.3**	**20**	**0**	**0.0**	**24:59**	**6**	**3**	**4**	**7**	**4**	**2**	**0**	**0**	**27:26**
	Canada	Olympics	7	0	2	2	2	....	....	....	....	....	....	....	....	....	....	....	....	....	....	....	....	....	....
2010-11	**Los Angeles**	**NHL**	**76**	**11**	**29**	**40**	**68**	**5**	**0**	**3**	**139**	**7.9**	**13**	**0**	**0.0**	**25:39**	**6**	**2**	**2**	**4**	**8**	**1**	**0**	**0**	**27:08**
	NHL Totals		**239**	**33**	**93**	**126**	**178**	**17**	**0**	**9**	**407**	**8.1**		**0**	**0.0**	**24:48**	**12**	**5**	**6**	**11**	**12**	**3**	**0**	**0**	**27:17**

OHL All-Rookie Team (2006) • OHL First All-Star Team (2007, 2008) • Canadian Major Junior First All-Star Team (2008) • NHL All-Rookie Team (2009) • NHL Second All-Star Team (2010)

DOWELL, Jake
(DOW-uhl, JAYK) **DAL**

Center. Shoots left. 6', 199 lbs. Born, Eau Claire, WI, March 4, 1985. Chicago's 10th choice, 140th overall, in 2004 Entry Draft.

Season	Club	League	GP	G	A	Pts	PIM	PP	SH	GW	S	%	+/-	TF	F%	Min	GP	G	A	Pts	PIM	PP	SH	GW	Min
2000-01	Eau Claire Mem.	High-WI	24	25	30	55	....	....	....	....	....	....	....	....	....	....	....	....	....	....	....	....	....	....	....
2001-02	USNTDP	U-17	11	5	1	6	14	....	....	....	....	....	....	....	....	....	....	....	....	....	....	....	....	....	....
	USNTDP	NAHL	44	5	12	17	51	....	....	....	....	....	....	....	....	....	....	....	....	....	....	....	....	....	....
2002-03	USNTDP	U-18	54	8	17	25	54	....	....	....	....	....	....	....	....	....	....	....	....	....	....	....	....	....	....
	USNTDP	NAHL	9	2	2	4	13	....	....	....	....	....	....	....	....	....	....	....	....	....	....	....	....	....	....
2003-04	U. of Wisconsin	WCHA	37	6	13	19	48	....	....	....	....	....	....	....	....	....	....	....	....	....	....	....	....	....	....
2004-05	U. of Wisconsin	WCHA	38	12	14	26	74	....	....	....	....	....	....	....	....	....	....	....	....	....	....	....	....	....	....
2005-06	U. of Wisconsin	WCHA	43	5	15	20	42	....	....	....	....	....	....	....	....	....	....	....	....	....	....	....	....	....	....
2006-07	U. of Wisconsin	WCHA	41	19	6	25	54	....	....	....	....	....	....	....	....	....	....	....	....	....	....	....	....	....	....
	Norfolk Admirals	AHL	9	2	3	5	8	....	....	....	....	....	....	....	....	....	6	0	3	3	4	....	....	....	....
2007-08	**Chicago**	**NHL**	**19**	**2**	**1**	**3**	**10**	**0**	**1**	**0**	**19**	**10.5**	**1**	**170**	**46.5**	**11:56**	....	....	....	....	....	....	....	....	....
	Rockford IceHogs	AHL	49	7	10	17	64	....	....	....	....	....	....	....	....	....	12	1	1	2	6	....	....	....	....

			Regular Season														Playoffs								
Season	Club	League	GP	G	A	Pts	PIM	PP	SH	GW	S	%	+/-	TF	F%	Min	GP	G	A	Pts	PIM	PP	SH	GW	Min
2008-09	Chicago	NHL	1	0	0	0	2	0	0	0	0	0.0	1	12	66.7	13:37	....	....	....	....	....	....	....	....	....
	Rockford IceHogs	AHL	75	6	14	20	128	....	....	....	....	....	....	....	....	....	4	0	0	0	0	....	....	....	....
2009-10	Chicago	NHL	3	1	1	2	5	0	0	0	4	25.0	1	4	50.0	6:56	....	....	....	....	....	....	....	....	....
	Rockford IceHogs	AHL	78	7	16	23	96	....	....	....	....	....	....	....	....	....	4	0	0	0	0	....	....	....	....
2010-11	Chicago	NHL	79	6	15	21	63	0	0	0	74	8.1	5	652	48.9	11:49	2	0	0	0	0	0	0	0	8:23
	NHL Totals		102	9	17	26	80	0	1	0	97	9.3		838	48.7	11:42	2	0	0	0	0	0	0	0	8:23

Signed as a free agent by **Dallas**, July 1, 2011.

DOWNIE, Steve

(DOW-nee, STEEV) **T.B.**

Right wing. Shoots right. 5'11", 191 lbs. Born, Newmarket, Ont., April 3, 1987. Philadelphia's 1st choice, 29th overall, in 2005 Entry Draft.

Season	Club	League	GP	G	A	Pts	PIM	PP	SH	GW	S	%	+/-	TF	F%	Min	GP	G	A	Pts	PIM	PP	SH	GW	Min
2002-03	Aurora Tigers	OPJHL	34	12	13	25	55	....	....	....	....	....	....	....	....	....	....	....	....	....	....	....	....	....	....
2003-04	Windsor Spitfires	OHL	49	7	9	16	90	....	....	....	....	....	....	....	....	....	4	0	1	1	27	....	....	....	....
2004-05	Windsor Spitfires	OHL	61	21	52	73	179	....	....	....	....	....	....	....	....	....	11	4	5	9	49	....	....	....	....
2005-06	Windsor Spitfires	OHL	1	3	0	3	4	....	....	....	....	....	....	....	....	....	....	....	....	....	....	....	....	....	....
	Peterborough	OHL	34	16	34	50	109	....	....	....	....	....	....	....	....	....	19	6	15	21	38	....	....	....	....
2006-07	Peterborough	OHL	28	23	36	59	92	....	....	....	....	....	....	....	....	....	....	....	....	....	....	....	....	....	....
	Kitchener Rangers	OHL	17	12	21	33	32	....	....	....	....	....	....	....	....	....	9	8	14	22	15	....	....	....	....
	Philadelphia	AHL	1	0	0	0	0	....	....	....	....	....	....	....	....	....	....	....	....	....	....	....	....	....	....
2007-08	Philadelphia	NHL	32	6	6	12	73	0	1	1	25	24.0	2	15	33.3	9:51	6	0	1	1	10	0	0	0	6:04
	Philadelphia	AHL	21	5	12	17	114	....	....	....	....	....	....	....	....	....	....	....	....	....	....	....	....	....	....
2008-09	Philadelphia	NHL	6	0	0	0	11	0	0	0	1	0.0	–4	13	15.4	5:57	....	....	....	....	....	....	....	....	....
	Philadelphia	AHL	4	1	7	8	23	....	....	....	....	....	....	....	....	....	....	....	....	....	....	....	....	....	....
	Tampa Bay	NHL	23	3	3	6	54	0	0	1	25	12.0	2	7	42.9	9:04	....	....	....	....	....	....	....	....	....
	Norfolk Admirals	AHL	23	8	17	25	107	....	....	....	....	....	....	....	....	....	....	....	....	....	....	....	....	....	....
2009-10	Tampa Bay	NHL	79	22	24	46	208	7	0	1	116	19.0	14	34	50.0	14:43	....	....	....	....	....	....	....	....	....
2010-11	Tampa Bay	NHL	57	10	22	32	171	2	0	1	83	12.0	8	96	44.8	14:31	17	2	12	14	40	0	0	1	12:35
	NHL Totals		197	41	55	96	517	9	1	4	250	16.4		165	42.4	12:56	23	2	13	15	50	0	0	1	10:54

Traded to **Tampa Bay** by **Philadelphia** with Steve Eminger and Tampa Bay's 4th round choice (previously acquired, Tampa Bay selected Alex Hutchings) in 2009 Entry Draft for Matt Carle and San Jose's 3rd round choice (previously acquired, Philadelphia selected Simon Bertilsson) in 2009 Entry Draft, November 7, 2008.

DRAPER, Kris

(DRAY-puhr, KRIHS)

Center. Shoots left. 5'10", 188 lbs. Born, Toronto, Ont., May 24, 1971. Winnipeg's 4th choice, 62nd overall, in 1989 Entry Draft.

Season	Club	League	GP	G	A	Pts	PIM	PP	SH	GW	S	%	+/-	TF	F%	Min	GP	G	A	Pts	PIM	PP	SH	GW	Min
1987-88	Don Mills Flyers	MTHL	40	35	32	67	46	....	....	....	....	....	....	....	....	....	....	....	....	....	....	....	....	....	....
1988-89	Canada	Nat-Tm	60	11	15	26	16	....	....	....	....	....	....	....	....	....	....	....	....	....	....	....	....	....	....
1989-90	Canada	Nat-Tm	61	12	22	34	44	....	....	....	....	....	....	....	....	....	....	....	....	....	....	....	....	....	....
1990-91	Ottawa 67's	OHL	39	19	42	61	35	....	....	....	....	....	....	....	....	....	17	8	11	19	20	....	....	....	....
	Winnipeg	NHL	3	1	0	1	5	0	0	0	1	100.0	0	....	....	....	....	....	....	....	....	....	....	....	....
	Moncton Hawks	AHL	7	2	1	3	2	....	....	....	....	....	....	....	....	....	....	....	....	....	....	....	....	....	....
1991-92	Winnipeg	NHL	10	2	0	2	2	0	0	0	19	10.5	0	....	....	....	2	0	0	0	0	0	0	0	....
	Moncton Hawks	AHL	61	11	18	29	113	....	....	....	....	....	....	....	....	....	4	0	1	1	6	....	....	....	....
1992-93	Winnipeg	NHL	7	0	0	0	2	0	0	0	5	0.0	–6	....	....	....	....	....	....	....	....	....	....	....	....
	Moncton Hawks	AHL	67	12	23	35	40	....	....	....	....	....	....	....	....	....	5	2	2	4	18	....	....	....	....
1993-94	Detroit	NHL	39	5	8	13	31	0	1	0	55	9.1	11	....	....	....	7	2	2	4	4	0	1	0	....
	Adirondack	AHL	46	20	23	43	49	....	....	....	....	....	....	....	....	....	....	....	....	....	....	....	....	....	....
1994-95	Detroit	NHL	36	2	6	8	22	0	0	0	44	4.5	1	....	....	....	18	4	1	5	12	0	1	1	....
1995-96	Detroit	NHL	52	7	9	16	32	0	1	0	51	13.7	2	....	....	....	18	4	2	6	18	0	1	0	....
1996-97♦	Detroit	NHL	76	8	5	13	73	1	0	1	85	9.4	–11	....	....	....	20	2	4	6	12	0	1	0	....
1997-98♦	Detroit	NHL	64	13	10	23	45	1	0	4	96	13.5	5	....	....	....	19	1	3	4	12	0	0	1	....
1998-99	Detroit	NHL	80	4	14	18	79	0	1	1	78	5.1	2	887	54.6	12:43	10	0	1	1	6	0	0	0	11:35
99-2000	Detroit	NHL	51	5	7	12	28	0	0	3	76	6.6	3	380	57.6	13:33	9	2	0	2	6	0	0	0	12:26
2000-01	Detroit	NHL	75	8	17	25	38	0	1	1	123	6.5	17	997	56.5	13:26	6	0	1	1	2	0	0	0	16:08
2001-02♦	Detroit	NHL	82	15	15	30	56	0	2	3	137	10.9	26	756	53.2	15:35	23	2	3	5	20	0	0	0	17:00
2002-03	Detroit	NHL	82	14	21	35	82	0	1	2	142	9.9	6	1059	56.9	16:12	4	0	0	0	4	0	0	0	17:29
2003-04	Detroit	NHL	67	24	16	40	31	2	5	1	149	16.1	22	1058	56.9	17:44	12	1	3	4	6	0	0	0	18:29
2004-05			DID NOT PLAY																						
2005-06	Detroit	NHL	80	10	22	32	58	0	1	1	153	6.5	3	1287	57.7	17:46	6	0	0	0	6	0	0	0	19:58
	Canada	Olympics	6	0	0	0	0	....	....	....	....	....	....	....	....	....	....	....	....	....	....	....	....	....	....
2006-07	Detroit	NHL	81	14	15	29	58	0	5	1	157	8.9	7	1242	57.3	16:45	18	2	0	2	24	0	0	0	16:36
2007-08♦	Detroit	NHL	65	9	8	17	68	0	2	2	97	9.3	–2	944	58.6	15:38	22	3	1	4	10	0	0	1	15:27
2008-09	Detroit	NHL	79	7	10	17	40	0	1	2	93	7.5	–13	1000	60.3	11:59	8	1	0	1	0	0	0	0	8:37
2009-10	Detroit	NHL	81	7	15	22	28	1	0	0	98	7.1	–2	319	52.0	11:32	12	0	0	0	16	0	0	0	7:24
2010-11	Detroit	NHL	47	6	5	11	12	0	0	1	57	10.5	1	168	56.6	10:27	8	0	1	1	2	0	0	0	9:19
	NHL Totals		1157	161	203	364	790	5	21	23	1716	9.4		10097	56.9	14:34	222	24	22	46	160	0	4	3	14:29

Frank J. Selke Trophy (2004)
Traded to **Detroit** by **Winnipeg** for future considerations, June 30, 1993. • Officially announced his retirement, July 26, 2011.

DRAZENOVIC, Nicholas

(DRAY-zehn-oh-vihk, NIH-koh-las) **CBJ**

Center. Shoots left. 6', 205 lbs. Born, Prince George, B.C., January 14, 1987. St. Louis' 6th choice, 171st overall, in 2005 Entry Draft.

Season	Club	League	GP	G	A	Pts	PIM	PP	SH	GW	S	%	+/-	TF	F%	Min	GP	G	A	Pts	PIM	PP	SH	GW	Min
2002-03	Prince George	WHL	15	4	4	8	....	....	....	....	....	....	....	....	....	....	4	0	0	0	....	....	....	....	....
2003-04	Prince George	WHL	65	7	30	37	38	....	....	....	....	....	....	....	....	....	....	....	....	....	....	....	....	....	....
2004-05	Prince George	WHL	72	18	38	56	24	....	....	....	....	....	....	....	....	....	....	....	....	....	....	....	....	....	....
2005-06	Prince George	WHL	71	30	33	63	51	....	....	....	....	....	....	....	....	....	5	0	0	0	4	....	....	....	....
2006-07	Prince George	WHL	58	18	32	50	63	....	....	....	....	....	....	....	....	....	15	9	10	19	6	....	....	....	....
2007-08	Peoria Rivermen	AHL	69	16	26	42	38	....	....	....	....	....	....	....	....	....	....	....	....	....	....	....	....	....	....
2008-09	Peoria Rivermen	AHL	76	12	21	33	43	....	....	....	....	....	....	....	....	....	5	1	0	1	2	....	....	....	....
2009-10	Peoria Rivermen	AHL	58	19	20	39	40	....	....	....	....	....	....	....	....	....	....	....	....	....	....	....	....	....	....
2010-11	St. Louis	NHL	3	0	0	0	0	0	0	0	2	0.0	–3	11	54.6	8:59	....	....	....	....	....	....	....	....	....
	Peoria Rivermen	AHL	75	23	23	46	24	....	....	....	....	....	....	....	....	....	4	0	1	1	2	....	....	....	....
	NHL Totals		3	0	0	0	0	0	0	0	2	0.0		11	54.5	8:59	....	....	....	....	....	....	....	....	....

Signed as a free agent by **Columbus**, July 1, 2011.

DREWISKE, Davis

(droo-WIHS-kee, DAY-vihs) **L.A.**

Defense. Shoots left. 6'2", 218 lbs. Born, Hudson, WI, November 22, 1984.

Season	Club	League	GP	G	A	Pts	PIM	PP	SH	GW	S	%	+/-	TF	F%	Min	GP	G	A	Pts	PIM	PP	SH	GW	Min
2003-04	Des Moines	USHL	60	4	19	23	63	....	....	....	....	....	....	....	....	....	3	0	0	0	4	....	....	....	....
2004-05	U. of Wisconsin	WCHA	34	1	5	6	20	....	....	....	....	....	....	....	....	....	....	....	....	....	....	....	....	....	....
2005-06	U. of Wisconsin	WCHA	35	2	2	4	22	....	....	....	....	....	....	....	....	....	....	....	....	....	....	....	....	....	....
2006-07	U. of Wisconsin	WCHA	41	4	6	10	46	....	....	....	....	....	....	....	....	....	....	....	....	....	....	....	....	....	....
2007-08	U. of Wisconsin	WCHA	40	5	16	21	46	....	....	....	....	....	....	....	....	....	....	....	....	....	....	....	....	....	....
	Manchester	AHL	5	0	0	0	6	....	....	....	....	....	....	....	....	....	4	0	1	1	6	....	....	....	....
2008-09	Los Angeles	NHL	17	0	3	3	18	0	0	0	21	0.0	1	0	0.0	17:19	....	....	....	....	....	....	....	....	....
	Manchester	AHL	61	1	13	14	95	....	....	....	....	....	....	....	....	....	....	....	....	....	....	....	....	....	....
2009-10	Los Angeles	NHL	42	1	7	8	14	0	0	0	32	3.1	–4	0	0.0	15:15	....	....	....	....	....	....	....	....	....
2010-11	Los Angeles	NHL	38	0	5	5	19	0	0	0	27	0.0	–1	0	0.0	14:21	....	....	....	....	....	....	....	....	....
	NHL Totals		97	1	15	16	51	0	0	0	80	1.3		0	0.0	15:16	....	....	....	....	....	....	....	....	....

Signed as a free agent by **Los Angeles**, April 1, 2008. • Missed majority of 2010-11 as a healthy reserve.

DRURY, Chris

(DROO-ree, KRIHS)

Center. Shoots right. 5'10", 191 lbs. Born, Trumbull, CT, August 20, 1976. Quebec's 5th choice, 72nd overall, in 1994 Entry Draft.

Season	Club	League	GP	G	A	Pts	PIM	PP	SH	GW	S	%	+/-	TF	F%	Min	GP	G	A	Pts	PIM	PP	SH	GW	Min
1991-92	Fairfield Prep	High-CT	25	22	27	49	....	....	....	....	....	....	....	....	....	....	....	....	....	....	....	....	....	....	....
1992-93	Fairfield Prep	High-CT	24	25	32	57	15	....	....	....	....	....	....	....	....	....	....	....	....	....	....	....	....	....	....
1993-94	Fairfield Prep	High-CT	24	37	18	55	....	....	....	....	....	....	....	....	....	....	....	....	....	....	....	....	....	....	....
1994-95	Boston University	H-East	39	12	15	27	38	....	....	....	....	....	....	....	....	....	....	....	....	....	....	....	....	....	....
1995-96	Boston University	H-East	37	35	33	*68	46	....	....	....	....	....	....	....	....	....	....	....	....	....	....	....	....	....	....
1996-97	Boston University	H-East	41	*38	24	62	64	....	....	....	....	....	....	....	....	....	....	....	....	....	....	....	....	....	....

Season	Club	League	GP	G	A	Pts	PIM	PP	SH	GW	S	%	+/-	TF	F%	Min	GP	G	A	Pts	PIM	PP	SH	GW	Min
			Regular Season														Playoffs								
1997-98	Boston University	H-East	38	28	29	57	88	....	....	....	....	....	....	....	....	....	....	....	....	....	....	....	....	....	....
1998-99	**Colorado**	**NHL**	**79**	**20**	**24**	**44**	**62**	**6**	**0**	**3**	**138**	**14.5**	**9**	**418**	**46.9**	**13:15**	**19**	**6**	**2**	**8**	**4**	**0**	**0**	**4**	**11:28**
99-2000	**Colorado**	**NHL**	**82**	**20**	**47**	**67**	**42**	**7**	**0**	**2**	**213**	**9.4**	**8**	**1321**	**53.1**	**18:33**	**17**	**4**	**10**	**14**	**4**	**1**	**0**	**2**	**18:30**
2000-01 ◆	**Colorado**	**NHL**	**71**	**24**	**41**	**65**	**47**	**11**	**0**	**5**	**204**	**11.8**	**6**	**552**	**55.1**	**18:03**	**23**	**11**	**5**	**16**	**4**	**2**	**0**	**2**	**19:06**
2001-02	**Colorado**	**NHL**	**82**	**21**	**25**	**46**	**38**	**5**	**0**	**6**	**236**	**8.9**	**1**	**1139**	**53.2**	**17:57**	**21**	**5**	**7**	**12**	**10**	**1**	**0**	**3**	**17:01**
	United States	Olympics	6	0	0	0	0	....	....	....	....	....	....	....	....	....	....	....	....	....	....	....	....	....	....
2002-03	**Calgary**	**NHL**	**80**	**23**	**30**	**53**	**33**	**5**	**1**	**5**	**224**	**10.3**	**-9**	**942**	**53.8**	**18:33**	....	....	....	....	....	....	....	....	....
2003-04	**Buffalo**	**NHL**	**76**	**18**	**35**	**53**	**68**	**5**	**1**	**2**	**152**	**11.8**	**8**	**1491**	**54.9**	**18:04**	....	....	....	....	....	....	....	....	....
2004-05			DID NOT PLAY																						
2005-06	**Buffalo**	**NHL**	**81**	**30**	**37**	**67**	**32**	**16**	**2**	**5**	**172**	**17.4**	**-11**	**1641**	**55.5**	**18:06**	**18**	**9**	**9**	**18**	**10**	**5**	**1**	**1**	**19:20**
	United States	Olympics	6	0	3	3	2	....	....	....	....	....	....	....	....	....	....	....	....	....	....	....	....	....	....
2006-07	**Buffalo**	**NHL**	**77**	**37**	**32**	**69**	**30**	**17**	**3**	**9**	**199**	**18.6**	**1**	**1613**	**58.8**	**18:47**	**16**	**8**	**5**	**13**	**2**	**3**	**0**	**3**	**20:45**
2007-08	**NY Rangers**	**NHL**	**82**	**25**	**33**	**58**	**45**	**12**	**0**	**7**	**220**	**11.4**	**-3**	**1359**	**54.9**	**19:48**	**10**	**3**	**3**	**6**	**8**	**0**	**0**	**1**	**18:27**
2008-09	**NY Rangers**	**NHL**	**81**	**22**	**34**	**56**	**32**	**10**	**1**	**2**	**219**	**10.0**	**-8**	**1183**	**51.0**	**20:15**	**6**	**1**	**0**	**1**	**2**	**0**	**0**	**1**	**13:32**
2009-10	**NY Rangers**	**NHL**	**77**	**14**	**18**	**32**	**31**	**2**	**0**	**1**	**148**	**9.5**	**-10**	**1206**	**52.9**	**17:47**	....	....	....	....	....	....	....	....	....
	United States	Olympics	6	2	0	2	0	....	....	....	....	....	....	....	....	....	....	....	....	....	....	....	....	....	....
2010-11	**NY Rangers**	**NHL**	**24**	**1**	**4**	**5**	**8**	**0**	**0**	**0**	**26**	**3.8**	**2**	**225**	**56.4**	**12:01**	**5**	**0**	**1**	**1**	**2**	**0**	**0**	**0**	**10:36**
	NHL Totals		**892**	**255**	**360**	**615**	**468**	**96**	**8**	**47**	**2151**	**11.9**		**13090**	**54.3**	**17:57**	**135**	**47**	**42**	**89**	**46**	**12**	**1**	**17**	**17:15**

Hockey East Second All-Star Team (1996, 1997) • NCAA East Second All-American Team (1996) • Hockey East Player of the Year (1997, 1998) • NCAA East First All-American Team (1997, 1998) • NCAA Championship All-Tournament Team (1997) • Hockey East First All-Star Team (1998) • Hobey Baker Memorial Award (Top U.S. Collegiate Player) (1998) • NHL All-Rookie Team (1999) • Calder Memorial Trophy (1999)

• Rights transferred to **Colorado** after **Quebec** franchise relocated, June 21, 1995. Traded to **Calgary** by **Colorado** with Stephane Yelle for Derek Morris, Jeff Shantz and Dean McAmmond, October 1, 2002. Traded to **Buffalo** by **Calgary** with Steve Begin for Steve Reinprecht and Rhett Warrener, July 3, 2003. Signed as a free agent by **NY Rangers**, July 1, 2007. • Missed majority of 2010-11 season due to hand and knee injuries.

DUBINSKY, Brandon
(DOO-bihn-skee, BRAN-duhn) **NYR**

Center. Shoots left. 6'1", 210 lbs. Born, Anchorage, AK, April 29, 1986. NY Rangers' 6th choice, 60th overall, in 2004 Entry Draft.

Season	Club	League	GP	G	A	Pts	PIM	PP	SH	GW	S	%	+/-	TF	F%	Min	GP	G	A	Pts	PIM	PP	SH	GW	Min
2001-02	Alaska All-Stars	AASHA	37	14	24	38	....	....	....	....	....	....	....	....	....	....	....	....	....	....	....	....	....	....	....
2002-03	Portland	WHL	44	8	18	26	35	....	....	....	....	....	....	....	....	....	7	2	2	4	10	....	....	....	....
2003-04	Portland	WHL	71	30	48	78	137	....	....	....	....	....	....	....	....	....	5	0	2	2	6	....	....	....	....
2004-05	Portland	WHL	68	23	36	59	160	....	....	....	....	....	....	....	....	....	7	4	5	9	8	....	....	....	....
2005-06	Portland	WHL	51	21	46	67	98	....	....	....	....	....	....	....	....	....	12	5	10	15	24	....	....	....	....
	Hartford	AHL	....	....	....	....	....	....	....	....	....	....	....	....	....	....	11	5	5	10	14	....	....	....	....
2006-07	**NY Rangers**	**NHL**	**6**	**0**	**0**	**0**	**2**	**0**	**0**	**0**	**9**	**0.0**	**0**	**26**	**46.2**	**8:10**	....	....	....	....	....	....	....	....	....
	Hartford	AHL	71	21	22	43	115	....	....	....	....	....	....	....	....	....	7	1	3	4	12	....	....	....	....
2007-08	**NY Rangers**	**NHL**	**82**	**14**	**26**	**40**	**79**	**1**	**0**	**0**	**157**	**8.9**	**8**	**995**	**51.5**	**14:30**	**10**	**4**	**4**	**8**	**12**	**2**	**0**	**0**	**18:59**
2008-09	**NY Rangers**	**NHL**	**82**	**13**	**28**	**41**	**112**	**3**	**1**	**7**	**188**	**6.9**	**-6**	**870**	**53.6**	**16:38**	**7**	**1**	**3**	**4**	**18**	**0**	**0**	**1**	**18:14**
2009-10	**NY Rangers**	**NHL**	**69**	**20**	**24**	**44**	**54**	**6**	**2**	**5**	**165**	**12.1**	**9**	**675**	**51.4**	**19:33**	....	....	....	....	....	....	....	....	....
2010-11	**NY Rangers**	**NHL**	**77**	**24**	**30**	**54**	**100**	**4**	**2**	**2**	**202**	**11.9**	**-3**	**875**	**52.5**	**20:14**	**5**	**2**	**1**	**3**	**2**	**0**	**0**	**1**	**24:56**
	NHL Totals		**316**	**71**	**108**	**179**	**347**	**14**	**5**	**14**	**721**	**9.8**		**3441**	**52.2**	**17:26**	**22**	**7**	**8**	**15**	**32**	**2**	**0**	**2**	**20:06**

WHL West Second All-Star Team (2004, 2006)

DUCHENE, Matt
(DOO-shayn, MAT) **COL**

Center. Shoots left. 5'11", 200 lbs. Born, Haliburton, Ont., January 16, 1991. Colorado's 1st choice, 3rd overall, in 2009 Entry Draft.

Season	Club	League	GP	G	A	Pts	PIM	PP	SH	GW	S	%	+/-	TF	F%	Min	GP	G	A	Pts	PIM	PP	SH	GW	Min
2006-07	Cent. Ont. Wolves	Minor-ON	52	69	37	106	36	....	....	....	....	....	....	....	....	....	....	....	....	....	....	....	....	....	....
2007-08	Brampton	OHL	64	30	20	50	22	....	....	....	....	....	....	....	....	....	5	1	1	2	10	....	....	....	....
2008-09	Brampton	OHL	57	31	48	79	42	....	....	....	....	....	....	....	....	....	21	14	12	26	21	....	....	....	....
2009-10	**Colorado**	**NHL**	**81**	**24**	**31**	**55**	**16**	**10**	**1**	**2**	**180**	**13.3**	**1**	**1088**	**44.0**	**17:44**	**6**	**0**	**3**	**3**	**0**	**0**	**0**	**0**	**19:20**
2010-11	**Colorado**	**NHL**	**80**	**27**	**40**	**67**	**33**	**3**	**0**	**2**	**202**	**13.4**	**-8**	**1246**	**50.4**	**18:57**	....	....	....	....	....	....	....	....	....
	NHL Totals		**161**	**51**	**71**	**122**	**49**	**13**	**1**	**4**	**382**	**13.4**		**2334**	**47.4**	**18:20**	**6**	**0**	**3**	**3**	**0**	**0**	**0**	**0**	**19:20**

NHL All-Rookie Team (2010)
Played in NHL All-Star Game (2011)

DUCO, Mike
(DOO-koh, MIGHK) **VAN**

Left wing. Shoots left. 5'10", 200 lbs. Born, Toronto, Ont., July 8, 1987.

Season	Club	League	GP	G	A	Pts	PIM	PP	SH	GW	S	%	+/-	TF	F%	Min	GP	G	A	Pts	PIM	PP	SH	GW	Min
2003-04	Kitchener Rangers	OHL	5	1	2	3	4	....	....	....	....	....	....	....	....	....	4	0	1	1	4	....	....	....	....
2004-05	Kitchener Rangers	OHL	62	24	26	50	78	....	....	....	....	....	....	....	....	....	15	0	0	0	11	....	....	....	....
2005-06	Kitchener Rangers	OHL	59	22	22	44	113	....	....	....	....	....	....	....	....	....	5	2	1	3	10	....	....	....	....
2006-07	Kitchener Rangers	OHL	54	20	20	40	121	....	....	....	....	....	....	....	....	....	9	1	1	2	12	....	....	....	....
2007-08	Kitchener Rangers	OHL	62	32	22	54	173	....	....	....	....	....	....	....	....	....	20	*16	6	22	37	....	....	....	....
2008-09	Rochester	AHL	68	14	14	28	147	....	....	....	....	....	....	....	....	....	....	....	....	....	....	....	....	....	....
2009-10	**Florida**	**NHL**	**10**	**0**	**0**	**0**	**50**	**0**	**0**	**0**	**6**	**0.0**	**-3**	**0**	**0.0**	**7:43**	....	....	....	....	....	....	....	....	....
	Rochester	AHL	59	9	10	19	111	....	....	....	....	....	....	....	....	....	7	1	0	1	18	....	....	....	....
2010-11	**Florida**	**NHL**	**2**	**0**	**0**	**0**	**10**	**0**	**0**	**0**	**0**	**0.0**	**-1**	**0**	**0.0**	**8:33**	....	....	....	....	....	....	....	....	....
	Rochester	AHL	67	20	11	31	126	....	....	....	....	....	....	....	....	....	....	....	....	....	....	....	....	....	....
	NHL Totals		**12**	**0**	**0**	**0**	**60**	**0**	**0**	**0**	**6**	**0.0**		**0**	**0.0**	**7:52**	....	....	....	....	....	....	....	....	....

Signed as a free agent by **Florida**, October 8, 2007. Traded to **Vancouver** by **Florida** for Sergei Shirokov, July 8, 2011.

DUMONT, J.P.
(DOO-mawnt, JAY-PEE)

Right wing. Shoots left. 6'1", 205 lbs. Born, Montreal, Que., April 1, 1978. NY Islanders' 1st choice, 3rd overall, in 1996 Entry Draft.

Season	Club	League	GP	G	A	Pts	PIM	PP	SH	GW	S	%	+/-	TF	F%	Min	GP	G	A	Pts	PIM	PP	SH	GW	Min
1993-94	Mtl-Bourassa	QAAA	44	27	20	47	44	....	....	....	....	....	....	....	....	....	4	2	3	5	4	....	....	....	....
1994-95	Mtl-Bourassa	QAAA	10	2	7	9	12	....	....	....	....	....	....	....	....	....	....	....	....	....	....	....	....	....	....
	Val-d'Or Foreurs	QMJHL	48	5	14	19	22	....	....	....	....	....	....	....	....	....	....	....	....	....	....	....	....	....	....
1995-96	Val-d'Or Foreurs	QMJHL	66	48	57	105	109	....	....	....	....	....	....	....	....	....	13	12	8	20	22	....	....	....	....
1996-97	Val-d'Or Foreurs	QMJHL	62	44	64	108	88	....	....	....	....	....	....	....	....	....	13	9	7	16	12	....	....	....	....
1997-98	Val-d'Or Foreurs	QMJHL	55	57	42	99	63	....	....	....	....	....	....	....	....	....	19	31	15	46	18	....	....	....	....
1998-99	**Chicago**	**NHL**	**25**	**9**	**6**	**15**	**10**	**0**	**0**	**2**	**42**	**21.4**	**7**	**10**	**50.0**	**14:14**	....	....	....	....	....	....	....	....	....
	Portland Pirates	AHL	50	32	14	46	39	....	....	....	....	....	....	....	....	....	....	....	....	....	....	....	....	....	....
	Chicago Wolves	IHL	....	....	....	....	....	....	....	....	....	....	....	....	....	....	10	4	1	5	6	....	....	....	....
99-2000	**Chicago**	**NHL**	**47**	**10**	**8**	**18**	**18**	**0**	**0**	**1**	**86**	**11.6**	**-6**	**12**	**33.3**	**12:54**	....	....	....	....	....	....	....	....	....
	Cleveland	IHL	7	5	2	7	8	....	....	....	....	....	....	....	....	....	....	....	....	....	....	....	....	....	....
	Rochester	AHL	13	7	10	17	18	....	....	....	....	....	....	....	....	....	21	14	7	21	32	....	....	....	....
2000-01	**Buffalo**	**NHL**	**79**	**23**	**28**	**51**	**54**	**9**	**0**	**5**	**156**	**14.7**	**1**	**3**	**33.3**	**15:01**	**13**	**4**	**3**	**7**	**8**	**0**	**0**	**0**	**14:32**
2001-02	**Buffalo**	**NHL**	**76**	**23**	**21**	**44**	**42**	**7**	**0**	**3**	**154**	**14.9**	**-10**	**4**	**50.0**	**15:14**	....	....	....	....	....	....	....	....	....
2002-03	**Buffalo**	**NHL**	**76**	**14**	**21**	**35**	**44**	**2**	**0**	**2**	**135**	**10.4**	**-14**	**15**	**20.0**	**15:04**	....	....	....	....	....	....	....	....	....
2003-04	**Buffalo**	**NHL**	**77**	**22**	**31**	**53**	**40**	**10**	**0**	**1**	**156**	**14.1**	**-9**	**32**	**43.8**	**17:00**	....	....	....	....	....	....	....	....	....
2004-05	SC Bern	Swiss	3	2	2	4	6	....	....	....	....	....	....	....	....	....	10	4	1	5	16	....	....	....	....
2005-06	**Buffalo**	**NHL**	**54**	**20**	**20**	**40**	**38**	**9**	**0**	**4**	**116**	**17.2**	**-1**	**9**	**11.1**	**16:00**	**18**	**7**	**7**	**14**	**14**	**3**	**0**	**1**	**16:39**
2006-07	**Nashville**	**NHL**	**82**	**21**	**45**	**66**	**28**	**5**	**0**	**3**	**143**	**14.7**	**14**	**6**	**16.7**	**16:12**	**5**	**4**	**2**	**6**	**0**	**1**	**1**	**1**	**21:03**
2007-08	**Nashville**	**NHL**	**80**	**29**	**43**	**72**	**34**	**7**	**0**	**8**	**192**	**15.1**	**5**	**13**	**23.1**	**18:30**	**6**	**0**	**2**	**2**	**4**	**0**	**0**	**0**	**17:23**
2008-09	**Nashville**	**NHL**	**82**	**16**	**49**	**65**	**20**	**5**	**0**	**4**	**176**	**9.1**	**1**	**6**	**50.0**	**17:30**	....	....	....	....	....	....	....	....	....
2009-10	**Nashville**	**NHL**	**74**	**17**	**28**	**45**	**20**	**3**	**1**	**3**	**112**	**15.2**	**8**	**0**	**0.0**	**14:46**	**6**	**2**	**2**	**4**	**0**	**0**	**0**	**1**	**14:18**
2010-11	**Nashville**	**NHL**	**70**	**10**	**9**	**19**	**16**	**1**	**0**	**2**	**89**	**11.2**	**2**	**2**	**50.0**	**11:11**	**3**	**0**	**1**	**1**	**2**	**0**	**0**	**0**	**6:48**
	NHL Totals		**822**	**214**	**309**	**523**	**364**	**58**	**1**	**38**	**1557**	**13.7**		**112**	**33.9**	**15:30**	**51**	**17**	**17**	**34**	**28**	**4**	**1**	**3**	**15:46**

QMJHL Second All-Star Team (1997) • AHL All-Rookie Team (1999)

• Rights traded to **Chicago** by **NY Islanders** with NY Islanders' 5th round choice (later traded to Philadelphia – Philadelphia selected Francis Belanger) in 1998 Entry Draft for Dmitri Nabokov, May 30, 1998. Traded to **Buffalo** by **Chicago** with Doug Gilmour for Michal Grosek, March 10, 2000. Signed as a free agent by **Bern** (Swiss), February 9, 2005. Signed as a free agent by **Nashville**, August 29, 2006.

DUPONT, Brodie

(DOO-pawnt, BROH-dee) **NSH**

Center. Shoots left. 6'2", 212 lbs. Born, Russell, Man., February 17, 1987. NY Rangers' 4th choice, 66th overall, in 2005 Entry Draft.

Season	Club	League	GP	G	A	Pts	PIM	PP	SH	GW	S	%	+/-	TF	F%	Min	Playoffs GP	G	A	Pts	PIM	PP	SH	GW	Min
2003-04	Swan Valley	MJHL	51	25	16	41	88										12	5	1	6	36				
	Calgary Hitmen	WHL	2	0	1	1	0																		
2004-05	Calgary Hitmen	WHL	70	14	11	25	111										12	2	8	10	21				
2005-06	Calgary Hitmen	WHL	72	30	23	53	123										13	4	5	9	24				
2006-07	Calgary Hitmen	WHL	70	37	33	70	90										18	9	7	16	33				
2007-08	Hartford	AHL	66	9	13	22	75										1	0	0	0	0				
2008-09	Hartford	AHL	79	18	24	42	112										6	0	2	2	15				
2009-10	Hartford	AHL	80	17	22	39	124																		
2010-11	**NY Rangers**	**NHL**	**1**	**0**	**0**	**0**	**0**	**0**	**0**	**0**	**1**	**0.0**	**0**	**0**	**0.0**	**5:34**									
	Connecticut	AHL	72	14	31	45	78										6	1	2	3	6				
	NHL Totals		**1**	**0**	**0**	**0**	**0**	**0**	**0**	**0**	**1**	**0.0**		**0**	**0.0**	**5:34**									

Traded to **Nashville** by **NY Rangers** for Andreas Thuresson, July 2, 2011.

DUPUIS, Pascal

(doo-PWEE, pas-KAL) **PIT**

Left wing. Shoots left. 6'1", 205 lbs. Born, Laval, Que., April 7, 1979.

Season	Club	League	GP	G	A	Pts	PIM	PP	SH	GW	S	%	+/-	TF	F%	Min	Playoffs GP	G	A	Pts	PIM	PP	SH	GW	Min
1995-96	Laval-Laurentides	QAAA	41	10	15	25											14	11	11	22					
1996-97	Rouyn-Noranda	QMJHL	44	9	15	24	20																		
1997-98	Rouyn-Noranda	QMJHL	42	10	19	29	36																		
	Shawinigan	QMJHL	25	6	11	17	10										6	2	0	2	4				
1998-99	Shawinigan	QMJHL	57	30	42	72	118										6	1	8	9	18				
99-2000	Shawinigan	QMJHL	61	50	55	105	164										13	*15	7	22	4				
2000-01	**Minnesota**	**NHL**	**4**	**1**	**0**	**1**	**4**	**1**	**0**	**0**	**8**	**12.5**	**0**	**0**	**0.0**	**15:36**									
	Cleveland	IHL	70	19	24	43	37										4	0	0	0	0				
2001-02	**Minnesota**	**NHL**	**76**	**15**	**12**	**27**	**16**	**3**	**2**	**0**	**154**	**9.7**	**–10**	**40**	**32.5**	**15:08**									
2002-03	**Minnesota**	**NHL**	**80**	**20**	**28**	**48**	**44**	**6**	**0**	**4**	**183**	**10.9**	**17**	**186**	**40.9**	**17:30**	**16**	**4**	**4**	**8**	**8**	**2**	**0**	**1**	**16:58**
2003-04	**Minnesota**	**NHL**	**59**	**11**	**15**	**26**	**20**	**2**	**0**	**1**	**127**	**8.7**	**5**	**129**	**45.7**	**15:48**									
2004-05	HC Ajoie	Swiss-2	8	5	5	10	26										6	6	8	14	8				
2005-06	**Minnesota**	**NHL**	**67**	**10**	**16**	**26**	**40**	**4**	**0**	**2**	**151**	**6.6**	**–10**	**93**	**29.0**	**16:30**									
2006-07	**Minnesota**	**NHL**	**48**	**10**	**3**	**13**	**38**	**2**	**2**	**0**	**106**	**9.4**	**–7**	**110**	**27.3**	**15:07**									
	NY Rangers	**NHL**	**6**	**1**	**0**	**1**	**0**	**0**	**0**	**0**	**10**	**10.0**	**–4**	**2**	**50.0**	**15:30**									
	Atlanta	**NHL**	**17**	**3**	**2**	**5**	**4**	**0**	**0**	**1**	**40**	**7.5**	**–6**	**19**	**52.6**	**16:44**	**4**	**1**	**2**	**3**	**4**	**0**	**0**	**0**	**20:28**
2007-08	**Atlanta**	**NHL**	**62**	**10**	**5**	**15**	**24**	**0**	**3**	**1**	**111**	**9.0**	**–4**	**13**	**38.5**	**14:46**									
	Pittsburgh	**NHL**	**16**	**2**	**10**	**12**	**8**	**0**	**0**	**0**	**32**	**6.3**	**4**	**3**	**0.0**	**16:50**	**20**	**2**	**5**	**7**	**18**	**0**	**0**	**0**	**16:14**
2008-09♦	**Pittsburgh**	**NHL**	**71**	**12**	**16**	**28**	**30**	**0**	**0**	**2**	**145**	**8.3**	**1**	**16**	**18.8**	**14:13**	**16**	**0**	**0**	**0**	**8**	**0**	**0**	**0**	**8:23**
2009-10	**Pittsburgh**	**NHL**	**81**	**18**	**20**	**38**	**16**	**0**	**0**	**5**	**157**	**11.5**	**5**	**33**	**39.4**	**14:11**	**13**	**2**	**6**	**8**	**4**	**0**	**0**	**1**	**16:51**
2010-11	**Pittsburgh**	**NHL**	**81**	**17**	**20**	**37**	**59**	**0**	**4**	**3**	**171**	**9.9**	**16**	**28**	**21.4**	**16:52**	**7**	**1**	**0**	**1**	**2**	**0**	**0**	**0**	**16:36**
	NHL Totals		**668**	**130**	**147**	**277**	**303**	**18**	**11**	**19**	**1395**	**9.3**		**672**	**36.2**	**15:40**	**76**	**10**	**17**	**27**	**44**	**2**	**0**	**2**	**15:06**

Signed as a free agent by **Minnesota**, August 18, 2000. Signed as a free agent by **Ajoie** (Swiss-2), January 14, 2005. Traded to **NY Rangers** by **Minnesota** for Adam Hall, February 9, 2007. Traded to **Atlanta** by **NY Rangers** with NY Rangers' 3rd round choice (later traded to Pittsburgh - Pittsburgh selected Robert Bortuzzo) in 2007 Entry Draft for Alex Bourret, February 27, 2007. Traded to **Pittsburgh** by **Atlanta** with Marian Hossa for Colby Armstrong, Erik Christensen, Angelo Esposito and Pittsburgh's 1st round choice (Daulton Leveille) in 2008 Entry Draft, February 26, 2008.

DUPUIS, Philippe

(doo-PWEE, fihl-EEP) **TOR**

Center. Shoots right. 6', 196 lbs. Born, Laval, Que., April 24, 1985. Columbus' 5th choice, 104th overall, in 2003 Entry Draft.

Season	Club	League	GP	G	A	Pts	PIM	PP	SH	GW	S	%	+/-	TF	F%	Min	Playoffs GP	G	A	Pts	PIM	PP	SH	GW	Min
2000-01	Laval-Laurentides	QAAA	46	16	27	43	74										8	1	5	6	30				
2001-02	Hull Olympiques	QMJHL	67	7	14	21	59										12	6	5	11	14				
2002-03	Hull Olympiques	QMJHL	68	22	34	56	89										20	2	4	6	22				
2003-04	Gatineau	QMJHL	60	18	37	55	77										15	6	10	16	14				
2004-05	Rouyn-Noranda	QMJHL	62	34	50	84	60										10	5	3	8	8				
2005-06	Moncton Wildcats	QMJHL	56	32	76	108	52										19	14	18	32	14				
2006-07	Syracuse Crunch	AHL	51	11	11	22	18																		
	Dayton Bombers	ECHL	8	3	2	5	8										19	6	9	15	28				
2007-08	Syracuse Crunch	AHL	29	7	4	11	2																		
	Lake Erie	AHL	17	5	3	8	12																		
2008-09	**Colorado**	**NHL**	**8**	**0**	**0**	**0**	**4**	**0**	**0**	**0**	**11**	**0.0**	**–1**	**50**	**52.0**	**9:34**									
	Lake Erie	AHL	67	17	29	46	42																		
2009-10	**Colorado**	**NHL**	**4**	**0**	**1**	**1**	**2**	**0**	**0**	**0**	**4**	**0.0**	**1**	**20**	**45.0**	**8:14**									
	Lake Erie	AHL	68	16	19	35	47																		
2010-11	**Colorado**	**NHL**	**74**	**6**	**11**	**17**	**40**	**0**	**1**	**0**	**101**	**5.9**	**–4**	**331**	**46.2**	**9:07**									
	NHL Totals		**86**	**6**	**12**	**18**	**46**	**0**	**1**	**0**	**116**	**5.2**		**401**	**46.9**	**9:07**									

Traded to **Colorado** by **Columbus** with Darcy Campbell for Mark Rycroft, January 22, 2008. Signed as a free agent by **Toronto**, July 7, 2011.

DURNO, Chris

(DUHR-noh, KRIHS) **CAR**

Center. Shoots left. 6'4", 223 lbs. Born, Scarborough, Ont., October 31, 1980.

Season	Club	League	GP	G	A	Pts	PIM	PP	SH	GW	S	%	+/-	TF	F%	Min	Playoffs GP	G	A	Pts	PIM	PP	SH	GW	Min
99-2000	Michigan Tech	WCHA	24	1	1	2	30																		
2000-01	Michigan Tech	WCHA	35	9	6	15	46																		
2001-02	Michigan Tech	WCHA	36	7	8	15	48																		
2002-03	Michigan Tech	WCHA	35	5	11	16	60																		
2003-04	Gwinnett	ECHL	68	20	26	46	46										13	7	5	12	10				
2004-05	Gwinnett	ECHL	66	20	36	56	101										8	5	2	7	8				
2005-06	Gwinnett	ECHL	13	12	10	22	19																		
	Milwaukee	AHL	57	20	20	40	52										21	2	2	4	18				
2006-07	Norfolk Admirals	AHL	22	4	1	5	61																		
	Portland Pirates	AHL	12	1	1	2	2																		
	Milwaukee	AHL	29	13	3	16	24										4	1	2	3	10				
2007-08	San Antonio	AHL	80	23	26	49	109										7	0	2	2	26				
2008-09	**Colorado**	**NHL**	**2**	**0**	**0**	**0**	**0**	**0**	**0**	**0**	**3**	**0.0**	**0**	**0**	**0.0**	**6:02**									
	Lake Erie	AHL	76	18	27	45	131																		
2009-10	**Colorado**	**NHL**	**41**	**4**	**4**	**8**	**47**	**0**	**0**	**0**	**27**	**14.8**	**3**	**40**	**52.5**	**7:28**	**1**	**0**	**0**	**0**	**0**	**0**	**0**	**0**	**6:09**
	Lake Erie	AHL	17	10	8	18	20																		
2010-11	Norfolk Admirals	AHL	73	19	17	36	120										3	0	0	0	4				
	NHL Totals		**43**	**4**	**4**	**8**	**47**	**0**	**0**	**0**	**30**	**13.3**		**40**	**52.5**	**7:24**	**1**	**0**	**0**	**0**	**0**	**0**	**0**	**0**	**6:09**

Signed as a free agent by **Chicago**, September 25, 2006. Traded to **Anaheim** by **Chicago** with Sebastiien Caron and Matt Keith for P.A. Parenteau and Bruno St. Jacques, December 28, 2006. Traded to **Nashville** by **Anaheim** for Shane Endicott, January 26, 2007. Signed as a free agent by **Colorado**, July 3, 2008. Signed as a free agent by **Tampa Bay**, July 25, 2010. Signed as a free agent by **Carolina**, July 15, 2011.

DVORAK, Radek

(duh-VOHR-ak, RA-dehk) **DAL**

Right wing. Shoots right. 6'2", 200 lbs. Born, Tabor, Czech., March 9, 1977. Florida's 1st choice, 10th overall, in 1995 Entry Draft.

Season	Club	League	GP	G	A	Pts	PIM	PP	SH	GW	S	%	+/-	TF	F%	Min	Playoffs GP	G	A	Pts	PIM	PP	SH	GW	Min
1992-93	C. Budejovice Jr.	Czech-Jr.	35	44	46	90																			
1993-94	C. Budejovice Jr.	CzRep-Jr.	20	17	18	35																			
	C. Budejovice	CzRep	8	0	0	0	0																		
1994-95	C. Budejovice	CzRep	10	3	5	8	2										9	5	1	6					
1995-96	**Florida**	**NHL**	**77**	**13**	**14**	**27**	**20**	**0**	**0**	**4**	**126**	**10.3**	**5**				**16**	**1**	**3**	**4**	**0**	**0**	**0**	**0**	
1996-97	**Florida**	**NHL**	**78**	**18**	**21**	**39**	**30**	**2**	**0**	**1**	**139**	**12.9**	**–2**				**3**	**0**	**0**	**0**	**0**	**0**	**0**	**0**	
1997-98	**Florida**	**NHL**	**64**	**12**	**24**	**36**	**33**	**2**	**3**	**0**	**112**	**10.7**	**–1**												
1998-99	**Florida**	**NHL**	**82**	**19**	**24**	**43**	**29**	**0**	**4**	**0**	**182**	**10.4**	**7**	**98**	**46.9**	**16:13**									
99-2000	**Florida**	**NHL**	**35**	**7**	**10**	**17**	**6**	**0**	**0**	**1**	**67**	**10.4**	**5**	**16**	**37.5**	**15:25**									
	NY Rangers	**NHL**	**46**	**11**	**22**	**33**	**10**	**2**	**1**	**0**	**90**	**12.2**	**0**	**34**	**35.3**	**18:24**									
2000-01	**NY Rangers**	**NHL**	**82**	**31**	**36**	**67**	**20**	**5**	**2**	**3**	**230**	**13.5**	**9**	**20**	**30.0**	**19:04**									
2001-02	**NY Rangers**	**NHL**	**65**	**17**	**20**	**37**	**14**	**3**	**3**	**1**	**210**	**8.1**	**–20**	**5**	**0.0**	**19:44**									
	Czech Republic	Olympics	4	0	0	0	0																		
2002-03	**NY Rangers**	**NHL**	**63**	**6**	**21**	**27**	**16**	**2**	**0**	**0**	**134**	**4.5**	**–3**	**9**	**44.4**	**15:42**									
	Edmonton	**NHL**	**12**	**4**	**4**	**8**	**14**	**1**	**0**	**0**	**32**	**12.5**	**–3**	**1**	**0.0**	**16:07**	**4**	**1**	**0**	**1**	**0**	**0**	**0**	**1**	**15:05**
2003-04	**Edmonton**	**NHL**	**78**	**15**	**35**	**50**	**26**	**6**	**0**	**0**	**188**	**8.0**	**18**	**24**	**29.2**	**16:56**									

			Regular Season														Playoffs								
Season	Club	League	GP	G	A	Pts	PIM	PP	SH	GW	S	%	+/-	TF	F%	Min	GP	G	A	Pts	PIM	PP	SH	GW	Min
2004-05	C. Budejovice	CzRep-2	32	23	35	58	18	....	....	....	....	....	....	....	....	....	16	5	13	18	20	....	....	....	....
2005-06	**Edmonton**	**NHL**	64	8	20	28	26	2	0	2	131	6.1	–2	14	28.6	16:34	16	0	2	2	4	0	0	0	13:29
2006-07	**St. Louis**	**NHL**	82	10	27	37	48	1	1	1	139	7.2	–6	26	38.5	15:38	....	....	....	....	....	....	....	....	....
2007-08	**Florida**	**NHL**	67	8	9	17	16	0	1	1	146	5.5	–1	12	16.7	15:07	....	....	....	....	....	....	....	....	....
2008-09	**Florida**	**NHL**	81	15	21	36	42	0	4	3	136	11.0	0	17	35.3	16:26	....	....	....	....	....	....	....	....	....
2009-10	**Florida**	**NHL**	76	14	18	32	20	1	3	1	140	10.0	–7	17	17.7	17:26	....	....	....	....	....	....	....	....	....
2010-11	**Florida**	**NHL**	53	7	14	21	20	0	1	3	89	7.9	2	10	20.0	16:33	....	....	....	....	....	....	....	....	....
	Atlanta	**NHL**	13	0	1	1	4	0	0	0	20	0.0	0	9	55.6	14:08	....	....	....	....	....	....	....	....	....
	NHL Totals		1118	215	341	556	394	27	23	21	2311	9.3		312	36.2	16:50	39	2	5	7	4	0	0	1	13:48

Traded to **San Jose** by **Florida** for Mike Vernon and San Jose's 3rd round choice (Sean O'Connor) in 2000 Entry Draft, December 30, 1999. Traded to **NY Rangers** by **San Jose** for Todd Harvey and NY Rangers' 4th round choice (Dimitri Patzold) in 2001 Entry Draft, December 30, 1999. Traded to **Edmonton** by **NY Rangers** with Cory Cross for Anson Carter and Ales Pisa, March 11, 2003. Signed as a free agent by **Ceske Budejovice** (CzRep-2), September 15, 2004. Signed as a free agent by **St. Louis**, September 14, 2006. Signed as a free agent by **Florida**, July 1, 2007. Traded to **Atlanta** by **Florida** with Carolina's 5th round choice (previously acquired, later traded to San Jose – San Jose selected Sean Kuraly) in 2011 Entry Draft for Niclas Bergfors and Patrick Rissmiller, February 28, 2011. • Transferred to **Winnipeg** after **Atlanta** franchise relocated, June 21, 2011. Signed as a free agent by **Dallas**, July 1, 2011.

DWYER, Patrick

(DWIGH-uhr, PAT-rihk) **CAR**

Right wing. Shoots right. 5'11", 175 lbs. Born, Spokane, WA, June 22, 1983. Atlanta's 3rd choice, 116th overall, in 2002 Entry Draft.

Season	Club	League	GP	G	A	Pts	PIM	PP	SH	GW	S	%	+/-	TF	F%	Min	GP	G	A	Pts	PIM	PP	SH	GW	Min
2000-01	Great Falls	NWJHL	40	33	57	90	106	....	....	....	....	....	....	....	....	....	12	10	12	22	....	....	....	....	....
2001-02	Western Mich.	CCHA	38	17	17	34	26	....	....	....	....	....	....	....	....	....	....	....	....	....	....	....	....	....	....
2002-03	Western Mich.	CCHA	33	9	10	19	20	....	....	....	....	....	....	....	....	....	....	....	....	....	....	....	....	....	....
2003-04	Western Mich.	CCHA	35	13	13	26	22	....	....	....	....	....	....	....	....	....	....	....	....	....	....	....	....	....	....
2004-05	Western Mich.	CCHA	36	6	16	22	56	....	....	....	....	....	....	....	....	....	....	....	....	....	....	....	....	....	....
2005-06	Chicago Wolves	AHL	73	16	29	45	49	....	....	....	....	....	....	....	....	....	....	....	....	....	....	....	....	....	....
2006-07	Albany River Rats	AHL	79	16	25	41	39	....	....	....	....	....	....	....	....	....	5	0	1	1	5	....	....	....	....
2007-08	Albany River Rats	AHL	59	13	12	25	29	....	....	....	....	....	....	....	....	....	7	0	2	2	0	....	....	....	....
2008-09	**Carolina**	**NHL**	13	1	0	1	0	0	0	0	9	11.1	–2	12	41.7	8:34	2	0	1	1	0	0	0	0	4:48
	Albany River Rats	AHL	62	24	16	40	29	....	....	....	....	....	....	....	....	....	....	....	....	....	....	....	....	....	....
2009-10	**Carolina**	**NHL**	58	7	5	12	6	0	0	2	80	8.8	–3	224	34.8	12:30	....	....	....	....	....	....	....	....	....
2010-11	**Carolina**	**NHL**	80	8	10	18	12	0	1	2	104	7.7	–6	238	33.6	12:35	....	....	....	....	....	....	....	....	....
	NHL Totals		151	16	15	31	18	0	1	4	193	8.3		474	34.4	12:12	2	0	1	1	0	0	0	0	4:48

CCHA All-Rookie Team (2002) • CCHA Rookie of the Year (2002)

Signed as a free agent by **Carolina**, July 7, 2006.

EAGER, Ben

(EE-guhr, BEHN) **EDM**

Left wing. Shoots left. 6'2", 235 lbs. Born, Ottawa, Ont., January 22, 1984. Phoenix's 2nd choice, 23rd overall, in 2002 Entry Draft.

Season	Club	League	GP	G	A	Pts	PIM	PP	SH	GW	S	%	+/-	TF	F%	Min	GP	G	A	Pts	PIM	PP	SH	GW	Min
99-2000	Ott. Jr. Senators	CJHL	50	8	11	19	119	....	....	....	....	....	....	....	....	....	....	....	....	....	....	....	....	....	....
2000-01	Oshawa Generals	OHL	61	4	6	10	120	....	....	....	....	....	....	....	....	....	....	....	....	....	....	....	....	....	....
2001-02	Oshawa Generals	OHL	63	14	23	37	255	....	....	....	....	....	....	....	....	....	5	0	1	1	13	....	....	....	....
2002-03	Oshawa Generals	OHL	58	16	24	40	216	....	....	....	....	....	....	....	....	....	8	0	4	4	8	....	....	....	....
2003-04	Oshawa Generals	OHL	61	25	27	52	204	....	....	....	....	....	....	....	....	....	7	2	3	5	31	....	....	....	....
	Philadelphia	AHL	5	0	0	0	0	....	....	....	....	....	....	....	....	....	3	0	1	1	8	....	....	....	....
2004-05	Philadelphia	AHL	66	7	10	17	232	....	....	....	....	....	....	....	....	....	16	1	1	2	71	....	....	....	....
2005-06	**Philadelphia**	**NHL**	25	3	5	8	18	0	0	0	21	14.3	0	0	0.0	7:24	2	0	0	0	26	0	0	0	7:06
	Philadelphia	AHL	49	6	12	18	256	....	....	....	....	....	....	....	....	....	....	....	....	....	....	....	....	....	....
2006-07	**Philadelphia**	**NHL**	63	6	5	11	*233	0	0	0	48	12.5	–13	1	100.0	8:14	....	....	....	....	....	....	....	....	....
	Philadelphia	AHL	3	0	0	0	21	....	....	....	....	....	....	....	....	....	....	....	....	....	....	....	....	....	....
2007-08	**Philadelphia**	**NHL**	23	0	0	0	62	0	0	0	11	0.0	–8	5	20.0	5:29	....	....	....	....	....	....	....	....	....
	Chicago	**NHL**	9	0	2	2	27	0	0	0	5	0.0	–1	0	0.0	6:37	....	....	....	....	....	....	....	....	....
2008-09	**Chicago**	**NHL**	75	11	4	15	161	0	0	0	80	13.8	1	0	0.0	8:31	17	1	1	2	*61	0	0	1	8:32
2009-10 ♦	**Chicago**	**NHL**	60	7	9	16	120	0	0	2	68	10.3	9	1	0.0	8:20	18	1	2	3	20	0	0	1	6:02
2010-11	**Atlanta**	**NHL**	34	3	7	10	77	0	0	1	41	7.3	4	2	0.0	12:15	....	....	....	....	....	....	....	....	....
	San Jose	**NHL**	34	4	3	7	43	0	0	0	43	9.3	0	0	0.0	9:02	10	1	0	1	41	0	0	0	4:53
	NHL Totals		323	34	35	69	741	0	0	3	317	10.7		9	22.2	8:31	47	3	3	6	148	0	0	2	6:44

Traded to **Philadelphia** by **Phoenix** with Sean Burke and Branko Radivojevic for Mike Comrie, February 9, 2004. Traded to **Chicago** by **Philadelphia** for Jim Vandermeer, December 18, 2007. Traded to **Atlanta** by **Chicago** with Brent Sopel, Dustin Byfuglien and Akim Aliu for Marty Reasoner, Joey Crabb, Jeremy Morin and New Jersey's 1st (previously acquired, Chicago selected Kevin Hayes) and 2nd (previously acquired, Chicago selected Justin Holl) round choices in 2010 Entry Draft, June 24, 2010. Traded to **San Jose** by **Atlanta** for San Jose's 5th round choice (Austen Brassard) in 2011 Entry Draft, January 18, 2011. Signed as a free agent by **Edmonton**, July 1, 2011.

EARL, Robbie

(UHRL, RAW-bee)

Left wing. Shoots left. 6'1", 195 lbs. Born, Chicago, IL, June 2, 1985. Toronto's 4th choice, 187th overall, in 2004 Entry Draft.

Season	Club	League	GP	G	A	Pts	PIM	PP	SH	GW	S	%	+/-	TF	F%	Min	GP	G	A	Pts	PIM	PP	SH	GW	Min
2000-01	L.A. Jr. Kings	Minor-CA	29	48	22	70	....	....	....	....	....	....	....	....	....	....	....	....	....	....	....	....	....	....	....
2001-02	USNTDP	U-17	15	8	9	17	....	....	....	....	....	....	....	....	....	....	....	....	....	....	....	....	....	....	....
	USNTDP	NAHL	43	14	7	21	43	....	....	....	....	....	....	....	....	....	....	....	....	....	....	....	....	....	....
2002-03	USNTDP	U-18	43	16	8	24	58	....	....	....	....	....	....	....	....	....	....	....	....	....	....	....	....	....	....
	USNTDP	NAHL	10	4	5	9	18	....	....	....	....	....	....	....	....	....	....	....	....	....	....	....	....	....	....
2003-04	U. of Wisconsin	WCHA	42	14	13	27	46	....	....	....	....	....	....	....	....	....	....	....	....	....	....	....	....	....	....
2004-05	U. of Wisconsin	WCHA	41	20	24	44	62	....	....	....	....	....	....	....	....	....	....	....	....	....	....	....	....	....	....
2005-06	U. of Wisconsin	WCHA	42	24	26	50	56	....	....	....	....	....	....	....	....	....	....	....	....	....	....	....	....	....	....
	Toronto Marlies	AHL	1	0	0	0	0	....	....	....	....	....	....	....	....	....	3	0	0	0	0	....	....	....	....
2006-07	Toronto Marlies	AHL	67	12	18	30	50	....	....	....	....	....	....	....	....	....	....	....	....	....	....	....	....	....	....
2007-08	**Toronto**	**NHL**	9	0	1	1	0	0	0	0	9	0.0	–2	2	100.0	9:14	....	....	....	....	....	....	....	....	....
	Toronto Marlies	AHL	66	14	33	47	56	....	....	....	....	....	....	....	....	....	....	....	....	....	....	....	....	....	....
2008-09	Toronto Marlies	AHL	36	2	8	10	28	....	....	....	....	....	....	....	....	....	....	....	....	....	....	....	....	....	....
	Houston Aeros	AHL	33	4	5	9	26	....	....	....	....	....	....	....	....	....	20	5	4	9	14	....	....	....	....
2009-10	**Minnesota**	**NHL**	32	6	0	6	6	0	0	0	29	20.7	1	2	0.0	8:56	....	....	....	....	....	....	....	....	....
	Houston Aeros	AHL	41	10	8	18	16	....	....	....	....	....	....	....	....	....	....	....	....	....	....	....	....	....	....
2010-11	**Minnesota**	**NHL**	6	0	0	0	0	0	0	0	6	0.0	–3	2	0.0	8:46	....	....	....	....	....	....	....	....	....
	Houston Aeros	AHL	69	24	31	55	42	....	....	....	....	....	....	....	....	....	24	5	7	12	20	....	....	....	....
	NHL Totals		47	6	1	7	6	0	0	0	44	13.6		6	33.3	8:58	....	....	....	....	....	....	....	....	....

WCHA All-Rookie Team (2004) • WCHA Second All-Star Team (2005) • NCAA Championship All-Tournament Team (2006) • NCAA Championship Tournament MVP (2006)

Traded to **Minnesota** by **Toronto** for Ryan Hamilton, January 21, 2009. Signed as a free agent by **Riga** (Russia-KHL), August 5, 2011.

EATON, Mark

(EE-tohn, MAHRK) **NYI**

Defense. Shoots left. 6'1", 214 lbs. Born, Wilmington, DE, May 6, 1977.

Season	Club	League	GP	G	A	Pts	PIM	PP	SH	GW	S	%	+/-	TF	F%	Min	GP	G	A	Pts	PIM	PP	SH	GW	Min
1995-96	Waterloo	USHL	50	4	21	25	....	....	....	....	....	....	....	....	....	....	....	....	....	....	....	....	....	....	....
1996-97	Waterloo	USHL	50	6	32	38	62	....	....	....	....	....	....	....	....	....	....	....	....	....	....	....	....	....	....
1997-98	U. of Notre Dame	CCHA	41	12	17	29	32	....	....	....	....	....	....	....	....	....	....	....	....	....	....	....	....	....	....
1998-99	Philadelphia	AHL	74	9	27	36	38	....	....	....	....	....	....	....	....	....	16	4	8	12	0	....	....	....	....
99-2000	**Philadelphia**	**NHL**	27	1	1	2	8	0	0	1	25	4.0	1	0	0.0	18:17	7	0	0	0	0	0	0	0	13:36
	Philadelphia	AHL	47	9	17	26	6	....	....	....	....	....	....	....	....	....	....	....	....	....	....	....	....	....	....
2000-01	**Nashville**	**NHL**	34	3	8	11	14	1	0	1	32	9.4	7	0	0.0	17:13	....	....	....	....	....	....	....	....	....
	Milwaukee	IHL	34	3	12	15	27	....	....	....	....	....	....	....	....	....	....	....	....	....	....	....	....	....	....
2001-02	**Nashville**	**NHL**	58	3	5	8	24	0	0	0	52	5.8	–12	0	0.0	17:12	....	....	....	....	....	....	....	....	....
2002-03	**Nashville**	**NHL**	50	2	7	9	22	0	0	0	52	3.8	1	0	0.0	15:45	....	....	....	....	....	....	....	....	....
	Milwaukee	AHL	3	1	0	1	2	....	....	....	....	....	....	....	....	....	....	....	....	....	....	....	....	....	....
2003-04	**Nashville**	**NHL**	75	4	9	13	26	0	0	1	82	4.9	16	0	0.0	20:56	6	0	0	0	2	0	0	0	19:51
2004-05	Grand Rapids	AHL	29	3	3	6	21	....	....	....	....	....	....	....	....	....	....	....	....	....	....	....	....	....	....
2005-06	**Nashville**	**NHL**	69	3	1	4	44	0	0	0	28	10.7	–2	0	0.0	19:43	5	0	0	0	8	0	0	0	17:49
2006-07	**Pittsburgh**	**NHL**	35	0	3	3	16	0	0	0	22	0.0	–6	0	0.0	19:12	5	0	0	0	0	0	0	0	18:31
2007-08	**Pittsburgh**	**NHL**	36	0	3	3	4	0	0	0	28	0.0	6	0	0.0	19:40	....	....	....	....	....	....	....	....	....
2008-09 ♦	**Pittsburgh**	**NHL**	68	4	5	9	36	1	0	0	34	11.8	3	1	100.0	17:46	24	4	3	7	10	1	0	0	18:07

								Regular Season									Playoffs								
Season	Club	League	GP	G	A	Pts	PIM	PP	SH	GW	S	%	+/-	TF	F%	Min	GP	G	A	Pts	PIM	PP	SH	GW	Min
2009-10	**Pittsburgh**	**NHL**	**79**	**3**	**13**	**16**	**26**	**0**	**0**	**1**	**65**	**4.6**	**5**	**0**	**0.0**	**19:45**	**13**	**0**	**3**	**3**	**4**	**0**	**0**	**0**	**20:43**
2010-11	**NY Islanders**	**NHL**	**34**	**0**	**3**	**3**	**8**	**0**	**0**	**0**	**29**	**0.0**	**–2**	**0**	**0.0**	**20:22**	....	....	....	....	....	....	....	....	....
	NHL Totals		**565**	**23**	**58**	**81**	**228**	**2**	**0**	**4**	**449**	**5.1**		**1**	**100.0**	**18:50**	**60**	**4**	**6**	**10**	**24**	**1**	**0**	**0**	**18:20**

USHL Second All-Star Team (1997) • Curt Hammer Award (USHL – Most Gentlemanly Player) (1997) • CCHA Rookie of the Year (1998)

Signed as a free agent by **Philadelphia**, August 4, 1998. Traded to **Nashville** by **Philadelphia** for Detroit's 3rd round choice (previously acquired, Philadelphia selected Patrick Sharp) in 2001 Entry Draft, September 29, 2000. Signed as a free agent by **Grand Rapids** (AHL), February 16, 2005. Signed as a free agent by **Pittsburgh**, July 3, 2006. Signed as a free agent by **NY Islanders**, July 2, 2010. • Missed majority of 2010-11 due to hip injury at Calgary, January 3, 2011.

EAVES, Patrick

(EEVZ, PAT-rihk) **DET**

Right wing. Shoots right. 6', 191 lbs. Born, Calgary, Alta., May 1, 1984. Ottawa's 1st choice, 29th overall, in 2003 Entry Draft.

99-2000	Shat.-St. Mary's	High-MN	50	23	24	47	....	....	....	....	....	....	....	....	....	....	....	....	....	....	....	....	....	....	....
2000-01	USNTDP	U-17	13	7	8	15	3	....	....	....	....	....	....	....	....	....	....	....	....	....	....	....	....	....	....
	USNTDP	NAHL	34	12	11	23	75	....	....	....	....	....	....	....	....	....	....	....	....	....	....	....	....	....	....
2001-02	USNTDP	U-18	32	19	21	40	87	....	....	....	....	....	....	....	....	....	....	....	....	....	....	....	....	....	....
	USNTDP	USHL	9	1	4	5	18	....	....	....	....	....	....	....	....	....	....	....	....	....	....	....	....	....	....
	USNTDP	NAHL	8	5	3	8	37	....	....	....	....	....	....	....	....	....	....	....	....	....	....	....	....	....	....
2002-03	Boston College	H-East	14	10	8	18	61	....	....	....	....	....	....	....	....	....	....	....	....	....	....	....	....	....	....
2003-04	Boston College	H-East	34	18	23	41	66	....	....	....	....	....	....	....	....	....	....	....	....	....	....	....	....	....	....
2004-05	Boston College	H-East	36	19	29	48	36	....	....	....	....	....	....	....	....	....	....	....	....	....	....	....	....	....	....
2005-06	**Ottawa**	**NHL**	**58**	**20**	**9**	**29**	**22**	**5**	**1**	**4**	**100**	**20.0**	**7**	**14**	**21.4**	**12:29**	**10**	**1**	**0**	**1**	**10**	**0**	**0**	**0**	**11:40**
	Binghamton	AHL	18	5	8	13	10	....	....	....	....	....	....	....	....	....	....	....	....	....	....	....	....	....	....
2006-07	**Ottawa**	**NHL**	**73**	**14**	**18**	**32**	**36**	**3**	**1**	**1**	**130**	**10.8**	**1**	**9**	**11.1**	**12:13**	**7**	**0**	**2**	**2**	**2**	**0**	**0**	**0**	**7:23**
2007-08	**Ottawa**	**NHL**	**26**	**4**	**6**	**10**	**6**	**1**	**0**	**1**	**59**	**6.8**	**0**	**1**	**100.0**	**12:44**	....	....	....	....	....	....	....	....	....
	Carolina	**NHL**	**11**	**1**	**4**	**5**	**4**	**1**	**0**	**0**	**22**	**4.5**	**–2**	**2**	**0.0**	**12:51**	....	....	....	....	....	....	....	....	....
2008-09	**Carolina**	**NHL**	**74**	**6**	**8**	**14**	**31**	**1**	**1**	**1**	**115**	**5.2**	**7**	**12**	**41.7**	**11:15**	**18**	**1**	**2**	**3**	**13**	**0**	**0**	**0**	**9:29**
2009-10	**Detroit**	**NHL**	**65**	**12**	**10**	**22**	**26**	**0**	**1**	**1**	**120**	**10.0**	**0**	**14**	**28.6**	**13:26**	**8**	**0**	**0**	**0**	**2**	**0**	**0**	**0**	**11:58**
2010-11	**Detroit**	**NHL**	**63**	**13**	**7**	**20**	**14**	**2**	**1**	**1**	**108**	**12.0**	**–2**	**10**	**30.0**	**12:42**	**11**	**3**	**1**	**4**	**6**	**0**	**0**	**0**	**11:24**
	NHL Totals		**370**	**70**	**62**	**132**	**139**	**13**	**5**	**9**	**654**	**10.7**		**62**	**27.4**	**12:25**	**54**	**5**	**5**	**10**	**33**	**0**	**0**	**0**	**10:23**

Hockey East Second All-Star Team (2004) • NCAA East Second All-American Team (2004) • Hockey East First All-Star Team (2005) • NCAA East First All-American Team (2005)

• Missed majority of 2002-03 due to neck injury vs. University of Maine (Hockey East), December 7, 2002. Traded to **Carolina** by **Ottawa** with Joe Corvo for Cory Stillman and Mike Commodore, February 11, 2008. • Missed majority of 2007-08 due to shoulder injury at Buffalo, November 21, 2007. Traded to **Boston** by **Carolina** with Carolina's 4th round choice (Craig Cunningham) in 2010 Entry Draft for Aaron Ward, July 24, 2009. Signed as a free agent by **Detroit**, August 4, 2009.

EBBETT, Andrew

(EH-beht, AN-droo) **VAN**

Center. Shoots left. 5'9", 174 lbs. Born, Calgary, Alta., January 2, 1983.

2002-03	U. of Michigan	CCHA	43	9	18	27	22	....	....	....	....	....	....	....	....	....	....	....	....	....	....	....	....	....	....
2003-04	U. of Michigan	CCHA	43	9	28	37	56	....	....	....	....	....	....	....	....	....	....	....	....	....	....	....	....	....	....
2004-05	U. of Michigan	CCHA	40	6	31	37	28	....	....	....	....	....	....	....	....	....	....	....	....	....	....	....	....	....	....
2005-06	U. of Michigan	CCHA	41	14	28	42	25	....	....	....	....	....	....	....	....	....	....	....	....	....	....	....	....	....	....
2006-07	Binghamton	AHL	71	26	39	65	44	....	....	....	....	....	....	....	....	....	....	....	....	....	....	....	....	....	....
2007-08	**Anaheim**	**NHL**	**3**	**0**	**0**	**0**	**2**	**0**	**0**	**0**	**3**	**0.0**	**3**	**29**	**58.6**	**13:18**	....	....	....	....	....	....	....	....	....
	Portland Pirates	AHL	74	18	54	72	66	....	....	....	....	....	....	....	....	....	18	6	11	17	4	....	....	....	....
2008-09	**Anaheim**	**NHL**	**48**	**8**	**24**	**32**	**24**	**6**	**0**	**0**	**100**	**8.0**	**8**	**455**	**48.6**	**13:52**	**13**	**1**	**2**	**3**	**8**	**0**	**0**	**0**	**13:11**
	Iowa Chops	AHL	28	10	19	29	6	....	....	....	....	....	....	....	....	....	....	....	....	....	....	....	....	....	....
2009-10	**Anaheim**	**NHL**	**2**	**0**	**0**	**0**	**0**	**0**	**0**	**0**	**1**	**0.0**	**–1**	**17**	**35.3**	**12:55**	....	....	....	....	....	....	....	....	....
	Chicago	**NHL**	**10**	**1**	**0**	**1**	**2**	**0**	**0**	**0**	**14**	**7.1**	**1**	**72**	**50.0**	**10:43**	....	....	....	....	....	....	....	....	....
	Minnesota	**NHL**	**49**	**8**	**6**	**14**	**6**	**2**	**0**	**2**	**57**	**14.0**	**–8**	**464**	**50.0**	**13:06**	....	....	....	....	....	....	....	....	....
2010-11	**Phoenix**	**NHL**	**33**	**2**	**3**	**5**	**4**	**0**	**1**	**1**	**23**	**8.7**	**–1**	**229**	**45.4**	**10:01**	**3**	**0**	**0**	**0**	**0**	**0**	**0**	**0**	**7:58**
	San Antonio	AHL	37	11	27	38	12	....	....	....	....	....	....	....	....	....	....	....	....	....	....	....	....	....	....
	NHL Totals		**145**	**19**	**33**	**52**	**38**	**8**	**1**	**3**	**198**	**9.6**		**1266**	**48.7**	**12:29**	**16**	**1**	**2**	**3**	**8**	**0**	**0**	**0**	**12:13**

Signed as a free agent by **Anaheim**, May 16, 2007. Claimed on waivers by **Chicago** from **Anaheim**, October 17, 2009. Claimed on waivers by **Minnesota** from **Chicago**, November 21, 2009. Signed as a free agent by **Phoenix**, July 2, 2010. Signed as a free agent by **Vancouver**, July 5, 2011.

EBERLE, Jordan

(EH-buhr-lee, JOHR-dahn) **EDM**

Center. Shoots right. 6', 185 lbs. Born, Regina, Sask., May 15, 1990. Edmonton's 1st choice, 22nd overall, in 2008 Entry Draft.

2005-06	Calgary Buffaloes	AMHL	31	14	20	34	6	....	....	....	....	....	....	....	....	....	11	7	1	8	8	....	....	....	....
2006-07	Regina Pats	WHL	66	28	27	55	32	....	....	....	....	....	....	....	....	....	6	2	5	7	2	....	....	....	....
2007-08	Regina Pats	WHL	70	42	33	75	20	....	....	....	....	....	....	....	....	....	5	2	4	6	7	....	....	....	....
2008-09	Regina Pats	WHL	61	35	39	74	20	....	....	....	....	....	....	....	....	....	....	....	....	....	....	....	....	....	....
	Springfield	AHL	9	3	6	9	4	....	....	....	....	....	....	....	....	....	....	....	....	....	....	....	....	....	....
2009-10	Regina Pats	WHL	57	50	56	106	32	....	....	....	....	....	....	....	....	....	....	....	....	....	....	....	....	....	....
	Springfield	AHL	11	6	8	14	0	....	....	....	....	....	....	....	....	....	....	....	....	....	....	....	....	....	....
2010-11	**Edmonton**	**NHL**	**69**	**18**	**25**	**43**	**22**	**4**	**2**	**5**	**158**	**11.4**	**–12**	**26**	**42.3**	**17:41**	....	....	....	....	....	....	....	....	....
	NHL Totals		**69**	**18**	**25**	**43**	**22**	**4**	**2**	**5**	**158**	**11.4**		**26**	**42.3**	**17:41**	....	....	....	....	....	....	....	....	....

WHL East First All-Star Team (2008, 2010) • WHL Player of the Year (2010) • Canadian Major Junior First All-Star Team (2010) • Canadian Major Junior Player of the Year (2010)

ECKFORD, Tyler

(EHK-fuhrd, TIGH-luhr) **PHX**

Defense. Shoots left. 6'1", 205 lbs. Born, Vancouver, B.C., September 8, 1985. New Jersey's 5th choice, 217th overall, in 2004 Entry Draft.

2003-04	Surrey Eagles	BCHL	58	7	30	37	101	....	....	....	....	....	....	....	....	....	13	2	8	10	34	....	....	....	....
2004-05	Surrey Eagles	BCHL	60	22	43	65	93	....	....	....	....	....	....	....	....	....	25	4	15	19	46	....	....	....	....
2005-06	Alaska	CCHA	38	3	15	18	43	....	....	....	....	....	....	....	....	....	....	....	....	....	....	....	....	....	....
2006-07	Alaska	CCHA	39	5	17	22	54	....	....	....	....	....	....	....	....	....	....	....	....	....	....	....	....	....	....
2007-08	Alaska	CCHA	35	8	23	31	55	....	....	....	....	....	....	....	....	....	....	....	....	....	....	....	....	....	....
2008-09	Lowell Devils	AHL	72	2	25	27	59	....	....	....	....	....	....	....	....	....	....	....	....	....	....	....	....	....	....
2009-10	**New Jersey**	**NHL**	**3**	**0**	**1**	**1**	**4**	**0**	**0**	**0**	**1**	**0.0**	**0**	**0**	**0.0**	**7:23**	....	....	....	....	....	....	....	....	....
	Lowell Devils	AHL	61	8	23	31	26	....	....	....	....	....	....	....	....	....	5	1	0	1	2	....	....	....	....
2010-11	**New Jersey**	**NHL**	**4**	**0**	**0**	**0**	**0**	**0**	**0**	**0**	**1**	**0.0**	**–1**	**0**	**0.0**	**8:43**	....	....	....	....	....	....	....	....	....
	Albany Devils	AHL	37	2	10	12	12	....	....	....	....	....	....	....	....	....	....	....	....	....	....	....	....	....	....
	NHL Totals		**7**	**0**	**1**	**1**	**4**	**0**	**0**	**0**	**2**	**0.0**		**0**	**0.0**	**8:09**	....	....	....	....	....	....	....	....	....

CCHA All-Rookie Team (2006) • CCHA First All-Star Team (2008) • NCAA West First All-American Team (2008)

Signed as a free agent by **Phoenix**, July 4, 2011.

EDLER, Alexander

(EHD-luhr, al-EHX-AN-duhr) **VAN**

Defense. Shoots left. 6'4", 215 lbs. Born, Ostersund, Sweden, April 21, 1986. Vancouver's 2nd choice, 91st overall, in 2004 Entry Draft.

2001-02	Jamtland	Exhib.	8	0	1	1	2	....	....	....	....	....	....	....	....	....	....	....	....	....	....	....	....	....	....
2002-03	Jamtland	Exhib.	8	2	1	3	0	....	....	....	....	....	....	....	....	....	....	....	....	....	....	....	....	....	....
2003-04	Jamtland Jr.	Swe-Jr.	6	0	3	3	6	....	....	....	....	....	....	....	....	....	....	....	....	....	....	....	....	....	....
	Jamtland	Sweden-3	24	3	6	9	20	....	....	....	....	....	....	....	....	....	....	....	....	....	....	....	....	....	....
2004-05	MODO Jr.	Swe-Jr.	33	8	15	23	40	....	....	....	....	....	....	....	....	....	5	1	0	1	6	....	....	....	....
2005-06	Kelowna Rockets	WHL	62	13	40	53	44	....	....	....	....	....	....	....	....	....	12	3	5	8	12	....	....	....	....
2006-07	**Vancouver**	**NHL**	**22**	**1**	**2**	**3**	**6**	**0**	**0**	**0**	**10**	**10.0**	**3**	**0**	**0.0**	**11:27**	**3**	**0**	**0**	**0**	**2**	**0**	**0**	**0**	**11:51**
	Manitoba Moose	AHL	49	5	21	26	28	....	....	....	....	....	....	....	....	....	8	0	0	0	2	....	....	....	....
2007-08	**Vancouver**	**NHL**	**75**	**8**	**12**	**20**	**42**	**4**	**0**	**0**	**124**	**6.5**	**6**	**1**	**100.0**	**21:20**	....	....	....	....	....	....	....	....	....
	Manitoba Moose	AHL	2	0	1	1	0	....	....	....	....	....	....	....	....	....	....	....	....	....	....	....	....	....	....
2008-09	**Vancouver**	**NHL**	**80**	**10**	**27**	**37**	**54**	**5**	**0**	**1**	**145**	**6.9**	**11**	**1**	**100.0**	**21:08**	**10**	**1**	**7**	**8**	**6**	**1**	**0**	**0**	**22:09**
2009-10	**Vancouver**	**NHL**	**76**	**5**	**37**	**42**	**40**	**2**	**0**	**0**	**161**	**3.1**	**0**	**2**	**0.0**	**22:39**	**12**	**2**	**4**	**6**	**10**	**1**	**0**	**0**	**23:07**
2010-11	**Vancouver**	**NHL**	**51**	**8**	**25**	**33**	**24**	**5**	**0**	**1**	**121**	**6.6**	**13**	**2**	**0.0**	**24:17**	**25**	**2**	**9**	**11**	**8**	**0**	**0**	**0**	**24:46**
	NHL Totals		**304**	**32**	**103**	**135**	**166**	**16**	**0**	**2**	**561**	**5.7**		**6**	**33.3**	**21:23**	**50**	**5**	**20**	**25**	**26**	**2**	**0**	**0**	**23:04**

Season	Club	League	Regular Season GP	G	A	Pts	PIM	PP	SH	GW	S	%	+/-	TF	F%	Min	Playoffs GP	G	A	Pts	PIM	PP	SH	GW	Min

EHRHOFF, Christian

(AIR-hawf, KRIHS-tyehn) **BUF**

Defense. Shoots left. 6'2", 203 lbs. Born, Moers, West Germany, July 6, 1982. San Jose's 2nd choice, 106th overall, in 2001 Entry Draft.

Season	Club	League	GP	G	A	Pts	PIM	PP	SH	GW	S	%	+/-	TF	F%	Min	GP	G	A	Pts	PIM	PP	SH	GW	Min
1998-99	Krefelder EV Jr.	Ger-Jr.	22	10	14	24	46	....	....	....	....	....	....	....	....	....	....	....	....	....	....	....	....	....	....
99-2000	EV Duisburg	German-3	41	3	12	15	50	....	....	....	....	....	....	....	....	....	....	....	....	....	....	....	....	....	....
	Krefeld Pinguine	Germany	9	1	0	1	6	....	....	....	....	....	....	....	....	....	3	0	0	0	0	....	....	....	....
2000-01	EV Duisburg	German-3	6	1	2	3	12	....	....	....	....	....	....	....	....	....	....	....	....	....	....	....	....	....	....
	Krefeld Pinguine	Germany	58	3	11	14	73	....	....	....	....	....	....	....	....	....	....	....	....	....	....	....	....	....	....
2001-02	Krefeld Pinguine	Germany	46	7	17	24	81	....	....	....	....	....	....	....	....	....	3	0	0	0	2	....	....	....	....
	Germany	Olympics	7	0	0	0	8	....	....	....	....	....	....	....	....	....	....	....	....	....	....	....	....	....	....
2002-03	Krefeld Pinguine	Germany	48	10	17	27	54	....	....	....	....	....	....	....	....	....	14	3	6	9	24	....	....	....	....
2003-04	**San Jose**	**NHL**	**41**	**1**	**11**	**12**	**14**	**0**	**0**	**1**	**58**	**1.7**	**4**	**0**	**0.0**	**15:23**	....	....	....	....	....	....	....	....	....
	Cleveland Barons	AHL	27	4	10	14	43	....	....	....	....	....	....	....	....	....	9	2	6	8	11	....	....	....	....
2004-05	Cleveland Barons	AHL	79	12	23	35	103	....	....	....	....	....	....	....	....	....	....	....	....	....	....	....	....	....	....
2005-06	**San Jose**	**NHL**	**64**	**5**	**18**	**23**	**32**	**2**	**0**	**2**	**124**	**4.0**	**10**	**0**	**0.0**	**17:48**	**11**	**2**	**6**	**8**	**18**	**1**	**0**	**1**	**19:47**
	Germany	Olympics	5	1	1	2	4	....	....	....	....	....	....	....	....	....	....	....	....	....	....	....	....	....	....
2006-07	**San Jose**	**NHL**	**82**	**10**	**23**	**33**	**63**	**6**	**0**	**2**	**164**	**6.1**	**8**	**1**	**0.0**	**18:34**	**11**	**0**	**2**	**2**	**6**	**0**	**0**	**0**	**17:47**
2007-08	**San Jose**	**NHL**	**77**	**1**	**21**	**22**	**72**	**1**	**0**	**1**	**97**	**1.0**	**9**	**0**	**0.0**	**21:44**	**10**	**0**	**5**	**5**	**14**	**0**	**0**	**0**	**23:04**
2008-09	**San Jose**	**NHL**	**77**	**8**	**34**	**42**	**63**	**5**	**0**	**2**	**165**	**4.8**	**−12**	**0**	**0.0**	**21:14**	**6**	**0**	**0**	**0**	**2**	**0**	**0**	**0**	**24:47**
2009-10	**Vancouver**	**NHL**	**80**	**14**	**30**	**44**	**42**	**6**	**0**	**3**	**181**	**7.7**	**36**	**0**	**0.0**	**22:47**	**12**	**3**	**4**	**7**	**8**	**1**	**0**	**0**	**24:09**
	Germany	Olympics	4	0	0	0	4	....	....	....	....	....	....	....	....	....	....	....	....	....	....	....	....	....	....
2010-11	**Vancouver**	**NHL**	**79**	**14**	**36**	**50**	**52**	**6**	**0**	**3**	**209**	**6.7**	**19**	**0**	**0.0**	**23:59**	**23**	**2**	**10**	**12**	**16**	**1**	**0**	**0**	**22:26**
	NHL Totals		**500**	**53**	**173**	**226**	**338**	**26**	**0**	**14**	**998**	**5.3**		**1**	**0.0**	**20:38**	**73**	**7**	**27**	**34**	**64**	**3**	**0**	**1**	**21:54**

Traded to **Vancouver** by **San Jose** with Brad Lukowich for Patrick White and Daniel Rahimi, August 28, 2009. Traded to **NY Islanders** by **Vancouver** for NY Islanders' 4th round choice in 2012 Entry Draft, June 28, 2011. Traded to **Buffalo** by **NY Islanders** for Buffalo's 4th round choice in 2012 Entry Draft, June 29, 2011.

EKMAN-LARSSON, Oliver

(EHK-man-LAHR-suhn, AW-lih-vuhr) **PHX**

Defense. Shoots left. 6'2", 190 lbs. Born, Karlskrona, Sweden, July 17, 1991. Phoenix's 1st choice, 6th overall, in 2009 Entry Draft.

Season	Club	League	GP	G	A	Pts	PIM	PP	SH	GW	S	%	+/-	TF	F%	Min	GP	G	A	Pts	PIM	PP	SH	GW	Min
2005-06	Tingsryds AIF Jr.	Swe-Jr.	1	0	0	0	2	....	....	....	....	....	....	....	....	....	....	....	....	....	....	....	....	....	....
2006-07	Tingsryds AIF U18	Swe-U18	23	0	3	3	28	....	....	....	....	....	....	....	....	....	....	....	....	....	....	....	....	....	....
2007-08	Tingsryds AIF U18	Swe-U18	12	2	3	5	57	....	....	....	....	....	....	....	....	....	....	....	....	....	....	....	....	....	....
	Tingsryds AIF Jr.	Swe-Jr.	7	2	4	6	16	....	....	....	....	....	....	....	....	....	....	....	....	....	....	....	....	....	....
	Tingsryds AIF	Sweden-3	27	3	5	8	10	....	....	....	....	....	....	....	....	....	....	....	....	....	....	....	....	....	....
2008-09	Leksands IF	Sweden-2	47	5	16	21	38	....	....	....	....	....	....	....	....	....	....	....	....	....	....	....	....	....	....
2009-10	Leksands IF	Sweden-2	52	11	22	33	106	....	....	....	....	....	....	....	....	....	....	....	....	....	....	....	....	....	....
2010-11	**Phoenix**	**NHL**	**48**	**1**	**10**	**11**	**24**	**0**	**0**	**0**	**50**	**2.0**	**3**	**0**	**0.0**	**15:02**	....	....	....	....	....	....	....	....	....
	San Antonio	AHL	15	3	7	10	16	....	....	....	....	....	....	....	....	....	....	....	....	....	....	....	....	....	....
	NHL Totals		**48**	**1**	**10**	**11**	**24**	**0**	**0**	**0**	**50**	**2.0**		**0**	**0.0**	**15:02**	....	....	....	....	....	....	....	....	....

ELIAS, Patrik

(ehl-EE-ahsh, PAT-rihk) **N.J.**

Center. Shoots left. 6'1", 195 lbs. Born, Trebic, Czech., April 13, 1976. New Jersey's 2nd choice, 51st overall, in 1994 Entry Draft.

Season	Club	League	GP	G	A	Pts	PIM	PP	SH	GW	S	%	+/-	TF	F%	Min	GP	G	A	Pts	PIM	PP	SH	GW	Min
1992-93	Poldi Kladno	Czech	2	0	0	0	....	....	....	....	....	....	....	....	....	....	....	....	....	....	....	....	....	....	....
1993-94	HC Kladno	CzRep	15	1	2	3	....	....	....	....	....	....	....	....	....	....	11	2	2	4	....	....	....	....	....
1994-95	HC Kladno	CzRep	28	4	3	7	37	....	....	....	....	....	....	....	....	....	7	1	2	3	12	....	....	....	....
1995-96	**New Jersey**	**NHL**	**1**	**0**	**0**	**0**	**0**	**0**	**0**	**0**	**2**	**0.0**	**−1**	....	....	....	....	....	....	....	....	....	....	....	....
	Albany River Rats	AHL	74	27	36	63	83	....	....	....	....	....	....	....	....	....	4	1	1	2	2	....	....	....	....
1996-97	**New Jersey**	**NHL**	**17**	**2**	**3**	**5**	**2**	**0**	**0**	**0**	**23**	**8.7**	**−4**	....	....	....	**8**	**2**	**3**	**5**	**4**	**1**	**0**	**0**	....
	Albany River Rats	AHL	57	24	43	67	76	....	....	....	....	....	....	....	....	....	6	1	2	3	8	....	....	....	....
1997-98	**New Jersey**	**NHL**	**74**	**18**	**19**	**37**	**28**	**5**	**0**	**6**	**147**	**12.2**	**18**	....	....	....	**4**	**0**	**1**	**1**	**0**	**0**	**0**	**0**	....
	Albany River Rats	AHL	3	3	0	3	2	....	....	....	....	....	....	....	....	....	....	....	....	....	....	....	....	....	....
1998-99	**New Jersey**	**NHL**	**74**	**17**	**33**	**50**	**34**	**3**	**0**	**2**	**157**	**10.8**	**19**	**99**	**38.4**	**15:50**	**7**	**0**	**5**	**5**	**6**	**0**	**0**	**0**	**18:07**
99-2000	Trebic	CzRep-2	2	2	1	3	2	....	....	....	....	....	....	....	....	....	....	....	....	....	....	....	....	....	....
	Pardubice	CzRep	5	1	4	5	31	....	....	....	....	....	....	....	....	....	....	....	....	....	....	....	....	....	....
	♦ **New Jersey**	**NHL**	**72**	**35**	**37**	**72**	**58**	**9**	**0**	**9**	**183**	**19.1**	**16**	**134**	**45.5**	**17:28**	**23**	**7**	***13**	**20**	**9**	**2**	**1**	**1**	**17:44**
2000-01	**New Jersey**	**NHL**	**82**	**40**	**56**	**96**	**51**	**8**	**3**	**6**	**220**	**18.2**	***45**	**155**	**41.3**	**18:44**	**25**	**9**	**14**	**23**	**10**	**3**	**1**	**2**	**18:14**
2001-02	**New Jersey**	**NHL**	**75**	**29**	**32**	**61**	**36**	**8**	**1**	**8**	**199**	**14.6**	**4**	**128**	**45.3**	**18:57**	**6**	**2**	**4**	**6**	**6**	**2**	**0**	**0**	**20:33**
	Czech Republic	Olympics	4	1	1	2	0	....	....	....	....	....	....	....	....	....	....	....	....	....	....	....	....	....	....
2002-03 ♦	**New Jersey**	**NHL**	**81**	**28**	**29**	**57**	**22**	**6**	**0**	**4**	**255**	**11.0**	**17**	**427**	**43.8**	**18:05**	**24**	**5**	**8**	**13**	**26**	**2**	**0**	**2**	**17:14**
2003-04	**New Jersey**	**NHL**	**82**	**38**	**43**	**81**	**44**	**9**	**3**	**9**	**300**	**12.7**	**26**	**49**	**36.7**	**18:46**	**5**	**3**	**2**	**5**	**2**	**1**	**0**	**1**	**18:59**
2004-05	Znojmo	CzRep	28	8	20	28	65	....	....	....	....	....	....	....	....	....	....	....	....	....	....	....	....	....	....
	Magnitogorsk	Russia	17	5	9	14	28	....	....	....	....	....	....	....	....	....	....	....	....	....	....	....	....	....	....
2005-06	**New Jersey**	**NHL**	**38**	**16**	**29**	**45**	**20**	**6**	**0**	**3**	**142**	**11.3**	**11**	**10**	**20.0**	**18:34**	**9**	**6**	**10**	**16**	**4**	**4**	**0**	**0**	**18:43**
	Czech Republic	Olympics	1	0	0	0	2	....	....	....	....	....	....	....	....	....	....	....	....	....	....	....	....	....	....
2006-07	**New Jersey**	**NHL**	**75**	**21**	**48**	**69**	**38**	**8**	**0**	**5**	**267**	**7.9**	**1**	**18**	**38.9**	**18:37**	**10**	**1**	**9**	**10**	**4**	**1**	**0**	**0**	**19:13**
2007-08	**New Jersey**	**NHL**	**74**	**20**	**35**	**55**	**38**	**7**	**0**	**8**	**263**	**7.6**	**10**	**776**	**45.6**	**18:28**	**5**	**4**	**2**	**6**	**4**	**3**	**0**	**0**	**20:30**
2008-09	**New Jersey**	**NHL**	**77**	**31**	**47**	**78**	**32**	**12**	**2**	**6**	**247**	**12.6**	**18**	**87**	**29.9**	**18:34**	**7**	**1**	**2**	**3**	**2**	**0**	**0**	**0**	**17:53**
2009-10	**New Jersey**	**NHL**	**58**	**19**	**29**	**48**	**40**	**3**	**1**	**4**	**145**	**13.1**	**18**	**457**	**44.9**	**17:37**	**5**	**0**	**4**	**4**	**2**	**0**	**0**	**0**	**18:41**
	Czech Republic	Olympics	5	2	2	4	2	....	....	....	....	....	....	....	....	....	....	....	....	....	....	....	....	....	....
2010-11	**New Jersey**	**NHL**	**81**	**21**	**41**	**62**	**16**	**7**	**1**	**5**	**204**	**10.3**	**−4**	**498**	**45.0**	**18:38**	....	....	....	....	....	....	....	....	....
	NHL Totals		**961**	**335**	**481**	**816**	**459**	**91**	**11**	**75**	**2754**	**12.2**		**2838**	**43.8**	**18:12**	**138**	**40**	**77**	**117**	**79**	**19**	**2**	**6**	**18:17**

NHL All-Rookie Team (1998) • NHL First All-Star Team (2001) • Bud Light Plus/Minus Award (2001) (tied with Joe Sakic)

Played in NHL All-Star Game (2000, 2002, 2011)

Signed as a free agent by **Znojmo** (CzRep), September 6, 2004. Signed as a free agent by **Magnitogorsk** (Russia), December 9, 2004. • Missed majority of 2005-06 due to hepatitis-A..

ELKINS, Corey

(EHL-kihns, KOH-ree) **L.A.**

Left wing. Shoots left. 6'2", 214 lbs. Born, West Bloomfield, MI, February 23, 1985.

Season	Club	League	GP	G	A	Pts	PIM	PP	SH	GW	S	%	+/-	TF	F%	Min	GP	G	A	Pts	PIM	PP	SH	GW	Min
2002-03	Det. Compuware	NAHL	49	8	11	19	37	....	....	....	....	....	....	....	....	....	....	....	....	....	....	....	....	....	....
2003-04	St. Louis	USHL	57	12	17	29	36	....	....	....	....	....	....	....	....	....	....	....	....	....	....	....	....	....	....
2004-05	Sioux City	USHL	58	19	23	42	27	....	....	....	....	....	....	....	....	....	13	4	1	5	8	....	....	....	....
2005-06	Ohio State	CCHA	9	0	0	0	0	....	....	....	....	....	....	....	....	....	....	....	....	....	....	....	....	....	....
2006-07	Ohio State	CCHA	26	7	7	14	10	....	....	....	....	....	....	....	....	....	....	....	....	....	....	....	....	....	....
2007-08	Ohio State	CCHA	25	2	3	5	12	....	....	....	....	....	....	....	....	....	....	....	....	....	....	....	....	....	....
2008-09	Ohio State	CCHA	42	18	23	41	18	....	....	....	....	....	....	....	....	....	....	....	....	....	....	....	....	....	....
2009-10	**Los Angeles**	**NHL**	**3**	**1**	**0**	**1**	**0**	**0**	**0**	**0**	**5**	**20.0**	**−2**	**18**	**33.3**	**11:54**	....	....	....	....	....	....	....	....	....
	Manchester	AHL	73	21	22	43	24	....	....	....	....	....	....	....	....	....	14	3	5	8	0	....	....	....	....
2010-11	Manchester	AHL	76	18	26	44	29	....	....	....	....	....	....	....	....	....	7	2	3	5	2	....	....	....	....
	NHL Totals		**3**	**1**	**0**	**1**	**0**	**0**	**0**	**0**	**5**	**20.0**		**18**	**33.3**	**11:54**	....	....	....	....	....	....	....	....	....

Signed as a free agent by **Los Angeles**, March 31, 2009.

ELLER, Lars

(EHL-uhr, LARZ) **MTL**

Center. Shoots left. 6'2", 198 lbs. Born, Rodovre, Denmark, May 8, 1989. St. Louis' 1st choice, 13th overall, in 2007 Entry Draft.

Season	Club	League	GP	G	A	Pts	PIM	PP	SH	GW	S	%	+/-	TF	F%	Min	GP	G	A	Pts	PIM	PP	SH	GW	Min
2004-05	Rodovre IK Jr.	Den-Jr.	28	21	26	47	20	....	....	....	....	....	....	....	....	....	....	....	....	....	....	....	....	....	....
	Rodovre	Denmark	1	3	1	4	0	....	....	....	....	....	....	....	....	....	....	....	....	....	....	....	....	....	....
2005-06	Frolunda U18	Swe-U18	8	2	4	6	10	....	....	....	....	....	....	....	....	....	2	0	0	0	0	....	....	....	....
	Frolunda Jr.	Swe-Jr.	36	7	7	14	6	....	....	....	....	....	....	....	....	....	2	0	0	0	0	....	....	....	....
2006-07	Frolunda U18	Swe-U18	3	1	4	5	6	....	....	....	....	....	....	....	....	....	6	3	2	5	8	....	....	....	....
	Frolunda Jr.	Swe-Jr.	39	18	37	55	58	....	....	....	....	....	....	....	....	....	8	4	1	5	24	....	....	....	....
2007-08	Boras HC	Sweden-2	19	2	6	8	8	....	....	....	....	....	....	....	....	....	....	....	....	....	....	....	....	....	....
	Frolunda Jr.	Swe-Jr.	9	4	4	8	10	....	....	....	....	....	....	....	....	....	7	5	6	11	14	....	....	....	....
	Frolunda	Sweden	14	0	2	2	4	....	....	....	....	....	....	....	....	....	7	0	1	1	2	....	....	....	....
2008-09	Frolunda	Sweden	48	12	17	29	28	....	....	....	....	....	....	....	....	....	10	3	1	4	12	....	....	....	....

Season	Club	League	Regular Season GP	G	A	Pts	PIM	PP	SH	GW	S	%	+/-	TF	F%	Min	Playoffs GP	G	A	Pts	PIM	PP	SH	GW	Min
2009-10	**St. Louis**	**NHL**	**7**	**2**	**0**	**2**	**4**	1	0	0	8	25.0	2	19	47.4	10:49	....	....	....	....	....	....	....	....	....
	Peoria Rivermen	AHL	70	18	39	57	84	....	....	....	....	....	....	....	....	....	....	....	....	....	....	....	....	....	....
2010-11	**Montreal**	**NHL**	**77**	**7**	**10**	**17**	**48**	0	0	2	79	8.9	–4	431	42.5	11:08	7	0	2	2	4	0	0	0	13:04
	NHL Totals		**84**	**9**	**10**	**19**	**52**	1	0	2	87	10.3		450	42.7	11:07	7	0	2	2	4	0	0	0	13:05

AHL All-Rookie Team (2010)

Traded to **Montreal** by **St. Louis** with Ian Schultz for Jaroslav Halak, June 17, 2010.

ELLERBY, Keaton

(EHL-uhr-bee, KEE-tuhn) **FLA**

Defense. Shoots left. 6'4", 186 lbs. Born, Strathmore, Alta., November 5, 1988. Florida's 1st choice, 10th overall, in 2007 Entry Draft.

Season	Club	League	GP	G	A	Pts	PIM	PP	SH	GW	S	%	+/-	TF	F%	Min	GP	G	A	Pts	PIM	PP	SH	GW	Min
2003-04	Okotoks Oilers	AMHA	30	7	32	39	69	....	....	....	....	....	....	....	....	....	....	....	....	....	....	....	....	....	....
2004-05	Kamloops Blazers	WHL	60	0	1	1	77	....	....	....	....	....	....	....	....	....	6	0	0	0	16	....	....	....	....
2005-06	Kamloops Blazers	WHL	68	2	6	8	121	....	....	....	....	....	....	....	....	....	....	....	....	....	....	....	....	....	....
2006-07	Kamloops Blazers	WHL	69	2	23	25	120	....	....	....	....	....	....	....	....	....	4	1	2	3	12	....	....	....	....
2007-08	Kamloops Blazers	WHL	16	0	3	3	29	....	....	....	....	....	....	....	....	....	....	....	....	....	....	....	....	....	....
	Moose Jaw	WHL	53	2	21	23	81	....	....	....	....	....	....	....	....	....	5	0	2	2	15	....	....	....	....
2008-09	Rochester	AHL	75	3	20	23	44	....	....	....	....	....	....	....	....	....	....	....	....	....	....	....	....	....	....
2009-10	**Florida**	**NHL**	**22**	**0**	**0**	**0**	**2**	0	0	0	5	0.0	–1	0	0.0	5:26	....	....	....	....	....	....	....	....	....
	Rochester	AHL	58	6	13	19	34	....	....	....	....	....	....	....	....	....	7	1	0	1	4	....	....	....	....
2010-11	**Florida**	**NHL**	**54**	**2**	**10**	**12**	**22**	0	0	0	56	3.6	–15	0	0.0	16:06	....	....	....	....	....	....	....	....	....
	Rochester	AHL	17	2	3	5	8	....	....	....	....	....	....	....	....	....	....	....	....	....	....	....	....	....	....
	NHL Totals		**76**	**2**	**10**	**12**	**24**	0	0	0	61	3.3		0	0.0	13:00	....	....	....	....	....	....	....	....	....

ELLIS, Matt

(EHL-ihs, MAT) **BUF**

Left wing. Shoots left. 6', 212 lbs. Born, Welland, Ont., August 31, 1981.

Season	Club	League	GP	G	A	Pts	PIM	PP	SH	GW	S	%	+/-	TF	F%	Min	GP	G	A	Pts	PIM	PP	SH	GW	Min
1998-99	St. Michael's	OHL	47	10	8	18	6	....	....	....	....	....	....	....	....	....	....	....	....	....	....	....	....	....	....
99-2000	St. Michael's	OHL	59	15	20	35	20	....	....	....	....	....	....	....	....	....	....	....	....	....	....	....	....	....	....
2000-01	St. Michael's	OHL	68	21	24	45	19	....	....	....	....	....	....	....	....	....	18	4	8	12	6	....	....	....	....
2001-02	St. Michael's	OHL	66	38	51	89	20	....	....	....	....	....	....	....	....	....	15	8	6	14	6	....	....	....	....
2002-03	Toledo Storm	ECHL	71	27	32	59	34	....	....	....	....	....	....	....	....	....	7	3	5	8	0	....	....	....	....
2003-04	Grand Rapids	AHL	64	5	10	15	23	....	....	....	....	....	....	....	....	....	4	0	0	0	2	....	....	....	....
2004-05	Grand Rapids	AHL	79	18	23	41	59	....	....	....	....	....	....	....	....	....	....	....	....	....	....	....	....	....	....
2005-06	Grand Rapids	AHL	74	20	28	48	61	....	....	....	....	....	....	....	....	....	16	4	1	5	20	....	....	....	....
2006-07	**Detroit**	**NHL**	**16**	**0**	**0**	**0**	**6**	0	0	0	22	0.0	–1	48	47.9	5:35	....	....	....	....	....	....	....	....	....
	Grand Rapids	AHL	65	26	23	49	44	....	....	....	....	....	....	....	....	....	7	4	3	7	4	....	....	....	....
2007-08	**Detroit**	**NHL**	**35**	**2**	**4**	**6**	**12**	0	0	1	28	7.1	1	87	49.4	5:23	....	....	....	....	....	....	....	....	....
	Los Angeles	**NHL**	**19**	**1**	**1**	**2**	**14**	0	1	0	38	2.6	2	27	37.0	12:41	....	....	....	....	....	....	....	....	....
2008-09	**Buffalo**	**NHL**	**45**	**7**	**5**	**12**	**12**	0	0	2	73	9.6	4	239	46.9	8:50	....	....	....	....	....	....	....	....	....
	Portland Pirates	AHL	12	2	2	4	4	....	....	....	....	....	....	....	....	....	....	....	....	....	....	....	....	....	....
2009-10	**Buffalo**	**NHL**	**72**	**3**	**10**	**13**	**12**	0	0	1	112	2.7	–1	282	50.0	9:03	3	1	0	1	0	0	0	0	9:44
2010-11	**Buffalo**	**NHL**	**14**	**0**	**0**	**0**	**0**	0	0	0	20	0.0	–4	58	48.3	10:03	1	0	0	0	0	0	0	0	11:32
	Portland Pirates	AHL	52	10	21	31	12	....	....	....	....	....	....	....	....	....	11	1	5	6	4	....	....	....	....
	NHL Totals		**201**	**13**	**20**	**33**	**56**	0	1	4	293	4.4		741	48.2	8:30	4	1	0	1	0	0	0	0	10:11

Signed as a free agent by **Detroit**, May 10, 2002. Claimed on waivers by **Los Angeles** from **Detroit**, February 21, 2008. Claimed on waivers by **Buffalo** from **Los Angeles**, October 1, 2008.

EMINGER, Steve

(EH-mihn-juhr, STEEV) **NYR**

Defense. Shoots right. 6'2", 203 lbs. Born, Woodbridge, Ont., October 31, 1983. Washington's 1st choice, 12th overall, in 2002 Entry Draft.

Season	Club	League	GP	G	A	Pts	PIM	PP	SH	GW	S	%	+/-	TF	F%	Min	GP	G	A	Pts	PIM	PP	SH	GW	Min
1998-99	Bramalea Blues	OPJHL	47	6	9	15	81	....	....	....	....	....	....	....	....	....	....	....	....	....	....	....	....	....	....
99-2000	Kitchener Rangers	OHL	50	2	14	16	74	....	....	....	....	....	....	....	....	....	5	0	0	0	0	....	....	....	....
2000-01	Kitchener Rangers	OHL	54	6	26	32	66	....	....	....	....	....	....	....	....	....	....	....	....	....	....	....	....	....	....
2001-02	Kitchener Rangers	OHL	64	19	39	58	93	....	....	....	....	....	....	....	....	....	4	0	2	2	10	....	....	....	....
2002-03	**Washington**	**NHL**	**17**	**0**	**2**	**2**	**24**	0	0	0	6	0.0	–3	0	0.0	10:08	....	....	....	....	....	....	....	....	....
	Kitchener Rangers	OHL	23	2	27	29	40	....	....	....	....	....	....	....	....	....	21	3	8	11	44	....	....	....	....
2003-04	**Washington**	**NHL**	**41**	**0**	**4**	**4**	**45**	0	0	0	12	0.0	–11	0	0.0	17:32	....	....	....	....	....	....	....	....	....
	Portland Pirates	AHL	41	0	4	4	40	....	....	....	....	....	....	....	....	....	7	0	1	1	2	....	....	....	....
2004-05	Portland Pirates	AHL	62	3	17	20	40	....	....	....	....	....	....	....	....	....	....	....	....	....	....	....	....	....	....
2005-06	**Washington**	**NHL**	**66**	**5**	**13**	**18**	**81**	1	0	0	50	10.0	–12	1	100.0	21:21	....	....	....	....	....	....	....	....	....
2006-07	**Washington**	**NHL**	**68**	**1**	**16**	**17**	**63**	0	0	0	27	3.7	–14	1	100.0	18:56	....	....	....	....	....	....	....	....	....
2007-08	**Washington**	**NHL**	**20**	**0**	**2**	**2**	**8**	0	0	0	14	0.0	–4	0	0.0	11:08	5	1	0	1	2	0	0	0	16:06
2008-09	**Philadelphia**	**NHL**	**12**	**0**	**2**	**2**	**8**	0	0	0	9	0.0	0	0	0.0	17:53	....	....	....	....	....	....	....	....	....
	Tampa Bay	**NHL**	**50**	**4**	**19**	**23**	**36**	2	0	0	63	6.3	–4	1	0.0	23:33	....	....	....	....	....	....	....	....	....
	Florida	**NHL**	**9**	**1**	**0**	**1**	**6**	0	0	1	13	7.7	1	0	0.0	15:49	....	....	....	....	....	....	....	....	....
2009-10	**Anaheim**	**NHL**	**63**	**4**	**12**	**16**	**30**	0	0	1	45	8.9	1	0	0.0	19:29	....	....	....	....	....	....	....	....	....
2010-11	**NY Rangers**	**NHL**	**65**	**2**	**4**	**6**	**22**	0	0	1	23	8.7	–5	0	0.0	15:51	....	....	....	....	....	....	....	....	....
	NHL Totals		**411**	**17**	**74**	**91**	**323**	3	0	3	262	6.5		3	66.7	18:30	5	1	0	1	2	0	0	0	16:06

OHL Second All-Star Team (2002, 2003) • Canadian Major Junior Second All-Star Team (2002) • Memorial Cup All-Star Team (2003)

Traded to **Philadelphia** by **Washington** with Washington's 3rd round choice (Jacob Deserres) in 2008 Entry Draft for Philadelphia's 1st round choice (John Carlson) in 2008 Entry Draft, June 20, 2008. Traded to **Tampa Bay** by **Philadelphia** with Steve Downie and Tampa Bay's 4th round choice (previously acquired, Tampa Bay selected Alex Hutchings) in 2009 Entry Draft for Matt Carle and San Jose's 3rd round choice (previously acquired, Philadelphia selected Simon Bertilsson) in 2009 Entry Draft, November 7, 2008. Traded to **Florida** by **Tampa Bay** for Noah Welch and Florida's 3rd round choice (later traded to Detroit – Detroit selected Andrej Nestrasil) in 2009 Entry Draft, March 4, 2009. Signed as a free agent by **Anaheim**, September 4, 2009. Traded to **NY Rangers** by **Anaheim** for Aaron Voros and Ryan Hillier, July 9, 2010.

EMMERTON, Cory

(EHM-uhr-tuhn, KOH-ree) **DET**

Center. Shoots left. 6', 190 lbs. Born, St. Thomas, Ont., June 1, 1988. Detroit's 1st choice, 41st overall, in 2006 Entry Draft.

Season	Club	League	GP	G	A	Pts	PIM	PP	SH	GW	S	%	+/-	TF	F%	Min	GP	G	A	Pts	PIM	PP	SH	GW	Min
2003-04	Elgin-Mid. Chiefs	Minor-ON	32	33	24	57	26	....	....	....	....	....	....	....	....	....	....	....	....	....	....	....	....	....	....
2004-05	Kingston	OHL	58	17	21	38	8	....	....	....	....	....	....	....	....	....	....	....	....	....	....	....	....	....	....
2005-06	Kingston	OHL	66	26	64	90	32	....	....	....	....	....	....	....	....	....	6	2	0	2	6	....	....	....	....
2006-07	Kingston	OHL	40	29	37	66	22	....	....	....	....	....	....	....	....	....	5	5	2	7	2	....	....	....	....
	Grand Rapids	AHL	....	....	....	....	....	....	....	....	....	....	....	....	....	....	2	0	0	0	0	....	....	....	....
2007-08	Kingston	OHL	24	13	18	31	6	....	....	....	....	....	....	....	....	....	....	....	....	....	....	....	....	....	....
	Brampton	OHL	30	12	18	30	10	....	....	....	....	....	....	....	....	....	5	0	2	2	2	....	....	....	....
	Grand Rapids	AHL	7	0	1	1	0	....	....	....	....	....	....	....	....	....	....	....	....	....	....	....	....	....	....
2008-09	Grand Rapids	AHL	69	10	25	35	18	....	....	....	....	....	....	....	....	....	9	1	0	1	2	....	....	....	....
2009-10	Grand Rapids	AHL	76	12	25	37	22	....	....	....	....	....	....	....	....	....	....	....	....	....	....	....	....	....	....
2010-11	**Detroit**	**NHL**	**2**	**1**	**0**	**1**	**0**	0	0	0	3	33.3	1	1	0.0	8:20	....	....	....	....	....	....	....	....	....
	Grand Rapids	AHL	65	12	26	38	26	....	....	....	....	....	....	....	....	....	....	....	....	....	....	....	....	....	....
	NHL Totals		**2**	**1**	**0**	**1**	**0**	0	0	0	3	33.3		1	0.0	8:21									

ENGELLAND, Deryk

(ehn-GUHL-uhnd, DEH-rihk) **PIT**

Defense. Shoots right. 6'2", 202 lbs. Born, Edmonton, Alta., April 5, 1982. New Jersey's 11th choice, 194th overall, in 2000 Entry Draft.

Season	Club	League	GP	G	A	Pts	PIM	PP	SH	GW	S	%	+/-	TF	F%	Min	GP	G	A	Pts	PIM	PP	SH	GW	Min
1998-99	Moose Jaw	WHL	2	0	0	0	0	....	....	....	....	....	....	....	....	....	....	....	....	....	....	....	....	....	....
99-2000	Moose Jaw	WHL	55	0	5	5	62	....	....	....	....	....	....	....	....	....	4	0	0	0	0	....	....	....	....
2000-01	Moose Jaw	WHL	65	4	11	15	157	....	....	....	....	....	....	....	....	....	4	0	0	0	10	....	....	....	....
2001-02	Moose Jaw	WHL	56	7	10	17	102	....	....	....	....	....	....	....	....	....	12	0	2	2	27	....	....	....	....
2002-03	Moose Jaw	WHL	65	3	8	11	199	....	....	....	....	....	....	....	....	....	13	1	1	2	20	....	....	....	....
2003-04	Lowell	AHL	26	0	0	0	34	....	....	....	....	....	....	....	....	....	....	....	....	....	....	....	....	....	....
	Las Vegas	ECHL	35	2	11	13	63	....	....	....	....	....	....	....	....	....	2	0	0	0	0	....	....	....	....
2004-05	Las Vegas	ECHL	72	5	16	21	138	....	....	....	....	....	....	....	....	....	....	....	....	....	....	....	....	....	....
2005-06	Hershey Bears	AHL	37	0	4	4	77	....	....	....	....	....	....	....	....	....	1	0	0	0	0	....	....	....	....
	South Carolina	ECHL	35	3	13	16	20	....	....	....	....	....	....	....	....	....	....	....	....	....	....	....	....	....	....
2006-07	Hershey Bears	AHL	44	4	6	10	95	....	....	....	....	....	....	....	....	....	14	0	0	0	14	....	....	....	....
	Reading Royals	ECHL	6	0	3	3	8	....	....	....	....	....	....	....	....	....	....	....	....	....	....	....	....	....	....
2007-08	Wilkes-Barre	AHL	80	2	15	17	141	....	....	....	....	....	....	....	....	....	23	1	3	4	14	....	....	....	....
2008-09	Wilkes-Barre	AHL	80	3	11	14	143	....	....	....	....	....	....	....	....	....	12	0	2	2	6	....	....	....	....

			Regular Season														Playoffs								
Season	Club	League	GP	G	A	Pts	PIM	PP	SH	GW	S	%	+/-	TF	F%	Min	GP	G	A	Pts	PIM	PP	SH	GW	Min
2009-10	**Pittsburgh**	**NHL**	**9**	**0**	**2**	**2**	**17**	**0**	**0**	**0**	**4**	**0.0**	**–2**	**0**	**0.0**	**16:08**	....	....	....	....	....	....	....	....	....
	Wilkes-Barre	AHL	71	5	6	11	121	....	....	....	....	....	....	....	....	....	4	0	1	1	7	....	....	....	....
2010-11	**Pittsburgh**	**NHL**	**63**	**3**	**7**	**10**	**123**	**0**	**0**	**0**	**49**	**6.1**	**–5**	**0**	**0.0**	**13:20**	....	....	....	....	....	....	....	....	....
	NHL Totals		**72**	**3**	**9**	**12**	**140**	**0**	**0**	**0**	**53**	**5.7**		**0**	**0.0**	**13:41**	....	....	....	....	....	....	....	....	....

Signed as a free agent by **Calgary**, July, 2003. Signed as a free agent by **Pittsburgh**, July 16, 2007.

ENGQVIST, Andreas

(ENG-kvihst, awn-DRAY-uhs) **MTL**

Center. Shoots right. 6'4", 199 lbs. Born, Stockholm, Sweden, December 23, 1987.

Season	Club	League	GP	G	A	Pts	PIM	PP	SH	GW	S	%	+/-	TF	F%	Min	GP	G	A	Pts	PIM	PP	SH	GW	Min
2004-05	Spanga U18	Swe-U18	6	3	6	9	6	....	....	....	....	....	....	....	....	....	....	....	....	....	....	....	....	....	....
	Spanga Jr.	Swe-Jr.	13	15	9	24	12	....	....	....	....	....	....	....	....	....	....	....	....	....	....	....	....	....	....
2005-06	Djurgarden Jr.	Swe-Jr.	26	6	13	19	6	....	....	....	....	....	....	....	....	....	4	1	1	2	2	....	....	....	....
	Djurgarden	Sweden	1	0	0	0	0	....	....	....	....	....	....	....	....	....	....	....	....	....	....	....	....	....	....
2006-07	Djurgarden Jr.	Swe-Jr.	5	1	3	4	4	....	....	....	....	....	....	....	....	....	7	3	4	7	10	....	....	....	....
	Djurgarden	Sweden	43	1	3	4	16	....	....	....	....	....	....	....	....	....	....	....	....	....	....	....	....	....	....
2007-08	Djurgarden Jr.	Swe-Jr.	1	1	0	1	0	....	....	....	....	....	....	....	....	....	....	....	....	....	....	....	....	....	....
	Djurgarden	Sweden	51	5	7	12	16	....	....	....	....	....	....	....	....	....	5	0	0	0	0	....	....	....	....
2008-09	Djurgarden	Sweden	31	9	7	16	12	....	....	....	....	....	....	....	....	....	....	....	....	....	....	....	....	....	....
2009-10	Djurgarden	Sweden	55	14	12	26	30	....	....	....	....	....	....	....	....	....	16	5	8	13	10	....	....	....	....
2010-11	**Montreal**	**NHL**	**3**	**0**	**0**	**0**	**0**	**0**	**0**	**0**	**1**	**0.0**	**0**	**19**	**36.8**	**8:46**	....	....	....	....	....	....	....	....	....
	Hamilton	AHL	71	10	15	25	18	....	....	....	....	....	....	....	....	....	20	4	5	9	0	....	....	....	....
	NHL Totals		**3**	**0**	**0**	**0**	**0**	**0**	**0**	**0**	**1**	**0.0**		**19**	**36.8**	**8:46**	....	....	....	....	....	....	....	....	....

Signed as a free agent by **Montreal**, July 13, 2009.

ENNIS, Tyler

(EH-nihs, TIGH-luhr) **BUF**

Center. Shoots left. 5'9", 157 lbs. Born, Edmonton, Alta., October 6, 1989. Buffalo's 2nd choice, 26th overall, in 2008 Entry Draft.

Season	Club	League	GP	G	A	Pts	PIM	PP	SH	GW	S	%	+/-	TF	F%	Min	GP	G	A	Pts	PIM	PP	SH	GW	Min
2004-05	K of C Pats	AMHL	36	15	17	32	10	....	....	....	....	....	....	....	....	....	....	....	....	....	....	....	....	....	....
2005-06	Medicine Hat	WHL	43	3	7	10	10	....	....	....	....	....	....	....	....	....	7	0	0	0	0	....	....	....	....
2006-07	Medicine Hat	WHL	71	26	24	50	30	....	....	....	....	....	....	....	....	....	22	8	4	12	6	....	....	....	....
2007-08	Medicine Hat	WHL	70	43	48	91	42	....	....	....	....	....	....	....	....	....	5	0	4	4	6	....	....	....	....
2008-09	Medicine Hat	WHL	61	43	42	85	21	....	....	....	....	....	....	....	....	....	11	8	11	19	10	....	....	....	....
2009-10	**Buffalo**	**NHL**	**10**	**3**	**6**	**9**	**6**	**0**	**0**	**0**	**23**	**13.0**	**1**	**31**	**41.9**	**15:20**	**6**	**1**	**3**	**4**	**0**	**0**	**0**	**0**	**17:09**
	Portland Pirates	AHL	69	23	42	65	12	....	....	....	....	....	....	....	....	....	....	....	....	....	....	....	....	....	....
2010-11	**Buffalo**	**NHL**	**82**	**20**	**29**	**49**	**30**	**5**	**0**	**1**	**210**	**9.5**	**0**	**9**	**22.2**	**15:40**	**7**	**2**	**2**	**4**	**4**	**0**	**0**	**1**	**16:38**
	NHL Totals		**92**	**23**	**35**	**58**	**36**	**5**	**0**	**1**	**233**	**9.9**		**40**	**37.5**	**15:38**	**13**	**3**	**5**	**8**	**4**	**0**	**0**	**1**	**16:52**

WHL East First All-Star Team (2008, 2009) • AHL All-Rookie Team (2010) • Dudley "Red" Garrett Memorial Award (AHL – Rookie of the Year) (2010)

ENSTROM, Tobias

(EHN-struhm, toh-BYE-uhs) **WPG**

Defense. Shoots left. 5'10", 180 lbs. Born, Nordingra, Sweden, November 5, 1984. Atlanta's 8th choice, 239th overall, in 2003 Entry Draft.

Season	Club	League	GP	G	A	Pts	PIM	PP	SH	GW	S	%	+/-	TF	F%	Min	GP	G	A	Pts	PIM	PP	SH	GW	Min
99-2000	MoDo U18	Swe-U18	3	0	0	0	0	....	....	....	....	....	....	....	....	....	....	....	....	....	....	....	....	....	....
2000-01	MoDo U18	Swe-U18	16	7	6	13	18	....	....	....	....	....	....	....	....	....	....	....	....	....	....	....	....	....	....
	MoDo Jr.	Swe-Jr.	1	0	0	0	0	....	....	....	....	....	....	....	....	....	....	....	....	....	....	....	....	....	....
2001-02	MODO Jr.	Swe-Jr.	21	1	7	8	10	....	....	....	....	....	....	....	....	....	2	1	1	2	2	....	....	....	....
2002-03	MODO Jr.	Swe-Jr.	7	4	6	10	31	....	....	....	....	....	....	....	....	....	....	....	....	....	....	....	....	....	....
	MODO	Sweden	42	1	5	6	16	....	....	....	....	....	....	....	....	....	6	0	1	1	4	....	....	....	....
2003-04	MODO	Sweden	33	1	4	5	6	....	....	....	....	....	....	....	....	....	6	1	1	2	2	....	....	....	....
2004-05	MODO	Sweden	49	4	10	14	24	....	....	....	....	....	....	....	....	....	2	0	0	0	0	....	....	....	....
2005-06	MODO	Sweden	47	4	7	11	48	....	....	....	....	....	....	....	....	....	4	0	1	1	25	....	....	....	....
2006-07	MODO	Sweden	55	7	21	28	52	....	....	....	....	....	....	....	....	....	20	1	11	12	37	....	....	....	....
2007-08	**Atlanta**	**NHL**	**82**	**5**	**33**	**38**	**42**	**4**	**0**	**0**	**105**	**4.8**	**–5**	**0**	**0.0**	**24:28**	....	....	....	....	....	....	....	....	....
2008-09	**Atlanta**	**NHL**	**82**	**5**	**27**	**32**	**52**	**2**	**1**	**1**	**86**	**5.8**	**14**	**2**	**50.0**	**23:32**	....	....	....	....	....	....	....	....	....
2009-10	**Atlanta**	**NHL**	**82**	**6**	**44**	**50**	**30**	**2**	**0**	**0**	**109**	**5.5**	**–5**	**0**	**0.0**	**22:16**	....	....	....	....	....	....	....	....	....
	Sweden	Olympics	4	0	2	2	4	....	....	....	....	....	....	....	....	....	....	....	....	....	....	....	....	....	....
2010-11	**Atlanta**	**NHL**	**72**	**10**	**41**	**51**	**54**	**6**	**0**	**0**	**113**	**8.8**	**–10**	**0**	**0.0**	**23:41**	....	....	....	....	....	....	....	....	....
	NHL Totals		**318**	**26**	**145**	**171**	**178**	**14**	**1**	**1**	**413**	**6.3**		**2**	**50.0**	**23:29**	....	....	....	....	....	....	....	....	....

NHL All-Rookie Team (2008)

• Transferred to **Winnipeg** after **Atlanta** franchise relocated, June 21, 2011.

ERAT, Martin

(EE-rat, MAHR-tihn) **NSH**

Right wing. Shoots left. 6', 200 lbs. Born, Trebic, Czech., August 29, 1981. Nashville's 12th choice, 191st overall, in 1999 Entry Draft.

Season	Club	League	GP	G	A	Pts	PIM	PP	SH	GW	S	%	+/-	TF	F%	Min	GP	G	A	Pts	PIM	PP	SH	GW	Min
1997-98	HC ZPS Zlin Jr.	CzRep-Jr.	46	35	30	65	....	....	....	....	....	....	....	....	....	....	....	....	....	....	....	....	....	....	....
1998-99	HC ZPS Zlin Jr.	CzRep-Jr.	35	21	23	44	....	....	....	....	....	....	....	....	....	....	....	....	....	....	....	....	....	....	....
	Zlin	CzRep	5	0	0	0	2	....	....	....	....	....	....	....	....	....	....	....	....	....	....	....	....	....	....
99-2000	Saskatoon Blades	WHL	66	27	26	53	82	....	....	....	....	....	....	....	....	....	11	4	8	12	16	....	....	....	....
2000-01	Saskatoon Blades	WHL	31	19	35	54	48	....	....	....	....	....	....	....	....	....	....	....	....	....	....	....	....	....	....
	Red Deer Rebels	WHL	17	4	24	28	24	....	....	....	....	....	....	....	....	....	22	*15	*21	*36	32	....	....	....	....
2001-02	**Nashville**	**NHL**	**80**	**9**	**24**	**33**	**32**	**2**	**0**	**2**	**84**	**10.7**	**–11**	**3**	**66.7**	**13:10**	....	....	....	....	....	....	....	....	....
2002-03	**Nashville**	**NHL**	**27**	**1**	**7**	**8**	**14**	**1**	**0**	**0**	**39**	**2.6**	**–9**	**1**	**0.0**	**12:47**	....	....	....	....	....	....	....	....	....
	Milwaukee	AHL	45	10	22	32	41	....	....	....	....	....	....	....	....	....	6	5	4	9	4	....	....	....	....
2003-04	**Nashville**	**NHL**	**76**	**16**	**33**	**49**	**38**	**4**	**0**	**2**	**137**	**11.7**	**10**	**31**	**29.0**	**15:00**	**6**	**0**	**1**	**1**	**6**	**0**	**0**	**0**	**14:09**
2004-05	HC Hame Zlin	CzRep	48	20	23	43	129	....	....	....	....	....	....	....	....	....	16	*7	5	12	12	....	....	....	....
2005-06	**Nashville**	**NHL**	**80**	**20**	**29**	**49**	**76**	**5**	**0**	**1**	**143**	**14.0**	**0**	**25**	**16.0**	**14:45**	**5**	**1**	**1**	**2**	**6**	**1**	**0**	**0**	**19:31**
	Czech Republic	Olympics	8	1	1	2	4	....	....	....	....	....	....	....	....	....	....	....	....	....	....	....	....	....	....
2006-07	**Nashville**	**NHL**	**68**	**16**	**41**	**57**	**50**	**5**	**1**	**3**	**132**	**12.1**	**13**	**43**	**44.2**	**18:59**	**3**	**0**	**1**	**1**	**0**	**0**	**0**	**0**	**14:13**
2007-08	**Nashville**	**NHL**	**76**	**23**	**34**	**57**	**40**	**4**	**0**	**6**	**163**	**14.1**	**–3**	**41**	**36.6**	**18:39**	**6**	**1**	**3**	**4**	**8**	**0**	**0**	**0**	**20:56**
2008-09	**Nashville**	**NHL**	**71**	**17**	**33**	**50**	**48**	**3**	**0**	**3**	**149**	**11.4**	**–7**	**38**	**29.0**	**18:34**	....	....	....	....	....	....	....	....	....
2009-10	**Nashville**	**NHL**	**74**	**21**	**28**	**49**	**50**	**5**	**0**	**2**	**168**	**12.5**	**–7**	**73**	**32.9**	**17:59**	**6**	**4**	**1**	**5**	**4**	**0**	**0**	**0**	**18:56**
	Czech Republic	Olympics	5	0	1	1	2	....	....	....	....	....	....	....	....	....	....	....	....	....	....	....	....	....	....
2010-11	**Nashville**	**NHL**	**64**	**17**	**33**	**50**	**22**	**7**	**0**	**3**	**135**	**12.6**	**14**	**44**	**43.2**	**18:06**	**10**	**1**	**5**	**6**	**6**	**1**	**0**	**0**	**19:15**
	NHL Totals		**616**	**140**	**262**	**402**	**370**	**36**	**1**	**22**	**1150**	**12.2**		**299**	**34.4**	**16:37**	**36**	**7**	**12**	**19**	**30**	**2**	**0**	**0**	**18:15**

Signed as a free agent by **Zlin** (CzRep), September 5, 2004.

ERICSSON, Jonathan

(AIR-ihk-suhn, JAWN-ah-thuhn) **DET**

Defense. Shoots left. 6'4", 220 lbs. Born, Karlskrona, Sweden, March 2, 1984. Detroit's 10th choice, 291st overall, in 2002 Entry Draft.

Season	Club	League	GP	G	A	Pts	PIM	PP	SH	GW	S	%	+/-	TF	F%	Min	GP	G	A	Pts	PIM	PP	SH	GW	Min
2001-02	Hasten Jr.	Swe-Jr.	STATISTICS NOT AVAILABLE																						
2002-03	Vita Hasten	Sweden-3	40	2	4	6	36	....	....	....	....	....	....	....	....	....	....	....	....	....	....	....	....	....	....
2003-04	Sodertalje SK	Sweden	42	1	0	1	12	....	....	....	....	....	....	....	....	....	....	....	....	....	....	....	....	....	....
2004-05	Sodertalje SK	Sweden	15	0	0	0	4	....	....	....	....	....	....	....	....	....	1	0	0	0	0	....	....	....	....
2005-06	Sodertalje SK Jr.	Swe-Jr.	1	0	0	0	2	....	....	....	....	....	....	....	....	....	....	....	....	....	....	....	....	....	....
	Almtuna	Sweden-2	19	2	3	5	44	....	....	....	....	....	....	....	....	....	....	....	....	....	....	....	....	....	....
	Sodertalje SK	Sweden	24	0	0	0	20	....	....	....	....	....	....	....	....	....	....	....	....	....	....	....	....	....	....
	Sodertalje SK	Sweden-Q	7	0	1	1	4	....	....	....	....	....	....	....	....	....	....	....	....	....	....	....	....	....	....
2006-07	Grand Rapids	AHL	67	5	24	29	102	....	....	....	....	....	....	....	....	....	7	0	0	0	8	....	....	....	....
2007-08	**Detroit**	**NHL**	**8**	**1**	**0**	**1**	**4**	**1**	**0**	**0**	**19**	**5.3**	**–3**	**0**	**0.0**	**15:58**	....	....	....	....	....	....	....	....	....
	Grand Rapids	AHL	69	10	24	34	83	....	....	....	....	....	....	....	....	....	....	....	....	....	....	....	....	....	....
2008-09	**Detroit**	**NHL**	**19**	**1**	**3**	**4**	**15**	**0**	**0**	**0**	**25**	**4.0**	**–1**	**0**	**0.0**	**17:40**	**22**	**4**	**4**	**8**	**25**	**0**	**0**	**1**	**18:44**
	Grand Rapids	AHL	40	2	13	15	48	....	....	....	....	....	....	....	....	....	....	....	....	....	....	....	....	....	....
2009-10	**Detroit**	**NHL**	**62**	**4**	**9**	**13**	**44**	**0**	**1**	**1**	**55**	**7.3**	**–15**	**0**	**0.0**	**16:42**	**12**	**0**	**2**	**2**	**8**	**0**	**0**	**0**	**14:17**
2010-11	**Detroit**	**NHL**	**74**	**3**	**12**	**15**	**87**	**1**	**0**	**0**	**89**	**3.4**	**8**	**0**	**0.0**	**18:50**	**11**	**1**	**2**	**3**	**4**	**0**	**0**	**0**	**18:47**
	NHL Totals		**163**	**9**	**24**	**33**	**150**	**2**	**1**	**1**	**188**	**4.8**		**0**	**0.0**	**17:45**	**45**	**5**	**8**	**13**	**37**	**0**	**0**	**1**	**17:34**

Season	Club	League	GP	G	A	Pts	PIM	PP	SH	GW	S	%	+/-	TF	F%	Min	GP	G	A	Pts	PIM	PP	SH	GW	Min
			Regular Season														Playoffs								

ERIKSSON, Anders

(AIR-ihk-suhn, AND-uhrs)

Defense. Shoots left. 6'3", 224 lbs. Born, Bollnas, Sweden, January 9, 1975. Detroit's 1st choice, 22nd overall, in 1993 Entry Draft.

Season	Club	League	GP	G	A	Pts	PIM	PP	SH	GW	S	%	+/-	TF	F%	Min	GP	G	A	Pts	PIM	PP	SH	GW	Min
1992-93	MoDo Jr.	Swe-Jr.	10	5	3	8	14	....	....	....	....	....	....	....	....	....	....	....	....	....	....	....	....	....	....
	MoDo	Sweden	20	0	2	2	2	....	....	....	....	....	....	....	....	....	1	0	0	0	0	....	....	....	....
1993-94	MoDo	Sweden	38	2	8	10	42	....	....	....	....	....	....	....	....	....	11	0	0	0	8	....	....	....	....
	MoDo Jr.	Swe-Jr.	3	1	2	3	34	....	....	....	....	....	....	....	....	....	....	....	....	....	....	....	....	....	....
1994-95	MoDo	Sweden	39	3	6	9	54	....	....	....	....	....	....	....	....	....	....	....	....	....	....	....	....	....	....
1995-96	**Detroit**	**NHL**	**1**	**0**	**0**	**0**	**2**	**0**	**0**	**0**	**0**	**0.0**	**1**	....	....	....	**3**	**0**	**0**	**0**	**0**	**0**	**0**	**0**	....
	Adirondack	AHL	75	6	36	42	64	....	....	....	....	....	....	....	....	....	3	0	0	0	0	....	....	....	....
1996-97	**Detroit**	**NHL**	**23**	**0**	**6**	**6**	**10**	**0**	**0**	**0**	**27**	**0.0**	**5**	....	....	....	....	....	....	....	....	....	....	....	....
	Adirondack	AHL	44	3	25	28	36	....	....	....	....	....	....	....	....	....	4	0	1	1	4	....	....	....	....
1997-98♦	**Detroit**	**NHL**	**66**	**7**	**14**	**21**	**32**	**1**	**0**	**2**	**91**	**7.7**	**21**	....	....	....	**18**	**0**	**5**	**5**	**16**	**0**	**0**	**0**	....
1998-99	**Detroit**	**NHL**	**61**	**2**	**10**	**12**	**34**	**0**	**0**	**1**	**67**	**3.0**	**5**	**0**	**0.0**	**15:54**	....	....	....	....	....	....	....	....	....
	Chicago	**NHL**	**11**	**0**	**8**	**8**	**0**	**0**	**0**	**0**	**12**	**0.0**	**6**	**0**	**0.0**	**22:51**	....	....	....	....	....	....	....	....	....
99-2000	**Chicago**	**NHL**	**73**	**3**	**25**	**28**	**20**	**0**	**0**	**1**	**86**	**3.5**	**4**	**1**	**100.0**	**21:03**	....	....	....	....	....	....	....	....	....
2000-01	**Chicago**	**NHL**	**13**	**2**	**3**	**5**	**2**	**1**	**0**	**0**	**19**	**10.5**	**-4**	**0**	**0.0**	**21:20**	....	....	....	....	....	....	....	....	....
	Florida	**NHL**	**60**	**0**	**21**	**21**	**28**	**0**	**0**	**0**	**80**	**0.0**	**2**	**1**	**0.0**	**21:02**	....	....	....	....	....	....	....	....	....
2001-02	**Toronto**	**NHL**	**34**	**0**	**2**	**2**	**12**	**0**	**0**	**0**	**31**	**0.0**	**-1**	**0**	**0.0**	**15:55**	**10**	**0**	**0**	**0**	**0**	**0**	**0**	**0**	**17:24**
	St. John's	AHL	25	4	6	10	14	....	....	....	....	....	....	....	....	....	11	0	5	5	6	....	....	....	....
2002-03	**Toronto**	**NHL**	**4**	**0**	**0**	**0**	**0**	**0**	**0**	**0**	**7**	**0.0**	**1**	**0**	**0.0**	**19:02**	....	....	....	....	....	....	....	....	....
	St. John's	AHL	72	5	34	39	133	....	....	....	....	....	....	....	....	....	....	....	....	....	....	....	....	....	....
2003-04	**Columbus**	**NHL**	**66**	**7**	**20**	**27**	**18**	**2**	**0**	**1**	**84**	**8.3**	**-6**	**0**	**0.0**	**20:42**	....	....	....	....	....	....	....	....	....
	Syracuse Crunch	AHL	9	1	3	4	12	....	....	....	....	....	....	....	....	....	....	....	....	....	....	....	....	....	....
2004-05	HV 71 Jonkoping	Sweden	32	1	9	10	54	....	....	....	....	....	....	....	....	....	....	....	....	....	....	....	....	....	....
2005-06	Magnitogorsk	Russia	17	2	7	9	10	....	....	....	....	....	....	....	....	....	11	3	2	5	16	....	....	....	....
	Springfield	AHL	12	1	8	9	10	....	....	....	....	....	....	....	....	....	....	....	....	....	....	....	....	....	....
2006-07	**Columbus**	**NHL**	**79**	**0**	**23**	**23**	**46**	**0**	**0**	**0**	**78**	**0.0**	**12**	**1**	**100.0**	**20:12**	....	....	....	....	....	....	....	....	....
2007-08	**Calgary**	**NHL**	**61**	**1**	**17**	**18**	**36**	**1**	**0**	**0**	**50**	**2.0**	**-5**	**0**	**0.0**	**20:47**	**3**	**0**	**1**	**1**	**2**	**0**	**0**	**0**	**18:16**
2008-09	Quad City Flames	AHL	64	4	45	49	60	....	....	....	....	....	....	....	....	....	....	....	....	....	....	....	....	....	....
	Calgary	**NHL**	....	....	....	....	....	....	....	....	....	....	....	....	....	....	**2**	**0**	**0**	**0**	**0**	**0**	**0**	**0**	**18:42**
2009-10	San Antonio	AHL	10	1	3	4	2	....	....	....	....	....	....	....	....	....	....	....	....	....	....	....	....	....	....
	Phoenix	**NHL**	**12**	**0**	**3**	**3**	**2**	**0**	**0**	**0**	**4**	**0.0**	**0**	**0**	**0.0**	**15:45**	....	....	....	....	....	....	....	....	....
	NY Rangers	**NHL**	**8**	**0**	**2**	**2**	**0**	**0**	**0**	**0**	**2**	**0.0**	**2**	**0**	**0.0**	**14:30**	....	....	....	....	....	....	....	....	....
	Hartford	AHL	8	0	3	3	4	....	....	....	....	....	....	....	....	....	....	....	....	....	....	....	....	....	....
2010-11	Timra IK	Sweden	6	0	1	1	6	....	....	....	....	....	....	....	....	....	....	....	....	....	....	....	....	....	....
	MODO	Sweden	25	2	10	12	46	....	....	....	....	....	....	....	....	....	....	....	....	....	....	....	....	....	....
	MODO	Sweden-Q	10	0	3	3	12	....	....	....	....	....	....	....	....	....	....	....	....	....	....	....	....	....	....
	NHL Totals		**572**	**22**	**154**	**176**	**242**	**5**	**0**	**5**	**638**	**3.4**		**3**	**66.7**	**19:36**	**36**	**0**	**6**	**6**	**18**	**0**	**0**	**0**	**17:45**

Traded to **Chicago** by **Detroit** with Detroit's 1st round choices in 1999 (Steve McCarthy) and 2001 (Adam Munro) Entry Drafts for Chris Chelios, March 23, 1999. Traded to **Florida** by **Chicago** for Jaroslav Spacek, November 6, 2000. Signed as a free agent by **Toronto**, July 4, 2001. Signed as a free agent by **Columbus**, October 10, 2003. Signed as a free agent by **Calgary**, September 16, 2004. Signed as a free agent by **Jonkoping** (Sweden), October 29, 2004. Signed as a fee agent by **Columbus**, July 1, 2006. Signed as a free agent by **Calgary**, July 5, 2007. Signed as a free agent by **San Antonio** (AHL), December 4, 2009. Signed as a free agent by **Phoenix**, December 21, 2009. Traded to **NY Rangers** by **Phoenix** for Miika Wiikman and NY Rangers' 7th round choice (Zac Larraza) in 2011 Entry Draft, March 3, 2010. Signed as a free agent by **Timra** (Sweden), November 25, 2010. Signed as a free agent by **MODO** (Sweden), December 19, 2010.

ERIKSSON, Loui

(AIR-ihk-suhn, LOO-ee) **DAL**

Left wing. Shoots left. 6'3", 193 lbs. Born, Goteborg, Sweden, July 17, 1985. Dallas' 1st choice, 33rd overall, in 2003 Entry Draft.

Season	Club	League	GP	G	A	Pts	PIM	PP	SH	GW	S	%	+/-	TF	F%	Min	GP	G	A	Pts	PIM	PP	SH	GW	Min
2000-01	V.Frolunda U18	Swe-U18	9	5	3	8	4	....	....	....	....	....	....	....	....	....	....	....	....	....	....	....	....	....	....
	V.Frolunda Jr.	Swe-Jr.	1	0	0	0	0	....	....	....	....	....	....	....	....	....	....	....	....	....	....	....	....	....	....
2001-02	V.Frolunda U18	Swe-U18	1	1	0	1	0	....	....	....	....	....	....	....	....	....	....	....	....	....	....	....	....	....	....
	V.Frolunda Jr.	Swe-Jr.	35	7	15	22	2	....	....	....	....	....	....	....	....	....	8	2	3	5	2	....	....	....	....
2002-03	V.Frolunda Jr.	Swe-Jr.	30	16	15	31	10	....	....	....	....	....	....	....	....	....	8	4	6	10	4	....	....	....	....
2003-04	V.Frolunda	Sweden	46	8	5	13	4	....	....	....	....	....	....	....	....	....	10	1	5	6	0	....	....	....	....
2004-05	Frolunda	Sweden	39	5	9	14	4	....	....	....	....	....	....	....	....	....	12	0	0	0	0	....	....	....	....
2005-06	Iowa Stars	AHL	78	31	29	60	27	....	....	....	....	....	....	....	....	....	7	2	5	7	0	....	....	....	....
2006-07	**Dallas**	**NHL**	**59**	**6**	**13**	**19**	**18**	**2**	**0**	**0**	**78**	**7.7**	**-3**	**9**	**44.4**	**13:11**	**4**	**0**	**1**	**1**	**0**	**0**	**0**	**0**	**15:47**
	Iowa Stars	AHL	15	5	3	8	13	....	....	....	....	....	....	....	....	....	9	2	5	7	0	....	....	....	....
2007-08	**Dallas**	**NHL**	**69**	**14**	**17**	**31**	**28**	**4**	**0**	**0**	**120**	**11.7**	**5**	**13**	**15.4**	**14:02**	**18**	**4**	**4**	**8**	**8**	**1**	**0**	**0**	**18:12**
	Iowa Stars	AHL	2	1	2	3	2	....	....	....	....	....	....	....	....	....	....	....	....	....	....	....	....	....	....
2008-09	**Dallas**	**NHL**	**82**	**36**	**27**	**63**	**14**	**7**	**1**	**4**	**178**	**20.2**	**14**	**11**	**18.2**	**19:50**	....	....	....	....	....	....	....	....	....
2009-10	**Dallas**	**NHL**	**82**	**29**	**42**	**71**	**26**	**6**	**2**	**4**	**214**	**13.6**	**-4**	**11**	**36.4**	**19:46**	....	....	....	....	....	....	....	....	....
	Sweden	Olympics	4	3	1	4	0	....	....	....	....	....	....	....	....	....	....	....	....	....	....	....	....	....	....
2010-11	**Dallas**	**NHL**	**79**	**27**	**46**	**73**	**8**	**10**	**1**	**6**	**179**	**15.1**	**10**	**4**	**25.0**	**20:34**	....	....	....	....	....	....	....	....	....
	NHL Totals		**371**	**112**	**145**	**257**	**94**	**29**	**4**	**14**	**769**	**14.6**		**48**	**27.1**	**17:50**	**22**	**4**	**5**	**9**	**8**	**1**	**0**	**0**	**17:46**

Played in NHL All-Star Game (2011)

ERSKINE, John

(UHR-skihn, JAWN) **WSH**

Defense. Shoots left. 6'4", 220 lbs. Born, Kingston, Ont., June 26, 1980. Dallas' 1st choice, 39th overall, in 1998 Entry Draft.

Season	Club	League	GP	G	A	Pts	PIM	PP	SH	GW	S	%	+/-	TF	F%	Min	GP	G	A	Pts	PIM	PP	SH	GW	Min
1996-97	Quinte Hawks	ON-Jr.A	48	4	16	20	241	....	....	....	....	....	....	....	....	....	....	....	....	....	....	....	....	....	....
1997-98	London Knights	OHL	55	0	9	9	205	....	....	....	....	....	....	....	....	....	16	0	5	5	25	....	....	....	....
1998-99	London Knights	OHL	57	8	12	20	208	....	....	....	....	....	....	....	....	....	25	5	10	15	38	....	....	....	....
99-2000	London Knights	OHL	58	12	31	43	177	....	....	....	....	....	....	....	....	....	....	....	....	....	....	....	....	....	....
2000-01	Utah Grizzlies	IHL	77	1	8	9	284	....	....	....	....	....	....	....	....	....	....	....	....	....	....	....	....	....	....
2001-02	**Dallas**	**NHL**	**33**	**0**	**1**	**1**	**62**	**0**	**0**	**0**	**16**	**0.0**	**-8**	**0**	**0.0**	**10:44**	....	....	....	....	....	....	....	....	....
	Utah Grizzlies	AHL	39	2	6	8	118	....	....	....	....	....	....	....	....	....	3	0	0	0	10	....	....	....	....
2002-03	**Dallas**	**NHL**	**16**	**2**	**0**	**2**	**29**	**0**	**0**	**0**	**12**	**16.7**	**1**	**0**	**0.0**	**10:45**	....	....	....	....	....	....	....	....	....
	Utah Grizzlies	AHL	52	2	8	10	274	....	....	....	....	....	....	....	....	....	1	0	1	1	15	....	....	....	....
2003-04	**Dallas**	**NHL**	**32**	**0**	**1**	**1**	**84**	**0**	**0**	**0**	**23**	**0.0**	**-9**	**0**	**0.0**	**12:36**	....	....	....	....	....	....	....	....	....
	Utah Grizzlies	AHL	5	0	0	0	18	....	....	....	....	....	....	....	....	....	....	....	....	....	....	....	....	....	....
2004-05	Houston Aeros	AHL	61	3	7	10	238	....	....	....	....	....	....	....	....	....	5	0	1	1	20	....	....	....	....
2005-06	**Dallas**	**NHL**	**26**	**0**	**0**	**0**	**62**	**0**	**0**	**0**	**9**	**0.0**	**-3**	**0**	**0.0**	**11:00**	....	....	....	....	....	....	....	....	....
	NY Islanders	**NHL**	**34**	**1**	**0**	**1**	**99**	**0**	**0**	**0**	**23**	**4.3**	**-12**	**0**	**0.0**	**14:37**	....	....	....	....	....	....	....	....	....
2006-07	**Washington**	**NHL**	**29**	**1**	**6**	**7**	**69**	**0**	**0**	**0**	**14**	**7.1**	**-13**	**0**	**0.0**	**18:03**	....	....	....	....	....	....	....	....	....
	Hershey Bears	AHL	4	0	2	2	9	....	....	....	....	....	....	....	....	....	....	....	....	....	....	....	....	....	....
2007-08	**Washington**	**NHL**	**51**	**2**	**7**	**9**	**96**	**0**	**0**	**1**	**48**	**4.2**	**1**	**0**	**0.0**	**15:43**	**7**	**0**	**2**	**2**	**6**	**0**	**0**	**0**	**17:07**
2008-09	**Washington**	**NHL**	**52**	**0**	**4**	**4**	**63**	**0**	**0**	**0**	**50**	**0.0**	**1**	**0**	**0.0**	**16:48**	**12**	**0**	**1**	**1**	**16**	**0**	**0**	**0**	**19:06**
2009-10	**Washington**	**NHL**	**50**	**1**	**5**	**6**	**66**	**0**	**0**	**0**	**50**	**2.0**	**16**	**0**	**0.0**	**15:59**	....	....	....	....	....	....	....	....	....
2010-11	**Washington**	**NHL**	**73**	**4**	**7**	**11**	**94**	**0**	**0**	**1**	**58**	**6.9**	**1**	**0**	**0.0**	**14:50**	**9**	**1**	**1**	**2**	**6**	**0**	**0**	**0**	**13:26**
	NHL Totals		**396**	**11**	**31**	**42**	**724**	**0**	**0**	**2**	**303**	**3.6**		**0**	**0.0**	**14:38**	**28**	**1**	**4**	**5**	**28**	**0**	**0**	**0**	**16:47**

OHL First All-Star Team (2000)

• Missed majority of 2003-04 due to ankle (December 27, 2003 vs. Columbus) and hernia (January 24, 2004 vs. St. Louis) injuries. Traded to **NY Islanders** by **Dallas** with Dallas' 2nd round choice (Jesse Joensuu) in 2006 Entry Draft for Janne Niinimaa and NY Islanders' 5th round choice (Ondrej Roman) in 2007 Entry Draft, January 10, 2005. Signed as a free agent by **Washington**, September 14, 2006. • Missed majority of 2006-07 due to foot (December 16, 2006 vs. Philadelphia) and thumb (March 9, 2007 vs. Carolina) injuries.

EVANS, Brennan

(EH-vans, BREH-nuhn) **ST.L.**

Defense. Shoots left. 6'3", 230 lbs. Born, North Battleford, Sask., January 6, 1982.

Season	Club	League	GP	G	A	Pts	PIM	PP	SH	GW	S	%	+/-	TF	F%	Min	GP	G	A	Pts	PIM	PP	SH	GW	Min
1998-99	Camrose Kodiaks	AJHL	47	1	6	7	98	....	....	....	....	....	....	....	....	....	5	0	2	2	0	....	....	....	....
	Seattle	WHL	....	....	....	....	....	....	....	....	....	....	....	....	....	....	1	0	0	0	0	....	....	....	....
99-2000	Seattle	WHL	52	1	2	3	40	....	....	....	....	....	....	....	....	....	1	0	0	0	0	....	....	....	....
2000-01	Seattle	WHL	11	1	0	1	25	....	....	....	....	....	....	....	....	....	....	....	....	....	....	....	....	....	....
	Kootenay Ice	WHL	55	2	7	9	105	....	....	....	....	....	....	....	....	....	11	0	0	0	25	....	....	....	....
2001-02	Kootenay Ice	WHL	72	2	3	5	121	....	....	....	....	....	....	....	....	....	22	0	6	6	38	....	....	....	....
2002-03	Kootenay Ice	WHL	67	6	17	23	182	....	....	....	....	....	....	....	....	....	11	1	1	2	24	....	....	....	....
2003-04	Lowell	AHL	64	1	9	10	65	....	....	....	....	....	....	....	....	....	....	....	....	....	....	....	....	....	....
	Calgary	**NHL**	....	....	....	....	....	....	....	....	....	....	....	....	....	....	**2**	**0**	**0**	**0**	**0**	**0**	**0**	**0**	**2:52**
2004-05	Lowell	AHL	51	0	7	7	79	....	....	....	....	....	....	....	....	....	5	0	0	0	2	....	....	....	....
2005-06	Binghamton	AHL	70	3	6	9	198	....	....	....	....	....	....	....	....	....	....	....	....	....	....	....	....	....	....
2006-07	Worcester Sharks	AHL	75	2	14	16	170	....	....	....	....	....	....	....	....	....	5	0	1	1	21	....	....	....	....

			Regular Season														Playoffs								
Season	Club	League	GP	G	A	Pts	PIM	PP	SH	GW	S	%	+/-	TF	F%	Min	GP	G	A	Pts	PIM	PP	SH	GW	Min
2007-08	Worcester Sharks	AHL	80	1	13	14	211	....	....	....	....	....	....	....	....	....	....	....	....	....	....	....	....	....	....
2008-09	Iowa Chops	AHL	75	1	14	15	189	....	....	....	....	....	....	....	....	....	....	....	....	....	....	....	....	....	....
2009-10	Toronto Marlies	AHL	79	1	7	8	199	....	....	....	....	....	....	....	....	....	....	....	....	....	....	....	....	....	....
2010-11	Peoria Rivermen	AHL	66	3	11	14	113	....	....	....	....	....	....	....	....	....	4	0	0	0	6	....	....	....	....
	NHL Totals		....	....	....	....	....	....	....	....	....	....	....	....	....	....	**2**	**0**	**0**	**0**	**0**	**0**	**0**	**0**	**2:52**

Signed as a free agent by **Calgary**, September 30, 2003. Signed as a free agent by **San Jose**, July 18, 2007. Signed as a free agent by **Anaheim**, July 11, 2008. • Assigned to **Toronto** (AHL) by **Anaheim**, October 2, 2009. Signed as a free agent by **St. Louis**, July 12, 2010.

EXELBY, Garnet (EHX-uhl-bee, GAHR-neht) DET

Defense. Shoots left. 6'1", 215 lbs. Born, Ste. Anne, Man., August 16, 1981. Atlanta's 9th choice, 217th overall, in 1999 Entry Draft.

1997-98	Wpg. South Blues	MJHL	46	5	11	16	110	....	....	....	....	....	....	....	....	....	....	....	....	....	....	....	....	....	....
1998-99	Saskatoon Blades	WHL	61	5	3	8	91	....	....	....	....	....	....	....	....	....	....	....	....	....	....	....	....	....	....
99-2000	Saskatoon Blades	WHL	63	1	8	9	79	....	....	....	....	....	....	....	....	....	11	0	2	2	21	....	....	....	....
2000-01	Saskatoon Blades	WHL	43	5	10	15	110	....	....	....	....	....	....	....	....	....	....	....	....	....	....	....	....	....	....
	Regina Pats	WHL	22	2	8	10	51	....	....	....	....	....	....	....	....	....	6	0	2	2	2	....	....	....	....
2001-02	Chicago Wolves	AHL	75	3	4	7	257	....	....	....	....	....	....	....	....	....	25	0	4	4	49	....	....	....	....
2002-03	**Atlanta**	**NHL**	**15**	**0**	**2**	**2**	**41**	**0**	**0**	**0**	**9**	**0.0**	**0**	**0**	**0.0**	**18:04**	....	....	....	....	....	....	....	....	....
	Chicago Wolves	AHL	53	3	6	9	140	....	....	....	....	....	....	....	....	....	9	0	1	1	27	....	....	....	....
2003-04	**Atlanta**	**NHL**	**71**	**1**	**9**	**10**	**134**	**0**	**0**	**0**	**42**	**2.4**	**–10**	**0**	**0.0**	**19:32**	....	....	....	....	....	....	....	....	....
2004-05			DID NOT PLAY																						
2005-06	**Atlanta**	**NHL**	**75**	**1**	**9**	**10**	**75**	**0**	**0**	**0**	**44**	**2.3**	**11**	**0**	**0.0**	**15:41**	....	....	....	....	....	....	....	....	....
2006-07	**Atlanta**	**NHL**	**58**	**2**	**8**	**10**	**56**	**0**	**1**	**0**	**57**	**3.5**	**2**	**0**	**0.0**	**18:00**	**4**	**0**	**0**	**0**	**6**	**0**	**0**	**0**	**15:38**
2007-08	**Atlanta**	**NHL**	**79**	**2**	**5**	**7**	**85**	**0**	**0**	**0**	**37**	**5.4**	**–21**	**0**	**0.0**	**18:53**	....	....	....	....	....	....	....	....	....
2008-09	**Atlanta**	**NHL**	**59**	**0**	**7**	**7**	**120**	**0**	**0**	**0**	**42**	**0.0**	**–2**	**0**	**0.0**	**16:43**	....	....	....	....	....	....	....	....	....
2009-10	**Toronto**	**NHL**	**51**	**1**	**3**	**4**	**73**	**0**	**0**	**0**	**14**	**7.1**	**–8**	**0**	**0.0**	**10:06**	....	....	....	....	....	....	....	....	....
2010-11	Rockford IceHogs	AHL	77	3	10	13	128	....	....	....	....	....	....	....	....	....	....	....	....	....	....	....	....	....	....
	NHL Totals		**408**	**7**	**43**	**50**	**584**	**0**	**1**	**0**	**245**	**2.9**		**0**	**0.0**	**16:51**	**4**	**0**	**0**	**0**	**6**	**0**	**0**	**0**	**15:38**

Traded to **Toronto** by **Atlanta** with Colin Stuart for Pavel Kubina and Tim Stapleton, July 1, 2009. Signed to a PTO (professional tryout) contract by **Rockford** (AHL), October 9, 2010. Signed as a free agent by **Chicago**, November 26, 2010. Signed as a free agent by **Detroit**, July 5, 2011.

FAHEY, Brian (FAY-hee, BRIGH-uhn)

Defense. Shoots right. 6'1", 216 lbs. Born, Des Plaines, IL, March 2, 1981. Colorado's 7th choice, 119th overall, in 2000 Entry Draft.

1997-98	USNTDP	U-18	17	1	10	11	12	....	....	....	....	....	....	....	....	....	....	....	....	....	....	....	....	....	....
	USNTDP	USHL	5	1	1	2	8	....	....	....	....	....	....	....	....	....	....	....	....	....	....	....	....	....	....
	USNTDP	NAHL	39	5	10	15	35	....	....	....	....	....	....	....	....	....	7	0	0	0	2	....	....	....	....
1998-99	USNTDP	U-18	6	1	0	1	4	....	....	....	....	....	....	....	....	....	....	....	....	....	....	....	....	....	....
	USNTDP	USHL	52	9	9	18	34	....	....	....	....	....	....	....	....	....	....	....	....	....	....	....	....	....	....
99-2000	U. of Wisconsin	WCHA	41	6	11	17	42	....	....	....	....	....	....	....	....	....	....	....	....	....	....	....	....	....	....
2000-01	U. of Wisconsin	WCHA	38	1	5	6	16	....	....	....	....	....	....	....	....	....	....	....	....	....	....	....	....	....	....
2001-02	U. of Wisconsin	WCHA	38	2	8	10	55	....	....	....	....	....	....	....	....	....	....	....	....	....	....	....	....	....	....
2002-03	U. of Wisconsin	WCHA	39	5	4	9	34	....	....	....	....	....	....	....	....	....	....	....	....	....	....	....	....	....	....
2003-04	Worcester IceCats	AHL	2	0	0	0	2	....	....	....	....	....	....	....	....	....	....	....	....	....	....	....	....	....	....
	Hershey Bears	AHL	12	0	1	1	6	....	....	....	....	....	....	....	....	....	....	....	....	....	....	....	....	....	....
	Atlantic City	ECHL	55	11	26	37	49	....	....	....	....	....	....	....	....	....	2	0	0	0	2	....	....	....	....
2004-05	Worcester IceCats	AHL	20	0	4	4	12	....	....	....	....	....	....	....	....	....	....	....	....	....	....	....	....	....	....
	Atlantic City	ECHL	46	10	16	26	47	....	....	....	....	....	....	....	....	....	3	0	2	2	0	....	....	....	....
2005-06	Iowa Stars	AHL	64	6	11	17	74	....	....	....	....	....	....	....	....	....	7	0	1	1	8	....	....	....	....
	Idaho Steelheads	ECHL	3	1	1	2	4	....	....	....	....	....	....	....	....	....	....	....	....	....	....	....	....	....	....
2006-07	Chicago Wolves	AHL	75	11	18	29	81	....	....	....	....	....	....	....	....	....	15	3	2	5	20	....	....	....	....
2007-08	Chicago Wolves	AHL	76	14	23	37	123	....	....	....	....	....	....	....	....	....	24	2	8	10	24	....	....	....	....
2008-09	Hartford	AHL	66	4	20	24	67	....	....	....	....	....	....	....	....	....	5	0	1	1	6	....	....	....	....
2009-10	Lake Erie	AHL	71	11	14	25	97	....	....	....	....	....	....	....	....	....	....	....	....	....	....	....	....	....	....
2010-11	**Washington**	**NHL**	**7**	**0**	**1**	**1**	**2**	**0**	**0**	**0**	**4**	**0.0**	**–1**	**0**	**0.0**	**11:49**	....	....	....	....	....	....	....	....	....
	Hershey Bears	AHL	60	4	26	30	64	....	....	....	....	....	....	....	....	....	6	1	0	1	4	....	....	....	....
	NHL Totals		**7**	**0**	**1**	**1**	**2**	**0**	**0**	**0**	**4**	**0.0**		**0**	**0.0**	**11:49**	....	....	....	....	....	....	....	....	....

WCHA All-Rookie Team (2000) • ECHL All-Rookie Team (2004)

Signed as a free agent by **Chicago** (AHL), August 31, 2006. Signed as a free agent by **NY Rangers**, July 17, 2008. Traded to **Colorado** by **NY Rangers** for Nigel Wiliams, July 16, 2009. Signed as a free agent by **Washington**, July 7, 2010.

FALK, Justin (FAWLK, JUHS-tihn) MIN

Defense. Shoots left. 6'5", 215 lbs. Born, Snowflake, Man., October 11, 1988. Minnesota's 2nd choice, 110th overall, in 2007 Entry Draft.

2004-05	Swan Valley	MJHL	56	0	8	8	46	....	....	....	....	....	....	....	....	....	....	....	....	....	....	....	....	....	....
	Calgary Hitmen	WHL	4	0	0	0	2	....	....	....	....	....	....	....	....	....	5	0	0	0	0	....	....	....	....
2005-06	Calgary Hitmen	WHL	5	0	2	2	0	....	....	....	....	....	....	....	....	....	....	....	....	....	....	....	....	....	....
	Spokane Chiefs	WHL	48	0	8	8	35	....	....	....	....	....	....	....	....	....	....	....	....	....	....	....	....	....	....
2006-07	Spokane Chiefs	WHL	62	3	12	15	88	....	....	....	....	....	....	....	....	....	6	0	0	0	8	....	....	....	....
2007-08	Spokane Chiefs	WHL	72	4	22	26	98	....	....	....	....	....	....	....	....	....	21	1	4	5	12	....	....	....	....
2008-09	Houston Aeros	AHL	65	0	3	3	44	....	....	....	....	....	....	....	....	....	20	0	2	2	4	....	....	....	....
2009-10	**Minnesota**	**NHL**	**3**	**0**	**0**	**0**	**0**	**0**	**0**	**0**	**1**	**0.0**	**–2**	**0**	**0.0**	**7:33**	....	....	....	....	....	....	....	....	....
	Houston Aeros	AHL	69	3	6	9	87	....	....	....	....	....	....	....	....	....	....	....	....	....	....	....	....	....	....
2010-11	**Minnesota**	**NHL**	**22**	**0**	**3**	**3**	**6**	**0**	**0**	**0**	**7**	**0.0**	**–4**	**0**	**0.0**	**14:09**	....	....	....	....	....	....	....	....	....
	Houston Aeros	AHL	55	3	11	14	41	....	....	....	....	....	....	....	....	....	24	0	5	5	33	....	....	....	....
	NHL Totals		**25**	**0**	**3**	**3**	**6**	**0**	**0**	**0**	**8**	**0.0**		**0**	**0.0**	**13:22**	....	....	....	....	....	....	....	....	....

Memorial Cup All-Star Team (2008)

FAYNE, Mark (FAYN, MAHRK) N.J.

Defense. Shoots right. 6'3", 215 lbs. Born, Nashua, NH, May 15, 1987. New Jersey's 5th choice, 155th overall, in 2005 Entry Draft.

2003-04	Nobles	High-MA	20	3	5	8	14	....	....	....	....	....	....	....	....	....	....	....	....	....	....	....	....	....	....
2004-05	Nobles	High-MA	24	1	17	18	16	....	....	....	....	....	....	....	....	....	....	....	....	....	....	....	....	....	....
2005-06	Nobles	High-MA	29	10	24	34	....	....	....	....	....	....	....	....	....	....	....	....	....	....	....	....	....	....	....
2006-07	Providence	H-East	36	5	7	12	43	....	....	....	....	....	....	....	....	....	....	....	....	....	....	....	....	....	....
2007-08	Providence	H-East	36	2	4	6	18	....	....	....	....	....	....	....	....	....	....	....	....	....	....	....	....	....	....
2008-09	Providence	H-East	33	4	5	9	30	....	....	....	....	....	....	....	....	....	....	....	....	....	....	....	....	....	....
2009-10	Providence	H-East	34	5	17	22	14	....	....	....	....	....	....	....	....	....	....	....	....	....	....	....	....	....	....
2010-11	**New Jersey**	**NHL**	**57**	**4**	**10**	**14**	**27**	**0**	**0**	**0**	**77**	**5.2**	**10**	**0**	**0.0**	**17:50**	....	....	....	....	....	....	....	....	....
	Albany Devils	AHL	19	1	3	4	6	....	....	....	....	....	....	....	....	....	....	....	....	....	....	....	....	....	....
	NHL Totals		**57**	**4**	**10**	**14**	**27**	**0**	**0**	**0**	**77**	**5.2**		**0**	**0.0**	**17:50**	....	....	....	....	....	....	....	....	....

FEDORUK, Todd (FEH-duh-ruhk, TAWD) VAN

Left wing. Shoots left. 6'2", 232 lbs. Born, Redwater, Alta., February 13, 1979. Philadelphia's 6th choice, 164th overall, in 1997 Entry Draft.

1994-95	Ft. Saskatchewan	AMHL	STATISTICS NOT AVAILABLE																						
1995-96	Kelowna Rockets	WHL	44	1	1	2	83	....	....	....	....	....	....	....	....	....	4	0	0	0	6	....	....	....	....
1996-97	Kelowna Rockets	WHL	31	1	5	6	43	....	....	....	....	....	....	....	....	....	6	0	0	0	13	....	....	....	....
1997-98	Kelowna Rockets	WHL	31	3	5	8	120	....	....	....	....	....	....	....	....	....	....	....	....	....	....	....	....	....	....
	Regina Pats	WHL	21	4	3	7	80	....	....	....	....	....	....	....	....	....	9	1	2	3	23	....	....	....	....
1998-99	Regina Pats	WHL	39	12	12	24	107	....	....	....	....	....	....	....	....	....	....	....	....	....	....	....	....	....	....
	Prince Albert	WHL	28	6	4	10	75	....	....	....	....	....	....	....	....	....	13	1	6	7	49	....	....	....	....
99-2000	Trenton Titans	ECHL	18	2	5	7	118	....	....	....	....	....	....	....	....	....	....	....	....	....	....	....	....	....	....
	Philadelphia	AHL	19	1	2	3	40	....	....	....	....	....	....	....	....	....	5	0	1	1	2	....	....	....	....
2000-01	**Philadelphia**	**NHL**	**53**	**5**	**5**	**10**	**109**	**0**	**0**	**0**	**28**	**17.9**	**0**	**0**	**0.0**	**7:02**	**2**	**0**	**0**	**0**	**20**	**0**	**0**	**0**	**5:57**
	Philadelphia	AHL	14	0	1	1	49	....	....	....	....	....	....	....	....	....	....	....	....	....	....	....	....	....	....
2001-02	**Philadelphia**	**NHL**	**55**	**3**	**4**	**7**	**141**	**0**	**0**	**0**	**21**	**14.3**	**–2**	**5**	**0.0**	**6:21**	**3**	**0**	**0**	**0**	**0**	**0**	**0**	**0**	**2:46**
	Philadelphia	AHL	7	0	1	1	54	....	....	....	....	....	....	....	....	....	....	....	....	....	....	....	....	....	....
2002-03	**Philadelphia**	**NHL**	**63**	**1**	**5**	**6**	**105**	**0**	**0**	**0**	**33**	**3.0**	**1**	**1**	**0.0**	**6:30**	**1**	**0**	**0**	**0**	**0**	**0**	**0**	**0**	**4:52**

Season	Club	League	GP	G	A	Pts	PIM	PP	SH	GW	S	%	+/-	TF	F%	Min	GP	G	A	Pts	PIM	PP	SH	GW	Min
			Regular Season														Playoffs								
2003-04	**Philadelphia**	**NHL**	**49**	**1**	**4**	**5**	**136**	0	0	1	33	3.0	–4	0	0.0	6:47	1	0	0	0	2	0	0	0	6:42
	Philadelphia	AHL	2	0	2	2	2	....	....	....	....	....	....	....	....	....	....	....	....	....	....	....	....	....	....
2004-05	Philadelphia	AHL	42	4	12	16	142	....	....	....	....	....	....	....	....	....	16	2	2	4	33	....	....	....	....
2005-06	**Anaheim**	**NHL**	**76**	**4**	**19**	**23**	**174**	0	0	1	69	5.8	6	8	37.5	8:24	12	0	0	0	16	0	0	0	8:19
2006-07	**Anaheim**	**NHL**	**10**	**0**	**3**	**3**	**36**	0	0	0	2	0.0	2	1	0.0	7:30	....	....	....	....	....	....	....	....	....
	Philadelphia	**NHL**	**48**	**3**	**8**	**11**	**84**	0	0	0	28	10.7	–11	2	0.0	9:03	....	....	....	....	....	....	....	....	....
2007-08	**Dallas**	**NHL**	**11**	**0**	**2**	**2**	**33**	0	0	0	6	0.0	2	0	0.0	6:50	....	....	....	....	....	....	....	....	....
	Minnesota	**NHL**	**58**	**6**	**5**	**11**	**106**	2	0	0	51	11.8	0	4	0.0	10:59	6	1	1	2	16	1	0	0	13:38
2008-09	**Phoenix**	**NHL**	**72**	**6**	**7**	**13**	**72**	0	0	0	56	10.7	–9	15	26.7	10:36	....	....	....	....	....	....	....	....	....
2009-10	**Tampa Bay**	**NHL**	**50**	**3**	**3**	**6**	**54**	0	0	0	22	13.6	–12	2	100.0	7:31	....	....	....	....	....	....	....	....	....
2010-11			DID NOT PLAY																						
	NHL Totals		**545**	**32**	**65**	**97**	**1050**	2	0	2	349	9.2		38	23.7	8:11	25	1	1	2	54	1	0	0	8:32

Traded to **Anaheim** by **Philadelphia** for Anaheim's 2nd round choice (later traded to Phoenix - Phoenix selected Pier-Olivier Pelletier) in 2005 Entry Draft, July 29, 2005. Traded to **Philadelphia** by **Anaheim** for Philadelphia's 4th round choice (Justin Vaive) in 2007 Entry Draft, November 13, 2006. Signed as a free agent by **Dallas**, July 9, 2007. Claimed on waivers by **Minnesota** from **Dallas**, November 22, 2007. Signed as a free agent by **Phoenix**, July 1, 2008. Traded to **Tampa Bay** by **Phoenix** with David Hale for Radim Vrbata, July 21, 2009. Signed to a PTO (professional tryout) contract by **Vancouver**, August 4, 2011.

FEDOTENKO, Ruslan

(feh-doh-TEHN-koh, roos-LAHN) **NYR**

Left wing. Shoots left. 6'1", 200 lbs. Born, Kiev, USSR, January 18, 1979.

Season	Club	League	GP	G	A	Pts	PIM	PP	SH	GW	S	%	+/-	TF	F%	Min	GP	G	A	Pts	PIM	PP	SH	GW	Min
1995-96	Kiev 2	EEHL	33	9	11	20	12	....	....	....	....	....	....	....	....	....	....	....	....	....	....	....	....	....	....
	Sokol Kiev	CIS	2	0	0	0	0	....	....	....	....	....	....	....	....	....	....	....	....	....	....	....	....	....	....
1996-97	TPS Turku U18	Fin-U18	3	3	2	5	2	....	....	....	....	....	....	....	....	....	....	....	....	....	....	....	....	....	....
	TPS Turku Jr.	Fin-Jr.	11	1	1	2	2	....	....	....	....	....	....	....	....	....	....	....	....	....	....	....	....	....	....
	Kiekko-67 Turku	Finland-2	22	4	3	7	16	....	....	....	....	....	....	....	....	....	....	....	....	....	....	....	....	....	....
	Kiekko Turku	Finland-3	....	....	....	....	....	....	....	....	....	....	....	....	....	....	3	1	0	1	2				
1997-98	Melfort Mustangs	SJHL	68	35	31	66	55	....	....	....	....	....	....	....	....	....	....	....	....	....	....	....	....	....	....
1998-99	Sioux City	USHL	55	43	34	77	139	....	....	....	....	....	....	....	....	....	5	5	1	6	9				
99-2000	Trenton Titans	ECHL	8	5	3	8	9	....	....	....	....	....	....	....	....	....	....	....	....	....	....	....	....	....	....
	Philadelphia	AHL	67	16	34	50	42	....	....	....	....	....	....	....	....	....	2	0	0	0	0				
2000-01	**Philadelphia**	**NHL**	**74**	**16**	**20**	**36**	**72**	3	0	4	119	13.4	8	7	71.4	14:38	6	0	1	1	4	0	0	0	11:18
	Philadelphia	AHL	8	1	0	1	8	....	....	....	....	....	....	....	....	....	....	....	....	....	....	....	....	....	....
2001-02	**Philadelphia**	**NHL**	**78**	**17**	**9**	**26**	**43**	0	1	3	121	14.0	15	41	43.9	13:56	5	1	0	1	2	0	0	1	14:11
	Ukraine	Olympics	1	1	0	1	4	....	....	....	....	....	....	....	....	....	....	....	....	....	....	....	....	....	....
2002-03	**Tampa Bay**	**NHL**	**76**	**19**	**13**	**32**	**44**	6	0	6	114	16.7	–7	90	48.9	16:01	11	0	1	1	2	0	0	0	13:58
2003-04♦	**Tampa Bay**	**NHL**	**77**	**17**	**22**	**39**	**30**	0	0	3	116	14.7	14	58	55.2	14:39	22	12	2	14	14	5	0	3	16:40
2004-05			DID NOT PLAY																						
2005-06	**Tampa Bay**	**NHL**	**80**	**26**	**15**	**41**	**44**	4	0	6	164	15.9	–4	28	42.9	15:21	5	0	0	0	20	0	0	0	14:38
2006-07	**Tampa Bay**	**NHL**	**80**	**12**	**20**	**32**	**52**	2	0	1	154	7.8	–3	8	25.0	16:15	4	0	0	0	4	0	0	0	17:27
2007-08	**NY Islanders**	**NHL**	**67**	**16**	**17**	**33**	**40**	8	0	2	121	13.2	–9	28	39.3	16:42	....	....	....	....	....	....	....	....	....
2008-09♦	**Pittsburgh**	**NHL**	**65**	**16**	**23**	**39**	**44**	1	0	3	117	13.7	18	18	22.2	14:06	24	7	7	14	4	0	0	0	14:31
2009-10	**Pittsburgh**	**NHL**	**80**	**11**	**19**	**30**	**50**	3	0	3	158	7.0	–17	28	35.7	14:39	6	0	0	0	4	0	0	0	12:31
2010-11	**NY Rangers**	**NHL**	**66**	**10**	**15**	**25**	**25**	0	1	0	120	8.3	9	32	37.5	15:00	5	0	2	2	4	0	0	0	20:55
	NHL Totals		**743**	**160**	**173**	**333**	**444**	27	2	31	1304	12.3		338	44.4	15:08	88	20	13	33	58	5	0	4	15:07

USHL First All-Star Team (1999)

Signed as a free agent by **Philadelphia**, August 3, 1999. Traded to **Tampa Bay** by **Philadelphia** with Tampa Bay's 2nd round choice (previously acquired, later traded to Dallas – Dallas selected Tobias Stephan) in 2002 Entry Draft and Phoenix's 2nd round choice (previously acquired, later traded to San Jose – San Jose selected Dan Spang) in 2002 Entry Draft for Tampa Bay's 1st round choice (Joni Pitkanen) in 2002 Entry Draft, June 21, 2002. Signed as a free agent by **NY Islanders**, July 4, 2007. Signed as a free agent by **Pittsburgh**, July 3, 2008. Signed as a free agent by **NY Rangers**, October 4, 2010.

FEHR, Eric

(FAIR, AIR-ihk) **WPG**

Right wing. Shoots right. 6'4", 212 lbs. Born, Winkler, Man., September 7, 1985. Washington's 1st choice, 18th overall, in 2003 Entry Draft.

Season	Club	League	GP	G	A	Pts	PIM	PP	SH	GW	S	%	+/-	TF	F%	Min	GP	G	A	Pts	PIM	PP	SH	GW	Min
2000-01	Pembina Valley	MMMHL	36	45	13	58	30	....	....	....	....	....	....	....	....	....	....	....	....	....	....	....	....	....	....
	Brandon	WHL	4	0	0	0	0	....	....	....	....	....	....	....	....	....	....	....	....	....	....	....	....	....	....
2001-02	Brandon	WHL	63	11	16	27	29	....	....	....	....	....	....	....	....	....	12	1	1	2	0				
2002-03	Brandon	WHL	70	26	29	55	76	....	....	....	....	....	....	....	....	....	17	4	8	12	26				
2003-04	Brandon	WHL	71	50	34	84	129	....	....	....	....	....	....	....	....	....	7	5	0	5	16				
2004-05	Brandon	WHL	71	*59	52	*111	91	....	....	....	....	....	....	....	....	....	24	16	16	*32	47				
2005-06	**Washington**	**NHL**	**11**	**0**	**0**	**0**	**2**	0	0	0	10	0.0	0	4	25.0	5:45	....	....	....	....	....	....	....	....	....
	Hershey Bears	AHL	70	25	28	53	70	....	....	....	....	....	....	....	....	....	19	8	3	11	8				
2006-07	**Washington**	**NHL**	**14**	**2**	**1**	**3**	**8**	0	0	1	25	8.0	3	6	16.7	10:43	....	....	....	....	....	....	....	....	....
	Hershey Bears	AHL	40	22	19	41	63	....	....	....	....	....	....	....	....	....	....	....	....	....	....	....	....	....	....
2007-08	**Washington**	**NHL**	**23**	**1**	**5**	**6**	**6**	0	0	0	40	2.5	4	2	0.0	10:31	5	1	0	1	0	0	0	0	9:41
	Hershey Bears	AHL	11	3	4	7	4	....	....	....	....	....	....	....	....	....	2	1	3	4	2				
2008-09	**Washington**	**NHL**	**61**	**12**	**13**	**25**	**22**	1	0	2	134	9.0	8	3	33.3	11:15	9	0	0	0	0	0	0	0	7:22
2009-10	**Washington**	**NHL**	**69**	**21**	**18**	**39**	**24**	3	0	3	145	14.5	18	2	50.0	12:08	7	3	1	4	4	0	0	0	11:24
2010-11	**Washington**	**NHL**	**52**	**10**	**10**	**20**	**16**	3	0	1	120	8.3	0	1	0.0	12:35	5	1	0	1	0	0	0	0	13:28
	NHL Totals		**230**	**46**	**47**	**93**	**78**	7	0	7	474	9.7		18	22.2	11:27	26	5	1	6	4	0	0	0	10:05

WHL East First All-Star Team (2005) • WHL Player of the Year (2005) • Canadian Major Junior Second All-Star Team (2005)

Traded to **Winnipeg** by **Washington** for Danick Paquette and Winnipeg's 4th round choice in 2012 Entry Draft, July 8, 2011.

FERENCE, Andrew

(FAIR-ehns, AN-droo) **BOS**

Defense. Shoots left. 5'11", 189 lbs. Born, Edmonton, Alta., March 17, 1979. Pittsburgh's 8th choice, 208th overall, in 1997 Entry Draft.

Season	Club	League	GP	G	A	Pts	PIM	PP	SH	GW	S	%	+/-	TF	F%	Min	GP	G	A	Pts	PIM	PP	SH	GW	Min
1994-95	Sherwood Park	AMHL	31	4	14	18	74	....	....	....	....	....	....	....	....	....	....	....	....	....	....	....	....	....	....
	Portland	WHL	2	0	0	0	4	....	....	....	....	....	....	....	....	....	....	....	....	....	....	....	....	....	....
1995-96	Portland	WHL	72	9	31	40	159	....	....	....	....	....	....	....	....	....	7	1	3	4	12				
1996-97	Portland	WHL	72	12	32	44	149	....	....	....	....	....	....	....	....	....	6	1	2	3	12				
1997-98	Portland	WHL	72	11	57	68	142	....	....	....	....	....	....	....	....	....	16	2	18	20	28				
1998-99	Portland	WHL	40	11	21	32	104	....	....	....	....	....	....	....	....	....	4	1	4	5	10				
	Kansas City	IHL	5	1	2	3	4	....	....	....	....	....	....	....	....	....	3	0	0	0	9				
99-2000	**Pittsburgh**	**NHL**	**30**	**2**	**4**	**6**	**20**	0	0	1	26	7.7	3	0	0.0	16:19	....	....	....	....	....	....	....	....	....
	Wilkes-Barre	AHL	44	8	20	28	58	....	....	....	....	....	....	....	....	....	....	....	....	....	....	....	....	....	....
2000-01	**Pittsburgh**	**NHL**	**36**	**4**	**11**	**15**	**28**	1	0	1	47	8.5	6	0	0.0	18:51	18	3	7	10	16	1	0	1	22:02
	Wilkes-Barre	AHL	43	6	18	24	95	....	....	....	....	....	....	....	....	....	3	1	0	1	12				
2001-02	**Pittsburgh**	**NHL**	**75**	**4**	**7**	**11**	**73**	1	0	0	82	4.9	–12	2	0.0	18:34	....	....	....	....	....	....	....	....	....
2002-03	**Pittsburgh**	**NHL**	**22**	**1**	**3**	**4**	**36**	1	0	0	22	4.5	–16	1	100.0	19:33	....	....	....	....	....	....	....	....	....
	Wilkes-Barre	AHL	1	0	0	0	2	....	....	....	....	....	....	....	....	....	....	....	....	....	....	....	....	....	....
	Calgary	**NHL**	**16**	**0**	**4**	**4**	**6**	0	0	0	17	0.0	1	0	0.0	17:38	....	....	....	....	....	....	....	....	....
2003-04	**Calgary**	**NHL**	**72**	**4**	**12**	**16**	**53**	1	0	0	86	4.7	5	0	0.0	18:40	26	0	3	3	25	0	0	0	24:13
2004-05	C. Budejovice	CzRep-2	19	5	6	11	45	....	....	....	....	....	....	....	....	....	12	2	7	9	10				
2005-06	**Calgary**	**NHL**	**82**	**4**	**27**	**31**	**85**	2	0	0	111	3.6	–12	1	0.0	20:08	7	0	4	4	12	0	0	0	23:09
2006-07	**Calgary**	**NHL**	**54**	**2**	**10**	**12**	**66**	1	0	0	51	3.9	7	3	33.3	18:29	....	....	....	....	....	....	....	....	....
	Boston	**NHL**	**26**	**1**	**2**	**3**	**31**	0	0	0	29	3.4	–2	0	0.0	22:22	....	....	....	....	....	....	....	....	....
2007-08	**Boston**	**NHL**	**59**	**1**	**14**	**15**	**50**	0	0	0	71	1.4	–14	1	100.0	22:15	7	0	4	4	6	0	0	0	21:39
2008-09	**Boston**	**NHL**	**47**	**1**	**15**	**16**	**40**	1	0	0	72	1.4	7	0	0.0	21:32	3	0	0	0	4	0	0	0	15:30
2009-10	**Boston**	**NHL**	**51**	**0**	**8**	**8**	**16**	0	0	0	60	0.0	–7	0	0.0	19:42	13	0	1	1	18	0	0	0	14:58
2010-11♦	**Boston**	**NHL**	**70**	**3**	**12**	**15**	**60**	0	0	0	78	3.8	22	0	0.0	17:59	25	4	6	10	37	1	0	1	20:36
	NHL Totals		**640**	**27**	**129**	**156**	**564**	8	0	2	752	3.6		8	37.5	19:26	99	7	25	32	118	2	0	2	21:10

WHL West First All-Star Team (1998) • WHL West Second All-Star Team (1999)

• Missed majority of 2002-03 due to groin (November 18, 2002 vs. Montreal) and ankle (March 20, 2003 vs. Los Angeles) injuries. Traded to **Calgary** by **Pittsburgh** for Calgary's 3rd round choice (Brian Gifford) in 2004 Entry Draft, February 9, 2003. Signed as a free agent by **Ceske Budejovice** (CzRep-2), December 1, 2004. Traded to **Boston** by **Calgary** with Chuck Kobasew for Brad Stuart, Wayne Primeau and Washington's 4th round choice (previously acquired, Calgary selected T.J. Brodie) in 2008 Entry Draft, February 10, 2007.

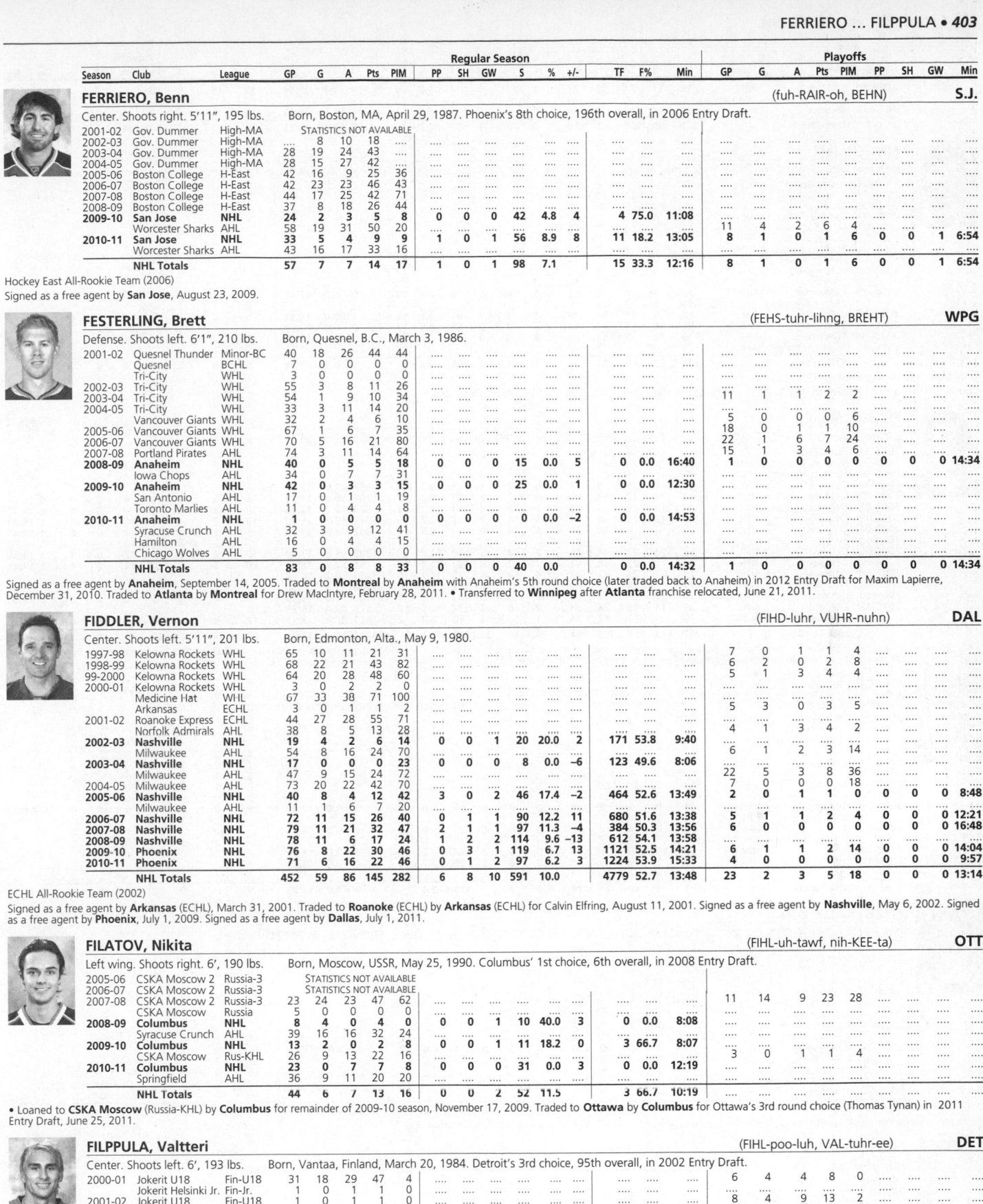

FERRIERO, Benn
(fuh-RAIR-oh, BEHN) **S.J.**

Center. Shoots right. 5'11", 195 lbs. Born, Boston, MA, April 29, 1987. Phoenix's 8th choice, 196th overall, in 2006 Entry Draft.

Season	Club	League	GP	G	A	Pts	PIM	PP	SH	GW	S	%	+/-	TF	F%	Min	GP	G	A	Pts	PIM	PP	SH	GW	Min
			Regular Season														Playoffs								
2001-02	Gov. Dummer	High-MA	STATISTICS NOT AVAILABLE					....	....	....	....	....	....	....	....	....	....	....	....	....	....	....	....	....	....
2002-03	Gov. Dummer	High-MA	....	8	10	18	....	....	....	....	....	....	....	....	....	....	....	....	....	....	....	....	....	....	....
2003-04	Gov. Dummer	High-MA	28	19	24	43	....	....	....	....	....	....	....	....	....	....	....	....	....	....	....	....	....	....	....
2004-05	Gov. Dummer	High-MA	28	15	27	42	....	....	....	....	....	....	....	....	....	....	....	....	....	....	....	....	....	....	....
2005-06	Boston College	H-East	42	16	9	25	36	....	....	....	....	....	....	....	....	....	....	....	....	....	....	....	....	....	....
2006-07	Boston College	H-East	42	23	23	46	43	....	....	....	....	....	....	....	....	....	....	....	....	....	....	....	....	....	....
2007-08	Boston College	H-East	44	17	25	42	71	....	....	....	....	....	....	....	....	....	....	....	....	....	....	....	....	....	....
2008-09	Boston College	H-East	37	8	18	26	44	....	....	....	....	....	....	....	....	....	....	....	....	....	....	....	....	....	....
2009-10	**San Jose**	**NHL**	**24**	**2**	**3**	**5**	**8**	**0**	**0**	**0**	**42**	**4.8**	**4**	**4**	**75.0**	**11:08**	....	....	....	....	....	....	....	....	....
	Worcester Sharks	AHL	58	19	31	50	20	....	....	....	....	....	....	....	....	....	11	4	2	6	4	....	....	....	....
2010-11	**San Jose**	**NHL**	**33**	**5**	**4**	**9**	**9**	**1**	**0**	**1**	**56**	**8.9**	**8**	**11**	**18.2**	**13:05**	**8**	**1**	**0**	**1**	**6**	**0**	**0**	**1**	**6:54**
	Worcester Sharks	AHL	43	16	17	33	16	....	....	....	....	....	....	....	....	....	....	....	....	....	....	....	....	....	....
	NHL Totals		**57**	**7**	**7**	**14**	**17**	**1**	**0**	**1**	**98**	**7.1**		**15**	**33.3**	**12:16**	**8**	**1**	**0**	**1**	**6**	**0**	**0**	**1**	**6:54**

Hockey East All-Rookie Team (2006)
Signed as a free agent by **San Jose**, August 23, 2009.

FESTERLING, Brett
(FEHS-tuhr-lihng, BREHT) **WPG**

Defense. Shoots left. 6'1", 210 lbs. Born, Quesnel, B.C., March 3, 1986.

Season	Club	League	GP	G	A	Pts	PIM	PP	SH	GW	S	%	+/-	TF	F%	Min	GP	G	A	Pts	PIM	PP	SH	GW	Min
2001-02	Quesnel Thunder	Minor-BC	40	18	26	44	44	....	....	....	....	....	....	....	....	....	....	....	....	....	....	....	....	....	....
	Quesnel	BCHL	7	0	0	0	0	....	....	....	....	....	....	....	....	....	....	....	....	....	....	....	....	....	....
	Tri-City	WHL	3	0	0	0	0	....	....	....	....	....	....	....	....	....	....	....	....	....	....	....	....	....	....
2002-03	Tri-City	WHL	55	3	8	11	26	....	....	....	....	....	....	....	....	....	....	....	....	....	....	....	....	....	....
2003-04	Tri-City	WHL	54	1	9	10	34	....	....	....	....	....	....	....	....	....	11	1	1	2	2	....	....	....	....
2004-05	Tri-City	WHL	33	3	11	14	20	....	....	....	....	....	....	....	....	....	....	....	....	....	....	....	....	....	....
	Vancouver Giants	WHL	32	2	4	6	10	....	....	....	....	....	....	....	....	....	5	0	0	0	6	....	....	....	....
2005-06	Vancouver Giants	WHL	67	1	6	7	35	....	....	....	....	....	....	....	....	....	18	0	1	1	10	....	....	....	....
2006-07	Vancouver Giants	WHL	70	5	16	21	80	....	....	....	....	....	....	....	....	....	22	1	6	7	24	....	....	....	....
2007-08	Portland Pirates	AHL	74	3	11	14	64	....	....	....	....	....	....	....	....	....	15	1	3	4	6	....	....	....	....
2008-09	**Anaheim**	**NHL**	**40**	**0**	**5**	**5**	**18**	**0**	**0**	**0**	**15**	**0.0**	**5**	**0**	**0.0**	**16:40**	**1**	**0**	**0**	**0**	**0**	**0**	**0**	**0**	**14:34**
	Iowa Chops	AHL	34	0	7	7	31	....	....	....	....	....	....	....	....	....	....	....	....	....	....	....	....	....	....
2009-10	**Anaheim**	**NHL**	**42**	**0**	**3**	**3**	**15**	**0**	**0**	**0**	**25**	**0.0**	**1**	**0**	**0.0**	**12:30**	....	....	....	....	....	....	....	....	....
	San Antonio	AHL	17	0	1	1	19	....	....	....	....	....	....	....	....	....	....	....	....	....	....	....	....	....	....
	Toronto Marlies	AHL	11	0	4	4	8	....	....	....	....	....	....	....	....	....	....	....	....	....	....	....	....	....	....
2010-11	**Anaheim**	**NHL**	**1**	**0**	**0**	**0**	**0**	**0**	**0**	**0**	**0**	**0.0**	**-2**	**0**	**0.0**	**14:53**	....	....	....	....	....	....	....	....	....
	Syracuse Crunch	AHL	32	3	9	12	41	....	....	....	....	....	....	....	....	....	....	....	....	....	....	....	....	....	....
	Hamilton	AHL	16	0	4	4	15	....	....	....	....	....	....	....	....	....	....	....	....	....	....	....	....	....	....
	Chicago Wolves	AHL	5	0	0	0	0	....	....	....	....	....	....	....	....	....	....	....	....	....	....	....	....	....	....
	NHL Totals		**83**	**0**	**8**	**8**	**33**	**0**	**0**	**0**	**40**	**0.0**		**0**	**0.0**	**14:32**	**1**	**0**	**0**	**0**	**0**	**0**	**0**	**0**	**14:34**

Signed as a free agent by **Anaheim**, September 14, 2005. Traded to **Montreal** by **Anaheim** with Anaheim's 5th round choice (later traded back to Anaheim) in 2012 Entry Draft for Maxim Lapierre, December 31, 2010. Traded to **Atlanta** by **Montreal** for Drew MacIntyre, February 28, 2011. • Transferred to **Winnipeg** after **Atlanta** franchise relocated, June 21, 2011.

FIDDLER, Vernon
(FIHD-luhr, VUHR-nuhn) **DAL**

Center. Shoots left. 5'11", 201 lbs. Born, Edmonton, Alta., May 9, 1980.

Season	Club	League	GP	G	A	Pts	PIM	PP	SH	GW	S	%	+/-	TF	F%	Min	GP	G	A	Pts	PIM	PP	SH	GW	Min
1997-98	Kelowna Rockets	WHL	65	10	11	21	31	....	....	....	....	....	....	....	....	....	7	0	1	1	4	....	....	....	....
1998-99	Kelowna Rockets	WHL	68	22	21	43	82	....	....	....	....	....	....	....	....	....	6	2	0	2	8	....	....	....	....
99-2000	Kelowna Rockets	WHL	64	20	28	48	60	....	....	....	....	....	....	....	....	....	5	1	3	4	4	....	....	....	....
2000-01	Kelowna Rockets	WHL	3	0	2	2	0	....	....	....	....	....	....	....	....	....	....	....	....	....	....	....	....	....	....
	Medicine Hat	WHL	67	33	38	71	100	....	....	....	....	....	....	....	....	....	....	....	....	....	....	....	....	....	....
	Arkansas	ECHL	3	0	1	1	2	....	....	....	....	....	....	....	....	....	5	3	0	3	5	....	....	....	....
2001-02	Roanoke Express	ECHL	44	27	28	55	71	....	....	....	....	....	....	....	....	....	....	....	....	....	....	....	....	....	....
	Norfolk Admirals	AHL	38	8	5	13	28	....	....	....	....	....	....	....	....	....	4	1	3	4	2	....	....	....	....
2002-03	**Nashville**	**NHL**	**19**	**4**	**2**	**6**	**14**	**0**	**0**	**1**	**20**	**20.0**	**2**	**171**	**53.8**	**9:40**	....	....	....	....	....	....	....	....	....
	Milwaukee	AHL	54	8	16	24	70	....	....	....	....	....	....	....	....	....	6	1	2	3	14	....	....	....	....
2003-04	**Nashville**	**NHL**	**17**	**0**	**0**	**0**	**23**	**0**	**0**	**0**	**8**	**0.0**	**-6**	**123**	**49.6**	**8:06**	....	....	....	....	....	....	....	....	....
	Milwaukee	AHL	47	9	15	24	72	....	....	....	....	....	....	....	....	....	22	5	3	8	36	....	....	....	....
2004-05	Milwaukee	AHL	73	20	22	42	70	....	....	....	....	....	....	....	....	....	7	0	0	0	18	....	....	....	....
2005-06	**Nashville**	**NHL**	**40**	**8**	**4**	**12**	**42**	**3**	**0**	**2**	**46**	**17.4**	**-2**	**464**	**52.6**	**13:49**	**2**	**0**	**1**	**1**	**0**	**0**	**0**	**0**	**8:48**
	Milwaukee	AHL	11	1	6	7	20	....	....	....	....	....	....	....	....	....	....	....	....	....	....	....	....	....	....
2006-07	**Nashville**	**NHL**	**72**	**11**	**15**	**26**	**40**	**0**	**1**	**1**	**90**	**12.2**	**11**	**680**	**51.6**	**13:38**	**5**	**1**	**1**	**2**	**4**	**0**	**0**	**0**	**12:21**
2007-08	**Nashville**	**NHL**	**79**	**11**	**21**	**32**	**47**	**2**	**1**	**1**	**97**	**11.3**	**-4**	**384**	**50.3**	**13:56**	**6**	**0**	**0**	**0**	**0**	**0**	**0**	**0**	**16:48**
2008-09	**Nashville**	**NHL**	**78**	**11**	**6**	**17**	**24**	**1**	**2**	**2**	**114**	**9.6**	**-13**	**612**	**54.1**	**13:58**	....	....	....	....	....	....	....	....	....
2009-10	**Phoenix**	**NHL**	**76**	**8**	**22**	**30**	**46**	**0**	**3**	**1**	**119**	**6.7**	**13**	**1121**	**52.5**	**14:21**	**6**	**1**	**1**	**2**	**14**	**0**	**0**	**0**	**14:04**
2010-11	**Phoenix**	**NHL**	**71**	**6**	**16**	**22**	**46**	**0**	**1**	**2**	**97**	**6.2**	**3**	**1224**	**53.9**	**15:33**	**4**	**0**	**0**	**0**	**0**	**0**	**0**	**0**	**9:57**
	NHL Totals		**452**	**59**	**86**	**145**	**282**	**6**	**8**	**10**	**591**	**10.0**		**4779**	**52.7**	**13:48**	**23**	**2**	**3**	**5**	**18**	**0**	**0**	**0**	**13:14**

ECHL All-Rookie Team (2002)
Signed as a free agent by **Arkansas** (ECHL), March 31, 2001. Traded to **Roanoke** (ECHL) by **Arkansas** (ECHL) for Calvin Elfring, August 11, 2001. Signed as a free agent by **Nashville**, May 6, 2002. Signed as a free agent by **Phoenix**, July 1, 2009. Signed as a free agent by **Dallas**, July 1, 2011.

FILATOV, Nikita
(FIHL-uh-tawf, nih-KEE-ta) **OTT**

Left wing. Shoots right. 6', 190 lbs. Born, Moscow, USSR, May 25, 1990. Columbus' 1st choice, 6th overall, in 2008 Entry Draft.

Season	Club	League	GP	G	A	Pts	PIM	PP	SH	GW	S	%	+/-	TF	F%	Min	GP	G	A	Pts	PIM	PP	SH	GW	Min
2005-06	CSKA Moscow 2	Russia-3	STATISTICS NOT AVAILABLE																						
2006-07	CSKA Moscow 2	Russia-3	STATISTICS NOT AVAILABLE																						
2007-08	CSKA Moscow 2	Russia-3	23	24	23	47	62	....	....	....	....	....	....	....	....	....	11	14	9	23	28	....	....	....	....
	CSKA Moscow	Russia	5	0	0	0	0	....	....	....	....	....	....	....	....	....	....	....	....	....	....	....	....	....	....
2008-09	**Columbus**	**NHL**	**8**	**4**	**0**	**4**	**0**	**0**	**0**	**1**	**10**	**40.0**	**3**	**0**	**0.0**	**8:08**	....	....	....	....	....	....	....	....	....
	Syracuse Crunch	AHL	39	16	16	32	24	....	....	....	....	....	....	....	....	....	....	....	....	....	....	....	....	....	....
2009-10	**Columbus**	**NHL**	**13**	**2**	**0**	**2**	**8**	**0**	**0**	**1**	**11**	**18.2**	**0**	**3**	**66.7**	**8:07**	....	....	....	....	....	....	....	....	....
	CSKA Moscow	Rus-KHL	26	9	13	22	16	....	....	....	....	....	....	....	....	....	3	0	1	1	4	....	....	....	....
2010-11	**Columbus**	**NHL**	**23**	**0**	**7**	**7**	**8**	**0**	**0**	**0**	**31**	**0.0**	**3**	**0**	**0.0**	**12:19**	....	....	....	....	....	....	....	....	....
	Springfield	AHL	36	9	11	20	20	....	....	....	....	....	....	....	....	....	....	....	....	....	....	....	....	....	....
	NHL Totals		**44**	**6**	**7**	**13**	**16**	**0**	**0**	**2**	**52**	**11.5**		**3**	**66.7**	**10:19**	....	....	....	....	....	....	....	....	....

• Loaned to **CSKA Moscow** (Russia-KHL) by **Columbus** for remainder of 2009-10 season, November 17, 2009. Traded to **Ottawa** by **Columbus** for Ottawa's 3rd round choice (Thomas Tynan) in 2011 Entry Draft, June 25, 2011.

FILPPULA, Valtteri
(FIHL-poo-luh, VAL-tuhr-ee) **DET**

Center. Shoots left. 6', 193 lbs. Born, Vantaa, Finland, March 20, 1984. Detroit's 3rd choice, 95th overall, in 2002 Entry Draft.

Season	Club	League	GP	G	A	Pts	PIM	PP	SH	GW	S	%	+/-	TF	F%	Min	GP	G	A	Pts	PIM	PP	SH	GW	Min
2000-01	Jokerit U18	Fin-U18	31	18	29	47	4	....	....	....	....	....	....	....	....	....	6	4	4	8	0	....	....	....	....
	Jokerit Helsinki Jr.	Fin-Jr.	1	0	1	1	0	....	....	....	....	....	....	....	....	....	....	....	....	....	....	....	....	....	....
2001-02	Jokerit U18	Fin-U18	1	0	1	1	0	....	....	....	....	....	....	....	....	....	8	4	9	13	2	....	....	....	....
	Jokerit Helsinki Jr.	Fin-Jr.	40	8	15	23	14	....	....	....	....	....	....	....	....	....	1	0	0	0	0	....	....	....	....
2002-03	Jokerit Helsinki Jr.	Fin-Jr.	35	16	37	53	14	....	....	....	....	....	....	....	....	....	11	4	10	14	4	....	....	....	....
2003-04	Suomi U20	Finland-2	1	0	0	0	2	....	....	....	....	....	....	....	....	....	....	....	....	....	....	....	....	....	....
	Jokerit Helsinki	Finland	49	5	13	18	6	....	....	....	....	....	....	....	....	....	....	....	....	....	....	....	....	....	....
2004-05	Jokerit Helsinki	Finland	55	10	20	30	20	....	....	....	....	....	....	....	....	....	12	5	6	11	2	....	....	....	....
2005-06	**Detroit**	**NHL**	**4**	**0**	**1**	**1**	**2**	**0**	**0**	**0**	**1**	**0.0**	**1**	**21**	**47.6**	**7:19**	....	....	....	....	....	....	....	....	....
	Grand Rapids	AHL	74	20	51	71	30	....	....	....	....	....	....	....	....	....	16	7	9	16	4	....	....	....	....
2006-07	**Detroit**	**NHL**	**73**	**10**	**7**	**17**	**20**	**0**	**0**	**1**	**76**	**13.2**	**8**	**267**	**55.8**	**11:16**	**18**	**3**	**2**	**5**	**2**	**0**	**0**	**0**	**12:12**
	Grand Rapids	AHL	3	2	2	4	2	....	....	....	....	....	....	....	....	....	....	....	....	....	....	....	....	....	....
2007-08 ♦	**Detroit**	**NHL**	**78**	**19**	**17**	**36**	**28**	**3**	**0**	**3**	**122**	**15.6**	**16**	**621**	**50.6**	**16:58**	**22**	**5**	**6**	**11**	**2**	**0**	**0**	**0**	**16:40**
2008-09	**Detroit**	**NHL**	**80**	**12**	**28**	**40**	**42**	**1**	**0**	**1**	**129**	**9.3**	**9**	**785**	**52.1**	**16:06**	**23**	**3**	**13**	**16**	**8**	**1**	**0**	**1**	**17:38**

Season	Club	League	GP	G	A	Pts	PIM	PP	SH	GW	S	%	+/-	TF	F%	Min	GP	G	A	Pts	PIM	PP	SH	GW	Min
			Regular Season														Playoffs								
2009-10	Detroit	NHL	55	11	24	35	24	1	1	1	114	9.6	−4	573	51.7	18:14	12	4	5	9	6	2	0	0	18:34
	Finland	Olympics	6	3	0	3	0	....	....	....	....	....	....	....	....	....	....	....	....	....	....	....	....	....	....
2010-11	Detroit	NHL	71	16	23	39	22	4	0	5	115	13.9	−1	928	51.5	16:43	11	2	6	8	6	0	0	2	17:47
	NHL Totals		361	68	100	168	138	9	1	11	557	12.2		3195	51.8	15:39	86	17	32	49	24	3	0	3	16:24

FINGER, Jeff

(FIHN-guhr, JEHF) **TOR**

Defense. Shoots right. 6'1", 209 lbs. Born, Houghton, MI, December 18, 1979. Colorado's 11th choice, 240th overall, in 1999 Entry Draft.

Season	Club	League	GP	G	A	Pts	PIM	PP	SH	GW	S	%	+/-	TF	F%	Min	GP	G	A	Pts	PIM	PP	SH	GW	Min
1997-98	Green Bay	USHL	51	5	9	14	208	....	....	....	....	....	....	....	....	....	4	0	0	0	18	....	....	....	....
1998-99	Green Bay	USHL	54	11	28	39	199	....	....	....	....	....	....	....	....	....	6	0	3	3	14	....	....	....	....
99-2000	Green Bay	USHL	55	13	35	48	15	....	....	....	....	....	....	....	....	....	14	3	11	14	40	....	....	....	....
2000-01	St. Cloud State	WCHA	41	4	5	9	84	....	....	....	....	....	....	....	....	....	....	....	....	....	....	....	....	....	....
2001-02	St. Cloud State	WCHA	42	6	20	26	105	....	....	....	....	....	....	....	....	....	....	....	....	....	....	....	....	....	....
2002-03	St. Cloud State	WCHA	24	5	8	13	46	....	....	....	....	....	....	....	....	....	....	....	....	....	....	....	....	....	....
2003-04	Reading Royals	ECHL	10	2	5	7	24	....	....	....	....	....	....	....	....	....	....	....	....	....	....	....	....	....	....
	Hershey Bears	AHL	63	2	9	11	88	....	....	....	....	....	....	....	....	....	....	....	....	....	....	....	....	....	....
2004-05	Hershey Bears	AHL	75	4	12	16	125	....	....	....	....	....	....	....	....	....	....	....	....	....	....	....	....	....	....
2005-06	Lowell	AHL	70	3	20	23	116	....	....	....	....	....	....	....	....	....	....	....	....	....	....	....	....	....	....
2006-07	**Colorado**	**NHL**	**22**	**1**	**4**	**5**	**11**	**0**	**0**	**0**	**16**	**6.3**	**10**	**0**	**0.0**	**13:48**	....	....	....	....	....	....	....	....	....
	Albany River Rats	AHL	44	3	10	13	65	....	....	....	....	....	....	....	....	....	5	1	1	2	4	....	....	....	....
2007-08	**Colorado**	**NHL**	**72**	**8**	**11**	**19**	**40**	**1**	**1**	**1**	**93**	**8.6**	**12**	**1**	**100.0**	**19:57**	**5**	**0**	**2**	**2**	**4**	**0**	**0**	**0**	**22:05**
2008-09	**Toronto**	**NHL**	**66**	**6**	**17**	**23**	**43**	**0**	**0**	**0**	**68**	**8.8**	**−7**	**0**	**0.0**	**20:29**	....	....	....	....	....	....	....	....	....
2009-10	**Toronto**	**NHL**	**39**	**2**	**8**	**10**	**20**	**0**	**0**	**0**	**29**	**6.9**	**−11**	**0**	**0.0**	**13:47**	....	....	....	....	....	....	....	....	....
2010-11	Toronto Marlies	AHL	23	0	5	5	8	....	....	....	....	....	....	....	....	....	....	....	....	....	....	....	....	....	....
	NHL Totals		**199**	**17**	**40**	**57**	**114**	**1**	**1**	**1**	**206**	**8.3**		**1**	**100.0**	**18:14**	**5**	**0**	**2**	**2**	**4**	**0**	**0**	**0**	**22:05**

USHL Defenseman of the Year (2000)

Signed as a free agent by **Toronto**, July 1, 2008. • Missed majority of 2009-10 and 2010-11 as a healthy reserve.

FISHER, Mike

(FIH-shuhr, MIGHK) **NSH**

Center. Shoots right. 6'1", 208 lbs. Born, Peterborough, Ont., June 5, 1980. Ottawa's 2nd choice, 44th overall, in 1998 Entry Draft.

Season	Club	League	GP	G	A	Pts	PIM	PP	SH	GW	S	%	+/-	TF	F%	Min	GP	G	A	Pts	PIM	PP	SH	GW	Min
1996-97	Peterborough	OPJHL	51	26	30	56	35	....	....	....	....	....	....	....	....	....	....	....	....	....	....	....	....	....	....
1997-98	Sudbury Wolves	OHL	66	24	25	49	65	....	....	....	....	....	....	....	....	....	9	2	2	4	13	....	....	....	....
1998-99	Sudbury Wolves	OHL	68	41	65	106	55	....	....	....	....	....	....	....	....	....	4	2	1	3	4	....	....	....	....
99-2000	**Ottawa**	**NHL**	**32**	**4**	**5**	**9**	**15**	**0**	**0**	**1**	**49**	**8.2**	**−6**	**356**	**47.8**	**12:57**	....	....	....	....	....	....	....	....	....
2000-01	**Ottawa**	**NHL**	**60**	**7**	**12**	**19**	**46**	**0**	**0**	**3**	**83**	**8.4**	**−1**	**709**	**50.2**	**11:38**	**4**	**0**	**1**	**1**	**4**	**0**	**0**	**0**	**13:41**
2001-02	**Ottawa**	**NHL**	**58**	**15**	**9**	**24**	**55**	**0**	**3**	**4**	**123**	**12.2**	**8**	**848**	**48.7**	**14:05**	**10**	**2**	**1**	**3**	**0**	**0**	**0**	**0**	**16:17**
2002-03	**Ottawa**	**NHL**	**74**	**18**	**20**	**38**	**54**	**5**	**1**	**3**	**142**	**12.7**	**13**	**1077**	**48.1**	**15:59**	**18**	**2**	**2**	**4**	**16**	**0**	**1**	**1**	**16:58**
2003-04	**Ottawa**	**NHL**	**24**	**4**	**6**	**10**	**39**	**1**	**0**	**0**	**47**	**8.5**	**−3**	**357**	**42.0**	**17:26**	**7**	**1**	**0**	**1**	**4**	**0**	**0**	**1**	**16:11**
2004-05	EV Zug	Swiss	21	9	18	27	34	....	....	....	....	....	....	....	....	....	9	2	3	5	10	....	....	....	....
2005-06	**Ottawa**	**NHL**	**68**	**22**	**22**	**44**	**64**	**2**	**4**	**3**	**150**	**14.7**	**23**	**883**	**50.3**	**17:09**	**10**	**2**	**2**	**4**	**12**	**0**	**1**	**0**	**18:50**
2006-07	**Ottawa**	**NHL**	**68**	**22**	**26**	**48**	**41**	**7**	**2**	**3**	**193**	**11.4**	**15**	**1191**	**52.1**	**18:25**	**20**	**5**	**5**	**10**	**24**	**2**	**1**	**1**	**17:43**
2007-08	**Ottawa**	**NHL**	**79**	**23**	**24**	**47**	**82**	**6**	**2**	**4**	**215**	**10.7**	**−10**	**1230**	**50.2**	**19:46**	....	....	....	....	....	....	....	....	....
2008-09	**Ottawa**	**NHL**	**78**	**13**	**19**	**32**	**66**	**1**	**2**	**3**	**182**	**7.1**	**0**	**1044**	**51.3**	**18:30**	....	....	....	....	....	....	....	....	....
2009-10	**Ottawa**	**NHL**	**79**	**25**	**28**	**53**	**59**	**10**	**0**	**6**	**212**	**11.8**	**1**	**1307**	**52.0**	**18:58**	**6**	**2**	**3**	**5**	**6**	**2**	**0**	**0**	**23:04**
2010-11	**Ottawa**	**NHL**	**55**	**14**	**10**	**24**	**33**	**3**	**0**	**1**	**132**	**10.6**	**−19**	**825**	**48.4**	**18:25**	....	....	....	....	....	....	....	....	....
	Nashville	**NHL**	**27**	**5**	**7**	**12**	**10**	**1**	**0**	**1**	**60**	**8.3**	**2**	**421**	**48.2**	**18:15**	**12**	**3**	**4**	**7**	**11**	**0**	**0**	**1**	**20:43**
	NHL Totals		**702**	**172**	**188**	**360**	**564**	**36**	**14**	**32**	**1588**	**10.8**		**10248**	**49.8**	**17:02**	**87**	**17**	**18**	**35**	**77**	**4**	**3**	**4**	**18:00**

• Missed majority of 1999-2000 due to knee injury vs. Boston, December 30, 1999. • Missed majority of 2003-04 due to elbow injury in practice, October 4, 2003. Signed as a free agent by **Zug** (Swiss), November 1, 2004. Traded to **Nashville** by **Ottawa** for Nashville's 1st round choice (Stefan Noesen) in 2011 Entry Draft and future considerations, February 10, 2011.

FISTRIC, Mark

(FIHST-rihc, MAHRK) **DAL**

Defense. Shoots left. 6'3", 231 lbs. Born, Edmonton, Alta., June 1, 1986. Dallas' 1st choice, 28th overall, in 2004 Entry Draft.

Season	Club	League	GP	G	A	Pts	PIM	PP	SH	GW	S	%	+/-	TF	F%	Min	GP	G	A	Pts	PIM	PP	SH	GW	Min
2000-01	Edmonton MLAC	AMBHL	34	13	13	26	144	....	....	....	....	....	....	....	....	....	....	....	....	....	....	....	....	....	....
2001-02	Edmonton MLAC	AMHL	30	8	10	18	85	....	....	....	....	....	....	....	....	....	....	....	....	....	....	....	....	....	....
	Vancouver Giants	WHL	4	0	2	2	0	....	....	....	....	....	....	....	....	....	....	....	....	....	....	....	....	....	....
2002-03	Vancouver Giants	WHL	63	2	7	9	81	....	....	....	....	....	....	....	....	....	4	0	0	0	8	....	....	....	....
2003-04	Vancouver Giants	WHL	72	1	11	12	192	....	....	....	....	....	....	....	....	....	11	0	2	2	10	....	....	....	....
2004-05	Vancouver Giants	WHL	15	1	5	6	32	....	....	....	....	....	....	....	....	....	6	1	1	2	16	....	....	....	....
2005-06	Vancouver Giants	WHL	60	7	22	29	148	....	....	....	....	....	....	....	....	....	18	1	9	10	30	....	....	....	....
2006-07	Iowa Stars	AHL	80	2	22	24	83	....	....	....	....	....	....	....	....	....	12	0	0	0	16	....	....	....	....
2007-08	**Dallas**	**NHL**	**37**	**0**	**2**	**2**	**24**	**0**	**0**	**0**	**17**	**0.0**	**3**	**0**	**0.0**	**12:44**	**9**	**0**	**0**	**0**	**6**	**0**	**0**	**0**	**14:51**
	Iowa Stars	AHL	30	1	4	5	48	....	....	....	....	....	....	....	....	....	....	....	....	....	....	....	....	....	....
2008-09	**Dallas**	**NHL**	**36**	**0**	**4**	**4**	**42**	**0**	**0**	**0**	**35**	**0.0**	**−1**	**0**	**0.0**	**15:57**	....	....	....	....	....	....	....	....	....
	Manitoba Moose	AHL	35	0	8	8	26	....	....	....	....	....	....	....	....	....	22	2	5	7	26	....	....	....	....
2009-10	**Dallas**	**NHL**	**67**	**1**	**9**	**10**	**69**	**0**	**0**	**0**	**46**	**2.2**	**27**	**0**	**0.0**	**14:56**	....	....	....	....	....	....	....	....	....
2010-11	**Dallas**	**NHL**	**57**	**2**	**3**	**5**	**44**	**0**	**0**	**1**	**26**	**7.7**	**−10**	**0**	**0.0**	**14:23**	....	....	....	....	....	....	....	....	....
	Texas Stars	AHL	3	0	0	0	2	....	....	....	....	....	....	....	....	....	....	....	....	....	....	....	....	....	....
	NHL Totals		**197**	**3**	**18**	**21**	**179**	**0**	**0**	**1**	**124**	**2.4**		**0**	**0.0**	**14:33**	**9**	**0**	**0**	**0**	**6**	**0**	**0**	**0**	**14:51**

FITZGERALD, Zack

(fihtz-JAIR-uhld, ZAK)

Defense. Shoots left. 6'2", 205 lbs. Born, Two Harbors, MN, June 16, 1985. St. Louis' 4th choice, 88th overall, in 2003 Entry Draft.

Season	Club	League	GP	G	A	Pts	PIM	PP	SH	GW	S	%	+/-	TF	F%	Min	GP	G	A	Pts	PIM	PP	SH	GW	Min
2000-01	Duluth East	High-MN	26	1	7	8	44	....	....	....	....	....	....	....	....	....	....	....	....	....	....	....	....	....	....
2001-02	Seattle	WHL	61	3	7	10	214	....	....	....	....	....	....	....	....	....	10	0	2	2	19	....	....	....	....
2002-03	Seattle	WHL	64	8	14	22	232	....	....	....	....	....	....	....	....	....	15	0	4	4	33	....	....	....	....
2003-04	Seattle	WHL	58	4	15	19	163	....	....	....	....	....	....	....	....	....	....	....	....	....	....	....	....	....	....
2004-05	Seattle	WHL	65	7	18	25	*244	....	....	....	....	....	....	....	....	....	9	0	3	3	24	....	....	....	....
2005-06	Peoria Rivermen	AHL	13	1	1	2	47	....	....	....	....	....	....	....	....	....	....	....	....	....	....	....	....	....	....
	Alaska Aces	ECHL	12	1	1	2	108	....	....	....	....	....	....	....	....	....	....	....	....	....	....	....	....	....	....
2006-07	Peoria Rivermen	AHL	29	0	2	2	86	....	....	....	....	....	....	....	....	....	....	....	....	....	....	....	....	....	....
	Alaska Aces	ECHL	10	0	1	1	48	....	....	....	....	....	....	....	....	....	14	2	3	5	*82	....	....	....	....
2007-08	**Vancouver**	**NHL**	**1**	**0**	**0**	**0**	**0**	**0**	**0**	**0**	**1**	**0.0**	**0**	**0**	**0.0**	**13:20**	....	....	....	....	....	....	....	....	....
	Manitoba Moose	AHL	48	5	3	8	158	....	....	....	....	....	....	....	....	....	3	0	0	0	14	....	....	....	....
2008-09	Manitoba Moose	AHL	56	0	8	8	209	....	....	....	....	....	....	....	....	....	16	0	1	1	14	....	....	....	....
2009-10	Albany River Rats	AHL	77	2	12	14	*311	....	....	....	....	....	....	....	....	....	2	0	0	0	0	....	....	....	....
2010-11	Charlotte	AHL	76	0	8	8	229	....	....	....	....	....	....	....	....	....	10	0	1	1	32	....	....	....	....
	NHL Totals		**1**	**0**	**0**	**0**	**0**	**0**	**0**	**0**	**1**	**0.0**		**0**	**0.0**	**13:20**	....	....	....	....	....	....	....	....	....

Traded to **Vancouver** by **St. Louis** for Francois-Pierre Guenette, August 1, 2007. Signed as a free agent by **Carolina**, July 15, 2009.

FLEISCHMANN, Tomas

(FLIGHSH-muhn, TAW-mahsh) **FLA**

Left wing. Shoots left. 6'1", 192 lbs. Born, Koprivnice, Czech., May 16, 1984. Detroit's 2nd choice, 63rd overall, in 2002 Entry Draft.

Season	Club	League	GP	G	A	Pts	PIM	PP	SH	GW	S	%	+/-	TF	F%	Min	GP	G	A	Pts	PIM	PP	SH	GW	Min
99-2000	HC Vitkovice Jr.	CzRep-Jr.	46	9	13	22	6	....	....	....	....	....	....	....	....	....	....	....	....	....	....	....	....	....	....
2000-01	HC Vitkovice U17	CzR-U17	30	28	34	62	8	....	....	....	....	....	....	....	....	....	....	....	....	....	....	....	....	....	....
	HC Vitkovice Jr.	CzRep-Jr.	21	4	9	13	8	....	....	....	....	....	....	....	....	....	....	....	....	....	....	....	....	....	....
2001-02	HC Vitkovice Jr.	CzRep-Jr.	46	26	35	51	16	....	....	....	....	....	....	....	....	....	....	....	....	....	....	....	....	....	....
	TJ Novy Jicin	CzRep-3	8	3	2	5	8	....	....	....	....	....	....	....	....	....	7	3	4	7	35	....	....	....	....
2002-03	Moose Jaw	WHL	65	21	50	71	36	....	....	....	....	....	....	....	....	....	12	4	11	15	6	....	....	....	....
2003-04	Moose Jaw	WHL	60	33	42	75	32	....	....	....	....	....	....	....	....	....	10	3	4	7	10	....	....	....	....
2004-05	Portland Pirates	AHL	53	7	12	19	14	....	....	....	....	....	....	....	....	....	....	....	....	....	....	....	....	....	....
2005-06	**Washington**	**NHL**	**14**	**0**	**2**	**2**	**0**	**0**	**0**	**0**	**11**	**0.0**	**−7**	**5**	**40.0**	**6:45**	....	....	....	....	....	....	....	....	....
	Hershey Bears	AHL	57	30	33	63	32	....	....	....	....	....	....	....	....	....	20	11	*21	32	15	....	....	....	....
2006-07	**Washington**	**NHL**	**29**	**4**	**4**	**8**	**8**	**1**	**0**	**1**	**52**	**7.7**	**−6**	**14**	**35.7**	**11:38**	....	....	....	....	....	....	....	....	....
	Hershey Bears	AHL	45	22	29	51	22	....	....	....	....	....	....	....	....	....	19	5	16	21	10	....	....	....	....
2007-08	**Washington**	**NHL**	**75**	**10**	**20**	**30**	**18**	**1**	**0**	**1**	**107**	**9.3**	**−7**	**30**	**50.0**	**12:37**	**2**	**0**	**0**	**0**	**0**	**0**	**0**	**0**	**9:49**
2008-09	**Washington**	**NHL**	**73**	**19**	**18**	**37**	**20**	**7**	**0**	**4**	**131**	**14.5**	**−3**	**34**	**26.5**	**15:05**	**14**	**3**	**1**	**4**	**4**	**1**	**0**	**1**	**14:19**

											Regular Season						Playoffs							
Season	Club	League	GP	G	A	Pts	PIM	PP	SH	GW	S	%	+/-	TF	F%	Min	GP	G	A	Pts	PIM	PP	SH	GW	Min
2009-10	Washington	NHL	69	23	28	51	28	7	0	4	121	19.0	9	371	43.1	16:02	6	0	1	1	6	0	0	0	13:21
	Hershey Bears	AHL	2	0	1	1	0																		
	Czech Republic	Olympics	5	1	2	3	2																		
2010-11	Washington	NHL	23	4	6	10	10	0	0	1	44	9.1	3	225	43.1	14:20									
	Colorado	NHL	22	8	13	21	8	3	0	1	54	14.8	–1	11	18.2	18:28									
	NHL Totals		305	68	91	159	92	19	0	12	520	13.1		690	42.0	14:10	22	3	2	5	10	1	0	1	13:39

WHL East Second All-Star Team (2004)

Traded to **Washington** by **Detroit** with Detroit's 1st round choice (Mike Green) in 2004 Entry Draft and Detroit's 4th round choice (Luke Lynes) in 2006 Entry Draft for Robert Lang, February 27, 2004. Traded to **Colorado** by **Washington** for Scott Hannan, November 30, 2010. Signed as a free agent by **Florida**, July 1, 2011.

FLOOD, Mark

(FLUD, MAHRK) **WPG**

Defense. Shoots right. 6'1", 190 lbs. Born, Charlottetown, P.E.I., September 29, 1984. Montreal's 8th choice, 188th overall, in 2003 Entry Draft.

2000-01	Charlotwn AAA	PEIHA	STATISTICS NOT AVAILABLE																						
	Charlotwn Abbies	MJrHL	11	0	2	2	2																		
2001-02	Peterborough	OHL	57	1	4	5	21										6	0	0	0	2				
2002-03	Peterborough	OHL	68	5	24	29	18										7	1	2	3	0				
2003-04	Peterborough	OHL	68	15	29	44	30																		
2004-05	Peterborough	OHL	60	4	38	42	14										14	2	7	9	0				
2005-06	Syracuse Crunch	AHL	9	1	1	2	2																		
	Dayton Bombers	ECHL	50	11	14	25	20																		
2006-07	Syracuse Crunch	AHL	8	1	1	2	2																		
	Albany River Rats	AHL	36	3	7	10	20																		
2007-08	Albany River Rats	AHL	53	10	12	22	18																		
2008-09	Albany River Rats	AHL	76	6	25	31	27																		
2009-10	NY Islanders	NHL	6	0	1	1	0	0	0	0	5	0.0	–4	0	0.0	12:43									
	Bridgeport	AHL	61	10	23	33	39										5	0	2	2	6				
2010-11	Manitoba Moose	AHL	63	11	29	40	29										14	0	6	6	2				
	NHL Totals		6	0	1	1	0	0	0	0	5	0.0		0	0.0	12:43									

Signed as a free agent by **Columbus**, August 22, 2005. Traded to **Carolina** by **Columbus** for Derrick Walser, November 29, 2006. Signed as a free agent by **NY Islanders**, July 6, 2009. Signed as a free agent by **Manitoba** (AHL), September 8, 2010. Signed as a free agent by **Winnipeg**, July 3. 2011.

FOLIGNO, Nick

(foh-LEE-noh, NIHK) **OTT**

Left wing. Shoots left. 6', 208 lbs. Born, Buffalo, NY, October 31, 1987. Ottawa's 1st choice, 28th overall, in 2006 Entry Draft.

2003-04	USNTDP	U-17	18	7	9	16	28																		
	USNTDP	NAHL	43	8	12	20	44										7	2	1	3	8				
2004-05	USNTDP	U-18	4	2	1	3	0																		
	Sudbury Wolves	OHL	65	10	28	38	111										12	5	5	10	16				
2005-06	Sudbury Wolves	OHL	65	24	46	70	146										10	1	3	4	28				
2006-07	Sudbury Wolves	OHL	66	31	57	88	135										21	12	17	29	36				
2007-08	Ottawa	NHL	45	6	3	9	20	0	0	0	44	13.6	0	49	44.9	9:10	4	1	0	1	2	0	0	0	12:50
	Binghamton	AHL	28	6	13	19	16																		
2008-09	Ottawa	NHL	81	17	15	32	59	7	0	2	145	11.7	–10	47	44.7	13:41									
2009-10	Ottawa	NHL	61	9	17	26	53	2	0	2	83	10.8	6	50	34.0	14:19	6	0	1	1	2	0	0	0	17:07
2010-11	Ottawa	NHL	82	14	20	34	43	5	0	3	149	9.4	–19	138	47.1	15:35									
	NHL Totals		269	46	55	101	175	14	0	7	421	10.9		284	44.0	13:39	10	1	1	2	4	0	0	0	15:24

FOOTE, Adam

(FUT, A-duhm)

Defense. Shoots right. 6'2", 220 lbs. Born, Toronto, Ont., July 10, 1971. Quebec's 2nd choice, 22nd overall, in 1989 Entry Draft.

1987-88	Whitby Midgets	Minor-ON	65	25	43	68	108																		
1988-89	Sault Ste. Marie	OHL	66	7	32	39	120																		
1989-90	Sault Ste. Marie	OHL	61	12	43	55	199																		
1990-91	Sault Ste. Marie	OHL	59	18	51	69	93										14	5	12	17	28				
1991-92	Quebec	NHL	46	2	5	7	44	0	0	0	55	3.6	–4												
	Halifax Citadels	AHL	6	0	1	1	2																		
1992-93	Quebec	NHL	81	4	12	16	168	0	1	0	54	7.4	6				6	0	1	1	2	0	0	0	
1993-94	Quebec	NHL	45	2	6	8	67	0	0	0	42	4.8	3												
1994-95	Quebec	NHL	35	0	7	7	52	0	0	0	24	0.0	17				6	0	1	1	14	0	0	0	
1995-96 ♦	Colorado	NHL	73	5	11	16	88	1	0	1	49	10.2	27				22	1	3	4	36	0	0	0	
1996-97	Colorado	NHL	78	2	19	21	135	0	0	0	60	3.3	16				17	0	4	4	62	0	0	0	
1997-98	Colorado	NHL	77	3	14	17	124	0	0	1	64	4.7	–3				7	0	0	0	23	0	0	0	
	Canada	Olympics	6	0	1	1	4																		
1998-99	Colorado	NHL	64	5	16	21	92	3	0	0	83	6.0	20	0	0.0	24:50	19	2	3	5	24	1	0	0	28:34
99-2000	Colorado	NHL	59	5	13	18	98	1	0	2	63	7.9	5	0	0.0	25:51	16	0	7	7	28	0	0	0	26:05
2000-01 ♦	Colorado	NHL	35	3	12	15	42	1	1	1	59	5.1	6	0	0.0	25:22	23	3	4	7	*47	1	0	1	28:22
2001-02	Colorado	NHL	55	5	22	27	55	1	1	0	85	5.9	7	0	0.0	25:59	21	1	6	7	28	0	0	0	27:46
	Canada	Olympics	6	1	0	1	2																		
2002-03	Colorado	NHL	78	11	20	31	88	3	0	2	106	10.4	30	0	0.0	25:43	6	0	1	1	8	0	0	0	24:12
2003-04	Colorado	NHL	73	8	22	30	87	5	0	1	105	7.6	13	0	0.0	24:03	11	0	4	4	10	0	0	0	25:06
2004-05			DID NOT PLAY																						
2005-06	Columbus	NHL	65	6	16	22	89	2	2	1	67	9.0	–16	0	0.0	24:34									
	Canada	Olympics	6	0	1	1	6																		
2006-07	Columbus	NHL	59	3	9	12	71	2	0	0	78	3.8	–17	0	0.0	24:44									
2007-08	Columbus	NHL	63	1	14	15	95	0	1	0	57	1.8	3	0	0.0	24:02									
	Colorado	NHL	12	0	1	1	12	0	0	0	9	0.0	–1	0	0.0	20:01	10	0	0	0	6	0	0	0	21:14
2008-09	Colorado	NHL	42	1	6	7	30	0	0	1	19	5.3	–12	0	0.0	19:41									
2009-10	Colorado	NHL	67	0	9	9	64	0	0	0	26	0.0	8	0	0.0	19:22	6	0	1	1	10	0	0	0	21:23
2010-11	Colorado	NHL	47	0	8	8	33	0	0	0	23	0.0	–9	0	0.0	17:56									
	NHL Totals		1154	66	242	308	1534	19	6	10	1128	5.9		0	0.0	23:36	170	7	35	42	298	2	0	1	26:24

OHL First All-Star Team (1991)

• Transferred to **Colorado** after **Quebec** franchise relocated, June 21, 1995. • Missed majority of 2000-01 due to shoulder injury vs. Carolina, January 6, 2001. Signed as a free agent by **Columbus**, August 2, 2005. Traded to **Colorado** by **Columbus** for Colorado's 1st round choice (later traded to Philadelphia - Philadelphia selected Luca Sbisa) in 2008 Entry Draft and Colorado's 4th round choice (David Savard) in 2009 Entry Draft, February 26, 2008. • Officially announced his retirement, April 8, 2011.

FORSBERG, Peter

(FOHRS-buhrg, PEE-tuhr)

Center. Shoots left. 6', 205 lbs. Born, Ornskoldsvik, Sweden, July 20, 1973. Philadelphia's 1st choice, 6th overall, in 1991 Entry Draft.

1989-90	MoDo Jr.	Swe-Jr.	30	15	12	27	42																		
	MoDo	Sweden	1	0	1	1	4																		
1990-91	MoDo Jr.	Swe-Jr.	39	38	64	102	56																		
	MoDo	Sweden	23	7	10	17	22																		
1991-92	MoDo	Sweden	39	9	18	27	78																		
1992-93	MoDo Jr.	Swe-Jr.	2	0	3	3	4																		
	MoDo	Sweden	39	23	24	47	92										3	4	1	5	0				
1993-94	MoDo	Sweden	39	18	26	44	82										11	9	7	16	14				
	Sweden	Olympics	8	2	6	8	6																		
1994-95	MoDo	Sweden	11	5	9	14	20																		
	Quebec	NHL	47	15	35	50	16	3	0	3	86	17.4	17				6	2	4	6	4	1	0	0	
1995-96 ♦	Colorado	NHL	82	30	86	116	47	7	3	3	217	13.8	26				22	10	11	21	18	3	0	1	
1996-97	Colorado	NHL	65	28	58	86	73	5	4	4	188	14.9	31				14	5	12	17	10	3	0	0	
1997-98	Colorado	NHL	72	25	66	91	94	7	3	7	202	12.4	6				7	6	5	11	12	2	0	0	
	Sweden	Olympics	4	1	4	5	6																		
1998-99	Colorado	NHL	78	30	67	97	108	9	2	7	217	13.8	27	895	54.4	23:29	19	8	16	*24	31	1	1	0	21:39
99-2000	Colorado	NHL	49	14	37	51	52	3	0	2	105	13.3	9	519	46.6	20:55	16	7	8	15	12	2	1	*4	20:59
2000-01 ♦	Colorado	NHL	73	27	62	89	54	12	2	5	178	15.2	23	755	46.6	20:48	11	4	10	14	6	1	0	2	21:55
2001-02	Colorado	NHL															20	9	*18	*27	20	0	0	*4	18:10
2002-03	Colorado	NHL	75	29	*77	*106	70	8	0	2	166	17.5	*52	709	47.0	19:20	7	2	6	8	6	1	0	0	20:01
2003-04	Colorado	NHL	39	18	37	55	30	3	1	5	85	21.2	16	549	42.3	19:12	11	4	7	11	12	1	0	1	19:02

			Regular Season														Playoffs								
Season	Club	League	GP	G	A	Pts	PIM	PP	SH	GW	S	%	+/-	TF	F%	Min	GP	G	A	Pts	PIM	PP	SH	GW	Min
2004-05	MODO	Sweden	33	13	26	39	88	....	....	....	....	....	....	....	....	....	1	0	0	0	2	....	....	....	....
2005-06	**Philadelphia**	**NHL**	**60**	**19**	**56**	**75**	**46**	**8**	**1**	**2**	**132**	**14.4**	**21**	**941**	**50.6**	**18:47**	**6**	**4**	**4**	**8**	**6**	**1**	**0**	**2**	**18:55**
	Sweden	Olympics	6	0	6	6	0	....	....	....	....	....	....	....	....	....	....	....	....	....	....	....	....	....	....
2006-07	**Philadelphia**	**NHL**	**40**	**11**	**29**	**40**	**72**	**5**	**0**	**2**	**63**	**17.5**	**2**	**690**	**50.9**	**17:44**	....	....	....	....	....	....	....	....	....
	Nashville	**NHL**	**17**	**2**	**13**	**15**	**16**	**1**	**0**	**1**	**36**	**5.6**	**5**	**267**	**47.6**	**19:36**	**5**	**2**	**2**	**4**	**12**	**0**	**0**	**0**	**20:57**
2007-08	**Colorado**	**NHL**	**9**	**1**	**13**	**14**	**8**	**0**	**0**	**0**	**15**	**6.7**	**7**	**4**	**100.0**	**19:15**	**7**	**1**	**4**	**5**	**14**	**0**	**0**	**0**	**18:17**
2008-09	MODO	Sweden	3	1	2	3	0	....	....	....	....	....	....	....	....	....	....	....	....	....	....	....	....	....	....
2009-10	MODO	Sweden	23	11	19	30	66	....	....	....	....	....	....	....	....	....	....	....	....	....	....	....	....	....	....
	Sweden	Olympics	4	0	1	1	2	....	....	....	....	....	....	....	....	....	....	....	....	....	....	....	....	....	....
2010-11	**Colorado**	**NHL**	**2**	**0**	**0**	**0**	**4**	**0**	**0**	**0**	**3**	**0.0**	**–4**	**0**	**0.0**	**17:35**	....	....	....	....	....	....	....	....	....
	NHL Totals		**708**	**249**	**636**	**885**	**690**	**71**	**16**	**43**	**1693**	**14.7**		**5329**	**48.9**	**20:15**	**151**	**64**	**107**	**171**	**163**	**16**	**2**	**14**	**20:04**

NHL All-Rookie Team (1995) • Calder Memorial Trophy (1995) • NHL First All-Star Team (1998, 1999, 2003) • Bud Light Plus/Minus Award (2003) (tied with Milan Hejduk) • Art Ross Trophy (2003) • Hart Memorial Trophy (2003).

Played in NHL All-Star Game (1996, 1998, 1999, 2001, 2003)

Traded to **Quebec** by **Philadelphia** with Steve Duchesne, Kerry Huffman, Mike Ricci, Ron Hextall, Philadelphia's 1st round choice (Jocelyn Thibault) in 1993 Entry Draft, $15,000,000 and future considerations (Chris Simon and Philadelphia's 1st round choice (later traded to Toronto – later traded to Washington – Washington selected Nolan Baumgartner) in 1994 Entry Draft, July 21, 1992) for Eric Lindros, June 30, 1992. Transferred to **Colorado** after **Quebec** franchise relocated, June 21, 1995. • Missed entire 2001-02 regular due to spleen (May 9, 2001 vs. Los Angeles) and ankle (January 10, 2002 in practice) injuries. • Missed majority of 2003-04 due to groin (October 28, 2003 vs. Calgary) and hip (February 16, 2004 vs. Vancouver) injuries. Signed as a free agent by **MODO** (Sweden), September 18, 2004. Signed as a free agent by **Philadelphia**, August 3, 2005. Traded to **Nashville** by **Philadelphia** for Scottie Upshall, Ryan Parent and Nashville's 1st (later traded back to Nashville - Nashville selected Jonathon Blum) and 3rd (later traded to Washington - Washington selected Phil Desimone) round choices in 2007 Entry Draft, February 15, 2007. Signed as a free agent by **Colorado**, February 25, 2008. Signed as a free agent by **MODO** (Sweden), November 16, 2009. Signed as a free agent by **Colorado**, February 6, 2011. • Officially announced his retirement, February 14, 2011.

FORTUNUS, Maxime

(fohr-TOON-uhs, MAX-eem) **DAL**

Defense. Shoots right. 6'1", 198 lbs. Born, Longueil, Que., July 28, 1983.

Season	Club	League	GP	G	A	Pts	PIM	PP	SH	GW	S	%	+/-	TF	F%	Min	GP	G	A	Pts	PIM	PP	SH	GW	Min
99-2000	Baie-Comeau	QMJHL	68	6	15	21	36	....	....	....	....	....	....	....	....	....	6	0	0	0	2	....	....	....	....
2000-01	Baie-Comeau	QMJHL	71	10	31	41	106	....	....	....	....	....	....	....	....	....	11	2	4	6	6	....	....	....	....
2001-02	Baie-Comeau	QMJHL	72	11	30	41	76	....	....	....	....	....	....	....	....	....	5	0	1	1	2	....	....	....	....
2002-03	Baie-Comeau	QMJHL	69	12	32	44	44	....	....	....	....	....	....	....	....	....	12	2	4	6	6	....	....	....	....
2003-04	Baie-Comeau	QMJHL	5	1	0	1	15	....	....	....	....	....	....	....	....	....	....	....	....	....	....	....	....	....	....
	Houston Aeros	AHL	12	0	2	2	2	....	....	....	....	....	....	....	....	....	1	0	0	0	0	....	....	....	....
	Louisiana	ECHL	64	3	15	18	27	....	....	....	....	....	....	....	....	....	4	1	1	2	0	....	....	....	....
2004-05	Houston Aeros	AHL	13	0	0	0	4	....	....	....	....	....	....	....	....	....	....	....	....	....	....	....	....	....	....
	Louisiana	ECHL	59	8	16	24	26	....	....	....	....	....	....	....	....	....	....	....	....	....	....	....	....	....	....
2005-06	Manitoba Moose	AHL	76	3	10	13	36	....	....	....	....	....	....	....	....	....	13	0	0	0	10	....	....	....	....
2006-07	Manitoba Moose	AHL	72	2	18	20	64	....	....	....	....	....	....	....	....	....	13	1	4	5	10	....	....	....	....
2007-08	Manitoba Moose	AHL	65	8	13	21	28	....	....	....	....	....	....	....	....	....	6	0	1	1	4	....	....	....	....
2008-09	Manitoba Moose	AHL	58	7	12	19	18	....	....	....	....	....	....	....	....	....	22	3	7	10	2	....	....	....	....
2009-10	**Dallas**	**NHL**	**8**	**0**	**0**	**0**	**4**	**0**	**0**	**0**	**5**	**0.0**	**–6**	**0**	**0.0**	**15:09**	....	....	....	....	....	....	....	....	....
	Texas Stars	AHL	72	11	12	23	28	....	....	....	....	....	....	....	....	....	24	2	7	9	14	....	....	....	....
2010-11	Texas Stars	AHL	73	5	29	34	20	....	....	....	....	....	....	....	....	....	6	0	1	1	2	....	....	....	....
	NHL Totals		**8**	**0**	**0**	**0**	**4**	**0**	**0**	**0**	**5**	**0.0**		**0**	**0.0**	**15:09**	....	....	....	....	....	....	....	....	....

Signed as a free agent by **Dallas**, July 3, 2008.

FOSTER, Alex

(FAW-stuhr, AL-ehx)

Center. Shoots left. 6', 200 lbs. Born, Canton, MI, August 26, 1984.

Season	Club	League	GP	G	A	Pts	PIM	PP	SH	GW	S	%	+/-	TF	F%	Min	GP	G	A	Pts	PIM	PP	SH	GW	Min
2001-02	Sioux Falls	USHL	57	6	15	21	72	....	....	....	....	....	....	....	....	....	3	0	1	1	8	....	....	....	....
2002-03	Cleveland Barons	NAHL	43	9	18	27	38	....	....	....	....	....	....	....	....	....	....	....	....	....	....	....	....	....	....
	Sioux Falls	USHL	5	0	1	1	0	....	....	....	....	....	....	....	....	....	....	....	....	....	....	....	....	....	....
2003-04	Danville Wings	USHL	55	23	30	53	91	....	....	....	....	....	....	....	....	....	6	1	2	3	6	....	....	....	....
2004-05	Bowling Green	CCHA	34	8	23	31	31	....	....	....	....	....	....	....	....	....	....	....	....	....	....	....	....	....	....
2005-06	Bowling Green	CCHA	38	11	40	51	40	....	....	....	....	....	....	....	....	....	....	....	....	....	....	....	....	....	....
2006-07	Toronto Marlies	AHL	57	8	9	17	31	....	....	....	....	....	....	....	....	....	....	....	....	....	....	....	....	....	....
	Columbia Inferno	ECHL	9	1	10	11	6	....	....	....	....	....	....	....	....	....	....	....	....	....	....	....	....	....	....
2007-08	**Toronto**	**NHL**	**3**	**0**	**0**	**0**	**0**	**0**	**0**	**0**	**1**	**0.0**	**0**	**1**	**0.0**	**3:32**	....	....	....	....	....	....	....	....	....
	Toronto Marlies	AHL	67	18	28	46	30	....	....	....	....	....	....	....	....	....	19	2	6	8	12	....	....	....	....
2008-09	Toronto Marlies	AHL	80	12	23	35	88	....	....	....	....	....	....	....	....	....	6	2	3	5	8	....	....	....	....
2009-10	Toronto Marlies	AHL	30	9	8	17	20	....	....	....	....	....	....	....	....	....	....	....	....	....	....	....	....	....	....
2010-11	Toronto Marlies	AHL	70	10	24	34	28	....	....	....	....	....	....	....	....	....	....	....	....	....	....	....	....	....	....
	NHL Totals		**3**	**0**	**0**	**0**	**0**	**0**	**0**	**0**	**1**	**0.0**		**1**	**0.0**	**3:32**	....	....	....	....	....	....	....	....	....

CCHA Second All-Star Team (2006)

Signed as a free agent by **Toronto**, March 8, 2006. • Missed majority of 2009-10 due to various injuries.

FOSTER, Kurtis

(FAW-stuhr, KUHR-this) **ANA**

Defense. Shoots right. 6'5", 226 lbs. Born, Carp, Ont., November 24, 1981. Calgary's 2nd choice, 40th overall, in 2000 Entry Draft.

Season	Club	League	GP	G	A	Pts	PIM	PP	SH	GW	S	%	+/-	TF	F%	Min	GP	G	A	Pts	PIM	PP	SH	GW	Min
1996-97	Ottawa Valley	ODMHA	36	7	18	25	88	....	....	....	....	....	....	....	....	....	....	....	....	....	....	....	....	....	....
1997-98	Peterborough	OHL	39	1	1	2	45	....	....	....	....	....	....	....	....	....	4	0	0	0	2	....	....	....	....
1998-99	Peterborough	OHL	54	2	13	15	59	....	....	....	....	....	....	....	....	....	5	0	0	0	6	....	....	....	....
99-2000	Peterborough	OHL	68	6	18	24	116	....	....	....	....	....	....	....	....	....	5	1	2	3	4	....	....	....	....
2000-01	Peterborough	OHL	62	17	24	41	78	....	....	....	....	....	....	....	....	....	7	1	1	2	10	....	....	....	....
2001-02	Peterborough	OHL	33	10	4	14	58	....	....	....	....	....	....	....	....	....	....	....	....	....	....	....	....	....	....
	Chicago Wolves	AHL	39	6	9	15	59	....	....	....	....	....	....	....	....	....	14	1	1	2	21	....	....	....	....
2002-03	**Atlanta**	**NHL**	**2**	**0**	**0**	**0**	**0**	**0**	**0**	**0**	**1**	**0.0**	**–2**	**0**	**0.0**	**11:06**	....	....	....	....	....	....	....	....	....
	Chicago Wolves	AHL	75	15	27	42	159	....	....	....	....	....	....	....	....	....	9	1	3	4	14	....	....	....	....
2003-04	**Atlanta**	**NHL**	**3**	**0**	**1**	**1**	**0**	**0**	**0**	**0**	**1**	**0.0**	**0**	**0**	**0.0**	**6:58**	....	....	....	....	....	....	....	....	....
	Chicago Wolves	AHL	67	11	19	30	95	....	....	....	....	....	....	....	....	....	10	0	3	3	12	....	....	....	....
2004-05	Cincinnati	AHL	78	17	25	42	71	....	....	....	....	....	....	....	....	....	9	2	3	5	28	....	....	....	....
2005-06	**Minnesota**	**NHL**	**58**	**10**	**18**	**28**	**60**	**6**	**0**	**2**	**124**	**8.1**	**–3**	**0**	**0.0**	**19:13**	....	....	....	....	....	....	....	....	....
	Houston Aeros	AHL	19	4	11	15	32	....	....	....	....	....	....	....	....	....	....	....	....	....	....	....	....	....	....
2006-07	**Minnesota**	**NHL**	**57**	**3**	**20**	**23**	**52**	**0**	**0**	**0**	**135**	**2.2**	**–3**	**1**	**100.0**	**17:59**	**3**	**0**	**2**	**2**	**0**	**0**	**0**	**0**	**18:38**
2007-08	**Minnesota**	**NHL**	**56**	**7**	**12**	**19**	**37**	**3**	**0**	**2**	**118**	**5.9**	**0**	**3**	**66.7**	**16:24**	....	....	....	....	....	....	....	....	....
2008-09	**Minnesota**	**NHL**	**10**	**1**	**5**	**6**	**6**	**0**	**0**	**0**	**10**	**10.0**	**7**	**0**	**0.0**	**13:35**	....	....	....	....	....	....	....	....	....
	Houston Aeros	AHL	6	1	5	6	6	....	....	....	....	....	....	....	....	....	....	....	....	....	....	....	....	....	....
2009-10	**Tampa Bay**	**NHL**	**71**	**8**	**34**	**42**	**48**	**3**	**0**	**1**	**165**	**4.8**	**–5**	**0**	**0.0**	**17:11**	....	....	....	....	....	....	....	....	....
2010-11	**Edmonton**	**NHL**	**74**	**8**	**14**	**22**	**45**	**5**	**0**	**0**	**182**	**4.4**	**–12**	**0**	**0.0**	**17:40**	....	....	....	....	....	....	....	....	....
	NHL Totals		**331**	**37**	**104**	**141**	**248**	**17**	**0**	**5**	**736**	**5.0**		**4**	**75.0**	**17:25**	**3**	**0**	**2**	**2**	**0**	**0**	**0**	**0**	**18:38**

Yanick Dupre Memorial Award (AHL - Outstanding Humanitarian Contribution) (2004)

• Rights traded to **Atlanta** by **Calgary** with Jeff Cowan for Petr Buzek and Atlanta's 6th round choice (Adam Pardy) in 2004 Entry Draft, December 18, 2001. Traded to **Anaheim** by **Atlanta** for Niclas Havelid, June 26, 2004. Signed as a free agent by **Minnesota**, August 4, 2005. • Missed majority of 2008-09 due to leg injury vs. San Jose, March 20, 2008. Signed as a free agent by **Tampa Bay**, July 8, 2009. Signed as a free agent by **Edmonton**, July 1, 2010. Traded to **Anaheim** by **Edmonton** for Andy Sutton, July 1, 2011.

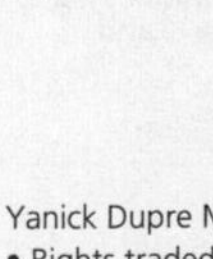

FOWLER, Cam

(FOW-luhr, KAM) **ANA**

Defense. Shoots left. 6'1", 196 lbs. Born, Windsor, Ont., December 5, 1991. Anaheim's 1st choice, 12th overall, in 2010 Entry Draft.

Season	Club	League	GP	G	A	Pts	PIM	PP	SH	GW	S	%	+/-	TF	F%	Min	GP	G	A	Pts	PIM	PP	SH	GW	Min
2006-07	Det. Honeybaked	MWEHL	21	5	13	18	18	....	....	....	....	....	....	....	....	....	....	....	....	....	....	....	....	....	....
	Det. Honeybaked	Minor-MI	31	3	7	10	....	....	....	....	....	....	....	....	....	....	....	....	....	....	....	....	....	....	....
2007-08	USNTDP	NAHL	38	3	10	13	2	....	....	....	....	....	....	....	....	....	3	0	0	0	2	....	....	....	....
	USNTDP	U-17	18	0	2	2	8	....	....	....	....	....	....	....	....	....	....	....	....	....	....	....	....	....	....
	USNTDP	U-18	1	0	0	0	0	....	....	....	....	....	....	....	....	....	....	....	....	....	....	....	....	....	....
2008-09	USNTDP	NAHL	14	2	7	9	12	....	....	....	....	....	....	....	....	....	....	....	....	....	....	....	....	....	....
	USNTDP	U-18	33	6	25	31	32	....	....	....	....	....	....	....	....	....	....	....	....	....	....	....	....	....	....
2009-10	Windsor Spitfires	OHL	55	8	47	55	14	....	....	....	....	....	....	....	....	....	19	3	11	14	10	....	....	....	....
	Windsor Spitfires	M-Cup	....	....	....	....	....	....	....	....	....	....	....	....	....	....	4	2	4	6	0	....	....	....	....
2010-11	**Anaheim**	**NHL**	**76**	**10**	**30**	**40**	**20**	**6**	**0**	**3**	**123**	**8.1**	**–25**	**0**	**0.0**	**22:08**	**6**	**1**	**3**	**4**	**2**	**1**	**0**	**0**	**22:13**
	NHL Totals		**76**	**10**	**30**	**40**	**20**	**6**	**0**	**3**	**123**	**8.1**		**0**	**0.0**	**22:08**	**6**	**1**	**3**	**4**	**2**	**1**	**0**	**0**	**22:14**

Memorial Cup All-Star Team (2010)

FRANSON, Cody

(FRAN-suhn, KOH-dee) **TOR**

Defense. Shoots right. 6'5", 213 lbs. Born, Salmon Arm, B.C., August 8, 1987. Nashville's 3rd choice, 79th overall, in 2005 Entry Draft.

			Regular Season														Playoffs								
Season	Club	League	GP	G	A	Pts	PIM	PP	SH	GW	S	%	+/-	TF	F%	Min	GP	G	A	Pts	PIM	PP	SH	GW	Min
2002-03	Sicamous	Minor-BC	65	44	82	126	42	....	....	....	....	....	....	....	....	....	....	....	....	....	....	....	....	....	....
	Vancouver Giants	WHL	3	0	0	0	2	....	....	....	....	....	....	....	....	....	....	....	....	....	....	....	....	....	....
2003-04	Beaver Valley	KIJHL	48	10	22	32	70	....	....	....	....	....	....	....	....	....	....	....	....	....	....	....	....	....	....
	Trail	BCHL	2	0	1	1	0	....	....	....	....	....	....	....	....	....	....	....	....	....	....	....	....	....	....
	Vancouver Giants	WHL	2	0	0	0	0	....	....	....	....	....	....	....	....	....	....	....	....	....	....	....	....	....	....
2004-05	Vancouver Giants	WHL	64	2	11	13	44	....	....	....	....	....	....	....	....	....	4	0	1	1	0	....	....	....	....
2005-06	Vancouver Giants	WHL	71	15	40	55	61	....	....	....	....	....	....	....	....	....	18	5	15	20	12	....	....	....	....
2006-07	Vancouver Giants	WHL	59	17	34	51	88	....	....	....	....	....	....	....	....	....	19	3	4	7	10	....	....	....	....
2007-08	Milwaukee	AHL	76	11	25	36	40	....	....	....	....	....	....	....	....	....	6	0	2	2	2	....	....	....	....
2008-09	Milwaukee	AHL	76	11	41	52	47	....	....	....	....	....	....	....	....	....	11	3	5	8	8	....	....	....	....
2009-10	**Nashville**	**NHL**	**61**	**6**	**15**	**21**	**16**	**1**	**0**	**3**	**90**	**6.7**	**15**	**0**	**0.0**	**14:12**	**4**	**0**	**1**	**1**	**2**	**0**	**0**	**0**	**9:02**
	Milwaukee	AHL	6	2	5	7	4	....	....	....	....	....	....	....	....	....	....	....	....	....	....	....	....	....	....
2010-11	**Nashville**	**NHL**	**80**	**8**	**21**	**29**	**30**	**2**	**0**	**2**	**156**	**5.1**	**10**	**0**	**0.0**	**15:10**	**12**	**1**	**5**	**6**	**0**	**0**	**0**	**0**	**15:19**
	NHL Totals		**141**	**14**	**36**	**50**	**46**	**3**	**0**	**5**	**246**	**5.7**		**0**	**0.0**	**14:45**	**16**	**1**	**6**	**7**	**2**	**0**	**0**	**0**	**13:45**

WHL West Second All-Star Team (2006) • WHL West First All-Star Team (2007) • Memorial Cup All-Star Team (2007) • AHL All-Rookie Team (2008) • AHL Second All-Star Team (2009)

Traded to **Toronto** by **Nashville** with Matthew Lombardi and future considerations for Brett Lebda, Robert Slaney and future considerations, July 3, 2011.

FRANZEN, Johan

(FRAN-zehn, YOH-han) **DET**

Left wing. Shoots left. 6'3", 222 lbs. Born, Landsbro, Sweden, December 23, 1979. Detroit's 1st choice, 97th overall, in 2004 Entry Draft.

			Regular Season														Playoffs								
Season	Club	League	GP	G	A	Pts	PIM	PP	SH	GW	S	%	+/-	TF	F%	Min	GP	G	A	Pts	PIM	PP	SH	GW	Min
2001-02	Linkopings HC	Sweden	36	2	6	8	64	....	....	....	....	....	....	....	....	....	....	....	....	....	....	....	....	....	....
2002-03	Linkopings HC	Sweden	37	2	4	6	14	....	....	....	....	....	....	....	....	....	....	....	....	....	....	....	....	....	....
2003-04	Linkopings HC	Sweden	49	12	18	30	26	....	....	....	....	....	....	....	....	....	5	0	1	1	8	....	....	....	....
2004-05	Linkopings HC	Sweden	43	7	7	14	45	....	....	....	....	....	....	....	....	....	6	2	0	2	16	....	....	....	....
2005-06	**Detroit**	**NHL**	**80**	**12**	**4**	**16**	**36**	**0**	**2**	**2**	**119**	**10.1**	**4**	**171**	**41.5**	**12:27**	**6**	**1**	**2**	**3**	**4**	**0**	**0**	**0**	**12:00**
2006-07	**Detroit**	**NHL**	**69**	**10**	**20**	**30**	**37**	**0**	**1**	**2**	**151**	**6.6**	**20**	**45**	**40.0**	**15:35**	**18**	**3**	**4**	**7**	**10**	**0**	**0**	**2**	**16:47**
2007-08 ♦	**Detroit**	**NHL**	**72**	**27**	**11**	**38**	**51**	**14**	**0**	**8**	**199**	**13.6**	**12**	**390**	**48.5**	**17:44**	**16**	***13**	**5**	**18**	**14**	***6**	***2**	***5**	**18:49**
2008-09	**Detroit**	**NHL**	**71**	**34**	**25**	**59**	**44**	**11**	**1**	**8**	**246**	**13.8**	**21**	**241**	**56.0**	**18:06**	**23**	**12**	**11**	**23**	**12**	**4**	**0**	**3**	**19:41**
2009-10	**Detroit**	**NHL**	**27**	**10**	**11**	**21**	**22**	**6**	**0**	**1**	**91**	**11.0**	**1**	**27**	**55.6**	**18:42**	**12**	**6**	**12**	**18**	**16**	**1**	**0**	**1**	**17:34**
	Sweden	Olympics	4	1	1	2	2	....	....	....	....	....	....	....	....	....	....	....	....	....	....	....	....	....	....
2010-11	**Detroit**	**NHL**	**76**	**28**	**27**	**55**	**58**	**10**	**0**	**5**	**248**	**11.3**	**5**	**147**	**50.3**	**17:26**	**8**	**2**	**1**	**3**	**6**	**0**	**0**	**0**	**15:47**
	NHL Totals		**395**	**121**	**98**	**219**	**248**	**41**	**4**	**26**	**1054**	**11.5**		**1021**	**49.2**	**16:22**	**83**	**37**	**35**	**72**	**62**	**11**	**2**	**11**	**17:39**

• Missed majority of 2009-10 due to knee injury vs. Chicago, October 8, 2009.

FRASER, Colin

(FRAY-zuhr, KAW-lihn) **L.A.**

Center. Shoots left. 6'1", 193 lbs. Born, Surrey, B.C., January 28, 1985. Philadelphia's 3rd choice, 69th overall, in 2003 Entry Draft.

			Regular Season														Playoffs								
Season	Club	League	GP	G	A	Pts	PIM	PP	SH	GW	S	%	+/-	TF	F%	Min	GP	G	A	Pts	PIM	PP	SH	GW	Min
2000-01	Port Coquitlam	PIJHL	38	16	24	40	90	....	....	....	....	....	....	....	....	....	8	2	2	4	21	....	....	....	....
2001-02	Red Deer Rebels	WHL	67	11	31	42	126	....	....	....	....	....	....	....	....	....	23	2	1	3	39	....	....	....	....
2002-03	Red Deer Rebels	WHL	69	15	37	52	192	....	....	....	....	....	....	....	....	....	22	7	6	13	40	....	....	....	....
2003-04	Red Deer Rebels	WHL	70	24	29	53	174	....	....	....	....	....	....	....	....	....	19	5	9	14	24	....	....	....	....
2004-05	Red Deer Rebels	WHL	63	24	43	67	148	....	....	....	....	....	....	....	....	....	7	2	5	7	8	....	....	....	....
	Norfolk Admirals	AHL	3	0	0	0	20	....	....	....	....	....	....	....	....	....	6	1	0	1	2	....	....	....	....
2005-06	Norfolk Admirals	AHL	75	12	13	25	145	....	....	....	....	....	....	....	....	....	4	0	0	0	7	....	....	....	....
2006-07	**Chicago**	**NHL**	**1**	**0**	**0**	**0**	**2**	**0**	**0**	**0**	**0**	**0.0**	**–1**	**2**	**0.0**	**3:18**	....	....	....	....	....	....	....	....	....
	Norfolk Admirals	AHL	67	12	24	36	158	....	....	....	....	....	....	....	....	....	6	1	0	1	21	....	....	....	....
2007-08	**Chicago**	**NHL**	**5**	**0**	**0**	**0**	**7**	**0**	**0**	**0**	**4**	**0.0**	**–2**	**38**	**36.8**	**10:19**	....	....	....	....	....	....	....	....	....
	Rockford IceHogs	AHL	75	17	24	41	165	....	....	....	....	....	....	....	....	....	12	1	2	3	28	....	....	....	....
2008-09	**Chicago**	**NHL**	**81**	**6**	**11**	**17**	**55**	**0**	**1**	**0**	**67**	**9.0**	**3**	**787**	**47.8**	**10:54**	**2**	**0**	**0**	**0**	**2**	**0**	**0**	**0**	**11:31**
2009-10 ♦	**Chicago**	**NHL**	**70**	**7**	**12**	**19**	**44**	**0**	**0**	**0**	**92**	**7.6**	**6**	**445**	**48.8**	**9:36**	**3**	**0**	**0**	**0**	**0**	**0**	**0**	**0**	**8:24**
2010-11	**Edmonton**	**NHL**	**67**	**3**	**2**	**5**	**60**	**0**	**1**	**0**	**57**	**5.3**	**–2**	**552**	**44.6**	**10:17**	....	....	....	....	....	....	....	....	....
	NHL Totals		**224**	**16**	**25**	**41**	**168**	**0**	**2**	**0**	**220**	**7.3**		**1824**	**46.8**	**10:16**	**5**	**0**	**0**	**0**	**2**	**0**	**0**	**0**	**9:38**

Canadian Major Junior Humanitarian Player of the Year (2005)

Traded to **Chicago** by **Philadelphia** with Jim Vandermeer and Los Angeles' 2nd round choice (previously acquired, Chicago selected Bryan Bickell) in 2004 Entry Draft for Alex Zhamnov and Washington's 4th round choice (previously acquired, Philadelphia selected R.J. Anderson) in 2004 Entry Draft, February 19, 2004. Traded to **Edmonton** by **Chicago** for Edmonton's 6th round choice (Mirko Hoefflin) in 2010 Entry Draft, June 24, 2010. Traded to **Los Angeles** by **Edmonton** with Los Angeles' 7th round choice in 2012 Entry Draft for Ryan Smyth, June 26, 2011.

FRASER, Jamie

(FRAY-zuhr, JAY-mee)

Defense. Shoots left. 6', 198 lbs. Born, Sarnia, Ont., November 17, 1985.

			Regular Season														Playoffs								
Season	Club	League	GP	G	A	Pts	PIM	PP	SH	GW	S	%	+/-	TF	F%	Min	GP	G	A	Pts	PIM	PP	SH	GW	Min
2002-03	Brampton	OHL	57	3	11	14	13	....	....	....	....	....	....	....	....	....	10	0	2	2	2	....	....	....	....
2003-04	Brampton	OHL	61	4	13	17	36	....	....	....	....	....	....	....	....	....	12	3	1	4	6	....	....	....	....
2004-05	Sarnia Sting	OHL	66	10	21	31	22	....	....	....	....	....	....	....	....	....	....	....	....	....	....	....	....	....	....
2005-06	Sarnia Sting	OHL	65	16	26	42	68	....	....	....	....	....	....	....	....	....	....	....	....	....	....	....	....	....	....
	South Carolina	ECHL	3	1	0	1	2	....	....	....	....	....	....	....	....	....	6	1	1	2	2	....	....	....	....
2006-07	Syracuse Crunch	AHL	2	0	0	0	0	....	....	....	....	....	....	....	....	....	....	....	....	....	....	....	....	....	....
	South Carolina	ECHL	27	5	23	28	6	....	....	....	....	....	....	....	....	....	....	....	....	....	....	....	....	....	....
	Bridgeport	AHL	43	3	11	14	16	....	....	....	....	....	....	....	....	....	....	....	....	....	....	....	....	....	....
2007-08	Bridgeport	AHL	70	11	13	24	20	....	....	....	....	....	....	....	....	....	....	....	....	....	....	....	....	....	....
2008-09	**NY Islanders**	**NHL**	**1**	**0**	**0**	**0**	**0**	**0**	**0**	**0**	**0**	**0.0**	**0**	**0**	**0.0**	**11:00**	....	....	....	....	....	....	....	....	....
	Bridgeport	AHL	66	7	14	21	30	....	....	....	....	....	....	....	....	....	....	....	....	....	....	....	....	....	....
2009-10	Houston Aeros	AHL	59	6	16	22	36	....	....	....	....	....	....	....	....	....	....	....	....	....	....	....	....	....	....
2010-11	Houston Aeros	AHL	22	0	1	1	6	....	....	....	....	....	....	....	....	....	....	....	....	....	....	....	....	....	....
	Elmira Jackals	ECHL	8	0	4	4	0	....	....	....	....	....	....	....	....	....	....	....	....	....	....	....	....	....	....
	NHL Totals		**1**	**0**	**0**	**0**	**0**	**0**	**0**	**0**	**0**	**0.0**		**0**	**0.0**	**11:00**	....	....	....	....	....	....	....	....	....

Signed as a free agent by **NY Islanders**, February 22, 2007. Signed as a free agent by **Minnesota**, July 8, 2009. • Missed majority of 2010-11 due to abdominal and hip injuries.

FRASER, Mark

(FRAY-zuhr, MAHRK) **N.J.**

Defense. Shoots left. 6'3", 220 lbs. Born, Ottawa, Ont., September 29, 1986. New Jersey's 3rd choice, 84th overall, in 2005 Entry Draft.

			Regular Season														Playoffs								
Season	Club	League	GP	G	A	Pts	PIM	PP	SH	GW	S	%	+/-	TF	F%	Min	GP	G	A	Pts	PIM	PP	SH	GW	Min
2004-05	Gloucester	CJHL	STATISTICS NOT AVAILABLE																						
	Kitchener Rangers	OHL	58	0	8	8	96	....	....	....	....	....	....	....	....	....	15	0	3	3	26	....	....	....	....
2005-06	Kitchener Rangers	OHL	59	0	5	5	129	....	....	....	....	....	....	....	....	....	5	0	1	1	4	....	....	....	....
	Albany River Rats	AHL	4	0	0	0	2	....	....	....	....	....	....	....	....	....	....	....	....	....	....	....	....	....	....
2006-07	**New Jersey**	**NHL**	**7**	**0**	**0**	**0**	**7**	**0**	**0**	**0**	**1**	**0.0**	**–1**	**0**	**0.0**	**3:34**	....	....	....	....	....	....	....	....	....
	Lowell Devils	AHL	71	1	8	9	73	....	....	....	....	....	....	....	....	....	....	....	....	....	....	....	....	....	....
2007-08	Lowell Devils	AHL	79	1	17	18	96	....	....	....	....	....	....	....	....	....	....	....	....	....	....	....	....	....	....
2008-09	Lowell Devils	AHL	74	3	14	17	152	....	....	....	....	....	....	....	....	....	....	....	....	....	....	....	....	....	....
2009-10	**New Jersey**	**NHL**	**61**	**3**	**3**	**6**	**36**	**0**	**0**	**0**	**24**	**12.5**	**3**	**0**	**0.0**	**12:23**	**1**	**0**	**0**	**0**	**0**	**0**	**0**	**0**	**5:52**
2010-11	**New Jersey**	**NHL**	**26**	**0**	**2**	**2**	**29**	**0**	**0**	**0**	**16**	**0.0**	**2**	**0**	**0.0**	**13:59**	....	....	....	....	....	....	....	....	....
	Albany Devils	AHL	5	0	1	1	0	....	....	....	....	....	....	....	....	....	....	....	....	....	....	....	....	....	....
	NHL Totals		**94**	**3**	**5**	**8**	**72**	**0**	**0**	**0**	**41**	**7.3**		**0**	**0.0**	**12:10**	**1**	**0**	**0**	**0**	**0**	**0**	**0**	**0**	**5:52**

• Missed majority of 2010-11 due to hand injury at Buffalo, October 13. 2010 and as a healthy reserve.

FRATTIN, Matt

(FRA-tihn, MAT) **TOR**

Right wing. Shoots right. 6', 200 lbs. Born, Edmonton, Alta., January 3, 1988. Toronto's 2nd choice, 99th overall, in 2007 Entry Draft.

			Regular Season														Playoffs								
Season	Club	League	GP	G	A	Pts	PIM	PP	SH	GW	S	%	+/-	TF	F%	Min	GP	G	A	Pts	PIM	PP	SH	GW	Min
2004-05	Gregg Distributors	AMHL	34	12	13	25	14	....	....	....	....	....	....	....	....	....	....	....	....	....	....	....	....	....	....
2005-06	Gregg Distributors	AMHL	34	20	17	37	48	....	....	....	....	....	....	....	....	....	6	5	1	6	4	....	....	....	....
	Ft. Saskatchewan	AJHL	3	2	0	2	0	....	....	....	....	....	....	....	....	....	....	....	....	....	....	....	....	....	....
2006-07	Ft. Saskatchewan	AJHL	58	49	34	83	75	....	....	....	....	....	....	....	....	....	15	5	6	11	10	....	....	....	....
2007-08	North Dakota	WCHA	43	4	11	15	18	....	....	....	....	....	....	....	....	....	....	....	....	....	....	....	....	....	....
2008-09	North Dakota	WCHA	42	13	12	25	48	....	....	....	....	....	....	....	....	....	....	....	....	....	....	....	....	....	....
2009-10	North Dakota	WCHA	24	11	8	19	21	....	....	....	....	....	....	....	....	....	....	....	....	....	....	....	....	....	....

			Regular Season													Playoffs								
Season	Club	League	GP	G	A	Pts	PIM	PP	SH	GW	S	%	+/-	TF	F%	Min	GP	G	A	Pts	PIM	PP	SH	GW	Min
2010-11	North Dakota	WCHA	44	*36	24	*60	42	....	....	....	....	....	....	....	....	....	....	....	....	....	....	....	....	....	....
	Toronto	NHL	1	0	0	0	0	0	0	0	5	0.0	–1	0	0.0	15:34	....	....	....	....	....	....	....	....	....
	NHL Totals		1	0	0	0	0	0	0	0	5	0.0		0	0.0	15:34	....	....	....	....	....	....	....	....	....

WCHA First All-Star Team (2011) • NCAA West First All-American Team (2011) • WCHA Player of the Year (2011)

FRISCHMON, Trevor
(FRIHCH-muhn, TREH-vuhr) **NYI**

Center. Shoots left. 6', 202 lbs. Born, Ham Lake, MN, August 5, 1981.

Season	Club	League	GP	G	A	Pts	PIM	PP	SH	GW	S	%	+/-	TF	F%	Min	GP	G	A	Pts	PIM	PP	SH	GW	Min
99-2000	Lincoln Stars	USHL	4	1	1	2	48	....	....	....	....	....	....	....	....	....	8	0	2	2	0	....	....	....	....
2000-01	Lincoln Stars	USHL	55	13	18	31	49	....	....	....	....	....	....	....	....	....	11	4	1	5	0	....	....	....	....
2001-02	Lincoln Stars	USHL	58	17	28	45	38	....	....	....	....	....	....	....	....	....	4	0	2	2	2	....	....	....	....
2002-03	Colorado College	WCHA	38	3	4	7	22	....	....	....	....	....	....	....	....	....	....	....	....	....	....	....	....	....	....
2003-04	Colorado College	WCHA	39	10	7	17	34	....	....	....	....	....	....	....	....	....	....	....	....	....	....	....	....	....	....
2004-05	Colorado College	WCHA	42	10	16	26	24	....	....	....	....	....	....	....	....	....	....	....	....	....	....	....	....	....	....
2005-06	Colorado College	WCHA	41	7	9	16	41	....	....	....	....	....	....	....	....	....	....	....	....	....	....	....	....	....	....
2006-07	Syracuse Crunch	AHL	33	0	7	7	10	....	....	....	....	....	....	....	....	....	....	....	....	....	....	....	....	....	....
	Dayton Bombers	ECHL	24	5	8	13	14	....	....	....	....	....	....	....	....	....	20	3	5	8	24	....	....	....	....
2007-08	Syracuse Crunch	AHL	59	5	11	16	38	....	....	....	....	....	....	....	....	....	13	1	2	3	10	....	....	....	....
	Charlotte	ECHL	7	1	4	5	2	....	....	....	....	....	....	....	....	....	....	....	....	....	....	....	....	....	....
2008-09	Syracuse Crunch	AHL	80	5	20	25	57	....	....	....	....	....	....	....	....	....	....	....	....	....	....	....	....	....	....
2009-10	Columbus	NHL	3	0	0	0	4	0	0	0	1	0.0	0	6	66.7	6:06	....	....	....	....	....	....	....	....	....
	Syracuse Crunch	AHL	75	7	18	25	34	....	....	....	....	....	....	....	....	....	....	....	....	....	....	....	....	....	....
2010-11	Springfield	AHL	80	4	25	29	39	....	....	....	....	....	....	....	....	....	....	....	....	....	....	....	....	....	....
	NHL Totals		3	0	0	0	4	0	0	0	1	0.0		6	66.7	6:06	....	....	....	....	....	....	....	....	....

Signed as a free agent by **Columbus**, July 3, 2009. Signed as a free agent by **NY Islanders**, July 5, 2011.

FRITSCHE, Dan
(FRIH-tchee, DAN)

Center. Shoots right. 6'1", 204 lbs. Born, Parma, OH, July 13, 1985. Columbus' 2nd choice, 46th overall, in 2003 Entry Draft.

Season	Club	League	GP	G	A	Pts	PIM	PP	SH	GW	S	%	+/-	TF	F%	Min	GP	G	A	Pts	PIM	PP	SH	GW	Min
2000-01	Cleveland Barons	NAHL	49	23	29	52	47	....	....	....	....	....	....	....	....	....	1	1	1	2	0	....	....	....	....
2001-02	Sarnia Sting	OHL	17	5	13	18	20	....	....	....	....	....	....	....	....	....	....	....	....	....	....	....	....	....	....
2002-03	Sarnia Sting	OHL	61	32	39	71	79	....	....	....	....	....	....	....	....	....	5	2	2	4	4	....	....	....	....
2003-04	Sarnia Sting	OHL	27	16	13	29	26	....	....	....	....	....	....	....	....	....	5	1	5	6	0	....	....	....	....
	Columbus	NHL	19	1	0	1	12	0	0	0	19	5.3	–5	139	38.1	8:24	....	....	....	....	....	....	....	....	....
	Syracuse Crunch	AHL	4	2	0	2	0	....	....	....	....	....	....	....	....	....	4	0	1	1	4	....	....	....	....
2004-05	Sarnia Sting	OHL	2	1	1	2	0	....	....	....	....	....	....	....	....	....	....	....	....	....	....	....	....	....	....
	London Knights	OHL	28	17	18	35	18	....	....	....	....	....	....	....	....	....	17	9	13	22	12	....	....	....	....
2005-06	Columbus	NHL	59	6	7	13	22	0	0	0	93	6.5	–14	270	48.9	10:17	....	....	....	....	....	....	....	....	....
	Syracuse Crunch	AHL	19	5	4	9	12	....	....	....	....	....	....	....	....	....	6	2	2	4	8	....	....	....	....
2006-07	Columbus	NHL	59	12	15	27	35	5	1	4	81	14.8	3	296	49.3	14:02	....	....	....	....	....	....	....	....	....
2007-08	Columbus	NHL	69	10	12	22	22	1	1	4	109	9.2	2	121	48.8	12:21	....	....	....	....	....	....	....	....	....
2008-09	NY Rangers	NHL	16	1	3	4	2	0	0	0	20	5.0	–2	7	71.4	9:33	....	....	....	....	....	....	....	....	....
	Minnesota	NHL	34	4	5	9	10	1	1	0	34	11.8	–3	87	41.4	11:09	....	....	....	....	....	....	....	....	....
2009-10	Syracuse Crunch	AHL	67	13	29	42	12	....	....	....	....	....	....	....	....	....	....	....	....	....	....	....	....	....	....
2010-11	Geneve	Swiss	39	15	18	33	66	....	....	....	....	....	....	....	....	....	....	....	....	....	....	....	....	....	....
	NHL Totals		256	34	42	76	103	7	3	8	356	9.6		920	46.8	11:38	....	....	....	....	....	....	....	....	....

Memorial Cup All-Star Team (2005)

• Missed majority of 2001-02 due to shoulder surgery, December 12, 2001. Traded to **NY Rangers** by **Columbus** with Nikolai Zherdev for Fedor Tyutin and Christian Backman, July 2, 2008. Traded to **Minnesota** by **NY Rangers** for Erik Reitz, January 29, 2009. Signed as a free agent by **Syracuse** (AHL), October 6, 2009. Signed as a free agent b **Geneve** (Swiss), October 3, 2010.

FROLIK, Michael
(FROH-lihk, MIGH-kuhl) **CHI**

Left wing. Shoots left. 6'1", 185 lbs. Born, Kladno, Czech., February 17, 1988. Florida's 1st choice, 10th overall, in 2006 Entry Draft.

Season	Club	League	GP	G	A	Pts	PIM	PP	SH	GW	S	%	+/-	TF	F%	Min	GP	G	A	Pts	PIM	PP	SH	GW	Min
2002-03	HC Kladno U17	CzR-U17	46	37	21	58	36	....	....	....	....	....	....	....	....	....	9	9	1	10	18	....	....	....	....
	HC Kladno Jr.	CzRep-Jr.	....	....	....	....	....	....	....	....	....	....	....	....	....	....	1	0	0	0	2	....	....	....	....
2003-04	HC Kladno U17	CzR-U17	1	0	1	1	2	....	....	....	....	....	....	....	....	....	....	....	....	....	....	....	....	....	....
	HC Kladno Jr.	CzRep-Jr.	53	21	23	44	22	....	....	....	....	....	....	....	....	....	7	3	1	4	6	....	....	....	....
2004-05	HC Kladno U17	CzR-U17	....	....	....	....	....	....	....	....	....	....	....	....	....	....	1	1	0	1	0	....	....	....	....
	HC Kladno Jr.	CzRep-Jr.	15	9	11	20	18	....	....	....	....	....	....	....	....	....	5	1	0	1	0	....	....	....	....
	HC Rabat Kladno	CzRep	27	3	1	4	6	....	....	....	....	....	....	....	....	....	1	0	0	0	0	....	....	....	....
2005-06	HC Kladno Jr.	CzRep-Jr.	3	1	2	3	0	....	....	....	....	....	....	....	....	....	6	3	9	12	6	....	....	....	....
	HC Rabat Kladno	CzRep	48	2	7	9	32	....	....	....	....	....	....	....	....	....	....	....	....	....	....	....	....	....	....
2006-07	Rimouski Oceanic	QMJHL	52	31	42	73	40	....	....	....	....	....	....	....	....	....	....	....	....	....	....	....	....	....	....
2007-08	Rimouski Oceanic	QMJHL	45	24	41	65	22	....	....	....	....	....	....	....	....	....	9	2	4	6	12	....	....	....	....
2008-09	Florida	NHL	79	21	24	45	22	1	0	2	158	13.3	10	67	40.3	14:48	....	....	....	....	....	....	....	....	....
2009-10	Florida	NHL	82	21	22	43	43	5	0	1	219	9.6	–4	35	37.1	17:29	....	....	....	....	....	....	....	....	....
2010-11	Florida	NHL	52	8	21	29	16	1	0	1	158	5.1	2	12	41.7	16:02	....	....	....	....	....	....	....	....	....
	Chicago	NHL	28	3	6	9	14	0	0	0	93	3.2	0	107	40.2	14:46	7	2	3	5	2	0	0	0	17:28
	NHL Totals		241	53	73	126	95	7	0	4	628	8.4		221	39.8	15:59	7	2	3	5	2	0	0	0	17:28

QMJHL All-Rookie Team (2007)

Traded to **Chicago** by **Florida** with Alexander Salak for Jack Skille, Hugh Jessiman and David Pacan, February 9, 2011.

FROLOV, Alex
(FROH-lawf, AL-ehx)

Left wing. Shoots right. 6'2", 210 lbs. Born, Moscow, USSR, June 19, 1982. Los Angeles' 1st choice, 20th overall, in 2000 Entry Draft.

Season	Club	League	GP	G	A	Pts	PIM	PP	SH	GW	S	%	+/-	TF	F%	Min	GP	G	A	Pts	PIM	PP	SH	GW	Min
1998-99	Spartak Moscow	Russia	1	0	0	0	0	....	....	....	....	....	....	....	....	....	....	....	....	....	....	....	....	....	....
99-2000	Yaroslavl 2	Russia-3	36	27	13	40	30	....	....	....	....	....	....	....	....	....	....	....	....	....	....	....	....	....	....
2000-01	Krylja Sovetov	Russia-2	44	20	19	39	8	....	....	....	....	....	....	....	....	....	....	....	....	....	....	....	....	....	....
2001-02	Krylja Sovetov	Russia	43	18	12	30	16	....	....	....	....	....	....	....	....	....	3	1	0	1	0	....	....	....	....
	Krylja Sovetov 2	Russia-3	2	0	0	0	4	....	....	....	....	....	....	....	....	....	....	....	....	....	....	....	....	....	....
2002-03	Los Angeles	NHL	79	14	17	31	34	1	0	3	141	9.9	12	9	22.2	14:23	....	....	....	....	....	....	....	....	....
2003-04	Los Angeles	NHL	77	24	24	48	24	5	2	3	168	14.3	8	34	32.4	17:13	....	....	....	....	....	....	....	....	....
	Nizhny Novgorod	Russia	1	0	0	0	0	....	....	....	....	....	....	....	....	....	....	....	....	....	....	....	....	....	....
2004-05	CSKA Moscow	Russia	42	20	17	37	10	....	....	....	....	....	....	....	....	....	....	....	....	....	....	....	....	....	....
	Dynamo Moscow	Russia	6	2	1	3	2	....	....	....	....	....	....	....	....	....	6	2	1	3	0	....	....	....	....
2005-06	Los Angeles	NHL	69	21	33	54	40	4	3	4	174	12.1	17	4	50.0	19:18	....	....	....	....	....	....	....	....	....
	Russia	Olympics	3	0	1	1	0	....	....	....	....	....	....	....	....	....	....	....	....	....	....	....	....	....	....
2006-07	Los Angeles	NHL	82	35	36	71	34	10	1	6	195	17.9	–8	19	36.8	19:56	....	....	....	....	....	....	....	....	....
2007-08	Los Angeles	NHL	71	23	44	67	22	5	0	7	160	14.4	1	11	18.2	18:48	....	....	....	....	....	....	....	....	....
2008-09	Los Angeles	NHL	77	32	27	59	30	12	1	1	176	18.2	–6	11	45.5	19:55	....	....	....	....	....	....	....	....	....
2009-10	Los Angeles	NHL	81	19	32	51	26	5	0	1	182	10.4	–1	12	58.3	18:26	6	1	3	4	0	0	0	0	16:49
2010-11	NY Rangers	NHL	43	7	9	16	8	0	0	2	78	9.0	4	7	14.3	14:26	....	....	....	....	....	....	....	....	....
	NHL Totals		579	175	222	397	218	42	7	27	1274	13.7		107	34.6	17:59	6	1	3	4	0	0	0	0	16:49

Signed as a free agent by **CSKA Moscow** (Russia), July 14, 2004. Signed as a free agent by **Dynamo Moscow** (Russia), February 17, 2005. Signed as a free agent by **NY Rangers**, July 27, 2010. Signed as a free agent by **Omsk** (Russia-KHL), May 12, 2011.

GABORIK, Marian
(GAB-uhr-ihk, MAIR-ee-uhn) **NYR**

Right wing. Shoots left. 6'1", 204 lbs. Born, Trencin, Czech., February 14, 1982. Minnesota's 1st choice, 3rd overall, in 2000 Entry Draft.

Season	Club	League	GP	G	A	Pts	PIM	PP	SH	GW	S	%	+/-	TF	F%	Min	GP	G	A	Pts	PIM	PP	SH	GW	Min
1997-98	Dukla Trencin Jr.	Slovak-Jr.	36	37	22	59	28	....	....	....	....	....	....	....	....	....	....	....	....	....	....	....	....	....	....
	Dukla Trencin	Slovakia	1	1	0	1	0	....	....	....	....	....	....	....	....	....	....	....	....	....	....	....	....	....	....
1998-99	Dukla Trencin	Slovakia	33	11	9	20	6	....	....	....	....	....	....	....	....	....	3	1	0	1	2	....	....	....	....
99-2000	Dukla Trencin	Slovakia	50	25	21	46	34	....	....	....	....	....	....	....	....	....	5	1	2	3	2	....	....	....	....
2000-01	Minnesota	NHL	71	18	18	36	32	6	0	3	179	10.1	–6	3	33.3	15:26	....	....	....	....	....	....	....	....	....
2001-02	Minnesota	NHL	78	30	37	67	34	10	0	4	221	13.6	0	4	25.0	16:47	....	....	....	....	....	....	....	....	....
2002-03	Minnesota	NHL	81	30	35	65	46	5	1	8	280	10.7	12	16	25.0	17:24	18	9	8	17	6	4	0	0	18:12
2003-04	Dukla Trencin	Slovakia	9	10	3	13	10	....	....	....	....	....	....	....	....	....	....	....	....	....	....	....	....	....	....
	Minnesota	NHL	65	18	22	40	20	3	0	4	220	8.2	10	11	45.5	18:17	....	....	....	....	....	....	....	....	....

			Regular Season														Playoffs								
Season	Club	League	GP	G	A	Pts	PIM	PP	SH	GW	S	%	+/-	TF	F%	Min	GP	G	A	Pts	PIM	PP	SH	GW	Min
2004-05	Dukla Trencin	Slovakia	29	25	27	52	46	....	....	....	....	....	....	....	....	....	12	8	9	17	26	....	....	....	....
	Farjestad	Sweden	12	6	4	10	45	....	....	....	....	....	....	....	....	....	....	....	....	....	....	....	....	....	....
2005-06	**Minnesota**	**NHL**	**65**	**38**	**28**	**66**	**64**	**10**	**2**	**7**	**252**	**15.1**	**6**	**11**	**27.3**	**18:26**	....	....	....	....	....	....	....	....	....
	Slovakia	Olympics	6	3	4	7	4	....	....	....	....	....	....	....	....	....	....	....	....	....	....	....	....	....	....
2006-07	**Minnesota**	**NHL**	**48**	**30**	**27**	**57**	**40**	**12**	**1**	**7**	**196**	**15.3**	**12**	**4**	**0.0**	**19:38**	**5**	**3**	**1**	**4**	**8**	**1**	**1**	**1**	**19:32**
2007-08	**Minnesota**	**NHL**	**77**	**42**	**41**	**83**	**63**	**11**	**1**	**8**	**278**	**15.1**	**17**	**21**	**28.6**	**19:36**	**6**	**0**	**1**	**1**	**4**	**0**	**0**	**0**	**21:51**
2008-09	**Minnesota**	**NHL**	**17**	**13**	**10**	**23**	**2**	**2**	**1**	**2**	**68**	**19.1**	**3**	**5**	**0.0**	**20:00**	....	....	....	....	....	....	....	....	....
2009-10	**NY Rangers**	**NHL**	**76**	**42**	**44**	**86**	**37**	**14**	**1**	**4**	**272**	**15.4**	**15**	**7**	**28.6**	**21:15**	....	....	....	....	....	....	....	....	....
	Slovakia	Olympics	7	4	1	5	6	....	....	....	....	....	....	....	....	....	....	....	....	....	....	....	....	....	....
2010-11	**NY Rangers**	**NHL**	**62**	**22**	**26**	**48**	**18**	**7**	**0**	**4**	**192**	**11.5**	**8**	**0**	**0.0**	**18:05**	**5**	**1**	**1**	**2**	**2**	**0**	**0**	**0**	**23:55**
	NHL Totals		**640**	**283**	**288**	**571**	**356**	**80**	**7**	**51**	**2158**	**13.1**		**82**	**26.8**	**18:19**	**34**	**13**	**11**	**24**	**20**	**5**	**1**	**1**	**19:53**

Played in NHL All-Star Game (2003, 2008)

Signed as a free agent by **Trencin** (Slovakia), July 5, 2004. Signed as a free agent by **Farjestad** (Sweden), December 21, 2004. • Missed majority of 2008-09 due to hip surgery, January 5, 2009. Signed as a free agent by **NY Rangers**, July 1, 2009.

GAGNE, Simon
(gah-N'YAY, see-MOHN) **L.A.**

Left wing. Shoots left. 6'1", 193 lbs. Born, Ste-Foy, Que., February 29, 1980. Philadelphia's 1st choice, 22nd overall, in 1998 Entry Draft.

Season	Club	League	GP	G	A	Pts	PIM	PP	SH	GW	S	%	+/-	TF	F%	Min	GP	G	A	Pts	PIM	PP	SH	GW	Min
1995-96	Ste-Foy	QAAA	27	13	9	22	18	....	....	....	....	....	....	....	....	....	15	7	8	15	8	....	....	....	....
1996-97	Beauport	QMJHL	51	9	22	31	39	....	....	....	....	....	....	....	....	....	....	....	....	....	....	....	....	....	....
1997-98	Quebec Remparts	QMJHL	53	30	39	69	26	....	....	....	....	....	....	....	....	....	12	11	5	16	23	....	....	....	....
1998-99	Quebec Remparts	QMJHL	61	50	*70	*120	42	....	....	....	....	....	....	....	....	....	13	9	8	17	4	....	....	....	....
99-2000	**Philadelphia**	**NHL**	**80**	**20**	**28**	**48**	**22**	**8**	**1**	**4**	**159**	**12.6**	**11**	**443**	**42.2**	**14:59**	**17**	**5**	**5**	**10**	**2**	**2**	**0**	**1**	**16:46**
2000-01	**Philadelphia**	**NHL**	**69**	**27**	**32**	**59**	**18**	**6**	**0**	**7**	**191**	**14.1**	**24**	**21**	**28.6**	**18:05**	**6**	**3**	**0**	**3**	**0**	**2**	**0**	**0**	**19:09**
2001-02	**Philadelphia**	**NHL**	**79**	**33**	**33**	**66**	**32**	**4**	**1**	**7**	**199**	**16.6**	**31**	**6**	**83.3**	**18:09**	**5**	**0**	**0**	**0**	**2**	**0**	**0**	**0**	**19:16**
	Canada	Olympics	6	1	3	4	0	....	....	....	....	....	....	....	....	....	....	....	....	....	....	....	....	....	....
2002-03	**Philadelphia**	**NHL**	**46**	**9**	**18**	**27**	**16**	**1**	**1**	**3**	**115**	**7.8**	**20**	**70**	**42.9**	**17:24**	**13**	**4**	**1**	**5**	**6**	**0**	**1**	**1**	**18:13**
2003-04	**Philadelphia**	**NHL**	**80**	**24**	**21**	**45**	**29**	**6**	**0**	**6**	**211**	**11.4**	**12**	**104**	**39.4**	**16:27**	**18**	**5**	**4**	**9**	**12**	**0**	**0**	**1**	**16:48**
2004-05			DID NOT PLAY																						
2005-06	**Philadelphia**	**NHL**	**72**	**47**	**32**	**79**	**38**	**12**	**2**	**7**	**334**	**14.1**	**31**	**18**	**38.9**	**20:46**	**6**	**3**	**1**	**4**	**2**	**1**	**0**	**0**	**21:45**
	Canada	Olympics	6	1	2	3	6	....	....	....	....	....	....	....	....	....	....	....	....	....	....	....	....	....	....
2006-07	**Philadelphia**	**NHL**	**76**	**41**	**27**	**68**	**30**	**13**	**2**	**4**	**291**	**14.1**	**2**	**49**	**42.9**	**21:02**	....	....	....	....	....	....	....	....	....
2007-08	**Philadelphia**	**NHL**	**25**	**7**	**11**	**18**	**4**	**5**	**0**	**2**	**76**	**9.2**	**-8**	**2**	**50.0**	**18:09**	....	....	....	....	....	....	....	....	....
2008-09	**Philadelphia**	**NHL**	**79**	**34**	**40**	**74**	**42**	**12**	**4**	**3**	**221**	**15.4**	**21**	**10**	**30.0**	**19:01**	**6**	**3**	**1**	**4**	**2**	**1**	**1**	**1**	**20:29**
2009-10	**Philadelphia**	**NHL**	**58**	**17**	**23**	**40**	**47**	**5**	**0**	**4**	**183**	**9.3**	**-1**	**4**	**25.0**	**18:37**	**19**	**9**	**3**	**12**	**0**	**5**	**0**	**2**	**17:35**
2010-11	**Tampa Bay**	**NHL**	**63**	**17**	**23**	**40**	**20**	**7**	**0**	**3**	**154**	**11.0**	**-12**	**16**	**37.5**	**16:53**	**15**	**5**	**7**	**12**	**4**	**0**	**0**	**1**	**15:52**
	NHL Totals		**727**	**276**	**288**	**564**	**298**	**79**	**11**	**50**	**2134**	**12.9**		**743**	**41.5**	**18:09**	**105**	**37**	**22**	**59**	**30**	**11**	**2**	**7**	**17:43**

QMJHL Second All-Star Team (1999) • NHL All-Rookie Team (2000)

Played in NHL ALL-Star Game (2001, 2007)

• Missed majority of 2007-08 due to concussion at Pittsburgh, February 10, 2008. Traded to **Tampa Bay** by **Philadelphia** for Matt Walker and Tampa Bay's 4th round choice (Marcel Noebels) in 2011 Entry Draft, July 19, 2010. Signed as a free agent by **Los Angeles**, July 2, 2011.

GAGNER, Sam
(GAH-n'yay, SAM) **EDM**

Center/Wing. Shoots right. 5'11", 191 lbs. Born, London, Ont., August 10, 1989. Edmonton's 1st choice, 6th overall, in 2007 Entry Draft.

Season	Club	League	GP	G	A	Pts	PIM	PP	SH	GW	S	%	+/-	TF	F%	Min	GP	G	A	Pts	PIM	PP	SH	GW	Min
2001-02	Tor. Marlboros	GTHL	68	56	61	117	42	....	....	....	....	....	....	....	....	....	....	....	....	....	....	....	....	....	....
2002-03	Tor. Marlboros	GTHL	72	68	86	154	35	....	....	....	....	....	....	....	....	....	....	....	....	....	....	....	....	....	....
2003-04	Tor. Marlboros	GTHL	85	64	108	171	36	....	....	....	....	....	....	....	....	....	....	....	....	....	....	....	....	....	....
2004-05	Tor. Marlboros	GTHL	70	62	118	180	56	....	....	....	....	....	....	....	....	....	....	....	....	....	....	....	....	....	....
	Milton Icehawks	OPJHL	13	5	10	15	10	....	....	....	....	....	....	....	....	....	....	....	....	....	....	....	....	....	....
2005-06	Sioux City	USHL	56	11	35	46	60	....	....	....	....	....	....	....	....	....	....	....	....	....	....	....	....	....	....
2006-07	London Knights	OHL	53	35	83	118	36	....	....	....	....	....	....	....	....	....	16	7	*22	29	22	....	....	....	....
2007-08	**Edmonton**	**NHL**	**79**	**13**	**36**	**49**	**23**	**4**	**0**	**1**	**135**	**9.6**	**-21**	**299**	**41.8**	**15:41**	....	....	....	....	....	....	....	....	....
2008-09	**Edmonton**	**NHL**	**76**	**16**	**25**	**41**	**51**	**6**	**0**	**1**	**156**	**10.3**	**-1**	**690**	**42.0**	**16:46**	....	....	....	....	....	....	....	....	....
2009-10	**Edmonton**	**NHL**	**68**	**15**	**26**	**41**	**33**	**6**	**0**	**1**	**170**	**8.8**	**-8**	**709**	**47.4**	**16:17**	....	....	....	....	....	....	....	....	....
2010-11	**Edmonton**	**NHL**	**68**	**15**	**27**	**42**	**37**	**3**	**1**	**2**	**138**	**10.9**	**-17**	**935**	**43.9**	**17:45**	....	....	....	....	....	....	....	....	....
	NHL Totals		**291**	**59**	**114**	**173**	**144**	**19**	**1**	**5**	**599**	**9.8**		**2633**	**44.1**	**16:35**	....	....	....	....	....	....	....	....	....

USHL All-Rookie Team (2006) • OHL All-Rookie Team (2007)

GAGNON, Aaron
(GAN-YAWN, AIR-ruhn) **WPG**

Center. Shoots right. 5'11", 186 lbs. Born, Quesnel, B.C., April 24, 1986. Phoenix's 8th choice, 240th overall, in 2004 Entry Draft.

Season	Club	League	GP	G	A	Pts	PIM	PP	SH	GW	S	%	+/-	TF	F%	Min	GP	G	A	Pts	PIM	PP	SH	GW	Min
2001-02	North Okanoghan	Minor-BC	41	59	59	118	60	....	....	....	....	....	....	....	....	....	....	....	....	....	....	....	....	....	....
	Seattle	WHL	2	0	0	0	0	....	....	....	....	....	....	....	....	....	....	....	....	....	....	....	....	....	....
2002-03	Seattle	WHL	60	5	13	18	14	....	....	....	....	....	....	....	....	....	15	3	2	5	4	....	....	....	....
2003-04	Seattle	WHL	63	21	15	36	29	....	....	....	....	....	....	....	....	....	....	....	....	....	....	....	....	....	....
2004-05	Seattle	WHL	72	31	34	65	29	....	....	....	....	....	....	....	....	....	12	4	5	9	16	....	....	....	....
2005-06	Seattle	WHL	62	24	21	45	40	....	....	....	....	....	....	....	....	....	7	5	3	8	6	....	....	....	....
2006-07	Seattle	WHL	59	42	38	80	58	....	....	....	....	....	....	....	....	....	11	6	2	8	10	....	....	....	....
2007-08	Iowa Stars	AHL	25	0	1	1	8	....	....	....	....	....	....	....	....	....	....	....	....	....	....	....	....	....	....
	Idaho Steelheads	ECHL	22	7	14	21	4	....	....	....	....	....	....	....	....	....	4	1	1	2	2	....	....	....	....
2008-09	Grand Rapids	AHL	61	8	11	19	28	....	....	....	....	....	....	....	....	....	10	1	2	3	2	....	....	....	....
2009-10	**Dallas**	**NHL**	**2**	**0**	**0**	**0**	**0**	**0**	**0**	**0**	**2**	**0.0**	**0**	**11**	**72.7**	**8:49**	....	....	....	....	....	....	....	....	....
	Texas Stars	AHL	78	27	31	58	42	....	....	....	....	....	....	....	....	....	24	8	4	12	18	....	....	....	....
2010-11	**Dallas**	**NHL**	**19**	**0**	**2**	**2**	**0**	**0**	**0**	**0**	**9**	**0.0**	**-3**	**55**	**54.6**	**8:04**	....	....	....	....	....	....	....	....	....
	Texas Stars	AHL	58	14	22	36	24	....	....	....	....	....	....	....	....	....	6	2	2	4	4	....	....	....	....
	NHL Totals		**21**	**0**	**2**	**2**	**0**	**0**	**0**	**0**	**11**	**0.0**		**66**	**57.6**	**8:08**	....	....	....	....	....	....	....	....	....

WHL West First All-Star Team (2005, 2007)

Signed as a free agent by **Dallas**, February 2, 2007. Signed as a free agent by **Winnipeg**, July 4, 2011.

GALIARDI, T.J.
(gal-ee-AR-dee, TEE-JAY) **COL**

Left wing. Shoots left. 6'2", 190 lbs. Born, Calgary, Alta., April 22, 1988. Colorado's 4th choice, 55th overall, in 2007 Entry Draft.

Season	Club	League	GP	G	A	Pts	PIM	PP	SH	GW	S	%	+/-	TF	F%	Min	GP	G	A	Pts	PIM	PP	SH	GW	Min
2004-05	Cgy. North Stars	AMHL	36	14	16	30	32	....	....	....	....	....	....	....	....	....	....	....	....	....	....	....	....	....	....
2005-06	Calgary Royals	AJHL	56	19	37	56	60	....	....	....	....	....	....	....	....	....	....	....	....	....	....	....	....	....	....
2006-07	Dartmouth	ECAC	33	14	17	31	30	....	....	....	....	....	....	....	....	....	....	....	....	....	....	....	....	....	....
2007-08	Calgary Hitmen	WHL	72	18	52	70	77	....	....	....	....	....	....	....	....	....	16	5	*19	*24	20	....	....	....	....
2008-09	**Colorado**	**NHL**	**11**	**3**	**1**	**4**	**6**	**0**	**0**	**0**	**14**	**21.4**	**-4**	**133**	**42.1**	**16:21**	....	....	....	....	....	....	....	....	....
	Lake Erie	AHL	66	10	17	27	32	....	....	....	....	....	....	....	....	....	....	....	....	....	....	....	....	....	....
2009-10	**Colorado**	**NHL**	**70**	**15**	**24**	**39**	**28**	**2**	**1**	**3**	**120**	**12.5**	**6**	**327**	**50.5**	**18:11**	**6**	**0**	**2**	**2**	**6**	**0**	**0**	**0**	**20:50**
2010-11	**Colorado**	**NHL**	**35**	**7**	**8**	**15**	**12**	**0**	**0**	**1**	**62**	**11.3**	**-6**	**134**	**46.3**	**16:12**	....	....	....	....	....	....	....	....	....
	Lake Erie	AHL	1	0	1	1	0	....	....	....	....	....	....	....	....	....	....	....	....	....	....	....	....	....	....
	NHL Totals		**116**	**25**	**33**	**58**	**46**	**2**	**1**	**4**	**196**	**12.8**		**594**	**47.6**	**17:25**	**6**	**0**	**2**	**2**	**6**	**0**	**0**	**0**	**20:50**

ECAC All-Rookie Team (2007)

• Missed majority of 2010-11 due to wrist injury vs. Calgary, November 9. 2010.

GARRISON, Jason
(GAIR-ih-suhn, JAY-suhn) **FLA**

Defense. Shoots left. 6'2", 220 lbs. Born, White Rock, B.C., November 13, 1984.

Season	Club	League	GP	G	A	Pts	PIM	PP	SH	GW	S	%	+/-	TF	F%	Min	GP	G	A	Pts	PIM	PP	SH	GW	Min
2003-04	Nanaimo Clippers	BCHL	52	7	20	27	31	....	....	....	....	....	....	....	....	....	24	3	10	13	12	....	....	....	....
2004-05	Nanaimo Clippers	BCHL	57	22	40	62	42	....	....	....	....	....	....	....	....	....	....	....	....	....	....	....	....	....	....
2005-06	U. Minn-Duluth	WCHA	40	3	9	12	26	....	....	....	....	....	....	....	....	....	....	....	....	....	....	....	....	....	....
2006-07	U. Minn-Duluth	WCHA	21	1	2	3	16	....	....	....	....	....	....	....	....	....	....	....	....	....	....	....	....	....	....
2007-08	U. Minn-Duluth	WCHA	26	5	9	14	26	....	....	....	....	....	....	....	....	....	....	....	....	....	....	....	....	....	....
2008-09	**Florida**	**NHL**	**1**	**0**	**0**	**0**	**0**	**0**	**0**	**0**	**0**	**0.0**	**0**	**0**	**0.0**	**11:57**	....	....	....	....	....	....	....	....	....
	Rochester	AHL	75	8	27	35	68	....	....	....	....	....	....	....	....	....	....	....	....	....	....	....	....	....	....

Season	Club	League	GP	G	A	Pts	PIM	PP	SH	GW	S	%	+/-	TF	F%	Min	GP	G	A	Pts	PIM	PP	SH	GW	Min
2009-10	Florida	NHL	39	2	6	8	23	0	0	0	24	8.3	5	0	0.0	15:08	....								
	Rochester	AHL	38	3	16	19	33									....	7	2	7	9	0				
2010-11	Florida	NHL	73	5	13	18	26	0	0	3	116	4.3	-2	0	0.0	22:18	....								
	NHL Totals		113	7	19	26	49	0	0	3	140	5.0		0	0.0	19:44	....								

Signed as a free agent by **Florida**, April 2, 2008.

GAUNCE, Cameron
(GAWNS, KAM-ih-RUHN) **COL**

Defense. Shoots left. 6'1", 203 lbs. Born, Sudbury, Ont., March 19, 1990. Colorado's 1st choice, 50th overall, in 2008 Entry Draft.

Season	Club	League	GP	G	A	Pts	PIM	PP	SH	GW	S	%	+/-	TF	F%	Min	GP	G	A	Pts	PIM	PP	SH	GW	Min
2005-06	Markham Waxers	Minor-ON	72	11	60	71	122									....									
2006-07	Markham Waxers	OPJHL	45	2	12	14	68									....	11	0	3	3	26				
2007-08	St. Michael's	OHL	63	10	30	40	99									....	4	0	1	1	6				
2008-09	St. Michael's	OHL	67	17	47	64	110									....	11	4	6	10	20				
2009-10	St. Michael's	OHL	55	6	31	37	112									....	16	0	13	13	34				
2010-11	Colorado	NHL	11	1	0	1	16	0	0	0	4	25.0	-3	0	0.0	12:44	....								
	Lake Erie	AHL	61	2	20	22	84									....									
	NHL Totals		11	1	0	1	16	0	0	0	4	25.0		0	0.0	12:44	....								

OHL Second All-Star Team (2009, 2010)

GAUSTAD, Paul
(GAW-stad, PAWL) **BUF**

Center. Shoots left. 6'5", 212 lbs. Born, Fargo, ND, February 3, 1982. Buffalo's 6th choice, 220th overall, in 2000 Entry Draft.

Season	Club	League	GP	G	A	Pts	PIM	PP	SH	GW	S	%	+/-	TF	F%	Min	GP	G	A	Pts	PIM	PP	SH	GW	Min
1998-99	Portland Hawks	USAHA	45	47	53	100	81									....									
99-2000	Portland	WHL	56	6	8	14	110									....									
2000-01	Portland	WHL	70	11	30	41	168									....	16	10	6	16	59				
2001-02	Portland	WHL	72	36	44	80	202									....	6	3	1	4	16				
2002-03	Buffalo	NHL	1	0	0	0	0	0	0	0	0	0.0	0	7	42.9	5:48	....								
	Rochester	AHL	80	14	39	53	137									....	3	0	0	0	4				
2003-04	Rochester	AHL	78	9	22	31	169									....	16	3	10	13	30				
2004-05	Rochester	AHL	76	18	25	43	192									....	9	6	5	11	16				
2005-06	Buffalo	NHL	78	9	15	24	65	0	0	0	113	8.0	4	829	52.2	12:08	18	0	4	4	14	0	0	0	12:21
2006-07	Buffalo	NHL	54	9	13	22	74	3	0	0	75	12.0	11	386	52.9	13:19	7	0	1	1	2	0	0	0	11:00
2007-08	Buffalo	NHL	82	10	26	36	85	5	0	2	136	7.4	-4	1165	54.9	17:10	....								
2008-09	Buffalo	NHL	62	12	17	29	108	3	1	1	122	9.8	4	858	52.7	16:06	....								
2009-10	Buffalo	NHL	65	12	10	22	82	3	0	1	111	10.8	-7	1043	57.4	15:45	6	0	1	1	4	0	0	0	18:40
2010-11	Buffalo	NHL	81	12	19	31	101	1	0	3	117	10.3	7	1158	59.8	15:08	7	0	2	2	13	0	0	0	19:19
	NHL Totals		423	64	100	164	515	15	1	7	674	9.5		5446	55.5	14:57	38	0	8	8	37	0	0	0	14:23

GEOFFRION, Blake
(JEHF-REE-ohn, BLAYK) **NSH**

Left wing. Shoots left. 6'1", 192 lbs. Born, Plantation, FL, February 3, 1988. Nashville's 1st choice, 56th overall, in 2006 Entry Draft.

Season	Club	League	GP	G	A	Pts	PIM	PP	SH	GW	S	%	+/-	TF	F%	Min	GP	G	A	Pts	PIM	PP	SH	GW	Min
2003-04	Culver Academy	High-IN	45			65										....									
2004-05	USNTDP	U-17	11	2	3	5	24									....									
	USNTDP	NAHL	37	7	15	22	62									....	10	2	5	7	23				
2005-06	USNTDP	U-18	41	12	14	26	38									....									
	USNTDP	NAHL	13	6	9	15	30									....									
2006-07	U. of Wisconsin	WCHA	36	2	4	6	62									....									
2007-08	U. of Wisconsin	WCHA	36	10	20	30	52									....									
2008-09	U. of Wisconsin	WCHA	35	15	13	28	73									....									
2009-10	U. of Wisconsin	WCHA	40	*28	22	50	56									....									
	Milwaukee	AHL														....	3	2	0	2	0				
2010-11	Nashville	NHL	20	6	2	8	7	0	0	1	24	25.0	3	99	46.5	8:16	12	0	2	2	4	0	0	0	7:37
	Milwaukee	AHL	45	11	26	37	38									....	1	0	2	2	2				
	NHL Totals		20	6	2	8	7	0	0	1	24	25.0		99	46.5	8:16	12	0	2	2	4	0	0	0	7:37

WCHA First All-Star Team (2010) • NCAA West First All-American Team (2010) • Hobey Baker Memorial Award (Top U.S. Collegiate Player) (2010)

GERBE, Nathan
(GUHR-bee, NAY-thuhn) **BUF**

Center. Shoots left. 5'5", 178 lbs. Born, Oxford, MI, July 24, 1987. Buffalo's 5th choice, 142nd overall, in 2005 Entry Draft.

Season	Club	League	GP	G	A	Pts	PIM	PP	SH	GW	S	%	+/-	TF	F%	Min	GP	G	A	Pts	PIM	PP	SH	GW	Min
2002-03	River City Lancers	USHL	25	3	3	6	49									....	7	1	1	2	2				
2003-04	USNTDP	U-17	32	14	12	26	66									....									
	USNTDP	NAHL	26	11	7	18	87									....									
2004-05	USNTDP	U-18	26	6	11	17	48									....									
	USNTDP	NAHL	12	7	5	12	25									....									
2005-06	Boston College	H-East	39	11	7	18	75									....									
2006-07	Boston College	H-East	41	*25	22	47	76									....									
2007-08	Boston College	H-East	43	*35	33	*68	65									....									
2008-09	Buffalo	NHL	10	0	1	1	4	0	0	0	24	0.0	3		1100.0	13:37	....								
	Portland Pirates	AHL	57	30	26	56	63									....	5	0	0	0	4				
2009-10	Buffalo	NHL	10	2	3	5	4	2	0	1	29	6.9	1	3	33.3	14:39	2	1	1	2	0	0	0	0	14:38
	Portland Pirates	AHL	44	11	27	38	46									....	4	1	1	2	4				
2010-11	Buffalo	NHL	64	16	15	31	34	2	0	3	171	9.4	11	17	23.5	13:20	7	2	0	2	18	0	0	0	13:20
	NHL Totals		84	18	19	37	42	4	0	4	224	8.0		21	28.6	13:31	9	3	1	4	18	0	0	0	13:38

Hockey East Second Alll-Star Team (2007) • NCAA Championship All-Tournament Team (2007, 2008) • Hockey East First All-Star Team (2008) • NCAA East First All-American Team (2008) • NCAA Championship Tournament MVP (2008) • AHL All-Rookie Team (2009) • Dudley "Red" Garrett Memorial Award (AHL – Rookie of the Year) (2009)

GERVAIS, Bruno
(ZHUR-vay, BROO-noh) **T.B.**

Defense. Shoots right. 6'1", 200 lbs. Born, Longueuil, Que., October 3, 1984. NY Islanders' 6th choice, 182nd overall, in 2003 Entry Draft.

Season	Club	League	GP	G	A	Pts	PIM	PP	SH	GW	S	%	+/-	TF	F%	Min	GP	G	A	Pts	PIM	PP	SH	GW	Min
99-2000	Antoine-Girouard	QAAA	6	0	0	0	0									....	4	0	0	0	0				
2000-01	Antoine-Girouard	QAAA	40	8	27	35	46									....	7	4	2	6	8				
2001-02	Acadie-Bathurst	QMJHL	65	4	12	16	42									....	16	3	2	5	8				
2002-03	Acadie-Bathurst	QMJHL	72	22	28	50	73									....	11	3	5	8	14				
2003-04	Acadie-Bathurst	QMJHL	23	4	6	10	28									....									
2004-05	Bridgeport	AHL	76	8	22	30	58									....									
2005-06	NY Islanders	NHL	27	3	4	7	8	1	0	0	21	14.3	-1	0	0.0	16:47	....								
	Bridgeport	AHL	55	17	25	42	70									....	7	1	2	3	0				
2006-07	NY Islanders	NHL	51	0	6	6	28	0	0	0	47	0.0	-10	0	0.0	15:23	5	1	1	2	2	0	0	0	15:36
	Bridgeport	AHL	3	0	0	0	6									....									
2007-08	NY Islanders	NHL	60	0	13	13	34	0	0	0	59	0.0	-5	0	0.0	20:00	....								
2008-09	NY Islanders	NHL	69	3	16	19	33	0	0	0	82	3.7	-15	1	0.0	21:36	....								
2009-10	NY Islanders	NHL	71	3	14	17	31	1	0	1	83	3.6	-15	0	0.0	20:01	....								
2010-11	NY Islanders	NHL	53	0	6	6	30	0	0	0	43	0.0	-14	0	0.0	15:41	....								
	NHL Totals		331	9	59	68	164	2	0	2	335	2.7		1	0.0	18:40	5	1	1	2	2	0	0	0	15:36

QMJHL Second All-Star Team (2003)
• Missed majority of 2003-04 due to knee injury in Team Canada Jr. training camp, December 12, 2003. Traded to **Tampa Bay** by **NY Islanders** for future considerations, June 25, 2011.

GETZLAF, Ryan
(GEHTZ-laf, RIGH-uhn) **ANA**

Center. Shoots right. 6'4", 220 lbs. Born, Regina, Sask., May 10, 1985. Anaheim's 1st choice, 19th overall, in 2003 Entry Draft.

Season	Club	League	GP	G	A	Pts	PIM	PP	SH	GW	S	%	+/-	TF	F%	Min	GP	G	A	Pts	PIM	PP	SH	GW	Min
2000-01	Regina Rangers	SBHL	41	33	41	74	189									....									
	Reg. Pat Cdns.	SMHL	8	4	3	7	8									....									
2001-02	Calgary Hitmen	WHL	63	9	9	18	34									....	7	2	1	3	4				
2002-03	Calgary Hitmen	WHL	70	29	39	68	121									....	5	1	1	2	6				
2003-04	Calgary Hitmen	WHL	49	28	47	75	97									....	7	5	1	6	12				
2004-05	Calgary Hitmen	WHL	51	29	25	54	102									....	12	4	13	17	18				
	Cincinnati	AHL														....	10	1	4	5	4				
2005-06	Anaheim	NHL	57	14	25	39	22	10	0	1	116	12.1	6	534	44.0	12:35	16	3	4	7	13	2	0	1	15:49
	Portland Pirates	AHL	17	8	25	33	36									....	1	0	0	0	4				

Season	Club	League	GP	G	A	Pts	PIM	PP	SH	GW	S	%	+/-	TF	F%	Min	GP	G	A	Pts	PIM	PP	SH	GW	Min
			Regular Season														Playoffs								
2006-07♦	Anaheim	NHL	82	25	33	58	66	11	1	6	203	12.3	17	888	49.4	15:04	21	7	10	17	32	3	1	3	21:43
2007-08	Anaheim	NHL	77	24	58	82	94	4	1	2	185	13.0	32	1152	47.3	19:39	6	2	3	5	6	1	0	0	20:29
2008-09	Anaheim	NHL	81	25	66	91	121	9	0	2	227	11.0	5	1128	50.2	20:08	13	4	14	18	25	1	0	0	24:08
2009-10	Anaheim	NHL	66	19	50	69	79	8	0	5	149	12.8	4	1124	47.4	21:40	....	....	....	....	....	....	....	....	....
	Canada	Olympics	7	3	4	7	2	....	....	....	....	....	....	....	....	....	....	....	....	....	....	....	....	....	....
2010-11	Anaheim	NHL	67	19	57	76	35	7	0	4	117	16.2	14	1183	45.8	21:51	6	2	4	6	9	0	0	1	24:01
	NHL Totals		430	126	289	415	417	49	2	20	997	12.6		6009	47.6	18:35	62	18	35	53	85	7	1	5	20:49

WHL East First All-Star Team (2004) • WHL East Second All-Star Team (2005)
Played in NHL All-Star Game (2008, 2009)

GILBERT, Tom

(GIHL-buhrt, TAWM) **EDM**

Defense. Shoots right. 6'3", 206 lbs. Born, Bloomington, MN, January 10, 1983. Colorado's 5th choice, 129th overall, in 2002 Entry Draft.

Season	Club	League	GP	G	A	Pts	PIM	PP	SH	GW	S	%	+/-	TF	F%	Min	GP	G	A	Pts	PIM	PP	SH	GW	Min
99-2000	Bloomington-Jeff.	High-MN	18	7	18	25	....	....	....	....	....	....	....	....	....	....	....	....	....	....	....	....	....	....	....
2000-01	Bloomington-Jeff.	High-MN	23	20	18	38	....	....	....	....	....	....	....	....	....	....	....	....	....	....	....	....	....	....	....
	Chicago Steel	USHL	1	0	0	0	0	....	....	....	....	....	....	....	....	....	....	....	....	....	....	....	....	....	....
2001-02	Chicago Steel	USHL	57	13	15	28	62	....	....	....	....	....	....	....	....	....	4	0	0	0	4	....	....	....	....
2002-03	U. of Wisconsin	WCHA	39	7	13	20	36	....	....	....	....	....	....	....	....	....	....	....	....	....	....	....	....	....	....
2003-04	U. of Wisconsin	WCHA	39	6	15	21	36	....	....	....	....	....	....	....	....	....	....	....	....	....	....	....	....	....	....
2004-05	U. of Wisconsin	WCHA	41	8	9	17	48	....	....	....	....	....	....	....	....	....	....	....	....	....	....	....	....	....	....
2005-06	U. of Wisconsin	WCHA	43	12	19	31	32	....	....	....	....	....	....	....	....	....	....	....	....	....	....	....	....	....	....
2006-07	Edmonton	NHL	12	1	5	6	0	0	0	0	13	7.7	-1	0	0.0	20:05	....	....	....	....	....	....	....	....	....
	Wilkes-Barre	AHL	48	4	26	30	32	....	....	....	....	....	....	....	....	....	10	1	7	8	10	....	....	....	....
2007-08	Edmonton	NHL	82	13	20	33	20	3	0	1	98	13.3	-6	0	0.0	22:12	....	....	....	....	....	....	....	....	....
2008-09	Edmonton	NHL	82	5	40	45	26	2	0	1	107	4.7	6	0	0.0	21:58	....	....	....	....	....	....	....	....	....
2009-10	Edmonton	NHL	82	5	26	31	16	1	1	0	98	5.1	-10	0	0.0	22:25	....	....	....	....	....	....	....	....	....
2010-11	Edmonton	NHL	79	6	20	26	32	3	0	0	106	5.7	-14	0	0.0	24:30	....	....	....	....	....	....	....	....	....
	NHL Totals		337	30	111	141	94	9	1	2	422	7.1		0	0.0	22:40	....	....	....	....	....	....	....	....	....

WCHA First All-Star Team (2006) • NCAA West Second All-American Team (2006) • NCAA Championship All-Tournament Team (2006) • NHL All-Rookie Team (2008)
Traded to **Edmonton** by **Colorado** for Tommy Salo and Edmonton's 6th round choice (Justin Mercier) in 2005 Entry Draft, March 8, 2004.

GILL, Hal

(GIHL, HAL) **MTL**

Defense. Shoots left. 6'7", 241 lbs. Born, Concord, MA, April 6, 1975. Boston's 8th choice, 207th overall, in 1993 Entry Draft.

Season	Club	League	GP	G	A	Pts	PIM	PP	SH	GW	S	%	+/-	TF	F%	Min	GP	G	A	Pts	PIM	PP	SH	GW	Min
1992-93	Nashoba	High-MA	20	25	25	50	....	....	....	....	....	....	....	....	....	....	....	....	....	....	....	....	....	....	....
1993-94	Providence	H-East	31	1	2	3	26	....	....	....	....	....	....	....	....	....	....	....	....	....	....	....	....	....	....
1994-95	Providence	H-East	26	1	3	4	22	....	....	....	....	....	....	....	....	....	....	....	....	....	....	....	....	....	....
1995-96	Providence	H-East	39	5	12	17	54	....	....	....	....	....	....	....	....	....	....	....	....	....	....	....	....	....	....
1996-97	Providence	H-East	35	5	16	21	52	....	....	....	....	....	....	....	....	....	....	....	....	....	....	....	....	....	....
1997-98	Boston	NHL	68	2	4	6	47	0	0	0	56	3.6	4	....	....	....	6	0	0	0	4	0	0	0	....
	Providence Bruins	AHL	4	1	0	1	23	....	....	....	....	....	....	....	....	....	....	....	....	....	....	....	....	....	....
1998-99	Boston	NHL	80	3	7	10	63	0	0	2	102	2.9	-10	1	100.0	20:54	12	0	0	0	14	0	0	0	20:41
99-2000	Boston	NHL	81	3	9	12	51	0	0	0	120	2.5	0	0	0.0	17:15	....	....	....	....	....	....	....	....	....
2000-01	Boston	NHL	80	1	10	11	71	0	0	0	79	1.3	-2	0	0.0	18:21	....	....	....	....	....	....	....	....	....
2001-02	Boston	NHL	79	4	18	22	77	0	0	0	137	2.9	16	0	0.0	24:13	6	0	1	1	2	0	0	0	23:04
2002-03	Boston	NHL	76	4	13	17	56	0	0	0	114	3.5	21	0	0.0	20:42	5	0	0	0	4	0	0	0	20:19
2003-04	Boston	NHL	82	2	7	9	99	0	0	0	104	1.9	16	0	0.0	18:24	7	0	1	1	4	0	0	0	19:03
2004-05	Lukko Rauma	Finland	31	2	8	10	110	....	....	....	....	....	....	....	....	....	8	0	0	0	*57	....	....	....	....
2005-06	Boston	NHL	80	1	9	10	124	0	0	0	68	1.5	-4	0	0.0	18:37	....	....	....	....	....	....	....	....	....
2006-07	Toronto	NHL	82	6	14	20	91	0	0	1	79	7.6	11	1	0.0	18:53	....	....	....	....	....	....	....	....	....
2007-08	Toronto	NHL	63	2	18	20	52	0	0	0	69	2.9	0	1	0.0	20:42	....	....	....	....	....	....	....	....	....
	Pittsburgh	NHL	18	1	3	4	16	0	0	0	17	5.9	6	0	0.0	17:31	20	0	1	1	12	0	0	0	19:17
2008-09♦	Pittsburgh	NHL	62	2	8	10	53	0	0	0	40	5.0	11	0	0.0	17:54	24	0	2	2	6	0	0	0	19:26
2009-10	Montreal	NHL	68	2	9	11	68	0	0	0	41	4.9	-10	1	0.0	18:21	18	0	1	1	20	0	0	0	19:54
2010-11	Montreal	NHL	75	2	7	9	43	0	0	1	62	3.2	-9	0	0.0	19:49	7	0	0	0	2	0	0	0	23:21
	NHL Totals		994	35	136	171	911	0	0	4	1088	3.2		3	33.3	19:28	105	0	6	6	68	0	0	0	20:09

Signed as a free agent by **Rauma** (Finland), November 25, 2004. Signed as a free agent by **Toronto**, July 1, 2006. Traded to **Pittsburgh** by **Toronto** for Pittsburgh's 2nd round choice (Jimmy Hayes) in 2008 Entry Draft and Pittsburgh's 5th round choice (later traded to NY Rangers, later traded back to Pittsburgh – Pittsburgh selected Andy Bathgate) in 2009 Entry Draft, February 26, 2008. Signed as a free agent by **Montreal**, July 1, 2009.

GILLIES, Colton

(GIHL-eez, KOHL-tuhn) **MIN**

Left wing. Shoots left. 6'4", 208 lbs. Born, White Rock, B.C., February 12, 1989. Minnesota's 1st choice, 16th overall, in 2007 Entry Draft.

Season	Club	League	GP	G	A	Pts	PIM	PP	SH	GW	S	%	+/-	TF	F%	Min	GP	G	A	Pts	PIM	PP	SH	GW	Min
2004-05	North Delta Flyers	PIJHL	44	9	17	26	....	....	....	....	....	....	....	....	....	....	6	2	1	3	....	....	....	....	....
	Surrey Eagles	BCHL	3	1	0	1	0	....	....	....	....	....	....	....	....	....	....	....	....	....	....	....	....	....	....
	Saskatoon Blades	WHL	9	1	1	2	8	....	....	....	....	....	....	....	....	....	2	0	0	0	0	....	....	....	....
2005-06	Saskatoon Blades	WHL	63	6	6	12	57	....	....	....	....	....	....	....	....	....	8	0	0	0	4	....	....	....	....
2006-07	Saskatoon Blades	WHL	65	13	17	30	148	....	....	....	....	....	....	....	....	....	....	....	....	....	....	....	....	....	....
2007-08	Saskatoon Blades	WHL	58	24	23	47	97	....	....	....	....	....	....	....	....	....	....	....	....	....	....	....	....	....	....
	Houston Aeros	AHL	11	1	7	8	4	....	....	....	....	....	....	....	....	....	5	0	0	0	2	....	....	....	....
2008-09	Minnesota	NHL	45	2	5	7	18	0	0	1	22	9.1	-2	2	50.0	8:14	....	....	....	....	....	....	....	....	....
2009-10	Houston Aeros	AHL	72	7	13	20	73	....	....	....	....	....	....	....	....	....	....	....	....	....	....	....	....	....	....
2010-11	Minnesota	NHL	7	1	0	1	2	0	0	0	3	33.3	-2	2	50.0	10:22	....	....	....	....	....	....	....	....	....
	Houston Aeros	AHL	64	11	15	26	82	....	....	....	....	....	....	....	....	....	24	7	5	12	32	....	....	....	....
	NHL Totals		52	3	5	8	20	0	0	1	25	12.0		4	50.0	8:31	....	....	....	....	....	....	....	....	....

GILLIES, Trevor

(GIHL-eez, TREH-vuhr) **NYI**

Left wing. Shoots left. 6'3", 227 lbs. Born, Cambridge, Ont., January 30, 1979.

Season	Club	League	GP	G	A	Pts	PIM	PP	SH	GW	S	%	+/-	TF	F%	Min	GP	G	A	Pts	PIM	PP	SH	GW	Min
1996-97	North Bay	OHL	26	0	3	3	72	....	....	....	....	....	....	....	....	....	....	....	....	....	....	....	....	....	....
1997-98	North Bay	OHL	2	0	0	0	4	....	....	....	....	....	....	....	....	....	....	....	....	....	....	....	....	....	....
	Sarnia Sting	OHL	17	0	1	1	33	....	....	....	....	....	....	....	....	....	....	....	....	....	....	....	....	....	....
	Oshawa Generals	OHL	45	1	2	3	184	....	....	....	....	....	....	....	....	....	7	0	1	1	12	....	....	....	....
1998-99	Oshawa Generals	OHL	66	6	9	15	270	....	....	....	....	....	....	....	....	....	11	0	2	2	28	....	....	....	....
99-2000	Lowell	AHL	8	0	0	0	38	....	....	....	....	....	....	....	....	....	....	....	....	....	....	....	....	....	....
	Mississippi	ECHL	53	0	6	6	202	....	....	....	....	....	....	....	....	....	....	....	....	....	....	....	....	....	....
2000-01	Greensboro	ECHL	63	1	6	7	303	....	....	....	....	....	....	....	....	....	....	....	....	....	....	....	....	....	....
	Worcester IceCats	AHL	....	....	....	....	....	....	....	....	....	....	....	....	....	....	6	0	0	0	24	....	....	....	....
2001-02	Providence Bruins	AHL	5	0	0	0	21	....	....	....	....	....	....	....	....	....	....	....	....	....	....	....	....	....	....
	Augusta Lynx	ECHL	46	0	1	1	*269	....	....	....	....	....	....	....	....	....	....	....	....	....	....	....	....	....	....
	Richmond	ECHL	18	0	1	1	*51	....	....	....	....	....	....	....	....	....	....	....	....	....	....	....	....	....	....
2002-03	Lowell	AHL	25	0	1	1	132	....	....	....	....	....	....	....	....	....	....	....	....	....	....	....	....	....	....
	Richmond	ECHL	6	0	0	0	20	....	....	....	....	....	....	....	....	....	....	....	....	....	....	....	....	....	....
	Peoria Rivermen	ECHL	24	0	1	1	180	....	....	....	....	....	....	....	....	....	....	....	....	....	....	....	....	....	....
2003-04	Springfield	AHL	61	2	1	3	277	....	....	....	....	....	....	....	....	....	....	....	....	....	....	....	....	....	....
2004-05	Hartford	AHL	49	0	2	2	277	....	....	....	....	....	....	....	....	....	....	....	....	....	....	....	....	....	....
2005-06	Anaheim	NHL	1	0	0	0	21	0	0	0	1	0.0	0	0	0.0	2:40	....	....	....	....	....	....	....	....	....
	Portland Pirates	AHL	50	2	3	5	169	....	....	....	....	....	....	....	....	....	4	0	0	0	0	....	....	....	....
2006-07	Portland Pirates	AHL	51	1	6	7	151	....	....	....	....	....	....	....	....	....	....	....	....	....	....	....	....	....	....
	Augusta Lynx	ECHL	7	0	2	2	23	....	....	....	....	....	....	....	....	....	....	....	....	....	....	....	....	....	....
2007-08	Albany River Rats	AHL	51	1	1	2	112	....	....	....	....	....	....	....	....	....	7	0	0	0	19	....	....	....	....
2008-09	Albany River Rats	AHL	30	0	0	0	125	....	....	....	....	....	....	....	....	....	....	....	....	....	....	....	....	....	....

Season	Club	League	GP	G	A	Pts	PIM	PP	SH	GW	S	%	+/-	TF	F%	Min	GP	G	A	Pts	PIM	PP	SH	GW	Min
			Regular Season														Playoffs								
2009-10	Bridgeport	AHL	24	1	0	1	169	....	....	....	....	....	....	....	....	....	....	....	....	....	....	....	....	....	....
	NY Islanders	**NHL**	**14**	**0**	**1**	**1**	**75**	**0**	**0**	**0**	**6**	**0.0**	**–2**	**0**	**0.0**	**3:49**	....	....	....	....	....	....	....	....	....
2010-11	**NY Islanders**	**NHL**	**39**	**2**	**0**	**2**	**165**	**0**	**0**	**0**	**9**	**22.2**	**–3**	**1**	**0.0**	**3:04**	....	....	....	....	....	....	....	....	....
	NHL Totals		**54**	**2**	**1**	**3**	**261**	**0**	**0**	**0**	**16**	**12.5**		**1**	**0.0**	**3:15**	....	....	....	....	....	....	....	....	....

Signed as a free agent by **NY Rangers**, July 20, 2004. Traded to **Anaheim** by **NY Rangers** with NY Rangers' 4th round choice (later traded back to NY Rangers, later traded to Washington - Washington selected Brett Bruneteau) in 2007 Entry Draft for Steve Rucchin, August 23, 2005. Signed as a free agent by **Carolina**, July 2, 2007. • Missed majority of 2008-09 due to injury at Wilkes-Barre (AHL), December 20, 2008. Signed as a free agent by **Bridgeport** (AHL), October 2, 2009. Signed as a free agent by **NY Islanders**, January 29, 2010. • Suspended nine games by NHL for deliberate attempt to injure Eric Tangradi in game vs, Pittsburgh, February 11, 2011 and suspended an additional ten games for deliberate attempt to injure Cal Clutterbuck in game vs. Minnesota, March 2, 2011. • Missed majority of 2010-11 as a healthy reserve.

GILROY, Matt

(GIHL-roy, MAT) **T.B.**

Defense. Shoots right. 6'1", 201 lbs. Born, North Bellmore, NY, July 30, 1984.

Season	Club	League	GP	G	A	Pts	PIM	PP	SH	GW	S	%	+/-	TF	F%	Min	GP	G	A	Pts	PIM	PP	SH	GW	Min
2000-01	St. Mary's Gaels	High-NY	STATISTICS NOT AVAILABLE																						
2001-02	St. Mary's Gaels	High-NY	STATISTICS NOT AVAILABLE																						
2002-03	St. Mary's Gaels	High-NY	STATISTICS NOT AVAILABLE																						
2003-04	NY Apple Core	EJHL	STATISTICS NOT AVAILABLE																						
2004-05	Walpole Stars	EJHL	55	24	29	53	20	....	....	....	....	....	....	....	....	....	....	....	....	....	....	....	....	....	....
2005-06	Boston University	H-East	36	2	6	8	10	....	....	....	....	....	....	....	....	....	....	....	....	....	....	....	....	....	....
2006-07	Boston University	H-East	39	9	17	26	14	....	....	....	....	....	....	....	....	....	....	....	....	....	....	....	....	....	....
2007-08	Boston University	H-East	40	6	15	21	12	....	....	....	....	....	....	....	....	....	....	....	....	....	....	....	....	....	....
2008-09	Boston University	H-East	45	8	29	37	12	....	....	....	....	....	....	....	....	....	....	....	....	....	....	....	....	....	....
2009-10	**NY Rangers**	**NHL**	**69**	**4**	**11**	**15**	**23**	**0**	**0**	**1**	**82**	**4.9**	**0**	**1**	**100.0**	**16:19**	....	....	....	....	....	....	....	....	....
	Hartford	AHL	5	0	4	4	4	....	....	....	....	....	....	....	....	....	....	....	....	....	....	....	....	....	....
2010-11	**NY Rangers**	**NHL**	**58**	**3**	**8**	**11**	**14**	**0**	**0**	**1**	**75**	**4.0**	**5**	**0**	**0.0**	**14:11**	**5**	**1**	**0**	**1**	**2**	**0**	**0**	**0**	**15:40**
	NHL Totals		**127**	**7**	**19**	**26**	**37**	**0**	**0**	**2**	**157**	**4.5**		**1**	**100.0**	**15:20**	**5**	**1**	**0**	**1**	**2**	**0**	**0**	**0**	**15:40**

Hockey East First All-Star Team (2008, 2009) • NCAA East First All-American Team (2008, 2009) • Hobey Baker Memorial Award (Top U.S. Collegiate Player) (2009)

Signed as a free agent by **NY Rangers**, April 17, 2009. Signed as a free agent by **Tampa Bay**, July 2, 2011.

GIONTA, Brian

(jee-OHN-tuh, BRIGH-uhn) **MTL**

Right wing. Shoots right. 5'7", 173 lbs. Born, Rochester, NY, January 18, 1979. New Jersey's 4th choice, 82nd overall, in 1998 Entry Draft.

Season	Club	League	GP	G	A	Pts	PIM	PP	SH	GW	S	%	+/-	TF	F%	Min	GP	G	A	Pts	PIM	PP	SH	GW	Min
1994-95	Rochester	EmJHL	28	*52	37	*89	....	....	....	....	....	....	....	....	....	....	....	....	....	....	....	....	....	....	....
1995-96	Niagara Scenic	ON-Jr.A	51	47	44	91	59	....	....	....	....	....	....	....	....	....	....	....	....	....	....	....	....	....	....
1996-97	Niagara Scenic	ON-Jr.A	50	57	70	127	101	....	....	....	....	....	....	....	....	....	6	6	11	17	21	....	....	....	....
1997-98	Boston College	H-East	40	30	32	62	44	....	....	....	....	....	....	....	....	....	....	....	....	....	....	....	....	....	....
1998-99	Boston College	H-East	39	27	33	60	46	....	....	....	....	....	....	....	....	....	....	....	....	....	....	....	....	....	....
99-2000	Boston College	H-East	42	*33	23	56	66	....	....	....	....	....	....	....	....	....	....	....	....	....	....	....	....	....	....
2000-01	Boston College	H-East	43	*33	21	*54	47	....	....	....	....	....	....	....	....	....	....	....	....	....	....	....	....	....	....
2001-02	**New Jersey**	**NHL**	**33**	**4**	**7**	**11**	**8**	**0**	**0**	**0**	**58**	**6.9**	**10**	**36**	**44.4**	**13:25**	**6**	**2**	**2**	**4**	**0**	**0**	**1**	**2**	**17:08**
	Albany River Rats	AHL	37	9	16	25	18	....	....	....	....	....	....	....	....	....	....	....	....	....	....	....	....	....	....
2002-03♦	**New Jersey**	**NHL**	**58**	**12**	**13**	**25**	**23**	**2**	**0**	**3**	**129**	**9.3**	**5**	**14**	**57.1**	**14:48**	**24**	**1**	**8**	**9**	**6**	**0**	**0**	**0**	**14:31**
2003-04	**New Jersey**	**NHL**	**75**	**21**	**8**	**29**	**36**	**0**	**0**	**8**	**174**	**12.1**	**19**	**60**	**58.3**	**14:44**	**5**	**2**	**3**	**5**	**0**	**1**	**0**	**0**	**15:41**
2004-05	Albany River Rats	AHL	15	5	7	12	10	....	....	....	....	....	....	....	....	....	....	....	....	....	....	....	....	....	....
2005-06	**New Jersey**	**NHL**	**82**	**48**	**41**	**89**	**46**	**24**	**1**	**10**	**291**	**16.5**	**18**	**73**	**38.4**	**19:49**	**9**	**3**	**4**	**7**	**2**	**1**	**1**	**2**	**20:06**
	United States	Olympics	6	4	0	4	2	....	....	....	....	....	....	....	....	....	....	....	....	....	....	....	....	....	....
2006-07	**New Jersey**	**NHL**	**62**	**25**	**20**	**45**	**36**	**11**	**0**	**4**	**194**	**12.9**	**–3**	**31**	**38.7**	**18:49**	**11**	**8**	**1**	**9**	**4**	**3**	**0**	**1**	**19:15**
2007-08	**New Jersey**	**NHL**	**82**	**22**	**31**	**53**	**46**	**8**	**1**	**4**	**257**	**8.6**	**1**	**55**	**54.6**	**18:16**	**5**	**1**	**0**	**1**	**2**	**0**	**0**	**0**	**17:52**
2008-09	**New Jersey**	**NHL**	**81**	**20**	**40**	**60**	**32**	**3**	**3**	**1**	**248**	**8.1**	**12**	**132**	**38.6**	**16:58**	**7**	**2**	**3**	**5**	**4**	**0**	**0**	**0**	**17:49**
2009-10	**Montreal**	**NHL**	**61**	**28**	**18**	**46**	**26**	**10**	**0**	**3**	**237**	**11.8**	**3**	**13**	**53.9**	**20:45**	**19**	**9**	**6**	**15**	**14**	**4**	**0**	**1**	**22:11**
2010-11	**Montreal**	**NHL**	**82**	**29**	**17**	**46**	**24**	**7**	**2**	**6**	**298**	**9.7**	**3**	**59**	**32.2**	**19:37**	**7**	**3**	**2**	**5**	**0**	**1**	**0**	**2**	**22:35**
	NHL Totals		**616**	**209**	**195**	**404**	**277**	**65**	**7**	**39**	**1886**	**11.1**		**473**	**43.6**	**17:46**	**93**	**31**	**29**	**60**	**32**	**10**	**2**	**8**	**18:27**

Hockey East Rookie of the Year (1998) • Hockey East Second All-Star Team (1998) • NCAA East Second All-American Team (1998) • Hockey East First All-Star Team (1999, 2000, 2001) • NCAA East First All-American Team (1999, 2000, 2001) • Hockey East Player of the Year (2001)

Signed as a free agent by **Montreal**, July 1, 2009.

GIONTA, Stephen

(jee-OHN-tuh, STEE-vehn) **N.J.**

Center. Shoots right. 5'7", 185 lbs. Born, Rochester, NY, October 9, 1983.

Season	Club	League	GP	G	A	Pts	PIM	PP	SH	GW	S	%	+/-	TF	F%	Min	GP	G	A	Pts	PIM	PP	SH	GW	Min
2002-03	Boston College	H-East	33	5	10	15	36	....	....	....	....	....	....	....	....	....	....	....	....	....	....	....	....	....	....
2003-04	Boston College	H-East	41	9	15	24	36	....	....	....	....	....	....	....	....	....	....	....	....	....	....	....	....	....	....
2004-05	Boston College	H-East	38	8	11	19	44	....	....	....	....	....	....	....	....	....	....	....	....	....	....	....	....	....	....
2005-06	Boston College	H-East	37	11	21	32	66	....	....	....	....	....	....	....	....	....	....	....	....	....	....	....	....	....	....
	Albany River Rats	AHL	3	5	1	6	2	....	....	....	....	....	....	....	....	....	....	....	....	....	....	....	....	....	....
2006-07	Lowell Devils	AHL	67	7	8	15	15	....	....	....	....	....	....	....	....	....	....	....	....	....	....	....	....	....	....
2007-08	Lowell Devils	AHL	63	16	13	29	33	....	....	....	....	....	....	....	....	....	....	....	....	....	....	....	....	....	....
2008-09	Lowell Devils	AHL	52	2	9	11	30	....	....	....	....	....	....	....	....	....	....	....	....	....	....	....	....	....	....
2009-10	Lowell Devils	AHL	68	15	19	34	26	....	....	....	....	....	....	....	....	....	5	0	1	1	0	....	....	....	....
2010-11	**New Jersey**	**NHL**	**12**	**0**	**0**	**0**	**6**	**0**	**0**	**0**	**13**	**0.0**	**–3**	**0**	**0.0**	**9:00**	....	....	....	....	....	....	....	....	....
	Albany Devils	AHL	54	10	20	30	21	....	....	....	....	....	....	....	....	....	....	....	....	....	....	....	....	....	....
	NHL Totals		**12**	**0**	**0**	**0**	**6**	**0**	**0**	**0**	**13**	**0.0**		**0**	**0.0**	**9:00**	....	....	....	....	....	....	....	....	....

Signed to an ATO (amateur tryout) contract by **Albany** (AHL), April 12, 2006. Signed as a free agent by **New Jersey**, August 26, 2010.

GIORDANO, Mark

(jee-ohr-DAN-oh, MAHRK) **CGY**

Defense. Shoots left. 6', 203 lbs. Born, Toronto, Ont., October 3, 1983.

Season	Club	League	GP	G	A	Pts	PIM	PP	SH	GW	S	%	+/-	TF	F%	Min	GP	G	A	Pts	PIM	PP	SH	GW	Min
2002-03	Owen Sound	OHL	68	18	30	48	109	....	....	....	....	....	....	....	....	....	4	1	3	4	2	....	....	....	....
2003-04	Owen Sound	OHL	65	14	35	49	72	....	....	....	....	....	....	....	....	....	7	1	3	4	5	....	....	....	....
2004-05	Lowell	AHL	66	6	10	16	85	....	....	....	....	....	....	....	....	....	11	0	1	1	41	....	....	....	....
2005-06	**Calgary**	**NHL**	**7**	**0**	**1**	**1**	**8**	**0**	**0**	**0**	**5**	**0.0**	**2**	**0**	**0.0**	**12:05**	....	....	....	....	....	....	....	....	....
	Omaha	AHL	73	16	42	58	141	....	....	....	....	....	....	....	....	....	....	....	....	....	....	....	....	....	....
2006-07	**Calgary**	**NHL**	**48**	**7**	**8**	**15**	**36**	**3**	**0**	**2**	**49**	**14.3**	**7**	**0**	**0.0**	**13:27**	**4**	**1**	**0**	**1**	**0**	**1**	**0**	**0**	**12:16**
	Omaha	AHL	5	0	2	2	8	....	....	....	....	....	....	....	....	....	3	0	1	1	2	....	....	....	....
2007-08	Dynamo Moscow	Russia	50	4	8	12	89	....	....	....	....	....	....	....	....	....	9	1	5	6	35	....	....	....	....
2008-09	**Calgary**	**NHL**	**58**	**2**	**17**	**19**	**59**	**2**	**0**	**0**	**82**	**2.4**	**2**	**0**	**0.0**	**16:13**	....	....	....	....	....	....	....	....	....
2009-10	**Calgary**	**NHL**	**82**	**11**	**19**	**30**	**81**	**5**	**0**	**1**	**111**	**9.9**	**17**	**0**	**0.0**	**20:50**	....	....	....	....	....	....	....	....	....
2010-11	**Calgary**	**NHL**	**82**	**8**	**35**	**43**	**67**	**5**	**0**	**1**	**165**	**4.8**	**–8**	**0**	**0.0**	**23:08**	....	....	....	....	....	....	....	....	....
	NHL Totals		**277**	**28**	**80**	**108**	**251**	**15**	**0**	**4**	**412**	**6.8**		**0**	**0.0**	**19:03**	**4**	**1**	**0**	**1**	**0**	**1**	**0**	**0**	**12:16**

Signed as a free agent by **Calgary**, July 6, 2004. Signed as a free agent by **Dynamo Moscow** (Russia) August 28, 2007. Signed as a free agent by **Calgary**, July 1, 2008.

GIRARDI, Dan

(jih-RAHR-dee, DAN) **NYR**

Defense. Shoots right. 6'1", 206 lbs. Born, Welland, Ont., April 29, 1984.

Season	Club	League	GP	G	A	Pts	PIM	PP	SH	GW	S	%	+/-	TF	F%	Min	GP	G	A	Pts	PIM	PP	SH	GW	Min
2000-01	Barrie Colts	OHL	6	0	0	0	0	....	....	....	....	....	....	....	....	....	....	....	....	....	....	....	....	....	....
2001-02	Barrie Colts	OHL	21	0	1	1	0	....	....	....	....	....	....	....	....	....	20	0	0	0	0	....	....	....	....
2002-03	Barrie Colts	OHL	31	3	13	16	24	....	....	....	....	....	....	....	....	....	....	....	....	....	....	....	....	....	....
	Guelph Storm	OHL	36	1	13	14	20	....	....	....	....	....	....	....	....	....	11	0	9	9	14	....	....	....	....
2003-04	Guelph Storm	OHL	68	8	39	47	55	....	....	....	....	....	....	....	....	....	22	2	17	19	10	....	....	....	....
2004-05	Guelph Storm	OHL	38	5	20	25	24	....	....	....	....	....	....	....	....	....	....	....	....	....	....	....	....	....	....
	London Knights	OHL	31	4	10	14	14	....	....	....	....	....	....	....	....	....	18	0	6	6	10	....	....	....	....
2005-06	Hartford	AHL	66	8	31	39	44	....	....	....	....	....	....	....	....	....	13	4	5	9	8	....	....	....	....
	Charlotte	ECHL	7	1	4	5	6	....	....	....	....	....	....	....	....	....	....	....	....	....	....	....	....	....	....
2006-07	**NY Rangers**	**NHL**	**34**	**0**	**6**	**6**	**8**	**0**	**0**	**0**	**33**	**0.0**	**7**	**0**	**0.0**	**15:50**	**10**	**0**	**0**	**0**	**4**	**0**	**0**	**0**	**19:52**
	Hartford	AHL	45	2	22	24	16	....	....	....	....	....	....	....	....	....	....	....	....	....	....	....	....	....	....
2007-08	**NY Rangers**	**NHL**	**82**	**10**	**18**	**28**	**14**	**5**	**0**	**1**	**147**	**6.8**	**0**	**1**	**0.0**	**21:12**	**10**	**0**	**3**	**3**	**6**	**0**	**0**	**0**	**20:42**
2008-09	**NY Rangers**	**NHL**	**82**	**4**	**18**	**22**	**53**	**2**	**0**	**1**	**122**	**3.3**	**–14**	**0**	**0.0**	**21:32**	**7**	**0**	**0**	**0**	**6**	**0**	**0**	**0**	**21:04**

			Regular Season														Playoffs								
Season	Club	League	GP	G	A	Pts	PIM	PP	SH	GW	S	%	+/-	TF	F%	Min	GP	G	A	Pts	PIM	PP	SH	GW	Min
2009-10	**NY Rangers**	**NHL**	**82**	**6**	**18**	**24**	**53**	**1**	**1**	**1**	**108**	**5.6**	**–2**	**0**	**0.0**	**21:29**	....	....	....	....	....	....	....	....	....
2010-11	**NY Rangers**	**NHL**	**80**	**4**	**27**	**31**	**37**	**2**	**0**	**1**	**110**	**3.6**	**7**	**0**	**0.0**	**24:35**	**5**	**0**	**0**	**0**	**0**	**0**	**0**	**0**	**27:01**
	NHL Totals		**360**	**24**	**87**	**111**	**165**	**10**	**1**	**4**	**520**	**4.6**		**1**	**0.0**	**21:35**	**32**	**0**	**3**	**3**	**16**	**0**	**0**	**0**	**21:30**

AHL All-Rookie Team (2006)
Signed as a free agent by **NY Rangers**, July 1, 2006.

GIROUX, Alexandre

(ZHIH-roo, al-ehx-AHN-druh) **CBJ**

Center/Left wing. Shoots left. 6'3", 203 lbs. Born, Quebec City, Que., June 16, 1981. Ottawa's 9th choice, 213th overall, in 1999 Entry Draft.

Season	Club	League	GP	G	A	Pts	PIM	PP	SH	GW	S	%	+/-	TF	F%	Min	GP	G	A	Pts	PIM	PP	SH	GW	Min
1997-98	Ste-Foy	QAAA	42	28	30	58	96	....	....	....	....	....	....	....	....	....	....	....	....	....	....	....	....	....	....
1998-99	Hull Olympiques	QMJHL	67	15	22	37	124	....	....	....	....	....	....	....	....	....	22	2	2	4	8	....	....	....	....
99-2000	Hull Olympiques	QMJHL	72	52	47	99	117	....	....	....	....	....	....	....	....	....	15	12	6	18	30	....	....	....	....
2000-01	Hull Olympiques	QMJHL	38	31	32	63	62	....	....	....	....	....	....	....	....	....	....	....	....	....	....	....	....	....	....
	Rouyn-Noranda	QMJHL	25	13	14	27	56	....	....	....	....	....	....	....	....	....	9	2	6	8	22	....	....	....	....
2001-02	Grand Rapids	AHL	70	11	16	27	74	....	....	....	....	....	....	....	....	....	....	....	....	....	....	....	....	....	....
2002-03	Binghamton	AHL	67	19	16	35	101	....	....	....	....	....	....	....	....	....	10	1	0	1	10	....	....	....	....
2003-04	Binghamton	AHL	59	19	23	42	79	....	....	....	....	....	....	....	....	....	....	....	....	....	....	....	....	....	....
	Hartford	AHL	16	6	3	9	13	....	....	....	....	....	....	....	....	....	16	3	4	7	28	....	....	....	....
2004-05	Hartford	AHL	78	32	22	54	128	....	....	....	....	....	....	....	....	....	6	3	3	6	23	....	....	....	....
2005-06	**NY Rangers**	**NHL**	**1**	**0**	**0**	**0**	**0**	**0**	**0**	**0**	**0**	**0.0**	**–1**	**0**	**0.0**	**2:50**	....	....	....	....	....	....	....	....	....
	Hartford	AHL	73	36	31	67	102	....	....	....	....	....	....	....	....	....	13	7	9	16	17	....	....	....	....
2006-07	**Washington**	**NHL**	**9**	**2**	**2**	**4**	**2**	**0**	**0**	**0**	**11**	**18.2**	**–4**	**2**	**50.0**	**10:11**	....	....	....	....	....	....	....	....	....
	Hershey Bears	AHL	67	42	28	70	82	....	....	....	....	....	....	....	....	....	19	4	7	11	27	....	....	....	....
2007-08	Chicago Wolves	AHL	44	19	22	41	47	....	....	....	....	....	....	....	....	....	....	....	....	....	....	....	....	....	....
	Hershey Bears	AHL	24	14	13	27	30	....	....	....	....	....	....	....	....	....	5	3	1	4	2	....	....	....	....
2008-09	**Washington**	**NHL**	**12**	**1**	**1**	**2**	**10**	**0**	**0**	**1**	**20**	**5.0**	**4**	**1**	**0.0**	**10:34**	....	....	....	....	....	....	....	....	....
	Hershey Bears	AHL	69	*60	37	*97	84	....	....	....	....	....	....	....	....	....	22	*15	13	*28	22	....	....	....	....
2009-10	**Washington**	**NHL**	**9**	**1**	**2**	**3**	**4**	**0**	**0**	**0**	**17**	**5.9**	**3**	**0**	**0.0**	**10:22**	....	....	....	....	....	....	....	....	....
	Hershey Bears	AHL	69	*50	53	103	34	....	....	....	....	....	....	....	....	....	21	*14	13	*27	22	....	....	....	....
2010-11	**Edmonton**	**NHL**	**8**	**1**	**1**	**2**	**2**	**0**	**0**	**0**	**13**	**7.7**	**–2**	**2**	**0.0**	**14:46**	....	....	....	....	....	....	....	....	....
	Oklahoma City	AHL	70	32	46	78	63	....	....	....	....	....	....	....	....	....	6	2	1	3	2	....	....	....	....
	NHL Totals		**39**	**5**	**6**	**11**	**18**	**0**	**0**	**1**	**61**	**8.2**		**5**	**20.0**	**11:06**	....	....	....	....	....	....	....	....	....

AHL First All-Star Team (2009, 2010, 2011) • Willie Marshall Award (AHL – Top Goal-scorer) (2009, 2010) • John B. Sollenberger Trophy (AHL – Leading Scorer) (2009) • Les Cunningham Award (AHL – MVP) (2009)

Traded to **NY Rangers** by **Ottawa** with Karel Rachunek for Greg De Vries, March 9, 2004. Signed as a free agent by **Washington**, July 14, 2006. Signed as a free agent by **Atlanta**, July 13, 2007. Traded to **Washington** by **Atlanta** for Joe Motzko, February 26, 2008. Signed as a free agent by **Edmonton**, July 3, 2010. Signed as a free agent by **Columbus**, July 4, 2011.

GIROUX, Claude

(zhih-ROO, KLOHD) **PHI**

Right wing. Shoots right. 5'11", 172 lbs. Born, Hearst, Ont., January 12, 1988. Philadelphia's 1st choice, 22nd overall, in 2006 Entry Draft.

Season	Club	League	GP	G	A	Pts	PIM	PP	SH	GW	S	%	+/-	TF	F%	Min	GP	G	A	Pts	PIM	PP	SH	GW	Min
2004-05	Cumberland	CJHL	48	13	27	40	30	....	....	....	....	....	....	....	....	....	....	....	....	....	....	....	....	....	....
2005-06	Gatineau	QMJHL	69	39	64	103	64	....	....	....	....	....	....	....	....	....	17	5	15	20	24	....	....	....	....
2006-07	Gatineau	QMJHL	63	48	64	112	49	....	....	....	....	....	....	....	....	....	5	2	5	7	2	....	....	....	....
	Philadelphia	AHL	5	1	1	2	6	....	....	....	....	....	....	....	....	....	....	....	....	....	....	....	....	....	....
2007-08	**Philadelphia**	**NHL**	**2**	**0**	**0**	**0**	**0**	**0**	**0**	**0**	**2**	**0.0**	**–2**	**0**	**0.0**	**9:35**	....	....	....	....	....	....	....	....	....
	Gatineau	QMJHL	55	38	68	106	37	....	....	....	....	....	....	....	....	....	19	17	*34	*51	6	....	....	....	....
2008-09	**Philadelphia**	**NHL**	**42**	**9**	**18**	**27**	**14**	**2**	**0**	**0**	**67**	**13.4**	**10**	**309**	**47.3**	**15:10**	**6**	**2**	**3**	**5**	**6**	**0**	**0**	**0**	**15:57**
	Philadelphia	AHL	33	17	17	34	22	....	....	....	....	....	....	....	....	....	....	....	....	....	....	....	....	....	....
2009-10	**Philadelphia**	**NHL**	**82**	**16**	**31**	**47**	**23**	**8**	**0**	**2**	**145**	**11.0**	**–9**	**600**	**49.5**	**16:37**	**23**	**10**	**11**	**21**	**4**	**3**	**0**	**2**	**18:45**
2010-11	**Philadelphia**	**NHL**	**82**	**25**	**51**	**76**	**47**	**8**	**3**	**5**	**169**	**14.8**	**20**	**1095**	**50.1**	**19:24**	**11**	**1**	**11**	**12**	**8**	**0**	**0**	**0**	**21:57**
	NHL Totals		**208**	**50**	**100**	**150**	**84**	**18**	**3**	**7**	**383**	**13.1**		**2004**	**49.5**	**17:21**	**40**	**13**	**25**	**38**	**18**	**3**	**0**	**2**	**19:13**

QMJHL All-Rookie Team (2006) • QMJHL First All-Star Team (2008) • Canadian Major Junior First All-Star Team (2008)
Played in NHL All-Star Game (2011)

GLASS, Tanner

(GLAS, TA-nuhr) **WPG**

Forward. Shoots left. 6'1", 210 lbs. Born, Regina, Sask., November 29, 1983. Florida's 13th choice, 265th overall, in 2003 Entry Draft.

Season	Club	League	GP	G	A	Pts	PIM	PP	SH	GW	S	%	+/-	TF	F%	Min	GP	G	A	Pts	PIM	PP	SH	GW	Min
2000-01	Yorkton Mallers	SMHL	39	31	29	60	120	....	....	....	....	....	....	....	....	....	4	3	1	4	10	....	....	....	....
2001-02	Penticton	BCHL	57	11	28	39	171	....	....	....	....	....	....	....	....	....	....	....	....	....	....	....	....	....	....
2002-03	Penticton	BCHL	32	15	25	40	108	....	....	....	....	....	....	....	....	....	....	....	....	....	....	....	....	....	....
	Nanaimo Clippers	BCHL	18	8	14	22	46	....	....	....	....	....	....	....	....	....	....	....	....	....	....	....	....	....	....
2003-04	Dartmouth	ECAC	26	4	7	11	18	....	....	....	....	....	....	....	....	....	....	....	....	....	....	....	....	....	....
2004-05	Dartmouth	ECAC	33	7	8	15	32	....	....	....	....	....	....	....	....	....	....	....	....	....	....	....	....	....	....
2005-06	Dartmouth	ECAC	33	12	16	28	56	....	....	....	....	....	....	....	....	....	....	....	....	....	....	....	....	....	....
2006-07	Dartmouth	ECAC	32	8	20	28	92	....	....	....	....	....	....	....	....	....	....	....	....	....	....	....	....	....	....
	Rochester	AHL	4	0	1	1	5	....	....	....	....	....	....	....	....	....	....	....	....	....	....	....	....	....	....
2007-08	**Florida**	**NHL**	**41**	**1**	**1**	**2**	**39**	**0**	**0**	**0**	**11**	**9.1**	**–5**	**2**	**0.0**	**4:25**	....	....	....	....	....	....	....	....	....
	Rochester	AHL	43	6	5	11	84	....	....	....	....	....	....	....	....	....	....	....	....	....	....	....	....	....	....
2008-09	**Florida**	**NHL**	**3**	**0**	**0**	**0**	**7**	**0**	**0**	**0**	**1**	**0.0**	**0**	**1**	**100.0**	**6:45**	....	....	....	....	....	....	....	....	....
	Rochester	AHL	44	4	9	13	100	....	....	....	....	....	....	....	....	....	....	....	....	....	....	....	....	....	....
2009-10	**Vancouver**	**NHL**	**67**	**4**	**7**	**11**	**115**	**0**	**0**	**0**	**52**	**7.7**	**5**	**18**	**16.7**	**10:28**	**4**	**0**	**0**	**0**	**0**	**0**	**0**	**0**	**3:08**
2010-11	**Vancouver**	**NHL**	**73**	**3**	**7**	**10**	**72**	**0**	**0**	**1**	**45**	**6.7**	**–5**	**62**	**40.3**	**8:56**	**20**	**0**	**0**	**0**	**18**	**0**	**0**	**0**	**7:28**
	NHL Totals		**184**	**8**	**15**	**23**	**233**	**0**	**0**	**1**	**109**	**7.3**		**83**	**34.9**	**8:27**	**24**	**0**	**0**	**0**	**18**	**0**	**0**	**0**	**6:45**

Signed as a free aget by **Vancouver**, July 22, 2009. Signed as a free agent by **Winnipeg**, July 2, 2011.

GLEASON, Tim

(GLEE-suhn, TIHM) **CAR**

Defense. Shoots left. 6', 217 lbs. Born, Clawson, MI, January 29, 1983. Ottawa's 2nd choice, 23rd overall, in 2001 Entry Draft.

Season	Club	League	GP	G	A	Pts	PIM	PP	SH	GW	S	%	+/-	TF	F%	Min	GP	G	A	Pts	PIM	PP	SH	GW	Min
1998-99	Leamington Flyers	ON-Jr.B	52	5	26	31	76	....	....	....	....	....	....	....	....	....	....	....	....	....	....	....	....	....	....
99-2000	Windsor Spitfires	OHL	55	5	13	18	101	....	....	....	....	....	....	....	....	....	12	2	4	6	14	....	....	....	....
2000-01	Windsor Spitfires	OHL	47	8	28	36	124	....	....	....	....	....	....	....	....	....	9	1	2	3	23	....	....	....	....
2001-02	Windsor Spitfires	OHL	67	17	42	59	109	....	....	....	....	....	....	....	....	....	16	7	13	20	40	....	....	....	....
2002-03	Windsor Spitfires	OHL	45	7	31	38	75	....	....	....	....	....	....	....	....	....	7	5	2	7	17	....	....	....	....
2003-04	**Los Angeles**	**NHL**	**47**	**0**	**7**	**7**	**21**	**0**	**0**	**0**	**45**	**0.0**	**1**	**0**	**0.0**	**14:59**	....	....	....	....	....	....	....	....	....
	Manchester	AHL	22	0	8	8	19	....	....	....	....	....	....	....	....	....	6	0	1	1	4	....	....	....	....
2004-05	Manchester	AHL	67	10	14	24	112	....	....	....	....	....	....	....	....	....	5	0	0	0	4	....	....	....	....
2005-06	**Los Angeles**	**NHL**	**78**	**2**	**19**	**21**	**77**	**0**	**0**	**0**	**72**	**2.8**	**0**	**0**	**0.0**	**17:41**	....	....	....	....	....	....	....	....	....
2006-07	**Carolina**	**NHL**	**57**	**2**	**4**	**6**	**57**	**1**	**0**	**0**	**72**	**2.8**	**–10**	**0**	**0.0**	**18:53**	....	....	....	....	....	....	....	....	....
2007-08	**Carolina**	**NHL**	**80**	**3**	**16**	**19**	**84**	**0**	**0**	**0**	**98**	**3.1**	**5**	**0**	**0.0**	**18:38**	....	....	....	....	....	....	....	....	....
2008-09	**Carolina**	**NHL**	**70**	**0**	**12**	**12**	**68**	**0**	**0**	**0**	**61**	**0.0**	**3**	**0**	**0.0**	**20:40**	**18**	**1**	**4**	**5**	**32**	**0**	**0**	**1**	**20:29**
2009-10	**Carolina**	**NHL**	**61**	**5**	**14**	**19**	**78**	**1**	**1**	**0**	**76**	**6.6**	**0**	**0**	**0.0**	**21:12**	....	....	....	....	....	....	....	....	....
	United States	Olympics	6	0	0	0	0	....	....	....	....	....	....	....	....	....	....	....	....	....	....	....	....	....	....
2010-11	**Carolina**	**NHL**	**82**	**2**	**14**	**16**	**85**	**0**	**0**	**0**	**84**	**2.4**	**–11**	**0**	**0.0**	**20:58**	....	....	....	....	....	....	....	....	....
	NHL Totals		**475**	**14**	**86**	**100**	**470**	**2**	**1**	**0**	**508**	**2.8**		**0**	**0.0**	**19:11**	**18**	**1**	**4**	**5**	**32**	**0**	**0**	**1**	**20:29**

• Rights traded to **Los Angeles** by **Ottawa** for Bryan Smolinski, March 11, 2003. Traded to **Carolina** by **Los Angeles** with Eric Belanger for Oleg Tverdovsky and Jack Johnson, September 29, 2006.

GLENCROSS, Curtis

(GLEHN-kraws, KUHR-tihs) **CGY**

Center. Shoots left. 6'1", 200 lbs. Born, Kindersley, Sask., December 28, 1982.

Season	Club	League	GP	G	A	Pts	PIM	PP	SH	GW	S	%	+/-	TF	F%	Min	GP	G	A	Pts	PIM	PP	SH	GW	Min
2001-02	Brooks Bandits	AJHL	....	42	26	68	....	....	....	....	....	....	....	....	....	....	....	....	....	....	....	....	....	....	....
2002-03	Alaska Anchorage	WCHA	35	11	12	23	79	....	....	....	....	....	....	....	....	....	....	....	....	....	....	....	....	....	....
2003-04	Alaska Anchorage	WCHA	37	21	13	34	79	....	....	....	....	....	....	....	....	....	....	....	....	....	....	....	....	....	....
	Cincinnati	AHL	7	2	1	3	6	....	....	....	....	....	....	....	....	....	9	1	6	7	10	....	....	....	....
2004-05	Cincinnati	AHL	51	6	3	9	63	....	....	....	....	....	....	....	....	....	12	2	0	2	10	....	....	....	....
2005-06	Portland Pirates	AHL	41	15	10	25	85	....	....	....	....	....	....	....	....	....	19	4	6	10	37	....	....	....	....
2006-07	**Anaheim**	**NHL**	**2**	**1**	**0**	**1**	**2**	**0**	**0**	**0**	**5**	**20.0**	**–1**	**0**	**0.0**	**10:43**	....	....	....	....	....	....	....	....	....
	Portland Pirates	AHL	31	6	10	16	74	....	....	....	....	....	....	....	....	....	....	....	....	....	....	....	....	....	....
	Columbus	**NHL**	**7**	**0**	**0**	**0**	**0**	**0**	**0**	**0**	**3**	**0.0**	**–4**	**2**	**0.0**	**8:43**	....	....	....	....	....	....	....	....	....
	Syracuse Crunch	AHL	29	19	16	35	53	....	....	....	....	....	....	....	....	....	....	....	....	....	....	....	....	....	....

			Regular Season														Playoffs								
Season	Club	League	GP	G	A	Pts	PIM	PP	SH	GW	S	%	+/-	TF	F%	Min	GP	G	A	Pts	PIM	PP	SH	GW	Min
2007-08	Columbus	NHL	36	6	6	12	25	1	0	1	63	9.5	3	14	57.1	12:07	....	....	....	....	....	....	....	....	....
	Edmonton	NHL	26	9	4	13	28	0	0	0	41	22.0	5	11	45.5	10:19	....	....	....	....	....	....	....	....	....
2008-09	Calgary	NHL	74	13	27	40	42	1	1	3	152	8.6	14	62	48.4	14:41	6	0	3	3	12	0	0	0	15:00
2009-10	Calgary	NHL	67	15	18	33	58	2	3	2	117	12.8	11	24	37.5	15:43	....	....	....	....	....	....	....	....	....
2010-11	Calgary	NHL	79	24	19	43	59	3	2	4	149	16.1	6	141	40.4	16:15	....	....	....	....	....	....	....	....	....
	NHL Totals		**291**	**68**	**74**	**142**	**214**	**7**	**6**	**10**	**530**	**12.8**		**254**	**42.9**	**14:28**	**6**	**0**	**3**	**3**	**12**	**0**	**0**	**0**	**15:00**

Signed as a free agent by **Anaheim**, March 25, 2004. Traded to **Columbus** by **Anaheim** with Zenon Konopka and Anaheim's 7th round choice (Trent Vogelhuber) in 2007 Entry Draft for Mark Hartigan, Joe Motzko and Columbus' 4th round choice (Sebastian Stefaniszin) in 2007 Entry Draft, January 26, 2007. Traded to **Edmonton** by **Columbus** for Dick Tarnstrom, February 1, 2008. Signed as a free agent by **Calgary**, July 2, 2008.

GLUMAC, Mike

(GLOO-kmak, MIGHK)

Right wing. Shoots right. 6'2", 209 lbs. Born, Niagara Falls, Ont., April 5, 1980.

Season	Club	League	GP	G	A	Pts	PIM	PP	SH	GW	S	%	+/-	TF	F%	Min	GP	G	A	Pts	PIM	PP	SH	GW	Min
1996-97	St. Mike's B's	OPJHL	50	13	25	38	33	....	....	....	....	....	....	....	....	....	6	1	0	1	2	....	....	....	....
1997-98	Newmarket	OPJHL	36	16	16	32	57	....	....	....	....	....	....	....	....	....	....	....	....	....	....	....	....	....	....
1998-99	Miami U.	CCHA	35	2	0	2	44	....	....	....	....	....	....	....	....	....	....	....	....	....	....	....	....	....	....
99-2000	Miami U.	CCHA	36	8	5	13	52	....	....	....	....	....	....	....	....	....	....	....	....	....	....	....	....	....	....
2000-01	Miami U.	CCHA	37	9	10	19	46	....	....	....	....	....	....	....	....	....	....	....	....	....	....	....	....	....	....
2001-02	Miami U.	CCHA	36	15	8	23	28	....	....	....	....	....	....	....	....	....	....	....	....	....	....	....	....	....	....
2002-03	Pee Dee Pride	ECHL	69	37	32	69	49	....	....	....	....	....	....	....	....	....	....	....	....	....	....	....	....	....	....
	Cleveland Barons	AHL	2	0	0	0	0	....	....	....	....	....	....	....	....	....	....	....	....	....	....	....	....	....	....
2003-04	Worcester IceCats	AHL	80	28	24	52	74	....	....	....	....	....	....	....	....	....	10	3	3	6	11	....	....	....	....
2004-05	Worcester IceCats	AHL	45	12	17	29	27	....	....	....	....	....	....	....	....	....	....	....	....	....	....	....	....	....	....
2005-06	**St. Louis**	**NHL**	**33**	**7**	**5**	**12**	**33**	**5**	**0**	**0**	**55**	**12.7**	**–8**	**5**	**40.0**	**12:25**	....	....	....	....	....	....	....	....	....
	Peoria Rivermen	AHL	49	25	32	57	64	....	....	....	....	....	....	....	....	....	4	1	1	2	5	....	....	....	....
2006-07	**St. Louis**	**NHL**	**3**	**0**	**1**	**1**	**0**	**0**	**0**	**0**	**4**	**0.0**	**1**	**0**	**0.0**	**8:24**	....	....	....	....	....	....	....	....	....
	Peoria Rivermen	AHL	72	27	30	57	115	....	....	....	....	....	....	....	....	....	....	....	....	....	....	....	....	....	....
2007-08	**St. Louis**	**NHL**	**4**	**0**	**0**	**0**	**5**	**0**	**0**	**0**	**3**	**0.0**	**–1**	**3**	**33.3**	**10:08**	....	....	....	....	....	....	....	....	....
	Peoria Rivermen	AHL	75	21	28	49	99	....	....	....	....	....	....	....	....	....	....	....	....	....	....	....	....	....	....
2008-09	Hamilton	AHL	66	33	19	52	60	....	....	....	....	....	....	....	....	....	6	1	3	4	4	....	....	....	....
2009-10	Hamilton	AHL	75	20	20	40	70	....	....	....	....	....	....	....	....	....	19	11	3	14	11	....	....	....	....
2010-11	Adler Mannheim	Germany	40	17	8	25	44	....	....	....	....	....	....	....	....	....	6	3	1	4	2	....	....	....	....
	NHL Totals		**40**	**7**	**6**	**13**	**38**	**5**	**0**	**0**	**62**	**11.3**		**8**	**37.5**	**11:53**	....	....	....	....	....	....	....	....	....

ECHL All-Rookie Team (2003)

Signed as a free agent by **Pee Dee** (ECHL), August 28, 2002. Signed as a free agent by **Worcester** (AHL), October 6, 2003. Signed as a free agent by **St. Louis**, June 29, 2004. Signed as a free agent by **Montreal**, July 16, 2008. Signed as a free agent by **Mannheim** (Germany), September 29, 2010.

GOC, Marcel

(GAWCH, MAHR-sehl) **FLA**

Center. Shoots left. 6'1", 202 lbs. Born, Calw, West Germany, August 24, 1983. San Jose's 1st choice, 20th overall, in 2001 Entry Draft.

Season	Club	League	GP	G	A	Pts	PIM	PP	SH	GW	S	%	+/-	TF	F%	Min	GP	G	A	Pts	PIM	PP	SH	GW	Min
1998-99	Schwenningen Jr.	Ger-Jr.	12	23	10	33	12	....	....	....	....	....	....	....	....	....	....	....	....	....	....	....	....	....	....
99-2000	Schwenningen	Germany	51	0	3	3	4	....	....	....	....	....	....	....	....	....	11	1	1	2	2	....	....	....	....
2000-01	Schwenningen	Germany	58	13	28	41	12	....	....	....	....	....	....	....	....	....	....	....	....	....	....	....	....	....	....
2001-02	Schwenningen	Germany	45	8	9	17	24	....	....	....	....	....	....	....	....	....	....	....	....	....	....	....	....	....	....
	Adler Mannheim	Germany	8	0	2	2	0	....	....	....	....	....	....	....	....	....	....	....	....	....	....	....	....	....	....
2002-03	Adler Mannheim	Germany	36	6	14	20	16	....	....	....	....	....	....	....	....	....	8	1	2	3	0	....	....	....	....
2003-04	Cleveland Barons	AHL	78	16	21	37	24	....	....	....	....	....	....	....	....	....	....	....	....	....	....	....	....	....	....
	San Jose	**NHL**	....	....	....	....	....	....	....	....	....	....	....	....	....	....	**5**	**1**	**1**	**2**	**0**	**0**	**0**	**1**	**7:08**
2004-05	Cleveland Barons	AHL	76	16	34	50	28	....	....	....	....	....	....	....	....	....	....	....	....	....	....	....	....	....	....
2005-06	**San Jose**	**NHL**	**81**	**8**	**14**	**22**	**22**	**2**	**0**	**2**	**96**	**8.3**	**–7**	**808**	**47.9**	**11:42**	**11**	**0**	**3**	**3**	**0**	**0**	**0**	**0**	**12:38**
	Germany	Olympics	5	1	0	1	0	....	....	....	....	....	....	....	....	....	....	....	....	....	....	....	....	....	....
2006-07	**San Jose**	**NHL**	**78**	**5**	**8**	**13**	**24**	**0**	**1**	**0**	**96**	**5.2**	**–2**	**659**	**55.2**	**12:01**	**11**	**2**	**1**	**3**	**4**	**0**	**0**	**0**	**14:49**
2007-08	**San Jose**	**NHL**	**51**	**5**	**3**	**8**	**12**	**0**	**0**	**0**	**87**	**5.7**	**–15**	**208**	**51.4**	**10:41**	**4**	**0**	**0**	**0**	**2**	**0**	**0**	**0**	**8:03**
2008-09	**San Jose**	**NHL**	**55**	**2**	**9**	**11**	**18**	**0**	**0**	**1**	**104**	**1.9**	**–6**	**570**	**58.3**	**13:55**	**6**	**0**	**0**	**0**	**2**	**0**	**0**	**0**	**10:33**
2009-10	**Nashville**	**NHL**	**73**	**12**	**18**	**30**	**14**	**0**	**0**	**1**	**118**	**10.2**	**10**	**912**	**52.1**	**14:41**	**6**	**0**	**1**	**1**	**2**	**0**	**0**	**0**	**16:07**
	Germany	Olympics	4	2	1	3	0	....	....	....	....	....	....	....	....	....	....	....	....	....	....	....	....	....	....
2010-11	**Nashville**	**NHL**	**51**	**9**	**15**	**24**	**6**	**0**	**1**	**2**	**111**	**8.1**	**10**	**693**	**49.9**	**16:02**	....	....	....	....	....	....	....	....	....
	NHL Totals		**389**	**41**	**67**	**108**	**96**	**2**	**2**	**6**	**612**	**6.7**		**3850**	**52.2**	**13:04**	**43**	**3**	**6**	**9**	**10**	**0**	**0**	**1**	**12:19**

Signed as a free agent by **Nashville**, August 21, 2009. Signed as a free agent by **Florida**, July 1, 2011.

GODARD, Eric

(GAW-duhrd, AIR-ihk) **DAL**

Right wing. Shoots right. 6'4", 214 lbs. Born, Vernon, B.C., March 7, 1980.

Season	Club	League	GP	G	A	Pts	PIM	PP	SH	GW	S	%	+/-	TF	F%	Min	GP	G	A	Pts	PIM	PP	SH	GW	Min
1997-98	Lethbridge	WHL	7	0	0	0	26	....	....	....	....	....	....	....	....	....	2	0	0	0	0	....	....	....	....
1998-99	Lethbridge	WHL	66	2	5	7	211	....	....	....	....	....	....	....	....	....	4	0	0	0	14	....	....	....	....
99-2000	Lethbridge	WHL	60	3	5	8	*310	....	....	....	....	....	....	....	....	....	....	....	....	....	....	....	....	....	....
	Louisville Panthers	AHL	4	0	1	1	16	....	....	....	....	....	....	....	....	....	....	....	....	....	....	....	....	....	....
2000-01	Louisville Panthers	AHL	45	0	0	0	132	....	....	....	....	....	....	....	....	....	....	....	....	....	....	....	....	....	....
2001-02	Bridgeport	AHL	67	1	4	5	198	....	....	....	....	....	....	....	....	....	20	0	4	4	30	....	....	....	....
2002-03	**NY Islanders**	**NHL**	**19**	**0**	**0**	**0**	**48**	**0**	**0**	**0**	**6**	**0.0**	**–3**	**0**	**0.0**	**4:32**	**2**	**0**	**1**	**1**	**4**	**0**	**0**	**0**	**1:09**
	Bridgeport	AHL	46	2	2	4	199	....	....	....	....	....	....	....	....	....	6	0	0	0	16	....	....	....	....
2003-04	**NY Islanders**	**NHL**	**31**	**0**	**1**	**1**	**97**	**0**	**0**	**0**	**5**	**0.0**	**–2**	**1**	**0.0**	**3:46**	....	....	....	....	....	....	....	....	....
	Bridgeport	AHL	7	0	0	0	13	....	....	....	....	....	....	....	....	....	....	....	....	....	....	....	....	....	....
2004-05	Bridgeport	AHL	75	7	11	18	295	....	....	....	....	....	....	....	....	....	....	....	....	....	....	....	....	....	....
2005-06	**NY Islanders**	**NHL**	**57**	**2**	**2**	**4**	**115**	**0**	**0**	**0**	**17**	**11.8**	**–2**	**1**	**0.0**	**3:34**	....	....	....	....	....	....	....	....	....
2006-07	**Calgary**	**NHL**	**19**	**0**	**1**	**1**	**50**	**0**	**0**	**0**	**3**	**0.0**	**0**	**0**	**0.0**	**3:47**	....	....	....	....	....	....	....	....	....
	Omaha	AHL	36	5	4	9	94	....	....	....	....	....	....	....	....	....	....	....	....	....	....	....	....	....	....
2007-08	**Calgary**	**NHL**	**74**	**1**	**1**	**2**	**171**	**0**	**0**	**1**	**14**	**7.1**	**–8**	**1**	**0.0**	**4:43**	**5**	**0**	**0**	**0**	**2**	**0**	**0**	**0**	**3:31**
2008-09♦	**Pittsburgh**	**NHL**	**71**	**2**	**2**	**4**	**171**	**0**	**0**	**0**	**20**	**10.0**	**–3**	**1**	**100.0**	**4:04**	....	....	....	....	....	....	....	....	....
2009-10	**Pittsburgh**	**NHL**	**45**	**1**	**2**	**3**	**76**	**0**	**0**	**0**	**17**	**5.9**	**2**	**1**	**100.0**	**4:11**	....	....	....	....	....	....	....	....	....
2010-11	**Pittsburgh**	**NHL**	**19**	**0**	**3**	**3**	**105**	**0**	**0**	**0**	**1**	**0.0**	**4**	**0**	**0.0**	**5:10**	....	....	....	....	....	....	....	....	....
	NHL Totals		**335**	**6**	**12**	**18**	**833**	**0**	**0**	**1**	**83**	**7.2**		**5**	**40.0**	**4:11**	**7**	**0**	**1**	**1**	**6**	**0**	**0**	**0**	**2:50**

Signed as a free agent by **Florida**, September 24, 1999. Traded to **NY Islanders** by **Florida** for Florida's 3rd round choice (previously acquired, Florida selected Gregory Campbell) in 2002 Entry Draft, June 22, 2002. • Missed majority of 2003-04 as a healthy reserve. Signed as a free agent by **Calgary**, August 14, 2006. Signed as a free agent by **Pittsburgh**, July 1, 2008. • Missed majority of 2010-11 due to facial injury at Ottawa, December 26, 2010, as a healthy reserve and serving a ten-game suspension for leaving the bench in game at NY Islanders, February 11, 2011. Signed as a free agent by **Dallas**. July 12, 2011.

GOERTZEN, Steven

(GUHRT-sehn, STEE-vehn)

Right wing. Shoots right. 6'2", 216 lbs. Born, Stony Plain, Alta., May 26, 1984. Columbus' 11th choice, 225th overall, in 2002 Entry Draft.

Season	Club	League	GP	G	A	Pts	PIM	PP	SH	GW	S	%	+/-	TF	F%	Min	GP	G	A	Pts	PIM	PP	SH	GW	Min
99-2000	Spruce Grove	AMBHL	36	16	17	33	30	....	....	....	....	....	....	....	....	....	....	....	....	....	....	....	....	....	....
2000-01	St. Albert Raiders	AMHL	34	11	19	30	70	....	....	....	....	....	....	....	....	....	....	....	....	....	....	....	....	....	....
	St. Albert Saints	AJHL	1	0	0	0	0	....	....	....	....	....	....	....	....	....	....	....	....	....	....	....	....	....	....
2001-02	Seattle	WHL	66	6	9	15	45	....	....	....	....	....	....	....	....	....	11	2	0	2	4	....	....	....	....
2002-03	Seattle	WHL	71	12	19	31	95	....	....	....	....	....	....	....	....	....	14	4	3	7	9	....	....	....	....
2003-04	Seattle	WHL	69	15	18	33	115	....	....	....	....	....	....	....	....	....	....	....	....	....	....	....	....	....	....
	Syracuse Crunch	AHL	8	0	3	3	4	....	....	....	....	....	....	....	....	....	1	0	0	0	0	....	....	....	....
2004-05	Syracuse Crunch	AHL	57	2	7	9	100	....	....	....	....	....	....	....	....	....	....	....	....	....	....	....	....	....	....
	Dayton Bombers	ECHL	11	0	3	3	2	....	....	....	....	....	....	....	....	....	....	....	....	....	....	....	....	....	....
2005-06	**Columbus**	**NHL**	**39**	**0**	**0**	**0**	**44**	**0**	**0**	**0**	**23**	**0.0**	**–17**	**11**	**54.6**	**8:32**	....	....	....	....	....	....	....	....	....
	Syracuse Crunch	AHL	40	7	8	15	55	....	....	....	....	....	....	....	....	....	6	0	1	1	34	....	....	....	....
2006-07	**Columbus**	**NHL**	**7**	**0**	**0**	**0**	**10**	**0**	**0**	**0**	**1**	**0.0**	**0**	**0**	**0.0**	**5:21**	....	....	....	....	....	....	....	....	....
	Syracuse Crunch	AHL	60	9	7	16	120	....	....	....	....	....	....	....	....	....	....	....	....	....	....	....	....	....	....
2007-08	Syracuse Crunch	AHL	59	8	5	13	72	....	....	....	....	....	....	....	....	....	....	....	....	....	....	....	....	....	....
	San Antonio	AHL	22	1	3	4	34	....	....	....	....	....	....	....	....	....	7	1	0	1	5	....	....	....	....
2008-09	**Phoenix**	**NHL**	**16**	**2**	**2**	**4**	**24**	**0**	**0**	**0**	**18**	**11.1**	**–2**	**2**	**50.0**	**9:42**	....	....	....	....	....	....	....	....	....
	San Antonio	AHL	57	6	8	14	90	....	....	....	....	....	....	....	....	....	....	....	....	....	....	....	....	....	....

			Regular Season														Playoffs								
Season	Club	League	GP	G	A	Pts	PIM	PP	SH	GW	S	%	+/-	TF	F%	Min	GP	G	A	Pts	PIM	PP	SH	GW	Min
2009-10	**Carolina**	**NHL**	**6**	**0**	**0**	**0**	**5**	**0**	**0**	**0**	**1**	**0.0**	**–2**	**0**	**0.0**	**7:44**									
	Albany River Rats	AHL	71	8	15	23	85										8	0	1	1	7				
2010-11	Springfield	AHL	65	7	9	16	48																		
	NHL Totals		**68**	**2**	**2**	**4**	**83**	**0**	**0**	**0**	**43**	**4.7**		**13**	**53.8**	**8:24**									

Traded to **Phoenix** by **Columbus** for Nat DiCasmirro, February 28, 2008. Signed as a free agent by **Carolina**, July 8, 2009. Signed to a PTO (professional tryout) contract by **Springfield** (AHL), October 6, 2010.

GOLIGOSKI, Alex

(goh-lih-GAW-skee, AL-ehx) **DAL**

Defense. Shoots left. 5'11", 180 lbs. Born, Grand Rapids, MN, July 30, 1985. Pittsburgh's 3rd choice, 61st overall, in 2004 Entry Draft.

Season	Club	League	GP	G	A	Pts	PIM	PP	SH	GW	S	%	+/-	TF	F%	Min	GP	G	A	Pts	PIM	PP	SH	GW	Min
2002-03	Grand Rapids	High-MN	28	14	20	34	22																		
2003-04	Grand Rapids	High-MN	26	25	31	56	16																		
	Sioux Falls	USHL	10	0	2	2	6																		
2004-05	U. of Minnesota	WCHA	33	5	15	20	44																		
2005-06	U. of Minnesota	WCHA	41	11	28	39	63																		
2006-07	U. of Minnesota	WCHA	44	9	30	39	51																		
2007-08	**Pittsburgh**	**NHL**	**3**	**0**	**2**	**2**	**2**	**0**	**0**	**0**	**2**	**0.0**	**2**	**0**	**0.0**	**13:56**									
	Wilkes-Barre	AHL	70	10	28	38	53										23	4	24	28	18				
2008-09 ♦	**Pittsburgh**	**NHL**	**45**	**6**	**14**	**20**	**16**	**4**	**0**	**0**	**61**	**9.8**	**5**	**0**	**0.0**	**18:18**	**2**	**0**	**1**	**1**	**0**	**0**	**0**	**0**	**10:22**
	Wilkes-Barre	AHL	26	2	16	18	16										9	1	5	6	10				
2009-10	**Pittsburgh**	**NHL**	**69**	**8**	**29**	**37**	**22**	**2**	**0**	**0**	**98**	**8.2**	**7**	**0**	**0.0**	**21:25**	**13**	**2**	**7**	**9**	**2**	**1**	**0**	**0**	**20:34**
2010-11	**Pittsburgh**	**NHL**	**60**	**9**	**22**	**31**	**28**	**4**	**0**	**4**	**101**	**8.9**	**20**	**0**	**0.0**	**20:46**									
	Dallas	**NHL**	**23**	**5**	**10**	**15**	**12**	**3**	**0**	**0**	**61**	**8.2**	**0**	**0**	**0.0**	**26:04**									
	NHL Totals		**200**	**28**	**77**	**105**	**80**	**13**	**0**	**4**	**323**	**8.7**		**0**	**0.0**	**20:57**	**15**	**2**	**8**	**10**	**2**	**1**	**0**	**0**	**19:13**

WCHA All-Rookie Team (2005) • WCHA Second All-Star Team (2006) • WCHA First All-Star Team (2007) • NCAA West First All-American Team (2007) • AHL All-Rookie Team (2008)

Traded to **Dallas** by **Pittsburgh** for James Neal and Matt Niskanen, February 21, 2011.

GOMEZ, Scott

(GOH-mehz, SKAWT) **MTL**

Center. Shoots left. 5'11", 198 lbs. Born, Anchorage, AK, December 23, 1979. New Jersey's 2nd choice, 27th overall, in 1998 Entry Draft.

Season	Club	League	GP	G	A	Pts	PIM	PP	SH	GW	S	%	+/-	TF	F%	Min	GP	G	A	Pts	PIM	PP	SH	GW	Min
1994-95	East High	High-AK	28	30	48	78																			
1995-96	East High	High-AK	27	*56	49	*101																			
	Anchorage	AAHL	40	*70	*67	*137	44																		
1996-97	South Surrey	BCHL	56	48	76	124	94										21	18	23	41	57				
1997-98	Tri-City	WHL	45	12	37	49	57																		
1998-99	Tri-City	WHL	58	30	*78	108	55										10	6	13	19	31				
99-2000 ♦	**New Jersey**	**NHL**	**82**	**19**	**51**	**70**	**78**	**7**	**0**	**1**	**204**	**9.3**	**14**	**341**	**44.6**	**16:21**	**23**	**4**	**6**	**10**	**4**	**1**	**0**	**2**	**14:08**
2000-01	**New Jersey**	**NHL**	**76**	**14**	**49**	**63**	**46**	**2**	**0**	**4**	**155**	**9.0**	**–1**	**1010**	**44.6**	**15:46**	**25**	**5**	**9**	**14**	**24**	**0**	**0**	**0**	**16:06**
2001-02	**New Jersey**	**NHL**	**76**	**10**	**38**	**48**	**36**	**1**	**0**	**1**	**156**	**6.4**	**–4**	**628**	**48.7**	**16:46**									
2002-03 ♦	**New Jersey**	**NHL**	**80**	**13**	**42**	**55**	**48**	**2**	**0**	**4**	**205**	**6.3**	**17**	**864**	**47.5**	**16:01**	**24**	**3**	**9**	**12**	**2**	**0**	**0**	**0**	**13:45**
2003-04	**New Jersey**	**NHL**	**80**	**14**	***56**	**70**	**70**	**3**	**0**	**1**	**189**	**7.4**	**18**	**1129**	**46.2**	**16:00**	**5**	**0**	**6**	**6**	**0**	**0**	**0**	**0**	**17:14**
2004-05	Alaska Aces	ECHL	61	13	*73	*86	69										4	1	3	4	4				
2005-06	**New Jersey**	**NHL**	**82**	**33**	**51**	**84**	**42**	**9**	**0**	**5**	**244**	**13.5**	**8**	**1434**	**52.6**	**18:47**	**9**	**5**	**4**	**9**	**6**	**4**	**0**	**1**	**18:14**
	United States	Olympics	6	1	4	5	10																		
2006-07	**New Jersey**	**NHL**	**72**	**13**	**47**	**60**	**42**	**4**	**0**	**1**	**248**	**5.2**	**7**	**1204**	**52.2**	**18:56**	**11**	**4**	**10**	**14**	**14**	**0**	**0**	**1**	**20:01**
2007-08	**NY Rangers**	**NHL**	**81**	**16**	**54**	**70**	**36**	**7**	**0**	**3**	**242**	**6.6**	**3**	**1165**	**52.5**	**19:54**	**10**	**4**	**7**	**11**	**8**	**1**	**0**	**0**	**20:53**
2008-09	**NY Rangers**	**NHL**	**77**	**16**	**42**	**58**	**60**	**3**	**1**	**7**	**271**	**5.9**	**–2**	**1312**	**52.4**	**21:04**	**7**	**2**	**3**	**5**	**4**	**1**	**0**	**0**	**19:58**
2009-10	**Montreal**	**NHL**	**78**	**12**	**47**	**59**	**60**	**5**	**0**	**1**	**180**	**6.7**	**1**	**1375**	**50.8**	**19:56**	**19**	**2**	**12**	**14**	**25**	**0**	**0**	**0**	**21:10**
2010-11	**Montreal**	**NHL**	**80**	**7**	**31**	**38**	**48**	**3**	**0**	**2**	**157**	**4.5**	**–15**	**1197**	**48.0**	**18:34**	**7**	**0**	**4**	**4**	**2**	**0**	**0**	**0**	**19:42**
	NHL Totals		**864**	**167**	**508**	**675**	**566**	**46**	**1**	**30**	**2251**	**7.4**		**11659**	**49.7**	**18:00**	**140**	**29**	**70**	**99**	**89**	**7**	**0**	**4**	**17:16**

WHL West First All-Star Team (1999) • NHL All-Rookie Team (2000) • Calder Memorial Trophy (2000) • ECHL First All-Star Team (2005) • ECHL Leading Scorer (2005) • ECHL MVP (2005)

Played in NHL All-Star Game (2000, 2008)

Signed as a free agent by **Alaska** (ECHL), October 25, 2004. Signed as a free agent by **NY Rangers**, July 1, 2007. Traded to **Montreal** by **NY Rangers** with Tom Pyatt and Michael Busto for Chris Higgins, Ryan McDonagh and Pavel Valentenko, June 30, 2009.

GONCHAR, Sergei

(gohn-CHAR, SAIR-gay) **OTT**

Defense. Shoots left. 6'2", 211 lbs. Born, Chelyabinsk, USSR, April 13, 1974. Washington's 1st choice, 14th overall, in 1992 Entry Draft.

Season	Club	League	GP	G	A	Pts	PIM	PP	SH	GW	S	%	+/-	TF	F%	Min	GP	G	A	Pts	PIM	PP	SH	GW	Min
1990-91	Mechel	USSR-2	2	0	0	0	0																		
	Chelyabinsk	USSR-Q	11	0	0	0	4																		
1991-92	Chelyabinsk	CIS	31	1	0	1	6																		
1992-93	Dynamo Moscow	CIS	31	1	3	4	70										10	0	0	0	12				
1993-94	Dynamo Moscow	CIS	44	4	5	9	36																		
	Portland Pirates	AHL															2	0	0	0	0				
1994-95	Portland Pirates	AHL	61	10	32	42	67																		
	Washington	**NHL**	**31**	**2**	**5**	**7**	**22**	**0**	**0**	**0**	**38**	**5.3**	**4**				**7**	**2**	**2**	**4**	**2**	**0**	**0**	**1**	
1995-96	**Washington**	**NHL**	**78**	**15**	**26**	**41**	**60**	**4**	**0**	**4**	**139**	**10.8**	**25**				**6**	**2**	**4**	**6**	**4**	**1**	**0**	**0**	
1996-97	**Washington**	**NHL**	**57**	**13**	**17**	**30**	**36**	**3**	**0**	**3**	**129**	**10.1**	**–11**												
1997-98	Lada Togliatti	Russia	7	3	2	5	4																		
	Washington	**NHL**	**72**	**5**	**16**	**21**	**66**	**2**	**0**	**0**	**134**	**3.7**	**2**				**21**	**7**	**4**	**11**	**30**	**3**	**1**	**2**	
	Russia	Olympics	6	0	2	2	0																		
1998-99	**Washington**	**NHL**	**53**	**21**	**10**	**31**	**57**	**13**	**1**	**3**	**180**	**11.7**	**1**	**0**	**0.0**	**23:55**									
99-2000	**Washington**	**NHL**	**73**	**18**	**36**	**54**	**52**	**5**	**0**	**3**	**181**	**9.9**	**26**	**0**	**0.0**	**21:46**	**5**	**1**	**0**	**1**	**6**	**0**	**0**	**0**	**19:58**
2000-01	**Washington**	**NHL**	**76**	**19**	**38**	**57**	**70**	**8**	**0**	**2**	**241**	**7.9**	**12**	**1**	**100.0**	**22:26**	**6**	**1**	**3**	**4**	**2**	**1**	**0**	**0**	**19:45**
2001-02	**Washington**	**NHL**	**76**	**26**	**33**	**59**	**58**	**7**	**0**	**2**	**216**	**12.0**	**–1**	**1**	**100.0**	**23:51**									
	Russia	Olympics	6	0	0	0	2																		
2002-03	**Washington**	**NHL**	**82**	**18**	**49**	**67**	**52**	**7**	**0**	**2**	**224**	**8.0**	**13**	**0**	**0.0**	**26:35**	**6**	**0**	**5**	**5**	**4**	**0**	**0**	**0**	**29:00**
2003-04	**Washington**	**NHL**	**56**	**7**	**42**	**49**	**44**	**4**	**0**	**0**	**127**	**5.5**	**–20**	**0**	**0.0**	**27:57**									
	Boston	**NHL**	**15**	**4**	**5**	**9**	**12**	**2**	**0**	**0**	**34**	**11.8**	**6**	**0**	**0.0**	**25:32**	**7**	**1**	**4**	**5**	**4**	**1**	**0**	**1**	**27:51**
2004-05	Magnitogorsk	Russia	40	2	17	19	54										4	1	1	2	6				
2005-06	**Pittsburgh**	**NHL**	**75**	**12**	**46**	**58**	**100**	**8**	**0**	**2**	**192**	**6.3**	**–13**	**0**	**0.0**	**24:40**									
	Russia	Olympics	8	0	2	2	8																		
2006-07	**Pittsburgh**	**NHL**	**82**	**13**	**54**	**67**	**72**	**10**	**1**	**3**	**191**	**6.8**	**–5**	**0**	**0.0**	**26:34**	**5**	**1**	**3**	**4**	**2**	**1**	**0**	**0**	**26:53**
2007-08	**Pittsburgh**	**NHL**	**78**	**12**	**53**	**65**	**66**	**8**	**0**	**2**	**173**	**6.9**	**13**	**0**	**0.0**	**25:55**	**20**	**1**	**13**	**14**	**8**	**1**	**0**	**0**	**25:13**
2008-09 ♦	**Pittsburgh**	**NHL**	**25**	**6**	**13**	**19**	**26**	**5**	**0**	**1**	**71**	**8.5**	**6**	**0**	**0.0**	**25:11**	**22**	**3**	**11**	**14**	**12**	**2**	**0**	**2**	**23:03**
2009-10	**Pittsburgh**	**NHL**	**62**	**11**	**39**	**50**	**49**	**6**	**0**	**3**	**138**	**8.0**	**–4**	**0**	**0.0**	**24:24**	**13**	**2**	**10**	**12**	**4**	**1**	**0**	**1**	**26:27**
	Russia	Olympics	4	1	0	1	2																		
2010-11	**Ottawa**	**NHL**	**67**	**7**	**20**	**27**	**20**	**5**	**0**	**0**	**107**	**6.5**	**–15**	**0**	**0.0**	**23:12**									
	NHL Totals		**1058**	**209**	**502**	**711**	**862**	**97**	**2**	**30**	**2515**	**8.3**		**2**	**100.0**	**24:42**	**118**	**21**	**59**	**80**	**78**	**11**	**1**	**7**	**24:43**

NHL Second All-Star Team (2002, 2003)

Played in NHL All-Star Game (2001, 2002, 2003, 2008)

Traded to **Boston** by **Washington** for Shaonne Morrisonn and Boston's 1st (Jeff Schultz) and 2nd (Michail Yunkov) round choices in 2004 Entry Draft, March 3, 2004. Signed as a free agent by **Magnitogorsk** (Russia), September 21, 2004. Signed as a free agent by **Pittsburgh**, August 3, 2005. Signed as a free agent by **Ottawa**, July 1, 2010.

GORDON, Andrew

(GOHR-duhn, AN-droo) **ANA**

Right wing. Shoots right. 6', 194 lbs. Born, Halifax, N.S., December 13, 1985. Washington's 11th choice, 197th overall, in 2004 Entry Draft.

Season	Club	League	GP	G	A	Pts	PIM	PP	SH	GW	S	%	+/-	TF	F%	Min	GP	G	A	Pts	PIM	PP	SH	GW	Min
2002-03	Notre Dame	SJHL	58	20	27	47	12																		
2003-04	Notre Dame	SJHL	55	20	44	64	12																		
2004-05	St. Cloud State	WCHA	38	9	8	17	6																		
2005-06	St. Cloud State	WCHA	42	20	20	40	22																		
2006-07	St. Cloud State	WCHA	40	22	23	45	16																		
2007-08	Hershey Bears	AHL	58	16	35	51	39										5	3	2	5	2				
	South Carolina	ECHL	11	8	6	14	6										9	5	3	8	8				
2008-09	**Washington**	**NHL**	**1**	**0**	**0**	**0**	**0**	**0**	**0**	**0**	**1**	**0.0**	**0**	**0**	**0.0**	**7:12**									
	Hershey Bears	AHL	80	21	24	45	47										22	6	4	10	6				
2009-10	**Washington**	**NHL**	**2**	**0**	**0**	**0**	**0**	**0**	**0**	**0**	**0**	**0.0**	**–2**	**0**	**0.0**	**6:41**									
	Hershey Bears	AHL	79	37	34	71	57										17	13	7	20	2				

			Regular Season														Playoffs								
Season	Club	League	GP	G	A	Pts	PIM	PP	SH	GW	S	%	+/-	TF	F%	Min	GP	G	A	Pts	PIM	PP	SH	GW	Min
2010-11	**Washington**	**NHL**	**9**	**1**	**1**	**2**	**0**	**0**	**0**	**0**	**5**	**20.0**	**–2**	**0**	**0.0**	**8:40**	....	....	....	....	....	....	....	....	....
	Hershey Bears	AHL	50	28	29	57	24	....	....	....	....	....	....	....	....	....	2	0	1	1	6	....	....	....	....
	NHL Totals		**12**	**1**	**1**	**2**	**0**	**0**	**0**	**0**	**6**	**16.7**		**0**	**0.0**	**8:13**	....	....	....	....	....	....	....	....	....

WCHA First All-Star Team (2007) • AHL Second All-Star Team (2010)

Signed as a free agent by **Anaheim**, July 2, 2011.

GORDON, Boyd

(GOHR-duhn, BOID) **PHX**

Center. Shoots right. 6'1", 200 lbs. Born, Unity, Sask., October 19, 1983. Washington's 3rd choice, 17th overall, in 2002 Entry Draft.

Season	Club	League	GP	G	A	Pts	PIM	PP	SH	GW	S	%	+/-	TF	F%	Min	GP	G	A	Pts	PIM	PP	SH	GW	Min
1998-99	Regina Rangers	SMBHL	60	70	102	172	53	....	....	....	....	....	....	....	....	....	....	....	....	....	....	....	....	....	....
99-2000	Red Deer Rebels	WHL	66	10	26	36	24	....	....	....	....	....	....	....	....	....	4	0	1	1	16	....	....	....	....
2000-01	Red Deer Rebels	WHL	72	12	27	39	39	....	....	....	....	....	....	....	....	....	22	3	6	9	2	....	....	....	....
2001-02	Red Deer Rebels	WHL	66	22	29	51	19	....	....	....	....	....	....	....	....	....	23	10	12	22	8	....	....	....	....
2002-03	Red Deer Rebels	WHL	56	33	48	81	28	....	....	....	....	....	....	....	....	....	23	8	12	20	14	....	....	....	....
2003-04	**Washington**	**NHL**	**41**	**1**	**5**	**6**	**8**	**0**	**0**	**0**	**42**	**2.4**	**–9**	**328**	**43.0**	**13:11**	....	....	....	....	....	....	....	....	....
	Portland Pirates	AHL	43	5	17	22	16	....	....	....	....	....	....	....	....	....	7	2	1	3	0	....	....	....	....
2004-05	Portland Pirates	AHL	80	17	22	39	35	....	....	....	....	....	....	....	....	....	....	....	....	....	....	....	....	....	....
2005-06	**Washington**	**NHL**	**25**	**0**	**1**	**1**	**4**	**0**	**0**	**0**	**12**	**0.0**	**–4**	**216**	**46.3**	**11:40**	....	....	....	....	....	....	....	....	....
	Hershey Bears	AHL	58	16	22	38	23	....	....	....	....	....	....	....	....	....	21	3	5	8	10	....	....	....	....
2006-07	**Washington**	**NHL**	**71**	**7**	**22**	**29**	**14**	**0**	**2**	**0**	**104**	**6.7**	**10**	**1214**	**52.1**	**15:53**	....	....	....	....	....	....	....	....	....
2007-08	**Washington**	**NHL**	**67**	**7**	**9**	**16**	**12**	**0**	**1**	**0**	**100**	**7.0**	**5**	**904**	**55.8**	**15:44**	**7**	**0**	**0**	**0**	**0**	**0**	**0**	**0**	**13:23**
2008-09	**Washington**	**NHL**	**63**	**5**	**9**	**14**	**16**	**0**	**1**	**2**	**69**	**7.2**	**–4**	**667**	**56.1**	**13:28**	**14**	**0**	**3**	**3**	**4**	**0**	**0**	**0**	**11:17**
2009-10	**Washington**	**NHL**	**36**	**4**	**6**	**10**	**12**	**0**	**0**	**0**	**40**	**10.0**	**4**	**205**	**61.0**	**10:17**	**6**	**1**	**1**	**2**	**0**	**0**	**1**	**0**	**11:02**
	Hershey Bears	AHL	2	0	2	2	0	....	....	....	....	....	....	....	....	....	....	....	....	....	....	....	....	....	....
2010-11	**Washington**	**NHL**	**60**	**3**	**6**	**9**	**16**	**0**	**1**	**1**	**77**	**3.9**	**–5**	**719**	**58.0**	**13:03**	**9**	**0**	**0**	**0**	**6**	**0**	**0**	**0**	**12:54**
	NHL Totals		**363**	**27**	**58**	**85**	**82**	**0**	**5**	**3**	**444**	**6.1**		**4253**	**53.9**	**13:49**	**36**	**1**	**4**	**5**	**10**	**0**	**1**	**0**	**12:03**

WHL East First All-Star Team (2003)

• Missed majority of 2009-10 due to recurring back injury. Signed as a free agent by **Phoeniix**, July 1, 2011.

GORGES, Josh

(GOHR-juhz, JAWSH) **MTL**

Defense. Shoots left. 6'1", 200 lbs. Born, Kelowna, B.C., August 14, 1984.

Season	Club	League	GP	G	A	Pts	PIM	PP	SH	GW	S	%	+/-	TF	F%	Min	GP	G	A	Pts	PIM	PP	SH	GW	Min
2000-01	Kelowna Rockets	WHL	57	4	6	10	24	....	....	....	....	....	....	....	....	....	6	1	1	2	4	....	....	....	....
2001-02	Kelowna Rockets	WHL	72	7	34	41	74	....	....	....	....	....	....	....	....	....	15	1	7	8	8	....	....	....	....
2002-03	Kelowna Rockets	WHL	54	11	48	59	76	....	....	....	....	....	....	....	....	....	19	3	17	20	16	....	....	....	....
2003-04	Kelowna Rockets	WHL	62	11	31	42	38	....	....	....	....	....	....	....	....	....	17	2	13	15	6	....	....	....	....
2004-05	Cleveland Barons	AHL	74	4	8	12	37	....	....	....	....	....	....	....	....	....	....	....	....	....	....	....	....	....	....
2005-06	**San Jose**	**NHL**	**49**	**0**	**6**	**6**	**31**	**0**	**0**	**0**	**25**	**0.0**	**5**	**0**	**0.0**	**17:38**	**11**	**0**	**1**	**1**	**4**	**0**	**0**	**0**	**18:56**
	Cleveland Barons	AHL	18	2	3	5	12	....	....	....	....	....	....	....	....	....	....	....	....	....	....	....	....	....	....
2006-07	**San Jose**	**NHL**	**47**	**1**	**3**	**4**	**26**	**0**	**0**	**0**	**37**	**2.7**	**–3**	**0**	**0.0**	**17:48**	....	....	....	....	....	....	....	....	....
	Worcester Sharks	AHL	7	0	1	1	2	....	....	....	....	....	....	....	....	....	....	....	....	....	....	....	....	....	....
	Montreal	**NHL**	**7**	**0**	**0**	**0**	**0**	**0**	**0**	**0**	**3**	**0.0**	**–1**	**0**	**0.0**	**12:28**	....	....	....	....	....	....	....	....	....
2007-08	**Montreal**	**NHL**	**62**	**0**	**9**	**9**	**32**	**0**	**0**	**0**	**41**	**0.0**	**0**	**0**	**0.0**	**16:20**	**12**	**0**	**3**	**3**	**0**	**0**	**0**	**0**	**18:20**
2008-09	**Montreal**	**NHL**	**81**	**4**	**19**	**23**	**37**	**2**	**0**	**0**	**63**	**6.3**	**12**	**1**	**0.0**	**20:08**	**4**	**0**	**1**	**1**	**7**	**0**	**0**	**0**	**23:46**
2009-10	**Montreal**	**NHL**	**82**	**3**	**7**	**10**	**39**	**0**	**0**	**1**	**52**	**5.8**	**2**	**0**	**0.0**	**21:01**	**19**	**0**	**2**	**2**	**14**	**0**	**0**	**0**	**22:42**
2010-11	**Montreal**	**NHL**	**36**	**1**	**6**	**7**	**18**	**1**	**0**	**1**	**20**	**5.0**	**–3**	**0**	**0.0**	**21:10**	....	....	....	....	....	....	....	....	....
	NHL Totals		**364**	**9**	**50**	**59**	**183**	**3**	**0**	**2**	**241**	**3.7**		**1**	**0.0**	**19:00**	**46**	**0**	**7**	**7**	**25**	**0**	**0**	**0**	**20:45**

WHL West Second All-Star Team (2003) • WHL West First All-Star Team (2004) • George Parsons Trophy (Memorial Cup - Most Sportsmanlike Player) (2004)

Signed as a free agent by **San Jose**, September 20, 2002. Traded to **Montreal** by **San Jose** with San Jose's 1st round choice (Max Pacioretty) in 2007 Entry Draft for Craig Rivet and Montreal's 5th round choice (Julien Demers) in 2008 Entry Draft, February 25, 2007. • Missed majority of 2010-11 due to knee injury at NY Islanders, December 26, 2010.

GRABNER, Michael

(GRAB-nuhr, MIGH-kuhl) **NYI**

Right wing. Shoots left. 6', 170 lbs. Born, Villach, Austria, October 5, 1987. Vancouver's 1st choice, 14th overall, in 2006 Entry Draft.

Season	Club	League	GP	G	A	Pts	PIM	PP	SH	GW	S	%	+/-	TF	F%	Min	GP	G	A	Pts	PIM	PP	SH	GW	Min
2002-03	EC Villacher SV Jr.	Austria-Jr.	13	6	4	10	4	....	....	....	....	....	....	....	....	....	....	....	....	....	....	....	....	....	....
2003-04	EC Villacher SV Jr.	Austria-Jr.	23	32	5	37	58	....	....	....	....	....	....	....	....	....	....	....	....	....	....	....	....	....	....
	EC Villacher SV	Austria	18	2	1	3	0	....	....	....	....	....	....	....	....	....	....	....	....	....	....	....	....	....	....
	Austria	WJ18-B	5	3	1	4	4	....	....	....	....	....	....	....	....	....	....	....	....	....	....	....	....	....	....
2004-05	Spokane Chiefs	WHL	58	13	11	24	18	....	....	....	....	....	....	....	....	....	....	....	....	....	....	....	....	....	....
2005-06	Spokane Chiefs	WHL	67	36	14	50	28	....	....	....	....	....	....	....	....	....	....	....	....	....	....	....	....	....	....
2006-07	Spokane Chiefs	WHL	55	39	16	55	34	....	....	....	....	....	....	....	....	....	6	0	1	1	2	....	....	....	....
	Manitoba Moose	AHL	2	1	1	2	0	....	....	....	....	....	....	....	....	....	6	0	0	0	0	....	....	....	....
2007-08	Manitoba Moose	AHL	74	22	22	44	8	....	....	....	....	....	....	....	....	....	6	3	0	3	2	....	....	....	....
2008-09	Manitoba Moose	AHL	66	30	18	48	20	....	....	....	....	....	....	....	....	....	20	10	7	17	2	....	....	....	....
2009-10	**Vancouver**	**NHL**	**20**	**5**	**6**	**11**	**8**	**2**	**0**	**1**	**63**	**7.9**	**2**	**2**	**50.0**	**13:54**	**9**	**1**	**0**	**1**	**0**	**0**	**0**	**0**	**9:06**
	Manitoba Moose	AHL	38	15	11	26	6	....	....	....	....	....	....	....	....	....	....	....	....	....	....	....	....	....	....
2010-11	**NY Islanders**	**NHL**	**76**	**34**	**18**	**52**	**10**	**2**	**6**	**3**	**228**	**14.9**	**13**	**6**	**33.3**	**15:05**	....	....	....	....	....	....	....	....	....
	NHL Totals		**96**	**39**	**24**	**63**	**18**	**4**	**6**	**4**	**291**	**13.4**		**8**	**37.5**	**14:50**	**9**	**1**	**0**	**1**	**0**	**0**	**0**	**0**	**9:06**

NHL All-Rookie Team (2011)

Traded to **Florida** by **Vancouver** with Steve Bernier and Vancouver's 1st round choice (Quinton Howden) in 2010 Entry Draft for Keith Ballard and Victor Oreskovich, June 25, 2010. Claimed on waivers by **NY Islanders** from **Florida**, October 5, 2010.

GRABOVSKI, Mikhail

(gra-BAWV-skee, mih-kigh-EHL) **TOR**

Center. Shoots left. 5'11", 183 lbs. Born, Potsdam, East Germany, January 31, 1984. Montreal's 4th choice, 150th overall, in 2004 Entry Draft.

Season	Club	League	GP	G	A	Pts	PIM	PP	SH	GW	S	%	+/-	TF	F%	Min	GP	G	A	Pts	PIM	PP	SH	GW	Min
2001-02	HC Minsk	Belarus	26	10	7	17	16	....	....	....	....	....	....	....	....	....	....	....	....	....	....	....	....	....	....
2002-03	HC Minsk	Belarus	STATISTICS NOT AVAILABLE																						
2003-04	Nizhnekamsk	Russia	45	6	11	17	26	....	....	....	....	....	....	....	....	....	5	0	0	0	4	....	....	....	....
2004-05	Nizhnekamsk	Russia	60	16	20	36	32	....	....	....	....	....	....	....	....	....	3	2	0	2	2	....	....	....	....
	Yunost-Minsk	BelOpen	....	....	....	....	....	....	....	....	....	....	....	....	....	....	5	2	4	6	6	....	....	....	....
2005-06	Dynamo Moscow	Russia	48	10	17	27	28	....	....	....	....	....	....	....	....	....	4	0	0	0	4	....	....	....	....
	Yunost-Minsk	BelOpen	8	6	8	14	10	....	....	....	....	....	....	....	....	....	....	....	....	....	....	....	....	....	....
2006-07	**Montreal**	**NHL**	**3**	**0**	**0**	**0**	**0**	**0**	**0**	**0**	**5**	**0.0**	**–2**	**31**	**41.9**	**13:18**	....	....	....	....	....	....	....	....	....
	Hamilton	AHL	66	17	37	54	34	....	....	....	....	....	....	....	....	....	20	4	7	11	21	....	....	....	....
2007-08	**Montreal**	**NHL**	**24**	**3**	**6**	**9**	**8**	**0**	**0**	**1**	**23**	**13.0**	**–4**	**154**	**33.1**	**11:14**	....	....	....	....	....	....	....	....	....
	Hamilton	AHL	12	8	12	20	6	....	....	....	....	....	....	....	....	....	....	....	....	....	....	....	....	....	....
2008-09	**Toronto**	**NHL**	**78**	**20**	**28**	**48**	**92**	**6**	**0**	**2**	**120**	**16.7**	**–8**	**957**	**44.5**	**16:13**	....	....	....	....	....	....	....	....	....
2009-10	**Toronto**	**NHL**	**59**	**10**	**25**	**35**	**10**	**2**	**1**	**3**	**126**	**7.9**	**3**	**735**	**49.8**	**16:48**	....	....	....	....	....	....	....	....	....
2010-11	**Toronto**	**NHL**	**81**	**29**	**29**	**58**	**60**	**10**	**0**	**4**	**239**	**12.1**	**14**	**1326**	**48.4**	**19:22**	....	....	....	....	....	....	....	....	....
	NHL Totals		**245**	**62**	**88**	**150**	**170**	**18**	**1**	**10**	**513**	**12.1**		**3203**	**46.8**	**16:52**	....	....	....	....	....	....	....	....	....

Traded to **Toronto** by **Montreal** for Greg Pateryn and Toronto's 2nd round choice (later traded to Chicago, later traded back to Toronto, later traded to Boston - Boston selected Jared Knight) in 2010 Entry Draft, July 3, 2008.

GRACHEV, Evgeny

(gra-CHAWF, ehv-GEH-nee) **ST.L.**

Center. Shoots left. 6'4", 224 lbs. Born, Khabarovsk, USSR, February 21, 1990. NY Rangers' 3rd choice, 75th overall, in 2008 Entry Draft.

Season	Club	League	GP	G	A	Pts	PIM	PP	SH	GW	S	%	+/-	TF	F%	Min	GP	G	A	Pts	PIM	PP	SH	GW	Min
2005-06	Yaroslavl 2	Russia-3	1	0	0	0	2	....	....	....	....	....	....	....	....	....	....	....	....	....	....	....	....	....	....
2006-07	Yaroslavl 2	Russia-3	28	7	6	13	6	....	....	....	....	....	....	....	....	....	....	....	....	....	....	....	....	....	....
2007-08	Yaroslavl 2	Russia-3	STATISTICS NOT AVAILABLE																						
	Yaroslavl	Russia	1	0	0	0	0	....	....	....	....	....	....	....	....	....	....	....	....	....	....	....	....	....	....
2008-09	Brampton	OHL	60	40	40	80	22	....	....	....	....	....	....	....	....	....	19	11	14	25	4	....	....	....	....
2009-10	Hartford	AHL	80	12	16	28	14	....	....	....	....	....	....	....	....	....	....	....	....	....	....	....	....	....	....
2010-11	**NY Rangers**	**NHL**	**8**	**0**	**0**	**0**	**0**	**0**	**0**	**0**	**3**	**0.0**	**–3**	**1**	**0.0**	**7:42**	....	....	....	....	....	....	....	....	....
	Connecticut	AHL	73	16	22	38	24	....	....	....	....	....	....	....	....	....	6	0	2	2	4	....	....	....	....
	NHL Totals		**8**	**0**	**0**	**0**	**0**	**0**	**0**	**0**	**3**	**0.0**		**1**	**0.0**	**7:42**	....	....	....	....	....	....	....	....	....

OHL Rookie of the Year (2009) • Canadian Major Junior All-Rookie Team (2009)

Traded to **St. Louis** by **NY Rangers** for St. Louis' 3rd round choice (Steven Fogarty) in 2011 Entry Draft, June 25, 2011.

GRAGNANI, Marc-Andre
(GRUH-na-nee, MAHRK-AWN-dray) **BUF**

Defense. Shoots left. 6'2", 201 lbs. Born, Montreal, Que., March 11, 1987. Buffalo's 3rd choice, 87th overall, in 2005 Entry Draft.

Season	Club	League	GP	G	A	Pts	PIM	PP	SH	GW	S	%	+/-	TF	F%	Min	GP	G	A	Pts	PIM	PP	SH	GW	Min
			Regular Season														Playoffs								
2002-03	West Island Lions	QAAA	34	3	15	18	22	....	....	....	....	....	....	....	....	....	....	....	....	....	....	....	....	....	....
2003-04	P.E.I. Rocket	QMJHL	61	2	13	15	42	....	....	....	....	....	....	....	....	....	11	0	0	0	4	....	....	....	....
2004-05	P.E.I. Rocket	QMJHL	68	10	29	39	48	....	....	....	....	....	....	....	....	....	....	....	....	....	....	....	....	....	....
2005-06	P.E.I. Rocket	QMJHL	62	16	55	71	75	....	....	....	....	....	....	....	....	....	6	1	4	5	14	....	....	....	....
2006-07	P.E.I. Rocket	QMJHL	65	22	46	68	58	....	....	....	....	....	....	....	....	....	7	5	8	13	4	....	....	....	....
2007-08	**Buffalo**	**NHL**	**2**	**0**	**0**	**0**	**4**	**0**	**0**	**0**	**1**	**0.0**	**–2**	**0**	**0.0**	**6:18**	....	....	....	....	....	....	....	....	....
	Rochester	AHL	78	14	38	52	38	....	....	....	....	....	....	....	....	....	....	....	....	....	....	....	....	....	....
2008-09	**Buffalo**	**NHL**	**4**	**0**	**0**	**0**	**2**	**0**	**0**	**0**	**3**	**0.0**	**2**	**0**	**0.0**	**15:23**	....	....	....	....	....	....	....	....	....
	Portland Pirates	AHL	76	9	42	51	59	....	....	....	....	....	....	....	....	....	5	0	2	2	4	....	....	....	....
2009-10	Portland Pirates	AHL	66	12	31	43	37	....	....	....	....	....	....	....	....	....	4	0	2	2	0	....	....	....	....
2010-11	**Buffalo**	**NHL**	**9**	**1**	**2**	**3**	**2**	**0**	**0**	**1**	**11**	**9.1**	**0**	**0**	**0.0**	**15:17**	**7**	**1**	**6**	**7**	**4**	**1**	**0**	**0**	**21:53**
	Portland Pirates	AHL	63	12	48	60	51	....	....	....	....	....	....	....	....	....	....	....	....	....	....	....	....	....	....
	NHL Totals		**15**	**1**	**2**	**3**	**8**	**0**	**0**	**1**	**15**	**6.7**		**0**	**0.0**	**14:07**	**7**	**1**	**6**	**7**	**4**	**1**	**0**	**0**	**21:54**

AHL First All-Star Team (2011) • Eddie Shore Award (AHL – Outstanding Defenseman) (2011)

GRANT, Triston
(GRANT, TRIHS-tuhn)

Left wing. Shoots left. 6'1", 211 lbs. Born, Neepawa, Man., February 2, 1984. Philadelphia's 10th choice, 286th overall, in 2004 Entry Draft.

Season	Club	League	GP	G	A	Pts	PIM	PP	SH	GW	S	%	+/-	TF	F%	Min	GP	G	A	Pts	PIM	PP	SH	GW	Min
2000-01	Neepawa Natives	MJHL	STATISTICS NOT AVAILABLE																						
	Lethbridge	WHL	23	2	0	2	75	....	....	....	....	....	....	....	....	....	5	0	0	0	11	....	....	....	....
2001-02	Lethbridge	WHL	36	8	1	9	110	....	....	....	....	....	....	....	....	....	....	....	....	....	....	....	....	....	....
	Vancouver Giants	WHL	21	2	4	6	53	....	....	....	....	....	....	....	....	....	....	....	....	....	....	....	....	....	....
2002-03	Vancouver Giants	WHL	72	10	10	20	200	....	....	....	....	....	....	....	....	....	4	0	0	0	10	....	....	....	....
2003-04	Vancouver Giants	WHL	69	10	8	18	267	....	....	....	....	....	....	....	....	....	11	1	1	2	33	....	....	....	....
2004-05	Vancouver Giants	WHL	70	20	12	32	193	....	....	....	....	....	....	....	....	....	6	1	0	1	8	....	....	....	....
2005-06	Philadelphia	AHL	64	2	3	5	190	....	....	....	....	....	....	....	....	....	....	....	....	....	....	....	....	....	....
2006-07	**Philadelphia**	**NHL**	**8**	**0**	**1**	**1**	**10**	**0**	**0**	**0**	**3**	**0.0**	**–1**	**0**	**0.0**	**4:32**	....	....	....	....	....	....	....	....	....
	Philadelphia	AHL	61	5	6	11	199	....	....	....	....	....	....	....	....	....	....	....	....	....	....	....	....	....	....
2007-08	Philadelphia	AHL	72	10	11	21	181	....	....	....	....	....	....	....	....	....	12	0	2	2	34	....	....	....	....
2008-09	Milwaukee	AHL	55	3	8	11	153	....	....	....	....	....	....	....	....	....	11	1	1	2	12	....	....	....	....
2009-10	**Nashville**	**NHL**	**3**	**0**	**0**	**0**	**9**	**0**	**0**	**0**	**2**	**0.0**	**–1**	**0**	**0.0**	**7:14**	....	....	....	....	....	....	....	....	....
	Milwaukee	AHL	74	12	13	25	236	....	....	....	....	....	....	....	....	....	5	0	2	2	16	....	....	....	....
2010-11	Rochester	AHL	56	7	6	13	144	....	....	....	....	....	....	....	....	....	....	....	....	....	....	....	....	....	....
	NHL Totals		**11**	**0**	**1**	**1**	**19**	**0**	**0**	**0**	**5**	**0.0**		**0**	**0.0**	**5:16**	....	....	....	....	....	....	....	....	....

Traded to **Nashville** by **Philadelphia** with Philadelphia's 7th round choice (later traded to St. Louis – St. Louis selected Maxwell Tardy) in 2009 Entry Draft for Janne Niskala, June 24, 2008. Signed as a free agent by **Florida**, July 2, 2010.

GREBESHKOV, Denis
(greh-behsh-KAHV, DEH-nihs)

Defense. Shoots left. 6', 209 lbs. Born, Yaroslavl, USSR, October 11, 1983. Los Angeles' 1st choice, 18th overall, in 2002 Entry Draft.

Season	Club	League	GP	G	A	Pts	PIM	PP	SH	GW	S	%	+/-	TF	F%	Min	GP	G	A	Pts	PIM	PP	SH	GW	Min
99-2000	Yaroslavl 2	Russia-3	42	2	1	3	12	....	....	....	....	....	....	....	....	....	6	0	0	0	2	....	....	....	....
2000-01	Yaroslavl 2	Russia-3	34	7	2	9	20	....	....	....	....	....	....	....	....	....	....	....	....	....	....	....	....	....	....
2001-02	Yaroslavl 2	Russia-3	7	1	1	2	2	....	....	....	....	....	....	....	....	....	....	....	....	....	....	....	....	....	....
	Yaroslavl	Russia	27	1	2	3	10	....	....	....	....	....	....	....	....	....	....	....	....	....	....	....	....	....	....
2002-03	Yaroslavl	Russia	48	0	7	7	26	....	....	....	....	....	....	....	....	....	10	0	1	1	2	....	....	....	....
2003-04	**Los Angeles**	**NHL**	**4**	**0**	**1**	**1**	**0**	**0**	**0**	**0**	**5**	**0.0**	**–4**	**0**	**0.0**	**18:29**	....	....	....	....	....	....	....	....	....
	Manchester	AHL	43	2	7	9	34	....	....	....	....	....	....	....	....	....	6	0	1	1	6	....	....	....	....
2004-05	Manchester	AHL	75	5	44	49	87	....	....	....	....	....	....	....	....	....	6	0	4	4	2	....	....	....	....
2005-06	**Los Angeles**	**NHL**	**8**	**0**	**2**	**2**	**12**	**0**	**0**	**0**	**10**	**0.0**	**–4**	**0**	**0.0**	**15:16**	....	....	....	....	....	....	....	....	....
	Manchester	AHL	48	2	25	27	59	....	....	....	....	....	....	....	....	....	....	....	....	....	....	....	....	....	....
	NY Islanders	**NHL**	**21**	**0**	**3**	**3**	**8**	**0**	**0**	**0**	**14**	**0.0**	**–8**	**0**	**0.0**	**17:11**	....	....	....	....	....	....	....	....	....
	Bridgeport	AHL	....	....	....	....	....	....	....	....	....	....	....	....	....	....	7	1	1	2	8	....	....	....	....
2006-07	Yaroslavl	Russia	47	8	9	17	79	....	....	....	....	....	....	....	....	....	7	0	2	2	6	....	....	....	....
2007-08	**Edmonton**	**NHL**	**71**	**3**	**15**	**18**	**22**	**1**	**0**	**0**	**34**	**8.8**	**2**	**0**	**0.0**	**16:53**	....	....	....	....	....	....	....	....	....
2008-09	**Edmonton**	**NHL**	**72**	**7**	**32**	**39**	**38**	**2**	**0**	**0**	**62**	**11.3**	**12**	**0**	**0.0**	**21:10**	....	....	....	....	....	....	....	....	....
2009-10	**Edmonton**	**NHL**	**47**	**6**	**13**	**19**	**26**	**1**	**0**	**0**	**43**	**14.0**	**–16**	**1**	**100.0**	**21:49**	....	....	....	....	....	....	....	....	....
	Russia	Olympics	4	0	1	1	2	....	....	....	....	....	....	....	....	....	....	....	....	....	....	....	....	....	....
	Nashville	**NHL**	**4**	**1**	**1**	**2**	**6**	**0**	**0**	**0**	**4**	**25.0**	**0**	**0**	**0.0**	**16:28**	**2**	**0**	**2**	**2**	**0**	**0**	**0**	**0**	**11:22**
2010-11	St. Petersburg	Rus-KHL	54	8	9	17	44	....	....	....	....	....	....	....	....	....	11	0	5	5	12	....	....	....	....
	NHL Totals		**227**	**17**	**67**	**84**	**112**	**4**	**0**	**0**	**172**	**9.9**		**1**	**100.0**	**19:15**	**2**	**0**	**2**	**2**	**0**	**0**	**0**	**0**	**11:22**

Traded to **NY Islanders** by **Los Angeles** with Jeff Tambellini for Mark Parrish and Brent Sopel, March 8, 2006. Signed as a free agent by **Yaroslavl** (Russia), July 10, 2006. Traded to **Edmonton** by **NY Islanders** for Marc-Andre Bergeron and Edmonton's 3rd round choice (later traded back to Edmonton, later traded to Anaheim, later traded back to NY Islanders - NY Islanders selected Kirill Petrov) in 2008 Entry Draft, February 18, 2007. Traded to **Nashville** by **Edmonton** for Nashville's 2nd round choice (Curtis Hamilton) in 2010 Entry Draft, March 1, 2010. Signed as a free agent by **St. Petersburg** (Russia-KHL), July 28, 2010.

GREEN, Josh
(GREEN, JAWSH) **EDM**

Left wing. Shoots left. 6'4", 225 lbs. Born, Camrose, Alta., November 16, 1977. Los Angeles' 1st choice, 30th overall, in 1996 Entry Draft.

Season	Club	League	GP	G	A	Pts	PIM	PP	SH	GW	S	%	+/-	TF	F%	Min	GP	G	A	Pts	PIM	PP	SH	GW	Min
1992-93	Camrose Kodiaks	Minor-AB	60	55	45	100	80	....	....	....	....	....	....	....	....	....	....	....	....	....	....	....	....	....	....
1993-94	Medicine Hat	WHL	63	22	22	44	43	....	....	....	....	....	....	....	....	....	3	0	0	0	4	....	....	....	....
1994-95	Medicine Hat	WHL	68	32	23	55	64	....	....	....	....	....	....	....	....	....	5	5	1	6	2	....	....	....	....
1995-96	Medicine Hat	WHL	46	18	25	43	55	....	....	....	....	....	....	....	....	....	5	2	2	4	4	....	....	....	....
1996-97	Medicine Hat	WHL	51	25	32	57	61	....	....	....	....	....	....	....	....	....	....	....	....	....	....	....	....	....	....
	Swift Current	WHL	23	10	15	25	33	....	....	....	....	....	....	....	....	....	10	9	7	16	19	....	....	....	....
1997-98	Swift Current	WHL	5	9	1	10	9	....	....	....	....	....	....	....	....	....	....	....	....	....	....	....	....	....	....
	Portland	WHL	26	26	18	44	27	....	....	....	....	....	....	....	....	....	....	....	....	....	....	....	....	....	....
	Fredericton	AHL	43	16	15	31	14	....	....	....	....	....	....	....	....	....	4	1	3	4	6	....	....	....	....
1998-99	**Los Angeles**	**NHL**	**27**	**1**	**3**	**4**	**8**	**1**	**0**	**0**	**35**	**2.9**	**–5**	**2**	**50.0**	**11:44**	....	....	....	....	....	....	....	....	....
	Springfield	AHL	41	15	15	30	29	....	....	....	....	....	....	....	....	....	....	....	....	....	....	....	....	....	....
99-2000	**NY Islanders**	**NHL**	**49**	**12**	**14**	**26**	**41**	**2**	**0**	**3**	**109**	**11.0**	**–7**	**12**	**50.0**	**13:36**	....	....	....	....	....	....	....	....	....
	Lowell	AHL	17	6	2	8	19	....	....	....	....	....	....	....	....	....	....	....	....	....	....	....	....	....	....
2000-01	Hamilton	AHL	2	2	0	2	2	....	....	....	....	....	....	....	....	....	....	....	....	....	....	....	....	....	....
	Edmonton	**NHL**	....	....	....	....	....	....	....	....	....	....	....	....	....	....	**3**	**0**	**0**	**0**	**0**	**0**	**0**	**0**	**7:55**
2001-02	**Edmonton**	**NHL**	**61**	**10**	**5**	**15**	**52**	**1**	**0**	**1**	**78**	**12.8**	**9**	**18**	**38.9**	**10:05**	....	....	....	....	....	....	....	....	....
2002-03	**Edmonton**	**NHL**	**20**	**0**	**2**	**2**	**12**	**0**	**0**	**0**	**20**	**0.0**	**–3**	**5**	**0.0**	**10:22**	....	....	....	....	....	....	....	....	....
	NY Rangers	**NHL**	**4**	**0**	**0**	**0**	**2**	**0**	**0**	**0**	**3**	**0.0**	**–1**	**0**	**0.0**	**9:07**	....	....	....	....	....	....	....	....	....
	Washington	**NHL**	**21**	**1**	**2**	**3**	**7**	**0**	**0**	**0**	**20**	**5.0**	**1**	**3**	**0.0**	**8:07**	....	....	....	....	....	....	....	....	....
2003-04	**Calgary**	**NHL**	**36**	**2**	**4**	**6**	**24**	**0**	**0**	**0**	**47**	**4.3**	**–3**	**39**	**30.8**	**11:18**	....	....	....	....	....	....	....	....	....
	Lowell	AHL	22	6	9	15	46	....	....	....	....	....	....	....	....	....	....	....	....	....	....	....	....	....	....
	NY Rangers	**NHL**	**14**	**3**	**2**	**5**	**8**	**0**	**0**	**1**	**29**	**10.3**	**0**	**9**	**55.6**	**14:16**	....	....	....	....	....	....	....	....	....
2004-05	Manitoba Moose	AHL	67	21	19	40	72	....	....	....	....	....	....	....	....	....	14	9	5	14	26	....	....	....	....
2005-06	**Vancouver**	**NHL**	**33**	**4**	**2**	**6**	**14**	**0**	**0**	**0**	**35**	**11.4**	**2**	**146**	**40.4**	**8:35**	....	....	....	....	....	....	....	....	....
	Manitoba Moose	AHL	35	7	24	31	33	....	....	....	....	....	....	....	....	....	10	5	5	10	23	....	....	....	....
2006-07	**Vancouver**	**NHL**	**57**	**2**	**5**	**7**	**25**	**0**	**0**	**2**	**74**	**2.7**	**0**	**266**	**40.6**	**11:25**	**9**	**0**	**1**	**1**	**12**	**0**	**0**	**0**	**10:13**
2007-08	Salzburg	Austria	43	20	22	42	100	....	....	....	....	....	....	....	....	....	....	....	....	....	....	....	....	....	....
2008-09	Iowa Chops	AHL	39	10	14	24	52	....	....	....	....	....	....	....	....	....	....	....	....	....	....	....	....	....	....
	Anaheim	**NHL**	....	....	....	....	....	....	....	....	....	....	....	....	....	....	**5**	**0**	**0**	**0**	**0**	**0**	**0**	**0**	**5:53**
2009-10	MODO	Sweden	47	12	8	20	79	....	....	....	....	....	....	....	....	....	....	....	....	....	....	....	....	....	....
2010-11	**Anaheim**	**NHL**	**12**	**0**	**0**	**0**	**6**	**0**	**0**	**0**	**10**	**0.0**	**–3**	**7**	**42.9**	**10:00**	....	....	....	....	....	....	....	....	....
	Syracuse Crunch	AHL	69	15	31	46	74	....	....	....	....	....	....	....	....	....	....	....	....	....	....	....	....	....	....
	NHL Totals		**334**	**35**	**39**	**74**	**199**	**4**	**0**	**7**	**460**	**7.6**		**507**	**39.6**	**11:00**	**17**	**0**	**1**	**1**	**12**	**0**	**0**	**0**	**8:32**

Traded to **NY Islanders** by **Los Angeles** with Olli Jokinen, Mathieu Biron and Los Angeles' 1st round choice (Taylor Pyatt) in 1999 Entry Draft for Ziggy Palffy, Brian Smolinski, Marcel Cousineau and New Jersey's 4th round choice (previously acquired, Los Angeles selected Daniel Johansson) in 1999 Entry Draft, June 20, 1999. Traded to **Edmonton** by **NY Islanders** with Eric Brewer and NY Islanders' 2nd round choice (Brad Winchester) in 2000 Entry Draft for Roman Hamrlik, June 24, 2000. • Missed majority of 2000-01 due to shoulder injury vs. Detroit, October 10, 2000. Traded to **NY Rangers** by **Edmonton** for future considerations, December 12, 2002. Claimed on waivers by **Washington** from **NY Rangers**, January 15, 2003. Signed as a free agent by **Calgary**, July 17, 2003. Claimed on waivers by **NY Rangers** from **Calgary**, March 6, 2004. Signed to a PTO (professional tryout) contract by **Manitoba** (AHL), September 27, 2004. Signed as a free agent by **Vancouver**, August 23, 2005. Signed as a free agent by **Salzburg** (Austria), July 30, 2007. Signed as a free agent by **Anaheim**, July 22, 2008. Signed as a free agent by **MODO** (Sweden). July 9, 2009. Signed as a free agent by **Anaheim**, July 12, 2010. Signed as a free agent by **Edmonton**, July 3, 2011.

GREEN, Mike

(GREEN, MIGHK) **WSH**

Defense. Shoots right. 6'1", 204 lbs. Born, Calgary, Alta., October 12, 1985. Washington's 3rd choice, 29th overall, in 2004 Entry Draft.

			Regular Season														Playoffs								
Season	Club	League	GP	G	A	Pts	PIM	PP	SH	GW	S	%	+/-	TF	F%	Min	GP	G	A	Pts	PIM	PP	SH	GW	Min
2000-01	Cgy. North Stars	AMHL	36	4	23	27	34	....	....	....	....	....	....	....	....	....	....	....	....	....	....	....	....	....	....
	Saskatoon Blades	WHL	5	0	2	2	0	....	....	....	....	....	....	....	....	....	....	....	....	....	....	....	....	....	....
2001-02	Saskatoon Blades	WHL	62	3	20	23	57	....	....	....	....	....	....	....	....	....	7	0	1	1	2	....	....	....	....
2002-03	Saskatoon Blades	WHL	72	6	36	42	70	....	....	....	....	....	....	....	....	....	6	0	2	2	6	....	....	....	....
2003-04	Saskatoon Blades	WHL	59	14	25	39	92	....	....	....	....	....	....	....	....	....	....	....	....	....	....	....	....	....	....
2004-05	Saskatoon Blades	WHL	67	14	52	66	105	....	....	....	....	....	....	....	....	....	4	0	0	0	6	....	....	....	....
2005-06	**Washington**	**NHL**	**22**	**1**	**2**	**3**	**18**	**0**	**0**	**0**	**13**	**7.7**	**–8**	**0**	**0.0**	**14:54**	....	....	....	....	....	....	....	....	....
	Hershey Bears	AHL	56	9	34	43	79	....	....	....	....	....	....	....	....	....	21	3	15	18	30	....	....	....	....
2006-07	**Washington**	**NHL**	**70**	**2**	**10**	**12**	**36**	**0**	**0**	**0**	**68**	**2.9**	**–10**	**0**	**0.0**	**15:29**	....	....	....	....	....	....	....	....	....
2007-08	**Washington**	**NHL**	**82**	**18**	**38**	**56**	**62**	**8**	**0**	**4**	**234**	**7.7**	**6**	**1**	**0.0**	**23:38**	**7**	**3**	**4**	**7**	**15**	**2**	**0**	**0**	**26:59**
2008-09	**Washington**	**NHL**	**68**	**31**	**42**	**73**	**68**	**18**	**1**	**4**	**243**	**12.8**	**24**	**0**	**0.0**	**25:46**	**14**	**1**	**8**	**9**	**12**	**1**	**0**	**0**	**24:59**
2009-10	**Washington**	**NHL**	**75**	**19**	**57**	**76**	**54**	**10**	**0**	**4**	**205**	**9.3**	**39**	**0**	**0.0**	**25:29**	**7**	**0**	**3**	**3**	**12**	**0**	**0**	**0**	**26:01**
2010-11	**Washington**	**NHL**	**49**	**8**	**16**	**24**	**48**	**5**	**0**	**1**	**115**	**7.0**	**6**	**0**	**0.0**	**25:12**	**8**	**1**	**5**	**6**	**8**	**1**	**0**	**0**	**21:27**
	NHL Totals		**366**	**79**	**165**	**244**	**286**	**41**	**1**	**13**	**878**	**9.0**		**1**	**0.0**	**22:32**	**36**	**5**	**20**	**25**	**47**	**4**	**0**	**0**	**24:47**

WHL East First All-Star Team (2005) • AHL All-Rookie Team (2006) • NHL First All-Star Team (2009, 2010) @ASG = Played in NHL All-Star Game (2011)

GREENE, Andy

(GREEN, AN-dee) **N.J.**

Defense. Shoots left. 5'11", 190 lbs. Born, Trenton, MI, October 30, 1982.

Season	Club	League	GP	G	A	Pts	PIM	PP	SH	GW	S	%	+/-	TF	F%	Min	GP	G	A	Pts	PIM	PP	SH	GW	Min
2002-03	Miami U.	CCHA	41	4	19	23	64	....	....	....	....	....	....	....	....	....	....	....	....	....	....	....	....	....	....
2003-04	Miami U.	CCHA	41	7	19	26	78	....	....	....	....	....	....	....	....	....	....	....	....	....	....	....	....	....	....
2004-05	Miami U.	CCHA	38	7	27	34	66	....	....	....	....	....	....	....	....	....	....	....	....	....	....	....	....	....	....
2005-06	Miami U.	CCHA	39	9	22	31	48	....	....	....	....	....	....	....	....	....	....	....	....	....	....	....	....	....	....
2006-07	**New Jersey**	**NHL**	**23**	**1**	**5**	**6**	**6**	**1**	**0**	**0**	**23**	**4.3**	**–1**	**0**	**0.0**	**14:15**	**11**	**2**	**1**	**3**	**2**	**0**	**0**	**1**	**17:04**
	Lowell Devils	AHL	52	5	16	21	28	....	....	....	....	....	....	....	....	....	....	....	....	....	....	....	....	....	....
2007-08	**New Jersey**	**NHL**	**59**	**2**	**8**	**10**	**22**	**2**	**0**	**0**	**50**	**4.0**	**0**	**0**	**0.0**	**19:30**	**2**	**0**	**0**	**0**	**0**	**0**	**0**	**0**	**15:11**
2008-09	**New Jersey**	**NHL**	**49**	**2**	**7**	**9**	**22**	**0**	**0**	**0**	**38**	**5.3**	**3**	**0**	**0.0**	**16:17**	**3**	**0**	**1**	**1**	**0**	**0**	**0**	**0**	**15:18**
2009-10	**New Jersey**	**NHL**	**78**	**6**	**31**	**37**	**14**	**4**	**0**	**4**	**86**	**7.0**	**9**	**0**	**0.0**	**23:32**	**5**	**1**	**1**	**2**	**6**	**1**	**0**	**0**	**19:42**
2010-11	**New Jersey**	**NHL**	**82**	**4**	**19**	**23**	**22**	**1**	**0**	**1**	**91**	**4.4**	**–23**	**0**	**0.0**	**22:22**	....	....	....	....	....	....	....	....	....
	NHL Totals		**291**	**15**	**70**	**85**	**86**	**8**	**0**	**5**	**288**	**5.2**		**0**	**0.0**	**20:26**	**21**	**3**	**3**	**6**	**8**	**1**	**0**	**1**	**17:16**

CCHA All-Rookie Team (2003) • CCHA First All-Star Team (2004, 2005, 2006) • NCAA West First All-American Team (2006)

Signed as a free agent by **New Jersey**, April 4, 2006.

GREENE, Matt

(GREEN, MAT) **L.A.**

Defense. Shoots right. 6'3", 231 lbs. Born, Grand Ledge, MI, May 13, 1983. Edmonton's 4th choice, 44th overall, in 2002 Entry Draft.

Season	Club	League	GP	G	A	Pts	PIM	PP	SH	GW	S	%	+/-	TF	F%	Min	GP	G	A	Pts	PIM	PP	SH	GW	Min
2000-01	USNTDP	U-18	34	0	9	9	8	....	....	....	....	....	....	....	....	....	....	....	....	....	....	....	....	....	....
	USNTDP	USHL	20	0	1	1	51	....	....	....	....	....	....	....	....	....	....	....	....	....	....	....	....	....	....
2001-02	Green Bay	USHL	55	4	20	24	150	....	....	....	....	....	....	....	....	....	7	0	1	1	31	....	....	....	....
2002-03	North Dakota	WCHA	39	0	4	4	*135	....	....	....	....	....	....	....	....	....	....	....	....	....	....	....	....	....	....
2003-04	North Dakota	WCHA	40	1	16	17	86	....	....	....	....	....	....	....	....	....	....	....	....	....	....	....	....	....	....
2004-05	North Dakota	WCHA	43	2	8	10	*126	....	....	....	....	....	....	....	....	....	....	....	....	....	....	....	....	....	....
2005-06	**Edmonton**	**NHL**	**27**	**0**	**2**	**2**	**43**	**0**	**0**	**0**	**10**	**0.0**	**–6**	**0**	**0.0**	**11:13**	**18**	**0**	**1**	**1**	**34**	**0**	**0**	**0**	**10:03**
	Iowa Stars	AHL	26	2	5	7	47	....	....	....	....	....	....	....	....	....	....	....	....	....	....	....	....	....	....
2006-07	**Edmonton**	**NHL**	**78**	**1**	**9**	**10**	**109**	**0**	**0**	**0**	**52**	**1.9**	**–22**	**0**	**0.0**	**17:36**	....	....	....	....	....	....	....	....	....
2007-08	**Edmonton**	**NHL**	**46**	**0**	**1**	**1**	**53**	**0**	**0**	**0**	**28**	**0.0**	**–3**	**0**	**0.0**	**16:42**	....	....	....	....	....	....	....	....	....
2008-09	**Los Angeles**	**NHL**	**82**	**2**	**12**	**14**	**111**	**0**	**0**	**0**	**76**	**2.6**	**1**	**1**	**100.0**	**19:44**	....	....	....	....	....	....	....	....	....
2009-10	**Los Angeles**	**NHL**	**75**	**2**	**7**	**9**	**83**	**0**	**0**	**1**	**57**	**3.5**	**4**	**0**	**0.0**	**17:29**	**6**	**0**	**1**	**1**	**0**	**0**	**0**	**0**	**18:45**
2010-11	**Los Angeles**	**NHL**	**71**	**2**	**9**	**11**	**70**	**0**	**0**	**1**	**50**	**4.0**	**3**	**0**	**0.0**	**16:59**	**6**	**0**	**0**	**0**	**14**	**0**	**0**	**0**	**16:44**
	NHL Totals		**379**	**7**	**40**	**47**	**469**	**0**	**0**	**2**	**273**	**2.6**		**1**	**100.0**	**17:22**	**30**	**0**	**2**	**2**	**48**	**0**	**0**	**0**	**13:08**

USHL Second All-Star Team (2002)

Traded to **Los Angeles** by **Edmonton** with Jarret Stoll for Lubomir Visnovsky, June 29, 2008.

GREENING, Colin

(GREEN-ihng, KAW-lihn) **OTT**

Center/Left wing. Shoots left. 6'3", 211 lbs. Born, St. John's, Nfld., March 9, 1986. Ottawa's 8th choice, 204th overall, in 2005 Entry Draft.

Season	Club	League	GP	G	A	Pts	PIM	PP	SH	GW	S	%	+/-	TF	F%	Min	GP	G	A	Pts	PIM	PP	SH	GW	Min
2002-03	St. John's	NFAHA	60	24	34	58	48	....	....	....	....	....	....	....	....	....	....	....	....	....	....	....	....	....	....
2003-04	Upper Canada	High-ON	53	30	43	73	40	....	....	....	....	....	....	....	....	....	....	....	....	....	....	....	....	....	....
2004-05	Upper Canada	High-ON	35	24	22	46	24	....	....	....	....	....	....	....	....	....	....	....	....	....	....	....	....	....	....
2005-06	Nanaimo Clippers	BCHL	56	27	35	62	46	....	....	....	....	....	....	....	....	....	5	3	0	3	2	....	....	....	....
2006-07	Cornell Big Red	ECAC	31	11	8	19	26	....	....	....	....	....	....	....	....	....	....	....	....	....	....	....	....	....	....
2007-08	Cornell Big Red	ECAC	36	14	19	33	41	....	....	....	....	....	....	....	....	....	....	....	....	....	....	....	....	....	....
2008-09	Cornell Big Red	ECAC	36	15	16	31	28	....	....	....	....	....	....	....	....	....	....	....	....	....	....	....	....	....	....
2009-10	Cornell Big Red	ECAC	34	15	20	35	31	....	....	....	....	....	....	....	....	....	....	....	....	....	....	....	....	....	....
2010-11	**Ottawa**	**NHL**	**24**	**6**	**7**	**13**	**10**	**0**	**0**	**2**	**57**	**10.5**	**2**	**24**	**45.8**	**15:05**	....	....	....	....	....	....	....	....	....
	Binghamton	AHL	59	15	25	40	41	....	....	....	....	....	....	....	....	....	23	1	4	5	13	....	....	....	....
	NHL Totals		**24**	**6**	**7**	**13**	**10**	**0**	**0**	**2**	**57**	**10.5**		**24**	**45.8**	**15:05**	....	....	....	....	....	....	....	....	....

ECAC Second All-Star Team (2008, 2009, 2010)

GREENTREE, Kyle

(GREEN-TREE, KIGHL) **WSH**

Left wing. Shoots left. 6'3", 215 lbs. Born, Victoria, B.C., November 15, 1983.

Season	Club	League	GP	G	A	Pts	PIM	PP	SH	GW	S	%	+/-	TF	F%	Min	GP	G	A	Pts	PIM	PP	SH	GW	Min
99-2000	Victoria Salsa	BCHL	28	7	6	13	11	....	....	....	....	....	....	....	....	....	....	....	....	....	....	....	....	....	....
2000-01	Victoria Salsa	BCHL	59	27	38	65	50	....	....	....	....	....	....	....	....	....	....	....	....	....	....	....	....	....	....
2001-02	Victoria Salsa	BCHL	57	42	43	85	125	....	....	....	....	....	....	....	....	....	....	....	....	....	....	....	....	....	....
2002-03	Victoria Salsa	BCHL	52	46	53	99	110	....	....	....	....	....	....	....	....	....	....	....	....	....	....	....	....	....	....
2003-04	Victoria Salsa	BCHL	59	62	53	115	170	....	....	....	....	....	....	....	....	....	5	4	5	9	29	....	....	....	....
2004-05	Alaska	CCHA	37	12	20	32	31	....	....	....	....	....	....	....	....	....	....	....	....	....	....	....	....	....	....
2005-06	Alaska	CCHA	39	8	19	27	58	....	....	....	....	....	....	....	....	....	....	....	....	....	....	....	....	....	....
2006-07	Alaska	CCHA	39	21	21	42	78	....	....	....	....	....	....	....	....	....	....	....	....	....	....	....	....	....	....
	Philadelphia	AHL	8	2	0	2	2	....	....	....	....	....	....	....	....	....	....	....	....	....	....	....	....	....	....
2007-08	**Philadelphia**	**NHL**	**2**	**0**	**0**	**0**	**0**	**0**	**0**	**0**	**3**	**0.0**	**–1**	**0**	**0.0**	**9:12**	....	....	....	....	....	....	....	....	....
	Philadelphia	AHL	72	24	24	48	83	....	....	....	....	....	....	....	....	....	12	1	3	4	11	....	....	....	....
2008-09	**Calgary**	**NHL**	**2**	**0**	**0**	**0**	**0**	**0**	**0**	**0**	**3**	**0.0**	**–1**	**0**	**0.0**	**9:18**	....	....	....	....	....	....	....	....	....
	Quad City Flames	AHL	79	39	37	76	63	....	....	....	....	....	....	....	....	....	....	....	....	....	....	....	....	....	....
2009-10	Rockford IceHogs	AHL	64	25	20	45	57	....	....	....	....	....	....	....	....	....	3	0	0	0	19	....	....	....	....
2010-11	Hershey Bears	AHL	74	30	33	63	110	....	....	....	....	....	....	....	....	....	6	1	1	2	4	....	....	....	....
	NHL Totals		**4**	**0**	**0**	**0**	**0**	**0**	**0**	**0**	**6**	**0.0**		**0**	**0.0**	**9:15**	....	....	....	....	....	....	....	....	....

Signed as a free agent by **Philadelphia**, March 14, 2007. Traded to **Calgary** by **Philadelphia** for Tim Ramholt, June 30, 2008. Traded to **Chicago** by **Calgary** for Aaron Johnson, October 7, 2009. Signed as a free agent by **Washington**, July 7, 2010.

GRIER, Mike

(GREER, MIGHK)

Right wing. Shoots right. 6'1", 224 lbs. Born, Detroit, MI, January 5, 1975. St. Louis' 7th choice, 219th overall, in 1993 Entry Draft.

Season	Club	League	GP	G	A	Pts	PIM	PP	SH	GW	S	%	+/-	TF	F%	Min	GP	G	A	Pts	PIM	PP	SH	GW	Min
1992-93	St. Sebastian's	High-MA	22	16	27	43	32	....	....	....	....	....	....	....	....	....	....	....	....	....	....	....	....	....	....
1993-94	Boston University	H-East	39	9	9	18	56	....	....	....	....	....	....	....	....	....	....	....	....	....	....	....	....	....	....
1994-95	Boston University	H-East	37	*29	26	55	85	....	....	....	....	....	....	....	....	....	....	....	....	....	....	....	....	....	....
1995-96	Boston University	H-East	38	21	25	46	82	....	....	....	....	....	....	....	....	....	....	....	....	....	....	....	....	....	....
1996-97	**Edmonton**	**NHL**	**79**	**15**	**17**	**32**	**45**	**4**	**0**	**2**	**89**	**16.9**	**7**	....	....	....	**12**	**3**	**1**	**4**	**4**	**1**	**0**	**1**	....
1997-98	**Edmonton**	**NHL**	**66**	**9**	**6**	**15**	**73**	**1**	**0**	**1**	**90**	**10.0**	**–3**	....	....	....	**12**	**2**	**2**	**4**	**13**	**0**	**0**	**1**	....
1998-99	**Edmonton**	**NHL**	**82**	**20**	**24**	**44**	**54**	**3**	**2**	**1**	**143**	**14.0**	**5**	**34**	**20.6**	**15:57**	**4**	**1**	**1**	**2**	**6**	**0**	**0**	**0**	**23:26**
99-2000	**Edmonton**	**NHL**	**65**	**9**	**22**	**31**	**68**	**0**	**3**	**2**	**115**	**7.8**	**9**	**32**	**46.8**	**15:45**	....	....	....	....	....	....	....	....	....
2000-01	**Edmonton**	**NHL**	**74**	**20**	**16**	**36**	**20**	**2**	**3**	**2**	**124**	**16.1**	**11**	**36**	**38.9**	**16:44**	**6**	**0**	**0**	**0**	**8**	**0**	**0**	**0**	**21:23**
2001-02	**Edmonton**	**NHL**	**82**	**8**	**17**	**25**	**32**	**0**	**2**	**3**	**112**	**7.1**	**1**	**38**	**47.4**	**15:01**	....	....	....	....	....	....	....	....	....
2002-03	**Washington**	**NHL**	**82**	**15**	**17**	**32**	**36**	**2**	**2**	**2**	**133**	**11.3**	**–14**	**98**	**43.9**	**17:48**	**6**	**1**	**1**	**2**	**2**	**0**	**0**	**0**	**17:59**

			Regular Season														Playoffs								
Season	Club	League	GP	G	A	Pts	PIM	PP	SH	GW	S	%	+/-	TF	F%	Min	GP	G	A	Pts	PIM	PP	SH	GW	Min
2003-04	Washington	NHL	68	8	12	20	32	1	1	0	115	7.0	–19	54	44.4	17:25									
	Buffalo	NHL	14	1	8	9	4	0	0	0	18	5.6	10	11	63.6	17:29									
2004-05			DID NOT PLAY																						
2005-06	Buffalo	NHL	81	7	16	23	28	0	0	4	109	6.4	–7	9	22.2	14:22	18	3	5	8	2	0	1	0	16:17
2006-07	San Jose	NHL	81	16	17	33	43	2	3	1	125	12.8	–5	46	41.3	16:26	11	2	2	4	27	0	0	0	17:16
2007-08	San Jose	NHL	78	9	13	22	24	1	3	4	132	6.8	–8	86	25.6	16:13	13	0	1	1	2	0	0	0	15:20
2008-09	San Jose	NHL	62	10	13	23	25	0	1	2	108	9.3	8	43	34.9	15:00	6	0	0	0	6	0	0	0	10:33
2009-10	Buffalo	NHL	73	10	12	22	14	0	0	2	123	8.1	–4	52	38.5	15:48	6	2	0	2	2	0	0	0	18:34
2010-11	Buffalo	NHL	73	5	11	16	12	0	0	0	107	4.7	0	31	32.3	14:24	7	0	1	1	0	0	0	0	9:29
	NHL Totals		1060	162	221	383	510	16	20	26	1643	9.9		570	37.9	15:56	101	14	14	28	72	1	1	2	16:17

Hockey East First All-Star Team (1995) • NCAA East First All-American Team (1995)

• Rights traded to **Edmonton** by **St. Louis** with Curtis Joseph for St. Louis' 1st round choices in 1996 (previously acquired, St. Louis selected Marty Reasoner) and 1997 (previously acquired, later traded to Los Angeles – Los Angeles selected Matt Zultek) Entry Drafts, August 4, 1995. Traded to **Washington** by **Edmonton** for Washington's 2nd round choice (later traded to NY Islanders – NY Islanders selected Evgeni Tunik) in 2003 Entry Draft and Vancouver's 3rd round choice (previously acquired, Edmonton selected Zachery Stortini) in 2003 Entry Draft, October 7, 2002. Traded to **Buffalo** by **Washington** for Jakub Klepis, March 9, 2004. Signed as a free agent by **San Jose**, July 3, 2006. Signed as a free agent by **Buffalo**, August 10, 2009.

GROSSMAN, Nicklas
(GROHS-man, NIHK-luhs) **DAL**

Defense. Shoots left. 6'3", 227 lbs. Born, Stockholm, Sweden, January 22, 1985. Dallas' 4th choice, 56th overall, in 2004 Entry Draft.

Season	Club	League	GP	G	A	Pts	PIM	PP	SH	GW	S	%	+/-	TF	F%	Min	GP	G	A	Pts	PIM	PP	SH	GW	Min
2002-03	Sodertalje SK Jr.	Swe-Jr.	34	1	1	2	32																		
2003-04	Sodertalje SK Jr.	Swe-Jr.	33	1	2	3	32										2	0	0	0	0				
	Sodertalje SK	Sweden	1	0	0	0	0																		
2004-05	Sodertalje SK Jr.	Swe-Jr.	12	3	6	9	8										1	0	0	0	0				
	Sodertalje SK	Sweden	31	0	2	2	14										9	0	0	0	0				
2005-06	Iowa Stars	AHL	61	2	3	5	49										7	0	1	1	4				
2006-07	Dallas	NHL	8	0	0	0	4	0	0	0	8	0.0	–1	0	0.0	12:49									
	Iowa Stars	AHL	67	2	8	10	40										8	0	0	0	10				
2007-08	Dallas	NHL	62	0	7	7	22	0	0	0	34	0.0	10	0	0.0	15:33	18	1	1	2	6	0	0	0	18:37
	Iowa Stars	AHL	10	0	0	0	10																		
2008-09	Dallas	NHL	81	2	10	12	51	0	0	1	60	3.3	–8	0	0.0	17:39									
2009-10	Dallas	NHL	71	0	7	7	32	0	0	0	58	0.0	–3	1	0.0	19:11									
2010-11	Dallas	NHL	59	1	9	10	35	0	0	0	38	2.6	7	0	0.0	18:12									
	NHL Totals		281	3	33	36	144	0	0	1	198	1.5		1	0.0	17:33	18	1	1	2	6	0	0	0	18:37

GUENIN, Nate
(GEH-nihn, NAYT) **ANA**

Defense. Shoots right. 6'2", 210 lbs. Born, Sewickley, PA, December 10, 1982. NY Rangers' 3rd choice, 127th overall, in 2002 Entry Draft.

Season	Club	League	GP	G	A	Pts	PIM	PP	SH	GW	S	%	+/-	TF	F%	Min	GP	G	A	Pts	PIM	PP	SH	GW	Min
99-2000	Pittsburgh	AAHA	40	3	10	13	122																		
2000-01	Green Bay	USHL	54	2	11	13	70										4	1	1	2	6				
2001-02	Green Bay	USHL	56	4	11	15	150										7	3	3	6	10				
2002-03	Ohio State	CCHA	42	2	9	11	85																		
2003-04	Ohio State	CCHA	29	2	15	17	92																		
2004-05	Ohio State	CCHA	41	2	12	14	136																		
2005-06	Ohio State	CCHA	39	0	11	11	87																		
2006-07	Philadelphia	NHL	9	0	2	2	4	0	0	0	0	0.0	0	0	0.0	8:40									
	Philadelphia	AHL	68	3	9	12	92																		
2007-08	Philadelphia	NHL	2	0	0	0	2	0	0	0	0	0.0	2	0	0.0	9:57									
	Philadelphia	AHL	77	4	13	17	146										12	0	1	1	18				
2008-09	Philadelphia	NHL	1	0	0	0	0	0	0	0	0	0.0	0	0	0.0	13:25									
	Philadelphia	AHL	62	0	14	14	95										4	0	0	0	10				
2009-10	Pittsburgh	NHL	2	0	0	0	0	0	0	0	1	0.0	–2	0	0.0	13:32									
	Wilkes-Barre	AHL	41	3	2	5	63																		
	Peoria Rivermen	AHL	27	2	11	13	35																		
2010-11	Columbus	NHL	3	0	0	0	2	0	0	0	2	0.0	–3	0	0.0	14:48									
	Springfield	AHL	30	0	5	5	21																		
	Syracuse Crunch	AHL	43	2	10	12	44																		
	NHL Totals		17	0	2	2	8	0	0	0	3	0.0		0	0.0	10:45									

USHL All-Rookie Team (2001) • CCHA Second All-Star Team (2005)

Signed as a free agent by **Philadelphia**, August 16, 2006. Signed as a free agent by **Pittsburgh**, July 3, 2009. Traded to **St. Louis** by **Pittsburgh** for Steve Wagner, February 11, 2010. Signed as a free agent by **Columbus**, July 2, 2010. Traded to **Anaheim** by **Columbus** for Trevor Smith, January 4, 2011.

GUITE, Ben
(GEE-tay, BEHN) **S.J.**

Right wing. Shoots right. 6'1", 210 lbs. Born, Montreal, Que., July 17, 1978. Montreal's 8th choice, 172nd overall, in 1997 Entry Draft.

Season	Club	League	GP	G	A	Pts	PIM	PP	SH	GW	S	%	+/-	TF	F%	Min	GP	G	A	Pts	PIM	PP	SH	GW	Min
1994-95	Lac St-Louis Lions	QAAA	40	9	12	21	....										4	0	0	0	0				
1995-96	Capital District	Exhib.	STATISTICS NOT AVAILABLE																						
1996-97	U. of Maine	H-East	34	7	7	14	21																		
1997-98	U. of Maine	H-East	32	6	12	18	20																		
1998-99	U. of Maine	H-East	40	12	16	28	30																		
99-2000	U. of Maine	H-East	40	22	14	36	36																		
2000-01	Tallahassee	ECHL	68	11	18	29	34																		
2001-02	Bridgeport	AHL	68	12	18	30	39																		
	Cincinnati	AHL	10	2	5	7	4										3	0	0	0	2				
2002-03	Cincinnati	AHL	80	13	16	29	44																		
2003-04	Bridgeport	AHL	79	6	18	24	73										7	0	0	0	6				
2004-05	Providence Bruins	AHL	77	9	15	24	69										17	3	4	7	34				
2005-06	Boston	NHL	1	0	0	0	0	0	0	0	2	0.0	0	11	18.2	8:53									
	Providence Bruins	AHL	73	22	30	52	87										6	1	3	4	14				
2006-07	Colorado	NHL	39	3	8	11	16	0	1	1	63	4.8	–4	388	49.5	12:17									
	Albany River Rats	AHL	36	10	19	29	22																		
2007-08	Colorado	NHL	79	11	11	22	47	0	0	2	103	10.7	1	805	48.0	13:05	10	1	0	1	14	0	1	0	12:02
2008-09	Colorado	NHL	50	5	7	12	30	0	0	1	63	7.9	2	555	51.5	12:43									
2009-10	Nashville	NHL	6	0	0	0	4	0	0	0	5	0.0	–3	34	44.1	8:30									
	Milwaukee	AHL	64	8	13	21	56										7	3	1	4	6				
2010-11	Springfield	AHL	72	17	30	47	91																		
	NHL Totals		175	19	26	45	97	0	1	4	236	8.1		1793	49.1	12:37	10	1	0	1	14	0	1	0	12:02

Signed as a free agent by **NY Islanders**, August, 2001. Traded to **Anaheim** by **NY Islanders** with the rights to Bjorn Mellin for Dave Roche, March 19, 2002. Signed as a free agent by **NY Rangers**, September 16, 2003. Signed as a free agent by **Bridgeport** (AHL), October 10, 2003. Signed to a PTO (professional tryout) contract by **Providence** (AHL), September 28, 2004. Signed as a free agent by **Boston**, August 15, 2005. Signed as a free agent by **Colorado**, July 12, 2006. Signed as a free agent by **Nashville**, July 14, 2009. Signed as a free agent by **Columbus**, August 18, 2010. Signed as a free agent by **San Jose**, July 8, 2011.

GUNNARSSON, Carl
(GUHN-nuhr-suhn, KARL) **TOR**

Defense. Shoots left. 6'2", 196 lbs. Born, Orebro, Sweden, November 9, 1986. Toronto's 6th choice, 194th overall, in 2007 Entry Draft.

Season	Club	League	GP	G	A	Pts	PIM	PP	SH	GW	S	%	+/-	TF	F%	Min	GP	G	A	Pts	PIM	PP	SH	GW	Min
2003-04	HC Orebro 90	Sweden-2	43	0	4	4	16																		
2004-05	Linkoping U18	Swe-U18	1	0	1	1	2																		
	Linkopings HC Jr.	Swe-Jr.	22	2	5	7	24																		
2005-06	Linkopings HC Jr.	Swe-Jr.	30	7	6	13	26										4	1	0	1	4				
	IFK Arboga IK	Sweden-2	12	1	5	6	8																		
	Linkopings HC	Sweden	14	0	0	0	0																		
2006-07	Linkopings HC Jr.	Swe-Jr.	6	0	5	5	6																		
	VIK Vasteras HK	Sweden-2	15	2	3	5	14																		
	Linkopings HC	Sweden	30	2	2	4	8										15	0	4	4	4				
2007-08	Linkopings HC	Sweden	53	2	7	9	26										16	0	4	4	10				
2008-09	Linkopings HC	Sweden	53	6	10	16	26										7	0	1	1	2				
2009-10	Toronto	NHL	43	3	12	15	10	0	0	0	45	6.7	8	1	0.0	21:26									
	Toronto Marlies	AHL	12	0	2	2	2																		
2010-11	Toronto	NHL	68	4	16	20	14	1	0	1	69	5.8	–2	0	0.0	18:15									
	NHL Totals		111	7	28	35	24	1	0	1	114	6.1		1	0.0	19:29									

GUSTAFSSON, Erik

(GOOS-tahf-suhn, AIR-ihk) **PHI**

Defense. Shoots left. 5'10", 180 lbs. Born, Kvissleby, Sweden, December 15, 1988.

Season	Club	League	GP	G	A	Pts	PIM	PP	SH	GW	S	%	+/-	TF	F%	Min	GP	G	A	Pts	PIM	PP	SH	GW	Min
			Regular Season														Playoffs								
2004-05	Timra IK U18	Swe-U18	14	4	2	6	12	....	....	....	....	....	....	....	....	....	3	0	0	0	0	....	....	....	....
2005-06	Timra IK U18	Swe-U18	8	2	1	3	8	....	....	....	....	....	....	....	....	....	....	....	....	....	....	....	....	....	....
	Timra IK Jr.	Swe-Jr.	38	3	4	7	26	....	....	....	....	....	....	....	....	....	1	0	0	0	0	....	....	....	....
2006-07	Timra IK Jr.	Swe-Jr.	41	7	13	20	93	....	....	....	....	....	....	....	....	....	3	0	0	0	14	....	....	....	....
2007-08	Northern Mich.	CCHA	44	0	27	27	12	....	....	....	....	....	....	....	....	....	....	....	....	....	....	....	....	....	....
2008-09	Northern Mich.	CCHA	40	4	30	34	10	....	....	....	....	....	....	....	....	....	....	....	....	....	....	....	....	....	....
2009-10	Northern Mich.	CCHA	39	3	29	32	26	....	....	....	....	....	....	....	....	....	....	....	....	....	....	....	....	....	....
	Adirondack	AHL	5	2	5	7	0	....	....	....	....	....	....	....	....	....	....	....	....	....	....	....	....	....	....
2010-11	**Philadelphia**	**NHL**	**3**	**0**	**0**	**0**	**4**	**0**	**0**	**0**	**2**	**0.0**	**–1**	**0**	**0.0**	**10:57**	....	....	....	....	....	....	....	....	....
	Adirondack	AHL	72	5	44	49	14	....	....	....	....	....	....	....	....	....	....	....	....	....	....	....	....	....	....
	NHL Totals		**3**	**0**	**0**	**0**	**4**	**0**	**0**	**0**	**2**	**0.0**		**0**	**0.0**	**10:57**	....	....	....	....	....	....	....	....	....

CCHA All-Rookie Team (2008) • CCHA First All-Star Team (2009, 2010) • NCAA West Second All-American Team (2009, 2010) • AHL All-Rookie Team (2011)

Signed as a free agent by **Philadelphia**, March 31, 2010.

HAGMAN, Niklas

(HAG-muhn, NIHK-luhs) **CGY**

Left wing. Shoots left. 6', 210 lbs. Born, Espoo, Finland, December 5, 1979. Florida's 3rd choice, 70th overall, in 1999 Entry Draft.

1995-96	HIFK Helsinki U18	Fin-U18	26	12	21	33	32	....	....	....	....	....	....	....	....	....	4	3	0	3	2	....	....	....	....
	HIFK Helsinki Jr.	Fin-Jr.	12	3	1	4	0	....	....	....	....	....	....	....	....	....	....	....	....	....	....	....	....	....	....
1996-97	HIFK Helsinki Jr.	Fin-Jr.	30	13	12	25	30	....	....	....	....	....	....	....	....	....	....	....	....	....	....	....	....	....	....
	HIFK Helsinki U18	Fin-U18	21	19	12	31	46	....	....	....	....	....	....	....	....	....	4	1	1	2	0	....	....	....	....
1997-98	HIFK Helsinki U18	Fin-U18	1	0	1	1	0	....	....	....	....	....	....	....	....	....	....	....	....	....	....	....	....	....	....
	HIFK Helsinki Jr.	Fin-Jr.	26	9	5	14	16	....	....	....	....	....	....	....	....	....	....	....	....	....	....	....	....	....	....
	HIFK Helsinki	Finland	8	1	0	1	0	....	....	....	....	....	....	....	....	....	....	....	....	....	....	....	....	....	....
1998-99	HIFK Helsinki	Finland	17	1	1	2	14	....	....	....	....	....	....	....	....	....	....	....	....	....	....	....	....	....	....
	HIFK Helsinki Jr.	Fin-Jr.	15	4	10	14	43	....	....	....	....	....	....	....	....	....	....	....	....	....	....	....	....	....	....
	HIFK Helsinki	EuroHL	1	0	1	1	0	....	....	....	....	....	....	....	....	....	....	....	....	....	....	....	....	....	....
	Blues Espoo	Finland	14	1	1	2	2	....	....	....	....	....	....	....	....	....	4	1	0	1	0	....	....	....	....
99-2000	Karpat Oulu Jr.	Fin-Jr.	4	7	3	10	0	....	....	....	....	....	....	....	....	....	....	....	....	....	....	....	....	....	....
	Karpat Oulu	Finland-2	41	17	18	35	12	....	....	....	....	....	....	....	....	....	7	4	2	6	0	....	....	....	....
2000-01	Karpat Oulu	Finland	56	28	18	46	32	....	....	....	....	....	....	....	....	....	8	3	1	4	0	....	....	....	....
2001-02	**Florida**	**NHL**	**78**	**10**	**18**	**28**	**8**	**0**	**1**	**2**	**134**	**7.5**	**–6**	**32**	**28.1**	**13:50**	....	....	....	....	....	....	....	....	....
	Finland	Olympics	4	1	2	3	0	....	....	....	....	....	....	....	....	....	....	....	....	....	....	....	....	....	....
2002-03	**Florida**	**NHL**	**80**	**8**	**15**	**23**	**20**	**2**	**0**	**0**	**132**	**6.1**	**–8**	**17**	**11.8**	**13:31**	....	....	....	....	....	....	....	....	....
2003-04	**Florida**	**NHL**	**75**	**10**	**13**	**23**	**22**	**0**	**1**	**2**	**122**	**8.2**	**–5**	**19**	**21.1**	**14:47**	....	....	....	....	....	....	....	....	....
2004-05	HC Davos	Swiss	44	17	22	39	20	....	....	....	....	....	....	....	....	....	15	10	7	17	6	....	....	....	....
2005-06	**Florida**	**NHL**	**30**	**2**	**4**	**6**	**2**	**0**	**0**	**0**	**52**	**3.8**	**–8**	**10**	**10.0**	**14:00**	....	....	....	....	....	....	....	....	....
	Dallas	**NHL**	**54**	**6**	**9**	**15**	**16**	**0**	**1**	**0**	**74**	**8.1**	**–2**	**6**	**66.7**	**11:17**	**5**	**2**	**1**	**3**	**4**	**0**	**0**	**1**	**10:50**
	Finland	Olympics	8	0	1	1	2	....	....	....	....	....	....	....	....	....	....	....	....	....	....	....	....	....	....
2006-07	**Dallas**	**NHL**	**82**	**17**	**12**	**29**	**34**	**2**	**1**	**2**	**152**	**11.2**	**3**	**15**	**20.0**	**14:26**	**7**	**0**	**1**	**1**	**10**	**0**	**0**	**0**	**16:26**
2007-08	**Dallas**	**NHL**	**82**	**27**	**14**	**41**	**51**	**4**	**4**	**8**	**178**	**15.2**	**4**	**19**	**10.5**	**15:36**	**18**	**2**	**1**	**3**	**14**	**0**	**0**	**0**	**13:25**
2008-09	**Toronto**	**NHL**	**65**	**22**	**20**	**42**	**4**	**6**	**0**	**3**	**168**	**13.1**	**–5**	**1**	**0.0**	**17:05**	....	....	....	....	....	....	....	....	....
2009-10	**Toronto**	**NHL**	**55**	**20**	**13**	**33**	**23**	**4**	**0**	**1**	**148**	**13.5**	**–3**	**31**	**32.3**	**16:09**	....	....	....	....	....	....	....	....	....
	Finland	Olympics	6	4	2	6	2	....	....	....	....	....	....	....	....	....	....	....	....	....	....	....	....	....	....
	Calgary	**NHL**	**27**	**5**	**6**	**11**	**2**	**0**	**0**	**1**	**68**	**7.4**	**–1**	**7**	**28.6**	**16:05**	....	....	....	....	....	....	....	....	....
2010-11	**Calgary**	**NHL**	**71**	**11**	**16**	**27**	**24**	**4**	**0**	**0**	**140**	**7.9**	**–2**	**25**	**12.0**	**13:38**	....	....	....	....	....	....	....	....	....
	NHL Totals		**699**	**138**	**140**	**278**	**206**	**22**	**8**	**19**	**1368**	**10.1**		**182**	**22.0**	**14:32**	**30**	**4**	**3**	**7**	**28**	**0**	**0**	**1**	**13:41**

Signed as a free agent by **Davos** (Swiss), July 23, 2004. Traded to **Dallas** by **Florida** for Dallas' 7th round choice (Sergei Gayduchenko) in 2007 Entry Draft, December 12, 2005. Signed as a free agent by **Toronto**, July 1, 2008. Traded to **Calgary** by **Toronto** with Matt Stajan, Jamal Mayers and Ian White for Dion Phaneuf, Fredrik Sjostrom and Keith Aulie, January 31, 2010.

HAINSEY, Ron

(HAYN-zee, RAWN) **WPG**

Defense. Shoots left. 6'3", 210 lbs. Born, Bolton, CT, March 24, 1981. Montreal's 1st choice, 13th overall, in 2000 Entry Draft.

1997-98	USNTDP	U-17	18	2	7	9	28	....	....	....	....	....	....	....	....	....	....	....	....	....	....	....	....	....	....
	USNTDP	USHL	3	0	0	0	0	....	....	....	....	....	....	....	....	....	....	....	....	....	....	....	....	....	....
	USNTDP	NAHL	40	4	7	11	16	....	....	....	....	....	....	....	....	....	5	0	1	1	0	....	....	....	....
1998-99	USNTDP	USHL	48	5	12	17	45	....	....	....	....	....	....	....	....	....	....	....	....	....	....	....	....	....	....
99-2000	U. Mass-Lowell	H-East	30	3	8	11	20	....	....	....	....	....	....	....	....	....	....	....	....	....	....	....	....	....	....
2000-01	U. Mass-Lowell	H-East	33	10	26	36	51	....	....	....	....	....	....	....	....	....	....	....	....	....	....	....	....	....	....
	Quebec Citadelles	AHL	4	1	0	1	0	....	....	....	....	....	....	....	....	....	1	0	0	0	0	....	....	....	....
2001-02	Quebec Citadelles	AHL	63	7	24	31	26	....	....	....	....	....	....	....	....	....	3	0	0	0	0	....	....	....	....
2002-03	**Montreal**	**NHL**	**21**	**0**	**0**	**0**	**2**	**0**	**0**	**0**	**12**	**0.0**	**–1**	**0**	**0.0**	**12:25**	....	....	....	....	....	....	....	....	....
	Hamilton	AHL	33	2	11	13	26	....	....	....	....	....	....	....	....	....	23	1	10	11	20	....	....	....	....
2003-04	**Montreal**	**NHL**	**11**	**1**	**1**	**2**	**4**	**0**	**0**	**0**	**11**	**9.1**	**3**	**0**	**0.0**	**13:15**	....	....	....	....	....	....	....	....	....
	Hamilton	AHL	54	7	24	31	35	....	....	....	....	....	....	....	....	....	10	0	5	5	6	....	....	....	....
2004-05	Hamilton	AHL	68	9	14	23	45	....	....	....	....	....	....	....	....	....	4	1	1	2	0	....	....	....	....
2005-06	Hamilton	AHL	22	3	14	17	19	....	....	....	....	....	....	....	....	....	....	....	....	....	....	....	....	....	....
	Columbus	**NHL**	**55**	**2**	**15**	**17**	**43**	**1**	**0**	**0**	**81**	**2.5**	**13**	**1**	**0.0**	**17:47**	....	....	....	....	....	....	....	....	....
2006-07	**Columbus**	**NHL**	**80**	**9**	**25**	**34**	**69**	**7**	**0**	**0**	**136**	**6.6**	**–19**	**2**	**50.0**	**22:53**	....	....	....	....	....	....	....	....	....
2007-08	**Columbus**	**NHL**	**78**	**8**	**24**	**32**	**25**	**8**	**0**	**0**	**161**	**5.0**	**–7**	**0**	**0.0**	**22:34**	....	....	....	....	....	....	....	....	....
2008-09	**Atlanta**	**NHL**	**81**	**6**	**33**	**39**	**32**	**4**	**0**	**0**	**148**	**4.1**	**–16**	**0**	**0.0**	**22:22**	....	....	....	....	....	....	....	....	....
2009-10	**Atlanta**	**NHL**	**80**	**5**	**21**	**26**	**39**	**0**	**0**	**0**	**121**	**4.1**	**–6**	**0**	**0.0**	**22:08**	....	....	....	....	....	....	....	....	....
2010-11	**Atlanta**	**NHL**	**82**	**3**	**16**	**19**	**24**	**0**	**0**	**2**	**83**	**3.6**	**3**	**0**	**0.0**	**18:05**	....	....	....	....	....	....	....	....	....
	NHL Totals		**488**	**34**	**135**	**169**	**238**	**20**	**0**	**2**	**753**	**4.5**		**3**	**33.3**	**20:35**	....	....	....	....	....	....	....	....	....

Hockey East First All-Star Team (2001) • NCAA East Second All-American Team (2001) • AHL All-Rookie Team (2002)

Claimed on waivers by **Columbus** from **Montreal**, November 29, 2005. Signed as a free agent by **Atlanta**, July 2, 2008. • Transferred to **Winnipeg** after **Atlanta** franchise relocated, June 21, 2011.

HALE, David

(HAYL, DAY-vihd)

Defense. Shoots left. 6'1", 215 lbs. Born, Colorado Springs, CO, June 18, 1981. New Jersey's 1st choice, 22nd overall, in 2000 Entry Draft.

1997-98	Colorado North	High-CO	25	11	33	44	154	....	....	....	....	....	....	....	....	....	....	....	....	....	....	....	....	....	....
1998-99	Sioux City	USHL	56	3	15	18	127	....	....	....	....	....	....	....	....	....	5	0	0	0	18	....	....	....	....
99-2000	Sioux City	USHL	54	6	18	24	187	....	....	....	....	....	....	....	....	....	5	0	2	2	6	....	....	....	....
2000-01	North Dakota	WCHA	44	4	5	9	79	....	....	....	....	....	....	....	....	....	....	....	....	....	....	....	....	....	....
2001-02	North Dakota	WCHA	34	4	5	9	63	....	....	....	....	....	....	....	....	....	....	....	....	....	....	....	....	....	....
2002-03	North Dakota	WCHA	26	2	6	8	49	....	....	....	....	....	....	....	....	....	....	....	....	....	....	....	....	....	....
2003-04	**New Jersey**	**NHL**	**65**	**0**	**4**	**4**	**72**	**0**	**0**	**0**	**45**	**0.0**	**12**	**0**	**0.0**	**15:01**	**1**	**0**	**0**	**0**	**0**	**0**	**0**	**0**	**8:59**
2004-05	Albany River Rats	AHL	30	2	3	5	39	....	....	....	....	....	....	....	....	....	....	....	....	....	....	....	....	....	....
2005-06	**New Jersey**	**NHL**	**38**	**0**	**4**	**4**	**21**	**0**	**0**	**0**	**19**	**0.0**	**5**	**0**	**0.0**	**12:03**	**8**	**0**	**2**	**2**	**12**	**0**	**0**	**0**	**12:06**
	Albany River Rats	AHL	30	2	5	7	64	....	....	....	....	....	....	....	....	....	....	....	....	....	....	....	....	....	....
2006-07	**New Jersey**	**NHL**	**43**	**0**	**1**	**1**	**26**	**0**	**0**	**0**	**21**	**0.0**	**2**	**0**	**0.0**	**9:41**	....	....	....	....	....	....	....	....	....
	Lowell Devils	AHL	2	0	1	1	0	....	....	....	....	....	....	....	....	....	....	....	....	....	....	....	....	....	....
	Calgary	**NHL**	**11**	**0**	**0**	**0**	**10**	**0**	**0**	**0**	**12**	**0.0**	**–2**	**0**	**0.0**	**15:47**	**2**	**0**	**0**	**0**	**6**	**0**	**0**	**0**	**12:42**
2007-08	**Calgary**	**NHL**	**58**	**0**	**2**	**2**	**46**	**0**	**0**	**0**	**35**	**0.0**	**0**	**0**	**0.0**	**13:53**	**6**	**0**	**0**	**0**	**2**	**0**	**0**	**0**	**12:48**
2008-09	**Phoenix**	**NHL**	**48**	**3**	**6**	**9**	**36**	**0**	**0**	**0**	**22**	**13.6**	**–11**	**0**	**0.0**	**15:08**	....	....	....	....	....	....	....	....	....
2009-10	**Tampa Bay**	**NHL**	**39**	**0**	**4**	**4**	**25**	**0**	**0**	**0**	**25**	**0.0**	**–2**	**0**	**0.0**	**14:03**	....	....	....	....	....	....	....	....	....
	Norfolk Admirals	AHL	4	1	1	2	0	....	....	....	....	....	....	....	....	....	....	....	....	....	....	....	....	....	....
2010-11	**Ottawa**	**NHL**	**25**	**1**	**4**	**5**	**6**	**0**	**0**	**1**	**20**	**5.0**	**7**	**0**	**0.0**	**16:19**	....	....	....	....	....	....	....	....	....
	Binghamton	AHL	36	2	4	6	32	....	....	....	....	....	....	....	....	....	....	....	....	....	....	....	....	....	....
	NHL Totals		**327**	**4**	**25**	**29**	**242**	**0**	**0**	**1**	**199**	**2.0**		**0**	**0.0**	**13:48**	**17**	**0**	**2**	**2**	**20**	**0**	**0**	**0**	**12:14**

USHL First All-Star Team (2000)

Traded to **Calgary** by **New Jersey** with New Jersey's 5th round choice (later traded to Buffalo - Buffalo selected Jean-Simon Allard) in 2007 Entry Draft for Calgary's 3rd round choice (Nick Palmieri) in 2007 Entry Draft, February 27, 2007. Signed as a free agent by **Phoenix**, July 3, 2008. Traded to **Tampa Bay** by **Phoenix** with Todd Fedoruk for Radim Vrbata, July 21, 2009. Signed as a free agent by **Ottawa**, August 4, 2010.

HALEY, Micheal (HAY-lee, MIGH-kuhl) NYI

Center. Shoots left. 5'10", 204 lbs. Born, Guelph, Ont., March 30, 1986.

Season	Club	League	GP	G	A	Pts	PIM	PP	SH	GW	S	%	+/-	TF	F%	Min	GP	G	A	Pts	PIM	PP	SH	GW	Min
2002-03	Sarnia Sting	OHL	43	3	3	6	32										6	0	0	0	2				
2003-04	Sarnia Sting	OHL	51	8	8	16	69																		
2004-05	Sarnia Sting	OHL	61	14	16	30	122																		
2005-06	Sarnia Sting	OHL	23	2	6	8	83																		
	St. Michael's	OHL	30	12	0	12	78										4	0	1	1	11				
2006-07	St. Michael's	OHL	68	30	24	54	174																		
	South Carolina	ECHL	7	5	1	6	13																		
2007-08	Bridgeport	AHL	36	2	2	4	75																		
	Utah Grizzlies	ECHL	28	11	8	19	115										14	7	6	13	49				
2008-09	Bridgeport	AHL	45	5	3	8	99										5	1	0	1	10				
2009-10	**NY Islanders**	**NHL**	**2**	**0**	**0**	**0**	**9**	**0**	**0**	**0**	**0**	**0.0**	**-3**	**5**	**20.0**	**7:37**									
	Bridgeport	AHL	65	6	8	14	196										3	0	0	0	4				
2010-11	**NY Islanders**	**NHL**	**27**	**2**	**1**	**3**	**85**	**0**	**0**	**0**	**13**	**15.4**	**-4**	**20**	**35.0**	**8:02**									
	Bridgeport	AHL	50	12	10	22	144																		
	NHL Totals		**29**	**2**	**1**	**3**	**94**	**0**	**0**	**0**	**13**	**15.4**		**25**	**32.0**	**8:00**									

Signed as a free agent by **NY Islanders**, May 19, 2008.

HALISCHUK, Matt (huh-LIHS-chuhk, MAT) NSH

Right wing. Shoots right. 6', 185 lbs. Born, Toronto, Ont., June 1, 1988. New Jersey's 4th choice, 117th overall, in 2007 Entry Draft.

Season	Club	League	GP	G	A	Pts	PIM	PP	SH	GW	S	%	+/-	TF	F%	Min	GP	G	A	Pts	PIM	PP	SH	GW	Min
2003-04	Tor. Jr. Canadiens	GTHL	53	37	48	85	27																		
2004-05	St. Michael's	OHL	30	3	3	6	4																		
	St. Mike's B's	OPJHL	17	5	11	16	8										32	10	15	25	4				
2005-06	St. Michael's	OHL	61	13	18	31	16										4	1	1	2	0				
2006-07	Kitchener Rangers	OHL	67	33	33	66	20										9	4	1	5	10				
2007-08	Kitchener Rangers	OHL	40	13	46	59	16										20	*16	16	32	0				
2008-09	**New Jersey**	**NHL**	**1**	**0**	**1**	**1**	**0**	**0**	**0**	**0**	**0**	**0.0**	**-1**	**0**	**0.0**	**9:47**									
	Lowell Devils	AHL	47	14	15	29	10																		
2009-10	**New Jersey**	**NHL**	**20**	**1**	**1**	**2**	**2**	**0**	**0**	**0**	**22**	**4.5**	**-4**	**4**	**25.0**	**11:18**									
	Lowell Devils	AHL	32	11	11	22	2										1	0	0	0	0				
2010-11	**Nashville**	**NHL**	**27**	**4**	**8**	**12**	**2**	**0**	**0**	**1**	**29**	**13.8**	**5**	**4**	**0.0**	**10:08**	**12**	**2**	**0**	**2**	**0**	**0**	**0**	**1**	**11:45**
	Milwaukee	AHL	37	11	12	23	12										1	1	1	2	0				
	NHL Totals		**48**	**5**	**10**	**15**	**4**	**0**	**0**	**1**	**51**	**9.8**		**8**	**12.5**	**10:37**	**12**	**2**	**0**	**2**	**0**	**0**	**0**	**1**	**11:45**

OHL First All-Star Team (2008) • George Parsons Trophy (Memorial Cup - Most Sportsmanlike Player) (2008)

Traded to **Nashville** by **New Jersey** with New Jersey's 2nd round choice (Magnus Hellberg) in 2011 Entry Draft for Jason Arnott, June 19, 2010.

HALL, Adam (HAWL, A-duhm) T.B.

Right wing. Shoots right. 6'3", 213 lbs. Born, Kalamazoo, MI, August 14, 1980. Nashville's 3rd choice, 52nd overall, in 1999 Entry Draft.

Season	Club	League	GP	G	A	Pts	PIM	PP	SH	GW	S	%	+/-	TF	F%	Min	GP	G	A	Pts	PIM	PP	SH	GW	Min
1996-97	Bramalea Blues	OPJHL	43	9	14	23	92																		
1997-98	USNTDP	U-18	29	18	9	27	19																		
	USNTDP	USHL	21	9	11	20	20																		
	USNTDP	NAHL	15	12	1	13	20										6	3	2	5	4				
1998-99	Michigan State	CCHA	36	16	7	23	74																		
99-2000	Michigan State	CCHA	40	*26	13	39	38																		
2000-01	Michigan State	CCHA	42	18	12	30	42																		
2001-02	Michigan State	CCHA	41	19	15	34	36																		
	Nashville	**NHL**	**1**	**0**	**1**	**1**	**0**	**0**	**0**	**0**	**2**	**0.0**	**0**	**0**	**0.0**	**14:04**									
	Milwaukee	AHL	6	2	2	4	4																		
2002-03	**Nashville**	**NHL**	**79**	**16**	**12**	**28**	**31**	**8**	**0**	**2**	**146**	**11.0**	**-8**	**17**	**52.9**	**14:09**									
	Milwaukee	AHL	1	0	0	0	2																		
2003-04	**Nashville**	**NHL**	**79**	**13**	**14**	**27**	**37**	**6**	**0**	**1**	**151**	**8.6**	**-8**	**348**	**56.3**	**16:14**	**6**	**2**	**1**	**3**	**2**	**0**	**0**	**1**	**18:29**
2004-05	KalPa Kuopio	Finland-2	36	23	17	40	28										9	2	3	5	4				
2005-06	**Nashville**	**NHL**	**75**	**14**	**15**	**29**	**40**	**10**	**0**	**5**	**122**	**11.5**	**0**	**470**	**48.9**	**16:47**	**5**	**1**	**0**	**1**	**0**	**1**	**0**	**1**	**12:10**
2006-07	**NY Rangers**	**NHL**	**49**	**4**	**8**	**12**	**18**	**3**	**0**	**0**	**61**	**6.6**	**-13**	**59**	**45.8**	**12:27**									
	Minnesota	**NHL**	**23**	**2**	**3**	**5**	**8**	**0**	**0**	**0**	**42**	**4.8**	**2**	**11**	**72.7**	**12:13**	**3**	**0**	**0**	**0**	**7**	**0**	**0**	**0**	**10:06**
2007-08	**Pittsburgh**	**NHL**	**46**	**2**	**4**	**6**	**24**	**0**	**0**	**0**	**39**	**5.1**	**-2**	**290**	**50.3**	**11:52**	**17**	**3**	**1**	**4**	**8**	**0**	**0**	**1**	**10:59**
2008-09	**Tampa Bay**	**NHL**	**74**	**5**	**5**	**10**	**29**	**1**	**0**	**0**	**90**	**5.6**	**-9**	**338**	**50.0**	**11:12**									
2009-10	Norfolk Admirals	AHL	79	16	25	41	47																		
2010-11	**Tampa Bay**	**NHL**	**82**	**7**	**11**	**18**	**32**	**0**	**0**	**1**	**167**	**4.2**	**-12**	**655**	**55.0**	**14:51**	**18**	**1**	**4**	**5**	**8**	**0**	**0**	**0**	**13:53**
	NHL Totals		**508**	**63**	**73**	**136**	**219**	**28**	**0**	**9**	**820**	**7.7**		**2188**	**52.3**	**14:05**	**49**	**7**	**6**	**13**	**25**	**1**	**0**	**3**	**13:02**

CCHA Second All-Star Team (2000)

Signed as a free agent by **Kuopio** (Finland-2), October 11, 2004. Traded to **NY Rangers** by **Nashville** for Dominic Moore, July 19, 2006. Traded to **Minnesota** by **NY Rangers** for Pascal Dupuis, February 9, 2007. Signed as a free agent by **Pittsburgh**, October 1, 2007. Signed as a free agent by **Tampa Bay**, July 1, 2008.

HALL, Taylor (HAWL, TAY-luhr) EDM

Left wing. Shoots left. 6'1", 194 lbs. Born, Calgary, Alta., November 14, 1991. Edmonton's 1st choice, 1st overall, in 2010 Entry Draft.

Season	Club	League	GP	G	A	Pts	PIM	PP	SH	GW	S	%	+/-	TF	F%	Min	GP	G	A	Pts	PIM	PP	SH	GW	Min
2006-07	King. Jr. Front.	Minor-ON	29	44	41	85	10																		
2007-08	Windsor Spitfires	OHL	63	45	39	84	22										5	2	3	5	2				
2008-09	Windsor Spitfires	OHL	63	38	52	90	60										20	*16	20	*36	12				
2009-10	Windsor Spitfires	OHL	57	40	*66	*106	56										19	17	18	*35	32				
2010-11	**Edmonton**	**NHL**	**65**	**22**	**20**	**42**	**27**	**8**	**0**	**4**	**186**	**11.8**	**-9**	**105**	**40.0**	**18:13**									
	NHL Totals		**65**	**22**	**20**	**42**	**27**	**8**	**0**	**4**	**186**	**11.8**		**105**	**40.0**	**18:13**									

Canadian Major Junior All-Rookie Team (2008) • Canadian Major Junior Rookie of the Year (2008) • OHL First All-Star Team (2009, 2010) • Canadian Major Junior Second All-Star Team (2010) • Memorial Cup All-Star Team (2009, 2010) • Ed Chynoweth Trophy (Memorial Cup - Leading Scorer) (2010) • Stafford Smythe Memorial Trophy (Memorial Cup - MVP) (2009, 2010)

HALPERN, Jeff (HAL-pehrn, JEHF) WSH

Center. Shoots right. 5'11", 198 lbs. Born, Potomac, MD, May 3, 1976.

Season	Club	League	GP	G	A	Pts	PIM	PP	SH	GW	S	%	+/-	TF	F%	Min	GP	G	A	Pts	PIM	PP	SH	GW	Min
1994-95	Stratford Cullitons	ON-Jr.B	44	29	54	83	43																		
1995-96	Princeton	ECAC	29	3	11	14	30																		
1996-97	Princeton	ECAC	33	7	24	31	35																		
1997-98	Princeton	ECAC	36	*28	25	*53	46																		
1998-99	Princeton	ECAC	33	*22	22	44	32																		
	Portland Pirates	AHL	6	2	1	3	4																		
99-2000	**Washington**	**NHL**	**79**	**18**	**11**	**29**	**39**	**4**	**4**	**1**	**108**	**16.7**	**21**	**812**	**51.1**	**13:14**	**5**	**2**	**1**	**3**	**0**	**1**	**0**	**1**	**15:16**
2000-01	**Washington**	**NHL**	**80**	**21**	**21**	**42**	**60**	**2**	**1**	**5**	**110**	**19.1**	**13**	**1293**	**52.4**	**16:08**	**6**	**2**	**3**	**5**	**17**	**1**	**0**	**1**	**20:02**
2001-02	**Washington**	**NHL**	**48**	**5**	**14**	**19**	**29**	**0**	**0**	**4**	**74**	**6.8**	**-9**	**661**	**56.0**	**15:19**									
2002-03	**Washington**	**NHL**	**82**	**13**	**21**	**34**	**88**	**1**	**2**	**2**	**126**	**10.3**	**6**	**1492**	**54.1**	**17:25**	**6**	**0**	**1**	**1**	**2**	**0**	**0**	**0**	**19:59**
2003-04	**Washington**	**NHL**	**79**	**19**	**27**	**46**	**56**	**7**	**0**	**2**	**114**	**16.7**	**-21**	**1509**	**54.3**	**19:03**									
2004-05	HC Ajoie	Swiss-2	15	5	12	17	52																		
	Kloten Flyers	Swiss	9	7	4	11	6																		
2005-06	**Washington**	**NHL**	**70**	**11**	**33**	**44**	**79**	**6**	**0**	**1**	**151**	**7.3**	**-8**	**1454**	**55.2**	**20:00**									
2006-07	**Dallas**	**NHL**	**76**	**8**	**17**	**25**	**78**	**1**	**0**	**4**	**106**	**7.5**	**-7**	**1135**	**51.8**	**16:48**	**7**	**2**	**1**	**3**	**4**	**0**	**0**	**1**	**18:57**
2007-08	**Dallas**	**NHL**	**64**	**10**	**14**	**24**	**40**	**1**	**1**	**0**	**86**	**11.6**	**-2**	**548**	**54.0**	**16:21**									
	Tampa Bay	**NHL**	**19**	**10**	**8**	**18**	**14**	**3**	**0**	**2**	**46**	**21.7**	**2**	**185**	**46.0**	**18:12**									
2008-09	**Tampa Bay**	**NHL**	**52**	**7**	**9**	**16**	**32**	**1**	**1**	**1**	**60**	**11.7**	**-13**	**822**	**52.8**	**17:01**									

Season	Club	League	GP	G	A	Pts	PIM	PP	SH	GW	S	%	+/-	TF	F%	Min	GP	G	A	Pts	PIM	PP	SH	GW	Min
			Regular Season														Playoffs								
2009-10	**Tampa Bay**	**NHL**	**55**	**9**	**8**	**17**	**27**	**2**	**0**	**1**	**65**	**13.8**	**–13**	**479**	**52.0**	**15:39**	....	....	....	....	....	....	....	....	....
	Los Angeles	**NHL**	**16**	**0**	**2**	**2**	**12**	**0**	**0**	**0**	**6**	**0.0**	**–1**	**91**	**49.5**	**10:41**	**6**	**0**	**0**	**0**	**4**	**0**	**0**	**0**	**10:12**
2010-11	**Montreal**	**NHL**	**72**	**11**	**15**	**26**	**29**	**0**	**1**	**3**	**62**	**17.7**	**6**	**594**	**56.9**	**12:44**	**4**	**1**	**0**	**1**	**0**	**0**	**0**	**0**	**17:46**
	NHL Totals		**792**	**142**	**200**	**342**	**583**	**28**	**10**	**26**	**1114**	**12.7**		**11075**	**53.5**	**16:18**	**34**	**7**	**6**	**13**	**27**	**2**	**0**	**3**	**17:06**

ECAC Second All-Star Team (1998, 1999)

Signed as a free agent by **Washington**, March 29, 1999. Signed as a free agent by **Ajoie** (Swiss-2), October 8, 2004. Signed as a free agent by **Kloten** (Swiss), December 30, 2004. Signed as a free agent by **Dallas**, July 5, 2006. Traded to **Tampa Bay** by **Dallas** with Jussi Jokinen, Mike Smith and Dallas' 4th round choice (later traded to Minnesota, later traded to Edmonton – Edmonton selected Kyle Bigos) in 2009 Entry Draft for Brad Richards and Johan Holmqvist, February 26, 2008. Traded to **Los Angeles** by **Tampa Bay** for Teddy Purcell and Florida's 3rd round choice (previously acquired, Tampa Bay selected Brock Beukeboom) in 2010 Entry Draft, March 3, 2010. Signed as a free agent by **Montreal**, September 7, 2010. Signed as a free agent by **Washington**, July 1, 2011.

HAMEL, Denis

(ha-MEHL, deh-NEE)

Left wing. Shoots left. 6'1", 201 lbs. Born, Lachute, Que., May 10, 1977. St. Louis' 5th choice, 153rd overall, in 1995 Entry Draft.

Season	Club	League	GP	G	A	Pts	PIM	PP	SH	GW	S	%	+/-	TF	F%	Min	GP	G	A	Pts	PIM	PP	SH	GW	Min
1992-93	Lachute Regents	QAAA	32	18	24	42	....	....	....	....	....	....	....	....	....	....	....	....	....	....	....	....	....	....	....
1993-94	Lac St-Louis Lions	QAAA	28	10	11	21	50	....	....	....	....	....	....	....	....	....	....	....	....	....	....	....	....	....	....
	Abitibi Forestiers	QAAA	15	5	7	12	29	....	....	....	....	....	....	....	....	....	5	0	3	3	16	....	....	....	....
1994-95	Chicoutimi	QMJHL	66	15	12	27	155	....	....	....	....	....	....	....	....	....	13	2	0	2	29	....	....	....	....
1995-96	Chicoutimi	QMJHL	65	40	49	89	199	....	....	....	....	....	....	....	....	....	17	10	14	24	64	....	....	....	....
1996-97	Chicoutimi	QMJHL	70	50	50	100	339	....	....	....	....	....	....	....	....	....	20	15	10	25	65	....	....	....	....
1997-98	Rochester	AHL	74	10	15	25	98	....	....	....	....	....	....	....	....	....	4	1	2	3	0	....	....	....	....
1998-99	Rochester	AHL	74	16	17	33	121	....	....	....	....	....	....	....	....	....	20	3	4	7	10	....	....	....	....
99-2000	**Buffalo**	**NHL**	**3**	**1**	**0**	**1**	**0**	**0**	**0**	**0**	**3**	**33.3**	**–1**	**0**	**0.0**	**9:45**	....	....	....	....	....	....	....	....	....
	Rochester	AHL	76	34	24	58	122	....	....	....	....	....	....	....	....	....	21	6	7	13	49	....	....	....	....
2000-01	**Buffalo**	**NHL**	**41**	**8**	**3**	**11**	**22**	**1**	**1**	**3**	**55**	**14.5**	**–2**	**171**	**33.9**	**10:58**	....	....	....	....	....	....	....	....	....
2001-02	**Buffalo**	**NHL**	**61**	**2**	**6**	**8**	**28**	**0**	**0**	**0**	**80**	**2.5**	**–1**	**94**	**39.4**	**11:00**	....	....	....	....	....	....	....	....	....
2002-03	**Buffalo**	**NHL**	**25**	**2**	**0**	**2**	**17**	**0**	**0**	**1**	**41**	**4.9**	**–4**	**4**	**25.0**	**12:40**	....	....	....	....	....	....	....	....	....
	Rochester	AHL	48	27	20	47	64	....	....	....	....	....	....	....	....	....	3	3	2	5	4	....	....	....	....
2003-04	**Ottawa**	**NHL**	**5**	**0**	**0**	**0**	**0**	**0**	**0**	**0**	**6**	**0.0**	**–3**	**1**	**100.0**	**6:16**	....	....	....	....	....	....	....	....	....
	Binghamton	AHL	78	29	38	67	116	....	....	....	....	....	....	....	....	....	2	0	0	0	2	....	....	....	....
2004-05	Binghamton	AHL	80	39	39	78	75	....	....	....	....	....	....	....	....	....	5	1	0	1	4	....	....	....	....
2005-06	**Ottawa**	**NHL**	**4**	**1**	**0**	**1**	**0**	**0**	**0**	**0**	**9**	**11.1**	**1**	**1**	**0.0**	**9:10**	....	....	....	....	....	....	....	....	....
	Binghamton	AHL	77	*56	35	91	65	....	....	....	....	....	....	....	....	....	....	....	....	....	....	....	....	....	....
2006-07	**Ottawa**	**NHL**	**43**	**4**	**3**	**7**	**10**	**0**	**0**	**0**	**36**	**11.1**	**4**	**9**	**33.3**	**5:38**	....	....	....	....	....	....	....	....	....
	Atlanta	**NHL**	**3**	**1**	**0**	**1**	**0**	**0**	**0**	**0**	**3**	**33.3**	**0**	**2**	**0.0**	**10:25**	....	....	....	....	....	....	....	....	....
	Philadelphia	**NHL**	**7**	**0**	**0**	**0**	**0**	**0**	**0**	**0**	**3**	**0.0**	**–4**	**0**	**0.0**	**6:58**	....	....	....	....	....	....	....	....	....
2007-08	Binghamton	AHL	67	32	23	55	60	....	....	....	....	....	....	....	....	....	....	....	....	....	....	....	....	....	....
2008-09	Binghamton	AHL	63	25	25	50	36	....	....	....	....	....	....	....	....	....	....	....	....	....	....	....	....	....	....
2009-10	Binghamton	AHL	73	22	29	51	45	....	....	....	....	....	....	....	....	....	....	....	....	....	....	....	....	....	....
2010-11	Adirondack	AHL	66	25	25	50	50	....	....	....	....	....	....	....	....	....	....	....	....	....	....	....	....	....	....
	NHL Totals		**192**	**19**	**12**	**31**	**77**	**1**	**1**	**4**	**236**	**8.1**		**282**	**35.5**	**9:40**	....	....	....	....	....	....	....	....	....

QMJHL All-Rookie Team (1995) • AHL First All-Star Team (2004) • Willie Marshall Award (AHL - Top Goal-scorer) (2006) (tied with Don MacLean) • Yanick Dupre Memorial Award (AHL - Outstanding Humanitarian Contribution) (2008)

Traded to **Buffalo** by **St. Louis** for Charlie Huddy and Buffalo's 7th round choice (Daniel Corso) in 1996 Entry Draft, March 19, 1996. • Missed majority of 2000-01 due to knee injury vs. NY Islanders, January 27, 2001. Signed as a free agent by **Ottawa**, July 5, 2003. Claimed by **Washington** from **Ottawa** in Waiver Draft, October 3, 2003. Traded to **Ottawa** by **Washington** for future considerations, October 5, 2003. Claimed on waivers by **Atlanta** from **Ottawa**, February 10, 2007. Claimed on waivers by **Philadelphia** from **Atlanta**, February 27, 2007. Signed as a free agent by **Ottawa**, July 6, 2007. Signed to a PTO (professional tryout) contract by **Adirondack** (AHL), November 1, 2010.

HAMHUIS, Dan

(HAM-HOOS, DAN) **VAN**

Defense. Shoots left. 6', 209 lbs. Born, Smithers, B.C., December 13, 1982. Nashville's 1st choice, 12th overall, in 2001 Entry Draft.

Season	Club	League	GP	G	A	Pts	PIM	PP	SH	GW	S	%	+/-	TF	F%	Min	GP	G	A	Pts	PIM	PP	SH	GW	Min
1997-98	Smithers A's	Minor-BC	59	59	72	131	59	....	....	....	....	....	....	....	....	....	....	....	....	....	....	....	....	....	....
1998-99	Prince George	WHL	56	1	3	4	45	....	....	....	....	....	....	....	....	....	7	1	2	3	8	....	....	....	....
99-2000	Prince George	WHL	70	10	23	33	140	....	....	....	....	....	....	....	....	....	13	2	3	5	35	....	....	....	....
2000-01	Prince George	WHL	62	13	47	60	125	....	....	....	....	....	....	....	....	....	6	2	3	5	15	....	....	....	....
2001-02	Prince George	WHL	59	10	50	60	135	....	....	....	....	....	....	....	....	....	7	0	5	5	16	....	....	....	....
2002-03	Milwaukee	AHL	68	6	21	27	81	....	....	....	....	....	....	....	....	....	6	0	3	3	2	....	....	....	....
2003-04	**Nashville**	**NHL**	**80**	**7**	**19**	**26**	**57**	**2**	**0**	**4**	**115**	**6.1**	**–12**	**0**	**0.0**	**22:08**	**6**	**0**	**2**	**2**	**6**	**0**	**0**	**0**	**20:29**
2004-05	Milwaukee	AHL	76	13	38	51	85	....	....	....	....	....	....	....	....	....	7	0	2	2	10	....	....	....	....
2005-06	**Nashville**	**NHL**	**82**	**7**	**31**	**38**	**70**	**4**	**1**	**1**	**135**	**5.2**	**11**	**0**	**0.0**	**22:34**	**5**	**0**	**2**	**2**	**2**	**0**	**0**	**0**	**19:41**
2006-07	**Nashville**	**NHL**	**81**	**6**	**14**	**20**	**66**	**0**	**0**	**1**	**84**	**7.1**	**8**	**1**	**0.0**	**21:20**	**5**	**0**	**1**	**1**	**2**	**0**	**0**	**0**	**21:36**
2007-08	**Nashville**	**NHL**	**80**	**4**	**23**	**27**	**66**	**1**	**0**	**1**	**127**	**3.1**	**–4**	**0**	**0.0**	**22:44**	**6**	**1**	**1**	**2**	**6**	**1**	**0**	**0**	**22:47**
2008-09	**Nashville**	**NHL**	**82**	**3**	**23**	**26**	**67**	**1**	**1**	**1**	**135**	**2.2**	**–4**	**0**	**0.0**	**22:50**	....	....	....	....	....	....	....	....	....
2009-10	**Nashville**	**NHL**	**78**	**5**	**19**	**24**	**49**	**0**	**0**	**0**	**115**	**4.3**	**4**	**0**	**0.0**	**21:15**	**6**	**0**	**2**	**2**	**2**	**0**	**0**	**0**	**22:25**
2010-11	**Vancouver**	**NHL**	**64**	**6**	**17**	**23**	**34**	**2**	**0**	**1**	**109**	**5.5**	**29**	**0**	**0.0**	**22:41**	**19**	**1**	**5**	**6**	**6**	**1**	**0**	**0**	**24:50**
	NHL Totals		**547**	**38**	**146**	**184**	**409**	**10**	**2**	**9**	**820**	**4.6**		**1**	**0.0**	**22:13**	**47**	**2**	**13**	**15**	**24**	**2**	**0**	**0**	**22:49**

WHL West First All-Star Team (2001, 2002) • WHL Player of the Year (2002) • Canadian Major Junior First All-Star Team (2002) • Canadian Major Junior Defenseman of the Year (2002) • AHL Second All-Star Team (2005)

Traded to **Philadelphia** by **Nashville** for Ryan Parent and future considerations, June 19, 2010. Traded to **Pittsburgh** by **Philadelphia** for Pittsburgh's 3rd round choice (later traded to Phoenix – Phoenix selected Harrison Ruopp) in 2011 Entry Draft, June 25, 2010. Signed as a free agent by **Vancouver**, July 1, 2010.

HAMILL, Zach

(HA-mihl, ZAK) **BOS**

Center. Shoots right. 5'11", 180 lbs. Born, Vancouver, B.C., September 23, 1988. Boston's 1st choice, 8th overall, in 2007 Entry Draft.

Season	Club	League	GP	G	A	Pts	PIM	PP	SH	GW	S	%	+/-	TF	F%	Min	GP	G	A	Pts	PIM	PP	SH	GW	Min
2002-03	Port Coquitlam	Minor-BC	61	120	83	203	....	....	....	....	....	....	....	....	....	....	....	....	....	....	....	....	....	....	....
2003-04	Port Coquitlam	PIJHL	39	30	31	51	50	....	....	....	....	....	....	....	....	....	....	....	....	....	....	....	....	....	....
	Everett Silvertips	WHL	4	0	2	2	0	....	....	....	....	....	....	....	....	....	20	3	2	5	2	....	....	....	....
2004-05	Everett Silvertips	WHL	57	8	25	33	29	....	....	....	....	....	....	....	....	....	11	2	3	5	8	....	....	....	....
2005-06	Everett Silvertips	WHL	53	21	38	59	28	....	....	....	....	....	....	....	....	....	15	3	11	14	4	....	....	....	....
2006-07	Everett Silvertips	WHL	69	32	*61	*93	90	....	....	....	....	....	....	....	....	....	12	2	8	10	16	....	....	....	....
2007-08	Everett Silvertips	WHL	67	26	49	75	88	....	....	....	....	....	....	....	....	....	4	0	3	3	2	....	....	....	....
	Providence Bruins	AHL	7	0	5	5	6	....	....	....	....	....	....	....	....	....	9	1	3	4	0	....	....	....	....
2008-09	Providence Bruins	AHL	65	13	13	26	40	....	....	....	....	....	....	....	....	....	16	1	5	6	4	....	....	....	....
2009-10	**Boston**	**NHL**	**1**	**0**	**1**	**1**	**0**	**0**	**0**	**0**	**1**	**0.0**	**1**	**4**	**25.0**	**12:08**	....	....	....	....	....	....	....	....	....
	Providence Bruins	AHL	75	14	30	44	24	....	....	....	....	....	....	....	....	....	....	....	....	....	....	....	....	....	....
2010-11	**Boston**	**NHL**	**3**	**0**	**1**	**1**	**0**	**0**	**0**	**0**	**1**	**0.0**	**1**	**16**	**31.3**	**10:28**	....	....	....	....	....	....	....	....	....
	Providence Bruins	AHL	68	9	34	43	66	....	....	....	....	....	....	....	....	....	....	....	....	....	....	....	....	....	....
	NHL Totals		**4**	**0**	**2**	**2**	**0**	**0**	**0**	**0**	**2**	**0.0**		**20**	**30.0**	**10:53**	....	....	....	....	....	....	....	....	....

WHL West First All-Star Team (2007) • Canadian Major Junior First All-Star Team (2007)

HAMONIC, Travis

(HA-mohn-ihk, TRA-vihs) **NYI**

Defense. Shoots right. 6'2", 208 lbs. Born, Winnipeg, Man., August 16, 1990. NY Islanders' 4th choice, 53rd overall, in 2008 Entry Draft.

Season	Club	League	GP	G	A	Pts	PIM	PP	SH	GW	S	%	+/-	TF	F%	Min	GP	G	A	Pts	PIM	PP	SH	GW	Min
2006-07	Winnipeg Saints	MJHL	....	2	13	15	....	....	....	....	....	....	....	....	....	....	....	....	....	....	....	....	....	....	....
	Moose Jaw	WHL	22	0	3	3	30	....	....	....	....	....	....	....	....	....	....	....	....	....	....	....	....	....	....
2007-08	Moose Jaw	WHL	61	5	17	22	101	....	....	....	....	....	....	....	....	....	6	0	1	1	6	....	....	....	....
2008-09	Moose Jaw	WHL	57	13	27	40	126	....	....	....	....	....	....	....	....	....	....	....	....	....	....	....	....	....	....
2009-10	Moose Jaw	WHL	31	10	29	39	48	....	....	....	....	....	....	....	....	....	....	....	....	....	....	....	....	....	....
	Brandon	WHL	10	1	4	5	17	....	....	....	....	....	....	....	....	....	15	4	7	11	23	....	....	....	....
	Brandon	M-Cup	....	....	....	....	....	....	....	....	....	....	....	....	....	....	5	1	2	3	11	....	....	....	....
2010-11	**NY Islanders**	**NHL**	**62**	**5**	**21**	**26**	**103**	**1**	**0**	**0**	**118**	**4.2**	**4**	**0**	**0.0**	**21:34**	....	....	....	....	....	....	....	....	....
	Bridgeport	AHL	19	2	5	7	45	....	....	....	....	....	....	....	....	....	....	....	....	....	....	....	....	....	....
	NHL Totals		**62**	**5**	**21**	**26**	**103**	**1**	**0**	**0**	**118**	**4.2**		**0**	**0.0**	**21:34**	....	....	....	....	....	....	....	....	....

WHL East Second All-Star Team (2010) • Memorial Cup All-Star Team (2010)

HAMRLIK, Roman
(HAHM-reh-lik, ROH-muhn) **WSH**

Defense. Shoots left. 6'2", 207 lbs. Born, Zlin, Czech., April 12, 1974. Tampa Bay's 1st choice, 1st overall, in 1992 Entry Draft.

			Regular Season														Playoffs								
Season	Club	League	GP	G	A	Pts	PIM	PP	SH	GW	S	%	+/-	TF	F%	Min	GP	G	A	Pts	PIM	PP	SH	GW	Min
1990-91	AC ZPS Zlin	Czech	14	2	2	4	18	....	....	....	....	....	....	....	....	....	....	....	....	....	....	....	....	....	....
1991-92	AC ZPS Zlin	Czech	34	5	5	10	50	....	....	....	....	....	....	....	....	....	....	....	....	....	....	....	....	....	....
1992-93	**Tampa Bay**	**NHL**	**67**	**6**	**15**	**21**	**71**	**1**	**0**	**1**	**113**	**5.3**	**-21**	....	....	....	....	....	....	....	....	....	....	....	....
	Atlanta Knights	IHL	2	1	1	2	2	....	....	....	....	....	....	....	....	....	....	....	....	....	....	....	....	....	....
1993-94	**Tampa Bay**	**NHL**	**64**	**3**	**18**	**21**	**135**	**0**	**0**	**0**	**158**	**1.9**	**-14**	....	....	....	....	....	....	....	....	....	....	....	....
1994-95	AC ZPS Zlin	CzRep	2	1	0	1	10	....	....	....	....	....	....	....	....	....	....	....	....	....	....	....	....	....	....
	Tampa Bay	**NHL**	**48**	**12**	**11**	**23**	**86**	**7**	**1**	**2**	**134**	**9.0**	**-18**	....	....	....	....	....	....	....	....	....	....	....	....
1995-96	**Tampa Bay**	**NHL**	**82**	**16**	**49**	**65**	**103**	**12**	**0**	**2**	**281**	**5.7**	**-24**	....	....	....	**5**	**0**	**1**	**1**	**4**	**0**	**0**	**0**	....
1996-97	**Tampa Bay**	**NHL**	**79**	**12**	**28**	**40**	**57**	**6**	**0**	**0**	**238**	**5.0**	**-29**	....	....	....	....	....	....	....	....	....	....	....	....
1997-98	**Tampa Bay**	**NHL**	**37**	**3**	**12**	**15**	**22**	**1**	**0**	**0**	**86**	**3.5**	**-18**	....	....	....	....	....	....	....	....	....	....	....	....
	Edmonton	**NHL**	**41**	**6**	**20**	**26**	**48**	**4**	**1**	**3**	**112**	**5.4**	**3**	....	....	....	**12**	**0**	**6**	**6**	**12**	**0**	**0**	**0**	....
	Czech Republic	Olympics	6	1	0	1	2	....	....	....	....	....	....	....	....	....	....	....	....	....	....	....	....	....	....
1998-99	**Edmonton**	**NHL**	**75**	**8**	**24**	**32**	**70**	**3**	**0**	**0**	**172**	**4.7**	**9**	**0**	**0.0**	**23:49**	**3**	**0**	**0**	**0**	**2**	**0**	**0**	**0**	**16:23**
99-2000	Zlin	CzRep	6	0	3	3	4	....	....	....	....	....	....	....	....	....	....	....	....	....	....	....	....	....	....
	Edmonton	**NHL**	**80**	**8**	**37**	**45**	**68**	**5**	**0**	**0**	**180**	**4.4**	**1**	**0**	**0.0**	**25:18**	**5**	**0**	**1**	**1**	**4**	**0**	**0**	**0**	**24:44**
2000-01	**NY Islanders**	**NHL**	**76**	**16**	**30**	**46**	**92**	**5**	**1**	**4**	**232**	**6.9**	**-20**	**1**	**100.0**	**25:12**	....	....	....	....	....	....	....	....	....
2001-02	**NY Islanders**	**NHL**	**70**	**11**	**26**	**37**	**78**	**4**	**1**	**1**	**169**	**6.5**	**7**	**1**	**0.0**	**25:32**	**7**	**1**	**6**	**7**	**6**	**0**	**0**	**0**	**29:09**
	Czech Republic	Olympics	4	0	1	1	2	....	....	....	....	....	....	....	....	....	....	....	....	....	....	....	....	....	....
2002-03	**NY Islanders**	**NHL**	**73**	**9**	**32**	**41**	**87**	**3**	**0**	**2**	**151**	**6.0**	**21**	**0**	**0.0**	**26:34**	**5**	**0**	**2**	**2**	**2**	**0**	**0**	**0**	**29:24**
2003-04	**NY Islanders**	**NHL**	**81**	**7**	**22**	**29**	**68**	**2**	**0**	**2**	**182**	**3.8**	**2**	**0**	**0.0**	**24:35**	**5**	**0**	**1**	**1**	**2**	**0**	**0**	**0**	**25:30**
2004-05	HC Hame Zlin	CzRep	45	2	14	16	70	....	....	....	....	....	....	....	....	....	17	1	3	4	24	....	....	....	....
2005-06	**Calgary**	**NHL**	**51**	**7**	**19**	**26**	**56**	**1**	**1**	**0**	**89**	**7.9**	**8**	**0**	**0.0**	**21:51**	**7**	**0**	**2**	**2**	**2**	**0**	**0**	**0**	**19:44**
2006-07	**Calgary**	**NHL**	**75**	**7**	**31**	**38**	**88**	**1**	**0**	**1**	**125**	**5.6**	**22**	**0**	**0.0**	**24:52**	**6**	**0**	**1**	**1**	**8**	**0**	**0**	**0**	**26:53**
2007-08	**Montreal**	**NHL**	**77**	**5**	**21**	**26**	**38**	**3**	**0**	**3**	**129**	**3.9**	**7**	**0**	**0.0**	**23:08**	**12**	**1**	**2**	**3**	**8**	**0**	**0**	**0**	**22:55**
2008-09	**Montreal**	**NHL**	**81**	**6**	**27**	**33**	**62**	**0**	**0**	**0**	**143**	**4.2**	**4**	**0**	**0.0**	**21:55**	**4**	**0**	**0**	**0**	**2**	**0**	**0**	**0**	**25:19**
2009-10	**Montreal**	**NHL**	**75**	**6**	**20**	**26**	**56**	**2**	**0**	**1**	**100**	**6.0**	**-2**	**0**	**0.0**	**23:26**	**19**	**0**	**9**	**9**	**15**	**0**	**0**	**0**	**20:08**
2010-11	**Montreal**	**NHL**	**79**	**5**	**29**	**34**	**81**	**2**	**0**	**0**	**129**	**3.9**	**6**	**0**	**0.0**	**22:17**	**7**	**0**	**3**	**3**	**6**	**0**	**0**	**0**	**23:20**
	NHL Totals		**1311**	**153**	**471**	**624**	**1366**	**62**	**5**	**22**	**2923**	**5.2**		**2**	**50.0**	**24:04**	**97**	**2**	**34**	**36**	**73**	**0**	**0**	**0**	**23:25**

Played in NHL All-Star Game (1996, 1999, 2003)

Traded to **Edmonton** by **Tampa Bay** with Paul Comrie for Bryan Marchment, Steve Kelly and Jason Bonsignore, December 30, 1997. Traded to **NY Islanders** by **Edmonton** for Eric Brewer, Josh Green and NY Islanders' 2nd round choice (Brad Winchester) in 2000 Entry Draft, June 24, 2000. Signed as a free agent by **Zlin** (CzRep), August 4, 2004. Signed as a free agent by **Calgary**, August 14, 2005 Signed as a free agent by **Montreal**, July 2, 2007. Signed as a free agent by **Washington**, July 1, 2011.

HANDZUS, Michal
(HAHND-zoos, MIGH-kuhl) **S.J.**

Center. Shoots left. 6'4", 220 lbs. Born, Banska Bystrica, Czech., March 11, 1977. St. Louis' 3rd choice, 101st overall, in 1995 Entry Draft.

			Regular Season														Playoffs								
Season	Club	League	GP	G	A	Pts	PIM	PP	SH	GW	S	%	+/-	TF	F%	Min	GP	G	A	Pts	PIM	PP	SH	GW	Min
1993-94	B. Bystrica Jr.	Slovak-Jr.	40	23	36	59		....	....	....	....	....	....	....	....	....	....	....	....	....	....	....	....	....	....
1994-95	B. Bystrica	Slovak-2	22	15	14	29	10	....	....	....	....	....	....	....	....	....	....	....	....	....	....	....	....	....	....
1995-96	B. Bystrica	Slovakia	19	3	1	4	8	....	....	....	....	....	....	....	....	....	....	....	....	....	....	....	....	....	....
1996-97	HC SKP PS Poprad	Slovakia	44	15	18	33		....	....	....	....	....	....	....	....	....	....	....	....	....	....	....	....	....	....
1997-98	Worcester IceCats	AHL	69	27	36	63	54	....	....	....	....	....	....	....	....	....	11	2	6	8	10	....	....	....	....
1998-99	**St. Louis**	**NHL**	**66**	**4**	**12**	**16**	**30**	**0**	**0**	**0**	**78**	**5.1**	**-9**	**794**	**49.9**	**14:48**	**11**	**0**	**2**	**2**	**8**	**0**	**0**	**0**	**16:52**
99-2000	**St. Louis**	**NHL**	**81**	**25**	**28**	**53**	**44**	**3**	**4**	**5**	**166**	**15.1**	**19**	**1243**	**51.5**	**17:43**	**7**	**0**	**3**	**3**	**6**	**0**	**0**	**0**	**16:35**
2000-01	**St. Louis**	**NHL**	**36**	**10**	**14**	**24**	**12**	**3**	**2**	**2**	**58**	**17.2**	**11**	**581**	**50.6**	**18:00**	....	....	....	....	....	....	....	....	....
	Phoenix	**NHL**	**10**	**4**	**4**	**8**	**21**	**0**	**1**	**0**	**14**	**28.6**	**5**	**111**	**60.4**	**15:26**	....	....	....	....	....	....	....	....	....
2001-02	**Phoenix**	**NHL**	**79**	**15**	**30**	**45**	**34**	**3**	**1**	**1**	**94**	**16.0**	**-8**	**1227**	**48.7**	**16:09**	**5**	**0**	**0**	**0**	**2**	**0**	**0**	**0**	**15:01**
	Slovakia	Olympics	2	1	0	1	6	....	....	....	....	....	....	....	....	....	....	....	....	....	....	....	....	....	....
2002-03	**Philadelphia**	**NHL**	**82**	**23**	**21**	**44**	**46**	**1**	**1**	**9**	**133**	**17.3**	**13**	**1350**	**52.3**	**17:33**	**13**	**2**	**6**	**8**	**6**	**0**	**0**	**1**	**18:23**
2003-04	**Philadelphia**	**NHL**	**82**	**20**	**38**	**58**	**82**	**7**	**1**	**2**	**135**	**14.8**	**18**	**1457**	**49.9**	**18:43**	**18**	**5**	**5**	**10**	**10**	**0**	**0**	**0**	**18:33**
2004-05	HKm Zvolen	Slovakia	33	14	24	38	34	....	....	....	....	....	....	....	....	....	17	5	10	15	6	....	....	....	....
2005-06	**Philadelphia**	**NHL**	**73**	**11**	**33**	**44**	**38**	**2**	**1**	**1**	**113**	**9.7**	**-2**	**1143**	**53.2**	**18:28**	**6**	**0**	**2**	**2**	**2**	**0**	**0**	**0**	**15:56**
2006-07	**Chicago**	**NHL**	**8**	**3**	**5**	**8**	**6**	**1**	**0**	**0**	**9**	**33.3**	**4**	**173**	**51.5**	**20:59**	....	....	....	....	....	....	....	....	....
2007-08	**Los Angeles**	**NHL**	**82**	**7**	**14**	**21**	**45**	**0**	**3**	**0**	**89**	**7.9**	**-21**	**1167**	**45.6**	**15:14**	....	....	....	....	....	....	....	....	....
2008-09	**Los Angeles**	**NHL**	**82**	**18**	**24**	**42**	**32**	**7**	**1**	**4**	**143**	**12.6**	**-7**	**1320**	**54.5**	**18:54**	....	....	....	....	....	....	....	....	....
2009-10	**Los Angeles**	**NHL**	**81**	**20**	**22**	**42**	**38**	**5**	**1**	**6**	**117**	**17.1**	**4**	**1363**	**50.9**	**18:18**	**6**	**3**	**2**	**5**	**4**	**3**	**0**	**0**	**19:31**
	Slovakia	Olympics	7	3	3	6	0	....	....	....	....	....	....	....	....	....	....	....	....	....	....	....	....	....	....
2010-11	**Los Angeles**	**NHL**	**82**	**12**	**18**	**30**	**20**	**4**	**0**	**3**	**94**	**12.8**	**-5**	**1312**	**51.7**	**17:21**	**6**	**1**	**1**	**2**	**0**	**0**	**0**	**0**	**20:21**
	NHL Totals		**844**	**172**	**263**	**435**	**448**	**36**	**16**	**33**	**1243**	**13.8**		**13241**	**51.0**	**17:24**	**72**	**11**	**21**	**32**	**38**	**3**	**0**	**1**	**17:50**

Traded to **Phoenix** by **St. Louis** with Ladislav Nagy, the rights to Jeff Taffe and St. Louis' 1st round choice (Ben Eager) in 2002 Entry Draft for Keith Tkachuk, March 13, 2001. Traded to **Philadelphia** by **Phoenix** with Robert Esche for Brian Boucher and Nashville's 3rd round choice (previously acquired, Phoenix selected Joe Callahan) in 2002 Entry Draft, June 12, 2002. Signed as a free agent by **Zvolen** (Slovakia), October 27, 2004. Traded to **Chicago** by **Philadelphia** for Kyle Calder, August 4, 2006. • Missed remainder of 2006-07 due to knee injury vs. St. Louis, October 21, 2006. Signed as a free agent by **Los Angeles**, July 2, 2007. Signed as a free agent by **San Jose**, July 1, 2011.

HANNAN, Scott
(HAN-nan, SKAWT)

Defense. Shoots left. 6'1", 225 lbs. Born, Richmond, B.C., January 23, 1979. San Jose's 2nd choice, 23rd overall, in 1997 Entry Draft.

			Regular Season														Playoffs								
Season	Club	League	GP	G	A	Pts	PIM	PP	SH	GW	S	%	+/-	TF	F%	Min	GP	G	A	Pts	PIM	PP	SH	GW	Min
1994-95	Surrey Wolves	Minor-BC	70	54	54	108	200	....	....	....	....	....	....	....	....	....	....	....	....	....	....	....	....	....	....
	Tacoma Rockets	WHL	2	0	0	0	0	....	....	....	....	....	....	....	....	....	....	....	....	....	....	....	....	....	....
1995-96	Kelowna Rockets	WHL	69	4	5	9	76	....	....	....	....	....	....	....	....	....	6	0	1	1	4	....	....	....	....
1996-97	Kelowna Rockets	WHL	70	17	26	43	84	....	....	....	....	....	....	....	....	....	6	0	0	0	8	....	....	....	....
1997-98	Kelowna Rockets	WHL	47	10	30	40	70	....	....	....	....	....	....	....	....	....	7	2	7	9	14	....	....	....	....
1998-99	**San Jose**	**NHL**	**5**	**0**	**2**	**2**	**6**	**0**	**0**	**0**	**4**	**0.0**	**0**	**0**	**0.0**	**7:15**	....	....	....	....	....	....	....	....	....
	Kelowna Rockets	WHL	47	15	30	45	92	....	....	....	....	....	....	....	....	....	6	1	2	3	14	....	....	....	....
	Kentucky	AHL	2	0	0	0	2	....	....	....	....	....	....	....	....	....	12	0	2	2	10	....	....	....	....
99-2000	**San Jose**	**NHL**	**30**	**1**	**2**	**3**	**10**	**0**	**0**	**0**	**28**	**3.6**	**7**	**1**	**0.0**	**17:09**	**1**	**0**	**1**	**1**	**0**	**0**	**0**	**0**	**18:14**
	Kentucky	AHL	41	5	12	17	40	....	....	....	....	....	....	....	....	....	....	....	....	....	....	....	....	....	....
2000-01	**San Jose**	**NHL**	**75**	**3**	**14**	**17**	**51**	**0**	**0**	**1**	**96**	**3.1**	**10**	**0**	**0.0**	**19:02**	**6**	**0**	**1**	**1**	**6**	**0**	**0**	**0**	**25:10**
2001-02	**San Jose**	**NHL**	**75**	**2**	**12**	**14**	**57**	**0**	**0**	**1**	**68**	**2.9**	**10**	**1**	**100.0**	**20:19**	**12**	**0**	**2**	**2**	**12**	**0**	**0**	**0**	**20:46**
2002-03	**San Jose**	**NHL**	**81**	**3**	**19**	**22**	**61**	**1**	**0**	**0**	**103**	**2.9**	**0**	**3**	**33.3**	**24:16**	....	....	....	....	....	....	....	....	....
2003-04	**San Jose**	**NHL**	**82**	**6**	**15**	**21**	**48**	**0**	**0**	**0**	**114**	**5.3**	**10**	**0**	**0.0**	**23:41**	**17**	**1**	**5**	**6**	**22**	**1**	**0**	**1**	**26:38**
2004-05			DID NOT PLAY																						
2005-06	**San Jose**	**NHL**	**81**	**6**	**18**	**24**	**58**	**2**	**0**	**1**	**104**	**5.8**	**7**	**0**	**0.0**	**24:34**	**11**	**0**	**1**	**1**	**6**	**0**	**0**	**0**	**25:16**
2006-07	**San Jose**	**NHL**	**79**	**4**	**20**	**24**	**38**	**0**	**1**	**1**	**79**	**5.1**	**1**	**0**	**0.0**	**22:49**	**11**	**0**	**2**	**2**	**33**	**0**	**0**	**0**	**21:42**
2007-08	**Colorado**	**NHL**	**82**	**2**	**19**	**21**	**55**	**0**	**0**	**0**	**79**	**2.5**	**-5**	**1**	**100.0**	**22:41**	**9**	**0**	**1**	**1**	**4**	**0**	**0**	**0**	**19:15**
2008-09	**Colorado**	**NHL**	**81**	**1**	**9**	**10**	**26**	**0**	**0**	**0**	**70**	**1.4**	**-21**	**1**	**0.0**	**22:22**	....	....	....	....	....	....	....	....	....
2009-10	**Colorado**	**NHL**	**81**	**2**	**14**	**16**	**40**	**0**	**0**	**0**	**53**	**3.8**	**2**	**2**	**100.0**	**21:56**	**6**	**0**	**0**	**0**	**4**	**0**	**0**	**0**	**22:33**
2010-11	**Colorado**	**NHL**	**23**	**0**	**6**	**6**	**6**	**0**	**0**	**0**	**21**	**0.0**	**1**	**0**	**0.0**	**18:38**	....	....	....	....	....	....	....	....	....
	Washington	**NHL**	**55**	**1**	**4**	**5**	**28**	**0**	**0**	**0**	**35**	**2.9**	**3**	**0**	**0.0**	**20:16**	**9**	**0**	**1**	**1**	**2**	**0**	**0**	**0**	**23:37**
	NHL Totals		**830**	**31**	**154**	**185**	**484**	**3**	**1**	**4**	**854**	**3.6**		**9**	**55.6**	**21:55**	**82**	**1**	**14**	**15**	**89**	**1**	**0**	**1**	**23:17**

WHL West First All-Star Team (1999)

Signed as a free agent by **Colorado**, July 1, 2007. Traded to **Washington** by **Colorado** for Tomas Fleischmann, November 30, 2010.

HANSEN, Jannik
(HAHN-suhn, YAH-nihk) **VAN**

Left wing. Shoots right. 6'1", 195 lbs. Born, Herlev, Denmark, March 15, 1986. Vancouver's 7th choice, 287th overall, in 2004 Entry Draft.

			Regular Season														Playoffs								
Season	Club	League	GP	G	A	Pts	PIM	PP	SH	GW	S	%	+/-	TF	F%	Min	GP	G	A	Pts	PIM	PP	SH	GW	Min
2002-03	Rodovre	Denmark	15	0	0	0	0	....	....	....	....	....	....	....	....	....	....	....	....	....	....	....	....	....	....
	Malmo U18	Swe-U18	12	8	7	15	2	....	....	....	....	....	....	....	....	....	3	2	0	2	0	....	....	....	....
	Denmark	WJ18-B	5	2	5	7	14	....	....	....	....	....	....	....	....	....	....	....	....	....	....	....	....	....	....
2003-04	Rodovre	Denmark	35	12	7	19	48	....	....	....	....	....	....	....	....	....	....	....	....	....	....	....	....	....	....
2004-05	Rodovre	Denmark	32	17	17	34	40	....	....	....	....	....	....	....	....	....	5	3	1	4	24	....	....	....	....
2005-06	Portland	WHL	64	24	40	64	67	....	....	....	....	....	....	....	....	....	12	7	6	13	16	....	....	....	....
2006-07	Manitoba Moose	AHL	72	12	22	34	38	....	....	....	....	....	....	....	....	....	6	0	0	0	2	....	....	....	....
	Vancouver	**NHL**															**10**	**0**	**1**	**1**	**4**	**0**	**0**	**0**	**12:41**
2007-08	**Vancouver**	**NHL**	**5**	**0**	**0**	**0**	**2**	**0**	**0**	**0**	**3**	**0.0**	**0**	**1**	**100.0**	**11:34**	....	....	....	....	....	....	....	....	....
	Manitoba Moose	AHL	50	21	22	43	22	....	....	....	....	....	....	....	....	....	6	2	2	4	0	....	....	....	....
2008-09	**Vancouver**	**NHL**	**55**	**6**	**15**	**21**	**37**	**0**	**0**	**1**	**64**	**9.4**	**5**	**12**	**16.7**	**12:31**	**2**	**0**	**0**	**0**	**0**	**0**	**0**	**0**	**10:16**
	Manitoba Moose	AHL	2	1	0	1	2	....	....	....	....	....	....	....	....	....	....	....	....	....	....	....	....	....	....

			Regular Season														Playoffs								
Season	Club	League	GP	G	A	Pts	PIM	PP	SH	GW	S	%	+/-	TF	F%	Min	GP	G	A	Pts	PIM	PP	SH	GW	Min
2009-10	**Vancouver**	**NHL**	**47**	**9**	**6**	**15**	**18**	**0**	**1**	**3**	**67**	**13.4**	**–5**	**14**	**42.9**	**12:20**	**12**	**1**	**2**	**3**	**4**	**0**	**0**	**0**	**10:05**
	Manitoba Moose	AHL	5	0	2	2	5	....	....	....	....	....	....	....	....	....	....	....	....	....	....	....	....	....	....
2010-11	**Vancouver**	**NHL**	**82**	**9**	**20**	**29**	**32**	**0**	**0**	**2**	**113**	**8.0**	**13**	**19**	**42.1**	**14:43**	**25**	**3**	**6**	**9**	**18**	**0**	**0**	**0**	**15:50**
	NHL Totals		**189**	**24**	**41**	**65**	**89**	**0**	**1**	**6**	**247**	**9.7**		**46**	**37.0**	**13:24**	**49**	**4**	**9**	**13**	**26**	**0**	**0**	**0**	**13:33**

HANSON, Christian

(HAN-suhn, KRIHST-chehn) **WSH**

Center. Shoots right. 6'4", 228 lbs. Born, Venetia, PA, March 10, 1986.

2003-04	Tri-City Storm	USHL	58	11	8	19	35	....	....	....	....	....	....	....	....	....	11	2	2	4	4	....	....	....	....
2004-05	Tri-City Storm	USHL	60	19	33	52	23	....	....	....	....	....	....	....	....	....	9	1	2	3	8	....	....	....	....
2005-06	U. of Notre Dame	CCHA	23	1	2	3	14	....	....	....	....	....	....	....	....	....	....	....	....	....	....	....	....	....	....
2006-07	U. of Notre Dame	CCHA	33	6	2	8	24	....	....	....	....	....	....	....	....	....	....	....	....	....	....	....	....	....	....
2007-08	U. of Notre Dame	CCHA	47	13	9	22	57	....	....	....	....	....	....	....	....	....	....	....	....	....	....	....	....	....	....
2008-09	U. of Notre Dame	CCHA	37	16	15	31	28	....	....	....	....	....	....	....	....	....	....	....	....	....	....	....	....	....	....
	Toronto	**NHL**	**5**	**1**	**1**	**2**	**2**	**0**	**0**	**0**	**9**	**11.1**	**–1**	**4**	**25.0**	**16:19**	....	....	....	....	....	....	....	....	....
2009-10	**Toronto**	**NHL**	**31**	**2**	**5**	**7**	**16**	**0**	**1**	**0**	**45**	**4.4**	**–2**	**177**	**55.4**	**13:22**	....	....	....	....	....	....	....	....	....
	Toronto Marlies	AHL	38	12	19	31	35	....	....	....	....	....	....	....	....	....	....	....	....	....	....	....	....	....	....
2010-11	**Toronto**	**NHL**	**6**	**0**	**0**	**0**	**4**	**0**	**0**	**0**	**2**	**0.0**	**0**	**17**	**41.2**	**8:26**	....	....	....	....	....	....	....	....	....
	Toronto Marlies	AHL	58	13	21	34	51	....	....	....	....	....	....	....	....	....	....	....	....	....	....	....	....	....	....
	NHL Totals		**42**	**3**	**6**	**9**	**22**	**0**	**1**	**0**	**56**	**5.4**		**198**	**53.5**	**13:01**	....	....	....	....	....	....	....	....	....

CCHA Second All-Star Team (2009)

Signed as a free agent by **Toronto**, March 31, 2009. Signed as a free agent by **Washington**, July 11, 2011.

HANZAL, Martin

(HAHN-zuhl, MAHR-tihn) **PHX**

Center. Shoots left. 6'5", 220 lbs. Born, Pisek, Czech., February 20, 1987. Phoenix's 1st choice, 17th overall, in 2005 Entry Draft.

2002-03	C. Budejovice U17	CzR-U17	47	24	30	54	28	....	....	....	....	....	....	....	....	....	7	1	3	4	25	....	....	....	....
2003-04	C. Budejovice U17	CzR-U17	2	0	2	2	2	....	....	....	....	....	....	....	....	....	2	1	0	1	4	....	....	....	....
	C. Budejovice Jr.	CzRep-Jr.	53	15	7	22	32	....	....	....	....	....	....	....	....	....	....	....	....	....	....	....	....	....	....
2004-05	C. Budejovice Jr.	CzRep-Jr.	37	22	22	44	80	....	....	....	....	....	....	....	....	....	2	1	2	3	2	....	....	....	....
	C. Budejovice	CzRep-2	15	1	2	3	2	....	....	....	....	....	....	....	....	....	6	0	0	0	6	....	....	....	....
2005-06	C. Budejovice Jr.	CzRep-Jr.	7	3	5	8	20	....	....	....	....	....	....	....	....	....	....	....	....	....	....	....	....	....	....
	C. Budejovice	CzRep	19	0	1	1	10	....	....	....	....	....	....	....	....	....	....	....	....	....	....	....	....	....	....
	BK Mlada Boleslav	CzRep-2	5	2	0	2	0	....	....	....	....	....	....	....	....	....	....	....	....	....	....	....	....	....	....
	Omaha Lancers	USHL	19	4	15	19	30	....	....	....	....	....	....	....	....	....	5	1	0	1	4	....	....	....	....
2006-07	Red Deer Rebels	WHL	60	26	59	85	94	....	....	....	....	....	....	....	....	....	6	2	7	9	19	....	....	....	....
2007-08	**Phoenix**	**NHL**	**72**	**8**	**27**	**35**	**28**	**1**	**1**	**3**	**111**	**7.2**	**–7**	**1019**	**46.1**	**16:45**	....	....	....	....	....	....	....	....	....
2008-09	**Phoenix**	**NHL**	**74**	**11**	**20**	**31**	**40**	**0**	**2**	**2**	**97**	**11.3**	**–4**	**1078**	**48.3**	**16:21**	....	....	....	....	....	....	....	....	....
2009-10	**Phoenix**	**NHL**	**81**	**11**	**22**	**33**	**104**	**2**	**0**	**0**	**147**	**7.5**	**0**	**1104**	**50.6**	**18:29**	**7**	**0**	**3**	**3**	**10**	**0**	**0**	**0**	**18:58**
2010-11	**Phoenix**	**NHL**	**61**	**16**	**10**	**26**	**54**	**7**	**0**	**5**	**149**	**10.7**	**4**	**1029**	**50.3**	**19:30**	**4**	**1**	**2**	**3**	**8**	**1**	**0**	**0**	**19:50**
	NHL Totals		**288**	**46**	**79**	**125**	**226**	**10**	**3**	**10**	**504**	**9.1**		**4230**	**48.9**	**17:43**	**11**	**1**	**5**	**6**	**18**	**1**	**0**	**0**	**19:17**

WHL East Second All-Star Team (2007)

HARJU, Johan

(HAHR-yoo, YOH-hahn) **T.B.**

Left wing. Shoots left. 6'3", 210 lbs. Born, Overtornea, Sweden, May 15, 1986. Tampa Bay's 6th choice, 167th overall, in 2007 Entry Draft.

2002-03	Lulea HF U18	Swe-U18	11	7	2	9	14	....	....	....	....	....	....	....	....	....	....	....	....	....	....	....	....	....	....
	Lulea HF Jr.	Swe-Jr.	7	2	0	2	0	....	....	....	....	....	....	....	....	....	....	....	....	....	....	....	....	....	....
2003-04	Lulea HF U18	Swe-U18	3	1	3	4	0	....	....	....	....	....	....	....	....	....	7	4	3	7	8	....	....	....	....
	Lulea HF Jr.	Swe-Jr.	35	14	12	26	8	....	....	....	....	....	....	....	....	....	....	....	....	....	....	....	....	....	....
2004-05	Lulea HF Jr.	Swe-Jr.	33	18	13	31	14	....	....	....	....	....	....	....	....	....	7	2	2	4	2	....	....	....	....
	Pitea HC	Sweden-2	1	0	0	0	0	....	....	....	....	....	....	....	....	....	....	....	....	....	....	....	....	....	....
	Lulea HF	Sweden	4	0	0	0	0	....	....	....	....	....	....	....	....	....	....	....	....	....	....	....	....	....	....
2005-06	Lulea HF Jr.	Swe-Jr.	17	14	9	23	4	....	....	....	....	....	....	....	....	....	4	3	1	4	8	....	....	....	....
	Lulea HF	Sweden	39	3	1	4	8	....	....	....	....	....	....	....	....	....	4	0	0	0	20	....	....	....	....
2006-07	Lulea HF	Sweden	55	12	10	22	30	....	....	....	....	....	....	....	....	....	4	2	0	2	4	....	....	....	....
2007-08	Lulea HF	Sweden	51	20	8	28	55	....	....	....	....	....	....	....	....	....	....	....	....	....	....	....	....	....	....
2008-09	Lulea HF	Sweden	55	27	22	49	30	....	....	....	....	....	....	....	....	....	5	4	1	5	0	....	....	....	....
2009-10	Dynamo Moscow	Rus-KHL	55	4	14	18	38	....	....	....	....	....	....	....	....	....	2	1	0	1	8	....	....	....	....
2010-11	**Tampa Bay**	**NHL**	**10**	**1**	**2**	**3**	**2**	**0**	**0**	**0**	**14**	**7.1**	**–2**	**5**	**40.0**	**8:28**	....	....	....	....	....	....	....	....	....
	Norfolk Admirals	AHL	63	23	30	53	20	....	....	....	....	....	....	....	....	....	6	1	0	1	6	....	....	....	....
	NHL Totals		**10**	**1**	**2**	**3**	**2**	**0**	**0**	**0**	**14**	**7.1**		**5**	**40.0**	**8:28**	....	....	....	....	....	....	....	....	....

Signed as a free agent by **Dynamo Moscow** (Russia-KHL), April 8, 2009.

HARRISON, Jay

(HAIR-ih-suhn, JAY) **CAR**

Defense. Shoots left. 6'4", 211 lbs. Born, Oshawa, Ont., November 3, 1982. Toronto's 4th choice, 82nd overall, in 2001 Entry Draft.

1997-98	Oshawa	ON-Jr.A	42	1	11	12	143	....	....	....	....	....	....	....	....	....	....	....	....	....	....	....	....	....	....
1998-99	Brampton	OHL	63	1	14	15	108	....	....	....	....	....	....	....	....	....	....	....	....	....	....	....	....	....	....
99-2000	Brampton	OHL	68	2	18	20	139	....	....	....	....	....	....	....	....	....	6	0	2	2	15	....	....	....	....
2000-01	Brampton	OHL	53	4	15	19	112	....	....	....	....	....	....	....	....	....	9	1	1	2	17	....	....	....	....
2001-02	Brampton	OHL	61	12	31	43	116	....	....	....	....	....	....	....	....	....	....	....	....	....	....	....	....	....	....
	St. John's	AHL	7	0	1	1	2	....	....	....	....	....	....	....	....	....	10	0	0	0	4	....	....	....	....
	Memphis	CHL	....	....	....	....	....	....	....	....	....	....	....	....	....	....	1	0	0	0	2	....	....	....	....
2002-03	St. John's	AHL	72	2	8	10	72	....	....	....	....	....	....	....	....	....	....	....	....	....	....	....	....	....	....
2003-04	St. John's	AHL	70	4	5	9	141	....	....	....	....	....	....	....	....	....	....	....	....	....	....	....	....	....	....
2004-05	St. John's	AHL	60	0	4	4	108	....	....	....	....	....	....	....	....	....	4	0	1	1	14	....	....	....	....
2005-06	**Toronto**	**NHL**	**8**	**0**	**1**	**1**	**2**	**0**	**0**	**0**	**7**	**0.0**	**5**	**0**	**0.0**	**18:50**	....	....	....	....	....	....	....	....	....
	Toronto Marlies	AHL	57	9	20	29	100	....	....	....	....	....	....	....	....	....	5	1	3	4	8	....	....	....	....
2006-07	**Toronto**	**NHL**	**5**	**0**	**0**	**0**	**6**	**0**	**0**	**0**	**3**	**0.0**	**–5**	**0**	**0.0**	**8:22**	....	....	....	....	....	....	....	....	....
	Toronto Marlies	AHL	41	4	14	18	68	....	....	....	....	....	....	....	....	....	....	....	....	....	....	....	....	....	....
2007-08	Toronto Marlies	AHL	69	13	14	27	73	....	....	....	....	....	....	....	....	....	18	2	10	12	35	....	....	....	....
2008-09	EV Zug	Swiss	41	6	9	15	96	....	....	....	....	....	....	....	....	....	7	1	2	3	33	....	....	....	....
	Toronto	**NHL**	**7**	**0**	**1**	**1**	**10**	**0**	**0**	**0**	**6**	**0.0**	**–2**	**0**	**0.0**	**17:16**	....	....	....	....	....	....	....	....	....
2009-10	**Carolina**	**NHL**	**38**	**1**	**5**	**6**	**50**	**0**	**0**	**0**	**30**	**3.3**	**–8**	**0**	**0.0**	**14:43**	....	....	....	....	....	....	....	....	....
	Albany River Rats	AHL	32	2	12	14	22	....	....	....	....	....	....	....	....	....	8	0	3	3	23	....	....	....	....
2010-11	**Carolina**	**NHL**	**72**	**3**	**7**	**10**	**72**	**0**	**0**	**0**	**49**	**6.1**	**5**	**0**	**0.0**	**15:16**	....	....	....	....	....	....	....	....	....
	NHL Totals		**130**	**4**	**14**	**18**	**140**	**0**	**0**	**0**	**95**	**4.2**		**0**	**0.0**	**15:10**	....	....	....	....	....	....	....	....	....

OHL All-Rookie Team (1999)

Signed as a free agent by **Zug** (Swiss), June 16, 2008. Signed as a free agent by **Toronto**, March 27, 2009. Signed as a free agent by **Carolina**, July 9, 2009.

HARROLD, Peter

(HAIR-ohld, PEE-tuhr) **N.J.**

Defense. Shoots right. 6', 185 lbs. Born, Kirtland Hills, OH, June 8, 1983.

2003-04	Boston College	H-East	40	2	12	14	12	....	....	....	....	....	....	....	....	....	....	....	....	....	....	....	....	....	....
2004-05	Boston College	H-East	35	4	10	14	22	....	....	....	....	....	....	....	....	....	....	....	....	....	....	....	....	....	....
2005-06	Boston College	H-East	42	7	23	30	32	....	....	....	....	....	....	....	....	....	....	....	....	....	....	....	....	....	....
2006-07	**Los Angeles**	**NHL**	**12**	**0**	**2**	**2**	**8**	**0**	**0**	**0**	**11**	**0.0**	**0**	**1**	**0.0**	**15:12**	....	....	....	....	....	....	....	....	....
	Manchester	AHL	62	7	27	34	43	....	....	....	....	....	....	....	....	....	16	3	8	11	18	....	....	....	....
2007-08	**Los Angeles**	**NHL**	**25**	**2**	**3**	**5**	**2**	**0**	**0**	**0**	**16**	**12.5**	**3**	**2**	**50.0**	**16:23**	....	....	....	....	....	....	....	....	....
	Manchester	AHL	49	7	36	43	25	....	....	....	....	....	....	....	....	....	4	0	1	1	4	....	....	....	....
2008-09	**Los Angeles**	**NHL**	**69**	**4**	**8**	**12**	**28**	**1**	**0**	**1**	**95**	**4.2**	**–13**	**16**	**37.5**	**13:10**	....	....	....	....	....	....	....	....	....
2009-10	**Los Angeles**	**NHL**	**39**	**1**	**2**	**3**	**8**	**0**	**0**	**0**	**23**	**4.3**	**–2**	**14**	**14.3**	**9:15**	**2**	**0**	**0**	**0**	**0**	**0**	**0**	**0**	**11:58**
2010-11	**Los Angeles**	**NHL**	**19**	**1**	**3**	**4**	**4**	**0**	**0**	**0**	**12**	**8.3**	**3**	**0**	**0.0**	**12:15**	....	....	....	....	....	....	....	....	....
	NHL Totals		**164**	**8**	**18**	**26**	**50**	**1**	**0**	**1**	**157**	**5.1**		**33**	**27.3**	**12:46**	**2**	**0**	**0**	**0**	**0**	**0**	**0**	**0**	**11:58**

Hockey East First All-Star Team (2006) • NCAA East First All-American Team (2006)

Signed as a free agent by **Los Angeles**, April 12, 2006. • Missed majority of 2009-10 and 2010-11 as a healthy reserve.

HARTIKAINEN, Teemu
(har-tih-KIGH-nehn, TEE-moo) **EDM**

Center. Shoots left. 6'1", 215 lbs. Born, Kuopio, Finland, May 3, 1990. Edmonton's 4th choice, 163rd overall, in 2008 Entry Draft.

			Regular Season														Playoffs								
Season	Club	League	GP	G	A	Pts	PIM	PP	SH	GW	S	%	+/-	TF	F%	Min	GP	G	A	Pts	PIM	PP	SH	GW	Min
2006-07	KalPa Kuopio U18	Fin-U18	19	24	13	37	51	....	....	....	....	....	....	....	....	....	....	....	....	....	....	....	....	....	....
	KalPa Kuopio Jr.	Fin-Jr.	11	2	1	3	0	....	....	....	....	....	....	....	....	....	3	0	0	0	4	....	....	....	....
2007-08	KalPa Kuopio U18	Fin-U18	7	9	6	15	6	....	....	....	....	....	....	....	....	....	....	....	....	....	....	....	....	....	....
	KalPa Kuopio Jr.	Fin-Jr.	37	10	7	17	24	....	....	....	....	....	....	....	....	....	11	1	4	5	6	....	....	....	....
	KalPa Kuopio	Finland	1	0	0	0	0	....	....	....	....	....	....	....	....	....	....	....	....	....	....	....	....	....	....
2008-09	Suomi U20	Finland-2	3	0	2	2	8	....	....	....	....	....	....	....	....	....	....	....	....	....	....	....	....	....	....
	KalPa Kuopio	Finland	51	17	6	23	12	....	....	....	....	....	....	....	....	....	12	3	0	3	0	....	....	....	....
2009-10	KalPa Kuopio	Finland	53	15	18	33	22	....	....	....	....	....	....	....	....	....	13	6	1	7	28	....	....	....	....
	Suomi U20	Finland-2	1	0	0	0	0	....	....	....	....	....	....	....	....	....	....	....	....	....	....	....	....	....	....
2010-11	**Edmonton**	**NHL**	**12**	**3**	**2**	**5**	**4**	**1**	**0**	**0**	**21**	**14.3**	**-3**	**18**	**33.3**	**17:25**	....	....	....	....	....	....	....	....	....
	Oklahoma City	AHL	66	17	25	42	27	....	....	....	....	....	....	....	....	....	6	0	1	1	4	....	....	....	....
	NHL Totals		**12**	**3**	**2**	**5**	**4**	**1**	**0**	**0**	**21**	**14.3**		**18**	**33.3**	**17:25**	....	....	....	....	....	....	....	....	....

HARTNELL, Scott
(HAHRT-nuhl, SKAWT) **PHI**

Left wing. Shoots left. 6'2", 210 lbs. Born, Regina, Sask., April 18, 1982. Nashville's 1st choice, 6th overall, in 2000 Entry Draft.

Season	Club	League	GP	G	A	Pts	PIM	PP	SH	GW	S	%	+/-	TF	F%	Min	GP	G	A	Pts	PIM	PP	SH	GW	Min
1997-98	Lloydminster	AJHL	56	9	25	34	82	....	....	....	....	....	....	....	....	....	4	2	1	3	8	....	....	....	....
	Prince Albert	WHL	1	0	1	1	2	....	....	....	....	....	....	....	....	....	....	....	....	....	....	....	....	....	....
1998-99	Prince Albert	WHL	65	10	34	44	104	....	....	....	....	....	....	....	....	....	14	0	5	5	22	....	....	....	....
99-2000	Prince Albert	WHL	62	27	55	82	124	....	....	....	....	....	....	....	....	....	6	3	2	5	6	....	....	....	....
2000-01	**Nashville**	**NHL**	**75**	**2**	**14**	**16**	**48**	**0**	**0**	**0**	**92**	**2.2**	**-8**	**3**	**33.3**	**10:54**	....	....	....	....	....	....	....	....	....
2001-02	**Nashville**	**NHL**	**75**	**14**	**27**	**41**	**111**	**3**	**0**	**4**	**162**	**8.6**	**5**	**12**	**25.0**	**16:58**	....	....	....	....	....	....	....	....	....
2002-03	**Nashville**	**NHL**	**82**	**12**	**22**	**34**	**101**	**2**	**0**	**2**	**221**	**5.4**	**-3**	**23**	**30.4**	**15:17**	....	....	....	....	....	....	....	....	....
2003-04	**Nashville**	**NHL**	**59**	**18**	**15**	**33**	**87**	**5**	**0**	**3**	**154**	**11.7**	**-5**	**48**	**37.5**	**16:16**	**6**	**1**	**2**	**3**	**2**	**0**	**0**	**0**	**15:37**
2004-05	Valerengen	Norway	28	17	12	29	103	....	....	....	....	....	....	....	....	....	11	12	7	19	24	....	....	....	....
2005-06	**Nashville**	**NHL**	**81**	**25**	**23**	**48**	**101**	**10**	**2**	**8**	**211**	**11.8**	**8**	**58**	**37.9**	**16:05**	**5**	**1**	**0**	**1**	**4**	**0**	**0**	**0**	**12:12**
2006-07	**Nashville**	**NHL**	**64**	**22**	**17**	**39**	**96**	**10**	**0**	**2**	**150**	**14.7**	**19**	**134**	**47.0**	**15:43**	**5**	**1**	**1**	**2**	**28**	**1**	**0**	**0**	**14:23**
2007-08	**Philadelphia**	**NHL**	**80**	**24**	**19**	**43**	**159**	**10**	**1**	**6**	**176**	**13.6**	**2**	**32**	**40.6**	**16:11**	**17**	**3**	**4**	**7**	**20**	**0**	**0**	**0**	**15:28**
2008-09	**Philadelphia**	**NHL**	**82**	**30**	**30**	**60**	**143**	**6**	**1**	**5**	**210**	**14.3**	**14**	**36**	**50.0**	**17:48**	**6**	**1**	**1**	**2**	**23**	**1**	**0**	**0**	**18:36**
2009-10	**Philadelphia**	**NHL**	**81**	**14**	**30**	**44**	**155**	**8**	**0**	**4**	**171**	**8.2**	**-6**	**5**	**20.0**	**15:43**	**23**	**8**	**9**	**17**	**25**	**3**	**0**	**0**	**16:14**
2010-11	**Philadelphia**	**NHL**	**82**	**24**	**25**	**49**	**142**	**4**	**0**	**4**	**177**	**13.6**	**14**	**10**	**50.0**	**16:36**	**11**	**1**	**3**	**4**	**23**	**0**	**0**	**0**	**16:18**
	NHL Totals		**761**	**185**	**222**	**407**	**1143**	**58**	**4**	**38**	**1724**	**10.7**		**361**	**41.8**	**15:46**	**73**	**16**	**20**	**36**	**125**	**5**	**0**	**0**	**15:48**

Signed as a free agent by **Oslo** (Norway), October 21, 2004. Traded to **Philadelphia** by **Nashville** with Kimmo Timmonen for Nashville's 1st round choice (previously acquired, Nashville selected Jonathon Blum) in 2007 Entry Draft, June 18, 2007.

HAVLAT, Martin
(HAV-lat, MAHR-tihn) **S.J.**

Right wing. Shoots left. 6'2", 217 lbs. Born, Mlada Boleslav, Czech., April 19, 1981. Ottawa's 1st choice, 26th overall, in 1999 Entry Draft.

Season	Club	League	GP	G	A	Pts	PIM	PP	SH	GW	S	%	+/-	TF	F%	Min	GP	G	A	Pts	PIM	PP	SH	GW	Min
1997-98	Ytong Brno Jr.	CzRep-Jr.	32	38	29	67	....	....	....	....	....	....	....	....	....	....	....	....	....	....	....	....	....	....	....
1998-99	HC Trinec Jr.	CzRep-Jr.	31	28	23	51	....	....	....	....	....	....	....	....	....	....	....	....	....	....	....	....	....	....	....
	Trinec	CzRep	24	2	3	5	4	....	....	....	....	....	....	....	....	....	8	0	0	0		....	....	....	....
99-2000	HC Ocelari Trinec	CzRep	46	13	29	42	42	....	....	....	....	....	....	....	....	....	4	0	2	2	8	....	....	....	....
2000-01	**Ottawa**	**NHL**	**73**	**19**	**23**	**42**	**20**	**7**	**0**	**5**	**133**	**14.3**	**8**	**40**	**30.0**	**13:47**	**4**	**0**	**0**	**0**	**2**	**0**	**0**	**0**	**14:04**
2001-02	**Ottawa**	**NHL**	**72**	**22**	**28**	**50**	**66**	**9**	**0**	**6**	**145**	**15.2**	**-7**	**15**	**40.0**	**14:46**	**12**	**2**	**5**	**7**	**14**	**2**	**0**	**2**	**16:19**
	Czech Republic	Olympics	4	3	1	4	27	....	....	....	....	....	....	....	....	....	....	....	....	....	....	....	....	....	....
2002-03	**Ottawa**	**NHL**	**67**	**24**	**35**	**59**	**30**	**9**	**0**	**4**	**179**	**13.4**	**20**	**7**	**14.3**	**16:27**	**18**	**5**	**6**	**11**	**14**	**1**	**0**	**2**	**16:27**
2003-04	HC Sparta Praha	CzRep	5	1	3	4	8	....	....	....	....	....	....	....	....	....	....	....	....	....	....	....	....	....	....
	Ottawa	**NHL**	**68**	**31**	**37**	**68**	**46**	**13**	**0**	**7**	**175**	**17.7**	**12**	**11**	**36.4**	**16:44**	**7**	**0**	**3**	**3**	**2**	**0**	**0**	**0**	**16:10**
2004-05	Znojmo	CzRep	12	10	4	14	16	....	....	....	....	....	....	....	....	....	....	....	....	....	....	....	....	....	....
	Dynamo Moscow	Russia	10	2	0	2	14	....	....	....	....	....	....	....	....	....	....	....	....	....	....	....	....	....	....
	HC Sparta Praha	CzRep	9	5	4	9	37	....	....	....	....	....	....	....	....	....	5	0	0	0	20	....	....	....	....
2005-06	**Ottawa**	**NHL**	**18**	**9**	**7**	**16**	**4**	**2**	**1**	**1**	**57**	**15.8**	**6**	**25**	**36.0**	**18:11**	**10**	**7**	**6**	**13**	**4**	**3**	**0**	**1**	**17:13**
2006-07	**Chicago**	**NHL**	**56**	**25**	**32**	**57**	**28**	**5**	**0**	**1**	**176**	**14.2**	**15**	**12**	**33.3**	**21:24**	....	....	....	....	....	....	....	....	....
2007-08	**Chicago**	**NHL**	**35**	**10**	**17**	**27**	**22**	**3**	**0**	**2**	**87**	**11.5**	**4**	**3**	**0.0**	**18:35**	....	....	....	....	....	....	....	....	....
2008-09	**Chicago**	**NHL**	**81**	**29**	**48**	**77**	**30**	**5**	**0**	**5**	**249**	**11.6**	**29**	**8**	**25.0**	**17:25**	**16**	**5**	**10**	**15**	**8**	**0**	**0**	**1**	**15:34**
2009-10	**Minnesota**	**NHL**	**73**	**18**	**36**	**54**	**34**	**4**	**0**	**3**	**169**	**10.7**	**-19**	**12**	**50.0**	**17:56**	....	....	....	....	....	....	....	....	....
	Czech Republic	Olympics	5	0	2	2	0	....	....	....	....	....	....	....	....	....	....	....	....	....	....	....	....	....	....
2010-11	**Minnesota**	**NHL**	**78**	**22**	**40**	**62**	**52**	**3**	**0**	**4**	**229**	**9.6**	**-10**	**10**	**30.0**	**18:21**	....	....	....	....	....	....	....	....	....
	NHL Totals		**621**	**209**	**303**	**512**	**332**	**60**	**1**	**38**	**1599**	**13.1**		**143**	**32.9**	**17:08**	**67**	**19**	**30**	**49**	**44**	**6**	**0**	**6**	**16:10**

NHL All-Rookie Team (2001)

Played in NHL All-Star Game (2007, 2011)

Signed as a free agent by **Znojmo** (CzRep), September 24, 2004. Signed as a free agent by **Dynamo Moscow** (Russia), November 10, 2004. Signed as a free agent by **Sparta Praha** (CzRep), January 31, 2005. • Missed majority of 2005-06 due to shoulder injury vs. Montreal, November 29, 2005. Traded to **Chicago** by **Ottawa** with Bryan Smolinski for Tom Preissing, Josh Hennessy, Michal Barinka and Chicago's 2nd round choice (Patrick Wiercioch) in 2008 Entry Draft, July 10, 2006. • Missed majority of 2007-08 due to shoulder (October 4, 2007 at Minnesota) and groin (December 22, 2007 at Ottawa) injuries. Signed as a free agent by **Minnesota**, July 1, 2009. Traded to **San Jose** by **Minnesota** for Dany Heatley, July 3, 2011.

HAYDAR, Darren
(HAY-duhr, DAIR-ehn)

Right wing. Shoots right. 5'9", 170 lbs. Born, Toronto, Ont., October 22, 1979. Nashville's 15th choice, 248th overall, in 1999 Entry Draft.

Season	Club	League	GP	G	A	Pts	PIM	PP	SH	GW	S	%	+/-	TF	F%	Min	GP	G	A	Pts	PIM	PP	SH	GW	Min
1995-96	Milton Merchants	OPJHL	6	1	2	3	4	....	....	....	....	....	....	....	....	....	....	....	....	....	....	....	....	....	....
1996-97	Milton Merchants	OPJHL	51	32	68	100	68	....	....	....	....	....	....	....	....	....	....	....	....	....	....	....	....	....	....
1997-98	Milton Merchants	OPJHL	51	*71	*69	*140	65	....	....	....	....	....	....	....	....	....	....	....	....	....	....	....	....	....	....
1998-99	New Hampshire	H-East	41	31	30	61	34	....	....	....	....	....	....	....	....	....	....	....	....	....	....	....	....	....	....
99-2000	New Hampshire	H-East	38	22	19	41	42	....	....	....	....	....	....	....	....	....	....	....	....	....	....	....	....	....	....
2000-01	New Hampshire	H-East	39	18	23	41	38	....	....	....	....	....	....	....	....	....	....	....	....	....	....	....	....	....	....
2001-02	New Hampshire	H-East	40	31	*45	*76	28	....	....	....	....	....	....	....	....	....	....	....	....	....	....	....	....	....	....
2002-03	**Nashville**	**NHL**	**2**	**0**	**0**	**0**	**0**	**0**	**0**	**0**	**1**	**0.0**	**-1**	**0**	**0.0**	**8:54**	....	....	....	....	....	....	....	....	....
	Milwaukee	AHL	75	29	46	75	36	....	....	....	....	....	....	....	....	....	6	1	4	5	2	....	....	....	....
2003-04	Milwaukee	AHL	79	22	37	59	35	....	....	....	....	....	....	....	....	....	22	*11	15	*26	10	....	....	....	....
2004-05	Milwaukee	AHL	59	24	26	50	42	....	....	....	....	....	....	....	....	....	7	3	4	7	14	....	....	....	....
2005-06	Milwaukee	AHL	80	35	57	92	50	....	....	....	....	....	....	....	....	....	21	*18	17	*35	18	....	....	....	....
2006-07	**Atlanta**	**NHL**	**4**	**0**	**0**	**0**	**0**	**0**	**0**	**0**	**4**	**0.0**	**0**	**3**	**66.7**	**8:01**	....	....	....	....	....	....	....	....	....
	Chicago Wolves	AHL	73	41	*81	*122	55	....	....	....	....	....	....	....	....	....	15	*10	*14	*24	14	....	....	....	....
2007-08	**Atlanta**	**NHL**	**16**	**1**	**7**	**8**	**2**	**0**	**0**	**0**	**14**	**7.1**	**4**	**2**	**0.0**	**11:46**	....	....	....	....	....	....	....	....	....
	Chicago Wolves	AHL	51	19	39	58	52	....	....	....	....	....	....	....	....	....	24	*12	15	27	8	....	....	....	....
2008-09	Grand Rapids	AHL	79	31	49	80	26	....	....	....	....	....	....	....	....	....	10	4	7	11	4	....	....	....	....
2009-10	**Colorado**	**NHL**	**1**	**0**	**0**	**0**	**0**	**0**	**0**	**0**	**2**	**0.0**	**0**	**0**	**0.0**	**5:22**	....	....	....	....	....	....	....	....	....
	Lake Erie	AHL	66	23	41	64	60	....	....	....	....	....	....	....	....	....	....	....	....	....	....	....	....	....	....
2010-11	Chicago Wolves	AHL	77	27	47	74	60	....	....	....	....	....	....	....	....	....	....	....	....	....	....	....	....	....	....
	NHL Totals		**23**	**1**	**7**	**8**	**2**	**0**	**0**	**0**	**21**	**4.8**		**5**	**40.0**	**10:35**	....	....	....	....	....	....	....	....	....

Hockey East Second All-Star Team (1999, 2000) • Hockey East Rookie of the Year (1999) • Hockey East First All-Star Team (2002) • Hockey East Player of the Year (2002) • AHL All-Rookie Team (2003) • Dudley "Red" Garrett Memorial Award (AHL – Rookie of the Year) (2003) • AHL First All-Star Team (2007) • John P. Sollenberger Trophy (AHL – Top Scorer) (2007) • Les Cunningham Award (AHL – MVP) (2007) • AHL Second All-Star Team (2009, 2011)

Signed as a free agent by **Atlanta**, July 4, 2006. Signed as a free agent by **Detroit**, July 23, 2008. Signed as a free agent by **Colorado**, July 6, 2009. Signed as a free agent by **Chicago** (AHL), July 29, 2010.

HEATLEY, Dany
(HEET-lee, DA-nee) **MIN**

Left wing. Shoots left. 6'4", 220 lbs. Born, Freiburg, West Germany, January 21, 1981. Atlanta's 1st choice, 2nd overall, in 2000 Entry Draft.

Season	Club	League	GP	G	A	Pts	PIM	PP	SH	GW	S	%	+/-	TF	F%	Min	GP	G	A	Pts	PIM	PP	SH	GW	Min
1996-97	Calgary Blazers	AMHL	25	30	42	72	26	....	....	....	....	....	....	....	....	....	....	....	....	....	....	....	....	....	....
1997-98	Calgary Buffaloes	AMHL	36	39	42	*81	34	....	....	....	....	....	....	....	....	....	10	10	12	*22	30	....	....	....	....
1998-99	Calgary Canucks	AJHL	60	*70	56	*126	91	....	....	....	....	....	....	....	....	....	13	*22	13	*35	6	....	....	....	....
99-2000	U. of Wisconsin	WCHA	38	28	28	56	32	....	....	....	....	....	....	....	....	....	....	....	....	....	....	....	....	....	....
2000-01	U. of Wisconsin	WCHA	39	24	33	57	74	....	....	....	....	....	....	....	....	....	....	....	....	....	....	....	....	....	....
2001-02	**Atlanta**	**NHL**	**82**	**26**	**41**	**67**	**56**	**7**	**0**	**4**	**202**	**12.9**	**-19**	**116**	**32.8**	**19:53**	....	....	....	....	....	....	....	....	....
2002-03	**Atlanta**	**NHL**	**77**	**41**	**48**	**89**	**58**	**19**	**1**	**6**	**252**	**16.3**	**-8**	**49**	**36.7**	**21:57**	....	....	....	....	....	....	....	....	....
2003-04	**Atlanta**	**NHL**	**31**	**13**	**12**	**25**	**18**	**5**	**0**	**3**	**83**	**15.7**	**-8**	**41**	**24.4**	**19:53**	....	....	....	....	....	....	....	....	....

			Regular Season														Playoffs								
Season	Club	League	GP	G	A	Pts	PIM	PP	SH	GW	S	%	+/-	TF	F%	Min	GP	G	A	Pts	PIM	PP	SH	GW	Min
2004-05	SC Bern	Swiss	16	14	10	24	58	....	....	....	....	....	....	....	....	....	....	....	....	....	....	....	....	....	....
	Ak Bars Kazan	Russia	11	3	1	4	22	....	....	....	....	....	....	....	....	....	4	2	1	3	4	....	....	....	....
2005-06	**Ottawa**	**NHL**	**82**	**50**	**53**	**103**	**86**	**23**	**2**	**7**	**300**	**16.7**	**29**	**166**	**53.6**	**21:09**	**10**	**3**	**9**	**12**	**11**	**3**	**0**	**1**	**18:56**
	Canada	Olympics	6	2	1	3	8	....	....	....	....	....	....	....	....	....	....	....	....	....	....	....	....	....	....
2006-07	**Ottawa**	**NHL**	**82**	**50**	**55**	**105**	**74**	**17**	**3**	***10**	**310**	**16.1**	**31**	**60**	**38.3**	**21:02**	**20**	**7**	***15**	***22**	**14**	**2**	**0**	**2**	**21:18**
2007-08	**Ottawa**	**NHL**	**71**	**41**	**41**	**82**	**76**	**13**	**0**	**8**	**224**	**18.3**	**33**	**26**	**57.7**	**21:44**	**4**	**0**	**1**	**1**	**6**	**0**	**0**	**0**	**21:41**
2008-09	**Ottawa**	**NHL**	**82**	**39**	**33**	**72**	**88**	**15**	**0**	**6**	**258**	**15.1**	**–11**	**30**	**46.7**	**20:07**	....	....	....	....	....	....	....	....	....
2009-10	**San Jose**	**NHL**	**82**	**39**	**43**	**82**	**54**	**18**	**1**	**9**	**280**	**13.9**	**14**	**35**	**40.0**	**20:14**	**14**	**2**	**11**	**13**	**16**	**1**	**0**	**0**	**20:41**
	Canada	Olympics	7	4	3	7	4	....	....	....	....	....	....	....	....	....	....	....	....	....	....	....	....	....	....
2010-11	**San Jose**	**NHL**	**80**	**26**	**38**	**64**	**56**	**11**	**1**	**5**	**217**	**12.0**	**8**	**20**	**45.0**	**19:39**	**18**	**3**	**6**	**9**	**12**	**0**	**0**	**0**	**18:56**
	NHL Totals		**669**	**325**	**364**	**689**	**566**	**128**	**8**	**58**	**2126**	**15.3**		**543**	**42.4**	**20:39**	**66**	**15**	**42**	**57**	**59**	**6**	**0**	**3**	**20:12**

WCHA First All-Star Team (2000) • WCHA Rookie of the Year (2000) • NCAA West Second All-American Team (2000) • WCHA Second All-Star Team (2001) • NCAA West First All-American Team (2001) • NHL All-Rookie Team (2002) • Calder Memorial Trophy (2002) • NHL Second All-Star Team (2006) • NHL First All-Star Team (2007)

Played in NHL All-Star Game (2003, 2007, 2009)

• Missed majority of 2003-04 due to automobile accident, September 29, 2003. Signed as a free agent by **Bern** (Swiss), October 13, 2004. Signed as a free agent by **Kazan** (Russia), February 9, 2005. Traded to **Ottawa** by **Atlanta** for Marian Hossa and Greg de Vries, August 23, 2005. Traded to **San Jose** by **Ottawa** with Ottawa's 5th round choice (Isaac MacLeod) in 2010 Entry Draft for Milan Michalek, Jonathan Cheechoo and San Jose's 2nd round choice (later traded to NY Islanders, later traded to Chicago – Chicago selected Kent Simpson) in 2010 Entry Draft, September 12, 2009. Traded to **Minnesota** by **San Jose** for Martin Havlat, July 3, 2011.

HECHT, Jochen

(HEHSHT, YOH-khehn) **BUF**

Left wing. Shoots left. 6'1", 198 lbs. Born, Mannheim, West Germany, June 21, 1977. St. Louis' 1st choice, 49th overall, in 1995 Entry Draft.

Season	Club	League	GP	G	A	Pts	PIM	PP	SH	GW	S	%	+/-	TF	F%	Min	GP	G	A	Pts	PIM	PP	SH	GW	Min
1993-94	Mannheim Jr.	Ger-Jr.	28	27	13	40	103	....	....	....	....	....	....	....	....	....	....	....	....	....	....	....	....	....	....
1994-95	Adler Mannheim	Germany	43	11	12	23	68	....	....	....	....	....	....	....	....	....	10	5	4	9	12	....	....	....	....
1995-96	Adler Mannheim	Germany	44	12	16	28	68	....	....	....	....	....	....	....	....	....	8	3	2	5	6	....	....	....	....
1996-97	Adler Mannheim	Germany	46	21	21	42	36	....	....	....	....	....	....	....	....	....	9	3	3	6	4	....	....	....	....
1997-98	Adler Mannheim	Germany	44	7	19	26	42	....	....	....	....	....	....	....	....	....	10	1	1	2	14	....	....	....	....
	Adler Mannheim	EuroHL	5	0	4	4	8	....	....	....	....	....	....	....	....	....	....	....	....	....	....	....	....	....	....
	Germany	Olympics	4	1	0	1	6	....	....	....	....	....	....	....	....	....	....	....	....	....	....	....	....	....	....
1998-99	**St. Louis**	**NHL**	**3**	**0**	**0**	**0**	**0**	**0**	**0**	**0**	**4**	**0.0**	**–2**	**19**	**21.1**	**13:16**	**5**	**2**	**0**	**2**	**0**	**0**	**0**	**0**	**16:40**
	Worcester IceCats	AHL	74	21	35	56	48	....	....	....	....	....	....	....	....	....	4	1	1	2	2	....	....	....	....
99-2000	**St. Louis**	**NHL**	**63**	**13**	**21**	**34**	**28**	**5**	**0**	**1**	**140**	**9.3**	**20**	**75**	**49.3**	**15:25**	**7**	**4**	**6**	**10**	**2**	**1**	**0**	**1**	**17:02**
2000-01	**St. Louis**	**NHL**	**72**	**19**	**25**	**44**	**48**	**8**	**3**	**1**	**208**	**9.1**	**11**	**160**	**43.8**	**17:56**	**15**	**2**	**4**	**6**	**4**	**0**	**0**	**0**	**17:19**
2001-02	**Edmonton**	**NHL**	**82**	**16**	**24**	**40**	**60**	**5**	**0**	**3**	**211**	**7.6**	**4**	**26**	**53.9**	**15:00**	....	....	....	....	....	....	....	....	....
	Germany	Olympics	4	1	1	2	2	....	....	....	....	....	....	....	....	....	....	....	....	....	....	....	....	....	....
2002-03	**Buffalo**	**NHL**	**49**	**10**	**16**	**26**	**30**	**2**	**0**	**2**	**145**	**6.9**	**4**	**33**	**30.3**	**17:55**	....	....	....	....	....	....	....	....	....
2003-04	**Buffalo**	**NHL**	**64**	**15**	**37**	**52**	**49**	**2**	**1**	**0**	**174**	**8.6**	**17**	**141**	**43.3**	**19:00**	....	....	....	....	....	....	....	....	....
2004-05	Adler Mannheim	Germany	48	16	34	50	151	....	....	....	....	....	....	....	....	....	14	10	10	*20	14	....	....	....	....
2005-06	**Buffalo**	**NHL**	**64**	**18**	**24**	**42**	**34**	**4**	**2**	**4**	**179**	**10.1**	**10**	**156**	**39.7**	**18:07**	**15**	**2**	**6**	**8**	**8**	**0**	**0**	**1**	**17:29**
2006-07	**Buffalo**	**NHL**	**76**	**19**	**37**	**56**	**39**	**3**	**0**	**1**	**197**	**9.6**	**19**	**145**	**39.3**	**18:51**	**16**	**4**	**1**	**5**	**10**	**0**	**0**	**1**	**17:41**
2007-08	**Buffalo**	**NHL**	**75**	**22**	**27**	**49**	**38**	**3**	**1**	**2**	**229**	**9.6**	**1**	**905**	**42.0**	**19:19**	....	....	....	....	....	....	....	....	....
2008-09	**Buffalo**	**NHL**	**70**	**12**	**15**	**27**	**33**	**3**	**1**	**1**	**173**	**6.9**	**–9**	**538**	**43.7**	**17:24**	....	....	....	....	....	....	....	....	....
2009-10	Germany	Olympics	4	0	1	1	2	....	....	....	....	....	....	....	....	....	....	....	....	....	....	....	....	....	....
	Buffalo	**NHL**	**79**	**21**	**21**	**42**	**35**	**3**	**0**	**2**	**224**	**9.4**	**14**	**322**	**45.3**	**17:11**	....	....	....	....	....	....	....	....	....
2010-11	**Buffalo**	**NHL**	**67**	**12**	**17**	**29**	**40**	**0**	**0**	**4**	**172**	**7.0**	**4**	**729**	**43.1**	**17:05**	**1**	**0**	**1**	**1**	**0**	**0**	**0**	**0**	**15:22**
	NHL Totals		**764**	**177**	**264**	**441**	**434**	**38**	**8**	**21**	**2056**	**8.6**		**3249**	**42.8**	**17:31**	**59**	**14**	**18**	**32**	**24**	**1**	**0**	**3**	**17:20**

Traded to **Edmonton** by **St. Louis** with Marty Reasoner and Jan Horacek for Doug Weight and Michel Riesen, July 1, 2001. Traded to **Buffalo** by **Edmonton** for Atlanta's 2nd round choice (previously acquired, Edmonton selected Jeff Deslauriers) in 2002 Entry Draft and Nashville's 2nd round choice (previously acquired, Edmonton selected Jarret Stoll) in 2002 Entry Draft, June 22, 2002. Signed as a free agent by **Mannheim** (Germany), August 2, 2004.

HEDMAN, Victor

(HEHD-muhn, VIHK-tohr) **T.B.**

Defense. Shoots left. 6'6", 229 lbs. Born, Ornskoldsvik, Sweden, December 18, 1990. Tampa Bay's 1st choice, 2nd overall, in 2009 Entry Draft.

Season	Club	League	GP	G	A	Pts	PIM	PP	SH	GW	S	%	+/-	TF	F%	Min	GP	G	A	Pts	PIM	PP	SH	GW	Min
2005-06	MODO U18	Swe-U18	8	3	3	6	14	....	....	....	....	....	....	....	....	....	2	0	0	0	0	....	....	....	....
	MODO Jr.	Swe-Jr.	10	0	1	1	8	....	....	....	....	....	....	....	....	....	....	....	....	....	....	....	....	....	....
2006-07	MODO U18	Swe-U18	3	3	0	3	29	....	....	....	....	....	....	....	....	....	....	....	....	....	....	....	....	....	....
	MODO Jr.	Swe-Jr.	34	13	12	25	30	....	....	....	....	....	....	....	....	....	5	1	1	2	44	....	....	....	....
2007-08	MODO Jr.	Swe-Jr.	6	2	1	3	26	....	....	....	....	....	....	....	....	....	3	2	0	2	4	....	....	....	....
	MODO	Sweden	39	2	2	4	44	....	....	....	....	....	....	....	....	....	5	1	0	1	4	....	....	....	....
2008-09	MODO Jr.	Swe-Jr.	2	0	2	2	10	....	....	....	....	....	....	....	....	....	5	0	1	1	2	....	....	....	....
	MODO	Sweden	43	7	14	21	52	....	....	....	....	....	....	....	....	....	....	....	....	....	....	....	....	....	....
2009-10	**Tampa Bay**	**NHL**	**74**	**4**	**16**	**20**	**79**	**0**	**0**	**0**	**90**	**4.4**	**–3**	**0**	**0.0**	**20:51**	....	....	....	....	....	....	....	....	....
2010-11	**Tampa Bay**	**NHL**	**79**	**3**	**23**	**26**	**70**	**0**	**0**	**0**	**101**	**3.0**	**3**	**0**	**0.0**	**21:01**	**18**	**0**	**6**	**6**	**8**	**0**	**0**	**0**	**22:16**
	NHL Totals		**153**	**7**	**39**	**46**	**149**	**0**	**0**	**0**	**191**	**3.7**		**0**	**0.0**	**20:56**	**18**	**0**	**6**	**6**	**8**	**0**	**0**	**0**	**22:16**

HEIKKINEN, Ilkka

(HAY-kih-nehn, IHL-ka) **NYR**

Defense. Shoots left. 6'2", 205 lbs. Born, Rauma, Finland, November 13, 1984.

Season	Club	League	GP	G	A	Pts	PIM	PP	SH	GW	S	%	+/-	TF	F%	Min	GP	G	A	Pts	PIM	PP	SH	GW	Min
2004-05	Lukko Rauma	Finland	48	0	2	2	8	....	....	....	....	....	....	....	....	....	9	0	0	0	0	....	....	....	....
2005-06	Lukko Rauma	Finland	55	5	10	15	46	....	....	....	....	....	....	....	....	....	....	....	....	....	....	....	....	....	....
2006-07	Lukko Rauma	Finland	55	7	17	24	71	....	....	....	....	....	....	....	....	....	3	0	0	0	0	....	....	....	....
2007-08	HIFK Helsinki	Finland	51	11	26	37	96	....	....	....	....	....	....	....	....	....	7	0	2	2	6	....	....	....	....
2008-09	HIFK Helsinki	Finland	54	8	26	34	22	....	....	....	....	....	....	....	....	....	2	0	1	1	0	....	....	....	....
2009-10	**NY Rangers**	**NHL**	**7**	**0**	**0**	**0**	**0**	**0**	**0**	**0**	**4**	**0.0**	**2**	**0**	**0.0**	**8:52**	....	....	....	....	....	....	....	....	....
	Hartford	AHL	72	8	30	38	27	....	....	....	....	....	....	....	....	....	....	....	....	....	....	....	....	....	....
2010-11	Sibir Novosibirsk	Rus-KHL	49	7	15	22	19	....	....	....	....	....	....	....	....	....	4	0	0	0	4	....	....	....	....
	NHL Totals		**7**	**0**	**0**	**0**	**0**	**0**	**0**	**0**	**4**	**0.0**		**0**	**0.0**	**8:52**	....	....	....	....	....	....	....	....	....

Signed as a free agent by **NY Rangers**, May 20, 2009. Signed as a free agent by **Novosibirsk** (Russia-KHL), May 21, 2010.

HEJDA, Jan

(HAY-dah, YAHN) **COL**

Defense. Shoots left. 6'4", 237 lbs. Born, Prague, Czech., June 18, 1978. Buffalo's 4th choice, 106th overall, in 2003 Entry Draft.

Season	Club	League	GP	G	A	Pts	PIM	PP	SH	GW	S	%	+/-	TF	F%	Min	GP	G	A	Pts	PIM	PP	SH	GW	Min
1997-98	HC Slavia Praha	CzRep	44	2	5	7	51	....	....	....	....	....	....	....	....	....	5	0	0	0	6	....	....	....	....
1998-99	HC Slavia Praha	CzRep	34	1	2	3	38	....	....	....	....	....	....	....	....	....	....	....	....	....	....	....	....	....	....
99-2000	HC Slavia Praha	CzRep	26	1	2	3	14	....	....	....	....	....	....	....	....	....	....	....	....	....	....	....	....	....	....
	HC Femax Havirov	CzRep	7	0	2	2	6	....	....	....	....	....	....	....	....	....	....	....	....	....	....	....	....	....	....
	Liberec	CzRep-2	1	0	0	0	4	....	....	....	....	....	....	....	....	....	....	....	....	....	....	....	....	....	....
2000-01	HC Slavia Praha	CzRep	38	2	6	8	70	....	....	....	....	....	....	....	....	....	11	3	0	3	12	....	....	....	....
	SK Kadan	CzRep-2	8	1	0	1	6	....	....	....	....	....	....	....	....	....	....	....	....	....	....	....	....	....	....
2001-02	HC Slavia Praha	CzRep	42	9	8	17	52	....	....	....	....	....	....	....	....	....	9	1	1	2	14	....	....	....	....
2002-03	HC Slavia Praha	CzRep	52	6	11	17	44	....	....	....	....	....	....	....	....	....	17	5	8	13	12	....	....	....	....
2003-04	CSKA Moscow	Russia	60	1	5	6	26	....	....	....	....	....	....	....	....	....	....	....	....	....	....	....	....	....	....
2004-05	CSKA Moscow	Russia	60	2	11	13	59	....	....	....	....	....	....	....	....	....	....	....	....	....	....	....	....	....	....
2005-06	Mytischi	Russia	50	3	12	15	56	....	....	....	....	....	....	....	....	....	9	2	3	5	24	....	....	....	....
2006-07	**Edmonton**	**NHL**	**39**	**1**	**8**	**9**	**20**	**0**	**0**	**1**	**33**	**3.0**	**–6**	**0**	**0.0**	**20:23**	....	....	....	....	....	....	....	....	....
	Hamilton	AHL	5	0	3	3	21	....	....	....	....	....	....	....	....	....	....	....	....	....	....	....	....	....	....
2007-08	**Columbus**	**NHL**	**81**	**0**	**13**	**13**	**61**	**0**	**0**	**0**	**71**	**0.0**	**20**	**0**	**0.0**	**21:08**	....	....	....	....	....	....	....	....	....
2008-09	**Columbus**	**NHL**	**82**	**3**	**18**	**21**	**38**	**0**	**0**	**1**	**66**	**4.5**	**23**	**1**	**0.0**	**22:23**	**3**	**0**	**0**	**0**	**2**	**0**	**0**	**0**	**16:53**
2009-10	**Columbus**	**NHL**	**62**	**3**	**10**	**13**	**36**	**1**	**0**	**0**	**63**	**4.8**	**–14**	**2**	**50.0**	**20:39**	....	....	....	....	....	....	....	....	....
	Czech Republic	Olympics	5	0	0	0	4	....	....	....	....	....	....	....	....	....	....	....	....	....	....	....	....	....	....
2010-11	**Columbus**	**NHL**	**77**	**5**	**15**	**20**	**28**	**0**	**0**	**0**	**79**	**6.3**	**–6**	**1**	**100.0**	**21:07**	....	....	....	....	....	....	....	....	....
	NHL Totals		**341**	**12**	**64**	**76**	**183**	**1**	**0**	**2**	**312**	**3.8**		**4**	**50.0**	**21:15**	**3**	**0**	**0**	**0**	**2**	**0**	**0**	**0**	**16:53**

• Rights traded to **Edmonton** by **Buffalo** for Edmonton's 7th round choice (Nick Eno) in 2007 Entry Draft, July 10, 2006. Signed as a free agent by **Columbus**, July 5, 2007. Signed as a free agent by **Colorado**, July 1, 2011.

HEJDUK, Milan

(HAY-dook, MEE-lan) **COL**

Right wing. Shoots right. 6', 190 lbs. Born, Usti nad Labem, Czech., February 14, 1976. Quebec's 6th choice, 87th overall, in 1994 Entry Draft.

			Regular Season														Playoffs								
Season	Club	League	GP	G	A	Pts	PIM	PP	SH	GW	S	%	+/-	TF	F%	Min	GP	G	A	Pts	PIM	PP	SH	GW	Min
1993-94	HC Pardubice	CzRep	22	6	3	9	....	....	....	....	....	....	....	....	....	....	10	5	1	6	....	....	....	....	....
1994-95	HC Pardubice	CzRep	43	11	13	24	6	....	....	....	....	....	....	....	....	....	6	3	1	4	0	....	....	....	....
1995-96	Pardubice	CzRep	37	13	7	20	....	....	....	....	....	....	....	....	....	....	....	....	....	....	....	....	....	....	....
1996-97	Pardubice	CzRep	51	27	11	38	10	....	....	....	....	....	....	....	....	....	10	6	0	6	27	....	....	....	....
1997-98	Pardubice	CzRep	48	26	19	45	20	....	....	....	....	....	....	....	....	....	3	0	0	0	2	....	....	....	....
	Czech Republic	Olympics	4	0	0	0	2	....	....	....	....	....	....	....	....	....	....	....	....	....	....	....	....	....	....
1998-99	**Colorado**	**NHL**	82	14	34	48	26	4	0	5	178	7.9	8	2	50.0	15:45	16	6	6	12	4	1	0	3	15:53
99-2000	**Colorado**	**NHL**	82	36	36	72	16	13	0	9	228	15.8	14	3	100.0	19:58	17	5	4	9	6	3	0	1	19:56
2000-01 ♦	**Colorado**	**NHL**	80	41	38	79	36	12	1	9	213	19.2	32	3	33.3	19:52	23	7	*16	23	6	4	0	1	21:33
2001-02	**Colorado**	**NHL**	62	21	23	44	24	7	1	5	139	15.1	0	5	40.0	20:11	16	3	3	6	4	1	0	0	18:24
	Czech Republic	Olympics	4	1	0	1	0	....	....	....	....	....	....	....	....	....	....	....	....	....	....	....	....	....	....
2002-03	**Colorado**	**NHL**	82	*50	48	98	32	18	0	4	244	20.5	*52	43	44.2	19:50	7	2	2	4	2	1	0	0	20:42
2003-04	**Colorado**	**NHL**	82	35	40	75	20	16	0	6	237	14.8	19	69	47.8	18:46	11	5	2	7	0	2	0	0	18:40
2004-05	Pardubice	CzRep	48	25	26	51	14	....	....	....	....	....	....	....	....	....	16	6	2	8	6	....	....	....	....
2005-06	**Colorado**	**NHL**	74	24	34	58	24	14	1	2	221	10.9	13	23	17.4	18:33	9	2	6	8	2	0	0	0	20:56
	Czech Republic	Olympics	8	2	1	3	2	....	....	....	....	....	....	....	....	....	....	....	....	....	....	....	....	....	....
2006-07	**Colorado**	**NHL**	80	35	35	70	44	12	1	6	257	13.6	10	109	45.0	17:53	....	....	....	....	....	....	....	....	....
2007-08	**Colorado**	**NHL**	77	29	25	54	36	8	1	4	205	14.1	8	136	39.7	19:21	10	3	3	6	4	2	0	0	19:05
2008-09	**Colorado**	**NHL**	82	27	32	59	16	10	1	2	211	12.8	–19	160	45.0	19:56	....	....	....	....	....	....	....	....	....
2009-10	**Colorado**	**NHL**	56	23	21	44	10	8	0	4	153	15.0	6	14	28.6	19:01	3	1	0	1	0	0	0	0	12:58
2010-11	**Colorado**	**NHL**	71	22	34	56	18	10	0	2	170	12.9	–23	5	40.0	17:55	....	....	....	....	....	....	....	....	....
	NHL Totals		910	357	400	757	302	132	6	58	2456	14.5		572	42.7	18:54	112	34	42	76	28	14	0	5	19:13

NHL All-Rookie Team (1999) • NHL Second All-Star Team (2003) • Bud Light Plus/Minus Award (2003) (tied with Peter Forsberg) • Maurice "Rocket" Richard Trophy (2003)
Played in NHL All-Star Game (2000, 2001, 2009)
• Rights transferred to **Colorado** after **Quebec** franchise relocated, June 21, 1995. Signed as a free agent by **Pardubice** (CzRep), September 18, 2004.

HELM, Darren

(HEHLM, DAIR-ehn) **DET**

Center/Left wing. Shoots left. 5'11", 195 lbs. Born, Winnipeg, Man., January 21, 1987. Detroit's 5th choice, 132nd overall, in 2005 Entry Draft.

			Regular Season														Playoffs								
Season	Club	League	GP	G	A	Pts	PIM	PP	SH	GW	S	%	+/-	TF	F%	Min	GP	G	A	Pts	PIM	PP	SH	GW	Min
2003-04	Selkirk Fishermen	MJBHL	34	39	32	71	34	....	....	....	....	....	....	....	....	....	....	....	....	....	....	....	....	....	....
2004-05	Medicine Hat	WHL	72	10	14	24	27	....	....	....	....	....	....	....	....	....	13	2	6	8	10	....	....	....	....
2005-06	Medicine Hat	WHL	70	41	38	79	37	....	....	....	....	....	....	....	....	....	13	5	4	9	2	....	....	....	....
2006-07	Medicine Hat	WHL	59	25	39	64	53	....	....	....	....	....	....	....	....	....	23	10	12	22	14	....	....	....	....
2007-08 ♦	**Detroit**	**NHL**	7	0	0	0	2	0	0	0	7	0.0	–2	23	21.7	7:00	18	2	2	4	2	0	0	0	7:30
	Grand Rapids	AHL	67	16	15	31	30	....	....	....	....	....	....	....	....	....	....	....	....	....	....	....	....	....	....
2008-09	**Detroit**	**NHL**	16	0	1	1	4	0	0	0	29	0.0	–7	132	56.1	12:26	23	4	1	5	4	0	0	1	12:06
	Grand Rapids	AHL	55	13	24	37	24	....	....	....	....	....	....	....	....	....	....	....	....	....	....	....	....	....	....
2009-10	**Detroit**	**NHL**	75	11	13	24	18	0	3	3	165	6.7	–2	875	51.1	14:30	12	1	0	1	4	0	0	0	13:56
2010-11	**Detroit**	**NHL**	82	12	20	32	16	0	2	2	177	6.8	9	938	52.6	13:18	11	3	3	6	8	0	0	1	13:28
	NHL Totals		180	23	34	57	40	0	5	5	378	6.1		1968	51.8	13:29	64	10	6	16	18	0	0	2	11:23

WHL East First All-Star Team (2006) • WHL East Second All-Star Team (2007) • Memorial Cup All-Star Team (2007)

HELMINEN, Dwight

(HEHL-mih-nehn, DWIGHT)

Center. Shoots left. 5'10", 190 lbs. Born, Hancock, MI, June 22, 1983. Edmonton's 12th choice, 244th overall, in 2002 Entry Draft.

			Regular Season														Playoffs								
Season	Club	League	GP	G	A	Pts	PIM	PP	SH	GW	S	%	+/-	TF	F%	Min	GP	G	A	Pts	PIM	PP	SH	GW	Min
1998-99	Det. Compuware	MNHL	32	9	7	16	....	....	....	....	....	....	....	....	....	....	....	....	....	....	....	....	....	....	....
99-2000	USNTDP	USHL	30	5	7	12	10	....	....	....	....	....	....	....	....	....	....	....	....	....	....	....	....	....	....
	USNTDP	NAHL	30	7	10	17	8	....	....	....	....	....	....	....	....	....	....	....	....	....	....	....	....	....	....
2000-01	USNTDP	U-18	42	9	36	45	20	....	....	....	....	....	....	....	....	....	....	....	....	....	....	....	....	....	....
	USNTDP	USHL	24	12	7	19	8	....	....	....	....	....	....	....	....	....	....	....	....	....	....	....	....	....	....
	USNTDP	NAHL	1	0	1	1	2	....	....	....	....	....	....	....	....	....	....	....	....	....	....	....	....	....	....
2001-02	U. of Michigan	CCHA	39	10	8	18	10	....	....	....	....	....	....	....	....	....	....	....	....	....	....	....	....	....	....
2002-03	U. of Michigan	CCHA	39	17	16	33	34	....	....	....	....	....	....	....	....	....	....	....	....	....	....	....	....	....	....
2003-04	U. of Michigan	CCHA	41	17	11	28	4	....	....	....	....	....	....	....	....	....	....	....	....	....	....	....	....	....	....
2004-05	Hartford	AHL	41	2	7	9	10	....	....	....	....	....	....	....	....	....	....	....	....	....	....	....	....	....	....
	Charlotte	ECHL	28	5	16	21	10	....	....	....	....	....	....	....	....	....	15	7	3	10	2	....	....	....	....
2005-06	Hartford	AHL	77	32	24	56	40	....	....	....	....	....	....	....	....	....	13	3	5	8	10	....	....	....	....
2006-07	Hartford	AHL	80	15	24	39	32	....	....	....	....	....	....	....	....	....	7	1	1	2	2	....	....	....	....
2007-08	JYP Jyvaskyla	Finland	52	20	25	45	10	....	....	....	....	....	....	....	....	....	6	3	3	6	0	....	....	....	....
2008-09	**Carolina**	**NHL**	23	1	1	2	0	0	0	0	15	6.7	–2	131	46.6	6:50	1	0	0	0	0	0	0	0	3:08
	Albany River Rats	AHL	54	15	15	30	26	....	....	....	....	....	....	....	....	....	....	....	....	....	....	....	....	....	....
2009-10	**San Jose**	**NHL**	4	1	0	1	0	0	0	0	1	100.0	–1	9	22.2	10:59	7	1	0	1	4	0	0	0	6:01
	Worcester Sharks	AHL	74	12	10	22	16	....	....	....	....	....	....	....	....	....	2	0	0	0	0	....	....	....	....
2010-11	Pelicans Lahti	Finland	60	12	16	28	40	....	....	....	....	....	....	....	....	....	....	....	....	....	....	....	....	....	....
	Pelicans Lahti	Finland-Q	....	....	....	....	....	....	....	....	....	....	....	....	....	....	4	3	0	3	0	....	....	....	....
	NHL Totals		27	2	1	3	0	0	0	0	16	12.5		140	45.0	7:27	8	1	0	1	4	0	0	0	5:40

Traded to **NY Rangers** by **Edmonton** with Steve Valiquette and Edmonton's 2nd round compensatory choice (Dane Byers) in 2004 Entry Draft for Petr Nedved and Jussi Markkanen, March 3, 2004. Signed as a free agent by **Jyvaskyla** (Finland), July 7, 2007. Signed as a free agent by **Carolina**, July 3, 2008. Signed as a free agent by **San Jose**, July 16, 2009. Signed as a free agent by **Lahti** (Finland), June 21, 2010.

HEMSKY, Ales

(HEHM-skee, ahl-EHSH) **EDM**

Right wing. Shoots right. 6', 184 lbs. Born, Pardubice, Czech., August 13, 1983. Edmonton's 1st choice, 13th overall, in 2001 Entry Draft.

			Regular Season														Playoffs								
Season	Club	League	GP	G	A	Pts	PIM	PP	SH	GW	S	%	+/-	TF	F%	Min	GP	G	A	Pts	PIM	PP	SH	GW	Min
99-2000	HC Pardubice Jr.	CzRep-Jr.	45	20	36	56	54	....	....	....	....	....	....	....	....	....	7	4	14	18	36	....	....	....	....
	Pardubice	CzRep	4	0	1	1	0	....	....	....	....	....	....	....	....	....	....	....	....	....	....	....	....	....	....
2000-01	Hull Olympiques	QMJHL	68	36	64	100	67	....	....	....	....	....	....	....	....	....	5	2	3	5	2	....	....	....	....
2001-02	Hull Olympiques	QMJHL	53	27	70	97	86	....	....	....	....	....	....	....	....	....	10	6	10	16	6	....	....	....	....
2002-03	**Edmonton**	**NHL**	59	6	24	30	14	0	0	1	50	12.0	5	3	33.3	12:04	6	0	0	0	0	0	0	0	12:46
2003-04	**Edmonton**	**NHL**	71	12	22	34	14	4	0	3	87	13.8	–7	3	33.3	14:26	....	....	....	....	....	....	....	....	....
2004-05	Pardubice	CzRep	47	13	18	31	28	....	....	....	....	....	....	....	....	....	16	4	*10	*14	26	....	....	....	....
2005-06	**Edmonton**	**NHL**	81	19	58	77	64	7	1	4	178	10.7	–5	7	42.9	16:59	24	6	11	17	14	4	0	2	16:06
	Czech Republic	Olympics	8	1	2	3	2	....	....	....	....	....	....	....	....	....	....	....	....	....	....	....	....	....	....
2006-07	**Edmonton**	**NHL**	64	13	40	53	40	5	0	1	122	10.7	–7	10	30.0	16:59	....	....	....	....	....	....	....	....	....
2007-08	**Edmonton**	**NHL**	74	20	51	71	34	8	0	2	184	10.9	–9	5	20.0	18:35	....	....	....	....	....	....	....	....	....
2008-09	**Edmonton**	**NHL**	72	23	43	66	32	4	0	2	185	12.4	1	4	0.0	18:39	....	....	....	....	....	....	....	....	....
2009-10	**Edmonton**	**NHL**	22	7	15	22	8	3	0	0	57	12.3	7	1	100.0	17:56	....	....	....	....	....	....	....	....	....
2010-11	**Edmonton**	**NHL**	47	14	28	42	18	1	1	1	100	14.0	3	7	14.3	18:17	....	....	....	....	....	....	....	....	....
	NHL Totals		490	114	281	395	224	32	2	14	963	11.8		40	27.5	16:41	30	6	11	17	14	4	0	2	15:26

QMJHL Second All-Star Team (2002)
Signed as a free agent by **Pardubice** (CzRep), September 18, 2004. • Missed majority of 2009-10 due to shoulder injury vs. Los Angeles, November 25, 2009.

HENDRICKS, Matt

(HEHN-drihks, MAT) **WSH**

Center. Shoots left. 6', 215 lbs. Born, Blaine, MN, June 17, 1981. Nashville's 5th choice, 131st overall, in 2000 Entry Draft.

			Regular Season														Playoffs								
Season	Club	League	GP	G	A	Pts	PIM	PP	SH	GW	S	%	+/-	TF	F%	Min	GP	G	A	Pts	PIM	PP	SH	GW	Min
1998-99	Blaine Bengals	High-MN	22	23	34	57	42	....	....	....	....	....	....	....	....	....	....	....	....	....	....	....	....	....	....
99-2000	Blaine Bengals	High-MN	21	23	30	53	28	....	....	....	....	....	....	....	....	....	....	....	....	....	....	....	....	....	....
2000-01	St. Cloud State	WCHA	37	3	9	12	23	....	....	....	....	....	....	....	....	....	....	....	....	....	....	....	....	....	....
2001-02	St. Cloud State	WCHA	42	19	20	39	74	....	....	....	....	....	....	....	....	....	....	....	....	....	....	....	....	....	....
2002-03	St. Cloud State	WCHA	37	18	18	36	64	....	....	....	....	....	....	....	....	....	....	....	....	....	....	....	....	....	....
2003-04	St. Cloud State	WCHA	37	14	11	25	32	....	....	....	....	....	....	....	....	....	....	....	....	....	....	....	....	....	....
	Milwaukee	AHL	1	0	0	0	2	....	....	....	....	....	....	....	....	....	....	....	....	....	....	....	....	....	....
2004-05	Lowell	AHL	15	1	2	3	10	....	....	....	....	....	....	....	....	....	....	....	....	....	....	....	....	....	....
	Florida Everblades	ECHL	54	24	26	50	94	....	....	....	....	....	....	....	....	....	4	0	0	0	4	....	....	....	....
2005-06	Rochester	AHL	56	13	14	27	84	....	....	....	....	....	....	....	....	....	....	....	....	....	....	....	....	....	....
2006-07	Hershey Bears	AHL	65	18	26	44	105	....	....	....	....	....	....	....	....	....	19	8	4	12	18	....	....	....	....
2007-08	Providence Bruins	AHL	67	22	30	52	121	....	....	....	....	....	....	....	....	....	10	0	3	3	6	....	....	....	....

			Regular Season														Playoffs								
Season	Club	League	GP	G	A	Pts	PIM	PP	SH	GW	S	%	+/-	TF	F%	Min	GP	G	A	Pts	PIM	PP	SH	GW	Min
2008-09	**Colorado**	**NHL**	**4**	**0**	**0**	**0**	**13**	**0**	**0**	**0**	**5**	**0.0**	**1**	**1**	**0.0**	**8:30**									
	Lake Erie	AHL	43	14	15	29	71																		
2009-10	**Colorado**	**NHL**	**56**	**9**	**7**	**16**	**74**	**0**	**1**	**1**	**63**	**14.3**	**1**	**83**	**39.8**	**9:16**	**6**	**0**	**0**	**0**	**0**	**0**	**0**	**0**	**9:52**
2010-11	**Washington**	**NHL**	**77**	**9**	**16**	**25**	**110**	**1**	**0**	**3**	**113**	**8.0**	**-2**	**98**	**53.1**	**11:28**	**7**	**0**	**0**	**0**	**4**	**0**	**0**	**0**	**9:08**
	NHL Totals		**137**	**18**	**23**	**41**	**197**	**1**	**1**	**4**	**181**	**9.9**		**182**	**46.7**	**10:28**	**13**	**0**	**0**	**0**	**4**	**0**	**0**	**0**	**9:28**

Signed as a free agent by **Boston**, July 9, 2007. Traded to **Colorado** by **Boston** for Johnny Boychuk, June 24, 2008. Signed as a free agent by **Washington**, September 27, 2010.

HENDRY, Jordan

(HEHN-dree, JOHR-dahn)

Defense. Shoots left. 6', 197 lbs. Born, Nokomis, Sask., February 23, 1984.

Season	Club	League	GP	G	A	Pts	PIM	PP	SH	GW	S	%	+/-	TF	F%	Min	GP	G	A	Pts	PIM	PP	SH	GW	Min
2002-03	Alaska	CCHA	35	3	5	8	10																		
2003-04	Alaska	CCHA	36	4	9	13	38																		
2004-05	Alaska	CCHA	3	0	1	1	21																		
2005-06	Alaska	CCHA	38	4	10	14	74																		
	Norfolk Admirals	AHL	13	1	4	5	13										3	0	0	0	2				
2006-07	Norfolk Admirals	AHL	80	4	12	16	84										6	0	2	2	6				
2007-08	**Chicago**	**NHL**	**40**	**1**	**3**	**4**	**22**	**0**	**0**	**0**	**32**	**3.1**	**0**	**0**	**0.0**	**17:13**									
	Rockford IceHogs	AHL	45	3	4	7	58										1	0	0	0	2				
2008-09	**Chicago**	**NHL**	**9**	**0**	**0**	**0**	**4**	**0**	**0**	**0**	**1**	**0.0**	**-1**	**0**	**0.0**	**10:06**									
	Rockford IceHogs	AHL	53	3	6	9	45										4	0	0	0	2				
2009-10♦	**Chicago**	**NHL**	**43**	**2**	**6**	**8**	**10**	**0**	**0**	**1**	**42**	**4.8**	**5**	**0**	**0.0**	**11:51**	**15**	**0**	**0**	**0**	**2**	**0**	**0**	**0**	**8:09**
2010-11	**Chicago**	**NHL**	**37**	**1**	**0**	**1**	**4**	**0**	**0**	**0**	**35**	**2.9**	**-2**	**1**	**0.0**	**10:42**									
	NHL Totals		**129**	**4**	**9**	**13**	**40**	**0**	**0**	**1**	**110**	**3.6**		**1**	**0.0**	**13:04**	**15**	**0**	**0**	**0**	**2**	**0**	**0**	**0**	**8:09**

Signed as a free agent by **Chicago**, July 17, 2006. • Missed majority of 2010-11 due to knee injury and as a healthy reserve.

HENNESSY, Josh

(HEHN-eh-see, JAWSH) **BOS**

Center. Shoots left. 6', 192 lbs. Born, Brockton, MA, February 7, 1985. San Jose's 3rd choice, 43rd overall, in 2003 Entry Draft.

Season	Club	League	GP	G	A	Pts	PIM	PP	SH	GW	S	%	+/-	TF	F%	Min	GP	G	A	Pts	PIM	PP	SH	GW	Min
2000-01	Milton Academy	High-MA	28	20	30	50	20																		
2001-02	Quebec Remparts	QMJHL	70	20	20	40	24										9	3	9	12	8				
2002-03	Quebec Remparts	QMJHL	72	33	51	84	44										11	6	9	15	10				
2003-04	Quebec Remparts	QMJHL	59	40	42	82	55																		
2004-05	Quebec Remparts	QMJHL	68	35	50	85	39										12	2	9	11	6				
2005-06	Cleveland Barons	AHL	80	24	39	63	60																		
2006-07	**Ottawa**	**NHL**	**10**	**1**	**0**	**1**	**4**	**0**	**0**	**0**	**6**	**16.7**	**0**	**43**	**37.2**	**5:39**									
	Binghamton	AHL	76	27	30	57	54																		
2007-08	**Ottawa**	**NHL**	**5**	**0**	**0**	**0**	**0**	**0**	**0**	**0**	**2**	**0.0**	**-1**	**12**	**41.7**	**3:46**									
	Binghamton	AHL	76	22	29	51	49																		
2008-09	**Ottawa**	**NHL**	**1**	**0**	**0**	**0**	**0**	**0**	**0**	**0**	**0**	**0.0**	**0**	**7**	**28.6**	**13:40**									
	Binghamton	AHL	59	20	17	37	26																		
2009-10	**Ottawa**	**NHL**	**4**	**0**	**0**	**0**	**0**	**0**	**0**	**0**	**2**	**0.0**	**-1**	**13**	**61.5**	**5:59**									
	Binghamton	AHL	78	30	38	68	26																		
2010-11	HC Lugano	Swiss	36	9	10	19	22										1	0	0	0	0				
	NHL Totals		**20**	**1**	**0**	**1**	**4**	**0**	**0**	**0**	**10**	**10.0**		**75**	**41.3**	**5:39**									

Traded to **Chicago** by **San Jose** with Tom Preissing for Mark Bell, July 9, 2006. Traded to **Ottawa** by **Chicago** with Tom Preissing, Michal Barinka and Chicago's 2nd round choice (Patrick Wiercioch) in 2008 Entry Draft for Martin Havlat and Bryan Smolinski, July 10, 2006. Signed as a free agent by **Lugano** (Swiss), May 6, 2010. Signed as a free agent by **Boston**, July 5, 2011.

HENRIQUE, Adam

(HEHN-reek, A-duhm) **N.J.**

Center. Shoots left. 6', 200 lbs. Born, Brantford, Ont., February 6, 1990. New Jersey's 4th choice, 82nd overall, in 2008 Entry Draft.

Season	Club	League	GP	G	A	Pts	PIM	PP	SH	GW	S	%	+/-	TF	F%	Min	GP	G	A	Pts	PIM	PP	SH	GW	Min
2006-07	Windsor Spitfires	OHL	62	23	21	44	20																		
2007-08	Windsor Spitfires	OHL	66	20	24	44	28										5	2	3	5	4				
2008-09	Windsor Spitfires	OHL	56	30	33	63	47										20	8	9	17	19				
2009-10	Windsor Spitfires	OHL	54	38	39	77	57										19	*20	5	25	12				
2010-11	**New Jersey**	**NHL**	**1**	**0**	**0**	**0**	**0**	**0**	**0**	**0**	**3**	**0.0**	**1**	**1**	**0.0**	**13:21**									
	Albany Devils	AHL	73	25	25	50	26																		
	NHL Totals		**1**	**0**	**0**	**0**	**0**	**0**	**0**	**0**	**3**	**0.0**		**1**	**0.0**	**13:21**									

HENRY, Alex

(HEHN-ree, AL-ehx) **MTL**

Defense. Shoots left. 6'6", 231 lbs. Born, Elliot Lake, Ont., October 18, 1979. Edmonton's 2nd choice, 67th overall, in 1998 Entry Draft.

Season	Club	League	GP	G	A	Pts	PIM	PP	SH	GW	S	%	+/-	TF	F%	Min	GP	G	A	Pts	PIM	PP	SH	GW	Min
1995-96	Timmins Majors	NOHA	30	4	11	15	6																		
	Timmins	NOJHA	2	0	0	0	0																		
1996-97	London Knights	OHL	61	1	10	11	65																		
1997-98	London Knights	OHL	62	5	9	14	97										16	0	3	3	14				
1998-99	London Knights	OHL	68	5	23	28	105										25	3	10	13	22				
99-2000	Hamilton	AHL	60	1	0	1	69																		
2000-01	Hamilton	AHL	56	2	3	5	87																		
2001-02	Hamilton	AHL	69	4	8	12	143										15	1	2	3	16				
2002-03	**Edmonton**	**NHL**	**3**	**0**	**0**	**0**	**0**	**0**	**0**	**0**	**0**	**0.0**	**-1**	**0**	**0.0**	**7:02**									
	Washington	**NHL**	**38**	**0**	**0**	**0**	**80**	**0**	**0**	**0**	**8**	**0.0**	**-4**	**1**	**0.0**	**3:39**									
	Portland Pirates	AHL	3	0	1	1	0																		
2003-04	**Minnesota**	**NHL**	**71**	**2**	**4**	**6**	**106**	**0**	**0**	**0**	**37**	**5.4**	**4**	**2**	**0.0**	**14:53**									
2004-05	ESV Kaufbeuren	German-2	26	6	6	12	32																		
2005-06	**Minnesota**	**NHL**	**63**	**0**	**5**	**5**	**73**	**0**	**0**	**0**	**41**	**0.0**	**-4**	**2**	**50.0**	**11:26**									
2006-07	Milwaukee	AHL	64	1	6	7	66										2	0	0	0	7				
2007-08	Milwaukee	AHL	80	3	13	16	142										6	0	1	1	10				
2008-09	**Montreal**	**NHL**	**2**	**0**	**0**	**0**	**10**	**0**	**0**	**0**	**0**	**0.0**	**-2**	**0**	**0.0**	**6:34**									
	Hamilton	AHL	79	3	7	10	127										6	0	0	0	8				
2009-10	Hamilton	AHL	68	0	13	13	154										19	2	2	4	22				
2010-11	Hamilton	AHL	80	1	13	14	96										20	0	3	3	34				
	NHL Totals		**177**	**2**	**9**	**11**	**269**	**0**	**0**	**0**	**86**	**2.3**		**5**	**20.0**	**11:01**									

Claimed on waivers by **Washington** from **Edmonton**, October 24, 2002. Claimed on waivers by **Minnesota** from **Washington**, October 9, 2003. Signed as a free agent by **Kaufbeuren** (German-2), January 15, 2005. Signed as a free agent by **Nashville**, August 22, 2006. Signed as a free agent by **Montreal**, July 3, 2008.

HENSICK, T.J.

(HEHN-sihk, TEE-JAY) **ST.L.**

Center. Shoots right. 5'10", 190 lbs. Born, Lansing, MI, December 10, 1985. Colorado's 5th choice, 88th overall, in 2005 Entry Draft.

Season	Club	League	GP	G	A	Pts	PIM	PP	SH	GW	S	%	+/-	TF	F%	Min	GP	G	A	Pts	PIM	PP	SH	GW	Min
2001-02	USNTDP	U-17	17	10	5	15	....																		
	USNTDP	NAHL	46	15	25	40	10																		
2002-03	USNTDP	U-18	48	24	24	48	11																		
	USNTDP	NAHL	10	6	7	13	0																		
2003-04	U. of Michigan	CCHA	43	12	*34	46	38																		
2004-05	U. of Michigan	CCHA	39	23	32	55	24																		
2005-06	U. of Michigan	CCHA	41	17	35	52	44																		
2006-07	U. of Michigan	CCHA	41	23	*46	*69	38																		
2007-08	**Colorado**	**NHL**	**31**	**6**	**5**	**11**	**2**	**4**	**0**	**1**	**52**	**11.5**	**-4**	**256**	**42.2**	**11:59**	**2**	**0**	**1**	**1**	**0**	**0**	**0**	**0**	**15:29**
	Lake Erie	AHL	50	12	33	45	18																		
2008-09	**Colorado**	**NHL**	**61**	**4**	**17**	**21**	**14**	**1**	**0**	**0**	**116**	**3.4**	**-7**	**510**	**47.3**	**12:54**									
	Lake Erie	AHL	12	7	9	16	2																		
2009-10	**Colorado**	**NHL**	**7**	**1**	**2**	**3**	**0**	**0**	**0**	**0**	**13**	**7.7**	**0**	**14**	**42.9**	**9:27**									
	Lake Erie	AHL	58	20	50	70	25																		
2010-11	**St. Louis**	**NHL**	**13**	**1**	**2**	**3**	**2**	**0**	**0**	**0**	**12**	**8.3**	**-5**	**29**	**37.9**	**9:05**									
	Peoria Rivermen	AHL	59	21	48	69	27										4	2	1	3	2				
	NHL Totals		**112**	**12**	**26**	**38**	**18**	**5**	**0**	**1**	**193**	**6.2**		**809**	**45.2**	**11:59**	**2**	**0**	**1**	**1**	**0**	**0**	**0**	**0**	**15:29**

CCHA All-Rookie Team (2004) • CCHA First All-Star Team (2004, 2005, 2007) • CCHA Rookie of the Year (2004) • NCAA West First All-American Team (2005, 2007) • CCHA Second All-Star Team (2006)
Traded to **St. Louis** by **Colorado** for Julian Talbot, June 17, 2010.

HESHKA, Shaun

(HEHSH-kah, SHAWN) **PHX**

Defense. Shoots right. 6'1", 208 lbs. Born, Melville, Sask., July 30, 1985.

			Regular Season														Playoffs								
Season	Club	League	GP	G	A	Pts	PIM	PP	SH	GW	S	%	+/-	TF	F%	Min	GP	G	A	Pts	PIM	PP	SH	GW	Min
2002-03	Melville	SJHL	53	6	14	20	53	....	....	....	....	....	....	....	....	....	....	....	....	....	....	....	....	....	....
2003-04	Everett Silvertips	WHL	66	3	7	10	25	....	....	....	....	....	....	....	....	....	21	0	2	2	8	....	....	....	....
2004-05	Everett Silvertips	WHL	72	12	26	38	21	....	....	....	....	....	....	....	....	....	11	2	0	2	6	....	....	....	....
2005-06	Everett Silvertips	WHL	66	10	49	59	91	....	....	....	....	....	....	....	....	....	14	3	10	13	10	....	....	....	....
2006-07	Manitoba Moose	AHL	57	2	4	6	14	....	....	....	....	....	....	....	....	....	7	0	0	0	8	....	....	....	....
	Victoria	ECHL	3	0	1	1	4	....	....	....	....	....	....	....	....	....	....	....	....	....	....	....	....	....	....
2007-08	Manitoba Moose	AHL	77	9	21	30	59	....	....	....	....	....	....	....	....	....	6	0	1	1	4	....	....	....	....
2008-09	Manitoba Moose	AHL	77	3	23	26	25	....	....	....	....	....	....	....	....	....	22	0	5	5	12	....	....	....	....
2009-10	**Phoenix**	**NHL**	**8**	**0**	**2**	**2**	**4**	**0**	**0**	**0**	**3**	**0.0**	**0**	**0**	**0.0**	**13:19**	....	....	....	....	....	....	....	....	....
	San Antonio	AHL	73	7	26	33	34	....	....	....	....	....	....	....	....	....	....	....	....	....	....	....	....	....	....
2010-11	Salzburg	Austria	50	6	18	24	32	....	....	....	....	....	....	....	....	....	....	....	....	....	....	....	....	....	....
	NHL Totals		**8**	**0**	**2**	**2**	**4**	**0**	**0**	**0**	**3**	**0.0**		**0**	**0.0**	**13:19**	....	....	....	....	....	....	....	....	....

WHL West First All-Star Team (2006)

Signed as a free agent by **Vancouver**, July 24, 2006. Traded to **Phoenix** by **Vancouver** for Phoenix's 7th round choice (Steven Anthony) in 2009 Entry Draft, June 27, 2009.

HIGGINS, Chris

(HIH-gihns, KRIHS) **VAN**

Left wing. Shoots left. 6', 205 lbs. Born, Smithtown, NY, June 2, 1983. Montreal's 1st choice, 14th overall, in 2002 Entry Draft.

			Regular Season														Playoffs								
Season	Club	League	GP	G	A	Pts	PIM	PP	SH	GW	S	%	+/-	TF	F%	Min	GP	G	A	Pts	PIM	PP	SH	GW	Min
99-2000	Avon Old Farms	High-CT	27	19	20	39	10	....	....	....	....	....	....	....	....	....	....	....	....	....	....	....	....	....	....
2000-01	Avon Old Farms	High-CT	24	22	14	36	29	....	....	....	....	....	....	....	....	....	....	....	....	....	....	....	....	....	....
2001-02	Yale	ECAC	27	14	17	31	32	....	....	....	....	....	....	....	....	....	....	....	....	....	....	....	....	....	....
2002-03	Yale	ECAC	28	20	21	41	41	....	....	....	....	....	....	....	....	....	....	....	....	....	....	....	....	....	....
2003-04	**Montreal**	**NHL**	**2**	**0**	**0**	**0**	**0**	**0**	**0**	**0**	**0**	**0.0**	**0**	**9**	**22.2**	**6:18**	....	....	....	....	....	....	....	....	....
	Hamilton	AHL	67	21	27	48	18	....	....	....	....	....	....	....	....	....	10	3	2	5	0	....	....	....	....
2004-05	Hamilton	AHL	76	28	23	51	33	....	....	....	....	....	....	....	....	....	4	3	3	6	4	....	....	....	....
2005-06	**Montreal**	**NHL**	**80**	**23**	**15**	**38**	**26**	**7**	**3**	**3**	**148**	**15.5**	**–1**	**45**	**51.1**	**14:25**	**6**	**1**	**3**	**4**	**0**	**0**	**0**	**0**	**17:04**
2006-07	**Montreal**	**NHL**	**61**	**22**	**16**	**38**	**26**	**8**	**3**	**3**	**159**	**13.8**	**–11**	**53**	**34.0**	**17:54**	....	....	....	....	....	....	....	....	....
2007-08	**Montreal**	**NHL**	**82**	**27**	**25**	**52**	**22**	**12**	**0**	**5**	**241**	**11.2**	**0**	**62**	**35.5**	**17:57**	**12**	**3**	**2**	**5**	**2**	**0**	**0**	**0**	**18:27**
2008-09	**Montreal**	**NHL**	**57**	**12**	**11**	**23**	**22**	**2**	**2**	**1**	**151**	**7.9**	**–1**	**57**	**50.9**	**17:00**	**4**	**2**	**0**	**2**	**2**	**0**	**0**	**0**	**17:35**
2009-10	**NY Rangers**	**NHL**	**55**	**6**	**8**	**14**	**32**	**0**	**0**	**1**	**137**	**4.4**	**–9**	**63**	**41.3**	**17:55**	....	....	....	....	....	....	....	....	....
	Calgary	**NHL**	**12**	**2**	**1**	**3**	**0**	**0**	**0**	**0**	**28**	**7.1**	**0**	**7**	**28.6**	**15:52**	....	....	....	....	....	....	....	....	....
2010-11	**Florida**	**NHL**	**48**	**11**	**12**	**23**	**10**	**1**	**0**	**0**	**126**	**8.7**	**5**	**65**	**46.2**	**16:39**	....	....	....	....	....	....	....	....	....
	Vancouver	**NHL**	**14**	**2**	**3**	**5**	**6**	**0**	**0**	**0**	**34**	**5.9**	**0**	**20**	**55.0**	**15:07**	**25**	**4**	**4**	**8**	**2**	**1**	**0**	**3**	**17:08**
	NHL Totals		**411**	**105**	**91**	**196**	**144**	**30**	**8**	**13**	**1024**	**10.3**		**381**	**42.8**	**16:45**	**47**	**10**	**9**	**19**	**6**	**1**	**0**	**3**	**17:30**

ECAC All-Rookie Team (2002) • ECAC Second All-Star Team (2002) • ECAC Rookie of the Year (2002) • ECAC First All-Star Team (2003) • ECAC Player of the Year (2003) (co-winner - David LeNeveu) • NCAA East First All-American Team (2003)

Traded to **NY Rangers** by **Montreal** with Ryan McDonagh and Pavel Valentenko for Scott Gomez, Tom Pyatt and Michael Busto, June 30, 2009. Traded to **Calgary** by **NY Rangers** with Ales Kotalik for Olli Jokinen and Brandon Prust, February 2, 2010. Signed as a free agent by **Florida**, July 2, 2010. Traded to **Vancouver** by **Florida** for Evan Oberg and Vancouver's 3rd round choice in 2013 Entry Draft, February 28, 2011.

HILLEN, Jack

(HIHL-uhn, JAK) **NSH**

Defense. Shoots left. 5'10", 190 lbs. Born, Minnetonka, MN, January 24, 1986.

			Regular Season														Playoffs								
Season	Club	League	GP	G	A	Pts	PIM	PP	SH	GW	S	%	+/-	TF	F%	Min	GP	G	A	Pts	PIM	PP	SH	GW	Min
2003-04	Tri-City Storm	USHL	21	2	2	4	16	....	....	....	....	....	....	....	....	....	8	0	1	1	4	....	....	....	....
2004-05	Colorado College	WCHA	30	2	9	11	20	....	....	....	....	....	....	....	....	....	....	....	....	....	....	....	....	....	....
2005-06	Colorado College	WCHA	42	4	9	13	48	....	....	....	....	....	....	....	....	....	....	....	....	....	....	....	....	....	....
2006-07	Colorado College	WCHA	38	7	8	15	38	....	....	....	....	....	....	....	....	....	....	....	....	....	....	....	....	....	....
2007-08	Colorado College	WCHA	41	6	*31	37	60	....	....	....	....	....	....	....	....	....	....	....	....	....	....	....	....	....	....
	NY Islanders	**NHL**	**2**	**0**	**1**	**1**	**4**	**0**	**0**	**0**	**3**	**0.0**	**1**	**0**	**0.0**	**15:32**	....	....	....	....	....	....	....	....	....
2008-09	**NY Islanders**	**NHL**	**40**	**1**	**5**	**6**	**16**	**0**	**0**	**0**	**47**	**2.1**	**–9**	**0**	**0.0**	**15:13**	....	....	....	....	....	....	....	....	....
	Bridgeport	AHL	33	4	13	17	31	....	....	....	....	....	....	....	....	....	5	0	2	2	2	....	....	....	....
2009-10	**NY Islanders**	**NHL**	**69**	**3**	**18**	**21**	**44**	**1**	**0**	**0**	**78**	**3.8**	**–5**	**1**	**100.0**	**20:42**	....	....	....	....	....	....	....	....	....
2010-11	**NY Islanders**	**NHL**	**64**	**4**	**18**	**22**	**45**	**0**	**0**	**1**	**81**	**4.9**	**–5**	**0**	**0.0**	**18:49**	....	....	....	....	....	....	....	....	....
	NHL Totals		**175**	**8**	**42**	**50**	**109**	**1**	**0**	**1**	**209**	**3.8**		**1**	**100.0**	**18:42**	....	....	....	....	....	....	....	....	....

WCHA First All-Star Team (2008) • NCAA West First All-American Team (2008)

Signed as a free agent by **NY Islanders**, April 1, 2008. Signed as a free agent by **Nashville**, August 8, 2011.

HJALMARSSON, Niklas

(JAHL-muhr-suhn, NIHK-luhs) **CHI**

Defense. Shoots left. 6'3", 205 lbs. Born, Eksjo, Sweden, June 6, 1987. Chicago's 5th choice, 108th overall, in 2005 Entry Draft.

			Regular Season														Playoffs								
Season	Club	League	GP	G	A	Pts	PIM	PP	SH	GW	S	%	+/-	TF	F%	Min	GP	G	A	Pts	PIM	PP	SH	GW	Min
2003-04	HV 71 Jr.	Swe-Jr.	15	1	3	4	14	....	....	....	....	....	....	....	....	....	2	0	0	0	8	....	....	....	....
2004-05	HV 71 U18	Swe-U18	3	0	2	2	4	....	....	....	....	....	....	....	....	....	....	....	....	....	....	....	....	....	....
	HV 71 Jr.	Swe-Jr.	31	4	11	15	87	....	....	....	....	....	....	....	....	....	....	....	....	....	....	....	....	....	....
	HV 71 Jonkoping	Sweden	14	0	0	0	0	....	....	....	....	....	....	....	....	....	....	....	....	....	....	....	....	....	....
2005-06	HV 71 Jr.	Swe-Jr.	7	3	2	5	12	....	....	....	....	....	....	....	....	....	....	....	....	....	....	....	....	....	....
	HV 71 Jonkoping	Sweden	4	1	2	3	0	....	....	....	....	....	....	....	....	....	12	0	1	1	4	....	....	....	....
2006-07	HV 71 Jonkoping	Sweden	37	2	0	2	24	....	....	....	....	....	....	....	....	....	14	1	1	2	0	....	....	....	....
	HV 71 Jr.	Swe-Jr.	7	0	2	2	14	....	....	....	....	....	....	....	....	....	....	....	....	....	....	....	....	....	....
	IK Oskarshamn	Sweden-2	8	1	2	3	6	....	....	....	....	....	....	....	....	....	....	....	....	....	....	....	....	....	....
2007-08	**Chicago**	**NHL**	**13**	**0**	**1**	**1**	**13**	**0**	**0**	**0**	**5**	**0.0**	**–2**	**0**	**0.0**	**13:37**	....	....	....	....	....	....	....	....	....
	Rockford IceHogs	AHL	47	4	9	13	31	....	....	....	....	....	....	....	....	....	12	0	4	4	8	....	....	....	....
2008-09	**Chicago**	**NHL**	**21**	**1**	**2**	**3**	**0**	**0**	**0**	**0**	**15**	**6.7**	**4**	**0**	**0.0**	**14:59**	**17**	**0**	**1**	**1**	**6**	**0**	**0**	**0**	**16:37**
	Rockford IceHogs	AHL	52	2	16	18	53	....	....	....	....	....	....	....	....	....	....	....	....	....	....	....	....	....	....
2009-10 ♦	**Chicago**	**NHL**	**77**	**2**	**15**	**17**	**20**	**0**	**0**	**1**	**62**	**3.2**	**9**	**0**	**0.0**	**19:40**	**22**	**1**	**7**	**8**	**6**	**0**	**0**	**0**	**21:01**
2010-11	**Chicago**	**NHL**	**80**	**3**	**7**	**10**	**39**	**0**	**0**	**0**	**64**	**4.7**	**13**	**0**	**0.0**	**18:29**	**7**	**0**	**2**	**2**	**2**	**0**	**0**	**0**	**18:55**
	NHL Totals		**191**	**6**	**25**	**31**	**72**	**0**	**0**	**1**	**146**	**4.1**		**0**	**0.0**	**18:14**	**46**	**1**	**10**	**11**	**14**	**0**	**0**	**0**	**19:04**

HNIDY, Shane

(NIGH-dee, SHAYN)

Defense. Shoots right. 6'2", 204 lbs. Born, Neepawa, Man., November 8, 1975. Buffalo's 7th choice, 173rd overall, in 1994 Entry Draft.

			Regular Season														Playoffs								
Season	Club	League	GP	G	A	Pts	PIM	PP	SH	GW	S	%	+/-	TF	F%	Min	GP	G	A	Pts	PIM	PP	SH	GW	Min
1990-91	Yellowhead	MMMHL	36	9	11	20	92	....	....	....	....	....	....	....	....	....	....	....	....	....	....	....	....	....	....
1991-92	Swift Current	WHL	56	1	3	4	11	....	....	....	....	....	....	....	....	....	4	0	0	0	0	....	....	....	....
1992-93	Swift Current	WHL	45	5	12	17	62	....	....	....	....	....	....	....	....	....	....	....	....	....	....	....	....	....	....
	Prince Albert	WHL	27	2	10	12	43	....	....	....	....	....	....	....	....	....	....	....	....	....	....	....	....	....	....
1993-94	Prince Albert	WHL	69	7	26	33	113	....	....	....	....	....	....	....	....	....	....	....	....	....	....	....	....	....	....
1994-95	Prince Albert	WHL	72	5	29	34	169	....	....	....	....	....	....	....	....	....	15	4	7	11	29	....	....	....	....
1995-96	Prince Albert	WHL	58	11	42	53	100	....	....	....	....	....	....	....	....	....	18	4	11	15	34	....	....	....	....
1996-97	Baton Rouge	ECHL	21	3	10	13	50	....	....	....	....	....	....	....	....	....	....	....	....	....	....	....	....	....	....
	Saint John Flames	AHL	44	2	12	14	112	....	....	....	....	....	....	....	....	....	....	....	....	....	....	....	....	....	....
1997-98	Grand Rapids	IHL	77	6	12	18	210	....	....	....	....	....	....	....	....	....	3	0	2	2	23	....	....	....	....
1998-99	Adirondack	AHL	68	9	20	29	121	....	....	....	....	....	....	....	....	....	3	0	1	1	0	....	....	....	....
99-2000	Cincinnati	AHL	68	9	19	28	153	....	....	....	....	....	....	....	....	....	....	....	....	....	....	....	....	....	....
2000-01	**Ottawa**	**NHL**	**52**	**3**	**2**	**5**	**84**	**0**	**0**	**1**	**47**	**6.4**	**8**	**0**	**0.0**	**13:05**	**1**	**0**	**0**	**0**	**0**	**0**	**0**	**0**	**13:23**
	Grand Rapids	IHL	2	0	0	0	2	....	....	....	....	....	....	....	....	....	....	....	....	....	....	....	....	....	....
2001-02	**Ottawa**	**NHL**	**33**	**1**	**1**	**2**	**57**	**0**	**0**	**0**	**34**	**2.9**	**–10**	**0**	**0.0**	**16:56**	**12**	**1**	**1**	**2**	**12**	**0**	**0**	**0**	**16:00**
2002-03	**Ottawa**	**NHL**	**67**	**0**	**8**	**8**	**130**	**0**	**0**	**0**	**58**	**0.0**	**–1**	**1**	**0.0**	**13:55**	**1**	**0**	**0**	**0**	**0**	**0**	**0**	**0**	**9:38**
2003-04	**Ottawa**	**NHL**	**37**	**0**	**5**	**5**	**72**	**0**	**0**	**0**	**16**	**0.0**	**2**	**0**	**0.0**	**11:19**	....	....	....	....	....	....	....	....	....
	Nashville	**NHL**	**9**	**0**	**2**	**2**	**10**	**0**	**0**	**0**	**12**	**0.0**	**3**	**0**	**0.0**	**18:11**	**5**	**0**	**0**	**0**	**6**	**0**	**0**	**0**	**12:31**
2004-05	Florida Everblades	ECHL	19	1	4	5	56	....	....	....	....	....	....	....	....	....	17	0	4	4	6	....	....	....	....
2005-06	**Atlanta**	**NHL**	**66**	**0**	**3**	**3**	**33**	**0**	**0**	**0**	**50**	**0.0**	**1**	**0**	**0.0**	**10:14**	....	....	....	....	....	....	....	....	....
2006-07	**Atlanta**	**NHL**	**72**	**5**	**7**	**12**	**63**	**0**	**1**	**1**	**86**	**5.8**	**15**	**0**	**0.0**	**15:38**	**4**	**1**	**0**	**1**	**0**	**0**	**0**	**0**	**15:48**
2007-08	**Anaheim**	**NHL**	**33**	**1**	**2**	**3**	**30**	**0**	**0**	**0**	**21**	**4.8**	**2**	**0**	**0.0**	**13:08**	....	....	....	....	....	....	....	....	....
	Boston	**NHL**	**43**	**1**	**4**	**5**	**41**	**0**	**1**	**0**	**28**	**3.6**	**–4**	**0**	**0.0**	**14:42**	**7**	**1**	**1**	**2**	**9**	**0**	**0**	**0**	**17:11**
2008-09	**Boston**	**NHL**	**65**	**3**	**9**	**12**	**45**	**1**	**0**	**1**	**49**	**6.1**	**6**	**0**	**0.0**	**15:38**	**7**	**1**	**0**	**1**	**0**	**0**	**0**	**0**	**14:06**

			Regular Season														Playoffs								
Season	Club	League	GP	G	A	Pts	PIM	PP	SH	GW	S	%	+/-	TF	F%	Min	GP	G	A	Pts	PIM	PP	SH	GW	Min
2009-10	**Minnesota**	**NHL**	**70**	**2**	**12**	**14**	**66**	**0**	**0**	**0**	**49**	**4.1**	**–6**	**0**	**0.0**	**13:32**	....	....	....	....	....	....	....	....	....
2010-11	**Boston**	**NHL**	**3**	**0**	**0**	**0**	**2**	**0**	**0**	**0**	**3**	**0.0**	**–2**	**0**	**0.0**	**14:47**	**3**	**0**	**0**	**0**	**7**	**0**	**0**	**0**	**3:09**
	NHL Totals		**550**	**16**	**55**	**71**	**633**	**1**	**2**	**3**	**453**	**3.5**		**1**	**0.0**	**13:52**	**40**	**4**	**2**	**6**	**34**	**0**	**0**	**0**	**14:14**

Signed as a free agent by **Detroit**, August 6, 1998. Traded to **Ottawa** by **Detroit** for Ottawa's 8th round choice (Todd Jackson) in 2000 Entry Draft, June 25, 2000. • Missed majority of 2001-02 due to ankle injury vs. Boston, December 26, 2001. Traded to **Nashville** by **Ottawa** for Colorado's 3rd round choice (previously acquired, Ottawa selected Peter Regin) in 2004 Entry Draft, March 9, 2004. Signed as a free agent by **Florida** (ECHL), December 6, 2004. Traded to **Atlanta** by **Nashville** for Atlanta's 4th round choice (Niko Snellman) in 2006 Entry Draft, July 30, 2005. Signed as a free agent by **Anaheim**, July 5, 2007. Traded to **Boston** by **Anaheim** with Anaheim's 6th round choice (Nicholas Tremblay) in 2008 Entry Draft for Brandon Bochenski, January 2, 2008. Signed as a free agent by **Minnesota**, July 3, 2009. Signed as a free agent by **Boston**, February 26, 2011. • Missed majority od 2010-11 due to shoulder injury in Phoenix training camp and as a healthy reserve with Boston.

HODGSON, Cody
(HAWJ-suhn, KOH-dee) **VAN**

Center. Shoots right. 6', 185 lbs. Born, Toronto, Ont., February 18, 1990. Vancouver's 1st choice, 10th overall, in 2008 Entry Draft.

Season	Club	League	GP	G	A	Pts	PIM	PP	SH	GW	S	%	+/-	TF	F%	Min	GP	G	A	Pts	PIM	PP	SH	GW	Min
2005-06	Markham Waxers	Minor-ON	30	27	24	51	22	....	....	....	....	....	....	....	....	....	15	13	14	27	8	....	....	....	....
2006-07	Brampton	OHL	63	23	23	46	24	....	....	....	....	....	....	....	....	....	4	1	3	4	0	....	....	....	....
2007-08	Brampton	OHL	68	40	45	85	36	....	....	....	....	....	....	....	....	....	5	5	0	5	2	....	....	....	....
2008-09	Brampton	OHL	53	43	49	92	33	....	....	....	....	....	....	....	....	....	21	11	20	31	18	....	....	....	....
	Manitoba Moose	AHL	....	....	....	....	....	....	....	....	....	....	....	....	....	....	11	2	4	6	4	....	....	....	....
2009-10	Brampton	OHL	13	8	12	20	9	....	....	....	....	....	....	....	....	....	11	3	7	10	4	....	....	....	....
2010-11	**Vancouver**	**NHL**	**8**	**1**	**1**	**2**	**0**	**0**	**0**	**0**	**9**	**11.1**	**1**	**42**	**38.1**	**7:44**	**12**	**0**	**1**	**1**	**2**	**0**	**0**	**0**	**6:45**
	Manitoba Moose	AHL	52	17	13	30	14	....	....	....	....	....	....	....	....	....	....	....	....	....	....	....	....	....	....
	NHL Totals		**8**	**1**	**1**	**2**	**0**	**0**	**0**	**0**	**9**	**11.1**		**42**	**38.1**	**7:45**	**12**	**0**	**1**	**1**	**2**	**0**	**0**	**0**	**6:46**

OHL First All-Star Team (2009) • OHL Player of the Year (2009) • Canadian Major Junior First All-Star Team (2009) • Canadian Major Junior Player of the Year (2009)

HOGGAN, Jeff
(HOH-guhn, JEHF)

Left wing. Shoots left. 6'1", 193 lbs. Born, Hope, B.C., February 1, 1978.

Season	Club	League	GP	G	A	Pts	PIM	PP	SH	GW	S	%	+/-	TF	F%	Min	GP	G	A	Pts	PIM	PP	SH	GW	Min
1998-99	Powell River Kings	BCHL	STATISTICS NOT AVAILABLE																						
99-2000	Nebraska-Omaha	CCHA	34	16	9	25	82	....	....	....	....	....	....	....	....	....	....	....	....	....	....	....	....	....	....
2000-01	Nebraska-Omaha	CCHA	42	12	17	29	78	....	....	....	....	....	....	....	....	....	....	....	....	....	....	....	....	....	....
2001-02	Nebraska-Omaha	CCHA	41	24	21	45	92	....	....	....	....	....	....	....	....	....	....	....	....	....	....	....	....	....	....
	Houston Aeros	AHL	....	....	....	....	....	....	....	....	....	....	....	....	....	....	4	0	0	0	2	....	....	....	....
2002-03	Houston Aeros	AHL	65	6	5	11	45	....	....	....	....	....	....	....	....	....	14	1	2	3	23	....	....	....	....
2003-04	Houston Aeros	AHL	77	21	15	36	88	....	....	....	....	....	....	....	....	....	2	0	1	1	4	....	....	....	....
2004-05	Worcester IceCats	AHL	47	16	9	25	55	....	....	....	....	....	....	....	....	....	....	....	....	....	....	....	....	....	....
2005-06	**St. Louis**	**NHL**	**52**	**2**	**6**	**8**	**34**	**0**	**0**	**0**	**60**	**3.3**	**–16**	**4**	**25.0**	**8:47**	....	....	....	....	....	....	....	....	....
2006-07	**Boston**	**NHL**	**46**	**0**	**2**	**2**	**33**	**0**	**0**	**0**	**53**	**0.0**	**–8**	**3**	**33.3**	**7:04**	....	....	....	....	....	....	....	....	....
	Providence Bruins	AHL	22	4	7	11	27	....	....	....	....	....	....	....	....	....	13	4	3	7	17	....	....	....	....
2007-08	**Boston**	**NHL**	**1**	**0**	**0**	**0**	**0**	**0**	**0**	**0**	**0**	**0.0**	**0**	**0**	**0.0**	**7:57**	....	....	....	....	....	....	....	....	....
	Providence Bruins	AHL	71	29	31	60	59	....	....	....	....	....	....	....	....	....	5	3	4	7	4	....	....	....	....
2008-09	**Phoenix**	**NHL**	**4**	**0**	**1**	**1**	**7**	**0**	**0**	**0**	**7**	**0.0**	**–1**	**2**	**0.0**	**12:00**	....	....	....	....	....	....	....	....	....
	San Antonio	AHL	60	22	13	35	64	....	....	....	....	....	....	....	....	....	....	....	....	....	....	....	....	....	....
2009-10	**Phoenix**	**NHL**	**4**	**0**	**0**	**0**	**2**	**0**	**0**	**0**	**5**	**0.0**	**–1**	**2**	**0.0**	**7:07**	....	....	....	....	....	....	....	....	....
	San Antonio	AHL	70	13	20	33	44	....	....	....	....	....	....	....	....	....	....	....	....	....	....	....	....	....	....
2010-11	Wolfsburg	Germany	38	11	10	21	63	....	....	....	....	....	....	....	....	....	2	0	0	0	2	....	....	....	....
	NHL Totals		**107**	**2**	**9**	**11**	**76**	**0**	**0**	**0**	**125**	**1.6**		**11**	**18.2**	**8:06**	....	....	....	....	....	....	....	....	....

CCHA First All-Star Team (2002) • NCAA West Second All-American Team (2002)

Signed to a PTO (professional tryout) contract by **Houston** (AHL), April 4, 2002. Signed as a free agent by **Minnesota**, August 20, 2002. Signed as a free agent by **Worcester** (AHL), September, 2004. Signed as a free agent by **St. Louis**, August 2, 2005. Signed as a free agent by **Boston**, July 21, 2006. Signed as a free agent by **Phoenix**, July 15, 2008. Signed as a free agent by **Wolfsburg** (Germany), July 29, 2010.

HOLDEN, Nick
(HOHL-dehn, NIHK) **CBJ**

Defense. Shoots left. 6'4", 210 lbs. Born, St. Albert, Alta., May 15, 1987.

Season	Club	League	GP	G	A	Pts	PIM	PP	SH	GW	S	%	+/-	TF	F%	Min	GP	G	A	Pts	PIM	PP	SH	GW	Min
2004-05	Camrose Kodiaks	AJHL	4	0	0	0	0	....	....	....	....	....	....	....	....	....	....	....	....	....	....	....	....	....	....
2005-06	Camrose Kodiaks	AJHL	29	5	8	13	27	....	....	....	....	....	....	....	....	....	....	....	....	....	....	....	....	....	....
	Sherwood Park	AJHL	28	2	15	17	19	....	....	....	....	....	....	....	....	....	....	....	....	....	....	....	....	....	....
2006-07	Chilliwack Bruins	WHL	67	8	23	31	62	....	....	....	....	....	....	....	....	....	5	1	1	2	6	....	....	....	....
2007-08	Chilliwack Bruins	WHL	70	22	38	60	54	....	....	....	....	....	....	....	....	....	4	1	3	4	0	....	....	....	....
	Syracuse Crunch	AHL	1	0	0	0	2	....	....	....	....	....	....	....	....	....	....	....	....	....	....	....	....	....	....
2008-09	Syracuse Crunch	AHL	61	4	18	22	46	....	....	....	....	....	....	....	....	....	....	....	....	....	....	....	....	....	....
2009-10	Syracuse Crunch	AHL	68	6	17	23	52	....	....	....	....	....	....	....	....	....	....	....	....	....	....	....	....	....	....
2010-11	**Columbus**	**NHL**	**5**	**0**	**0**	**0**	**0**	**0**	**0**	**0**	**6**	**0.0**	**0**	**0**	**0.0**	**17:11**	....	....	....	....	....	....	....	....	....
	Springfield	AHL	67	4	21	25	63	....	....	....	....	....	....	....	....	....	....	....	....	....	....	....	....	....	....
	NHL Totals		**5**	**0**	**0**	**0**	**0**	**0**	**0**	**0**	**6**	**0.0**		**0**	**0.0**	**17:11**	....	....	....	....	....	....	....	....	....

Signed as a free agent by **Columbus**, March 28, 2008.

HOLLWEG, Ryan
(HOHL-wehg, RIGH-uhn)

Center. Shoots left. 5'10", 212 lbs. Born, Downey, CA, April 23, 1983. NY Rangers' 10th choice, 238th overall, in 2001 Entry Draft.

Season	Club	League	GP	G	A	Pts	PIM	PP	SH	GW	S	%	+/-	TF	F%	Min	GP	G	A	Pts	PIM	PP	SH	GW	Min
1998-99	Langley Hornets	BCHL	58	14	40	54	187	....	....	....	....	....	....	....	....	....	....	....	....	....	....	....	....	....	....
99-2000	Medicine Hat	WHL	54	19	27	46	107	....	....	....	....	....	....	....	....	....	....	....	....	....	....	....	....	....	....
2000-01	Medicine Hat	WHL	65	19	39	58	125	....	....	....	....	....	....	....	....	....	....	....	....	....	....	....	....	....	....
2001-02	Medicine Hat	WHL	58	30	40	70	121	....	....	....	....	....	....	....	....	....	....	....	....	....	....	....	....	....	....
	Hartford	AHL	8	1	1	2	2	....	....	....	....	....	....	....	....	....	9	0	2	2	19	....	....	....	....
2002-03	Medicine Hat	WHL	4	1	1	2	8	....	....	....	....	....	....	....	....	....	....	....	....	....	....	....	....	....	....
2003-04	Medicine Hat	WHL	52	25	32	57	117	....	....	....	....	....	....	....	....	....	20	6	9	15	22	....	....	....	....
2004-05	Hartford	AHL	73	8	6	14	239	....	....	....	....	....	....	....	....	....	6	1	0	1	9	....	....	....	....
2005-06	**NY Rangers**	**NHL**	**52**	**2**	**3**	**5**	**84**	**0**	**0**	**0**	**32**	**6.3**	**–3**	**19**	**57.9**	**7:15**	**4**	**0**	**1**	**1**	**19**	**0**	**0**	**0**	**10:26**
	Hartford	AHL	7	2	1	3	11	....	....	....	....	....	....	....	....	....	....	....	....	....	....	....	....	....	....
2006-07	**NY Rangers**	**NHL**	**78**	**1**	**2**	**3**	**131**	**0**	**0**	**0**	**63**	**1.6**	**–11**	**86**	**39.5**	**8:14**	**2**	**0**	**0**	**0**	**2**	**0**	**0**	**0**	**5:19**
2007-08	**NY Rangers**	**NHL**	**70**	**2**	**2**	**4**	**96**	**0**	**0**	**0**	**59**	**3.4**	**–12**	**39**	**46.2**	**8:18**	**8**	**0**	**0**	**0**	**2**	**0**	**0**	**0**	**4:50**
2008-09	**Toronto**	**NHL**	**25**	**0**	**2**	**2**	**38**	**0**	**0**	**0**	**12**	**0.0**	**–7**	**3**	**33.3**	**6:28**	....	....	....	....	....	....	....	....	....
	Toronto Marlies	AHL	28	2	1	3	34	....	....	....	....	....	....	....	....	....	6	0	0	0	20	....	....	....	....
2009-10	San Antonio	AHL	53	4	6	10	93	....	....	....	....	....	....	....	....	....	....	....	....	....	....	....	....	....	....
2010-11	**Phoenix**	**NHL**	**3**	**0**	**0**	**0**	**0**	**0**	**0**	**0**	**0**	**0.0**	**–1**	**0**	**0.0**	**6:33**	....	....	....	....	....	....	....	....	....
	San Antonio	AHL	63	9	8	17	125	....	....	....	....	....	....	....	....	....	....	....	....	....	....	....	....	....	....
	NHL Totals		**228**	**5**	**9**	**14**	**349**	**0**	**0**	**0**	**166**	**3.0**		**147**	**43.5**	**7:49**	**14**	**0**	**1**	**1**	**23**	**0**	**0**	**0**	**6:30**

• Missed majority of 2002-03 due to concussion vs. Vancouver (WHL), October 8, 2002. Traded to **Toronto** by **NY Rangers** for Pittsburgh's 5th round choice (previously acquired, later traded back to Pittsburgh – Pittsburgh selected Andy Bathgate) in 2009 Entry Draft, July 14, 2008. Signed as a free agent by **Phoenix**, September 28, 2009.

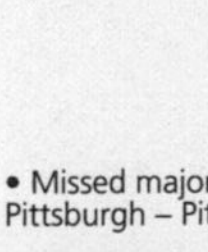

HOLMSTROM, Ben
(HOHLM-struhm, BEHN) **PHI**

Right wing. Shoots right. 6'1", 197 lbs. Born, Colorado Springs, CO, April 9, 1987.

Season	Club	League	GP	G	A	Pts	PIM	PP	SH	GW	S	%	+/-	TF	F%	Min	GP	G	A	Pts	PIM	PP	SH	GW	Min
2006-07	U. Mass-Lowell	H-East	30	4	9	13	18	....	....	....	....	....	....	....	....	....	....	....	....	....	....	....	....	....	....
2007-08	U. Mass-Lowell	H-East	37	7	20	27	62	....	....	....	....	....	....	....	....	....	....	....	....	....	....	....	....	....	....
2008-09	U. Mass-Lowell	H-East	38	6	15	21	52	....	....	....	....	....	....	....	....	....	....	....	....	....	....	....	....	....	....
2009-10	U. Mass-Lowell	H-East	39	9	14	23	69	....	....	....	....	....	....	....	....	....	....	....	....	....	....	....	....	....	....
	Adirondack	AHL	13	3	0	3	9	....	....	....	....	....	....	....	....	....	....	....	....	....	....	....	....	....	....
2010-11	**Philadelphia**	**NHL**	**2**	**0**	**0**	**0**	**5**	**0**	**0**	**0**	**0**	**0.0**	**–1**	**16**	**31.3**	**9:04**	....	....	....	....	....	....	....	....	....
	Adirondack	AHL	79	16	22	38	75	....	....	....	....	....	....	....	....	....	....	....	....	....	....	....	....	....	....
	NHL Totals		**2**	**0**	**0**	**0**	**5**	**0**	**0**	**0**	**0**	**0.0**		**16**	**31.3**	**9:04**	....	....	....	....	....	....	....	....	....

Signed as a free agent by **Philadelphia**, March 17, 2010.

			Regular Season														Playoffs								
Season	Club	League	GP	G	A	Pts	PIM	PP	SH	GW	S	%	+/-	TF	F%	Min	GP	G	A	Pts	PIM	PP	SH	GW	Min

HOLMSTROM, Tomas
(HOHLM-struhm, TAW-mas) **DET**

Left wing. Shoots left. 6', 198 lbs. Born, Pitea, Sweden, January 23, 1973. Detroit's 9th choice, 257th overall, in 1994 Entry Draft.

Season	Club	League	GP	G	A	Pts	PIM	PP	SH	GW	S	%	+/-	TF	F%	Min	GP	G	A	Pts	PIM	PP	SH	GW	Min
1989-90	Pitea HC	Sweden-2	9	1	0	1	4	....	....	....	....	....	....	....	....	....	....	....	....	....	....	....	....	....	....
1990-91	Pitea HC	Sweden-2	26	5	4	9	16	....	....	....	....	....	....	....	....	....	....	....	....	....	....	....	....	....	....
1991-92	Pitea HC	Sweden-2	31	15	12	27	44	....	....	....	....	....	....	....	....	....	....	....	....	....	....	....	....	....	....
1992-93	Pitea HC	Sweden-2	32	17	15	32	30	....	....	....	....	....	....	....	....	....	....	....	....	....	....	....	....	....	....
1993-94	Bodens IK	Sweden-2	34	23	16	39	86	....	....	....	....	....	....	....	....	....	9	3	3	6	24	....	....	....	....
1994-95	Lulea HF	Sweden	40	14	14	28	56	....	....	....	....	....	....	....	....	....	8	1	2	3	20	....	....	....	....
1995-96	Lulea HF	Sweden	34	12	11	23	78	....	....	....	....	....	....	....	....	....	11	6	2	8	22	....	....	....	....
1996-97♦	**Detroit**	**NHL**	**47**	**6**	**3**	**9**	**33**	**3**	**0**	**0**	**53**	**11.3**	**-10**	....	....	....	**1**	**0**	**0**	**0**	**0**	**0**	**0**	**0**	....
	Adirondack	AHL	6	3	1	4	7	....	....	....	....	....	....	....	....	....	....	....	....	....	....	....	....	....	....
1997-98♦	**Detroit**	**NHL**	**57**	**5**	**17**	**22**	**44**	**1**	**0**	**1**	**48**	**10.4**	**6**	....	....	....	**22**	**7**	**12**	**19**	**16**	**2**	**0**	**0**	....
1998-99	**Detroit**	**NHL**	**82**	**13**	**21**	**34**	**69**	**5**	**0**	**4**	**100**	**13.0**	**-11**	**0**	**0.0**	**12:22**	**10**	**4**	**3**	**7**	**4**	**2**	**0**	**1**	**12:32**
99-2000	**Detroit**	**NHL**	**72**	**13**	**22**	**35**	**43**	**4**	**0**	**1**	**71**	**18.3**	**4**	**0**	**0.0**	**12:06**	**9**	**3**	**1**	**4**	**16**	**1**	**0**	**1**	**11:42**
2000-01	**Detroit**	**NHL**	**73**	**16**	**24**	**40**	**40**	**9**	**0**	**2**	**74**	**21.6**	**-12**	**2**	**50.0**	**11:41**	**6**	**1**	**3**	**4**	**8**	**1**	**0**	**0**	**14:23**
2001-02♦	**Detroit**	**NHL**	**69**	**8**	**18**	**26**	**58**	**6**	**0**	**1**	**79**	**10.1**	**-12**	**2**	**0.0**	**12:23**	**23**	**8**	**3**	**11**	**8**	**3**	**0**	**2**	**11:31**
	Sweden	Olympics	4	1	0	1	0	....	....	....	....	....	....	....	....	....	....	....	....	....	....	....	....	....	....
2002-03	**Detroit**	**NHL**	**74**	**20**	**20**	**40**	**62**	**12**	**0**	**2**	**109**	**18.3**	**11**	**2**	**0.0**	**12:28**	**4**	**1**	**1**	**2**	**4**	**1**	**0**	**0**	**14:37**
2003-04	**Detroit**	**NHL**	**67**	**15**	**15**	**30**	**38**	**6**	**0**	**0**	**74**	**20.3**	**8**	**3**	**0.0**	**12:23**	**12**	**2**	**2**	**4**	**10**	**1**	**0**	**1**	**11:27**
2004-05	Lulea HF	Sweden	47	14	16	30	50	....	....	....	....	....	....	....	....	....	4	0	0	0	18	....	....	....	....
2005-06	**Detroit**	**NHL**	**81**	**29**	**30**	**59**	**66**	**11**	**0**	**8**	**140**	**20.7**	**14**	**0**	**0.0**	**13:59**	**6**	**1**	**2**	**3**	**12**	**1**	**0**	**0**	**17:04**
	Sweden	Olympics	8	1	3	4	10	....	....	....	....	....	....	....	....	....	....	....	....	....	....	....	....	....	....
2006-07	**Detroit**	**NHL**	**77**	**30**	**22**	**52**	**58**	**13**	**0**	**5**	**176**	**17.0**	**13**	**0**	**0.0**	**15:13**	**15**	**5**	**3**	**8**	**14**	**4**	**0**	**1**	**16:15**
2007-08♦	**Detroit**	**NHL**	**59**	**20**	**20**	**40**	**58**	**11**	**0**	**5**	**137**	**14.6**	**9**	**1**	**0.0**	**17:33**	**21**	**4**	**8**	**12**	**26**	**1**	**0**	**0**	**17:10**
2008-09	**Detroit**	**NHL**	**53**	**14**	**23**	**37**	**38**	**8**	**0**	**1**	**75**	**18.7**	**18**	**8**	**37.5**	**15:16**	**23**	**2**	**5**	**7**	**22**	**0**	**0**	**0**	**13:45**
2009-10	**Detroit**	**NHL**	**68**	**25**	**20**	**45**	**60**	**13**	**0**	**5**	**131**	**19.1**	**5**	**1**	**0.0**	**15:49**	**12**	**4**	**3**	**7**	**12**	**1**	**0**	**1**	**13:27**
2010-11	**Detroit**	**NHL**	**73**	**18**	**19**	**37**	**62**	**10**	**0**	**1**	**125**	**14.4**	**-6**	**1**	**100.0**	**14:48**	**11**	**3**	**4**	**7**	**8**	**0**	**0**	**2**	**14:27**
	NHL Totals		**952**	**232**	**274**	**506**	**729**	**112**	**0**	**36**	**1392**	**16.7**		**20**	**25.0**	**13:44**	**175**	**45**	**50**	**95**	**160**	**18**	**0**	**9**	**13:57**

Signed as a free agent by **Lulea** (Sweden), September 16, 2004.

HOLOS, Jonas
(hoh-LAWS, YOH-nuhs) **COL**

Defense. Shoots right. 5'11", 196 lbs. Born, Sarpsborg, Norway, August 27, 1987. Colorado's 6th choice, 170th overall, in 2008 Entry Draft.

Season	Club	League	GP	G	A	Pts	PIM	PP	SH	GW	S	%	+/-	TF	F%	Min	GP	G	A	Pts	PIM	PP	SH	GW	Min
2002-03	Sarpsborg Jr.	Norway-Jr.	20	1	1	2	0	....	....	....	....	....	....	....	....	....	....	....	....	....	....	....	....	....	....
2003-04	Sarpsborg Jr.	Norway-Jr.	35	10	7	17	24	....	....	....	....	....	....	....	....	....	1	0	1	1	2	....	....	....	....
	Sarpsborg	Norway	1	0	0	0	0	....	....	....	....	....	....	....	....	....	....	....	....	....	....	....	....	....	....
2004-05	Sarpsborg Jr.	Norway-Jr.	1	1	1	2	0	....	....	....	....	....	....	....	....	....	1	0	0	0	0	....	....	....	....
	Sarpsborg	Norway	41	3	2	5	18	....	....	....	....	....	....	....	....	....	4	0	0	0	2	....	....	....	....
2005-06	Sarpsborg	Norway	26	3	4	7	14	....	....	....	....	....	....	....	....	....	6	0	0	0	0	....	....	....	....
2006-07	Sarpsborg 2	Norway-2	1	2	0	2	0	....	....	....	....	....	....	....	....	....	....	....	....	....	....	....	....	....	....
	Sarpsborg	Norway	40	11	19	30	32	....	....	....	....	....	....	....	....	....	13	2	2	4	18	....	....	....	....
2007-08	Sarpsborg	Norway	40	2	20	22	67	....	....	....	....	....	....	....	....	....	6	1	0	1	2	....	....	....	....
2008-09	Farjestad	Sweden	55	8	8	16	12	....	....	....	....	....	....	....	....	....	13	3	3	6	8	....	....	....	....
2009-10	Farjestad	Sweden	51	1	13	14	24	....	....	....	....	....	....	....	....	....	7	0	0	0	2	....	....	....	....
	Norway	Olympics	4	0	1	1	2	....	....	....	....	....	....	....	....	....	....	....	....	....	....	....	....	....	....
2010-11	**Colorado**	**NHL**	**39**	**0**	**6**	**6**	**10**	**0**	**0**	**0**	**36**	**0.0**	**-3**	**0**	**0.0**	**18:03**	....	....	....	....	....	....	....	....	....
	Lake Erie	AHL	17	0	6	6	8	....	....	....	....	....	....	....	....	....	7	1	1	2	8	....	....	....	....
	NHL Totals		**39**	**0**	**6**	**6**	**10**	**0**	**0**	**0**	**36**	**0.0**		**0**	**0.0**	**18:03**	....	....	....	....	....	....	....	....	....

HOLZER, Korbinian
(HOHL-zuhr, kohr-BEEHN-yuhn) **TOR**

Defense. Shoots right. 6'3", 205 lbs. Born, Munich, West Germany, February 16, 1988. Toronto's 4th choice, 111th overall, in 2006 Entry Draft.

Season	Club	League	GP	G	A	Pts	PIM	PP	SH	GW	S	%	+/-	TF	F%	Min	GP	G	A	Pts	PIM	PP	SH	GW	Min
2004-05	EC Bad Tolz Jr.	Ger-Jr.	34	7	11	18	66	....	....	....	....	....	....	....	....	....	5	0	2	2	2	....	....	....	....
2005-06	EC Bad Tolz Jr.	Ger-Jr.	2	1	1	2	6	....	....	....	....	....	....	....	....	....	....	....	....	....	....	....	....	....	....
	Tolzer Lowen	German-2	46	3	3	6	94	....	....	....	....	....	....	....	....	....	....	....	....	....	....	....	....	....	....
2006-07	Regensburg	German-2	42	2	6	8	68	....	....	....	....	....	....	....	....	....	4	0	0	0	2	....	....	....	....
2007-08	Dusseldorf	Germany	35	2	5	7	66	....	....	....	....	....	....	....	....	....	13	0	2	2	20	....	....	....	....
2008-09	Dusseldorf	Germany	38	4	5	9	89	....	....	....	....	....	....	....	....	....	16	0	1	1	18	....	....	....	....
2009-10	Dusseldorf	Germany	52	6	16	22	96	....	....	....	....	....	....	....	....	....	3	0	0	0	4	....	....	....	....
	Germany	Olympics	4	0	0	0	2	....	....	....	....	....	....	....	....	....	....	....	....	....	....	....	....	....	....
2010-11	**Toronto**	**NHL**	**2**	**0**	**0**	**0**	**2**	**0**	**0**	**0**	**1**	**0.0**	**-1**	**0**	**0.0**	**13:01**	....	....	....	....	....	....	....	....	....
	Toronto Marlies	AHL	73	3	10	13	88	....	....	....	....	....	....	....	....	....	....	....	....	....	....	....	....	....	....
	NHL Totals		**2**	**0**	**0**	**0**	**2**	**0**	**0**	**0**	**1**	**0.0**		**0**	**0.0**	**13:01**	....	....	....	....	....	....	....	....	....

HORCOFF, Shawn
(hohr-KAWF, SHAWN) **EDM**

Center. Shoots left. 6'1", 208 lbs. Born, Trail, B.C., September 17, 1978. Edmonton's 3rd choice, 99th overall, in 1998 Entry Draft.

Season	Club	League	GP	G	A	Pts	PIM	PP	SH	GW	S	%	+/-	TF	F%	Min	GP	G	A	Pts	PIM	PP	SH	GW	Min
1994-95	Trail Smokies	RMJHL	47	50	46	96	26	....	....	....	....	....	....	....	....	....	....	....	....	....	....	....	....	....	....
1995-96	Chilliwack Chiefs	BCHL	58	49	96	*145	44	....	....	....	....	....	....	....	....	....	9	5	19	24	12	....	....	....	....
1996-97	Michigan State	CCHA	40	10	13	23	20	....	....	....	....	....	....	....	....	....	....	....	....	....	....	....	....	....	....
1997-98	Michigan State	CCHA	34	14	13	27	50	....	....	....	....	....	....	....	....	....	....	....	....	....	....	....	....	....	....
1998-99	Michigan State	CCHA	39	12	25	37	70	....	....	....	....	....	....	....	....	....	....	....	....	....	....	....	....	....	....
99-2000	Michigan State	CCHA	42	14	*51	*65	50	....	....	....	....	....	....	....	....	....	....	....	....	....	....	....	....	....	....
2000-01	**Edmonton**	**NHL**	**49**	**9**	**7**	**16**	**10**	**0**	**0**	**2**	**42**	**21.4**	**8**	**122**	**41.8**	**9:14**	**5**	**0**	**0**	**0**	**0**	**0**	**0**	**0**	**6:31**
	Hamilton	AHL	24	10	18	28	19	....	....	....	....	....	....	....	....	....	....	....	....	....	....	....	....	....	....
2001-02	**Edmonton**	**NHL**	**61**	**8**	**14**	**22**	**18**	**0**	**0**	**0**	**57**	**14.0**	**3**	**454**	**46.3**	**11:20**	....	....	....	....	....	....	....	....	....
	Hamilton	AHL	2	1	2	3	6	....	....	....	....	....	....	....	....	....	....	....	....	....	....	....	....	....	....
2002-03	**Edmonton**	**NHL**	**78**	**12**	**21**	**33**	**55**	**2**	**0**	**3**	**98**	**12.2**	**10**	**301**	**42.9**	**13:30**	**6**	**3**	**1**	**4**	**6**	**0**	**0**	**1**	**15:27**
2003-04	**Edmonton**	**NHL**	**80**	**15**	**25**	**40**	**73**	**0**	**2**	**3**	**110**	**13.6**	**0**	**1378**	**50.7**	**17:31**	....	....	....	....	....	....	....	....	....
2004-05	Mora IK	Sweden	50	19	27	46	117	....	....	....	....	....	....	....	....	....	....	....	....	....	....	....	....	....	....
2005-06	**Edmonton**	**NHL**	**79**	**22**	**51**	**73**	**85**	**3**	**3**	**5**	**167**	**13.2**	**0**	**1421**	**52.7**	**19:59**	**24**	**7**	**12**	**19**	**12**	**1**	**1**	**2**	**21:37**
2006-07	**Edmonton**	**NHL**	**80**	**16**	**35**	**51**	**56**	**5**	**0**	**5**	**168**	**9.5**	**-22**	**1422**	**50.6**	**20:50**	....	....	....	....	....	....	....	....	....
2007-08	**Edmonton**	**NHL**	**53**	**21**	**29**	**50**	**30**	**6**	**0**	**2**	**115**	**18.3**	**1**	**963**	**50.6**	**22:13**	....	....	....	....	....	....	....	....	....
2008-09	**Edmonton**	**NHL**	**80**	**17**	**36**	**53**	**39**	**8**	**0**	**2**	**178**	**9.6**	**7**	**1756**	**53.9**	**21:22**	....	....	....	....	....	....	....	....	....
2009-10	**Edmonton**	**NHL**	**77**	**13**	**23**	**36**	**51**	**4**	**0**	**1**	**123**	**10.6**	**-29**	**1337**	**46.5**	**19:26**	....	....	....	....	....	....	....	....	....
2010-11	**Edmonton**	**NHL**	**47**	**9**	**18**	**27**	**46**	**5**	**0**	**1**	**78**	**11.5**	**-1**	**813**	**48.3**	**18:41**	....	....	....	....	....	....	....	....	....
	NHL Totals		**684**	**142**	**259**	**401**	**463**	**33**	**5**	**24**	**1136**	**12.5**		**9967**	**50.2**	**17:42**	**35**	**10**	**13**	**23**	**18**	**1**	**1**	**3**	**18:24**

CCHA First All-Star Team (2000) • CCHA Player of the Year (2000) • NCAA West First All-American Team (2000)

Played in NHL All-Star Game (2008)

Signed as a free agent by **Mora** (Sweden), September 6, 2004.

HORDICHUK, Darcy
(HOHR-dih-chuhk, DAHR-see) **EDM**

Left wing. Shoots left. 6'1", 211 lbs. Born, Kamsack, Sask., August 10, 1980. Atlanta's 9th choice, 180th overall, in 2000 Entry Draft.

Season	Club	League	GP	G	A	Pts	PIM	PP	SH	GW	S	%	+/-	TF	F%	Min	GP	G	A	Pts	PIM	PP	SH	GW	Min
1996-97	Yorkton Mallers	SMHL	57	6	15	21	230	....	....	....	....	....	....	....	....	....	....	....	....	....	....	....	....	....	....
	Calgary Hitmen	WHL	3	0	0	0	2	....	....	....	....	....	....	....	....	....	....	....	....	....	....	....	....	....	....
1997-98	Dauphin Kings	MJHL	58	12	21	33	279	....	....	....	....	....	....	....	....	....	....	....	....	....	....	....	....	....	....
1998-99	Saskatoon Blades	WHL	66	3	2	5	246	....	....	....	....	....	....	....	....	....	....	....	....	....	....	....	....	....	....
99-2000	Saskatoon Blades	WHL	63	6	8	14	269	....	....	....	....	....	....	....	....	....	11	4	2	6	43	....	....	....	....
2000-01	**Atlanta**	**NHL**	**11**	**0**	**0**	**0**	**38**	**0**	**0**	**0**	**6**	**0.0**	**-3**	**0**	**0.0**	**7:18**	....	....	....	....	....	....	....	....	....
	Orlando	IHL	69	7	3	10	*369	....	....	....	....	....	....	....	....	....	16	3	3	6	*41	....	....	....	....
2001-02	**Atlanta**	**NHL**	**33**	**1**	**1**	**2**	**127**	**0**	**0**	**0**	**8**	**12.5**	**-5**	**4**	**25.0**	**6:03**	....	....	....	....	....	....	....	....	....
	Chicago Wolves	AHL	34	5	4	9	127	....	....	....	....	....	....	....	....	....	....	....	....	....	....	....	....	....	....
	Phoenix	**NHL**	**1**	**0**	**0**	**0**	**14**	**0**	**0**	**0**	**0**	**0.0**	**0**	**0**	**0.0**	**7:18**	....	....	....	....	....	....	....	....	....
2002-03	**Phoenix**	**NHL**	**25**	**0**	**0**	**0**	**82**	**0**	**0**	**0**	**5**	**0.0**	**-1**	**0**	**0.0**	**4:47**	....	....	....	....	....	....	....	....	....
	Springfield	AHL	22	1	3	4	38	....	....	....	....	....	....	....	....	....	....	....	....	....	....	....	....	....	....
	Florida	**NHL**	**3**	**0**	**0**	**0**	**15**	**0**	**0**	**0**	**2**	**0.0**	**-1**	**0**	**0.0**	**9:45**	....	....	....	....	....	....	....	....	....
2003-04	**Florida**	**NHL**	**57**	**3**	**1**	**4**	**158**	**0**	**0**	**1**	**27**	**11.1**	**-10**	**4**	**50.0**	**6:46**	....	....	....	....	....	....	....	....	....

			Regular Season														Playoffs								
Season	Club	League	GP	G	A	Pts	PIM	PP	SH	GW	S	%	+/-	TF	F%	Min	GP	G	A	Pts	PIM	PP	SH	GW	Min
2004-05			DID NOT PLAY																						
2005-06	**Nashville**	**NHL**	**74**	**7**	**6**	**13**	**163**	**0**	**0**	**1**	**52**	**13.5**	**9**	**1**	**0.0**	**6:09**									
2006-07	**Nashville**	**NHL**	**53**	**1**	**3**	**4**	**90**	**0**	**0**	**0**	**22**	**4.5**	**−2**	**0**	**0.0**	**4:48**	....	....	....	....	....	....	....	....	....
2007-08	**Nashville**	**NHL**	**45**	**1**	**2**	**3**	**60**	**0**	**0**	**1**	**18**	**5.6**	**−1**	**0**	**0.0**	**5:09**	**2**	**0**	**0**	**0**	**0**	**0**	**0**	**0**	**3:38**
2008-09	**Vancouver**	**NHL**	**73**	**4**	**1**	**5**	**109**	**0**	**0**	**.0**	**26**	**15.4**	**1**	**1**	**100.0**	**5:32**	**5**	**0**	**0**	**0**	**2**	**0**	**0**	**0**	**3:32**
2009-10	**Vancouver**	**NHL**	**56**	**1**	**1**	**2**	**142**	**0**	**0**	**0**	**21**	**4.8**	**−7**	**1**	**0.0**	**6:02**	**10**	**1**	**0**	**1**	**14**	**0**	**0**	**0**	**5:20**
2010-11	**Florida**	**NHL**	**64**	**1**	**4**	**5**	**76**	**0**	**0**	**0**	**32**	**3.1**	**−1**	**0**	**0.0**	**5:04**	....	....	....	....	....	....	....	....	....
	NHL Totals		**495**	**19**	**19**	**38**	**1074**	**0**	**0**	**3**	**219**	**8.7**		**11**	**36.4**	**5:43**	**17**	**1**	**0**	**1**	**16**	**0**	**0**	**0**	**4:36**

Traded to **Phoenix** by **Atlanta** with Atlanta's 4th (Lance Monych) and 5th (John Zeiler) round choices in 2002 Entry Draft for Kiril Safronov, the rights to Ruslan Zainullin and Phoenix's 4th round choice (Patrick Dwyer) in 2002 Entry Draft, March 19, 2002. Traded to **Florida** by **Phoenix** with Phoenix's 2nd round choice (later traded to Tampa Bay – Tampa Bay selected Matt Smaby) in 2003 Entry Draft for Brad Ference, March 8, 2003. Traded to **Nashville** by **Florida** for Nashville's 4th round choice (Matt Duffy) in 2005 Entry Draft, July 27, 2005. Traded to **Carolina** by **Nashville** with Nashville's 5th round choice (later traded to Phoenix – Phoenix selected Louis Domingue) in 2010 Entry Draft for Carolina's 5th round choice (later traded to Tampa Bay – Tampa Bay selected Michael Zador) in 2009 Entry Draft, June 19, 2008. Signed as a free agent by **Vancouver**, July 1, 2008. Traded to **Florida** by **Vancouver** for Andrew Peters, October 6, 2010. Signed as a free agent by **Edmonton**, July 1, 2011.

HORNQVIST, Patric

(HOHRN-kwihst, PAT-rihk) **NSH**

Right wing. Shoots left. 6', 188 lbs. Born, Sollentuna, Sweden, January 1, 1987. Nashville's 7th choice, 230th overall, in 2005 Entry Draft.

Season	Club	League	GP	G	A	Pts	PIM	PP	SH	GW	S	%	+/-	TF	F%	Min	GP	G	A	Pts	PIM	PP	SH	GW	Min
2003-04	Vasby Jr.	Swe-Jr.	10	7	10	17	30	....	....	....	....	....	....	....	....	....	....	....	....	....	....	....	....	....	....
	Vasby	Sweden-3	32	8	5	13	26	....	....	....	....	....	....	....	....	....	....	....	....	....	....	....	....	....	....
2004-05	Vasby	Sweden-3	28	12	12	24	36	....	....	....	....	....	....	....	....	....	....	....	....	....	....	....	....	....	....
	Djurgarden Jr.	Swe-Jr.	5	3	0	3	2	....	....	....	....	....	....	....	....	....	....	....	....	....	....	....	....	....	....
2005-06	Djurgarden Jr.	Swe-Jr.	4	2	1	3	2	....	....	....	....	....	....	....	....	....	....	....	....	....	....	....	....	....	....
	Djurgarden	Sweden	47	5	2	7	36	....	....	....	....	....	....	....	....	....	4	1	2	3	2	....	....	....	....
2006-07	Djurgarden	Sweden	49	23	11	34	38	....	....	....	....	....	....	....	....	....	....	....	....	....	....	....	....	....	....
	Djurgarden Jr.	Swe-Jr.	....	....	....	....	....	....	....	....	....	....	....	....	....	....	7	2	5	7	14	....	....	....	....
2007-08	Djurgarden	Sweden	53	18	12	30	58	....	....	....	....	....	....	....	....	....	5	0	1	1	6	....	....	....	....
2008-09	**Nashville**	**NHL**	**28**	**2**	**5**	**7**	**16**	**0**	**0**	**0**	**54**	**3.7**	**−3**	**5**	**20.0**	**11:24**	....	....	....	....	....	....	....	....	....
	Milwaukee	AHL	49	17	18	35	44	....	....	....	....	....	....	....	....	....	11	4	4	8	6	....	....	....	....
2009-10	**Nashville**	**NHL**	**80**	**30**	**21**	**51**	**40**	**10**	**0**	**8**	**275**	**10.9**	**18**	**18**	**27.8**	**15:41**	**2**	**0**	**1**	**1**	**4**	**0**	**0**	**0**	**13:10**
	Sweden	Olympics	4	1	0	1	4	....	....	....	....	....	....	....	....	....	....	....	....	....	....	....	....	....	....
2010-11	**Nashville**	**NHL**	**79**	**21**	**27**	**48**	**47**	**6**	**0**	**5**	**265**	**7.9**	**11**	**45**	**48.9**	**15:44**	**12**	**2**	**1**	**3**	**6**	**1**	**0**	**0**	**15:16**
	NHL Totals		**187**	**53**	**53**	**106**	**103**	**16**	**0**	**13**	**594**	**8.9**		**68**	**41.2**	**15:04**	**14**	**2**	**2**	**4**	**10**	**1**	**0**	**0**	**14:58**

HORTON, Nathan

(HOHR-tuhn, NAY-thuhn) **BOS**

Center. Shoots right. 6'2", 229 lbs. Born, Welland, Ont., May 29, 1985. Florida's 1st choice, 3rd overall, in 2003 Entry Draft.

Season	Club	League	GP	G	A	Pts	PIM	PP	SH	GW	S	%	+/-	TF	F%	Min	GP	G	A	Pts	PIM	PP	SH	GW	Min
2000-01	Thorold	ON-Jr.B	41	16	31	47	75	....	....	....	....	....	....	....	....	....	....	....	....	....	....	....	....	....	....
2001-02	Oshawa Generals	OHL	64	31	36	67	84	....	....	....	....	....	....	....	....	....	5	1	2	3	10	....	....	....	....
2002-03	Oshawa Generals	OHL	54	33	35	68	111	....	....	....	....	....	....	....	....	....	13	9	6	15	10	....	....	....	....
2003-04	**Florida**	**NHL**	**55**	**14**	**8**	**22**	**57**	**6**	**1**	**0**	**81**	**17.3**	**−5**	**270**	**41.9**	**13:20**	....	....	....	....	....	....	....	....	....
2004-05	San Antonio	AHL	21	5	4	9	21	....	....	....	....	....	....	....	....	....	....	....	....	....	....	....	....	....	....
2005-06	**Florida**	**NHL**	**71**	**28**	**19**	**47**	**89**	**3**	**0**	**1**	**162**	**17.3**	**8**	**24**	**45.8**	**16:53**	....	....	....	....	....	....	....	....	....
2006-07	**Florida**	**NHL**	**82**	**31**	**31**	**62**	**61**	**7**	**1**	**3**	**217**	**14.3**	**15**	**31**	**48.4**	**18:04**	....	....	....	....	....	....	....	....	....
2007-08	**Florida**	**NHL**	**82**	**27**	**35**	**62**	**85**	**9**	**0**	**3**	**212**	**12.7**	**15**	**73**	**39.7**	**18:44**	....	....	....	....	....	....	....	....	....
2008-09	**Florida**	**NHL**	**67**	**22**	**23**	**45**	**48**	**5**	**1**	**5**	**131**	**16.8**	**−5**	**863**	**43.7**	**17:51**	....	....	....	....	....	....	....	....	....
2009-10	**Florida**	**NHL**	**65**	**20**	**37**	**57**	**42**	**7**	**2**	**4**	**159**	**12.6**	**−1**	**85**	**56.5**	**20:53**	....	....	....	....	....	....	....	....	....
2010-11 ♦	**Boston**	**NHL**	**80**	**26**	**27**	**53**	**85**	**6**	**0**	**2**	**188**	**13.8**	**29**	**19**	**42.1**	**16:17**	**21**	**8**	**9**	**17**	**35**	**1**	**0**	**3**	**16:54**
	NHL Totals		**502**	**168**	**180**	**348**	**467**	**43**	**5**	**18**	**1150**	**14.6**		**1365**	**44.0**	**17:33**	**21**	**8**	**9**	**17**	**35**	**1**	**0**	**3**	**16:54**

OHL All-Rookie Team (2002)

Signed as a free agent by **San Antonio** (AHL), October 28, 2004. Traded to **Boston** by **Florida** with Gregory Campbell for Dennis Wideman, Boston's 1st round choice (later traded to Los Angeles – Los Angeles selected Derek Forbort) in 2010 Entry Draft and Boston's 3rd round choice (Kyle Rau) in 2011 Entry Draft, June 22, 2010.

HOSSA, Marian

(HOH-sa, MAIR-ee-uhn) **CHI**

Right wing. Shoots left. 6'1", 210 lbs. Born, Stara Lubovna, Czech., January 12, 1979. Ottawa's 1st choice, 12th overall, in 1997 Entry Draft.

Season	Club	League	GP	G	A	Pts	PIM	PP	SH	GW	S	%	+/-	TF	F%	Min	GP	G	A	Pts	PIM	PP	SH	GW	Min
1995-96	Dukla Trencin Jr.	Slovak-Jr.	53	42	49	91	26	....	....	....	....	....	....	....	....	....	....	....	....	....	....	....	....	....	....
1996-97	Dukla Trencin	Slovakia	46	25	19	44	33	....	....	....	....	....	....	....	....	....	7	5	5	10	....	....	....	....	....
1997-98	Portland	WHL	53	45	40	85	50	....	....	....	....	....	....	....	....	....	16	13	6	19	6	....	....	....	....
	Ottawa	**NHL**	**7**	**0**	**1**	**1**	**0**	**0**	**0**	**0**	**10**	**0.0**	**−1**	....	....	....	....	....	....	....	....	....	....	....	....
1998-99	**Ottawa**	**NHL**	**60**	**15**	**15**	**30**	**37**	**1**	**0**	**2**	**124**	**12.1**	**18**	**4**	**25.0**	**13:59**	**4**	**0**	**2**	**2**	**4**	**0**	**0**	**0**	**16:46**
99-2000	**Ottawa**	**NHL**	**78**	**29**	**27**	**56**	**32**	**5**	**0**	**4**	**240**	**12.1**	**5**	**7**	**57.1**	**17:12**	**6**	**0**	**0**	**0**	**2**	**0**	**0**	**0**	**15:22**
2000-01	**Ottawa**	**NHL**	**81**	**32**	**43**	**75**	**44**	**11**	**2**	**7**	**249**	**12.9**	**19**	**14**	**42.9**	**18:01**	**4**	**1**	**1**	**2**	**4**	**0**	**0**	**0**	**19:02**
2001-02	Dukla Trencin	Slovakia	8	3	4	7	16	....	....	....	....	....	....	....	....	....	....	....	....	....	....	....	....	....	....
	Ottawa	**NHL**	**80**	**31**	**35**	**66**	**50**	**9**	**1**	**4**	**278**	**11.2**	**11**	**12**	**33.3**	**18:29**	**12**	**4**	**6**	**10**	**2**	**1**	**0**	**0**	**19:04**
	Slovakia	Olympics	2	4	2	6	0	....	....	....	....	....	....	....	....	....	....	....	....	....	....	....	....	....	....
2002-03	**Ottawa**	**NHL**	**80**	**45**	**35**	**80**	**34**	**14**	**0**	**10**	**229**	**19.7**	**8**	**19**	**36.8**	**18:31**	**18**	**5**	**11**	**16**	**6**	**3**	**0**	**1**	**18:41**
2003-04	**Ottawa**	**NHL**	**81**	**36**	**46**	**82**	**46**	**14**	**1**	**5**	**233**	**15.5**	**4**	**25**	**40.0**	**18:37**	**7**	**3**	**1**	**4**	**0**	**1**	**0**	**2**	**21:24**
2004-05	Mora IK	Sweden	24	18	14	32	22	....	....	....	....	....	....	....	....	....	....	....	....	....	....	....	....	....	....
	Dukla Trencin	Slovakia	25	22	20	42	38	....	....	....	....	....	....	....	....	....	5	4	5	9	14	....	....	....	....
2005-06	**Atlanta**	**NHL**	**80**	**39**	**53**	**92**	**67**	**14**	***7**	**7**	**341**	**11.4**	**17**	**15**	**26.7**	**21:41**	....	....	....	....	....	....	....	....	....
	Slovakia	Olympics	6	5	5	10	4	....	....	....	....	....	....	....	....	....	....	....	....	....	....	....	....	....	....
2006-07	**Atlanta**	**NHL**	**82**	**43**	**57**	**100**	**49**	**17**	**3**	**5**	**340**	**12.6**	**18**	**18**	**22.2**	**21:41**	**4**	**0**	**1**	**1**	**6**	**0**	**0**	**0**	**18:55**
2007-08	**Atlanta**	**NHL**	**60**	**26**	**30**	**56**	**30**	**8**	**2**	**4**	**229**	**11.4**	**−14**	**14**	**28.6**	**21:55**	....	....	....	....	....	....	....	....	....
	Pittsburgh	**NHL**	**12**	**3**	**7**	**10**	**6**	**0**	**0**	**0**	**35**	**8.6**	**0**	**1**	**0.0**	**18:34**	**20**	**12**	**14**	**26**	**12**	**5**	**0**	**2**	**21:00**
2008-09	**Detroit**	**NHL**	**74**	**40**	**31**	**71**	**63**	**10**	**0**	**8**	**307**	**13.0**	**27**	**19**	**21.1**	**17:48**	**23**	**6**	**9**	**15**	**10**	**2**	**1**	**1**	**18:38**
2009-10 ♦	**Chicago**	**NHL**	**57**	**24**	**27**	**51**	**18**	**2**	**5**	**2**	**199**	**12.1**	**24**	**1**	**0.0**	**18:44**	**22**	**3**	**12**	**15**	**25**	**0**	**0**	**1**	**18:25**
	Slovakia	Olympics	7	3	6	9	6	....	....	....	....	....	....	....	....	....	....	....	....	....	....	....	....	....	....
2010-11	**Chicago**	**NHL**	**65**	**25**	**32**	**57**	**32**	**8**	**2**	**2**	**205**	**12.2**	**9**	**4**	**75.0**	**19:42**	**7**	**2**	**4**	**6**	**2**	**1**	**0**	**1**	**18:35**
	NHL Totals		**897**	**388**	**439**	**827**	**508**	**113**	**23**	**60**	**3019**	**12.9**		**153**	**33.3**	**18:54**	**127**	**36**	**61**	**97**	**73**	**13**	**1**	**8**	**18:58**

WHL West First All-Star Team (1998) • WHL Rookie of the Year (1998) • Canadian Major Junior First All-Star Team (1998) • Memorial Cup All-Star Team (1998) • NHL All-Rookie Team (1999) • NHL Second All-Star Team (2009)

Played in NHL All-Star Game (2001, 2003, 2007, 2008)

Signed as a free agent by **Trencin** (Slovakia), September 16, 2004. Signed as a free agent by **Mora** (Sweden), November 11, 2004. Signed as a free agent by **Trencin** (Slovakia), January 31, 2005. Traded to **Atlanta** by **Ottawa** with Greg de Vries for Dany Heatley, August 23, 2005. Traded to **Pittsburgh** by **Atlanta** with Pascal Dupuis for Colby Armstrong, Erik Christensen, Angelo Esposito and Pittsburgh's 1st round choice (Daulton Leveille) in 2008 Entry Draft , February 26, 2008. Signed as a free agent by **Detroit**, July 2, 2008. Signed as a free agent by **Chicago**, July 1, 2009.

HUDLER, Jiri

(HOOD-luhr, YIH-ree) **DET**

Center. Shoots left. 5'10", 182 lbs. Born, Olomouc, Czech., January 4, 1984. Detroit's 1st choice, 58th overall, in 2002 Entry Draft.

Season	Club	League	GP	G	A	Pts	PIM	PP	SH	GW	S	%	+/-	TF	F%	Min	GP	G	A	Pts	PIM	PP	SH	GW	Min
1998-99	HC Vsetin U17	CzR-U17	46	57	57	114	....	....	....	....	....	....	....	....	....	....	....	....	....	....	....	....	....	....	....
99-2000	HC Vsetin Jr.	CzRep-Jr.	53	29	31	60	75	....	....	....	....	....	....	....	....	....	....	....	....	....	....	....	....	....	....
	Vsetin	CzRep	2	0	1	1	0	....	....	....	....	....	....	....	....	....	....	....	....	....	....	....	....	....	....
2000-01	HC Vsetin Jr.	CzRep-Jr.	16	8	14	22	16	....	....	....	....	....	....	....	....	....	....	....	....	....	....	....	....	....	....
	HC Slovnaft Vsetin	CzRep	22	1	4	5	10	....	....	....	....	....	....	....	....	....	....	....	....	....	....	....	....	....	....
	HC Femax Havirov	CzRep	15	5	1	6	12	....	....	....	....	....	....	....	....	....	....	....	....	....	....	....	....	....	....
2001-02	HC Vsetin	CzRep	46	15	31	46	54	....	....	....	....	....	....	....	....	....	....	....	....	....	....	....	....	....	....
	Liberec	CzRep-2	13	9	7	16	10	....	....	....	....	....	....	....	....	....	....	....	....	....	....	....	....	....	....
	HC Olomouc	CzRep-3	1	0	2	2	4	....	....	....	....	....	....	....	....	....	....	....	....	....	....	....	....	....	....
2002-03	HC Vsetin	CzRep	30	19	27	46	22	....	....	....	....	....	....	....	....	....	....	....	....	....	....	....	....	....	....
	Ak Bars Kazan	Russia	11	1	5	6	12	....	....	....	....	....	....	....	....	....	1	0	0	0	0	....	....	....	....
2003-04	**Detroit**	**NHL**	**12**	**1**	**2**	**3**	**10**	**1**	**0**	**0**	**8**	**12.5**	**−1**	**50**	**30.0**	**8:10**	....	....	....	....	....	....	....	....	....
	Grand Rapids	AHL	57	17	32	49	46	....	....	....	....	....	....	....	....	....	4	1	5	6	2	....	....	....	....
2004-05	Grand Rapids	AHL	52	12	22	34	10	....	....	....	....	....	....	....	....	....	....	....	....	....	....	....	....	....	....
	HC Vsetin	CzRep	7	5	2	7	10	....	....	....	....	....	....	....	....	....	....	....	....	....	....	....	....	....	....
2005-06	**Detroit**	**NHL**	**4**	**0**	**0**	**0**	**2**	**0**	**0**	**0**	**3**	**0.0**	**0**	**0**	**0.0**	**7:13**	....	....	....	....	....	....	....	....	....
	Grand Rapids	AHL	76	36	61	97	56	....	....	....	....	....	....	....	....	....	16	6	16	22	20	....	....	....	....
2006-07	**Detroit**	**NHL**	**76**	**15**	**10**	**25**	**36**	**3**	**0**	**4**	**107**	**14.0**	**16**	**20**	**30.0**	**10:02**	**6**	**0**	**2**	**2**	**4**	**0**	**0**	**0**	**9:09**
2007-08 ♦	**Detroit**	**NHL**	**81**	**13**	**29**	**42**	**26**	**3**	**0**	**2**	**131**	**9.9**	**11**	**26**	**38.5**	**13:10**	**22**	**5**	**9**	**14**	**14**	**2**	**0**	**2**	**11:36**
2008-09	**Detroit**	**NHL**	**82**	**23**	**34**	**57**	**16**	**6**	**0**	**2**	**155**	**14.8**	**7**	**29**	**44.8**	**13:39**	**23**	**4**	**8**	**12**	**6**	**2**	**0**	**1**	**13:28**

			Regular Season														Playoffs								
Season	Club	League	GP	G	A	Pts	PIM	PP	SH	GW	S	%	+/-	TF	F%	Min	GP	G	A	Pts	PIM	PP	SH	GW	Min
2009-10	Dynamo Moscow	Rus-KHL	54	19	35	54	18										4	0	1	1	4				
2010-11	**Detroit**	**NHL**	**73**	**10**	**27**	**37**	**28**	**3**	**0**	**2**	**105**	**9.5**	**-7**	**70**	**44.3**	**13:40**	**10**	**1**	**2**	**3**	**6**	**0**	**0**	**0**	**11:57**
	NHL Totals		**328**	**62**	**102**	**164**	**118**	**16**	**0**	**10**	**509**	**12.2**		**195**	**38.5**	**12:25**	**61**	**10**	**21**	**31**	**30**	**4**	**0**	**3**	**12:07**

AHL Second All-Star Team (2006)

Signed as a free agent by **Vsetin** (CzRep), December 2, 2004. Signed as a free agent by **Dynamo Moscow** (Russia-KHL), July 10, 2009. Signed as a free agent by **Detroit**, May 24, 2010.

HUNTER, Trent

(HUHN-tuhr, TREHNT)

Right wing. Shoots right. 6'3", 217 lbs. Born, Red Deer, Alta., July 5, 1980. Anaheim's 4th choice, 150th overall, in 1998 Entry Draft.

Season	Club	League	GP	G	A	Pts	PIM	PP	SH	GW	S	%	+/-	TF	F%	Min	GP	G	A	Pts	PIM	PP	SH	GW	Min
1996-97	Red Deer	AMHL	42	30	25	55	50																		
1997-98	Prince George	WHL	60	13	14	27	34										8	1	0	1	4				
1998-99	Prince George	WHL	50	18	20	38	34										7	2	5	7	2				
99-2000	Prince George	WHL	67	46	49	95	47										13	7	15	22	6				
2000-01	Springfield	AHL	57	18	17	35	14																		
2001-02	Bridgeport	AHL	80	30	35	65	30										17	8	11	19	6				
	NY Islanders	**NHL**															**4**	**1**	**1**	**2**	**2**	**0**	**0**	**0**	**11:13**
2002-03	**NY Islanders**	**NHL**	**8**	**0**	**4**	**4**	**4**	**0**	**0**	**0**	**19**	**0.0**	**5**	**1**	**0.0**	**12:13**									
	Bridgeport	AHL	70	30	41	71	39										9	7	4	11	10				
2003-04	**NY Islanders**	**NHL**	**77**	**25**	**26**	**51**	**16**	**4**	**0**	**7**	**187**	**13.4**	**23**	**19**	**36.8**	**15:39**	**5**	**0**	**0**	**0**	**4**	**0**	**0**	**0**	**11:38**
2004-05	Nykoping	Sweden-2	33	13	12	25	73										4	5	3	8	2				
2005-06	**NY Islanders**	**NHL**	**82**	**16**	**19**	**35**	**34**	**5**	**0**	**3**	**221**	**7.2**	**-9**	**32**	**28.1**	**17:50**									
2006-07	**NY Islanders**	**NHL**	**77**	**20**	**15**	**35**	**22**	**5**	**1**	**2**	**168**	**11.9**	**5**	**14**	**42.9**	**16:00**	**5**	**3**	**0**	**3**	**0**	**0**	**0**	**0**	**15:05**
2007-08	**NY Islanders**	**NHL**	**82**	**12**	**29**	**41**	**43**	**2**	**0**	**1**	**222**	**5.4**	**-17**	**29**	**20.7**	**18:13**									
2008-09	**NY Islanders**	**NHL**	**55**	**14**	**17**	**31**	**41**	**5**	**0**	**2**	**154**	**9.1**	**-8**	**20**	**25.0**	**16:23**									
2009-10	**NY Islanders**	**NHL**	**61**	**11**	**17**	**28**	**18**	**3**	**0**	**1**	**159**	**6.9**	**3**	**9**	**22.2**	**15:11**									
2010-11	**NY Islanders**	**NHL**	**17**	**1**	**3**	**4**	**23**	**0**	**0**	**0**	**30**	**3.3**	**-3**	**2**	**0.0**	**12:40**									
	NHL Totals		**459**	**99**	**130**	**229**	**201**	**24**	**1**	**16**	**1160**	**8.5**		**126**	**27.8**	**16:25**	**14**	**4**	**1**	**5**	**6**	**0**	**0**	**0**	**12:45**

WHL West First All-Star Team (2000) • NHL All-Rookie Team (2004)

Traded to **NY Islanders** by **Anaheim** for Columbus' 4th round choice (previously acquired, Anaheim selected Jonas Ronnqvist) in 2000 Entry Draft, May 23, 2000. Signed as a free agent by **Nykoping** (Sweden-2), November 8, 2004. • Missed majority of 2010-11 due to knee injury vs. Columbus, November 24, 2010. Traded to **New Jersey** by **NY Islanders** for Brian Rolston, July 28, 2011.

HUNWICK, Matt

(HUHN-wihk, MAT) **COL**

Defense. Shoots left. 5'11", 190 lbs. Born, Warren, MI, May 21, 1985. Boston's 6th choice, 224th overall, in 2004 Entry Draft.

Season	Club	League	GP	G	A	Pts	PIM	PP	SH	GW	S	%	+/-	TF	F%	Min	GP	G	A	Pts	PIM	PP	SH	GW	Min
2001-02	USNTDP	U-17	14	3	4	7	6																		
	USNTDP	NAHL	29	2	1	3	30																		
2002-03	USNTDP	U-18	40	6	16	22	40																		
	USNTDP	NAHL	8	2	2	4	23																		
2003-04	U. of Michigan	CCHA	41	1	14	15	62																		
2004-05	U. of Michigan	CCHA	40	6	19	25	60																		
2005-06	U. of Michigan	CCHA	41	11	19	30	70																		
2006-07	U. of Michigan	CCHA	41	6	21	27	64																		
2007-08	**Boston**	**NHL**	**13**	**0**	**1**	**1**	**4**	**0**	**0**	**0**	**6**	**0.0**	**-1**	**0**	**0.0**	**10:36**									
	Providence Bruins	AHL	55	2	21	23	49										10	0	5	5	8				
2008-09	**Boston**	**NHL**	**53**	**6**	**21**	**27**	**31**	**0**	**0**	**1**	**58**	**10.3**	**15**	**0**	**0.0**	**16:59**	**1**	**0**	**0**	**0**	**0**	**0**	**0**	**0**	**15:59**
	Providence Bruins	AHL	3	0	3	3	0																		
2009-10	**Boston**	**NHL**	**76**	**6**	**8**	**14**	**32**	**1**	**1**	**1**	**60**	**10.0**	**-16**	**1**	**0.0**	**17:58**	**13**	**0**	**6**	**6**	**2**	**0**	**0**	**0**	**21:57**
2010-11	**Boston**	**NHL**	**22**	**1**	**2**	**3**	**9**	**0**	**0**	**0**	**26**	**3.8**	**4**	**0**	**0.0**	**16:13**									
	Colorado	**NHL**	**51**	**0**	**10**	**10**	**16**	**0**	**0**	**0**	**74**	**0.0**	**-19**	**0**	**0.0**	**19:30**									
	NHL Totals		**215**	**13**	**42**	**55**	**92**	**1**	**1**	**2**	**224**	**5.8**		**1**	**0.0**	**17:28**	**14**	**0**	**6**	**6**	**2**	**0**	**0**	**0**	**21:31**

CCHA All-Rookie Team (2004) • CCHA Second All-Star Team (2005, 2006) • CCHA First All-Star Team (2007) • NCAA West Second All-American Team (2007)

Traded to **Colorado** by **Boston** for Colby Cohen, November 29, 2010.

HUSELIUS, Kristian

(hoo-SAY-lee-uhs, KRIHST-yan) **CBJ**

Left wing. Shoots left. 6'2", 184 lbs. Born, Osterhaninge, Sweden, November 10, 1978. Florida's 2nd choice, 47th overall, in 1997 Entry Draft.

Season	Club	League	GP	G	A	Pts	PIM	PP	SH	GW	S	%	+/-	TF	F%	Min	GP	G	A	Pts	PIM	PP	SH	GW	Min
1994-95	Hammarby Jr.	Swe-Jr.	17	6	2	8	2																		
1995-96	Hammarby Jr.	Swe-Jr.	25	13	8	21	14																		
	Hammarby	Sweden-2	6	1	0	1	0																		
1996-97	Farjestad	Sweden	13	2	0	2	4										5	1	0	1	0				
1997-98	Farjestad	Sweden	34	2	1	3	2										11	0	0	0	0				
	Farjestad	EuroHL	5	2	3	5	0																		
1998-99	Farjestad	Sweden	28	4	4	8	4																		
	Farjestad	EuroHL	6	2	2	4	8										1	0	0	0	0				
	V.Frolunda	Sweden	20	2	2	4	2										4	1	0	1	0				
99-2000	V.Frolunda	Sweden	50	21	23	44	20										5	2	2	4	8				
2000-01	V.Frolunda	Sweden	49	*32	*35	*67	26										5	4	5	9	14				
2001-02	**Florida**	**NHL**	**79**	**23**	**22**	**45**	**14**	**6**	**1**	**3**	**169**	**13.6**	**-4**	**14**	**21.4**	**16:55**									
2002-03	**Florida**	**NHL**	**78**	**20**	**23**	**43**	**20**	**3**	**0**	**3**	**187**	**10.7**	**-6**	**6**	**33.3**	**17:20**									
2003-04	**Florida**	**NHL**	**76**	**10**	**21**	**31**	**24**	**2**	**0**	**2**	**168**	**6.0**	**-6**	**185**	**37.8**	**14:14**									
2004-05	Linkopings HC	Sweden	34	14	*35	49	10																		
	Rapperswil	Swiss															4	1	3	4	2				
2005-06	**Florida**	**NHL**	**24**	**5**	**3**	**8**	**4**	**2**	**0**	**0**	**57**	**8.8**	**-11**	**3**	**66.7**	**14:44**									
	Calgary	**NHL**	**54**	**15**	**24**	**39**	**36**	**6**	**0**	**4**	**107**	**14.0**	**2**	**3**	**33.3**	**14:55**	**7**	**2**	**4**	**6**	**4**	**2**	**0**	**0**	**15:35**
2006-07	**Calgary**	**NHL**	**81**	**34**	**43**	**77**	**26**	**14**	**2**	**6**	**173**	**19.7**	**21**	**14**	**28.6**	**17:23**	**6**	**0**	**2**	**2**	**4**	**0**	**0**	**0**	**15:08**
2007-08	**Calgary**	**NHL**	**81**	**25**	**41**	**66**	**40**	**6**	**0**	**5**	**202**	**12.4**	**10**	**4**	**25.0**	**17:42**	**7**	**0**	**4**	**4**	**6**	**0**	**0**	**0**	**13:45**
2008-09	**Columbus**	**NHL**	**74**	**21**	**35**	**56**	**44**	**5**	**0**	**2**	**212**	**9.9**	**1**	**45**	**28.9**	**19:31**	**4**	**1**	**1**	**2**	**4**	**1**	**0**	**0**	**17:52**
2009-10	**Columbus**	**NHL**	**74**	**23**	**40**	**63**	**36**	**8**	**1**	**5**	**162**	**14.2**	**-4**	**14**	**28.6**	**18:24**									
2010-11	**Columbus**	**NHL**	**39**	**14**	**9**	**23**	**10**	**6**	**0**	**1**	**94**	**14.9**	**-17**	**0**	**0.0**	**16:23**									
	NHL Totals		**660**	**190**	**261**	**451**	**254**	**58**	**4**	**31**	**1531**	**12.4**		**288**	**34.7**	**16:59**	**24**	**3**	**11**	**14**	**18**	**3**	**0**	**0**	**15:19**

NHL All-Rookie Team (2002)

Signed as a free agent by **Linkopings** (Sweden), July 29, 2004. Signed as a free agent by **Rapperswil** (Swiss), February 23, 2005. Traded to **Calgary** by **Florida** for Steve Montador and Dustin Johner, December 2, 2005. Signed as a free agent by **Columbus**, July 2, 2008. • Missed majority of 2010-11 due to ankle and lower body injuries.

HUSKINS, Kent

(HUHS-kihnz, KEHNT) **ST.L.**

Defense. Shoots left. 6'4", 210 lbs. Born, Ottawa, Ont., May 4, 1979. Chicago's 3rd choice, 156th overall, in 1998 Entry Draft.

Season	Club	League	GP	G	A	Pts	PIM	PP	SH	GW	S	%	+/-	TF	F%	Min	GP	G	A	Pts	PIM	PP	SH	GW	Min
1995-96	Kanata Valley	CJHL	49	6	21	27	18																		
1996-97	Kanata Valley	CJHL	53	11	36	47	89																		
1997-98	Clarkson Knights	ECAC	35	2	8	10	46																		
1998-99	Clarkson Knights	ECAC	37	5	11	16	28																		
99-2000	Clarkson Knights	ECAC	28	2	16	18	30																		
2000-01	Clarkson Knights	ECAC	35	6	28	34	22																		
2001-02	Norfolk Admirals	AHL	65	4	11	15	44										4	0	1	1	0				
2002-03	Norfolk Admirals	AHL	80	5	22	27	48										9	2	2	4	4				
2003-04	San Antonio	AHL	79	5	14	19	42																		
2004-05	Manitoba Moose	AHL	65	5	11	16	41										14	0	2	2	12				
2005-06	Portland Pirates	AHL	80	8	23	31	64										18	3	6	9	14				
2006-07♦	**Anaheim**	**NHL**	**33**	**0**	**3**	**3**	**14**	**0**	**0**	**0**	**16**	**0.0**	**-3**	**0**	**0.0**	**14:04**	**21**	**0**	**1**	**1**	**11**	**0**	**0**	**0**	**11:45**
	Portland Pirates	AHL	39	3	12	15	23																		
2007-08	**Anaheim**	**NHL**	**76**	**4**	**15**	**19**	**59**	**1**	**0**	**2**	**46**	**8.7**	**23**	**0**	**0.0**	**16:05**	**6**	**0**	**1**	**1**	**2**	**0**	**0**	**0**	**14:35**
2008-09	**Anaheim**	**NHL**	**33**	**2**	**4**	**6**	**27**	**0**	**0**	**0**	**20**	**10.0**	**6**	**1**	**0.0**	**18:47**									
2009-10	**San Jose**	**NHL**	**82**	**3**	**19**	**22**	**47**	**0**	**0**	**0**	**47**	**6.4**	**6**	**0**	**0.0**	**17:29**	**15**	**0**	**0**	**0**	**6**	**0**	**0**	**0**	**12:48**
2010-11	**San Jose**	**NHL**	**50**	**2**	**8**	**10**	**12**	**0**	**0**	**0**	**38**	**5.3**	**8**	**0**	**0.0**	**16:37**	**5**	**0**	**1**	**1**	**2**	**0**	**0**	**0**	**18:48**
	NHL Totals		**274**	**11**	**49**	**60**	**159**	**1**	**0**	**2**	**167**	**6.6**		**1**	**0.0**	**16:41**	**47**	**0**	**3**	**3**	**21**	**0**	**0**	**0**	**13:12**

ECAC First All-Star Team (2000, 2001) • NCAA East First All-American Team (2001)

Signed as a free agent by **Florida**, August 14, 2003. Signed as a free agent by **Manitoba** (AHL), September 16, 2004. Signed as a free agent by **Anaheim**, August 30, 2005. Traded to **San Jose** by **Anaheim** with Travis Moen for Timo Pielmeier, Nick Bonino and future considerations, March 4, 2009. Signed as a free agent by **St. Louis**, July 2, 2011.

HUTCHINSON, Andrew

(HUHT-chihn-suhn, AN-droo)

Defense. Shoots right. 6'2", 195 lbs. Born, Evanston, IL, March 24, 1980. Nashville's 4th choice, 54th overall, in 1999 Entry Draft.

			Regular Season														Playoffs								
Season	Club	League	GP	G	A	Pts	PIM	PP	SH	GW	S	%	+/-	TF	F%	Min	GP	G	A	Pts	PIM	PP	SH	GW	Min
1996-97	Det. L. Caesars	MNHL	82	15	41	56	....	....	....	....	....	....	....	....	....	....	....	....	....	....	....	....	....	....	....
1997-98	USNTDP	U-18	27	3	11	14	35	....	....	....	....	....	....	....	....	....	....	....	....	....	....	....	....	....	....
	USNTDP	USHL	15	0	7	7	8	....	....	....	....	....	....	....	....	....	....	....	....	....	....	....	....	....	....
	USNTDP	NAHL	12	2	0	2	8	....	....	....	....	....	....	....	....	....	5	2	3	5	2	....	....	....	....
1998-99	Michigan State	CCHA	37	3	12	15	26	....	....	....	....	....	....	....	....	....	....	....	....	....	....	....	....	....	....
99-2000	Michigan State	CCHA	42	5	12	17	64	....	....	....	....	....	....	....	....	....	....	....	....	....	....	....	....	....	....
2000-01	Michigan State	CCHA	42	5	19	24	46	....	....	....	....	....	....	....	....	....	....	....	....	....	....	....	....	....	....
2001-02	Michigan State	CCHA	39	6	16	22	24	....	....	....	....	....	....	....	....	....	....	....	....	....	....	....	....	....	....
	Milwaukee	AHL	5	0	1	1	0	....	....	....	....	....	....	....	....	....	....	....	....	....	....	....	....	....	....
2002-03	Milwaukee	AHL	63	9	17	26	40	....	....	....	....	....	....	....	....	....	3	1	0	1	0	....	....	....	....
	Toledo Storm	ECHL	10	2	5	7	4	....	....	....	....	....	....	....	....	....	....	....	....	....	....	....	....	....	....
2003-04	**Nashville**	**NHL**	**18**	**4**	**4**	**8**	**4**	**2**	**0**	**1**	**24**	**16.7**	**1**	**0**	**0.0**	**16:43**	....	....	....	....	....	....	....	....	....
	Milwaukee	AHL	46	12	12	24	39	....	....	....	....	....	....	....	....	....	22	5	11	16	33	....	....	....	....
2004-05	Milwaukee	AHL	76	10	35	45	79	....	....	....	....	....	....	....	....	....	7	1	3	4	8	....	....	....	....
2005-06♦	**Carolina**	**NHL**	**36**	**3**	**8**	**11**	**18**	**2**	**0**	**0**	**33**	**9.1**	**–2**	**0**	**0.0**	**10:22**	....	....	....	....	....	....	....	....	....
2006-07	**Carolina**	**NHL**	**41**	**3**	**11**	**14**	**30**	**2**	**0**	**0**	**45**	**6.7**	**0**	**0**	**0.0**	**12:13**	....	....	....	....	....	....	....	....	....
2007-08	Hartford	AHL	67	18	46	64	66	....	....	....	....	....	....	....	....	....	5	2	2	4	4	....	....	....	....
2008-09	**Tampa Bay**	**NHL**	**2**	**0**	**0**	**0**	**0**	**0**	**0**	**0**	**2**	**0.0**	**–5**	**0**	**0.0**	**14:44**	....	....	....	....	....	....	....	....	....
	Norfolk Admirals	AHL	20	1	12	13	14	....	....	....	....	....	....	....	....	....	....	....	....	....	....	....	....	....	....
	Dallas	**NHL**	**38**	**2**	**3**	**5**	**12**	**0**	**0**	**0**	**56**	**3.6**	**–4**	**0**	**0.0**	**14:20**	....	....	....	....	....	....	....	....	....
2009-10	Texas Stars	AHL	78	9	29	38	50	....	....	....	....	....	....	....	....	....	21	5	11	16	14	....	....	....	....
2010-11	**Pittsburgh**	**NHL**	**5**	**0**	**1**	**1**	**6**	**0**	**0**	**0**	**2**	**0.0**	**–3**	**0**	**0.0**	**15:18**	....	....	....	....	....	....	....	....	....
	Wilkes-Barre	AHL	54	7	29	36	29	....	....	....	....	....	....	....	....	....	12	0	5	5	0	....	....	....	....
	NHL Totals		**140**	**12**	**27**	**39**	**70**	**6**	**0**	**1**	**162**	**7.4**		**0**	**0.0**	**13:03**	....	....	....	....	....	....	....	....	....

CCHA Second All-Star Team (2001, 2002) • NCAA West Second All-American Team (2002) • AHL First All-Star Team (2008) • Eddie Shore Award (AHL – Outstanding Defenseman) (2008)

Traded to **Carolina** by **Nashville** for Phoenix's 3rd round choice (previously acquired, Nashville selected Teemu Laakso) in 2005 Entry Draft, July 29, 2005. Traded to **NY Rangers** by **Carolina** with Joe Barnes and Carolina's 3rd round choice (Evgeny Grachev) in 2008 Entry Draft for Matt Cullen, July 17, 2007. Signed as a free agent by **Tampa Bay**, July 9, 2008. Traded to **Dallas** by **Tampa Bay** for Lauri Tukonen, November 30, 2008. Signed as a free agent by **Pittsburgh**, July 7, 2010.

IGINLA, Jarome

(ih-GIHN-lah, jah-ROHM) **CGY**

Right wing. Shoots right. 6'1", 207 lbs. Born, Edmonton, Alta., July 1, 1977. Dallas' 1st choice, 11th overall, in 1995 Entry Draft.

1991-92	St. Albert Raiders	AMHL	36	26	30	56	22	....	....	....	....	....	....	....	....	....	....	....	....	....	....	....	....	....	....
1992-93	St. Albert Raiders	AMHL	36	34	53	*87	20	....	....	....	....	....	....	....	....	....	....	....	....	....	....	....	....	....	....
1993-94	Kamloops Blazers	WHL	48	6	23	29	33	....	....	....	....	....	....	....	....	....	19	3	6	9	10	....	....	....	....
1994-95	Kamloops Blazers	WHL	72	33	38	71	111	....	....	....	....	....	....	....	....	....	21	7	11	18	34	....	....	....	....
1995-96	Kamloops Blazers	WHL	63	63	73	136	120	....	....	....	....	....	....	....	....	....	16	16	13	29	44	....	....	....	....
	Calgary	**NHL**	....	....	....	....	....	....	....	....	....	....	....	....	....	....	**2**	**1**	**1**	**2**	**0**	**0**	**0**	**0**	....
1996-97	**Calgary**	**NHL**	**82**	**21**	**29**	**50**	**37**	**8**	**1**	**3**	**169**	**12.4**	**–4**	....	....	....	....	....	....	....	....	....	....	....	....
1997-98	**Calgary**	**NHL**	**70**	**13**	**19**	**32**	**29**	**0**	**2**	**1**	**154**	**8.4**	**–10**	....	....	....	....	....	....	....	....	....	....	....	....
1998-99	**Calgary**	**NHL**	**82**	**28**	**23**	**51**	**58**	**7**	**0**	**4**	**211**	**13.3**	**1**	**111**	**51.4**	**16:30**	....	....	....	....	....	....	....	....	....
99-2000	**Calgary**	**NHL**	**77**	**29**	**34**	**63**	**26**	**12**	**0**	**4**	**256**	**11.3**	**0**	**278**	**52.9**	**18:24**	....	....	....	....	....	....	....	....	....
2000-01	**Calgary**	**NHL**	**77**	**31**	**40**	**71**	**62**	**10**	**0**	**4**	**229**	**13.5**	**–2**	**638**	**51.7**	**19:58**	....	....	....	....	....	....	....	....	....
2001-02	**Calgary**	**NHL**	**82**	***52**	**44**	***96**	**77**	**16**	**1**	**7**	**311**	**16.7**	**27**	**308**	**55.2**	**22:22**	....	....	....	....	....	....	....	....	....
	Canada	Olympics	6	3	1	4	0	....	....	....	....	....	....	....	....	....	....	....	....	....	....	....	....	....	....
2002-03	**Calgary**	**NHL**	**75**	**35**	**32**	**67**	**49**	**11**	**3**	**6**	**316**	**11.1**	**–10**	**90**	**43.3**	**21:26**	....	....	....	....	....	....	....	....	....
2003-04	**Calgary**	**NHL**	**81**	***41**	**32**	**73**	**84**	**8**	**4**	***10**	**265**	**15.5**	**21**	**305**	**54.4**	**21:18**	**26**	***13**	**9**	**22**	**45**	**4**	***2**	**3**	**23:18**
2004-05			Did not play																						
2005-06	**Calgary**	**NHL**	**82**	**35**	**32**	**67**	**86**	**17**	**1**	**6**	**293**	**11.9**	**5**	**541**	**54.2**	**21:42**	**7**	**5**	**3**	**8**	**11**	**1**	**1**	**1**	**24:14**
	Canada	Olympics	6	2	1	3	4	....	....	....	....	....	....	....	....	....	....	....	....	....	....	....	....	....	....
2006-07	**Calgary**	**NHL**	**70**	**39**	**55**	**94**	**40**	**13**	**1**	**7**	**264**	**14.8**	**12**	**406**	**53.0**	**22:04**	**6**	**2**	**2**	**4**	**12**	**0**	**0**	**1**	**23:45**
2007-08	**Calgary**	**NHL**	**82**	**50**	**48**	**98**	**83**	**15**	**0**	**9**	**338**	**14.8**	**27**	**445**	**55.1**	**21:26**	**7**	**4**	**5**	**9**	**2**	**3**	**0**	**0**	**22:43**
2008-09	**Calgary**	**NHL**	**82**	**35**	**54**	**89**	**37**	**10**	**0**	**4**	**289**	**12.1**	**–2**	**501**	**52.5**	**21:37**	**6**	**3**	**1**	**4**	**0**	**2**	**0**	**0**	**20:56**
2009-10	**Calgary**	**NHL**	**82**	**32**	**37**	**69**	**58**	**10**	**0**	**5**	**257**	**12.5**	**–2**	**323**	**47.1**	**20:36**	....	....	....	....	....	....	....	....	....
	Canada	Olympics	7	*5	2	7	0	....	....	....	....	....	....	....	....	....	....	....	....	....	....	....	....	....	....
2010-11	**Calgary**	**NHL**	**82**	**43**	**43**	**86**	**40**	**14**	**0**	**6**	**289**	**14.9**	**0**	**420**	**54.1**	**20:56**	....	....	....	....	....	....	....	....	....
	NHL Totals		**1106**	**484**	**522**	**1006**	**766**	**151**	**13**	**76**	**3641**	**13.3**		**4366**	**52.8**	**20:41**	**54**	**28**	**21**	**49**	**70**	**10**	**3**	**5**	**23:08**

George Parsons Trophy (Memorial Cup - Most Sportsmanlike Player) (1995) • WHL West First All-Star Team (1996) • WHL Player of the Year (1996) • Canadian Major Junior First All-Star Team (1996) • NHL All-Rookie Team (1997) • NHL First All-Star Team (2002, 2008, 2009) • Maurice "Rocket" Richard Trophy (2002) • Art Ross Trophy (2002) • Lester B. Pearson Award (2002) • NHL Second All-Star Team (2004) • NHL Foundation Award (2004) • King Clancy Memorial Trophy (2004) • Maurice "Rocket" Richard Trophy (2004) (tied with Ilya Kovalchuk and Rick Nash) • Mark Messier NHL Leadership Award (2009)

Played in NHL All-Star Game (2002, 2003, 2004, 2008, 2009)

Traded to **Calgary** by **Dallas** with Corey Millen for Joe Nieuwendyk, December 19, 1995.

IRWIN, Brayden

(UHR-wihn, BRAY-duhn) **TOR**

Right wing. Shoots right. 6'5", 215 lbs. Born, Toronto, Ont., March 24, 1987.

2005-06	St. Michael's	OPJHL	21	8	12	20	44	....	....	....	....	....	....	....	....	....	20	11	10	21	22	....	....	....	....
2006-07	U. of Vermont	H-East	33	7	12	19	14	....	....	....	....	....	....	....	....	....	....	....	....	....	....	....	....	....	....
2007-08	U. of Vermont	H-East	39	10	8	18	48	....	....	....	....	....	....	....	....	....	....	....	....	....	....	....	....	....	....
2008-09	U. of Vermont	H-East	33	6	5	11	60	....	....	....	....	....	....	....	....	....	....	....	....	....	....	....	....	....	....
2009-10	U. of Vermont	H-East	39	15	19	34	72	....	....	....	....	....	....	....	....	....	....	....	....	....	....	....	....	....	....
	Toronto	**NHL**	**2**	**0**	**0**	**0**	**2**	**0**	**0**	**0**	**3**	**0.0**	**0**	**6**	**50.0**	**10:06**	....	....	....	....	....	....	....	....	....
2010-11	Toronto Marlies	AHL	45	7	8	15	37	....	....	....	....	....	....	....	....	....	....	....	....	....	....	....	....	....	....
	NHL Totals		**2**	**0**	**0**	**0**	**2**	**0**	**0**	**0**	**3**	**0.0**		**6**	**50.0**	**10:06**	....	....	....	....	....	....	....	....	....

Signed as a free agent by **Toronto**, March 30, 2010.

IVANANS, Raitis

(EE-vahn-ahns, RIGHT-uhs) **CGY**

Left wing. Shoots left. 6'4", 240 lbs. Born, Riga, Latvia, January 3, 1979.

1997-98	Flint Generals	UHL	18	0	1	1	20	....	....	....	....	....	....	....	....	....	....	....	....	....	....	....	....	....	....
1998-99	Macon Whoopee	CHL	16	1	1	2	20	....	....	....	....	....	....	....	....	....	....	....	....	....	....	....	....	....	....
	Tulsa Oilers	CHL	32	2	7	9	39	....	....	....	....	....	....	....	....	....	....	....	....	....	....	....	....	....	....
99-2000	Pensacola	ECHL	59	3	7	10	146	....	....	....	....	....	....	....	....	....	2	0	0	0	0	....	....	....	....
2000-01	Hershey Bears	AHL	2	0	0	0	0	....	....	....	....	....	....	....	....	....	....	....	....	....	....	....	....	....	....
	New Haven	UHL	66	4	10	14	270	....	....	....	....	....	....	....	....	....	8	1	0	1	4	....	....	....	....
2001-02	Toledo Storm	ECHL	16	2	2	4	59	....	....	....	....	....	....	....	....	....	....	....	....	....	....	....	....	....	....
	Baton Rouge	ECHL	40	4	5	9	180	....	....	....	....	....	....	....	....	....	....	....	....	....	....	....	....	....	....
2002-03	Milwaukee	AHL	17	0	0	0	38	....	....	....	....	....	....	....	....	....	1	0	0	0	15	....	....	....	....
	Rockford IceHogs	UHL	50	4	2	6	208	....	....	....	....	....	....	....	....	....	....	....	....	....	....	....	....	....	....
2003-04	Milwaukee	AHL	54	1	7	8	166	....	....	....	....	....	....	....	....	....	7	0	1	1	17	....	....	....	....
	Rockford IceHogs	UHL	1	0	0	0	0	....	....	....	....	....	....	....	....	....	....	....	....	....	....	....	....	....	....
2004-05	Hamilton	AHL	75	2	5	7	259	....	....	....	....	....	....	....	....	....	2	0	1	1	0	....	....	....	....
2005-06	**Montreal**	**NHL**	**4**	**0**	**0**	**0**	**9**	**0**	**0**	**0**	**0**	**0.0**	**–1**	**0**	**0.0**	**2:58**	....	....	....	....	....	....	....	....	....
	Hamilton	AHL	43	2	0	2	120	....	....	....	....	....	....	....	....	....	....	....	....	....	....	....	....	....	....
2006-07	**Los Angeles**	**NHL**	**66**	**4**	**4**	**8**	**140**	**0**	**0**	**0**	**37**	**10.8**	**–12**	**1**	**0.0**	**6:59**	....	....	....	....	....	....	....	....	....
2007-08	**Los Angeles**	**NHL**	**73**	**6**	**2**	**8**	**134**	**0**	**0**	**0**	**48**	**12.5**	**–10**	**0**	**0.0**	**7:30**	....	....	....	....	....	....	....	....	....
2008-09	**Los Angeles**	**NHL**	**76**	**2**	**0**	**2**	**145**	**0**	**0**	**2**	**25**	**8.0**	**–8**	**0**	**0.0**	**6:22**	....	....	....	....	....	....	....	....	....
2009-10	**Los Angeles**	**NHL**	**61**	**0**	**0**	**0**	**136**	**0**	**0**	**0**	**18**	**0.0**	**–8**	**0**	**0.0**	**4:54**	**1**	**0**	**0**	**0**	**0**	**0**	**0**	**0**	**5:48**
2010-11	**Calgary**	**NHL**	**1**	**0**	**0**	**0**	**5**	**0**	**0**	**0**	**0**	**0.0**	**–1**	**0**	**0.0**	**8:20**	....	....	....	....	....	....	....	....	....
	NHL Totals		**281**	**12**	**6**	**18**	**569**	**0**	**0**	**2**	**128**	**9.4**		**1**	**0.0**	**6:27**	**1**	**0**	**0**	**0**	**0**	**0**	**0**	**0**	**5:48**

Signed as a free agent by **Montreal**, July 16, 2004. Signed as a free agent by **Los Angeles**, July 13, 2006. Signed as a free agent by **Calgary**, July 2, 2010. • Missed remainder of 2010-11 due to concussion vs. Edmonton, October 11, 2010.

Season	Club	League	GP	G	A	Pts	PIM	PP	SH	GW	S	%	+/-	TF	F%	Min	GP	G	A	Pts	PIM	PP	SH	GW	Min
			Regular Season														Playoffs								

JACKMAN, Barret
(JAK-man, BAIR-reht) **ST.L.**

Defense. Shoots left. 6', 205 lbs. Born, Trail, B.C., March 5, 1981. St. Louis' 1st choice, 17th overall, in 1999 Entry Draft.

Season	Club	League	GP	G	A	Pts	PIM	PP	SH	GW	S	%	+/-	TF	F%	Min	GP	G	A	Pts	PIM	PP	SH	GW	Min
1996-97	Beaver Valley	VIJHL	32	22	25	47	180	....	....	....	....	....	....	....	....	....	....	....	....	....	....	....	....	....	....
1997-98	Regina Pats	WHL	68	2	11	13	224	....	....	....	....	....	....	....	....	....	9	0	3	3	32	....	....	....	....
1998-99	Regina Pats	WHL	70	8	36	44	259	....	....	....	....	....	....	....	....	....	....	....	....	....	....	....	....	....	....
99-2000	Regina Pats	WHL	53	9	37	46	175	....	....	....	....	....	....	....	....	....	6	1	1	2	19	....	....	....	....
	Worcester IceCats	AHL	....	....	....	....	....	....	....	....	....	....	....	....	....	....	2	0	0	0	13	....	....	....	....
2000-01	Regina Pats	WHL	43	9	27	36	138	....	....	....	....	....	....	....	....	....	6	0	3	3	8	....	....	....	....
2001-02	**St. Louis**	**NHL**	**1**	**0**	**0**	**0**	**0**	**0**	**0**	**0**	**1**	**0.0**	**0**	**0**	**0.0**	**18:56**	**1**	**0**	**0**	**0**	**2**	**0**	**0**	**0**	**18:24**
	Worcester IceCats	AHL	75	2	12	14	266	....	....	....	....	....	....	....	....	....	3	0	1	1	4	....	....	....	....
2002-03	**St. Louis**	**NHL**	**82**	**3**	**16**	**19**	**190**	**0**	**0**	**0**	**66**	**4.5**	**23**	**0**	**0.0**	**20:03**	**7**	**0**	**0**	**0**	**14**	**0**	**0**	**0**	**21:59**
2003-04	**St. Louis**	**NHL**	**15**	**1**	**2**	**3**	**41**	**0**	**0**	**0**	**11**	**9.1**	**–1**	**0**	**0.0**	**18:16**	....	....	....	....	....	....	....	....	....
2004-05	Missouri	UHL	28	3	17	20	61	....	....	....	....	....	....	....	....	....	3	0	0	0	4	....	....	....	....
2005-06	**St. Louis**	**NHL**	**63**	**4**	**6**	**10**	**156**	**0**	**0**	**2**	**56**	**7.1**	**–6**	**0**	**0.0**	**18:46**	....	....	....	....	....	....	....	....	....
2006-07	**St. Louis**	**NHL**	**70**	**3**	**24**	**27**	**82**	**1**	**0**	**1**	**86**	**3.5**	**20**	**0**	**0.0**	**21:30**	....	....	....	....	....	....	....	....	....
	Peoria Rivermen	AHL	1	0	0	0	0	....	....	....	....	....	....	....	....	....	....	....	....	....	....	....	....	....	....
2007-08	**St. Louis**	**NHL**	**78**	**2**	**14**	**16**	**93**	**1**	**0**	**0**	**80**	**2.5**	**–12**	**0**	**0.0**	**22:24**	....	....	....	....	....	....	....	....	....
2008-09	**St. Louis**	**NHL**	**82**	**4**	**17**	**21**	**86**	**1**	**1**	**0**	**89**	**4.5**	**–17**	**0**	**0.0**	**23:26**	**4**	**0**	**1**	**1**	**5**	**0**	**0**	**0**	**25:18**
2009-10	**St. Louis**	**NHL**	**66**	**2**	**15**	**17**	**81**	**0**	**1**	**0**	**73**	**2.7**	**3**	**1**	**0.0**	**22:41**	....	....	....	....	....	....	....	....	....
2010-11	**St. Louis**	**NHL**	**60**	**0**	**13**	**13**	**57**	**0**	**0**	**0**	**65**	**0.0**	**3**	**0**	**0.0**	**20:48**	....	....	....	....	....	....	....	....	....
	NHL Totals		**517**	**19**	**107**	**126**	**786**	**3**	**2**	**3**	**527**	**3.6**		**1**	**0.0**	**21:21**	**12**	**0**	**1**	**1**	**21**	**0**	**0**	**0**	**22:47**

WHL East Second All-Star Team (2000) • AHL All-Rookie Team (2002) • NHL All-Rookie Team (2003) • Calder Memorial Trophy (2003)

• Missed majority of 2003-04 due to shoulder injury vs. Vancouver, October 22, 2003. Signed as a free agent by **Missouri** (UHL), February 3, 2005.

JACKMAN, Tim
(JAK-man, TIHM) **CGY**

Right wing. Shoots right. 6'4", 220 lbs. Born, Minot, ND, November 14, 1981. Columbus' 2nd choice, 38th overall, in 2001 Entry Draft.

Season	Club	League	GP	G	A	Pts	PIM	PP	SH	GW	S	%	+/-	TF	F%	Min	GP	G	A	Pts	PIM	PP	SH	GW	Min
1998-99	Park Center	High-MN	22	22	22	44	....	....	....	....	....	....	....	....	....	....	....	....	....	....	....	....	....	....	....
99-2000	Park Center	High-MN	19	34	22	56	....	....	....	....	....	....	....	....	....	....	....	....	....	....	....	....	....	....	....
	Twin Cities	USHL	25	11	9	20	58	....	....	....	....	....	....	....	....	....	13	8	5	13	12	....	....	....	....
2000-01	Minnesota State	WCHA	37	11	14	25	92	....	....	....	....	....	....	....	....	....	....	....	....	....	....	....	....	....	....
2001-02	Minnesota State	WCHA	36	14	14	28	86	....	....	....	....	....	....	....	....	....	....	....	....	....	....	....	....	....	....
2002-03	Syracuse Crunch	AHL	77	9	7	16	48	....	....	....	....	....	....	....	....	....	....	....	....	....	....	....	....	....	....
2003-04	**Columbus**	**NHL**	**19**	**1**	**2**	**3**	**16**	**0**	**0**	**0**	**18**	**5.6**	**–7**	**1**	**100.0**	**9:56**	....	....	....	....	....	....	....	....	....
	Syracuse Crunch	AHL	64	23	13	36	61	....	....	....	....	....	....	....	....	....	7	2	3	5	12	....	....	....	....
2004-05	Syracuse Crunch	AHL	73	14	21	35	98	....	....	....	....	....	....	....	....	....	....	....	....	....	....	....	....	....	....
2005-06	**Phoenix**	**NHL**	**8**	**0**	**0**	**0**	**21**	**0**	**0**	**0**	**4**	**0.0**	**1**	**1**	**0.0**	**7:13**	....	....	....	....	....	....	....	....	....
	San Antonio	AHL	50	7	13	20	127	....	....	....	....	....	....	....	....	....	....	....	....	....	....	....	....	....	....
	Manchester	AHL	18	2	3	5	33	....	....	....	....	....	....	....	....	....	7	0	3	3	20	....	....	....	....
2006-07	**Los Angeles**	**NHL**	**5**	**0**	**0**	**0**	**10**	**0**	**0**	**0**	**3**	**0.0**	**–1**	**0**	**0.0**	**6:36**	....	....	....	....	....	....	....	....	....
	Manchester	AHL	69	19	14	33	143	....	....	....	....	....	....	....	....	....	16	3	3	6	26	....	....	....	....
2007-08	**NY Islanders**	**NHL**	**36**	**1**	**3**	**4**	**57**	**0**	**0**	**0**	**36**	**2.8**	**–3**	**2**	**100.0**	**6:37**	....	....	....	....	....	....	....	....	....
	Bridgeport	AHL	44	15	21	36	67	....	....	....	....	....	....	....	....	....	....	....	....	....	....	....	....	....	....
2008-09	**NY Islanders**	**NHL**	**69**	**5**	**7**	**12**	**155**	**0**	**1**	**0**	**99**	**5.1**	**–17**	**22**	**31.8**	**11:45**	....	....	....	....	....	....	....	....	....
	Bridgeport	AHL	12	6	1	7	35	....	....	....	....	....	....	....	....	....	....	....	....	....	....	....	....	....	....
2009-10	**NY Islanders**	**NHL**	**54**	**4**	**5**	**9**	**98**	**0**	**0**	**0**	**51**	**7.8**	**–4**	**7**	**42.9**	**9:39**	....	....	....	....	....	....	....	....	....
2010-11	**Calgary**	**NHL**	**82**	**10**	**13**	**23**	**86**	**1**	**0**	**1**	**131**	**7.6**	**4**	**16**	**37.5**	**9:49**	....	....	....	....	....	....	....	....	....
	NHL Totals		**273**	**21**	**30**	**51**	**443**	**1**	**1**	**1**	**342**	**6.1**		**49**	**38.8**	**9:43**	....	....	....	....	....	....	....	....	....

Traded to **Phoenix** by **Columbus** with Geoff Sanderson for Cale Hulse, Mike Rupp and Jason Chimera, October 8, 2005. Traded to **Los Angeles** by **Phoenix** for Yanick Lehoux, March 9, 2006. Signed as a free agent by **NY Islanders**, July 5, 2007. Signed as a free agent by **Calgary**, July 2, 2010.

JACKSON, Scott
(JAK-suhn, SKAWT) **T.B.**

Defense. Shoots left. 6'3", 219 lbs. Born, Salmon Arm, B.C., February 5, 1987. St. Louis' 2nd choice, 37th overall, in 2005 Entry Draft.

Season	Club	League	GP	G	A	Pts	PIM	PP	SH	GW	S	%	+/-	TF	F%	Min	GP	G	A	Pts	PIM	PP	SH	GW	Min
2002-03	Sicamous Eagles	KIJHL	45	2	20	22	20	....	....	....	....	....	....	....	....	....	....	....	....	....	....	....	....	....	....
	Seattle	WHL	2	0	0	0	2	....	....	....	....	....	....	....	....	....	....	....	....	....	....	....	....	....	....
2003-04	Seattle	WHL	66	4	9	13	17	....	....	....	....	....	....	....	....	....	....	....	....	....	....	....	....	....	....
2004-05	Seattle	WHL	72	6	16	22	46	....	....	....	....	....	....	....	....	....	12	1	2	3	4	....	....	....	....
2005-06	Seattle	WHL	57	3	23	26	48	....	....	....	....	....	....	....	....	....	7	1	4	5	12	....	....	....	....
2006-07	Seattle	WHL	71	4	31	35	52	....	....	....	....	....	....	....	....	....	11	0	5	5	9	....	....	....	....
2007-08	Seattle	WHL	58	6	17	23	44	....	....	....	....	....	....	....	....	....	12	2	2	4	8	....	....	....	....
2008-09	Norfolk Admirals	AHL	34	0	4	4	14	....	....	....	....	....	....	....	....	....	....	....	....	....	....	....	....	....	....
	Mississippi	ECHL	3	1	0	1	2	....	....	....	....	....	....	....	....	....	....	....	....	....	....	....	....	....	....
2009-10	**Tampa Bay**	**NHL**	**1**	**0**	**0**	**0**	**0**	**0**	**0**	**0**	**0**	**0.0**	**0**	**0**	**0.0**	**13:44**	....	....	....	....	....	....	....	....	....
	Norfolk Admirals	AHL	72	1	14	15	32	....	....	....	....	....	....	....	....	....	....	....	....	....	....	....	....	....	....
2010-11	Norfolk Admirals	AHL	68	1	4	5	47	....	....	....	....	....	....	....	....	....	6	0	0	0	0	....	....	....	....
	NHL Totals		**1**	**0**	**0**	**0**	**0**	**0**	**0**	**0**	**0**	**0.0**		**0**	**0.0**	**13:44**	....	....	....	....	....	....	....	....	....

Signed as a free agent by **Tampa Bay**, July 3, 2008.

JACQUES, Jean-Francois
(ZHAWK, ZHAWN-fran-SWUH) **ANA**

Left wing. Shoots left. 6'4", 217 lbs. Born, Montreal, Que., April 29, 1985. Edmonton's 3rd choice, 68th overall, in 2003 Entry Draft.

Season	Club	League	GP	G	A	Pts	PIM	PP	SH	GW	S	%	+/-	TF	F%	Min	GP	G	A	Pts	PIM	PP	SH	GW	Min
2000-01	Cap-d-Madeleine	QAAA	39	22	13	35	28	....	....	....	....	....	....	....	....	....	10	5	8	13	14	....	....	....	....
2001-02	Baie-Comeau	QMJHL	66	10	14	24	136	....	....	....	....	....	....	....	....	....	5	1	0	1	2	....	....	....	....
2002-03	Baie-Comeau	QMJHL	67	12	21	33	123	....	....	....	....	....	....	....	....	....	12	4	2	6	13	....	....	....	....
2003-04	Baie-Comeau	QMJHL	59	20	24	44	70	....	....	....	....	....	....	....	....	....	4	1	0	1	4	....	....	....	....
2004-05	Baie-Comeau	QMJHL	69	36	42	78	56	....	....	....	....	....	....	....	....	....	6	3	5	8	6	....	....	....	....
	Edmonton	AHL	6	0	0	0	5	....	....	....	....	....	....	....	....	....	....	....	....	....	....	....	....	....	....
2005-06	**Edmonton**	**NHL**	**7**	**0**	**0**	**0**	**0**	**0**	**0**	**0**	**8**	**0.0**	**–3**	**0**	**0.0**	**6:43**	....	....	....	....	....	....	....	....	....
	Hamilton	AHL	65	24	19	43	131	....	....	....	....	....	....	....	....	....	....	....	....	....	....	....	....	....	....
2006-07	**Edmonton**	**NHL**	**37**	**0**	**0**	**0**	**33**	**0**	**0**	**0**	**23**	**0.0**	**–11**	**2**	**0.0**	**7:55**	....	....	....	....	....	....	....	....	....
	Wilkes-Barre	AHL	29	10	17	27	53	....	....	....	....	....	....	....	....	....	11	1	2	3	43	....	....	....	....
2007-08	**Edmonton**	**NHL**	**9**	**0**	**0**	**0**	**2**	**0**	**0**	**0**	**2**	**0.0**	**–3**	**0**	**0.0**	**6:10**	....	....	....	....	....	....	....	....	....
	Springfield	AHL	38	11	14	25	63	....	....	....	....	....	....	....	....	....	....	....	....	....	....	....	....	....	....
2008-09	**Edmonton**	**NHL**	**7**	**1**	**0**	**1**	**9**	**0**	**0**	**0**	**3**	**33.3**	**0**	**0**	**0.0**	**7:22**	....	....	....	....	....	....	....	....	....
	Springfield	AHL	8	1	5	6	13	....	....	....	....	....	....	....	....	....	....	....	....	....	....	....	....	....	....
2009-10	**Edmonton**	**NHL**	**49**	**4**	**7**	**11**	**78**	**0**	**0**	**0**	**49**	**8.2**	**–15**	**5**	**40.0**	**11:12**	....	....	....	....	....	....	....	....	....
2010-11	**Edmonton**	**NHL**	**51**	**4**	**1**	**5**	**63**	**0**	**0**	**0**	**28**	**14.3**	**–6**	**16**	**31.3**	**7:04**	....	....	....	....	....	....	....	....	....
	Oklahoma City	AHL	4	1	0	1	15	....	....	....	....	....	....	....	....	....	....	....	....	....	....	....	....	....	....
	NHL Totals		**160**	**9**	**8**	**17**	**185**	**0**	**0**	**0**	**113**	**8.0**		**23**	**30.4**	**8:29**	....	....	....	....	....	....	....	....	....

• Missed majority of 2008-09 due to off-season back surgery. Signed as a free agent by **Anaheim**, July 6, 2011.

JAFFRAY, Jason
(JAF-ray, JAY-suhn) **WPG**

Left wing. Shoots left. 6'1", 195 lbs. Born, Olds, Alta., June 30, 1981.

Season	Club	League	GP	G	A	Pts	PIM	PP	SH	GW	S	%	+/-	TF	F%	Min	GP	G	A	Pts	PIM	PP	SH	GW	Min
1997-98	Edmonton Ice	WHL	6	0	1	1	0	....	....	....	....	....	....	....	....	....	....	....	....	....	....	....	....	....	....
1998-99	Kootenay Ice	WHL	57	14	12	26	50	....	....	....	....	....	....	....	....	....	7	1	2	3	6	....	....	....	....
99-2000	Kootenay Ice	WHL	71	24	28	52	102	....	....	....	....	....	....	....	....	....	21	10	9	19	17	....	....	....	....
2000-01	Kootenay Ice	WHL	70	31	42	73	108	....	....	....	....	....	....	....	....	....	11	5	7	12	10	....	....	....	....
2001-02	Kootenay Ice	WHL	32	15	19	34	38	....	....	....	....	....	....	....	....	....	....	....	....	....	....	....	....	....	....
	Swift Current	WHL	41	23	26	49	44	....	....	....	....	....	....	....	....	....	12	4	5	9	25	....	....	....	....
2002-03	Norfolk Admirals	AHL	2	0	0	0	0	....	....	....	....	....	....	....	....	....	....	....	....	....	....	....	....	....	....
	Roanoke Express	ECHL	64	34	51	85	89	....	....	....	....	....	....	....	....	....	4	0	3	3	4	....	....	....	....
2003-04	Wilkes-Barre	AHL	5	0	1	1	0	....	....	....	....	....	....	....	....	....	....	....	....	....	....	....	....	....	....
	Wheeling Nailers	ECHL	54	37	37	74	81	....	....	....	....	....	....	....	....	....	2	1	1	2	2	....	....	....	....
2004-05	Cleveland Barons	AHL	30	10	6	16	23	....	....	....	....	....	....	....	....	....	....	....	....	....	....	....	....	....	....
	Manitoba Moose	AHL	14	4	4	8	6	....	....	....	....	....	....	....	....	....	1	0	0	0	0	....	....	....	....
	Wheeling Nailers	ECHL	23	6	6	12	22	....	....	....	....	....	....	....	....	....	....	....	....	....	....	....	....	....	....
2005-06	Manitoba Moose	AHL	73	12	35	47	58	....	....	....	....	....	....	....	....	....	13	6	1	7	11	....	....	....	....

			Regular Season														Playoffs								
Season	Club	League	GP	G	A	Pts	PIM	PP	SH	GW	S	%	+/-	TF	F%	Min	GP	G	A	Pts	PIM	PP	SH	GW	Min
2006-07	Manitoba Moose	AHL	77	35	46	81	75	....	....	....	....	....	....	....	....	....	13	6	7	13	6	....	....	....	....
2007-08	**Vancouver**	**NHL**	**19**	**2**	**4**	**6**	**19**	**1**	**0**	**1**	**15**	**13.3**	**4**	**176**	**47.7**	**12:35**	....	....	....	....	....	....	....	....	....
	Manitoba Moose	AHL	43	21	27	48	51	....	....	....	....	....	....	....	....	....	3	1	4	5	0	....	....	....	....
2008-09	**Vancouver**	**NHL**	**14**	**2**	**2**	**4**	**14**	**0**	**0**	**2**	**11**	**18.2**	**–2**	**65**	**47.7**	**9:04**	....	....	....	....	....	....	....	....	....
	Manitoba Moose	AHL	56	23	26	49	52	....	....	....	....	....	....	....	....	....	22	9	10	19	12	....	....	....	....
2009-10	**Calgary**	**NHL**	**3**	**0**	**0**	**0**	**0**	**0**	**0**	**0**	**4**	**0.0**	**–1**	**14**	**35.7**	**6:39**	....	....	....	....	....	....	....	....	....
	Abbotsford Heat	AHL	72	25	29	54	70	....	....	....	....	....	....	....	....	....	9	2	1	3	8	....	....	....	....
2010-11	Manitoba Moose	AHL	6	1	1	2	2	....	....	....	....	....	....	....	....	....	14	3	6	9	6	....	....	....	....
	NHL Totals		**36**	**4**	**6**	**10**	**33**	**1**	**0**	**3**	**30**	**13.3**		**255**	**47.1**	**10:43**	....	....	....	....	....	....	....	....	....

ECHL Rookie of the Year (2003) • AHL Second All-Star Team (2007)

Signed as a free agent by **Vancouver**, July 3, 2007. Signed as a free agent by **Calgary**, July 7, 2009. Traded to **Anaheim** by **Calgary** with future considerations for Logan MacMillan and future considerations, June 30, 2010. Signed as a free agent by **Winnipeg**, July 19, 2011.

JAGR, Jaromir

(YAH-guhr, YAIR-oh-MEER) **PHI**

Right wing. Shoots left. 6'3", 240 lbs. Born, Kladno, Czech., February 15, 1972. Pittsburgh's 1st choice, 5th overall, in 1990 Entry Draft.

Season	Club	League	GP	G	A	Pts	PIM	PP	SH	GW	S	%	+/-	TF	F%	Min	GP	G	A	Pts	PIM	PP	SH	GW	Min
1984-85	Kladno Jr.	Czech-Jr.	34	24	17	41	....	....	....	....	....	....	....	....	....	....	....	....	....	....	....	....	....	....	....
1985-86	Kladno Jr.	Czech-Jr.	36	41	29	70	....	....	....	....	....	....	....	....	....	....	....	....	....	....	....	....	....	....	....
1986-87	Kladno Jr.	Czech-Jr.	30	35	35	70	....	....	....	....	....	....	....	....	....	....	....	....	....	....	....	....	....	....	....
1987-88	Kladno Jr.	Czech-Jr.	35	57	27	84	....	....	....	....	....	....	....	....	....	....	....	....	....	....	....	....	....	....	....
1988-89	Kladno	Czech	29	3	3	6	4	....	....	....	....	....	....	....	....	....	10	5	7	12	0	....	....	....	....
1989-90	Poldi Kladno	Czech	42	22	28	50	....	....	....	....	....	....	....	....	....	....	9	*8	2	10	....	....	....	....	....
1990-91♦	**Pittsburgh**	**NHL**	**80**	**27**	**30**	**57**	**42**	**7**	**0**	**4**	**136**	**19.9**	**–4**	....	....	....	**24**	**3**	**10**	**13**	**6**	**1**	**0**	**1**	....
1991-92♦	**Pittsburgh**	**NHL**	**70**	**32**	**37**	**69**	**34**	**4**	**0**	**4**	**194**	**16.5**	**12**	....	....	....	**21**	**11**	**13**	**24**	**6**	**2**	**0**	**4**	....
1992-93	**Pittsburgh**	**NHL**	**81**	**34**	**60**	**94**	**61**	**10**	**1**	**9**	**242**	**14.0**	**30**	....	....	....	**12**	**5**	**4**	**9**	**23**	**1**	**0**	**1**	....
1993-94	**Pittsburgh**	**NHL**	**80**	**32**	**67**	**99**	**61**	**9**	**0**	**6**	**298**	**10.7**	**15**	....	....	....	**6**	**2**	**4**	**6**	**16**	**0**	**0**	**1**	....
1994-95	HC Kladno	CzRep	11	8	14	22	10	....	....	....	....	....	....	....	....	....	....	....	....	....	....	....	....	....	....
	HC Bolzano	Euroliga	5	8	8	16	4	....	....	....	....	....	....	....	....	....	....	....	....	....	....	....	....	....	....
	HC Bolzano	Italy	1	0	0	0	0	....	....	....	....	....	....	....	....	....	....	....	....	....	....	....	....	....	....
	Schalke	German-2	1	1	10	11	0	....	....	....	....	....	....	....	....	....	....	....	....	....	....	....	....	....	....
	Pittsburgh	**NHL**	**48**	**32**	**38**	***70**	**37**	**8**	**3**	**7**	**192**	**16.7**	**23**	....	....	....	**12**	**10**	**5**	**15**	**6**	**2**	**1**	**1**	....
1995-96	**Pittsburgh**	**NHL**	**82**	**62**	**87**	**149**	**96**	**20**	**1**	***12**	**403**	**15.4**	**31**	....	....	....	**18**	**11**	**12**	**23**	**18**	**5**	**1**	**1**	....
1996-97	**Pittsburgh**	**NHL**	**63**	**47**	**48**	**95**	**40**	**11**	**2**	**6**	**234**	**20.1**	**22**	....	....	....	**5**	**4**	**4**	**8**	**4**	**2**	**0**	**0**	....
1997-98	**Pittsburgh**	**NHL**	**77**	**35**	***67**	***102**	**64**	**7**	**0**	**8**	**262**	**13.4**	**17**	....	....	....	**6**	**4**	**5**	**9**	**2**	**1**	**0**	**0**	....
	Czech Republic	Olympics	6	1	4	5	2	....	....	....	....	....	....	....	....	....	....	....	....	....	....	....	....	....	....
1998-99	**Pittsburgh**	**NHL**	**81**	**44**	***83**	***127**	**66**	**10**	**1**	**7**	**343**	**12.8**	**17**	**4**	**50.0**	**25:51**	**9**	**5**	**7**	**12**	**16**	**1**	**0**	**1**	**25:32**
99-2000	**Pittsburgh**	**NHL**	**63**	**42**	**54**	***96**	**50**	**10**	**0**	**5**	**290**	**14.5**	**25**	**9**	**22.2**	**23:12**	**11**	**8**	**8**	**16**	**6**	**2**	**0**	***4**	**24:32**
2000-01	**Pittsburgh**	**NHL**	**81**	**52**	***69**	***121**	**42**	**14**	**1**	**10**	**317**	**16.4**	**19**	**2**	**0.0**	**23:19**	**16**	**2**	**10**	**12**	**18**	**2**	**0**	**0**	**22:15**
2001-02	**Washington**	**NHL**	**69**	**31**	**48**	**79**	**30**	**10**	**0**	**3**	**197**	**15.7**	**0**	**2**	**50.0**	**21:43**	....	....	....	....	....	....	....	....	....
	Czech Republic	Olympics	4	2	3	5	4	....	....	....	....	....	....	....	....	....	....	....	....	....	....	....	....	....	....
2002-03	**Washington**	**NHL**	**75**	**36**	**41**	**77**	**38**	**13**	**2**	**9**	**290**	**12.4**	**5**	**5**	**20.0**	**21:18**	**6**	**2**	**5**	**7**	**2**	**1**	**0**	**0**	**25:13**
2003-04	**Washington**	**NHL**	**46**	**16**	**29**	**45**	**26**	**6**	**0**	**1**	**159**	**10.1**	**–4**	**1**	**0.0**	**21:05**	....	....	....	....	....	....	....	....	....
	NY Rangers	**NHL**	**31**	**15**	**14**	**29**	**12**	**4**	**0**	**2**	**98**	**15.3**	**–1**	**0**	**0.0**	**20:45**	....	....	....	....	....	....	....	....	....
2004-05	HC Rabat Kladno	CzRep	17	11	17	28	16	....	....	....	....	....	....	....	....	....	....	....	....	....	....	....	....	....	....
	Avangard Omsk	Russia	32	16	22	38	63	....	....	....	....	....	....	....	....	....	11	4	*10	*14	22	....	....	....	....
2005-06	**NY Rangers**	**NHL**	**82**	**54**	**69**	**123**	**72**	**24**	**0**	**9**	**368**	**14.7**	**34**	**6**	**16.7**	**22:05**	**3**	**0**	**1**	**1**	**2**	**0**	**0**	**0**	**13:47**
	Czech Republic	Olympics	8	2	5	7	6	....	....	....	....	....	....	....	....	....	....	....	....	....	....	....	....	....	....
2006-07	**NY Rangers**	**NHL**	**82**	**30**	**66**	**96**	**78**	**7**	**0**	**5**	**324**	**9.3**	**26**	**6**	**16.7**	**21:46**	**10**	**5**	**6**	**11**	**12**	**2**	**0**	**0**	**22:07**
2007-08	**NY Rangers**	**NHL**	**82**	**25**	**46**	**71**	**58**	**7**	**0**	**5**	**249**	**10.0**	**8**	**3**	**33.3**	**20:28**	**10**	**5**	**10**	**15**	**12**	**2**	**0**	**1**	**19:54**
2008-09	Omsk	Rus-KHL	55	25	28	53	62	....	....	....	....	....	....	....	....	....	9	4	5	9	4	....	....	....	....
2009-10	Omsk	Rus-KHL	51	22	20	42	50	....	....	....	....	....	....	....	....	....	3	1	1	2	0	....	....	....	....
	Czech Republic	Olympics	5	2	1	3	6	....	....	....	....	....	....	....	....	....	....	....	....	....	....	....	....	....	....
2010-11	Omsk	Rus-KHL	49	19	31	50	48	....	....	....	....	....	....	....	....	....	14	2	7	9	8	....	....	....	....
	NHL Totals		**1273**	**646**	**953**	**1599**	**907**	**181**	**11**	**112**	**4596**	**14.1**		**38**	**23.7**	**22:18**	**169**	**77**	**104**	**181**	**149**	**24**	**2**	**15**	**22:36**

NHL All-Rookie Team (1991) • NHL First All-Star Team (1995, 1996, 1998, 1999, 2000, 2001, 2006) • Art Ross Trophy (1995, 1998, 1999, 2000, 2001) • NHL Second All-Star Team (1997) • Lester B. Pearson Award (1999, 2000, 2006) • Hart Memorial Trophy (1999)

Played in NHL All-Star Game (1992, 1993, 1996, 1998, 1999, 2000, 2002, 2003, 2004)

Traded to **Washington** by **Pittsburgh** with Frantisek Kucera for Kris Beech, Michal Sivek, Ross Lupaschuk and future considerations, July 11, 2001. Traded to **NY Rangers** by **Washington** for Anson Carter, January 23, 2004. Signed as a free agent by **Kladno** (CzRep), September 17, 2004. Signed as a free agent by **Omsk** (Russia), November 7, 2004. Signed as a free agent by **Omsk** (Rus-KHL), July 4, 2008. Signed as a free agent by **Philadelphia**, July 1, 2011.

JANCEVSKI, Dan

(jan-SEHV-skee, DAN) **PHI**

Defense. Shoots left. 6'3", 222 lbs. Born, Windsor, Ont., June 15, 1981. Dallas' 2nd choice, 66th overall, in 1999 Entry Draft.

Season	Club	League	GP	G	A	Pts	PIM	PP	SH	GW	S	%	+/-	TF	F%	Min	GP	G	A	Pts	PIM	PP	SH	GW	Min
1995-96	Riverside Selects	Minor-ON	59	9	22	31	67	....	....	....	....	....	....	....	....	....	....	....	....	....	....	....	....	....	....
1996-97	Windsor Lions	Minor-ON	47	6	20	26	99	....	....	....	....	....	....	....	....	....	....	....	....	....	....	....	....	....	....
1997-98	Tecumseh	ON-Jr.B	49	3	11	14	145	....	....	....	....	....	....	....	....	....	....	....	....	....	....	....	....	....	....
1998-99	London Knights	OHL	68	2	12	14	115	....	....	....	....	....	....	....	....	....	25	1	7	8	24	....	....	....	....
99-2000	London Knights	OHL	59	8	15	23	138	....	....	....	....	....	....	....	....	....	....	....	....	....	....	....	....	....	....
2000-01	London Knights	OHL	39	4	23	27	95	....	....	....	....	....	....	....	....	....	....	....	....	....	....	....	....	....	....
	Sudbury Wolves	OHL	31	3	14	17	42	....	....	....	....	....	....	....	....	....	12	0	9	9	17	....	....	....	....
2001-02	Utah Grizzlies	AHL	77	0	13	13	147	....	....	....	....	....	....	....	....	....	5	0	0	0	4	....	....	....	....
2002-03	Utah Grizzlies	AHL	76	1	10	11	172	....	....	....	....	....	....	....	....	....	2	0	1	1	12	....	....	....	....
2003-04	Utah Grizzlies	AHL	80	5	17	22	171	....	....	....	....	....	....	....	....	....	....	....	....	....	....	....	....	....	....
2004-05	Hamilton	AHL	80	6	20	26	163	....	....	....	....	....	....	....	....	....	4	0	0	0	2	....	....	....	....
2005-06	**Dallas**	**NHL**	**2**	**0**	**0**	**0**	**0**	**0**	**0**	**0**	**0**	**0.0**	**1**	**0**	**0.0**	**9:13**	....	....	....	....	....	....	....	....	....
	Iowa Stars	AHL	77	9	29	38	91	....	....	....	....	....	....	....	....	....	7	1	1	2	6	....	....	....	....
2006-07	Hamilton	AHL	80	7	24	31	87	....	....	....	....	....	....	....	....	....	22	3	11	14	16	....	....	....	....
2007-08	**Tampa Bay**	**NHL**	**2**	**0**	**0**	**0**	**2**	**0**	**0**	**0**	**0**	**0.0**	**–1**	**0**	**0.0**	**2:23**	....	....	....	....	....	....	....	....	....
	Norfolk Admirals	AHL	37	4	16	20	52	....	....	....	....	....	....	....	....	....	....	....	....	....	....	....	....	....	....
	Dallas	**NHL**	**2**	**0**	**0**	**0**	**0**	**0**	**0**	**0**	**3**	**0.0**	**0**	**0**	**0.0**	**9:19**	....	....	....	....	....	....	....	....	....
	Iowa Stars	AHL	33	3	7	10	36	....	....	....	....	....	....	....	....	....	....	....	....	....	....	....	....	....	....
2008-09	**Dallas**	**NHL**	**3**	**0**	**0**	**0**	**0**	**0**	**0**	**0**	**4**	**0.0**	**0**	**0**	**0.0**	**15:20**	....	....	....	....	....	....	....	....	....
	Hamilton	AHL	76	1	27	28	76	....	....	....	....	....	....	....	....	....	6	0	3	3	6	....	....	....	....
2009-10	Texas Stars	AHL	78	3	20	23	71	....	....	....	....	....	....	....	....	....	24	1	11	12	20	....	....	....	....
2010-11	Adirondack	AHL	75	0	15	15	34	....	....	....	....	....	....	....	....	....	....	....	....	....	....	....	....	....	....
	NHL Totals		**9**	**0**	**0**	**0**	**2**	**0**	**0**	**0**	**7**	**0.0**		**0**	**0.0**	**9:45**	....	....	....	....	....	....	....	....	....

Signed as a free agent by **Montreal**, July 13, 2006. Signed as a free agent by **Tampa Bay**, July 6, 2007. Traded to **Dallas** by **Tampa Bay** for Junior Lessard, January 15, 2008. Signed as a free agent by **Philadelphia**, July 22, 2010.

JANIK, Doug

(JAN-nihk, DUHG) **DET**

Defense. Shoots left. 6'1", 214 lbs. Born, Agawam, MA, March 26, 1980. Buffalo's 3rd choice, 55th overall, in 1999 Entry Draft.

Season	Club	League	GP	G	A	Pts	PIM	PP	SH	GW	S	%	+/-	TF	F%	Min	GP	G	A	Pts	PIM	PP	SH	GW	Min
1995-96	N.E. Jr. Whalers	EJHL	48	16	38	54	....	....	....	....	....	....	....	....	....	....	....	....	....	....	....	....	....	....	....
1996-97	N.E. Jr. Whalers	EJHL	39	12	24	36	22	....	....	....	....	....	....	....	....	....	11	5	9	14	10	....	....	....	....
1997-98	USNTDP	U-18	29	6	13	19	43	....	....	....	....	....	....	....	....	....	....	....	....	....	....	....	....	....	....
	USNTDP	USHL	19	1	6	7	34	....	....	....	....	....	....	....	....	....	....	....	....	....	....	....	....	....	....
	USNTDP	NAHL	10	0	4	4	10	....	....	....	....	....	....	....	....	....	7	1	3	4	18	....	....	....	....
1998-99	U. of Maine	H-East	35	3	13	16	44	....	....	....	....	....	....	....	....	....	....	....	....	....	....	....	....	....	....
99-2000	U. of Maine	H-East	36	6	14	20	54	....	....	....	....	....	....	....	....	....	....	....	....	....	....	....	....	....	....
2000-01	U. of Maine	H-East	39	3	15	18	52	....	....	....	....	....	....	....	....	....	....	....	....	....	....	....	....	....	....
2001-02	Rochester	AHL	80	6	17	23	100	....	....	....	....	....	....	....	....	....	2	0	0	0	0	....	....	....	....
2002-03	**Buffalo**	**NHL**	**6**	**0**	**0**	**0**	**2**	**0**	**0**	**0**	**1**	**0.0**	**1**	**0**	**0.0**	**7:42**	....	....	....	....	....	....	....	....	....
	Rochester	AHL	75	3	13	16	120	....	....	....	....	....	....	....	....	....	3	0	0	0	6	....	....	....	....
2003-04	**Buffalo**	**NHL**	**4**	**0**	**0**	**0**	**19**	**0**	**0**	**0**	**3**	**0.0**	**0**	**0**	**0.0**	**8:26**	....	....	....	....	....	....	....	....	....
	Rochester	AHL	74	2	14	16	109	....	....	....	....	....	....	....	....	....	16	1	2	3	22	....	....	....	....
2004-05	Rochester	AHL	76	2	10	12	196	....	....	....	....	....	....	....	....	....	9	0	2	2	10	....	....	....	....
2005-06	Rochester	AHL	71	5	19	24	161	....	....	....	....	....	....	....	....	....	....	....	....	....	....	....	....	....	....
	Buffalo	**NHL**	....	....	....	....	....	....	....	....	....	....	....	....	....	....	**5**	**1**	**0**	**1**	**2**	**0**	**0**	**0**	**10:30**
2006-07	**Tampa Bay**	**NHL**	**75**	**2**	**9**	**11**	**53**	**0**	**0**	**0**	**49**	**4.1**	**–11**	**0**	**0.0**	**14:28**	**1**	**0**	**0**	**0**	**0**	**0**	**0**	**0**	**3:42**
2007-08	**Tampa Bay**	**NHL**	**61**	**1**	**3**	**4**	**45**	**0**	**0**	**0**	**23**	**4.3**	**–3**	**0**	**0.0**	**9:20**	....	....	....	....	....	....	....	....	....

			Regular Season														Playoffs								
Season	Club	League	GP	G	A	Pts	PIM	PP	SH	GW	S	%	+/-	TF	F%	Min	GP	G	A	Pts	PIM	PP	SH	GW	Min
2008-09	**Dallas**	**NHL**	13	0	1	1	2	0	0	0	1	0.0	–2	0	0.0	9:45	....	....	....	....	....	....	....	....	....
	Rockford IceHogs	AHL	4	0	2	2	4	....	....	....	....	....	....	....	....	....	....	....	....	....	....	....	....	....	....
	Montreal	**NHL**	2	0	0	0	2	0	0	0	0	0.0	–1	0	0.0	13:54	....	....	....	....	....	....	....	....	....
	Hamilton	AHL	18	0	5	5	10	....	....	....	....	....	....	....	....	....	6	0	0	0	7	....	....	....	....
2009-10	**Detroit**	**NHL**	13	0	2	2	18	0	0	0	5	0.0	–3	0	0.0	13:28	....	....	....	....	....	....	....	....	....
	Grand Rapids	AHL	66	6	31	37	84	....	....	....	....	....	....	....	....	....	....	....	....	....	....	....	....	....	....
2010-11	**Detroit**	**NHL**	7	0	0	0	7	0	0	0	8	0.0	–2	0	0.0	13:13	....	....	....	....	....	....	....	....	....
	Grand Rapids	AHL	60	5	17	22	77	....	....	....	....	....	....	....	....	....	....	....	....	....	....	....	....	....	....
	NHL Totals		**181**	**3**	**15**	**18**	**148**	**0**	**0**	**0**	**90**	**3.3**		**0**	**0.0**	**11:55**	**6**	**1**	**0**	**1**	**2**	**0**	**0**	**0**	**9:22**

Signed as a free agent by **Tampa Bay**, July 6, 2006. Signed as a free agent by **Chicago**, July 15, 2008. Claimed on waivers by **Dallas** from **Chicago**, October 2, 2008. Claimed on waivers by **Chicago** from **Dallas**, October 8, 2008. Traded to **Dallas** by **Chicago** for Dallas's 7th round choice (Mac Carruth) in 2010 Entry Draft, October 8, 2008. Traded to **Montreal** by **Dallas** for Steve Begin, February 26, 2009. Signed as a free agent by **Detroit**, July 8, 2009.

JANSSEN, Cam

(JAN-suhn, KAM) **N.J.**

Right wing. Shoots right. 6', 215 lbs. Born, St. Louis, MO, April 15, 1984. New Jersey's 6th choice, 117th overall, in 2002 Entry Draft.

Season	Club	League	GP	G	A	Pts	PIM	PP	SH	GW	S	%	+/-	TF	F%	Min	GP	G	A	Pts	PIM	PP	SH	GW	Min
2000-01	St. Louis Jr. Blues	CSJHL	45	1	2	3	244	....	....	....	....	....	....	....	....	....	....	....	....	....	....	....	....	....	....
2001-02	Windsor Spitfires	OHL	64	5	17	22	*268	....	....	....	....	....	....	....	....	....	10	0	0	0	13	....	....	....	....
2002-03	Windsor Spitfires	OHL	50	1	12	13	211	....	....	....	....	....	....	....	....	....	7	0	1	1	22	....	....	....	....
2003-04	Windsor Spitfires	OHL	35	4	9	13	144	....	....	....	....	....	....	....	....	....	....	....	....	....	....	....	....	....	....
	Guelph Storm	OHL	29	7	4	11	125	....	....	....	....	....	....	....	....	....	22	3	3	6	49	....	....	....	....
2004-05	Albany River Rats	AHL	70	1	3	4	337	....	....	....	....	....	....	....	....	....	....	....	....	....	....	....	....	....	....
2005-06	**New Jersey**	**NHL**	47	0	0	0	91	0	0	0	10	0.0	–3	2	100.0	4:44	9	0	0	0	26	0	0	0	3:43
	Albany River Rats	AHL	26	1	3	4	117	....	....	....	....	....	....	....	....	....	....	....	....	....	....	....	....	....	....
2006-07	**New Jersey**	**NHL**	48	1	0	1	114	0	0	0	9	11.1	–2	1	100.0	4:06	....	....	....	....	....	....	....	....	....
	Lowell Devils	AHL	9	0	1	1	29	....	....	....	....	....	....	....	....	....	....	....	....	....	....	....	....	....	....
2007-08	**St. Louis**	**NHL**	12	0	1	1	18	0	0	0	9	0.0	–1	0	0.0	7:07	....	....	....	....	....	....	....	....	....
	Lowell Devils	AHL	3	0	0	0	4	....	....	....	....	....	....	....	....	....	....	....	....	....	....	....	....	....	....
2008-09	**St. Louis**	**NHL**	56	1	3	4	131	0	0	0	22	4.5	–5	2	0.0	5:01	1	0	0	0	0	0	0	0	3:59
2009-10	**St. Louis**	**NHL**	43	0	0	0	190	0	0	0	11	0.0	–3	1	0.0	4:43	....	....	....	....	....	....	....	....	....
2010-11	**St. Louis**	**NHL**	54	1	3	4	131	0	0	0	16	6.3	–6	0	0.0	4:53	....	....	....	....	....	....	....	....	....
	NHL Totals		**260**	**3**	**7**	**10**	**675**	**0**	**0**	**0**	**77**	**3.9**		**6**	**50.0**	**4:49**	**10**	**0**	**0**	**0**	**26**	**0**	**0**	**0**	**3:45**

Traded to **St. Louis** by **New Jersey** for Bryce Salvador, February 26, 2008. Signed as a free agent by **New Jersey**, July 14, 2011.

JEFFREY, Dustin

(JEHF-ree, DUHS-tihn) **PIT**

Center. Shoots left. 6'1", 205 lbs. Born, Sarnia, Ont., February 27, 1988. Pittsburgh's 8th choice, 171st overall, in 2007 Entry Draft.

Season	Club	League	GP	G	A	Pts	PIM	PP	SH	GW	S	%	+/-	TF	F%	Min	GP	G	A	Pts	PIM	PP	SH	GW	Min
2003-04	Lambton Sting	Minor-ON	40	44	23	67	22	....	....	....	....	....	....	....	....	....	....	....	....	....	....	....	....	....	....
2004-05	Mississauga	OHL	53	10	15	25	20	....	....	....	....	....	....	....	....	....	....	....	....	....	....	....	....	....	....
2005-06	Mississauga	OHL	30	6	9	15	26	....	....	....	....	....	....	....	....	....	....	....	....	....	....	....	....	....	....
	Sault Ste. Marie	OHL	39	12	11	23	10	....	....	....	....	....	....	....	....	....	4	1	2	3	2	....	....	....	....
2006-07	Sault Ste. Marie	OHL	68	34	58	92	40	....	....	....	....	....	....	....	....	....	13	6	12	18	11	....	....	....	....
2007-08	Sault Ste. Marie	OHL	56	38	59	97	30	....	....	....	....	....	....	....	....	....	14	3	8	11	12	....	....	....	....
	Wilkes-Barre	AHL	....	....	....	....	....	....	....	....	....	....	....	....	....	....	15	2	1	3	4	....	....	....	....
2008-09	**Pittsburgh**	**NHL**	14	1	2	3	0	0	0	0	18	5.6	4	103	41.8	10:47	....	....	....	....	....	....	....	....	....
	Wilkes-Barre	AHL	63	11	26	37	31	....	....	....	....	....	....	....	....	....	12	5	5	10	8	....	....	....	....
2009-10	**Pittsburgh**	**NHL**	1	0	0	0	0	0	0	0	0	0.0	0	0	0.0	8:35	....	....	....	....	....	....	....	....	....
	Wilkes-Barre	AHL	77	24	47	71	16	....	....	....	....	....	....	....	....	....	4	0	1	1	6	....	....	....	....
2010-11	**Pittsburgh**	**NHL**	25	7	5	12	4	1	0	1	39	17.9	5	247	44.1	12:58	....	....	....	....	....	....	....	....	....
	Wilkes-Barre	AHL	40	17	28	45	8	....	....	....	....	....	....	....	....	....	....	....	....	....	....	....	....	....	....
	NHL Totals		**40**	**8**	**7**	**15**	**4**	**1**	**0**	**1**	**57**	**14.0**		**350**	**43.4**	**12:06**	....	....	....	....	....	....	....	....	....

JESSIMAN, Hugh

(JEHS-ih-muhn, HEW)

Right wing. Shoots right. 6'6", 221 lbs. Born, New York, NY, March 28, 1984. NY Rangers' 1st choice, 12th overall, in 2003 Entry Draft.

Season	Club	League	GP	G	A	Pts	PIM	PP	SH	GW	S	%	+/-	TF	F%	Min	GP	G	A	Pts	PIM	PP	SH	GW	Min
2001-02	Brunswick Bruins	High-CT	18	25	27	52	40	....	....	....	....	....	....	....	....	....	....	....	....	....	....	....	....	....	....
2002-03	Dartmouth	ECAC	34	23	24	47	48	....	....	....	....	....	....	....	....	....	....	....	....	....	....	....	....	....	....
2003-04	Dartmouth	ECAC	34	16	17	33	71	....	....	....	....	....	....	....	....	....	....	....	....	....	....	....	....	....	....
2004-05	Dartmouth	ECAC	12	1	1	2	18	....	....	....	....	....	....	....	....	....	....	....	....	....	....	....	....	....	....
2005-06	Hartford	AHL	46	7	12	19	66	....	....	....	....	....	....	....	....	....	2	0	0	0	0	....	....	....	....
	Charlotte	ECHL	25	13	10	23	56	....	....	....	....	....	....	....	....	....	....	....	....	....	....	....	....	....	....
2006-07	Hartford	AHL	49	7	6	13	79	....	....	....	....	....	....	....	....	....	7	1	0	1	9	....	....	....	....
	Charlotte	ECHL	20	12	10	22	52	....	....	....	....	....	....	....	....	....	....	....	....	....	....	....	....	....	....
2007-08	Hartford	AHL	71	18	24	42	154	....	....	....	....	....	....	....	....	....	5	0	1	1	21	....	....	....	....
2008-09	Hartford	AHL	6	0	0	0	2	....	....	....	....	....	....	....	....	....	....	....	....	....	....	....	....	....	....
	Milwaukee	AHL	63	20	7	27	100	....	....	....	....	....	....	....	....	....	10	2	0	2	10	....	....	....	....
2009-10	Milwaukee	AHL	78	20	22	42	111	....	....	....	....	....	....	....	....	....	....	....	....	....	....	....	....	....	....
2010-11	**Florida**	**NHL**	2	0	0	0	5	0	0	0	2	0.0	–1	0	0.0	7:21	....	....	....	....	....	....	....	....	....
	Rockford IceHogs	AHL	25	3	2	5	27	....	....	....	....	....	....	....	....	....	....	....	....	....	....	....	....	....	....
	Rochester	AHL	25	5	3	8	47	....	....	....	....	....	....	....	....	....	....	....	....	....	....	....	....	....	....
	NHL Totals		**2**	**0**	**0**	**0**	**5**	**0**	**0**	**0**	**2**	**0.0**		**0**	**0.0**	**7:21**	....	....	....	....	....	....	....	....	....

ECAC All-Rookie Team (2003) • ECAC Rookie of the Year (2003) • ECAC Second All-Star Team (2004)

Traded to **Nashville** by **NY Rangers** for future considerations, October 30, 2008. Signed as a free agent by **Chicago**, August 4, 2010. Traded to **Florida** by **Chicago** with Jack Skille and David Pacan for Michael Frolik and Alexander Salak, February 9, 2011.

JOENSUU, Jesse

(YOH-ehn-soo, JEH-see) **NYI**

Wing. Shoots left. 6'4", 209 lbs. Born, Pori, Finland, October 5, 1987. NY Islanders' 2nd choice, 60th overall, in 2006 Entry Draft.

Season	Club	League	GP	G	A	Pts	PIM	PP	SH	GW	S	%	+/-	TF	F%	Min	GP	G	A	Pts	PIM	PP	SH	GW	Min
2002-03	Assat Pori U18	Fin-U18	26	8	10	18	53	....	....	....	....	....	....	....	....	....	3	1	2	3	0	....	....	....	....
	Assat Pori Jr.	Fin-Jr.	3	0	1	1	2	....	....	....	....	....	....	....	....	....	....	....	....	....	....	....	....	....	....
2003-04	Assat Pori U18	Fin-U18	6	7	2	9	8	....	....	....	....	....	....	....	....	....	....	....	....	....	....	....	....	....	....
	Assat Pori Jr.	Fin-Jr.	28	7	9	16	18	....	....	....	....	....	....	....	....	....	3	0	1	1	2	....	....	....	....
	Assat Pori	Finland	6	0	0	0	0	....	....	....	....	....	....	....	....	....	....	....	....	....	....	....	....	....	....
2004-05	Assat Pori Jr.	Fin-Jr.	17	7	13	20	20	....	....	....	....	....	....	....	....	....	2	1	1	2	2	....	....	....	....
	Assat Pori	Finland	39	1	1	2	4	....	....	....	....	....	....	....	....	....	....	....	....	....	....	....	....	....	....
2005-06	Assat Pori	Finland	51	4	8	12	57	....	....	....	....	....	....	....	....	....	14	0	2	2	12	....	....	....	....
	Suomi U20	Finland-2	2	1	0	1	12	....	....	....	....	....	....	....	....	....	....	....	....	....	....	....	....	....	....
2006-07	Assat Pori Jr.	Fin-Jr.	5	2	1	3	6	....	....	....	....	....	....	....	....	....	....	....	....	....	....	....	....	....	....
	Suomi U20	Finland-2	2	0	2	2	6	....	....	....	....	....	....	....	....	....	....	....	....	....	....	....	....	....	....
	Assat Pori	Finland	52	9	17	26	74	....	....	....	....	....	....	....	....	....	....	....	....	....	....	....	....	....	....
2007-08	Assat Pori	Finland	56	17	18	35	89	....	....	....	....	....	....	....	....	....	....	....	....	....	....	....	....	....	....
	Bridgeport	AHL	1	0	0	0	0	....	....	....	....	....	....	....	....	....	....	....	....	....	....	....	....	....	....
2008-09	**NY Islanders**	**NHL**	7	1	2	3	4	0	0	0	9	11.1	–1	0	0.0	12:06	....	....	....	....	....	....	....	....	....
	Bridgeport	AHL	71	20	19	39	58	....	....	....	....	....	....	....	....	....	5	2	1	3	4	....	....	....	....
2009-10	**NY Islanders**	**NHL**	11	1	0	1	4	0	0	0	13	7.7	4	1	0.0	11:09	....	....	....	....	....	....	....	....	....
	Bridgeport	AHL	70	14	34	48	66	....	....	....	....	....	....	....	....	....	5	0	2	2	6	....	....	....	....
2010-11	**NY Islanders**	**NHL**	42	6	3	9	33	0	0	2	41	14.6	–6	9	55.6	11:35	....	....	....	....	....	....	....	....	....
	Bridgeport	AHL	35	8	16	24	31	....	....	....	....	....	....	....	....	....	....	....	....	....	....	....	....	....	....
	NHL Totals		**60**	**8**	**5**	**13**	**41**	**0**	**0**	**2**	**63**	**12.7**		**10**	**50.0**	**11:34**	....	....	....	....	....	....	....	....	....

JOHANSSON, Marcus

(yoh-HAHN-suhn, MAHR-kuhs) **WSH**

Center. Shoots left. 5'11", 189 lbs. Born, Landskrona, Sweden, October 6, 1990. Washington's 1st choice, 24th overall, in 2009 Entry Draft.

Season	Club	League	GP	G	A	Pts	PIM	PP	SH	GW	S	%	+/-	TF	F%	Min	GP	G	A	Pts	PIM	PP	SH	GW	Min
2005-06	Malmo U18	Swe-U18	12	0	7	7	0	....	....	....	....	....	....	....	....	....	6	0	4	4	0	....	....	....	....
2006-07	Farjestad U18	Swe-U18	12	5	9	14	8	....	....	....	....	....	....	....	....	....	8	7	3	10	2	....	....	....	....
2007-08	Farjestad U18	Swe-U18	24	12	26	38	16	....	....	....	....	....	....	....	....	....	8	4	8	12	0	....	....	....	....
	Skare BK	Sweden-3	19	2	10	12	10	....	....	....	....	....	....	....	....	....	....	....	....	....	....	....	....	....	....
	Farjestad	Sweden	....	....	....	....	....	....	....	....	....	....	....	....	....	....	3	0	0	0	0	....	....	....	....

								Regular Season									Playoffs								
Season	Club	League	GP	G	A	Pts	PIM	PP	SH	GW	S	%	+/-	TF	F%	Min	GP	G	A	Pts	PIM	PP	SH	GW	Min
2008-09	Farjestad U18	Swe-U18	2	2	0	2	0	....	....	....	....	....	....	....	....	....	....	....	....	....	....	....	....	....	....
	Skare BK Karlstad	Sweden-3	5	5	5	10	0	....	....	....	....	....	....	....	....	....	....	....	....	....	....	....	....	....	....
	Farjestad	Sweden	45	5	5	10	10	....	....	....	....	....	....	....	....	....	6	0	0	0	0	....	....	....	....
2009-10	Farjestad	Sweden	42	10	10	20	10	....	....	....	....	....	....	....	....	....	7	0	5	5	2	....	....	....	....
2010-11	**Washington**	**NHL**	**69**	**13**	**14**	**27**	**10**	**2**	**1**	**2**	**102**	**12.7**	**2**	**669**	**40.5**	**14:43**	**9**	**2**	**4**	**6**	**0**	**0**	**0**	**0**	**18:22**
	Hershey Bears	AHL	2	0	0	0	0	....	....	....	....	....	....	....	....	....	....	....	....	....	....	....	....	....	....
	NHL Totals		**69**	**13**	**14**	**27**	**10**	**2**	**1**	**2**	**102**	**12.7**		**669**	**40.5**	**14:43**	**9**	**2**	**4**	**6**	**0**	**0**	**0**	**0**	**18:22**

JOHNSON, Aaron

(JAWN-suhn, AIR-ruhn) **CBJ**

Defense. Shoots left. 6'2", 211 lbs. Born, Port Hawkesbury, N.S., April 30, 1983. Columbus' 4th choice, 85th overall, in 2001 Entry Draft.

1998-99	Cape Breton	NSAHA	56	28	42	70	98	....	....	....	....	....	....	....	....	....	....	....	....	....	....	....	....	....	....
99-2000	Rimouski Oceanic	QMJHL	63	1	14	15	57	....	....	....	....	....	....	....	....	....	8	0	0	0	0	....	....	....	....
2000-01	Rimouski Oceanic	QMJHL	64	12	41	53	128	....	....	....	....	....	....	....	....	....	11	2	4	6	35	....	....	....	....
2001-02	Rimouski Oceanic	QMJHL	68	17	49	66	172	....	....	....	....	....	....	....	....	....	7	1	2	3	12	....	....	....	....
2002-03	Rimouski Oceanic	QMJHL	25	4	20	24	41	....	....	....	....	....	....	....	....	....	....	....	....	....	....	....	....	....	....
	Quebec Remparts	QMJHL	32	6	31	37	41	....	....	....	....	....	....	....	....	....	11	4	4	8	25	....	....	....	....
2003-04	**Columbus**	**NHL**	**29**	**2**	**6**	**8**	**32**	**0**	**0**	**1**	**33**	**6.1**	**–2**	**0**	**0.0**	**15:02**	....	....	....	....	....	....	....	....	....
	Syracuse Crunch	AHL	49	6	15	21	83	....	....	....	....	....	....	....	....	....	7	2	3	5	27	....	....	....	....
2004-05	Syracuse Crunch	AHL	77	6	17	23	140	....	....	....	....	....	....	....	....	....	....	....	....	....	....	....	....	....	....
2005-06	**Columbus**	**NHL**	**26**	**2**	**6**	**8**	**23**	**1**	**0**	**1**	**28**	**7.1**	**9**	**0**	**0.0**	**14:12**	....	....	....	....	....	....	....	....	....
	Syracuse Crunch	AHL	49	5	24	29	122	....	....	....	....	....	....	....	....	....	6	1	3	4	19	....	....	....	....
2006-07	**Columbus**	**NHL**	**61**	**3**	**7**	**10**	**38**	**0**	**0**	**0**	**52**	**5.8**	**–9**	**0**	**0.0**	**12:44**	....	....	....	....	....	....	....	....	....
2007-08	**NY Islanders**	**NHL**	**30**	**0**	**2**	**2**	**30**	**0**	**0**	**0**	**16**	**0.0**	**2**	**0**	**0.0**	**13:52**	....	....	....	....	....	....	....	....	....
	Bridgeport	AHL	2	0	0	0	0	....	....	....	....	....	....	....	....	....	....	....	....	....	....	....	....	....	....
2008-09	**Chicago**	**NHL**	**38**	**3**	**5**	**8**	**33**	**0**	**0**	**1**	**27**	**11.1**	**19**	**0**	**0.0**	**14:09**	....	....	....	....	....	....	....	....	....
	Rockford IceHogs	AHL	2	0	1	1	4	....	....	....	....	....	....	....	....	....	....	....	....	....	....	....	....	....	....
2009-10	**Calgary**	**NHL**	**22**	**1**	**2**	**3**	**19**	**0**	**0**	**0**	**13**	**7.7**	**0**	**0**	**0.0**	**12:11**	....	....	....	....	....	....	....	....	....
	Edmonton	**NHL**	**19**	**3**	**4**	**7**	**16**	**1**	**0**	**0**	**23**	**13.0**	**–6**	**0**	**0.0**	**19:40**	....	....	....	....	....	....	....	....	....
2010-11	Milwaukee	AHL	72	9	26	35	70	....	....	....	....	....	....	....	....	....	13	1	2	3	16	....	....	....	....
	NHL Totals		**225**	**14**	**32**	**46**	**191**	**2**	**0**	**3**	**192**	**7.3**		**0**	**0.0**	**14:07**	....	....	....	....	....	....	....	....	....

Signed as a free agent by **NY Islanders**, July 12, 2007. • Missed majority of 2007-08 due to recurring knee injury and as a healthy reserve. Signed as a free agent by **Chicago**, July 15, 2008. Traded to **Calgary** by **Chicago** for Kyle Greentree, October 7, 2009. Traded to **Edmonton** by **Calgary** with Calgary's 3rd round choice (Travis Ewanyk) in 2011 Entry Draft for Steve Staios, March 3, 2010. Signed as a free agent by **Nashville**, August 31, 2010. Signed as a free agent by **Columbus**, July 5, 2011.

JOHNSON, Erik

(JAWN-suhn, AIR-ihk) **COL**

Defense. Shoots right. 6'4", 232 lbs. Born, Bloomington, MN, March 21, 1988. St. Louis' 1st choice, 1st overall, in 2006 Entry Draft.

2003-04	Holy Angels	High-MN	31	13	21	34	....	....	....	....	....	....	....	....	....	....	....	....	....	....	....	....	....	....	....
2004-05	USNTDP	U-17	26	5	9	14	14	....	....	....	....	....	....	....	....	....	....	....	....	....	....	....	....	....	....
	USNTDP	NAHL	31	6	6	12	12	....	....	....	....	....	....	....	....	....	....	....	....	....	....	....	....	....	....
2005-06	USNTDP	U-18	36	12	22	34	78	....	....	....	....	....	....	....	....	....	....	....	....	....	....	....	....	....	....
	USNTDP	NAHL	11	4	11	15	10	....	....	....	....	....	....	....	....	....	....	....	....	....	....	....	....	....	....
2006-07	U. of Minnesota	WCHA	41	4	20	24	50	....	....	....	....	....	....	....	....	....	....	....	....	....	....	....	....	....	....
2007-08	**St. Louis**	**NHL**	**69**	**5**	**28**	**33**	**28**	**4**	**0**	**3**	**105**	**4.8**	**–9**	**1**	**0.0**	**18:11**	....	....	....	....	....	....	....	....	....
	Peoria Rivermen	AHL	1	0	0	0	2	....	....	....	....	....	....	....	....	....	....	....	....	....	....	....	....	....	....
2008-09	**St. Louis**	**NHL**	DID NOT PLAY – INJURED					....	....	....	....	....	....	....	....	....	....	....	....	....	....	....	....	....	....
2009-10	**St. Louis**	**NHL**	**79**	**10**	**29**	**39**	**79**	**6**	**0**	**2**	**186**	**5.4**	**1**	**0**	**0.0**	**21:27**	....	....	....	....	....	....	....	....	....
	United States	Olympics	6	1	0	1	4	....	....	....	....	....	....	....	....	....	....	....	....	....	....	....	....	....	....
2010-11	**St. Louis**	**NHL**	**55**	**5**	**14**	**19**	**37**	**1**	**1**	**2**	**108**	**4.6**	**–8**	**0**	**0.0**	**22:08**	....	....	....	....	....	....	....	....	....
	Colorado	**NHL**	**22**	**3**	**7**	**10**	**19**	**2**	**0**	**0**	**53**	**5.7**	**–5**	**0**	**0.0**	**24:33**	....	....	....	....	....	....	....	....	....
	NHL Totals		**225**	**23**	**78**	**101**	**163**	**13**	**1**	**7**	**452**	**5.1**		**1**	**0.0**	**20:55**	....	....	....	....	....	....	....	....	....

WCHA All-Rookie Team (2007)

• Missed entire 2008-09 due to off-ice knee injury, September 16, 2008, November 20, 2008. Traded to **Colorado** by **St. Louis** with Jay McClement and St. Louis's 1st round choice (Duncan Siemens) in 2011 Entry Draft for Kevin Shattenkirk, Chris Stewart and Colorado's 2nd round choice (Ty Rattie) in 2011 Entry Draft, February 19, 2011.

JOHNSON, Jack

(JAHN-suhn, JAK) **L.A.**

Defense. Shoots left. 6'1", 219 lbs. Born, Indianapolis, IN, January 13, 1987. Carolina's 1st choice, 3rd overall, in 2005 Entry Draft.

2002-03	Shat.-St. Mary's	High-MN	48	15	27	42	....	....	....	....	....	....	....	....	....	....	....	....	....	....	....	....	....	....	....
2003-04	USNTDP	U-17	31	12	9	21	78	....	....	....	....	....	....	....	....	....	....	....	....	....	....	....	....	....	....
	USNTDP	NAHL	29	3	12	15	93	....	....	....	....	....	....	....	....	....	....	....	....	....	....	....	....	....	....
2004-05	USNTDP	U-18	26	5	9	14	86	....	....	....	....	....	....	....	....	....	....	....	....	....	....	....	....	....	....
	USNTDP	NAHL	12	7	10	17	57	....	....	....	....	....	....	....	....	....	....	....	....	....	....	....	....	....	....
2005-06	U. of Michigan	CCHA	38	10	22	32	*149	....	....	....	....	....	....	....	....	....	....	....	....	....	....	....	....	....	....
2006-07	U. of Michigan	CCHA	36	16	23	39	87	....	....	....	....	....	....	....	....	....	....	....	....	....	....	....	....	....	....
	Los Angeles	**NHL**	**5**	**0**	**0**	**0**	**18**	**0**	**0**	**0**	**5**	**0.0**	**–5**	**0**	**0.0**	**21:23**	....	....	....	....	....	....	....	....	....
2007-08	**Los Angeles**	**NHL**	**74**	**3**	**8**	**11**	**76**	**0**	**0**	**0**	**81**	**3.7**	**–19**	**5**	**60.0**	**21:42**	....	....	....	....	....	....	....	....	....
2008-09	**Los Angeles**	**NHL**	**41**	**6**	**5**	**11**	**46**	**3**	**0**	**0**	**50**	**12.0**	**–18**	**0**	**0.0**	**20:17**	....	....	....	....	....	....	....	....	....
2009-10	**Los Angeles**	**NHL**	**80**	**8**	**28**	**36**	**48**	**3**	**0**	**0**	**130**	**6.2**	**–15**	**0**	**0.0**	**22:37**	**6**	**0**	**7**	**7**	**6**	**0**	**0**	**0**	**23:42**
	United States	Olympics	6	0	1	1	2	....	....	....	....	....	....	....	....	....	....	....	....	....	....	....	....	....	....
2010-11	**Los Angeles**	**NHL**	**82**	**5**	**37**	**42**	**44**	**3**	**0**	**0**	**153**	**3.3**	**–21**	**0**	**0.0**	**23:12**	**6**	**1**	**4**	**5**	**0**	**1**	**0**	**1**	**22:48**
	NHL Totals		**282**	**22**	**78**	**100**	**232**	**9**	**0**	**0**	**419**	**5.3**		**5**	**60.0**	**22:11**	**12**	**1**	**11**	**12**	**6**	**1**	**0**	**1**	**23:15**

CCHA All-Rookie Team (2006) • CCHA First All-Star Team (2007) • NCAA West First All-American Team (2007)

Traded to **Los Angeles** by **Carolina** with Oleg Tverdovsky for Eric Belanger and Tim Gleason, September 29, 2006.

JOHNSON, Nick

(JAWN-suhn, NIHK) **PIT**

Right wing. Shoots right. 6'1", 183 lbs. Born, Calgary, Alta., December 24, 1985. Pittsburgh's 4th choice, 67th overall, in 2004 Entry Draft.

2002-03	St. Albert Saints	AJHL	60	21	30	51	10	....	....	....	....	....	....	....	....	....	....	....	....	....	....	....	....	....	....
2003-04	St. Albert Saints	AJHL	51	35	36	71	33	....	....	....	....	....	....	....	....	....	4	0	2	2	0	....	....	....	....
2004-05	Dartmouth	ECAC	35	18	17	35	16	....	....	....	....	....	....	....	....	....	....	....	....	....	....	....	....	....	....
2005-06	Dartmouth	ECAC	33	15	10	25	24	....	....	....	....	....	....	....	....	....	....	....	....	....	....	....	....	....	....
2006-07	Dartmouth	ECAC	33	14	16	30	46	....	....	....	....	....	....	....	....	....	....	....	....	....	....	....	....	....	....
2007-08	Dartmouth	ECAC	32	10	25	35	20	....	....	....	....	....	....	....	....	....	....	....	....	....	....	....	....	....	....
	Wilkes-Barre	AHL	4	0	1	1	0	....	....	....	....	....	....	....	....	....	10	0	1	1	2	....	....	....	....
2008-09	Wilkes-Barre	AHL	56	14	17	31	30	....	....	....	....	....	....	....	....	....	12	4	6	10	8	....	....	....	....
	Wheeling Nailers	ECHL	18	14	10	24	19	....	....	....	....	....	....	....	....	....	....	....	....	....	....	....	....	....	....
2009-10	**Pittsburgh**	**NHL**	**6**	**1**	**1**	**2**	**2**	**0**	**0**	**0**	**7**	**14.3**	**–2**	**1**	**100.0**	**10:06**	....	....	....	....	....	....	....	....	....
	Wilkes-Barre	AHL	61	16	27	43	50	....	....	....	....	....	....	....	....	....	4	4	0	4	2	....	....	....	....
2010-11	**Pittsburgh**	**NHL**	**4**	**1**	**2**	**3**	**5**	**0**	**0**	**0**	**10**	**10.0**	**1**	**0**	**0.0**	**16:44**	....	....	....	....	....	....	....	....	....
	Wilkes-Barre	AHL	48	20	19	39	49	....	....	....	....	....	....	....	....	....	....	....	....	....	....	....	....	....	....
	NHL Totals		**10**	**2**	**3**	**5**	**7**	**0**	**0**	**0**	**17**	**11.8**		**1**	**100.0**	**12:45**	....	....	....	....	....	....	....	....	....

ECAC All-Rookie Team (2005) • ECAC First All-Star Team (2008) • NCAA East Second All-American Team (2008)

JOHNSON, Ryan

(JAWN-suhn, RIGH-uhn)

Center. Shoots left. 6'1", 199 lbs. Born, Thunder Bay, Ont., June 14, 1976. Florida's 4th choice, 36th overall, in 1994 Entry Draft.

1992-93	Thunder Bay	TBAHA	60	25	33	58	....	....	....	....	....	....	....	....	....	....	....	....	....	....	....	....	....	....	....
1993-94	Thunder Bay	USHL	48	14	36	50	28	....	....	....	....	....	....	....	....	....	....	....	....	....	....	....	....	....	....
1994-95	North Dakota	WCHA	38	6	22	28	39	....	....	....	....	....	....	....	....	....	....	....	....	....	....	....	....	....	....
1995-96	North Dakota	WCHA	21	2	17	19	14	....	....	....	....	....	....	....	....	....	....	....	....	....	....	....	....	....	....
	Canada	Nat-Tm	28	5	12	17	14	....	....	....	....	....	....	....	....	....	....	....	....	....	....	....	....	....	....
1996-97	Carolina	AHL	79	18	24	42	28	....	....	....	....	....	....	....	....	....	....	....	....	....	....	....	....	....	....
1997-98	**Florida**	**NHL**	**10**	**0**	**2**	**2**	**0**	**0**	**0**	**0**	**6**	**0.0**	**–4**	....	....	....	....	....	....	....	....	....	....	....	....
	New Haven	AHL	64	19	48	67	12	....	....	....	....	....	....	....	....	....	3	0	1	1	0	....	....	....	....
1998-99	**Florida**	**NHL**	**1**	**1**	**0**	**1**	**0**	**0**	**0**	**0**	**1**	**100.0**	**0**	**16**	**37.5**	**15:26**	....	....	....	....	....	....	....	....	....
	New Haven	AHL	37	8	19	27	18	....	....	....	....	....	....	....	....	....	....	....	....	....	....	....	....	....	....

Season	Club	League	Regular Season														Playoffs								
Season	Club	League	GP	G	A	Pts	PIM	PP	SH	GW	S	%	+/-	TF	F%	Min	GP	G	A	Pts	PIM	PP	SH	GW	Min
99-2000	Florida	NHL	66	4	12	16	14	0	0	0	44	9.1	1	684	51.8	11:47	....	....	....	....	....	....	....	....	....
	Tampa Bay	NHL	14	0	2	2	2	0	0	0	5	0.0	-9	117	53.0	11:02	....	....	....	....	....	....	....	....	....
2000-01	Tampa Bay	NHL	80	7	14	21	44	1	0	0	71	9.9	-20	951	48.9	15:47	....	....	....	....	....	....	....	....	....
2001-02	Florida	NHL	29	1	3	4	10	0	0	0	24	4.2	-5	336	47.9	13:00	....	....	....	....	....	....	....	....	....
2002-03	Florida	NHL	58	2	5	7	26	0	0	0	54	3.7	-13	689	48.0	10:40	....	....	....	....	....	....	....	....	....
	St. Louis	NHL	17	0	0	0	12	0	0	0	13	0.0	0	180	51.7	10:34	6	0	2	2	6	0	0	0	8:14
2003-04	St. Louis	NHL	69	4	7	11	8	0	1	1	36	11.1	-2	537	53.6	9:54	3	0	0	0	0	0	0	0	6:11
2004-05	Missouri	UHL	29	7	14	21	12	....	....	....	....	....	....	....	....	....	6	1	0	1	13	....	....	....	....
2005-06	St. Louis	NHL	65	3	6	9	33	1	1	0	57	5.3	-21	569	55.9	11:24	....	....	....	....	....	....	....	....	....
2006-07	St. Louis	NHL	59	7	4	11	47	0	2	0	50	14.0	-7	525	55.4	12:21	....	....	....	....	....	....	....	....	....
2007-08	St. Louis	NHL	79	5	13	18	22	0	1	1	85	5.9	-2	803	54.6	14:22	....	....	....	....	....	....	....	....	....
2008-09	Vancouver	NHL	62	2	7	9	12	0	0	1	22	9.1	1	565	48.5	11:01	10	1	1	2	2	0	0	0	11:52
2009-10	Vancouver	NHL	58	1	4	5	12	0	0	1	19	5.3	-4	537	52.7	10:37	4	0	0	0	2	0	0	0	8:23
2010-11	Rockford IceHogs	AHL	1	0	0	0	0	....	....	....	....	....	....	....	....	....	....	....	....	....	....	....	....	....	....
	Chicago	NHL	34	1	5	6	8	0	0	1	25	4.0	-2	312	63.1	10:21	6	0	1	1	2	0	0	0	9:55
	NHL Totals		701	38	84	122	250	2	5	5	512	7.4		6821	52.2	12:03	29	1	4	5	12	0	0	0	9:39

Traded to **Tampa Bay** by **Florida** with Dwayne Hay for Mike Sillinger, March 14, 2000. Traded to **Florida** by **Tampa Bay** with Tampa Bay's 6th round choice (later traded back to Tampa Bay – Tampa Bay selected Doug O'Brien) in 2003 Entry Draft for Vaclav Prospal, July 10, 2001. • Missed majority of 2001-02 due to concussion vs. St. Louis, December 22, 2001. Claimed on waivers by **St. Louis** from **Florida**, February 19, 2003. Signed as a free agent by **Missouri** (UHL), February 3, 2005. Signed as a free agent by **Vancouver**, July 2, 2008. Signed to a PTO (professional tryout) contract by **Rockford** (AHL), December 10, 2010. Signed as a free agent by **Chicago**, December 17, 2010.

JOKINEN, Jussi

(YOH-kih-nihn, YEW-see) **CAR**

Center. Shoots left. 5'11", 198 lbs. Born, Kalajoki, Finland, April 1, 1983. Dallas' 7th choice, 192nd overall, in 2001 Entry Draft.

Season	Club	League	GP	G	A	Pts	PIM	PP	SH	GW	S	%	+/-	TF	F%	Min	GP	G	A	Pts	PIM	PP	SH	GW	Min
99-2000	Karpat Oulu U18	Fin-U18	15	6	25	31	14	....	....	....	....	....	....	....	....	....	6	2	3	5	0	....	....	....	....
	Karpat Oulu Jr.	Fin-Jr.	28	4	7	11	14	....	....	....	....	....	....	....	....	....	....	....	....	....	....	....	....	....	....
2000-01	Karpat Oulu U18	Fin-U18	1	2	1	3	0	....	....	....	....	....	....	....	....	....	....	....	....	....	....	....	....	....	....
	Karpat Oulu Jr.	Fin-Jr.	41	18	31	49	69	....	....	....	....	....	....	....	....	....	6	2	1	3	0	....	....	....	....
2001-02	Karpat Oulu Jr.	Fin-Jr.	2	4	1	5	2	....	....	....	....	....	....	....	....	....	1	1	1	2	0	....	....	....	....
	Karpat Oulu	Finland	54	10	6	16	38	....	....	....	....	....	....	....	....	....	4	1	0	1	0	....	....	....	....
2002-03	Karpat Oulu	Finland	51	14	23	37	10	....	....	....	....	....	....	....	....	....	15	2	1	3	33	....	....	....	....
2003-04	Karpat Oulu	Finland	55	15	23	38	20	....	....	....	....	....	....	....	....	....	15	3	4	7	6	....	....	....	....
2004-05	Karpat Oulu	Finland	56	23	24	47	24	....	....	....	....	....	....	....	....	....	12	3	4	7	2	....	....	....	....
2005-06	Dallas	NHL	81	17	38	55	30	8	0	2	107	15.9	2	23	30.4	13:34	5	2	1	3	0	1	0	0	13:40
	Finland	Olympics	8	1	3	4	2	....	....	....	....	....	....	....	....	....	....	....	....	....	....	....	....	....	....
2006-07	Dallas	NHL	82	14	34	48	18	6	0	1	121	11.6	8	278	52.2	13:54	4	0	1	1	0	0	0	0	13:22
2007-08	Dallas	NHL	52	14	14	28	14	5	0	2	93	15.1	2	295	53.2	12:44	....	....	....	....	....	....	....	....	....
	Tampa Bay	NHL	20	2	12	14	4	1	0	0	38	5.3	-16	46	45.7	18:57	....	....	....	....	....	....	....	....	....
2008-09	Tampa Bay	NHL	46	6	10	16	16	2	0	0	64	9.4	-8	510	52.2	15:38	....	....	....	....	....	....	....	....	....
	Carolina	NHL	25	1	10	11	12	0	0	1	37	2.7	-2	163	58.3	14:43	18	7	4	11	2	2	0	*3	15:35
2009-10	Carolina	NHL	81	30	35	65	36	10	0	6	160	18.8	3	265	51.3	16:49	....	....	....	....	....	....	....	....	....
2010-11	Carolina	NHL	70	19	33	52	24	8	0	1	136	14.0	3	320	52.8	17:13	....	....	....	....	....	....	....	....	....
	NHL Totals		457	103	186	289	154	40	0	13	756	13.6		1900	52.4	15:10	27	9	6	15	2	3	0	3	14:54

Traded to **Tampa Bay** by **Dallas** with Jeff Halpern, Mike Smith and Dallas' 4th round choice (later traded to Minnesota, later traded to Edmonton – Edmonton selected Kyle Bigos) in 2009 Entry Draft for Brad Richards and Johan Holmqvist, February 26, 2008. Traded to **Carolina** by **Tampa Bay** for Wade Brookbank, Josef Melichar and future considerations, February 7, 2009.

JOKINEN, Olli

(YOH-kih-nihn, OH-lee) **CGY**

Center. Shoots left. 6'3", 215 lbs. Born, Kuopio, Finland, December 5, 1978. Los Angeles' 1st choice, 3rd overall, in 1997 Entry Draft.

Season	Club	League	GP	G	A	Pts	PIM	PP	SH	GW	S	%	+/-	TF	F%	Min	GP	G	A	Pts	PIM	PP	SH	GW	Min
1994-95	KalPa Kuopio U18	Fin-U18	30	22	28	50	92	....	....	....	....	....	....	....	....	....	....	....	....	....	....	....	....	....	....
	KalPa Kuopio Jr.	Fin-Jr.	6	0	1	1	6	....	....	....	....	....	....	....	....	....	....	....	....	....	....	....	....	....	....
1995-96	KalPa Kuopio U18	Fin-U18	9	9	13	22	4	....	....	....	....	....	....	....	....	....	....	....	....	....	....	....	....	....	....
	KalPa Kuopio Jr.	Fin-Jr.	25	20	14	34	47	....	....	....	....	....	....	....	....	....	7	4	4	8	20	....	....	....	....
	KalPa Kuopio	Finland	15	1	1	2	2	....	....	....	....	....	....	....	....	....	....	....	....	....	....	....	....	....	....
1996-97	HIFK Helsinki Jr.	Fin-Jr.	2	1	0	1	6	....	....	....	....	....	....	....	....	....	....	....	....	....	....	....	....	....	....
	HIFK Helsinki	Finland	50	14	27	41	88	....	....	....	....	....	....	....	....	....	....	....	....	....	....	....	....	....	....
1997-98	Los Angeles	NHL	8	0	0	0	6	0	0	0	12	0.0	-5	....	....	....	....	....	....	....	....	....	....	....	....
	HIFK Helsinki	Finland	30	11	28	39	32	....	....	....	....	....	....	....	....	....	9	7	2	9	2	....	....	....	....
1998-99	Los Angeles	NHL	66	9	12	21	44	3	1	1	87	10.3	-10	779	43.9	14:42	....	....	....	....	....	....	....	....	....
	Springfield	AHL	9	3	6	9	6	....	....	....	....	....	....	....	....	....	....	....	....	....	....	....	....	....	....
99-2000	NY Islanders	NHL	82	11	10	21	80	1	2	3	138	8.0	0	841	46.1	16:15	....	....	....	....	....	....	....	....	....
2000-01	Florida	NHL	78	6	10	16	106	0	0	0	121	5.0	-22	638	42.3	13:23	....	....	....	....	....	....	....	....	....
2001-02	Florida	NHL	80	9	20	29	98	3	1	0	153	5.9	-16	1222	45.2	18:05	....	....	....	....	....	....	....	....	....
	Finland	Olympics	4	2	1	3	0	....	....	....	....	....	....	....	....	....	....	....	....	....	....	....	....	....	....
2002-03	Florida	NHL	81	36	29	65	79	13	3	6	240	15.0	-17	1925	46.7	22:02	....	....	....	....	....	....	....	....	....
2003-04	Florida	NHL	82	26	32	58	81	8	2	8	280	9.3	-16	1986	47.1	22:35	....	....	....	....	....	....	....	....	....
2004-05	Kloten Flyers	Swiss	8	6	1	7	14	....	....	....	....	....	....	....	....	....	....	....	....	....	....	....	....	....	....
	Sodertalje SK	Sweden	23	13	9	22	52	....	....	....	....	....	....	....	....	....	....	....	....	....	....	....	....	....	....
	HIFK Helsinki	Finland	14	9	8	17	10	....	....	....	....	....	....	....	....	....	5	2	0	2	24	....	....	....	....
2005-06	Florida	NHL	82	38	51	89	88	14	1	9	351	10.8	14	955	46.9	20:29	....	....	....	....	....	....	....	....	....
	Finland	Olympics	8	6	2	8	2	....	....	....	....	....	....	....	....	....	....	....	....	....	....	....	....	....	....
2006-07	Florida	NHL	82	39	52	91	78	9	1	8	351	11.1	18	1074	44.3	20:32	....	....	....	....	....	....	....	....	....
2007-08	Florida	NHL	82	34	37	71	67	18	0	5	341	10.0	-19	938	43.1	19:54	....	....	....	....	....	....	....	....	....
2008-09	Phoenix	NHL	57	21	21	42	49	6	2	2	169	12.4	-5	737	42.2	18:10	....	....	....	....	....	....	....	....	....
	Calgary	NHL	19	8	7	15	18	3	0	1	67	11.9	-7	215	47.4	21:03	6	2	3	5	4	0	0	0	19:24
2009-10	Calgary	NHL	56	11	24	35	53	2	0	2	162	6.8	2	739	49.3	18:30	....	....	....	....	....	....	....	....	....
	NY Rangers	NHL	26	4	11	15	22	1	0	1	74	5.4	1	234	49.6	16:29	....	....	....	....	....	....	....	....	....
	Finland	Olympics	6	3	1	4	2	....	....	....	....	....	....	....	....	....	....	....	....	....	....	....	....	....	....
2010-11	Calgary	NHL	79	17	37	54	44	5	0	1	208	8.2	-17	1165	47.4	17:47	....	....	....	....	....	....	....	....	....
	NHL Totals		960	269	353	622	913	86	13	47	2754	9.8		13448	45.8	18:37	6	2	3	5	4	0	0	0	19:24

Played in NHL All-Star Game (2003)

Traded to **NY Islanders** by **Los Angeles** with Josh Green, Mathieu Biron and Los Angeles' 1st round choice (Taylor Pyatt) in 1999 Entry Draft for Ziggy Palffy, Bryan Smolinski, Marcel Cousineau and New Jersey's 4th round choice (previously acquired, Los Angeles selected Daniel Johansson) in 1999 Entry Draft, June 20, 1999. Traded to **Florida** by **NY Islanders** with Roberto Luongo for Mark Parrish and Oleg Kvasha, June 24, 2000. Signed as a free agent by **Kloten** (Swiss), September 15, 2004. Signed as a free agent by **Sodertalje** (Sweden), November, 2004. Signed as a free agent by **HIFK Helsinki** (Finland), January 30, 2005.Traded to **Phoenix** by **Florida** for Keith Ballard, Nick Boynton and Ottawa's 2nd round choice (previously acquired, later traded back to Phoenix - Phoenix selected Jared Staal) in 2008 Entry Draft, June 20, 2008. Traded to **Calgary** by **Phoenix** with Phoenix's 3rd round choice (later traded to Florida – Florida selected Josh Birkholz) in 2009 Entry Draft for Matthew Lombardi, Brandon Prust and Calgary's 1st round choice (Brandon Gormley) in 2010 Entry Draft, March 4, 2009. Traded to **NY Rangers** by **Calgary** with Brandon Prust for Chris Higgins and Ales Kotalik, February 2, 2010. Signed as a free agent by **Calgary**, July 1, 2010.

JONES, Blair

(JOHNZ, BLAYR) **T.B.**

Center. Shoots right. 6'2", 216 lbs. Born, Central Butte, Sask., September 27, 1986. Tampa Bay's 5th choice, 102nd overall, in 2005 Entry Draft.

Season	Club	League	GP	G	A	Pts	PIM	PP	SH	GW	S	%	+/-	TF	F%	Min	GP	G	A	Pts	PIM	PP	SH	GW	Min
2002-03	Bethune	SBHL	STATISTICS NOT AVAILABLE																						
	Red Deer Rebels	WHL	37	3	4	7	17	....	....	....	....	....	....	....	....	....	10	1	0	1	0	....	....	....	....
2003-04	Red Deer Rebels	WHL	72	9	22	31	55	....	....	....	....	....	....	....	....	....	19	1	5	6	24	....	....	....	....
2004-05	Red Deer Rebels	WHL	39	7	18	25	48	....	....	....	....	....	....	....	....	....	....	....	....	....	....	....	....	....	....
	Moose Jaw	WHL	29	7	18	25	30	....	....	....	....	....	....	....	....	....	5	2	5	7	8	....	....	....	....
2005-06	Moose Jaw	WHL	72	35	50	85	85	....	....	....	....	....	....	....	....	....	22	9	12	21	45	....	....	....	....
2006-07	Tampa Bay	NHL	20	1	2	3	2	0	0	0	6	16.7	0	65	41.5	5:46	....	....	....	....	....	....	....	....	....
	Springfield	AHL	45	5	16	21	36	....	....	....	....	....	....	....	....	....	....	....	....	....	....	....	....	....	....
2007-08	Tampa Bay	NHL	4	0	0	0	0	0	0	0	1	0.0	0	8	12.5	1:55	....	....	....	....	....	....	....	....	....
	Norfolk Admirals	AHL	75	14	28	42	50	....	....	....	....	....	....	....	....	....	....	....	....	....	....	....	....	....	....
2008-09	Norfolk Admirals	AHL	80	20	34	54	61	....	....	....	....	....	....	....	....	....	....	....	....	....	....	....	....	....	....
2009-10	Tampa Bay	NHL	14	0	0	0	10	0	0	0	26	0.0	-5	28	53.6	12:50	....	....	....	....	....	....	....	....	....
	Norfolk Admirals	AHL	63	9	21	30	27	....	....	....	....	....	....	....	....	....	....	....	....	....	....	....	....	....	....
2010-11	Tampa Bay	NHL	18	1	2	3	2	0	0	0	20	5.0	-2	86	53.5	8:01	7	0	0	0	2	0	0	0	6:24
	Norfolk Admirals	AHL	56	24	31	55	75	....	....	....	....	....	....	....	....	....	4	1	0	1	8	....	....	....	....
	NHL Totals		56	2	4	6	14	0	0	0	53	3.8		187	47.6	7:59	7	0	0	0	2	0	0	0	6:24

WHL East Second All-Star Team (2006)

					Regular Season													Playoffs							
Season	Club	League	GP	G	A	Pts	PIM	PP	SH	GW	S	%	+/-	TF	F%	Min	GP	G	A	Pts	PIM	PP	SH	GW	Min

JONES, David
(JOHNZ, DAY-vihd)   COL

Right wing. Shoots right. 6'2", 210 lbs.   Born, Guelph, Ont., August 10, 1984. Colorado's 8th choice, 288th overall, in 2003 Entry Draft.

Season	Club	League	GP	G	A	Pts	PIM	PP	SH	GW	S	%	+/-	TF	F%	Min	GP	G	A	Pts	PIM	PP	SH	GW	Min
2000-01	Port Coquitlam	PIJHL	40	18	11	29	33	....	....	....	....	....	....	....	....	....	....	....	....	....	....	....	....	....	....
2001-02	Coquitlam	BCHL	59	19	32	51	62	....	....	....	....	....	....	....	....	....	....	....	....	....	....	....	....	....	....
2002-03	Coquitlam	BCHL	35	9	19	28	55	....	....	....	....	....	....	....	....	....	7	2	6	8	8	....	....	....	....
2003-04	Coquitlam	BCHL	53	33	60	93	78	....	....	....	....	....	....	....	....	....	7	3	6	9	4	....	....	....	....
2004-05	Dartmouth	ECAC	34	9	5	14	26	....	....	....	....	....	....	....	....	....	....	....	....	....	....	....	....	....	....
2005-06	Dartmouth	ECAC	33	17	17	34	38	....	....	....	....	....	....	....	....	....	....	....	....	....	....	....	....	....	....
2006-07	Dartmouth	ECAC	33	18	26	*44	22	....	....	....	....	....	....	....	....	....	....	....	....	....	....	....	....	....	....
2007-08	**Colorado**	**NHL**	**27**	**2**	**4**	**6**	**8**	**1**	**0**	**0**	**37**	**5.4**	**–5**	**8**	**37.5**	**11:22**	**10**	**0**	**1**	**1**	**6**	**0**	**0**	**0**	**11:50**
	Lake Erie	AHL	45	14	16	30	16	....	....	....	....	....	....	....	....	....	....	....	....	....	....	....	....	....	....
2008-09	**Colorado**	**NHL**	**40**	**8**	**5**	**13**	**8**	**1**	**0**	**1**	**47**	**17.0**	**–8**	**8**	**50.0**	**12:44**									
2009-10	**Colorado**	**NHL**	**23**	**10**	**6**	**16**	**2**	**1**	**2**	**3**	**39**	**25.6**	**1**	**7**	**28.6**	**17:56**									
2010-11	**Colorado**	**NHL**	**77**	**27**	**18**	**45**	**28**	**6**	**0**	**4**	**153**	**17.6**	**–2**	**21**	**47.6**	**17:41**									
	NHL Totals		**167**	**47**	**33**	**80**	**46**	**9**	**2**	**8**	**276**	**17.0**		**44**	**43.2**	**15:30**	**10**	**0**	**1**	**1**	**6**	**0**	**0**	**0**	**11:50**

ECAC Second All-Star Team (2006) • ECAC First All-Star Tearm (2007) • NCAA East First All-American Team (2007)
• Missed majority of 2008-09 due to shoulder injury vs. San Jose, January 27, 2009. • Missed remainder of 2009-10 due to knee injury vs. Minnesota, November 28, 2009.

JONES, Randy
(JOHNZ, RAN-dee)   WPG

Defense. Shoots left. 6'2", 210 lbs.   Born, Quispamsis, N.B., July 23, 1981.

Season	Club	League	GP	G	A	Pts	PIM	PP	SH	GW	S	%	+/-	TF	F%	Min	GP	G	A	Pts	PIM	PP	SH	GW	Min
99-2000	Cobourg Cougars	OPJHL	44	20	36	56	51	....	....	....	....	....	....	....	....	....	....	....	....	....	....	....	....	....	....
2000-01	Cobourg Cougars	OPJHL	28	15	21	36	46	....	....	....	....	....	....	....	....	....	....	....	....	....	....	....	....	....	....
2001-02	Clarkson Knights	ECAC	34	9	11	20	32	....	....	....	....	....	....	....	....	....	....	....	....	....	....	....	....	....	....
2002-03	Clarkson Knights	ECAC	33	13	20	33	65	....	....	....	....	....	....	....	....	....	....	....	....	....	....	....	....	....	....
2003-04	**Philadelphia**	**NHL**	**5**	**0**	**0**	**0**	**0**	**0**	**0**	**0**	**5**	**0.0**	**1**	**0**	**0.0**	**12:00**									
	Philadelphia	AHL	55	8	24	32	63	....	....	....	....	....	....	....	....	....	12	0	1	1	17	....	....	....	....
2004-05	Philadelphia	AHL	69	5	19	24	32	....	....	....	....	....	....	....	....	....	18	0	5	5	10	....	....	....	....
2005-06	**Philadelphia**	**NHL**	**28**	**0**	**8**	**8**	**16**	**0**	**0**	**0**	**21**	**0.0**	**–6**	**1**	**100.0**	**14:58**									
	Philadelphia	AHL	21	2	3	5	53	....	....	....	....	....	....	....	....	....	....	....	....	....	....	....	....	....	....
2006-07	**Philadelphia**	**NHL**	**66**	**4**	**18**	**22**	**38**	**0**	**0**	**0**	**67**	**6.0**	**–14**	**1**	**0.0**	**16:06**									
2007-08	**Philadelphia**	**NHL**	**71**	**5**	**26**	**31**	**58**	**1**	**0**	**0**	**103**	**4.9**	**8**	**0**	**0.0**	**19:24**	**16**	**0**	**2**	**2**	**4**	**0**	**0**	**0**	**21:24**
2008-09	**Philadelphia**	**NHL**	**47**	**4**	**4**	**8**	**22**	**1**	**0**	**2**	**45**	**8.9**	**8**	**0**	**0.0**	**19:07**	**6**	**0**	**1**	**1**	**0**	**0**	**0**	**0**	**14:38**
	Philadelphia	AHL	2	0	2	2	0	....	....	....	....	....	....	....	....	....	....	....	....	....	....	....	....	....	....
2009-10	Adirondack	AHL	6	0	1	1	6	....	....	....	....	....	....	....	....	....	....	....	....	....	....	....	....	....	....
	Los Angeles	**NHL**	**48**	**5**	**16**	**21**	**28**	**1**	**1**	**1**	**54**	**9.3**	**–3**	**0**	**0.0**	**18:10**	**4**	**0**	**0**	**0**	**2**	**0**	**0**	**0**	**17:42**
2010-11	**Tampa Bay**	**NHL**	**61**	**1**	**12**	**13**	**15**	**0**	**0**	**0**	**52**	**1.9**	**–4**	**0**	**0.0**	**17:03**	**5**	**0**	**1**	**1**	**2**	**0**	**0**	**0**	**6:58**
	NHL Totals		**326**	**19**	**84**	**103**	**177**	**3**	**1**	**3**	**347**	**5.5**		**2**	**50.0**	**17:35**	**31**	**0**	**4**	**4**	**8**	**0**	**0**	**0**	**17:17**

ECAC First All-Star Team (2003)
Signed as a free agent by **Philadelphia**, July 24, 2003. Claimed on waivers by **Los Angeles** from **Philadelphia**, October 29, 2009. Signed as a free agent by **Tampa Bay**, August 25, 2010. Signed as a free agent by **Winnipeg**, July 4, 2011.

JONES, Ryan
(JOHNZ, RIGH-uhn)   EDM

Right wing. Shoots left. 6', 205 lbs.   Born, Chatham, Ont., June 14, 1984. Minnesota's 5th choice, 111th overall, in 2004 Entry Draft.

Season	Club	League	GP	G	A	Pts	PIM	PP	SH	GW	S	%	+/-	TF	F%	Min	GP	G	A	Pts	PIM	PP	SH	GW	Min
2002-03	Chatham	ON-Jr.B	38	12	11	23	42	....	....	....	....	....	....	....	....	....	....	....	....	....	....	....	....	....	....
2003-04	Chatham	ON-Jr.B	46	39	30	69	64	....	....	....	....	....	....	....	....	....	17	17	9	26	25	....	....	....	....
2004-05	Miami U.	CCHA	38	8	7	15	79	....	....	....	....	....	....	....	....	....	....	....	....	....	....	....	....	....	....
2005-06	Miami U.	CCHA	39	22	13	35	72	....	....	....	....	....	....	....	....	....	....	....	....	....	....	....	....	....	....
2006-07	Miami U.	CCHA	42	29	19	48	88	....	....	....	....	....	....	....	....	....	....	....	....	....	....	....	....	....	....
2007-08	Miami U.	CCHA	42	31	18	49	83	....	....	....	....	....	....	....	....	....	....	....	....	....	....	....	....	....	....
	Houston Aeros	AHL	4	0	0	0	2	....	....	....	....	....	....	....	....	....	4	1	1	2	2	....	....	....	....
2008-09	**Nashville**	**NHL**	**46**	**7**	**10**	**17**	**22**	**2**	**0**	**1**	**63**	**11.1**	**1**	**10**	**10.0**	**11:26**									
	Milwaukee	AHL	25	13	9	22	30	....	....	....	....	....	....	....	....	....	11	4	3	7	10	....	....	....	....
2009-10	**Nashville**	**NHL**	**41**	**7**	**4**	**11**	**18**	**2**	**0**	**0**	**53**	**13.2**	**3**	**1**	**0.0**	**10:43**									
	Milwaukee	AHL	15	4	1	5	15	....	....	....	....	....	....	....	....	....	....	....	....	....	....	....	....	....	....
	Edmonton	**NHL**	**8**	**1**	**0**	**1**	**8**	**0**	**0**	**0**	**9**	**11.1**	**–3**	**0**	**0.0**	**10:21**									
2010-11	**Edmonton**	**NHL**	**81**	**18**	**7**	**25**	**34**	**2**	**1**	**2**	**126**	**14.3**	**–5**	**29**	**34.5**	**13:50**									
	NHL Totals		**176**	**33**	**21**	**54**	**82**	**6**	**1**	**3**	**251**	**13.1**		**40**	**27.5**	**12:19**									

CCHA Second All-Star Team (2006, 2007) • CCHA First All-Star Team (2008) • NCAA West First All-American Team (2008)
Traded to **Nashville** by **Minnesota** with Minnesota's 2nd round choice (Charles-Olivier Roussel) in 2009 Entry Draft for Marek Zidlicky, July 1, 2008. Claimed on waivers by **Edmonton** from **Nashville**, March 3, 2010.

JOSEFSON, Jacob
(JOH-sehf-suhn, YA-kuhb)   N.J.

Center. Shoots left. 6'1", 190 lbs.   Born, Stockholm, Sweden, March 2, 1991. New Jersey's 1st choice, 20th overall, in 2009 Entry Draft.

Season	Club	League	GP	G	A	Pts	PIM	PP	SH	GW	S	%	+/-	TF	F%	Min	GP	G	A	Pts	PIM	PP	SH	GW	Min
2005-06	Djurgarden U18	Swe-U18	5	1	1	2	0	....	....	....	....	....	....	....	....	....	....	....	....	....	....	....	....	....	....
2006-07	Djurgarden U18	Swe-U18	25	14	17	31	22	....	....	....	....	....	....	....	....	....	3	0	0	0	0	....	....	....	....
2007-08	Djurgarden U18	Swe-U18	4	1	2	3	12	....	....	....	....	....	....	....	....	....	6	0	6	6	4	....	....	....	....
	Djurgarden Jr.	Swe-Jr.	34	14	17	31	22	....	....	....	....	....	....	....	....	....	7	2	3	5	8	....	....	....	....
	Djurgarden	Sweden	1	0	0	0	0	....	....	....	....	....	....	....	....	....	....	....	....	....	....	....	....	....	....
2008-09	Djurgarden Jr.	Swe-Jr.	5	1	2	3	8	....	....	....	....	....	....	....	....	....	6	1	3	4	4	....	....	....	....
	Djurgarden	Sweden	50	5	11	16	14	....	....	....	....	....	....	....	....	....	....	....	....	....	....	....	....	....	....
	Djurgarden U18	Swe-U18						....	....	....	....	....	....	....	....	....	1	0	0	0	0	....	....	....	....
2009-10	Djurgarden	Sweden	43	8	12	20	20	....	....	....	....	....	....	....	....	....	14	3	2	5	4	....	....	....	....
2010-11	**New Jersey**	**NHL**	**28**	**3**	**7**	**10**	**6**	**0**	**0**	**1**	**31**	**9.7**	**5**	**202**	**47.0**	**13:14**									
	Albany Devils	AHL	18	3	9	12	4	....	....	....	....	....	....	....	....	....	....	....	....	....	....	....	....	....	....
	NHL Totals		**28**	**3**	**7**	**10**	**6**	**0**	**0**	**1**	**31**	**9.7**		**202**	**47.0**	**13:14**									

JOSLIN, Derek
(JAWS-lihn, DAIR-ihk)   CAR

Defense. Shoots left. 6'1", 210 lbs.   Born, Richmond Hill, Ont., March 17, 1987. San Jose's 5th choice, 149th overall, in 2005 Entry Draft.

Season	Club	League	GP	G	A	Pts	PIM	PP	SH	GW	S	%	+/-	TF	F%	Min	GP	G	A	Pts	PIM	PP	SH	GW	Min
2002-03	Vaughan Kings	GTHL	60	9	18	27	72	....	....	....	....	....	....	....	....	....	....	....	....	....	....	....	....	....	....
2003-04	Aurora Tigers	OPJHL	36	4	12	16		....	....	....	....	....	....	....	....	....	....	....	....	....	....	....	....	....	....
	Ottawa 67's	OHL	7	0	0	0	4	....	....	....	....	....	....	....	....	....	....	....	....	....	....	....	....	....	....
2004-05	Ottawa 67's	OHL	68	6	24	30	44	....	....	....	....	....	....	....	....	....	21	0	3	3	24	....	....	....	....
2005-06	Ottawa 67's	OHL	68	11	37	48	40	....	....	....	....	....	....	....	....	....	6	1	5	6	10	....	....	....	....
	Cleveland Barons	AHL	2	0	0	0	0	....	....	....	....	....	....	....	....	....	....	....	....	....	....	....	....	....	....
2006-07	Ottawa 67's	OHL	68	11	38	49	66	....	....	....	....	....	....	....	....	....	5	1	4	5	4	....	....	....	....
	Worcester Sharks	AHL	3	0	0	0	0	....	....	....	....	....	....	....	....	....	4	0	0	0	2	....	....	....	....
2007-08	Worcester Sharks	AHL	80	10	24	34	44	....	....	....	....	....	....	....	....	....	....	....	....	....	....	....	....	....	....
2008-09	**San Jose**	**NHL**	**12**	**0**	**0**	**0**	**6**	**0**	**0**	**0**	**9**	**0.0**	**–3**	**0**	**0.0**	**11:22**									
	Worcester Sharks	AHL	63	11	19	30	40	....	....	....	....	....	....	....	....	....	12	0	2	2	8	....	....	....	....
2009-10	**San Jose**	**NHL**	**24**	**0**	**3**	**3**	**12**	**0**	**0**	**0**	**19**	**0.0**	**1**	**0**	**0.0**	**13:53**									
	Worcester Sharks	AHL	55	5	27	32	29	....	....	....	....	....	....	....	....	....	11	4	1	5	4	....	....	....	....
2010-11	**San Jose**	**NHL**	**17**	**1**	**3**	**4**	**8**	**0**	**0**	**0**	**11**	**9.1**	**–2**	**0**	**0.0**	**12:28**									
	Carolina	**NHL**	**17**	**1**	**4**	**5**	**2**	**1**	**0**	**1**	**23**	**4.3**	**7**	**0**	**0.0**	**18:04**									
	NHL Totals		**70**	**2**	**10**	**12**	**28**	**1**	**0**	**1**	**62**	**3.2**		**0**	**0.0**	**14:07**									

Traded to **Carolina** by **San Jose** for future considerations, February 18, 2011. • Missed majority of 2010-11 due to recurring upper body injury and as a healthy reserve.

JOVANOVSKI, Ed
(joh-van-OHV-skee, EHD) **FLA**

Defense. Shoots left. 6'3", 221 lbs. Born, Windsor, Ont., June 26, 1976. Florida's 1st choice, 1st overall, in 1994 Entry Draft.

			Regular Season														Playoffs								
Season	Club	League	GP	G	A	Pts	PIM	PP	SH	GW	S	%	+/-	TF	F%	Min	GP	G	A	Pts	PIM	PP	SH	GW	Min
1991-92	Windsor	Minor-ON	50	25	40	65	88	....	....	....	....	....	....	....	....	....	....	....	....	....	....	....	....	....	....
1992-93	Windsor Bulldogs	ON-Jr.B	48	7	46	53	88	....	....	....	....	....	....	....	....	....	....	....	....	....	....	....	....	....	....
1993-94	Windsor Spitfires	OHL	62	15	36	51	221	....	....	....	....	....	....	....	....	....	4	0	0	0	15	....	....	....	....
1994-95	Windsor Spitfires	OHL	50	23	42	65	198	....	....	....	....	....	....	....	....	....	9	2	7	9	39	....	....	....	....
1995-96	**Florida**	**NHL**	**70**	**10**	**11**	**21**	**137**	**2**	**0**	**2**	**116**	**8.6**	**-3**	....	....	....	**22**	**1**	**8**	**9**	**52**	**0**	**0**	**0**	....
1996-97	**Florida**	**NHL**	**61**	**7**	**16**	**23**	**172**	**3**	**0**	**1**	**80**	**8.8**	**-1**	....	....	....	**5**	**0**	**0**	**0**	**4**	**0**	**0**	**0**	....
1997-98	**Florida**	**NHL**	**81**	**9**	**14**	**23**	**158**	**2**	**1**	**3**	**142**	**6.3**	**-12**	....	....	....	....	....	....	....	....	....	....	....	....
1998-99	**Florida**	**NHL**	**41**	**3**	**13**	**16**	**82**	**1**	**0**	**1**	**68**	**4.4**	**-4**	**0**	**0.0**	**22:35**	....	....	....	....	....	....	....	....	....
	Vancouver	**NHL**	**31**	**2**	**9**	**11**	**44**	**0**	**0**	**0**	**41**	**4.9**	**-5**	**0**	**0.0**	**21:16**	....	....	....	....	....	....	....	....	....
99-2000	**Vancouver**	**NHL**	**75**	**5**	**21**	**26**	**54**	**1**	**0**	**1**	**109**	**4.6**	**-3**	**0**	**0.0**	**24:03**	....	....	....	....	....	....	....	....	....
2000-01	**Vancouver**	**NHL**	**79**	**12**	**35**	**47**	**102**	**4**	**0**	**2**	**193**	**6.2**	**-1**	**0**	**0.0**	**24:57**	**4**	**1**	**1**	**2**	**0**	**0**	**0**	**0**	**25:54**
2001-02	**Vancouver**	**NHL**	**82**	**17**	**31**	**48**	**101**	**7**	**1**	**3**	**202**	**8.4**	**-7**	**0**	**0.0**	**25:11**	**6**	**1**	**4**	**5**	**8**	**1**	**0**	**0**	**25:48**
	Canada	Olympics	6	0	3	3	4	....	....	....	....	....	....	....	....	....	....	....	....	....	....	....	....	....	....
2002-03	**Vancouver**	**NHL**	**67**	**6**	**40**	**46**	**113**	**2**	**0**	**1**	**145**	**4.1**	**19**	**0**	**0.0**	**24:15**	**14**	**7**	**1**	**8**	**22**	**4**	**1**	**2**	**23:40**
2003-04	**Vancouver**	**NHL**	**56**	**7**	**16**	**23**	**64**	**2**	**0**	**1**	**143**	**4.9**	**2**	**0**	**0.0**	**23:11**	**7**	**0**	**4**	**4**	**6**	**0**	**0**	**0**	**26:36**
2004-05			DID NOT PLAY																						
2005-06	**Vancouver**	**NHL**	**44**	**8**	**25**	**33**	**58**	**6**	**0**	**2**	**87**	**9.2**	**-8**	**0**	**0.0**	**24:26**	....	....	....	....	....	....	....	....	....
	Canada	Olympics	DID NOT PLAY – INJURED																						
2006-07	**Phoenix**	**NHL**	**54**	**11**	**18**	**29**	**63**	**6**	**0**	**1**	**135**	**8.1**	**-6**	**0**	**0.0**	**23:09**	....	....	....	....	....	....	....	....	....
2007-08	**Phoenix**	**NHL**	**80**	**12**	**39**	**51**	**73**	**8**	**0**	**2**	**240**	**5.0**	**-13**	**0**	**0.0**	**22:33**	....	....	....	....	....	....	....	....	....
2008-09	**Phoenix**	**NHL**	**82**	**9**	**27**	**36**	**106**	**6**	**0**	**3**	**194**	**4.6**	**-15**	**1**	**0.0**	**22:10**	....	....	....	....	....	....	....	....	....
2009-10	**Phoenix**	**NHL**	**66**	**10**	**24**	**34**	**55**	**5**	**0**	**2**	**117**	**8.5**	**-12**	**1**	**0.0**	**21:38**	**7**	**1**	**0**	**1**	**4**	**0**	**0**	**0**	**21:13**
2010-11	**Phoenix**	**NHL**	**50**	**5**	**9**	**14**	**39**	**1**	**0**	**1**	**73**	**6.8**	**4**	**0**	**0.0**	**20:29**	**4**	**0**	**1**	**1**	**2**	**0**	**0**	**0**	**15:24**
	NHL Totals		**1019**	**133**	**348**	**481**	**1421**	**56**	**2**	**26**	**2085**	**6.4**		**2**	**0.0**	**23:14**	**69**	**11**	**19**	**30**	**98**	**5**	**1**	**2**	**23:29**

OHL All-Rookie Team (1994) • OHL Second All-Star Team (1994) • OHL First All-Star Team (1995) • NHL All-Rookie Team (1996)

Played in NHL All-Star Game (2001, 2002, 2003, 2007, 2008)

Traded to **Vancouver** by **Florida** with Dave Gagner, Mike Brown, Kevin Weekes and Florida's 1st round choice (Nathan Smith) in 2000 Entry Draft for Pavel Bure, Bret Hedican, Brad Ference and Vancouver's 3rd round choice (Robert Fried) in 2000 Entry Draft, January 17, 1999. Signed as a free agent by **Phoenix**, July 1, 2006. Signed as a free agent by **Florida**, July 1, 2011.

JUNLAND, Jonas
(YUHN-land, YOH-nuhs) **ST.L.**

Defense. Shoots left. 6'2", 200 lbs. Born, Linkoping, Sweden, November 15, 1987. St. Louis' 4th choice, 64th overall, in 2006 Entry Draft.

			Regular Season														Playoffs								
Season	Club	League	GP	G	A	Pts	PIM	PP	SH	GW	S	%	+/-	TF	F%	Min	GP	G	A	Pts	PIM	PP	SH	GW	Min
2002-03	Linkoping U18	Swe-U18	7	0	0	0	6	....	....	....	....	....	....	....	....	....	....	....	....	....	....	....	....	....	....
2003-04	Linkoping U18	Swe-U18	4	0	0	0	4	....	....	....	....	....	....	....	....	....	....	....	....	....	....	....	....	....	....
	Linkopings HC Jr.	Swe-Jr.	19	1	0	1	12	....	....	....	....	....	....	....	....	....	....	....	....	....	....	....	....	....	....
2004-05	Linkoping U18	Swe-U18	11	6	5	11	35	....	....	....	....	....	....	....	....	....	....	....	....	....	....	....	....	....	....
	Linkopings HC Jr.	Swe-Jr.	32	3	5	8	96	....	....	....	....	....	....	....	....	....	....	....	....	....	....	....	....	....	....
2005-06	Linkopings HC Jr.	Swe-Jr.	32	17	23	40	44	....	....	....	....	....	....	....	....	....	....	....	....	....	....	....	....	....	....
	Linkoping U18	Swe-U18	1	5	0	5	2	....	....	....	....	....	....	....	....	....	....	....	....	....	....	....	....	....	....
	Linkopings HC	Sweden	4	0	0	0	0	....	....	....	....	....	....	....	....	....	....	....	....	....	....	....	....	....	....
2006-07	Linkopings HC Jr.	Swe-Jr.	9	6	7	13	26	....	....	....	....	....	....	....	....	....	....	....	....	....	....	....	....	....	....
	IK Oskarshamn	Sweden-2	4	0	3	3	4	....	....	....	....	....	....	....	....	....	....	....	....	....	....	....	....	....	....
	Linkopings HC	Sweden	41	1	4	5	22	....	....	....	....	....	....	....	....	....	15	0	5	5	20	....	....	....	....
2007-08	Linkopings HC	Sweden	52	3	17	20	42	....	....	....	....	....	....	....	....	....	16	4	3	7	18	....	....	....	....
2008-09	**St. Louis**	**NHL**	**1**	**0**	**0**	**0**	**2**	**0**	**0**	**0**	**0**	**0.0**	**0**	**0**	**0.0**	**12:28**	....	....	....	....	....	....	....	....	....
	Peoria Rivermen	AHL	70	13	18	31	52	....	....	....	....	....	....	....	....	....	5	0	1	1	6	....	....	....	....
2009-10	**St. Louis**	**NHL**	**3**	**0**	**2**	**2**	**0**	**0**	**0**	**0**	**7**	**0.0**	**-3**	**0**	**0.0**	**17:11**	....	....	....	....	....	....	....	....	....
	Peoria Rivermen	AHL	74	14	30	44	49	....	....	....	....	....	....	....	....	....	....	....	....	....	....	....	....	....	....
2010-11	Farjestad	Sweden	41	5	17	22	18	....	....	....	....	....	....	....	....	....	14	3	3	6	12	....	....	....	....
	NHL Totals		**4**	**0**	**2**	**2**	**2**	**0**	**0**	**0**	**7**	**0.0**		**0**	**0.0**	**16:00**	....	....	....	....	....	....	....	....	....

Signed as a free agent by **Farjestad** (Sweden), May 1, 2010

JURCINA, Milan
(YEWR-chee-nah, MEE-lan) **NYI**

Defense. Shoots right. 6'4", 240 lbs. Born, Liptovsky Mikulas, Czech., June 7, 1983. Boston's 7th choice, 241st overall, in 2001 Entry Draft.

			Regular Season														Playoffs								
Season	Club	League	GP	G	A	Pts	PIM	PP	SH	GW	S	%	+/-	TF	F%	Min	GP	G	A	Pts	PIM	PP	SH	GW	Min
99-2000	L. Mikulas Jr.	Slovak-Jr.	STATISTICS NOT AVAILABLE																						
2000-01	Halifax	QMJHL	68	0	5	5	56	....	....	....	....	....	....	....	....	....	6	0	2	2	12	....	....	....	....
2001-02	Halifax	QMJHL	61	4	16	20	58	....	....	....	....	....	....	....	....	....	13	5	3	8	10	....	....	....	....
2002-03	Halifax	QMJHL	51	15	13	28	102	....	....	....	....	....	....	....	....	....	25	6	6	12	40	....	....	....	....
2003-04	Providence Bruins	AHL	73	5	12	17	52	....	....	....	....	....	....	....	....	....	2	0	1	1	2	....	....	....	....
2004-05	Providence Bruins	AHL	79	6	17	23	92	....	....	....	....	....	....	....	....	....	17	1	3	4	30	....	....	....	....
2005-06	**Boston**	**NHL**	**51**	**6**	**5**	**11**	**54**	**2**	**0**	**0**	**64**	**9.4**	**3**	**1**	**0.0**	**16:28**	....	....	....	....	....	....	....	....	....
	Providence Bruins	AHL	7	0	3	3	8	....	....	....	....	....	....	....	....	....	....	....	....	....	....	....	....	....	....
	Slovakia	Olympics	6	0	1	1	8	....	....	....	....	....	....	....	....	....	....	....	....	....	....	....	....	....	....
2006-07	**Boston**	**NHL**	**40**	**2**	**1**	**3**	**20**	**0**	**0**	**1**	**29**	**6.9**	**-5**	**0**	**0.0**	**10:42**	....	....	....	....	....	....	....	....	....
	Washington	**NHL**	**30**	**2**	**7**	**9**	**24**	**0**	**0**	**0**	**42**	**4.8**	**5**	**0**	**0.0**	**23:09**	....	....	....	....	....	....	....	....	....
2007-08	**Washington**	**NHL**	**75**	**1**	**8**	**9**	**30**	**1**	**0**	**0**	**58**	**1.7**	**4**	**0**	**0.0**	**16:38**	**7**	**0**	**0**	**0**	**6**	**0**	**0**	**0**	**16:26**
2008-09	**Washington**	**NHL**	**79**	**3**	**11**	**14**	**68**	**0**	**0**	**1**	**95**	**3.2**	**1**	**0**	**0.0**	**16:09**	**14**	**2**	**0**	**2**	**12**	**0**	**1**	**0**	**16:46**
2009-10	**Washington**	**NHL**	**27**	**0**	**4**	**4**	**14**	**0**	**0**	**0**	**32**	**0.0**	**0**	**0**	**0.0**	**17:26**	....	....	....	....	....	....	....	....	....
	Columbus	**NHL**	**17**	**1**	**2**	**3**	**10**	**0**	**0**	**1**	**17**	**5.9**	**2**	**0**	**0.0**	**18:02**	....	....	....	....	....	....	....	....	....
	Slovakia	Olympics	7	0	0	0	2	....	....	....	....	....	....	....	....	....	....	....	....	....	....	....	....	....	....
2010-11	**NY Islanders**	**NHL**	**46**	**4**	**13**	**17**	**30**	**1**	**1**	**0**	**76**	**5.3**	**-4**	**1**	**0.0**	**18:04**	....	....	....	....	....	....	....	....	....
	NHL Totals		**365**	**19**	**51**	**70**	**250**	**4**	**1**	**3**	**413**	**4.6**		**2**	**0.0**	**16:42**	**21**	**2**	**0**	**2**	**18**	**0**	**1**	**0**	**16:40**

Traded to **Washington** by **Boston** for Washington's 4th round choice (later traded to Calgary - Calgary selected T. J. Brodie) in 2008 Entry Draft, February 1, 2007. Traded to **Columbus** by **Washington** with Chris Clark for Jason Chimera, December 28, 2009. Traded to **Washington** by **Columbus** for future considerations, March 3, 2010. Signed as a free agent by **NY Islanders**, July 2, 2010.

KABERLE, Tomas
(KA-buhr-lay, TAW-mas) **CAR**

Defense. Shoots left. 6'1", 214 lbs. Born, Rakovnik, Czech., March 2, 1978. Toronto's 13th choice, 204th overall, in 1996 Entry Draft.

			Regular Season														Playoffs								
Season	Club	League	GP	G	A	Pts	PIM	PP	SH	GW	S	%	+/-	TF	F%	Min	GP	G	A	Pts	PIM	PP	SH	GW	Min
1994-95	HC Kladno Jr.	CzRep-Jr.	37	7	10	17	....	....	....	....	....	....	....	....	....	....	....	....	....	....	....	....	....	....	....
	HC Kladno	CzRep	4	0	1	1	0	....	....	....	....	....	....	....	....	....	....	....	....	....	....	....	....	....	....
1995-96	Kladno Jr.	CzRep-Jr.	23	6	13	19	....	....	....	....	....	....	....	....	....	....	....	....	....	....	....	....	....	....	....
	HC Poldi Kladno	CzRep	23	0	1	1	2	....	....	....	....	....	....	....	....	....	2	0	0	0	0	....	....	....	....
1996-97	HC Poldi Kladno	CzRep	49	0	5	5	26	....	....	....	....	....	....	....	....	....	3	0	0	0	0	....	....	....	....
1997-98	Kladno	CzRep	47	4	19	23	12	....	....	....	....	....	....	....	....	....	....	....	....	....	....	....	....	....	....
	St. John's	AHL	2	0	0	0	0	....	....	....	....	....	....	....	....	....	....	....	....	....	....	....	....	....	....
1998-99	**Toronto**	**NHL**	**57**	**4**	**18**	**22**	**12**	**0**	**0**	**2**	**71**	**5.6**	**3**	**0**	**0.0**	**18:42**	**14**	**0**	**3**	**3**	**2**	**0**	**0**	**0**	**17:10**
99-2000	**Toronto**	**NHL**	**82**	**7**	**33**	**40**	**24**	**2**	**0**	**0**	**82**	**8.5**	**3**	**0**	**0.0**	**22:55**	**12**	**1**	**4**	**5**	**0**	**0**	**0**	**1**	**23:01**
2000-01	**Toronto**	**NHL**	**82**	**6**	**39**	**45**	**24**	**0**	**0**	**1**	**96**	**6.3**	**10**	**2**	**0.0**	**22:41**	**11**	**1**	**3**	**4**	**0**	**0**	**0**	**1**	**21:33**
2001-02	Kladno	CzRep	9	1	7	8	4	....	....	....	....	....	....	....	....	....	....	....	....	....	....	....	....	....	....
	Toronto	**NHL**	**69**	**10**	**29**	**39**	**2**	**5**	**0**	**3**	**85**	**11.8**	**5**	**2**	**100.0**	**25:00**	**20**	**2**	**8**	**10**	**16**	**0**	**0**	**0**	**28:40**
	Czech Republic	Olympics	4	0	1	1	2	....	....	....	....	....	....	....	....	....	....	....	....	....	....	....	....	....	....
2002-03	**Toronto**	**NHL**	**82**	**11**	**36**	**47**	**30**	**4**	**1**	**2**	**119**	**9.2**	**20**	**3**	**66.7**	**24:50**	**7**	**2**	**1**	**3**	**0**	**1**	**0**	**1**	**30:04**
2003-04	**Toronto**	**NHL**	**71**	**3**	**28**	**31**	**18**	**0**	**0**	**1**	**88**	**3.4**	**16**	**2**	**0.0**	**23:12**	**13**	**0**	**3**	**3**	**6**	**0**	**0**	**0**	**20:16**
2004-05	HC Rabat Kladno	CzRep	49	8	31	39	38	....	....	....	....	....	....	....	....	....	7	1	0	1	0	....	....	....	....
2005-06	**Toronto**	**NHL**	**82**	**9**	**58**	**67**	**46**	**6**	**0**	**2**	**163**	**5.5**	**-1**	**0**	**0.0**	**28:10**	....	....	....	....	....	....	....	....	....
	Czech Republic	Olympics	8	2	2	4	2	....	....	....	....	....	....	....	....	....	....	....	....	....	....	....	....	....	....
2006-07	**Toronto**	**NHL**	**74**	**11**	**47**	**58**	**20**	**2**	**0**	**1**	**128**	**8.6**	**3**	**0**	**0.0**	**25:52**	....	....	....	....	....	....	....	....	....
2007-08	**Toronto**	**NHL**	**82**	**8**	**45**	**53**	**22**	**6**	**0**	**1**	**155**	**5.2**	**-8**	**2**	**50.0**	**24:52**	....	....	....	....	....	....	....	....	....
2008-09	**Toronto**	**NHL**	**57**	**4**	**27**	**31**	**8**	**3**	**0**	**1**	**93**	**4.3**	**-8**	**0**	**0.0**	**23:28**	....	....	....	....	....	....	....	....	....
2009-10	**Toronto**	**NHL**	**82**	**7**	**42**	**49**	**24**	**3**	**0**	**1**	**158**	**4.4**	**-16**	**0**	**0.0**	**22:21**	....	....	....	....	....	....	....	....	....
	Czech Republic	Olympics	5	1	2	3	0	....	....	....	....	....	....	....	....	....	....	....	....	....	....	....	....	....	....

Season	Club	League	Regular Season GP	G	A	Pts	PIM	PP	SH	GW	S	%	+/-	TF	F%	Min	Playoffs GP	G	A	Pts	PIM	PP	SH	GW	Min
2010-11	**Toronto**	**NHL**	**58**	**3**	**35**	**38**	**16**	**0**	**0**	**1**	**99**	**3.0**	**–2**	**0**	**0.0**	**22:28**	....	....	....	....	....	....	....	....	....
	♦ Boston	**NHL**	**24**	**1**	**8**	**9**	**2**	**0**	**0**	**0**	**31**	**3.2**	**6**	**0**	**0.0**	**21:15**	**25**	**0**	**11**	**11**	**4**	**0**	**0**	**0**	**16:01**
	NHL Totals		**902**	**84**	**445**	**529**	**248**	**31**	**1**	**16**	**1368**	**6.1**		**11**	**45.5**	**23:48**	**102**	**6**	**33**	**39**	**28**	**1**	**0**	**3**	**21:35**

Played in NHL All-Star Game (2002, 2007, 2008, 2009)

Signed as a restricted free agent by **Kladno** (CzRep) with **Toronto** retaining NHL rights, September 29, 2001. Signed as a free agent by **Kladno** (CzRep), September 17, 2004. Traded to **Boston** by **Toronto** for Joe Colborne, Boston's 1st round choice (later traded to Anaheim – Anaheim selected Rickard Rakell) in 2011 Entry Draft and Boston's 2nd round choice (later traded to Colorado) in 2012 Entry Draft, February 18, 2011. Signed as a free agent by **Carolina**, July 5, 2011.

KADRI, Nazem (KAH-dree, NA-zihm) TOR

Center. Shoots left. 6', 188 lbs. Born, London, Ont., October 6, 1990. Toronto's 1st choice, 7th overall, in 2009 Entry Draft.

2005-06	Lon. Jr. Knights	Minor-ON	62	49	43	92	82	....	....	....	....	....	....	....	....	....	....	....	....	....	....	....	....	....	....
2006-07	Kitchener Rangers	OHL	62	7	15	22	30	....	....	....	....	....	....	....	....	....	9	0	2	2	4	....	....	....	....
2007-08	Kitchener Rangers	OHL	68	25	40	65	57	....	....	....	....	....	....	....	....	....	20	9	17	26	26	....	....	....	....
	Kitchener Rangers	M-Cup	....	....	....	....	....	....	....	....	....	....	....	....	....	....	5	1	3	4	0	....	....	....	....
2008-09	London Knights	OHL	56	25	53	78	31	....	....	....	....	....	....	....	....	....	14	9	12	21	22	....	....	....	....
2009-10	London Knights	OHL	56	35	58	93	105	....	....	....	....	....	....	....	....	....	12	9	18	27	26	....	....	....	....
	Toronto	**NHL**	**1**	**0**	**0**	**0**	**0**	**0**	**0**	**0**	**0**	**0.0**	**–1**	**13**	**15.4**	**17:26**	....	....	....	....	....	....	....	....	....
2010-11	**Toronto**	**NHL**	**29**	**3**	**9**	**12**	**8**	**0**	**0**	**0**	**51**	**5.9**	**–3**	**121**	**40.5**	**15:47**	....	....	....	....	....	....	....	....	....
	Toronto Marlies	AHL	44	17	24	41	62	....	....	....	....	....	....	....	....	....	....	....	....	....	....	....	....	....	....
	NHL Totals		**30**	**3**	**9**	**12**	**8**	**0**	**0**	**0**	**51**	**5.9**		**134**	**38.1**	**15:50**	....	....	....	....	....	....	....	....	....

OHL Second All-Star Team (2010)

KALETA, Patrick (ka-LEH-tuh, PAT-rihk) BUF

Right wing. Shoots right. 6'1", 206 lbs. Born, Buffalo, NY, June 8, 1986. Buffalo's 5th choice, 176th overall, in 2004 Entry Draft.

2002-03	Peterborough	OHL	67	7	9	16	67	....	....	....	....	....	....	....	....	....	7	0	0	0	6	....	....	....	....
2003-04	Peterborough	OHL	67	14	14	28	124	....	....	....	....	....	....	....	....	....	....	....	....	....	....	....	....	....	....
2004-05	Peterborough	OHL	62	24	28	52	146	....	....	....	....	....	....	....	....	....	14	3	3	6	30	....	....	....	....
2005-06	Peterborough	OHL	68	16	35	51	121	....	....	....	....	....	....	....	....	....	19	8	10	18	43	....	....	....	....
2006-07	**Buffalo**	**NHL**	**7**	**0**	**2**	**2**	**21**	**0**	**0**	**0**	**6**	**0.0**	**3**	**0**	**0.0**	**6:49**	....	....	....	....	....	....	....	....	....
	Rochester	AHL	58	5	10	15	133	....	....	....	....	....	....	....	....	....	5	0	0	0	12	....	....	....	....
2007-08	**Buffalo**	**NHL**	**40**	**3**	**2**	**5**	**41**	**0**	**0**	**0**	**26**	**11.5**	**1**	**6**	**16.7**	**6:19**	....	....	....	....	....	....	....	....	....
	Rochester	AHL	29	1	3	4	109	....	....	....	....	....	....	....	....	....	....	....	....	....	....	....	....	....	....
2008-09	**Buffalo**	**NHL**	**51**	**4**	**5**	**9**	**89**	**0**	**0**	**0**	**35**	**11.4**	**1**	**5**	**20.0**	**8:55**	....	....	....	....	....	....	....	....	....
2009-10	**Buffalo**	**NHL**	**55**	**10**	**5**	**15**	**89**	**0**	**2**	**4**	**64**	**15.6**	**2**	**2**	**0.0**	**10:09**	**6**	**1**	**1**	**2**	**22**	**0**	**0**	**0**	**10:04**
2010-11	**Buffalo**	**NHL**	**51**	**4**	**5**	**9**	**78**	**0**	**1**	**0**	**65**	**6.2**	**–4**	**12**	**41.7**	**10:11**	**6**	**1**	**2**	**3**	**6**	**0**	**0**	**1**	**10:58**
	NHL Totals		**204**	**21**	**19**	**40**	**318**	**0**	**3**	**4**	**196**	**10.7**		**25**	**28.0**	**8:59**	**12**	**2**	**3**	**5**	**28**	**0**	**0**	**1**	**10:31**

KALINSKI, Jon (kuh-LIHN-skee, JAWN) PHI

Left wing. Shoots left. 6'1", 175 lbs. Born, Bonnyville , Alta., May 25, 1987. Philadelphia's 5th choice, 152nd overall, in 2007 Entry Draft.

2003-04	Bonnyville	AJHL	52	13	13	26	68	....	....	....	....	....	....	....	....	....	5	0	0	0	8	....	....	....	....
2004-05	Bonnyville	AJHL	58	16	25	41	195	....	....	....	....	....	....	....	....	....	4	2	0	2	6	....	....	....	....
2005-06	Minnesota State	WCHA	30	4	7	11	73	....	....	....	....	....	....	....	....	....	....	....	....	....	....	....	....	....	....
2006-07	Minnesota State	WCHA	37	17	10	27	74	....	....	....	....	....	....	....	....	....	....	....	....	....	....	....	....	....	....
2007-08	Minnesota State	WCHA	39	8	10	18	56	....	....	....	....	....	....	....	....	....	....	....	....	....	....	....	....	....	....
	Philadelphia	AHL	5	0	3	3	4	....	....	....	....	....	....	....	....	....	10	1	2	3	14	....	....	....	....
2008-09	**Philadelphia**	**NHL**	**12**	**1**	**2**	**3**	**0**	**0**	**0**	**1**	**7**	**14.3**	**–2**	**46**	**45.7**	**7:37**	....	....	....	....	....	....	....	....	....
	Philadelphia	AHL	46	10	7	17	49	....	....	....	....	....	....	....	....	....	4	1	2	3	4	....	....	....	....
2009-10	**Philadelphia**	**NHL**	**10**	**0**	**2**	**2**	**0**	**0**	**0**	**0**	**9**	**0.0**	**–2**	**30**	**36.7**	**6:57**	....	....	....	....	....	....	....	....	....
	Adirondack	AHL	69	10	18	28	29	....	....	....	....	....	....	....	....	....	....	....	....	....	....	....	....	....	....
2010-11	Adirondack	AHL	73	6	17	23	86	....	....	....	....	....	....	....	....	....	....	....	....	....	....	....	....	....	....
	NHL Totals		**22**	**1**	**4**	**5**	**0**	**0**	**0**	**1**	**16**	**6.3**		**76**	**42.1**	**7:19**	....	....	....	....	....	....	....	....	....

KALUS, Petr (KAY-lihs, PEE-tuhr)

Left wing. Shoots left. 6'1", 201 lbs. Born, Ostrava, Czech., June 29, 1987. Boston's 2nd choice, 39th overall, in 2005 Entry Draft.

2002-03	HC Ostrava U17	CzR-U17	18	3	19	22	14	....	....	....	....	....	....	....	....	....	....	....	....	....	....	....	....	....	....
	HC Vitkovice U17	CzR-U17	10	3	1	4	37	....	....	....	....	....	....	....	....	....	....	....	....	....	....	....	....	....	....
	HC Vitkovice Jr.	CzRep-Jr.	11	0	0	0	4	....	....	....	....	....	....	....	....	....	....	....	....	....	....	....	....	....	....
2003-04	HC Vitkovice U17	CzR-U17	9	7	5	12	60	....	....	....	....	....	....	....	....	....	7	3	5	8	2	....	....	....	....
	HC Vitkovice Jr.	CzRep-Jr.	41	8	8	16	67	....	....	....	....	....	....	....	....	....	....	....	....	....	....	....	....	....	....
2004-05	HC Vitkovice Jr.	CzRep-Jr.	39	20	11	31	161	....	....	....	....	....	....	....	....	....	2	2	0	2	25	....	....	....	....
	Vitkovice	CzRep	1	0	0	0	0	....	....	....	....	....	....	....	....	....	....	....	....	....	....	....	....	....	....
2005-06	Regina Pats	WHL	60	36	22	58	87	....	....	....	....	....	....	....	....	....	6	4	1	5	6	....	....	....	....
2006-07	**Boston**	**NHL**	**9**	**4**	**1**	**5**	**6**	**1**	**0**	**0**	**8**	**50.0**	**0**	**0**	**0.0**	**11:16**	....	....	....	....	....	....	....	....	....
	Providence Bruins	AHL	43	13	17	30	110	....	....	....	....	....	....	....	....	....	9	1	0	1	12	....	....	....	....
2007-08	Houston Aeros	AHL	58	8	10	18	57	....	....	....	....	....	....	....	....	....	....	....	....	....	....	....	....	....	....
2008-09	MVD	Rus-KHL	17	0	2	2	106	....	....	....	....	....	....	....	....	....	....	....	....	....	....	....	....	....	....
	Houston Aeros	AHL	2	0	0	0	0	....	....	....	....	....	....	....	....	....	....	....	....	....	....	....	....	....	....
2009-10	**Minnesota**	**NHL**	**2**	**0**	**0**	**0**	**0**	**0**	**0**	**0**	**0**	**0.0**	**0**	**1**	**0.0**	**7:44**	....	....	....	....	....	....	....	....	....
	Houston Aeros	AHL	66	12	11	23	77	....	....	....	....	....	....	....	....	....	....	....	....	....	....	....	....	....	....
2010-11	Houston Aeros	AHL	34	6	2	8	68	....	....	....	....	....	....	....	....	....	....	....	....	....	....	....	....	....	....
	Springfield	AHL	10	1	0	1	4	....	....	....	....	....	....	....	....	....	....	....	....	....	....	....	....	....	....
	NHL Totals		**11**	**4**	**1**	**5**	**6**	**1**	**0**	**0**	**8**	**50.0**		**1**	**0.0**	**10:38**	....	....	....	....	....	....	....	....	....

Traded to **Minnesota** by **Boston** with Boston's 4th round choice (Alexander Fallstrom) in 2009 Entry Draft for Manny Fernandez, July 1, 2007. Traded to **Columbus** by **Minnesota** for future considerations, March 1, 2011.

KAMPFER, Steven (KAMP-fuhr, STEE-vehn) BOS

Defense. Shoots right. 5'11", 197 lbs. Born, Ann Arbor, MI, September 24, 1988. Anaheim's 5th choice, 93rd overall, in 2007 Entry Draft.

2004-05	Sioux City	USHL	47	6	13	19	91	....	....	....	....	....	....	....	....	....	13	2	5	7	12	....	....	....	....
2005-06	Sioux City	USHL	56	6	10	16	99	....	....	....	....	....	....	....	....	....	....	....	....	....	....	....	....	....	....
2006-07	U. of Michigan	CCHA	35	1	3	4	24	....	....	....	....	....	....	....	....	....	....	....	....	....	....	....	....	....	....
2007-08	U. of Michigan	CCHA	42	2	15	17	36	....	....	....	....	....	....	....	....	....	....	....	....	....	....	....	....	....	....
2008-09	U. of Michigan	CCHA	25	1	12	13	24	....	....	....	....	....	....	....	....	....	....	....	....	....	....	....	....	....	....
2009-10	U. of Michigan	CCHA	45	3	23	26	50	....	....	....	....	....	....	....	....	....	....	....	....	....	....	....	....	....	....
	Providence Bruins	AHL	6	1	2	3	4	....	....	....	....	....	....	....	....	....	....	....	....	....	....	....	....	....	....
2010-11	**Boston**	**NHL**	**38**	**5**	**5**	**10**	**12**	**0**	**0**	**1**	**57**	**8.8**	**9**	**0**	**0.0**	**17:44**	....	....	....	....	....	....	....	....	....
	Providence Bruins	AHL	22	3	13	16	12	....	....	....	....	....	....	....	....	....	....	....	....	....	....	....	....	....	....
	NHL Totals		**38**	**5**	**5**	**10**	**12**	**0**	**0**	**1**	**57**	**8.8**		**0**	**0.0**	**17:44**	....	....	....	....	....	....	....	....	....

Traded to **Boston** by **Anaheim** for Boston's 4th round choice (later traded to Carolina - Carolina selected Justin Shugg) in 2010 Entry Draft, March 2, 2010.

KANA, Tomas (KA-nah, TAW-mahsh)

Center. Shoots right. 6', 204 lbs. Born, Opava, Czech., November 29, 1987. St. Louis' 3rd choice, 31st overall, in 2006 Entry Draft.

2002-03	HC Vitkovice U17	CzR-U17	44	20	14	34	72	....	....	....	....	....	....	....	....	....	2	2	0	2	4	....	....	....	....
	HC Vitkovice Jr.	CzRep-Jr.	3	2	0	2	4	....	....	....	....	....	....	....	....	....	....	....	....	....	....	....	....	....	....
2003-04	HC Vitkovice U17	CzR-U17	8	2	9	11	33	....	....	....	....	....	....	....	....	....	7	4	5	9	18	....	....	....	....
	HC Vitkovice Jr.	CzRep-Jr.	50	12	7	19	78	....	....	....	....	....	....	....	....	....	....	....	....	....	....	....	....	....	....
2004-05	HC Vitkovice Jr.	CzRep-Jr.	46	12	22	34	155	....	....	....	....	....	....	....	....	....	2	0	0	0	2	....	....	....	....
	Vitkovice	CzRep	1	0	0	0	0	....	....	....	....	....	....	....	....	....	....	....	....	....	....	....	....	....	....
2005-06	HC Vitkovice Jr.	CzRep-Jr.	5	4	3	7	16	....	....	....	....	....	....	....	....	....	....	....	....	....	....	....	....	....	....
	Vitkovice	CzRep	42	5	9	14	50	....	....	....	....	....	....	....	....	....	6	0	1	1	2	....	....	....	....
2006-07	Vitkovice	CzRep	44	9	7	16	54	....	....	....	....	....	....	....	....	....	....	....	....	....	....	....	....	....	....
	BK Mlada Boleslav	CzRep-2	6	2	1	3	16	....	....	....	....	....	....	....	....	....	6	1	0	1	16	....	....	....	....

			Regular Season														Playoffs								
Season	Club	League	GP	G	A	Pts	PIM	PP	SH	GW	S	%	+/-	TF	F%	Min	GP	G	A	Pts	PIM	PP	SH	GW	Min
2007-08	Alaska Aces	ECHL	12	2	0	2	4	....	....	....	....	....	....	....	....	....	....	....	....	....	....	....	....	....	....
	HC Sareza Ostrava	CzRep-2	8	3	0	3	6	....	....	....	....	....	....	....	....	....	....	....	....	....	....	....	....	....	....
	Vitkovice	CzRep	8	1	1	2	6	....	....	....	....	....	....	....	....	....	....	....	....	....	....	....	....	....	....
	Usti n. L.	CzRep	17	4	4	8	18	....	....	....	....	....	....	....	....	....	....	....	....	....	....	....	....	....	....
	Usti n. L.	CzRep-Q	....	....	....	....	....	....	....	....	....	....	....	....	....	....	3	0	0	0	2	....	....	....	....
2008-09	Peoria Rivermen	AHL	18	1	0	1	15	....	....	....	....	....	....	....	....	....	....	....	....	....	....	....	....	....	....
	Alaska Aces	ECHL	30	6	14	20	65	....	....	....	....	....	....	....	....	....	21	1	2	3	10	....	....	....	....
2009-10	Alaska Aces	ECHL	11	0	6	6	10	....	....	....	....	....	....	....	....	....	....	....	....	....	....	....	....	....	....
	Columbus	**NHL**	**6**	**0**	**2**	**2**	**2**	**0**	**0**	**0**	**4**	**0.0**	**2**	**0**	**0.0**	**8:41**	....	....	....	....	....	....	....	....	....
	Syracuse Crunch	AHL	50	15	13	28	47	....	....	....	....	....	....	....	....	....	....	....	....	....	....	....	....	....	....
2010-11	Springfield	AHL	31	2	4	6	43	....	....	....	....	....	....	....	....	....	....	....	....	....	....	....	....	....	....
	NHL Totals		**6**	**0**	**2**	**2**	**2**	**0**	**0**	**0**	**4**	**0.0**		**0**	**0.0**	**8:41**	....	....	....	....	....	....	....	....	....

Traded to **Columbus** by **St. Louis** with Brendan Bell for Pascal Pelletier, December 8, 2009. • Missed majority of 2010-11 due to broken hand.

KANE, Boyd

(KAYN, BOID)

Left wing. Shoots left. 6'2", 225 lbs. Born, Swift Current, Sask., April 18, 1978. NY Rangers' 4th choice, 114th overall, in 1998 Entry Draft.

1994-95	Regina Pats	WHL	25	6	5	11	6	....	....	....	....	....	....	....	....	....	4	0	0	0	0	....	....	....	....
1995-96	Regina Pats	WHL	72	21	42	63	155	....	....	....	....	....	....	....	....	....	11	5	7	12	12	....	....	....	....
1996-97	Regina Pats	WHL	66	25	50	75	119	....	....	....	....	....	....	....	....	....	5	1	1	2	15	....	....	....	....
1997-98	Regina Pats	WHL	68	48	45	93	133	....	....	....	....	....	....	....	....	....	9	5	7	12	29	....	....	....	....
1998-99	Hartford	AHL	56	3	5	8	23	....	....	....	....	....	....	....	....	....	....	....	....	....	....	....	....	....	....
	Charlotte	ECHL	12	5	6	11	14	....	....	....	....	....	....	....	....	....	....	....	....	....	....	....	....	....	....
99-2000	Hartford	AHL	8	0	0	0	9	....	....	....	....	....	....	....	....	....	....	....	....	....	....	....	....	....	....
	Charlotte	ECHL	47	10	19	29	110	....	....	....	....	....	....	....	....	....	....	....	....	....	....	....	....	....	....
	Binghamton	UHL	3	0	2	2	4	....	....	....	....	....	....	....	....	....	1	0	0	0	0	....	....	....	....
2000-01	Charlotte	ECHL	12	9	8	17	6	....	....	....	....	....	....	....	....	....	....	....	....	....	....	....	....	....	....
	Hartford	AHL	56	11	17	28	81	....	....	....	....	....	....	....	....	....	5	2	0	2	2	....	....	....	....
2001-02	Hartford	AHL	78	17	22	39	193	....	....	....	....	....	....	....	....	....	10	1	2	3	50	....	....	....	....
2002-03	Springfield	AHL	72	15	22	37	121	....	....	....	....	....	....	....	....	....	6	3	1	4	8	....	....	....	....
2003-04	**Philadelphia**	**NHL**	**7**	**0**	**0**	**0**	**7**	**0**	**0**	**0**	**6**	**0.0**	**–4**	**3**	**33.3**	**9:56**	....	....	....	....	....	....	....	....	....
	Philadelphia	AHL	73	13	22	35	177	....	....	....	....	....	....	....	....	....	12	0	1	1	39	....	....	....	....
2004-05	Philadelphia	AHL	58	9	15	24	112	....	....	....	....	....	....	....	....	....	21	0	7	7	28	....	....	....	....
2005-06	**Washington**	**NHL**	**5**	**0**	**1**	**1**	**2**	**0**	**0**	**0**	**1**	**0.0**	**1**	**0**	**0.0**	**4:04**	....	....	....	....	....	....	....	....	....
	Hershey Bears	AHL	74	20	29	49	185	....	....	....	....	....	....	....	....	....	21	4	9	13	14	....	....	....	....
2006-07	**Philadelphia**	**NHL**	**15**	**0**	**2**	**2**	**28**	**0**	**0**	**0**	**7**	**0.0**	**–4**	**4**	**25.0**	**6:58**	....	....	....	....	....	....	....	....	....
	Philadelphia	AHL	57	10	22	32	98	....	....	....	....	....	....	....	....	....	....	....	....	....	....	....	....	....	....
2007-08	Philadelphia	AHL	57	18	26	44	102	....	....	....	....	....	....	....	....	....	12	4	4	8	25	....	....	....	....
2008-09	**Philadelphia**	**NHL**	**1**	**0**	**0**	**0**	**0**	**0**	**0**	**0**	**0**	**0.0**	**0**	**0**	**0.0**	**8:12**	....	....	....	....	....	....	....	....	....
	Philadelphia	AHL	58	17	26	43	74	....	....	....	....	....	....	....	....	....	4	1	1	2	6	....	....	....	....
2009-10	**Washington**	**NHL**	**3**	**0**	**0**	**0**	**2**	**0**	**0**	**0**	**2**	**0.0**	**–1**	**0**	**0.0**	**8:13**	....	....	....	....	....	....	....	....	....
	Hershey Bears	AHL	76	24	20	44	77	....	....	....	....	....	....	....	....	....	21	1	6	7	34	....	....	....	....
2010-11	Hershey Bears	AHL	74	24	25	49	80	....	....	....	....	....	....	....	....	....	6	1	2	3	4	....	....	....	....
	NHL Totals		**31**	**0**	**3**	**3**	**39**	**0**	**0**	**0**	**16**	**0.0**		**7**	**28.6**	**7:20**	....	....	....	....	....	....	....	....	....

• Re-entered NHL Entry Draft. Originally Pittsburgh's 3rd choice, 72nd overall, in 1996 Entry Draft.

Traded to **Tampa Bay** by **NY Rangers** for Gordie Dwyer, October 10, 2002. Signed as a free agent by **Philadelphia**, July 14, 2003. Signed as a free agent by **Washington**, August 12, 2005. Signed as a free agent by **Philadelphia**, July 13, 2006. Signed as a free agent by **Washington**, July 13, 2009. Signed as a free agent by **Hershey** (AHL), July 29, 2010.

KANE, Evander

(KAYN, ee-VAN-duhr) **WPG**

Left wing. Shoots left. 6'2", 195 lbs. Born, Vancouver, B.C., August 2, 1991. Atlanta's 1st choice, 4th overall, in 2009 Entry Draft.

2006-07	Greater Van.	BCMML	30	22	32	54	150	....	....	....	....	....	....	....	....	....	....	....	....	....	....	....	....	....	....
	Vancouver Giants	WHL	8	1	0	1	11	....	....	....	....	....	....	....	....	....	5	0	0	0	0	....	....	....	....
2007-08	Vancouver Giants	WHL	65	24	17	41	66	....	....	....	....	....	....	....	....	....	10	1	2	3	8	....	....	....	....
2008-09	Vancouver Giants	WHL	61	48	48	96	89	....	....	....	....	....	....	....	....	....	17	7	8	15	45	....	....	....	....
2009-10	**Atlanta**	**NHL**	**66**	**14**	**12**	**26**	**62**	**0**	**1**	**3**	**127**	**11.0**	**2**	**26**	**53.9**	**14:00**	....	....	....	....	....	....	....	....	....
2010-11	**Atlanta**	**NHL**	**73**	**19**	**24**	**43**	**68**	**4**	**0**	**2**	**234**	**8.1**	**–12**	**64**	**40.6**	**17:52**	....	....	....	....	....	....	....	....	....
	NHL Totals		**139**	**33**	**36**	**69**	**130**	**4**	**1**	**5**	**361**	**9.1**		**90**	**44.4**	**16:02**	....	....	....	....	....	....	....	....	....

WHL West First All-Star Team (2009)

• Transferred to **Winnipeg** after **Atlanta** franchise relocated, June 21, 2011.

KANE, Patrick

(KAYN, PAT-rihk) **CHI**

Right wing. Shoots left. 5'10", 178 lbs. Born, Buffalo, NY, November 19, 1988. Chicago's 1st choice, 1st overall, in 2007 Entry Draft.

2003-04	Det. Honeybaked	MWEHL	70	83	77	160	....	....	....	....	....	....	....	....	....	....	....	....	....	....	....	....	....	....	....
2004-05	USNTDP	U-17	23	16	17	33	8	....	....	....	....	....	....	....	....	....	....	....	....	....	....	....	....	....	....
	USNTDP	NAHL	40	16	21	37	8	....	....	....	....	....	....	....	....	....	9	7	8	15	2	....	....	....	....
2005-06	USNTDP	U-18	43	35	33	68	10	....	....	....	....	....	....	....	....	....	....	....	....	....	....	....	....	....	....
	USNTDP	NAHL	15	17	17	34	12	....	....	....	....	....	....	....	....	....	....	....	....	....	....	....	....	....	....
2006-07	London Knights	OHL	58	62	83	*145	52	....	....	....	....	....	....	....	....	....	16	10	21	*31	16	....	....	....	....
2007-08	**Chicago**	**NHL**	**82**	**21**	**51**	**72**	**52**	**7**	**0**	**4**	**191**	**11.0**	**–5**	**26**	**61.5**	**18:22**	....	....	....	....	....	....	....	....	....
2008-09	**Chicago**	**NHL**	**80**	**25**	**45**	**70**	**42**	**13**	**0**	**4**	**254**	**9.8**	**–2**	**31**	**41.9**	**18:40**	**16**	**9**	**5**	**14**	**12**	**2**	**0**	**0**	**16:36**
2009-10♦	**Chicago**	**NHL**	**82**	**30**	**58**	**88**	**20**	**9**	**0**	**6**	**261**	**11.5**	**16**	**22**	**40.9**	**19:12**	**22**	**10**	**18**	**28**	**6**	**1**	**1**	**1**	**18:55**
	United States	Olympics	6	3	2	5	2	....	....	....	....	....	....	....	....	....	....	....	....	....	....	....	....	....	....
2010-11	**Chicago**	**NHL**	**73**	**27**	**46**	**73**	**28**	**5**	**0**	**2**	**216**	**12.5**	**7**	**14**	**14.3**	**19:17**	**7**	**1**	**5**	**6**	**2**	**1**	**0**	**0**	**21:50**
	NHL Totals		**317**	**103**	**200**	**303**	**142**	**34**	**0**	**16**	**922**	**11.2**		**93**	**43.0**	**18:52**	**45**	**20**	**28**	**48**	**20**	**4**	**1**	**1**	**18:33**

OHL All-Rookie Team (2007) • OHL First All-Star Team (2007) • OHL Rookie of the Year (2007) • Canadian Major Junior First All-Star Team (2007) • Canadian Major Junior Rookie of the Year (2007) • NHL All-Rookie Team (2008) • Calder Memorial Trophy (2008) • NHL First All-Star Team (2010)

Played in NHL All-Star Game (2009, 2011)

KARLSSON, Erik

(KAHRL-suhn, AIR-ihk) **OTT**

Defense. Shoots right. 6', 175 lbs. Born, Landsbro, Sweden, May 31, 1990. Ottawa's 1st choice, 15th overall, in 2008 Entry Draft.

2006-07	Sodertalje SK U18	Swe-U18	2	0	1	1	33	....	....	....	....	....	....	....	....	....	....	....	....	....	....	....	....	....	....
	Sodertalje SK Jr.	Swe-Jr.	10	2	8	10	8	....	....	....	....	....	....	....	....	....	....	....	....	....	....	....	....	....	....
2007-08	Frolunda U18	Swe-U18	3	1	2	3	2	....	....	....	....	....	....	....	....	....	2	0	1	1	10	....	....	....	....
	Frolunda Jr.	Swe-Jr.	38	13	24	37	68	....	....	....	....	....	....	....	....	....	5	1	0	1	4	....	....	....	....
	Frolunda	Sweden	7	1	0	1	0	....	....	....	....	....	....	....	....	....	6	0	0	0	0	....	....	....	....
2008-09	Frolunda Jr.	Swe-Jr.	1	0	2	2	2	....	....	....	....	....	....	....	....	....	....	....	....	....	....	....	....	....	....
	Boras HC	Sweden-2	7	0	1	1	14	....	....	....	....	....	....	....	....	....	....	....	....	....	....	....	....	....	....
	Frolunda	Sweden	45	5	5	10	10	....	....	....	....	....	....	....	....	....	11	1	2	3	24	....	....	....	....
2009-10	**Ottawa**	**NHL**	**60**	**5**	**21**	**26**	**24**	**1**	**0**	**0**	**112**	**4.5**	**–5**	**0**	**0.0**	**20:07**	**6**	**1**	**5**	**6**	**4**	**1**	**0**	**0**	**25:52**
	Binghamton	AHL	12	0	11	11	22	....	....	....	....	....	....	....	....	....	....	....	....	....	....	....	....	....	....
2010-11	**Ottawa**	**NHL**	**75**	**13**	**32**	**45**	**50**	**4**	**0**	**4**	**182**	**7.1**	**–30**	**0**	**0.0**	**23:31**	....	....	....	....	....	....	....	....	....
	NHL Totals		**135**	**18**	**53**	**71**	**74**	**5**	**0**	**4**	**294**	**6.1**		**0**	**0.0**	**22:00**	**6**	**1**	**5**	**6**	**4**	**1**	**0**	**0**	**25:52**

Played in NHL All-Star Game (2011)

KARSUMS, Martins

(KAHR-suhmz, MAHR-tihnsh) **T.B.**

Right wing. Shoots right. 5'10", 198 lbs. Born, Riga, Latvia, February 26, 1986. Boston's 2nd choice, 64th overall, in 2004 Entry Draft.

2000-01	Prizma '83 Riga Jr.	Latvia-Jr.	2	0	0	0	0	....	....	....	....	....	....	....	....	....	....	....	....	....	....	....	....	....	....
	Lido Nafta Jr.	Latvia-Jr.	18	8	6	14	....	....	....	....	....	....	....	....	....	....	....	....	....	....	....	....	....	....	....
2001-02	Prizma '83 Riga	EEHL-B	16	7	8	15	4	....	....	....	....	....	....	....	....	....	....	....	....	....	....	....	....	....	....
	Prizma '83 Riga	Latvia	6	4	1	5	4	....	....	....	....	....	....	....	....	....	....	....	....	....	....	....	....	....	....
2002-03	HK Riga 2000	EEHL	2	0	0	0	0	....	....	....	....	....	....	....	....	....	....	....	....	....	....	....	....	....	....
	Vilki Riga	Latvia	....	7	5	12	14	....	....	....	....	....	....	....	....	....	....	....	....	....	....	....	....	....	....
2003-04	Moncton Wildcats	QMJHL	60	30	23	53	76	....	....	....	....	....	....	....	....	....	20	8	9	17	14	....	....	....	....
2004-05	Moncton Wildcats	QMJHL	30	14	12	26	31	....	....	....	....	....	....	....	....	....	2	0	0	0	0	....	....	....	....
2005-06	Moncton Wildcats	QMJHL	49	34	31	65	89	....	....	....	....	....	....	....	....	....	21	15	11	26	22	....	....	....	....

Season	Club	League	GP	G	A	Pts	PIM	PP	SH	GW	S	%	+/-	TF	F%	Min	GP	G	A	Pts	PIM	PP	SH	GW	Min
									Regular Season											Playoffs					
2006-07	Providence Bruins	AHL	54	13	22	35	41	....	....	....	....	....	....	....			12	3	1	4	2	....			....
2007-08	Providence Bruins	AHL	79	20	43	63	57	....	....	....	....	....	....	....			10	7	3	10	6	....			....
2008-09	**Boston**	**NHL**	6	0	1	1	0	0	0	0	6	0.0	-3	1	0.0	9:45	....								
	Providence Bruins	AHL	43	17	24	41	20	....										
	Tampa Bay	**NHL**	18	1	4	5	6	0	0	0	22	4.5	-5	2	100.0	11:40	....								
2009-10	Norfolk Admirals	AHL	36	4	12	16	6	....										
	Dynamo Riga	Rus-KHL	12	4	4	8	16										9	2	1	3	4				
	Latvia	Olympics	4	0	2	2	2										
2010-11	Dynamo Riga	Rus-KHL	52	17	15	32	46										11	1	2	3	8				
	NHL Totals		24	1	5	6	6	0	0	0	28	3.6		3	66.7	11:11	....								

QMJHL All-Rookie Team (2004)

Traded to **Tampa Bay** by **Boston** with Matt Lashoff for Mark Recchi and Tampa Bay's 2nd round choice (later traded to Florida - Florida selected Alexander Petrovic) in 2010 Entry Draft, March 4, 2009. Signed as a free agent by **Riga** (Russia-KHL), January 17, 2010.

KASSIAN, Matt   (KAS-ee-uhn, MAT)   MIN

Left wing. Shoots left. 6'5", 252 lbs.   Born, Edmonton, Alta., October 28, 1986. Minnesota's 2nd choice, 57th overall, in 2005 Entry Draft.

Season	Club	League	GP	G	A	Pts	PIM	PP	SH	GW	S	%	+/-	TF	F%	Min	GP	G	A	Pts	PIM
2002-03	Sherwood Park	AJHL	33	5	7	12	38										
2003-04	Vancouver Giants	WHL	37	1	0	1	42										3	0	0	0	4
2004-05	Vancouver Giants	WHL	41	0	3	3	89										
	Kamloops Blazers	WHL	28	3	0	3	83										6	1	2	3	14
2005-06	Kamloops Blazers	WHL	67	5	6	11	147										
2006-07	Kamloops Blazers	WHL	72	8	10	18	162										4	0	1	1	0
2007-08	Houston Aeros	AHL	19	0	0	0	48										
	Texas Wildcatters	ECHL	47	6	4	10	90										
2008-09	Houston Aeros	AHL	56	1	2	3	130										4	0	0	0	10
2009-10	Houston Aeros	AHL	59	2	4	6	149										
2010-11	**Minnesota**	**NHL**	4	0	0	0	12	0	0	0	1	0.0	-1	0	0.0	5:29	
	Houston Aeros	AHL	60	4	4	8	132										8	0	0	0	2
	NHL Totals		4	0	0	0	12	0	0	0	1	0.0		0	0.0	5:29	

KATIC, Mark   (KA-tihk, MAHRK)   NYI

Defense. Shoots left. 5'10", 195 lbs.   Born, Timmins, Ont., May 9, 1989. NY Islanders' 1st choice, 62nd overall, in 2007 Entry Draft.

Season	Club	League	GP	G	A	Pts	PIM	PP	SH	GW	S	%	+/-	TF	F%	Min	GP	G	A	Pts	PIM
2003-04	Timmins Majors	GNMHL	40	12	20	32	35										
2004-05	Timmins Majors	GNMHL	35	11	21	32	74										
2005-06	Sarnia Sting	OHL	51	5	29	34	33										
2006-07	Sarnia Sting	OHL	68	5	35	40	31										4	1	3	4	8
2007-08	Sarnia Sting	OHL	45	5	26	31	28										6	0	3	3	8
2008-09	Sarnia Sting	OHL	63	13	41	54	45										4	1	0	1	6
2009-10	Bridgeport	AHL	48	3	11	14	16										
2010-11	**NY Islanders**	**NHL**	11	0	1	1	4	0	0	0	8	0.0	-9	0	0.0	16:26	
	Bridgeport	AHL	63	4	26	30	37										
	NHL Totals		11	0	1	1	4	0	0	0	8	0.0		0	0.0	16:26	

OHL All-Rookie Team (2006)

KEITH, Duncan   (KEETH, DUHN-kuhn)   CHI

Defense. Shoots left. 6'1", 196 lbs.   Born, Winnipeg, Man., July 16, 1983. Chicago's 2nd choice, 54th overall, in 2002 Entry Draft.

Season	Club	League	GP	G	A	Pts	PIM	PP	SH	GW	S	%	+/-	TF	F%	Min	GP	G	A	Pts	PIM	PP	SH	GW	Min
1998-99	Penticton	Minor-BC	44	51	57	108	45										
99-2000	Penticton	BCHL	59	9	27	36	37										
2000-01	Penticton	BCHL	60	18	64	82	61										9	4	6	10	18
2001-02	Michigan State	CCHA	41	3	12	15	18										
2002-03	Michigan State	CCHA	15	3	6	9	8										
	Kelowna Rockets	WHL	37	11	35	46	60										19	3	11	14	12
2003-04	Norfolk Admirals	AHL	75	7	18	25	44										8	1	1	2	6
2004-05	Norfolk Admirals	AHL	79	9	17	26	78										6	0	0	0	14
2005-06	**Chicago**	**NHL**	81	9	12	21	79	1	1	0	134	6.7	-11	0	0.0	23:26	
2006-07	**Chicago**	**NHL**	82	2	29	31	76	0	0	0	122	1.6	0	0	0.0	23:36	
2007-08	**Chicago**	**NHL**	82	12	20	32	56	1	1	0	148	8.1	30	0	0.0	25:34	
2008-09	**Chicago**	**NHL**	77	8	36	44	60	2	1	1	173	4.6	33	0	0.0	25:34	17	0	6	6	10	0	0	0	24:39
2009-10 ♦	**Chicago**	**NHL**	82	14	55	69	51	3	1	1	213	6.6	21	0	0.0	26:36	22	2	15	17	10	0	0	0	28:11
	Canada	Olympics	7	0	6	6	2										
2010-11	**Chicago**	**NHL**	82	7	38	45	22	3	1	1	173	4.0	-1	0	0.0	26:53	7	4	2	6	6	1	0	1	26:55
	NHL Totals		486	52	190	242	344	10	5	3	963	5.4		0	0.0	25:16	46	6	23	29	26	1	0	1	26:41

NHL First All-Star Team (2010) • James Norris Memorial Trophy (2010)

Played in NHL All-Star Game (2008, 2011)

• Left **Michigan State** (CCHA) and signed as a free agent by **Kelowna** (WHL), December 27, 2002.

KEITH, Matt   (KEETH, MAT)   CGY

Right wing. Shoots right. 6'2", 200 lbs.   Born, Edmonton, Alta., April 11, 1983. Chicago's 3rd choice, 59th overall, in 2001 Entry Draft.

Season	Club	League	GP	G	A	Pts	PIM	PP	SH	GW	S	%	+/-	TF	F%	Min	GP	G	A	Pts	PIM
1998-99	Banff Icemen	HJHL	STATISTICS NOT AVAILABLE														
	Spokane Chiefs	WHL	7	1	0	1	4										
99-2000	Spokane Chiefs	WHL	39	1	3	4	37										15	1	2	3	11
2000-01	Spokane Chiefs	WHL	33	13	14	27	63										12	1	3	4	14
2001-02	Spokane Chiefs	WHL	68	34	33	67	71										11	5	5	10	16
2002-03	Spokane Chiefs	WHL	7	2	2	4	11										
	Red Deer Rebels	WHL	49	25	26	51	32										23	6	7	13	30
2003-04	**Chicago**	**NHL**	20	2	3	5	10	1	0	0	21	9.5	-5	2	100.0	11:58	
	Norfolk Admirals	AHL	66	13	13	26	57										8	1	2	3	10
2004-05	Norfolk Admirals	AHL	80	18	31	49	74										6	0	1	1	0
2005-06	**Chicago**	**NHL**	2	0	0	0	0	0	0	0	6	0.0		0	0.0	11:42	
	Norfolk Admirals	AHL	72	26	19	45	61										3	0	1	1	0
2006-07	**Chicago**	**NHL**	2	0	0	0	4	0	0	0	0	0.0	-2	0	0.0	9:33	
	Norfolk Admirals	AHL	19	2	8	10	15										
	Portland Pirates	AHL	44	10	12	22	22										
2007-08	Portland Pirates	AHL	34	5	5	10	13										
	NY Islanders	**NHL**	3	0	0	0	0	0	0	0	3	0.0	-1	0	0.0	10:41	
	Bridgeport	AHL	42	6	16	22	17										
2008-09	ERC Ingolstadt	Germany	46	15	13	28	60										
2009-10	Rockford IceHogs	AHL	69	21	20	41	27										4	0	0	0	2
2010-11	Abbotsford Heat	AHL	77	20	15	35	45										
	NHL Totals		27	2	3	5	14	1	0	0	30	6.7		2	100.0	11:37	

• Missed majority of 2000-01 due to shoulder injury vs. Tri-City (WHL), September 22, 2000. Traded to **Anaheim** by **Chicago** with Sebastien Caron and Chris Durno for P.A. Parenteau and Bruno St. Jacques, December 28, 2006. Traded to **NY Islanders** by **Anaheim** for Darryl Bootland, January 9, 2008. Signed as a free agent by **Ingolstadt** (Germany), July 25, 2008. Signed as a free agent by **Rockford** (AHL), October 1, 2009. Signed as a free agent by **Abbotsford** (AHL), September 27, 2010.

KELLER, Ryan   (KEHL-uhr, RIGH-uhn)

Center. Shoots right. 5'10", 196 lbs.   Born, Saskatoon, Sask., January 6, 1984.

Season	Club	League	GP	G	A	Pts	PIM	PP	SH	GW	S	%	+/-	TF	F%	Min	GP	G	A	Pts	PIM
2001-02	Saskatoon Blades	WHL	52	18	23	41	58										7	1	2	3	14
2002-03	Saskatoon Blades	WHL	66	38	41	79	101										6	7	1	8	8
2003-04	Saskatoon Blades	WHL	72	24	20	44	59										
2004-05	Saskatoon Blades	WHL	67	40	33	73	63										4	1	1	2	9
2005-06	Grand Rapids	AHL	10	1	0	1	14										13	0	0	0	0
	Muskegon Fury	UHL	65	41	40	81	79										3	2	2	4	0
2006-07	Grand Rapids	AHL	38	9	8	17	26										
	Syracuse Crunch	AHL	22	5	9	14	14										

			Regular Season														Playoffs								
Season	Club	League	GP	G	A	Pts	PIM	PP	SH	GW	S	%	+/-	TF	F%	Min	GP	G	A	Pts	PIM	PP	SH	GW	Min
2007-08	Blues Espoo	Finland	47	22	22	44	24	....	....	....	....	....	....	....	....	....	17	3	6	9	22	....	....	....	....
2008-09	Blues Espoo	Finland	54	21	34	55	38	....	....	....	....	....	....	....	....	....	14	*9	7	16	4	....	....	....	....
2009-10	**Ottawa**	**NHL**	**6**	**0**	**0**	**0**	**0**	**0**	**0**	**0**	**5**	**0.0**	**–1**	**0**	**0.0**	**6:13**	....	....	....	....	....	....	....	....	....
	Binghamton	AHL	72	34	34	68	48	....	....	....	....	....	....	....	....	....	....	....	....	....	....	....	....	....	....
2010-11	Binghamton	AHL	71	32	19	51	38	....	....	....	....	....	....	....	....	....	23	10	*15	25	8	....	....	....	....
	NHL Totals		**6**	**0**	**0**	**0**	**0**	**0**	**0**	**0**	**5**	**0.0**		**0**	**0.0**	**6:13**	....	....	....	....	....	....	....	....	....

Signed as a free agent by **Ottawa**, June 1, 2009.

KELLY, Chris

(KEHL-lee, KRIHS) **BOS**

Center/Left wing. Shoots left. 6', 198 lbs. Born, Toronto, Ont., November 11, 1980. Ottawa's 4th choice, 94th overall, in 1999 Entry Draft.

Season	Club	League	GP	G	A	Pts	PIM	PP	SH	GW	S	%	+/-	TF	F%	Min	GP	G	A	Pts	PIM	PP	SH	GW	Min
1995-96	Toronto Marlies	MTHL	42	25	45	70	25	....	....	....	....	....	....	....	....	....	....	....	....	....	....	....	....	....	....
1996-97	Vaughan Vipers	OPJHL	5	0	0	0	5	....	....	....	....	....	....	....	....	....	....	....	....	....	....	....	....	....	....
	Aurora Tigers	ON-Jr.A	49	14	20	34	11	....	....	....	....	....	....	....	....	....	....	....	....	....	....	....	....	....	....
1997-98	London Knights	OHL	54	15	14	29	4	....	....	....	....	....	....	....	....	....	16	4	5	9	12	....	....	....	....
1998-99	London Knights	OHL	68	36	41	77	60	....	....	....	....	....	....	....	....	....	25	9	17	26	22	....	....	....	....
99-2000	London Knights	OHL	63	29	43	72	57	....	....	....	....	....	....	....	....	....	....	....	....	....	....	....	....	....	....
2000-01	London Knights	OHL	31	21	34	55	46	....	....	....	....	....	....	....	....	....	....	....	....	....	....	....	....	....	....
	Sudbury Wolves	OHL	19	5	16	21	17	....	....	....	....	....	....	....	....	....	12	11	5	16	14	....	....	....	....
2001-02	Grand Rapids	AHL	31	3	3	6	20	....	....	....	....	....	....	....	....	....	5	1	1	2	5	....	....	....	....
	Muskegon Fury	UHL	4	1	2	3	0	....	....	....	....	....	....	....	....	....	....	....	....	....	....	....	....	....	....
2002-03	Binghamton	AHL	77	17	14	31	73	....	....	....	....	....	....	....	....	....	14	2	3	5	8	....	....	....	....
2003-04	**Ottawa**	**NHL**	**4**	**0**	**0**	**0**	**0**	**0**	**0**	**0**	**4**	**0.0**	**–2**	**5**	**40.0**	**9:29**	....	....	....	....	....	....	....	....	....
	Binghamton	AHL	54	15	19	34	40	....	....	....	....	....	....	....	....	....	2	0	0	0	4	....	....	....	....
2004-05	Binghamton	AHL	77	24	36	60	57	....	....	....	....	....	....	....	....	....	6	1	2	3	11	....	....	....	....
2005-06	**Ottawa**	**NHL**	**82**	**10**	**20**	**30**	**76**	**1**	**0**	**2**	**112**	**8.9**	**21**	**808**	**45.8**	**12:20**	**10**	**0**	**0**	**0**	**2**	**0**	**0**	**0**	**11:49**
2006-07	**Ottawa**	**NHL**	**82**	**15**	**23**	**38**	**40**	**1**	**2**	**0**	**131**	**11.5**	**28**	**564**	**49.8**	**15:18**	**20**	**3**	**4**	**7**	**4**	**0**	**0**	**0**	**15:28**
2007-08	**Ottawa**	**NHL**	**75**	**11**	**19**	**30**	**30**	**0**	**1**	**1**	**124**	**8.9**	**3**	**162**	**53.1**	**16:36**	....	....	....	....	....	....	....	....	....
2008-09	**Ottawa**	**NHL**	**82**	**12**	**11**	**23**	**38**	**0**	**1**	**1**	**118**	**10.2**	**–10**	**494**	**47.4**	**15:36**	....	....	....	....	....	....	....	....	....
2009-10	**Ottawa**	**NHL**	**81**	**15**	**17**	**32**	**38**	**0**	**0**	**3**	**112**	**13.4**	**–7**	**894**	**45.6**	**14:58**	**6**	**1**	**5**	**6**	**2**	**1**	**0**	**0**	**18:46**
2010-11	**Ottawa**	**NHL**	**57**	**12**	**11**	**23**	**27**	**0**	**1**	**2**	**89**	**13.5**	**–12**	**726**	**50.1**	**15:39**	....	....	....	....	....	....	....	....	....
	♦ Boston	**NHL**	**24**	**2**	**3**	**5**	**6**	**0**	**0**	**0**	**24**	**8.3**	**–1**	**190**	**53.7**	**14:52**	**25**	**5**	**8**	**13**	**6**	**0**	**0**	**0**	**15:28**
	NHL Totals		**487**	**77**	**104**	**181**	**255**	**2**	**5**	**9**	**714**	**10.8**		**3843**	**48.1**	**14:58**	**61**	**9**	**17**	**26**	**14**	**1**	**0**	**0**	**15:12**

Traded to **Boston** by **Ottawa** for Boston's 2nd round choice (Shane Prince) in 2011 Entry Draft, February 15, 2011.

KENNEDY, Tim

(KEH-nuh-dee, TIHM) **FLA**

Left wing. Shoots left. 5'10", 173 lbs. Born, Buffalo, NY, April 30, 1986. Washington's 6th choice, 181st overall, in 2005 Entry Draft.

Season	Club	League	GP	G	A	Pts	PIM	PP	SH	GW	S	%	+/-	TF	F%	Min	GP	G	A	Pts	PIM	PP	SH	GW	Min
2003-04	Sioux City	USHL	56	9	10	19	42	....	....	....	....	....	....	....	....	....	7	2	2	4	6				
2004-05	Sioux City	USHL	54	30	31	61	112	....	....	....	....	....	....	....	....	....	13	*6	*11	*17	18	....	....	....	....
2005-06	Michigan State	CCHA	29	4	15	19	31	....	....	....	....	....	....	....	....	....	....	....	....	....	....	....	....	....	....
2006-07	Michigan State	CCHA	42	18	25	43	49	....	....	....	....	....	....	....	....	....	....	....	....	....	....	....	....	....	....
2007-08	Michigan State	CCHA	42	20	23	43	50	....	....	....	....	....	....	....	....	....	....	....	....	....	....	....	....	....	....
2008-09	**Buffalo**	**NHL**	**1**	**0**	**0**	**0**	**0**	**0**	**0**	**0**	**1**	**0.0**	**0**	**1**	**0.0**	**11:04**	....	....	....	....	....	....	....	....	....
	Portland Pirates	AHL	73	18	49	67	51	....	....	....	....	....	....	....	....	....	5	0	1	1	2	....	....	....	....
2009-10	**Buffalo**	**NHL**	**78**	**10**	**16**	**26**	**50**	**1**	**0**	**3**	**98**	**10.2**	**–3**	**397**	**33.5**	**12:57**	**6**	**1**	**2**	**3**	**4**	**0**	**0**	**0**	**14:25**
2010-11	Connecticut	AHL	53	12	30	42	44	....	....	....	....	....	....	....	....	....	....	....	....	....	....	....	....	....	....
	Florida	**NHL**	**6**	**0**	**1**	**1**	**0**	**0**	**0**	**0**	**2**	**0.0**	**0**	**30**	**40.0**	**10:23**	....	....	....	....	....	....	....	....	....
	Rochester	AHL	14	0	7	7	8	....	....	....	....	....	....	....	....	....	....	....	....	....	....	....	....	....	....
	NHL Totals		**85**	**10**	**17**	**27**	**50**	**1**	**0**	**3**	**101**	**9.9**		**428**	**33.9**	**12:45**	**6**	**1**	**2**	**3**	**4**	**0**	**0**	**0**	**14:25**

USHL Second All-Star Team (2005) • NCAA Championship All-Tournament Team (2007) • CCHA Second All-Star Team (2008) • AHL All-Rookie Team (2009)

Traded to **Buffalo** by **Washington** for Buffalo's 6th round choice (Mathieu Perreault) in 2006 Entry Draft, July 30, 2005. Signed as a free agent by **NY Rangers**, August 30, 2010. Traded to **Florida** by **NY Rangers** with NY Rangers' 3rd round choice (Logan Shaw) in 2011 Entry Draft for Bryan McCabe, February 26, 2011.

KENNEDY, Tyler

(KEH-nuh-dee, TIGH-luhr) **PIT**

Center. Shoots right. 5'11", 183 lbs. Born, Sault Ste. Marie, Ont., July 15, 1986. Pittsburgh's 6th choice, 99th overall, in 2004 Entry Draft.

Season	Club	League	GP	G	A	Pts	PIM	PP	SH	GW	S	%	+/-	TF	F%	Min	GP	G	A	Pts	PIM	PP	SH	GW	Min
2002-03	Sault Ste. Marie	OHL	61	5	10	15	28	....	....	....	....	....	....	....	....	....	4	0	0	0	0				
2003-04	Sault Ste. Marie	OHL	63	16	26	42	28	....	....	....	....	....	....	....	....	....	....	....	....	....	....	....	....	....	....
2004-05	Sault Ste. Marie	OHL	61	21	36	57	37	....	....	....	....	....	....	....	....	....	4	1	3	4	4	....	....	....	....
2005-06	Sault Ste. Marie	OHL	64	22	48	70	60	....	....	....	....	....	....	....	....	....	4	1	2	3	2	....	....	....	....
2006-07	Wilkes-Barre	AHL	40	12	25	37	20	....	....	....	....	....	....	....	....	....	....	....	....	....	....	....	....	....	....
2007-08	**Pittsburgh**	**NHL**	**55**	**10**	**9**	**19**	**35**	**1**	**0**	**4**	**104**	**9.6**	**2**	**8**	**25.0**	**12:13**	**20**	**0**	**4**	**4**	**13**	**0**	**0**	**0**	**10:18**
	Wilkes-Barre	AHL	10	5	4	9	10	....	....	....	....	....	....	....	....	....	....	....	....	....	....	....	....	....	....
2008-09♦	**Pittsburgh**	**NHL**	**67**	**15**	**20**	**35**	**30**	**0**	**0**	**3**	**171**	**8.8**	**15**	**78**	**53.9**	**13:46**	**24**	**5**	**4**	**9**	**4**	**0**	**0**	**3**	**13:40**
2009-10	**Pittsburgh**	**NHL**	**64**	**13**	**12**	**25**	**31**	**1**	**0**	**4**	**175**	**7.4**	**10**	**64**	**42.2**	**12:35**	**10**	**0**	**0**	**0**	**2**	**0**	**0**	**0**	**11:57**
2010-11	**Pittsburgh**	**NHL**	**80**	**21**	**24**	**45**	**37**	**7**	**0**	**2**	**234**	**9.0**	**1**	**60**	**45.0**	**14:32**	**7**	**2**	**1**	**3**	**2**	**1**	**0**	**1**	**17:32**
	NHL Totals		**266**	**59**	**65**	**124**	**133**	**9**	**0**	**13**	**684**	**8.6**		**210**	**46.7**	**13:23**	**61**	**7**	**9**	**16**	**21**	**1**	**0**	**4**	**12:43**

KESLER, Ryan

(KEHZ-luhr, RIGH-uhn) **VAN**

Center. Shoots right. 6'2", 202 lbs. Born, Livonia, MI, August 31, 1984. Vancouver's 1st choice, 23rd overall, in 2003 Entry Draft.

Season	Club	League	GP	G	A	Pts	PIM	PP	SH	GW	S	%	+/-	TF	F%	Min	GP	G	A	Pts	PIM	PP	SH	GW	Min
99-2000	Det. Honeybaked	MWEHL	72	44	73	117	....	....	....	....	....	....	....	....	....	....	....	....	....	....	....	....	....	....	....
2000-01	USNTDP	U-18	26	8	20	28	24	....	....	....	....	....	....	....	....	....	....	....	....	....	....	....	....	....	....
	USNTDP	NAHL	56	7	21	28	40	....	....	....	....	....	....	....	....	....	....	....	....	....	....	....	....	....	....
2001-02	USNTDP	U-18	46	11	33	44	23	....	....	....	....	....	....	....	....	....	....	....	....	....	....	....	....	....	....
	USNTDP	USHL	13	5	5	10	10	....	....	....	....	....	....	....	....	....	....	....	....	....	....	....	....	....	....
	USNTDP	NAHL	10	5	6	11	4	....	....	....	....	....	....	....	....	....	....	....	....	....	....	....	....	....	....
2002-03	Ohio State	CCHA	40	11	20	31	44	....	....	....	....	....	....	....	....	....	....	....	....	....	....	....	....	....	....
2003-04	**Vancouver**	**NHL**	**28**	**2**	**3**	**5**	**16**	**0**	**0**	**0**	**23**	**8.7**	**–2**	**194**	**40.2**	**10:42**	....	....	....	....	....	....	....	....	....
	Manitoba Moose	AHL	33	3	8	11	29	....	....	....	....	....	....	....	....	....	....	....	....	....	....	....	....	....	....
2004-05	Manitoba Moose	AHL	78	30	27	57	105	....	....	....	....	....	....	....	....	....	14	4	5	9	8	....	....	....	....
2005-06	**Vancouver**	**NHL**	**82**	**10**	**13**	**23**	**79**	**1**	**0**	**2**	**119**	**8.4**	**1**	**984**	**46.8**	**14:03**	....	....	....	....	....	....	....	....	....
2006-07	**Vancouver**	**NHL**	**48**	**6**	**10**	**16**	**40**	**0**	**0**	**0**	**88**	**6.8**	**1**	**690**	**46.1**	**16:26**	**1**	**0**	**0**	**0**	**0**	**0**	**0**	**0**	**27:51**
2007-08	**Vancouver**	**NHL**	**80**	**21**	**16**	**37**	**79**	**4**	**2**	**2**	**177**	**11.9**	**1**	**1358**	**53.0**	**19:03**	....	....	....	....	....	....	....	....	....
2008-09	**Vancouver**	**NHL**	**82**	**26**	**33**	**59**	**61**	**10**	**2**	**2**	**179**	**14.5**	**8**	**976**	**54.0**	**19:28**	**10**	**2**	**2**	**4**	**14**	**1**	**0**	**0**	**20:29**
2009-10	**Vancouver**	**NHL**	**82**	**25**	**50**	**75**	**104**	**12**	**1**	**5**	**214**	**11.7**	**1**	**1401**	**55.1**	**19:38**	**12**	**1**	**9**	**10**	**4**	**0**	**0**	**0**	**21:19**
	United States	Olympics	6	2	0	2	2	....	....	....	....	....	....	....	....	....	....	....	....	....	....	....	....	....	....
2010-11	**Vancouver**	**NHL**	**82**	**41**	**32**	**73**	**66**	**15**	**3**	**7**	**260**	**15.8**	**24**	**1496**	**57.4**	**20:30**	**25**	**7**	**12**	**19**	**47**	**4**	**0**	**2**	**22:34**
	NHL Totals		**484**	**131**	**157**	**288**	**445**	**42**	**8**	**18**	**1060**	**12.4**		**7099**	**52.6**	**17:52**	**48**	**10**	**23**	**33**	**65**	**5**	**0**	**2**	**21:56**

Frank J. Selke Trophy (2011)

Played in NHL All-Star Game (2011)

KESSEL, Phil

(KEH-suhl, FIHL) **TOR**

Center. Shoots right. 6', 202 lbs. Born, Madison, WI, October 2, 1987. Boston's 1st choice, 5th overall, in 2006 Entry Draft.

Season	Club	League	GP	G	A	Pts	PIM	PP	SH	GW	S	%	+/-	TF	F%	Min	GP	G	A	Pts	PIM	PP	SH	GW	Min
2003-04	USNTDP	U-17	32	31	18	49	8	....	....	....	....	....	....	....	....	....	....	....	....	....	....	....	....	....	....
	USNTDP	NAHL	30	21	12	33	18	....	....	....	....	....	....	....	....	....	....	....	....	....	....	....	....	....	....
2004-05	USNTDP	U-18	31	41	32	73	16	....	....	....	....	....	....	....	....	....	....	....	....	....	....	....	....	....	....
	USNTDP	NAHL	14	11	14	25	21	....	....	....	....	....	....	....	....	....	....	....	....	....	....	....	....	....	....
2005-06	U. of Minnesota	WCHA	39	18	33	51	28	....	....	....	....	....	....	....	....	....	....	....	....	....	....	....	....	....	....
2006-07	**Boston**	**NHL**	**70**	**11**	**18**	**29**	**12**	**1**	**0**	**0**	**170**	**6.5**	**–12**	**373**	**40.8**	**14:04**	....	....	....	....	....	....	....	....	....
	Providence Bruins	AHL	2	1	0	1	2	....	....	....	....	....	....	....	....	....	....	....	....	....	....	....	....	....	....
2007-08	**Boston**	**NHL**	**82**	**19**	**18**	**37**	**28**	**5**	**0**	**3**	**213**	**8.9**	**–6**	**326**	**42.3**	**15:14**	**4**	**3**	**1**	**4**	**2**	**1**	**0**	**0**	**14:31**
2008-09	**Boston**	**NHL**	**70**	**36**	**24**	**60**	**16**	**8**	**0**	**6**	**232**	**15.5**	**23**	**87**	**48.3**	**16:34**	**11**	**6**	**5**	**11**	**4**	**0**	**0**	**0**	**15:55**

			Regular Season														Playoffs								
Season	Club	League	GP	G	A	Pts	PIM	PP	SH	GW	S	%	+/-	TF	F%	Min	GP	G	A	Pts	PIM	PP	SH	GW	Min
2009-10	Toronto	NHL	70	30	25	55	21	8	0	5	297	10.1	–8	122	48.4	19:33	....	....	....	....	....	....	....	....	....
	United States	Olympics	6	1	1	2	0	....	....	....	....	....	....	....	....	....	....	....	....	....	....	....	....	....	....
2010-11	Toronto	NHL	82	32	32	64	24	12	1	6	325	9.8	–20	59	40.7	19:39	....	....	....	....	....	....	....	....	....
	NHL Totals		374	128	117	245	101	34	1	20	1237	10.3		967	42.9	17:02	15	9	6	15	6	1	0	0	15:33

WCHA All-Rookie Team (2006) • WCHA Rookie of the Year (2006) • Bill Masterton Memorial Trophy (2007) @ASG = Played in NHL All-Star Game (2011)

Traded to **Toronto** by **Boston** for Toronto's 1st (Tyler Seguin) and 2nd (Jared Knight) round choices in 2010 Entry Draft and Toronto's 1st round choice (Dougie Hamilton) in 2011 Entry Draft, September 18, 2009.

KINDL, Jakub
(KEEHN-duhl, YA-kuhb) **DET**

Defense. Shoots left. 6'3", 199 lbs. Born, Sumperk, Czech., February 10, 1987. Detroit's 1st choice, 19th overall, in 2005 Entry Draft.

Season	Club	League	GP	G	A	Pts	PIM	PP	SH	GW	S	%	+/-	TF	F%	Min	GP	G	A	Pts	PIM	PP	SH	GW	Min
2002-03	HC Pardubice U17	CzR-U17	3	0	3	3	10	....	....	....	....	....	....	....	....	....	....	....	....	....	....	....	....	....	....
	HC Pardubice Jr.	CzRep-Jr.	27	0	3	3	46	....	....	....	....	....	....	....	....	....	....	....	....	....	....	....	....	....	....
	Pardubice	CzRep	1	0	0	0	0	....	....	....	....	....	....	....	....	....	....	....	....	....	....	....	....	....	....
2003-04	HC Pardubice U17	CzR-U17	2	0	1	1	6	....	....	....	....	....	....	....	....	....	....	....	....	....	....	....	....	....	....
	HC Pardubice Jr.	CzRep-Jr.	48	4	14	18	108	....	....	....	....	....	....	....	....	....	....	....	....	....	....	....	....	....	....
	Hr. Kralove	CzRep-2	1	0	0	0	0	....	....	....	....	....	....	....	....	....	1	0	0	0	0	....	....	....	....
2004-05	Kitchener Rangers	OHL	62	3	11	14	92	....	....	....	....	....	....	....	....	....	12	0	0	0	22	....	....	....	....
2005-06	Kitchener Rangers	OHL	60	12	46	58	112	....	....	....	....	....	....	....	....	....	5	1	0	1	10	....	....	....	....
	Grand Rapids	AHL	3	0	1	1	2	....	....	....	....	....	....	....	....	....	....	....	....	....	....	....	....	....	....
2006-07	Kitchener Rangers	OHL	54	11	44	55	142	....	....	....	....	....	....	....	....	....	9	2	9	11	8	....	....	....	....
	Grand Rapids	AHL	....	....	....	....	....	....	....	....	....	....	....	....	....	....	7	0	2	2	0	....	....	....	....
2007-08	Grand Rapids	AHL	75	3	14	17	82	....	....	....	....	....	....	....	....	....	....	....	....	....	....	....	....	....	....
2008-09	Grand Rapids	AHL	78	6	27	33	76	....	....	....	....	....	....	....	....	....	10	2	1	3	2	....	....	....	....
2009-10	Detroit	NHL	3	0	0	0	0	0	0	0	1	0.0	–2	0	0.0	10:50	....	....	....	....	....	....	....	....	....
	Grand Rapids	AHL	73	3	30	33	59	....	....	....	....	....	....	....	....	....	....	....	....	....	....	....	....	....	....
2010-11	Detroit	NHL	48	2	2	4	36	0	0	0	62	3.2	–6	0	0.0	13:37	....	....	....	....	....	....	....	....	....
	Grand Rapids	AHL	8	1	4	5	6	....	....	....	....	....	....	....	....	....	....	....	....	....	....	....	....	....	....
	NHL Totals		51	2	2	4	36	0	0	0	63	3.2		0	0.0	13:27	....	....	....	....	....	....	....	....	....

OHL Second All-Star Team (2007)

KING, D.J.
(KIHNG, DEE-JAY) **WSH**

Center. Shoots left. 6'3", 230 lbs. Born, Meadow Lake, Sask., January 27, 1984. St. Louis' 6th choice, 190th overall, in 2002 Entry Draft.

Season	Club	League	GP	G	A	Pts	PIM	PP	SH	GW	S	%	+/-	TF	F%	Min	GP	G	A	Pts	PIM	PP	SH	GW	Min
2000-01	Beardy's	SMHL	52	30	28	58	120	....	....	....	....	....	....	....	....	....	....	....	....	....	....	....	....	....	....
2001-02	Lethbridge	WHL	65	10	14	24	104	....	....	....	....	....	....	....	....	....	4	1	0	1	2	....	....	....	....
2002-03	Lethbridge	WHL	55	15	17	32	139	....	....	....	....	....	....	....	....	....	....	....	....	....	....	....	....	....	....
2003-04	Lethbridge	WHL	35	8	15	23	102	....	....	....	....	....	....	....	....	....	....	....	....	....	....	....	....	....	....
	Kelowna Rockets	WHL	28	5	2	7	80	....	....	....	....	....	....	....	....	....	17	1	6	7	16	....	....	....	....
2004-05	Worcester IceCats	AHL	74	6	8	14	178	....	....	....	....	....	....	....	....	....	....	....	....	....	....	....	....	....	....
2005-06	Peoria Rivermen	AHL	67	5	6	11	160	....	....	....	....	....	....	....	....	....	2	0	0	0	2	....	....	....	....
	Alaska Aces	ECHL	5	0	4	4	4	....	....	....	....	....	....	....	....	....	....	....	....	....	....	....	....	....	....
2006-07	St. Louis	NHL	27	1	1	2	52	0	0	0	12	8.3	–3	2	50.0	5:31	....	....	....	....	....	....	....	....	....
	Peoria Rivermen	AHL	38	5	4	9	102	....	....	....	....	....	....	....	....	....	....	....	....	....	....	....	....	....	....
2007-08	St. Louis	NHL	61	3	3	6	100	0	0	1	36	8.3	–4	7	28.6	5:36	....	....	....	....	....	....	....	....	....
2008-09	St. Louis	NHL	1	0	1	1	0	0	0	0	0	0.0	0	0	0.0	8:20	....	....	....	....	....	....	....	....	....
2009-10	St. Louis	NHL	12	0	0	0	33	0	0	0	5	0.0	–4	0	0.0	4:30	....	....	....	....	....	....	....	....	....
	Peoria Rivermen	AHL	10	0	1	1	13	....	....	....	....	....	....	....	....	....	....	....	....	....	....	....	....	....	....
2010-11	Washington	NHL	16	0	2	2	30	0	0	0	6	0.0	–3	0	0.0	5:41	....	....	....	....	....	....	....	....	....
	NHL Totals		117	4	7	11	215	0	0	1	59	6.8		9	33.3	5:30	....	....	....	....	....	....	....	....	....

• Missed majority of 2008-09 due to recurring shoulder injury. • Missed majority of 2009-10 due to hand injury and as a healthy reserve. Traded to **Washigton** by **St. Louis** for Stefan Della Rovere, July 28, 2010. • Missed majority of 2010-11 as a healthy reserve.

KING, Dwight
(KIHNG, DWIGHT) **L.A.**

Center/Left wing. Shoots left. 6'3", 227 lbs. Born, Meadowlake, Sask., July 5, 1989. Los Angeles' 6th choice, 109th overall, in 2007 Entry Draft.

Season	Club	League	GP	G	A	Pts	PIM	PP	SH	GW	S	%	+/-	TF	F%	Min	GP	G	A	Pts	PIM	PP	SH	GW	Min
2004-05	Beardy's	SMHL	44	26	30	56	16	....	....	....	....	....	....	....	....	....	3	0	1	1	4	....	....	....	....
	Lethbridge	WHL	7	0	0	0	2	....	....	....	....	....	....	....	....	....	4	0	0	0	2	....	....	....	....
2005-06	Lethbridge	WHL	68	8	8	16	22	....	....	....	....	....	....	....	....	....	6	0	0	0	6	....	....	....	....
2006-07	Lethbridge	WHL	62	12	32	44	39	....	....	....	....	....	....	....	....	....	....	....	....	....	....	....	....	....	....
2007-08	Lethbridge	WHL	72	34	35	69	56	....	....	....	....	....	....	....	....	....	19	8	6	14	12	....	....	....	....
2008-09	Lethbridge	WHL	64	25	35	60	51	....	....	....	....	....	....	....	....	....	11	1	7	8	2	....	....	....	....
2009-10	Manchester	AHL	52	10	16	26	42	....	....	....	....	....	....	....	....	....	16	2	7	9	4	....	....	....	....
	Ontario Reign	ECHL	20	4	5	9	9	....	....	....	....	....	....	....	....	....	....	....	....	....	....	....	....	....	....
2010-11	Los Angeles	NHL	6	0	0	0	2	0	0	0	3	0.0	–2	0	0.0	11:43	....	....	....	....	....	....	....	....	....
	Manchester	AHL	72	24	28	52	58	....	....	....	....	....	....	....	....	....	7	2	3	5	2	....	....	....	....
	NHL Totals		6	0	0	0	2	0	0	0	3	0.0		0	0.0	11:43	....	....	....	....	....	....	....	....	....

KINRADE, Geoff
(KIHN-rayd, JEHF) **OTT**

Defense. Shoots left. 6', 207 lbs. Born, Nelson, B.C., July 29, 1985.

Season	Club	League	GP	G	A	Pts	PIM	PP	SH	GW	S	%	+/-	TF	F%	Min	GP	G	A	Pts	PIM	PP	SH	GW	Min
2003-04	Cowichan Valley	BCHL	48	2	3	5	34	....	....	....	....	....	....	....	....	....	6	1	2	3	4	....	....	....	....
2004-05	Cowichan Valley	BCHL	60	13	21	34	49	....	....	....	....	....	....	....	....	....	....	....	....	....	....	....	....	....	....
2005-06	Michigan Tech	WCHA	33	1	6	7	46	....	....	....	....	....	....	....	....	....	....	....	....	....	....	....	....	....	....
2006-07	Michigan Tech	WCHA	40	5	14	19	30	....	....	....	....	....	....	....	....	....	....	....	....	....	....	....	....	....	....
2007-08	Michigan Tech	WCHA	39	5	14	19	30	....	....	....	....	....	....	....	....	....	....	....	....	....	....	....	....	....	....
2008-09	Michigan Tech	WCHA	38	3	13	16	18	....	....	....	....	....	....	....	....	....	....	....	....	....	....	....	....	....	....
	Tampa Bay	NHL	1	0	0	0	0	0	0	0	1	0.0	–1	0	0.0	17:32	....	....	....	....	....	....	....	....	....
	Norfolk Admirals	AHL	10	1	4	5	12	....	....	....	....	....	....	....	....	....	....	....	....	....	....	....	....	....	....
2009-10	Binghamton	AHL	76	7	20	27	59	....	....	....	....	....	....	....	....	....	....	....	....	....	....	....	....	....	....
2010-11	Binghamton	AHL	78	6	19	25	43	....	....	....	....	....	....	....	....	....	23	1	4	5	6	....	....	....	....
	NHL Totals		1	0	0	0	0	0	0	0	1	0.0		0	0.0	17:32	....	....	....	....	....	....	....	....	....

Signed to an ATO (amateur tryout) contract by **Tampa Bay**, April 9, 2009. Signed as a free agent by **Ottawa**, July 10, 2009.

KLASEN, Linus
(KLAW-suhn, LEE-nuhs) **NSH**

Left wing. Shoots left. 5'8", 178 lbs. Born, Stockholm, Sweden, February 19, 1986.

Season	Club	League	GP	G	A	Pts	PIM	PP	SH	GW	S	%	+/-	TF	F%	Min	GP	G	A	Pts	PIM	PP	SH	GW	Min
2001-02	Huddinge IK U18	Swe-U18	14	7	5	12	4	....	....	....	....	....	....	....	....	....	7	0	0	0	0	....	....	....	....
2002-03	Huddinge IK U18	Swe-U18	13	3	4	7	4	....	....	....	....	....	....	....	....	....	2	0	0	0	0	....	....	....	....
	Huddinge IK Jr.	Swe-Jr.	2	0	0	0	0	....	....	....	....	....	....	....	....	....	....	....	....	....	....	....	....	....	....
2003-04	Huddinge IK U18	Swe-U18	11	8	12	20	14	....	....	....	....	....	....	....	....	....	....	....	....	....	....	....	....	....	....
	Huddinge IK Jr.	Swe-Jr.	21	3	2	5	6	....	....	....	....	....	....	....	....	....	2	0	0	0	0	....	....	....	....
2004-05	Lincoln Stars	USHL	26	7	9	16	13	....	....	....	....	....	....	....	....	....	....	....	....	....	....	....	....	....	....
	Huddinge IK	Sweden-2	2	0	0	0	0	....	....	....	....	....	....	....	....	....	....	....	....	....	....	....	....	....	....
	Huddinge IK Jr.	Swe-Jr.	9	4	5	9	27	....	....	....	....	....	....	....	....	....	3	0	2	2	0	....	....	....	....
2005-06	Huddinge IK Jr.	Swe-Jr.	8	3	6	9	29	....	....	....	....	....	....	....	....	....	....	....	....	....	....	....	....	....	....
	Huddinge IK	Sweden-3	43	24	51	75	38	....	....	....	....	....	....	....	....	....	5	3	3	6	2	....	....	....	....
2006-07	Huddinge IK	Sweden-2	52	19	44	63	30	....	....	....	....	....	....	....	....	....	....	....	....	....	....	....	....	....	....
2007-08	Sodertalje SK Jr.	Swe-Jr.	1	0	2	2	0	....	....	....	....	....	....	....	....	....	....	....	....	....	....	....	....	....	....
	Sodertalje SK	Sweden	52	14	20	34	24	....	....	....	....	....	....	....	....	....	....	....	....	....	....	....	....	....	....
2008-09	Sodertalje SK	Sweden	53	14	15	29	8	....	....	....	....	....	....	....	....	....	....	....	....	....	....	....	....	....	....
	Sodertalje SK	Sweden-Q	9	2	3	5	0	....	....	....	....	....	....	....	....	....	....	....	....	....	....	....	....	....	....
2009-10	Sodertalje SK	Sweden	51	19	32	51	20	....	....	....	....	....	....	....	....	....	....	....	....	....	....	....	....	....	....
	Sodertalje SK	Sweden-Q	10	4	4	8	4	....	....	....	....	....	....	....	....	....	....	....	....	....	....	....	....	....	....
2010-11	Nashville	NHL	4	0	0	0	0	0	0	0	4	0.0	–3	0	0.0	12:53	....	....	....	....	....	....	....	....	....
	Milwaukee	AHL	47	22	23	45	20	....	....	....	....	....	....	....	....	....	....	....	....	....	....	....	....	....	....
	NHL Totals		4	0	0	0	0	0	0	0	4	0.0		0	0.0	12:53	....	....	....	....	....	....	....	....	....

Signed as a free agent by **Nashville**, April 20, 2010.

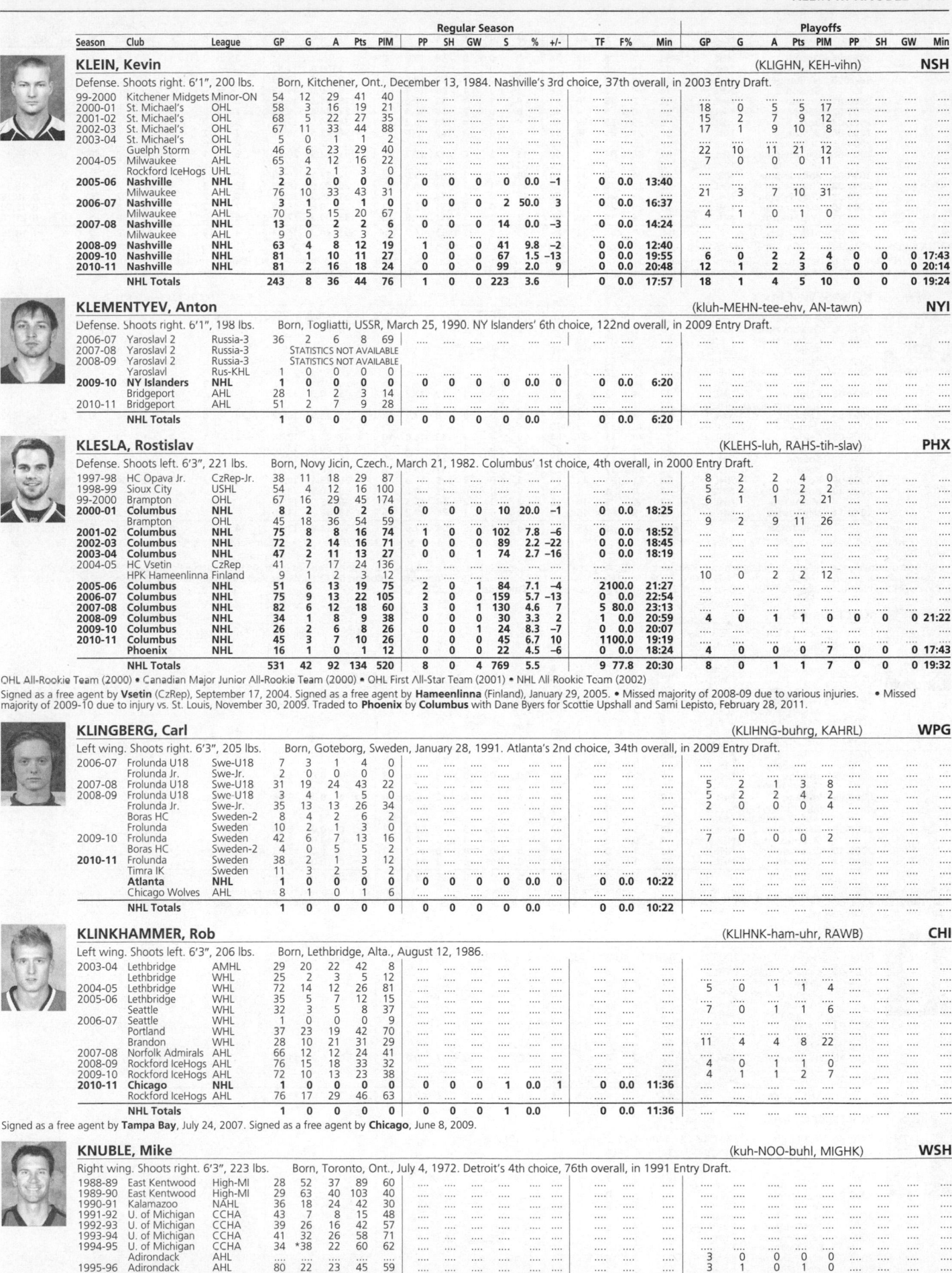

KLEIN, Kevin (KLIGHN, KEH-vihn) NSH

Defense. Shoots right. 6'1", 200 lbs. Born, Kitchener, Ont., December 13, 1984. Nashville's 3rd choice, 37th overall, in 2003 Entry Draft.

Season	Club	League	GP	G	A	Pts	PIM	PP	SH	GW	S	%	+/-	TF	F%	Min	GP	G	A	Pts	PIM	PP	SH	GW	Min
			Regular Season														Playoffs								
99-2000	Kitchener Midgets	Minor-ON	54	12	29	41	40	....	....	....	....	....	....	....	....	....	....	....	....	....	....	....	....	....	....
2000-01	St. Michael's	OHL	58	3	16	19	21	....	....	....	....	....	....	....	....	....	18	0	5	5	17	....	....	....	....
2001-02	St. Michael's	OHL	68	5	22	27	35	....	....	....	....	....	....	....	....	....	15	2	7	9	12	....	....	....	....
2002-03	St. Michael's	OHL	67	11	33	44	88	....	....	....	....	....	....	....	....	....	17	1	9	10	8	....	....	....	....
2003-04	St. Michael's	OHL	5	0	1	1	2	....	....	....	....	....	....	....	....	....	....	....	....	....	....	....	....	....	....
	Guelph Storm	OHL	46	6	23	29	40	....	....	....	....	....	....	....	....	....	22	10	11	21	12	....	....	....	....
2004-05	Milwaukee	AHL	65	4	12	16	22	....	....	....	....	....	....	....	....	....	7	0	0	0	11	....	....	....	....
	Rockford IceHogs	UHL	3	2	1	3	0	....	....	....	....	....	....	....	....	....	....	....	....	....	....	....	....	....	....
2005-06	**Nashville**	**NHL**	**2**	**0**	**0**	**0**	**0**	**0**	**0**	**0**	**0**	**0.0**	**–1**	**0**	**0.0**	**13:40**	....	....	....	....	....	....	....	....	....
	Milwaukee	AHL	76	10	33	43	31	....	....	....	....	....	....	....	....	....	21	3	7	10	31	....	....	....	....
2006-07	**Nashville**	**NHL**	**3**	**1**	**0**	**1**	**0**	**0**	**0**	**0**	**2**	**50.0**	**3**	**0**	**0.0**	**16:37**	....	....	....	....	....	....	....	....	....
	Milwaukee	AHL	70	5	15	20	67	....	....	....	....	....	....	....	....	....	4	1	0	1	0	....	....	....	....
2007-08	**Nashville**	**NHL**	**13**	**0**	**2**	**2**	**6**	**0**	**0**	**0**	**14**	**0.0**	**–3**	**0**	**0.0**	**14:24**	....	....	....	....	....	....	....	....	....
	Milwaukee	AHL	9	0	3	3	2	....	....	....	....	....	....	....	....	....	....	....	....	....	....	....	....	....	....
2008-09	**Nashville**	**NHL**	**63**	**4**	**8**	**12**	**19**	**1**	**0**	**0**	**41**	**9.8**	**–2**	**0**	**0.0**	**12:40**	....	....	....	....	....	....	....	....	....
2009-10	**Nashville**	**NHL**	**81**	**1**	**10**	**11**	**27**	**0**	**0**	**0**	**67**	**1.5**	**–13**	**0**	**0.0**	**19:55**	**6**	**0**	**2**	**2**	**4**	**0**	**0**	**0**	**17:43**
2010-11	**Nashville**	**NHL**	**81**	**2**	**16**	**18**	**24**	**0**	**0**	**0**	**99**	**2.0**	**9**	**0**	**0.0**	**20:48**	**12**	**1**	**2**	**3**	**6**	**0**	**0**	**0**	**20:14**
	NHL Totals		**243**	**8**	**36**	**44**	**76**	**1**	**0**	**0**	**223**	**3.6**		**0**	**0.0**	**17:57**	**18**	**1**	**4**	**5**	**10**	**0**	**0**	**0**	**19:24**

KLEMENTYEV, Anton (kluh-MEHN-tee-ehv, AN-tawn) NYI

Defense. Shoots right. 6'1", 198 lbs. Born, Togliatti, USSR, March 25, 1990. NY Islanders' 6th choice, 122nd overall, in 2009 Entry Draft.

Season	Club	League	GP	G	A	Pts	PIM	PP	SH	GW	S	%	+/-	TF	F%	Min	GP	G	A	Pts	PIM	PP	SH	GW	Min
2006-07	Yaroslavl 2	Russia-3	36	2	6	8	69	....	....	....	....	....	....	....	....	....	....	....	....	....	....	....	....	....	....
2007-08	Yaroslavl 2	Russia-3	STATISTICS NOT AVAILABLE																						
2008-09	Yaroslavl 2	Russia-3	STATISTICS NOT AVAILABLE																						
	Yaroslavl	Rus-KHL	1	0	0	0	0	....	....	....	....	....	....	....	....	....	....	....	....	....	....	....	....	....	....
2009-10	**NY Islanders**	**NHL**	**1**	**0**	**0**	**0**	**0**	**0**	**0**	**0**	**0**	**0.0**	**0**	**0**	**0.0**	**6:20**	....	....	....	....	....	....	....	....	....
	Bridgeport	AHL	28	1	2	3	14	....	....	....	....	....	....	....	....	....	....	....	....	....	....	....	....	....	....
2010-11	Bridgeport	AHL	51	2	7	9	28	....	....	....	....	....	....	....	....	....	....	....	....	....	....	....	....	....	....
	NHL Totals		**1**	**0**	**0**	**0**	**0**	**0**	**0**	**0**	**0**	**0.0**		**0**	**0.0**	**6:20**	....	....	....	....	....	....	....	....	....

KLESLA, Rostislav (KLEHS-luh, RAHS-tih-slav) PHX

Defense. Shoots left. 6'3", 221 lbs. Born, Novy Jicin, Czech., March 21, 1982. Columbus' 1st choice, 4th overall, in 2000 Entry Draft.

Season	Club	League	GP	G	A	Pts	PIM	PP	SH	GW	S	%	+/-	TF	F%	Min	GP	G	A	Pts	PIM	PP	SH	GW	Min
1997-98	HC Opava Jr.	CzRep-Jr.	38	11	18	29	87	....	....	....	....	....	....	....	....	....	8	2	2	4	0	....	....	....	....
1998-99	Sioux City	USHL	54	4	12	16	100	....	....	....	....	....	....	....	....	....	5	2	0	2	2	....	....	....	....
99-2000	Brampton	OHL	67	16	29	45	174	....	....	....	....	....	....	....	....	....	6	1	1	2	21	....	....	....	....
2000-01	**Columbus**	**NHL**	**8**	**2**	**0**	**2**	**6**	**0**	**0**	**0**	**10**	**20.0**	**–1**	**0**	**0.0**	**18:25**	....	....	....	....	....	....	....	....	....
	Brampton	OHL	45	18	36	54	59	....	....	....	....	....	....	....	....	....	9	2	9	11	26	....	....	....	....
2001-02	**Columbus**	**NHL**	**75**	**8**	**8**	**16**	**74**	**1**	**0**	**0**	**102**	**7.8**	**–6**	**0**	**0.0**	**18:52**	....	....	....	....	....	....	....	....	....
2002-03	**Columbus**	**NHL**	**72**	**2**	**14**	**16**	**71**	**0**	**0**	**0**	**89**	**2.2**	**–22**	**0**	**0.0**	**18:45**	....	....	....	....	....	....	....	....	....
2003-04	**Columbus**	**NHL**	**47**	**2**	**11**	**13**	**27**	**0**	**0**	**1**	**74**	**2.7**	**–16**	**0**	**0.0**	**18:19**	....	....	....	....	....	....	....	....	....
2004-05	HC Vsetin	CzRep	41	7	17	24	136	....	....	....	....	....	....	....	....	....	....	....	....	....	....	....	....	....	....
	HPK Hameenlinna	Finland	9	1	2	3	12	....	....	....	....	....	....	....	....	....	10	0	2	2	12	....	....	....	....
2005-06	**Columbus**	**NHL**	**51**	**6**	**13**	**19**	**75**	**2**	**0**	**1**	**84**	**7.1**	**–4**	**2**	**100.0**	**21:27**	....	....	....	....	....	....	....	....	....
2006-07	**Columbus**	**NHL**	**75**	**9**	**13**	**22**	**105**	**2**	**0**	**0**	**159**	**5.7**	**–13**	**0**	**0.0**	**22:54**	....	....	....	....	....	....	....	....	....
2007-08	**Columbus**	**NHL**	**82**	**6**	**12**	**18**	**60**	**3**	**0**	**1**	**130**	**4.6**	**7**	**5**	**80.0**	**23:13**	....	....	....	....	....	....	....	....	....
2008-09	**Columbus**	**NHL**	**34**	**1**	**8**	**9**	**38**	**0**	**0**	**0**	**30**	**3.3**	**2**	**1**	**0.0**	**20:59**	**4**	**0**	**1**	**1**	**0**	**0**	**0**	**0**	**21:22**
2009-10	**Columbus**	**NHL**	**26**	**2**	**6**	**8**	**26**	**0**	**0**	**1**	**24**	**8.3**	**–7**	**0**	**0.0**	**20:07**	....	....	....	....	....	....	....	....	....
2010-11	**Columbus**	**NHL**	**45**	**3**	**7**	**10**	**26**	**0**	**0**	**0**	**45**	**6.7**	**10**	**1**	**100.0**	**19:19**	....	....	....	....	....	....	....	....	....
	Phoenix	**NHL**	**16**	**1**	**0**	**1**	**12**	**0**	**0**	**0**	**22**	**4.5**	**–6**	**0**	**0.0**	**18:24**	**4**	**0**	**0**	**0**	**7**	**0**	**0**	**0**	**17:43**
	NHL Totals		**531**	**42**	**92**	**134**	**520**	**8**	**0**	**4**	**769**	**5.5**		**9**	**77.8**	**20:30**	**8**	**0**	**1**	**1**	**7**	**0**	**0**	**0**	**19:32**

OHL All-Rookie Team (2000) • Canadian Major Junior All-Rookie Team (2000) • OHL First All-Star Team (2001) • NHL All Rookie Team (2002)

Signed as a free agent by **Vsetin** (CzRep), September 17, 2004. Signed as a free agent by **Hameenlinna** (Finland), January 29, 2005. • Missed majority of 2008-09 due to various injuries. • Missed majority of 2009-10 due to injury vs. St. Louis, November 30, 2009. Traded to **Phoenix** by **Columbus** with Dane Byers for Scottie Upshall and Sami Lepisto, February 28, 2011.

KLINGBERG, Carl (KLIHNG-buhrg, KAHRL) WPG

Left wing. Shoots right. 6'3", 205 lbs. Born, Goteborg, Sweden, January 28, 1991. Atlanta's 2nd choice, 34th overall, in 2009 Entry Draft.

Season	Club	League	GP	G	A	Pts	PIM	PP	SH	GW	S	%	+/-	TF	F%	Min	GP	G	A	Pts	PIM	PP	SH	GW	Min
2006-07	Frolunda U18	Swe-U18	7	3	1	4	0	....	....	....	....	....	....	....	....	....	....	....	....	....	....	....	....	....	....
	Frolunda Jr.	Swe-Jr.	2	0	0	0	0	....	....	....	....	....	....	....	....	....	....	....	....	....	....	....	....	....	....
2007-08	Frolunda U18	Swe-U18	31	19	24	43	22	....	....	....	....	....	....	....	....	....	5	2	1	3	8	....	....	....	....
2008-09	Frolunda U18	Swe-U18	3	4	1	5	0	....	....	....	....	....	....	....	....	....	5	2	2	4	2	....	....	....	....
	Frolunda Jr.	Swe-Jr.	35	13	13	26	34	....	....	....	....	....	....	....	....	....	2	0	0	0	4	....	....	....	....
	Boras HC	Sweden-2	8	4	2	6	2	....	....	....	....	....	....	....	....	....	....	....	....	....	....	....	....	....	....
	Frolunda	Sweden	10	2	1	3	0	....	....	....	....	....	....	....	....	....	....	....	....	....	....	....	....	....	....
2009-10	Frolunda	Sweden	42	6	7	13	16	....	....	....	....	....	....	....	....	....	7	0	0	0	2	....	....	....	....
	Boras HC	Sweden-2	4	0	5	5	2	....	....	....	....	....	....	....	....	....	....	....	....	....	....	....	....	....	....
2010-11	Frolunda	Sweden	38	2	1	3	12	....	....	....	....	....	....	....	....	....	....	....	....	....	....	....	....	....	....
	Timra IK	Sweden	11	3	2	5	2	....	....	....	....	....	....	....	....	....	....	....	....	....	....	....	....	....	....
	Atlanta	**NHL**	**1**	**0**	**0**	**0**	**0**	**0**	**0**	**0**	**0**	**0.0**	**0**	**0**	**0.0**	**10:22**	....	....	....	....	....	....	....	....	....
	Chicago Wolves	AHL	8	1	0	1	6	....	....	....	....	....	....	....	....	....	....	....	....	....	....	....	....	....	....
	NHL Totals		**1**	**0**	**0**	**0**	**0**	**0**	**0**	**0**	**0**	**0.0**		**0**	**0.0**	**10:22**	....	....	....	....	....	....	....	....	....

KLINKHAMMER, Rob (KLIHNK-ham-uhr, RAWB) CHI

Left wing. Shoots left. 6'3", 206 lbs. Born, Lethbridge, Alta., August 12, 1986.

Season	Club	League	GP	G	A	Pts	PIM	PP	SH	GW	S	%	+/-	TF	F%	Min	GP	G	A	Pts	PIM	PP	SH	GW	Min
2003-04	Lethbridge	AMHL	29	20	22	42	8	....	....	....	....	....	....	....	....	....	....	....	....	....	....	....	....	....	....
	Lethbridge	WHL	25	2	3	5	12	....	....	....	....	....	....	....	....	....	....	....	....	....	....	....	....	....	....
2004-05	Lethbridge	WHL	72	14	12	26	81	....	....	....	....	....	....	....	....	....	5	0	1	1	4	....	....	....	....
2005-06	Lethbridge	WHL	35	5	7	12	15	....	....	....	....	....	....	....	....	....	....	....	....	....	....	....	....	....	....
	Seattle	WHL	32	3	5	8	37	....	....	....	....	....	....	....	....	....	7	0	1	1	6	....	....	....	....
2006-07	Seattle	WHL	1	0	0	0	9	....	....	....	....	....	....	....	....	....	....	....	....	....	....	....	....	....	....
	Portland	WHL	37	23	19	42	70	....	....	....	....	....	....	....	....	....	....	....	....	....	....	....	....	....	....
	Brandon	WHL	28	10	21	31	29	....	....	....	....	....	....	....	....	....	11	4	4	8	22	....	....	....	....
2007-08	Norfolk Admirals	AHL	66	12	12	24	41	....	....	....	....	....	....	....	....	....	....	....	....	....	....	....	....	....	....
2008-09	Rockford IceHogs	AHL	76	15	18	33	32	....	....	....	....	....	....	....	....	....	4	0	1	1	0	....	....	....	....
2009-10	Rockford IceHogs	AHL	72	10	13	23	38	....	....	....	....	....	....	....	....	....	4	1	1	2	7	....	....	....	....
2010-11	**Chicago**	**NHL**	**1**	**0**	**0**	**0**	**0**	**0**	**0**	**0**	**1**	**0.0**	**1**	**0**	**0.0**	**11:36**	....	....	....	....	....	....	....	....	....
	Rockford IceHogs	AHL	76	17	29	46	63	....	....	....	....	....	....	....	....	....	....	....	....	....	....	....	....	....	....
	NHL Totals		**1**	**0**	**0**	**0**	**0**	**0**	**0**	**0**	**1**	**0.0**		**0**	**0.0**	**11:36**	....	....	....	....	....	....	....	....	....

Signed as a free agent by **Tampa Bay**, July 24, 2007. Signed as a free agent by **Chicago**, June 8, 2009.

KNUBLE, Mike (kuh-NOO-buhl, MIGHK) WSH

Right wing. Shoots right. 6'3", 223 lbs. Born, Toronto, Ont., July 4, 1972. Detroit's 4th choice, 76th overall, in 1991 Entry Draft.

Season	Club	League	GP	G	A	Pts	PIM	PP	SH	GW	S	%	+/-	TF	F%	Min	GP	G	A	Pts	PIM	PP	SH	GW	Min
1988-89	East Kentwood	High-MI	28	52	37	89	60	....	....	....	....	....	....	....	....	....	....	....	....	....	....	....	....	....	....
1989-90	East Kentwood	High-MI	29	63	40	103	40	....	....	....	....	....	....	....	....	....	....	....	....	....	....	....	....	....	....
1990-91	Kalamazoo	NAHL	36	18	24	42	30	....	....	....	....	....	....	....	....	....	....	....	....	....	....	....	....	....	....
1991-92	U. of Michigan	CCHA	43	7	8	15	48	....	....	....	....	....	....	....	....	....	....	....	....	....	....	....	....	....	....
1992-93	U. of Michigan	CCHA	39	26	16	42	57	....	....	....	....	....	....	....	....	....	....	....	....	....	....	....	....	....	....
1993-94	U. of Michigan	CCHA	41	32	26	58	71	....	....	....	....	....	....	....	....	....	....	....	....	....	....	....	....	....	....
1994-95	U. of Michigan	CCHA	34	*38	22	60	62	....	....	....	....	....	....	....	....	....	....	....	....	....	....	....	....	....	....
	Adirondack	AHL	....	....	....	....	....	....	....	....	....	....	....	....	....	....	3	0	0	0	0	....	....	....	....
1995-96	Adirondack	AHL	80	22	23	45	59	....	....	....	....	....	....	....	....	....	3	1	0	1	0	....	....	....	....
1996-97	**Detroit**	**NHL**	**9**	**1**	**0**	**1**	**0**	**0**	**0**	**0**	**10**	**10.0**	**–1**	....	....	....	....	....	....	....	....	....	....	....	....
	Adirondack	AHL	68	28	35	63	54	....	....	....	....	....	....	....	....	....	....	....	....	....	....	....	....	....	....

			Regular Season														Playoffs								
Season	Club	League	GP	G	A	Pts	PIM	PP	SH	GW	S	%	+/-	TF	F%	Min	GP	G	A	Pts	PIM	PP	SH	GW	Min
1997-98♦	Detroit	NHL	53	7	6	13	16	0	0	0	54	13.0	2	....	....	....	3	0	1	1	0	0	0	0	....
1998-99	NY Rangers	NHL	82	15	20	35	26	3	0	1	113	13.3	−7	1	100.0	14:52	....	....	....	....	....	....	....	....	....
99-2000	NY Rangers	NHL	59	9	5	14	18	1	0	1	50	18.0	−5	9	55.6	10:39	....	....	....	....	....	....	....	....	....
	Boston	NHL	14	3	3	6	8	1	0	1	28	10.7	−2	3	0.0	19:29	....	....	....	....	....	....	....	....	....
2000-01	Boston	NHL	82	7	13	20	37	0	1	1	92	7.6	0	115	31.3	10:34	....	....	....	....	....	....	....	....	....
2001-02	Boston	NHL	54	8	6	14	42	0	0	2	77	10.4	9	27	44.4	9:45	2	0	0	0	0	0	0	0	3:30
2002-03	Boston	NHL	75	30	29	59	45	9	0	4	185	16.2	18	34	44.1	17:24	5	0	2	2	2	0	0	0	17:35
2003-04	Boston	NHL	82	21	25	46	32	4	0	3	192	10.9	19	54	31.5	18:47	7	2	0	2	0	1	0	0	19:45
2004-05	Linkopings HC	Sweden	49	*26	13	39	40	....	....	....	....	....	....	....	....	....	6	0	1	1	2	....	....	....	....
2005-06	Philadelphia	NHL	82	34	31	65	80	13	2	6	217	15.7	25	161	32.3	20:21	6	1	3	4	8	0	0	0	19:17
	United States	Olympics	6	1	1	2	4	....	....	....	....	....	....	....	....	....	....	....	....	....	....	....	....	....	....
2006-07	Philadelphia	NHL	64	24	30	54	56	10	0	1	160	15.0	2	62	37.1	19:38	....	....	....	....	....	....	....	....	....
2007-08	Philadelphia	NHL	82	29	26	55	72	15	1	3	177	16.4	−3	25	40.0	18:55	12	3	4	7	6	0	0	1	18:34
2008-09	Philadelphia	NHL	82	27	20	47	62	11	0	6	173	15.6	5	51	35.3	18:10	6	2	1	3	2	0	0	0	18:26
2009-10	Washington	NHL	69	29	24	53	59	6	0	5	151	19.2	23	6	0.0	16:53	7	2	4	6	6	0	1	0	17:50
2010-11	Washington	NHL	79	24	16	40	36	7	1	1	203	11.8	10	33	30.3	17:53	6	2	0	2	8	1	0	0	21:10
	NHL Totals		968	268	254	522	589	80	5	35	1882	14.2		581	34.3	16:27	54	12	15	27	32	2	1	1	18:19

CCHA Second All-Star Team (1994, 1995) • NCAA West Second All-American Team (1995)

Traded to **NY Rangers** by **Detroit** for NY Rangers' 2nd round choice (Tomas Kopecky) in 2000 Entry Draft, October 1, 1998. Traded to **Boston** by **NY Rangers** for Rob DiMaio, March 10, 2000. Signed as a free agent by **Philadelphia**, July 3, 2004. Signed as a free agent by **Linkopings** (Sweden), August 2, 2004. Signed as a free agent by **Washington**, July 1, 2009.

KOBASEW, Chuck (KOH-buh-soo, CHUHK) COL

Right wing. Shoots right. 6', 192 lbs. Born, Vancouver, B.C., April 17, 1982. Calgary's 1st choice, 14th overall, in 2001 Entry Draft.

1997-98	Osoyoos Heat	KIJHL	6	2	2	4	2	....	....	....	....	....	....	....	....	....	....	....	....	....	....	....	....	....	....
1998-99	Osoyoos Heat	KIJHL	23	25	24	49	....	....	....	....	....	....	....	....	....	....	....	....	....	....	....	....	....	....	....
	Penticton	BCHL	30	11	17	28	18	....	....	....	....	....	....	....	....	....	....	....	....	....	....	....	....	....	....
99-2000	Penticton	BCHL	58	*54	52	106	83	....	....	....	....	....	....	....	....	....	....	....	....	....	....	....	....	....	....
2000-01	Boston College	H-East	43	27	22	49	38	....	....	....	....	....	....	....	....	....	....	....	....	....	....	....	....	....	....
2001-02	Kelowna Rockets	WHL	55	41	21	62	114	....	....	....	....	....	....	....	....	....	15	10	5	15	22	....	....	....	....
2002-03	Calgary	NHL	23	4	2	6	8	1	0	1	29	13.8	−3	5	0.0	11:48	....	....	....	....	....	....	....	....	....
	Saint John Flames	AHL	48	21	12	33	61	....	....	....	....	....	....	....	....	....	....	....	....	....	....	....	....	....	....
2003-04	Calgary	NHL	70	6	11	17	51	3	0	0	78	7.7	−12	91	42.9	10:22	26	0	1	1	24	0	0	0	9:02
2004-05	Lowell	AHL	79	38	37	75	110	....	....	....	....	....	....	....	....	....	11	6	3	9	27	....	....	....	....
2005-06	Calgary	NHL	77	20	11	31	64	10	0	4	143	14.0	−10	47	25.5	12:16	7	1	0	1	0	0	0	1	12:29
2006-07	Calgary	NHL	40	4	13	17	37	1	0	1	69	5.8	7	26	30.8	13:13	....	....	....	....	....	....	....	....	....
	Boston	NHL	10	1	1	2	25	1	0	0	24	4.2	−6	6	16.7	18:51	....	....	....	....	....	....	....	....	....
2007-08	Boston	NHL	73	22	17	39	29	6	3	3	147	15.0	6	70	40.0	17:41	....	....	....	....	....	....	....	....	....
2008-09	Boston	NHL	68	21	21	42	56	6	0	3	129	16.3	5	26	23.1	14:41	11	3	3	6	14	0	0	1	16:09
2009-10	Boston	NHL	7	0	1	1	2	0	0	0	13	0.0	−2	0	0.0	14:22	....	....	....	....	....	....	....	....	....
	Minnesota	NHL	42	9	5	14	16	2	0	2	58	15.5	−9	8	25.0	13:50	....	....	....	....	....	....	....	....	....
2010-11	Minnesota	NHL	63	9	7	16	19	0	0	1	74	12.2	−6	13	46.2	11:50	....	....	....	....	....	....	....	....	....
	NHL Totals		473	96	89	185	307	30	3	15	764	12.6		292	34.9	13:29	44	4	4	8	38	0	0	2	11:21

Hockey East Second All-Star Team (2001) • Hockey East Rookie of the Year (2001) • NCAA Championship All-Tournament Team (2001) • NCAA Championship Tournament MVP (2001) • AHL First All-Star Team (2005)

• Left **Boston College** (Hockey East) and signed with **Kelowna** (WHL), August 13, 2001. Traded to **Boston** by **Calgary** with Andrew Ference for Brad Stuart, Wayne Primeau and Washington's 4th round choice (previously acquired, Calgary selected T.J. Brodie) in 2008 Entry Draft, February 10, 2007. Traded to **Minnesota** by **Boston** for Craig Weller, Alexander Fallstrom and Minnesota's 2nd round choice (Alexander Khokhlachev) in 2011 Entry Draft, October 18, 2009. Signed as a free agent by **Colorado**, July 1, 2011.

KOCI, David (KOH-chee, DAY-vihd)

Left wing. Shoots left. 6'6", 238 lbs. Born, Prague, Czech., May 12, 1981. Pittsburgh's 5th choice, 146th overall, in 2000 Entry Draft.

1997-98	Sparta Jr.	CzRep-Jr.	41	2	9	11	105	....	....	....	....	....	....	....	....	....	....	....	....	....	....	....	....	....	....
1998-99	Hvezda Praha Jr.	CzRep-Jr.	22	1	3	4	36	....	....	....	....	....	....	....	....	....	....	....	....	....	....	....	....	....	....
	Sparta Jr.	CzRep-Jr.	7	0	0	0	4	....	....	....	....	....	....	....	....	....	....	....	....	....	....	....	....	....	....
99-2000	Sparta Jr.	CzRep-Jr.	47	0	6	6	124	....	....	....	....	....	....	....	....	....	....	....	....	....	....	....	....	....	....
2000-01	Prince George	WHL	70	2	7	9	155	....	....	....	....	....	....	....	....	....	6	0	0	0	20	....	....	....	....
2001-02	Wilkes-Barre	AHL	26	1	3	4	98	....	....	....	....	....	....	....	....	....	....	....	....	....	....	....	....	....	....
	Wheeling Nailers	ECHL	33	2	4	6	105	....	....	....	....	....	....	....	....	....	....	....	....	....	....	....	....	....	....
2002-03	Wilkes-Barre	AHL	9	0	0	0	4	....	....	....	....	....	....	....	....	....	....	....	....	....	....	....	....	....	....
	Wheeling Nailers	ECHL	48	0	1	1	103	....	....	....	....	....	....	....	....	....	....	....	....	....	....	....	....	....	....
2003-04	Wilkes-Barre	AHL	78	1	7	8	298	....	....	....	....	....	....	....	....	....	10	0	0	0	24	....	....	....	....
2004-05	Wilkes-Barre	AHL	68	1	8	9	311	....	....	....	....	....	....	....	....	....	....	....	....	....	....	....	....	....	....
2005-06	Wilkes-Barre	AHL	13	0	0	0	59	....	....	....	....	....	....	....	....	....	....	....	....	....	....	....	....	....	....
2006-07	Chicago	NHL	9	0	0	0	88	0	0	0	3	0.0	−3	0	0.0	4:44	....	....	....	....	....	....	....	....	....
	Norfolk Admirals	AHL	44	0	1	1	223	....	....	....	....	....	....	....	....	....	....	....	....	....	....	....	....	....	....
2007-08	Chicago	NHL	18	0	0	0	68	0	0	0	2	0.0	−4	0	0.0	3:38	....	....	....	....	....	....	....	....	....
	Rockford IceHogs	AHL	7	0	0	0	25	....	....	....	....	....	....	....	....	....	....	....	....	....	....	....	....	....	....
	Norfolk Admirals	AHL	21	0	2	2	57	....	....	....	....	....	....	....	....	....	....	....	....	....	....	....	....	....	....
2008-09	Tampa Bay	NHL	33	1	1	2	132	0	0	0	8	12.5	3	0	0.0	6:14	....	....	....	....	....	....	....	....	....
	St. Louis	NHL	4	0	0	0	9	0	0	0	5	0.0	−2	0	0.0	3:37	....	....	....	....	....	....	....	....	....
2009-10	Colorado	NHL	43	1	0	1	84	0	0	0	6	16.7	−2	0	0.0	3:03	....	....	....	....	....	....	....	....	....
2010-11	Colorado	NHL	35	1	0	1	80	0	0	0	9	11.1	−5	0	0.0	4:05	....	....	....	....	....	....	....	....	....
	NHL Totals		142	3	1	4	461	0	0	0	33	9.1		0	0.0	4:15	....	....	....	....	....	....	....	....	....

• Missed majority of 2005-06 due to knee injury, November, 2006. Signed as a free agent by **Chicago**, July 17, 2006. Signed as a free agent by **Tampa Bay**, July 3, 2008. Claimed on waivers by **St. Louis** from **Tampa Bay**, October 21, 2008. Claimed on waivers by **Tampa Bay** from **St. Louis**, November 20, 2008. Signed as a free agent by **Colorado**, July 1, 2009. • Missed majority of 2010-11 due to facial injury and as a healthy reserve.

KOHN, Dustin (KOHN, DUHS-tihn)

Defense. Shoots left. 6'1", 200 lbs. Born, Edmonton, Alta., February 2, 1987. NY Islanders' 2nd choice, 46th overall, in 2005 Entry Draft.

2003-04	Calgary Hitmen	WHL	52	3	6	9	13	....	....	....	....	....	....	....	....	....	7	0	1	1	2	....	....	....	....
2004-05	Calgary Hitmen	WHL	71	8	35	43	61	....	....	....	....	....	....	....	....	....	12	0	4	4	6	....	....	....	....
2005-06	Calgary Hitmen	WHL	38	2	12	14	20	....	....	....	....	....	....	....	....	....	....	....	....	....	....	....	....	....	....
	Brandon	WHL	31	2	13	15	30	....	....	....	....	....	....	....	....	....	6	0	4	4	10	....	....	....	....
	Bridgeport	AHL	2	0	0	0	0	....	....	....	....	....	....	....	....	....	....	....	....	....	....	....	....	....	....
2006-07	Brandon	WHL	61	5	45	50	77	....	....	....	....	....	....	....	....	....	11	1	8	9	18	....	....	....	....
2007-08	Bridgeport	AHL	62	3	9	12	28	....	....	....	....	....	....	....	....	....	....	....	....	....	....	....	....	....	....
2008-09	Bridgeport	AHL	58	4	13	17	45	....	....	....	....	....	....	....	....	....	5	0	0	0	4	....	....	....	....
2009-10	NY Islanders	NHL	22	0	4	4	4	0	0	0	7	0.0	−2	0	0.0	11:36	....	....	....	....	....	....	....	....	....
	Bridgeport	AHL	45	2	15	17	53	....	....	....	....	....	....	....	....	....	5	2	2	4	2	....	....	....	....
2010-11	Bridgeport	AHL	45	2	13	15	42	....	....	....	....	....	....	....	....	....	....	....	....	....	....	....	....	....	....
	NHL Totals		22	0	4	4	4	0	0	0	7	0.0		0	0.0	11:36	....	....	....	....	....	....	....	....	....

KOISTINEN, Ville (KOIS-tih-nehn, VIHL-ee)

Defense. Shoots left. 5'11", 187 lbs. Born, Oulu, Finland, June 17, 1982.

1998-99	Ilves Tampere U18	Fin-U18	34	4	10	14	86	....	....	....	....	....	....	....	....	....	....	....	....	....	....	....	....	....	....
	Ilves Tampere Jr.	Fin-Jr.	1	0	0	0	2	....	....	....	....	....	....	....	....	....	....	....	....	....	....	....	....	....	....
99-2000	Ilves Tampere U18	Fin-U18	14	4	6	10	69	....	....	....	....	....	....	....	....	....	....	....	....	....	....	....	....	....	....
	Ilves Tampere Jr.	Fin-Jr.	34	4	2	6	40	....	....	....	....	....	....	....	....	....	....	....	....	....	....	....	....	....	....
2000-01	Ilves Tampere	Finland	6	0	0	0	0	....	....	....	....	....	....	....	....	....	5	0	1	1	0	....	....	....	....
	Ilves Tampere Jr.	Fin-Jr.	26	1	8	9	101	....	....	....	....	....	....	....	....	....	....	....	....	....	....	....	....	....	....
2001-02	Ilves Tampere	Finland	53	1	8	9	42	....	....	....	....	....	....	....	....	....	....	....	....	....	....	....	....	....	....
	Ilves Tampere Jr.	Fin-Jr.	6	2	2	4	16	....	....	....	....	....	....	....	....	....	....	....	....	....	....	....	....	....	....
2002-03	Ilves Tampere	Finland	18	4	1	5	8	....	....	....	....	....	....	....	....	....	....	....	....	....	....	....	....	....	....
	Ilves Tampere Jr.	Fin-Jr.	1	0	0	0	10	....	....	....	....	....	....	....	....	....	....	....	....	....	....	....	....	....	....
2003-04	Ilves Tampere	Finland	54	7	16	23	51	....	....	....	....	....	....	....	....	....	7	0	2	2	0	....	....	....	....
2004-05	Ilves Tampere	Finland	52	6	14	20	69	....	....	....	....	....	....	....	....	....	3	0	0	0	0	....	....	....	....
2005-06	Ilves Tampere	Finland	56	8	26	34	70	....	....	....	....	....	....	....	....	....	4	0	1	1	2	....	....	....	....
2006-07	Milwaukee	AHL	59	9	32	41	44	....	....	....	....	....	....	....	....	....	4	0	2	2	4	....	....	....	....

Season	Club	League	GP	G	A	Pts	PIM	PP	SH	GW	S	%	+/-	TF	F%	Min	GP	G	A	Pts	PIM	PP	SH	GW	Min
			Regular Season														Playoffs								
2007-08	Nashville	NHL	48	4	13	17	18	2	0	1	60	6.7	13	0	0.0	16:48									
2008-09	Nashville	NHL	38	3	8	11	14	1	0	2	42	7.1	0	1	0.0	14:42									
2009-10	Florida	NHL	17	1	3	4	8	0	0	0	12	8.3	1	0	0.0	7:50									
	Rochester	AHL	8	1	1	2	4																		
2010-11	Skelleftea AIK	Sweden	31	4	8	12	28																		
	NHL Totals		103	8	24	32	40	3	0	3	114	7.0		1	0.0	14:33									

Signed as a free agent by **Nashville**, May 11, 2006. • Missed majority of 2008-09 as a healthy reserve. • Missed majority of 2009-10 due to knee injury, December 28, 2010.

KOIVU, Mikko

(KOI-voo, MEE-koh) **MIN**

Center. Shoots left. 6'2", 219 lbs. Born, Turku, Finland, March 12, 1983. Minnesota's 1st choice, 6th overall, in 2001 Entry Draft.

Season	Club	League	GP	G	A	Pts	PIM	PP	SH	GW	S	%	+/-	TF	F%	Min	GP	G	A	Pts	PIM	PP	SH	GW	Min
99-2000	TPS Turku U18	Fin-U18	11	4	9	13	18																		
	TPS Turku Jr.	Fin-Jr.	30	4	8	12	22										13	1	4	5	8				
2000-01	TPS Turku U18	Fin-U18															7	2	10	12	2				
	TPS Turku Jr.	Fin-Jr.	26	9	36	45	26										3	1	1	2	6				
	TPS Turku	Finland	21	0	1	1	2																		
2001-02	TPS Turku Jr.	Fin-Jr.	2	0	1	1	12																		
	TPS Turku	Finland	48	4	3	7	34										8	0	3	3	4				
2002-03	TPS Turku	Finland	37	7	13	20	20										7	2	2	4	6				
2003-04	TPS Turku	Finland	45	6	24	30	36										13	1	7	8	8				
2004-05	Houston Aeros	AHL	67	20	28	48	47										5	1	0	1	2				
2005-06	Minnesota	NHL	64	6	15	21	40	3	0	0	96	6.3	–9	724	47.4	13:17									
	Finland	Olympics	8	0	0	0	6																		
2006-07	Minnesota	NHL	82	20	34	54	58	9	2	2	162	12.3	6	1165	50.9	17:29	5	1	0	1	4	0	0	0	17:43
2007-08	Minnesota	NHL	57	11	31	42	42	2	0	2	144	7.6	13	1032	52.5	20:53	6	4	1	5	4	0	1	0	21:56
2008-09	Minnesota	NHL	79	20	47	67	66	5	4	3	236	8.5	2	1625	52.7	21:29									
2009-10	Minnesota	NHL	80	22	49	71	50	8	1	2	246	8.9	–2	1518	56.9	20:45									
	Finland	Olympics	6	0	4	4	2																		
2010-11	Minnesota	NHL	71	17	45	62	50	7	1	3	191	8.9	4	1293	52.8	19:29									
	NHL Totals		433	96	221	317	306	34	8	12	1075	8.9		7357	52.8	18:58	11	5	1	6	8	0	1	0	20:01

KOIVU, Saku

(KOI-voo, SA-koo) **ANA**

Center. Shoots left. 5'10", 182 lbs. Born, Turku, Finland, November 23, 1974. Montreal's 1st choice, 21st overall, in 1993 Entry Draft.

Season	Club	League	GP	G	A	Pts	PIM	PP	SH	GW	S	%	+/-	TF	F%	Min	GP	G	A	Pts	PIM	PP	SH	GW	Min
1990-91	TPS Turku U18	Fin-U18	24	20	28	48	26																		
	TPS Turku Jr.	Fin-Jr.	13	3	7	10	6																		
1991-92	TPS Turku U18	Fin-U18	12	3	7	10	6																		
	TPS Turku Jr.	Fin-Jr.	34	25	28	53	57										8	5	9	14	6				
1992-93	TPS Turku	Finland	46	3	7	10	28										11	3	2	5	2				
1993-94	TPS Turku	Finland	47	23	30	53	42										11	4	8	12	16				
	Finland	Olympics	8	4	3	7	12																		
1994-95	TPS Turku	Finland	45	27	47	74	73										13	7	10	17	16				
1995-96	Montreal	NHL	82	20	25	45	40	8	3	2	136	14.7	–7				6	3	1	4	8	0	0	0	
1996-97	Montreal	NHL	50	17	39	56	38	5	0	3	135	12.6	7				5	1	3	4	10	0	0	0	
1997-98	Montreal	NHL	69	14	43	57	48	2	2	3	145	9.7	8				6	2	3	5	2	1	0	0	
	Finland	Olympics	6	2	8	10	4																		
1998-99	Montreal	NHL	65	14	30	44	38	4	2	0	145	9.7	–7	1427	52.6	20:02									
99-2000	Montreal	NHL	24	3	18	21	14	1	0	0	53	5.7	7	495	52.9	19:13									
2000-01	Montreal	NHL	54	17	30	47	40	7	0	3	113	15.0	2	1092	47.6	21:23									
2001-02	Montreal	NHL	3	0	2	2	0	0	0	0	2	0.0	0	13	61.5	13:57	12	4	6	10	4	1	0	1	15:54
2002-03	Montreal	NHL	82	21	50	71	72	5	1	5	147	14.3	5	1566	49.6	19:14									
2003-04	Montreal	NHL	68	14	41	55	52	5	0	3	112	12.5	–5	1194	53.9	19:18	11	3	8	11	10	2	0	0	20:34
2004-05	TPS Turku	Finland	20	8	8	16	28										6	3	2	5	30				
2005-06	Montreal	NHL	72	17	45	62	70	5	0	4	138	12.3	1	1412	53.8	18:31	3	0	2	2	2	0	0	0	14:24
	Finland	Olympics	8	3	*8	*11	12																		
2006-07	Montreal	NHL	81	22	53	75	74	11	1	4	154	14.3	–21	1453	54.9	18:07									
2007-08	Montreal	NHL	77	16	40	56	93	8	0	3	150	10.7	4	1341	52.3	18:07	7	3	6	9	4	2	0	0	19:33
2008-09	Montreal	NHL	65	16	34	50	44	5	0	5	123	13.0	4	1122	54.1	17:03	4	0	3	3	2	0	0	0	17:45
2009-10	Anaheim	NHL	71	19	33	52	36	5	1	6	124	15.3	14	1110	51.4	18:35									
	Finland	Olympics	6	0	2	2	6																		
2010-11	Anaheim	NHL	75	15	30	45	36	4	0	3	104	14.4	–8	1339	52.8	19:08	6	1	6	7	6	0	0	0	18:19
	NHL Totals		938	225	513	738	695	75	10	44	1781	12.6		13564	52.4	18:52	60	17	38	55	48	6	0	1	18:06

Bill Masterton Memorial Trophy (2002) • Olympic All-Star Team (2006) • King Clancy Memorial Trophy (2007)

Played in NHL All-Star Game (1998)

• Missed majority of 1999-2000 due to shoulder injury vs. NY Rangers, October 30, 1999. • Missed majority of 2001-02 due to non-Hodgkin 's lymphoma, September 6, 2001. Signed as a free agent by **Turku** (Finland), October 21, 2004. Signed as a free agent by **Anaheim**, July 8, 2009.

KOLARIK, Chad

(kah-LOHR-ihk, CHAD) **NYR**

Center. Shoots right. 5'11", 185 lbs. Born, Abington, PA, January 26, 1986. Phoenix's 7th choice, 199th overall, in 2004 Entry Draft.

Season	Club	League	GP	G	A	Pts	PIM	PP	SH	GW	S	%	+/-	TF	F%	Min	GP	G	A	Pts	PIM	PP	SH	GW	Min
2002-03	USNTDP	U-17	21	14	10	24	4																		
	USNTDP	NAHL	44	16	22	38	43																		
2003-04	USNTDP	U-18	45	18	20	38	16																		
	USNTDP	NAHL	10	3	4	7	4																		
2004-05	U. of Michigan	CCHA	42	18	17	35	53																		
2005-06	U. of Michigan	CCHA	41	12	26	38	30																		
2006-07	U. of Michigan	CCHA	41	18	27	45	24																		
2007-08	U. of Michigan	CCHA	39	30	26	56	24																		
	San Antonio	AHL															7	4	2	6	0				
2008-09	San Antonio	AHL	76	20	30	50	47																		
2009-10	San Antonio	AHL	59	17	18	35	41																		
	Columbus	NHL	2	0	0	0	0	0	0	0	2	0.0	–1	0	0.0	6:29									
	Syracuse Crunch	AHL	17	9	6	15	14																		
2010-11	Springfield	AHL	13	4	6	10	18																		
	NY Rangers	NHL	4	0	1	1	2	0	0	0	4	0.0	–1	0	0.0	9:08									
	Connecticut	AHL	36	17	14	31	36										3	3	2	5	0				
	NHL Totals		6	0	1	1	2	0	0	0	6	0.0		0	0.0	8:15									

CCHA First All-Star Team (2008) • NCAA West Second All-American Team (2008)

Traded to **Columbus** by **Phoenix** for Alexandre Picard, March 3, 2010. Traded to **NY Rangers** by **Columbus** for Dane Byers, November 11, 2010.

KOMISAREK, Mike

(koh-mih-SAIR-ehk, MIGHK) **TOR**

Defense. Shoots right. 6'4", 243 lbs. Born, West Islip, NY, January 19, 1982. Montreal's 1st choice, 7th overall, in 2001 Entry Draft.

Season	Club	League	GP	G	A	Pts	PIM	PP	SH	GW	S	%	+/-	TF	F%	Min	GP	G	A	Pts	PIM	PP	SH	GW	Min
1998-99	N.E. Jr. Coyotes	EJHL	53	17	24	51																			
99-2000	USNTDP	U-18	6	0	0	0	12																		
	USNTDP	USHL	51	5	8	13	124																		
	USNTDP	NAHL	1	0	0	0	16																		
2000-01	U. of Michigan	CCHA	41	4	12	16	77																		
2001-02	U. of Michigan	CCHA	40	11	19	30	70																		
2002-03	Montreal	NHL	21	0	1	1	28	0	0	0	26	0.0	–6	0	0.0	16:42									
	Hamilton	AHL	56	5	25	30	79										23	1	5	6	60				
2003-04	Montreal	NHL	46	0	4	4	34	0	0	0	40	0.0	4	0	0.0	12:00	7	0	0	0	8	0	0	0	14:09
	Hamilton	AHL	18	2	7	9	47																		
2004-05	Hamilton	AHL	20	1	4	5	49										4	0	1	1	8				
2005-06	Montreal	NHL	71	2	4	6	116	0	0	0	66	3.0	–1	0	0.0	14:40	6	0	0	0	10	0	0	0	18:35
2006-07	Montreal	NHL	82	4	15	19	96	0	2	1	78	5.1	7	0	0.0	19:16									
2007-08	Montreal	NHL	75	4	13	17	101	0	0	1	75	5.3	9	1	0.0	21:09	12	1	2	3	18	0	0	1	20:02
2008-09	Montreal	NHL	66	2	9	11	121	0	0	0	56	3.6	0	0	0.0	20:37	4	0	0	0	20	0	0	0	19:00

			Regular Season														Playoffs								
Season	Club	League	GP	G	A	Pts	PIM	PP	SH	GW	S	%	+/-	TF	F%	Min	GP	G	A	Pts	PIM	PP	SH	GW	Min
2009-10	**Toronto**	**NHL**	34	0	4	4	40	0	0	0	35	0.0	–9	0	0.0	19:56	....	....	....	....	....	....	....	....	....
2010-11	**Toronto**	**NHL**	75	1	9	10	86	0	0	0	48	2.1	–8	0	0.0	13:38	....	....	....	....	....	....	....	....	....
	NHL Totals		470	13	59	72	622	0	2	2	424	3.1		1	0.0	17:23	29	1	2	3	56	0	0	1	18:10

CCHA First All-Star Team (2002) • NCAA West First All-American Team (2002) • AHL All-Rookie Team (2003)
Played in NHL All-Star Game (2009)
Signed as a free agent by **Toronto**, July 1, 2009. • Missed majority of 2009-10 due to shoulder injury, February 10, 2010.

KONOPKA, Zenon

(kuh-NOHP-kah, ZEH-nohn) **OTT**

Center. Shoots left. 6', 209 lbs. Born, Niagara on the Lake, Ont., January 2, 1981.

Season	Club	League	GP	G	A	Pts	PIM	PP	SH	GW	S	%	+/-	TF	F%	Min	GP	G	A	Pts	PIM	PP	SH	GW	Min
1998-99	Ottawa 67's	OHL	56	7	8	15	62	....	....	....	....	....	....	....	....	....	7	0	0	0	2	....	....	....	....
99-2000	Ottawa 67's	OHL	59	8	11	19	107	....	....	....	....	....	....	....	....	....	11	1	2	3	8	....	....	....	....
2000-01	Ottawa 67's	OHL	66	20	45	65	120	....	....	....	....	....	....	....	....	....	20	7	13	20	47	....	....	....	....
2001-02	Ottawa 67's	OHL	61	18	68	86	100	....	....	....	....	....	....	....	....	....	13	8	6	14	49	....	....	....	....
2002-03	Wilkes-Barre	AHL	4	0	1	1	9	....	....	....	....	....	....	....	....	....	....	....	....	....	....	....	....	....	....
	Wheeling Nailers	ECHL	68	22	48	70	231	....	....	....	....	....	....	....	....	....	....	....	....	....	....	....	....	....	....
2003-04	Utah Grizzlies	AHL	43	7	4	11	198	....	....	....	....	....	....	....	....	....	....	....	....	....	....	....	....	....	....
	Idaho Steelheads	ECHL	23	6	22	28	82	....	....	....	....	....	....	....	....	....	17	9	8	17	30	....	....	....	....
2004-05	Cincinnati	AHL	75	17	29	46	212	....	....	....	....	....	....	....	....	....	12	3	3	6	26	....	....	....	....
2005-06	**Anaheim**	**NHL**	23	4	3	7	48	2	0	0	18	22.2	–4	142	53.5	7:19	....	....	....	....	....	....	....	....	....
	Portland Pirates	AHL	34	18	26	44	57	....	....	....	....	....	....	....	....	....	19	11	18	29	46	....	....	....	....
2006-07	Lada Togliatti	Russia	4	0	0	0	8	....	....	....	....	....	....	....	....	....	....	....	....	....	....	....	....	....	....
	Columbus	**NHL**	6	0	0	0	20	0	0	0	2	0.0	–2	22	63.6	5:00	....	....	....	....	....	....	....	....	....
	Portland Pirates	AHL	42	11	24	35	97	....	....	....	....	....	....	....	....	....	....	....	....	....	....	....	....	....	....
	Syracuse Crunch	AHL	20	9	11	20	70	....	....	....	....	....	....	....	....	....	....	....	....	....	....	....	....	....	....
2007-08	**Columbus**	**NHL**	3	0	0	0	15	0	0	0	4	0.0	0	21	52.4	7:54	....	....	....	....	....	....	....	....	....
	Syracuse Crunch	AHL	62	24	31	55	194	....	....	....	....	....	....	....	....	....	13	3	7	10	42	....	....	....	....
2008-09	**Tampa Bay**	**NHL**	7	0	1	1	29	0	0	0	6	0.0	–1	25	68.0	7:01	....	....	....	....	....	....	....	....	....
	Norfolk Admirals	AHL	70	17	40	57	186	....	....	....	....	....	....	....	....	....	....	....	....	....	....	....	....	....	....
2009-10	**Tampa Bay**	**NHL**	74	2	3	5	*265	0	0	1	41	4.9	–11	462	62.3	8:08	....	....	....	....	....	....	....	....	....
2010-11	**NY Islanders**	**NHL**	82	2	7	9	*307	0	0	0	56	3.6	–14	1075	57.7	10:11	....	....	....	....	....	....	....	....	....
	NHL Totals		195	8	14	22	684	2	0	1	127	6.3		1747	58.7	8:46	....	....	....	....	....	....	....	....	....

ECHL All-Rookie Team (2003)
Signed as a free agent by **Utah** (AHL), September 10, 2003. Signed as a free agent by **Anaheim**, September 1, 2004. Signed as a free agent by **Togliatti** (Russia), July 26, 2006. Traded to **Columbus** by **Anaheim** with Curtis Glencross and Anaheim's 7th round choice (Trent Vogelhuber) in 2007 Entry Draft for Mark Hartigan, Joe Motzko and Columbus' 4th round choice (Sebastian Stefaniszin) in 2007 Entry Draft, January 26, 2007. Signed as a free agent by **Tampa Bay**, July 10, 2008. Signed as a free agent by **NY Islanders**, July 2, 2010. Signed as a free agent by **Ottawa**, July 5, 2011.

KONTIOLA, Petri

(KAWN-tee-oh-la, PEH-tree) **ANA**

Center. Shoots right. 6', 204 lbs. Born, Seinajoki, Finland, October 4, 1984. Chicago's 12th choice, 196th overall, in 2004 Entry Draft.

Season	Club	League	GP	G	A	Pts	PIM	PP	SH	GW	S	%	+/-	TF	F%	Min	GP	G	A	Pts	PIM	PP	SH	GW	Min
2001-02	Tappara U18	Fin-U18	22	5	3	8	8	....	....	....	....	....	....	....	....	....	2	1	0	1	2	....	....	....	....
2002-03	Tappara Jr.	Fin-Jr.	36	7	10	17	12	....	....	....	....	....	....	....	....	....	8	3	3	6	0	....	....	....	....
2003-04	Suomi U20	Finland-2	6	1	1	2	4	....	....	....	....	....	....	....	....	....	....	....	....	....	....	....	....	....	....
	Tappara Jr.	Fin-Jr.	12	3	12	15	8	....	....	....	....	....	....	....	....	....	10	4	4	8	10	....	....	....	....
	Tappara Tampere	Finland	39	4	9	13	29	....	....	....	....	....	....	....	....	....	3	1	1	2	0	....	....	....	....
2004-05	Tappara Jr.	Fin-Jr.	1	1	0	1	0	....	....	....	....	....	....	....	....	....	....	....	....	....	....	....	....	....	....
	Tappara Tampere	Finland	54	8	17	25	24	....	....	....	....	....	....	....	....	....	8	2	2	4	2	....	....	....	....
2005-06	Tappara Tampere	Finland	56	9	*35	44	55	....	....	....	....	....	....	....	....	....	6	1	3	4	0	....	....	....	....
2006-07	Tappara Tampere	Finland	51	12	35	47	50	....	....	....	....	....	....	....	....	....	5	1	3	4	8	....	....	....	....
2007-08	**Chicago**	**NHL**	12	0	5	5	6	0	0	0	13	0.0	5	45	68.9	14:33	....	....	....	....	....	....	....	....	....
	Rockford IceHogs	AHL	66	18	50	68	32	....	....	....	....	....	....	....	....	....	12	5	5	10	4	....	....	....	....
2008-09	Rockford IceHogs	AHL	61	15	38	53	22	....	....	....	....	....	....	....	....	....	....	....	....	....	....	....	....	....	....
	Iowa Chops	AHL	20	4	5	9	8	....	....	....	....	....	....	....	....	....	....	....	....	....	....	....	....	....	....
2009-10	Magnitogorsk	Rus-KHL	54	7	15	22	24	....	....	....	....	....	....	....	....	....	10	2	2	4	0	....	....	....	....
2010-11	Magnitogorsk	Rus-KHL	54	14	34	48	36	....	....	....	....	....	....	....	....	....	16	2	6	8	14	....	....	....	....
	NHL Totals		12	0	5	5	6	0	0	0	13	0.0		45	68.9	14:33	....	....	....	....	....	....	....	....	....

Traded to **Anaheim** by **Chicago** with James Wisniewski for Samuel Pahlsson, Logan Stephenson and future considerations, March 4, 2009. Signed as a free agent by **Magnitogorsk** (Russia-KHL), May 26, 2009.

KOPECKY, Tomas

(koh-PEHTS-kee, TAW-mahsh) **FLA**

Center. Shoots left. 6'3", 203 lbs. Born, Ilava, Czech., February 5, 1982. Detroit's 2nd choice, 38th overall, in 2000 Entry Draft.

Season	Club	League	GP	G	A	Pts	PIM	PP	SH	GW	S	%	+/-	TF	F%	Min	GP	G	A	Pts	PIM	PP	SH	GW	Min
1997-98	Dukla Trencin Jr.	Slovak-Jr.	41	19	22	41	....	....	....	....	....	....	....	....	....	....	....	....	....	....	....	....	....	....	....
1998-99	Dukla Trencin Jr.	Slovak-Jr.	44	13	16	29	18	....	....	....	....	....	....	....	....	....	....	....	....	....	....	....	....	....	....
99-2000	Dukla Trencin Jr.	Slovak-Jr.	14	8	9	17	36	....	....	....	....	....	....	....	....	....	....	....	....	....	....	....	....	....	....
	Dukla Trencin	Slovakia	52	3	4	7	24	....	....	....	....	....	....	....	....	....	5	0	0	0	0	....	....	....	....
2000-01	Lethbridge	WHL	49	22	28	50	52	....	....	....	....	....	....	....	....	....	5	1	1	2	6	....	....	....	....
	Cincinnati	AHL	1	0	0	0	0	....	....	....	....	....	....	....	....	....	....	....	....	....	....	....	....	....	....
2001-02	Lethbridge	WHL	60	34	42	76	94	....	....	....	....	....	....	....	....	....	4	2	1	3	15	....	....	....	....
	Cincinnati	AHL	2	1	1	2	6	....	....	....	....	....	....	....	....	....	2	0	0	0	0	....	....	....	....
2002-03	Grand Rapids	AHL	70	17	21	38	32	....	....	....	....	....	....	....	....	....	14	0	0	0	6	....	....	....	....
2003-04	Grand Rapids	AHL	48	6	6	12	28	....	....	....	....	....	....	....	....	....	1	0	0	0	2	....	....	....	....
2004-05	Grand Rapids	AHL	48	8	8	16	35	....	....	....	....	....	....	....	....	....	....	....	....	....	....	....	....	....	....
2005-06	**Detroit**	**NHL**	1	0	0	0	2	0	0	0	1	0.0	1	0	0.0	9:41	....	....	....	....	....	....	....	....	....
	Grand Rapids	AHL	77	32	37	69	108	....	....	....	....	....	....	....	....	....	16	3	4	7	25	....	....	....	....
2006-07	**Detroit**	**NHL**	26	1	0	1	22	0	0	0	27	3.7	–2	5	40.0	7:15	4	0	0	0	6	0	0	0	3:38
2007-08♦	**Detroit**	**NHL**	77	5	7	12	43	0	0	1	87	5.7	2	109	40.4	9:37	....	....	....	....	....	....	....	....	....
2008-09	**Detroit**	**NHL**	79	6	13	19	46	1	1	2	110	5.5	–7	79	45.6	10:25	8	0	1	1	7	0	0	0	9:32
2009-10♦	**Chicago**	**NHL**	74	10	11	21	28	1	0	2	95	10.5	0	118	44.1	9:29	17	4	2	6	8	1	0	1	13:35
	Slovakia	Olympics	7	1	0	1	2	....	....	....	....	....	....	....	....	....	....	....	....	....	....	....	....	....	....
2010-11	**Chicago**	**NHL**	81	15	27	42	60	3	0	2	178	8.4	–13	284	42.3	15:19	1	0	0	0	0	0	0	0	2:22
	NHL Totals		338	37	58	95	201	5	1	7	498	7.4		595	42.7	10:57	30	4	3	7	21	1	0	1	10:48

• Missed majority of 2006-07 due to broken collarbone vs. Chicago, December 14, 2006. Signed as a free agent by **Chicago**, July 1, 2009. • Rights traded to **Florida** by **Chicago** for Florida's 7th round choice in 2012 or 2013 Entry Draft June 27, 2011.

KOPITAR, Anze

(KOH-pih-tahr, AHN-zheh) **L.A.**

Center. Shoots left. 6'3", 227 lbs. Born, Jesenice, Yugoslavia, August 24, 1987. Los Angeles' 1st choice, 11th overall, in 2005 Entry Draft.

Season	Club	League	GP	G	A	Pts	PIM	PP	SH	GW	S	%	+/-	TF	F%	Min	GP	G	A	Pts	PIM	PP	SH	GW	Min
2002-03	Jesenice U18	Sloven-U18	14	38	38	76	10	....	....	....	....	....	....	....	....	....	....	....	....	....	....	....	....	....	....
	Jesenice Jr.	Sloven-Jr.	20	15	12	27	8	....	....	....	....	....	....	....	....	....	....	....	....	....	....	....	....	....	....
	Kranjska Gora	Slovenia	11	4	4	8	4	....	....	....	....	....	....	....	....	....	....	....	....	....	....	....	....	....	....
2003-04	Jesenice Jr.	Sloven-Jr.	25	32	28	60	16	....	....	....	....	....	....	....	....	....	....	....	....	....	....	....	....	....	....
	Kranjska Gora	Slovenia	21	14	11	25	10	....	....	....	....	....	....	....	....	....	4	1	1	2	0	....	....	....	....
2004-05	Sodertalje SK U18	Swe-U18	1	1	2	3	0	....	....	....	....	....	....	....	....	....	1	0	0	0	2	....	....	....	....
	Sodertalje SK Jr.	Swe-Jr.	30	28	21	49	26	....	....	....	....	....	....	....	....	....	2	1	1	2	0	....	....	....	....
	Sodertalje SK	Sweden	5	0	0	0	0	....	....	....	....	....	....	....	....	....	10	0	0	0	0	....	....	....	....
2005-06	Sodertalje SK	Sweden	47	8	12	20	28	....	....	....	....	....	....	....	....	....	....	....	....	....	....	....	....	....	....
	Sodertalje SK	Sweden-Q	10	7	4	11	6	....	....	....	....	....	....	....	....	....	....	....	....	....	....	....	....	....	....
2006-07	**Los Angeles**	**NHL**	72	20	41	61	24	7	2	1	193	10.4	–12	1204	46.1	20:32	....	....	....	....	....	....	....	....	....
2007-08	**Los Angeles**	**NHL**	82	32	45	77	22	12	2	3	201	15.9	–15	1150	49.2	20:41	....	....	....	....	....	....	....	....	....
2008-09	**Los Angeles**	**NHL**	82	27	39	66	32	7	1	3	234	11.5	–17	1355	49.5	20:27	....	....	....	....	....	....	....	....	....
2009-10	**Los Angeles**	**NHL**	82	34	47	81	16	14	1	2	259	13.1	6	1211	49.7	21:47	6	2	3	5	2	1	0	1	21:13
2010-11	**Los Angeles**	**NHL**	75	25	48	73	20	6	1	6	233	10.7	25	1160	49.9	21:35	....	....	....	....	....	....	....	....	....
	NHL Totals		393	138	220	358	114	46	7	15	1120	12.3		6080	48.9	21:01	6	2	3	5	2	1	0	1	21:13

Played in NHL All-Star Game (2008, 2011)

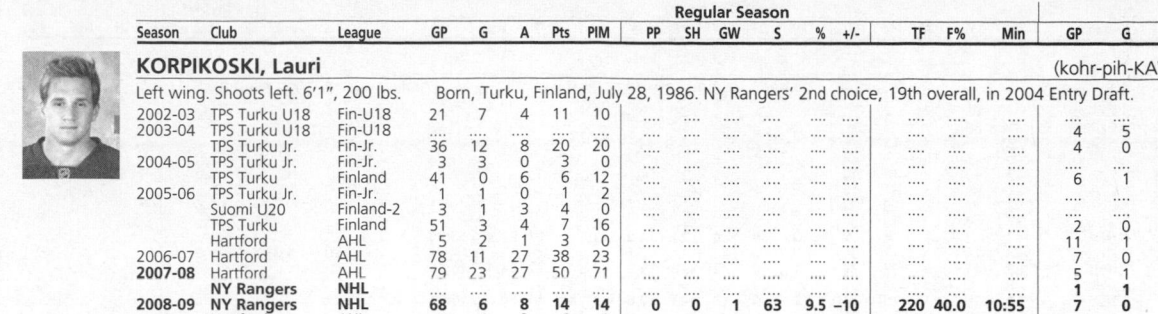

KORPIKOSKI, Lauri
(kohr-pih-KAWS-kee, LOW-ree) **PHX**

Left wing. Shoots left. 6'1", 200 lbs. Born, Turku, Finland, July 28, 1986. NY Rangers' 2nd choice, 19th overall, in 2004 Entry Draft.

Season	Club	League	GP	G	A	Pts	PIM	PP	SH	GW	S	%	+/-	TF	F%	Min	GP	G	A	Pts	PIM	PP	SH	GW	Min
			Regular Season														Playoffs								
2002-03	TPS Turku U18	Fin-U18	21	7	4	11	10	....	....	....	....	....	....	....	....	....	....	....	....	....	....	....	....	....	....
2003-04	TPS Turku U18	Fin-U18	....	....	....	....	....	....	....	....	....	....	....	....	....	....	4	5	3	8	16	....	....	....	....
	TPS Turku Jr.	Fin-Jr.	36	12	8	20	20	....	....	....	....	....	....	....	....	....	4	0	2	2	4	....	....	....	....
2004-05	TPS Turku Jr.	Fin-Jr.	3	3	0	3	0	....	....	....	....	....	....	....	....	....	....	....	....	....	....	....	....	....	....
	TPS Turku	Finland	41	0	6	6	12	....	....	....	....	....	....	....	....	....	6	1	0	1	0	....	....	....	....
2005-06	TPS Turku Jr.	Fin-Jr.	1	1	0	1	2	....	....	....	....	....	....	....	....	....	....	....	....	....	....	....	....	....	....
	Suomi U20	Finland-2	3	1	3	4	0	....	....	....	....	....	....	....	....	....	....	....	....	....	....	....	....	....	....
	TPS Turku	Finland	51	3	4	7	16	....	....	....	....	....	....	....	....	....	2	0	1	1	0	....	....	....	....
	Hartford	AHL	5	2	1	3	0	....	....	....	....	....	....	....	....	....	11	1	0	1	2	....	....	....	....
2006-07	Hartford	AHL	78	11	27	38	23	....	....	....	....	....	....	....	....	....	7	0	0	0	0	....	....	....	....
2007-08	Hartford	AHL	79	23	27	50	71	....	....	....	....	....	....	....	....	....	5	1	1	2	0	....	....	....	....
	NY Rangers	**NHL**	....	....	....	....	....	....	....	....	....	....	....	....	....	....	**1**	**1**	**0**	**1**	**0**	**0**	**0**	**0**	**7:14**
2008-09	**NY Rangers**	**NHL**	**68**	**6**	**8**	**14**	**14**	**0**	**0**	**1**	**63**	**9.5**	**–10**	**220**	**40.0**	**10:55**	**7**	**0**	**2**	**2**	**0**	**0**	**0**	**0**	**13:10**
	Hartford	AHL	4	4	2	6	0	....	....	....	....	....	....	....	....	....	....	....	....	....	....	....	....	....	....
2009-10	**Phoenix**	**NHL**	**71**	**5**	**6**	**11**	**16**	**0**	**0**	**1**	**68**	**7.4**	**–10**	**49**	**28.6**	**12:18**	**7**	**1**	**0**	**1**	**2**	**0**	**1**	**0**	**16:16**
2010-11	**Phoenix**	**NHL**	**79**	**19**	**21**	**40**	**20**	**0**	**2**	**4**	**103**	**18.4**	**17**	**244**	**43.9**	**15:32**	**4**	**0**	**1**	**1**	**2**	**0**	**0**	**0**	**16:33**
	NHL Totals		**218**	**30**	**35**	**65**	**50**	**0**	**2**	**6**	**234**	**12.8**		**513**	**40.7**	**13:02**	**19**	**2**	**3**	**5**	**4**	**0**	**1**	**0**	**14:42**

Traded to **Phoenix** by **NY Rangers** for Enver Lisin, July 13, 2009.

KOSTITSYN, Andrei
(kaws-TIHT-sihn, AWN-dray) **MTL**

Left wing. Shoots left. 6', 214 lbs. Born, Novopolotsk, USSR, February 3, 1985. Montreal's 1st choice, 10th overall, in 2003 Entry Draft.

Season	Club	League	GP	G	A	Pts	PIM	PP	SH	GW	S	%	+/-	TF	F%	Min	GP	G	A	Pts	PIM	PP	SH	GW	Min
99-2000	Belarus	WJ18-A	6	0	0	0	4	....	....	....	....	....	....	....	....	....	....	....	....	....	....	....	....	....	....
2000-01	Novopolotsk	Belarus	1	2	1	3	2	....	....	....	....	....	....	....	....	....	....	....	....	....	....	....	....	....	....
	Novopolotsk	EEHL	5	1	0	1	0	....	....	....	....	....	....	....	....	....	....	....	....	....	....	....	....	....	....
	Yunost Minsk	Belarus	3	1	4	5	8	....	....	....	....	....	....	....	....	....	....	....	....	....	....	....	....	....	....
	HC Vitebsk	Belarus	17	17	6	23	42	....	....	....	....	....	....	....	....	....	....	....	....	....	....	....	....	....	....
	Belarus	WJ18-B	5	7	7	*14	8	....	....	....	....	....	....	....	....	....	....	....	....	....	....	....	....	....	....
2001-02	Novopolotsk	Belarus	17	9	6	15	28	....	....	....	....	....	....	....	....	....	....	....	....	....	....	....	....	....	....
	Novopolotsk	EEHL	29	9	8	17	16	....	....	....	....	....	....	....	....	....	....	....	....	....	....	....	....	....	....
	Yunost Minsk	Belarus	6	2	0	2	8	....	....	....	....	....	....	....	....	....	....	....	....	....	....	....	....	....	....
2002-03	CSKA Moscow	Russia	6	0	0	0	2	....	....	....	....	....	....	....	....	....	....	....	....	....	....	....	....	....	....
	Voskresensk	Russia-2	2	1	1	2	0	....	....	....	....	....	....	....	....	....	....	....	....	....	....	....	....	....	....
	Yunost Minsk	Belarus	4	6	4	10	43	....	....	....	....	....	....	....	....	....	....	....	....	....	....	....	....	....	....
	CSKA Moscow 2	Russia-3	3	2	2	4	25	....	....	....	....	....	....	....	....	....	....	....	....	....	....	....	....	....	....
	Belarus	WC-A	2	1	0	1	2	....	....	....	....	....	....	....	....	....	....	....	....	....	....	....	....	....	....
2003-04	CSKA Moscow 2	Russia-3	STATISTICS NOT AVAILABLE																						
	CSKA Moscow	Russia	12	0	1	1	2	....	....	....	....	....	....	....	....	....	....	....	....	....	....	....	....	....	....
	Yunost Minsk	Belarus	STATISTICS NOT AVAILABLE																						
2004-05	Hamilton	AHL	66	12	11	23	24	....	....	....	....	....	....	....	....	....	3	0	0	0	0	....	....	....	....
2005-06	**Montreal**	**NHL**	**12**	**2**	**1**	**3**	**2**	**0**	**0**	**0**	**9**	**22.2**	**1**	**1**	**0.0**	**7:32**	....	....	....	....	....	....	....	....	....
	Hamilton	AHL	64	18	29	47	76	....	....	....	....	....	....	....	....	....	....	....	....	....	....	....	....	....	....
2006-07	**Montreal**	**NHL**	**22**	**1**	**10**	**11**	**6**	**0**	**0**	**0**	**38**	**2.6**	**3**	**1**	**0.0**	**13:17**	....	....	....	....	....	....	....	....	....
	Hamilton	AHL	50	21	31	52	50	....	....	....	....	....	....	....	....	....	....	....	....	....	....	....	....	....	....
2007-08	**Montreal**	**NHL**	**78**	**26**	**27**	**53**	**29**	**12**	**0**	**5**	**156**	**16.7**	**15**	**6**	**66.7**	**15:41**	**12**	**5**	**3**	**8**	**2**	**1**	**0**	**1**	**16:01**
2008-09	**Montreal**	**NHL**	**74**	**23**	**18**	**41**	**50**	**6**	**0**	**2**	**169**	**13.6**	**–7**	**6**	**50.0**	**15:35**	**4**	**1**	**0**	**1**	**2**	**0**	**0**	**0**	**14:15**
2009-10	**Montreal**	**NHL**	**59**	**15**	**18**	**33**	**32**	**6**	**0**	**2**	**136**	**11.0**	**1**	**6**	**16.7**	**15:59**	**19**	**3**	**5**	**8**	**12**	**1**	**0**	**0**	**14:15**
2010-11	**Montreal**	**NHL**	**81**	**20**	**25**	**45**	**36**	**5**	**0**	**6**	**196**	**10.2**	**3**	**2**	**0.0**	**15:53**	**6**	**2**	**0**	**2**	**6**	**0**	**0**	**0**	**18:19**
	NHL Totals		**326**	**87**	**99**	**186**	**155**	**29**	**0**	**15**	**704**	**12.4**		**22**	**36.4**	**15:18**	**41**	**11**	**8**	**19**	**22**	**2**	**0**	**1**	**15:22**

KOSTITSYN, Sergei
(kaws-TIHT-sihn, SAIR-gay) **NSH**

Left wing. Shoots left. 6', 207 lbs. Born, Novopolotsk, USSR, March 20, 1987. Montreal's 6th choice, 200th overall, in 2005 Entry Draft.

Season	Club	League	GP	G	A	Pts	PIM	PP	SH	GW	S	%	+/-	TF	F%	Min	GP	G	A	Pts	PIM	PP	SH	GW	Min
2003-04	HK Gomel	EEHL	6	0	1	1	0	....	....	....	....	....	....	....	....	....	....	....	....	....	....	....	....	....	....
	HK Gomel 2	EEHL-B	6	7	2	9	14	....	....	....	....	....	....	....	....	....	....	....	....	....	....	....	....	....	....
	Yunior Minsk	EEHL-B	STATISTICS NOT AVAILABLE																						
	Yunior Minsk	Belarus	3	0	0	0	0	....	....	....	....	....	....	....	....	....	....	....	....	....	....	....	....	....	....
	HK Gomel	Belarus	22	5	4	9	4	....	....	....	....	....	....	....	....	....	11	1	2	3	8	....	....	....	....
2004-05	HK Gomel	BelOpen	40	4	10	14	24	....	....	....	....	....	....	....	....	....	4	2	0	2	12	....	....	....	....
2005-06	London Knights	OHL	63	26	52	78	78	....	....	....	....	....	....	....	....	....	19	13	24	37	*44	....	....	....	....
2006-07	London Knights	OHL	59	40	*91	131	76	....	....	....	....	....	....	....	....	....	16	9	12	21	39	....	....	....	....
2007-08	**Montreal**	**NHL**	**52**	**9**	**18**	**27**	**51**	**3**	**1**	**0**	**49**	**18.4**	**9**	**23**	**34.8**	**14:21**	**12**	**3**	**5**	**8**	**14**	**0**	**0**	**0**	**15:09**
	Hamilton	AHL	22	6	16	22	18	....	....	....	....	....	....	....	....	....	....	....	....	....	....	....	....	....	....
2008-09	**Montreal**	**NHL**	**56**	**8**	**15**	**23**	**64**	**5**	**0**	**1**	**74**	**10.8**	**–3**	**9**	**33.3**	**14:08**	**1**	**0**	**0**	**0**	**2**	**0**	**0**	**0**	**12:10**
	Hamilton	AHL	16	5	8	13	18	....	....	....	....	....	....	....	....	....	....	....	....	....	....	....	....	....	....
2009-10	**Montreal**	**NHL**	**47**	**7**	**11**	**18**	**8**	**0**	**0**	**2**	**59**	**11.9**	**4**	**7**	**14.3**	**14:10**	**5**	**0**	**0**	**0**	**0**	**0**	**0**	**0**	**7:59**
	Hamilton	AHL	16	4	9	13	2	....	....	....	....	....	....	....	....	....	....	....	....	....	....	....	....	....	....
	Belarus	Olympics	4	2	3	5	0	....	....	....	....	....	....	....	....	....	....	....	....	....	....	....	....	....	....
2010-11	**Nashville**	**NHL**	**77**	**23**	**27**	**50**	**20**	**4**	**1**	**2**	**93**	**24.7**	**10**	**6**	**16.7**	**15:11**	**12**	**0**	**5**	**5**	**2**	**0**	**0**	**0**	**18:21**
	NHL Totals		**232**	**47**	**71**	**118**	**143**	**12**	**2**	**5**	**275**	**17.1**		**45**	**28.9**	**14:33**	**30**	**3**	**10**	**13**	**18**	**0**	**0**	**0**	**15:08**

OHL All-Rookie Team (2006)

Traded to **Nashville** by **Montreal** with future considerations for Dan Ellis, Dustin Boyd and future considerations, June 29, 2010.

KOSTOPOULOS, Tom
(kaw-STAWP-oh-lihs, TAWM) **CGY**

Right wing. Shoots right. 6', 200 lbs. Born, Mississauga, Ont., January 24, 1979. Pittsburgh's 9th choice, 204th overall, in 1999 Entry Draft.

Season	Club	League	GP	G	A	Pts	PIM	PP	SH	GW	S	%	+/-	TF	F%	Min	GP	G	A	Pts	PIM	PP	SH	GW	Min
1995-96	Brampton	OPJHL	24	9	9	18	28	....	....	....	....	....	....	....	....	....	....	....	....	....	....	....	....	....	....
1996-97	London Knights	OHL	64	13	12	25	67	....	....	....	....	....	....	....	....	....	....	....	....	....	....	....	....	....	....
1997-98	London Knights	OHL	66	24	26	50	108	....	....	....	....	....	....	....	....	....	16	6	4	10	26	....	....	....	....
1998-99	London Knights	OHL	66	27	60	87	114	....	....	....	....	....	....	....	....	....	25	19	16	35	32	....	....	....	....
99-2000	Wilkes-Barre	AHL	76	26	32	58	121	....	....	....	....	....	....	....	....	....	....	....	....	....	....	....	....	....	....
2000-01	Wilkes-Barre	AHL	80	16	36	52	120	....	....	....	....	....	....	....	....	....	21	3	9	12	6	....	....	....	....
2001-02	**Pittsburgh**	**NHL**	**11**	**1**	**2**	**3**	**9**	**0**	**0**	**0**	**8**	**12.5**	**–1**	**0**	**0.0**	**12:03**	....	....	....	....	....	....	....	....	....
	Wilkes-Barre	AHL	70	27	26	53	112	....	....	....	....	....	....	....	....	....	....	....	....	....	....	....	....	....	....
2002-03	**Pittsburgh**	**NHL**	**8**	**0**	**1**	**1**	**0**	**0**	**0**	**0**	**6**	**0.0**	**–4**	**2**	**0.0**	**4:33**	....	....	....	....	....	....	....	....	....
	Wilkes-Barre	AHL	71	21	42	63	131	....	....	....	....	....	....	....	....	....	6	1	2	3	7	....	....	....	....
2003-04	**Pittsburgh**	**NHL**	**60**	**9**	**13**	**22**	**67**	**2**	**1**	**1**	**101**	**8.9**	**–14**	**10**	**30.0**	**14:26**	....	....	....	....	....	....	....	....	....
	Wilkes-Barre	AHL	21	7	13	20	43	....	....	....	....	....	....	....	....	....	24	7	16	23	32	....	....	....	....
2004-05	Manchester	AHL	64	25	46	71	99	....	....	....	....	....	....	....	....	....	6	0	7	7	10	....	....	....	....
2005-06	**Los Angeles**	**NHL**	**76**	**8**	**14**	**22**	**100**	**0**	**0**	**1**	**74**	**10.8**	**–8**	**30**	**36.7**	**12:56**	....	....	....	....	....	....	....	....	....
2006-07	**Los Angeles**	**NHL**	**76**	**7**	**15**	**22**	**73**	**0**	**0**	**0**	**90**	**7.8**	**–2**	**62**	**29.0**	**11:34**	....	....	....	....	....	....	....	....	....
2007-08	**Montreal**	**NHL**	**67**	**7**	**6**	**13**	**113**	**0**	**3**	**1**	**98**	**7.1**	**–3**	**28**	**28.6**	**11:16**	**12**	**3**	**1**	**4**	**6**	**0**	**0**	**1**	**13:35**
2008-09	**Montreal**	**NHL**	**78**	**8**	**14**	**22**	**106**	**0**	**1**	**0**	**121**	**6.6**	**–1**	**16**	**31.3**	**14:09**	**4**	**0**	**1**	**1**	**4**	**0**	**0**	**0**	**14:01**
2009-10	**Carolina**	**NHL**	**82**	**8**	**13**	**21**	**106**	**0**	**2**	**0**	**103**	**7.8**	**4**	**21**	**47.6**	**12:31**	....	....	....	....	....	....	....	....	....
2010-11	**Carolina**	**NHL**	**17**	**1**	**3**	**4**	**30**	**0**	**0**	**0**	**13**	**7.7**	**–1**	**14**	**28.6**	**11:17**	....	....	....	....	....	....	....	....	....
	Calgary	**NHL**	**59**	**7**	**7**	**14**	**44**	**2**	**0**	**0**	**66**	**10.6**	**–3**	**53**	**26.4**	**12:38**	....	....	....	....	....	....	....	....	....
	NHL Totals		**534**	**56**	**88**	**144**	**648**	**4**	**7**	**3**	**680**	**8.2**		**236**	**30.9**	**12:35**	**16**	**3**	**2**	**5**	**10**	**0**	**0**	**1**	**13:41**

Signed as a free agent by **Manchester** (AHL), July 12, 2004. Signed as a free agent by **Los Angeles**, August 1, 2005. Signed as a free agent by **Montreal**, July 4, 2007. Signed as a free agent by **Carolina**, July 14, 2009. Traded to **Calgary** by **Carolina** with Anton Babchuk for Ian White and Brett Sutter, November 17, 2010.

KOTALIK, Ales

(KOH-tahl-eek, ahl-EHSH) **BUF**

Right wing. Shoots right. 6'1", 225 lbs. Born, Jindrichuv Hradec, Czech., December 23, 1978. Buffalo's 7th choice, 164th overall, in 1998 Entry Draft.

			Regular Season														Playoffs								
Season	Club	League	GP	G	A	Pts	PIM	PP	SH	GW	S	%	+/-	TF	F%	Min	GP	G	A	Pts	PIM	PP	SH	GW	Min
1993-94	C. Budejovice Jr.	CzRep-Jr.	28	12	12	24	....	....	....	....	....	....	....	....	....	....	....	....	....	....	....	....	....	....	....
1994-95	C. Budejovice Jr.	CzRep-Jr.	36	26	17	43	....	....	....	....	....	....	....	....	....	....	....	....	....	....	....	....	....	....	....
1995-96	C. Budejovice Jr.	CzRep-Jr.	28	6	7	13	....	....	....	....	....	....	....	....	....	....	....	....	....	....	....	....	....	....	....
1996-97	C. Budejovice Jr.	CzRep-Jr.	36	15	16	31	24	....	....	....	....	....	....	....	....	....	....	....	....	....	....	....	....	....	....
1997-98	C. Budejovice	CzRep	47	9	7	16	14	....	....	....	....	....	....	....	....	....	....	....	....	....	....	....	....	....	....
1998-99	C. Budejovice	CzRep	41	8	13	21	16	....	....	....	....	....	....	....	....	....	3	0	0	0	....	....	....	....	....
99-2000	C. Budejovice	CzRep	43	7	12	19	34	....	....	....	....	....	....	....	....	....	3	0	1	1	6	....	....	....	....
2000-01	C. Budejovice	CzRep	52	19	29	48	54	....	....	....	....	....	....	....	....	....	....	....	....	....	....	....	....	....	....
2001-02	**Buffalo**	**NHL**	**13**	**1**	**3**	**4**	**2**	**0**	**0**	**0**	**21**	**4.8**	**–1**	**11**	**27.3**	**12:35**	....	....	....	....	....	....	....	....	....
	Rochester	AHL	68	18	25	43	55	....	....	....	....	....	....	....	....	....	1	0	0	0	0	....	....	....	....
2002-03	**Buffalo**	**NHL**	**68**	**21**	**14**	**35**	**30**	**4**	**0**	**2**	**138**	**15.2**	**–2**	**37**	**51.4**	**15:15**	....	....	....	....	....	....	....	....	....
	Rochester	AHL	8	0	2	2	4	....	....	....	....	....	....	....	....	....	....	....	....	....	....	....	....	....	....
2003-04	**Buffalo**	**NHL**	**62**	**15**	**11**	**26**	**41**	**2**	**0**	**3**	**142**	**10.6**	**–1**	**14**	**50.0**	**15:11**	....	....	....	....	....	....	....	....	....
2004-05	Liberec	CzRep	25	8	8	16	46	....	....	....	....	....	....	....	....	....	12	2	5	7	12	....	....	....	....
2005-06	**Buffalo**	**NHL**	**82**	**25**	**37**	**62**	**62**	**10**	**0**	**5**	**261**	**9.6**	**–3**	**29**	**41.4**	**15:34**	**18**	**4**	**7**	**11**	**8**	**0**	**0**	**3**	**15:15**
	Czech Republic	Olympics	4	0	0	0	0	....	....	....	....	....	....	....	....	....	....	....	....	....	....	....	....	....	....
2006-07	**Buffalo**	**NHL**	**66**	**16**	**22**	**38**	**46**	**3**	**0**	**4**	**162**	**9.9**	**–5**	**35**	**48.6**	**14:31**	**16**	**2**	**2**	**4**	**8**	**0**	**0**	**0**	**12:29**
2007-08	**Buffalo**	**NHL**	**79**	**23**	**20**	**43**	**58**	**12**	**0**	**1**	**207**	**11.1**	**–5**	**220**	**44.6**	**15:21**	....	....	....	....	....	....	....	....	....
2008-09	**Buffalo**	**NHL**	**56**	**13**	**19**	**32**	**28**	**8**	**0**	**1**	**153**	**8.5**	**–7**	**77**	**39.0**	**15:14**	....	....	....	....	....	....	....	....	....
	Edmonton	**NHL**	**19**	**7**	**4**	**11**	**6**	**1**	**0**	**0**	**55**	**12.7**	**2**	**8**	**75.0**	**16:06**	....	....	....	....	....	....	....	....	....
2009-10	**NY Rangers**	**NHL**	**45**	**8**	**14**	**22**	**38**	**4**	**0**	**3**	**100**	**8.0**	**–18**	**2**	**0.0**	**13:56**	....	....	....	....	....	....	....	....	....
	Calgary	**NHL**	**26**	**3**	**2**	**5**	**29**	**1**	**0**	**1**	**72**	**4.2**	**1**	**8**	**62.5**	**14:36**	....	....	....	....	....	....	....	....	....
2010-11	**Calgary**	**NHL**	**26**	**4**	**2**	**6**	**8**	**1**	**0**	**2**	**62**	**6.5**	**–7**	**11**	**54.6**	**12:22**	....	....	....	....	....	....	....	....	....
	Abbotsford Heat	AHL	25	6	16	22	10	....	....	....	....	....	....	....	....	....	....	....	....	....	....	....	....	....	....
	NHL Totals		**542**	**136**	**148**	**284**	**348**	**46**	**0**	**22**	**1373**	**9.9**		**452**	**44.9**	**14:54**	**34**	**6**	**9**	**15**	**16**	**0**	**0**	**3**	**13:57**

Signed as a free agent by **Liberec** (CzRep), September 6, 2004. Traded to **Edmonton** by **Buffalo** for Carolina's 2nd round choice (previously acquired, later traded to Toronto – Toronto selected Jesse Blacker) in 2009 Entry Draft, March 4, 2009. Signed as a free agent by **NY Rangers**, July 9, 2009. Traded to **Calgary** by **NY Rangers** with Chris Higgins for Olli Jokinen and Brandon Prust, February 2, 2010. Traded to **Buffalo** by **Calgary** with Robyn Regehr and Calgary's 2nd round choice in 2012 Entry Draft for Chris Butler and Paul Byron, June 25, 2011.

KOVALCHUK, Ilya

(koh-vuhl-CHUHK, IHL-yah) **N.J.**

Left wing. Shoots right. 6'3", 230 lbs. Born, Tver, USSR, April 15, 1983. Atlanta's 1st choice, 1st overall, in 2001 Entry Draft.

Season	Club	League	GP	G	A	Pts	PIM	PP	SH	GW	S	%	+/-	TF	F%	Min	GP	G	A	Pts	PIM	PP	SH	GW	Min
99-2000	Spartak Moscow	Russia-2	49	12	5	17	75	....	....	....	....	....	....	....	....	....	....	....	....	....	....	....	....	....	....
	Spartak 2	Russia-3	2	2	1	3	14	....	....	....	....	....	....	....	....	....	....	....	....	....	....	....	....	....	....
2000-01	Spartak Moscow	Russia-2	40	28	18	46	78	....	....	....	....	....	....	....	....	....	12	14	4	18	38	....	....	....	....
2001-02	**Atlanta**	**NHL**	**65**	**29**	**22**	**51**	**28**	**7**	**0**	**4**	**184**	**15.8**	**–19**	**6**	**16.7**	**18:32**	....	....	....	....	....	....	....	....	....
	Russia	Olympics	6	1	2	3	14	....	....	....	....	....	....	....	....	....	....	....	....	....	....	....	....	....	....
2002-03	**Atlanta**	**NHL**	**81**	**38**	**29**	**67**	**57**	**9**	**0**	**3**	**257**	**14.8**	**–24**	**15**	**40.0**	**19:27**	....	....	....	....	....	....	....	....	....
2003-04	**Atlanta**	**NHL**	**81**	***41**	**46**	**87**	**63**	**16**	**1**	**6**	**341**	**12.0**	**–10**	**28**	**32.1**	**23:41**	....	....	....	....	....	....	....	....	....
2004-05	Ak Bars Kazan	Russia	53	19	23	42	72	....	....	....	....	....	....	....	....	....	4	0	1	1	0	....	....	....	....
2005-06	**Atlanta**	**NHL**	**78**	**52**	**46**	**98**	**68**	***27**	**0**	**7**	**323**	**16.1**	**–6**	**47**	**40.4**	**22:23**	....	....	....	....	....	....	....	....	....
	Russia	Olympics	8	4	1	5	31	....	....	....	....	....	....	....	....	....	....	....	....	....	....	....	....	....	....
2006-07	**Atlanta**	**NHL**	**82**	**42**	**34**	**76**	**66**	**18**	**0**	**7**	**336**	**12.5**	**–2**	**66**	**39.4**	**21:32**	**4**	**1**	**1**	**2**	**19**	**0**	**0**	**0**	**18:42**
2007-08	**Atlanta**	**NHL**	**79**	**52**	**35**	**87**	**52**	**16**	**2**	**4**	**283**	**18.4**	**–12**	**32**	**43.8**	**21:30**	....	....	....	....	....	....	....	....	....
2008-09	**Atlanta**	**NHL**	**79**	**43**	**48**	**91**	**50**	**12**	**0**	**6**	**275**	**15.6**	**–12**	**14**	**35.7**	**21:48**	....	....	....	....	....	....	....	....	....
2009-10	**Atlanta**	**NHL**	**49**	**31**	**27**	**58**	**45**	**10**	**0**	**3**	**179**	**17.3**	**1**	**23**	**21.7**	**22:14**	....	....	....	....	....	....	....	....	....
	New Jersey	**NHL**	**27**	**10**	**17**	**27**	**8**	**2**	**0**	**1**	**111**	**9.0**	**9**	**7**	**28.6**	**21:40**	**5**	**2**	**4**	**6**	**6**	**1**	**0**	**0**	**23:38**
	Russia	Olympics	4	1	2	3	0	....	....	....	....	....	....	....	....	....	....	....	....	....	....	....	....	....	....
2010-11	**New Jersey**	**NHL**	**81**	**31**	**29**	**60**	**28**	**9**	**0**	**9**	**245**	**12.7**	**–26**	**31**	**29.0**	**22:34**	....	....	....	....	....	....	....	....	....
	NHL Totals		**702**	**369**	**333**	**702**	**465**	**126**	**3**	**50**	**2534**	**14.6**		**269**	**35.7**	**21:33**	**9**	**3**	**5**	**8**	**25**	**1**	**0**	**0**	**21:26**

NHL All-Rookie Team (2002) • NHL Second All-Star Team (2004) • Maurice "Rocket" Richard Trophy (2004) (tied with Jarome Iginla and Rick Nash)

Played in NHL All-Star Game (2004, 2008, 2009)

Signed as a free agent by **Kazan** (Russia) August 22, 2004. Traded to **New Jersey** by **Atlanta** with Anssi Salmela and Atlanta's 2nd round choice (Jonathon Merrill) in 2010 Entry Draft for Johnny Oduya, Niclas Bergfors, Patrice Cormier and New Jersey's 1st (later traded to Chicago - Chicago selected Kevin Hayes) and 2nd (later traded to Chicago - Chicago selected Justin Holl) round choices in 2010 Entry Draft, February 4, 2010.

KOVALEV, Alex

(koh-VAH-lehv, AL-ehx)

Right wing. Shoots left. 6'2", 222 lbs. Born, Togliatti, USSR, February 24, 1973. NY Rangers' 1st choice, 15th overall, in 1991 Entry Draft.

Season	Club	League	GP	G	A	Pts	PIM	PP	SH	GW	S	%	+/-	TF	F%	Min	GP	G	A	Pts	PIM	PP	SH	GW	Min
1989-90	Dynamo Moscow	USSR	1	0	0	0	0	....	....	....	....	....	....	....	....	....	....	....	....	....	....	....	....	....	....
1990-91	Dyn'o Moscow 2	USSR-3	21	16	....	....	....	....	....	....	....	....	....	....	....	....	....	....	....	....	....	....	....	....	....
	Dynamo Moscow	USSR	18	1	2	3	4	....	....	....	....	....	....	....	....	....	....	....	....	....	....	....	....	....	....
	Dynamo Moscow	Super-S	1	0	0	0	0	....	....	....	....	....	....	....	....	....	....	....	....	....	....	....	....	....	....
1991-92	Dynamo Moscow	CIS	33	16	9	25	20	....	....	....	....	....	....	....	....	....	....	....	....	....	....	....	....	....	....
	Dyn'o Moscow 2	CIS-3	4	5	0	5	12	....	....	....	....	....	....	....	....	....	....	....	....	....	....	....	....	....	....
	Russia	Olympics	8	1	2	3	14	....	....	....	....	....	....	....	....	....	....	....	....	....	....	....	....	....	....
1992-93	**NY Rangers**	**NHL**	**65**	**20**	**18**	**38**	**79**	**3**	**0**	**3**	**134**	**14.9**	**–10**	....	....	....	....	....	....	....	....	....	....	....	....
	Binghamton	AHL	13	13	11	24	35	....	....	....	....	....	....	....	....	....	9	3	5	8	14	....	....	....	....
1993-94 ♦	**NY Rangers**	**NHL**	**76**	**23**	**33**	**56**	**154**	**7**	**0**	**3**	**184**	**12.5**	**18**	....	....	....	**23**	**9**	**12**	**21**	**18**	**5**	**0**	**2**	....
1994-95	Lada Togliatti	CIS	12	8	8	16	49	....	....	....	....	....	....	....	....	....	....	....	....	....	....	....	....	....	....
	NY Rangers	**NHL**	**48**	**13**	**15**	**28**	**30**	**1**	**1**	**1**	**103**	**12.6**	**–6**	....	....	....	**10**	**4**	**7**	**11**	**10**	**0**	**0**	**0**	....
1995-96	**NY Rangers**	**NHL**	**81**	**24**	**34**	**58**	**98**	**8**	**1**	**7**	**206**	**11.7**	**5**	....	....	....	**11**	**3**	**4**	**7**	**14**	**0**	**0**	**1**	....
1996-97	**NY Rangers**	**NHL**	**45**	**13**	**22**	**35**	**42**	**1**	**0**	**0**	**110**	**11.8**	**11**	....	....	....	....	....	....	....	....	....	....	....	....
1997-98	**NY Rangers**	**NHL**	**73**	**23**	**30**	**53**	**44**	**8**	**0**	**3**	**173**	**13.3**	**–22**	....	....	....	....	....	....	....	....	....	....	....	....
1998-99	**NY Rangers**	**NHL**	**14**	**3**	**4**	**7**	**12**	**1**	**0**	**1**	**35**	**8.6**	**–6**	**18**	**44.4**	**19:53**	....	....	....	....	....	....	....	....	....
	Pittsburgh	**NHL**	**63**	**20**	**26**	**46**	**37**	**5**	**1**	**4**	**156**	**12.8**	**8**	**226**	**43.4**	**20:30**	**10**	**5**	**7**	**12**	**14**	**0**	**0**	**1**	**20:24**
99-2000	**Pittsburgh**	**NHL**	**82**	**26**	**40**	**66**	**94**	**9**	**2**	**4**	**254**	**10.2**	**–3**	**306**	**47.4**	**22:53**	**11**	**1**	**5**	**6**	**10**	**0**	**0**	**0**	**26:35**
2000-01	**Pittsburgh**	**NHL**	**79**	**44**	**51**	**95**	**96**	**12**	**2**	**9**	**307**	**14.3**	**12**	**255**	**40.0**	**23:35**	**18**	**5**	**5**	**10**	**16**	**1**	**0**	**0**	**20:57**
2001-02	**Pittsburgh**	**NHL**	**67**	**32**	**44**	**76**	**80**	**8**	**1**	**3**	**266**	**12.0**	**2**	**179**	**45.3**	**24:03**	....	....	....	....	....	....	....	....	....
	Russia	Olympics	6	3	1	4	4	....	....	....	....	....	....	....	....	....	....	....	....	....	....	....	....	....	....
2002-03	**Pittsburgh**	**NHL**	**54**	**27**	**37**	**64**	**50**	**8**	**0**	**1**	**212**	**12.7**	**–11**	**19**	**31.6**	**24:03**	....	....	....	....	....	....	....	....	....
	NY Rangers	**NHL**	**24**	**10**	**3**	**13**	**20**	**3**	**0**	**2**	**59**	**16.9**	**2**	**19**	**42.1**	**20:09**	....	....	....	....	....	....	....	....	....
2003-04	**NY Rangers**	**NHL**	**66**	**13**	**29**	**42**	**54**	**3**	**0**	**0**	**178**	**7.3**	**–5**	**29**	**48.3**	**19:37**	....	....	....	....	....	....	....	....	....
	Montreal	**NHL**	**12**	**1**	**2**	**3**	**12**	**0**	**0**	**1**	**29**	**3.4**	**–4**	**2**	**50.0**	**15:36**	**11**	**6**	**4**	**10**	**8**	**1**	**0**	**1**	**20:11**
2004-05	Ak Bars Kazan	Russia	35	10	12	22	80	....	....	....	....	....	....	....	....	....	4	0	0	0	8	....	....	....	....
2005-06	**Montreal**	**NHL**	**69**	**23**	**42**	**65**	**76**	**9**	**0**	**5**	**206**	**11.2**	**–1**	**47**	**48.9**	**19:28**	**6**	**4**	**3**	**7**	**4**	**1**	**0**	**0**	**19:21**
	Russia	Olympics	8	4	2	6	4	....	....	....	....	....	....	....	....	....	....	....	....	....	....	....	....	....	....
2006-07	**Montreal**	**NHL**	**73**	**18**	**29**	**47**	**78**	**8**	**0**	**5**	**197**	**9.1**	**–19**	**162**	**46.3**	**18:15**	....	....	....	....	....	....	....	....	....
2007-08	**Montreal**	**NHL**	**82**	**35**	**49**	**84**	**70**	**17**	**0**	**5**	**230**	**15.2**	**18**	**58**	**55.2**	**19:33**	**12**	**5**	**6**	**11**	**8**	**2**	**1**	**1**	**21:41**
2008-09	**Montreal**	**NHL**	**78**	**26**	**39**	**65**	**74**	**11**	**1**	**4**	**209**	**12.4**	**–5**	**50**	**32.0**	**19:26**	**4**	**2**	**1**	**3**	**2**	**0**	**0**	**0**	**19:54**
2009-10	**Ottawa**	**NHL**	**77**	**18**	**31**	**49**	**54**	**4**	**0**	**5**	**165**	**10.9**	**–8**	**3**	**33.3**	**18:10**	....	....	....	....	....	....	....	....	....
2010-11	**Ottawa**	**NHL**	**54**	**14**	**13**	**27**	**28**	**6**	**0**	**3**	**123**	**11.4**	**–9**	**6**	**33.3**	**16:16**	....	....	....	....	....	....	....	....	....
	Pittsburgh	**NHL**	**20**	**2**	**5**	**7**	**16**	**0**	**0**	**0**	**28**	**7.1**	**3**	**4**	**25.0**	**17:10**	**7**	**1**	**1**	**2**	**10**	**0**	**0**	**1**	**16:02**
	NHL Totals		**1302**	**428**	**596**	**1024**	**1298**	**132**	**9**	**69**	**3564**	**12.0**		**1383**	**44.3**	**20:21**	**123**	**45**	**55**	**100**	**114**	**10**	**1**	**7**	**21:03**

NHL Second All-Star Team (2008)

Played in NHL All-Star Game (2001, 2003, 2009)

Traded to **Pittsburgh** by **NY Rangers** with Harry York for Petr Nedved, Chris Tamer and Sean Pronger, November 25, 1998. Traded to **NY Rangers** by **Pittsburgh** with Mike Wilson, Janne Laukkanen and Dan LaCouture for Joel Bouchard, Richard Lintner, Rico Fata and Mikael Samuelsson, February 10, 2003. Traded to **Montreal** by **NY Rangers** for Jozef Balej and Montreal's 2nd round choice (Bruce Graham) in 2004 Entry Draft, March 2, 2004. Signed as a free agent by **Kazan** (Russia), November 3, 2004. Signed as a free agent by **Ottawa**, July 6, 2009. Traded to **Pittsburgh** by **Ottawa** for Pittsburgh's 7th round choice (Ryan Dzingel) in 2011 Entry Draft, February 24, 2011. Signed as a free agent by **Mytischi** (Russia-KHL), July 29, 2011.

KRAJICEK, Lukas
(KRIGH-ih-chehk, LOO-kahsh)

Defense. Shoots left. 6'3", 205 lbs. Born, Prostejov, Czech., March 11, 1983. Florida's 2nd choice, 24th overall, in 2001 Entry Draft.

			Regular Season														Playoffs								
Season	Club	League	GP	G	A	Pts	PIM	PP	SH	GW	S	%	+/-	TF	F%	Min	GP	G	A	Pts	PIM	PP	SH	GW	Min
1998-99	HC ZPS Zlin Jr.	CzRep-Jr.	48	8	18	26	40	....	....	....	....	....	....	....	....	....	....	....	....	....	....	....	....	....	....
99-2000	Det. Compuware	NAHL	53	5	22	27	61	....	....	....	....	....	....	....	....	....	5	0	1	1	18	....	....	....	....
2000-01	Peterborough	OHL	61	8	27	35	53	....	....	....	....	....	....	....	....	....	7	0	5	5	0	....	....	....	....
2001-02	**Florida**	**NHL**	**5**	**0**	**0**	**0**	**0**	**0**	**0**	**0**	**3**	**0.0**	**0**	**0**	**0.0**	**13:23**	....	....	....	....	....	....	....	....	....
	Peterborough	OHL	55	10	32	42	56	....	....	....	....	....	....	....	....	....	6	0	5	5	6	....	....	....	....
2002-03	Peterborough	OHL	52	11	42	53	42	....	....	....	....	....	....	....	....	....	7	0	3	3	0	....	....	....	....
	San Antonio	AHL	3	0	1	1	0	....	....	....	....	....	....	....	....	....	3	0	0	0	0	....	....	....	....
2003-04	**Florida**	**NHL**	**18**	**1**	**6**	**7**	**12**	**1**	**0**	**0**	**16**	**6.3**	**–2**	**0**	**0.0**	**13:32**	....	....	....	....	....	....	....	....	....
	San Antonio	AHL	54	5	12	17	24	....	....	....	....	....	....	....	....	....	....	....	....	....	....	....	....	....	....
2004-05	San Antonio	AHL	78	2	22	24	57	....	....	....	....	....	....	....	....	....	....	....	....	....	....	....	....	....	....
2005-06	**Florida**	**NHL**	**67**	**2**	**14**	**16**	**50**	**2**	**0**	**0**	**89**	**2.2**	**1**	**0**	**0.0**	**18:30**	....	....	....	....	....	....	....	....	....
2006-07	**Vancouver**	**NHL**	**78**	**3**	**13**	**16**	**64**	**1**	**0**	**2**	**105**	**2.9**	**–4**	**0**	**0.0**	**18:31**	**12**	**0**	**2**	**2**	**12**	**0**	**0**	**0**	**18:50**
2007-08	**Vancouver**	**NHL**	**39**	**2**	**9**	**11**	**36**	**1**	**0**	**0**	**28**	**7.1**	**–3**	**0**	**0.0**	**18:10**	....	....	....	....	....	....	....	....	....
2008-09	**Tampa Bay**	**NHL**	**71**	**2**	**17**	**19**	**48**	**0**	**0**	**0**	**66**	**3.0**	**–8**	**0**	**0.0**	**19:37**	....	....	....	....	....	....	....	....	....
2009-10	**Tampa Bay**	**NHL**	**23**	**0**	**1**	**1**	**21**	**0**	**0**	**0**	**17**	**0.0**	**–4**	**0**	**0.0**	**17:32**	....	....	....	....	....	....	....	....	....
	Norfolk Admirals	AHL	15	0	6	6	8	....	....	....	....	....	....	....	....	....	....	....	....	....	....	....	....	....	....
	Philadelphia	**NHL**	**27**	**1**	**1**	**2**	**14**	**0**	**0**	**0**	**25**	**4.0**	**–10**	**0**	**0.0**	**16:58**	**22**	**0**	**3**	**3**	**8**	**0**	**0**	**0**	**10:01**
2010-11	HC Ocelari Trinec	CzRep	48	6	14	20	84	....	....	....	....	....	....	....	....	....	18	3	4	7	22	....	....	....	....
	NHL Totals		**328**	**11**	**61**	**72**	**245**	**5**	**0**	**2**	**349**	**3.2**		**0**	**0.0**	**18:10**	**34**	**0**	**5**	**5**	**20**	**0**	**0**	**0**	**13:08**

OHL All-Rookie Team (2001) • OHL First All-Star Team (2003) • Canadian Major Junior Second All-Star Team (2003)

Traded to **Vancouver** by **Florida** with Roberto Luongo and Florida's 6th round choice (Sergei Shirokov) in 2006 Entry Draft for Todd Bertuzzi, Bryan Allen and Alex Auld, June 23, 2006. Traded to **Tampa Bay** by **Vancouver** with Juraj Simek for Shane O'Brien and Michel Ouellet, October 6, 2008. Signed as a free agent by **Philadelphia**, January 31, 2010. Signed as a free agent by **Trinec** (Russia-KHL), September 16, 2010. Signed as a free agent by **MinskD (Russia-KHL), May 27, 2011.**

KREJCI, David
(KRAY-chee, DAY-vihd) **BOS**

Center. Shoots right. 6', 177 lbs. Born, Sternberk, Czech., April 28, 1986. Boston's 1st choice, 63rd overall, in 2004 Entry Draft.

2000-01	HC Olomouc U17	CzR-U17	26	2	6	8	4	....	....	....	....	....	....	....	....	....	3	1	1	2	0	....	....	....	....
2001-02	HC Trinec U17	CzR-U17	48	32	27	59	30	....	....	....	....	....	....	....	....	....	6	2	4	6	2	....	....	....	....
2002-03	HC Trinec U17	CzR-U17	22	12	24	36	42	....	....	....	....	....	....	....	....	....	....	....	....	....	....	....	....	....	....
	HC Trinec Jr.	CzRep-Jr.	12	4	5	9	2	....	....	....	....	....	....	....	....	....	12	5	5	10	8	....	....	....	....
2003-04	HC Kladno Jr.	CzRep-Jr.	50	23	37	60	37	....	....	....	....	....	....	....	....	....	7	3	6	9	4	....	....	....	....
2004-05	Gatineau	QMJHL	62	22	41	63	31	....	....	....	....	....	....	....	....	....	10	2	7	9	10	....	....	....	....
2005-06	Gatineau	QMJHL	55	27	54	81	54	....	....	....	....	....	....	....	....	....	17	10	22	32	24	....	....	....	....
2006-07	**Boston**	**NHL**	**6**	**0**	**0**	**0**	**2**	**0**	**0**	**0**	**2**	**0.0**	**–3**	**14**	**28.6**	**4:24**	....	....	....	....	....	....	....	....	....
	Providence Bruins	AHL	69	31	43	74	47	....	....	....	....	....	....	....	....	....	13	3	13	16	22	....	....	....	....
2007-08	**Boston**	**NHL**	**56**	**6**	**21**	**27**	**20**	**1**	**1**	**0**	**73**	**8.2**	**–3**	**635**	**48.2**	**14:55**	**7**	**1**	**4**	**5**	**2**	**1**	**0**	**0**	**19:09**
	Providence Bruins	AHL	25	7	21	28	19	....	....	....	....	....	....	....	....	....	....	....	....	....	....	....	....	....	....
2008-09	**Boston**	**NHL**	**82**	**22**	**51**	**73**	**26**	**5**	**2**	**6**	**146**	**15.1**	***37**	**1048**	**50.3**	**16:52**	**11**	**2**	**6**	**8**	**2**	**0**	**0**	**1**	**17:18**
2009-10	**Boston**	**NHL**	**79**	**17**	**35**	**52**	**26**	**6**	**0**	**3**	**156**	**10.9**	**8**	**1104**	**50.7**	**18:15**	**9**	**4**	**4**	**8**	**2**	**2**	**0**	**0**	**19:06**
	Czech Republic	Olympics	5	2	1	3	6	....	....	....	....	....	....	....	....	....	....	....	....	....	....	....	....	....	....
2010-11♦	**Boston**	**NHL**	**75**	**13**	**49**	**62**	**28**	**1**	**0**	**2**	**157**	**8.3**	**23**	**1149**	**48.7**	**18:51**	**25**	***12**	**11**	***23**	**10**	**2**	**0**	**4**	**20:07**
	NHL Totals		**298**	**58**	**156**	**214**	**102**	**13**	**3**	**11**	**534**	**10.9**		**3950**	**49.5**	**17:07**	**52**	**19**	**25**	**44**	**16**	**5**	**0**	**5**	**19:13**

KREPS, Kamil
(KREHPS, KA-mihl)

Center. Shoots right. 6'2", 194 lbs. Born, Litomerice, Czech., November 18, 1984. Florida's 3rd choice, 38th overall, in 2003 Entry Draft.

99-2000	Litvinov Jr.	CzRep-Jr.	48	18	16	34	10	....	....	....	....	....	....	....	....	....	....	....	....	....	....	....	....	....	....
2000-01	Litvinov Jr.	CzRep-Jr.	47	16	23	39	6	....	....	....	....	....	....	....	....	....	6	2	6	8	10	....	....	....	....
2001-02	Brampton	OHL	68	19	24	43	14	....	....	....	....	....	....	....	....	....	....	....	....	....	....	....	....	....	....
2002-03	Brampton	OHL	53	19	42	61	12	....	....	....	....	....	....	....	....	....	11	3	5	8	4	....	....	....	....
2003-04	Brampton	OHL	57	19	27	46	19	....	....	....	....	....	....	....	....	....	12	7	8	15	2	....	....	....	....
2004-05	San Antonio	AHL	58	5	6	11	11	....	....	....	....	....	....	....	....	....	....	....	....	....	....	....	....	....	....
	Texas Wildcatters	ECHL	12	5	6	11	6	....	....	....	....	....	....	....	....	....	....	....	....	....	....	....	....	....	....
2005-06	Rochester	AHL	61	13	19	32	20	....	....	....	....	....	....	....	....	....	....	....	....	....	....	....	....	....	....
2006-07	**Florida**	**NHL**	**14**	**1**	**1**	**2**	**6**	**0**	**0**	**0**	**20**	**5.0**	**–1**	**113**	**48.7**	**11:13**	....	....	....	....	....	....	....	....	....
	Rochester	AHL	50	14	21	35	16	....	....	....	....	....	....	....	....	....	6	1	0	1	0	....	....	....	....
2007-08	**Florida**	**NHL**	**76**	**8**	**17**	**25**	**29**	**1**	**0**	**2**	**99**	**8.1**	**10**	**763**	**53.9**	**12:59**	....	....	....	....	....	....	....	....	....
	Rochester	AHL	6	1	5	6	6	....	....	....	....	....	....	....	....	....	....	....	....	....	....	....	....	....	....
2008-09	**Florida**	**NHL**	**66**	**4**	**15**	**19**	**18**	**0**	**1**	**1**	**77**	**5.2**	**2**	**870**	**50.5**	**13:58**	....	....	....	....	....	....	....	....	....
2009-10	**Florida**	**NHL**	**76**	**5**	**9**	**14**	**18**	**1**	**0**	**1**	**83**	**6.0**	**–7**	**737**	**51.8**	**12:42**	....	....	....	....	....	....	....	....	....
2010-11	Karpat Oulu	Finland	55	14	15	29	43	....	....	....	....	....	....	....	....	....	3	1	1	2	0	....	....	....	....
	NHL Totals		**232**	**18**	**42**	**60**	**71**	**2**	**1**	**4**	**279**	**6.5**		**2483**	**51.8**	**13:04**	....	....	....	....	....	....	....	....	....

Signed as a free agent by **Oulu** (Finland), June 1, 2010.

KROG, Jason
(KROHG, JAY-suhn)

Center. Shoots right. 5'11", 185 lbs. Born, Fernie, B.C., October 9, 1975.

1992-93	Chilliwack Chiefs	BCJHL	52	30	27	57	52	....	....	....	....	....	....	....	....	....	....	....	....	....	....	....	....	....	....
1993-94	Chilliwack Chiefs	BCJHL	42	19	36	55	20	....	....	....	....	....	....	....	....	....	....	....	....	....	....	....	....	....	....
1994-95	Chilliwack Chiefs	BCJHL	60	47	81	128	36	....	....	....	....	....	....	....	....	....	....	....	....	....	....	....	....	....	....
1995-96	New Hampshire	H-East	34	4	16	20	20	....	....	....	....	....	....	....	....	....	....	....	....	....	....	....	....	....	....
1996-97	New Hampshire	H-East	39	23	*44	*67	28	....	....	....	....	....	....	....	....	....	....	....	....	....	....	....	....	....	....
1997-98	New Hampshire	H-East	38	*33	33	66	44	....	....	....	....	....	....	....	....	....	....	....	....	....	....	....	....	....	....
1998-99	New Hampshire	H-East	41	*34	*51	*85	38	....	....	....	....	....	....	....	....	....	....	....	....	....	....	....	....	....	....
99-2000	**NY Islanders**	**NHL**	**17**	**2**	**4**	**6**	**6**	**1**	**0**	**0**	**22**	**9.1**	**–1**	**81**	**53.1**	**10:03**	....	....	....	....	....	....	....	....	....
	Lowell	AHL	45	6	21	27	22	....	....	....	....	....	....	....	....	....	....	....	....	....	....	....	....	....	....
	Providence Bruins	AHL	11	9	8	17	4	....	....	....	....	....	....	....	....	....	6	2	2	4	0	....	....	....	....
2000-01	**NY Islanders**	**NHL**	**9**	**0**	**3**	**3**	**0**	**0**	**0**	**0**	**7**	**0.0**	**4**	**60**	**48.3**	**10:32**	....	....	....	....	....	....	....	....	....
	Lowell	AHL	26	11	16	27	6	....	....	....	....	....	....	....	....	....	....	....	....	....	....	....	....	....	....
	Springfield	AHL	24	7	23	30	4	....	....	....	....	....	....	....	....	....	....	....	....	....	....	....	....	....	....
2001-02	**NY Islanders**	**NHL**	**2**	**0**	**0**	**0**	**0**	**0**	**0**	**0**	**0**	**0.0**	**0**	**13**	**46.2**	**6:40**	....	....	....	....	....	....	....	....	....
	Bridgeport	AHL	64	26	36	62	13	....	....	....	....	....	....	....	....	....	20	10	13	23	8	....	....	....	....
2002-03	**Anaheim**	**NHL**	**67**	**10**	**15**	**25**	**12**	**0**	**1**	**1**	**92**	**10.9**	**1**	**634**	**60.4**	**13:47**	**21**	**3**	**1**	**4**	**4**	**0**	**0**	**0**	**12:10**
	Cincinnati	AHL	9	3	4	7	6	....	....	....	....	....	....	....	....	....	....	....	....	....	....	....	....	....	....
2003-04	**Anaheim**	**NHL**	**80**	**6**	**12**	**18**	**16**	**1**	**0**	**1**	**111**	**5.4**	**–4**	**769**	**58.5**	**11:58**	....	....	....	....	....	....	....	....	....
2004-05	EC Villacher SV	Austria	48	27	33	60	38	....	....	....	....	....	....	....	....	....	3	0	1	1	4	....	....	....	....
2005-06	Geneve	Swiss	29	15	14	29	32	....	....	....	....	....	....	....	....	....	....	....	....	....	....	....	....	....	....
	Frolunda	Sweden	7	5	1	6	6	....	....	....	....	....	....	....	....	....	17	5	3	8	10	....	....	....	....
2006-07	**Atlanta**	**NHL**	**14**	**1**	**3**	**4**	**6**	**0**	**0**	**0**	**14**	**7.1**	**3**	**165**	**55.2**	**13:58**	....	....	....	....	....	....	....	....	....
	Chicago Wolves	AHL	44	26	54	80	20	....	....	....	....	....	....	....	....	....	15	5	14	19	17	....	....	....	....
	NY Rangers	**NHL**	**9**	**2**	**0**	**2**	**4**	**0**	**0**	**1**	**8**	**25.0**	**2**	**66**	**56.1**	**9:58**	....	....	....	....	....	....	....	....	....
2007-08	Chicago Wolves	AHL	80	*39	*73	*112	30	....	....	....	....	....	....	....	....	....	24	*12	*26	*38	2	....	....	....	....
2008-09	**Vancouver**	**NHL**	**4**	**1**	**0**	**1**	**2**	**1**	**0**	**0**	**5**	**20.0**	**0**	**24**	**58.3**	**10:14**	....	....	....	....	....	....	....	....	....
	Manitoba Moose	AHL	74	30	56	86	30	....	....	....	....	....	....	....	....	....	22	8	15	23	0	....	....	....	....
2009-10	Chicago Wolves	AHL	78	14	61	75	34	....	....	....	....	....	....	....	....	....	14	5	6	11	6	....	....	....	....
2010-11	Chicago Wolves	AHL	80	19	56	75	22	....	....	....	....	....	....	....	....	....	....	....	....	....	....	....	....	....	....
	NHL Totals		**202**	**22**	**37**	**59**	**46**	**3**	**1**	**3**	**259**	**8.5**		**1812**	**58.1**	**12:19**	**21**	**3**	**1**	**4**	**4**	**0**	**0**	**0**	**12:10**

Hockey East First All-Star Team (1997, 1998, 1999) • NCAA East Second All-American Team (1997) • Hockey East Player of the Year (1999) • NCAA East First All-American Team (1999) • NCAA Championship All-Tournament Team (1999) • Hobey Baker Memorial Award (Top U.S. Collegiate Player) (1999) • AHL First All-Star Team (2008) • Willie Marshall Award (AHL – Top Goal-scorer) (2008) • John B. Sollenberger Trophy (AHL – Leading Scorer) (2008) • Les Cunningham Award (AHL – MVP) (2008) • Jack A. Butterfield Trophy (AHL – Playoff MVP) (2008) • AHL Second All-Star Team (2009)

Signed as a free agent by **NY Islanders**, May 14, 1999. • Loaned to **Providence** (AHL) by **NY Islanders**, March 1, 2000. Signed as a free agent by **Anaheim**, July 17, 2002. Signed as a free agent by **Villacher** (Austria), August 24, 2004. Signed as a free agent by **Geneve** (Swiss), May 19, 2005. Signed as a free agent by **Frolunda** (Sweden), January 31, 2006. Signed as a free agent by **Atlanta**, July 4, 2006. Claimed on waivers by **NY Rangers** from **Atlanta**, January 12, 2007. Claimed on waivers by **Atlanta** from **NY Rangers**, February 27, 2007. Signed as a free agent by **Vancouver**, July 14, 2008. Signed as a free agent by **Atlanta**, July 6, 2009. • Transferred to **Winnipeg** after **Atlanta** franchise relocated, June 21, 2011.

KRONWALL, Niklas

(KRAWN-wahl, NIHK-luhs) **DET**

Defense. Shoots left. 6', 192 lbs. Born, Stockholm, Sweden, January 12, 1981. Detroit's 1st choice, 29th overall, in 2000 Entry Draft.

			Regular Season														Playoffs								
Season	Club	League	GP	G	A	Pts	PIM	PP	SH	GW	S	%	+/-	TF	F%	Min	GP	G	A	Pts	PIM	PP	SH	GW	Min
1996-97	Djurgarden Jr.	Swe-Jr.	1	0	0	0	0	....	....	....	....	....	....	....	....	....	....	....	....	....	....	....	....	....	....
1997-98	Djurgarden Jr.	Swe-Jr.	27	4	3	7	71	....	....	....	....	....	....	....	....	....	2	0	0	0	2	....	....	....	....
1998-99	Huddinge IK	Sweden-2	14	0	1	1	10	....	....	....	....	....	....	....	....	....	....	....	....	....	....	....	....	....	....
	Huddinge IK Jr.	Swe-Jr.	2	0	0	0	6	....	....	....	....	....	....	....	....	....	....	....	....	....	....	....	....	....	....
99-2000	Djurgarden	Sweden	37	1	4	5	16	....	....	....	....	....	....	....	....	....	8	0	0	0	8	....	....	....	....
2000-01	Djurgarden	Sweden	31	1	9	10	32	....	....	....	....	....	....	....	....	....	15	0	1	1	8	....	....	....	....
2001-02	Djurgarden	Sweden	48	5	7	12	34	....	....	....	....	....	....	....	....	....	5	0	0	0	0	....	....	....	....
2002-03	Djurgarden	Sweden	50	5	13	18	46	....	....	....	....	....	....	....	....	....	12	3	2	5	18	....	....	....	....
2003-04	**Detroit**	**NHL**	**20**	**1**	**4**	**5**	**16**	**0**	**0**	**1**	**18**	**5.6**	**5**	**0**	**0.0**	**13:51**	....	....	....	....	....	....	....	....	....
	Grand Rapids	AHL	25	2	11	13	20	....	....	....	....	....	....	....	....	....	....	....	....	....	....	....	....	....	....
2004-05	Grand Rapids	AHL	76	13	40	53	53	....	....	....	....	....	....	....	....	....	....	....	....	....	....	....	....	....	....
2005-06	**Detroit**	**NHL**	**27**	**1**	**8**	**9**	**28**	**1**	**0**	**0**	**28**	**3.6**	**11**	**0**	**0.0**	**20:31**	**6**	**0**	**3**	**3**	**2**	**0**	**0**	**0**	**22:43**
	Grand Rapids	AHL	1	0	0	0	0	....	....	....	....	....	....	....	....	....	....	....	....	....	....	....	....	....	....
	Sweden	Olympics	2	1	1	2	8	....	....	....	....	....	....	....	....	....	....	....	....	....	....	....	....	....	....
2006-07	**Detroit**	**NHL**	**68**	**1**	**21**	**22**	**54**	**1**	**0**	**0**	**104**	**1.0**	**0**	**0**	**0.0**	**20:39**	....	....	....	....	....	....	....	....	....
2007-08♦	**Detroit**	**NHL**	**65**	**7**	**28**	**35**	**44**	**0**	**0**	**0**	**108**	**6.5**	**25**	**0**	**0.0**	**21:06**	**22**	**0**	**15**	**15**	**18**	**0**	**0**	**0**	**23:20**
2008-09	**Detroit**	**NHL**	**80**	**6**	**45**	**51**	**50**	**4**	**0**	**1**	**121**	**5.0**	**2**	**1**	**100.0**	**22:54**	**23**	**2**	**7**	**9**	**33**	**2**	**0**	**0**	**23:24**
2009-10	**Detroit**	**NHL**	**48**	**7**	**15**	**22**	**32**	**3**	**0**	**0**	**68**	**10.3**	**5**	**0**	**0.0**	**21:55**	**12**	**0**	**5**	**5**	**12**	**0**	**0**	**0**	**23:15**
	Sweden	Olympics	4	0	0	0	2	....	....	....	....	....	....	....	....	....	....	....	....	....	....	....	....	....	....
2010-11	**Detroit**	**NHL**	**77**	**11**	**26**	**37**	**36**	**5**	**0**	**3**	**131**	**8.4**	**5**	**0**	**0.0**	**22:52**	**11**	**2**	**4**	**6**	**4**	**1**	**0**	**0**	**23:04**
	NHL Totals		**385**	**34**	**147**	**181**	**260**	**14**	**0**	**5**	**578**	**5.9**		**1**	**100.0**	**21:26**	**74**	**4**	**34**	**38**	**69**	**3**	**0**	**0**	**23:15**

AHL First All-Star Team (2005) • Eddie Shore Award (AHL – Outstanding Defenseman) (2005)

• Missed majority of 2005-06 due to knee surgery.

KRONWALL, Staffan

(KRAWN-wahl, STAH-fuhn)

Defense. Shoots left. 6'3", 209 lbs. Born, Jarfalla, Sweden, September 10, 1982. Toronto's 9th choice, 285th overall, in 2002 Entry Draft.

Season	Club	League	GP	G	A	Pts	PIM	PP	SH	GW	S	%	+/-	TF	F%	Min	GP	G	A	Pts	PIM	PP	SH	GW	Min
99-2000	Huddinge IK Jr.	Swe-Jr.	34	2	0	2	38	....	....	....	....	....	....	....	....	....	....	....	....	....	....	....	....	....	....
	Huddinge IK U18	Swe-U18	7	0	3	3	0	....	....	....	....	....	....	....	....	....	....	....	....	....	....	....	....	....	....
2000-01	Huddinge IK Jr.	Swe-Jr.	23	6	1	7	16	....	....	....	....	....	....	....	....	....	....	....	....	....	....	....	....	....	....
	Huddinge IK	Sweden-3	1	0	0	0	0	....	....	....	....	....	....	....	....	....	....	....	....	....	....	....	....	....	....
2001-02	Huddinge IK	Sweden-2	42	4	7	11	30	....	....	....	....	....	....	....	....	....	....	....	....	....	....	....	....	....	....
	Huddinge IK Jr.	Swe-Jr.	1	0	0	0	0	....	....	....	....	....	....	....	....	....	4	2	1	3	27	....	....	....	....
2002-03	Djurgarden	Sweden	48	4	6	10	65	....	....	....	....	....	....	....	....	....	12	1	1	2	8	....	....	....	....
2003-04	Djurgarden	Sweden	44	1	5	6	54	....	....	....	....	....	....	....	....	....	4	0	1	1	2	....	....	....	....
2004-05	Brynas IF Gavle	Sweden	3	0	1	1	4	....	....	....	....	....	....	....	....	....	....	....	....	....	....	....	....	....	....
	Djurgarden Jr.	Swe-Jr.	5	2	4	6	0	....	....	....	....	....	....	....	....	....	....	....	....	....	....	....	....	....	....
	Djurgarden	Sweden	35	1	4	5	43	....	....	....	....	....	....	....	....	....	12	2	0	2	10	....	....	....	....
2005-06	**Toronto**	**NHL**	**34**	**0**	**1**	**1**	**14**	**0**	**0**	**0**	**18**	**0.0**	**–3**	**0**	**0.0**	**12:57**	....	....	....	....	....	....	....	....	....
	Toronto Marlies	AHL	16	1	10	11	12	....	....	....	....	....	....	....	....	....	4	0	2	2	2	....	....	....	....
2006-07	Toronto Marlies	AHL	47	3	14	17	32	....	....	....	....	....	....	....	....	....	....	....	....	....	....	....	....	....	....
2007-08	**Toronto**	**NHL**	**18**	**0**	**0**	**0**	**7**	**0**	**0**	**0**	**9**	**0.0**	**–2**	**0**	**0.0**	**11:07**	....	....	....	....	....	....	....	....	....
	Toronto Marlies	AHL	26	3	7	10	14	....	....	....	....	....	....	....	....	....	19	1	1	2	11	....	....	....	....
2008-09	Toronto Marlies	AHL	42	7	18	25	46	....	....	....	....	....	....	....	....	....	....	....	....	....	....	....	....	....	....
	Washington	**NHL**	**3**	**0**	**0**	**0**	**0**	**0**	**0**	**0**	**4**	**0.0**	**–1**	**0**	**0.0**	**13:13**	....	....	....	....	....	....	....	....	....
	Hershey Bears	AHL	17	2	7	9	13	....	....	....	....	....	....	....	....	....	21	3	9	12	6	....	....	....	....
2009-10	**Calgary**	**NHL**	**11**	**1**	**2**	**3**	**2**	**0**	**0**	**1**	**6**	**16.7**	**–1**	**0**	**0.0**	**9:54**	....	....	....	....	....	....	....	....	....
	Abbotsford Heat	AHL	44	5	23	28	24	....	....	....	....	....	....	....	....	....	9	0	2	2	0	....	....	....	....
2010-11	Abbotsford Heat	AHL	1	0	0	0	0	....	....	....	....	....	....	....	....	....	....	....	....	....	....	....	....	....	....
	Djurgarden	Sweden	45	7	13	20	14	....	....	....	....	....	....	....	....	....	7	0	1	1	2	....	....	....	....
	NHL Totals		**66**	**1**	**3**	**4**	**23**	**0**	**0**	**1**	**37**	**2.7**		**0**	**0.0**	**11:57**	....	....	....	....	....	....	....	....	....

Claimed on waivers by **Washington** from **Toronto**, February 6, 2009. Signed as a free agent by **Calgary**, July 14, 2009. • Loaned to **Djurgardens** (Sweden) by **Calgary**, October 11, 2010.

KRUGER, Marcus

(KROO-guhr, MAHR-kuhs) **CHI**

Center. Shoots left. 5'11", 172 lbs. Born, Stockholm, Sweden, May 27, 1990. Chicago's 5th choice, 149th overall, in 2009 Entry Draft.

Season	Club	League	GP	G	A	Pts	PIM	PP	SH	GW	S	%	+/-	TF	F%	Min	GP	G	A	Pts	PIM	PP	SH	GW	Min
2006-07	Djurgarden U18	Swe-U18	23	5	14	19	10	....	....	....	....	....	....	....	....	....	3	2	1	3	2	....	....	....	....
2007-08	Djurgarden U18	Swe-U18	22	11	20	31	22	....	....	....	....	....	....	....	....	....	7	3	8	11	6	....	....	....	....
	Djurgarden Jr.	Swe-Jr.	22	3	13	16	16	....	....	....	....	....	....	....	....	....	7	5	3	8	0	....	....	....	....
2008-09	Djurgarden Jr.	Swe-Jr.	34	9	30	39	24	....	....	....	....	....	....	....	....	....	6	1	5	6	2	....	....	....	....
	Djurgarden	Sweden	15	2	2	4	2	....	....	....	....	....	....	....	....	....	....	....	....	....	....	....	....	....	....
2009-10	Djurgarden	Sweden	38	11	20	31	14	....	....	....	....	....	....	....	....	....	16	3	7	10	6	....	....	....	....
2010-11	Djurgarden	Sweden	52	6	29	35	52	....	....	....	....	....	....	....	....	....	3	0	1	1	0	....	....	....	....
	Chicago	**NHL**	**7**	**0**	**0**	**0**	**4**	**0**	**0**	**0**	**7**	**0.0**	**–4**	**39**	**35.9**	**11:58**	**5**	**0**	**1**	**1**	**0**	**0**	**0**	**0**	**11:51**
	NHL Totals		**7**	**0**	**0**	**0**	**4**	**0**	**0**	**0**	**7**	**0.0**		**39**	**35.9**	**11:58**	**5**	**0**	**1**	**1**	**0**	**0**	**0**	**0**	**11:51**

KUBA, Filip

(KOO-bah, FIHL-ihp) **OTT**

Defense. Shoots left. 6'4", 229 lbs. Born, Ostrava, Czech., December 29, 1976. Florida's 8th choice, 192nd overall, in 1995 Entry Draft.

Season	Club	League	GP	G	A	Pts	PIM	PP	SH	GW	S	%	+/-	TF	F%	Min	GP	G	A	Pts	PIM	PP	SH	GW	Min
1994-95	HC Vitkovice Jr.	CzRep-Jr.	35	10	15	25	....	....	....	....	....	....	....	....	....	....	....	....	....	....	....	....	....	....	....
	HC Vitkovice	CzRep	....	....	....	....	....	....	....	....	....	....	....	....	....	....	4	0	0	0	2	....	....	....	....
1995-96	HC Vitkovice	CzRep	19	0	1	1	....	....	....	....	....	....	....	....	....	....	....	....	....	....	....	....	....	....	....
1996-97	Carolina	AHL	51	0	12	12	38	....	....	....	....	....	....	....	....	....	....	....	....	....	....	....	....	....	....
1997-98	New Haven	AHL	77	4	13	17	58	....	....	....	....	....	....	....	....	....	3	1	1	2	0	....	....	....	....
1998-99	**Florida**	**NHL**	**5**	**0**	**1**	**1**	**0**	**0**	**0**	**0**	**5**	**0.0**	**2**	**0**	**0.0**	**22:29**	....	....	....	....	....	....	....	....	....
	Kentucky	AHL	45	2	8	10	33	....	....	....	....	....	....	....	....	....	10	0	1	1	4	....	....	....	....
99-2000	**Florida**	**NHL**	**13**	**1**	**5**	**6**	**2**	**1**	**0**	**1**	**16**	**6.3**	**–3**	**0**	**0.0**	**13:52**	....	....	....	....	....	....	....	....	....
	Houston Aeros	IHL	27	3	6	9	13	....	....	....	....	....	....	....	....	....	11	1	2	3	4	....	....	....	....
2000-01	**Minnesota**	**NHL**	**75**	**9**	**21**	**30**	**28**	**4**	**0**	**4**	**141**	**6.4**	**–6**	**1**	**0.0**	**24:16**	....	....	....	....	....	....	....	....	....
2001-02	**Minnesota**	**NHL**	**62**	**5**	**19**	**24**	**32**	**3**	**0**	**1**	**101**	**5.0**	**–6**	**0**	**0.0**	**25:30**	....	....	....	....	....	....	....	....	....
2002-03	**Minnesota**	**NHL**	**78**	**8**	**21**	**29**	**29**	**4**	**2**	**1**	**129**	**6.2**	**0**	**1**	**0.0**	**23:56**	**18**	**3**	**5**	**8**	**24**	**3**	**0**	**0**	**26:46**
2003-04	**Minnesota**	**NHL**	**77**	**5**	**19**	**24**	**28**	**2**	**1**	**2**	**114**	**4.4**	**–7**	**2**	**0.0**	**24:06**	....	....	....	....	....	....	....	....	....
2004-05			DID NOT PLAY																						
2005-06	**Minnesota**	**NHL**	**65**	**6**	**19**	**25**	**44**	**1**	**1**	**1**	**69**	**8.7**	**0**	**2**	**0.0**	**21:46**	....	....	....	....	....	....	....	....	....
	Czech Republic	Olympics	8	1	0	1	0	....	....	....	....	....	....	....	....	....	....	....	....	....	....	....	....	....	....
2006-07	**Tampa Bay**	**NHL**	**81**	**15**	**22**	**37**	**36**	**5**	**1**	**2**	**106**	**14.2**	**–9**	**0**	**0.0**	**20:12**	**6**	**1**	**4**	**5**	**4**	**0**	**1**	**0**	**20:47**
2007-08	**Tampa Bay**	**NHL**	**75**	**6**	**25**	**31**	**40**	**2**	**0**	**0**	**113**	**5.3**	**–8**	**2**	**0.0**	**24:57**	....	....	....	....	....	....	....	....	....
2008-09	**Ottawa**	**NHL**	**71**	**3**	**37**	**40**	**28**	**2**	**0**	**0**	**111**	**2.7**	**4**	**0**	**0.0**	**23:17**	....	....	....	....	....	....	....	....	....
2009-10	**Ottawa**	**NHL**	**53**	**3**	**25**	**28**	**28**	**2**	**0**	**0**	**90**	**3.3**	**–5**	**1**	**0.0**	**22:51**	....	....	....	....	....	....	....	....	....
	Czech Republic	Olympics	5	0	1	1	0	....	....	....	....	....	....	....	....	....	....	....	....	....	....	....	....	....	....
2010-11	**Ottawa**	**NHL**	**64**	**2**	**14**	**16**	**16**	**0**	**0**	**1**	**76**	**2.6**	**–26**	**0**	**0.0**	**20:44**	....	....	....	....	....	....	....	....	....
	NHL Totals		**719**	**63**	**228**	**291**	**311**	**26**	**5**	**13**	**1071**	**5.9**		**9**	**0.0**	**22:59**	**24**	**4**	**9**	**13**	**28**	**3**	**1**	**0**	**25:16**

Played in NHL All-Star Game (2004)

Traded to **Calgary** by **Florida** for Rocky Thompson, March 16, 2000. Claimed by **Minnesota** from **Calgary** in Expansion Draft, June 23, 2000. Signed as a free agent by **Tampa Bay**, July 1, 2006. Traded to **Ottawa** by **Tampa Bay** with Alexandre Picard and San Jose's 1st round choice (previously acquired, later traded to NY Islanders, later traded to Columbus, later traded to Anaheim - Anaheim selected Kyle Palmieri) in 2009 Entry Draft for Andrej Meszaros, August 29, 2008.

KUBALIK, Tomas

(koo-BAHL-ihk, TAW-mahsh) **CBJ**

Right wing. Shoots right. 6'3", 209 lbs. Born, Plzen, Czech., May 1, 1990. Columbus' 6th choice, 135th overall, in 2008 Entry Draft.

Season	Club	League	GP	G	A	Pts	PIM	PP	SH	GW	S	%	+/-	TF	F%	Min	GP	G	A	Pts	PIM	PP	SH	GW	Min
2003-04	HC Plzen U17	CzR-U17	4	0	0	0	0	....	....	....	....	....	....	....	....	....	....	....	....	....	....	....	....	....	....
2004-05	HC Plzen U17	CzR-U17	37	4	1	5	18	....	....	....	....	....	....	....	....	....	....	....	....	....	....	....	....	....	....
2005-06	HC Plzen U17	CzR-U17	35	26	21	47	91	....	....	....	....	....	....	....	....	....	6	1	5	6	16	....	....	....	....
	HC Plzen Jr.	CzRep-Jr.	5	1	2	3	6	....	....	....	....	....	....	....	....	....	....	....	....	....	....	....	....	....	....
2006-07	HC Plzen U17	CzR-U17	2	4	1	5	6	....	....	....	....	....	....	....	....	....	8	5	5	10	30	....	....	....	....
	HC Plzen Jr.	CzRep-Jr.	34	23	15	38	76	....	....	....	....	....	....	....	....	....	3	1	2	3	24	....	....	....	....
	Plzen	CzRep	23	1	0	1	18	....	....	....	....	....	....	....	....	....	....	....	....	....	....	....	....	....	....

			Regular Season														Playoffs								
Season	Club	League	GP	G	A	Pts	PIM	PP	SH	GW	S	%	+/-	TF	F%	Min	GP	G	A	Pts	PIM	PP	SH	GW	Min
2007-08	HC Plzen Jr.	CzRep-Jr.	22	8	13	21	50	....	....	....	....	....	....	....	....	....	5	1	3	4	22	....	....	....	....
	Beroun	CzRep-2	7	0	0	0	2	....	....	....	....	....	....	....	....	....	....	....	....	....	....	....	....	....	....
	Plzen	CzRep	20	2	1	3	8	....	....	....	....	....	....	....	....	....	1	0	0	0	0	....	....	....	....
2008-09	HC Plzen Jr.	CzRep-Jr.	4	1	2	3	10	....	....	....	....	....	....	....	....	....	....	....	....	....	....	....	....	....	....
	Plzen	CzRep	32	1	1	2	64	....	....	....	....	....	....	....	....	....	17	1	0	1	8	....	....	....	....
2009-10	Victoriaville Tigres	QMJHL	58	33	42	75	95	....	....	....	....	....	....	....	....	....	16	4	10	14	8	....	....	....	....
2010-11	**Columbus**	**NHL**	**4**	**0**	**2**	**2**	**0**	**0**	**0**	**0**	**5**	**0.0**	**–3**	**1**	**100.0**	**14:45**	....	....	....	....	....	....	....	....	....
	Springfield	AHL	76	24	29	53	43	....	....	....	....	....	....	....	....	....	....	....	....	....	....	....	....	....	....
	NHL Totals		**4**	**0**	**2**	**2**	**0**	**0**	**0**	**0**	**5**	**0.0**		**1**	**100.0**	**14:45**	....	....	....	....	....	....	....	....	....

KUBINA, Pavel

(koo-BEE-nuh, PAH-vehl) **T.B.**

Defense. Shoots right. 6'4", 258 lbs. Born, Celadna, Czech., April 15, 1977. Tampa Bay's 6th choice, 179th overall, in 1996 Entry Draft.

Season	Club	League	GP	G	A	Pts	PIM	PP	SH	GW	S	%	+/-	TF	F%	Min	GP	G	A	Pts	PIM	PP	SH	GW	Min
1993-94	HC Vitkovice Jr.	CzRep-Jr.	35	4	3	7	....	....	....	....	....	....	....	....	....	....	....	....	....	....	....	....	....	....	....
	HC Vitkovice	CzRep	1	0	0	0	....	....	....	....	....	....	....	....	....	....	....	....	....	....	....	....	....	....	....
1994-95	HC Vitkovice Jr.	CzRep-Jr.	20	6	10	16	....	....	....	....	....	....	....	....	....	....	....	....	....	....	....	....	....	....	....
	HC Vitkovice	CzRep	8	2	0	2	10	....	....	....	....	....	....	....	....	....	4	0	0	0	0	....	....	....	....
1995-96	HC Vitkovice Jr.	CzRep-Jr.	16	5	10	15	....	....	....	....	....	....	....	....	....	....	....	....	....	....	....	....	....	....	....
	HC Vitkovice	CzRep	33	3	4	7	32	....	....	....	....	....	....	....	....	....	4	0	0	0	0	....	....	....	....
1996-97	HC Vitkovice	CzRep	1	0	0	0	0	....	....	....	....	....	....	....	....	....	....	....	....	....	....	....	....	....	....
	Moose Jaw	WHL	61	12	32	44	116	....	....	....	....	....	....	....	....	....	11	2	5	7	27	....	....	....	....
1997-98	**Tampa Bay**	**NHL**	**10**	**1**	**2**	**3**	**22**	**0**	**0**	**0**	**8**	**12.5**	**–1**	....	....	....	....	....	....	....	....	....	....	....	....
	Adirondack	AHL	55	4	8	12	86	....	....	....	....	....	....	....	....	....	1	1	0	1	14	....	....	....	....
1998-99	**Tampa Bay**	**NHL**	**68**	**9**	**12**	**21**	**80**	**3**	**1**	**1**	**119**	**7.6**	**–33**	**2**	**0.0**	**22:47**	....	....	....	....	....	....	....	....	....
	Cleveland	IHL	6	2	2	4	16	....	....	....	....	....	....	....	....	....	....	....	....	....	....	....	....	....	....
99-2000	**Tampa Bay**	**NHL**	**69**	**8**	**18**	**26**	**93**	**6**	**0**	**3**	**128**	**6.3**	**–19**	**0**	**0.0**	**22:32**	....	....	....	....	....	....	....	....	....
2000-01	**Tampa Bay**	**NHL**	**70**	**11**	**19**	**30**	**103**	**6**	**1**	**1**	**128**	**8.6**	**–14**	**2**	**0.0**	**24:06**	....	....	....	....	....	....	....	....	....
2001-02	**Tampa Bay**	**NHL**	**82**	**11**	**23**	**34**	**106**	**5**	**2**	**3**	**189**	**5.8**	**–22**	**1**	**100.0**	**23:39**	....	....	....	....	....	....	....	....	....
	Czech Republic	Olympics	4	0	1	1	0	....	....	....	....	....	....	....	....	....	....	....	....	....	....	....	....	....	....
2002-03	**Tampa Bay**	**NHL**	**75**	**3**	**19**	**22**	**78**	**0**	**0**	**0**	**139**	**2.2**	**–7**	**1**	**0.0**	**21:24**	**11**	**0**	**0**	**0**	**12**	**0**	**0**	**0**	**24:52**
2003-04♦	**Tampa Bay**	**NHL**	**81**	**17**	**18**	**35**	**85**	**8**	**1**	**4**	**153**	**11.1**	**9**	**1**	**0.0**	**21:09**	**22**	**0**	**4**	**4**	**50**	**0**	**0**	**0**	**22:54**
2004-05	Vitkovice	CzRep	28	6	5	11	46	....	....	....	....	....	....	....	....	....	12	4	6	10	34	....	....	....	....
2005-06	**Tampa Bay**	**NHL**	**76**	**5**	**33**	**38**	**96**	**4**	**0**	**3**	**155**	**3.2**	**–12**	**2**	**0.0**	**22:25**	**5**	**1**	**1**	**2**	**26**	**1**	**0**	**0**	**20:09**
	Czech Republic	Olympics	8	1	1	2	12	....	....	....	....	....	....	....	....	....	....	....	....	....	....	....	....	....	....
2006-07	**Toronto**	**NHL**	**61**	**7**	**14**	**21**	**48**	**4**	**0**	**1**	**97**	**7.2**	**7**	**0**	**0.0**	**21:19**	....	....	....	....	....	....	....	....	....
2007-08	**Toronto**	**NHL**	**72**	**11**	**29**	**40**	**116**	**6**	**0**	**4**	**136**	**8.1**	**5**	**1**	**0.0**	**23:55**	....	....	....	....	....	....	....	....	....
2008-09	**Toronto**	**NHL**	**82**	**14**	**26**	**40**	**94**	**9**	**0**	**4**	**184**	**7.6**	**–15**	**0**	**0.0**	**22:03**	....	....	....	....	....	....	....	....	....
2009-10	**Atlanta**	**NHL**	**76**	**6**	**32**	**38**	**66**	**2**	**0**	**1**	**159**	**3.8**	**0**	**0**	**0.0**	**22:38**	....	....	....	....	....	....	....	....	....
	Czech Republic	Olympics	5	0	0	0	2	....	....	....	....	....	....	....	....	....	....	....	....	....	....	....	....	....	....
2010-11	**Tampa Bay**	**NHL**	**79**	**4**	**19**	**23**	**62**	**1**	**0**	**2**	**78**	**5.1**	**2**	**0**	**0.0**	**19:14**	**8**	**2**	**1**	**3**	**10**	**2**	**0**	**0**	**15:17**
	NHL Totals		**901**	**107**	**264**	**371**	**1049**	**54**	**5**	**27**	**1673**	**6.4**		**10**	**10.0**	**22:15**	**46**	**3**	**6**	**9**	**98**	**3**	**0**	**0**	**21:45**

Played in NHL All-Star Game (2004)

Signed as a free agent by **Vitkovice** (CzRep), September 17, 2004. Signed as a free agent by **Toronto**, July 1, 2006. Traded to **Atlanta** by **Toronto** with Tim Stapleton for Garnet Exelby and Colin Stuart, July 1, 2009. Signed as a free agent by **Tampa Bay**, July 2, 2010.

KULDA , Arturs

(KOOL-da, AHR-tuhrs) **WPG**

Defense. Shoots left. 6'2", 215 lbs. Born, Riga, Latvia, July 25, 1988. Atlanta's 7th choice, 200th overall, in 2006 Entry Draft.

Season	Club	League	GP	G	A	Pts	PIM	PP	SH	GW	S	%	+/-	TF	F%	Min	GP	G	A	Pts	PIM	PP	SH	GW	Min
2003-04	Prizma/Riga 86	Latvia	11	0	0	0	8	....	....	....	....	....	....	....	....	....	2	0	0	0	0	....	....	....	....
2004-05	CSKA Moscow 2	Russia-3	STATISTICS NOT AVAILABLE																						
2005-06	CSKA Moscow 2	Russia-3	44	5	12	17	....	....	....	....	....	....	....	....	....	....	....	....	....	....	....	....	....	....	....
2006-07	Peterborough	OHL	58	2	9	11	83	....	....	....	....	....	....	....	....	....	....	....	....	....	....	....	....	....	....
2007-08	Peterborough	OHL	55	7	27	34	87	....	....	....	....	....	....	....	....	....	5	1	3	4	6	....	....	....	....
	Chicago Wolves	AHL	5	0	1	1	10	....	....	....	....	....	....	....	....	....	22	1	5	6	32	....	....	....	....
2008-09	Chicago Wolves	AHL	57	1	14	15	59	....	....	....	....	....	....	....	....	....	....	....	....	....	....	....	....	....	....
2009-10	**Atlanta**	**NHL**	**4**	**0**	**2**	**2**	**2**	**0**	**0**	**0**	**5**	**0.0**	**2**	**0**	**0.0**	**11:59**	....	....	....	....	....	....	....	....	....
	Chicago Wolves	AHL	66	6	19	25	46	....	....	....	....	....	....	....	....	....	14	1	4	5	8	....	....	....	....
2010-11	**Atlanta**	**NHL**	**2**	**0**	**0**	**0**	**2**	**0**	**0**	**0**	**3**	**0.0**	**–2**	**0**	**0.0**	**11:06**	....	....	....	....	....	....	....	....	....
	Chicago Wolves	AHL	69	5	12	17	73	....	....	....	....	....	....	....	....	....	....	....	....	....	....	....	....	....	....
	NHL Totals		**6**	**0**	**2**	**2**	**4**	**0**	**0**	**0**	**8**	**0.0**		**0**	**0.0**	**11:42**	....	....	....	....	....	....	....	....	....

• Transferred to **Winnipeg** after **Atlanta** franchise relocated, June 21, 2011.

KULEMIN, Nikolai

(KOOL-ay-mihn, NIH-koh-ligh) **TOR**

Wing. Shoots left. 6'1", 225 lbs. Born, Magnitogorsk, USSR, July 14, 1986. Toronto's 2nd choice, 44th overall, in 2006 Entry Draft.

Season	Club	League	GP	G	A	Pts	PIM	PP	SH	GW	S	%	+/-	TF	F%	Min	GP	G	A	Pts	PIM	PP	SH	GW	Min
2003-04	Magnitogorsk 2	Russia-3	43	8	18	26	91	....	....	....	....	....	....	....	....	....	....	....	....	....	....	....	....	....	....
2004-05	Magnitogorsk 2	Russia-3	43	9	13	22	44	....	....	....	....	....	....	....	....	....	....	....	....	....	....	....	....	....	....
2005-06	Magnitogorsk	Russia	31	5	7	12	8	....	....	....	....	....	....	....	....	....	11	2	4	6	6	....	....	....	....
	Magnitogorsk 2	Russia-3	4	3	1	4	6	....	....	....	....	....	....	....	....	....	....	....	....	....	....	....	....	....	....
2006-07	Magnitogorsk	Russia	54	27	12	39	42	....	....	....	....	....	....	....	....	....	15	10	1	11	10	....	....	....	....
2007-08	Magnitogorsk	Russia	57	21	12	33	63	....	....	....	....	....	....	....	....	....	11	2	2	4	29	....	....	....	....
2008-09	**Toronto**	**NHL**	**73**	**15**	**16**	**31**	**18**	**2**	**0**	**1**	**129**	**11.6**	**–8**	**66**	**53.0**	**13:48**	....	....	....	....	....	....	....	....	....
	Toronto Marlies	AHL	5	0	0	0	0	....	....	....	....	....	....	....	....	....	....	....	....	....	....	....	....	....	....
2009-10	**Toronto**	**NHL**	**78**	**16**	**20**	**36**	**16**	**0**	**1**	**3**	**145**	**11.0**	**0**	**66**	**40.9**	**16:22**	....	....	....	....	....	....	....	....	....
2010-11	**Toronto**	**NHL**	**82**	**30**	**27**	**57**	**26**	**5**	**1**	**5**	**173**	**17.3**	**7**	**111**	**54.1**	**17:19**	....	....	....	....	....	....	....	....	....
	NHL Totals		**233**	**61**	**63**	**124**	**60**	**7**	**2**	**9**	**447**	**13.6**		**243**	**50.2**	**15:54**	....	....	....	....	....	....	....	....	....

KULIKOV, Dmitry

(kool-YIH-kawf, dih-MEE-tree) **FLA**

Defense. Shoots left. 6'1", 183 lbs. Born, Lipetsk, USSR, October 29, 1990. Florida's 1st choice, 14th overall, in 2009 Entry Draft.

Season	Club	League	GP	G	A	Pts	PIM	PP	SH	GW	S	%	+/-	TF	F%	Min	GP	G	A	Pts	PIM	PP	SH	GW	Min
2007-08	Yaroslavl 2	Russia-3	STATISTICS NOT AVAILABLE																						
2008-09	Drummondville	QMJHL	57	12	50	62	46	....	....	....	....	....	....	....	....	....	19	2	18	20	16	....	....	....	....
2009-10	**Florida**	**NHL**	**68**	**3**	**13**	**16**	**32**	**1**	**0**	**0**	**87**	**3.4**	**–5**	**0**	**0.0**	**17:56**	....	....	....	....	....	....	....	....	....
2010-11	**Florida**	**NHL**	**72**	**6**	**20**	**26**	**45**	**1**	**0**	**1**	**83**	**7.2**	**–5**	**0**	**0.0**	**19:57**	....	....	....	....	....	....	....	....	....
	NHL Totals		**140**	**9**	**33**	**42**	**77**	**2**	**0**	**1**	**170**	**5.3**		**0**	**0.0**	**18:58**	....	....	....	....	....	....	....	....	....

QMJHL All-Rookie Team (2009) • QMJHL First All-Star Team (2009) • QMJHL Rookie of the Year (2009) • Canadian Major Junior Second All-Star Team (2009) • Canadian Major Junior All-Rookie Team (2009)

KUNITZ, Chris

(KOO-nihtz, KRIHS) **PIT**

Left wing. Shoots left. 6', 193 lbs. Born, Regina, Sask., September 26, 1979.

Season	Club	League	GP	G	A	Pts	PIM	PP	SH	GW	S	%	+/-	TF	F%	Min	GP	G	A	Pts	PIM	PP	SH	GW	Min
1996-97	Yorkton Mallers	SMHL	64	38	38	76	233	....	....	....	....	....	....	....	....	....	....	....	....	....	....	....	....	....	....
1997-98	Melville	SJHL	STATISTICS NOT AVAILABLE																						
1998-99	Melville	SJHL	63	57	32	89	222	....	....	....	....	....	....	....	....	....	....	....	....	....	....	....	....	....	....
99-2000	Ferris State	CCHA	38	20	9	29	70	....	....	....	....	....	....	....	....	....	....	....	....	....	....	....	....	....	....
2000-01	Ferris State	CCHA	37	16	13	29	81	....	....	....	....	....	....	....	....	....	....	....	....	....	....	....	....	....	....
2001-02	Ferris State	CCHA	35	*28	10	38	68	....	....	....	....	....	....	....	....	....	....	....	....	....	....	....	....	....	....
2002-03	Ferris State	CCHA	42	*35	*44	*79	56	....	....	....	....	....	....	....	....	....	....	....	....	....	....	....	....	....	....
2003-04	**Anaheim**	**NHL**	**21**	**0**	**6**	**6**	**12**	**0**	**0**	**0**	**31**	**0.0**	**1**	**7**	**14.3**	**9:07**	....	....	....	....	....	....	....	....	....
	Cincinnati	AHL	59	19	25	44	101	....	....	....	....	....	....	....	....	....	9	3	2	5	24	....	....	....	....
2004-05	Cincinnati	AHL	54	22	17	39	71	....	....	....	....	....	....	....	....	....	12	1	7	8	20	....	....	....	....
2005-06	**Atlanta**	**NHL**	**2**	**0**	**0**	**0**	**2**	**0**	**0**	**0**	**0**	**0.0**	**–3**	**0**	**0.0**	**5:43**	....	....	....	....	....	....	....	....	....
	Anaheim	**NHL**	**67**	**19**	**22**	**41**	**69**	**5**	**1**	**2**	**149**	**12.8**	**19**	**15**	**46.7**	**14:08**	**16**	**3**	**5**	**8**	**8**	**0**	**0**	**0**	**12:30**
	Portland Pirates	AHL	5	0	4	4	12	....	....	....	....	....	....	....	....	....	....	....	....	....	....	....	....	....	....
2006-07♦	**Anaheim**	**NHL**	**81**	**25**	**35**	**60**	**81**	**11**	**0**	**5**	**180**	**13.9**	**23**	**13**	**30.8**	**17:03**	**13**	**1**	**5**	**6**	**19**	**0**	**0**	**0**	**17:47**
2007-08	**Anaheim**	**NHL**	**82**	**21**	**29**	**50**	**80**	**7**	**1**	**6**	**196**	**10.7**	**8**	**49**	**32.7**	**16:54**	**6**	**0**	**2**	**2**	**8**	**0**	**0**	**0**	**18:30**
2008-09	**Anaheim**	**NHL**	**62**	**16**	**19**	**35**	**55**	**3**	**0**	**2**	**139**	**11.5**	**9**	**22**	**45.5**	**16:29**	....	....	....	....	....	....	....	....	....
	♦ Pittsburgh	**NHL**	**20**	**7**	**11**	**18**	**16**	**3**	**0**	**1**	**39**	**17.9**	**3**	**5**	**60.0**	**16:17**	**24**	**1**	**13**	**14**	**19**	**0**	**0**	**0**	**16:55**

			Regular Season														Playoffs								
Season	Club	League	GP	G	A	Pts	PIM	PP	SH	GW	S	%	+/-	TF	F%	Min	GP	G	A	Pts	PIM	PP	SH	GW	Min
2009-10	**Pittsburgh**	**NHL**	**50**	**13**	**19**	**32**	**39**	**2**	**1**	**0**	**131**	**9.9**	**3**	**15**	**40.0**	**16:26**	**13**	**4**	**7**	**11**	**8**	**1**	**0**	**0**	**17:26**
2010-11	**Pittsburgh**	**NHL**	**66**	**23**	**25**	**48**	**47**	**7**	**1**	**2**	**133**	**17.3**	**18**	**8**	**50.0**	**18:17**	**6**	**1**	**0**	**1**	**6**	**0**	**0**	**0**	**17:22**
	NHL Totals		**451**	**124**	**166**	**290**	**401**	**38**	**4**	**18**	**998**	**12.4**		**134**	**38.1**	**16:10**	**78**	**10**	**32**	**42**	**68**	**1**	**0**	**0**	**16:24**

CCHA First All-Star Team (2002, 2003) • CCHA Player of the Year (2003) • NCAA West First All-American Team (2003)

Signed as a free agent by **Anaheim**, April 1, 2003. Claimed on waivers by **Atlanta** from **Anaheim**, October 4, 2005. Claimed on waivers by **Anaheim** from **Atlanta**, October 18, 2005. Traded to **Pittsburgh** by **Anaheim** with Eric Tangradi for Ryan Whitney, February 26, 2009.

LAAKSO, Teemu

(LAK-soh, TEE-moo) **NSH**

Defense. Shoots right. 6'1", 215 lbs. Born, Tuusula, Finland, August 27, 1987. Nashville's 2nd choice, 78th overall, in 2005 Entry Draft.

Season	Club	League	GP	G	A	Pts	PIM	PP	SH	GW	S	%	+/-	TF	F%	Min	GP	G	A	Pts	PIM	PP	SH	GW	Min
2002-03	KJT U18	Fin-U18	18	2	5	7	24	....	....	....	....	....	....	....	....	....	....	....	....	....	....	....	....	....	....
2003-04	HIFK Helsinki Jr.	Fin-Jr.	41	3	6	9	20	....	....	....	....	....	....	....	....	....	3	0	1	1	0	....	....	....	....
2004-05	HIFK Helsinki U18	Fin-U18	....	....	....	....	....	....	....	....	....	....	....	....	....	....	1	0	0	0	0	....	....	....	....
	HIFK Helsinki Jr.	Fin-Jr.	20	5	4	9	18	....	....	....	....	....	....	....	....	....	....	....	....	....	....	....	....	....	....
	HIFK Helsinki	Finland	15	0	2	2	2	....	....	....	....	....	....	....	....	....	....	....	....	....	....	....	....	....	....
2005-06	HIFK Helsinki Jr.	Fin-Jr.	6	1	2	3	32	....	....	....	....	....	....	....	....	....	....	....	....	....	....	....	....	....	....
	Suomi U20	Finland-2	6	2	0	2	10	....	....	....	....	....	....	....	....	....	....	....	....	....	....	....	....	....	....
	HIFK Helsinki	Finland	47	2	1	3	20	....	....	....	....	....	....	....	....	....	8	1	0	1	0	....	....	....	....
2006-07	Suomi U20	Finland-2	2	0	1	1	4	....	....	....	....	....	....	....	....	....	....	....	....	....	....	....	....	....	....
	HIFK Helsinki	Finland	50	3	6	9	70	....	....	....	....	....	....	....	....	....	5	0	1	1	0	....	....	....	....
2007-08	HIFK Helsinki	Finland	53	3	7	10	40	....	....	....	....	....	....	....	....	....	7	0	0	0	2	....	....	....	....
2008-09	Milwaukee	AHL	42	2	7	9	50	....	....	....	....	....	....	....	....	....	....	....	....	....	....	....	....	....	....
2009-10	**Nashville**	**NHL**	**7**	**0**	**0**	**0**	**2**	**0**	**0**	**0**	**5**	**0.0**	**–2**	**0**	**0.0**	**10:48**	....	....	....	....	....	....	....	....	....
	Milwaukee	AHL	46	4	9	13	42	....	....	....	....	....	....	....	....	....	7	1	2	3	4	....	....	....	....
2010-11	**Nashville**	**NHL**	**1**	**0**	**0**	**0**	**0**	**0**	**0**	**0**	**0**	**0.0**	**0**	**0**	**0.0**	**2:43**	....	....	....	....	....	....	....	....	....
	Milwaukee	AHL	74	8	22	30	46	....	....	....	....	....	....	....	....	....	8	1	1	2	0	....	....	....	....
	NHL Totals		**8**	**0**	**0**	**0**	**2**	**0**	**0**	**0**	**5**	**0.0**		**0**	**0.0**	**9:47**	....	....	....	....	....	....	....	....	....

LADD, Andrew

(LAD, AN-droo) **WPG**

Left wing. Shoots left. 6'3", 205 lbs. Born, Maple Ridge, B.C., December 12, 1985. Carolina's 1st choice, 4th overall, in 2004 Entry Draft.

Season	Club	League	GP	G	A	Pts	PIM	PP	SH	GW	S	%	+/-	TF	F%	Min	GP	G	A	Pts	PIM	PP	SH	GW	Min
2000-01	Okanagan Chiefs	Minor-BC	6	4	8	12	10	....	....	....	....	....	....	....	....	....	....	....	....	....	....	....	....	....	....
2001-02	Port Coquitlam	Minor-BC	50	50	41	91	49	....	....	....	....	....	....	....	....	....	....	....	....	....	....	....	....	....	....
	Vancouver Giants	WHL	1	0	0	0	0	....	....	....	....	....	....	....	....	....	....	....	....	....	....	....	....	....	....
2002-03	Coquitlam	BCHL	58	15	40	55	61	....	....	....	....	....	....	....	....	....	....	....	....	....	....	....	....	....	....
2003-04	Calgary Hitmen	WHL	71	30	45	75	119	....	....	....	....	....	....	....	....	....	7	1	6	7	10	....	....	....	....
2004-05	Calgary Hitmen	WHL	65	19	26	45	167	....	....	....	....	....	....	....	....	....	12	7	4	11	18	....	....	....	....
2005-06♦	**Carolina**	**NHL**	**29**	**6**	**5**	**11**	**4**	**3**	**0**	**0**	**43**	**14.0**	**0**	**0**	**0.0**	**11:10**	**17**	**2**	**3**	**5**	**4**	**0**	**0**	**1**	**9:27**
	Lowell	AHL	25	11	8	19	28	....	....	....	....	....	....	....	....	....	....	....	....	....	....	....	....	....	....
2006-07	**Carolina**	**NHL**	**65**	**11**	**10**	**21**	**46**	**2**	**0**	**3**	**109**	**10.1**	**1**	**1**	**0.0**	**11:12**	....	....	....	....	....	....	....	....	....
2007-08	**Carolina**	**NHL**	**43**	**9**	**9**	**18**	**31**	**0**	**0**	**1**	**76**	**11.8**	**9**	**5**	**60.0**	**11:45**	....	....	....	....	....	....	....	....	....
	Albany River Rats	AHL	2	1	0	1	4	....	....	....	....	....	....	....	....	....	....	....	....	....	....	....	....	....	....
	Chicago	**NHL**	**20**	**5**	**7**	**12**	**4**	**1**	**0**	**0**	**55**	**9.1**	**4**	**3**	**33.3**	**14:58**	....	....	....	....	....	....	....	....	....
2008-09	**Chicago**	**NHL**	**82**	**15**	**34**	**49**	**28**	**0**	**0**	**2**	**195**	**7.7**	**26**	**42**	**23.8**	**14:24**	**17**	**3**	**1**	**4**	**12**	**0**	**0**	**1**	**12:55**
2009-10♦	**Chicago**	**NHL**	**82**	**17**	**21**	**38**	**67**	**0**	**0**	**1**	**148**	**11.5**	**2**	**12**	**41.7**	**13:42**	**19**	**3**	**3**	**6**	**12**	**0**	**0**	**0**	**12:48**
2010-11	**Atlanta**	**NHL**	**81**	**29**	**30**	**59**	**39**	**9**	**2**	**2**	**195**	**14.9**	**–10**	**44**	**34.1**	**20:04**	....	....	....	....	....	....	....	....	....
	NHL Totals		**402**	**92**	**116**	**208**	**219**	**15**	**2**	**9**	**821**	**11.2**		**107**	**31.8**	**14:23**	**53**	**8**	**7**	**15**	**28**	**0**	**0**	**2**	**11:46**

Traded to **Chicago** by **Carolina** for Tuomo Ruutu, February 26, 2008. Traded to **Atlanta** by **Chicago** for Ivan Vishnevskiy and Winnipeg/Atlanta's 2nd round choice (Adam Clendening) in 2011 Entry Draft, July 1, 2010. • Transferred to **Winnipeg** after **Atlanta** franchise relocated, June 21, 2011.

LAICH, Brooks

(LIGHK, BRUKS) **WSH**

Center. Shoots left. 6'2", 200 lbs. Born, Wawota, Sask., June 23, 1983. Ottawa's 7th choice, 193rd overall, in 2001 Entry Draft.

Season	Club	League	GP	G	A	Pts	PIM	PP	SH	GW	S	%	+/-	TF	F%	Min	GP	G	A	Pts	PIM	PP	SH	GW	Min
99-2000	Tisdale Trojans	SMHL	57	51	52	103	....	....	....	....	....	....	....	....	....	....	....	....	....	....	....	....	....	....	....
2000-01	Moose Jaw	WHL	71	9	21	30	28	....	....	....	....	....	....	....	....	....	4	0	0	0	5	....	....	....	....
2001-02	Moose Jaw	WHL	28	6	14	20	12	....	....	....	....	....	....	....	....	....	....	....	....	....	....	....	....	....	....
	Seattle	WHL	47	22	36	58	42	....	....	....	....	....	....	....	....	....	11	5	3	8	11	....	....	....	....
2002-03	Seattle	WHL	60	41	53	94	65	....	....	....	....	....	....	....	....	....	15	5	14	19	24	....	....	....	....
2003-04	**Ottawa**	**NHL**	**1**	**0**	**0**	**0**	**2**	**0**	**0**	**0**	**1**	**0.0**	**0**	**7**	**42.9**	**9:34**	....	....	....	....	....	....	....	....	....
	Binghamton	AHL	44	15	18	33	16	....	....	....	....	....	....	....	....	....	....	....	....	....	....	....	....	....	....
	Washington	**NHL**	**4**	**0**	**1**	**1**	**0**	**0**	**0**	**0**	**2**	**0.0**	**–1**	**49**	**51.0**	**10:50**	....	....	....	....	....	....	....	....	....
	Portland Pirates	AHL	22	1	3	4	12	....	....	....	....	....	....	....	....	....	6	0	0	0	0	....	....	....	....
2004-05	Portland Pirates	AHL	68	16	10	26	33	....	....	....	....	....	....	....	....	....	....	....	....	....	....	....	....	....	....
2005-06	**Washington**	**NHL**	**73**	**7**	**14**	**21**	**26**	**1**	**0**	**1**	**118**	**5.9**	**–9**	**666**	**49.7**	**11:13**	....	....	....	....	....	....	....	....	....
	Hershey Bears	AHL	10	7	6	13	8	....	....	....	....	....	....	....	....	....	21	8	7	15	29	....	....	....	....
2006-07	**Washington**	**NHL**	**73**	**8**	**10**	**18**	**29**	**2**	**3**	**0**	**119**	**6.7**	**–2**	**563**	**51.9**	**13:36**	....	....	....	....	....	....	....	....	....
2007-08	**Washington**	**NHL**	**82**	**21**	**16**	**37**	**35**	**8**	**2**	**4**	**122**	**17.2**	**–3**	**596**	**47.2**	**14:03**	**7**	**1**	**5**	**6**	**4**	**0**	**0**	**0**	**18:37**
2008-09	**Washington**	**NHL**	**82**	**23**	**30**	**53**	**31**	**9**	**1**	**3**	**185**	**12.4**	**–1**	**511**	**51.1**	**17:17**	**14**	**3**	**4**	**7**	**10**	**2**	**0**	**0**	**17:27**
2009-10	**Washington**	**NHL**	**78**	**25**	**34**	**59**	**34**	**12**	**1**	**4**	**222**	**11.3**	**16**	**337**	**45.1**	**18:17**	**7**	**2**	**1**	**3**	**4**	**0**	**0**	**1**	**19:57**
2010-11	**Washington**	**NHL**	**82**	**16**	**32**	**48**	**46**	**4**	**1**	**3**	**207**	**7.7**	**14**	**524**	**51.3**	**18:25**	**9**	**1**	**6**	**7**	**2**	**0**	**0**	**0**	**21:54**
	NHL Totals		**475**	**100**	**137**	**237**	**203**	**36**	**8**	**15**	**976**	**10.2**		**3253**	**49.6**	**15:31**	**37**	**7**	**16**	**23**	**20**	**2**	**0**	**1**	**19:14**

WHL West First All-Star Team (2003)

Traded to **Washington** by **Ottawa** with Ottawa's 2nd round choice (later traded to Colorado - Colorado selected Chris Durand) in 2005 Entry Draft for Peter Bondra, February 18, 2004.

LAING, Quintin

(LANG, QUIHN-tihn) **CGY**

Left wing. Shoots left. 6'3", 183 lbs. Born, Rosetown, Sask., June 8, 1979. Detroit's 3rd choice, 102nd overall, in 1997 Entry Draft.

Season	Club	League	GP	G	A	Pts	PIM	PP	SH	GW	S	%	+/-	TF	F%	Min	GP	G	A	Pts	PIM	PP	SH	GW	Min
1993-94	Delisle Contacts	SAHA	30	25	50	75	25	....	....	....	....	....	....	....	....	....	....	....	....	....	....	....	....	....	....
1994-95	Delisle Contacts	SAHA	30	30	45	75	15	....	....	....	....	....	....	....	....	....	....	....	....	....	....	....	....	....	....
1995-96	Sask. Contacts	SMHL	44	18	12	30	20	....	....	....	....	....	....	....	....	....	....	....	....	....	....	....	....	....	....
1996-97	Kelowna Rockets	WHL	63	13	24	37	54	....	....	....	....	....	....	....	....	....	1	0	0	0	0	....	....	....	....
1997-98	Kelowna Rockets	WHL	59	11	24	35	47	....	....	....	....	....	....	....	....	....	7	0	1	1	8	....	....	....	....
1998-99	Kelowna Rockets	WHL	70	11	10	21	107	....	....	....	....	....	....	....	....	....	6	3	0	3	0	....	....	....	....
99-2000	Kelowna Rockets	WHL	68	22	30	52	61	....	....	....	....	....	....	....	....	....	5	1	1	2	8	....	....	....	....
2000-01	Norfolk Admirals	AHL	10	0	1	1	10	....	....	....	....	....	....	....	....	....	....	....	....	....	....	....	....	....	....
	Jackson Bandits	ECHL	60	13	24	37	39	....	....	....	....	....	....	....	....	....	5	0	0	0	0	....	....	....	....
2001-02	Jackson Bandits	ECHL	16	4	6	10	12	....	....	....	....	....	....	....	....	....	....	....	....	....	....	....	....	....	....
	Norfolk Admirals	AHL	61	6	15	21	32	....	....	....	....	....	....	....	....	....	4	0	0	0	2	....	....	....	....
2002-03	Norfolk Admirals	AHL	69	5	12	17	33	....	....	....	....	....	....	....	....	....	8	2	2	4	0	....	....	....	....
2003-04	**Chicago**	**NHL**	**3**	**0**	**1**	**1**	**0**	**0**	**0**	**0**	**3**	**0.0**	**1**	**0**	**0.0**	**11:57**	....	....	....	....	....	....	....	....	....
	Norfolk Admirals	AHL	78	12	10	22	74	....	....	....	....	....	....	....	....	....	8	5	1	6	4	....	....	....	....
2004-05	Norfolk Admirals	AHL	66	10	13	23	54	....	....	....	....	....	....	....	....	....	4	0	0	0	0	....	....	....	....
2005-06	Norfolk Admirals	AHL	73	14	31	45	70	....	....	....	....	....	....	....	....	....	4	0	0	0	0	....	....	....	....
2006-07	Hershey Bears	AHL	75	15	28	43	44	....	....	....	....	....	....	....	....	....	19	2	5	7	21	....	....	....	....
2007-08	**Washington**	**NHL**	**39**	**1**	**5**	**6**	**10**	**0**	**0**	**1**	**48**	**2.1**	**4**	**6**	**33.3**	**11:33**	....	....	....	....	....	....	....	....	....
	Hershey Bears	AHL	20	2	6	8	28	....	....	....	....	....	....	....	....	....	....	....	....	....	....	....	....	....	....
2008-09	**Washington**	**NHL**	**1**	**0**	**0**	**0**	**0**	**0**	**0**	**0**	**2**	**0.0**	**1**	**0**	**0.0**	**10:19**	....	....	....	....	....	....	....	....	....
	Hershey Bears	AHL	55	9	16	25	21	....	....	....	....	....	....	....	....	....	9	2	2	4	0	....	....	....	....
2009-10	**Washington**	**NHL**	**36**	**2**	**2**	**4**	**21**	**0**	**0**	**0**	**38**	**5.3**	**2**	**7**	**57.1**	**9:38**	....	....	....	....	....	....	....	....	....
	Hershey Bears	AHL	2	0	0	0	0	....	....	....	....	....	....	....	....	....	....	....	....	....	....	....	....	....	....
2010-11	Abbotsford Heat	AHL	59	7	19	26	40	....	....	....	....	....	....	....	....	....	....	....	....	....	....	....	....	....	....
	Victoria	ECHL	4	0	1	1	0	....	....	....	....	....	....	....	....	....	....	....	....	....	....	....	....	....	....
	NHL Totals		**79**	**3**	**8**	**11**	**31**	**0**	**0**	**1**	**91**	**3.3**		**13**	**46.2**	**10:41**	....	....	....	....	....	....	....	....	....

Signed as a free agent by **Chicago**, June 4, 2003. Signed as a free agent by **Washington**, July 18, 2006. • Missed majority of 2009-10 due to broken jaw at NY Rangers, November 17, 2009 and as a healthy reserve. Signed to a PTO (professional tryout) contract by **Abbotsford** (AHL), November 10, 2010. Signed as a free agent by **Calgary**, July 1, 2011.

LALIBERTE, David
(la-lih-BUHR-tee, DAY-vihd)

Right wing. Shoots right. 6'1", 194 lbs. Born, St-Jean-Sur-Richelieu, Que., March 17, 1986. Philadelphia's 3rd choice, 124th overall, in 2004 Entry Draft.

			Regular Season														Playoffs								
Season	Club	League	GP	G	A	Pts	PIM	PP	SH	GW	S	%	+/-	TF	F%	Min	GP	G	A	Pts	PIM	PP	SH	GW	Min
2001-02	Antoine-Girouard	QAAA	41	21	21	42	14	....	....	....	....	....	....	....	....	....	15	8	9	17	6	....	....	....	....
2002-03	Montreal Rocket	QMJHL	66	15	14	29	10	....	....	....	....	....	....	....	....	....	6	3	0	3	2	....	....	....	....
2003-04	P.E.I. Rocket	QMJHL	70	21	22	43	51	....	....	....	....	....	....	....	....	....	11	1	3	4	6	....	....	....	....
2004-05	P.E.I. Rocket	QMJHL	41	23	13	36	36	....	....	....	....	....	....	....	....	....	....	....	....	....	....	....	....	....	....
2005-06	P.E.I. Rocket	QMJHL	34	12	11	23	41	....	....	....	....	....	....	....	....	....	6	3	1	4	6	....	....	....	....
2006-07	P.E.I. Rocket	QMJHL	68	50	48	98	86	....	....	....	....	....	....	....	....	....	7	5	4	9	4	....	....	....	....
2007-08	Philadelphia	AHL	27	3	6	9	13	....	....	....	....	....	....	....	....	....	....	....	....	....	....	....	....	....	....
	Wheeling Nailers	ECHL	27	10	14	24	16	....	....	....	....	....	....	....	....	....	....	....	....	....	....	....	....	....	....
2008-09	Philadelphia	AHL	70	28	20	48	43	....	....	....	....	....	....	....	....	....	4	0	1	1	4	....	....	....	....
2009-10	**Philadelphia**	**NHL**	**11**	**2**	**1**	**3**	**6**	**0**	**0**	**1**	**8**	**25.0**	**1**	**1**	**100.0**	**7:47**	**1**	**0**	**0**	**0**	**2**	**0**	**0**	**0**	**5:32**
	Adirondack	AHL	66	18	28	46	39	....	....	....	....	....	....	....	....	....	....	....	....	....	....	....	....	....	....
2010-11	Adirondack	AHL	19	3	6	9	20	....	....	....	....	....	....	....	....	....	....	....	....	....	....	....	....	....	....
	Syracuse Crunch	AHL	30	5	4	9	32	....	....	....	....	....	....	....	....	....	....	....	....	....	....	....	....	....	....
	Providence Bruins	AHL	17	1	5	6	14	....	....	....	....	....	....	....	....	....	....	....	....	....	....	....	....	....	....
	NHL Totals		**11**	**2**	**1**	**3**	**6**	**0**	**0**	**1**	**8**	**25.0**		**1**	**100.0**	**7:47**	**1**	**0**	**0**	**0**	**2**	**0**	**0**	**0**	**5:32**

Traded to **Anaheim** by **Philadelphia** with Patrick Maroon for Danny Syvret and Rob Bordson, November 21, 2010. Traded to **Boston** by **Anaheim** with Stefan Chaput for Brian McGrattan and Sean Zimmerman, February 27, 2011.

LANGENBRUNNER, Jamie
(lan-gehn-BRUH-nuhr, JAY-mee) **ST.L.**

Right wing. Shoots right. 6'1", 205 lbs. Born, Cloquet, MN, July 24, 1975. Dallas' 2nd choice, 35th overall, in 1993 Entry Draft.

			Regular Season														Playoffs								
Season	Club	League	GP	G	A	Pts	PIM	PP	SH	GW	S	%	+/-	TF	F%	Min	GP	G	A	Pts	PIM	PP	SH	GW	Min
1990-91	Cloquet	High-MN	20	6	16	22	8	....	....	....	....	....	....	....	....	....	....	....	....	....	....	....	....	....	....
1991-92	Cloquet	High-MN	23	16	23	39	24	....	....	....	....	....	....	....	....	....	....	....	....	....	....	....	....	....	....
1992-93	Cloquet	High-MN	27	27	62	89	18	....	....	....	....	....	....	....	....	....	....	....	....	....	....	....	....	....	....
1993-94	Peterborough	OHL	62	33	58	91	53	....	....	....	....	....	....	....	....	....	7	4	6	10	2	....	....	....	....
1994-95	Peterborough	OHL	62	42	57	99	84	....	....	....	....	....	....	....	....	....	11	8	14	22	12	....	....	....	....
	Dallas	**NHL**	**2**	**0**	**0**	**0**	**2**	**0**	**0**	**0**	**1**	**0.0**	**0**	....	....	....	....	....	....	....	....	....	....	....	....
	Kalamazoo Wings	IHL	....	....	....	....	....	....	....	....	....	....	....	....	....	....	11	1	3	4	2	....	....	....	....
1995-96	**Dallas**	**NHL**	**12**	**2**	**2**	**4**	**6**	**1**	**0**	**0**	**15**	**13.3**	**–2**	....	....	....	....	....	....	....	....	....	....	....	....
	Michigan	IHL	59	25	40	65	129	....	....	....	....	....	....	....	....	....	10	3	10	13	8	....	....	....	....
1996-97	**Dallas**	**NHL**	**76**	**13**	**26**	**39**	**51**	**3**	**0**	**3**	**112**	**11.6**	**–2**	....	....	....	**5**	**1**	**1**	**2**	**14**	**0**	**0**	**1**	....
1997-98	**Dallas**	**NHL**	**81**	**23**	**29**	**52**	**61**	**8**	**0**	**6**	**159**	**14.5**	**9**	....	....	....	**16**	**1**	**4**	**5**	**14**	**0**	**0**	**1**	....
	United States	Olympics	3	0	0	0	4	....	....	....	....	....	....	....	....	....	....	....	....	....	....	....	....	....	....
1998-99 ♦	**Dallas**	**NHL**	**75**	**12**	**33**	**45**	**62**	**4**	**0**	**1**	**145**	**8.3**	**10**	**217**	**46.1**	**15:51**	**23**	**10**	**7**	**17**	**16**	***4**	**0**	**3**	**17:43**
99-2000	**Dallas**	**NHL**	**65**	**18**	**21**	**39**	**68**	**4**	**2**	**6**	**153**	**11.8**	**16**	**40**	**50.0**	**17:33**	**15**	**1**	**7**	**8**	**18**	**1**	**0**	**0**	**15:28**
2000-01	**Dallas**	**NHL**	**53**	**12**	**18**	**30**	**57**	**3**	**2**	**4**	**104**	**11.5**	**4**	**316**	**45.3**	**16:30**	**10**	**2**	**2**	**4**	**6**	**0**	**0**	**1**	**19:26**
2001-02	**Dallas**	**NHL**	**68**	**10**	**16**	**26**	**54**	**0**	**1**	**2**	**132**	**7.6**	**–11**	**120**	**45.0**	**15:45**	....	....	....	....	....	....	....	....	....
	New Jersey	**NHL**	**14**	**3**	**3**	**6**	**23**	**0**	**0**	**2**	**31**	**9.7**	**2**	**2**	**50.0**	**15:27**	**5**	**0**	**1**	**1**	**8**	**0**	**0**	**0**	**14:57**
2002-03 ♦	**New Jersey**	**NHL**	**78**	**22**	**33**	**55**	**65**	**5**	**1**	**5**	**197**	**11.2**	**17**	**72**	**47.2**	**17:48**	**24**	***11**	**7**	***18**	**16**	**1**	**0**	***4**	**17:34**
2003-04	**New Jersey**	**NHL**	**53**	**10**	**16**	**26**	**43**	**1**	**2**	**2**	**130**	**7.7**	**9**	**31**	**51.6**	**16:01**	**5**	**0**	**2**	**2**	**2**	**0**	**0**	**0**	**15:04**
2004-05	ERC Ingolstadt	Germany	11	2	2	4	22	....	....	....	....	....	....	....	....	....	11	1	6	7	6	....	....	....	....
2005-06	**New Jersey**	**NHL**	**80**	**19**	**34**	**53**	**74**	**8**	**1**	**1**	**243**	**7.8**	**–1**	**41**	**43.9**	**18:36**	**9**	**3**	**10**	**13**	**16**	**1**	**0**	**1**	**19:46**
2006-07	**New Jersey**	**NHL**	**82**	**23**	**37**	**60**	**64**	**12**	**0**	**7**	**243**	**9.5**	**–9**	**23**	**34.8**	**18:33**	**11**	**2**	**6**	**8**	**7**	**1**	**0**	**1**	**19:16**
2007-08	**New Jersey**	**NHL**	**64**	**13**	**28**	**41**	**30**	**5**	**1**	**2**	**152**	**8.6**	**–1**	**18**	**55.6**	**18:18**	**5**	**0**	**4**	**4**	**4**	**0**	**0**	**0**	**18:30**
2008-09	**New Jersey**	**NHL**	**81**	**29**	**40**	**69**	**56**	**6**	**3**	**7**	**229**	**12.7**	**25**	**25**	**40.0**	**18:06**	**4**	**2**	**1**	**3**	**2**	**0**	**0**	**0**	**16:13**
2009-10	**New Jersey**	**NHL**	**81**	**19**	**42**	**61**	**44**	**6**	**2**	**4**	**228**	**8.3**	**6**	**60**	**48.3**	**19:33**	**5**	**0**	**1**	**1**	**4**	**0**	**0**	**0**	**18:38**
	United States	Olympics	6	1	3	4	0	....	....	....	....	....	....	....	....	....	....	....	....	....	....	....	....	....	....
2010-11	**New Jersey**	**NHL**	**31**	**4**	**10**	**14**	**16**	**0**	**0**	**2**	**76**	**5.3**	**–15**	**10**	**10.0**	**18:33**	....	....	....	....	....	....	....	....	....
	Dallas	**NHL**	**39**	**5**	**13**	**18**	**29**	**1**	**0**	**1**	**77**	**6.5**	**–3**	**18**	**55.6**	**16:33**	....	....	....	....	....	....	....	....	....
	NHL Totals		**1035**	**237**	**401**	**638**	**805**	**67**	**15**	**55**	**2427**	**9.8**		**993**	**45.7**	**17:34**	**137**	**33**	**53**	**86**	**127**	**8**	**0**	**12**	**17:38**

Traded to **New Jersey** by **Dallas** with Joe Nieuwendyk for Jason Arnott, Randy McKay and New Jersey's 1st round choice (later traded to Columbus, later traded to Buffalo – Buffalo selected Daniel Paille) in 2002 Entry Draft, March 19, 2002. Signed as a free agent by **Ingolstadt** (Germany), January 24, 2005. Traded to **Dallas** by **New Jersey** for Dallas's 3rd round choice (Blake Coleman) in 2011 Entry Draft and future considerations, January 6, 2011. Signed as a free agent by **St. Louis**, July 6, 2011.

LANGKOW, Daymond
(LANG-kow, DAY-muhn) **CGY**

Center. Shoots left. 5'10", 183 lbs. Born, Edmonton, Alta., September 27, 1976. Tampa Bay's 1st choice, 5th overall, in 1995 Entry Draft.

			Regular Season														Playoffs								
Season	Club	League	GP	G	A	Pts	PIM	PP	SH	GW	S	%	+/-	TF	F%	Min	GP	G	A	Pts	PIM	PP	SH	GW	Min
1991-92	Edmonton Pats	AMHL	35	36	45	81	100	....	....	....	....	....	....	....	....	....	....	....	....	....	....	....	....	....	....
	Tri-City	WHL	1	0	0	0	0	....	....	....	....	....	....	....	....	....	....	....	....	....	....	....	....	....	....
1992-93	Tri-City	WHL	64	22	42	64	100	....	....	....	....	....	....	....	....	....	4	1	0	1	4	....	....	....	....
1993-94	Tri-City	WHL	61	40	43	83	174	....	....	....	....	....	....	....	....	....	4	2	2	4	15	....	....	....	....
1994-95	Tri-City	WHL	72	*67	73	*140	142	....	....	....	....	....	....	....	....	....	17	12	15	27	52	....	....	....	....
1995-96	Tri-City	WHL	48	30	61	91	103	....	....	....	....	....	....	....	....	....	11	14	13	27	20	....	....	....	....
	Tampa Bay	**NHL**	**4**	**0**	**1**	**1**	**0**	**0**	**0**	**0**	**4**	**0.0**	**–1**	....	....	....	....	....	....	....	....	....	....	....	....
1996-97	**Tampa Bay**	**NHL**	**79**	**15**	**13**	**28**	**35**	**3**	**1**	**1**	**170**	**8.8**	**1**	....	....	....	....	....	....	....	....	....	....	....	....
	Adirondack	AHL	2	1	1	2	0	....	....	....	....	....	....	....	....	....	....	....	....	....	....	....	....	....	....
1997-98	**Tampa Bay**	**NHL**	**68**	**8**	**14**	**22**	**62**	**2**	**0**	**1**	**156**	**5.1**	**–9**	....	....	....	....	....	....	....	....	....	....	....	....
1998-99	**Tampa Bay**	**NHL**	**22**	**4**	**6**	**10**	**15**	**1**	**0**	**1**	**40**	**10.0**	**0**	**399**	**48.4**	**17:10**	....	....	....	....	....	....	....	....	....
	Cleveland	IHL	4	1	1	2	18	....	....	....	....	....	....	....	....	....	....	....	....	....	....	....	....	....	....
	Philadelphia	**NHL**	**56**	**10**	**13**	**23**	**24**	**3**	**1**	**1**	**109**	**9.2**	**–8**	**738**	**48.0**	**15:12**	**6**	**0**	**2**	**2**	**2**	**0**	**0**	**0**	**16:50**
99-2000	**Philadelphia**	**NHL**	**82**	**18**	**32**	**50**	**56**	**5**	**0**	**7**	**222**	**8.1**	**1**	**1263**	**45.1**	**16:57**	**16**	**5**	**5**	**10**	**23**	**1**	**1**	**2**	**20:03**
2000-01	**Philadelphia**	**NHL**	**71**	**13**	**41**	**54**	**50**	**3**	**0**	**2**	**190**	**6.8**	**12**	**1181**	**47.2**	**18:38**	**6**	**2**	**4**	**6**	**2**	**1**	**0**	**0**	**20:17**
2001-02	**Phoenix**	**NHL**	**80**	**27**	**35**	**62**	**36**	**6**	**3**	**2**	**171**	**15.8**	**18**	**1379**	**46.2**	**19:11**	**5**	**1**	**0**	**1**	**0**	**0**	**0**	**0**	**21:06**
2002-03	**Phoenix**	**NHL**	**82**	**20**	**32**	**52**	**56**	**4**	**2**	**2**	**196**	**10.2**	**20**	**1972**	**46.5**	**21:00**	....	....	....	....	....	....	....	....	....
2003-04	**Phoenix**	**NHL**	**81**	**21**	**31**	**52**	**40**	**4**	**1**	**2**	**174**	**12.1**	**4**	**1472**	**43.1**	**21:07**	....	....	....	....	....	....	....	....	....
2004-05			DID NOT PLAY																						
2005-06	**Calgary**	**NHL**	**82**	**25**	**34**	**59**	**46**	**11**	**0**	**7**	**171**	**14.6**	**2**	**1130**	**47.4**	**18:07**	**7**	**1**	**5**	**6**	**6**	**1**	**0**	**0**	**19:42**
2006-07	**Calgary**	**NHL**	**81**	**33**	**44**	**77**	**44**	**10**	**1**	**6**	**247**	**13.4**	**23**	**1173**	**45.9**	**20:07**	**6**	**2**	**2**	**4**	**4**	**2**	**0**	**1**	**20:06**
2007-08	**Calgary**	**NHL**	**80**	**30**	**35**	**65**	**19**	**14**	**1**	**4**	**201**	**14.9**	**16**	**817**	**43.7**	**18:50**	**7**	**3**	**2**	**5**	**0**	**2**	**0**	**0**	**18:21**
2008-09	**Calgary**	**NHL**	**73**	**21**	**28**	**49**	**20**	**4**	**0**	**3**	**161**	**13.0**	**1**	**753**	**46.9**	**17:11**	**6**	**0**	**3**	**3**	**2**	**0**	**0**	**0**	**17:06**
2009-10	**Calgary**	**NHL**	**72**	**14**	**23**	**37**	**30**	**1**	**1**	**2**	**126**	**11.1**	**2**	**1130**	**43.5**	**18:55**	....	....	....	....	....	....	....	....	....
2010-11	**Calgary**	**NHL**	**4**	**0**	**1**	**1**	**0**	**0**	**0**	**0**	**6**	**0.0**	**3**	**43**	**53.5**	**14:46**	....	....	....	....	....	....	....	....	....
	NHL Totals		**1017**	**259**	**383**	**642**	**533**	**71**	**11**	**41**	**2344**	**11.0**		**13450**	**45.8**	**18:43**	**59**	**14**	**23**	**37**	**39**	**7**	**1**	**3**	**19:18**

WHL West First All-Star Team (1995) • Canadian Major Junior First All-Star Team (1995) • WHL West Second All-Star Team (1996)

Traded to **Philadelphia** by **Tampa Bay** with Mikael Renberg for Chris Gratton and Mike Sillinger, December 12, 1998. Traded to **Phoenix** by **Philadelphia** for Phoenix's 2nd round choice (later traded to Tampa Bay, later traded to San Jose – San Jose selected Dan Spang) in 2002 Entry Draft and Phoenix's 1st round choice (Jeff Carter) in 2003 Entry Draft, July 2, 2001. Traded to **Calgary** by **Phoenix** for Denis Gauthier and Oleg Saprykin, August 26, 2004. • Missed remainder of 2009-10 and majority of 2010-11 due to neck injury vs. Minnesota, March 21, 2010.

LAPIERRE, Maxim
(la-PEE-air, max-EEM) **VAN**

Center. Shoots right. 6'2", 207 lbs. Born, St. Leonard, Que., March 29, 1985. Montreal's 3rd choice, 61st overall, in 2003 Entry Draft.

			Regular Season														Playoffs								
Season	Club	League	GP	G	A	Pts	PIM	PP	SH	GW	S	%	+/-	TF	F%	Min	GP	G	A	Pts	PIM	PP	SH	GW	Min
2001-02	Cap-d-Madeleine	QAAA	42	14	27	41	44	....	....	....	....	....	....	....	....	....	10	3	5	8	16	....	....	....	....
	Montreal Rocket	QMJHL	9	2	0	2	2	....	....	....	....	....	....	....	....	....	....	....	....	....	....	....	....	....	....
2002-03	Montreal Rocket	QMJHL	72	22	21	43	55	....	....	....	....	....	....	....	....	....	7	1	3	4	6	....	....	....	....
2003-04	P.E.I. Rocket	QMJHL	67	25	36	61	138	....	....	....	....	....	....	....	....	....	11	7	2	9	14	....	....	....	....
2004-05	P.E.I. Rocket	QMJHL	69	25	27	52	139	....	....	....	....	....	....	....	....	....	....	....	....	....	....	....	....	....	....
2005-06	**Montreal**	**NHL**	**1**	**0**	**0**	**0**	**0**	**0**	**0**	**0**	**0**	**0.0**	**–1**	**2**	**50.0**	**3:04**	....	....	....	....	....	....	....	....	....
	Hamilton	AHL	73	13	23	36	214	....	....	....	....	....	....	....	....	....	....	....	....	....	....	....	....	....	....
2006-07	**Montreal**	**NHL**	**46**	**6**	**6**	**12**	**24**	**0**	**1**	**2**	**82**	**7.3**	**–7**	**425**	**45.2**	**11:25**	....	....	....	....	....	....	....	....	....
	Hamilton	AHL	37	11	13	24	59	....	....	....	....	....	....	....	....	....	22	6	6	12	41	....	....	....	....
2007-08	**Montreal**	**NHL**	**53**	**7**	**11**	**18**	**60**	**0**	**0**	**0**	**68**	**10.3**	**5**	**527**	**49.2**	**13:10**	**12**	**0**	**3**	**3**	**6**	**0**	**0**	**0**	**11:38**
	Hamilton	AHL	19	7	7	14	63	....	....	....	....	....	....	....	....	....	....	....	....	....	....	....	....	....	....
2008-09	**Montreal**	**NHL**	**79**	**15**	**13**	**28**	**76**	**1**	**2**	**2**	**165**	**9.1**	**9**	**987**	**53.2**	**14:48**	**4**	**0**	**0**	**0**	**26**	**0**	**0**	**0**	**14:56**
2009-10	**Montreal**	**NHL**	**76**	**7**	**7**	**14**	**61**	**0**	**0**	**1**	**101**	**6.9**	**–14**	**425**	**48.9**	**12:16**	**19**	**3**	**1**	**4**	**20**	**0**	**0**	**1**	**12:20**

			Regular Season														Playoffs								
Season	Club	League	GP	G	A	Pts	PIM	PP	SH	GW	S	%	+/-	TF	F%	Min	GP	G	A	Pts	PIM	PP	SH	GW	Min
2010-11	**Montreal**	**NHL**	**38**	**5**	**3**	**8**	**63**	**0**	**0**	**0**	**78**	**6.4**	**–7**	**50**	**58.0**	**11:42**	....	....	....	....	....	....	....	....	....
	Anaheim	**NHL**	**21**	**0**	**3**	**3**	**9**	**0**	**0**	**0**	**28**	**0.0**	**–6**	**133**	**53.4**	**11:35**	....	....	....	....	....	....	....	....	....
	Vancouver	**NHL**	**19**	**1**	**0**	**1**	**8**	**0**	**0**	**0**	**23**	**4.3**	**–1**	**157**	**46.5**	**11:32**	**25**	**3**	**2**	**5**	***66**	**0**	**0**	**1**	**13:34**
	NHL Totals		**333**	**41**	**43**	**84**	**301**	**1**	**3**	**5**	**545**	**7.5**		**2706**	**50.2**	**12:43**	**60**	**6**	**6**	**12**	**118**	**0**	**0**	**2**	**12:53**

Traded to **Anaheim** by **Montreal** for Brett Festerling and Anaheim's 5th round choice (later traded back to Anaheim) in 2012 Entry Draft, December 31, 2010. Traded to **Vancouver** by **Anaheim** with MacGregor Sharp for Joel Perrault and Vancouver's 3rd round choice in 2012 Entry Draft, February 28, 2011.

LARMAN, Drew

(LAHR-man, DROO)

Center. Shoots right. 6'3", 195 lbs. Born, Canton, MI, May 15, 1985.

Season	Club	League	GP	G	A	Pts	PIM	PP	SH	GW	S	%	+/-	TF	F%	Min	GP	G	A	Pts	PIM	PP	SH	GW	Min
2002-03	Sarnia Sting	OHL	67	4	14	18	25	....	....	....	....	....	....	....	....	....	....	....	....	....	....	....	....	....	....
2003-04	Sarnia Sting	OHL	68	9	18	27	13	....	....	....	....	....	....	....	....	....	5	0	1	1	0	....	....	....	....
2004-05	Sarnia Sting	OHL	12	2	0	2	6	....	....	....	....	....	....	....	....	....	....	....	....	....	....	....	....	....	....
	London Knights	OHL	58	11	10	21	28	....	....	....	....	....	....	....	....	....	18	3	4	7	8	....	....	....	....
2005-06	Rochester	AHL	44	7	8	15	24	....	....	....	....	....	....	....	....	....	....	....	....	....	....	....	....	....	....
	Florida Everblades	ECHL	6	0	0	0	4	....	....	....	....	....	....	....	....	....	8	4	2	6	4	....	....	....	....
2006-07	**Florida**	**NHL**	**16**	**2**	**0**	**2**	**2**	**0**	**0**	**0**	**15**	**13.3**	**–3**	**97**	**46.4**	**7:23**	....	....	....	....	....	....	....	....	....
	Rochester	AHL	54	17	11	28	35	....	....	....	....	....	....	....	....	....	....	....	....	....	....	....	....	....	....
2007-08	**Florida**	**NHL**	**6**	**0**	**1**	**1**	**2**	**0**	**0**	**0**	**1**	**0.0**	**1**	**26**	**38.5**	**6:00**	....	....	....	....	....	....	....	....	....
	Rochester	AHL	54	10	12	22	44	....	....	....	....	....	....	....	....	....	....	....	....	....	....	....	....	....	....
2008-09	Rochester	AHL	61	10	13	23	40	....	....	....	....	....	....	....	....	....	....	....	....	....	....	....	....	....	....
2009-10	**Boston**	**NHL**	**4**	**0**	**0**	**0**	**0**	**0**	**0**	**0**	**5**	**0.0**	**–1**	**2**	**50.0**	**8:05**	....	....	....	....	....	....	....	....	....
	Providence Bruins	AHL	55	6	6	12	26	....	....	....	....	....	....	....	....	....	....	....	....	....	....	....	....	....	....
2010-11	Florida Everblades	ECHL	57	3	8	11	30	....	....	....	....	....	....	....	....	....	4	0	2	2	2	....	....	....	....
	NHL Totals		**26**	**2**	**1**	**3**	**4**	**0**	**0**	**0**	**21**	**9.5**		**125**	**44.8**	**7:10**	....	....	....	....	....	....	....	....	....

Signed as a free agent by **Florida**, September 28, 2005. Signed as a free agent by **Boston** July 13, 2009. Signed as a free agent by **Florida** (ECHL), November 11, 2010.

LaROSE, Chad

(lah-ROHZ, CHAD) **CAR**

Right wing. Shoots right. 5'10", 181 lbs. Born, Fraser, MI, March 27, 1982.

Season	Club	League	GP	G	A	Pts	PIM	PP	SH	GW	S	%	+/-	TF	F%	Min	GP	G	A	Pts	PIM	PP	SH	GW	Min
99-2000	Sioux Falls	USHL	54	29	26	55	28	....	....	....	....	....	....	....	....	....	3	0	1	1	0	....	....	....	....
2000-01	Sioux Falls	USHL	24	11	22	33	50	....	....	....	....	....	....	....	....	....	....	....	....	....	....	....	....	....	....
	Plymouth Whalers	OHL	32	18	7	25	24	....	....	....	....	....	....	....	....	....	19	10	10	20	22	....	....	....	....
2001-02	Plymouth Whalers	OHL	53	32	27	59	40	....	....	....	....	....	....	....	....	....	6	3	4	7	16	....	....	....	....
2002-03	Plymouth Whalers	OHL	67	61	56	117	52	....	....	....	....	....	....	....	....	....	15	9	8	17	25	....	....	....	....
2003-04	Lowell	AHL	36	7	9	16	29	....	....	....	....	....	....	....	....	....	....	....	....	....	....	....	....	....	....
	Florida Everblades	ECHL	41	16	19	35	16	....	....	....	....	....	....	....	....	....	14	3	4	7	20	....	....	....	....
2004-05	Lowell	AHL	66	20	22	42	32	....	....	....	....	....	....	....	....	....	11	3	5	8	10	....	....	....	....
2005-06♦	**Carolina**	**NHL**	**49**	**1**	**12**	**13**	**35**	**0**	**0**	**1**	**62**	**1.6**	**7**	**5**	**40.0**	**10:35**	**21**	**0**	**1**	**1**	**10**	**0**	**0**	**0**	**8:58**
	Lowell	AHL	23	14	11	25	10	....	....	....	....	....	....	....	....	....	....	....	....	....	....	....	....	....	....
2006-07	**Carolina**	**NHL**	**80**	**6**	**12**	**18**	**10**	**0**	**2**	**0**	**94**	**6.4**	**–2**	**50**	**30.0**	**10:13**	....	....	....	....	....	....	....	....	....
2007-08	**Carolina**	**NHL**	**58**	**11**	**12**	**23**	**46**	**0**	**1**	**2**	**117**	**9.4**	**6**	**19**	**31.6**	**14:03**	....	....	....	....	....	....	....	....	....
2008-09	**Carolina**	**NHL**	**81**	**19**	**12**	**31**	**35**	**0**	**2**	**4**	**171**	**11.1**	**6**	**18**	**27.8**	**15:08**	**18**	**4**	**7**	**11**	**16**	**0**	**0**	**0**	**17:48**
2009-10	**Carolina**	**NHL**	**56**	**11**	**17**	**28**	**24**	**0**	**1**	**0**	**138**	**8.0**	**–2**	**12**	**16.7**	**15:42**	....	....	....	....	....	....	....	....	....
2010-11	**Carolina**	**NHL**	**82**	**16**	**15**	**31**	**59**	**2**	**1**	**0**	**176**	**9.1**	**–21**	**33**	**33.3**	**16:01**	....	....	....	....	....	....	....	....	....
	NHL Totals		**406**	**64**	**80**	**144**	**209**	**2**	**7**	**7**	**758**	**8.4**		**137**	**29.9**	**13:43**	**39**	**4**	**8**	**12**	**26**	**0**	**0**	**0**	**13:02**

OHL Second All-Star Team (2003)

Signed as a free agent by **Carolina**, August 6, 2003.

LARSEN, Philip

(LAHR-suhn, FIHL-ihp) **DAL**

Defense. Shoots right. 6'1", 183 lbs. Born, Esbjerg, Denmark, December 7, 1989. Dallas' 3rd choice, 149th overall, in 2008 Entry Draft.

Season	Club	League	GP	G	A	Pts	PIM	PP	SH	GW	S	%	+/-	TF	F%	Min	GP	G	A	Pts	PIM	PP	SH	GW	Min
2004-05	Esbjerg IK Jr.	Den-Jr.	10	1	0	1	2	....	....	....	....	....	....	....	....	....	....	....	....	....	....	....	....	....	....
2005-06	Rogle Jr.	Swe-Jr.	32	1	4	5	24	....	....	....	....	....	....	....	....	....	....	....	....	....	....	....	....	....	....
	Rogle	Sweden-2	13	0	0	0	0	....	....	....	....	....	....	....	....	....	....	....	....	....	....	....	....	....	....
2006-07	Frolunda U18	Swe-U18	3	1	2	3	2	....	....	....	....	....	....	....	....	....	4	2	1	3	8	....	....	....	....
	Frolunda Jr.	Swe-Jr.	37	3	15	18	50	....	....	....	....	....	....	....	....	....	8	0	1	1	6	....	....	....	....
	Frolunda	Sweden	5	0	0	0	0	....	....	....	....	....	....	....	....	....	....	....	....	....	....	....	....	....	....
2007-08	Frolunda Jr.	Swe-Jr.	8	1	4	5	12	....	....	....	....	....	....	....	....	....	7	0	4	4	6	....	....	....	....
	Boras HC	Sweden-2	24	5	5	10	32	....	....	....	....	....	....	....	....	....	....	....	....	....	....	....	....	....	....
	Frolunda	Sweden	16	0	0	0	2	....	....	....	....	....	....	....	....	....	....	....	....	....	....	....	....	....	....
2008-09	Frolunda Jr.	Swe-Jr.	1	1	0	1	0	....	....	....	....	....	....	....	....	....	....	....	....	....	....	....	....	....	....
	Frolunda	Sweden	53	2	15	17	18	....	....	....	....	....	....	....	....	....	11	2	1	3	4	....	....	....	....
2009-10	Frolunda	Sweden	42	1	9	10	20	....	....	....	....	....	....	....	....	....	7	0	0	0	4	....	....	....	....
	Dallas	**NHL**	**2**	**0**	**1**	**1**	**0**	**0**	**0**	**0**	**1**	**0.0**	**1**	**0**	**0.0**	**12:27**	....	....	....	....	....	....	....	....	....
2010-11	**Dallas**	**NHL**	**6**	**0**	**2**	**2**	**0**	**0**	**0**	**0**	**11**	**0.0**	**1**	**0**	**0.0**	**13:26**	....	....	....	....	....	....	....	....	....
	Texas Stars	AHL	54	4	18	22	12	....	....	....	....	....	....	....	....	....	6	2	3	5	4	....	....	....	....
	NHL Totals		**8**	**0**	**3**	**3**	**0**	**0**	**0**	**0**	**12**	**0.0**		**0**	**0.0**	**13:11**	....	....	....	....	....	....	....	....	....

• Assigned to **Frolunda** (Sweden) by **Dallas**, September 20. 2009.

LASHOFF, Matt

(LASH-awf, MAT) **TOR**

Defense. Shoots left. 6'2", 204 lbs. Born, East Greenbush, NY, September 29, 1986. Boston's 1st choice, 22nd overall, in 2005 Entry Draft.

Season	Club	League	GP	G	A	Pts	PIM	PP	SH	GW	S	%	+/-	TF	F%	Min	GP	G	A	Pts	PIM	PP	SH	GW	Min
2002-03	USNTDP	U-17	16	1	3	4	14	....	....	....	....	....	....	....	....	....	....	....	....	....	....	....	....	....	....
	USNTDP	NAHL	46	2	5	7	53	....	....	....	....	....	....	....	....	....	....	....	....	....	....	....	....	....	....
2003-04	Kitchener Rangers	OHL	62	5	19	24	94	....	....	....	....	....	....	....	....	....	5	0	1	1	0	....	....	....	....
2004-05	Kitchener Rangers	OHL	44	4	18	22	44	....	....	....	....	....	....	....	....	....	13	0	3	3	18	....	....	....	....
2005-06	Kitchener Rangers	OHL	56	7	40	47	146	....	....	....	....	....	....	....	....	....	5	1	1	2	12	....	....	....	....
	Providence Bruins	AHL	7	1	1	2	6	....	....	....	....	....	....	....	....	....	6	0	0	0	6	....	....	....	....
2006-07	**Boston**	**NHL**	**12**	**0**	**2**	**2**	**12**	**0**	**0**	**0**	**8**	**0.0**	**–6**	**0**	**0.0**	**14:55**	....	....	....	....	....	....	....	....	....
	Providence Bruins	AHL	64	11	26	37	60	....	....	....	....	....	....	....	....	....	....	....	....	....	....	....	....	....	....
2007-08	**Boston**	**NHL**	**18**	**1**	**4**	**5**	**0**	**1**	**0**	**0**	**11**	**9.1**	**–2**	**0**	**0.0**	**13:35**	....	....	....	....	....	....	....	....	....
	Providence Bruins	AHL	60	9	27	36	79	....	....	....	....	....	....	....	....	....	9	0	4	4	6	....	....	....	....
2008-09	**Boston**	**NHL**	**16**	**0**	**1**	**1**	**10**	**0**	**0**	**0**	**6**	**0.0**	**1**	**0**	**0.0**	**13:07**	....	....	....	....	....	....	....	....	....
	Providence Bruins	AHL	33	5	16	21	36	....	....	....	....	....	....	....	....	....	....	....	....	....	....	....	....	....	....
	Tampa Bay	**NHL**	**12**	**0**	**7**	**7**	**10**	**0**	**0**	**0**	**19**	**0.0**	**–7**	**0**	**0.0**	**23:46**	....	....	....	....	....	....	....	....	....
	Norfolk Admirals	AHL	2	0	0	0	2	....	....	....	....	....	....	....	....	....	....	....	....	....	....	....	....	....	....
2009-10	**Tampa Bay**	**NHL**	**5**	**0**	**0**	**0**	**21**	**0**	**0**	**0**	**2**	**0.0**	**–2**	**0**	**0.0**	**8:53**	....	....	....	....	....	....	....	....	....
	Norfolk Admirals	AHL	68	8	16	24	105	....	....	....	....	....	....	....	....	....	....	....	....	....	....	....	....	....	....
2010-11	**Toronto**	**NHL**	**11**	**0**	**1**	**1**	**6**	**0**	**0**	**0**	**8**	**0.0**	**1**	**0**	**0.0**	**13:50**	....	....	....	....	....	....	....	....	....
	Toronto Marlies	AHL	69	7	21	28	137	....	....	....	....	....	....	....	....	....	....	....	....	....	....	....	....	....	....
	NHL Totals		**74**	**1**	**15**	**16**	**59**	**1**	**0**	**0**	**54**	**1.9**		**0**	**0.0**	**15:04**	....	....	....	....	....	....	....	....	....

AHL All-Rookie Team (2007)

Traded to **Tampa Bay** by **Boston** with Martins Karsums for Mark Recchi and Tampa Bay's 2nd round choice (later traded to Florida – Florida selected Alexander Petrovic) in 2010 Entry Draft, March 4, 2009. Traded to **Toronto** by **Tampa Bay** for Alex Berry and Stefano Giliati, August 27, 2010.

LATENDRESSE, Guillaume

(lah-TEHN-drehs, GEE-OHM) **MIN**

Left wing. Shoots left. 6'2", 240 lbs. Born, Ste-Catherine, Que., May 24, 1987. Montreal's 2nd choice, 45th overall, in 2005 Entry Draft.

Season	Club	League	GP	G	A	Pts	PIM	PP	SH	GW	S	%	+/-	TF	F%	Min	GP	G	A	Pts	PIM	PP	SH	GW	Min
2003-04	Drummondville	QMJHL	53	24	25	49	66	....	....	....	....	....	....	....	....	....	....	....	....	....	....	....	....	....	....
2004-05	Drummondville	QMJHL	65	29	49	78	76	....	....	....	....	....	....	....	....	....	6	6	4	10	7	....	....	....	....
2005-06	Drummondville	QMJHL	51	43	40	83	105	....	....	....	....	....	....	....	....	....	5	3	2	5	8	....	....	....	....
2006-07	**Montreal**	**NHL**	**80**	**16**	**13**	**29**	**47**	**5**	**0**	**3**	**121**	**13.2**	**–20**	**16**	**12.5**	**12:36**	....	....	....	....	....	....	....	....	....
2007-08	**Montreal**	**NHL**	**73**	**16**	**11**	**27**	**41**	**2**	**0**	**3**	**116**	**13.8**	**–2**	**8**	**25.0**	**12:15**	**8**	**0**	**1**	**1**	**19**	**0**	**0**	**0**	**10:43**
2008-09	**Montreal**	**NHL**	**56**	**14**	**12**	**26**	**45**	**1**	**0**	**2**	**117**	**12.0**	**4**	**2**	**50.0**	**13:37**	**4**	**0**	**0**	**0**	**12**	**0**	**0**	**0**	**11:44**

			Regular Season														Playoffs								
Season	Club	League	GP	G	A	Pts	PIM	PP	SH	GW	S	%	+/-	TF	F%	Min	GP	G	A	Pts	PIM	PP	SH	GW	Min
2009-10	**Montreal**	**NHL**	**23**	**2**	**1**	**3**	**4**	**0**	**0**	**0**	**27**	**7.4**	**–4**	**0**	**0.0**	**11:21**	....	....	....	....	....	....	....	....	....
	Minnesota	**NHL**	**55**	**25**	**12**	**37**	**12**	**7**	**0**	**4**	**133**	**18.8**	**1**	**9**	**11.1**	**16:28**	....	....	....	....	....	....	....	....	....
2010-11	**Minnesota**	**NHL**	**11**	**3**	**3**	**6**	**8**	**1**	**0**	**1**	**18**	**16.7**	**2**	**6**	**0.0**	**12:43**	....	....	....	....	....	....	....	....	....
	NHL Totals		**298**	**76**	**52**	**128**	**157**	**16**	**0**	**13**	**532**	**14.3**		**41**	**14.6**	**13:20**	**12**	**0**	**1**	**1**	**31**	**0**	**0**	**0**	**11:03**

QMJHL All-Rookie Team (2004)

Traded to **Minnesota** by **Montreal** for Benoit Pouliot, November 23, 2009. • Missed majority of 2010-11 due to groin injury,

LEACH, Jay
(LEECH, JAY) **N.J.**

Defense. Shoots left. 6'5", 220 lbs. Born, Syracuse, NY, September 2, 1979. Phoenix's 5th choice, 115th overall, in 1998 Entry Draft.

Season	Club	League	GP	G	A	Pts	PIM	PP	SH	GW	S	%	+/-	TF	F%	Min	GP	G	A	Pts	PIM	PP	SH	GW	Min
1994-95	John Marshall	High-MN	10	0	0	0	14	....	....	....	....	....	....	....	....	....	....	....	....	....	....	....	....	....	....
1995-96	John Marshall	High-MN	11	1	2	3	8	....	....	....	....	....	....	....	....	....	4	0	0	0	0	....	....	....	....
	Capital District	Exhib.	53	3	8	11	33	....	....	....	....	....	....	....	....	....	....	....	....	....	....	....	....	....	....
1996-97	Capital District	Exhib.	57	8	50	58	140	....	....	....	....	....	....	....	....	....	....	....	....	....	....	....	....	....	....
1997-98	Providence	H-East	32	0	8	8	29	....	....	....	....	....	....	....	....	....	....	....	....	....	....	....	....	....	....
1998-99	Providence	H-East	33	1	8	9	42	....	....	....	....	....	....	....	....	....	....	....	....	....	....	....	....	....	....
99-2000	Providence	H-East	37	1	9	10	101	....	....	....	....	....	....	....	....	....	....	....	....	....	....	....	....	....	....
2000-01	Providence	H-East	40	4	21	25	104	....	....	....	....	....	....	....	....	....	....	....	....	....	....	....	....	....	....
2001-02	Mississippi	ECHL	70	3	13	16	116	....	....	....	....	....	....	....	....	....	10	1	1	2	8	....	....	....	....
2002-03	Springfield	AHL	9	0	0	0	0	....	....	....	....	....	....	....	....	....	....	....	....	....	....	....	....	....	....
	Augusta Lynx	ECHL	65	8	11	19	162	....	....	....	....	....	....	....	....	....	....	....	....	....	....	....	....	....	....
2003-04	Providence Bruins	AHL	3	0	0	0	4	....	....	....	....	....	....	....	....	....	....	....	....	....	....	....	....	....	....
	Long Beach	ECHL	3	0	1	1	4	....	....	....	....	....	....	....	....	....	....	....	....	....	....	....	....	....	....
	Bridgeport	AHL	23	0	1	1	33	....	....	....	....	....	....	....	....	....	7	0	1	1	10	....	....	....	....
	Trenton Titans	ECHL	31	2	11	13	45	....	....	....	....	....	....	....	....	....	....	....	....	....	....	....	....	....	....
2004-05	Providence Bruins	AHL	62	4	5	9	92	....	....	....	....	....	....	....	....	....	17	0	0	0	28	....	....	....	....
	Trenton Titans	ECHL	11	0	2	2	17	....	....	....	....	....	....	....	....	....	....	....	....	....	....	....	....	....	....
2005-06	**Boston**	**NHL**	**2**	**0**	**0**	**0**	**7**	**0**	**0**	**0**	**0**	**0.0**	**1**	**0**	**0.0**	**6:20**	....	....	....	....	....	....	....	....	....
	Providence Bruins	AHL	72	5	11	16	100	....	....	....	....	....	....	....	....	....	6	0	1	1	15	....	....	....	....
2006-07	Providence Bruins	AHL	73	2	5	7	128	....	....	....	....	....	....	....	....	....	13	0	4	4	13	....	....	....	....
2007-08	**Tampa Bay**	**NHL**	**2**	**0**	**0**	**0**	**0**	**0**	**0**	**0**	**0**	**0.0**	**–1**	**0**	**0.0**	**4:37**	....	....	....	....	....	....	....	....	....
	Norfolk Admirals	AHL	55	3	8	11	54	....	....	....	....	....	....	....	....	....	....	....	....	....	....	....	....	....	....
	Portland Pirates	AHL	20	3	6	9	30	....	....	....	....	....	....	....	....	....	18	1	0	1	7	....	....	....	....
2008-09	**New Jersey**	**NHL**	**24**	**0**	**1**	**1**	**21**	**0**	**0**	**0**	**5**	**0.0**	**0**	**0**	**0.0**	**14:50**	....	....	....	....	....	....	....	....	....
	Lowell Devils	AHL	24	2	4	6	29	....	....	....	....	....	....	....	....	....	....	....	....	....	....	....	....	....	....
2009-10	Lowell Devils	AHL	12	0	3	3	10	....	....	....	....	....	....	....	....	....	....	....	....	....	....	....	....	....	....
	Montreal	**NHL**	**7**	**0**	**0**	**0**	**5**	**0**	**0**	**0**	**4**	**0.0**	**0**	**0**	**0.0**	**13:02**	....	....	....	....	....	....	....	....	....
	San Jose	**NHL**	**28**	**1**	**1**	**2**	**20**	**0**	**0**	**0**	**26**	**3.8**	**3**	**0**	**0.0**	**15:11**	....	....	....	....	....	....	....	....	....
2010-11	Worcester Sharks	AHL	50	1	4	5	45	....	....	....	....	....	....	....	....	....	....	....	....	....	....	....	....	....	....
	New Jersey	**NHL**	**7**	**0**	**0**	**0**	**7**	**0**	**0**	**0**	**2**	**0.0**	**0**	**0**	**0.0**	**14:15**	....	....	....	....	....	....	....	....	....
	Albany Devils	AHL	16	1	3	4	8	....	....	....	....	....	....	....	....	....	....	....	....	....	....	....	....	....	....
	NHL Totals		**70**	**1**	**2**	**3**	**60**	**0**	**0**	**0**	**37**	**2.7**		**0**	**0.0**	**14:12**	....	....	....	....	....	....	....	....	....

Signed as a free agent by **Boston**, September 26, 2003. Signed as a free agent by **Tampa Bay**, July 3, 2007. Traded to **Anaheim** by **Tampa Bay** for Brandon Segal and Anaheim's 7th round choice (David Carle) in 2008 Entry Draft, February 26, 2008. Signed as a free agent by **New Jersey**, July 17, 2008. Claimed on waivers by **Montreal** from **New Jersey**, November 6, 2009. Claimed on waivers by **San Jose** from **Montreal**, December 1, 2009. Traded to **New Jersey** by **San Jose** with Steven Zalewski for Michael Swift and Patrick Davis, February 9, 2011.

LEBDA, Brett
(LEHB-dah, BREHT)

Defense. Shoots left. 5'9", 195 lbs. Born, Buffalo Grove, IL, January 15, 1982.

Season	Club	League	GP	G	A	Pts	PIM	PP	SH	GW	S	%	+/-	TF	F%	Min	GP	G	A	Pts	PIM	PP	SH	GW	Min
1998-99	USNTDP	U-17	11	1	7	8	4	....	....	....	....	....	....	....	....	....	....	....	....	....	....	....	....	....	....
	USNTDP	USHL	3	0	0	0	0	....	....	....	....	....	....	....	....	....	....	....	....	....	....	....	....	....	....
	USNTDP	NAHL	52	11	17	28	56	....	....	....	....	....	....	....	....	....	....	....	....	....	....	....	....	....	....
99-2000	USNTDP	U-18	4	0	0	0	6	....	....	....	....	....	....	....	....	....	....	....	....	....	....	....	....	....	....
	USNTDP	USHL	22	6	7	13	28	....	....	....	....	....	....	....	....	....	....	....	....	....	....	....	....	....	....
2000-01	U. of Notre Dame	CCHA	39	7	19	26	109	....	....	....	....	....	....	....	....	....	....	....	....	....	....	....	....	....	....
2001-02	U. of Notre Dame	CCHA	34	6	8	14	54	....	....	....	....	....	....	....	....	....	....	....	....	....	....	....	....	....	....
2002-03	U. of Notre Dame	CCHA	40	7	14	21	48	....	....	....	....	....	....	....	....	....	....	....	....	....	....	....	....	....	....
2003-04	U. of Notre Dame	CCHA	39	6	18	24	42	....	....	....	....	....	....	....	....	....	....	....	....	....	....	....	....	....	....
	Grand Rapids	AHL	6	0	1	1	0	....	....	....	....	....	....	....	....	....	4	0	0	0	2	....	....	....	....
2004-05	Grand Rapids	AHL	80	2	10	12	34	....	....	....	....	....	....	....	....	....	....	....	....	....	....	....	....	....	....
2005-06	**Detroit**	**NHL**	**46**	**3**	**9**	**12**	**20**	**1**	**0**	**1**	**50**	**6.0**	**9**	**2**	**0.0**	**12:38**	**6**	**0**	**0**	**0**	**4**	**0**	**0**	**0**	**13:09**
	Grand Rapids	AHL	25	4	14	18	42	....	....	....	....	....	....	....	....	....	11	1	4	5	8	....	....	....	....
2006-07	**Detroit**	**NHL**	**74**	**5**	**13**	**18**	**61**	**1**	**0**	**2**	**107**	**4.7**	**16**	**0**	**0.0**	**14:54**	**12**	**0**	**2**	**2**	**8**	**0**	**0**	**0**	**16:23**
2007-08 ♦	**Detroit**	**NHL**	**78**	**3**	**11**	**14**	**48**	**0**	**0**	**1**	**110**	**2.7**	**–1**	**1**	**0.0**	**16:29**	**19**	**0**	**2**	**2**	**6**	**0**	**0**	**0**	**12:33**
2008-09	**Detroit**	**NHL**	**65**	**6**	**10**	**16**	**48**	**0**	**0**	**1**	**69**	**8.7**	**9**	**1**	**100.0**	**13:39**	**23**	**0**	**6**	**6**	**22**	**0**	**0**	**0**	**13:21**
2009-10	**Detroit**	**NHL**	**63**	**1**	**7**	**8**	**24**	**0**	**0**	**0**	**61**	**1.6**	**–2**	**0**	**0.0**	**14:59**	**2**	**0**	**0**	**0**	**0**	**0**	**0**	**0**	**5:56**
2010-11	**Toronto**	**NHL**	**41**	**1**	**3**	**4**	**14**	**0**	**0**	**0**	**34**	**2.9**	**–14**	**2**	**0.0**	**13:20**	....	....	....	....	....	....	....	....	....
	NHL Totals		**367**	**19**	**53**	**72**	**215**	**2**	**0**	**5**	**431**	**4.4**		**6**	**16.7**	**14:34**	**62**	**0**	**10**	**10**	**40**	**0**	**0**	**0**	**13:26**

CCHA All-Rookie Team (2001) • CCHA Second All-Star Team (2004)

Signed as a free agent by **Detroit**, April 3, 2004. Signed as a free agent by **Toronto**, July 7, 2010. Traded to **Nashville** by **Toronto** with Robert Slaney and future considerations for Cody Franson, Matthew Lombardi and future consideratons, July 3, 2011.

LECAVALIER, Vincent
(luh-KAV-uhl-YAY, VIHN-sihnt) **T.B.**

Center. Shoots left. 6'4", 208 lbs. Born, Ile Bizard, Que., April 21, 1980. Tampa Bay's 1st choice, 1st overall, in 1998 Entry Draft.

Season	Club	League	GP	G	A	Pts	PIM	PP	SH	GW	S	%	+/-	TF	F%	Min	GP	G	A	Pts	PIM	PP	SH	GW	Min
1995-96	Notre Dame	SMHL	22	52	52	104	....	....	....	....	....	....	....	....	....	....	....	....	....	....	....	....	....	....	....
1996-97	Rimouski Oceanic	QMJHL	64	42	60	102	36	....	....	....	....	....	....	....	....	....	4	4	3	7	2	....	....	....	....
1997-98	Rimouski Oceanic	QMJHL	58	44	71	115	117	....	....	....	....	....	....	....	....	....	18	*15	*26	*41	46	....	....	....	....
1998-99	**Tampa Bay**	**NHL**	**82**	**13**	**15**	**28**	**23**	**2**	**0**	**2**	**125**	**10.4**	**–19**	**953**	**40.3**	**13:40**	....	....	....	....	....	....	....	....	....
99-2000	**Tampa Bay**	**NHL**	**80**	**25**	**42**	**67**	**43**	**6**	**0**	**3**	**166**	**15.1**	**–25**	**1288**	**44.4**	**19:18**	....	....	....	....	....	....	....	....	....
2000-01	**Tampa Bay**	**NHL**	**68**	**23**	**28**	**51**	**66**	**7**	**0**	**3**	**165**	**13.9**	**–26**	**1278**	**44.9**	**19:57**	....	....	....	....	....	....	....	....	....
2001-02	**Tampa Bay**	**NHL**	**76**	**20**	**17**	**37**	**61**	**5**	**0**	**3**	**164**	**12.2**	**–18**	**931**	**41.5**	**17:09**	....	....	....	....	....	....	....	....	....
2002-03	**Tampa Bay**	**NHL**	**80**	**33**	**45**	**78**	**39**	**11**	**2**	**3**	**274**	**12.0**	**0**	**1200**	**43.9**	**19:33**	**11**	**3**	**3**	**6**	**22**	**1**	**0**	**1**	**22:36**
2003-04 ♦	**Tampa Bay**	**NHL**	**81**	**32**	**34**	**66**	**52**	**5**	**2**	**6**	**242**	**13.2**	**24**	**1119**	**41.4**	**18:04**	**23**	**9**	**7**	**16**	**25**	**2**	**0**	**0**	**19:39**
2004-05	Ak Bars Kazan	Russia	30	7	9	16	78	....	....	....	....	....	....	....	....	....	4	1	0	1	6	....	....	....	....
2005-06	**Tampa Bay**	**NHL**	**80**	**35**	**40**	**75**	**90**	**13**	**2**	**7**	**309**	**11.3**	**0**	**1366**	**51.2**	**20:08**	**5**	**1**	**3**	**4**	**7**	**1**	**0**	**0**	**22:17**
	Canada	Olympics	6	0	3	3	16	....	....	....	....	....	....	....	....	....	....	....	....	....	....	....	....	....	....
2006-07	**Tampa Bay**	**NHL**	**82**	***52**	**56**	**108**	**44**	**16**	**5**	**7**	**339**	**15.3**	**2**	**1653**	**46.6**	**22:36**	**6**	**5**	**2**	**7**	**10**	**1**	**0**	**1**	**26:29**
2007-08	**Tampa Bay**	**NHL**	**81**	**40**	**52**	**92**	**89**	**10**	**1**	**7**	**318**	**12.6**	**–17**	**1671**	**48.8**	**22:57**	....	....	....	....	....	....	....	....	....
2008-09	**Tampa Bay**	**NHL**	**77**	**29**	**38**	**67**	**54**	**10**	**1**	**6**	**291**	**10.0**	**–9**	**1395**	**50.9**	**20:15**	....	....	....	....	....	....	....	....	....
2009-10	**Tampa Bay**	**NHL**	**82**	**24**	**46**	**70**	**63**	**5**	**0**	**3**	**295**	**8.1**	**–16**	**1449**	**53.2**	**19:47**	....	....	....	....	....	....	....	....	....
2010-11	**Tampa Bay**	**NHL**	**65**	**25**	**29**	**54**	**43**	**12**	**0**	**5**	**210**	**11.9**	**–5**	**1161**	**50.9**	**18:27**	**18**	**6**	**13**	**19**	**16**	**3**	**0**	**3**	**19:51**
	NHL Totals		**934**	**351**	**442**	**793**	**667**	**102**	**13**	**55**	**2898**	**12.1**		**15464**	**47.0**	**19:20**	**63**	**24**	**28**	**52**	**80**	**8**	**0**	**5**	**21:05**

QMJHL All-Rookie Team (1997) • QMJHL Offensive Rookie of the Year (1997) • Canadian Major Junior Rookie of the Year (1997) • QMJHL First All-Star Team (1998) • Canadian Major Junior First All-Star Team (1998) • NHL Second All-Star Team (2007) • Maurice "Rocket" Richard Trophy (2007) • NHL Foundation Award (2008) • King Clancy Memorial Trophy (2008)

Played in NHL All-Star Game (2003, 2007, 2008, 2009)

Signed as a free agent by **Kazan** (Russia), November 4, 2004.

LEDDY, Nick
(LEH-dee, NIHK) **CHI**

Defense. Shoots left. 5'11", 179 lbs. Born, Eden Prairie, MN, March 20, 1991. Minnesota's 1st choice, 16th overall, in 2009 Entry Draft.

Season	Club	League	GP	G	A	Pts	PIM	PP	SH	GW	S	%	+/-	TF	F%	Min	GP	G	A	Pts	PIM	PP	SH	GW	Min
2006-07	Eden Prairie	High-MN	28	2	16	18	10	....	....	....	....	....	....	....	....	....	....	....	....	....	....	....	....	....	....
2007-08	Eden Prairie	High-MN	27	6	22	28	14	....	....	....	....	....	....	....	....	....	....	....	....	....	....	....	....	....	....
	USNTDP	U-18	4	0	2	2	....	....	....	....	....	....	....	....	....	....	....	....	....	....	....	....	....	....	....
2008-09	Eden Prairie	High-MN	31	12	33	45	26	....	....	....	....	....	....	....	....	....	....	....	....	....	....	....	....	....	....
	Team Southwest	UMHSEL	24	9	11	20	....	....	....	....	....	....	....	....	....	....	....	....	....	....	....	....	....	....	....
2009-10	U. of Minnesota	WCHA	30	3	8	11	4	....	....	....	....	....	....	....	....	....	....	....	....	....	....	....	....	....	....

Season	Club	League	GP	G	A	Pts	PIM	PP	SH	GW	S	%	+/-	TF	F%	Min	GP	G	A	Pts	PIM	PP	SH	GW	Min
			Regular Season														Playoffs								
2010-11	**Chicago**	**NHL**	**46**	**4**	**3**	**7**	**4**	**0**	**0**	**0**	**37**	**10.8**	**–3**	**0**	**0.0**	**14:19**	**7**	**0**	**0**	**0**	**0**	**0**	**0**	**0**	**14:36**
	Rockford IceHogs	AHL	22	2	8	10	2	....	....	....	....	....	....	....	....	....	....	....	....	....	....	....	....	....	....
	NHL Totals		**46**	**4**	**3**	**7**	**4**	**0**	**0**	**0**	**37**	**10.8**		**0**	**0.0**	**14:19**	**7**	**0**	**0**	**0**	**0**	**0**	**0**	**0**	**14:36**

Traded to **Chicago** by **Minnesota** with Kim Johnsson for Cam Barker, February 12, 2010.

LEE, Brian

(LEE, BRIGH-uhn) **OTT**

Defense. Shoots right. 6'3", 208 lbs. Born, Moorhead, MN, March 26, 1987. Ottawa's 1st choice, 9th overall, in 2005 Entry Draft.

Season	Club	League	GP	G	A	Pts	PIM	PP	SH	GW	S	%	+/-	TF	F%	Min	GP	G	A	Pts	PIM	PP	SH	GW	Min
2003-04	Moorhead Spuds	High-MN	29	10	38	48	....	....	....	....	....	....	....	....	....	....	....	....	....	....	....	....	....	....	....
2004-05	Moorhead Spuds	High-MN	25	12	26	38	....	....	....	....	....	....	....	....	....	....	....	....	....	....	....	....	....	....	....
	Lincoln Stars	USHL	12	0	3	3	4	....	....	....	....	....	....	....	....	....	4	2	3	5	2	....	....	....	....
2005-06	North Dakota	WCHA	44	4	23	27	44	....	....	....	....	....	....	....	....	....	....	....	....	....	....	....	....	....	....
2006-07	North Dakota	WCHA	38	2	24	26	69	....	....	....	....	....	....	....	....	....	....	....	....	....	....	....	....	....	....
2007-08	**Ottawa**	**NHL**	**6**	**0**	**1**	**1**	**4**	**0**	**0**	**0**	**6**	**0.0**	**1**	**0**	**0.0**	**16:49**	**4**	**0**	**0**	**0**	**2**	**0**	**0**	**0**	**14:31**
	Binghamton	AHL	55	3	22	25	51	....	....	....	....	....	....	....	....	....	....	....	....	....	....	....	....	....	....
2008-09	**Ottawa**	**NHL**	**53**	**2**	**11**	**13**	**33**	**1**	**0**	**1**	**51**	**3.9**	**–2**	**0**	**0.0**	**18:53**	....	....	....	....	....	....	....	....	....
	Binghamton	AHL	27	2	10	12	41	....	....	....	....	....	....	....	....	....	....	....	....	....	....	....	....	....	....
2009-10	**Ottawa**	**NHL**	**23**	**2**	**1**	**3**	**12**	**0**	**0**	**0**	**22**	**9.1**	**–5**	**0**	**0.0**	**15:33**	....	....	....	....	....	....	....	....	....
	Binghamton	AHL	41	3	12	15	52	....	....	....	....	....	....	....	....	....	....	....	....	....	....	....	....	....	....
2010-11	**Ottawa**	**NHL**	**50**	**0**	**3**	**3**	**24**	**0**	**0**	**0**	**35**	**0.0**	**–10**	**0**	**0.0**	**17:17**	....	....	....	....	....	....	....	....	....
	NHL Totals		**132**	**4**	**16**	**20**	**73**	**1**	**0**	**1**	**114**	**3.5**		**0**	**0.0**	**17:36**	**4**	**0**	**0**	**0**	**2**	**0**	**0**	**0**	**14:31**

WCHA All-Rookie Team (2006)

LEGWAND, David

(LEHG-wawnd, DAY-vihd) **NSH**

Center. Shoots left. 6'2", 204 lbs. Born, Detroit, MI, August 17, 1980. Nashville's 1st choice, 2nd overall, in 1998 Entry Draft.

Season	Club	League	GP	G	A	Pts	PIM	PP	SH	GW	S	%	+/-	TF	F%	Min	GP	G	A	Pts	PIM	PP	SH	GW	Min
1996-97	Det. Compuware	MNHL	44	21	41	62	58	....	....	....	....	....	....	....	....	....	....	....	....	....	....	....	....	....	....
1997-98	Plymouth Whalers	OHL	59	54	51	105	56	....	....	....	....	....	....	....	....	....	15	8	12	20	24	....	....	....	....
1998-99	Plymouth Whalers	OHL	55	31	49	80	65	....	....	....	....	....	....	....	....	....	11	3	8	11	8	....	....	....	....
	Nashville	**NHL**	**1**	**0**	**0**	**0**	**0**	**0**	**0**	**0**	**2**	**0.0**	**0**	**9**	**55.6**	**12:50**	....	....	....	....	....	....	....	....	....
99-2000	**Nashville**	**NHL**	**71**	**13**	**15**	**28**	**30**	**4**	**0**	**2**	**111**	**11.7**	**–6**	**637**	**41.6**	**14:43**	....	....	....	....	....	....	....	....	....
2000-01	**Nashville**	**NHL**	**81**	**13**	**28**	**41**	**38**	**3**	**0**	**3**	**172**	**7.6**	**1**	**888**	**40.3**	**15:14**	....	....	....	....	....	....	....	....	....
2001-02	**Nashville**	**NHL**	**63**	**11**	**19**	**30**	**54**	**1**	**1**	**1**	**121**	**9.1**	**1**	**843**	**40.5**	**16:25**	....	....	....	....	....	....	....	....	....
2002-03	**Nashville**	**NHL**	**64**	**17**	**31**	**48**	**34**	**3**	**1**	**4**	**167**	**10.2**	**–2**	**1095**	**46.6**	**19:14**	....	....	....	....	....	....	....	....	....
2003-04	**Nashville**	**NHL**	**82**	**18**	**29**	**47**	**46**	**5**	**1**	**5**	**165**	**10.9**	**9**	**1109**	**45.1**	**17:17**	**6**	**1**	**0**	**1**	**8**	**0**	**1**	**0**	**15:41**
2004-05	EHC Basel	Swiss-2	3	6	2	8	2	....	....	....	....	....	....	....	....	....	19	16	23	39	20	....	....	....	....
2005-06	**Nashville**	**NHL**	**44**	**7**	**19**	**26**	**34**	**0**	**0**	**5**	**109**	**6.4**	**3**	**580**	**44.7**	**16:50**	**5**	**0**	**1**	**1**	**8**	**0**	**0**	**0**	**17:21**
	Milwaukee	AHL	3	0	0	0	0	....	....	....	....	....	....	....	....	....	....	....	....	....	....	....	....	....	....
2006-07	**Nashville**	**NHL**	**78**	**27**	**36**	**63**	**44**	**3**	**1**	**7**	**153**	**17.6**	**23**	**1108**	**45.3**	**18:22**	**5**	**0**	**3**	**3**	**2**	**0**	**0**	**0**	**22:23**
2007-08	**Nashville**	**NHL**	**65**	**15**	**29**	**44**	**38**	**4**	**0**	**1**	**144**	**10.4**	**–4**	**700**	**43.6**	**18:01**	**3**	**1**	**0**	**1**	**2**	**0**	**0**	**0**	**18:15**
2008-09	**Nashville**	**NHL**	**73**	**20**	**22**	**42**	**32**	**1**	**3**	**1**	**175**	**11.4**	**–3**	**1023**	**49.8**	**19:27**	....	....	....	....	....	....	....	....	....
2009-10	**Nashville**	**NHL**	**82**	**11**	**27**	**38**	**24**	**0**	**1**	**3**	**151**	**7.3**	**–5**	**1124**	**47.9**	**18:42**	**6**	**2**	**5**	**7**	**8**	**0**	**0**	**1**	**19:16**
2010-11	**Nashville**	**NHL**	**64**	**17**	**24**	**41**	**24**	**0**	**2**	**3**	**130**	**13.1**	**13**	**837**	**47.2**	**18:48**	**12**	**6**	**3**	**9**	**8**	**1**	***2**	**0**	**22:06**
	NHL Totals		**768**	**169**	**279**	**448**	**398**	**24**	**10**	**35**	**1600**	**10.6**		**9953**	**45.1**	**17:33**	**37**	**10**	**12**	**22**	**36**	**1**	**3**	**1**	**19:41**

OHL All-Rookie Team (1998) • OHL First All-Star Team (1998) • OHL Rookie of the Year (1998) • OHL MVP (1998) • Canadian Major Junior Rookie of the Year (1998)
Signed as a free agent by **Basel** (Swiss-2), January 27, 2005.

LEHMAN, Scott

(LAY-man, SKAWT)

Defense. Shoots left. 6'1", 194 lbs. Born, Fort McMurray, Alta., January 6, 1986. Atlanta's 3rd choice, 76th overall, in 2004 Entry Draft.

Season	Club	League	GP	G	A	Pts	PIM	PP	SH	GW	S	%	+/-	TF	F%	Min	GP	G	A	Pts	PIM	PP	SH	GW	Min
2002-03	St. Michael's	OHL	53	3	10	13	50	....	....	....	....	....	....	....	....	....	19	1	3	4	34	....	....	....	....
2003-04	St. Michael's	OHL	66	5	27	32	189	....	....	....	....	....	....	....	....	....	18	2	2	4	38	....	....	....	....
2004-05	St. Michael's	OHL	57	2	19	21	189	....	....	....	....	....	....	....	....	....	10	2	2	4	31	....	....	....	....
2005-06	St. Michael's	OHL	68	5	50	55	175	....	....	....	....	....	....	....	....	....	4	0	2	2	15	....	....	....	....
2006-07	Chicago Wolves	AHL	3	0	0	0	14	....	....	....	....	....	....	....	....	....	....	....	....	....	....	....	....	....	....
	Gwinnett	ECHL	72	2	12	14	86	....	....	....	....	....	....	....	....	....	4	0	0	0	11	....	....	....	....
2007-08	Chicago Wolves	AHL	40	2	5	7	109	....	....	....	....	....	....	....	....	....	....	....	....	....	....	....	....	....	....
	Gwinnett	ECHL	6	0	2	2	18	....	....	....	....	....	....	....	....	....	....	....	....	....	....	....	....	....	....
2008-09	**Atlanta**	**NHL**	**1**	**0**	**0**	**0**	**0**	**0**	**0**	**0**	**0**	**0.0**	**0**	**0**	**0.0**	**3:03**	....	....	....	....	....	....	....	....	....
	Chicago Wolves	AHL	50	2	3	5	86	....	....	....	....	....	....	....	....	....	....	....	....	....	....	....	....	....	....
2009-10	Chicago Wolves	AHL	11	0	2	2	16	....	....	....	....	....	....	....	....	....	....	....	....	....	....	....	....	....	....
2010-11	Cincinnati	ECHL	49	7	10	17	104	....	....	....	....	....	....	....	....	....	4	1	1	2	2	....	....	....	....
	Milwaukee	AHL	2	0	0	0	4	....	....	....	....	....	....	....	....	....	....	....	....	....	....	....	....	....	....
	NHL Totals		**1**	**0**	**0**	**0**	**0**	**0**	**0**	**0**	**0**	**0.0**		**0**	**0.0**	**3:03**	....	....	....	....	....	....	....	....	....

• Missed majority of 2009-10 due to shoulder injury at Rockford (AHL), December 2, 2009. Signed as a free agent by **Milwaukee** (AHL), July 21, 2010.

LEHTONEN, Mikko

(LEH-tuh-nehn, MEE-koh) **MIN**

Right wing. Shoots right. 6'3", 196 lbs. Born, Espoo, Finland, April 1, 1987. Boston's 3rd choice, 83rd overall, in 2005 Entry Draft.

Season	Club	League	GP	G	A	Pts	PIM	PP	SH	GW	S	%	+/-	TF	F%	Min	GP	G	A	Pts	PIM	PP	SH	GW	Min
2002-03	Blues Espoo U18	Fin-U18	11	1	3	4	2	....	....	....	....	....	....	....	....	....	1	0	0	0	0	....	....	....	....
2003-04	Blues Espoo U18	Fin-U18	20	8	7	15	22	....	....	....	....	....	....	....	....	....	....	....	....	....	....	....	....	....	....
	Blues Espoo Jr.	Fin-Jr.	8	3	0	3	0	....	....	....	....	....	....	....	....	....	5	0	0	0	0	....	....	....	....
2004-05	Blues Espoo U18	Fin-U18	2	0	2	2	0	....	....	....	....	....	....	....	....	....	....	....	....	....	....	....	....	....	....
	Blues Espoo Jr.	Fin-Jr.	37	6	9	15	38	....	....	....	....	....	....	....	....	....	6	3	1	4	0	....	....	....	....
	Blues Espoo	Finland	1	0	0	0	0	....	....	....	....	....	....	....	....	....	....	....	....	....	....	....	....	....	....
2005-06	Blues Espoo Jr.	Fin-Jr.	15	3	4	7	12	....	....	....	....	....	....	....	....	....	10	5	2	7	6	....	....	....	....
	Suomi U20	Finland-2	3	1	0	1	2	....	....	....	....	....	....	....	....	....	....	....	....	....	....	....	....	....	....
	Blues Espoo	Finland	25	4	0	4	0	....	....	....	....	....	....	....	....	....	....	....	....	....	....	....	....	....	....
2006-07	Suomi U20	Finland-2	3	0	3	3	0	....	....	....	....	....	....	....	....	....	....	....	....	....	....	....	....	....	....
	Blues Espoo	Finland	39	6	9	15	24	....	....	....	....	....	....	....	....	....	9	1	1	2	4	....	....	....	....
2007-08	Blues Espoo	Finland	42	8	12	20	12	....	....	....	....	....	....	....	....	....	17	1	8	9	4	....	....	....	....
2008-09	**Boston**	**NHL**	**1**	**0**	**0**	**0**	**0**	**0**	**0**	**0**	**1**	**0.0**	**0**	**0**	**0.0**	**16:14**	....	....	....	....	....	....	....	....	....
	Providence Bruins	AHL	72	28	25	53	39	....	....	....	....	....	....	....	....	....	14	2	5	7	4	....	....	....	....
2009-10	**Boston**	**NHL**	**1**	**0**	**0**	**0**	**0**	**0**	**0**	**0**	**1**	**0.0**	**–1**	**0**	**0.0**	**7:08**	....	....	....	....	....	....	....	....	....
	Providence Bruins	AHL	78	23	27	50	58	....	....	....	....	....	....	....	....	....	....	....	....	....	....	....	....	....	....
2010-11	Skelleftea AIK	Sweden	55	*30	28	58	34	....	....	....	....	....	....	....	....	....	18	4	7	11	16	....	....	....	....
	NHL Totals		**2**	**0**	**0**	**0**	**0**	**0**	**0**	**0**	**2**	**0.0**		**0**	**0.0**	**11:41**	....	....	....	....	....	....	....	....	....

Signed as a free agent by **Skelleftea** (Sweden), August 17, 2010. Traded to **Minnesota** by **Boston** with Jeff Penner for Anton Khudobin, February 28, 2011. Signed as a free agent by **Cherepovets** (Russia-KHL), May 4, 2011.

LEINO, Ville

(LAY-noh, VIHL-ee) **BUF**

Left wing. Shoots left. 6'1", 190 lbs. Born, Savonlinna, Finland, October 6, 1983.

Season	Club	League	GP	G	A	Pts	PIM	PP	SH	GW	S	%	+/-	TF	F%	Min	GP	G	A	Pts	PIM	PP	SH	GW	Min
2002-03	Ilves Tampere Jr.	Fin-Jr.	26	14	21	35	24	....	....	....	....	....	....	....	....	....	....	....	....	....	....	....	....	....	....
	Ilves Tampere	Finland	23	1	1	2	0	....	....	....	....	....	....	....	....	....	....	....	....	....	....	....	....	....	....
2003-04	Ilves Tampere Jr.	Fin-Jr.	5	4	6	10	6	....	....	....	....	....	....	....	....	....	....	....	....	....	....	....	....	....	....
	Ilves Tampere	Finland	54	9	15	24	26	....	....	....	....	....	....	....	....	....	7	1	1	2	4	....	....	....	....
2004-05	Ilves Tampere	Finland	56	8	11	19	32	....	....	....	....	....	....	....	....	....	7	1	0	1	2	....	....	....	....
2005-06	HPK Hameenlinna	Finland	56	12	31	43	65	....	....	....	....	....	....	....	....	....	13	3	*9	12	4	....	....	....	....
2006-07	HPK Hameenlinna	Finland	50	11	29	40	73	....	....	....	....	....	....	....	....	....	8	1	9	10	31	....	....	....	....
2007-08	Jokerit Helsinki	Finland	55	28	*49	77	18	....	....	....	....	....	....	....	....	....	14	8	11	19	8	....	....	....	....
2008-09	**Detroit**	**NHL**	**13**	**5**	**4**	**9**	**6**	**0**	**0**	**1**	**17**	**29.4**	**5**	**12**	**58.3**	**12:42**	**7**	**0**	**2**	**2**	**0**	**0**	**0**	**0**	**8:44**
	Grand Rapids	AHL	57	15	31	46	18	....	....	....	....	....	....	....	....	....	10	3	10	13	10	....	....	....	....
2009-10	**Detroit**	**NHL**	**42**	**4**	**3**	**7**	**6**	**1**	**0**	**1**	**54**	**7.4**	**–10**	**5**	**20.0**	**13:13**	....	....	....	....	....	....	....	....	....
	Philadelphia	**NHL**	**13**	**2**	**2**	**4**	**4**	**0**	**0**	**1**	**23**	**8.7**	**2**	**9**	**55.6**	**12:40**	**19**	**7**	**14**	**21**	**6**	**0**	**0**	**2**	**16:16**
2010-11	**Philadelphia**	**NHL**	**81**	**19**	**34**	**53**	**22**	**5**	**0**	**2**	**117**	**16.2**	**14**	**136**	**57.4**	**16:01**	**11**	**3**	**2**	**5**	**0**	**1**	**0**	**1**	**16:46**
	NHL Totals		**149**	**30**	**43**	**73**	**38**	**6**	**0**	**5**	**211**	**14.2**		**162**	**56.2**	**14:39**	**37**	**10**	**18**	**28**	**6**	**1**	**0**	**3**	**15:00**

Signed as a free agent by **Detroit**, May 10, 2008. Traded to **Philadelpia** by **Detroit** for Ole-Kristian Tollefsen and Philadelphia's 5th round choice (Mattias Backman) in 2011 Entry Draft, February 6, 2010. Signed as a free agent by **Buffalo**, July 1, 2011.

LEOPOLD, Jordan (LEE-oh-pohld, JOHR-dahn) BUF

Defense. Shoots left. 6'1", 206 lbs. Born, Golden Valley, MN, August 3, 1980. Anaheim's 1st choice, 44th overall, in 1999 Entry Draft.

Season	Club	League	GP	G	A	Pts	PIM	PP	SH	GW	S	%	+/-	TF	F%	Min	GP	G	A	Pts	PIM	PP	SH	GW	Min
			Regular Season														Playoffs								
1995-96	Armstrong	High-MN	19	11	14	25	30	....	....	....	....	....	....	....	....	....	....	....	....	....	....	....	....	....	....
1996-97	Armstrong	High-MN	30	24	36	60	....	....	....	....	....	....	....	....	....	....	....	....	....	....	....	....	....	....	....
1997-98	USNTDP	U-18	25	7	3	10	2	....	....	....	....	....	....	....	....	....	....	....	....	....	....	....	....	....	....
	USNTDP	USHL	19	2	4	6	6	....	....	....	....	....	....	....	....	....	....	....	....	....	....	....	....	....	....
	USNTDP	NAHL	16	2	5	7	8	....	....	....	....	....	....	....	....	....	....	....	....	....	....	....	....	....	....
1998-99	U. of Minnesota	WCHA	39	7	16	23	20	....	....	....	....	....	....	....	....	....	....	....	....	....	....	....	....	....	....
99-2000	U. of Minnesota	WCHA	39	6	18	24	20	....	....	....	....	....	....	....	....	....	....	....	....	....	....	....	....	....	....
2000-01	U. of Minnesota	WCHA	42	12	37	49	38	....	....	....	....	....	....	....	....	....	....	....	....	....	....	....	....	....	....
2001-02	U. of Minnesota	WCHA	44	20	28	48	28	....	....	....	....	....	....	....	....	....	....	....	....	....	....	....	....	....	....
2002-03	**Calgary**	**NHL**	**58**	**4**	**10**	**14**	**12**	**3**	**0**	**0**	**78**	**5.1**	**-15**	**0**	**0.0**	**20:36**	....	....	....	....	....	....	....	....	....
	Saint John Flames	AHL	3	1	2	3	0	....	....	....	....	....	....	....	....	....	....	....	....	....	....	....	....	....	....
2003-04	**Calgary**	**NHL**	**82**	**9**	**24**	**33**	**24**	**6**	**0**	**1**	**138**	**6.5**	**8**	**0**	**0.0**	**22:14**	**26**	**0**	**10**	**10**	**6**	**0**	**0**	**0**	**25:41**
2004-05		DID NOT PLAY																							
2005-06	**Calgary**	**NHL**	**74**	**2**	**18**	**20**	**68**	**2**	**0**	**1**	**87**	**2.3**	**6**	**0**	**0.0**	**22:20**	**7**	**0**	**1**	**1**	**4**	**0**	**0**	**0**	**19:13**
	United States	Olympics	6	1	0	1	4	....	....	....	....	....	....	....	....	....	....	....	....	....	....	....	....	....	....
2006-07	**Colorado**	**NHL**	**15**	**2**	**3**	**5**	**14**	**1**	**1**	**0**	**19**	**10.5**	**-4**	**0**	**0.0**	**19:47**	....	....	....	....	....	....	....	....	....
2007-08	**Colorado**	**NHL**	**43**	**5**	**8**	**13**	**20**	**2**	**0**	**1**	**35**	**14.3**	**5**	**0**	**0.0**	**15:59**	**7**	**0**	**3**	**3**	**0**	**0**	**0**	**0**	**17:00**
2008-09	**Colorado**	**NHL**	**64**	**6**	**14**	**20**	**18**	**1**	**0**	**1**	**82**	**7.3**	**-10**	**0**	**0.0**	**18:10**	....	....	....	....	....	....	....	....	....
	Calgary	**NHL**	**19**	**1**	**3**	**4**	**6**	**0**	**0**	**0**	**25**	**4.0**	**-5**	**0**	**0.0**	**20:58**	**6**	**0**	**1**	**1**	**8**	**0**	**0**	**0**	**23:10**
2009-10	**Florida**	**NHL**	**61**	**7**	**11**	**18**	**22**	**1**	**0**	**1**	**69**	**10.1**	**-7**	**0**	**0.0**	**22:25**	....	....	....	....	....	....	....	....	....
	Pittsburgh	**NHL**	**20**	**4**	**4**	**8**	**6**	**0**	**0**	**2**	**26**	**15.4**	**5**	**0**	**0.0**	**20:27**	**8**	**0**	**0**	**0**	**2**	**0**	**0**	**0**	**16:31**
2010-11	**Buffalo**	**NHL**	**71**	**13**	**22**	**35**	**36**	**5**	**0**	**1**	**134**	**9.7**	**-11**	**0**	**0.0**	**23:20**	**5**	**0**	**1**	**1**	**4**	**0**	**0**	**0**	**20:57**
	NHL Totals		**507**	**53**	**117**	**170**	**226**	**21**	**1**	**8**	**693**	**7.6**		**0**	**0.0**	**21:00**	**59**	**0**	**16**	**16**	**24**	**0**	**0**	**0**	**21:59**

WCHA All-Rookie Team (1999) • WCHA Second All-Star Team (2000) • WCHA First All-Star Team (2001, 2002) • NCAA West First All-American Team (2001) • Hobey Baker Memorial Award (Top U.S. Collegiate Player) (2002)

Traded to **Calgary** by **Anaheim** for Andrei Nazarov and Calgary's 2nd round choice (later traded to Phoenix, later traded back to Calgary – Calgary selected Andrei Taratukhin) in 2001 Entry Draft, September 26, 2000. Traded to **Colorado** by **Calgary** with Calgary's 2nd round choice (Codey Burki) in 2006 Entry Draft and Calgary's 2nd round choice (Trevor Cann) in 2007 Entry Draft for Alex Tanguay, June 24, 2006. • Missed majority of 2006-07 due to off-season hernia surgery, groin injury and wrist injury vs. Calgary, February 15, 2007. Traded to **Calgary** by **Colorado** for Ryan Wilson, Lawrence Nycholat and Montreal's 2nd round choice (previously acquired, Colorado selected Stefan Elliott) in 2009 Entry Draft, March 4, 2009. Traded to **Florida** by **Calgary** with Phoenix's 3rd round choice (previously acquired, Florida selected Josh Birkholz) in 2009 Entry Draft for Jay Bouwmeester, June 27, 2009. Traded to **Pittsburgh** by **Florida** for Pittsburgh's 2nd round choice (Connor Brickley) in 2010 Entry Draft, March 1, 2010. Signed as a free agent by **Buffalo**, July 1, 2010.

LEPISTO, Sami (LEH-pihs-toh, SA-mee) CHI

Defense. Shoots left. 6', 195 lbs. Born, Espoo, Finland, October 17, 1984. Washington's 6th choice, 66th overall, in 2004 Entry Draft.

Season	Club	League	GP	G	A	Pts	PIM	PP	SH	GW	S	%	+/-	TF	F%	Min	GP	G	A	Pts	PIM	PP	SH	GW	Min
2001-02	Jokerit U18	Fin-U18	20	8	14	22	36	....	....	....	....	....	....	....	....	....	8	4	8	12	12	....	....	....	....
	Jokerit Helsinki Jr.	Fin-Jr.	14	0	5	5	2	....	....	....	....	....	....	....	....	....	....	....	....	....	....	....	....	....	....
2002-03	Jokerit Helsinki Jr.	Fin-Jr.	36	5	14	19	34	....	....	....	....	....	....	....	....	....	11	1	5	6	8	....	....	....	....
2003-04	Suomi U20	Finland-2	1	0	0	0	0	....	....	....	....	....	....	....	....	....	....	....	....	....	....	....	....	....	....
	Jokerit Helsinki	Finland	53	3	4	7	20	....	....	....	....	....	....	....	....	....	8	0	1	1	4	....	....	....	....
2004-05	Jokerit Helsinki	Finland	55	7	18	25	44	....	....	....	....	....	....	....	....	....	12	1	7	8	12	....	....	....	....
2005-06	Jokerit Helsinki	Finland	56	8	21	29	68	....	....	....	....	....	....	....	....	....	....	....	....	....	....	....	....	....	....
2006-07	Jokerit Helsinki	Finland	26	1	9	10	32	....	....	....	....	....	....	....	....	....	10	2	2	4	4	....	....	....	....
2007-08	**Washington**	**NHL**	**7**	**0**	**1**	**1**	**12**	**0**	**0**	**0**	**8**	**0.0**	**-1**	**0**	**0.0**	**13:17**	....	....	....	....	....	....	....	....	....
	Hershey Bears	AHL	55	4	41	45	51	....	....	....	....	....	....	....	....	....	5	0	1	1	4	....	....	....	....
2008-09	**Washington**	**NHL**	**7**	**0**	**4**	**4**	**6**	**0**	**0**	**0**	**7**	**0.0**	**-3**	**0**	**0.0**	**19:36**	....	....	....	....	....	....	....	....	....
	Hershey Bears	AHL	70	4	38	42	80	....	....	....	....	....	....	....	....	....	....	....	....	....	....	....	....	....	....
2009-10	**Phoenix**	**NHL**	**66**	**1**	**10**	**11**	**60**	**0**	**0**	**1**	**68**	**1.5**	**14**	**1**	**100.0**	**18:14**	**7**	**1**	**0**	**1**	**6**	**0**	**0**	**0**	**15:50**
	Finland	Olympics	6	0	1	1	6	....	....	....	....	....	....	....	....	....	....	....	....	....	....	....	....	....	....
2010-11	**Phoenix**	**NHL**	**51**	**4**	**7**	**11**	**37**	**0**	**0**	**0**	**31**	**12.9**	**7**	**1**	**100.0**	**16:38**	....	....	....	....	....	....	....	....	....
	Columbus	**NHL**	**19**	**0**	**5**	**5**	**18**	**0**	**0**	**0**	**25**	**0.0**	**3**	**0**	**0.0**	**20:01**	....	....	....	....	....	....	....	....	....
	NHL Totals		**150**	**5**	**27**	**32**	**133**	**0**	**0**	**1**	**139**	**3.6**		**2**	**100.0**	**17:45**	**7**	**1**	**0**	**1**	**6**	**0**	**0**	**0**	**15:50**

Traded to **Phoenix** by **Washington** for Phoenix's 5th round choice (Caleb Herbert) in 2010 Entry Draft, June 27, 2009. Traded to **Columbus** by **Phoenix** with Scottie Upshall for Rostislav Klesla and Dane Byers, February 28, 2011. Signed as a free agent by **Chicago**, July 15, 2011.

LESSARD, Francis (leh-SAHR, FRAN-sihs) OTT

Right wing. Shoots right. 6'3", 235 lbs. Born, Montreal, Que., May 30, 1979. Carolina's 3rd choice, 80th overall, in 1997 Entry Draft.

Season	Club	League	GP	G	A	Pts	PIM	PP	SH	GW	S	%	+/-	TF	F%	Min	GP	G	A	Pts	PIM	PP	SH	GW	Min
1994-95	Laval-Laurentides	QAAA	1	0	0	0	0	....	....	....	....	....	....	....	....	....	....	....	....	....	....	....	....	....	....
1995-96	Laval-Laurentides	QAAA	41	5	7	12	73	....	....	....	....	....	....	....	....	....	13	1	3	4		....	....	....	....
1996-97	Val-d'Or Foreurs	QMJHL	66	1	9	10	312	....	....	....	....	....	....	....	....	....	....	....	....	....	....	....	....	....	....
1997-98	Val-d'Or Foreurs	QMJHL	63	3	20	23	338	....	....	....	....	....	....	....	....	....	19	1	6	7	*101	....	....	....	....
1998-99	Drummondville	QMJHL	53	12	36	48	295	....	....	....	....	....	....	....	....	....	....	....	....	....	....	....	....	....	....
99-2000	Philadelphia	AHL	78	4	8	12	416	....	....	....	....	....	....	....	....	....	5	0	1	1	7	....	....	....	....
2000-01	Philadelphia	AHL	64	3	7	10	330	....	....	....	....	....	....	....	....	....	10	0	0	0	33	....	....	....	....
2001-02	Philadelphia	AHL	60	0	6	6	251	....	....	....	....	....	....	....	....	....	....	....	....	....	....	....	....	....	....
	Atlanta	**NHL**	**5**	**0**	**0**	**0**	**26**	**0**	**0**	**0**	**2**	**0.0**	**0**	**0**	**0.0**	**12:45**	....	....	....	....	....	....	....	....	....
	Chicago Wolves	AHL	7	2	1	3	34	....	....	....	....	....	....	....	....	....	15	0	1	1	40	....	....	....	....
2002-03	**Atlanta**	**NHL**	**18**	**0**	**2**	**2**	**61**	**0**	**0**	**0**	**7**	**0.0**	**1**	**0**	**0.0**	**5:40**	....	....	....	....	....	....	....	....	....
	Chicago Wolves	AHL	50	2	5	7	194	....	....	....	....	....	....	....	....	....	1	0	0	0	0	....	....	....	....
2003-04	**Atlanta**	**NHL**	**62**	**1**	**1**	**2**	**181**	**0**	**0**	**0**	**19**	**5.3**	**-5**	**1**	**0.0**	**4:28**	....	....	....	....	....	....	....	....	....
2004-05		DID NOT PLAY																							
2005-06	**Atlanta**	**NHL**	**6**	**0**	**0**	**0**	**0**	**0**	**0**	**0**	**0**	**0.0**	**-2**	**0**	**0.0**	**2:33**	....	....	....	....	....	....	....	....	....
	Chicago Wolves	AHL	36	2	3	5	161	....	....	....	....	....	....	....	....	....	....	....	....	....	....	....	....	....	....
2006-07	Hartford	AHL	58	3	6	9	*309	....	....	....	....	....	....	....	....	....	....	....	....	....	....	....	....	....	....
2007-08	Hartford	AHL	14	4	1	5	49	....	....	....	....	....	....	....	....	....	....	....	....	....	....	....	....	....	....
2008-09	San Antonio	AHL	59	2	2	4	*324	....	....	....	....	....	....	....	....	....	....	....	....	....	....	....	....	....	....
2009-10	San Antonio	AHL	61	2	2	4	289	....	....	....	....	....	....	....	....	....	....	....	....	....	....	....	....	....	....
2010-11	**Ottawa**	**NHL**	**24**	**0**	**0**	**0**	**78**	**0**	**0**	**0**	**6**	**0.0**	**0**	**1**	**100.0**	**3:51**	....	....	....	....	....	....	....	....	....
	Binghamton	AHL	36	2	1	3	187	....	....	....	....	....	....	....	....	....	....	....	....	....	....	....	....	....	....
	NHL Totals		**115**	**1**	**3**	**4**	**346**	**0**	**0**	**0**	**34**	**2.9**		**2**	**50.0**	**4:47**	....	....	....	....	....	....	....	....	....

Memorial Cup All-Star Team (1998)

Traded to **Philadelphia** by **Carolina** for Philadelphia's 8th round choice (Antti Jokella) in 1999 Entry Draft, May 25, 1999. Traded to **Atlanta** by **Philadelphia** for David Harlock and Atlanta's 3rd (later traded to Phoenix – Phoenix selected Tyler Redenbach) and 7th (later traded to San Jose – San Jose selected Joe Pavelski) round choices in 2003 Entry Draft, March 15, 2002. Signed as a free agent by **Phoenix**, July 31, 2008. Signed as a free agent by **Ottawa**, August 4, 2010.

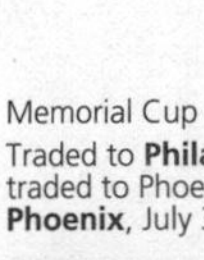

LETANG, Kris (leh-TANG, KRIHS) PIT

Defense. Shoots right. 6', 201 lbs. Born, Montreal, Que., April 24, 1987. Pittsburgh's 3rd choice, 62nd overall, in 2005 Entry Draft.

Season	Club	League	GP	G	A	Pts	PIM	PP	SH	GW	S	%	+/-	TF	F%	Min	GP	G	A	Pts	PIM	PP	SH	GW	Min
2002-03	Antoine-Girouard	QAAA	42	2	10	12	34	....	....	....	....	....	....	....	....	....	....	....	....	....	....	....	....	....	....
2003-04	Antoine-Girouard	QAAA	39	12	41	53	94	....	....	....	....	....	....	....	....	....	13	7	9	16	38	....	....	....	....
2004-05	Val-d'Or Foreurs	QMJHL	70	13	19	32	79	....	....	....	....	....	....	....	....	....	....	....	....	....	....	....	....	....	....
2005-06	Val-d'Or Foreurs	QMJHL	60	25	43	68	156	....	....	....	....	....	....	....	....	....	5	1	5	6	20	....	....	....	....
2006-07	**Pittsburgh**	**NHL**	**7**	**2**	**0**	**2**	**4**	**2**	**0**	**0**	**8**	**25.0**	**-3**	**0**	**0.0**	**11:33**	....	....	....	....	....	....	....	....	....
	Val-d'Or Foreurs	QMJHL	40	14	38	52	74	....	....	....	....	....	....	....	....	....	19	12	19	31	48	....	....	....	....
	Wilkes-Barre	AHL	....	....	....	....	....	....	....	....	....	....	....	....	....	....	1	0	1	1	2	....	....	....	....
2007-08	**Pittsburgh**	**NHL**	**63**	**6**	**11**	**17**	**23**	**1**	**0**	**3**	**68**	**8.8**	**-1**	**0**	**0.0**	**18:10**	**16**	**0**	**2**	**2**	**12**	**0**	**0**	**0**	**17:07**
	Wilkes-Barre	AHL	10	1	6	7	4	....	....	....	....	....	....	....	....	....	....	....	....	....	....	....	....	....	....
2008-09◆	**Pittsburgh**	**NHL**	**74**	**10**	**23**	**33**	**24**	**4**	**1**	**3**	**138**	**7.2**	**-7**	**1**	**0.0**	**21:09**	**23**	**4**	**9**	**13**	**26**	**2**	**0**	**1**	**19:18**
2009-10	**Pittsburgh**	**NHL**	**73**	**3**	**24**	**27**	**51**	**0**	**0**	**0**	**174**	**1.7**	**1**	**0**	**0.0**	**21:34**	**13**	**5**	**2**	**7**	**6**	**4**	**0**	**1**	**23:15**
2010-11	**Pittsburgh**	**NHL**	**82**	**8**	**42**	**50**	**101**	**4**	**0**	**2**	**236**	**3.4**	**15**	**1**	**100.0**	**24:02**	**7**	**0**	**4**	**4**	**10**	**0**	**0**	**0**	**26:32**
	NHL Totals		**299**	**29**	**100**	**129**	**203**	**11**	**1**	**8**	**624**	**4.6**		**2**	**50.0**	**21:11**	**59**	**9**	**17**	**26**	**54**	**6**	**0**	**2**	**20:26**

QMJHL All-Rookie Team (2005) • Canadian Major Junior All-Rookie Team (2005) • QMJHL First All-Star Team (2006, 2007) • Canadian Major Junior Second All-Star Team (2006, 2007)

Played in NHL All-Star Game (2011)

LETESTU, Mark
(luh-TEHS- too, MAHRK) **PIT**

Center. Shoots right. 5'11", 195 lbs. Born, Elk Point, Alta., February 4, 1985.

			Regular Season														Playoffs								
Season	Club	League	GP	G	A	Pts	PIM	PP	SH	GW	S	%	+/-	TF	F%	Min	GP	G	A	Pts	PIM	PP	SH	GW	Min
2003-04	Bonnyville	AJHL	58	22	27	49	24	....	....	....	....	....	....	....	....	....	....	....	....	....	....	....	....	....	....
2004-05	Bonnyville	AJHL	63	39	47	86	32	....	....	....	....	....	....	....	....	....	....	....	....	....	....	....	....	....	....
2005-06	Bonnyville	AJHL	58	50	55	105	59	....	....	....	....	....	....	....	....	....	....	....	....	....	....	....	....	....	....
2006-07	Western Mich.	CCHA	37	24	22	46	14	....	....	....	....	....	....	....	....	....	....	....	....	....	....	....	....	....	....
	Wilkes-Barre	AHL	3	0	0	0	0	....	....	....	....	....	....	....	....	....	2	0	0	0	2	....	....	....	....
2007-08	Wilkes-Barre	AHL	52	6	12	18	28	....	....	....	....	....	....	....	....	....	13	0	3	3	0	....	....	....	....
	Wheeling Nailers	ECHL	6	1	2	3	4	....	....	....	....	....	....	....	....	....	....	....	....	....	....	....	....	....	....
2008-09	Wilkes-Barre	AHL	73	24	37	61	6	....	....	....	....	....	....	....	....	....	12	2	8	10	4	....	....	....	....
2009-10	**Pittsburgh**	**NHL**	**10**	**1**	**0**	**1**	**2**	**0**	**0**	**0**	**9**	**11.1**	**–2**	**74**	**55.4**	**9:38**	**4**	**0**	**1**	**1**	**0**	**0**	**0**	**0**	**9:39**
	Wilkes-Barre	AHL	63	21	34	55	21	....	....	....	....	....	....	....	....	....	4	0	3	3	0	....	....	....	....
2010-11	**Pittsburgh**	**NHL**	**64**	**14**	**13**	**27**	**13**	**4**	**0**	**3**	**128**	**10.9**	**4**	**734**	**55.5**	**14:15**	**7**	**0**	**1**	**1**	**0**	**0**	**0**	**0**	**15:29**
	NHL Totals		**74**	**15**	**13**	**28**	**15**	**4**	**0**	**3**	**137**	**10.9**		**808**	**55.4**	**13:38**	**11**	**0**	**2**	**2**	**0**	**0**	**0**	**0**	**13:22**

Signed as a free agent by **Pittsburgh**, March 22, 2007.

LETOURNEAU-LEBLOND, Pierre-Luc
(leh-TOOR-noh-leh-BLAWN) **CGY**

Left wing. Shoots left. 6'2", 210 lbs. Born, Levis, Que., June 4, 1985. New Jersey's 4th choice, 216th overall, in 2004 Entry Draft.

			Regular Season														Playoffs								
Season	Club	League	GP	G	A	Pts	PIM	PP	SH	GW	S	%	+/-	TF	F%	Min	GP	G	A	Pts	PIM	PP	SH	GW	Min
2003-04	Baie-Comeau	QMJHL	62	2	3	5	198	....	....	....	....	....	....	....	....	....	4	0	0	0	6	....	....	....	....
2004-05	Baie-Comeau	QMJHL	67	1	6	7	229	....	....	....	....	....	....	....	....	....	6	0	1	1	10	....	....	....	....
2005-06	Albany River Rats	AHL	27	1	1	2	130	....	....	....	....	....	....	....	....	....	....	....	....	....	....	....	....	....	....
	Adirondack	UHL	31	3	6	9	165	....	....	....	....	....	....	....	....	....	6	0	1	1	29	....	....	....	....
2006-07	Trenton Titans	ECHL	52	4	9	13	183	....	....	....	....	....	....	....	....	....	4	0	0	0	15	....	....	....	....
2007-08	Lowell Devils	AHL	36	3	3	6	98	....	....	....	....	....	....	....	....	....	....	....	....	....	....	....	....	....	....
	Trenton Devils	ECHL	6	0	1	1	46	....	....	....	....	....	....	....	....	....	....	....	....	....	....	....	....	....	....
2008-09	**New Jersey**	**NHL**	**8**	**0**	**1**	**1**	**22**	**0**	**0**	**0**	**3**	**0.0**	**3**	**0**	**0.0**	**4:51**	....	....	....	....	....	....	....	....	....
	Lowell Devils	AHL	60	5	5	10	216	....	....	....	....	....	....	....	....	....	....	....	....	....	....	....	....	....	....
2009-10	**New Jersey**	**NHL**	**27**	**0**	**2**	**2**	**48**	**0**	**0**	**0**	**9**	**0.0**	**–4**	**2**	**50.0**	**5:31**	**5**	**0**	**0**	**0**	**10**	**0**	**0**	**0**	**4:34**
	Lowell Devils	AHL	5	0	2	2	18	....	....	....	....	....	....	....	....	....	....	....	....	....	....	....	....	....	....
2010-11	**New Jersey**	**NHL**	**2**	**0**	**0**	**0**	**21**	**0**	**0**	**0**	**0**	**0.0**	**–2**	**0**	**0.0**	**3:28**	....	....	....	....	....	....	....	....	....
	Albany Devils	AHL	64	8	5	13	*334	....	....	....	....	....	....	....	....	....	....	....	....	....	....	....	....	....	....
	NHL Totals		**37**	**0**	**3**	**3**	**91**	**0**	**0**	**0**	**12**	**0.0**		**2**	**50.0**	**5:16**	**5**	**0**	**0**	**0**	**10**	**0**	**0**	**0**	**4:34**

• Missed majority of 2009-10 due to upper body injury and as a healthy reserve. Traded to **Calgary** by **New Jersey** for Calgary's 5th round choice in 2012 Entry Draft, July 12, 2011.

LEWIS, Grant
(LOO-ihs, GRANT)

Defense. Shoots right. 6'3", 190 lbs. Born, Pittsburgh, PA, January 20, 1985. Atlanta's 2nd choice, 40th overall, in 2004 Entry Draft.

			Regular Season														Playoffs								
Season	Club	League	GP	G	A	Pts	PIM	PP	SH	GW	S	%	+/-	TF	F%	Min	GP	G	A	Pts	PIM	PP	SH	GW	Min
2002-03	Pittsburgh Forge	NAHL	50	2	7	9	59	....	....	....	....	....	....	....	....	....	....	....	....	....	....	....	....	....	....
2003-04	Dartmouth	ECAC	34	3	22	25	57	....	....	....	....	....	....	....	....	....	....	....	....	....	....	....	....	....	....
2004-05	Dartmouth	ECAC	33	5	17	22	32	....	....	....	....	....	....	....	....	....	....	....	....	....	....	....	....	....	....
2005-06	Dartmouth	ECAC	29	4	11	15	53	....	....	....	....	....	....	....	....	....	....	....	....	....	....	....	....	....	....
2006-07	Dartmouth	ECAC	24	1	14	15	30	....	....	....	....	....	....	....	....	....	....	....	....	....	....	....	....	....	....
2007-08	Chicago Wolves	AHL	43	2	14	16	44	....	....	....	....	....	....	....	....	....	2	0	0	0	2	....	....	....	....
2008-09	**Atlanta**	**NHL**	**1**	**0**	**0**	**0**	**0**	**0**	**0**	**0**	**1**	**0.0**	**0**	**0**	**0.0**	**15:29**	....	....	....	....	....	....	....	....	....
	Chicago Wolves	AHL	54	0	22	22	72	....	....	....	....	....	....	....	....	....	....	....	....	....	....	....	....	....	....
2009-10	Chicago Wolves	AHL	26	1	2	3	23	....	....	....	....	....	....	....	....	....	....	....	....	....	....	....	....	....	....
	Hershey Bears	AHL	10	0	3	3	6	....	....	....	....	....	....	....	....	....	1	0	0	0	0	....	....	....	....
2010-11	Milwaukee	AHL	47	8	15	23	40	....	....	....	....	....	....	....	....	....	11	0	4	4	18	....	....	....	....
	NHL Totals		**1**	**0**	**0**	**0**	**0**	**0**	**0**	**0**	**1**	**0.0**		**0**	**0.0**	**15:29**	....	....	....	....	....	....	....	....	....

ECAC All-Rookie Team (2004) • ECAC First All-Star Team (2004) • ECAC Second All-Star Team (2006) @FNOT = Traded to **Nashville** by **Atlanta** for Ian McKenzie, September 1, 2010.

LEWIS, Trevor
(LOO-ihs, TREH-vuhr) **L.A.**

Center. Shoots right. 6'1", 195 lbs. Born, Salt Lake City, UT, January 8, 1987. Los Angeles' 2nd choice, 17th overall, in 2006 Entry Draft.

			Regular Season														Playoffs								
Season	Club	League	GP	G	A	Pts	PIM	PP	SH	GW	S	%	+/-	TF	F%	Min	GP	G	A	Pts	PIM	PP	SH	GW	Min
2004-05	Des Moines	USHL	52	10	12	22	70	....	....	....	....	....	....	....	....	....	....	....	....	....	....	....	....	....	....
2005-06	Des Moines	USHL	56	35	40	75	69	....	....	....	....	....	....	....	....	....	11	3	*13	*16	16	....	....	....	....
2006-07	Owen Sound	OHL	62	29	44	73	51	....	....	....	....	....	....	....	....	....	4	1	2	3	0	....	....	....	....
	Manchester	AHL	8	4	2	6	2	....	....	....	....	....	....	....	....	....	2	0	0	0	0	....	....	....	....
2007-08	Manchester	AHL	76	12	16	28	43	....	....	....	....	....	....	....	....	....	4	0	0	0	2	....	....	....	....
2008-09	**Los Angeles**	**NHL**	**6**	**1**	**2**	**3**	**0**	**0**	**0**	**0**	**10**	**10.0**	**0**	**4**	**25.0**	**11:36**	....	....	....	....	....	....	....	....	....
	Manchester	AHL	75	20	31	51	30	....	....	....	....	....	....	....	....	....	....	....	....	....	....	....	....	....	....
2009-10	**Los Angeles**	**NHL**	**5**	**0**	**0**	**0**	**0**	**0**	**0**	**0**	**4**	**0.0**	**–3**	**5**	**0.0**	**9:08**	....	....	....	....	....	....	....	....	....
	Manchester	AHL	23	5	2	7	6	....	....	....	....	....	....	....	....	....	16	5	4	9	10	....	....	....	....
2010-11	**Los Angeles**	**NHL**	**72**	**3**	**10**	**13**	**6**	**0**	**0**	**2**	**105**	**2.9**	**–11**	**385**	**39.2**	**11:29**	**6**	**1**	**3**	**4**	**2**	**1**	**0**	**0**	**16:39**
	NHL Totals		**83**	**4**	**12**	**16**	**6**	**0**	**0**	**2**	**119**	**3.4**		**394**	**38.6**	**11:21**	**6**	**1**	**3**	**4**	**2**	**1**	**0**	**0**	**16:39**

USHL Player of the Year (2006)
• Missed majority of 2009-10 due to upper body injury and as a healthy reserve.

LIDSTROM, Nicklas
(LID-struhm, NIHK-luhs) **DET**

Defense. Shoots left. 6'1", 190 lbs. Born, Vasteras, Sweden, April 28, 1970. Detroit's 3rd choice, 53rd overall, in 1989 Entry Draft.

			Regular Season														Playoffs								
Season	Club	League	GP	G	A	Pts	PIM	PP	SH	GW	S	%	+/-	TF	F%	Min	GP	G	A	Pts	PIM	PP	SH	GW	Min
1987-88	Vasteras	Sweden-2	3	0	0	0	0	....	....	....	....	....	....	....	....	....	5	0	0	0	6	....	....	....	....
1988-89	Vasteras IK	Sweden	34	1	6	7	4	....	....	....	....	....	....	....	....	....	5	0	2	2	0	....	....	....	....
1989-90	Vasteras IK	Sweden	39	8	8	16	14	....	....	....	....	....	....	....	....	....	2	0	1	1	2	....	....	....	....
1990-91	Vasteras IK	Sweden	38	4	19	23	2	....	....	....	....	....	....	....	....	....	4	0	0	0	4	....	....	....	....
1991-92	**Detroit**	**NHL**	**80**	**11**	**49**	**60**	**22**	**5**	**0**	**1**	**168**	**6.5**	**36**	....	....	....	**11**	**1**	**2**	**3**	**0**	**1**	**0**	**0**	....
1992-93	**Detroit**	**NHL**	**84**	**7**	**34**	**41**	**28**	**3**	**0**	**2**	**156**	**4.5**	**7**	....	....	....	**7**	**1**	**0**	**1**	**0**	**1**	**0**	**0**	....
1993-94	**Detroit**	**NHL**	**84**	**10**	**46**	**56**	**26**	**4**	**0**	**3**	**200**	**5.0**	**43**	....	....	....	**7**	**3**	**2**	**5**	**0**	**1**	**1**	**0**	....
1994-95	Vasteras IK	Sweden	13	2	10	12	4	....	....	....	....	....	....	....	....	....	....	....	....	....	....	....	....	....	....
	Detroit	**NHL**	**43**	**10**	**16**	**26**	**6**	**7**	**0**	**0**	**90**	**11.1**	**15**	....	....	....	**18**	**4**	**12**	**16**	**8**	**3**	**0**	**2**	....
1995-96	**Detroit**	**NHL**	**81**	**17**	**50**	**67**	**20**	**8**	**1**	**1**	**211**	**8.1**	**29**	....	....	....	**19**	**5**	**9**	**14**	**10**	**1**	**0**	**0**	....
1996-97♦	**Detroit**	**NHL**	**79**	**15**	**42**	**57**	**30**	**8**	**0**	**1**	**214**	**7.0**	**11**	....	....	....	**20**	**2**	**6**	**8**	**2**	**0**	**0**	**0**	....
1997-98♦	**Detroit**	**NHL**	**80**	**17**	**42**	**59**	**18**	**7**	**1**	**1**	**205**	**8.3**	**22**	....	....	....	**22**	**6**	**13**	**19**	**8**	**2**	**0**	**2**	....
	Sweden	Olympics	4	1	1	2	2	....	....	....	....	....	....	....	....	....	....	....	....	....	....	....	....	....	....
1998-99	**Detroit**	**NHL**	**81**	**14**	**43**	**57**	**14**	**6**	**2**	**3**	**205**	**6.8**	**14**	**0**	**0.0**	**26:31**	**10**	**2**	**9**	**11**	**4**	**2**	**0**	**0**	**30:21**
99-2000	**Detroit**	**NHL**	**81**	**20**	**53**	**73**	**18**	**9**	**4**	**3**	**218**	**9.2**	**19**	**0**	**0.0**	**28:45**	**9**	**2**	**4**	**6**	**4**	**1**	**0**	**0**	**30:28**
2000-01	**Detroit**	**NHL**	**82**	**15**	**56**	**71**	**18**	**8**	**0**	**0**	**272**	**5.5**	**9**	**0**	**0.0**	**28:27**	**6**	**1**	**7**	**8**	**0**	**0**	**0**	**0**	**29:17**
2001-02♦	**Detroit**	**NHL**	**78**	**9**	**50**	**59**	**20**	**6**	**0**	**0**	**215**	**4.2**	**13**	**0**	**0.0**	**28:49**	**23**	**5**	**11**	**16**	**2**	**2**	**1**	**2**	**31:10**
	Sweden	Olympics	4	1	5	6	0	....	....	....	....	....	....	....	....	....	....	....	....	....	....	....	....	....	....
2002-03	**Detroit**	**NHL**	**82**	**18**	**44**	**62**	**38**	**8**	**1**	**4**	**175**	**10.3**	**40**	**0**	**0.0**	**29:20**	**4**	**0**	**2**	**2**	**0**	**0**	**0**	**0**	**33:35**
2003-04	**Detroit**	**NHL**	**81**	**10**	**28**	**38**	**18**	**3**	**1**	**3**	**194**	**5.2**	**19**	**0**	**0.0**	**27:39**	**12**	**2**	**5**	**7**	**4**	**2**	**0**	**0**	**27:01**
2004-05			DID NOT PLAY																						
2005-06	**Detroit**	**NHL**	**80**	**16**	**64**	**80**	**50**	**9**	**0**	**2**	**243**	**6.6**	**21**	**0**	**0.0**	**28:07**	**6**	**1**	**1**	**2**	**2**	**1**	**0**	**1**	**31:55**
	Sweden	Olympics	8	2	4	6	2	....	....	....	....	....	....	....	....	....	....	....	....	....	....	....	....	....	....
2006-07	**Detroit**	**NHL**	**80**	**13**	**49**	**62**	**46**	**10**	**0**	**1**	**224**	**5.8**	**40**	**0**	**0.0**	**27:29**	**18**	**4**	**14**	**18**	**6**	**4**	**0**	**2**	**30:37**
2007-08♦	**Detroit**	**NHL**	**76**	**10**	**60**	**70**	**40**	**5**	**0**	**4**	**188**	**5.3**	**40**	**0**	**0.0**	**26:43**	**22**	**3**	**10**	**13**	**14**	**1**	**1**	**1**	**26:49**
2008-09	**Detroit**	**NHL**	**78**	**16**	**43**	**59**	**30**	**10**	**0**	**4**	**180**	**8.9**	**31**	**0**	**0.0**	**24:49**	**21**	**4**	**12**	**16**	**6**	**3**	**0**	**1**	**25:39**
2009-10	**Detroit**	**NHL**	**82**	**9**	**40**	**49**	**24**	**5**	**0**	**1**	**194**	**4.6**	**22**	**0**	**0.0**	**25:26**	**12**	**4**	**6**	**10**	**2**	**3**	**0**	**0**	**26:22**
	Sweden	Olympics	4	0	0	0	2	....	....	....	....	....	....	....	....	....	....	....	....	....	....	....	....	....	....
2010-11	**Detroit**	**NHL**	**82**	**16**	**46**	**62**	**20**	**7**	**0**	**1**	**175**	**9.1**	**–2**	**0**	**0.0**	**23:28**	**11**	**4**	**4**	**8**	**4**	**2**	**0**	**0**	**21:49**
	NHL Totals		**1494**	**253**	**855**	**1108**	**486**	**128**	**10**	**35**	**3727**	**6.8**		**0**	**0.0**	**27:08**	**258**	**54**	**129**	**183**	**76**	**30**	**3**	**11**	**28:17**

NHL All-Rookie Team (1992) • NHL First All-Star Team (1998, 1999, 2000, 2001, 2002, 2003, 2006, 2007, 2008, 2011) • James Norris Memorial Trophy (2001, 2002, 2003, 2006, 2007, 2008, 2011) • Conn Smythe Trophy (2002) • Olympic All-Star Team (2006) • NHL Second All-Star Team (2009, 2010)

Played in NHL All-Star Game (1996, 1998, 1999, 2000, 2001, 2002, 2003, 2004, 2007, 2008, 2011)

LIFFITON, David
(LIH-fih-tuhn, DAY-vihd) **COL**

Defense. Shoots left. 6'2", 210 lbs. Born, Windsor, Ont., October 18, 1984. Colorado's 1st choice, 63rd overall, in 2003 Entry Draft.

Season	Club	League	GP	G	A	Pts	PIM	PP	SH	GW	S	%	+/-	TF	F%	Min	GP	G	A	Pts	PIM	PP	SH	GW	Min
			Regular Season														Playoffs								
2000-01	Aylmer Aces	ON-Jr.B	51	1	9	10	51	....	....	....	....	....	....	....	....	....	....	....	....	....	....	....	....	....	....
2001-02	Plymouth Whalers	OHL	62	3	9	12	65	....	....	....	....	....	....	....	....	....	6	0	0	0	0	....	....	....	....
2002-03	Plymouth Whalers	OHL	64	5	11	16	139	....	....	....	....	....	....	....	....	....	18	1	3	4	29	....	....	....	....
2003-04	Plymouth Whalers	OHL	44	2	9	11	85	....	....	....	....	....	....	....	....	....	9	0	0	0	12	....	....	....	....
2004-05	Hartford	AHL	33	0	1	1	74	....	....	....	....	....	....	....	....	....	....	....	....	....	....	....	....	....	....
	Charlotte	ECHL	16	0	2	2	18	....	....	....	....	....	....	....	....	....	15	1	4	5	27	....	....	....	....
2005-06	**NY Rangers**	**NHL**	**1**	**0**	**0**	**0**	**2**	**0**	**0**	**0**	**0**	**0.0**	**0**	**0**	**0.0**	**8:42**	....	....	....	....	....	....	....	....	....
	Hartford	AHL	50	2	7	9	158	....	....	....	....	....	....	....	....	....	....	....	....	....	....	....	....	....	....
2006-07	**NY Rangers**	**NHL**	**2**	**0**	**0**	**0**	**7**	**0**	**0**	**0**	**2**	**0.0**	**1**	**0**	**0.0**	**11:31**	....	....	....	....	....	....	....	....	....
	Hartford	AHL	72	2	11	13	189	....	....	....	....	....	....	....	....	....	7	1	1	2	18	....	....	....	....
2007-08	Hartford	AHL	21	0	2	2	52	....	....	....	....	....	....	....	....	....	....	....	....	....	....	....	....	....	....
2008-09	Esbjerg	Denmark	25	3	6	9	84	....	....	....	....	....	....	....	....	....	4	0	0	0	4	....	....	....	....
2009-10	Syracuse Crunch	AHL	72	5	15	20	118	....	....	....	....	....	....	....	....	....	....	....	....	....	....	....	....	....	....
2010-11	**Colorado**	**NHL**	**4**	**1**	**0**	**1**	**17**	**0**	**0**	**0**	**2**	**50.0**	**3**	**0**	**0.0**	**7:28**	....	....	....	....	....	....	....	....	....
	Lake Erie	AHL	18	1	3	4	57	....	....	....	....	....	....	....	....	....	....	....	....	....	....	....	....	....	....
	NHL Totals		**7**	**1**	**0**	**1**	**26**	**0**	**0**	**0**	**4**	**25.0**		**0**	**0.0**	**8:48**	....	....	....	....	....	....	....	....	....

Traded to **NY Rangers** by **Colorado** with Chris McAllister and Florida's 2nd round choice (previously acquired, later traded back to Florida – Florida selected David Shantz) in 2004 Entry Draft for Matthew Barnaby and NY Rangers' 3rd round choice (Denis Parshin) in 2004 Entry Draft, March 8, 2004. • Missed majority of 2007-08 due to post-concussion syndrome. Signed as a free agent by **New Jersey**, September 29, 2009. Signed as a free agent by **Colorado**, July 2, 2010. • Missed majority of 2010-11 due to upper body injury vs. Houston (AHL), December 12, 2010.

LILES, John-Michael
(LIGH-uhls, JAWN-MIGHK-uhl) **TOR**

Defense. Shoots left. 5'10", 185 lbs. Born, Indianapolis, IN, November 25, 1980. Colorado's 8th choice, 159th overall, in 2000 Entry Draft.

Season	Club	League	GP	G	A	Pts	PIM	PP	SH	GW	S	%	+/-	TF	F%	Min	GP	G	A	Pts	PIM	PP	SH	GW	Min
1997-98	USNTDP	U-17	15	0	6	6	4	....	....	....	....	....	....	....	....	....	....	....	....	....	....	....	....	....	....
	USNTDP	USHL	5	0	1	1	0	....	....	....	....	....	....	....	....	....	....	....	....	....	....	....	....	....	....
	USNTDP	NAHL	42	4	7	11	40	....	....	....	....	....	....	....	....	....	5	2	0	2	0	....	....	....	....
1998-99	USNTDP	USHL	46	4	14	18	47	....	....	....	....	....	....	....	....	....	....	....	....	....	....	....	....	....	....
	USNTDP	NAHL	13	2	5	7	6	....	....	....	....	....	....	....	....	....	....	....	....	....	....	....	....	....	....
99-2000	Michigan State	CCHA	40	8	20	28	26	....	....	....	....	....	....	....	....	....	....	....	....	....	....	....	....	....	....
2000-01	Michigan State	CCHA	42	7	18	25	28	....	....	....	....	....	....	....	....	....	....	....	....	....	....	....	....	....	....
2001-02	Michigan State	CCHA	41	13	22	35	18	....	....	....	....	....	....	....	....	....	....	....	....	....	....	....	....	....	....
2002-03	Michigan State	CCHA	39	16	34	50	46	....	....	....	....	....	....	....	....	....	....	....	....	....	....	....	....	....	....
	Hershey Bears	AHL	5	0	1	1	4	....	....	....	....	....	....	....	....	....	5	0	0	0	2	....	....	....	....
2003-04	**Colorado**	**NHL**	**79**	**10**	**24**	**34**	**28**	**2**	**0**	**1**	**115**	**8.7**	**7**	**0**	**0.0**	**16:14**	**11**	**0**	**1**	**1**	**4**	**0**	**0**	**0**	**16:41**
2004-05	Iserlohn Roosters	Germany	17	5	6	11	24	....	....	....	....	....	....	....	....	....	....	....	....	....	....	....	....	....	....
2005-06	**Colorado**	**NHL**	**82**	**14**	**35**	**49**	**44**	**6**	**0**	**1**	**154**	**9.1**	**5**	**1**	**100.0**	**18:31**	**9**	**1**	**2**	**3**	**6**	**1**	**0**	**0**	**17:35**
	United States	Olympics	6	0	2	2	2	....	....	....	....	....	....	....	....	....	....	....	....	....	....	....	....	....	....
2006-07	**Colorado**	**NHL**	**71**	**14**	**30**	**44**	**24**	**8**	**0**	**3**	**128**	**10.9**	**0**	**0**	**0.0**	**17:46**	....	....	....	....	....	....	....	....	....
2007-08	**Colorado**	**NHL**	**81**	**6**	**26**	**32**	**26**	**5**	**0**	**1**	**163**	**3.7**	**2**	**0**	**0.0**	**19:40**	**10**	**2**	**3**	**5**	**2**	**1**	**0**	**0**	**19:08**
2008-09	**Colorado**	**NHL**	**75**	**12**	**27**	**39**	**31**	**6**	**0**	**1**	**146**	**8.2**	**-19**	**0**	**0.0**	**21:33**	....	....	....	....	....	....	....	....	....
2009-10	**Colorado**	**NHL**	**59**	**6**	**25**	**31**	**30**	**3**	**0**	**2**	**96**	**6.3**	**-2**	**0**	**0.0**	**18:28**	**6**	**1**	**1**	**2**	**4**	**1**	**0**	**0**	**19:01**
2010-11	**Colorado**	**NHL**	**76**	**6**	**40**	**46**	**35**	**3**	**0**	**0**	**163**	**3.7**	**-9**	**0**	**0.0**	**22:01**	....	....	....	....	....	....	....	....	....
	NHL Totals		**523**	**68**	**207**	**275**	**218**	**33**	**0**	**9**	**965**	**7.0**		**1**	**100.0**	**19:11**	**36**	**4**	**7**	**11**	**16**	**3**	**0**	**0**	**17:59**

CCHA Second All-Star Team (2001) • CCHA First All-Star Team (2002, 2003) • NCAA West Second All-American Team (2002) • NCAA West First All-American Team (2003) • NHL All-Rookie Team (2004)

Signed as a free agent by **Iserlohn** (Germany), December 29, 2004. Traded to **Toronto** by **Colorado** for Boston's 2nd round choice (previously acquired) in 2012 Entry Draft, June 24, 2011..

LILJA, Andreas
(LIHL-yuh, awn-DRAY-uhs) **PHI**

Defense. Shoots left. 6'3", 220 lbs. Born, Helsingborg, Sweden, July 13, 1975. Los Angeles' 2nd choice, 54th overall, in 2000 Entry Draft.

Season	Club	League	GP	G	A	Pts	PIM	PP	SH	GW	S	%	+/-	TF	F%	Min	GP	G	A	Pts	PIM	PP	SH	GW	Min
1993-94	Malmo IF Jr.	Swe-Jr.	14	3	7	10	38	....	....	....	....	....	....	....	....	....	....	....	....	....	....	....	....	....	....
1994-95	Malmo IF Jr.	Swe-Jr.	30	7	13	20	82	....	....	....	....	....	....	....	....	....	....	....	....	....	....	....	....	....	....
	Malmo IF	Sweden	4	0	0	0	2	....	....	....	....	....	....	....	....	....	....	....	....	....	....	....	....	....	....
1995-96	Malmo IF Jr.	Swe-Jr.	3	0	1	1	6	....	....	....	....	....	....	....	....	....	....	....	....	....	....	....	....	....	....
	Malmo IF	Sweden	40	1	5	6	63	....	....	....	....	....	....	....	....	....	5	0	1	1	2	....	....	....	....
1996-97	Malmo	Sweden	47	1	0	1	22	....	....	....	....	....	....	....	....	....	4	0	0	0	10	....	....	....	....
1997-98	Malmo	Sweden	10	0	0	0	0	....	....	....	....	....	....	....	....	....	....	....	....	....	....	....	....	....	....
	Mora IK	Sweden-2	13	1	4	5	30	....	....	....	....	....	....	....	....	....	4	1	0	1	14	....	....	....	....
1998-99	Malmo	Sweden	41	0	3	3	44	....	....	....	....	....	....	....	....	....	1	0	0	0	4	....	....	....	....
99-2000	Malmo	Sweden	49	8	11	19	88	....	....	....	....	....	....	....	....	....	6	0	0	0	8	....	....	....	....
2000-01	**Los Angeles**	**NHL**	**2**	**0**	**0**	**0**	**4**	**0**	**0**	**0**	**1**	**0.0**	**-2**	**0**	**0.0**	**12:22**	**1**	**0**	**0**	**0**	**0**	**0**	**0**	**0**	**6:56**
	Lowell	AHL	61	7	29	36	149	....	....	....	....	....	....	....	....	....	4	0	6	6	6	....	....	....	....
2001-02	**Los Angeles**	**NHL**	**26**	**1**	**4**	**5**	**22**	**1**	**0**	**0**	**12**	**8.3**	**3**	**0**	**0.0**	**11:27**	**5**	**0**	**0**	**0**	**6**	**0**	**0**	**0**	**10:26**
	Manchester	AHL	4	0	1	1	4	....	....	....	....	....	....	....	....	....	....	....	....	....	....	....	....	....	....
2002-03	**Los Angeles**	**NHL**	**17**	**0**	**3**	**3**	**14**	**0**	**0**	**0**	**13**	**0.0**	**5**	**0**	**0.0**	**20:04**	....	....	....	....	....	....	....	....	....
	Florida	**NHL**	**56**	**4**	**8**	**12**	**56**	**0**	**0**	**0**	**59**	**6.8**	**8**	**0**	**0.0**	**19:11**	....	....	....	....	....	....	....	....	....
2003-04	**Florida**	**NHL**	**79**	**3**	**4**	**7**	**90**	**0**	**0**	**0**	**79**	**3.8**	**-8**	**1**	**0.0**	**19:34**	....	....	....	....	....	....	....	....	....
2004-05	Mora IK	Sweden	44	3	8	11	67	....	....	....	....	....	....	....	....	....	....	....	....	....	....	....	....	....	....
	HC Ambri-Piotta	Swiss	....	....	....	....	....	....	....	....	....	....	....	....	....	....	5	0	2	2	6	....	....	....	....
2005-06	**Detroit**	**NHL**	**82**	**2**	**13**	**15**	**98**	**0**	**0**	**1**	**78**	**2.6**	**18**	**1**	**0.0**	**19:01**	**6**	**0**	**1**	**1**	**6**	**0**	**0**	**0**	**19:21**
2006-07	**Detroit**	**NHL**	**57**	**0**	**5**	**5**	**54**	**0**	**0**	**0**	**37**	**0.0**	**6**	**1**	**0.0**	**15:25**	**18**	**1**	**0**	**1**	**10**	**0**	**0**	**0**	**19:02**
2007-08•	**Detroit**	**NHL**	**79**	**2**	**10**	**12**	**93**	**0**	**0**	**2**	**72**	**2.8**	**-2**	**1**	**0.0**	**18:14**	**12**	**0**	**1**	**1**	**16**	**0**	**0**	**0**	**14:05**
2008-09	**Detroit**	**NHL**	**60**	**2**	**11**	**13**	**66**	**0**	**0**	**0**	**60**	**3.3**	**13**	**1**	**0.0**	**17:00**	....	....	....	....	....	....	....	....	....
2009-10	**Detroit**	**NHL**	**20**	**1**	**1**	**2**	**4**	**0**	**0**	**0**	**19**	**5.3**	**-2**	**0**	**0.0**	**14:08**	**11**	**0**	**0**	**0**	**14**	**0**	**0**	**0**	**11:00**
	Grand Rapids	AHL	4	0	0	0	6	....	....	....	....	....	....	....	....	....	....	....	....	....	....	....	....	....	....
2010-11	**Anaheim**	**NHL**	**52**	**1**	**6**	**7**	**28**	**0**	**0**	**0**	**31**	**3.2**	**-15**	**0**	**0.0**	**17:26**	**3**	**0**	**0**	**0**	**0**	**0**	**0**	**0**	**11:02**
	NHL Totals		**530**	**16**	**65**	**81**	**529**	**1**	**0**	**3**	**461**	**3.5**		**5**	**0.0**	**17:41**	**56**	**1**	**2**	**3**	**52**	**0**	**0**	**0**	**15:01**

• Missed majority of 2001-02 as a healthy reserve. Traded to **Florida** by **Los Angeles** with Jaroslav Bednar for Dmitry Yushkevich and Florida's 5th round choice (previously acquired, Los Angeles selected Brady Murray) in 2003 Entry Draft, November 26, 2002. Signed as a free agent by **Nashville**, July 26, 2004. Signed as a free agent by **Mora** (Sweden), September 15, 2004. Signed as a free agent by **Ambri-Piotta** (Swiss), February 25, 2005. Signed as a free agent by **Detroit**, August 24, 2005. • Missed remainder of 2008-09 season and majority of 2009-10 due to concussion at Nashville, February 28, 2009. Signed as a free agent by **Anaheim**, October 11, 2010. Signed as a free agent by **Philadelphia**, July 1, 2011.

LINDGREN, Perttu
(LIHND-gruhn, PUHR-too)

Center. Shoots left. 6', 188 lbs. Born, Tampere, Finland, August 26, 1987. Dallas' 4th choice, 75th overall, in 2005 Entry Draft.

Season	Club	League	GP	G	A	Pts	PIM	PP	SH	GW	S	%	+/-	TF	F%	Min	GP	G	A	Pts	PIM	PP	SH	GW	Min
2003-04	Ilves Tampere U18	Fin-U18	24	11	17	28	26	....	....	....	....	....	....	....	....	....	....	....	....	....	....	....	....	....	....
	Ilves Tampere Jr.	Fin-Jr.	2	0	0	0	0	....	....	....	....	....	....	....	....	....	....	....	....	....	....	....	....	....	....
2004-05	Ilves Tampere Jr.	Fin-Jr.	38	12	29	41	2	....	....	....	....	....	....	....	....	....	10	7	10	17	4	....	....	....	....
	Ilves Tampere	Finland	2	0	0	0	0	....	....	....	....	....	....	....	....	....	....	....	....	....	....	....	....	....	....
2005-06	Ilves Tampere Jr.	Fin-Jr.	2	1	0	1	0	....	....	....	....	....	....	....	....	....	....	....	....	....	....	....	....	....	....
	Suomi U20	Finland-2	3	0	3	3	0	....	....	....	....	....	....	....	....	....	....	....	....	....	....	....	....	....	....
	Ilves Tampere	Finland	51	13	24	37	16	....	....	....	....	....	....	....	....	....	4	0	0	0	0	....	....	....	....
2006-07	Suomi U20	Finland-2	2	1	1	2	2	....	....	....	....	....	....	....	....	....	....	....	....	....	....	....	....	....	....
	Ilves Tampere	Finland	43	4	22	26	38	....	....	....	....	....	....	....	....	....	7	4	2	6	2	....	....	....	....
2007-08	Iowa Stars	AHL	69	10	24	34	6	....	....	....	....	....	....	....	....	....	....	....	....	....	....	....	....	....	....
2008-09	Lukko Rauma	Finland	49	5	19	24	16	....	....	....	....	....	....	....	....	....	7	1	0	1	6	....	....	....	....
2009-10	**Dallas**	**NHL**	**1**	**0**	**0**	**0**	**0**	**0**	**0**	**0**	**0**	**0.0**	**0**	**5**	**40.0**	**8:33**	....	....	....	....	....	....	....	....	....
	Texas Stars	AHL	74	14	33	47	14	....	....	....	....	....	....	....	....	....	24	7	10	17	2	....	....	....	....
2010-11	Lukko Rauma	Finland	56	23	*43	*66	30	....	....	....	....	....	....	....	....	....	12	4	5	9	2	....	....	....	....
	NHL Totals		**1**	**0**	**0**	**0**	**0**	**0**	**0**	**0**	**0**	**0.0**		**5**	**40.0**	**8:33**	....	....	....	....	....	....	....	....	....

• Assigned to **Rauma** (Finland) by **Dallas**, October 2, 2008. Signed as a free agent by **Rauma** (Finland), April 19, 2010.

LINDSTROM, Joakim

(LIHND-struhm, YOH-ah-kihm) **COL**

Center. Shoots left. 6', 187 lbs. Born, Skelleftea, Sweden, December 5, 1983. Columbus' 2nd choice, 41st overall, in 2002 Entry Draft.

			Regular Season														Playoffs								
Season	Club	League	GP	G	A	Pts	PIM	PP	SH	GW	S	%	+/-	TF	F%	Min	GP	G	A	Pts	PIM	PP	SH	GW	Min
99-2000	MoDo U18	Swe-U18	17	6	*14	20	32	....	....	....	....	....	....	....	....	....	....	....	....	....	....	....	....	....	....
	Malmo Jr.	Swe-Jr.	10	4	4	8	2	....	....	....	....	....	....	....	....	....	....	....	....	....	....	....	....	....	....
2000-01	Malmo Jr.	Swe-Jr.	12	7	14	21	46	....	....	....	....	....	....	....	....	....	4	2	3	5	24	....	....	....	....
	MoDo	Sweden	10	2	3	5	2	....	....	....	....	....	....	....	....	....	7	0	1	1	0	....	....	....	....
2001-02	Malmo Jr.	Swe-Jr.	10	9	6	15	67	....	....	....	....	....	....	....	....	....	....	....	....	....	....	....	....	....	....
	IF Troja-Ljungby	Sweden-2	3	0	0	0	12	....	....	....	....	....	....	....	....	....	....	....	....	....	....	....	....	....	....
	MODO	Sweden	42	4	3	7	20	....	....	....	....	....	....	....	....	....	14	3	5	8	8	....	....	....	....
2002-03	MODO	Sweden	29	4	2	6	14	....	....	....	....	....	....	....	....	....	6	1	1	2	2	....	....	....	....
	Malmo Jr.	Swe-Jr.	2	5	1	6	8	....	....	....	....	....	....	....	....	....	....	....	....	....	....	....	....	....	....
	Ornskoldsviks SK	Sweden-2	2	1	1	2	4	....	....	....	....	....	....	....	....	....	....	....	....	....	....	....	....	....	....
2003-04	MODO	Sweden	15	0	2	2	0	....	....	....	....	....	....	....	....	....	....	....	....	....	....	....	....	....	....
	Sundsvall	Sweden-2	2	0	5	5	0	....	....	....	....	....	....	....	....	....	....	....	....	....	....	....	....	....	....
2004-05	MODO Jr.	Swe-Jr.	2	4	1	5	0	....	....	....	....	....	....	....	....	....	....	....	....	....	....	....	....	....	....
	MODO	Sweden	37	2	3	5	24	....	....	....	....	....	....	....	....	....	....	....	....	....	....	....	....	....	....
	Syracuse Crunch	AHL	13	4	4	8	0	....	....	....	....	....	....	....	....	....	....	....	....	....	....	....	....	....	....
2005-06	**Columbus**	**NHL**	**3**	**0**	**0**	**0**	**0**	**0**	**0**	**0**	**4**	**0.0**	**0**	**0**	**0.0**	**5:11**	....	....	....	....	....	....	....	....	....
	Syracuse Crunch	AHL	64	14	29	43	52	....	....	....	....	....	....	....	....	....	6	1	1	2	0	....	....	....	....
2006-07	**Columbus**	**NHL**	**9**	**1**	**0**	**1**	**4**	**0**	**0**	**0**	**9**	**11.1**	**–3**	**0**	**0.0**	**8:28**	....	....	....	....	....	....	....	....	....
	Syracuse Crunch	AHL	50	22	26	48	34	....	....	....	....	....	....	....	....	....	....	....	....	....	....	....	....	....	....
2007-08	**Columbus**	**NHL**	**25**	**3**	**4**	**7**	**14**	**2**	**0**	**1**	**25**	**12.0**	**0**	**7**	**28.6**	**9:26**	....	....	....	....	....	....	....	....	....
	Syracuse Crunch	AHL	49	25	35	60	68	....	....	....	....	....	....	....	....	....	13	4	3	7	6	....	....	....	....
2008-09	Iowa Chops	AHL	21	7	14	21	33	....	....	....	....	....	....	....	....	....	....	....	....	....	....	....	....	....	....
	Phoenix	**NHL**	**44**	**9**	**11**	**20**	**28**	**3**	**0**	**2**	**77**	**11.7**	**–6**	**14**	**35.7**	**14:52**	....	....	....	....	....	....	....	....	....
	San Antonio	AHL	3	1	1	2	2	....	....	....	....	....	....	....	....	....	....	....	....	....	....	....	....	....	....
2009-10	Nizhny Novgorod	Rus-KHL	55	10	20	30	62	....	....	....	....	....	....	....	....	....	....	....	....	....	....	....	....	....	....
2010-11	Skelleftea AIK	Sweden	54	28	32	*60	134	....	....	....	....	....	....	....	....	....	18	4	7	11	16	....	....	....	....
	NHL Totals		**81**	**13**	**15**	**28**	**46**	**5**	**0**	**3**	**115**	**11.3**		**21**	**33.3**	**12:07**	....	....	....	....	....	....	....	....	....

Traded to **Anaheim** by **Columbus** for Anaheim's 4th round choice (Mathieu Corbeil-Theriault) in 2010 Entry Draft, July 14, 2008. Claimed on waivers by **Chicago** from **Anaheim**, October 3, 2008. Claimed on waivers by **Anaheim** from **Chicago**, October 7, 2008. Traded to **Phoenix** by **Anaheim** for Logan Stephenson, December 3, 2008. Signed as a free agent by **Novgorod** (Russia-KHL). June 30, 2009. Signed as a free agent by **Skelleftea** (Sweden), May 18, 2010. Signed as a free agent by **Colorado**, June 16, 2011.

LINGLET, Charles

(LIHNG-leht, CHAHR-uhlz)

Left wing. Shoots left. 6'2", 205 lbs. Born, Montreal, Que., June 22, 1982.

			Regular Season														Playoffs								
Season	Club	League	GP	G	A	Pts	PIM	PP	SH	GW	S	%	+/-	TF	F%	Min	GP	G	A	Pts	PIM	PP	SH	GW	Min
99-2000	Baie-Comeau	QMJHL	64	14	20	34	13	....	....	....	....	....	....	....	....	....	6	3	3	6	4	....	....	....	....
2000-01	Baie-Comeau	QMJHL	70	21	34	55	61	....	....	....	....	....	....	....	....	....	11	2	2	4	10	....	....	....	....
2001-02	Baie-Comeau	QMJHL	72	52	71	123	34	....	....	....	....	....	....	....	....	....	5	1	3	4	2	....	....	....	....
2002-03	Baie-Comeau	QMJHL	47	21	27	48	35	....	....	....	....	....	....	....	....	....	12	3	8	11	18	....	....	....	....
2003-04	Utah Grizzlies	AHL	7	0	0	0	2	....	....	....	....	....	....	....	....	....	....	....	....	....	....	....	....	....	....
	Alaska Aces	ECHL	62	20	35	55	61	....	....	....	....	....	....	....	....	....	7	2	5	7	4	....	....	....	....
2004-05	Alaska Aces	ECHL	72	28	34	62	44	....	....	....	....	....	....	....	....	....	15	6	10	16	14	....	....	....	....
2005-06	Peoria Rivermen	AHL	38	14	7	21	10	....	....	....	....	....	....	....	....	....	....	....	....	....	....	....	....	....	....
	Las Vegas	ECHL	16	5	9	14	15	....	....	....	....	....	....	....	....	....	12	5	4	9	20	....	....	....	....
2006-07	Peoria Rivermen	AHL	73	31	29	60	30	....	....	....	....	....	....	....	....	....	....	....	....	....	....	....	....	....	....
2007-08	Peoria Rivermen	AHL	80	24	42	66	65	....	....	....	....	....	....	....	....	....	....	....	....	....	....	....	....	....	....
2008-09	Peoria Rivermen	AHL	37	1	8	9	23	....	....	....	....	....	....	....	....	....	....	....	....	....	....	....	....	....	....
	Springfield	AHL	21	7	9	16	6	....	....	....	....	....	....	....	....	....	....	....	....	....	....	....	....	....	....
2009-10	Springfield	AHL	75	19	55	74	36	....	....	....	....	....	....	....	....	....	....	....	....	....	....	....	....	....	....
	Edmonton	**NHL**	**5**	**0**	**0**	**0**	**2**	**0**	**0**	**0**	**7**	**0.0**	**–5**	**1**	**0.0**	**10:16**	....	....	....	....	....	....	....	....	....
2010-11	Nizhny Novgorod	Rus-KHL	53	20	25	45	30	....	....	....	....	....	....	....	....	....	....	....	....	....	....	....	....	....	....
	NHL Totals		**5**	**0**	**0**	**0**	**2**	**0**	**0**	**0**	**7**	**0.0**		**1**	**0.0**	**10:16**	....	....	....	....	....	....	....	....	....

QMJHL First All-Star Team (2002) • AHL Second All-Star Team (2010)

Signed as a free agent by **St. Louis**, January 1, 2007. • Loaned to **Springfield** (AHL) by **St. Louis** (Peoria-AHL), February 18, 2009. Signed as a free agent by **Springfield** (AHL), September, 2009. Signed as a free agent by **Edmonton**, March 31, 2010. Signed as a free agent by **Novgorod** (Russia-KHL), June 28, 2010.

LISIN, Enver

(LEE-sihn, EHN-vuhr)

Right wing. Shoots left. 6'2", 200 lbs. Born, Moscow, USSR, April 22, 1986. Phoenix's 3rd choice, 50th overall, in 2004 Entry Draft.

			Regular Season														Playoffs								
Season	Club	League	GP	G	A	Pts	PIM	PP	SH	GW	S	%	+/-	TF	F%	Min	GP	G	A	Pts	PIM	PP	SH	GW	Min
2001-02	Dyn'o Moscow 2	Russia-3	6	3	0	3	14	....	....	....	....	....	....	....	....	....	....	....	....	....	....	....	....	....	....
2002-03	Dyn'o Moscow 2	Russia-3	STATISTICS NOT AVAILABLE																						
2003-04	Dyn'o Moscow 2	Russia-3	STATISTICS NOT AVAILABLE																						
	Kristall Saratov	Russia-2	35	10	6	16	30	....	....	....	....	....	....	....	....	....	4	1	0	1	0	....	....	....	....
2004-05	Ak Bars Kazan 2	Russia-3	....	4	3	7		....	....	....	....	....	....	....	....	....	....	....	....	....	....	....	....	....	....
	Ak Bars Kazan	Russia	53	8	4	12	4	....	....	....	....	....	....	....	....	....	3	0	0	0	0	....	....	....	....
2005-06	Ak Bars Kazan	Russia	43	7	5	12	26	....	....	....	....	....	....	....	....	....	13	3	1	4	6	....	....	....	....
2006-07	**Phoenix**	**NHL**	**17**	**1**	**1**	**2**	**16**	**1**	**0**	**0**	**35**	**2.9**	**–18**	**7**	**28.6**	**15:02**	....	....	....	....	....	....	....	....	....
	San Antonio	AHL	2	2	0	2	4	....	....	....	....	....	....	....	....	....	....	....	....	....	....	....	....	....	....
	Ak Bars Kazan	Russia	20	6	2	8	18	....	....	....	....	....	....	....	....	....	1	0	0	0	0	....	....	....	....
2007-08	**Phoenix**	**NHL**	**13**	**4**	**1**	**5**	**6**	**1**	**0**	**0**	**27**	**14.8**	**–5**	**2**	**50.0**	**14:27**	....	....	....	....	....	....	....	....	....
	San Antonio	AHL	58	16	19	35	26	....	....	....	....	....	....	....	....	....	6	1	2	3	0	....	....	....	....
2008-09	**Phoenix**	**NHL**	**48**	**13**	**8**	**21**	**24**	**1**	**0**	**2**	**105**	**12.4**	**–13**	**6**	**33.3**	**14:50**	....	....	....	....	....	....	....	....	....
	San Antonio	AHL	10	2	4	6	6	....	....	....	....	....	....	....	....	....	....	....	....	....	....	....	....	....	....
2009-10	**NY Rangers**	**NHL**	**57**	**6**	**8**	**14**	**18**	**0**	**0**	**0**	**91**	**6.6**	**–1**	**3**	**66.7**	**11:11**	....	....	....	....	....	....	....	....	....
2010-11	Magnitogorsk	Rus-KHL	44	12	13	25	44	....	....	....	....	....	....	....	....	....	15	2	5	7	18	....	....	....	....
	NHL Totals		**135**	**24**	**18**	**42**	**64**	**3**	**0**	**2**	**258**	**9.3**		**18**	**38.9**	**13:17**	....	....	....	....	....	....	....	....	....

Traded to **NY Rangers** by **Phoenix** for Lauri Korpikoski, July 13, 2009. Signed as a free agent by **Magnitogorsk** (Russia-KHL), October 5, 2010.

LITTLE, Bryan

(LIH-tuhl, BRIGH-uhn) **WPG**

Right wing. Shoots right. 5'11", 185 lbs. Born, Edmonton, Alta., November 12, 1987. Atlanta's 1st choice, 12th overall, in 2006 Entry Draft.

			Regular Season														Playoffs								
Season	Club	League	GP	G	A	Pts	PIM	PP	SH	GW	S	%	+/-	TF	F%	Min	GP	G	A	Pts	PIM	PP	SH	GW	Min
2003-04	Barrie Colts	OHL	64	34	24	58	18	....	....	....	....	....	....	....	....	....	12	5	5	10	7	....	....	....	....
2004-05	Barrie Colts	OHL	62	36	32	68	34	....	....	....	....	....	....	....	....	....	4	5	1	6	2	....	....	....	....
2005-06	Barrie Colts	OHL	64	42	67	109	99	....	....	....	....	....	....	....	....	....	14	8	15	23	19	....	....	....	....
2006-07	Barrie Colts	OHL	57	41	66	107	77	....	....	....	....	....	....	....	....	....	8	4	5	9	8	....	....	....	....
	Chicago Wolves	AHL	....	....	....	....	....	....	....	....	....	....	....	....	....	....	2	0	0	0	0	....	....	....	....
2007-08	**Atlanta**	**NHL**	**48**	**6**	**10**	**16**	**18**	**2**	**0**	**1**	**76**	**7.9**	**–2**	**505**	**45.2**	**15:37**	....	....	....	....	....	....	....	....	....
	Chicago Wolves	AHL	34	9	16	25	10	....	....	....	....	....	....	....	....	....	24	8	5	13	10	....	....	....	....
2008-09	**Atlanta**	**NHL**	**79**	**31**	**20**	**51**	**24**	**12**	**0**	**4**	**172**	**18.0**	**–5**	**214**	**43.5**	**16:55**	....	....	....	....	....	....	....	....	....
2009-10	**Atlanta**	**NHL**	**79**	**13**	**21**	**34**	**20**	**3**	**0**	**1**	**165**	**7.9**	**–6**	**154**	**44.2**	**15:45**	....	....	....	....	....	....	....	....	....
2010-11	**Atlanta**	**NHL**	**76**	**18**	**30**	**48**	**33**	**2**	**2**	**1**	**158**	**11.4**	**11**	**1331**	**46.3**	**18:27**	....	....	....	....	....	....	....	....	....
	NHL Totals		**282**	**68**	**81**	**149**	**95**	**19**	**2**	**7**	**571**	**11.9**		**2204**	**45.6**	**16:47**	....	....	....	....	....	....	....	....	....

OHL Second All-Star Team (2007)

• Transferred to **Winnipeg** after **Atlanta** franchise relocated, June 21, 2011.

LOCKE, Corey

(LAWK, KOH-ree) **OTT**

Center. Shoots left. 5'9", 185 lbs. Born, Toronto, Ont., May 8, 1984. Montreal's 5th choice, 113th overall, in 2003 Entry Draft.

			Regular Season														Playoffs								
Season	Club	League	GP	G	A	Pts	PIM	PP	SH	GW	S	%	+/-	TF	F%	Min	GP	G	A	Pts	PIM	PP	SH	GW	Min
2000-01	Newmarket	OPJHL	49	34	51	85	16	....	....	....	....	....	....	....	....	....	16	10	12	22	14	....	....	....	....
2001-02	Ottawa 67's	OHL	55	18	25	43	18	....	....	....	....	....	....	....	....	....	13	6	7	13	10	....	....	....	....
2002-03	Ottawa 67's	OHL	66	*63	*88	*151	83	....	....	....	....	....	....	....	....	....	23	*19	19	*38	30	....	....	....	....
2003-04	Ottawa 67's	OHL	65	*51	67	*118	82	....	....	....	....	....	....	....	....	....	7	7	3	10	10	....	....	....	....
2004-05	Hamilton	AHL	78	16	27	43	20	....	....	....	....	....	....	....	....	....	4	0	0	0	2	....	....	....	....
2005-06	Hamilton	AHL	77	19	40	59	67	....	....	....	....	....	....	....	....	....	....	....	....	....	....	....	....	....	....
2006-07	Hamilton	AHL	80	20	35	55	54	....	....	....	....	....	....	....	....	....	22	*10	12	22	10	....	....	....	....
2007-08	**Montreal**	**NHL**	**1**	**0**	**0**	**0**	**0**	**0**	**0**	**0**	**1**	**0.0**	**–1**	**5**	**40.0**	**5:59**	....	....	....	....	....	....	....	....	....
	Hamilton	AHL	78	30	42	72	50	....	....	....	....	....	....	....	....	....	....	....	....	....	....	....	....	....	....
2008-09	Houston Aeros	AHL	77	25	54	79	60	....	....	....	....	....	....	....	....	....	20	12	11	23	32	....	....	....	....

Season	Club	League	GP	G	A	Pts	PIM	PP	SH	GW	S	%	+/-	TF	F%	Min	Playoffs GP	G	A	Pts	PIM	PP	SH	GW	Min
2009-10	NY Rangers	NHL	3	0	0	0	0	0	0	0	2	0.0	1	7	14.3	6:18	....	....	....	....	....	....	....	....	....
	Hartford	AHL	76	31	54	85	44	....	....	....	....	....	....	....	....	....	....	....	....	....	....	....	....	....	....
2010-11	Ottawa	NHL	5	0	1	1	0	0	0	0	6	0.0	–1	32	21.9	9:10	....	....	....	....	....	....	....	....	....
	Binghamton	AHL	69	21	*65	*86	42	....	....	....	....	....	....	....	....	....	16	3	12	15	12	....	....	....	....
	NHL Totals		9	0	1	1	0	0	0	0	9	0.0		44	22.7	7:52	....	....	....	....	....	....	....	....	....

OHL First All-Star Team (2003, 2004) • OHL Player of the Year (2003, 2004) • Canadian Major Junior First All-Star Team (2003, 2004) • Canadian Major Junior Player of the Year (2003) • AHL Second All-Star Team (2010) • AHL First All-Star Team (2011) • John B. Sollenberger Trophy (AHL – Leading Scorer) (2011) • Les Cunningham Award (AHL – MVP) (2011)

Traded to **Minnesota** by **Montreal** for Shawn Belle, July 11, 2008. Signed as a free agent by **NY Rangers**, July 3, 2009. Signed as a free agent by **Ottawa**, July 7, 2010.

LOKTIONOV, Andrei

(lawk-too-OH-nawf, ahn-DRAY) **L.A.**

Center. Shoots left. 5'10", 180 lbs. Born, Voskresensk, USSR, May 30, 1990. Los Angeles' 7th choice, 123rd overall, in 2008 Entry Draft.

Season	Club	League	GP	G	A	Pts	PIM	PP	SH	GW	S	%	+/-	TF	F%	Min	Playoffs GP	G	A	Pts	PIM	PP	SH	GW	Min
2005-06	Spartak 2	Russia-3	4	1	1	2	2	....	....	....	....	....	....	....	....	....	....	....	....	....	....	....	....	....	....
2006-07	Yaroslavl 2	Russia-3	31	7	21	28	26	....	....	....	....	....	....	....	....	....	....	....	....	....	....	....	....	....	....
2007-08	Yaroslavl 2	Russia-3	STATISTICS NOT AVAILABLE																						
	Yaroslavl	Russia	5	0	1	1	0	....	....	....	....	....	....	....	....	....	1	0	0	0	0	....	....	....	....
2008-09	Windsor Spitfires	OHL	51	24	42	66	16	....	....	....	....	....	....	....	....	....	20	11	22	33	2	....	....	....	....
2009-10	Los Angeles	NHL	1	0	0	0	0	0	0	0	1	0.0	0	8	12.5	11:52	....	....	....	....	....	....	....	....	....
	Manchester	AHL	29	9	15	24	12	....	....	....	....	....	....	....	....	....	16	1	8	9	2	....	....	....	....
2010-11	Los Angeles	NHL	19	4	3	7	2	0	0	2	26	15.4	2	55	41.8	14:46	....	....	....	....	....	....	....	....	....
	Manchester	AHL	34	8	23	31	6	....	....	....	....	....	....	....	....	....	....	....	....	....	....	....	....	....	....
	NHL Totals		20	4	3	7	2	0	0	2	27	14.8		63	38.1	14:37	....	....	....	....	....	....	....	....	....

• Missed majority of 2009-10 due to shoulder injury at Vancouver, November 26, 2009, November 29, 2009.

LOMBARDI, Matthew

(lawm-BAHR-dee, MA-thew) **TOR**

Center. Shoots left. 5'11", 195 lbs. Born, Montreal, Que., March 18, 1982. Calgary's 3rd choice, 90th overall, in 2002 Entry Draft.

Season	Club	League	GP	G	A	Pts	PIM	PP	SH	GW	S	%	+/-	TF	F%	Min	Playoffs GP	G	A	Pts	PIM	PP	SH	GW	Min
1997-98	Gatineau	QAAA	42	10	13	23	....	....	....	....	....	....	....	....	....	....	13	4	7	11	....	....	....	....	....
1998-99	Victoriaville Tigres	QMJHL	47	6	10	16	8	....	....	....	....	....	....	....	....	....	5	0	0	0	0	....	....	....	....
99-2000	Victoriaville Tigres	QMJHL	65	18	26	44	28	....	....	....	....	....	....	....	....	....	6	0	0	0	6	....	....	....	....
2000-01	Victoriaville Tigres	QMJHL	72	28	39	67	66	....	....	....	....	....	....	....	....	....	13	12	6	18	10	....	....	....	....
2001-02	Victoriaville Tigres	QMJHL	66	57	73	130	70	....	....	....	....	....	....	....	....	....	22	*17	18	35	18	....	....	....	....
2002-03	Saint John Flames	AHL	76	25	21	46	41	....	....	....	....	....	....	....	....	....	....	....	....	....	....	....	....	....	....
2003-04	Calgary	NHL	79	16	13	29	32	3	2	4	130	12.3	4	992	47.9	14:26	13	1	5	6	4	0	0	1	14:46
2004-05	Lowell	AHL	9	3	1	4	9	....	....	....	....	....	....	....	....	....	11	0	3	3	16	....	....	....	....
2005-06	Calgary	NHL	55	6	20	26	48	1	2	2	72	8.3	–1	499	52.9	14:09	7	0	2	2	2	0	0	0	15:51
	Omaha	AHL	1	1	1	2	0	....	....	....	....	....	....	....	....	....	....	....	....	....	....	....	....	....	....
2006-07	Calgary	NHL	81	20	26	46	48	5	4	5	176	11.4	10	965	49.1	16:22	6	1	1	2	0	1	0	0	15:19
2007-08	Calgary	NHL	82	14	22	36	67	2	2	4	181	7.7	–6	955	47.6	17:19	7	0	0	0	4	0	0	0	17:14
2008-09	Calgary	NHL	50	9	21	30	30	0	1	2	119	7.6	11	459	53.4	16:27	....	....	....	....	....	....	....	....	....
	Phoenix	NHL	19	5	11	16	14	1	0	0	58	8.6	2	384	50.3	20:54	....	....	....	....	....	....	....	....	....
2009-10	Phoenix	NHL	78	19	34	53	36	4	0	2	174	10.9	8	910	49.7	17:56	7	1	5	6	2	0	0	0	17:36
2010-11	Nashville	NHL	2	0	0	0	0	0	0	0	6	0.0	–1	29	55.2	14:50	....	....	....	....	....	....	....	....	....
	NHL Totals		446	89	147	236	275	16	11	19	916	9.7		5193	49.6	16:24	40	3	13	16	12	1	0	1	15:58

• Re-entered NHL Entry Draft. Originally Edmonton's 7th choice, 215th overall, in 2000 Entry Draft.

Memorial Cup All-Star Team (2002) • Ed Chynoweth Trophy (Memorial Cup - Leading Scorer) (2002)

Traded to **Phoenix** by **Calgary** with Brandon Prust and Calgary's 1st round choice (Brandon Gormley) in 2010 Entry Draft for Olli Jokinen and Phoenix's 3rd round choice (later traded to Florida – Florida selected Josh Birkholz) in 2009 Entry Draft, March 4, 2009. Signed as a free agent by **Nashville**, July 2, 2010. • Missed majority of 2010-11 due to concussion at Chicago, October 13, 2010. Traded to **Toronto** by **Nashville** with Cody Franson and future considerations for Brett Lebda, Robert Slaney and future considerations, July 3, 2011.

LOVEJOY, Ben

(LUHV-joi, BEHN) **PIT**

Defense. Shoots right. 6'2", 215 lbs. Born, Concord, NH, February 20, 1984.

Season	Club	League	GP	G	A	Pts	PIM	PP	SH	GW	S	%	+/-	TF	F%	Min	Playoffs GP	G	A	Pts	PIM	PP	SH	GW	Min
2002-03	Boston College	H-East	22	0	6	6	6	....	....	....	....	....	....	....	....	....	....	....	....	....	....	....	....	....	....
2003-04	Dartmouth	ECAC	DID NOT PLAY – TRANSFERRED COLLEGES																						
2004-05	Dartmouth	ECAC	32	2	11	13	28	....	....	....	....	....	....	....	....	....	....	....	....	....	....	....	....	....	....
2005-06	Dartmouth	ECAC	32	2	16	18	24	....	....	....	....	....	....	....	....	....	....	....	....	....	....	....	....	....	....
2006-07	Dartmouth	ECAC	32	7	16	23	28	....	....	....	....	....	....	....	....	....	....	....	....	....	....	....	....	....	....
	Norfolk Admirals	AHL	5	0	0	0	6	....	....	....	....	....	....	....	....	....	....	....	....	....	....	....	....	....	....
2007-08	Wilkes-Barre	AHL	72	2	18	20	63	....	....	....	....	....	....	....	....	....	23	2	8	10	18	....	....	....	....
2008-09	Pittsburgh	NHL	2	0	0	0	0	0	0	0	1	0.0	0	0	0.0	11:53	....	....	....	....	....	....	....	....	....
	Wilkes-Barre	AHL	76	7	24	31	84	....	....	....	....	....	....	....	....	....	12	1	1	2	14	....	....	....	....
2009-10	Pittsburgh	NHL	12	0	3	3	2	0	0	0	14	0.0	8	0	0.0	16:37	....	....	....	....	....	....	....	....	....
	Wilkes-Barre	AHL	65	9	20	29	92	....	....	....	....	....	....	....	....	....	2	0	2	2	2	....	....	....	....
2010-11	Pittsburgh	NHL	47	3	14	17	48	0	0	0	60	5.0	11	0	0.0	15:00	7	0	2	2	4	0	0	0	10:54
	NHL Totals		61	3	17	20	50	0	0	0	75	4.0		0	0.0	15:13	7	0	2	2	4	0	0	0	10:54

AHL Second All-Star Team (2009)

Signed as a free agent by **Wilkes-Barre** (AHL), June 14, 2007. Signed as a free agent by **Pittsburgh**, July 7, 2008.

LUCIC, Milan

(LOO-cheech, MEE-lahn) **BOS**

Left wing. Shoots left. 6'4", 220 lbs. Born, Vancouver, B.C., June 7, 1988. Boston's 3rd choice, 50th overall, in 2006 Entry Draft.

Season	Club	League	GP	G	A	Pts	PIM	PP	SH	GW	S	%	+/-	TF	F%	Min	Playoffs GP	G	A	Pts	PIM	PP	SH	GW	Min
2004-05	Coquitlam	BCHL	50	9	14	23	100	....	....	....	....	....	....	....	....	....	....	....	....	....	....	....	....	....	....
	Vancouver Giants	WHL	1	0	0	0	2	....	....	....	....	....	....	....	....	....	2	0	0	0	0	....	....	....	....
2005-06	Vancouver Giants	WHL	62	9	10	19	149	....	....	....	....	....	....	....	....	....	18	3	4	7	23	....	....	....	....
2006-07	Vancouver Giants	WHL	70	30	38	68	147	....	....	....	....	....	....	....	....	....	22	7	12	19	26	....	....	....	....
2007-08	Boston	NHL	77	8	19	27	89	1	0	4	88	9.1	–2	8	50.0	12:07	7	2	0	2	4	0	0	0	16:24
2008-09	Boston	NHL	72	17	25	42	136	2	0	3	97	17.5	17	10	60.0	14:57	10	3	6	9	43	0	0	0	15:14
2009-10	Boston	NHL	50	9	11	20	44	0	0	2	72	12.5	–7	14	21.4	14:21	13	5	4	9	19	2	0	1	16:27
2010-11 ♦	Boston	NHL	79	30	32	62	121	5	0	7	173	17.3	28	54	38.9	16:35	25	5	7	12	63	1	0	0	17:54
	NHL Totals		278	64	87	151	390	8	0	16	430	14.9		86	39.5	14:31	55	15	17	32	129	3	0	1	16:53

Memorial Cup All-Star Team (2007) • Stafford Smythe Memorial Trophy (Memorial Cup - MVP) (2007)

LUKOWICH, Brad

(loo-KUH-which, BRAD) **DAL**

Defense. Shoots left. 6'1", 200 lbs. Born, Cranbrook, B.C., August 12, 1976. NY Islanders' 4th choice, 90th overall, in 1994 Entry Draft.

Season	Club	League	GP	G	A	Pts	PIM	PP	SH	GW	S	%	+/-	TF	F%	Min	Playoffs GP	G	A	Pts	PIM	PP	SH	GW	Min
1992-93	Cranbrook Colts	RMJHL	54	21	41	62	162	....	....	....	....	....	....	....	....	....	....	....	....	....	....	....	....	....	....
	Kamloops Blazers	WHL	1	0	0	0	0	....	....	....	....	....	....	....	....	....	....	....	....	....	....	....	....	....	....
1993-94	Kamloops Blazers	WHL	42	5	11	16	166	....	....	....	....	....	....	....	....	....	16	0	1	1	35	....	....	....	....
1994-95	Kamloops Blazers	WHL	63	10	35	45	125	....	....	....	....	....	....	....	....	....	18	0	7	7	21	....	....	....	....
1995-96	Kamloops Blazers	WHL	65	14	55	69	114	....	....	....	....	....	....	....	....	....	13	2	10	12	29	....	....	....	....
1996-97	Michigan	IHL	69	2	6	8	77	....	....	....	....	....	....	....	....	....	4	0	1	1	2	....	....	....	....
1997-98	Dallas	NHL	4	0	1	1	2	0	0	0	2	0.0	–2	....	....	....	....	....	....	....	....	....	....	....	....
	Michigan	IHL	60	6	27	33	104	....	....	....	....	....	....	....	....	....	4	0	4	4	14	....	....	....	....
1998-99	Dallas	NHL	14	1	2	3	19	0	0	0	8	12.5	3	0	0.0	16:18	8	0	1	1	4	0	0	0	10:00
	Michigan	IHL	67	8	21	29	95	....	....	....	....	....	....	....	....	....	....	....	....	....	....	....	....	....	....
99-2000	Dallas	NHL	60	3	1	4	50	0	0	1	33	9.1	–14	1	0.0	11:44	....	....	....	....	....	....	....	....	....
2000-01	Dallas	NHL	80	4	10	14	76	0	0	2	43	9.3	28	1	100.0	14:48	10	1	0	1	4	0	0	0	17:28
2001-02	Dallas	NHL	66	1	6	7	40	0	0	0	56	1.8	–1	0	0.0	13:14	....	....	....	....	....	....	....	....	....
2002-03	Tampa Bay	NHL	70	1	14	15	46	0	0	0	52	1.9	4	1	0.0	17:34	9	0	1	1	2	0	0	0	17:48
2003-04 ♦	Tampa Bay	NHL	79	5	14	19	24	0	0	1	86	5.8	29	3	0.0	18:45	18	0	2	2	6	0	0	0	15:51
2004-05	Fort Worth	CHL	16	3	5	8	33	....	....	....	....	....	....	....	....	....	....	....	....	....	....	....	....	....	....
2005-06	NY Islanders	NHL	57	1	12	13	32	0	0	1	36	2.8	–3	0	0.0	19:15	....	....	....	....	....	....	....	....	....
	New Jersey	NHL	18	1	7	8	8	0	0	0	13	7.7	3	0	0.0	19:11	9	0	0	0	4	0	0	0	21:28
2006-07	New Jersey	NHL	75	4	8	12	36	0	1	2	50	8.0	1	0	0.0	20:13	11	0	1	1	2	0	0	0	19:57
2007-08	Tampa Bay	NHL	59	1	6	7	20	0	0	0	28	3.6	–15	0	0.0	16:36	....	....	....	....	....	....	....	....	....
2008-09	San Jose	NHL	58	0	8	8	12	0	0	0	43	0.0	5	0	0.0	16:13	6	0	0	0	0	0	0	0	14:30

			Regular Season														Playoffs								
Season	Club	League	GP	G	A	Pts	PIM	PP	SH	GW	S	%	+/-	TF	F%	Min	GP	G	A	Pts	PIM	PP	SH	GW	Min
2009-10	Texas Stars	AHL	29	3	15	18	10	....	....	....	....	....	....	....	....	....	....	....	....	....	....	....	....	....	....
	Vancouver	**NHL**	**13**	**1**	**1**	**2**	**4**	**0**	**0**	**1**	**1**	**100.0**	**5**	**0**	**0.0**	**11:13**	....	....	....	....	....	....	....	....	....
2010-11	**Dallas**	**NHL**	**5**	**0**	**0**	**0**	**0**	**0**	**0**	**0**	**3**	**0.0**	**2**	**0**	**0.0**	**10:16**	....	....	....	....	....	....	....	....	....
	Texas Stars	AHL	67	4	23	27	59	....	....	....	....	....	....	....	....	....	6	1	0	1	2	....	....	....	....
	NHL Totals		**658**	**23**	**90**	**113**	**369**	**0**	**1**	**8**	**454**	**5.1**		**6**	**16.7**	**16:29**	**71**	**1**	**5**	**6**	**22**	**0**	**0**	**0**	**16:54**

Traded to **Dallas** by **NY Islanders** for Dallas' 3rd round choice (Robert Schnabel) in 1997 Entry Draft, June 1, 1996. Traded to **Minnesota** by **Dallas** with Manny Fernandez for Minnesota's 3rd round choice (Joel Lundqvist) in 2000 Entry Draft and Minnesota's 4th round choice (later traded back to Minnesota, later traded to Los Angeles – Los Angeles selected Aaron Rome) in 2002 Entry Draft, June 12, 2000. Traded to **Dallas** by **Minnesota** with Minnesota's 3rd (Yared Hagos) and 9th (Dale Sullivan) round choices in 2001 Entry Draft for Aaron Gavey, Pavel Patera, Dallas' 8th round choice (Eric Johansson) in 2000 Entry Draft and Minnesota's 4th round choice (previously acquired, later traded to Los Angeles – Los Angeles selected Aaron Rome) in 2002 Entry Draft, June 25, 2000. Traded to **Tampa Bay** by **Dallas** with Dallas' 7th round choice (Jay Rosehill) in 2003 Entry Draft for Tampa Bay's 2nd round choice (previously acquired, later traded back to Tampa Bay, later traded to Dallas – Dallas selected Tobias Stephan) in 2002 Entry Draft, June 22, 2002. Signed as a free agent by **Fort Worth** (CHL), September 21, 2004. Signed as a free agent by **NY Islanders**, August 11, 2005. Traded to **New Jersey** by **NY Islanders** for New Jersey's 3rd round choice (later traded to Phoenix - Phoenix selected Jonas Ahnelov) in 2006 Entry Draft, March 9, 2006. Signed as a free agent by **Tampa Bay**, July 3, 2007. Traded to **San Jose** by **Tampa Bay** with Dan Boyle for Matt Carle, Ty Wishart, San Jose's 1st round choice (later traded to Ottawa, later traded to NY Islanders, later traded to Columbus, later traded to Anahaim - Anaheim selected Kyle Palmieri) in 2009 Entry Draft and San Jose's 4th round choice (James Mullin) in 2010 Entry Draft, July 4, 2008. Traded to **Vancouver** by **San Jose** with Christian Ehrhoff for Patrick White and Daniel Rahimi, August 28, 2009. • Assigned to **Texas** (AHL) by **Vancouver**, October 1, 2009. Signed as a free agent by **Dallas**, July 16, 2010.

LUNDIN, Mike

(LUHN-dihn, MIGHK) **MIN**

Defense. Shoots left. 6'2", 191 lbs. Born, Burnsville, MN, September 24, 1984. Tampa Bay's 3rd choice, 102nd overall, in 2004 Entry Draft.

Season	Club	League	GP	G	A	Pts	PIM	PP	SH	GW	S	%	+/-	TF	F%	Min	GP	G	A	Pts	PIM	PP	SH	GW	Min
2002-03	Apple Valley	High-MN	27	8	20	27	....	....	....	....	....	....	....	....	....	....	....	....	....	....	....	....	....	....	....
2003-04	U. of Maine	H-East	44	3	16	19	34	....	....	....	....	....	....	....	....	....	....	....	....	....	....	....	....	....	....
2004-05	U. of Maine	H-East	40	1	13	14	2	....	....	....	....	....	....	....	....	....	....	....	....	....	....	....	....	....	....
2005-06	U. of Maine	H-East	36	3	13	16	4	....	....	....	....	....	....	....	....	....	....	....	....	....	....	....	....	....	....
2006-07	U. of Maine	H-East	40	6	14	20	2	....	....	....	....	....	....	....	....	....	....	....	....	....	....	....	....	....	....
2007-08	**Tampa Bay**	**NHL**	**81**	**0**	**6**	**6**	**16**	**0**	**0**	**0**	**33**	**0.0**	**3**	**0**	**0.0**	**13:48**	....	....	....	....	....	....	....	....	....
2008-09	**Tampa Bay**	**NHL**	**25**	**0**	**2**	**2**	**4**	**0**	**0**	**0**	**8**	**0.0**	**–4**	**1**	**0.0**	**16:39**	....	....	....	....	....	....	....	....	....
	Norfolk Admirals	AHL	51	4	25	29	18	....	....	....	....	....	....	....	....	....	....	....	....	....	....	....	....	....	....
2009-10	**Tampa Bay**	**NHL**	**49**	**3**	**10**	**13**	**18**	**0**	**0**	**0**	**42**	**7.1**	**–4**	**0**	**0.0**	**21:57**	....	....	....	....	....	....	....	....	....
	Norfolk Admirals	AHL	27	2	14	16	4	....	....	....	....	....	....	....	....	....	....	....	....	....	....	....	....	....	....
2010-11	**Tampa Bay**	**NHL**	**69**	**1**	**11**	**12**	**12**	**0**	**0**	**0**	**55**	**1.8**	**–3**	**0**	**0.0**	**20:24**	**18**	**0**	**2**	**2**	**2**	**0**	**0**	**0**	**14:40**
	NHL Totals		**224**	**4**	**29**	**33**	**50**	**0**	**0**	**0**	**138**	**2.9**		**1**	**0.0**	**17:56**	**18**	**0**	**2**	**2**	**2**	**0**	**0**	**0**	**14:41**

Hockey East Second All-Star Team (2007)

Signed as a free agent by **Minnesota**, July 9, 2011.

LUNDMARK, Jamie

(LUHND-mahrk, JAY-mee)

Center. Shoots right. 6', 197 lbs. Born, Edmonton, Alta., January 16, 1981. NY Rangers' 2nd choice, 9th overall, in 1999 Entry Draft.

Season	Club	League	GP	G	A	Pts	PIM	PP	SH	GW	S	%	+/-	TF	F%	Min	GP	G	A	Pts	PIM	PP	SH	GW	Min
1996-97	St. Albert Saints	AJHL	35	10	9	19	8	....	....	....	....	....	....	....	....	....	....	....	....	....	....	....	....	....	....
1997-98	St. Albert Saints	AJHL	57	33	58	91	171	....	....	....	....	....	....	....	....	....	19	13	18	31	5	....	....	....	....
1998-99	Moose Jaw	WHL	70	40	51	91	123	....	....	....	....	....	....	....	....	....	11	5	4	9	24	....	....	....	....
99-2000	Moose Jaw	WHL	37	21	27	48	33	....	....	....	....	....	....	....	....	....	....	....	....	....	....	....	....	....	....
2000-01	Seattle	WHL	52	35	42	77	49	....	....	....	....	....	....	....	....	....	9	4	4	8	16	....	....	....	....
2001-02	Hartford	AHL	79	27	32	59	56	....	....	....	....	....	....	....	....	....	10	3	4	7	16	....	....	....	....
2002-03	**NY Rangers**	**NHL**	**55**	**8**	**11**	**19**	**16**	**0**	**0**	**0**	**78**	**10.3**	**–3**	**62**	**43.6**	**12:04**	....	....	....	....	....	....	....	....	....
	Hartford	AHL	22	9	9	18	18	....	....	....	....	....	....	....	....	....	2	0	0	0	0	....	....	....	....
2003-04	**NY Rangers**	**NHL**	**56**	**2**	**8**	**10**	**33**	**0**	**0**	**1**	**68**	**2.9**	**–8**	**379**	**40.4**	**12:46**	....	....	....	....	....	....	....	....	....
2004-05	HC Forst Bolzano	Italy	14	9	9	18	22	....	....	....	....	....	....	....	....	....	....	....	....	....	....	....	....	....	....
	Hartford	AHL	64	14	27	41	146	....	....	....	....	....	....	....	....	....	6	2	4	6	8	....	....	....	....
2005-06	**NY Rangers**	**NHL**	**3**	**1**	**0**	**1**	**6**	**0**	**0**	**0**	**1**	**100.0**	**–2**	**2**	**0.0**	**9:49**	....	....	....	....	....	....	....	....	....
	Phoenix	**NHL**	**38**	**5**	**13**	**18**	**36**	**1**	**0**	**0**	**61**	**8.2**	**–1**	**366**	**58.7**	**12:37**	....	....	....	....	....	....	....	....	....
	San Antonio	AHL	4	1	2	3	2	....	....	....	....	....	....	....	....	....	....	....	....	....	....	....	....	....	....
	Calgary	**NHL**	**12**	**4**	**6**	**10**	**20**	**1**	**0**	**1**	**16**	**25.0**	**2**	**103**	**53.4**	**12:32**	**4**	**0**	**1**	**1**	**7**	**0**	**0**	**0**	**9:44**
2006-07	**Calgary**	**NHL**	**39**	**0**	**4**	**4**	**31**	**0**	**0**	**0**	**28**	**0.0**	**–4**	**233**	**55.4**	**8:37**	....	....	....	....	....	....	....	....	....
	Los Angeles	**NHL**	**29**	**7**	**2**	**9**	**25**	**0**	**0**	**0**	**53**	**13.2**	**–8**	**410**	**47.6**	**16:03**	....	....	....	....	....	....	....	....	....
2007-08	Dynamo Moscow	Russia	17	2	1	3	31	....	....	....	....	....	....	....	....	....	....	....	....	....	....	....	....	....	....
	Lake Erie	AHL	51	13	20	33	71	....	....	....	....	....	....	....	....	....	....	....	....	....	....	....	....	....	....
2008-09	**Calgary**	**NHL**	**27**	**8**	**8**	**16**	**17**	**0**	**0**	**0**	**50**	**16.0**	**2**	**120**	**51.7**	**13:59**	**2**	**0**	**0**	**0**	**0**	**0**	**0**	**0**	**7:06**
	Quad City Flames	AHL	54	15	37	52	31	....	....	....	....	....	....	....	....	....	....	....	....	....	....	....	....	....	....
2009-10	**Calgary**	**NHL**	**21**	**4**	**5**	**9**	**4**	**1**	**0**	**1**	**36**	**11.1**	**–6**	**62**	**48.4**	**15:22**	....	....	....	....	....	....	....	....	....
	Abbotsford Heat	AHL	32	9	12	21	64	....	....	....	....	....	....	....	....	....	....	....	....	....	....	....	....	....	....
	Toronto	**NHL**	**15**	**1**	**2**	**3**	**16**	**0**	**0**	**0**	**16**	**6.3**	**–1**	**30**	**50.0**	**11:34**	....	....	....	....	....	....	....	....	....
2010-11	Milwaukee	AHL	34	6	12	18	22	....	....	....	....	....	....	....	....	....	....	....	....	....	....	....	....	....	....
	Timra IK	Sweden	18	3	7	10	12	....	....	....	....	....	....	....	....	....	....	....	....	....	....	....	....	....	....
	NHL Totals		**295**	**40**	**59**	**99**	**204**	**3**	**0**	**3**	**407**	**9.8**		**1767**	**49.9**	**12:35**	**6**	**0**	**1**	**1**	**7**	**0**	**0**	**0**	**8:51**

WHL All-Rookie Team (1999) • WHL East Second All-Star Team (1999) • WHL West First All-Star Team (2001)

Signed as a free agent by **Bolzano** (Italy), September 21, 2004. Signed as a free agent by **Hartford** (AHL), November 16, 2004. Traded to **Phoenix** by **NY Rangers** for Jeff Taffe, October 18, 2005. Traded to **Calgary** by **Phoenix** for Calgary's 4th round choice (later traded to NY Islanders - NY Islanders selected Doug Rogers) in 2006 Entry Draft, March 9, 2006. Traded to **Los Angeles** by **Calgary** with Calgary's 4th round choice (Dwight King) in 2007 Entry Draft and Calgary's 2nd round choice (later traded back to Calgary - Calgary selected Mitch Wahl) in 2008 Entry Draft for Craig Conroy, January 29, 2007. Signed as a free agent by **Dynamo Moscow** (Russia), July 27, 2007. Signed as a free agent by **Lake Erie** (AHL), December 8, 2007. Signed as a free agent by **Calgary**, July 16, 2008. Claimed on waivers by **Toronto** from **Calgary**, February 16, 2010. Signed as a free agent by **Nashville**, July 16, 2010. Signed as a free agent by **Timra**, January 10. 2011.

LUPUL, Joffrey

(LOO-puhl, JAWF-ree) **TOR**

Right wing. Shoots right. 6'1", 206 lbs. Born, Fort Saskatchewan, Alta., September 23, 1983. Anaheim's 1st choice, 7th overall, in 2002 Entry Draft.

Season	Club	League	GP	G	A	Pts	PIM	PP	SH	GW	S	%	+/-	TF	F%	Min	GP	G	A	Pts	PIM	PP	SH	GW	Min
1998-99	Ft. Saskatchewan	Minor-AB	36	40	50	90	40	....	....	....	....	....	....	....	....	....	....	....	....	....	....	....	....	....	....
99-2000	Ft. Saskatchewan	AMHL	34	43	30	*73	47	....	....	....	....	....	....	....	....	....	4	0	1	1	2	....	....	....	....
2000-01	Medicine Hat	WHL	69	30	26	56	39	....	....	....	....	....	....	....	....	....	22	3	6	9	2	....	....	....	....
2001-02	Medicine Hat	WHL	72	*56	50	106	95	....	....	....	....	....	....	....	....	....	....	....	....	....	....	....	....	....	....
2002-03	Medicine Hat	WHL	50	41	37	78	82	....	....	....	....	....	....	....	....	....	11	4	11	15	20	....	....	....	....
2003-04	**Anaheim**	**NHL**	**75**	**13**	**21**	**34**	**28**	**4**	**0**	**2**	**137**	**9.5**	**–6**	**11**	**9.1**	**13:37**	....	....	....	....	....	....	....	....	....
	Cincinnati	AHL	3	3	2	5	2	....	....	....	....	....	....	....	....	....	....	....	....	....	....	....	....	....	....
2004-05	Cincinnati	AHL	65	30	26	56	58	....	....	....	....	....	....	....	....	....	12	3	9	12	27	....	....	....	....
2005-06	**Anaheim**	**NHL**	**81**	**28**	**25**	**53**	**48**	**12**	**2**	**2**	**296**	**9.5**	**–13**	**101**	**37.6**	**16:38**	**16**	**9**	**2**	**11**	**31**	**1**	**0**	**1**	**16:43**
2006-07	**Edmonton**	**NHL**	**81**	**16**	**12**	**28**	**45**	**5**	**0**	**1**	**172**	**9.3**	**–29**	**14**	**35.7**	**15:36**	....	....	....	....	....	....	....	....	....
2007-08	**Philadelphia**	**NHL**	**56**	**20**	**26**	**46**	**35**	**7**	**0**	**3**	**176**	**11.4**	**2**	**4**	**75.0**	**18:13**	**17**	**4**	**6**	**10**	**2**	**2**	**0**	**1**	**16:13**
2008-09	**Philadelphia**	**NHL**	**79**	**25**	**25**	**50**	**58**	**6**	**0**	**4**	**194**	**12.9**	**1**	**21**	**47.6**	**15:41**	**6**	**1**	**1**	**2**	**2**	**0**	**0**	**0**	**17:07**
2009-10	**Anaheim**	**NHL**	**23**	**10**	**4**	**14**	**18**	**0**	**0**	**0**	**66**	**15.2**	**3**	**5**	**20.0**	**15:58**	....	....	....	....	....	....	....	....	....
2010-11	**Anaheim**	**NHL**	**26**	**5**	**8**	**13**	**14**	**2**	**0**	**1**	**54**	**9.3**	**–4**	**14**	**50.0**	**13:13**	....	....	....	....	....	....	....	....	....
	Syracuse Crunch	AHL	3	1	3	4	0	....	....	....	....	....	....	....	....	....	....	....	....	....	....	....	....	....	....
	Toronto	**NHL**	**28**	**9**	**9**	**18**	**19**	**2**	**0**	**1**	**75**	**12.0**	**–7**	**18**	**27.8**	**17:51**	....	....	....	....	....	....	....	....	....
	NHL Totals		**449**	**126**	**130**	**256**	**265**	**38**	**2**	**14**	**1170**	**10.8**		**188**	**37.2**	**15:49**	**39**	**14**	**9**	**23**	**35**	**3**	**0**	**2**	**16:34**

WHL East First All-Star Team (2002) • Canadian Major Junior First All-Star Team (2002)

Traded to **Edmonton** by **Anaheim** with Ladislav Smid, Anaheim's 1st round choice (later traded to Phoenix - Phoenix selected Nick Ross) in 2007 Entry Draft and Anaheim's 1st (Jordan Eberle) and 2nd (later traded to NY Islanders - NY Islanders selected Travis Hamonic) round choices in 2008 Entry Draft for Chris Pronger, July 3, 2006. Traded to **Philadelphia** by **Edmonton** with Jason Smith for Joni Pitkanen, Geoff Sanderson and Philadelphia's 3rd round choice (Cameron Abney) in 2009 Entry Draft, July 1, 2007. Traded to **Anaheim** by **Philadelphia** with Luca Sbisa, Philadelphia's 1st round choices in 2009 (later traded to Columbus - Columbus selected John Moore) and 2010 (Emerson Etem) Entry Drafts and future considerations for Chris Pronger and Ryan Dingle, June 26, 2009. • Missed majority of 2009-10 due to recurring back injury, December 16, 2009. Traded to **Toronto** by **Anaheim** with Jake Gardiner for Francois Beauchemin, February 9, 2011.

LYDMAN, Toni

(LEWD-man, TOH-nee) **ANA**

Defense. Shoots left. 6'1", 202 lbs. Born, Lahti, Finland, September 25, 1977. Calgary's 5th choice, 89th overall, in 1996 Entry Draft.

Season	Club	League	GP	G	A	Pts	PIM	PP	SH	GW	S	%	+/-	TF	F%	Min	GP	G	A	Pts	PIM	PP	SH	GW	Min
1993-94	K-Reipas U18	Fin-U18	9	3	1	4	4	....	....	....	....	....	....	....	....	....	....	....	....	....	....	....	....	....	....
	K-Reipas Jr.	Fin-Jr.	1	0	0	0	0	....	....	....	....	....	....	....	....	....	....	....	....	....	....	....	....	....	....
1994-95	K-Reipas U18	Fin-U18	9	7	4	11	12	....	....	....	....	....	....	....	....	....	....	....	....	....	....	....	....	....	....
	K-Reipas Jr.	Fin-Jr.	26	6	4	10	10	....	....	....	....	....	....	....	....	....	....	....	....	....	....	....	....	....	....
1995-96	Reipas Lahti Jr.	Fin-Jr.	9	2	2	4	6	....	....	....	....	....	....	....	....	....	....	....	....	....	....	....	....	....	....
	Reipas Lahti	Finland-2	39	5	2	7	30	....	....	....	....	....	....	....	....	....	3	0	1	1	0	....	....	....	....
1996-97	Tappara Tampere	Finland	49	1	2	3	65	....	....	....	....	....	....	....	....	....	3	0	0	0	6	....	....	....	....
1997-98	Tappara Tampere	Finland	48	4	10	14	48	....	....	....	....	....	....	....	....	....	4	0	2	2	0	....	....	....	....

			Regular Season														Playoffs								
Season	Club	League	GP	G	A	Pts	PIM	PP	SH	GW	S	%	+/-	TF	F%	Min	GP	G	A	Pts	PIM	PP	SH	GW	Min
1998-99	HIFK Helsinki	Finland	42	4	7	11	36	....	....	....	....	....	....	....	....	....	11	0	3	3	2	....	....	....	....
	HIFK Helsinki	EuroHL	6	0	2	2	29	....	....	....	....	....	....	....	....	....	4	1	....	....	....	....	....	....	....
99-2000	HIFK Helsinki	Finland	46	4	18	22	36	....	....	....	....	....	....	....	....	....	9	0	4	4	6	....	....	....	....
2000-01	**Calgary**	**NHL**	**62**	**3**	**16**	**19**	**30**	**1**	**0**	**0**	**80**	**3.8**	**–7**	**0**	**0.0**	**20:36**	....	....	....	....	....	....	....	....	....
2001-02	**Calgary**	**NHL**	**79**	**6**	**22**	**28**	**52**	**1**	**0**	**0**	**126**	**4.8**	**–8**	**0**	**0.0**	**21:10**	....	....	....	....	....	....	....	....	....
2002-03	**Calgary**	**NHL**	**81**	**6**	**20**	**26**	**28**	**3**	**0**	**0**	**143**	**4.2**	**–7**	**0**	**0.0**	**25:47**	....	....	....	....	....	....	....	....	....
2003-04	**Calgary**	**NHL**	**67**	**4**	**16**	**20**	**30**	**2**	**0**	**1**	**93**	**4.3**	**6**	**0**	**0.0**	**21:13**	**6**	**0**	**1**	**1**	**2**	**0**	**0**	**0**	**14:30**
2004-05	HIFK Helsinki	Finland	8	1	2	3	2	....	....	....	....	....	....	....	....	....	5	0	3	3	0	....	....	....	....
2005-06	**Buffalo**	**NHL**	**75**	**1**	**16**	**17**	**82**	**0**	**0**	**0**	**68**	**1.5**	**9**	**0**	**0.0**	**21:38**	**18**	**1**	**4**	**5**	**18**	**0**	**0**	**0**	**23:03**
	Finland	Olympics	8	1	0	1	10	....	....	....	....	....	....	....	....	....	....	....	....	....	....	....	....	....	....
2006-07	**Buffalo**	**NHL**	**67**	**2**	**17**	**19**	**55**	**0**	**0**	**1**	**44**	**4.5**	**10**	**0**	**0.0**	**20:36**	**16**	**2**	**2**	**4**	**14**	**0**	**0**	**0**	**23:41**
2007-08	**Buffalo**	**NHL**	**82**	**4**	**22**	**26**	**74**	**3**	**0**	**0**	**86**	**4.7**	**1**	**1**	**0.0**	**21:40**	....	....	....	....	....	....	....	....	....
2008-09	**Buffalo**	**NHL**	**80**	**3**	**20**	**23**	**70**	**0**	**0**	**0**	**99**	**3.0**	**0**	**0**	**0.0**	**21:47**	....	....	....	....	....	....	....	....	....
2009-10	**Buffalo**	**NHL**	**67**	**4**	**16**	**20**	**30**	**0**	**0**	**1**	**77**	**5.2**	**10**	**0**	**0.0**	**18:52**	**6**	**0**	**1**	**1**	**6**	**0**	**0**	**0**	**26:15**
	Finland	Olympics	6	0	0	0	2	....	....	....	....	....	....	....	....	....	....	....	....	....	....	....	....	....	....
2010-11	**Anaheim**	**NHL**	**78**	**3**	**22**	**25**	**42**	**0**	**0**	**0**	**99**	**3.0**	**32**	**0**	**0.0**	**22:10**	**6**	**0**	**0**	**0**	**2**	**0**	**0**	**0**	**20:09**
	NHL Totals		**738**	**36**	**187**	**223**	**493**	**10**	**0**	**3**	**915**	**3.9**		**1**	**0.0**	**21:39**	**52**	**3**	**8**	**11**	**42**	**0**	**0**	**0**	**22:18**

Signed as a free agent by **HIFK Helsinki** (Finland), January 31, 2005. Traded to **Buffalo** by **Calgary** for Buffalo's 3rd round choice (John Armstrong) in 2006 Entry Draft, August 25, 2005. Signed as a free agent by **Anaheim**, July 1, 2010.

MacARTHUR, Clarke

(muh-KAR-thuhr, KLAHRK) **TOR**

Left wing. Shoots left. 6', 191 lbs. Born, Lloydminster, Alta., April 6, 1985. Buffalo's 3rd choice, 74th overall, in 2003 Entry Draft.

99-2000	Lloydminster	CABHL	24	19	45	64	51	....	....	....	....	....	....	....	....	....	5	9	6	15	4	....	....	....	....
2000-01	Strathcona	AMBHL	38	36	63	99	44	....	....	....	....	....	....	....	....	....	8	6	2	8	10	....	....	....	....
2001-02	Drayton Valley	AJHL	61	22	40	62	33	....	....	....	....	....	....	....	....	....	16	5	8	13	34	....	....	....	....
2002-03	Medicine Hat	WHL	70	23	52	75	104	....	....	....	....	....	....	....	....	....	11	3	6	9	8	....	....	....	....
2003-04	Medicine Hat	WHL	62	35	40	75	93	....	....	....	....	....	....	....	....	....	20	8	10	18	16	....	....	....	....
2004-05	Medicine Hat	WHL	58	30	44	74	100	....	....	....	....	....	....	....	....	....	13	3	8	11	18	....	....	....	....
	Rochester	AHL	....	....	....	....	....	....	....	....	....	....	....	....	....	....	3	0	1	1	0	....	....	....	....
2005-06	Rochester	AHL	69	21	32	53	71	....	....	....	....	....	....	....	....	....	....	....	....	....	....	....	....	....	....
2006-07	**Buffalo**	**NHL**	**19**	**3**	**4**	**7**	**4**	**0**	**0**	**0**	**16**	**18.8**	**4**	**50**	**46.0**	**8:54**	....	....	....	....	....	....	....	....	....
	Rochester	AHL	51	21	42	63	57	....	....	....	....	....	....	....	....	....	6	2	4	6	4	....	....	....	....
2007-08	**Buffalo**	**NHL**	**37**	**8**	**7**	**15**	**20**	**0**	**0**	**1**	**51**	**15.7**	**3**	**14**	**28.6**	**14:34**	....	....	....	....	....	....	....	....	....
	Rochester	AHL	43	14	28	42	26	....	....	....	....	....	....	....	....	....	....	....	....	....	....	....	....	....	....
2008-09	**Buffalo**	**NHL**	**71**	**17**	**14**	**31**	**56**	**5**	**0**	**0**	**108**	**15.7**	**–4**	**218**	**34.9**	**13:50**	....	....	....	....	....	....	....	....	....
2009-10	**Buffalo**	**NHL**	**60**	**13**	**13**	**26**	**47**	**3**	**0**	**3**	**99**	**13.1**	**–14**	**143**	**43.4**	**14:22**	....	....	....	....	....	....	....	....	....
	Atlanta	**NHL**	**21**	**3**	**6**	**9**	**2**	**1**	**1**	**0**	**30**	**10.0**	**–2**	**10**	**50.0**	**15:37**	....	....	....	....	....	....	....	....	....
2010-11	**Toronto**	**NHL**	**82**	**21**	**41**	**62**	**37**	**6**	**0**	**3**	**154**	**13.6**	**–3**	**16**	**56.3**	**17:07**	....	....	....	....	....	....	....	....	....
	NHL Totals		**290**	**65**	**85**	**150**	**166**	**15**	**1**	**7**	**458**	**14.2**		**451**	**39.7**	**14:46**	....	....	....	....	....	....	....	....	....

Memorial Cup All-Star Team (2004) • WHL East First All-Star Team (2005)

Traded to **Atlanta** by **Buffalo** for Atlanta's 3rd (Jerome Gauthier-Leduc) and 4th (Steven Shipley) round choices in 2010 Entry Draft, March 3, 2010. Signed as a free agent by **Toronto**, August 28, 2010.

MacDONALD, Andrew

(MAK-DAWN-uhld, AN-droo) **NYI**

Defense. Shoots left. 6'1", 201 lbs. Born, Judique, N.S., September 7, 1986. NY Islanders' 10th choice, 160th overall, in 2006 Entry Draft.

2003-04	Truro Bearcats	MJrHL	50	8	20	28	43	....	....	....	....	....	....	....	....	....	10	0	0	0	....	....	....	....	....
2004-05	Truro Bearcats	MJrHL	56	11	22	33	60	....	....	....	....	....	....	....	....	....	17	6	7	13	....	....	....	....	....
2005-06	Moncton Wildcats	QMJHL	68	6	40	46	62	....	....	....	....	....	....	....	....	....	21	2	11	13	10	....	....	....	....
2006-07	Moncton Wildcats	QMJHL	65	14	44	58	81	....	....	....	....	....	....	....	....	....	7	1	5	6	4	....	....	....	....
	Bridgeport	AHL	3	0	0	0	0	....	....	....	....	....	....	....	....	....	....	....	....	....	....	....	....	....	....
2007-08	Bridgeport	AHL	21	2	3	5	10	....	....	....	....	....	....	....	....	....	....	....	....	....	....	....	....	....	....
	Utah Grizzlies	ECHL	37	1	11	12	39	....	....	....	....	....	....	....	....	....	15	3	9	12	12	....	....	....	....
2008-09	**NY Islanders**	**NHL**	**3**	**0**	**0**	**0**	**2**	**0**	**0**	**0**	**1**	**0.0**	**2**	**0**	**0.0**	**10:10**	....	....	....	....	....	....	....	....	....
	Bridgeport	AHL	69	9	24	33	46	....	....	....	....	....	....	....	....	....	5	1	1	2	4	....	....	....	....
2009-10	**NY Islanders**	**NHL**	**46**	**1**	**6**	**7**	**20**	**0**	**0**	**0**	**43**	**2.3**	**4**	**1**	**0.0**	**20:05**	....	....	....	....	....	....	....	....	....
	Bridgeport	AHL	21	2	6	8	29	....	....	....	....	....	....	....	....	....	5	3	1	4	10	....	....	....	....
2010-11	**NY Islanders**	**NHL**	**60**	**4**	**23**	**27**	**37**	**1**	**0**	**1**	**72**	**5.6**	**9**	**0**	**0.0**	**23:25**	....	....	....	....	....	....	....	....	....
	NHL Totals		**109**	**5**	**29**	**34**	**59**	**1**	**0**	**1**	**116**	**4.3**		**1**	**0.0**	**21:39**	....	....	....	....	....	....	....	....	....

QMJHL First All-Star Team (2007)

MACHACEK, Spencer

(muh-HA-chehk, SPEHN-suhr) **WPG**

Right wing. Shoots right. 6'1", 200 lbs. Born, Lethbridge, Alta., October 14, 1988. Atlanta's 1st choice, 67th overall, in 2007 Entry Draft.

2004-05	Brooks Bandits	AJHL	59	16	20	36	41	....	....	....	....	....	....	....	....	....	10	2	2	4	8	....	....	....	....
2005-06	Vancouver Giants	WHL	70	23	22	45	53	....	....	....	....	....	....	....	....	....	18	6	8	14	8	....	....	....	....
2006-07	Vancouver Giants	WHL	63	21	24	45	32	....	....	....	....	....	....	....	....	....	22	9	11	20	14	....	....	....	....
2007-08	Vancouver Giants	WHL	70	33	45	78	69	....	....	....	....	....	....	....	....	....	10	5	2	7	6	....	....	....	....
2008-09	**Atlanta**	**NHL**	**2**	**0**	**0**	**0**	**0**	**0**	**0**	**0**	**1**	**0.0**	**0**	**0**	**0.0**	**8:12**	....	....	....	....	....	....	....	....	....
	Chicago Wolves	AHL	77	23	25	48	23	....	....	....	....	....	....	....	....	....	....	....	....	....	....	....	....	....	....
2009-10	Chicago Wolves	AHL	79	20	29	49	68	....	....	....	....	....	....	....	....	....	13	7	4	11	8	....	....	....	....
2010-11	**Atlanta**	**NHL**	**10**	**0**	**0**	**0**	**0**	**0**	**0**	**0**	**7**	**0.0**	**–2**	**0**	**0.0**	**7:41**	....	....	....	....	....	....	....	....	....
	Chicago Wolves	AHL	67	21	32	53	45	....	....	....	....	....	....	....	....	....	....	....	....	....	....	....	....	....	....
	NHL Totals		**12**	**0**	**0**	**0**	**0**	**0**	**0**	**0**	**8**	**0.0**		**0**	**0.0**	**7:46**	....	....	....	....	....	....	....	....	....

• Transferred to **Winnipeg** after **Atlanta** franchise relocated, June 21, 2011.

MACIAS, Ray

(mah-CHEE-ahs, RAY)

Defense. Shoots right. 6'2", 195 lbs. Born, Long Beach, CA, September 18, 1986. Colorado's 6th choice, 124th overall, in 2005 Entry Draft.

2002-03	L.A. Jr. Kings	Minor-CA	49	37	26	63	100	....	....	....	....	....	....	....	....	....	....	....	....	....	....	....	....	....	....
	Kamloops Blazers	WHL	4	0	0	0	0	....	....	....	....	....	....	....	....	....	2	0	0	0	0	....	....	....	....
2003-04	Kamloops Blazers	WHL	69	12	17	29	14	....	....	....	....	....	....	....	....	....	5	2	0	2	0	....	....	....	....
2004-05	Kamloops Blazers	WHL	69	12	35	47	18	....	....	....	....	....	....	....	....	....	2	0	0	0	0	....	....	....	....
2005-06	Kamloops Blazers	WHL	68	12	26	38	34	....	....	....	....	....	....	....	....	....	....	....	....	....	....	....	....	....	....
2006-07	Kamloops Blazers	WHL	70	30	40	70	58	....	....	....	....	....	....	....	....	....	....	....	....	....	....	....	....	....	....
2007-08	Lake Erie	AHL	42	4	9	13	18	....	....	....	....	....	....	....	....	....	....	....	....	....	....	....	....	....	....
	Johnstown Chiefs	ECHL	5	0	5	5	0	....	....	....	....	....	....	....	....	....	6	1	3	4	2	....	....	....	....
2008-09	**Colorado**	**NHL**	**6**	**0**	**1**	**1**	**0**	**0**	**0**	**0**	**4**	**0.0**	**0**	**0**	**0.0**	**17:59**	....	....	....	....	....	....	....	....	....
	Lake Erie	AHL	36	3	15	18	20	....	....	....	....	....	....	....	....	....	....	....	....	....	....	....	....	....	....
	Johnstown Chiefs	ECHL	8	1	5	6	4	....	....	....	....	....	....	....	....	....	....	....	....	....	....	....	....	....	....
2009-10	Lake Erie	AHL	52	7	10	17	16	....	....	....	....	....	....	....	....	....	....	....	....	....	....	....	....	....	....
2010-11	**Colorado**	**NHL**	**2**	**0**	**0**	**0**	**2**	**0**	**0**	**0**	**0**	**0.0**	**–1**	**0**	**0.0**	**15:06**	....	....	....	....	....	....	....	....	....
	Lake Erie	AHL	43	3	11	14	28	....	....	....	....	....	....	....	....	....	4	0	0	0	0	....	....	....	....
	NHL Totals		**8**	**0**	**1**	**1**	**2**	**0**	**0**	**0**	**4**	**0.0**		**0**	**0.0**	**17:16**	....	....	....	....	....	....	....	....	....

WHL West First All-Star Team (2007)

MacINTYRE, Steve

(MAK-ihn-tighr, STEEV) **PIT**

Left wing. Shoots left. 6'5", 250 lbs. Born, Brock, Sask., August 8, 1980.

2002-03	St. Jean Mission	QSPHL	10	1	1	2	68	....	....	....	....	....	....	....	....	....	....	....	....	....	....	....	....	....	....
	Muskegon Fury	UHL	54	2	1	3	279	....	....	....	....	....	....	....	....	....	5	0	0	0	24	....	....	....	....
2003-04	Hartford	AHL	3	0	0	0	0	....	....	....	....	....	....	....	....	....	....	....	....	....	....	....	....	....	....
	Charlotte	ECHL	61	1	4	5	217	....	....	....	....	....	....	....	....	....	....	....	....	....	....	....	....	....	....
	Jacksonville	WHA2	6	0	2	2	18	....	....	....	....	....	....	....	....	....	5	0	1	1	17	....	....	....	....
2004-05	Hartford	AHL	27	1	1	2	207	....	....	....	....	....	....	....	....	....	....	....	....	....	....	....	....	....	....
	Charlotte	ECHL	46	1	4	5	214	....	....	....	....	....	....	....	....	....	11	0	4	4	17	....	....	....	....
2005-06	Charlotte	ECHL	61	3	2	5	238	....	....	....	....	....	....	....	....	....	1	0	0	0	4	....	....	....	....
2006-07	Quad City	UHL	46	2	1	3	168	....	....	....	....	....	....	....	....	....	5	0	0	0	6	....	....	....	....
2007-08	Providence Bruins	AHL	62	2	3	5	213	....	....	....	....	....	....	....	....	....	5	0	0	0	9	....	....	....	....

			Regular Season														Playoffs								
Season	**Club**	**League**	**GP**	**G**	**A**	**Pts**	**PIM**	**PP**	**SH**	**GW**	**S**	**%**	**+/-**	**TF**	**F%**	**Min**	**GP**	**G**	**A**	**Pts**	**PIM**	**PP**	**SH**	**GW**	**Min**
2008-09	**Edmonton**	**NHL**	**22**	**2**	**0**	**2**	**40**	**0**	**0**	**1**	**6**	**33.3**	**–2**	**0**	**0.0**	**3:55**	....	....	....	....	....	....	....	....	....
2009-10	**Edmonton**	**NHL**	**4**	**0**	**0**	**0**	**7**	**0**	**0**	**0**	**0**	**0.0**	**0**	**0**	**0.0**	**1:35**	....	....	....	....	....	....	....	....	....
	Florida	**NHL**	**18**	**0**	**1**	**1**	**17**	**0**	**0**	**0**	**3**	**0.0**	**–3**	**0**	**0.0**	**3:10**	....	....	....	....	....	....	....	....	....
	Rochester	AHL	34	0	2	2	86	....	....	....	....	....	....	....	....	....	6	0	0	0	23	....	....	....	....
2010-11	**Edmonton**	**NHL**	**34**	**0**	**1**	**1**	**93**	**0**	**0**	**0**	**6**	**0.0**	**–1**	**0**	**0.0**	**3:32**	....	....	....	....	....	....	....	....	....
	NHL Totals		**78**	**2**	**2**	**4**	**157**	**0**	**0**	**1**	**15**	**13.3**		**0**	**0.0**	**3:27**	....	....	....	....	....	....	....	....	....

Signed as a free agent by **NY Rangers**, August 15, 2005. Signed as a free agent by **Quad City** (UHL), August 24, 2006. Signed as a free agent by **Florida**, July 3, 2008. Claimed on waivers by **Edmonton** from **Florida**, September 30, 2008. • Missed majority of 2008-09 due to facial injury and as a healthy reserve. Claimed on waivers by **Florida** from **Edmonton**, November 10, 2009. Signed as a free agent by **Edmonton**, July 2, 2010. • Missed majority of 2010-11 as a healthy reserve.

MacKENZIE, Derek
(muh-KEHN-zee, DAIR-ihk) **CBJ**

Center. Shoots left. 5'11", 178 lbs. Born, Sudbury, Ont., June 11, 1981. Atlanta's 6th choice, 128th overall, in 1999 Entry Draft.

Season	Club	League	GP	G	A	Pts	PIM	PP	SH	GW	S	%	+/-	TF	F%	Min	GP	G	A	Pts	PIM	PP	SH	GW	Min
1996-97	Rayside-Balfour	NOJHA	40	23	32	55	40	....	....	....	....	....	....	....	....	....	....	....	....	....	....	....	....	....	....
1997-98	Sudbury Wolves	OHL	59	9	11	20	26	....	....	....	....	....	....	....	....	....	....	....	....	....	....	....	....	....	....
1998-99	Sudbury Wolves	OHL	68	22	65	87	74	....	....	....	....	....	....	....	....	....	4	2	4	6	2	....	....	....	....
99-2000	Sudbury Wolves	OHL	68	24	33	57	110	....	....	....	....	....	....	....	....	....	12	5	9	14	16	....	....	....	....
2000-01	Sudbury Wolves	OHL	62	40	49	89	89	....	....	....	....	....	....	....	....	....	12	6	8	14	16	....	....	....	....
2001-02	**Atlanta**	**NHL**	**1**	**0**	**0**	**0**	**2**	**0**	**0**	**0**	**1**	**0.0**	**–1**	**16**	**56.3**	**13:51**	....	....	....	....	....	....	....	....	....
	Chicago Wolves	AHL	68	13	12	25	80	....	....	....	....	....	....	....	....	....	25	4	2	6	20	....	....	....	....
2002-03	Chicago Wolves	AHL	80	14	18	32	97	....	....	....	....	....	....	....	....	....	9	0	0	0	4	....	....	....	....
2003-04	**Atlanta**	**NHL**	**12**	**0**	**1**	**1**	**10**	**0**	**0**	**0**	**7**	**0.0**	**0**	**63**	**46.0**	**6:38**	....	....	....	....	....	....	....	....	....
	Chicago Wolves	AHL	63	19	16	35	67	....	....	....	....	....	....	....	....	....	10	7	1	8	13	....	....	....	....
2004-05	Chicago Wolves	AHL	78	13	20	33	87	....	....	....	....	....	....	....	....	....	18	5	6	11	33	....	....	....	....
2005-06	**Atlanta**	**NHL**	**11**	**0**	**1**	**1**	**8**	**0**	**0**	**0**	**11**	**0.0**	**0**	**59**	**55.9**	**6:33**	....	....	....	....	....	....	....	....	....
	Chicago Wolves	AHL	36	10	12	22	48	....	....	....	....	....	....	....	....	....	....	....	....	....	....	....	....	....	....
2006-07	**Atlanta**	**NHL**	**4**	**0**	**0**	**0**	**0**	**0**	**0**	**0**	**3**	**0.0**	**1**	**16**	**56.3**	**5:00**	....	....	....	....	....	....	....	....	....
	Chicago Wolves	AHL	52	14	23	37	62	....	....	....	....	....	....	....	....	....	....	....	....	....	....	....	....	....	....
2007-08	**Columbus**	**NHL**	**17**	**2**	**0**	**2**	**8**	**0**	**0**	**0**	**19**	**10.5**	**–2**	**73**	**34.3**	**7:47**	....	....	....	....	....	....	....	....	....
	Syracuse Crunch	AHL	62	25	24	49	46	....	....	....	....	....	....	....	....	....	13	6	8	14	22	....	....	....	....
2008-09	**Columbus**	**NHL**	**1**	**0**	**0**	**0**	**2**	**0**	**0**	**0**	**1**	**0.0**	**–1**	**4**	**50.0**	**7:15**	....	....	....	....	....	....	....	....	....
	Syracuse Crunch	AHL	64	22	30	52	50	....	....	....	....	....	....	....	....	....	....	....	....	....	....	....	....	....	....
2009-10	**Columbus**	**NHL**	**18**	**1**	**3**	**4**	**0**	**0**	**0**	**0**	**14**	**7.1**	**3**	**104**	**54.8**	**8:42**	....	....	....	....	....	....	....	....	....
	Syracuse Crunch	AHL	47	17	30	47	30	....	....	....	....	....	....	....	....	....	....	....	....	....	....	....	....	....	....
2010-11	**Columbus**	**NHL**	**63**	**9**	**14**	**23**	**22**	**0**	**1**	**1**	**76**	**11.8**	**14**	**473**	**52.0**	**10:51**	....	....	....	....	....	....	....	....	....
	NHL Totals		**127**	**12**	**19**	**31**	**52**	**0**	**1**	**1**	**132**	**9.1**		**808**	**50.7**	**9:10**	....	....	....	....	....	....	....	....	....

Signed as a free agent by **Columbus**, July 11, 2007.

MACLEAN, Brett
(muh-KLAIN, BREHT) **PHX**

Left wing. Shoots right. 6'1", 200 lbs. Born, Port Elgin, Ont., December 24, 1988. Phoenix's 3rd choice, 32nd overall, in 2007 Entry Draft.

Season	Club	League	GP	G	A	Pts	PIM	PP	SH	GW	S	%	+/-	TF	F%	Min	GP	G	A	Pts	PIM	PP	SH	GW	Min
2003-04	Listowel Cyclones	ON-Jr.B	9	4	6	10	10	....	....	....	....	....	....	....	....	....	2	3	2	5	12	....	....	....	....
	Grey-Bruce	Minor-ON	66	71	47	118	117	....	....	....	....	....	....	....	....	....	....	....	....	....	....	....	....	....	....
2004-05	Erie Otters	OHL	68	7	16	23	31	....	....	....	....	....	....	....	....	....	6	1	1	2	6	....	....	....	....
2005-06	Erie Otters	OHL	13	3	5	8	6	....	....	....	....	....	....	....	....	....	....	....	....	....	....	....	....	....	....
	Oshawa Generals	OHL	35	13	25	38	29	....	....	....	....	....	....	....	....	....	....	....	....	....	....	....	....	....	....
2006-07	Oshawa Generals	OHL	68	47	53	100	43	....	....	....	....	....	....	....	....	....	7	6	9	15	9	....	....	....	....
2007-08	Oshawa Generals	OHL	61	*61	58	119	42	....	....	....	....	....	....	....	....	....	15	5	11	16	12	....	....	....	....
2008-09	San Antonio	AHL	74	21	19	40	33	....	....	....	....	....	....	....	....	....	....	....	....	....	....	....	....	....	....
2009-10	San Antonio	AHL	76	30	35	65	43	....	....	....	....	....	....	....	....	....	....	....	....	....	....	....	....	....	....
2010-11	**Phoenix**	**NHL**	**13**	**2**	**1**	**3**	**2**	**1**	**0**	**2**	**16**	**12.5**	**0**	**2**	**50.0**	**8:46**	....	....	....	....	....	....	....	....	....
	San Antonio	AHL	51	23	27	50	28	....	....	....	....	....	....	....	....	....	....	....	....	....	....	....	....	....	....
	NHL Totals		**13**	**2**	**1**	**3**	**2**	**1**	**0**	**2**	**16**	**12.5**		**2**	**50.0**	**8:46**	....	....	....	....	....	....	....	....	....

OHL Second All-Star Team (2007) • OHL First All-Star Team (2008) • Canadian Major Junior Second All-Star Team (2008)

MADDEN, John
(MA-dehn, JAWN)

Center. Shoots left. 5'11", 190 lbs. Born, Barrie, Ont., May 4, 1973.

Season	Club	League	GP	G	A	Pts	PIM	PP	SH	GW	S	%	+/-	TF	F%	Min	GP	G	A	Pts	PIM	PP	SH	GW	Min
1989-90	Alliston Hornets	ON-Jr.C	31	24	25	49	26	....	....	....	....	....	....	....	....	....	....	....	....	....	....	....	....	....	....
1990-91	Alliston Hornets	ON-Jr.C	14	15	21	36	10	....	....	....	....	....	....	....	....	....	....	....	....	....	....	....	....	....	....
	Barrie Colts	ON-Jr.B	1	0	0	0	0	....	....	....	....	....	....	....	....	....	....	....	....	....	....	....	....	....	....
1991-92	Barrie Colts	ON-Jr.B	42	50	54	104	46	....	....	....	....	....	....	....	....	....	13	10	9	19	14	....	....	....	....
1992-93	Barrie Colts	COJHL	43	49	75	124	62	....	....	....	....	....	....	....	....	....	....	....	....	....	....	....	....	....	....
1993-94	U. of Michigan	CCHA	36	6	11	17	14	....	....	....	....	....	....	....	....	....	....	....	....	....	....	....	....	....	....
1994-95	U. of Michigan	CCHA	39	21	22	43	8	....	....	....	....	....	....	....	....	....	....	....	....	....	....	....	....	....	....
1995-96	U. of Michigan	CCHA	43	27	30	57	45	....	....	....	....	....	....	....	....	....	....	....	....	....	....	....	....	....	....
1996-97	U. of Michigan	CCHA	42	26	37	63	56	....	....	....	....	....	....	....	....	....	....	....	....	....	....	....	....	....	....
1997-98	Albany River Rats	AHL	74	20	36	56	40	....	....	....	....	....	....	....	....	....	13	3	13	16	14	....	....	....	....
1998-99	**New Jersey**	**NHL**	**4**	**0**	**1**	**1**	**0**	**0**	**0**	**0**	**4**	**0.0**	**–2**	**0**	**0.0**	**9:13**	....	....	....	....	....	....	....	....	....
	Albany River Rats	AHL	75	38	60	98	44	....	....	....	....	....	....	....	....	....	5	2	2	4	6	....	....	....	....
99-2000♦	**New Jersey**	**NHL**	**74**	**16**	**9**	**25**	**6**	**0**	***6**	**3**	**115**	**13.9**	**7**	**770**	**47.5**	**11:40**	**20**	**3**	**4**	**7**	**0**	**0**	**1**	**2**	**15:30**
2000-01	**New Jersey**	**NHL**	**80**	**23**	**15**	**38**	**12**	**0**	**3**	**4**	**163**	**14.1**	**24**	**974**	**46.6**	**15:35**	**25**	**4**	**3**	**7**	**6**	**0**	**0**	**0**	**15:15**
2001-02	**New Jersey**	**NHL**	**82**	**15**	**8**	**23**	**25**	**0**	**0**	**2**	**170**	**8.8**	**6**	**1001**	**47.0**	**15:36**	**6**	**0**	**0**	**0**	**0**	**0**	**0**	**0**	**17:25**
2002-03♦	**New Jersey**	**NHL**	**80**	**19**	**22**	**41**	**26**	**2**	**2**	**3**	**207**	**9.2**	**13**	**1502**	**50.9**	**18:18**	**24**	**6**	**10**	**16**	**2**	**2**	**1**	**1**	**19:38**
2003-04	**New Jersey**	**NHL**	**80**	**12**	**23**	**35**	**22**	**1**	**1**	**1**	**210**	**5.7**	**7**	**1377**	**53.3**	**17:17**	**5**	**0**	**0**	**0**	**0**	**0**	**0**	**0**	**14:51**
2004-05	HIFK Helsinki	Finland	3	0	0	0	0	....	....	....	....	....	....	....	....	....	....	....	....	....	....	....	....	....	....
2005-06	**New Jersey**	**NHL**	**82**	**16**	**20**	**36**	**36**	**0**	**1**	**0**	**194**	**8.2**	**–7**	**1613**	**51.5**	**18:59**	**9**	**4**	**1**	**5**	**8**	**0**	***2**	**0**	**18:56**
2006-07	**New Jersey**	**NHL**	**74**	**12**	**20**	**32**	**14**	**0**	**0**	**1**	**153**	**7.8**	**–7**	**1366**	**49.8**	**18:53**	**11**	**1**	**1**	**2**	**2**	**0**	**0**	**0**	**21:17**
2007-08	**New Jersey**	**NHL**	**80**	**20**	**23**	**43**	**26**	**3**	**3**	**3**	**185**	**10.8**	**1**	**1463**	**53.7**	**19:27**	**5**	**2**	**1**	**3**	**2**	**0**	**0**	**1**	**21:18**
2008-09	**New Jersey**	**NHL**	**76**	**7**	**16**	**23**	**26**	**0**	**1**	**2**	**132**	**5.3**	**–7**	**1160**	**51.6**	**16:25**	**7**	**0**	**1**	**1**	**4**	**0**	**0**	**0**	**18:24**
2009-10♦	**Chicago**	**NHL**	**79**	**10**	**13**	**23**	**12**	**0**	**0**	**0**	**127**	**7.9**	**–2**	**1156**	**53.0**	**15:25**	**22**	**1**	**1**	**2**	**2**	**0**	**0**	**0**	**11:35**
2010-11	**Minnesota**	**NHL**	**76**	**12**	**13**	**25**	**10**	**1**	**1**	**4**	**107**	**11.2**	**–9**	**988**	**51.0**	**15:20**	....	....	....	....	....	....	....	....	....
	NHL Totals		**867**	**162**	**183**	**345**	**215**	**7**	**18**	**23**	**1767**	**9.2**		**13370**	**50.9**	**16:38**	**134**	**21**	**22**	**43**	**26**	**2**	**4**	**4**	**16:41**

CCHA First All-Star Team (1997) • NCAA West First All-American Team (1997) • Frank J. Selke Trophy (2001)

Signed as a free agent by **New Jersey**, June 26, 1997. Signed as a free agent by **HIFK Helsinki** (Finland), November 29, 2004. Signed as a free agent by **Chicago**, July 2, 2009. Signed as a free agent by **Minnesota**, August 6, 2010.

MAGNAN, Olivier
(MAHG-nan, oh-LIHV-ee-ay)

Defense. Shoots left. 6'2", 210 lbs. Born, Sherbrooke, Que., May 1, 1986. New Jersey's 6th choice, 148th overall, in 2006 Entry Draft.

Season	Club	League	GP	G	A	Pts	PIM	PP	SH	GW	S	%	+/-	TF	F%	Min	GP	G	A	Pts	PIM	PP	SH	GW	Min
2002-03	Val-d'Or Foreurs	QMJHL	2	0	0	0	0	....	....	....	....	....	....	....	....	....	....	....	....	....	....	....	....	....	....
2003-04	Rouyn-Noranda	QMJHL	69	1	8	9	67	....	....	....	....	....	....	....	....	....	11	0	2	2	6	....	....	....	....
2004-05	Rouyn-Noranda	QMJHL	70	5	15	20	82	....	....	....	....	....	....	....	....	....	10	0	2	2	14	....	....	....	....
2005-06	Rouyn-Noranda	QMJHL	69	14	27	41	97	....	....	....	....	....	....	....	....	....	5	0	1	1	6	....	....	....	....
2006-07	Lowell Devils	AHL	24	1	1	2	13	....	....	....	....	....	....	....	....	....	....	....	....	....	....	....	....	....	....
	Trenton Titans	ECHL	45	1	9	10	63	....	....	....	....	....	....	....	....	....	1	0	0	0	0	....	....	....	....
2007-08	Lowell Devils	AHL	75	1	15	16	69	....	....	....	....	....	....	....	....	....	....	....	....	....	....	....	....	....	....
2008-09	Lowell Devils	AHL	76	2	8	10	66	....	....	....	....	....	....	....	....	....	....	....	....	....	....	....	....	....	....
2009-10	Lowell Devils	AHL	71	3	16	19	68	....	....	....	....	....	....	....	....	....	5	0	0	0	4	....	....	....	....
2010-11	**New Jersey**	**NHL**	**18**	**0**	**0**	**0**	**4**	**0**	**0**	**0**	**8**	**0.0**	**–4**	**1**	**0.0**	**15:43**	....	....	....	....	....	....	....	....	....
	Albany Devils	AHL	50	2	11	13	35	....	....	....	....	....	....	....	....	....	....	....	....	....	....	....	....	....	....
	NHL Totals		**18**	**0**	**0**	**0**	**4**	**0**	**0**	**0**	**8**	**0.0**		**1**	**0.0**	**15:43**	....	....	....	....	....	....	....	....	....

Signed as a free agent by **Minsk** (Russia-KHL), July 22, 2011.

MAIR, Adam
(MAIR, A-duhm)

Center. Shoots right. 6'1", 208 lbs. Born, Hamilton, Ont., February 15, 1979. Toronto's 2nd choice, 84th overall, in 1997 Entry Draft.

			Regular Season														Playoffs								
Season	Club	League	GP	G	A	Pts	PIM	PP	SH	GW	S	%	+/-	TF	F%	Min	GP	G	A	Pts	PIM	PP	SH	GW	Min
1994-95	Ohsweken	ON-Jr.B	39	21	23	44	91	....	....	....	....	....	....	....	....	....	....	....	....	....	....	....	....	....	....
1995-96	Owen Sound	OHL	62	12	15	27	63	....	....	....	....	....	....	....	....	....	6	0	0	0	2	....	....	....	....
1996-97	Owen Sound	OHL	65	16	35	51	113	....	....	....	....	....	....	....	....	....	4	1	0	1	2	....	....	....	....
1997-98	Owen Sound	OHL	56	25	27	52	179	....	....	....	....	....	....	....	....	....	11	6	3	9	31	....	....	....	....
1998-99	Owen Sound	OHL	43	23	41	64	109	....	....	....	....	....	....	....	....	....	16	10	10	20	*47	....	....	....	....
	Toronto	NHL	....	....	....	....	....	....	....	....	....	....	....	....	....	....	5	1	0	1	14	0	0	0	5:37
	St. John's	AHL	....	....	....	....	....	....	....	....	....	....	....	....	....	....	3	1	0	1	6	....	....	....	....
99-2000	Toronto	NHL	8	1	0	1	6	0	0	0	7	14.3	-1	9	33.3	11:33	5	0	0	0	8	0	0	0	10:15
	St. John's	AHL	66	22	27	49	124	....	....	....	....	....	....	....	....	....	....	....	....	....	....	....	....	....	....
2000-01	Toronto	NHL	16	0	2	2	14	0	0	0	17	0.0	3	56	51.8	9:01	....	....	....	....	....	....	....	....	....
	St. John's	AHL	47	18	27	45	69	....	....	....	....	....	....	....	....	....	....	....	....	....	....	....	....	....	....
	Los Angeles	NHL	10	0	0	0	6	0	0	0	5	0.0	-3	21	61.9	6:14	....	....	....	....	....	....	....	....	....
2001-02	Los Angeles	NHL	18	1	1	2	57	0	0	0	10	10.0	1	31	58.1	7:11	....	....	....	....	....	....	....	....	....
	Manchester	AHL	27	10	9	19	48	....	....	....	....	....	....	....	....	....	5	5	1	6	10	....	....	....	....
2002-03	Buffalo	NHL	79	6	11	17	146	0	1	1	83	7.2	-4	572	51.2	10:37	....	....	....	....	....	....	....	....	....
2003-04	Buffalo	NHL	81	6	14	20	146	1	0	1	82	7.3	-3	340	45.9	9:38	....	....	....	....	....	....	....	....	....
2004-05			DID NOT PLAY																						
2005-06	Buffalo	NHL	40	2	5	7	47	0	0	0	40	5.0	-2	12	41.7	7:59	3	0	0	0	0	0	0	0	9:17
2006-07	Buffalo	NHL	82	2	9	11	128	0	0	0	73	2.7	-1	130	46.2	7:33	16	1	4	5	10	0	0	0	7:33
2007-08	Buffalo	NHL	72	5	12	17	66	0	0	2	62	8.1	-2	361	45.4	8:52	....	....	....	....	....	....	....	....	....
2008-09	Buffalo	NHL	75	8	11	19	95	0	0	1	75	10.7	4	414	48.3	10:35	....	....	....	....	....	....	....	....	....
2009-10	Buffalo	NHL	69	6	8	14	73	0	0	0	67	9.0	-2	178	52.3	9:14	6	1	1	2	4	0	0	0	12:01
2010-11	New Jersey	NHL	65	1	3	4	45	0	0	0	58	1.7	-16	112	50.9	9:06	....	....	....	....	....	....	....	....	....
	NHL Totals		615	38	76	114	829	1	1	5	579	6.6		2236	48.8	9:11	35	3	5	8	36	0	0	0	8:34

Traded to **Los Angeles** by **Toronto** with Toronto's 2nd round choice (Michael Cammalleri) in 2001 Entry Draft for Aki Berg, March 13, 2001. Traded to **Buffalo** by **Los Angeles** with Los Angeles' 5th round choice (Thomas Morrow) in 2003 Entry Draft for Erik Rasmussen, July 24, 2002. • Missed majority of 2005-06 season due to groin (training camp) and head (January 12, 2006 vs. Phoenix) injuries. Signed as a free agent by **New Jersey**, October 12, 2010.

MALHOTRA, Manny
(mal-HOH-truh, MAN-ee) **VAN**

Center. Shoots left. 6'2", 208 lbs. Born, Mississauga, Ont., May 18, 1980. NY Rangers' 1st choice, 7th overall, in 1998 Entry Draft.

			Regular Season														Playoffs								
Season	Club	League	GP	G	A	Pts	PIM	PP	SH	GW	S	%	+/-	TF	F%	Min	GP	G	A	Pts	PIM	PP	SH	GW	Min
1995-96	Mississauga Reps	MTHL	54	27	44	71	62	....	....	....	....	....	....	....	....	....	....	....	....	....	....	....	....	....	....
1996-97	Guelph Storm	OHL	61	16	28	44	26	....	....	....	....	....	....	....	....	....	18	7	7	14	11	....	....	....	....
1997-98	Guelph Storm	OHL	57	16	35	51	29	....	....	....	....	....	....	....	....	....	12	7	6	13	8	....	....	....	....
1998-99	NY Rangers	NHL	73	8	8	16	13	1	0	2	61	13.1	-2	588	43.9	8:36	....	....	....	....	....	....	....	....	....
99-2000	NY Rangers	NHL	27	0	0	0	4	0	0	0	18	0.0	-6	132	44.7	6:42	....	....	....	....	....	....	....	....	....
	Guelph Storm	OHL	5	2	2	4	4	....	....	....	....	....	....	....	....	....	6	0	2	2	4	....	....	....	....
	Hartford	AHL	12	1	5	6	2	....	....	....	....	....	....	....	....	....	23	1	2	3	10	....	....	....	....
2000-01	NY Rangers	NHL	50	4	8	12	31	0	0	2	46	8.7	-10	248	44.4	9:03	....	....	....	....	....	....	....	....	....
	Hartford	AHL	28	5	6	11	69	....	....	....	....	....	....	....	....	....	5	0	0	0	0	....	....	....	....
2001-02	NY Rangers	NHL	56	7	6	13	42	0	1	1	41	17.1	-1	310	42.9	10:14	....	....	....	....	....	....	....	....	....
	Dallas	NHL	16	1	0	1	5	0	0	0	19	5.3	-3	121	48.8	10:37	....	....	....	....	....	....	....	....	....
2002-03	Dallas	NHL	59	3	7	10	42	0	0	1	62	4.8	-2	447	47.0	9:22	5	1	0	1	0	0	0	0	8:13
2003-04	Dallas	NHL	9	0	0	0	4	0	0	0	4	0.0	-2	13	61.5	7:48	....	....	....	....	....	....	....	....	....
	Columbus	NHL	56	12	13	25	24	1	0	2	103	11.7	-5	840	53.8	14:47	....	....	....	....	....	....	....	....	....
2004-05	Ljubljana	Slovenia	13	6	7	13	20	....	....	....	....	....	....	....	....	....	....	....	....	....	....	....	....	....	....
	Ljubljana	Interliga	13	7	7	14	16	....	....	....	....	....	....	....	....	....	....	....	....	....	....	....	....	....	....
	HV 71 Jonkoping	Sweden	20	5	2	7	16	....	....	....	....	....	....	....	....	....	....	....	....	....	....	....	....	....	....
2005-06	Columbus	NHL	58	10	21	31	41	1	1	0	102	9.8	1	827	56.4	16:21	....	....	....	....	....	....	....	....	....
2006-07	Columbus	NHL	82	9	16	25	76	2	0	3	109	8.3	-8	1127	55.1	14:48	....	....	....	....	....	....	....	....	....
2007-08	Columbus	NHL	71	11	18	29	34	2	0	2	112	9.8	-3	1158	59.0	16:28	....	....	....	....	....	....	....	....	....
2008-09	Columbus	NHL	77	11	24	35	28	0	0	3	116	9.5	9	1380	58.0	18:01	4	0	0	0	0	0	0	0	17:54
2009-10	San Jose	NHL	71	14	19	33	41	2	0	4	111	12.6	17	664	62.5	15:37	15	1	0	1	0	1	0	0	16:55
2010-11	Vancouver	NHL	72	11	19	30	22	3	1	2	111	9.9	9	1261	61.7	16:10	6	0	0	0	0	0	0	0	11:50
	NHL Totals		777	101	159	260	407	12	3	22	1015	10.0		9116	55.4	13:27	30	2	0	2	0	1	0	0	14:35

Memorial Cup All-Star Team (1998) • George Parsons Trophy (Memorial Cup - Most Sportsmanlike Player) (1998)

Traded to **Dallas** by **NY Rangers** with Barrett Heisten for Martin Rucinsky and Roman Lyashenko, March 12, 2002. Claimed on waivers by **Columbus** from **Dallas**, November 21, 2003. Signed as a free agent by **Ljubljana** (Slovenia), October 8, 2004. Signed as a free agent by **Jonkoping** (Sweden), December 20, 2004. Signed as a free agent by **San Jose**, September 23, 2009. Signed as a free agent by **Vancouver**, July 1, 2010.

MALKIN, Evgeni
(MAHL-kihn, ehv-GEH-nee) **PIT**

Center. Shoots left. 6'3", 195 lbs. Born, Magnitogorsk, USSR, July 31, 1986. Pittsburgh's 1st choice, 2nd overall, in 2004 Entry Draft.

			Regular Season														Playoffs								
Season	Club	League	GP	G	A	Pts	PIM	PP	SH	GW	S	%	+/-	TF	F%	Min	GP	G	A	Pts	PIM	PP	SH	GW	Min
2003-04	Magnitogorsk 2	Russia-3	2	1	0	1	8	....	....	....	....	....	....	....	....	....	....	....	....	....	....	....	....	....	....
	Magnitogorsk	Russia	34	3	9	12	12	....	....	....	....	....	....	....	....	....	....	....	....	....	....	....	....	....	....
2004-05	Magnitogorsk 2	Russia-3	2	1	1	2	2	....	....	....	....	....	....	....	....	....	....	....	....	....	....	....	....	....	....
	Magnitogorsk	Russia	52	12	20	32	24	....	....	....	....	....	....	....	....	....	5	0	4	4	0	....	....	....	....
2005-06	Magnitogorsk	Russia	46	21	26	47	46	....	....	....	....	....	....	....	....	....	11	5	10	15	41	....	....	....	....
	Russia	Olympics	7	2	4	6	31	....	....	....	....	....	....	....	....	....	....	....	....	....	....	....	....	....	....
2006-07	Pittsburgh	NHL	78	33	52	85	80	16	0	6	242	13.6	2	728	43.3	19:10	5	0	4	4	8	0	0	0	19:34
2007-08	Pittsburgh	NHL	82	47	59	106	78	17	0	5	272	17.3	16	890	39.3	21:19	20	10	12	22	24	5	1	3	20:48
2008-09♦	Pittsburgh	NHL	82	35	*78	*113	80	14	2	4	290	12.1	17	668	42.4	22:31	24	14	*22	*36	51	*7	0	*3	20:57
2009-10	Pittsburgh	NHL	67	28	49	77	100	13	2	7	268	10.4	-6	498	40.0	20:51	13	5	6	11	6	4	0	1	21:54
	Russia	Olympics	4	3	3	6	0	....	....	....	....	....	....	....	....	....	....	....	....	....	....	....	....	....	....
2010-11	Pittsburgh	NHL	43	15	22	37	18	5	0	3	182	8.2	-4	200	38.5	19:49	....	....	....	....	....	....	....	....	....
	NHL Totals		352	158	260	418	356	65	4	25	1254	12.6		2984	41.0	20:51	62	29	44	73	89	16	1	7	20:59

NHL All-Rookie Team (2007) • Calder Memorial Trophy (2007) • NHL First All-Star Team (2008, 2009) • Art Ross Trophy (2009) • Conn Smythe Trophy (2009)

Played in NHL All-Star Game (2008, 2009)

MALONE, Ryan
(MA-lohn, RIGH-uhn) **T.B.**

Left wing. Shoots left. 6'4", 219 lbs. Born, Pittsburgh, PA, December 1, 1979. Pittsburgh's 5th choice, 115th overall, in 1999 Entry Draft.

			Regular Season														Playoffs								
Season	Club	League	GP	G	A	Pts	PIM	PP	SH	GW	S	%	+/-	TF	F%	Min	GP	G	A	Pts	PIM	PP	SH	GW	Min
1997-98	Shat.-St. Mary's	High-MN	50	41	44	85	69	....	....	....	....	....	....	....	....	....	....	....	....	....	....	....	....	....	....
1998-99	Omaha Lancers	USHL	51	14	22	36	81	....	....	....	....	....	....	....	....	....	12	2	4	6	23	....	....	....	....
99-2000	St. Cloud State	WCHA	38	9	21	30	68	....	....	....	....	....	....	....	....	....	....	....	....	....	....	....	....	....	....
2000-01	St. Cloud State	WCHA	36	7	18	25	52	....	....	....	....	....	....	....	....	....	....	....	....	....	....	....	....	....	....
2001-02	St. Cloud State	WCHA	41	24	25	49	76	....	....	....	....	....	....	....	....	....	....	....	....	....	....	....	....	....	....
2002-03	St. Cloud State	WCHA	27	16	20	36	85	....	....	....	....	....	....	....	....	....	....	....	....	....	....	....	....	....	....
	Wilkes-Barre	AHL	3	0	1	1	2	....	....	....	....	....	....	....	....	....	....	....	....	....	....	....	....	....	....
2003-04	Pittsburgh	NHL	81	22	21	43	64	5	3	4	139	15.8	-23	230	27.4	18:54	....	....	....	....	....	....	....	....	....
2004-05	Blues Espoo	Finland	9	2	1	3	36	....	....	....	....	....	....	....	....	....	....	....	....	....	....	....	....	....	....
	SV Renon	Italy	10	6	2	8	20	....	....	....	....	....	....	....	....	....	6	4	4	8	36	....	....	....	....
	HC Ambri-Piotta	Swiss	....	....	....	....	....	....	....	....	....	....	....	....	....	....	1	0	0	0	2	....	....	....	....
2005-06	Pittsburgh	NHL	77	22	22	44	63	10	5	1	153	14.4	-22	728	39.6	18:06	....	....	....	....	....	....	....	....	....
2006-07	Pittsburgh	NHL	64	16	15	31	71	1	1	0	125	12.8	4	109	44.0	16:15	5	0	0	0	0	0	0	0	13:48
2007-08	Pittsburgh	NHL	77	27	24	51	103	11	2	6	159	17.0	14	38	31.6	19:05	20	6	10	16	25	3	0	2	18:43
2008-09	Tampa Bay	NHL	70	26	19	45	98	7	0	3	124	21.0	4	47	29.8	17:45	....	....	....	....	....	....	....	....	....
2009-10	Tampa Bay	NHL	69	21	26	47	68	7	0	7	172	12.2	-8	97	39.2	18:46	....	....	....	....	....	....	....	....	....
	United States	Olympics	6	3	2	5	6	....	....	....	....	....	....	....	....	....	....	....	....	....	....	....	....	....	....
2010-11	Tampa Bay	NHL	54	14	24	38	51	9	0	1	149	9.4	-3	143	39.2	16:02	18	3	3	6	24	1	0	1	15:35
	NHL Totals		492	148	151	299	518	50	11	22	1021	14.5		1392	37.3	17:58	43	9	13	22	49	4	0	3	16:50

NHL All-Rookie Team (2004)

Signed as a free agent by **Espoo** (Finland), September 29, 2004. Signed as a free agent by **Renon** (Italy), January 3, 2005. Signed as a free agent by **Ambri-Piotta** (Swiss), February 25, 2005. Traded to **Tampa Bay** by **Pittsburgh** with Gary Roberts for Tampa Bay's 3rd round choice (Ben Hanowski) in 2009 Entry Draft, June 28, 2008.

MANCARI, Mark

(man-KAH-ree, MAHRK) **VAN**

Right wing. Shoots right. 6'3", 225 lbs. Born, London, Ont., July 11, 1985. Buffalo's 6th choice, 207th overall, in 2004 Entry Draft.

			Regular Season														Playoffs								
Season	Club	League	GP	G	A	Pts	PIM	PP	SH	GW	S	%	+/-	TF	F%	Min	GP	G	A	Pts	PIM	PP	SH	GW	Min
2001-02	Ottawa 67's	OHL	34	3	3	6	10										2	0	1	1	0				
2002-03	Ottawa 67's	OHL	61	8	11	19	20										11	2	1	3	2				
2003-04	Ottawa 67's	OHL	67	29	36	65	56										7	5	3	8	11				
2004-05	Ottawa 67's	OHL	64	36	32	68	86										21	*14	10	24	24				
2005-06	Rochester	AHL	71	18	24	42	80																		
2006-07	**Buffalo**	**NHL**	**3**	**0**	**1**	**1**	**2**	**0**	**0**	**0**	**1**	**0.0**	**–1**	**0**	**0.0**	**6:12**									
	Rochester	AHL	64	23	34	57	49										6	1	5	6	6				
2007-08	Rochester	AHL	80	21	36	57	78																		
2008-09	**Buffalo**	**NHL**	**7**	**1**	**1**	**2**	**4**	**0**	**0**	**0**	**21**	**4.8**	**–4**	**7**	**57.1**	**13:16**									
	Portland Pirates	AHL	73	29	38	67	61										5	1	2	3	2				
2009-10	**Buffalo**	**NHL**	**6**	**1**	**1**	**2**	**4**	**0**	**0**	**0**	**19**	**5.3**	**3**	**3**	**0.0**	**14:04**									
	Portland Pirates	AHL	74	28	46	74	55										4	1	1	2	2				
2010-11	**Buffalo**	**NHL**	**20**	**1**	**7**	**8**	**12**	**1**	**0**	**0**	**43**	**2.3**	**–1**	**6**	**50.0**	**12:19**	**1**	**0**	**0**	**0**	**0**	**0**	**0**	**0**	**9:50**
	Portland Pirates	AHL	56	32	32	64	57										9	6	6	12	0				
	NHL Totals		**36**	**3**	**10**	**13**	**22**	**1**	**0**	**0**	**84**	**3.6**		**16**	**43.8**	**12:17**	**1**	**0**	**0**	**0**	**0**	**0**	**0**	**0**	**9:50**

AHL First All-Star Team (2011)

Signed as a free agent by **Vancouver**, July 1, 2011.

MARA, Paul

(MAIR-uh, PAWL)

Defense. Shoots left. 6'4", 207 lbs. Born, Ridgewood, NJ, September 7, 1979. Tampa Bay's 1st choice, 7th overall, in 1997 Entry Draft.

Season	Club	League	GP	G	A	Pts	PIM	PP	SH	GW	S	%	+/-	TF	F%	Min	GP	G	A	Pts	PIM	PP	SH	GW	Min
1994-95	Belmont Hill	High-MA	28	5	17	22	28																		
1995-96	Belmont Hill	High-MA	28	18	20	38	40																		
1996-97	Sudbury Wolves	OHL	44	9	34	43	61																		
1997-98	Sudbury Wolves	OHL	25	8	18	26	79																		
	Plymouth Whalers	OHL	25	8	15	23	30										15	3	14	17	30				
1998-99	Plymouth Whalers	OHL	52	13	41	54	95										11	5	7	12	28				
	Tampa Bay	**NHL**	**1**	**1**	**1**	**2**	**0**	**1**	**0**	**0**	**1**	**100.0**	**–3**	**0**	**0.0**	**19:34**									
99-2000	**Tampa Bay**	**NHL**	**54**	**7**	**11**	**18**	**73**	**4**	**0**	**1**	**78**	**9.0**	**–27**	**0**	**0.0**	**22:13**									
	Detroit Vipers	IHL	15	3	5	8	22																		
2000-01	**Tampa Bay**	**NHL**	**46**	**6**	**10**	**16**	**40**	**2**	**0**	**1**	**58**	**10.3**	**–17**	**0**	**0.0**	**23:06**									
	Detroit Vipers	IHL	10	3	3	6	22																		
	Phoenix	**NHL**	**16**	**0**	**4**	**4**	**14**	**0**	**0**	**0**	**20**	**0.0**	**1**	**0**	**0.0**	**19:22**									
2001-02	**Phoenix**	**NHL**	**75**	**7**	**17**	**24**	**58**	**2**	**0**	**0**	**112**	**6.3**	**–6**	**2**	**100.0**	**21:34**	**5**	**0**	**0**	**0**	**4**	**0**	**0**	**0**	**22:57**
2002-03	**Phoenix**	**NHL**	**73**	**10**	**15**	**25**	**78**	**1**	**0**	**0**	**95**	**10.5**	**–7**	**1**	**0.0**	**21:06**									
2003-04	**Phoenix**	**NHL**	**81**	**6**	**36**	**42**	**48**	**1**	**0**	**0**	**140**	**4.3**	**–11**	**2**	**0.0**	**23:37**									
2004-05	Hannover	Germany	35	5	13	18	89																		
2005-06	**Phoenix**	**NHL**	**78**	**15**	**32**	**47**	**70**	**8**	**0**	**0**	**157**	**9.6**	**–12**	**1**	**0.0**	**21:29**									
2006-07	**Boston**	**NHL**	**59**	**3**	**15**	**18**	**95**	**0**	**0**	**0**	**60**	**5.0**	**–22**	**0**	**0.0**	**21:53**									
	NY Rangers	**NHL**	**19**	**2**	**3**	**5**	**18**	**1**	**0**	**0**	**40**	**5.0**	**6**	**0**	**0.0**	**22:56**	**10**	**2**	**2**	**4**	**18**	**2**	**0**	**0**	**19:43**
2007-08	**NY Rangers**	**NHL**	**61**	**1**	**16**	**17**	**52**	**0**	**0**	**0**	**80**	**1.3**	**1**	**1**	**0.0**	**17:53**	**10**	**0**	**1**	**1**	**20**	**0**	**0**	**0**	**17:48**
2008-09	**NY Rangers**	**NHL**	**76**	**5**	**16**	**21**	**94**	**1**	**0**	**0**	**102**	**4.9**	**2**	**2**	**50.0**	**18:58**	**7**	**1**	**1**	**2**	**8**	**0**	**0**	**0**	**14:43**
2009-10	**Montreal**	**NHL**	**42**	**0**	**8**	**8**	**48**	**0**	**0**	**0**	**30**	**0.0**	**–16**	**0**	**0.0**	**18:44**									
2010-11	**Anaheim**	**NHL**	**33**	**1**	**1**	**2**	**40**	**0**	**0**	**1**	**34**	**2.9**	**–1**	**0**	**0.0**	**20:10**									
	Montreal	**NHL**	**20**	**0**	**4**	**4**	**48**	**0**	**0**	**0**	**16**	**0.0**	**2**	**0**	**0.0**	**15:09**	**1**	**0**	**0**	**0**	**0**	**0**	**0**	**0**	**13:11**
	NHL Totals		**734**	**64**	**189**	**253**	**776**	**21**	**0**	**3**	**1023**	**6.3**		**9**	**33.3**	**20:55**	**33**	**3**	**4**	**7**	**50**	**2**	**0**	**0**	**18:22**

Traded to **Phoenix** by **Tampa Bay** with Mike Johnson, Ruslan Zainullin and NY Islanders' 2nd round choice (previously acquired, Phoenix selected Matthew Spiller) in 2001 Entry Draft for Nikolai Khabibulin and Stan Neckar, March 5, 2001. Signed as a free agent by **Hannover** (Germany), October 29, 2004. Traded to **Boston** by **Phoenix** with Phoenix's 3rd round choice (later traded to Anaheim - Anaheim selected Maxime Macenauer) in 2007 Entry Draft for Nick Boynton and Boston's 4th round choice (later traded to Toronto - Toronto selected Matt Frattin) in 2007 Entry Draft, June 26, 2006. Traded to **NY Rangers** by **Boston** for Aaron Ward, February 27, 2007. Signed as a free agent by **Montreal**, July 10, 2009. Signed as a free agent by **Anaheim**, September 16, 2010. Traded to **Montreal** by **Anaheim** for Anaheim's 5th round choice (previously acquired) in 2012 Entry Draft, February 17, 2011.

MARCHAND, Brad

(mahr-SHAND, BRAD) **BOS**

Center. Shoots left. 5'9", 183 lbs. Born, Halifax, N.S., May 11, 1988. Boston's 4th choice, 71st overall, in 2006 Entry Draft.

Season	Club	League	GP	G	A	Pts	PIM	PP	SH	GW	S	%	+/-	TF	F%	Min	GP	G	A	Pts	PIM	PP	SH	GW	Min
2003-04	Dartmouth	NSMHL	60	47	47	94	104																		
2004-05	Moncton Wildcats	QMJHL	61	9	20	29	52										11	1	0	1	7				
2005-06	Moncton Wildcats	QMJHL	68	29	37	66	83										20	5	14	19	34				
2006-07	Val-d'Or Foreurs	QMJHL	57	33	47	80	108										20	*16	*24	*40	36				
2007-08	Val-d'Or Foreurs	QMJHL	33	21	23	44	36																		
	Halifax	QMJHL	26	10	19	29	40										14	3	16	19	18				
2008-09	Providence Bruins	AHL	79	18	41	59	67										16	7	8	15	26				
2009-10	**Boston**	**NHL**	**20**	**0**	**1**	**1**	**20**	**0**	**0**	**0**	**32**	**0.0**	**–3**	**11**	**27.3**	**11:58**									
	Providence Bruins	AHL	34	13	19	32	51																		
2010-11♦	**Boston**	**NHL**	**77**	**21**	**20**	**41**	**51**	**2**	**5**	**2**	**149**	**14.1**	**25**	**25**	**32.0**	**13:59**	**25**	**11**	**8**	**19**	**40**	**0**	**1**	**1**	**16:46**
	NHL Totals		**97**	**21**	**21**	**42**	**71**	**2**	**5**	**2**	**181**	**11.6**		**36**	**30.6**	**13:34**	**25**	**11**	**8**	**19**	**40**	**0**	**1**	**1**	**16:46**

MARCHANT, Todd

(mahr-SHAHNT, TAWD)

Center. Shoots left. 5'10", 179 lbs. Born, Buffalo, NY, August 12, 1973. NY Rangers' 8th choice, 164th overall, in 1993 Entry Draft.

Season	Club	League	GP	G	A	Pts	PIM	PP	SH	GW	S	%	+/-	TF	F%	Min	GP	G	A	Pts	PIM	PP	SH	GW	Min
1990-91	Niagara Scenics	NAHL	37	31	47	78																			
1991-92	Clarkson Knights	ECAC	32	20	12	32	32																		
1992-93	Clarkson Knights	ECAC	33	18	28	46	38																		
1993-94	United States	Nat-Tm	59	28	39	67	48																		
	United States	Olympics	8	1	1	2	6																		
	NY Rangers	**NHL**	**1**	**0**	**0**	**0**	**0**	**0**	**0**	**0**	**1**	**0.0**	**–1**												
	Binghamton	AHL	8	2	7	9	6																		
	Edmonton	**NHL**	**3**	**0**	**1**	**1**	**2**	**0**	**0**	**0**	**5**	**0.0**	**–1**												
	Cape Breton	AHL	3	1	4	5	2										5	1	1	2	0				
1994-95	Cape Breton	AHL	38	22	25	47	25																		
	Edmonton	**NHL**	**45**	**13**	**14**	**27**	**32**	**3**	**2**	**2**	**95**	**13.7**	**–3**												
1995-96	**Edmonton**	**NHL**	**81**	**19**	**19**	**38**	**66**	**2**	**3**	**2**	**221**	**8.6**	**–19**												
1996-97	**Edmonton**	**NHL**	**79**	**14**	**19**	**33**	**44**	**0**	**4**	**3**	**202**	**6.9**	**11**				**12**	**4**	**2**	**6**	**12**	**0**	***3**	**1**	
1997-98	**Edmonton**	**NHL**	**76**	**14**	**21**	**35**	**71**	**2**	**1**	**3**	**194**	**7.2**	**9**				**12**	**1**	**1**	**2**	**10**	**0**	**0**	**0**	
1998-99	**Edmonton**	**NHL**	**82**	**14**	**22**	**36**	**65**	**3**	**1**	**2**	**183**	**7.7**	**3**	**1449**	**50.0**	**16:47**	**4**	**1**	**1**	**2**	**12**	**0**	**0**	**0**	**24:21**
99-2000	**Edmonton**	**NHL**	**82**	**17**	**23**	**40**	**70**	**0**	**1**	**0**	**170**	**10.0**	**7**	**1593**	**52.9**	**17:08**	**3**	**1**	**0**	**1**	**2**	**0**	**0**	**0**	**18:07**
2000-01	**Edmonton**	**NHL**	**71**	**13**	**26**	**39**	**51**	**0**	**4**	**2**	**113**	**11.5**	**1**	**1549**	**53.8**	**17:54**	**6**	**0**	**0**	**0**	**4**	**0**	**0**	**0**	**22:57**
2001-02	**Edmonton**	**NHL**	**82**	**12**	**22**	**34**	**41**	**0**	**3**	**1**	**124**	**9.7**	**7**	**1523**	**52.4**	**16:58**									
2002-03	**Edmonton**	**NHL**	**77**	**20**	**40**	**60**	**48**	**7**	**1**	**3**	**146**	**13.7**	**13**	**1336**	**58.0**	**19:54**	**6**	**0**	**2**	**2**	**2**	**0**	**0**	**0**	**20:03**
2003-04	**Columbus**	**NHL**	**77**	**9**	**25**	**34**	**34**	**4**	**0**	**2**	**163**	**5.5**	**–17**	**1412**	**50.9**	**20:39**									
2004-05			DID NOT PLAY																						
2005-06	**Columbus**	**NHL**	**18**	**3**	**6**	**9**	**20**	**0**	**0**	**0**	**42**	**7.1**	**–1**	**289**	**50.2**	**20:05**									
	Anaheim	**NHL**	**61**	**6**	**19**	**25**	**46**	**0**	**0**	**0**	**90**	**6.7**	**3**	**743**	**51.7**	**16:25**	**16**	**3**	**10**	**13**	**14**	**0**	**0**	**0**	**17:34**
2006-07♦	**Anaheim**	**NHL**	**56**	**8**	**15**	**23**	**44**	**0**	**3**	**2**	**115**	**7.0**	**7**	**647**	**54.3**	**15:10**	**11**	**0**	**3**	**3**	**12**	**0**	**0**	**0**	**15:44**
2007-08	**Anaheim**	**NHL**	**75**	**9**	**7**	**16**	**48**	**0**	**0**	**0**	**93**	**9.7**	**–3**	**673**	**49.2**	**14:49**	**6**	**2**	**0**	**2**	**0**	**0**	**0**	**0**	**17:40**
2008-09	**Anaheim**	**NHL**	**72**	**5**	**13**	**18**	**34**	**0**	**2**	**0**	**101**	**5.0**	**–2**	**593**	**50.3**	**14:32**	**13**	**1**	**1**	**2**	**16**	**0**	**0**	**1**	**19:56**
2009-10	**Anaheim**	**NHL**	**78**	**9**	**13**	**22**	**32**	**0**	**3**	**1**	**83**	**10.8**	**–16**	**569**	**49.9**	**15:49**									
2010-11	**Anaheim**	**NHL**	**79**	**1**	**7**	**8**	**26**	**0**	**0**	**0**	**63**	**1.6**	**–18**	**548**	**48.0**	**13:17**	**6**	**0**	**1**	**1**	**4**	**0**	**0**	**0**	**14:22**
	NHL Totals		**1195**	**186**	**312**	**498**	**774**	**21**	**28**	**23**	**2204**	**8.4**		**12924**	**52.2**	**16:43**	**95**	**13**	**21**	**34**	**88**	**0**	**3**	**2**	**18:31**

ECAC Second All-Star Team (1993)

Traded to **Edmonton** by **NY Rangers** for Craig MacTavish, March 21, 1994. Signed as a free agent by **Columbus**, July 3, 2003. Claimed on waivers by **Anaheim** from **Columbus**, November 21, 2005.

MARKOV, Andrei

(MAHR-kahf, AHN-dray) **MTL**

Defense. Shoots left. 6', 207 lbs. Born, Voskresensk, USSR, December 20, 1978. Montreal's 6th choice, 162nd overall, in 1998 Entry Draft.

			Regular Season														Playoffs								
Season	Club	League	GP	G	A	Pts	PIM	PP	SH	GW	S	%	+/-	TF	F%	Min	GP	G	A	Pts	PIM	PP	SH	GW	Min
1995-96	Voskresensk	CIS	38	0	0	0	14	....	....	....	....	....	....	....	....	....	....	....	....	....	....	....	....	....	....
1996-97	Voskresensk	Russia	43	8	4	12	32	....	....	....	....	....	....	....	....	....	2	1	1	2	0	....	....	....	....
1997-98	Voskresensk	Russia	43	10	5	15	83	....	....	....	....	....	....	....	....	....	....	....	....	....	....	....	....	....	....
1998-99	Dynamo Moscow	Russia	38	10	11	21	32	....	....	....	....	....	....	....	....	....	16	3	6	9	6	....	....	....	....
	Dynamo Moscow	EuroHL	12	7	5	12	12	....	....	....	....	....	....	....	....	....	6	2	2	4	4	....	....	....	....
99-2000	Dynamo Moscow	Russia	29	11	12	23	28	....	....	....	....	....	....	....	....	....	17	4	3	7	8	....	....	....	....
2000-01	Montreal	NHL	63	6	17	23	18	2	0	0	82	7.3	-6	2	50.0	16:53	....	....	....	....	....	....	....	....	....
	Quebec Citadelles	AHL	14	0	5	5	4	....	....	....	....	....	....	....	....	....	7	1	1	2	2	....	....	....	....
2001-02	Montreal	NHL	56	5	19	24	24	2	0	1	73	6.8	-1	0	0.0	17:15	12	1	3	4	8	0	0	1	15:53
	Quebec Citadelles	AHL	12	4	6	10	7	....	....	....	....	....	....	....	....	....	....	....	....	....	....	....	....	....	....
2002-03	Montreal	NHL	79	13	24	37	34	3	0	2	159	8.2	13	1	0.0	23:17	....	....	....	....	....	....	....	....	....
2003-04	Montreal	NHL	69	6	22	28	20	2	0	0	105	5.7	-2	2	50.0	21:29	11	1	4	5	8	0	0	1	22:52
2004-05	Dynamo Moscow	Russia	42	7	16	23	76	....	....	....	....	....	....	....	....	....	10	2	0	2	22	....	....	....	....
2005-06	Montreal	NHL	67	10	36	46	74	6	1	1	88	11.4	13	1	0.0	23:33	6	0	1	1	4	0	0	0	25:29
	Russia	Olympics	8	1	2	3	6	....	....	....	....	....	....	....	....	....	....	....	....	....	....	....	....	....	....
2006-07	Montreal	NHL	77	6	43	49	56	5	0	2	128	4.7	2	1	0.0	24:29	....	....	....	....	....	....	....	....	....
2007-08	Montreal	NHL	82	16	42	58	63	10	1	2	145	11.0	1	0	0.0	24:58	12	1	3	4	8	0	0	0	24:54
2008-09	Montreal	NHL	78	12	52	64	36	7	0	3	165	7.3	-2	0	0.0	24:38	....	....	....	....	....	....	....	....	....
2009-10	Montreal	NHL	45	6	28	34	32	4	0	1	85	7.1	11	0	0.0	23:48	8	0	4	4	0	0	0	0	23:47
	Russia	Olympics	4	0	2	2	0	....	....	....	....	....	....	....	....	....	....	....	....	....	....	....	....	....	....
2010-11	Montreal	NHL	7	1	2	3	4	0	0	1	20	5.0	2	0	0.0	22:55	....	....	....	....	....	....	....	....	....
	NHL Totals		623	81	285	366	361	41	2	13	1050	7.7		7	28.6	22:30	49	3	15	18	28	0	0	2	22:07

Played in NHL All-Star Game (2008, 2009)

Signed as a free agent by **Dynamo Moscow** (Russia), June 19, 2004. • Missed majority of 2010-11 due to knee injury vs. Carolina, November 13, 2010.

MARLEAU, Patrick

(mahr-LOH, PAT-rihk) **S.J.**

Center. Shoots left. 6'2", 220 lbs. Born, Aneroid, Sask., September 15, 1979. San Jose's 1st choice, 2nd overall, in 1997 Entry Draft.

			Regular Season														Playoffs								
Season	Club	League	GP	G	A	Pts	PIM	PP	SH	GW	S	%	+/-	TF	F%	Min	GP	G	A	Pts	PIM	PP	SH	GW	Min
1993-94	Swift Current	SMHL	53	72	95	167	....	....	....	....	....	....	....	....	....	....	....	....	....	....	....	....	....	....	....
1994-95	Swift Current	SMHL	31	30	22	52	18	....	....	....	....	....	....	....	....	....	....	....	....	....	....	....	....	....	....
1995-96	Seattle	WHL	72	32	42	74	22	....	....	....	....	....	....	....	....	....	5	3	4	7	4	....	....	....	....
1996-97	Seattle	WHL	71	51	74	125	37	....	....	....	....	....	....	....	....	....	15	7	16	23	12	....	....	....	....
1997-98	San Jose	NHL	74	13	19	32	14	1	0	2	90	14.4	5	....	....	....	5	0	1	1	0	0	0	0	....
1998-99	San Jose	NHL	81	21	24	45	24	4	0	4	134	15.7	10	1121	43.4	15:11	6	2	1	3	4	2	0	0	11:08
99-2000	San Jose	NHL	81	17	23	40	36	3	0	3	161	10.6	-9	851	42.0	14:11	5	1	1	2	2	1	0	0	11:51
2000-01	San Jose	NHL	81	25	27	52	22	5	0	6	146	17.1	7	1088	44.8	16:17	6	2	0	2	4	0	0	0	14:50
2001-02	San Jose	NHL	79	21	23	44	40	3	0	5	121	17.4	9	897	47.3	14:04	12	6	5	11	6	1	0	3	15:50
2002-03	San Jose	NHL	82	28	29	57	33	8	1	3	172	16.3	-10	1403	47.3	18:31	....	....	....	....	....	....	....	....	....
2003-04	San Jose	NHL	80	28	29	57	24	9	0	5	220	12.7	-5	1014	41.6	18:12	17	8	4	12	6	4	1	2	19:16
2004-05			DID NOT PLAY																						
2005-06	San Jose	NHL	82	34	52	86	26	20	1	4	260	13.1	-12	1216	46.8	19:56	11	9	5	14	8	4	0	2	21:07
2006-07	San Jose	NHL	77	32	46	78	33	14	0	9	180	17.8	9	693	50.5	18:34	11	3	3	6	2	1	0	1	18:59
2007-08	San Jose	NHL	78	19	29	48	33	7	0	2	185	10.3	-19	605	52.4	18:14	13	4	4	8	2	0	*2	0	23:04
2008-09	San Jose	NHL	76	38	33	71	18	11	5	10	251	15.1	16	591	52.5	21:21	6	2	1	3	8	1	0	2	20:29
2009-10	San Jose	NHL	82	44	39	83	22	12	4	6	274	16.1	21	615	51.4	21:13	14	8	5	13	8	3	1	2	22:07
	Canada	Olympics	7	2	3	5	0	....	....	....	....	....	....	....	....	....	....	....	....	....	....	....	....	....	....
2010-11	San Jose	NHL	82	37	36	73	16	11	2	9	279	13.3	-3	549	52.5	20:47	18	7	6	13	9	3	0	1	22:21
	NHL Totals		1035	357	409	766	341	108	13	68	2473	14.4		10643	46.9	18:02	124	52	36	88	59	20	4	13	19:24

WHL West First All-Star Team (1997)
Played in NHL All-Star Game (2004, 2007, 2009)

MARTIN, Matt

(MAHR-tihn, MAT) **NYI**

Left wing. Shoots left. 6'3", 210 lbs. Born, Windsor, Ont., May 8, 1989. NY Islanders' 11th choice, 148th overall, in 2008 Entry Draft.

			Regular Season														Playoffs								
Season	Club	League	GP	G	A	Pts	PIM	PP	SH	GW	S	%	+/-	TF	F%	Min	GP	G	A	Pts	PIM	PP	SH	GW	Min
2005-06	Blenheim Blast	ON-Jr.C	40	11	12	23	102	....	....	....	....	....	....	....	....	....	....	....	....	....	....	....	....	....	....
2006-07	Sarnia Blast	ON-Jr.B	9	2	5	7	16	....	....	....	....	....	....	....	....	....	....	....	....	....	....	....	....	....	....
	Sarnia Sting	OHL	39	3	3	6	52	....	....	....	....	....	....	....	....	....	4	0	0	0	0	....	....	....	....
2007-08	Sarnia Sting	OHL	66	25	13	38	155	....	....	....	....	....	....	....	....	....	9	3	3	6	16	....	....	....	....
2008-09	Sarnia Sting	OHL	61	35	30	65	142	....	....	....	....	....	....	....	....	....	5	3	0	3	10	....	....	....	....
2009-10	NY Islanders	NHL	5	0	2	2	26	0	0	0	10	0.0	-1	0	0.0	13:14	....	....	....	....	....	....	....	....	....
	Bridgeport	AHL	76	12	19	31	113	....	....	....	....	....	....	....	....	....	5	1	2	3	4	....	....	....	....
2010-11	NY Islanders	NHL	68	5	9	14	147	0	0	1	60	8.3	-13	27	37.0	10:57	....	....	....	....	....	....	....	....	....
	Bridgeport	AHL	7	1	2	3	11	....	....	....	....	....	....	....	....	....	....	....	....	....	....	....	....	....	....
	NHL Totals		73	5	11	16	173	0	0	1	70	7.1		27	37.0	11:07	....	....	....	....	....	....	....	....	....

MARTIN, Paul

(MAHR-tihn, PAWL) **PIT**

Defense. Shoots left. 6'1", 200 lbs. Born, Minneapolis, MN, March 5, 1981. New Jersey's 5th choice, 62nd overall, in 2000 Entry Draft.

			Regular Season														Playoffs								
Season	Club	League	GP	G	A	Pts	PIM	PP	SH	GW	S	%	+/-	TF	F%	Min	GP	G	A	Pts	PIM	PP	SH	GW	Min
1998-99	Elk River Elks	High-MN	24	9	11	20	....	....	....	....	....	....	....	....	....	....	....	....	....	....	....	....	....	....	....
99-2000	Elk River Elks	High-MN	24	15	35	50	26	....	....	....	....	....	....	....	....	....	....	....	....	....	....	....	....	....	....
2000-01	U. of Minnesota	WCHA	38	3	17	20	8	....	....	....	....	....	....	....	....	....	....	....	....	....	....	....	....	....	....
2001-02	U. of Minnesota	WCHA	44	8	30	38	22	....	....	....	....	....	....	....	....	....	....	....	....	....	....	....	....	....	....
2002-03	U. of Minnesota	WCHA	45	9	30	39	32	....	....	....	....	....	....	....	....	....	....	....	....	....	....	....	....	....	....
2003-04	New Jersey	NHL	70	6	18	24	4	2	0	2	82	7.3	12	0	0.0	20:08	5	1	1	2	4	1	0	0	23:40
2004-05	Fribourg	Swiss	11	3	4	7	2	....	....	....	....	....	....	....	....	....	....	....	....	....	....	....	....	....	....
2005-06	New Jersey	NHL	80	5	32	37	32	3	0	0	97	5.2	1	0	0.0	23:37	9	0	3	3	4	0	0	0	24:17
2006-07	New Jersey	NHL	82	3	23	26	18	1	0	0	84	3.6	-9	0	0.0	25:13	11	0	4	4	6	0	0	0	25:09
2007-08	New Jersey	NHL	73	5	27	32	22	2	0	2	93	5.4	20	0	0.0	23:53	5	1	2	3	2	1	0	0	25:35
2008-09	New Jersey	NHL	73	5	28	33	36	2	0	1	107	4.7	21	0	0.0	24:22	7	0	4	4	2	0	0	0	26:20
2009-10	New Jersey	NHL	22	2	9	11	2	1	0	0	21	9.5	10	0	0.0	22:30	5	0	0	0	0	0	0	0	22:24
2010-11	Pittsburgh	NHL	77	3	21	24	16	2	0	1	104	2.9	9	0	0.0	23:22	7	0	2	2	2	0	0	0	24:42
	NHL Totals		477	29	158	187	130	13	0	6	588	4.9		0	0.0	23:27	49	2	16	18	20	2	0	0	24:42

Minnesota High School Player of the Year (1999) • WCHA All-Rookie Team (2001) • WCHA Second All-Star Team (2002, 2003) • NCAA West Second All-American Team (2003) • NCAA Championship All-Tournament Team (2003)

Signed as a free agent by **Fribourg** (Swiss), November 4, 2004. • Missed majority of 2009-10 due to arm injury at Pittsburgh, October 24, 2009. Signed as a free agent by **Pittsburgh**, July 1, 2010.

MARTINEK, Radek

(MAHR-tee-nihk, RA-dehk) **CBJ**

Defense. Shoots right. 6'2", 210 lbs. Born, Havlicko Brod, Czech., August 31, 1976. NY Islanders' 12th choice, 228th overall, in 1999 Entry Draft.

			Regular Season														Playoffs								
Season	Club	League	GP	G	A	Pts	PIM	PP	SH	GW	S	%	+/-	TF	F%	Min	GP	G	A	Pts	PIM	PP	SH	GW	Min
1996-97	C. Budejovice	CzRep	52	3	5	8	40	....	....	....	....	....	....	....	....	....	5	0	1	1	2	....	....	....	....
	C. Budejovice	EuroHL	6	0	0	0	0	....	....	....	....	....	....	....	....	....	2	0	0	0	0	....	....	....	....
1997-98	C. Budejovice	CzRep	42	2	7	9	36	....	....	....	....	....	....	....	....	....	....	....	....	....	....	....	....	....	....
1998-99	C. Budejovice	CzRep	52	12	13	25	50	....	....	....	....	....	....	....	....	....	3	0	2	2	....	....	....	....	....
99-2000	C. Budejovice	CzRep	45	5	18	23	24	....	....	....	....	....	....	....	....	....	3	0	0	0	6	....	....	....	....
2000-01	C. Budejovice	CzRep	44	8	10	18	45	....	....	....	....	....	....	....	....	....	....	....	....	....	....	....	....	....	....
2001-02	NY Islanders	NHL	23	1	4	5	16	0	0	1	25	4.0	5	0	0.0	21:07	....	....	....	....	....	....	....	....	....
2002-03	NY Islanders	NHL	66	2	11	13	26	0	0	1	67	3.0	15	0	0.0	17:15	4	0	0	0	4	0	0	0	10:16
	Bridgeport	AHL	3	0	3	3	2	....	....	....	....	....	....	....	....	....	....	....	....	....	....	....	....	....	....
2003-04	NY Islanders	NHL	47	4	3	7	43	0	0	1	48	8.3	-9	0	0.0	13:03	5	0	1	1	0	0	0	0	12:12
2004-05	C. Budejovice	CzRep-2	30	12	18	30	80	....	....	....	....	....	....	....	....	....	12	2	3	5	6	....	....	....	....
2005-06	NY Islanders	NHL	74	1	16	17	32	0	0	0	79	1.3	-9	1	0.0	18:16	....	....	....	....	....	....	....	....	....
2006-07	NY Islanders	NHL	43	2	15	17	40	0	0	0	44	4.5	19	1	100.0	19:54	....	....	....	....	....	....	....	....	....
2007-08	NY Islanders	NHL	69	0	15	15	40	0	0	0	98	0.0	-9	0	0.0	22:52	....	....	....	....	....	....	....	....	....
2008-09	NY Islanders	NHL	51	6	4	10	28	1	0	1	54	11.1	-16	0	0.0	21:34	....	....	....	....	....	....	....	....	....

Season	Club	League	GP	G	A	Pts	PIM	PP	SH	GW	S	%	+/-	TF	F%	Min	GP	G	A	Pts	PIM	PP	SH	GW	Min
			Regular Season														Playoffs								
2009-10	**NY Islanders**	**NHL**	**16**	**2**	**1**	**3**	**12**	**0**	**1**	**0**	**24**	**8.3**	**–1**	**0**	**0.0**	**22:48**	....	....	....	....	....	....	....	....	....
2010-11	**NY Islanders**	**NHL**	**64**	**3**	**13**	**16**	**35**	**1**	**0**	**0**	**97**	**3.1**	**–5**	**0**	**0.0**	**20:51**	....	....	....	....	....	....	....	....	....
	NHL Totals		**453**	**21**	**82**	**103**	**272**	**2**	**1**	**4**	**536**	**3.9**		**2**	**50.0**	**19:28**	**9**	**0**	**1**	**1**	**4**	**0**	**0**	**0**	**11:20**

• Missed majority of 2001-02 due to knee injury vs. NY Rangers, November 11, 2001. Signed as a free agent by **Ceske Budejovice** (CzRep-2), September 17, 2004. • Missed majority of 2009-10 due to knee injury at New Jersey, November 7, 2009. Signed as a free agent by **Columbus**, July 6, 2011.

MARTINEZ, Alec

(mar-TEE-nehz, AL-ehk) **L.A.**

Defense. Shoots left. 6', 205 lbs. Born, Rochester Hills, MI, July 26, 1987. Los Angeles' 5th choice, 95th overall, in 2007 Entry Draft.

Season	Club	League	GP	G	A	Pts	PIM	PP	SH	GW	S	%	+/-	TF	F%	Min	GP	G	A	Pts	PIM	PP	SH	GW	Min
2004-05	Cedar Rapids	USHL	58	10	11	21	30	....	....	....	....	....	....	....	....	....	11	1	2	3	8	....	....	....	....
2005-06	Miami U.	CCHA	39	3	8	11	31	....	....	....	....	....	....	....	....	....	....	....	....	....	....	....	....	....	....
2006-07	Miami U.	CCHA	42	9	15	24	40	....	....	....	....	....	....	....	....	....	....	....	....	....	....	....	....	....	....
2007-08	Miami U.	CCHA	42	9	23	32	42	....	....	....	....	....	....	....	....	....	....	....	....	....	....	....	....	....	....
2008-09	Manchester	AHL	72	8	15	23	42	....	....	....	....	....	....	....	....	....	....	....	....	....	....	....	....	....	....
2009-10	**Los Angeles**	**NHL**	**4**	**0**	**0**	**0**	**2**	**0**	**0**	**0**	**6**	**0.0**	**–2**	**0**	**0.0**	**15:25**	....	....	....	....	....	....	....	....	....
	Manchester	AHL	55	7	23	30	26	....	....	....	....	....	....	....	....	....	16	0	3	3	10	....	....	....	....
2010-11	**Los Angeles**	**NHL**	**60**	**5**	**11**	**16**	**18**	**1**	**0**	**0**	**74**	**6.8**	**11**	**0**	**0.0**	**15:17**	**6**	**0**	**1**	**1**	**2**	**0**	**0**	**0**	**13:29**
	Manchester	AHL	20	5	11	16	14	....	....	....	....	....	....	....	....	....	....	....	....	....	....	....	....	....	....
	NHL Totals		**64**	**5**	**11**	**16**	**20**	**1**	**0**	**0**	**80**	**6.3**		**0**	**0.0**	**15:17**	**6**	**0**	**1**	**1**	**2**	**0**	**0**	**0**	**13:30**

CCHA First All-Star Team (2008) • NCAA West Second All-American Team (2008)

MASHINTER, Brandon

(ma-SHIHN-tuhr, BRAN-duhn) **S.J.**

Center. Shoots left. 6'4", 220 lbs. Born, Bradford, Ont., September 20, 1988.

Season	Club	League	GP	G	A	Pts	PIM	PP	SH	GW	S	%	+/-	TF	F%	Min	GP	G	A	Pts	PIM	PP	SH	GW	Min
2004-05	Tor. T-Birds	OPJHL	49	3	6	9	19	....	....	....	....	....	....	....	....	....	....	....	....	....	....	....	....	....	....
	Sarnia Sting	OHL	8	0	0	0	9	....	....	....	....	....	....	....	....	....	....	....	....	....	....	....	....	....	....
2005-06	Sarnia Sting	OHL	65	6	1	7	65	....	....	....	....	....	....	....	....	....	....	....	....	....	....	....	....	....	....
2006-07	Sarnia Sting	OHL	55	7	8	15	49	....	....	....	....	....	....	....	....	....	4	0	2	2	0	....	....	....	....
2007-08	Kitchener Rangers	OHL	62	10	10	20	84	....	....	....	....	....	....	....	....	....	20	2	2	4	16	....	....	....	....
2008-09	Kitchener Rangers	OHL	21	14	12	26	24	....	....	....	....	....	....	....	....	....	....	....	....	....	....	....	....	....	....
	Belleville Bulls	OHL	31	20	12	32	32	....	....	....	....	....	....	....	....	....	17	8	3	11	13	....	....	....	....
2009-10	Worcester Sharks	AHL	79	22	15	37	117	....	....	....	....	....	....	....	....	....	11	1	5	6	6	....	....	....	....
2010-11	**San Jose**	**NHL**	**13**	**0**	**0**	**0**	**17**	**0**	**0**	**0**	**5**	**0.0**	**–2**	**0**	**0.0**	**6:23**	....	....	....	....	....	....	....	....	....
	Worcester Sharks	AHL	62	14	19	33	96	....	....	....	....	....	....	....	....	....	....	....	....	....	....	....	....	....	....
	NHL Totals		**13**	**0**	**0**	**0**	**17**	**0**	**0**	**0**	**5**	**0.0**		**0**	**0.0**	**6:23**	....	....	....	....	....	....	....	....	....

Signed as a free agent by **San Jose**, March 3, ,2009.

MATSUMOTO, Jon

(mat-suh-MOH-toh, JAWN) **CAR**

Center. Shoots left. 6', 184 lbs. Born, Ottawa, Ont., October 13, 1986. Philadelphia's 5th choice, 79th overall, in 2006 Entry Draft.

Season	Club	League	GP	G	A	Pts	PIM	PP	SH	GW	S	%	+/-	TF	F%	Min	GP	G	A	Pts	PIM	PP	SH	GW	Min
2002-03	Cumberland	CJHL	8	2	3	5	2	....	....	....	....	....	....	....	....	....	10	4	7	11	2	....	....	....	....
2003-04	Cumberland	CJHL	51	31	32	63	26	....	....	....	....	....	....	....	....	....	7	5	5	10	6	....	....	....	....
2004-05	Bowling Green	CCHA	36	18	14	32	22	....	....	....	....	....	....	....	....	....	....	....	....	....	....	....	....	....	....
2005-06	Bowling Green	CCHA	36	20	28	48	43	....	....	....	....	....	....	....	....	....	....	....	....	....	....	....	....	....	....
2006-07	Bowling Green	CCHA	38	11	22	33	70	....	....	....	....	....	....	....	....	....	....	....	....	....	....	....	....	....	....
	Philadelphia	AHL	16	2	2	4	10	....	....	....	....	....	....	....	....	....	....	....	....	....	....	....	....	....	....
2007-08	Philadelphia	AHL	77	20	24	44	52	....	....	....	....	....	....	....	....	....	12	2	2	4	10	....	....	....	....
2008-09	Philadelphia	AHL	78	29	34	63	77	....	....	....	....	....	....	....	....	....	4	1	2	3	4	....	....	....	....
2009-10	Adirondack	AHL	80	30	32	62	50	....	....	....	....	....	....	....	....	....	....	....	....	....	....	....	....	....	....
2010-11	**Carolina**	**NHL**	**13**	**2**	**0**	**2**	**4**	**0**	**0**	**0**	**11**	**18.2**	**–4**	**83**	**36.1**	**7:04**	....	....	....	....	....	....	....	....	....
	Charlotte	AHL	65	20	28	48	36	....	....	....	....	....	....	....	....	....	15	3	5	8	12	....	....	....	....
	NHL Totals		**13**	**2**	**0**	**2**	**4**	**0**	**0**	**0**	**11**	**18.2**		**83**	**36.1**	**7:04**	....	....	....	....	....	....	....	....	....

Traded to **Carolina** by **Philadelphia** for Washington's 7th round choice (previously acquired, Philadelphia selected Ricard Blidstrand) in 2010 Entry Draft, June 25, 2010.

MATTHIAS, Shawn

(muh-TIGH-uhs, SHAWN) **FLA**

Center. Shoots left. 6'2", 213 lbs. Born, Mississauga, Ont., February 19, 1988. Detroit's 2nd choice, 47th overall, in 2006 Entry Draft.

Season	Club	League	GP	G	A	Pts	PIM	PP	SH	GW	S	%	+/-	TF	F%	Min	GP	G	A	Pts	PIM	PP	SH	GW	Min
2004-05	Belleville Bulls	OHL	37	1	1	2	15	....	....	....	....	....	....	....	....	....	3	0	0	0	0	....	....	....	....
2005-06	Belleville Bulls	OHL	67	13	21	34	42	....	....	....	....	....	....	....	....	....	6	3	0	3	2	....	....	....	....
2006-07	Belleville Bulls	OHL	64	38	35	73	61	....	....	....	....	....	....	....	....	....	15	13	5	18	10	....	....	....	....
2007-08	**Florida**	**NHL**	**4**	**2**	**0**	**2**	**2**	**1**	**0**	**0**	**5**	**40.0**	**–2**	**38**	**44.7**	**13:08**	....	....	....	....	....	....	....	....	....
	Belleville Bulls	OHL	53	32	47	79	50	....	....	....	....	....	....	....	....	....	1	1	0	1	0	....	....	....	....
2008-09	**Florida**	**NHL**	**16**	**0**	**2**	**2**	**2**	**0**	**0**	**0**	**11**	**0.0**	**–3**	**91**	**50.6**	**9:10**	....	....	....	....	....	....	....	....	....
	Rochester	AHL	61	10	10	20	16	....	....	....	....	....	....	....	....	....	....	....	....	....	....	....	....	....	....
2009-10	**Florida**	**NHL**	**55**	**7**	**9**	**16**	**10**	**0**	**0**	**2**	**67**	**10.4**	**–3**	**313**	**38.0**	**10:48**	....	....	....	....	....	....	....	....	....
	Rochester	AHL	27	6	7	13	12	....	....	....	....	....	....	....	....	....	7	2	5	7	7	....	....	....	....
2010-11	**Florida**	**NHL**	**51**	**6**	**10**	**16**	**16**	**0**	**0**	**0**	**90**	**6.7**	**0**	**370**	**50.8**	**11:50**	....	....	....	....	....	....	....	....	....
	NHL Totals		**126**	**15**	**21**	**36**	**30**	**1**	**0**	**2**	**173**	**8.7**		**812**	**45.6**	**11:05**	....	....	....	....	....	....	....	....	....

Traded to **Florida** by **Detroit** with Detroit's 2nd round choice (later traded to Nashville - Nashville selected Nick Spaling) in 2007 Entry Draft for Todd Bertuzzi, February 27, 2007.

MAULDIN, Greg

(MAWL-dihn, GREHG) **COL**

Center. Shoots right. 5'11", 195 lbs. Born, Boston, MA, June 10, 1982. Columbus' 10th choice, 199th overall, in 2002 Entry Draft.

Season	Club	League	GP	G	A	Pts	PIM	PP	SH	GW	S	%	+/-	TF	F%	Min	GP	G	A	Pts	PIM	PP	SH	GW	Min
99-2000	Bos. Jr. Bruins	EJHL	58	45	42	87	14	....	....	....	....	....	....	....	....	....	....	....	....	....	....	....	....	....	....
2000-01	Bos. Jr. Bruins	EJHL	53	48	58	106	73	....	....	....	....	....	....	....	....	....	....	....	....	....	....	....	....	....	....
2001-02	Massachusetts	H-East	33	12	12	24	10	....	....	....	....	....	....	....	....	....	....	....	....	....	....	....	....	....	....
2002-03	Massachusetts	H-East	36	21	20	41	26	....	....	....	....	....	....	....	....	....	....	....	....	....	....	....	....	....	....
2003-04	Massachusetts	H-East	29	15	14	29	15	....	....	....	....	....	....	....	....	....	....	....	....	....	....	....	....	....	....
	Columbus	**NHL**	**6**	**0**	**0**	**0**	**4**	**0**	**0**	**0**	**6**	**0.0**	**–2**	**0**	**0.0**	**8:47**	....	....	....	....	....	....	....	....	....
	Syracuse Crunch	AHL	2	0	0	0	0	....	....	....	....	....	....	....	....	....	1	0	0	0	0	....	....	....	....
2004-05	Syracuse Crunch	AHL	66	7	20	27	49	....	....	....	....	....	....	....	....	....	....	....	....	....	....	....	....	....	....
2005-06	Syracuse Crunch	AHL	56	12	17	29	53	....	....	....	....	....	....	....	....	....	....	....	....	....	....	....	....	....	....
	Houston Aeros	AHL	11	1	3	4	0	....	....	....	....	....	....	....	....	....	8	1	1	2	2	....	....	....	....
2006-07	Bloomington	UHL	2	0	0	0	2	....	....	....	....	....	....	....	....	....	....	....	....	....	....	....	....	....	....
	Huddinge IK	Sweden-2	6	1	2	3	0	....	....	....	....	....	....	....	....	....	....	....	....	....	....	....	....	....	....
	IK Oskarshamn	Sweden-2	26	5	8	13	31	....	....	....	....	....	....	....	....	....	....	....	....	....	....	....	....	....	....
2007-08	Binghamton	AHL	71	15	18	33	37	....	....	....	....	....	....	....	....	....	....	....	....	....	....	....	....	....	....
2008-09	Binghamton	AHL	80	24	27	51	41	....	....	....	....	....	....	....	....	....	....	....	....	....	....	....	....	....	....
2009-10	**NY Islanders**	**NHL**	**1**	**0**	**0**	**0**	**0**	**0**	**0**	**0**	**2**	**0.0**	**–1**	**11**	**72.7**	**10:02**	....	....	....	....	....	....	....	....	....
	Bridgeport	AHL	77	25	29	54	35	....	....	....	....	....	....	....	....	....	5	1	2	3	0	....	....	....	....
2010-11	**Colorado**	**NHL**	**29**	**5**	**5**	**10**	**8**	**0**	**2**	**1**	**46**	**10.9**	**5**	**7**	**28.6**	**10:33**	....	....	....	....	....	....	....	....	....
	Lake Erie	AHL	43	18	17	35	20	....	....	....	....	....	....	....	....	....	7	0	2	2	2	....	....	....	....
	NHL Totals		**36**	**5**	**5**	**10**	**12**	**0**	**2**	**1**	**54**	**9.3**		**18**	**55.6**	**10:14**	....	....	....	....	....	....	....	....	....

EJHL First All-Star Team (2000, 2001) • EJHL MVP (2000)

Signed as a free agent by **Oskarshamn** (Sweden-2), October 23, 2006. Signed as a free agent by **Binghamton** (AHL), August 9, 2007. Signed as a free agent by **Ottawa**, July 7, 2008. Signed as a free agent by **NY Islanders**, July 6, 2009. Signed as a free agent by **Colorado**, July 2, 2010.

MAXWELL, Ben

(MAX-wehl, BEHN) **WPG**

Center. Shoots left. 6'1", 195 lbs. Born, North Vancouver, B.C., March 30, 1988. Montreal's 2nd choice, 49th overall, in 2006 Entry Draft.

Season	Club	League	GP	G	A	Pts	PIM	PP	SH	GW	S	%	+/-	TF	F%	Min	GP	G	A	Pts	PIM	PP	SH	GW	Min
2003-04	North Delta Ice	PIJHL	40	17	28	45	46	....	....	....	....	....	....	....	....	....	5	3	6	9	0	....	....	....	....
	Surrey Eagles	BCHL	2	0	0	0	0	....	....	....	....	....	....	....	....	....	....	....	....	....	....	....	....	....	....
	Kootenay Ice	WHL	3	0	1	1	2	....	....	....	....	....	....	....	....	....	1	0	0	0	0	....	....	....	....
2004-05	Kootenay Ice	WHL	68	8	10	18	37	....	....	....	....	....	....	....	....	....	16	0	1	1	6	....	....	....	....
2005-06	Kootenay Ice	WHL	69	28	32	60	52	....	....	....	....	....	....	....	....	....	6	3	5	8	0	....	....	....	....
2006-07	Kootenay Ice	WHL	39	19	34	53	42	....	....	....	....	....	....	....	....	....	7	1	4	5	21	....	....	....	....
2007-08	Kootenay Ice	WHL	31	9	18	27	26	....	....	....	....	....	....	....	....	....	10	6	3	9	14	....	....	....	....

			Regular Season														Playoffs								
Season	Club	League	GP	G	A	Pts	PIM	PP	SH	GW	S	%	+/-	TF	F%	Min	GP	G	A	Pts	PIM	PP	SH	GW	Min
2008-09	**Montreal**	**NHL**	**7**	**0**	**0**	**0**	**2**	**0**	**0**	**0**	**2**	**0.0**	**–1**	**53**	**37.7**	**9:55**	....	....	....	....	....	....	....	....	....
	Hamilton	AHL	73	22	36	58	58	....	....	....	....	....	....	....	....	....	6	3	1	4	4	....	....	....	....
2009-10	**Montreal**	**NHL**	**13**	**0**	**0**	**0**	**6**	**0**	**0**	**0**	**6**	**0.0**	**–2**	**16**	**50.0**	**8:47**	**1**	**0**	**0**	**0**	**0**	**0**	**0**	**0**	**1:03**
	Hamilton	AHL	57	16	28	44	22	....	....	....	....	....	....	....	....	....	1	0	0	0	0	....	....	....	....
2010-11	Hamilton	AHL	47	11	29	40	32	....	....	....	....	....	....	....	....	....	....	....	....	....	....	....	....	....	....
	Atlanta	**NHL**	**12**	**1**	**1**	**2**	**9**	**0**	**0**	**0**	**13**	**7.7**	**–7**	**36**	**44.4**	**12:00**	....	....	....	....	....	....	....	....	....
	Chicago Wolves	AHL	2	0	1	1	0	....	....	....	....	....	....	....	....	....	....	....	....	....	....	....	....	....	....
	NHL Totals		**32**	**1**	**1**	**2**	**17**	**0**	**0**	**0**	**21**	**4.8**		**105**	**41.9**	**10:14**	**1**	**0**	**0**	**0**	**0**	**0**	**0**	**0**	**1:03**

Traded to **Atlanta** by **Montreal** with Montreal's 4th round choice (later traded back to Montreal - Montreal selected Olivier Archambault) in 2011 Entry Draft for Brent Sopel and Nigel Dawes, February 24, 2011. • Transferred to **Winnipeg** after **Atlanta** franchise relocated, June 21, 2011.

MAYERS, Jamal

(MAI-uhrz, JUH-MAHL) **CHI**

Right wing. Shoots right. 6'1", 215 lbs. Born, Toronto, Ont., October 24, 1974. St. Louis' 3rd choice, 89th overall, in 1993 Entry Draft.

			Regular Season														Playoffs								
Season	Club	League	GP	G	A	Pts	PIM	PP	SH	GW	S	%	+/-	TF	F%	Min	GP	G	A	Pts	PIM	PP	SH	GW	Min
1990-91	Markham	ON-Jr.B	44	12	24	36	78	....	....	....	....	....	....	....	....	....	....	....	....	....	....	....	....	....	....
1991-92	Thornhill	ON-Jr.A	56	38	69	107	36	....	....	....	....	....	....	....	....	....	....	....	....	....	....	....	....	....	....
1992-93	Western Mich.	CCHA	38	8	17	25	26	....	....	....	....	....	....	....	....	....	....	....	....	....	....	....	....	....	....
1993-94	Western Mich.	CCHA	40	17	32	49	40	....	....	....	....	....	....	....	....	....	....	....	....	....	....	....	....	....	....
1994-95	Western Mich.	CCHA	39	13	32	45	40	....	....	....	....	....	....	....	....	....	....	....	....	....	....	....	....	....	....
1995-96	Western Mich.	CCHA	38	17	22	39	75	....	....	....	....	....	....	....	....	....	....	....	....	....	....	....	....	....	....
1996-97	**St. Louis**	**NHL**	**6**	**0**	**1**	**1**	**2**	**0**	**0**	**0**	**7**	**0.0**	**–3**	....	....	....	....	....	....	....	....	....	....	....	....
	Worcester IceCats	AHL	62	12	14	26	104	....	....	....	....	....	....	....	....	....	5	4	5	9	4	....	....	....	....
1997-98	Worcester IceCats	AHL	61	19	24	43	117	....	....	....	....	....	....	....	....	....	11	3	4	7	10	....	....	....	....
1998-99	**St. Louis**	**NHL**	**34**	**4**	**5**	**9**	**40**	**0**	**0**	**0**	**48**	**8.3**	**–3**	**2**	**50.0**	**8:08**	**11**	**0**	**1**	**1**	**8**	**0**	**0**	**0**	**8:34**
	Worcester IceCats	AHL	20	9	7	16	34	....	....	....	....	....	....	....	....	....	....	....	....	....	....	....	....	....	....
99-2000	**St. Louis**	**NHL**	**79**	**7**	**10**	**17**	**90**	**0**	**0**	**0**	**99**	**7.1**	**0**	**77**	**52.0**	**9:46**	**7**	**0**	**4**	**4**	**2**	**0**	**0**	**0**	**10:42**
2000-01	**St. Louis**	**NHL**	**77**	**8**	**13**	**21**	**117**	**0**	**0**	**0**	**132**	**6.1**	**–3**	**273**	**51.3**	**11:04**	**15**	**2**	**3**	**5**	**8**	**0**	**0**	**0**	**11:28**
2001-02	**St. Louis**	**NHL**	**77**	**9**	**8**	**17**	**99**	**0**	**1**	**0**	**105**	**8.6**	**9**	**761**	**52.6**	**11:36**	**10**	**3**	**0**	**3**	**2**	**0**	**0**	**2**	**11:14**
2002-03	**St. Louis**	**NHL**	**15**	**2**	**5**	**7**	**8**	**0**	**0**	**0**	**26**	**7.7**	**1**	**111**	**51.4**	**14:21**	....	....	....	....	....	....	....	....	....
2003-04	**St. Louis**	**NHL**	**80**	**6**	**5**	**11**	**91**	**0**	**1**	**3**	**130**	**4.6**	**–19**	**681**	**48.6**	**13:01**	**5**	**0**	**0**	**0**	**0**	**0**	**0**	**0**	**12:55**
2004-05	Hammarby	Sweden-2	19	9	13	22	36	....	....	....	....	....	....	....	....	....	....	....	....	....	....	....	....	....	....
	Missouri	UHL	13	5	2	7	68	....	....	....	....	....	....	....	....	....	....	....	....	....	....	....	....	....	....
2005-06	**St. Louis**	**NHL**	**67**	**15**	**11**	**26**	**129**	**0**	**2**	**1**	**111**	**13.5**	**–22**	**363**	**48.5**	**15:07**	....	....	....	....	....	....	....	....	....
2006-07	**St. Louis**	**NHL**	**80**	**8**	**14**	**22**	**89**	**0**	**2**	**0**	**129**	**6.2**	**–19**	**432**	**57.4**	**14:37**	....	....	....	....	....	....	....	....	....
2007-08	**St. Louis**	**NHL**	**80**	**12**	**15**	**27**	**91**	**0**	**1**	**3**	**153**	**7.8**	**–19**	**683**	**56.2**	**15:56**	....	....	....	....	....	....	....	....	....
2008-09	**Toronto**	**NHL**	**71**	**7**	**9**	**16**	**82**	**0**	**0**	**1**	**72**	**9.7**	**–7**	**429**	**57.3**	**10:33**	....	....	....	....	....	....	....	....	....
2009-10	**Toronto**	**NHL**	**44**	**2**	**6**	**8**	**78**	**0**	**0**	**0**	**47**	**4.3**	**–5**	**264**	**56.8**	**8:55**	....	....	....	....	....	....	....	....	....
	Calgary	**NHL**	**27**	**1**	**5**	**6**	**53**	**0**	**0**	**1**	**28**	**3.6**	**2**	**115**	**55.7**	**9:11**	....	....	....	....	....	....	....	....	....
2010-11	**San Jose**	**NHL**	**78**	**3**	**11**	**14**	**124**	**0**	**0**	**0**	**62**	**4.8**	**3**	**98**	**54.1**	**8:53**	**12**	**0**	**0**	**0**	**12**	**0**	**0**	**0**	**5:37**
	NHL Totals		**815**	**84**	**118**	**202**	**1093**	**0**	**7**	**9**	**1149**	**7.3**		**4289**	**53.4**	**11:51**	**60**	**5**	**8**	**13**	**32**	**0**	**0**	**2**	**9:46**

• Missed majority of 2002-03 due to knee injury vs. Calgary, November 16, 2002. Signed as a free agent by **Hammarby** (Sweden-2), November 16, 2004. Signed as a free agent by **Missouri** (UHL), March 11, 2005. Traded to **Toronto** by **St. Louis** for Florida's 3rd round choice (previously acquired, St. Louis selected James Livingston) in 2008 Entry Draft, June 19, 2008. Traded to **Calgary** by **Toronto** with Matt Stajan, Niklas Hagman and Ian White for Dion Phaneuf, Fredrik Sjostrom and Keith Aulie, January 31, 2010. Signed as a free agent by **San Jose**, August 4, 2010. Signed as a free agent by **Chicago**, July 1, 2011.

MAYOROV, Maksim

(may-YOHR-ahv, mahx-EEM) **CBJ**

Left wing. Shoots left. 6'2", 202 lbs. Born, Andizhan, USSR, March 26, 1989. Columbus' 5th choice, 94th overall, in 2007 Entry Draft.

			Regular Season														Playoffs								
Season	Club	League	GP	G	A	Pts	PIM	PP	SH	GW	S	%	+/-	TF	F%	Min	GP	G	A	Pts	PIM	PP	SH	GW	Min
2005-06	Ak Bars Kazan 2	Russia-3	STATISTICS NOT AVAILABLE																						
2006-07	Leninogorsk	Russia-2	28	6	4	10	6	....	....	....	....	....	....	....	....	....	....	....	....	....	....	....	....	....	....
	Almetjevsk	Russia-2	6	1	1	2	0	....	....	....	....	....	....	....	....	....	4	0	0	0	2	....	....	....	....
2007-08	Ak Bars Kazan	Russia	11	1	0	1	16	....	....	....	....	....	....	....	....	....	....	....	....	....	....	....	....	....	....
2008-09	**Columbus**	**NHL**	**3**	**0**	**0**	**0**	**0**	**0**	**0**	**0**	**1**	**0.0**	**0**	**0**	**0.0**	**5:44**	....	....	....	....	....	....	....	....	....
	Syracuse Crunch	AHL	71	17	14	31	30	....	....	....	....	....	....	....	....	....	....	....	....	....	....	....	....	....	....
2009-10	**Columbus**	**NHL**	**4**	**0**	**0**	**0**	**0**	**0**	**0**	**0**	**4**	**0.0**	**–1**	**0**	**0.0**	**7:40**	....	....	....	....	....	....	....	....	....
	Syracuse Crunch	AHL	74	17	15	32	24	....	....	....	....	....	....	....	....	....	....	....	....	....	....	....	....	....	....
2010-11	**Columbus**	**NHL**	**5**	**1**	**0**	**1**	**0**	**0**	**0**	**0**	**3**	**33.3**	**0**	**0**	**0.0**	**8:42**	....	....	....	....	....	....	....	....	....
	Springfield	AHL	69	19	14	33	16	....	....	....	....	....	....	....	....	....	....	....	....	....	....	....	....	....	....
	NHL Totals		**12**	**1**	**0**	**1**	**0**	**0**	**0**	**0**	**8**	**12.5**		**0**	**0.0**	**7:37**	....	....	....	....	....	....	....	....	....

McARDLE, Kenndal

(muh-KAHR-duhl, KEHN-dahl) **WPG**

Left wing. Shoots left. 5'11", 190 lbs. Born, Toronto, Ont., January 4, 1987. Florida's 1st choice, 20th overall, in 2005 Entry Draft.

			Regular Season														Playoffs								
Season	Club	League	GP	G	A	Pts	PIM	PP	SH	GW	S	%	+/-	TF	F%	Min	GP	G	A	Pts	PIM	PP	SH	GW	Min
2002-03	Burnaby W.C.	Minor-BC	30	1	9	10	131	....	....	....	....	....	....	....	....	....	....	....	....	....	....	....	....	....	....
	Moose Jaw	WHL	2	0	0	0	0	....	....	....	....	....	....	....	....	....	....	....	....	....	....	....	....	....	....
2003-04	Moose Jaw	WHL	54	8	8	16	57	....	....	....	....	....	....	....	....	....	10	3	2	5	6	....	....	....	....
2004-05	Moose Jaw	WHL	70	37	37	74	122	....	....	....	....	....	....	....	....	....	5	1	0	1	16	....	....	....	....
2005-06	Moose Jaw	WHL	72	28	43	71	135	....	....	....	....	....	....	....	....	....	22	6	10	16	43	....	....	....	....
2006-07	Moose Jaw	WHL	26	10	10	20	75	....	....	....	....	....	....	....	....	....	....	....	....	....	....	....	....	....	....
	Vancouver Giants	WHL	37	9	13	22	54	....	....	....	....	....	....	....	....	....	22	*11	9	20	49	....	....	....	....
2007-08	Rochester	AHL	36	5	5	10	31	....	....	....	....	....	....	....	....	....	....	....	....	....	....	....	....	....	....
	Florida Everblades	ECHL	6	3	1	4	26	....	....	....	....	....	....	....	....	....	3	0	0	0	2	....	....	....	....
2008-09	**Florida**	**NHL**	**3**	**0**	**0**	**0**	**2**	**0**	**0**	**0**	**1**	**0.0**	**–1**	**0**	**0.0**	**7:30**	....	....	....	....	....	....	....	....	....
	Rochester	AHL	58	12	12	24	79	....	....	....	....	....	....	....	....	....	....	....	....	....	....	....	....	....	....
2009-10	**Florida**	**NHL**	**19**	**1**	**2**	**3**	**29**	**0**	**0**	**0**	**10**	**10.0**	**–4**	**0**	**0.0**	**8:54**	....	....	....	....	....	....	....	....	....
	Rochester	AHL	18	3	5	8	63	....	....	....	....	....	....	....	....	....	....	....	....	....	....	....	....	....	....
2010-11	**Florida**	**NHL**	**11**	**0**	**0**	**0**	**16**	**0**	**0**	**0**	**6**	**0.0**	**–3**	**3**	**33.3**	**9:57**	....	....	....	....	....	....	....	....	....
	Rochester	AHL	54	14	12	26	106	....	....	....	....	....	....	....	....	....	....	....	....	....	....	....	....	....	....
	NHL Totals		**33**	**1**	**2**	**3**	**47**	**0**	**0**	**0**	**17**	**5.9**		**3**	**33.3**	**9:07**	....	....	....	....	....	....	....	....	....

• Missed majority of 2009-10 due to shoulder injury at Nashville, November 28, 2010. Traded to **Winnipeg** by **Florida** for Angelo Esposito, July 9, 2011.

McBAIN, Jamie

(muhk-BAYN, JAY-mee) **CAR**

Defense. Shoots right. 6'2", 200 lbs. Born, Edina, MN, February 25, 1988. Carolina's 1st choice, 63rd overall, in 2006 Entry Draft.

			Regular Season														Playoffs								
Season	Club	League	GP	G	A	Pts	PIM	PP	SH	GW	S	%	+/-	TF	F%	Min	GP	G	A	Pts	PIM	PP	SH	GW	Min
2003-04	Shat.-St. Mary's	High-MN	73	6	27	33	....	....	....	....	....	....	....	....	....	....	....	....	....	....	....	....	....	....	....
2004-05	USNTDP	U-17	14	1	6	7	16	....	....	....	....	....	....	....	....	....	....	....	....	....	....	....	....	....	....
	USNTDP	NAHL	38	2	7	9	22	....	....	....	....	....	....	....	....	....	10	0	3	3	4	....	....	....	....
2005-06	USNTDP	U-18	41	9	16	25	35	....	....	....	....	....	....	....	....	....	....	....	....	....	....	....	....	....	....
	USNTDP	NAHL	14	0	5	5	6	....	....	....	....	....	....	....	....	....	....	....	....	....	....	....	....	....	....
2006-07	U. of Wisconsin	WCHA	36	3	15	18	36	....	....	....	....	....	....	....	....	....	....	....	....	....	....	....	....	....	....
2007-08	U. of Wisconsin	WCHA	35	5	19	24	18	....	....	....	....	....	....	....	....	....	....	....	....	....	....	....	....	....	....
2008-09	U. of Wisconsin	WCHA	40	7	30	37	30	....	....	....	....	....	....	....	....	....	....	....	....	....	....	....	....	....	....
	Albany River Rats	AHL	10	1	1	2	2	....	....	....	....	....	....	....	....	....	....	....	....	....	....	....	....	....	....
2009-10	**Carolina**	**NHL**	**14**	**3**	**7**	**10**	**0**	**1**	**0**	**1**	**29**	**10.3**	**6**	**0**	**0.0**	**25:47**	....	....	....	....	....	....	....	....	....
	Albany River Rats	AHL	68	7	33	40	10	....	....	....	....	....	....	....	....	....	8	4	2	6	8	....	....	....	....
2010-11	**Carolina**	**NHL**	**76**	**7**	**23**	**30**	**32**	**1**	**0**	**2**	**95**	**7.4**	**–8**	**0**	**0.0**	**19:06**	....	....	....	....	....	....	....	....	....
	NHL Totals		**90**	**10**	**30**	**40**	**32**	**2**	**0**	**3**	**124**	**8.1**		**0**	**0.0**	**20:08**	....	....	....	....	....	....	....	....	....

WCHA All-Rookie Team (2007) • WCHA First All-Star Team (2009) • WCHA Player of the Year (2009) • NCAA West First All-American Team (2009)

McCABE, Bryan

(muh-KAYB, BRIGH-uhn)

Defense. Shoots left. 6'2", 220 lbs. Born, St. Catharines, Ont., June 8, 1975. NY Islanders' 2nd choice, 40th overall, in 1993 Entry Draft.

			Regular Season														Playoffs								
Season	Club	League	GP	G	A	Pts	PIM	PP	SH	GW	S	%	+/-	TF	F%	Min	GP	G	A	Pts	PIM	PP	SH	GW	Min
1990-91	Calgary Canucks	AMHL	33	14	34	48	55	....	....	....	....	....	....	....	....	....	....	....	....	....	....	....	....	....	....
1991-92	Medicine Hat	WHL	68	6	24	30	157	....	....	....	....	....	....	....	....	....	4	0	0	0	6	....	....	....	....
1992-93	Medicine Hat	WHL	14	0	13	13	83	....	....	....	....	....	....	....	....	....	....	....	....	....	....	....	....	....	....
	Spokane Chiefs	WHL	46	3	44	47	134	....	....	....	....	....	....	....	....	....	6	1	5	6	28	....	....	....	....
1993-94	Spokane Chiefs	WHL	64	22	62	84	218	....	....	....	....	....	....	....	....	....	3	0	4	4	4	....	....	....	....
1994-95	Spokane Chiefs	WHL	42	14	39	53	115	....	....	....	....	....	....	....	....	....	....	....	....	....	....	....	....	....	....
	Brandon	WHL	20	6	10	16	38	....	....	....	....	....	....	....	....	....	18	4	13	17	59	....	....	....	....
1995-96	**NY Islanders**	**NHL**	**82**	**7**	**16**	**23**	**156**	**3**	**0**	**1**	**130**	**5.4**	**–24**	....	....	....	....	....	....	....	....	....	....	....	....

			Regular Season														Playoffs								
Season	Club	League	GP	G	A	Pts	PIM	PP	SH	GW	S	%	+/-	TF	F%	Min	GP	G	A	Pts	PIM	PP	SH	GW	Min
1996-97	NY Islanders	NHL	82	8	20	28	165	2	1	2	117	6.8	-2	....	....	....	....	....	....	....	....	....	....	....	....
1997-98	NY Islanders	NHL	56	3	9	12	145	1	0	0	81	3.7	9	....	....	....	....	....	....	....	....	....	....	....	....
	Vancouver	NHL	26	1	11	12	64	0	1	0	42	2.4	10	....	....	....	....	....	....	....	....	....	....	....	....
1998-99	Vancouver	NHL	69	7	14	21	120	1	2	0	98	7.1	-11	1	0.0	24:13	....	....	....	....	....	....	....	....	....
99-2000	Chicago	NHL	79	6	19	25	139	2	0	2	119	5.0	-8	1	0.0	23:23	....	....	....	....	....	....	....	....	....
2000-01	Toronto	NHL	82	5	24	29	123	3	0	2	159	3.1	16	0	0.0	23:49	11	2	3	5	16	1	0	0	23:56
2001-02	Toronto	NHL	82	17	26	43	129	8	0	1	157	10.8	16	1	0.0	24:34	20	5	5	10	30	3	0	1	29:33
2002-03	Toronto	NHL	75	6	18	24	135	3	0	1	149	4.0	9	1	0.0	23:39	7	0	3	3	10	0	0	0	27:28
2003-04	Toronto	NHL	75	16	37	53	86	8	0	2	168	9.5	22	2	50.0	25:44	13	3	5	8	14	2	0	0	28:47
2004-05	HV 71 Jonkoping	Sweden	10	1	0	1	30	....	....	....	....	....	....	....	....	....	....	....	....	....	....	....	....	....	....
2005-06	Toronto	NHL	73	19	49	68	116	13	0	6	207	9.2	-1	1	0.0	28:18	....	....	....	....	....	....	....	....	....
	Canada	Olympics	6	0	0	0	18	....	....	....	....	....	....	....	....	....	....	....	....	....	....	....	....	....	....
2006-07	Toronto	NHL	82	15	42	57	115	11	0	1	207	7.2	3	0	0.0	26:50	....	....	....	....	....	....	....	....	....
2007-08	Toronto	NHL	54	5	18	23	81	4	0	2	107	4.7	-2	0	0.0	25:55	....	....	....	....	....	....	....	....	....
2008-09	Florida	NHL	69	15	24	39	41	8	0	3	153	9.8	-1	0	0.0	23:08	....	....	....	....	....	....	....	....	....
2009-10	Florida	NHL	82	8	35	43	83	3	0	1	169	4.7	-4	0	0.0	23:20	....	....	....	....	....	....	....	....	....
2010-11	Florida	NHL	48	5	17	22	28	2	0	0	88	5.7	3	0	0.0	21:01	....	....	....	....	....	....	....	....	....
	NY Rangers	NHL	19	2	4	6	6	2	0	0	34	5.9	-1	0	0.0	15:54	5	0	2	2	14	0	0	0	19:13
	NHL Totals		1135	145	383	528	1732	74	4	24	2185	6.6		7	14.3	24:23	56	10	18	28	84	6	0	1	27:05

WHL West Second All-Star Team (1993) • WHL West First All-Star Team (1994) • WHL East First All-Star Team (1995) • Memorial Cup All-Star Team (1995) • NHL Second All-Star Team (2004)

Traded to **Vancouver** by **NY Islanders** with Todd Bertuzzi and NY Islanders' 3rd round choice (Jarkko Ruutu) in 1998 Entry Draft for Trevor Linden, February 6, 1998. Traded to **Chicago** by **Vancouver** with Vancouver's 1st round choice (Pavel Vorobiev) in 2000 Entry Draft for Chicago's 1st round choice (later traded to Tampa Bay, later traded to NY Rangers – NY Rangers selected Pavel Brendl) in 1999 Entry Draft, June 25, 1999. Traded to **Toronto** by **Chicago** for Alexander Karpovtsev and Toronto's 4th round choice (Vladimir Gusev) in 2001 Entry Draft, October 2, 2000. Signed as a free agent by **Jonkoping** (Sweden), October 29, 2004. Traded to **Florida** by **Toronto** with Toronto's 4th round choice (Sam Brittain) in 2010 Entry Draft for Mike Van Ryn, September 2, 2008. Traded to **NY Rangers** by **Florida** for Tim Kennedy and NY Rangers' 3rd round choice (Logan Shaw) in 2011 Entry Draft, February 26, 2011.

McCARTHY, John

(muh-KAHR-thee, JAWN) **S.J.**

Left wing. Shoots left. 6'1", 200 lbs. Born, Boston, MA, August 9, 1986. San Jose's 5th choice, 202nd overall, in 2006 Entry Draft.

2004-05	Des Moines	USHL	60	8	10	18	32	....	....	....	....	....	....	....	....	....	....	....	....	....	....	....	....	....	....
2005-06	Boston University	H-East	32	2	2	4	12	....	....	....	....	....	....	....	....	....	....	....	....	....	....	....	....	....	....
2006-07	Boston University	H-East	39	2	3	5	18	....	....	....	....	....	....	....	....	....	....	....	....	....	....	....	....	....	....
2007-08	Boston University	H-East	38	4	3	7	24	....	....	....	....	....	....	....	....	....	....	....	....	....	....	....	....	....	....
2008-09	Boston University	H-East	45	6	23	29	24	....	....	....	....	....	....	....	....	....	....	....	....	....	....	....	....	....	....
2009-10	San Jose	NHL	4	0	0	0	0	0	0	0	3	0.0	-3	0	0.0	9:08	....	....	....	....	....	....	....	....	....
	Worcester Sharks	AHL	74	15	27	42	39	....	....	....	....	....	....	....	....	....	11	2	3	5	10	....	....	....	....
2010-11	San Jose	NHL	37	2	2	4	8	0	0	0	41	4.9	-8	36	36.1	8:45	....	....	....	....	....	....	....	....	....
	Worcester Sharks	AHL	25	7	5	12	13	....	....	....	....	....	....	....	....	....	....	....	....	....	....	....	....	....	....
	NHL Totals		41	2	2	4	8	0	0	0	44	4.5		36	36.1	8:47	....	....	....	....	....	....	....	....	....

McCLEMENT, Jay

(muh-KLEHM-ehnt, JAY) **COL**

Center. Shoots left. 6'1", 205 lbs. Born, Kingston, Ont., March 2, 1983. St. Louis' 1st choice, 57th overall, in 2001 Entry Draft.

1997-98	Kingston	OPJHL	48	3	8	11	15	....	....	....	....	....	....	....	....	....	....	....	....	....	....	....	....	....	....
1998-99	Kingston	OPJHL	51	25	28	53	34	....	....	....	....	....	....	....	....	....	....	....	....	....	....	....	....	....	....
99-2000	Brampton	OHL	63	13	16	29	34	....	....	....	....	....	....	....	....	....	6	0	4	4	8	....	....	....	....
2000-01	Brampton	OHL	66	30	19	49	61	....	....	....	....	....	....	....	....	....	9	4	2	6	10	....	....	....	....
2001-02	Brampton	OHL	61	26	29	55	43	....	....	....	....	....	....	....	....	....	....	....	....	....	....	....	....	....	....
2002-03	Brampton	OHL	45	22	27	49	37	....	....	....	....	....	....	....	....	....	11	3	4	7	11	....	....	....	....
	Worcester IceCats	AHL	....	....	....	....	....	....	....	....	....	....	....	....	....	....	1	0	0	0	0	....	....	....	....
2003-04	Worcester IceCats	AHL	69	12	13	25	20	....	....	....	....	....	....	....	....	....	10	0	3	3	0	....	....	....	....
2004-05	Worcester IceCats	AHL	79	17	34	51	45	....	....	....	....	....	....	....	....	....	....	....	....	....	....	....	....	....	....
2005-06	St. Louis	NHL	67	6	21	27	30	1	0	2	76	7.9	-23	691	46.9	13:56	....	....	....	....	....	....	....	....	....
	Peoria Rivermen	AHL	11	4	5	9	4	....	....	....	....	....	....	....	....	....	4	0	2	2	2	....	....	....	....
2006-07	St. Louis	NHL	81	8	28	36	55	0	0	0	104	7.7	3	839	52.7	13:53	....	....	....	....	....	....	....	....	....
2007-08	St. Louis	NHL	81	9	13	22	26	0	0	2	110	8.2	-17	700	52.3	13:55	....	....	....	....	....	....	....	....	....
2008-09	St. Louis	NHL	82	12	14	26	29	0	3	3	137	8.8	-10	1451	52.1	16:36	4	0	0	0	4	0	0	0	16:28
2009-10	St. Louis	NHL	82	11	18	29	22	0	0	3	109	10.1	0	1412	49.7	16:44	....	....	....	....	....	....	....	....	....
2010-11	St. Louis	NHL	56	6	10	16	18	1	0	1	89	6.7	-13	831	51.4	17:08	....	....	....	....	....	....	....	....	....
	Colorado	NHL	24	1	3	4	12	0	0	0	38	2.6	-8	321	52.3	15:39	....	....	....	....	....	....	....	....	....
	NHL Totals		473	53	107	160	192	2	3	11	663	8.0		6245	51.0	15:20	4	0	0	0	4	0	0	0	16:28

Traded to **Colorado** by **St. Louis** with Erik Johnson and St. Louis's 1st round choice (Duncan Siemens) in 2011 Entry Draft for Kevin Shattenkirk, Chris Stewart and Colorado's 2nd round choice (Ty Rattie) in 2011 Entry Draft, February 19, 2011.

McCORMICK, Cody

(muh-KOHR-mihk, KOH-dee) **BUF**

Center/Right wing. Shoots right. 6'3", 221 lbs. Born, London, Ont., April 18, 1983. Colorado's 5th choice, 144th overall, in 2001 Entry Draft.

1998-99	Elgin-Middlesex	MHAO	58	22	40	62	81	....	....	....	....	....	....	....	....	....	....	....	....	....	....	....	....	....	....
99-2000	Belleville Bulls	OHL	45	3	4	7	42	....	....	....	....	....	....	....	....	....	9	1	0	1	10	....	....	....	....
2000-01	Belleville Bulls	OHL	66	7	16	23	135	....	....	....	....	....	....	....	....	....	10	1	1	2	23	....	....	....	....
2001-02	Belleville Bulls	OHL	63	10	17	27	118	....	....	....	....	....	....	....	....	....	11	2	4	6	24	....	....	....	....
2002-03	Belleville Bulls	OHL	61	36	33	69	166	....	....	....	....	....	....	....	....	....	7	4	7	11	11	....	....	....	....
2003-04	Colorado	NHL	44	2	3	5	73	0	0	1	33	6.1	-4	110	32.7	8:07	....	....	....	....	....	....	....	....	....
	Hershey Bears	AHL	32	3	6	9	60	....	....	....	....	....	....	....	....	....	....	....	....	....	....	....	....	....	....
2004-05	Hershey Bears	AHL	40	5	6	11	68	....	....	....	....	....	....	....	....	....	....	....	....	....	....	....	....	....	....
2005-06	Colorado	NHL	45	4	4	8	29	0	0	1	43	9.3	1	16	25.0	7:42	....	....	....	....	....	....	....	....	....
	Lowell	AHL	13	1	6	7	34	....	....	....	....	....	....	....	....	....	....	....	....	....	....	....	....	....	....
2006-07	Colorado	NHL	6	0	1	1	6	0	0	0	6	0.0	1	3	33.3	6:44	....	....	....	....	....	....	....	....	....
	Albany River Rats	AHL	42	8	8	16	64	....	....	....	....	....	....	....	....	....	5	1	0	1	4	....	....	....	....
2007-08	Colorado	NHL	40	2	2	4	50	0	0	1	45	4.4	5	17	35.3	10:58	4	0	1	1	7	0	0	0	11:53
	Lake Erie	AHL	13	2	4	6	16	....	....	....	....	....	....	....	....	....	....	....	....	....	....	....	....	....	....
2008-09	Colorado	NHL	55	1	11	12	92	0	0	0	66	1.5	-5	107	35.5	9:36	....	....	....	....	....	....	....	....	....
2009-10	Portland Pirates	AHL	66	17	12	29	168	....	....	....	....	....	....	....	....	....	3	0	0	0	9	....	....	....	....
	Buffalo	NHL	....	....	....	....	....	....	....	....	....	....	....	....	....	....	3	0	2	2	14	0	0	0	10:41
2010-11	Buffalo	NHL	81	8	12	20	142	0	0	1	104	7.7	2	316	41.8	10:57	7	1	0	1	2	0	0	0	8:11
	NHL Totals		271	17	33	50	392	0	0	4	297	5.7		569	38.1	9:35	14	1	3	4	23	0	0	0	9:47

OHL First All-Star Team (2003)

Signed as a free agent by **Buffalo**, August 1, 2009.

McDONAGH, Ryan

(muhk-DUHN-uh, RIGH-uhn) **NYR**

Defense. Shoots left. 6'1", 213 lbs. Born, St.Paul, MN, June 13, 1989. Montreal's 1st choice, 12th overall, in 2007 Entry Draft.

2004-05	Cretin-Derham	High-MN	28	12	18	30	....	....	....	....	....	....	....	....	....	....	....	....	....	....	....	....	....	....	....
2005-06	Cretin-Derham	High-MN	25	12	33	45	....	....	....	....	....	....	....	....	....	....	....	....	....	....	....	....	....	....	....
2006-07	Cretin-Derham	High-MN	26	14	26	40	....	....	....	....	....	....	....	....	....	....	....	....	....	....	....	....	....	....	....
2007-08	U. of Wisconsin	WCHA	40	5	7	12	42	....	....	....	....	....	....	....	....	....	....	....	....	....	....	....	....	....	....
2008-09	U. of Wisconsin	WCHA	36	5	11	16	59	....	....	....	....	....	....	....	....	....	....	....	....	....	....	....	....	....	....
2009-10	U. of Wisconsin	WCHA	43	4	14	18	73	....	....	....	....	....	....	....	....	....	....	....	....	....	....	....	....	....	....
2010-11	NY Rangers	NHL	40	1	8	9	14	0	0	1	27	3.7	16	0	0.0	18:44	5	0	0	0	4	0	0	0	22:49
	Connecticut	AHL	38	1	7	8	12	....	....	....	....	....	....	....	....	....	....	....	....	....	....	....	....	....	....
	NHL Totals		40	1	8	9	14	0	0	1	27	3.7		0	0.0	18:44	5	0	0	0	4	0	0	0	22:49

WCHA All-Rookie Team (2008) • WCHA Second All-Star Team (2010)

Traded to **NY Rangers** by **Montreal** with Chris Higgins and Pavel Valentenko for Scott Gomez, Tom Pyatt and Michael Busto, June 30, 2009.

McDONALD, Andy
(muhk-DAWN-uhld, AN-dee) **ST.L.**

Center. Shoots left. 5'11", 190 lbs. Born, Strathroy, Ont., August 25, 1977.

Season	Club	League	GP	G	A	Pts	PIM	PP	SH	GW	S	%	+/-	TF	F%	Min	Playoffs GP	G	A	Pts	PIM	PP	SH	GW	Min
1993-94	Strathroy Blades	ON-Jr.B	7	2	2	4	0	....	....	....	....	....	....	....	....	....	....	....	....	....	....	....	....	....	....
1994-95	Strathroy Rockets	ON-Jr.B	50	32	41	73	24	....	....	....	....	....	....	....	....	....	....	....	....	....	....	....	....	....	....
1995-96	Strathroy Rockets	ON-Jr.B	52	31	56	87	103	....	....	....	....	....	....	....	....	....	....	....	....	....	....	....	....	....	....
1996-97	Colgate	ECAC	33	9	10	19	16	....	....	....	....	....	....	....	....	....	....	....	....	....	....	....	....	....	....
1997-98	Colgate	ECAC	35	13	19	32	26	....	....	....	....	....	....	....	....	....	....	....	....	....	....	....	....	....	....
1998-99	Colgate	ECAC	35	20	26	46	42	....	....	....	....	....	....	....	....	....	....	....	....	....	....	....	....	....	....
99-2000	Colgate	ECAC	34	25	*33	*58	49	....	....	....	....	....	....	....	....	....	....	....	....	....	....	....	....	....	....
2000-01	**Anaheim**	**NHL**	**16**	**1**	**0**	**1**	**6**	**0**	**0**	**0**	**21**	**4.8**	**0**	**139**	**48.9**	**11:11**	....	....	....	....	....	....	....	....	....
	Cincinnati	AHL	46	15	25	40	21	....	....	....	....	....	....	....	....	....	3	0	1	1	2	....	....	....	....
2001-02	**Anaheim**	**NHL**	**53**	**7**	**21**	**28**	**10**	**2**	**0**	**3**	**79**	**8.9**	**2**	**818**	**53.7**	**15:59**	....	....	....	....	....	....	....	....	....
	Cincinnati	AHL	21	7	25	32	6	....	....	....	....	....	....	....	....	....	....	....	....	....	....	....	....	....	....
2002-03	**Anaheim**	**NHL**	**46**	**10**	**11**	**21**	**14**	**3**	**0**	**1**	**92**	**10.9**	**–1**	**604**	**56.0**	**18:31**	....	....	....	....	....	....	....	....	....
2003-04	**Anaheim**	**NHL**	**79**	**9**	**21**	**30**	**24**	**2**	**1**	**1**	**162**	**5.6**	**–13**	**282**	**54.3**	**16:34**	....	....	....	....	....	....	....	....	....
2004-05	ERC Ingolstadt	Germany	36	13	17	30	26	....	....	....	....	....	....	....	....	....	10	5	2	7	35	....	....	....	....
2005-06	**Anaheim**	**NHL**	**82**	**34**	**51**	**85**	**32**	**13**	**0**	**7**	**229**	**14.8**	**24**	**1095**	**56.3**	**16:48**	**16**	**2**	**7**	**9**	**10**	**2**	**0**	**0**	**16:33**
2006-07 ♦	**Anaheim**	**NHL**	**82**	**27**	**51**	**78**	**46**	**8**	**0**	**3**	**252**	**10.7**	**16**	**908**	**55.4**	**17:35**	**21**	**10**	**4**	**14**	**10**	**5**	**0**	**0**	**18:37**
2007-08	**Anaheim**	**NHL**	**33**	**4**	**12**	**16**	**30**	**0**	**0**	**0**	**79**	**5.1**	**–4**	**392**	**55.4**	**16:41**	....	....	....	....	....	....	....	....	....
	St. Louis	**NHL**	**49**	**14**	**22**	**36**	**32**	**3**	**0**	**1**	**103**	**13.6**	**–17**	**556**	**55.8**	**18:40**	....	....	....	....	....	....	....	....	....
2008-09	**St. Louis**	**NHL**	**46**	**15**	**29**	**44**	**24**	**6**	**1**	**1**	**128**	**11.7**	**–13**	**367**	**58.0**	**19:05**	**4**	**1**	**3**	**4**	**0**	**0**	**0**	**0**	**23:35**
2009-10	**St. Louis**	**NHL**	**79**	**24**	**33**	**57**	**18**	**6**	**0**	**3**	**191**	**12.6**	**–9**	**447**	**53.9**	**18:08**	....	....	....	....	....	....	....	....	....
2010-11	**St. Louis**	**NHL**	**58**	**20**	**30**	**50**	**26**	**5**	**1**	**3**	**180**	**11.1**	**18**	**349**	**59.3**	**20:02**	....	....	....	....	....	....	....	....	....
	NHL Totals		**623**	**165**	**281**	**446**	**262**	**48**	**3**	**23**	**1516**	**10.9**		**5957**	**55.5**	**17:34**	**41**	**13**	**14**	**27**	**20**	**7**	**0**	**0**	**18:18**

ECAC Second All-Star Team (1999) • ECAC First All-Star Team (2000) • ECAC Player of the Year (2000) • NCAA East First All-American Team (2000)

Played in NHL All-Star Game (2007)

Signed as a free agent by **Anaheim**, April 3, 2000. Signed as a free agent by **Ingolstadt** (Germany), September 17, 2004. Traded to **St. Louis** by **Anaheim** for Doug Weight, Michal Birner and St. Louis' 7th round choice (later traded to Los Angeles, later traded back to St. Louis - St. Louis selected Paul Karpowich) in 2008 Entry Draft, December 14, 2007.

McDONALD, Colin
(muhk-DAWN-uhld, KAW-lihn) **PIT**

Right wing. Shoots right. 6'2", 190 lbs. Born, New Haven, CT, September 30, 1984. Edmonton's 2nd choice, 51st overall, in 2003 Entry Draft.

Season	Club	League	GP	G	A	Pts	PIM	PP	SH	GW	S	%	+/-	TF	F%	Min	Playoffs GP	G	A	Pts	PIM	PP	SH	GW	Min
2001-02	N.E. Jr. Coyotes	EJHL	39	16	20	36	50	....	....	....	....	....	....	....	....	....	....	....	....	....	....	....	....	....	....
2002-03	N.E. Jr. Coyotes	EJHL	44	28	40	*68	59	....	....	....	....	....	....	....	....	....	....	....	....	....	....	....	....	....	....
2003-04	Providence	H-East	37	10	6	16	47	....	....	....	....	....	....	....	....	....	....	....	....	....	....	....	....	....	....
2004-05	Providence	H-East	26	11	5	16	14	....	....	....	....	....	....	....	....	....	....	....	....	....	....	....	....	....	....
2005-06	Providence	H-East	36	9	19	28	29	....	....	....	....	....	....	....	....	....	....	....	....	....	....	....	....	....	....
2006-07	Providence	H-East	36	13	4	17	30	....	....	....	....	....	....	....	....	....	....	....	....	....	....	....	....	....	....
2007-08	Springfield	AHL	73	12	11	23	46	....	....	....	....	....	....	....	....	....	....	....	....	....	....	....	....	....	....
2008-09	Springfield	AHL	77	10	12	22	65	....	....	....	....	....	....	....	....	....	....	....	....	....	....	....	....	....	....
	Stockton Thunder	ECHL	3	0	2	2	0	....	....	....	....	....	....	....	....	....	....	....	....	....	....	....	....	....	....
2009-10	**Edmonton**	**NHL**	**2**	**1**	**0**	**1**	**0**	**0**	**0**	**0**	**3**	**33.3**	**1**	**0**	**0.0**	**6:42**	....	....	....	....	....	....	....	....	....
	Springfield	AHL	76	12	11	23	38	....	....	....	....	....	....	....	....	....	....	....	....	....	....	....	....	....	....
2010-11	Oklahoma City	AHL	80	*42	16	58	63	....	....	....	....	....	....	....	....	....	6	1	1	2	6	....	....	....	....
	NHL Totals		**2**	**1**	**0**	**1**	**0**	**0**	**0**	**0**	**3**	**33.3**		**0**	**0.0**	**6:42**	....	....	....	....	....	....	....	....	....

Hockey East All-Rookie Team (2004) • Willie Marshall Award (AHL – Top Goal-scorer) (2011)

Signed as a free agent by **Oklahoma City** (AHL). July 9, 2010. Signed as a free agent by **Pittsburgh**, July 1, 2011.

McGINN, Jamie
(muh-GIHN, JAY-mee) **S.J.**

Left wing. Shoots left. 6'1", 205 lbs. Born, Fergus, Ont., August 5, 1988. San Jose's 2nd choice, 36th overall, in 2006 Entry Draft.

Season	Club	League	GP	G	A	Pts	PIM	PP	SH	GW	S	%	+/-	TF	F%	Min	Playoffs GP	G	A	Pts	PIM	PP	SH	GW	Min
2003-04	Tor. Jr. Canadiens	GTHL	31	....	....	48	....	....	....	....	....	....	....	....	....	....	18	14	18	32	....	....	....	....	....
2004-05	Ottawa 67's	OHL	59	10	12	22	35	....	....	....	....	....	....	....	....	....	18	4	7	11	0	....	....	....	....
2005-06	Ottawa 67's	OHL	65	26	31	57	113	....	....	....	....	....	....	....	....	....	6	2	2	4	4	....	....	....	....
2006-07	Ottawa 67's	OHL	68	46	43	89	49	....	....	....	....	....	....	....	....	....	5	5	1	6	2	....	....	....	....
	Worcester Sharks	AHL	4	1	1	2	4	....	....	....	....	....	....	....	....	....	6	0	0	0	8	....	....	....	....
2007-08	Ottawa 67's	OHL	51	29	29	58	54	....	....	....	....	....	....	....	....	....	4	2	2	4	4	....	....	....	....
	Worcester Sharks	AHL	8	0	2	2	0	....	....	....	....	....	....	....	....	....	....	....	....	....	....	....	....	....	....
2008-09	**San Jose**	**NHL**	**35**	**4**	**2**	**6**	**2**	**1**	**0**	**1**	**27**	**14.8**	**–6**	**7**	**85.7**	**8:55**	....	....	....	....	....	....	....	....	....
	Worcester Sharks	AHL	47	19	11	30	52	....	....	....	....	....	....	....	....	....	6	4	0	4	19	....	....	....	....
2009-10	**San Jose**	**NHL**	**59**	**10**	**3**	**13**	**38**	**0**	**0**	**2**	**76**	**13.2**	**–3**	**16**	**43.8**	**10:00**	**15**	**0**	**0**	**0**	**8**	**0**	**0**	**0**	**7:45**
	Worcester Sharks	AHL	27	7	14	21	15	....	....	....	....	....	....	....	....	....	....	....	....	....	....	....	....	....	....
2010-11	**San Jose**	**NHL**	**49**	**1**	**5**	**6**	**33**	**0**	**0**	**0**	**63**	**1.6**	**–6**	**11**	**72.7**	**11:35**	**7**	**0**	**1**	**1**	**30**	**0**	**0**	**0**	**6:33**
	Worcester Sharks	AHL	30	9	11	20	27	....	....	....	....	....	....	....	....	....	....	....	....	....	....	....	....	....	....
	NHL Totals		**143**	**15**	**10**	**25**	**73**	**1**	**0**	**3**	**166**	**9.0**		**34**	**61.8**	**10:17**	**22**	**0**	**1**	**1**	**38**	**0**	**0**	**0**	**7:22**

McGRATTAN, Brian
(muh-GRA-tuhn, BRIGH-uhn) **ANA**

Right wing. Shoots right. 6'4", 235 lbs. Born, Hamilton, Ont., September 2, 1981. Los Angeles' 5th choice, 104th overall, in 1999 Entry Draft.

Season	Club	League	GP	G	A	Pts	PIM	PP	SH	GW	S	%	+/-	TF	F%	Min	Playoffs GP	G	A	Pts	PIM	PP	SH	GW	Min
1997-98	Guelph Fire	ON-Jr.B	15	4	3	7	94	....	....	....	....	....	....	....	....	....	....	....	....	....	....	....	....	....	....
	Guelph Storm	OHL	25	3	2	5	11	....	....	....	....	....	....	....	....	....	....	....	....	....	....	....	....	....	....
1998-99	Guelph Storm	OHL	6	1	3	4	15	....	....	....	....	....	....	....	....	....	....	....	....	....	....	....	....	....	....
	Sudbury Wolves	OHL	53	7	10	17	153	....	....	....	....	....	....	....	....	....	4	0	0	0	8	....	....	....	....
99-2000	Sudbury Wolves	OHL	25	2	8	10	79	....	....	....	....	....	....	....	....	....	....	....	....	....	....	....	....	....	....
	Mississauga	OHL	42	9	13	22	166	....	....	....	....	....	....	....	....	....	....	....	....	....	....	....	....	....	....
2000-01	Mississauga	OHL	31	20	9	29	83	....	....	....	....	....	....	....	....	....	....	....	....	....	....	....	....	....	....
2001-02	Mississauga	OHL	7	2	3	5	16	....	....	....	....	....	....	....	....	....	....	....	....	....	....	....	....	....	....
	Owen Sound	OHL	2	0	0	0	0	....	....	....	....	....	....	....	....	....	....	....	....	....	....	....	....	....	....
	Oshawa Generals	OHL	25	10	5	15	72	....	....	....	....	....	....	....	....	....	....	....	....	....	....	....	....	....	....
	Sault Ste. Marie	OHL	26	8	7	15	71	....	....	....	....	....	....	....	....	....	6	2	0	2	20	....	....	....	....
2002-03	Binghamton	AHL	59	9	10	19	173	....	....	....	....	....	....	....	....	....	1	0	0	0	0	....	....	....	....
2003-04	Binghamton	AHL	66	9	11	20	327	....	....	....	....	....	....	....	....	....	1	0	0	0	0	....	....	....	....
2004-05	Binghamton	AHL	71	7	1	8	*551	....	....	....	....	....	....	....	....	....	6	0	2	2	28	....	....	....	....
2005-06	**Ottawa**	**NHL**	**60**	**2**	**3**	**5**	**141**	**0**	**0**	**0**	**36**	**5.6**	**0**	**0**	**0.0**	**4:14**	....	....	....	....	....	....	....	....	....
2006-07	**Ottawa**	**NHL**	**45**	**0**	**2**	**2**	**100**	**0**	**0**	**0**	**22**	**0.0**	**–1**	**1**	**100.0**	**3:51**	....	....	....	....	....	....	....	....	....
2007-08	**Ottawa**	**NHL**	**38**	**0**	**3**	**3**	**46**	**0**	**0**	**0**	**11**	**0.0**	**0**	**0**	**0.0**	**2:52**	....	....	....	....	....	....	....	....	....
2008-09	**Phoenix**	**NHL**	**5**	**0**	**0**	**0**	**22**	**0**	**0**	**0**	**2**	**0.0**	**–2**	**0**	**0.0**	**5:31**	....	....	....	....	....	....	....	....	....
	San Antonio	AHL	1	0	0	0	2	....	....	....	....	....	....	....	....	....	....	....	....	....	....	....	....	....	....
2009-10	**Calgary**	**NHL**	**34**	**1**	**3**	**4**	**86**	**0**	**0**	**0**	**19**	**5.3**	**3**	**0**	**0.0**	**3:26**	....	....	....	....	....	....	....	....	....
2010-11	Providence Bruins	AHL	39	4	1	5	97	....	....	....	....	....	....	....	....	....	....	....	....	....	....	....	....	....	....
	Syracuse Crunch	AHL	20	6	4	10	56	....	....	....	....	....	....	....	....	....	....	....	....	....	....	....	....	....	....
	NHL Totals		**182**	**3**	**11**	**14**	**395**	**0**	**0**	**0**	**90**	**3.3**		**1**	**100.0**	**3:45**	....	....	....	....	....	....	....	....	....

• Missed majority of 2000-01 due to knee injury vs. Kingston (OHL), January 1, 2001. Signed as a free agent by **Ottawa**, June 2, 2002. • Missed majority of 2007-08 as a healthy reserve. Traded to **Phoenix** by **Ottawa** for Boston's 5th round choice (previously acquired, Ottawa selected Jeff Costello) in 2009 Entry Draft, June 25, 2008. Signed as a free agent by **Calgary**, July 11, 2009. • Missed majority of 2009-10 as a healthy reserve. Signed as a free agent by **Boston**, October 11, 2010. Traded to **Anaheim** by **Boston** with Sean Zimmerman for David Laliberte and Stefan Chaput, February 27, 2011.

McIVER, Nathan
(muh-KEE-vuhr, NAY-thuhn) **BOS**

Defense. Shoots left. 6'3", 205 lbs. Born, Summerside, P.E.I., January 6, 1985. Vancouver's 9th choice, 254th overall, in 2003 Entry Draft.

Season	Club	League	GP	G	A	Pts	PIM	PP	SH	GW	S	%	+/-	TF	F%	Min	Playoffs GP	G	A	Pts	PIM	PP	SH	GW	Min
2001-02	Summerside	MJrHL	47	4	4	8	91	....	....	....	....	....	....	....	....	....	5	0	0	0	9	....	....	....	....
2002-03	St. Michael's	OHL	68	5	10	15	121	....	....	....	....	....	....	....	....	....	19	0	4	4	41	....	....	....	....
2003-04	St. Michael's	OHL	57	4	11	15	183	....	....	....	....	....	....	....	....	....	16	0	1	1	22	....	....	....	....
2004-05	St. Michael's	OHL	67	4	22	26	160	....	....	....	....	....	....	....	....	....	3	0	1	1	13	....	....	....	....
2005-06	Manitoba Moose	AHL	66	1	6	7	155	....	....	....	....	....	....	....	....	....	12	0	0	0	28	....	....	....	....
2006-07	**Vancouver**	**NHL**	**1**	**0**	**0**	**0**	**7**	**0**	**0**	**0**	**0**	**0.0**	**–3**	**0**	**0.0**	**11:20**	....	....	....	....	....	....	....	....	....
	Manitoba Moose	AHL	63	1	2	3	139	....	....	....	....	....	....	....	....	....	2	0	0	0	0	....	....	....	....
2007-08	**Vancouver**	**NHL**	**17**	**0**	**0**	**0**	**52**	**0**	**0**	**0**	**9**	**0.0**	**–8**	**0**	**0.0**	**10:28**	....	....	....	....	....	....	....	....	....
	Manitoba Moose	AHL	43	3	3	6	108	....	....	....	....	....	....	....	....	....	6	0	1	1	11	....	....	....	....

			Regular Season														Playoffs								
Season	Club	League	GP	G	A	Pts	PIM	PP	SH	GW	S	%	+/-	TF	F%	Min	GP	G	A	Pts	PIM	PP	SH	GW	Min
2008-09	**Anaheim**	**NHL**	**18**	**0**	**1**	**1**	**36**	**0**	**0**	**0**	**5**	**0.0**	**2**	**0**	**0.0**	**9:24**	....	....	....	....	....	....	....	....	....
	Manitoba Moose	AHL	28	0	2	2	59	....	....	....	....	....	....	....	....	....	10	0	0	0	10	....	....	....	....
2009-10	Manitoba Moose	AHL	44	1	4	5	109	....	....	....	....	....	....	....	....	....	....	....	....	....	....	....	....	....	....
2010-11	Providence Bruins	AHL	60	0	3	3	176	....	....	....	....	....	....	....	....	....	....	....	....	....	....	....	....	....	....
	NHL Totals		**36**	**0**	**1**	**1**	**95**	**0**	**0**	**0**	**14**	**0.0**		**0**	**0.0**	**9:57**	....	....	....	....	....	....	....	....	....

Claimed on waivers by **Anaheim** from **Vancouver**, October 4, 2008. Traded to **Vancouver** by **Anaheim** for Mike Brown, February 4, 2009. Signed as a free agent by **Boston**, July 5, 2010.

McLAREN, Frazer

(muh-KLAIR-uhn, FRAY-zuhr) **S.J.**

Left wing. Shoots left. 6'5", 250 lbs. Born, Winnipeg, Man., October 29, 1987. San Jose's 8th choice, 203rd overall, in 2007 Entry Draft.

2002-03	Kelvin	High-MB	56	27	24	51	136	....	....	....	....	....	....	....	....	....	....	....	....	....	....	....	....	....	....
2003-04	Portland	WHL	50	0	3	3	44	....	....	....	....	....	....	....	....	....	1	0	0	0	0	....	....	....	....
2004-05	Portland	WHL	71	6	5	11	124	....	....	....	....	....	....	....	....	....	7	0	0	0	10	....	....	....	....
2005-06	Portland	WHL	70	12	6	18	194	....	....	....	....	....	....	....	....	....	12	0	2	2	27	....	....	....	....
2006-07	Portland	WHL	61	19	12	31	186	....	....	....	....	....	....	....	....	....	....	....	....	....	....	....	....	....	....
2007-08	Portland	WHL	18	4	3	7	45	....	....	....	....	....	....	....	....	....	....	....	....	....	....	....	....	....	....
	Moose Jaw	WHL	48	15	18	33	119	....	....	....	....	....	....	....	....	....	6	1	1	2	8	....	....	....	....
	Worcester Sharks	AHL	4	0	1	1	17	....	....	....	....	....	....	....	....	....	....	....	....	....	....	....	....	....	....
2008-09	Worcester Sharks	AHL	75	7	1	8	181	....	....	....	....	....	....	....	....	....	12	1	4	5	*50	....	....	....	....
2009-10	**San Jose**	**NHL**	**23**	**1**	**5**	**6**	**54**	**0**	**0**	**0**	**13**	**7.7**	**6**	**0**	**0.0**	**6:02**	....	....	....	....	....	....	....	....	....
	Worcester Sharks	AHL	52	4	11	15	148	....	....	....	....	....	....	....	....	....	11	0	0	0	37	....	....	....	....
2010-11	**San Jose**	**NHL**	**9**	**0**	**0**	**0**	**22**	**0**	**0**	**0**	**1**	**0.0**	**–1**	**0**	**0.0**	**4:15**	....	....	....	....	....	....	....	....	....
	Worcester Sharks	AHL	40	2	2	4	71	....	....	....	....	....	....	....	....	....	....	....	....	....	....	....	....	....	....
	NHL Totals		**32**	**1**	**5**	**6**	**76**	**0**	**0**	**0**	**14**	**7.1**		**0**	**0.0**	**5:32**	....	....	....	....	....	....	....	....	....

McLEAN, Brett

(muh-KLAYN, BREHT) **CHI**

Center. Shoots left. 5'11", 185 lbs. Born, Comox, B.C., August 14, 1978. Dallas' 9th choice, 242nd overall, in 1997 Entry Draft.

1993-94	Notre Dame	SMBHL	71	109	124	233	70	....	....	....	....	....	....	....	....	....	....	....	....	....	....	....	....	....	....
1994-95	Tacoma Rockets	WHL	67	11	23	34	33	....	....	....	....	....	....	....	....	....	4	0	1	1	0	....	....	....	....
1995-96	Kelowna Rockets	WHL	71	37	42	79	60	....	....	....	....	....	....	....	....	....	6	2	2	4	6	....	....	....	....
1996-97	Kelowna Rockets	WHL	72	44	60	104	89	....	....	....	....	....	....	....	....	....	6	4	2	6	12	....	....	....	....
1997-98	Kelowna Rockets	WHL	54	42	45	87	91	....	....	....	....	....	....	....	....	....	7	4	5	9	17	....	....	....	....
1998-99	Kelowna Rockets	WHL	44	32	38	70	46	....	....	....	....	....	....	....	....	....	....	....	....	....	....	....	....	....	....
	Brandon	WHL	21	15	16	31	20	....	....	....	....	....	....	....	....	....	5	1	6	7	8	....	....	....	....
	Cincinnati	AHL	7	0	3	3	6	....	....	....	....	....	....	....	....	....	....	....	....	....	....	....	....	....	....
99-2000	Johnstown Chiefs	ECHL	8	4	7	11	6	....	....	....	....	....	....	....	....	....	....	....	....	....	....	....	....	....	....
	Saint John Flames	AHL	72	15	23	38	115	....	....	....	....	....	....	....	....	....	3	0	1	1	2	....	....	....	....
2000-01	Cleveland	IHL	74	20	24	44	54	....	....	....	....	....	....	....	....	....	4	0	0	0	18	....	....	....	....
2001-02	Houston Aeros	AHL	78	24	21	45	71	....	....	....	....	....	....	....	....	....	14	1	6	7	12	....	....	....	....
2002-03	**Chicago**	**NHL**	**2**	**0**	**0**	**0**	**0**	**0**	**0**	**0**	**1**	**0.0**	**–1**	**19**	**26.3**	**10:47**	....	....	....	....	....	....	....	....	....
	Norfolk Admirals	AHL	77	23	38	61	60	....	....	....	....	....	....	....	....	....	9	2	6	8	9	....	....	....	....
2003-04	**Chicago**	**NHL**	**76**	**11**	**20**	**31**	**54**	**5**	**1**	**0**	**125**	**8.8**	**–11**	**1135**	**51.1**	**17:33**	....	....	....	....	....	....	....	....	....
	Norfolk Admirals	AHL	4	3	3	6	6	....	....	....	....	....	....	....	....	....	....	....	....	....	....	....	....	....	....
2004-05	Malmo	Sweden	38	7	6	13	102	....	....	....	....	....	....	....	....	....	....	....	....	....	....	....	....	....	....
	Malmo	Sweden-Q	9	1	1	2	16	....	....	....	....	....	....	....	....	....	....	....	....	....	....	....	....	....	....
2005-06	**Colorado**	**NHL**	**82**	**9**	**31**	**40**	**51**	**1**	**0**	**0**	**115**	**7.8**	**–7**	**770**	**50.7**	**12:12**	**8**	**0**	**1**	**1**	**4**	**0**	**0**	**0**	**10:40**
2006-07	**Colorado**	**NHL**	**78**	**15**	**20**	**35**	**36**	**0**	**0**	**3**	**134**	**11.2**	**8**	**413**	**50.1**	**13:38**	....	....	....	....	....	....	....	....	....
2007-08	**Florida**	**NHL**	**67**	**14**	**23**	**37**	**34**	**3**	**1**	**1**	**140**	**10.0**	**–5**	**624**	**47.4**	**16:14**	....	....	....	....	....	....	....	....	....
2008-09	**Florida**	**NHL**	**80**	**7**	**12**	**19**	**29**	**0**	**0**	**2**	**114**	**6.1**	**–12**	**456**	**43.2**	**12:26**	....	....	....	....	....	....	....	....	....
2009-10	SC Bern	Swiss	34	13	20	33	24	....	....	....	....	....	....	....	....	....	15	5	7	12	8	....	....	....	....
2010-11	SC Bern	Swiss	50	10	17	27	22	....	....	....	....	....	....	....	....	....	6	3	0	3	6	....	....	....	....
	NHL Totals		**385**	**56**	**106**	**162**	**204**	**9**	**2**	**6**	**629**	**8.9**		**3417**	**49.0**	**14:17**	**8**	**0**	**1**	**1**	**4**	**0**	**0**	**0**	**10:40**

WHL West Second All-Star Team (1998)

Signed as a free agent by **Calgary**, September 1, 1999. Signed as a free agent by **Minnesota**, July 13, 2000. Signed as a free agent by **Chicago**, July 23, 2002. Signed as a free agent by **Colorado**, July 22, 2004. Signed as a free agent by **Malmo** (Sweden), September 24, 2004. Signed as a free agent by **Florida**, July 1, 2007. Signed as a free agent by **Bern** (Swiss), October 10, 2009. Signed as a free agent by **Chicago**, July 1, 2011.

McLEAN, Kurtis

(muh-KLAYN, KUHR-this)

Center. Shoots right. 5'11", 175 lbs. Born, Kirkland Lake, Ont., November 2, 1980.

99-2000	Trenton Sting	OPJHL	49	31	56	87	33	....	....	....	....	....	....	....	....	....	....	....	....	....	....	....	....	....	....
2000-01	Trenton Sting	OPJHL	47	37	38	75	16	....	....	....	....	....	....	....	....	....	....	....	....	....	....	....	....	....	....
2001-02	Norwich U.	NCAA-3	32	28	24	52	12	....	....	....	....	....	....	....	....	....	....	....	....	....	....	....	....	....	....
2002-03	Norwich U.	NCAA-3	29	25	23	48	26	....	....	....	....	....	....	....	....	....	....	....	....	....	....	....	....	....	....
2003-04	Norwich U.	NCAA-3	28	36	21	57	16	....	....	....	....	....	....	....	....	....	....	....	....	....	....	....	....	....	....
2004-05	Norwich U.	NCAA-3	26	29	26	55	6	....	....	....	....	....	....	....	....	....	....	....	....	....	....	....	....	....	....
2005-06	Wilkes-Barre	AHL	32	4	11	15	8	....	....	....	....	....	....	....	....	....	....	....	....	....	....	....	....	....	....
	Wheeling Nailers	ECHL	41	31	25	56	32	....	....	....	....	....	....	....	....	....	5	4	4	8	4	....	....	....	....
2006-07	Wilkes-Barre	AHL	55	16	16	32	24	....	....	....	....	....	....	....	....	....	10	4	3	7	4	....	....	....	....
	Wheeling Nailers	ECHL	16	11	12	23	21	....	....	....	....	....	....	....	....	....	....	....	....	....	....	....	....	....	....
2007-08	Wilkes-Barre	AHL	76	22	32	54	58	....	....	....	....	....	....	....	....	....	23	4	15	19	8	....	....	....	....
2008-09	**NY Islanders**	**NHL**	**4**	**1**	**0**	**1**	**0**	**0**	**0**	**1**	**5**	**20.0**	**1**	**1**	**0.0**	**10:34**	....	....	....	....	....	....	....	....	....
	Bridgeport	AHL	62	15	37	52	30	....	....	....	....	....	....	....	....	....	....	....	....	....	....	....	....	....	....
2009-10	Lukko Rauma	Finland	42	18	25	43	28	....	....	....	....	....	....	....	....	....	4	0	1	1	10	....	....	....	....
2010-11	Lukko Rauma	Finland	60	16	39	55	24	....	....	....	....	....	....	....	....	....	13	6	4	10	4	....	....	....	....
	NHL Totals		**4**	**1**	**0**	**1**	**0**	**0**	**0**	**1**	**5**	**20.0**		**1**	**0.0**	**10:34**	....	....	....	....	....	....	....	....	....

Signed as a free agent by **Wilkes-Barre** (AHL), September 29, 2005. Signed as a free agent by **Pittsburgh**, September 7, 2006. Signed as a free agent by **NY Islanders**, July 3, 2008. Signed as a free agent by **Rauma** (Finland), May 29, 2009.

McLEOD, Cody

(muh-KLOWD, KOH-dee) **COL**

Left wing. Shoots left. 6'2", 210 lbs. Born, Binscarth, Man., June 26, 1984.

2001-02	Portland	WHL	47	10	3	13	86	....	....	....	....	....	....	....	....	....	5	0	0	0	0	....	....	....	....
2002-03	Portland	WHL	71	15	18	33	153	....	....	....	....	....	....	....	....	....	7	1	1	2	13	....	....	....	....
2003-04	Portland	WHL	69	13	18	31	227	....	....	....	....	....	....	....	....	....	5	2	2	4	6	....	....	....	....
2004-05	Portland	WHL	70	31	29	60	195	....	....	....	....	....	....	....	....	....	7	0	3	3	8	....	....	....	....
	Adirondack	UHL	1	0	0	0	0	....	....	....	....	....	....	....	....	....	5	0	0	0	11	....	....	....	....
2005-06	Lowell	AHL	33	4	5	9	87	....	....	....	....	....	....	....	....	....	....	....	....	....	....	....	....	....	....
	San Diego Gulls	ECHL	16	4	5	9	48	....	....	....	....	....	....	....	....	....	2	2	1	3	14	....	....	....	....
2006-07	Albany River Rats	AHL	73	11	8	19	180	....	....	....	....	....	....	....	....	....	5	0	0	0	4	....	....	....	....
2007-08	**Colorado**	**NHL**	**49**	**4**	**5**	**9**	**120**	**0**	**0**	**0**	**60**	**6.7**	**–6**	**3**	**0.0**	**10:07**	**10**	**1**	**1**	**2**	**26**	**0**	**0**	**0**	**12:23**
	Lake Erie	AHL	27	6	7	13	101	....	....	....	....	....	....	....	....	....	....	....	....	....	....	....	....	....	....
2008-09	**Colorado**	**NHL**	**79**	**15**	**5**	**20**	**162**	**0**	**0**	**3**	**118**	**12.7**	**–11**	**5**	**40.0**	**11:35**	....	....	....	....	....	....	....	....	....
2009-10	**Colorado**	**NHL**	**74**	**7**	**11**	**18**	**138**	**0**	**0**	**1**	**117**	**6.0**	**–13**	**13**	**30.8**	**12:56**	**6**	**0**	**0**	**0**	**5**	**0**	**0**	**0**	**11:03**
2010-11	**Colorado**	**NHL**	**71**	**5**	**3**	**8**	**189**	**2**	**0**	**0**	**73**	**6.8**	**–7**	**8**	**37.5**	**9:47**	....	....	....	....	....	....	....	....	....
	NHL Totals		**273**	**31**	**24**	**55**	**609**	**2**	**0**	**4**	**368**	**8.4**		**29**	**31.0**	**11:13**	**16**	**1**	**1**	**2**	**31**	**0**	**0**	**0**	**11:53**

Signed as a free agent by **Colorado**, July 6, 2006.

McMILLAN, Brandon

(muhk-MIHL-uhn, BRAN-duhn) **ANA**

Center. Shoots left. 5'11", 192 lbs. Born, Richmond, B.C., March 22, 1990. Anaheim's 7th choice, 85th overall, in 2008 Entry Draft.

2006-07	Kelowna Rockets	WHL	55	2	10	12	27	....	....	....	....	....	....	....	....	....	....	....	....	....	....	....	....	....	....
2007-08	Kelowna Rockets	WHL	71	15	26	41	56	....	....	....	....	....	....	....	....	....	7	0	0	0	6	....	....	....	....
2008-09	Kelowna Rockets	WHL	70	14	35	49	75	....	....	....	....	....	....	....	....	....	22	0	5	5	20	....	....	....	....
2009-10	Kelowna Rockets	WHL	55	25	42	67	63	....	....	....	....	....	....	....	....	....	12	5	10	15	14	....	....	....	....
2010-11	**Anaheim**	**NHL**	**60**	**11**	**10**	**21**	**18**	**2**	**2**	**2**	**77**	**14.3**	**–5**	**293**	**38.9**	**14:04**	**6**	**1**	**1**	**2**	**0**	**0**	**0**	**0**	**13:08**
	Syracuse Crunch	AHL	16	4	2	6	10	....	....	....	....	....	....	....	....	....	....	....	....	....	....	....	....	....	....
	NHL Totals		**60**	**11**	**10**	**21**	**18**	**2**	**2**	**2**	**77**	**14.3**		**293**	**38.9**	**14:04**	**6**	**1**	**1**	**2**	**0**	**0**	**0**	**0**	**13:09**

McMILLAN, Carson

(muhk-MIHL-lihn, KAHR-suhn) **MIN**

Right wing. Shoots right. 6'1", 193 lbs. Born, Brandon, Man., September 10, 1988. Minnesota's 5th choice, 200th overall, in 2007 Entry Draft.

			Regular Season														Playoffs								
Season	Club	League	GP	G	A	Pts	PIM	PP	SH	GW	S	%	+/-	TF	F%	Min	GP	G	A	Pts	PIM	PP	SH	GW	Min
2003-04	Crocus Plains	High-MB	STATISTICS NOT AVAILABLE																						
	Brandon	MMHL	4	0	0	0	0																		
2004-05	Brandon	MMHL	40	17	19	36	34										5	3	4	7	8				
	Winkler Flyers	MJHL	4	1	1	2	2																		
2005-06	Calgary Hitmen	WHL	59	3	2	5	42										13	0	0	0	2				
2006-07	Calgary Hitmen	WHL	72	7	15	22	76										18	2	0	2	17				
2007-08	Calgary Hitmen	WHL	72	16	26	42	87										16	1	0	1	22				
2008-09	Calgary Hitmen	WHL	68	31	41	72	93										18	3	8	11	18				
2009-10	Houston Aeros	AHL	56	4	4	8	70																		
2010-11	**Minnesota**	**NHL**	**4**	**1**	**1**	**2**	**0**	**0**	**0**	**0**	**5**	**20.0**	**1**	**23**	**39.1**	**9:20**									
	Houston Aeros	AHL	78	12	10	22	80										21	3	2	5	14				
	NHL Totals		**4**	**1**	**1**	**2**	**0**	**0**	**0**	**0**	**5**	**20.0**		**23**	**39.1**	**9:20**									

McQUAID, Adam

(muh-KWAYD, A-duhm) **BOS**

Defense. Shoots right. 6'4", 197 lbs. Born, Charlottetown, P.E.I., October 12, 1986. Columbus' 2nd choice, 55th overall, in 2005 Entry Draft.

Season	Club	League	GP	G	A	Pts	PIM	PP	SH	GW	S	%	+/-	TF	F%	Min	GP	G	A	Pts	PIM	PP	SH	GW	Min
2003-04	Sudbury Wolves	OHL	47	3	6	9	25										7	0	1	1	2				
2004-05	Sudbury Wolves	OHL	66	3	16	19	98										8	0	2	2	10				
2005-06	Sudbury Wolves	OHL	68	3	14	17	107										10	0	1	1	16				
2006-07	Sudbury Wolves	OHL	65	9	22	31	110										21	1	5	6	24				
2007-08	Providence Bruins	AHL	68	1	8	9	73										10	0	0	0	9				
2008-09	Providence Bruins	AHL	78	4	11	15	141										16	0	3	3	26				
2009-10	**Boston**	**NHL**	**19**	**1**	**0**	**1**	**21**	**0**	**0**	**1**	**10**	**10.0**	**-5**	**0**	**0.0**	**10:44**	**9**	**0**	**0**	**0**	**6**	**0**	**0**	**0**	**10:12**
	Providence Bruins	AHL	32	3	7	10	66																		
2010-11♦	**Boston**	**NHL**	**67**	**3**	**12**	**15**	**96**	**0**	**0**	**0**	**46**	**6.5**	**30**	**0**	**0.0**	**14:52**	**23**	**0**	**4**	**4**	**14**	**0**	**0**	**0**	**13:01**
	NHL Totals		**86**	**4**	**12**	**16**	**117**	**0**	**0**	**1**	**56**	**7.1**		**0**	**0.0**	**13:57**	**32**	**0**	**4**	**4**	**20**	**0**	**0**	**0**	**12:14**

Traded to **Boston** by **Columbus** for Boston's 5th round choice (later traded to Dallas – Dallas selected Jamie Benn) in 2007 Entry Draft, May 16, 2007.

McRAE, Philip

(muh-KRAY, FIHL-ihp) **ST.L.**

Center. Shoots left. 6'2", 200 lbs. Born, Minneapolis, MN, March 15, 1990. St. Louis' 2nd choice, 33rd overall, in 2008 Entry Draft.

Season	Club	League	GP	G	A	Pts	PIM	PP	SH	GW	S	%	+/-	TF	F%	Min	GP	G	A	Pts	PIM	PP	SH	GW	Min
2005-06	USNTDP	U-17	15	1	1	2	0																		
	USNTDP	NAHL	33	8	8	16	9										10	1	2	3	2				
2006-07	London Knights	OHL	63	2	8	10	27										16	0	0	0	6				
2007-08	London Knights	OHL	66	18	28	46	61										4	0	0	0	7				
2008-09	London Knights	OHL	59	29	31	60	54										14	5	5	10	12				
2009-10	London Knights	OHL	33	11	26	37	43																		
	Plymouth Whalers	OHL	19	5	9	14	21										9	6	9	15	11				
2010-11	**St. Louis**	**NHL**	**15**	**1**	**2**	**3**	**2**	**0**	**0**	**0**	**13**	**7.7**	**-10**	**64**	**53.1**	**9:02**									
	Peoria Rivermen	AHL	46	12	14	26	23																		
	NHL Totals		**15**	**1**	**2**	**3**	**2**	**0**	**0**	**0**	**13**	**7.7**		**64**	**53.1**	**9:02**									

MEECH, Derek

(MEECH, DAIR-ihk) **WPG**

Defense. Shoots left. 5'11", 205 lbs. Born, Winnipeg, Man., April 21, 1984. Detroit's 7th choice, 229th overall, in 2002 Entry Draft.

Season	Club	League	GP	G	A	Pts	PIM	PP	SH	GW	S	%	+/-	TF	F%	Min	GP	G	A	Pts	PIM	PP	SH	GW	Min
99-2000	Wpg. Warriors	MMMHL	36	15	40	55	24																		
	Red Deer Rebels	WHL	5	1	0	1	2																		
2000-01	Red Deer Rebels	WHL	60	2	7	9	40										22	0	0	0	9				
2001-02	Red Deer Rebels	WHL	71	8	19	27	33										13	1	1	2	6				
2002-03	Red Deer Rebels	WHL	65	6	16	22	53										12	1	1	2	12				
2003-04	Red Deer Rebels	WHL	62	10	28	38	40										19	4	7	11	10				
2004-05	Grand Rapids	AHL	78	6	8	14	40																		
2005-06	Grand Rapids	AHL	79	4	16	20	85										16	0	2	2	4				
2006-07	**Detroit**	**NHL**	**4**	**0**	**0**	**0**	**2**	**0**	**0**	**0**	**3**	**0.0**	**1**	**0**	**0.0**	**5:47**									
	Grand Rapids	AHL	67	6	23	29	40										7	0	1	1	4				
2007-08	**Detroit**	**NHL**	**32**	**0**	**3**	**3**	**6**	**0**	**0**	**0**	**44**	**0.0**	**-5**	**0**	**0.0**	**12:08**									
	Grand Rapids	AHL	6	1	1	2	0																		
2008-09	**Detroit**	**NHL**	**41**	**2**	**5**	**7**	**12**	**0**	**0**	**0**	**44**	**4.5**	**-12**	**2**	**0.0**	**10:03**	**2**	**0**	**0**	**0**	**0**	**0**	**0**	**0**	**4:04**
2009-10	**Detroit**	**NHL**	**49**	**2**	**4**	**6**	**19**	**1**	**0**	**2**	**57**	**3.5**	**-12**	**0**	**0.0**	**11:55**									
2010-11	Grand Rapids	AHL	74	10	27	37	81																		
	NHL Totals		**126**	**4**	**12**	**16**	**39**	**1**	**0**	**2**	**148**	**2.7**		**2**	**0.0**	**11:10**	**2**	**0**	**0**	**0**	**0**	**0**	**0**	**0**	**4:04**

WHL East Second All-Star Team (2004)

• Missed majority of 2007-08 as a healthy reserve. Signed as a free agent by **Winnipeg**, July 2, 2011.

MERCIER, Justin

(MUHR-see-uhr, JUHS-tihn) **COL**

Forward. Shoots left. 5'11", 190 lbs. Born, Erie, PA, June 25, 1987. Colorado's 8th choice, 168th overall, in 2005 Entry Draft.

Season	Club	League	GP	G	A	Pts	PIM	PP	SH	GW	S	%	+/-	TF	F%	Min	GP	G	A	Pts	PIM	PP	SH	GW	Min
2003-04	St. Louis	USHL	60	12	9	21	49																		
2004-05	USNTDP	U-18	26	1	7	8	31																		
	USNTDP	NAHL	16	4	3	7	33																		
2005-06	Miami U.	CCHA	35	3	7	10	32																		
2006-07	Miami U.	CCHA	40	10	15	25	59																		
2007-08	Miami U.	CCHA	42	25	15	40	42																		
2008-09	Miami U.	CCHA	40	14	15	29	58																		
2009-10	**Colorado**	**NHL**	**9**	**1**	**1**	**2**	**0**	**0**	**0**	**0**	**5**	**20.0**	**2**	**1**	**100.0**	**7:11**									
	Lake Erie	AHL	64	13	10	23	54																		
2010-11	Lake Erie	AHL	80	12	16	28	66										7	3	2	5	2				
	NHL Totals		**9**	**1**	**1**	**2**	**0**	**0**	**0**	**0**	**5**	**20.0**		**1**	**100.0**	**7:11**									

MESZAROS, Andrej

(MEHT-zahr-ohsh, AWN-dray) **PHI**

Defense. Shoots left. 6'2", 223 lbs. Born, Povazska Bystrica, Czech., October 13, 1985. Ottawa's 1st choice, 23rd overall, in 2004 Entry Draft.

Season	Club	League	GP	G	A	Pts	PIM	PP	SH	GW	S	%	+/-	TF	F%	Min	GP	G	A	Pts	PIM	PP	SH	GW	Min
2002-03	Dukla Trencin Jr.	Slovak-Jr.	33	6	10	16	12																		
	Dukla Trencin	Slovakia	23	0	1	1	4																		
2003-04	Dukla Trencin	Slovakia	44	3	3	6	8										14	3	1	4	2				
	Dukla Trencin Jr.	Slovak-Jr.	5	2	2	4	0																		
2004-05	Vancouver Giants	WHL	59	11	30	41	94										6	1	3	4	14				
2005-06	**Ottawa**	**NHL**	**82**	**10**	**29**	**39**	**61**	**5**	**0**	**2**	**137**	**7.3**	**34**	**1**	**0.0**	**18:11**	**10**	**1**	**0**	**1**	**18**	**0**	**0**	**0**	**17:50**
	Slovakia	Olympics	6	0	2	2	4																		
2006-07	**Ottawa**	**NHL**	**82**	**7**	**28**	**35**	**102**	**0**	**0**	**1**	**147**	**4.8**	**-15**	**0**	**0.0**	**21:41**	**20**	**1**	**6**	**7**	**12**	**0**	**0**	**0**	**20:29**
2007-08	**Ottawa**	**NHL**	**82**	**9**	**27**	**36**	**50**	**6**	**1**	**1**	**160**	**5.6**	**5**	**1**	**0.0**	**21:02**	**4**	**0**	**1**	**1**	**6**	**0**	**0**	**0**	**18:59**
2008-09	**Tampa Bay**	**NHL**	**52**	**2**	**14**	**16**	**36**	**1**	**0**	**1**	**87**	**2.3**	**-4**	**1**	**0.0**	**24:11**									
2009-10	**Tampa Bay**	**NHL**	**81**	**6**	**11**	**17**	**50**	**2**	**0**	**1**	**145**	**4.1**	**-14**	**0**	**0.0**	**20:11**									
	Slovakia	Olympics	7	0	0	0	4																		
2010-11	**Philadelphia**	**NHL**	**81**	**8**	**24**	**32**	**42**	**3**	**0**	**2**	**144**	**5.6**	**30**	**0**	**0.0**	**21:07**	**11**	**2**	**4**	**6**	**8**	**0**	**0**	**0**	**26:01**
	NHL Totals		**460**	**42**	**133**	**175**	**341**	**17**	**1**	**8**	**820**	**5.1**		**3**	**0.0**	**20:52**	**45**	**4**	**11**	**15**	**44**	**0**	**0**	**0**	**21:07**

WHL West Second All-Star Team (2005) • NHL All-Rookie Team (2006)

Traded to **Tampa Bay** by **Ottawa** for Filip Kuba, Alexandre Picard and San Jose's 1st round choice (previously acquired, later traded to NY Islanders, later traded to Columbus, later traded to Anaheim - Anaheim selected Kyle Palmieri) in 2009 Entry Draft, August 29, 2008. Traded to **Philadelphia** by **Tampa Bay** for Philadelphia's 2nd round choice (Nikita Kucharev) in 2011 Entry Draft, July 1, 2010.

METHOT, Marc

(meh-THAWT, MAHRK) **CBJ**

Defense. Shoots left. 6'3", 222 lbs. Born, Ottawa, Ont., June 21, 1985. Columbus' 7th choice, 168th overall, in 2003 Entry Draft.

Season	Club	League	GP	G	A	Pts	PIM	PP	SH	GW	S	%	+/-	TF	F%	Min	Playoffs GP	G	A	Pts	PIM	PP	SH	GW	Min
2001-02	Kanata Laser	CJHL	50	3	10	13	22																		
2002-03	London Knights	OHL	68	2	13	15	46										14	2	4	6	6				
2003-04	London Knights	OHL	63	2	9	11	66										15	0	3	3	18				
2004-05	London Knights	OHL	67	4	12	16	88										18	2	1	3	32				
2005-06	Syracuse Crunch	AHL	70	2	11	13	75										5	0	0	0	8				
2006-07	**Columbus**	**NHL**	20	0	4	4	12	0	0	0	11	0.0	5	0	0.0	14:38									
	Syracuse Crunch	AHL	59	1	15	16	58																		
2007-08	**Columbus**	**NHL**	9	0	0	0	8	0	0	0	9	0.0	–1	0	0.0	14:14									
	Syracuse Crunch	AHL	66	7	6	13	130										13	0	6	6	14				
2008-09	**Columbus**	**NHL**	66	4	13	17	55	0	0	0	58	6.9	7	0	0.0	17:57	4	0	0	0	2	0	0	0	16:15
2009-10	**Columbus**	**NHL**	60	2	6	8	51	0	0	0	42	4.8	–8	0	0.0	19:31									
2010-11	**Columbus**	**NHL**	74	0	15	15	58	0	0	0	58	0.0	2	0	0.0	19:53									
	NHL Totals		**229**	**6**	**38**	**44**	**184**	**0**	**0**	**0**	**178**	**3.4**		**0**	**0.0**	**18:33**	**4**	**0**	**0**	**0**	**2**	**0**	**0**	**0**	**16:15**

METROPOLIT, Glen

(meh-troh-PAW-liht, GLEHN)

Center. Shoots right. 5'10", 196 lbs. Born, Toronto, Ont., June 25, 1974.

Season	Club	League	GP	G	A	Pts	PIM	PP	SH	GW	S	%	+/-	TF	F%	Min	Playoffs GP	G	A	Pts	PIM	PP	SH	GW	Min
1992-93	Richmond Hill	ON-Jr.A	43	27	36	63	36																		
1993-94	Richmond Hill	ON-Jr.A	49	38	62	100	83																		
1994-95	Vernon Vipers	BCJHL	60	43	74	117	92																		
1995-96	Nashville Knights	ECHL	58	30	31	61	62										5	3	8	11	2				
	Atlanta Knights	IHL	1	0	0	0	0																		
1996-97	Pensacola	ECHL	54	35	47	82	45										12	9	16	25	28				
	Quebec Rafales	IHL	22	5	4	9	14										5	0	0	0	2				
1997-98	Grand Rapids	IHL	79	20	35	55	90										3	1	1	2	0				
1998-99	Grand Rapids	IHL	77	28	53	81	92																		
99-2000	**Washington**	**NHL**	30	6	13	19	4	1	0	1	57	10.5	5	37	46.0	13:17	2	0	0	0	2	0	0	0	7:07
	Portland Pirates	AHL	48	18	42	60	73										1	1	0	1	0				
2000-01	**Washington**	**NHL**	15	1	5	6	10	0	0	0	20	5.0	–2	3	33.3	11:50	1	0	0	0	0	0	0	0	7:03
	Portland Pirates	AHL	51	25	42	67	59																		
2001-02	**Tampa Bay**	**NHL**	2	0	0	0	0	0	0	0	1	0.0	–2	2	50.0	10:26									
	Washington	**NHL**	33	1	16	17	6	0	0	0	51	2.0	3	145	49.7	14:24									
	Portland Pirates	AHL	32	17	22	39	20																		
2002-03	**Washington**	**NHL**	23	2	3	5	6	0	0	1	22	9.1	4	99	49.5	10:07									
	Portland Pirates	AHL	33	7	23	30	23										3	1	1	2	0				
2003-04	Jokerit Helsinki	Finland	55	15	35	50	77										7	6	1	7	33				
2004-05	Jokerit Helsinki	Finland	51	16	31	47	42										12	5	6	11	20				
2005-06	HC Lugano	Swiss	44	24	*39	*63	60										17	9	18	27	8				
2006-07	**Atlanta**	**NHL**	57	12	16	28	20	4	0	2	92	13.0	9	206	49.0	11:47									
	St. Louis	**NHL**	20	2	3	5	14	1	0	0	31	6.5	0	154	50.0	12:58									
2007-08	**Boston**	**NHL**	82	11	22	33	36	1	0	5	141	7.8	–3	1242	49.4	16:26	7	1	0	1	4	0	0	1	16:27
2008-09	**Philadelphia**	**NHL**	55	4	10	14	15	1	0	0	63	6.3	–1	562	50.2	12:59									
	Montreal	**NHL**	21	2	1	3	13	0	0	0	19	10.5	–4	215	46.5	11:37	4	0	2	2	2	0	0	0	16:04
2009-10	**Montreal**	**NHL**	69	16	13	29	24	10	0	1	115	13.9	–1	661	49.5	13:34	16	0	2	2	4	0	0	0	6:43
2010-11	EV Zug	Swiss	47	15	38	*53	32										10	2	10	12	8				
	NHL Totals		**407**	**57**	**102**	**159**	**148**	**18**	**0**	**10**	**612**	**9.3**		**3326**	**49.3**	**13:27**	**30**	**1**	**4**	**5**	**12**	**0**	**0**	**1**	**10:16**

Signed as a free agent by **Washington**, July 19, 1999. Claimed by **Tampa Bay** from **Washington** in Waiver Draft, September 28, 2001. Claimed on waivers by **Washington** from **Tampa Bay**, October 20, 2001. Signed as a free agent by **Jokerit Helsinki** (Finland), April 22, 2003. Claimed by **Ottawa** from **Washington** in Waiver Draft, October 3, 2003. Signed as a free agent by **Atlanta**, July 3, 2006. Traded to **St. Louis** by **Atlanta** with Atlanta's 1st (later traded to Calgary – Calgary selected Mikael Backlund) and 3rd (Brett Sonne) round choices in 2007 Entry Draft and Atlanta's 1st (later traded back to Atlanta – Atlanta selected Zach Bogosian) and 2nd (Philip McRae) round choices in 2008 Entry Draft for Keith Tkachuk, February 25, 2007. Signed as a free agent by **Boston**, October 3, 2007. Signed as a free agent by **Philadelphia**, July 1, 2008. Claimed on waivers by **Montreal** from **Philadelphia**, February 27, 2009. Signed as a free agent by **Zug** (Swiss), August 2, 2010.

MEYER, Freddy

(MAY-uhr, FREH-dee)

Defense. Shoots left. 5'10", 185 lbs. Born, Sanbornville, NH, January 4, 1981.

Season	Club	League	GP	G	A	Pts	PIM	PP	SH	GW	S	%	+/-	TF	F%	Min	Playoffs GP	G	A	Pts	PIM	PP	SH	GW	Min
1996-97	Cardigan Mtn.	High-NH	STATISTICS NOT AVAILABLE																						
1997-98	USNTDP	NAHL															2	1	0	1	37				
1998-99	USNTDP	U-18	6	1	4	5	8																		
	USNTDP	USHL	54	10	23	33	151																		
99-2000	USNTDP	USHL	28	3	8	11	60																		
	USNTDP	NAHL	3	0	2	2	0																		
	Boston University	H-East	25	1	11	12	52																		
2000-01	Boston University	H-East	28	6	13	19	82																		
2001-02	Boston University	H-East	37	5	15	20	78																		
2002-03	Boston University	H-East	36	5	16	21	76																		
2003-04	**Philadelphia**	**NHL**	1	0	0	0	0	0	0	0	1	0.0	0	0	0.0	15:24									
	Philadelphia	AHL	59	14	14	28	50										12	0	3	3	8				
2004-05	Philadelphia	AHL	59	6	9	15	71										21	3	9	12	34				
2005-06	**Philadelphia**	**NHL**	57	6	21	27	33	2	0	0	68	8.8	10	0	0.0	17:56	6	0	1	1	8	0	0	0	18:23
	Philadelphia	AHL	11	3	3	6	22																		
2006-07	**Philadelphia**	**NHL**	25	2	3	5	14	1	0	0	27	7.4	–4	0	0.0	18:36									
	NY Islanders	**NHL**	35	0	3	3	24	0	0	0	14	0.0	0	0	0.0	16:39									
2007-08	**Phoenix**	**NHL**	5	0	0	0	0	0	0	0	2	0.0	–4	0	0.0	6:43									
	San Antonio	AHL	8	0	2	2	12																		
	NY Islanders	**NHL**	52	3	9	12	22	0	0	2	49	6.1	6	0	0.0	19:54									
2008-09	**NY Islanders**	**NHL**	27	4	5	9	14	0	0	1	36	11.1	–19	0	0.0	21:00									
2009-10	**NY Islanders**	**NHL**	64	4	11	15	40	0	0	0	56	7.1	–2	0	0.0	16:46									
2010-11	**Atlanta**	**NHL**	15	1	1	2	8	0	0	0	11	9.1	–7	0	0.0	15:16									
	NHL Totals		**281**	**20**	**53**	**73**	**155**	**3**	**0**	**3**	**264**	**7.6**		**0**	**0.0**	**17:53**	**6**	**0**	**1**	**1**	**8**	**0**	**0**	**0**	**18:23**

Hockey East All-Rookie Team (2000) • Hockey East First All-Star Team (2003) • NCAA East First All-American Team (2003)

Signed as a free agent by **Philadelphia**, May 21, 2003. Traded to **NY Islanders** by **Philadelphia** with Philadelphia's 3rd round choice (Mark Katic) in 2007 Entry Draft for Alexei Zhitnik, December 16, 2006. Claimed on waivers by **Phoenix** from **NY Islanders**, October 8, 2007. Claimed on waivers by **NY Islanders** from **Phoenix**, November 10, 2007. • Missed majority of 2008-09 due to abdominal and groin injuries. Signed as a free agent by **Atlanta**, August 19, 2010. • Missed majority of 2010-11 due to upper body injury. • Transferred to **Winnipeg** after **Atlanta** franchise relocated, June 21, 2011.

MEYER, Stefan

(MAY-uhr, STEH-fan) **CGY**

Left wing. Shoots left. 6'2", 200 lbs. Born, Medicine Hat, Alta., July 20, 1985. Florida's 4th choice, 55th overall, in 2003 Entry Draft.

Season	Club	League	GP	G	A	Pts	PIM	PP	SH	GW	S	%	+/-	TF	F%	Min	Playoffs GP	G	A	Pts	PIM	PP	SH	GW	Min
2000-01	Notre Dame	SBHL	50	36	52	88	71																		
	Medicine Hat	WHL	4	1	1	2	0																		
2001-02	Medicine Hat	WHL	67	18	22	40	48																		
2002-03	Medicine Hat	WHL	70	36	16	52	90										11	3	3	6	14				
2003-04	Medicine Hat	WHL	72	34	41	75	69										19	7	10	17	27				
2004-05	Medicine Hat	WHL	69	34	43	77	104										13	2	4	6	8				
2005-06	Rochester	AHL	68	12	16	28	139																		
2006-07	Rochester	AHL	63	13	9	22	90										6	0	2	2	8				
2007-08	**Florida**	**NHL**	4	0	0	0	0	0	0	0	0	0.0	–1	6	50.0	2:26									
	Rochester	AHL	70	21	19	40	77																		
2008-09	Rochester	AHL	65	18	22	40	57																		
2009-10	San Antonio	AHL	67	10	8	18	86																		
2010-11	**Calgary**	**NHL**	16	0	2	2	17	0	0	0	12	0.0	0	17	41.2	7:45									
	Abbotsford Heat	AHL	42	12	5	17	50																		
	NHL Totals		**20**	**0**	**2**	**2**	**17**	**0**	**0**	**0**	**12**	**0.0**		**23**	**43.5**	**6:41**									

Traded to **Phoenix** by **Florida** for Steve Reinprecht, June 19, 2009. Signed as a free agent by **Calgary**, July 20, 2010.

MICHALEK, Milan
(mih-KHAL-ihk, MEE-lan) **OTT**

Right wing. Shoots left. 6'2", 217 lbs. Born, Jindrichuv Hradec, Czech., December 7, 1984. San Jose's 1st choice, 6th overall, in 2003 Entry Draft.

			Regular Season														Playoffs								
Season	Club	League	GP	G	A	Pts	PIM	PP	SH	GW	S	%	+/-	TF	F%	Min	GP	G	A	Pts	PIM	PP	SH	GW	Min
99-2000	C. Budejovice Jr.	CzRep-Jr.	48	16	26	42	42	....	....	....	....	....	....	....	....	....	6	3	1	4	4	....	....	....	....
2000-01	C. Budejovice Jr.	CzRep-Jr.	30	10	13	23	30	....	....	....	....	....	....	....	....	....	4	1	3	4	2	....	....	....	....
	C. Budejovice	CzRep	5	0	0	0	0	....	....	....	....	....	....	....	....	....	....	....	....	....	....	....	....	....	....
2001-02	C. Budejovice	CzRep	47	6	11	17	12	....	....	....	....	....	....	....	....	....	....	....	....	....	....	....	....	....	....
	C. Budejovice Jr.	CzRep-Jr.	5	3	2	5	4	....	....	....	....	....	....	....	....	....	7	5	4	9	14	....	....	....	....
2002-03	C. Budejovice	CzRep	46	3	5	8	14	....	....	....	....	....	....	....	....	....	4	1	0	1	2	....	....	....	....
	Kladno	CzRep-2	....	....	....	....	....	....	....	....	....	....	....	....	....	....	6	2	2	4	16	....	....	....	....
2003-04	**San Jose**	**NHL**	**2**	**1**	**0**	**1**	**4**	**0**	**0**	**0**	**1**	**100.0**	**1**	**0**	**0.0**	**9:05**	....	....	....	....	....	....	....	....	....
	Cleveland Barons	AHL	7	2	2	4	4	....	....	....	....	....	....	....	....	....	....	....	....	....	....	....	....	....	....
2004-05			DID NOT PLAY																						
2005-06	**San Jose**	**NHL**	**81**	**17**	**18**	**35**	**45**	**4**	**0**	**2**	**159**	**10.7**	**1**	**4**	**0.0**	**15:46**	**9**	**1**	**4**	**5**	**8**	**1**	**0**	**0**	**15:11**
2006-07	**San Jose**	**NHL**	**78**	**26**	**40**	**66**	**36**	**11**	**0**	**9**	**191**	**13.6**	**17**	**11**	**18.2**	**16:46**	**11**	**4**	**2**	**6**	**4**	**0**	**0**	**1**	**18:50**
2007-08	**San Jose**	**NHL**	**79**	**24**	**31**	**55**	**47**	**5**	**1**	**8**	**233**	**10.3**	**19**	**10**	**60.0**	**18:05**	**13**	**4**	**0**	**4**	**4**	**1**	**0**	**1**	**17:34**
2008-09	**San Jose**	**NHL**	**77**	**23**	**34**	**57**	**52**	**6**	**0**	**6**	**179**	**12.8**	**11**	**30**	**46.7**	**18:27**	**6**	**1**	**0**	**1**	**2**	**1**	**0**	**0**	**19:22**
2009-10	**Ottawa**	**NHL**	**66**	**22**	**12**	**34**	**18**	**8**	**2**	**3**	**163**	**13.5**	**–12**	**8**	**50.0**	**18:15**	**1**	**0**	**0**	**0**	**0**	**0**	**0**	**0**	**12:08**
	Czech Republic	Olympics	5	2	0	2	0	....	....	....	....	....	....	....	....	....	....	....	....	....	....	....	....	....	....
2010-11	**Ottawa**	**NHL**	**66**	**18**	**15**	**33**	**49**	**1**	**4**	**0**	**167**	**10.8**	**–12**	**13**	**30.8**	**18:04**	....	....	....	....	....	....	....	....	....
	NHL Totals		**449**	**131**	**150**	**281**	**251**	**35**	**7**	**28**	**1093**	**12.0**		**76**	**39.5**	**17:29**	**40**	**10**	**6**	**16**	**18**	**3**	**0**	**2**	**17:31**

• Missed majority of 2003-04 due to knee injury vs. Calgary, October 11, 2003. Traded to **Ottawa** by **San Jose** with Jonathan Cheechoo and San Jose's 2nd round choice (later traded to NY Islanders, later traded to Chicago - Chicago selected Kent Simpson) in 2010 Entry Draft for Dany Heatley and Ottawa's 5th round choice (Isaac MacLeod) in 2010 Entry Draft, September 12, 2009.

MICHALEK, Zbynek
(mih-KHAL-ihk, z'BIGH-nehk) **PIT**

Defense. Shoots right. 6'2", 210 lbs. Born, Jindrichuv Hradec, Czech., December 23, 1982.

Season	Club	League	GP	G	A	Pts	PIM	PP	SH	GW	S	%	+/-	TF	F%	Min	GP	G	A	Pts	PIM	PP	SH	GW	Min
99-2000	Karlovy Vary Jr.	CzRep-Jr.	40	2	10	12	20	....	....	....	....	....	....	....	....	....	....	....	....	....	....	....	....	....	....
2000-01	Shawinigan	QMJHL	69	10	29	39	52	....	....	....	....	....	....	....	....	....	3	0	0	0	0	....	....	....	....
2001-02	Shawinigan	QMJHL	68	16	35	51	54	....	....	....	....	....	....	....	....	....	12	8	9	17	17	....	....	....	....
2002-03	Houston Aeros	AHL	62	4	10	14	26	....	....	....	....	....	....	....	....	....	23	1	1	2	6	....	....	....	....
2003-04	**Minnesota**	**NHL**	**22**	**1**	**1**	**2**	**4**	**0**	**0**	**0**	**17**	**5.9**	**–7**	**0**	**0.0**	**14:13**	....	....	....	....	....	....	....	....	....
	Houston Aeros	AHL	55	5	16	21	32	....	....	....	....	....	....	....	....	....	2	1	0	1	0	....	....	....	....
2004-05	Houston Aeros	AHL	76	7	17	24	48	....	....	....	....	....	....	....	....	....	5	1	2	3	4	....	....	....	....
2005-06	**Phoenix**	**NHL**	**82**	**9**	**15**	**24**	**62**	**5**	**0**	**2**	**105**	**8.6**	**4**	**0**	**0.0**	**22:50**	....	....	....	....	....	....	....	....	....
2006-07	**Phoenix**	**NHL**	**82**	**4**	**24**	**28**	**34**	**3**	**0**	**0**	**144**	**2.8**	**–20**	**1**	**100.0**	**23:40**	....	....	....	....	....	....	....	....	....
2007-08	**Phoenix**	**NHL**	**75**	**4**	**13**	**17**	**34**	**0**	**0**	**2**	**92**	**4.3**	**9**	**0**	**0.0**	**21:36**	....	....	....	....	....	....	....	....	....
2008-09	**Phoenix**	**NHL**	**82**	**6**	**21**	**27**	**28**	**0**	**0**	**0**	**106**	**5.7**	**–13**	**0**	**0.0**	**22:43**	....	....	....	....	....	....	....	....	....
2009-10	**Phoenix**	**NHL**	**72**	**3**	**14**	**17**	**30**	**2**	**0**	**1**	**104**	**2.9**	**5**	**0**	**0.0**	**22:39**	**7**	**0**	**2**	**2**	**2**	**0**	**0**	**0**	**20:28**
	Czech Republic	Olympics	5	0	0	0	2	....	....	....	....	....	....	....	....	....	....	....	....	....	....	....	....	....	....
2010-11	**Pittsburgh**	**NHL**	**73**	**5**	**14**	**19**	**30**	**1**	**0**	**2**	**104**	**4.8**	**0**	**0**	**0.0**	**21:50**	**7**	**0**	**1**	**1**	**0**	**0**	**0**	**0**	**27:20**
	NHL Totals		**488**	**32**	**102**	**134**	**222**	**11**	**0**	**7**	**672**	**4.8**		**1**	**100.0**	**22:12**	**14**	**0**	**3**	**3**	**2**	**0**	**0**	**0**	**23:54**

Signed as a free agent by **Minnesota**, September 29, 2001. Traded to **Phoenix** by **Minnesota** for Erik Westrum and Dustin Wood, August 26, 2005. Signed as a free agent by **Pittsburgh**, July 1, 2010.

MIETTINEN, Antti
(mih-EHT-tih-nehn, AN-tee)

Right wing. Shoots right. 6', 190 lbs. Born, Hameenlinna, Finland, July 3, 1980. Dallas' 10th choice, 224th overall, in 2000 Entry Draft.

Season	Club	League	GP	G	A	Pts	PIM	PP	SH	GW	S	%	+/-	TF	F%	Min	GP	G	A	Pts	PIM	PP	SH	GW	Min
1996-97	HPK U18	Fin-U18	36	24	29	53	34	....	....	....	....	....	....	....	....	....	....	....	....	....	....	....	....	....	....
1997-98	HPK U18	Fin-U18	34	13	28	41	63	....	....	....	....	....	....	....	....	....	....	....	....	....	....	....	....	....	....
	HPK Jr.	Fin-Jr.	8	1	0	1	2	....	....	....	....	....	....	....	....	....	....	....	....	....	....	....	....	....	....
1998-99	HPK Jr.	Fin-Jr.	35	17	22	39	28	....	....	....	....	....	....	....	....	....	3	2	3	5	2	....	....	....	....
	FPS Forssa	Finland-2	4	3	1	4	6	....	....	....	....	....	....	....	....	....	....	....	....	....	....	....	....	....	....
	HPK Hameenlinna	Finland	13	0	0	0	2	....	....	....	....	....	....	....	....	....	4	0	0	0	0	....	....	....	....
99-2000	HPK Jr.	Fin-Jr.	31	24	53	77	28	....	....	....	....	....	....	....	....	....	2	1	6	7	2	....	....	....	....
	HPK Hameenlinna	Finland	39	2	1	3	8	....	....	....	....	....	....	....	....	....	7	1	0	1	0	....	....	....	....
2000-01	HPK Jr.	Fin-Jr.	4	3	10	13	2	....	....	....	....	....	....	....	....	....	....	....	....	....	....	....	....	....	....
	HPK Hameenlinna	Finland	55	13	11	24	20	....	....	....	....	....	....	....	....	....	....	....	....	....	....	....	....	....	....
2001-02	HPK Hameenlinna	Finland	56	19	37	56	50	....	....	....	....	....	....	....	....	....	8	2	4	6	8	....	....	....	....
2002-03	HPK Hameenlinna	Finland	53	25	25	50	54	....	....	....	....	....	....	....	....	....	10	1	7	8	29	....	....	....	....
2003-04	**Dallas**	**NHL**	**16**	**1**	**0**	**1**	**0**	**0**	**0**	**1**	**17**	**5.9**	**–9**	**1**	**0.0**	**9:51**	....	....	....	....	....	....	....	....	....
	Utah Grizzlies	AHL	48	7	23	30	20	....	....	....	....	....	....	....	....	....	....	....	....	....	....	....	....	....	....
2004-05	Hamilton	AHL	35	8	20	28	21	....	....	....	....	....	....	....	....	....	4	1	1	2	6	....	....	....	....
2005-06	**Dallas**	**NHL**	**79**	**11**	**20**	**31**	**46**	**4**	**0**	**1**	**107**	**10.3**	**0**	**1**	**100.0**	**12:06**	**5**	**0**	**1**	**1**	**8**	**0**	**0**	**0**	**12:10**
2006-07	**Dallas**	**NHL**	**74**	**11**	**14**	**25**	**38**	**6**	**0**	**1**	**141**	**7.8**	**–5**	**11**	**18.2**	**14:20**	**4**	**1**	**1**	**2**	**2**	**0**	**0**	**0**	**12:16**
2007-08	**Dallas**	**NHL**	**69**	**15**	**19**	**34**	**34**	**5**	**0**	**3**	**136**	**11.0**	**4**	**23**	**60.9**	**13:59**	**15**	**1**	**1**	**2**	**0**	**0**	**0**	**0**	**9:33**
2008-09	**Minnesota**	**NHL**	**82**	**15**	**29**	**44**	**32**	**4**	**2**	**3**	**186**	**8.1**	**–1**	**60**	**46.7**	**18:17**	....	....	....	....	....	....	....	....	....
2009-10	**Minnesota**	**NHL**	**79**	**20**	**22**	**42**	**44**	**5**	**0**	**4**	**175**	**11.4**	**–2**	**83**	**42.2**	**18:03**	....	....	....	....	....	....	....	....	....
	Finland	Olympics	6	1	0	1	0	....	....	....	....	....	....	....	....	....	....	....	....	....	....	....	....	....	....
2010-11	**Minnesota**	**NHL**	**73**	**16**	**19**	**35**	**38**	**8**	**0**	**4**	**168**	**9.5**	**–3**	**100**	**36.0**	**17:02**	....	....	....	....	....	....	....	....	....
	NHL Totals		**472**	**89**	**123**	**212**	**232**	**32**	**2**	**17**	**930**	**9.6**		**279**	**41.6**	**15:29**	**24**	**2**	**3**	**5**	**10**	**0**	**0**	**0**	**10:33**

Signed as a free agent by **Minnesota**, July 3, 2008.

MIHALIK, Vladimir
(mih-HAHL-ihk, vla-DIH-meer)

Defense. Shoots left. 6'8", 246 lbs. Born, Presov, Czech., January 29, 1987. Tampa Bay's 1st choice, 30th overall, in 2005 Entry Draft.

Season	Club	League	GP	G	A	Pts	PIM	PP	SH	GW	S	%	+/-	TF	F%	Min	GP	G	A	Pts	PIM	PP	SH	GW	Min
2003-04	Presov	Svk-U18	6	4	4	8	4	....	....	....	....	....	....	....	....	....	....	....	....	....	....	....	....	....	....
	Presov Jr.	Slovak-Jr.	23	6	10	16	44	....	....	....	....	....	....	....	....	....	....	....	....	....	....	....	....	....	....
2004-05	PHK Presov Jr.	Slovak-Jr.	23	6	10	16	44	....	....	....	....	....	....	....	....	....	....	....	....	....	....	....	....	....	....
	PHK Presov	Slovak-2	32	3	1	4	24	....	....	....	....	....	....	....	....	....	6	0	1	1	2	....	....	....	....
2005-06	Red Deer Rebels	WHL	62	3	9	12	86	....	....	....	....	....	....	....	....	....	....	....	....	....	....	....	....	....	....
2006-07	Prince George	WHL	53	7	19	26	91	....	....	....	....	....	....	....	....	....	15	1	2	3	17	....	....	....	....
2007-08	Norfolk Admirals	AHL	68	1	15	16	68	....	....	....	....	....	....	....	....	....	....	....	....	....	....	....	....	....	....
2008-09	**Tampa Bay**	**NHL**	**11**	**0**	**3**	**3**	**6**	**0**	**0**	**0**	**7**	**0.0**	**–3**	**0**	**0.0**	**13:24**	....	....	....	....	....	....	....	....	....
	Norfolk Admirals	AHL	61	2	13	15	58	....	....	....	....	....	....	....	....	....	....	....	....	....	....	....	....	....	....
2009-10	**Tampa Bay**	**NHL**	**4**	**0**	**0**	**0**	**2**	**0**	**0**	**0**	**1**	**0.0**	**–4**	**0**	**0.0**	**11:32**	....	....	....	....	....	....	....	....	....
	Norfolk Admirals	AHL	75	2	16	18	67	....	....	....	....	....	....	....	....	....	....	....	....	....	....	....	....	....	....
2010-11	Norfolk Admirals	AHL	66	1	8	9	107	....	....	....	....	....	....	....	....	....	6	0	2	2	8	....	....	....	....
	NHL Totals		**15**	**0**	**3**	**3**	**8**	**0**	**0**	**0**	**8**	**0.0**		**0**	**0.0**	**12:54**	....	....	....	....	....	....	....	....	....

MIKKELSON, Brendan
(MIGHK-ehl-sohn, BREHN-duhn) **CGY**

Defense. Shoots left. 6'2", 202 lbs. Born, Regina, Sask., June 22, 1987. Anaheim's 2nd choice, 31st overall, in 2005 Entry Draft.

Season	Club	League	GP	G	A	Pts	PIM	PP	SH	GW	S	%	+/-	TF	F%	Min	GP	G	A	Pts	PIM	PP	SH	GW	Min
2003-04	Portland	WHL	65	3	12	15	43	....	....	....	....	....	....	....	....	....	5	1	0	1	0	....	....	....	....
2004-05	Portland	WHL	70	5	10	15	60	....	....	....	....	....	....	....	....	....	7	1	2	3	0	....	....	....	....
2005-06	Portland	WHL	3	1	1	2	4	....	....	....	....	....	....	....	....	....	....	....	....	....	....	....	....	....	....
	Vancouver Giants	WHL	19	1	8	9	37	....	....	....	....	....	....	....	....	....	....	....	....	....	....	....	....	....	....
2006-07	Vancouver Giants	WHL	69	6	23	29	60	....	....	....	....	....	....	....	....	....	21	3	7	10	10	....	....	....	....
2007-08	Portland Pirates	AHL	66	6	10	16	50	....	....	....	....	....	....	....	....	....	14	2	6	8	2	....	....	....	....
2008-09	**Anaheim**	**NHL**	**34**	**0**	**2**	**2**	**17**	**0**	**0**	**0**	**19**	**0.0**	**0**	**0**	**0.0**	**13:56**	....	....	....	....	....	....	....	....	....
	Iowa Chops	AHL	31	2	8	10	18	....	....	....	....	....	....	....	....	....	....	....	....	....	....	....	....	....	....
2009-10	**Anaheim**	**NHL**	**28**	**0**	**2**	**2**	**14**	**0**	**0**	**0**	**21**	**0.0**	**–5**	**0**	**0.0**	**15:00**	....	....	....	....	....	....	....	....	....
	Toronto Marlies	AHL	49	7	15	22	43	....	....	....	....	....	....	....	....	....	....	....	....	....	....	....	....	....	....
2010-11	**Anaheim**	**NHL**	**5**	**0**	**1**	**1**	**7**	**0**	**0**	**0**	**4**	**0.0**	**–1**	**0**	**0.0**	**19:24**	....	....	....	....	....	....	....	....	....
	Calgary	**NHL**	**19**	**0**	**1**	**1**	**2**	**0**	**0**	**0**	**10**	**0.0**	**–5**	**0**	**0.0**	**12:52**	....	....	....	....	....	....	....	....	....
	Abbotsford Heat	AHL	4	0	1	1	4	....	....	....	....	....	....	....	....	....	....	....	....	....	....	....	....	....	....
	NHL Totals		**86**	**0**	**6**	**6**	**40**	**0**	**0**	**0**	**54**	**0.0**		**0**	**0.0**	**14:22**	....	....	....	....	....	....	....	....	....

Memorial Cup All-Star Team (2007)

• Missed majority of 2005-06 due to shoulder and knee injuries. Claimed on waivers by **Calgary** from **Anaheim**, October 19, 2010.

MILLER, Drew

(MIH-luhr, DROO) **DET**

Left wing. Shoots left. 6'2", 178 lbs. Born, Dover, NJ, February 17, 1984. Anaheim's 6th choice, 186th overall, in 2003 Entry Draft.

			Regular Season														Playoffs								
Season	Club	League	GP	G	A	Pts	PIM	PP	SH	GW	S	%	+/-	TF	F%	Min	GP	G	A	Pts	PIM	PP	SH	GW	Min
2000-01	Capital Centre	NAHL	37	4	3	7	22	....	....	....	....	....	....	....	....	....	....	....	....	....	....	....	....	....	....
2001-02	Capital Centre	NAHL	54	18	16	34	56	....	....	....	....	....	....	....	....	....	....	....	....	....	....	....	....	....	....
2002-03	Capital Centre	NAHL	11	10	9	19	....	....	....	....	....	....	....	....	....	....	....	....	....	....	....	....	....	....	....
	River City Lancers	USHL	49	14	11	25	22	....	....	....	....	....	....	....	....	....	11	5	4	9	6	....	....	....	....
2003-04	Michigan State	CCHA	41	4	6	10	39	....	....	....	....	....	....	....	....	....	....	....	....	....	....	....	....	....	....
2004-05	Michigan State	CCHA	40	17	16	33	20	....	....	....	....	....	....	....	....	....	....	....	....	....	....	....	....	....	....
2005-06	Michigan State	CCHA	44	18	25	43	30	....	....	....	....	....	....	....	....	....	....	....	....	....	....	....	....	....	....
2006-07	Portland Pirates	AHL	79	16	20	36	51	....	....	....	....	....	....	....	....	....	....	....	....	....	....	....	....	....	....
	♦ **Anaheim**	**NHL**	....	....	....	....	....	....	....	....	....	....	....	....	....	....	**3**	**0**	**0**	**0**	**2**	**0**	**0**	**0**	**7:00**
2007-08	**Anaheim**	**NHL**	**26**	**2**	**3**	**5**	**6**	**0**	**0**	**0**	**30**	**6.7**	**–1**	**9**	**33.3**	**11:11**	....	....	....	....	....	....	....	....	....
	Portland Pirates	AHL	31	16	20	36	12	....	....	....	....	....	....	....	....	....	16	1	7	8	12	....	....	....	....
2008-09	**Anaheim**	**NHL**	**27**	**4**	**6**	**10**	**17**	**0**	**0**	**0**	**45**	**8.9**	**0**	**14**	**21.4**	**12:59**	**13**	**2**	**1**	**3**	**2**	**0**	**0**	**1**	**16:09**
	Iowa Chops	AHL	53	23	15	38	10	....	....	....	....	....	....	....	....	....	....	....	....	....	....	....	....	....	....
2009-10	**Tampa Bay**	**NHL**	**14**	**0**	**0**	**0**	**2**	**0**	**0**	**0**	**10**	**0.0**	**–3**	**2**	**0.0**	**12:14**	....	....	....	....	....	....	....	....	....
	Detroit	**NHL**	**66**	**10**	**9**	**19**	**10**	**1**	**1**	**3**	**93**	**10.8**	**5**	**41**	**34.2**	**12:42**	**12**	**1**	**1**	**2**	**4**	**0**	**0**	**0**	**12:35**
2010-11	**Detroit**	**NHL**	**67**	**10**	**8**	**18**	**13**	**0**	**1**	**2**	**85**	**11.8**	**–2**	**17**	**23.5**	**11:45**	**9**	**1**	**1**	**2**	**4**	**0**	**0**	**0**	**10:17**
	NHL Totals		**200**	**26**	**26**	**52**	**48**	**1**	**2**	**5**	**263**	**9.9**		**83**	**28.9**	**12:12**	**37**	**4**	**3**	**7**	**12**	**0**	**0**	**1**	**12:49**

Traded to **Tampa Bay** by **Anaheim** with Anaheim's 3rd round choice (Adam Janosik) in 2010 Entry Draft for Evgeny Artyukhin, August 13, 2009. Claimed on waivers by **Detroit** from **Tampa Bay**, November 11, 2009.

MILLS, Brad

(MIHLS, BRAD) **N.J.**

Right wing. Shoots right. 6', 195 lbs. Born, Terrace, B.C., May 3, 1983.

Season	Club	League	GP	G	A	Pts	PIM	PP	SH	GW	S	%	+/-	TF	F%	Min	GP	G	A	Pts	PIM	PP	SH	GW	Min
2002-03	Fort McMurray	AJHL	62	20	47	67	73	....	....	....	....	....	....	....	....	....	....	....	....	....	....	....	....	....	....
2003-04	Yale	ECAC	27	4	7	11	18	....	....	....	....	....	....	....	....	....	....	....	....	....	....	....	....	....	....
2004-05	Yale	ECAC	27	12	14	26	30	....	....	....	....	....	....	....	....	....	....	....	....	....	....	....	....	....	....
2005-06	Yale	ECAC	22	8	8	16	65	....	....	....	....	....	....	....	....	....	....	....	....	....	....	....	....	....	....
2006-07	Yale	ECAC	20	2	6	8	39	....	....	....	....	....	....	....	....	....	....	....	....	....	....	....	....	....	....
	Lowell Devils	AHL	8	0	1	1	4	....	....	....	....	....	....	....	....	....	....	....	....	....	....	....	....	....	....
2007-08	Lowell Devils	AHL	16	1	2	3	44	....	....	....	....	....	....	....	....	....	....	....	....	....	....	....	....	....	....
	Trenton Devils	ECHL	26	9	7	16	67	....	....	....	....	....	....	....	....	....	....	....	....	....	....	....	....	....	....
2008-09	Lowell Devils	AHL	75	5	16	21	108	....	....	....	....	....	....	....	....	....	....	....	....	....	....	....	....	....	....
2009-10	Lowell Devils	AHL	51	12	7	19	67	....	....	....	....	....	....	....	....	....	2	1	2	3	4	....	....	....	....
2010-11	**New Jersey**	**NHL**	**4**	**1**	**0**	**1**	**5**	**0**	**0**	**0**	**6**	**16.7**	**1**	**17**	**41.2**	**8:16**	....	....	....	....	....	....	....	....	....
	Albany Devils	AHL	53	15	9	24	102	....	....	....	....	....	....	....	....	....	....	....	....	....	....	....	....	....	....
	NHL Totals		**4**	**1**	**0**	**1**	**5**	**0**	**0**	**0**	**6**	**16.7**		**17**	**41.2**	**8:17**	....	....	....	....	....	....	....	....	....

Signed as a free agent by **Lowell** (AHL), March 16, 2007. Signed as a free agent by **New Jersey**, June 1, 2009.

MINARD, Chris

(mih-NAHRD, KRIHS) **DET**

Center. Shoots left. 6'1", 205 lbs. Born, Thompson, Man., November 18, 1981.

Season	Club	League	GP	G	A	Pts	PIM	PP	SH	GW	S	%	+/-	TF	F%	Min	GP	G	A	Pts	PIM	PP	SH	GW	Min
1997-98	Owen Sound	OHL	9	0	1	1	1	....	....	....	....	....	....	....	....	....	1	0	0	0	2	....	....	....	....
1998-99	Owen Sound	OHL	43	6	9	15	18	....	....	....	....	....	....	....	....	....	....	....	....	....	....	....	....	....	....
99-2000	Owen Sound	OHL	38	12	14	26	39	....	....	....	....	....	....	....	....	....	....	....	....	....	....	....	....	....	....
	St. Michael's	OHL	28	5	14	19	6	....	....	....	....	....	....	....	....	....	....	....	....	....	....	....	....	....	....
2000-01	St. Michael's	OHL	40	11	8	19	28	....	....	....	....	....	....	....	....	....	....	....	....	....	....	....	....	....	....
	Oshawa Generals	OHL	28	12	12	24	18	....	....	....	....	....	....	....	....	....	....	....	....	....	....	....	....	....	....
2001-02	Oshawa Generals	OHL	67	36	35	71	20	....	....	....	....	....	....	....	....	....	5	2	3	5	6	....	....	....	....
2002-03	Pensacola	ECHL	72	15	17	32	71	....	....	....	....	....	....	....	....	....	4	0	0	0	6	....	....	....	....
2003-04	San Angelo Saints	CHL	64	39	36	75	51	....	....	....	....	....	....	....	....	....	5	1	1	2	2	....	....	....	....
2004-05	Alaska Aces	ECHL	69	*49	29	78	54	....	....	....	....	....	....	....	....	....	15	4	4	8	12	....	....	....	....
	Milwaukee	AHL	1	0	0	0	0	....	....	....	....	....	....	....	....	....	....	....	....	....	....	....	....	....	....
2005-06	Albany River Rats	AHL	37	7	12	19	26	....	....	....	....	....	....	....	....	....	....	....	....	....	....	....	....	....	....
	Alaska Aces	ECHL	33	26	16	42	38	....	....	....	....	....	....	....	....	....	22	*14	5	19	*54	....	....	....	....
2006-07	Lowell Devils	AHL	65	32	17	49	30	....	....	....	....	....	....	....	....	....	....	....	....	....	....	....	....	....	....
2007-08	**Pittsburgh**	**NHL**	**15**	**1**	**1**	**2**	**10**	**0**	**0**	**0**	**9**	**11.1**	**–1**	**0**	**0.0**	**3:53**	....	....	....	....	....	....	....	....	....
	Wilkes-Barre	AHL	56	25	17	42	33	....	....	....	....	....	....	....	....	....	23	11	6	17	10	....	....	....	....
2008-09	**Pittsburgh**	**NHL**	**20**	**1**	**2**	**3**	**4**	**0**	**0**	**1**	**33**	**3.0**	**0**	**2**	**100.0**	**9:25**	....	....	....	....	....	....	....	....	....
	Wilkes-Barre	AHL	54	34	23	57	38	....	....	....	....	....	....	....	....	....	12	6	3	9	12	....	....	....	....
2009-10	**Edmonton**	**NHL**	**5**	**0**	**1**	**1**	**0**	**0**	**0**	**0**	**4**	**0.0**	**–3**	**0**	**0.0**	**9:44**	....	....	....	....	....	....	....	....	....
	Springfield	AHL	40	22	16	38	18	....	....	....	....	....	....	....	....	....	....	....	....	....	....	....	....	....	....
2010-11	Grand Rapids	AHL	79	18	17	35	45	....	....	....	....	....	....	....	....	....	....	....	....	....	....	....	....	....	....
	NHL Totals		**40**	**2**	**4**	**6**	**14**	**0**	**0**	**1**	**46**	**4.3**		**2**	**100.0**	**7:23**	....	....	....	....	....	....	....	....	....

Signed as a free agent by **Albany** (AHL), August 16, 2005. Signed as a free agent by **Pittsburgh**, July 12, 2007. Signed as a free agent by **Edmonton**, July 13, 2009. Signed as a free agent by **Detroit**, July 6, 2010.

MINK, Graham

(MIHNK, GRAY-uhm)

Right wing. Shoots right. 6'2", 225 lbs. Born, Stowe, VT, May 21, 1979.

Season	Club	League	GP	G	A	Pts	PIM	PP	SH	GW	S	%	+/-	TF	F%	Min	GP	G	A	Pts	PIM	PP	SH	GW	Min
1997-98	NMH School	High-MA	25	17	25	42	....	....	....	....	....	....	....	....	....	....	....	....	....	....	....	....	....	....	....
1998-99	U. of Vermont	ECAC	27	4	2	6	34	....	....	....	....	....	....	....	....	....	....	....	....	....	....	....	....	....	....
99-2000	U. of Vermont	ECAC	17	7	4	11	14	....	....	....	....	....	....	....	....	....	....	....	....	....	....	....	....	....	....
2000-01	U. of Vermont	ECAC	32	17	12	29	52	....	....	....	....	....	....	....	....	....	....	....	....	....	....	....	....	....	....
2001-02	Richmond	ECHL	29	8	9	17	78	....	....	....	....	....	....	....	....	....	....	....	....	....	....	....	....	....	....
	Portland Pirates	AHL	56	17	17	34	50	....	....	....	....	....	....	....	....	....	....	....	....	....	....	....	....	....	....
2002-03	Portland Pirates	AHL	71	22	15	37	115	....	....	....	....	....	....	....	....	....	....	....	....	....	....	....	....	....	....
2003-04	**Washington**	**NHL**	**2**	**0**	**0**	**0**	**2**	**0**	**0**	**0**	**0**	**0.0**	**–1**	**1**	**0.0**	**5:32**	....	....	....	....	....	....	....	....	....
	Portland Pirates	AHL	68	18	19	37	74	....	....	....	....	....	....	....	....	....	3	0	1	1	4	....	....	....	....
2004-05	Portland Pirates	AHL	63	18	21	39	86	....	....	....	....	....	....	....	....	....	....	....	....	....	....	....	....	....	....
2005-06	**Washington**	**NHL**	**3**	**0**	**0**	**0**	**0**	**0**	**0**	**0**	**1**	**0.0**	**0**	**0**	**0.0**	**5:32**	....	....	....	....	....	....	....	....	....
	Hershey Bears	AHL	43	21	19	40	50	....	....	....	....	....	....	....	....	....	21	8	13	21	29	....	....	....	....
2006-07	Worcester Sharks	AHL	61	31	32	63	52	....	....	....	....	....	....	....	....	....	6	1	5	6	8	....	....	....	....
2007-08	Worcester Sharks	AHL	71	24	31	55	67	....	....	....	....	....	....	....	....	....	....	....	....	....	....	....	....	....	....
2008-09	**Washington**	**NHL**	**2**	**0**	**0**	**0**	**0**	**0**	**0**	**0**	**4**	**0.0**	**0**	**0**	**0.0**	**8:03**	....	....	....	....	....	....	....	....	....
	Hershey Bears	AHL	68	32	27	59	101	....	....	....	....	....	....	....	....	....	22	7	8	15	16	....	....	....	....
2009-10	Rochester	AHL	67	20	17	37	86	....	....	....	....	....	....	....	....	....	6	3	2	5	23	....	....	....	....
2010-11	Peoria Rivermen	AHL	70	24	26	50	122	....	....	....	....	....	....	....	....	....	4	0	0	0	10	....	....	....	....
	NHL Totals		**7**	**0**	**0**	**0**	**2**	**0**	**0**	**0**	**5**	**0.0**		**1**	**0.0**	**6:15**	....	....	....	....	....	....	....	....	....

Signed as a free agent by **Portland** (AHL), September 30, 2001. Signed as a free agent by **Washington**, April 9, 2002. Signed as a free agent by **San Jose**, July 14, 2006. Signed as a free agent by **Washington**, July 2, 2008. Signed as a free agent by **Florida**, July 10, 2009. Traded to **St. Louis** by **Florida** for T.J. Fast, August 3, 2010.

MITCHELL, John

(MIH-chuhl, JAWN) **NYR**

Center. Shoots left. 6'1", 204 lbs. Born, Oakville, Ont., January 22, 1985. Toronto's 4th choice, 158th overall, in 2003 Entry Draft.

Season	Club	League	GP	G	A	Pts	PIM	PP	SH	GW	S	%	+/-	TF	F%	Min	GP	G	A	Pts	PIM	PP	SH	GW	Min
2000-01	Waterloo Siskens	OPJHL	47	15	29	44	33	....	....	....	....	....	....	....	....	....	....	....	....	....	....	....	....	....	....
2001-02	Plymouth Whalers	OHL	62	9	9	18	23	....	....	....	....	....	....	....	....	....	6	1	0	1	4	....	....	....	....
2002-03	Plymouth Whalers	OHL	68	18	37	55	31	....	....	....	....	....	....	....	....	....	18	2	10	12	8	....	....	....	....
2003-04	Plymouth Whalers	OHL	65	28	54	82	45	....	....	....	....	....	....	....	....	....	9	6	6	12	6	....	....	....	....
2004-05	Plymouth Whalers	OHL	63	25	50	75	59	....	....	....	....	....	....	....	....	....	4	1	1	2	0	....	....	....	....
	St. John's	AHL	2	0	0	0	0	....	....	....	....	....	....	....	....	....	....	....	....	....	....	....	....	....	....
2005-06	Toronto Marlies	AHL	51	5	12	17	22	....	....	....	....	....	....	....	....	....	2	0	0	0	0	....	....	....	....
2006-07	Toronto Marlies	AHL	73	16	20	36	46	....	....	....	....	....	....	....	....	....	....	....	....	....	....	....	....	....	....
2007-08	Toronto Marlies	AHL	79	20	31	51	56	....	....	....	....	....	....	....	....	....	19	8	4	12	12	....	....	....	....
2008-09	**Toronto**	**NHL**	**76**	**12**	**17**	**29**	**33**	**2**	**0**	**0**	**98**	**12.2**	**–16**	**669**	**48.7**	**13:48**	....	....	....	....	....	....	....	....	....
2009-10	**Toronto**	**NHL**	**60**	**6**	**17**	**23**	**31**	**1**	**0**	**1**	**90**	**6.7**	**–7**	**477**	**51.2**	**15:49**	....	....	....	....	....	....	....	....	....

			Regular Season														Playoffs								
Season	Club	League	GP	G	A	Pts	PIM	PP	SH	GW	S	%	+/-	TF	F%	Min	GP	G	A	Pts	PIM	PP	SH	GW	Min
2010-11	Toronto	NHL	23	2	1	3	12	1	0	1	28	7.1	–7	149	55.7	12:31	....	....	....	....	....	....	....	....	....
	Toronto Marlies	AHL	10	1	4	5	2	....	....	....	....	....	....	....	....	....	....	....	....	....	....	....	....	....	....
	Connecticut	AHL	14	7	5	12	10	....	....	....	....	....	....	....	....	....	6	3	3	6	0	....	....	....	....
	NHL Totals		159	20	35	55	76	4	0	2	216	9.3		1295	50.4	14:23	....	....	....	....	....	....	....	....	....

Traded to **NY Rangers** by **Toronto** for NY Rangers' 7th round choice in 2012 Entry Draft, February 28, 2011.

MITCHELL, Torrey

(MIH-chuhl, TOH-ree) **S.J.**

Center. Shoots right. 5'11", 190 lbs. Born, Montreal, Que., January 30, 1985. San Jose's 3rd choice, 126th overall, in 2004 Entry Draft.

Season	Club	League	GP	G	A	Pts	PIM	PP	SH	GW	S	%	+/-	TF	F%	Min	GP	G	A	Pts	PIM	PP	SH	GW	Min
2002-03	Hotchkiss School	High-CT	26	19	30	49	33	....	....	....	....	....	....	....	....	....	....	....	....	....	....	....	....	....	....
2003-04	Hotchkiss School	High-CT	25	25	37	62	42	....	....	....	....	....	....	....	....	....	....	....	....	....	....	....	....	....	....
2004-05	U. of Vermont	ECAC	38	11	19	30	74	....	....	....	....	....	....	....	....	....	....	....	....	....	....	....	....	....	....
2005-06	U. of Vermont	H-East	38	12	28	40	34	....	....	....	....	....	....	....	....	....	....	....	....	....	....	....	....	....	....
2006-07	U. of Vermont	H-East	39	12	23	35	46	....	....	....	....	....	....	....	....	....	....	....	....	....	....	....	....	....	....
	Worcester Sharks	AHL	11	2	5	7	27	....	....	....	....	....	....	....	....	....	6	1	1	2	15	....	....	....	....
2007-08	San Jose	NHL	82	10	10	20	50	1	2	0	110	9.1	–3	692	49.4	14:19	13	1	2	3	10	1	0	0	14:00
2008-09	Worcester Sharks	AHL	2	1	0	1	0	....	....	....	....	....	....	....	....	....	....	....	....	....	....	....	....	....	....
	San Jose	NHL	....	....	....	....	....	....	....	....	....	....	....	....	....	....	4	0	0	0	2	0	0	0	9:38
2009-10	San Jose	NHL	56	2	9	11	27	0	0	0	59	3.4	6	205	43.4	11:26	15	0	2	2	2	0	0	0	13:05
	Worcester Sharks	AHL	5	1	2	3	10	....	....	....	....	....	....	....	....	....	....	....	....	....	....	....	....	....	....
2010-11	San Jose	NHL	66	9	14	23	46	0	0	1	116	7.8	10	203	48.8	13:21	18	1	4	5	10	0	0	0	15:02
	NHL Totals		204	21	33	54	123	1	2	1	285	7.4		1100	48.2	13:13	50	2	8	10	24	1	0	0	13:45

ECAC All-Rookie Team (2005)

• Missed majority of 2008-09 due to leg injury in training camp, September 18, 2008.

MITCHELL, Willie

(MIH-chuhl, WIH-lee) **L.A.**

Defense. Shoots left. 6'3", 212 lbs. Born, Port McNeill, B.C., April 23, 1977. New Jersey's 12th choice, 199th overall, in 1996 Entry Draft.

Season	Club	League	GP	G	A	Pts	PIM	PP	SH	GW	S	%	+/-	TF	F%	Min	GP	G	A	Pts	PIM	PP	SH	GW	Min
1993-94	Notre Dame	SMHL	31	4	11	15	81	....	....	....	....	....	....	....	....	....	....	....	....	....	....	....	....	....	....
1994-95	Kelowna Spartans	BCHL	42	3	8	11	71	....	....	....	....	....	....	....	....	....	....	....	....	....	....	....	....	....	....
1995-96	Melfort Mustangs	SJHL	19	2	6	8	....	....	....	....	....	....	....	....	....	....	14	0	2	2	12	....	....	....	....
1996-97	Melfort Mustangs	SJHL	64	14	42	56	227	....	....	....	....	....	....	....	....	....	4	0	1	1	23	....	....	....	....
1997-98	Clarkson Knights	ECAC	34	9	17	26	105	....	....	....	....	....	....	....	....	....	....	....	....	....	....	....	....	....	....
1998-99	Clarkson Knights	ECAC	34	10	19	29	40	....	....	....	....	....	....	....	....	....	....	....	....	....	....	....	....	....	....
	Albany River Rats	AHL	6	1	3	4	29	....	....	....	....	....	....	....	....	....	....	....	....	....	....	....	....	....	....
99-2000	New Jersey	NHL	2	0	0	0	0	0	0	0	2	0.0	1	0	0.0	16:04	....	....	....	....	....	....	....	....	....
	Albany River Rats	AHL	63	5	14	19	71	....	....	....	....	....	....	....	....	....	5	1	2	3	4	....	....	....	....
2000-01	New Jersey	NHL	16	0	2	2	29	0	0	0	14	0.0	0	0	0.0	14:52	....	....	....	....	....	....	....	....	....
	Albany River Rats	AHL	41	3	13	16	94	....	....	....	....	....	....	....	....	....	....	....	....	....	....	....	....	....	....
	Minnesota	NHL	17	1	7	8	11	0	0	0	16	6.3	4	0	0.0	20:49	....	....	....	....	....	....	....	....	....
2001-02	Minnesota	NHL	68	3	10	13	68	0	0	1	67	4.5	–16	0	0.0	21:25	....	....	....	....	....	....	....	....	....
2002-03	Minnesota	NHL	69	2	12	14	84	0	1	1	67	3.0	13	0	0.0	21:28	18	1	3	4	14	0	0	0	24:48
2003-04	Minnesota	NHL	70	1	13	14	83	0	0	0	58	1.7	12	2	50.0	22:36	....	....	....	....	....	....	....	....	....
2004-05			DID NOT PLAY																						
2005-06	Minnesota	NHL	64	2	6	8	87	0	0	0	48	4.2	15	0	0.0	20:52	....	....	....	....	....	....	....	....	....
	Dallas	NHL	16	0	2	2	26	0	0	0	10	0.0	4	0	0.0	20:46	5	0	0	0	2	0	0	0	23:21
2006-07	Vancouver	NHL	62	1	10	11	45	0	0	0	54	1.9	1	0	0.0	22:13	12	0	1	1	12	0	0	0	27:14
2007-08	Vancouver	NHL	72	2	10	12	81	0	0	1	65	3.1	6	0	0.0	23:12	....	....	....	....	....	....	....	....	....
2008-09	Vancouver	NHL	82	3	20	23	59	0	0	1	88	3.4	29	1	0.0	22:55	10	0	2	2	22	0	0	0	24:13
2009-10	Vancouver	NHL	48	4	8	12	48	0	0	1	47	8.5	13	0	0.0	22:37	....	....	....	....	....	....	....	....	....
2010-11	Los Angeles	NHL	57	5	5	10	21	0	1	1	59	8.5	4	0	0.0	21:49	6	1	1	2	4	0	0	0	24:17
	NHL Totals		643	24	105	129	642	0	2	6	595	4.0		3	33.3	21:53	51	2	7	9	54	0	0	0	25:03

SJHL First All-Star Team (1997) • SJHL Top Defenseman Award (1997) • ECAC Second All-Star Team (1998) • ECAC Rookie of the Year (1998) (co-winner - Erik Cole) • ECAC First All-Star Team (1999) • NCAA East Second All-American Team (1999)

Traded to **Minnesota** by **New Jersey** for Sean O'Donnell, March 4, 2001. Traded to **Dallas** by **Minnesota** with Minnesota's 2nd round choice (Nico Saccheti) in 2007 Entry Draft for Martin Skoula and Shawn Belle, March 9, 2006. Signed as a free agent by **Vancouver**, July 1, 2006. Signed as a free agent by **Los Angeles**, August 25, 2010.

MODANO, Mike

(moh-DA-noh, MIGHK)

Center. Shoots left. 6'3", 212 lbs. Born, Livonia, MI, June 7, 1970. Minnesota's 1st choice, 1st overall, in 1988 Entry Draft.

Season	Club	League	GP	G	A	Pts	PIM	PP	SH	GW	S	%	+/-	TF	F%	Min	GP	G	A	Pts	PIM	PP	SH	GW	Min
1985-86	Det. L. Caesars	MNHL	69	66	65	131	32	....	....	....	....	....	....	....	....	....	....	....	....	....	....	....	....	....	....
1986-87	Prince Albert	WHL	70	32	30	62	96	....	....	....	....	....	....	....	....	....	8	1	4	5	4	....	....	....	....
1987-88	Prince Albert	WHL	65	47	80	127	80	....	....	....	....	....	....	....	....	....	9	7	11	18	18	....	....	....	....
1988-89	Prince Albert	WHL	41	39	66	105	74	....	....	....	....	....	....	....	....	....	....	....	....	....	....	....	....	....	....
	Minnesota	NHL	....	....	....	....	....	....	....	....	....	....	....	....	....	....	2	0	0	0	0	0	0	0	....
1989-90	Minnesota	NHL	80	29	46	75	63	12	0	2	172	16.9	–7	....	....	....	7	1	1	2	12	0	0	0	....
1990-91	Minnesota	NHL	79	28	36	64	65	9	0	2	232	12.1	2	....	....	....	23	8	12	20	16	3	0	1	....
1991-92	Minnesota	NHL	76	33	44	77	46	5	0	8	256	12.9	–9	....	....	....	7	3	2	5	4	1	0	0	....
1992-93	Minnesota	NHL	82	33	60	93	83	9	0	7	307	10.7	–7	....	....	....	....	....	....	....	....	....	....	....	....
1993-94	Dallas	NHL	76	50	43	93	54	18	0	4	281	17.8	–8	....	....	....	9	7	3	10	16	2	0	2	....
1994-95	Dallas	NHL	30	12	17	29	8	4	1	0	100	12.0	7	....	....	....	....	....	....	....	....	....	....	....	....
1995-96	Dallas	NHL	78	36	45	81	63	8	4	4	320	11.3	–12	....	....	....	....	....	....	....	....	....	....	....	....
1996-97	Dallas	NHL	80	35	48	83	42	9	5	9	291	12.0	43	....	....	....	7	4	1	5	0	1	1	2	....
1997-98	Dallas	NHL	52	21	38	59	32	7	5	2	191	11.0	25	....	....	....	17	4	10	14	12	1	0	1	....
	United States	Olympics	4	2	0	2	0	....	....	....	....	....	....	....	....	....	....	....	....	....	....	....	....	....	....
1998-99 ♦	Dallas	NHL	77	34	47	81	44	6	4	7	224	15.2	29	1572	51.1	20:50	23	5	*18	23	16	1	1	1	24:40
99-2000	Dallas	NHL	77	38	43	81	48	11	1	8	188	20.2	0	1763	51.4	22:55	23	10	*13	23	10	*4	0	2	25:26
2000-01	Dallas	NHL	81	33	51	84	52	8	3	7	208	15.9	26	1791	52.0	22:24	9	3	4	7	0	2	0	0	25:43
2001-02	Dallas	NHL	78	34	43	77	38	6	2	5	219	15.5	14	1710	53.7	22:27	....	....	....	....	....	....	....	....	....
	United States	Olympics	6	0	*6	6	4	....	....	....	....	....	....	....	....	....	....	....	....	....	....	....	....	....	....
2002-03	Dallas	NHL	79	28	57	85	30	5	2	6	193	14.5	34	1808	51.4	20:53	12	5	10	15	4	1	0	2	23:53
2003-04	Dallas	NHL	76	14	30	44	46	6	0	0	152	9.2	–21	1523	52.6	20:27	5	1	2	3	8	1	0	0	23:17
2004-05			DID NOT PLAY																						
2005-06	Dallas	NHL	78	27	50	77	58	12	1	4	207	13.0	23	1421	51.1	19:34	5	1	3	4	4	1	0	0	22:14
	United States	Olympics	6	2	0	2	6	....	....	....	....	....	....	....	....	....	....	....	....	....	....	....	....	....	....
2006-07	Dallas	NHL	59	22	21	43	34	9	0	7	141	15.6	9	918	52.2	18:24	7	1	1	2	4	1	0	1	26:14
2007-08	Dallas	NHL	82	21	36	57	48	5	1	4	200	10.5	–11	1145	49.2	19:14	18	5	7	12	22	5	0	3	19:42
2008-09	Dallas	NHL	80	15	31	46	46	4	0	4	197	7.6	–13	1176	52.5	18:18	....	....	....	....	....	....	....	....	....
2009-10	Dallas	NHL	59	14	16	30	22	3	0	2	115	12.2	–6	847	50.4	14:18	....	....	....	....	....	....	....	....	....
2010-11	Detroit	NHL	40	4	11	15	8	1	0	0	79	5.1	–4	274	48.5	12:27	2	0	1	1	0	0	0	0	10:13
	NHL Totals		1499	561	813	1374	930	157	29	92	4273	13.1		15948	51.6	19:47	176	58	88	146	128	24	2	15	23:37

WHL East First All-Star Team (1989) • NHL All-Rookie Team (1990) • NHL Second All-Star Team (2000)

Played in NHL All-Star Game (1993, 1998, 1999, 2000, 2003, 2004, 2009)

• Transferred to **Dallas** after **Minnesota** franchise relocated, June 9, 1993. Signed as a free agent by **Detroit**, August 5, 2010. • Missed majority of 2010-11 due to arm injury vs. Columbus, November 26, 2010.

MODIN, Fredrik

(moh-DEEN, FREHD-rihk)

Left wing. Shoots left. 6'4", 220 lbs. Born, Sundsvall, Sweden, October 8, 1974. Toronto's 3rd choice, 64th overall, in 1994 Entry Draft.

Season	Club	League	GP	G	A	Pts	PIM	PP	SH	GW	S	%	+/-	TF	F%	Min	GP	G	A	Pts	PIM	PP	SH	GW	Min
1991-92	Sundsvall/Timra	Sweden-2	11	1	0	1	0	....	....	....	....	....	....	....	....	....	....	....	....	....	....	....	....	....	....
1992-93	Sundsvall/Timra	Sweden-2	30	5	7	12	12	....	....	....	....	....	....	....	....	....	5	1	0	1	0	....	....	....	....
1993-94	Sundsvall/Timra	Sweden-2	30	16	15	31	36	....	....	....	....	....	....	....	....	....	2	0	1	1	6	....	....	....	....
1994-95	Brynas IF Gavle	Sweden	38	9	10	19	33	....	....	....	....	....	....	....	....	....	14	4	4	8	6	....	....	....	....
1995-96	Brynas IF Gavle	Sweden	22	4	8	12	22	....	....	....	....	....	....	....	....	....	....	....	....	....	....	....	....	....	....
1996-97	Toronto	NHL	76	6	7	13	24	0	0	0	85	7.1	–14	....	....	....	....	....	....	....	....	....	....	....	....
1997-98	Toronto	NHL	74	16	16	32	32	1	0	4	137	11.7	–5	....	....	....	....	....	....	....	....	....	....	....	....
1998-99	Toronto	NHL	67	16	15	31	35	1	0	3	108	14.8	14	2	50.0	13:34	8	0	0	0	6	0	0	0	9:50
99-2000	Tampa Bay	NHL	80	22	26	48	18	3	0	5	167	13.2	–26	6	50.0	15:32	....	....	....	....	....	....	....	....	....
2000-01	Tampa Bay	NHL	76	32	24	56	48	8	0	4	217	14.7	–1	21	42.9	17:15	....	....	....	....	....	....	....	....	....

Season	Club	League	Regular Season														Playoffs								
			GP	G	A	Pts	PIM	PP	SH	GW	S	%	+/-	TF	F%	Min	GP	G	A	Pts	PIM	PP	SH	GW	Min
2001-02	Tampa Bay	NHL	54	14	17	31	27	2	0	4	141	9.9	0	25	40.0	19:05	....	....	....	....	....	....	....	....	....
2002-03	Tampa Bay	NHL	76	17	23	40	43	2	1	4	179	9.5	7	35	28.6	17:35	11	2	0	2	18	0	0	0	19:18
2003-04♦	Tampa Bay	NHL	82	29	28	57	32	5	1	2	206	14.1	31	138	38.4	18:12	23	8	11	19	10	3	0	2	20:47
2004-05	Timra IK	Sweden	43	12	24	36	58	....	....	....	....	....	....	....	....	....	7	1	1	2	8	....	....	....	....
2005-06	Tampa Bay	NHL	77	31	23	54	56	12	1	4	221	14.0	5	171	51.5	19:35	5	0	0	0	6	0	0	0	18:46
	Sweden	Olympics	8	2	1	3	6	....	....	....	....	....	....	....	....	....	....	....	....	....	....	....	....	....	....
2006-07	Columbus	NHL	79	22	20	42	50	6	0	4	220	10.0	–3	508	46.5	19:07	....	....	....	....	....	....	....	....	....
2007-08	Columbus	NHL	23	6	6	12	20	2	0	1	41	14.6	1	103	44.7	16:51	....	....	....	....	....	....	....	....	....
2008-09	Columbus	NHL	50	9	16	25	28	2	0	0	113	8.0	2	122	40.2	16:53	4	1	0	1	0	0	0	0	13:07
2009-10	Columbus	NHL	24	2	4	6	12	0	0	2	35	5.7	–6	12	58.3	14:41	....	....	....	....	....	....	....	....	....
	Sweden	Olympics	3	0	1	1	0	....	....	....	....	....	....	....	....	....	....	....	....	....	....	....	....	....	....
	Los Angeles	NHL	20	3	2	5	14	2	0	0	32	9.4	–2	16	68.8	14:55	6	3	1	4	2	2	0	0	17:22
2010-11	Atlanta	NHL	36	7	3	10	12	0	1	0	51	13.7	–11	16	43.8	11:57	....	....	....	....	....	....	....	....	....
	Calgary	NHL	4	0	0	0	2	0	0	0	3	0.0	–3	4	25.0	8:28	....	....	....	....	....	....	....	....	....
	NHL Totals		898	232	230	462	453	46	4	37	1956	11.9		1179	45.0	16:58	57	14	12	26	42	5	0	2	17:53

Played in NHL All-Star Game (2001)

Traded to **Tampa Bay** by **Toronto** for Cory Cross and Tampa Bay's 7th round choice (Ivan Kolozvary) in 2001 Entry Draft, October 1, 1999. Signed as a free agent by **Timra** (Sweden), October 5, 2004. Traded to **Columbus** by **Tampa Bay** with Fredrik Norrena for Marc Denis, June 30, 2006. • Missed majority of 2007-08 due to shoulder injury at Anaheim, November 1, 2007. Traded to **Los Angeles** by **Columbus** for future considerations, March 3, 2010. Signed as a free agent by **Atlanta**, September 6, 2010. Traded to **Calgary** by **Atlanta** for Calgary's 7th round choice (later traded to San Jose – San Jose selected Colin Blackwell) in 2011 Entry Draft, February 28, 2011. • Missed majority of 2010-11 due to various injuries. • Officially announced his retirement, May 19, 2011.

MOEN, Travis

(MOH-ehn, TRA-vihs) **MTL**

Left wing. Shoots left. 6'2", 215 lbs. Born, Stewart Valley, Sask., April 6, 1982. Calgary's 6th choice, 155th overall, in 2000 Entry Draft.

Season	Club	League	GP	G	A	Pts	PIM	PP	SH	GW	S	%	+/-	TF	F%	Min	GP	G	A	Pts	PIM	PP	SH	GW	Min
1998-99	Swift Current	SMHL	STATISTICS NOT AVAILABLE																						
	Kelowna Rockets	WHL	4	0	0	0	0	....	....	....	....	....	....	....	....	....	....	....	....	....	....	....	....	....	....
99-2000	Kelowna Rockets	WHL	66	9	6	15	96	....	....	....	....	....	....	....	....	....	5	1	1	2	2	....	....	....	....
2000-01	Kelowna Rockets	WHL	40	8	8	16	106	....	....	....	....	....	....	....	....	....	....	....	....	....	....	....	....	....	....
2001-02	Kelowna Rockets	WHL	71	10	17	27	197	....	....	....	....	....	....	....	....	....	13	1	0	1	28	....	....	....	....
2002-03	Norfolk Admirals	AHL	42	1	2	3	62	....	....	....	....	....	....	....	....	....	9	0	0	0	20	....	....	....	....
2003-04	Chicago	NHL	82	4	2	6	142	0	0	2	51	7.8	–17	19	15.8	10:57	....	....	....	....	....	....	....	....	....
2004-05	Norfolk Admirals	AHL	79	8	12	20	187	....	....	....	....	....	....	....	....	....	6	0	1	1	6	....	....	....	....
2005-06	Anaheim	NHL	39	4	1	5	72	0	0	0	28	14.3	–3	8	12.5	11:03	9	1	0	1	10	0	0	0	8:25
2006-07♦	Anaheim	NHL	82	11	10	21	101	0	0	0	124	8.9	–4	10	30.0	14:48	21	7	5	12	22	0	0	3	17:19
2007-08	Anaheim	NHL	77	3	5	8	81	0	1	1	98	3.1	–10	25	32.0	15:50	6	1	1	2	2	0	0	0	14:09
2008-09	Anaheim	NHL	63	4	7	11	77	0	2	1	77	5.2	–17	7	28.6	14:53	....	....	....	....	....	....	....	....	....
	San Jose	NHL	19	3	2	5	14	0	1	1	24	12.5	–1	11	18.2	15:21	6	0	0	0	2	0	0	0	12:54
2009-10	Montreal	NHL	81	8	11	19	57	1	2	0	107	7.5	–2	12	25.0	15:00	19	2	1	3	4	0	1	1	13:15
2010-11	Montreal	NHL	79	6	10	16	96	0	1	0	99	6.1	–4	22	36.4	13:11	7	0	1	1	2	0	0	0	16:33
	NHL Totals		522	43	48	91	640	1	7	5	608	7.1		114	26.3	13:53	68	11	8	19	42	0	1	4	14:15

Signed as a free agent by **Chicago**, October 21, 2002. Traded to **Anaheim** by **Chicago** for Michael Holmqvist, July 30, 2005. • Missed majority of 2005-06 due to knee and shoulder injuries and as a healthy reserve. Traded to **San Jose** by **Anaheim** with Kent Huskins for Timo Pielmeier, Nick Bonino and future considerations, March 4, 2009. Signed as a free agent by **Montreal**, July 10, 2009.

MOLLER, Oscar

(MOH-luhr, AH-skuhr) **L.A.**

Center. Shoots right. 5'10", 189 lbs. Born, Stockholm, Sweden, January 22, 1989. Los Angeles' 2nd choice, 52nd overall, in 2007 Entry Draft.

Season	Club	League	GP	G	A	Pts	PIM	PP	SH	GW	S	%	+/-	TF	F%	Min	GP	G	A	Pts	PIM	PP	SH	GW	Min
2003-04	Spanga U18	Swe-U18	32	28	12	40	68	....	....	....	....	....	....	....	....	....	....	....	....	....	....	....	....	....	....
2004-05	Spanga U18	Swe-U18	24	28	16	44	52	....	....	....	....	....	....	....	....	....	....	....	....	....	....	....	....	....	....
	Spanga Jr.	Swe-Jr.	4	6	1	7	6	....	....	....	....	....	....	....	....	....	....	....	....	....	....	....	....	....	....
	Spanga	Sweden-4	6	6	4	10	0	....	....	....	....	....	....	....	....	....	....	....	....	....	....	....	....	....	....
2005-06	Djurgarden U18	Swe-U18	8	8	5	13	6	....	....	....	....	....	....	....	....	....	2	1	0	1	0	....	....	....	....
	Djurgarden Jr.	Swe-Jr.	25	8	5	13	41	....	....	....	....	....	....	....	....	....	4	2	0	2	0	....	....	....	....
2006-07	Chilliwack Bruins	WHL	68	32	37	69	50	....	....	....	....	....	....	....	....	....	5	0	3	3	6	....	....	....	....
2007-08	Chilliwack Bruins	WHL	63	39	43	82	42	....	....	....	....	....	....	....	....	....	4	2	1	3	4	....	....	....	....
	Manchester	AHL	....	....	....	....	....	....	....	....	....	....	....	....	....	....	2	0	1	1	0	....	....	....	....
2008-09	Los Angeles	NHL	40	7	8	15	16	5	0	0	81	8.6	–3	86	43.0	13:22	....	....	....	....	....	....	....	....	....
	Manchester	AHL	8	2	3	5	6	....	....	....	....	....	....	....	....	....	....	....	....	....	....	....	....	....	....
2009-10	Los Angeles	NHL	34	4	3	7	4	1	0	0	42	9.5	–6	104	30.8	8:35	....	....	....	....	....	....	....	....	....
	Manchester	AHL	43	15	18	33	20	....	....	....	....	....	....	....	....	....	16	2	5	7	0	....	....	....	....
2010-11	Los Angeles	NHL	13	1	3	4	2	0	0	0	27	3.7	–1	5	80.0	14:36	1	0	0	0	0	0	0	0	10:37
	Manchester	AHL	59	23	27	50	34	....	....	....	....	....	....	....	....	....	....	....	....	....	....	....	....	....	....
	NHL Totals		87	12	14	26	22	6	0	0	150	8.0		195	37.4	11:41	1	0	0	0	0	0	0	0	10:37

WHL West First All-Star Team (2008)

MONTADOR, Steve

(MAWN-tuh-dohr, STEEV) **CHI**

Defense. Shoots right. 6', 207 lbs. Born, Vancouver, B.C., December 21, 1979.

Season	Club	League	GP	G	A	Pts	PIM	PP	SH	GW	S	%	+/-	TF	F%	Min	GP	G	A	Pts	PIM	PP	SH	GW	Min
1995-96	St. Mike's B's	OPJHL	46	3	16	19	145	....	....	....	....	....	....	....	....	....	7	1	2	3	10	....	....	....	....
1996-97	North Bay	OHL	63	7	28	35	129	....	....	....	....	....	....	....	....	....	....	....	....	....	....	....	....	....	....
1997-98	North Bay	OHL	37	5	16	21	54	....	....	....	....	....	....	....	....	....	....	....	....	....	....	....	....	....	....
	Erie Otters	OHL	26	3	17	20	35	....	....	....	....	....	....	....	....	....	7	1	1	2	9	....	....	....	....
1998-99	Erie Otters	OHL	61	9	33	42	114	....	....	....	....	....	....	....	....	....	5	0	2	2	4	....	....	....	....
99-2000	Peterborough	OHL	64	14	42	56	97	....	....	....	....	....	....	....	....	....	5	0	2	2	4	....	....	....	....
	Saint John Flames	AHL	....	....	....	....	....	....	....	....	....	....	....	....	....	....	2	0	0	0	0	....	....	....	....
2000-01	Saint John Flames	AHL	58	1	6	7	95	....	....	....	....	....	....	....	....	....	19	0	8	8	13	....	....	....	....
2001-02	Calgary	NHL	11	1	2	3	26	0	0	0	10	10.0	–2	0	0.0	12:12	....	....	....	....	....	....	....	....	....
	Saint John Flames	AHL	67	9	16	25	107	....	....	....	....	....	....	....	....	....	....	....	....	....	....	....	....	....	....
2002-03	Calgary	NHL	50	1	1	2	114	0	0	0	64	1.6	–9	0	0.0	15:11	....	....	....	....	....	....	....	....	....
	Saint John Flames	AHL	11	1	7	8	20	....	....	....	....	....	....	....	....	....	....	....	....	....	....	....	....	....	....
2003-04	Calgary	NHL	26	1	2	3	50	0	0	1	31	3.2	–1	1	0.0	11:46	20	1	2	3	6	0	0	1	17:43
2004-05	HC Mulhouse	France	15	1	7	8	69	....	....	....	....	....	....	....	....	....	....	....	....	....	....	....	....	....	....
2005-06	Calgary	NHL	7	1	0	1	11	0	0	0	13	7.7	0	0	0.0	11:49	....	....	....	....	....	....	....	....	....
	Florida	NHL	51	1	5	6	68	0	0	0	42	2.4	4	0	0.0	14:04	....	....	....	....	....	....	....	....	....
2006-07	Florida	NHL	72	1	8	9	119	0	0	0	88	1.1	1	0	0.0	13:08	....	....	....	....	....	....	....	....	....
2007-08	Florida	NHL	73	8	15	23	73	2	0	0	96	8.3	1	0	0.0	11:39	....	....	....	....	....	....	....	....	....
2008-09	Anaheim	NHL	65	4	16	20	125	0	0	0	100	4.0	14	0	0.0	16:12	....	....	....	....	....	....	....	....	....
	Boston	NHL	13	0	1	1	18	0	0	0	17	0.0	3	1	0.0	15:55	11	1	2	3	18	0	0	0	19:33
2009-10	Buffalo	NHL	78	5	18	23	75	0	0	2	134	3.7	0	1	0.0	17:06	6	1	0	1	4	0	0	0	23:54
2010-11	Buffalo	NHL	73	5	21	26	83	0	0	0	118	4.2	16	1	0.0	19:43	6	0	1	1	8	0	0	0	15:45
	NHL Totals		519	28	89	117	762	2	0	3	713	3.9		4	0.0	15:05	43	3	5	8	36	0	0	1	18:47

Signed as a free agent by **Calgary**, April 10, 2000. • Missed majority of 2003-04 as a healthy reserve. Signed as a free agent by **Mulhouse** (France), September 17, 2004. Traded to **Florida** by **Calgary** with Dustin Johner for Kristian Huselius, December 2, 2005. Signed as a free agent by **Anaheim**, July 11, 2008. Traded to **Boston** by **Anaheim** for Petteri Nokelainen, March 4, 2009. Signed as a free agent by **Buffalo**, July 1, 2009. Traded to **Chicago** by **Buffalo** for Florida's 7th round choice (previously acquired) in 2012 or 2013 Entry Draft, June 29, 2011.

MOORE, Dominic

(MOOR, DOHM-ihn-ihk) **T.B.**

Center. Shoots left. 6', 192 lbs. Born, Sarnia, Ont., August 3, 1980. NY Rangers' 2nd choice, 95th overall, in 2000 Entry Draft.

Season	Club	League	GP	G	A	Pts	PIM	PP	SH	GW	S	%	+/-	TF	F%	Min	GP	G	A	Pts	PIM	PP	SH	GW	Min
1996-97	Thornhill Rattlers	ON-Jr.A	29	4	6	10	48	....	....	....	....	....	....	....	....	....	1	0	1	1	0	....	....	....	....
1997-98	Aurora Tigers	OPJHL	51	10	15	25	16	....	....	....	....	....	....	....	....	....	....	....	....	....	....	....	....	....	....
1998-99	Aurora Tigers	OPJHL	51	34	53	87	70	....	....	....	....	....	....	....	....	....	....	....	....	....	....	....	....	....	....
99-2000	Harvard Crimson	ECAC	30	12	12	24	28	....	....	....	....	....	....	....	....	....	....	....	....	....	....	....	....	....	....
2000-01	Harvard Crimson	ECAC	32	15	28	43	40	....	....	....	....	....	....	....	....	....	....	....	....	....	....	....	....	....	....
2001-02	Harvard Crimson	ECAC	32	13	16	29	37	....	....	....	....	....	....	....	....	....	....	....	....	....	....	....	....	....	....
2002-03	Harvard Crimson	ECAC	34	*24	27	*51	30	....	....	....	....	....	....	....	....	....	....	....	....	....	....	....	....	....	....
2003-04	NY Rangers	NHL	5	0	3	3	0	0	0	0	3	0.0	0	36	30.6	9:18	....	....	....	....	....	....	....	....	....
	Hartford	AHL	70	14	25	39	60	....	....	....	....	....	....	....	....	....	16	3	3	6	8	....	....	....	....
2004-05	Hartford	AHL	78	19	31	50	78	....	....	....	....	....	....	....	....	....	6	1	1	2	4	....	....	....	....
2005-06	NY Rangers	NHL	82	9	9	18	28	2	0	1	139	6.5	4	814	46.3	12:28	4	0	0	0	2	0	0	0	11:21
2006-07	Pittsburgh	NHL	59	6	9	15	46	0	0	0	100	6.0	1	678	51.6	13:04	....	....	....	....	....	....	....	....	....
	Minnesota	NHL	10	2	0	2	10	0	0	1	11	18.2	3	66	62.1	10:12	....	....	....	....	....	....	....	....	....

			Regular Season														Playoffs								
Season	Club	League	GP	G	A	Pts	PIM	PP	SH	GW	S	%	+/-	TF	F%	Min	GP	G	A	Pts	PIM	PP	SH	GW	Min
2007-08	**Minnesota**	**NHL**	**30**	**1**	**2**	**3**	**10**	**0**	**0**	**0**	**28**	**3.6**	**–11**	**311**	**52.4**	**11:57**	....	....	....	....	....	....	....	....	....
	Toronto	**NHL**	**38**	**4**	**10**	**14**	**14**	**1**	**0**	**0**	**72**	**5.6**	**7**	**393**	**50.6**	**14:21**	....	....	....	....	....	....	....	....	....
2008-09	**Toronto**	**NHL**	**63**	**12**	**29**	**41**	**69**	**4**	**1**	**1**	**132**	**9.1**	**–1**	**1007**	**54.8**	**17:18**	....	....	....	....	....	....	....	....	....
	Buffalo	**NHL**	**18**	**1**	**3**	**4**	**23**	**0**	**0**	**0**	**33**	**3.0**	**–1**	**237**	**51.1**	**15:12**	....	....	....	....	....	....	....	....	....
2009-10	**Florida**	**NHL**	**48**	**8**	**9**	**17**	**35**	**2**	**1**	**0**	**81**	**9.9**	**–7**	**462**	**55.8**	**14:55**	....	....	....	....	....	....	....	....	....
	Montreal	**NHL**	**21**	**2**	**9**	**11**	**8**	**0**	**1**	**0**	**38**	**5.3**	**4**	**201**	**53.2**	**14:40**	**19**	**4**	**1**	**5**	**6**	**0**	**0**	**1**	**14:34**
2010-11	**Tampa Bay**	**NHL**	**77**	**18**	**14**	**32**	**52**	**6**	**0**	**3**	**175**	**10.3**	**–12**	**892**	**53.3**	**15:36**	**18**	**3**	**8**	**11**	**18**	**1**	**0**	**0**	**17:46**
	NHL Totals		**451**	**63**	**97**	**160**	**295**	**15**	**3**	**6**	**812**	**7.8**		**5097**	**52.1**	**14:16**	**41**	**7**	**9**	**16**	**26**	**1**	**0**	**1**	**15:40**

ECAC All-Rookie Team (2000) • ECAC Second All-Star Team (2001) • ECAC First All-Star Team (2003) • NCAA East First All-American Team (2003)

Traded to **Nashville** by **NY Rangers** for Adam Hall, July 19, 2006. Traded to **Pittsburgh** by **Nashville** with Libor Pivko for Pittsburgh's 3rd round choice (Ryan Thang) in 2007 Entry Draft, July 19, 2006. Traded to **Minnesota** by **Pittsburgh** for Minnesota's 3rd round choice (Casey Pierro-Zabotel) in 2007 Entry Draft, February 27, 2007. Claimed on waivers by **Toronto** from **Minnesota**, January 11, 2008. Traded to **Buffalo** by **Toronto** for Carolina's 2nd round choice (previously acquired, Toronto selected Jesse Blacker) in 2009 Entry Draft, March 4, 2009. Signed as a free agent by **Florida**, October 5, 2009. Traded to **Montreal** by **Florida** for Montreal's 2nd round choice (later traded to San Jose – San Jose selected Matthew Nieto) in 2011 Entry Draft, February 11, 2010. Signed as a free agent by **Tampa Bay**, July 30, 2010.

MOORE, Greg

(MOOR, GREHG)

Right wing. Shoots right. 6'1", 225 lbs. Born, Lisbon, ME, March 26, 1984. Calgary's 5th choice, 143rd overall, in 2003 Entry Draft.

Season	Club	League	GP	G	A	Pts	PIM	PP	SH	GW	S	%	+/-	TF	F%	Min	GP	G	A	Pts	PIM	PP	SH	GW	Min
99-2000	St. Dominic	High-ME	31	32	40	72		....	....	....	....	....	....	....	....	....	....	....	....	....	....	....	....	....	....
2000-01	USNTDP	U-17	13	4	6	10	1	....	....	....	....	....	....	....	....	....	....	....	....	....	....	....	....	....	....
	USNTDP	NAHL	56	8	12	20	22	....	....	....	....	....	....	....	....	....	....	....	....	....	....	....	....	....	....
2001-02	USNTDP	U-18	35	8	20	28	14	....	....	....	....	....	....	....	....	....	....	....	....	....	....	....	....	....	....
	USNTDP	USHL	12	2	2	4	4	....	....	....	....	....	....	....	....	....	....	....	....	....	....	....	....	....	....
	USNTDP	NAHL	6	3	2	5	2	....	....	....	....	....	....	....	....	....	....	....	....	....	....	....	....	....	....
2002-03	U. of Maine	H-East	33	9	7	16	10	....	....	....	....	....	....	....	....	....	....	....	....	....	....	....	....	....	....
2003-04	U. of Maine	H-East	39	15	8	23	44	....	....	....	....	....	....	....	....	....	....	....	....	....	....	....	....	....	....
2004-05	U. of Maine	H-East	40	14	9	23	16	....	....	....	....	....	....	....	....	....	....	....	....	....	....	....	....	....	....
2005-06	U. of Maine	H-East	42	28	17	45	47	....	....	....	....	....	....	....	....	....	....	....	....	....	....	....	....	....	....
	Hartford	AHL	2	1	1	2	2	....	....	....	....	....	....	....	....	....	13	2	5	7	6	....	....	....	....
2006-07	Hartford	AHL	79	8	17	25	41	....	....	....	....	....	....	....	....	....	7	0	1	1	4	....	....	....	....
2007-08	**NY Rangers**	**NHL**	**6**	**0**	**0**	**0**	**0**	**0**	**0**	**0**	**13**	**0.0**	**–2**	**8**	**37.5**	**11:49**	....	....	....	....	....	....	....	....	....
	Hartford	AHL	72	26	40	66	31	....	....	....	....	....	....	....	....	....	5	1	2	3	2	....	....	....	....
2008-09	Hartford	AHL	71	23	16	39	28	....	....	....	....	....	....	....	....	....	6	0	2	2	0	....	....	....	....
2009-10	Bridgeport	AHL	62	14	17	31	28	....	....	....	....	....	....	....	....	....	....	....	....	....	....	....	....	....	....
	Columbus	**NHL**	**4**	**0**	**0**	**0**	**0**	**0**	**0**	**0**	**2**	**0.0**	**0**	**8**	**50.0**	**5:54**	....	....	....	....	....	....	....	....	....
	Syracuse Crunch	AHL	16	5	5	10	10	....	....	....	....	....	....	....	....	....	....	....	....	....	....	....	....	....	....
2010-11	Adirondack	AHL	57	7	13	20	18	....	....	....	....	....	....	....	....	....	....	....	....	....	....	....	....	....	....
	Springfield	AHL	18	2	2	4	4	....	....	....	....	....	....	....	....	....	....	....	....	....	....	....	....	....	....
	NHL Totals		**10**	**0**	**0**	**0**	**0**	**0**	**0**	**0**	**15**	**0.0**		**16**	**43.8**	**9:27**	....	....	....	....	....	....	....	....	....

Hockey East First All-Star Team (2006) • NCAA East First All-American Team (2006)

Traded to **NY Rangers** by **Calgary** with Jamie McLennan and Blair Betts for Chris Simon and NY Rangers' 7th round choice (Matt Schneider) in 2004 Entry Draft, March 6, 2004. Signed as a free agent by **NY Islanders**, July 6, 2009. Traded to **Columbus** by **NY Islanders** for Dylan Reese, March 1, 2010. Traded to **Columbus** by **Philadelphia** with Michael Chaput for Tom Sestito, February 28, 2011.

MOORE, John

(MOOR, JAWN) **CBJ**

Defense. Shoots left. 6'3", 198 lbs. Born, Winnetka, IL, November 19, 1990. Columbus' 1st choice, 21st overall, in 2009 Entry Draft.

Season	Club	League	GP	G	A	Pts	PIM	PP	SH	GW	S	%	+/-	TF	F%	Min	GP	G	A	Pts	PIM	PP	SH	GW	Min
2006-07	Chicago Mission	MWEHL	31	1	12	13	26	....	....	....	....	....	....	....	....	....	....	....	....	....	....	....	....	....	....
	Chicago Mission	Exhib.	30	13	37	50	14	....	....	....	....	....	....	....	....	....	....	....	....	....	....	....	....	....	....
2007-08	Chicago Steel	USHL	56	4	11	15	26	....	....	....	....	....	....	....	....	....	7	0	2	2	2	....	....	....	....
2008-09	Chicago Steel	USHL	57	14	25	39	50	....	....	....	....	....	....	....	....	....	....	....	....	....	....	....	....	....	....
2009-10	Kitchener Rangers	OHL	61	10	37	47	53	....	....	....	....	....	....	....	....	....	20	4	12	16	2	....	....	....	....
2010-11	**Columbus**	**NHL**	**2**	**0**	**0**	**0**	**0**	**0**	**0**	**0**	**0**	**0.0**	**0**	**0**	**0.0**	**11:28**	....	....	....	....	....	....	....	....	....
	Springfield	AHL	73	5	19	24	23	....	....	....	....	....	....	....	....	....	....	....	....	....	....	....	....	....	....
	NHL Totals		**2**	**0**	**0**	**0**	**0**	**0**	**0**	**0**	**0**	**0.0**		**0**	**0.0**	**11:29**	....	....	....	....	....	....	....	....	....

USHL First All-Star Team (2009) • USHL Defenseman of the Year (2009)

MOORE, Mike

(MOOR, MIGHK) **S.J.**

Defense. Shoots left. 6'1", 190 lbs. Born, Calgary, Alta., December 12, 1984.

Season	Club	League	GP	G	A	Pts	PIM	PP	SH	GW	S	%	+/-	TF	F%	Min	GP	G	A	Pts	PIM	PP	SH	GW	Min
2003-04	Surrey Eagles	BCHL	52	6	21	27	148	....	....	....	....	....	....	....	....	....	10	0	2	2	6	....	....	....	....
2004-05	Princeton	ECAC	25	3	7	10	22	....	....	....	....	....	....	....	....	....	....	....	....	....	....	....	....	....	....
2005-06	Princeton	ECAC	30	0	4	4	42	....	....	....	....	....	....	....	....	....	....	....	....	....	....	....	....	....	....
2006-07	Princeton	ECAC	32	4	10	14	50	....	....	....	....	....	....	....	....	....	....	....	....	....	....	....	....	....	....
2007-08	Princeton	ECAC	34	7	17	24	40	....	....	....	....	....	....	....	....	....	....	....	....	....	....	....	....	....	....
	Worcester Sharks	AHL	3	0	0	0	16	....	....	....	....	....	....	....	....	....	....	....	....	....	....	....	....	....	....
2008-09	Worcester Sharks	AHL	76	5	13	18	132	....	....	....	....	....	....	....	....	....	12	0	1	1	17	....	....	....	....
2009-10	Worcester Sharks	AHL	64	3	19	22	82	....	....	....	....	....	....	....	....	....	11	0	0	0	14	....	....	....	....
2010-11	**San Jose**	**NHL**	**6**	**1**	**0**	**1**	**7**	**0**	**0**	**0**	**5**	**20.0**	**–1**	**0**	**0.0**	**10:07**	....	....	....	....	....	....	....	....	....
	Worcester Sharks	AHL	49	2	10	12	50	....	....	....	....	....	....	....	....	....	....	....	....	....	....	....	....	....	....
	NHL Totals		**6**	**1**	**0**	**1**	**7**	**0**	**0**	**0**	**5**	**20.0**		**0**	**0.0**	**10:07**	....	....	....	....	....	....	....	....	....

ECAC First All-Star Team (2008) • NCAA East First All-American Team (2008)

Signed as a free agent by **San Jose**, April 8, 2008.

MORAN, Brad

(moh-RAN, BRAD)

Center. Shoots left. 5'11", 182 lbs. Born, Abbotsford, B.C., March 20, 1979. Buffalo's 8th choice, 191st overall, in 1998 Entry Draft.

Season	Club	League	GP	G	A	Pts	PIM	PP	SH	GW	S	%	+/-	TF	F%	Min	GP	G	A	Pts	PIM	PP	SH	GW	Min
1994-95	Abbotsford	Minor-BC	56	66	93	159	40	....	....	....	....	....	....	....	....	....	....	....	....	....	....	....	....	....	....
1995-96	Calgary Hitmen	WHL	70	13	31	44	28	....	....	....	....	....	....	....	....	....	....	....	....	....	....	....	....	....	....
1996-97	Calgary Hitmen	WHL	72	30	36	66	61	....	....	....	....	....	....	....	....	....	....	....	....	....	....	....	....	....	....
1997-98	Calgary Hitmen	WHL	72	53	49	102	64	....	....	....	....	....	....	....	....	....	18	10	8	18	20	....	....	....	....
1998-99	Calgary Hitmen	WHL	71	60	58	118	96	....	....	....	....	....	....	....	....	....	21	17	*25	42	26	....	....	....	....
99-2000	Calgary Hitmen	WHL	72	48	*72	*120	84	....	....	....	....	....	....	....	....	....	13	7	15	22	18	....	....	....	....
2000-01	Syracuse Crunch	AHL	71	11	19	30	30	....	....	....	....	....	....	....	....	....	5	3	4	7	2	....	....	....	....
2001-02	**Columbus**	**NHL**	**3**	**0**	**0**	**0**	**0**	**0**	**0**	**0**	**2**	**0.0**	**0**	**22**	**40.9**	**7:39**	....	....	....	....	....	....	....	....	....
	Syracuse Crunch	AHL	64	25	24	49	51	....	....	....	....	....	....	....	....	....	10	5	8	13	2	....	....	....	....
2002-03	Syracuse Crunch	AHL	47	12	19	31	22	....	....	....	....	....	....	....	....	....	....	....	....	....	....	....	....	....	....
2003-04	**Columbus**	**NHL**	**2**	**1**	**1**	**2**	**2**	**0**	**0**	**0**	**4**	**25.0**	**–1**	**25**	**64.0**	**10:03**	....	....	....	....	....	....	....	....	....
	Syracuse Crunch	AHL	72	24	35	59	44	....	....	....	....	....	....	....	....	....	7	5	3	8	2	....	....	....	....
2004-05	Syracuse Crunch	AHL	80	26	46	72	70	....	....	....	....	....	....	....	....	....	....	....	....	....	....	....	....	....	....
2005-06	Langnau	Swiss	18	4	4	8	18	....	....	....	....	....	....	....	....	....	6	4	6	10	10	....	....	....	....
2006-07	**Vancouver**	**NHL**	**3**	**0**	**1**	**1**	**2**	**0**	**0**	**0**	**3**	**0.0**	**0**	**24**	**58.3**	**12:38**	....	....	....	....	....	....	....	....	....
	Manitoba Moose	AHL	69	25	47	72	52	....	....	....	....	....	....	....	....	....	13	5	6	11	12	....	....	....	....
2007-08	Manitoba Moose	AHL	74	22	55	77	44	....	....	....	....	....	....	....	....	....	6	1	4	5	4	....	....	....	....
2008-09	Skelleftea AIK	Sweden	55	11	31	42	28	....	....	....	....	....	....	....	....	....	9	2	2	4	6	....	....	....	....
2009-10	Skelleftea AIK	Sweden	55	14	26	40	32	....	....	....	....	....	....	....	....	....	12	0	5	5	6	....	....	....	....
2010-11	Oklahoma City	AHL	79	20	52	72	40	....	....	....	....	....	....	....	....	....	6	1	2	3	2	....	....	....	....
	NHL Totals		**8**	**1**	**2**	**3**	**4**	**0**	**0**	**0**	**9**	**11.1**		**71**	**54.9**	**10:07**	....	....	....	....	....	....	....	....	....

WHL East First All-Star Team (1999, 2000) • WHL Player of the Year (2000)

Signed as a free agent by **Columbus**, June 5, 2000. Signed as a free agent by **Vancouver**, June 19, 2006. Signed as a free agent by **Skelleftea** (Sweden), June 15, 2008. Signed as a free agent by **Edmonton**, July 7, 2010.

MOREAU, Ethan
(moh-ROH, EE-thuhn)

Left wing. Shoots left. 6'3", 219 lbs. Born, Huntsville, Ont., September 22, 1975. Chicago's 1st choice, 14th overall, in 1994 Entry Draft.

			Regular Season														Playoffs								
Season	Club	League	GP	G	A	Pts	PIM	PP	SH	GW	S	%	+/-	TF	F%	Min	GP	G	A	Pts	PIM	PP	SH	GW	Min
1990-91	Orillia Terriers	ON-Jr.B	42	17	22	39	26	....	....	....	....	....	....	....	....	....	12	6	6	12	18	....	....	....	....
1991-92	Niagara Falls	OHL	62	20	35	55	39	....	....	....	....	....	....	....	....	....	17	4	6	10	4	....	....	....	....
1992-93	Niagara Falls	OHL	65	32	41	73	69	....	....	....	....	....	....	....	....	....	4	0	3	3	4	....	....	....	....
1993-94	Niagara Falls	OHL	59	44	54	98	100	....	....	....	....	....	....	....	....	....	....	....	....	....	....	....	....	....	....
1994-95	Niagara Falls	OHL	39	25	41	66	69	....	....	....	....	....	....	....	....	....	....	....	....	....	....	....	....	....	....
	Sudbury Wolves	OHL	23	13	17	30	22	....	....	....	....	....	....	....	....	....	18	6	12	18	26	....	....	....	....
1995-96	Chicago	NHL	8	0	1	1	4	0	0	0	1	0.0	1	....	....	....	....	....	....	....	....	....	....	....	....
	Indianapolis Ice	IHL	71	21	20	41	126	....	....	....	....	....	....	....	....	....	5	4	0	4	8	....	....	....	....
1996-97	Chicago	NHL	82	15	16	31	123	0	0	1	114	13.2	13	....	....	....	6	1	0	1	9	0	0	0	....
1997-98	Chicago	NHL	54	9	9	18	73	2	0	0	87	10.3	0	....	....	....	....	....	....	....	....	....	....	....	....
1998-99	Chicago	NHL	66	9	6	15	84	0	0	1	80	11.3	-5	3	33.3	12:30	....	....	....	....	....	....	....	....	....
	Edmonton	NHL	14	1	5	6	8	0	0	1	16	6.3	2	1	0.0	11:47	4	0	3	3	6	0	0	0	17:26
99-2000	Edmonton	NHL	73	17	10	27	62	1	0	3	106	16.0	8	8	62.5	15:07	5	0	1	1	0	0	0	0	15:46
2000-01	Edmonton	NHL	68	9	10	19	90	0	1	3	97	9.3	-6	2	0.0	14:11	4	0	0	0	2	0	0	0	10:35
2001-02	Edmonton	NHL	80	11	5	16	81	0	2	1	129	8.5	4	11	54.6	12:43	....	....	....	....	....	....	....	....	....
2002-03	Edmonton	NHL	78	14	17	31	112	2	3	2	137	10.2	-7	25	12.0	13:30	6	0	1	1	16	0	0	0	12:23
2003-04	Edmonton	NHL	81	20	12	32	96	0	3	5	180	11.1	7	59	44.1	15:04	....	....	....	....	....	....	....	....	....
2004-05	EC Villacher SV	Austria	16	10	6	16	73	....	....	....	....	....	....	....	....	....	3	4	0	4	0	....	....	....	....
2005-06	Edmonton	NHL	74	11	16	27	87	2	4	4	151	7.3	6	29	48.3	15:59	21	2	1	3	19	0	0	0	14:35
2006-07	Edmonton	NHL	7	1	0	1	12	0	0	0	18	5.6	-4	20	50.0	15:08	....	....	....	....	....	....	....	....	....
2007-08	Edmonton	NHL	25	5	4	9	39	1	0	0	54	9.3	-4	23	43.5	15:55	....	....	....	....	....	....	....	....	....
2008-09	Edmonton	NHL	77	14	12	26	133	0	1	2	159	8.8	0	36	30.6	15:22	....	....	....	....	....	....	....	....	....
2009-10	Edmonton	NHL	76	9	9	18	62	0	3	2	143	6.3	-18	17	41.2	14:24	....	....	....	....	....	....	....	....	....
2010-11	Columbus	NHL	37	1	5	6	24	0	0	1	56	1.8	-9	17	29.4	12:29	....	....	....	....	....	....	....	....	....
	NHL Totals		900	146	137	283	1090	8	17	26	1528	9.6		251	39.0	14:15	46	3	6	9	52	0	0	0	14:17

OHL All-Rookie Team (1992) • King Clancy Memorial Trophy (2009)

Traded to **Edmonton** by **Chicago** with Daniel Cleary, Chad Kilger and Christian Laflamme for Boris Mironov, Dean McAmmond and Jonas Elofsson, March 20, 1999. Signed as a free agent by **Villacher** (Austria), December 20, 2004. • Missed majority of 2006-07 due to shoulder injury sustained in game vs. Detroit, October 21, 2006. • Missed majority of 2007-08 due to foot injury in training camp. Claimed on waivers by **Columbus** from **Edmonton**, June 30, 2010. • Missed majority of 2010-11 due to various injuries.

MORIN, Jeremy
(moh-REHN, JAIR-eh-mee) **CHI**

Left wing. Shoots right. 6'1", 189 lbs. Born, Auburn, NY, April 16, 1991. Atlanta's 3rd choice, 45th overall, in 2009 Entry Draft.

Season	Club	League	GP	G	A	Pts	PIM	PP	SH	GW	S	%	+/-	TF	F%	Min	GP	G	A	Pts	PIM	PP	SH	GW	Min
2006-07	Syracuse Stars	EJHL	45	26	28	54	80	....	....	....	....	....	....	....	....	....	....	....	....	....	....	....	....	....	....
2007-08	USNTDP	NAHL	30	17	17	34	26	....	....	....	....	....	....	....	....	....	....	....	....	....	....	....	....	....	....
	USNTDP	U-17	7	11	1	12	4	....	....	....	....	....	....	....	....	....	....	....	....	....	....	....	....	....	....
	USNTDP	U-18	28	20	14	34	36	....	....	....	....	....	....	....	....	....	....	....	....	....	....	....	....	....	....
2008-09	USNTDP	NAHL	14	12	15	27	28	....	....	....	....	....	....	....	....	....	....	....	....	....	....	....	....	....	....
	USNTDP	U-18	41	21	11	32	79	....	....	....	....	....	....	....	....	....	....	....	....	....	....	....	....	....	....
2009-10	Kitchener Rangers	OHL	58	47	36	83	76	....	....	....	....	....	....	....	....	....	20	12	9	21	32	....	....	....	....
2010-11	Chicago	NHL	9	2	1	3	9	0	0	0	13	15.4	2	0	0.0	12:06	....	....	....	....	....	....	....	....	....
	Rockford IceHogs	AHL	22	8	4	12	34	....	....	....	....	....	....	....	....	....	....	....	....	....	....	....	....	....	....
	NHL Totals		9	2	1	3	9	0	0	0	13	15.4		0	0.0	12:06	....	....	....	....	....	....	....	....	....

OHL Second All-Star Team (2010)

Traded to **Chicago** by **Atlanta** with Marty Reasoner, Joey Crabb and New Jersey's 1st (previously acquired, Chicago selected Kevin Hayes) and 2nd (previously acquired, Chicago selected Justin Holl) round choices in 2010 Entry Draft for Dustin Byfuglien, Brent Sopel, Ben Eager and Akim Aliu, June 24, 2010. • Missed majority of 2010-11 due to upper body injury.

MORIN, Travis
(moh-REHN, TRA-vihs)

Center. Shoots left. 6'2", 195 lbs. Born, Minneapolis, MN, January 9, 1984. Washington's 13th choice, 263rd overall, in 2004 Entry Draft.

Season	Club	League	GP	G	A	Pts	PIM	PP	SH	GW	S	%	+/-	TF	F%	Min	GP	G	A	Pts	PIM	PP	SH	GW	Min
2001-02	Chicago Steel	USHL	20	5	8	13	....	....	....	....	....	....	....	....	....	....	4	0	0	0	2	....	....	....	....
2002-03	Chicago Steel	USHL	60	21	26	47	46	....	....	....	....	....	....	....	....	....	....	....	....	....	....	....	....	....	....
2003-04	Minnesota State	WCHA	38	9	12	21	14	....	....	....	....	....	....	....	....	....	....	....	....	....	....	....	....	....	....
2004-05	Minnesota State	WCHA	36	12	19	31	20	....	....	....	....	....	....	....	....	....	....	....	....	....	....	....	....	....	....
2005-06	Minnesota State	WCHA	39	20	22	42	16	....	....	....	....	....	....	....	....	....	....	....	....	....	....	....	....	....	....
2006-07	Minnesota State	WCHA	38	17	22	39	34	....	....	....	....	....	....	....	....	....	....	....	....	....	....	....	....	....	....
	South Carolina	ECHL	8	2	1	3	0	....	....	....	....	....	....	....	....	....	....	....	....	....	....	....	....	....	....
2007-08	Hershey Bears	AHL	4	0	0	0	0	....	....	....	....	....	....	....	....	....	....	....	....	....	....	....	....	....	....
	South Carolina	ECHL	68	34	50	84	30	....	....	....	....	....	....	....	....	....	20	*10	7	17	18	....	....	....	....
2008-09	Hershey Bears	AHL	1	0	1	1	0	....	....	....	....	....	....	....	....	....	....	....	....	....	....	....	....	....	....
	South Carolina	ECHL	71	26	*62	88	46	....	....	....	....	....	....	....	....	....	19	4	*18	22	12	....	....	....	....
2009-10	Texas Stars	AHL	80	21	31	52	30	....	....	....	....	....	....	....	....	....	24	4	12	16	6	....	....	....	....
2010-11	Dallas	NHL	3	0	0	0	0	0	0	0	2	0.0	0	14	57.1	8:52	....	....	....	....	....	....	....	....	....
	Texas Stars	AHL	64	21	24	45	30	....	....	....	....	....	....	....	....	....	6	3	4	7	0	....	....	....	....
	NHL Totals		3	0	0	0	0	0	0	0	2	0.0		14	57.1	8:52	....	....	....	....	....	....	....	....	....

WCHA Second All-Star Team (2007) • ECHL First All-Star Team (2009)

Signed as a free agent by **Texas** (AHL), October 21, 2009. Signed as a free agent by **Dallas**, July 12, 2010.

MORMINA, Joey
(mohr-MEE-nah, JOH-ee)

Defense. Shoots left. 6'6", 220 lbs. Born, Montreal, Que., June 29, 1982. Philadelphia's 6th choice, 193rd overall, in 2002 Entry Draft.

Season	Club	League	GP	G	A	Pts	PIM	PP	SH	GW	S	%	+/-	TF	F%	Min	GP	G	A	Pts	PIM	PP	SH	GW	Min
2000-01	Holderness	High-NH	29	15	15	30	....	....	....	....	....	....	....	....	....	....	....	....	....	....	....	....	....	....	....
2001-02	Colgate	ECAC	34	2	13	15	28	....	....	....	....	....	....	....	....	....	....	....	....	....	....	....	....	....	....
2002-03	Colgate	ECAC	40	4	9	13	52	....	....	....	....	....	....	....	....	....	....	....	....	....	....	....	....	....	....
2003-04	Colgate	ECAC	28	2	10	12	26	....	....	....	....	....	....	....	....	....	....	....	....	....	....	....	....	....	....
2004-05	Colgate	ECAC	39	8	8	16	50	....	....	....	....	....	....	....	....	....	....	....	....	....	....	....	....	....	....
2005-06	Manchester	AHL	61	0	13	13	70	....	....	....	....	....	....	....	....	....	7	0	0	0	4	....	....	....	....
2006-07	Manchester	AHL	62	2	9	11	108	....	....	....	....	....	....	....	....	....	1	0	0	0	2	....	....	....	....
2007-08	Carolina	NHL	1	0	0	0	0	0	0	0	1	0.0	0	0	0.0	7:45	....	....	....	....	....	....	....	....	....
	Albany River Rats	AHL	77	4	9	13	96	....	....	....	....	....	....	....	....	....	7	0	0	0	4	....	....	....	....
2008-09	Wilkes-Barre	AHL	70	2	9	11	71	....	....	....	....	....	....	....	....	....	12	0	0	0	12	....	....	....	....
2009-10	Adirondack	AHL	77	5	18	23	102	....	....	....	....	....	....	....	....	....	....	....	....	....	....	....	....	....	....
2010-11	Wilkes-Barre	AHL	50	2	9	11	44	....	....	....	....	....	....	....	....	....	12	0	0	0	16	....	....	....	....
	NHL Totals		1	0	0	0	0	0	0	0	1	0.0		0	0.0	7:45	....	....	....	....	....	....	....	....	....

Signed as a free agent by **Los Angeles**, August 24, 2005. Signed as a free agent by **Carolina**, July 2, 2007. Signed as a free agent by **Pittsburgh**, July 10, 2008. Signed as a free agent by **Philadelphia**, July 23, 2009. Signed to a PTO (professional tryout) contract by **Wilkes-Barre/Scranton** (AHL), October 11, 2010.

MORRIS, Derek
(MOH-rihs, DAIR-ihk) **PHX**

Defense. Shoots right. 6', 215 lbs. Born, Edmonton, Alta., August 24, 1978. Calgary's 1st choice, 13th overall, in 1996 Entry Draft.

Season	Club	League	GP	G	A	Pts	PIM	PP	SH	GW	S	%	+/-	TF	F%	Min	GP	G	A	Pts	PIM	PP	SH	GW	Min
1994-95	Red Deer Vipers	AMHL	31	6	35	41	74	....	....	....	....	....	....	....	....	....	....	....	....	....	....	....	....	....	....
1995-96	Regina Pats	WHL	67	8	44	52	70	....	....	....	....	....	....	....	....	....	11	1	7	8	26	....	....	....	....
1996-97	Regina Pats	WHL	67	18	57	75	147	....	....	....	....	....	....	....	....	....	5	0	3	3	9	....	....	....	....
	Saint John Flames	AHL	7	0	3	3	7	....	....	....	....	....	....	....	....	....	5	0	3	3	7	....	....	....	....
1997-98	Calgary	NHL	82	9	20	29	88	5	1	1	120	7.5	1	....	....	....	....	....	....	....	....	....	....	....	....
1998-99	Calgary	NHL	71	7	27	34	73	3	0	2	150	4.7	4	0	0.0	20:44	....	....	....	....	....	....	....	....	....
99-2000	Calgary	NHL	78	9	29	38	80	3	0	2	193	4.7	2	0	0.0	24:51	....	....	....	....	....	....	....	....	....
2000-01	Calgary	NHL	51	5	23	28	56	3	1	4	142	3.5	-15	0	0.0	25:51	....	....	....	....	....	....	....	....	....
	Saint John Flames	AHL	3	1	2	3	2	....	....	....	....	....	....	....	....	....	....	....	....	....	....	....	....	....	....
2001-02	Calgary	NHL	61	4	30	34	88	2	0	1	166	2.4	-4	1	100.0	24:40	....	....	....	....	....	....	....	....	....
2002-03	Colorado	NHL	75	11	37	48	68	9	0	7	191	5.8	16	0	0.0	23:49	7	0	3	3	6	0	0	0	22:44
2003-04	Colorado	NHL	69	6	22	28	47	2	0	1	139	4.3	4	0	0.0	20:53	....	....	....	....	....	....	....	....	....
	Phoenix	NHL	14	0	4	4	2	0	0	0	28	0.0	-5	0	0.0	25:02	....	....	....	....	....	....	....	....	....
2004-05			DID NOT PLAY																						
2005-06	Phoenix	NHL	53	6	21	27	54	4	1	2	91	6.6	-7	1	0.0	20:52	....	....	....	....	....	....	....	....	....
2006-07	Phoenix	NHL	82	6	19	25	115	2	0	1	129	4.7	-18	1	100.0	20:29	....	....	....	....	....	....	....	....	....
2007-08	Phoenix	NHL	82	8	17	25	83	2	0	0	135	5.9	8	1	0.0	21:43	....	....	....	....	....	....	....	....	....

			Regular Season														Playoffs								
Season	Club	League	GP	G	A	Pts	PIM	PP	SH	GW	S	%	+/-	TF	F%	Min	GP	G	A	Pts	PIM	PP	SH	GW	Min
2008-09	Phoenix	NHL	57	5	7	12	24	0	1	0	89	5.6	–13	0	0.0	21:16	....	....	....	....	....	....	....	....	....
	NY Rangers	NHL	18	0	8	8	16	0	0	0	31	0.0	3	0	0.0	19:41	7	0	2	2	0	0	0	0	16:24
2009-10	Boston	NHL	58	3	22	25	26	2	0	0	95	3.2	–2	1	0.0	22:00	....	....	....	....	....	....	....	....	....
	Phoenix	NHL	18	1	3	4	11	0	0	0	25	4.0	4	0	0.0	19:39	7	1	3	4	11	1	0	1	19:35
2010-11	Phoenix	NHL	77	5	11	16	58	1	0	1	83	6.0	–2	3	66.7	21:04	....	....	....	....	....	....	....	....	....
	NHL Totals		946	85	300	385	889	38	4	22	1807	4.7		8	50.0	22:13	21	1	8	9	17	1	0	1	19:34

WHL East First All-Star Team (1997) • NHL All-Rookie Team (1998)

Traded to **Colorado** by **Calgary** with Jeff Shantz and Dean McAmmond for Chris Drury and Stephane Yelle, October 1, 2002. Traded to **Phoenix** by **Colorado** with Keith Ballard for Ossi Vaananen, Chris Gratton and Phoenix's 2nd round choice (Paul Stastny) in 2005 Entry Draft, March 9, 2004. Traded to **NY Rangers** by **Phoenix** for Dmitri Kalinin, Nigel Dawes and Petr Prucha, March 4, 2009. Signed as a free agent by **Boston**, July 25, 2009. Traded to **Phoenix** by **Boston** for Phoenix's 3rd round choice (Anthony Camera) in 2011 Entry Draft, March 3, 2010.

MORRISON, Brendan

(MOHR-ih-suhn, BREHN-duhn) **CGY**

Center. Shoots left. 5'11", 185 lbs. Born, Pitt Meadows, B.C., August 15, 1975. New Jersey's 3rd choice, 39th overall, in 1993 Entry Draft.

Season	Club	League	GP	G	A	Pts	PIM	PP	SH	GW	S	%	+/-	TF	F%	Min	GP	G	A	Pts	PIM	PP	SH	GW	Min
1990-91	Ridge Meadows	Minor-BC	77	126	127	253	88	....	....	....	....	....	....	....	....	....	....	....	....	....	....	....	....	....	....
1991-92	Ridge Meadows	Minor-BC	55	56	111	167	56	....	....	....	....	....	....	....	....	....	....	....	....	....	....	....	....	....	....
1992-93	Penticton	BCJHL	56	35	59	94	45	....	....	....	....	....	....	....	....	....	....	....	....	....	....	....	....	....	....
1993-94	U. of Michigan	CCHA	38	20	28	48	24	....	....	....	....	....	....	....	....	....	....	....	....	....	....	....	....	....	....
1994-95	U. of Michigan	CCHA	39	23	*53	*76	42	....	....	....	....	....	....	....	....	....	....	....	....	....	....	....	....	....	....
1995-96	U. of Michigan	CCHA	35	28	44	*72	41	....	....	....	....	....	....	....	....	....	....	....	....	....	....	....	....	....	....
1996-97	U. of Michigan	CCHA	43	31	*57	*88	52	....	....	....	....	....	....	....	....	....	....	....	....	....	....	....	....	....	....
1997-98	New Jersey	NHL	11	5	4	9	0	0	0	1	19	26.3	3	....	....	....	3	0	1	1	0	0	0	0	....
	Albany River Rats	AHL	72	35	49	84	44	....	....	....	....	....	....	....	....	....	8	3	4	7	19	....	....	....	....
1998-99	New Jersey	NHL	76	13	33	46	18	5	0	2	111	11.7	–4	920	51.1	13:55	7	0	2	2	0	0	0	0	13:04
99-2000	Trebic	CzRep-2	2	0	0	0	0	....	....	....	....	....	....	....	....	....	....	....	....	....	....	....	....	....	....
	Pardubice	CzRep	6	5	2	7	2	....	....	....	....	....	....	....	....	....	....	....	....	....	....	....	....	....	....
	New Jersey	NHL	44	5	21	26	8	2	0	1	79	6.3	8	572	51.1	16:09	....	....	....	....	....	....	....	....	....
	Vancouver	NHL	12	2	7	9	10	0	0	0	17	11.8	4	48	54.2	14:41	....	....	....	....	....	....	....	....	....
2000-01	Vancouver	NHL	82	16	38	54	42	3	2	3	179	8.9	2	1685	50.1	18:22	4	1	2	3	0	1	0	0	20:50
2001-02	Vancouver	NHL	82	23	44	67	26	6	0	4	183	12.6	18	1307	49.9	19:21	6	0	2	2	6	0	0	0	19:44
2002-03	Vancouver	NHL	82	25	46	71	36	6	2	8	167	15.0	18	1585	48.3	21:13	14	4	7	11	18	1	0	1	20:18
2003-04	Vancouver	NHL	82	22	38	60	50	5	1	4	161	13.7	16	1486	51.0	20:08	7	2	3	5	8	1	0	1	22:00
2004-05	Linkopings HC	Sweden	45	16	28	44	50	....	....	....	....	....	....	....	....	....	6	0	2	2	10	....	....	....	....
2005-06	Vancouver	NHL	82	19	37	56	84	8	0	5	156	12.2	–1	1328	50.5	19:31	....	....	....	....	....	....	....	....	....
2006-07	Vancouver	NHL	82	20	31	51	60	6	2	3	139	14.4	–9	1230	50.8	17:57	12	1	3	4	6	0	0	0	23:09
2007-08	Vancouver	NHL	39	9	16	25	18	3	0	3	54	16.7	–3	370	45.1	15:23	....	....	....	....	....	....	....	....	....
2008-09	Anaheim	NHL	62	10	12	22	16	1	0	2	82	12.2	0	350	46.0	13:51	....	....	....	....	....	....	....	....	....
	Dallas	NHL	19	6	3	9	16	2	0	2	29	20.7	3	100	43.0	15:23	....	....	....	....	....	....	....	....	....
2009-10	Washington	NHL	74	12	30	42	40	3	0	3	105	11.4	23	978	51.2	15:44	5	0	1	1	2	0	0	0	12:00
2010-11	Calgary	NHL	66	9	34	43	16	3	1	1	89	10.1	13	762	49.6	16:42	....	....	....	....	....	....	....	....	....
	NHL Totals		895	196	394	590	440	53	8	42	1570	12.5		12721	49.9	17:33	58	8	21	29	40	3	0	2	19:26

CCHA Rookie of the Year (1994) • CCHA First All-Star Team (1995, 1996, 1997) • NCAA West First All-American Team (1995, 1996, 1997) • CCHA Player of the Year (1996, 1997) • NCAA Championship All-Tournament Team (1996) • NCAA Championship Tournament MVP (1996) • Hobey Baker Memorial Award (Top U.S. Collegiate Player) (1997) • AHL All-Rookie Team (1998)

Traded to **Vancouver** by **New Jersey** with Denis Pederson for Alexander Mogilny, March 14, 2000. Signed as a free agent by **Linkopings** (Sweden), September, 2004. Signed as a free agent by **Anaheim**, July 8, 2008. Claimed on waivers by **Dallas** from **Anaheim**, March 4, 2009. Signed as a free agent by **Washington**, July 10, 2009. Signed as a free agent by **Calgary**, October 4, 2010.

MORRISONN, Shaone

(MOHR-ih-suhn, SHAWN) **BUF**

Defense. Shoots left. 6'4", 210 lbs. Born, Vancouver, B.C., December 23, 1982. Boston's 1st choice, 19th overall, in 2001 Entry Draft.

Season	Club	League	GP	G	A	Pts	PIM	PP	SH	GW	S	%	+/-	TF	F%	Min	GP	G	A	Pts	PIM	PP	SH	GW	Min
1997-98	Vancouver T-Birds	Minor-BC	45	16	44	60	75	....	....	....	....	....	....	....	....	....	....	....	....	....	....	....	....	....	....
1998-99	South Surrey	BCHL	19	0	2	2	13	....	....	....	....	....	....	....	....	....	....	....	....	....	....	....	....	....	....
99-2000	Kamloops Blazers	WHL	57	1	6	7	80	....	....	....	....	....	....	....	....	....	4	0	0	0	6	....	....	....	....
2000-01	Kamloops Blazers	WHL	61	13	25	38	132	....	....	....	....	....	....	....	....	....	4	0	0	0	6	....	....	....	....
2001-02	Kamloops Blazers	WHL	61	11	26	37	106	....	....	....	....	....	....	....	....	....	4	0	2	2	2	....	....	....	....
2002-03	Boston	NHL	11	0	0	0	8	0	0	0	4	0.0	0	0	0.0	8:57	....	....	....	....	....	....	....	....	....
	Providence Bruins	AHL	60	5	16	21	103	....	....	....	....	....	....	....	....	....	4	0	0	0	6	....	....	....	....
2003-04	Boston	NHL	30	1	7	8	10	0	0	0	13	7.7	10	0	0.0	18:11	....	....	....	....	....	....	....	....	....
	Providence Bruins	AHL	18	0	2	2	16	....	....	....	....	....	....	....	....	....	....	....	....	....	....	....	....	....	....
	Washington	NHL	3	0	0	0	0	0	0	0	1	0.0	0	0	0.0	18:52	....	....	....	....	....	....	....	....	....
	Portland Pirates	AHL	13	1	4	5	10	....	....	....	....	....	....	....	....	....	7	0	1	1	4	....	....	....	....
2004-05	Portland Pirates	AHL	71	4	14	18	63	....	....	....	....	....	....	....	....	....	....	....	....	....	....	....	....	....	....
2005-06	Washington	NHL	80	1	13	14	91	0	0	0	56	1.8	7	4	0.0	20:44	....	....	....	....	....	....	....	....	....
2006-07	Washington	NHL	78	3	10	13	106	0	0	0	46	6.5	3	2	0.0	20:57	....	....	....	....	....	....	....	....	....
2007-08	Washington	NHL	76	1	9	10	63	0	0	1	47	2.1	4	1	100.0	20:16	7	0	1	1	6	0	0	0	21:18
2008-09	Washington	NHL	72	3	10	13	77	0	0	1	50	6.0	4	0	0.0	17:59	14	0	1	1	8	0	0	0	18:03
2009-10	Washington	NHL	68	1	11	12	68	0	0	1	32	3.1	8	0	0.0	17:34	5	0	0	0	2	0	0	0	15:54
2010-11	Buffalo	NHL	62	1	4	5	32	0	0	1	44	2.3	–2	0	0.0	16:10	1	0	0	0	2	0	0	0	13:22
	NHL Totals		480	11	64	75	455	0	0	4	293	3.8		7	14.3	18:48	27	0	2	2	18	0	0	0	18:19

Traded to **Washington** by **Boston** with Boston's 1st (Jeff Schultz) and 2nd (Michail Yunkov) round choices in 2004 Entry Draft for Sergei Gonchar, March 3, 2004. Signed as a free agent by **Buffalo**, August 2, 2010.

MORROW, Brenden

(MOHR-roh, BREHN-duhn) **DAL**

Left wing. Shoots left. 6', 209 lbs. Born, Carlyle, Sask., January 16, 1979. Dallas' 1st choice, 25th overall, in 1997 Entry Draft.

Season	Club	League	GP	G	A	Pts	PIM	PP	SH	GW	S	%	+/-	TF	F%	Min	GP	G	A	Pts	PIM	PP	SH	GW	Min
1994-95	Estevan	SMBHL	60	117	72	189	45	....	....	....	....	....	....	....	....	....	....	....	....	....	....	....	....	....	....
1995-96	Portland	WHL	65	13	12	25	61	....	....	....	....	....	....	....	....	....	7	0	0	0	8	....	....	....	....
1996-97	Portland	WHL	71	39	49	88	149	....	....	....	....	....	....	....	....	....	6	2	1	3	4	....	....	....	....
1997-98	Portland	WHL	68	34	52	86	184	....	....	....	....	....	....	....	....	....	16	10	8	18	65	....	....	....	....
1998-99	Portland	WHL	61	41	44	85	248	....	....	....	....	....	....	....	....	....	4	0	4	4	18	....	....	....	....
99-2000	Dallas	NHL	64	14	19	33	81	3	0	3	113	12.4	8	25	48.0	15:51	21	2	4	6	22	1	0	0	15:04
	Michigan	IHL	9	2	0	2	18	....	....	....	....	....	....	....	....	....	....	....	....	....	....	....	....	....	....
2000-01	Dallas	NHL	82	20	24	44	128	7	0	6	121	16.5	18	22	45.5	15:29	10	0	3	3	12	0	0	0	17:00
2001-02	Dallas	NHL	72	17	18	35	109	4	0	3	102	16.7	12	39	41.0	16:52	....	....	....	....	....	....	....	....	....
2002-03	Dallas	NHL	71	21	22	43	134	2	3	4	105	20.0	20	29	27.6	15:43	12	3	5	8	16	2	0	0	21:03
2003-04	Dallas	NHL	81	25	24	49	121	9	0	3	132	18.9	10	38	47.4	19:24	5	0	1	1	4	0	0	0	21:29
2004-05	Oklahoma City	CHL	19	8	14	22	31	....	....	....	....	....	....	....	....	....	....	....	....	....	....	....	....	....	....
2005-06	Dallas	NHL	81	23	42	65	183	8	1	4	146	15.8	30	32	37.5	19:15	5	1	5	6	6	0	0	0	21:57
2006-07	Dallas	NHL	40	16	15	31	33	8	0	3	101	15.8	–2	51	39.2	18:16	7	2	1	3	18	2	0	1	21:54
2007-08	Dallas	NHL	82	32	42	74	105	12	2	7	207	15.5	23	41	39.0	20:00	18	9	6	15	22	4	0	2	23:17
2008-09	Dallas	NHL	18	5	10	15	49	2	0	0	52	9.6	–4	9	33.3	21:21	....	....	....	....	....	....	....	....	....
2009-10	Dallas	NHL	76	20	26	46	69	9	1	2	155	12.9	–3	31	29.0	19:10	....	....	....	....	....	....	....	....	....
	Canada	Olympics	7	2	1	3	2	....	....	....	....	....	....	....	....	....	....	....	....	....	....	....	....	....	....
2010-11	Dallas	NHL	82	33	23	56	76	9	1	5	209	15.8	–3	11	9.1	19:14	....	....	....	....	....	....	....	....	....
	NHL Totals		749	226	265	491	1088	73	8	40	1443	15.7		328	38.1	18:04	78	17	25	42	100	9	0	3	19:36

WHL West First All-Star Team (1999)

Signed as a free agent by **Oklahoma City** (CHL), October 19, 2004. • Missed majority of 2006-07 due to groin (November 22, 2006 vs. Nashville) and wrist (December 26, 2006 at Chicago) injuries. • Missed majority of 2008-09 due to knee injury vs. Chicago, November 20, 2008.

MOSS, Dave

(MAWS, DAYV) **CGY**

Left wing. Shoots left. 6'3", 200 lbs. Born, Livonia, MI, December 28, 1981. Calgary's 9th choice, 220th overall, in 2001 Entry Draft.

Season	Club	League	GP	G	A	Pts	PIM	PP	SH	GW	S	%	+/-	TF	F%	Min	GP	G	A	Pts	PIM	PP	SH	GW	Min
99-2000	Catholic Central	High-MI	28	18	20	28	20	....	....	....	....	....	....	....	....	....	....	....	....	....	....	....	....	....	....
2000-01	St. Louis Jr. Blues	CSJHL	9	2	2	4	2	....	....	....	....	....	....	....	....	....	....	....	....	....	....	....	....	....	....
	Cedar Rapids	USHL	51	20	18	38	14	....	....	....	....	....	....	....	....	....	4	0	1	1	2	....	....	....	....
2001-02	U. of Michigan	CCHA	43	4	9	13	10	....	....	....	....	....	....	....	....	....	....	....	....	....	....	....	....	....	....
2002-03	U. of Michigan	CCHA	43	14	17	31	37	....	....	....	....	....	....	....	....	....	....	....	....	....	....	....	....	....	....
2003-04	U. of Michigan	CCHA	38	8	12	20	18	....	....	....	....	....	....	....	....	....	....	....	....	....	....	....	....	....	....
2004-05	U. of Michigan	CCHA	38	10	20	30	26	....	....	....	....	....	....	....	....	....	....	....	....	....	....	....	....	....	....
2005-06	Omaha	AHL	63	21	27	48	28	....	....	....	....	....	....	....	....	....	....	....	....	....	....	....	....	....	....

			Regular Season														Playoffs								
Season	Club	League	GP	G	A	Pts	PIM	PP	SH	GW	S	%	+/-	TF	F%	Min	GP	G	A	Pts	PIM	PP	SH	GW	Min
2006-07	Calgary	NHL	41	10	8	18	12	3	0	1	70	14.3	5	11	36.4	11:13	6	0	1	1	0	0	0	0	10:30
	Omaha	AHL	28	9	12	21	22	....	....	....	....	....	....	....	....	....	....	....	....	....	....	....	....	....	....
2007-08	Calgary	NHL	41	4	7	11	10	0	0	0	60	6.7	–4	17	41.2	12:24	5	1	1	2	4	0	0	0	10:20
2008-09	Calgary	NHL	81	20	19	39	22	8	0	4	194	10.3	–5	46	50.0	13:36	6	3	0	3	0	0	0	1	12:50
2009-10	Calgary	NHL	64	8	9	17	20	3	0	2	133	6.0	–9	43	34.9	13:43	....	....	....	....	....	....	....	....	....
2010-11	Calgary	NHL	58	17	13	30	18	5	0	3	127	13.4	9	364	43.1	13:41	....	....	....	....	....	....	....	....	....
	NHL Totals		285	59	56	115	82	19	0	10	584	10.1		481	42.8	13:08	17	4	2	6	4	0	0	1	11:16

MOTIN, Johan

(MOH-tihn, YOH-han) **EDM**

Defense. Shoots right. 6'2", 220 lbs. Born, Karlskoga, Sweden, October 10, 1989. Edmonton's 2nd choice, 103rd overall, in 2008 Entry Draft.

2005-06	Farjestad U18	Swe-U18	14	0	7	7	6	....	....	....	....	....	....	....	....	....	8	0	2	2	8	....	....	....	....
2006-07	Farjestad U18	Swe-U18	1	0	0	0	0	....	....	....	....	....	....	....	....	....	1	1	1	2	0	....	....	....	....
	Skare BK Karlstad	Sweden-3	18	0	4	4	30	....	....	....	....	....	....	....	....	....	....	....	....	....	....	....	....	....	....
	Farjestad	Sweden	22	0	4	4	8	....	....	....	....	....	....	....	....	....	9	0	0	0	2	....	....	....	....
2007-08	Farjestad	Sweden	28	0	2	2	10	....	....	....	....	....	....	....	....	....	....	....	....	....	....	....	....	....	....
	Bofors	Sweden-2	15	2	3	5	18	....	....	....	....	....	....	....	....	....	....	....	....	....	....	....	....	....	....
	Skare BK	Sweden-3	3	0	2	2	2	....	....	....	....	....	....	....	....	....	....	....	....	....	....	....	....	....	....
2008-09	Skare BK Karlstad	Sweden-3	8	0	3	3	8	....	....	....	....	....	....	....	....	....	....	....	....	....	....	....	....	....	....
	Farjestad	Sweden	52	0	3	3	28	....	....	....	....	....	....	....	....	....	13	0	1	1	6	....	....	....	....
2009-10	Edmonton	NHL	1	0	0	0	0	0	0	0	0	0.0	–1	0	0.0	14:08	....	....	....	....	....	....	....	....	....
	Springfield	AHL	55	1	5	6	33	....	....	....	....	....	....	....	....	....	....	....	....	....	....	....	....	....	....
2010-11	Stockton Thunder	ECHL	14	1	1	2	12	....	....	....	....	....	....	....	....	....	1	0	1	1	0	....	....	....	....
	Oklahoma City	AHL	34	1	3	4	30	....	....	....	....	....	....	....	....	....	....	....	....	....	....	....	....	....	....
	NHL Totals		1	0	0	0	0	0	0	0	0	0.0		0	0.0	14:08	....	....	....	....	....	....	....	....	....

MOTTAU, Mike

(MAW-tuh, MIGHK) **NYI**

Defense. Shoots left. 6', 190 lbs. Born, Quincy, MA, March 19, 1978. NY Rangers' 10th choice, 182nd overall, in 1997 Entry Draft.

1994-95	Thayer Academy	High-MA	29	7	19	26	....	....	....	....	....	....	....	....	....	....	....	....	....	....	....	....	....	....	....
1995-96	Thayer Academy	High-MA	31	6	20	26	14	....	....	....	....	....	....	....	....	....	....	....	....	....	....	....	....	....	....
1996-97	Boston College	H-East	38	5	18	23	77	....	....	....	....	....	....	....	....	....	....	....	....	....	....	....	....	....	....
1997-98	Boston College	H-East	40	13	36	49	50	....	....	....	....	....	....	....	....	....	....	....	....	....	....	....	....	....	....
1998-99	Boston College	H-East	43	3	39	42	44	....	....	....	....	....	....	....	....	....	....	....	....	....	....	....	....	....	....
99-2000	Boston College	H-East	42	6	37	43	61	....	....	....	....	....	....	....	....	....	....	....	....	....	....	....	....	....	....
2000-01	NY Rangers	NHL	18	0	3	3	13	0	0	0	17	0.0	–6	0	0.0	15:18	....	....	....	....	....	....	....	....	....
	Hartford	AHL	61	10	33	43	45	....	....	....	....	....	....	....	....	....	5	0	1	1	19	....	....	....	....
2001-02	NY Rangers	NHL	1	0	0	0	0	0	0	0	0	0.0	0	0	0.0	6:20	....	....	....	....	....	....	....	....	....
	Hartford	AHL	80	9	42	51	56	....	....	....	....	....	....	....	....	....	10	0	5	5	4	....	....	....	....
2002-03	Hartford	AHL	29	1	18	19	24	....	....	....	....	....	....	....	....	....	....	....	....	....	....	....	....	....	....
	Calgary	NHL	4	0	0	0	0	0	0	0	0	0.0	–1	0	0.0	9:50	....	....	....	....	....	....	....	....	....
	Saint John Flames	AHL	32	5	12	17	14	....	....	....	....	....	....	....	....	....	....	....	....	....	....	....	....	....	....
2003-04	Cincinnati	AHL	69	9	22	31	79	....	....	....	....	....	....	....	....	....	9	1	2	3	8	....	....	....	....
2004-05	Worcester IceCats	AHL	73	4	31	35	23	....	....	....	....	....	....	....	....	....	....	....	....	....	....	....	....	....	....
2005-06	Peoria Rivermen	AHL	76	8	48	56	81	....	....	....	....	....	....	....	....	....	4	0	1	1	6	....	....	....	....
2006-07	Lowell Devils	AHL	43	1	26	27	33	....	....	....	....	....	....	....	....	....	....	....	....	....	....	....	....	....	....
2007-08	New Jersey	NHL	76	4	13	17	48	1	0	1	68	5.9	–11	0	0.0	20:39	5	1	0	1	0	0	0	0	21:24
2008-09	New Jersey	NHL	80	1	14	15	35	0	0	0	71	1.4	24	0	0.0	17:47	7	1	1	2	0	0	0	0	17:59
2009-10	New Jersey	NHL	79	2	16	18	41	0	0	0	74	2.7	4	0	0.0	22:16	5	0	1	1	0	0	0	0	17:57
2010-11	NY Islanders	NHL	20	0	3	3	8	0	0	0	21	0.0	–12	0	0.0	20:20	....	....	....	....	....	....	....	....	....
	NHL Totals		278	7	49	56	145	1	0	1	251	2.8		0	0.0	19:42	17	2	2	4	0	0	0	0	18:59

Hockey East First All-Star Team (1998, 2000) • NCAA East Second All-American Team (1998) • NCAA Championship All-Tournament Team (1998, 2000) • Hockey East Second All-Star Team (1999) • NCAA East First All-American Team (1999, 2000) • Hockey East Player of the Year (2000) (co-winner - Ty Conklin) • Hobey Baker Memorial Award (Top U.S. Collegiate Player) (2000) • AHL All-Rookie Team (2001)

Traded to **Calgary** by **NY Rangers** for Calgary's 6th round choice (Ivan Dornic) in 2003 Entry Draft and future considerations, January 22, 2003. Signed as a free agent by **Anaheim**, July 25, 2003. Signed as a free agent by **Worcester** (AHL), September 30, 2004. Signed as a free agent by **New Jersey**, July 17, 2006. Signed as a free agent by **NY Islanders**, September 28, 2010. • Missed majority of 2010-11 due to recurring hip injury.

MOULSON, Matt

(MOHL-suhn, MAT) **NYI**

Left wing. Shoots left. 6'1", 210 lbs. Born, North York, Ont., November 1, 1983. Pittsburgh's 11th choice, 263rd overall, in 2003 Entry Draft.

2001-02	Guelph	ON-Jr.B	42	56	46	102	80	....	....	....	....	....	....	....	....	....	....	....	....	....	....	....	....	....	....
2002-03	Cornell Big Red	ECAC	33	13	10	23	22	....	....	....	....	....	....	....	....	....	....	....	....	....	....	....	....	....	....
2003-04	Cornell Big Red	ECAC	32	18	17	35	37	....	....	....	....	....	....	....	....	....	....	....	....	....	....	....	....	....	....
2004-05	Cornell Big Red	ECAC	34	22	20	42	33	....	....	....	....	....	....	....	....	....	....	....	....	....	....	....	....	....	....
2005-06	Cornell Big Red	ECAC	35	18	20	38	14	....	....	....	....	....	....	....	....	....	....	....	....	....	....	....	....	....	....
2006-07	Manchester	AHL	77	25	32	57	23	....	....	....	....	....	....	....	....	....	16	2	3	5	8	....	....	....	....
2007-08	Los Angeles	NHL	22	5	4	9	4	0	0	0	35	14.3	2	4	25.0	12:05	....	....	....	....	....	....	....	....	....
	Manchester	AHL	57	28	28	56	29	....	....	....	....	....	....	....	....	....	4	2	0	2	4	....	....	....	....
2008-09	Los Angeles	NHL	7	1	0	1	2	0	0	1	6	16.7	–4	0	0.0	14:30	....	....	....	....	....	....	....	....	....
	Manchester	AHL	54	21	26	47	35	....	....	....	....	....	....	....	....	....	....	....	....	....	....	....	....	....	....
2009-10	NY Islanders	NHL	82	30	18	48	16	8	0	5	208	14.4	–1	4	75.0	16:38	....	....	....	....	....	....	....	....	....
2010-11	NY Islanders	NHL	82	31	22	53	24	9	0	3	237	13.1	–10	9	55.6	18:52	....	....	....	....	....	....	....	....	....
	NHL Totals		193	67	44	111	46	17	0	9	486	13.8		17	52.9	16:59	....	....	....	....	....	....	....	....	....

ECAC First All-Star Team (2005) • NCAA East Second All-American Team (2005) • ECAC Second All-Star Team (2006)

Signed as a free agent by **Los Angeles**, September 1, 2006. Signed as a free agent by **NY Islanders**, July 6, 2009.

MUELLER, Chris

(MEW-luhr, KRIHS) **NSH**

Center. Shoots right. 5'10", 180 lbs. Born, West Seneca, NY, March 6, 1986.

2007-08	Grand Rapids	AHL	2	0	0	0	0	....	....	....	....	....	....	....	....	....	....	....	....	....	....	....	....	....	....
2008-09	Johnstown Chiefs	ECHL	3	3	3	6	2	....	....	....	....	....	....	....	....	....	....	....	....	....	....	....	....	....	....
	Lake Erie	AHL	59	5	11	16	23	....	....	....	....	....	....	....	....	....	....	....	....	....	....	....	....	....	....
2009-10	Cincinnati	ECHL	5	4	1	5	0	....	....	....	....	....	....	....	....	....	....	....	....	....	....	....	....	....	....
	Milwaukee	AHL	67	13	14	27	37	....	....	....	....	....	....	....	....	....	....	....	....	....	....	....	....	....	....
2010-11	Nashville	NHL	15	0	3	3	2	0	0	0	7	0.0	0	89	48.3	8:38	....	....	....	....	....	....	....	....	....
	Milwaukee	AHL	67	24	26	50	34	....	....	....	....	....	....	....	....	....	13	4	7	11	13	....	....	....	....
	NHL Totals		15	0	3	3	2	0	0	0	7	0.0		89	48.3	8:38	....	....	....	....	....	....	....	....	....

Signed to a ATO (amateur tryout) contract by **Grand Rapids** (AHL), April 9, 2008. Signed as a free agent by **Lake Erie**, October 8, 2008. Signed as a free agent by **Milwaukee** (AHL), October 13, 2009. Signed as a free agent by **Nashville**, December 27, 2010.

MUELLER, Marcel

(MEW-luhr, MAHR-sehl) **TOR**

Left wing. Shoots left. 6'3", 232 lbs. Born, Berlin, East Germany, July 10, 1988.

2003-04	Mannheim Jr.	Ger-Jr.	27	3	5	8	51	....	....	....	....	....	....	....	....	....	4	1	2	3	4	....	....	....	....
2004-05	Mannheim Jr.	Ger-Jr.	26	21	13	34	100	....	....	....	....	....	....	....	....	....	....	....	....	....	....	....	....	....	....
	Mannheimer ERC	German-5	3	1	1	2	4	....	....	....	....	....	....	....	....	....	....	....	....	....	....	....	....	....	....
2005-06	Eisb. Jrs. Berl. Jr.	Ger-Jr.	8	9	4	13	50	....	....	....	....	....	....	....	....	....	1	0	0	0	0	....	....	....	....
	Eisb. Jrs. Berlin	German-3	27	7	8	15	91	....	....	....	....	....	....	....	....	....	....	....	....	....	....	....	....	....	....
	Eisbaren Berlin	Germany	24	1	1	2	20	....	....	....	....	....	....	....	....	....	....	....	....	....	....	....	....	....	....
2006-07	Eisb. Jrs. Berlin	German-3	9	1	3	4	18	....	....	....	....	....	....	....	....	....	....	....	....	....	....	....	....	....	....
	Eisbaren Berlin	Germany	36	1	7	8	53	....	....	....	....	....	....	....	....	....	3	0	0	0	14	....	....	....	....
2007-08	Kolner Haie	Germany	44	6	7	13	61	....	....	....	....	....	....	....	....	....	14	1	1	2	6	....	....	....	....
2008-09	Kolner Haie	Germany	41	11	14	25	60	....	....	....	....	....	....	....	....	....	....	....	....	....	....	....	....	....	....
2009-10	Kolner Haie	Germany	53	24	32	56	122	....	....	....	....	....	....	....	....	....	3	0	4	4	2	....	....	....	....
2010-11	Toronto	NHL	3	0	0	0	2	0	0	0	5	0.0	0	1	0.0	10:07	....	....	....	....	....	....	....	....	....
	Toronto Marlies	AHL	57	14	18	32	44	....	....	....	....	....	....	....	....	....	....	....	....	....	....	....	....	....	....
	NHL Totals		3	0	0	0	2	0	0	0	5	0.0		1	0.0	10:07	....	....	....	....	....	....	....	....	....

Signed as a free agent by **Toronto**, July 14, 2010.

MUELLER, Peter

(MEW-luhr, PEE-tuhr) **COL**

Center. Shoots right. 6'2", 204 lbs. Born, Bloomington, MN, April 14, 1988. Phoenix's 1st choice, 8th overall, in 2006 Entry Draft.

Season	Club	League	GP	G	A	Pts	PIM	PP	SH	GW	S	%	+/-	TF	F%	Min	Playoffs GP	G	A	Pts	PIM	PP	SH	GW	Min
2003-04	USNTDP	U-17	17	4	9	13	25	....	....	....	....	....	....	....	....	....	....	....	....	....	....	....	....	....	....
	USNTDP	NAHL	43	10	16	26	26	....	....	....	....	....	....	....	....	....	7	3	2	5	4	....	....	....	....
2004-05	USNTDP	U-18	43	27	27	64	75	....	....	....	....	....	....	....	....	....	....	....	....	....	....	....	....	....	....
	USNTDP	NAHL	14	11	13	24	16	....	....	....	....	....	....	....	....	....	....	....	....	....	....	....	....	....	....
2005-06	Everett Silvertips	WHL	52	26	32	58	44	....	....	....	....	....	....	....	....	....	15	7	6	13	10	....	....	....	....
2006-07	Everett Silvertips	WHL	51	21	57	78	45	....	....	....	....	....	....	....	....	....	12	7	9	16	12	....	....	....	....
2007-08	**Phoenix**	**NHL**	81	22	32	54	32	7	0	3	201	10.9	–13	251	41.8	17:16	....	....	....	....	....	....	....	....	....
2008-09	**Phoenix**	**NHL**	72	13	23	36	24	5	0	4	138	9.4	–7	92	44.6	16:05	....	....	....	....	....	....	....	....	....
2009-10	**Phoenix**	**NHL**	54	4	13	17	8	1	0	1	89	4.5	–5	42	42.9	12:55	....	....	....	....	....	....	....	....	....
	Colorado	**NHL**	15	9	11	20	8	3	0	1	35	25.7	4	2	0.0	17:50	....	....	....	....	....	....	....	....	....
2010-11			DID NOT PLAY – INJURED																						
	NHL Totals		**222**	**48**	**79**	**127**	**72**	**16**	**0**	**9**	**463**	**10.4**		**387**	**42.4**	**15:52**	....	....	....	....	....	....	....	....	....

WHL Rookie ot the Year (2006) • WHL West First All-Star Team (2007) • Canadian Major Junior Second All-Star Team (2007)

Traded to **Colorado** by **Phoenix** with Kevin Porter for Wojtek Wolski, March 3, 2010. • Missed 2010-11 due to concussion in training camp.

MURPHY, Cory

(MUHR-fee, KOH-ree)

Defense. Shoots left. 5'9", 175 lbs. Born, Kanata, Ont., February 13, 1978.

Season	Club	League	GP	G	A	Pts	PIM	PP	SH	GW	S	%	+/-	TF	F%	Min	Playoffs GP	G	A	Pts	PIM	PP	SH	GW	Min
1997-98	Colgate	ECAC	35	8	19	27	38	....	....	....	....	....	....	....	....	....	....	....	....	....	....	....	....	....	....
1998-99	Colgate	ECAC	34	3	23	26	26	....	....	....	....	....	....	....	....	....	....	....	....	....	....	....	....	....	....
99-2000	Colgate	ECAC	35	10	19	29	26	....	....	....	....	....	....	....	....	....	....	....	....	....	....	....	....	....	....
2000-01	Colgate	ECAC	34	7	22	29	34	....	....	....	....	....	....	....	....	....	....	....	....	....	....	....	....	....	....
2001-02	Blues Espoo	Finland	46	9	15	24	38	....	....	....	....	....	....	....	....	....	3	0	1	1	0	....	....	....	....
2002-03	Blues Espoo	Finland	45	11	4	15	49	....	....	....	....	....	....	....	....	....	7	1	0	1	2	....	....	....	....
2003-04	Ilves Tampere	Finland	56	18	26	44	22	....	....	....	....	....	....	....	....	....	7	1	2	3	2	....	....	....	....
2004-05	Ilves Tampere	Finland	56	12	23	35	36	....	....	....	....	....	....	....	....	....	7	1	3	4	18	....	....	....	....
2005-06	Fribourg	Swiss	44	13	22	35	52	....	....	....	....	....	....	....	....	....	....	....	....	....	....	....	....	....	....
2006-07	HIFK Helsinki	Finland	45	13	37	50	46	....	....	....	....	....	....	....	....	....	5	0	1	1	4	....	....	....	....
2007-08	**Florida**	**NHL**	47	2	15	17	22	1	0	0	65	3.1	0	0	0.0	15:23	....	....	....	....	....	....	....	....	....
2008-09	**Florida**	**NHL**	7	0	1	1	2	0	0	0	8	0.0	–1	0	0.0	10:10	....	....	....	....	....	....	....	....	....
	Rochester	AHL	5	2	4	6	2	....	....	....	....	....	....	....	....	....	....	....	....	....	....	....	....	....	....
	Tampa Bay	**NHL**	25	5	10	15	12	4	0	0	47	10.6	–3	0	0.0	20:08	....	....	....	....	....	....	....	....	....
2009-10	**New Jersey**	**NHL**	12	2	1	3	2	0	0	0	9	22.2	–2	0	0.0	12:26	....	....	....	....	....	....	....	....	....
	Lowell Devils	AHL	64	6	38	44	30	....	....	....	....	....	....	....	....	....	5	0	0	0	2	....	....	....	....
2010-11	ZSC Lions Zurich	Swiss	49	10	25	35	30	....	....	....	....	....	....	....	....	....	5	0	3	3	0	....	....	....	....
	NHL Totals		**91**	**9**	**27**	**36**	**38**	**5**	**0**	**0**	**129**	**7.0**		**0**	**0.0**	**15:54**	....	....	....	....	....	....	....	....	....

ECAC First All-Star Team (2000) • ECAC Second All-Star Team (2001)

Signed as a free agent by **Florida**, March 26, 2007. Claimed on wiavers by **Tampa Bay** from **Florida**, January 19, 2009. Signed as a free agent by **New Jersey**, July 17, 2009. Signed as a free agent by **ZSC Lions** (Swiss), June 4, 2010.

MURRAY, Andrew

(MUHR-ree, AN-droo) **S.J.**

Center. Shoots left. 6'2", 210 lbs. Born, Selkirk, Man., November 6, 1981. Columbus' 11th choice, 242nd overall, in 2001 Entry Draft.

Season	Club	League	GP	G	A	Pts	PIM	PP	SH	GW	S	%	+/-	TF	F%	Min	Playoffs GP	G	A	Pts	PIM	PP	SH	GW	Min
99-2000	Selkirk Steelers	MJHL	63	29	48	77	....	....	....	....	....	....	....	....	....	....	....	....	....	....	....	....	....	....	....
2000-01	Selkirk Steelers	MJHL	64	46	56	102	72	....	....	....	....	....	....	....	....	....	5	3	0	3	6	....	....	....	....
2001-02	Bemidji State	CHA	35	15	15	30	22	....	....	....	....	....	....	....	....	....	....	....	....	....	....	....	....	....	....
2002-03	Bemidji State	CHA	36	9	18	27	38	....	....	....	....	....	....	....	....	....	....	....	....	....	....	....	....	....	....
2003-04	Bemidji State	CHA	25	6	14	20	41	....	....	....	....	....	....	....	....	....	....	....	....	....	....	....	....	....	....
2004-05	Bemidji State	CHA	32	16	22	38	30	....	....	....	....	....	....	....	....	....	....	....	....	....	....	....	....	....	....
2005-06	Syracuse Crunch	AHL	77	13	16	29	73	....	....	....	....	....	....	....	....	....	6	0	1	1	17	....	....	....	....
2006-07	Syracuse Crunch	AHL	72	10	12	22	62	....	....	....	....	....	....	....	....	....	....	....	....	....	....	....	....	....	....
2007-08	**Columbus**	**NHL**	39	6	4	10	12	0	0	0	45	13.3	0	32	46.9	11:42	....	....	....	....	....	....	....	....	....
	Syracuse Crunch	AHL	34	13	2	15	15	....	....	....	....	....	....	....	....	....	....	....	....	....	....	....	....	....	....
2008-09	**Columbus**	**NHL**	67	8	3	11	10	1	0	3	89	9.0	–6	85	45.9	11:16	....	....	....	....	....	....	....	....	....
2009-10	**Columbus**	**NHL**	46	5	2	7	6	0	0	0	73	6.8	–6	118	41.5	10:22	....	....	....	....	....	....	....	....	....
2010-11	**Columbus**	**NHL**	29	4	4	8	4	0	0	1	48	8.3	2	41	46.3	11:23	....	....	....	....	....	....	....	....	....
	NHL Totals		**181**	**23**	**13**	**36**	**32**	**1**	**0**	**4**	**255**	**9.0**		**276**	**44.2**	**11:09**	....	....	....	....	....	....	....	....	....

CHA All-Rookie Team (2002)

• Missed majority of 2010-11 due to lower body injury. Signed as a free agent by **San Jose**, July 19, 2011.

MURRAY, Brady

(MUHR-ree, BRAY-dee) **L.A.**

Center. Shoots left. 5'10", 185 lbs. Born, Brandon, Man., August 17, 1984. Los Angeles' 6th choice, 152nd overall, in 2003 Entry Draft.

Season	Club	League	GP	G	A	Pts	PIM	PP	SH	GW	S	%	+/-	TF	F%	Min	Playoffs GP	G	A	Pts	PIM	PP	SH	GW	Min
2001-02	Shat.-St. Mary's	High-MN	60	58	92	150	50	....	....	....	....	....	....	....	....	....	....	....	....	....	....	....	....	....	....
2002-03	Salmon Arm	BCHL	59	42	59	101	30	....	....	....	....	....	....	....	....	....	....	....	....	....	....	....	....	....	....
2003-04	North Dakota	WCHA	37	19	27	46	32	....	....	....	....	....	....	....	....	....	....	....	....	....	....	....	....	....	....
2004-05	North Dakota	WCHA	25	8	12	20	22	....	....	....	....	....	....	....	....	....	....	....	....	....	....	....	....	....	....
2005-06	Rapperswil	Swiss	36	3	9	12	28	....	....	....	....	....	....	....	....	....	10	3	2	5	10	....	....	....	....
2006-07	Rapperswil	Swiss	38	12	20	32	38	....	....	....	....	....	....	....	....	....	7	4	2	6	6	....	....	....	....
2007-08	**Los Angeles**	**NHL**	4	1	0	1	6	0	0	0	2	50.0	–2	31	51.6	11:18	....	....	....	....	....	....	....	....	....
	Manchester	AHL	58	14	13	27	50	....	....	....	....	....	....	....	....	....	4	1	0	1	2	....	....	....	....
2008-09	HC Lugano	Swiss	36	*26	14	40	26	....	....	....	....	....	....	....	....	....	7	1	4	5	0	....	....	....	....
2009-10	HC Lugano	Swiss	47	6	13	19	12	....	....	....	....	....	....	....	....	....	4	1	0	1	2	....	....	....	....
2010-11	HC Lugano	Swiss	25	5	5	10	10	....	....	....	....	....	....	....	....	....	4	2	1	3	0	....	....	....	....
	NHL Totals		**4**	**1**	**0**	**1**	**6**	**0**	**0**	**0**	**2**	**50.0**		**31**	**51.6**	**11:18**	....	....	....	....	....	....	....	....	....

WCHA All-Rookie Team (2004) • WCHA Rookie of the Year (2004)

• Assigned to **Lugano** (Swiss) by **Los Angeles**, October 9, 2008.

MURRAY, Douglas

(MUHR-ree, DUHG-luhs) **S.J.**

Defense. Shoots left. 6'3", 240 lbs. Born, Bromma, Sweden, March 12, 1980. San Jose's 6th choice, 241st overall, in 1999 Entry Draft.

Season	Club	League	GP	G	A	Pts	PIM	PP	SH	GW	S	%	+/-	TF	F%	Min	Playoffs GP	G	A	Pts	PIM	PP	SH	GW	Min
1998-99	NY Apple Core	EJHL	60	17	47	64	62	....	....	....	....	....	....	....	....	....	....	....	....	....	....	....	....	....	....
99-2000	Cornell Big Red	ECAC	32	3	6	9	38	....	....	....	....	....	....	....	....	....	....	....	....	....	....	....	....	....	....
2000-01	Cornell Big Red	ECAC	25	5	13	18	39	....	....	....	....	....	....	....	....	....	....	....	....	....	....	....	....	....	....
2001-02	Cornell Big Red	ECAC	35	11	21	32	67	....	....	....	....	....	....	....	....	....	....	....	....	....	....	....	....	....	....
2002-03	Cornell Big Red	ECAC	35	5	20	25	30	....	....	....	....	....	....	....	....	....	....	....	....	....	....	....	....	....	....
2003-04	Cleveland Barons	AHL	72	10	12	22	75	....	....	....	....	....	....	....	....	....	9	3	0	3	37	....	....	....	....
2004-05	Cleveland Barons	AHL	54	6	17	23	56	....	....	....	....	....	....	....	....	....	....	....	....	....	....	....	....	....	....
2005-06	**San Jose**	**NHL**	34	0	1	1	27	0	0	0	21	0.0	3	0	0.0	13:53	....	....	....	....	....	....	....	....	....
	Cleveland Barons	AHL	20	1	7	8	37	....	....	....	....	....	....	....	....	....	....	....	....	....	....	....	....	....	....
2006-07	**San Jose**	**NHL**	35	0	3	3	31	0	0	0	18	0.0	0	0	0.0	10:46	....	....	....	....	....	....	....	....	....
	Worcester Sharks	AHL	5	2	1	3	8	....	....	....	....	....	....	....	....	....	....	....	....	....	....	....	....	....	....
2007-08	**San Jose**	**NHL**	66	1	9	10	98	0	0	0	48	2.1	20	2	50.0	17:28	13	1	1	2	2	0	0	0	18:09
2008-09	**San Jose**	**NHL**	75	0	7	7	38	0	0	0	56	0.0	6	0	0.0	16:39	6	0	0	0	9	0	0	0	16:51
2009-10	**San Jose**	**NHL**	79	4	13	17	66	1	0	1	85	4.7	3	0	0.0	20:20	15	1	6	7	8	0	0	0	20:21
	Sweden	Olympics	4	0	0	0	0	....	....	....	....	....	....	....	....	....	....	....	....	....	....	....	....	....	....
2010-11	**San Jose**	**NHL**	73	1	13	14	44	0	0	0	102	1.0	5	0	0.0	19:37	18	0	1	1	8	0	0	0	19:30
	NHL Totals		**362**	**6**	**46**	**52**	**304**	**1**	**0**	**1**	**330**	**1.8**		**2**	**50.0**	**17:22**	**52**	**2**	**8**	**10**	**27**	**0**	**0**	**0**	**19:06**

ECAC First All-Star Team (2002, 2003) • NCAA East First All-American Team (2003)

• Missed majority of 2006-07 due to respiratory infection.

MURRAY, Garth
(MUHR-ree, GARTH)

Center. Shoots left. 6'2", 210 lbs. Born, Regina, Sask., September 17, 1982. NY Rangers' 3rd choice, 79th overall, in 2001 Entry Draft.

			Regular Season														Playoffs								
Season	Club	League	GP	G	A	Pts	PIM	PP	SH	GW	S	%	+/-	TF	F%	Min	GP	G	A	Pts	PIM	PP	SH	GW	Min
1997-98	Calgary Buffaloes	AMHL	56	26	34	60	110																		
	Regina Pats	WHL	4	0	0	0	2										2	0	0	0	0				
1998-99	Regina Pats	WHL	60	3	5	8	101																		
99-2000	Regina Pats	WHL	68	14	26	40	155										7	1	1	2	7				
2000-01	Regina Pats	WHL	72	28	16	44	183										6	1	1	2	10				
2001-02	Regina Pats	WHL	62	33	30	63	154										6	2	3	5	9				
	Hartford	AHL	4	0	0	0	0										9	1	3	4	6				
2002-03	Hartford	AHL	64	10	14	24	121										2	0	0	0	6				
2003-04	**NY Rangers**	**NHL**	**20**	**1**	**0**	**1**	**24**	**0**	**0**	**0**	**18**	**5.6**	**–5**	**5**	**20.0**	**9:16**									
	Hartford	AHL	63	11	11	22	159										16	0	4	4	29				
2004-05	Hartford	AHL	55	4	5	9	182										5	1	0	1	8				
2005-06	**Montreal**	**NHL**	**36**	**5**	**1**	**6**	**44**	**0**	**0**	**1**	**25**	**20.0**	**–2**	**99**	**46.5**	**9:15**	**6**	**0**	**0**	**0**	**0**	**0**	**0**	**0**	**12:39**
	Hamilton	AHL	26	1	1	2	46																		
2006-07	**Montreal**	**NHL**	**43**	**2**	**1**	**3**	**32**	**0**	**0**	**0**	**28**	**7.1**	**–10**	**107**	**42.1**	**8:23**									
2007-08	**Montreal**	**NHL**	**1**	**0**	**0**	**0**	**0**	**0**	**0**	**0**	**0**	**0.0**	**0**	**1**	**0.0**	**12:46**									
	Florida	**NHL**	**6**	**0**	**0**	**0**	**19**	**0**	**0**	**0**	**3**	**0.0**	**0**	**2**	**0.0**	**5:09**									
2008-09	**Phoenix**	**NHL**	**10**	**0**	**0**	**0**	**12**	**0**	**0**	**0**	**12**	**0.0**	**–2**	**80**	**45.0**	**9:20**									
	San Antonio	AHL	64	11	10	21	146																		
2009-10	Abbotsford Heat	AHL	80	9	22	31	169										13	1	2	3	34				
2010-11	Victoria	ECHL	8	2	1	3	23																		
	Manitoba Moose	AHL	55	6	5	11	90										13	0	1	1	*42				
	NHL Totals		**116**	**8**	**2**	**10**	**131**	**0**	**0**	**1**	**86**	**9.3**		**294**	**43.5**	**8:45**	**6**	**0**	**0**	**0**	**0**	**0**	**0**	**0**	**12:39**

Traded to **Montreal** by **NY Rangers** for Marcel Hossa, September 30, 2005. Claimed on waivers by **Florida** from **Montreal**, November 13, 2007. Signed as a free agent by **Phoenix**, July 18, 2008. Signed as a free agent by **Calgary**, July 2, 2009. Signed to a PTO (professional tryout) contract by **Manitoba** (AHL), December 11, 2010.

MURSAK , Jan
(MUHR-sak, YAHN) **DET**

Left wing. Shoots right. 5'11", 190 lbs. Born, Maribor, Yugoslavia, January 20, 1988. Detroit's 5th choice, 182nd overall, in 2006 Entry Draft.

Season	Club	League	GP	G	A	Pts	PIM	PP	SH	GW	S	%	+/-	TF	F%	Min	GP	G	A	Pts	PIM	PP	SH	GW	Min
2002-03	HK Maribor U18	Sloven-U18	13	27	18	45	14																		
2003-04	HK Maribor U18	Sloven-U18	22	27	17	44	14																		
	HK Maribor Jr.	Sloven-Jr.	19	8	8	16	37																		
	HK Maribor	Slovenia	14	3	3	6	16																		
2004-05	HK Maribor Jr.	Sloven-Jr.	19	17	16	33	39																		
	HK Maribor	Slovenia	24	16	29	45	10																		
2005-06	C. Budejovice Jr.	CzRep-Jr.	43	15	15	30	32										5	0	2	2	2				
2006-07	Saginaw Spirit	OHL	62	27	53	80	50										6	1	2	3	10				
	Grand Rapids	AHL															7	0	2	2	2				
2007-08	Saginaw Spirit	OHL	26	6	20	26	15																		
	Belleville Bulls	OHL	31	11	27	38	8										21	9	15	24	10				
2008-09	Grand Rapids	AHL	51	2	7	9	25										6	0	1	1	0				
2009-10	Grand Rapids	AHL	79	24	18	42	46																		
2010-11	**Detroit**	**NHL**	**19**	**1**	**0**	**1**	**4**	**0**	**0**	**0**	**20**	**5.0**	**–3**	**6**	**50.0**	**8:12**									
	Grand Rapids	AHL	54	13	22	35	35																		
	NHL Totals		**19**	**1**	**0**	**1**	**4**	**0**	**0**	**0**	**20**	**5.0**		**6**	**50.0**	**8:12**									

MUZZIN, Jake
(MUH-zihn, JAYK) **L.A.**

Defense. Shoots left. 6'3", 213 lbs. Born, Woodstock, Ont., February 21, 1989. Pittsburgh's 7th choice, 141st overall, in 2007 Entry Draft.

Season	Club	League	GP	G	A	Pts	PIM	PP	SH	GW	S	%	+/-	TF	F%	Min	GP	G	A	Pts	PIM	PP	SH	GW	Min
2004-05	Brantford 99ers	Minor-ON	57	20	23	43	78																		
2005-06	Sault Ste. Marie	OHL	DID NOT PLAY – INJURED																						
2006-07	Soo Thunderbirds	NOJHL	4	0	3	3	2																		
	Sault Ste. Marie	OHL	37	1	3	4	10										13	0	4	4	6				
2007-08	Sault Ste. Marie	OHL	67	6	12	18	53										10	1	3	4	4				
2008-09	Sault Ste. Marie	OHL	62	6	23	29	57																		
2009-10	Sault Ste. Marie	OHL	64	15	52	67	76										5	0	1	1	2				
	Manchester	AHL	1	0	1	1	0										13	1	3	4	6				
2010-11	**Los Angeles**	**NHL**	**11**	**0**	**1**	**1**	**0**	**0**	**0**	**0**	**8**	**0.0**	**–2**	**0**	**0.0**	**13:43**									
	Manchester	AHL	45	3	15	18	39										7	3	1	4	2				
	NHL Totals		**11**	**0**	**1**	**1**	**0**	**0**	**0**	**0**	**8**	**0.0**		**0**	**0.0**	**13:43**									

OHL First All-Star Team (2010) • Canadian Major Junior First All-Star Team (2010)

• Missed 2005-06 due to off-season back surgery. Signed as a free agent by **Los Angeles**, January 4, 2010.

MYERS, Tyler
(MIGH-uhrz, TIGH-luhr) **BUF**

Defense. Shoots right. 6'8", 227 lbs. Born, Houston, TX, February 1, 1990. Buffalo's 1st choice, 12th overall, in 2008 Entry Draft.

Season	Club	League	GP	G	A	Pts	PIM	PP	SH	GW	S	%	+/-	TF	F%	Min	GP	G	A	Pts	PIM	PP	SH	GW	Min
2005-06	Notre Dame	SMHL	34	4	6	10	78																		
	Kelowna Rockets	WHL	9	0	1	1	2										8	1	0	1	2				
2006-07	Kelowna Rockets	WHL	59	2	13	15	78																		
2007-08	Kelowna Rockets	WHL	65	6	13	19	97										7	1	2	3	12				
2008-09	Kelowna Rockets	WHL	58	9	33	42	105										22	5	15	20	29				
2009-10	**Buffalo**	**NHL**	**82**	**11**	**37**	**48**	**32**	**3**	**0**	**1**	**104**	**10.6**	**13**	**0**	**0.0**	**23:44**	**6**	**1**	**0**	**1**	**4**	**0**	**0**	**0**	**25:54**
2010-11	**Buffalo**	**NHL**	**80**	**10**	**27**	**37**	**40**	**3**	**0**	**5**	**122**	**8.2**	**0**	**0**	**0.0**	**22:27**	**7**	**1**	**5**	**6**	**16**	**0**	**0**	**0**	**23:52**
	NHL Totals		**162**	**21**	**64**	**85**	**72**	**6**	**0**	**6**	**226**	**9.3**		**0**	**0.0**	**23:06**	**13**	**2**	**5**	**7**	**20**	**0**	**0**	**0**	**24:48**

WHL West Second All-Star Team (2009) • NHL All-Rookie Team (2010) • Calder Memorial Trophy (2010)

NASH, Brendon
(NASH, BREHN-duhn) **MTL**

Defense. Shoots left. 6'3", 212 lbs. Born, Kamloops, B.C., March 31, 1987.

Season	Club	League	GP	G	A	Pts	PIM	PP	SH	GW	S	%	+/-	TF	F%	Min	GP	G	A	Pts	PIM	PP	SH	GW	Min
2005-06	Salmon Arm	BCHL	53	9	33	42	80																		
2006-07	Cornell Big Red	ECAC	29	2	12	14	38																		
2007-08	Cornell Big Red	ECAC	24	2	14	16	49																		
2008-09	Cornell Big Red	ECAC	34	2	16	18	38																		
2009-10	Cornell Big Red	ECAC	33	2	17	19	48																		
2010-11	**Montreal**	**NHL**	**2**	**0**	**0**	**0**	**0**	**0**	**0**	**0**	**2**	**0.0**	**–1**	**0**	**0.0**	**10:12**									
	Hamilton	AHL	75	5	25	30	58										19	0	4	4	14				
	NHL Totals		**2**	**0**	**0**	**0**	**0**	**0**	**0**	**0**	**2**	**0.0**		**0**	**0.0**	**10:12**									

ECAC Second All-Star Team (2009) • ECAC First All-Star Team (2010) • NCAA East First All-American Team (2010)

Signed as a free agent by **Montreal**, March 30, 2010.

NASH, Rick
(NASH, RIHK) **CBJ**

Left wing. Shoots left. 6'4", 216 lbs. Born, Brampton, Ont., June 16, 1984. Columbus' 1st choice, 1st overall, in 2002 Entry Draft.

Season	Club	League	GP	G	A	Pts	PIM	PP	SH	GW	S	%	+/-	TF	F%	Min	GP	G	A	Pts	PIM	PP	SH	GW	Min
99-2000	Tor. Marlboros	GTHL	34	61	54	115	34																		
2000-01	London Knights	OHL	58	31	35	66	56										4	3	3	6	8				
2001-02	London Knights	OHL	54	32	40	72	88										12	10	9	19	21				
2002-03	**Columbus**	**NHL**	**74**	**17**	**22**	**39**	**78**	**6**	**0**	**2**	**154**	**11.0**	**–27**	**14**	**35.7**	**13:57**									
2003-04	**Columbus**	**NHL**	**80**	***41**	**16**	**57**	**87**	***19**	**0**	**7**	**269**	**15.2**	**–35**	**21**	**28.6**	**17:38**									
2004-05	HC Davos	Swiss	44	26	20	46	83										15	9	2	11	26				
2005-06	**Columbus**	**NHL**	**54**	**31**	**23**	**54**	**51**	**11**	**0**	**4**	**170**	**18.2**	**5**	**38**	**50.0**	**18:16**									
	Canada	Olympics	6	0	1	1	10																		
2006-07	**Columbus**	**NHL**	**75**	**27**	**30**	**57**	**73**	**9**	**1**	**5**	**228**	**11.8**	**–8**	**143**	**42.7**	**19:12**									
2007-08	**Columbus**	**NHL**	**80**	**38**	**31**	**69**	**95**	**10**	**4**	**6**	**329**	**11.6**	**2**	**44**	**31.8**	**20:29**									
2008-09	**Columbus**	**NHL**	**78**	**40**	**39**	**79**	**52**	**6**	**5**	**5**	**263**	**15.2**	**11**	**18**	**27.8**	**21:10**	**4**	**1**	**2**	**3**	**2**	**0**	**0**	**0**	**20:52**

			Regular Season														Playoffs								
Season	Club	League	GP	G	A	Pts	PIM	PP	SH	GW	S	%	+/-	TF	F%	Min	GP	G	A	Pts	PIM	PP	SH	GW	Min
2009-10	**Columbus**	**NHL**	**76**	**33**	**34**	**67**	**58**	**10**	**2**	**6**	**254**	**13.0**	**-2**	**22**	**50.0**	**20:56**	....	....	....	....	....	....	....	....	....
	Canada	Olympics	7	2	3	5	0	....	....	....	....	....	....	....	....	....	....	....	....	....	....	....	....	....	....
2010-11	**Columbus**	**NHL**	**75**	**32**	**34**	**66**	**34**	**6**	**0**	**7**	**305**	**10.5**	**2**	**24**	**29.2**	**18:56**	....	....	....	....	....	....	....	....	....
	NHL Totals		**592**	**259**	**229**	**488**	**528**	**77**	**12**	**42**	**1972**	**13.1**		**324**	**39.5**	**18:52**	**4**	**1**	**2**	**3**	**2**	**0**	**0**	**0**	**20:52**

OHL All-Rookie Team (2001) • OHL Rookie of the Year (2001) • CHL All-Rookie Team (2001) • NHL All-Rookie Team (2003) • Maurice "Rocket" Richard Trophy (2004) (tied with Jarome Iginla and Ilya Kovalchuk) • NHL Foundation Award (2009)

Played in NHL All-Star Game (2004, 2007, 2008, 2009, 2011)

Signed as a free agent by **Davos** (Swiss), August 3, 2004.

NEAL, James

(NEEL, JAYMS) **PIT**

Left wing. Shoots left. 6'2", 208 lbs. Born, Whitby, Ont., September 3, 1987. Dallas' 2nd choice, 33rd overall, in 2005 Entry Draft.

Season	Club	League	GP	G	A	Pts	PIM	PP	SH	GW	S	%	+/-	TF	F%	Min	GP	G	A	Pts	PIM	PP	SH	GW	Min
2003-04	Bowmanville	OPJHL	43	28	27	55	....	....	....	....	....	....	....	....	....	....	....	....	....	....	....	....	....	....	....
	Plymouth Whalers	OHL	9	2	4	6	0	....	....	....	....	....	....	....	....	....	....	....	....	....	....	....	....	....	....
2004-05	Plymouth Whalers	OHL	67	18	26	44	32	....	....	....	....	....	....	....	....	....	4	1	1	2	6	....	....	....	....
2005-06	Plymouth Whalers	OHL	66	21	37	58	109	....	....	....	....	....	....	....	....	....	13	9	7	16	33	....	....	....	....
2006-07	Plymouth Whalers	OHL	45	27	38	65	94	....	....	....	....	....	....	....	....	....	20	13	12	25	54	....	....	....	....
2007-08	Iowa Stars	AHL	62	18	19	37	63	....	....	....	....	....	....	....	....	....	....	....	....	....	....	....	....	....	....
2008-09	**Dallas**	**NHL**	**77**	**24**	**13**	**37**	**51**	**9**	**0**	**2**	**171**	**14.0**	**-11**	**31**	**35.5**	**15:52**	....	....	....	....	....	....	....	....	....
	Manitoba Moose	AHL	5	4	1	5	2	....	....	....	....	....	....	....	....	....	....	....	....	....	....	....	....	....	....
2009-10	**Dallas**	**NHL**	**78**	**27**	**28**	**55**	**64**	**2**	**1**	**4**	**200**	**13.5**	**-5**	**60**	**31.7**	**18:12**	....	....	....	....	....	....	....	....	....
2010-11	**Dallas**	**NHL**	**59**	**21**	**18**	**39**	**60**	**5**	**0**	**3**	**160**	**13.1**	**8**	**17**	**41.2**	**17:42**	....	....	....	....	....	....	....	....	....
	Pittsburgh	**NHL**	**20**	**1**	**5**	**6**	**6**	**0**	**0**	**0**	**52**	**1.9**	**-1**	**6**	**16.7**	**16:54**	**7**	**1**	**1**	**2**	**6**	**0**	**0**	**1**	**17:25**
	NHL Totals		**234**	**73**	**64**	**137**	**181**	**16**	**1**	**9**	**583**	**12.5**		**114**	**33.3**	**17:12**	**7**	**1**	**1**	**2**	**6**	**0**	**0**	**1**	**17:25**

OHL First All-Star Team (2007) • Canadian Major Junior Second All-Star Team (2007)

Traded to **Pittsburgh** by **Dallas** with Matt Niskanen for Alex Goligoski, February 21, 2011.

NEGRIN, John

(NEH-grihn, JAWN) **CGY**

Defense. Shoots left. 6'2", 195 lbs. Born, West Vancouver, B.C., March 25, 1989. Calgary's 2nd choice, 70th overall, in 2007 Entry Draft.

Season	Club	League	GP	G	A	Pts	PIM	PP	SH	GW	S	%	+/-	TF	F%	Min	GP	G	A	Pts	PIM	PP	SH	GW	Min
2004-05	North Delta Flyers	PIJHL	45	3	12	15	53	....	....	....	....	....	....	....	....	....	....	....	....	....	....	....	....	....	....
	Kootenay Ice	WHL	2	0	0	0	0	....	....	....	....	....	....	....	....	....	....	....	....	....	....	....	....	....	....
2005-06	Kootenay Ice	WHL	55	3	7	10	48	....	....	....	....	....	....	....	....	....	6	0	0	0	6	....	....	....	....
2006-07	Kootenay Ice	WHL	44	1	15	16	57	....	....	....	....	....	....	....	....	....	7	0	2	2	8	....	....	....	....
2007-08	Kootenay Ice	WHL	71	1	41	42	68	....	....	....	....	....	....	....	....	....	10	1	1	2	8	....	....	....	....
2008-09	Kootenay Ice	WHL	38	5	26	31	27	....	....	....	....	....	....	....	....	....	....	....	....	....	....	....	....	....	....
	Swift Current	WHL	25	3	15	18	22	....	....	....	....	....	....	....	....	....	7	2	4	6	8	....	....	....	....
	Calgary	**NHL**	**3**	**0**	**1**	**1**	**2**	**0**	**0**	**0**	**3**	**0.0**	**-2**	**0**	**0.0**	**9:59**	....	....	....	....	....	....	....	....	....
2009-10	Abbotsford Heat	AHL	45	5	10	15	28	....	....	....	....	....	....	....	....	....	....	....	....	....	....	....	....	....	....
2010-11	Abbotsford Heat	AHL	24	0	6	6	24	....	....	....	....	....	....	....	....	....	....	....	....	....	....	....	....	....	....
	NHL Totals		**3**	**0**	**1**	**1**	**2**	**0**	**0**	**0**	**3**	**0.0**		**0**	**0.0**	**9:59**	....	....	....	....	....	....	....	....	....

WHL East Second All-Star Team (2009)

NEIL, Chris

(NEEL, KRIHS) **OTT**

Right wing. Shoots right. 6'1", 215 lbs. Born, Markdale, Ont., June 18, 1979. Ottawa's 7th choice, 161st overall, in 1998 Entry Draft.

Season	Club	League	GP	G	A	Pts	PIM	PP	SH	GW	S	%	+/-	TF	F%	Min	GP	G	A	Pts	PIM	PP	SH	GW	Min
1995-96	Orangeville	ON-Jr.B	43	15	15	30	50	....	....	....	....	....	....	....	....	....	....	....	....	....	....	....	....	....	....
1996-97	North Bay	OHL	65	13	16	29	150	....	....	....	....	....	....	....	....	....	....	....	....	....	....	....	....	....	....
1997-98	North Bay	OHL	59	26	29	55	231	....	....	....	....	....	....	....	....	....	....	....	....	....	....	....	....	....	....
1998-99	North Bay	OHL	66	26	46	72	215	....	....	....	....	....	....	....	....	....	4	1	0	1	15	....	....	....	....
99-2000	Mobile Mysticks	ECHL	4	0	2	2	39	....	....	....	....	....	....	....	....	....	....	....	....	....	....	....	....	....	....
	Grand Rapids	IHL	51	9	10	19	301	....	....	....	....	....	....	....	....	....	8	0	2	2	24	....	....	....	....
2000-01	Grand Rapids	IHL	78	15	21	36	354	....	....	....	....	....	....	....	....	....	10	2	2	4	22	....	....	....	....
2001-02	**Ottawa**	**NHL**	**72**	**10**	**7**	**17**	**231**	**1**	**0**	**0**	**56**	**17.9**	**5**	**0**	**0.0**	**8:22**	**12**	**0**	**0**	**0**	**12**	**0**	**0**	**0**	**7:12**
2002-03	**Ottawa**	**NHL**	**68**	**6**	**4**	**10**	**147**	**0**	**0**	**0**	**62**	**9.7**	**8**	**5**	**60.0**	**7:40**	**15**	**1**	**0**	**1**	**24**	**0**	**0**	**0**	**7:57**
2003-04	**Ottawa**	**NHL**	**82**	**8**	**8**	**16**	**194**	**0**	**0**	**1**	**76**	**10.5**	**13**	**14**	**42.9**	**8:51**	**7**	**0**	**1**	**1**	**19**	**0**	**0**	**0**	**6:45**
2004-05	Binghamton	AHL	22	4	6	10	132	....	....	....	....	....	....	....	....	....	6	1	1	2	26	....	....	....	....
2005-06	**Ottawa**	**NHL**	**79**	**16**	**17**	**33**	**204**	**8**	**0**	**0**	**126**	**12.7**	**9**	**9**	**22.2**	**12:18**	**10**	**1**	**0**	**1**	**14**	**0**	**0**	**0**	**6:58**
2006-07	**Ottawa**	**NHL**	**82**	**12**	**16**	**28**	**177**	**3**	**0**	**3**	**139**	**8.6**	**6**	**13**	**38.5**	**13:08**	**20**	**2**	**2**	**4**	**20**	**0**	**0**	**0**	**10:40**
2007-08	**Ottawa**	**NHL**	**68**	**6**	**14**	**20**	**199**	**0**	**0**	**1**	**78**	**7.7**	**-3**	**0**	**0.0**	**12:46**	**4**	**0**	**1**	**1**	**22**	**0**	**0**	**0**	**11:17**
2008-09	**Ottawa**	**NHL**	**60**	**3**	**7**	**10**	**146**	**0**	**0**	**0**	**59**	**5.1**	**-13**	**6**	**16.7**	**10:58**	....	....	....	....	....	....	....	....	....
2009-10	**Ottawa**	**NHL**	**68**	**10**	**12**	**22**	**175**	**1**	**0**	**2**	**100**	**10.0**	**-1**	**4**	**50.0**	**11:59**	**6**	**3**	**1**	**4**	**20**	**0**	**0**	**0**	**14:11**
2010-11	**Ottawa**	**NHL**	**80**	**6**	**10**	**16**	**210**	**0**	**0**	**2**	**105**	**5.7**	**-14**	**6**	**50.0**	**12:46**	....	....	....	....	....	....	....	....	....
	NHL Totals		**659**	**77**	**95**	**172**	**1683**	**13**	**0**	**9**	**801**	**9.6**		**57**	**38.6**	**11:01**	**74**	**7**	**5**	**12**	**131**	**0**	**0**	**0**	**9:00**

Signed as a free agent by **Binghamton** (AHL), March 2, 2005.

NEMISZ, Greg

(NEH-mihtz, GREHG) **CGY**

Center. Shoots right. 6'3", 197 lbs. Born, Courtice, Ont., June 5, 1990. Calgary's 1st choice, 25th overall, in 2008 Entry Draft.

Season	Club	League	GP	G	A	Pts	PIM	PP	SH	GW	S	%	+/-	TF	F%	Min	GP	G	A	Pts	PIM	PP	SH	GW	Min
2005-06	Clarington	Minor-ON	32	29	24	53	24	....	....	....	....	....	....	....	....	....	....	....	....	....	....	....	....	....	....
2006-07	Windsor Spitfires	OHL	62	11	23	34	23	....	....	....	....	....	....	....	....	....	....	....	....	....	....	....	....	....	....
2007-08	Windsor Spitfires	OHL	68	34	33	67	52	....	....	....	....	....	....	....	....	....	5	2	1	3	8	....	....	....	....
2008-09	Windsor Spitfires	OHL	65	36	41	77	48	....	....	....	....	....	....	....	....	....	20	8	12	20	22	....	....	....	....
2009-10	Windsor Spitfires	OHL	51	34	36	70	50	....	....	....	....	....	....	....	....	....	15	2	10	12	12	....	....	....	....
2010-11	**Calgary**	**NHL**	**6**	**0**	**1**	**1**	**0**	**0**	**0**	**0**	**5**	**0.0**	**-1**	**3**	**33.3**	**5:06**	....	....	....	....	....	....	....	....	....
	Abbotsford Heat	AHL	68	14	19	33	28	....	....	....	....	....	....	....	....	....	....	....	....	....	....	....	....	....	....
	NHL Totals		**6**	**0**	**1**	**1**	**0**	**0**	**0**	**0**	**5**	**0.0**		**3**	**33.3**	**5:06**	....	....	....	....	....	....	....	....	....

OHL Second All-Star Team (2009)

NEWBURY, Kris

(new-BUHR-ee, KRIHS) **NYR**

Center. Shoots left. 5'11", 213 lbs. Born, Brampton, Ont., February 19, 1982. San Jose's 4th choice, 139th overall, in 2002 Entry Draft.

Season	Club	League	GP	G	A	Pts	PIM	PP	SH	GW	S	%	+/-	TF	F%	Min	GP	G	A	Pts	PIM	PP	SH	GW	Min
1996-97	Brampton	OPJHL	28	9	4	13	36	....	....	....	....	....	....	....	....	....	....	....	....	....	....	....	....	....	....
1997-98	Brampton	OPJHL	46	11	21	32	161	....	....	....	....	....	....	....	....	....	....	....	....	....	....	....	....	....	....
1998-99	Belleville Bulls	OHL	51	6	8	14	89	....	....	....	....	....	....	....	....	....	....	....	....	....	....	....	....	....	....
99-2000	Belleville Bulls	OHL	34	6	18	24	72	....	....	....	....	....	....	....	....	....	....	....	....	....	....	....	....	....	....
	Sarnia Sting	OHL	27	6	8	14	44	....	....	....	....	....	....	....	....	....	7	0	3	3	16	....	....	....	....
2000-01	Sarnia Sting	OHL	64	28	30	58	126	....	....	....	....	....	....	....	....	....	4	1	3	4	20	....	....	....	....
2001-02	Sarnia Sting	OHL	66	42	62	104	141	....	....	....	....	....	....	....	....	....	5	1	3	4	15	....	....	....	....
2002-03	Sarnia Sting	OHL	64	34	58	92	149	....	....	....	....	....	....	....	....	....	6	4	4	8	16	....	....	....	....
2003-04	St. John's	AHL	72	5	15	20	153	....	....	....	....	....	....	....	....	....	....	....	....	....	....	....	....	....	....
2004-05	St. John's	AHL	55	4	9	13	103	....	....	....	....	....	....	....	....	....	5	0	0	0	36	....	....	....	....
	Pensacola	ECHL	6	2	4	6	20	....	....	....	....	....	....	....	....	....	....	....	....	....	....	....	....	....	....
2005-06	Toronto Marlies	AHL	74	22	37	59	215	....	....	....	....	....	....	....	....	....	5	0	1	1	12	....	....	....	....
2006-07	**Toronto**	**NHL**	**15**	**2**	**2**	**4**	**26**	**0**	**0**	**0**	**30**	**6.7**	**4**	**20**	**45.0**	**7:42**	....	....	....	....	....	....	....	....	....
	Toronto Marlies	AHL	37	12	24	36	87	....	....	....	....	....	....	....	....	....	....	....	....	....	....	....	....	....	....
2007-08	**Toronto**	**NHL**	**28**	**1**	**1**	**2**	**32**	**0**	**0**	**0**	**14**	**7.1**	**-7**	**55**	**40.0**	**4:22**	....	....	....	....	....	....	....	....	....
	Toronto Marlies	AHL	54	16	27	43	101	....	....	....	....	....	....	....	....	....	19	4	9	13	*73	....	....	....	....
2008-09	**Toronto**	**NHL**	**1**	**0**	**0**	**0**	**2**	**0**	**0**	**0**	**0**	**0.0**	**0**	**3**	**33.3**	**4:55**	....	....	....	....	....	....	....	....	....
	Toronto Marlies	AHL	33	6	23	29	72	....	....	....	....	....	....	....	....	....	....	....	....	....	....	....	....	....	....
2009-10	**Detroit**	**NHL**	**4**	**1**	**0**	**1**	**4**	**0**	**0**	**0**	**3**	**33.3**	**1**	**18**	**38.9**	**8:41**	....	....	....	....	....	....	....	....	....
	Grand Rapids	AHL	52	11	22	33	144	....	....	....	....	....	....	....	....	....	....	....	....	....	....	....	....	....	....
	Hartford	AHL	18	4	14	18	61	....	....	....	....	....	....	....	....	....	....	....	....	....	....	....	....	....	....

			Regular Season														Playoffs								
Season	Club	League	GP	G	A	Pts	PIM	PP	SH	GW	S	%	+/-	TF	F%	Min	GP	G	A	Pts	PIM	PP	SH	GW	Min
2010-11	**NY Rangers**	**NHL**	**11**	**0**	**1**	**1**	**35**	**0**	**0**	**0**	**6**	**0.0**	**–1**	**56**	**60.7**	**7:38**	....	....	....	....	....	....	....	....	....
	Connecticut	AHL	69	17	44	61	139	....	....	....	....	....	....	....	....	....	6	2	2	4	2	....	....	....	....
	NHL Totals		**59**	**4**	**4**	**8**	**99**	**0**	**0**	**0**	**53**	**7.5**		**152**	**48.0**	**6:08**	....	....	....	....	....	....	....	....	....

OHL Second All-Star Team (2002)

Signed as a free agent by **St. John's** (AHL), October 2, 2003. Signed as a free agent by **Toronto**, July 17, 2006. Signed as a free agent by **Detroit**, July 7, 2009. Traded to **NY Rangers** by **Detroit** for Jordan Owens, March 3, 2010.

NICHOL, Scott

(NIH-KOHL, SKAWT) **ST.L.**

Center. Shoots right. 5'9", 180 lbs. Born, Edmonton, Alta., December 31, 1974. Buffalo's 9th choice, 272nd overall, in 1993 Entry Draft.

Season	Club	League	GP	G	A	Pts	PIM	PP	SH	GW	S	%	+/-	TF	F%	Min	GP	G	A	Pts	PIM	PP	SH	GW	Min
1991-92	Calgary Flames	AMHL	23	26	16	42	132	....	....	....	....	....	....	....	....	....	....	....	....	....	....	....	....	....	....
1992-93	Portland	WHL	67	31	33	64	146	....	....	....	....	....	....	....	....	....	16	8	8	16	41	....	....	....	....
1993-94	Portland	WHL	65	40	53	93	144	....	....	....	....	....	....	....	....	....	10	3	8	11	16	....	....	....	....
1994-95	Rochester	AHL	71	11	16	27	136	....	....	....	....	....	....	....	....	....	5	0	3	3	14	....	....	....	....
1995-96	**Buffalo**	**NHL**	**2**	**0**	**0**	**0**	**10**	**0**	**0**	**0**	**4**	**0.0**	**0**	....	....	....	....	....	....	....	....	....	....	....	....
	Rochester	AHL	62	14	18	32	170	....	....	....	....	....	....	....	....	....	19	7	6	13	36	....	....	....	....
1996-97	Rochester	AHL	68	22	21	43	133	....	....	....	....	....	....	....	....	....	10	2	1	3	26	....	....	....	....
1997-98	**Buffalo**	**NHL**	**3**	**0**	**0**	**0**	**4**	**0**	**0**	**0**	**5**	**0.0**	**0**	....	....	....	....	....	....	....	....	....	....	....	....
	Rochester	AHL	35	13	7	20	113	....	....	....	....	....	....	....	....	....	17	0	6	6	18	....	....	....	....
1998-99	Rochester	AHL	52	13	20	33	120	....	....	....	....	....	....	....	....	....	....	....	....	....	....	....	....	....	....
99-2000	Rochester	AHL	37	7	11	18	141	....	....	....	....	....	....	....	....	....	12	0	3	3	10	....	....	....	....
2000-01	Detroit Vipers	IHL	67	7	24	31	198	....	....	....	....	....	....	....	....	....	11	1	1	2	12	....	....	....	....
2001-02	**Calgary**	**NHL**	**60**	**8**	**9**	**17**	**107**	**2**	**1**	**0**	**49**	**16.3**	**–9**	**458**	**53.1**	**12:41**	....	....	....	....	....	....	....	....	....
2002-03	**Calgary**	**NHL**	**68**	**5**	**5**	**10**	**149**	**0**	**1**	**0**	**66**	**7.6**	**–7**	**357**	**58.3**	**10:47**	....	....	....	....	....	....	....	....	....
2003-04	**Chicago**	**NHL**	**75**	**7**	**11**	**18**	**145**	**0**	**0**	**1**	**112**	**6.3**	**–16**	**1178**	**57.4**	**15:46**	....	....	....	....	....	....	....	....	....
2004-05	London Racers	Britain	16	7	12	19	86	....	....	....	....	....	....	....	....	....	....	....	....	....	....	....	....	....	....
2005-06	**Nashville**	**NHL**	**34**	**3**	**3**	**6**	**79**	**0**	**1**	**0**	**32**	**9.4**	**3**	**242**	**58.3**	**10:30**	**3**	**0**	**0**	**0**	**2**	**0**	**0**	**0**	**7:45**
	Milwaukee	AHL	6	3	5	8	18	....	....	....	....	....	....	....	....	....	....	....	....	....	....	....	....	....	....
2006-07	**Nashville**	**NHL**	**59**	**7**	**6**	**13**	**79**	**1**	**1**	**2**	**58**	**12.1**	**7**	**623**	**58.0**	**12:32**	**5**	**0**	**0**	**0**	**17**	**0**	**0**	**0**	**10:22**
2007-08	**Nashville**	**NHL**	**73**	**10**	**8**	**18**	**72**	**0**	**2**	**1**	**101**	**9.9**	**12**	**738**	**59.8**	**13:16**	**2**	**0**	**0**	**0**	**0**	**0**	**0**	**0**	**7:31**
2008-09	**Nashville**	**NHL**	**43**	**4**	**6**	**10**	**41**	**0**	**0**	**0**	**42**	**9.5**	**0**	**359**	**54.6**	**11:04**	....	....	....	....	....	....	....	....	....
2009-10	**San Jose**	**NHL**	**79**	**4**	**15**	**19**	**72**	**0**	**1**	**0**	**93**	**4.3**	**0**	**832**	**60.6**	**13:04**	**15**	**1**	**1**	**2**	**17**	**0**	**0**	**0**	**8:54**
2010-11	**San Jose**	**NHL**	**56**	**4**	**3**	**7**	**50**	**0**	**0**	**0**	**61**	**6.6**	**–3**	**485**	**59.4**	**9:45**	**15**	**0**	**0**	**0**	**26**	**0**	**0**	**0**	**6:22**
	NHL Totals		**552**	**52**	**66**	**118**	**808**	**3**	**7**	**4**	**623**	**8.3**		**5272**	**58.0**	**12:25**	**40**	**1**	**1**	**2**	**62**	**0**	**0**	**0**	**7:59**

• Missed majority of 1999-2000 due to knee injury vs. Saint John (AHL), February 16, 2000. Signed as a free agent by **Calgary**, July 1, 2001. Signed as a free agent by **Chicago**, July 1, 2003. Signed as a free agent by **London** (Britain), October 26, 2004. Signed as a free agent by **Nashville**, August 6, 2005. Signed as a free agent by **San Jose**, July 15, 2009. Signed as a free agent by **St. Louis**, July 5, 2011.

NIEDERMAYER, Rob

(NEE-duhr-MIGH-uhr, RAWB)

Center. Shoots left. 6'2", 203 lbs. Born, Cassiar, B.C., December 28, 1974. Florida's 1st choice, 5th overall, in 1993 Entry Draft.

Season	Club	League	GP	G	A	Pts	PIM	PP	SH	GW	S	%	+/-	TF	F%	Min	GP	G	A	Pts	PIM	PP	SH	GW	Min
1989-90	Cranbrook Blazers	Minor-BC	35	42	40	82	30	....	....	....	....	....	....	....	....	....	....	....	....	....	....	....	....	....	....
1990-91	Medicine Hat	WHL	71	24	26	50	8	....	....	....	....	....	....	....	....	....	12	3	7	10	2	....	....	....	....
1991-92	Medicine Hat	WHL	71	32	46	78	77	....	....	....	....	....	....	....	....	....	4	2	3	5	2	....	....	....	....
1992-93	Medicine Hat	WHL	52	43	34	77	67	....	....	....	....	....	....	....	....	....	....	....	....	....	....	....	....	....	....
1993-94	**Florida**	**NHL**	**65**	**9**	**17**	**26**	**51**	**3**	**0**	**2**	**67**	**13.4**	**–11**	....	....	....	....	....	....	....	....	....	....	....	....
1994-95	Medicine Hat	WHL	13	9	15	24	14	....	....	....	....	....	....	....	....	....	....	....	....	....	....	....	....	....	....
	Florida	**NHL**	**48**	**4**	**6**	**10**	**36**	**1**	**0**	**0**	**58**	**6.9**	**–13**	....	....	....	....	....	....	....	....	....	....	....	....
1995-96	**Florida**	**NHL**	**82**	**26**	**35**	**61**	**107**	**11**	**0**	**6**	**155**	**16.8**	**1**	....	....	....	**22**	**5**	**3**	**8**	**12**	**2**	**0**	**2**	....
1996-97	**Florida**	**NHL**	**60**	**14**	**24**	**38**	**54**	**3**	**0**	**2**	**136**	**10.3**	**4**	....	....	....	**5**	**2**	**1**	**3**	**6**	**1**	**0**	**0**	....
1997-98	**Florida**	**NHL**	**33**	**8**	**7**	**15**	**41**	**5**	**0**	**2**	**64**	**12.5**	**–9**	....	....	....	....	....	....	....	....	....	....	....	....
1998-99	**Florida**	**NHL**	**82**	**18**	**33**	**51**	**50**	**6**	**1**	**3**	**142**	**12.7**	**–13**	**1895**	**47.1**	**21:17**	....	....	....	....	....	....	....	....	....
99-2000	**Florida**	**NHL**	**81**	**10**	**23**	**33**	**46**	**1**	**0**	**4**	**135**	**7.4**	**–5**	**1632**	**47.9**	**19:04**	**4**	**1**	**0**	**1**	**6**	**0**	**0**	**0**	**15:55**
2000-01	**Florida**	**NHL**	**67**	**12**	**20**	**32**	**50**	**3**	**1**	**0**	**115**	**10.4**	**–12**	**997**	**45.0**	**20:30**	....	....	....	....	....	....	....	....	....
2001-02	**Calgary**	**NHL**	**57**	**6**	**14**	**20**	**49**	**1**	**2**	**1**	**87**	**6.9**	**–15**	**777**	**48.4**	**18:01**	....	....	....	....	....	....	....	....	....
2002-03	**Calgary**	**NHL**	**54**	**8**	**10**	**18**	**42**	**2**	**0**	**1**	**104**	**7.7**	**–13**	**139**	**48.9**	**17:29**	....	....	....	....	....	....	....	....	....
	Anaheim	**NHL**	**12**	**2**	**2**	**4**	**15**	**1**	**0**	**0**	**21**	**9.5**	**3**	**14**	**42.9**	**15:21**	**21**	**3**	**7**	**10**	**18**	**0**	***2**	**0**	**23:35**
2003-04	**Anaheim**	**NHL**	**55**	**12**	**16**	**28**	**34**	**6**	**0**	**2**	**111**	**10.8**	**–6**	**45**	**64.4**	**19:28**	....	....	....	....	....	....	....	....	....
2004-05	Ferencvaros	Hungary	5	2	1	3	14	....	....	....	....	....	....	....	....	....	....	....	....	....	....	....	....	....	....
2005-06	**Anaheim**	**NHL**	**76**	**15**	**24**	**39**	**89**	**4**	**1**	**2**	**140**	**10.7**	**–5**	**447**	**45.6**	**17:52**	**16**	**1**	**3**	**4**	**10**	**1**	**0**	**0**	**19:36**
2006-07 ♦	**Anaheim**	**NHL**	**82**	**5**	**11**	**16**	**77**	**0**	**0**	**0**	**106**	**4.7**	**–8**	**76**	**40.8**	**16:39**	**21**	**5**	**5**	**10**	**39**	**0**	**1**	**1**	**18:35**
2007-08	**Anaheim**	**NHL**	**78**	**8**	**8**	**16**	**54**	**0**	**1**	**1**	**111**	**7.2**	**1**	**69**	**33.3**	**17:43**	**2**	**0**	**0**	**0**	**0**	**0**	**0**	**0**	**13:47**
2008-09	**Anaheim**	**NHL**	**79**	**14**	**7**	**21**	**42**	**1**	**1**	**2**	**88**	**15.9**	**–17**	**68**	**38.2**	**15:34**	**13**	**0**	**3**	**3**	**12**	**0**	**0**	**0**	**16:13**
2009-10	**New Jersey**	**NHL**	**71**	**10**	**12**	**22**	**45**	**0**	**1**	**0**	**93**	**10.8**	**3**	**945**	**50.6**	**16:49**	**5**	**0**	**0**	**0**	**6**	**0**	**0**	**0**	**12:39**
2010-11	**Buffalo**	**NHL**	**71**	**5**	**14**	**19**	**22**	**0**	**0**	**1**	**80**	**6.3**	**–8**	**276**	**46.7**	**12:46**	**7**	**1**	**3**	**4**	**2**	**0**	**0**	**0**	**14:06**
	NHL Totals		**1153**	**186**	**283**	**469**	**904**	**48**	**8**	**29**	**1813**	**10.3**		**7380**	**47.3**	**17:43**	**116**	**18**	**25**	**43**	**111**	**4**	**3**	**3**	**18:41**

WHL East First All-Star Team (1993)

• Missed majority of 1997-98 due to thumb (November 26, 1997 vs. Boston) and head (March 19, 1998 vs. Buffalo) injuries. Traded to **Calgary** by **Florida** with Philadelphia's 2nd round choice (previously acquired, Calgary selected Andrei Medvedev) in 2001 Entry Draft for Valeri Bure and Jason Wiemer, June 23, 2001. Traded to **Anaheim** by **Calgary** for Mike Commodore and Jean-Francois Damphousse, March 11, 2003. Signed as a free agent by **Ferencvaros** (Hungary), January 17, 2005. Signed as a free agent by **New Jersey**, September 25, 2009. Signed as a free agent by **Buffalo**, July 7, 2010.

NIEDERREITER, Nino

(nee-duhr-RIGH-tuhr, NEE-noh) **NYI**

Right wing. Shoots left. 6'2", 205 lbs. Born, Chur, Switzerland, September 8, 1992. NY Islanders' 1st choice, 5th overall, in 2010 Entry Draft.

Season	Club	League	GP	G	A	Pts	PIM	PP	SH	GW	S	%	+/-	TF	F%	Min	GP	G	A	Pts	PIM	PP	SH	GW	Min
2006-07	HC Davos U18	Swiss-U18	32	43	19	62	38	....	....	....	....	....	....	....	....	....	....	....	....	....	....	....	....	....	....
	HC Davos Jr.	Swiss-Jr.	....	....	....	....	....	....	....	....	....	....	....	....	....	....	1	0	0	0	4	....	....	....	....
2007-08	HC Davos U18	Swiss-U18	32	39	26	65	62	....	....	....	....	....	....	....	....	....	5	6	3	9	4	....	....	....	....
	HC Davos Jr.	Swiss-Jr.	8	7	3	10	4	....	....	....	....	....	....	....	....	....	3	0	1	1	8	....	....	....	....
2008-09	HC Davos U18	Swiss-U18	6	6	6	12	6	....	....	....	....	....	....	....	....	....	....	....	....	....	....	....	....	....	....
	HC Davos Jr.	Swiss-Jr.	30	20	14	34	44	....	....	....	....	....	....	....	....	....	8	5	6	11	12	....	....	....	....
	HC Davos	Swiss	....	....	....	....	....	....	....	....	....	....	....	....	....	....	3	0	1	1	0	....	....	....	....
2009-10	Portland	WHL	65	36	24	60	68	....	....	....	....	....	....	....	....	....	13	8	8	16	16	....	....	....	....
2010-11	**NY Islanders**	**NHL**	**9**	**1**	**1**	**2**	**8**	**0**	**0**	**0**	**12**	**8.3**	**–1**	**0**	**0.0**	**13:36**	....	....	....	....	....	....	....	....	....
	Portland	WHL	55	41	29	70	67	....	....	....	....	....	....	....	....	....	21	9	18	27	30	....	....	....	....
	NHL Totals		**9**	**1**	**1**	**2**	**8**	**0**	**0**	**0**	**12**	**8.3**		**0**	**0.0**	**13:36**	....	....	....	....	....	....	....	....	....

WHL West Second All-Star Team (2010)

NIELSEN, Frans

(NEEL-sehn, FRAHNZ) **NYI**

Center. Shoots left. 6', 187 lbs. Born, Herning, Denmark, April 24, 1984. NY Islanders' 2nd choice, 87th overall, in 2002 Entry Draft.

Season	Club	League	GP	G	A	Pts	PIM	PP	SH	GW	S	%	+/-	TF	F%	Min	GP	G	A	Pts	PIM	PP	SH	GW	Min
99-2000	Herning IK Jr.	Den-Jr.	36	18	16	34	6	....	....	....	....	....	....	....	....	....	....	....	....	....	....	....	....	....	....
	Denmark	WJ18-B	5	3	4	7	0	....	....	....	....	....	....	....	....	....	....	....	....	....	....	....	....	....	....
2000-01	Herning IK	Denmark	38	18	19	37	6	....	....	....	....	....	....	....	....	....	....	....	....	....	....	....	....	....	....
	Denmark	WJ18-B	3	2	1	3	0	....	....	....	....	....	....	....	....	....	....	....	....	....	....	....	....	....	....
2001-02	Malmo	Sweden	20	0	1	1	0	....	....	....	....	....	....	....	....	....	....	....	....	....	....	....	....	....	....
	Malmo Jr.	Swe-Jr.	29	15	27	42	8	....	....	....	....	....	....	....	....	....	7	3	7	10	2	....	....	....	....
2002-03	Malmo	Sweden	47	3	6	9	10	....	....	....	....	....	....	....	....	....	....	....	....	....	....	....	....	....	....
	Malmo Jr.	Swe-Jr.	2	1	3	4	0	....	....	....	....	....	....	....	....	....	....	....	....	....	....	....	....	....	....
2003-04	Malmo	Sweden	50	9	7	16	28	....	....	....	....	....	....	....	....	....	....	....	....	....	....	....	....	....	....
	Malmo	Sweden-Q	10	3	5	8	2	....	....	....	....	....	....	....	....	....	....	....	....	....	....	....	....	....	....
2004-05	Malmo	Sweden	49	8	7	15	6	....	....	....	....	....	....	....	....	....	....	....	....	....	....	....	....	....	....
	Malmo	Sweden-Q	10	7	2	9	0	....	....	....	....	....	....	....	....	....	....	....	....	....	....	....	....	....	....
2005-06	Timra IK	Sweden	50	5	13	18	22	....	....	....	....	....	....	....	....	....	....	....	....	....	....	....	....	....	....
2006-07	**NY Islanders**	**NHL**	**15**	**1**	**1**	**2**	**0**	**0**	**0**	**1**	**16**	**6.3**	**–2**	**53**	**45.3**	**5:13**	....	....	....	....	....	....	....	....	....
	Bridgeport	AHL	54	20	24	44	10	....	....	....	....	....	....	....	....	....	....	....	....	....	....	....	....	....	....
2007-08	**NY Islanders**	**NHL**	**16**	**2**	**1**	**3**	**0**	**0**	**0**	**0**	**17**	**11.8**	**1**	**111**	**48.7**	**8:42**	....	....	....	....	....	....	....	....	....
	Bridgeport	AHL	48	10	28	38	18	....	....	....	....	....	....	....	....	....	....	....	....	....	....	....	....	....	....
2008-09	**NY Islanders**	**NHL**	**59**	**9**	**24**	**33**	**18**	**3**	**1**	**2**	**101**	**8.9**	**–4**	**758**	**47.2**	**16:32**	....	....	....	....	....	....	....	....	....

			Regular Season														Playoffs								
Season	Club	League	GP	G	A	Pts	PIM	PP	SH	GW	S	%	+/-	TF	F%	Min	GP	G	A	Pts	PIM	PP	SH	GW	Min
2009-10	**NY Islanders**	**NHL**	**76**	**12**	**26**	**38**	**6**	**0**	**1**	**1**	**136**	**8.8**	**4**	**1165**	**50.0**	**17:13**	....	....	....	....	....	....	....	....	....
2010-11	**NY Islanders**	**NHL**	**71**	**13**	**31**	**44**	**38**	**0**	***7**	**1**	**156**	**8.3**	**13**	**965**	**46.2**	**17:46**	....	....	....	....	....	....	....	....	....
	NHL Totals		**237**	**37**	**83**	**120**	**62**	**3**	**9**	**5**	**426**	**8.7**		**3052**	**48.0**	**15:53**	....	....	....	....	....	....	....	....	....

NIKITIN, Nikita

(nih-KEE-tihn, nih-KEE-tuh) **ST.L.**

Defense. Shoots left. 6'3", 217 lbs. Born, Omsk, USSR, June 16, 1986. St. Louis' 5th choice, 136th overall, in 2004 Entry Draft.

2002-03	Omsk 2	Russia-3	34	3	7	10	4	....	....	....	....	....	....	....	....	....	....	....	....	....	....	....	....	....	....
2003-04	Omsk 2	Russia-3	34	3	8	11	22	....	....	....	....	....	....	....	....	....	....	....	....	....	....	....	....	....	....
2004-05	Omsk 2	Russia-3	31	3	8	11	20	....	....	....	....	....	....	....	....	....	....	....	....	....	....	....	....	....	....
	Avangard Omsk	Russia	12	0	0	0	2	....	....	....	....	....	....	....	....	....	3	0	0	0	0	....	....	....	....
2005-06	Avangard Omsk	Russia	43	1	2	3	22	....	....	....	....	....	....	....	....	....	13	1	2	3	6	....	....	....	....
	Omsk 2	Russia-3	1	0	0	0	0	....	....	....	....	....	....	....	....	....	....	....	....	....	....	....	....	....	....
2006-07	Avangard Omsk	Russia	54	1	15	16	99	....	....	....	....	....	....	....	....	....	9	0	4	4	35	....	....	....	....
2007-08	Avangard Omsk	Russia	57	3	11	14	48	....	....	....	....	....	....	....	....	....	4	0	1	1	2	....	....	....	....
2008-09	Omsk	Rus-KHL	53	4	11	15	28	....	....	....	....	....	....	....	....	....	9	1	2	3	8	....	....	....	....
2009-10	Omsk	Rus-KHL	43	4	9	13	14	....	....	....	....	....	....	....	....	....	3	0	0	0	0	....	....	....	....
2010-11	**St. Louis**	**NHL**	**41**	**1**	**8**	**9**	**10**	**0**	**0**	**0**	**46**	**2.2**	**1**	**0**	**0.0**	**16:24**	....	....	....	....	....	....	....	....	....
	Peoria Rivermen	AHL	22	3	11	14	12	....	....	....	....	....	....	....	....	....	....	....	....	....	....	....	....	....	....
	NHL Totals		**41**	**1**	**8**	**9**	**10**	**0**	**0**	**0**	**46**	**2.2**		**0**	**0.0**	**16:24**	....	....	....	....	....	....	....	....	....

NIKULIN, Alexander

(nih-KOO-lihn, al-EHX-AN-duhr) **PHX**

Center. Shoots left. 6'1", 205 lbs. Born, Moscow, USSR, August 25, 1985. Ottawa's 6th choice, 122nd overall, in 2004 Entry Draft.

2002-03	CSKA Moscow 2	Russia-3	46	22	14	36	....	....	....	....	....	....	....	....	....	....	....	....	....	....	....	....	....	....	....
2003-04	CSKA Moscow 2	Russia-3	47	21	20	41	46	....	....	....	....	....	....	....	....	....	....	....	....	....	....	....	....	....	....
2004-05	CSKA Moscow	Russia	16	3	3	6	0	....	....	....	....	....	....	....	....	....	....	....	....	....	....	....	....	....	....
2005-06	CSKA Moscow	Russia	51	10	12	22	22	....	....	....	....	....	....	....	....	....	7	1	0	1	2	....	....	....	....
2006-07	CSKA Moscow	Russia	33	5	11	16	8	....	....	....	....	....	....	....	....	....	12	4	2	6	4	....	....	....	....
2007-08	**Ottawa**	**NHL**	**2**	**0**	**0**	**0**	**0**	**0**	**0**	**0**	**0**	**0.0**	**–2**	**1**	**100.0**	**4:56**	....	....	....	....	....	....	....	....	....
	Binghamton	AHL	71	14	36	50	34	....	....	....	....	....	....	....	....	....	....	....	....	....	....	....	....	....	....
2008-09	Binghamton	AHL	5	2	0	2	0	....	....	....	....	....	....	....	....	....	....	....	....	....	....	....	....	....	....
	Phoenix	**NHL**	**1**	**0**	**0**	**0**	**0**	**0**	**0**	**0**	**1**	**0.0**	**–1**	**3**	**0.0**	**5:35**	....	....	....	....	....	....	....	....	....
	San Antonio	AHL	64	7	16	23	20	....	....	....	....	....	....	....	....	....	....	....	....	....	....	....	....	....	....
2009-10	CSKA Moscow	Rus-KHL	42	5	17	22	2	....	....	....	....	....	....	....	....	....	3	0	0	0	0	....	....	....	....
2010-11	CSKA Moscow	Rus-KHL	7	0	1	1	0	....	....	....	....	....	....	....	....	....	....	....	....	....	....	....	....	....	....
	Amur Khabarovsk	Rus-KHL	45	5	17	22	4	....	....	....	....	....	....	....	....	....	....	....	....	....	....	....	....	....	....
	NHL Totals		**3**	**0**	**0**	**0**	**0**	**0**	**0**	**0**	**1**	**0.0**		**4**	**25.0**	**5:09**	....	....	....	....	....	....	....	....	....

Traded to **Phoenix** by **Ottawa** for Drew Fata, November 3, 2008. Signed as a free agent by **CSKA Moscow** (Russia-KHL), June 24. 2009. Signed as a free agent by **Khabarovsk** (Russia-KHL), September 29. 2010.

NILSSON, Robert

(NIHL-suhn, RAW-buhrt)

Center. Shoots left. 5'11", 185 lbs. Born, Calgary, Alta., January 10, 1985. NY Islanders' 1st choice, 15th overall, in 2003 Entry Draft.

2000-01	Leksands IF Jr.	Swe-Jr.	23	14	28	42	26	....	....	....	....	....	....	....	....	....	2	0	0	0	2	....	....	....	....
	Leksands IF U18	Swe-U18	4	6	3	9	6	....	....	....	....	....	....	....	....	....	2	0	2	2	2	....	....	....	....
2001-02	Leksands IF Jr.	Swe-Jr.	21	13	18	31	24	....	....	....	....	....	....	....	....	....	5	0	5	5	8	....	....	....	....
	Leksands IF	Sweden-2	14	1	4	5	8	....	....	....	....	....	....	....	....	....	....	....	....	....	....	....	....	....	....
2002-03	Leksands IF	Sweden	41	8	13	21	10	....	....	....	....	....	....	....	....	....	5	0	1	1	2	....	....	....	....
	Leksands IF Jr.	Swe-Jr.	....	....	....	....	....	....	....	....	....	....	....	....	....	....	2	1	1	2	2	....	....	....	....
2003-04	Leksands IF Jr.	Swe-Jr.	4	2	8	10	4	....	....	....	....	....	....	....	....	....	....	....	....	....	....	....	....	....	....
	Leksands IF	Sweden	34	2	4	6	6	....	....	....	....	....	....	....	....	....	....	....	....	....	....	....	....	....	....
	Fribourg	Swiss	7	1	3	4	2	....	....	....	....	....	....	....	....	....	4	1	0	1	2	....	....	....	....
2004-05	Almtuna	Sweden-2	3	0	1	1	2	....	....	....	....	....	....	....	....	....	....	....	....	....	....	....	....	....	....
	Hammarby	Sweden-2	7	0	4	4	4	....	....	....	....	....	....	....	....	....	....	....	....	....	....	....	....	....	....
	Djurgarden Jr.	Swe-Jr.	8	8	4	12	12	....	....	....	....	....	....	....	....	....	....	....	....	....	....	....	....	....	....
	Djurgarden	Sweden	23	2	4	6	6	....	....	....	....	....	....	....	....	....	3	0	0	0	0	....	....	....	....
2005-06	**NY Islanders**	**NHL**	**53**	**6**	**14**	**20**	**26**	**1**	**0**	**1**	**70**	**8.6**	**–6**	**31**	**29.0**	**11:52**	....	....	....	....	....	....	....	....	....
	Bridgeport	AHL	29	8	20	28	12	....	....	....	....	....	....	....	....	....	7	1	4	5	0	....	....	....	....
2006-07	Bridgeport	AHL	50	12	34	46	34	....	....	....	....	....	....	....	....	....	....	....	....	....	....	....	....	....	....
	Edmonton	**NHL**	**4**	**1**	**0**	**1**	**4**	**0**	**0**	**0**	**8**	**12.5**	**–1**	**2**	**50.0**	**17:21**	....	....	....	....	....	....	....	....	....
	Wilkes-Barre	AHL	19	6	14	20	14	....	....	....	....	....	....	....	....	....	11	3	12	15	8	....	....	....	....
2007-08	**Edmonton**	**NHL**	**71**	**10**	**31**	**41**	**22**	**3**	**0**	**0**	**102**	**9.8**	**8**	**15**	**46.7**	**13:56**	....	....	....	....	....	....	....	....	....
	Springfield	AHL	5	2	2	4	4	....	....	....	....	....	....	....	....	....	....	....	....	....	....	....	....	....	....
2008-09	**Edmonton**	**NHL**	**64**	**9**	**20**	**29**	**26**	**4**	**0**	**1**	**77**	**11.7**	**1**	**10**	**40.0**	**15:11**	....	....	....	....	....	....	....	....	....
2009-10	**Edmonton**	**NHL**	**60**	**11**	**16**	**27**	**12**	**3**	**0**	**1**	**104**	**10.6**	**–17**	**3**	**33.3**	**14:45**	....	....	....	....	....	....	....	....	....
2010-11	Ufa	Rus-KHL	41	5	22	27	28	....	....	....	....	....	....	....	....	....	21	3	7	10	2	....	....	....	....
	NHL Totals		**252**	**37**	**81**	**118**	**90**	**11**	**0**	**3**	**361**	**10.2**		**61**	**36.1**	**14:04**	....	....	....	....	....	....	....	....	....

Traded to **Edmonton** by **NY Islanders** with Ryan O'Marra and NY Islanders' 1st round choice (Alex Plante) in 2007 Entry Draft for Ryan Smyth, February 27, 2007. Signed as a free agent by **Ufa** (Russia-KHL), July 25, 2010.

NISKANEN, Matt

(NIHS-kah-nehn, MAT) **PIT**

Defense. Shoots right. 6', 200 lbs. Born, Virginia, MN, December 6, 1986. Dallas' 1st choice, 28th overall, in 2005 Entry Draft.

2003-04	Virginia	High-MN	....	24	37	61	....	....	....	....	....	....	....	....	....	....	....	....	....	....	....	....	....	....	....
2004-05	Virginia	High-MN	29	27	38	65	34	....	....	....	....	....	....	....	....	....	....	....	....	....	....	....	....	....	....
2005-06	U. Minn-Duluth	WCHA	38	1	13	14	40	....	....	....	....	....	....	....	....	....	....	....	....	....	....	....	....	....	....
2006-07	U. Minn-Duluth	WCHA	39	9	22	31	42	....	....	....	....	....	....	....	....	....	....	....	....	....	....	....	....	....	....
	Iowa Stars	AHL	13	0	3	3	6	....	....	....	....	....	....	....	....	....	12	2	5	7	10	....	....	....	....
2007-08	**Dallas**	**NHL**	**78**	**7**	**19**	**26**	**36**	**2**	**0**	**0**	**99**	**7.1**	**22**	**0**	**0.0**	**20:30**	**16**	**0**	**3**	**3**	**10**	**0**	**0**	**0**	**16:23**
2008-09	**Dallas**	**NHL**	**80**	**6**	**29**	**35**	**52**	**2**	**0**	**0**	**111**	**5.4**	**–11**	**0**	**0.0**	**19:58**	....	....	....	....	....	....	....	....	....
2009-10	**Dallas**	**NHL**	**74**	**3**	**12**	**15**	**18**	**0**	**0**	**2**	**110**	**2.7**	**–15**	**0**	**0.0**	**18:16**	....	....	....	....	....	....	....	....	....
2010-11	**Dallas**	**NHL**	**45**	**0**	**6**	**6**	**30**	**0**	**0**	**0**	**51**	**0.0**	**–1**	**0**	**0.0**	**15:44**	....	....	....	....	....	....	....	....	....
	Pittsburgh	**NHL**	**18**	**1**	**3**	**4**	**20**	**0**	**0**	**0**	**26**	**3.8**	**–2**	**0**	**0.0**	**18:31**	**7**	**0**	**1**	**1**	**0**	**0**	**0**	**0**	**12:58**
	NHL Totals		**295**	**17**	**69**	**86**	**156**	**4**	**0**	**2**	**397**	**4.3**		**0**	**0.0**	**18:57**	**23**	**0**	**4**	**4**	**10**	**0**	**0**	**0**	**15:21**

WCHA First All-Star Team (2007)

Traded to **Pittsburgh** by **Dallas** with James Neal for Alex Goligoski, February 21, 2011.

NODL, Andreas

(NOHD'L, awn-DRAY-uhs) **PHI**

Right wing. Shoots left. 6'1", 196 lbs. Born, Vienna, Austria, February 28, 1987. Philadelphia's 2nd choice, 39th overall, in 2006 Entry Draft.

2001-02	Wien Jr.	Austria-Jr.	1	0	0	0	0	....	....	....	....	....	....	....	....	....	....	....	....	....	....	....	....	....	....
2002-03	Wien Jr.	Austria-Jr.	STATISTICS NOT AVAILABLE																						
	Austria	WJ18-B	5	2	2	4	4	....	....	....	....	....	....	....	....	....	....	....	....	....	....	....	....	....	....
2003-04	Wien Jr.	Austria-Jr.	15	11	10	21	47	....	....	....	....	....	....	....	....	....	....	....	....	....	....	....	....	....	....
	Vienna Capitals	Austria	25	15	22	37	26	....	....	....	....	....	....	....	....	....	....	....	....	....	....	....	....	....	....
	Austria	WJ18-B	5	2	3	5	26	....	....	....	....	....	....	....	....	....	....	....	....	....	....	....	....	....	....
2004-05	Sioux Falls	USHL	44	7	9	16	24	....	....	....	....	....	....	....	....	....	....	....	....	....	....	....	....	....	....
2005-06	Sioux Falls	USHL	58	29	30	59	16	....	....	....	....	....	....	....	....	....	14	6	9	15	6	....	....	....	....
2006-07	St. Cloud State	WCHA	40	18	28	46	32	....	....	....	....	....	....	....	....	....	....	....	....	....	....	....	....	....	....
2007-08	St. Cloud State	WCHA	40	18	26	44	22	....	....	....	....	....	....	....	....	....	....	....	....	....	....	....	....	....	....
	Philadelphia	AHL	3	1	0	1	0	....	....	....	....	....	....	....	....	....	10	1	0	1	2	....	....	....	....
2008-09	**Philadelphia**	**NHL**	**38**	**1**	**3**	**4**	**2**	**0**	**0**	**0**	**33**	**3.0**	**–15**	**0**	**0.0**	**11:09**	....	....	....	....	....	....	....	....	....
	Philadelphia	AHL	39	6	14	20	20	....	....	....	....	....	....	....	....	....	4	0	1	1	2	....	....	....	....
2009-10	**Philadelphia**	**NHL**	**10**	**0**	**1**	**1**	**0**	**0**	**0**	**0**	**2**	**0.0**	**–2**	**0**	**0.0**	**8:55**	**10**	**0**	**0**	**0**	**0**	**0**	**0**	**0**	**8:28**
	Adirondack	AHL	65	14	20	34	24	....	....	....	....	....	....	....	....	....	....	....	....	....	....	....	....	....	....
2010-11	**Philadelphia**	**NHL**	**67**	**11**	**11**	**22**	**16**	**1**	**1**	**2**	**100**	**11.0**	**14**	**19**	**57.9**	**13:16**	**2**	**0**	**0**	**0**	**0**	**0**	**0**	**0**	**7:25**
	NHL Totals		**115**	**12**	**15**	**27**	**18**	**1**	**1**	**2**	**135**	**8.9**		**19**	**57.9**	**12:12**	**12**	**0**	**0**	**0**	**0**	**0**	**0**	**0**	**8:17**

USHL First All-Star Team (2006) • WCHA All-Rookie Team (2007) • WCHA Rookie of the Year (2007) • NCAA Rookie of the Year (2007) • WCHA Second All-Star Team (2008)

NOKELAINEN, Petteri

(noh-kuh-LAY-nehn, PEH-tuh-ree) **PHX**

Center. Shoots right. 6'1", 200 lbs. Born, Imatra, Finland, January 16, 1986. NY Islanders' 1st choice, 16th overall, in 2004 Entry Draft.

			Regular Season														Playoffs								
Season	Club	League	GP	G	A	Pts	PIM	PP	SH	GW	S	%	+/-	TF	F%	Min	GP	G	A	Pts	PIM	PP	SH	GW	Min
2001-02	SaiPa U18	Fin-U18	6	2	1	3	14	....	....	....	....	....	....	....	....	....	....	....	....	....	....	....	....	....	....
2002-03	SaiPa U18	Fin-U18	10	3	8	11	18	....	....	....	....	....	....	....	....	....	....	....	....	....	....	....	....	....	....
	SaiPa Jr.	Fin-Jr.	28	7	4	11	28	....	....	....	....	....	....	....	....	....	3	1	0	1	4	....	....	....	....
	SaiPa	Finland	2	1	0	1	2	....	....	....	....	....	....	....	....	....	....	....	....	....	....	....	....	....	....
2003-04	Suomi U20	Finland-2	3	0	1	1	0	....	....	....	....	....	....	....	....	....	....	....	....	....	....	....	....	....	....
	SaiPa Jr.	Fin-Jr.	10	5	3	8	4	....	....	....	....	....	....	....	....	....	4	0	1	1	0	....	....	....	....
	SaiPa	Finland	40	4	4	8	16	....	....	....	....	....	....	....	....	....	....	....	....	....	....	....	....	....	....
2004-05	SaiPa	Finland	52	15	5	20	34	....	....	....	....	....	....	....	....	....	....	....	....	....	....	....	....	....	....
2005-06	**NY Islanders**	**NHL**	15	1	1	2	4	0	0	1	13	7.7	–1	82	48.8	7:47	....	....	....	....	....	....	....	....	....
2006-07	Bridgeport	AHL	60	6	10	16	51	....	....	....	....	....	....	....	....	....	....	....	....	....	....	....	....	....	....
2007-08	**Boston**	**NHL**	57	7	3	10	19	0	0	1	40	17.5	0	288	52.8	8:16	7	0	2	2	4	0	0	0	12:38
	Providence Bruins	AHL	8	3	5	8	4	....	....	....	....	....	....	....	....	....	6	4	1	5	0	....	....	....	....
2008-09	**Boston**	**NHL**	33	0	3	3	10	0	0	0	30	0.0	–1	87	62.1	9:40	....	....	....	....	....	....	....	....	....
	Anaheim	**NHL**	17	4	2	6	6	0	1	0	26	15.4	3	205	49.8	14:20	9	0	0	0	2	0	0	0	8:42
2009-10	**Anaheim**	**NHL**	50	4	7	11	21	0	0	0	70	5.7	–7	354	43.5	12:56	....	....	....	....	....	....	....	....	....
	Phoenix	**NHL**	17	1	1	2	6	0	0	0	18	5.6	–2	90	51.1	10:24	5	0	0	0	2	0	0	0	8:22
2010-11	Jokerit Helsinki	Finland	46	11	16	27	116	....	....	....	....	....	....	....	....	....	7	2	0	2	12	....	....	....	....
	NHL Totals		189	17	17	34	66	0	1	2	197	8.6		1106	49.5	10:27	21	0	2	2	8	0	0	0	9:56

• Missed majority of 2005-06 due to knee injury vs. Pittsburgh, November 3, 2005. Traded to **Boston** by **NY Islanders** for Ben Walter and Boston's 2nd round choice (later traded to Columbus – Columbus selected Kevin Lynch) in 2009 Entry Draft, September 11, 2007. Traded to **Anaheim** by **Boston** for Steve Montador, March 4, 2009. Traded to **Phoenix** by **Anaheim** for Phoenix's 6th round choice (later traded to Ottawa – Ottawa selected Max McCormick) in 2011 Entry Draft, March 3, 2010. Signed as a free agent by **Jokerit Helsinki** (Finland), August 28, 2010.

NOLAN, Owen

(NOH-lan, OH-wehn) **VAN**

Right wing. Shoots right. 6'1", 214 lbs. Born, Belfast, N.Ireland, February 12, 1972. Quebec's 1st choice, 1st overall, in 1990 Entry Draft.

Season	Club	League	GP	G	A	Pts	PIM	PP	SH	GW	S	%	+/-	TF	F%	Min	GP	G	A	Pts	PIM	PP	SH	GW	Min
1987-88	Thorold	Minor-ON	28	53	32	85	24	....	....	....	....	....	....	....	....	....	....	....	....	....	....	....	....	....	....
	Thorold	ON-Jr.B	3	1	0	1	2	....	....	....	....	....	....	....	....	....	....	....	....	....	....	....	....	....	....
1988-89	Cornwall Royals	OHL	62	34	25	59	213	....	....	....	....	....	....	....	....	....	18	5	11	16	41	....	....	....	....
1989-90	Cornwall Royals	OHL	58	51	59	110	240	....	....	....	....	....	....	....	....	....	6	7	5	12	26	....	....	....	....
1990-91	**Quebec**	**NHL**	59	3	10	13	109	0	0	0	54	5.6	–19	....	....	....	....	....	....	....	....	....	....	....	....
	Halifax Citadels	AHL	6	4	4	8	11	....	....	....	....	....	....	....	....	....	....	....	....	....	....	....	....	....	....
1991-92	**Quebec**	**NHL**	75	42	31	73	183	17	0	0	190	22.1	–9	....	....	....	....	....	....	....	....	....	....	....	....
1992-93	**Quebec**	**NHL**	73	36	41	77	185	15	0	4	241	14.9	–1	....	....	....	5	1	0	1	2	0	0	0	....
1993-94	**Quebec**	**NHL**	6	2	2	4	8	0	0	0	15	13.3	2	....	....	....	....	....	....	....	....	....	....	....	....
1994-95	**Quebec**	**NHL**	46	30	19	49	46	13	2	*8	137	21.9	21	....	....	....	6	2	3	5	6	0	0	0	....
1995-96	**Colorado**	**NHL**	9	4	4	8	9	4	0	0	23	17.4	–3	....	....	....	....	....	....	....	....	....	....	....	....
	San Jose	**NHL**	72	29	32	61	137	12	1	2	184	15.8	–30	....	....	....	....	....	....	....	....	....	....	....	....
1996-97	**San Jose**	**NHL**	72	31	32	63	155	10	0	3	225	13.8	–19	....	....	....	....	....	....	....	....	....	....	....	....
1997-98	**San Jose**	**NHL**	75	14	27	41	144	3	1	1	192	7.3	–2	....	....	....	6	2	2	4	26	2	0	1	....
1998-99	**San Jose**	**NHL**	78	19	26	45	129	6	2	3	207	9.2	16	657	49.3	19:09	6	1	1	2	6	0	0	0	20:15
99-2000	**San Jose**	**NHL**	78	44	40	84	110	*18	4	6	261	16.9	–1	357	50.7	21:07	10	8	2	10	6	2	*2	3	22:14
2000-01	**San Jose**	**NHL**	57	24	25	49	75	10	1	4	191	12.6	0	407	46.9	21:49	6	1	1	2	8	0	0	1	22:45
2001-02	**San Jose**	**NHL**	75	23	43	66	93	8	2	2	217	10.6	7	545	47.0	19:23	12	3	6	9	8	0	0	0	19:46
	Canada	Olympics	6	0	3	3	2	....	....	....	....	....	....	....	....	....	....	....	....	....	....	....	....	....	....
2002-03	**San Jose**	**NHL**	61	22	20	42	91	8	3	4	192	11.5	–5	226	50.4	18:08	....	....	....	....	....	....	....	....	....
	Toronto	**NHL**	14	7	5	12	16	5	0	1	29	24.1	2	56	48.2	17:00	7	0	2	2	2	0	0	0	23:19
2003-04	**Toronto**	**NHL**	65	19	29	48	110	7	2	3	154	12.3	4	242	53.3	17:57	....	....	....	....	....	....	....	....	....
2004-05			DID NOT PLAY																						
2005-06			DID NOT PLAY – INJURED																						
2006-07	**Phoenix**	**NHL**	76	16	24	40	56	2	3	1	154	10.4	–2	238	52.5	15:25	....	....	....	....	....	....	....	....	....
2007-08	**Calgary**	**NHL**	77	16	16	32	71	1	1	3	163	9.8	6	346	52.3	16:33	7	3	2	5	2	0	0	2	19:11
2008-09	**Minnesota**	**NHL**	59	25	20	45	26	12	0	5	148	16.9	5	161	46.6	16:24	....	....	....	....	....	....	....	....	....
2009-10	**Minnesota**	**NHL**	73	16	17	33	40	4	1	3	151	10.6	–12	390	47.2	16:36	....	....	....	....	....	....	....	....	....
2010-11	ZSC Lions Zurich	Swiss	24	7	19	26	53	....	....	....	....	....	....	....	....	....	5	2	2	4	2	....	....	....	....
	NHL Totals		1200	422	463	885	1793	155	23	53	3128	13.5		3625	49.3	18:12	65	21	19	40	66	4	2	7	21:09

OHL Rookie of the Year (1989) • OHL First All-Star Team (1990)

Played in NHL All-Star Game (1992, 1996, 1997, 2000, 2002)

• Missed majority of 1993-94 due to shoulder injury vs. Tampa Bay, November 13, 1993. • Transferred to **Colorado** after **Quebec** franchise relocated, June 21, 1995. Traded to **San Jose** by **Colorado** for Sandis Ozolinsh, October 26, 1995. Traded to **Toronto** by **San Jose** for Alyn McCauley, Brad Boyes and Toronto's 1st round choice (later traded to Boston – Boston selected Mark Stuart) in 2003 Entry Draft, March 5, 2003. • Missed 2005-06 recovering from knee surgery, July, 2005. Signed as a free agent by **Phoenix**, August 16, 2006. Signed as a free agent by **Calgary**, July 3, 2007. Signed as a free agent by **Minnesota**, July 6, 2008. Signed as a free agent by **Zurich** (Swiss), October 21, 2010. Signed to a PTO (professional tryout) contract by **Vancouver**, August 4, 2011.

NOREAU, Maxim

(NOHR-oh, max-EEM) **N.J.**

Defense. Shoots right. 6', 195 lbs. Born, Montreal, Que., May 14, 1987.

Season	Club	League	GP	G	A	Pts	PIM	PP	SH	GW	S	%	+/-	TF	F%	Min	GP	G	A	Pts	PIM	PP	SH	GW	Min
2004-05	Victoriaville Tigres	QMJHL	65	5	8	13	47	....	....	....	....	....	....	....	....	....	7	0	0	0	8	....	....	....	....
2005-06	Victoriaville Tigres	QMJHL	69	22	43	65	116	....	....	....	....	....	....	....	....	....	5	2	4	6	7	....	....	....	....
2006-07	Victoriaville Tigres	QMJHL	69	17	53	70	106	....	....	....	....	....	....	....	....	....	6	2	1	3	8	....	....	....	....
2007-08	Houston Aeros	AHL	50	8	8	16	48	....	....	....	....	....	....	....	....	....	5	0	0	0	4	....	....	....	....
	Texas Wildcatters	ECHL	2	0	3	3	0	....	....	....	....	....	....	....	....	....	....	....	....	....	....	....	....	....	....
2008-09	Houston Aeros	AHL	77	14	25	39	49	....	....	....	....	....	....	....	....	....	20	4	7	11	2	....	....	....	....
2009-10	**Minnesota**	**NHL**	1	0	0	0	0	0	0	0	0	0.0	0	0	0.0	7:01	....	....	....	....	....	....	....	....	....
	Houston Aeros	AHL	76	18	34	52	60	....	....	....	....	....	....	....	....	....	....	....	....	....	....	....	....	....	....
2010-11	**Minnesota**	**NHL**	5	0	0	0	0	0	0	0	8	0.0	–1	0	0.0	14:17	....	....	....	....	....	....	....	....	....
	Houston Aeros	AHL	76	10	44	54	58	....	....	....	....	....	....	....	....	....	24	2	10	12	23	....	....	....	....
	NHL Totals		6	0	0	0	0	0	0	0	8	0.0		0	0.0	13:04	....	....	....	....	....	....	....	....	....

AHL Second All-Star Team (2010) • AHL First All-Star Team (2011)

Signed as a free agent by **Minnesota**, May 22, 2008. Traded to **New Jersey** by **Minnesota** for David McIntyre, June 16, 2011. Signed as a free agent by **Ambri-Piotta** (Swiss), July 31, 2011.

NYCHOLAT, Lawrence

(NIH-koh-lat, LAW-rehnts)

Defense. Shoots left. 6', 200 lbs. Born, Calgary, Alta., May 7, 1979.

Season	Club	League	GP	G	A	Pts	PIM	PP	SH	GW	S	%	+/-	TF	F%	Min	GP	G	A	Pts	PIM	PP	SH	GW	Min
1995-96	Notre Dame	SMHL	42	10	36	46	66	....	....	....	....	....	....	....	....	....	....	....	....	....	....	....	....	....	....
1996-97	Swift Current	WHL	67	8	13	21	64	....	....	....	....	....	....	....	....	....	10	0	0	0	24	....	....	....	....
1997-98	Swift Current	WHL	71	13	35	48	108	....	....	....	....	....	....	....	....	....	1	0	0	0	0	....	....	....	....
1998-99	Swift Current	WHL	72	16	44	60	122	....	....	....	....	....	....	....	....	....	6	2	2	4	12	....	....	....	....
99-2000	Swift Current	WHL	70	22	58	80	92	....	....	....	....	....	....	....	....	....	2	0	0	0	0	....	....	....	....
2000-01	Jackson Bandits	ECHL	5	1	2	3	5	....	....	....	....	....	....	....	....	....	....	....	....	....	....	....	....	....	....
	Cleveland	IHL	42	3	7	10	69	....	....	....	....	....	....	....	....	....	4	0	0	0	2	....	....	....	....
2001-02	Houston Aeros	AHL	72	3	11	14	92	....	....	....	....	....	....	....	....	....	14	1	0	1	23	....	....	....	....
2002-03	Houston Aeros	AHL	66	11	28	39	155	....	....	....	....	....	....	....	....	....	....	....	....	....	....	....	....	....	....
	Hartford	AHL	15	2	9	11	6	....	....	....	....	....	....	....	....	....	2	2	0	2	0	....	....	....	....
2003-04	**NY Rangers**	**NHL**	9	0	0	0	6	0	0	0	6	0.0	–2	0	0.0	17:09	....	....	....	....	....	....	....	....	....
	Hartford	AHL	72	6	26	32	130	....	....	....	....	....	....	....	....	....	16	0	5	5	28	....	....	....	....
2004-05	Hartford	AHL	79	5	38	43	132	....	....	....	....	....	....	....	....	....	6	0	3	3	11	....	....	....	....
2005-06	Hershey Bears	AHL	73	13	44	57	94	....	....	....	....	....	....	....	....	....	16	2	12	14	12	....	....	....	....
2006-07	**Washington**	**NHL**	18	2	6	8	12	0	0	0	22	9.1	–3	0	0.0	20:32	....	....	....	....	....	....	....	....	....
	Hershey Bears	AHL	29	3	25	28	39	....	....	....	....	....	....	....	....	....	....	....	....	....	....	....	....	....	....
	Ottawa	**NHL**	1	0	0	0	0	0	0	0	3	0.0	0	0	0.0	12:48	....	....	....	....	....	....	....	....	....
2007-08	**Ottawa**	**NHL**	3	0	0	0	0	0	0	0	4	0.0	1	0	0.0	11:57	....	....	....	....	....	....	....	....	....
	Binghamton	AHL	77	12	37	49	74	....	....	....	....	....	....	....	....	....	....	....	....	....	....	....	....	....	....
2008-09	**Vancouver**	**NHL**	14	0	1	1	6	0	0	0	8	0.0	3	0	0.0	9:41	....	....	....	....	....	....	....	....	....
	Manitoba Moose	AHL	3	0	3	3	4	....	....	....	....	....	....	....	....	....	....	....	....	....	....	....	....	....	....
	Colorado	**NHL**	5	0	0	0	0	0	0	0	1	0.0	–2	0	0.0	10:33	....	....	....	....	....	....	....	....	....

			Regular Season														Playoffs								
Season	Club	League	GP	G	A	Pts	PIM	PP	SH	GW	S	%	+/-	TF	F%	Min	GP	G	A	Pts	PIM	PP	SH	GW	Min
2009-10	Manitoba Moose	AHL	37	5	17	22	49	....	....	....	....	....	....	....	....	....	4	0	1	1	4	....	....	....	....
2010-11	Hershey Bears	AHL	32	5	23	28	21	....	....	....	....	....	....	....	....	....	....	....	....	....	....	....	....	....	....
	NHL Totals		**50**	**2**	**7**	**9**	**24**	**0**	**0**	**0**	**44**	**4.5**		**0**	**0.0**	**15:13**	....	....	....	....	....	....	....	....	....

AHL First All-Star Team (2008)

Signed as a free agent by **Minnesota**, August 31, 2000. Traded to **NY Rangers** by **Minnesota** for Johan Holmqvist, March 11, 2003. Signed as a free agent by **Washington**, August 9, 2005. Traded to **Ottawa** by **Washington** for Andy Hedlund and Ottawa's 6th round choice (Justin Taylor) in 2007 Entry Draft, February 26, 2007. Traded to **Vancouver** by **Ottawa** for Ryan Shannon, September 2, 2008. Claimed on waivers by **Calgary** from **Vancouver**, March 3, 2009. Traded to **Colorado** by **Calgary** with Ryan Wilson and and Montreal's 2nd round choice (previously acquired, Colorado selected Stefan Elliott) in 2009 Entry Draft for Jordan Leopold, March 4, 2009. Signed as a free agent by **Vancouver**, July 2, 2009. • Missed majority of 2009-10 and 2010-11 due to various injuries. Signed as a free agent by **Hershey** (AHL), July 9, 2010.

NYSTROM, Eric (NIGH-stuhm, AIR-ihk) MIN

Left wing. Shoots left. 6'1", 197 lbs. Born, Syosset, NY, February 14, 1983. Calgary's 1st choice, 10th overall, in 2002 Entry Draft.

Season	Club	League	GP	G	A	Pts	PIM	PP	SH	GW	S	%	+/-	TF	F%	Min	GP	G	A	Pts	PIM	PP	SH	GW	Min
99-2000	USNTDP	NAHL	55	7	16	23	57	....	....	....	....	....	....	....	....	....	3	0	0	0	0	....	....	....	....
2000-01	USNTDP	U-18	43	10	12	22	52	....	....	....	....	....	....	....	....	....	....	....	....	....	....	....	....	....	....
	USNTDP	USHL	23	5	5	10	50	....	....	....	....	....	....	....	....	....	....	....	....	....	....	....	....	....	....
2001-02	U. of Michigan	CCHA	40	18	13	31	42	....	....	....	....	....	....	....	....	....	....	....	....	....	....	....	....	....	....
2002-03	U. of Michigan	CCHA	39	15	11	26	24	....	....	....	....	....	....	....	....	....	....	....	....	....	....	....	....	....	....
2003-04	U. of Michigan	CCHA	43	10	12	22	50	....	....	....	....	....	....	....	....	....	....	....	....	....	....	....	....	....	....
2004-05	U. of Michigan	CCHA	38	13	19	32	33	....	....	....	....	....	....	....	....	....	....	....	....	....	....	....	....	....	....
2005-06	**Calgary**	**NHL**	**2**	**0**	**0**	**0**	**0**	**0**	**0**	**0**	**0**	**0.0**	**−1**	**5**	**60.0**	**12:01**	....	....	....	....	....	....	....	....	....
	Omaha	AHL	78	15	18	33	37	....	....	....	....	....	....	....	....	....	....	....	....	....	....	....	....	....	....
2006-07	Omaha	AHL	12	2	0	2	0	....	....	....	....	....	....	....	....	....	5	0	0	0	2	....	....	....	....
2007-08	**Calgary**	**NHL**	**44**	**3**	**7**	**10**	**48**	**0**	**0**	**0**	**42**	**7.1**	**−5**	**14**	**50.0**	**11:30**	**7**	**0**	**0**	**0**	**2**	**0**	**0**	**0**	**7:39**
	Quad City Flames	AHL	18	4	3	7	15	....	....	....	....	....	....	....	....	....	....	....	....	....	....	....	....	....	....
2008-09	**Calgary**	**NHL**	**76**	**5**	**5**	**10**	**89**	**0**	**1**	**3**	**83**	**6.0**	**−7**	**29**	**37.9**	**9:16**	**6**	**2**	**2**	**4**	**0**	**0**	**0**	**1**	**10:57**
2009-10	**Calgary**	**NHL**	**82**	**11**	**8**	**19**	**54**	**0**	**0**	**2**	**91**	**12.1**	**0**	**279**	**45.5**	**13:11**	....	....	....	....	....	....	....	....	....
2010-11	**Minnesota**	**NHL**	**82**	**4**	**8**	**12**	**30**	**1**	**0**	**0**	**83**	**4.8**	**−16**	**131**	**34.4**	**13:19**	....	....	....	....	....	....	....	....	....
	NHL Totals		**286**	**23**	**28**	**51**	**221**	**1**	**1**	**5**	**299**	**7.7**		**458**	**42.1**	**11:54**	**13**	**2**	**2**	**4**	**2**	**0**	**0**	**1**	**9:10**

CCHA All-Rookie Team (2002)

• Missed majority of 2006-07 due to shoulder injury in pre-season. Signed as a free agent by **Minnesota**, July 1, 2010.

OBERG, Evan (OH-buhrg, EH-vuhn) FLA

Defense. Shoots left. 6', 165 lbs. Born, Forestburg, Alta., February 16, 1988.

Season	Club	League	GP	G	A	Pts	PIM	PP	SH	GW	S	%	+/-	TF	F%	Min	GP	G	A	Pts	PIM	PP	SH	GW	Min
2005-06	Camrose Kodiaks	AJHL	44	4	9	13	56	....	....	....	....	....	....	....	....	....	14	1	1	2	14	....	....	....	....
2006-07	Camrose Kodiaks	AJHL	52	9	14	23	86	....	....	....	....	....	....	....	....	....	16	3	11	14	24	....	....	....	....
2007-08	U. Minn-Duluth	WCHA	24	1	2	3	10	....	....	....	....	....	....	....	....	....	....	....	....	....	....	....	....	....	....
2008-09	U. Minn-Duluth	WCHA	43	7	20	27	50	....	....	....	....	....	....	....	....	....	....	....	....	....	....	....	....	....	....
2009-10	**Vancouver**	**NHL**	**2**	**0**	**0**	**0**	**0**	**0**	**0**	**0**	**0**	**0.0**	**0**	**0**	**0.0**	**6:17**	....	....	....	....	....	....	....	....	....
	Manitoba Moose	AHL	70	3	23	26	64	....	....	....	....	....	....	....	....	....	5	1	1	2	4	....	....	....	....
2010-11	**Vancouver**	**NHL**	**2**	**0**	**0**	**0**	**0**	**0**	**0**	**0**	**1**	**0.0**	**0**	**0**	**0.0**	**9:50**	....	....	....	....	....	....	....	....	....
	Manitoba Moose	AHL	38	6	5	11	28	....	....	....	....	....	....	....	....	....	....	....	....	....	....	....	....	....	....
	Rochester	AHL	5	1	1	2	0	....	....	....	....	....	....	....	....	....	....	....	....	....	....	....	....	....	....
	NHL Totals		**4**	**0**	**0**	**0**	**0**	**0**	**0**	**0**	**1**	**0.0**		**0**	**0.0**	**8:03**	....	....	....	....	....	....	....	....	....

Signed as a free agent by **Vancouver**, April 10, 2009. Traded to **Florida** by **Vancouver** with Vancouver's 3rd round choice in 2013 Entry Draft for Chris Higgins, February 28, 2011.

O'BRIEN, Jim (oh-BRIGH-uhn, JIHM) OTT

Center. Shoots right. 6'2", 200 lbs. Born, Maplewood, MN, January 29, 1989. Ottawa's 1st choice, 29th overall, in 2007 Entry Draft.

Season	Club	League	GP	G	A	Pts	PIM	PP	SH	GW	S	%	+/-	TF	F%	Min	GP	G	A	Pts	PIM	PP	SH	GW	Min
2003-04	Det. Caesars	MWEHL	68	19	24	43	72	....	....	....	....	....	....	....	....	....	....	....	....	....	....	....	....	....	....
2004-05	USNTDP	U-17	13	6	6	12	10	....	....	....	....	....	....	....	....	....	....	....	....	....	....	....	....	....	....
	USNTDP	NAHL	40	10	12	22	41	....	....	....	....	....	....	....	....	....	1	0	0	0	0	....	....	....	....
2005-06	USNTDP	U-18	38	11	14	25	62	....	....	....	....	....	....	....	....	....	....	....	....	....	....	....	....	....	....
	USNTDP	NAHL	13	6	10	16	14	....	....	....	....	....	....	....	....	....	....	....	....	....	....	....	....	....	....
2006-07	U. of Minnesota	WCHA	43	7	8	15	51	....	....	....	....	....	....	....	....	....	....	....	....	....	....	....	....	....	....
2007-08	Seattle	WHL	70	21	34	55	66	....	....	....	....	....	....	....	....	....	12	2	6	8	14	....	....	....	....
2008-09	Seattle	WHL	63	27	35	62	55	....	....	....	....	....	....	....	....	....	5	1	0	1	10	....	....	....	....
	Binghamton	AHL	6	0	1	1	0	....	....	....	....	....	....	....	....	....	....	....	....	....	....	....	....	....	....
2009-10	Binghamton	AHL	76	8	9	17	49	....	....	....	....	....	....	....	....	....	....	....	....	....	....	....	....	....	....
2010-11	**Ottawa**	**NHL**	**6**	**0**	**0**	**0**	**2**	**0**	**0**	**0**	**11**	**0.0**	**−3**	**16**	**50.0**	**9:40**	....	....	....	....	....	....	....	....	....
	Binghamton	AHL	74	24	32	56	67	....	....	....	....	....	....	....	....	....	23	3	4	7	12	....	....	....	....
	NHL Totals		**6**	**0**	**0**	**0**	**2**	**0**	**0**	**0**	**11**	**0.0**		**16**	**50.0**	**9:40**	....	....	....	....	....	....	....	....	....

O'BRIEN, Shane (oh-BRIGH-uhn, SHAYN) COL

Defense. Shoots left. 6'3", 230 lbs. Born, Port Hope, Ont., August 9, 1983. Anaheim's 8th choice, 250th overall, in 2003 Entry Draft.

Season	Club	League	GP	G	A	Pts	PIM	PP	SH	GW	S	%	+/-	TF	F%	Min	GP	G	A	Pts	PIM	PP	SH	GW	Min
99-2000	Port Hope	OPJHL	47	6	27	33	110	....	....	....	....	....	....	....	....	....	....	....	....	....	....	....	....	....	....
2000-01	Kingston	OHL	61	2	12	14	89	....	....	....	....	....	....	....	....	....	4	0	1	1	6	....	....	....	....
2001-02	Kingston	OHL	67	10	23	33	132	....	....	....	....	....	....	....	....	....	1	0	0	0	2	....	....	....	....
2002-03	Kingston	OHL	28	8	15	23	100	....	....	....	....	....	....	....	....	....	....	....	....	....	....	....	....	....	....
	St. Michael's	OHL	34	8	11	19	108	....	....	....	....	....	....	....	....	....	19	4	10	14	*79	....	....	....	....
2003-04	Cincinnati	AHL	60	2	8	10	163	....	....	....	....	....	....	....	....	....	9	0	2	2	20	....	....	....	....
2004-05	Cincinnati	AHL	77	5	20	25	319	....	....	....	....	....	....	....	....	....	12	1	3	4	57	....	....	....	....
2005-06	Portland Pirates	AHL	77	8	33	41	287	....	....	....	....	....	....	....	....	....	19	6	16	22	*81	....	....	....	....
2006-07	**Anaheim**	**NHL**	**62**	**2**	**12**	**14**	**140**	**1**	**0**	**2**	**55**	**3.6**	**5**	**0**	**0.0**	**14:04**	....	....	....	....	....	....	....	....	....
	Tampa Bay	**NHL**	**18**	**0**	**2**	**2**	**36**	**0**	**0**	**0**	**17**	**0.0**	**−8**	**0**	**0.0**	**18:08**	**6**	**0**	**0**	**0**	**12**	**0**	**0**	**0**	**17:12**
2007-08	**Tampa Bay**	**NHL**	**77**	**4**	**17**	**21**	**154**	**0**	**0**	**1**	**69**	**5.8**	**−2**	**0**	**0.0**	**21:13**	....	....	....	....	....	....	....	....	....
2008-09	**Tampa Bay**	**NHL**	**1**	**0**	**0**	**0**	**0**	**0**	**0**	**0**	**0**	**0.0**	**−1**	**0**	**0.0**	**14:04**	....	....	....	....	....	....	....	....	....
	Vancouver	**NHL**	**76**	**0**	**10**	**10**	**196**	**0**	**0**	**0**	**39**	**0.0**	**6**	**0**	**0.0**	**14:56**	**10**	**1**	**1**	**2**	**24**	**0**	**0**	**0**	**12:06**
2009-10	**Vancouver**	**NHL**	**65**	**2**	**6**	**8**	**79**	**0**	**0**	**0**	**37**	**5.4**	**15**	**0**	**0.0**	**17:01**	**12**	**1**	**2**	**3**	**25**	**0**	**0**	**0**	**17:44**
2010-11	**Nashville**	**NHL**	**80**	**2**	**7**	**9**	**83**	**0**	**0**	**0**	**50**	**4.0**	**1**	**0**	**0.0**	**17:07**	**12**	**0**	**0**	**0**	**18**	**0**	**0**	**0**	**16:47**
	NHL Totals		**379**	**10**	**54**	**64**	**688**	**1**	**0**	**3**	**267**	**3.7**		**0**	**0.0**	**17:02**	**40**	**2**	**3**	**5**	**79**	**0**	**0**	**0**	**15:58**

Traded to **Tampa Bay** by **Anaheim** with Colorado's 3rd round choice (previously acquired, Tampa Bay selected Luca Cunti) in 2007 Entry Draft for Gerald Coleman and Tampa Bay's 1st round choice (later traded to Minnesota - Minnesota selected Colton Gillies) in 2007 Entry Draft, February 24, 2007. Traded to **Vancouver** by **Tampa Bay** with Michel Ouellet for Lukas Krajicek and Juraj Simek, October 6, 2008. Traded to **Nashville** by **Vancouver** with Dan Gendur for Ryan Parent and Jonas Andersson, October 5, 2010. Signed as a free agent by **Colorado**, July 13, 2011.

O'BYRNE, Ryan (oh-BUHRN, RIGH-uhn) COL

Defense. Shoots right. 6'5", 234 lbs. Born, Victoria, B.C., July 19, 1984. Montreal's 4th choice, 79th overall, in 2003 Entry Draft.

Season	Club	League	GP	G	A	Pts	PIM	PP	SH	GW	S	%	+/-	TF	F%	Min	GP	G	A	Pts	PIM	PP	SH	GW	Min
2001-02	Victoria Salsa	BCHL	52	2	9	11	91	....	....	....	....	....	....	....	....	....	....	....	....	....	....	....	....	....	....
2002-03	Victoria Salsa	BCHL	32	3	6	9	94	....	....	....	....	....	....	....	....	....	....	....	....	....	....	....	....	....	....
	Nanaimo Clippers	BCHL	9	2	4	6	24	....	....	....	....	....	....	....	....	....	....	....	....	....	....	....	....	....	....
2003-04	Cornell Big Red	ECAC	31	0	2	2	71	....	....	....	....	....	....	....	....	....	....	....	....	....	....	....	....	....	....
2004-05	Cornell Big Red	ECAC	33	3	7	10	68	....	....	....	....	....	....	....	....	....	....	....	....	....	....	....	....	....	....
2005-06	Cornell Big Red	ECAC	28	7	6	13	69	....	....	....	....	....	....	....	....	....	....	....	....	....	....	....	....	....	....
2006-07	Hamilton	AHL	80	0	12	12	129	....	....	....	....	....	....	....	....	....	22	2	5	7	32	....	....	....	....
2007-08	**Montreal**	**NHL**	**33**	**1**	**6**	**7**	**45**	**0**	**0**	**0**	**10**	**10.0**	**7**	**0**	**0.0**	**13:24**	**4**	**0**	**0**	**0**	**0**	**0**	**0**	**0**	**10:46**
	Hamilton	AHL	20	2	6	8	49	....	....	....	....	....	....	....	....	....	....	....	....	....	....	....	....	....	....
2008-09	**Montreal**	**NHL**	**37**	**0**	**5**	**5**	**58**	**0**	**0**	**0**	**14**	**0.0**	**−7**	**0**	**0.0**	**15:06**	**2**	**0**	**0**	**0**	**2**	**0**	**0**	**0**	**13:04**
	Hamilton	AHL	18	1	5	6	35	....	....	....	....	....	....	....	....	....	....	....	....	....	....	....	....	....	....
2009-10	**Montreal**	**NHL**	**55**	**1**	**3**	**4**	**74**	**0**	**0**	**1**	**27**	**3.7**	**−3**	**0**	**0.0**	**15:16**	**13**	**0**	**0**	**0**	**10**	**0**	**0**	**0**	**12:43**
2010-11	**Montreal**	**NHL**	**3**	**0**	**0**	**0**	**4**	**0**	**0**	**0**	**3**	**0.0**	**0**	**0**	**0.0**	**14:55**	....	....	....	....	....	....	....	....	....
	Colorado	**NHL**	**64**	**0**	**10**	**10**	**71**	**0**	**0**	**0**	**42**	**0.0**	**−7**	**0**	**0.0**	**20:24**	....	....	....	....	....	....	....	....	....
	NHL Totals		**192**	**2**	**24**	**26**	**252**	**0**	**0**	**1**	**96**	**2.1**		**0**	**0.0**	**16:37**	**19**	**0**	**0**	**0**	**12**	**0**	**0**	**0**	**12:20**

Traded to **Colorado** by **Montreal** for the rights to Michael Bournival, November 11, 2010.

			Regular Season															Playoffs								
Season	Club	League	GP	G	A	Pts	PIM	PP	SH	GW	S	%	+/-	TF	F%	Min	GP	G	A	Pts	PIM	PP	SH	GW	Min

O'DONNELL, Sean

(oh-DAHN-uhl, SHAWN) **CHI**

Defense. Shoots left. 6'2", 237 lbs. Born, Ottawa, Ont., October 13, 1971. Buffalo's 6th choice, 123rd overall, in 1991 Entry Draft.

Season	Club	League	GP	G	A	Pts	PIM	PP	SH	GW	S	%	+/-	TF	F%	Min	GP	G	A	Pts	PIM	PP	SH	GW	Min
1987-88	Kanata Valley	CJHL	54	4	25	29	96	....	....	....	....	....	....	....	....	....	....	....	....	....	....	....	....	....	....
1988-89	Sudbury Wolves	OHL	56	1	9	10	49	....	....	....	....	....	....	....	....	....	....	....	....	....	....	....	....	....	....
1989-90	Sudbury Wolves	OHL	64	7	19	26	84	....	....	....	....	....	....	....	....	....	7	1	2	3	8	....	....	....	....
1990-91	Sudbury Wolves	OHL	66	8	23	31	114	....	....	....	....	....	....	....	....	....	5	1	4	5	10	....	....	....	....
1991-92	Rochester	AHL	73	4	9	13	193	....	....	....	....	....	....	....	....	....	16	1	2	3	21	....	....	....	....
1992-93	Rochester	AHL	74	3	18	21	203	....	....	....	....	....	....	....	....	....	17	1	6	7	38	....	....	....	....
1993-94	Rochester	AHL	64	2	10	12	242	....	....	....	....	....	....	....	....	....	4	0	1	1	21	....	....	....	....
1994-95	Phoenix	IHL	61	2	18	20	132	....	....	....	....	....	....	....	....	....	9	0	1	1	21	....	....	....	....
	Los Angeles	**NHL**	**15**	**0**	**2**	**2**	**49**	**0**	**0**	**0**	**12**	**0.0**	**-2**	....	....	....	....	....	....	....	....	....	....	....	....
1995-96	**Los Angeles**	**NHL**	**71**	**2**	**5**	**7**	**127**	**0**	**0**	**0**	**65**	**3.1**	**3**	....	....	....	....	....	....	....	....	....	....	....	....
1996-97	**Los Angeles**	**NHL**	**55**	**5**	**12**	**17**	**144**	**2**	**0**	**0**	**68**	**7.4**	**-13**	....	....	....	....	....	....	....	....	....	....	....	....
1997-98	**Los Angeles**	**NHL**	**80**	**2**	**15**	**17**	**179**	**0**	**0**	**1**	**71**	**2.8**	**7**	....	....	....	**4**	**1**	**0**	**1**	**36**	**0**	**0**	**0**	....
1998-99	**Los Angeles**	**NHL**	**80**	**1**	**13**	**14**	**186**	**0**	**0**	**0**	**64**	**1.6**	**1**	**0**	**0.0**	**19:10**	....	....	....	....	....	....	....	....	....
99-2000	**Los Angeles**	**NHL**	**80**	**2**	**12**	**14**	**114**	**0**	**0**	**1**	**51**	**3.9**	**4**	**0**	**0.0**	**17:41**	**4**	**1**	**0**	**1**	**4**	**0**	**0**	**0**	**16:26**
2000-01	**Minnesota**	**NHL**	**63**	**4**	**12**	**16**	**128**	**1**	**0**	**2**	**58**	**6.9**	**-2**	**12**	**50.0**	**23:00**	....	....	....	....	....	....	....	....	....
	New Jersey	**NHL**	**17**	**0**	**1**	**1**	**33**	**0**	**0**	**0**	**9**	**0.0**	**2**	**0**	**0.0**	**16:27**	**23**	**1**	**2**	**3**	**41**	**0**	**0**	**0**	**16:21**
2001-02	**Boston**	**NHL**	**80**	**3**	**22**	**25**	**89**	**1**	**0**	**2**	**112**	**2.7**	**27**	**0**	**0.0**	**24:50**	**6**	**0**	**2**	**2**	**4**	**0**	**0**	**0**	**24:58**
2002-03	**Boston**	**NHL**	**70**	**1**	**15**	**16**	**76**	**1**	**0**	**1**	**61**	**1.6**	**8**	**1**	**0.0**	**22:05**	....	....	....	....	....	....	....	....	....
2003-04	**Boston**	**NHL**	**82**	**1**	**10**	**11**	**110**	**0**	**0**	**0**	**72**	**1.4**	**10**	**3**	**33.3**	**20:36**	**7**	**0**	**0**	**0**	**0**	**0**	**0**	**0**	**19:53**
2004-05			DID NOT PLAY																						
2005-06	**Phoenix**	**NHL**	**57**	**1**	**7**	**8**	**121**	**0**	**0**	**0**	**23**	**4.3**	**3**	**0**	**0.0**	**16:18**	....	....	....	....	....	....	....	....	....
	Anaheim	**NHL**	**21**	**1**	**2**	**3**	**26**	**0**	**0**	**0**	**10**	**10.0**	**3**	**0**	**0.0**	**17:13**	**16**	**2**	**3**	**5**	**23**	**0**	**0**	**1**	**16:44**
2006-07♦	**Anaheim**	**NHL**	**79**	**2**	**15**	**17**	**92**	**0**	**0**	**1**	**47**	**4.3**	**9**	**1**	**0.0**	**19:55**	**21**	**0**	**2**	**2**	**10**	**0**	**0**	**0**	**20:20**
2007-08	**Anaheim**	**NHL**	**82**	**2**	**7**	**9**	**84**	**0**	**1**	**0**	**25**	**8.0**	**9**	**2**	**100.0**	**17:14**	**6**	**1**	**1**	**2**	**2**	**0**	**0**	**0**	**15:32**
2008-09	**Los Angeles**	**NHL**	**82**	**0**	**12**	**12**	**71**	**0**	**0**	**0**	**32**	**0.0**	**2**	**1**	**0.0**	**20:29**	....	....	....	....	....	....	....	....	....
2009-10	**Los Angeles**	**NHL**	**78**	**3**	**12**	**15**	**70**	**0**	**0**	**1**	**44**	**6.8**	**14**	**1**	**0.0**	**18:44**	**6**	**0**	**1**	**1**	**4**	**0**	**0**	**0**	**18:27**
2010-11	**Philadelphia**	**NHL**	**81**	**1**	**17**	**18**	**87**	**0**	**0**	**0**	**34**	**2.9**	**8**	**0**	**0.0**	**15:33**	**11**	**0**	**2**	**2**	**5**	**0**	**0**	**0**	**12:43**
	NHL Totals		**1173**	**31**	**191**	**222**	**1786**	**4**	**1**	**9**	**858**	**3.6**		**21**	**42.9**	**19:31**	**104**	**6**	**13**	**19**	**129**	**0**	**0**	**1**	**17:42**

Traded to **Los Angeles** by **Buffalo** for Doug Houda, July 26, 1994. Claimed by **Minnesota** from **Los Angeles** in Expansion Draft, June 23, 2000. Traded to **New Jersey** by **Minnesota** for Willie Mitchell, March 4, 2001. Signed as a free agent by **Boston**, July 2, 2001. Signed as a free agent by **Phoenix**, July 6, 2004. Traded to **Anaheim** by **Phoenix** for Joel Perreault, March 9, 2006. Traded to **Los Angeles** by **Anaheim** for future considerations, September 30, 2008. Signed as a free agent by **Philadelphia**, July 1, 2010. Signed as a free agent by **Chicago**, July 1, 2011.

ODUYA, Johnny

(oh-DOO-yuh, JAW-nee) **WPG**

Defense. Shoots left. 6', 190 lbs. Born, Stockholm, Sweden, October 1, 1981. Washington's 6th choice, 221st overall, in 2001 Entry Draft.

Season	Club	League	GP	G	A	Pts	PIM	PP	SH	GW	S	%	+/-	TF	F%	Min	GP	G	A	Pts	PIM	PP	SH	GW	Min
1996-97	Hammarby Jr.	Swe-Jr.	13	0	0	0	....	....	....	....	....	....	....	....	....	....	....	....	....	....	....	....	....	....	....
1997-98	Hammarby Jr.	Swe-Jr.	26	3	11	14	70	....	....	....	....	....	....	....	....	....	....	....	....	....	....	....	....	....	....
1998-99	Hammarby Jr.	Swe-Jr.	38	14	31	45	45	....	....	....	....	....	....	....	....	....	....	....	....	....	....	....	....	....	....
99-2000	Hammarby Jr.	Swe-Jr.	32	3	18	21	48	....	....	....	....	....	....	....	....	....	6	1	2	3	4	....	....	....	....
	Hammarby	Sweden-2	1	0	0	0	0	....	....	....	....	....	....	....	....	....	1	0	0	0	0	....	....	....	....
2000-01	Moncton Wildcats	QMJHL	44	11	38	49	147	....	....	....	....	....	....	....	....	....	....	....	....	....	....	....	....	....	....
	Victoriaville Tigres	QMJHL	24	3	16	19	112	....	....	....	....	....	....	....	....	....	13	4	9	13	10	....	....	....	....
2001-02	Hammarby	Sweden-2	46	11	14	25	66	....	....	....	....	....	....	....	....	....	2	1	0	1	4	....	....	....	....
2002-03	Hammarby	Sweden-2	48	15	25	40	200	....	....	....	....	....	....	....	....	....	....	....	....	....	....	....	....	....	....
2003-04	Djurgarden	Sweden	42	4	4	8	*173	....	....	....	....	....	....	....	....	....	4	0	0	0	6	....	....	....	....
2004-05	Djurgarden	Sweden	49	2	4	6	139	....	....	....	....	....	....	....	....	....	12	0	2	2	39	....	....	....	....
2005-06	Frolunda	Sweden	47	8	11	19	95	....	....	....	....	....	....	....	....	....	17	1	2	3	16	....	....	....	....
2006-07	**New Jersey**	**NHL**	**76**	**2**	**9**	**11**	**61**	**0**	**0**	**0**	**55**	**3.6**	**-5**	**0**	**0.0**	**18:31**	**6**	**0**	**1**	**1**	**6**	**0**	**0**	**0**	**12:59**
2007-08	**New Jersey**	**NHL**	**75**	**6**	**20**	**26**	**46**	**2**	**0**	**0**	**63**	**9.5**	**27**	**0**	**0.0**	**19:02**	**5**	**0**	**1**	**1**	**6**	**0**	**0**	**0**	**20:40**
2008-09	**New Jersey**	**NHL**	**82**	**7**	**22**	**29**	**30**	**1**	**1**	**4**	**108**	**6.5**	**21**	**0**	**0.0**	**20:52**	**7**	**0**	**0**	**0**	**2**	**0**	**0**	**0**	**20:19**
2009-10	**New Jersey**	**NHL**	**40**	**2**	**2**	**4**	**18**	**0**	**0**	**0**	**44**	**4.5**	**2**	**0**	**0.0**	**21:11**	....	....	....	....	....	....	....	....	....
	Atlanta	**NHL**	**27**	**1**	**8**	**9**	**12**	**0**	**0**	**0**	**24**	**4.2**	**6**	**0**	**0.0**	**21:22**	....	....	....	....	....	....	....	....	....
	Sweden	Olympics	4	0	0	0	12	....	....	....	....	....	....	....	....	....	....	....	....	....	....	....	....	....	....
2010-11	**Atlanta**	**NHL**	**82**	**2**	**15**	**17**	**22**	**0**	**0**	**0**	**90**	**2.2**	**-15**	**0**	**0.0**	**20:43**	....	....	....	....	....	....	....	....	....
	NHL Totals		**382**	**20**	**76**	**96**	**189**	**3**	**1**	**4**	**384**	**5.2**		**0**	**0.0**	**20:05**	**18**	**0**	**2**	**2**	**14**	**0**	**0**	**0**	**17:58**

Signed as a free agent by **New Jersey**, July 24, 2006. Traded to **Atlanta** by **New Jersey** with Niclas Bergfors, Patrice Cormier and New Jersey's 1st (later traded to Chicago - Chicago selected Kevin Hayes) and 2nd (later traded to Chicago - Chicago selected Justin Holl) round choices in 2010 Entry Draft for Ilya Kovalchuk, Anssi Salmela and Atlanta's 2nd round choice (Jonathon Merrill) in 2010 Entry Draft, February 4, 2010. • Transferred to **Winnipeg** after **Atlanta** franchise relocated, June 21, 2011.

OHLUND, Mattias

(OH-luhnd, mat-TEE-uhs) **T.B.**

Defense. Shoots left. 6'4", 229 lbs. Born, Pitea, Sweden, September 9, 1976. Vancouver's 1st choice, 13th overall, in 1994 Entry Draft.

Season	Club	League	GP	G	A	Pts	PIM	PP	SH	GW	S	%	+/-	TF	F%	Min	GP	G	A	Pts	PIM	PP	SH	GW	Min
1992-93	Pitea HC	Sweden-2	22	0	6	6	16	....	....	....	....	....	....	....	....	....	....	....	....	....	....	....	....	....	....
1993-94	Pitea HC	Sweden-2	28	7	10	17	66	....	....	....	....	....	....	....	....	....	....	....	....	....	....	....	....	....	....
1994-95	Lulea HF	Sweden	34	6	10	16	34	....	....	....	....	....	....	....	....	....	9	4	0	4	16	....	....	....	....
1995-96	Lulea HF	Sweden	38	4	10	14	26	....	....	....	....	....	....	....	....	....	13	1	3	4	47	....	....	....	....
1996-97	Lulea HF	Sweden	47	7	9	16	38	....	....	....	....	....	....	....	....	....	10	1	2	3	8	....	....	....	....
	Lulea HF	EuroHL	6	0	3	3	0	....	....	....	....	....	....	....	....	....	....	....	....	....	....	....	....	....	....
1997-98	**Vancouver**	**NHL**	**77**	**7**	**23**	**30**	**76**	**1**	**0**	**0**	**172**	**4.1**	**3**	....	....	....	....	....	....	....	....	....	....	....	....
	Sweden	Olympics	4	0	1	1	4	....	....	....	....	....	....	....	....	....	....	....	....	....	....	....	....	....	....
1998-99	**Vancouver**	**NHL**	**74**	**9**	**26**	**35**	**83**	**2**	**1**	**1**	**129**	**7.0**	**-19**	**0**	**0.0**	**26:04**	....	....	....	....	....	....	....	....	....
99-2000	**Vancouver**	**NHL**	**42**	**4**	**16**	**20**	**24**	**2**	**1**	**1**	**63**	**6.3**	**6**	**0**	**0.0**	**27:41**	....	....	....	....	....	....	....	....	....
2000-01	**Vancouver**	**NHL**	**65**	**8**	**20**	**28**	**46**	**1**	**1**	**4**	**136**	**5.9**	**-16**	**0**	**0.0**	**25:00**	**4**	**1**	**3**	**4**	**6**	**1**	**0**	**0**	**26:32**
2001-02	**Vancouver**	**NHL**	**81**	**10**	**26**	**36**	**56**	**4**	**1**	**3**	**193**	**5.2**	**16**	**0**	**0.0**	**25:17**	**6**	**1**	**1**	**2**	**6**	**0**	**0**	**0**	**28:48**
	Sweden	Olympics	4	0	2	2	2	....	....	....	....	....	....	....	....	....	....	....	....	....	....	....	....	....	....
2002-03	**Vancouver**	**NHL**	**59**	**2**	**27**	**29**	**42**	**0**	**0**	**0**	**100**	**2.0**	**1**	**0**	**0.0**	**25:23**	**13**	**3**	**4**	**7**	**12**	**0**	**0**	**0**	**24:01**
2003-04	**Vancouver**	**NHL**	**82**	**14**	**20**	**34**	**73**	**5**	**0**	**3**	**129**	**10.9**	**14**	**0**	**0.0**	**25:47**	**7**	**1**	**4**	**5**	**13**	**0**	**0**	**1**	**27:25**
2004-05	Lulea HF	Sweden	2	1	0	1	4	....	....	....	....	....	....	....	....	....	....	....	....	....	....	....	....	....	....
2005-06	**Vancouver**	**NHL**	**78**	**13**	**20**	**33**	**92**	**8**	**1**	**2**	**183**	**7.1**	**-6**	**1**	**0.0**	**25:40**	....	....	....	....	....	....	....	....	....
	Sweden	Olympics	6	0	2	2	2	....	....	....	....	....	....	....	....	....	....	....	....	....	....	....	....	....	....
2006-07	**Vancouver**	**NHL**	**77**	**11**	**20**	**31**	**80**	**6**	**0**	**2**	**170**	**6.5**	**-3**	**1**	**0.0**	**24:47**	**12**	**2**	**5**	**7**	**12**	**1**	**0**	**0**	**28:18**
2007-08	**Vancouver**	**NHL**	**53**	**9**	**15**	**24**	**79**	**4**	**0**	**2**	**128**	**7.0**	**-1**	**0**	**0.0**	**23:46**	....	....	....	....	....	....	....	....	....
2008-09	**Vancouver**	**NHL**	**82**	**6**	**19**	**25**	**105**	**3**	**0**	**1**	**131**	**4.6**	**14**	**0**	**0.0**	**21:34**	**10**	**1**	**2**	**3**	**6**	**1**	**0**	**0**	**23:54**
2009-10	**Tampa Bay**	**NHL**	**67**	**0**	**13**	**13**	**59**	**0**	**0**	**0**	**71**	**0.0**	**-8**	**0**	**0.0**	**22:49**	....	....	....	....	....	....	....	....	....
	Sweden	Olympics	4	1	0	1	2	....	....	....	....	....	....	....	....	....	....	....	....	....	....	....	....	....	....
2010-11	**Tampa Bay**	**NHL**	**72**	**0**	**5**	**5**	**70**	**0**	**0**	**0**	**39**	**0.0**	**-7**	**0**	**0.0**	**18:43**	**18**	**1**	**2**	**3**	**8**	**0**	**1**	**0**	**20:12**
	NHL Totals		**909**	**93**	**250**	**343**	**885**	**36**	**5**	**19**	**1644**	**5.7**		**2**	**0.0**	**24:16**	**70**	**10**	**21**	**31**	**63**	**3**	**1**	**1**	**24:39**

NHL All-Rookie Team (1998)

Played in NHL All-Star Game (1999)

Signed as a free agent by **Lulea** (Sweden), December 21, 2004. Signed as a free agent by **Tampa Bay**, July 1, 2009.

OKPOSO, Kyle

(OH-poh-soh, KIGHL) **NYI**

Right wing. Shoots right. 6', 210 lbs. Born, St. Paul, MN, April 16, 1988. NY Islanders' 1st choice, 7th overall, in 2006 Entry Draft.

Season	Club	League	GP	G	A	Pts	PIM	PP	SH	GW	S	%	+/-	TF	F%	Min	GP	G	A	Pts	PIM	PP	SH	GW	Min
2004-05	Shat.-St. Mary's	High-MN	65	47	45	92	72	....	....	....	....	....	....	....	....	....	....	....	....	....	....	....	....	....	....
2005-06	Des Moines	USHL	50	27	31	58	56	....	....	....	....	....	....	....	....	....	11	5	11	*16	8	....	....	....	....
2006-07	U. of Minnesota	WCHA	40	19	21	40	34	....	....	....	....	....	....	....	....	....	....	....	....	....	....	....	....	....	....
2007-08	U. of Minnesota	WCHA	18	7	4	11	6	....	....	....	....	....	....	....	....	....	....	....	....	....	....	....	....	....	....
	NY Islanders	**NHL**	**9**	**2**	**3**	**5**	**2**	**1**	**0**	**1**	**15**	**13.3**	**3**	**0**	**0.0**	**16:28**	....	....	....	....	....	....	....	....	....
	Bridgeport	AHL	35	9	19	28	12	....	....	....	....	....	....	....	....	....	....	....	....	....	....	....	....	....	....
2008-09	**NY Islanders**	**NHL**	**65**	**18**	**21**	**39**	**36**	**9**	**0**	**3**	**165**	**10.9**	**-6**	**15**	**33.3**	**18:01**	....	....	....	....	....	....	....	....	....
	Bridgeport	AHL	....	....	....	....	....	....	....	....	....	....	....	....	....	....	2	1	0	1	2	....	....	....	....
2009-10	**NY Islanders**	**NHL**	**80**	**19**	**33**	**52**	**34**	**4**	**0**	**4**	**249**	**7.6**	**-22**	**69**	**47.8**	**20:32**	....	....	....	....	....	....	....	....	....
2010-11	**NY Islanders**	**NHL**	**38**	**5**	**15**	**20**	**40**	**0**	**0**	**2**	**72**	**6.9**	**3**	**87**	**41.4**	**16:35**	....	....	....	....	....	....	....	....	....
	NHL Totals		**192**	**44**	**72**	**116**	**112**	**14**	**0**	**10**	**501**	**8.8**		**171**	**43.3**	**18:43**	....	....	....	....	....	....	....	....	....

USHL All-Rookie Team (2006) • USHL First All-Star Team (2006) • USHL Rookie of the Year (2006) • WCHA All-Rookie Team (2007) • WCHA Second All-Star Team (2007)
• Missed majority of 2010-11 due to shoulder surgery.

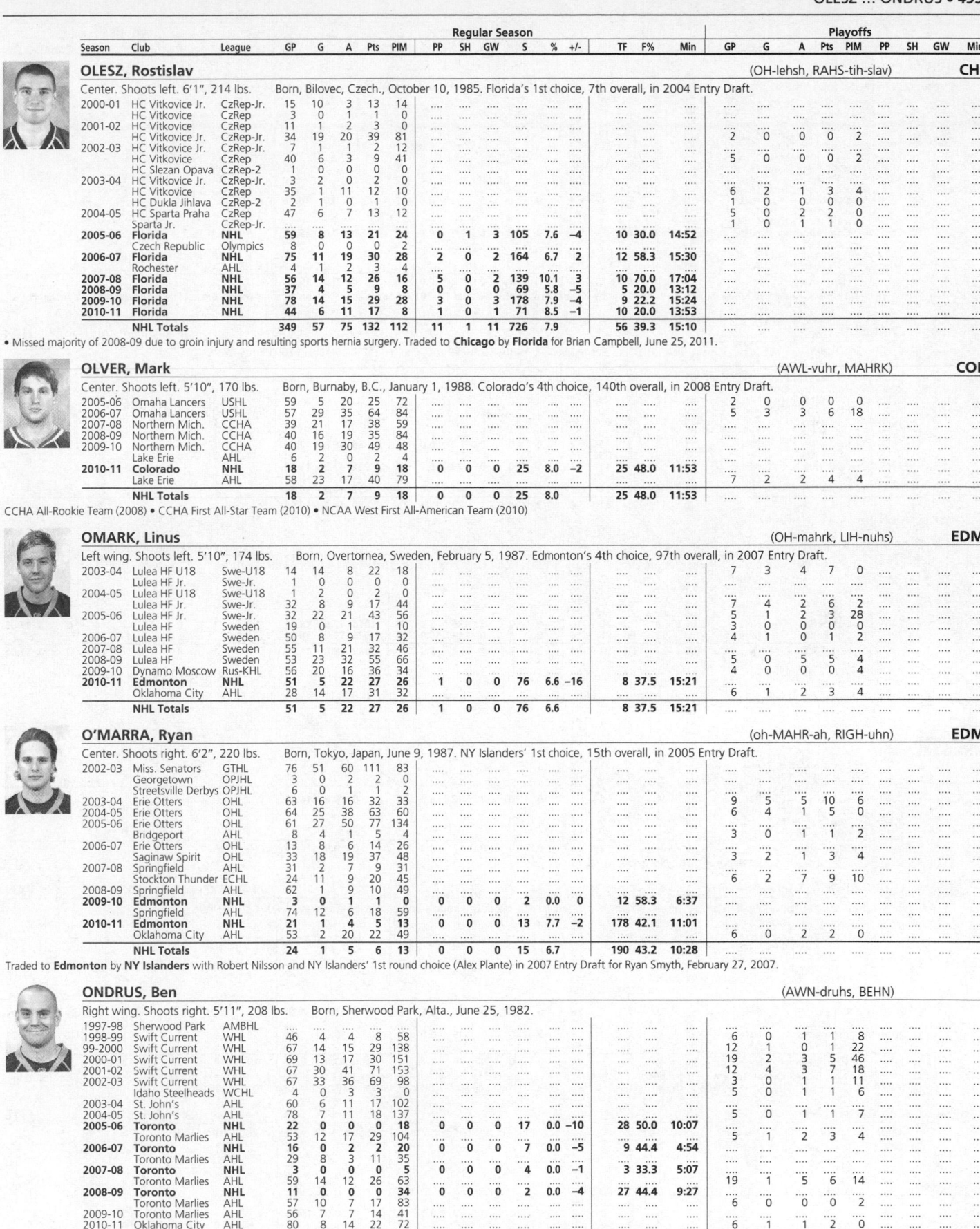

OLESZ, Rostislav

(OH-lehsh, RAHS-tih-slav) **CHI**

Center. Shoots left. 6'1", 214 lbs. Born, Bilovec, Czech., October 10, 1985. Florida's 1st choice, 7th overall, in 2004 Entry Draft.

			Regular Season														Playoffs								
Season	Club	League	GP	G	A	Pts	PIM	PP	SH	GW	S	%	+/-	TF	F%	Min	GP	G	A	Pts	PIM	PP	SH	GW	Min
2000-01	HC Vitkovice Jr.	CzRep-Jr.	15	10	3	13	14	....	....	....	....	....	....	....	....	....	....	....	....	....	....	....	....	....	....
	HC Vitkovice	CzRep	3	0	1	1	0	....	....	....	....	....	....	....	....	....	....	....	....	....	....	....	....	....	....
2001-02	HC Vitkovice	CzRep	11	1	2	3	0	....	....	....	....	....	....	....	....	....	....	....	....	....	....	....	....	....	....
	HC Vitkovice Jr.	CzRep-Jr.	34	19	20	39	81	....	....	....	....	....	....	....	....	....	2	0	0	0	2	....	....	....	....
2002-03	HC Vitkovice Jr.	CzRep-Jr.	7	1	1	2	12	....	....	....	....	....	....	....	....	....	....	....	....	....	....	....	....	....	....
	HC Vitkovice	CzRep	40	6	3	9	41	....	....	....	....	....	....	....	....	....	5	0	0	0	2	....	....	....	....
	HC Slezan Opava	CzRep-2	1	0	0	0	0	....	....	....	....	....	....	....	....	....	....	....	....	....	....	....	....	....	....
2003-04	HC Vitkovice Jr.	CzRep-Jr.	3	2	0	2	0	....	....	....	....	....	....	....	....	....	....	....	....	....	....	....	....	....	....
	HC Vitkovice	CzRep	35	1	11	12	10	....	....	....	....	....	....	....	....	....	6	2	1	3	4	....	....	....	....
	HC Dukla Jihlava	CzRep-2	2	1	0	1	0	....	....	....	....	....	....	....	....	....	1	0	0	0	0	....	....	....	....
2004-05	HC Sparta Praha	CzRep	47	6	7	13	12	....	....	....	....	....	....	....	....	....	5	0	2	2	0	....	....	....	....
	Sparta Jr.	CzRep-Jr.	....	....	....	....	....	....	....	....	....	....	....	....	....	....	1	0	1	1	0	....	....	....	....
2005-06	**Florida**	**NHL**	**59**	**8**	**13**	**21**	**24**	**0**	**1**	**3**	**105**	**7.6**	**–4**	**10**	**30.0**	**14:52**	....	....	....	....	....	....	....	....	....
	Czech Republic	Olympics	8	0	0	0	2	....	....	....	....	....	....	....	....	....	....	....	....	....	....	....	....	....	....
2006-07	**Florida**	**NHL**	**75**	**11**	**19**	**30**	**28**	**2**	**0**	**2**	**164**	**6.7**	**2**	**12**	**58.3**	**15:30**	....	....	....	....	....	....	....	....	....
	Rochester	AHL	4	1	2	3	4	....	....	....	....	....	....	....	....	....	....	....	....	....	....	....	....	....	....
2007-08	**Florida**	**NHL**	**56**	**14**	**12**	**26**	**16**	**5**	**0**	**2**	**139**	**10.1**	**3**	**10**	**70.0**	**17:04**	....	....	....	....	....	....	....	....	....
2008-09	**Florida**	**NHL**	**37**	**4**	**5**	**9**	**8**	**0**	**0**	**0**	**69**	**5.8**	**–5**	**5**	**20.0**	**13:12**	....	....	....	....	....	....	....	....	....
2009-10	**Florida**	**NHL**	**78**	**14**	**15**	**29**	**28**	**3**	**0**	**3**	**178**	**7.9**	**–4**	**9**	**22.2**	**15:24**	....	....	....	....	....	....	....	....	....
2010-11	**Florida**	**NHL**	**44**	**6**	**11**	**17**	**8**	**1**	**0**	**1**	**71**	**8.5**	**–1**	**10**	**20.0**	**13:53**	....	....	....	....	....	....	....	....	....
	NHL Totals		**349**	**57**	**75**	**132**	**112**	**11**	**1**	**11**	**726**	**7.9**		**56**	**39.3**	**15:10**	....	....	....	....	....	....	....	....	....

• Missed majority of 2008-09 due to groin injury and resulting sports hernia surgery. Traded to **Chicago** by **Florida** for Brian Campbell, June 25, 2011.

OLVER, Mark

(AWL-vuhr, MAHRK) **COL**

Center. Shoots left. 5'10", 170 lbs. Born, Burnaby, B.C., January 1, 1988. Colorado's 4th choice, 140th overall, in 2008 Entry Draft.

			Regular Season														Playoffs								
Season	Club	League	GP	G	A	Pts	PIM	PP	SH	GW	S	%	+/-	TF	F%	Min	GP	G	A	Pts	PIM	PP	SH	GW	Min
2005-06	Omaha Lancers	USHL	59	5	20	25	72	....	....	....	....	....	....	....	....	....	2	0	0	0	0	....	....	....	....
2006-07	Omaha Lancers	USHL	57	29	35	64	84	....	....	....	....	....	....	....	....	....	5	3	3	6	18	....	....	....	....
2007-08	Northern Mich.	CCHA	39	21	17	38	59	....	....	....	....	....	....	....	....	....	....	....	....	....	....	....	....	....	....
2008-09	Northern Mich.	CCHA	40	16	19	35	84	....	....	....	....	....	....	....	....	....	....	....	....	....	....	....	....	....	....
2009-10	Northern Mich.	CCHA	40	19	30	49	48	....	....	....	....	....	....	....	....	....	....	....	....	....	....	....	....	....	....
	Lake Erie	AHL	6	2	0	2	4	....	....	....	....	....	....	....	....	....	....	....	....	....	....	....	....	....	....
2010-11	**Colorado**	**NHL**	**18**	**2**	**7**	**9**	**18**	**0**	**0**	**0**	**25**	**8.0**	**–2**	**25**	**48.0**	**11:53**	....	....	....	....	....	....	....	....	....
	Lake Erie	AHL	58	23	17	40	79	....	....	....	....	....	....	....	....	....	7	2	2	4	4	....	....	....	....
	NHL Totals		**18**	**2**	**7**	**9**	**18**	**0**	**0**	**0**	**25**	**8.0**		**25**	**48.0**	**11:53**	....	....	....	....	....	....	....	....	....

CCHA All-Rookie Team (2008) • CCHA First All-Star Team (2010) • NCAA West First All-American Team (2010)

OMARK, Linus

(OH-mahrk, LIH-nuhs) **EDM**

Left wing. Shoots left. 5'10", 174 lbs. Born, Overtornea, Sweden, February 5, 1987. Edmonton's 4th choice, 97th overall, in 2007 Entry Draft.

			Regular Season														Playoffs								
Season	Club	League	GP	G	A	Pts	PIM	PP	SH	GW	S	%	+/-	TF	F%	Min	GP	G	A	Pts	PIM	PP	SH	GW	Min
2003-04	Lulea HF U18	Swe-U18	14	14	8	22	18	....	....	....	....	....	....	....	....	....	7	3	4	7	0	....	....	....	....
	Lulea HF Jr.	Swe-Jr.	1	0	0	0	0	....	....	....	....	....	....	....	....	....	....	....	....	....	....	....	....	....	....
2004-05	Lulea HF U18	Swe-U18	1	2	0	2	0	....	....	....	....	....	....	....	....	....	....	....	....	....	....	....	....	....	....
	Lulea HF Jr.	Swe-Jr.	32	8	9	17	44	....	....	....	....	....	....	....	....	....	7	4	2	6	2	....	....	....	....
2005-06	Lulea HF Jr.	Swe-Jr.	32	22	21	43	56	....	....	....	....	....	....	....	....	....	5	1	2	3	28	....	....	....	....
	Lulea HF	Sweden	19	0	1	1	10	....	....	....	....	....	....	....	....	....	3	0	0	0	0	....	....	....	....
2006-07	Lulea HF	Sweden	50	8	9	17	32	....	....	....	....	....	....	....	....	....	4	1	0	1	2	....	....	....	....
2007-08	Lulea HF	Sweden	55	11	21	32	46	....	....	....	....	....	....	....	....	....	....	....	....	....	....	....	....	....	....
2008-09	Lulea HF	Sweden	53	23	32	55	66	....	....	....	....	....	....	....	....	....	5	0	5	5	4	....	....	....	....
2009-10	Dynamo Moscow	Rus-KHL	56	20	16	36	34	....	....	....	....	....	....	....	....	....	4	0	0	0	4	....	....	....	....
2010-11	**Edmonton**	**NHL**	**51**	**5**	**22**	**27**	**26**	**1**	**0**	**0**	**76**	**6.6**	**–16**	**8**	**37.5**	**15:21**	....	....	....	....	....	....	....	....	....
	Oklahoma City	AHL	28	14	17	31	32	....	....	....	....	....	....	....	....	....	6	1	2	3	4	....	....	....	....
	NHL Totals		**51**	**5**	**22**	**27**	**26**	**1**	**0**	**0**	**76**	**6.6**		**8**	**37.5**	**15:21**	....	....	....	....	....	....	....	....	....

O'MARRA, Ryan

(oh-MAHR-ah, RIGH-uhn) **EDM**

Center. Shoots right. 6'2", 220 lbs. Born, Tokyo, Japan, June 9, 1987. NY Islanders' 1st choice, 15th overall, in 2005 Entry Draft.

			Regular Season														Playoffs								
Season	Club	League	GP	G	A	Pts	PIM	PP	SH	GW	S	%	+/-	TF	F%	Min	GP	G	A	Pts	PIM	PP	SH	GW	Min
2002-03	Miss. Senators	GTHL	76	51	60	111	83	....	....	....	....	....	....	....	....	....	....	....	....	....	....	....	....	....	....
	Georgetown	OPJHL	3	0	2	2	0	....	....	....	....	....	....	....	....	....	....	....	....	....	....	....	....	....	....
	Streetsville Derbys	OPJHL	6	0	1	1	2	....	....	....	....	....	....	....	....	....	....	....	....	....	....	....	....	....	....
2003-04	Erie Otters	OHL	63	16	16	32	33	....	....	....	....	....	....	....	....	....	9	5	5	10	6	....	....	....	....
2004-05	Erie Otters	OHL	64	25	38	63	60	....	....	....	....	....	....	....	....	....	6	4	1	5	0	....	....	....	....
2005-06	Erie Otters	OHL	61	27	50	77	134	....	....	....	....	....	....	....	....	....	....	....	....	....	....	....	....	....	....
	Bridgeport	AHL	8	4	1	5	4	....	....	....	....	....	....	....	....	....	3	0	1	1	2	....	....	....	....
2006-07	Erie Otters	OHL	13	8	6	14	26	....	....	....	....	....	....	....	....	....	....	....	....	....	....	....	....	....	....
	Saginaw Spirit	OHL	33	18	19	37	48	....	....	....	....	....	....	....	....	....	3	2	1	3	4	....	....	....	....
2007-08	Springfield	AHL	31	2	7	9	31	....	....	....	....	....	....	....	....	....	....	....	....	....	....	....	....	....	....
	Stockton Thunder	ECHL	24	11	9	20	45	....	....	....	....	....	....	....	....	....	6	2	7	9	10	....	....	....	....
2008-09	Springfield	AHL	62	1	9	10	49	....	....	....	....	....	....	....	....	....	....	....	....	....	....	....	....	....	....
2009-10	**Edmonton**	**NHL**	**3**	**0**	**1**	**1**	**0**	**0**	**0**	**0**	**2**	**0.0**	**0**	**12**	**58.3**	**6:37**	....	....	....	....	....	....	....	....	....
	Springfield	AHL	74	12	6	18	59	....	....	....	....	....	....	....	....	....	....	....	....	....	....	....	....	....	....
2010-11	**Edmonton**	**NHL**	**21**	**1**	**4**	**5**	**13**	**0**	**0**	**0**	**13**	**7.7**	**–2**	**178**	**42.1**	**11:01**	....	....	....	....	....	....	....	....	....
	Oklahoma City	AHL	53	2	20	22	49	....	....	....	....	....	....	....	....	....	6	0	2	2	0	....	....	....	....
	NHL Totals		**24**	**1**	**5**	**6**	**13**	**0**	**0**	**0**	**15**	**6.7**		**190**	**43.2**	**10:28**	....	....	....	....	....	....	....	....	....

Traded to **Edmonton** by **NY Islanders** with Robert Nilsson and NY Islanders' 1st round choice (Alex Plante) in 2007 Entry Draft for Ryan Smyth, February 27, 2007.

ONDRUS, Ben

(AWN-druhs, BEHN)

Right wing. Shoots right. 5'11", 208 lbs. Born, Sherwood Park, Alta., June 25, 1982.

			Regular Season														Playoffs								
Season	Club	League	GP	G	A	Pts	PIM	PP	SH	GW	S	%	+/-	TF	F%	Min	GP	G	A	Pts	PIM	PP	SH	GW	Min
1997-98	Sherwood Park	AMBHL	....	....	....	....	....	....	....	....	....	....	....	....	....	....	....	....	....	....	....	....	....	....	....
1998-99	Swift Current	WHL	46	4	4	8	58	....	....	....	....	....	....	....	....	....	6	0	1	1	8	....	....	....	....
99-2000	Swift Current	WHL	67	14	15	29	138	....	....	....	....	....	....	....	....	....	12	1	0	1	22	....	....	....	....
2000-01	Swift Current	WHL	69	13	17	30	151	....	....	....	....	....	....	....	....	....	19	2	3	5	46	....	....	....	....
2001-02	Swift Current	WHL	67	30	41	71	153	....	....	....	....	....	....	....	....	....	12	4	3	7	18	....	....	....	....
2002-03	Swift Current	WHL	67	33	36	69	98	....	....	....	....	....	....	....	....	....	3	0	1	1	11	....	....	....	....
	Idaho Steelheads	WCHL	4	0	3	3	0	....	....	....	....	....	....	....	....	....	5	0	1	1	6	....	....	....	....
2003-04	St. John's	AHL	60	6	11	17	102	....	....	....	....	....	....	....	....	....	....	....	....	....	....	....	....	....	....
2004-05	St. John's	AHL	78	7	11	18	137	....	....	....	....	....	....	....	....	....	5	0	1	1	7	....	....	....	....
2005-06	**Toronto**	**NHL**	**22**	**0**	**0**	**0**	**18**	**0**	**0**	**0**	**17**	**0.0**	**–10**	**28**	**50.0**	**10:07**	....	....	....	....	....	....	....	....	....
	Toronto Marlies	AHL	53	12	17	29	104	....	....	....	....	....	....	....	....	....	5	1	2	3	4	....	....	....	....
2006-07	**Toronto**	**NHL**	**16**	**0**	**2**	**2**	**20**	**0**	**0**	**0**	**7**	**0.0**	**–5**	**9**	**44.4**	**4:54**	....	....	....	....	....	....	....	....	....
	Toronto Marlies	AHL	29	8	3	11	35	....	....	....	....	....	....	....	....	....	....	....	....	....	....	....	....	....	....
2007-08	**Toronto**	**NHL**	**3**	**0**	**0**	**0**	**5**	**0**	**0**	**0**	**4**	**0.0**	**–1**	**3**	**33.3**	**5:07**	....	....	....	....	....	....	....	....	....
	Toronto Marlies	AHL	59	14	12	26	63	....	....	....	....	....	....	....	....	....	19	1	5	6	14	....	....	....	....
2008-09	**Toronto**	**NHL**	**11**	**0**	**0**	**0**	**34**	**0**	**0**	**0**	**2**	**0.0**	**–4**	**27**	**44.4**	**9:27**	....	....	....	....	....	....	....	....	....
	Toronto Marlies	AHL	57	10	7	17	83	....	....	....	....	....	....	....	....	....	6	0	0	0	2	....	....	....	....
2009-10	Toronto Marlies	AHL	56	7	7	14	41	....	....	....	....	....	....	....	....	....	....	....	....	....	....	....	....	....	....
2010-11	Oklahoma City	AHL	80	8	14	22	72	....	....	....	....	....	....	....	....	....	6	1	1	2	0	....	....	....	....
	NHL Totals		**52**	**0**	**2**	**2**	**77**	**0**	**0**	**0**	**30**	**0.0**		**67**	**46.3**	**8:05**	....	....	....	....	....	....	....	....	....

Signed as a free agent by **Idaho** (WCHL), March 23, 2003. Signed as a free agent by **St. John's** (AHL), September 1, 2003. Signed as a free agent by **Toronto**, May 27, 2004. Signed as a free agent by **Edmonton**, July 9, 2010.

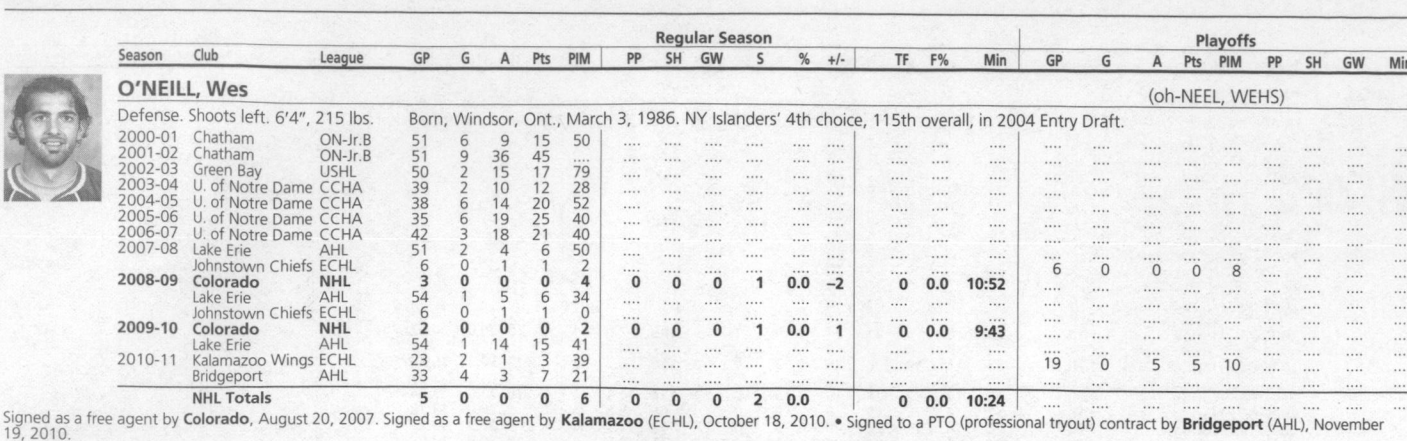

							Regular Season										Playoffs							
Season	Club	League	GP	G	A	Pts	PIM	PP	SH	GW	S	%	+/-	TF	F%	Min	GP	G	A	Pts	PIM	PP	SH	GW	Min

O'NEILL, Wes (oh-NEEL, WEHS)

Defense. Shoots left. 6'4", 215 lbs. Born, Windsor, Ont., March 3, 1986. NY Islanders' 4th choice, 115th overall, in 2004 Entry Draft.

Season	Club	League	GP	G	A	Pts	PIM	PP	SH	GW	S	%	+/-	TF	F%	Min	GP	G	A	Pts	PIM	PP	SH	GW	Min
2000-01	Chatham	ON-Jr.B	51	6	9	15	50	....	....	....	....	....	....	....	....	....	....	....	....	....	....				
2001-02	Chatham	ON-Jr.B	51	9	36	45	....	....	....	....	....	....	....	....	....	....	....	....	....	....	....				
2002-03	Green Bay	USHL	50	2	15	17	79	....	....	....	....	....	....	....	....	....	....	....	....	....	....				
2003-04	U. of Notre Dame	CCHA	39	2	10	12	28	....	....	....	....	....	....	....	....	....	....	....	....	....	....				
2004-05	U. of Notre Dame	CCHA	38	6	14	20	52	....	....	....	....	....	....	....	....	....	....	....	....	....	....				
2005-06	U. of Notre Dame	CCHA	35	6	19	25	40	....	....	....	....	....	....	....	....	....	....	....	....	....	....				
2006-07	U. of Notre Dame	CCHA	42	3	18	21	40	....	....	....	....	....	....	....	....	....	....	....	....	....	....				
2007-08	Lake Erie	AHL	51	2	4	6	50	....	....	....	....	....	....	....	....	....	6	0	0	0	8				
	Johnstown Chiefs	ECHL	6	0	1	1	2	....	....	....	....	....	....	....	....	....	....	....	....	....	....				
2008-09	**Colorado**	**NHL**	**3**	**0**	**0**	**0**	**4**	0	0	0	1	0.0	–2	0	0.0	10:52	....	....	....	....	....				
	Lake Erie	AHL	54	1	5	6	34	....	....	....	....	....	....	....	....	....	....	....	....	....	....				
	Johnstown Chiefs	ECHL	6	0	1	1	0	....	....	....	....	....	....	....	....	....	....	....	....	....	....				
2009-10	**Colorado**	**NHL**	**2**	**0**	**0**	**0**	**2**	0	0	0	1	0.0	1	0	0.0	9:43	....	....	....	....	....				
	Lake Erie	AHL	54	1	14	15	41	....	....	....	....	....	....	....	....	....	....	....	....	....	....				
2010-11	Kalamazoo Wings	ECHL	23	2	1	3	39	....	....	....	....	....	....	....	....	....	19	0	5	5	10				
	Bridgeport	AHL	33	4	3	7	21	....	....	....	....	....	....	....	....	....	....	....	....	....	....				
	NHL Totals		**5**	**0**	**0**	**0**	**6**	0	0	0	2	0.0		0	0.0	10:24									

Signed as a free agent by **Colorado**, August 20, 2007. Signed as a free agent by **Kalamazoo** (ECHL), October 18, 2010. • Signed to a PTO (professional tryout) contract by **Bridgeport** (AHL), November 19, 2010.

O'REILLY, Cal (oh-RIGH-lee, KAL) **NSH**

Center. Shoots left. 6', 188 lbs. Born, Toronto, Ont., September 30, 1986. Nashville's 4th choice, 150th overall, in 2005 Entry Draft.

Season	Club	League	GP	G	A	Pts	PIM	PP	SH	GW	S	%	+/-	TF	F%	Min	GP	G	A	Pts	PIM	PP	SH	GW	Min
2002-03	St. Mary's Lincolns	ON-Jr.B	46	11	19	30	2	....	....	....	....	....	....	....	....	....	....	....	....	....	....				
2003-04	Windsor Spitfires	OHL	61	3	18	21	2	....	....	....	....	....	....	....	....	....	3	0	1	1	0				
2004-05	Windsor Spitfires	OHL	68	24	50	74	16	....	....	....	....	....	....	....	....	....	11	4	5	9	4				
2005-06	Windsor Spitfires	OHL	68	18	81	99	8	....	....	....	....	....	....	....	....	....	7	3	8	11	0				
	Milwaukee	AHL	2	0	0	0	0	....	....	....	....	....	....	....	....	....	10	0	1	1	0				
2006-07	Milwaukee	AHL	78	18	47	65	20	....	....	....	....	....	....	....	....	....	4	1	2	3	0				
2007-08	Milwaukee	AHL	80	16	63	79	22	....	....	....	....	....	....	....	....	....	6	1	2	3	0				
2008-09	**Nashville**	**NHL**	**11**	**3**	**2**	**5**	**2**	0	0	0	6	50.0	2	88	39.8	12:36	....	....	....	....	....				
	Milwaukee	AHL	67	13	56	69	20	....	....	....	....	....	....	....	....	....	11	2	6	8	0				
2009-10	**Nashville**	**NHL**	**31**	**2**	**9**	**11**	**4**	1	0	0	23	8.7	1	281	47.3	13:38	....	....	....	....	....				
	Milwaukee	AHL	35	9	31	40	8	....	....	....	....	....	....	....	....	....	....	....	....	....	....				
2010-11	**Nashville**	**NHL**	**38**	**6**	**12**	**18**	**2**	1	0	1	44	13.6	4	497	46.5	16:54	....	....	....	....	....				
	NHL Totals		**80**	**11**	**23**	**34**	**8**	2	0	1	73	15.1		866	46.1	15:03									

• Missed majority of 2010-11 due to leg injury.

O'REILLY, Ryan (oh-RIGH-lee, RIGH-uhn) **COL**

Center. Shoots left. 6', 200 lbs. Born, Clinton, Ont., February 7, 1991. Colorado's 2nd choice, 33rd overall, in 2009 Entry Draft.

Season	Club	League	GP	G	A	Pts	PIM	PP	SH	GW	S	%	+/-	TF	F%	Min	GP	G	A	Pts	PIM	PP	SH	GW	Min
2006-07	Tor. Jr. Canadiens	GTHL	50	31	43	74	....	....	....	....	....	....	....	....	....	....	....	....	....	....	....				
	Tor. Canadiens	OPJHL	1	1	0	1	0	....	....	....	....	....	....	....	....	....	....	....	....	....	....				
2007-08	Erie Otters	OHL	61	19	33	52	14	....	....	....	....	....	....	....	....	....	5	0	5	5	2				
2008-09	Erie Otters	OHL	68	16	50	66	26	....	....	....	....	....	....	....	....	....	....	....	....	....	....				
2009-10	**Colorado**	**NHL**	**81**	**8**	**18**	**26**	**18**	0	2	1	135	5.9	4	1014	47.8	16:46	6	1	0	1	2	0	0	1	17:05
2010-11	**Colorado**	**NHL**	**74**	**13**	**13**	**26**	**16**	2	1	0	119	10.9	–7	1025	51.8	16:03	....	....	....	....	....				
	NHL Totals		**155**	**21**	**31**	**52**	**34**	2	3	2	254	8.3		2039	49.8	16:26	6	1	0	1	2	0	0	1	17:05

ORESKOVIC, Phil (oh-rehs-KOH-vihch, FIHL)

Defense. Shoots right. 6'4", 217 lbs. Born, North York, Ont., January 26, 1987. Toronto's 2nd choice, 82nd overall, in 2005 Entry Draft.

Season	Club	League	GP	G	A	Pts	PIM	PP	SH	GW	S	%	+/-	TF	F%	Min	GP	G	A	Pts	PIM	PP	SH	GW	Min
2003-04	Brampton	OHL	66	0	7	7	64	....	....	....	....	....	....	....	....	....	12	0	2	2	16				
2004-05	Brampton	OHL	61	1	6	7	147	....	....	....	....	....	....	....	....	....	6	0	0	0	4				
2005-06	Brampton	OHL	65	3	9	12	202	....	....	....	....	....	....	....	....	....	11	0	0	0	34				
2006-07	Brampton	OHL	36	2	12	14	113	....	....	....	....	....	....	....	....	....	....	....	....	....	....				
	Owen Sound	OHL	26	1	7	8	66	....	....	....	....	....	....	....	....	....	4	0	0	0	2				
	Toronto Marlies	AHL	3	0	1	1	2	....	....	....	....	....	....	....	....	....	....	....	....	....	....				
2007-08	Toronto Marlies	AHL	54	1	9	10	68	....	....	....	....	....	....	....	....	....	7	0	1	1	11				
	Columbia Inferno	ECHL	13	0	4	4	19	....	....	....	....	....	....	....	....	....	....	....	....	....	....				
2008-09	**Toronto**	**NHL**	**10**	**1**	**1**	**2**	**21**	0	0	0	12	8.3	–2	0	0.0	16:14	....	....	....	....	....				
	Toronto Marlies	AHL	65	1	10	11	103	....	....	....	....	....	....	....	....	....	6	0	0	0	12				
2009-10	Toronto Marlies	AHL	74	2	7	9	142	....	....	....	....	....	....	....	....	....	....	....	....	....	....				
2010-11	Hershey Bears	AHL	14	0	0	0	22	....	....	....	....	....	....	....	....	....	1	0	0	0	0				
	NHL Totals		**10**	**1**	**1**	**2**	**21**	0	0	0	12	8.3		0	0.0	16:14	....	....	....	....	....				

Signed to a PTO (professional tryout) contract by **Hershey** (AHL), November 11, 2010.

ORESKOVICH, Victor (oh-rehs-KOH-vihch, VIHK-tohr) **VAN**

Right wing. Shoots right. 6'3", 215 lbs. Born, Whitby, Ont., August 15, 1986. Colorado's 2nd choice, 55th overall, in 2004 Entry Draft.

Season	Club	League	GP	G	A	Pts	PIM	PP	SH	GW	S	%	+/-	TF	F%	Min	GP	G	A	Pts	PIM	PP	SH	GW	Min
2002-03	Milton IceHawks	OPJHL	49	28	46	74	51	....	....	....	....	....	....	....	....	....	....	....	....	....	....				
2003-04	Green Bay	USHL	58	11	26	37	33	....	....	....	....	....	....	....	....	....	....	....	....	....	....				
2004-05	U. of Notre Dame	CCHA	37	1	2	3	69	....	....	....	....	....	....	....	....	....	....	....	....	....	....				
2005-06	U. of Notre Dame	CCHA	9	2	1	3	8	....	....	....	....	....	....	....	....	....	....	....	....	....	....				
	Kitchener Rangers	OHL	19	6	10	16	16	....	....	....	....	....	....	....	....	....	5	0	2	2	4				
2006-07	Kitchener Rangers	OHL	62	28	32	60	48	....	....	....	....	....	....	....	....	....	5	2	0	2	4				
2007-08				OUT OF HOCKEY – RETIRED																					
2008-09				OUT OF HOCKEY – RETIRED																					
2009-10	**Florida**	**NHL**	**50**	**2**	**4**	**6**	**26**	0	0	0	55	3.6	–8	3	33.3	8:53	....	....	....	....	....				
	Rochester	AHL	34	6	9	15	18	....	....	....	....	....	....	....	....	....	6	0	0	0	10				
2010-11	**Vancouver**	**NHL**	**16**	**0**	**3**	**3**	**8**	0	0	0	19	0.0	1	2	50.0	7:54	19	0	0	0	12	0	0	0	6:21
	Manitoba Moose	AHL	40	4	8	12	38	....	....	....	....	....	....	....	....	....	....	....	....	....	....				
	NHL Totals		**66**	**2**	**7**	**9**	**34**	0	0	0	74	2.7		5	40.0	8:39	19	0	0	0	12	0	0	0	6:21

• Assigned to **Lake Erie** (AHL) but failed to report. He was suspended by Colorado and then announced his retirement, September 17, 2007. Signed as a free agent by **Florida**, October 9, 2009. Traded to **Vancouver** by **Florida** with Keith Ballard for Steve Bernier, Michael Grabner and Vancouver's 1st round choice (Quinton Howden) in 2010 Entry Draft, June 25, 2010.

ORPIK, Brooks (OHR-pihk, BRUKS) **PIT**

Defense. Shoots left. 6'2", 219 lbs. Born, San Francisco, CA, September 26, 1980. Pittsburgh's 1st choice, 18th overall, in 2000 Entry Draft.

Season	Club	League	GP	G	A	Pts	PIM	PP	SH	GW	S	%	+/-	TF	F%	Min	GP	G	A	Pts	PIM	PP	SH	GW	Min
1996-97	Thayer Academy	High-MA	20	4	1	5	....	....	....	....	....	....	....	....	....	....	....	....	....	....	....				
1997-98	Thayer Academy	High-MA	22	0	7	7	....	....	....	....	....	....	....	....	....	....	....	....	....	....	....				
1998-99	Boston College	H-East	41	1	10	11	*96	....	....	....	....	....	....	....	....	....	....	....	....	....	....				
99-2000	Boston College	H-East	38	1	9	10	102	....	....	....	....	....	....	....	....	....	....	....	....	....	....				
2000-01	Boston College	H-East	40	0	20	20	*124	....	....	....	....	....	....	....	....	....	....	....	....	....	....				
2001-02	Wilkes-Barre	AHL	78	2	18	20	99	....	....	....	....	....	....	....	....	....	....	....	....	....	....				
2002-03	**Pittsburgh**	**NHL**	**6**	**0**	**0**	**0**	**2**	0	0	0	2	0.0	–5	0	0.0	18:19	....	....	....	....	....				
	Wilkes-Barre	AHL	71	4	14	18	105	....	....	....	....	....	....	....	....	....	6	0	0	0	14				
2003-04	**Pittsburgh**	**NHL**	**79**	**1**	**9**	**10**	**127**	0	0	0	56	1.8	–36	0	0.0	18:25	....	....	....	....	....				
	Wilkes-Barre	AHL	3	0	0	0	2	....	....	....	....	....	....	....	....	....	24	0	4	4	53				
2005-06	**Pittsburgh**	**NHL**	**64**	**2**	**7**	**9**	**124**	0	0	0	32	6.3	–3	0	0.0	18:50	....	....	....	....	....				
2006-07	**Pittsburgh**	**NHL**	**70**	**0**	**6**	**6**	**82**	0	0	0	59	0.0	4	0	0.0	16:37	5	0	0	0	8	0	0	0	15:43
2007-08	**Pittsburgh**	**NHL**	**78**	**1**	**10**	**11**	**57**	0	0	0	50	2.0	11	0	0.0	16:58	20	0	2	2	18	0	0	0	20:47
2008-09 ◆	**Pittsburgh**	**NHL**	**79**	**2**	**17**	**19**	**73**	1	0	0	39	5.1	10	0	0.0	20:20	24	0	4	4	22	0	0	0	20:04

			Regular Season														Playoffs								
Season	Club	League	GP	G	A	Pts	PIM	PP	SH	GW	S	%	+/-	TF	F%	Min	GP	G	A	Pts	PIM	PP	SH	GW	Min
2009-10	Pittsburgh	NHL	73	2	23	25	64	0	0	0	61	3.3	6	0	0.0	20:06	13	0	2	2	12	0	0	0	21:40
	United States	Olympics	6	0	0	0	0	....	....	....	....	....	....	....	....	....	....	....	....	....	....	....	....	....	....
2010-11	Pittsburgh	NHL	63	1	12	13	66	0	0	0	56	1.8	12	1	100.0	20:53	7	0	3	3	14	0	0	0	24:11
	NHL Totals		512	9	84	93	595	1	0	0	355	2.5		1	100.0	18:50	69	0	11	11	74	0	0	0	20:41

ORR, Colton

(OHR, KOHL-tuhn) **TOR**

Right wing. Shoots right. 6'3", 222 lbs. Born, Winnipeg, Man., March 3, 1982.

Season	Club	League	GP	G	A	Pts	PIM	PP	SH	GW	S	%	+/-	TF	F%	Min	GP	G	A	Pts	PIM	PP	SH	GW	Min
1998-99	St. Boniface	MJHL	STATISTICS NOT AVAILABLE																						
	Swift Current	WHL	2	0	0	0	0	....	....	....	....	....	....	....	....	....	....	....	....	....	....	....	....	....	....
99-2000	Swift Current	WHL	61	3	2	5	130	....	....	....	....	....	....	....	....	....	12	1	0	1	25	....	....	....	....
2000-01	Swift Current	WHL	19	0	4	4	67	....	....	....	....	....	....	....	....	....	....	....	....	....	....	....	....	....	....
	Kamloops Blazers	WHL	41	8	1	9	179	....	....	....	....	....	....	....	....	....	3	0	0	0	20	....	....	....	....
2001-02	Kamloops Blazers	WHL	1	0	0	0	7	....	....	....	....	....	....	....	....	....	2	0	0	0	2	....	....	....	....
2002-03	Kamloops Blazers	WHL	3	2	0	2	17	....	....	....	....	....	....	....	....	....	....	....	....	....	....	....	....	....	....
	Regina Pats	WHL	37	6	2	8	170	....	....	....	....	....	....	....	....	....	3	0	0	0	19	....	....	....	....
	Providence Bruins	AHL	1	0	0	0	7	....	....	....	....	....	....	....	....	....	....	....	....	....	....	....	....	....	....
2003-04	Boston	NHL	1	0	0	0	0	0	0	0	0	0.0	–1	0	0.0	2:13	....	....	....	....	....	....	....	....	....
	Providence Bruins	AHL	64	1	4	5	257	....	....	....	....	....	....	....	....	....	2	0	0	0	9	....	....	....	....
2004-05	Providence Bruins	AHL	61	1	6	7	279	....	....	....	....	....	....	....	....	....	17	1	0	1	44	....	....	....	....
2005-06	Boston	NHL	20	0	0	0	27	0	0	0	1	0.0	0	0	0.0	1:49	....	....	....	....	....	....	....	....	....
	NY Rangers	NHL	15	0	1	1	44	0	0	0	0	0.0	1	0	0.0	4:19	1	0	0	0	2	0	0	0	4:17
2006-07	NY Rangers	NHL	53	2	1	3	126	0	0	1	23	8.7	–2	0	0.0	5:20	4	0	0	0	12	0	0	0	4:57
2007-08	NY Rangers	NHL	74	1	1	2	159	0	0	1	24	4.2	–13	2	50.0	7:49	2	0	0	0	0	0	0	0	4:26
2008-09	NY Rangers	NHL	82	1	4	5	193	0	0	0	40	2.5	–15	16	25.0	6:29	5	0	0	0	16	0	0	0	3:50
2009-10	Toronto	NHL	82	4	2	6	239	0	0	1	43	9.3	–4	2	50.0	6:52	....	....	....	....	....	....	....	....	....
2010-11	Toronto	NHL	46	2	0	2	128	0	0	1	14	14.3	–1	1	0.0	5:04	....	....	....	....	....	....	....	....	....
	NHL Totals		373	10	9	19	916	0	0	4	145	6.9		21	28.6	6:09	12	0	0	0	30	0	0	0	4:21

Signed as a free agent by **Boston**, September 19, 2001. • Missed majority of 2001-02 due to wrist injury vs. Red Deer (WHL), October 20, 2001. Claimed on waivers by **NY Rangers** from **Boston**, November 29, 2005. Signed as a free agent by **Toronto**, July 1, 2009.

ORTMEYER, Jed

(OHRT-migh-uhr, JEHD) **MIN**

Center. Shoots right. 6', 200 lbs. Born, Omaha, NE, September 3, 1978.

Season	Club	League	GP	G	A	Pts	PIM	PP	SH	GW	S	%	+/-	TF	F%	Min	GP	G	A	Pts	PIM	PP	SH	GW	Min
1997-98	Omaha Lancers	USHL	54	23	25	48	52	....	....	....	....	....	....	....	....	....	14	3	4	7	31	....	....	....	....
1998-99	Omaha Lancers	USHL	52	23	36	59	81	....	....	....	....	....	....	....	....	....	12	5	6	11	16	....	....	....	....
99-2000	U. of Michigan	CCHA	41	8	16	24	40	....	....	....	....	....	....	....	....	....	....	....	....	....	....	....	....	....	....
2000-01	U. of Michigan	CCHA	27	10	11	21	52	....	....	....	....	....	....	....	....	....	....	....	....	....	....	....	....	....	....
2001-02	U. of Michigan	CCHA	41	15	23	38	40	....	....	....	....	....	....	....	....	....	....	....	....	....	....	....	....	....	....
2002-03	U. of Michigan	CCHA	36	18	16	34	48	....	....	....	....	....	....	....	....	....	....	....	....	....	....	....	....	....	....
2003-04	NY Rangers	NHL	58	2	4	6	16	0	0	0	48	4.2	–10	16	31.3	9:52	....	....	....	....	....	....	....	....	....
	Hartford	AHL	13	2	8	10	4	....	....	....	....	....	....	....	....	....	16	5	2	7	6	....	....	....	....
2004-05	Hartford	AHL	61	7	20	27	63	....	....	....	....	....	....	....	....	....	6	0	1	1	4	....	....	....	....
2005-06	NY Rangers	NHL	78	5	2	7	38	0	0	1	90	5.6	2	21	23.8	11:06	4	1	0	1	4	0	0	0	11:40
2006-07	NY Rangers	NHL	41	2	9	11	22	0	1	0	67	3.0	7	8	12.5	12:35	9	0	0	0	2	0	0	0	9:37
	Hartford	AHL	8	1	3	4	6	....	....	....	....	....	....	....	....	....	....	....	....	....	....	....	....	....	....
2007-08	Nashville	NHL	51	4	4	8	32	0	1	0	68	5.9	–8	12	50.0	12:27	....	....	....	....	....	....	....	....	....
2008-09	Nashville	NHL	2	0	0	0	0	0	0	0	4	0.0	0	0	0.0	11:01	....	....	....	....	....	....	....	....	....
	Milwaukee	AHL	55	10	13	23	51	....	....	....	....	....	....	....	....	....	11	1	6	7	8	....	....	....	....
2009-10	San Jose	NHL	76	8	11	19	37	0	0	1	131	6.1	4	18	27.8	11:31	4	0	1	1	0	0	0	0	6:59
2010-11	San Antonio	AHL	20	2	1	3	16	....	....	....	....	....	....	....	....	....	....	....	....	....	....	....	....	....	....
	Houston Aeros	AHL	40	6	10	16	29	....	....	....	....	....	....	....	....	....	24	6	7	13	4	....	....	....	....
	Minnesota	NHL	4	0	0	0	2	0	0	0	5	0.0	–1	0	0.0	9:24	....	....	....	....	....	....	....	....	....
	NHL Totals		310	21	30	51	147	0	2	2	413	5.1		75	29.3	11:22	17	1	1	2	6	0	0	0	9:29

Signed as a free agent by **NY Rangers**, May 10, 2003. Signed as a free agent by **Nashville**, July 2, 2007. Signed as a free agent by **San Jose**, July 16, 2009. Signed to a PTO (professional tryout) contract by **San Antonio** (AHL), October 29, 2010. Signed to a PTO (professional tryout) contract by **Houston** (AHL), January 1, 2011. Signed as a free agent by **Minnesota**, January 4, 2011.

OSALA, Oskar

(OH-sa-la, AWZ-kuhr) **CAR**

Left wing. Shoots left. 6'4", 219 lbs. Born, Vaasa, Finland, December 26, 1987. Washington's 6th choice, 97th overall, in 2006 Entry Draft.

Season	Club	League	GP	G	A	Pts	PIM	PP	SH	GW	S	%	+/-	TF	F%	Min	GP	G	A	Pts	PIM	PP	SH	GW	Min
2003-04	Sport Vaasa U18	Fin-U18	25	19	18	37	32	....	....	....	....	....	....	....	....	....	....	....	....	....	....	....	....	....	....
	Sport Vaasa Jr.	Fin-Jr.	2	0	0	0	4	....	....	....	....	....	....	....	....	....	....	....	....	....	....	....	....	....	....
	Sport Vaasa	Finland-2	5	0	0	0	0	....	....	....	....	....	....	....	....	....	....	....	....	....	....	....	....	....	....
2004-05	Sport Vaasa U18	Fin-U18	4	4	2	6	16	....	....	....	....	....	....	....	....	....	....	....	....	....	....	....	....	....	....
	Sport Vaasa Jr.	Fin-Jr.	19	13	14	27	28	....	....	....	....	....	....	....	....	....	2	0	0	0	2	....	....	....	....
	Sport Vaasa	Finland-2	21	1	4	5	6	....	....	....	....	....	....	....	....	....	7	0	0	0	6	....	....	....	....
2005-06	Mississauga	OHL	68	17	26	43	86	....	....	....	....	....	....	....	....	....	....	....	....	....	....	....	....	....	....
2006-07	Suomi U20	Finland-2	2	1	0	1	0	....	....	....	....	....	....	....	....	....	....	....	....	....	....	....	....	....	....
	Mississauga	OHL	54	22	22	44	81	....	....	....	....	....	....	....	....	....	5	2	2	4	0	....	....	....	....
2007-08	Blues Espoo	Finland	53	18	17	35	62	....	....	....	....	....	....	....	....	....	17	7	3	10	8	....	....	....	....
2008-09	Washington	NHL	2	0	0	0	0	0	0	0	1	0.0	–1	0	0.0	8:44	....	....	....	....	....	....	....	....	....
	Hershey Bears	AHL	75	23	14	37	47	....	....	....	....	....	....	....	....	....	22	6	4	10	17	....	....	....	....
2009-10	Carolina	NHL	1	0	0	0	0	0	0	0	1	0.0	0	0	0.0	6:46	....	....	....	....	....	....	....	....	....
	Hershey Bears	AHL	53	15	14	29	57	....	....	....	....	....	....	....	....	....	....	....	....	....	....	....	....	....	....
	Albany River Rats	AHL	16	9	3	12	11	....	....	....	....	....	....	....	....	....	8	2	1	3	2	....	....	....	....
2010-11	Charlotte	AHL	59	13	29	42	55	....	....	....	....	....	....	....	....	....	15	3	2	5	29	....	....	....	....
	NHL Totals		3	0	0	0	0	0	0	0	2	0.0		0	0.0	8:04	....	....	....	....	....	....	....	....	....

Signed as a free agent by **Espoo** (Finland), July 23, 2007. Traded to **Carolina** by **Washington** with Brian Pothier and Washington's 2nd round choice (later traded to NY Rangers, later traded to Calgary – Calgary selected Tyler Wotherspoon) in 2011 Entry Draft for Joe Corvo, March 3, 2010.

OSHIE, T.J.

(OH-shee, TEE-JAY) **ST.L.**

Center. Shoots right. 5'11", 195 lbs. Born, Mt. Vernon, WA, December 23, 1986. St. Louis' 1st choice, 24th overall, in 2005 Entry Draft.

Season	Club	League	GP	G	A	Pts	PIM	PP	SH	GW	S	%	+/-	TF	F%	Min	GP	G	A	Pts	PIM	PP	SH	GW	Min
2004-05	Warroad Warriors	High-MN	31	37	62	99	22	....	....	....	....	....	....	....	....	....	....	....	....	....	....	....	....	....	....
	Sioux Falls	USHL	11	3	2	5	6	....	....	....	....	....	....	....	....	....	....	....	....	....	....	....	....	....	....
2005-06	North Dakota	WCHA	44	24	21	45	33	....	....	....	....	....	....	....	....	....	....	....	....	....	....	....	....	....	....
2006-07	North Dakota	WCHA	43	17	*35	52	30	....	....	....	....	....	....	....	....	....	....	....	....	....	....	....	....	....	....
2007-08	North Dakota	WCHA	42	18	27	45	57	....	....	....	....	....	....	....	....	....	....	....	....	....	....	....	....	....	....
2008-09	St. Louis	NHL	57	14	25	39	30	6	1	1	101	13.9	16	109	43.1	16:35	4	0	0	0	2	0	0	0	19:01
2009-10	St. Louis	NHL	76	18	30	48	36	1	1	3	158	11.4	–1	153	41.8	18:19	....	....	....	....	....	....	....	....	....
2010-11	St. Louis	NHL	49	12	22	34	15	3	1	3	103	11.7	10	227	44.1	19:11	....	....	....	....	....	....	....	....	....
	NHL Totals		182	44	77	121	81	10	3	7	362	12.2		489	43.1	18:01	4	0	0	0	2	0	0	0	19:01

WCHA All-Rookie Team (2006) • WCHA First All-Star Team (2008) • NCAA West First All-American Team (2008)

O'SULLIVAN, Patrick

(Oh-SUHL-ih-vihn, PAT-rihk) **PHX**

Center. Shoots left. 5'11", 190 lbs. Born, Toronto, Ont., February 1, 1985. Minnesota's 2nd choice, 56th overall, in 2003 Entry Draft.

Season	Club	League	GP	G	A	Pts	PIM	PP	SH	GW	S	%	+/-	TF	F%	Min	GP	G	A	Pts	PIM	PP	SH	GW	Min
99-2000	Strathroy Rockets	ON-Jr.B	45	6	13	19	53	....	....	....	....	....	....	....	....	....	....	....	....	....	....	....	....	....	....
2000-01	USNTDP	U-17	8	8	10	18	12	....	....	....	....	....	....	....	....	....	....	....	....	....	....	....	....	....	....
	USNTDP	NAHL	56	22	35	57	57	....	....	....	....	....	....	....	....	....	....	....	....	....	....	....	....	....	....
2001-02	Mississauga	OHL	68	34	58	92	61	....	....	....	....	....	....	....	....	....	....	....	....	....	....	....	....	....	....
	USNTDP	USHL	1	1	0	1	2	....	....	....	....	....	....	....	....	....	....	....	....	....	....	....	....	....	....
2002-03	Mississauga	OHL	56	40	41	81	57	....	....	....	....	....	....	....	....	....	5	2	9	11	18	....	....	....	....
2003-04	Mississauga	OHL	53	43	39	82	32	....	....	....	....	....	....	....	....	....	24	12	11	23	16	....	....	....	....
2004-05	Mississauga	OHL	57	31	59	90	63	....	....	....	....	....	....	....	....	....	5	0	4	4	6	....	....	....	....
2005-06	Houston Aeros	AHL	78	47	46	93	64	....	....	....	....	....	....	....	....	....	8	5	5	10	4	....	....	....	....
2006-07	Los Angeles	NHL	44	5	14	19	14	2	0	1	92	5.4	–6	127	46.5	14:04	....	....	....	....	....	....	....	....	....
	Manchester	AHL	41	18	21	39	12	....	....	....	....	....	....	....	....	....	16	8	9	17	10	....	....	....	....
2007-08	Los Angeles	NHL	82	22	31	53	36	3	3	2	220	10.0	–8	461	44.0	18:42	....	....	....	....	....	....	....	....	....

			Regular Season														Playoffs								
Season	Club	League	GP	G	A	Pts	PIM	PP	SH	GW	S	%	+/-	TF	F%	Min	GP	G	A	Pts	PIM	PP	SH	GW	Min
2008-09	Los Angeles	NHL	62	14	23	37	16	2	1	1	200	7.0	1	39	46.2	19:26	....	....	....	....	....	....	....	....	....
	Edmonton	NHL	19	2	4	6	12	0	0	0	59	3.4	–7	60	38.3	18:14	....	....	....	....	....	....	....	....	....
2009-10	Edmonton	NHL	73	11	23	34	32	3	1	3	191	5.8	–35	195	36.4	17:31	....	....	....	....	....	....	....	....	....
2010-11	Carolina	NHL	10	1	0	1	2	0	0	0	13	7.7	–1	11	27.3	8:52	....	....	....	....	....	....	....	....	....
	Minnesota	NHL	21	1	6	7	2	0	0	0	37	2.7	–1	40	42.5	13:46	....	....	....	....	....	....	....	....	....
	Houston Aeros	AHL	36	19	29	48	22	....	....	....	....	....	....	....	....	....	24	4	14	18	16	....	....	....	....
	NHL Totals		311	56	101	157	114	10	5	7	812	6.9		933	42.2	17:14	....	....	....	....	....	....	....	....	....

Canadian Major Junior Rookie of the Year (2002) • AHL All-Rookie Team (2006) • Dudley "Red" Garrett Memorial Trophy (AHL - Top Rookie) (2006)

Traded to **Los Angeles** by **Minnesota** with Edmonton's 1st round choice (previously acquired, Los Angeles selected Trevor Lewis) in 2006 Entry Draft for Pavol Demitra, June 24, 2006. Traded to **Carolina** by **Los Angeles** with Calgary's 2nd round choice (previously acquired, Carolina selected Brian Dumoulin) in 2009 Entry Draft for Justin Williams, March 4, 2009. Traded to **Edmonton** by **Carolina** with Carolina's 2nd round choice (later traded to Buffalo, later traded to Toronto – Toronto selected Jesse Blacker) in 2009 Entry Draft for Erik Cole and Edmonton's 5th round choice (Matt Kennedy) in 2009 Entry Draft, March 4, 2009. Traded to **Phoenix** by **Edmonton** for Jim Vandermeer, June 30, 2010. Signed as a free agent by **Carolina**, September 17, 2010. Claimed on waivers by **Minnesota** from **Carolina**, November 23, 2010. Signed as a free agent by **Phoenix**, August 5, 2011.

OTT, Steve
(AWT, STEEV) **DAL**

Center. Shoots left. 6', 192 lbs. Born, Summerside, P.E.I., August 19, 1982. Dallas' 1st choice, 25th overall, in 2000 Entry Draft.

Season	Club	League	GP	G	A	Pts	PIM	PP	SH	GW	S	%	+/-	TF	F%	Min	GP	G	A	Pts	PIM	PP	SH	GW	Min
1998-99	Leamington Flyers	ON-Jr.B	48	14	30	44	110	....	....	....	....	....	....	....	....	....	....	....	....	....	....	....	....	....	....
99-2000	Windsor Spitfires	OHL	66	23	39	62	131	....	....	....	....	....	....	....	....	....	12	3	5	8	21	....	....	....	....
2000-01	Windsor Spitfires	OHL	55	50	37	87	164	....	....	....	....	....	....	....	....	....	9	3	8	11	27	....	....	....	....
2001-02	Windsor Spitfires	OHL	53	43	45	88	178	....	....	....	....	....	....	....	....	....	14	6	10	16	49	....	....	....	....
2002-03	Dallas	NHL	26	3	4	7	31	0	0	0	25	12.0	6	4	50.0	8:46	1	0	0	0	0	0	0	0	6:57
	Utah Grizzlies	AHL	40	9	11	20	98	....	....	....	....	....	....	....	....	....	....	....	....	....	....	....	....	....	....
2003-04	Dallas	NHL	73	2	10	12	152	0	0	1	74	2.7	–2	59	49.2	10:14	4	1	0	1	0	0	0	1	6:55
2004-05	Hamilton	AHL	67	18	21	39	279	....	....	....	....	....	....	....	....	....	4	0	0	0	20	....	....	....	....
2005-06	Dallas	NHL	82	5	17	22	178	0	0	1	89	5.6	1	535	49.2	11:54	5	0	1	1	2	0	0	0	7:41
2006-07	Dallas	NHL	19	0	4	4	35	0	0	0	17	0.0	–4	39	59.0	9:11	6	0	0	0	8	0	0	0	6:43
	Iowa Stars	AHL	3	0	0	0	8	....	....	....	....	....	....	....	....	....	....	....	....	....	....	....	....	....	....
2007-08	Dallas	NHL	73	11	11	22	147	0	1	2	89	12.4	2	311	58.8	14:28	18	2	1	3	22	1	0	1	13:46
2008-09	Dallas	NHL	64	19	27	46	135	5	0	0	132	14.4	3	172	46.5	17:35	....	....	....	....	....	....	....	....	....
2009-10	Dallas	NHL	73	22	14	36	153	8	1	2	146	15.1	–14	352	56.8	16:28	....	....	....	....	....	....	....	....	....
2010-11	Dallas	NHL	82	12	20	32	183	3	2	4	120	10.0	–9	1138	56.6	17:09	....	....	....	....	....	....	....	....	....
	NHL Totals		492	74	107	181	1014	16	4	10	692	10.7		2610	54.6	14:03	34	3	2	5	32	1	0	2	10:37

Canadian Major Junior Second All-Star Team (2001) • OHL Second All-Star Team (2002)

• Missed majority of 2006-07 due to ankle injury vs. Los Angeles, October 28, 2006.

OUELLET, Michel
(oo-LEHT, mee-SHEHL) **T.B.**

Right wing. Shoots right. 6', 200 lbs. Born, Rimouski, Que., March 5, 1982. Pittsburgh's 4th choice, 124th overall, in 2000 Entry Draft.

Season	Club	League	GP	G	A	Pts	PIM	PP	SH	GW	S	%	+/-	TF	F%	Min	GP	G	A	Pts	PIM	PP	SH	GW	Min
1997-98	Jonquiere Elites	QAAA	33	20	32	52	52	....	....	....	....	....	....	....	....	....	....	....	....	....	....	....	....	....	....
1998-99	Rimouski Oceanic	QMJHL	28	7	13	20	10	....	....	....	....	....	....	....	....	....	11	0	1	1	6	....	....	....	....
99-2000	Rimouski Oceanic	QMJHL	72	36	53	89	38	....	....	....	....	....	....	....	....	....	14	4	5	9	14	....	....	....	....
2000-01	Rimouski Oceanic	QMJHL	63	42	50	92	50	....	....	....	....	....	....	....	....	....	11	6	7	13	8	....	....	....	....
2001-02	Rimouski Oceanic	QMJHL	61	40	58	98	66	....	....	....	....	....	....	....	....	....	7	3	6	9	4	....	....	....	....
2002-03	Wilkes-Barre	AHL	4	0	2	2	0	....	....	....	....	....	....	....	....	....	....	....	....	....	....	....	....	....	....
	Wheeling Nailers	ECHL	55	20	26	46	40	....	....	....	....	....	....	....	....	....	....	....	....	....	....	....	....	....	....
2003-04	Wilkes-Barre	AHL	79	30	19	49	34	....	....	....	....	....	....	....	....	....	22	2	10	12	6	....	....	....	....
2004-05	Wilkes-Barre	AHL	80	31	32	63	56	....	....	....	....	....	....	....	....	....	11	2	3	5	6	....	....	....	....
2005-06	Pittsburgh	NHL	50	16	16	32	16	11	0	0	87	18.4	–13	16	37.5	14:02	....	....	....	....	....	....	....	....	....
	Wilkes-Barre	AHL	19	10	20	30	12	....	....	....	....	....	....	....	....	....	....	....	....	....	....	....	....	....	....
2006-07	Pittsburgh	NHL	73	19	29	48	30	11	0	2	148	12.8	–3	8	37.5	13:20	5	0	2	2	6	0	0	0	12:54
2007-08	Tampa Bay	NHL	64	17	19	36	12	5	0	0	132	12.9	11	42	45.2	13:38	....	....	....	....	....	....	....	....	....
2008-09	Vancouver	NHL	3	0	0	0	0	0	0	0	3	0.0	1	1	0.0	9:39	....	....	....	....	....	....	....	....	....
	Manitoba Moose	AHL	46	13	27	40	30	....	....	....	....	....	....	....	....	....	....	....	....	....	....	....	....	....	....
2009-10	Fribourg	Swiss	11	1	4	5	4	....	....	....	....	....	....	....	....	....	5	1	1	2	4	....	....	....	....
2010-11	Hamburg Freezers	Germany	39	11	17	28	24	....	....	....	....	....	....	....	....	....	....	....	....	....	....	....	....	....	....
	NHL Totals		190	52	64	116	58	27	0	2	370	14.1		67	41.8	13:33	5	0	2	2	6	0	0	0	12:54

AHL All-Rookie Team (2004)

Signed as a free agent by **Tampa Bay**, July 1, 2007. Traded to **Vancouver** by **Tampa Bay** with Shane O'Brien for Lukas Krajicek and Juraj Simek, October 6, 2008. Signed as a free agent by **Fribourg** (Swiss), October 5, 2009. Signed as a free agent by **Hamburg** (Germany), April 14, 2010. Signed as a free agent by **Tampa Bay**, July 1, 2011.

OVECHKIN, Alex
(oh-VEHCH-kihn, AL-ehx) **WSH**

Left wing. Shoots right. 6'2", 233 lbs. Born, Moscow, USSR, September 17, 1985. Washington's 1st choice, 1st overall, in 2004 Entry Draft.

Season	Club	League	GP	G	A	Pts	PIM	PP	SH	GW	S	%	+/-	TF	F%	Min	GP	G	A	Pts	PIM	PP	SH	GW	Min
2001-02	Dyn'o Moscow 2	Russia-3	19	18	8	26	20	....	....	....	....	....	....	....	....	....	....	....	....	....	....	....	....	....	....
	Dynamo Moscow	Russia	22	2	2	4	4	....	....	....	....	....	....	....	....	....	3	0	0	0	0	....	....	....	....
2002-03	Dynamo Moscow	Russia	40	8	7	15	28	....	....	....	....	....	....	....	....	....	5	0	0	0	2	....	....	....	....
2003-04	Dynamo Moscow	Russia	53	13	11	24	40	....	....	....	....	....	....	....	....	....	3	0	0	0	2	....	....	....	....
2004-05	Dynamo Moscow	Russia	37	13	13	26	32	....	....	....	....	....	....	....	....	....	10	2	4	6	31	....	....	....	....
2005-06	Washington	NHL	81	52	54	106	52	21	3	5	425	12.2	2	16	12.5	21:37	....	....	....	....	....	....	....	....	....
	Russia	Olympics	8	5	0	5	8	....	....	....	....	....	....	....	....	....	....	....	....	....	....	....	....	....	....
2006-07	Washington	NHL	82	46	46	92	52	16	0	8	392	11.7	–19	17	47.1	21:23	....	....	....	....	....	....	....	....	....
2007-08	Washington	NHL	82	*65	47	*112	40	*22	0	*11	446	14.6	28	18	38.9	23:06	7	4	5	9	0	1	0	2	24:03
2008-09	Washington	NHL	79	*56	54	110	72	19	1	10	528	10.6	8	32	25.0	23:00	14	11	10	21	8	3	0	1	23:21
2009-10	Washington	NHL	72	50	59	109	89	13	0	7	368	13.6	45	22	45.5	21:48	7	5	5	10	0	1	0	0	23:06
	Russia	Olympics	4	2	2	4	2	....	....	....	....	....	....	....	....	....	....	....	....	....	....	....	....	....	....
2010-11	Washington	NHL	79	32	53	85	41	7	0	*11	367	8.7	24	18	33.3	21:22	9	5	5	10	10	1	0	1	23:30
	NHL Totals		475	301	313	614	346	98	4	52	2526	11.9		123	33.3	22:03	37	25	25	50	18	6	0	4	23:29

Olympic All-Star Team (2006) • NHL All-Rookie Team (2006) • NHL First All-Star Team (2006, 2007, 2008, 2009, 2010) • Calder Memorial Trophy (2006) • Maurice "Rocket" Richard Trophy (2008, 2009) • Art Ross Trophy (2008) • Lester B. Pearson Award (2008, 2009) • Hart Memorial Trophy (2008, 2009) • Ted Lindsay Award (2010) • NHL Second All-Star Team (2011)

Played in NHL All-Star Game (2007, 2008, 2009, 2011)

OYSTRICK, Nathan
(OI-strihk, NAY-thuhn) **PHX**

Defense. Shoots left. 6', 210 lbs. Born, Regina, Sask., December 17, 1982. Atlanta's 7th choice, 198th overall, in 2002 Entry Draft.

Season	Club	League	GP	G	A	Pts	PIM	PP	SH	GW	S	%	+/-	TF	F%	Min	GP	G	A	Pts	PIM	PP	SH	GW	Min
99-2000	Reg. Pat Cdns.	SMHL	43	6	22	28	214	....	....	....	....	....	....	....	....	....	....	....	....	....	....	....	....	....	....
2000-01	South Surrey	BCHL	STATISTICS NOT AVAILABLE																						
2001-02	South Surrey	BCHL	50	15	42	57	142	....	....	....	....	....	....	....	....	....	....	....	....	....	....	....	....	....	....
2002-03	Northern Mich.	CCHA	34	2	10	12	26	....	....	....	....	....	....	....	....	....	....	....	....	....	....	....	....	....	....
2003-04	Northern Mich.	CCHA	39	8	20	28	98	....	....	....	....	....	....	....	....	....	....	....	....	....	....	....	....	....	....
2004-05	Northern Mich.	CCHA	40	7	13	20	87	....	....	....	....	....	....	....	....	....	....	....	....	....	....	....	....	....	....
2005-06	Northern Mich.	CCHA	38	9	20	29	58	....	....	....	....	....	....	....	....	....	....	....	....	....	....	....	....	....	....
	Chicago Wolves	AHL	2	0	1	1	4	....	....	....	....	....	....	....	....	....	....	....	....	....	....	....	....	....	....
2006-07	Chicago Wolves	AHL	80	15	32	47	105	....	....	....	....	....	....	....	....	....	15	0	6	6	16	....	....	....	....
2007-08	Chicago Wolves	AHL	80	15	28	43	112	....	....	....	....	....	....	....	....	....	24	3	8	11	35	....	....	....	....
2008-09	Atlanta	NHL	53	4	8	12	50	0	0	0	43	9.3	–2	0	0.0	15:45	....	....	....	....	....	....	....	....	....
2009-10	Anaheim	NHL	3	0	0	0	2	0	0	0	1	0.0	–1	0	0.0	10:35	....	....	....	....	....	....	....	....	....
	Chicago Wolves	AHL	43	7	16	23	96	....	....	....	....	....	....	....	....	....	14	2	8	10	8	....	....	....	....
2010-11	St. Louis	NHL	9	1	2	3	9	1	0	0	11	9.1	1	0	0.0	12:10	....	....	....	....	....	....	....	....	....
	Peoria Rivermen	AHL	61	15	30	45	125	....	....	....	....	....	....	....	....	....	4	1	1	2	7	....	....	....	....
	NHL Totals		65	5	10	15	61	1	0	0	55	9.1		0	0.0	15:01	....	....	....	....	....	....	....	....	....

CCHA Second All-Star Team (2004) • CCHA First All-Star Team (2005, 2006) • NCAA West Second All-American Team (2006) • AHL All-Rookie Team (2007) • AHL Second All-Star Team (2007)

Traded to **Anaheim** by **Atlanta** with future considerations for Evgeny Artyukhin, March 1, 2010. Signed as a free agent by **St. Louis**, July 12, 2010. Signed as a free agent by **Phoenix**, July 6, 2011.

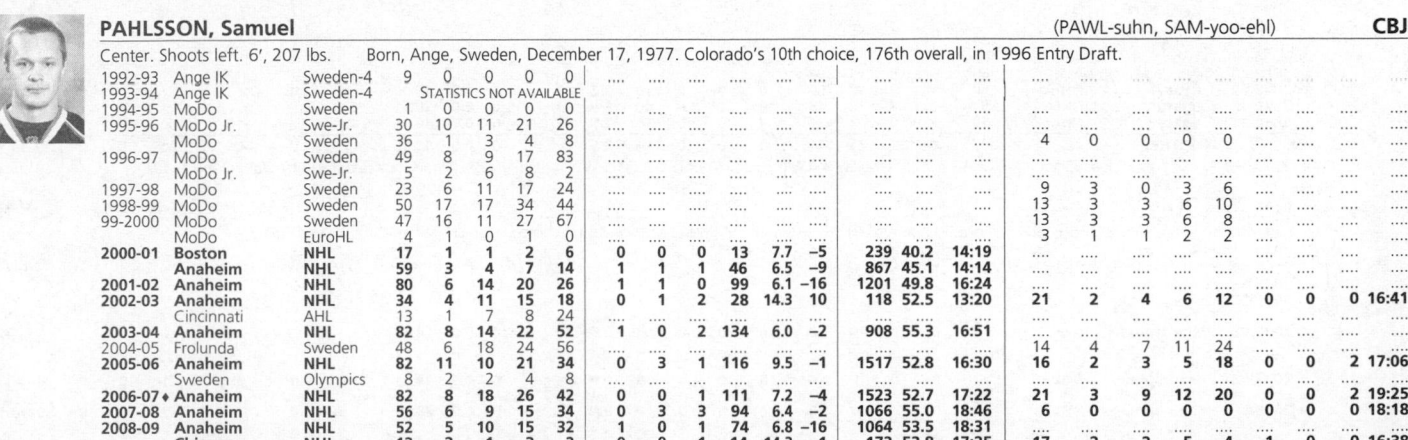

PAAJARVI, Magnus

(pe-ya-YAR-vee, MAG-nuhs) **EDM**

Left wing. Shoots left. 6'3", 200 lbs. Born, Norrkoping, Sweden, April 12, 1991. Edmonton's 1st choice, 10th overall, in 2009 Entry Draft.

			Regular Season														Playoffs								
Season	Club	League	GP	G	A	Pts	PIM	PP	SH	GW	S	%	+/-	TF	F%	Min	GP	G	A	Pts	PIM	PP	SH	GW	Min
2005-06	Malmo U18	Swe-U18	13	2	3	5	4	....	....	....	....	....	....	....	....	....	1	0	0	0	0	....	....	....	....
	Malmo Jr.	Swe-Jr.	2	0	0	0	0	....	....	....	....	....	....	....	....	....	....	....	....	....	....	....	....	....	....
2006-07	Malmo U18	Swe-U18	3	3	3	6	0	....	....	....	....	....	....	....	....	....	....	....	....	....	....	....	....	....	....
	Malmo Jr.	Swe-Jr.	20	4	2	6	6	....	....	....	....	....	....	....	....	....	4	0	1	1	0	....	....	....	....
2007-08	Timra IK U18	Swe-U18	5	1	6	7	4	....	....	....	....	....	....	....	....	....	....	....	....	....	....	....	....	....	....
	Timra IK Jr.	Swe-Jr.	18	7	15	22	6	....	....	....	....	....	....	....	....	....	....	....	....	....	....	....	....	....	....
	Timra IK	Sweden	35	1	2	3	2	....	....	....	....	....	....	....	....	....	11	0	0	0	2	....	....	....	....
2008-09	Timra IK Jr.	Swe-Jr.	1	0	0	0	0	....	....	....	....	....	....	....	....	....	....	....	....	....	....	....	....	....	....
	Timra IK	Sweden	50	7	10	17	4	....	....	....	....	....	....	....	....	....	7	1	0	1	0	....	....	....	....
2009-10	Timra IK	Sweden	49	12	17	29	6	....	....	....	....	....	....	....	....	....	5	0	1	1	2	....	....	....	....
2010-11	**Edmonton**	**NHL**	**80**	**15**	**19**	**34**	**16**	**3**	**0**	**0**	**180**	**8.3**	**–13**	**5**	**20.0**	**15:23**	....	....	....	....	....	....	....	....	....
	NHL Totals		**80**	**15**	**19**	**34**	**16**	**3**	**0**	**0**	**180**	**8.3**		**5**	**20.0**	**15:23**	....	....	....	....	....	....	....	....	....

PACIORETTY, Max

(pahk-OHR-eht-tee, MAX) **MTL**

Left wing. Shoots left. 6'2", 196 lbs. Born, New Canaan, CT, November 20, 1988. Montreal's 2nd choice, 22nd overall, in 2007 Entry Draft.

			Regular Season														Playoffs								
Season	Club	League	GP	G	A	Pts	PIM	PP	SH	GW	S	%	+/-	TF	F%	Min	GP	G	A	Pts	PIM	PP	SH	GW	Min
2004-05	Taft Rhinos	High-CT	23	5	14	19	....	....	....	....	....	....	....	....	....	....	....	....	....	....	....	....	....	....	....
2005-06	Taft Rhinos	High-CT	26	7	26	33	....	....	....	....	....	....	....	....	....	....	....	....	....	....	....	....	....	....	....
2006-07	Sioux City	USHL	60	21	42	63	119	....	....	....	....	....	....	....	....	....	7	4	6	10	10	....	....	....	....
2007-08	U. of Michigan	CCHA	37	15	24	39	59	....	....	....	....	....	....	....	....	....	....	....	....	....	....	....	....	....	....
2008-09	**Montreal**	**NHL**	**34**	**3**	**8**	**11**	**27**	**1**	**0**	**0**	**57**	**5.3**	**–3**	**2**	**50.0**	**12:37**	....	....	....	....	....	....	....	....	....
	Hamilton	AHL	37	6	23	29	43	....	....	....	....	....	....	....	....	....	....	....	....	....	....	....	....	....	....
2009-10	**Montreal**	**NHL**	**52**	**3**	**11**	**14**	**20**	**0**	**0**	**0**	**74**	**4.1**	**–5**	**7**	**14.3**	**12:43**	....	....	....	....	....	....	....	....	....
	Hamilton	AHL	18	2	9	11	10	....	....	....	....	....	....	....	....	....	5	1	0	1	2	....	....	....	....
2010-11	**Montreal**	**NHL**	**37**	**14**	**10**	**24**	**39**	**7**	**0**	**2**	**112**	**12.5**	**–1**	**1**	**0.0**	**15:54**	....	....	....	....	....	....	....	....	....
	Hamilton	AHL	27	17	15	32	20	....	....	....	....	....	....	....	....	....	....	....	....	....	....	....	....	....	....
	NHL Totals		**123**	**20**	**29**	**49**	**86**	**8**	**0**	**2**	**243**	**8.2**		**10**	**20.0**	**13:39**	....	....	....	....	....	....	....	....	....

USHL All-Rookie Team (2007) • USHL Rookie of the Year (2007) • CCHA All-Rookie Team (2008) • CCHA Rookie of the Year (2008)

PADDOCK, Cam

(PA-dawk, KAM)

Center. Shoots right. 6'1", 190 lbs. Born, Vancouver, B.C., March 22, 1983. Pittsburgh's 6th choice, 137th overall, in 2002 Entry Draft.

			Regular Season														Playoffs								
Season	Club	League	GP	G	A	Pts	PIM	PP	SH	GW	S	%	+/-	TF	F%	Min	GP	G	A	Pts	PIM	PP	SH	GW	Min
99-2000	Kelowna Rockets	WHL	46	5	5	10	42	....	....	....	....	....	....	....	....	....	5	0	0	0	0	....	....	....	....
2000-01	Kelowna Rockets	WHL	72	14	10	24	110	....	....	....	....	....	....	....	....	....	6	0	0	0	4	....	....	....	....
2001-02	Kelowna Rockets	WHL	72	38	35	73	122	....	....	....	....	....	....	....	....	....	15	8	6	14	35	....	....	....	....
2002-03	Kelowna Rockets	WHL	71	33	26	59	107	....	....	....	....	....	....	....	....	....	19	11	8	19	18	....	....	....	....
2003-04	Kelowna Rockets	WHL	62	17	22	39	86	....	....	....	....	....	....	....	....	....	16	3	4	7	22	....	....	....	....
	Wilkes-Barre	AHL	1	0	0	0	2	....	....	....	....	....	....	....	....	....	....	....	....	....	....	....	....	....	....
2004-05	Wilkes-Barre	AHL	16	0	0	0	13	....	....	....	....	....	....	....	....	....	....	....	....	....	....	....	....	....	....
	Wheeling Nailers	ECHL	53	11	18	29	70	....	....	....	....	....	....	....	....	....	....	....	....	....	....	....	....	....	....
2005-06	Wilkes-Barre	AHL	4	0	0	0	2	....	....	....	....	....	....	....	....	....	....	....	....	....	....	....	....	....	....
	Wheeling Nailers	ECHL	61	14	24	38	90	....	....	....	....	....	....	....	....	....	9	0	0	0	12	....	....	....	....
2006-07	San Antonio	AHL	22	0	2	2	13	....	....	....	....	....	....	....	....	....	....	....	....	....	....	....	....	....	....
	Phoenix	ECHL	46	11	20	31	117	....	....	....	....	....	....	....	....	....	3	2	0	2	9	....	....	....	....
2007-08	San Antonio	AHL	78	12	13	25	107	....	....	....	....	....	....	....	....	....	7	0	2	2	18	....	....	....	....
2008-09	**St. Louis**	**NHL**	**16**	**2**	**1**	**3**	**0**	**0**	**0**	**0**	**17**	**11.8**	**–4**	**87**	**46.0**	**10:41**	....	....	....	....	....	....	....	....	....
	Peoria Rivermen	AHL	60	8	7	15	96	....	....	....	....	....	....	....	....	....	7	2	2	4	0	....	....	....	....
2009-10	Peoria Rivermen	AHL	80	15	12	27	95	....	....	....	....	....	....	....	....	....	....	....	....	....	....	....	....	....	....
2010-11	Iserlohn Roosters	Germany	46	5	12	17	40	....	....	....	....	....	....	....	....	....	....	....	....	....	....	....	....	....	....
	NHL Totals		**16**	**2**	**1**	**3**	**0**	**0**	**0**	**0**	**17**	**11.8**		**87**	**46.0**	**10:41**	....	....	....	....	....	....	....	....	....

Signed as a free agent by **San Antonio** (AHL), December 26, 2006. Signed as a free agent by **St. Louis**, July 15, 2008. Signed as a free agent by **Iserlohn** (Germany), August 27, 2010.

PAETSCH, Nathan

(PASH, NAY-thuhn)

Defense. Shoots left. 6'1", 198 lbs. Born, Humboldt, Sask., March 30, 1983. Buffalo's 8th choice, 202nd overall, in 2003 Entry Draft.

			Regular Season														Playoffs								
Season	Club	League	GP	G	A	Pts	PIM	PP	SH	GW	S	%	+/-	TF	F%	Min	GP	G	A	Pts	PIM	PP	SH	GW	Min
1998-99	Tisdale Trojans	SMHL	74	20	55	75	120	....	....	....	....	....	....	....	....	....	....	....	....	....	....	....	....	....	....
	Moose Jaw	WHL	2	0	0	0	0	....	....	....	....	....	....	....	....	....	1	0	0	0	0	....	....	....	....
99-2000	Moose Jaw	WHL	68	9	35	44	49	....	....	....	....	....	....	....	....	....	4	0	1	1	0	....	....	....	....
2000-01	Moose Jaw	WHL	70	8	54	62	118	....	....	....	....	....	....	....	....	....	4	1	2	3	6	....	....	....	....
2001-02	Moose Jaw	WHL	59	16	36	52	86	....	....	....	....	....	....	....	....	....	12	0	4	4	16	....	....	....	....
2002-03	Moose Jaw	WHL	59	15	39	54	81	....	....	....	....	....	....	....	....	....	13	3	10	13	6	....	....	....	....
2003-04	Rochester	AHL	54	5	5	10	49	....	....	....	....	....	....	....	....	....	16	1	1	2	28	....	....	....	....
2004-05	Rochester	AHL	80	4	19	23	150	....	....	....	....	....	....	....	....	....	9	1	1	2	16	....	....	....	....
2005-06	**Buffalo**	**NHL**	**1**	**0**	**1**	**1**	**0**	**0**	**0**	**0**	**0**	**0.0**	**–1**	**0**	**0.0**	**15:38**	**1**	**0**	**0**	**0**	**0**	**0**	**0**	**0**	**12:06**
	Rochester	AHL	72	11	39	50	90	....	....	....	....	....	....	....	....	....	....	....	....	....	....	....	....	....	....
2006-07	**Buffalo**	**NHL**	**63**	**2**	**22**	**24**	**50**	**0**	**0**	**0**	**62**	**3.2**	**10**	**0**	**0.0**	**15:15**	....	....	....	....	....	....	....	....	....
2007-08	**Buffalo**	**NHL**	**59**	**2**	**7**	**9**	**27**	**0**	**0**	**0**	**49**	**4.1**	**3**	**0**	**0.0**	**13:38**	....	....	....	....	....	....	....	....	....
2008-09	**Buffalo**	**NHL**	**23**	**2**	**4**	**6**	**25**	**0**	**0**	**0**	**21**	**9.5**	**3**	**0**	**0.0**	**12:11**	....	....	....	....	....	....	....	....	....
2009-10	**Buffalo**	**NHL**	**11**	**1**	**1**	**2**	**6**	**0**	**0**	**0**	**9**	**11.1**	**2**	**0**	**0.0**	**9:39**	....	....	....	....	....	....	....	....	....
	Columbus	**NHL**	**10**	**0**	**0**	**0**	**6**	**0**	**0**	**0**	**8**	**0.0**	**–5**	**0**	**0.0**	**11:14**	....	....	....	....	....	....	....	....	....
2010-11	Rochester	AHL	9	1	2	3	2	....	....	....	....	....	....	....	....	....	....	....	....	....	....	....	....	....	....
	Syracuse Crunch	AHL	34	8	9	17	12	....	....	....	....	....	....	....	....	....	....	....	....	....	....	....	....	....	....
	NHL Totals		**167**	**7**	**35**	**42**	**114**	**0**	**0**	**0**	**149**	**4.7**		**0**	**0.0**	**13:39**	**1**	**0**	**0**	**0**	**0**	**0**	**0**	**0**	**12:06**

• Re-entered NHL Entry Draft. Originally Washington's 1st choice, 58th overall, in 2001 Entry Draft.

WHL East Second All-Star Team (2003)

• Missed majority of 2008-09 as a healthy reserve. Traded to **Columbus** by **Buffalo** with Vancouver's 2nd round choice (previously acquired, Columbus selected Petr Straka) in 2010 Entry Draft for Raffi Torres, March 3, 2010. • Missed majority of 2009-10 as a healthy reserve. Signed as a free agent by **Florida**, July 7, 2010. Traded to **Vancouver** by **Florida** for Sean Zimmerman, October 7, 2010. • Reassigned to **Syracuse** (AHL) by **Vancouver**, November 1, 2010.

PAHLSSON, Samuel

(PAWL-suhn, SAM-yoo-ehl) **CBJ**

Center. Shoots left. 6', 207 lbs. Born, Ange, Sweden, December 17, 1977. Colorado's 10th choice, 176th overall, in 1996 Entry Draft.

			Regular Season														Playoffs								
Season	Club	League	GP	G	A	Pts	PIM	PP	SH	GW	S	%	+/-	TF	F%	Min	GP	G	A	Pts	PIM	PP	SH	GW	Min
1992-93	Ange IK	Sweden-4	9	0	0	0	0	....	....	....	....	....	....	....	....	....	....	....	....	....	....	....	....	....	....
1993-94	Ange IK	Sweden-4	STATISTICS NOT AVAILABLE					....	....	....	....	....	....	....	....	....	....	....	....	....	....	....	....	....	....
1994-95	MoDo	Sweden	1	0	0	0	0	....	....	....	....	....	....	....	....	....	....	....	....	....	....	....	....	....	....
1995-96	MoDo Jr.	Swe-Jr.	30	10	11	21	26	....	....	....	....	....	....	....	....	....	....	....	....	....	....	....	....	....	....
	MoDo	Sweden	36	1	3	4	8	....	....	....	....	....	....	....	....	....	4	0	0	0	0	....	....	....	....
1996-97	MoDo	Sweden	49	8	9	17	83	....	....	....	....	....	....	....	....	....	....	....	....	....	....	....	....	....	....
	MoDo Jr.	Swe-Jr.	5	2	6	8	2	....	....	....	....	....	....	....	....	....	....	....	....	....	....	....	....	....	....
1997-98	MoDo	Sweden	23	6	11	17	24	....	....	....	....	....	....	....	....	....	9	3	0	3	6	....	....	....	....
1998-99	MoDo	Sweden	50	17	17	34	44	....	....	....	....	....	....	....	....	....	13	3	3	6	10	....	....	....	....
99-2000	MoDo	Sweden	47	16	11	27	67	....	....	....	....	....	....	....	....	....	13	3	3	6	8	....	....	....	....
	MoDo	EuroHL	4	1	0	1	0	....	....	....	....	....	....	....	....	....	3	1	1	2	2	....	....	....	....
2000-01	**Boston**	**NHL**	**17**	**1**	**1**	**2**	**6**	**0**	**0**	**0**	**13**	**7.7**	**–5**	**239**	**40.2**	**14:19**	....	....	....	....	....	....	....	....	....
	Anaheim	**NHL**	**59**	**3**	**4**	**7**	**14**	**1**	**1**	**1**	**46**	**6.5**	**–9**	**867**	**45.1**	**14:14**	....	....	....	....	....	....	....	....	....
2001-02	**Anaheim**	**NHL**	**80**	**6**	**14**	**20**	**26**	**1**	**1**	**0**	**99**	**6.1**	**–16**	**1201**	**49.8**	**16:24**	....	....	....	....	....	....	....	....	....
2002-03	**Anaheim**	**NHL**	**34**	**4**	**11**	**15**	**18**	**0**	**1**	**2**	**28**	**14.3**	**10**	**118**	**52.5**	**13:20**	**21**	**2**	**4**	**6**	**12**	**0**	**0**	**0**	**16:41**
	Cincinnati	AHL	13	1	7	8	24	....	....	....	....	....	....	....	....	....	....	....	....	....	....	....	....	....	....
2003-04	**Anaheim**	**NHL**	**82**	**8**	**14**	**22**	**52**	**1**	**0**	**2**	**134**	**6.0**	**–2**	**908**	**55.3**	**16:51**	....	....	....	....	....	....	....	....	....
2004-05	Frolunda	Sweden	48	6	18	24	56	....	....	....	....	....	....	....	....	....	14	4	7	11	24	....	....	....	....
2005-06	**Anaheim**	**NHL**	**82**	**11**	**10**	**21**	**34**	**0**	**3**	**1**	**116**	**9.5**	**–1**	**1517**	**52.8**	**16:30**	**16**	**2**	**3**	**5**	**18**	**0**	**0**	**2**	**17:06**
	Sweden	Olympics	8	2	2	4	8	....	....	....	....	....	....	....	....	....	....	....	....	....	....	....	....	....	....
2006-07 ♦	**Anaheim**	**NHL**	**82**	**8**	**18**	**26**	**42**	**0**	**0**	**1**	**111**	**7.2**	**–4**	**1523**	**52.7**	**17:22**	**21**	**3**	**9**	**12**	**20**	**0**	**0**	**2**	**19:25**
2007-08	**Anaheim**	**NHL**	**56**	**6**	**9**	**15**	**34**	**0**	**3**	**3**	**94**	**6.4**	**–2**	**1066**	**55.0**	**18:46**	**6**	**0**	**0**	**0**	**0**	**0**	**0**	**0**	**18:18**
2008-09	**Anaheim**	**NHL**	**52**	**5**	**10**	**15**	**32**	**1**	**0**	**1**	**74**	**6.8**	**–16**	**1064**	**53.5**	**18:31**									
	Chicago	**NHL**	**13**	**2**	**1**	**3**	**2**	**0**	**0**	**1**	**14**	**14.3**	**–1**	**173**	**53.8**	**17:25**	**17**	**2**	**3**	**5**	**4**	**1**	**0**	**0**	**16:38**

			Regular Season														Playoffs								
Season	Club	League	GP	G	A	Pts	PIM	PP	SH	GW	S	%	+/-	TF	F%	Min	GP	G	A	Pts	PIM	PP	SH	GW	Min
2009-10	**Columbus**	**NHL**	**79**	**3**	**13**	**16**	**32**	**0**	**0**	**0**	**93**	**3.2**	**–9**	**1273**	**52.9**	**16:17**									
	Sweden	Olympics	3	0	1	1	2																		
2010-11	**Columbus**	**NHL**	**82**	**7**	**13**	**20**	**30**	**0**	**1**	**1**	**108**	**6.5**	**–13**	**1298**	**52.0**	**15:20**									
	NHL Totals		**718**	**64**	**118**	**182**	**322**	**4**	**10**	**13**	**930**	**6.9**		**11247**	**52.0**	**16:25**	**81**	**9**	**19**	**28**	**54**	**1**	**0**	**4**	**17:35**

Traded to **Boston** by **Colorado** with Brian Rolston, Martin Grenier and New Jersey's 1st round choice (previously acquired, Boston selected Martin Samuelsson) in 2000 Entry Draft for Raymond Bourque and Dave Andreychuk, March 6, 2000. Traded to **Anaheim** by **Boston** for Patrick Traverse and Andrei Nazarov, November 18, 2000. Signed as a free agent by **Frolunda** (Sweden), September, 2004. Traded to **Chicago** by **Anaheim** with Logan Stephenson and future considerations for James Wisniewski and Petri Kontiola, March 4, 2009. Signed as a free agent by **Columbus**, July 1, 2009.

PAILLE, Daniel

(PIGH-yay, DAN-yehl) **BOS**

Left wing. Shoots left. 6', 200 lbs. Born, Welland, Ont., April 15, 1984. Buffalo's 2nd choice, 20th overall, in 2002 Entry Draft.

Season	Club	League	GP	G	A	Pts	PIM	PP	SH	GW	S	%	+/-	TF	F%	Min	GP	G	A	Pts	PIM	PP	SH	GW	Min
99-2000	Welland Cougars	ON-Jr.B	42	14	17	31	19										16	16	16	32					
2000-01	Guelph Storm	OHL	64	22	31	53	57										4	2	0	2	2				
2001-02	Guelph Storm	OHL	62	27	30	57	54										9	5	2	7	9				
2002-03	Guelph Storm	OHL	54	30	27	57	28										11	8	6	14	6				
2003-04	Guelph Storm	OHL	59	37	43	80	63										22	9	9	18	14				
2004-05	Rochester	AHL	79	14	15	29	54										9	2	2	4	6				
2005-06	**Buffalo**	**NHL**	**14**	**1**	**2**	**3**	**2**	**0**	**0**	**0**	**15**	**6.7**	**5**	**4**	**25.0**	**10:24**									
	Rochester	AHL	45	14	13	27	29																		
2006-07	**Buffalo**	**NHL**	**29**	**3**	**8**	**11**	**18**	**0**	**0**	**0**	**45**	**6.7**	**5**	**6**	**33.3**	**12:47**	**1**	**0**	**0**	**0**	**0**	**0**	**0**	**0**	**4:52**
	Rochester	AHL	29	7	14	21	12																		
2007-08	**Buffalo**	**NHL**	**77**	**19**	**16**	**35**	**14**	**0**	**3**	**2**	**110**	**17.3**	**9**	**41**	**36.6**	**13:16**									
2008-09	**Buffalo**	**NHL**	**73**	**12**	**15**	**27**	**20**	**0**	**0**	**2**	**80**	**15.0**	**0**	**17**	**17.7**	**11:54**									
2009-10	**Buffalo**	**NHL**	**2**	**0**	**1**	**1**	**0**	**0**	**0**	**0**	**2**	**0.0**	**1**	**0**	**0.0**	**10:22**									
	Boston	**NHL**	**74**	**10**	**9**	**19**	**12**	**0**	**1**	**0**	**118**	**8.5**	**–4**	**13**	**30.8**	**13:49**	**13**	**0**	**2**	**2**	**2**	**0**	**0**	**0**	**16:01**
2010-11 ♦	**Boston**	**NHL**	**43**	**6**	**7**	**13**	**28**	**0**	**1**	**0**	**48**	**12.5**	**3**	**0**	**0.0**	**11:18**	**25**	**3**	**3**	**6**	**4**	**0**	**1**	**0**	**8:43**
	NHL Totals		**312**	**51**	**58**	**109**	**94**	**0**	**5**	**4**	**418**	**12.2**		**81**	**30.9**	**12:37**	**39**	**3**	**5**	**8**	**6**	**0**	**1**	**0**	**11:03**

Traded to **Boston** by **Buffalo** for Boston's 3rd round choice (Kevin Sundher) in 2010 Entry Draft, October 20, 2009.

PALMIERI, Kyle

(pawl-mee-AIR-ee, KIGHL) **ANA**

Right wing. Shoots right. 5'11", 193 lbs. Born, Smithtown, NY, February 1, 1991. Anaheim's 2nd choice, 26th overall, in 2009 Entry Draft.

Season	Club	League	GP	G	A	Pts	PIM	PP	SH	GW	S	%	+/-	TF	F%	Min	GP	G	A	Pts	PIM	PP	SH	GW	Min
2007-08	USNTDP	NAHL	32	15	10	25	43																		
	USNTDP	U-17	7	5	0	5	8																		
	USNTDP	U-18	27	9	9	18	20																		
2008-09	USNTDP	NAHL	5	1	1	2	2																		
	USNTDP	U-18	28	14	14	28	49																		
2009-10	U. of Notre Dame	CCHA	33	9	8	17	36																		
2010-11	**Anaheim**	**NHL**	**10**	**1**	**0**	**1**	**0**	**0**	**0**	**0**	**10**	**10.0**	**–1**	**0**	**0.0**	**8:41**	**1**	**0**	**0**	**0**	**0**	**0**	**0**	**0**	**10:07**
	Syracuse Crunch	AHL	62	29	22	51	56																		
	NHL Totals		**10**	**1**	**0**	**1**	**0**	**0**	**0**	**0**	**10**	**10.0**		**0**	**0.0**	**8:41**	**1**	**0**	**0**	**0**	**0**	**0**	**0**	**0**	**10:07**

PALMIERI, Nick

(pawl-mee-AIR-ee, NIHK) **N.J.**

Right wing. Shoots right. 6'3", 220 lbs. Born, Utica, NY, July 12, 1989. New Jersey's 2nd choice, 79th overall, in 2007 Entry Draft.

Season	Club	League	GP	G	A	Pts	PIM	PP	SH	GW	S	%	+/-	TF	F%	Min	GP	G	A	Pts	PIM	PP	SH	GW	Min
2004-05	Northwood	High-NY	STATISTICS NOT AVAILABLE																						
2005-06	Erie Otters	OHL	68	13	10	23	79																		
2006-07	Erie Otters	OHL	56	24	21	45	99																		
2007-08	Erie Otters	OHL	50	28	18	46	122																		
	Lowell Devils	AHL	9	1	0	1	4																		
2008-09	Erie Otters	OHL	18	7	5	12	41																		
	Belleville Bulls	OHL	43	20	9	29	75										17	14	3	17	27				
2009-10	**New Jersey**	**NHL**	**6**	**0**	**1**	**1**	**0**	**0**	**0**	**0**	**10**	**0.0**	**0**	**2**	**50.0**	**11:45**									
	Lowell Devils	AHL	69	21	15	36	36										5	1	3	4	2				
2010-11	**New Jersey**	**NHL**	**43**	**9**	**8**	**17**	**6**	**1**	**0**	**2**	**66**	**13.6**	**9**	**2**	**100.0**	**14:20**									
	Albany Devils	AHL	26	6	5	11	28																		
	NHL Totals		**49**	**9**	**9**	**18**	**6**	**1**	**0**	**2**	**76**	**11.8**		**4**	**75.0**	**14:01**									

PALUSHAJ, Aaron

(puh-LOO-shigh, AIR-ruhn) **MTL**

Right wing. Shoots right. 5'11", 187 lbs. Born, Livonia, MI, September 7, 1989. St. Louis' 5th choice, 44th overall, in 2007 Entry Draft.

Season	Club	League	GP	G	A	Pts	PIM	PP	SH	GW	S	%	+/-	TF	F%	Min	GP	G	A	Pts	PIM	PP	SH	GW	Min
2005-06	Des Moines	USHL	58	10	23	33	53										11	2	4	6	15				
2006-07	Des Moines	USHL	56	22	45	67	62										8	6	5	11	6				
2007-08	U. of Michigan	CCHA	43	10	*34	44	22																		
2008-09	U. of Michigan	CCHA	39	13	*37	*50	26																		
	Peoria Rivermen	AHL	4	2	0	2	4										4	0	1	1	2				
2009-10	Peoria Rivermen	AHL	44	5	17	22	22																		
	Hamilton	AHL	18	3	7	10	8										19	2	10	12	28				
2010-11	**Montreal**	**NHL**	**3**	**0**	**0**	**0**	**2**	**0**	**0**	**0**	**3**	**0.0**	**1**	**1**	**0.0**	**8:31**									
	Hamilton	AHL	68	22	35	57	42										19	7	12	19	14				
	NHL Totals		**3**	**0**	**0**	**0**	**2**	**0**	**0**	**0**	**3**	**0.0**		**1**	**0.0**	**8:31**									

CCHA First All-Star Team (2009) • NCAA West First All-American Team (2009)

Traded to **Montreal** by **St. Louis** for Matt D'Agostini, March 2, 2010.

PARDY, Adam

(PAHR-dee, A-duhm) **DAL**

Defense. Shoots left. 6'2", 220 lbs. Born, Bonavista, Nfld., March 29, 1984. Calgary's 6th choice, 173rd overall, in 2004 Entry Draft.

Season	Club	League	GP	G	A	Pts	PIM	PP	SH	GW	S	%	+/-	TF	F%	Min	GP	G	A	Pts	PIM	PP	SH	GW	Min
2002-03	Yarmouth	MJrHL	1	0	0	0	2																		
	Antigonish	MJrHL	31	5	16	21	42																		
	Cape Breton	QMJHL	7	0	1	1	2										2	0	0	0	0				
2003-04	Cape Breton	QMJHL	68	4	12	16	137										5	0	1	1	8				
2004-05	Cape Breton	QMJHL	69	12	27	39	163										5	2	2	4	8				
2005-06	Omaha	AHL	24	0	0	0	18																		
	Las Vegas	ECHL	41	1	11	12	55										10	2	1	3	12				
2006-07	Omaha	AHL	70	2	6	8	60										6	1	1	2	0				
2007-08	Quad City Flames	AHL	65	5	13	18	67																		
2008-09	**Calgary**	**NHL**	**60**	**1**	**9**	**10**	**69**	**0**	**0**	**0**	**38**	**2.6**	**3**	**0**	**0.0**	**15:00**	**6**	**0**	**2**	**2**	**5**	**0**	**0**	**0**	**14:51**
2009-10	**Calgary**	**NHL**	**57**	**2**	**7**	**9**	**48**	**0**	**0**	**0**	**40**	**5.0**	**–3**	**0**	**0.0**	**15:51**									
2010-11	**Calgary**	**NHL**	**30**	**1**	**6**	**7**	**24**	**0**	**0**	**0**	**36**	**2.8**	**3**	**0**	**0.0**	**14:41**									
	NHL Totals		**147**	**4**	**22**	**26**	**141**	**0**	**0**	**0**	**114**	**3.5**		**0**	**0.0**	**15:16**	**6**	**0**	**2**	**2**	**5**	**0**	**0**	**0**	**14:51**

• Missed majority of 2010-11 due to shoulder (October 10, 2010 vs. Los Angeles) and upper body (February 7, 2011 vs. Chicago) injuries. Signed as a free agent by **Dallas**, July 1, 2011.

PARENT, Ryan

(PAIR-ehnt, RIGH-uhn) **VAN**

Defense. Shoots left. 6'3", 198 lbs. Born, Prince Albert, Sask., March 17, 1987. Nashville's 1st choice, 18th overall, in 2005 Entry Draft.

Season	Club	League	GP	G	A	Pts	PIM	PP	SH	GW	S	%	+/-	TF	F%	Min	GP	G	A	Pts	PIM	PP	SH	GW	Min
2002-03	Waterloo Siskins	ON-Jr.B	41	2	8	10	35																		
2003-04	Guelph Storm	OHL	58	1	5	6	18										22	0	0	0	2				
2004-05	Guelph Storm	OHL	66	2	17	19	36										4	0	1	1	4				
2005-06	Guelph Storm	OHL	60	4	17	21	122										15	1	4	5	24				
	Milwaukee	AHL															10	0	0	0	4				
2006-07	**Philadelphia**	**NHL**	**1**	**0**	**0**	**0**	**0**	**0**	**0**	**0**	**1**	**0.0**	**0**	**0**	**0.0**	**14:10**									
	Philadelphia	AHL	6	1	0	1	4																		
	Guelph Storm	OHL	43	3	7	10	86										4	0	1	1	14				
2007-08	**Philadelphia**	**NHL**	**22**	**0**	**0**	**0**	**6**	**0**	**0**	**0**	**9**	**0.0**	**–4**	**0**	**0.0**	**14:59**	**4**	**0**	**1**	**1**	**0**	**0**	**0**	**0**	**16:36**
	Philadelphia	AHL	53	1	7	8	42																		
2008-09	**Philadelphia**	**NHL**	**31**	**0**	**4**	**4**	**10**	**0**	**0**	**0**	**9**	**0.0**	**3**	**0**	**0.0**	**18:12**	**6**	**0**	**0**	**0**	**6**	**0**	**0**	**0**	**18:52**
	Philadelphia	AHL	15	0	1	1	18																		
2009-10	**Philadelphia**	**NHL**	**48**	**1**	**2**	**3**	**20**	**0**	**0**	**0**	**27**	**3.7**	**–14**	**0**	**0.0**	**14:46**	**17**	**1**	**0**	**1**	**2**	**0**	**0**	**0**	**7:28**

			Regular Season														Playoffs								
Season	Club	League	GP	G	A	Pts	PIM	PP	SH	GW	S	%	+/-	TF	F%	Min	GP	G	A	Pts	PIM	PP	SH	GW	Min
2010-11	**Vancouver**	**NHL**	**4**	**0**	**0**	**0**	**0**	**0**	**0**	**0**	**3**	**0.0**	**–3**	**0**	**0.0**	**13:54**									
	Manitoba Moose	AHL	39	1	1	2	56																		
	NHL Totals		**106**	**1**	**6**	**7**	**36**	**0**	**0**	**0**	**49**	**2.0**		**0**	**0.0**	**15:47**	**27**	**1**	**1**	**2**	**8**	**0**	**0**	**0**	**11:21**

OHL Second All-Star Team (2006, 2007)

Traded to **Philadelphia** by **Nashville** with Scottie Upshall and Nashville's 1st (later traded back to Nashville - Nashville selected Jonathon Blum) and 3rd (later traded to Washington - Washington selected Phil Desimone) round choices in 2007 Entry Draft for Peter Forsberg, February 15, 2007. Traded to **Nashville** by **Philadelphia** with future considerations for Dan Hamhuis, June 19, 2010. Traded to **Vancouver** by **Nashville** with Jonas Andersson for Shane O'Brien and Dan Gendur, October 5, 2010.

PARENTEAU, P.A.

(pair-ehn-TOH, PEE-AY) **NYI**

Left wing. Shoots right. 6', 198 lbs. Born, Hull, Que., March 24, 1983. Anaheim's 11th choice, 264th overall, in 2001 Entry Draft.

99-2000	Charles-Lemoyne	QAAA	40	25	40	65	18										16	4	9	13	8				
2000-01	Moncton Wildcats	QMJHL	45	10	19	29	38																		
	Chicoutimi	QMJHL	28	10	13	23	14										7	4	7	11	2				
2001-02	Chicoutimi	QMJHL	68	51	67	118	120										4	3	1	4	10				
2002-03	Chicoutimi	QMJHL	31	20	35	55	56																		
	Sherbrooke	QMJHL	28	13	35	48	84										12	8	11	19	6				
2003-04	Cincinnati	AHL	66	14	16	30	20										7	1	2	3	6				
2004-05	Cincinnati	AHL	76	17	24	41	58										9	2	0	2	8				
2005-06	Portland Pirates	AHL	56	22	27	49	42										19	5	17	22	24				
	Augusta Lynx	ECHL	2	0	1	1	0																		
2006-07	Portland Pirates	AHL	28	15	13	28	35																		
	Chicago	**NHL**	**5**	**0**	**1**	**1**	**2**	**0**	**0**	**0**	**7**	**0.0**	**–1**	**2**	**50.0**	**11:05**									
	Norfolk Admirals	AHL	40	15	36	51	12										6	2	1	3	2				
2007-08	Hartford	AHL	75	34	47	81	81										5	3	2	5	13				
2008-09	Hartford	AHL	74	29	49	78	142																		
2009-10	**NY Rangers**	**NHL**	**22**	**3**	**5**	**8**	**4**	**1**	**0**	**0**	**38**	**7.9**	**–2**	**12**	**33.3**	**13:42**									
	Hartford	AHL	35	20	25	45	63																		
2010-11	**NY Islanders**	**NHL**	**81**	**20**	**33**	**53**	**46**	**9**	**0**	**2**	**161**	**12.4**	**–8**	**30**	**36.7**	**18:13**									
	NHL Totals		**108**	**23**	**39**	**62**	**52**	**10**	**0**	**2**	**206**	**11.2**		**44**	**36.4**	**16:58**									

AHL Second All-Star Team (2008) • AHL First All-Star Team (2009)

Traded to **Chicago** by **Anaheim** with Bruno St. Jacques for Sebastien Caron, Matt Keith and Chris Durno, December 28, 2006. Traded to **NY Rangers** by **Chicago** for future considerations, October 11, 2007. Signed as a free agent by **NY Islanders**, July 2, 2010.

PARISE, Zach

(pah-REE-say, ZAK) **N.J.**

Left wing. Shoots left. 5'11", 195 lbs. Born, Minneapolis, MN, July 28, 1984. New Jersey's 1st choice, 17th overall, in 2003 Entry Draft.

2000-01	Shat.-St. Mary's	High-MN	58	69	93	162																			
2001-02	Shat.-St. Mary's	High-MN	67	77	101	178	58																		
	USNTDP	U-18	12	7	7	14	6																		
2002-03	North Dakota	WCHA	39	26	35	61	34																		
2003-04	North Dakota	WCHA	37	23	32	55	24																		
2004-05	Albany River Rats	AHL	73	18	40	58	56																		
2005-06	**New Jersey**	**NHL**	**81**	**14**	**18**	**32**	**28**	**2**	**0**	**5**	**133**	**10.5**	**–1**	**162**	**42.6**	**13:08**	**9**	**1**	**2**	**3**	**2**	**0**	**0**	**0**	**15:03**
2006-07	**New Jersey**	**NHL**	**82**	**31**	**31**	**62**	**30**	**9**	**0**	**7**	**247**	**12.6**	**–3**	**52**	**44.2**	**17:32**	**11**	**7**	**3**	**10**	**8**	**2**	**0**	**1**	**19:08**
2007-08	**New Jersey**	**NHL**	**81**	**32**	**33**	**65**	**25**	**10**	**1**	**8**	**266**	**12.0**	**13**	**104**	**48.1**	**18:04**	**5**	**1**	**4**	**5**	**2**	**1**	**0**	**0**	**18:29**
2008-09	**New Jersey**	**NHL**	**82**	**45**	**49**	**94**	**24**	**14**	**0**	**8**	**364**	**12.4**	**30**	**121**	**44.6**	**18:45**	**7**	**3**	**3**	**6**	**2**	**1**	**0**	**1**	**19:02**
2009-10	**New Jersey**	**NHL**	**81**	**38**	**44**	**82**	**32**	**9**	**1**	**5**	**347**	**11.0**	**24**	**48**	**37.5**	**19:46**	**5**	**1**	**3**	**4**	**0**	**0**	**1**	**0**	**20:44**
	United States	Olympics	6	4	4	8	0																		
2010-11	**New Jersey**	**NHL**	**13**	**3**	**3**	**6**	**6**	**0**	**0**	**1**	**49**	**6.1**	**–1**	**11**	**36.4**	**19:51**									
	NHL Totals		**420**	**163**	**178**	**341**	**145**	**44**	**2**	**34**	**1406**	**11.6**		**498**	**43.8**	**17:32**	**37**	**13**	**15**	**28**	**14**	**4**	**1**	**2**	**18:15**

WCHA All-Rookie Team (2003) • WCHA First All-Star Team (2004) • NCAA West First All-American Team (2004) • NHL Second All-Star Team (2009) • Olympic All-Star Team (2010)

Played in NHL All-Star Game (2009)

• Missed majority of 2010-11 due to knee injury at Los Angeles, October 30, 2010.

PARK, Richard

(PAHRK, RIH-chuhrd)

Right wing. Shoots right. 5'11", 190 lbs. Born, Seoul, South Korea, May 27, 1976. Pittsburgh's 2nd choice, 50th overall, in 1994 Entry Draft.

1991-92	Tor. Young Nats	MTHL	76	49	58	107	91																		
1992-93	Belleville Bulls	OHL	66	23	38	61	38										5	0	0	0	14				
1993-94	Belleville Bulls	OHL	59	27	49	76	70										12	3	5	8	18				
1994-95	Belleville Bulls	OHL	45	28	51	79	35										16	9	18	27	12				
	Pittsburgh	**NHL**	**1**	**0**	**1**	**1**	**2**	**0**	**0**	**0**	**4**	**0.0**	**1**				**3**	**0**	**0**	**0**	**2**	**0**	**0**	**0**	
1995-96	Belleville Bulls	OHL	6	7	6	13	2										14	18	12	30	10				
	Pittsburgh	**NHL**	**56**	**4**	**6**	**10**	**36**	**0**	**1**	**1**	**62**	**6.5**	**3**				**1**	**0**	**0**	**0**	**0**	**0**	**0**	**0**	
1996-97	**Pittsburgh**	**NHL**	**1**	**0**	**0**	**0**	**0**	**0**	**0**	**0**	**1**	**0.0**	**–1**												
	Cleveland	IHL	50	12	15	27	30																		
	Anaheim	**NHL**	**11**	**1**	**1**	**2**	**10**	**0**	**0**	**0**	**9**	**11.1**	**0**				**11**	**0**	**1**	**1**	**2**	**0**	**0**	**0**	
1997-98	**Anaheim**	**NHL**	**15**	**0**	**2**	**2**	**8**	**0**	**0**	**0**	**14**	**0.0**	**–3**												
	Cincinnati	AHL	56	17	26	43	36																		
1998-99	**Philadelphia**	**NHL**	**7**	**0**	**0**	**0**	**0**	**0**	**0**	**0**	**5**	**0.0**	**–1**	**15**	**53.3**	**9:21**									
	Philadelphia	AHL	75	41	42	83	33										16	9	6	15	4				
99-2000	Utah Grizzlies	IHL	82	28	32	60	36										5	1	0	1	0				
2000-01	Cleveland	IHL	75	27	21	48	29										4	0	2	2	4				
2001-02	**Minnesota**	**NHL**	**63**	**10**	**15**	**25**	**10**	**2**	**1**	**2**	**115**	**8.7**	**–1**	**79**	**41.8**	**16:28**									
	Houston Aeros	AHL	13	4	10	14	6																		
2002-03	**Minnesota**	**NHL**	**81**	**14**	**10**	**24**	**16**	**2**	**2**	**3**	**149**	**9.4**	**–3**	**178**	**48.9**	**16:36**	**18**	**3**	**3**	**6**	**4**	**0**	**0**	**1**	**17:03**
2003-04	**Minnesota**	**NHL**	**73**	**13**	**12**	**25**	**28**	**4**	**0**	**1**	**142**	**9.2**	**0**	**379**	**40.1**	**16:30**									
2004-05	Malmo	Sweden	9	1	3	4	4																		
	Langnau	Swiss	10	3	0	3	8										6	4	1	5	6				
2005-06	**Vancouver**	**NHL**	**60**	**8**	**10**	**18**	**29**	**0**	**1**	**2**	**97**	**8.2**	**–2**	**26**	**26.9**	**11:00**									
2006-07	**NY Islanders**	**NHL**	**82**	**10**	**16**	**26**	**33**	**0**	**2**	**2**	**93**	**10.8**	**4**	**218**	**39.0**	**11:39**	**5**	**0**	**1**	**1**	**2**	**0**	**0**	**0**	**9:16**
2007-08	**NY Islanders**	**NHL**	**82**	**12**	**20**	**32**	**20**	**1**	**4**	**2**	**132**	**9.1**	**–4**	**626**	**50.2**	**15:14**									
2008-09	**NY Islanders**	**NHL**	**71**	**14**	**17**	**31**	**34**	**4**	**2**	**1**	**138**	**10.1**	**–13**	**809**	**49.0**	**17:10**									
2009-10	**NY Islanders**	**NHL**	**81**	**9**	**22**	**31**	**28**	**0**	**1**	**4**	**146**	**6.2**	**–9**	**1040**	**51.5**	**15:45**									
2010-11	Geneve	Swiss	47	15	19	34	16										3	2	1	3	2				
	NHL Totals		**684**	**95**	**132**	**227**	**254**	**13**	**14**	**18**	**1107**	**8.6**		**3370**	**48.0**	**15:01**	**38**	**3**	**5**	**8**	**10**	**0**	**0**	**1**	**15:22**

OHL All-Rookie Team (1993) • AHL Second All-Star Team (1999)

Traded to **Anaheim** by **Pittsburgh** for Roman Oksiuta, March 18, 1997. Signed as a free agent by **Philadelphia**, August 24, 1998. Signed as a free agent by **Utah** (IHL), September 22, 1999. Signed as a free agent by **Minnesota**, June 6, 2000. Signed as a free agent by **Malmo** (Sweden), November 8, 2004. Signed as a free agent by **Langnau** (Swiss), January 4, 2005. Signed as a free agent by **Vancouver**, August 8, 2005. Signed as a free agent by **NY Islanders**, October 2, 2006. Signed as a free agent by **Geneva** (Swiss), September 9, 2010.

PARRISH, Mark

(PAIR-ihsh, MAHRK) **OTT**

Right wing. Shoots right. 5'11", 199 lbs. Born, Bloomington, MN, February 2, 1977. Colorado's 3rd choice, 79th overall, in 1996 Entry Draft.

1994-95	Jefferson Jaguars	High-MN	27	40	20	60	42																		
1995-96	St. Cloud State	WCHA	39	15	13	28	30																		
1996-97	St. Cloud State	WCHA	35	*27	15	42	60																		
1997-98	Seattle	WHL	54	54	38	92	29										5	2	3	5	2				
	New Haven	AHL	1	1	0	1	2																		
1998-99	**Florida**	**NHL**	**73**	**24**	**13**	**37**	**25**	**5**	**0**	**5**	**129**	**18.6**	**–6**	**1**	**0.0**	**13:59**									
	New Haven	AHL	2	1	0	1	0																		
99-2000	**Florida**	**NHL**	**81**	**26**	**18**	**44**	**39**	**6**	**0**	**3**	**152**	**17.1**	**1**	**8**	**75.0**	**14:04**	**4**	**0**	**1**	**1**	**0**	**0**	**0**	**0**	**12:37**
2000-01	**NY Islanders**	**NHL**	**70**	**17**	**13**	**30**	**28**	**6**	**0**	**3**	**123**	**13.8**	**–27**	**3**	**33.3**	**15:27**									
2001-02	**NY Islanders**	**NHL**	**78**	**30**	**30**	**60**	**32**	**9**	**1**	**6**	**162**	**18.5**	**10**	**10**	**40.0**	**16:48**	**7**	**2**	**1**	**3**	**6**	**2**	**0**	**0**	**17:27**
2002-03	**NY Islanders**	**NHL**	**81**	**23**	**25**	**48**	**28**	**9**	**0**	**5**	**147**	**15.6**	**–11**	**9**	**44.4**	**16:12**	**5**	**1**	**0**	**1**	**4**	**1**	**0**	**0**	**16:02**
2003-04	**NY Islanders**	**NHL**	**59**	**24**	**11**	**35**	**18**	**6**	**0**	**6**	**105**	**22.9**	**8**	**5**	**20.0**	**17:20**	**5**	**1**	**2**	**3**	**0**	**0**	**0**	**0**	**20:35**

Season	Club	League	GP	G	A	Pts	PIM	PP	SH	GW	S	%	+/-	TF	F%	Min	GP	G	A	Pts	PIM	PP	SH	GW	Min
			Regular Season														Playoffs								
2004-05			DID NOT PLAY																						
2005-06	**NY Islanders**	**NHL**	**57**	**24**	**17**	**41**	**16**	**13**	**0**	**5**	**102**	**23.5**	**−14**	**12**	**16.7**	**19:34**	....	....	....	....	....	....	....	....	....
	Los Angeles	**NHL**	**19**	**5**	**3**	**8**	**4**	**3**	**0**	**0**	**35**	**14.3**	**−9**	**0**	**0.0**	**15:29**	....	....	....	....	....	....	....	....	....
	United States	Olympics	6	0	0	0	4	....	....	....	....	....	....	....	....	....	....	....	....	....	....	....	....	....	....
2006-07	**Minnesota**	**NHL**	**76**	**19**	**20**	**39**	**18**	**5**	**0**	**4**	**141**	**13.5**	**9**	**13**	**30.8**	**14:20**	**5**	**1**	**0**	**1**	**0**	**0**	**0**	**0**	**15:46**
2007-08	**Minnesota**	**NHL**	**66**	**16**	**14**	**30**	**16**	**7**	**0**	**0**	**95**	**16.8**	**2**	**10**	**40.0**	**14:56**	**1**	**0**	**0**	**0**	**0**	**0**	**0**	**0**	**5:04**
2008-09	**Dallas**	**NHL**	**44**	**8**	**5**	**13**	**18**	**4**	**0**	**3**	**46**	**17.4**	**−3**	**5**	**20.0**	**11:16**	....	....	....	....	....	....	....	....	....
	Bridgeport	AHL	3	1	1	2	2	....	....	....	....	....	....	....	....	....	....	....	....	....	....	....	....	....	....
2009-10	Norfolk Admirals	AHL	56	17	21	38	32	....	....	....	....	....	....	....	....	....	....	....	....	....	....	....	....	....	....
	Tampa Bay	**NHL**	**16**	**0**	**2**	**2**	**4**	**0**	**0**	**0**	**10**	**0.0**	**−5**	**10**	**40.0**	**15:10**	....	....	....	....	....	....	....	....	....
2010-11	**Buffalo**	**NHL**	**2**	**0**	**0**	**0**	**0**	**0**	**0**	**0**	**0**	**0.0**	**−2**	**0**	**0.0**	**11:46**	....	....	....	....	....	....	....	....	....
	Portland Pirates	AHL	56	17	34	51	12	....	....	....	....	....	....	....	....	....	12	3	3	6	0	....	....	....	....
	NHL Totals		**722**	**216**	**171**	**387**	**246**	**73**	**1**	**40**	**1247**	**17.3**		**86**	**36.0**	**15:25**	**27**	**5**	**4**	**9**	**10**	**3**	**0**	**0**	**16:17**

NCAA West Second All-American Team (1997) • WHL West First All-Star Team (1998)

Played in NHL All-Star Game (2002)

• Rights traded to **Florida** by **Colorado** with Anaheim's 3rd round choice (previously acquired, Florida selected Lance Ward) in 1998 Entry Draft for Tom Fitzgerald, March 24, 1998. Traded to **NY Islanders** by **Florida** with Oleg Kvasha for Roberto Luongo and Olli Jokinen, June 24, 2000. Traded to **Los Angeles** by **NY Islanders** with Brent Sopel for Denis Grebeshkov and Jeff Tambellini, March 8, 2006. Signed as a free agent by **Minnesota**, July 1, 2006. Signed as a free agent by **Dallas**, November 5, 2008. Signed as a free agent by **Norfolk** (AHL), October 8, 2009. Signed as a free agent by **Tampa Bay**, February 9, 2010. Signed as a free agent by **Buffalo**, October 6, 2010. Signed as a free agent by **Ottawa**, July 8, 2011.

PARROS, George

(PAIR-ohs, JOHRJ) **ANA**

Right wing. Shoots right. 6'5", 228 lbs. Born, Washington, PA, December 29, 1979. Los Angeles' 9th choice, 222nd overall, in 1999 Entry Draft.

Season	Club	League	GP	G	A	Pts	PIM	PP	SH	GW	S	%	+/-	TF	F%	Min	GP	G	A	Pts	PIM	PP	SH	GW	Min
1996-97	Delbarton	High-NJ	14	15	8	23	....	....	....	....	....	....	....	....	....	....	....	....	....	....	....	....	....	....	....
1997-98	Delbarton	High-NJ	15	22	17	39	....	....	....	....	....	....	....	....	....	....	....	....	....	....	....	....	....	....	....
1998-99	Chicago Freeze	NAHL	54	30	20	50	126	....	....	....	....	....	....	....	....	....	....	....	....	....	....	....	....	....	....
99-2000	Princeton	ECAC	27	4	2	6	14	....	....	....	....	....	....	....	....	....	....	....	....	....	....	....	....	....	....
2000-01	Princeton	ECAC	31	7	10	17	38	....	....	....	....	....	....	....	....	....	....	....	....	....	....	....	....	....	....
2001-02	Princeton	ECAC	31	9	13	22	36	....	....	....	....	....	....	....	....	....	....	....	....	....	....	....	....	....	....
2002-03	Princeton	ECAC	22	0	7	7	29	....	....	....	....	....	....	....	....	....	....	....	....	....	....	....	....	....	....
	Manchester	AHL	9	0	1	1	7	....	....	....	....	....	....	....	....	....	....	....	....	....	....	....	....	....	....
2003-04	Manchester	AHL	57	3	6	9	126	....	....	....	....	....	....	....	....	....	5	0	0	0	4	....	....	....	....
2004-05	Manchester	AHL	67	14	8	22	247	....	....	....	....	....	....	....	....	....	6	1	1	2	27	....	....	....	....
	Reading Royals	ECHL	3	0	0	0	9	....	....	....	....	....	....	....	....	....	....	....	....	....	....	....	....	....	....
2005-06	**Los Angeles**	**NHL**	**55**	**2**	**3**	**5**	**138**	**0**	**0**	**0**	**23**	**8.7**	**1**	**1**	**0.0**	**4:56**	....	....	....	....	....	....	....	....	....
2006-07	**Colorado**	**NHL**	**2**	**0**	**0**	**0**	**0**	**0**	**0**	**0**	**1**	**0.0**	**−1**	**0**	**0.0**	**3:33**	....	....	....	....	....	....	....	....	....
	♦ **Anaheim**	**NHL**	**32**	**1**	**0**	**1**	**102**	**0**	**0**	**0**	**18**	**5.6**	**−2**	**0**	**0.0**	**5:09**	**5**	**0**	**0**	**0**	**10**	**0**	**0**	**0**	**3:49**
2007-08	**Anaheim**	**NHL**	**69**	**1**	**4**	**5**	**183**	**0**	**0**	**0**	**30**	**3.3**	**3**	**10**	**30.0**	**5:57**	**1**	**0**	**0**	**0**	**0**	**0**	**0**	**0**	**2:42**
2008-09	**Anaheim**	**NHL**	**74**	**5**	**5**	**10**	**135**	**0**	**0**	**0**	**47**	**10.6**	**8**	**3**	**0.0**	**6:16**	**7**	**0**	**0**	**0**	**9**	**0**	**0**	**0**	**5:33**
2009-10	**Anaheim**	**NHL**	**57**	**4**	**0**	**4**	**136**	**0**	**0**	**0**	**25**	**16.0**	**4**	**7**	**14.3**	**6:00**	....	....	....	....	....	....	....	....	....
2010-11	**Anaheim**	**NHL**	**78**	**3**	**1**	**4**	**171**	**0**	**0**	**1**	**33**	**9.1**	**−4**	**4**	**25.0**	**6:25**	**6**	**0**	**0**	**0**	**16**	**0**	**0**	**0**	**4:06**
	NHL Totals		**367**	**16**	**13**	**29**	**865**	**0**	**0**	**1**	**177**	**9.0**		**25**	**20.0**	**5:53**	**19**	**0**	**0**	**0**	**35**	**0**	**0**	**0**	**4:29**

Claimed on waivers by **Colorado** from **Los Angeles**, October 3, 2006. Traded to **Anaheim** by **Colorado** with Colorado's 3rd round choice (later traded to Tampa Bay - Tampa Bay selected Luca Cunti) in 2007 Entry Draft for Atlanta's 2nd round choice (previously acquired, Colorado selected T.J. Galiardi) in 2007 Entry Draft and Anaheim's 3rd round choice (later traded to San Jose - San Jose selected Tyson Sexsmith) in 2007 Entry Draft, November 13, 2006.

PARSE, Scott

(PARS, SKAWT) **L.A.**

Center. Shoots right. 5'11", 188 lbs. Born, Portage, MI, September 5, 1984. Los Angeles' 5th choice, 174th overall, in 2004 Entry Draft.

Season	Club	League	GP	G	A	Pts	PIM	PP	SH	GW	S	%	+/-	TF	F%	Min	GP	G	A	Pts	PIM	PP	SH	GW	Min
2002-03	Tri-City Storm	USHL	48	21	23	44	32	....	....	....	....	....	....	....	....	....	3	2	1	3	8	....	....	....	....
2003-04	Nebraska-Omaha	CCHA	39	16	19	35	52	....	....	....	....	....	....	....	....	....	....	....	....	....	....	....	....	....	....
2004-05	Nebraska-Omaha	CCHA	39	19	30	49	32	....	....	....	....	....	....	....	....	....	....	....	....	....	....	....	....	....	....
2005-06	Nebraska-Omaha	CCHA	41	20	*41	*61	40	....	....	....	....	....	....	....	....	....	....	....	....	....	....	....	....	....	....
2006-07	Nebraska-Omaha	CCHA	40	24	28	52	36	....	....	....	....	....	....	....	....	....	....	....	....	....	....	....	....	....	....
	Grand Rapids	AHL	10	2	5	7	6	....	....	....	....	....	....	....	....	....	7	1	0	1	8	....	....	....	....
2007-08	Manchester	AHL	14	0	3	3	4	....	....	....	....	....	....	....	....	....	....	....	....	....	....	....	....	....	....
	Reading Royals	ECHL	18	5	11	16	14	....	....	....	....	....	....	....	....	....	....	....	....	....	....	....	....	....	....
2008-09	Manchester	AHL	74	15	24	39	38	....	....	....	....	....	....	....	....	....	....	....	....	....	....	....	....	....	....
2009-10	**Los Angeles**	**NHL**	**59**	**11**	**13**	**24**	**22**	**0**	**0**	**1**	**78**	**14.1**	**13**	**11**	**54.6**	**10:32**	**4**	**0**	**0**	**0**	**0**	**0**	**0**	**0**	**6:38**
	Manchester	AHL	14	4	11	15	21	....	....	....	....	....	....	....	....	....	....	....	....	....	....	....	....	....	....
2010-11	**Los Angeles**	**NHL**	**5**	**1**	**3**	**4**	**0**	**0**	**0**	**0**	**6**	**16.7**	**5**	**0**	**0.0**	**13:47**	**2**	**0**	**0**	**0**	**0**	**0**	**0**	**0**	**8:47**
	NHL Totals		**64**	**12**	**16**	**28**	**22**	**0**	**0**	**1**	**84**	**14.3**		**11**	**54.5**	**10:47**	**6**	**0**	**0**	**0**	**0**	**0**	**0**	**0**	**7:21**

USHL All-Rookie Team (2003) • CCHA First All-Star Team (2005, 2007) • CCHA Player of the Year (2006) • NCAA West First All-American Team (2006) • NCAA West Second All-American Team (2007)

• Missed majority of 2010-11 due to hip injury at San Jose, November 15, 2010.

PAVELSKI, Joe

(pah-VEHL-skee, JOH) **S.J.**

Center. Shoots right. 5'11", 195 lbs. Born, Plover, WI, July 11, 1984. San Jose's 7th choice, 205th overall, in 2003 Entry Draft.

Season	Club	League	GP	G	A	Pts	PIM	PP	SH	GW	S	%	+/-	TF	F%	Min	GP	G	A	Pts	PIM	PP	SH	GW	Min
2002-03	Waterloo	USHL	60	36	33	69	32	....	....	....	....	....	....	....	....	....	7	5	7	12	8	....	....	....	....
2003-04	Waterloo	USHL	54	21	31	52	58	....	....	....	....	....	....	....	....	....	12	6	6	12	10	....	....	....	....
2004-05	U. of Wisconsin	WCHA	41	16	29	45	26	....	....	....	....	....	....	....	....	....	....	....	....	....	....	....	....	....	....
2005-06	U. of Wisconsin	WCHA	43	23	33	56	34	....	....	....	....	....	....	....	....	....	....	....	....	....	....	....	....	....	....
2006-07	**San Jose**	**NHL**	**46**	**14**	**14**	**28**	**18**	**5**	**0**	**3**	**111**	**12.6**	**4**	**389**	**48.6**	**15:02**	**6**	**1**	**0**	**1**	**0**	**0**	**0**	**0**	**10:27**
	Worcester Sharks	AHL	16	8	18	26	8	....	....	....	....	....	....	....	....	....	....	....	....	....	....	....	....	....	....
2007-08	**San Jose**	**NHL**	**82**	**19**	**21**	**40**	**28**	**8**	**1**	**4**	**207**	**9.2**	**1**	**501**	**53.5**	**14:07**	**13**	**5**	**4**	**9**	**0**	**2**	**0**	**3**	**22:03**
2008-09	**San Jose**	**NHL**	**80**	**25**	**34**	**59**	**46**	**8**	**3**	**3**	**266**	**9.4**	**5**	**1274**	**56.3**	**18:58**	**6**	**0**	**1**	**1**	**9**	**0**	**0**	**0**	**19:21**
2009-10	**San Jose**	**NHL**	**67**	**25**	**26**	**51**	**26**	**3**	**1**	**5**	**228**	**11.0**	**1**	**821**	**58.1**	**19:29**	**15**	**9**	**8**	**17**	**6**	**5**	**0**	**3**	**21:32**
	United States	Olympics	6	0	3	3	4	....	....	....	....	....	....	....	....	....	....	....	....	....	....	....	....	....	....
2010-11	**San Jose**	**NHL**	**74**	**20**	**46**	**66**	**24**	**11**	**1**	**5**	**282**	**7.1**	**10**	**1020**	**54.3**	**19:39**	**18**	**5**	**5**	**10**	**10**	**1**	**0**	**1**	**21:08**
	NHL Totals		**349**	**103**	**141**	**244**	**142**	**35**	**6**	**20**	**1094**	**9.4**		**4005**	**55.1**	**17:33**	**58**	**20**	**18**	**38**	**25**	**8**	**0**	**7**	**20:09**

USHL All-Rookie Team (2003) • USHL First All-Star Team (2003) • USHL Rookie of the Year (2003) • WCHA All-Rookie Team (2005) • WCHA Second All-Star Team (2006) • NCAA West Second All-American Team (2006)

PECKHAM, Theo

(PEHK-uhm, THEE-oh) **EDM**

Defense. Shoots left. 6'2", 234 lbs. Born, Richmond Hill, Ont., November 10, 1987. Edmonton's 2nd choice, 75th overall, in 2006 Entry Draft.

Season	Club	League	GP	G	A	Pts	PIM	PP	SH	GW	S	%	+/-	TF	F%	Min	GP	G	A	Pts	PIM	PP	SH	GW	Min
2003-04	North York	OPJHL	29	1	4	5	46	....	....	....	....	....	....	....	....	....	....	....	....	....	....	....	....	....	....
2004-05	Owen Sound	OHL	61	1	9	10	209	....	....	....	....	....	....	....	....	....	8	0	0	0	8	....	....	....	....
2005-06	Owen Sound	OHL	67	6	9	15	236	....	....	....	....	....	....	....	....	....	11	1	6	7	32	....	....	....	....
2006-07	Owen Sound	OHL	53	10	25	35	173	....	....	....	....	....	....	....	....	....	4	0	1	1	0	....	....	....	....
2007-08	**Edmonton**	**NHL**	**1**	**0**	**0**	**0**	**2**	**0**	**0**	**0**	**0**	**0.0**	**0**	**0**	**0.0**	**13:22**	....	....	....	....	....	....	....	....	....
	Springfield	AHL	59	6	7	13	174	....	....	....	....	....	....	....	....	....	....	....	....	....	....	....	....	....	....
2008-09	**Edmonton**	**NHL**	**15**	**0**	**0**	**0**	**59**	**0**	**0**	**0**	**8**	**0.0**	**−1**	**0**	**0.0**	**11:38**	....	....	....	....	....	....	....	....	....
	Springfield	AHL	47	6	13	19	107	....	....	....	....	....	....	....	....	....	....	....	....	....	....	....	....	....	....
2009-10	**Edmonton**	**NHL**	**15**	**0**	**1**	**1**	**43**	**0**	**0**	**0**	**9**	**0.0**	**−8**	**0**	**0.0**	**16:04**	....	....	....	....	....	....	....	....	....
	Springfield	AHL	37	0	6	6	106	....	....	....	....	....	....	....	....	....	....	....	....	....	....	....	....	....	....
2010-11	**Edmonton**	**NHL**	**71**	**3**	**10**	**13**	**198**	**0**	**0**	**0**	**41**	**7.3**	**−5**	**0**	**0.0**	**18:36**	....	....	....	....	....	....	....	....	....
	NHL Totals		**102**	**3**	**11**	**14**	**302**	**0**	**0**	**0**	**58**	**5.2**		**0**	**0.0**	**17:09**	....	....	....	....	....	....	....	....	....

PELECH, Matt

(PEH-lihk, MAT) **S.J.**

Defense. Shoots right. 6'3", 220 lbs. Born, Toronto, Ont., September 4, 1987. Calgary's 1st choice, 26th overall, in 2005 Entry Draft.

Season	Club	League	GP	G	A	Pts	PIM	PP	SH	GW	S	%	+/-	TF	F%	Min	GP	G	A	Pts	PIM	PP	SH	GW	Min
2002-03	Vaughan Kings	GTHL	44	3	13	16	113	....	....	....	....	....	....	....	....	....	....	....	....	....	....	....	....	....	....
2003-04	Sarnia Sting	OHL	62	4	6	10	39	....	....	....	....	....	....	....	....	....	5	0	1	1	12	....	....	....	....
2004-05	Sarnia Sting	OHL	31	1	5	6	74	....	....	....	....	....	....	....	....	....	....	....	....	....	....	....	....	....	....
2005-06	Sarnia Sting	OHL	18	0	2	2	59	....	....	....	....	....	....	....	....	....	....	....	....	....	....	....	....	....	....
	London Knights	OHL	34	1	7	8	80	....	....	....	....	....	....	....	....	....	19	0	0	0	48	....	....	....	....
2006-07	Belleville Bulls	OHL	58	5	30	35	171	....	....	....	....	....	....	....	....	....	12	0	3	3	22	....	....	....	....
2007-08	Quad City Flames	AHL	77	3	6	9	141	....	....	....	....	....	....	....	....	....	....	....	....	....	....	....	....	....	....

Season	Club	League	GP	G	A	Pts	PIM	PP	SH	GW	S	%	+/-	TF	F%	Min	GP	G	A	Pts	PIM	PP	SH	GW	Min
						Regular Season													Playoffs						
2008-09	Calgary	NHL	5	0	3	3	9	0	0	0	4	0.0	1	0	0.0	13:16	....	....	....	....	....				....
	Quad City Flames	AHL	59	3	6	9	130										....								
2009-10	Abbotsford Heat	AHL	42	2	8	10	125										13	0	4	4	31				
2010-11	Abbotsford Heat	AHL	59	3	2	5	198										....								
	NHL Totals		5	0	3	3	9	0	0	0	4	0.0		0	0.0	13:16	....								

Signed as a free agent by **San Jose**, July 6, 2011.

PELLETIER, Pascal (PEHL-tyay, pas-KAL)

Left wing. Shoots right. 5'11", 191 lbs. Born, Labrador City, Nfld., June 16, 1983.

Season	Club	League	GP	G	A	Pts	PIM	PP	SH	GW	S	%	+/-	TF	F%	Min	GP	G	A	Pts	PIM	PP	SH	GW	Min
2000-01	Baie-Comeau	QMJHL	70	15	44	59	176										11	2	11	13	6				
2001-02	Baie-Comeau	QMJHL	56	12	25	37	115										5	3	4	7	0				
2002-03	Baie-Comeau	QMJHL	67	46	55	101	113										12	5	7	12	14				
2003-04	Shawinigan	QMJIL	64	39	52	91	85										11	3	9	12	20				
2004-05	Louisiana	ECHL	61	10	28	38	75																		
	Gwinnett	ECHL	6	0	1	1	2										5	0	2	2	2				
2005-06	Providence Bruins	AHL	53	20	26	46	42										6	2	4	6	23				
	Gwinnett	ECHL	21	18	12	30	18																		
2006-07	Providence Bruins	AHL	80	14	35	49	60										13	5	4	9	16				
2007-08	**Boston**	**NHL**	6	0	0	0	0	0	0	0	8	0.0	-2	1	100.0	11:04	....								
	Providence Bruins	AHL	73	37	38	75	66										10	6	6	12	4				
2008-09	**Chicago**	**NHL**	7	0	0	0	0	0	0	0	7	0.0	-4	33	39.4	9:08	....								
	Rockford IceHogs	AHL	71	29	26	55	45										4	1	0	1	6				
2009-10	Syracuse Crunch	AHL	25	3	13	16	23																		
	Peoria Rivermen	AHL	55	14	28	42	41																		
2010-11	Langnau	Swiss	47	17	21	38	95										4	1	1	2	29				
	NHL Totals		13	0	0	0	0	0	0	0	15	0.0		34	41.2	10:01	....								

AHL First All-Star Team (2008)
Signed as a free agent by **Boston**, August 7, 2006. Traded to **Chicago** by **Boston** for Martin St. Pierre, July 24, 2008. Signed as a free agent by **Columbus**, July 6, 2009. Traded to **St. Louis** by **Columbus** for Tomas Kana and Brendan Bell, December 8, 2009. Signed as a free agent by **Langnau** (Swiss), May 20, 2010.

PELLEY, Rod (PEHL-lee, RAWD) N.J.

Center. Shoots left. 5'11", 195 lbs. Born, Kitimat, B.C., September 1, 1984.

Season	Club	League	GP	G	A	Pts	PIM	PP	SH	GW	S	%	+/-	TF	F%	Min	GP	G	A	Pts	PIM	PP	SH	GW	Min
2002-03	Ohio State	CCHA	43	8	3	11	26																		
2003-04	Ohio State	CCHA	42	10	12	22	38																		
2004-05	Ohio State	CCHA	41	22	19	41	54																		
2005-06	Ohio State	CCHA	39	7	7	14	42																		
2006-07	**New Jersey**	**NHL**	9	0	0	0	0	0	0	0	8	0.0	-3	98	40.8	11:00	....								
	Lowell Devils	AHL	65	17	12	29	35																		
2007-08	**New Jersey**	**NHL**	58	2	4	6	19	0	0	1	59	3.4	-3	321	46.7	9:19	....								
	Lowell Devils	AHL	11	2	1	3	18																		
2008-09	Lowell Devils	AHL	75	15	23	38	78																		
2009-10	**New Jersey**	**NHL**	63	2	8	10	40	0	0	0	74	2.7	-4	198	49.5	7:52	3	0	0	0	2	0	0	0	9:12
2010-11	**New Jersey**	**NHL**	74	3	7	10	27	1	0	0	88	3.4	-9	320	52.8	11:48	....								
	NHL Totals		204	7	19	26	86	1	0	1	229	3.1		937	48.8	9:51	3	0	0	0	2	0	0	0	9:12

CCHA Second All-Star Team (2005)
Signed as a free agent by **New Jersey**, July 17, 2006.

PELTIER, Derek (PEHL-tyay, DAIR-ihk)

Defense. Shoots left. 5'11", 195 lbs. Born, Plymouth, MN, March 14, 1985. Colorado's 5th choice, 184th overall, in 2004 Entry Draft.

Season	Club	League	GP	G	A	Pts	PIM	PP	SH	GW	S	%	+/-	TF	F%	Min	GP	G	A	Pts	PIM	PP	SH	GW	Min
2003-04	Cedar Rapids	USHL	55	7	26	33	34										4	0	0	0	4				
2004-05	U. of Minnesota	WCHA	43	6	13	19	22																		
2005-06	U. of Minnesota	WCHA	41	1	17	18	30																		
2006-07	U. of Minnesota	WCHA	44	4	11	15	28																		
2007-08	U. of Minnesota	WCHA	45	4	17	21	38																		
	Lake Erie	AHL	6	0	1	1	4																		
2008-09	**Colorado**	**NHL**	11	0	0	0	2	0	0	0	7	0.0	-4	0	0.0	13:15	....								
	Lake Erie	AHL	63	2	17	19	32																		
2009-10	**Colorado**	**NHL**	3	0	0	0	0	0	0	0	1	0.0	0	0	0.0	9:00	....								
	Lake Erie	AHL	44	1	12	13	26																		
2010-11	Peoria Rivermen	AHL	61	3	10	13	28										4	0	1	1	0				
	NHL Totals		14	0	0	0	2	0	0	0	8	0.0		0	0.0	12:21	....								

Signed to a PTO (professional tryout) contract by **Peoria** (AHL), October 7, 2010.

PENNER, Dustin (PEH-nuhr, DUHS-tihn) L.A.

Right wing. Shoots left. 6'4", 245 lbs. Born, Winkler, Man., September 28, 1982.

Season	Club	League	GP	G	A	Pts	PIM	PP	SH	GW	S	%	+/-	TF	F%	Min	GP	G	A	Pts	PIM	PP	SH	GW	Min
2001-02	MSU - Bottineau	NJCAA	23	20	12	32	30																		
2002-03	U. of Maine	H-East	DID NOT PLAY – FRESHMAN																						
2003-04	U. of Maine	H-East	43	11	12	23	52																		
2004-05	Cincinnati	AHL	77	10	18	28	82										9	2	3	5	13				
2005-06	**Anaheim**	**NHL**	19	4	3	7	14	2	0	1	46	8.7	3	1	0.0	11:58	13	3	6	9	12	0	0	0	13:16
	Portland Pirates	AHL	57	39	45	84	68										5	4	3	7	0				
2006-07	**Anaheim** ◆	**NHL**	82	29	16	45	58	9	0	5	204	14.2	-2	58	46.6	13:59	21	3	5	8	2	0	0	2	14:05
2007-08	**Edmonton**	**NHL**	82	23	24	47	45	13	0	4	201	11.4	-12	189	55.0	17:12	....								
2008-09	**Edmonton**	**NHL**	78	17	20	37	61	5	0	5	137	12.4	7	114	47.4	15:23	....								
2009-10	**Edmonton**	**NHL**	82	32	31	63	38	9	0	1	203	15.8	6	421	47.7	18:23	....								
2010-11	**Edmonton**	**NHL**	62	21	18	39	45	6	1	3	137	15.3	-12	294	43.2	18:28	....								
	Los Angeles	**NHL**	19	2	4	6	2	0	0	0	36	5.6	0	12	33.3	17:01	6	1	1	2	4	0	0	0	14:32
	NHL Totals		424	128	116	244	263	44	1	19	964	13.3		1089	47.5	16:25	40	7	12	19	18	0	0	2	13:53

NCAA Championship All-Tournament Team (2004) • AHL Second All-Star Team (2006)
Signed as a free agent by **Anaheim**, May 12, 2004. Signed as a free agent by **Edmonton**, August 2, 2007. Traded to **Los Angeles** by **Edmonton** for Colten Teubert, Los Angeles' 1st round choice (Oscar Klefborn) in 2011 Entry Draft and future considerations, February 28, 2011.

PENNER, Jeff (PEH-nuhr, JEHF) MIN

Defense. Shoots left. 5'10", 183 lbs. Born, Winnipeg, Man., April 13, 1987.

Season	Club	League	GP	G	A	Pts	PIM	PP	SH	GW	S	%	+/-	TF	F%	Min	GP	G	A	Pts	PIM	PP	SH	GW	Min
2005-06	Dauphin Kings	MJHL	44	8	27	35	46																		
2006-07	Dauphin Kings	MJHL	45	9	44	53	....																		
2007-08	Alaska	CCHA	35	5	7	12	49																		
	Providence Bruins	AHL	2	0	0	0	0																		
2008-09	Providence Bruins	AHL	80	10	18	28	50										16	6	5	11	8				
2009-10	**Boston**	**NHL**	2	0	0	0	0	0	0	0	1	0.0	0	0	0.0	14:01	....								
	Providence Bruins	AHL	68	7	28	35	28																		
2010-11	Providence Bruins	AHL	57	5	14	19	30										5	0	4	4	2				
	Houston Aeros	AHL	10	0	4	4	8																		
	NHL Totals		2	0	0	0	0	0	0	0	1	0.0		0	0.0	14:01	....								

MJHL Rookie All-Star Team (2006) • MJHL First All-Star Team (2007)
Signed as a free agent by **Boston**, March 29, 2008. Traded to **Minnesota** by **Boston** with Mikko Lehtonen for Anton Khudobin, February 28, 2011.

			Regular Season														Playoffs								
Season	Club	League	GP	G	A	Pts	PIM	PP	SH	GW	S	%	+/-	TF	F%	Min	GP	G	A	Pts	PIM	PP	SH	GW	Min

PERRAULT, Joel (pair-OH, JOHL)

Center. Shoots right. 6'2", 212 lbs.　　Born, Montreal, Que., April 6, 1983. Anaheim's 7th choice, 137th overall, in 2001 Entry Draft.

Season	Club	League	GP	G	A	Pts	PIM	PP	SH	GW	S	%	+/-	TF	F%	Min	GP	G	A	Pts	PIM	PP	SH	GW	Min
99-2000	Antoine-Girouard	QAAA	19	4	7	11	6	....	....	....	....	....	....	....	....	....	....	....	....	....	....	....	....	....	....
2000-01	Baie-Comeau	QMJHL	68	10	14	24	46	....	....	....	....	....	....	....	....	....	11	1	1	2	10	....	....	....	....
2001-02	Baie-Comeau	QMJHL	57	18	44	62	96	....	....	....	....	....	....	....	....	....	5	2	0	2	6	....	....	....	....
2002-03	Baie-Comeau	QMJHL	70	51	65	*116	93	....	....	....	....	....	....	....	....	....	12	3	7	10	14	....	....	....	....
2003-04	Cincinnati	AHL	65	14	14	28	38	....	....	....	....	....	....	....	....	....	9	1	1	2	2	....	....	....	....
2004-05	Cincinnati	AHL	51	9	19	28	40	....	....	....	....	....	....	....	....	....	....	....	....	....	....	....	....	....	....
2005-06	Portland Pirates	AHL	25	12	12	24	20	....	....	....	....	....	....	....	....	....	....	....	....	....	....	....	....	....	....
	Phoenix	**NHL**	5	1	1	2	2	0	0	0	7	14.3	0	47	34.0	11:29	....	....	....	....	....	....	....	....	....
	San Antonio	AHL	12	1	6	7	4	....	....	....	....	....	....	....	....	....	....	....	....	....	....	....	....	....	....
2006-07	**Phoenix**	**NHL**	15	1	2	3	14	0	0	0	18	9.1	–3	109	82.6	11:29	....	....	....	....	....	....	....	....	....
	St. Louis	**NHL**	11	0	0	0	0	0	0	0	13	0.0	–4	20	25.0	8:19	....	....	....	....	....	....	....	....	....
	Peoria Rivermen	AHL	2	0	2	2	7	....	....	....	....	....	....	....	....	....	....	....	....	....	....	....	....	....	....
	San Antonio	AHL	21	10	4	14	8	....	....	....	....	....	....	....	....	....	....	....	....	....	....	....	....	....	....
2007-08	**Phoenix**	**NHL**	49	7	10	17	48	3	0	2	87	8.0	–11	599	49.1	14:26	....	....	....	....	....	....	....	....	....
	San Antonio	AHL	28	14	13	27	36	....	....	....	....	....	....	....	....	....	....	....	....	....	....	....	....	....	....
2008-09	**Phoenix**	**NHL**	7	2	1	3	4	0	0	0	15	13.3	2	76	44.7	12:52	....	....	....	....	....	....	....	....	....
	San Antonio	AHL	46	18	31	49	46	....	....	....	....	....	....	....	....	....	....	....	....	....	....	....	....	....	....
2009-10	**Phoenix**	**NHL**	2	1	0	1	0	0	0	0	7	14.3	–1	25	40.0	9:55	....	....	....	....	....	....	....	....	....
	San Antonio	AHL	47	17	19	36	38	....	....	....	....	....	....	....	....	....	....	....	....	....	....	....	....	....	....
2010-11	**Vancouver**	**NHL**	7	0	0	0	0	0	0	0	3	0.0	–1	31	41.9	7:12	....	....	....	....	....	....	....	....	....
	Manitoba Moose	AHL	37	5	18	23	43	....	....	....	....	....	....	....	....	....	....	....	....	....	....	....	....	....	....
	NHL Totals		96	12	14	26	68	3	0	2	150	8.0		907	50.9	12:23	....	....	....	....	....	....	....	....	....

QMJHL First All-Star Team (2003) • Canadian Major Junior First All-Star Team (2003)

Traded to **Phoenix** by **Anaheim** for Sean O'Donnell, March 9, 2006. Claimed on waivers by **St. Louis** from **Phoenix**, October 31, 2006. Claimed on waivers by **Phoenix** from **St. Louis**, December 19, 2006. Signed as a free agent by **Vancouver**, July 1, 2010. Traded to **Anaheim** by **Vancouver** with Vancouver's 3rd round choice in 2012 Entry Draft for Maxim Lapierre and MacGregor Sharp, February 28, 2011.

PERREAULT, Mathieu (pair-OH, MA-tyew)　　**WSH**

Center. Shoots left. 5'10", 174 lbs.　　Born, Drummondville, Que., January 5, 1988. Washington's 10th choice, 177th overall, in 2006 Entry Draft.

Season	Club	League	GP	G	A	Pts	PIM	PP	SH	GW	S	%	+/-	TF	F%	Min	GP	G	A	Pts	PIM	PP	SH	GW	Min
2004-05	Magog	QAAA	41	25	47	72	68	....	....	....	....	....	....	....	....	....	9	5	10	15	12	....	....	....	....
2005-06	Acadie-Bathurst	QMJHL	62	18	34	52	42	....	....	....	....	....	....	....	....	....	17	10	11	21	8	....	....	....	....
2006-07	Acadie-Bathurst	QMJHL	67	41	78	119	66	....	....	....	....	....	....	....	....	....	12	6	8	14	8	....	....	....	....
2007-08	Acadie-Bathurst	QMJHL	65	34	*80	*114	61	....	....	....	....	....	....	....	....	....	12	3	19	22	6	....	....	....	....
	Hershey Bears	AHL	....	....	....	....	....	....	....	....	....	....	....	....	....	....	3	0	0	0	0	....	....	....	....
2008-09	Hershey Bears	AHL	77	11	39	50	36	....	....	....	....	....	....	....	....	....	21	2	6	8	8	....	....	....	....
2009-10	**Washington**	**NHL**	21	4	5	9	6	1	0	0	27	14.8	4	210	45.2	11:21	....	....	....	....	....	....	....	....	....
	Hershey Bears	AHL	56	16	34	50	34	....	....	....	....	....	....	....	....	....	21	7	12	19	18	....	....	....	....
2010-11	**Washington**	**NHL**	35	7	7	14	20	1	0	1	41	17.1	–3	305	45.6	11:53	....	....	....	....	....	....	....	....	....
	Hershey Bears	AHL	34	11	24	35	38	....	....	....	....	....	....	....	....	....	6	3	3	6	6	....	....	....	....
	NHL Totals		56	11	12	23	26	2	0	1	68	16.2		515	45.4	11:41	....	....	....	....	....	....	....	....	....

QMJHL First All-Star Team (2007) • QMJHL Player of the Year (2007) • QMJHL Second All-Star Team (2008) • Canadian Major Junior Second All-Star Team (2007, 2008)

PERRON, David (peh-RAWN, DAY-vihd)　　**ST.L.**

Left wing. Shoots right. 6', 200 lbs.　　Born, Sherbrooke, Que., May 28, 1988. St. Louis' 3rd choice, 26th overall, in 2007 Entry Draft.

Season	Club	League	GP	G	A	Pts	PIM	PP	SH	GW	S	%	+/-	TF	F%	Min	GP	G	A	Pts	PIM	PP	SH	GW	Min
2005-06	St-Jerome	QJHL	51	24	45	69	92	....	....	....	....	....	....	....	....	....	8	4	5	9	8	....	....	....	....
2006-07	Lewiston	QMJHL	70	39	44	83	75	....	....	....	....	....	....	....	....	....	17	12	16	28	22	....	....	....	....
2007-08	**St. Louis**	**NHL**	62	13	14	27	38	3	0	1	68	19.1	16	14	35.7	12:33	....	....	....	....	....	....	....	....	....
2008-09	**St. Louis**	**NHL**	81	15	35	50	50	4	0	3	161	9.3	13	6	16.7	14:32	4	1	1	2	4	0	0	0	17:12
2009-10	**St. Louis**	**NHL**	82	20	27	47	60	5	1	2	166	12.0	–10	21	38.1	16:09	....	....	....	....	....	....	....	....	....
2010-11	**St. Louis**	**NHL**	10	5	2	7	12	0	0	0	29	17.2	7	0	0.0	18:25	....	....	....	....	....	....	....	....	....
	NHL Totals		235	53	78	131	160	12	1	6	424	12.5		41	34.1	14:44	4	1	1	2	4	0	0	0	17:12

• Missed majority of 2010-11 due to concussion vs. San Jose, November 4, 2010.

PERRY, Corey (PAIR-ee, KOH-ree)　　**ANA**

Right wing. Shoots right. 6'3", 212 lbs.　　Born, Peterborough, Ont., May 16, 1985. Anaheim's 2nd choice, 28th overall, in 2003 Entry Draft.

Season	Club	League	GP	G	A	Pts	PIM	PP	SH	GW	S	%	+/-	TF	F%	Min	GP	G	A	Pts	PIM	PP	SH	GW	Min
2000-01	Peterborough	Minor-ON	64	69	46	115	20	....	....	....	....	....	....	....	....	....	3	3	0	3	0	....	....	....	....
2001-02	London Knights	OHL	67	28	31	59	56	....	....	....	....	....	....	....	....	....	12	2	3	5	30	....	....	....	....
2002-03	London Knights	OHL	67	25	53	78	145	....	....	....	....	....	....	....	....	....	14	7	16	23	27	....	....	....	....
2003-04	London Knights	OHL	66	40	*73	113	98	....	....	....	....	....	....	....	....	....	15	7	15	22	20	....	....	....	....
	Cincinnati	AHL	....	....	....	....	....	....	....	....	....	....	....	....	....	....	3	1	1	2	4	....	....	....	....
2004-05	London Knights	OHL	60	*47	*83	*130	117	....	....	....	....	....	....	....	....	....	18	11	*27	*38	46	....	....	....	....
2005-06	**Anaheim**	**NHL**	56	13	12	25	50	4	0	2	98	13.3	1	11	27.3	11:34	11	0	3	3	16	0	0	0	9:33
	Portland Pirates	AHL	19	16	18	34	32	....	....	....	....	....	....	....	....	....	1	1	0	1	0	....	....	....	....
2006-07 ♦	**Anaheim**	**NHL**	82	17	27	44	55	4	0	3	194	8.8	12	21	42.9	12:28	21	6	9	15	37	1	0	1	16:30
2007-08	**Anaheim**	**NHL**	70	29	25	54	108	11	0	4	200	14.5	12	16	18.8	17:57	3	2	1	3	8	0	0	0	14:55
2008-09	**Anaheim**	**NHL**	78	32	40	72	109	10	0	8	283	11.3	10	31	29.0	18:36	13	8	6	14	36	2	0	1	22:00
2009-10	**Anaheim**	**NHL**	82	27	49	76	111	6	1	2	270	10.0	0	28	21.4	21:04	....	....	....	....	....	....	....	....	....
	Canada	Olympics	7	4	1	5	2	....	....	....	....	....	....	....	....	....	....	....	....	....	....	....	....	....	....
2010-11	**Anaheim**	**NHL**	82	*50	48	98	104	14	4	*11	290	17.2	9	22	40.9	22:19	6	2	6	8	4	1	1	1	25:15
	NHL Totals		450	168	201	369	537	49	5	30	1335	12.6		129	30.2	17:38	54	18	25	43	101	4	1	3	17:17

OHL First All-Star Team (2004, 2005) • Canadian Major Junior Second All-Star Team (2004) • Canadian Major Junior First All-Star Team (2005) • Memorial Cup All-Star Team (2005) • Stafford Smythe Memorial Trophy (Memorial Cup - MVP) (2005) • NHL First All-Star Team (2011) • Maurice "Rocket" Richard Trophy (2011) • Hart Memorial Trophy (2011) • Played in NHL All-Star Game (2008, 2011)

PETERS, Warren (PEE-tuhrz, WAHR-ihn)　　**MIN**

Center. Shoots left. 6', 203 lbs.　　Born, Saskatoon, Sask., July 10, 1982.

Season	Club	League	GP	G	A	Pts	PIM	PP	SH	GW	S	%	+/-	TF	F%	Min	GP	G	A	Pts	PIM	PP	SH	GW	Min
1997-98	Saskatoon Blades	WHL	1	0	0	0	0	....	....	....	....	....	....	....	....	....	....	....	....	....	....	....	....	....	....
1998-99	Saskatoon Blades	WHL	53	8	6	14	111	....	....	....	....	....	....	....	....	....	....	....	....	....	....	....	....	....	....
99-2000	Saskatoon Blades	WHL	70	11	17	28	97	....	....	....	....	....	....	....	....	....	10	1	2	3	13	....	....	....	....
2000-01	Saskatoon Blades	WHL	63	27	14	41	111	....	....	....	....	....	....	....	....	....	....	....	....	....	....	....	....	....	....
2001-02	Saskatoon Blades	WHL	72	34	26	60	115	....	....	....	....	....	....	....	....	....	7	1	4	5	13	....	....	....	....
2002-03	Saskatoon Blades	WHL	71	31	44	75	108	....	....	....	....	....	....	....	....	....	6	1	6	7	6	....	....	....	....
	Portland Pirates	AHL	1	0	0	0	0	....	....	....	....	....	....	....	....	....	....	....	....	....	....	....	....	....	....
2003-04	Utah Grizzlies	AHL	55	4	4	8	63	....	....	....	....	....	....	....	....	....	....	....	....	....	....	....	....	....	....
	Idaho Steelheads	ECHL	21	6	7	13	33	....	....	....	....	....	....	....	....	....	....	....	....	....	....	....	....	....	....
2004-05	Idaho Steelheads	ECHL	69	23	23	46	131	....	....	....	....	....	....	....	....	....	4	0	1	1	12	....	....	....	....
2005-06	Omaha	AHL	77	15	10	25	133	....	....	....	....	....	....	....	....	....	....	....	....	....	....	....	....	....	....
2006-07	Omaha	AHL	79	17	16	33	95	....	....	....	....	....	....	....	....	....	6	2	1	3	4	....	....	....	....
2007-08	Quad City Flames	AHL	75	11	13	24	74	....	....	....	....	....	....	....	....	....	....	....	....	....	....	....	....	....	....
2008-09	**Calgary**	**NHL**	16	1	0	1	12	0	0	0	13	7.7	–2	69	58.0	7:05	4	0	0	0	0	0	0	0	7:03
	Quad City Flames	AHL	62	11	6	17	51	....	....	....	....	....	....	....	....	....	....	....	....	....	....	....	....	....	....
2009-10	**Dallas**	**NHL**	11	1	0	1	2	0	0	0	8	12.5	1	80	48.8	7:13	....	....	....	....	....	....	....	....	....
	Texas Stars	AHL	61	20	14	34	52	....	....	....	....	....	....	....	....	....	23	4	4	8	*56	....	....	....	....
2010-11	**Minnesota**	**NHL**	11	1	0	1	4	0	0	0	11	9.1	–2	79	62.0	8:43	....	....	....	....	....	....	....	....	....
	Houston Aeros	AHL	62	15	17	32	47	....	....	....	....	....	....	....	....	....	24	4	8	12	16	....	....	....	....
	NHL Totals		38	3	0	3	18	0	0	0	32	9.4		228	56.1	7:35	4	0	0	0	0	0	0	0	7:03

Signed as a free agent by **Calgary**, August 5, 2005. Signed as a free agent by **Dallas**, July 6, 2009. Signed as a free agent by **Minnesota**, July 2, 2010.

			Regular Season														Playoffs								
Season	Club	League	GP	G	A	Pts	PIM	PP	SH	GW	S	%	+/-	TF	F%	Min	GP	G	A	Pts	PIM	PP	SH	GW	Min

PETERSEN, Toby

(PEE-tuhr-suhn, TOH-bee) **DAL**

Center. Shoots left. 5'10", 197 lbs. Born, Minneapolis, MN, October 27, 1978. Pittsburgh's 9th choice, 244th overall, in 1998 Entry Draft.

Season	Club	League	GP	G	A	Pts	PIM	PP	SH	GW	S	%	+/-	TF	F%	Min	GP	G	A	Pts	PIM	PP	SH	GW	Min
1995-96	Jefferson Jaguars	High-MN	25	29	30	59	....	....	....	....	....	....	....	....	....	....	....	....	....	....	....	....	....	....	....
1996-97	Colorado College	WCHA	40	17	21	38	18	....	....	....	....	....	....	....	....	....	....	....	....	....	....	....	....	....	....
1997-98	Colorado College	WCHA	40	16	17	33	34	....	....	....	....	....	....	....	....	....	....	....	....	....	....	....	....	....	....
1998-99	Colorado College	WCHA	21	12	12	24	2	....	....	....	....	....	....	....	....	....	....	....	....	....	....	....	....	....	....
99-2000	Colorado College	WCHA	37	14	19	33	8	....	....	....	....	....	....	....	....	....	....	....	....	....	....	....	....	....	....
2000-01	**Pittsburgh**	**NHL**	**12**	**2**	**6**	**8**	**4**	**0**	**0**	**1**	**25**	**8.0**	**3**	**39**	**35.9**	**13:22**	....	....	....	....	....	....	....	....	....
	Wilkes-Barre	AHL	73	26	41	67	22	....	....	....	....	....	....	....	....	....	21	7	6	13	4	....	....	....	....
2001-02	**Pittsburgh**	**NHL**	**79**	**8**	**10**	**18**	**4**	**1**	**1**	**0**	**116**	**6.9**	**–15**	**338**	**45.6**	**12:16**	....	....	....	....	....	....	....	....	....
2002-03	Wilkes-Barre	AHL	80	31	35	66	24	....	....	....	....	....	....	....	....	....	6	1	3	4	4	....	....	....	....
2003-04	Wilkes-Barre	AHL	62	15	29	44	4	....	....	....	....	....	....	....	....	....	21	2	10	12	12	....	....	....	....
2004-05	Edmonton	AHL	78	14	15	29	21	....	....	....	....	....	....	....	....	....	....	....	....	....	....	....	....	....	....
2005-06	**Edmonton**	**NHL**	....	....	....	....	....	....	....	....	....	....	....	....	....	....	**2**	**1**	**0**	**1**	**0**	**0**	**0**	**0**	**6:23**
	Iowa Stars	AHL	79	26	47	73	48	....	....	....	....	....	....	....	....	....	7	2	4	6	2	....	....	....	....
2006-07	**Edmonton**	**NHL**	**64**	**6**	**9**	**15**	**4**	**0**	**2**	**1**	**92**	**6.5**	**–18**	**214**	**48.1**	**13:40**	....	....	....	....	....	....	....	....	....
	Iowa Stars	AHL	7	2	6	8	0	....	....	....	....	....	....	....	....	....	....	....	....	....	....	....	....	....	....
2007-08	**Dallas**	**NHL**	**8**	**0**	**3**	**3**	**4**	**0**	**0**	**0**	**6**	**0.0**	**0**	**44**	**50.0**	**7:50**	**16**	**0**	**0**	**0**	**2**	**0**	**0**	**0**	**9:45**
	Iowa Stars	AHL	63	21	30	51	24	....	....	....	....	....	....	....	....	....	....	....	....	....	....	....	....	....	....
2008-09	**Dallas**	**NHL**	**57**	**4**	**7**	**11**	**14**	**0**	**0**	**0**	**80**	**5.0**	**1**	**283**	**45.2**	**11:25**	....	....	....	....	....	....	....	....	....
2009-10	**Dallas**	**NHL**	**78**	**9**	**6**	**15**	**6**	**0**	**1**	**0**	**110**	**8.2**	**3**	**171**	**44.4**	**10:55**	....	....	....	....	....	....	....	....	....
2010-11	**Dallas**	**NHL**	**60**	**2**	**4**	**6**	**8**	**0**	**2**	**0**	**58**	**3.4**	**–7**	**120**	**38.3**	**10:02**	....	....	....	....	....	....	....	....	....
	Texas Stars	AHL	1	0	1	1	2	....	....	....	....	....	....	....	....	....	....	....	....	....	....	....	....	....	....
	NHL Totals		**358**	**31**	**45**	**76**	**44**	**1**	**6**	**2**	**487**	**6.4**		**1209**	**44.9**	**11:39**	**18**	**1**	**0**	**1**	**2**	**0**	**0**	**0**	**9:23**

WCHA All-Rookie Team (1997) • AHL All-Rookie Team (2001)

Signed as a free agent by **Edmonton**, July 30, 2004. Signed as a free agent by **Dallas**, July 6, 2007.

PETIOT, Richard

(PEH-tee-awt, RIH-chuhrd) **T.B.**

Defense. Shoots left. 6'3", 215 lbs. Born, Daysland, Alta., August 20, 1982. Los Angeles' 6th choice, 116th overall, in 2001 Entry Draft.

Season	Club	League	GP	G	A	Pts	PIM	PP	SH	GW	S	%	+/-	TF	F%	Min	GP	G	A	Pts	PIM	PP	SH	GW	Min
2000-01	Camrose Kodiaks	AJHL	55	8	16	24	81	....	....	....	....	....	....	....	....	....	8	2	1	3	8	....	....	....	....
2001-02	Colorado College	WCHA	39	4	6	10	35	....	....	....	....	....	....	....	....	....	....	....	....	....	....	....	....	....	....
2002-03	Colorado College	WCHA	38	1	6	7	86	....	....	....	....	....	....	....	....	....	....	....	....	....	....	....	....	....	....
2003-04	Colorado College	WCHA	39	3	5	8	61	....	....	....	....	....	....	....	....	....	....	....	....	....	....	....	....	....	....
2004-05	Colorado College	WCHA	26	3	5	8	42	....	....	....	....	....	....	....	....	....	....	....	....	....	....	....	....	....	....
2005-06	**Los Angeles**	**NHL**	**2**	**0**	**0**	**0**	**2**	**0**	**0**	**0**	**1**	**0.0**	**–2**	**0**	**0.0**	**4:47**	....	....	....	....	....	....	....	....	....
	Manchester	AHL	63	4	10	14	52	....	....	....	....	....	....	....	....	....	7	1	0	1	6	....	....	....	....
2006-07	Manchester	AHL	13	1	1	2	25	....	....	....	....	....	....	....	....	....	2	0	0	0	2	....	....	....	....
2007-08	Manchester	AHL	40	2	5	7	56	....	....	....	....	....	....	....	....	....	....	....	....	....	....	....	....	....	....
2008-09	Toronto Marlies	AHL	45	3	11	14	59	....	....	....	....	....	....	....	....	....	....	....	....	....	....	....	....	....	....
	Tampa Bay	**NHL**	**11**	**0**	**3**	**3**	**21**	**0**	**0**	**0**	**10**	**0.0**	**5**	**0**	**0.0**	**20:37**	....	....	....	....	....	....	....	....	....
	Norfolk Admirals	AHL	1	0	0	0	0	....	....	....	....	....	....	....	....	....	....	....	....	....	....	....	....	....	....
2009-10	Rockford IceHogs	AHL	80	8	29	37	88	....	....	....	....	....	....	....	....	....	4	0	0	0	4	....	....	....	....
2010-11	**Edmonton**	**NHL**	**2**	**0**	**0**	**0**	**2**	**0**	**0**	**0**	**1**	**0.0**	**1**	**0**	**0.0**	**13:05**	....	....	....	....	....	....	....	....	....
	Oklahoma City	AHL	66	0	15	15	52	....	....	....	....	....	....	....	....	....	6	0	0	0	4	....	....	....	....
	NHL Totals		**15**	**0**	**3**	**3**	**25**	**0**	**0**	**0**	**12**	**0.0**		**0**	**0.0**	**17:30**	....	....	....	....	....	....	....	....	....

AJHL All-Rookie Team (2001) • AJHL South Second All-Star Team (2001)

• Missed majority of 2006-07 due to knee injury in rookie training camp, October 6, 2006. Signed as a free agent by **Toronto**, July 15, 2008. Traded to **Tampa Bay** by **Toronto** for Olaf Kolzig, Jamie Heward, Andy Rogers and Carolina's 4th round choice (previously acquired – later forfeited) in 2009 Entry Draft, March 4, 2009. Signed as a free agent by **Chicago**, July 9, 2009. Signed as a free agent by **Edmonton**, July 2, 2010. Signed as a free agent by **Tampa Bay**, July 2, 2011.

PETRY, Jeff

(PEH-tree, JEHF) **EDM**

Defense. Shoots right. 6'3", 196 lbs. Born, Ann Arbor, MI, December 9, 1987. Edmonton's 1st choice, 45th overall, in 2006 Entry Draft.

Season	Club	League	GP	G	A	Pts	PIM	PP	SH	GW	S	%	+/-	TF	F%	Min	GP	G	A	Pts	PIM	PP	SH	GW	Min
2004-05	St. Mary's Prep	High-MI	23	2	8	10	....	....	....	....	....	....	....	....	....	....	6	2	5	7	....	....	....	....	....
2005-06	Det. Caesers	MWEHL	33	7	21	28	24	....	....	....	....	....	....	....	....	....	....	....	....	....	....	....	....	....	....
	Des Moines	USHL	48	1	14	15	68	....	....	....	....	....	....	....	....	....	11	2	5	7	8	....	....	....	....
2006-07	Des Moines	USHL	55	18	27	45	71	....	....	....	....	....	....	....	....	....	8	0	6	6	10	....	....	....	....
2007-08	Michigan State	CCHA	42	3	21	24	28	....	....	....	....	....	....	....	....	....	....	....	....	....	....	....	....	....	....
2008-09	Michigan State	CCHA	38	2	12	14	32	....	....	....	....	....	....	....	....	....	....	....	....	....	....	....	....	....	....
2009-10	Springfield	AHL	8	0	3	3	2	....	....	....	....	....	....	....	....	....	....	....	....	....	....	....	....	....	....
	Michigan State	CCHA	38	4	25	29	26	....	....	....	....	....	....	....	....	....	....	....	....	....	....	....	....	....	....
2010-11	**Edmonton**	**NHL**	**35**	**1**	**4**	**5**	**10**	**0**	**0**	**0**	**41**	**2.4**	**–12**	**0**	**0.0**	**20:22**	....	....	....	....	....	....	....	....	....
	Oklahoma City	AHL	41	7	17	24	18	....	....	....	....	....	....	....	....	....	6	0	1	1	4	....	....	....	....
	NHL Totals		**35**	**1**	**4**	**5**	**10**	**0**	**0**	**0**	**41**	**2.4**		**0**	**0.0**	**20:22**	....	....	....	....	....	....	....	....	....

USHL First All-Star Team (2007) • USHL Defenseman of the Year (2007) • CCHA All-Rookie Team (2008) • CCHA Second All-Star Team (2010) • NCAA West Second All-American Team (2010)

PETTINGER, Matt

(PEH-tihn-juhr, MAT)

Left wing. Shoots left. 6'1", 205 lbs. Born, Edmonton, Alta., October 22, 1980. Washington's 2nd choice, 43rd overall, in 2000 Entry Draft.

Season	Club	League	GP	G	A	Pts	PIM	PP	SH	GW	S	%	+/-	TF	F%	Min	GP	G	A	Pts	PIM	PP	SH	GW	Min
1994-95	Victoria Racquet	Minor-BC	55	52	48	100	41	....	....	....	....	....	....	....	....	....	....	....	....	....	....	....	....	....	....
1995-96	Victoria Racquet	Minor-BC	60	80	65	145	45	....	....	....	....	....	....	....	....	....	....	....	....	....	....	....	....	....	....
1996-97	Victoria Salsa	BCHL	49	22	14	36	31	....	....	....	....	....	....	....	....	....	....	....	....	....	....	....	....	....	....
1997-98	Victoria Salsa	BCHL	55	22	20	42	56	....	....	....	....	....	....	....	....	....	7	5	1	6	8	....	....	....	....
1998-99	U. of Denver	WCHA	33	6	14	20	44	....	....	....	....	....	....	....	....	....	....	....	....	....	....	....	....	....	....
99-2000	U. of Denver	WCHA	19	2	6	8	49	....	....	....	....	....	....	....	....	....	....	....	....	....	....	....	....	....	....
	Calgary Hitmen	WHL	27	14	6	20	41	....	....	....	....	....	....	....	....	....	11	2	6	8	30	....	....	....	....
2000-01	**Washington**	**NHL**	**10**	**0**	**0**	**0**	**2**	**0**	**0**	**0**	**6**	**0.0**	**–1**	**2**	**50.0**	**7:47**	....	....	....	....	....	....	....	....	....
	Portland Pirates	AHL	64	19	17	36	92	....	....	....	....	....	....	....	....	....	2	0	0	0	4	....	....	....	....
2001-02	**Washington**	**NHL**	**61**	**7**	**3**	**10**	**44**	**1**	**0**	**1**	**73**	**9.6**	**–8**	**5**	**20.0**	**9:39**	....	....	....	....	....	....	....	....	....
	Portland Pirates	AHL	9	3	3	6	24	....	....	....	....	....	....	....	....	....	....	....	....	....	....	....	....	....	....
2002-03	**Washington**	**NHL**	**1**	**0**	**0**	**0**	**0**	**0**	**0**	**0**	**0**	**0.0**	**0**	**1**	**0.0**	**3:30**	....	....	....	....	....	....	....	....	....
	Portland Pirates	AHL	69	14	13	27	72	....	....	....	....	....	....	....	....	....	3	0	2	2	2	....	....	....	....
2003-04	**Washington**	**NHL**	**71**	**7**	**5**	**12**	**37**	**1**	**0**	**1**	**92**	**7.6**	**–9**	**18**	**44.4**	**11:25**	....	....	....	....	....	....	....	....	....
2004-05	Ljubljana	Slovenia	1	0	1	1	0	....	....	....	....	....	....	....	....	....	....	....	....	....	....	....	....	....	....
	Ljubljana	Interliga	7	2	4	6	41	....	....	....	....	....	....	....	....	....	....	....	....	....	....	....	....	....	....
2005-06	**Washington**	**NHL**	**71**	**20**	**18**	**38**	**39**	**4**	**5**	**2**	**134**	**14.9**	**–2**	**39**	**12.8**	**15:29**	....	....	....	....	....	....	....	....	....
2006-07	**Washington**	**NHL**	**64**	**16**	**16**	**32**	**22**	**4**	**3**	**2**	**111**	**14.4**	**–13**	**23**	**30.4**	**16:53**	....	....	....	....	....	....	....	....	....
2007-08	**Washington**	**NHL**	**56**	**2**	**5**	**7**	**25**	**1**	**0**	**1**	**98**	**2.0**	**–11**	**12**	**58.3**	**14:43**	....	....	....	....	....	....	....	....	....
	Vancouver	**NHL**	**20**	**4**	**2**	**6**	**11**	**0**	**0**	**2**	**29**	**13.8**	**0**	**7**	**57.1**	**13:10**	....	....	....	....	....	....	....	....	....
2008-09	Manitoba Moose	AHL	2	3	0	3	0	....	....	....	....	....	....	....	....	....	....	....	....	....	....	....	....	....	....
	Tampa Bay	**NHL**	**59**	**8**	**7**	**15**	**24**	**2**	**0**	**1**	**82**	**9.8**	**–14**	**18**	**16.7**	**12:19**	....	....	....	....	....	....	....	....	....
2009-10	**Vancouver**	**NHL**	**9**	**1**	**2**	**3**	**6**	**0**	**0**	**0**	**8**	**12.5**	**3**	**13**	**23.1**	**10:45**	**1**	**0**	**0**	**0**	**0**	**0**	**0**	**0**	**4:12**
	Manitoba Moose	AHL	54	14	16	30	31	....	....	....	....	....	....	....	....	....	....	....	....	....	....	....	....	....	....
2010-11	Kolner Haie	Germany	44	14	31	45	32	....	....	....	....	....	....	....	....	....	5	1	2	3	2	....	....	....	....
	NHL Totals		**422**	**65**	**58**	**123**	**210**	**13**	**8**	**10**	**633**	**10.3**		**138**	**28.3**	**13:12**	**1**	**0**	**0**	**0**	**0**	**0**	**0**	**0**	**4:12**

• Left **University of Denver** (WCHA) and signed as a free agent with **Calgary** (WHL), January 10, 2000. Signed as a free agent by **Ljubljana** (Slovenia), December 6, 2004. Traded to **Vancouver** by **Washington** for Matt Cooke, February 26, 2008. Claimed on waivers by **Tampa Bay** from **Vancouver**, October 21, 2008. Signed as a free agent by **Vancouver**, November 2, 2009. Signed as a free agent by **Koln** (Germany). August 6, 2010.

PEVERLEY, Rich

(PEH-vuhr-lee, RIHTCH) **BOS**

Center. Shoots right. 6', 195 lbs. Born, Guelph, Ont., July 8, 1982.

Season	Club	League	GP	G	A	Pts	PIM	PP	SH	GW	S	%	+/-	TF	F%	Min	GP	G	A	Pts	PIM	PP	SH	GW	Min
1998-99	Kitchener	ON-Jr.B	STATISTICS NOT AVAILABLE																						
99-2000	Milton Merchants	OPJHL	STATISTICS NOT AVAILABLE																						
2000-01	St. Lawrence	ECAC	29	2	4	6	4	....	....	....	....	....	....	....	....	....	....	....	....	....	....	....	....	....	....
2001-02	St. Lawrence	ECAC	34	10	21	31	18	....	....	....	....	....	....	....	....	....	....	....	....	....	....	....	....	....	....
2002-03	St. Lawrence	ECAC	34	15	23	38	12	....	....	....	....	....	....	....	....	....	....	....	....	....	....	....	....	....	....
2003-04	St. Lawrence	ECAC	41	17	25	42	34	....	....	....	....	....	....	....	....	....	....	....	....	....	....	....	....	....	....

			Regular Season														Playoffs								
Season	Club	League	GP	G	A	Pts	PIM	PP	SH	GW	S	%	+/-	TF	F%	Min	GP	G	A	Pts	PIM	PP	SH	GW	Min
2004-05	Portland Pirates	AHL	1	0	0	0	0	....	....	....	....	....	....	....	....	....	....	....	....	....	....	....	....	....	....
	South Carolina	ECHL	69	30	28	58	72	....	....	....	....	....	....	....	....	....	4	2	2	4	6	....	....	....	....
2005-06	Milwaukee	AHL	65	12	34	46	44	....	....	....	....	....	....	....	....	....	21	2	9	11	18	....	....	....	....
	Reading Royals	ECHL	11	4	11	15	4	....	....	....	....	....	....	....	....	....	....	....	....	....	....	....	....	....	....
2006-07	Milwaukee	AHL	66	30	38	68	62	....	....	....	....	....	....	....	....	....	4	1	2	3	8	....	....	....	....
	Nashville	**NHL**	13	0	1	1	0	0	0	0	9	0.0	–1	45	48.9	7:31	....	....	....	....	....	....	....	....	....
2007-08	**Nashville**	**NHL**	33	5	5	10	8	0	0	2	43	11.6	4	132	46.2	10:20	6	0	2	2	0	0	0	0	8:52
	Milwaukee	AHL	45	14	40	54	50	....	....	....	....	....	....	....	....	....	3	1	0	1	0	....	....	....	....
2008-09	**Nashville**	**NHL**	27	2	7	9	15	0	0	0	42	4.8	–3	130	49.2	12:08	....	....	....	....	....	....	....	....	....
	Atlanta	**NHL**	39	13	22	35	18	2	1	5	75	17.3	16	554	52.4	18:49	....	....	....	....	....	....	....	....	....
2009-10	**Atlanta**	**NHL**	82	22	33	55	36	7	2	7	166	13.3	–14	1193	54.2	18:40	....	....	....	....	....	....	....	....	....
2010-11	**Atlanta**	**NHL**	59	14	20	34	35	6	1	2	161	8.7	–16	1020	55.5	19:13	....	....	....	....	....	....	....	....	....
	♦ **Boston**	**NHL**	23	4	3	7	2	0	1	1	40	10.0	–1	156	58.3	15:46	25	4	8	12	17	0	0	2	16:11
	NHL Totals		276	60	91	151	114	15	5	17	536	11.2		3230	53.9	16:24	31	4	10	14	17	0	0	2	14:46

Signed as a free agent by **Nashville**, January 18, 2007. Claimed on waivers by **Atlanta** from **Nashville**, January 10, 2009. Traded to **Boston** by **Atlanta** with Boris Valabik for Blake Wheeler and Mark Stuart, February 18, 2011.

PHANEUF, Dion

(fah-NUF, DEE-awn) **TOR**

Defense. Shoots left. 6'3", 214 lbs. Born, Edmonton, Alta., April 10, 1985. Calgary's 1st choice, 9th overall, in 2003 Entry Draft.

2000-01	Southgate Lions	AMBHL	35	15	50	65	208	....	....	....	....	....	....	....	....	....	4	3	4	7	15	....	....	....	....
2001-02	Red Deer Rebels	WHL	67	5	12	17	170	....	....	....	....	....	....	....	....	....	21	0	2	2	14	....	....	....	....
2002-03	Red Deer Rebels	WHL	71	16	14	30	185	....	....	....	....	....	....	....	....	....	23	7	7	14	34	....	....	....	....
2003-04	Red Deer Rebels	WHL	62	19	24	43	126	....	....	....	....	....	....	....	....	....	19	2	9	11	30	....	....	....	....
2004-05	Red Deer Rebels	WHL	55	24	32	56	73	....	....	....	....	....	....	....	....	....	7	1	4	5	12	....	....	....	....
2005-06	**Calgary**	**NHL**	82	20	29	49	93	16	0	7	242	8.3	5	0	0.0	21:44	7	1	0	1	7	1	0	0	18:37
2006-07	**Calgary**	**NHL**	79	17	33	50	98	13	0	4	230	7.4	10	0	0.0	25:40	6	1	0	1	7	1	0	0	26:24
2007-08	**Calgary**	**NHL**	82	17	43	60	182	10	1	4	263	6.5	12	0	0.0	26:25	7	3	4	7	4	1	0	0	27:07
2008-09	**Calgary**	**NHL**	80	11	36	47	100	4	0	4	277	4.0	–11	0	0.0	26:32	5	0	3	3	4	0	0	0	24:48
2009-10	**Calgary**	**NHL**	55	10	12	22	49	5	0	2	138	7.2	3	0	0.0	23:14	....	....	....	....	....	....	....	....	....
	Toronto	**NHL**	26	2	8	10	34	0	0	1	87	2.3	–2	0	0.0	26:22	....	....	....	....	....	....	....	....	....
2010-11	**Toronto**	**NHL**	66	8	22	30	88	3	0	1	190	4.2	–2	0	0.0	25:18	....	....	....	....	....	....	....	....	....
	NHL Totals		470	85	183	268	644	51	1	23	1427	6.0		0	0.0	24:58	25	5	7	12	22	3	0	0	24:06

WHL East First All-Star Team (2004, 2005) • WHL Defenseman of the Year (2004, 2005) • Canadian Major Junior First All-Star Team (2004, 2005) • NHL All-Rookie Team (2006) • NHL First All-Star Team (2008)

Played in NHL All-Star Game (2007, 2008)

Traded to **Toronto** by **Calgary** with Fredrik Sjostrom and Keith Aulie for Matt Stajan, Niklas Hagman, Jamal Mayers and Ian White, January 31, 2010.

PHILLIPS, Chris

(FIHL-ihps, KRIHS) **OTT**

Defense. Shoots left. 6'3", 220 lbs. Born, Calgary, Alta., March 9, 1978. Ottawa's 1st choice, 1st overall, in 1996 Entry Draft.

1993-94	Fort McMurray	AJHL	56	6	16	22	72	....	....	....	....	....	....	....	....	....	10	0	3	3	16	....	....	....	....
1994-95	Fort McMurray	AJHL	48	16	32	48	127	....	....	....	....	....	....	....	....	....	11	4	2	6	10	....	....	....	....
1995-96	Prince Albert	WHL	61	10	30	40	97	....	....	....	....	....	....	....	....	....	18	2	12	14	30	....	....	....	....
1996-97	Prince Albert	WHL	32	3	23	26	58	....	....	....	....	....	....	....	....	....	....	....	....	....	....	....	....	....	....
	Lethbridge	WHL	26	4	18	22	28	....	....	....	....	....	....	....	....	....	19	4	*21	25	20	....	....	....	....
1997-98	**Ottawa**	**NHL**	72	5	11	16	38	2	0	2	107	4.7	2	....	....	....	11	0	2	2	2	0	0	0	....
1998-99	**Ottawa**	**NHL**	34	3	3	6	32	2	0	0	51	5.9	–5	0	0.0	18:06	3	0	0	0	0	0	0	0	13:50
99-2000	**Ottawa**	**NHL**	65	5	14	19	39	0	0	1	96	5.2	12	0	0.0	16:50	6	0	1	1	4	0	0	0	18:17
2000-01	**Ottawa**	**NHL**	73	2	12	14	31	2	0	0	77	2.6	8	1	0.0	21:28	1	1	0	1	0	0	0	0	20:52
2001-02	**Ottawa**	**NHL**	63	6	16	22	29	1	0	1	103	5.8	5	0	0.0	19:31	12	0	0	0	12	0	0	0	21:44
2002-03	**Ottawa**	**NHL**	78	3	16	19	71	2	0	1	97	3.1	7	0	0.0	20:13	18	2	4	6	12	0	0	1	21:36
2003-04	**Ottawa**	**NHL**	82	7	16	23	46	0	0	1	93	7.5	15	1	100.0	20:50	7	1	0	1	12	1	0	0	20:26
2004-05	Brynas IF Gavle	Sweden	27	5	3	8	45	....	....	....	....	....	....	....	....	....	....	....	....	....	....	....	....	....	....
	Brynas IF Gavle	Sweden-Q	9	1	2	3	2	....	....	....	....	....	....	....	....	....	....	....	....	....	....	....	....	....	....
2005-06	**Ottawa**	**NHL**	69	1	18	19	90	0	0	0	79	1.3	19	0	0.0	20:52	9	2	0	2	6	0	0	0	21:41
2006-07	**Ottawa**	**NHL**	82	8	18	26	80	0	1	3	94	8.5	36	2	0.0	22:22	20	0	0	0	24	0	0	0	23:11
2007-08	**Ottawa**	**NHL**	81	5	13	18	56	1	0	1	80	6.3	15	1	0.0	22:29	4	0	0	0	4	0	0	0	22:00
2008-09	**Ottawa**	**NHL**	82	6	16	22	66	0	1	0	88	6.8	–14	0	0.0	21:52	....	....	....	....	....	....	....	....	....
2009-10	**Ottawa**	**NHL**	82	8	16	24	45	1	1	2	82	9.8	8	0	0.0	22:21	6	0	0	0	4	0	0	0	24:57
2010-11	**Ottawa**	**NHL**	82	1	8	9	32	0	0	0	81	1.2	–35	0	0.0	21:31	....	....	....	....	....	....	....	....	....
	NHL Totals		945	60	177	237	655	11	3	12	1128	5.3		5	20.0	20:56	97	6	7	13	80	1	0	1	21:39

WHL Rookie of the Year (1996) • WHL East First All-Star Team (1997) • Canadian Major Junior First All-Star Team (1997) • Memorial Cup All-Star Team (1997)

• Missed majority of 1998-99 due to ankle injury vs. Buffalo, December 30, 1998. Signed as a free agent by **Gavle** (Sweden), November 2, 2004.

PICARD, Alexandre

(pee-KARD, al-ehx-AHN-druh) **PIT**

Defense. Shoots left. 6'3", 215 lbs. Born, Gatineau, Que., July 5, 1985. Philadelphia's 5th choice, 85th overall, in 2003 Entry Draft.

2000-01	Gatineau	QAAA	42	6	15	21	38	....	....	....	....	....	....	....	....	....	11	0	1	1	8	....	....	....	....
2001-02	Halifax	QMJHL	59	2	12	14	28	....	....	....	....	....	....	....	....	....	13	2	3	5	6	....	....	....	....
2002-03	Halifax	QMJHL	71	4	30	34	64	....	....	....	....	....	....	....	....	....	25	1	5	6	14	....	....	....	....
2003-04	Cape Breton	QMJHL	57	10	26	36	44	....	....	....	....	....	....	....	....	....	5	0	0	0	0	....	....	....	....
2004-05	Halifax	QMJHL	68	15	23	38	46	....	....	....	....	....	....	....	....	....	13	1	5	6	14	....	....	....	....
	Philadelphia	AHL	....	....	....	....	....	....	....	....	....	....	....	....	....	....	2	0	0	0	0	....	....	....	....
2005-06	**Philadelphia**	**NHL**	6	0	0	0	4	0	0	0	9	0.0	–2	0	0.0	9:33	....	....	....	....	....	....	....	....	....
	Philadelphia	AHL	75	7	26	33	82	....	....	....	....	....	....	....	....	....	....	....	....	....	....	....	....	....	....
2006-07	**Philadelphia**	**NHL**	62	3	19	22	17	1	0	0	56	5.4	–19	0	0.0	18:29	....	....	....	....	....	....	....	....	....
	Philadelphia	AHL	6	1	2	3	2	....	....	....	....	....	....	....	....	....	....	....	....	....	....	....	....	....	....
2007-08	**Philadelphia**	**NHL**	4	0	0	0	2	0	0	0	3	0.0	–3	0	0.0	13:02	....	....	....	....	....	....	....	....	....
	Philadelphia	AHL	53	8	30	38	31	....	....	....	....	....	....	....	....	....	....	....	....	....	....	....	....	....	....
	Tampa Bay	**NHL**	20	3	3	6	8	1	0	1	21	14.3	–9	0	0.0	21:54	....	....	....	....	....	....	....	....	....
	Norfolk Admirals	AHL	1	0	0	0	0	....	....	....	....	....	....	....	....	....	....	....	....	....	....	....	....	....	....
2008-09	**Ottawa**	**NHL**	47	6	8	14	8	6	0	1	72	8.3	–2	0	0.0	18:52	....	....	....	....	....	....	....	....	....
2009-10	**Ottawa**	**NHL**	45	4	11	15	20	1	0	1	64	6.3	–2	0	0.0	19:03	....	....	....	....	....	....	....	....	....
	Carolina	**NHL**	9	0	0	0	6	0	0	0	7	0.0	2	0	0.0	15:04	....	....	....	....	....	....	....	....	....
2010-11	**Montreal**	**NHL**	43	3	5	8	17	2	0	1	49	6.1	0	0	0.0	16:26	....	....	....	....	....	....	....	....	....
	NHL Totals		236	19	46	65	82	11	0	4	281	6.8		0	0.0	18:08	....	....	....	....	....	....	....	....	....

QMJHL Second All-Star Team (2005)

Traded to **Tampa Bay** by **Philadelphia** with Philadelphia's 2nd round choice (Richard Panik) in 2009 Entry Draft for Vaclav Prospal, February 25, 2008. Traded to **Ottawa** by **Tampa Bay** with Filip Kuba and San Jose's 1st round choice (previously acquired, later traded to Columbus, later traded to NY Islanders, later traded to Anaheim - Anaheim selected Kyle Palmieri) in 2009 Entry Draft for Andrej Meszaros, August 29, 2008. Traded to **Carolina** by **Ottawa** with Ottawa's 2nd round choice (later traded to Edmonton - Edmonton selected Martin Marincin) in 2010 Entry Draft for Matt Cullen, February 12, 2010. Signed as a free agent by **Montreal**, July 31, 2010. Signed as a free agent by **Pittsburgh**, July 5, 2011.

PICARD, Alexandre

(pee-KARD, al-ehx-AHN-druh) **T.B.**

Left wing. Shoots left. 6'2", 206 lbs. Born, Les Saules, Que., October 9, 1985. Columbus' 1st choice, 8th overall, in 2004 Entry Draft.

2000-01	St-Francois	QAAA	5	1	1	2	0	....	....	....	....	....	....	....	....	....	....	....	....	....	....	....	....	....	....
2001-02	St-Francois	QAAA	41	21	30	51	48	....	....	....	....	....	....	....	....	....	8	2	7	9	8	....	....	....	....
	Sherbrooke	QMJHL	6	0	3	3	0	....	....	....	....	....	....	....	....	....	....	....	....	....	....	....	....	....	....
2002-03	Sherbrooke	QMJHL	66	14	15	29	41	....	....	....	....	....	....	....	....	....	12	4	0	4	10	....	....	....	....
2003-04	Lewiston	QMJHL	69	39	41	80	88	....	....	....	....	....	....	....	....	....	7	7	4	11	6	....	....	....	....
2004-05	Lewiston	QMJHL	65	40	45	85	160	....	....	....	....	....	....	....	....	....	8	5	2	7	18	....	....	....	....
2005-06	**Columbus**	**NHL**	17	0	0	0	14	0	0	0	10	0.0	–2	3	33.3	9:09	....	....	....	....	....	....	....	....	....
	Syracuse Crunch	AHL	45	15	15	30	52	....	....	....	....	....	....	....	....	....	6	1	0	1	19	....	....	....	....
2006-07	**Columbus**	**NHL**	23	0	1	1	6	0	0	0	20	0.0	–3	0	0.0	7:49	....	....	....	....	....	....	....	....	....
	Syracuse Crunch	AHL	48	11	18	29	73	....	....	....	....	....	....	....	....	....	....	....	....	....	....	....	....	....	....
2007-08	**Columbus**	**NHL**	3	0	0	0	2	0	0	0	1	0.0	0	0	0.0	6:46	....	....	....	....	....	....	....	....	....
	Syracuse Crunch	AHL	50	7	13	20	116	....	....	....	....	....	....	....	....	....	13	2	1	3	14	....	....	....	....
2008-09	**Columbus**	**NHL**	15	0	1	1	26	0	0	0	10	0.0	–1	0	0.0	6:53	....	....	....	....	....	....	....	....	....
	Syracuse Crunch	AHL	49	22	10	32	107	....	....	....	....	....	....	....	....	....	....	....	....	....	....	....	....	....	....

			Regular Season														Playoffs								
Season	Club	League	GP	G	A	Pts	PIM	PP	SH	GW	S	%	+/-	TF	F%	Min	GP	G	A	Pts	PIM	PP	SH	GW	Min
2009-10	**Columbus**	**NHL**	**9**	**0**	**0**	**0**	**10**	**0**	**0**	**0**	**12**	**0.0**	**–3**	**0**	**0.0**	**7:13**	....	....	....	....	....	....	....	....	....
	Syracuse Crunch	AHL	42	17	18	35	111	....	....	....	....	....	....	....	....	....	....	....	....	....	....	....	....	....	....
	San Antonio	AHL	16	9	6	15	14	....	....	....	....	....	....	....	....	....	....	....	....	....	....	....	....	....	....
2010-11	San Antonio	AHL	59	24	22	46	84	....	....	....	....	....	....	....	....	....	....	....	....	....	....	....	....	....	....
	NHL Totals		**67**	**0**	**2**	**2**	**58**	**0**	**0**	**0**	**53**	**0.0**		**3**	**33.3**	**7:49**	....	....	....	....	....	....	....	....	....

QMJHL Second All-Star Team (2004)

Traded to **Phoenix** by **Columbus** for Chad Kolarik, March 3, 2010. Signed as a free agent by **Tampa Bay**, July 7, 2011.

PIETRANGELO, Alex

(puh-TRAN-geh-loh, AL-ehx) **ST.L.**

Defense. Shoots right. 6'3", 206 lbs. Born, King City, Ont., January 18, 1990. St. Louis' 1st choice, 4th overall, in 2008 Entry Draft.

Season	Club	League	GP	G	A	Pts	PIM	PP	SH	GW	S	%	+/-	TF	F%	Min	GP	G	A	Pts	PIM	PP	SH	GW	Min
2005-06	Tor. Jr. Canadiens	GTHL	44	13	31	44	33	....	....	....	....	....	....	....	....	....	....	....	....	....	....	....	....	....	....
2006-07	Mississauga	OHL	59	7	45	52	45	....	....	....	....	....	....	....	....	....	4	0	0	0	8	....	....	....	....
2007-08	Niagara Ice Dogs	OHL	60	13	40	53	94	....	....	....	....	....	....	....	....	....	6	5	4	9	4	....	....	....	....
2008-09	Niagara Ice Dogs	OHL	36	8	21	29	32	....	....	....	....	....	....	....	....	....	12	1	5	6	20	....	....	....	....
	St. Louis	**NHL**	**8**	**0**	**1**	**1**	**2**	**0**	**0**	**0**	**7**	**0.0**	**0**	**0**	**0.0**	**16:31**	....	....	....	....	....	....	....	....	....
	Peoria Rivermen	AHL	1	0	0	0	4	....	....	....	....	....	....	....	....	....	7	0	3	3	2	....	....	....	....
2009-10	**St. Louis**	**NHL**	**9**	**1**	**1**	**2**	**6**	**0**	**0**	**0**	**7**	**14.3**	**–9**	**0**	**0.0**	**16:34**	....	....	....	....	....	....	....	....	....
	Barrie Colts	OHL	25	9	20	29	27	....	....	....	....	....	....	....	....	....	17	2	12	14	8	....	....	....	....
2010-11	**St. Louis**	**NHL**	**79**	**11**	**32**	**43**	**19**	**4**	**0**	**1**	**161**	**6.8**	**18**	**0**	**0.0**	**22:00**	....	....	....	....	....	....	....	....	....
	NHL Totals		**96**	**12**	**34**	**46**	**27**	**4**	**0**	**1**	**175**	**6.9**		**0**	**0.0**	**21:02**	....	....	....	....	....	....	....	....	....

• Missed majority of 2009-10 as a healthy reserve.

PIHLSTROM, Antti

(PIHL-stuhm, AN-tee) **NSH**

Left wing. Shoots left. 5'11", 190 lbs. Born, Vanntaa, Finland, October 22, 1984.

Season	Club	League	GP	G	A	Pts	PIM	PP	SH	GW	S	%	+/-	TF	F%	Min	GP	G	A	Pts	PIM	PP	SH	GW	Min
2001-02	Jokerit U18	Fin-U18	26	15	14	29	41	....	....	....	....	....	....	....	....	....	8	0	5	5	18	....	....	....	....
	Jokerit Helsinki Jr.	Fin-Jr.	1	0	0	0	0	....	....	....	....	....	....	....	....	....	....	....	....	....	....	....	....	....	....
2002-03	Blues Espoo Jr.	Fin-Jr.	36	10	16	26	38	....	....	....	....	....	....	....	....	....	10	1	1	2	8	....	....	....	....
2003-04	Blues Espoo Jr.	Fin-Jr.	23	9	19	28	42	....	....	....	....	....	....	....	....	....	1	0	2	2	0	....	....	....	....
	Suomi U20	Finland-2	4	0	1	1	2	....	....	....	....	....	....	....	....	....	....	....	....	....	....	....	....	....	....
	Blues Espoo	Finland	49	1	3	4	18	....	....	....	....	....	....	....	....	....	9	0	0	0	0	....	....	....	....
2004-05	Blues Espoo	Finland	53	4	3	7	30	....	....	....	....	....	....	....	....	....	....	....	....	....	....	....	....	....	....
	Blues Espoo Jr.	Fin-Jr.	11	7	3	10	36	....	....	....	....	....	....	....	....	....	7	0	2	2	26	....	....	....	....
2005-06	SaiPa	Finland	54	10	11	21	60	....	....	....	....	....	....	....	....	....	8	1	0	1	2	....	....	....	....
2006-07	HPK Hameenlinna	Finland	56	16	23	39	63	....	....	....	....	....	....	....	....	....	9	3	5	8	4	....	....	....	....
2007-08	**Nashville**	**NHL**	**1**	**0**	**0**	**0**	**0**	**0**	**0**	**0**	**1**	**0.0**	**–1**	**0**	**0.0**	**9:08**	....	....	....	....	....	....	....	....	....
	Milwaukee	AHL	78	27	18	45	62	....	....	....	....	....	....	....	....	....	6	1	0	1	8	....	....	....	....
2008-09	**Nashville**	**NHL**	**53**	**2**	**5**	**7**	**10**	**1**	**0**	**0**	**88**	**2.3**	**–1**	**1**	**0.0**	**11:27**	....	....	....	....	....	....	....	....	....
	Milwaukee	AHL	15	8	4	12	10	....	....	....	....	....	....	....	....	....	....	....	....	....	....	....	....	....	....
2009-10	Farjestad	Sweden	43	4	6	10	44	....	....	....	....	....	....	....	....	....	....	....	....	....	....	....	....	....	....
	JYP Jyvaskyla	Finland	19	7	14	21	14	....	....	....	....	....	....	....	....	....	14	4	4	8	18	....	....	....	....
2010-11	JYP Jyvaskyla	Finland	59	30	23	53	51	....	....	....	....	....	....	....	....	....	10	1	3	4	26	....	....	....	....
	NHL Totals		**54**	**2**	**5**	**7**	**10**	**1**	**0**	**0**	**89**	**2.2**		**1**	**0.0**	**11:24**	....	....	....	....	....	....	....	....	....

Signed as a free agent by **Nashville**, June 1, 2007. Signed as a free agent by **Farjestad** (Sweden), August 6, 2009. • Loaned to **Jyvaskyla** (Finland) by **Farjestad** (Sweden), January 29, 2010.

PIRRI, Brandon

(PIHR-ee, BRAN-duhn) **CHI**

Center. Shoots left. 6', 180 lbs. Born, Toronto, Ont., April 10, 1991. Chicago's 2nd choice, 59th overall, in 2009 Entry Draft.

Season	Club	League	GP	G	A	Pts	PIM	PP	SH	GW	S	%	+/-	TF	F%	Min	GP	G	A	Pts	PIM	PP	SH	GW	Min
2006-07	Tor. Young Nats	GTHL	44	54	72	128	18	....	....	....	....	....	....	....	....	....	....	....	....	....	....	....	....	....	....
2007-08	Streetsville Derbys	OPJHL	40	18	32	50	42	....	....	....	....	....	....	....	....	....	....	....	....	....	....	....	....	....	....
2008-09	Streetsville Derbys	ON-Jr.A	18	21	28	49	24	....	....	....	....	....	....	....	....	....	....	....	....	....	....	....	....	....	....
	Georgetown	ON-Jr.A	26	25	20	45	22	....	....	....	....	....	....	....	....	....	14	8	13	21	10	....	....	....	....
2009-10	RPI Engineers	ECAC	39	11	*32	43	67	....	....	....	....	....	....	....	....	....	....	....	....	....	....	....	....	....	....
2010-11	**Chicago**	**NHL**	**1**	**0**	**0**	**0**	**0**	**0**	**0**	**0**	**1**	**0.0**	**–1**	**6**	**33.3**	**8:56**	....	....	....	....	....	....	....	....	....
	Rockford IceHogs	AHL	70	12	31	43	50	....	....	....	....	....	....	....	....	....	....	....	....	....	....	....	....	....	....
	NHL Totals		**1**	**0**	**0**	**0**	**0**	**0**	**0**	**0**	**1**	**0.0**		**6**	**33.3**	**8:56**	....	....	....	....	....	....	....	....	....

ECAC All-Rookie Team (2010)

PISANI, Fernando

(pih-ZAN-ee, FUHR-nan-DOH)

Right wing. Shoots left. 6'1", 205 lbs. Born, Edmonton, Alta., December 27, 1976. Edmonton's 9th choice, 195th overall, in 1996 Entry Draft.

Season	Club	League	GP	G	A	Pts	PIM	PP	SH	GW	S	%	+/-	TF	F%	Min	GP	G	A	Pts	PIM	PP	SH	GW	Min
1993-94	St. Albert Saints	AJHL	50	6	21	27	24	....	....	....	....	....	....	....	....	....	....	....	....	....	....	....	....	....	....
1994-95	Bonnyville	AJHL	16	4	34	37	97	....	....	....	....	....	....	....	....	....	....	....	....	....	....	....	....	....	....
	St. Albert Saints	AJHL	40	26	21	47	16	....	....	....	....	....	....	....	....	....	....	....	....	....	....	....	....	....	....
1995-96	St. Albert Saints	AJHL	58	40	63	103	134	....	....	....	....	....	....	....	....	....	18	7	22	29	28	....	....	....	....
1996-97	Providence	H-East	35	12	18	30	36	....	....	....	....	....	....	....	....	....	....	....	....	....	....	....	....	....	....
1997-98	Providence	H-East	36	16	18	34	20	....	....	....	....	....	....	....	....	....	....	....	....	....	....	....	....	....	....
1998-99	Providence	H-East	38	14	37	51	42	....	....	....	....	....	....	....	....	....	....	....	....	....	....	....	....	....	....
99-2000	Providence	H-East	38	14	24	38	56	....	....	....	....	....	....	....	....	....	....	....	....	....	....	....	....	....	....
2000-01	Hamilton	AHL	52	12	13	25	28	....	....	....	....	....	....	....	....	....	....	....	....	....	....	....	....	....	....
2001-02	Hamilton	AHL	79	26	34	60	60	....	....	....	....	....	....	....	....	....	15	4	6	10	4	....	....	....	....
2002-03	**Edmonton**	**NHL**	**35**	**8**	**5**	**13**	**10**	**0**	**1**	**0**	**32**	**25.0**	**9**	**1**	**100.0**	**10:43**	**6**	**1**	**0**	**1**	**2**	**0**	**0**	**0**	**13:48**
	Hamilton	AHL	41	17	15	32	24	....	....	....	....	....	....	....	....	....	....	....	....	....	....	....	....	....	....
2003-04	**Edmonton**	**NHL**	**76**	**16**	**14**	**30**	**46**	**4**	**1**	**1**	**99**	**16.2**	**14**	**10**	**20.0**	**12:46**	....	....	....	....	....	....	....	....	....
2004-05	Langnau	Swiss	7	1	3	4	0	....	....	....	....	....	....	....	....	....	....	....	....	....	....	....	....	....	....
	Asiago	Italy	12	1	5	6	6	....	....	....	....	....	....	....	....	....	9	4	6	10	0	....	....	....	....
2005-06	**Edmonton**	**NHL**	**80**	**18**	**19**	**37**	**42**	**4**	**1**	**2**	**131**	**13.7**	**5**	**35**	**22.9**	**13:51**	**24**	***14**	**4**	**18**	**10**	**3**	**1**	***5**	**17:12**
2006-07	**Edmonton**	**NHL**	**77**	**14**	**14**	**28**	**40**	**2**	**1**	**0**	**142**	**9.9**	**–1**	**20**	**40.0**	**16:54**	....	....	....	....	....	....	....	....	....
2007-08	**Edmonton**	**NHL**	**56**	**13**	**9**	**22**	**28**	**4**	**0**	**3**	**96**	**13.5**	**–5**	**7**	**28.6**	**16:32**	....	....	....	....	....	....	....	....	....
2008-09	**Edmonton**	**NHL**	**38**	**7**	**8**	**15**	**14**	**0**	**0**	**0**	**72**	**9.7**	**–1**	**123**	**40.7**	**15:19**	....	....	....	....	....	....	....	....	....
2009-10	**Edmonton**	**NHL**	**40**	**4**	**4**	**8**	**10**	**0**	**0**	**0**	**54**	**7.4**	**–16**	**16**	**18.8**	**14:35**	....	....	....	....	....	....	....	....	....
2010-11	**Chicago**	**NHL**	**60**	**7**	**9**	**16**	**10**	**1**	**0**	**1**	**72**	**9.7**	**0**	**66**	**51.5**	**12:34**	**3**	**0**	**0**	**0**	**0**	**0**	**0**	**0**	**7:54**
	NHL Totals		**462**	**87**	**82**	**169**	**200**	**15**	**4**	**7**	**698**	**12.5**		**278**	**38.8**	**14:17**	**33**	**15**	**4**	**19**	**12**	**3**	**1**	**5**	**15:44**

Signed as a free agent by **Langnau** (Swiss), October 24, 2004. Signed as a free agent by **Asiago** (Italy), December 23, 2004. • Missed majority of 2008-09 due to ankle injury at Detroit, November 17, 2008. Signed as a free agent by **Chicago**, August 24, 2010.

PISKULA, Joe

(pihs-KOO-luh, JOH) **CGY**

Defense. Shoots left. 6'3", 214 lbs. Born, Antigo, WI, July 5, 1984.

Season	Club	League	GP	G	A	Pts	PIM	PP	SH	GW	S	%	+/-	TF	F%	Min	GP	G	A	Pts	PIM	PP	SH	GW	Min
2002-03	Chicago Steel	USHL	13	0	0	0	18	....	....	....	....	....	....	....	....	....	....	....	....	....	....	....	....	....	....
	Des Moines	USHL	32	2	6	8	18	....	....	....	....	....	....	....	....	....	4	0	1	1	4	....	....	....	....
2003-04	Des Moines	USHL	58	2	4	6	68	....	....	....	....	....	....	....	....	....	3	0	1	1	0	....	....	....	....
2004-05	U. of Wisconsin	WCHA	40	0	6	6	24	....	....	....	....	....	....	....	....	....	....	....	....	....	....	....	....	....	....
2005-06	U. of Wisconsin	WCHA	34	2	9	11	22	....	....	....	....	....	....	....	....	....	....	....	....	....	....	....	....	....	....
2006-07	U. of Wisconsin	WCHA	38	1	4	5	34	....	....	....	....	....	....	....	....	....	....	....	....	....	....	....	....	....	....
	Los Angeles	**NHL**	**5**	**0**	**0**	**0**	**6**	**0**	**0**	**0**	**4**	**0.0**	**–3**	**0**	**0.0**	**9:59**	....	....	....	....	....	....	....	....	....
2007-08	Manchester	AHL	55	0	7	7	57	....	....	....	....	....	....	....	....	....	4	0	0	0	4	....	....	....	....
2008-09	Manchester	AHL	67	0	12	12	40	....	....	....	....	....	....	....	....	....	....	....	....	....	....	....	....	....	....
2009-10	Manchester	AHL	72	2	10	12	51	....	....	....	....	....	....	....	....	....	16	2	2	4	12	....	....	....	....
2010-11	Abbotsford Heat	AHL	71	1	11	12	73	....	....	....	....	....	....	....	....	....	....	....	....	....	....	....	....	....	....
	NHL Totals		**5**	**0**	**0**	**0**	**6**	**0**	**0**	**0**	**4**	**0.0**		**0**	**0.0**	**9:59**	....	....	....	....	....	....	....	....	....

Signed as a free agent by **Los Angeles**, March 21, 2007. Signed as a free agent by **Abbotsford** (AHL), October 6, 2010. Signed as a free agent by **Calgary**, July 1, 2011.

PITKANEN, Joni

(PIHT-ka-nuhn, YOH-nee) **CAR**

Defense. Shoots left. 6'3", 210 lbs. Born, Oulu, Finland, September 19, 1983. Philadelphia's 1st choice, 4th overall, in 2002 Entry Draft.

			Regular Season														Playoffs								
Season	Club	League	GP	G	A	Pts	PIM	PP	SH	GW	S	%	+/-	TF	F%	Min	GP	G	A	Pts	PIM	PP	SH	GW	Min
1998-99	Karpat Oulu U18	Fin-U18	30	1	5	6	12	....	....	....	....	....	....	....	....	....	....	....	....	....	....	....	....	....	....
99-2000	Karpat Oulu U18	Fin-U18	36	12	14	26	26	....	....	....	....	....	....	....	....	....	6	1	4	5	2	....	....	....	....
	Karpat Oulu Jr.	Fin-Jr.	2	0	0	0	0	....	....	....	....	....	....	....	....	....	....	....	....	....	....	....	....	....	....
2000-01	Karpat Oulu Jr.	Fin-Jr.	24	6	11	17	77	....	....	....	....	....	....	....	....	....	....	....	....	....	....	....	....	....	....
	Karpat Oulu	Finland	21	0	0	0	10	....	....	....	....	....	....	....	....	....	2	0	0	0	2	....	....	....	....
2001-02	Karpat Oulu Jr.	Fin-Jr.	....	....	....	....	....	....	....	....	....	....	....	....	....	....	1	0	0	0	0	....	....	....	....
	Karpat Oulu	Finland	49	4	15	19	65	....	....	....	....	....	....	....	....	....	4	0	0	0	12	....	....	....	....
2002-03	Karpat Oulu	Finland	35	5	15	20	38	....	....	....	....	....	....	....	....	....	....	....	....	....	....	....	....	....	....
2003-04	**Philadelphia**	**NHL**	**71**	**8**	**19**	**27**	**44**	**5**	**0**	**2**	**133**	**6.0**	**15**	**0**	**0.0**	**16:35**	**15**	**0**	**3**	**3**	**6**	**0**	**0**	**0**	**12:13**
2004-05	Philadelphia	AHL	76	6	35	41	105	....	....	....	....	....	....	....	....	....	21	3	4	7	16	....	....	....	....
2005-06	**Philadelphia**	**NHL**	**58**	**13**	**33**	**46**	**78**	**5**	**0**	**3**	**118**	**11.0**	**22**	**0**	**0.0**	**23:43**	**6**	**0**	**2**	**2**	**2**	**0**	**0**	**0**	**24:12**
	Finland	Olympics	DID NOT PLAY – INJURED																						
2006-07	**Philadelphia**	**NHL**	**77**	**4**	**39**	**43**	**88**	**1**	**0**	**0**	**137**	**2.9**	**–25**	**0**	**0.0**	**24:33**	....	....	....	....	....	....	....	....	....
2007-08	**Edmonton**	**NHL**	**63**	**8**	**18**	**26**	**56**	**1**	**1**	**1**	**101**	**7.9**	**–5**	**0**	**0.0**	**24:07**	....	....	....	....	....	....	....	....	....
2008-09	**Carolina**	**NHL**	**71**	**7**	**26**	**33**	**58**	**2**	**0**	**3**	**147**	**4.8**	**11**	**0**	**0.0**	**24:48**	**18**	**0**	**8**	**8**	**16**	**0**	**0**	**0**	**26:29**
2009-10	**Carolina**	**NHL**	**71**	**6**	**40**	**46**	**72**	**1**	**0**	**1**	**161**	**3.7**	**–11**	**0**	**0.0**	**27:23**	....	....	....	....	....	....	....	....	....
	Finland	Olympics	5	1	2	3	*29	....	....	....	....	....	....	....	....	....	....	....	....	....	....	....	....	....	....
2010-11	**Carolina**	**NHL**	**72**	**5**	**30**	**35**	**60**	**1**	**0**	**1**	**144**	**3.5**	**–2**	**0**	**0.0**	**25:01**	....	....	....	....	....	....	....	....	....
	NHL Totals		**483**	**51**	**205**	**256**	**456**	**16**	**1**	**11**	**941**	**5.4**		**0**	**0.0**	**23:45**	**39**	**0**	**13**	**13**	**24**	**0**	**0**	**0**	**20:39**

NHL All-Rookie Team (2004)

Traded to **Edmonton** by **Philadelphia** with Geoff Sanderson and Philadelphia's 3rd round choice (Cameron Abney) in 2009 Entry Draft for Joffrey Lupul and Jason Smith, July 1, 2007. Traded to **Carolina** by **Edmonton** for Erik Cole, July 1, 2008.

PLANTE, Alex

(PLAWNT, AL-ehx) **EDM**

Defense. Shoots right. 6'4", 230 lbs. Born, Brandon, Man., May 9, 1989. Edmonton's 2nd choice, 15th overall, in 2007 Entry Draft.

			Regular Season														Playoffs								
Season	Club	League	GP	G	A	Pts	PIM	PP	SH	GW	S	%	+/-	TF	F%	Min	GP	G	A	Pts	PIM	PP	SH	GW	Min
2004-05	Brandon	MMHL	37	5	21	26	120	....	....	....	....	....	....	....	....	....	....	....	....	....	....	....	....	....	....
	Calgary Hitmen	WHL	8	0	0	0	6	....	....	....	....	....	....	....	....	....	11	0	0	0	17	....	....	....	....
2005-06	Calgary Hitmen	WHL	54	1	3	4	72	....	....	....	....	....	....	....	....	....	13	0	0	0	6	....	....	....	....
2006-07	Calgary Hitmen	WHL	58	8	30	38	81	....	....	....	....	....	....	....	....	....	13	5	6	11	14	....	....	....	....
2007-08	Calgary Hitmen	WHL	36	1	1	2	28	....	....	....	....	....	....	....	....	....	15	0	4	4	10	....	....	....	....
2008-09	Calgary Hitmen	WHL	68	8	37	45	157	....	....	....	....	....	....	....	....	....	18	6	9	15	41	....	....	....	....
2009-10	**Edmonton**	**NHL**	**4**	**0**	**1**	**1**	**2**	**0**	**0**	**0**	**4**	**0.0**	**1**	**0**	**0.0**	**13:36**	....	....	....	....	....	....	....	....	....
	Springfield	AHL	49	2	7	9	122	....	....	....	....	....	....	....	....	....	....	....	....	....	....	....	....	....	....
2010-11	**Edmonton**	**NHL**	**3**	**0**	**0**	**0**	**11**	**0**	**0**	**0**	**5**	**0.0**	**–2**	**0**	**0.0**	**15:03**	....	....	....	....	....	....	....	....	....
	Oklahoma City	AHL	73	2	15	17	138	....	....	....	....	....	....	....	....	....	5	0	0	0	12	....	....	....	....
	NHL Totals		**7**	**0**	**1**	**1**	**13**	**0**	**0**	**0**	**9**	**0.0**		**0**	**0.0**	**14:13**	....	....	....	....	....	....	....	....	....

PLATT, Geoff

(PLAT, JEHF) **ANA**

Center. Shoots left. 5'9", 175 lbs. Born, Toronto, Ont., July 10, 1985.

			Regular Season														Playoffs								
Season	Club	League	GP	G	A	Pts	PIM	PP	SH	GW	S	%	+/-	TF	F%	Min	GP	G	A	Pts	PIM	PP	SH	GW	Min
2000-01	St. Mike's B's	OPJHL	6	2	0	2	4	....	....	....	....	....	....	....	....	....	....	....	....	....	....	....	....	....	....
2001-02	North Bay	OHL	63	4	6	10	34	....	....	....	....	....	....	....	....	....	5	0	0	0	6	....	....	....	....
2002-03	Saginaw Spirit	OHL	62	32	22	54	81	....	....	....	....	....	....	....	....	....	....	....	....	....	....	....	....	....	....
2003-04	Saginaw Spirit	OHL	27	7	13	20	49	....	....	....	....	....	....	....	....	....	....	....	....	....	....	....	....	....	....
	Erie Otters	OHL	28	18	11	29	22	....	....	....	....	....	....	....	....	....	9	9	1	10	22	....	....	....	....
2004-05	Erie Otters	OHL	68	45	34	79	84	....	....	....	....	....	....	....	....	....	6	2	3	5	16	....	....	....	....
	Atlantic City	ECHL	2	0	2	2	0	....	....	....	....	....	....	....	....	....	3	0	0	0	0	....	....	....	....
2005-06	Syracuse Crunch	AHL	66	31	34	65	58	....	....	....	....	....	....	....	....	....	6	3	0	3	6	....	....	....	....
	Columbus	**NHL**	**15**	**0**	**5**	**5**	**16**	**0**	**0**	**0**	**29**	**0.0**	**–4**	**53**	**45.3**	**11:12**	....	....	....	....	....	....	....	....	....
2006-07	**Columbus**	**NHL**	**26**	**4**	**5**	**9**	**10**	**0**	**0**	**0**	**40**	**10.0**	**1**	**168**	**56.6**	**10:04**	....	....	....	....	....	....	....	....	....
	Syracuse Crunch	AHL	53	28	21	49	59	....	....	....	....	....	....	....	....	....	....	....	....	....	....	....	....	....	....
2007-08	Syracuse Crunch	AHL	15	4	3	7	6	....	....	....	....	....	....	....	....	....	....	....	....	....	....	....	....	....	....
	Anaheim	**NHL**	**5**	**0**	**0**	**0**	**2**	**0**	**0**	**0**	**4**	**0.0**	**2**	**7**	**28.6**	**11:17**	....	....	....	....	....	....	....	....	....
	Portland Pirates	AHL	60	28	30	58	49	....	....	....	....	....	....	....	....	....	18	8	9	17	24	....	....	....	....
2008-09	Ilves Tampere	Finland	45	19	18	37	54	....	....	....	....	....	....	....	....	....	3	1	0	1	4	....	....	....	....
	Dynamo Minsk	Rus-KHL	13	2	3	5	8	....	....	....	....	....	....	....	....	....	....	....	....	....	....	....	....	....	....
2009-10	Dynamo Minsk	Rus-KHL	56	26	18	44	77	....	....	....	....	....	....	....	....	....	....	....	....	....	....	....	....	....	....
2010-11	Dynamo Minsk	Rus-KHL	54	18	15	33	46	....	....	....	....	....	....	....	....	....	7	4	3	7	4	....	....	....	....
	NHL Totals		**46**	**4**	**10**	**14**	**28**	**0**	**0**	**0**	**73**	**5.5**		**228**	**53.1**	**10:34**	....	....	....	....	....	....	....	....	....

Signed as a free agent by **Syracuse** (AHL), September 23, 2005. Signed as a free agent by **Columbus**, November 25, 2005. Traded to **Anaheim** by **Columbus** for Aaron Rome and Clay Wilson, November 15, 2007. Signed as a free agent by **Minsk** (Russia-KHL), May 15, 2009.

PLEKANEC, Tomas

(pleh-KA-nehts, TAW-muhs) **MTL**

Left wing. Shoots left. 5'11", 198 lbs. Born, Kladno, Czech., October 31, 1982. Montreal's 4th choice, 71st overall, in 2001 Entry Draft.

			Regular Season														Playoffs								
Season	Club	League	GP	G	A	Pts	PIM	PP	SH	GW	S	%	+/-	TF	F%	Min	GP	G	A	Pts	PIM	PP	SH	GW	Min
1996-97	Kladno U17	CzR-U17	13	1	3	4	....	....	....	....	....	....	....	....	....	....	....	....	....	....	....	....	....	....	....
1997-98	HC Kladno U17	CzR-U17	45	38	26	64	....	....	....	....	....	....	....	....	....	....	....	....	....	....	....	....	....	....	....
1998-99	HC Kladno Jr.	CzRep-Jr.	53	22	20	42	....	....	....	....	....	....	....	....	....	....	....	....	....	....	....	....	....	....	....
99-2000	HC Kladno Jr.	CzRep-Jr.	43	14	16	30	....	....	....	....	....	....	....	....	....	....	....	....	....	....	....	....	....	....	....
	Kralupy	CzRep-3	6	2	2	4	2	....	....	....	....	....	....	....	....	....	....	....	....	....	....	....	....	....	....
	HC CKD Slany	CzRep-3	3	0	1	1	6	....	....	....	....	....	....	....	....	....	....	....	....	....	....	....	....	....	....
2000-01	Kladno	CzRep	47	9	9	18	24	....	....	....	....	....	....	....	....	....	....	....	....	....	....	....	....	....	....
	HC Kladno Jr.	CzRep-Jr.	9	6	4	10	4	....	....	....	....	....	....	....	....	....	....	....	....	....	....	....	....	....	....
2001-02	Kladno	CzRep	48	7	16	23	28	....	....	....	....	....	....	....	....	....	....	....	....	....	....	....	....	....	....
	BK Mlada Boleslav	CzRep-3	6	6	3	9	14	....	....	....	....	....	....	....	....	....	....	....	....	....	....	....	....	....	....
	Kladno	CzRep-Q	5	0	1	1	0	....	....	....	....	....	....	....	....	....	....	....	....	....	....	....	....	....	....
2002-03	Hamilton	AHL	77	19	27	46	74	....	....	....	....	....	....	....	....	....	13	3	2	5	8	....	....	....	....
2003-04	**Montreal**	**NHL**	**2**	**0**	**0**	**0**	**0**	**0**	**0**	**0**	**0**	**0.0**	**0**	**11**	**45.5**	**9:02**	....	....	....	....	....	....	....	....	....
	Hamilton	AHL	74	23	43	66	90	....	....	....	....	....	....	....	....	....	10	2	5	7	6	....	....	....	....
2004-05	Hamilton	AHL	80	29	35	64	68	....	....	....	....	....	....	....	....	....	4	2	4	6	6	....	....	....	....
2005-06	**Montreal**	**NHL**	**67**	**9**	**20**	**29**	**32**	**1**	**0**	**0**	**99**	**9.1**	**4**	**708**	**50.3**	**13:15**	**6**	**0**	**4**	**4**	**6**	**0**	**0**	**0**	**18:00**
	Hamilton	AHL	2	0	0	0	2	....	....	....	....	....	....	....	....	....	....	....	....	....	....	....	....	....	....
2006-07	**Montreal**	**NHL**	**81**	**20**	**27**	**47**	**36**	**5**	**2**	**1**	**150**	**13.3**	**10**	**1159**	**48.3**	**15:59**	....	....	....	....	....	....	....	....	....
2007-08	**Montreal**	**NHL**	**81**	**29**	**40**	**69**	**42**	**12**	**2**	**6**	**186**	**15.6**	**15**	**1381**	**49.5**	**18:05**	**12**	**4**	**5**	**9**	**2**	**2**	**0**	**0**	**18:02**
2008-09	**Montreal**	**NHL**	**80**	**20**	**19**	**39**	**54**	**6**	**3**	**2**	**202**	**9.9**	**–9**	**1351**	**50.6**	**17:15**	**3**	**0**	**0**	**0**	**4**	**0**	**0**	**0**	**13:36**
2009-10	**Montreal**	**NHL**	**82**	**25**	**45**	**70**	**50**	**3**	**1**	**4**	**216**	**11.6**	**5**	**1615**	**49.0**	**19:58**	**19**	**4**	**7**	**11**	**20**	**1**	**0**	**1**	**19:57**
	Czech Republic	Olympics	5	2	1	3	2	....	....	....	....	....	....	....	....	....	....	....	....	....	....	....	....	....	....
2010-11	**Montreal**	**NHL**	**77**	**22**	**35**	**57**	**60**	**3**	**1**	**4**	**227**	**9.7**	**8**	**1577**	**50.0**	**20:15**	**7**	**2**	**3**	**5**	**2**	**0**	**1**	**0**	**23:20**
	NHL Totals		**470**	**125**	**186**	**311**	**274**	**30**	**9**	**17**	**1080**	**11.6**		**7802**	**49.6**	**17:32**	**47**	**10**	**19**	**29**	**34**	**3**	**1**	**1**	**19:19**

POLAK, Roman

(POH-lahk, ROH-muhn) **ST.L.**

Defense. Shoots right. 6'1", 227 lbs. Born, Ostrava, Czech., April 28, 1986. St. Louis' 6th choice, 180th overall, in 2004 Entry Draft.

			Regular Season														Playoffs								
Season	Club	League	GP	G	A	Pts	PIM	PP	SH	GW	S	%	+/-	TF	F%	Min	GP	G	A	Pts	PIM	PP	SH	GW	Min
2001-02	HC Ostrava Jr.	CzRep-Jr.	46	4	9	13	84	....	....	....	....	....	....	....	....	....	....	....	....	....	....	....	....	....	....
2002-03	HC Ostrava Jr.	CzRep-Jr.	32	3	12	15	34	....	....	....	....	....	....	....	....	....	....	....	....	....	....	....	....	....	....
2003-04	HC Vitkovice Jr.	CzRep-Jr.	52	4	8	12	48	....	....	....	....	....	....	....	....	....	....	....	....	....	....	....	....	....	....
2004-05	Kootenay Ice	WHL	65	5	18	23	85	....	....	....	....	....	....	....	....	....	9	0	0	0	6	....	....	....	....
2005-06	HC Vitkovice Jr.	CzRep-Jr.	1	0	0	0	4	....	....	....	....	....	....	....	....	....	....	....	....	....	....	....	....	....	....
	Vitkovice	CzRep	37	0	1	1	16	....	....	....	....	....	....	....	....	....	6	0	0	0	6	....	....	....	....
2006-07	**St. Louis**	**NHL**	**19**	**0**	**0**	**0**	**6**	**0**	**0**	**0**	**13**	**0.0**	**–3**	**0**	**0.0**	**13:38**	....	....	....	....	....	....	....	....	....
	Peoria Rivermen	AHL	53	4	8	12	66	....	....	....	....	....	....	....	....	....	....	....	....	....	....	....	....	....	....
2007-08	**St. Louis**	**NHL**	**6**	**0**	**1**	**1**	**0**	**0**	**0**	**0**	**2**	**0.0**	**1**	**0**	**0.0**	**11:32**	....	....	....	....	....	....	....	....	....
	Peoria Rivermen	AHL	34	0	7	7	33	....	....	....	....	....	....	....	....	....	....	....	....	....	....	....	....	....	....
2008-09	**St. Louis**	**NHL**	**69**	**1**	**14**	**15**	**45**	**0**	**0**	**1**	**73**	**1.4**	**–15**	**1**	**0.0**	**21:32**	**4**	**0**	**0**	**0**	**0**	**0**	**0**	**0**	**21:49**

Season	Club	League	GP	G	A	Pts	PIM	PP	SH	GW	S	%	+/-	TF	F%	Min	GP	G	A	Pts	PIM	PP	SH	GW	Min
2009-10	St. Louis	NHL	78	4	17	21	59	0	0	1	73	5.5	7	0	0.0	19:59	....	....	....	....	....	....	....	....	....
	Czech Republic	Olympics	5	0	0	0	4																		
2010-11	St. Louis	NHL	55	3	9	12	33	0	0	1	54	5.6	–4	1	0.0	19:57	....	....	....	....	....	....	....	....	....
	NHL Totals		227	8	41	49	143	0	0	3	215	3.7		2	0.0	19:41	4	0	0	0	0	0	0	0	21:49

POMINVILLE, Jason   (paw-MIHN-vihl, JAY-suhn)   BUF

Right wing. Shoots right. 6', 185 lbs.   Born, Repentigny, Que., November 30, 1982. Buffalo's 4th choice, 55th overall, in 2001 Entry Draft.

Season	Club	League	GP	G	A	Pts	PIM	PP	SH	GW	S	%	+/-	TF	F%	Min	GP	G	A	Pts	PIM	PP	SH	GW	Min
1997-98	Cap-d-Madeleine	QAAA	13	3	7	10																			
1998-99	Cap-d-Madeleine	QAAA	41	18	38	56	16										7	2	7	9	0				
	Shawinigan	QMJHL	2	0	0	0	0																		
99-2000	Shawinigan	QMJHL	60	4	17	21	12										13	2	3	5	0				
2000-01	Shawinigan	QMJHL	71	46	67	113	24										10	6	6	12	0				
2001-02	Shawinigan	QMJHL	66	57	64	121	32										2	0	0	0	0				
2002-03	Rochester	AHL	73	13	21	34	16										3	1	1	2	0				
2003-04	Buffalo	NHL	1	0	0	0	0	0	0	0	3	0.0	0	0	0.0	14:22									
	Rochester	AHL	66	34	30	64	30										16	9	10	19	6				
2004-05	Rochester	AHL	78	30	38	68	43																		
	Rochester	AHL	18	19	7	26	11																		
2005-06	Buffalo	NHL	57	18	12	30	22	10	2	2	124	14.5	–4	5	20.0	14:07	18	5	5	10	8	0	1	1	12:11
2006-07	Buffalo	NHL	82	34	34	68	30	2	2	5	212	16.0	25	14	42.9	17:25	16	4	6	10	0	0		0	17:54
2007-08	Buffalo	NHL	82	27	53	80	20	2	1	1	232	11.6	16	67	37.3	19:58									
2008-09	Buffalo	NHL	82	20	46	66	18	6	1	2	239	8.4	–4	67	37.3	19:46									
2009-10	Buffalo	NHL	82	24	38	62	22	8	0	2	252	9.5	13	120	35.0	18:45	6	2	2	4	2	0	0	1	20:17
2010-11	Buffalo	NHL	73	22	30	52	15	5	1	2	215	10.2	1	155	43.2	18:09	5	1	3	4	2	0	0	1	15:51
	NHL Totals		459	145	213	358	127	33	7	14	1277	11.4		428	38.8	18:14	45	12	16	28	12	0	1	3	15:42

QMJHL First All-Star Team (2002)

PONIKAROVSKY, Alexei   (poh-nih-kahr-OHV-skee, al-EHX-ay)   CAR

Left wing. Shoots left. 6'4", 226 lbs.   Born, Kiev, USSR, April 9, 1980. Toronto's 4th choice, 87th overall, in 1998 Entry Draft.

Season	Club	League	GP	G	A	Pts	PIM	PP	SH	GW	S	%	+/-	TF	F%	Min	GP	G	A	Pts	PIM	PP	SH	GW	Min
1996-97	Dyn'o Moscow 2	Russia-3	60	12	15	27	30																		
	Dyn'o Moscow 2	Russia-3	2	0	0	0	2																		
1997-98	Dynamo Moscow	Russia	24	1	2	3	30																		
1998-99	Krylja Sovetov	Russia	13	2	1	3	2																		
	Dynamo Moscow	Russia															3	0	0	0	0				
99-2000	THK Tver	Russia-2	29	8	14	22	26																		
	Dynamo Moscow	Russia	19	1	0	1	8										1	0	0	0	0				
	Dynamo Moscow	EuroHL	2	0	2	2	0																		
2000-01	Toronto	NHL	22	1	3	4	14	0	0	0	21	4.8	–1	7	28.6	8:32									
	St. John's	AHL	49	12	24	36	44										4	0	0	0	4				
2001-02	Toronto	NHL	8	2	0	2	0	0	0	1	8	25.0	2	2	50.0	8:03	10	0	0	0	4	0	0	0	8:15
	St. John's	AHL	72	21	27	48	74										5	2	1	3	8				
	Ukraine	Olympics	4	1	1	2	6																		
2002-03	Toronto	NHL	13	0	3	3	11	0	0	0	13	0.0	4	4	25.0	10:43									
	St. John's	AHL	63	24	22	46	68																		
2003-04	Toronto	NHL	73	9	19	28	44	1	0	2	110	8.2	14	20	30.0	11:36	13	1	3	4	8	0	0	1	14:20
2004-05	Voskresensk	Russia	19	1	5	6	16																		
2005-06	Toronto	NHL	81	21	17	38	68	2	4	3	157	13.4	15	13	30.8	14:06									
2006-07	Toronto	NHL	71	21	24	45	63	6	0	1	198	10.6	8	4	25.0	17:06									
2007-08	Toronto	NHL	66	18	17	35	36	1	0	1	150	12.0	3	4	25.0	15:58									
2008-09	Toronto	NHL	82	23	38	61	38	5	0	3	185	12.4	6	11	54.6	15:47									
2009-10	Toronto	NHL	61	19	22	41	44	4	0	1	147	12.9	5	37	32.4	16:50									
	Pittsburgh	NHL	16	2	7	9	17	1	0	0	37	5.4	–6	1	0.0	15:05	11	1	4	5	4	0	0	0	13:13
2010-11	Los Angeles	NHL	61	5	10	15	36	1	0	0	94	5.3	1	5	20.0	12:36	4	1	0	1	0	0	0	0	10:10
	NHL Totals		554	121	160	281	371	21	4	13	1120	10.8		108	32.4	14:24	38	3	7	10	16	0	0	1	11:58

Signed as a free agent by **Voskresensk** (Russia), November 13, 2004. Traded to **Pittsburgh** by **Toronto** for Martin Skoula and Luca Caputi, March 2, 2010. Signed as a free agent by **Los Angeles**, July 27, 2010. Signed as a free agent by **Carolina**, July 1, 2011.

POPOVIC, Mark   (poh-PUH-vihk, MAHRK)

Defense. Shoots left. 6'1", 205 lbs.   Born, Stoney Creek, Ont., October 11, 1982. Anaheim's 2nd choice, 35th overall, in 2001 Entry Draft.

Season	Club	League	GP	G	A	Pts	PIM	PP	SH	GW	S	%	+/-	TF	F%	Min	GP	G	A	Pts	PIM	PP	SH	GW	Min
1997-98	Mississauga	OPJHL	51	10	16	26	32																		
1998-99	St. Michael's	OHL	60	6	26	32	46																		
99-2000	St. Michael's	OHL	68	11	29	40	68																		
2000-01	St. Michael's	OHL	61	7	35	42	54										18	3	5	8	22				
2001-02	St. Michael's	OHL	58	12	29	41	42										15	1	11	12	10				
2002-03	Cincinnati	AHL	73	3	21	24	46																		
2003-04	Anaheim	NHL	1	0	0	0	0	0	0	0	1	0.0	0	0	0.0	13:48									
	Cincinnati	AHL	74	4	10	14	63										9	1	2	3	4				
2004-05	Cincinnati	AHL	74	1	17	18	47										11	2	3	5	6				
2005-06	Atlanta	NHL	7	0	0	0	0	0	0	0	6	0.0	–5	0	0.0	11:04									
	Chicago Wolves	AHL	73	12	26	38	51																		
2006-07	Atlanta	NHL	3	0	1	1	0	0	0	0	1	0.0	1	0	0.0	10:15									
	Chicago Wolves	AHL	65	16	24	40	51										15	3	6	9	4				
2007-08	Atlanta	NHL	33	0	2	2	10	0	0	0	25	0.0	–4	0	0.0	14:28									
2008-09	St. Petersburg	Rus-KHL	52	8	15	23	40										3	0	0	2	0				
2009-10	Atlanta	NHL	37	2	2	4	10	0	0	0	24	8.3	0	0	0.0	14:48									
2010-11	HC Lugano	Swiss	33	4	12	16	20										4	0	4	4	2				
	NHL Totals		81	2	5	7	20	0	0	0	57	3.5		0	0.0	14:10									

OHL First All-Star Team (2002)

Traded to **Atlanta** by **Anaheim** for Kip Brennan, August 23, 2005. Signed as a free agent by **St. Petersburg** (Russia-KHL), August 29, 2008. • Missed majority of 2009-10 due to foot and upper body injuries. Signed as a free agent by **Lugano** (Swiss), September 21, 2010.

PORTER, Chris   (POHR-tuhr, KRIHS)   ST.L.

Center. Shoots left. 6'1", 200 lbs.   Born, Toronto, Ont., May 29, 1984. Chicago's 10th choice, 282nd overall, in 2003 Entry Draft.

Season	Club	League	GP	G	A	Pts	PIM	PP	SH	GW	S	%	+/-	TF	F%	Min	GP	G	A	Pts	PIM	PP	SH	GW	Min
2001-02	Shat.-St. Mary's	High-MN	75	10	25	35	32																		
2002-03	Lincoln Stars	USHL	59	13	22	35	74										10	4	3	7	10				
2003-04	North Dakota	WCHA	41	10	15	25	46																		
2004-05	North Dakota	WCHA	45	12	3	15	36																		
2005-06	North Dakota	WCHA	46	7	16	23	40																		
2006-07	North Dakota	WCHA	43	13	17	30	38																		
2007-08	Peoria Rivermen	AHL	80	12	25	37	72																		
2008-09	St. Louis	NHL	6	1	1	2	0	0	0	0	7	14.3	–1	3	33.3	10:32									
	Peoria Rivermen	AHL	74	7	16	23	72										7	1	1	2	0				
2009-10	Peoria Rivermen	AHL	80	13	18	31	53																		
2010-11	St. Louis	NHL	45	3	4	7	16	0	0	1	55	5.5	–4	22	54.6	10:23									
	Peoria Rivermen	AHL	36	9	11	20	63																		
	NHL Totals		51	4	5	9	16	0	0	1	62	6.5		25	52.0	10:24									

Signed as a free agent by **St. Louis**, August 21, 2007.

PORTER, Kevin

(POHR-tuhr, KEH-vihn) **COL**

Center. Shoots left. 6', 190 lbs. Born, Detroit, MI, March 12, 1986. Phoenix's 5th choice, 119th overall, in 2004 Entry Draft.

			Regular Season														Playoffs								
Season	Club	League	GP	G	A	Pts	PIM	PP	SH	GW	S	%	+/-	TF	F%	Min	GP	G	A	Pts	PIM	PP	SH	GW	Min
2002-03	USNTDP	U-17	19	9	11	20	8	....	....	....	....	....	....	....	....	....	....	....	....	....	....	....	....	....	....
	USNTDP	U-18	13	1	2	3	2	....	....	....	....	....	....	....	....	....	....	....	....	....	....	....	....	....	....
	USNTDP	NAHL	40	19	9	28	17	....	....	....	....	....	....	....	....	....	....	....	....	....	....	....	....	....	....
2003-04	USNTDP	U-18	44	5	21	26	26	....	....	....	....	....	....	....	....	....	....	....	....	....	....	....	....	....	....
	USNTDP	NAHL	11	3	8	11	4	....	....	....	....	....	....	....	....	....	....	....	....	....	....	....	....	....	....
2004-05	U. of Michigan	CCHA	39	11	13	24	51	....	....	....	....	....	....	....	....	....	....	....	....	....	....	....	....	....	....
2005-06	U. of Michigan	CCHA	39	17	21	38	30	....	....	....	....	....	....	....	....	....	....	....	....	....	....	....	....	....	....
2006-07	U. of Michigan	CCHA	41	24	34	58	16	....	....	....	....	....	....	....	....	....	....	....	....	....	....	....	....	....	....
2007-08	U. of Michigan	CCHA	43	*33	30	*63	18	....	....	....	....	....	....	....	....	....	....	....	....	....	....	....	....	....	....
	San Antonio	AHL	....	....	....	....	....	....	....	....	....	....	....	....	....	....	7	0	4	4	0	....	....	....	....
2008-09	**Phoenix**	**NHL**	**34**	**5**	**5**	**10**	**4**	**1**	**0**	**2**	**39**	**12.8**	**–2**	**95**	**29.5**	**13:38**	....	....	....	....	....	....	....	....	....
	San Antonio	AHL	42	13	22	35	14	....	....	....	....	....	....	....	....	....	....	....	....	....	....	....	....	....	....
2009-10	**Phoenix**	**NHL**	**4**	**0**	**0**	**0**	**0**	**0**	**0**	**0**	**3**	**0.0**	**1**	**15**	**33.3**	**7:22**	....	....	....	....	....	....	....	....	....
	San Antonio	AHL	52	15	25	40	31	....	....	....	....	....	....	....	....	....	....	....	....	....	....	....	....	....	....
	Colorado	**NHL**	**16**	**2**	**1**	**3**	**0**	**0**	**1**	**0**	**18**	**11.1**	**–4**	**27**	**48.2**	**13:13**	**4**	**0**	**0**	**0**	**0**	**0**	**0**	**0**	**10:38**
	Lake Erie	AHL	4	1	0	1	2	....	....	....	....	....	....	....	....	....	....	....	....	....	....	....	....	....	....
2010-11	**Colorado**	**NHL**	**74**	**14**	**11**	**25**	**27**	**1**	**0**	**3**	**102**	**13.7**	**–11**	**58**	**32.8**	**13:49**	....	....	....	....	....	....	....	....	....
	NHL Totals		**128**	**21**	**17**	**38**	**31**	**2**	**1**	**5**	**162**	**13.0**		**195**	**33.3**	**13:29**	**4**	**0**	**0**	**0**	**0**	**0**	**0**	**0**	**10:38**

CCHA Second All-Star Team (2007) • CCHA First All-Star Team (2008) • CCHA Player of the Year (2008) • NCAA West First All-American Team (2008)

Traded to **Colorado** by **Phoenix** with Peter Mueller for Wojtek Wolski, March 3, 2010.

POSTMA, Paul

(POHST-muh, PAWL) **WPG**

Defense. Shoots right. 6'3", 195 lbs. Born, Red Deer, Alta., February 22, 1989. Atlanta's 4th choice, 205th overall, in 2007 Entry Draft.

			Regular Season														Playoffs								
Season	Club	League	GP	G	A	Pts	PIM	PP	SH	GW	S	%	+/-	TF	F%	Min	GP	G	A	Pts	PIM	PP	SH	GW	Min
2004-05	Red Deer	AMHL	36	6	5	11	24	....	....	....	....	....	....	....	....	....	....	....	....	....	....	....	....	....	....
	Swift Current	WHL	4	0	0	0	0	....	....	....	....	....	....	....	....	....	....	....	....	....	....	....	....	....	....
2005-06	Swift Current	WHL	58	2	9	11	6	....	....	....	....	....	....	....	....	....	4	0	0	0	0	....	....	....	....
2006-07	Swift Current	WHL	70	5	19	24	42	....	....	....	....	....	....	....	....	....	6	0	1	1	0	....	....	....	....
2007-08	Swift Current	WHL	2	0	0	0	2	....	....	....	....	....	....	....	....	....	....	....	....	....	....	....	....	....	....
	Calgary Hitmen	WHL	66	14	28	42	30	....	....	....	....	....	....	....	....	....	16	6	4	10	4	....	....	....	....
2008-09	Calgary Hitmen	WHL	70	23	61	84	28	....	....	....	....	....	....	....	....	....	18	5	8	13	10	....	....	....	....
2009-10	Chicago Wolves	AHL	63	15	14	29	24	....	....	....	....	....	....	....	....	....	7	0	2	2	0	....	....	....	....
2010-11	**Atlanta**	**NHL**	**1**	**0**	**0**	**0**	**0**	**0**	**0**	**0**	**1**	**0.0**	**0**	**0**	**0.0**	**9:55**	....	....	....	....	....	....	....	....	....
	Chicago Wolves	AHL	69	12	33	45	20	....	....	....	....	....	....	....	....	....	....	....	....	....	....	....	....	....	....
	NHL Totals		**1**	**0**	**0**	**0**	**0**	**0**	**0**	**0**	**1**	**0.0**		**0**	**0.0**	**9:55**	....	....	....	....	....	....	....	....	....

WHL East First All-Star Team (2009) • Canadian Major Junior Second All-Star Team (2009)

• Transferred to **Winnipeg** after **Atlanta** franchise relocated, June 21, 2011.

POTHIER, Brian

(POH-thee-uhr, BRIGH-uhn)

Defense. Shoots right. 6', 204 lbs. Born, New Bedford, MA, April 15, 1977.

			Regular Season														Playoffs								
Season	Club	League	GP	G	A	Pts	PIM	PP	SH	GW	S	%	+/-	TF	F%	Min	GP	G	A	Pts	PIM	PP	SH	GW	Min
1995-96	NMH School	High-MA	27	11	22	33	36	....	....	....	....	....	....	....	....	....	....	....	....	....	....	....	....	....	....
1996-97	RPI Engineers	ECAC	34	1	11	12	42	....	....	....	....	....	....	....	....	....	....	....	....	....	....	....	....	....	....
1997-98	RPI Engineers	ECAC	35	2	9	11	28	....	....	....	....	....	....	....	....	....	....	....	....	....	....	....	....	....	....
1998-99	RPI Engineers	ECAC	37	5	13	18	36	....	....	....	....	....	....	....	....	....	....	....	....	....	....	....	....	....	....
99-2000	RPI Engineers	ECAC	36	9	24	33	44	....	....	....	....	....	....	....	....	....	....	....	....	....	....	....	....	....	....
2000-01	**Atlanta**	**NHL**	**3**	**0**	**0**	**0**	**2**	**0**	**0**	**0**	**0**	**0.0**	**4**	**0**	**0.0**	**20:38**	....	....	....	....	....	....	....	....	....
	Orlando	IHL	76	12	29	41	69	....	....	....	....	....	....	....	....	....	16	3	5	8	11	....	....	....	....
2001-02	**Atlanta**	**NHL**	**33**	**3**	**6**	**9**	**22**	**1**	**0**	**1**	**65**	**4.6**	**–19**	**0**	**0.0**	**21:41**	....	....	....	....	....	....	....	....	....
	Chicago Wolves	AHL	39	6	13	19	30	....	....	....	....	....	....	....	....	....	....	....	....	....	....	....	....	....	....
2002-03	**Ottawa**	**NHL**	**14**	**2**	**4**	**6**	**6**	**0**	**0**	**1**	**23**	**8.7**	**11**	**0**	**0.0**	**15:23**	**1**	**0**	**0**	**0**	**2**	**0**	**0**	**0**	**13:11**
	Binghamton	AHL	68	7	40	47	58	....	....	....	....	....	....	....	....	....	8	2	8	10	4	....	....	....	....
2003-04	**Ottawa**	**NHL**	**55**	**2**	**6**	**8**	**24**	**1**	**0**	**1**	**78**	**2.6**	**6**	**0**	**0.0**	**16:43**	**7**	**0**	**0**	**0**	**6**	**0**	**0**	**0**	**17:15**
2004-05	Binghamton	AHL	77	12	36	48	64	....	....	....	....	....	....	....	....	....	6	0	1	1	6	....	....	....	....
2005-06	**Ottawa**	**NHL**	**77**	**5**	**30**	**35**	**59**	**3**	**0**	**0**	**133**	**3.8**	**29**	**0**	**0.0**	**16:46**	**8**	**2**	**1**	**3**	**2**	**0**	**0**	**0**	**15:02**
2006-07	**Washington**	**NHL**	**72**	**3**	**25**	**28**	**44**	**2**	**0**	**0**	**118**	**2.5**	**–11**	**0**	**0.0**	**23:59**	....	....	....	....	....	....	....	....	....
2007-08	**Washington**	**NHL**	**38**	**5**	**9**	**14**	**20**	**1**	**0**	**1**	**65**	**7.7**	**5**	**0**	**0.0**	**18:42**	....	....	....	....	....	....	....	....	....
2008-09	**Washington**	**NHL**	**9**	**1**	**2**	**3**	**4**	**0**	**0**	**1**	**8**	**12.5**	**0**	**0**	**0.0**	**16:35**	**13**	**0**	**2**	**2**	**8**	**0**	**0**	**0**	**16:48**
	Hershey Bears	AHL	4	0	0	0	2	....	....	....	....	....	....	....	....	....	....	....	....	....	....	....	....	....	....
2009-10	**Washington**	**NHL**	**41**	**4**	**7**	**11**	**10**	**1**	**0**	**1**	**57**	**7.0**	**12**	**0**	**0.0**	**18:03**	....	....	....	....	....	....	....	....	....
	Carolina	**NHL**	**20**	**1**	**3**	**4**	**11**	**0**	**0**	**1**	**24**	**4.2**	**–8**	**0**	**0.0**	**21:01**	....	....	....	....	....	....	....	....	....
2010-11	Geneve	Swiss	44	8	25	33	26	....	....	....	....	....	....	....	....	....	6	2	4	6	10	....	....	....	....
	NHL Totals		**362**	**26**	**92**	**118**	**202**	**9**	**0**	**7**	**571**	**4.6**		**0**	**0.0**	**19:12**	**29**	**2**	**3**	**5**	**18**	**0**	**0**	**0**	**16:18**

ECAC Second All-Star Team (2000) • ECAC All-Tournament Team (2000) • NCAA East Second All-American Team (2000) • Ken McKenzie Trophy (IHL – U.S. - Born Rookie of the Year) (2001) • Garry F. Longman Memorial Trophy (IHL – Rookie of the Year) (2001) • AHL Second All-Star Team (2003, 2005)

Signed as a free agent by **Atlanta**, March 27, 2000. Traded to **Ottawa** by **Atlanta** for Shawn McEachern and Ottawa's 6th round choice (Dan Turple) in 2004 Entry Draft, June 29, 2002. Signed as a free agent by **Washington**, July 1, 2006. • Missed remainder of 2007-08 and majority of 2008-09 due to concussion at Boston, January 3, 2008. Traded to **Carolina** by **Washington** with Oskar Osala and Washington's 2nd round choice (later traded to NY Rangers, later traded to Calgary – Calgary selected Tyler Wotherspoon) in 2011 Entry Draft for Joe Corvo, March 3, 2010. Signed as a free agent by **Geneve** (Swiss), July 27, 2010.

POTI, Tom

(POH-tee, TAWM) **WSH**

Defense. Shoots left. 6'3", 197 lbs. Born, Worcester, MA, March 22, 1977. Edmonton's 4th choice, 59th overall, in 1996 Entry Draft.

			Regular Season														Playoffs								
Season	Club	League	GP	G	A	Pts	PIM	PP	SH	GW	S	%	+/-	TF	F%	Min	GP	G	A	Pts	PIM	PP	SH	GW	Min
1992-93	St. Peter's Marian	High-MA	55	25	46	71	....	....	....	....	....	....	....	....	....	....	....	....	....	....	....	....	....	....	....
1993-94	Cushing	High-MA	30	10	35	45	....	....	....	....	....	....	....	....	....	....	....	....	....	....	....	....	....	....	....
1994-95	Cushing	High-MA	36	17	54	71	35	....	....	....	....	....	....	....	....	....	....	....	....	....	....	....	....	....	....
	Central-Mass	MBAHL	8	8	10	18	....	....	....	....	....	....	....	....	....	....	....	....	....	....	....	....	....	....	....
1995-96	Cushing	High-MA	29	14	59	73	18	....	....	....	....	....	....	....	....	....	....	....	....	....	....	....	....	....	....
1996-97	Boston University	H-East	38	4	17	21	54	....	....	....	....	....	....	....	....	....	....	....	....	....	....	....	....	....	....
1997-98	Boston University	H-East	38	13	29	42	60	....	....	....	....	....	....	....	....	....	....	....	....	....	....	....	....	....	....
1998-99	**Edmonton**	**NHL**	**73**	**5**	**16**	**21**	**42**	**2**	**0**	**3**	**94**	**5.3**	**10**	**0**	**0.0**	**19:33**	**4**	**0**	**1**	**1**	**2**	**0**	**0**	**0**	**28:02**
99-2000	**Edmonton**	**NHL**	**76**	**9**	**26**	**35**	**65**	**2**	**1**	**1**	**125**	**7.2**	**8**	**0**	**0.0**	**24:10**	**5**	**0**	**1**	**1**	**0**	**0**	**0**	**0**	**23:53**
2000-01	**Edmonton**	**NHL**	**81**	**12**	**20**	**32**	**60**	**6**	**0**	**3**	**161**	**7.5**	**–4**	**0**	**0.0**	**22:44**	**6**	**0**	**2**	**2**	**2**	**0**	**0**	**0**	**20:25**
2001-02	**Edmonton**	**NHL**	**55**	**1**	**16**	**17**	**42**	**1**	**0**	**0**	**100**	**1.0**	**–6**	**0**	**0.0**	**24:32**	....	....	....	....	....	....	....	....	....
	United States	Olympics	6	0	1	1	4	....	....	....	....	....	....	....	....	....	....	....	....	....	....	....	....	....	....
	NY Rangers	**NHL**	**11**	**1**	**7**	**8**	**2**	**1**	**0**	**1**	**9**	**11.1**	**–4**	**0**	**0.0**	**21:45**	....	....	....	....	....	....	....	....	....
2002-03	**NY Rangers**	**NHL**	**80**	**11**	**37**	**48**	**58**	**3**	**0**	**2**	**148**	**7.4**	**–6**	**0**	**0.0**	**24:43**	....	....	....	....	....	....	....	....	....
2003-04	**NY Rangers**	**NHL**	**67**	**10**	**14**	**24**	**47**	**4**	**0**	**5**	**124**	**8.1**	**–1**	**0**	**0.0**	**22:28**	....	....	....	....	....	....	....	....	....
2004-05			DID NOT PLAY																						
2005-06	**NY Rangers**	**NHL**	**73**	**3**	**20**	**23**	**70**	**2**	**0**	**2**	**122**	**2.5**	**16**	**4**	**25.0**	**20:46**	**4**	**0**	**0**	**0**	**2**	**0**	**0**	**0**	**19:39**
2006-07	**NY Islanders**	**NHL**	**78**	**6**	**38**	**44**	**74**	**6**	**0**	**1**	**134**	**4.5**	**–1**	**0**	**0.0**	**25:43**	**5**	**0**	**3**	**3**	**6**	**0**	**0**	**0**	**27:34**
2007-08	**Washington**	**NHL**	**71**	**2**	**27**	**29**	**46**	**0**	**0**	**0**	**99**	**2.0**	**9**	**0**	**0.0**	**23:29**	**7**	**0**	**1**	**1**	**8**	**0**	**0**	**0**	**24:01**
2008-09	**Washington**	**NHL**	**52**	**3**	**10**	**13**	**28**	**0**	**0**	**1**	**48**	**6.3**	**3**	**0**	**0.0**	**21:09**	**14**	**2**	**5**	**7**	**4**	**1**	**0**	**0**	**21:37**
2009-10	**Washington**	**NHL**	**70**	**4**	**20**	**24**	**42**	**2**	**0**	**0**	**69**	**5.8**	**26**	**0**	**0.0**	**21:24**	**6**	**0**	**4**	**4**	**5**	**0**	**0**	**0**	**21:23**
2010-11	**Washington**	**NHL**	**21**	**2**	**5**	**7**	**8**	**0**	**0**	**0**	**20**	**10.0**	**–4**	**0**	**0.0**	**18:22**	....	....	....	....	....	....	....	....	....
	NHL Totals		**808**	**69**	**256**	**325**	**584**	**29**	**1**	**19**	**1253**	**5.5**		**4**	**25.0**	**22:43**	**51**	**2**	**17**	**19**	**29**	**1**	**0**	**0**	**22:56**

NCAA Championship All-Tournament Team (1997) • Hockey East First All-Star Team (1998) • NCAA East First All-American Team (1998) • NHL All-Rookie Team (1999)

Played in NHL All-Star Game (2003)

Traded to **NY Rangers** by **Edmonton** with Rem Murray for Mike York and NY Rangers' 4th round choice (Ivan Koltsov) in 2002 Entry Draft, March 19, 2002. Signed as a free agent by **NY Islanders**, July 8, 2006. Signed as a free agent by **Washington**, July 1, 2007. • Missed majority of 2010-11 due to recurring lower body injury.

			Regular Season														Playoffs								
Season	Club	League	GP	G	A	Pts	PIM	PP	SH	GW	S	%	+/-	TF	F%	Min	GP	G	A	Pts	PIM	PP	SH	GW	Min

POTTER, Corey
(PAW-tuhr, KOHR-ee) **EDM**

Defense. Shoots right. 6'3", 206 lbs. Born, Lansing, MI, January 5, 1984. NY Rangers' 4th choice, 122nd overall, in 2003 Entry Draft.

99-2000	Det. Honeybaked	MWEHL	58	10	38	48	....	....	....	....	....	....	....	....	....	....	....	....	....	....	....	....	....	....	....
2000-01	USNTDP	U-17	13	0	0	0	6	....	....	....	....	....	....	....	....	....	....	....	....	....	....	....	....	....	....
	USNTDP	NAHL	53	4	4	8	20	....	....	....	....	....	....	....	....	....	....	....	....	....	....	....	....	....	....
2001-02	USNTDP	U-18	38	4	6	10	49	....	....	....	....	....	....	....	....	....	....	....	....	....	....	....	....	....	....
	USNTDP	USHL	13	2	2	4	12	....	....	....	....	....	....	....	....	....	....	....	....	....	....	....	....	....	....
	USNTDP	NAHL	10	0	3	3	4	....	....	....	....	....	....	....	....	....	....	....	....	....	....	....	....	....	....
2002-03	Michigan State	CCHA	35	4	4	8	30	....	....	....	....	....	....	....	....	....	....	....	....	....	....	....	....	....	....
2003-04	Michigan State	CCHA	38	0	8	8	63	....	....	....	....	....	....	....	....	....	....	....	....	....	....	....	....	....	....
2004-05	Michigan State	CCHA	32	0	6	6	73	....	....	....	....	....	....	....	....	....	....	....	....	....	....	....	....	....	....
2005-06	Michigan State	CCHA	45	4	18	22	117	....	....	....	....	....	....	....	....	....	....	....	....	....	....	....	....	....	....
2006-07	Hartford	AHL	30	2	8	10	21	....	....	....	....	....	....	....	....	....	7	1	4	5	12	....	....	....	....
	Charlotte	ECHL	43	6	13	19	56	....	....	....	....	....	....	....	....	....	....	....	....	....	....	....	....	....	....
2007-08	Hartford	AHL	80	5	27	32	102	....	....	....	....	....	....	....	....	....	5	0	1	1	14	....	....	....	....
2008-09	**NY Rangers**	**NHL**	**5**	**1**	**1**	**2**	**0**	**0**	**0**	**0**	**4**	**25.0**	**-1**	**0**	**0.0**	**13:15**	....	....	....	....	....	....	....	....	....
	Hartford	AHL	67	10	22	32	82	....	....	....	....	....	....	....	....	....	6	1	3	4	23	....	....	....	....
2009-10	**NY Rangers**	**NHL**	**3**	**0**	**0**	**0**	**2**	**0**	**0**	**0**	**2**	**0.0**	**0**	**0**	**0.0**	**12:07**	....	....	....	....	....	....	....	....	....
	Hartford	AHL	69	4	24	28	54	....	....	....	....	....	....	....	....	....	....	....	....	....	....	....	....	....	....
2010-11	**Pittsburgh**	**NHL**	**1**	**0**	**0**	**0**	**0**	**0**	**0**	**0**	**1**	**0.0**	**0**	**0**	**0.0**	**16:43**	....	....	....	....	....	....	....	....	....
	Wilkes-Barre	AHL	75	7	30	37	52	....	....	....	....	....	....	....	....	....	12	2	7	9	10	....	....	....	....
	NHL Totals		**9**	**1**	**1**	**2**	**2**	**0**	**0**	**0**	**7**	**14.3**		**0**	**0.0**	**13:15**	....	....	....	....	....	....	....	....	....

Signed as a free agent by **Pittsburgh**, July 16, 2010. Signed as a free agent by **Edmonton**, July 1, 2011.

POTULNY, Ryan
(poh-TUHL-nee, RIGH-uhn) **WSH**

Center. Shoots left. 6', 190 lbs. Born, Grand Forks, ND, September 5, 1984. Philadelphia's 6th choice, 87th overall, in 2003 Entry Draft.

2001-02	Lincoln Stars	USHL	60	23	34	57	65	....	....	....	....	....	....	....	....	....	4	0	1	1	2	....	....	....	....
2002-03	Lincoln Stars	USHL	54	35	*43	*78	18	....	....	....	....	....	....	....	....	....	10	6	*11	*17	8	....	....	....	....
2003-04	U. of Minnesota	WCHA	15	6	8	14	10	....	....	....	....	....	....	....	....	....	....	....	....	....	....	....	....	....	....
2004-05	U. of Minnesota	WCHA	44	24	17	41	20	....	....	....	....	....	....	....	....	....	....	....	....	....	....	....	....	....	....
2005-06	U. of Minnesota	WCHA	41	*38	25	*63	31	....	....	....	....	....	....	....	....	....	....	....	....	....	....	....	....	....	....
	Philadelphia	**NHL**	**2**	**0**	**1**	**1**	**0**	**0**	**0**	**0**	**0**	**0.0**	**1**	**9**	**44.4**	**6:09**	....	....	....	....	....	....	....	....	....
2006-07	**Philadelphia**	**NHL**	**35**	**7**	**5**	**12**	**22**	**0**	**0**	**2**	**56**	**12.5**	**1**	**278**	**43.5**	**11:00**	....	....	....	....	....	....	....	....	....
	Philadelphia	AHL	30	12	14	26	34	....	....	....	....	....	....	....	....	....	....	....	....	....	....	....	....	....	....
2007-08	**Philadelphia**	**NHL**	**7**	**0**	**1**	**1**	**4**	**0**	**0**	**0**	**5**	**0.0**	**0**	**32**	**43.8**	**6:30**	....	....	....	....	....	....	....	....	....
	Philadelphia	AHL	58	21	26	47	51	....	....	....	....	....	....	....	....	....	12	3	5	8	10	....	....	....	....
2008-09	**Edmonton**	**NHL**	**8**	**0**	**3**	**3**	**0**	**0**	**0**	**0**	**9**	**0.0**	**2**	**10**	**10.0**	**10:29**	....	....	....	....	....	....	....	....	....
	Springfield	AHL	70	38	24	62	48	....	....	....	....	....	....	....	....	....	....	....	....	....	....	....	....	....	....
2009-10	**Edmonton**	**NHL**	**64**	**15**	**17**	**32**	**28**	**7**	**1**	**2**	**152**	**9.9**	**-21**	**820**	**47.4**	**16:17**	....	....	....	....	....	....	....	....	....
	Springfield	AHL	14	3	5	8	8	....	....	....	....	....	....	....	....	....	....	....	....	....	....	....	....	....	....
2010-11	**Chicago**	**NHL**	**3**	**0**	**0**	**0**	**0**	**0**	**0**	**0**	**2**	**0.0**	**-1**	**26**	**38.5**	**10:07**	....	....	....	....	....	....	....	....	....
	Rockford IceHogs	AHL	58	18	23	41	30	....	....	....	....	....	....	....	....	....	....	....	....	....	....	....	....	....	....
	Ottawa	**NHL**	**7**	**0**	**0**	**0**	**0**	**0**	**0**	**0**	**5**	**0.0**	**0**	**0**	**0.0**	**6:57**	....	....	....	....	....	....	....	....	....
	Binghamton	AHL	13	3	5	8	4	....	....	....	....	....	....	....	....	....	23	*14	12	*26	12	....	....	....	....
	NHL Totals		**126**	**22**	**27**	**49**	**54**	**7**	**1**	**4**	**229**	**9.6**		**1175**	**45.9**	**13:05**	....	....	....	....	....	....	....	....	....

USHL First All-Star Team (2003) • USHL Player of the Year (2003) • WCHA First All-Star Team (2006) • NCAA West First All-American Team (2006)

• Missed majority of 2003-04 due to knee injury vs. North Dakota (WCHA), November 7, 2003. Traded to **Edmonton** by **Philadelphia** for Danny Syvret, June 6, 2008. Signed as a free agent by **Chicago**, September 9, 2010. Traded to **Ottawa** by **Chicago** with Chicago's 2nd round choice (later traded to Detroit – Detroit selected Xavier Ouellet) in 2011 Entry Draft for Chris Campoli and future considerations, February 28, 2011. Signed as a free agent by **Washington**, July 1, 2011.

POULIOT, Benoit
(POO lee oh, BEHN wah) **BOS**

Left wing. Shoots Left. 6'3", 199 lbs. Born, Alfred, Ont., September 29, 1986. Minnesota's 1st choice, 4th overall, in 2005 Entry Draft.

2002-03	Clarence Beavers	ON-Jr.B	38	13	17	30	86	....	....	....	....	....	....	....	....	....	5	0	2	2	8	....	....	....	....
	Hawkesbury	CJHL	1	1	0	1	0	....	....	....	....	....	....	....	....	....	....	....	....	....	....	....	....	....	....
2003-04	Hawkesbury	CJHL	45	21	21	42	85	....	....	....	....	....	....	....	....	....	6	3	7	10	10	....	....	....	....
	Sudbury Wolves	OHL	4	2	2	4	0	....	....	....	....	....	....	....	....	....	4	2	1	3	0	....	....	....	....
2004-05	Sudbury Wolves	OHL	67	29	38	67	102	....	....	....	....	....	....	....	....	....	12	6	8	14	20	....	....	....	....
2005-06	Sudbury Wolves	OHL	51	35	30	65	141	....	....	....	....	....	....	....	....	....	8	8	3	11	16	....	....	....	....
	Houston Aeros	AHL	....	....	....	....	....	....	....	....	....	....	....	....	....	....	2	0	0	0	2	....	....	....	....
2006-07	**Minnesota**	**NHL**	**3**	**0**	**0**	**0**	**0**	**0**	**0**	**0**	**1**	**0.0**	**-1**	**2**	**0.0**	**6:58**	....	....	....	....	....	....	....	....	....
	Houston Aeros	AHL	67	19	17	36	109	....	....	....	....	....	....	....	....	....	....	....	....	....	....	....	....	....	....
2007-08	**Minnesota**	**NHL**	**11**	**2**	**1**	**3**	**0**	**0**	**0**	**0**	**10**	**20.0**	**-1**	**65**	**40.0**	**8:49**	**1**	**0**	**0**	**0**	**0**	**0**	**0**	**0**	**10:16**
	Houston Aeros	AHL	46	10	14	24	67	....	....	....	....	....	....	....	....	....	3	0	0	0	2	....	....	....	....
2008-09	**Minnesota**	**NHL**	**37**	**5**	**6**	**11**	**18**	**2**	**0**	**1**	**34**	**14.7**	**1**	**217**	**42.9**	**11:51**	....	....	....	....	....	....	....	....	....
	Houston Aeros	AHL	30	9	15	24	20	....	....	....	....	....	....	....	....	....	20	1	7	8	28	....	....	....	....
2009-10	**Minnesota**	**NHL**	**14**	**2**	**2**	**4**	**12**	**0**	**0**	**0**	**19**	**10.5**	**0**	**8**	**50.0**	**11:56**	....	....	....	....	....	....	....	....	....
	Montreal	**NHL**	**39**	**15**	**9**	**24**	**31**	**4**	**0**	**3**	**92**	**16.3**	**8**	**3**	**33.3**	**16:44**	**18**	**0**	**2**	**2**	**6**	**0**	**0**	**0**	**11:45**
	Hamilton	AHL	3	1	2	3	4	....	....	....	....	....	....	....	....	....	....	....	....	....	....	....	....	....	....
2010-11	**Montreal**	**NHL**	**79**	**13**	**17**	**30**	**87**	**0**	**0**	**4**	**129**	**10.1**	**2**	**22**	**45.5**	**11:32**	**3**	**0**	**0**	**0**	**7**	**0**	**0**	**0**	**6:12**
	NHL Totals		**183**	**37**	**35**	**72**	**148**	**7**	**0**	**8**	**285**	**13.0**		**317**	**42.3**	**12:30**	**22**	**0**	**2**	**2**	**13**	**0**	**0**	**0**	**10:56**

OHL All-Rookie Team (2005) • OHL First All-Star Team (2005) • OHL Rookie of the Year (2005) • Canadian Major Junior All-Rookie Team (2005) • Canadian Major Junior Rookie of the Year (2005)

Traded to **Montreal** by **Minnesota** for Guillaume Latendresse, November 23, 2009. Signed as a free agent by **Boston**, July 1, 2011.

POULIOT, Marc
(POO-lee-oh, MAHRK) **PHX**

Center. Shoots right. 6'2", 193 lbs. Born, Quebec, Que., May 22, 1985. Edmonton's 1st choice, 22nd overall, in 2003 Entry Draft.

2000-01	Ste-Foy	QAAA	38	16	39	55	52	....	....	....	....	....	....	....	....	....	16	8	12	20	16	....	....	....	....
2001-02	Rimouski Oceanic	QMJHL	28	9	14	23	32	....	....	....	....	....	....	....	....	....	5	0	0	0	4	....	....	....	....
2002-03	Rimouski Oceanic	QMJHL	65	32	41	73	100	....	....	....	....	....	....	....	....	....	....	....	....	....	....	....	....	....	....
2003-04	Rimouski Oceanic	QMJHL	42	25	33	58	62	....	....	....	....	....	....	....	....	....	9	5	7	12	12	....	....	....	....
2004-05	Rimouski Oceanic	QMJHL	70	45	69	114	83	....	....	....	....	....	....	....	....	....	13	4	15	19	8	....	....	....	....
2005-06	**Edmonton**	**NHL**	**8**	**1**	**0**	**1**	**0**	**0**	**0**	**0**	**5**	**20.0**	**1**	**56**	**55.4**	**8:30**	....	....	....	....	....	....	....	....	....
	Hamilton	AHL	65	15	31	46	63	....	....	....	....	....	....	....	....	....	....	....	....	....	....	....	....	....	....
2006-07	**Edmonton**	**NHL**	**46**	**4**	**7**	**11**	**18**	**0**	**0**	**0**	**73**	**5.5**	**-2**	**353**	**48.7**	**13:03**	....	....	....	....	....	....	....	....	....
	Wilkes-Barre	AHL	33	14	17	31	20	....	....	....	....	....	....	....	....	....	11	5	5	10	4	....	....	....	....
2007-08	**Edmonton**	**NHL**	**24**	**1**	**6**	**7**	**12**	**0**	**0**	**0**	**32**	**3.1**	**-1**	**44**	**47.7**	**10:20**	....	....	....	....	....	....	....	....	....
	Springfield	AHL	55	21	26	47	47	....	....	....	....	....	....	....	....	....	....	....	....	....	....	....	....	....	....
2008-09	**Edmonton**	**NHL**	**63**	**8**	**12**	**20**	**23**	**0**	**0**	**2**	**94**	**8.5**	**1**	**211**	**48.3**	**11:30**	....	....	....	....	....	....	....	....	....
2009-10	**Edmonton**	**NHL**	**35**	**7**	**7**	**14**	**21**	**1**	**0**	**1**	**60**	**11.7**	**-4**	**235**	**44.3**	**12:48**	....	....	....	....	....	....	....	....	....
	Springfield	AHL	4	1	5	6	12	....	....	....	....	....	....	....	....	....	....	....	....	....	....	....	....	....	....
2010-11	**Tampa Bay**	**NHL**	**3**	**0**	**0**	**0**	**0**	**0**	**0**	**0**	**2**	**0.0**	**-2**	**13**	**38.5**	**10:46**	....	....	....	....	....	....	....	....	....
	Norfolk Admirals	AHL	69	25	47	72	53	....	....	....	....	....	....	....	....	....	6	4	3	7	4	....	....	....	....
	NHL Totals		**179**	**21**	**32**	**53**	**74**	**1**	**0**	**3**	**266**	**7.9**		**912**	**47.7**	**11:51**	....	....	....	....	....	....	....	....	....

QMJHL First All-Star Team (2005) • George Parsons Trophy (Memorial Cup - Most Sportsmanlike Player) (2005)

• Missed majority of 2009-10 due to lower body injury. Signed as a free agent by **Tampa Bay**, July 23, 2010. Traded to **Phoenix** by **Tampa Bay** for Phoenix's 7th round choice (Matthew Peca) in 2011 Entry Draft, June 25, 2011.

POWE, Darroll
(POW, DAIR-ohl) **MIN**

Left wing. Shoots left. 5'11", 212 lbs. Born, Saskatoon, Sask., June 22, 1985.

2003-04	Princeton	ECAC	29	4	5	9	28	....	....	....	....	....	....	....	....	....	....	....	....	....	....	....	....	....	....
2004-05	Princeton	ECAC	30	5	2	7	41	....	....	....	....	....	....	....	....	....	....	....	....	....	....	....	....	....	....
2005-06	Princeton	ECAC	27	6	10	16	48	....	....	....	....	....	....	....	....	....	....	....	....	....	....	....	....	....	....
2006-07	Princeton	ECAC	34	13	15	28	63	....	....	....	....	....	....	....	....	....	....	....	....	....	....	....	....	....	....
	Philadelphia	AHL	11	2	2	4	20	....	....	....	....	....	....	....	....	....	....	....	....	....	....	....	....	....	....
2007-08	Philadelphia	AHL	76	9	14	23	133	....	....	....	....	....	....	....	....	....	10	1	0	1	6	....	....	....	....

			Regular Season														Playoffs								
Season	Club	League	GP	G	A	Pts	PIM	PP	SH	GW	S	%	+/-	TF	F%	Min	GP	G	A	Pts	PIM	PP	SH	GW	Min
2008-09	**Philadelphia**	**NHL**	**60**	**6**	**5**	**11**	**35**	**0**	**0**	**0**	**72**	**8.3**	**–8**	**263**	**48.7**	**10:32**	**6**	**1**	**2**	**3**	**7**	**0**	**0**	**0**	**14:02**
	Philadelphia	AHL	8	4	3	7	20	....	....	....	....	....	....	....	....	....	....	....	....	....	....	....	....	....	....
2009-10	**Philadelphia**	**NHL**	**63**	**9**	**6**	**15**	**54**	**0**	**0**	**0**	**103**	**8.7**	**0**	**210**	**45.2**	**12:05**	**23**	**0**	**1**	**1**	**6**	**0**	**0**	**0**	**12:33**
2010-11	**Philadelphia**	**NHL**	**81**	**7**	**10**	**17**	**41**	**0**	**2**	**2**	**87**	**8.0**	**–6**	**134**	**49.3**	**12:17**	**11**	**0**	**1**	**1**	**4**	**0**	**0**	**0**	**12:10**
	NHL Totals		**204**	**22**	**21**	**43**	**130**	**0**	**2**	**2**	**262**	**8.4**		**607**	**47.6**	**11:43**	**40**	**1**	**4**	**5**	**17**	**0**	**0**	**0**	**12:40**

Signed as a free agent by **Philadelphia**, April 17, 2008. Traded to **Minnesota** by **Philadelphia** for Minnesota's 3rd round choice in 2013 Entry Draft, June 27, 2011.

PREISSING, Tom

(PRIGH-sihng, TAHM)

Defense. Shoots right. 6', 197 lbs. Born, Arlington Heights, IL, December 3, 1978.

Season	Club	League	GP	G	A	Pts	PIM	PP	SH	GW	S	%	+/-	TF	F%	Min	GP	G	A	Pts	PIM	PP	SH	GW	Min
1997-98	Green Bay	USHL	56	8	13	21	30	....	....	....	....	....	....	....	....	....	4	0	2	2	2	....	....	....	....
1998-99	Green Bay	USHL	53	18	37	55	40	....	....	....	....	....	....	....	....	....	6	3	6	9	2	....	....	....	....
99-2000	Colorado College	WCHA	36	4	14	18	20	....	....	....	....	....	....	....	....	....	....	....	....	....	....	....	....	....	....
2000-01	Colorado College	WCHA	33	6	18	24	26	....	....	....	....	....	....	....	....	....	....	....	....	....	....	....	....	....	....
2001-02	Colorado College	WCHA	43	6	26	32	42	....	....	....	....	....	....	....	....	....	....	....	....	....	....	....	....	....	....
2002-03	Colorado College	WCHA	42	23	29	52	16	....	....	....	....	....	....	....	....	....	....	....	....	....	....	....	....	....	....
2003-04	**San Jose**	**NHL**	**69**	**2**	**17**	**19**	**12**	**2**	**0**	**1**	**89**	**2.2**	**8**	**0**	**0.0**	**18:12**	**11**	**0**	**1**	**1**	**0**	**0**	**0**	**0**	**12:49**
2004-05	Krefeld Pinguine	Germany	33	1	6	7	32	....	....	....	....	....	....	....	....	....	....	....	....	....	....	....	....	....	....
2005-06	**San Jose**	**NHL**	**74**	**11**	**32**	**43**	**26**	**2**	**0**	**2**	**131**	**8.4**	**17**	**1**	**0.0**	**20:30**	**11**	**1**	**6**	**7**	**4**	**0**	**0**	**0**	**23:50**
2006-07	**Ottawa**	**NHL**	**80**	**7**	**31**	**38**	**18**	**3**	**0**	**0**	**94**	**7.4**	**40**	**0**	**0.0**	**15:15**	**20**	**2**	**5**	**7**	**10**	**1**	**0**	**1**	**15:02**
2007-08	**Los Angeles**	**NHL**	**77**	**8**	**16**	**24**	**16**	**6**	**0**	**1**	**93**	**8.6**	**–6**	**9**	**22.2**	**17:53**	....	....	....	....	....	....	....	....	....
2008-09	**Los Angeles**	**NHL**	**22**	**3**	**4**	**7**	**6**	**2**	**0**	**0**	**40**	**7.5**	**–7**	**0**	**0.0**	**16:45**	....	....	....	....	....	....	....	....	....
	Manchester	AHL	14	2	4	6	6	....	....	....	....	....	....	....	....	....	....	....	....	....	....	....	....	....	....
2009-10	**Colorado**	**NHL**	**4**	**0**	**1**	**1**	**0**	**0**	**0**	**0**	**6**	**0.0**	**–6**	**0**	**0.0**	**13:05**	....	....	....	....	....	....	....	....	....
	Lake Erie	AHL	49	9	22	31	38	....	....	....	....	....	....	....	....	....	....	....	....	....	....	....	....	....	....
2010-11	Barys Astana	Rus-KHL	2	1	0	1	0	....	....	....	....	....	....	....	....	....	....	....	....	....	....	....	....	....	....
	NHL Totals		**326**	**31**	**101**	**132**	**78**	**15**	**0**	**4**	**453**	**6.8**		**10**	**20.0**	**17:46**	**42**	**3**	**12**	**15**	**14**	**1**	**0**	**1**	**16:45**

USHL First All-Star Team (1999) • USHL Defenseman of the Year (1999) • WCHA First All-Star Team (2003) • NCAA West First All-American Team (2003)

Signed as a free agent by **San Jose**, April 4, 2003. Signed as a free agent by **Krefeld** (Germany), November 15, 2004. Traded to **Chicago** by **San Jose** with Josh Hennessy for Mark Bell, July 9, 2006. Traded to **Ottawa** by **Chicago** with Josh Hennessy, Michal Barinka and Chicago's 2nd round choice (Patrick Wiercioch) in 2008 Entry Draft for Martin Havlat and Bryan Smolinski, July 10, 2006. Signed as a free agent by **Los Angeles**, July 2, 2007. Traded to **Colorado** by **Los Angeles** with Kyle Quincey and Los Angeles' 5th round choice (Luke Walker) in 2010 Entry Draft for Ryan Smyth, July 3, 2009. Signed as a free agent by **Oulu** (Finland), September 16, 2010. • Loaned to **Astana** (Russia-KHL) by **Oulu** (Finland). September 17, 2010. • Missed remainder of 2010-11 due to knee injury vs. Novokuznetsk, September 19, 2010. Signed as a free agent by **Biel** (Swiss), July 11, 2011.

PRONGER, Chris

(PRAWN-guhr, KRIHS) **PHI**

Defense. Shoots left. 6'6", 220 lbs. Born, Dryden, Ont., October 10, 1974. Hartford's 1st choice, 2nd overall, in 1993 Entry Draft.

Season	Club	League	GP	G	A	Pts	PIM	PP	SH	GW	S	%	+/-	TF	F%	Min	GP	G	A	Pts	PIM	PP	SH	GW	Min
1990-91	Stratford Cullitons	ON-Jr.B	48	15	37	52	132	....	....	....	....	....	....	....	....	....	....	....	....	....	....	....	....	....	....
1991-92	Peterborough	OHL	63	17	45	62	90	....	....	....	....	....	....	....	....	....	10	1	8	9	28	....	....	....	....
1992-93	Peterborough	OHL	61	15	62	77	108	....	....	....	....	....	....	....	....	....	21	15	25	40	51	....	....	....	....
1993-94	**Hartford**	**NHL**	**81**	**5**	**25**	**30**	**113**	**2**	**0**	**0**	**174**	**2.9**	**–3**	....	....	....	....	....	....	....	....	....	....	....	....
1994-95	**Hartford**	**NHL**	**43**	**5**	**9**	**14**	**54**	**3**	**0**	**1**	**94**	**5.3**	**–12**	....	....	....	....	....	....	....	....	....	....	....	....
1995-96	**St. Louis**	**NHL**	**78**	**7**	**18**	**25**	**110**	**3**	**1**	**1**	**138**	**5.1**	**–18**	....	....	....	**13**	**1**	**5**	**6**	**16**	**0**	**0**	**0**	....
1996-97	**St. Louis**	**NHL**	**79**	**11**	**24**	**35**	**143**	**4**	**0**	**0**	**147**	**7.5**	**15**	....	....	....	**6**	**1**	**1**	**2**	**22**	**0**	**0**	**0**	....
1997-98	**St. Louis**	**NHL**	**81**	**9**	**27**	**36**	**180**	**1**	**0**	**2**	**145**	**6.2**	***47**	....	....	....	**10**	**1**	**9**	**10**	**26**	**0**	**0**	**0**	....
	Canada	Olympics	6	0	0	0	4	....	....	....	....	....	....	....	....	....	....	....	....	....	....	....	....	....	....
1998-99	**St. Louis**	**NHL**	**67**	**13**	**33**	**46**	**113**	**8**	**0**	**0**	**172**	**7.6**	**3**	**0**	**0.0**	**30:36**	**13**	**1**	**4**	**5**	**28**	**1**	**0**	**0**	**35:53**
99-2000	**St. Louis**	**NHL**	**79**	**14**	**48**	**62**	**92**	**8**	**0**	**3**	**192**	**7.3**	***52**	**1**	**0.0**	**30:14**	**7**	**3**	**4**	**7**	**32**	**2**	**0**	**2**	**30:14**
2000-01	**St. Louis**	**NHL**	**51**	**8**	**39**	**47**	**75**	**4**	**0**	**0**	**121**	**6.6**	**21**	**0**	**0.0**	**27:45**	**15**	**1**	**7**	**8**	**32**	**0**	**0**	**0**	**33:50**
2001-02	**St. Louis**	**NHL**	**78**	**7**	**40**	**47**	**120**	**4**	**1**	**3**	**204**	**3.4**	**23**	**0**	**0.0**	**29:28**	**9**	**1**	**7**	**8**	**24**	**0**	**0**	**0**	**27:51**
	Canada	Olympics	6	0	1	1	2	....	....	....	....	....	....	....	....	....	....	....	....	....	....	....	....	....	....
2002-03	**St. Louis**	**NHL**	**5**	**1**	**3**	**4**	**10**	**0**	**0**	**0**	**11**	**9.1**	**–2**	**1**	**0.0**	**21:39**	**7**	**1**	**3**	**4**	**14**	**0**	**0**	**0**	**24:36**
2003-04	**St. Louis**	**NHL**	**80**	**14**	**40**	**54**	**88**	**7**	**0**	**3**	**203**	**6.9**	**–1**	**2**	**0.0**	**27:28**	**5**	**0**	**1**	**1**	**16**	**0**	**0**	**0**	**27:54**
2004-05			DID NOT PLAY																						
2005-06	**Edmonton**	**NHL**	**80**	**12**	**44**	**56**	**74**	**10**	**0**	**3**	**155**	**7.7**	**2**	**1**	**0.0**	**27:59**	**24**	**5**	**16**	**21**	**26**	**3**	**0**	**0**	**30:57**
	Canada	Olympics	6	1	2	3	16	....	....	....	....	....	....	....	....	....	....	....	....	....	....	....	....	....	....
2006-07 ♦	**Anaheim**	**NHL**	**66**	**13**	**46**	**59**	**69**	**8**	**0**	**2**	**166**	**7.8**	**27**	**4**	**25.0**	**27:06**	**19**	**3**	**12**	**15**	**26**	**1**	**0**	**0**	**30:11**
2007-08	**Anaheim**	**NHL**	**72**	**12**	**31**	**43**	**128**	**8**	**0**	**4**	**182**	**6.6**	**–1**	**7**	**57.1**	**26:00**	**6**	**2**	**3**	**5**	**12**	**2**	**0**	**1**	**24:14**
2008-09	**Anaheim**	**NHL**	**82**	**11**	**37**	**48**	**88**	**4**	**0**	**2**	**196**	**5.6**	**0**	**7**	**28.6**	**26:56**	**13**	**2**	**8**	**10**	**12**	**1**	**0**	**0**	**27:13**
2009-10	**Philadelphia**	**NHL**	**82**	**10**	**45**	**55**	**79**	**5**	**0**	**2**	**175**	**5.7**	**22**	**0**	**0.0**	**25:56**	**23**	**4**	**14**	**18**	***36**	**3**	**0**	**0**	**29:03**
	Canada	Olympics	7	0	5	5	2	....	....	....	....	....	....	....	....	....	....	....	....	....	....	....	....	....	....
2010-11	**Philadelphia**	**NHL**	**50**	**4**	**21**	**25**	**44**	**3**	**0**	**1**	**112**	**3.6**	**7**	**0**	**0.0**	**22:30**	**3**	**0**	**1**	**1**	**4**	**0**	**0**	**0**	**13:55**
	NHL Totals		**1154**	**156**	**530**	**686**	**1580**	**82**	**2**	**27**	**2587**	**6.0**		**23**	**30.4**	**27:33**	**173**	**26**	**95**	**121**	**326**	**13**	**0**	**3**	**29:41**

OHL All-Rookie Team (1992) • OHL First All-Star Team (1993) • Canadian Major Junior First All-Star Team (1993) • Canadian Major Junior Defenseman of the Year (1993) • NHL All-Rookie Team (1994) • NHL Second All-Star Team (1998, 2004, 2007) • Bud Ice Plus/Minus Award (1998) • NHL First All-Star Team (2000) • Bud Light Plus/Minus Award (2000) • James Norris Memorial Trophy (2000) • Hart Memorial Trophy (2000)

Played in NHL All-Star Game (1999, 2000, 2002, 2004, 2008)

Traded to **St. Louis** by **Hartford** for Brendan Shanahan, July 27, 1995. • Missed majority of 2002-03 due to wrist and knee surgeries, September 10, 2002. Traded to **Edmonton** by **St. Louis** for Eric Brewer, Doug Lynch and Jeff Woywitka, August 2, 2005. Traded to **Anaheim** by **Edmonton** for Joffrey Lupul, Ladislav Smid, Anaheim's 1st round choice (later traded to Phoenix - Phoenix selected Nick Ross) in 2007 Entry Draft and Anaheim's 1st (Jordan Eberle) and 2nd (later traded to NY Islanders - NY Islanders selected Travis Hamonic) round choices in 2008 Entry Draft, July 3, 2006. Traded to **Philadelphia** by **Anaheim** with Ryan Dingle for Joffrey Lupul, Luca Sbisa, Philadelphia's 1st round choices in 2009 (later traded to Columbus - Columbus selected John Moore) and 2010 (Emerson Etem) Entry Drafts and future considerations, June 26, 2009.

PROSPAL, Vinny

(PRAWS-puhl, vih-NEE) **CBJ**

Center. Shoots left. 6'2", 198 lbs. Born, Ceske Budejovice, Czech., February 17, 1975. Philadelphia's 2nd choice, 71st overall, in 1993 Entry Draft.

Season	Club	League	GP	G	A	Pts	PIM	PP	SH	GW	S	%	+/-	TF	F%	Min	GP	G	A	Pts	PIM	PP	SH	GW	Min
1991-92	C. Budejovice Jr.	Czech-Jr.	36	16	16	32	12	....	....	....	....	....	....	....	....	....	....	....	....	....	....	....	....	....	....
1992-93	C. Budejovice Jr.	Czech-Jr.	32	26	31	57	24	....	....	....	....	....	....	....	....	....	....	....	....	....	....	....	....	....	....
1993-94	Hershey Bears	AHL	55	14	21	35	38	....	....	....	....	....	....	....	....	....	2	0	0	0	2	....	....	....	....
1994-95	Hershey Bears	AHL	69	13	32	45	36	....	....	....	....	....	....	....	....	....	2	1	0	1	4	....	....	....	....
1995-96	Hershey Bears	AHL	68	15	36	51	59	....	....	....	....	....	....	....	....	....	5	2	4	6	2	....	....	....	....
1996-97	**Philadelphia**	**NHL**	**18**	**5**	**10**	**15**	**4**	**0**	**0**	**0**	**35**	**14.3**	**3**	....	....	....	**5**	**1**	**3**	**4**	**4**	**0**	**0**	**0**	....
	Philadelphia	AHL	63	32	63	95	70	....	....	....	....	....	....	....	....	....	....	....	....	....	....	....	....	....	....
1997-98	**Philadelphia**	**NHL**	**41**	**5**	**13**	**18**	**17**	**4**	**0**	**0**	**60**	**8.3**	**–10**	....	....	....	....	....	....	....	....	....	....	....	....
	Ottawa	**NHL**	**15**	**1**	**6**	**7**	**4**	**0**	**0**	**0**	**28**	**3.6**	**–1**	....	....	....	**6**	**0**	**0**	**0**	**0**	**0**	**0**	**0**	....
1998-99	**Ottawa**	**NHL**	**79**	**10**	**26**	**36**	**58**	**2**	**0**	**3**	**114**	**8.8**	**8**	**997**	**56.2**	**13:03**	**4**	**0**	**0**	**0**	**0**	**0**	**0**	**0**	**12:37**
99-2000	**Ottawa**	**NHL**	**79**	**22**	**33**	**55**	**40**	**5**	**0**	**4**	**204**	**10.8**	**–2**	**1331**	**49.6**	**16:26**	**6**	**0**	**4**	**4**	**4**	**0**	**0**	**0**	**17:40**
2000-01	**Ottawa**	**NHL**	**40**	**1**	**12**	**13**	**12**	**0**	**0**	**0**	**68**	**1.5**	**1**	**501**	**50.1**	**12:57**	....	....	....	....	....	....	....	....	....
	Florida	**NHL**	**34**	**4**	**12**	**16**	**10**	**1**	**0**	**0**	**68**	**5.9**	**–2**	**487**	**54.6**	**16:36**	....	....	....	....	....	....	....	....	....
2001-02	**Tampa Bay**	**NHL**	**81**	**18**	**37**	**55**	**38**	**7**	**0**	**2**	**166**	**10.8**	**–11**	**555**	**52.8**	**17:31**	....	....	....	....	....	....	....	....	....
2002-03	**Tampa Bay**	**NHL**	**80**	**22**	**57**	**79**	**53**	**9**	**0**	**4**	**134**	**16.4**	**9**	**161**	**51.6**	**18:39**	**11**	**4**	**2**	**6**	**8**	**2**	**0**	**0**	**21:15**
2003-04	**Anaheim**	**NHL**	**82**	**19**	**35**	**54**	**54**	**7**	**0**	**4**	**185**	**10.3**	**–9**	**45**	**46.7**	**18:37**	....	....	....	....	....	....	....	....	....
2004-05	C. Budejovice	CzRep-2	39	28	60	88	82	....	....	....	....	....	....	....	....	....	16	15	15	30	32	....	....	....	....
2005-06	**Tampa Bay**	**NHL**	**81**	**25**	**55**	**80**	**50**	**10**	**0**	**3**	**236**	**10.6**	**–3**	**267**	**45.3**	**19:10**	**5**	**0**	**2**	**2**	**0**	**0**	**0**	**0**	**15:56**
	Czech Republic	Olympics	8	4	2	6	2	....	....	....	....	....	....	....	....	....	....	....	....	....	....	....	....	....	....
2006-07	**Tampa Bay**	**NHL**	**82**	**14**	**41**	**55**	**36**	**2**	**0**	**1**	**219**	**6.4**	**–24**	**124**	**52.4**	**19:04**	**6**	**1**	**4**	**5**	**4**	**0**	**0**	**1**	**22:19**
2007-08	**Tampa Bay**	**NHL**	**62**	**29**	**28**	**57**	**39**	**9**	**0**	**4**	**175**	**16.6**	**–7**	**176**	**54.6**	**20:00**	....	....	....	....	....	....	....	....	....
	Philadelphia	**NHL**	**18**	**4**	**10**	**14**	**6**	**1**	**0**	**1**	**40**	**10.0**	**7**	**86**	**58.1**	**17:15**	**17**	**3**	**10**	**13**	**6**	**1**	**0**	**0**	**16:49**
2008-09	**Tampa Bay**	**NHL**	**82**	**19**	**26**	**45**	**52**	**7**	**0**	**2**	**194**	**9.8**	**–20**	**202**	**53.0**	**17:41**	....	....	....	....	....	....	....	....	....
2009-10	**NY Rangers**	**NHL**	**75**	**20**	**38**	**58**	**32**	**6**	**1**	**4**	**180**	**11.1**	**8**	**639**	**51.2**	**20:06**	....	....	....	....	....	....	....	....	....
2010-11	**NY Rangers**	**NHL**	**29**	**9**	**14**	**23**	**8**	**2**	**0**	**0**	**61**	**14.8**	**4**	**128**	**53.9**	**15:20**	**5**	**1**	**0**	**1**	**0**	**0**	**0**	**0**	**19:30**
	NHL Totals		**978**	**227**	**453**	**680**	**513**	**72**	**1**	**32**	**2167**	**10.5**		**5699**	**52.1**	**17:37**	**65**	**10**	**25**	**35**	**26**	**3**	**0**	**1**	**18:17**

AHL First All-Star Team (1997)

Traded to **Ottawa** by **Philadelphia** with Pat Falloon and Dallas' 2nd round choice (previously acquired, Ottawa selected Chris Bala) in 1998 Entry Draft for Alexandre Daigle, January 17, 1998. Traded to **Florida** by **Ottawa** for future considerations, January 20, 2001. Traded to **Tampa Bay** by **Florida** for Ryan Johnson and Tampa Bay's 6th round choice (later traded back to Tampa Bay – Tampa Bay selected Doug O'Brien) in 2003 Entry Draft, July 10, 2001. Signed as a free agent by **Anaheim**, July 17, 2003. Traded to **Tampa Bay** by **Anaheim** for Tampa Bay's 2nd round choice (Brendan Mikkelson) in 2005 Entry Draft, August 16, 2004. Signed as a free agent by **Ceske Budejovice** (CzRep-2), September 17, 2004. Traded to **Philadelphia** by **Tampa Bay** for Alexandre Picard and Philadelphia's 2nd round choice (Richard Panik) in 2009 Entry Draft, February 25, 2008. Traded to **Tampa Bay** by **Philadelphia** for Nashville's 7th round choice (previously acquired, Philadelphia selected Joacim Eriksson) in 2008 Entry Draft and future considerations, June 18, 2008. Signed as a free agent by **NY Rangers**, August 17, 2009. • Missed majority of 2010-11 due to knee surgery, October 6, 2010. Signed as a free agent by **Columbus**, July 23. 2011.

PROSSER, Nate

(PRAW-suhr, NAYT) **MIN**

Defense. Shoots right. 6'2", 207 lbs. Born, Elk River, MN, May 7, 1986.

Season	Club	League	GP	G	A	Pts	PIM	PP	SH	GW	S	%	+/-	TF	F%	Min	GP	G	A	Pts	PIM	PP	SH	GW	Min
			Regular Season														Playoffs								
2006-07	Colorado College	WCHA	21	0	3	3	8	....	....	....	....	....	....	....	....	....	....	....	....	....	....	....	....	....	....
2007-08	Colorado College	WCHA	39	3	17	20	51	....	....	....	....	....	....	....	....	....	....	....	....	....	....	....	....	....	....
2008-09	Colorado College	WCHA	38	5	8	13	61	....	....	....	....	....	....	....	....	....	....	....	....	....	....	....	....	....	....
2009-10	**Minnesota**	**NHL**	3	0	1	1	8	0	0	0	4	0.0	2	0	0.0	19:37	....	....	....	....	....	....	....	....	....
	Colorado College	WCHA	39	4	24	28	58	....	....	....	....	....	....	....	....	....	....	....	....	....	....	....	....	....	....
2010-11	**Minnesota**	**NHL**	2	0	0	0	0	0	0	0	1	0.0	0	0	0.0	14:48	....	....	....	....	....	....	....	....	....
	Houston Aeros	AHL	73	8	19	27	31	....	....	....	....	....	....	....	....	....	24	2	2	4	16	....	....	....	....
	NHL Totals		5	0	1	1	8	0	0	0	5	0.0		0	0.0	17:41	....	....	....	....	....	....	....	....	....

WCHA Second All-Star Team (2010)

Signed as a free agent by **Minnesota**, March 18, 2010.

PRUCHA, Petr

(PROO-khah, PEE-tuhr)

Right wing. Shoots right. 6', 175 lbs. Born, Chrudim, Czech., September 14, 1982. NY Rangers' 8th choice, 240th overall, in 2002 Entry Draft.

Season	Club	League	GP	G	A	Pts	PIM	PP	SH	GW	S	%	+/-	TF	F%	Min	GP	G	A	Pts	PIM	PP	SH	GW	Min
99-2000	HC Chrudim Jr.	CzRep-Jr.	43	35	27	62	62	....	....	....	....	....	....	....	....	....	....	....	....	....	....	....	....	....	....
2000-01	HC Pardubice Jr.	CzRep-Jr.	54	39	22	61	18	....	....	....	....	....	....	....	....	....	....	....	....	....	....	....	....	....	....
2001-02	HC Pardubice Jr.	CzRep-Jr.	28	38	28	66	18	....	....	....	....	....	....	....	....	....	3	2	6	8	0	....	....	....	....
	Sumperk	CzRep-2	8	6	4	10	0	....	....	....	....	....	....	....	....	....	....	....	....	....	....	....	....	....	....
	Sumperk	CzRep-Q	5	5	3	8	0	....	....	....	....	....	....	....	....	....	....	....	....	....	....	....	....	....	....
	Pardubice	CzRep	20	1	1	2	2	....	....	....	....	....	....	....	....	....	5	0	0	0	0	....	....	....	....
2002-03	Pardubice	CzRep	49	7	9	16	12	....	....	....	....	....	....	....	....	....	17	2	6	8	8	....	....	....	....
	HC Pardubice Jr.	CzRep-Jr.	4	5	4	9	25	....	....	....	....	....	....	....	....	....	....	....	....	....	....	....	....	....	....
	Hr. Kralove	CzRep-2	11	3	5	8	35	....	....	....	....	....	....	....	....	....	....	....	....	....	....	....	....	....	....
2003-04	Pardubice	CzRep	48	11	13	24	24	....	....	....	....	....	....	....	....	....	7	4	3	7	2	....	....	....	....
	Hr. Kralove	CzRep-2	3	1	0	1	25	....	....	....	....	....	....	....	....	....	....	....	....	....	....	....	....	....	....
2004-05	Pardubice	CzRep	47	7	10	17	24	....	....	....	....	....	....	....	....	....	16	6	7	13	2	....	....	....	....
2005-06	**NY Rangers**	**NHL**	68	30	17	47	32	16	0	2	130	23.1	3	150	52.0	13:42	4	1	0	1	0	1	0	0	14:13
	Hartford	AHL	2	2	1	3	0	....	....	....	....	....	....	....	....	....	....	....	....	....	....	....	....	....	....
2006-07	**NY Rangers**	**NHL**	79	22	18	40	30	8	0	2	136	16.2	–7	70	50.0	13:00	10	0	1	1	4	0	0	0	13:35
2007-08	**NY Rangers**	**NHL**	62	7	10	17	22	2	0	1	89	7.9	3	3	66.7	11:38	3	0	0	0	0	0	0	0	8:13
2008-09	**NY Rangers**	**NHL**	28	4	5	9	16	0	0	0	44	9.1	–2	0	0.0	12:09	....	....	....	....	....	....	....	....	....
	Phoenix	**NHL**	19	2	8	10	6	1	0	1	23	8.7	1	8	12.5	18:26	....	....	....	....	....	....	....	....	....
2009-10	**Phoenix**	**NHL**	79	13	9	22	23	4	0	2	128	10.2	–2	151	45.0	14:02	7	1	2	3	4	0	0	1	13:31
2010-11	**Phoenix**	**NHL**	11	0	1	1	4	0	0	0	10	0.0	0	5	60.0	11:28	....	....	....	....	....	....	....	....	....
	San Antonio	AHL	20	8	13	21	2	....	....	....	....	....	....	....	....	....	....	....	....	....	....	....	....	....	....
	St. Petersburg	Rus-KHL	11	1	2	3	4	....	....	....	....	....	....	....	....	....	11	5	1	6	14	....	....	....	....
	NHL Totals		346	78	68	146	133	31	0	8	560	13.9		387	48.3	13:19	24	2	3	5	8	1	0	1	13:00

Traded to **Phoenix** by **NY Rangers** with Dmitri Kalinin and Nigel Dawes for Derek Morris, March 4, 2009. Signed as a free agent by **St. Petersburg** (Russia-KHL), January 11, 2011.

PRUST, Brandon

(PROOST, BRAN-duhn) **NYR**

Left wing. Shoots left. 6'2", 192 lbs. Born, London, Ont., March 16, 1984. Calgary's 2nd choice, 70th overall, in 2004 Entry Draft.

Season	Club	League	GP	G	A	Pts	PIM	PP	SH	GW	S	%	+/-	TF	F%	Min	GP	G	A	Pts	PIM	PP	SH	GW	Min
2001-02	London Nationals	ON-Jr.B	52	17	35	52	38	....	....	....	....	....	....	....	....	....	....	....	....	....	....	....	....	....	....
2002-03	London Knights	OHL	65	12	17	29	94	....	....	....	....	....	....	....	....	....	14	2	1	3	21	....	....	....	....
2003-04	London Knights	OHL	64	19	33	52	269	....	....	....	....	....	....	....	....	....	15	7	13	20	33	....	....	....	....
2004-05	London Knights	OHL	48	10	20	30	174	....	....	....	....	....	....	....	....	....	15	3	5	8	*71	....	....	....	....
2005-06	Omaha	AHL	79	12	14	26	294	....	....	....	....	....	....	....	....	....	....	....	....	....	....	....	....	....	....
2006-07	**Calgary**	**NHL**	10	0	0	0	25	0	0	0	1	0.0	1	0	0.0	6:03	....	....	....	....	....	....	....	....	....
	Omaha	AHL	63	17	10	27	211	....	....	....	....	....	....	....	....	....	6	0	3	3	20	....	....	....	....
2007-08	Quad City Flames	AHL	79	10	27	37	248	....	....	....	....	....	....	....	....	....	....	....	....	....	....	....	....	....	....
2008-09	**Calgary**	**NHL**	25	1	1	2	79	0	0	1	15	6.7	–4	15	53.3	6:21	....	....	....	....	....	....	....	....	....
	Phoenix	**NHL**	11	0	1	1	29	0	0	0	8	0.0	–4	16	56.3	9:59	....	....	....	....	....	....	....	....	....
2009-10	**Calgary**	**NHL**	43	1	4	5	98	0	0	1	23	4.3	6	29	37.9	6:33	....	....	....	....	....	....	....	....	....
	NY Rangers	**NHL**	26	4	5	9	65	0	0	2	21	19.0	3	2	100.0	9:20	....	....	....	....	....	....	....	....	....
2010-11	**NY Rangers**	**NHL**	82	13	16	29	160	0	5	1	87	14.9	2	9	44.4	13:49	5	0	1	1	4	0	0	0	16:24
	NHL Totals		197	19	27	46	456	0	5	5	155	12.3		71	47.9	10:05	5	0	1	1	4	0	0	0	16:24

Traded to **Phoenix** by **Calgary** with Matthew Lombardi and Calgary's 1st round choice (Brandon Gormley) in 2010 Entry Draft for Olli Jokinen and Phoenix's 3rd round choice (later traded to Florida – Florida selected Josh Birkholz) in 2009 Entry Draft, March 4, 2009. Traded to **Calgary** by **Phoenix** for Jim Vandermeer, June 27, 2009. Traded to **NY Rangers** by **Calgary** with Olli Jokinen for Chris Higgins and Ales Kotalik, February 2, 2010.

PURCELL, Teddy

(PUHR-sihl, TEH-dee) **T.B.**

Right wing. Shoots right. 6'2", 201 lbs. Born, St. Johns, Nfld., September 8, 1985.

Season	Club	League	GP	G	A	Pts	PIM	PP	SH	GW	S	%	+/-	TF	F%	Min	GP	G	A	Pts	PIM	PP	SH	GW	Min
2003-04	Notre Dame	SJHL	51	21	25	46	8	....	....	....	....	....	....	....	....	....	....	....	....	....	....	....	....	....	....
2004-05	Cedar Rapids	USHL	58	20	47	67	22	....	....	....	....	....	....	....	....	....	11	5	9	14	4	....	....	....	....
2005-06	Cedar Rapids	USHL	55	19	*52	71	14	....	....	....	....	....	....	....	....	....	8	3	8	11	4	....	....	....	....
2006-07	U. of Maine	H-East	40	16	27	43	34	....	....	....	....	....	....	....	....	....	....	....	....	....	....	....	....	....	....
2007-08	**Los Angeles**	**NHL**	10	1	2	3	0	0	0	0	10	10.0	2	0	0.0	11:59	....	....	....	....	....	....	....	....	....
	Manchester	AHL	67	25	58	83	34	....	....	....	....	....	....	....	....	....	4	0	3	3	0	....	....	....	....
2008-09	**Los Angeles**	**NHL**	40	4	12	16	4	2	0	1	68	5.9	–4	29	17.2	13:31	....	....	....	....	....	....	....	....	....
	Manchester	AHL	38	16	22	38	12	....	....	....	....	....	....	....	....	....	....	....	....	....	....	....	....	....	....
2009-10	**Los Angeles**	**NHL**	41	3	3	6	4	1	0	1	55	5.5	–1	3	33.3	11:22	....	....	....	....	....	....	....	....	....
	Tampa Bay	**NHL**	19	3	6	9	6	1	0	0	46	6.5	–8	1	100.0	16:05	....	....	....	....	....	....	....	....	....
2010-11	**Tampa Bay**	**NHL**	81	17	34	51	10	3	0	1	196	8.7	5	37	32.4	14:06	18	6	11	17	2	1	0	1	13:42
	NHL Totals		191	28	57	85	24	7	0	3	375	7.5		70	27.1	13:29	18	6	11	17	2	1	0	1	13:42

AHL All-Rookie Team (2008) • AHL First All-Star Team (2008)

Signed as a free agent by **Los Angeles**, April 27, 2007. Traded to **Tampa Bay** by **Los Angeles** with Florida's 3rd round choice (previously acquired, Tampa Bay selected Brock Beukeboom) in 2010 Entry Draft for Jeff Halpern, March 3, 2010.

PYATT, Taylor

(PIGH-at, TAY-luhr) **PHX**

Left wing. Shoots left. 6'3", 226 lbs. Born, Thunder Bay, Ont., August 19, 1981. NY Islanders' 2nd choice, 8th overall, in 1999 Entry Draft.

Season	Club	League	GP	G	A	Pts	PIM	PP	SH	GW	S	%	+/-	TF	F%	Min	GP	G	A	Pts	PIM	PP	SH	GW	Min
1996-97	Thunder Bay	TBAHA	60	52	61	113	72	....	....	....	....	....	....	....	....	....	....	....	....	....	....	....	....	....	....
1997-98	Sudbury Wolves	OHL	58	14	17	31	104	....	....	....	....	....	....	....	....	....	10	3	1	4	8	....	....	....	....
1998-99	Sudbury Wolves	OHL	68	37	38	75	95	....	....	....	....	....	....	....	....	....	4	0	4	4	6	....	....	....	....
99-2000	Sudbury Wolves	OHL	68	40	49	89	98	....	....	....	....	....	....	....	....	....	12	8	7	15	25	....	....	....	....
2000-01	**NY Islanders**	**NHL**	78	4	14	18	39	1	0	2	86	4.7	–17	1	0.0	12:14	....	....	....	....	....	....	....	....	....
2001-02	**Buffalo**	**NHL**	48	10	10	20	35	0	0	0	61	16.4	4	0	0.0	13:30	....	....	....	....	....	....	....	....	....
	Rochester	AHL	27	6	4	10	36	....	....	....	....	....	....	....	....	....	....	....	....	....	....	....	....	....	....
2002-03	**Buffalo**	**NHL**	78	14	14	28	38	2	0	0	110	12.7	–8	8	25.0	14:06	....	....	....	....	....	....	....	....	....
2003-04	**Buffalo**	**NHL**	63	8	12	20	25	1	2	4	98	8.2	–7	19	26.3	15:36	....	....	....	....	....	....	....	....	....
2004-05	Hammarby	Sweden-2	24	11	9	20	20	....	....	....	....	....	....	....	....	....	....	....	....	....	....	....	....	....	....
2005-06	**Buffalo**	**NHL**	41	6	6	12	33	0	0	1	62	9.7	–1	11	18.2	11:14	14	0	5	5	10	0	0	0	11:08
2006-07	**Vancouver**	**NHL**	76	23	14	37	42	9	0	4	150	15.3	5	4	0.0	13:58	12	2	4	6	6	0	0	1	18:02
2007-08	**Vancouver**	**NHL**	79	16	21	37	60	7	0	2	167	9.6	9	36	33.3	15:47	....	....	....	....	....	....	....	....	....
2008-09	**Vancouver**	**NHL**	69	10	9	19	43	0	0	1	99	10.1	0	33	48.5	14:43	4	0	0	0	2	0	0	0	14:13
2009-10	**Phoenix**	**NHL**	74	12	11	23	39	1	0	3	121	9.9	13	1	0.0	13:27	7	1	1	2	2	1	0	0	14:22
2010-11	**Phoenix**	**NHL**	76	18	13	31	27	2	0	6	126	14.3	11	20	30.0	15:30	4	1	0	1	0	0	0	0	14:56
	NHL Totals		682	121	124	245	381	23	2	23	1080	11.2		133	32.3	14:08	41	4	10	14	20	1	0	1	14:23

OHL First All-Star Team (2000)

Traded to **Buffalo** by **NY Islanders** with Tim Connolly for Michael Peca, June 24, 2001. Signed as a free agent by **Hammarby** (Sweden-2), November 16, 2004. • Rights traded to **Vancouver** by **Buffalo** for Vancouver's 4th round choice (later traded to Calgary - Calgary selected Keith Aulie) in 2007 Entry Draft, July 14, 2006. Signed as a free agent by **Phoenix**, September 2, 2009.

			Regular Season															Playoffs							
Season	Club	League	GP	G	A	Pts	PIM	PP	SH	GW	S	%	+/-	TF	F%	Min	GP	G	A	Pts	PIM	PP	SH	GW	Min

PYATT, Tom
(PIGH-at, TAWM)   **T.B.**

Center. Shoots left. 5'11", 187 lbs.   Born, Thunder Bay, Ont., February 14, 1987. NY Rangers' 6th choice, 107th overall, in 2005 Entry Draft.

Season	Club	League	GP	G	A	Pts	PIM	PP	SH	GW	S	%	+/-	TF	F%	Min	GP	G	A	Pts	PIM	PP	SH	GW	Min
2003-04	Saginaw Spirit	OHL	67	9	9	18	21	....	....	....	....	....	....	....	....	....	....	....	....	....	....	....	....	....	....
2004-05	Saginaw Spirit	OHL	57	18	30	48	14	....	....	....	....	....	....	....	....	....	....	....	....	....	....	....	....	....	....
2005-06	Saginaw Spirit	OHL	58	24	29	53	29	....	....	....	....	....	....	....	....	....	4	1	2	3	4	....	....	....	....
2006-07	Saginaw Spirit	OHL	58	43	38	81	18	....	....	....	....	....	....	....	....	....	6	3	5	8	0	....	....	....	....
	Hartford	AHL	1	0	0	0	0	....	....	....	....	....	....	....	....	....	....	....	....	....	....	....	....	....	....
2007-08	Hartford	AHL	41	4	7	11	6	....	....	....	....	....	....	....	....	....	3	0	0	0	0	....	....	....	....
	Charlotte	ECHL	16	6	9	15	8	....	....	....	....	....	....	....	....	....	3	0	0	0	0	....	....	....	....
2008-09	Hartford	AHL	73	15	22	37	22	....	....	....	....	....	....	....	....	....	4	0	0	0	2	....	....	....	....
2009-10	**Montreal**	**NHL**	40	2	3	5	10	0	0	0	48	4.2	–5	50	42.0	11:04	18	2	2	4	2	0	0	1	13:03
	Hamilton	AHL	41	13	22	35	8	....	....	....	....	....	....	....	....	....	....	....	....	....	....	....	....	....	....
2010-11	**Montreal**	**NHL**	61	2	5	7	9	0	0	0	65	3.1	–1	110	50.0	10:38	7	0	0	0	0	0	0	0	9:54
	NHL Totals		101	4	8	12	19	0	0	0	113	3.5		160	47.5	10:49	25	2	2	4	2	0	0	1	12:10

Traded to **Montreal** by **NY Rangers** with Scott Gomez and Michael Busto for Chris Higgins, Ryan McDonagh and Pavel Valentenko, June 30, 2009. Signed as a free agent by **Tampa Bay**, July 6, 2011.

PYORALA, Mika
(P'YOHR-ah-lah, MEE-kah)

Center. Shoots left. 6', 190 lbs.   Born, Oulu, Finland, July 13, 1981.

Season	Club	League	GP	G	A	Pts	PIM	PP	SH	GW	S	%	+/-	TF	F%	Min	GP	G	A	Pts	PIM	PP	SH	GW	Min
2001-02	Karpat Oulu	Finland	51	4	2	6	35	....	....	....	....	....	....	....	....	....	4	0	1	1	2	....	....	....	....
2002-03	Karpat Oulu	Finland	56	17	11	28	22	....	....	....	....	....	....	....	....	....	15	2	3	5	6	....	....	....	....
2003-04	Karpat Oulu	Finland	53	12	19	31	8	....	....	....	....	....	....	....	....	....	13	0	1	1	0	....	....	....	....
2004-05	Karpat Oulu	Finland	56	9	13	22	18	....	....	....	....	....	....	....	....	....	11	3	1	4	4	....	....	....	....
2005-06	Karpat Oulu	Finland	41	13	8	21	10	....	....	....	....	....	....	....	....	....	11	5	6	11	0	....	....	....	....
2006-07	Karpat Oulu	Finland	56	28	17	45	30	....	....	....	....	....	....	....	....	....	10	4	2	6	2	....	....	....	....
2007-08	Timra IK	Sweden	46	17	16	33	18	....	....	....	....	....	....	....	....	....	11	6	4	10	0	....	....	....	....
2008-09	Timra IK	Sweden	55	21	22	43	10	....	....	....	....	....	....	....	....	....	7	2	1	3	6	....	....	....	....
2009-10	**Philadelphia**	**NHL**	36	2	2	4	10	0	0	0	41	4.9	–3	207	45.9	13:36	....	....	....	....	....	....	....	....	....
	Adirondack	AHL	35	8	10	18	10	....	....	....	....	....	....	....	....	....	....	....	....	....	....	....	....	....	....
2010-11	Frolunda	Sweden	47	14	9	23	8	....	....	....	....	....	....	....	....	....	....	....	....	....	....	....	....	....	....
	NHL Totals		36	2	2	4	10	0	0	0	41	4.9		207	45.9	13:36									

Signed as a free agent by **Philadelphia**, July 23, 2009. Signed as a free agent by **Frolunda** (Sweden), July 29, 2010.

QUICK, Kevin
(KWIHK, KEH-vihn)

Defense. Shoots left. 6', 181 lbs.   Born, Buffalo, NY, March 29, 1988. Tampa Bay's 2nd choice, 78th overall, in 2006 Entry Draft.

Season	Club	League	GP	G	A	Pts	PIM	PP	SH	GW	S	%	+/-	TF	F%	Min	GP	G	A	Pts	PIM	PP	SH	GW	Min
2004-05	Salisbury School	High-CT	27	3	9	12	3	....	....	....	....	....	....	....	....	....	....	....	....	....	....	....	....	....	....
2005-06	Salisbury School	High-CT	28	3	20	23	6	....	....	....	....	....	....	....	....	....	....	....	....	....	....	....	....	....	....
2006-07	Salisbury School	High-CT	25	1	10	11	10	....	....	....	....	....	....	....	....	....	....	....	....	....	....	....	....	....	....
2007-08	U. of Michigan	CCHA	21	2	2	4	12	....	....	....	....	....	....	....	....	....	....	....	....	....	....	....	....	....	....
	Norfolk Admirals	AHL	18	0	4	4	6	....	....	....	....	....	....	....	....	....	....	....	....	....	....	....	....	....	....
2008-09	**Tampa Bay**	**NHL**	6	0	1	1	0	0	0	0	7	0.0	0	0	0.0	13:23	....	....	....	....	....	....	....	....	....
	Norfolk Admirals	AHL	49	1	8	9	8	....	....	....	....	....	....	....	....	....	....	....	....	....	....	....	....	....	....
	Elmira Jackals	ECHL	....	....	....	....	....	....	....	....	....	....	....	....	....	....	9	0	1	1	0	....	....	....	....
2009-10	Norfolk Admirals	AHL	47	0	4	4	10	....	....	....	....	....	....	....	....	....	....	....	....	....	....	....	....	....	....
2010-11	Norfolk Admirals	AHL	45	0	15	15	0	....	....	....	....	....	....	....	....	....	2	0	0	0	2	....	....	....	....
	NHL Totals		6	0	1	1	0	0	0	0	7	0.0		0	0.0	13:23	....								

QUINCEY, Kyle
(KWIHN-see, KIGHL)   **COL**

Defense. Shoots left. 6'2", 207 lbs.   Born, Kitchener, Ont., August 12, 1985. Detroit's 2nd choice, 132nd overall, in 2003 Entry Draft.

Season	Club	League	GP	G	A	Pts	PIM	PP	SH	GW	S	%	+/-	TF	F%	Min	GP	G	A	Pts	PIM	PP	SH	GW	Min
2001-02	Mississauga	OPJHL	27	5	14	19	31	....	....	....	....	....	....	....	....	....	....	....	....	....	....	....	....	....	....
2002-03	London Knights	OHL	66	6	12	18	77	....	....	....	....	....	....	....	....	....	14	3	4	7	11	....	....	....	....
2003-04	London Knights	OHL	3	0	2	2	4	....	....	....	....	....	....	....	....	....	....	....	....	....	....	....	....	....	....
	Mississauga	OHL	61	14	23	37	135	....	....	....	....	....	....	....	....	....	24	3	13	16	32	....	....	....	....
2004-05	Mississauga	OHL	59	15	31	46	111	....	....	....	....	....	....	....	....	....	5	0	3	3	4	....	....	....	....
2005-06	**Detroit**	**NHL**	1	0	0	0	0	0	0	0	1	0.0	0	0	0.0	11:37	....	....	....	....	....	....	....	....	....
	Grand Rapids	AHL	70	7	26	33	107	....	....	....	....	....	....	....	....	....	16	0	1	1	27	....	....	....	....
2006-07	**Detroit**	**NHL**	6	1	0	1	0	0	0	0	7	14.3	0	0	0.0	11:26	13	0	0	0	2	0	0	0	8:11
	Grand Rapids	AHL	65	4	18	22	126	....	....	....	....	....	....	....	....	....	2	0	0	0	0	....	....	....	....
2007-08	**Detroit**	**NHL**	6	0	0	0	4	0	0	0	5	0.0	–3	0	0.0	13:58	....	....	....	....	....	....	....	....	....
	Grand Rapids	AHL	66	5	15	20	149	....	....	....	....	....	....	....	....	....	....	....	....	....	....	....	....	....	....
2008-09	**Los Angeles**	**NHL**	72	4	34	38	63	2	0	2	150	2.7	–5	0	0.0	20:59	....	....	....	....	....	....	....	....	....
2009-10	**Colorado**	**NHL**	79	6	23	29	76	1	0	0	139	4.3	9	1	0.0	23:37	6	0	0	0	8	0	0	0	22:06
2010-11	**Colorado**	**NHL**	21	0	1	1	18	0	0	0	39	0.0	–5	0	0.0	19:35	....	....	....	....	....	....	....	....	....
	NHL Totals		185	11	58	69	161	3	0	2	341	3.2		1	0.0	21:21	19	0	0	0	10	0	0	0	12:35

OHL Second All-Star Team (2005)

Claimed on waivers by **Los Angeles** from **Detroit**, October 13, 2008. Traded to **Colorado** by **Los Angeles** with Tom Preissing and Los Angeles' 5th round choice (Luke Walker) in 2010 Entry Draft for Ryan Smyth, July 3, 2009. • Missed majority of 2010-11 due to shoulder injury at Atlanta, December 10, 2010.

RADULOV, Alexander
(ra-DEW-lahf, al-EHX-AN-duhr)   **NSH**

Right wing. Shoots left. 6'1", 188 lbs.   Born, Nizhny Tagil, USSR, July 5, 1986. Nashville's 1st choice, 15th overall, in 2004 Entry Draft.

Season	Club	League	GP	G	A	Pts	PIM	PP	SH	GW	S	%	+/-	TF	F%	Min	GP	G	A	Pts	PIM	PP	SH	GW	Min
2002-03	Dyn'o Moscow 2	Russia-3	STATISTICS NOT AVAILABLE																						
2003-04	Dyn'o Moscow 2	Russia-3	STATISTICS NOT AVAILABLE																						
	THK Tver	Russia-2	42	15	16	31	102	....	....	....	....	....	....	....	....	....	....	....	....	....	....	....	....	....	....
	Dynamo Moscow	Russia	1	0	0	0	2	....	....	....	....	....	....	....	....	....	....	....	....	....	....	....	....	....	....
2004-05	Quebec Remparts	QMJHL	65	32	43	75	64	....	....	....	....	....	....	....	....	....	13	6	5	11	15	....	....	....	....
2005-06	Quebec Remparts	QMJHL	62	61	*91	*152	101	....	....	....	....	....	....	....	....	....	23	21	*34	*55	30	....	....	....	....
2006-07	**Nashville**	**NHL**	64	18	19	37	26	5	0	4	96	18.8	19	0	0.0	11:38	4	3	1	4	19	0	0	0	13:10
	Milwaukee	AHL	11	6	12	18	26	....	....	....	....	....	....	....	....	....	....	....	....	....	....	....	....	....	....
2007-08	**Nashville**	**NHL**	81	26	32	58	44	4	0	2	183	14.2	7	1	0.0	16:24	6	2	2	4	6	1	0	0	15:59
2008-09	Ufa	Rus-KHL	52	22	26	48	92	....	....	....	....	....	....	....	....	....	4	0	2	2	4	....	....	....	....
2009-10	Ufa	Rus-KHL	54	24	39	63	62	....	....	....	....	....	....	....	....	....	16	8	*11	*19	10	....	....	....	....
	Russia	Olympics	4	1	1	2	4	....	....	....	....	....	....	....	....	....	....	....	....	....	....	....	....	....	....
2010-11	Ufa	Rus-KHL	54	20	*60	*80	83	....	....	....	....	....	....	....	....	....	21	3	*15	18	42	....	....	....	....
	NHL Totals		145	44	51	95	70	9	0	6	279	15.8		1	0.0	14:18	10	5	3	8	25	1	0	0	14:51

QMJHL All-Rookie Team (2005) • QMJHL First All-Star Team (2006) • QMJHL Player of the Year (2006) • Canadian Major Junior First All-Star Team (2006) • Canadian Major Junior Player of the Year (2006) • Memorial Cup All-Star Team (2006) • Stafford Smythe Memorial Trophy (Memorial Cup - MVP) (2006)

Signed as a free agent by **Ufa** (Russia-KHL), July 11, 2008.

RAFALSKI, Brian
(ra-FAWL-skee, BRIGH-uhn)

Defense. Shoots right. 5'10", 194 lbs.   Born, Dearborn, MI, September 28, 1973.

Season	Club	League	GP	G	A	Pts	PIM	PP	SH	GW	S	%	+/-	TF	F%	Min	GP	G	A	Pts	PIM	PP	SH	GW	Min
1990-91	Madison Capitols	USHL	47	12	11	23	28	....	....	....	....	....	....	....	....	....	....	....	....	....	....	....	....	....	....
1991-92	U. of Wisconsin	WCHA	34	3	14	17	34	....	....	....	....	....	....	....	....	....	....	....	....	....	....	....	....	....	....
1992-93	U. of Wisconsin	WCHA	32	0	13	13	10	....	....	....	....	....	....	....	....	....	....	....	....	....	....	....	....	....	....
1993-94	U. of Wisconsin	WCHA	37	6	17	23	26	....	....	....	....	....	....	....	....	....	....	....	....	....	....	....	....	....	....
1994-95	U. of Wisconsin	WCHA	43	11	34	45	48	....	....	....	....	....	....	....	....	....	....	....	....	....	....	....	....	....	....
1995-96	Brynas IF Gavle	Sweden	40	4	14	18	26	....	....	....	....	....	....	....	....	....	9	0	1	1	2	....	....	....	....
1996-97	HPK Hameenlinna	Finland	49	11	24	35	26	....	....	....	....	....	....	....	....	....	10	6	5	11	4	....	....	....	....
1997-98	HIFK Helsinki	Finland	40	13	10	23	20	....	....	....	....	....	....	....	....	....	9	5	6	11	0	....	....	....	....
1998-99	HIFK Helsinki	Finland	53	19	34	53	18	....	....	....	....	....	....	....	....	....	11	5	*9	*14	4	....	....	....	....
	HIFK Helsinki	EuroHL	6	4	6	10	10	....	....	....	....	....	....	....	....	....	4	1	0	1	2	....	....	....	....
99-2000♦	**New Jersey**	**NHL**	75	5	27	32	28	1	0	1	128	3.9	21	1	0.0	18:51	23	2	6	8	8	0	0	1	21:25
2000-01	**New Jersey**	**NHL**	78	9	43	52	26	6	0	1	142	6.3	36	2100.0	21:41	25	7	11	18	7	1	0	*3	22:08
2001-02	**New Jersey**	**NHL**	76	7	40	47	18	2	0	4	125	5.6	15	0	0.0	22:08	6	3	2	5	4	3	0	0	21:45
	United States	Olympics	6	1	2	3	2	....	....	....	....	....	....	....	....	....	....	....	....	....	....	....	....	....	....

			Regular Season														Playoffs								
Season	Club	League	GP	G	A	Pts	PIM	PP	SH	GW	S	%	+/-	TF	F%	Min	GP	G	A	Pts	PIM	PP	SH	GW	Min
2002-03 ♦	New Jersey	NHL	79	3	37	40	14	2	0	0	178	1.7	18	1	0.0	23:09	23	2	9	11	8	2	0	0	25:46
2003-04	New Jersey	NHL	69	6	30	36	24	2	0	1	130	4.6	6	0	0.0	22:48	5	0	1	1	0	0	0	0	22:22
2004-05			DID NOT PLAY																						
2005-06	New Jersey	NHL	82	6	43	49	36	3	0	2	126	4.8	0	1	0.0	25:32	9	1	8	9	2	1	0	0	27:26
	United States	Olympics	5	0	2	2	0	....	....	....	....	....	....	....	....	....	....	....	....	....	....	....	....	....	....
2006-07	New Jersey	NHL	82	8	47	55	34	3	1	4	148	5.4	4	0	0.0	25:29	11	2	6	8	8	2	0	0	22:54
2007-08 ♦	Detroit	NHL	73	13	42	55	34	10	0	1	175	7.4	27	0	0.0	24:04	22	4	10	14	12	2	0	0	24:53
2008-09	Detroit	NHL	78	10	49	59	20	5	0	1	141	7.1	17	0	0.0	23:10	18	3	9	12	11	3	0	1	22:27
2009-10	Detroit	NHL	78	8	34	42	26	5	0	1	134	6.0	23	0	0.0	24:14	12	3	8	11	2	1	0	0	23:58
	United States	Olympics	6	4	4	8	2	....	....	....	....	....	....	....	....	....	....	....	....	....	....	....	....	....	....
2010-11	Detroit	NHL	63	4	44	48	22	0	0	0	106	3.8	11	0	0.0	20:25	11	2	1	3	4	2	0	1	21:03
	NHL Totals		833	79	436	515	282	39	1	16	1533	5.2		5	40.0	22:57	165	29	71	100	66	17	0	6	23:20

WCHA First All-Star Team (1995) • NCAA West First All-American Team (1995) • NHL All-Rookie Team (2000) • Olympic All-Star Team (2010) • Olympics Best Defenseman (2010)

Played in NHL All-Star Game (2004, 2007)

Signed as a free agent by **New Jersey**, June 18, 1999. Signed as a free agent by **Detroit**, July 1, 2007. • Officially announced his retirement, May 25, 2011.

RAKHSHANI, Rhett (rahk-SHAH-nee, REHT) NYI

Right wing. Shoots right. 5'10", 190 lbs. Born, Orange, CA, March 6, 1988. NY Islanders' 4th choice, 100th overall, in 2006 Entry Draft.

Season	Club	League	GP	G	A	Pts	PIM	PP	SH	GW	S	%	+/-	TF	F%	Min	GP	G	A	Pts	PIM	PP	SH	GW	Min
2003-04	California Wave	Minor-CA	56	54	67	121	....	....	....	....	....	....	....	....	....	....	....	....	....	....	....	....	....	....	....
2004-05	USNTDP	U-17	14	6	5	11	32	....	....	....	....	....	....	....	....	....	....	....	....	....	....	....	....	....	....
	USNTDP	NAHL	40	12	15	27	21	....	....	....	....	....	....	....	....	....	9	1	4	5	2	....	....	....	....
2005-06	USNTDP	U-18	43	11	12	23	30	....	....	....	....	....	....	....	....	....	....	....	....	....	....	....	....	....	....
	USNTDP	NAHL	16	13	13	26	35	....	....	....	....	....	....	....	....	....	....	....	....	....	....	....	....	....	....
2006-07	U. of Denver	WCHA	40	10	26	36	38	....	....	....	....	....	....	....	....	....	....	....	....	....	....	....	....	....	....
2007-08	U. of Denver	WCHA	37	14	14	28	52	....	....	....	....	....	....	....	....	....	....	....	....	....	....	....	....	....	....
2008-09	U. of Denver	WCHA	38	15	22	37	50	....	....	....	....	....	....	....	....	....	....	....	....	....	....	....	....	....	....
2009-10	U. of Denver	WCHA	41	21	29	50	40	....	....	....	....	....	....	....	....	....	....	....	....	....	....	....	....	....	....
	Bridgeport	AHL	5	0	2	2	2	....	....	....	....	....	....	....	....	....	5	0	0	0	2	....	....	....	....
2010-11	NY Islanders	NHL	2	0	0	0	0	0	0	0	2	0.0	–1	0	0.0	11:42	....	....	....	....	....	....	....	....	....
	Bridgeport	AHL	66	24	38	62	32	....	....	....	....	....	....	....	....	....	....	....	....	....	....	....	....	....	....
	NHL Totals		2	0	0	0	0	0	0	0	2	0.0		0	0.0	11:43	....	....	....	....	....	....	....	....	....

WCHA First All-Star Team (2010) • NCAA West First All-American Team (2010) • AHL All-Rookie Team (2011)

RANGER, Paul (RAIN-juhr, PAWL) T.B.

Defense. Shoots left. 6'3", 210 lbs. Born, Whitby, Ont., September 12, 1984. Tampa Bay's 7th choice, 183rd overall, in 2002 Entry Draft.

Season	Club	League	GP	G	A	Pts	PIM	PP	SH	GW	S	%	+/-	TF	F%	Min	GP	G	A	Pts	PIM	PP	SH	GW	Min
2000-01	Oshawa Generals	OHL	32	0	1	1	2	....	....	....	....	....	....	....	....	....	....	....	....	....	....	....	....	....	....
2001-02	Oshawa Generals	OHL	62	0	9	9	49	....	....	....	....	....	....	....	....	....	5	0	0	0	4	....	....	....	....
2002-03	Oshawa Generals	OHL	68	10	28	38	70	....	....	....	....	....	....	....	....	....	13	0	3	3	10	....	....	....	....
2003-04	Oshawa Generals	OHL	62	12	31	43	72	....	....	....	....	....	....	....	....	....	7	0	1	1	10	....	....	....	....
2004-05	Springfield	AHL	69	3	8	11	46	....	....	....	....	....	....	....	....	....	....	....	....	....	....	....	....	....	....
2005-06	Tampa Bay	NHL	76	1	17	18	58	0	0	1	73	1.4	5	0	0.0	17:07	5	2	4	6	0	1	0	0	21:43
	Springfield	AHL	1	1	2	3	0	....	....	....	....	....	....	....	....	....	....	....	....	....	....	....	....	....	....
2006-07	Tampa Bay	NHL	72	4	24	28	42	0	0	2	90	4.4	5	0	0.0	20:19	6	0	1	1	4	0	0	0	21:22
2007-08	Tampa Bay	NHL	72	10	21	31	56	0	1	0	105	9.5	–13	0	0.0	25:13	....	....	....	....	....	....	....	....	....
2008-09	Tampa Bay	NHL	42	2	11	13	56	0	0	0	69	2.9	–5	0	0.0	24:30	....	....	....	....	....	....	....	....	....
2009-10	Tampa Bay	NHL	8	1	1	2	6	0	0	0	11	9.1	–2	0	0.0	20:19	....	....	....	....	....	....	....	....	....
2010-11			DID NOT PLAY																						
	NHL Totals		270	18	74	92	218	0	1	3	348	5.2		0	0.0	21:23	11	2	5	7	4	1	0	0	21:31

• Missed majority of 2009-10 and all of 2010-11 for personal reasons.

RAYMOND, Mason (RAY-muhnd, MAY-sohn) VAN

Left wing. Shoots left. 6', 185 lbs. Born, Cochrane, Alta., September 17, 1985. Vancouver's 2nd choice, 51st overall, in 2005 Entry Draft.

Season	Club	League	GP	G	A	Pts	PIM	PP	SH	GW	S	%	+/-	TF	F%	Min	GP	G	A	Pts	PIM	PP	SH	GW	Min
2003-04	Camrose Kodiaks	AJHL	....	27	35	62	....	....	....	....	....	....	....	....	....	....	....	....	....	....	....	....	....	....	....
2004-05	Camrose Kodiaks	AJHL	55	*41	41	82	80	....	....	....	....	....	....	....	....	....	15	8	*12	20	....	....	....	....	....
2005-06	U. Minn-Duluth	WCHA	40	11	17	28	30	....	....	....	....	....	....	....	....	....	....	....	....	....	....	....	....	....	....
2006-07	U. Minn-Duluth	WCHA	39	14	32	46	45	....	....	....	....	....	....	....	....	....	....	....	....	....	....	....	....	....	....
	Manitoba Moose	AHL	11	2	2	4	6	....	....	....	....	....	....	....	....	....	13	0	1	1	0	....	....	....	....
2007-08	Vancouver	NHL	49	9	12	21	2	1	0	0	80	11.3	1	63	38.1	12:31	....	....	....	....	....	....	....	....	....
	Manitoba Moose	AHL	20	7	10	17	6	....	....	....	....	....	....	....	....	....	....	....	....	....	....	....	....	....	....
2008-09	Vancouver	NHL	72	11	12	23	24	4	0	0	145	7.6	2	50	34.0	13:43	10	2	1	3	2	0	0	0	15:12
2009-10	Vancouver	NHL	82	25	28	53	48	8	0	4	217	11.5	0	23	34.8	17:20	12	3	1	4	6	0	0	1	17:36
2010-11	Vancouver	NHL	70	15	24	39	10	2	1	5	197	7.6	8	65	40.0	15:48	24	2	6	8	6	0	0	0	17:29
	NHL Totals		273	60	76	136	84	15	1	9	639	9.4		201	37.3	15:07	46	7	8	15	14	0	0	1	17:01

AJHL MVP (2005) • WCHA All-Rookie Team (2006) • WCHA First All-Star Team (2007)

REASONER, Marty (REE-suh-nuhr, MAHR-tee) NYI

Center. Shoots left. 6'1", 205 lbs. Born, Honeoye Falls, NY, February 26, 1977. St. Louis' 1st choice, 14th overall, in 1996 Entry Draft.

Season	Club	League	GP	G	A	Pts	PIM	PP	SH	GW	S	%	+/-	TF	F%	Min	GP	G	A	Pts	PIM	PP	SH	GW	Min
1993-94	Deerfield	High-MA	22	27	25	52	....	....	....	....	....	....	....	....	....	....	....	....	....	....	....	....	....	....	....
1994-95	Deerfield	High-MA	26	25	32	57	14	....	....	....	....	....	....	....	....	....	....	....	....	....	....	....	....	....	....
1995-96	Boston College	H-East	34	16	29	45	32	....	....	....	....	....	....	....	....	....	....	....	....	....	....	....	....	....	....
1996-97	Boston College	H-East	35	20	24	44	31	....	....	....	....	....	....	....	....	....	....	....	....	....	....	....	....	....	....
1997-98	Boston College	H-East	42	*33	40	*73	56	....	....	....	....	....	....	....	....	....	....	....	....	....	....	....	....	....	....
1998-99	St. Louis	NHL	22	3	7	10	8	1	0	0	33	9.1	2	224	53.6	13:55	....	....	....	....	....	....	....	....	....
	Worcester IceCats	AHL	44	17	22	39	24	....	....	....	....	....	....	....	....	....	4	2	1	3	6	....	....	....	....
99-2000	St. Louis	NHL	32	10	14	24	20	3	0	0	51	19.6	9	379	49.6	15:20	7	2	1	3	4	1	0	0	13:12
	Worcester IceCats	AHL	44	23	28	51	39	....	....	....	....	....	....	....	....	....	....	....	....	....	....	....	....	....	....
2000-01	St. Louis	NHL	41	4	9	13	14	0	0	0	65	6.2	–5	454	53.1	14:00	10	3	1	4	0	0	0	1	12:21
	Worcester IceCats	AHL	34	17	18	35	25	....	....	....	....	....	....	....	....	....	....	....	....	....	....	....	....	....	....
2001-02	Edmonton	NHL	52	6	5	11	41	3	0	2	66	9.1	0	470	55.5	11:44	....	....	....	....	....	....	....	....	....
2002-03	Edmonton	NHL	70	11	20	31	28	2	2	0	102	10.8	19	968	53.5	14:50	6	1	0	1	2	1	0	0	14:22
	Hamilton	AHL	2	0	2	2	2	....	....	....	....	....	....	....	....	....	....	....	....	....	....	....	....	....	....
2003-04	Edmonton	NHL	17	2	6	8	10	0	1	0	28	7.1	5	321	52.7	16:30	....	....	....	....	....	....	....	....	....
2004-05	Salzburg	Austria	11	5	4	9	12	....	....	....	....	....	....	....	....	....	....	....	....	....	....	....	....	....	....
2005-06	Edmonton	NHL	58	9	17	26	20	5	0	1	63	14.3	–12	524	52.5	12:45	....	....	....	....	....	....	....	....	....
	Boston	NHL	19	2	6	8	8	1	0	0	39	5.1	–2	227	46.7	15:09	....	....	....	....	....	....	....	....	....
2006-07	Edmonton	NHL	72	6	14	20	60	0	0	1	84	7.1	–15	765	54.6	13:52	....	....	....	....	....	....	....	....	....
2007-08	Edmonton	NHL	82	11	14	25	50	0	0	0	113	9.7	–17	906	52.8	14:58	....	....	....	....	....	....	....	....	....
2008-09	Atlanta	NHL	79	14	16	30	36	0	1	2	131	10.7	11	1141	52.9	15:19	....	....	....	....	....	....	....	....	....
2009-10	Atlanta	NHL	80	4	13	17	24	0	0	0	86	4.7	–3	1006	50.9	12:30	....	....	....	....	....	....	....	....	....
2010-11	Florida	NHL	82	14	18	32	22	0	0	4	124	11.3	2	1284	54.5	17:10	....	....	....	....	....	....	....	....	....
	NHL Totals		706	96	159	255	341	15	4	10	985	9.7		8669	52.9	14:24	23	6	2	8	6	2	0	1	13:08

Hockey East Rookie of the Year (1996) • Hockey East First All-Star Team (1997, 1998) • NCAA East First All-American Team (1998) • NCAA Championship All-Tournament Team (1998)

Traded to **Edmonton** by **St. Louis** with Jochen Hecht and Jan Horacek for Doug Weight and Michel Riesen, July 1, 2001. • Missed majority of 2003-04 due to ankle (November 8, 2003 vs. Toronto) and knee (January 13, 2004 vs. Florida) injuries. Signed as a free agent by **Salzburg** (Austria), January 30, 2005. Traded to **Boston** by **Edmonton** with Yan Stastny and Edmonton's 2nd round choice (Milan Lucic) in 2006 Entry Draft for Sergei Samsonov, March 9, 2006. Signed as a free agent by **Edmonton**, July 4, 2006. Signed as a free agent by **Atlanta**, July 17, 2008. Traded to **Chicago** by **Atlanta** with Joey Crabb, Jeremy Morin and New Jersey's 1st (prevously acquired, Chicago selected Kevin Hayes) and 2nd (previously acquired, Chicago selected Justin Holl) round choices in 2010 Entry Draft for Brent Sopel, Dustin Byfuglien, Ben Eager and Akim Aliu, June 24, 2010. Traded to **Florida** by **Chicago** for Jeff Taffe, July 22, 2010. Signed as a free agent by **NY Islanders**, July 1, 2011.

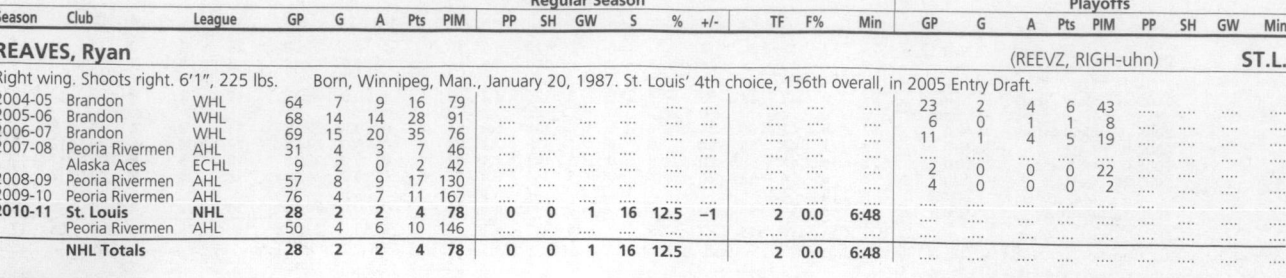

			Regular Season														Playoffs								
Season	Club	League	GP	G	A	Pts	PIM	PP	SH	GW	S	%	+/-	TF	F%	Min	GP	G	A	Pts	PIM	PP	SH	GW	Min

REAVES, Ryan

(REEVZ, RIGH-uhn) **ST.L.**

Right wing. Shoots right. 6'1", 225 lbs. Born, Winnipeg, Man., January 20, 1987. St. Louis' 4th choice, 156th overall, in 2005 Entry Draft.

Season	Club	League	GP	G	A	Pts	PIM	PP	SH	GW	S	%	+/-	TF	F%	Min	GP	G	A	Pts	PIM	PP	SH	GW	Min
2004-05	Brandon	WHL	64	7	9	16	79										23	2	4	6	43				
2005-06	Brandon	WHL	68	14	14	28	91										6	0	1	1	8				
2006-07	Brandon	WHL	69	15	20	35	76										11	1	4	5	19				
2007-08	Peoria Rivermen	AHL	31	4	3	7	46																		
	Alaska Aces	ECHL	9	2	0	2	42										2	0	0	0	22				
2008-09	Peoria Rivermen	AHL	57	8	9	17	130										4	0	0	0	2				
2009-10	Peoria Rivermen	AHL	76	4	7	11	167																		
2010-11	**St. Louis**	**NHL**	**28**	**2**	**2**	**4**	**78**	**0**	**0**	**1**	**16**	**12.5**	**–1**	**2**	**0.0**	**6:48**									
	Peoria Rivermen	AHL	50	4	6	10	146																		
	NHL Totals		**28**	**2**	**2**	**4**	**78**	**0**	**0**	**1**	**16**	**12.5**		**2**	**0.0**	**6:48**									

RECCHI, Mark

(REH-kee, MAHRK)

Right wing. Shoots left. 5'10", 195 lbs. Born, Kamloops, B.C., February 1, 1968. Pittsburgh's 4th choice, 67th overall, in 1988 Entry Draft.

Season	Club	League	GP	G	A	Pts	PIM	PP	SH	GW	S	%	+/-	TF	F%	Min	GP	G	A	Pts	PIM	PP	SH	GW	Min
1984-85	Langley Eagles	BCJHL	51	26	39	65	39																		
	New Westminster	WHL	4	1	0	1	0																		
1985-86	New Westminster	WHL	72	21	40	61	55																		
1986-87	Kamloops Blazers	WHL	40	26	50	76	63										13	3	16	19	17				
1987-88	Kamloops Blazers	WHL	62	61	*93	154	75										17	10	*21	*31	18				
1988-89	**Pittsburgh**	**NHL**	**15**	**1**	**1**	**2**	**0**	**0**	**0**	**0**	**11**	**9.1**	**–2**												
	Muskegon	IHL	63	50	49	99	86										14	7	*14	*21	28				
1989-90	**Pittsburgh**	**NHL**	**74**	**30**	**37**	**67**	**44**	**6**	**2**	**4**	**143**	**21.0**	**6**												
	Muskegon	IHL	4	7	4	11	2																		
1990-91 ♦	**Pittsburgh**	**NHL**	**78**	**40**	**73**	**113**	**48**	**12**	**0**	**9**	**184**	**21.7**	**0**				**24**	**10**	**24**	**34**	**33**	**5**	**0**	**2**	
1991-92	**Pittsburgh**	**NHL**	**58**	**33**	**37**	**70**	**78**	**16**	**1**	**4**	**156**	**21.2**	**–16**												
	Philadelphia	**NHL**	**22**	**10**	**17**	**27**	**18**	**4**	**0**	**1**	**54**	**18.5**	**–5**												
1992-93	**Philadelphia**	**NHL**	**84**	**53**	**70**	**123**	**95**	**15**	**4**	**6**	**274**	**19.3**	**1**												
1993-94	**Philadelphia**	**NHL**	**84**	**40**	**67**	**107**	**46**	**11**	**0**	**5**	**217**	**18.4**	**–2**												
1994-95	**Philadelphia**	**NHL**	**10**	**2**	**3**	**5**	**12**	**1**	**0**	**2**	**17**	**11.8**	**–6**												
	Montreal	**NHL**	**39**	**14**	**29**	**43**	**16**	**8**	**0**	**1**	**104**	**13.5**	**–3**												
1995-96	**Montreal**	**NHL**	**82**	**28**	**50**	**78**	**69**	**11**	**2**	**6**	**191**	**14.7**	**20**				**6**	**3**	**3**	**6**	**0**	**3**	**0**	**0**	
1996-97	**Montreal**	**NHL**	**82**	**34**	**46**	**80**	**58**	**7**	**2**	**3**	**202**	**16.8**	**–1**				**5**	**4**	**2**	**6**	**2**	**0**	**0**	**0**	
1997-98	**Montreal**	**NHL**	**82**	**32**	**42**	**74**	**51**	**9**	**1**	**6**	**216**	**14.8**	**11**				**10**	**4**	**8**	**12**	**6**	**0**	**0**	**2**	
	Canada	Olympics	5	0	2	2	0																		
1998-99	**Montreal**	**NHL**	**61**	**12**	**35**	**47**	**28**	**3**	**0**	**2**	**152**	**7.9**	**–4**	**239**	**44.8**	**20:37**									
	Philadelphia	**NHL**	**10**	**4**	**2**	**6**	**6**	**0**	**0**	**0**	**19**	**21.1**	**–3**	**4**	**25.0**	**19:30**	**6**	**0**	**1**	**1**	**2**	**0**	**0**	**0**	**19:35**
99-2000	**Philadelphia**	**NHL**	**82**	**28**	***63**	**91**	**50**	**7**	**1**	**5**	**223**	**12.6**	**20**	**353**	**49.6**	**21:43**	**18**	**6**	**12**	**18**	**6**	**2**	**0**	**1**	**23:10**
2000-01	**Philadelphia**	**NHL**	**69**	**27**	**50**	**77**	**33**	**7**	**1**	**8**	**191**	**14.1**	**15**	**138**	**42.8**	**21:40**	**6**	**2**	**2**	**4**	**2**	**1**	**0**	**1**	**23:01**
2001-02	**Philadelphia**	**NHL**	**80**	**22**	**42**	**64**	**46**	**7**	**2**	**4**	**205**	**10.7**	**5**	**82**	**53.7**	**20:40**	**4**	**0**	**0**	**0**	**2**	**0**	**0**	**0**	**21:10**
2002-03	**Philadelphia**	**NHL**	**79**	**20**	**32**	**52**	**35**	**8**	**1**	**3**	**171**	**11.7**	**0**	**168**	**52.4**	**18:50**	**13**	**7**	**3**	**10**	**2**	**1**	**0**	**1**	**18:00**
2003-04	**Philadelphia**	**NHL**	**82**	**26**	**49**	**75**	**47**	**14**	**1**	**5**	**167**	**15.6**	**18**	**298**	**52.4**	**17:12**	**18**	**4**	**2**	**6**	**4**	**2**	**0**	**0**	**16:46**
2004-05			DID NOT PLAY																						
2005-06	**Pittsburgh**	**NHL**	**63**	**24**	**33**	**57**	**56**	**11**	**0**	**2**	**164**	**14.6**	**–28**	**387**	**48.3**	**21:17**									
	♦ **Carolina**	**NHL**	**20**	**4**	**3**	**7**	**12**	**2**	**0**	**1**	**35**	**11.4**	**–8**	**6**	**33.3**	**17:37**	**25**	**7**	**9**	**16**	**18**	**2**	**0**	**2**	**16:34**
2006-07	**Pittsburgh**	**NHL**	**82**	**24**	**44**	**68**	**62**	**14**	**0**	**3**	**190**	**12.6**	**1**	**26**	**46.2**	**19:42**	**5**	**0**	**4**	**4**	**0**	**0**	**0**	**0**	**19:09**
2007-08	**Pittsburgh**	**NHL**	**19**	**2**	**6**	**8**	**12**	**2**	**0**	**0**	**36**	**5.6**	**–2**	**9**	**44.4**	**16:25**									
	Atlanta	**NHL**	**53**	**12**	**28**	**40**	**20**	**5**	**0**	**0**	**85**	**14.1**	**–16**	**49**	**46.9**	**18:23**									
2008-09	**Tampa Bay**	**NHL**	**62**	**13**	**32**	**45**	**20**	**2**	**0**	**1**	**97**	**13.4**	**–15**	**54**	**40.7**	**16:53**									
	Boston	**NHL**	**18**	**10**	**6**	**16**	**2**	**4**	**0**	**2**	**32**	**31.3**	**–3**	**2**	**100.0**	**16:22**	**11**	**3**	**3**	**6**	**2**	**1**	**0**	**1**	**16:57**
2009-10	**Boston**	**NHL**	**81**	**18**	**25**	**43**	**34**	**8**	**0**	**2**	**152**	**11.8**	**4**	**146**	**37.0**	**17:03**	**13**	**6**	**4**	**10**	**6**	**3**	**0**	**0**	**19:29**
2010-11 ♦	**Boston**	**NHL**	**81**	**14**	**34**	**48**	**35**	**6**	**0**	**6**	**132**	**10.6**	**13**	**97**	**53.6**	**16:06**	**25**	**5**	**9**	**14**	**8**	**2**	**0**	**1**	**16:09**
	NHL Totals		**1652**	**577**	**956**	**1533**	**1033**	**200**	**18**	**91**	**3820**	**15.1**		**2058**	**48.0**	**19:00**	**189**	**61**	**86**	**147**	**93**	**22**	**0**	**11**	**18:23**

WHL West First All-Star Team (1988) • IHL Second All-Star Team (1989) • NHL Second All-Star Team (1992)

Played in NHL All-Star Game (1991, 1993, 1994, 1997, 1998, 1999, 2000)

Traded to **Philadelphia** by **Pittsburgh** with Brian Benning and Los Angeles' 1st round choice (previously acquired, Philadelphia selected Jason Bowen) in 1992 Entry Draft for Rick Tocchet, Kjell Samuelsson, Ken Wregget and Philadelphia's 3rd round choice (Dave Roche) in 1993 Entry Draft, February 19, 1992. Traded to **Montreal** by **Philadelphia** with Philadelphia's 3rd round choice (Martin Hohenberger) in 1995 Entry Draft for Eric Desjardins, Gilbert Dionne and John LeClair, February 9, 1995. Traded to **Philadelphia** by **Montreal** for Danius Zubrus, Philadelphia's 2nd round choice (Matt Carkner) in 1999 Entry Draft and NY Islanders' 6th round choice (previously acquired, Montreal selected Scott Selig) in 2000 Entry Draft, March 10, 1999. Signed as a free agent by **Pittsburgh**, July 9, 2004. Traded to **Carolina** by **Pittsburgh** for Niklas Nordgren, Krys Kolanos and Carolina's 2nd round choice (later traded to San Jose, later traded to Philadelphia - Philadelphia selected Kevin Marshall) in 2007 Entry Draft, March 9, 2006. Signed as a free agent by **Pittsburgh**, July 25, 2006. Claimed on waivers by **Atlanta** from **Pittsburgh**, December 8, 2007. Signed as a free agent by **Tampa Bay**, July 8, 2008. Traded to **Boston** by **Tampa Bay** with Tampa Bay's 2nd round choice (later traded to Florida - Florida selected Alexander Petrovic) in 2010 Entry Draft for Matt Lashoff and Martins Karsums, March 4, 2009. • Officially announced his retirement, June 15, 2011.

RECHLICZ, Joel

(REHK-lihj, JOHL)

Right wing. Shoots right. 6'4", 220 lbs. Born, Brookfield, WI, June 14, 1987.

Season	Club	League	GP	G	A	Pts	PIM	PP	SH	GW	S	%	+/-	TF	F%	Min	GP	G	A	Pts	PIM	PP	SH	GW	Min
2004-05	Santa Fe	NAHL	3	0	1	1	29																		
2005-06	Des Moines	USHL	2	0	0	0	4																		
	Indiana Ice	USHL	2	0	0	0	16																		
	Gatineau	QMJHL	3	0	0	0	17																		
2006-07	Chicoutimi	QMJHL	55	0	1	1	159										1	0	0	0	2				
	Chicago Hounds	UHL	2	0	0	0	9																		
2007-08	Albany River Rats	AHL	25	0	1	1	106																		
	Kalamazoo Wings	IHL	25	1	0	1	100																		
2008-09	**NY Islanders**	**NHL**	**17**	**0**	**1**	**1**	**68**	**0**	**0**	**0**	**7**	**0.0**	**–1**	**0**	**0.0**	**4:52**									
	Bridgeport	AHL	4	0	0	0	12																		
	Utah Grizzlies	ECHL	45	0	1	1	110																		
2009-10	**NY Islanders**	**NHL**	**6**	**0**	**0**	**0**	**27**	**0**	**0**	**0**	**1**	**0.0**	**–2**	**0**	**0.0**	**2:41**									
	Bridgeport	AHL	21	0	0	0	128																		
2010-11	Hershey Bears	AHL	28	1	0	1	132																		
	NHL Totals		**23**	**0**	**1**	**1**	**95**	**0**	**0**	**0**	**8**	**0.0**		**0**	**0.0**	**4:18**									

Signed as a free agent by **NY Islanders**, May 6, 2008. • Missed majority of 2009-10 as a healthy reserve. Signed as a free agent by **Hershey** (AHL), July 29, 2010.

REDDEN, Wade

(REH-duhn, WAYD) **NYR**

Defense. Shoots left. 6'2", 205 lbs. Born, Lloydminster, Sask., June 12, 1977. NY Islanders' 1st choice, 2nd overall, in 1995 Entry Draft.

Season	Club	League	GP	G	A	Pts	PIM	PP	SH	GW	S	%	+/-	TF	F%	Min	GP	G	A	Pts	PIM	PP	SH	GW	Min
1992-93	Lloydminster	AJHL	34	4	11	15	64																		
1993-94	Brandon	WHL	63	4	35	39	98										14	2	4	6	10				
1994-95	Brandon	WHL	64	14	46	60	83										18	5	10	15	8				
1995-96	Brandon	WHL	51	9	45	54	55										19	5	10	15	19				
1996-97	**Ottawa**	**NHL**	**82**	**6**	**24**	**30**	**41**	**2**	**0**	**1**	**102**	**5.9**	**1**				**7**	**1**	**3**	**4**	**2**	**0**	**0**	**0**	
1997-98	**Ottawa**	**NHL**	**80**	**8**	**14**	**22**	**27**	**3**	**0**	**2**	**103**	**7.8**	**17**				**9**	**0**	**2**	**2**	**2**	**0**	**0**	**0**	
1998-99	**Ottawa**	**NHL**	**72**	**8**	**21**	**29**	**54**	**3**	**0**	**1**	**127**	**6.3**	**7**	**0**	**0.0**	**23:27**	**4**	**1**	**2**	**3**	**2**	**1**	**0**	**0**	**26:39**
99-2000	**Ottawa**	**NHL**	**81**	**10**	**26**	**36**	**49**	**3**	**0**	**2**	**163**	**6.1**	**–1**	**0**	**0.0**	**23:43**									
2000-01	**Ottawa**	**NHL**	**78**	**10**	**37**	**47**	**49**	**4**	**0**	**0**	**159**	**6.3**	**22**	**0**	**0.0**	**25:17**	**4**	**0**	**0**	**0**	**0**	**0**	**0**	**0**	**27:29**
2001-02	**Ottawa**	**NHL**	**79**	**9**	**25**	**34**	**48**	**4**	**1**	**1**	**156**	**5.8**	**22**	**1**	**0.0**	**25:06**	**12**	**3**	**2**	**5**	**6**	**1**	**0**	**1**	**27:56**
2002-03	**Ottawa**	**NHL**	**76**	**10**	**35**	**45**	**70**	**4**	**0**	**3**	**154**	**6.5**	**23**	**0**	**0.0**	**25:24**	**18**	**1**	**8**	**9**	**10**	**0**	**0**	**1**	**25:28**
2003-04	**Ottawa**	**NHL**	**81**	**17**	**26**	**43**	**65**	**12**	**0**	**3**	**175**	**9.7**	**21**	**0**	**0.0**	**24:54**	**7**	**1**	**0**	**1**	**2**	**1**	**0**	**0**	**26:47**
2004-05			DID NOT PLAY																						
2005-06	**Ottawa**	**NHL**	**65**	**10**	**40**	**50**	**63**	**8**	**0**	**4**	**153**	**6.5**	***35**	**1**	**100.0**	**23:28**	**9**	**2**	**8**	**10**	**10**	**2**	**0**	**1**	**25:06**
	Canada	Olympics	6	1	0	1	0																		
2006-07	**Ottawa**	**NHL**	**64**	**7**	**29**	**36**	**50**	**4**	**0**	**3**	**122**	**5.7**	**1**	**0**	**0.0**	**22:54**	**20**	**3**	**7**	**10**	**10**	**3**	**0**	**1**	**23:37**
2007-08	**Ottawa**	**NHL**	**80**	**6**	**32**	**38**	**60**	**4**	**0**	**1**	**136**	**4.4**	**11**	**0**	**0.0**	**22:13**	**4**	**0**	**1**	**1**	**11**	**0**	**0**	**0**	**19:21**
2008-09	**NY Rangers**	**NHL**	**81**	**3**	**23**	**26**	**51**	**2**	**0**	**0**	**161**	**1.9**	**–5**	**0**	**0.0**	**22:20**	**7**	**0**	**2**	**2**	**0**	**0**	**0**	**0**	**23:24**

			Regular Season														Playoffs								
Season	Club	League	GP	G	A	Pts	PIM	PP	SH	GW	S	%	+/-	TF	F%	Min	GP	G	A	Pts	PIM	PP	SH	GW	Min
2009-10	**NY Rangers**	**NHL**	**75**	**2**	**12**	**14**	**27**	**0**	**0**	**0**	**66**	**3.0**	**8**	**1**	**100.0**	**17:31**									
2010-11	Connecticut	AHL	70	8	34	42	46										6	0	6	6	0				
	NHL Totals		**994**	**106**	**344**	**450**	**654**	**53**	**1**	**21**	**1777**	**6.0**		**3**	**66.7**	**23:19**	**101**	**12**	**35**	**47**	**55**	**8**	**0**	**4**	**25:08**

WHL Rookie of the Year (1994) • WHL East Second All-Star Team (1995) • WHL East First All-Star Team (1996) • Memorial Cup All-Star Team (1996)
Played in NHL All-Star Game (2002)
Traded to **Ottawa** by **NY Islanders** with Damian Rhodes for Don Beaupre, Martin Straka and Bryan Berard, January 23, 1996. Signed as a free agent by **NY Rangers**, July 1, 2008.

REDDOX, Liam

(REH-dawks, LEE-uhm)

Left wing. Shoots left. 5'11", 178 lbs. Born, East York, Ont., January 27, 1986. Edmonton's 5th choice, 112th overall, in 2004 Entry Draft.

Season	Club	League	GP	G	A	Pts	PIM	PP	SH	GW	S	%	+/-	TF	F%	Min	GP	G	A	Pts	PIM	PP	SH	GW	Min
2002-03	Wellington Dukes	OPJHL	45	32	32	64	29																		
	Peterborough	OHL	4	0	0	0	0																		
2003-04	Peterborough	OHL	68	31	33	64	24																		
2004-05	Peterborough	OHL	68	36	46	82	38										14	3	10	13	10				
2005-06	Peterborough	OHL	68	19	45	64	74										19	5	9	14	20				
2006-07	Stockton Thunder	ECHL	70	8	18	26	49										6	2	1	3	4				
2007-08	**Edmonton**	**NHL**	**1**	**0**	**0**	**0**	**0**	**0**	**0**	**0**	**1**	**0.0**	**–1**	**0**	**0.0**	**5:55**									
	Springfield	AHL	65	16	28	44	48																		
2008-09	**Edmonton**	**NHL**	**46**	**5**	**7**	**12**	**10**	**1**	**0**	**0**	**39**	**12.8**	**–6**	**25**	**44.0**	**10:28**									
	Springfield	AHL	14	5	4	9	2																		
2009-10	**Edmonton**	**NHL**	**9**	**0**	**2**	**2**	**4**	**0**	**0**	**0**	**11**	**0.0**	**–2**	**0**	**0.0**	**12:32**									
	Springfield	AHL	70	18	17	35	24																		
2010-11	**Edmonton**	**NHL**	**44**	**1**	**9**	**10**	**20**	**0**	**0**	**0**	**85**	**1.2**	**–8**	**124**	**33.1**	**15:00**									
	Oklahoma City	AHL	37	18	15	33	16																		
	NHL Totals		**100**	**6**	**18**	**24**	**34**	**1**	**0**	**0**	**136**	**4.4**		**149**	**34.9**	**12:36**									

OHL All-Rookie Team (2004)
Signed as a free agent by **Vaxjo** (Sweden), May 25, 2011.

REESE, Dylan

(REES, DIH-luhn) **NYI**

Defense. Shoots right. 6'1", 201 lbs. Born, Pittsburgh, PA, August 29, 1984. NY Rangers' 9th choice, 209th overall, in 2003 Entry Draft.

Season	Club	League	GP	G	A	Pts	PIM	PP	SH	GW	S	%	+/-	TF	F%	Min	GP	G	A	Pts	PIM	PP	SH	GW	Min
2000-01	Pittsburgh	MWEHL	66	14	42	66	....																		
2001-02	Pittsburgh Forge	NAHL	48	7	16	23	70										7	0	2	2	4				
2002-03	Pittsburgh Forge	NAHL	56	11	30	41	98										5	2	3	5	6				
2003-04	Harvard Crimson	ECAC	21	1	4	5	18																		
2004-05	Harvard Crimson	ECAC	34	7	12	19	44																		
2005-06	Harvard Crimson	ECAC	33	4	15	19	36																		
2006-07	Harvard Crimson	ECAC	33	9	9	18	26																		
	Hartford	AHL	10	0	4	4	12										2	0	0	0	2				
2007-08	San Antonio	AHL	59	1	6	7	49										3	1	1	2	4				
2008-09	San Antonio	AHL	75	1	27	28	64																		
2009-10	**NY Islanders**	**NHL**	**19**	**2**	**2**	**4**	**14**	**0**	**0**	**1**	**16**	**12.5**	**4**	**0**	**0.0**	**15:02**									
	Syracuse Crunch	AHL	51	4	18	22	31																		
	Bridgeport	AHL	1	1	1	2	0										5	1	3	4	0				
2010-11	**NY Islanders**	**NHL**	**27**	**0**	**6**	**6**	**15**	**0**	**0**	**0**	**23**	**0.0**	**–12**	**0**	**0.0**	**14:49**									
	Bridgeport	AHL	37	4	14	18	30																		
	NHL Totals		**46**	**2**	**8**	**10**	**29**	**0**	**0**	**1**	**39**	**5.1**		**0**	**0.0**	**14:55**									

ECAC Second All-Star Team (2006, 2007)
Signed as a free agent by **San Antonio** (AHL), September 5, 2007. Signed as a free agent by **Columbus**, September 29, 2009. Traded to **NY Islanders** by **Columbus** for Greg Moore, March 1, 2010.

REGEHR, Robyn

(reh-GEER, RAW-bihn) **BUF**

Defense. Shoots left. 6'3", 225 lbs. Born, Recife, Brazil, April 19, 1980. Colorado's 3rd choice, 19th overall, in 1998 Entry Draft.

Season	Club	League	GP	G	A	Pts	PIM	PP	SH	GW	S	%	+/-	TF	F%	Min	GP	G	A	Pts	PIM	PP	SH	GW	Min
1995-96	Prince Albert	SMHL	59	8	24	32	157																		
1996-97	Kamloops Blazers	WHL	64	4	19	23	67										5	0	1	1	18				
1997-98	Kamloops Blazers	WHL	65	4	10	14	120										5	0	3	3	8				
1998-99	Kamloops Blazers	WHL	54	12	20	32	130										12	1	4	5	21				
99-2000	**Calgary**	**NHL**	**57**	**5**	**7**	**12**	**46**	**2**	**0**	**0**	**64**	**7.8**	**–2**	**0**	**0.0**	**18:24**									
	Saint John Flames	AHL	5	0	0	0	0																		
2000-01	**Calgary**	**NHL**	**71**	**1**	**3**	**4**	**70**	**0**	**0**	**0**	**62**	**1.6**	**–7**	**1**	**0.0**	**19:43**									
2001-02	**Calgary**	**NHL**	**77**	**2**	**6**	**8**	**93**	**0**	**0**	**0**	**82**	**2.4**	**–24**	**0**	**0.0**	**20:54**									
2002-03	**Calgary**	**NHL**	**76**	**0**	**12**	**12**	**87**	**0**	**0**	**0**	**109**	**0.0**	**–9**	**1**	**100.0**	**22:45**									
2003-04	**Calgary**	**NHL**	**82**	**4**	**14**	**18**	**74**	**2**	**0**	**1**	**106**	**3.8**	**14**	**2**	**50.0**	**22:21**	**26**	**2**	**7**	**9**	**20**	**0**	**0**	**0**	**26:27**
2004-05			DID NOT PLAY																						
2005-06	**Calgary**	**NHL**	**68**	**6**	**20**	**26**	**67**	**5**	**0**	**2**	**89**	**6.7**	**6**	**1**	**100.0**	**23:08**	**7**	**1**	**3**	**4**	**6**	**1**	**0**	**0**	**22:22**
	Canada	Olympics	6	0	1	1	2																		
2006-07	**Calgary**	**NHL**	**78**	**2**	**19**	**21**	**75**	**0**	**0**	**0**	**66**	**3.0**	**27**	**1**	**0.0**	**21:55**	**1**	**0**	**0**	**0**	**0**	**0**	**0**	**0**	**11:15**
2007-08	**Calgary**	**NHL**	**82**	**5**	**15**	**20**	**79**	**1**	**1**	**0**	**93**	**5.4**	**11**	**0**	**0.0**	**21:20**	**7**	**0**	**2**	**2**	**2**	**0**	**0**	**0**	**21:50**
2008-09	**Calgary**	**NHL**	**75**	**0**	**8**	**8**	**73**	**0**	**0**	**0**	**79**	**0.0**	**10**	**0**	**0.0**	**21:09**									
2009-10	**Calgary**	**NHL**	**81**	**2**	**15**	**17**	**80**	**0**	**0**	**0**	**78**	**2.6**	**2**	**1**	**0.0**	**21:38**									
2010-11	**Calgary**	**NHL**	**79**	**2**	**15**	**17**	**58**	**1**	**0**	**0**	**72**	**2.8**	**2**	**0**	**0.0**	**21:29**									
	NHL Totals		**826**	**29**	**134**	**163**	**802**	**11**	**1**	**3**	**900**	**3.2**		**7**	**42.9**	**21:25**	**41**	**3**	**12**	**15**	**28**	**1**	**0**	**0**	**24:36**

WHL West First All-Star Team (1999)
Traded to **Calgary** by **Colorado** with Rene Corbet, Wade Belak and Colorado's 2nd round compensatory choice (Jarret Stoll) in 2000 Entry Draft for Theoren Fleury and Chris Dingman, February 28, 1999. Traded to **Buffalo** by **Calgary** with Ales Kotalik and Calgary's 2nd round choice in 2012 Entry Draft for Chris Butler and Paul Byron, June 25, 2011.

REGIN, Peter

(REE-gihn, PEE-tuhr) **OTT**

Center. Shoots left. 6'2", 205 lbs. Born, Herning, Denmark, April 16, 1986. Ottawa's 4th choice, 87th overall, in 2004 Entry Draft.

Season	Club	League	GP	G	A	Pts	PIM	PP	SH	GW	S	%	+/-	TF	F%	Min	GP	G	A	Pts	PIM	PP	SH	GW	Min
2002-03	Herning IK	Denmark	24	0	1	1	4										10	1	3	4	4				
2003-04	Herning IK	Denmark	33	9	11	20	14																		
2004-05	Herning Blue Fox	Denmark	36	19	27	46	43										16	5	8	13	2				
2005-06	Timra IK	Sweden	44	4	7	11	14																		
2006-07	Timra IK	Sweden	51	9	7	16	16										7	2	2	4	2				
2007-08	Timra IK	Sweden	55	12	19	31	36										11	2	7	9	2				
2008-09	**Ottawa**	**NHL**	**11**	**1**	**1**	**2**	**2**	**0**	**0**	**1**	**7**	**14.3**	**0**	**77**	**53.3**	**10:32**									
	Binghamton	AHL	56	18	29	47	36																		
2009-10	**Ottawa**	**NHL**	**75**	**13**	**16**	**29**	**20**	**1**	**0**	**1**	**135**	**9.6**	**10**	**538**	**44.6**	**12:54**	**6**	**3**	**1**	**4**	**6**	**0**	**0**	**0**	**18:06**
2010-11	**Ottawa**	**NHL**	**55**	**3**	**14**	**17**	**12**	**0**	**0**	**1**	**87**	**3.4**	**–4**	**316**	**41.8**	**13:23**									
	NHL Totals		**141**	**17**	**31**	**48**	**34**	**1**	**0**	**3**	**229**	**7.4**		**931**	**44.4**	**12:54**	**6**	**3**	**1**	**4**	**6**	**0**	**0**	**0**	**18:06**

REICH, Jeremy

(REECH, JAIR-eh-mee)

Left wing. Shoots left. 6'1", 203 lbs. Born, Craik, Sask., February 11, 1979. Chicago's 3rd choice, 39th overall, in 1997 Entry Draft.

Season	Club	League	GP	G	A	Pts	PIM	PP	SH	GW	S	%	+/-	TF	F%	Min	GP	G	A	Pts	PIM	PP	SH	GW	Min
1993-94	Pilote Butte	SAHA	80	70	65	135	120																		
1994-95	Sask. Contacts	SMHL	35	13	20	33	81																		
1995-96	Seattle	WHL	65	11	11	22	88										5	0	1	1	10				
1996-97	Seattle	WHL	62	19	31	50	104										15	2	5	7	36				
1997-98	Seattle	WHL	43	24	23	47	121																		
	Swift Current	WHL	22	8	8	16	47										12	5	6	11	37				
1998-99	Swift Current	WHL	67	21	28	49	220										6	0	3	3	26				
99-2000	Swift Current	WHL	72	33	58	91	167										12	2	10	12	19				
2000-01	Syracuse Crunch	AHL	56	6	9	15	108										5	0	0	0	6				
2001-02	Syracuse Crunch	AHL	59	9	7	16	178										10	4	0	4	16				
2002-03	Syracuse Crunch	AHL	78	14	13	27	195																		
2003-04	**Columbus**	**NHL**	**9**	**0**	**1**	**1**	**20**	**0**	**0**	**0**	**3**	**0.0**	**–3**	**0**	**0.0**	**7:38**									
	Syracuse Crunch	AHL	72	14	37	51	150										6	1	1	2	13				

			Regular Season														Playoffs								
Season	Club	League	GP	G	A	Pts	PIM	PP	SH	GW	S	%	+/-	TF	F%	Min	GP	G	A	Pts	PIM	PP	SH	GW	Min
2004-05	Syracuse Crunch	AHL	50	4	5	9	189	....	....	....	....	....	....	....	....	....	....	....	....	....	....	....	....	....	....
	Houston Aeros	AHL	18	3	4	7	34	....	....	....	....	....	....	....	....	....	5	0	1	1	28	....	....	....	....
2005-06	Providence Bruins	AHL	77	8	15	23	235	....	....	....	....	....	....	....	....	....	6	0	0	0	27	....	....	....	....
2006-07	**Boston**	**NHL**	**32**	**0**	**1**	**1**	**63**	**0**	**0**	**0**	**27**	**0.0**	**−10**	**4**	**25.0**	**8:14**	....	....	....	....	....	....	....	....	....
	Providence Bruins	AHL	46	4	7	11	105	....	....	....	....	....	....	....	....	....	....	....	....	....	....	....	....	....	....
2007-08	**Boston**	**NHL**	**58**	**2**	**2**	**4**	**78**	**0**	**0**	**1**	**39**	**5.1**	**−5**	**31**	**48.4**	**8:15**	**4**	**0**	**0**	**0**	**8**	**0**	**0**	**0**	**10:27**
2008-09	Providence Bruins	AHL	76	21	13	34	139	....	....	....	....	....	....	....	....	....	16	3	5	8	21	....	....	....	....
2009-10	Bridgeport	AHL	33	12	8	20	24	....	....	....	....	....	....	....	....	....	5	1	2	3	4	....	....	....	....
2010-11	Providence Bruins	AHL	72	14	9	23	52	....	....	....	....	....	....	....	....	....	....	....	....	....	....	....	....	....	....
	NHL Totals		**99**	**2**	**4**	**6**	**161**	**0**	**0**	**1**	**69**	**2.9**		**35**	**45.7**	**8:12**	**4**	**0**	**0**	**0**	**8**	**0**	**0**	**0**	**10:27**

Signed as a free agent by **Columbus**, May 17, 2000. • Loaned to **Houston** (AHL) by **Syracuse** (AHL) for the loan of Jason Beckett, March 10, 2005. Signed as a free agent by **Boston**, September 7, 2005. Signed as a free agent by **NY Islanders**, July 2, 2009. Signed as a free agent by **Boston**, July 1, 2010.

REINPRECHT, Steve

(RIGHN-prehkt, STEEV) **FLA**

Center. Shoots left. 6', 195 lbs. Born, Edmonton, Alta., May 7, 1976.

1993-94	Edmonton SSAC	AMHL	71	48	77	125	....	....	....	....	....	....	....	....	....	....	....	....	....	....	....	....	....	....	....
1994-95	St. Albert Saints	AJHL	56	35	44	79	14	....	....	....	....	....	....	....	....	....	....	....	....	....	....	....	....	....	....
1995-96	St. Albert Saints	AJHL	39	24	33	57	16	....	....	....	....	....	....	....	....	....	....	....	....	....	....	....	....	....	....
1996-97	U. of Wisconsin	WCHA	38	11	9	20	12	....	....	....	....	....	....	....	....	....	....	....	....	....	....	....	....	....	....
1997-98	U. of Wisconsin	WCHA	41	19	24	43	18	....	....	....	....	....	....	....	....	....	....	....	....	....	....	....	....	....	....
1998-99	U. of Wisconsin	WCHA	38	16	17	33	14	....	....	....	....	....	....	....	....	....	....	....	....	....	....	....	....	....	....
99-2000	U. of Wisconsin	WCHA	37	26	40	*66	14	....	....	....	....	....	....	....	....	....	....	....	....	....	....	....	....	....	....
	Los Angeles	**NHL**	**1**	**0**	**0**	**0**	**2**	**0**	**0**	**0**	**0**	**0.0**	**0**	**6**	**50.0**	**6:01**	....	....	....	....	....	....	....	....	....
2000-01	**Los Angeles**	**NHL**	**59**	**12**	**17**	**29**	**12**	**3**	**2**	**3**	**72**	**16.7**	**11**	**676**	**41.4**	**12:39**	....	....	....	....	....	....	....	....	....
	♦ Colorado	**NHL**	**21**	**3**	**4**	**7**	**2**	**0**	**0**	**0**	**28**	**10.7**	**−1**	**209**	**51.2**	**15:38**	**22**	**2**	**3**	**5**	**2**	**0**	**0**	**0**	**12:09**
2001-02	**Colorado**	**NHL**	**67**	**19**	**27**	**46**	**18**	**4**	**0**	**3**	**111**	**17.1**	**14**	**413**	**52.1**	**16:32**	**21**	**7**	**5**	**12**	**8**	**0**	**0**	**2**	**16:23**
2002-03	**Colorado**	**NHL**	**77**	**18**	**33**	**51**	**18**	**2**	**1**	**1**	**146**	**12.3**	**−6**	**928**	**46.4**	**17:22**	**7**	**1**	**2**	**3**	**0**	**0**	**0**	**0**	**15:32**
2003-04	**Calgary**	**NHL**	**44**	**7**	**22**	**29**	**4**	**3**	**0**	**1**	**68**	**10.3**	**1**	**120**	**40.0**	**17:05**	....	....	....	....	....	....	....	....	....
2004-05	HC Mulhouse	France	22	20	27	47	6	....	....	....	....	....	....	....	....	....	10	7	6	13	2	....	....	....	....
2005-06	**Calgary**	**NHL**	**52**	**10**	**19**	**29**	**24**	**5**	**0**	**1**	**72**	**13.9**	**10**	**340**	**49.4**	**14:49**	....	....	....	....	....	....	....	....	....
	Phoenix	**NHL**	**28**	**12**	**11**	**23**	**8**	**4**	**1**	**2**	**58**	**20.7**	**1**	**526**	**47.3**	**19:06**	....	....	....	....	....	....	....	....	....
2006-07	**Phoenix**	**NHL**	**49**	**9**	**24**	**33**	**28**	**2**	**0**	**1**	**71**	**12.7**	**−3**	**537**	**52.3**	**15:40**	....	....	....	....	....	....	....	....	....
2007-08	**Phoenix**	**NHL**	**81**	**16**	**30**	**46**	**26**	**5**	**1**	**0**	**105**	**15.2**	**−3**	**1020**	**50.6**	**15:42**	....	....	....	....	....	....	....	....	....
2008-09	**Phoenix**	**NHL**	**73**	**14**	**27**	**41**	**20**	**3**	**0**	**3**	**95**	**14.7**	**0**	**886**	**46.3**	**15:54**	....	....	....	....	....	....	....	....	....
2009-10	**Florida**	**NHL**	**82**	**16**	**22**	**38**	**18**	**3**	**0**	**1**	**124**	**12.9**	**−1**	**989**	**47.7**	**16:05**	....	....	....	....	....	....	....	....	....
2010-11	**Florida**	**NHL**	**29**	**4**	**6**	**10**	**6**	**1**	**0**	**1**	**31**	**12.9**	**−2**	**172**	**51.7**	**11:46**	....	....	....	....	....	....	....	....	....
	Adler Mannheim	Germany	18	4	9	13	2	....	....	....	....	....	....	....	....	....	6	1	2	3	2	....	....	....	....
	NHL Totals		**663**	**140**	**242**	**382**	**186**	**35**	**5**	**17**	**981**	**14.3**		**6822**	**47.9**	**15:45**	**50**	**10**	**10**	**20**	**10**	**0**	**0**	**2**	**14:24**

WCHA Second All-Star Team (1998) • WCHA First All-Star Team (2000) • WCHA Player of the Year (2000) • NCAA West First All-American Team (2000)

Signed as a free agent by **Los Angeles**, March 31, 2000. Traded to **Colorado** by **Los Angeles** with Rob Blake for Adam Deadmarsh, Aaron Miller, a player to be named later (Jared Aulin, March 22, 2001) and Colorado's 1st round choices in 2001 (Dave Steckel) and 2003 (Brian Boyle) Entry Drafts, February 21, 2001. Traded to **Buffalo** by **Colorado** for Keith Ballard, July 3, 2003. Traded to **Calgary** by **Buffalo** with Rhett Warrener for Chris Drury and Steve Begin, July 3, 2003. Signed as a free agent by **Mulhouse** (France), September 28, 2004. Traded to **Phoenix** by **Calgary** with Philippe Sauve for Brian Boucher and Mike Leclerc, February 2, 2006. Traded to **Florida** by **Phoenix** for Stefan Meyer, June 19, 2009. • Loaned to **Mannheim** (Germany) by **Florida**, January 6, 2011.

REPIK, Michal

(REH-pihk, MEE-khahl) **FLA**

Right wing. Shoots right. 5'10", 180 lbs. Born, Vlasim, Czech., December 31, 1988. Florida's 2nd choice, 40th overall, in 2007 Entry Draft.

2002-03	Sparta U17	CzR-U17	18	7	10	17	6	....	....	....	....	....	....	....	....	....	2	0	0	0	0	....	....	....	....
2003-04	Sparta U17	CzR-U17	33	25	17	42	42	....	....	....	....	....	....	....	....	....	3	0	0	0	0	....	....	....	....
	Sparta Jr.	CzRep-Jr.	23	12	5	17	10	....	....	....	....	....	....	....	....	....	....	....	....	....	....	....	....	....	....
2004-05	Sparta U17	CzR-U17	2	2	3	5	6	....	....	....	....	....	....	....	....	....	....	....	....	....	....	....	....	....	....
	Sparta Jr.	CzRep-Jr.	45	26	31	57	24	....	....	....	....	....	....	....	....	....	8	2	4	6	10	....	....	....	....
2005-06	Vancouver Giants	WHL	69	24	28	52	55	....	....	....	....	....	....	....	....	....	14	3	3	6	19	....	....	....	....
2006-07	Vancouver Giants	WHL	56	24	31	55	56	....	....	....	....	....	....	....	....	....	22	10	*16	*26	24	....	....	....	....
2007-08	Vancouver Giants	WHL	51	27	34	61	62	....	....	....	....	....	....	....	....	....	10	5	6	11	18	....	....	....	....
2008-09	**Florida**	**NHL**	**5**	**2**	**0**	**2**	**2**	**0**	**0**	**0**	**7**	**28.6**	**1**	**1**	**100.0**	**7:32**	....	....	....	....	....	....	....	....	....
	Rochester	AHL	75	19	30	49	58	....	....	....	....	....	....	....	....	....	....	....	....	....	....	....	....	....	....
2009-10	**Florida**	**NHL**	**19**	**3**	**2**	**5**	**6**	**0**	**0**	**0**	**23**	**13.0**	**1**	**1**	**100.0**	**8:35**	....	....	....	....	....	....	....	....	....
	Rochester	AHL	60	22	31	53	57	....	....	....	....	....	....	....	....	....	7	1	1	2	4	....	....	....	....
2010-11	**Florida**	**NHL**	**31**	**2**	**6**	**8**	**22**	**0**	**0**	**0**	**54**	**3.7**	**−6**	**7**	**42.9**	**12:47**	....	....	....	....	....	....	....	....	....
	Rochester	AHL	53	11	34	45	38	....	....	....	....	....	....	....	....	....	....	....	....	....	....	....	....	....	....
	NHL Totals		**55**	**7**	**8**	**15**	**30**	**0**	**0**	**0**	**84**	**8.3**		**9**	**55.6**	**10:51**	....	....	....	....	....	....	....	....	....

Memorial Cup All-Star Team (2007) • Ed Chynoweth Trophy (Memorial Cup - Leading Scorer) (2007)

RIBEIRO, Mike

(rih-BAIR-roh, MIGHK) **DAL**

Center. Shoots left. 6', 179 lbs. Born, Montreal, Que., February 10, 1980. Montreal's 2nd choice, 45th overall, in 1998 Entry Draft.

1996-97	Mtl-Bourassa	QAAA	43	32	57	89	48	....	....	....	....	....	....	....	....	....	16	15	23	38	14	....	....	....	....
1997-98	Rouyn-Noranda	QMJHL	67	40	*85	125	55	....	....	....	....	....	....	....	....	....	6	3	1	4	0	....	....	....	....
1998-99	Rouyn-Noranda	QMJHL	69	*67	*100	*167	137	....	....	....	....	....	....	....	....	....	11	5	11	16	12	....	....	....	....
	Fredericton	AHL	....	....	....	....	....	....	....	....	....	....	....	....	....	....	5	0	1	1	2	....	....	....	....
99-2000	**Montreal**	**NHL**	**19**	**1**	**1**	**2**	**2**	**1**	**0**	**0**	**18**	**5.6**	**−6**	**95**	**34.7**	**10:40**	....	....	....	....	....	....	....	....	....
	Quebec Citadelles	AHL	3	0	0	0	2	....	....	....	....	....	....	....	....	....	....	....	....	....	....	....	....	....	....
	Rouyn-Noranda	QMJHL	2	1	3	4	0	....	....	....	....	....	....	....	....	....	....	....	....	....	....	....	....	....	....
	Quebec Remparts	QMJHL	21	17	28	45	30	....	....	....	....	....	....	....	....	....	11	3	20	23	38	....	....	....	....
2000-01	**Montreal**	**NHL**	**2**	**0**	**0**	**0**	**2**	**0**	**0**	**0**	**3**	**0.0**	**0**	**11**	**18.2**	**10:38**	....	....	....	....	....	....	....	....	....
	Quebec Citadelles	AHL	74	26	40	66	44	....	....	....	....	....	....	....	....	....	9	1	5	6	23	....	....	....	....
2001-02	**Montreal**	**NHL**	**43**	**8**	**10**	**18**	**12**	**3**	**0**	**0**	**48**	**16.7**	**−11**	**141**	**44.0**	**13:55**	....	....	....	....	....	....	....	....	....
	Quebec Citadelles	AHL	23	9	14	23	36	....	....	....	....	....	....	....	....	....	3	0	3	3	0	....	....	....	....
2002-03	**Montreal**	**NHL**	**52**	**5**	**12**	**17**	**6**	**2**	**0**	**0**	**57**	**8.8**	**−3**	**358**	**50.3**	**11:07**	....	....	....	....	....	....	....	....	....
	Hamilton	AHL	3	0	1	1	0	....	....	....	....	....	....	....	....	....	....	....	....	....	....	....	....	....	....
2003-04	**Montreal**	**NHL**	**81**	**20**	**45**	**65**	**34**	**7**	**0**	**5**	**103**	**19.4**	**15**	**913**	**44.8**	**17:05**	**11**	**2**	**1**	**3**	**18**	**0**	**0**	**0**	**16:31**
2004-05	Blues Espoo	Finland	17	8	9	17	4	....	....	....	....	....	....	....	....	....	....	....	....	....	....	....	....	....	....
2005-06	**Montreal**	**NHL**	**79**	**16**	**35**	**51**	**36**	**8**	**0**	**2**	**130**	**12.3**	**−6**	**843**	**44.7**	**16:35**	**6**	**0**	**2**	**2**	**0**	**0**	**0**	**0**	**18:22**
2006-07	**Dallas**	**NHL**	**81**	**18**	**41**	**59**	**22**	**6**	**0**	**3**	**111**	**16.2**	**3**	**678**	**46.6**	**14:56**	**7**	**0**	**3**	**3**	**4**	**0**	**0**	**0**	**18:28**
2007-08	**Dallas**	**NHL**	**76**	**27**	**56**	**83**	**46**	**7**	**0**	**5**	**107**	**25.2**	**21**	**883**	**45.0**	**18:26**	**18**	**3**	**14**	**17**	**16**	**0**	**0**	**0**	**21:45**
2008-09	**Dallas**	**NHL**	**82**	**22**	**56**	**78**	**52**	**7**	**0**	**1**	**163**	**13.5**	**−4**	**1240**	**45.5**	**20:57**	....	....	....	....	....	....	....	....	....
2009-10	**Dallas**	**NHL**	**66**	**19**	**34**	**53**	**38**	**8**	**2**	**0**	**155**	**12.3**	**−5**	**1102**	**44.8**	**19:32**	....	....	....	....	....	....	....	....	....
2010-11	**Dallas**	**NHL**	**82**	**19**	**52**	**71**	**28**	**7**	**0**	**4**	**161**	**11.8**	**−4**	**1213**	**46.6**	**19:58**	....	....	....	....	....	....	....	....	....
	NHL Totals		**663**	**155**	**342**	**497**	**278**	**56**	**2**	**20**	**1056**	**14.7**		**7477**	**45.5**	**17:07**	**42**	**5**	**20**	**25**	**38**	**0**	**0**	**0**	**19:21**

QMJHL Second All-Star Team (1998) • QMJHL First All-Star Team (1999) • Canadian Major Junior First All-Star Team (1999)

Played in NHL All-Star Game (2008)

Signed as a free agent by **Espoo** (Finland), January 17, 2005. Traded to **Dallas** by **Montreal** with Montreal's 6th round choice (Matthew Tassone) in 2008 Entry Draft for Janne Niinimaa and Dallas' 5th round choice (Andrew Conboy) in 2007 Entry Draft, September 30, 2006.

RICHARDS, Brad

(RIH-chuhrds, BRAD) **NYR**

Center. Shoots left. 6', 195 lbs. Born, Murray Harbour, P.E.I., May 2, 1980. Tampa Bay's 2nd choice, 64th overall, in 1998 Entry Draft.

1996-97	Notre Dame	SJHL	63	39	48	87	73	....	....	....	....	....	....	....	....	....	....	....	....	....	....	....	....	....	....
1997-98	Rimouski Oceanic	QMJHL	68	33	82	115	44	....	....	....	....	....	....	....	....	....	19	8	24	32	2	....	....	....	....
1998-99	Rimouski Oceanic	QMJHL	59	39	92	131	55	....	....	....	....	....	....	....	....	....	11	9	12	21	6	....	....	....	....
99-2000	Rimouski Oceanic	QMJHL	63	*71	*115	*186	69	....	....	....	....	....	....	....	....	....	12	13	*24	*37	16	....	....	....	....
2000-01	**Tampa Bay**	**NHL**	**82**	**21**	**41**	**62**	**14**	**7**	**0**	**3**	**179**	**11.7**	**−10**	**955**	**41.4**	**16:54**	....	....	....	....	....	....	....	....	....
2001-02	**Tampa Bay**	**NHL**	**82**	**20**	**42**	**62**	**13**	**5**	**0**	**0**	**251**	**8.0**	**−18**	**911**	**41.2**	**19:48**	....	....	....	....	....	....	....	....	....
2002-03	**Tampa Bay**	**NHL**	**80**	**17**	**57**	**74**	**24**	**4**	**0**	**2**	**277**	**6.1**	**3**	**1007**	**47.5**	**19:56**	**11**	**0**	**5**	**5**	**12**	**0**	**0**	**0**	**22:21**
2003-04	**♦ Tampa Bay**	**NHL**	**82**	**26**	**53**	**79**	**12**	**5**	**1**	**6**	**244**	**10.7**	**13**	**1167**	**46.7**	**20:26**	**23**	**12**	**14**	***26**	**4**	***7**	**0**	***7**	**23:28**
2004-05	Ak Bars Kazan	Russia	6	2	5	7	16	....	....	....	....	....	....	....	....	....	....	....	....	....	....	....	....	....	....
2005-06	**Tampa Bay**	**NHL**	**82**	**23**	**68**	**91**	**32**	**7**	**4**	**0**	**282**	**8.2**	**0**	**1288**	**50.2**	**22:45**	**5**	**3**	**5**	**8**	**6**	**0**	**0**	**0**	**24:11**
	Canada	Olympics	6	2	2	4	6	....	....	....	....	....	....	....	....	....	....	....	....	....	....	....	....	....	....

			Regular Season														Playoffs								
Season	Club	League	GP	G	A	Pts	PIM	PP	SH	GW	S	%	+/-	TF	F%	Min	GP	G	A	Pts	PIM	PP	SH	GW	Min
2006-07	**Tampa Bay**	**NHL**	**82**	**25**	**45**	**70**	**23**	**12**	**1**	**3**	**272**	**9.2**	**–19**	**1580**	**51.4**	**24:07**	**6**	**3**	**5**	**8**	**6**	**2**	**0**	**0**	**25:39**
2007-08	**Tampa Bay**	**NHL**	**62**	**18**	**33**	**51**	**15**	**9**	**1**	**4**	**228**	**7.9**	**–25**	**944**	**48.1**	**24:17**	....	....	....	....	....	....	....	....	....
	Dallas	**NHL**	**12**	**2**	**9**	**11**	**0**	**0**	**1**	**0**	**21**	**9.5**	**–2**	**130**	**56.2**	**19:15**	**18**	**3**	**12**	**15**	**8**	**0**	**0**	**0**	**21:06**
2008-09	**Dallas**	**NHL**	**56**	**16**	**32**	**48**	**6**	**5**	**0**	**2**	**180**	**8.9**	**–4**	**911**	**50.6**	**20:29**	....	....	....	....	....	....	....	....	....
2009-10	**Dallas**	**NHL**	**80**	**24**	**67**	**91**	**14**	**13**	**0**	**2**	**284**	**8.5**	**–12**	**1140**	**51.5**	**20:52**	....	....	....	....	....	....	....	....	....
2010-11	**Dallas**	**NHL**	**72**	**28**	**49**	**77**	**24**	**7**	**0**	**3**	**272**	**10.3**	**1**	**990**	**50.6**	**21:43**	....	....	....	....	....	....	....	....	....
	NHL Totals		**772**	**220**	**496**	**716**	**177**	**74**	**8**	**25**	**2490**	**8.8**		**11023**	**48.3**	**21:02**	**63**	**21**	**41**	**62**	**36**	**9**	**0**	**7**	**22:52**

QMJHL First All-Star Team (2000) • Canadian Major Junior First All-Star Team (2000) • Canadian Major Junior Player of the Year (2000) • Memorial Cup All-Star Team (2000) • Stafford Smythe Memorial Trophy (Memorial Cup - MVP) (2000) • NHL All-Rookie Team (2001) • Lady Byng Memorial Trophy (2004) • Conn Smythe Trophy (2004)

Played in NHL All-Star Game (2011)

Signed as a free agent by **Kazan** (Russia), November 8, 2004. Traded to **Dallas** by **Tampa Bay** with Johan Holmqvist for Jussi Jokinen, Jeff Halpern, Mike Smith and Dallas' 4th round choice (later traded to Minnesota, later traded to Edmonton – Edmonton selected Kyle Bigos) in 2009 Entry Draft, February 26, 2008. Signed as a free agent by **NY Rangers**, July 2, 2011.

RICHARDS, Mike

(RIH-chuhrds, MIGHK) **L.A.**

Center. Shoots left. 5'11", 195 lbs. Born, Kenora, Ont., February 11, 1985. Philadelphia's 2nd choice, 24th overall, in 2003 Entry Draft.

Season	Club	League	GP	G	A	Pts	PIM	PP	SH	GW	S	%	+/-	TF	F%	Min	GP	G	A	Pts	PIM	PP	SH	GW	Min
2000-01	Kenora Stars	NOHA	85	76	73	149	20	....	....	....	....	....	....	....	....	....	....	....	....	....	....	....	....	....	....
2001-02	Kitchener Rangers	OHL	65	20	38	58	52	....	....	....	....	....	....	....	....	....	4	0	1	1	6	....	....	....	....
2002-03	Kitchener Rangers	OHL	67	37	50	87	99	....	....	....	....	....	....	....	....	....	21	9	18	27	24	....	....	....	....
2003-04	Kitchener Rangers	OHL	58	36	53	89	82	....	....	....	....	....	....	....	....	....	1	0	0	0	0	....	....	....	....
2004-05	Kitchener Rangers	OHL	43	22	36	58	75	....	....	....	....	....	....	....	....	....	15	11	17	28	36	....	....	....	....
	Philadelphia	AHL	....	....	....	....	....	....	....	....	....	....	....	....	....	....	14	7	8	15	28	....	....	....	....
2005-06	**Philadelphia**	**NHL**	**79**	**11**	**23**	**34**	**65**	**1**	**3**	**1**	**168**	**6.5**	**6**	**914**	**45.7**	**15:23**	**6**	**0**	**1**	**1**	**0**	**0**	**0**	**0**	**15:41**
2006-07	**Philadelphia**	**NHL**	**59**	**10**	**22**	**32**	**52**	**1**	**4**	**3**	**130**	**7.7**	**–12**	**978**	**47.8**	**17:50**	....	....	....	....	....	....	....	....	....
2007-08	**Philadelphia**	**NHL**	**73**	**28**	**47**	**75**	**76**	**8**	**5**	**6**	**212**	**13.2**	**14**	**1381**	**50.5**	**21:31**	**17**	**7**	**7**	**14**	**10**	**1**	***2**	**0**	**20:55**
2008-09	**Philadelphia**	**NHL**	**79**	**30**	**50**	**80**	**63**	**8**	***7**	**4**	**238**	**12.6**	**22**	**1660**	**49.0**	**21:44**	**6**	**1**	**4**	**5**	**6**	**1**	**0**	**0**	**22:58**
2009-10	**Philadelphia**	**NHL**	**82**	**31**	**31**	**62**	**79**	**13**	**1**	**3**	**237**	**13.1**	**–2**	**1373**	**50.7**	**20:24**	**23**	**7**	**16**	**23**	**18**	**2**	**1**	**1**	**21:45**
	Canada	Olympics	7	2	3	5	0	....	....	....	....	....	....	....	....	....	....	....	....	....	....	....	....	....	....
2010-11	**Philadelphia**	**NHL**	**81**	**23**	**43**	**66**	**62**	**5**	**3**	**4**	**184**	**12.5**	**11**	**1216**	**49.8**	**18:53**	**11**	**1**	**6**	**7**	**15**	**1**	**0**	**0**	**19:19**
	NHL Totals		**453**	**133**	**216**	**349**	**397**	**36**	**23**	**21**	**1169**	**11.4**		**7522**	**49.2**	**19:20**	**63**	**16**	**34**	**50**	**49**	**5**	**3**	**1**	**20:38**

Memorial Cup All-Star Team (2003) • OHL Second All-Star Team (2005) • Canadian Major Junior Second All-Star Team (2005)

Played in NHL All-Star Game (2008)

Traded to **Los Angeles** by **Philadelphia** with Rob Bordson for Brayden Schenn, Wayne Simmonds and Los Angeles' 2nd round choice in 2012 Entry Draft, June 23, 2011.

RICHARDSON, Brad

(RIH-chuhrd-suhn, BRAD) **L.A.**

Center. Shoots left. 5'11", 192 lbs. Born, Belleville, Ont., February 4, 1985. Colorado's 4th choice, 163rd overall, in 2003 Entry Draft.

Season	Club	League	GP	G	A	Pts	PIM	PP	SH	GW	S	%	+/-	TF	F%	Min	GP	G	A	Pts	PIM	PP	SH	GW	Min
2001-02	Owen Sound	OHL	58	12	21	33	20	....	....	....	....	....	....	....	....	....	....	....	....	....	....	....	....	....	....
2002-03	Owen Sound	OHL	67	27	40	67	54	....	....	....	....	....	....	....	....	....	4	1	1	2	10	....	....	....	....
2003-04	Owen Sound	OHL	15	7	9	16	4	....	....	....	....	....	....	....	....	....	....	....	....	....	....	....	....	....	....
2004-05	Owen Sound	OHL	68	41	56	97	60	....	....	....	....	....	....	....	....	....	8	6	4	10	8	....	....	....	....
2005-06	**Colorado**	**NHL**	**41**	**3**	**10**	**13**	**12**	**1**	**0**	**0**	**51**	**5.9**	**0**	**305**	**41.0**	**10:44**	**9**	**1**	**0**	**1**	**6**	**0**	**0**	**0**	**11:41**
	Lowell	AHL	29	4	13	17	20	....	....	....	....	....	....	....	....	....	....	....	....	....	....	....	....	....	....
2006-07	**Colorado**	**NHL**	**73**	**14**	**8**	**22**	**28**	**0**	**3**	**3**	**129**	**10.9**	**4**	**358**	**40.8**	**13:10**	....	....	....	....	....	....	....	....	....
	Albany River Rats	AHL	3	0	1	1	2	....	....	....	....	....	....	....	....	....	....	....	....	....	....	....	....	....	....
2007-08	**Colorado**	**NHL**	**22**	**2**	**3**	**5**	**8**	**0**	**0**	**0**	**32**	**6.3**	**–3**	**60**	**43.3**	**13:29**	....	....	....	....	....	....	....	....	....
	Lake Erie	AHL	38	14	26	40	18	....	....	....	....	....	....	....	....	....	....	....	....	....	....	....	....	....	....
2008-09	**Los Angeles**	**NHL**	**31**	**0**	**5**	**5**	**11**	**0**	**0**	**0**	**37**	**0.0**	**–6**	**95**	**54.7**	**10:48**	....	....	....	....	....	....	....	....	....
	Manchester	AHL	3	1	2	3	0	....	....	....	....	....	....	....	....	....	....	....	....	....	....	....	....	....	....
2009-10	**Los Angeles**	**NHL**	**81**	**11**	**16**	**27**	**37**	**0**	**1**	**4**	**148**	**7.4**	**1**	**391**	**48.1**	**12:51**	**6**	**1**	**1**	**2**	**2**	**0**	**0**	**1**	**14:41**
2010-11	**Los Angeles**	**NHL**	**68**	**7**	**12**	**19**	**47**	**0**	**1**	**1**	**103**	**6.8**	**–13**	**181**	**50.8**	**11:46**	**6**	**2**	**3**	**5**	**2**	**0**	**0**	**0**	**15:37**
	NHL Totals		**316**	**37**	**54**	**91**	**143**	**1**	**5**	**8**	**500**	**7.4**		**1390**	**45.3**	**12:15**	**21**	**4**	**4**	**8**	**10**	**0**	**0**	**1**	**13:40**

Traded to **Los Angeles** by **Colorado** for Detroit's 2nd round choice (previously acquired, Colorado selected Peter Delmas) in 2008 Entry Draft, June 21, 2008.

RICHMOND, Danny

(RIHCH-muhnd, DA-nee) **WSH**

Defense. Shoots left. 6', 192 lbs. Born, Chicago, IL, August 1, 1984. Carolina's 2nd choice, 31st overall, in 2003 Entry Draft.

Season	Club	League	GP	G	A	Pts	PIM	PP	SH	GW	S	%	+/-	TF	F%	Min	GP	G	A	Pts	PIM	PP	SH	GW	Min
2000-01	Team Illinois	MWEHL	79	25	40	65	....	....	....	....	....	....	....	....	....	....	....	....	....	....	....	....	....	....	....
2001-02	Chicago Steel	USHL	56	8	45	53	129	....	....	....	....	....	....	....	....	....	4	0	4	4	20	....	....	....	....
2002-03	U. of Michigan	CCHA	43	3	19	22	48	....	....	....	....	....	....	....	....	....	....	....	....	....	....	....	....	....	....
2003-04	London Knights	OHL	59	13	22	35	92	....	....	....	....	....	....	....	....	....	15	5	6	11	10	....	....	....	....
2004-05	Lowell	AHL	63	4	9	13	139	....	....	....	....	....	....	....	....	....	6	0	2	2	8	....	....	....	....
2005-06	**Carolina**	**NHL**	**10**	**0**	**1**	**1**	**7**	**0**	**0**	**0**	**7**	**0.0**	**–3**	**0**	**0.0**	**9:00**	....	....	....	....	....	....	....	....	....
	Lowell	AHL	32	4	11	15	60	....	....	....	....	....	....	....	....	....	....	....	....	....	....	....	....	....	....
	Chicago	**NHL**	**10**	**0**	**0**	**0**	**18**	**0**	**0**	**0**	**6**	**0.0**	**–3**	**0**	**0.0**	**13:36**	....	....	....	....	....	....	....	....	....
	Norfolk Admirals	AHL	31	4	8	12	42	....	....	....	....	....	....	....	....	....	3	0	1	1	2	....	....	....	....
2006-07	**Chicago**	**NHL**	**22**	**0**	**2**	**2**	**48**	**0**	**0**	**0**	**13**	**0.0**	**–1**	**0**	**0.0**	**12:20**	....	....	....	....	....	....	....	....	....
	Norfolk Admirals	AHL	57	10	24	34	144	....	....	....	....	....	....	....	....	....	6	0	0	0	8	....	....	....	....
2007-08	**Chicago**	**NHL**	**7**	**0**	**0**	**0**	**2**	**0**	**0**	**0**	**2**	**0.0**	**–5**	**0**	**0.0**	**9:24**	....	....	....	....	....	....	....	....	....
	Rockford IceHogs	AHL	40	2	12	14	156	....	....	....	....	....	....	....	....	....	....	....	....	....	....	....	....	....	....
2008-09	Wilkes-Barre	AHL	55	3	14	17	108	....	....	....	....	....	....	....	....	....	....	....	....	....	....	....	....	....	....
	Peoria Rivermen	AHL	18	1	4	5	21	....	....	....	....	....	....	....	....	....	7	0	4	4	2	....	....	....	....
2009-10	Peoria Rivermen	AHL	54	1	15	16	135	....	....	....	....	....	....	....	....	....	....	....	....	....	....	....	....	....	....
	Rockford IceHogs	AHL	15	0	6	6	31	....	....	....	....	....	....	....	....	....	4	0	1	1	5	....	....	....	....
2010-11	Toronto Marlies	AHL	68	3	20	23	121	....	....	....	....	....	....	....	....	....	....	....	....	....	....	....	....	....	....
	NHL Totals		**49**	**0**	**3**	**3**	**75**	**0**	**0**	**0**	**28**	**0.0**		**0**	**0.0**	**11:29**	....	....	....	....	....	....	....	....	....

USHL All-Rookie Team (2002) • USHL First All-Star Team (2002) • USHL Rookie of the Year (2002) • CCHA All-Rookie Team (2003)

• Left **University of Michigan** (CCHA) and signed with **London** (OHL), June 6, 2003. Traded to **Chicago** by **Carolina** with Columbus' 4th round choice (previously acquired, later traded to Toronto – Toronto selected James Reimer) in 2006 Entry Draft for Anton Babchuk and Chicago's 4th round choice (later traded to St. Louis – St. Louis selected Cade Fairchild) in 2007 Entry Draft, January 20, 2006. Traded to **Pittsburgh** by **Chicago** for Tim Brent, July 17, 2008. Traded to **St. Louis** by **Pittsburgh** for Andy Wozniewski, March 4, 2009. Traded to **Chicago** by **St. Louis** with Hannu Toivonen for Joe Fallon and Daryl Boyle, March 1, 2010. Signed as a free agent by **Toronto**, July 15, 2010. Signed as a free agent by **Washington**, July 4, 2011.

RINALDO, Zac

(rih-NAL-doh, ZAK) **PHI**

Center. Shoots left. 5'11", 169 lbs. Born, Mississauga, Ont., June 15, 1990. Philadelphia's 4th choice, 178th overall, in 2008 Entry Draft.

Season	Club	League	GP	G	A	Pts	PIM	PP	SH	GW	S	%	+/-	TF	F%	Min	GP	G	A	Pts	PIM	PP	SH	GW	Min
2006-07	Hamilton	OPJHL	44	16	16	32	193	....	....	....	....	....	....	....	....	....	16	4	4	8	48	....	....	....	....
	St. Michael's	OHL	6	0	0	0	2	....	....	....	....	....	....	....	....	....	....	....	....	....	....	....	....	....	....
2007-08	St. Michael's	OHL	63	7	7	14	191	....	....	....	....	....	....	....	....	....	4	0	0	0	9	....	....	....	....
2008-09	St. Michael's	OHL	34	6	7	13	*112	....	....	....	....	....	....	....	....	....	....	....	....	....	....	....	....	....	....
	London Knights	OHL	22	4	13	17	*89	....	....	....	....	....	....	....	....	....	8	1	1	2	26	....	....	....	....
2009-10	London Knights	OHL	34	8	7	15	*148	....	....	....	....	....	....	....	....	....	....	....	....	....	....	....	....	....	....
	Barrie Colts	OHL	26	2	8	10	*107	....	....	....	....	....	....	....	....	....	4	2	0	2	11	....	....	....	....
2010-11	Adirondack	AHL	60	3	6	9	331	....	....	....	....	....	....	....	....	....	....	....	....	....	....	....	....	....	....
	Philadelphia	**NHL**	....	....	....	....	....	....	....	....	....	....	....	....	....	....	**2**	**0**	**0**	**0**	**12**	**0**	**0**	**0**	**2:53**
	NHL Totals		....	....	....	....	....	....	....	....	....	....		....	....	....	**2**	**0**	**0**	**0**	**12**	**0**	**0**	**0**	**2:53**

RISSMILLER, Patrick

(RIGHZ-mih-luhr, PAT-rihk) **COL**

Left wing. Shoots left. 6'4", 225 lbs. Born, Belmont, MA, October 26, 1978.

Season	Club	League	GP	G	A	Pts	PIM	PP	SH	GW	S	%	+/-	TF	F%	Min	GP	G	A	Pts	PIM	PP	SH	GW	Min
1997-98	The Hill School	High-PA	STATISTICS NOT AVAILABLE																						
1998-99	Holy Cross	MAAC	34	13	28	41	23	....	....	....	....	....	....	....	....	....	....	....	....	....	....	....	....	....	....
99-2000	Holy Cross	MAAC	35	10	17	27	22	....	....	....	....	....	....	....	....	....	....	....	....	....	....	....	....	....	....
2000-01	Holy Cross	MAAC	29	14	15	29	40	....	....	....	....	....	....	....	....	....	....	....	....	....	....	....	....	....	....
2001-02	Holy Cross	MAAC	33	16	*30	*46	31	....	....	....	....	....	....	....	....	....	....	....	....	....	....	....	....	....	....
2002-03	Cleveland Barons	AHL	72	14	26	40	24	....	....	....	....	....	....	....	....	....	....	....	....	....	....	....	....	....	....
	Cincinnati	ECHL	2	2	2	4	0	....	....	....	....	....	....	....	....	....	....	....	....	....	....	....	....	....	....
2003-04	**San Jose**	**NHL**	**4**	**0**	**0**	**0**	**0**	**0**	**0**	**0**	**2**	**0.0**	**0**	**26**	**53.9**	**7:07**	....	....	....	....	....	....	....	....	....
	Cleveland Barons	AHL	75	14	31	45	66	....	....	....	....	....	....	....	....	....	9	0	1	1	8	....	....	....	....

			Regular Season														Playoffs								
Season	Club	League	GP	G	A	Pts	PIM	PP	SH	GW	S	%	+/-	TF	F%	Min	GP	G	A	Pts	PIM	PP	SH	GW	Min
2004-05	Cleveland Barons	AHL	69	21	23	44	50	....	....	....	....	....	....	....	....	....	....	....	....	....	....	....	....	....	....
2005-06	**San Jose**	**NHL**	18	3	3	6	8	1	0	1	26	11.5	1	3	0.0	9:22	11	2	1	3	6	0	0	0	8:06
	Cleveland Barons	AHL	68	15	37	52	30	....	....	....	....	....	....	....	....	....	....	....	....	....	....	....	....	....	....
2006-07	**San Jose**	**NHL**	79	7	15	22	22	1	0	0	100	7.0	1	25	36.0	12:10	11	1	3	4	0	0	0	1	12:40
2007-08	**San Jose**	**NHL**	79	8	9	17	30	0	0	2	119	6.7	–8	214	50.9	13:10	8	0	0	0	4	0	0	0	11:25
2008-09	**NY Rangers**	**NHL**	2	0	0	0	0	0	0	0	2	0.0	–2	0	0.0	9:13	....	....	....	....	....	....	....	....	....
	Hartford	AHL	64	14	40	54	24	....	....	....	....	....	....	....	....	....	6	0	1	1	6	....	....	....	....
2009-10	Hartford	AHL	6	0	2	2	8	....	....	....	....	....	....	....	....	....	....	....	....	....	....	....	....	....	....
	Grand Rapids	AHL	63	20	25	45	18	....	....	....	....	....	....	....	....	....	....	....	....	....	....	....	....	....	....
2010-11	**Atlanta**	**NHL**	1	0	0	0	0	0	0	0	2	0.0	–1	3	33.3	13:07	....	....	....	....	....	....	....	....	....
	Chicago Wolves	AHL	6	1	0	1	6	....	....	....	....	....	....	....	....	....	....	....	....	....	....	....	....	....	....
	Lake Erie	AHL	43	11	19	30	10	....	....	....	....	....	....	....	....	....	....	....	....	....	....	....	....	....	....
	Florida	**NHL**	9	0	1	1	0	0	0	0	12	0.0	0	1	100.0	10:04	....	....	....	....	....	....	....	....	....
	Rochester	AHL	8	2	8	10	6	....	....	....	....	....	....	....	....	....	....	....	....	....	....	....	....	....	....
	NHL Totals		**192**	**18**	**28**	**46**	**60**	**2**	**0**	**3**	**263**	**6.8**		**272**	**49.3**	**12:05**	**30**	**3**	**4**	**7**	**10**	**0**	**0**	**1**	**10:40**

MAAC All-Rookie Team (1999) • MAAC First All-Star Team (2002) • MAAC Offensive Player of the Year (2002)

Signed as a free agent by **Cleveland** (AHL), September 23, 2002. Signed as a free agent by **San Jose**, June 30, 2003. Signed as a free agent by **NY Rangers**, July 1, 2008. Traded to **Atlanta** by **NY Rangers** with Donald Brashear for Todd White, August 2, 2010. • Reassigned to **Lake Erie** (AHL) by **Atlanta**, November 19, 2010. Traded to **Florida** by **Atlanta** with Niclas Bergfors for Radek Dvorak and Carolina's 5th round choice (previously acquired, later traded to San Jose – San Jose selected Sean Kuraly) in 2011 Entry Draft, February 28, 2011. Signed as a free agent by **Colorado**. July 12, 2011.

RITOLA, Mattias

(RIH-toh-lah, mat-TEE-uhs) **T.B.**

Right wing. Shoots left. 6', 192 lbs. Born, Borlange, Sweden, March 14, 1987. Detroit's 4th choice, 103rd overall, in 2005 Entry Draft.

Season	Club	League	GP	G	A	Pts	PIM	PP	SH	GW	S	%	+/-	TF	F%	Min	GP	G	A	Pts	PIM	PP	SH	GW	Min
2003-04	V.Frolunda U18	Swe-U18	11	4	11	15	35	....	....	....	....	....	....	....	....	....	7	2	7	9	12	....	....	....	....
	V.Frolunda Jr.	Swe-Jr.	24	7	4	11	8	....	....	....	....	....	....	....	....	....	5	0	1	1	0	....	....	....	....
2004-05	Frolunda Jr.	Swe-Jr.	9	2	6	8	6	....	....	....	....	....	....	....	....	....	....	....	....	....	....	....	....	....	....
	Leksands IF U18	Swe-U18	STATISTICS NOT AVAILABLE																						
	Leksands IF Jr.	Swe-Jr.	18	8	10	18	14	....	....	....	....	....	....	....	....	....	5	1	1	2	2	....	....	....	....
2005-06	Leksands IF Jr.	Swe-Jr.	14	4	2	6	16	....	....	....	....	....	....	....	....	....	....	....	....	....	....	....	....	....	....
	Leksands IF	Sweden	30	0	3	3	10	....	....	....	....	....	....	....	....	....	....	....	....	....	....	....	....	....	....
	Leksands IF	Sweden-Q	8	0	0	0	4	....	....	....	....	....	....	....	....	....	....	....	....	....	....	....	....	....	....
2006-07	Leksands IF Jr.	Swe-Jr.	12	5	7	12	16	....	....	....	....	....	....	....	....	....	....	....	....	....	....	....	....	....	....
	Leksands IF	Sweden-2	23	1	4	5	4	....	....	....	....	....	....	....	....	....	....	....	....	....	....	....	....	....	....
	IFK Arboga IK	Sweden-2	3	1	0	1	2	....	....	....	....	....	....	....	....	....	....	....	....	....	....	....	....	....	....
	Borlange HF	Sweden-3	11	4	6	10	14	....	....	....	....	....	....	....	....	....	....	....	....	....	....	....	....	....	....
2007-08	**Detroit**	**NHL**	2	0	1	1	0	0	0	0	2	0.0	0	0	0.0	5:47	....	....	....	....	....	....	....	....	....
	Grand Rapids	AHL	72	7	15	22	62	....	....	....	....	....	....	....	....	....	....	....	....	....	....	....	....	....	....
2008-09	Grand Rapids	AHL	66	15	27	42	32	....	....	....	....	....	....	....	....	....	8	0	2	2	0	....	....	....	....
2009-10	**Detroit**	**NHL**	5	0	0	0	0	0	0	0	9	0.0	0	3	0.0	11:42	1	0	0	0	0	0	0	0	7:45
	Grand Rapids	AHL	73	19	23	42	50	....	....	....	....	....	....	....	....	....	....	....	....	....	....	....	....	....	....
2010-11	**Tampa Bay**	**NHL**	31	4	4	8	11	0	0	2	42	9.5	–5	44	43.2	10:04	1	0	0	0	0	0	0	0	2:23
	Norfolk Admirals	AHL	17	9	18	27	8	....	....	....	....	....	....	....	....	....	4	1	4	5	0	....	....	....	....
	NHL Totals		**38**	**4**	**5**	**9**	**11**	**0**	**0**	**2**	**53**	**7.5**		**47**	**40.4**	**10:03**	**2**	**0**	**0**	**0**	**0**	**0**	**0**	**0**	**5:04**

Claimed on waivers by **Tampa Bay** from **Detroit**, October 5, 2010.

RIVET, Craig

(rih-VAY, KRAYG)

Defense. Shoots right. 6'2", 207 lbs. Born, North Bay, Ont., September 13, 1974. Montreal's 4th choice, 68th overall, in 1992 Entry Draft.

Season	Club	League	GP	G	A	Pts	PIM	PP	SH	GW	S	%	+/-	TF	F%	Min	GP	G	A	Pts	PIM	PP	SH	GW	Min
1990-91	Barrie Colts	ON-Jr.B	42	9	17	26	55	....	....	....	....	....	....	....	....	....	....	....	....	....	....	....	....	....	....
1991-92	Kingston	OHL	66	5	21	26	97	....	....	....	....	....	....	....	....	....	....	....	....	....	....	....	....	....	....
1992-93	Kingston	OHL	64	19	55	74	117	....	....	....	....	....	....	....	....	....	16	5	7	12	39	....	....	....	....
1993-94	Kingston	OHL	61	12	52	64	100	....	....	....	....	....	....	....	....	....	6	0	3	3	6	....	....	....	....
	Fredericton	AHL	4	0	2	2	2	....	....	....	....	....	....	....	....	....	....	....	....	....	....	....	....	....	....
1994-95	Fredericton	AHL	78	5	27	32	126	....	....	....	....	....	....	....	....	....	12	0	4	4	17	....	....	....	....
	Montreal	**NHL**	5	0	1	1	5	0	0	0	2	0.0	2	....	....	....	....	....	....	....	....	....	....	....	....
1995-96	**Montreal**	**NHL**	19	1	4	5	54	0	0	0	9	11.1	4	....	....	....	....	....	....	....	....	....	....	....	....
	Fredericton	AHL	49	5	18	23	189	....	....	....	....	....	....	....	....	....	6	0	0	0	12	....	....	....	....
1996-97	**Montreal**	**NHL**	35	0	4	4	54	0	0	0	24	0.0	7	....	....	....	5	0	1	1	14	0	0	0	....
	Fredericton	AHL	23	3	12	15	99	....	....	....	....	....	....	....	....	....	....	....	....	....	....	....	....	....	....
1997-98	**Montreal**	**NHL**	61	0	2	2	93	0	0	0	26	0.0	–3	....	....	....	5	0	0	0	2	0	0	0	....
1998-99	**Montreal**	**NHL**	66	2	8	10	66	0	0	0	39	5.1	–3	0	0.0	14:20	....	....	....	....	....	....	....	....	....
99-2000	**Montreal**	**NHL**	61	3	14	17	76	0	0	1	71	4.2	11	0	0.0	19:03	....	....	....	....	....	....	....	....	....
2000-01	**Montreal**	**NHL**	26	1	2	3	36	0	0	0	22	4.5	–8	0	0.0	19:04	....	....	....	....	....	....	....	....	....
2001-02	**Montreal**	**NHL**	82	8	17	25	76	0	0	0	90	8.9	1	1	0.0	19:00	12	0	3	3	4	0	0	0	21:26
2002-03	**Montreal**	**NHL**	82	7	15	22	71	3	0	2	118	5.9	1	0	0.0	22:00	....	....	....	....	....	....	....	....	....
2003-04	**Montreal**	**NHL**	80	4	8	12	98	2	0	1	96	4.2	–1	0	0.0	19:28	11	1	4	5	2	1	0	0	24:07
2004-05	TPS Turku	Finland	18	3	1	4	28	....	....	....	....	....	....	....	....	....	6	0	0	0	39	....	....	....	....
2005-06	**Montreal**	**NHL**	82	7	27	34	109	5	0	1	122	5.7	–5	2	0.0	22:27	6	0	2	2	2	0	0	0	24:09
2006-07	**Montreal**	**NHL**	54	6	10	16	57	2	0	0	58	10.3	–7	0	0.0	21:04	....	....	....	....	....	....	....	....	....
	San Jose	**NHL**	17	1	7	8	12	0	0	0	31	3.2	8	0	0.0	23:31	11	2	3	5	18	1	0	0	25:18
2007-08	**San Jose**	**NHL**	74	5	30	35	104	2	0	0	105	4.8	3	0	0.0	21:12	13	0	6	6	16	0	0	0	23:01
2008-09	**Buffalo**	**NHL**	64	2	22	24	125	1	0	0	80	2.5	4	0	0.0	20:14	....	....	....	....	....	....	....	....	....
2009-10	**Buffalo**	**NHL**	78	1	14	15	100	0	0	0	63	1.6	–6	0	0.0	18:13	6	1	0	1	11	0	0	1	14:35
2010-11	**Buffalo**	**NHL**	23	1	2	3	12	0	0	0	20	5.0	–5	0	0.0	13:02	....	....	....	....	....	....	....	....	....
	Columbus	**NHL**	14	1	0	1	23	0	0	0	13	7.7	–7	0	0.0	17:22	....	....	....	....	....	....	....	....	....
	NHL Totals		**923**	**50**	**187**	**237**	**1171**	**15**	**0**	**5**	**989**	**5.1**		**3**	**0.0**	**19:35**	**69**	**4**	**19**	**23**	**69**	**2**	**0**	**1**	**22:35**

• Missed majority of 2000-01 due to shoulder injury vs. Vancouver, October 30, 2000. Signed as a free agent by **Turku** (Finland), January 11, 2005. Traded to **San Jose** by **Montreal** with Montreal's 5th round choice (Julien Demers) in 2008 Entry Draft for Josh Gorges and San Jose's 1st round choice (Max Pacioretty) in 2007 Entry Draft, February 25, 2007. Traded to **Buffalo** by **San Jose** with San Jose's 7th round choice (Riley Boychuk) in 2010 Entry Draft for Buffalo's 2nd round choices in 2009 (William Wrenn) and 2010 (later traded to Carolina - Carolina selected Mark Alt) Entry Drafts, July 4, 2008. Claimed on waivers by **Columbus** from **Buffalo**, February 26, 2011. • Missed majority of 2010-11 as a healthy reserve.

ROBIDAS, Stephane

(ROH-bih-dah, STEH-fan) **DAL**

Defense. Shoots right. 5'11", 190 lbs. Born, Sherbrooke, Que., March 3, 1977. Montreal's 7th choice, 164th overall, in 1995 Entry Draft.

Season	Club	League	GP	G	A	Pts	PIM	PP	SH	GW	S	%	+/-	TF	F%	Min	GP	G	A	Pts	PIM	PP	SH	GW	Min
1992-93	Magog	QAAA	41	3	12	15	16	....	....	....	....	....	....	....	....	....	5	1	1	2	2	....	....	....	....
1993-94	Shawinigan	QMJHL	67	3	19	22	33	....	....	....	....	....	....	....	....	....	1	0	0	0	0	....	....	....	....
1994-95	Shawinigan	QMJHL	71	13	56	69	44	....	....	....	....	....	....	....	....	....	15	7	12	19	4	....	....	....	....
1995-96	Shawinigan	QMJHL	67	23	56	79	53	....	....	....	....	....	....	....	....	....	6	1	5	6	10	....	....	....	....
1996-97	Shawinigan	QMJHL	67	24	51	75	59	....	....	....	....	....	....	....	....	....	7	4	6	10	14	....	....	....	....
1997-98	Fredericton	AHL	79	10	21	31	50	....	....	....	....	....	....	....	....	....	4	0	2	2	0	....	....	....	....
1998-99	Fredericton	AHL	79	8	33	41	59	....	....	....	....	....	....	....	....	....	15	1	5	6	10	....	....	....	....
99-2000	**Montreal**	**NHL**	1	0	0	0	0	0	0	0	0	0.0	0	0	0.0	15:54	....	....	....	....	....	....	....	....	....
	Quebec Citadelles	AHL	76	14	31	45	36	....	....	....	....	....	....	....	....	....	3	0	1	1	0	....	....	....	....
2000-01	**Montreal**	**NHL**	65	6	6	12	14	1	0	0	77	7.8	0	1	100.0	20:44	....	....	....	....	....	....	....	....	....
2001-02	**Montreal**	**NHL**	56	1	10	11	14	1	0	0	68	1.5	–25	3	33.3	18:58	2	0	0	0	4	0	0	0	13:07
2002-03	**Dallas**	**NHL**	76	3	7	10	35	0	0	1	47	6.4	15	1	100.0	12:54	12	0	1	1	20	0	0	0	13:54
2003-04	**Dallas**	**NHL**	14	1	0	1	8	1	0	0	8	12.5	–2	1	100.0	12:57	....	....	....	....	....	....	....	....	....
	Chicago	**NHL**	45	2	10	12	33	0	1	1	55	3.6	6	0	0.0	20:56	....	....	....	....	....	....	....	....	....
2004-05	Frankfurt Lions	Germany	51	15	32	47	64	....	....	....	....	....	....	....	....	....	6	1	2	3	6	....	....	....	....
2005-06	**Dallas**	**NHL**	75	5	15	20	67	1	1	0	95	5.3	15	0	0.0	16:59	5	0	2	2	4	0	0	0	16:42
2006-07	**Dallas**	**NHL**	75	0	17	17	86	0	0	0	106	0.0	–1	0	0.0	18:04	7	0	1	1	2	0	0	0	19:02
2007-08	**Dallas**	**NHL**	82	9	17	26	85	7	0	2	153	5.9	0	0	0.0	20:39	18	3	8	11	12	3	0	0	25:31
2008-09	**Dallas**	**NHL**	72	3	23	26	76	1	0	0	158	1.9	10	1	100.0	24:32	....	....	....	....	....	....	....	....	....

Season	Club	League	Regular Season GP	G	A	Pts	PIM	PP	SH	GW	S	%	+/-	TF	F%	Min	Playoffs GP	G	A	Pts	PIM	PP	SH	GW	Min
2009-10	**Dallas**	**NHL**	**82**	**10**	**31**	**41**	**70**	**7**	**0**	**1**	**199**	**5.0**	**–10**	**0**	**0.0**	**24:29**	....	....	....	....	....	....	....	....	....
2010-11	**Dallas**	**NHL**	**81**	**5**	**25**	**30**	**67**	**1**	**0**	**1**	**106**	**4.7**	**–7**	**0**	**0.0**	**24:32**	....	....	....	....	....	....	....	....	....
	NHL Totals		**724**	**45**	**161**	**206**	**555**	**20**	**2**	**6**	**1072**	**4.2**		**7**	**71.4**	**20:11**	**44**	**3**	**12**	**15**	**42**	**3**	**0**	**0**	**19:45**

QMJHL First All-Star Team (1996, 1997)

Played in NHL All-Star Game (2009)

Claimed by **Atlanta** from **Montreal** in Waiver Draft, October 4, 2002. Traded to **Dallas** by **Atlanta** for future considerations, October 4, 2002. Traded to **Chicago** by **Dallas** with Dallas' 2nd round choice (Jakub Sindel) in 2004 Entry Draft for Jon Klemm and NY Rangers' 4th round choice (previously acquired, Dallas selected Fredrik Naslund) in 2004 Entry Draft, November 17, 2003. Signed as a free agent by **Frankfurt** (Germany), September 17, 2004. Signed as a free agent by **Dallas**, August 6, 2005.

ROBITAILLE, Louis

(ROH-buh-tigh, LOO-ee)

Left wing. Shoots left. 6'2", 215 lbs. Born, Montreal, Que., March 16, 1982.

Season	Club	League	GP	G	A	Pts	PIM	PP	SH	GW	S	%	+/-	TF	F%	Min	GP	G	A	Pts	PIM	PP	SH	GW	Min
99-2000	Montreal Rocket	QMJHL	71	3	21	24	266	....	....	....	....	....	....	....	....	....	5	1	1	2	18	....	....	....	....
2000-01	Montreal Rocket	QMJHL	69	2	10	12	269	....	....	....	....	....	....	....	....	....	....	....	....	....	....	....	....	....	....
2001-02	Montreal Rocket	QMJHL	71	3	28	31	294	....	....	....	....	....	....	....	....	....	7	3	0	3	41	....	....	....	....
2002-03	Montreal Rocket	QMJHL	60	7	23	30	191	....	....	....	....	....	....	....	....	....	7	0	10	10	12	....	....	....	....
2003-04	Portland Pirates	AHL	58	1	5	6	103	....	....	....	....	....	....	....	....	....	5	1	0	1	17	....	....	....	....
	Quad City	UHL	2	0	1	1	10	....	....	....	....	....	....	....	....	....	....	....	....	....	....	....	....	....	....
2004-05	Portland Pirates	AHL	59	2	3	5	186	....	....	....	....	....	....	....	....	....	....	....	....	....	....	....	....	....	....
2005-06	**Washington**	**NHL**	**2**	**0**	**0**	**0**	**5**	**0**	**0**	**0**	**0**	**0.0**	**–1**	**0**	**0.0**	**4:42**	....	....	....	....	....	....	....	....	....
	Hershey Bears	AHL	65	7	12	19	334	....	....	....	....	....	....	....	....	....	21	0	2	2	64	....	....	....	....
2006-07	Hershey Bears	AHL	67	6	8	14	254	....	....	....	....	....	....	....	....	....	13	0	1	1	30	....	....	....	....
2007-08	Hershey Bears	AHL	68	4	8	12	*350	....	....	....	....	....	....	....	....	....	5	0	0	0	30	....	....	....	....
2008-09	St-Hyacinthe	QNAHL	19	0	8	8	137	....	....	....	....	....	....	....	....	....	....	....	....	....	....	....	....	....	....
	SG Cortina	Italy	16	0	12	12	103	....	....	....	....	....	....	....	....	....	....	....	....	....	....	....	....	....	....
2009-10	Lowell Devils	AHL	73	2	11	13	286	....	....	....	....	....	....	....	....	....	5	0	0	0	22	....	....	....	....
2010-11	Albany Devils	AHL	50	2	6	8	246	....	....	....	....	....	....	....	....	....	....	....	....	....	....	....	....	....	....
	NHL Totals		**2**	**0**	**0**	**0**	**5**	**0**	**0**	**0**	**0**	**0.0**		**0**	**0.0**	**4:42**	....	....	....	....	....	....	....	....	....

Signed as a free agent by **Washington**, August 24, 2004. Signed as a free agent by **Lowell** (AHL), August 10, 2009.

RODNEY, Bryan

(ROHD-nee, BRIGH-uhn) **ANA**

Defense. Shoots right. 6', 204 lbs. Born, London, Ont., April 22, 1984.

Season	Club	League	GP	G	A	Pts	PIM	PP	SH	GW	S	%	+/-	TF	F%	Min	GP	G	A	Pts	PIM	PP	SH	GW	Min
2000-01	Ottawa 67's	OHL	65	0	15	15	26	....	....	....	....	....	....	....	....	....	20	1	4	5	20	....	....	....	....
2001-02	Ottawa 67's	OHL	30	3	8	11	14	....	....	....	....	....	....	....	....	....	....	....	....	....	....	....	....	....	....
	Kingston	OHL	18	2	8	10	8	....	....	....	....	....	....	....	....	....	1	0	0	0	0	....	....	....	....
2002-03	Kingston	OHL	67	8	52	60	60	....	....	....	....	....	....	....	....	....	....	....	....	....	....	....	....	....	....
2003-04	Kingston	OHL	67	11	65	76	68	....	....	....	....	....	....	....	....	....	5	1	4	5	8	....	....	....	....
2004-05	London Knights	OHL	64	23	39	62	48	....	....	....	....	....	....	....	....	....	12	5	10	15	20	....	....	....	....
2005-06	Hartford	AHL	8	1	2	3	0	....	....	....	....	....	....	....	....	....	....	....	....	....	....	....	....	....	....
	Charlotte	ECHL	59	4	21	25	47	....	....	....	....	....	....	....	....	....	3	0	1	1	0	....	....	....	....
2006-07	Charlotte	ECHL	31	2	19	21	14	....	....	....	....	....	....	....	....	....	....	....	....	....	....	....	....	....	....
	Columbia Inferno	ECHL	14	2	9	11	12	....	....	....	....	....	....	....	....	....	....	....	....	....	....	....	....	....	....
2007-08	Albany River Rats	AHL	42	4	11	15	22	....	....	....	....	....	....	....	....	....	7	3	3	6	2	....	....	....	....
	Columbia Inferno	ECHL	17	2	9	11	10	....	....	....	....	....	....	....	....	....	....	....	....	....	....	....	....	....	....
	Elmira Jackals	ECHL	6	5	5	10	2	....	....	....	....	....	....	....	....	....	....	....	....	....	....	....	....	....	....
2008-09	**Carolina**	**NHL**	**8**	**0**	**2**	**2**	**2**	**0**	**0**	**0**	**3**	**0.0**	**–3**	**0**	**0.0**	**12:38**	....	....	....	....	....	....	....	....	....
	Albany River Rats	AHL	58	3	33	36	28	....	....	....	....	....	....	....	....	....	....	....	....	....	....	....	....	....	....
2009-10	**Carolina**	**NHL**	**22**	**1**	**10**	**11**	**8**	**0**	**0**	**0**	**24**	**4.2**	**–4**	**0**	**0.0**	**16:44**	....	....	....	....	....	....	....	....	....
	Albany River Rats	AHL	54	7	28	35	42	....	....	....	....	....	....	....	....	....	8	0	4	4	8	....	....	....	....
2010-11	**Carolina**	**NHL**	**3**	**0**	**0**	**0**	**2**	**0**	**0**	**0**	**3**	**0.0**	**0**	**0**	**0.0**	**8:44**	....	....	....	....	....	....	....	....	....
	Charlotte	AHL	77	9	38	47	38	....	....	....	....	....	....	....	....	....	16	0	4	4	12	....	....	....	....
	NHL Totals		**33**	**1**	**12**	**13**	**12**	**0**	**0**	**0**	**30**	**3.3**		**0**	**0.0**	**15:01**	....	....	....	....	....	....	....	....	....

Signed as a free agent by **Charlotte** (ECHL), October 21, 2005. Signed as a free agent by **Albany** (AHL), December 16, 2007. Signed as a free agent by **Carolina**, May 12, 2008. Signed as a free agent by **Anaheim**, July 5, 2011.

ROLSTON, Brian

(ROHL-stuhn, BRIGH-uhn) **NYI**

Center. Shoots left. 6'2", 215 lbs. Born, Flint, MI, February 21, 1973. New Jersey's 2nd choice, 11th overall, in 1991 Entry Draft.

Season	Club	League	GP	G	A	Pts	PIM	PP	SH	GW	S	%	+/-	TF	F%	Min	GP	G	A	Pts	PIM	PP	SH	GW	Min
1989-90	Det. Compuware	NAHL	40	36	37	73	57	....	....	....	....	....	....	....	....	....	....	....	....	....	....	....	....	....	....
1990-91	Det. Compuware	NAHL	36	49	46	95	14	....	....	....	....	....	....	....	....	....	....	....	....	....	....	....	....	....	....
1991-92	Lake Superior	CCHA	37	14	23	37	14	....	....	....	....	....	....	....	....	....	....	....	....	....	....	....	....	....	....
1992-93	Lake Superior	CCHA	39	33	31	64	20	....	....	....	....	....	....	....	....	....	....	....	....	....	....	....	....	....	....
1993-94	United States	Nat-Tm	41	20	28	48	36	....	....	....	....	....	....	....	....	....	....	....	....	....	....	....	....	....	....
	United States	Olympics	8	7	0	7	8	....	....	....	....	....	....	....	....	....	....	....	....	....	....	....	....	....	....
	Albany River Rats	AHL	17	5	5	10	8	....	....	....	....	....	....	....	....	....	5	1	2	3	0	....	....	....	....
1994-95	Albany River Rats	AHL	18	9	11	20	10	....	....	....	....	....	....	....	....	....	....	....	....	....	....	....	....	....	....
	♦ New Jersey	**NHL**	**40**	**7**	**11**	**18**	**17**	**2**	**0**	**3**	**92**	**7.6**	**5**	....	....	....	**6**	**2**	**1**	**3**	**4**	**1**	**0**	**0**	....
1995-96	**New Jersey**	**NHL**	**58**	**13**	**11**	**24**	**8**	**3**	**1**	**4**	**139**	**9.4**	**9**	....	....	....	....	....	....	....	....	....	....	....	....
1996-97	**New Jersey**	**NHL**	**81**	**18**	**27**	**45**	**20**	**2**	**2**	**3**	**237**	**7.6**	**6**	....	....	....	**10**	**4**	**1**	**5**	**6**	**1**	**2**	**0**	....
1997-98	**New Jersey**	**NHL**	**76**	**16**	**14**	**30**	**16**	**0**	**2**	**1**	**185**	**8.6**	**7**	....	....	....	**6**	**1**	**0**	**1**	**2**	**0**	**1**	**0**	....
1998-99	**New Jersey**	**NHL**	**82**	**24**	**33**	**57**	**14**	**5**	***5**	**3**	**210**	**11.4**	**11**	**51**	**45.1**	**18:49**	**7**	**1**	**0**	**1**	**2**	**0**	**1**	**0**	**17:36**
99-2000	**New Jersey**	**NHL**	**11**	**3**	**1**	**4**	**0**	**1**	**0**	**2**	**33**	**9.1**	**–2**	**37**	**37.8**	**19:09**	....	....	....	....	....	....	....	....	....
	Colorado	**NHL**	**50**	**8**	**10**	**18**	**12**	**1**	**0**	**3**	**107**	**7.5**	**–6**	**65**	**41.5**	**16:18**	....	....	....	....	....	....	....	....	....
	Boston	**NHL**	**16**	**5**	**4**	**9**	**6**	**3**	**0**	**1**	**66**	**7.6**	**–4**	**265**	**41.1**	**22:13**	....	....	....	....	....	....	....	....	....
2000-01	**Boston**	**NHL**	**77**	**19**	**39**	**58**	**28**	**5**	**0**	**4**	**286**	**6.6**	**6**	**666**	**45.7**	**19:19**	....	....	....	....	....	....	....	....	....
2001-02	**Boston**	**NHL**	**82**	**31**	**31**	**62**	**30**	**6**	***9**	**7**	**331**	**9.4**	**11**	**1289**	**46.6**	**20:24**	**6**	**4**	**1**	**5**	**0**	**1**	**1**	**0**	**20:37**
	United States	Olympics	6	0	3	3	0	....	....	....	....	....	....	....	....	....	....	....	....	....	....	....	....	....	....
2002-03	**Boston**	**NHL**	**81**	**27**	**32**	**59**	**32**	**6**	**5**	**5**	**281**	**9.6**	**1**	**1148**	**47.6**	**20:28**	**5**	**0**	**2**	**2**	**0**	**0**	**0**	**0**	**18:39**
2003-04	**Boston**	**NHL**	**82**	**19**	**29**	**48**	**40**	**3**	**2**	**3**	**257**	**7.4**	**9**	**1205**	**50.7**	**19:38**	**7**	**1**	**0**	**1**	**8**	**0**	**0**	**0**	**16:33**
2004-05			DID NOT PLAY																						
2005-06	**Minnesota**	**NHL**	**82**	**34**	**45**	**79**	**50**	**15**	**5**	**7**	**293**	**11.6**	**14**	**403**	**46.4**	**20:21**	....	....	....	....	....	....	....	....	....
	United States	Olympics	6	3	1	4	4	....	....	....	....	....	....	....	....	....	....	....	....	....	....	....	....	....	....
2006-07	**Minnesota**	**NHL**	**78**	**31**	**33**	**64**	**46**	**13**	**1**	**6**	**305**	**10.2**	**6**	**295**	**45.4**	**21:16**	**5**	**1**	**1**	**2**	**4**	**0**	**0**	**0**	**20:25**
2007-08	**Minnesota**	**NHL**	**81**	**31**	**28**	**59**	**53**	**11**	**1**	**8**	**289**	**10.7**	**–1**	**165**	**40.6**	**20:04**	**6**	**2**	**4**	**6**	**8**	**0**	**1**	**0**	**22:27**
2008-09	**New Jersey**	**NHL**	**64**	**15**	**17**	**32**	**30**	**8**	**0**	**3**	**174**	**8.6**	**2**	**180**	**46.1**	**15:06**	**7**	**1**	**1**	**2**	**4**	**1**	**0**	**0**	**14:09**
2009-10	**New Jersey**	**NHL**	**80**	**20**	**17**	**37**	**22**	**7**	**0**	**3**	**232**	**8.6**	**2**	**63**	**50.8**	**16:56**	**5**	**2**	**1**	**3**	**0**	**2**	**0**	**0**	**14:48**
2010-11	**New Jersey**	**NHL**	**65**	**14**	**20**	**34**	**34**	**6**	**0**	**4**	**168**	**8.3**	**–6**	**135**	**38.5**	**17:36**	....	....	....	....	....	....	....	....	....
	NHL Totals		**1186**	**335**	**402**	**737**	**458**	**97**	**33**	**70**	**3685**	**9.1**		**5967**	**46.7**	**19:05**	**70**	**19**	**12**	**31**	**38**	**6**	**6**	**0**	**18:03**

NCAA Championship All-Tournament Team (1992, 1993) • CCHA First All-Star Team (1993) • NCAA West Second All-American Team (1993)

Played in NHL All-Star Game (2007)

Traded to **Colorado** by **New Jersey** with New Jersey's 1st round choice (later traded to Boston – Boston selected Martin Samuelsson) in 2000 Entry Draft for Claude Lemieux and Colorado's 1st (David Hale) and 2nd (Matt DeMarchi) round choices in 2000 Entry Draft, November 3, 1999. Traded to **Boston** by **Colorado** with Martin Grenier, Samuel Pahlsson and New Jersey's 1st round choice (previously acquired, Boston selected Martin Samuelsson) in 2000 Entry Draft for Raymond Bourque and Dave Andreychuk, March 6, 2000. Signed as a free agent by **Minnesota**, July 8, 2004. Traded to **Tampa Bay** by **Minnesota** for Dallas' 4th round choice (previously acquired, later traded to Edmonton – Edmonton selected Kyle Bigos) in 2009 Entry Draft, June 29, 2008. Signed as a free agent by **New Jersey**, July 1, 2008. Traded to **NY Islanders** by **New Jersey** for Trent Hunter, July 28, 2011.

ROME, Aaron

(ROHM, AIR-uhn) **VAN**

Defense. Shoots left. 6'1", 218 lbs. Born, Nesbitt, Man., September 27, 1983. Los Angeles' 4th choice, 104th overall, in 2002 Entry Draft.

Season	Club	League	GP	G	A	Pts	PIM	PP	SH	GW	S	%	+/-	TF	F%	Min	GP	G	A	Pts	PIM	PP	SH	GW	Min
1998-99	Sask. Contacts	SMHL	STATISTICS NOT AVAILABLE																						
	Saskatoon Blades	WHL	1	0	0	0	0	....	....	....	....	....	....	....	....	....	....	....	....	....	....	....	....	....	....
99-2000	Saskatoon Blades	WHL	47	0	6	6	22	....	....	....	....	....	....	....	....	....	1	0	0	0	0	....	....	....	....
2000-01	Saskatoon Blades	WHL	3	0	0	0	2	....	....	....	....	....	....	....	....	....	....	....	....	....	....	....	....	....	....
	Kootenay Ice	WHL	53	2	8	10	43	....	....	....	....	....	....	....	....	....	11	1	3	4	6	....	....	....	....
2001-02	Kootenay Ice	WHL	33	4	13	17	55	....	....	....	....	....	....	....	....	....	....	....	....	....	....	....	....	....	....
	Swift Current	WHL	37	3	11	14	113	....	....	....	....	....	....	....	....	....	10	1	4	5	23	....	....	....	....
2002-03	Swift Current	WHL	61	12	44	56	201	....	....	....	....	....	....	....	....	....	4	1	0	1	20	....	....	....	....

			Regular Season														Playoffs								
Season	Club	League	GP	G	A	Pts	PIM	PP	SH	GW	S	%	+/-	TF	F%	Min	GP	G	A	Pts	PIM	PP	SH	GW	Min
2003-04	Swift Current	WHL	41	7	26	33	122	....	....	....	....	....	....	....	....	....	....	....	....	....	....	....	....	....	....
	Moose Jaw	WHL	28	3	16	19	88	....	....	....	....	....	....	....	....	....	8	0	6	6	17	....	....	....	....
2004-05	Cincinnati	AHL	75	2	14	16	130	....	....	....	....	....	....	....	....	....	12	3	3	6	33	....	....	....	....
2005-06	Portland Pirates	AHL	64	5	19	24	87	....	....	....	....	....	....	....	....	....	18	1	4	5	33	....	....	....	....
2006-07 ♦	**Anaheim**	**NHL**	**1**	**0**	**0**	**0**	**0**	**0**	**0**	**0**	**1**	**0.0**	**–1**	**0**	**0.0**	**14:31**	**1**	**0**	**0**	**0**	**0**	**0**	**0**	**0**	**11:01**
	Portland Pirates	AHL	76	8	17	25	139	....	....	....	....	....	....	....	....	....	....	....	....	....	....	....	....	....	....
2007-08	**Columbus**	**NHL**	**17**	**1**	**1**	**2**	**33**	**0**	**0**	**0**	**15**	**6.7**	**–4**	**0**	**0.0**	**18:11**	....	....	....	....	....	....	....	....	....
	Portland Pirates	AHL	14	2	3	5	31	....	....	....	....	....	....	....	....	....	....	....	....	....	....	....	....	....	....
	Syracuse Crunch	AHL	41	3	21	24	126	....	....	....	....	....	....	....	....	....	....	....	....	....	....	....	....	....	....
2008-09	**Columbus**	**NHL**	**8**	**0**	**1**	**1**	**0**	**0**	**0**	**0**	**7**	**0.0**	**1**	**0**	**0.0**	**15:28**	**1**	**0**	**1**	**1**	**0**	**0**	**0**	**0**	**15:24**
	Syracuse Crunch	AHL	48	7	21	28	153	....	....	....	....	....	....	....	....	....	....	....	....	....	....	....	....	....	....
2009-10	**Vancouver**	**NHL**	**49**	**0**	**4**	**4**	**24**	**0**	**0**	**0**	**49**	**0.0**	**–2**	**0**	**0.0**	**15:11**	**1**	**0**	**0**	**0**	**0**	**0**	**0**	**0**	**9:32**
	Manitoba Moose	AHL	7	6	1	7	15	....	....	....	....	....	....	....	....	....	....	....	....	....	....	....	....	....	....
2010-11	**Vancouver**	**NHL**	**56**	**1**	**4**	**5**	**53**	**0**	**0**	**0**	**50**	**2.0**	**1**	**0**	**0.0**	**17:25**	**14**	**1**	**0**	**1**	**37**	**0**	**0**	**0**	**13:01**
	NHL Totals		**131**	**2**	**10**	**12**	**110**	**0**	**0**	**0**	**122**	**1.6**		**0**	**0.0**	**16:32**	**17**	**1**	**1**	**2**	**37**	**0**	**0**	**0**	**12:51**

WHL East Second All-Star Team (2004)

Signed as a free agent by **Anaheim**, June 7, 2004. Traded to **Columbus** by **Anaheim** with Clay Wilson for Geoff Platt, November 15, 2007. Signed as a free agent by **Vancouver**, July 1, 2009.

ROSEHILL, Jay

(ROHZ-hihl, JAY) **TOR**

Left wing. Shoots left. 6'3", 215 lbs. Born, Olds, Alta., July 16, 1985. Tampa Bay's 6th choice, 227th overall, in 2003 Entry Draft.

Season	Club	League	GP	G	A	Pts	PIM	PP	SH	GW	S	%	+/-	TF	F%	Min	GP	G	A	Pts	PIM	PP	SH	GW	Min
2002-03	Olds Grizzlys	AJHL	59	1	4	5	219	....	....	....	....	....	....	....	....	....	....	....	....	....	....	....	....	....	....
2003-04	Olds Grizzlys	AJHL	42	4	12	16	172	....	....	....	....	....	....	....	....	....	14	2	2	4	....	....	....	....	....
2004-05	U. Minn-Duluth	WCHA	34	0	5	5	103	....	....	....	....	....	....	....	....	....	....	....	....	....	....	....	....	....	....
2005-06	Springfield	AHL	45	1	2	3	68	....	....	....	....	....	....	....	....	....	....	....	....	....	....	....	....	....	....
	Johnstown Chiefs	ECHL	5	0	0	0	13	....	....	....	....	....	....	....	....	....	5	0	0	0	4	....	....	....	....
2006-07	Springfield	AHL	64	0	6	6	85	....	....	....	....	....	....	....	....	....	....	....	....	....	....	....	....	....	....
	Johnstown Chiefs	ECHL	1	0	0	0	2	....	....	....	....	....	....	....	....	....	....	....	....	....	....	....	....	....	....
2007-08	Norfolk Admirals	AHL	66	3	4	7	194	....	....	....	....	....	....	....	....	....	....	....	....	....	....	....	....	....	....
	Mississippi	ECHL	2	0	0	0	6	....	....	....	....	....	....	....	....	....	....	....	....	....	....	....	....	....	....
2008-09	Norfolk Admirals	AHL	57	5	7	12	221	....	....	....	....	....	....	....	....	....	....	....	....	....	....	....	....	....	....
	Toronto Marlies	AHL	13	2	1	3	54	....	....	....	....	....	....	....	....	....	6	0	0	0	4	....	....	....	....
2009-10	**Toronto**	**NHL**	**15**	**1**	**1**	**2**	**67**	**0**	**0**	**0**	**6**	**16.7**	**–2**	**3**	**33.3**	**6:14**	....	....	....	....	....	....	....	....	....
	Toronto Marlies	AHL	46	1	2	3	172	....	....	....	....	....	....	....	....	....	....	....	....	....	....	....	....	....	....
2010-11	**Toronto**	**NHL**	**26**	**1**	**2**	**3**	**71**	**0**	**0**	**0**	**12**	**8.3**	**–6**	**0**	**0.0**	**5:12**	....	....	....	....	....	....	....	....	....
	Toronto Marlies	AHL	32	7	6	13	114	....	....	....	....	....	....	....	....	....	....	....	....	....	....	....	....	....	....
	NHL Totals		**41**	**2**	**3**	**5**	**138**	**0**	**0**	**0**	**18**	**11.1**		**3**	**33.3**	**5:35**	....	....	....	....	....	....	....	....	....

Signed as a free agent by **Toronto**, July 6 2009.

ROSS, Jared

(RAWS, JAIR-uhd)

Center. Shoots left. 5'10", 175 lbs. Born, Huntsville, AL, September 18, 1982.

Season	Club	League	GP	G	A	Pts	PIM	PP	SH	GW	S	%	+/-	TF	F%	Min	GP	G	A	Pts	PIM	PP	SH	GW	Min
2001-02	AL-Huntsville	CHA	37	11	17	28	8	....	....	....	....	....	....	....	....	....	....	....	....	....	....	....	....	....	....
2002-03	AL-Huntsville	CHA	35	21	20	41	30	....	....	....	....	....	....	....	....	....	....	....	....	....	....	....	....	....	....
2003-04	AL-Huntsville	CHA	31	19	31	50	46	....	....	....	....	....	....	....	....	....	....	....	....	....	....	....	....	....	....
2004-05	AL-Huntsville	CHA	30	22	18	40	53	....	....	....	....	....	....	....	....	....	....	....	....	....	....	....	....	....	....
	Motor City	UHL	12	3	5	8	2	....	....	....	....	....	....	....	....	....	....	....	....	....	....	....	....	....	....
2005-06	Chicago Wolves	AHL	62	10	27	37	37	....	....	....	....	....	....	....	....	....	....	....	....	....	....	....	....	....	....
	Gwinnett	ECHL	1	0	0	0	0	....	....	....	....	....	....	....	....	....	....	....	....	....	....	....	....	....	....
2006-07	Chicago Wolves	AHL	41	7	8	15	14	....	....	....	....	....	....	....	....	....	....	....	....	....	....	....	....	....	....
	Philadelphia	AHL	21	4	10	14	6	....	....	....	....	....	....	....	....	....	....	....	....	....	....	....	....	....	....
2007-08	Philadelphia	AHL	67	23	39	62	56	....	....	....	....	....	....	....	....	....	12	5	4	9	4	....	....	....	....
2008-09	**Philadelphia**	**NHL**	**10**	**0**	**0**	**0**	**2**	**0**	**0**	**0**	**12**	**0.0**	**–4**	**48**	**56.3**	**7:44**	**6**	**1**	**0**	**1**	**0**	**0**	**0**	**0**	**4:10**
	Philadelphia	AHL	64	29	40	69	26	....	....	....	....	....	....	....	....	....	....	....	....	....	....	....	....	....	....
2009-10	**Philadelphia**	**NHL**	**3**	**0**	**0**	**0**	**0**	**0**	**0**	**0**	**4**	**0.0**	**–1**	**11**	**54.6**	**7:39**	**3**	**0**	**0**	**0**	**0**	**0**	**0**	**0**	**5:37**
	Adirondack	AHL	73	12	34	46	40	....	....	....	....	....	....	....	....	....	....	....	....	....	....	....	....	....	....
2010-11	Chicago Wolves	AHL	66	15	40	55	38	....	....	....	....	....	....	....	....	....	....	....	....	....	....	....	....	....	....
	NHL Totals		**13**	**0**	**0**	**0**	**2**	**0**	**0**	**0**	**16**	**0.0**		**59**	**55.9**	**7:43**	**9**	**1**	**0**	**1**	**0**	**0**	**0**	**0**	**4:39**

Traded to **Philadelphia** (AHL) by **Chicago** (AHL) for the loan of Niko Dimitrakos, March 1, 2007. Signed as a free agent by **Philadelphia**, April 8, 2008. Signed as a free agent by **Atlanta**, July 7, 2010. • Transferred to **Winnipeg** after **Atlanta** franchise relocated, June 21, 2011.

ROY, Derek

(ROI, DAIR-ihk) **BUF**

Center. Shoots left. 5'9", 184 lbs. Born, Ottawa, Ont., May 4, 1983. Buffalo's 2nd choice, 32nd overall, in 2001 Entry Draft.

Season	Club	League	GP	G	A	Pts	PIM	PP	SH	GW	S	%	+/-	TF	F%	Min	GP	G	A	Pts	PIM	PP	SH	GW	Min
1998-99	Ontario East	Minor-ON	34	61	31	92	42	....	....	....	....	....	....	....	....	....	....	....	....	....	....	....	....	....	....
99-2000	Kitchener Rangers	OHL	66	34	53	87	44	....	....	....	....	....	....	....	....	....	5	4	1	5	6	....	....	....	....
2000-01	Kitchener Rangers	OHL	65	42	39	81	114	....	....	....	....	....	....	....	....	....	....	....	....	....	....	....	....	....	....
2001-02	Kitchener Rangers	OHL	62	43	46	89	92	....	....	....	....	....	....	....	....	....	4	1	2	3	2	....	....	....	....
2002-03	Kitchener Rangers	OHL	49	28	50	78	73	....	....	....	....	....	....	....	....	....	21	9	*23	32	14	....	....	....	....
2003-04	**Buffalo**	**NHL**	**49**	**9**	**10**	**19**	**12**	**1**	**0**	**4**	**71**	**12.7**	**–8**	**715**	**47.4**	**15:19**	....	....	....	....	....	....	....	....	....
	Rochester	AHL	26	10	16	26	20	....	....	....	....	....	....	....	....	....	16	6	8	14	18	....	....	....	....
2004-05	Rochester	AHL	67	16	45	61	60	....	....	....	....	....	....	....	....	....	9	6	5	11	6	....	....	....	....
2005-06	**Buffalo**	**NHL**	**70**	**18**	**28**	**46**	**57**	**5**	**1**	**1**	**151**	**11.9**	**1**	**807**	**48.0**	**17:02**	**18**	**5**	**10**	**15**	**16**	**1**	**1**	**0**	**17:03**
	Rochester	AHL	8	7	13	20	10	....	....	....	....	....	....	....	....	....	....	....	....	....	....	....	....	....	....
2006-07	**Buffalo**	**NHL**	**75**	**21**	**42**	**63**	**60**	**6**	**1**	**3**	**130**	**16.2**	**37**	**1129**	**48.5**	**18:28**	**16**	**2**	**5**	**7**	**14**	**0**	**0**	**0**	**18:03**
2007-08	**Buffalo**	**NHL**	**78**	**32**	**49**	**81**	**46**	**6**	**3**	**4**	**218**	**14.7**	**13**	**1393**	**51.2**	**20:58**	....	....	....	....	....	....	....	....	....
2008-09	**Buffalo**	**NHL**	**82**	**28**	**42**	**70**	**38**	**9**	**1**	**9**	**221**	**12.7**	**–5**	**1469**	**50.7**	**21:12**	....	....	....	....	....	....	....	....	....
2009-10	**Buffalo**	**NHL**	**80**	**26**	**43**	**69**	**48**	**10**	**1**	**6**	**215**	**12.1**	**9**	**1225**	**50.4**	**19:23**	**6**	**0**	**2**	**2**	**4**	**0**	**0**	**0**	**22:59**
2010-11	**Buffalo**	**NHL**	**35**	**10**	**25**	**35**	**16**	**2**	**0**	**1**	**89**	**11.2**	**–1**	**528**	**46.4**	**19:32**	**1**	**0**	**1**	**1**	**0**	**0**	**0**	**0**	**20:01**
	NHL Totals		**469**	**144**	**239**	**383**	**277**	**39**	**7**	**28**	**1095**	**13.2**		**7266**	**49.5**	**19:03**	**41**	**7**	**18**	**25**	**34**	**1**	**1**	**0**	**18:23**

OHL All-Rookie Team (2000) • OHL Rookie of the Year (2000) • CHL All-Rookie Team (2000) • CHL Plus/Minus Award (2000) • CHL Most Sportsmanlike Player (2000) • Memorial Cup All-Star Team (2003) • Stafford Smythe Memorial Trophy (Memorial Cup - MVP) (2003)

• Missed majority of 2010-11 due to leg injury vs. Florida, December 23, 2010.

ROY, Mathieu

(WAH, MA-tyew)

Defense. Shoots right. 6'2", 208 lbs. Born, St-Georges, Que., August 10, 1983. Edmonton's 10th choice, 215th overall, in 2003 Entry Draft.

Season	Club	League	GP	G	A	Pts	PIM	PP	SH	GW	S	%	+/-	TF	F%	Min	GP	G	A	Pts	PIM	PP	SH	GW	Min
1998-99	Levis	QAAA	11	4	1	5	16	....	....	....	....	....	....	....	....	....	....	....	....	....	....	....	....	....	....
99-2000	Levis	QAAA	24	3	4	7	88	....	....	....	....	....	....	....	....	....	6	1	1	2	22	....	....	....	....
	Val-d'Or Foreurs	QMJHL	48	1	4	5	66	....	....	....	....	....	....	....	....	....	....	....	....	....	....	....	....	....	....
2000-01	Val-d'Or Foreurs	QMJHL	30	0	7	7	60	....	....	....	....	....	....	....	....	....	17	0	0	0	4	....	....	....	....
2001-02	Val-d'Or Foreurs	QMJHL	53	7	26	33	103	....	....	....	....	....	....	....	....	....	7	0	2	2	19	....	....	....	....
2002-03	Val-d'Or Foreurs	QMJHL	52	11	21	32	164	....	....	....	....	....	....	....	....	....	7	1	0	1	8	....	....	....	....
2003-04	Toronto	AHL	30	0	2	2	46	....	....	....	....	....	....	....	....	....	....	....	....	....	....	....	....	....	....
	Columbus	ECHL	10	1	2	3	13	....	....	....	....	....	....	....	....	....	....	....	....	....	....	....	....	....	....
2004-05	Edmonton	AHL	51	3	22	25	68	....	....	....	....	....	....	....	....	....	....	....	....	....	....	....	....	....	....
2005-06	**Edmonton**	**NHL**	**1**	**0**	**0**	**0**	**0**	**0**	**0**	**0**	**0**	**0.0**	**–1**	**0**	**0.0**	**13:00**	....	....	....	....	....	....	....	....	....
	Hamilton	AHL	50	3	16	19	82	....	....	....	....	....	....	....	....	....	....	....	....	....	....	....	....	....	....
2006-07	**Edmonton**	**NHL**	**16**	**2**	**0**	**2**	**30**	**0**	**0**	**0**	**18**	**11.1**	**–7**	**0**	**0.0**	**14:06**	....	....	....	....	....	....	....	....	....
	Hamilton	AHL	31	6	12	18	40	....	....	....	....	....	....	....	....	....	....	....	....	....	....	....	....	....	....
2007-08	**Edmonton**	**NHL**	**13**	**0**	**1**	**1**	**27**	**0**	**0**	**0**	**8**	**0.0**	**0**	**0**	**0.0**	**10:23**	....	....	....	....	....	....	....	....	....
	Springfield	AHL	20	2	8	10	34	....	....	....	....	....	....	....	....	....	....	....	....	....	....	....	....	....	....
2008-09	Springfield	AHL	59	2	15	17	120	....	....	....	....	....	....	....	....	....	....	....	....	....	....	....	....	....	....
2009-10	**Columbus**	**NHL**	**31**	**0**	**10**	**10**	**17**	**0**	**0**	**0**	**32**	**0.0**	**–2**	**1**	**100.0**	**18:19**	....	....	....	....	....	....	....	....	....
	Syracuse Crunch	AHL	14	0	4	4	32	....	....	....	....	....	....	....	....	....	....	....	....	....	....	....	....	....	....
	Rochester	AHL	1	0	0	0	0	....	....	....	....	....	....	....	....	....	6	0	0	0	11	....	....	....	....

			Regular Season														Playoffs								
Season	Club	League	GP	G	A	Pts	PIM	PP	SH	GW	S	%	+/-	TF	F%	Min	GP	G	A	Pts	PIM	PP	SH	GW	Min
2010-11	Tampa Bay	NHL	4	0	0	0	2	0	0	0	1	0.0	–2	0	0.0	4:43	....	....	....	....	....	....	....	....	....
	Norfolk Admirals	AHL	45	4	18	22	68	....	....	....	....	....	....	....	....	....	6	0	1	1	4	....	....	....	....
	NHL Totals		65	2	11	13	76	0	0	0	59	3.4		1	100.0	14:47	....	....	....	....	....	....	....	....	....

• Missed majority of 2007-08 due to recurring shoulder injury and as a healthy reserve. Signed as a free agent by **Columbus**, July 14, 2009. Traded to **Florida** by **Columbus** for Matt Rust, March 3, 2010. Signed as a free agent by **Tampa Bay**, July 29, 2010.

ROZSIVAL, Michal

(roh-ZIH-vahl, MEE-khahl) **PHX**

Defense. Shoots right. 6'2", 212 lbs. Born, Vlasim, Czech., September 3, 1978. Pittsburgh's 5th choice, 105th overall, in 1996 Entry Draft.

Season	Club	League	GP	G	A	Pts	PIM	PP	SH	GW	S	%	+/-	TF	F%	Min	GP	G	A	Pts	PIM	PP	SH	GW	Min
1994-95	Jihlava Jr.	CzRep-Jr.	31	8	13	21	....	....	....	....	....	....	....	....	....	....	....	....	....	....	....	....	....	....	....
1995-96	HC Dukla Jihlava	CzRep	36	3	4	7	....	....	....	....	....	....	....	....	....	....	....	....	....	....	....	....	....	....	....
1996-97	Swift Current	WHL	63	8	31	39	69	....	....	....	....	....	....	....	....	....	10	0	6	6	15	....	....	....	....
1997-98	Swift Current	WHL	71	14	55	69	122	....	....	....	....	....	....	....	....	....	12	0	5	5	33	....	....	....	....
1998-99	Syracuse Crunch	AHL	49	3	22	25	72	....	....	....	....	....	....	....	....	....	....	....	....	....	....	....	....	....	....
99-2000	**Pittsburgh**	**NHL**	**75**	**4**	**17**	**21**	**48**	**1**	**0**	**1**	**73**	**5.5**	**11**	**1**	**0.0**	**19:01**	**2**	**0**	**0**	**0**	**4**	**0**	**0**	**0**	**30:56**
2000-01	**Pittsburgh**	**NHL**	**30**	**1**	**4**	**5**	**26**	**0**	**0**	**0**	**17**	**5.9**	**3**	**1**	**100.0**	**17:06**	....	....	....	....	....	....	....	....	....
	Wilkes-Barre	AHL	29	8	8	16	32	....	....	....	....	....	....	....	....	....	21	3	*19	22	23	....	....	....	....
2001-02	**Pittsburgh**	**NHL**	**79**	**9**	**20**	**29**	**47**	**4**	**0**	**4**	**89**	**10.1**	**–6**	**0**	**0.0**	**20:01**	....	....	....	....	....	....	....	....	....
2002-03	**Pittsburgh**	**NHL**	**53**	**4**	**6**	**10**	**40**	**1**	**0**	**0**	**61**	**6.6**	**–5**	**0**	**0.0**	**20:25**	....	....	....	....	....	....	....	....	....
2003-04	Wilkes-Barre	AHL	1	0	0	0	2	....	....	....	....	....	....	....	....	....	....	....	....	....	....	....	....	....	....
2004-05	HC Ocelari Trinec	CzRep	35	1	10	11	40	....	....	....	....	....	....	....	....	....	....	....	....	....	....	....	....	....	....
	Pardubice	CzRep	16	1	3	4	30	....	....	....	....	....	....	....	....	....	16	1	2	3	34	....	....	....	....
2005-06	**NY Rangers**	**NHL**	**82**	**5**	**25**	**30**	**90**	**3**	**0**	**3**	**115**	**4.3**	***35**	**1**	**0.0**	**22:27**	**4**	**0**	**1**	**1**	**8**	**0**	**0**	**0**	**24:31**
2006-07	**NY Rangers**	**NHL**	**80**	**10**	**30**	**40**	**52**	**7**	**0**	**3**	**104**	**9.6**	**10**	**3**	**0.0**	**23:46**	**10**	**3**	**4**	**7**	**10**	**2**	**0**	**1**	**24:45**
2007-08	**NY Rangers**	**NHL**	**80**	**13**	**25**	**38**	**80**	**6**	**2**	**0**	**127**	**10.2**	**0**	**0**	**0.0**	**24:33**	**10**	**1**	**5**	**6**	**10**	**0**	**0**	**0**	**25:05**
2008-09	**NY Rangers**	**NHL**	**76**	**8**	**22**	**30**	**52**	**3**	**0**	**2**	**120**	**6.7**	**–7**	**0**	**0.0**	**22:31**	**7**	**0**	**0**	**0**	**4**	**0**	**0**	**0**	**22:41**
2009-10	**NY Rangers**	**NHL**	**82**	**3**	**20**	**23**	**78**	**1**	**0**	**1**	**80**	**3.8**	**3**	**1**	**100.0**	**21:26**	....	....	....	....	....	....	....	....	....
2010-11	**NY Rangers**	**NHL**	**32**	**3**	**12**	**15**	**22**	**0**	**0**	**1**	**24**	**12.5**	**3**	**0**	**0.0**	**22:03**	....	....	....	....	....	....	....	....	....
	Phoenix	**NHL**	**33**	**3**	**3**	**6**	**20**	**2**	**0**	**2**	**31**	**9.7**	**3**	**0**	**0.0**	**19:59**	**4**	**0**	**0**	**0**	**2**	**0**	**0**	**0**	**19:54**
	NHL Totals		**702**	**63**	**184**	**247**	**555**	**28**	**2**	**17**	**841**	**7.5**		**7**	**28.6**	**21:34**	**37**	**4**	**10**	**14**	**38**	**2**	**0**	**1**	**24:14**

WHL East First All-Star Team (1998)

• Missed majority of 2003-04 due to knee injury in training camp, September 18, 2003. Signed as a free agent by **Trinec** (CzRep), September 17, 2004. Signed as a free agent by **Pardubice** (CzRep), January, 2005. Signed as a free agent by **NY Rangers**, August 29, 2005. Traded to **Phoenix** by **NY Rangers** for Wojtek Wolski, January 10, 2011.

RUPP, Mike

(RUHP, MIGHK) **NYR**

Center. Shoots left. 6'5", 230 lbs. Born, Cleveland, OH, January 13, 1980. New Jersey's 7th choice, 76th overall, in 2000 Entry Draft.

Season	Club	League	GP	G	A	Pts	PIM	PP	SH	GW	S	%	+/-	TF	F%	Min	GP	G	A	Pts	PIM	PP	SH	GW	Min
1996-97	St. Edward's	High-OH	20	26	24	50	....	....	....	....	....	....	....	....	....	....	....	....	....	....	....	....	....	....	....
1997-98	Windsor Spitfires	OHL	38	9	8	17	60	....	....	....	....	....	....	....	....	....	....	....	....	....	....	....	....	....	....
	Erie Otters	OHL	26	7	3	10	57	....	....	....	....	....	....	....	....	....	7	3	1	4	6	....	....	....	....
1998-99	Erie Otters	OHL	63	22	25	47	102	....	....	....	....	....	....	....	....	....	5	0	2	2	25	....	....	....	....
99-2000	Erie Otters	OHL	58	32	21	53	134	....	....	....	....	....	....	....	....	....	13	5	5	10	22	....	....	....	....
2000-01	Albany River Rats	AHL	71	10	10	20	63	....	....	....	....	....	....	....	....	....	....	....	....	....	....	....	....	....	....
2001-02	Albany River Rats	AHL	78	13	17	30	90	....	....	....	....	....	....	....	....	....	....	....	....	....	....	....	....	....	....
2002-03 ♦	**New Jersey**	**NHL**	**26**	**5**	**3**	**8**	**21**	**2**	**0**	**3**	**34**	**14.7**	**0**	**150**	**44.7**	**11:39**	**4**	**1**	**3**	**4**	**0**	**0**	**0**	**1**	**11:28**
	Albany River Rats	AHL	47	8	11	19	74	....	....	....	....	....	....	....	....	....	....	....	....	....	....	....	....	....	....
2003-04	**New Jersey**	**NHL**	**51**	**6**	**5**	**11**	**41**	**1**	**0**	**1**	**64**	**9.4**	**–1**	**386**	**47.9**	**10:38**	....	....	....	....	....	....	....	....	....
	Phoenix	**NHL**	**6**	**0**	**1**	**1**	**6**	**0**	**0**	**0**	**12**	**0.0**	**–3**	**94**	**57.5**	**16:59**	....	....	....	....	....	....	....	....	....
2004-05	Danbury Trashers	UHL	14	5	5	10	30	....	....	....	....	....	....	....	....	....	11	3	4	7	38	....	....	....	....
2005-06	**Phoenix**	**NHL**	**1**	**0**	**0**	**0**	**0**	**0**	**0**	**0**	**1**	**0.0**	**0**	**1**	**0.0**	**6:30**	....	....	....	....	....	....	....	....	....
	Columbus	**NHL**	**39**	**4**	**2**	**6**	**58**	**0**	**0**	**0**	**38**	**10.5**	**–3**	**264**	**48.1**	**9:04**	....	....	....	....	....	....	....	....	....
	Syracuse Crunch	AHL	3	1	2	3	12	....	....	....	....	....	....	....	....	....	....	....	....	....	....	....	....	....	....
2006-07	**New Jersey**	**NHL**	**76**	**6**	**3**	**9**	**92**	**0**	**0**	**1**	**60**	**10.0**	**–10**	**33**	**45.5**	**6:27**	**9**	**0**	**1**	**1**	**7**	**0**	**0**	**0**	**2:46**
2007-08	**New Jersey**	**NHL**	**64**	**3**	**6**	**9**	**58**	**1**	**0**	**0**	**69**	**4.3**	**–8**	**155**	**48.4**	**8:04**	**5**	**0**	**1**	**1**	**2**	**0**	**0**	**0**	**7:48**
2008-09	**New Jersey**	**NHL**	**72**	**3**	**6**	**9**	**136**	**0**	**0**	**0**	**76**	**3.9**	**–2**	**90**	**51.1**	**8:44**	**7**	**0**	**0**	**0**	**14**	**0**	**0**	**0**	**6:55**
2009-10	**Pittsburgh**	**NHL**	**81**	**13**	**6**	**19**	**120**	**0**	**0**	**1**	**87**	**14.9**	**5**	**143**	**44.1**	**9:03**	**11**	**0**	**0**	**0**	**8**	**0**	**0**	**0**	**7:28**
2010-11	**Pittsburgh**	**NHL**	**81**	**9**	**8**	**17**	**124**	**0**	**0**	**1**	**81**	**11.1**	**–4**	**162**	**50.6**	**10:03**	**7**	**1**	**1**	**2**	**4**	**0**	**0**	**0**	**9:07**
	NHL Totals		**497**	**49**	**40**	**89**	**656**	**4**	**0**	**7**	**522**	**9.4**		**1478**	**48.3**	**9:02**	**43**	**2**	**6**	**8**	**35**	**0**	**0**	**1**	**7:05**

• Re-entered NHL Entry Draft. Originally NY Islanders' 1st choice, 9th overall, in 1998 Entry Draft.

Traded to **Phoenix** by **New Jersey** with New Jersey's 2nd round choice (later traded to Edmonton – Edmonton selected Geoff Paukovich) in 2004 Entry Draft for Jan Hrdina, March 5, 2004. Signed as a free agent by **Danbury** (UHL), February 10, 2005. Traded to **Columbus** by **Phoenix** with Cale Hulse and Jason Chimera for Geoff Sanderson and Tim Jackman, October 8, 2005. Signed as a free agent by **New Jersey**, July 10, 2006. Signed as a free agent by **Pittsburgh**, July 1, 2009. Signed as a free agent by **NY Rangers**, July 1, 2011.

RUSSELL, Kris

(RUH-sehl, KRIHS) **CBJ**

Defense. Shoots left. 5'10", 174 lbs. Born, Red Deer, Alta., May 2, 1987. Columbus' 3rd choice, 67th overall, in 2005 Entry Draft.

Season	Club	League	GP	G	A	Pts	PIM	PP	SH	GW	S	%	+/-	TF	F%	Min	GP	G	A	Pts	PIM	PP	SH	GW	Min
2003-04	Medicine Hat	WHL	55	4	15	19	30	....	....	....	....	....	....	....	....	....	20	3	2	5	4	....	....	....	....
2004-05	Medicine Hat	WHL	72	26	35	61	37	....	....	....	....	....	....	....	....	....	10	2	1	3	4	....	....	....	....
2005-06	Medicine Hat	WHL	55	14	33	47	18	....	....	....	....	....	....	....	....	....	13	4	8	12	11	....	....	....	....
2006-07	Medicine Hat	WHL	59	32	37	69	56	....	....	....	....	....	....	....	....	....	23	4	15	19	24	....	....	....	....
2007-08	**Columbus**	**NHL**	**67**	**2**	**8**	**10**	**14**	**1**	**0**	**1**	**90**	**2.2**	**–12**	**0**	**0.0**	**14:47**	....	....	....	....	....	....	....	....	....
2008-09	**Columbus**	**NHL**	**66**	**2**	**19**	**21**	**28**	**1**	**0**	**1**	**86**	**2.3**	**–10**	**0**	**0.0**	**16:07**	**4**	**1**	**1**	**2**	**2**	**0**	**0**	**0**	**16:40**
	Syracuse Crunch	AHL	14	3	5	8	0	....	....	....	....	....	....	....	....	....	....	....	....	....	....	....	....	....	....
2009-10	**Columbus**	**NHL**	**70**	**7**	**15**	**22**	**32**	**0**	**0**	**1**	**108**	**6.5**	**3**	**0**	**0.0**	**18:35**	....	....	....	....	....	....	....	....	....
2010-11	**Columbus**	**NHL**	**73**	**5**	**18**	**23**	**37**	**1**	**0**	**0**	**88**	**5.7**	**–9**	**0**	**0.0**	**17:31**	....	....	....	....	....	....	....	....	....
	NHL Totals		**276**	**16**	**60**	**76**	**111**	**3**	**0**	**3**	**372**	**4.3**		**0**	**0.0**	**16:47**	**4**	**1**	**1**	**2**	**2**	**0**	**0**	**0**	**16:40**

WHL East Second All-Star Team (2005) • WHL East First All-Star Team (2006, 2007) • WHL Defenseman of the Year (2006, 2007) • Canadian Major Junior Second All-Star Team (2006) • Canadian Major Junior Sportsman of the Year (2006) • WHL Player of the Year (2007) • Canadian Major Junior First All-Star Team (2007) • Canadian Major Junior Defenseman of the Year (2007)

RUUTU, Jarkko

(ROO-too, YAHR-koh)

Right wing. Shoots left. 6'1", 204 lbs. Born, Vantaa, Finland, August 23, 1975. Vancouver's 3rd choice, 68th overall, in 1998 Entry Draft.

Season	Club	League	GP	G	A	Pts	PIM	PP	SH	GW	S	%	+/-	TF	F%	Min	GP	G	A	Pts	PIM	PP	SH	GW	Min
1991-92	HIFK Helsinki Jr.	Fin-Jr.	1	0	0	0	0	....	....	....	....	....	....	....	....	....	....	....	....	....	....	....	....	....	....
1992-93	HIFK Helsinki U18	Fin-U18	33	26	21	47	53	....	....	....	....	....	....	....	....	....	....	....	....	....	....	....	....	....	....
	HIFK Helsinki Jr.	Fin-Jr.	1	0	0	0	0	....	....	....	....	....	....	....	....	....	....	....	....	....	....	....	....	....	....
1993-94	HIFK Helsinki Jr.	Fin-Jr.	19	9	12	21	44	....	....	....	....	....	....	....	....	....	....	....	....	....	....	....	....	....	....
1994-95	HIFK Helsinki Jr.	Fin-Jr.	35	26	22	48	117	....	....	....	....	....	....	....	....	....	....	....	....	....	....	....	....	....	....
1995-96	Michigan Tech	WCHA	39	12	10	22	96	....	....	....	....	....	....	....	....	....	....	....	....	....	....	....	....	....	....
1996-97	HIFK Helsinki	Finland	48	11	10	21	155	....	....	....	....	....	....	....	....	....	....	....	....	....	....	....	....	....	....
1997-98	HIFK Helsinki	Finland	37	10	10	20	166	....	....	....	....	....	....	....	....	....	9	7	4	11	10	....	....	....	....
1998-99	HIFK Helsinki	Finland	25	10	4	14	136	....	....	....	....	....	....	....	....	....	9	0	2	2	43	....	....	....	....
	HIFK Helsinki	EuroHL	5	1	2	3	8	....	....	....	....	....	....	....	....	....	....	....	....	....	....	....	....	....	....
99-2000	**Vancouver**	**NHL**	**8**	**0**	**1**	**1**	**6**	**0**	**0**	**0**	**4**	**0.0**	**–1**	**0**	**0.0**	**8:47**	....	....	....	....	....	....	....	....	....
	Syracuse Crunch	AHL	65	26	32	58	164	....	....	....	....	....	....	....	....	....	4	3	1	4	8	....	....	....	....
2000-01	**Vancouver**	**NHL**	**21**	**3**	**3**	**6**	**32**	**0**	**1**	**0**	**23**	**13.0**	**1**	**0**	**0.0**	**10:39**	**4**	**0**	**1**	**1**	**8**	**0**	**0**	**0**	**10:18**
	Kansas City	IHL	46	11	18	29	111	....	....	....	....	....	....	....	....	....	....	....	....	....	....	....	....	....	....
2001-02	**Vancouver**	**NHL**	**49**	**2**	**7**	**9**	**74**	**0**	**0**	**0**	**37**	**5.4**	**–1**	**5**	**0.0**	**10:11**	**1**	**0**	**0**	**0**	**0**	**0**	**0**	**0**	**8:53**
	Finland	Olympics	4	0	0	0	4	....	....	....	....	....	....	....	....	....	....	....	....	....	....	....	....	....	....
2002-03	**Vancouver**	**NHL**	**36**	**2**	**2**	**4**	**66**	**0**	**0**	**1**	**36**	**5.6**	**–7**	**6**	**16.7**	**8:58**	**13**	**0**	**2**	**2**	**14**	**0**	**0**	**0**	**11:59**
2003-04	**Vancouver**	**NHL**	**71**	**6**	**8**	**14**	**133**	**1**	**0**	**0**	**70**	**8.6**	**–13**	**20**	**30.0**	**11:29**	**6**	**1**	**0**	**1**	**10**	**0**	**0**	**0**	**9:13**
2004-05	HIFK Helsinki	Finland	50	10	18	28	215	....	....	....	....	....	....	....	....	....	3	0	0	0	41	....	....	....	....
2005-06	**Vancouver**	**NHL**	**82**	**10**	**7**	**17**	**142**	**2**	**0**	**2**	**85**	**11.8**	**1**	**11**	**0.0**	**11:42**	....	....	....	....	....	....	....	....	....
	Finland	Olympics	8	0	0	0	31	....	....	....	....	....	....	....	....	....	....	....	....	....	....	....	....	....	....
2006-07	**Pittsburgh**	**NHL**	**81**	**7**	**9**	**16**	**125**	**0**	**0**	**2**	**63**	**11.1**	**0**	**3**	**100.0**	**9:20**	**5**	**0**	**0**	**0**	**10**	**0**	**0**	**0**	**6:38**
2007-08	**Pittsburgh**	**NHL**	**71**	**6**	**10**	**16**	**138**	**0**	**1**	**1**	**55**	**10.9**	**3**	**10**	**40.0**	**10:12**	**20**	**2**	**1**	**3**	**26**	**0**	**0**	**1**	**10:37**
2008-09	**Ottawa**	**NHL**	**78**	**7**	**14**	**21**	**144**	**0**	**1**	**0**	**89**	**7.9**	**0**	**8**	**25.0**	**11:43**	....	....	....	....	....	....	....	....	....
2009-10	**Ottawa**	**NHL**	**82**	**12**	**14**	**26**	**121**	**0**	**0**	**1**	**106**	**11.3**	**–2**	**24**	**20.8**	**13:21**	**6**	**2**	**1**	**3**	**34**	**0**	**0**	**1**	**18:20**
	Finland	Olympics	6	2	1	3	14	....	....	....	....	....	....	....	....	....	....	....	....	....	....	....	....	....	....

Season	Club	League	GP	G	A	Pts	PIM	PP	SH	GW	S	%	+/-	TF	F%	Min	GP	G	A	Pts	PIM	PP	SH	GW	Min
			Regular Season														Playoffs								
2010-11	**Ottawa**	**NHL**	**50**	**2**	**8**	**10**	**59**	**0**	**0**	**1**	**46**	**4.3**	**−2**	**15**	**40.0**	**12:28**	....	....	....	....	....	....	....	....	....
	Anaheim	**NHL**	**23**	**1**	**1**	**2**	**38**	**0**	**0**	**0**	**20**	**5.0**	**0**	**5**	**40.0**	**8:59**	**3**	**0**	**0**	**0**	**12**	**0**	**0**	**0**	**5:31**
	NHL Totals		**652**	**58**	**84**	**142**	**1078**	**3**	**3**	**8**	**634**	**9.1**		**107**	**27.1**	**11:04**	**58**	**5**	**5**	**10**	**114**	**0**	**0**	**2**	**10:55**

• Missed majority of 2002-03 as a healthy reserve. Signed as a free agent by **HIFK Helsinki** (Finland), September 23, 2004. Signed as a free agent by **Pittsburgh**, July 4, 2006. Signed as a free agent by **Ottawa**, July 2, 2008. Traded to **Anaheim** by **Ottawa** for Phoenix's 6th round choice (previously acquired, Ottawa selected Max McCormick) in 2011 Entry Draft, February 17, 2011.

RUUTU, Tuomo

(ROO-too, TOO-oh-moh) **CAR**

Center/Left wing. Shoots left. 6', 205 lbs. Born, Vantaa, Finland, February 16, 1983. Chicago's 1st choice, 9th overall, in 2001 Entry Draft.

Season	Club	League	GP	G	A	Pts	PIM	PP	SH	GW	S	%	+/-	TF	F%	Min	GP	G	A	Pts	PIM	PP	SH	GW	Min
1998-99	HIFK Helsinki U18	Fin-U18	25	9	11	20	88	....	....	....	....	....	....	....	....	....	2	1	1	2	2	....	....	....	....
99-2000	HIFK Helsinki U18	Fin-U18	5	0	3	3	12	....	....	....	....	....	....	....	....	....	3	1	2	3	2	....	....	....	....
	HIFK Helsinki Jr.	Fin-Jr.	35	11	16	27	32	....	....	....	....	....	....	....	....	....	3	0	1	1	4	....	....	....	....
	HIFK Helsinki	Finland	1	0	0	0	2	....	....	....	....	....	....	....	....	....	....	....	....	....	....	....	....	....	....
2000-01	Jokerit Helsinki Jr.	Fin-Jr.	2	1	0	1	0	....	....	....	....	....	....	....	....	....	....	....	....	....	....	....	....	....	....
	Jokerit Helsinki	Finland	47	11	11	22	94	....	....	....	....	....	....	....	....	....	5	0	0	0	4	....	....	....	....
2001-02	Jokerit Helsinki	Finland	51	7	16	23	69	....	....	....	....	....	....	....	....	....	10	0	6	6	29	....	....	....	....
2002-03	HIFK Helsinki	Finland	30	12	15	27	24	....	....	....	....	....	....	....	....	....	....	....	....	....	....	....	....	....	....
2003-04	**Chicago**	**NHL**	**82**	**23**	**21**	**44**	**58**	**10**	**0**	**3**	**174**	**13.2**	**−31**	**317**	**46.4**	**16:24**	....	....	....	....	....	....	....	....	....
2004-05			DID NOT PLAY																						
2005-06	**Chicago**	**NHL**	**15**	**2**	**3**	**5**	**31**	**1**	**0**	**0**	**30**	**6.7**	**−7**	**90**	**46.7**	**14:43**	....	....	....	....	....	....	....	....	....
2006-07	**Chicago**	**NHL**	**71**	**17**	**21**	**38**	**95**	**1**	**0**	**1**	**115**	**14.8**	**4**	**347**	**42.7**	**17:21**	....	....	....	....	....	....	....	....	....
2007-08	**Chicago**	**NHL**	**60**	**6**	**15**	**21**	**75**	**1**	**0**	**1**	**71**	**8.5**	**3**	**49**	**53.1**	**15:35**	....	....	....	....	....	....	....	....	....
	Carolina	**NHL**	**17**	**4**	**7**	**11**	**16**	**3**	**0**	**0**	**29**	**13.8**	**1**	**17**	**11.8**	**17:01**	....	....	....	....	....	....	....	....	....
2008-09	**Carolina**	**NHL**	**79**	**26**	**28**	**54**	**79**	**10**	**0**	**4**	**190**	**13.7**	**0**	**37**	**51.4**	**18:19**	**16**	**1**	**3**	**4**	**8**	**0**	**0**	**0**	**14:16**
2009-10	**Carolina**	**NHL**	**54**	**14**	**21**	**35**	**50**	**5**	**0**	**1**	**122**	**11.5**	**−4**	**47**	**40.4**	**16:23**	....	....	....	....	....	....	....	....	....
	Finland	Olympics	6	1	0	1	2	....	....	....	....	....	....	....	....	....	....	....	....	....	....	....	....	....	....
2010-11	**Carolina**	**NHL**	**82**	**19**	**38**	**57**	**54**	**7**	**0**	**1**	**148**	**12.8**	**1**	**643**	**41.2**	**16:50**	....	....	....	....	....	....	....	....	....
	NHL Totals		**460**	**111**	**154**	**265**	**458**	**38**	**0**	**11**	**879**	**12.6**		**1547**	**43.2**	**16:49**	**16**	**1**	**3**	**4**	**8**	**0**	**0**	**0**	**14:16**

• Missed majority of 2005-06 due to back (October 15, 2005 at San Jose) and ankle (January 8, 2006 vs. Nashville) injuries. Traded to **Carolina** by **Chicago** for Andrew Ladd, February 26, 2008.

RUZICKA, Stefan

(roo-ZHEECH-kuh, STEH-fan) **PHI**

Right wing. Shoots right. 6'1", 196 lbs. Born, Nitra, Czech., February 17, 1985. Philadelphia's 4th choice, 81st overall, in 2003 Entry Draft.

Season	Club	League	GP	G	A	Pts	PIM	PP	SH	GW	S	%	+/-	TF	F%	Min	GP	G	A	Pts	PIM	PP	SH	GW	Min
2000-01	Nitra Jr.	Slovak-Jr.	38	30	15	45	....	....	....	....	....	....	....	....	....	....	....	....	....	....	....	....	....	....	....
2001-02	HKM Nitra Jr.	Slovak-Jr.	29	27	25	52	....	....	....	....	....	....	....	....	....	....	....	....	....	....	....	....	....	....	....
	HKM Nitra	Slovakia	19	0	5	5	29	....	....	....	....	....	....	....	....	....	....	....	....	....	....	....	....	....	....
2002-03	HKM Nitra Jr.	Slovak-Jr.	30	18	22	40	64	....	....	....	....	....	....	....	....	....	....	....	....	....	....	....	....	....	....
	HKM Nitra	Slovak-2	17	5	7	12	4	....	....	....	....	....	....	....	....	....	....	....	....	....	....	....	....	....	....
2003-04	Owen Sound	OHL	62	34	38	72	63	....	....	....	....	....	....	....	....	....	7	1	6	7	8	....	....	....	....
	Philadelphia	AHL	2	0	0	0	0	....	....	....	....	....	....	....	....	....	3	1	0	1	2	....	....	....	....
2004-05	Owen Sound	OHL	62	37	33	70	61	....	....	....	....	....	....	....	....	....	8	3	3	6	14	....	....	....	....
2005-06	**Philadelphia**	**NHL**	**1**	**0**	**0**	**0**	**2**	**0**	**0**	**0**	**1**	**0.0**	**0**	**1**	**0.0**	**4:48**	....	....	....	....	....	....	....	....	....
	Philadelphia	AHL	73	16	32	48	88	....	....	....	....	....	....	....	....	....	....	....	....	....	....	....	....	....	....
2006-07	**Philadelphia**	**NHL**	**40**	**3**	**10**	**13**	**18**	**1**	**0**	**0**	**75**	**4.0**	**−6**	**3**	**0.0**	**12:44**	....	....	....	....	....	....	....	....	....
	Philadelphia	AHL	32	16	11	27	29	....	....	....	....	....	....	....	....	....	....	....	....	....	....	....	....	....	....
2007-08	**Philadelphia**	**NHL**	**14**	**1**	**3**	**4**	**27**	**0**	**0**	**0**	**10**	**10.0**	**5**	**5**	**0.0**	**8:40**	....	....	....	....	....	....	....	....	....
	Philadelphia	AHL	59	19	31	50	105	....	....	....	....	....	....	....	....	....	....	....	....	....	....	....	....	....	....
2008-09	Spartak Moscow	Rus-KHL	55	18	19	37	81	....	....	....	....	....	....	....	....	....	12	4	9	13	30	....	....	....	....
2009-10	Spartak Moscow	Rus-KHL	56	16	20	36	72	....	....	....	....	....	....	....	....	....	6	3	4	7	6	....	....	....	....
2010-11	Spartak Moscow	Rus-KHL	47	17	15	32	47	....	....	....	....	....	....	....	....	....	10	3	1	4	24	....	....	....	....
	Spartak Moscow	Rus-KHL															4	3	0	3	2	....	....	....	....
	NHL Totals		**55**	**4**	**13**	**17**	**47**	**1**	**0**	**0**	**86**	**4.7**		**9**	**0.0**	**11:33**	....	....	....	....	....	....	....	....	....

OHL All-Rookie Team (2004) • OHL Second All-Star Team (2004)

Signed as a free agent by **Spartak Moscow** (Russia-KHL), July 3, 2008.

RYAN, Bobby

(RIGH-uhn, BAW-bee) **ANA**

Right wing. Shoots right. 6'2", 209 lbs. Born, Cherry Hill, NJ, March 17, 1987. Anaheim's 1st choice, 2nd overall, in 2005 Entry Draft.

Season	Club	League	GP	G	A	Pts	PIM	PP	SH	GW	S	%	+/-	TF	F%	Min	GP	G	A	Pts	PIM	PP	SH	GW	Min
2003-04	Owen Sound	OHL	65	22	17	39	52	....	....	....	....	....	....	....	....	....	7	1	2	3	2	....	....	....	....
2004-05	Owen Sound	OHL	62	37	52	89	51	....	....	....	....	....	....	....	....	....	8	2	7	9	8	....	....	....	....
2005-06	Owen Sound	OHL	59	31	64	95	44	....	....	....	....	....	....	....	....	....	11	5	7	12	14	....	....	....	....
	Portland Pirates	AHL	....	....	....	....	....	....	....	....	....	....	....	....	....	....	19	1	7	8	22	....	....	....	....
2006-07	Owen Sound	OHL	63	43	59	102	63	....	....	....	....	....	....	....	....	....	4	1	1	2	2	....	....	....	....
	Portland Pirates	AHL	8	3	6	9	6	....	....	....	....	....	....	....	....	....	....	....	....	....	....	....	....	....	....
2007-08	**Anaheim**	**NHL**	**23**	**5**	**5**	**10**	**6**	**3**	**0**	**0**	**37**	**13.5**	**−1**	**1**	**100.0**	**11:16**	**2**	**0**	**0**	**0**	**2**	**0**	**0**	**0**	**11:09**
	Portland Pirates	AHL	48	21	28	49	38	....	....	....	....	....	....	....	....	....	16	8	12	20	18	....	....	....	....
2008-09	**Anaheim**	**NHL**	**64**	**31**	**26**	**57**	**33**	**12**	**0**	**3**	**174**	**17.8**	**13**	**13**	**46.2**	**15:26**	**13**	**5**	**2**	**7**	**0**	**2**	**0**	**1**	**19:41**
	Iowa Chops	AHL	14	9	10	19	19	....	....	....	....	....	....	....	....	....	....	....	....	....	....	....	....	....	....
2009-10	**Anaheim**	**NHL**	**81**	**35**	**29**	**64**	**81**	**11**	**0**	**3**	**258**	**13.6**	**9**	**93**	**44.1**	**18:29**	....	....	....	....	....	....	....	....	....
	United States	Olympics	6	1	1	2	2	....	....	....	....	....	....	....	....	....	....	....	....	....	....	....	....	....	....
2010-11	**Anaheim**	**NHL**	**82**	**34**	**37**	**71**	**61**	**5**	**1**	**5**	**270**	**12.6**	**15**	**219**	**39.7**	**20:11**	**4**	**3**	**1**	**4**	**2**	**0**	**0**	**0**	**20:29**
	NHL Totals		**250**	**105**	**97**	**202**	**181**	**31**	**1**	**11**	**739**	**14.2**		**326**	**41.4**	**17:36**	**19**	**8**	**3**	**11**	**4**	**2**	**0**	**1**	**18:57**

OHL First All-Star Team (2005) • AHL All-Rookie Team (2008) • NHL All-Rookie Team (2009)

RYAN, Michael

(RIGH-uhn, MIGH-kuhl) **BUF**

Center. Shoots left. 6'1", 188 lbs. Born, Boston, MA, May 16, 1980. Dallas' 1st choice, 32nd overall, in 1999 Entry Draft.

Season	Club	League	GP	G	A	Pts	PIM	PP	SH	GW	S	%	+/-	TF	F%	Min	GP	G	A	Pts	PIM	PP	SH	GW	Min
1997-98	Bos. College High	High-MA	23	22	14	36	28	....	....	....	....	....	....	....	....	....	....	....	....	....	....	....	....	....	....
1998-99	Bos. College High	High-MA	21	20	24	44	22	....	....	....	....	....	....	....	....	....	....	....	....	....	....	....	....	....	....
99-2000	Northeastern	H-East	32	4	9	13	47	....	....	....	....	....	....	....	....	....	....	....	....	....	....	....	....	....	....
2000-01	Northeastern	H-East	33	17	12	29	52	....	....	....	....	....	....	....	....	....	....	....	....	....	....	....	....	....	....
2001-02	Northeastern	H-East	36	24	15	39	54	....	....	....	....	....	....	....	....	....	....	....	....	....	....	....	....	....	....
2002-03	Northeastern	H-East	34	18	14	32	30	....	....	....	....	....	....	....	....	....	....	....	....	....	....	....	....	....	....
2003-04	Rochester	AHL	45	3	9	12	31	....	....	....	....	....	....	....	....	....	....	....	....	....	....	....	....	....	....
2004-05	Rochester	AHL	59	11	11	22	20	....	....	....	....	....	....	....	....	....	....	....	....	....	....	....	....	....	....
2005-06	Rochester	AHL	56	15	22	37	70	....	....	....	....	....	....	....	....	....	5	0	1	1	4	....	....	....	....
2006-07	**Buffalo**	**NHL**	**19**	**3**	**2**	**5**	**2**	**0**	**1**	**0**	**34**	**8.8**	**−8**	**2**	**0.0**	**13:40**	....	....	....	....	....	....	....	....	....
	Rochester	AHL	50	28	23	51	68	....	....	....	....	....	....	....	....	....	6	4	0	4	4	....	....	....	....
2007-08	**Buffalo**	**NHL**	**46**	**4**	**4**	**8**	**30**	**0**	**0**	**0**	**60**	**6.7**	**−4**	**2**	**0.0**	**9:53**	....	....	....	....	....	....	....	....	....
2008-09	**Carolina**	**NHL**	**18**	**0**	**2**	**2**	**2**	**0**	**0**	**0**	**24**	**0.0**	**−3**	**6**	**16.7**	**8:12**	....	....	....	....	....	....	....	....	....
	Albany River Rats	AHL	40	25	17	42	34	....	....	....	....	....	....	....	....	....	....	....	....	....	....	....	....	....	....
2009-10	Albany River Rats	AHL	3	0	0	0	2	....	....	....	....	....	....	....	....	....	....	....	....	....	....	....	....	....	....
2010-11	Springfield	AHL	6	1	2	3	0	....	....	....	....	....	....	....	....	....	....	....	....	....	....	....	....	....	....
	Adirondack	AHL	52	25	16	41	47	....	....	....	....	....	....	....	....	....	....	....	....	....	....	....	....	....	....
	NHL Totals		**83**	**7**	**8**	**15**	**34**	**0**	**1**	**0**	**118**	**5.9**		**10**	**10.0**	**10:23**	....	....	....	....	....	....	....	....	....

Traded to **Buffalo** by **Dallas** with Dallas's 2nd round choice (Branislav Fabry) in 2003 Entry Draft for Stu Barnes, March 10, 2003. Signed as a free agent by **Carolina**, October 31, 2008. • Missed majority of 2009-10 due to concussion in pre-season (September 21, 2009) vs. Atlanta and lower body injury (December 30, 2009) vs. Adirondack (AHL). Signed to a professional tryout (PTO) contract by **Springfield** (AHL), October 24, 2010. Signed as a free agent by **Philadelphia**, November 22, 2010. Signed as a free agent by **Buffalo**, August 9, 2011.

RYDER, Michael

(RIGH-duhr, MIGH-kuhl) **DAL**

Right wing. Shoots right. 6', 186 lbs. Born, St. John's, Nfld., March 31, 1980. Montreal's 9th choice, 216th overall, in 1998 Entry Draft.

Season	Club	League	GP	G	A	Pts	PIM	PP	SH	GW	S	%	+/-	TF	F%	Min	GP	G	A	Pts	PIM	PP	SH	GW	Min
1996-97	Bonavista Saints	NFAHA	23	31	17	48	....	....	....	....	....	....	....	....	....	....	....	....	....	....	....	....	....	....	....
1997-98	Hull Olympiques	QMJHL	69	34	28	62	41	....	....	....	....	....	....	....	....	....	10	4	2	6	4	....	....	....	....
1998-99	Hull Olympiques	QMJHL	69	44	43	87	65	....	....	....	....	....	....	....	....	....	23	*20	16	36	39	....	....	....	....
99-2000	Hull Olympiques	QMJHL	63	50	58	108	50	....	....	....	....	....	....	....	....	....	15	11	17	28	28	....	....	....	....
2000-01	Tallahassee	ECHL	5	4	5	9	6	....	....	....	....	....	....	....	....	....	....	....	....	....	....	....	....	....	....
	Quebec Citadelles	AHL	61	6	9	15	14	....	....	....	....	....	....	....	....	....	....	....	....	....	....	....	....	....	....
2001-02	Mississippi	ECHL	20	14	13	27	2	....	....	....	....	....	....	....	....	....	....	....	....	....	....	....	....	....	....
	Quebec Citadelles	AHL	50	11	17	28	9	....	....	....	....	....	....	....	....	....	3	0	1	1	2	....	....	....	....

			Regular Season														Playoffs								
Season	Club	League	GP	G	A	Pts	PIM	PP	SH	GW	S	%	+/-	TF	F%	Min	GP	G	A	Pts	PIM	PP	SH	GW	Min
2002-03	Hamilton	AHL	69	34	33	67	43	....	....	....	....	....	....	....	....	....	23	11	6	17	8	....	....	....	....
2003-04	**Montreal**	**NHL**	**81**	**25**	**38**	**63**	**26**	**10**	**0**	**4**	**215**	**11.6**	**10**	**25**	**24.0**	**16:00**	**11**	**1**	**2**	**3**	**4**	**0**	**0**	**0**	**16:52**
2004-05	Leksands IF	Sweden-2	42	34	27	61	32	....	....	....	....	....	....	....	....	....	....	....	....	....	....	....	....	....	....
2005-06	**Montreal**	**NHL**	**81**	**30**	**25**	**55**	**40**	**18**	**0**	**6**	**243**	**12.3**	**–5**	**17**	**52.9**	**16:10**	**6**	**2**	**3**	**5**	**0**	**1**	**0**	**1**	**16:09**
2006-07	**Montreal**	**NHL**	**82**	**30**	**28**	**58**	**60**	**17**	**2**	**3**	**221**	**13.6**	**–25**	**28**	**42.9**	**16:17**	....	....	....	....	....	....	....	....	....
2007-08	**Montreal**	**NHL**	**70**	**14**	**17**	**31**	**30**	**1**	**0**	**2**	**134**	**10.4**	**–4**	**19**	**26.3**	**13:15**	**4**	**0**	**0**	**0**	**2**	**0**	**0**	**0**	**10:46**
2008-09	**Boston**	**NHL**	**74**	**27**	**26**	**53**	**26**	**10**	**0**	**7**	**185**	**14.6**	**28**	**15**	**46.7**	**14:55**	**11**	**5**	**8**	**13**	**8**	**1**	**0**	**1**	**15:45**
2009-10	**Boston**	**NHL**	**82**	**18**	**15**	**33**	**35**	**7**	**0**	**1**	**191**	**9.4**	**3**	**15**	**13.3**	**15:18**	**13**	**4**	**1**	**5**	**2**	**1**	**0**	**0**	**15:47**
2010-11♦	**Boston**	**NHL**	**79**	**18**	**23**	**41**	**26**	**8**	**0**	**6**	**165**	**10.9**	**–1**	**8**	**62.5**	**14:29**	**25**	**8**	**9**	**17**	**8**	**2**	**0**	**2**	**14:34**
	NHL Totals		**549**	**162**	**172**	**334**	**243**	**71**	**2**	**29**	**1354**	**12.0**		**127**	**36.2**	**15:15**	**70**	**20**	**23**	**43**	**24**	**5**	**0**	**4**	**15:16**

NHL All-Rookie Team (2004)

Signed as a free agent by **Leksands** (Sweden-2), September 19, 2004. Signed as a free agent by **Boston**, July 1, 2008. Signed as a free agent by **Dallas**, July 1, 2011.

RYPIEN, Rick

(RIH-pihn, RIHK) **WPG**

Center. Shoots right. 5'11", 190 lbs. Born, Coleman, Alta., May 16, 1984.

Season	Club	League	GP	G	A	Pts	PIM	PP	SH	GW	S	%	+/-	TF	F%	Min	GP	G	A	Pts	PIM	PP	SH	GW	Min
2001-02	Crowsnest Pass	AJHL	57	12	10	22	143	....	....	....	....	....	....	....	....	....	....	....	....	....	....	....	....	....	....
	Regina Pats	WHL	1	0	0	0	0	....	....	....	....	....	....	....	....	....	....	....	....	....	....	....	....	....	....
2002-03	Regina Pats	WHL	50	6	12	18	159	....	....	....	....	....	....	....	....	....	5	1	1	2	21	....	....	....	....
2003-04	Regina Pats	WHL	65	19	26	45	186	....	....	....	....	....	....	....	....	....	4	0	1	1	18	....	....	....	....
2004-05	Regina Pats	WHL	63	22	29	51	148	....	....	....	....	....	....	....	....	....	....	....	....	....	....	....	....	....	....
	Manitoba Moose	AHL	8	1	1	2	5	....	....	....	....	....	....	....	....	....	14	0	0	0	35	....	....	....	....
2005-06	Manitoba Moose	AHL	49	9	6	15	122	....	....	....	....	....	....	....	....	....	13	1	1	2	22	....	....	....	....
	Vancouver	**NHL**	**5**	**1**	**0**	**1**	**4**	**0**	**0**	**0**	**6**	**16.7**	**1**	**22**	**36.4**	**6:19**	....	....	....	....	....	....	....	....	....
2006-07	**Vancouver**	**NHL**	**2**	**0**	**0**	**0**	**5**	**0**	**0**	**0**	**0**	**0.0**	**0**	**6**	**66.7**	**4:46**	....	....	....	....	....	....	....	....	....
	Manitoba Moose	AHL	14	3	3	6	35	....	....	....	....	....	....	....	....	....	....	....	....	....	....	....	....	....	....
2007-08	**Vancouver**	**NHL**	**22**	**1**	**2**	**3**	**41**	**0**	**0**	**0**	**8**	**12.5**	**–5**	**106**	**41.5**	**8:07**	....	....	....	....	....	....	....	....	....
	Manitoba Moose	AHL	34	3	11	14	81	....	....	....	....	....	....	....	....	....	6	0	0	0	10	....	....	....	....
2008-09	**Vancouver**	**NHL**	**12**	**3**	**0**	**3**	**19**	**0**	**1**	**0**	**16**	**18.8**	**–3**	**18**	**50.0**	**9:20**	**10**	**0**	**2**	**2**	**40**	**0**	**0**	**0**	**7:30**
2009-10	**Vancouver**	**NHL**	**69**	**4**	**4**	**8**	**126**	**0**	**0**	**1**	**61**	**6.6**	**–3**	**153**	**43.1**	**7:14**	**7**	**0**	**1**	**1**	**7**	**0**	**0**	**0**	**4:40**
2010-11	**Vancouver**	**NHL**	**9**	**0**	**1**	**1**	**31**	**0**	**0**	**0**	**6**	**0.0**	**–5**	**14**	**64.3**	**5:07**	....	....	....	....	....	....	....	....	....
	Manitoba Moose	AHL	11	0	2	2	9	....	....	....	....	....	....	....	....	....	7	1	0	1	10	....	....	....	....
	NHL Totals		**119**	**9**	**7**	**16**	**226**	**0**	**1**	**1**	**97**	**9.3**		**319**	**43.9**	**7:22**	**17**	**0**	**3**	**3**	**47**	**0**	**0**	**0**	**6:20**

Signed to an ATO (amateur tryout) contract by **Manitoba** (AHL), March 22, 2005. Signed as a free agent by **Vancouver**, November 9, 2005. • Missed majority of 2006-07 due to recurring groin injury. • Missed majority of 2008-09 due to viral infection. • Granted indefinte leave of absence by **Vancouver**, November 25, 2010. Signed as a free agent by **Winnipeg**, July 4, 2011.

ST. LOUIS, Martin

(SAINT loo-EE, mahr-TEHN) **T.B.**

Right wing. Shoots left. 5'8", 176 lbs. Born, Laval, Que., June 18, 1975.

Season	Club	League	GP	G	A	Pts	PIM	PP	SH	GW	S	%	+/-	TF	F%	Min	GP	G	A	Pts	PIM	PP	SH	GW	Min
1991-92	Laval-Laurentides	QAAA	42	29	*74	*103	38	....	....	....	....	....	....	....	....	....	12	7	15	22	16	....	....	....	....
1992-93	Hawkesbury	CJHL	31	37	50	87	70	....	....	....	....	....	....	....	....	....	....	....	....	....	....	....	....	....	....
1993-94	U. of Vermont	ECAC	33	15	36	51	24	....	....	....	....	....	....	....	....	....	....	....	....	....	....	....	....	....	....
1994-95	U. of Vermont	ECAC	35	23	48	71	36	....	....	....	....	....	....	....	....	....	....	....	....	....	....	....	....	....	....
1995-96	U. of Vermont	ECAC	35	29	56	85	38	....	....	....	....	....	....	....	....	....	....	....	....	....	....	....	....	....	....
1996-97	U. of Vermont	ECAC	36	24	*36	60	65	....	....	....	....	....	....	....	....	....	....	....	....	....	....	....	....	....	....
1997-98	Cleveland	IHL	56	16	34	50	24	....	....	....	....	....	....	....	....	....	....	....	....	....	....	....	....	....	....
	Saint John Flames	AHL	25	15	11	26	20	....	....	....	....	....	....	....	....	....	20	5	15	20	16	....	....	....	....
1998-99	**Calgary**	**NHL**	**13**	**1**	**1**	**2**	**10**	**0**	**0**	**0**	**14**	**7.1**	**–2**	**0**	**0.0**	**8:15**	....	....	....	....	....	....	....	....	....
	Saint John Flames	AHL	53	28	34	62	30	....	....	....	....	....	....	....	....	....	7	4	4	8	2	....	....	....	....
99-2000	**Calgary**	**NHL**	**56**	**3**	**15**	**18**	**22**	**0**	**0**	**1**	**73**	**4.1**	**–5**	**3**	**0.0**	**14:41**	....	....	....	....	....	....	....	....	....
	Saint John Flames	AHL	17	15	11	26	14	....	....	....	....	....	....	....	....	....	....	....	....	....	....	....	....	....	....
2000-01	**Tampa Bay**	**NHL**	**78**	**18**	**22**	**40**	**12**	**3**	**3**	**4**	**141**	**12.8**	**–4**	**48**	**41.7**	**15:14**	....	....	....	....	....	....	....	....	....
2001-02	**Tampa Bay**	**NHL**	**53**	**16**	**19**	**35**	**20**	**6**	**1**	**2**	**105**	**15.2**	**4**	**33**	**39.4**	**18:41**	....	....	....	....	....	....	....	....	....
2002-03	**Tampa Bay**	**NHL**	**82**	**33**	**37**	**70**	**32**	**12**	**3**	**5**	**201**	**16.4**	**10**	**37**	**37.8**	**19:43**	**11**	**7**	**5**	**12**	**0**	**1**	***2**	**3**	**22:21**
2003-04♦	**Tampa Bay**	**NHL**	**82**	**38**	***56**	***94**	**24**	**8**	***8**	**7**	**212**	**17.9**	***35**	**24**	**33.3**	**20:35**	**23**	**9**	***15**	**24**	**14**	**3**	**1**	**3**	**22:52**
2004-05	Lausanne HC	Swiss	23	9	16	25	16	....	....	....	....	....	....	....	....	....	....	....	....	....	....	....	....	....	....
2005-06	**Tampa Bay**	**NHL**	**80**	**31**	**30**	**61**	**38**	**9**	**3**	**7**	**221**	**14.0**	**–3**	**13**	**23.1**	**20:59**	**5**	**4**	**0**	**4**	**2**	**1**	**0**	**1**	**22:53**
	Canada	Olympics	6	2	1	3	0	....	....	....	....	....	....	....	....	....	....	....	....	....	....	....	....	....	....
2006-07	**Tampa Bay**	**NHL**	**82**	**43**	**59**	**102**	**28**	**14**	**5**	**7**	**273**	**15.8**	**7**	**20**	**35.0**	**24:09**	**6**	**3**	**5**	**8**	**8**	**1**	**0**	**0**	**28:07**
2007-08	**Tampa Bay**	**NHL**	**82**	**25**	**58**	**83**	**26**	**10**	**2**	**5**	**241**	**10.4**	**–23**	**12**	**25.0**	**24:17**	....	....	....	....	....	....	....	....	....
2008-09	**Tampa Bay**	**NHL**	**82**	**30**	**50**	**80**	**14**	**7**	**2**	**3**	**262**	**11.5**	**4**	**30**	**46.7**	**21:17**	....	....	....	....	....	....	....	....	....
2009-10	**Tampa Bay**	**NHL**	**82**	**29**	**65**	**94**	**12**	**7**	**1**	**7**	**242**	**12.0**	**–8**	**157**	**45.2**	**21:49**	....	....	....	....	....	....	....	....	....
2010-11	**Tampa Bay**	**NHL**	**82**	**31**	**68**	**99**	**12**	**4**	**0**	**7**	**254**	**12.2**	**0**	**131**	**38.2**	**20:59**	**18**	**10**	**10**	**20**	**4**	**4**	**0**	**1**	**21:11**
	NHL Totals		**854**	**298**	**480**	**778**	**250**	**80**	**28**	**55**	**2239**	**13.3**		**508**	**40.0**	**20:17**	**63**	**33**	**35**	**68**	**28**	**10**	**3**	**8**	**22:48**

ECAC First All-Star Team (1995, 1996, 1997) • ECAC Player of the Year (1995) • NCAA East First All-American Team (1995, 1996, 1997) • NCAA Championship All-Tournament Team (1996) • NHL First All-Star Team (2004) • Art Ross Trophy (2004) • Lester B. Pearson Award (2004) • Hart Memorial Trophy (2004) • NHL Second All-Star Team (2007, 2010, 2011) • Lady Byng Memorial Trophy (2010, 2011)

Played in NHL All-Star Game (2003, 2004, 2007, 2008, 2009, 2011)

Signed as a free agent by **Calgary**, February 19, 1998. Signed as a free agent by **Tampa Bay**, July 31, 2000. Signed as a free agent by **Lausanne** (Swiss), November 4, 2004.

ST. PIERRE, Martin

(SAINT PEE-aihr, mahr-TEHN) **CBJ**

Center. Shoots left. 5'9", 187 lbs. Born, Ottawa, Ont., August 11, 1983.

Season	Club	League	GP	G	A	Pts	PIM	PP	SH	GW	S	%	+/-	TF	F%	Min	GP	G	A	Pts	PIM	PP	SH	GW	Min
2000-01	Guelph Storm	OHL	68	20	49	69	40	....	....	....	....	....	....	....	....	....	4	0	0	0	4	....	....	....	....
2001-02	Guelph Storm	OHL	66	32	53	85	68	....	....	....	....	....	....	....	....	....	9	3	9	12	12	....	....	....	....
2002-03	Guelph Storm	OHL	55	11	45	56	74	....	....	....	....	....	....	....	....	....	11	5	11	16	4	....	....	....	....
2003-04	Guelph Storm	OHL	68	45	65	110	95	....	....	....	....	....	....	....	....	....	22	8	*27	*35	20	....	....	....	....
2004-05	Greenville	ECHL	45	14	39	53	55	....	....	....	....	....	....	....	....	....	7	2	5	7	6	....	....	....	....
	Edmonton	AHL	18	4	3	7	8	....	....	....	....	....	....	....	....	....	....	....	....	....	....	....	....	....	....
2005-06	**Chicago**	**NHL**	**2**	**0**	**0**	**0**	**0**	**0**	**0**	**0**	**1**	**0.0**	**–1**	**15**	**33.3**	**12:02**	....	....	....	....	....	....	....	....	....
	Norfolk Admirals	AHL	77	23	50	73	98	....	....	....	....	....	....	....	....	....	4	0	3	3	2	....	....	....	....
2006-07	**Chicago**	**NHL**	**14**	**1**	**3**	**4**	**8**	**1**	**0**	**0**	**13**	**7.7**	**–3**	**129**	**48.1**	**12:29**	....	....	....	....	....	....	....	....	....
	Norfolk Admirals	AHL	65	27	72	99	100	....	....	....	....	....	....	....	....	....	6	0	1	1	6	....	....	....	....
2007-08	Mytischi	Russia	14	1	6	7	16	....	....	....	....	....	....	....	....	....	....	....	....	....	....	....	....	....	....
	Chicago	**NHL**	**5**	**0**	**0**	**0**	**0**	**0**	**0**	**0**	**2**	**0.0**	**–3**	**59**	**55.9**	**15:17**	....	....	....	....	....	....	....	....	....
	Rockford IceHogs	AHL	69	21	67	88	80	....	....	....	....	....	....	....	....	....	12	2	12	14	12	....	....	....	....
2008-09	**Boston**	**NHL**	**14**	**2**	**2**	**4**	**4**	**0**	**1**	**1**	**15**	**13.3**	**–1**	**101**	**42.6**	**11:24**	....	....	....	....	....	....	....	....	....
	Providence Bruins	AHL	61	15	51	66	58	....	....	....	....	....	....	....	....	....	16	5	11	16	26	....	....	....	....
2009-10	**Ottawa**	**NHL**	**3**	**0**	**0**	**0**	**0**	**0**	**0**	**0**	**0**	**0.0**	**–2**	**20**	**45.0**	**9:37**	....	....	....	....	....	....	....	....	....
	Binghamton	AHL	77	24	48	72	50	....	....	....	....	....	....	....	....	....	....	....	....	....	....	....	....	....	....
2010-11	Nizhnekamsk	Rus-KHL	8	1	1	2	8	....	....	....	....	....	....	....	....	....	....	....	....	....	....	....	....	....	....
	Karpat Oulu	Finland	27	8	6	14	6	....	....	....	....	....	....	....	....	....	....	....	....	....	....	....	....	....	....
	Salzburg	Austria	11	3	9	12	18	....	....	....	....	....	....	....	....	....	....	....	....	....	....	....	....	....	....
	NHL Totals		**38**	**3**	**5**	**8**	**12**	**1**	**1**	**1**	**31**	**9.7**		**324**	**46.9**	**12:12**	....	....	....	....	....	....	....	....	....

AHL All-Rookie Team (2006) • AHL First All-Star Team (2007) • AHL Second All-Star Team (2008)

Signed as a free agent by **Chicago**, November 3, 2005. Signed as a free agent by **Mytischi** (Russia), June 22, 2007. Traded to **Boston** by **Chicago** for Pascal Pelletier, July 24, 2008. Signed as a free agent by **Ottawa**, July 1, 2009. Signed as a free agent by **Nizhnekamsk** (Russia-KHL), June 6, 2010. Signed as a free agent by **Oulu** (Finland), October 19, 2010. Signed as a free agent by **Salzburg** (Austria), January 22, 2011.

SALCIDO, Brian

(sal-SEE-doh, BRIGH-uhn)

Defense. Shoots left. 6'2", 188 lbs. Born, Los Angeles, CA, April 14, 1985. Anaheim's 5th choice, 141st overall, in 2005 Entry Draft.

Season	Club	League	GP	G	A	Pts	PIM	PP	SH	GW	S	%	+/-	TF	F%	Min	GP	G	A	Pts	PIM	PP	SH	GW	Min
2002-03	Shat.-St. Mary's	High-MN	53	8	35	43	....	....	....	....	....	....	....	....	....	....	....	....	....	....	....	....	....	....	....
2003-04	Colorado College	WCHA	12	1	0	1	48	....	....	....	....	....	....	....	....	....	....	....	....	....	....	....	....	....	....
2004-05	Colorado College	WCHA	38	7	23	30	52	....	....	....	....	....	....	....	....	....	....	....	....	....	....	....	....	....	....
2005-06	Colorado College	WCHA	42	8	32	40	69	....	....	....	....	....	....	....	....	....	....	....	....	....	....	....	....	....	....
2006-07	Portland Pirates	AHL	76	7	20	27	80	....	....	....	....	....	....	....	....	....	....	....	....	....	....	....	....	....	....
2007-08	Portland Pirates	AHL	71	11	42	53	58	....	....	....	....	....	....	....	....	....	18	0	6	6	18	....	....	....	....
2008-09	**Anaheim**	**NHL**	**2**	**0**	**1**	**1**	**0**	**0**	**0**	**0**	**1**	**0.0**	**2**	**0**	**0.0**	**12:18**	....	....	....	....	....	....	....	....	....
	Iowa Chops	AHL	76	10	33	43	108	....	....	....	....	....	....	....	....	....	....	....	....	....	....	....	....	....	....

								Regular Season									Playoffs								
Season	Club	League	GP	G	A	Pts	PIM	PP	SH	GW	S	%	+/-	TF	F%	Min	GP	G	A	Pts	PIM	PP	SH	GW	Min
2009-10	Manitoba Moose	AHL	68	8	10	18	50	....	....	....	....	....	....	....	....	....	5	0	1	1	6	....	....	....	....
2010-11	HC Sparta Praha	CzRep	23	2	1	3	38	....	....	....	....	....	....	....	....	....	....	....	....	....	....	....	....	....	....
	SaiPa	Finland	11	1	4	5	12	....	....	....	....	....	....	....	....	....	....	....	....	....	....	....	....	....	....
	NHL Totals		2	0	1	1	0	0	0	0	1	0.0		0	0.0	12:18	....	....	....	....	....	....	....	....	....

WCHA Second All-Star Team (2006) • AHL Second All-Star Team (2008)

• Assigned to **Manitoba** (AHL) by **Anaheim**, September 19, 2009. Signed as a free agent by **Sparta Praha** (CzRep), July 14, 2010. Signed as a free agent by **SaiPa** (Finland), November 29, 2010.

SALEI, Ruslan

(sah-LAY, roos-LAHN)

Defense. Shoots left. 6'1", 212 lbs. Born, Minsk, USSR, November 2, 1974. Anaheim's 1st choice, 9th overall, in 1996 Entry Draft.

Season	Club	League	GP	G	A	Pts	PIM	PP	SH	GW	S	%	+/-	TF	F%	Min	GP	G	A	Pts	PIM	PP	SH	GW	Min
1992-93	Dynamo Moscow	CIS	9	1	0	1	10	....	....	....	....	....	....	....	....	....	....	....	....	....	....	....	....	....	....
1993-94	Tivali Minsk	CIS	39	2	3	5	50	....	....	....	....	....	....	....	....	....	....	....	....	....	....	....	....	....	....
1994-95	Tivali Minsk	CIS	51	4	2	6	44	....	....	....	....	....	....	....	....	....	....	....	....	....	....	....	....	....	....
1995-96	Las Vegas	IHL	76	7	23	30	123	....	....	....	....	....	....	....	....	....	15	3	7	10	18	....	....	....	....
1996-97	Anaheim	NHL	30	0	1	1	37	0	0	0	14	0.0	–8	....	....	....	....	....	....	....	....	....	....	....	....
	Baltimore Bandits	AHL	12	1	4	5	12	....	....	....	....	....	....	....	....	....	....	....	....	....	....	....	....	....	....
	Las Vegas	IHL	8	0	2	2	24	....	....	....	....	....	....	....	....	....	3	2	1	3	6	....	....	....	....
1997-98	Anaheim	NHL	66	5	10	15	70	1	0	0	104	4.8	7	....	....	....	....	....	....	....	....	....	....	....	....
	Cincinnati	AHL	6	3	6	9	14	....	....	....	....	....	....	....	....	....	....	....	....	....	....	....	....	....	....
	Belarus	Olympics	7	1	0	1	4	....	....	....	....	....	....	....	....	....	....	....	....	....	....	....	....	....	....
1998-99	Anaheim	NHL	74	2	14	16	65	1	0	0	123	1.6	1	0	0.0	22:03	3	0	0	0	4	0	0	0	15:40
99-2000	Anaheim	NHL	71	5	5	10	94	1	0	0	116	4.3	3	0	0.0	20:21	....	....	....	....	....	....	....	....	....
2000-01	Anaheim	NHL	50	1	5	6	70	0	0	0	73	1.4	–14	0	0.0	20:40	....	....	....	....	....	....	....	....	....
2001-02	Anaheim	NHL	82	4	7	11	97	0	0	1	96	4.2	–10	0	0.0	21:25	....	....	....	....	....	....	....	....	....
	Belarus	Olympics	6	2	1	3	4	....	....	....	....	....	....	....	....	....	....	....	....	....	....	....	....	....	....
2002-03	Anaheim	NHL	61	4	8	12	78	0	0	0	93	4.3	2	0	0.0	21:53	21	2	3	5	26	0	0	1	26:05
2003-04	Anaheim	NHL	82	4	11	15	110	0	1	2	145	2.8	–1	0	0.0	23:42	....	....	....	....	....	....	....	....	....
2004-05	Ak Bars Kazan	Russia	35	8	12	20	36	....	....	....	....	....	....	....	....	....	4	0	0	0	2	....	....	....	....
2005-06	Anaheim	NHL	78	1	18	19	114	0	0	0	108	0.9	17	2	100.0	22:31	16	3	2	5	18	0	0	1	22:08
2006-07	Florida	NHL	82	6	26	32	102	2	0	0	148	4.1	–13	0	0.0	23:20	....	....	....	....	....	....	....	....	....
2007-08	Florida	NHL	65	3	20	23	75	1	0	0	81	3.7	–5	1	0.0	23:17	....	....	....	....	....	....	....	....	....
	Colorado	NHL	17	3	4	7	23	0	0	1	30	10.0	1	0	0.0	19:17	10	1	4	5	4	1	0	0	20:52
2008-09	Colorado	NHL	70	4	17	21	72	1	0	0	93	4.3	–4	0	0.0	21:06	....	....	....	....	....	....	....	....	....
2009-10	Colorado	NHL	14	1	5	6	10	0	0	0	22	4.5	–1	0	0.0	18:46	1	0	0	0	0	0	0	0	21:54
	Belarus	Olympics	4	1	0	1	0	....	....	....	....	....	....	....	....	....	....	....	....	....	....	....	....	....	....
2010-11	Detroit	NHL	75	2	8	10	48	0	0	0	75	2.7	0	0	0.0	17:58	11	1	0	1	0	0	0	0	16:40
	NHL Totals		917	45	159	204	1065	7	1	4	1321	3.4		3	66.7	21:37	62	7	9	16	52	1	0	2	21:59

Signed as a free agent by **Kazan** (Russia), October 20, 2004. Signed as a free agent by **Florida**, July 2, 2006. Traded to **Colorado** by **Florida** for Karlis Skrastins and Colorado's 3rd round choice (Adam Comrie) in 2008 Entry Draft, February 26, 2008. • Missed majority of 2009-10 due to back injury at Nashville, October 8, 2009. Signed as a free agent by **Detroit**, August 9, 2010. Signed as a free agent by **Yaroslavl** (Russia-KHL), July 5, 2011.

SALMELA, Anssi

(sahl-MEHL-ah, AN-see)

Defense. Shoots left. 6'1", 200 lbs. Born, Nokia, Finland, August 13, 1984.

Season	Club	League	GP	G	A	Pts	PIM	PP	SH	GW	S	%	+/-	TF	F%	Min	GP	G	A	Pts	PIM	PP	SH	GW	Min
2000-01	Tappara U18	Fin-U18	32	7	3	10	24	....	....	....	....	....	....	....	....	....	2	0	1	1	4	....	....	....	....
2001-02	Tappara U18	Fin-U18	11	6	4	10	12	....	....	....	....	....	....	....	....	....	....	....	....	....	....	....	....	....	....
	Tappara Jr.	Fin-Jr.	26	3	4	7	22	....	....	....	....	....	....	....	....	....	2	2	1	3	0	....	....	....	....
2002-03	Tappara Jr.	Fin-Jr.	23	5	9	14	22	....	....	....	....	....	....	....	....	....	....	....	....	....	....	....	....	....	....
2003-04	Suomi U20	Finland-2	5	2	2	4	0	....	....	....	....	....	....	....	....	....	....	....	....	....	....	....	....	....	....
	Tappara Jr.	Fin-Jr.	27	10	9	19	22	....	....	....	....	....	....	....	....	....	12	5	3	8	4	....	....	....	....
	Tappara Tampere	Finland	10	0	0	0	2	....	....	....	....	....	....	....	....	....	3	0	0	0	2	....	....	....	....
2004-05	Tappara Jr.	Fin-Jr.	10	2	4	6	6	....	....	....	....	....	....	....	....	....	1	0	0	0	0	....	....	....	....
	Tappara Tampere	Finland	48	1	5	6	49	....	....	....	....	....	....	....	....	....	8	0	0	0	0	....	....	....	....
2005-06	Tappara Tampere	Finland	8	0	1	1	0	....	....	....	....	....	....	....	....	....	....	....	....	....	....	....	....	....	....
	Pelicans Lahti	Finland	40	8	7	15	59	....	....	....	....	....	....	....	....	....	....	....	....	....	....	....	....	....	....
2006-07	Pelicans Lahti	Finland	56	11	12	23	58	....	....	....	....	....	....	....	....	....	6	1	1	2	4	....	....	....	....
2007-08	Tappara Tampere	Finland	56	16	16	32	40	....	....	....	....	....	....	....	....	....	11	0	6	6	14	....	....	....	....
2008-09	New Jersey	NHL	17	0	3	3	6	0	0	0	33	0.0	1	0	0.0	15:10	....	....	....	....	....	....	....	....	....
	Lowell Devils	AHL	38	8	16	24	41	....	....	....	....	....	....	....	....	....	....	....	....	....	....	....	....	....	....
	Atlanta	NHL	9	1	2	3	2	1	0	0	8	12.5	0	0	0.0	17:31	....	....	....	....	....	....	....	....	....
	Chicago Wolves	AHL	2	0	0	0	0	....	....	....	....	....	....	....	....	....	....	....	....	....	....	....	....	....	....
2009-10	Atlanta	NHL	29	1	4	5	22	0	0	0	27	3.7	4	0	0.0	13:10	....	....	....	....	....	....	....	....	....
	New Jersey	NHL	9	1	2	3	0	0	1	0	14	7.1	–5	0	0.0	14:27	....	....	....	....	....	....	....	....	....
2010-11	New Jersey	NHL	48	1	6	7	14	0	0	1	57	1.8	–11	0	0.0	17:24	....	....	....	....	....	....	....	....	....
	Albany Devils	AHL	2	0	0	0	0	....	....	....	....	....	....	....	....	....	....	....	....	....	....	....	....	....	....
	NHL Totals		112	4	17	21	44	1	1	1	139	2.9		0	0.0	15:44	....	....	....	....	....	....	....	....	....

Signed as a free agent by **New Jersey**, May 30, 2008. Traded to **Atlanta** by **New Jersey** for Niclas Havelid and Myles Stoesz, March 2, 2009. Traded to **New Jersey** by **Atlanta** with Ilya Kovalchuk and Atlanta's 2nd round choice (Jonathon Merrill) in 2010 Entry Draft for Johnny Oduya, Niclas Bergfors, Patrice Cormier and New Jersey's 1st (later traded to Chicago - Chicago selected Kevin Hayes) and 2nd (later traded to Chicago - Chicago selected Justin Holl) round choices in 2010 Entry Draft, February 4, 2010. • Missed majority of 2009-10 as a healthy reserve.

SALO, Sami

(SA-loh, SA-mee) **VAN**

Defense. Shoots right. 6'3", 212 lbs. Born, Turku, Finland, September 2, 1974. Ottawa's 7th choice, 239th overall, in 1996 Entry Draft.

Season	Club	League	GP	G	A	Pts	PIM	PP	SH	GW	S	%	+/-	TF	F%	Min	GP	G	A	Pts	PIM	PP	SH	GW	Min
1991-92	Kiekko-67 Jr.	Fin-Jr.	23	4	5	9	26	....	....	....	....	....	....	....	....	....	....	....	....	....	....	....	....	....	....
1992-93	Kiekko-67 Jr.	Fin-Jr.	21	9	4	13	4	....	....	....	....	....	....	....	....	....	....	....	....	....	....	....	....	....	....
1993-94	TPS Turku Jr.	Fin-Jr.	36	7	13	20	16	....	....	....	....	....	....	....	....	....	7	0	1	1	10	....	....	....	....
1994-95	TPS Turku Jr.	Fin-Jr.	14	1	3	4	6	....	....	....	....	....	....	....	....	....	....	....	....	....	....	....	....	....	....
	Kiekko-67 Turku	Finland-2	19	4	2	6	4	....	....	....	....	....	....	....	....	....	....	....	....	....	....	....	....	....	....
	TPS Turku	Finland	7	1	2	3	6	....	....	....	....	....	....	....	....	....	1	0	0	0	0	....	....	....	....
1995-96	TPS Turku	Finland	47	7	14	21	32	....	....	....	....	....	....	....	....	....	11	1	3	4	8	....	....	....	....
1996-97	TPS Turku	Finland	48	9	6	15	10	....	....	....	....	....	....	....	....	....	10	2	3	5	4	....	....	....	....
	TPS Turku	EuroHL	6	0	2	2	6	....	....	....	....	....	....	....	....	....	2	0	0	0	2	....	....	....	....
1997-98	Jokerit Helsinki	Finland	35	3	5	8	24	....	....	....	....	....	....	....	....	....	8	0	1	1	2	....	....	....	....
	Jokerit Helsinki	EuroHL	6	1	1	2	2	....	....	....	....	....	....	....	....	....	....	....	....	....	....	....	....	....	....
1998-99	Ottawa	NHL	61	7	12	19	24	2	0	1	106	6.6	20	0	0.0	19:42	4	0	0	0	0	0	0	0	21:32
	Detroit Vipers	IHL	5	0	2	2	0	....	....	....	....	....	....	....	....	....	....	....	....	....	....	....	....	....	....
99-2000	Ottawa	NHL	37	6	8	14	2	3	0	1	85	7.1	6	0	0.0	20:18	6	1	1	2	0	1	0	0	24:11
2000-01	Ottawa	NHL	31	2	16	18	10	1	0	0	61	3.3	9	0	0.0	19:44	4	0	0	0	0	0	0	0	22:30
2001-02	Ottawa	NHL	66	4	14	18	14	1	1	2	122	3.3	1	0	0.0	19:52	12	2	1	3	4	0	0	0	20:23
	Finland	Olympics	4	0	0	0	0	....	....	....	....	....	....	....	....	....	....	....	....	....	....	....	....	....	....
2002-03	Vancouver	NHL	79	9	21	30	10	4	0	1	126	7.1	9	0	0.0	20:08	12	1	3	4	0	0	0	0	20:52
2003-04	Vancouver	NHL	74	7	19	26	22	5	0	2	143	4.9	8	1	100.0	22:14	7	1	2	3	2	1	0	0	22:59
2004-05	Frolunda	Sweden	41	6	8	14	18	....	....	....	....	....	....	....	....	....	14	1	6	7	2	....	....	....	....
2005-06	Vancouver	NHL	59	10	23	33	38	9	0	2	140	7.1	9	0	0.0	24:30	....	....	....	....	....	....	....	....	....
	Finland	Olympics	6	1	3	4	0	....	....	....	....	....	....	....	....	....	....	....	....	....	....	....	....	....	....
2006-07	Vancouver	NHL	67	14	23	37	26	5	0	6	143	9.8	21	0	0.0	21:27	10	0	1	1	4	0	0	0	25:53
2007-08	Vancouver	NHL	63	8	17	25	38	6	0	1	122	6.6	8	0	0.0	23:39	....	....	....	....	....	....	....	....	....
2008-09	Vancouver	NHL	60	5	20	25	26	5	0	2	110	4.5	5	0	0.0	20:11	7	3	4	7	2	2	0	2	18:36
2009-10	Vancouver	NHL	68	9	19	28	18	6	0	3	119	7.6	14	0	0.0	20:41	12	1	5	6	2	1	0	0	20:40
	Finland	Olympics	6	1	1	2	4	....	....	....	....	....	....	....	....	....	....	....	....	....	....	....	....	....	....
2010-11	Vancouver	NHL	27	3	4	7	14	1	0	0	39	7.7	–3	0	0.0	20:21	21	3	2	5	2	3	0	1	19:13
	Manitoba Moose	AHL	3	2	0	2	2	....	....	....	....	....	....	....	....	....	....	....	....	....	....	....	....	....	....
	NHL Totals		692	84	196	280	242	48	1	21	1316	6.4		1	100.0	21:10	95	12	19	31	16	8	0	3	21:14

NHL All-Rookie Team (1999)

• Missed majority of 1999-2000 due to wrist injury vs. Philadelphia, November 28, 1999. • Missed majority of 2000-01 due to shoulder injury vs. Atlanta, December 14, 2000. Traded to **Vancouver** by **Ottawa** for Peter Schaefer, September 21, 2002. Signed as a free agent by **Frolunda** (Sweden), September 24, 2004. • Missed majority of 2010-11 due to torn Achilles tendon during off-season training, July 22, 2010.

SALVADOR, Bryce
(SAL-vuh-dohr, BRIGHS) **N.J.**

Defense. Shoots left. 6'3", 215 lbs. Born, Brandon, Man., February 11, 1976. Tampa Bay's 6th choice, 138th overall, in 1994 Entry Draft.

			Regular Season														Playoffs								
Season	Club	League	GP	G	A	Pts	PIM	PP	SH	GW	S	%	+/-	TF	F%	Min	GP	G	A	Pts	PIM	PP	SH	GW	Min
1991-92	Brandon	MAHA	52	6	23	29	38																		
1992-93	Lethbridge	WHL	64	1	4	5	29										4	0	0	0	0				
1993-94	Lethbridge	WHL	61	4	14	18	36										9	0	1	1	2				
1994-95	Lethbridge	WHL	67	1	9	10	88																		
1995-96	Lethbridge	WHL	56	4	12	16	75										3	0	1	1	2				
1996-97	Lethbridge	WHL	63	8	32	40	81										19	0	7	7	14				
1997-98	Worcester IceCats	AHL	46	2	8	10	74										11	0	1	1	45				
1998-99	Worcester IceCats	AHL	69	5	13	18	129										4	0	1	1	2				
99-2000	Worcester IceCats	AHL	55	0	13	13	53										9	0	1	1	2				
2000-01	**St. Louis**	**NHL**	**75**	**2**	**8**	**10**	**69**	**0**	**0**	**1**	**60**	**3.3**	**-4**	**1**	**0.0**	**16:38**	**14**	**2**	**0**	**2**	**18**	**0**	**0**	**1**	**14:41**
2001-02	**St. Louis**	**NHL**	**66**	**5**	**7**	**12**	**78**	**1**	**0**	**2**	**37**	**13.5**	**3**	**0**	**0.0**	**16:55**	**10**	**0**	**1**	**1**	**4**	**0**	**0**	**0**	**12:34**
2002-03	**St. Louis**	**NHL**	**71**	**2**	**8**	**10**	**95**	**1**	**0**	**0**	**73**	**2.7**	**7**	**0**	**0.0**	**18:57**	**7**	**0**	**0**	**0**	**2**	**0**	**0**	**0**	**17:17**
2003-04	**St. Louis**	**NHL**	**69**	**3**	**5**	**8**	**47**	**0**	**0**	**1**	**60**	**5.0**	**-4**	**0**	**0.0**	**17:29**	**5**	**0**	**0**	**0**	**2**	**0**	**0**	**0**	**14:31**
	Worcester IceCats	AHL	2	0	1	1	0																		
2004-05	Missouri	UHL	7	0	0	0	16										3	0	0	0	0				
2005-06	**St. Louis**	**NHL**	**46**	**1**	**4**	**5**	**26**	**0**	**0**	**0**	**23**	**4.3**	**-24**	**1**	**0.0**	**19:48**									
2006-07	**St. Louis**	**NHL**	**64**	**2**	**5**	**7**	**55**	**0**	**0**	**0**	**40**	**5.0**	**-5**	**0**	**0.0**	**19:44**									
2007-08	**St. Louis**	**NHL**	**56**	**1**	**10**	**11**	**43**	**0**	**0**	**1**	**29**	**3.4**	**12**	**1**	**0.0**	**19:38**									
	New Jersey	**NHL**	**8**	**0**	**0**	**0**	**11**	**0**	**0**	**0**	**0**	**0.0**	**0**	**0**	**0.0**	**20:54**	**5**	**1**	**0**	**1**	**2**	**0**	**0**	**0**	**17:55**
2008-09	**New Jersey**	**NHL**	**76**	**3**	**13**	**16**	**78**	**0**	**0**	**2**	**68**	**4.4**	**-1**	**1**	**100.0**	**19:29**	**4**	**0**	**0**	**0**	**4**	**0**	**0**	**0**	**15:29**
2009-10	**New Jersey**	**NHL**	**79**	**4**	**10**	**14**	**57**	**0**	**0**	**2**	**47**	**8.5**	**8**	**0**	**0.0**	**18:52**	**5**	**0**	**0**	**0**	**6**	**0**	**0**	**0**	**16:04**
2010-11			DID NOT PLAY – INJURED																						
	NHL Totals		**610**	**23**	**70**	**93**	**559**	**2**	**0**	**9**	**437**	**5.3**		**4**	**25.0**	**18:34**	**50**	**3**	**1**	**4**	**38**	**0**	**0**	**1**	**15:08**

Signed as a free agent by **St. Louis**, December 16, 1996. Signed as a free agent by **Missouri** (UHL), March 11, 2005. Traded to **New Jersey** by **St. Louis** for Cam Janssen, February 26, 2008. • Missed 2010-11 due to concussion in pre-season game vs. Philadelphia, September 28, 2010.

SAMSON, Jerome
(SAM-sohn, jeh-ROHM) **CAR**

Right wing. Shoots right. 6', 195 lbs. Born, Greenfield Park, Que., September 4, 1987.

			Regular Season														Playoffs								
Season	Club	League	GP	G	A	Pts	PIM	PP	SH	GW	S	%	+/-	TF	F%	Min	GP	G	A	Pts	PIM	PP	SH	GW	Min
2004-05	Moncton Wildcats	QMJHL	63	6	11	17	22										12	1	4	5	8				
2005-06	Moncton Wildcats	QMJHL	62	20	32	52	46										21	6	12	18	15				
2006-07	Moncton Wildcats	QMJHL	38	19	33	52	20																		
	Val-d'Or Foreurs	QMJHL	33	25	22	47	16										20	14	12	26	10				
2007-08	Albany River Rats	AHL	65	21	18	39	38										7	1	1	2	2				
2008-09	Albany River Rats	AHL	70	22	32	54	56																		
2009-10	**Carolina**	**NHL**	**7**	**0**	**2**	**2**	**10**	**0**	**0**	**0**	**17**	**0.0**	**-1**	**1**	**0.0**	**8:27**									
	Albany River Rats	AHL	74	37	41	78	66										8	6	3	9	8				
2010-11	**Carolina**	**NHL**	**23**	**0**	**2**	**2**	**0**	**0**	**0**	**0**	**28**	**0.0**	**0**	**3**	**66.7**	**6:51**									
	Charlotte	AHL	53	26	28	54	44																		
	NHL Totals		**30**	**0**	**4**	**4**	**10**	**0**	**0**	**0**	**45**	**0.0**		**4**	**50.0**	**7:13**									

AHL First All-Star Team (2010)

Signed as a free agent by **Carolina**, July 2, 2007.

SAMSONOV, Sergei
(sam-SAW-nahf, SAIR-gay)

Left wing. Shoots right. 5'8", 188 lbs. Born, Moscow, USSR, October 27, 1978. Boston's 2nd choice, 8th overall, in 1997 Entry Draft.

			Regular Season														Playoffs								
Season	Club	League	GP	G	A	Pts	PIM	PP	SH	GW	S	%	+/-	TF	F%	Min	GP	G	A	Pts	PIM	PP	SH	GW	Min
1994-95	CSKA Moscow 2	CIS-2	50	110	72	182																			
	CSKA Moscow	CIS	13	2	2	4	14										2	0	0	0	0				
1995-96	CSKA Moscow	CIS	51	21	17	38	12										3	1	1	2	4				
1996-97	Detroit Vipers	IHL	73	29	35	64	18										19	8	4	12	12				
1997-98	**Boston**	**NHL**	**81**	**22**	**25**	**47**	**8**	**7**	**0**	**3**	**159**	**13.8**	**9**				**6**	**2**	**5**	**7**	**0**	**0**	**0**	**1**	
1998-99	**Boston**	**NHL**	**79**	**25**	**26**	**51**	**18**	**6**	**0**	**8**	**160**	**15.6**	**-6**	**0**	**0.0**	**16:23**	**11**	**3**	**1**	**4**	**0**	**0**	**0**	**0**	**16:11**
99-2000	**Boston**	**NHL**	**77**	**19**	**26**	**45**	**4**	**6**	**0**	**3**	**145**	**13.1**	**-6**	**3**	**0.0**	**16:32**									
2000-01	**Boston**	**NHL**	**82**	**29**	**46**	**75**	**18**	**3**	**0**	**3**	**215**	**13.5**	**6**	**14**	**42.9**	**19:23**									
2001-02	**Boston**	**NHL**	**74**	**29**	**41**	**70**	**27**	**3**	**0**	**4**	**192**	**15.1**	**21**	**1**	**0.0**	**18:47**	**6**	**2**	**2**	**4**	**0**	**0**	**0**	**0**	**17:41**
	Russia	Olympics	6	1	2	3	4																		
2002-03	**Boston**	**NHL**	**8**	**5**	**6**	**11**	**2**	**1**	**0**	**3**	**23**	**21.7**	**8**	**0**	**0.0**	**20:20**	**5**	**0**	**2**	**2**	**0**	**0**	**0**	**0**	**17:07**
2003-04	**Boston**	**NHL**	**58**	**17**	**23**	**40**	**4**	**3**	**0**	**5**	**132**	**12.9**	**12**	**4**	**25.0**	**17:27**	**7**	**2**	**5**	**7**	**0**	**0**	**0**	**0**	**17:18**
2004-05	Dynamo Moscow	Russia	3	1	0	1	0										3	1	2	3	0				
2005-06	**Boston**	**NHL**	**55**	**18**	**19**	**37**	**22**	**6**	**0**	**1**	**107**	**16.8**	**-3**	**1**	**100.0**	**16:53**									
	Edmonton	**NHL**	**19**	**5**	**11**	**16**	**6**	**4**	**0**	**0**	**36**	**13.9**	**0**	**2**	**0.0**	**15:26**	**24**	**4**	**11**	**15**	**14**	**1**	**0**	**0**	**14:30**
2006-07	**Montreal**	**NHL**	**63**	**9**	**17**	**26**	**10**	**0**	**0**	**0**	**114**	**7.9**	**-4**	**14**	**14.3**	**13:59**									
2007-08	**Chicago**	**NHL**	**23**	**0**	**4**	**4**	**6**	**0**	**0**	**0**	**38**	**0.0**	**-7**	**1**	**0.0**	**12:21**									
	Rockford IceHogs	AHL	2	1	0	1	0																		
	Carolina	**NHL**	**38**	**14**	**18**	**32**	**10**	**3**	**0**	**2**	**71**	**19.7**	**6**	**2**	**0.0**	**18:02**									
2008-09	**Carolina**	**NHL**	**81**	**16**	**32**	**48**	**28**	**3**	**0**	**3**	**155**	**10.3**	**-8**	**7**	**57.1**	**17:19**	**17**	**5**	**3**	**8**	**6**	**0**	**0**	**0**	**15:48**
2009-10	**Carolina**	**NHL**	**72**	**14**	**15**	**29**	**32**	**2**	**0**	**2**	**104**	**13.5**	**-15**	**4**	**0.0**	**13:23**									
2010-11	**Carolina**	**NHL**	**58**	**10**	**16**	**26**	**12**	**4**	**0**	**0**	**87**	**11.5**	**0**	**6**	**50.0**	**14:09**									
	Florida	**NHL**	**20**	**3**	**11**	**14**	**2**	**0**	**0**	**1**	**36**	**8.3**	**-2**	**5**	**0.0**	**19:14**									
	NHL Totals		**888**	**235**	**336**	**571**	**209**	**51**	**0**	**38**	**1774**	**13.2**		**64**	**26.6**	**16:34**	**76**	**18**	**29**	**47**	**20**	**1**	**0**	**1**	**15:49**

Garry F. Longman Memorial Trophy (IHL – Rookie of the Year) (1997) • NHL All-Rookie Team (1998) • Calder Memorial Trophy (1998)

Played in NHL All-Star Game (2001)

• Missed majority of 2002-03 due to wrist injury vs. Columbus, October 18, 2002. Signed as a free agent by **Dynamo Moscow** (Russia), February 2, 2005. Traded to **Edmonton** by **Boston** for Marty Reasoner, Yan Stastny and Edmonton's 2nd round choice (Milan Lucic) in 2006 Entry Draft, March 9, 2006. Signed as a free agent by **Montreal**, July 12, 2006. Traded to **Chicago** by **Montreal** for Jassen Cullimore and Tony Salmelainen, June 16, 2007. Claimed on waivers by **Carolina** from **Chicago**, January 8, 2008. Traded to **Florida** by **Carolina** for Bryan Allen, February 28, 2011.

SAMUELSSON, Mikael
(SAM-yuhl-suhn, MIH-kigh-ehl) **VAN**

Right wing. Shoots right. 6'1", 218 lbs. Born, Mariefred, Sweden, December 23, 1976. San Jose's 7th choice, 145th overall, in 1998 Entry Draft.

			Regular Season														Playoffs								
Season	Club	League	GP	G	A	Pts	PIM	PP	SH	GW	S	%	+/-	TF	F%	Min	GP	G	A	Pts	PIM	PP	SH	GW	Min
1994-95	Sodertalje SK Jr.	Swe-Jr.	30	8	6	14	12																		
1995-96	Sodertalje SK Jr.	Swe-Jr.	22	13	12	25	20																		
	Sodertalje SK	Sweden-2	18	5	1	6	0										4	0	0	0	0				
1996-97	Sodertalje SK Jr.	Swe-Jr.	2	2	1	3																			
	Sodertalje SK	Sweden	29	3	2	5	10										10	0	0	0	4				
1997-98	Nykoping	Sweden-2	10	5	1	6	14																		
	Sodertalje SK	Sweden	41	11	9	20	66																		
1998-99	Sodertalje SK	Sweden-2	18	13	10	23	26										10	2	2	4	12				
	V.Frolunda	Sweden	27	0	5	5	10																		
99-2000	Brynas IF Gavle	Sweden	40	4	3	7	76										11	7	2	9	6				
	Brynas IF Gavle	EuroHL	4	0	2	2	4																		
2000-01	**San Jose**	**NHL**	**4**	**0**	**0**	**0**	**0**	**0**	**0**	**0**	**3**	**0.0**	**0**	**0**	**0.0**	**4:41**									
	Kentucky	AHL	66	32	46	78	58										3	1	0	1	0				
2001-02	**NY Rangers**	**NHL**	**67**	**6**	**10**	**16**	**23**	**1**	**2**	**1**	**94**	**6.4**	**10**	**5**	**40.0**	**11:52**									
	Hartford	AHL	8	3	6	9	12																		
2002-03	**NY Rangers**	**NHL**	**58**	**8**	**14**	**22**	**32**	**1**	**1**	**2**	**118**	**6.8**	**0**	**35**	**42.9**	**15:32**									
	Pittsburgh	**NHL**	**22**	**2**	**0**	**2**	**8**	**1**	**0**	**0**	**36**	**5.6**	**-21**	**8**	**75.0**	**14:04**									
2003-04	**Florida**	**NHL**	**37**	**3**	**6**	**9**	**35**	**0**	**0**	**1**	**50**	**6.0**	**0**	**28**	**28.6**	**12:15**									
2004-05	Geneve	Swiss	12	2	4	6	14																		
	Sodertalje SK	Sweden	29	7	13	20	45										10	3	3	6	24				
2005-06	Rapperswil	Swiss	1	0	0	0	0																		
	Detroit	**NHL**	**71**	**23**	**22**	**45**	**42**	**7**	**0**	**3**	**187**	**12.3**	**27**	**11**	**27.3**	**13:31**	**6**	**0**	**1**	**1**	**6**	**0**	**0**	**0**	**15:33**
	Sweden	Olympics	8	1	3	4	2																		
2006-07	**Detroit**	**NHL**	**53**	**14**	**20**	**34**	**28**	**6**	**0**	**2**	**189**	**7.4**	**1**	**3**	**66.7**	**15:09**	**18**	**3**	**8**	**11**	**14**	**1**	**0**	**1**	**15:27**
2007-08 ♦	**Detroit**	**NHL**	**73**	**11**	**29**	**40**	**26**	**3**	**0**	**1**	**249**	**4.4**	**21**	**14**	**42.9**	**16:16**	**22**	**5**	**8**	**13**	**8**	**0**	**0**	**1**	**15:56**
2008-09	**Detroit**	**NHL**	**81**	**19**	**21**	**40**	**50**	**7**	**0**	**1**	**257**	**7.4**	**0**	**8**	**25.0**	**15:22**	**23**	**5**	**5**	**10**	**6**	**0**	**0**	**2**	**15:08**

Season	Club	League	GP	G	A	Pts	PIM	PP	SH	GW	S	%	+/-	TF	F%	Min	Playoffs GP	G	A	Pts	PIM	PP	SH	GW	Min
2009-10	**Vancouver**	**NHL**	**74**	**30**	**23**	**53**	**64**	**7**	**0**	**4**	**219**	**13.7**	**10**	**31**	**35.5**	**17:10**	**12**	**8**	**7**	**15**	**16**	**3**	**0**	**1**	**17:58**
2010-11	**Vancouver**	**NHL**	**75**	**18**	**32**	**50**	**36**	**5**	**0**	**2**	**215**	**8.4**	**8**	**28**	**32.1**	**16:38**	**11**	**1**	**2**	**3**	**8**	**0**	**0**	**1**	**16:26**
	NHL Totals		**615**	**134**	**177**	**311**	**344**	**38**	**3**	**17**	**1617**	**8.3**		**171**	**37.4**	**14:57**	**92**	**22**	**31**	**53**	**58**	**4**	**0**	**6**	**15:56**

Traded to **NY Rangers** by **San Jose** with Christian Gosselin for Adam Graves and future considerations, June 24, 2001. Traded to **Pittsburgh** by **NY Rangers** with Joel Bouchard, Richard Lintner and Rico Fata for Mike Wilson, Alex Kovalev, Janne Laukkanen and Dan LaCouture, February 10, 2003. Traded to **Florida** by **Pittsburgh** with Pittsburgh's 1st round choice (Nathan Horton) and 2nd round compensatory choice (Stefan Meyer) in 2003 Entry Draft for Florida's 1st (Marc-Andre Fleury) and 3rd (Daniel Carcillo) round choices in 2003 Entry Draft, June 21, 2003. • Missed majority of 2003-04 due to jaw (November 21, 2003 vs. Washington) and hand (January 21, 2004 vs. Columbus) injuries. Signed as a free agent by **Geneve** (Swiss), September 8, 2004. Signed as a free agent by **Sodertalje** (Sweden), October 26, 2004. Signed as a free agent by **Detroit**, September 17, 2005. Signed as a free agent by **Vancouver**, July 3, 2009.

SANGUINETTI, Bobby
(san-GIH-neh-tee, BAW-bee) **CAR**

Defense. Shoots right. 6'3", 190 lbs. Born, Trenton, NJ, February 29, 1988. NY Rangers' 1st choice, 21st overall, in 2006 Entry Draft.

Season	Club	League	GP	G	A	Pts	PIM	PP	SH	GW	S	%	+/-	TF	F%	Min	Playoffs GP	G	A	Pts	PIM	PP	SH	GW	Min
2003-04	Lawrenceville	High-NJ	26	4	17	21																			
2004-05	Owen Sound	OHL	67	4	20	24	12										5	0	2	2	0				
2005-06	Owen Sound	OHL	68	14	51	65	44										11	5	10	15	4				
2006-07	Owen Sound	OHL	67	23	30	53	48										4	3	3	6	2				
	Hartford	AHL	5	0	3	3	2										7	0	1	1	2				
2007-08	Brampton	OHL	61	29	41	70	38										5	1	3	4	10				
	Hartford	AHL	6	0	1	1	2										5	0	0	0	2				
2008-09	Hartford	AHL	78	6	36	42	42										6	1	4	5	6				
2009-10	**NY Rangers**	**NHL**	**5**	**0**	**0**	**0**	**4**	**0**	**0**	**0**	**5**	**0.0**	**0**	**0**	**0.0**	**11:32**									
	Hartford	AHL	61	9	29	38	22																		
2010-11	Charlotte	AHL	31	3	12	15	6										10	0	2	2	6				
	NHL Totals		**5**	**0**	**0**	**0**	**4**	**0**	**0**	**0**	**5**	**0.0**		**0**	**0.0**	**11:32**									

OHL Second All-Star Team (2008)

Traded to **Carolina** by **NY Rangers** for Carolina's 6th round choice (Jesper Fasth) in 2010 Entry Draft and Washington's 2nd round choice (previously acquired, later traded to Calgary – Calgary selected Tyler Wotherspoon) in 2011 Entry Draft, June 25, 2010. • Missed majority of 2010-11 due to hip injury.

SANTORELLI, Mike
(san-toh-REHL-ee, MIGHK) **FLA**

Center. Shoots right. 6', 189 lbs. Born, Vancouver, B.C., December 14, 1985. Nashville's 6th choice, 178th overall, in 2004 Entry Draft.

Season	Club	League	GP	G	A	Pts	PIM	PP	SH	GW	S	%	+/-	TF	F%	Min	Playoffs GP	G	A	Pts	PIM	PP	SH	GW	Min
2003-04	Vernon Vipers	BCHL	60	43	53	96	26										5	0	2	2	0				
2004-05	Northern Mich.	CCHA	40	16	14	30	22																		
2005-06	Northern Mich.	CCHA	40	15	18	33	24																		
2006-07	Northern Mich.	CCHA	41	*30	17	47	28																		
2007-08	Milwaukee	AHL	80	21	21	42	60										6	0	0	0	2				
2008-09	**Nashville**	**NHL**	**7**	**0**	**0**	**0**	**2**	**0**	**0**	**0**	**11**	**0.0**	**–5**	**47**	**44.7**	**12:15**									
	Milwaukee	AHL	70	27	43	70	36										11	6	5	11	6				
2009-10	**Nashville**	**NHL**	**25**	**2**	**1**	**3**	**8**	**0**	**0**	**0**	**36**	**5.6**	**–8**	**105**	**45.7**	**10:57**									
	Milwaukee	AHL	57	26	33	59	20										7	3	4	7	2				
2010-11	**Florida**	**NHL**	**82**	**20**	**21**	**41**	**20**	**5**	**1**	**1**	**193**	**10.4**	**–17**	**1032**	**50.2**	**16:41**									
	NHL Totals		**114**	**22**	**22**	**44**	**30**	**5**	**1**	**1**	**240**	**9.2**		**1184**	**49.6**	**15:09**									

CCHA All-Rookie Team (2005) • CCHA First All-Star Team (2007) • NCAA West Second All-American Team (2007)

Traded to **Florida** by **Nashville** for Florida's 4th round choice (Josh Shalla) in 2011 Entry Draft, August 5, 2010.

SARICH, Cory
(SAHR-ihch, KOH-ree) **CGY**

Defense. Shoots right. 6'4", 207 lbs. Born, Saskatoon, Sask., August 16, 1978. Buffalo's 2nd choice, 27th overall, in 1996 Entry Draft.

Season	Club	League	GP	G	A	Pts	PIM	PP	SH	GW	S	%	+/-	TF	F%	Min	Playoffs GP	G	A	Pts	PIM	PP	SH	GW	Min
1994-95	Sask. Contacts	SMHL	31	5	22	27	99																		
	Saskatoon Blades	WHL	6	0	0	0	4										3	0	1	1	0				
1995-96	Saskatoon Blades	WHL	59	5	18	23	54										3	0	0	0	4				
1996-97	Saskatoon Blades	WHL	58	6	27	33	133																		
1997-98	Saskatoon Blades	WHL	33	5	24	29	90																		
	Seattle	WHL	13	3	16	19	47																		
1998-99	**Buffalo**	**NHL**	**4**	**0**	**0**	**0**	**0**	**0**	**0**	**0**	**2**	**0.0**	**3**	**0**	**0.0**	**13:11**									
	Rochester	AHL	77	3	26	29	82										20	2	4	6	14				
99-2000	**Buffalo**	**NHL**	**42**	**0**	**4**	**4**	**35**	**0**	**0**	**0**	**49**	**0.0**	**2**	**0**	**0.0**	**17:42**									
	Rochester	AHL	15	0	6	6	44																		
	Tampa Bay	**NHL**	**17**	**0**	**2**	**2**	**42**	**0**	**0**	**0**	**20**	**0.0**	**–8**	**0**	**0.0**	**20:42**									
2000-01	**Tampa Bay**	**NHL**	**73**	**1**	**8**	**9**	**106**	**0**	**0**	**1**	**66**	**1.5**	**–25**	**3**	**0.0**	**18:44**									
	Detroit Vipers	IHL	3	0	2	2	2																		
2001-02	**Tampa Bay**	**NHL**	**72**	**0**	**11**	**11**	**105**	**0**	**0**	**0**	**55**	**0.0**	**–4**	**2**	**50.0**	**16:06**									
	Springfield	AHL	2	0	0	0	0																		
2002-03	**Tampa Bay**	**NHL**	**82**	**5**	**9**	**14**	**63**	**0**	**0**	**2**	**79**	**6.3**	**–3**	**3**	**0.0**	**19:36**	**11**	**0**	**2**	**2**	**6**	**0**	**0**	**0**	**21:18**
2003-04♦	**Tampa Bay**	**NHL**	**82**	**3**	**16**	**19**	**89**	**0**	**1**	**1**	**93**	**3.2**	**5**	**1**	**0.0**	**18:31**	**23**	**0**	**2**	**2**	**25**	**0**	**0**	**0**	**19:11**
2004-05			DID NOT PLAY																						
2005-06	**Tampa Bay**	**NHL**	**82**	**1**	**14**	**15**	**79**	**0**	**0**	**0**	**88**	**1.1**	**–2**	**0**	**0.0**	**18:34**	**5**	**0**	**1**	**1**	**4**	**0**	**0**	**0**	**15:46**
2006-07	**Tampa Bay**	**NHL**	**82**	**0**	**15**	**15**	**70**	**0**	**0**	**0**	**64**	**0.0**	**–6**	**1**	**0.0**	**18:07**	**6**	**0**	**0**	**0**	**2**	**0**	**0**	**0**	**16:37**
2007-08	**Calgary**	**NHL**	**80**	**2**	**5**	**7**	**135**	**0**	**0**	**0**	**57**	**3.5**	**2**	**0**	**0.0**	**18:49**	**7**	**0**	**1**	**1**	**4**	**0**	**0**	**0**	**19:35**
2008-09	**Calgary**	**NHL**	**76**	**2**	**18**	**20**	**112**	**0**	**0**	**0**	**57**	**3.5**	**12**	**0**	**0.0**	**17:53**	**5**	**0**	**1**	**1**	**4**	**0**	**0**	**0**	**18:44**
2009-10	**Calgary**	**NHL**	**57**	**1**	**5**	**6**	**58**	**0**	**0**	**1**	**46**	**2.2**	**4**	**0**	**0.0**	**15:57**									
2010-11	**Calgary**	**NHL**	**76**	**4**	**13**	**17**	**75**	**0**	**0**	**1**	**75**	**5.3**	**11**	**1**	**0.0**	**17:53**									
	NHL Totals		**825**	**19**	**120**	**139**	**969**	**0**	**1**	**6**	**751**	**2.5**		**11**	**9.1**	**18:07**	**57**	**0**	**7**	**7**	**45**	**0**	**0**	**0**	**19:02**

WHL West Second All-Star Team (1998) • AHL All-Rookie Team (1999)

Traded to **Tampa Bay** by **Buffalo** with Wayne Primeau, Brian Holzinger and Buffalo's 3rd round choice (Alexander Kharitonov) in 2000 Entry Draft for Chris Gratton and Tampa Bay's 2nd round choice (Derek Roy) in 2001 Entry Draft, March 9, 2000. Signed as a free agent by **Calgary**, July 1, 2007.

SAUER, Michael
(SAW-uhr, MIGH-kuhl) **NYR**

Defense. Shoots right. 6'3", 213 lbs. Born, St. Cloud, MN, August 7, 1987. NY Rangers' 2nd choice, 40th overall, in 2005 Entry Draft.

Season	Club	League	GP	G	A	Pts	PIM	PP	SH	GW	S	%	+/-	TF	F%	Min	Playoffs GP	G	A	Pts	PIM	PP	SH	GW	Min
2003-04	St. Cloud Tech	High-MN	18	12	16	28	34																		
2004-05	Portland	WHL	32	2	11	13	10																		
2005-06	Portland	WHL	59	8	23	31	68										12	4	2	6	8				
2006-07	Portland	WHL	33	4	8	12	46																		
	Medicine Hat	WHL	32	1	10	11	29										23	1	5	6	34				
2007-08	Hartford	AHL	71	4	7	11	80										2	0	0	0	0				
2008-09	**NY Rangers**	**NHL**	**3**	**0**	**0**	**0**	**0**	**0**	**0**	**0**	**2**	**0.0**	**–1**	**0**	**0.0**	**9:21**									
	Hartford	AHL	64	6	17	23	35										6	0	0	0	10				
2009-10	Hartford	AHL	42	3	9	12	45																		
2010-11	**NY Rangers**	**NHL**	**76**	**3**	**12**	**15**	**75**	**1**	**0**	**2**	**54**	**5.6**	**20**	**0**	**0.0**	**17:31**	**5**	**0**	**1**	**1**	**0**	**0**	**0**	**0**	**23:16**
	NHL Totals		**79**	**3**	**12**	**15**	**75**	**1**	**0**	**2**	**56**	**5.4**		**0**	**0.0**	**17:12**	**5**	**0**	**1**	**1**	**0**	**0**	**0**	**0**	**23:16**

• Missed majority of 2004-05 due to recurring hip injury.

SAUVE, Yann
(soh-VAY, YAHN) **VAN**

Defense. Shoots left. 6'3", 209 lbs. Born, Montreal, Que., February 18, 1990. Vancouver's 2nd choice, 41st overall, in 2008 Entry Draft.

Season	Club	League	GP	G	A	Pts	PIM	PP	SH	GW	S	%	+/-	TF	F%	Min	Playoffs GP	G	A	Pts	PIM	PP	SH	GW	Min
2005-06	Chateauguay	QAAA	42	14	15	29	63										19	2	12	14	44				
2006-07	Saint John	QMJHL	60	2	13	15	75																		
2007-08	Saint John	QMJHL	69	6	15	21	92										14	1	2	3	23				
2008-09	Saint John	QMJHL	61	5	25	30	64										4	0	2	2	8				
2009-10	Saint John	QMJHL	61	7	29	36	65										21	5	10	15	36				
2010-11	**Vancouver**	**NHL**	**5**	**0**	**0**	**0**	**0**	**0**	**0**	**0**	**6**	**0.0**	**–2**	**0**	**0.0**	**13:00**									
	Manitoba Moose	AHL	39	3	11	14	24										13	0	1	1	4				
	Victoria	ECHL	8	0	2	2	4																		
	NHL Totals		**5**	**0**	**0**	**0**	**0**	**0**	**0**	**0**	**6**	**0.0**		**0**	**0.0**	**13:00**									

SAVARD, Marc
(suh-VAHRD, MAHRK) **BOS**

Center. Shoots left. 5'10", 191 lbs. Born, Ottawa, Ont., July 17, 1977. NY Rangers' 3rd choice, 91st overall, in 1995 Entry Draft.

			Regular Season														Playoffs								
Season	Club	League	GP	G	A	Pts	PIM	PP	SH	GW	S	%	+/-	TF	F%	Min	GP	G	A	Pts	PIM	PP	SH	GW	Min
1992-93	Metcalfe Jets	ON-Jr.B	36	*44	55	*99	38	....	....	....	....	....	....	....	....	....	....	....	....	....	....	....	....	....	....
1993-94	Oshawa Generals	OHL	61	18	39	57	20	....	....	....	....	....	....	....	....	....	5	4	3	7	8	....	....	....	....
1994-95	Oshawa Generals	OHL	66	43	96	*139	78	....	....	....	....	....	....	....	....	....	7	5	6	11	8	....	....	....	....
1995-96	Oshawa Generals	OHL	48	28	59	87	77	....	....	....	....	....	....	....	....	....	5	4	5	9	6	....	....	....	....
1996-97	Oshawa Generals	OHL	64	43	*87	*130	94	....	....	....	....	....	....	....	....	....	18	13	*24	*37	20	....	....	....	....
1997-98	**NY Rangers**	**NHL**	28	1	5	6	4	0	0	0	32	3.1	–4	....	....	....	....	....	....	....	....	....	....	....	....
	Hartford	AHL	58	21	53	74	66	....	....	....	....	....	....	....	....	....	15	8	19	27	24	....	....	....	....
1998-99	**NY Rangers**	**NHL**	70	9	36	45	38	4	0	1	116	7.8	–7	956	48.4	14:35	....	....	....	....	....	....	....	....	....
	Hartford	AHL	9	3	10	13	16	....	....	....	....	....	....	....	....	....	7	1	12	13	16	....	....	....	....
99-2000	**Calgary**	**NHL**	78	22	31	53	56	4	0	3	184	12.0	–2	1021	49.6	16:36	....	....	....	....	....	....	....	....	....
2000-01	**Calgary**	**NHL**	77	23	42	65	46	10	1	5	197	11.7	–12	1050	53.1	19:13	....	....	....	....	....	....	....	....	....
2001-02	**Calgary**	**NHL**	56	14	19	33	48	7	0	3	140	10.0	–18	577	54.8	17:20	....	....	....	....	....	....	....	....	....
2002-03	**Calgary**	**NHL**	10	1	2	3	8	0	0	0	21	4.8	–3	89	52.8	14:41	....	....	....	....	....	....	....	....	....
	Atlanta	**NHL**	57	16	31	47	77	6	0	4	127	12.6	–11	1247	50.9	19:50	....	....	....	....	....	....	....	....	....
2003-04	**Atlanta**	**NHL**	45	19	33	52	85	6	1	3	133	14.3	–8	1083	49.9	22:19	....	....	....	....	....	....	....	....	....
2004-05	HC Thurgau	Swiss-2	13	9	19	28	10	....	....	....	....	....	....	....	....	....	....	....	....	....	....	....	....	....	....
	SC Bern	Swiss	5	1	2	3	0	....	....	....	....	....	....	....	....	....	....	....	....	....	....	....	....	....	....
2005-06	**Atlanta**	**NHL**	82	28	69	97	100	14	1	4	212	13.2	7	1529	51.6	20:30	....	....	....	....	....	....	....	....	....
2006-07	**Boston**	**NHL**	82	22	74	96	96	10	1	3	221	10.0	–19	1420	50.1	20:13	....	....	....	....	....	....	....	....	....
2007-08	**Boston**	**NHL**	74	15	63	78	66	4	0	2	196	7.7	3	1555	51.6	20:31	7	1	5	6	6	0	0	1	17:06
2008-09	**Boston**	**NHL**	82	25	63	88	70	9	0	5	213	11.7	25	1289	49.9	19:32	11	6	7	13	4	3	0	2	19:36
2009-10	**Boston**	**NHL**	41	10	23	33	14	6	0	2	90	11.1	2	648	48.8	18:35	7	1	2	3	12	0	0	1	17:22
2010-11 ♦	**Boston**	**NHL**	25	2	8	10	29	0	0	1	50	4.0	–7	328	50.9	15:48	....	....	....	....	....	....	....	....	....
	NHL Totals		**807**	**207**	**499**	**706**	**737**	**80**	**4**	**36**	**1932**	**10.7**		**12792**	**50.8**	**18:49**	**25**	**8**	**14**	**22**	**22**	**3**	**0**	**4**	**18:16**

OHL Second All-Star Team (1995) • AHL All-Rookie Team (1998)

Played in NHL All-Star Game (2008, 2009)

Traded to **Calgary** by **NY Rangers** with NY Rangers 1st round choice (Oleg Saprykin) in 1999 Entry Draft for the rights to Jan Hlavac and Calgary's 1st (Jamie Lundmark) and 3rd (later traded back to Calgary – Calgary selected Craig Andersson) round choices in 1999 Entry Draft, June 26, 1999. Traded to **Atlanta** by **Calgary** for Ruslan Zainullin, November 15, 2002. Signed as a free agent by **Thurgau** (Swiss-2), October 11, 2004. Signed as a free agent by **Bern** (Swiss), November 23, 2004. Signed as a free agent by **Boston**, July 1, 2006. • Missed majority of 2010-11 due to concussions at Pittsburgh, March 7, 2010, and at Colorado, January 22, 2011.

SAWADA, Raymond
(suh-WAW-duh, RAY-muhnd) **DAL**

Right wing. Shoots right. 6'2", 207 lbs. Born, Richmond, B.C., February 19, 1985. Dallas' 3rd choice, 52nd overall, in 2004 Entry Draft.

Season	Club	League	GP	G	A	Pts	PIM	PP	SH	GW	S	%	+/-	TF	F%	Min	GP	G	A	Pts	PIM	PP	SH	GW	Min
2002-03	Richmond	PIJHL	36	7	17	24	155	....	....	....	....	....	....	....	....	....	....	....	....	....	....	....	....	....	....
2003-04	Nanaimo Clippers	BCHL	54	20	32	52	93	....	....	....	....	....	....	....	....	....	25	6	16	22	22	....	....	....	....
2004-05	Cornell Big Red	ECAC	35	4	5	9	48	....	....	....	....	....	....	....	....	....	....	....	....	....	....	....	....	....	....
2005-06	Cornell Big Red	ECAC	35	7	13	20	20	....	....	....	....	....	....	....	....	....	....	....	....	....	....	....	....	....	....
2006-07	Cornell Big Red	ECAC	31	10	11	21	29	....	....	....	....	....	....	....	....	....	....	....	....	....	....	....	....	....	....
2007-08	Cornell Big Red	ECAC	36	10	16	26	34	....	....	....	....	....	....	....	....	....	....	....	....	....	....	....	....	....	....
	Iowa Stars	AHL	10	2	7	9	14	....	....	....	....	....	....	....	....	....	....	....	....	....	....	....	....	....	....
2008-09	**Dallas**	**NHL**	5	1	0	1	0	0	0	0	2	50.0	–1	0	0.0	8:42	....	....	....	....	....	....	....	....	....
	Manitoba Moose	AHL	52	6	15	21	31	....	....	....	....	....	....	....	....	....	22	4	4	8	4	....	....	....	....
2009-10	**Dallas**	**NHL**	5	0	0	0	0	0	0	0	2	0.0	1	0	0.0	8:09	....	....	....	....	....	....	....	....	....
	Texas Stars	AHL	60	8	11	19	92	....	....	....	....	....	....	....	....	....	24	3	5	8	20	....	....	....	....
2010-11	**Dallas**	**NHL**	1	0	0	0	0	0	0	0	1	0.0	–1	0	0.0	5:50	....	....	....	....	....	....	....	....	....
	Texas Stars	AHL	57	11	18	29	91	....	....	....	....	....	....	....	....	....	6	1	5	6	2	....	....	....	....
	NHL Totals		**11**	**1**	**0**	**1**	**0**	**0**	**0**	**0**	**5**	**20.0**		**0**	**0.0**	**8:11**	....	....	....	....	....	....	....	....	....

SBISA, Luca
(S'BEE-za, LOO-ka) **ANA**

Defense. Shoots left. 6'2", 207 lbs. Born, Ozieri, Italy, January 30, 1990. Philadelphia's 1st choice, 19th overall, in 2008 Entry Draft.

Season	Club	League	GP	G	A	Pts	PIM	PP	SH	GW	S	%	+/-	TF	F%	Min	GP	G	A	Pts	PIM	PP	SH	GW	Min
2005-06	EV Zug Jr.	Swiss-Jr.	18	0	3	3	18	....	....	....	....	....	....	....	....	....	....	....	....	....	....	....	....	....	....
2006-07	EV Zug Jr.	Swiss-Jr.	STATISTICS NOT AVAILABLE																						
	EHC Seewen	Swiss-3	6	1	2	3	4	....	....	....	....	....	....	....	....	....	....	....	....	....	....	....	....	....	....
	EV Zug	Swiss	7	0	0	0	0	....	....	....	....	....	....	....	....	....	1	0	0	0	0	....	....	....	....
2007-08	Lethbridge	WHL	62	6	27	33	63	....	....	....	....	....	....	....	....	....	19	3	12	15	17	....	....	....	....
2008-09	**Philadelphia**	**NHL**	39	0	7	7	36	0	0	0	38	0.0	–6	0	0.0	17:29	1	0	0	0	2	0	0	0	5:37
	Lethbridge	WHL	18	4	11	15	19	....	....	....	....	....	....	....	....	....	11	2	1	3	12	....	....	....	....
	Philadelphia	AHL	2	1	1	2	2	....	....	....	....	....	....	....	....	....	....	....	....	....	....	....	....	....	....
2009-10	**Anaheim**	**NHL**	8	0	0	0	6	0	0	0	3	0.0	–1	0	0.0	12:38	....	....	....	....	....	....	....	....	....
	Lethbridge	WHL	17	1	12	13	18	....	....	....	....	....	....	....	....	....	....	....	....	....	....	....	....	....	....
	Portland	WHL	12	3	2	5	11	....	....	....	....	....	....	....	....	....	13	2	2	4	26	....	....	....	....
	Switzerland	Olympics	5	0	0	0	0	....	....	....	....	....	....	....	....	....	....	....	....	....	....	....	....	....	....
2010-11	**Anaheim**	**NHL**	68	2	9	11	43	1	0	0	76	2.6	–11	0	0.0	16:48	6	0	1	1	8	0	0	0	16:29
	Syracuse Crunch	AHL	8	2	7	9	4	....	....	....	....	....	....	....	....	....	....	....	....	....	....	....	....	....	....
	NHL Totals		**115**	**2**	**16**	**18**	**85**	**1**	**0**	**0**	**117**	**1.7**		**0**	**0.0**	**16:44**	**7**	**0**	**1**	**1**	**10**	**0**	**0**	**0**	**14:57**

Traded to **Anaheim** by **Philadelphia** with Joffrey Lupul, Philadelphia's 1st round choices in 2009 (later traded to Columbus - Columbus selected John Moore) and 2010 (Emerson Etem) Entry Drafts and future considerations for Chris Pronger and Ryan Dingle, June 26, 2009.

SCANDELLA, Marco
(skan-DEHL-a, MAHR-koh) **MIN**

Defense. Shoots left. 6'3", 217 lbs. Born, Montreal, Que., February 23, 1990. Minnesota's 2nd choice, 55th overall, in 2008 Entry Draft.

Season	Club	League	GP	G	A	Pts	PIM	PP	SH	GW	S	%	+/-	TF	F%	Min	GP	G	A	Pts	PIM	PP	SH	GW	Min
2005-06	Ecole Montpetit	QAAA	42	3	4	7	40	....	....	....	....	....	....	....	....	....	3	0	0	0	2	....	....	....	....
2006-07	Mtl. Predators	QAAA	42	7	13	20	66	....	....	....	....	....	....	....	....	....	3	0	1	1	10	....	....	....	....
2007-08	Val-d'Or Foreurs	QMJHL	65	4	10	14	35	....	....	....	....	....	....	....	....	....	4	0	1	1	4	....	....	....	....
2008-09	Val-d'Or Foreurs	QMJHL	58	10	27	37	64	....	....	....	....	....	....	....	....	....	....	....	....	....	....	....	....	....	....
	Houston Aeros	AHL	2	0	0	0	0	....	....	....	....	....	....	....	....	....	6	0	0	0	2	....	....	....	....
2009-10	Val-d'Or Foreurs	QMJHL	31	9	22	31	41	....	....	....	....	....	....	....	....	....	6	2	4	6	4	....	....	....	....
	Houston Aeros	AHL	7	0	1	1	7	....	....	....	....	....	....	....	....	....	....	....	....	....	....	....	....	....	....
2010-11	**Minnesota**	**NHL**	20	0	2	2	2	0	0	0	13	0.0	–9	0	0.0	14:58	....	....	....	....	....	....	....	....	....
	Houston Aeros	AHL	33	3	16	19	17	....	....	....	....	....	....	....	....	....	20	2	6	8	8	....	....	....	....
	NHL Totals		**20**	**0**	**2**	**2**	**2**	**0**	**0**	**0**	**13**	**0.0**		**0**	**0.0**	**14:58**	....	....	....	....	....	....	....	....	....

SCATCHARD, Dave
(SKAT-chuhrd, DAYV)

Center. Shoots right. 6'3", 220 lbs. Born, Hinton, Alta., February 20, 1976. Vancouver's 3rd choice, 42nd overall, in 1994 Entry Draft.

Season	Club	League	GP	G	A	Pts	PIM	PP	SH	GW	S	%	+/-	TF	F%	Min	GP	G	A	Pts	PIM	PP	SH	GW	Min
1991-92	Salmon Arm	Minor-BC	65	98	100	198	167	....	....	....	....	....	....	....	....	....	....	....	....	....	....	....	....	....	....
1992-93	Kimberley	RMJHL	51	20	23	43	61	....	....	....	....	....	....	....	....	....	....	....	....	....	....	....	....	....	....
1993-94	Portland	WHL	47	9	11	20	46	....	....	....	....	....	....	....	....	....	10	2	1	3	4	....	....	....	....
1994-95	Portland	WHL	71	20	30	50	148	....	....	....	....	....	....	....	....	....	8	0	3	3	21	....	....	....	....
1995-96	Portland	WHL	59	19	28	47	146	....	....	....	....	....	....	....	....	....	7	1	8	9	14	....	....	....	....
	Syracuse Crunch	AHL	1	0	0	0	0	....	....	....	....	....	....	....	....	....	15	2	5	7	29	....	....	....	....
1996-97	Syracuse Crunch	AHL	26	8	7	15	65	....	....	....	....	....	....	....	....	....	....	....	....	....	....	....	....	....	....
1997-98	**Vancouver**	**NHL**	76	13	11	24	165	0	0	1	85	15.3	–4	....	....	....	....	....	....	....	....	....	....	....	....
1998-99	**Vancouver**	**NHL**	82	13	13	26	140	0	2	2	130	10.0	–12	1007	56.3	13:46	....	....	....	....	....	....	....	....	....
99-2000	**Vancouver**	**NHL**	21	0	4	4	24	0	0	0	25	0.0	–3	190	59.5	10:12	....	....	....	....	....	....	....	....	....
	NY Islanders	**NHL**	44	12	14	26	93	0	1	1	103	11.7	0	710	55.8	13:42	....	....	....	....	....	....	....	....	....
2000-01	**NY Islanders**	**NHL**	81	21	24	45	114	4	0	5	176	11.9	–9	1322	55.1	16:50	....	....	....	....	....	....	....	....	....
2001-02	**NY Islanders**	**NHL**	80	12	15	27	111	3	1	4	117	10.3	–4	788	53.8	12:31	7	1	1	2	22	0	0	0	12:38
2002-03	**NY Islanders**	**NHL**	81	27	18	45	108	5	0	2	165	16.4	9	1147	52.7	14:30	5	1	0	1	6	0	0	1	15:58
2003-04	**NY Islanders**	**NHL**	61	9	16	25	78	1	1	1	111	8.1	12	1052	52.7	16:13	5	0	1	1	6	0	0	0	16:18
2004-05			DID NOT PLAY																						
2005-06	**Boston**	**NHL**	16	4	6	10	28	1	0	0	40	10.0	–2	272	54.8	16:56	....	....	....	....	....	....	....	....	....
	Phoenix	**NHL**	47	11	12	23	84	4	0	3	81	13.6	–11	594	53.2	14:44	....	....	....	....	....	....	....	....	....
2006-07	**Phoenix**	**NHL**	46	3	5	8	72	0	0	1	77	3.9	–18	385	52.5	13:31	....	....	....	....	....	....	....	....	....

			Regular Season														Playoffs								
Season	Club	League	GP	G	A	Pts	PIM	PP	SH	GW	S	%	+/-	TF	F%	Min	GP	G	A	Pts	PIM	PP	SH	GW	Min
2007-08	Hartford	AHL	3	0	1	1	0	....	....	....	....	....	....	....	....	....	....	....	....	....	....	....	....	....	....
	Milwaukee	AHL	8	1	2	3	14	....	....	....	....	....	....	....	....	....	....	....	....	....	....	....	....	....	....
2008-09			DID NOT PLAY – INJURED																						
2009-10	**Nashville**	**NHL**	**16**	**3**	**2**	**5**	**17**	**0**	**0**	**0**	**25**	**12.0**	**3**	**81**	**51.9**	**10:42**	....	....	....	....	....	....	....	....	....
	Milwaukee	AHL	36	20	10	30	59	....	....	....	....	....	....	....	....	....	3	0	0	0	2	....	....	....	....
2010-11	**St. Louis**	**NHL**	**8**	**0**	**1**	**1**	**6**	**0**	**0**	**0**	**6**	**0.0**	**1**	**26**	**46.2**	**4:45**	....	....	....	....	....	....	....	....	....
	Peoria Rivermen	AHL	41	7	11	18	50	....	....	....	....	....	....	....	....	....	....	....	....	....	....	....	....	....	....
	NHL Totals		**659**	**128**	**141**	**269**	**1040**	**18**	**5**	**20**	**1141**	**11.2**		**7574**	**54.2**	**14:11**	**17**	**2**	**2**	**4**	**34**	**0**	**0**	**1**	**14:41**

Traded to **NY Islanders** by **Vancouver** with Kevin Weekes and Bill Muckalt for Felix Potvin, NY Islanders' 2nd round compensatory choice (later traded to New Jersey – New Jersey selected Teemu Laine) in 2000 Entry Draft and NY Islanders' 3rd round choice (Thatcher Bell) in 2000 Entry Draft, December 19, 1999. Signed as a free agent by **Boston**, August 2, 2005. Traded to **Phoenix** by **Boston** for David Tanabe, November 18, 2005. • Missed remainder of 2006-07 season, majority of 2007-08 season and entire 2008-09 due to concussion vs. Pittsburgh, January 27, 2007. Signed to a PTO (professional tryout) contract by **Hartford** (AHL), October 17, 2007. Signed to a PTO (professional tryout) contract by **Milwaukee** (AHL), November 15, 2007. Signed as a free agent by **Nashville**, October 7, 2009. Signed as a free agent by **St. Louis**, August 4, 2010.

SCEVIOUR, Colton
(SEE-vee-yuhr, KOHL-tuhn) **DAL**

Center/Right wing. Shoots right. 6', 201 lbs. Born, Red Deer, Alta., April 20, 1989. Dallas' 3rd choice, 112th overall, in 2007 Entry Draft.

2004-05	Red Deer	AMHL	36	15	22	37	32	....	....	....	....	....	....	....	....	....	....	....	....	....	....	....	....	....	....
	Portland	WHL	6	1	0	1	6	....	....	....	....	....	....	....	....	....	4	0	0	0	0	....	....	....	....
2005-06	Portland	WHL	58	3	6	9	25	....	....	....	....	....	....	....	....	....	12	0	1	1	4	....	....	....	....
2006-07	Portland	WHL	49	12	26	38	38	....	....	....	....	....	....	....	....	....	....	....	....	....	....	....	....	....	....
2007-08	Portland	WHL	17	2	8	10	9	....	....	....	....	....	....	....	....	....	....	....	....	....	....	....	....	....	....
	Lethbridge	WHL	52	31	23	54	36	....	....	....	....	....	....	....	....	....	19	3	10	13	15	....	....	....	....
2008-09	Lethbridge	WHL	69	29	51	80	48	....	....	....	....	....	....	....	....	....	11	4	3	7	12	....	....	....	....
2009-10	Texas Stars	AHL	80	9	22	31	19	....	....	....	....	....	....	....	....	....	24	1	7	8	12	....	....	....	....
2010-11	**Dallas**	**NHL**	**1**	**0**	**0**	**0**	**0**	**0**	**0**	**0**	**0**	**0.0**	**–1**	**0**	**0.0**	**5:09**	....	....	....	....	....	....	....	....	....
	Texas Stars	AHL	77	16	25	41	17	....	....	....	....	....	....	....	....	....	6	1	0	1	0	....	....	....	....
	NHL Totals		**1**	**0**	**0**	**0**	**0**	**0**	**0**	**0**	**0**	**0.0**		**0**	**0.0**	**5:09**	....	....	....	....	....	....	....	....	....

SCHENN, Brayden
(SHEHN, BRAY-duhn) **PHI**

Center. Shoots left. 6', 193 lbs. Born, Saskatoon, Sask., August 22, 1991. Los Angeles' 1st choice, 5th overall, in 2009 Entry Draft.

2006-07	Sask. Contacts	SMHL	41	27	43	70	63	....	....	....	....	....	....	....	....	....	....	....	....	....	....	....	....	....	....
2007-08	Brandon	WHL	66	28	43	71	48	....	....	....	....	....	....	....	....	....	6	2	1	3	14	....	....	....	....
2008-09	Brandon	WHL	70	32	56	88	82	....	....	....	....	....	....	....	....	....	12	8	10	18	12	....	....	....	....
2009-10	**Los Angeles**	**NHL**	**1**	**0**	**0**	**0**	**0**	**0**	**0**	**0**	**0**	**0.0**	**–1**	**14**	**28.6**	**12:31**	....	....	....	....	....	....	....	....	....
	Brandon	WHL	59	34	65	99	55	....	....	....	....	....	....	....	....	....	15	8	11	19	2	....	....	....	....
2010-11	**Los Angeles**	**NHL**	**8**	**0**	**2**	**2**	**0**	**0**	**0**	**0**	**11**	**0.0**	**–1**	**51**	**33.3**	**11:15**	....	....	....	....	....	....	....	....	....
	Brandon	WHL	2	1	3	4	2	....	....	....	....	....	....	....	....	....	....	....	....	....	....	....	....	....	....
	Saskatoon Blades	WHL	27	21	32	53	23	....	....	....	....	....	....	....	....	....	10	6	5	11	14	....	....	....	....
	Manchester	AHL	7	3	4	7	4	....	....	....	....	....	....	....	....	....	5	1	3	4	0	....	....	....	....
	NHL Totals		**9**	**0**	**2**	**2**	**0**	**0**	**0**	**0**	**11**	**0.0**		**65**	**32.3**	**11:23**	....	....	....	....	....	....	....	....	....

WHL Rookie of the Year (2008) • Canadian Major Junior All-Rookie Team (2008) • WHL East Second All-Star Team (2009, 2011) • WHL East First All-Star Team (2010)

Traded to **Philadelphia** by **Los Angeles** with Wayne Simmonds and Los Angeles' 2nd round choice in 2012 Entry Draft for Mike Richards and Rob Bordson, June 23, 2011.

SCHENN, Luke
(SHEHN, LEWK) **TOR**

Defense. Shoots right. 6'2", 229 lbs. Born, Saskatoon, Sask., November 2, 1989. Toronto's 1st choice, 5th overall, in 2008 Entry Draft.

2004-05	Sask. Contacts	SMHL	41	5	22	27	69	....	....	....	....	....	....	....	....	....	....	....	....	....	....	....	....	....	....
2005-06	Kelowna Rockets	WHL	60	3	8	11	86	....	....	....	....	....	....	....	....	....	12	0	0	0	14	....	....	....	....
2006-07	Kelowna Rockets	WHL	72	2	27	29	139	....	....	....	....	....	....	....	....	....	....	....	....	....	....	....	....	....	....
2007-08	Kelowna Rockets	WHL	57	7	21	28	100	....	....	....	....	....	....	....	....	....	7	2	2	4	6	....	....	....	....
2008-09	**Toronto**	**NHL**	**70**	**2**	**12**	**14**	**71**	**1**	**0**	**0**	**102**	**2.0**	**–12**	**0**	**0.0**	**21:32**	....	....	....	....	....	....	....	....	....
2009-10	**Toronto**	**NHL**	**79**	**5**	**12**	**17**	**50**	**0**	**0**	**1**	**101**	**5.0**	**2**	**0**	**0.0**	**16:53**	....	....	....	....	....	....	....	....	....
2010-11	**Toronto**	**NHL**	**82**	**5**	**17**	**22**	**34**	**0**	**0**	**0**	**128**	**3.9**	**–7**	**0**	**0.0**	**22:22**	....	....	....	....	....	....	....	....	....
	NHL Totals		**231**	**12**	**41**	**53**	**155**	**1**	**0**	**1**	**331**	**3.6**		**0**	**0.0**	**20:14**	....	....	....	....	....	....	....	....	....

WHL West Second All-Star Team (2008) • NHL All-Rookie Team (2009)

SCHLEMKO, David
(SHLEHM-koh, DAY-vihd) **PHX**

Defense. Shoots left. 6'1", 201 lbs. Born, Edmonton, Alta., May 7, 1987.

2004-05	Medicine Hat	WHL	65	5	24	29	23	....	....	....	....	....	....	....	....	....	13	0	3	3	10	....	....	....	....
2005-06	Medicine Hat	WHL	69	9	35	44	44	....	....	....	....	....	....	....	....	....	13	2	5	7	15	....	....	....	....
2006-07	Medicine Hat	WHL	64	8	50	58	78	....	....	....	....	....	....	....	....	....	23	3	13	16	12	....	....	....	....
2007-08	San Antonio	AHL	1	0	0	0	4	....	....	....	....	....	....	....	....	....	....	....	....	....	....	....	....	....	....
	Arizona Sundogs	CHL	58	10	29	39	24	....	....	....	....	....	....	....	....	....	14	3	5	8	6	....	....	....	....
2008-09	**Phoenix**	**NHL**	**3**	**0**	**1**	**1**	**0**	**0**	**0**	**0**	**3**	**0.0**	**–2**	**0**	**0.0**	**19:16**	....	....	....	....	....	....	....	....	....
	San Antonio	AHL	68	7	22	29	20	....	....	....	....	....	....	....	....	....	....	....	....	....	....	....	....	....	....
2009-10	**Phoenix**	**NHL**	**17**	**1**	**4**	**5**	**8**	**0**	**0**	**0**	**19**	**5.3**	**1**	**0**	**0.0**	**17:49**	....	....	....	....	....	....	....	....	....
	San Antonio	AHL	55	5	26	31	30	....	....	....	....	....	....	....	....	....	....	....	....	....	....	....	....	....	....
2010-11	**Phoenix**	**NHL**	**43**	**4**	**10**	**14**	**24**	**0**	**0**	**0**	**47**	**8.5**	**8**	**0**	**0.0**	**16:02**	**4**	**1**	**0**	**1**	**4**	**1**	**0**	**0**	**15:54**
	San Antonio	AHL	3	0	0	0	2	....	....	....	....	....	....	....	....	....	....	....	....	....	....	....	....	....	....
	NHL Totals		**63**	**5**	**15**	**20**	**32**	**0**	**0**	**0**	**69**	**7.2**		**0**	**0.0**	**16:40**	**4**	**1**	**0**	**1**	**4**	**1**	**0**	**0**	**15:55**

WHL East Second All-Star Team (2007)

Signed as a free agent by **Phoenix**, July 19, 2007.

SCHREMP, Rob
(SHREHMP, RAWB)

Center. Shoots left. 5'10", 184 lbs. Born, Syracuse, NY, July 1, 1986. Edmonton's 2nd choice, 25th overall, in 2004 Entry Draft.

2000-01	Syracuse	OPJHL	49	32	46	78	....	....	....	....	....	....	....	....	....	....	....	....	....	....	....	....	....	....	....
2001-02	Syracuse	OPJHL	47	41	47	88	93	....	....	....	....	....	....	....	....	....	1	1	2	3	0	....	....	....	....
2002-03	Mississauga	OHL	65	26	48	74	25	....	....	....	....	....	....	....	....	....	2	1	0	1	0	....	....	....	....
2003-04	USNTDP	U-18	2	0	0	0	8	....	....	....	....	....	....	....	....	....	....	....	....	....	....	....	....	....	....
	Mississauga	OHL	3	2	4	6	0	....	....	....	....	....	....	....	....	....	....	....	....	....	....	....	....	....	....
	London Knights	OHL	60	28	41	69	18	....	....	....	....	....	....	....	....	....	15	7	6	13	2	....	....	....	....
2004-05	London Knights	OHL	62	41	49	90	54	....	....	....	....	....	....	....	....	....	18	13	16	29	16	....	....	....	....
2005-06	London Knights	OHL	57	*57	*88	*145	74	....	....	....	....	....	....	....	....	....	19	10	*37	*47	35	....	....	....	....
2006-07	**Edmonton**	**NHL**	**1**	**0**	**0**	**0**	**0**	**0**	**0**	**0**	**2**	**0.0**	**0**	**12**	**50.0**	**13:50**	....	....	....	....	....	....	....	....	....
	Wilkes-Barre	AHL	69	17	36	53	36	....	....	....	....	....	....	....	....	....	....	....	....	....	....	....	....	....	....
2007-08	**Edmonton**	**NHL**	**2**	**0**	**0**	**0**	**0**	**0**	**0**	**0**	**3**	**0.0**	**–1**	**1**	**0.0**	**6:57**	....	....	....	....	....	....	....	....	....
	Springfield	AHL	78	23	53	76	64	....	....	....	....	....	....	....	....	....	....	....	....	....	....	....	....	....	....
2008-09	**Edmonton**	**NHL**	**4**	**0**	**3**	**3**	**2**	**0**	**0**	**0**	**3**	**0.0**	**2**	**2**	**50.0**	**13:35**	....	....	....	....	....	....	....	....	....
	Springfield	AHL	69	7	35	42	50	....	....	....	....	....	....	....	....	....	....	....	....	....	....	....	....	....	....
2009-10	**NY Islanders**	**NHL**	**44**	**7**	**18**	**25**	**8**	**5**	**0**	**0**	**74**	**9.5**	**–4**	**395**	**47.3**	**13:54**	....	....	....	....	....	....	....	....	....
2010-11	**NY Islanders**	**NHL**	**45**	**10**	**12**	**22**	**12**	**2**	**0**	**1**	**64**	**15.6**	**–19**	**379**	**47.8**	**15:03**	....	....	....	....	....	....	....	....	....
	Bridgeport	AHL	1	0	1	1	0	....	....	....	....	....	....	....	....	....	....	....	....	....	....	....	....	....	....
	Atlanta	**NHL**	**18**	**3**	**1**	**4**	**4**	**2**	**0**	**2**	**19**	**15.8**	**–1**	**107**	**40.2**	**11:32**	....	....	....	....	....	....	....	....	....
	NHL Totals		**114**	**20**	**34**	**54**	**26**	**9**	**0**	**3**	**165**	**12.1**		**896**	**46.7**	**13:51**	....	....	....	....	....	....	....	....	....

OPJHL Rookie of the Year (2001) • OHL All-Rookie Team (2003) • OHL Rookie of the Year (2003) • OHL First All-Star Team (2006) • Canadian Major Junior First All-Star Team (2006)

Claimed on waivers by **NY Islanders** from **Edmonton**, September 29, 2009. Claimed on waivers by **Atlanta** from **NY Islanders**, February 28, 2011. • Transferred to **Winnipeg** after **Atlanta** franchise relocated, June 21, 2011. Signed as a free agent by **MODO** (Sweden), August 10, 2011.

			Regular Season														Playoffs								
Season	Club	League	GP	G	A	Pts	PIM	PP	SH	GW	S	%	+/-	TF	F%	Min	GP	G	A	Pts	PIM	PP	SH	GW	Min

SCHUBERT, Christoph

(SHOO-buhrt, KRIHS-tawf)

Defense. Shoots left. 6'3", 230 lbs. Born, Munich, West Germany, February 5, 1982. Ottawa's 5th choice, 127th overall, in 2001 Entry Draft.

Season	Club	League	GP	G	A	Pts	PIM	PP	SH	GW	S	%	+/-	TF	F%	Min	GP	G	A	Pts	PIM	PP	SH	GW	Min
1998-99	EV Landshut Jr.	Ger-Jr.	28	15	20	35	77	....	....	....	....	....	....	....	....	....	....	....	....	....	....	....	....	....	....
99-2000	EV Landshut Jr.	Ger-Jr.	11	14	11	25	51	....	....	....	....	....	....	....	....	....	....	....	....	....	....	....	....	....	....
	EV Landshut	German-3	55	7	5	12	68	....	....	....	....	....	....	....	....	....	....	....	....	....	....	....	....	....	....
2000-01	Munchen Barons	Germany	55	6	3	9	80	....	....	....	....	....	....	....	....	....	10	0	2	2	27	....	....	....	....
2001-02	Munchen Barons	Germany	50	5	11	16	125	....	....	....	....	....	....	....	....	....	9	3	4	7	32	....	....	....	....
2002-03	Binghamton	AHL	70	2	8	10	102	....	....	....	....	....	....	....	....	....	8	0	1	1	2	....	....	....	....
2003-04	Binghamton	AHL	70	2	10	12	69	....	....	....	....	....	....	....	....	....	1	0	0	0	0	....	....	....	....
2004-05	Binghamton	AHL	76	10	22	32	110	....	....	....	....	....	....	....	....	....	6	2	2	4	20	....	....	....	....
2005-06	**Ottawa**	**NHL**	**56**	**4**	**6**	**10**	**48**	**0**	**1**	**0**	**72**	**5.6**	**4**	**5**	**0.0**	**11:06**	**7**	**0**	**1**	**1**	**4**	**0**	**0**	**0**	**7:53**
	Germany	Olympics	5	0	1	1	2	....	....	....	....	....	....	....	....	....	....	....	....	....	....	....	....	....	....
2006-07	**Ottawa**	**NHL**	**80**	**8**	**17**	**25**	**56**	**1**	**0**	**1**	**97**	**8.2**	**30**	**1**	**0.0**	**11:13**	**20**	**0**	**1**	**1**	**22**	**0**	**0**	**0**	**9:10**
2007-08	**Ottawa**	**NHL**	**82**	**8**	**16**	**24**	**64**	**1**	**0**	**0**	**137**	**5.8**	**7**	**4**	**25.0**	**13:34**	**4**	**0**	**0**	**0**	**8**	**0**	**0**	**0**	**11:58**
2008-09	**Ottawa**	**NHL**	**50**	**3**	**3**	**6**	**26**	**1**	**0**	**0**	**57**	**5.3**	**–8**	**0**	**0.0**	**13:36**	....	....	....	....	....	....	....	....	....
2009-10	**Atlanta**	**NHL**	**47**	**2**	**5**	**7**	**69**	**0**	**0**	**0**	**73**	**2.7**	**–6**	**0**	**0.0**	**15:47**	....	....	....	....	....	....	....	....	....
2010-11	Frolunda	Sweden	23	0	4	4	49	....	....	....	....	....	....	....	....	....	....	....	....	....	....	....	....	....	....
	Hamburg Freezers	Germany	26	3	14	17	20	....	....	....	....	....	....	....	....	....	....	....	....	....	....	....	....	....	....
	NHL Totals		**315**	**25**	**47**	**72**	**263**	**3**	**1**	**1**	**436**	**5.7**		**10**	**10.0**	**12:52**	**31**	**0**	**2**	**2**	**34**	**0**	**0**	**0**	**9:14**

Claimed on waivers by **Atlanta** from **Ottawa**, October 2, 2009. Signed as a free agent by **Frolunda** (Sweden), September 15. 2010. Signed as a free agent by **Hamburg** (Germany), December 8, 2010.

SCHULTZ, Jeff

(SHUHLTZ, JEHF) **WSH**

Defense. Shoots left. 6'6", 230 lbs. Born, Calgary, Alta., February 25, 1986. Washington's 2nd choice, 27th overall, in 2004 Entry Draft.

Season	Club	League	GP	G	A	Pts	PIM	PP	SH	GW	S	%	+/-	TF	F%	Min	GP	G	A	Pts	PIM	PP	SH	GW	Min
2000-01	Calgary Hawks	CBHL	27	7	8	15	20	....	....	....	....	....	....	....	....	....	....	....	....	....	....	....	....	....	....
2001-02	Calgary Rangers	CBHL	27	5	18	23	42	....	....	....	....	....	....	....	....	....	....	....	....	....	....	....	....	....	....
2002-03	Calgary Hitmen	WHL	50	2	1	3	4	....	....	....	....	....	....	....	....	....	4	0	0	0	0	....	....	....	....
2003-04	Calgary Hitmen	WHL	72	11	24	35	33	....	....	....	....	....	....	....	....	....	7	1	1	2	0	....	....	....	....
2004-05	Calgary Hitmen	WHL	72	2	27	29	31	....	....	....	....	....	....	....	....	....	12	2	1	3	6	....	....	....	....
2005-06	Calgary Hitmen	WHL	68	7	33	40	36	....	....	....	....	....	....	....	....	....	13	4	6	10	6	....	....	....	....
	Hershey Bears	AHL	....	....	....	....	....	....	....	....	....	....	....	....	....	....	7	1	3	4	4	....	....	....	....
2006-07	**Washington**	**NHL**	**38**	**0**	**3**	**3**	**16**	**0**	**0**	**0**	**22**	**0.0**	**5**	**0**	**0.0**	**18:13**	....	....	....	....	....	....	....	....	....
	Hershey Bears	AHL	44	2	10	12	39	....	....	....	....	....	....	....	....	....	19	0	1	1	18	....	....	....	....
2007-08	**Washington**	**NHL**	**72**	**5**	**13**	**18**	**28**	**0**	**0**	**0**	**36**	**13.9**	**12**	**1**	**100.0**	**18:05**	**2**	**0**	**0**	**0**	**2**	**0**	**0**	**0**	**10:25**
	Hershey Bears	AHL	1	0	0	0	0	....	....	....	....	....	....	....	....	....	....	....	....	....	....	....	....	....	....
2008-09	**Washington**	**NHL**	**64**	**1**	**11**	**12**	**21**	**0**	**1**	**0**	**40**	**2.5**	**13**	**0**	**0.0**	**19:46**	**1**	**0**	**0**	**0**	**0**	**0**	**0**	**0**	**12:26**
2009-10	**Washington**	**NHL**	**73**	**3**	**20**	**23**	**32**	**0**	**0**	**0**	**43**	**7.0**	**50**	**0**	**0.0**	**19:52**	**7**	**0**	**1**	**1**	**4**	**0**	**0**	**0**	**19:43**
2010-11	**Washington**	**NHL**	**72**	**1**	**9**	**10**	**12**	**0**	**0**	**1**	**34**	**2.9**	**6**	**0**	**0.0**	**19:47**	**9**	**0**	**0**	**0**	**6**	**0**	**0**	**0**	**20:45**
	NHL Totals		**319**	**10**	**56**	**66**	**109**	**0**	**1**	**1**	**175**	**5.7**		**1**	**100.0**	**19:14**	**19**	**0**	**1**	**1**	**12**	**0**	**0**	**0**	**18:51**

WHL East Second All-Star Team (2006)

SCHULTZ, Nick

(SHUHLTZ, NIHK) **MIN**

Defense. Shoots left. 6'1", 206 lbs. Born, Strasbourg, Sask., August 25, 1982. Minnesota's 2nd choice, 33rd overall, in 2000 Entry Draft.

Season	Club	League	GP	G	A	Pts	PIM	PP	SH	GW	S	%	+/-	TF	F%	Min	GP	G	A	Pts	PIM	PP	SH	GW	Min
1997-98	Yorkton Mallers	SMHL	59	10	30	40	74	....	....	....	....	....	....	....	....	....	....	....	....	....	....	....	....	....	....
1998-99	Prince Albert	WHL	58	5	18	23	37	....	....	....	....	....	....	....	....	....	14	0	7	7	0	....	....	....	....
99-2000	Prince Albert	WHL	72	11	33	44	38	....	....	....	....	....	....	....	....	....	6	0	3	3	2	....	....	....	....
2000-01	Prince Albert	WHL	59	17	30	47	120	....	....	....	....	....	....	....	....	....	....	....	....	....	....	....	....	....	....
	Cleveland	IHL	4	1	1	2	2	....	....	....	....	....	....	....	....	....	3	0	1	1	0	....	....	....	....
2001-02	**Minnesota**	**NHL**	**52**	**4**	**6**	**10**	**14**	**1**	**0**	**1**	**47**	**8.5**	**0**	**0**	**0.0**	**16:08**	....	....	....	....	....	....	....	....	....
	Houston Aeros	AHL	....	....	....	....	....	....	....	....	....	....	....	....	....	....	14	1	5	6	2	....	....	....	....
2002-03	**Minnesota**	**NHL**	**75**	**3**	**7**	**10**	**23**	**0**	**0**	**1**	**70**	**4.3**	**11**	**0**	**0.0**	**18:28**	**18**	**0**	**1**	**1**	**10**	**0**	**0**	**0**	**19:39**
2003-04	**Minnesota**	**NHL**	**79**	**6**	**10**	**16**	**16**	**1**	**0**	**0**	**72**	**8.3**	**12**	**0**	**0.0**	**20:19**	....	....	....	....	....	....	....	....	....
2004-05	Kassel Huskies	Germany	46	7	15	22	26	....	....	....	....	....	....	....	....	....	7	0	4	4	6	....	....	....	....
2005-06	**Minnesota**	**NHL**	**79**	**2**	**12**	**14**	**43**	**0**	**0**	**0**	**45**	**4.4**	**2**	**0**	**0.0**	**17:58**	....	....	....	....	....	....	....	....	....
2006-07	**Minnesota**	**NHL**	**82**	**2**	**10**	**12**	**42**	**0**	**0**	**1**	**69**	**2.9**	**0**	**0**	**0.0**	**20:13**	**5**	**0**	**1**	**1**	**0**	**0**	**0**	**0**	**18:06**
2007-08	**Minnesota**	**NHL**	**81**	**2**	**13**	**15**	**42**	**0**	**0**	**0**	**52**	**3.8**	**9**	**0**	**0.0**	**20:10**	**1**	**0**	**0**	**0**	**0**	**0**	**0**	**0**	**16:11**
2008-09	**Minnesota**	**NHL**	**79**	**2**	**9**	**11**	**31**	**0**	**0**	**0**	**48**	**4.2**	**–4**	**1**	**0.0**	**20:33**	....	....	....	....	....	....	....	....	....
2009-10	**Minnesota**	**NHL**	**80**	**1**	**19**	**20**	**43**	**1**	**0**	**0**	**83**	**1.2**	**–8**	**0**	**0.0**	**20:58**	....	....	....	....	....	....	....	....	....
2010-11	**Minnesota**	**NHL**	**74**	**3**	**14**	**17**	**38**	**0**	**0**	**0**	**46**	**6.5**	**–4**	**1**	**100.0**	**20:13**	....	....	....	....	....	....	....	....	....
	NHL Totals		**681**	**25**	**100**	**125**	**292**	**3**	**0**	**3**	**532**	**4.7**		**2**	**50.0**	**19:35**	**24**	**0**	**2**	**2**	**10**	**0**	**0**	**0**	**19:11**

Signed as a free agent by **Kassel** (Germany), September 24, 2004.

SCOTT, John

(SKAWT, JAWN) **CHI**

Defense. Shoots left. 6'8", 258 lbs. Born, St. Catharines, Ont., September 26, 1982.

Season	Club	League	GP	G	A	Pts	PIM	PP	SH	GW	S	%	+/-	TF	F%	Min	GP	G	A	Pts	PIM	PP	SH	GW	Min
2002-03	Michigan Tech	WCHA	31	1	3	4	64	....	....	....	....	....	....	....	....	....	....	....	....	....	....	....	....	....	....
2003-04	Michigan Tech	WCHA	35	1	3	4	100	....	....	....	....	....	....	....	....	....	....	....	....	....	....	....	....	....	....
2004-05	Michigan Tech	WCHA	36	2	4	6	101	....	....	....	....	....	....	....	....	....	....	....	....	....	....	....	....	....	....
2005-06	Michigan Tech	WCHA	24	3	2	5	87	....	....	....	....	....	....	....	....	....	....	....	....	....	....	....	....	....	....
2006-07	Houston Aeros	AHL	65	1	5	6	107	....	....	....	....	....	....	....	....	....	....	....	....	....	....	....	....	....	....
2007-08	Houston Aeros	AHL	64	3	0	3	184	....	....	....	....	....	....	....	....	....	5	0	0	0	13	....	....	....	....
2008-09	**Minnesota**	**NHL**	**20**	**0**	**1**	**1**	**21**	**0**	**0**	**0**	**6**	**0.0**	**–1**	**0**	**0.0**	**9:14**	....	....	....	....	....	....	....	....	....
	Houston Aeros	AHL	44	2	2	4	111	....	....	....	....	....	....	....	....	....	....	....	....	....	....	....	....	....	....
2009-10	**Minnesota**	**NHL**	**51**	**1**	**1**	**2**	**90**	**0**	**0**	**0**	**22**	**4.5**	**–3**	**0**	**0.0**	**8:36**	....	....	....	....	....	....	....	....	....
2010-11	**Chicago**	**NHL**	**40**	**0**	**1**	**1**	**72**	**0**	**0**	**0**	**15**	**0.0**	**0**	**3**	**0.0**	**6:15**	**4**	**0**	**0**	**0**	**22**	**0**	**0**	**0**	**6:37**
	NHL Totals		**111**	**1**	**3**	**4**	**183**	**0**	**0**	**0**	**43**	**2.3**		**3**	**0.0**	**7:52**	**4**	**0**	**0**	**0**	**22**	**0**	**0**	**0**	**6:38**

Signed as a free agent by **Houston** (AHL), September 26, 2006. Signed as a free agent by **Minnesota**, December 31, 2006. Signed as a free agent by **Chicago**, July 2, 2010. • Missed majority of 2010-11 as a healthy reserve.

SCUDERI, Rob

(SKUD-uh-ree, RAWB) **L.A.**

Defense. Shoots left. 6'1", 216 lbs. Born, Syosset, NY, December 30, 1978. Pittsburgh's 5th choice, 134th overall, in 1998 Entry Draft.

Season	Club	League	GP	G	A	Pts	PIM	PP	SH	GW	S	%	+/-	TF	F%	Min	GP	G	A	Pts	PIM	PP	SH	GW	Min
1995-96	NY Apple Core	MtJHL	76	18	60	78	....	....	....	....	....	....	....	....	....	....	....	....	....	....	....	....	....	....	....
1996-97	NY Apple Core	MtJHL	82	42	70	112	64	....	....	....	....	....	....	....	....	....	....	....	....	....	....	....	....	....	....
1997-98	Boston College	H-East	42	0	24	24	12	....	....	....	....	....	....	....	....	....	....	....	....	....	....	....	....	....	....
1998-99	Boston College	H-East	41	2	8	10	20	....	....	....	....	....	....	....	....	....	....	....	....	....	....	....	....	....	....
99-2000	Boston College	H-East	42	1	12	13	22	....	....	....	....	....	....	....	....	....	....	....	....	....	....	....	....	....	....
2000-01	Boston College	H-East	43	4	19	23	42	....	....	....	....	....	....	....	....	....	....	....	....	....	....	....	....	....	....
2001-02	Wilkes-Barre	AHL	75	1	22	23	66	....	....	....	....	....	....	....	....	....	....	....	....	....	....	....	....	....	....
2002-03	Wilkes-Barre	AHL	74	4	17	21	44	....	....	....	....	....	....	....	....	....	6	0	1	1	4	....	....	....	....
2003-04	**Pittsburgh**	**NHL**	**13**	**1**	**2**	**3**	**4**	**0**	**0**	**0**	**4**	**25.0**	**2**	**0**	**0.0**	**20:06**	....	....	....	....	....	....	....	....	....
	Wilkes-Barre	AHL	64	1	15	16	54	....	....	....	....	....	....	....	....	....	24	0	3	3	14	....	....	....	....
2004-05	Wilkes-Barre	AHL	79	2	18	20	34	....	....	....	....	....	....	....	....	....	11	2	1	3	2	....	....	....	....
2005-06	**Pittsburgh**	**NHL**	**57**	**0**	**4**	**4**	**36**	**0**	**0**	**0**	**28**	**0.0**	**–18**	**0**	**0.0**	**20:15**	....	....	....	....	....	....	....	....	....
	Wilkes-Barre	AHL	13	0	8	8	8	....	....	....	....	....	....	....	....	....	....	....	....	....	....	....	....	....	....
2006-07	**Pittsburgh**	**NHL**	**78**	**1**	**10**	**11**	**28**	**0**	**0**	**0**	**31**	**3.2**	**3**	**0**	**0.0**	**18:49**	**5**	**0**	**0**	**0**	**2**	**0**	**0**	**0**	**17:14**
2007-08	**Pittsburgh**	**NHL**	**71**	**0**	**5**	**5**	**26**	**0**	**0**	**0**	**28**	**0.0**	**3**	**0**	**0.0**	**18:45**	**20**	**0**	**3**	**3**	**2**	**0**	**0**	**0**	**19:02**
2008-09 ♦	**Pittsburgh**	**NHL**	**81**	**1**	**15**	**16**	**18**	**0**	**0**	**0**	**51**	**2.0**	**23**	**0**	**0.0**	**19:10**	**24**	**1**	**4**	**5**	**6**	**0**	**0**	**0**	**20:30**
2009-10	**Los Angeles**	**NHL**	**73**	**0**	**11**	**11**	**21**	**0**	**0**	**0**	**38**	**0.0**	**16**	**0**	**0.0**	**19:16**	**6**	**0**	**0**	**0**	**6**	**0**	**0**	**0**	**20:40**
2010-11	**Los Angeles**	**NHL**	**82**	**2**	**13**	**15**	**16**	**0**	**0**	**1**	**46**	**4.3**	**1**	**0**	**0.0**	**20:17**	**6**	**0**	**2**	**2**	**0**	**0**	**0**	**0**	**20:49**
	NHL Totals		**455**	**5**	**60**	**65**	**149**	**0**	**0**	**1**	**226**	**2.2**		**0**	**0.0**	**19:25**	**61**	**1**	**9**	**10**	**16**	**0**	**0**	**0**	**19:48**

NCAA Championship All-Tournament Team (2001)
Signed as a free agent by **Los Angeles** July 2, 2009.

SEABROOK, Brent
(SEE-bruk, BREHNT) **CHI**

Defense. Shoots right. 6'3", 218 lbs. Born, Richmond, B.C., April 20, 1985. Chicago's 1st choice, 14th overall, in 2003 Entry Draft.

			Regular Season														Playoffs								
Season	Club	League	GP	G	A	Pts	PIM	PP	SH	GW	S	%	+/-	TF	F%	Min	GP	G	A	Pts	PIM	PP	SH	GW	Min
2000-01	Delta Ice Hawks	PIJHL	54	16	26	42	55																		
	Lethbridge	WHL	4	0	0	0	0	....	....	....	....	....	....	....	....	....	....	....	....	....	....	....	....	....	....
2001-02	Lethbridge	WHL	67	6	33	39	70	....	....	....	....	....	....	....	....	....	4	1	1	2	2	....	....	....	....
2002-03	Lethbridge	WHL	69	9	33	42	113	....	....	....	....	....	....	....	....	....	....	....	....	....	....	....	....	....	....
2003-04	Lethbridge	WHL	61	12	29	41	107	....	....	....	....	....	....	....	....	....	....	....	....	....	....	....	....	....	....
2004-05	Lethbridge	WHL	63	12	42	54	107	....	....	....	....	....	....	....	....	....	5	1	2	3	10	....	....	....	....
	Norfolk Admirals	AHL	3	0	0	0	2	....	....	....	....	....	....	....	....	....	6	0	1	1	6	....	....	....	....
2005-06	**Chicago**	**NHL**	**69**	**5**	**27**	**32**	**60**	**1**	**0**	**2**	**114**	**4.4**	**5**	**0**	**0.0**	**20:02**	....	....	....	....	....	....	....	....	....
2006-07	**Chicago**	**NHL**	**81**	**4**	**20**	**24**	**104**	**0**	**0**	**0**	**144**	**2.8**	**–6**	**2**	**50.0**	**20:46**	....	....	....	....	....	....	....	....	....
2007-08	**Chicago**	**NHL**	**82**	**9**	**23**	**32**	**90**	**4**	**0**	**2**	**152**	**5.9**	**13**	**1**	**0.0**	**21:30**	....	....	....	....	....	....	....	....	....
2008-09	**Chicago**	**NHL**	**82**	**8**	**18**	**26**	**62**	**3**	**1**	**1**	**132**	**6.1**	**23**	**0**	**0.0**	**23:19**	**17**	**1**	**11**	**12**	**14**	**1**	**0**	**0**	**26:00**
2009-10♦	**Chicago**	**NHL**	**78**	**4**	**26**	**30**	**59**	**0**	**0**	**2**	**129**	**3.1**	**20**	**0**	**0.0**	**23:13**	**22**	**4**	**7**	**11**	**14**	**1**	**0**	**0**	**24:11**
	Canada	Olympics	7	0	1	1	2	....	....	....	....	....	....	....	....	....	....	....	....	....	....	....	....	....	....
2010-11	**Chicago**	**NHL**	**82**	**9**	**39**	**48**	**47**	**5**	**0**	**1**	**135**	**6.7**	**0**	**0**	**0.0**	**24:23**	**5**	**0**	**1**	**1**	**6**	**0**	**0**	**0**	**22:57**
	NHL Totals		**474**	**39**	**153**	**192**	**422**	**13**	**1**	**8**	**806**	**4.8**		**3**	**33.3**	**22:16**	**44**	**5**	**19**	**24**	**34**	**2**	**0**	**0**	**24:45**

WHL East Second All-Star Team (2005)

SEDIN, Daniel
(suh-DEEN, DAN-yehl) **VAN**

Left wing. Shoots left. 6'1", 187 lbs. Born, Ornskoldsvik, Sweden, September 26, 1980. Vancouver's 1st choice, 2nd overall, in 1999 Entry Draft.

Season	Club	League	GP	G	A	Pts	PIM	PP	SH	GW	S	%	+/-	TF	F%	Min	GP	G	A	Pts	PIM	PP	SH	GW	Min
1997-98	Malmo Jr.	Swe-Jr.	4	3	3	6	4	....	....	....	....	....	....	....	....	....	....	....	....	....	....	....	....	....	....
	MoDo Jr.	Swe-Jr.	26	26	14	40	....	....	....	....	....	....	....	....	....	....	....	....	....	....	....	....	....	....	....
	MoDo	Sweden	45	4	8	12	26	....	....	....	....	....	....	....	....	....	9	0	0	0	2	....	....	....	....
1998-99	MoDo	Sweden	50	21	21	42	20	....	....	....	....	....	....	....	....	....	13	4	8	12	14	....	....	....	....
99-2000	MoDo	Sweden	50	19	26	45	28	....	....	....	....	....	....	....	....	....	13	*8	6	14	18	....	....	....	....
	MoDo	EuroHL	4	3	3	6	0	....	....	....	....	....	....	....	....	....	2	0	0	0	0	....	....	....	....
2000-01	**Vancouver**	**NHL**	**75**	**20**	**14**	**34**	**24**	**10**	**0**	**3**	**127**	**15.7**	**–3**	**10**	**60.0**	**13:00**	**4**	**1**	**2**	**3**	**0**	**0**	**0**	**0**	**16:15**
2001-02	**Vancouver**	**NHL**	**79**	**9**	**23**	**32**	**32**	**4**	**0**	**2**	**117**	**7.7**	**1**	**18**	**33.3**	**12:22**	**6**	**0**	**1**	**1**	**0**	**0**	**0**	**0**	**10:44**
2002-03	**Vancouver**	**NHL**	**79**	**14**	**17**	**31**	**34**	**4**	**0**	**2**	**134**	**10.4**	**8**	**24**	**45.8**	**12:26**	**14**	**1**	**5**	**6**	**8**	**1**	**0**	**1**	**12:23**
2003-04	**Vancouver**	**NHL**	**82**	**18**	**36**	**54**	**18**	**1**	**0**	**3**	**153**	**11.8**	**18**	**71**	**47.9**	**13:33**	**7**	**1**	**2**	**3**	**0**	**1**	**0**	**0**	**16:03**
2004-05	MODO	Sweden	49	13	20	33	40	....	....	....	....	....	....	....	....	....	6	0	3	3	6	....	....	....	....
2005-06	**Vancouver**	**NHL**	**82**	**22**	**49**	**71**	**34**	**11**	**0**	**4**	**204**	**10.8**	**7**	**49**	**42.9**	**16:40**	....	....	....	....	....	....	....	....	....
	Sweden	Olympics	8	1	3	4	2	....	....	....	....	....	....	....	....	....	....	....	....	....	....	....	....	....	....
2006-07	**Vancouver**	**NHL**	**81**	**36**	**48**	**84**	**36**	**16**	**0**	**8**	**236**	**15.3**	**19**	**44**	**22.7**	**18:04**	**12**	**2**	**3**	**5**	**4**	**0**	**0**	**0**	**21:31**
2007-08	**Vancouver**	**NHL**	**82**	**29**	**45**	**74**	**50**	**12**	**0**	**7**	**247**	**11.7**	**6**	**38**	**44.7**	**19:03**	....	....	....	....	....	....	....	....	....
2008-09	**Vancouver**	**NHL**	**82**	**31**	**51**	**82**	**36**	**9**	**0**	**7**	**285**	**10.9**	**24**	**35**	**40.0**	**18:48**	**10**	**4**	**6**	**10**	**8**	**2**	**0**	**0**	**18:37**
2009-10	**Vancouver**	**NHL**	**63**	**29**	**56**	**85**	**28**	**8**	**0**	**8**	**225**	**12.9**	**36**	**33**	**33.3**	**19:08**	**12**	**5**	**9**	**14**	**12**	**1**	**0**	**2**	**19:46**
	Sweden	Olympics	4	1	2	3	0	....	....	....	....	....	....	....	....	....	....	....	....	....	....	....	....	....	....
2010-11	**Vancouver**	**NHL**	**82**	**41**	**63**	***104**	**32**	***18**	**0**	**10**	**266**	**15.4**	**30**	**17**	**23.5**	**18:33**	**25**	**9**	**11**	**20**	**32**	***5**	**0**	**2**	**20:12**
	NHL Totals		**787**	**249**	**402**	**651**	**324**	**93**	**0**	**54**	**1994**	**12.5**		**339**	**39.5**	**16:09**	**90**	**23**	**39**	**62**	**64**	**10**	**0**	**5**	**17:48**

NHL Second All-Star Team (2010) • NHL First All-Star Team (2011) • Art Ross Trophy (2011) • Ted Lindsay Award (2011)
Played in NHL All-Star Game (2011)
Signed as a free agent by **MODO** (Sweden), September 18, 2004.

SEDIN, Henrik
(suh-DEEN, HEHN-rihk) **VAN**

Center. Shoots left. 6'2", 188 lbs. Born, Ornskoldsvik, Sweden, September 26, 1980. Vancouver's 2nd choice, 3rd overall, in 1999 Entry Draft.

Season	Club	League	GP	G	A	Pts	PIM	PP	SH	GW	S	%	+/-	TF	F%	Min	GP	G	A	Pts	PIM	PP	SH	GW	Min
1997-98	Malmo Jr.	Swe-Jr.	8	4	7	11	6	....	....	....	....	....	....	....	....	....	....	....	....	....	....	....	....	....	....
	MoDo Jr.	Swe-Jr.	26	14	22	36	....	....	....	....	....	....	....	....	....	....	....	....	....	....	....	....	....	....	....
	MoDo	Sweden	39	1	4	5	8	....	....	....	....	....	....	....	....	....	7	0	0	0	0	....	....	....	....
1998-99	MoDo	Sweden	49	12	22	34	32	....	....	....	....	....	....	....	....	....	13	2	8	10	6	....	....	....	....
99-2000	MoDo	Sweden	50	9	38	47	22	....	....	....	....	....	....	....	....	....	13	5	9	14	2	....	....	....	....
2000-01	**Vancouver**	**NHL**	**82**	**9**	**20**	**29**	**38**	**2**	**0**	**1**	**98**	**9.2**	**–2**	**1020**	**44.1**	**13:31**	**4**	**0**	**4**	**4**	**0**	**0**	**0**	**0**	**16:31**
2001-02	**Vancouver**	**NHL**	**82**	**16**	**20**	**36**	**36**	**3**	**0**	**1**	**78**	**20.5**	**9**	**785**	**47.4**	**12:48**	**6**	**3**	**0**	**3**	**0**	**0**	**0**	**1**	**11:55**
2002-03	**Vancouver**	**NHL**	**78**	**8**	**31**	**39**	**38**	**4**	**1**	**1**	**81**	**9.9**	**9**	**995**	**48.2**	**13:58**	**14**	**3**	**2**	**5**	**8**	**1**	**0**	**0**	**13:01**
2003-04	**Vancouver**	**NHL**	**76**	**11**	**31**	**42**	**32**	**2**	**0**	**2**	**99**	**11.1**	**23**	**961**	**50.0**	**14:02**	**7**	**2**	**2**	**4**	**2**	**2**	**0**	**0**	**16:02**
2004-05	MODO	Sweden	44	14	22	36	50	....	....	....	....	....	....	....	....	....	6	1	3	4	6	....	....	....	....
2005-06	**Vancouver**	**NHL**	**82**	**18**	**57**	**75**	**56**	**5**	**1**	**0**	**113**	**15.9**	**11**	**1238**	**50.7**	**16:54**	....	....	....	....	....	....	....	....	....
	Sweden	Olympics	8	3	1	4	2	....	....	....	....	....	....	....	....	....	....	....	....	....	....	....	....	....	....
2006-07	**Vancouver**	**NHL**	**82**	**10**	**71**	**81**	**66**	**1**	**0**	**2**	**134**	**7.5**	**19**	**1220**	**52.5**	**18:26**	**12**	**2**	**2**	**4**	**14**	**1**	**0**	**1**	**22:12**
2007-08	**Vancouver**	**NHL**	**82**	**15**	**61**	**76**	**56**	**4**	**1**	**2**	**141**	**10.6**	**6**	**1369**	**47.0**	**19:31**	....	....	....	....	....	....	....	....	....
2008-09	**Vancouver**	**NHL**	**82**	**22**	**60**	**82**	**48**	**4**	**0**	**8**	**143**	**15.4**	**22**	**1364**	**49.6**	**19:31**	**10**	**4**	**6**	**10**	**2**	**1**	**0**	**0**	**20:07**
2009-10	**Vancouver**	**NHL**	**82**	**29**	***83**	***112**	**48**	**4**	**2**	**5**	**166**	**17.5**	**35**	**1527**	**49.5**	**19:41**	**12**	**3**	**11**	**14**	**6**	**0**	**0**	**1**	**20:38**
	Sweden	Olympics	4	0	2	2	2	....	....	....	....	....	....	....	....	....	....	....	....	....	....	....	....	....	....
2010-11	**Vancouver**	**NHL**	**82**	**19**	***75**	**94**	**40**	**8**	**0**	**4**	**157**	**12.1**	**26**	**1387**	**52.0**	**19:16**	**25**	**3**	***19**	**22**	**16**	**2**	**0**	**1**	**20:56**
	NHL Totals		**810**	**157**	**509**	**666**	**458**	**37**	**5**	**26**	**1210**	**13.0**		**11866**	**49.3**	**16:48**	**90**	**20**	**46**	**66**	**48**	**7**	**0**	**4**	**18:34**

NHL First All-Star Team (2010, 2011) • Art Ross Trophy (2010) • Hart Memorial Trophy (2010)
Played in NHL All-Star Game (2008, 2011)
Signed as a free agent by **MODO** (Sweden), September 18, 2004.

SEGAL, Brandon
(SEE-guhl, BRAN-duhn)

Right wing. Shoots right. 6'2", 212 lbs. Born, Richmond, B.C., July 12, 1983. Nashville's 2nd choice, 102nd overall, in 2002 Entry Draft.

Season	Club	League	GP	G	A	Pts	PIM	PP	SH	GW	S	%	+/-	TF	F%	Min	GP	G	A	Pts	PIM	PP	SH	GW	Min
99-2000	Calgary Hitmen	WHL	44	2	6	8	76	....	....	....	....	....	....	....	....	....	13	1	1	2	13	....	....	....	....
	Delta Ice Hawks	PIJHL	....	....	....	....	....	....	....	....	....	....	....	....	....	....	3	0	1	1	2	....	....	....	....
2000-01	Calgary Hitmen	WHL	72	16	11	27	103	....	....	....	....	....	....	....	....	....	12	1	1	2	17	....	....	....	....
2001-02	Calgary Hitmen	WHL	71	43	40	83	122	....	....	....	....	....	....	....	....	....	7	1	4	5	16	....	....	....	....
2002-03	Calgary Hitmen	WHL	71	31	27	58	104	....	....	....	....	....	....	....	....	....	5	2	2	4	4	....	....	....	....
2003-04	Calgary Hitmen	WHL	28	18	12	30	29	....	....	....	....	....	....	....	....	....	....	....	....	....	....	....	....	....	....
	Milwaukee	AHL	44	11	10	21	54	....	....	....	....	....	....	....	....	....	13	2	1	3	21	....	....	....	....
2004-05	Milwaukee	AHL	59	7	8	15	45	....	....	....	....	....	....	....	....	....	3	1	0	1	11	....	....	....	....
	Rockford IceHogs	UHL	10	5	4	9	27	....	....	....	....	....	....	....	....	....	11	11	5	16	10	....	....	....	....
2005-06	Milwaukee	AHL	79	18	15	33	126	....	....	....	....	....	....	....	....	....	21	1	2	3	16	....	....	....	....
2006-07	Milwaukee	AHL	77	20	9	29	84	....	....	....	....	....	....	....	....	....	4	1	0	1	2	....	....	....	....
2007-08	Portland Pirates	AHL	54	5	9	14	46	....	....	....	....	....	....	....	....	....	....	....	....	....	....	....	....	....	....
	Norfolk Admirals	AHL	22	7	6	13	25	....	....	....	....	....	....	....	....	....	....	....	....	....	....	....	....	....	....
2008-09	**Tampa Bay**	**NHL**	**2**	**0**	**0**	**0**	**0**	**0**	**0**	**0**	**2**	**0.0**	**0**	**0**	**0.0**	**13:48**	....	....	....	....	....	....	....	....	....
	Norfolk Admirals	AHL	69	26	26	52	95	....	....	....	....	....	....	....	....	....	....	....	....	....	....	....	....	....	....
2009-10	**Los Angeles**	**NHL**	**25**	**1**	**1**	**2**	**20**	**0**	**0**	**0**	**24**	**4.2**	**0**	**3**	**0.0**	**6:47**	....	....	....	....	....	....	....	....	....
	Manchester	AHL	21	6	8	14	34	....	....	....	....	....	....	....	....	....	....	....	....	....	....	....	....	....	....
	Dallas	**NHL**	**19**	**5**	**5**	**10**	**18**	**0**	**0**	**2**	**31**	**16.1**	**3**	**0**	**0.0**	**11:20**	....	....	....	....	....	....	....	....	....
2010-11	**Dallas**	**NHL**	**46**	**5**	**5**	**10**	**41**	**0**	**0**	**1**	**40**	**12.5**	**0**	**4**	**50.0**	**8:17**	....	....	....	....	....	....	....	....	....
	Texas Stars	AHL	30	7	10	17	38	....	....	....	....	....	....	....	....	....	....	....	....	....	....	....	....	....	....
	NHL Totals		**92**	**11**	**11**	**22**	**79**	**0**	**0**	**3**	**97**	**11.3**		**7**	**28.6**	**8:38**	....	....	....	....	....	....	....	....	....

Traded to **Anaheim** by **Nashville** for future considerations, June 25, 2007. Traded to **Tampa Bay** by **Anaheim** with Anaheim's 7th round choice (David Carle) in 2008 Entry Draft for Jay Leach, February 26, 2008. Signed as a free agent by **Los Angeles**, July 13, 2009. Claimed on waivers by **Dallas** from **Los Angeles**, February 11, 2010.

SEGUIN, Tyler
(SAY-gihn, TIGH-luhr) **BOS**

Center. Shoots right. 6'1", 182 lbs. Born, Brampton, Ont., January 31, 1992. Boston's 1st choice, 2nd overall, in 2010 Entry Draft.

Season	Club	League	GP	G	A	Pts	PIM	PP	SH	GW	S	%	+/-	TF	F%	Min	GP	G	A	Pts	PIM	PP	SH	GW	Min
2007-08	Tor. Young Nats	GTHL	51	39	47	86	56										....	....	....	....	....	....	....	....	....
2008-09	Plymouth Whalers	OHL	61	21	46	67	28	....	....	....	....	....	....	....	....	....	11	5	11	16	8	....	....	....	....
2009-10	Plymouth Whalers	OHL	63	48	58	*106	54	....	....	....	....	....	....	....	....	....	9	5	5	10	8	....	....	....	....
2010-11♦	**Boston**	**NHL**	**74**	**11**	**11**	**22**	**18**	**1**	**0**	**0**	**131**	**8.4**	**–4**	**303**	**49.5**	**12:13**	**13**	**3**	**4**	**7**	**2**	**0**	**0**	**0**	**10:35**
	NHL Totals		**74**	**11**	**11**	**22**	**18**	**1**	**0**	**0**	**131**	**8.4**		**303**	**49.5**	**12:13**	**13**	**3**	**4**	**7**	**2**	**0**	**0**	**0**	**10:35**

OHL First All-Star Team (2010) • OHL Player of the Year (2010) • Canadian Major Junior First All-Star Team (2010)

								Regular Season									Playoffs								
Season	Club	League	GP	G	A	Pts	PIM	PP	SH	GW	S	%	+/-	TF	F%	Min	GP	G	A	Pts	PIM	PP	SH	GW	Min

SEIDENBERG, Dennis (SIGH-dehn-buhrg, DEH-nihs) **BOS**

Defense. Shoots left. 6'1", 210 lbs. Born, Schwenningen, West Germany, July 18, 1981. Philadelphia's 6th choice, 172nd overall, in 2001 Entry Draft.

Season	Club	League	GP	G	A	Pts	PIM	PP	SH	GW	S	%	+/-	TF	F%	Min	GP	G	A	Pts	PIM	PP	SH	GW	Min
99-2000	Mannheim Jr.	Ger-Jr.	52	12	28	40	28																		
	Adler Mannheim	Germany	3	0	0	0	0																		
2000-01	Mannheim Jr.	Ger-Jr.	9	3	8	11	20										12	0	1	1	10				
	Adler Mannheim	Germany	55	2	5	7	6										8	0	0	0	2				
2001-02	Adler Mannheim	Germany	55	7	13	20	56																		
2002-03	Philadelphia	NHL	58	4	9	13	20	1	0	0	123	3.3	8	1	0.0	16:50									
	Philadelphia	AHL	19	5	6	11	17																		
2003-04	Philadelphia	NHL	5	0	0	0	2	0	0	0	14	0.0	-4	0	0.0	17:20	3	0	0	0	0	0	0	0	7:36
	Philadelphia	AHL	33	7	12	19	31										9	2	2	4	4				
2004-05	Philadelphia	AHL	79	13	28	41	47										18	2	8	10	19				
2005-06	Philadelphia	NHL	29	2	5	7	4	1	0	0	34	5.9	-4	1	0.0	14:22									
	Phoenix	NHL	34	1	10	11	14	1	0	0	49	2.0	-9	0	0.0	19:13									
	Germany	Olympics	5	0	0	0	6																		
2006-07	Phoenix	NHL	32	1	1	2	16	0	0	0	36	2.8	-4	0	0.0	14:43									
	Carolina	NHL	20	1	5	6	2	0	0	0	47	2.1	-12	0	0.0	18:29									
2007-08	Carolina	NHL	47	0	15	15	18	0	0	0	80	0.0	6	1	100.0	18:50									
2008-09	Carolina	NHL	70	5	25	30	37	2	0	1	129	3.9	-9	0	0.0	22:20	16	1	5	6	16	0	0	0	22:25
2009-10	Florida	NHL	62	2	21	23	33	1	0	0	116	1.7	-3	1	0.0	22:55									
	Boston	NHL	17	2	7	9	6	1	0	1	37	5.4	9	0	0.0	22:57									
	Germany	Olympics	4	1	0	1	2																		
2010-11♦	Boston	NHL	81	7	25	32	41	2	0	1	166	4.2	3	0	0.0	23:33	25	1	10	11	31	0	0	0	27:37
	NHL Totals		455	25	123	148	193	8	0	4	831	3.0		4	25.0	20:05	44	2	15	17	47	0	0	0	24:22

• Missed majority of 2003-04 due to leg injury vs. Edmonton, January 10, 2004. Traded to **Phoenix** by **Philadelphia** with Philadelphia's 4th round choice (later traded to NY Islanders - NY Islanders selected Tomas Marcinko) in 2006 Entry Draft for Petr Nedved and Phoenix's 4th round choice (Joonas Lehtivuori) in 2006 Entry Draft, January 20, 2006. Traded to **Carolina** by **Phoenix** for Kevyn Adams, January 8, 2007. Signed as a free agent by **Florida**, September 14, 2009. Traded to **Boston** by **Florida** with Matt Bartkowski for Byron Bitz, Craig Weller and Tampa Bay's 2nd round choice (previously acquired, Florida selected Alexander Petrovic) in 2010 Entry Draft, March 3, 2010

SEKERA, Andrej (seh-KAIR-ah, AWN-dray) **BUF**

Defense. Shoots left. 6', 201 lbs. Born, Bojnice, Czech., June 8, 1986. Buffalo's 3rd choice, 71st overall, in 2004 Entry Draft.

Season	Club	League	GP	G	A	Pts	PIM	PP	SH	GW	S	%	+/-	TF	F%	Min	GP	G	A	Pts	PIM	PP	SH	GW	Min
2001-02	Dukla Trencin Jr.	Slovak-Jr.	52	5	10	15	10																		
2002-03	Dukla Trencin Jr.	Slovak-Jr.	48	9	15	24	20																		
2003-04	Dukla Trencin Jr.	Slovak-Jr	42	5	12	17	40										2	0	1	1	4				
	Dukla Trencin	Slovakia	3	0	0	0	2																		
	Dukla Trencin U18	Svk-U18	5	0	0	0	0																		
2004-05	Owen Sound	OHL	51	7	21	28	18										6	0	4	4	4				
2005-06	Owen Sound	OHL	51	21	34	55	54										11	5	8	13	9				
2006-07	Buffalo	NHL	2	0	0	0	2	0	0	0	0	0.0	1	0	0.0	7:31									
	Rochester	AHL	54	3	16	19	28																		
2007-08	Buffalo	NHL	37	2	6	8	16	0	0	1	28	7.1	5	0	0.0	19:37									
	Rochester	AHL	40	2	15	17	22																		
2008-09	Buffalo	NHL	69	3	16	19	22	1	0	1	84	3.6	-11	1	0.0	20:42									
2009-10	Buffalo	NHL	49	4	7	11	6	0	0	0	59	6.8	-1	0	0.0	17:27	6	0	0	0	7	0	0	0	13:55
	Slovakia	Olympics	7	1	0	1	0																		
2010-11	Buffalo	NHL	76	3	26	29	34	0	0	0	88	3.4	11	0	0.0	21:06	2	1	0	1	4	0	0	0	16:18
	NHL Totals		233	12	55	67	80	1	0	2	259	4.6		2	0.0	19:52	8	1	0	1	11	0	0	0	14:31

OHL All-Rookie Team (2005) • OHL First All-Star Team (2006)

SELANNE, Teemu (seh-LAH-nee, TEE-moo) **ANA**

Right wing. Shoots right. 6', 199 lbs. Born, Helsinki, Finland, July 3, 1970. Winnipeg's 1st choice, 10th overall, in 1988 Entry Draft.

Season	Club	League	GP	G	A	Pts	PIM	PP	SH	GW	S	%	+/-	TF	F%	Min	GP	G	A	Pts	PIM	PP	SH	GW	Min
1986-87	Jokerit U18	Fin-U18															7	10	3	13	2				
	Jokerit Helsinki Jr.	Fin-Jr.	33	10	12	22	8																		
1987-88	Jokerit Helsinki Jr.	Fin-Jr.	33	43	23	66	18										5	4	3	7	2				
	Jokerit Helsinki	Finland-2	5	1	1	2	0																		
1988-89	PvUK Lahti Jr.	Fin-Jr.	3	3	1	4	2																		
	Jokerit Helsinki Jr.	Fin-Jr.		8	8	16	4																		
	Jokerit Helsinki	Finland-2	35	36	33	69	14										5	7	3	10	4				
1989-90	Jokerit Helsinki	Finland	11	4	8	12	0																		
1990-91	Jokerit Helsinki Jr.	Fin-Jr.	4	3	2	5	10																		
	Jokerit Helsinki	Finland	42	33	25	58	12										10	10	7	17	18				
1991-92	Jokerit Helsinki	Finland	44	39	23	62	20																		
	Finland	Olympics	8	7	4	11	6																		
1992-93	Winnipeg	NHL	84	*76	56	132	45	24	0	7	387	19.6	8				6	4	2	6	2				
1993-94	Winnipeg	NHL	51	25	29	54	22	11	0	2	191	13.1	-23												
1994-95	Jokerit Helsinki	Finland	20	7	12	19	6																		
	Winnipeg	NHL	45	22	26	48	2	8	2	1	167	13.2	1												
1995-96	Winnipeg	NHL	51	24	48	72	18	6	1	4	163	14.7	3												
	Anaheim	NHL	28	16	20	36	4	3	0	1	104	15.4	2												
1996-97	Anaheim	NHL	78	51	58	109	34	11	1	8	273	18.7	28				11	7	3	10	4	3	0	1	
1997-98	Anaheim	NHL	73	*52	34	86	30	10	1	10	268	19.4	12												
	Finland	Olympics	5	4	6	10	4																		
1998-99	Anaheim	NHL	75	*47	60	107	30	*25	0	7	281	16.7	18	5	20.0	22:47	4	2	2	4	2	0	0	0	22:23
99-2000	Anaheim	NHL	79	33	52	85	12	8	0	6	236	14.0	6	13	23.1	22:44									
2000-01	Anaheim	NHL	61	26	33	59	36	10	0	5	202	12.9	-9	4	50.0	21:51									
	San Jose	NHL	12	7	6	13	0	2	0	2	31	22.6	1	4	75.0	18:14								0	17:13
2001-02	San Jose	NHL	82	29	25	54	40	9	1	8	202	14.4	-11	12	25.0	16:58	12	5	3	8	2	2	0	1	16:51
	Finland	Olympics	4	3	0	3	2																		
2002-03	San Jose	NHL	82	28	36	64	30	7	0	5	253	11.1	-6	107	42.1	19:14									
2003-04	Colorado	NHL	78	16	16	32	32	6	1	4	182	8.8	2	80	43.8	16:10	10	0	3	3	2	0	0	0	12:53
2004-05						DID NOT PLAY																			
2005-06	Anaheim	NHL	80	40	50	90	44	18	0	5	267	15.0	28	209	41.6	17:48	16	6	8	14	6	1	0	2	17:56
	Finland	Olympics	8	*6	5	*11	4																		
2006-07♦	Anaheim	NHL	82	48	46	94	82	*25	0	*10	257	18.7	26	351	50.7	17:42	21	5	10	15	10	2	0	2	19:08
2007-08	Anaheim	NHL	26	12	11	23	8	7	0	2	87	13.8	5	67	50.8	18:07	6	2	2	4	2	0	1	1	19:35
2008-09	Anaheim	NHL	65	27	27	54	36	16	0	5	186	14.5	-3	224	49.1	16:29	13	4	2	6	4	2	0	1	15:08
2009-10	Anaheim	NHL	54	27	21	48	16	14	0	5	173	15.6	3	131	47.3	17:19									
	Finland	Olympics	6	0	2	2	0																		
2010-11	Anaheim	NHL	73	31	49	80	49	16	0	5	213	14.6	6	218	44.5	17:56	6	6	1	7	12	4	0	0	18:58
	NHL Totals		1259	637	703	1340	570	236	7	102	4123	15.4		1425	46.3	18:47	111	41	38	79	52	17	0	10	17:27

NHL All-Rookie Team (1993) • NHL First All-Star Team (1993, 1997) • Calder Memorial Trophy (1993) • NHL Second All-Star Team (1998, 1999) • Maurice "Rocket" Richard Trophy (1999) • Olympic All-Star Team (2006) • Best Forward - Olympics (2006) • Bill Masterton Memorial Trophy (2006)
Played in NHL All-Star Game (1993, 1994, 1996, 1997, 1998, 1999, 2000, 2002, 2003, 2007)
• Missed majority of 1989-90 due to leg injury vs. HIFK Helsinki (Finland), October 19, 1989. Traded to **Anaheim** by **Winnipeg** with Marc Chouinard and Winnipeg's 4th round choice (later traded to Toronto, later traded to Montreal – Montreal selected Kim Staal) in 1996 Entry Draft for Chad Kilger, Oleg Tverdovsky and Anaheim's 3rd round choice (Per-Anton Lundstrom) in 1996 Entry Draft, February 7, 1996. Traded to **San Jose** by **Anaheim** for Jeff Friesen, Steve Shields and San Jose's 2nd round choice (later traded to Dallas – Dallas selected Vojtech Polak) in 2003 Entry Draft, March 5, 2001. Signed as a free agent by **Colorado**, July 3, 2003. Signed as a free agent by **Anaheim**, August 22, 2005. • Missed majority of 2007-08 season contemplating retirement.

SEMIN, Alexander (SEH-min, al-EHX-AN-duhr) **WSH**

Left wing. Shoots left. 6'2", 208 lbs. Born, Krasnoyarsk, USSR, March 3, 1984. Washington's 2nd choice, 13th overall, in 2002 Entry Draft.

Season	Club	League	GP	G	A	Pts	PIM	PP	SH	GW	S	%	+/-	TF	F%	Min	GP	G	A	Pts	PIM	PP	SH	GW	Min
2001-02	Chelyabinsk	Russia-2	46	13	8	21	52										2	0	2	2	0				
2002-03	Lada Togliatti	Russia	47	10	7	17	36										10	*5	3	8	10				
2003-04	Washington	NHL	52	10	12	22	36	4	0	2	92	10.9	-2	6	50.0	12:37	7	4	7	11	19				
	Portland Pirates	AHL	4	3	1	4	6																		
2004-05	Lada Togliatti	Russia	50	19	11	30	56										10	1	1	2	10				
2005-06	Lada Togliatti	Russia	16	5	4	9	52																		
	Mytischi	Russia	26	3	7	10	24										8	3	2	5	6				

			Regular Season														Playoffs								
Season	Club	League	GP	G	A	Pts	PIM	PP	SH	GW	S	%	+/-	TF	F%	Min	GP	G	A	Pts	PIM	PP	SH	GW	Min
2006-07	Washington	NHL	77	38	35	73	90	17	0	6	243	15.6	−7	44	27.3	18:24	....	....	....	....	....	....	....	....	....
2007-08	Washington	NHL	63	26	16	42	54	10	0	2	185	14.1	−18	11	36.4	16:55	7	3	5	8	8	2	0	1	19:45
2008-09	Washington	NHL	62	34	45	79	77	8	0	8	223	15.2	25	24	50.0	19:14	14	5	9	14	16	1	0	1	19:58
2009-10	Washington	NHL	73	40	44	84	66	8	2	5	278	14.4	36	16	37.5	19:07	7	0	2	2	4	0	0	0	19:21
	Russia	Olympics	4	0	2	2	4	....	....	....	....	....	....	....	....	....	....	....	....	....	....	....	....	....	....
2010-11	Washington	NHL	65	28	26	54	71	6	1	4	196	14.3	22	13	30.8	18:04	9	4	2	6	8	0	0	1	18:36
	NHL Totals		392	176	178	354	394	53	3	27	1217	14.5		114	36.0	17:36	37	12	18	30	36	3	0	3	19:29

Signed as a free agent by **Togliatti** (Russia), September 25, 2004. • Suspended by **Washington** for failing to report to **Portland** (AHL), September 28, 2004. Signed as a free agent by **Mytischi** (Russia), November 22, 2005.

SESTITO, Tim

(sehs-TEE-toh, TIHM) **N.J.**

Center. Shoots left. 5'11", 195 lbs. Born, Rome, NY, August 28, 1984.

Season	Club	League	GP	G	A	Pts	PIM	PP	SH	GW	S	%	+/-	TF	F%	Min	GP	G	A	Pts	PIM	PP	SH	GW	Min
2001-02	Plymouth Whalers	OHL	51	10	11	21	40	....	....	....	....	....	....	....	....	....	6	0	0	0	0	....	....	....	....
2002-03	Plymouth Whalers	OHL	61	11	7	18	49	....	....	....	....	....	....	....	....	....	18	2	3	5	4	....	....	....	....
2003-04	Plymouth Whalers	OHL	57	10	20	30	68	....	....	....	....	....	....	....	....	....	9	4	1	5	14	....	....	....	....
2004-05	Plymouth Whalers	OHL	67	14	18	32	93	....	....	....	....	....	....	....	....	....	4	0	0	0	14	....	....	....	....
	Bridgeport	AHL	9	2	1	3	12	....	....	....	....	....	....	....	....	....	....	....	....	....	....	....	....	....	....
2005-06	Greenville	ECHL	72	21	23	44	127	....	....	....	....	....	....	....	....	....	6	2	2	4	24	....	....	....	....
2006-07	Wilkes-Barre	AHL	4	0	0	0	6	....	....	....	....	....	....	....	....	....	....	....	....	....	....	....	....	....	....
	Stockton Thunder	ECHL	66	13	13	26	132	....	....	....	....	....	....	....	....	....	6	2	1	3	6	....	....	....	....
2007-08	Springfield	AHL	77	7	10	17	175	....	....	....	....	....	....	....	....	....	....	....	....	....	....	....	....	....	....
2008-09	Edmonton	NHL	1	0	0	0	0	0	0	0	1	0.0	0	2	50.0	5:53	....	....	....	....	....	....	....	....	....
	Springfield	AHL	51	5	3	8	77	....	....	....	....	....	....	....	....	....	....	....	....	....	....	....	....	....	....
2009-10	New Jersey	NHL	9	0	1	1	2	0	0	0	7	0.0	−2	64	53.1	12:16	....	....	....	....	....	....	....	....	....
	Lowell Devils	AHL	66	18	17	35	38	....	....	....	....	....	....	....	....	....	5	0	0	0	8	....	....	....	....
2010-11	New Jersey	NHL	36	0	2	2	9	0	0	0	22	0.0	−5	253	45.9	10:49	....	....	....	....	....	....	....	....	....
	Albany Devils	AHL	23	5	8	13	28	....	....	....	....	....	....	....	....	....	....	....	....	....	....	....	....	....	....
	NHL Totals		46	0	3	3	11	0	0	0	30	0.0		319	47.3	11:00	....	....	....	....	....	....	....	....	....

Signed as a free agent by **Edmonton**, August 28, 2006. Traded to **New Jersey** by **Edmonton** for future considerations, July 9, 2009.

SESTITO, Tom

(sehs-TEE-toh, TAWM) **PHI**

Left wing. Shoots left. 6'5", 228 lbs. Born, Rome, NY, September 28, 1987. Columbus' 3rd choice, 85th overall, in 2006 Entry Draft.

Season	Club	League	GP	G	A	Pts	PIM	PP	SH	GW	S	%	+/-	TF	F%	Min	GP	G	A	Pts	PIM	PP	SH	GW	Min
2003-04	Syracuse Jr. Stars	EmJHL	31	13	16	29	137	....	....	....	....	....	....	....	....	....	6	5	6	11	32	....	....	....	....
2004-05	Plymouth Whalers	OHL	35	1	3	4	88	....	....	....	....	....	....	....	....	....	....	....	....	....	....	....	....	....	....
2005-06	Plymouth Whalers	OHL	57	10	10	20	176	....	....	....	....	....	....	....	....	....	13	5	2	7	29	....	....	....	....
2006-07	Plymouth Whalers	OHL	60	42	22	64	135	....	....	....	....	....	....	....	....	....	19	11	6	17	57	....	....	....	....
2007-08	Columbus	NHL	1	0	0	0	17	0	0	0	0	0.0	0	0	0.0	4:36	....	....	....	....	....	....	....	....	....
	Syracuse Crunch	AHL	66	7	16	23	202	....	....	....	....	....	....	....	....	....	9	3	0	3	57	....	....	....	....
2008-09	Syracuse Crunch	AHL	52	8	12	20	168	....	....	....	....	....	....	....	....	....	....	....	....	....	....	....	....	....	....
2009-10	Columbus	NHL	3	0	0	0	7	0	0	0	0	0.0	0	0	0.0	5:34	....	....	....	....	....	....	....	....	....
	Syracuse Crunch	AHL	36	10	7	17	138	....	....	....	....	....	....	....	....	....	....	....	....	....	....	....	....	....	....
2010-11	Columbus	NHL	9	2	2	4	40	1	0	0	7	28.6	−4	1	100.0	9:32	....	....	....	....	....	....	....	....	....
	Springfield	AHL	46	11	21	32	192	....	....	....	....	....	....	....	....	....	....	....	....	....	....	....	....	....	....
	Adirondack	AHL	11	2	1	3	45	....	....	....	....	....	....	....	....	....	....	....	....	....	....	....	....	....	....
	NHL Totals		13	2	2	4	64	1	0	0	7	28.6		1	100.0	8:14	....	....	....	....	....	....	....	....	....

Traded to **Philadelphia** by **Columbus** for Michael Chaput and Greg Moore, February 28, 2011.

SETOGUCHI, Devin

(SEHT-oh-GOO-chee, DEH-vihn) **MIN**

Right wing. Shoots right. 6', 200 lbs. Born, Taber, Alta., January 1, 1987. San Jose's 1st choice, 8th overall, in 2005 Entry Draft.

Season	Club	League	GP	G	A	Pts	PIM	PP	SH	GW	S	%	+/-	TF	F%	Min	GP	G	A	Pts	PIM	PP	SH	GW	Min
2003-04	Saskatoon Blades	WHL	66	13	18	31	53	....	....	....	....	....	....	....	....	....	....	....	....	....	....	....	....	....	....
2004-05	Saskatoon Blades	WHL	69	33	31	64	34	....	....	....	....	....	....	....	....	....	4	0	1	1	0	....	....	....	....
2005-06	Saskatoon Blades	WHL	65	36	47	83	69	....	....	....	....	....	....	....	....	....	10	8	4	12	8	....	....	....	....
2006-07	Prince George	WHL	55	36	29	65	55	....	....	....	....	....	....	....	....	....	15	*11	10	21	24	....	....	....	....
2007-08	San Jose	NHL	44	11	6	17	8	3	0	2	105	10.5	6	17	64.7	14:15	9	1	1	2	2	0	0	0	10:25
	Worcester Sharks	AHL	23	8	11	19	25	....	....	....	....	....	....	....	....	....	....	....	....	....	....	....	....	....	....
2008-09	San Jose	NHL	81	31	34	65	25	11	0	3	246	12.6	16	21	28.6	16:13	6	1	2	3	2	0	0	0	16:21
2009-10	San Jose	NHL	70	20	16	36	19	8	0	4	165	12.1	0	10	30.0	15:18	15	5	4	9	6	1	0	1	18:25
2010-11	San Jose	NHL	72	22	19	41	37	4	0	5	199	11.1	−2	11	45.5	15:12	18	7	3	10	12	3	0	2	17:26
	NHL Totals		267	84	75	159	89	26	0	14	715	11.7		59	42.4	15:23	48	14	10	24	22	4	0	3	16:18

WHL East Second All-Star Team (2006)

Traded to **Minnesota** by **San Jose** with Charlie Coyle and San Jose's 1st round choice (Zack Phillips) in 2011 Entry Draft for Brent Burns and Minnesota's 2nd round choice in 2012 Entry Draft, June 24, 2011.

SEXTON, Dan

(SEHKS-tuhn, DAN) **ANA**

Right wing. Shoots right. 5'10", 174 lbs. Born, Apple Valley, MN, April 29, 1987.

Season	Club	League	GP	G	A	Pts	PIM	PP	SH	GW	S	%	+/-	TF	F%	Min	GP	G	A	Pts	PIM	PP	SH	GW	Min
2005-06	Wichita Falls	NAHL	58	22	37	59	16	....	....	....	....	....	....	....	....	....	5	2	1	3	0	....	....	....	....
2006-07	Sioux Falls	USHL	58	14	10	24	20	....	....	....	....	....	....	....	....	....	8	*8	1	9	0	....	....	....	....
2007-08	Bowling Green	CCHA	38	7	14	21	42	....	....	....	....	....	....	....	....	....	....	....	....	....	....	....	....	....	....
2008-09	Bowling Green	CCHA	38	17	22	39	20	....	....	....	....	....	....	....	....	....	....	....	....	....	....	....	....	....	....
2009-10	Anaheim	NHL	41	9	10	19	16	2	0	0	93	9.7	−3	1	0.0	13:30	....	....	....	....	....	....	....	....	....
	Manitoba Moose	AHL	13	5	7	12	2	....	....	....	....	....	....	....	....	....	6	2	3	5	2	....	....	....	....
	Bakersfield	ECHL	18	13	13	26	14	....	....	....	....	....	....	....	....	....	....	....	....	....	....	....	....	....	....
2010-11	Anaheim	NHL	47	4	9	13	4	1	0	0	78	5.1	−6	4	25.0	11:35	1	0	0	0	2	0	0	0	8:47
	Syracuse Crunch	AHL	17	9	8	17	4	....	....	....	....	....	....	....	....	....	....	....	....	....	....	....	....	....	....
	NHL Totals		88	13	19	32	20	3	0	0	171	7.6		5	20.0	12:29	1	0	0	0	2	0	0	0	8:47

Signed as a free agent by **Anaheim**, April 7, 2009.

SHANNON, Ryan

(SHA-nuhn, RIGH-uhn) **T.B.**

Center. Shoots right. 5'9", 175 lbs. Born, Darien, CT, March 2, 1983.

Season	Club	League	GP	G	A	Pts	PIM	PP	SH	GW	S	%	+/-	TF	F%	Min	GP	G	A	Pts	PIM	PP	SH	GW	Min
2001-02	Boston College	H-East	38	8	17	25	12	....	....	....	....	....	....	....	....	....	....	....	....	....	....	....	....	....	....
2002-03	Boston College	H-East	36	14	24	38	4	....	....	....	....	....	....	....	....	....	....	....	....	....	....	....	....	....	....
2003-04	Boston College	H-East	42	15	27	42	22	....	....	....	....	....	....	....	....	....	....	....	....	....	....	....	....	....	....
2004-05	Boston College	H-East	38	14	31	45	22	....	....	....	....	....	....	....	....	....	....	....	....	....	....	....	....	....	....
	Cincinnati	AHL	4	1	0	1	2	....	....	....	....	....	....	....	....	....	....	....	....	....	....	....	....	....	....
2005-06	Portland Pirates	AHL	71	27	59	86	44	....	....	....	....	....	....	....	....	....	19	11	11	22	8	....	....	....	....
2006-07♦	Anaheim	NHL	53	2	9	11	10	0	0	0	77	2.6	−2	25	52.0	10:39	11	0	0	0	6	0	0	0	4:04
	Portland Pirates	AHL	14	2	7	9	12	....	....	....	....	....	....	....	....	....	....	....	....	....	....	....	....	....	....
2007-08	Vancouver	NHL	27	5	8	13	24	4	0	0	34	14.7	−1	82	39.0	12:53	....	....	....	....	....	....	....	....	....
	Manitoba Moose	AHL	13	1	7	8	10	....	....	....	....	....	....	....	....	....	....	....	....	....	....	....	....	....	....
2008-09	Ottawa	NHL	35	8	12	20	2	3	0	1	61	13.1	−1	6	33.3	15:04	....	....	....	....	....	....	....	....	....
	Binghamton	AHL	36	10	25	35	16	....	....	....	....	....	....	....	....	....	....	....	....	....	....	....	....	....	....
2009-10	Ottawa	NHL	66	5	11	16	20	1	0	1	109	4.6	−12	51	37.3	12:40	2	0	0	0	0	0	0	0	6:13
2010-11	Ottawa	NHL	79	11	16	27	24	5	1	1	118	9.3	3	207	42.0	12:56	....	....	....	....	....	....	....	....	....
	NHL Totals		260	31	56	87	80	13	1	3	399	7.8		371	41.2	12:41	13	0	0	0	6	0	0	0	4:24

Hockey East First All-Star Team (2004) • NCAA East Second All-American Team (2004) • AHL All-Rookie Team (2006)

Signed as a free agent by **Anaheim**, November 28, 2005. Traded to **Vancouver** by **Anaheim** for Jason King and future considerations, June 23, 2007. Traded to **Ottawa** by **Vancouver** for Lawrence Nycholat, September 2, 2008. Signed as a free agent by **Tampa Bay**, July 7, 2011.

SHARP, MacGregor
(SHAHRP, muh-GREHG-uhr)

Center. Shoots left. 6'1", 185 lbs. Born, Vancouver, B.C., October 1, 1985.

Season	Club	League	GP	G	A	Pts	PIM	PP	SH	GW	S	%	+/-	TF	F%	Min	GP	G	A	Pts	PIM	PP	SH	GW	Min
			Regular Season														Playoffs								
2002-03	Camrose Kodiaks	AJHL	60	23	25	48	96																		
2003-04	Camrose Kodiaks	AJHL	44	20	26	46	45																		
2004-05	Camrose Kodiaks	AJHL	57	19	30	49	32																		
2005-06	U. Minn-Duluth	WCHA	40	6	8	14	31																		
2006-07	U. Minn-Duluth	WCHA	38	11	16	27	35																		
2007-08	U. Minn-Duluth	WCHA	36	7	10	17	14																		
2008-09	U. Minn-Duluth	WCHA	43	*26	24	*50	20																		
	Iowa Chops	AHL	6	1	1	2	4																		
2009-10	Anaheim	NHL	8	0	0	0	0	0	0	0	6	0.0	0	28	53.6	4:10									
	San Antonio	AHL	40	9	9	18	16																		
	Bakersfield	ECHL	17	4	12	16	10										10	3	5	8	10				
2010-11	Syracuse Crunch	AHL	50	6	7	13	26																		
	Abbotsford Heat	AHL	17	1	1	2	7																		
	NHL Totals		8	0	0	0	0	0	0	0	6	0.0		28	53.6	4:10									

Signed as a free agent by **Anaheim**, April 1, 2009. Traded to **Vancouver** by **Anaheim** with Maxim Lapierre for Joel Perrault and Vancouver's 3rd round choice in 2012 Entry Draft, February 28, 2011.

SHARP, Patrick
(SHAHRP, PAT-rihk) **CHI**

Center. Shoots right. 6'1", 199 lbs. Born, Winnipeg, Man., December 27, 1981. Philadelphia's 2nd choice, 95th overall, in 2001 Entry Draft.

Season	Club	League	GP	G	A	Pts	PIM	PP	SH	GW	S	%	+/-	TF	F%	Min	GP	G	A	Pts	PIM	PP	SH	GW	Min
1998-99	Thunder Bay	USHL	55	19	24	43	48										3	1	1	2	0				
99-2000	Thunder Bay	USHL	56	20	35	55	41																		
2000-01	U. of Vermont	ECAC	34	12	15	27	36																		
2001-02	U. of Vermont	ECAC	31	13	13	26	50																		
2002-03	Philadelphia	NHL	3	0	0	0	2	0	0	0	3	0.0	0	7	42.9	5:59									
	Philadelphia	AHL	53	14	19	33	39																		
2003-04	Philadelphia	NHL	41	5	2	7	55	0	0	1	44	11.4	–3	272	46.7	9:56	12	1	0	1	2	0	0	0	6:12
	Philadelphia	AHL	35	15	14	29	45										1	2	0	2	0				
2004-05	Philadelphia	AHL	75	23	29	52	80										21	8	13	*21	20				
2005-06	Philadelphia	NHL	22	5	3	8	10	1	0	3	33	15.2	4	38	52.6	7:43									
	Chicago	NHL	50	9	14	23	36	0	1	2	111	8.1	1	664	48.0	16:19									
2006-07	Chicago	NHL	80	20	15	35	74	5	3	1	160	12.5	–15	1008	46.5	17:04									
2007-08	Chicago	NHL	80	36	26	62	55	9	*7	7	209	17.2	23	594	51.4	18:47									
2008-09	Chicago	NHL	61	26	18	44	41	9	0	4	184	14.1	6	566	45.8	17:57	17	7	4	11	6	3	0	2	16:17
2009-10♦	Chicago	NHL	82	25	41	66	28	4	2	4	266	9.4	24	466	51.7	18:07	22	11	11	22	16	3	1	1	17:52
2010-11	Chicago	NHL	74	34	37	71	38	12	2	6	268	12.7	–1	508	48.0	19:25	7	3	2	5	2	3	0	0	18:55
	NHL Totals		493	160	156	316	339	40	15	28	1278	12.5		4123	48.2	16:50	58	22	17	39	26	9	1	3	15:07

Traded to **Chicago** by **Philadelphia** with Eric Meloche for Matt Ellison and Chicago's 3rd round choice (later traded to Montreal - Montreal selected Ryan White) in 2006 Entry Draft, December 5, 2005.
Played in NHL All-Star Game (2011)

SHATTENKIRK, Kevin
(SHAH-tehn-kuhrk, KEH-vihn) **ST.L.**

Defense. Shoots right. 5'11", 193 lbs. Born, Greenwich, CT, January 29, 1989. Colorado's 1st choice, 14th overall, in 2007 Entry Draft.

Season	Club	League	GP	G	A	Pts	PIM	PP	SH	GW	S	%	+/-	TF	F%	Min	GP	G	A	Pts	PIM	PP	SH	GW	Min
2004-05	Brunswick Bruins	High-CT	22	10	18	28																			
2005-06	USNTDP	U-17	13	4	4	8	4																		
	USNTDP	NAHL	28	6	9	15	17										12	3	7	10	10				
2006-07	USNTDP	U-18	43	8	19	27	36																		
	USNTDP	NAHL	14	5	8	13	26																		
2007-08	Boston University	H-East	40	4	17	21	38																		
2008-09	Boston University	H-East	43	7	21	28	40																		
2009-10	Boston University	H-East	38	7	22	29	38																		
	Lake Erie	AHL	3	0	2	2	0																		
2010-11	Colorado	NHL	46	7	19	26	20	2	0	1	67	10.4	–11	0	0.0	19:50									
	Lake Erie	AHL	10	0	0	0	10																		
	St. Louis	NHL	26	2	15	17	16	1	0	1	41	4.9	7	0	0.0	19:51									
	NHL Totals		72	9	34	43	36	3	0	2	108	8.3		0	0.0	19:50									

Hockey East All-Rookie Team (2008) • Hockey East Second All-Star Team (2009) • NCAA East Second All-American Team (2009)
Traded to **St. Louis** by **Colorado** with Chris Stewart and Colorado's 2nd round choice (Ty Rattie) in 2011 Entry Draft for Erik Johnson, Jay McClement and St. Louis's 1st round choice (Duncan Siemens) in 2011 Entry Draft, February 19, 2011.

SHELLEY, Jody
(SHEH-lee, JOH-dee) **PHI**

Left wing. Shoots left. 6'3", 230 lbs. Born, Thompson, Man., February 7, 1976.

Season	Club	League	GP	G	A	Pts	PIM	PP	SH	GW	S	%	+/-	TF	F%	Min	GP	G	A	Pts	PIM	PP	SH	GW	Min
1994-95	Halifax	QMJHL	72	10	12	22	194										7	0	1	1	12				
1995-96	Halifax	QMJHL	50	13	19	32	319										6	0	2	2	36				
1996-97	Halifax	QMJHL	59	25	19	44	*420										17	6	6	12	*125				
1997-98	Dalhousie	AUAA	19	6	11	17	145																		
	Saint John Flames	AHL	18	1	1	2	50																		
1998-99	Saint John Flames	AHL	8	0	0	0	46																		
	Johnstown Chiefs	ECHL	52	12	17	29	325																		
99-2000	Johnstown Chiefs	ECHL	36	9	17	26	256																		
	Saint John Flames	AHL	22	1	4	5	93										3	0	0	0	2				
2000-01	Syracuse Crunch	AHL	69	1	7	8	*357										5	0	0	0	21				
	Columbus	NHL	1	0	0	0	10	0	0	0	0	0.0	0	0	0.0	1:33									
2001-02	Columbus	NHL	52	3	3	6	206	0	0	0	35	8.6	1	0	0.0	6:32									
	Syracuse Crunch	AHL	22	3	5	8	165																		
2002-03	Columbus	NHL	68	1	4	5	*249	0	0	0	39	2.6	–5	1	0.0	6:08									
2003-04	Columbus	NHL	76	3	3	6	228	1	0	0	62	4.8	–10	3	0.0	7:14									
2004-05	JYP Jyvaskyla	Finland	11	0	1	1	20										3	0	0	0	25				
2005-06	Columbus	NHL	80	3	7	10	163	0	0	1	39	7.7	–4	7	14.3	5:58									
2006-07	Columbus	NHL	72	1	1	2	125	0	0	0	32	3.1	–6	2	0.0	4:52									
2007-08	Columbus	NHL	31	0	0	0	44	0	0	0	10	0.0	–2	1	0.0	4:20									
	San Jose	NHL	31	1	6	7	91	0	0	0	31	3.2	–2	1	0.0	7:24	6	0	0	0	2	0	0	0	3:16
2008-09	San Jose	NHL	70	2	2	4	116	0	0	1	44	4.5	–6	7	42.9	6:11	1	0	0	0	0	0	0	0	2:02
2009-10	San Jose	NHL	36	0	3	3	78	0	0	0	20	0.0	1	5	40.0	6:34									
	NY Rangers	NHL	21	2	4	6	37	0	0	0	29	6.9	4	1	0.0	7:07									
2010-11	Philadelphia	NHL	58	2	2	4	127	0	0	0	31	6.5	0	4	50.0	6:11	2	0	0	0	2	0	0	0	3:58
	NHL Totals		596	18	35	53	1474	1	0	2	372	4.8		32	25.0	6:10	9	0	0	0	4	0	0	0	3:17

Signed as a free agent by **Calgary**, September 1, 1998. Signed as a free agent by **Syracuse** (AHL), September 15, 2000. Signed as a free agent by **Columbus**, January 31, 2001. Signed as a free agent by **Jyvaskyla** (Finland), January 17, 2005. Traded to **San Jose** by **Columbus** for San Jose's 6th round choice (later traded to Atlanta, later traded to Chicago – Chicago selected David Pacan) in 2009 Entry Draft, January 29, 2008. Traded to **NY Rangers** by **San Jose** for NY Rangers' 6th round choice in 2011 Entry Draft, February 12, 2010. Signed as a free agent by **Philadelphia**, July 1, 2010.

SHEPPARD, James
(sheh-PUHRD, JAYMZ) **S.J.**

Center. Shoots left. 6'2", 210 lbs. Born, Halifax, N.S., April 25, 1988. Minnesota's 1st choice, 9th overall, in 2006 Entry Draft.

Season	Club	League	GP	G	A	Pts	PIM	PP	SH	GW	S	%	+/-	TF	F%	Min	GP	G	A	Pts	PIM	PP	SH	GW	Min
2003-04	Dartmouth	NSMHL	61	38	54	92	46																		
2004-05	Cape Breton	QMJHL	65	14	31	45	40										5	1	3	4	2				
2005-06	Cape Breton	QMJHL	66	30	54	84	78										9	2	5	7	12				
2006-07	Cape Breton	QMJHL	56	33	63	96	62										16	8	12	20	14				
2007-08	Minnesota	NHL	78	4	15	19	29	0	0	1	57	7.0	0	655	41.5	10:37	6	0	1	1	4	0	0	0	10:37
2008-09	Minnesota	NHL	82	5	19	24	41	0	0	1	88	5.7	–14	870	41.5	15:11									
2009-10	Minnesota	NHL	64	2	4	6	38	0	0	0	64	3.1	–14	343	45.2	11:59									
2010-11		DID NOT PLAY – INJURED																							
	NHL Totals		224	11	38	49	108	0	0	2	209	5.3		1868	42.2	12:41	6	0	1	1	4	0	0	0	10:37

QMJHL Second All-Star Team (2007)
• Did not play in 2010-11 due to off-season knee injury, September 4. 2010. Traded to **San Jose** by **Minnesota** for San Jose's 3rd round choice in 2013 Entry Draft, August 7, 2011.

SHIROKOV, Sergei

(sheer-OH-kawv, SAIR-gay) **FLA**

Right wing. Shoots right. 5'10", 195 lbs. Born, Ozery, USSR, March 10, 1986. Vancouver's 3rd choice, 163rd overall, in 2006 Entry Draft.

			Regular Season														Playoffs								
Season	Club	League	GP	G	A	Pts	PIM	PP	SH	GW	S	%	+/-	TF	F%	Min	GP	G	A	Pts	PIM	PP	SH	GW	Min
2001-02	HK CSKA 2	Russia-3	18	2	3	5	0	....	....	....	....	....	....	....	....	....	....	....	....	....	....	....	....	....	....
2002-03	CSKA Moscow 2	Russia-3	2	0	0	0	0	....	....	....	....	....	....	....	....	....	....	....	....	....	....	....	....	....	....
2003-04	CSKA Moscow 2	Russia-3	66	39	41	80	66	....	....	....	....	....	....	....	....	....	....	....	....	....	....	....	....	....	....
2004-05	CSKA Moscow 2	Russia-3	25	16	13	29	47	....	....	....	....	....	....	....	....	....	....	....	....	....	....	....	....	....	....
	CSKA Moscow	Russia	8	0	0	0	0	....	....	....	....	....	....	....	....	....	....	....	....	....	....	....	....	....	....
	CSKA Moscow	Russia	8	0	0	0	0	....	....	....	....	....	....	....	....	....	....	....	....	....	....	....	....	....	....
2005-06	CSKA Moscow	Russia	39	7	7	14	26	....	....	....	....	....	....	....	....	....	4	0	0	0	0	....	....	....	....
2006-07	CSKA Moscow	Russia	52	16	19	35	36	....	....	....	....	....	....	....	....	....	12	4	6	10	4	....	....	....	....
2007-08	CSKA Moscow	Russia	57	12	21	33	28	....	....	....	....	....	....	....	....	....	6	0	3	3	4	....	....	....	....
2008-09	CSKA Moscow	Rus-KHL	56	17	23	40	36	....	....	....	....	....	....	....	....	....	8	1	3	4	4	....	....	....	....
2009-10	**Vancouver**	**NHL**	**6**	**0**	**0**	**0**	**2**	**0**	**0**	**0**	**4**	**0.0**	**–4**	**2**	**50.0**	**12:50**	....	....	....	....	....	....	....	....	....
	Manitoba Moose	AHL	76	22	23	45	32	....	....	....	....	....	....	....	....	....	6	0	2	2	4	....	....	....	....
2010-11	**Vancouver**	**NHL**	**2**	**1**	**0**	**1**	**0**	**0**	**0**	**0**	**6**	**16.7**	**1**	**0**	**0.0**	**10:18**	....	....	....	....	....	....	....	....	....
	Manitoba Moose	AHL	76	22	36	58	51	....	....	....	....	....	....	....	....	....	14	7	3	10	4	....	....	....	....
	NHL Totals		**8**	**1**	**0**	**1**	**2**	**0**	**0**	**0**	**10**	**10.0**		**2**	**50.0**	**12:12**	....	....	....	....	....	....	....	....	....

Traded to **Florida** by **Vancouver** for Mike Duco, July 8, 2011.

SIFERS, Jaime

(SIH-fuhrs, JAY-mee)

Defense. Shoots right. 5'11", 205 lbs. Born, Stratford, CT, January 18, 1983.

Season	Club	League	GP	G	A	Pts	PIM	PP	SH	GW	S	%	+/-	TF	F%	Min	GP	G	A	Pts	PIM	PP	SH	GW	Min
2002-03	U. of Vermont	ECAC	34	4	14	18	66	....	....	....	....	....	....	....	....	....	....	....	....	....	....	....	....	....	....
2003-04	U. of Vermont	ECAC	35	4	14	18	93	....	....	....	....	....	....	....	....	....	....	....	....	....	....	....	....	....	....
2004-05	U. of Vermont	ECAC	36	4	12	16	57	....	....	....	....	....	....	....	....	....	....	....	....	....	....	....	....	....	....
2005-06	U. of Vermont	H-East	38	3	15	18	60	....	....	....	....	....	....	....	....	....	....	....	....	....	....	....	....	....	....
	Toronto Marlies	AHL	2	0	0	0	2	....	....	....	....	....	....	....	....	....	....	....	....	....	....	....	....	....	....
2006-07	Toronto Marlies	AHL	80	7	18	25	75	....	....	....	....	....	....	....	....	....	....	....	....	....	....	....	....	....	....
2007-08	Toronto Marlies	AHL	80	3	10	13	57	....	....	....	....	....	....	....	....	....	19	2	3	5	6	....	....	....	....
2008-09	**Toronto**	**NHL**	**23**	**0**	**2**	**2**	**18**	**0**	**0**	**0**	**25**	**0.0**	**–4**	**0**	**0.0**	**12:50**	....	....	....	....	....	....	....	....	....
	Toronto Marlies	AHL	43	4	16	20	47	....	....	....	....	....	....	....	....	....	4	0	1	1	4	....	....	....	....
2009-10	**Minnesota**	**NHL**	**14**	**0**	**0**	**0**	**6**	**0**	**0**	**0**	**9**	**0.0**	**1**	**0**	**0.0**	**12:59**	....	....	....	....	....	....	....	....	....
	Houston Aeros	AHL	54	3	5	8	58	....	....	....	....	....	....	....	....	....	....	....	....	....	....	....	....	....	....
2010-11	Chicago Wolves	AHL	68	4	18	22	66	....	....	....	....	....	....	....	....	....	....	....	....	....	....	....	....	....	....
	NHL Totals		**37**	**0**	**2**	**2**	**24**	**0**	**0**	**0**	**34**	**0.0**		**0**	**0.0**	**12:53**	....	....	....	....	....	....	....	....	....

ECAC Second All-Star Team (2005)

Signed as a free agent by **Toronto**, July 20, 2006. Signed as a free agent by **Minnesota**, July 8, 2009. Signed as a free agent by **Atlanta**, July 7, 2010. • Transferred to **Winnipeg** after **Atlanta** franchise relocated, June 21, 2011.

SIGALET, Jonathan

(SIH-ga-leht, JAWN-ah-thuhn)

Defense. Shoots left. 6'1", 185 lbs. Born, Vancouver, B.C., February 12, 1986. Boston's 4th choice, 100th overall, in 2005 Entry Draft.

Season	Club	League	GP	G	A	Pts	PIM	PP	SH	GW	S	%	+/-	TF	F%	Min	GP	G	A	Pts	PIM	PP	SH	GW	Min
2002-03	Salmon Arm	BCHL	52	13	39	52	34	....	....	....	....	....	....	....	....	....	....	....	....	....	....	....	....	....	....
2003-04	Bowling Green	CCHA	37	3	12	15	26	....	....	....	....	....	....	....	....	....	....	....	....	....	....	....	....	....	....
2004-05	Bowling Green	CCHA	35	3	13	16	36	....	....	....	....	....	....	....	....	....	....	....	....	....	....	....	....	....	....
2005-06	Providence Bruins	AHL	75	9	27	36	59	....	....	....	....	....	....	....	....	....	6	2	1	3	9	....	....	....	....
2006-07	**Boston**	**NHL**	**1**	**0**	**0**	**0**	**4**	**0**	**0**	**0**	**1**	**0.0**	**–2**	**0**	**0.0**	**14:41**	....	....	....	....	....	....	....	....	....
	Providence Bruins	AHL	50	9	13	22	37	....	....	....	....	....	....	....	....	....	....	....	....	....	....	....	....	....	....
2007-08	Providence Bruins	AHL	74	3	20	23	58	....	....	....	....	....	....	....	....	....	10	0	3	3	12	....	....	....	....
2008-09	Syracuse Crunch	AHL	19	5	6	11	16	....	....	....	....	....	....	....	....	....	....	....	....	....	....	....	....	....	....
2009-10	Syracuse Crunch	AHL	69	8	11	19	66	....	....	....	....	....	....	....	....	....	....	....	....	....	....	....	....	....	....
2010-11	Springfield	AHL	67	4	18	22	57	....	....	....	....	....	....	....	....	....	....	....	....	....	....	....	....	....	....
	NHL Totals		**1**	**0**	**0**	**0**	**4**	**0**	**0**	**0**	**1**	**0.0**		**0**	**0.0**	**14:41**	....	....	....	....	....	....	....	....	....

Traded to **Columbus** by **Boston** for Matt Marquardt, May 27, 2008. Signed as a free agent by **Poprad** (Russia-KHL), July 22, 2011.

SIM, Jon

(SIHM, JAWN)

Left wing. Shoots left. 5'10", 195 lbs. Born, New Glasgow, N.S., September 29, 1977. Dallas' 2nd choice, 70th overall, in 1996 Entry Draft.

Season	Club	League	GP	G	A	Pts	PIM	PP	SH	GW	S	%	+/-	TF	F%	Min	GP	G	A	Pts	PIM	PP	SH	GW	Min
1994-95	Laval Titan	QMJHL	9	0	1	1	6	....	....	....	....	....	....	....	....	....	....	....	....	....	....	....	....	....	....
	Sarnia Sting	OHL	25	9	12	21	19	....	....	....	....	....	....	....	....	....	4	3	2	5	2	....	....	....	....
1995-96	Sarnia Sting	OHL	63	56	46	102	130	....	....	....	....	....	....	....	....	....	10	8	7	15	26	....	....	....	....
1996-97	Sarnia Sting	OHL	64	*56	39	95	109	....	....	....	....	....	....	....	....	....	12	9	5	14	32	....	....	....	....
1997-98	Sarnia Sting	OHL	59	44	50	94	95	....	....	....	....	....	....	....	....	....	5	1	4	5	14	....	....	....	....
1998-99♦	**Dallas**	**NHL**	**7**	**1**	**0**	**1**	**12**	**0**	**0**	**0**	**8**	**12.5**	**1**	**6**	**50.0**	**11:26**	**4**	**0**	**0**	**0**	**0**	**0**	**0**	**0**	**6:27**
	Michigan	IHL	68	24	27	51	91	....	....	....	....	....	....	....	....	....	5	3	1	4	18	....	....	....	....
99-2000	**Dallas**	**NHL**	**25**	**5**	**3**	**8**	**10**	**2**	**0**	**1**	**44**	**11.4**	**4**	**4**	**75.0**	**10:51**	**7**	**1**	**0**	**1**	**6**	**0**	**0**	**0**	**11:11**
	Michigan	IHL	35	14	16	30	65	....	....	....	....	....	....	....	....	....	....	....	....	....	....	....	....	....	....
2000-01	**Dallas**	**NHL**	**15**	**0**	**3**	**3**	**6**	**0**	**0**	**0**	**18**	**0.0**	**–2**	**1**	**100.0**	**8:47**	....	....	....	....	....	....	....	....	....
	Utah Grizzlies	IHL	39	16	13	29	44	....	....	....	....	....	....	....	....	....	....	....	....	....	....	....	....	....	....
2001-02	**Dallas**	**NHL**	**26**	**3**	**0**	**3**	**10**	**1**	**0**	**0**	**43**	**7.0**	**–3**	**3**	**0.0**	**9:30**	....	....	....	....	....	....	....	....	....
	Utah Grizzlies	AHL	31	21	6	27	63	....	....	....	....	....	....	....	....	....	....	....	....	....	....	....	....	....	....
2002-03	**Dallas**	**NHL**	**4**	**0**	**0**	**0**	**0**	**0**	**0**	**0**	**7**	**0.0**	**–1**	**2**	**50.0**	**9:10**	....	....	....	....	....	....	....	....	....
	Utah Grizzlies	AHL	42	16	31	47	85	....	....	....	....	....	....	....	....	....	....	....	....	....	....	....	....	....	....
	Nashville	**NHL**	**4**	**1**	**0**	**1**	**0**	**0**	**0**	**0**	**3**	**33.3**	**0**	**14**	**35.7**	**9:18**	....	....	....	....	....	....	....	....	....
	Los Angeles	**NHL**	**14**	**0**	**2**	**2**	**19**	**0**	**0**	**0**	**29**	**0.0**	**–3**	**3**	**33.3**	**12:05**	....	....	....	....	....	....	....	....	....
2003-04	**Los Angeles**	**NHL**	**48**	**6**	**7**	**13**	**27**	**0**	**0**	**1**	**73**	**8.2**	**0**	**19**	**31.6**	**10:01**	....	....	....	....	....	....	....	....	....
	Pittsburgh	**NHL**	**15**	**2**	**3**	**5**	**6**	**0**	**0**	**1**	**27**	**7.4**	**–4**	**0**	**0.0**	**13:39**	....	....	....	....	....	....	....	....	....
2004-05	Utah Grizzlies	AHL	10	2	2	4	12	....	....	....	....	....	....	....	....	....	....	....	....	....	....	....	....	....	....
	Philadelphia	AHL	63	35	26	61	66	....	....	....	....	....	....	....	....	....	21	*10	7	17	44	....	....	....	....
2005-06	**Philadelphia**	**NHL**	**39**	**7**	**7**	**14**	**28**	**4**	**0**	**2**	**80**	**8.8**	**–6**	**1**	**0.0**	**10:59**	....	....	....	....	....	....	....	....	....
	Florida	**NHL**	**33**	**10**	**8**	**18**	**26**	**4**	**0**	**3**	**92**	**10.9**	**–1**	**0**	**0.0**	**12:28**	....	....	....	....	....	....	....	....	....
2006-07	**Atlanta**	**NHL**	**77**	**17**	**12**	**29**	**60**	**2**	**0**	**1**	**141**	**12.1**	**–1**	**9**	**22.2**	**11:45**	**4**	**0**	**0**	**0**	**0**	**0**	**0**	**0**	**5:29**
2007-08	**NY Islanders**	**NHL**	**2**	**0**	**1**	**1**	**2**	**0**	**0**	**0**	**8**	**0.0**	**–1**	**0**	**0.0**	**14:19**	....	....	....	....	....	....	....	....	....
2008-09	**NY Islanders**	**NHL**	**49**	**9**	**6**	**15**	**42**	**3**	**0**	**0**	**90**	**10.0**	**–12**	**6**	**16.7**	**12:10**	....	....	....	....	....	....	....	....	....
	Bridgeport	AHL	18	13	10	23	12	....	....	....	....	....	....	....	....	....	5	2	3	5	10	....	....	....	....
2009-10	**NY Islanders**	**NHL**	**77**	**13**	**9**	**22**	**44**	**1**	**0**	**0**	**128**	**10.2**	**–4**	**18**	**50.0**	**11:39**	....	....	....	....	....	....	....	....	....
2010-11	**NY Islanders**	**NHL**	**34**	**1**	**3**	**4**	**22**	**0**	**0**	**0**	**38**	**2.6**	**–10**	**11**	**45.5**	**11:24**	....	....	....	....	....	....	....	....	....
	Bridgeport	AHL	8	7	2	9	6	....	....	....	....	....	....	....	....	....	....	....	....	....	....	....	....	....	....
	Fribourg	Swiss	7	1	0	1	2	....	....	....	....	....	....	....	....	....	3	0	0	0	12	....	....	....	....
	NHL Totals		**469**	**75**	**64**	**139**	**314**	**17**	**0**	**9**	**829**	**9.0**		**97**	**38.1**	**11:20**	**15**	**1**	**0**	**1**	**6**	**0**	**0**	**0**	**8:24**

OHL Second All-Star Team (1998)

Traded to **Nashville** by **Dallas** for Bubba Berenzweig and future considerations, February 17, 2003. Claimed on waivers by **Los Angeles** from **Nashville**, March 8, 2003. Claimed on waivers by **Pittsburgh** from **Los Angeles**, March 4, 2004. Signed as a free agent by **Phoenix**, September 2, 2004. • Loaned to **Philadelphia** (AHL) by **Phoenix** (Utah – AHL) for the loan of Peter White, November 14, 2004. Signed as a free agent by **Philadelphia**, August 2, 2005. Traded to **Florida** by **Philadelphia** for Florida's 6th round choice (Patrick Maroon) in 2007 Entry Draft, January 23, 2006. Signed as a free agent by **Atlanta**, July 14, 2006. Signed as a free agent by **NY Islanders**, July 1, 2007. Signed as a free agent by **Fribourg-Gotteron** (Swiss), January 16, 2011.

SIMMONDS, Wayne

(SIH-muhnds, WAYN) **PHI**

Right wing. Shoots right. 6'2", 183 lbs. Born, Scarborough, Ont., August 26, 1988. Los Angeles' 3rd choice, 61st overall, in 2007 Entry Draft.

Season	Club	League	GP	G	A	Pts	PIM	PP	SH	GW	S	%	+/-	TF	F%	Min	GP	G	A	Pts	PIM	PP	SH	GW	Min
2004-05	Tor. Jr. Canadiens	GTHL	67	32	40	72	97	....	....	....	....	....	....	....	....	....	....	....	....	....	....	....	....	....	....
2005-06	Brockville Braves	CJHL	49	24	19	43	127	....	....	....	....	....	....	....	....	....	7	4	2	6	12	....	....	....	....
2006-07	Owen Sound	OHL	66	23	26	49	112	....	....	....	....	....	....	....	....	....	4	1	1	2	4	....	....	....	....
2007-08	Owen Sound	OHL	29	17	22	39	43	....	....	....	....	....	....	....	....	....	....	....	....	....	....	....	....	....	....
	Sault Ste. Marie	OHL	31	16	20	36	68	....	....	....	....	....	....	....	....	....	14	5	9	14	22	....	....	....	....
2008-09	**Los Angeles**	**NHL**	**82**	**9**	**14**	**23**	**73**	**2**	**0**	**2**	**127**	**7.1**	**–8**	**25**	**36.0**	**13:50**	....	....	....	....	....	....	....	....	....

			Regular Season														Playoffs								
Season	Club	League	GP	G	A	Pts	PIM	PP	SH	GW	S	%	+/-	TF	F%	Min	GP	G	A	Pts	PIM	PP	SH	GW	Min
2009-10	**Los Angeles**	**NHL**	**78**	**16**	**24**	**40**	**116**	**0**	**0**	**2**	**127**	**12.6**	**22**	**10**	**30.0**	**14:29**	**6**	**2**	**1**	**3**	**9**	**0**	**0**	**0**	**14:21**
2010-11	**Los Angeles**	**NHL**	**80**	**14**	**16**	**30**	**75**	**1**	**0**	**3**	**117**	**12.0**	**–2**	**19**	**36.8**	**13:27**	**6**	**1**	**2**	**3**	**20**	**0**	**0**	**0**	**14:44**
	NHL Totals		**240**	**39**	**54**	**93**	**264**	**3**	**0**	**7**	**371**	**10.5**		**54**	**35.2**	**13:55**	**12**	**3**	**3**	**6**	**29**	**0**	**0**	**0**	**14:33**

Traded to **Philadelphia** by **Los Angeles** with Brayden Schenn and Los Angeles' 2nd round choice in 2012 Entry Draft for Mike Richards and Rob Bordson, June 23, 2011.

SIMS, Shane

(SIHMZ, SHAYN) **NYI**

Defense. Shoots right. 6'1", 195 lbs. Born, East Amherst, NY, April 30, 1988. NY Islanders' 8th choice, 126th overall, in 2006 Entry Draft.

Season	Club	League	GP	G	A	Pts	PIM	PP	SH	GW	S	%	+/-	TF	F%	Min	GP	G	A	Pts	PIM	PP	SH	GW	Min
2004-05	Buffalo Lightning	OPJHL	48	14	26	40	47	....	....	....	....	....	....	....	....	....	....	....	....	....	....	....	....	....	....
2005-06	Des Moines	USHL	59	10	12	22	80	....	....	....	....	....	....	....	....	....	11	2	0	2	12	....	....	....	....
2006-07	Des Moines	USHL	59	10	19	29	137	....	....	....	....	....	....	....	....	....	8	1	3	4	8	....	....	....	....
2007-08	Ohio State	CCHA	39	1	10	11	45	....	....	....	....	....	....	....	....	....	....	....	....	....	....	....	....	....	....
2008-09	Ohio State	CCHA	42	7	17	24	42	....	....	....	....	....	....	....	....	....	....	....	....	....	....	....	....	....	....
2009-10	Ohio State	CCHA	34	5	12	17	22	....	....	....	....	....	....	....	....	....	....	....	....	....	....	....	....	....	....
2010-11	Ohio State	CCHA	37	3	16	19	24	....	....	....	....	....	....	....	....	....	....	....	....	....	....	....	....	....	....
	NY Islanders	**NHL**	**1**	**0**	**0**	**0**	**0**	**0**	**0**	**0**	**0**	**0.0**	**0**	**0**	**0.0**	**6:34**	....	....	....	....	....	....	....	....	....
	NHL Totals		**1**	**0**	**0**	**0**	**0**	**0**	**0**	**0**	**0**	**0.0**		**0**	**0.0**	**6:34**	....	....	....	....	....	....	....	....	....

USHL All-Rookie Team (2006)

SJOSTROM, Fredrik

(SHAW-strahm, FREHD-rihk)

Right wing. Shoots left. 6'1", 218 lbs. Born, Fargelanda, Sweden, May 6, 1983. Phoenix's 1st choice, 11th overall, in 2001 Entry Draft.

Season	Club	League	GP	G	A	Pts	PIM	PP	SH	GW	S	%	+/-	TF	F%	Min	GP	G	A	Pts	PIM	PP	SH	GW	Min
99-2000	MoDo U18	Swe-U18	4	0	2	2	6	....	....	....	....	....	....	....	....	....	....	....	....	....	....	....	....	....	....
	Malmo Jr.	Swe-Jr.	18	4	6	10	8	....	....	....	....	....	....	....	....	....	....	....	....	....	....	....	....	....	....
2000-01	V.Frolunda Jr.	Swe-Jr.	11	3	7	10	12	....	....	....	....	....	....	....	....	....	4	1	2	3	6	....	....	....	....
	V.Frolunda	Sweden	31	3	2	5	6	....	....	....	....	....	....	....	....	....	5	0	0	0	2	....	....	....	....
2001-02	Calgary Hitmen	WHL	58	19	31	50	51	....	....	....	....	....	....	....	....	....	4	1	1	2	8	....	....	....	....
2002-03	Calgary Hitmen	WHL	63	34	43	77	95	....	....	....	....	....	....	....	....	....	5	1	3	4	4	....	....	....	....
	Springfield	AHL	2	1	0	1	0	....	....	....	....	....	....	....	....	....	6	2	0	2	12	....	....	....	....
2003-04	**Phoenix**	**NHL**	**57**	**7**	**6**	**13**	**22**	**0**	**0**	**1**	**73**	**9.6**	**–7**	**7**	**28.6**	**11:35**	....	....	....	....	....	....	....	....	....
	Springfield	AHL	17	0	7	7	8	....	....	....	....	....	....	....	....	....	....	....	....	....	....	....	....	....	....
2004-05	Utah Grizzlies	AHL	80	14	24	38	57	....	....	....	....	....	....	....	....	....	....	....	....	....	....	....	....	....	....
2005-06	**Phoenix**	**NHL**	**75**	**6**	**17**	**23**	**42**	**1**	**0**	**1**	**109**	**5.5**	**1**	**8**	**12.5**	**13:20**	....	....	....	....	....	....	....	....	....
2006-07	**Phoenix**	**NHL**	**78**	**9**	**9**	**18**	**48**	**2**	**0**	**1**	**125**	**7.2**	**–11**	**15**	**13.3**	**14:07**	....	....	....	....	....	....	....	....	....
2007-08	**Phoenix**	**NHL**	**51**	**10**	**9**	**19**	**14**	**2**	**2**	**1**	**84**	**11.9**	**–2**	**33**	**18.2**	**13:33**	....	....	....	....	....	....	....	....	....
	NY Rangers	**NHL**	**18**	**2**	**0**	**2**	**8**	**0**	**0**	**1**	**26**	**7.7**	**0**	**3**	**0.0**	**8:05**	**10**	**0**	**1**	**1**	**2**	**0**	**0**	**0**	**6:28**
2008-09	**NY Rangers**	**NHL**	**79**	**7**	**6**	**13**	**30**	**0**	**2**	**0**	**95**	**7.4**	**–11**	**5**	**60.0**	**12:10**	**7**	**0**	**1**	**1**	**0**	**0**	**0**	**0**	**11:46**
2009-10	**Calgary**	**NHL**	**46**	**1**	**5**	**6**	**8**	**0**	**0**	**0**	**33**	**3.0**	**2**	**2**	**0.0**	**9:31**	....	....	....	....	....	....	....	....	....
	Toronto	**NHL**	**19**	**2**	**3**	**5**	**4**	**0**	**0**	**0**	**31**	**6.5**	**–4**	**5**	**0.0**	**13:52**	....	....	....	....	....	....	....	....	....
2010-11	**Toronto**	**NHL**	**66**	**2**	**3**	**5**	**14**	**0**	**0**	**0**	**62**	**3.2**	**–5**	**15**	**33.3**	**11:13**	....	....	....	....	....	....	....	....	....
	NHL Totals		**489**	**46**	**58**	**104**	**190**	**5**	**4**	**5**	**638**	**7.2**		**93**	**20.4**	**12:16**	**17**	**0**	**2**	**2**	**2**	**0**	**0**	**0**	**8:39**

Traded to **NY Rangers** by **Phoenix** with Josh Gratton, David LeNeveu and Phoenix's 5th round choice (Roman Horak) in 2009 Entry Draft for Marcel Hossa and Al Montoya, February 26, 2008. Signed as a free agent by **Calgary**, July 1, 2009. Traded to **Toronto** by **Calgary** with Dion Phaneuf and Keith Aulie for Matt Stajan, Niklas Hagman, Jamal Mayers and Ian White, January 31, 2010. Signed as a free agent by **Farjestad** (Sweden), July 29, 2011.

SKILLE, Jack

(SKIH-lee, JAK) **FLA**

Right wing. Shoots right. 6'1", 215 lbs. Born, Madison, WI, May 19, 1987. Chicago's 1st choice, 7th overall, in 2005 Entry Draft.

Season	Club	League	GP	G	A	Pts	PIM	PP	SH	GW	S	%	+/-	TF	F%	Min	GP	G	A	Pts	PIM	PP	SH	GW	Min
2003-04	USNTDP	U-17	33	14	10	24	30	....	....	....	....	....	....	....	....	....	....	....	....	....	....	....	....	....	....
	USNTDP	NAHL	28	11	9	20	31	....	....	....	....	....	....	....	....	....	....	....	....	....	....	....	....	....	....
2004-05	USNTDP	U-18	26	9	11	20	36	....	....	....	....	....	....	....	....	....	....	....	....	....	....	....	....	....	....
	USNTDP	NAHL	16	6	11	17	20	....	....	....	....	....	....	....	....	....	....	....	....	....	....	....	....	....	....
2005-06	U. of Wisconsin	WCHA	41	13	8	21	37	....	....	....	....	....	....	....	....	....	....	....	....	....	....	....	....	....	....
2006-07	U. of Wisconsin	WCHA	26	8	10	18	12	....	....	....	....	....	....	....	....	....	....	....	....	....	....	....	....	....	....
	Norfolk Admirals	AHL	9	4	4	8	0	....	....	....	....	....	....	....	....	....	3	0	0	0	2	....	....	....	....
2007-08	**Chicago**	**NHL**	**16**	**3**	**2**	**5**	**0**	**0**	**0**	**0**	**23**	**13.0**	**1**	**4**	**50.0**	**11:59**	....	....	....	....	....	....	....	....	....
	Rockford IceHogs	AHL	59	16	18	34	44	....	....	....	....	....	....	....	....	....	12	2	1	3	6	....	....	....	....
2008-09	**Chicago**	**NHL**	**8**	**1**	**0**	**1**	**5**	**0**	**0**	**0**	**14**	**7.1**	**–3**	**0**	**0.0**	**9:26**	....	....	....	....	....	....	....	....	....
	Rockford IceHogs	AHL	58	20	25	45	56	....	....	....	....	....	....	....	....	....	....	....	....	....	....	....	....	....	....
2009-10	**Chicago**	**NHL**	**6**	**1**	**1**	**2**	**0**	**0**	**0**	**0**	**9**	**11.1**	**–3**	**0**	**0.0**	**7:40**	....	....	....	....	....	....	....	....	....
	Rockford IceHogs	AHL	63	23	26	49	50	....	....	....	....	....	....	....	....	....	4	0	0	0	0	....	....	....	....
2010-11	**Chicago**	**NHL**	**49**	**7**	**10**	**17**	**25**	**1**	**0**	**1**	**121**	**5.8**	**3**	**4**	**50.0**	**10:44**	....	....	....	....	....	....	....	....	....
	Florida	**NHL**	**13**	**1**	**1**	**2**	**4**	**0**	**0**	**0**	**33**	**3.0**	**–12**	**6**	**16.7**	**16:25**	....	....	....	....	....	....	....	....	....
	NHL Totals		**92**	**13**	**14**	**27**	**34**	**1**	**0**	**1**	**200**	**6.5**		**14**	**35.7**	**11:26**	....	....	....	....	....	....	....	....	....

Traded to **Florida** by **Chicago** with Hugh Jessiman and David Pacan for Michael Frolik and Alexander Salak, February 9, 2011.

SKINNER, Brett

(SKIH-nuhr, BREHT)

Defense. Shoots left. 6'1", 183 lbs. Born, Brandon, Man., June 28, 1983. Vancouver's 3rd choice, 68th overall, in 2002 Entry Draft.

Season	Club	League	GP	G	A	Pts	PIM	PP	SH	GW	S	%	+/-	TF	F%	Min	GP	G	A	Pts	PIM	PP	SH	GW	Min
1998-99	Brandon Kings	MMBHL	29	3	18	21	20	....	....	....	....	....	....	....	....	....	....	....	....	....	....	....	....	....	....
99-2000	Brandon Kings	MMMHL	40	8	27	35	48	....	....	....	....	....	....	....	....	....	....	....	....	....	....	....	....	....	....
2000-01	Trail	BCHL	59	11	24	35	43	....	....	....	....	....	....	....	....	....	....	....	....	....	....	....	....	....	....
2001-02	Des Moines	USHL	44	9	38	47	25	....	....	....	....	....	....	....	....	....	3	0	1	1	0	....	....	....	....
2002-03	U. of Denver	WCHA	37	4	13	17	27	....	....	....	....	....	....	....	....	....	....	....	....	....	....	....	....	....	....
2003-04	U. of Denver	WCHA	44	7	23	30	32	....	....	....	....	....	....	....	....	....	....	....	....	....	....	....	....	....	....
2004-05	U. of Denver	WCHA	43	4	36	40	30	....	....	....	....	....	....	....	....	....	....	....	....	....	....	....	....	....	....
2005-06	Manitoba Moose	AHL	65	4	21	25	33	....	....	....	....	....	....	....	....	....	13	0	4	4	19	....	....	....	....
2006-07	Portland Pirates	AHL	41	6	12	18	24	....	....	....	....	....	....	....	....	....	....	....	....	....	....	....	....	....	....
	Augusta Lynx	ECHL	5	1	3	4	8	....	....	....	....	....	....	....	....	....	....	....	....	....	....	....	....	....	....
	Omaha	AHL	21	0	6	6	2	....	....	....	....	....	....	....	....	....	5	0	3	3	2	....	....	....	....
2007-08	Providence Bruins	AHL	68	7	40	47	47	....	....	....	....	....	....	....	....	....	10	0	1	1	0	....	....	....	....
2008-09	**NY Islanders**	**NHL**	**11**	**0**	**0**	**0**	**4**	**0**	**0**	**0**	**5**	**0.0**	**3**	**0**	**0.0**	**11:43**	....	....	....	....	....	....	....	....	....
	Bridgeport	AHL	24	1	11	12	10	....	....	....	....	....	....	....	....	....	....	....	....	....	....	....	....	....	....
	Chicago Wolves	AHL	37	3	20	23	4	....	....	....	....	....	....	....	....	....	....	....	....	....	....	....	....	....	....
2009-10	Lake Erie	AHL	73	3	25	28	43	....	....	....	....	....	....	....	....	....	....	....	....	....	....	....	....	....	....
2010-11	Amur Khabarovsk	Rus-KHL	34	2	4	6	12	....	....	....	....	....	....	....	....	....	....	....	....	....	....	....	....	....	....
	NHL Totals		**11**	**0**	**0**	**0**	**4**	**0**	**0**	**0**	**5**	**0.0**		**0**	**0.0**	**11:43**	....	....	....	....	....	....	....	....	....

USHL First All-Star Team (2002) • USHL Defenseman of the Year (2002) • WCHA First All-Star Team (2005) • NCAA West Second All-American Team (2005) • NCAA Championship All-Tournament Team (2005)

Traded to **Anaheim** by **Vancouver** with NY Islanders' 2nd round choice (previously acquired, Anaheim selected Bryce Swan) in 2006 Entry Draft for Keith Carney and Juha Alen, March 9, 2006. Traded to **Boston** by **Anaheim** with Nathan Saunders for Mark Mowers, September 24, 2007. Signed as a free agent by **NY Islanders**, July 3, 2008. Traded to **Atlanta** by **NY Islanders** for Junior Lessard, January 13, 2009. Signed as a free agent by **Colorado**, July 8, 2009. Signed as a free agent by **Amur** (Russia-KHL), August 13, 2010.

SKINNER, Jeff

(SKIH-nuhr, JEHF) **CAR**

Center. Shoots left. 5'11", 193 lbs. Born, Markham, Ont., May 16, 1992. Carolina's 1st choice, 7th overall, in 2010 Entry Draft.

Season	Club	League	GP	G	A	Pts	PIM	PP	SH	GW	S	%	+/-	TF	F%	Min	GP	G	A	Pts	PIM	PP	SH	GW	Min
2007-08	Tor. Young Nats	GTHL	56	65	44	109	163	....	....	....	....	....	....	....	....	....	....	....	....	....	....	....	....	....	....
2008-09	Kitchener Rangers	OHL	63	27	24	51	34	....	....	....	....	....	....	....	....	....	....	....	....	....	....	....	....	....	....
2009-10	Kitchener Rangers	OHL	64	50	40	90	72	....	....	....	....	....	....	....	....	....	20	*20	13	33	14	....	....	....	....
2010-11	**Carolina**	**NHL**	**82**	**31**	**32**	**63**	**46**	**6**	**0**	**2**	**215**	**14.4**	**3**	**157**	**36.9**	**16:44**	....	....	....	....	....	....	....	....	....
	NHL Totals		**82**	**31**	**32**	**63**	**46**	**6**	**0**	**2**	**215**	**14.4**		**157**	**36.9**	**16:44**	....	....	....	....	....	....	....	....	....

NHL All-Rookie Team (2011) • Calder Memorial Trophy (2011)

Played in NHL All-Star Game (2011)

			Regular Season															Playoffs							
Season	Club	League	GP	G	A	Pts	PIM	PP	SH	GW	S	%	+/-	TF	F%	Min	GP	G	A	Pts	PIM	PP	SH	GW	Min

SKOULA, Martin — (SKOO-la, MAHR-tihn)

Defense. Shoots left. 6'3", 226 lbs. Born, Litomerice, Czech., October 28, 1979. Colorado's 2nd choice, 17th overall, in 1998 Entry Draft.

Season	Club	League	GP	G	A	Pts	PIM	PP	SH	GW	S	%	+/-	TF	F%	Min	GP	G	A	Pts	PIM	PP	SH	GW	Min
1995-96	Litvinov Jr.	CzRep-Jr.	38	0	4	4	....																		
	Litvinov	CzRep															1	0	0	0	0				
1996-97	Litvinov Jr.	CzRep-Jr.	38	2	9	11	....																		
	Litvinov	CzRep	1	0	0	0	0																		
1997-98	Barrie Colts	OHL	66	8	36	44	36										6	1	3	4	4				
1998-99	Barrie Colts	OHL	67	13	46	59	46										12	3	10	13	13				
	Hershey Bears	AHL															1	0	0	0	0				
99-2000	Colorado	NHL	80	3	13	16	20	2	0	0	66	4.5	5	0	0.0	18:15	17	0	2	2	4	0	0	0	18:45
2000-01 ◆	Colorado	NHL	82	8	17	25	38	3	0	2	108	7.4	8	1100.0	20:41	23	1	4	5	8	0	0	0	11:59
2001-02	Colorado	NHL	82	10	21	31	42	5	0	1	100	10.0	-3	0	0.0	22:18	21	0	6	6	2	0	0	0	14:37
	Czech Republic	Olympics	4	0	0	0	0																		
2002-03	Colorado	NHL	81	4	21	25	68	2	0	0	93	4.3	11	1100.0	18:27	7	0	1	1	4	0	0	0	11:05
2003-04	Colorado	NHL	58	2	14	16	30	0	0	0	54	3.7	2	0	0.0	17:21									
	Anaheim	NHL	21	2	7	9	2	1	0	0	30	6.7	3	1	0.0	21:14									
2004-05	Litvinov	CzRep	47	4	15	19	101										6	0	0	0	6				
2005-06	Dallas	NHL	61	4	11	15	36	3	0	1	78	5.1	6	0	0.0	18:41									
	Minnesota	NHL	17	1	5	6	10	0	0	0	14	7.1	0	0	0.0	20:49									
2006-07	Minnesota	NHL	81	0	15	15	36	0	0	0	91	0.0	9	0	0.0	20:14	5	0	0	0	4	0	0	0	19:02
2007-08	Minnesota	NHL	80	3	8	11	26	0	0	1	63	4.8	-16	0	0.0	20:29	6	0	0	0	0	0	0	0	26:41
2008-09	Minnesota	NHL	81	4	12	16	10	0	0	0	55	7.3	-12	0	0.0	19:58									
2009-10	Pittsburgh	NHL	33	3	5	8	6	1	0	0	23	13.0	-4	0	0.0	16:43									
	New Jersey	NHL	19	0	3	3	4	0	0	0	11	0.0	7	0	0.0	18:37	4	0	0	0	0	0	0	0	16:39
2010-11	Omsk	Rus-KHL	52	3	19	22	21										14	0	3	3	4				
	NHL Totals		**776**	**44**	**152**	**196**	**328**	**17**	**0**	**5**	**786**	**5.6**		**3**	**66.7**	**19:37**	**83**	**1**	**13**	**14**	**22**	**0**	**0**	**0**	**15:40**

OHL All-Rookie Team (1998) • OHL Second All-Star Team (1999)

Traded to **Anaheim** by **Colorado** for Kurt Sauer and Anaheim's 4th round choice (Raymond Macias) in 2005 Entry Draft, February 21, 2004. Signed as a free agent by **Litvinov** (CzRep), September 17, 2004. Signed as a free agent by **Dallas**, August 3, 2005. Traded to **Minnesota** by **Dallas** with Shawn Belle for Willie Mitchell and Minnesota's 2nd round choice (Nico Saccheti) in 2007 Entry Draft, March 8, 2006. Signed as a free agent by **Pittsburgh**, September 29, 2009. Traded to **Toronto** by **Pittsburgh** with Luca Caputi for Alexei Ponikarovsky, March 2, 2010. Traded to **New Jersey** by **Toronto** for New Jersey's 5th round choice (Sam Carrick) in 2010 Entry Draft, March 3, 2010. Signed as a free agent by **Omsk** (Russia-KHL), June 23, 2010.

SKRASTINS, Karlis — (SKRAS-tihnz, KAR-lihs)

Defense. Shoots left. 6'2", 208 lbs. Born, Riga, Latvia, July 9, 1974. Nashville's 8th choice, 230th overall, in 1998 Entry Draft.

Season	Club	League	GP	G	A	Pts	PIM	PP	SH	GW	S	%	+/-	TF	F%	Min	GP	G	A	Pts	PIM	PP	SH	GW	Min
1992-93	Pardaugava Riga	CIS	40	3	5	8	16										2	0	0	0	0				
1993-94	Pardaugava Riga	CIS	42	7	5	12	18										2	1	0	1	4				
1994-95	Pardaugava Riga	CIS	52	4	14	18	69																		
1995-96	TPS Turku	Finland	50	4	11	15	32										11	2	2	4	10				
1996-97	TPS Turku	Finland	50	2	8	10	20										12	0	4	4	2				
	TPS Turku	EuroHL	6	0	1	1	4										4	0	0	0	14				
1997-98	TPS Turku	Finland	48	4	15	19	67										4	0	0	0	0				
	TPS Turku	EuroHL	6	0	1	1	6																		
1998-99	Nashville	NHL	2	0	1	1	0	0	0	0	0	0.0	0	0	0.0	11:47									
	Milwaukee	IHL	75	8	36	44	47										2	0	1	1	2				
99-2000	Nashville	NHL	59	5	6	11	20	1	0	2	51	9.8	-7	0	0.0	20:51									
	Milwaukee	IHL	19	3	8	11	10																		
2000-01	Nashville	NHL	82	1	11	12	30	0	0	1	66	1.5	-12	0	0.0	19:12									
2001-02	Nashville	NHL	82	4	13	17	36	0	0	0	84	4.8	-12	0	0.0	20:29									
	Latvia	Olympics	1	0	0	0	0																		
2002-03	Nashville	NHL	82	3	10	13	44	0	1	0	86	3.5	-18	0	0.0	20:17									
2003-04	Colorado	NHL	82	5	8	13	26	0	1	1	102	4.9	18	0	0.0	21:49	11	0	2	2	2	0	0	0	23:07
2004-05	HK Riga 2000	Latvia	4	0	4	4	0										9	3	10	13	33				
	HK Riga 2000	BelOpen	34	8	17	25	30										3	0	0	0	25				
2005-06	Colorado	NHL	82	3	11	14	65	0	2	0	58	5.2	-7	0	0.0	21:49	9	0	1	1	10	0	0	0	23:24
	Latvia	Olympics	5	0	1	1	0																		
2006-07	Colorado	NHL	68	0	11	11	30	0	0	0	65	0.0	0	0	0.0	21:14									
2007-08	Colorado	NHL	43	1	3	4	20	0	0	0	34	2.9	-2	0	0.0	18:02									
	Florida	NHL	17	1	0	1	12	0	0	0	11	9.1	-9	0	0.0	20:03									
2008-09	Florida	NHL	80	4	14	18	30	0	0	0	55	7.3	9	0	0.0	20:34									
2009-10	Dallas	NHL	79	2	11	13	24	0	0	0	53	3.8	-4	0	0.0	19:34									
	Latvia	Olympics	4	0	0	0	0																		
2010-11	Dallas	NHL	74	3	5	8	38	0	0	1	30	10.0	-1	1	0.0	17:57									
	NHL Totals		**832**	**32**	**104**	**136**	**375**	**1**	**4**	**8**	**695**	**4.6**		**1**	**0.0**	**20:14**	**20**	**0**	**3**	**3**	**12**	**0**	**0**	**0**	**23:15**

Traded to **Colorado** by **Nashville** for Colorado's 3rd round choice (later traded to Ottawa – Ottawa selected Peter Regin Jensen) in 2004 Entry Draft, June 30, 2003. Signed as a free agent by **Riga** (Latvia), September 25, 2004. Traded to **Florida** by **Colorado** with Colorado's 3rd round choice (Adam Comrie) in 2008 Entry Draft for Ruslan Salei, February 26, 2008. Signed as a free agent by **Dallas**, July 2, 2009.

SLATER, Jim — (SLAY-tuhr, JIHM) **WPG**

Center. Shoots left. 6', 200 lbs. Born, Lapeer, MI, December 9, 1982. Atlanta's 2nd choice, 30th overall, in 2002 Entry Draft.

Season	Club	League	GP	G	A	Pts	PIM	PP	SH	GW	S	%	+/-	TF	F%	Min	GP	G	A	Pts	PIM	PP	SH	GW	Min
1998-99	USNTDP	U-18	3	0	1	1	0																		
	Cleveland Barons	NAHL	50	13	20	33	58										2	0	0	0	2				
99-2000	Cleveland Barons	NAHL	56	35	50	85	129										3	1	3	4	4				
2000-01	Cleveland Barons	NAHL	48	27	37	64	122										6	6	6	12	6				
2001-02	Michigan State	CCHA	37	11	21	32	50																		
2002-03	Michigan State	CCHA	37	18	26	44	26																		
2003-04	Michigan State	CCHA	42	19	29	*48	38																		
2004-05	Michigan State	CCHA	41	16	32	48	30																		
2005-06	Atlanta	NHL	71	10	10	20	46	1	0	0	108	9.3	1	287	56.5	10:06									
	Chicago Wolves	AHL	4	0	2	2	2																		
2006-07	Atlanta	NHL	74	5	14	19	62	0	0	2	90	5.6	8	373	54.4	10:14	4	0	0	0	2	0	0	0	5:10
2007-08	Atlanta	NHL	69	8	5	13	41	0	2	0	95	8.4	-10	367	52.0	10:24									
	Chicago Wolves	AHL	3	0	0	0	0																		
2008-09	Atlanta	NHL	60	8	10	18	52	0	2	0	94	8.5	0	462	53.0	11:15									
2009-10	Atlanta	NHL	61	11	7	18	60	1	0	2	107	10.3	1	431	58.9	12:12									
2010-11	Atlanta	NHL	36	5	7	12	19	0	0	1	53	9.4	4	301	61.5	10:35									
	NHL Totals		**371**	**47**	**53**	**100**	**280**	**2**	**4**	**5**	**547**	**8.6**		**2221**	**55.8**	**10:45**	**4**	**0**	**0**	**0**	**2**	**0**	**0**	**0**	**5:10**

CCHA All-Rookie Team (2002) • CCHA First All-Star Team (2003, 2004) • NCAA West Second All-American Team (2004)

• Missed majority of 2010-11 due to concussion at New Jersey, December 31, 2010. • Transferred to **Winnipeg** after **Atlanta** franchise relocated, June 21, 2011.

SLOAN, Tyler — (SLOHN, TIGH-luhr) **NSH**

Defense. Shoots left. 6'4", 214 lbs. Born, Calgary, Alta., March 15, 1981.

Season	Club	League	GP	G	A	Pts	PIM	PP	SH	GW	S	%	+/-	TF	F%	Min	GP	G	A	Pts	PIM	PP	SH	GW	Min
1997-98	Calgary Buffaloes	AMHL	36	2	11	13	24										10	0	4	4	2				
1998-99	Calgary Royals	AJHL				STATISTICS NOT AVAILABLE																			
99-2000	Calgary Royals	AJHL	45	5	26	31	80																		
2000-01	Kamloops Blazers	WHL	70	5	28	33	146										4	0	0	0	4				
2001-02	Kamloops Blazers	WHL	70	3	29	32	89										4	0	0	0	15				
	Syracuse Crunch	AHL	2	0	0	0	5																		
2002-03	Syracuse Crunch	AHL	39	2	1	3	46																		
	Dayton Bombers	ECHL	14	1	2	3	22																		
2003-04	Syracuse Crunch	AHL	69	2	4	6	50										7	0	0	0	8				
2004-05	Syracuse Crunch	AHL	14	0	2	2	18																		
	Dayton Bombers	ECHL	43	6	11	17	84																		
2005-06	Las Vegas	ECHL	48	4	16	20	71										13	0	4	4	27				
	Manitoba Moose	AHL	4	0	0	0	0										2	0	1	1	2				
	Hershey Bears	AHL																							
2006-07	Hershey Bears	AHL	68	2	9	11	104										17	0	7	7	30				
2007-08	Hershey Bears	AHL	56	1	7	8	90										5	0	0	0	8				

			Regular Season														Playoffs								
Season	Club	League	GP	G	A	Pts	PIM	PP	SH	GW	S	%	+/-	TF	F%	Min	GP	G	A	Pts	PIM	PP	SH	GW	Min
2008-09	**Washington**	**NHL**	**26**	**1**	**4**	**5**	**14**	**0**	**0**	**0**	**8**	**12.5**	**4**	**0**	**0.0**	**16:39**	**2**	**0**	**1**	**1**	**0**	**0**	**0**	**0**	**18:24**
	Hershey Bears	AHL	46	2	10	12	61	....	....	....	....	....	....	....	....	....	16	0	5	5	14	....	....	....	....
2009-10	**Washington**	**NHL**	**40**	**2**	**4**	**6**	**22**	**0**	**0**	**0**	**34**	**5.9**	**–1**	**3**	**66.7**	**14:15**	**2**	**0**	**0**	**0**	**0**	**0**	**0**	**0**	**13:06**
	Hershey Bears	AHL	2	0	1	1	0	....	....	....	....	....	....	....	....	....	....	....	....	....	....	....	....	....	....
2010-11	**Washington**	**NHL**	**33**	**1**	**5**	**6**	**14**	**0**	**0**	**0**	**12**	**8.3**	**–6**	**0**	**0.0**	**12:30**	....	....	....	....	....	....	....	....	....
	Hershey Bears	AHL	6	0	2	2	6	....	....	....	....	....	....	....	....	....	....	....	....	....	....	....	....	....	....
	NHL Totals		**99**	**4**	**13**	**17**	**50**	**0**	**0**	**0**	**54**	**7.4**		**3**	**66.7**	**14:18**	**4**	**0**	**1**	**1**	**0**	**0**	**0**	**0**	**15:45**

Signed as a free agent by **Columbus**, September 24, 2000. Signed as a free agent by **Hershey** (AHL), August 15, 2007. Signed as a free agent by **Washington**, July 2, 2008. • Missed majority of 2010-11 due to recurring hip injury and as a healthy reserve. Signed as a free agent by **Nashville**, July 29, 2011.

SMABY, Matt
(SMA-bee, MAT) **ANA**

Defense. Shoots left. 6'4", 239 lbs. Born, Minneapolis, MN, October 14, 1984. Tampa Bay's 2nd choice, 41st overall, in 2003 Entry Draft.

2001-02	Shat.-St. Mary's	High-MN	65	7	18	25	134	....	....	....	....	....	....	....	....	....	....	....	....	....	....	....	....	....	....
2002-03	Shat.-St. Mary's	High-MN	57	3	20	23	114	....	....	....	....	....	....	....	....	....	....	....	....	....	....	....	....	....	....
2003-04	North Dakota	WCHA	39	1	6	7	81	....	....	....	....	....	....	....	....	....	....	....	....	....	....	....	....	....	....
2004-05	North Dakota	WCHA	44	1	2	3	86	....	....	....	....	....	....	....	....	....	....	....	....	....	....	....	....	....	....
2005-06	North Dakota	WCHA	46	4	15	19	*113	....	....	....	....	....	....	....	....	....	....	....	....	....	....	....	....	....	....
2006-07	Springfield	AHL	66	2	14	16	43	....	....	....	....	....	....	....	....	....	....	....	....	....	....	....	....	....	....
2007-08	**Tampa Bay**	**NHL**	**14**	**0**	**0**	**0**	**12**	**0**	**0**	**0**	**7**	**0.0**	**–6**	**0**	**0.0**	**12:08**	....	....	....	....	....	....	....	....	....
	Norfolk Admirals	AHL	58	1	5	6	66	....	....	....	....	....	....	....	....	....	....	....	....	....	....	....	....	....	....
2008-09	**Tampa Bay**	**NHL**	**43**	**0**	**4**	**4**	**50**	**0**	**0**	**0**	**28**	**0.0**	**–11**	**1**	**100.0**	**19:05**	....	....	....	....	....	....	....	....	....
	Norfolk Admirals	AHL	25	2	4	6	30	....	....	....	....	....	....	....	....	....	....	....	....	....	....	....	....	....	....
2009-10	**Tampa Bay**	**NHL**	**33**	**0**	**2**	**2**	**27**	**0**	**0**	**0**	**17**	**0.0**	**–4**	**0**	**0.0**	**13:29**	....	....	....	....	....	....	....	....	....
	Norfolk Admirals	AHL	7	0	2	2	9	....	....	....	....	....	....	....	....	....	....	....	....	....	....	....	....	....	....
2010-11	**Tampa Bay**	**NHL**	**32**	**0**	**0**	**0**	**17**	**0**	**0**	**0**	**9**	**0.0**	**2**	**0**	**0.0**	**6:59**	....	....	....	....	....	....	....	....	....
	NHL Totals		**122**	**0**	**6**	**6**	**106**	**0**	**0**	**0**	**61**	**0.0**		**1**	**100.0**	**13:36**	....	....	....	....	....	....	....	....	....

• Missed majority of 2009-10 due to various injuries and as a healthy reserve. • Missed majority of 2010-11 due to off-ice ankle injury and as a healthy reserve. Signed as a free agent by **Anaheim**. July 14, 2011.

SMID, Ladislav
(SHMIHD, LA-dih-slahv) **EDM**

Defense. Shoots left. 6'3", 226 lbs. Born, Frydlant V Cechach, Czech., February 1, 1986. Anaheim's 1st choice, 9th overall, in 2004 Entry Draft.

2001-02	HC Liberec Jr.	CzRep-Jr.	43	6	10	16	87	....	....	....	....	....	....	....	....	....	....	....	....	....	....	....	....	....	....
2002-03	HC Liberec Jr.	CzRep-Jr.	32	1	14	15	12	....	....	....	....	....	....	....	....	....	8	2	1	3	31	....	....	....	....
	Liberec	CzRep	4	0	0	0	0	....	....	....	....	....	....	....	....	....	....	....	....	....	....	....	....	....	....
2003-04	HC Liberec Jr.	CzRep-Jr.	14	4	10	14	38	....	....	....	....	....	....	....	....	....	2	1	0	1	6	....	....	....	....
	Liberec	CzRep	45	1	1	2	51	....	....	....	....	....	....	....	....	....	....	....	....	....	....	....	....	....	....
	Beroun	CzRep-2	....	....	....	....	....	....	....	....	....	....	....	....	....	....	3	1	1	2	4	....	....	....	....
2004-05	HC Liberec Jr.	CzRep-Jr.	3	0	1	1	4	....	....	....	....	....	....	....	....	....	....	....	....	....	....	....	....	....	....
	Liberec	CzRep	39	1	3	4	14	....	....	....	....	....	....	....	....	....	12	0	0	0	6	....	....	....	....
2005-06	Portland Pirates	AHL	71	3	25	28	48	....	....	....	....	....	....	....	....	....	16	0	1	1	16	....	....	....	....
2006-07	**Edmonton**	**NHL**	**77**	**3**	**7**	**10**	**37**	**0**	**0**	**0**	**53**	**5.7**	**–16**	**0**	**0.0**	**19:14**	....	....	....	....	....	....	....	....	....
2007-08	**Edmonton**	**NHL**	**65**	**0**	**4**	**4**	**58**	**0**	**0**	**0**	**45**	**0.0**	**–15**	**0**	**0.0**	**17:52**	....	....	....	....	....	....	....	....	....
	Springfield	AHL	8	1	4	5	15	....	....	....	....	....	....	....	....	....	....	....	....	....	....	....	....	....	....
2008-09	**Edmonton**	**NHL**	**60**	**0**	**11**	**11**	**57**	**0**	**0**	**0**	**33**	**0.0**	**–6**	**0**	**0.0**	**14:57**	....	....	....	....	....	....	....	....	....
2009-10	**Edmonton**	**NHL**	**51**	**1**	**8**	**9**	**39**	**0**	**0**	**0**	**36**	**2.8**	**5**	**0**	**0.0**	**19:11**	....	....	....	....	....	....	....	....	....
2010-11	**Edmonton**	**NHL**	**78**	**0**	**10**	**10**	**85**	**0**	**0**	**0**	**48**	**0.0**	**–10**	**0**	**0.0**	**20:17**	....	....	....	....	....	....	....	....	....
	NHL Totals		**331**	**4**	**40**	**44**	**276**	**0**	**0**	**0**	**215**	**1.9**		**0**	**0.0**	**18:26**	....	....	....	....	....	....	....	....	....

Traded to **Edmonton** by **Anaheim** with Joffrey Lupul, Anaheim's 1st round choice (later traded to Phoenix - Phoenix selected Nick Ross) in 2007 Entry Draft and Anaheim's 1st (Jordan Eberle) and 2nd (later traded to NY Islanders - NY Islanders selected Travis Hamonic) round choices in 2008 Entry Draft for Chris Pronger, July 3, 2006.

SMITH, Ben
(SMIHTH, BEHN) **CHI**

Right wing. Shoots right. 5'11", 205 lbs. Born, Winston-Salem, NC, July 11, 1988. Chicago's 5th choice, 169th overall, in 2008 Entry Draft.

2006-07	Boston College	H-East	42	10	8	18	10	....	....	....	....	....	....	....	....	....	....	....	....	....	....	....	....	....	....
2007-08	Boston College	H-East	44	25	25	50	12	....	....	....	....	....	....	....	....	....	....	....	....	....	....	....	....	....	....
2008-09	Boston College	H-East	37	6	11	17	6	....	....	....	....	....	....	....	....	....	....	....	....	....	....	....	....	....	....
2009-10	Boston College	H-East	42	16	21	37	8	....	....	....	....	....	....	....	....	....	....	....	....	....	....	....	....	....	....
	Rockford IceHogs	AHL	....	....	....	....	....	....	....	....	....	....	....	....	....	....	3	1	0	1	0	....	....	....	....
2010-11	**Chicago**	**NHL**	**6**	**1**	**0**	**1**	**0**	**0**	**0**	**0**	**6**	**16.7**	**1**	**8**	**75.0**	**13:47**	**7**	**3**	**0**	**3**	**0**	**0**	**0**	**1**	**14:50**
	Rockford IceHogs	AHL	63	19	12	31	16	....	....	....	....	....	....	....	....	....	....	....	....	....	....	....	....	....	....
	NHL Totals		**6**	**1**	**0**	**1**	**0**	**0**	**0**	**0**	**6**	**16.7**		**8**	**75.0**	**13:47**	**7**	**3**	**0**	**3**	**0**	**0**	**0**	**1**	**14:50**

NCAA Championship All-Tournament Team (2008, 2010) • NCAA Championship Tournament MVP (2010)

SMITH, Derek
(SMIHTH, DAIR-ihk) **CGY**

Defense. Shoots left. 6'2", 200 lbs. Born, Belleville, Ont., October 13, 1984.

2002-03	Wellington Dukes	OPJHL	21	6	10	16	26	....	....	....	....	....	....	....	....	....	....	....	....	....	....	....	....	....	....
2003-04	Wellington Dukes	OPJHL	44	8	26	34	34	....	....	....	....	....	....	....	....	....	....	....	....	....	....	....	....	....	....
2004-05	Lake Superior	CCHA	38	1	4	5	28	....	....	....	....	....	....	....	....	....	....	....	....	....	....	....	....	....	....
2005-06	Lake Superior	CCHA	36	2	8	10	18	....	....	....	....	....	....	....	....	....	....	....	....	....	....	....	....	....	....
2006-07	Lake Superior	CCHA	43	10	20	30	10	....	....	....	....	....	....	....	....	....	....	....	....	....	....	....	....	....	....
2007-08	Binghamton	AHL	52	2	11	13	18	....	....	....	....	....	....	....	....	....	....	....	....	....	....	....	....	....	....
	Elmira Jackals	ECHL	1	0	1	1	0	....	....	....	....	....	....	....	....	....	....	....	....	....	....	....	....	....	....
2008-09	Binghamton	AHL	75	7	17	24	49	....	....	....	....	....	....	....	....	....	....	....	....	....	....	....	....	....	....
2009-10	**Ottawa**	**NHL**	**2**	**0**	**0**	**0**	**0**	**0**	**0**	**0**	**4**	**0.0**	**–4**	**0**	**0.0**	**12:20**	....	....	....	....	....	....	....	....	....
	Binghamton	AHL	74	14	37	51	24	....	....	....	....	....	....	....	....	....	....	....	....	....	....	....	....	....	....
2010-11	**Ottawa**	**NHL**	**9**	**0**	**1**	**1**	**0**	**0**	**0**	**0**	**13**	**0.0**	**3**	**0**	**0.0**	**15:19**	....	....	....	....	....	....	....	....	....
	Binghamton	AHL	71	10	44	54	21	....	....	....	....	....	....	....	....	....	6	1	1	2	6	....	....	....	....
	NHL Totals		**11**	**0**	**1**	**1**	**0**	**0**	**0**	**0**	**17**	**0.0**		**0**	**0.0**	**14:46**	....	....	....	....	....	....	....	....	....

Signed as a free agent by **Ottawa**, April 12, 2007. Signed as a free agent by **Calgary**, July 13, 2011.

SMITH, Nathan
(SMIHTH, NAY-thun)

Center. Shoots left. 6'2", 190 lbs. Born, Edmonton, Alta., February 9, 1982. Vancouver's 1st choice, 23rd overall, in 2000 Entry Draft.

1997-98	Sherwood Park	AMHL	35	15	13	28	24	....	....	....	....	....	....	....	....	....	....	....	....	....	....	....	....	....	....
1998-99	Swift Current	WHL	47	5	8	13	26	....	....	....	....	....	....	....	....	....	....	....	....	....	....	....	....	....	....
99-2000	Swift Current	WHL	70	21	28	49	72	....	....	....	....	....	....	....	....	....	12	1	6	7	4	....	....	....	....
2000-01	Swift Current	WHL	67	28	62	90	78	....	....	....	....	....	....	....	....	....	19	4	3	7	20	....	....	....	....
2001-02	Swift Current	WHL	47	22	38	60	52	....	....	....	....	....	....	....	....	....	12	3	6	9	18	....	....	....	....
2002-03	Manitoba Moose	AHL	53	9	8	17	30	....	....	....	....	....	....	....	....	....	14	1	3	4	25	....	....	....	....
2003-04	**Vancouver**	**NHL**	**2**	**0**	**0**	**0**	**0**	**0**	**0**	**0**	**1**	**0.0**	**–1**	**12**	**33.3**	**5:16**	....	....	....	....	....	....	....	....	....
	Manitoba Moose	AHL	76	4	16	20	71	....	....	....	....	....	....	....	....	....	....	....	....	....	....	....	....	....	....
2004-05	Manitoba Moose	AHL	72	7	9	16	67	....	....	....	....	....	....	....	....	....	14	2	4	6	20	....	....	....	....
2005-06	**Vancouver**	**NHL**	**1**	**0**	**0**	**0**	**0**	**0**	**0**	**0**	**2**	**0.0**	**0**	**9**	**33.3**	**10:52**	....	....	....	....	....	....	....	....	....
	Manitoba Moose	AHL	20	5	4	9	57	....	....	....	....	....	....	....	....	....	....	....	....	....	....	....	....	....	....
2006-07	**Vancouver**	**NHL**	**1**	**0**	**0**	**0**	**0**	**0**	**0**	**0**	**0**	**0.0**	**0**	**9**	**66.7**	**8:45**	**4**	**0**	**0**	**0**	**0**	**0**	**0**	**0**	**6:57**
	Manitoba Moose	AHL	72	19	21	40	76	....	....	....	....	....	....	....	....	....	6	0	1	1	12	....	....	....	....
2007-08	**Pittsburgh**	**NHL**	**13**	**0**	**0**	**0**	**2**	**0**	**0**	**0**	**3**	**0.0**	**0**	**75**	**53.3**	**7:41**	....	....	....	....	....	....	....	....	....
	Wilkes-Barre	AHL	68	22	28	50	61	....	....	....	....	....	....	....	....	....	22	7	11	18	40	....	....	....	....
2008-09	Lake Erie	AHL	44	6	10	16	42	....	....	....	....	....	....	....	....	....	....	....	....	....	....	....	....	....	....
2009-10	**Minnesota**	**NHL**	**9**	**0**	**0**	**0**	**12**	**0**	**0**	**0**	**4**	**0.0**	**–4**	**49**	**53.1**	**7:51**	....	....	....	....	....	....	....	....	....
	Houston Aeros	AHL	67	14	23	37	83	....	....	....	....	....	....	....	....	....	....	....	....	....	....	....	....	....	....
2010-11	Augsburg	Germany	52	4	12	16	42	....	....	....	....	....	....	....	....	....	....	....	....	....	....	....	....	....	....
	NHL Totals		**26**	**0**	**0**	**0**	**14**	**0**	**0**	**0**	**10**	**0.0**		**154**	**51.3**	**7:43**	**4**	**0**	**0**	**0**	**0**	**0**	**0**	**0**	**6:57**

• Missed remainder of 2005-06 due to knee injury vs. Cleveland (AHL), November 27, 2005. Signed as a free agent by **Pittsburgh**, July 12, 2007. Signed as a free agent by **Colorado**, July 14, 2008. Signed as a free agent by **Minnesota**, July 22, 2009. Signed as a free agent by **Augsburg** (Germany), August 6, 2010. Signed as a free agent by **Syracuse** (AHL), August 11, 2011.

SMITH, Trevor
(SMIHTH, TREH-vuhr) **T.B.**

Center. Shoots left. 6'1", 195 lbs. Born, North Vancouver, B.C., February 8, 1985.

			Regular Season													Playoffs								
Season	Club	League	GP	G	A	Pts	PIM	PP	SH	GW	S	%	+/-	TF	F%	Min	GP	G	A	Pts	PIM	PP	SH	GW	Min
2003-04	Quesnel	BCHL	44	28	19	47	50	....	....	....	....	....	....	....	....	....	....	....	....	....	....	....	....	....	....
2004-05	Omaha Lancers	USHL	60	29	39	68	78	....	....	....	....	....	....	....	....	....	5	3	1	4	2	....	....	....	....
2005-06	New Hampshire	H-East	39	10	10	20	34	....	....	....	....	....	....	....	....	....	....	....	....	....	....	....	....	....	....
2006-07	New Hampshire	H-East	39	21	22	43	39	....	....	....	....	....	....	....	....	....	....	....	....	....	....	....	....	....	....
	Bridgeport	AHL	8	1	2	3	2	....	....	....	....	....	....	....	....	....	....	....	....	....	....	....	....	....	....
2007-08	Bridgeport	AHL	53	20	17	37	16	....	....	....	....	....	....	....	....	....	....	....	....	....	....	....	....	....	....
	Utah Grizzlies	ECHL	22	11	14	25	28	....	....	....	....	....	....	....	....	....	....	....	....	....	....	....	....	....	....
2008-09	**NY Islanders**	**NHL**	**7**	**1**	**0**	**1**	**0**	**0**	**0**	**0**	**7**	**14.3**	**–3**	**9**	**66.7**	**11:48**	....	....	....	....	....	....	....	....	....
	Bridgeport	AHL	76	30	32	62	40	....	....	....	....	....	....	....	....	....	5	1	3	4	0	....	....	....	....
2009-10	Bridgeport	AHL	77	21	26	47	73	....	....	....	....	....	....	....	....	....	5	1	2	3	2	....	....	....	....
2010-11	Syracuse Crunch	AHL	35	12	15	27	16	....	....	....	....	....	....	....	....	....	....	....	....	....	....	....	....	....	....
	Springfield	AHL	33	8	8	16	10	....	....	....	....	....	....	....	....	....	....	....	....	....	....	....	....	....	....
	NHL Totals		**7**	**1**	**0**	**1**	**0**	**0**	**0**	**0**	**7**	**14.3**		**9**	**66.7**	**11:48**	....	....	....	....	....	....	....	....	....

NCAA East Second All-American Team (2007)

Signed as a free agent by **NY Islanders**, April 2, 2007. Signed as a free agent by **Anaheim**, July 2, 2010. Traded to **Columbus** by **Anaheim** for Nate Guenin, January 4, 2011. Signed as a free agent by **Tampa Bay**, July 5, 2011.

SMITH, Wyatt
(SMIHTH, WIGH-uht)

Center. Shoots left. 5'11", 205 lbs. Born, Thief River Falls, MN, February 13, 1977. Phoenix's 6th choice, 233rd overall, in 1997 Entry Draft.

Season	Club	League	GP	G	A	Pts	PIM	PP	SH	GW	S	%	+/-	TF	F%	Min	GP	G	A	Pts	PIM	PP	SH	GW	Min
1994-95	Warroad Warriors	High-MN	28	29	31	60	28	....	....	....	....	....	....	....	....	....	....	....	....	....	....	....	....	....	....
1995-96	U. of Minnesota	WCHA	32	4	5	9	32	....	....	....	....	....	....	....	....	....	....	....	....	....	....	....	....	....	....
1996-97	U. of Minnesota	WCHA	38	16	14	30	44	....	....	....	....	....	....	....	....	....	....	....	....	....	....	....	....	....	....
1997-98	U. of Minnesota	WCHA	39	24	23	47	62	....	....	....	....	....	....	....	....	....	....	....	....	....	....	....	....	....	....
1998-99	U. of Minnesota	WCHA	43	23	20	43	37	....	....	....	....	....	....	....	....	....	....	....	....	....	....	....	....	....	....
99-2000	**Phoenix**	**NHL**	**2**	**0**	**0**	**0**	**0**	**0**	**0**	**0**	**0**	**0.0**	**–2**	**20**	**30.0**	**11:39**	....	....	....	....	....	....	....	....	....
	Springfield	AHL	60	14	26	40	26	....	....	....	....	....	....	....	....	....	5	2	3	5	13	....	....	....	....
2000-01	**Phoenix**	**NHL**	**42**	**3**	**7**	**10**	**13**	**0**	**1**	**0**	**40**	**7.5**	**7**	**335**	**40.9**	**12:20**	....	....	....	....	....	....	....	....	....
	Springfield	AHL	18	5	7	12	11	....	....	....	....	....	....	....	....	....	....	....	....	....	....	....	....	....	....
2001-02	**Phoenix**	**NHL**	**10**	**0**	**0**	**0**	**0**	**0**	**0**	**0**	**4**	**0.0**	**–5**	**81**	**48.2**	**10:36**	....	....	....	....	....	....	....	....	....
	Springfield	AHL	69	23	32	55	69	....	....	....	....	....	....	....	....	....	....	....	....	....	....	....	....	....	....
2002-03	**Nashville**	**NHL**	**11**	**1**	**0**	**1**	**0**	**0**	**0**	**0**	**8**	**12.5**	**–1**	**123**	**49.6**	**11:56**	....	....	....	....	....	....	....	....	....
	Milwaukee	AHL	56	24	27	51	89	....	....	....	....	....	....	....	....	....	4	1	0	1	2	....	....	....	....
2003-04	**Nashville**	**NHL**	**18**	**3**	**1**	**4**	**2**	**0**	**1**	**0**	**21**	**14.3**	**2**	**193**	**57.0**	**10:22**	....	....	....	....	....	....	....	....	....
	Milwaukee	AHL	40	9	7	16	40	....	....	....	....	....	....	....	....	....	22	5	7	12	25	....	....	....	....
2004-05	Milwaukee	AHL	69	19	28	47	89	....	....	....	....	....	....	....	....	....	7	1	4	5	10	....	....	....	....
2005-06	**NY Islanders**	**NHL**	**42**	**0**	**8**	**8**	**26**	**0**	**0**	**0**	**37**	**0.0**	**–7**	**384**	**48.4**	**11:14**	....	....	....	....	....	....	....	....	....
	Bridgeport	AHL	39	13	16	29	40	....	....	....	....	....	....	....	....	....	....	....	....	....	....	....	....	....	....
2006-07	**Minnesota**	**NHL**	**61**	**3**	**3**	**6**	**16**	**1**	**0**	**0**	**44**	**6.8**	**–8**	**508**	**43.5**	**9:31**	**4**	**0**	**0**	**0**	**0**	**0**	**0**	**0**	**11:02**
	Houston Aeros	AHL	12	4	3	7	12	....	....	....	....	....	....	....	....	....	....	....	....	....	....	....	....	....	....
2007-08	**Colorado**	**NHL**	**25**	**0**	**3**	**3**	**8**	**0**	**0**	**0**	**25**	**0.0**	**–4**	**108**	**50.9**	**11:38**	**1**	**0**	**0**	**0**	**0**	**0**	**0**	**0**	**10:47**
	Lake Erie	AHL	40	17	18	35	34	....	....	....	....	....	....	....	....	....	....	....	....	....	....	....	....	....	....
2008-09	Norfolk Admirals	AHL	18	3	4	7	12	....	....	....	....	....	....	....	....	....	....	....	....	....	....	....	....	....	....
	San Antonio	AHL	53	16	24	40	59	....	....	....	....	....	....	....	....	....	....	....	....	....	....	....	....	....	....
2009-10	Wilkes-Barre	AHL	76	13	35	48	70	....	....	....	....	....	....	....	....	....	4	1	0	1	4	....	....	....	....
2010-11	Providence Bruins	AHL	30	2	7	9	23	....	....	....	....	....	....	....	....	....	....	....	....	....	....	....	....	....	....
	ERC Ingolstadt	Germany	22	4	12	16	18	....	....	....	....	....	....	....	....	....	4	1	0	1	2	....	....	....	....
	NHL Totals		**211**	**10**	**22**	**32**	**65**	**1**	**2**	**0**	**179**	**5.6**		**1752**	**46.5**	**10:56**	**5**	**0**	**0**	**0**	**0**	**0**	**0**	**0**	**10:59**

Signed as a free agent by **Nashville**, July 15, 2002. Signed as a free agent by **NY Islanders**, August 10, 2005. Signed as a free agent by **Minnesota**, July 19, 2006. Signed as a free agent by **Colorado** , August 20, 2007. Signed as a free agent by **Tampa Bay**, July 3, 2008. Traded to **Phoenix** by **Tampa Bay** for future consideratons, November 25, 2008. Signed as a free agent by **Pittsburgh**, July 31, 2009. Signed as a free agent by **Boston**, September 3, 2010. Signed as a free agent by **Ingolstadt** (Germany), December 31, 2010.

SMITH, Zack
(SMIHTH, ZAK) **OTT**

Center. Shoots left. 6'2", 210 lbs. Born, Medicine Hat, Alta., April 5, 1988. Ottawa's 3rd choice, 79th overall, in 2008 Entry Draft.

Season	Club	League	GP	G	A	Pts	PIM	PP	SH	GW	S	%	+/-	TF	F%	Min	GP	G	A	Pts	PIM	PP	SH	GW	Min
2004-05	Swift Current	SMHL	43	15	27	42	83	....	....	....	....	....	....	....	....	....	....	....	....	....	....	....	....	....	....
	Swift Current	WHL	14	1	1	2	0	....	....	....	....	....	....	....	....	....	....	....	....	....	....	....	....	....	....
2005-06	Swift Current	WHL	64	2	5	7	78	....	....	....	....	....	....	....	....	....	3	0	0	0	9	....	....	....	....
2006-07	Swift Current	WHL	71	16	15	31	130	....	....	....	....	....	....	....	....	....	6	0	2	2	11	....	....	....	....
2007-08	Swift Current	WHL	72	22	47	69	136	....	....	....	....	....	....	....	....	....	12	5	5	10	29	....	....	....	....
	Manitoba Moose	AHL	....	....	....	....	....	....	....	....	....	....	....	....	....	....	6	0	1	1	0	....	....	....	....
2008-09	**Ottawa**	**NHL**	**1**	**0**	**0**	**0**	**0**	**0**	**0**	**0**	**0**	**0.0**	**0**	**1**	**0.0**	**7:01**	....	....	....	....	....	....	....	....	....
	Binghamton	AHL	79	24	24	48	132	....	....	....	....	....	....	....	....	....	....	....	....	....	....	....	....	....	....
2009-10	**Ottawa**	**NHL**	**15**	**2**	**1**	**3**	**14**	**0**	**1**	**0**	**11**	**18.2**	**1**	**61**	**47.5**	**9:03**	**6**	**0**	**0**	**0**	**5**	**0**	**0**	**0**	**7:25**
	Binghamton	AHL	68	14	27	41	100	....	....	....	....	....	....	....	....	....	....	....	....	....	....	....	....	....	....
2010-11	**Ottawa**	**NHL**	**55**	**4**	**5**	**9**	**120**	**0**	**0**	**0**	**78**	**5.1**	**–11**	**388**	**53.9**	**12:36**	....	....	....	....	....	....	....	....	....
	Binghamton	AHL	22	7	5	12	32	....	....	....	....	....	....	....	....	....	23	8	12	20	36	....	....	....	....
	NHL Totals		**71**	**6**	**6**	**12**	**134**	**0**	**1**	**0**	**89**	**6.7**		**450**	**52.9**	**11:47**	**6**	**0**	**0**	**0**	**5**	**0**	**0**	**0**	**7:25**

SMITHSON, Jerred
(SMIHTH-suhn, JEHR-rehd) **NSH**

Center. Shoots right. 6'3", 209 lbs. Born, Vernon, B.C., February 4, 1979.

Season	Club	League	GP	G	A	Pts	PIM	PP	SH	GW	S	%	+/-	TF	F%	Min	GP	G	A	Pts	PIM	PP	SH	GW	Min
1994-95	Vernon	Minor-BC	64	39	46	85	120	....	....	....	....	....	....	....	....	....	....	....	....	....	....	....	....	....	....
1995-96	Calgary Hitmen	WHL	60	4	2	6	16	....	....	....	....	....	....	....	....	....	....	....	....	....	....	....	....	....	....
1996-97	Calgary Hitmen	WHL	65	3	6	9	49	....	....	....	....	....	....	....	....	....	....	....	....	....	....	....	....	....	....
1997-98	Calgary Hitmen	WHL	65	12	9	21	65	....	....	....	....	....	....	....	....	....	18	0	2	2	25	....	....	....	....
1998-99	Calgary Hitmen	WHL	63	14	22	36	108	....	....	....	....	....	....	....	....	....	21	3	7	10	17	....	....	....	....
99-2000	Calgary Hitmen	WHL	66	14	25	39	111	....	....	....	....	....	....	....	....	....	10	1	1	2	16	....	....	....	....
2000-01	Lowell	AHL	24	1	1	2	10	....	....	....	....	....	....	....	....	....	4	0	0	0	2	....	....	....	....
	Trenton Titans	ECHL	3	0	1	1	2	....	....	....	....	....	....	....	....	....	....	....	....	....	....	....	....	....	....
2001-02	Manchester	AHL	78	5	13	18	45	....	....	....	....	....	....	....	....	....	5	0	1	1	4	....	....	....	....
2002-03	**Los Angeles**	**NHL**	**22**	**0**	**2**	**2**	**21**	**0**	**0**	**0**	**9**	**0.0**	**–5**	**175**	**48.0**	**8:50**	....	....	....	....	....	....	....	....	....
	Manchester	AHL	38	4	21	25	60	....	....	....	....	....	....	....	....	....	3	0	0	0	4	....	....	....	....
2003-04	**Los Angeles**	**NHL**	**8**	**0**	**1**	**1**	**4**	**0**	**0**	**0**	**2**	**0.0**	**0**	**86**	**64.0**	**10:39**	....	....	....	....	....	....	....	....	....
	Manchester	AHL	66	7	13	20	51	....	....	....	....	....	....	....	....	....	6	0	1	1	10	....	....	....	....
2004-05	Milwaukee	AHL	80	11	11	22	92	....	....	....	....	....	....	....	....	....	5	0	0	0	4	....	....	....	....
2005-06	**Nashville**	**NHL**	**66**	**5**	**9**	**14**	**54**	**0**	**0**	**1**	**50**	**10.0**	**9**	**613**	**54.3**	**11:50**	**3**	**0**	**0**	**0**	**4**	**0**	**0**	**0**	**9:26**
	Milwaukee	AHL	8	0	0	0	12	....	....	....	....	....	....	....	....	....	....	....	....	....	....	....	....	....	....
2006-07	**Nashville**	**NHL**	**64**	**5**	**7**	**12**	**42**	**1**	**1**	**2**	**47**	**10.6**	**–8**	**420**	**56.4**	**11:03**	**5**	**0**	**0**	**0**	**17**	**0**	**0**	**0**	**11:30**
2007-08	**Nashville**	**NHL**	**81**	**7**	**9**	**16**	**50**	**0**	**2**	**2**	**61**	**11.5**	**–9**	**572**	**52.1**	**12:05**	**6**	**0**	**0**	**0**	**2**	**0**	**0**	**0**	**11:52**
2008-09	**Nashville**	**NHL**	**82**	**4**	**9**	**13**	**49**	**0**	**0**	**0**	**74**	**5.4**	**–6**	**722**	**52.6**	**13:51**	....	....	....	....	....	....	....	....	....
2009-10	**Nashville**	**NHL**	**69**	**9**	**4**	**13**	**54**	**0**	**2**	**1**	**54**	**16.7**	**–4**	**548**	**54.9**	**13:58**	**6**	**1**	**0**	**1**	**6**	**0**	**0**	**0**	**15:36**
2010-11	**Nashville**	**NHL**	**82**	**5**	**8**	**13**	**34**	**0**	**0**	**0**	**73**	**6.8**	**–6**	**1006**	**57.5**	**14:51**	**11**	**1**	**1**	**2**	**8**	**0**	**0**	**1**	**14:09**
	NHL Totals		**474**	**35**	**49**	**84**	**308**	**1**	**5**	**6**	**370**	**9.5**		**4142**	**54.7**	**12:47**	**31**	**2**	**1**	**3**	**37**	**0**	**0**	**1**	**13:06**

Signed as a free agent by **Los Angeles**, February 18, 2000. Signed as a free agent by **Nashville**, July 22, 2004.

SMOTHERMAN, Jordan
(SMAW-thuhr-man, JOHR-dahn)

Left wing. Shoots left. 6'3", 225 lbs. Born, Corvallis, OR, May 11, 1986. Atlanta's 5th choice, 116th overall, in 2005 Entry Draft.

Season	Club	League	GP	G	A	Pts	PIM	PP	SH	GW	S	%	+/-	TF	F%	Min	GP	G	A	Pts	PIM	PP	SH	GW	Min
2002-03	Quebec Remparts	QMJHL	55	3	6	9	54	....	....	....	....	....	....	....	....	....	11	0	1	1	0	....	....	....	....
2003-04	Quebec Remparts	QMJHL	69	11	16	27	111	....	....	....	....	....	....	....	....	....	5	2	0	2	6	....	....	....	....
2004-05	Quebec Remparts	QMJHL	64	40	26	66	108	....	....	....	....	....	....	....	....	....	13	5	2	7	26	....	....	....	....
2005-06	Quebec Remparts	QMJHL	37	18	19	37	34	....	....	....	....	....	....	....	....	....	23	7	8	15	30	....	....	....	....
2006-07	Chicago Wolves	AHL	79	16	18	34	90	....	....	....	....	....	....	....	....	....	14	7	1	8	8	....	....	....	....
2007-08	**Atlanta**	**NHL**	**2**	**1**	**1**	**2**	**0**	**0**	**0**	**0**	**1**	**100.0**	**2**	**0**	**0.0**	**11:28**	....	....	....	....	....	....	....	....	....
	Chicago Wolves	AHL	76	20	22	42	73	....	....	....	....	....	....	....	....	....	24	3	5	8	16	....	....	....	....
2008-09	**Atlanta**	**NHL**	**2**	**0**	**0**	**0**	**0**	**0**	**0**	**0**	**1**	**0.0**	**–1**	**0**	**0.0**	**6:40**	....	....	....	....	....	....	....	....	....
	Chicago Wolves	AHL	64	19	12	31	94	....	....	....	....	....	....	....	....	....	....	....	....	....	....	....	....	....	....

Season	Club	League	GP	G	A	Pts	PIM	PP	SH	GW	S	%	+/-	TF	F%	Min	GP	G	A	Pts	PIM	PP	SH	GW	Min
			Regular Season														Playoffs								
2009-10	Syracuse Crunch	AHL	78	10	22	32	75	....	....	....	....	....	....	....	....	....	....	....	....	....	....	....	....	....	....
2010-11	Providence Bruins	AHL	71	14	12	26	68	....	....	....	....	....	....	....	....	....	....	....	....	....	....	....	....	....	....
	NHL Totals		**4**	**1**	**1**	**2**	**0**	**0**	**0**	**0**	**2**	**50.0**		**0**	**0.0**	**9:04**	....	....	....	....	....	....	....	....	....

• Previously went by his mother's maiden name (LaVallee). Traded to **Columbus** by **Atlanta** for future considerations, October 8, 2009. Signed as a free agent by **Providence** (AHL), September 19, 2010.

SMYTH, Ryan

(SMIHTH, RIGH-uhn) **EDM**

Left wing. Shoots left. 6'2", 192 lbs. Born, Banff, Alta., February 21, 1976. Edmonton's 2nd choice, 6th overall, in 1994 Entry Draft.

Season	Club	League	GP	G	A	Pts	PIM	PP	SH	GW	S	%	+/-	TF	F%	Min	GP	G	A	Pts	PIM	PP	SH	GW	Min
1990-91	Banff Blazers	Minor-AB	25	100	50	150	....	....	....	....	....	....	....	....	....	....	....	....	....	....	....	....	....	....	....
	Lethbridge	AMHL	34	8	21	29	....	....	....	....	....	....	....	....	....	....	....	....	....	....	....	....	....	....	....
1991-92	Caronport	SMHL	35	55	61	116	98	....	....	....	....	....	....	....	....	....	....	....	....	....	....	....	....	....	....
	Moose Jaw	WHL	2	0	0	0	0	....	....	....	....	....	....	....	....	....	....	....	....	....	....	....	....	....	....
1992-93	Moose Jaw	WHL	64	19	14	33	59	....	....	....	....	....	....	....	....	....	....	....	....	....	....	....	....	....	....
1993-94	Moose Jaw	WHL	72	50	55	105	88	....	....	....	....	....	....	....	....	....	....	....	....	....	....	....	....	....	....
1994-95	Moose Jaw	WHL	50	41	45	86	66	....	....	....	....	....	....	....	....	....	10	6	9	15	22	....	....	....	....
	Edmonton	**NHL**	**3**	**0**	**0**	**0**	**0**	**0**	**0**	**0**	**2**	**0.0**	**-1**	....	....	....	....	....	....	....	....	....	....	....	....
1995-96	**Edmonton**	**NHL**	**48**	**2**	**9**	**11**	**28**	**1**	**0**	**0**	**65**	**3.1**	**-10**	....	....	....	....	....	....	....	....	....	....	....	....
	Cape Breton	AHL	9	6	5	11	4	....	....	....	....	....	....	....	....	....	....	....	....	....	....	....	....	....	....
1996-97	**Edmonton**	**NHL**	**82**	**39**	**22**	**61**	**76**	***20**	**0**	**4**	**265**	**14.7**	**-7**	....	....	....	**12**	**5**	**5**	**10**	**12**	**1**	**0**	**2**	....
1997-98	**Edmonton**	**NHL**	**65**	**20**	**13**	**33**	**44**	**10**	**0**	**2**	**205**	**9.8**	**-24**	....	....	....	**12**	**1**	**3**	**4**	**16**	**1**	**0**	**0**	....
1998-99	**Edmonton**	**NHL**	**71**	**13**	**18**	**31**	**62**	**6**	**0**	**2**	**161**	**8.1**	**0**	**5**	**20.0**	**14:26**	**3**	**3**	**0**	**3**	**0**	**2**	**0**	**0**	**24:35**
99-2000	**Edmonton**	**NHL**	**82**	**28**	**26**	**54**	**58**	**11**	**0**	**4**	**238**	**11.8**	**-2**	**24**	**54.2**	**19:12**	**5**	**1**	**0**	**1**	**6**	**0**	**1**	**0**	**19:18**
2000-01	**Edmonton**	**NHL**	**82**	**31**	**39**	**70**	**58**	**11**	**0**	**6**	**245**	**12.7**	**10**	**17**	**35.3**	**19:58**	**6**	**3**	**4**	**7**	**4**	**0**	**0**	**0**	**24:46**
2001-02	**Edmonton**	**NHL**	**61**	**15**	**35**	**50**	**48**	**7**	**1**	**5**	**150**	**10.0**	**7**	**12**	**41.7**	**19:27**	....	....	....	....	....	....	....	....	....
	Canada	Olympics	6	0	1	1	0	....	....	....	....	....	....	....	....	....	....	....	....	....	....	....	....	....	....
2002-03	**Edmonton**	**NHL**	**66**	**27**	**34**	**61**	**67**	**10**	**0**	**3**	**199**	**13.6**	**5**	**42**	**42.9**	**19:21**	**6**	**2**	**0**	**2**	**16**	**0**	**1**	**0**	**17:39**
2003-04	**Edmonton**	**NHL**	**82**	**23**	**36**	**59**	**70**	**8**	**2**	**6**	**245**	**9.4**	**11**	**484**	**47.1**	**19:39**	....	....	....	....	....	....	....	....	....
2004-05			DID NOT PLAY																						
2005-06	**Edmonton**	**NHL**	**75**	**36**	**30**	**66**	**58**	**19**	**2**	**3**	**230**	**15.7**	**-5**	**159**	**47.8**	**20:13**	**24**	**7**	**9**	**16**	**22**	**4**	**0**	**1**	**21:27**
	Canada	Olympics	6	0	1	1	4	....	....	....	....	....	....	....	....	....	....	....	....	....	....	....	....	....	....
2006-07	**Edmonton**	**NHL**	**53**	**31**	**22**	**53**	**38**	**14**	**1**	**5**	**161**	**19.3**	**2**	**63**	**47.6**	**20:09**	....	....	....	....	....	....	....	....	....
	NY Islanders	**NHL**	**18**	**5**	**10**	**15**	**14**	**1**	**0**	**0**	**49**	**10.2**	**0**	**9**	**22.2**	**22:26**	**5**	**1**	**3**	**4**	**4**	**0**	**0**	**0**	**22:42**
2007-08	**Colorado**	**NHL**	**55**	**14**	**23**	**37**	**50**	**2**	**0**	**3**	**168**	**8.3**	**-4**	**33**	**39.4**	**19:37**	**8**	**2**	**3**	**5**	**2**	**1**	**0**	**1**	**17:29**
2008-09	**Colorado**	**NHL**	**77**	**26**	**33**	**59**	**62**	**10**	**1**	**3**	**257**	**10.1**	**-15**	**174**	**51.2**	**20:17**	....	....	....	....	....	....	....	....	....
2009-10	**Los Angeles**	**NHL**	**67**	**22**	**31**	**53**	**42**	**11**	**0**	**3**	**206**	**10.7**	**8**	**62**	**50.0**	**19:41**	**6**	**1**	**1**	**2**	**6**	**0**	**0**	**0**	**18:39**
2010-11	**Los Angeles**	**NHL**	**82**	**23**	**24**	**47**	**35**	**9**	**0**	**2**	**195**	**11.8**	**-1**	**132**	**43.2**	**18:02**	**6**	**2**	**3**	**5**	**0**	**0**	**0**	**0**	**18:20**
	NHL Totals		**1069**	**355**	**405**	**760**	**810**	**150**	**7**	**51**	**3041**	**11.7**		**1216**	**46.8**	**19:13**	**93**	**28**	**31**	**59**	**88**	**9**	**2**	**4**	**20:30**

WHL East Second All-Star Team (1995)

Played in NHL All-Star Game (2007)

Traded to **NY Islanders** by **Edmonton** for Ryan O'Marra, Robert Nilsson and NY Islanders' 1st round choice (Alex Plante) in 2007 Entry Draft, February 27, 2007. Signed as a free agent by **Colorado**, July 1, 2007. Traded to **Los Angeles** by **Colorado** for Kyle Quincey, Tom Preissing and Los Angeles' 5th round choice (Luke Walker) in 2010 Entry Draft, July 3, 2009. Traded to **Edmonton** by **Los Angeles** for Colin Fraser and a 7th round choice in 2012 Entry Draft, June 26, 2011.

SOBOTKA, Vladimir

(suh-BOHT-kah, vla-DIH-meer) **ST.L.**

Center. Shoots left. 5'10", 183 lbs. Born, Trebic, Czech., July 2, 1987. Boston's 5th choice, 106th overall, in 2005 Entry Draft.

Season	Club	League	GP	G	A	Pts	PIM	PP	SH	GW	S	%	+/-	TF	F%	Min	GP	G	A	Pts	PIM	PP	SH	GW	Min
2002-03	Slavia U17	CzR-U17	46	16	24	40	48	....	....	....	....	....	....	....	....	....	8	1	1	2	29	....	....	....	....
2003-04	Slavia U17	CzR-U17	35	24	41	65	109	....	....	....	....	....	....	....	....	....	7	7	12	19	8	....	....	....	....
	Slavia Jr.	CzRep-Jr.	18	6	6	12	16	....	....	....	....	....	....	....	....	....	....	....	....	....	....	....	....	....	....
	HC Slavia Praha	CzRep	1	0	0	0	0	....	....	....	....	....	....	....	....	....	....	....	....	....	....	....	....	....	....
2004-05	Slavia Jr.	CzRep-Jr.	27	12	21	33	93	....	....	....	....	....	....	....	....	....	....	....	....	....	....	....	....	....	....
	HC Slavia Praha	CzRep	18	0	1	1	8	....	....	....	....	....	....	....	....	....	....	....	....	....	....	....	....	....	....
	Havl. Brod	CzRep-3	7	3	0	3	31	....	....	....	....	....	....	....	....	....	7	1	5	6	0	....	....	....	....
2005-06	Slavia Jr.	CzRep-Jr.	8	10	4	14	42	....	....	....	....	....	....	....	....	....	....	....	....	....	....	....	....	....	....
	HC Slavia Praha	CzRep	33	1	9	10	28	....	....	....	....	....	....	....	....	....	11	2	3	5	10	....	....	....	....
2006-07	HC Slavia Praha	CzRep	33	7	6	13	38	....	....	....	....	....	....	....	....	....	....	....	....	....	....	....	....	....	....
2007-08	**Boston**	**NHL**	**48**	**1**	**6**	**7**	**24**	**0**	**0**	**1**	**40**	**2.5**	**1**	**247**	**48.6**	**8:50**	**6**	**2**	**0**	**2**	**0**	**0**	**0**	**0**	**8:37**
	Providence Bruins	AHL	18	10	10	20	37	....	....	....	....	....	....	....	....	....	6	0	4	4	0	....	....	....	....
2008-09	**Boston**	**NHL**	**25**	**1**	**4**	**5**	**10**	**0**	**0**	**0**	**19**	**5.3**	**-10**	**52**	**57.7**	**10:33**	....	....	....	....	....	....	....	....	....
	Providence Bruins	AHL	44	20	24	44	83	....	....	....	....	....	....	....	....	....	14	2	11	13	43	....	....	....	....
2009-10	**Boston**	**NHL**	**61**	**4**	**6**	**10**	**30**	**0**	**0**	**0**	**67**	**6.0**	**-7**	**361**	**54.3**	**11:06**	**13**	**0**	**2**	**2**	**15**	**0**	**0**	**0**	**13:20**
	Providence Bruins	AHL	6	4	6	10	4	....	....	....	....	....	....	....	....	....	....	....	....	....	....	....	....	....	....
2010-11	**St. Louis**	**NHL**	**65**	**7**	**22**	**29**	**69**	**1**	**1**	**0**	**75**	**9.3**	**-4**	**419**	**51.6**	**16:11**	....	....	....	....	....	....	....	....	....
	NHL Totals		**199**	**13**	**38**	**51**	**133**	**1**	**1**	**1**	**201**	**6.5**		**1079**	**52.1**	**12:09**	**19**	**2**	**2**	**4**	**15**	**0**	**0**	**0**	**11:51**

Traded to **St. Louis** by **Boston** for David Warsofsky, June 26, 2010.

SOPEL, Brent

(SOH-puhl, BREHNT)

Defense. Shoots right. 6'2", 205 lbs. Born, Calgary, Alta., January 7, 1977. Vancouver's 6th choice, 144th overall, in 1995 Entry Draft.

Season	Club	League	GP	G	A	Pts	PIM	PP	SH	GW	S	%	+/-	TF	F%	Min	GP	G	A	Pts	PIM	PP	SH	GW	Min
1992-93	Sask. Legion	SMHL	36	7	17	24	95	....	....	....	....	....	....	....	....	....	....	....	....	....	....	....	....	....	....
1993-94	Saskatoon Blazers	SMHL	34	9	30	39	180	....	....	....	....	....	....	....	....	....	....	....	....	....	....	....	....	....	....
	Saskatoon Blades	WHL	11	2	2	4	2	....	....	....	....	....	....	....	....	....	....	....	....	....	....	....	....	....	....
1994-95	Saskatoon Blades	WHL	22	1	10	11	31	....	....	....	....	....	....	....	....	....	....	....	....	....	....	....	....	....	....
	Swift Current	WHL	41	4	19	23	50	....	....	....	....	....	....	....	....	....	3	0	3	3	0	....	....	....	....
1995-96	Swift Current	WHL	71	13	48	61	87	....	....	....	....	....	....	....	....	....	6	1	2	3	4	....	....	....	....
	Syracuse Crunch	AHL	1	0	0	0	0	....	....	....	....	....	....	....	....	....	....	....	....	....	....	....	....	....	....
1996-97	Swift Current	WHL	62	15	41	56	109	....	....	....	....	....	....	....	....	....	10	5	11	16	32	....	....	....	....
	Syracuse Crunch	AHL	2	0	0	0	0	....	....	....	....	....	....	....	....	....	3	0	0	0	0	....	....	....	....
1997-98	Syracuse Crunch	AHL	76	10	33	43	70	....	....	....	....	....	....	....	....	....	5	0	7	7	12	....	....	....	....
1998-99	**Vancouver**	**NHL**	**5**	**1**	**0**	**1**	**4**	**1**	**0**	**0**	**5**	**20.0**	**-1**	**0**	**0.0**	**11:58**	....	....	....	....	....	....	....	....	....
	Syracuse Crunch	AHL	53	10	21	31	59	....	....	....	....	....	....	....	....	....	....	....	....	....	....	....	....	....	....
99-2000	**Vancouver**	**NHL**	**18**	**2**	**4**	**6**	**12**	**0**	**0**	**1**	**11**	**18.2**	**9**	**0**	**0.0**	**10:31**	....	....	....	....	....	....	....	....	....
	Syracuse Crunch	AHL	50	6	25	31	67	....	....	....	....	....	....	....	....	....	4	0	2	2	8	....	....	....	....
2000-01	**Vancouver**	**NHL**	**52**	**4**	**10**	**14**	**10**	**0**	**0**	**1**	**57**	**7.0**	**4**	**0**	**0.0**	**16:01**	**4**	**0**	**0**	**0**	**2**	**0**	**0**	**0**	**19:05**
	Kansas City	IHL	4	0	1	1	0	....	....	....	....	....	....	....	....	....	....	....	....	....	....	....	....	....	....
2001-02	**Vancouver**	**NHL**	**66**	**8**	**17**	**25**	**44**	**1**	**0**	**3**	**116**	**6.9**	**21**	**0**	**0.0**	**19:01**	**6**	**0**	**2**	**2**	**2**	**0**	**0**	**0**	**24:45**
2002-03	**Vancouver**	**NHL**	**81**	**7**	**30**	**37**	**23**	**6**	**0**	**1**	**167**	**4.2**	**-15**	**0**	**0.0**	**21:42**	**14**	**2**	**6**	**8**	**4**	**1**	**0**	**1**	**22:33**
2003-04	**Vancouver**	**NHL**	**80**	**10**	**32**	**42**	**36**	**6**	**0**	**2**	**173**	**5.8**	**11**	**0**	**0.0**	**21:56**	**7**	**0**	**1**	**1**	**0**	**0**	**0**	**0**	**23:55**
2004-05			DID NOT PLAY																						
2005-06	**NY Islanders**	**NHL**	**57**	**2**	**25**	**27**	**64**	**2**	**0**	**0**	**121**	**1.7**	**-9**	**0**	**0.0**	**23:35**	....	....	....	....	....	....	....	....	....
	Los Angeles	**NHL**	**11**	**0**	**1**	**1**	**6**	**0**	**0**	**0**	**12**	**0.0**	**-4**	**0**	**0.0**	**22:02**	....	....	....	....	....	....	....	....	....
2006-07	**Los Angeles**	**NHL**	**44**	**4**	**19**	**23**	**14**	**2**	**0**	**2**	**104**	**3.8**	**2**	**3**	**33.3**	**21:06**	....	....	....	....	....	....	....	....	....
	Vancouver	**NHL**	**20**	**1**	**4**	**5**	**10**	**0**	**0**	**0**	**27**	**3.7**	**0**	**0**	**0.0**	**18:25**	**11**	**0**	**0**	**0**	**2**	**0**	**0**	**0**	**19:44**
2007-08	**Chicago**	**NHL**	**58**	**1**	**19**	**20**	**28**	**0**	**0**	**0**	**56**	**1.8**	**9**	**0**	**0.0**	**20:18**	....	....	....	....	....	....	....	....	....
2008-09	**Chicago**	**NHL**	**23**	**1**	**1**	**2**	**8**	**0**	**0**	**1**	**15**	**6.7**	**-4**	**0**	**0.0**	**13:49**	....	....	....	....	....	....	....	....	....
2009-10 •	**Chicago**	**NHL**	**73**	**1**	**7**	**8**	**34**	**0**	**0**	**0**	**48**	**2.1**	**3**	**0**	**0.0**	**14:52**	**22**	**1**	**5**	**6**	**8**	**0**	**0**	**0**	**18:30**
2010-11	**Atlanta**	**NHL**	**59**	**2**	**5**	**7**	**16**	**0**	**0**	**0**	**40**	**5.0**	**7**	**0**	**0.0**	**16:26**	....	....	....	....	....	....	....	....	....
	Montreal	**NHL**	**12**	**0**	**0**	**0**	**0**	**0**	**0**	**0**	**4**	**0.0**	**-1**	**0**	**0.0**	**15:54**	**7**	**1**	**0**	**1**	**2**	**0**	**0**	**0**	**14:51**
	NHL Totals		**659**	**44**	**174**	**218**	**309**	**18**	**0**	**11**	**956**	**4.6**		**3**	**33.3**	**18:56**	**71**	**4**	**14**	**18**	**20**	**1**	**0**	**1**	**20:14**

Traded to **NY Islanders** by **Vancouver** for NY Islanders' 2nd round choice (later traded to Anaheim - Anaheim selected Bryce Swan) in 2006 Entry Draft, August 3, 2005. Traded to **Los Angeles** by **NY Islanders** with Mark Parrish for Denis Grebeshkov and Jeff Tambellini, March 8, 2006. Traded to **Vancouver** by **Los Angeles** for Anaheim's 2nd round choice (previously acquired, Los Angeles selected Wayne Simmonds) in 2007 Entry Draft and and Vancouver's 4th round choice (later traded to Buffalo - Buffalo selected Justin Jokinen) in 2008 Entry Draft, February 26, 2006. Signed as a free agent by **Chicago**, October 3, 2007. • Missed majority of 2008-09 due to recurring elbow injury. Traded to **Atlanta** by **Chicago** with Dustin Byfuglien, Ben Eager and Akim Aliu for Marty Reasoner, Joey Crabb, Jeremy Morin and New Jersey's 1st (previously acquired, Chicago selected Kevin Hayes) and 2nd (previously acquired, Chicago selected Justin Holl) round choices in 2010 Entry Draft, June 24, 2010. Traded to **Montreal** by **Atlanta** with Nigel Dawes for Ben Maxwell and Montreal's 4th round choice (later traded back to Montreal - Montreal selected Olivier Archambault) in 2011 Entry Draft, February 24, 2011. Signed as a free agent by **Novokuznetsk** (Russia-KHL), July 29, 2011.

SOURAY, Sheldon

(SOO-ray, SHEHL-duhn) **DAL**

Defense. Shoots left. 6'4", 233 lbs. Born, Elk Point, Alta., July 13, 1976. New Jersey's 3rd choice, 71st overall, in 1994 Entry Draft.

			Regular Season														Playoffs								
Season	Club	League	GP	G	A	Pts	PIM	PP	SH	GW	S	%	+/-	TF	F%	Min	GP	G	A	Pts	PIM	PP	SH	GW	Min
1990-91	Bonnyville Sabres	AAHA	30	15	20	35	100	....	....	....	....	....	....	....	....	....	....	....	....	....	....	....	....	....	....
1991-92	Quesnel	Minor-BC	20	5	15	20	200	....	....	....	....	....	....	....	....	....	....	....	....	....	....	....	....	....	....
	Alberta Cycle	AMHL	11	0	5	5	67	....	....	....	....	....	....	....	....	....	....	....	....	....	....	....	....	....	....
1992-93	Ft. Saskatchewan	AJHL	35	0	12	12	125	....	....	....	....	....	....	....	....	....	....	....	....	....	....	....	....	....	....
	Tri-City	WHL	2	0	0	0	0	....	....	....	....	....	....	....	....	....	....	....	....	....	....	....	....	....	....
1993-94	Tri-City	WHL	42	3	6	9	122	....	....	....	....	....	....	....	....	....	....	....	....	....	....	....	....	....	....
1994-95	Tri-City	WHL	40	2	24	26	140	....	....	....	....	....	....	....	....	....	....	....	....	....	....	....	....	....	....
	Prince George	WHL	11	2	3	5	23	....	....	....	....	....	....	....	....	....	....	....	....	....	....	....	....	....	....
	Albany River Rats	AHL	7	0	2	2	8	....	....	....	....	....	....	....	....	....	....	....	....	....	....	....	....	....	....
1995-96	Prince George	WHL	32	9	18	27	91	....	....	....	....	....	....	....	....	....	....	....	....	....	....	....	....	....	....
	Kelowna Rockets	WHL	27	7	20	27	94	....	....	....	....	....	....	....	....	....	6	0	5	5	2	....	....	....	....
	Albany River Rats	AHL	6	0	2	2	12	....	....	....	....	....	....	....	....	....	4	0	1	1	4	....	....	....	....
1996-97	Albany River Rats	AHL	70	2	11	13	160	....	....	....	....	....	....	....	....	....	16	2	3	5	47	....	....	....	....
1997-98	**New Jersey**	**NHL**	**60**	**3**	**7**	**10**	**85**	**0**	**0**	**1**	**74**	**4.1**	**18**	....	....	....	**3**	**0**	**1**	**1**	**2**	**0**	**0**	**0**	....
	Albany River Rats	AHL	6	0	0	0	8	....	....	....	....	....	....	....	....	....	....	....	....	....	....	....	....	....	....
1998-99	**New Jersey**	**NHL**	**70**	**1**	**7**	**8**	**110**	**0**	**0**	**0**	**101**	**1.0**	**5**	**0**	**0.0**	**14:56**	**2**	**0**	**1**	**1**	**0**	**0**	**0**	**0**	**12:57**
99-2000	**New Jersey**	**NHL**	**52**	**0**	**8**	**8**	**70**	**0**	**0**	**0**	**74**	**0.0**	**–6**	**0**	**0.0**	**17:12**	....	....	....	....	....	....	....	....	....
	Montreal	**NHL**	**19**	**3**	**0**	**3**	**44**	**0**	**0**	**0**	**39**	**7.7**	**7**	**0**	**0.0**	**19:18**	....	....	....	....	....	....	....	....	....
2000-01	**Montreal**	**NHL**	**52**	**3**	**8**	**11**	**95**	**0**	**0**	**2**	**103**	**2.9**	**–11**	**0**	**0.0**	**20:36**	....	....	....	....	....	....	....	....	....
2001-02	**Montreal**	**NHL**	**34**	**3**	**5**	**8**	**62**	**1**	**0**	**0**	**56**	**5.4**	**–5**	**1**	**100.0**	**18:11**	**12**	**0**	**1**	**1**	**16**	**0**	**0**	**0**	**19:01**
2002-03	**Montreal**	**NHL**	DID NOT PLAY – INJURED																						
2003-04	**Montreal**	**NHL**	**63**	**15**	**20**	**35**	**104**	**6**	**1**	**3**	**186**	**8.1**	**4**	**0**	**0.0**	**23:26**	**11**	**0**	**2**	**2**	**39**	**0**	**0**	**0**	**23:55**
2004-05	Farjestad	Sweden	39	9	8	17	117	....	....	....	....	....	....	....	....	....	15	1	6	7	77	....	....	....	....
2005-06	**Montreal**	**NHL**	**75**	**12**	**27**	**39**	**116**	**7**	**1**	**0**	**202**	**5.9**	**–11**	**0**	**0.0**	**22:15**	**6**	**3**	**2**	**5**	**8**	**2**	**0**	**0**	**18:47**
2006-07	**Montreal**	**NHL**	**81**	**26**	**38**	**64**	**135**	**19**	**1**	**6**	**224**	**11.6**	**–28**	**2**	**100.0**	**23:11**	....	....	....	....	....	....	....	....	....
2007-08	**Edmonton**	**NHL**	**26**	**3**	**7**	**10**	**36**	**2**	**0**	**1**	**71**	**4.2**	**–7**	**0**	**0.0**	**24:21**	....	....	....	....	....	....	....	....	....
2008-09	**Edmonton**	**NHL**	**81**	**23**	**30**	**53**	**98**	**12**	**1**	**5**	**268**	**8.6**	**1**	**0**	**0.0**	**24:51**	....	....	....	....	....	....	....	....	....
2009-10	**Edmonton**	**NHL**	**37**	**4**	**9**	**13**	**65**	**0**	**0**	**0**	**113**	**3.5**	**–19**	**0**	**0.0**	**22:37**	....	....	....	....	....	....	....	....	....
2010-11	Hershey Bears	AHL	40	4	15	19	85	....	....	....	....	....	....	....	....	....	6	1	1	2	16	....	....	....	....
	NHL Totals		**650**	**96**	**166**	**262**	**1020**	**47**	**4**	**18**	**1511**	**6.4**		**3**	**100.0**	**21:11**	**34**	**3**	**7**	**10**	**65**	**2**	**0**	**0**	**20:19**

WHL West Second All-Star Team (1996)

Played in NHL All-Star Game (2004, 2007, 2009)

Traded to **Montreal** by **New Jersey** with Josh DeWolf and New Jersey's 2nd round choice (later traded to Washington, later traded to Tampa Bay – Tampa Bay selected Andreas Holmqvist) in 2001 Entry Draft for Vladimir Malakhov, March 1, 2000. • Missed remainder of 2001-02 season and entire 2002-03 due to wrist injury vs. Tampa Bay, November 17, 2001. Signed as a free agent by **Farjestad** (Sweden), September 22, 2004. Signed as a free agent by **Edmonton**, July 12, 2007. • Missed majority of 2007-08 due to shoulder injury at Vancouver, October 13, 2007, February 8, 2008. • Missed majority of 2009-10 due to head (October 8, 2009 vs. Calgary) and hand (January 30, 2010 at Calgary) injuries. • Loaned to **Hershey** (AHL) by **Edmonton**, October 6, 2010. Signed as a free agent by **Dallas**, July 1, 2011.

SPACEK, Jaroslav

(SPAH-chehk, YAHR-roh-slav) **MTL**

Defense. Shoots left. 6', 210 lbs. Born, Rokycany, Czech., February 11, 1974. Florida's 5th choice, 117th overall, in 1998 Entry Draft.

			Regular Season														Playoffs								
Season	Club	League	GP	G	A	Pts	PIM	PP	SH	GW	S	%	+/-	TF	F%	Min	GP	G	A	Pts	PIM	PP	SH	GW	Min
1992-93	HC Skoda Plzen	Czech	16	1	3	4	....	....	....	....	....	....	....	....	....	....	....	....	....	....	....	....	....	....	....
1993-94	HC Skoda Plzen	CzRep	34	2	6	8	....	....	....	....	....	....	....	....	....	....	....	....	....	....	....	....	....	....	....
1994-95	Plzen	CzRep	38	4	8	12	14	....	....	....	....	....	....	....	....	....	3	1	0	1	2	....	....	....	....
1995-96	HC ZKZ Plzen	CzRep	40	3	10	13	42	....	....	....	....	....	....	....	....	....	3	0	1	1	4	....	....	....	....
1996-97	HC ZKZ Plzen	CzRep	52	9	29	38	44	....	....	....	....	....	....	....	....	....	....	....	....	....	....	....	....	....	....
1997-98	Farjestad	Sweden	45	10	16	26	63	....	....	....	....	....	....	....	....	....	12	2	5	7	14	....	....	....	....
	Farjestad	EuroHL	6	2	3	5	2	....	....	....	....	....	....	....	....	....	....	....	....	....	....	....	....	....	....
1998-99	**Florida**	**NHL**	**63**	**3**	**12**	**15**	**28**	**2**	**1**	**0**	**92**	**3.3**	**15**	**1**	**100.0**	**19:27**	....	....	....	....	....	....	....	....	....
	New Haven	AHL	14	4	8	12	15	....	....	....	....	....	....	....	....	....	....	....	....	....	....	....	....	....	....
99-2000	**Florida**	**NHL**	**82**	**10**	**26**	**36**	**53**	**4**	**0**	**1**	**111**	**9.0**	**7**	**1**	**0.0**	**22:40**	**4**	**0**	**0**	**0**	**0**	**0**	**0**	**0**	**20:29**
2000-01	**Florida**	**NHL**	**12**	**2**	**1**	**3**	**8**	**1**	**0**	**0**	**21**	**9.5**	**–4**	**0**	**0.0**	**19:12**	....	....	....	....	....	....	....	....	....
	Chicago	**NHL**	**50**	**5**	**18**	**23**	**20**	**2**	**0**	**1**	**85**	**5.9**	**7**	**0**	**0.0**	**21:31**	....	....	....	....	....	....	....	....	....
2001-02	**Chicago**	**NHL**	**60**	**3**	**10**	**13**	**29**	**0**	**0**	**1**	**64**	**4.7**	**5**	**0**	**0.0**	**16:25**	....	....	....	....	....	....	....	....	....
	Czech Republic	Olympics	4	0	0	0	0	....	....	....	....	....	....	....	....	....	....	....	....	....	....	....	....	....	....
	Columbus	**NHL**	**14**	**2**	**3**	**5**	**24**	**1**	**1**	**1**	**29**	**6.9**	**–9**	**0**	**0.0**	**23:35**	....	....	....	....	....	....	....	....	....
2002-03	**Columbus**	**NHL**	**81**	**9**	**36**	**45**	**70**	**5**	**0**	**1**	**166**	**5.4**	**–23**	**0**	**0.0**	**24:47**	....	....	....	....	....	....	....	....	....
2003-04	**Columbus**	**NHL**	**58**	**5**	**17**	**22**	**45**	**2**	**1**	**2**	**108**	**4.6**	**–13**	**0**	**0.0**	**23:26**	....	....	....	....	....	....	....	....	....
2004-05	Plzen	CzRep	30	3	8	11	26	....	....	....	....	....	....	....	....	....	....	....	....	....	....	....	....	....	....
	HC Slavia Praha	CzRep	17	4	9	13	29	....	....	....	....	....	....	....	....	....	7	0	2	2	8	....	....	....	....
2005-06	**Chicago**	**NHL**	**45**	**7**	**17**	**24**	**72**	**1**	**0**	**0**	**80**	**8.8**	**8**	**0**	**0.0**	**23:00**	....	....	....	....	....	....	....	....	....
	Edmonton	**NHL**	**31**	**5**	**14**	**19**	**24**	**3**	**0**	**0**	**70**	**7.1**	**3**	**0**	**0.0**	**24:37**	**24**	**3**	**11**	**14**	**24**	**2**	**0**	**0**	**25:53**
2006-07	**Buffalo**	**NHL**	**65**	**5**	**16**	**21**	**62**	**1**	**0**	**2**	**78**	**6.4**	**20**	**0**	**0.0**	**19:09**	**16**	**0**	**0**	**0**	**10**	**0**	**0**	**0**	**14:39**
2007-08	**Buffalo**	**NHL**	**60**	**9**	**23**	**32**	**42**	**7**	**0**	**1**	**95**	**9.5**	**7**	**0**	**0.0**	**22:59**	....	....	....	....	....	....	....	....	....
2008-09	**Buffalo**	**NHL**	**80**	**8**	**37**	**45**	**38**	**4**	**0**	**0**	**130**	**6.2**	**2**	**0**	**0.0**	**22:17**	....	....	....	....	....	....	....	....	....
2009-10	**Montreal**	**NHL**	**74**	**3**	**18**	**21**	**50**	**1**	**0**	**0**	**99**	**3.0**	**9**	**0**	**0.0**	**21:48**	**10**	**1**	**3**	**4**	**6**	**0**	**0**	**0**	**18:28**
2010-11	**Montreal**	**NHL**	**59**	**1**	**15**	**16**	**45**	**0**	**0**	**0**	**65**	**1.5**	**9**	**0**	**0.0**	**19:15**	**7**	**0**	**0**	**0**	**4**	**0**	**0**	**0**	**17:42**
	NHL Totals		**834**	**77**	**263**	**340**	**610**	**34**	**3**	**10**	**1293**	**6.0**		**2**	**50.0**	**21:37**	**61**	**4**	**14**	**18**	**44**	**2**	**0**	**0**	**20:26**

Traded to **Chicago** by **Florida** for Anders Eriksson, November 6, 2000. Traded to **Columbus** by **Chicago** with Chicago's 2nd round choice (Dan Fritsche) in 2003 Entry Draft for Lyle Odelein, March 19, 2002. Signed as a free agent by **Plzen** (CzRep), September 17, 2004. Signed as a free agent by **Slavia Praha** (CzRep), January 4, 2005. Signed as a free agent by **Chicago**, August 3, 2005. Traded to **Edmonton** by **Chicago** for Tony Salmelainen, January 26, 2006. Signed as a free agent by **Buffalo**, July 5, 2006. Signed as a free agent by **Montreal**, July 1, 2009.

SPALING, Nick

(SPAHL-ihng, NIHK) **NSH**

Center. Shoots left. 6'1", 198 lbs. Born, Palmerston, Ont., September 19, 1988. Nashville's 3rd choice, 58th overall, in 2007 Entry Draft.

			Regular Season														Playoffs								
Season	Club	League	GP	G	A	Pts	PIM	PP	SH	GW	S	%	+/-	TF	F%	Min	GP	G	A	Pts	PIM	PP	SH	GW	Min
2004-05	Listowel Cyclones	ON-Jr.B	61	25	27	52	58	....	....	....	....	....	....	....	....	....	....	....	....	....	....	....	....	....	....
2005-06	Kitchener Rangers	OHL	62	10	15	25	22	....	....	....	....	....	....	....	....	....	5	0	3	3	0	....	....	....	....
2006-07	Kitchener Rangers	OHL	61	23	36	59	41	....	....	....	....	....	....	....	....	....	9	2	3	5	4	....	....	....	....
2007-08	Kitchener Rangers	OHL	56	38	34	72	18	....	....	....	....	....	....	....	....	....	20	14	16	30	9	....	....	....	....
2008-09	Milwaukee	AHL	79	12	23	35	28	....	....	....	....	....	....	....	....	....	11	0	3	3	8	....	....	....	....
2009-10	**Nashville**	**NHL**	**28**	**0**	**3**	**3**	**0**	**0**	**0**	**0**	**26**	**0.0**	**3**	**95**	**41.1**	**11:03**	**6**	**0**	**0**	**0**	**0**	**0**	**0**	**0**	**8:24**
	Milwaukee	AHL	48	7	10	17	21	....	....	....	....	....	....	....	....	....	....	....	....	....	....	....	....	....	....
2010-11	**Nashville**	**NHL**	**74**	**8**	**6**	**14**	**20**	**1**	**0**	**2**	**75**	**10.7**	**–10**	**497**	**50.9**	**13:56**	**12**	**2**	**4**	**6**	**0**	**0**	**0**	**1**	**15:19**
	Milwaukee	AHL	4	1	1	2	2	....	....	....	....	....	....	....	....	....	....	....	....	....	....	....	....	....	....
	NHL Totals		**102**	**8**	**9**	**17**	**20**	**1**	**0**	**2**	**101**	**7.9**		**592**	**49.3**	**13:08**	**18**	**2**	**4**	**6**	**0**	**0**	**0**	**1**	**13:01**

SPEZZA, Jason

(SPEHT-zuh, JAY-suhn) **OTT**

Center. Shoots right. 6'3", 216 lbs. Born, Mississauga, Ont., June 13, 1983. Ottawa's 1st choice, 2nd overall, in 2001 Entry Draft.

			Regular Season														Playoffs								
Season	Club	League	GP	G	A	Pts	PIM	PP	SH	GW	S	%	+/-	TF	F%	Min	GP	G	A	Pts	PIM	PP	SH	GW	Min
1997-98	Toronto Marlies	MTHL	54	53	61	114	42	....	....	....	....	....	....	....	....	....	....	....	....	....	....	....	....	....	....
1998-99	Brampton	OHL	67	22	49	71	18	....	....	....	....	....	....	....	....	....	....	....	....	....	....	....	....	....	....
99-2000	Mississauga	OHL	52	24	37	61	33	....	....	....	....	....	....	....	....	....	....	....	....	....	....	....	....	....	....
2000-01	Mississauga	OHL	15	7	23	30	11	....	....	....	....	....	....	....	....	....	....	....	....	....	....	....	....	....	....
	Windsor Spitfires	OHL	41	36	50	86	32	....	....	....	....	....	....	....	....	....	9	4	5	9	10	....	....	....	....
2001-02	Windsor Spitfires	OHL	27	19	26	45	16	....	....	....	....	....	....	....	....	....	....	....	....	....	....	....	....	....	....
	Belleville Bulls	OHL	26	23	37	60	26	....	....	....	....	....	....	....	....	....	11	5	6	11	18	....	....	....	....
	Grand Rapids	AHL	....	....	....	....	....	....	....	....	....	....	....	....	....	....	3	1	0	1	2	....	....	....	....
2002-03	**Ottawa**	**NHL**	**33**	**7**	**14**	**21**	**8**	**3**	**0**	**0**	**65**	**10.8**	**–3**	**330**	**45.8**	**12:40**	**3**	**1**	**1**	**2**	**0**	**1**	**0**	**0**	**11:34**
	Binghamton	AHL	43	22	32	54	71	....	....	....	....	....	....	....	....	....	2	1	2	3	4	....	....	....	....
2003-04	**Ottawa**	**NHL**	**78**	**22**	**33**	**55**	**71**	**5**	**0**	**3**	**142**	**15.5**	**22**	**956**	**47.7**	**14:38**	**3**	**0**	**0**	**0**	**2**	**0**	**0**	**0**	**9:44**
2004-05	Binghamton	AHL	80	32	*85	*117	50	....	....	....	....	....	....	....	....	....	6	1	3	4	6	....	....	....	....
2005-06	**Ottawa**	**NHL**	**68**	**19**	**71**	**90**	**33**	**7**	**0**	**5**	**156**	**12.2**	**23**	**1220**	**52.6**	**19:00**	**10**	**5**	**9**	**14**	**2**	**3**	**0**	**1**	**17:59**
2006-07	**Ottawa**	**NHL**	**67**	**34**	**53**	**87**	**45**	**13**	**1**	**5**	**162**	**21.0**	**19**	**1261**	**53.0**	**19:17**	**20**	**7**	***15**	***22**	**10**	**3**	**0**	**0**	**20:58**
2007-08	**Ottawa**	**NHL**	**76**	**34**	**58**	**92**	**66**	**11**	**0**	**6**	**210**	**16.2**	**26**	**1445**	**50.5**	**20:40**	**4**	**0**	**1**	**1**	**0**	**0**	**0**	**0**	**19:45**
2008-09	**Ottawa**	**NHL**	**82**	**32**	**41**	**73**	**79**	**13**	**1**	**3**	**246**	**13.0**	**–14**	**1477**	**53.3**	**19:41**	....	....	....	....	....	....	....	....	....

			Regular Season														Playoffs								
Season	Club	League	GP	G	A	Pts	PIM	PP	SH	GW	S	%	+/-	TF	F%	Min	GP	G	A	Pts	PIM	PP	SH	GW	Min
2009-10	Ottawa	NHL	60	23	34	57	20	11	0	5	165	13.9	0	1018	50.5	19:04	6	1	6	7	4	1	0	0	22:46
2010-11	Ottawa	NHL	62	21	36	57	28	7	0	2	188	11.2	-7	1210	56.3	20:12	....	....	....	....	....	....	....	....	....
	NHL Totals		526	192	340	532	350	70	2	29	1334	14.4		8917	51.9	18:29	46	14	32	46	18	8	0	1	19:06

OHL All-Rookie Team (1999) • AHL All-Rookie Team (2003) • AHL First All-Star Team (2005) • John P. Sollenberger Trophy (AHL - Top Scorer) (2005) • Les Cunningham Award (AHL – MVP) (2005)
Played in NHL All-Star Game (2008)

SPURGEON, Jared (SPUHR-juhn, JAIR-uhd) MIN

Defense. Shoots right. 5'9", 175 lbs. Born, Edmonton, Alta., November 29, 1989. NY Islanders' 12th choice, 156th overall, in 2008 Entry Draft.

Season	Club	League	GP	G	A	Pts	PIM	PP	SH	GW	S	%	+/-	TF	F%	Min	GP	G	A	Pts	PIM	PP	SH	GW	Min
2004-05	K of C Pats	AMHL	26	9	21	30	16	....	....	....	....	....	....	....	....	....	....	....	....	....	....	....	....	....	....
2005-06	Spokane Chiefs	WHL	46	3	9	12	28	....	....	....	....	....	....	....	....	....	....	....	....	....	....	....	....	....	....
2006-07	Spokane Chiefs	WHL	38	4	15	19	16	....	....	....	....	....	....	....	....	....	....	....	....	....	....	....	....	....	....
2007-08	Spokane Chiefs	WHL	69	12	31	43	19	....	....	....	....	....	....	....	....	....	21	0	5	5	16	....	....	....	....
2008-09	Spokane Chiefs	WHL	59	10	35	45	37	....	....	....	....	....	....	....	....	....	12	2	3	5	10	....	....	....	....
2009-10	Spokane Chiefs	WHL	54	8	43	51	18	....	....	....	....	....	....	....	....	....	7	0	4	4	2	....	....	....	....
2010-11	Minnesota	NHL	53	4	8	12	2	2	0	1	38	10.5	-1	0	0.0	15:04	....	....	....	....	....	....	....	....	....
	Houston Aeros	AHL	23	2	7	9	10	....	....	....	....	....	....	....	....	....	23	1	10	11	10	....	....	....	....
	NHL Totals		53	4	8	12	2	2	0	1	38	10.5		0	0.0	15:04	....	....	....	....	....	....	....	....	....

Signed as a free agent by **Minnesota**, September 23, 2010.

STAAL, Eric (STAHL, AIR-ihk) CAR

Center. Shoots left. 6'4", 205 lbs. Born, Thunder Bay, Ont., October 29, 1984. Carolina's 1st choice, 2nd overall, in 2003 Entry Draft.

Season	Club	League	GP	G	A	Pts	PIM	PP	SH	GW	S	%	+/-	TF	F%	Min	GP	G	A	Pts	PIM	PP	SH	GW	Min
99-2000	Thunder Bay	Exhib.	7	4	8	12	0	....	....	....	....	....	....	....	....	....	....	....	....	....	....	....	....	....	....
2000-01	Peterborough	OHL	63	19	30	49	23	....	....	....	....	....	....	....	....	....	7	2	5	7	4	....	....	....	....
2001-02	Peterborough	OHL	56	23	39	62	40	....	....	....	....	....	....	....	....	....	6	3	6	9	10	....	....	....	....
2002-03	Peterborough	OHL	66	39	59	98	36	....	....	....	....	....	....	....	....	....	7	9	5	14	6	....	....	....	....
2003-04	Carolina	NHL	81	11	20	31	40	2	1	3	164	6.7	-6	669	43.1	16:40	....	....	....	....	....	....	....	....	....
2004-05	Lowell	AHL	77	26	51	77	88	....	....	....	....	....	....	....	....	....	11	2	8	10	12	....	....	....	....
2005-06♦	Carolina	NHL	82	45	55	100	81	19	4	4	279	16.1	-8	1309	42.6	19:39	25	9	*19	*28	8	*7	0	1	19:48
2006-07	Carolina	NHL	82	30	40	70	68	12	1	1	288	10.4	-6	1238	45.2	20:08	....	....	....	....	....	....	....	....	....
2007-08	Carolina	NHL	82	38	44	82	50	14	0	7	310	12.3	-2	1708	44.9	21:38	....	....	....	....	....	....	....	....	....
2008-09	Carolina	NHL	82	40	35	75	50	14	1	8	372	10.8	15	1586	45.3	21:03	18	10	5	15	4	3	0	1	21:31
2009-10	Carolina	NHL	70	29	41	70	68	13	0	5	277	10.5	4	1162	41.8	20:43	....	....	....	....	....	....	....	....	....
	Canada	Olympics	7	1	5	6	6	....	....	....	....	....	....	....	....	....	....	....	....	....	....	....	....	....	....
2010-11	Carolina	NHL	81	33	43	76	72	12	3	8	296	11.1	-10	1751	48.0	21:56	....	....	....	....	....	....	....	....	....
	NHL Totals		560	226	278	504	429	86	10	36	1986	11.4		9423	44.7	20:15	43	19	24	43	12	10	0	2	20:31

OHL Second All-Star Team (2003) • Canadian Major Junior First All-Star Team (2003) • NHL Second All-Star Team (2006)
Played in NHL All-Star Game (2007, 2008, 2009, 2011)

STAAL, Jordan (STAHL, JOHR-dahn) PIT

Center. Shoots left. 6'4", 220 lbs. Born, Thunder Bay, Ont., September 10, 1988. Pittsburgh's 1st choice, 2nd overall, in 2006 Entry Draft.

Season	Club	League	GP	G	A	Pts	PIM	PP	SH	GW	S	%	+/-	TF	F%	Min	GP	G	A	Pts	PIM	PP	SH	GW	Min
2004-05	Peterborough	OHL	66	9	19	28	29	....	....	....	....	....	....	....	....	....	14	5	5	10	16	....	....	....	....
2005-06	Peterborough	OHL	68	28	40	68	69	....	....	....	....	....	....	....	....	....	19	10	6	16	16	....	....	....	....
2006-07	Pittsburgh	NHL	81	29	13	42	24	4	*7	4	131	22.1	16	383	37.1	14:56	5	3	0	3	2	0	0	0	16:00
2007-08	Pittsburgh	NHL	82	12	16	28	55	3	0	4	183	6.6	-5	1202	42.2	18:16	20	6	1	7	14	1	0	1	18:16
2008-09♦	Pittsburgh	NHL	82	22	27	49	37	2	1	3	166	13.3	5	1206	47.0	19:51	24	4	5	9	8	0	1	0	19:13
2009-10	Pittsburgh	NHL	82	21	28	49	57	1	2	1	195	10.8	19	1324	48.3	19:24	11	3	2	5	6	2	0	0	18:14
2010-11	Pittsburgh	NHL	42	11	19	30	24	3	0	4	91	12.1	7	801	46.9	21:21	7	1	2	3	2	0	0	0	21:28
	NHL Totals		369	95	103	198	197	13	10	16	766	12.4		4916	45.4	18:29	67	17	10	27	32	3	1	1	18:46

NHL All-Rookie Team (2007)

STAAL, Marc (STAHL, MAHRK) NYR

Defense. Shoots left. 6'4", 208 lbs. Born, Thunder Bay, Ont., January 13, 1987. NY Rangers' 1st choice, 12th overall, in 2005 Entry Draft.

Season	Club	League	GP	G	A	Pts	PIM	PP	SH	GW	S	%	+/-	TF	F%	Min	GP	G	A	Pts	PIM	PP	SH	GW	Min
2003-04	Sudbury Wolves	OHL	61	1	13	14	34	....	....	....	....	....	....	....	....	....	7	1	2	3	2	....	....	....	....
2004-05	Sudbury Wolves	OHL	65	6	20	26	53	....	....	....	....	....	....	....	....	....	12	0	4	4	15	....	....	....	....
2005-06	Sudbury Wolves	OHL	57	11	38	49	60	....	....	....	....	....	....	....	....	....	10	0	8	8	8	....	....	....	....
	Hartford	AHL	....	....	....	....	....	....	....	....	....	....	....	....	....	....	12	0	2	2	8	....	....	....	....
2006-07	Sudbury Wolves	OHL	53	5	29	34	68	....	....	....	....	....	....	....	....	....	21	5	15	20	22	....	....	....	....
2007-08	NY Rangers	NHL	80	2	8	10	42	0	0	0	78	2.6	2	0	0.0	18:48	10	1	2	3	8	0	0	1	22:21
2008-09	NY Rangers	NHL	82	3	12	15	64	0	0	1	96	3.1	-7	0	0.0	21:08	7	1	0	1	0	0	0	0	21:33
2009-10	NY Rangers	NHL	82	8	19	27	44	0	0	2	78	10.3	11	0	0.0	23:08	....	....	....	....	....	....	....	....	....
2010-11	NY Rangers	NHL	77	7	22	29	50	4	2	2	116	6.0	8	0	0.0	25:44	5	0	1	1	0	0	0	0	28:01
	NHL Totals		321	20	61	81	200	4	2	5	368	5.4		0	0.0	22:10	22	2	3	5	8	0	0	1	23:23

OHL First All-Star Team (2006, 2007) • Canadian Major Junior First All-Star Team (2006, 2007)
Played in NHL All-Star Game (2011)

STAFFORD, Drew (STA-fuhrd, DROO) BUF

Right wing. Shoots right. 6'2", 214 lbs. Born, Milwaukee, WI, October 30, 1985. Buffalo's 1st choice, 13th overall, in 2004 Entry Draft.

Season	Club	League	GP	G	A	Pts	PIM	PP	SH	GW	S	%	+/-	TF	F%	Min	GP	G	A	Pts	PIM	PP	SH	GW	Min
2001-02	Shat.-St. Mary's	High-MN	45	35	53	88	30	....	....	....	....	....	....	....	....	....	....	....	....	....	....	....	....	....	....
2002-03	Shat.-St. Mary's	High-MN	65	49	67	116	....	....	....	....	....	....	....	....	....	....	....	....	....	....	....	....	....	....	....
2003-04	North Dakota	WCHA	36	11	21	32	30	....	....	....	....	....	....	....	....	....	....	....	....	....	....	....	....	....	....
2004-05	North Dakota	WCHA	42	13	25	38	34	....	....	....	....	....	....	....	....	....	....	....	....	....	....	....	....	....	....
2005-06	North Dakota	WCHA	42	24	24	48	63	....	....	....	....	....	....	....	....	....	....	....	....	....	....	....	....	....	....
2006-07	Buffalo	NHL	41	13	14	27	33	3	0	3	67	19.4	5	13	46.2	13:08	10	2	2	4	4	0	0	0	11:52
	Rochester	AHL	34	22	22	44	30	....	....	....	....	....	....	....	....	....	....	....	....	....	....	....	....	....	....
2007-08	Buffalo	NHL	64	16	22	38	51	1	0	5	103	15.5	3	21	38.1	13:32	....	....	....	....	....	....	....	....	....
2008-09	Buffalo	NHL	79	20	25	45	29	9	0	0	183	10.9	3	20	20.0	15:38	....	....	....	....	....	....	....	....	....
2009-10	Buffalo	NHL	71	14	20	34	35	5	0	1	181	7.7	4	86	47.7	14:28	3	0	0	0	0	0	0	0	14:06
2010-11	Buffalo	NHL	62	31	21	52	34	11	0	4	179	17.3	13	56	30.4	16:32	7	1	2	3	2	1	0	0	20:01
	NHL Totals		317	94	102	196	182	29	0	13	713	13.2		196	38.8	14:48	20	3	4	7	6	1	0	0	15:03

STAFFORD, Garrett (STA-fuhrd, GAIR-reht) PHX

Defense. Shoots right. 6'1", 207 lbs. Born, Los Angeles, CA, January 28, 1980.

Season	Club	League	GP	G	A	Pts	PIM	PP	SH	GW	S	%	+/-	TF	F%	Min	GP	G	A	Pts	PIM	PP	SH	GW	Min
1996-97	Des Moines	USHL	37	1	10	11	40	....	....	....	....	....	....	....	....	....	5	0	0	0	0	....	....	....	....
1997-98	Des Moines	USHL	53	6	17	23	89	....	....	....	....	....	....	....	....	....	12	1	3	4	42	....	....	....	....
1998-99	Des Moines	USHL	56	8	33	41	54	....	....	....	....	....	....	....	....	....	13	2	2	4	18	....	....	....	....
99-2000	New Hampshire	H-East	38	3	9	12	28	....	....	....	....	....	....	....	....	....	....	....	....	....	....	....	....	....	....
2000-01	New Hampshire	H-East	37	5	21	26	44	....	....	....	....	....	....	....	....	....	....	....	....	....	....	....	....	....	....
2001-02	New Hampshire	H-East	36	5	22	27	42	....	....	....	....	....	....	....	....	....	....	....	....	....	....	....	....	....	....
2002-03	New Hampshire	H-East	23	1	15	16	24	....	....	....	....	....	....	....	....	....	....	....	....	....	....	....	....	....	....
2003-04	Cleveland Barons	AHL	73	12	34	46	71	....	....	....	....	....	....	....	....	....	6	0	0	0	6	....	....	....	....
2004-05	Cleveland Barons	AHL	68	6	18	24	55	....	....	....	....	....	....	....	....	....	....	....	....	....	....	....	....	....	....
2005-06	Cleveland Barons	AHL	80	11	28	39	86	....	....	....	....	....	....	....	....	....	....	....	....	....	....	....	....	....	....
2006-07	Worcester Sharks	AHL	77	11	30	41	58	....	....	....	....	....	....	....	....	....	6	0	3	3	2	....	....	....	....
2007-08	Detroit	NHL	2	0	0	0	0	0	0	0	1	0.0	0	0	0.0	6:45	....	....	....	....	....	....	....	....	....
	Grand Rapids	AHL	69	11	33	44	36	....	....	....	....	....	....	....	....	....	....	....	....	....	....	....	....	....	....
2008-09	Dallas	NHL	3	0	2	2	0	0	0	0	5	0.0	0	0	0.0	18:00	....	....	....	....	....	....	....	....	....
	Grand Rapids	AHL	70	11	34	45	50	....	....	....	....	....	....	....	....	....	10	0	5	5	4	....	....	....	....
2009-10	Texas Stars	AHL	60	7	25	32	22	....	....	....	....	....	....	....	....	....	21	4	6	10	10	....	....	....	....

			Regular Season														Playoffs								
Season	Club	League	GP	G	A	Pts	PIM	PP	SH	GW	S	%	+/-	TF	F%	Min	GP	G	A	Pts	PIM	PP	SH	GW	Min
2010-11	**Phoenix**	**NHL**	**2**	**0**	**0**	**0**	**0**	**0**	**0**	**0**	**2**	**0.0**	**0**	**0**	**0.0**	**12:24**	....	....	....	....	....	....	....	....	....
	San Antonio	AHL	65	14	32	46	74	....	....	....	....	....	....	....	....	....	....	....	....	....	....	....	....	....	....
	NHL Totals		**7**	**0**	**2**	**2**	**0**	**0**	**0**	**0**	**8**	**0.0**		**0**	**0.0**	**13:11**	....	....	....	....	....	....	....	....	....

Hockey East Second All-Star Team (2002) • AHL All-Rookie Team (2004) • AHL Second All-Star Team (2004)

Signed as a free agent by **Cleveland** (AHL), October 10, 2003. Signed as a free agent by **San Jose**, December 9, 2003. Signed as a free agent by **Detroit**, July 16, 2007. Signed as a free agent by **Dallas**, July 3, 2008. Signed as a free agent by **Phoenix**, July 3, 2010.

STAIOS, Steve

(STAY-ohs, STEEV)

Defense. Shoots right. 6'1", 200 lbs. Born, Hamilton, Ont., July 28, 1973. St. Louis' 1st choice, 27th overall, in 1991 Entry Draft.

Season	Club	League	GP	G	A	Pts	PIM	PP	SH	GW	S	%	+/-	TF	F%	Min	GP	G	A	Pts	PIM	PP	SH	GW	Min
1988-89	Hamilton Huskies	Minor-ON	58	13	39	52	78	....	....	....	....	....	....	....	....	....	....	....	....	....	....	....	....	....	....
1989-90	Hamilton Kilty B's	ON-Jr.B	40	9	27	36	66	....	....	....	....	....	....	....	....	....	....	....	....	....	....	....	....	....	....
1990-91	Niagara Falls	OHL	66	17	29	46	115	....	....	....	....	....	....	....	....	....	12	2	3	5	10	....	....	....	....
1991-92	Niagara Falls	OHL	65	11	42	53	122	....	....	....	....	....	....	....	....	....	17	7	8	15	27	....	....	....	....
1992-93	Niagara Falls	OHL	12	4	14	18	30	....	....	....	....	....	....	....	....	....	....	....	....	....	....	....	....	....	....
	Sudbury Wolves	OHL	53	13	44	57	67	....	....	....	....	....	....	....	....	....	11	5	6	11	22	....	....	....	....
1993-94	Peoria Rivermen	IHL	38	3	9	12	42	....	....	....	....	....	....	....	....	....	....	....	....	....	....	....	....	....	....
1994-95	Peoria Rivermen	IHL	60	3	13	16	64	....	....	....	....	....	....	....	....	....	6	0	0	0	10	....	....	....	....
1995-96	Peoria Rivermen	IHL	6	0	1	1	14	....	....	....	....	....	....	....	....	....	....	....	....	....	....	....	....	....	....
	Worcester IceCats	AHL	57	1	11	12	114	....	....	....	....	....	....	....	....	....	....	....	....	....	....	....	....	....	....
	Boston	**NHL**	**12**	**0**	**0**	**0**	**4**	**0**	**0**	**0**	**4**	**0.0**	**–5**	....	....	....	**3**	**0**	**0**	**0**	**0**	**0**	**0**	**0**	....
	Providence Bruins	AHL	7	1	4	5	8	....	....	....	....	....	....	....	....	....	....	....	....	....	....	....	....	....	....
1996-97	**Boston**	**NHL**	**54**	**3**	**8**	**11**	**71**	**0**	**0**	**0**	**56**	**5.4**	**–26**	....	....	....	....	....	....	....	....	....	....	....	....
	Vancouver	**NHL**	**9**	**0**	**6**	**6**	**20**	**0**	**0**	**0**	**10**	**0.0**	**2**	....	....	....	....	....	....	....	....	....	....	....	....
1997-98	**Vancouver**	**NHL**	**77**	**3**	**4**	**7**	**134**	**0**	**0**	**1**	**45**	**6.7**	**–3**	....	....	....	....	....	....	....	....	....	....	....	....
1998-99	**Vancouver**	**NHL**	**57**	**0**	**2**	**2**	**54**	**0**	**0**	**0**	**33**	**0.0**	**–12**	**4**	**25.0**	**6:53**	....	....	....	....	....	....	....	....	....
99-2000	**Atlanta**	**NHL**	**27**	**2**	**3**	**5**	**66**	**0**	**0**	**0**	**38**	**5.3**	**–5**	**2**	**50.0**	**13:01**	....	....	....	....	....	....	....	....	....
2000-01	**Atlanta**	**NHL**	**70**	**9**	**13**	**22**	**137**	**4**	**0**	**0**	**156**	**5.8**	**–23**	**1**	**0.0**	**21:45**	....	....	....	....	....	....	....	....	....
2001-02	**Edmonton**	**NHL**	**73**	**5**	**5**	**10**	**108**	**0**	**0**	**1**	**101**	**5.0**	**10**	**0**	**0.0**	**18:05**	....	....	....	....	....	....	....	....	....
2002-03	**Edmonton**	**NHL**	**76**	**5**	**21**	**26**	**96**	**1**	**3**	**0**	**126**	**4.0**	**13**	**1**	**0.0**	**22:17**	**6**	**0**	**0**	**0**	**4**	**0**	**0**	**0**	**23:27**
2003-04	**Edmonton**	**NHL**	**82**	**6**	**22**	**28**	**86**	**1**	**0**	**1**	**153**	**3.9**	**17**	**0**	**0.0**	**23:03**	....	....	....	....	....	....	....	....	....
2004-05	Lulea HF	Sweden	7	2	1	3	12	....	....	....	....	....	....	....	....	....	....	....	....	....	....	....	....	....	....
2005-06	**Edmonton**	**NHL**	**82**	**8**	**20**	**28**	**84**	**1**	**0**	**1**	**140**	**5.7**	**10**	**0**	**0.0**	**20:53**	**24**	**1**	**5**	**6**	**28**	**1**	**0**	**0**	**21:31**
2006-07	**Edmonton**	**NHL**	**58**	**2**	**15**	**17**	**97**	**0**	**0**	**0**	**71**	**2.8**	**–5**	**0**	**0.0**	**21:23**	....	....	....	....	....	....	....	....	....
2007-08	**Edmonton**	**NHL**	**82**	**7**	**9**	**16**	**121**	**1**	**0**	**0**	**73**	**9.6**	**–14**	**1**	**100.0**	**22:01**	....	....	....	....	....	....	....	....	....
2008-09	**Edmonton**	**NHL**	**80**	**2**	**12**	**14**	**92**	**0**	**0**	**0**	**78**	**2.6**	**–5**	**0**	**0.0**	**19:48**	....	....	....	....	....	....	....	....	....
2009-10	**Edmonton**	**NHL**	**40**	**0**	**7**	**7**	**59**	**0**	**0**	**0**	**45**	**0.0**	**–19**	**0**	**0.0**	**18:51**	....	....	....	....	....	....	....	....	....
	Calgary	**NHL**	**18**	**1**	**2**	**3**	**16**	**1**	**0**	**0**	**16**	**6.3**	**–8**	**0**	**0.0**	**18:23**	....	....	....	....	....	....	....	....	....
2010-11	**Calgary**	**NHL**	**39**	**3**	**7**	**10**	**24**	**0**	**1**	**0**	**23**	**13.0**	**6**	**1**	**100.0**	**14:43**	....	....	....	....	....	....	....	....	....
	NHL Totals		**936**	**56**	**156**	**212**	**1269**	**9**	**4**	**4**	**1168**	**4.8**		**10**	**40.0**	**19:21**	**33**	**1**	**5**	**6**	**32**	**1**	**0**	**0**	**21:54**

Traded to **Boston** by **St. Louis** with Kevin Sawyer for Steve Leach, March 8, 1996. Claimed on waivers by **Vancouver** from **Boston**, March 18, 1997. Claimed by **Atlanta** from **Vancouver** in Expansion Draft, June 25, 1999. • Missed majority of 1999-2000 due to knee injury vs. Colorado, October 23, 1999. Traded to **New Jersey** by **Atlanta** for New Jersey's 9th round choice (Simon Gamache) in 2000 Entry Draft, June 12, 2000. Traded to **Atlanta** by **New Jersey** for future considerations, July 10, 2000. Signed as a free agent by **Edmonton**, July 12, 2001. Signed as a free agent by **Lulea** (Sweden), January 28, 2005. Traded to **Calgary** by **Edmonton** for Aaron Johnson and Calgary's 3rd round choice (Travis Ewayyk) in 2011 Entry Draft, March 3, 2010. • Missed majority of 2010-11 due to recurring upper body injury.

STAJAN, Matt

(STAY-juhn, MAT) **CGY**

Center. Shoots left. 6'1", 200 lbs. Born, Mississauga, Ont., December 19, 1983. Toronto's 2nd choice, 57th overall, in 2002 Entry Draft.

Season	Club	League	GP	G	A	Pts	PIM	PP	SH	GW	S	%	+/-	TF	F%	Min	GP	G	A	Pts	PIM	PP	SH	GW	Min
99-2000	Miss. Senators	GTHL	STATISTICS NOT AVAILABLE																						
2000-01	Belleville Bulls	OHL	57	9	18	27	27	....	....	....	....	....	....	....	....	....	7	1	6	7	5	....	....	....	....
2001-02	Belleville Bulls	OHL	68	33	52	85	50	....	....	....	....	....	....	....	....	....	11	3	8	11	14	....	....	....	....
2002-03	Belleville Bulls	OHL	57	34	60	94	75	....	....	....	....	....	....	....	....	....	7	5	8	13	16	....	....	....	....
	St. John's	AHL	1	0	1	1	0	....	....	....	....	....	....	....	....	....	....	....	....	....	....	....	....	....	....
	Toronto	**NHL**	**1**	**1**	**0**	**1**	**0**	**0**	**0**	**0**	**1**	**100.0**	**1**	**12**	**33.3**	**11:00**	....	....	....	....	....	....	....	....	....
2003-04	**Toronto**	**NHL**	**69**	**14**	**13**	**27**	**22**	**0**	**0**	**0**	**63**	**22.2**	**7**	**450**	**38.9**	**11:00**	**3**	**0**	**0**	**0**	**2**	**0**	**0**	**0**	**11:13**
2004-05	St. John's	AHL	80	23	43	66	43	....	....	....	....	....	....	....	....	....	5	2	2	4	6	....	....	....	....
2005-06	**Toronto**	**NHL**	**80**	**15**	**12**	**27**	**50**	**3**	**4**	**5**	**83**	**18.1**	**5**	**373**	**44.5**	**11:38**	....	....	....	....	....	....	....	....	....
2006-07	**Toronto**	**NHL**	**82**	**10**	**29**	**39**	**44**	**1**	**1**	**1**	**132**	**7.6**	**3**	**985**	**46.1**	**16:09**	....	....	....	....	....	....	....	....	....
2007-08	**Toronto**	**NHL**	**82**	**16**	**17**	**33**	**47**	**2**	**1**	**3**	**127**	**12.6**	**–11**	**1293**	**47.6**	**18:54**	....	....	....	....	....	....	....	....	....
2008-09	**Toronto**	**NHL**	**76**	**15**	**40**	**55**	**54**	**5**	**1**	**1**	**114**	**13.2**	**–4**	**1177**	**51.4**	**16:56**	....	....	....	....	....	....	....	....	....
2009-10	**Toronto**	**NHL**	**55**	**16**	**25**	**41**	**30**	**7**	**0**	**2**	**99**	**16.2**	**–3**	**926**	**51.6**	**18:47**	....	....	....	....	....	....	....	....	....
	Calgary	**NHL**	**27**	**3**	**13**	**16**	**2**	**0**	**0**	**2**	**33**	**9.1**	**–3**	**408**	**52.0**	**19:11**	....	....	....	....	....	....	....	....	....
2010-11	**Calgary**	**NHL**	**76**	**6**	**25**	**31**	**32**	**0**	**1**	**0**	**81**	**7.4**	**1**	**845**	**51.6**	**14:14**	....	....	....	....	....	....	....	....	....
	NHL Totals		**548**	**96**	**174**	**270**	**281**	**18**	**8**	**14**	**733**	**13.1**		**6469**	**48.6**	**15:30**	**3**	**0**	**0**	**0**	**2**	**0**	**0**	**0**	**11:13**

• Scored a goal in his first NHL game (April 5, 2003 vs. Ottawa).

Traded to **Calgary** by **Toronto** with Niklas Hagman, Jamal Mayers and Ian White for Dion Phaneuf, Fredrik Sjostrom and Keith Aulie, January 31, 2010.

STALBERG, Viktor

(STAHL-buhrg, VIHK-tohr) **CHI**

Left wing. Shoots left. 6'3", 210 lbs. Born, Stockholm, Sweden, January 17, 1986. Toronto's 5th choice, 161st overall, in 2006 Entry Draft.

Season	Club	League	GP	G	A	Pts	PIM	PP	SH	GW	S	%	+/-	TF	F%	Min	GP	G	A	Pts	PIM	PP	SH	GW	Min
2003-04	Molndal U18	Swe-U18	13	14	13	27	....	....	....	....	....	....	....	....	....	....	....	....	....	....	....	....	....	....	....
	Molndal Jr.	Swe-Jr.	18	25	10	35	....	....	....	....	....	....	....	....	....	....	....	....	....	....	....	....	....	....	....
	Molndal	Sweden-4	....	11	9	20	....	....	....	....	....	....	....	....	....	....	....	....	....	....	....	....	....	....	....
2004-05	Molndal Jr.	Swe-Jr.	11	16	7	23	....	....	....	....	....	....	....	....	....	....	....	....	....	....	....	....	....	....	....
	Molndal	Sweden-3	29	6	9	15	54	....	....	....	....	....	....	....	....	....	....	....	....	....	....	....	....	....	....
2005-06	Frolunda Jr.	Swe-Jr.	41	27	26	53	89	....	....	....	....	....	....	....	....	....	7	6	5	11	6	....	....	....	....
2006-07	U. of Vermont	H-East	39	7	8	15	53	....	....	....	....	....	....	....	....	....	....	....	....	....	....	....	....	....	....
2007-08	U. of Vermont	H-East	39	10	13	23	34	....	....	....	....	....	....	....	....	....	....	....	....	....	....	....	....	....	....
2008-09	U. of Vermont	H-East	39	24	22	46	32	....	....	....	....	....	....	....	....	....	....	....	....	....	....	....	....	....	....
	Toronto Marlies	AHL	....	....	....	....	....	....	....	....	....	....	....	....	....	....	2	0	1	1	0	....	....	....	....
2009-10	**Toronto**	**NHL**	**40**	**9**	**5**	**14**	**30**	**0**	**0**	**0**	**117**	**7.7**	**–13**	**9**	**33.3**	**14:37**	....	....	....	....	....	....	....	....	....
	Toronto Marlies	AHL	39	12	21	33	36	....	....	....	....	....	....	....	....	....	....	....	....	....	....	....	....	....	....
2010-11	**Chicago**	**NHL**	**77**	**12**	**12**	**24**	**43**	**0**	**0**	**3**	**135**	**8.9**	**2**	**9**	**55.6**	**10:42**	**7**	**1**	**0**	**1**	**5**	**0**	**0**	**0**	**12:17**
	NHL Totals		**117**	**21**	**17**	**38**	**73**	**0**	**0**	**3**	**252**	**8.3**		**18**	**44.4**	**12:02**	**7**	**1**	**0**	**1**	**5**	**0**	**0**	**0**	**12:18**

Hockey East First All-Star Team (2009) • NCAA East First All-American Team (2009)

Traded to **Chicago** by **Toronto** with Chris Didomenico and Phillipe Paradis for Kris Versteeg and Bill Sweatt, June 30, 2010.

STAMKOS, Steven

(STAM-kohs, STEE-vehn) **T.B.**

Center. Shoots right. 6'1", 188 lbs. Born, Markham, Ont., February 7, 1990. Tampa Bay's 1st choice, 1st overall, in 2008 Entry Draft.

Season	Club	League	GP	G	A	Pts	PIM	PP	SH	GW	S	%	+/-	TF	F%	Min	GP	G	A	Pts	PIM	PP	SH	GW	Min
2005-06	Markham Waxers	Minor-ON	66	105	92	197	87	....	....	....	....	....	....	....	....	....	....	....	....	....	....	....	....	....	....
2006-07	Sarnia Sting	OHL	63	42	50	92	56	....	....	....	....	....	....	....	....	....	4	3	3	6	0	....	....	....	....
2007-08	Sarnia Sting	OHL	61	58	47	105	88	....	....	....	....	....	....	....	....	....	9	11	0	11	20	....	....	....	....
2008-09	**Tampa Bay**	**NHL**	**79**	**23**	**23**	**46**	**39**	**9**	**0**	**1**	**181**	**12.7**	**–13**	**557**	**45.4**	**14:56**	....	....	....	....	....	....	....	....	....
2009-10	**Tampa Bay**	**NHL**	**82**	***51**	**44**	**95**	**38**	**24**	**1**	**5**	**297**	**17.2**	**–2**	**1004**	**47.9**	**20:33**	....	....	....	....	....	....	....	....	....
2010-11	**Tampa Bay**	**NHL**	**82**	**45**	**46**	**91**	**74**	**17**	**0**	**8**	**272**	**16.5**	**3**	**927**	**46.5**	**20:12**	**18**	**6**	**7**	**13**	**6**	**3**	**0**	**1**	**19:43**
	NHL Totals		**243**	**119**	**113**	**232**	**151**	**50**	**1**	**14**	**750**	**15.9**		**2488**	**46.8**	**18:36**	**18**	**6**	**7**	**13**	**6**	**3**	**0**	**1**	**19:44**

OHL Second All-Star Team (2008) • Canadian Major Junior First All-Star Team (2008) • Maurice "Rocket" Richard Trophy (2010) (tied with Sidney Crosby) • NHL Second All-Star Team (2011)

Played in NHL All-Star Game (2011)

STAPLETON, Tim

(STAY-puhl-TOHN, TIHM)

Center. Shoots right. 5'9", 160 lbs. Born, La Grange, IL, July 9, 1982.

			Regular Season														Playoffs								
Season	Club	League	GP	G	A	Pts	PIM	PP	SH	GW	S	%	+/-	TF	F%	Min	GP	G	A	Pts	PIM	PP	SH	GW	Min
2000-01	Green Bay	USHL	52	7	15	22	8	....	....	....	....	....	....	....	....	....	4	1	2	3	4	....	....	....	....
2001-02	Green Bay	USHL	61	24	36	60	10	....	....	....	....	....	....	....	....	....	7	4	7	11	0	....	....	....	....
2002-03	U. Minn-Duluth	WCHA	42	14	28	42	6	....	....	....	....	....	....	....	....	....	....	....	....	....	....	....	....	....	....
2003-04	U. Minn-Duluth	WCHA	43	16	25	41	18	....	....	....	....	....	....	....	....	....	....	....	....	....	....	....	....	....	....
2004-05	U. Minn-Duluth	WCHA	38	19	20	39	6	....	....	....	....	....	....	....	....	....	....	....	....	....	....	....	....	....	....
2005-06	U. Minn-Duluth	WCHA	39	14	16	30	4	....	....	....	....	....	....	....	....	....	....	....	....	....	....	....	....	....	....
	Portland Pirates	AHL	9	0	5	5	4	....	....	....	....	....	....	....	....	....	4	0	0	0	2	....	....	....	....
2006-07	Jokerit Helsinki	Finland	56	19	29	48	24	....	....	....	....	....	....	....	....	....	10	6	4	10	8	....	....	....	....
2007-08	Jokerit Helsinki	Finland	55	29	33	62	36	....	....	....	....	....	....	....	....	....	14	*9	8	17	8	....	....	....	....
2008-09	**Toronto**	**NHL**	**4**	**1**	**0**	**1**	**0**	**0**	**0**	**0**	**9**	**11.1**	**–3**	**5**	**20.0**	**15:06**	....	....	....	....	....	....	....	....	....
	Toronto Marlies	AHL	70	28	51	79	26	....	....	....	....	....	....	....	....	....	6	2	0	2	2	....	....	....	....
2009-10	**Atlanta**	**NHL**	**6**	**2**	**0**	**2**	**2**	**1**	**0**	**0**	**6**	**33.3**	**1**	**36**	**61.1**	**11:53**	....	....	....	....	....	....	....	....	....
	Chicago Wolves	AHL	73	30	29	59	18	....	....	....	....	....	....	....	....	....	14	4	9	13	12	....	....	....	....
2010-11	San Antonio	AHL	20	8	7	15	2	....	....	....	....	....	....	....	....	....	....	....	....	....	....	....	....	....	....
	Atlanta	**NHL**	**45**	**5**	**2**	**7**	**12**	**1**	**0**	**1**	**44**	**11.4**	**–10**	**225**	**48.4**	**11:07**	....	....	....	....	....	....	....	....	....
	Chicago Wolves	AHL	4	1	3	4	2	....	....	....	....	....	....	....	....	....	....	....	....	....	....	....	....	....	....
	NHL Totals		**55**	**8**	**2**	**10**	**14**	**2**	**0**	**1**	**59**	**13.6**		**266**	**49.6**	**11:29**	....	....	....	....	....	....	....	....	....

Signed as a free agent by **Toronto**, June 6, 2008. Traded to **Atlanta** by **Toronto** with Pavel Kubina for Garnet Exelby and Colin Stuart, July 1, 2009. Signed to a PTO (professional tryout) contract by **San Antonio** (AHL), September 28, 2010.

STASTNY, Paul

(STAS-nee, PAWL) **COL**

Center. Shoots left. 6', 205 lbs. Born, Quebec City, Que., December 27, 1985. Colorado's 2nd choice, 44th overall, in 2005 Entry Draft.

			Regular Season														Playoffs								
Season	Club	League	GP	G	A	Pts	PIM	PP	SH	GW	S	%	+/-	TF	F%	Min	GP	G	A	Pts	PIM	PP	SH	GW	Min
2003-04	River City Lancers	USHL	56	30	*47	77	46	....	....	....	....	....	....	....	....	....	3	1	2	3	0	....	....	....	....
2004-05	U. of Denver	WCHA	42	17	28	45	30	....	....	....	....	....	....	....	....	....	....	....	....	....	....	....	....	....	....
2005-06	U. of Denver	WCHA	39	19	34	53	79	....	....	....	....	....	....	....	....	....	....	....	....	....	....	....	....	....	....
2006-07	**Colorado**	**NHL**	**82**	**28**	**50**	**78**	**42**	**11**	**0**	**6**	**185**	**15.1**	**4**	**1226**	**48.5**	**18:10**	....	....	....	....	....	....	....	....	....
2007-08	**Colorado**	**NHL**	**66**	**24**	**47**	**71**	**24**	**3**	**0**	**4**	**138**	**17.4**	**22**	**1101**	**51.0**	**21:05**	**9**	**2**	**1**	**3**	**6**	**0**	**0**	**1**	**19:56**
2008-09	**Colorado**	**NHL**	**45**	**11**	**25**	**36**	**22**	**7**	**0**	**2**	**118**	**9.3**	**–9**	**850**	**51.8**	**21:14**	....	....	....	....	....	....	....	....	....
2009-10	**Colorado**	**NHL**	**81**	**20**	**59**	**79**	**50**	**9**	**0**	**2**	**199**	**10.1**	**2**	**1703**	**50.0**	**21:24**	**6**	**1**	**4**	**5**	**4**	**1**	**0**	**0**	**20:23**
	United States	Olympics	6	1	2	3	0	....	....	....	....	....	....	....	....	....	....	....	....	....	....	....	....	....	....
2010-11	**Colorado**	**NHL**	**74**	**22**	**35**	**57**	**56**	**4**	**1**	**3**	**181**	**12.2**	**–7**	**1524**	**53.2**	**19:44**	....	....	....	....	....	....	....	....	....
	NHL Totals		**348**	**105**	**216**	**321**	**194**	**34**	**1**	**17**	**821**	**12.8**		**6404**	**50.8**	**20:12**	**15**	**3**	**5**	**8**	**10**	**1**	**0**	**1**	**20:06**

WCHA All-Rookie Team (2005) • WCHA Rookie of the Year (2005) • NCAA Championship All-Tournament Team (2005) • WCHA First All-Star Team (2006) • NCAA West Second All-American Team (2006) • NHL All-Rookie Team (2007)

Played in NHL All-Star Game (2011)

STASTNY, Yan

(STAS-nee, YAHN)

Center. Shoots left. 5'10", 191 lbs. Born, Quebec City, Que., September 30, 1982. Boston's 6th choice, 259th overall, in 2002 Entry Draft.

			Regular Season														Playoffs								
Season	Club	League	GP	G	A	Pts	PIM	PP	SH	GW	S	%	+/-	TF	F%	Min	GP	G	A	Pts	PIM	PP	SH	GW	Min
99-2000	St. Louis Sting	NAHL	45	12	23	35	77	....	....	....	....	....	....	....	....	....	....	....	....	....	....	....	....	....	....
2000-01	St. Louis Jr. Blues	CSJHL	6	0	2	2	23	....	....	....	....	....	....	....	....	....	....	....	....	....	....	....	....	....	....
	Omaha Lancers	USHL	44	17	14	31	101	....	....	....	....	....	....	....	....	....	11	6	6	12	12	....	....	....	....
2001-02	U. of Notre Dame	CCHA	33	6	11	17	38	....	....	....	....	....	....	....	....	....	....	....	....	....	....	....	....	....	....
2002-03	U. of Notre Dame	CCHA	39	14	9	23	44	....	....	....	....	....	....	....	....	....	....	....	....	....	....	....	....	....	....
2003-04	Nurnberg	Germany	44	9	20	29	83	....	....	....	....	....	....	....	....	....	6	0	1	1	6	....	....	....	....
2004-05	Nurnberg	Germany	51	24	30	54	60	....	....	....	....	....	....	....	....	....	6	2	1	3	8	....	....	....	....
2005-06	**Edmonton**	**NHL**	**3**	**0**	**0**	**0**	**0**	**0**	**0**	**0**	**1**	**0.0**	**–2**	**17**	**41.2**	**6:53**	....	....	....	....	....	....	....	....	....
	Iowa Stars	AHL	51	14	17	31	42	....	....	....	....	....	....	....	....	....	....	....	....	....	....	....	....	....	....
	Boston	**NHL**	**17**	**1**	**3**	**4**	**10**	**0**	**0**	**0**	**13**	**7.7**	**–2**	**122**	**42.6**	**10:16**	....	....	....	....	....	....	....	....	....
	Providence Bruins	AHL	....	....	....	....	....	....	....	....	....	....	....	....	....	....	6	0	5	5	12	....	....	....	....
2006-07	**Boston**	**NHL**	**21**	**0**	**2**	**2**	**19**	**0**	**0**	**0**	**7**	**0.0**	**–3**	**51**	**45.1**	**7:28**	....	....	....	....	....	....	....	....	....
	Providence Bruins	AHL	11	3	9	12	12	....	....	....	....	....	....	....	....	....	....	....	....	....	....	....	....	....	....
	Peoria Rivermen	AHL	39	11	17	28	35	....	....	....	....	....	....	....	....	....	....	....	....	....	....	....	....	....	....
2007-08	**St. Louis**	**NHL**	**12**	**1**	**1**	**2**	**9**	**0**	**0**	**0**	**10**	**10.0**	**0**	**61**	**44.3**	**10:59**	....	....	....	....	....	....	....	....	....
	Peoria Rivermen	AHL	43	13	11	24	69	....	....	....	....	....	....	....	....	....	....	....	....	....	....	....	....	....	....
2008-09	**St. Louis**	**NHL**	**34**	**3**	**4**	**7**	**20**	**0**	**0**	**0**	**30**	**10.0**	**–14**	**102**	**45.1**	**12:45**	....	....	....	....	....	....	....	....	....
	Peoria Rivermen	AHL	30	12	7	19	21	....	....	....	....	....	....	....	....	....	6	2	2	4	2	....	....	....	....
2009-10	**St. Louis**	**NHL**	**4**	**1**	**0**	**1**	**0**	**0**	**0**	**0**	**7**	**14.3**	**1**	**15**	**60.0**	**9:30**	....	....	....	....	....	....	....	....	....
	Peoria Rivermen	AHL	49	10	17	27	51	....	....	....	....	....	....	....	....	....	....	....	....	....	....	....	....	....	....
	Manitoba Moose	AHL	16	2	4	6	18	....	....	....	....	....	....	....	....	....	6	2	2	4	8	....	....	....	....
2010-11	CSKA Moscow	Rus-KHL	49	5	7	12	52	....	....	....	....	....	....	....	....	....	....	....	....	....	....	....	....	....	....
	NHL Totals		**91**	**6**	**10**	**16**	**58**	**0**	**0**	**0**	**68**	**8.8**		**368**	**44.6**	**10:30**	....	....	....	....	....	....	....	....	....

Signed as a free agent by **Nurnberg** (Germany), September 18, 2003. Traded to **Edmonton** by **Boston** for Boston's 4th round choice (previously acquired, later traded to San Jose - San Jose selected James Delory) in 2006 Entry Draft, August 30, 2005. Traded to **Boston** by **Edmonton** with Marty Reasoner and Edmonton's 2nd round choice (Milan Lucic) in 2006 Entry Draft for Sergei Samsonov, March 9, 2006. Traded to **St. Louis** by **Boston** for St. Louis' 5th round choice (Denis Reul) in 2007 Entry Draft, January 16, 2006. Traded to **Vancouver** by **St. Louis** for Pierre-Cedric Labrie, March 3, 2010. Signed as a free agent by **CSKA Moscow** (Russia-KHL), June 29, 2010.

STAUBITZ, Brad

(STAW-bihtz, BRAD) **MIN**

Right wing. Shoots right. 6'1", 205 lbs. Born, Bright's Grove, Ont., July 28, 1984.

			Regular Season														Playoffs								
Season	Club	League	GP	G	A	Pts	PIM	PP	SH	GW	S	%	+/-	TF	F%	Min	GP	G	A	Pts	PIM	PP	SH	GW	Min
2001-02	Sault Ste. Marie	OHL	45	0	3	3	46	....	....	....	....	....	....	....	....	....	3	0	0	0	2	....	....	....	....
2002-03	Sault Ste. Marie	OHL	55	2	6	8	116	....	....	....	....	....	....	....	....	....	4	0	0	0	7	....	....	....	....
2003-04	Sault Ste. Marie	OHL	66	6	18	24	140	....	....	....	....	....	....	....	....	....	....	....	....	....	....	....	....	....	....
2004-05	Sault Ste. Marie	OHL	40	2	11	13	101	....	....	....	....	....	....	....	....	....	....	....	....	....	....	....	....	....	....
	Ottawa 67's	OHL	30	5	8	13	80	....	....	....	....	....	....	....	....	....	21	4	16	20	70	....	....	....	....
2005-06	Cleveland Barons	AHL	71	0	6	6	245	....	....	....	....	....	....	....	....	....	....	....	....	....	....	....	....	....	....
2006-07	Worcester Sharks	AHL	51	1	4	5	137	....	....	....	....	....	....	....	....	....	5	0	0	0	13	....	....	....	....
2007-08	Worcester Sharks	AHL	73	6	14	20	195	....	....	....	....	....	....	....	....	....	....	....	....	....	....	....	....	....	....
2008-09	**San Jose**	**NHL**	**35**	**1**	**2**	**3**	**76**	**0**	**0**	**1**	**22**	**4.5**	**0**	**2**	**0.0**	**6:13**	....	....	....	....	....	....	....	....	....
	Worcester Sharks	AHL	38	0	5	5	130	....	....	....	....	....	....	....	....	....	10	0	2	2	15	....	....	....	....
2009-10	**San Jose**	**NHL**	**47**	**3**	**3**	**6**	**110**	**0**	**0**	**1**	**24**	**12.5**	**0**	**4**	**0.0**	**6:13**	....	....	....	....	....	....	....	....	....
2010-11	**Minnesota**	**NHL**	**71**	**4**	**5**	**9**	**173**	**0**	**0**	**1**	**29**	**13.8**	**–5**	**4**	**0.0**	**6:31**	....	....	....	....	....	....	....	....	....
	NHL Totals		**153**	**8**	**10**	**18**	**359**	**0**	**0**	**3**	**75**	**10.7**		**10**	**0.0**	**6:21**	....	....	....	....	....	....	....	....	....

Signed as a free agent by **San Jose**, September 19, 2005. Traded to **Minnesota** by **San Jose** for Minnesota's 5th round choice (Freddie Hamiton) in 2010 Entry Draft, June 21, 2010.

STECKEL, David

(STEH-kuhl, DAY-vihd) **N.J.**

Center. Shoots left. 6'5", 215 lbs. Born, Milwaukee, WI, March 15, 1982. Los Angeles' 2nd choice, 30th overall, in 2001 Entry Draft.

			Regular Season														Playoffs								
Season	Club	League	GP	G	A	Pts	PIM	PP	SH	GW	S	%	+/-	TF	F%	Min	GP	G	A	Pts	PIM	PP	SH	GW	Min
1998-99	USNTDP	USHL	2	0	0	0	2	....	....	....	....	....	....	....	....	....	....	....	....	....	....	....	....	....	....
	USNTDP	NAHL	51	3	14	17	18	....	....	....	....	....	....	....	....	....	....	....	....	....	....	....	....	....	....
99-2000	USNTDP	U-18	6	2	5	7	14	....	....	....	....	....	....	....	....	....	....	....	....	....	....	....	....	....	....
	USNTDP	USHL	52	13	13	26	94	....	....	....	....	....	....	....	....	....	....	....	....	....	....	....	....	....	....
2000-01	Ohio State	CCHA	33	17	18	35	80	....	....	....	....	....	....	....	....	....	....	....	....	....	....	....	....	....	....
2001-02	Ohio State	CCHA	36	6	16	22	75	....	....	....	....	....	....	....	....	....	....	....	....	....	....	....	....	....	....
2002-03	Ohio State	CCHA	36	10	8	18	50	....	....	....	....	....	....	....	....	....	....	....	....	....	....	....	....	....	....
2003-04	Ohio State	CCHA	41	17	13	30	44	....	....	....	....	....	....	....	....	....	....	....	....	....	....	....	....	....	....
2004-05	Manchester	AHL	63	10	7	17	26	....	....	....	....	....	....	....	....	....	6	1	1	2	4	....	....	....	....
2005-06	**Washington**	**NHL**	**7**	**0**	**0**	**0**	**0**	**0**	**0**	**0**	**6**	**0.0**	**1**	**48**	**35.4**	**7:39**	....	....	....	....	....	....	....	....	....
	Hershey Bears	AHL	74	14	20	34	58	....	....	....	....	....	....	....	....	....	21	10	5	15	20	....	....	....	....
2006-07	**Washington**	**NHL**	**5**	**0**	**0**	**0**	**2**	**0**	**0**	**0**	**4**	**0.0**	**–2**	**43**	**65.1**	**12:26**	....	....	....	....	....	....	....	....	....
	Hershey Bears	AHL	71	30	31	61	46	....	....	....	....	....	....	....	....	....	19	6	9	15	16	....	....	....	....
2007-08	**Washington**	**NHL**	**67**	**5**	**7**	**12**	**34**	**0**	**0**	**1**	**66**	**7.6**	**1**	**900**	**56.3**	**13:34**	**7**	**1**	**1**	**2**	**4**	**0**	**0**	**0**	**14:23**
2008-09	**Washington**	**NHL**	**76**	**8**	**11**	**19**	**34**	**0**	**2**	**1**	**103**	**7.8**	**2**	**886**	**57.9**	**13:49**	**14**	**3**	**2**	**5**	**4**	**0**	**0**	**1**	**16:03**
2009-10	**Washington**	**NHL**	**79**	**5**	**11**	**16**	**19**	**1**	**0**	**1**	**90**	**5.6**	**4**	**1076**	**59.2**	**12:24**	**3**	**0**	**0**	**0**	**0**	**0**	**0**	**0**	**10:28**

Season	Club	League	GP	G	A	Pts	PIM	PP	SH	GW	S	%	+/-	TF	F%	Min	GP	G	A	Pts	PIM	PP	SH	GW	Min
			Regular Season														Playoffs								
2010-11	**Washington**	**NHL**	**57**	**5**	**6**	**11**	**24**	**0**	**1**	**1**	**61**	**8.2**	**–3**	**670**	**63.7**	**11:34**	....	....	....	....	....	....	....	....	....
	New Jersey	**NHL**	**18**	**1**	**0**	**1**	**2**	**0**	**0**	**0**	**18**	**5.6**	**–3**	**150**	**56.0**	**12:50**	....	....	....	....	....	....	....	....	....
	NHL Totals		**309**	**24**	**35**	**59**	**115**	**1**	**3**	**4**	**348**	**6.9**		**3773**	**58.7**	**12:46**	**24**	**4**	**3**	**7**	**8**	**0**	**0**	**1**	**14:52**

CCHA All-Rookie Team (2001)

Signed as a free agent by **Washington**, August 25, 2005. Traded to **New Jersey** by **Washington** with Washington's 2nd round choice in 2012 Entry Draft for Jason Arnott, February 28, 2011.

STEEN, Alex

(STEEN, AL-ehx) **ST.L.**

Center. Shoots left. 6'1", 200 lbs. Born, Winnipeg, Man., March 1, 1984. Toronto's 1st choice, 24th overall, in 2002 Entry Draft.

Season	Club	League	GP	G	A	Pts	PIM	PP	SH	GW	S	%	+/-	TF	F%	Min	GP	G	A	Pts	PIM	PP	SH	GW	Min
99-2000	V.Frolunda Jr.	Swe-Jr.	8	5	7	12	0	....	....	....	....	....	....	....	....	....	....	....	....	....	....	....	....	....	....
	V.Frolunda U18	Swe-U18	14	3	5	8	16	....	....	....	....	....	....	....	....	....	....	....	....	....	....	....	....	....	....
2000-01	V.Frolunda Jr.	Swe-Jr.	23	11	12	23	15	....	....	....	....	....	....	....	....	....	3	1	0	1	2	....	....	....	....
	V.Frolunda U18	Swe-U18	6	3	3	6	9	....	....	....	....	....	....	....	....	....	....	....	....	....	....	....	....	....	....
2001-02	V.Frolunda Jr.	Swe-Jr.	23	21	17	38	47	....	....	....	....	....	....	....	....	....	2	1	1	2	2	....	....	....	....
	V.Frolunda	Sweden	26	0	3	3	14	....	....	....	....	....	....	....	....	....	10	1	2	3	0	....	....	....	....
2002-03	V.Frolunda	Sweden	45	5	10	15	18	....	....	....	....	....	....	....	....	....	16	2	3	5	4	....	....	....	....
	V.Frolunda Jr.	Swe-Jr.	2	0	2	2	0	....	....	....	....	....	....	....	....	....	....	....	....	....	....	....	....	....	....
2003-04	V.Frolunda	Sweden	48	10	14	24	50	....	....	....	....	....	....	....	....	....	10	4	6	10	14	....	....	....	....
2004-05	MODO	Sweden	50	9	8	17	26	....	....	....	....	....	....	....	....	....	6	1	0	1	4	....	....	....	....
2005-06	**Toronto**	**NHL**	**75**	**18**	**27**	**45**	**42**	**9**	**1**	**3**	**176**	**10.2**	**–9**	**29**	**24.1**	**17:37**	....	....	....	....	....	....	....	....	....
2006-07	**Toronto**	**NHL**	**82**	**15**	**20**	**35**	**26**	**4**	**0**	**5**	**192**	**7.8**	**5**	**44**	**34.1**	**15:42**	....	....	....	....	....	....	....	....	....
2007-08	**Toronto**	**NHL**	**76**	**15**	**27**	**42**	**32**	**2**	**1**	**2**	**169**	**8.9**	**0**	**179**	**33.0**	**18:05**	....	....	....	....	....	....	....	....	....
2008-09	**Toronto**	**NHL**	**20**	**2**	**2**	**4**	**6**	**1**	**0**	**0**	**31**	**6.5**	**–4**	**82**	**52.4**	**15:38**	....	....	....	....	....	....	....	....	....
	St. Louis	**NHL**	**61**	**6**	**18**	**24**	**24**	**2**	**1**	**0**	**117**	**5.1**	**–6**	**154**	**41.6**	**16:34**	**4**	**0**	**1**	**1**	**0**	**0**	**0**	**0**	**17:47**
2009-10	**St. Louis**	**NHL**	**68**	**24**	**23**	**47**	**30**	**7**	**2**	**4**	**189**	**12.7**	**6**	**73**	**41.1**	**16:17**	....	....	....	....	....	....	....	....	....
2010-11	**St. Louis**	**NHL**	**72**	**20**	**31**	**51**	**26**	**1**	**2**	**5**	**218**	**9.2**	**–3**	**106**	**38.7**	**19:33**	....	....	....	....	....	....	....	....	....
	NHL Totals		**454**	**100**	**148**	**248**	**186**	**26**	**7**	**19**	**1092**	**9.2**		**667**	**38.8**	**17:14**	**4**	**0**	**1**	**1**	**0**	**0**	**0**	**0**	**17:47**

Traded to **St. Louis** by **Toronto** with Carlo Colaiacovo for Lee Stempniak, November 24, 2008.

STEMPNIAK, Lee

(STEHMP-nee-ak, LEE) **PHX**

Right wing. Shoots right. 6', 201 lbs. Born, Buffalo, NY, February 4, 1983. St. Louis' 7th choice, 148th overall, in 2003 Entry Draft.

Season	Club	League	GP	G	A	Pts	PIM	PP	SH	GW	S	%	+/-	TF	F%	Min	GP	G	A	Pts	PIM	PP	SH	GW	Min
2000-01	Buffalo Lightning	OPJHL	48	34	51	86	36	....	....	....	....	....	....	....	....	....	....	....	....	....	....	....	....	....	....
2001-02	Dartmouth	ECAC	32	12	9	21	8	....	....	....	....	....	....	....	....	....	....	....	....	....	....	....	....	....	....
2002-03	Dartmouth	ECAC	34	21	28	49	32	....	....	....	....	....	....	....	....	....	....	....	....	....	....	....	....	....	....
2003-04	Dartmouth	ECAC	34	16	22	38	42	....	....	....	....	....	....	....	....	....	....	....	....	....	....	....	....	....	....
2004-05	Dartmouth	ECAC	35	14	*29	43	34	....	....	....	....	....	....	....	....	....	....	....	....	....	....	....	....	....	....
2005-06	**St. Louis**	**NHL**	**57**	**14**	**13**	**27**	**22**	**5**	**0**	**2**	**100**	**14.0**	**–10**	**7**	**42.9**	**14:22**	....	....	....	....	....	....	....	....	....
	Peoria Rivermen	AHL	26	8	7	15	32	....	....	....	....	....	....	....	....	....	3	0	3	3	2	....	....	....	....
2006-07	**St. Louis**	**NHL**	**82**	**27**	**25**	**52**	**33**	**8**	**0**	**4**	**166**	**16.3**	**–2**	**7**	**14.3**	**14:43**	....	....	....	....	....	....	....	....	....
2007-08	**St. Louis**	**NHL**	**80**	**13**	**25**	**38**	**40**	**3**	**0**	**2**	**162**	**8.0**	**0**	**11**	**36.4**	**15:53**	....	....	....	....	....	....	....	....	....
2008-09	**St. Louis**	**NHL**	**14**	**3**	**10**	**13**	**2**	**0**	**0**	**1**	**43**	**7.0**	**–3**	**1**	**0.0**	**19:28**	....	....	....	....	....	....	....	....	....
	Toronto	**NHL**	**61**	**11**	**20**	**31**	**31**	**3**	**0**	**0**	**128**	**8.6**	**–9**	**12**	**33.3**	**15:52**	....	....	....	....	....	....	....	....	....
2009-10	**Toronto**	**NHL**	**62**	**14**	**16**	**30**	**18**	**5**	**1**	**1**	**164**	**8.5**	**–10**	**25**	**36.0**	**17:53**	....	....	....	....	....	....	....	....	....
	Phoenix	**NHL**	**18**	**14**	**4**	**18**	**8**	**4**	**0**	**1**	**48**	**29.2**	**10**	**14**	**57.1**	**15:22**	**7**	**0**	**2**	**2**	**0**	**0**	**0**	**0**	**14:28**
2010-11	**Phoenix**	**NHL**	**82**	**19**	**19**	**38**	**19**	**2**	**0**	**0**	**199**	**9.5**	**4**	**45**	**40.0**	**15:15**	**4**	**0**	**0**	**0**	**0**	**0**	**0**	**0**	**12:13**
	NHL Totals		**456**	**115**	**132**	**247**	**173**	**30**	**1**	**11**	**1010**	**11.4**		**122**	**38.5**	**15:44**	**11**	**0**	**2**	**2**	**0**	**0**	**0**	**0**	**13:39**

ECAC All-Rookie Team (2002) • ECAC First All-Star Team (2004, 2005) • NCAA East First All-American Team (2004) • NCAA East Second All-American Team (2005)

Traded to **Toronto** by **St. Louis** for Alex Steen and Carlo Colaiacovo, November 24, 2008. Traded to **Phoenix** by **Toronto** for Matt Jones and Phoenix's 4th (later traded to Washington – Washington selected Philipp Grubauer) and 7th (later traded to Edmonton – Edmonton selected Kellen Jones) round choices in 2010 Entry Draft, March 3, 2010.

STEPAN, Derek

(STEH-pan, DAIR-ihk) **NYR**

Center. Shoots right. 6', 182 lbs. Born, Hastings, MN, June 18, 1990. NY Rangers' 2nd choice, 51st overall, in 2008 Entry Draft.

Season	Club	League	GP	G	A	Pts	PIM	PP	SH	GW	S	%	+/-	TF	F%	Min	GP	G	A	Pts	PIM	PP	SH	GW	Min
2006-07	Shat.-St. Mary's	High-MN	63	38	32	70	22	....	....	....	....	....	....	....	....	....	....	....	....	....	....	....	....	....	....
2007-08	Shat.-St. Mary's	High-MN	60	44	67	111	22	....	....	....	....	....	....	....	....	....	....	....	....	....	....	....	....	....	....
2008-09	U. of Wisconsin	WCHA	40	9	24	33	6	....	....	....	....	....	....	....	....	....	....	....	....	....	....	....	....	....	....
2009-10	U. of Wisconsin	WCHA	41	12	*42	*54	8	....	....	....	....	....	....	....	....	....	....	....	....	....	....	....	....	....	....
2010-11	**NY Rangers**	**NHL**	**82**	**21**	**24**	**45**	**20**	**3**	**0**	**3**	**166**	**12.7**	**8**	**719**	**38.5**	**16:27**	**5**	**0**	**0**	**0**	**2**	**0**	**0**	**0**	**20:29**
	NHL Totals		**82**	**21**	**24**	**45**	**20**	**3**	**0**	**3**	**166**	**12.7**		**719**	**38.5**	**16:27**	**5**	**0**	**0**	**0**	**2**	**0**	**0**	**0**	**20:30**

STERLING, Brett

(STUHR-lihng, BREHT) **ST.L.**

Left wing. Shoots left. 5'7", 175 lbs. Born, Los Angeles, CA, April 24, 1984. Atlanta's 5th choice, 145th overall, in 2003 Entry Draft.

Season	Club	League	GP	G	A	Pts	PIM	PP	SH	GW	S	%	+/-	TF	F%	Min	GP	G	A	Pts	PIM	PP	SH	GW	Min
99-2000	L.A. Jr. Kings	SCAHA	35	45	25	70	....	....	....	....	....	....	....	....	....	....	....	....	....	....	....	....	....	....	....
2000-01	USNTDP	U-17	13	....	....	....	....	....	....	....	....	....	....	....	....	....	....	....	....	....	....	....	....	....	....
	USNTDP	NAHL	47	29	15	44	72	....	....	....	....	....	....	....	....	....	....	....	....	....	....	....	....	....	....
2001-02	USNTDP	U-18	31	21	15	36	18	....	....	....	....	....	....	....	....	....	....	....	....	....	....	....	....	....	....
	USNTDP	USHL	10	6	3	9	8	....	....	....	....	....	....	....	....	....	....	....	....	....	....	....	....	....	....
	USNTDP	NAHL	9	2	1	3	10	....	....	....	....	....	....	....	....	....	....	....	....	....	....	....	....	....	....
2002-03	Colorado College	WCHA	36	27	11	38	30	....	....	....	....	....	....	....	....	....	....	....	....	....	....	....	....	....	....
2003-04	Colorado College	WCHA	30	16	12	28	40	....	....	....	....	....	....	....	....	....	....	....	....	....	....	....	....	....	....
2004-05	Colorado College	WCHA	43	*34	29	63	74	....	....	....	....	....	....	....	....	....	....	....	....	....	....	....	....	....	....
2005-06	Colorado College	WCHA	42	31	24	55	66	....	....	....	....	....	....	....	....	....	....	....	....	....	....	....	....	....	....
2006-07	Chicago Wolves	AHL	77	*55	42	97	96	....	....	....	....	....	....	....	....	....	15	7	5	12	24	....	....	....	....
2007-08	**Atlanta**	**NHL**	**13**	**1**	**2**	**3**	**14**	**0**	**0**	**0**	**14**	**7.1**	**–2**	**3**	**66.7**	**12:24**	....	....	....	....	....	....	....	....	....
	Chicago Wolves	AHL	70	38	33	71	116	....	....	....	....	....	....	....	....	....	16	4	5	9	18	....	....	....	....
2008-09	**Atlanta**	**NHL**	**6**	**1**	**0**	**1**	**2**	**0**	**0**	**0**	**11**	**9.1**	**–3**	**0**	**0.0**	**13:53**	....	....	....	....	....	....	....	....	....
	Chicago Wolves	AHL	52	16	23	39	84	....	....	....	....	....	....	....	....	....	....	....	....	....	....	....	....	....	....
2009-10	Chicago Wolves	AHL	55	34	22	56	38	....	....	....	....	....	....	....	....	....	9	4	6	10	4	....	....	....	....
2010-11	**Pittsburgh**	**NHL**	**7**	**3**	**2**	**5**	**16**	**1**	**0**	**0**	**14**	**21.4**	**1**	**3**	**66.7**	**15:07**	....	....	....	....	....	....	....	....	....
	Wilkes-Barre	AHL	65	27	26	53	88	....	....	....	....	....	....	....	....	....	12	2	4	6	10	....	....	....	....
	NHL Totals		**26**	**5**	**4**	**9**	**32**	**1**	**0**	**0**	**39**	**12.8**		**6**	**66.7**	**13:28**									

WCHA All-Rookie Team (2003) • WCHA First All-Star Team (2005, 2006) • NCAA West First All-American Team (2005, 2006) • AHL All-Rookie Team (2007) • AHL First All-Star Team (2007) • Dudley "Red" Garrett Memorial Award (AHL - Rookie of the Year) (2007) • Willie Marshall Award (AHL - Top Goal-scorer) (2007) • AHL Second All-Star Team (2008)

Traded to **San Jose** by **Atlanta** with Michael Vernace and Atlanta's 7th round choice (Lee Moffie) in 2010 Entry Draft for future considerations, June 23, 2010. Signed as a free agent by **Pittsburgh**, July 3, 2010. Signed as a free agent by **St. Louis**, July 4, 2011.

STEWART, Anthony

(STEW-ahrt, AN-thu-nee) **CAR**

Right wing. Shoots right. 6'3", 230 lbs. Born, LaSalle, Que., January 5, 1985. Florida's 2nd choice, 25th overall, in 2003 Entry Draft.

Season	Club	League	GP	G	A	Pts	PIM	PP	SH	GW	S	%	+/-	TF	F%	Min	GP	G	A	Pts	PIM	PP	SH	GW	Min
2000-01	North York	MTHL	34	30	70	100	....	....	....	....	....	....	....	....	....	....	....	....	....	....	....	....	....	....	....
	St. Mike's B's	OPJHL	5	0	2	2	0	....	....	....	....	....	....	....	....	....	....	....	....	....	....	....	....	....	....
2001-02	Kingston	OHL	65	19	24	43	12	....	....	....	....	....	....	....	....	....	1	0	0	0	0	....	....	....	....
2002-03	Kingston	OHL	68	32	38	70	47	....	....	....	....	....	....	....	....	....	....	....	....	....	....	....	....	....	....
2003-04	Kingston	OHL	53	35	23	58	76	....	....	....	....	....	....	....	....	....	5	3	4	7	7	....	....	....	....
2004-05	Kingston	OHL	62	32	35	67	70	....	....	....	....	....	....	....	....	....	....	....	....	....	....	....	....	....	....
	San Antonio	AHL	10	1	2	3	14	....	....	....	....	....	....	....	....	....	....	....	....	....	....	....	....	....	....
2005-06	**Florida**	**NHL**	**10**	**2**	**1**	**3**	**2**	**1**	**0**	**0**	**16**	**12.5**	**2**	**1**	**0.0**	**7:13**	....	....	....	....	....	....	....	....	....
	Rochester	AHL	4	2	3	5	0	....	....	....	....	....	....	....	....	....	....	....	....	....	....	....	....	....	....
2006-07	**Florida**	**NHL**	**10**	**0**	**1**	**1**	**2**	**0**	**0**	**0**	**8**	**0.0**	**1**	**0**	**0.0**	**6:51**	....	....	....	....	....	....	....	....	....
	Rochester	AHL	62	13	14	27	64	....	....	....	....	....	....	....	....	....	6	2	0	2	2	....	....	....	....
2007-08	**Florida**	**NHL**	**26**	**0**	**1**	**1**	**0**	**0**	**0**	**0**	**21**	**0.0**	**–1**	**0**	**0.0**	**6:08**	....	....	....	....	....	....	....	....	....
	Rochester	AHL	54	13	18	31	61	....	....	....	....	....	....	....	....	....	....	....	....	....	....	....	....	....	....
2008-09	**Florida**	**NHL**	**59**	**2**	**5**	**7**	**34**	**0**	**0**	**0**	**56**	**3.6**	**–6**	**3**	**33.3**	**7:39**	....	....	....	....	....	....	....	....	....

			Regular Season														Playoffs								
Season	Club	League	GP	G	A	Pts	PIM	PP	SH	GW	S	%	+/-	TF	F%	Min	GP	G	A	Pts	PIM	PP	SH	GW	Min
2009-10	Chicago Wolves	AHL	77	12	19	31	67	....	....	....	....	....	....	....	....	....	13	9	3	12	6	....	....	....	....
2010-11	**Atlanta**	**NHL**	80	14	25	39	55	5	0	2	141	9.9	–10	18	38.9	14:58	....	....	....	....	....	....	....	....	....
	NHL Totals		185	18	33	51	93	6	0	2	242	7.4		22	36.4	10:32	....	....	....	....	....	....	....	....	....

• Missed remainder of 2005-06 due to wrist injury vs. Carolina, November 11, 2005. Signed as a free agent by **Atlanta**, July 13, 2009. Signed as a free agent by **Carolina**, July 2, 2011.

STEWART, Chris
(STEW-ahrt, KRIHS) **ST.L.**

Right wing. Shoots right. 6'2", 228 lbs. Born, Toronto, Ont., October 30, 1987. Colorado's 1st choice, 18th overall, in 2006 Entry Draft.

Season	Club	League	GP	G	A	Pts	PIM	PP	SH	GW	S	%	+/-	TF	F%	Min	GP	G	A	Pts	PIM	PP	SH	GW	Min
2004-05	Kingston	OHL	64	18	12	30	45	....	....	....	....	....	....	....	....	....	....	....	....	....	....	....	....	....	....
2005-06	Kingston	OHL	62	37	50	87	118	....	....	....	....	....	....	....	....	....	6	2	0	2	13	....	....	....	....
2006-07	Kingston	OHL	61	36	46	82	108	....	....	....	....	....	....	....	....	....	5	4	2	6	6	....	....	....	....
	Albany River Rats	AHL	5	1	2	3	2	....	....	....	....	....	....	....	....	....	1	0	0	0	0	....	....	....	....
2007-08	Lake Erie	AHL	77	25	19	44	93	....	....	....	....	....	....	....	....	....	....	....	....	....	....	....	....	....	....
2008-09	**Colorado**	**NHL**	53	11	8	19	54	1	1	1	98	11.2	–18	21	33.3	12:20	....	....	....	....	....	....	....	....	....
	Lake Erie	AHL	19	5	6	11	23	....	....	....	....	....	....	....	....	....	....	....	....	....	....	....	....	....	....
2009-10	**Colorado**	**NHL**	77	28	36	64	73	3	0	5	221	12.7	4	8	37.5	16:42	6	3	0	3	4	0	0	1	18:00
	Lake Erie	AHL	2	0	0	0	2	....	....	....	....	....	....	....	....	....	....	....	....	....	....	....	....	....	....
2010-11	**Colorado**	**NHL**	36	13	17	30	38	5	0	3	95	13.7	–10	6	33.3	16:56	....	....	....	....	....	....	....	....	....
	St. Louis	**NHL**	26	15	8	23	15	7	0	2	67	22.4	4	26	42.3	18:16	....	....	....	....	....	....	....	....	....
	NHL Totals		192	67	69	136	180	16	1	11	481	13.9		61	37.7	15:45	6	3	0	3	4	0	0	1	18:00

Traded to **St. Louis** by **Colorado** with Kevin Shattenkirk and Colorado's 2nd round choice (Ty Rattie) in 2011 Entry Draft for Erik Johnson, Jay McClement and St. Louis's 1st round choice (Duncan Siemens) in 2011 Entry Draft, February 19, 2011.

STEWART, Greg
(STEW-ahrt, GREHG)

Left wing. Shoots left. 6'2", 202 lbs. Born, Kitchener, Ont., May 21, 1986. Montreal's 7th choice, 246th overall, in 2004 Entry Draft.

Season	Club	League	GP	G	A	Pts	PIM	PP	SH	GW	S	%	+/-	TF	F%	Min	GP	G	A	Pts	PIM	PP	SH	GW	Min
2003-04	Peterborough	OHL	58	4	6	10	76	....	....	....	....	....	....	....	....	....	....	....	....	....	....	....	....	....	....
2004-05	Peterborough	OHL	68	16	18	34	111	....	....	....	....	....	....	....	....	....	14	3	3	6	20	....	....	....	....
2005-06	Peterborough	OHL	60	24	15	39	83	....	....	....	....	....	....	....	....	....	19	1	6	7	30	....	....	....	....
2006-07	Cincinnati	ECHL	62	8	15	23	126	....	....	....	....	....	....	....	....	....	10	5	2	7	36	....	....	....	....
2007-08	**Montreal**	**NHL**	1	0	0	0	5	0	0	0	2	0.0	0	0	0.0	11:26	....	....	....	....	....	....	....	....	....
	Hamilton	AHL	69	10	7	17	137	....	....	....	....	....	....	....	....	....	....	....	....	....	....	....	....	....	....
2008-09	**Montreal**	**NHL**	20	0	1	1	32	0	0	0	16	0.0	–4	1	100.0	8:37	2	0	0	0	2	0	0	0	8:31
	Hamilton	AHL	51	7	10	17	170	....	....	....	....	....	....	....	....	....	2	1	0	1	9	....	....	....	....
2009-10	**Montreal**	**NHL**	5	0	0	0	11	0	0	0	4	0.0	–3	1	0.0	4:12	....	....	....	....	....	....	....	....	....
	Hamilton	AHL	45	5	5	10	90	....	....	....	....	....	....	....	....	....	....	....	....	....	....	....	....	....	....
	Chicago Wolves	AHL	9	1	0	1	39	....	....	....	....	....	....	....	....	....	10	0	1	1	20	....	....	....	....
2010-11	Oklahoma City	AHL	74	6	10	16	108	....	....	....	....	....	....	....	....	....	6	0	2	2	21	....	....	....	....
	NHL Totals		26	0	1	1	48	0	0	0	22	0.0		2	50.0	7:52	2	0	0	0	2	0	0	0	8:31

• Reassigned to **Chicago** (AHL) by **Montreal**, March 10, 2010. Signed as a free agent by **Edmonton**, July 16, 2010.

STILLMAN, Cory
(STIHL-mahn, KOHR-ee)

Left wing. Shoots left. 6', 200 lbs. Born, Peterborough, Ont., December 20, 1973. Calgary's 1st choice, 6th overall, in 1992 Entry Draft.

Season	Club	League	GP	G	A	Pts	PIM	PP	SH	GW	S	%	+/-	TF	F%	Min	GP	G	A	Pts	PIM	PP	SH	GW	Min
1989-90	Peterborough	ON-Jr.B	41	30	*54	84	76	....	....	....	....	....	....	....	....	....	....	....	....	....	....	....	....	....	....
1990-91	Windsor Spitfires	OHL	64	31	70	101	31	....	....	....	....	....	....	....	....	....	11	3	6	9	8	....	....	....	....
1991-92	Windsor Spitfires	OHL	53	29	61	90	59	....	....	....	....	....	....	....	....	....	7	2	4	6	8	....	....	....	....
1992-93	Peterborough	OHL	61	25	55	80	55	....	....	....	....	....	....	....	....	....	18	3	8	11	18	....	....	....	....
1993-94	Saint John Flames	AHL	79	35	48	83	52	....	....	....	....	....	....	....	....	....	7	2	4	6	16	....	....	....	....
1994-95	Saint John Flames	AHL	63	28	53	81	70	....	....	....	....	....	....	....	....	....	5	0	2	2	2	....	....	....	....
	Calgary	**NHL**	10	0	2	2	2	0	0	0	7	0.0	1	....	....	....	....	....	....	....	....	....	....	....	....
1995-96	**Calgary**	**NHL**	74	16	19	35	41	4	1	3	132	12.1	–5	....	....	....	2	1	1	2	0	0	0	0	
1996-97	**Calgary**	**NHL**	58	6	20	26	14	2	0	0	112	5.4	–6	....	....	....	....	....	....	....	....	....	....	....	....
1997-98	**Calgary**	**NHL**	72	27	22	49	40	9	4	1	178	15.2	–9	....	....	....	....	....	....	....	....	....	....	....	....
1998-99	**Calgary**	**NHL**	76	27	30	57	38	9	3	5	175	15.4	7	535	46.5	16:19	....	....	....	....	....	....	....	....	....
99-2000	**Calgary**	**NHL**	37	12	9	21	12	6	0	3	59	20.3	–9	283	54.4	17:45	....	....	....	....	....	....	....	....	....
2000-01	**Calgary**	**NHL**	66	21	24	45	45	7	0	4	148	14.2	–6	346	43.9	18:50	....	....	....	....	....	....	....	....	....
	St. Louis	**NHL**	12	3	4	7	6	3	0	0	26	11.5	–2	36	61.1	18:37	15	3	5	8	8	1	0	1	14:58
2001-02	**St. Louis**	**NHL**	80	23	22	45	36	6	0	4	140	16.4	8	196	46.4	15:03	9	0	2	2	2	0	0	0	12:46
2002-03	**St. Louis**	**NHL**	79	24	43	67	56	6	0	4	157	15.3	12	266	41.7	18:20	6	2	2	4	2	2	0	1	18:05
2003-04♦	**Tampa Bay**	**NHL**	81	25	55	80	36	11	1	6	178	14.0	18	38	31.6	19:32	21	2	5	7	15	0	1	0	17:22
2004-05			DID NOT PLAY																						
2005-06♦	**Carolina**	**NHL**	72	21	55	76	32	10	0	3	177	11.9	–9	11	27.3	18:40	25	9	17	26	14	4	0	3	18:42
2006-07	**Carolina**	**NHL**	43	5	22	27	24	1	0	0	85	5.9	–8	7	28.6	17:25	....	....	....	....	....	....	....	....	....
2007-08	**Carolina**	**NHL**	55	21	25	46	14	10	0	6	124	16.9	–7	11	54.6	19:53	....	....	....	....	....	....	....	....	....
	Ottawa	**NHL**	24	3	16	19	10	1	0	0	42	7.1	–8	6	16.7	16:54	4	2	0	2	2	1	0	0	18:26
2008-09	**Florida**	**NHL**	63	17	32	49	37	8	0	2	115	14.8	1	30	36.7	16:35	....	....	....	....	....	....	....	....	....
2009-10	**Florida**	**NHL**	58	15	22	37	22	3	0	4	126	11.9	–3	29	62.1	17:34	....	....	....	....	....	....	....	....	....
2010-11	**Florida**	**NHL**	44	7	16	23	20	1	0	1	81	8.6	3	25	44.0	15:56	....	....	....	....	....	....	....	....	....
	Carolina	**NHL**	21	5	11	16	4	2	0	1	35	14.3	2	12	50.0	18:58	....	....	....	....	....	....	....	....	....
	NHL Totals		1025	278	449	727	489	99	9	47	2097	13.3		1831	46.4	17:42	82	19	32	51	43	8	1	5	16:55

OHL Rookie of the Year (1991)

• Missed majority of 1999-2000 due to shoulder injury vs. Philadelphia, December 27, 1999. Traded to **St. Louis by Calgary** for Craig Conroy and St. Louis' 7th round choice (David Moss) in 2001 Entry Draft, March 13, 2001. Traded to **Tampa Bay** by **St. Louis** for Tampa Bay's 2nd round choice (David Backes) in 2003 Entry Draft, June 21, 2003. Signed as a free agent by **Carolina**, August 2, 2005. Traded to **Ottawa** by **Carolina** with Mike Commodore for Joe Corvo and Patrick Eaves, February 11, 2008. Signed as a free agent by **Florida**, July 1, 2008. Traded to **Carolina** by **Florida** for Ryan Carter and Carolina's 5th round choice (later traded to Atlanta, later traded to San Jose – San Jose selected Sean Kuraly) in 2011 Entry Draft, February 24, 2011.

STOA, Ryan
(STOH-ah, RIGH-uhn) **COL**

Center. Shoots left. 6'3", 200 lbs. Born, Bloomington, MN, April 13, 1987. Colorado's 1st choice, 34th overall, in 2005 Entry Draft.

Season	Club	League	GP	G	A	Pts	PIM	PP	SH	GW	S	%	+/-	TF	F%	Min	GP	G	A	Pts	PIM	PP	SH	GW	Min
2003-04	USNTDP	U-17	18	9	8	17		....	....	....	....	....	....	....	....	....	....	....	....	....	....	....	....	....	....
	USNTDP	NAHL	42	10	12	22	26	....	....	....	....	....	....	....	....	....	7	7	1	8	2	....	....	....	....
2004-05	USNTDP	U-18	23	4	11	15	16	....	....	....	....	....	....	....	....	....	....	....	....	....	....	....	....	....	....
	USNTDP	NAHL	15	10	13	23	20	....	....	....	....	....	....	....	....	....	....	....	....	....	....	....	....	....	....
2005-06	U. of Minnesota	WCHA	41	10	15	25	43	....	....	....	....	....	....	....	....	....	....	....	....	....	....	....	....	....	....
2006-07	U. of Minnesota	WCHA	41	12	12	24	44	....	....	....	....	....	....	....	....	....	....	....	....	....	....	....	....	....	....
2007-08	U. of Minnesota	WCHA	2	1	1	2	2	....	....	....	....	....	....	....	....	....	....	....	....	....	....	....	....	....	....
2008-09	U. of Minnesota	WCHA	36	24	22	46	76	....	....	....	....	....	....	....	....	....	....	....	....	....	....	....	....	....	....
2009-10	**Colorado**	**NHL**	12	2	1	3	0	0	0	0	26	7.7	–3	0	0.0	11:04	1	0	0	0	2	0	0	0	8:45
	Lake Erie	AHL	54	23	17	40	42	....	....	....	....	....	....	....	....	....	....	....	....	....	....	....	....	....	....
2010-11	**Colorado**	**NHL**	25	2	2	4	20	0	0	1	45	4.4	–4	5	40.0	13:21	....	....	....	....	....	....	....	....	....
	Lake Erie	AHL	48	16	17	33	55	....	....	....	....	....	....	....	....	....	7	1	0	1	4	....	....	....	....
	NHL Totals		37	4	3	7	20	0	0	1	71	5.6		5	40.0	12:36	1	0	0	0	2	0	0	0	8:45

WCHA First All-Star Team (2009) • NCAA West First All-American Team (2009)

• Missed remainder of 2007-08 due to knee injury vs. University of Michigan (CCHA), October 13, 2007.

STOLL, Jarret
(STOHL, JAIR-iht) **L.A.**

Center. Shoots right. 6'1", 210 lbs. Born, Melville, Sask., June 25, 1982. Edmonton's 3rd choice, 36th overall, in 2002 Entry Draft.

Season	Club	League	GP	G	A	Pts	PIM	PP	SH	GW	S	%	+/-	TF	F%	Min	GP	G	A	Pts	PIM	PP	SH	GW	Min
1997-98	Saskatoon Blazers	SMHL	44	45	44	*89	78	....	....	....	....	....	....	....	....	....	....	....	....	....	....	....	....	....	....
	Edmonton Ice	WHL	8	2	3	5	4	....	....	....	....	....	....	....	....	....	....	....	....	....	....	....	....	....	....
1998-99	Kootenay Ice	WHL	57	13	21	34	38	....	....	....	....	....	....	....	....	....	4	0	0	0	2	....	....	....	....
99-2000	Kootenay Ice	WHL	71	37	38	75	64	....	....	....	....	....	....	....	....	....	20	7	9	16	24	....	....	....	....
2000-01	Kootenay Ice	WHL	62	40	66	106	105	....	....	....	....	....	....	....	....	....	11	5	9	14	22	....	....	....	....
2001-02	Kootenay Ice	WHL	47	32	34	66	64	....	....	....	....	....	....	....	....	....	22	6	14	20	35	....	....	....	....
2002-03	**Edmonton**	**NHL**	4	0	1	1	0	0	0	0	5	0.0	–3	30	63.3	7:44	....	....	....	....	....	....	....	....	....
	Hamilton	AHL	76	21	33	54	86	....	....	....	....	....	....	....	....	....	23	5	8	13	25	....	....	....	....
2003-04	**Edmonton**	**NHL**	68	10	11	21	42	1	1	2	107	9.3	8	1019	54.1	13:54	....	....	....	....	....	....	....	....	....
2004-05	Edmonton	AHL	66	21	17	38	92	....	....	....	....	....	....	....	....	....	....	....	....	....	....	....	....	....	....

Season	Club	League	GP	G	A	Pts	PIM	PP	SH	GW	S	%	+/-	TF	F%	Min	GP	G	A	Pts	PIM	PP	SH	GW	Min
													Regular Season								Playoffs				
2005-06	Edmonton	NHL	82	22	46	68	74	11	1	4	243	9.1	4	1348	56.8	18:23	24	4	6	10	24	2	0	1	17:06
2006-07	Edmonton	NHL	51	13	26	39	48	6	1	2	115	11.3	2	901	55.6	18:12	....	....	....	....	....				
2007-08	Edmonton	NHL	81	14	22	36	74	8	3	1	187	7.5	-23	1229	55.1	17:56	....	....	....	....	....				
2008-09	Los Angeles	NHL	74	18	23	41	68	10	0	1	155	11.6	-7	1047	57.2	17:05	....	....	....	....	....				
2009-10	Los Angeles	NHL	73	16	31	47	40	4	0	4	164	9.8	13	1105	56.0	17:25	6	1	0	1	4	1	0	0	15:51
2010-11	Los Angeles	NHL	82	20	23	43	42	4	1	5	187	10.7	-6	1310	57.5	17:10	5	0	3	3	0	0	0	0	18:44
	NHL Totals		**515**	**113**	**183**	**296**	**388**	**44**	**7**	**19**	**1163**	**9.7**		**7989**	**56.1**	**17:06**	**35**	**5**	**9**	**14**	**28**	**3**	**0**	**1**	**17:07**

• Re-entered NHL Entry Draft. Originally Calgary's 3rd choice, 46th overall, in 2000 Entry Draft.
WHL East First All-Star Team (2001) • Canadian Major Junior First All-Star Team (2001) • WHL West First All-Star Team (2002)
Traded to **Los Angeles** by **Edmonton** with Matt Greene for Lubomir Visnovsky, June 29, 2008.

STONE, Ryan

Center. Shoots left. 6'2", 207 lbs.   Born, Calgary, Alta., March 20, 1985. Pittsburgh's 2nd choice, 32nd overall, in 2003 Entry Draft.   (STOHN, RIGH-uhn)

Season	Club	League	GP	G	A	Pts	PIM	PP	SH	GW	S	%	+/-	TF	F%	Min	GP	G	A	Pts	PIM
2000-01	Cgy. North Stars	AMHL	34	37	28	55	90										19	0	3	3	39
2001-02	Brandon	WHL	65	11	27	38	128										12	4	2	6	20
2002-03	Brandon	WHL	54	14	31	45	158										11	1	3	4	24
2003-04	Brandon	WHL	50	20	38	58	125										24	4	*23	27	48
2004-05	Brandon	WHL	70	33	*66	99	127										11	4	7	11	12
2005-06	Wilkes-Barre	AHL	75	14	22	36	109										10	2	3	5	21
2006-07	Wilkes-Barre	AHL	41	7	26	33	86														
2007-08	**Pittsburgh**	**NHL**	6	0	1	1	5	0	0	0	3	0.0	-1	5	60.0	6:25					
	Wilkes-Barre	AHL	65	11	28	39	129										23	5	12	17	33
2008-09	**Pittsburgh**	**NHL**	2	0	0	0	2	0	0	0	5	0.0	1	0	0.0	10:20					
	Wilkes-Barre	AHL	38	9	19	28	53														
	Springfield	AHL	39	8	21	29	64														
2009-10	**Edmonton**	**NHL**	27	0	6	6	48	0	0	0	25	0.0	2	21	33.3	10:52					
2010-11	Abbotsford Heat	AHL	51	11	14	25	72														
	NHL Totals		**35**	**0**	**7**	**7**	**55**	**0**	**0**	**0**	**33**	**0.0**		**26**	**38.5**	**10:04**					

WHL East First All-Star Team (2005)
Traded to **Edmonton** by **Pittsburgh** with Dany Sabourin and Pittsburgh's 4th round choice (Tobias Rieder) in 2011 Entry Draft for Mathieu Garon, January 17, 2009. • Missed majority of 2009-10 due to knee inury vs. Vancouver (October 19, 2009) and reinjured vs. Pittsburgh (January 14, 2010). Signed as a free agent by **Calgary**, July 7, 2010.

STONER, Clayton   MIN

Defense. Shoots left. 6'3", 220 lbs.   Born, Port McNeill, B.C., February 19, 1985. Minnesota's 4th choice, 79th overall, in 2004 Entry Draft.   (STOH-nuhr, KLAY-tuhn)

Season	Club	League	GP	G	A	Pts	PIM	PP	SH	GW	S	%	+/-	TF	F%	Min	GP	G	A	Pts	PIM
2000-01	Campbell River	VIJHL	47	4	16	20	57														
2001-02	Campbell River	VIJHL	42	12	35	47	199														
2002-03	Tri-City	WHL	58	4	12	16	85														
2003-04	Tri-City	WHL	71	7	24	31	109										11	1	1	2	8
2004-05	Tri-City	WHL	60	12	34	46	81										4	0	3	3	2
2005-06	Houston Aeros	AHL	73	6	18	24	92										3	1	1	2	7
2006-07	Houston Aeros	AHL	65	1	6	7	104														
2007-08	Houston Aeros	AHL	56	3	12	15	78														
2008-09	Houston Aeros	AHL	63	2	22	24	81										20	1	4	5	27
2009-10	**Minnesota**	**NHL**	8	0	2	2	12	0	0	0	5	0.0	1	0	0.0	13:19					
	Houston Aeros	AHL	26	3	7	10	52														
2010-11	**Minnesota**	**NHL**	57	2	7	9	96	0	0	1	40	5.0	5	0	0.0	16:52					
	NHL Totals		**65**	**2**	**9**	**11**	**108**	**0**	**0**	**1**	**45**	**4.4**		**0**	**0.0**	**16:26**					

WHL West Second All-Star Team (2005)
• Missed majority of 2009-10 due to recurring groin injury.

STORTINI, Zack   NSH

Right wing. Shoots right. 6'4", 215 lbs.   Born, Elliot Lake, Ont., September 11, 1985. Edmonton's 5th choice, 94th overall, in 2003 Entry Draft.   (stohr-TEE-nee, ZAK)

Season	Club	League	GP	G	A	Pts	PIM	PP	SH	GW	S	%	+/-	TF	F%	Min	GP	G	A	Pts	PIM
2000-01	Newmarket	OPJHL	34	3	10	13	68														
2001-02	Sudbury Wolves	OHL	65	8	6	14	187										5	1	0	1	24
2002-03	Sudbury Wolves	OHL	62	13	16	29	222														
2003-04	Sudbury Wolves	OHL	62	21	16	37	151										7	1	1	2	14
	Toronto	AHL	2	0	0	0	7										3	0	0	0	4
2004-05	Sudbury Wolves	OHL	58	13	27	40	186										12	2	5	7	27
2005-06	Iowa Stars	AHL	27	2	1	3	108														
	Milwaukee	AHL	37	0	7	7	153										17	2	0	2	19
2006-07	**Edmonton**	**NHL**	29	1	0	1	105	0	0	0	17	5.9	-7	3	100.0	7:09					
	Hamilton	AHL	47	9	6	15	195										22	3	0	3	*56
2007-08	**Edmonton**	**NHL**	66	3	9	12	201	0	0	0	38	7.9	3	7	42.9	8:10					
	Springfield	AHL	4	3	2	5	21														
2008-09	**Edmonton**	**NHL**	52	6	5	11	181	0	0	0	23	26.1	-3	11	63.6	7:17					
2009-10	**Edmonton**	**NHL**	77	4	9	13	155	1	0	1	46	8.7	3	183	47.5	9:17					
2010-11	**Edmonton**	**NHL**	32	0	4	4	76	0	0	0	16	0.0	-2	33	42.4	7:06					
	Oklahoma City	AHL	29	1	2	3	53										5	1	0	1	6
	NHL Totals		**256**	**14**	**27**	**41**	**718**	**1**	**0**	**1**	**140**	**10.0**		**237**	**48.1**	**8:05**					

Signed as a free agent by **Nashville**, July 5, 2011.

STRACHAN, Tyson   FLA

Defense. Shoots right. 6'2", 215 lbs.   Born, Melfort, Sask., October 30, 1984. Carolina's 6th choice, 137th overall, in 2003 Entry Draft.   (STRAWN, TIGH-suhn)

Season	Club	League	GP	G	A	Pts	PIM	PP	SH	GW	S	%	+/-	TF	F%	Min	GP	G	A	Pts	PIM
2001-02	Tisdale Trojans	SMHL	42	5	18	23	70														
	Melville	SJHL	2	0	0	0	0														
2002-03	Vernon Vipers	BCHL	56	6	22	28	99														
2003-04	Ohio State	CCHA	30	2	5	7	8														
2004-05	Ohio State	CCHA	31	1	4	5	32														
2005-06	Ohio State	CCHA	23	3	2	5	37														
2006-07	Ohio State	CCHA	35	7	11	18	55														
	Albany River Rats	AHL	1	0	0	0	0														
2007-08	Peoria Rivermen	AHL	34	1	2	3	61										16	0	4	4	12
	Las Vegas	ECHL	25	2	7	9	68														
2008-09	**St. Louis**	**NHL**	30	0	3	3	39	0	0	0	21	0.0	8	0	0.0	13:26					
	Peoria Rivermen	AHL	29	2	3	5	67										3	0	0	0	11
2009-10	**St. Louis**	**NHL**	8	0	2	2	4	0	0	0	7	0.0	3	0	0.0	14:02					
	Peoria Rivermen	AHL	65	5	21	26	75														
2010-11	**St. Louis**	**NHL**	29	0	1	1	39	0	0	0	28	0.0	-10	0	0.0	12:08					
	Peoria Rivermen	AHL	13	0	8	8	4										1	0	0	0	2
	NHL Totals		**67**	**0**	**6**	**6**	**82**	**0**	**0**	**0**	**56**	**0.0**		**0**	**0.0**	**12:57**					

Signed as a free agent by **St. Louis**, October 9, 2008. Signed as a free agent by **Florida**, July 12, 2011.

STRAIT, Brian   PIT

Defense. Shoots left. 6'1", 200 lbs.   Born, Boston, MA, January 4, 1988. Pittsburgh's 3rd choice, 65th overall, in 2006 Entry Draft.   (STRAYT, BRIGH-uhn)

Season	Club	League	GP	G	A	Pts	PIM	GP	G	A	Pts	PIM
2003-04	NMH School	High-MA	30	5	15	20	....					
2004-05	USNTDP	U-17	18	1	5	6	8					
	USNTDP	NAHL	42	4	8	12	42	10	0	2	2	4
2005-06	USNTDP	U-18	40	2	7	9	31					
	USNTDP	NAHL	15	0	5	5	41					
2006-07	Boston University	H-East	36	3	3	6	47					
2007-08	Boston University	H-East	37	0	10	10	20					
2008-09	Boston University	H-East	38	2	5	7	67					
2009-10	Wilkes-Barre	AHL	78	2	12	14	73	4	0	1	1	0

			Regular Season														Playoffs								
Season	Club	League	GP	G	A	Pts	PIM	PP	SH	GW	S	%	+/-	TF	F%	Min	GP	G	A	Pts	PIM	PP	SH	GW	Min
2010-11	**Pittsburgh**	**NHL**	**3**	**0**	**0**	**0**	**0**	**0**	**0**	**0**	**0**	**0.0**	**−1**	**0**	**0.0**	**13:32**	....	....	....	....	....	....	....	....	....
	Wilkes-Barre	AHL	75	2	8	10	49	....	....	....	....	....	....	....	....	....	12	1	3	4	10	....	....	....	....
	NHL Totals		**3**	**0**	**0**	**0**	**0**	**0**	**0**	**0**	**0**	**0.0**		**0**	**0.0**	**13:32**	....	....	....	....	....	....	....	....	....

STRALMAN, Anton

(STROHL-muhn, AN-tawn)

Defense. Shoots right. 5'11", 193 lbs. Born, Tibro, Sweden, August 1, 1986. Toronto's 5th choice, 216th overall, in 2005 Entry Draft.

Season	Club	League	GP	G	A	Pts	PIM	PP	SH	GW	S	%	+/-	TF	F%	Min	GP	G	A	Pts	PIM	PP	SH	GW	Min
2002-03	Skovde IK Jr.	Swe-Jr.	46	20	9	29	38	....	....	....	....	....	....	....	....	....	....	....	....	....	....	....	....	....	....
2003-04	Skovde IK	Sweden-3	27	4	8	12	18	....	....	....	....	....	....	....	....	....	....	....	....	....	....	....	....	....	....
2004-05	Skovde IK	Sweden-2	50	10	11	21	40	....	....	....	....	....	....	....	....	....	....	....	....	....	....	....	....	....	....
2005-06	Timra IK	Sweden	45	1	4	5	28	....	....	....	....	....	....	....	....	....	....	....	....	....	....	....	....	....	....
	Timra IK Jr.	Swe-Jr.	....	....	....	....	....	....	....	....	....	....	....	....	....	....	3	0	0	0	4	....	....	....	....
2006-07	Timra IK	Sweden	53	10	11	21	34	....	....	....	....	....	....	....	....	....	7	1	3	4	10	....	....	....	....
2007-08	**Toronto**	**NHL**	**50**	**3**	**6**	**9**	**18**	**0**	**0**	**0**	**40**	**7.5**	**−10**	**0**	**0.0**	**12:49**	....	....	....	....	....	....	....	....	....
	Toronto Marlies	AHL	21	0	11	11	22	....	....	....	....	....	....	....	....	....	....	....	....	....	....	....	....	....	....
2008-09	**Toronto**	**NHL**	**38**	**1**	**12**	**13**	**20**	**0**	**0**	**1**	**43**	**2.3**	**−2**	**1**	**100.0**	**15:34**	....	....	....	....	....	....	....	....	....
	Toronto Marlies	AHL	36	7	9	16	24	....	....	....	....	....	....	....	....	....	6	1	2	3	0	....	....	....	....
2009-10	**Columbus**	**NHL**	**73**	**6**	**28**	**34**	**37**	**4**	**0**	**0**	**121**	**5.0**	**−17**	**0**	**0.0**	**20:29**	....	....	....	....	....	....	....	....	....
2010-11	**Columbus**	**NHL**	**51**	**1**	**17**	**18**	**22**	**1**	**0**	**1**	**80**	**1.3**	**−11**	**0**	**0.0**	**19:44**	....	....	....	....	....	....	....	....	....
	NHL Totals		**212**	**11**	**63**	**74**	**97**	**5**	**0**	**2**	**284**	**3.9**		**1**	**100.0**	**17:37**	....	....	....	....	....	....	....	....	....

Traded to **Calgary** by **Toronto** with Colin Stuart and Toronto's 7th round choice in 2012 Entry Draft for Wayne Primeau and Calgary's 2nd round choice (later traded to Chicago – Chicago selected Brandon Saad) in 2011 Entry Draft, July 27, 2009. Traded to **Columbus** by **Calgary** for Columbus' 3rd round choice (Max Reinhart) in 2010 Entry Draft, September 29, 2009.

STREIT, Mark

(STRIGHT, MAHRK) **NYI**

Defense. Shoots left. 5'11", 202 lbs. Born, Bern, Switz., December 11, 1977. Montreal's 8th choice, 262nd overall, in 2004 Entry Draft.

Season	Club	League	GP	G	A	Pts	PIM	PP	SH	GW	S	%	+/-	TF	F%	Min	GP	G	A	Pts	PIM	PP	SH	GW	Min
1995-96	Fribourg	Swiss	34	2	2	4	6	....	....	....	....	....	....	....	....	....	4	0	0	0	2	....	....	....	....
1996-97	HC Davos	Swiss	46	2	9	11	18	....	....	....	....	....	....	....	....	....	6	0	0	0	0	....	....	....	....
1997-98	HC Ambri-Piotta	Swiss	2	0	0	0	0	....	....	....	....	....	....	....	....	....	....	....	....	....	....	....	....	....	....
	HC Davos	Swiss	38	4	10	14	14	....	....	....	....	....	....	....	....	....	18	1	5	6	20	....	....	....	....
1998-99	HC Davos	Swiss	44	7	18	25	42	....	....	....	....	....	....	....	....	....	6	3	3	6	8	....	....	....	....
99-2000	Springfield	AHL	43	3	12	15	18	....	....	....	....	....	....	....	....	....	5	0	0	0	2	....	....	....	....
	Utah Grizzlies	IHL	1	0	1	1	2	....	....	....	....	....	....	....	....	....	....	....	....	....	....	....	....	....	....
	Tallahassee	ECHL	14	0	5	5	16	....	....	....	....	....	....	....	....	....	....	....	....	....	....	....	....	....	....
2000-01	ZSC Lions Zurich	Swiss	44	5	11	16	48	....	....	....	....	....	....	....	....	....	16	2	5	7	37	....	....	....	....
2001-02	ZSC Lions Zurich	Swiss	28	6	17	23	36	....	....	....	....	....	....	....	....	....	16	0	6	6	14	....	....	....	....
	Switzerland	Olympics	4	1	1	2	0	....	....	....	....	....	....	....	....	....	....	....	....	....	....	....	....	....	....
2002-03	ZSC Lions Zurich	Swiss	37	4	19	23	62	....	....	....	....	....	....	....	....	....	12	1	7	8	2	....	....	....	....
2003-04	ZSC Lions Zurich	Swiss	48	12	24	36	78	....	....	....	....	....	....	....	....	....	13	5	2	7	14	....	....	....	....
2004-05	ZSC Lions Zurich	Swiss	44	14	29	43	46	....	....	....	....	....	....	....	....	....	15	4	11	15	20	....	....	....	....
2005-06	**Montreal**	**NHL**	**48**	**2**	**9**	**11**	**28**	**2**	**0**	**0**	**52**	**3.8**	**−6**	**1**	**0.0**	**14:36**	**1**	**0**	**0**	**0**	**0**	**0**	**0**	**0**	**3:29**
	Switzerland	Olympics	6	2	1	3	6	....	....	....	....	....	....	....	....	....	....	....	....	....	....	....	....	....	....
2006-07	**Montreal**	**NHL**	**76**	**10**	**26**	**36**	**14**	**2**	**1**	**1**	**102**	**9.8**	**−5**	**12**	**33.3**	**14:01**	....	....	....	....	....	....	....	....	....
2007-08	**Montreal**	**NHL**	**81**	**13**	**49**	**62**	**28**	**7**	**0**	**3**	**165**	**7.9**	**−6**	**1**	**0.0**	**17:31**	**11**	**1**	**3**	**4**	**8**	**0**	**0**	**0**	**14:48**
2008-09	**NY Islanders**	**NHL**	**74**	**16**	**40**	**56**	**62**	**10**	**1**	**1**	**150**	**10.7**	**5**	**0**	**0.0**	**25:13**	....	....	....	....	....	....	....	....	....
2009-10	**NY Islanders**	**NHL**	**82**	**11**	**38**	**49**	**48**	**9**	**0**	**2**	**187**	**5.9**	**0**	**1**	**0.0**	**25:42**	....	....	....	....	....	....	....	....	....
	Switzerland	Olympics	5	0	3	3	0	....	....	....	....	....	....	....	....	....	....	....	....	....	....	....	....	....	....
2010-11			DID NOT PLAY – INJURED																						
	NHL Totals		**361**	**52**	**162**	**214**	**180**	**30**	**2**	**7**	**656**	**7.9**		**15**	**26.7**	**19:50**	**12**	**1**	**3**	**4**	**8**	**0**	**0**	**0**	**13:51**

Played in NHL All-Star Game (2009)

Signed as a free agent by **NY Islanders**, July 1, 2008. • Did not play in 2010-11 due to shoulder injury in training camp, September 25, 2010.

STRUDWICK, Jason

(STRUHD-wihk, JAY-suhn)

Defense. Shoots left. 6'4", 226 lbs. Born, Edmonton, Alta., July 17, 1975. NY Islanders' 3rd choice, 63rd overall, in 1994 Entry Draft.

Season	Club	League	GP	G	A	Pts	PIM	PP	SH	GW	S	%	+/-	TF	F%	Min	GP	G	A	Pts	PIM	PP	SH	GW	Min
1991-92	Edmonton Legion	AMHL	35	3	8	11	67	....	....	....	....	....	....	....	....	....	....	....	....	....	....	....	....	....	....
1992-93	Edmonton Pats	AMHL	33	8	20	28	135	....	....	....	....	....	....	....	....	....	....	....	....	....	....	....	....	....	....
1993-94	Kamloops Blazers	WHL	61	6	8	14	118	....	....	....	....	....	....	....	....	....	19	0	4	4	24	....	....	....	....
1994-95	Kamloops Blazers	WHL	72	3	11	14	183	....	....	....	....	....	....	....	....	....	21	1	1	2	39	....	....	....	....
1995-96	**NY Islanders**	**NHL**	**1**	**0**	**0**	**0**	**7**	**0**	**0**	**0**	**0**	**0.0**	**0**	....	....	....	....	....	....	....	....	....	....	....	....
	Worcester IceCats	AHL	60	2	7	9	119	....	....	....	....	....	....	....	....	....	4	0	1	1	0	....	....	....	....
1996-97	Kentucky	AHL	80	1	9	10	198	....	....	....	....	....	....	....	....	....	4	0	0	0	0	....	....	....	....
1997-98	**NY Islanders**	**NHL**	**17**	**0**	**1**	**1**	**36**	**0**	**0**	**0**	**3**	**0.0**	**1**	....	....	....	....	....	....	....	....	....	....	....	....
	Kentucky	AHL	39	3	1	4	87	....	....	....	....	....	....	....	....	....	....	....	....	....	....	....	....	....	....
	Vancouver	**NHL**	**11**	**0**	**1**	**1**	**29**	**0**	**0**	**0**	**5**	**0.0**	**−3**	....	....	....	....	....	....	....	....	....	....	....	....
	Syracuse Crunch	AHL	....	....	....	....	....	....	....	....	....	....	....	....	....	....	3	0	0	0	6	....	....	....	....
1998-99	**Vancouver**	**NHL**	**65**	**0**	**3**	**3**	**114**	**0**	**0**	**0**	**25**	**0.0**	**−19**	**0**	**0.0**	**12:49**	....	....	....	....	....	....	....	....	....
99-2000	**Vancouver**	**NHL**	**63**	**1**	**3**	**4**	**64**	**0**	**0**	**0**	**18**	**5.6**	**−13**	**0**	**0.0**	**15:12**	....	....	....	....	....	....	....	....	....
2000-01	**Vancouver**	**NHL**	**60**	**1**	**4**	**5**	**64**	**0**	**0**	**1**	**21**	**4.8**	**16**	**0**	**0.0**	**9:59**	**2**	**0**	**0**	**0**	**0**	**0**	**0**	**0**	**2:15**
2001-02	**Vancouver**	**NHL**	**44**	**2**	**4**	**6**	**96**	**0**	**0**	**0**	**13**	**15.4**	**4**	**0**	**0.0**	**9:45**	....	....	....	....	....	....	....	....	....
2002-03	**Chicago**	**NHL**	**48**	**2**	**3**	**5**	**87**	**0**	**0**	**0**	**19**	**10.5**	**−4**	**3**	**0.0**	**8:32**	....	....	....	....	....	....	....	....	....
2003-04	**Chicago**	**NHL**	**54**	**1**	**3**	**4**	**73**	**0**	**0**	**0**	**32**	**3.1**	**−16**	**1**	**0.0**	**14:55**	....	....	....	....	....	....	....	....	....
2004-05	Ferencvaros	Hungary	6	1	2	3	8	....	....	....	....	....	....	....	....	....	....	....	....	....	....	....	....	....	....
2005-06	**NY Rangers**	**NHL**	**65**	**3**	**4**	**7**	**66**	**0**	**0**	**0**	**31**	**9.7**	**−10**	**3**	**33.3**	**15:31**	**3**	**0**	**0**	**0**	**0**	**0**	**0**	**0**	**13:35**
2006-07	HC Lugano	Swiss	34	2	3	5	28	....	....	....	....	....	....	....	....	....	6	0	0	0	4	....	....	....	....
	NY Rangers	**NHL**	**8**	**0**	**0**	**0**	**2**	**0**	**0**	**0**	**3**	**0.0**	**0**	**0**	**0.0**	**13:40**	....	....	....	....	....	....	....	....	....
2007-08	**NY Rangers**	**NHL**	**52**	**1**	**1**	**2**	**40**	**0**	**0**	**1**	**21**	**4.8**	**0**	**0**	**0.0**	**12:57**	**2**	**0**	**0**	**0**	**0**	**0**	**0**	**0**	**9:41**
2008-09	**Edmonton**	**NHL**	**71**	**2**	**7**	**9**	**60**	**0**	**0**	**0**	**32**	**6.3**	**−4**	**0**	**0.0**	**12:38**	....	....	....	....	....	....	....	....	....
2009-10	**Edmonton**	**NHL**	**72**	**0**	**6**	**6**	**50**	**0**	**0**	**0**	**19**	**0.0**	**−18**	**0**	**0.0**	**16:56**	....	....	....	....	....	....	....	....	....
2010-11	**Edmonton**	**NHL**	**43**	**0**	**2**	**2**	**23**	**0**	**0**	**0**	**9**	**0.0**	**−16**	**0**	**0.0**	**15:04**	....	....	....	....	....	....	....	....	....
	NHL Totals		**674**	**13**	**42**	**55**	**811**	**0**	**0**	**2**	**251**	**5.2**		**7**	**14.3**	**13:19**	**7**	**0**	**0**	**0**	**0**	**0**	**0**	**0**	**9:14**

Traded to **Vancouver** by **NY Islanders** for Gino Odjick, March 23, 1998. Signed as a free agent by **Chicago**, July 15, 2002. Signed as a free agent by **NY Rangers**, July 20, 2004. Signed as a free agent by **Ferencvaros** (Hungary), January 17, 2005. Signed as a free agent by **Lugano**, September 12, 2006. Signed as a free agent by **NY Rangers**, March 19, 2007. Signed as a free agent by **Edmonton**, July 10, 2008.

STUART, Brad

(STEW-ahrt, BRAD) **DET**

Defense. Shoots left. 6'2", 210 lbs. Born, Rocky Mountain House, Alta., November 6, 1979. San Jose's 1st choice, 3rd overall, in 1998 Entry Draft.

Season	Club	League	GP	G	A	Pts	PIM	PP	SH	GW	S	%	+/-	TF	F%	Min	GP	G	A	Pts	PIM	PP	SH	GW	Min
1995-96	Red Deer	AMHL	35	12	25	37	83	....	....	....	....	....	....	....	....	....	....	....	....	....	....	....	....	....	....
	Regina Pats	WHL	3	0	0	0	0	....	....	....	....	....	....	....	....	....	....	....	....	....	....	....	....	....	....
1996-97	Regina Pats	WHL	57	7	36	43	49	....	....	....	....	....	....	....	....	....	5	0	4	4	14	....	....	....	....
1997-98	Regina Pats	WHL	72	20	45	65	82	....	....	....	....	....	....	....	....	....	9	3	4	7	10	....	....	....	....
1998-99	Regina Pats	WHL	29	10	19	29	43	....	....	....	....	....	....	....	....	....	....	....	....	....	....	....	....	....	....
	Calgary Hitmen	WHL	30	11	22	33	26	....	....	....	....	....	....	....	....	....	21	8	15	23	59	....	....	....	....
99-2000	**San Jose**	**NHL**	**82**	**10**	**26**	**36**	**32**	**5**	**1**	**3**	**133**	**7.5**	**3**	**0**	**0.0**	**20:24**	**12**	**1**	**0**	**1**	**6**	**1**	**0**	**0**	**16:30**
2000-01	**San Jose**	**NHL**	**77**	**5**	**18**	**23**	**56**	**1**	**0**	**2**	**119**	**4.2**	**10**	**0**	**0.0**	**20:06**	**5**	**1**	**0**	**1**	**0**	**0**	**0**	**0**	**20:19**
2001-02	**San Jose**	**NHL**	**82**	**6**	**23**	**29**	**39**	**2**	**0**	**2**	**96**	**6.3**	**13**	**0**	**0.0**	**21:41**	**12**	**0**	**3**	**3**	**8**	**0**	**0**	**0**	**19:42**
2002-03	**San Jose**	**NHL**	**36**	**4**	**10**	**14**	**46**	**2**	**0**	**1**	**63**	**6.3**	**−6**	**0**	**0.0**	**20:53**	....	....	....	....	....	....	....	....	....
2003-04	**San Jose**	**NHL**	**77**	**9**	**30**	**39**	**34**	**5**	**0**	**0**	**129**	**7.0**	**9**	**0**	**0.0**	**22:09**	**17**	**1**	**5**	**6**	**13**	**0**	**0**	**0**	**23:23**
2004-05			DID NOT PLAY																						
2005-06	**San Jose**	**NHL**	**23**	**2**	**10**	**12**	**14**	**1**	**0**	**0**	**41**	**4.9**	**−2**	**0**	**0.0**	**23:15**	....	....	....	....	....	....	....	....	....
	Boston	**NHL**	**55**	**10**	**21**	**31**	**38**	**6**	**0**	**2**	**122**	**8.2**	**−6**	**0**	**0.0**	**25:40**	....	....	....	....	....	....	....	....	....
2006-07	**Boston**	**NHL**	**48**	**7**	**10**	**17**	**26**	**1**	**0**	**2**	**74**	**9.5**	**−22**	**0**	**0.0**	**22:55**	....	....	....	....	....	....	....	....	....
	Calgary	**NHL**	**27**	**0**	**5**	**5**	**18**	**0**	**0**	**0**	**35**	**0.0**	**12**	**0**	**0.0**	**22:48**	**6**	**0**	**1**	**1**	**6**	**0**	**0**	**0**	**25:16**
2007-08	**Los Angeles**	**NHL**	**63**	**5**	**16**	**21**	**67**	**2**	**0**	**1**	**111**	**4.5**	**−16**	**4**	**0.0**	**21:13**	....	....	....	....	....	....	....	....	....
	♦ **Detroit**	**NHL**	**9**	**1**	**1**	**2**	**2**	**0**	**0**	**0**	**21**	**4.8**	**6**	**0**	**0.0**	**20:46**	**21**	**1**	**6**	**7**	**14**	**0**	**0**	**1**	**21:40**
2008-09	**Detroit**	**NHL**	**67**	**2**	**13**	**15**	**26**	**1**	**0**	**0**	**105**	**1.9**	**−3**	**0**	**0.0**	**20:13**	**23**	**3**	**6**	**9**	**12**	**1**	**0**	**0**	**24:09**

			Regular Season														Playoffs								
Season	Club	League	GP	G	A	Pts	PIM	PP	SH	GW	S	%	+/-	TF	F%	Min	GP	G	A	Pts	PIM	PP	SH	GW	Min
2009-10	**Detroit**	**NHL**	**82**	**4**	**16**	**20**	**22**	**1**	**0**	**2**	**153**	**2.6**	**–12**	**2**	**50.0**	**23:10**	**12**	**2**	**4**	**6**	**8**	**0**	**0**	**0**	**22:04**
2010-11	**Detroit**	**NHL**	**67**	**3**	**17**	**20**	**40**	**1**	**0**	**1**	**81**	**3.7**	**4**	**0**	**0.0**	**21:32**	**11**	**0**	**2**	**2**	**8**	**0**	**0**	**0**	**21:33**
	NHL Totals		**795**	**68**	**216**	**284**	**460**	**28**	**1**	**16**	**1283**	**5.3**		**6**	**16.7**	**21:49**	**119**	**9**	**27**	**36**	**75**	**2**	**0**	**1**	**21:50**

WHL East Second All-Star Team (1998) • WHL East First All-Star Team (1999) • Canadian Major Junior First All-Star Team (1999) • Canadian Major Junior Defenseman of the Year (1999) • NHL All-Rookie Team (2000)

• Missed majority of 2002-03 due to ankle (January 4, 2003 vs. Los Angeles) and head (February 21, 2003 vs. Columbus) injuries. Traded to **Boston** by **San Jose** with Marco Sturm and Wayne Primeau for Joe Thornton, November 30, 2005. Traded to **Calgary** by **Boston** with Wayne Primeau and Washington's 4th round choice (previously acquired, Calgary selected T.J. Brodie) in 2008 Entry Draft for Andrew Ference and Chuck Kobasew, February 10, 2007. Signed as a free agent by **Los Angeles**, July 3, 2007. Traded to **Detroit** by **Los Angeles** for Detroit's 2nd round choice (later traded to Colorado – Colorado selected Peter Delmas) in 2008 Entry Draft and Detroit's 4th round choice (later traded to Atlanta – Atlanta selected Ben Chiarot) in 2009 Entry Draft, February 26, 2008.

STUART, Colin

(STEW-ahrt, KAW-lihn) **BUF**

Left wing. Shoots left. 6'2", 205 lbs. Born, Rochester, MN, July 8, 1982. Atlanta's 5th choice, 135th overall, in 2001 Entry Draft.

Season	Club	League	GP	G	A	Pts	PIM	PP	SH	GW	S	%	+/-	TF	F%	Min	GP	G	A	Pts	PIM	PP	SH	GW	Min
1998-99	Roch. Lourdes	High-MN	23	22	32	54	....	....	....	....	....	....	....	....	....	....	....	....	....	....	....	....	....	....	....
99-2000	Lincoln Stars	USHL	53	18	19	37	38	....	....	....	....	....	....	....	....	....	9	1	3	4	2	....	....	....	....
2000-01	Colorado College	WCHA	41	2	7	9	26	....	....	....	....	....	....	....	....	....	....	....	....	....	....	....	....	....	....
2001-02	Colorado College	WCHA	43	13	9	22	34	....	....	....	....	....	....	....	....	....	....	....	....	....	....	....	....	....	....
2002-03	Colorado College	WCHA	42	13	11	24	56	....	....	....	....	....	....	....	....	....	....	....	....	....	....	....	....	....	....
2003-04	Colorado College	WCHA	30	10	12	22	38	....	....	....	....	....	....	....	....	....	....	....	....	....	....	....	....	....	....
2004-05	Chicago Wolves	AHL	39	3	2	5	12	....	....	....	....	....	....	....	....	....	....	....	....	....	....	....	....	....	....
	Gwinnett	ECHL	5	1	3	4	4	....	....	....	....	....	....	....	....	....	....	....	....	....	....	....	....	....	....
2005-06	Chicago Wolves	AHL	78	13	14	27	65	....	....	....	....	....	....	....	....	....	....	....	....	....	....	....	....	....	....
2006-07	Chicago Wolves	AHL	67	18	11	29	75	....	....	....	....	....	....	....	....	....	15	2	5	7	10	....	....	....	....
2007-08	**Atlanta**	**NHL**	**18**	**3**	**2**	**5**	**6**	**0**	**1**	**1**	**19**	**15.8**	**2**	**7**	**57.1**	**12:20**	....	....	....	....	....	....	....	....	....
	Chicago Wolves	AHL	58	8	8	16	45	....	....	....	....	....	....	....	....	....	24	3	3	6	18	....	....	....	....
2008-09	**Atlanta**	**NHL**	**33**	**5**	**3**	**8**	**18**	**0**	**3**	**0**	**54**	**9.3**	**3**	**12**	**41.7**	**12:29**	....	....	....	....	....	....	....	....	....
	Chicago Wolves	AHL	42	9	6	15	38	....	....	....	....	....	....	....	....	....	....	....	....	....	....	....	....	....	....
2009-10	Abbotsford Heat	AHL	67	17	19	36	36	....	....	....	....	....	....	....	....	....	3	0	0	0	6	....	....	....	....
2010-11	**Buffalo**	**NHL**	**3**	**0**	**0**	**0**	**2**	**0**	**0**	**0**	**5**	**0.0**	**1**	**2**	**50.0**	**13:09**	....	....	....	....	....	....	....	....	....
	Portland Pirates	AHL	72	16	28	44	53	....	....	....	....	....	....	....	....	....	12	3	4	7	8	....	....	....	....
	NHL Totals		**54**	**8**	**5**	**13**	**26**	**0**	**4**	**1**	**78**	**10.3**		**21**	**47.6**	**12:28**	....	....	....	....	....	....	....	....	....

Traded to **Toronto** by **Atlanta** with Garnet Exelby for Pavel Kubina and Tim Stapleton, July 1, 2009. Traded to **Calgary** by **Toronto** with Anton Stralman and Toronto's 7th round choice in 2012 Entry Draft for Wayne Primeau and Calgary's 2nd round choice (later traded to Chicago – Chicago selected Brandon Saad) in 2011 Entry Draft, July 27, 2009. Signed as a free agent by **Buffalo**, August 26, 2010.

STUART, Mark

(STEW-uhrt, MAHRK) **WPG**

Defense. Shoots left. 6'2", 213 lbs. Born, Rochester, MN, April 27, 1984. Boston's 1st choice, 21st overall, in 2003 Entry Draft.

Season	Club	League	GP	G	A	Pts	PIM	PP	SH	GW	S	%	+/-	TF	F%	Min	GP	G	A	Pts	PIM	PP	SH	GW	Min
99-2000	Roch. Lourdes	High-MN	28	19	22	41	....	....	....	....	....	....	....	....	....	....	....	....	....	....	....	....	....	....	....
2000-01	USNTDP	U-17	12	1	5	6	6	....	....	....	....	....	....	....	....	....	....	....	....	....	....	....	....	....	....
	USNTDP	NAHL	52	2	11	13	114	....	....	....	....	....	....	....	....	....	....	....	....	....	....	....	....	....	....
2001-02	USNTDP	U-18	40	9	9	18	....	....	....	....	....	....	....	....	....	....	....	....	....	....	....	....	....	....	....
	USNTDP	USHL	12	0	1	1	25	....	....	....	....	....	....	....	....	....	....	....	....	....	....	....	....	....	....
	USNTDP	NAHL	9	0	1	1	18	....	....	....	....	....	....	....	....	....	....	....	....	....	....	....	....	....	....
2002-03	Colorado College	WCHA	38	3	17	20	81	....	....	....	....	....	....	....	....	....	....	....	....	....	....	....	....	....	....
2003-04	Colorado College	WCHA	37	4	11	15	100	....	....	....	....	....	....	....	....	....	....	....	....	....	....	....	....	....	....
2004-05	Colorado College	WCHA	43	5	14	19	94	....	....	....	....	....	....	....	....	....	....	....	....	....	....	....	....	....	....
2005-06	**Boston**	**NHL**	**17**	**1**	**1**	**2**	**10**	**0**	**0**	**0**	**9**	**11.1**	**–1**	**0**	**0.0**	**17:46**	....	....	....	....	....	....	....	....	....
	Providence Bruins	AHL	60	4	3	7	76	....	....	....	....	....	....	....	....	....	6	0	0	0	25	....	....	....	....
2006-07	**Boston**	**NHL**	**15**	**0**	**1**	**1**	**14**	**0**	**0**	**0**	**4**	**0.0**	**7**	**0**	**0.0**	**10:23**	....	....	....	....	....	....	....	....	....
	Providence Bruins	AHL	49	4	16	20	62	....	....	....	....	....	....	....	....	....	3	0	1	1	9	....	....	....	....
2007-08	**Boston**	**NHL**	**82**	**4**	**4**	**8**	**81**	**0**	**0**	**1**	**60**	**6.7**	**2**	**0**	**0.0**	**15:22**	**7**	**0**	**1**	**1**	**8**	**0**	**0**	**0**	**16:00**
2008-09	**Boston**	**NHL**	**82**	**5**	**12**	**17**	**76**	**0**	**0**	**1**	**61**	**8.2**	**20**	**0**	**0.0**	**15:25**	**11**	**0**	**1**	**1**	**7**	**0**	**0**	**0**	**17:57**
2009-10	**Boston**	**NHL**	**56**	**2**	**5**	**7**	**80**	**0**	**0**	**0**	**53**	**3.8**	**1**	**0**	**0.0**	**17:01**	**4**	**0**	**0**	**0**	**6**	**0**	**0**	**0**	**14:39**
2010-11	**Boston**	**NHL**	**31**	**1**	**4**	**5**	**23**	**0**	**0**	**1**	**20**	**5.0**	**8**	**1**	**100.0**	**16:15**	....	....	....	....	....	....	....	....	....
	Atlanta	**NHL**	**23**	**1**	**0**	**1**	**21**	**0**	**0**	**0**	**21**	**4.8**	**–8**	**0**	**0.0**	**14:51**	....	....	....	....	....	....	....	....	....
	NHL Totals		**306**	**14**	**27**	**41**	**308**	**0**	**0**	**3**	**228**	**6.1**		**1**	**100.0**	**15:38**	**22**	**0**	**2**	**2**	**21**	**0**	**0**	**0**	**16:44**

WCHA All-Rookie Team (2003) • WCHA Second All-Star Team (2005) • NCAA West First All-American Team (2005)

Traded to **Atlanta** by **Boston** with Blake Wheeler for Rich Peverley and Boris Valabik, February 18, 2011. • Transferred to **Winnipeg** after **Atlanta** franchise relocated, June 21, 2011.

STURM, Marco

(STUHRM, MAHR-koh) **VAN**

Left wing. Shoots left. 6', 194 lbs. Born, Dingolfing, West Germany, September 8, 1978. San Jose's 2nd choice, 21st overall, in 1996 Entry Draft.

Season	Club	League	GP	G	A	Pts	PIM	PP	SH	GW	S	%	+/-	TF	F%	Min	GP	G	A	Pts	PIM	PP	SH	GW	Min
1995-96	EV Landshut	Germany	47	12	20	32	50	....	....	....	....	....	....	....	....	....	11	1	3	4	18	....	....	....	....
1996-97	EV Landshut	Germany	46	16	27	43	40	....	....	....	....	....	....	....	....	....	7	1	4	5	6	....	....	....	....
1997-98	**San Jose**	**NHL**	**74**	**10**	**20**	**30**	**40**	**2**	**0**	**3**	**118**	**8.5**	**–2**	....	....	....	**2**	**0**	**0**	**0**	**0**	**0**	**0**	**0**	....
	Germany	Olympics	2	0	0	0	0	....	....	....	....	....	....	....	....	....	....	....	....	....	....	....	....	....	....
1998-99	**San Jose**	**NHL**	**78**	**16**	**22**	**38**	**52**	**3**	**2**	**3**	**140**	**11.4**	**7**	**576**	**45.0**	**15:23**	**6**	**2**	**2**	**4**	**4**	**0**	**0**	**1**	**14:16**
99-2000	**San Jose**	**NHL**	**74**	**12**	**15**	**27**	**22**	**2**	**4**	**3**	**120**	**10.0**	**4**	**183**	**45.4**	**14:07**	**12**	**1**	**3**	**4**	**6**	**0**	**0**	**0**	**13:00**
2000-01	**San Jose**	**NHL**	**81**	**14**	**18**	**32**	**28**	**2**	**3**	**5**	**153**	**9.2**	**9**	**517**	**40.2**	**16:06**	**6**	**0**	**2**	**2**	**0**	**0**	**0**	**0**	**18:18**
2001-02	**San Jose**	**NHL**	**77**	**21**	**20**	**41**	**32**	**4**	**3**	**5**	**174**	**12.1**	**23**	**105**	**47.6**	**15:39**	**12**	**3**	**2**	**5**	**2**	**0**	**0**	**0**	**15:33**
	Germany	Olympics	5	0	1	1	0	....	....	....	....	....	....	....	....	....	....	....	....	....	....	....	....	....	....
2002-03	**San Jose**	**NHL**	**82**	**28**	**20**	**48**	**16**	**6**	**0**	**2**	**208**	**13.5**	**9**	**83**	**48.2**	**16:31**	....	....	....	....	....	....	....	....	....
2003-04	**San Jose**	**NHL**	**64**	**21**	**20**	**41**	**36**	**10**	**2**	**6**	**158**	**13.3**	**0**	**7**	**42.9**	**16:25**	....	....	....	....	....	....	....	....	....
2004-05	ERC Ingolstadt	Germany	45	22	16	38	56	....	....	....	....	....	....	....	....	....	11	3	4	7	12	....	....	....	....
2005-06	**San Jose**	**NHL**	**23**	**6**	**10**	**16**	**16**	**3**	**0**	**0**	**48**	**12.5**	**–8**	**9**	**44.4**	**17:28**	....	....	....	....	....	....	....	....	....
	Boston	**NHL**	**51**	**23**	**20**	**43**	**32**	**5**	**0**	**6**	**132**	**17.4**	**14**	**3**	**33.3**	**18:44**	....	....	....	....	....	....	....	....	....
2006-07	**Boston**	**NHL**	**76**	**27**	**17**	**44**	**46**	**10**	**2**	**1**	**224**	**12.1**	**–24**	**13**	**61.5**	**18:36**	....	....	....	....	....	....	....	....	....
2007-08	**Boston**	**NHL**	**80**	**27**	**29**	**56**	**40**	**10**	**1**	**5**	**229**	**11.8**	**11**	**34**	**29.4**	**18:00**	**7**	**2**	**2**	**4**	**6**	**0**	**1**	**1**	**18:20**
2008-09	**Boston**	**NHL**	**19**	**7**	**6**	**13**	**8**	**4**	**0**	**0**	**45**	**15.6**	**9**	**4**	**75.0**	**16:01**	....	....	....	....	....	....	....	....	....
2009-10	**Boston**	**NHL**	**76**	**22**	**15**	**37**	**30**	**4**	**1**	**2**	**203**	**10.8**	**14**	**11**	**18.2**	**16:46**	**7**	**0**	**0**	**0**	**4**	**0**	**0**	**0**	**14:15**
	Germany	Olympics	4	0	1	1	0	....	....	....	....	....	....	....	....	....	....	....	....	....	....	....	....	....	....
2010-11	**Los Angeles**	**NHL**	**17**	**4**	**5**	**9**	**17**	**1**	**0**	**0**	**27**	**14.8**	**6**	**1**	**100.0**	**14:28**	....	....	....	....	....	....	....	....	....
	Washington	**NHL**	**18**	**1**	**6**	**7**	**6**	**0**	**0**	**1**	**30**	**3.3**	**0**	**14**	**35.7**	**14:01**	**9**	**1**	**2**	**3**	**4**	**1**	**0**	**0**	**14:38**
	NHL Totals		**890**	**239**	**243**	**482**	**421**	**66**	**18**	**42**	**2009**	**11.9**		**1560**	**43.4**	**16:29**	**61**	**9**	**13**	**22**	**26**	**1**	**1**	**2**	**15:13**

Played in NHL All-Star Game (1999)

Signed as a free agent by **Ingolstadt** (Germany), August 8, 2004. Traded to **Boston** by **San Jose** with Brad Stuart and Wayne Primeau for Joe Thornton, November 30, 2005. • Missed majority of 2008-09 due to knee injury vs. Toronto, December 18, 2008. Traded to **Los Angeles** by **Boston** for future considerations, December 11, 2010. Claimed on waivers by **Washington** from **Los Angeles**, February 26, 2011. • Missed majority of 2010-11 due to knee injury in playoffs vs. Philadelphia, May 1, 2010. Signed as a free agent by **Vancouver**, July 1, 2011.

SUBBAN, P.K.

(soo-BAHN, PEE-KAY) **MTL**

Defense. Shoots right. 6', 206 lbs. Born, Toronto, Ont., May 13, 1989. Montreal's 3rd choice, 43rd overall, in 2007 Entry Draft.

Season	Club	League	GP	G	A	Pts	PIM	PP	SH	GW	S	%	+/-	TF	F%	Min	GP	G	A	Pts	PIM	PP	SH	GW	Min
2004-05	Markham	GTHL	67	15	28	43	179	....	....	....	....	....	....	....	....	....	....	....	....	....	....	....	....	....	....
2005-06	Belleville Bulls	OHL	52	5	7	12	70	....	....	....	....	....	....	....	....	....	3	0	0	0	2	....	....	....	....
2006-07	Belleville Bulls	OHL	68	15	41	56	89	....	....	....	....	....	....	....	....	....	15	5	8	13	26	....	....	....	....
2007-08	Belleville Bulls	OHL	58	8	38	46	100	....	....	....	....	....	....	....	....	....	21	8	15	23	28	....	....	....	....
2008-09	Belleville Bulls	OHL	56	14	62	76	94	....	....	....	....	....	....	....	....	....	17	3	12	15	22	....	....	....	....
2009-10	**Montreal**	**NHL**	**2**	**0**	**2**	**2**	**2**	**0**	**0**	**0**	**4**	**0.0**	**1**	**0**	**0.0**	**20:06**	**14**	**1**	**7**	**8**	**6**	**0**	**0**	**0**	**20:44**
	Hamilton	AHL	77	18	35	53	82	....	....	....	....	....	....	....	....	....	7	3	7	10	6	....	....	....	....
2010-11	**Montreal**	**NHL**	**77**	**14**	**24**	**38**	**124**	**9**	**0**	**3**	**197**	**7.1**	**–8**	**0**	**0.0**	**22:16**	**7**	**2**	**2**	**4**	**2**	**2**	**0**	**0**	**28:33**
	NHL Totals		**79**	**14**	**26**	**40**	**126**	**9**	**0**	**3**	**201**	**7.0**		**0**	**0.0**	**22:13**	**21**	**3**	**9**	**12**	**8**	**2**	**0**	**0**	**23:21**

OHL First All-Star Team (2009) • AHL All-Rookie Team (2010) • AHL First All-Star Team (2010) • NHL All-Rookie Team (2011)

			Regular Season														Playoffs								
Season	Club	League	GP	G	A	Pts	PIM	PP	SH	GW	S	%	+/-	TF	F%	Min	GP	G	A	Pts	PIM	PP	SH	GW	Min

SULLIVAN, Steve

(SUHL-ih-vuhn, STEEV) **PIT**

Right wing. Shoots right. 5'8", 161 lbs. Born, Timmins, Ont., July 6, 1974. New Jersey's 10th choice, 233rd overall, in 1994 Entry Draft.

Season	Club	League	GP	G	A	Pts	PIM	PP	SH	GW	S	%	+/-	TF	F%	Min	GP	G	A	Pts	PIM	PP	SH	GW	Min
1991-92	Timmins	NOJHA	47	66	55	121	141																		
1992-93	Sault Ste. Marie	OHL	62	36	27	63	44										16	3	8	11	18				
1993-94	Sault Ste. Marie	OHL	63	51	62	113	82										14	9	16	25	22				
1994-95	Albany River Rats	AHL	75	31	50	81	124										14	4	7	11	10				
1995-96	**New Jersey**	**NHL**	**16**	**5**	**4**	**9**	**8**	**2**	**0**	**1**	**23**	**21.7**	**3**												
	Albany River Rats	AHL	53	33	42	75	127										4	3	0	3	6				
1996-97	**New Jersey**	**NHL**	**33**	**8**	**14**	**22**	**14**	**2**	**0**	**2**	**63**	**12.7**	**9**												
	Albany River Rats	AHL	15	8	7	15	16																		
	Toronto	**NHL**	**21**	**5**	**11**	**16**	**23**	**1**	**0**	**1**	**45**	**11.1**	**5**												
1997-98	**Toronto**	**NHL**	**63**	**10**	**18**	**28**	**40**	**1**	**0**	**1**	**112**	**8.9**	**–8**												
1998-99	**Toronto**	**NHL**	**63**	**20**	**20**	**40**	**28**	**4**	**0**	**5**	**110**	**18.2**	**12**	**685**	**44.4**	**14:12**	**13**	**3**	**3**	**6**	**14**	**2**	**0**	**0**	**16:20**
99-2000	**Toronto**	**NHL**	**7**	**0**	**1**	**1**	**4**	**0**	**0**	**0**	**11**	**0.0**	**–1**	**47**	**48.9**	**11:52**									
	Chicago	**NHL**	**73**	**22**	**42**	**64**	**52**	**2**	**1**	**6**	**169**	**13.0**	**20**	**692**	**48.0**	**18:05**									
2000-01	**Chicago**	**NHL**	**81**	**34**	**41**	**75**	**54**	**6**	***8**	**3**	**204**	**16.7**	**3**	**649**	**42.4**	**20:32**									
2001-02	**Chicago**	**NHL**	**78**	**21**	**39**	**60**	**67**	**3**	**0**	**8**	**155**	**13.5**	**23**	**758**	**48.9**	**19:10**	**5**	**1**	**0**	**1**	**2**	**0**	**0**	**0**	**18:04**
2002-03	**Chicago**	**NHL**	**82**	**26**	**35**	**61**	**42**	**4**	**2**	**3**	**190**	**13.7**	**15**	**382**	**46.1**	**19:15**									
2003-04	**Chicago**	**NHL**	**56**	**15**	**28**	**43**	**36**	**4**	**2**	**4**	**140**	**10.7**	**–7**	**103**	**44.7**	**21:19**									
	Nashville	**NHL**	**24**	**9**	**21**	**30**	**12**	**7**	**0**	**0**	**78**	**11.5**	**8**	**124**	**43.6**	**20:02**	**6**	**1**	**1**	**2**	**6**	**0**	**0**	**1**	**18:58**
2004-05			DID NOT PLAY																						
2005-06	**Nashville**	**NHL**	**69**	**31**	**37**	**68**	**50**	**13**	**4**	**5**	**192**	**16.1**	**2**	**42**	**52.4**	**19:06**	**5**	**0**	**2**	**2**	**0**	**0**	**0**	**0**	**17:02**
2006-07	**Nashville**	**NHL**	**57**	**22**	**38**	**60**	**20**	**6**	**3**	**4**	**122**	**18.0**	**16**	**39**	**38.5**	**19:25**									
2007-08	**Nashville**	**NHL**	DID NOT PLAY – INJURED																						
2008-09	**Nashville**	**NHL**	**41**	**11**	**21**	**32**	**30**	**3**	**0**	**2**	**83**	**13.3**	**2**	**4**	**0.0**	**18:29**									
2009-10	**Nashville**	**NHL**	**82**	**17**	**34**	**51**	**35**	**5**	**0**	**4**	**152**	**11.2**	**2**	**10**	**10.0**	**17:55**	**6**	**0**	**3**	**3**	**2**	**0**	**0**	**0**	**17:59**
2010-11	**Nashville**	**NHL**	**44**	**10**	**12**	**22**	**28**	**3**	**0**	**1**	**79**	**12.7**	**4**	**13**	**38.5**	**16:02**	**9**	**2**	**1**	**3**	**2**	**0**	**0**	**1**	**9:23**
	NHL Totals		**890**	**266**	**416**	**682**	**543**	**66**	**20**	**50**	**1928**	**13.8**		**3548**	**45.8**	**18:35**	**44**	**7**	**10**	**17**	**26**	**2**	**0**	**2**	**15:46**

AHL First All-Star Team (1996) • Bill Masterton Memorial Trophy (2009)

Traded to **Toronto** by **New Jersey** with Jason Smith and the rights to Alyn McCauley for Doug Gilmour, Dave Ellett and New Jersey's 3rd round choice (previously acquired, New Jersey selected Andre Lakos) in 1999 Entry Draft, February 25, 1997. Claimed on waivers by **Chicago** from **Toronto**, October 23, 1999. Traded to **Nashville** by **Chicago** for Nashville's 2nd round choices in 2004 (Ryan Garlock) and 2005 (Michael Blunden) Entry Drafts, February 16, 2004. • Missed remainder of 2006-07, 2007-08 and start of 2008-09 due to back injury vs. Montreal, February 22, 2006. Signed as a free agent by **Pittsburgh**, July 1, 2011.

SULZER, Alexander

(ZUHLT-suhr, al-EHX-AN-duhr) **VAN**

Defense. Shoots left. 6'1", 204 lbs. Born, Kaufbeuren, West Germany, May 30, 1984. Nashville's 7th choice, 92nd overall, in 2003 Entry Draft.

Season	Club	League	GP	G	A	Pts	PIM	PP	SH	GW	S	%	+/-	TF	F%	Min	GP	G	A	Pts	PIM	PP	SH	GW	Min
2000-01	ESV Kaufbeuren	German-3	38	3	6	9	20																		
	Kaufbeuren Jr.	Ger-Jr.	1	0	2	2	2																		
2001-02	ESV Kaufbeuren	German-3	19	1	9	10	14																		
	Kaufbeuren Jr.	Ger-Jr.	1	0	0	0	4																		
2002-03	ESV Kaufbeuren	German-2	26	5	3	8	38										1	0	1	1	4				
	Hamburg Freezers	Germany	18	0	1	1	18										5	0	0	0	12				
2003-04	Dusseldorf	Germany	46	4	1	5	56										4	0	0	0	8				
2004-05	Dusseldorf	Germany	42	5	6	11	68																		
	EV Duisburg	German-2															7	0	3	3	6				
2005-06	Dusseldorf	Germany	48	3	15	18	82										13	3	6	9	22				
	Germany	Olympics	5	0	1	1	2																		
2006-07	Dusseldorf	Germany	44	4	11	15	82										9	2	1	3	20				
2007-08	Milwaukee	AHL	61	7	25	32	47																		
2008-09	**Nashville**	**NHL**	**2**	**0**	**0**	**0**	**0**	**0**	**0**	**0**	**0**	**0.0**	**0**	**0**	**0.0**	**6:34**									
	Milwaukee	AHL	48	8	26	34	36																		
2009-10	**Nashville**	**NHL**	**20**	**0**	**2**	**2**	**4**	**0**	**0**	**0**	**15**	**0.0**	**4**	**0**	**0.0**	**13:23**									
	Milwaukee	AHL	36	7	23	30	8										7	1	5	6	2				
	Germany	Olympics	4	0	0	0	4																		
2010-11	**Nashville**	**NHL**	**31**	**1**	**3**	**4**	**14**	**0**	**0**	**0**	**30**	**3.3**	**–5**	**1**	**100.0**	**17:42**									
	Florida	**NHL**	**9**	**0**	**1**	**1**	**0**	**0**	**0**	**0**	**7**	**0.0**	**–3**	**0**	**0.0**	**17:00**									
	NHL Totals		**62**	**1**	**6**	**7**	**18**	**0**	**0**	**0**	**52**	**1.9**		**1**	**100.0**	**15:51**									

Traded to **Florida** by **Nashville** for future considerations, February 25, 2011. • Missed majority of 2010-11 as a healthy reserve. Signed as a free agent by **Vancouver**, July 7, 2011.

SUMMERS, Chris

(SUHM-mehrs, KRIHS) **PHX**

Defense. Shoots left. 6'2", 210 lbs. Born, Ann Arbor, MI, February 5, 1988. Phoenix's 2nd choice, 29th overall, in 2006 Entry Draft.

Season	Club	League	GP	G	A	Pts	PIM	PP	SH	GW	S	%	+/-	TF	F%	Min	GP	G	A	Pts	PIM	PP	SH	GW	Min
2004-05	USNTDP	U-17	13	2	2	4	10																		
	USNTDP	NAHL	31	2	5	7	20										7	1	0	1	0				
2005-06	USNTDP	U-18	42	4	9	13	67																		
	USNTDP	NAHL	17	2	2	4	20																		
2006-07	U. of Michigan	CCHA	41	6	8	14	58																		
2007-08	U. of Michigan	CCHA	41	2	11	13	65																		
2008-09	U. of Michigan	CCHA	41	4	13	17	40																		
2009-10	U. of Michigan	CCHA	40	4	12	16	28																		
	San Antonio	AHL	6	1	0	1	0																		
2010-11	**Phoenix**	**NHL**	**2**	**0**	**0**	**0**	**4**	**0**	**0**	**0**	**0**	**0.0**	**–3**	**0**	**0.0**	**13:52**									
	San Antonio	AHL	75	1	9	10	54																		
	NHL Totals		**2**	**0**	**0**	**0**	**4**	**0**	**0**	**0**	**0**	**0.0**		**0**	**0.0**	**13:52**									

SUTER, Ryan

(SOO-tuhr, RIGH-uhn) **NSH**

Defense. Shoots left. 6'1", 198 lbs. Born, Madison, WI, January 21, 1985. Nashville's 1st choice, 7th overall, in 2003 Entry Draft.

Season	Club	League	GP	G	A	Pts	PIM	PP	SH	GW	S	%	+/-	TF	F%	Min	GP	G	A	Pts	PIM	PP	SH	GW	Min
2000-01	Culver Academy	High-IN	26	13	32	45																			
2001-02	USNTDP	U-17	8	2	11	13	21																		
	USNTDP	U-18	27	4	10	14	6																		
	USNTDP	NAHL	35	2	10	12	75																		
2002-03	USNTDP	NAHL	9	2	5	7	12																		
	USNTDP	U-18	42	7	17	24	124																		
2003-04	U. of Wisconsin	WCHA	39	3	16	19	93																		
2004-05	Milwaukee	AHL	63	7	16	23	70										7	1	5	6	16				
2005-06	**Nashville**	**NHL**	**71**	**1**	**15**	**16**	**66**	**0**	**0**	**0**	**84**	**1.2**	**7**	**0**	**0.0**	**17:21**									
2006-07	**Nashville**	**NHL**	**82**	**8**	**16**	**24**	**54**	**1**	**0**	**0**	**87**	**9.2**	**10**	**0**	**0.0**	**20:09**	**5**	**1**	**0**	**1**	**8**	**0**	**0**	**0**	**23:19**
2007-08	**Nashville**	**NHL**	**76**	**7**	**24**	**31**	**71**	**1**	**0**	**1**	**138**	**5.1**	**3**	**0**	**0.0**	**20:35**	**6**	**1**	**1**	**2**	**4**	**0**	**0**	**0**	**21:12**
2008-09	**Nashville**	**NHL**	**82**	**7**	**38**	**45**	**73**	**3**	**0**	**3**	**143**	**4.9**	**–16**	**0**	**0.0**	**24:16**									
2009-10	**Nashville**	**NHL**	**82**	**4**	**33**	**37**	**48**	**2**	**0**	**1**	**125**	**3.2**	**4**	**1**	**0.0**	**23:59**	**6**	**0**	**0**	**0**	**0**	**0**	**0**	**0**	**24:09**
	United States	Olympics	6	0	4	4	2																		
2010-11	**Nashville**	**NHL**	**70**	**4**	**35**	**39**	**54**	**1**	**0**	**1**	**115**	**3.5**	**20**	**1**	**0.0**	**25:12**	**12**	**1**	**5**	**6**	**6**	**0**	**0**	**0**	**28:51**
	NHL Totals		**463**	**31**	**161**	**192**	**366**	**8**	**0**	**6**	**692**	**4.5**		**2**	**0.0**	**21:58**	**29**	**3**	**6**	**9**	**18**	**0**	**0**	**0**	**25:21**

WCHA All-Rookie Team (2004)

SUTHERBY, Brian

(SUH-thur-bee, BRIGH-uhn)

Center. Shoots left. 6'2", 208 lbs. Born, Edmonton, Alta., March 1, 1982. Washington's 1st choice, 26th overall, in 2000 Entry Draft.

Season	Club	League	GP	G	A	Pts	PIM	PP	SH	GW	S	%	+/-	TF	F%	Min	GP	G	A	Pts	PIM	PP	SH	GW	Min
1997-98	CAC Cement	AMHL	36	36	23	59	60																		
1998-99	Moose Jaw	WHL	66	9	12	21	47										11	0	1	1	0				
99-2000	Moose Jaw	WHL	47	18	17	35	102										4	1	1	2	12				
2000-01	Moose Jaw	WHL	59	34	43	77	138										4	2	1	3	10				
2001-02	**Washington**	**NHL**	**7**	**0**	**0**	**0**	**2**	**0**	**0**	**0**	**3**	**0.0**	**–3**	**39**	**35.9**	**7:17**									
	Moose Jaw	WHL	36	18	27	45	75										12	7	5	12	33				
2002-03	**Washington**	**NHL**	**72**	**2**	**9**	**11**	**93**	**0**	**0**	**0**	**38**	**5.3**	**7**	**288**	**43.8**	**9:44**	**5**	**0**	**0**	**0**	**10**	**0**	**0**	**0**	**4:10**
	Portland Pirates	AHL	5	0	5	5	11																		

			Regular Season														Playoffs								
Season	Club	League	GP	G	A	Pts	PIM	PP	SH	GW	S	%	+/-	TF	F%	Min	GP	G	A	Pts	PIM	PP	SH	GW	Min
2003-04	Washington	NHL	30	2	0	2	28	0	0	0	24	8.3	–5	116	41.4	10:15	....	....	....	....	....	....	....	....	....
	Portland Pirates	AHL	6	2	4	6	16	....	....	....	....	....	....	....	....	....	....	....	....	....	....	....	....	....	....
2004-05	Portland Pirates	AHL	53	10	19	29	115	....	....	....	....	....	....	....	....	....	....	....	....	....	....	....	....	....	....
2005-06	Washington	NHL	76	14	16	30	73	0	2	0	85	16.5	–17	904	48.7	13:44	....	....	....	....	....	....	....	....	....
2006-07	Washington	NHL	69	7	10	17	78	1	0	0	87	8.0	–9	762	50.1	13:41	....	....	....	....	....	....	....	....	....
2007-08	Washington	NHL	5	1	0	1	7	0	0	0	3	33.3	–2	23	52.2	6:49	....	....	....	....	....	....	....	....	....
	Anaheim	NHL	45	0	1	1	57	0	0	0	46	0.0	–2	255	45.5	8:47	5	0	0	0	2	0	0	0	5:29
2008-09	Anaheim	NHL	17	3	3	6	19	0	0	0	17	17.6	6	45	48.9	7:12	....	....	....	....	....	....	....	....	....
	Dallas	NHL	42	5	4	9	52	0	1	0	50	10.0	–5	219	41.1	12:25	....	....	....	....	....	....	....	....	....
2009-10	Dallas	NHL	46	5	4	9	66	0	0	0	49	10.2	8	41	43.9	8:37	....	....	....	....	....	....	....	....	....
2010-11	Dallas	NHL	51	2	2	4	58	0	0	0	32	6.3	–10	32	59.4	7:25	....	....	....	....	....	....	....	....	....
	NHL Totals		460	41	49	90	533	1	3	0	434	9.4		2724	47.2	10:39	10	0	0	0	12	0	0	0	4:49

• Missed majority of 2003-04 due to groin injury vs. St. Louis, October 18, 2003. Traded to **Anaheim** by **Washington** for Anaheim's 2nd round choice (later traded to Montreal, later traded to Atlanta – Atlanta selected Jeremy Morin) in 2009 Entry Draft, November 19, 2007. Traded to **Dallas** by **Anaheim** for David McIntyre and Dallas' 6th round choice (Andreas Dahlstrom) in 2010 Entry Draft, December 14, 2008.

SUTTER, Brandon
(SUH-tuhr, BRAN-duhn) **CAR**

Center/Right wing. Shoots right. 6'3", 183 lbs. Born, Huntington, NY, February 14, 1989. Carolina's 1st choice, 11th overall, in 2007 Entry Draft.

Season	Club	League	GP	G	A	Pts	PIM	PP	SH	GW	S	%	+/-	TF	F%	Min	GP	G	A	Pts	PIM	PP	SH	GW	Min
2003-04	Red Deer Chiefs	AMBHL	35	25	34	59	28	....	....	....	....	....	....	....	....	....	11	5	4	9	....	....	....	....	....
2004-05	Red Deer	AMHL	34	4	16	20	28	....	....	....	....	....	....	....	....	....	....	....	....	....	....	....	....	....	....
	Red Deer Rebels	WHL	7	0	2	2	8	....	....	....	....	....	....	....	....	....	7	1	4	5	2	....	....	....	....
2005-06	Red Deer Rebels	WHL	68	22	24	46	36	....	....	....	....	....	....	....	....	....	....	....	....	....	....	....	....	....	....
2006-07	Red Deer Rebels	WHL	71	20	37	57	54	....	....	....	....	....	....	....	....	....	7	0	3	3	14	....	....	....	....
2007-08	Red Deer Rebels	WHL	59	26	23	49	38	....	....	....	....	....	....	....	....	....	....	....	....	....	....	....	....	....	....
	Albany River Rats	AHL	7	1	1	2	2	....	....	....	....	....	....	....	....	....	7	0	2	2	4	....	....	....	....
2008-09	Carolina	NHL	50	1	5	6	16	0	0	0	57	1.8	–1	332	38.6	8:50	....	....	....	....	....	....	....	....	....
	Albany River Rats	AHL	22	4	8	12	6	....	....	....	....	....	....	....	....	....	....	....	....	....	....	....	....	....	....
2009-10	Carolina	NHL	72	21	19	40	2	5	0	3	168	12.5	–1	997	49.1	16:33	....	....	....	....	....	....	....	....	....
	Albany River Rats	AHL	7	1	3	4	2	....	....	....	....	....	....	....	....	....	....	....	....	....	....	....	....	....	....
2010-11	Carolina	NHL	82	14	15	29	25	1	0	3	145	9.7	13	1349	44.3	16:51	....	....	....	....	....	....	....	....	....
	NHL Totals		204	36	39	75	43	6	0	6	370	9.7		2678	45.4	14:46	....	....	....	....	....	....	....	....	....

SUTTER, Brett
(SUH-tuhr, BREHT) **CAR**

Left wing. Shoots left. 6', 200 lbs. Born, Viking, Alta., June 2, 1987. Calgary's 7th choice, 179th overall, in 2005 Entry Draft.

Season	Club	League	GP	G	A	Pts	PIM	PP	SH	GW	S	%	+/-	TF	F%	Min	GP	G	A	Pts	PIM	PP	SH	GW	Min
2003-04	Kootenay Ice	WHL	44	5	7	12	26	....	....	....	....	....	....	....	....	....	4	0	0	0	4	....	....	....	....
2004-05	Kootenay Ice	WHL	70	8	11	19	70	....	....	....	....	....	....	....	....	....	16	1	2	3	16	....	....	....	....
2005-06	Kootenay Ice	WHL	16	8	7	15	21	....	....	....	....	....	....	....	....	....	....	....	....	....	....	....	....	....	....
	Red Deer Rebels	WHL	57	9	26	35	80	....	....	....	....	....	....	....	....	....	....	....	....	....	....	....	....	....	....
2006-07	Red Deer Rebels	WHL	67	28	29	57	77	....	....	....	....	....	....	....	....	....	7	3	4	7	11	....	....	....	....
2007-08	Quad City Flames	AHL	75	4	6	10	63	....	....	....	....	....	....	....	....	....	....	....	....	....	....	....	....	....	....
2008-09	Calgary	NHL	4	1	0	1	2	0	0	0	6	16.7	–2	1	0.0	8:04	....	....	....	....	....	....	....	....	....
	Quad City Flames	AHL	71	10	15	25	50	....	....	....	....	....	....	....	....	....	....	....	....	....	....	....	....	....	....
2009-10	Calgary	NHL	10	0	0	0	5	0	0	0	9	0.0	–1	5	20.0	9:40	....	....	....	....	....	....	....	....	....
	Abbotsford Heat	AHL	66	9	15	24	69	....	....	....	....	....	....	....	....	....	13	4	7	11	20	....	....	....	....
2010-11	Calgary	NHL	4	0	1	1	5	0	0	0	3	0.0	–1	23	52.2	10:07	....	....	....	....	....	....	....	....	....
	Carolina	NHL	1	0	0	0	0	0	0	0	0	0.0	0	3	33.3	4:09	....	....	....	....	....	....	....	....	....
	Charlotte	AHL	60	9	12	21	84	....	....	....	....	....	....	....	....	....	16	4	10	14	15	....	....	....	....
	NHL Totals		19	1	1	2	12	0	0	0	18	5.6		32	43.8	9:08	....	....	....	....	....	....	....	....	....

Traded to **Carolina** by **Calgary** with Ian White for Anton Babchuk and Tom Kostopoulos, November 17, 2010.

SUTTON, Andy
(SUH-tuhn, AN-dee) **EDM**

Defense. Shoots left. 6'6", 245 lbs. Born, Kingston, Ont., March 10, 1975.

Season	Club	League	GP	G	A	Pts	PIM	PP	SH	GW	S	%	+/-	TF	F%	Min	GP	G	A	Pts	PIM	PP	SH	GW	Min
1991-92	Gananoque	ON-Jr.B	36	11	9	20	....	....	....	....	....	....	....	....	....	....	14	9	21	30	....	....	....	....	....
1992-93	Gananoque	ON-Jr.B	38	14	9	23	....	....	....	....	....	....	....	....	....	....	12	16	13	29	....	....	....	....	....
1993-94	St. Mike's B's	ON-Jr.A	48	17	23	40	161	....	....	....	....	....	....	....	....	....	3	0	0	0	20	....	....	....	....
1994-95	Michigan Tech	WCHA	19	2	1	3	42	....	....	....	....	....	....	....	....	....	....	....	....	....	....	....	....	....	....
1995-96	Michigan Tech	WCHA	33	2	2	4	58	....	....	....	....	....	....	....	....	....	....	....	....	....	....	....	....	....	....
1996-97	Michigan Tech	WCHA	32	2	7	9	73	....	....	....	....	....	....	....	....	....	....	....	....	....	....	....	....	....	....
1997-98	Michigan Tech	WCHA	38	16	24	40	97	....	....	....	....	....	....	....	....	....	....	....	....	....	....	....	....	....	....
	Kentucky	AHL	7	0	0	0	33	....	....	....	....	....	....	....	....	....	....	....	....	....	....	....	....	....	....
1998-99	San Jose	NHL	31	0	3	3	65	0	0	0	24	0.0	–4	0	0.0	12:58	....	....	....	....	....	....	....	....	....
	Kentucky	AHL	21	5	10	15	53	....	....	....	....	....	....	....	....	....	5	0	0	0	23	....	....	....	....
99-2000	San Jose	NHL	40	1	1	2	80	0	0	0	29	3.4	–5	0	0.0	12:57	....	....	....	....	....	....	....	....	....
	Kentucky	AHL	3	0	1	1	0	....	....	....	....	....	....	....	....	....	....	....	....	....	....	....	....	....	....
2000-01	Minnesota	NHL	69	3	4	7	131	2	0	0	64	4.7	–11	3	33.3	12:55	....	....	....	....	....	....	....	....	....
2001-02	Minnesota	NHL	19	2	4	6	35	1	0	0	21	9.5	–4	2	0.0	10:57	....	....	....	....	....	....	....	....	....
	Atlanta	NHL	24	0	4	4	46	0	0	0	20	0.0	0	0	0.0	15:25	....	....	....	....	....	....	....	....	....
2002-03	Atlanta	NHL	53	3	18	21	114	1	1	0	65	4.6	–8	3	33.3	18:00	....	....	....	....	....	....	....	....	....
2003-04	Atlanta	NHL	65	8	13	21	94	7	1	1	102	7.8	0	1	0.0	23:21	....	....	....	....	....	....	....	....	....
2004-05	GCK Lions Zurich	Swiss-2	18	8	18	26	58	....	....	....	....	....	....	....	....	....	6	2	4	6	16	....	....	....	....
	ZSC Lions Zurich	Swiss	8	2	2	4	32	....	....	....	....	....	....	....	....	....	1	0	1	1	2	....	....	....	....
2005-06	Atlanta	NHL	76	8	17	25	144	2	1	3	86	9.3	13	1	0.0	21:05	....	....	....	....	....	....	....	....	....
2006-07	Atlanta	NHL	55	2	14	16	76	0	1	0	51	3.9	6	0	0.0	19:28	4	0	0	0	10	0	0	0	17:34
2007-08	NY Islanders	NHL	58	1	7	8	86	0	0	1	57	1.8	–6	0	0.0	18:10	....	....	....	....	....	....	....	....	....
2008-09	NY Islanders	NHL	23	2	8	10	40	0	0	0	19	10.5	3	0	0.0	20:14	....	....	....	....	....	....	....	....	....
2009-10	NY Islanders	NHL	54	4	8	12	73	0	0	0	58	6.9	–3	0	0.0	20:49	....	....	....	....	....	....	....	....	....
	Ottawa	NHL	18	1	0	1	34	0	0	0	19	5.3	–7	0	0.0	19:13	6	0	0	0	8	0	0	0	23:02
2010-11	Anaheim	NHL	39	0	4	4	87	0	0	0	31	0.0	1	0	0.0	14:45	1	0	0	0	2	0	0	0	8:18
	NHL Totals		624	35	105	140	1105	13	4	5	646	5.4		10	20.0	17:47	11	0	0	0	20	0	0	0	19:42

WCHA Second All-Star Team (1998)

Signed as a free agent by **San Jose**, March 20, 1998. Traded to **Minnesota** by **San Jose** with San Jose's 7th round choice (Peter Bartos) in 2000 Entry Draft and San Jose's 3rd round choice (later traded to Atlanta, later traded to Pittsburgh, later traded to Columbus – Columbus selected Aaron Johnson) in 2001 Entry Draft for Minnesota's 8th round choice (later traded to Calgary – Calgary selected Joe Campbell) in 2001 Entry Draft and future considerations, June 12, 2000. Traded to **Atlanta** by **Minnesota** for Hnat Domenichelli, January 22, 2002. Signed as a free agent by **GCK Zurich** (Swiss-2), September 24, 2004. • Loaned to **ZSC Zurich** (Swiss) by **GCK Zurich** (Swiss-2), February 22, 2005. Signed as a free agent by **NY Islanders**, August 10, 2007. • Missed majority of 2008-09 due to broken foot at Minnesota, December 19, 2008. Traded to **Ottawa** by **NY Islanders** for San Jose's 2nd round choice (previously acquired, later traded to Chicago – Chicago selected Kent Simpson) in 2010 Entry Draft, March 2, 2010. Signed as a free agent by **Anaheim**, August 2, 2010. • Missed majority of 2010-11 due to thumb injury at Detroit, October 8, 2011. Traded to **Edmonton** by **Anaheim** for Kurtis Foster, July 1, 2011.

SVATOS, Marek
(SVA-tohs, MAIR-ehk)

Right wing. Shoots right. 5'10", 185 lbs. Born, Kosice, Czech., June 17, 1982. Colorado's 10th choice, 227th overall, in 2001 Entry Draft.

Season	Club	League	GP	G	A	Pts	PIM	PP	SH	GW	S	%	+/-	TF	F%	Min	GP	G	A	Pts	PIM	PP	SH	GW	Min
99-2000	HC VSZ Kosice Jr.	Slovak-Jr.	39	43	30	73	28	....	....	....	....	....	....	....	....	....	....	....	....	....	....	....	....	....	....
	HC VSZ Kosice	Slovakia	19	2	2	4	0	....	....	....	....	....	....	....	....	....	....	....	....	....	....	....	....	....	....
2000-01	Kootenay Ice	WHL	39	23	18	41	47	....	....	....	....	....	....	....	....	....	11	7	2	9	26	....	....	....	....
2001-02	Kootenay Ice	WHL	53	38	39	77	58	....	....	....	....	....	....	....	....	....	21	12	6	18	40	....	....	....	....
2002-03	Hershey Bears	AHL	30	9	4	13	10	....	....	....	....	....	....	....	....	....	....	....	....	....	....	....	....	....	....
2003-04	Colorado	NHL	4	2	0	2	0	1	0	1	6	33.3	1	0	0.0	10:18	11	1	5	6	2	0	0	1	12:29
2004-05	Hershey Bears	AHL	72	18	28	46	69	....	....	....	....	....	....	....	....	....	....	....	....	....	....	....	....	....	....
2005-06	Colorado	NHL	61	32	18	50	60	12	0	9	165	19.4	0	5	20.0	13:45	....	....	....	....	....	....	....	....	....
	Slovakia	Olympics	6	0	0	0	0	....	....	....	....	....	....	....	....	....	....	....	....	....	....	....	....	....	....
2006-07	Colorado	NHL	66	15	15	30	46	8	0	2	179	8.4	1	1	100.0	12:30	....	....	....	....	....	....	....	....	....
2007-08	Colorado	NHL	62	26	11	37	32	3	0	6	140	18.6	13	3	33.3	13:39	....	....	....	....	....	....	....	....	....
2008-09	Colorado	NHL	69	14	20	34	34	6	0	1	140	10.0	–6	3	0.0	13:06	....	....	....	....	....	....	....	....	....
2009-10	Colorado	NHL	54	7	4	11	35	3	0	1	84	8.3	–13	0	0.0	11:25	3	1	0	1	2	0	0	0	13:17

			Regular Season														Playoffs								
Season	Club	League	GP	G	A	Pts	PIM	PP	SH	GW	S	%	+/-	TF	F%	Min	GP	G	A	Pts	PIM	PP	SH	GW	Min
2010-11	Omsk	Rus-KHL	19	3	5	8	14	....	....	....	....	....	....	....	....	....	....	....	....	....	....	....	....	....	....
	Nashville	**NHL**	**9**	**1**	**2**	**3**	**2**	**0**	**0**	**0**	**17**	**5.9**	**1**	**0**	**0.0**	**11:14**	....	....	....	....	....	....	....	....	....
	Ottawa	**NHL**	**19**	**3**	**2**	**5**	**8**	**0**	**0**	**0**	**33**	**9.1**	**–1**	**0**	**0.0**	**11:57**	....	....	....	....	....	....	....	....	....
	NHL Totals		**344**	**100**	**72**	**172**	**217**	**33**	**0**	**20**	**764**	**13.1**		**12**	**25.0**	**12:47**	**14**	**2**	**5**	**7**	**4**	**0**	**0**	**1**	**12:39**

WHL West Second All-Star Team (2002)

• Missed majority of 2002-03 due to recurring shoulder injury, January 28, 2003. • Missed majority of 2003-04 due to shoulder injury vs. St. Louis, October 12, 2003. Signed as a free agent by **Omsk** (Russia-KHL), September 24, 2010. Signed as a free agent by **St. Louis**, December 28, 2010. Claimed on waivers by **Nashville** from **St. Louis**, December 29, 2010. Claimed on waivers by **Ottawa** from **Nashville**, February 24, 2011.

SWEATT, Lee (SWEHT, LEE) OTT

Defense. Shoots right. 5'9", 195 lbs. Born, Elburn, IL, August 13, 1985.

Season	Club	League	GP	G	A	Pts	PIM	PP	SH	GW	S	%	+/-	TF	F%	Min	GP	G	A	Pts	PIM	PP	SH	GW	Min
2003-04	Colorado College	WCHA	37	4	12	16	20	....	....	....	....	....	....	....	....	....	....	....	....	....	....	....	....	....	....
2004-05	Colorado College	WCHA	42	3	25	28	34	....	....	....	....	....	....	....	....	....	....	....	....	....	....	....	....	....	....
2005-06	Colorado College	WCHA	41	5	16	21	36	....	....	....	....	....	....	....	....	....	....	....	....	....	....	....	....	....	....
2006-07	Colorado College	WCHA	37	9	15	24	51	....	....	....	....	....	....	....	....	....	....	....	....	....	....	....	....	....	....
	San Antonio	AHL	11	0	1	1	8	....	....	....	....	....	....	....	....	....	....	....	....	....	....	....	....	....	....
2007-08	TPS Turku	Finland	56	15	18	33	42	....	....	....	....	....	....	....	....	....	2	0	0	0	2	....	....	....	....
2008-09	Salzburg	Austria	52	10	26	36	99	....	....	....	....	....	....	....	....	....	12	2	4	6	14	....	....	....	....
2009-10	Dynamo Riga	Rus-KHL	37	2	5	7	18	....	....	....	....	....	....	....	....	....	....	....	....	....	....	....	....	....	....
	TPS Turku	Finland	21	9	7	16	8	....	....	....	....	....	....	....	....	....	15	*7	6	13	8	....	....	....	....
2010-11	**Vancouver**	**NHL**	**3**	**1**	**1**	**2**	**2**	**0**	**0**	**1**	**4**	**25.0**	**4**	**0**	**0.0**	**13:23**	....	....	....	....	....	....	....	....	....
	Manitoba Moose	AHL	41	5	9	14	18	....	....	....	....	....	....	....	....	....	....	....	....	....	....	....	....	....	....
	NHL Totals		**3**	**1**	**1**	**2**	**2**	**0**	**0**	**1**	**4**	**25.0**		**0**	**0.0**	**13:23**	....	....	....	....	....	....	....	....	....

Signed as a free agent by **Vancouver**, May 31, 2010. Signed as a free agent by **Ottawa**, July 11, 2011.

SYVRET, Danny (SIHV-reht, DA-nee) ST.L.

Defense. Shoots left. 5'11", 203 lbs. Born, Millgrove, Ont., June 13, 1985. Edmonton's 3rd choice, 81st overall, in 2005 Entry Draft.

Season	Club	League	GP	G	A	Pts	PIM	PP	SH	GW	S	%	+/-	TF	F%	Min	GP	G	A	Pts	PIM	PP	SH	GW	Min
2001-02	Cambridge	ON-Jr.B	43	6	41	47	23	....	....	....	....	....	....	....	....	....	....	....	....	....	....	....	....	....	....
	London Knights	OHL	1	0	0	0	0	....	....	....	....	....	....	....	....	....	....	....	....	....	....	....	....	....	....
2002-03	London Knights	OHL	68	8	14	22	31	....	....	....	....	....	....	....	....	....	14	1	6	7	11	....	....	....	....
2003-04	London Knights	OHL	68	3	28	31	32	....	....	....	....	....	....	....	....	....	15	1	6	7	4	....	....	....	....
2004-05	London Knights	OHL	62	23	46	69	33	....	....	....	....	....	....	....	....	....	18	5	15	20	4	....	....	....	....
2005-06	**Edmonton**	**NHL**	**10**	**0**	**0**	**0**	**6**	**0**	**0**	**0**	**8**	**0.0**	**–1**	**0**	**0.0**	**12:19**	....	....	....	....	....	....	....	....	....
	Hamilton	AHL	62	0	21	21	38	....	....	....	....	....	....	....	....	....	....	....	....	....	....	....	....	....	....
2006-07	**Edmonton**	**NHL**	**16**	**0**	**1**	**1**	**6**	**0**	**0**	**0**	**15**	**0.0**	**–10**	**0**	**0.0**	**18:28**	....	....	....	....	....	....	....	....	....
	Grand Rapids	AHL	57	4	16	20	16	....	....	....	....	....	....	....	....	....	....	....	....	....	....	....	....	....	....
2007-08	Springfield	AHL	36	1	7	8	14	....	....	....	....	....	....	....	....	....	....	....	....	....	....	....	....	....	....
	Hershey Bears	AHL	27	1	11	12	29	....	....	....	....	....	....	....	....	....	5	0	0	0	0	....	....	....	....
2008-09	**Philadelphia**	**NHL**	**2**	**0**	**0**	**0**	**0**	**0**	**0**	**0**	**0**	**0.0**	**–1**	**0**	**0.0**	**9:26**	....	....	....	....	....	....	....	....	....
	Philadelphia	AHL	76	12	45	57	44	....	....	....	....	....	....	....	....	....	4	0	1	1	0	....	....	....	....
2009-10	**Philadelphia**	**NHL**	**21**	**2**	**2**	**4**	**12**	**0**	**0**	**0**	**14**	**14.3**	**1**	**0**	**0.0**	**12:29**	....	....	....	....	....	....	....	....	....
	Adirondack	AHL	15	5	8	13	6	....	....	....	....	....	....	....	....	....	....	....	....	....	....	....	....	....	....
2010-11	**Anaheim**	**NHL**	**6**	**1**	**1**	**2**	**4**	**0**	**0**	**0**	**8**	**12.5**	**–3**	**0**	**0.0**	**16:27**	....	....	....	....	....	....	....	....	....
	Syracuse Crunch	AHL	8	0	4	4	11	....	....	....	....	....	....	....	....	....	....	....	....	....	....	....	....	....	....
	Philadelphia	**NHL**	**4**	**0**	**0**	**0**	**2**	**0**	**0**	**0**	**3**	**0.0**	**0**	**0**	**0.0**	**12:58**	**10**	**0**	**0**	**0**	**0**	**0**	**0**	**0**	**6:49**
	Adirondack	AHL	51	10	26	36	27	....	....	....	....	....	....	....	....	....	....	....	....	....	....	....	....	....	....
	NHL Totals		**59**	**3**	**4**	**7**	**30**	**0**	**0**	**0**	**48**	**6.3**		**0**	**0.0**	**14:24**	**10**	**0**	**0**	**0**	**0**	**0**	**0**	**0**	**6:49**

OHL First All-Star Team (2005) • Canadian Major Junior Defenseman of the Year (2005) • Canadian Major Junior First All-Star Team (2005) • Memorial Cup All-Star Team.. (2005) • AHL First All-Star Team (2009)

Traded to **Philadelphia** by **Edmonton** for Ryan Potulny, June 6, 2008. • Missed majority of 2009-10 due to upper body injury and as a healthy reserve. Signed as a free agent by **Anaheim**, July 21, 2010. Traded to **Philadelphia** by **Anaheim** with Rob Bordson for Patrick Maroon and David Laliberte, November 21, 2010. Signed as a free agent by **St. Louis**, August 8, 2011.

SZCZECHURA, Paul (sha-HUR-uh, PAWL) BUF

Right wing. Shoots right. 5'10", 186 lbs. Born, Brantford, Ont., November 30, 1985.

Season	Club	League	GP	G	A	Pts	PIM	PP	SH	GW	S	%	+/-	TF	F%	Min	GP	G	A	Pts	PIM	PP	SH	GW	Min
2003-04	Western Mich.	CCHA	39	9	11	20	12	....	....	....	....	....	....	....	....	....	....	....	....	....	....	....	....	....	....
2004-05	Western Mich.	CCHA	37	6	23	29	22	....	....	....	....	....	....	....	....	....	....	....	....	....	....	....	....	....	....
2005-06	Western Mich.	CCHA	40	10	26	36	47	....	....	....	....	....	....	....	....	....	....	....	....	....	....	....	....	....	....
2006-07	Western Mich.	CCHA	37	19	26	45	26	....	....	....	....	....	....	....	....	....	....	....	....	....	....	....	....	....	....
	Iowa Stars	AHL	14	3	4	7	19	....	....	....	....	....	....	....	....	....	10	3	1	4	8	....	....	....	....
2007-08	Iowa Stars	AHL	29	2	3	5	15	....	....	....	....	....	....	....	....	....	....	....	....	....	....	....	....	....	....
	Norfolk Admirals	AHL	24	14	12	26	16	....	....	....	....	....	....	....	....	....	....	....	....	....	....	....	....	....	....
2008-09	**Tampa Bay**	**NHL**	**31**	**4**	**5**	**9**	**12**	**1**	**0**	**0**	**51**	**7.8**	**–1**	**232**	**40.5**	**13:33**	....	....	....	....	....	....	....	....	....
	Norfolk Admirals	AHL	33	13	16	29	26	....	....	....	....	....	....	....	....	....	....	....	....	....	....	....	....	....	....
2009-10	**Tampa Bay**	**NHL**	**52**	**5**	**2**	**7**	**18**	**1**	**0**	**1**	**83**	**6.0**	**–15**	**403**	**46.2**	**13:05**	....	....	....	....	....	....	....	....	....
	Norfolk Admirals	AHL	35	8	21	29	24	....	....	....	....	....	....	....	....	....	....	....	....	....	....	....	....	....	....
2010-11	Norfolk Admirals	AHL	79	21	30	51	43	....	....	....	....	....	....	....	....	....	3	1	0	1	4	....	....	....	....
	NHL Totals		**83**	**9**	**7**	**16**	**30**	**2**	**0**	**1**	**134**	**6.7**		**635**	**44.1**	**13:16**	....	....	....	....	....	....	....	....	....

Signed as a free agent by **Tampa Bay**, April 24, 2008. Signed as a free agent by **Buffalo**, August 9, 2011.

TAFFE, Jeff (TAYF, JEHF) MIN

Center. Shoots left. 6'3", 207 lbs. Born, Hastings, MN, February 19, 1981. St. Louis' 1st choice, 30th overall, in 2000 Entry Draft.

Season	Club	League	GP	G	A	Pts	PIM	PP	SH	GW	S	%	+/-	TF	F%	Min	GP	G	A	Pts	PIM	PP	SH	GW	Min
1996-97	Hastings Huskies	High-MN	25	21	37	58	....	....	....	....	....	....	....	....	....	....	....	....	....	....	....	....	....	....	....
1997-98	Hastings Huskies	High-MN	28	37	29	66	....	....	....	....	....	....	....	....	....	....	....	....	....	....	....	....	....	....	....
1998-99	Hastings Huskies	High-MN	28	39	51	90	....	....	....	....	....	....	....	....	....	....	....	....	....	....	....	....	....	....	....
	Rochester	USHL	17	12	9	21	26	....	....	....	....	....	....	....	....	....	....	....	....	....	....	....	....	....	....
99-2000	U. of Minnesota	WCHA	39	10	10	20	22	....	....	....	....	....	....	....	....	....	....	....	....	....	....	....	....	....	....
2000-01	U. of Minnesota	WCHA	38	12	23	35	56	....	....	....	....	....	....	....	....	....	....	....	....	....	....	....	....	....	....
2001-02	U. of Minnesota	WCHA	43	34	24	58	86	....	....	....	....	....	....	....	....	....	....	....	....	....	....	....	....	....	....
2002-03	**Phoenix**	**NHL**	**20**	**3**	**1**	**4**	**4**	**1**	**0**	**1**	**18**	**16.7**	**–4**	**113**	**29.2**	**11:34**	....	....	....	....	....	....	....	....	....
	Springfield	AHL	57	23	26	49	44	....	....	....	....	....	....	....	....	....	5	0	3	3	8	....	....	....	....
2003-04	**Phoenix**	**NHL**	**59**	**8**	**10**	**18**	**20**	**5**	**0**	**0**	**67**	**11.9**	**–8**	**219**	**43.4**	**11:02**	....	....	....	....	....	....	....	....	....
	Springfield	AHL	15	10	6	16	19	....	....	....	....	....	....	....	....	....	....	....	....	....	....	....	....	....	....
2004-05	Utah Grizzlies	AHL	27	9	10	19	35	....	....	....	....	....	....	....	....	....	....	....	....	....	....	....	....	....	....
2005-06	**NY Rangers**	**NHL**	**2**	**0**	**0**	**0**	**0**	**0**	**0**	**0**	**1**	**0.0**	**0**	**0**	**0.0**	**3:49**	....	....	....	....	....	....	....	....	....
	Hartford	AHL	36	6	16	22	34	....	....	....	....	....	....	....	....	....	....	....	....	....	....	....	....	....	....
	Phoenix	**NHL**	**2**	**0**	**0**	**0**	**0**	**0**	**0**	**0**	**2**	**0.0**	**0**	**1**	**100.0**	**9:06**	....	....	....	....	....	....	....	....	....
	San Antonio	AHL	33	5	6	11	29	....	....	....	....	....	....	....	....	....	....	....	....	....	....	....	....	....	....
2006-07	**Phoenix**	**NHL**	**17**	**4**	**2**	**6**	**2**	**1**	**0**	**0**	**34**	**11.8**	**–7**	**64**	**39.1**	**14:12**	....	....	....	....	....	....	....	....	....
	San Antonio	AHL	59	20	20	40	22	....	....	....	....	....	....	....	....	....	....	....	....	....	....	....	....	....	....
2007-08	**Pittsburgh**	**NHL**	**45**	**5**	**7**	**12**	**8**	**1**	**0**	**1**	**56**	**8.9**	**2**	**152**	**48.7**	**9:35**	....	....	....	....	....	....	....	....	....
	Wilkes-Barre	AHL	27	11	10	21	22	....	....	....	....	....	....	....	....	....	....	....	....	....	....	....	....	....	....
2008-09	**Pittsburgh**	**NHL**	**8**	**0**	**2**	**2**	**2**	**0**	**0**	**0**	**5**	**0.0**	**–4**	**40**	**52.5**	**8:30**	....	....	....	....	....	....	....	....	....
	Wilkes-Barre	AHL	74	25	50	75	65	....	....	....	....	....	....	....	....	....	12	5	6	11	22	....	....	....	....
2009-10	**Florida**	**NHL**	**21**	**1**	**1**	**2**	**4**	**0**	**0**	**0**	**18**	**5.6**	**–1**	**74**	**44.6**	**8:25**	....	....	....	....	....	....	....	....	....
	Rochester	AHL	61	28	28	56	47	....	....	....	....	....	....	....	....	....	7	1	6	7	9	....	....	....	....
2010-11	**Chicago**	**NHL**	**1**	**0**	**0**	**0**	**0**	**0**	**0**	**0**	**0**	**0.0**	**0**	**5**	**40.0**	**4:05**	....	....	....	....	....	....	....	....	....
	Rockford IceHogs	AHL	74	30	37	67	22	....	....	....	....	....	....	....	....	....	....	....	....	....	....	....	....	....	....
	NHL Totals		**175**	**21**	**23**	**44**	**40**	**8**	**0**	**2**	**201**	**10.4**		**668**	**42.5**	**10:27**	....	....	....	....	....	....	....	....	....

• Rights traded to **Phoenix** by **St. Louis** with Michal Handzus, Ladislav Nagy and St. Louis' 1st round choice (Ben Eager) in 2002 Entry Draft for Keith Tkachuk, March 13, 2001. Traded to **NY Rangers** by **Phoenix** for Jamie Lundmark, October 18, 2005. Traded to **Phoenix** by **NY Rangers** for Martin Sonnenberg, January 24, 2006. Signed as a free agent by **Pittsburgh**, July 13, 2007. Signed as a free agent by **Florida**, July 6, 2009. Traded to **Chicago** by **Florida** for Marty Reasoner, July 22, 2010. Signed as a free agent by **Minnesota**, July 5, 2011.

TALBOT, Maxime
(TAL-buht, max-EEM) **PHI**

Center. Shoots left. 5'11", 190 lbs. Born, Lemoyne, Que., February 11, 1984. Pittsburgh's 9th choice, 234th overall, in 2002 Entry Draft.

			Regular Season														Playoffs								
Season	Club	League	GP	G	A	Pts	PIM	PP	SH	GW	S	%	+/-	TF	F%	Min	GP	G	A	Pts	PIM	PP	SH	GW	Min
99-2000	Antoine-Girouard	QAAA	42	19	21	40	32	....	....	....	....	....	....	....	....	....	7	3	6	9	0	....	....	....	....
2000-01	Rouyn-Noranda	QMJHL	40	9	15	24	78	....	....	....	....	....	....	....	....	....	....	....	....	....	....	....	....	....	....
	Hull Olympiques	QMJHL	24	6	7	13	60	....	....	....	....	....	....	....	....	....	5	1	0	1	2	....	....	....	....
2001-02	Hull Olympiques	QMJHL	65	24	36	60	174	....	....	....	....	....	....	....	....	....	12	4	6	10	51	....	....	....	....
2002-03	Hull Olympiques	QMJHL	69	46	58	104	130	....	....	....	....	....	....	....	....	....	20	14	*30	*44	33	....	....	....	....
2003-04	Gatineau	QMJHL	51	25	73	98	41	....	....	....	....	....	....	....	....	....	15	*11	*16	*27	0	....	....	....	....
2004-05	Wilkes-Barre	AHL	75	7	12	19	62	....	....	....	....	....	....	....	....	....	11	0	1	1	22	....	....	....	....
2005-06	**Pittsburgh**	**NHL**	48	5	3	8	59	0	2	1	45	11.1	−12	473	42.9	10:58	....	....	....	....	....	....	....	....	....
	Wilkes-Barre	AHL	42	12	20	32	80	....	....	....	....	....	....	....	....	....	11	3	6	9	16	....	....	....	....
2006-07	**Pittsburgh**	**NHL**	75	13	11	24	53	0	4	4	88	14.8	−2	903	44.4	13:54	5	0	1	1	7	0	0	0	15:51
	Wilkes-Barre	AHL	5	4	0	4	2	....	....	....	....	....	....	....	....	....	....	....	....	....	....	....	....	....	....
2007-08	**Pittsburgh**	**NHL**	63	12	14	26	53	0	2	1	80	15.0	8	513	45.0	15:28	17	3	6	9	36	0	0	1	14:27
2008-09♦	**Pittsburgh**	**NHL**	75	12	10	22	63	0	2	1	102	11.8	−9	542	51.1	14:08	24	8	5	13	19	0	0	2	15:14
2009-10	**Pittsburgh**	**NHL**	45	2	5	7	30	0	0	0	49	4.1	−9	165	41.2	12:13	13	2	4	6	11	0	1	1	14:15
2010-11	**Pittsburgh**	**NHL**	82	8	13	21	66	0	2	2	117	6.8	−3	874	48.6	15:04	7	1	3	4	14	0	0	0	16:53
	NHL Totals		388	52	56	108	324	0	12	9	481	10.8		3470	46.3	13:53	66	14	19	33	87	0	1	4	15:04

QMJHL Second All-Star Team (2003, 2004)
Signed as a free agent by **Philadelphia**, July 1, 2011.

TALLACKSON, Barry
(TAL-ak-suhn, BAIR-ee)

Right wing. Shoots right. 6'5", 215 lbs. Born, Grafton, ND, April 14, 1983. New Jersey's 2nd choice, 53rd overall, in 2002 Entry Draft.

99-2000	USNTDP	NAHL	53	14	6	20	90	....	....	....	....	....	....	....	....	....	3	1	0	1	8	....	....	....	....
2000-01	USNTDP	U-18	40	16	17	33	45	....	....	....	....	....	....	....	....	....	....	....	....	....	....	....	....	....	....
	USNTDP	USHL	23	7	7	14	32	....	....	....	....	....	....	....	....	....	....	....	....	....	....	....	....	....	....
2001-02	U. of Minnesota	WCHA	44	13	10	23	44	....	....	....	....	....	....	....	....	....	....	....	....	....	....	....	....	....	....
2002-03	U. of Minnesota	WCHA	32	9	14	23	18	....	....	....	....	....	....	....	....	....	....	....	....	....	....	....	....	....	....
2003-04	U. of Minnesota	WCHA	44	10	15	25	46	....	....	....	....	....	....	....	....	....	....	....	....	....	....	....	....	....	....
2004-05	U. of Minnesota	WCHA	36	11	8	19	54	....	....	....	....	....	....	....	....	....	....	....	....	....	....	....	....	....	....
	Albany River Rats	AHL	4	1	1	2	0	....	....	....	....	....	....	....	....	....	....	....	....	....	....	....	....	....	....
2005-06	**New Jersey**	**NHL**	10	1	1	2	2	0	0	0	11	9.1	−2	2	0.0	8:04	....	....	....	....	....	....	....	....	....
	Albany River Rats	AHL	60	14	23	37	62	....	....	....	....	....	....	....	....	....	....	....	....	....	....	....	....	....	....
2006-07	**New Jersey**	**NHL**	3	0	0	0	0	0	0	0	3	0.0	−1	0	0.0	12:06	....	....	....	....	....	....	....	....	....
	Lowell Devils	AHL	58	10	24	34	33	....	....	....	....	....	....	....	....	....	....	....	....	....	....	....	....	....	....
2007-08	**New Jersey**	**NHL**	3	0	0	0	0	0	0	0	0	0.0	0	0	0.0	7:03	....	....	....	....	....	....	....	....	....
	Lowell Devils	AHL	63	22	23	45	54	....	....	....	....	....	....	....	....	....	....	....	....	....	....	....	....	....	....
2008-09	**New Jersey**	**NHL**	4	0	0	0	0	0	0	0	2	0.0	−1	1	0.0	4:29	....	....	....	....	....	....	....	....	....
	Lowell Devils	AHL	56	11	10	21	29	....	....	....	....	....	....	....	....	....	....	....	....	....	....	....	....	....	....
2009-10	Peoria Rivermen	AHL	74	19	8	27	34	....	....	....	....	....	....	....	....	....	....	....	....	....	....	....	....	....	....
2010-11	Augsburg	Germany	51	29	26	55	46	....	....	....	....	....	....	....	....	....	....	....	....	....	....	....	....	....	....
	NHL Totals		20	1	1	2	2	0	0	0	16	6.3		3	0.0	7:48	....	....	....	....	....	....	....	....	....

Signed as a free agent by **St. Louis**, July 23, 2009. Signed as a free agent by **Augsburg** (Germany), July 17, 2010.

TALLINDER, Henrik
(tah-LIHN-duhr, HEHN-rihk) **N.J.**

Defense. Shoots left. 6'4", 210 lbs. Born, Stockholm, Sweden, January 10, 1979. Buffalo's 2nd choice, 48th overall, in 1997 Entry Draft.

1996-97	AIK Solna Jr.	Swe-Jr.	40	4	13	17	55	....	....	....	....	....	....	....	....	....	....	....	....	....	....	....	....	....	....
	AIK Solna	Sweden	1	0	0	0	0	....	....	....	....	....	....	....	....	....	....	....	....	....	....	....	....	....	....
1997-98	AIK Solna	Sweden	34	0	0	0	26	....	....	....	....	....	....	....	....	....	....	....	....	....	....	....	....	....	....
1998-99	AIK Solna	Sweden	36	0	0	0	30	....	....	....	....	....	....	....	....	....	....	....	....	....	....	....	....	....	....
99-2000	AIK Solna	Sweden	50	0	2	2	59	....	....	....	....	....	....	....	....	....	....	....	....	....	....	....	....	....	....
2000-01	TPS Turku	Finland	56	5	9	14	62	....	....	....	....	....	....	....	....	....	10	2	1	3	8	....	....	....	....
2001-02	**Buffalo**	**NHL**	2	0	0	0	0	0	0	0	4	0.0	−1	0	0.0	18:10	....	....	....	....	....	....	....	....	....
	Rochester	AHL	73	6	14	20	26	....	....	....	....	....	....	....	....	....	2	0	0	0	0	....	....	....	....
2002-03	**Buffalo**	**NHL**	46	3	10	13	28	1	0	0	37	8.1	−3	0	0.0	19:53	....	....	....	....	....	....	....	....	....
2003-04	**Buffalo**	**NHL**	72	1	9	10	26	0	0	0	63	1.6	5	1	0.0	18:23	....	....	....	....	....	....	....	....	....
2004-05	Linkopings HC	Sweden	44	6	10	16	63	....	....	....	....	....	....	....	....	....	....	....	....	....	....	....	....	....	....
	SC Bern	Swiss	....	....	....	....	....	....	....	....	....	....	....	....	....	....	10	1	1	2	4	....	....	....	....
2005-06	**Buffalo**	**NHL**	82	6	15	21	74	0	1	1	79	7.6	10	0	0.0	20:21	14	2	6	8	16	0	0	0	22:16
2006-07	**Buffalo**	**NHL**	47	4	10	14	34	0	0	0	34	11.8	19	1	0.0	21:07	16	0	2	2	10	0	0	0	23:40
2007-08	**Buffalo**	**NHL**	71	1	17	18	48	0	0	0	70	1.4	5	0	0.0	21:02	....	....	....	....	....	....	....	....	....
2008-09	**Buffalo**	**NHL**	66	1	11	12	36	0	0	1	35	2.9	−2	0	0.0	18:26	....	....	....	....	....	....	....	....	....
2009-10	**Buffalo**	**NHL**	82	4	16	20	32	0	0	0	53	7.5	13	0	0.0	20:37	6	0	2	2	2	0	0	0	22:41
	Sweden	Olympics	4	0	0	0	4	....	....	....	....	....	....	....	....	....	....	....	....	....	....	....	....	....	....
2010-11	**New Jersey**	**NHL**	82	5	11	16	40	0	1	2	102	4.9	−6	0	0.0	22:32	....	....	....	....	....	....	....	....	....
	NHL Totals		550	25	99	124	318	1	2	4	477	5.2		2	0.0	20:20	36	2	10	12	28	0	0	0	22:57

Signed as a free agent by **Linkopings** (Sweden), September 9, 2004. Signed as a free agent by **Bern** (Swiss), February 22, 2005. Signed as a free agent by **New Jersey**, July 1, 2010.

TAMBELLINI, Jeff
(tam-buh-LEE-nee, JEHF)

Left wing. Shoots left. 5'11", 186 lbs. Born, Calgary, Alta., April 13, 1984. Los Angeles' 3rd choice, 27th overall, in 2003 Entry Draft.

99-2000	Port Coquitlam	PIJHL	41	30	34	64	....	....	....	....	....	....	....	....	....	....	....	....	....	....	....	....	....	....	....
2000-01	Chilliwack Chiefs	BCHL	54	21	30	51	13	....	....	....	....	....	....	....	....	....	....	....	....	....	....	....	....	....	....
2001-02	Chilliwack Chiefs	BCHL	34	46	71	117	23	....	....	....	....	....	....	....	....	....	29	27	27	54	....	....	....	....	....
2002-03	U. of Michigan	CCHA	43	26	19	45	24	....	....	....	....	....	....	....	....	....	....	....	....	....	....	....	....	....	....
2003-04	U. of Michigan	CCHA	39	15	12	27	18	....	....	....	....	....	....	....	....	....	....	....	....	....	....	....	....	....	....
2004-05	U. of Michigan	CCHA	42	*24	33	*57	32	....	....	....	....	....	....	....	....	....	....	....	....	....	....	....	....	....	....
2005-06	**Los Angeles**	**NHL**	4	0	0	0	2	0	0	0	6	0.0	−1	1	0.0	9:23	....	....	....	....	....	....	....	....	....
	Manchester	AHL	56	25	31	56	26	....	....	....	....	....	....	....	....	....	....	....	....	....	....	....	....	....	....
	NY Islanders	**NHL**	21	1	3	4	8	0	0	0	11	9.1	2	3	33.3	9:54	....	....	....	....	....	....	....	....	....
	Bridgeport	AHL	....	....	....	....	....	....	....	....	....	....	....	....	....	....	7	1	2	3	2	....	....	....	....
2006-07	**NY Islanders**	**NHL**	23	2	7	9	6	0	0	0	20	10.0	6	1	0.0	7:14	....	....	....	....	....	....	....	....	....
	Bridgeport	AHL	50	30	29	59	46	....	....	....	....	....	....	....	....	....	....	....	....	....	....	....	....	....	....
2007-08	**NY Islanders**	**NHL**	31	1	3	4	8	0	0	0	43	2.3	−9	0	0.0	10:25	....	....	....	....	....	....	....	....	....
	Bridgeport	AHL	57	38	38	76	38	....	....	....	....	....	....	....	....	....	....	....	....	....	....	....	....	....	....
2008-09	**NY Islanders**	**NHL**	65	7	8	15	32	0	0	0	98	7.1	−20	5	60.0	13:07	....	....	....	....	....	....	....	....	....
	Bridgeport	AHL	6	3	0	3	2	....	....	....	....	....	....	....	....	....	....	....	....	....	....	....	....	....	....
2009-10	**NY Islanders**	**NHL**	36	7	7	14	14	3	0	0	55	12.7	−8	4	0.0	11:28	....	....	....	....	....	....	....	....	....
2010-11	**Vancouver**	**NHL**	62	9	8	17	18	1	0	0	114	7.9	10	35	54.3	11:47	6	0	0	0	2	0	0	0	7:12
	Manitoba Moose	AHL	7	5	2	7	0	....	....	....	....	....	....	....	....	....	....	....	....	....	....	....	....	....	....
	NHL Totals		242	27	36	63	88	4	0	0	347	7.8		49	46.9	11:17	6	0	0	0	2	0	0	0	7:12

CCHA All-Rookie Team (2003) • CCHA Second All-Star Team (2003) • CCHA Rookie of the Year (2003) • CCHA First All-Star Team (2005) • NCAA West Second All-American Team (2005)
Traded to **NY Islanders** by **Los Angeles** with Denis Grebeshkov for Mark Parrish and Brent Sopel, March 8, 2006. • Missed majority of 2009-10 as a healthy reserve. Signed as a free agent by **Vancouver**, July 1, 2010.

TANEV, Chris
(TA-nehv, KRIHS) **VAN**

Defense. Shoots right. 6'2", 199 lbs. Born, Toronto, Ont., December 20, 1989.

2006-07	Durham Fury	OPJHL	40	0	9	9	8	....	....	....	....	....	....	....	....	....	4	0	3	3	6	....	....	....	....
2007-08	Durham Fury	OPJHL	19	1	6	7	12	....	....	....	....	....	....	....	....	....	....	....	....	....	....	....	....	....	....
	Stouffville Spirit	OPJHL	4	0	0	0	0	....	....	....	....	....	....	....	....	....	....	....	....	....	....	....	....	....	....
	Markham Waxers	OPJHL	26	1	9	10	12	....	....	....	....	....	....	....	....	....	23	1	2	3	4	....	....	....	....
2008-09	Markham Waxers	ON-Jr.A	50	4	37	41	33	....	....	....	....	....	....	....	....	....	14	1	5	6	8	....	....	....	....
2009-10	RIT Tigers	AH	41	10	18	28	4	....	....	....	....	....	....	....	....	....	....	....	....	....	....	....	....	....	....

			Regular Season															Playoffs								
Season	Club	League	GP	G	A	Pts	PIM	PP	SH	GW	S	%	+/-	TF	F%	Min	GP	G	A	Pts	PIM	PP	SH	GW	Min
2010-11	**Vancouver**	**NHL**	**29**	**0**	**1**	**1**	**0**	**0**	**0**	**0**	**15**	**0.0**	**0**	**0**	**0.0**	**13:47**	**5**	**0**	**0**	**0**	**0**	**0**	**0**	**0**	**14:40**
	Manitoba Moose	AHL	39	1	8	9	16	....	....	....	....	....	....	....	....	....	14	1	2	3	4	....	....	....	....
	NHL Totals		**29**	**0**	**1**	**1**	**0**	**0**	**0**	**0**	**15**	**0.0**		**0**	**0.0**	**13:47**	**5**	**0**	**0**	**0**	**0**	**0**	**0**	**0**	**14:40**

Signed as a free agent by **Vancouver**, May 31, 2010.

TANGRADI, Eric

(tan-GRAY-dee, AIR-ihk) **PIT**

Center. Shoots left. 6'4", 221 lbs. Born, Philadelphia, PA, February 10, 1989. Anaheim's 2nd choice, 42nd overall, in 2007 Entry Draft.

Season	Club	League	GP	G	A	Pts	PIM	PP	SH	GW	S	%	+/-	TF	F%	Min	GP	G	A	Pts	PIM	PP	SH	GW	Min
2005-06	Wyoming Prep	High-PA	38	21	23	44	120	....	....	....	....	....	....	....	....	....	....	....	....	....	....	....	....	....	....
2006-07	Belleville Bulls	OHL	65	5	15	20	32	....	....	....	....	....	....	....	....	....	15	8	9	17	14	....	....	....	....
2007-08	Belleville Bulls	OHL	56	24	36	60	41	....	....	....	....	....	....	....	....	....	21	7	11	18	20	....	....	....	....
2008-09	Belleville Bulls	OHL	55	38	50	88	61	....	....	....	....	....	....	....	....	....	16	8	13	21	12	....	....	....	....
2009-10	**Pittsburgh**	**NHL**	**1**	**0**	**0**	**0**	**0**	**0**	**0**	**0**	**3**	**0.0**	**0**	**0**	**0.0**	**13:49**	....	....	....	....	....	....	....	....	....
	Wilkes-Barre	AHL	65	17	22	39	31	....	....	....	....	....	....	....	....	....	4	1	1	2	6	....	....	....	....
2010-11	**Pittsburgh**	**NHL**	**15**	**1**	**2**	**3**	**10**	**0**	**0**	**0**	**18**	**5.6**	**-4**	**3**	**33.3**	**11:12**	**1**	**0**	**0**	**0**	**0**	**0**	**0**	**0**	**15:12**
	Wilkes-Barre	AHL	42	18	15	33	86	....	....	....	....	....	....	....	....	....	....	....	....	....	....	....	....	....	....
	NHL Totals		**16**	**1**	**2**	**3**	**10**	**0**	**0**	**0**	**21**	**4.8**		**3**	**33.3**	**11:22**	**1**	**0**	**0**	**0**	**0**	**0**	**0**	**0**	**15:12**

Traded to **Pittsburgh** by **Anaheim** with Chris Kunitz for Ryan Whitney, February 26, 2009.

TANGUAY, Alex

(TAHNG-ay, AL-ehx) **CGY**

Left wing. Shoots left. 6'1", 195 lbs. Born, Ste-Justine, Que., November 21, 1979. Colorado's 1st choice, 12th overall, in 1998 Entry Draft.

Season	Club	League	GP	G	A	Pts	PIM	PP	SH	GW	S	%	+/-	TF	F%	Min	GP	G	A	Pts	PIM	PP	SH	GW	Min
1994-95	Cap-d-Madeleine	QAAA	1	0	1	1	0	....	....	....	....	....	....	....	....	....	....	....	....	....	....	....	....	....	....
1995-96	Cap-d-Madeleine	QAAA	44	29	34	63	64	....	....	....	....	....	....	....	....	....	5	2	4	6	14	....	....	....	....
1996-97	Halifax	QMJHL	70	27	41	68	50	....	....	....	....	....	....	....	....	....	12	4	8	12	8	....	....	....	....
1997-98	Halifax	QMJHL	51	47	38	85	32	....	....	....	....	....	....	....	....	....	5	7	6	13	4	....	....	....	....
1998-99	Halifax	QMJHL	31	27	34	61	30	....	....	....	....	....	....	....	....	....	5	1	2	3	2	....	....	....	....
	Hershey Bears	AHL	5	1	2	3	2	....	....	....	....	....	....	....	....	....	5	0	2	2	0	....	....	....	....
99-2000	**Colorado**	**NHL**	**76**	**17**	**34**	**51**	**22**	**5**	**0**	**3**	**74**	**23.0**	**6**	**11**	**45.5**	**15:38**	**17**	**2**	**1**	**3**	**2**	**1**	**0**	**1**	**10:49**
2000-01♦	**Colorado**	**NHL**	**82**	**27**	**50**	**77**	**37**	**7**	**1**	**3**	**135**	**20.0**	**35**	**30**	**43.3**	**17:51**	**23**	**6**	**15**	**21**	**8**	**1**	**0**	**2**	**19:18**
2001-02	**Colorado**	**NHL**	**70**	**13**	**35**	**48**	**36**	**7**	**0**	**2**	**90**	**14.4**	**8**	**37**	**40.5**	**18:20**	**19**	**5**	**8**	**13**	**0**	**3**	**0**	**0**	**17:25**
2002-03	**Colorado**	**NHL**	**82**	**26**	**41**	**67**	**36**	**3**	**0**	**5**	**142**	**18.3**	**34**	**123**	**39.0**	**17:48**	**7**	**1**	**2**	**3**	**4**	**0**	**0**	**1**	**19:06**
2003-04	**Colorado**	**NHL**	**69**	**25**	**54**	**79**	**42**	**7**	**0**	**5**	**117**	**21.4**	**30**	**71**	**40.9**	**18:21**	**8**	**2**	**2**	**4**	**2**	**1**	**0**	**1**	**15:46**
2004-05	HC Lugano	Swiss	6	3	3	6	4	....	....	....	....	....	....	....	....	....	....	....	....	....	....	....	....	....	....
2005-06	**Colorado**	**NHL**	**71**	**29**	**49**	**78**	**46**	**8**	**0**	**4**	**125**	**23.2**	**8**	**20**	**30.0**	**18:22**	**9**	**2**	**4**	**6**	**12**	**0**	**0**	**1**	**18:20**
2006-07	**Calgary**	**NHL**	**81**	**22**	**59**	**81**	**44**	**5**	**0**	**0**	**107**	**20.6**	**12**	**24**	**25.0**	**17:40**	**6**	**1**	**3**	**4**	**8**	**1**	**0**	**0**	**17:56**
2007-08	**Calgary**	**NHL**	**78**	**18**	**40**	**58**	**48**	**3**	**2**	**3**	**121**	**14.9**	**11**	**20**	**35.0**	**18:46**	**7**	**0**	**4**	**4**	**4**	**0**	**0**	**0**	**18:15**
2008-09	**Montreal**	**NHL**	**50**	**16**	**25**	**41**	**34**	**5**	**0**	**3**	**76**	**21.1**	**13**	**9**	**33.3**	**16:05**	**2**	**0**	**1**	**1**	**2**	**0**	**0**	**0**	**15:29**
2009-10	**Tampa Bay**	**NHL**	**80**	**10**	**27**	**37**	**32**	**3**	**0**	**2**	**91**	**11.0**	**-2**	**25**	**44.0**	**15:47**	....	....	....	....	....	....	....	....	....
2010-11	**Calgary**	**NHL**	**79**	**22**	**47**	**69**	**24**	**3**	**0**	**2**	**120**	**18.3**	**0**	**107**	**39.3**	**19:46**	....	....	....	....	....	....	....	....	....
	NHL Totals		**818**	**225**	**461**	**686**	**401**	**56**	**3**	**32**	**1198**	**18.8**		**477**	**38.8**	**17:43**	**98**	**19**	**40**	**59**	**42**	**7**	**0**	**6**	**16:50**

QMJHL All-Rookie Team (1997)

Played in NHL All-Star Game (2004)

Signed as a free agent by **Lugano** (Swiss), October 7, 2004. Traded to **Calgary** by **Colorado** for Jordan Leopold, Calgary's 2nd round choice (Codey Burki) in 2006 Entry Draft and Calgary's 2nd round choice (Trevor Cann) in 2007 Entry Draft, June 24, 2006. Traded to **Montreal** by **Calgary** with Calgary's 5th round choice (Maxim Trunev) in 2008 Entry Draft for Montreal's 1st round choice (Greg Nemisz) in 2008 Entry Draft and Montreal's 2nd round choice (later traded to Colorado – Colorado selected Stefan Elliott) in 2009 Entry Draft, June 20, 2008. Signed as a free agent by **Tampa Bay**, September 1, 2009. Signed as a free agent by **Calgary**, July 1, 2010.

TAORMINA, Matt

(tah'ohr-MEE-nah, MAT) **N.J.**

Defense. Shoots left. 5'10", 185 lbs. Born, Warren, MI, October 20, 1986.

Season	Club	League	GP	G	A	Pts	PIM	PP	SH	GW	S	%	+/-	TF	F%	Min	GP	G	A	Pts	PIM	PP	SH	GW	Min
2004-05	Texarkana Bandits	NAHL	52	14	30	44	44	....	....	....	....	....	....	....	....	....	....	....	....	....	....	....	....	....	....
2005-06	Providence	H-East	36	1	10	11	16	....	....	....	....	....	....	....	....	....	....	....	....	....	....	....	....	....	....
2006-07	Providence	H-East	35	5	2	7	6	....	....	....	....	....	....	....	....	....	....	....	....	....	....	....	....	....	....
2007-08	Providence	H-East	36	9	18	27	12	....	....	....	....	....	....	....	....	....	....	....	....	....	....	....	....	....	....
2008-09	Providence	H-East	34	5	15	20	16	....	....	....	....	....	....	....	....	....	....	....	....	....	....	....	....	....	....
	Binghamton	AHL	11	2	3	5	4	....	....	....	....	....	....	....	....	....	....	....	....	....	....	....	....	....	....
2009-10	Lowell Devils	AHL	75	10	40	50	45	....	....	....	....	....	....	....	....	....	5	1	3	4	4	....	....	....	....
2010-11	**New Jersey**	**NHL**	**17**	**3**	**2**	**5**	**2**	**1**	**0**	**0**	**38**	**7.9**	**-2**	**0**	**0.0**	**20:40**	....	....	....	....	....	....	....	....	....
	NHL Totals		**17**	**3**	**2**	**5**	**2**	**1**	**0**	**0**	**38**	**7.9**		**0**	**0.0**	**20:40**	....	....	....	....	....	....	....	....	....

Signed as a free agent by **Lowell** (AHL), August 20, 2009. Signed as a free agent by **New Jersey**, February 26, 2010. • Missed majority of 2010-11 due to ankle injury at Boston, November 15, 2010.

TARNASKY, Nick

(tahr-NAS-kee, NIHK)

Center. Shoots left. 6'2", 224 lbs. Born, Rocky Mtn. House, Alta., November 25, 1984. Tampa Bay's 11th choice, 287th overall, in 2003 Entry Draft.

Season	Club	League	GP	G	A	Pts	PIM	PP	SH	GW	S	%	+/-	TF	F%	Min	GP	G	A	Pts	PIM	PP	SH	GW	Min
99-2000	Leduc Oil Kings	AMBHL	36	21	11	32	59	....	....	....	....	....	....	....	....	....	....	....	....	....	....	....	....	....	....
2000-01	Leduc Oil Kings	AMHL	35	39	29	68	95	....	....	....	....	....	....	....	....	....	....	....	....	....	....	....	....	....	....
2001-02	Drayton Valley	AJHL	20	7	4	11	10	....	....	....	....	....	....	....	....	....	....	....	....	....	....	....	....	....	....
	Vancouver Giants	WHL	10	1	0	1	5	....	....	....	....	....	....	....	....	....	....	....	....	....	....	....	....	....	....
2002-03	Kelowna Rockets	WHL	39	4	12	16	39	....	....	....	....	....	....	....	....	....	....	....	....	....	....	....	....	....	....
	Lethbridge	WHL	30	5	8	13	45	....	....	....	....	....	....	....	....	....	....	....	....	....	....	....	....	....	....
2003-04	Lethbridge	WHL	71	26	23	49	108	....	....	....	....	....	....	....	....	....	....	....	....	....	....	....	....	....	....
2004-05	Springfield	AHL	80	7	10	17	176	....	....	....	....	....	....	....	....	....	....	....	....	....	....	....	....	....	....
2005-06	**Tampa Bay**	**NHL**	**12**	**0**	**1**	**1**	**4**	**0**	**0**	**0**	**9**	**0.0**	**-3**	**15**	**40.0**	**4:40**	....	....	....	....	....	....	....	....	....
	Springfield	AHL	68	14	9	23	100	....	....	....	....	....	....	....	....	....	....	....	....	....	....	....	....	....	....
2006-07	**Tampa Bay**	**NHL**	**77**	**5**	**4**	**9**	**80**	**0**	**0**	**1**	**41**	**12.2**	**-6**	**13**	**30.8**	**6:30**	**6**	**0**	**0**	**0**	**10**	**0**	**0**	**0**	**6:13**
2007-08	**Tampa Bay**	**NHL**	**80**	**6**	**4**	**10**	**78**	**1**	**0**	**1**	**91**	**6.6**	**-15**	**9**	**44.4**	**8:15**	....	....	....	....	....	....	....	....	....
2008-09	**Nashville**	**NHL**	**11**	**0**	**1**	**1**	**17**	**0**	**0**	**0**	**6**	**0.0**	**1**	**0**	**0.0**	**5:38**	....	....	....	....	....	....	....	....	....
	Florida	**NHL**	**34**	**1**	**5**	**6**	**33**	**0**	**0**	**0**	**32**	**3.1**	**-2**	**1**	**0.0**	**7:52**	....	....	....	....	....	....	....	....	....
2009-10	**Florida**	**NHL**	**31**	**1**	**2**	**3**	**85**	**0**	**0**	**0**	**19**	**5.3**	**-5**	**0**	**0.0**	**6:49**	....	....	....	....	....	....	....	....	....
	Rochester	AHL	5	3	0	3	7	....	....	....	....	....	....	....	....	....	....	....	....	....	....	....	....	....	....
2010-11	Springfield	AHL	66	7	13	20	150	....	....	....	....	....	....	....	....	....	....	....	....	....	....	....	....	....	....
	Florida Everblades	ECHL	3	1	2	3	0	....	....	....	....	....	....	....	....	....	....	....	....	....	....	....	....	....	....
	NHL Totals		**245**	**13**	**17**	**30**	**297**	**1**	**0**	**2**	**198**	**6.6**		**38**	**36.8**	**7:10**	**6**	**0**	**0**	**0**	**10**	**0**	**0**	**0**	**6:13**

Traded to **Nashville** by **Tampa Bay** for Nashville's 6th round choice (Jaroslav Janus) in 2009 Entry Draft, September 29, 2008. Traded to **Florida** by **Nashville** for Wade Belak, November 27, 2008. • Missed majority of 2009-10 due to eye injury in pre-season at Ottawa, September 16, 2009. Signed as a free agent by **Florida** (ECHL), November 5, 2010. Signed to a PTO (professional tryout) contract by **Springfield** (AHL), November 11, 2010.

TATAR, Tomas

(TAH-tahr, TAW-mahsh) **DET**

Center. Shoots left. 5'11", 179 lbs. Born, Ilava, Czech., December 1, 1990. Detroit's 2nd choice, 60th overall, in 2009 Entry Draft.

Season	Club	League	GP	G	A	Pts	PIM	PP	SH	GW	S	%	+/-	TF	F%	Min	GP	G	A	Pts	PIM	PP	SH	GW	Min
2004-05	Dubnica U18	Svk-U18	1	0	0	0	0	....	....	....	....	....	....	....	....	....	....	....	....	....	....	....	....	....	....
2005-06	Dubnica U18	Svk-U18	43	11	15	26	18	....	....	....	....	....	....	....	....	....	....	....	....	....	....	....	....	....	....
2006-07	Dubnica Jr.	Slovak-Jr.	6	3	0	3	2	....	....	....	....	....	....	....	....	....	....	....	....	....	....	....	....	....	....
	Dukla Trencin U18	Svk-U18	48	33	44	77	42	....	....	....	....	....	....	....	....	....	....	....	....	....	....	....	....	....	....
2007-08	Dukla Trencin U18	Svk-U18	4	9	4	13	0	....	....	....	....	....	....	....	....	....	....	....	....	....	....	....	....	....	....
	Dukla Trencin Jr.	Slovak-Jr.	42	41	35	76	32	....	....	....	....	....	....	....	....	....	....	....	....	....	....	....	....	....	....
2008-09	HC 07 Detva	Slovak-2	1	1	1	2	2	....	....	....	....	....	....	....	....	....	....	....	....	....	....	....	....	....	....
	HKm Zvolen	Slovakia	48	7	8	15	20	....	....	....	....	....	....	....	....	....	13	5	3	8	4	....	....	....	....
2009-10	Grand Rapids	AHL	58	16	16	32	12	....	....	....	....	....	....	....	....	....	....	....	....	....	....	....	....	....	....
2010-11	**Detroit**	**NHL**	**9**	**1**	**0**	**1**	**0**	**0**	**0**	**0**	**6**	**16.7**	**0**	**0**	**0.0**	**9:36**	....	....	....	....	....	....	....	....	....
	Grand Rapids	AHL	70	24	33	57	45	....	....	....	....	....	....	....	....	....	....	....	....	....	....	....	....	....	....
	NHL Totals		**9**	**1**	**0**	**1**	**0**	**0**	**0**	**0**	**6**	**16.7**		**0**	**0.0**	**9:36**	....	....	....	....	....	....	....	....	....

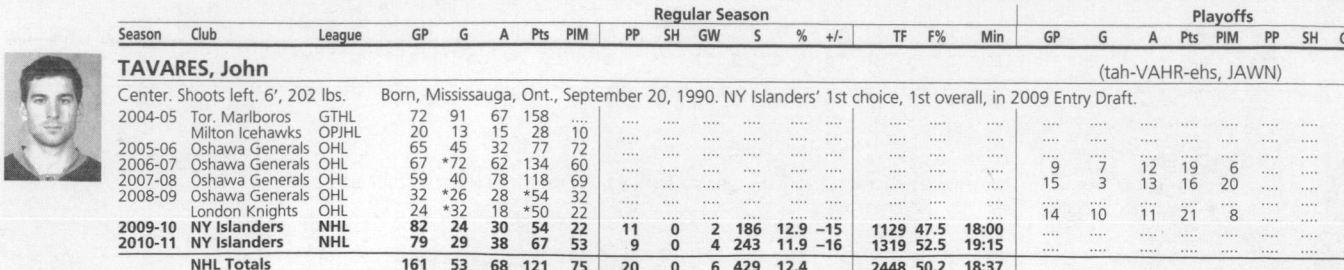

TAVARES, John
(tah-VAHR-ehs, JAWN) **NYI**

Center. Shoots left. 6', 202 lbs. Born, Mississauga, Ont., September 20, 1990. NY Islanders' 1st choice, 1st overall, in 2009 Entry Draft.

			Regular Season														Playoffs								
Season	Club	League	GP	G	A	Pts	PIM	PP	SH	GW	S	%	+/-	TF	F%	Min	GP	G	A	Pts	PIM	PP	SH	GW	Min
2004-05	Tor. Marlboros	GTHL	72	91	67	158	....	....	....	....	....	....	....	....	....	....	....	....	....	....	....	....	....	....	....
	Milton Icehawks	OPJHL	20	13	15	28	10	....	....	....	....	....	....	....	....	....	....	....	....	....	....	....	....	....	....
2005-06	Oshawa Generals	OHL	65	45	32	77	72	....	....	....	....	....	....	....	....	....	....	....	....	....	....	....	....	....	....
2006-07	Oshawa Generals	OHL	67	*72	62	134	60	....	....	....	....	....	....	....	....	....	9	7	12	19	6	....	....	....	....
2007-08	Oshawa Generals	OHL	59	40	78	118	69	....	....	....	....	....	....	....	....	....	15	3	13	16	20	....	....	....	....
2008-09	Oshawa Generals	OHL	32	*26	28	*54	32	....	....	....	....	....	....	....	....	....	....	....	....	....	....	....	....	....	....
	London Knights	OHL	24	*32	18	*50	22	....	....	....	....	....	....	....	....	....	14	10	11	21	8	....	....	....	....
2009-10	**NY Islanders**	**NHL**	**82**	**24**	**30**	**54**	**22**	**11**	**0**	**2**	**186**	**12.9**	**–15**	**1129**	**47.5**	**18:00**	....	....	....	....	....	....	....	....	....
2010-11	**NY Islanders**	**NHL**	**79**	**29**	**38**	**67**	**53**	**9**	**0**	**4**	**243**	**11.9**	**–16**	**1319**	**52.5**	**19:15**	....	....	....	....	....	....	....	....	....
	NHL Totals		**161**	**53**	**68**	**121**	**75**	**20**	**0**	**6**	**429**	**12.4**		**2448**	**50.2**	**18:37**	....	....	....	....	....	....	....	....	....

OHL All-Rookie Team (2006) • Canadian Major Junior Rookie of the Year (2006) • OHL First All-Star Team (2007) • Canadian Major Junior First All-Star Team (2007, 2009) • Canadian Major Junior Player of the Year (2007) • OHL Second All-Star Team (2009) • NHL All-Rookie Team (2010)

TEDENBY, Mattias
(TEH-dehn-bew, muh-TIGH-uhs) **N.J.**

Left wing. Shoots left. 5'10", 175 lbs. Born, Vetlanda, Sweden, February 21, 1990. New Jersey's 1st choice, 24th overall, in 2008 Entry Draft.

Season	Club	League	GP	G	A	Pts	PIM	PP	SH	GW	S	%	+/-	TF	F%	Min	GP	G	A	Pts	PIM	PP	SH	GW	Min
2005-06	HV 71 U18	Swe-U18	13	8	7	15	24	....	....	....	....	....	....	....	....	....	5	1	0	1	10	....	....	....	....
2006-07	HV 71 U18	Swe-U18	2	4	0	4	2	....	....	....	....	....	....	....	....	....	5	7	2	9	14	....	....	....	....
	HV 71 Jr.	Swe-Jr.	27	10	10	20	43	....	....	....	....	....	....	....	....	....	4	3	1	4	2	....	....	....	....
2007-08	HV 71 U18	Swe-U18	1	1	0	1	0	....	....	....	....	....	....	....	....	....	....	....	....	....	....	....	....	....	....
	HV 71 Jr.	Swe-Jr.	25	14	16	30	14	....	....	....	....	....	....	....	....	....	2	0	0	0	0	....	....	....	....
	HV 71 Jonkoping	Sweden	23	3	3	6	6	....	....	....	....	....	....	....	....	....	5	0	0	0	0	....	....	....	....
2008-09	IK Oskarshamn	Sweden-2	13	2	9	11	6	....	....	....	....	....	....	....	....	....	....	....	....	....	....	....	....	....	....
	HV 71 Jonkoping	Sweden	32	3	1	4	6	....	....	....	....	....	....	....	....	....	18	6	3	9	6	....	....	....	....
2009-10	HV 71 Jonkoping	Sweden	44	12	7	19	30	....	....	....	....	....	....	....	....	....	16	2	3	5	6	....	....	....	....
2010-11	**New Jersey**	**NHL**	**58**	**8**	**14**	**22**	**14**	**2**	**0**	**2**	**87**	**9.2**	**3**	**0**	**0.0**	**12:33**	....	....	....	....	....	....	....	....	....
	Albany Devils	AHL	12	3	2	5	6	....	....	....	....	....	....	....	....	....	....	....	....	....	....	....	....	....	....
	NHL Totals		**58**	**8**	**14**	**22**	**14**	**2**	**0**	**2**	**87**	**9.2**		**0**	**0.0**	**12:33**	....	....	....	....	....	....	....	....	....

THOMAS, Bill
(TAW-mas, BIHL)

Right wing. Shoots right. 6'1", 185 lbs. Born, Pittsburgh, PA, June 20, 1983.

Season	Club	League	GP	G	A	Pts	PIM	PP	SH	GW	S	%	+/-	TF	F%	Min	GP	G	A	Pts	PIM	PP	SH	GW	Min
2002-03	Tri-City Storm	USHL	60	29	21	50	20	....	....	....	....	....	....	....	....	....	3	0	3	3	4	....	....	....	....
2003-04	Tri-City Storm	USHL	60	31	38	69	30	....	....	....	....	....	....	....	....	....	11	*9	7	*16	4	....	....	....	....
2004-05	Nebraska-Omaha	CCHA	39	19	26	45	12	....	....	....	....	....	....	....	....	....	....	....	....	....	....	....	....	....	....
2005-06	Nebraska-Omaha	CCHA	41	*27	23	50	43	....	....	....	....	....	....	....	....	....	....	....	....	....	....	....	....	....	....
	Phoenix	**NHL**	**9**	**1**	**2**	**3**	**8**	**1**	**0**	**0**	**15**	**6.7**	**–2**	**2**	**50.0**	**13:30**	....	....	....	....	....	....	....	....	....
2006-07	**Phoenix**	**NHL**	**24**	**8**	**6**	**14**	**2**	**4**	**0**	**1**	**60**	**13.3**	**–6**	**0**	**0.0**	**13:29**	....	....	....	....	....	....	....	....	....
	San Antonio	AHL	47	13	20	33	20	....	....	....	....	....	....	....	....	....	....	....	....	....	....	....	....	....	....
2007-08	**Phoenix**	**NHL**	**7**	**0**	**0**	**0**	**0**	**0**	**0**	**0**	**9**	**0.0**	**–2**	**0**	**0.0**	**13:08**	....	....	....	....	....	....	....	....	....
	San Antonio	AHL	75	24	28	52	40	....	....	....	....	....	....	....	....	....	7	1	2	3	0	....	....	....	....
2008-09	**Pittsburgh**	**NHL**	**16**	**2**	**1**	**3**	**2**	**0**	**1**	**0**	**17**	**11.8**	**–4**	**101**	**51.5**	**9:31**	....	....	....	....	....	....	....	....	....
	Wilkes-Barre	AHL	39	8	10	18	24	....	....	....	....	....	....	....	....	....	12	1	4	5	12	....	....	....	....
2009-10	Springfield	AHL	33	5	12	17	14	....	....	....	....	....	....	....	....	....	....	....	....	....	....	....	....	....	....
	HC Lugano	Swiss	6	2	1	3	2	....	....	....	....	....	....	....	....	....	2	0	0	0	0	....	....	....	....
2010-11	**Florida**	**NHL**	**24**	**4**	**3**	**7**	**6**	**0**	**0**	**2**	**33**	**12.1**	**1**	**22**	**59.1**	**8:30**	....	....	....	....	....	....	....	....	....
	Rochester	AHL	53	16	20	36	12	....	....	....	....	....	....	....	....	....	....	....	....	....	....	....	....	....	....
	NHL Totals		**80**	**15**	**12**	**27**	**18**	**5**	**1**	**3**	**134**	**11.2**		**125**	**52.8**	**11:10**	....	....	....	....	....	....	....	....	....

CCHA All-Rookie Team (2005) • CCHA Rookie of the Year (2005) • CCHA Second All-Star Team (2005) • CCHA First All-Star Team (2006)

Signed as a free agent by **Phoenix**. March 27, 2006. Signed as a free agent by **Pittsburgh**. July 15, 2008. Signed to a PTO (professional tryout) contract by **Springfield** (AHL), November 3, 2009. Signed as a free agent by **Lugano** (Swiss), January 12, 2010. Signed as a free agent by **Florida**, July 2, 2010.

THOMPSON, Nate
(TAWM-suhn, NAYT) **T.B.**

Center. Shoots left. 6', 210 lbs. Born, Anchorage, AK, October 5, 1984. Boston's 8th choice, 183rd overall, in 2003 Entry Draft.

Season	Club	League	GP	G	A	Pts	PIM	PP	SH	GW	S	%	+/-	TF	F%	Min	GP	G	A	Pts	PIM	PP	SH	GW	Min
2001-02	Seattle	WHL	69	13	26	39	42	....	....	....	....	....	....	....	....	....	11	1	3	4	13	....	....	....	....
2002-03	Seattle	WHL	61	10	24	34	48	....	....	....	....	....	....	....	....	....	15	5	4	9	6	....	....	....	....
2003-04	Seattle	WHL	65	13	23	36	24	....	....	....	....	....	....	....	....	....	....	....	....	....	....	....	....	....	....
2004-05	Seattle	WHL	58	19	15	34	39	....	....	....	....	....	....	....	....	....	12	1	2	3	2	....	....	....	....
	Providence Bruins	AHL	....	....	....	....	....	....	....	....	....	....	....	....	....	....	11	0	1	1	6	....	....	....	....
2005-06	Providence Bruins	AHL	74	8	10	18	58	....	....	....	....	....	....	....	....	....	3	0	0	0	10	....	....	....	....
2006-07	**Boston**	**NHL**	**4**	**0**	**0**	**0**	**0**	**0**	**0**	**0**	**5**	**0.0**	**0**	**10**	**40.0**	**4:46**	....	....	....	....	....	....	....	....	....
	Providence Bruins	AHL	67	8	15	23	74	....	....	....	....	....	....	....	....	....	13	0	2	2	9	....	....	....	....
2007-08	Providence Bruins	AHL	75	19	20	39	83	....	....	....	....	....	....	....	....	....	10	2	3	5	4	....	....	....	....
2008-09	**NY Islanders**	**NHL**	**43**	**2**	**2**	**4**	**49**	**0**	**1**	**0**	**56**	**3.6**	**–11**	**429**	**50.4**	**12:05**	....	....	....	....	....	....	....	....	....
2009-10	**NY Islanders**	**NHL**	**39**	**1**	**5**	**6**	**39**	**0**	**0**	**0**	**48**	**2.1**	**–14**	**210**	**49.5**	**12:56**	....	....	....	....	....	....	....	....	....
	Tampa Bay	**NHL**	**32**	**1**	**3**	**4**	**17**	**0**	**0**	**0**	**44**	**2.3**	**–3**	**385**	**56.9**	**13:58**	....	....	....	....	....	....	....	....	....
2010-11	**Tampa Bay**	**NHL**	**79**	**10**	**15**	**25**	**29**	**0**	**1**	**2**	**123**	**8.1**	**–6**	**664**	**54.2**	**15:05**	**18**	**1**	**3**	**4**	**4**	**0**	**0**	**0**	**15:37**
	NHL Totals		**197**	**14**	**25**	**39**	**134**	**0**	**2**	**2**	**276**	**5.1**		**1698**	**53.2**	**13:37**	**18**	**1**	**3**	**4**	**4**	**0**	**0**	**0**	**15:38**

Claimed on waivers by **NY Islanders** from **Boston**, October 8, 2008. Claimed on waivers by **Tampa Bay** from **NY Islanders**, January 21, 2010.

THORBURN, Chris
(THOHR-buhrn, KRIHS) **WPG**

Right wing. Shoots right. 6'3", 230 lbs. Born, Sault Ste. Marie, Ont., June 3, 1983. Buffalo's 3rd choice, 50th overall, in 2001 Entry Draft.

Season	Club	League	GP	G	A	Pts	PIM	PP	SH	GW	S	%	+/-	TF	F%	Min	GP	G	A	Pts	PIM	PP	SH	GW	Min
1998-99	Elliot Lake Vikings	NOJHA	40	21	12	33	28	....	....	....	....	....	....	....	....	....	....	....	....	....	....	....	....	....	....
99-2000	North Bay	OHL	56	12	8	20	33	....	....	....	....	....	....	....	....	....	6	0	2	2	0	....	....	....	....
2000-01	North Bay	OHL	66	22	32	54	64	....	....	....	....	....	....	....	....	....	4	0	1	1	9	....	....	....	....
2001-02	North Bay	OHL	67	15	43	58	112	....	....	....	....	....	....	....	....	....	5	1	2	3	8	....	....	....	....
2002-03	Saginaw Spirit	OHL	37	19	19	38	68	....	....	....	....	....	....	....	....	....	....	....	....	....	....	....	....	....	....
	Plymouth Whalers	OHL	27	11	22	33	56	....	....	....	....	....	....	....	....	....	18	11	9	20	10	....	....	....	....
2003-04	Rochester	AHL	58	6	16	22	77	....	....	....	....	....	....	....	....	....	16	3	2	5	18	....	....	....	....
2004-05	Rochester	AHL	73	12	17	29	185	....	....	....	....	....	....	....	....	....	4	0	1	1	2	....	....	....	....
2005-06	**Buffalo**	**NHL**	**2**	**0**	**1**	**1**	**7**	**0**	**0**	**0**	**1**	**0.0**	**–1**	**1**	**0.0**	**6:52**	....	....	....	....	....	....	....	....	....
	Rochester	AHL	77	23	27	50	134	....	....	....	....	....	....	....	....	....	....	....	....	....	....	....	....	....	....
2006-07	**Pittsburgh**	**NHL**	**39**	**3**	**2**	**5**	**69**	**0**	**0**	**1**	**40**	**7.5**	**1**	**8**	**25.0**	**7:54**	....	....	....	....	....	....	....	....	....
	Wilkes-Barre	AHL	3	0	1	1	2	....	....	....	....	....	....	....	....	....	....	....	....	....	....	....	....	....	....
2007-08	**Atlanta**	**NHL**	**73**	**5**	**13**	**18**	**92**	**0**	**0**	**1**	**72**	**6.9**	**–4**	**20**	**60.0**	**8:56**	....	....	....	....	....	....	....	....	....
2008-09	**Atlanta**	**NHL**	**82**	**7**	**8**	**15**	**104**	**0**	**0**	**1**	**85**	**8.2**	**–10**	**37**	**40.5**	**9:35**	....	....	....	....	....	....	....	....	....
2009-10	**Atlanta**	**NHL**	**76**	**4**	**9**	**13**	**89**	**0**	**3**	**0**	**63**	**6.3**	**6**	**29**	**55.2**	**9:59**	....	....	....	....	....	....	....	....	....
2010-11	**Atlanta**	**NHL**	**82**	**9**	**10**	**19**	**77**	**2**	**0**	**0**	**114**	**7.9**	**–4**	**251**	**49.8**	**13:48**	....	....	....	....	....	....	....	....	....
	NHL Totals		**354**	**28**	**43**	**71**	**438**	**2**	**3**	**3**	**375**	**7.5**		**346**	**49.1**	**10:19**	....	....	....	....	....	....	....	....	....

Claimed on waivers by **Pittsburgh** from **Buffalo**, October 3, 2006. Traded to **Atlanta** by **Pittsburgh** for NY Rangers' 3rd round choice (previously acquired, Pittsburgh selected Robert Bortuzzo) in 2007 Entry Draft, June 22, 2007. • Transferred to **Winnipeg** after **Atlanta** franchise relocated, June 21, 2011.

THORESEN, Patrick
(THOR-eh-sehn, PAT-rihk)

Center. Shoots left. 5'11", 188 lbs. Born, Oslo, Norway, November 7, 1983.

Season	Club	League	GP	G	A	Pts	PIM	PP	SH	GW	S	%	+/-	TF	F%	Min	GP	G	A	Pts	PIM	PP	SH	GW	Min
99-2000	Storhamar	Norway	25	1	8	9	4	....	....	....	....	....	....	....	....	....	....	....	....	....	....	....	....	....	....
	Norway	WJ18-B	5	3	2	5	6	....	....	....	....	....	....	....	....	....	....	....	....	....	....	....	....	....	....
2000-01	Storhamar	Norway	40	18	27	45	24	....	....	....	....	....	....	....	....	....	....	....	....	....	....	....	....	....	....
2001-02	Moncton Wildcats	QMJHL	60	30	43	73	50	....	....	....	....	....	....	....	....	....	....	....	....	....	....	....	....	....	....
2002-03	Baie-Comeau	QMJHL	71	33	*75	108	57	....	....	....	....	....	....	....	....	....	12	2	8	10	8	....	....	....	....
2003-04	Morrums GoIS IK	Sweden-2	38	19	22	41	40	....	....	....	....	....	....	....	....	....	....	....	....	....	....	....	....	....	....
	Djurgarden	Sweden	3	0	0	0	2	....	....	....	....	....	....	....	....	....	....	....	....	....	....	....	....	....	....
2004-05	Djurgarden	Sweden	30	10	7	17	33	....	....	....	....	....	....	....	....	....	12	2	2	4	29	....	....	....	....

			Regular Season														Playoffs								
Season	Club	League	GP	G	A	Pts	PIM	PP	SH	GW	S	%	+/-	TF	F%	Min	GP	G	A	Pts	PIM	PP	SH	GW	Min
2005-06	Djurgarden	Sweden	50	17	19	36	44	....	....	....	....	....	....	....	....	....	....	....	....	....	....	....	....	....	....
	Salzburg	Austria	....	....	....	....	....	....	....	....	....	....	....	....	....	....	9	4	7	11	12	....	....	....	....
2006-07	**Edmonton**	**NHL**	**68**	**4**	**12**	**16**	**52**	**0**	**1**	**2**	**73**	**5.5**	**–1**	**82**	**51.2**	**11:25**	....	....	....	....	....	....	....	....	....
	Wilkes-Barre	AHL	5	1	5	6	4	....	....	....	....	....	....	....	....	....	....	....	....	....	....	....	....	....	....
2007-08	**Edmonton**	**NHL**	**17**	**2**	**1**	**3**	**6**	**0**	**0**	**0**	**18**	**11.1**	**–4**	**19**	**52.6**	**10:43**	....	....	....	....	....	....	....	....	....
	Springfield	AHL	29	13	13	26	13	....	....	....	....	....	....	....	....	....	....	....	....	....	....	....	....	....	....
	Philadelphia	**NHL**	**21**	**0**	**5**	**5**	**8**	**0**	**0**	**0**	**21**	**0.0**	**–6**	**81**	**38.3**	**12:36**	**14**	**0**	**2**	**2**	**4**	**0**	**0**	**0**	**9:22**
2008-09	HC Lugano	Swiss	48	22	41	63	83	....	....	....	....	....	....	....	....	....	7	1	7	8	2	....	....	....	....
2009-10	Ufa	Rus-KHL	56	24	33	57	71	....	....	....	....	....	....	....	....	....	15	5	9	14	37	....	....	....	....
	Norway	Olympics	4	0	5	5	0	....	....	....	....	....	....	....	....	....	....	....	....	....	....	....	....	....	....
2010-11	Ufa	Rus-KHL	54	29	37	66	30	....	....	....	....	....	....	....	....	....	21	3	*15	18	16	....	....	....	....
	NHL Totals		**106**	**6**	**18**	**24**	**66**	**0**	**1**	**2**	**112**	**5.4**		**182**	**45.6**	**11:32**	**14**	**0**	**2**	**2**	**4**	**0**	**0**	**0**	**9:22**

Signed as a free agent by **Edmonton**, June 12, 2006. Claimed on waivers by **Philadelphia** from **Edmonton**, February 22, 2008. Signed as a free agent by **Lugano** (Swiss), July 14, 2008. Signed as a free agent by **Ufa** (Russia-KHL), May 21, 2009.

THORNTON, Joe

(THOHRN-tuhn, JOH) **S.J.**

Center. Shoots left. 6'4", 230 lbs. Born, London, Ont., July 2, 1979. Boston's 1st choice, 1st overall, in 1997 Entry Draft.

1993-94	Elgin-Mid. Chiefs	Minor-ON	67	*83	*85	*168	45	....	....	....	....	....	....	....	....	....	....	....	....	....	....	....	....	....	....
	St. Thomas Stars	ON-Jr.B	6	2	6	8	2	....	....	....	....	....	....	....	....	....	....	....	....	....	....	....	....	....	....
1994-95	St. Thomas Stars	ON-Jr.B	50	40	64	104	53	....	....	....	....	....	....	....	....	....	....	....	....	....	....	....	....	....	....
1995-96	Sault Ste. Marie	OHL	66	30	46	76	53	....	....	....	....	....	....	....	....	....	4	1	1	2	11	....	....	....	....
1996-97	Sault Ste. Marie	OHL	59	41	81	122	123	....	....	....	....	....	....	....	....	....	11	11	8	19	24	....	....	....	....
1997-98	**Boston**	**NHL**	**55**	**3**	**4**	**7**	**19**	**0**	**0**	**1**	**33**	**9.1**	**–6**	....	....	....	**6**	**0**	**0**	**0**	**9**	**0**	**0**	**0**	....
1998-99	**Boston**	**NHL**	**81**	**16**	**25**	**41**	**69**	**7**	**0**	**1**	**128**	**12.5**	**3**	**1073**	**48.7**	**15:21**	**11**	**3**	**6**	**9**	**4**	**2**	**0**	**2**	**19:52**
99-2000	**Boston**	**NHL**	**81**	**23**	**37**	**60**	**82**	**5**	**0**	**3**	**171**	**13.5**	**–5**	**1861**	**49.5**	**21:18**	....	....	....	....	....	....	....	....	....
2000-01	**Boston**	**NHL**	**72**	**37**	**34**	**71**	**107**	**19**	**1**	**5**	**181**	**20.4**	**–4**	**1651**	**52.1**	**21:45**	....	....	....	....	....	....	....	....	....
2001-02	**Boston**	**NHL**	**66**	**22**	**46**	**68**	**127**	**6**	**0**	**5**	**152**	**14.5**	**7**	**1341**	**49.1**	**19:59**	**6**	**2**	**4**	**6**	**10**	**0**	**0**	**0**	**21:09**
2002-03	**Boston**	**NHL**	**77**	**36**	**65**	**101**	**109**	**12**	**2**	**4**	**196**	**18.4**	**12**	**1766**	**49.5**	**22:33**	**5**	**1**	**2**	**3**	**4**	**1**	**0**	**0**	**20:13**
2003-04	**Boston**	**NHL**	**77**	**23**	**50**	**73**	**98**	**4**	**0**	**6**	**187**	**12.3**	**18**	**1671**	**56.3**	**21:38**	**7**	**0**	**0**	**0**	**14**	**0**	**0**	**0**	**21:30**
2004-05	HC Davos	Swiss	40	10	44	54	80	....	....	....	....	....	....	....	....	....	14	4	*20	*24	29	....	....	....	....
2005-06	**Boston**	**NHL**	**23**	**9**	***24**	***33**	**6**	**3**	**0**	**2**	**60**	**15.0**	**0**	**511**	**52.3**	**21:33**	....	....	....	....	....	....	....	....	....
	San Jose	**NHL**	**58**	**20**	***72**	***92**	**55**	**8**	**0**	**4**	**135**	**14.8**	**31**	**1287**	**50.9**	**21:15**	**11**	**2**	**7**	**9**	**12**	**1**	**0**	**1**	**25:09**
	Canada	Olympics	6	1	2	3	0	....	....	....	....	....	....	....	....	....	....	....	....	....	....	....	....	....	....
2006-07	**San Jose**	**NHL**	**82**	**22**	***92**	**114**	**44**	**10**	**0**	**5**	**213**	**10.3**	**24**	**1522**	**51.1**	**20:19**	**11**	**1**	**10**	**11**	**10**	**0**	**0**	**0**	**22:00**
2007-08	**San Jose**	**NHL**	**82**	**29**	***67**	**96**	**59**	**11**	**0**	**5**	**178**	**16.3**	**18**	**1485**	**52.9**	**21:24**	**13**	**2**	**8**	**10**	**2**	**1**	**0**	**1**	**24:42**
2008-09	**San Jose**	**NHL**	**82**	**25**	**61**	**86**	**56**	**11**	**0**	**3**	**139**	**18.0**	**16**	**1295**	**55.4**	**19:28**	**6**	**1**	**4**	**5**	**5**	**1**	**0**	**0**	**19:14**
2009-10	**San Jose**	**NHL**	**79**	**20**	**69**	**89**	**54**	**4**	**1**	**2**	**141**	**14.2**	**17**	**1228**	**53.9**	**19:51**	**15**	**3**	**9**	**12**	**18**	**1**	**0**	**1**	**21:20**
	Canada	Olympics	7	1	1	2	0	....	....	....	....	....	....	....	....	....	....	....	....	....	....	....	....	....	....
2010-11	**San Jose**	**NHL**	**80**	**21**	**49**	**70**	**47**	**9**	**2**	**3**	**149**	**14.1**	**4**	**1240**	**54.4**	**19:52**	**18**	**3**	**14**	**17**	**16**	**0**	**0**	**2**	**22:15**
	NHL Totals		**995**	**306**	**695**	**1001**	**932**	**109**	**6**	**49**	**2063**	**14.8**		**17931**	**52.0**	**20:23**	**109**	**18**	**64**	**82**	**104**	**7**	**0**	**7**	**22:04**

OHL All-Rookie Team (1996) • OHL Rookie of the Year (1996) • Canadian Major Junior Rookie of the Year (1996) • OHL Second All-Star Team (1997) • NHL Second All-Star Team (2003, 2008) • NHL First All-Star Team (2006) • Art Ross Trophy (2006) • Hart Memorial Trophy (2006)

Played in NHL All-Star Game (2002, 2003, 2004, 2007, 2008, 2009)

Signed as a free agent by **Davos** (Swiss), July 8, 2004. Traded to **San Jose** by **Boston** for Brad Stuart, Marco Sturm and Wayne Primeau, November 30, 2005.

THORNTON, Shawn

(THOHRN-tuhn, SHAWN) **BOS**

Right wing. Shoots right. 6'2", 217 lbs. Born, Oshawa, Ont., July 23, 1977. Toronto's 6th choice, 190th overall, in 1997 Entry Draft.

1995-96	Peterborough	OHL	63	4	10	14	192	....	....	....	....	....	....	....	....	....	24	3	0	3	25	....	....	....	....
1996-97	Peterborough	OHL	61	19	10	29	204	....	....	....	....	....	....	....	....	....	11	2	4	6	20	....	....	....	....
1997-98	St. John's	AHL	59	0	3	3	225	....	....	....	....	....	....	....	....	....	....	....	....	....	....	....	....	....	....
1998-99	St. John's	AHL	78	8	11	19	354	....	....	....	....	....	....	....	....	....	5	0	0	0	9	....	....	....	....
99-2000	St. John's	AHL	60	4	12	16	316	....	....	....	....	....	....	....	....	....	....	....	....	....	....	....	....	....	....
2000-01	St. John's	AHL	79	5	12	17	320	....	....	....	....	....	....	....	....	....	3	1	2	3	2	....	....	....	....
2001-02	Norfolk Admirals	AHL	70	8	14	22	281	....	....	....	....	....	....	....	....	....	4	0	0	0	4	....	....	....	....
2002-03	**Chicago**	**NHL**	**13**	**1**	**1**	**2**	**31**	**0**	**0**	**0**	**15**	**6.7**	**–4**	**3**	**66.7**	**8:30**	....	....	....	....	....	....	....	....	....
	Norfolk Admirals	AHL	50	11	2	13	213	....	....	....	....	....	....	....	....	....	9	0	2	2	28	....	....	....	....
2003-04	**Chicago**	**NHL**	**8**	**1**	**0**	**1**	**23**	**0**	**0**	**0**	**14**	**7.1**	**2**	**19**	**42.1**	**11:14**	....	....	....	....	....	....	....	....	....
	Norfolk Admirals	AHL	64	6	11	17	259	....	....	....	....	....	....	....	....	....	8	1	1	2	6	....	....	....	....
2004-05	Norfolk Admirals	AHL	71	5	9	14	253	....	....	....	....	....	....	....	....	....	6	0	0	0	8	....	....	....	....
2005-06	**Chicago**	**NHL**	**10**	**0**	**0**	**0**	**16**	**0**	**0**	**0**	**16**	**0.0**	**–5**	**17**	**58.8**	**7:18**	....	....	....	....	....	....	....	....	....
	Norfolk Admirals	AHL	59	10	22	32	192	....	....	....	....	....	....	....	....	....	4	0	0	0	35	....	....	....	....
2006-07 ♦	**Anaheim**	**NHL**	**48**	**2**	**7**	**9**	**88**	**0**	**0**	**0**	**60**	**3.3**	**3**	**8**	**25.0**	**8:26**	**15**	**0**	**0**	**0**	**19**	**0**	**0**	**0**	**3:58**
	Portland Pirates	AHL	15	4	4	8	55	....	....	....	....	....	....	....	....	....	....	....	....	....	....	....	....	....	....
2007-08	**Boston**	**NHL**	**58**	**4**	**3**	**7**	**74**	**0**	**0**	**1**	**65**	**6.2**	**–1**	**7**	**28.6**	**7:24**	**7**	**0**	**0**	**0**	**6**	**0**	**0**	**0**	**8:04**
2008-09	**Boston**	**NHL**	**79**	**6**	**5**	**11**	**123**	**0**	**0**	**2**	**136**	**4.4**	**–2**	**5**	**20.0**	**10:02**	**10**	**1**	**0**	**1**	**6**	**0**	**0**	**0**	**9:07**
2009-10	**Boston**	**NHL**	**74**	**1**	**9**	**10**	**141**	**0**	**0**	**0**	**119**	**0.8**	**–9**	**23**	**47.8**	**9:03**	**12**	**0**	**0**	**0**	**4**	**0**	**0**	**0**	**7:08**
2010-11 ♦	**Boston**	**NHL**	**79**	**10**	**10**	**20**	**122**	**0**	**0**	**2**	**151**	**6.6**	**8**	**31**	**54.8**	**10:05**	**18**	**0**	**1**	**1**	**24**	**0**	**0**	**0**	**6:57**
	NHL Totals		**369**	**25**	**35**	**60**	**618**	**0**	**0**	**5**	**576**	**4.3**		**113**	**46.9**	**9:07**	**62**	**1**	**1**	**2**	**59**	**0**	**0**	**0**	**6:44**

Traded to **Chicago** by **Toronto** for Marty Wilford, September 30, 2001. Signed as a free agent by **Anaheim**, July 14, 2006. Signed as a free agent by **Boston**, July 1, 2007.

THURESSON, Andreas

(THUR-eh-suhn, an-DRAY-uhs) **NYR**

Center. Shoots right. 6'1", 212 lbs. Born, Kristianstad, Sweden, November 18, 1987. Nashville's 7th choice, 144th overall, in 2007 Entry Draft.

2003-04	Malmo Jr.	Swe-Jr.	19	2	2	4	16	....	....	....	....	....	....	....	....	....	8	0	0	0	6	....	....	....	....
	Tyringe SoSS	Sweden-3	12	0	1	1	0	....	....	....	....	....	....	....	....	....	....	....	....	....	....	....	....	....	....
	Malmo U18	Swe-U18	3	0	0	0	4	....	....	....	....	....	....	....	....	....	....	....	....	....	....	....	....	....	....
2004-05	Malmo U18	Swe-U18	3	1	1	2	4	....	....	....	....	....	....	....	....	....	....	....	....	....	....	....	....	....	....
	Malmo Jr.	Swe-Jr.	30	4	4	8	28	....	....	....	....	....	....	....	....	....	3	2	1	3	2	....	....	....	....
2005-06	Malmo U18	Swe-U18	2	1	0	1	4	....	....	....	....	....	....	....	....	....	....	....	....	....	....	....	....	....	....
	Malmo Jr.	Swe-Jr.	38	15	18	33	71	....	....	....	....	....	....	....	....	....	....	....	....	....	....	....	....	....	....
	Malmo	Sweden-2	20	0	2	2	10	....	....	....	....	....	....	....	....	....	....	....	....	....	....	....	....	....	....
2006-07	Malmo	Sweden	48	10	5	15	26	....	....	....	....	....	....	....	....	....	....	....	....	....	....	....	....	....	....
	Malmo	Sweden-Q	10	2	2	4	2	....	....	....	....	....	....	....	....	....	....	....	....	....	....	....	....	....	....
2007-08	Milwaukee	AHL	77	11	7	18	37	....	....	....	....	....	....	....	....	....	6	0	0	0	4	....	....	....	....
2008-09	Milwaukee	AHL	74	14	15	29	32	....	....	....	....	....	....	....	....	....	11	3	1	4	4	....	....	....	....
2009-10	**Nashville**	**NHL**	**22**	**1**	**2**	**3**	**4**	**0**	**0**	**0**	**30**	**3.3**	**–5**	**10**	**30.0**	**9:59**	....	....	....	....	....	....	....	....	....
	Milwaukee	AHL	50	14	19	33	24	....	....	....	....	....	....	....	....	....	7	2	7	9	16	....	....	....	....
2010-11	**Nashville**	**NHL**	**3**	**0**	**0**	**0**	**2**	**0**	**0**	**0**	**2**	**0.0**	**–1**	**2**	**0.0**	**10:09**	....	....	....	....	....	....	....	....	....
	Milwaukee	AHL	76	14	24	38	41	....	....	....	....	....	....	....	....	....	13	3	3	6	10	....	....	....	....
	NHL Totals		**25**	**1**	**2**	**3**	**6**	**0**	**0**	**0**	**32**	**3.1**		**12**	**25.0**	**10:00**	....	....	....	....	....	....	....	....	....

Traded to **NY Rangers** by **Nashville** for Brodie Dupont, July 2, 2011.

TIKHONOV, Viktor

(TIHK-uh-nawf, VIHK-tohr) **PHX**

Right wing. Shoots right. 6'2", 187 lbs. Born, Riga, Latvia, May 12, 1988. Phoenix's 2nd choice, 28th overall, in 2008 Entry Draft.

2004-05	CSKA Moscow 2	Russia-3	STATISTICS NOT AVAILABLE																						
2005-06	CSKA Moscow 2	Russia-3	STATISTICS NOT AVAILABLE																						
	HK Dmitrov	Russia-2	36	6	8	14	10	....	....	....	....	....	....	....	....	....	....	....	....	....	....	....	....	....	....
2006-07	Cherepovets 2	Russia-3	STATISTICS NOT AVAILABLE																						
	Cherepovets	Russia	4	0	0	0	0	....	....	....	....	....	....	....	....	....	....	....	....	....	....	....	....	....	....
2007-08	Cherepovets	Russia	43	7	5	12	43	....	....	....	....	....	....	....	....	....	8	0	1	1	4	....	....	....	....
2008-09	**Phoenix**	**NHL**	**61**	**8**	**8**	**16**	**20**	**1**	**0**	**1**	**71**	**11.3**	**–3**	**60**	**38.3**	**12:08**	....	....	....	....	....	....	....	....	....
	San Antonio	AHL	4	2	1	3	0	....	....	....	....	....	....	....	....	....	....	....	....	....	....	....	....	....	....

			Regular Season														Playoffs								
Season	Club	League	GP	G	A	Pts	PIM	PP	SH	GW	S	%	+/-	TF	F%	Min	GP	G	A	Pts	PIM	PP	SH	GW	Min
2009-10	San Antonio	AHL	18	2	6	8	12	....	....	....	....	....	....	....	....	....	....	....	....	....	....	....	....	....	....
	Cherepovets	Rus-KHL	25	14	1	15	12	....	....	....	....	....	....	....	....	....	....	....	....	....	....	....	....	....	....
2010-11	San Antonio	AHL	60	10	23	33	26	....	....	....	....	....	....	....	....	....	....	....	....	....	....	....	....	....	....
	NHL Totals		**61**	**8**	**8**	**16**	**20**	**1**	**0**	**1**	**71**	**11.3**		**60**	**38.3**	**12:08**	....	....	....	....	....	....	....	....	....

• Loaned to **Cherepovets** (Russia-KHL) by **Phoenix**, November 28, 2009.

TIMMINS, Scott

(TIHM-mihnz, SKAWT) **FLA**

Center. Shoots left. 5'11", 191 lbs. Born, Hamilton, Ont., September 11, 1989. Florida's 7th choice, 165th overall, in 2009 Entry Draft.

Season	Club	League	GP	G	A	Pts	PIM	PP	SH	GW	S	%	+/-	TF	F%	Min	GP	G	A	Pts	PIM	PP	SH	GW	Min
2005-06	Burlington	OPJHL	31	8	4	12	8	....	....	....	....	....	....	....	....	....	4	1	1	2	0	....	....	....	....
2006-07	Kitchener Rangers	OHL	42	2	5	7	8	....	....	....	....	....	....	....	....	....	....	....	....	....	....	....	....	....	....
2007-08	Kitchener Rangers	OHL	62	17	12	29	46	....	....	....	....	....	....	....	....	....	20	3	5	8	10	....	....	....	....
2008-09	Kitchener Rangers	OHL	38	25	24	49	28	....	....	....	....	....	....	....	....	....	....	....	....	....	....	....	....	....	....
	Windsor Spitfires	OHL	28	10	14	24	33	....	....	....	....	....	....	....	....	....	20	6	10	16	26	....	....	....	....
2009-10	Windsor Spitfires	OHL	56	30	24	54	47	....	....	....	....	....	....	....	....	....	19	11	11	22	18	....	....	....	....
2010-11	**Florida**	**NHL**	**19**	**1**	**0**	**1**	**8**	**0**	**0**	**0**	**13**	**7.7**	**–8**	**130**	**46.9**	**10:49**	....	....	....	....	....	....	....	....	....
	Rochester	AHL	45	10	12	22	18	....	....	....	....	....	....	....	....	....	....	....	....	....	....	....	....	....	....
	NHL Totals		**19**	**1**	**0**	**1**	**8**	**0**	**0**	**0**	**13**	**7.7**		**130**	**46.9**	**10:49**	....	....	....	....	....	....	....	....	....

TIMONEN, Kimmo

(TEEM-oh-nehn, KEE-moh) **PHI**

Defense. Shoots left. 5'10", 194 lbs. Born, Kuopio, Finland, March 18, 1975. Los Angeles' 11th choice, 250th overall, in 1993 Entry Draft.

Season	Club	League	GP	G	A	Pts	PIM	PP	SH	GW	S	%	+/-	TF	F%	Min	GP	G	A	Pts	PIM	PP	SH	GW	Min
1990-91	KalPa Kuopio Jr.	Fin-Jr.	4	0	1	1	2	....	....	....	....	....	....	....	....	....	....	....	....	....	....	....	....	....	....
1991-92	KalPa Kuopio Jr.	Fin-Jr.	32	7	10	17	4	....	....	....	....	....	....	....	....	....	....	....	....	....	....	....	....	....	....
	KalPa Kuopio	Finland	5	0	0	0	0	....	....	....	....	....	....	....	....	....	....	....	....	....	....	....	....	....	....
1992-93	KalPa Kuopio U18	Fin-U18	3	0	5	5	0	....	....	....	....	....	....	....	....	....	....	....	....	....	....	....	....	....	....
	KalPa Kuopio Jr.	Fin-Jr.	16	9	15	24	10	....	....	....	....	....	....	....	....	....	....	....	....	....	....	....	....	....	....
	KalPa Kuopio	Finland	33	0	2	2	4	....	....	....	....	....	....	....	....	....	....	....	....	....	....	....	....	....	....
1993-94	KalPa Kuopio Jr.	Fin-Jr.	5	4	7	11	0	....	....	....	....	....	....	....	....	....	....	....	....	....	....	....	....	....	....
	KalPa Kuopio	Finland	46	6	7	13	55	....	....	....	....	....	....	....	....	....	....	....	....	....	....	....	....	....	....
1994-95	TPS Turku Jr.	Fin-Jr.	1	0	0	0	0	....	....	....	....	....	....	....	....	....	....	....	....	....	....	....	....	....	....
	TPS Turku	Finland	45	3	4	7	10	....	....	....	....	....	....	....	....	....	13	0	1	1	6	....	....	....	....
1995-96	TPS Turku	Finland	48	3	21	24	22	....	....	....	....	....	....	....	....	....	9	1	2	3	12	....	....	....	....
1996-97	TPS Turku	Finland	50	10	14	24	18	....	....	....	....	....	....	....	....	....	12	2	7	9	6	....	....	....	....
	TPS Turku	EuroHL	6	1	0	1	27	....	....	....	....	....	....	....	....	....	4	0	1	1	0	....	....	....	....
1997-98	HIFK Helsinki	Finland	45	10	15	25	24	....	....	....	....	....	....	....	....	....	9	3	4	7	8	....	....	....	....
	Finland	Olympics	6	0	1	1	2	....	....	....	....	....	....	....	....	....	....	....	....	....	....	....	....	....	....
1998-99	**Nashville**	**NHL**	**50**	**4**	**8**	**12**	**30**	**1**	**0**	**0**	**75**	**5.3**	**–4**	**0**	**0.0**	**19:04**	....	....	....	....	....	....	....	....	....
	Milwaukee	IHL	29	2	13	15	22	....	....	....	....	....	....	....	....	....	....	....	....	....	....	....	....	....	....
99-2000	**Nashville**	**NHL**	**51**	**8**	**25**	**33**	**26**	**2**	**1**	**2**	**97**	**8.2**	**–5**	**0**	**0.0**	**21:06**	....	....	....	....	....	....	....	....	....
2000-01	**Nashville**	**NHL**	**82**	**12**	**13**	**25**	**50**	**6**	**0**	**3**	**151**	**7.9**	**–6**	**2**	**50.0**	**23:11**	....	....	....	....	....	....	....	....	....
2001-02	**Nashville**	**NHL**	**82**	**13**	**29**	**42**	**28**	**9**	**0**	**1**	**154**	**8.4**	**2**	**0**	**0.0**	**24:12**	....	....	....	....	....	....	....	....	....
	Finland	Olympics	4	0	1	1	2	....	....	....	....	....	....	....	....	....	....	....	....	....	....	....	....	....	....
2002-03	**Nashville**	**NHL**	**72**	**6**	**34**	**40**	**46**	**4**	**0**	**0**	**144**	**4.2**	**–3**	**0**	**0.0**	**22:25**	....	....	....	....	....	....	....	....	....
2003-04	**Nashville**	**NHL**	**77**	**12**	**32**	**44**	**52**	**8**	**0**	**1**	**180**	**6.7**	**–7**	**1**	**0.0**	**23:52**	**6**	**0**	**0**	**0**	**10**	**0**	**0**	**0**	**24:16**
2004-05	HC Lugano	Swiss	3	0	1	1	0	....	....	....	....	....	....	....	....	....	....	....	....	....	....	....	....	....	....
	Brynas IF Gavle	Sweden	10	5	3	8	8	....	....	....	....	....	....	....	....	....	....	....	....	....	....	....	....	....	....
	KalPa Kuopio	Finland-2	12	4	13	17	6	....	....	....	....	....	....	....	....	....	8	3	7	10	4	....	....	....	....
2005-06	**Nashville**	**NHL**	**79**	**11**	**39**	**50**	**74**	**8**	**0**	**1**	**156**	**7.1**	**–3**	**5**	**80.0**	**22:26**	**5**	**1**	**3**	**4**	**4**	**0**	**1**	**0**	**24:42**
	Finland	Olympics	8	1	4	5	2	....	....	....	....	....	....	....	....	....	....	....	....	....	....	....	....	....	....
2006-07	**Nashville**	**NHL**	**80**	**13**	**42**	**55**	**42**	**8**	**0**	**2**	**121**	**10.7**	**20**	**1**	**0.0**	**21:51**	**5**	**0**	**2**	**2**	**4**	**0**	**0**	**0**	**24:33**
2007-08	**Philadelphia**	**NHL**	**80**	**8**	**36**	**44**	**50**	**3**	**1**	**1**	**125**	**6.4**	**0**	**0**	**0.0**	**23:35**	**13**	**0**	**6**	**6**	**8**	**0**	**0**	**0**	**24:41**
2008-09	**Philadelphia**	**NHL**	**77**	**3**	**40**	**43**	**54**	**2**	**0**	**0**	**104**	**2.9**	**19**	**2**	**0.0**	**24:31**	**6**	**0**	**1**	**1**	**12**	**0**	**0**	**0**	**26:21**
2009-10	**Philadelphia**	**NHL**	**82**	**6**	**33**	**39**	**50**	**1**	**2**	**1**	**121**	**5.0**	**–2**	**0**	**0.0**	**22:53**	**23**	**1**	**10**	**11**	**20**	**0**	**0**	**0**	**26:38**
	Finland	Olympics	6	2	2	4	2	....	....	....	....	....	....	....	....	....	....	....	....	....	....	....	....	....	....
2010-11	**Philadelphia**	**NHL**	**82**	**6**	**31**	**37**	**36**	**1**	**2**	**0**	**147**	**4.1**	**11**	**1**	**0.0**	**22:28**	**11**	**1**	**5**	**6**	**14**	**0**	**0**	**0**	**24:53**
	NHL Totals		**894**	**102**	**362**	**464**	**538**	**53**	**6**	**12**	**1575**	**6.5**		**12**	**41.7**	**22:48**	**69**	**3**	**27**	**30**	**72**	**0**	**1**	**0**	**25:28**

Olympic All-Star Team (2006)

Played in NHL All-Star Game (2004, 2007, 2008)

Traded to **Nashville** by **Los Angeles** with Jan Vopat for future considerations, June 26, 1998. Signed as a free agent by **Lugano** (Swiss), October 31, 2004. Signed as a free agent by **Gavle** (Sweden), November 8, 2004. Signed as a free agent by **Kuopio** (Finland-2), January 3, 2005. Traded to **Philadelphia** by **Nashville** with Scott Hartnell for Nashville's 1st round choice (previously acquired, Nashville selected Jonathon Blum) in 2007 Entry Draft, June 18, 2007.

TLUSTY, Jiri

(T'LOO-stee, YIH-ree) **CAR**

Center. Shoots left. 6', 209 lbs. Born, Slany, Czech., March 16, 1988. Toronto's 1st choice, 13th overall, in 2006 Entry Draft.

Season	Club	League	GP	G	A	Pts	PIM	PP	SH	GW	S	%	+/-	TF	F%	Min	GP	G	A	Pts	PIM	PP	SH	GW	Min
2001-02	HC Kladno U17	CzR-U17	1	0	0	0	0	....	....	....	....	....	....	....	....	....	....	....	....	....	....	....	....	....	....
2002-03	HC Kladno U17	CzR-U17	48	28	17	45	22	....	....	....	....	....	....	....	....	....	10	5	4	9	12	....	....	....	....
2003-04	HC Kladno U17	CzR-U17	1	0	0	0	2	....	....	....	....	....	....	....	....	....	1	0	0	0	2	....	....	....	....
	HC Kladno Jr.	CzRep-Jr.	51	10	3	13	12	....	....	....	....	....	....	....	....	....	1	0	0	0	0	....	....	....	....
2004-05	HC Kladno Jr.	CzRep-Jr.	42	15	12	27	54	....	....	....	....	....	....	....	....	....	10	2	2	4	8	....	....	....	....
2005-06	HC Kladno Jr.	CzRep-Jr.	6	4	2	6	2	....	....	....	....	....	....	....	....	....	6	7	6	13	6	....	....	....	....
	HC Rabat Kladno	CzRep	44	7	3	10	51	....	....	....	....	....	....	....	....	....	....	....	....	....	....	....	....	....	....
2006-07	Sault Ste. Marie	OHL	37	13	21	34	28	....	....	....	....	....	....	....	....	....	13	9	8	17	14	....	....	....	....
	Toronto Marlies	AHL	6	3	1	4	4	....	....	....	....	....	....	....	....	....	....	....	....	....	....	....	....	....	....
2007-08	**Toronto**	**NHL**	**58**	**10**	**6**	**16**	**14**	**2**	**0**	**2**	**69**	**14.5**	**–12**	**2**	**50.0**	**10:55**	....	....	....	....	....	....	....	....	....
	Toronto Marlies	AHL	14	7	11	18	8	....	....	....	....	....	....	....	....	....	19	2	8	10	8	....	....	....	....
2008-09	**Toronto**	**NHL**	**14**	**0**	**4**	**4**	**0**	**0**	**0**	**0**	**22**	**0.0**	**0**	**3**	**33.3**	**12:42**	....	....	....	....	....	....	....	....	....
	Toronto Marlies	AHL	66	25	41	66	26	....	....	....	....	....	....	....	....	....	6	1	2	3	2	....	....	....	....
2009-10	**Toronto**	**NHL**	**2**	**0**	**0**	**0**	**0**	**0**	**0**	**0**	**2**	**0.0**	**–2**	**0**	**0.0**	**12:13**	....	....	....	....	....	....	....	....	....
	Toronto Marlies	AHL	19	8	7	15	4	....	....	....	....	....	....	....	....	....	....	....	....	....	....	....	....	....	....
	Carolina	**NHL**	**18**	**1**	**5**	**6**	**6**	**0**	**0**	**0**	**15**	**6.7**	**2**	**2**	**100.0**	**12:36**	....	....	....	....	....	....	....	....	....
	Albany River Rats	AHL	20	6	9	15	10	....	....	....	....	....	....	....	....	....	5	0	1	1	0	....	....	....	....
2010-11	**Carolina**	**NHL**	**57**	**6**	**6**	**12**	**14**	**0**	**0**	**0**	**53**	**11.3**	**1**	**15**	**13.3**	**9:52**	....	....	....	....	....	....	....	....	....
	Charlotte	AHL	5	1	1	2	4	....	....	....	....	....	....	....	....	....	....	....	....	....	....	....	....	....	....
	NHL Totals		**149**	**17**	**21**	**38**	**34**	**2**	**0**	**2**	**161**	**10.6**		**22**	**27.3**	**10:54**	....	....	....	....	....	....	....	....	....

Traded to **Carolina** by **Toronto** for Philippe Paradis, December 3, 2009.

TOEWS, Jonathan

(TAYVZ, JAWN-ah-thuhn) **CHI**

Center. Shoots left. 6'2", 210 lbs. Born, Winnipeg, Man., April 29, 1988. Chicago's 1st choice, 3rd overall, in 2006 Entry Draft.

Season	Club	League	GP	G	A	Pts	PIM	PP	SH	GW	S	%	+/-	TF	F%	Min	GP	G	A	Pts	PIM	PP	SH	GW	Min
2004-05	Shat.-St. Mary's	High-MN	64	48	62	110	38	....	....	....	....	....	....	....	....	....	....	....	....	....	....	....	....	....	....
2005-06	North Dakota	WCHA	42	22	17	39	22	....	....	....	....	....	....	....	....	....	....	....	....	....	....	....	....	....	....
2006-07	North Dakota	WCHA	34	18	28	46	10	....	....	....	....	....	....	....	....	....	....	....	....	....	....	....	....	....	....
2007-08	**Chicago**	**NHL**	**64**	**24**	**30**	**54**	**44**	**7**	**0**	**4**	**144**	**16.7**	**11**	**956**	**53.2**	**18:40**	....	....	....	....	....	....	....	....	....
2008-09	**Chicago**	**NHL**	**82**	**34**	**35**	**69**	**51**	**12**	**0**	**7**	**195**	**17.4**	**12**	**1287**	**54.7**	**18:38**	**17**	**7**	**6**	**13**	**26**	**5**	**0**	**2**	**16:14**
2009-10♦	**Chicago**	**NHL**	**76**	**25**	**43**	**68**	**47**	**9**	**1**	**3**	**202**	**12.4**	**22**	**1397**	**57.3**	**20:00**	**22**	**7**	***22**	**29**	**4**	**5**	**0**	**3**	**20:58**
	Canada	Olympics	7	1	*7	8	2	....	....	....	....	....	....	....	....	....	....	....	....	....	....	....	....	....	....
2010-11	**Chicago**	**NHL**	**80**	**32**	**44**	**76**	**26**	**10**	**1**	**8**	**233**	**13.7**	**25**	**1653**	**56.7**	**20:46**	**7**	**1**	**3**	**4**	**2**	**0**	**1**	**0**	**22:31**
	NHL Totals		**302**	**115**	**152**	**267**	**168**	**38**	**2**	**22**	**774**	**14.9**		**5293**	**55.8**	**19:33**	**46**	**15**	**31**	**46**	**32**	**10**	**1**	**5**	**19:27**

WCHA Second All-Star Team (2007) • NCAA West First All-American Team (2007) • NHL All-Rookie Team (2008) • Olympic All-Star Team (2010) • Olympics – Best Forward (2010) • Conn Smythe Trophy (2010)

Played in NHL All-Star Game (2009, 2011)

TOLLEFSEN, Ole-Kristian

(TOHL-uhf-suhn, OH-lay-KRIHS-tyahn)

Defense. Shoots left. 6'2", 211 lbs. Born, Oslo, Norway, March 29, 1984. Columbus' 3rd choice, 65th overall, in 2002 Entry Draft.

			Regular Season														Playoffs								
Season	Club	League	GP	G	A	Pts	PIM	PP	SH	GW	S	%	+/-	TF	F%	Min	GP	G	A	Pts	PIM	PP	SH	GW	Min
2000-01	Lillehammer IK	Norway	4	0	0	0	2	....	....	....	....	....	....	....	....	....	....	....	....	....	....	....	....	....	....
2001-02	Lillehammer IK	Norway	37	1	5	6	63	....	....	....	....	....	....	....	....	....	6	1	1	2	10	....	....	....	....
	Lillehammer IK	Nor-Jr.	....	....	....	....	....	....	....	....	....	....	....	....	....	....	1	0	2	2	4	....	....	....	....
2002-03	Brandon	WHL	43	6	14	20	73	....	....	....	....	....	....	....	....	....	17	0	2	2	38	....	....	....	....
2003-04	Brandon	WHL	53	3	27	30	94	....	....	....	....	....	....	....	....	....	11	0	4	4	15	....	....	....	....
2004-05	Syracuse Crunch	AHL	64	0	3	3	115	....	....	....	....	....	....	....	....	....	....	....	....	....	....	....	....	....	....
	Dayton Bombers	ECHL	2	0	0	0	0	....	....	....	....	....	....	....	....	....	....	....	....	....	....	....	....	....	....
2005-06	**Columbus**	**NHL**	**5**	**0**	**0**	**0**	**2**	**0**	**0**	**0**	**3**	**0.0**	**–2**	**0**	**0.0**	**16:18**	....	....	....	....	....	....	....	....	....
	Syracuse Crunch	AHL	58	2	16	18	155	....	....	....	....	....	....	....	....	....	1	0	0	0	6	....	....	....	....
2006-07	**Columbus**	**NHL**	**70**	**2**	**3**	**5**	**123**	**1**	**0**	**0**	**39**	**5.1**	**2**	**0**	**0.0**	**14:14**	....	....	....	....	....	....	....	....	....
2007-08	**Columbus**	**NHL**	**51**	**2**	**2**	**4**	**111**	**0**	**1**	**0**	**21**	**9.5**	**–3**	**0**	**0.0**	**12:18**	....	....	....	....	....	....	....	....	....
2008-09	**Columbus**	**NHL**	**19**	**0**	**1**	**1**	**37**	**0**	**0**	**0**	**12**	**0.0**	**–4**	**0**	**0.0**	**10:20**	....	....	....	....	....	....	....	....	....
2009-10	**Philadelphia**	**NHL**	**18**	**0**	**2**	**2**	**23**	**0**	**0**	**0**	**12**	**0.0**	**1**	**0**	**0.0**	**9:52**	....	....	....	....	....	....	....	....	....
	Grand Rapids	AHL	16	1	0	1	44	....	....	....	....	....	....	....	....	....	....	....	....	....	....	....	....	....	....
	Norway	Olympics	3	0	0	0	25	....	....	....	....	....	....	....	....	....	....	....	....	....	....	....	....	....	....
2010-11	MODO	Sweden	43	1	2	3	95	....	....	....	....	....	....	....	....	....	....	....	....	....	....	....	....	....	....
	NHL Totals		**163**	**4**	**8**	**12**	**296**	**1**	**1**	**0**	**87**	**4.6**		**0**	**0.0**	**12:45**	....	....	....	....	....	....	....	....	....

• Missed majority of 2008-09 due to knee surgery, December 17, 2008. Signed as a free agent by **Philadelphia**, July 30, 2009. Traded to **Detroit** by **Philadelphia** with Philadelphia's 5th round choice (Mattias Backman) in 2011 Entry Draft for Ville Leino, February 6, 2010. • Missed majority of 2009-10 due to head and knee injuries. Signed as a free agent by **MODO** (Sweden), May 13. 2010.

TOOTOO, Jordin

(TOO-TOO, JOHR-dahn) **NSH**

Right wing. Shoots right. 5'9", 199 lbs. Born, Churchill, Man., February 2, 1983. Nashville's 6th choice, 98th overall, in 2001 Entry Draft.

Season	Club	League	GP	G	A	Pts	PIM	PP	SH	GW	S	%	+/-	TF	F%	Min	GP	G	A	Pts	PIM	PP	SH	GW	Min
1997-98	Spruce Grove	AMBHL	STATISTICS NOT AVAILABLE														....	....	....	....	....	....	....	....	....
1998-99	OCN Blizzard	MJHL	47	16	21	37	251	....	....	....	....	....	....	....	....	....	....	....	....	....	....	....	....	....	....
99-2000	Brandon	WHL	45	6	10	16	214	....	....	....	....	....	....	....	....	....	....	....	....	....	....	....	....	....	....
2000-01	Brandon	WHL	60	20	28	48	172	....	....	....	....	....	....	....	....	....	6	2	4	6	18	....	....	....	....
2001-02	Brandon	WHL	64	32	39	71	272	....	....	....	....	....	....	....	....	....	16	4	3	7	*58	....	....	....	....
2002-03	Brandon	WHL	51	35	39	74	216	....	....	....	....	....	....	....	....	....	17	6	3	9	49	....	....	....	....
2003-04	**Nashville**	**NHL**	**70**	**4**	**4**	**8**	**137**	**2**	**0**	**0**	**92**	**4.3**	**–6**	**18**	**55.6**	**8:29**	**5**	**0**	**0**	**0**	**4**	**0**	**0**	**0**	**5:09**
2004-05	Milwaukee	AHL	59	10	12	22	266	....	....	....	....	....	....	....	....	....	6	0	0	0	41	....	....	....	....
2005-06	**Nashville**	**NHL**	**34**	**4**	**6**	**10**	**55**	**0**	**0**	**0**	**61**	**6.6**	**9**	**17**	**70.6**	**9:15**	**3**	**0**	**0**	**0**	**0**	**0**	**0**	**0**	**4:04**
	Milwaukee	AHL	41	13	14	27	133	....	....	....	....	....	....	....	....	....	15	9	2	11	35	....	....	....	....
2006-07	**Nashville**	**NHL**	**65**	**3**	**6**	**9**	**116**	**0**	**0**	**0**	**77**	**3.9**	**–11**	**12**	**33.3**	**8:24**	**4**	**0**	**1**	**1**	**21**	**0**	**0**	**0**	**9:32**
2007-08	**Nashville**	**NHL**	**63**	**11**	**7**	**18**	**100**	**0**	**0**	**1**	**98**	**11.2**	**–8**	**4**	**50.0**	**9:54**	**6**	**2**	**0**	**2**	**4**	**0**	**0**	**0**	**12:31**
2008-09	**Nashville**	**NHL**	**72**	**4**	**12**	**16**	**124**	**0**	**0**	**1**	**138**	**2.9**	**–15**	**16**	**56.3**	**12:05**	....	....	....	....	....	....	....	....	....
2009-10	**Nashville**	**NHL**	**51**	**6**	**10**	**16**	**40**	**0**	**0**	**1**	**101**	**5.9**	**2**	**8**	**25.0**	**10:50**	**6**	**0**	**1**	**1**	**2**	**0**	**0**	**0**	**7:58**
2010-11	**Nashville**	**NHL**	**54**	**8**	**10**	**18**	**61**	**0**	**0**	**1**	**85**	**9.4**	**8**	**3**	**66.7**	**11:53**	**12**	**1**	**5**	**6**	**28**	**0**	**0**	**0**	**13:26**
	NHL Totals		**409**	**40**	**55**	**95**	**633**	**2**	**0**	**4**	**652**	**6.1**		**78**	**52.6**	**10:08**	**36**	**3**	**7**	**10**	**59**	**0**	**0**	**0**	**10:00**

WHL East First All-Star Team (2003)

TORRES, Raffi

(TOHR-ehz, RA-fee) **PHX**

Left wing. Shoots left. 6', 216 lbs. Born, Toronto, Ont., October 8, 1981. NY Islanders' 2nd choice, 5th overall, in 2000 Entry Draft.

Season	Club	League	GP	G	A	Pts	PIM	PP	SH	GW	S	%	+/-	TF	F%	Min	GP	G	A	Pts	PIM	PP	SH	GW	Min
1997-98	Thornhill Rattlers	ON-Jr.A	46	17	16	33	90	....	....	....	....	....	....	....	....	....	....	....	....	....	....	....	....	....	....
1998-99	Brampton	OHL	62	35	27	62	32	....	....	....	....	....	....	....	....	....	....	....	....	....	....	....	....	....	....
99-2000	Brampton	OHL	68	43	48	91	40	....	....	....	....	....	....	....	....	....	6	5	2	7	23	....	....	....	....
2000-01	Brampton	OHL	55	33	37	70	76	....	....	....	....	....	....	....	....	....	8	7	4	11	19	....	....	....	....
2001-02	**NY Islanders**	**NHL**	**14**	**0**	**1**	**1**	**6**	**0**	**0**	**0**	**9**	**0.0**	**2**	**0**	**0.0**	**7:35**	....	....	....	....	....	....	....	....	....
	Bridgeport	AHL	59	20	10	30	45	....	....	....	....	....	....	....	....	....	20	8	9	17	26	....	....	....	....
2002-03	**NY Islanders**	**NHL**	**17**	**0**	**5**	**5**	**10**	**0**	**0**	**0**	**12**	**0.0**	**0**	**4**	**25.0**	**7:40**	....	....	....	....	....	....	....	....	....
	Bridgeport	AHL	49	17	15	32	54	....	....	....	....	....	....	....	....	....	....	....	....	....	....	....	....	....	....
	Hamilton	AHL	11	1	7	8	14	....	....	....	....	....	....	....	....	....	23	6	1	7	29	....	....	....	....
2003-04	**Edmonton**	**NHL**	**80**	**20**	**14**	**34**	**65**	**5**	**0**	**3**	**136**	**14.7**	**12**	**21**	**28.6**	**12:38**	....	....	....	....	....	....	....	....	....
2004-05	Edmonton	AHL	67	21	25	46	165	....	....	....	....	....	....	....	....	....	....	....	....	....	....	....	....	....	....
2005-06	**Edmonton**	**NHL**	**82**	**27**	**14**	**41**	**50**	**6**	**0**	**3**	**164**	**16.5**	**4**	**60**	**41.7**	**13:24**	**22**	**4**	**7**	**11**	**16**	**1**	**0**	**1**	**13:15**
2006-07	**Edmonton**	**NHL**	**82**	**15**	**19**	**34**	**88**	**1**	**0**	**0**	**154**	**9.7**	**–7**	**50**	**44.0**	**14:19**	....	....	....	....	....	....	....	....	....
2007-08	**Edmonton**	**NHL**	**32**	**5**	**6**	**11**	**36**	**1**	**0**	**2**	**87**	**5.7**	**–4**	**20**	**65.0**	**17:01**	....	....	....	....	....	....	....	....	....
2008-09	**Columbus**	**NHL**	**51**	**12**	**8**	**20**	**23**	**2**	**0**	**6**	**74**	**16.2**	**–4**	**19**	**57.9**	**12:06**	**4**	**0**	**2**	**2**	**2**	**0**	**0**	**0**	**12:04**
2009-10	**Columbus**	**NHL**	**60**	**19**	**12**	**31**	**32**	**7**	**0**	**3**	**99**	**19.2**	**–8**	**47**	**36.2**	**13:34**	....	....	....	....	....	....	....	....	....
	Buffalo	**NHL**	**14**	**0**	**5**	**5**	**2**	**0**	**0**	**0**	**21**	**0.0**	**–3**	**3**	**33.3**	**13:21**	**4**	**0**	**2**	**2**	**12**	**0**	**0**	**0**	**12:55**
2010-11	**Vancouver**	**NHL**	**80**	**14**	**15**	**29**	**78**	**3**	**0**	**4**	**115**	**12.2**	**4**	**32**	**31.3**	**12:29**	**23**	**3**	**4**	**7**	**28**	**0**	**0**	**1**	**11:51**
	NHL Totals		**512**	**112**	**99**	**211**	**390**	**25**	**0**	**21**	**871**	**12.9**		**256**	**41.4**	**13:03**	**53**	**7**	**15**	**22**	**58**	**1**	**0**	**2**	**12:32**

OHL All-Rookie Team (1999) • OHL Second All-Star Team (2000, 2001)

Traded to **Edmonton** by **NY Islanders** with Brad Isbister for Janne Niinimaa and Washington's 2nd round choice (previously acquired, NY Islanders selected Evgeni Tunik) in 2003 Entry Draft, March 11, 2003. • Missed majority of 2007-08 due to knee injury vs. Detroit, December 15, 2007. Traded to **Columbus** by **Edmonton** for Gilbert Brule, July 1, 2008. Traded to **Buffalo** by **Columbus** for Nathan Paetsch and Vancouver's 2nd round choice (previously acquired, Columbus selected Petr Straka) in 2010 Entry Draft, March 3, 2010. Signed as a free agent by **Vancouver**, August 25, 2010. Signed as a free agent by **Phoenix**, July 1, 2011.

TROTTER, Brock

(TRAW-tuhr, BRAWK) **MTL**

Center. Shoots right. 5'10", 180 lbs. Born, Brandon, Man., September 18, 1987.

Season	Club	League	GP	G	A	Pts	PIM	PP	SH	GW	S	%	+/-	TF	F%	Min	GP	G	A	Pts	PIM	PP	SH	GW	Min
2003-04	Dauphin Kings	MJHL	63	32	33	65	108	....	....	....	....	....	....	....	....	....	....	....	....	....	....	....	....	....	....
2004-05	Lincoln Stars	USHL	60	20	38	58	84	....	....	....	....	....	....	....	....	....	4	2	3	5	0	....	....	....	....
2005-06	U. of Denver	WCHA	5	3	2	5	2	....	....	....	....	....	....	....	....	....	....	....	....	....	....	....	....	....	....
2006-07	U. of Denver	WCHA	40	16	24	40	22	....	....	....	....	....	....	....	....	....	....	....	....	....	....	....	....	....	....
2007-08	U. of Denver	WCHA	24	13	18	31	18	....	....	....	....	....	....	....	....	....	....	....	....	....	....	....	....	....	....
	Hamilton	AHL	21	3	6	9	4	....	....	....	....	....	....	....	....	....	....	....	....	....	....	....	....	....	....
2008-09	Hamilton	AHL	76	18	31	49	32	....	....	....	....	....	....	....	....	....	6	0	1	1	13	....	....	....	....
2009-10	**Montreal**	**NHL**	**2**	**0**	**0**	**0**	**0**	**0**	**0**	**0**	**6**	**0.0**	**–1**	**0**	**0.0**	**9:03**	....	....	....	....	....	....	....	....	....
	Hamilton	AHL	75	36	41	77	56	....	....	....	....	....	....	....	....	....	19	8	11	19	14	....	....	....	....
2010-11	Dynamo Riga	Rus-KHL	49	9	17	26	38	....	....	....	....	....	....	....	....	....	11	4	5	9	10	....	....	....	....
	NHL Totals		**2**	**0**	**0**	**0**	**0**	**0**	**0**	**0**	**6**	**0.0**		**0**	**0.0**	**9:02**	....	....	....	....	....	....	....	....	....

• Missed majority of 2005-06 due to Achilles tendon injury vs. North Dakota (WCHA), October 29, 2005. Signed as a free agent by **Montreal**, February 7, 2008.

TURRIS, Kyle

(TUH-rihs, KIGHL) **PHX**

Center. Shoots right. 6'1", 185 lbs. Born, New Westminster, B.C., August 14, 1989. Phoenix's 1st choice, 3rd overall, in 2007 Entry Draft.

Season	Club	League	GP	G	A	Pts	PIM	PP	SH	GW	S	%	+/-	TF	F%	Min	GP	G	A	Pts	PIM	PP	SH	GW	Min
2004-05	Grandview	Minor-BC	30	13	20	33	....	....	....	....	....	....	....	....	....	....	12	3	6	9	....	....	....	....	....
2005-06	Burnaby Express	BCHL	57	36	36	72	32	....	....	....	....	....	....	....	....	....	20	10	13	23	6	....	....	....	....
2006-07	Burnaby Express	BCHL	53	66	55	121	83	....	....	....	....	....	....	....	....	....	14	12	14	26	16	....	....	....	....
2007-08	U. of Wisconsin	WCHA	36	11	24	35	38	....	....	....	....	....	....	....	....	....	....	....	....	....	....	....	....	....	....
	Phoenix	**NHL**	**3**	**0**	**1**	**1**	**2**	**0**	**0**	**0**	**11**	**0.0**	**–5**	**42**	**40.5**	**19:45**	....	....	....	....	....	....	....	....	....
2008-09	**Phoenix**	**NHL**	**63**	**8**	**12**	**20**	**21**	**3**	**0**	**3**	**91**	**8.8**	**–15**	**567**	**42.9**	**12:55**	....	....	....	....	....	....	....	....	....
	San Antonio	AHL	8	4	3	7	6	....	....	....	....	....	....	....	....	....	....	....	....	....	....	....	....	....	....
2009-10	San Antonio	AHL	76	24	39	63	60	....	....	....	....	....	....	....	....	....	....	....	....	....	....	....	....	....	....
2010-11	**Phoenix**	**NHL**	**65**	**11**	**14**	**25**	**16**	**0**	**0**	**1**	**116**	**9.5**	**0**	**540**	**50.0**	**11:16**	**4**	**1**	**2**	**3**	**2**	**0**	**0**	**0**	**13:49**
	San Antonio	AHL	2	0	1	1	2	....	....	....	....	....	....	....	....	....	....	....	....	....	....	....	....	....	....
	NHL Totals		**131**	**19**	**27**	**46**	**39**	**3**	**0**	**4**	**218**	**8.7**		**1149**	**46.1**	**12:16**	**4**	**1**	**2**	**3**	**2**	**0**	**0**	**0**	**13:50**

WCHA All-Rookie Team (2008)

TYRELL, Dana

(TIH-rehl, DAY-nuh) **T.B.**

Center/Right wing. Shoots left. 5'11", 185 lbs. Born, Airdrie, Alta., April 23, 1989. Tampa Bay's 1st choice, 47th overall, in 2007 Entry Draft.

			Regular Season														Playoffs								
Season	Club	League	GP	G	A	Pts	PIM	PP	SH	GW	S	%	+/-	TF	F%	Min	GP	G	A	Pts	PIM	PP	SH	GW	Min
2003-04	Airdrie Xtreme	AMHBL	35	21	47	68	28	....	....	....	....	....	....	....	....	....	7	6	4	10	....	....	....	....	....
2004-05	UFA Bisons	AMHL	34	16	23	39	32	....	....	....	....	....	....	....	....	....	16	8	9	*17	....	....	....	....	....
	Prince George	WHL	1	0	0	0	2	....	....	....	....	....	....	....	....	....	....	....	....	....	....	....	....	....	....
2005-06	Prince George	WHL	69	7	11	18	44	....	....	....	....	....	....	....	....	....	5	0	0	0	2	....	....	....	....
2006-07	Prince George	WHL	72	30	26	56	51	....	....	....	....	....	....	....	....	....	15	1	6	7	4	....	....	....	....
2007-08	Prince George	WHL	68	25	40	65	47	....	....	....	....	....	....	....	....	....	....	....	....	....	....	....	....	....	....
	Norfolk Admirals	AHL	11	1	5	6	6	....	....	....	....	....	....	....	....	....	....	....	....	....	....	....	....	....	....
2008-09	Prince George	WHL	30	19	21	40	27	....	....	....	....	....	....	....	....	....	....	....	....	....	....	....	....	....	....
2009-10	Norfolk Admirals	AHL	74	9	27	36	22	....	....	....	....	....	....	....	....	....	....	....	....	....	....	....	....	....	....
2010-11	**Tampa Bay**	**NHL**	**78**	**6**	**9**	**15**	**12**	**0**	**0**	**1**	**73**	**8.2**	**–5**	**11**	**45.5**	**12:03**	**7**	**0**	**0**	**0**	**2**	**0**	**0**	**0**	**7:24**
	NHL Totals		**78**	**6**	**9**	**15**	**12**	**0**	**0**	**1**	**73**	**8.2**		**11**	**45.5**	**12:03**	**7**	**0**	**0**	**0**	**2**	**0**	**0**	**0**	**7:25**

TYUTIN, Fedor

(T'YOO-tihn, FEH-duhr) **CBJ**

Defense. Shoots left. 6'2", 214 lbs. Born, Izhevsk, USSR, July 19, 1983. NY Rangers' 2nd choice, 40th overall, in 2001 Entry Draft.

Season	Club	League	GP	G	A	Pts	PIM	PP	SH	GW	S	%	+/-	TF	F%	Min	GP	G	A	Pts	PIM	PP	SH	GW	Min
1998-99	Magnitogorsk 2	Russia-4	7	0	1	1	2	....	....	....	....	....	....	....	....	....	....	....	....	....	....	....	....	....	....
99-2000	Izhstal Izhevsk 2	Russia-3	38	11	8	19	68	....	....	....	....	....	....	....	....	....	....	....	....	....	....	....	....	....	....
	Izhstal Izhevsk	Russia-2	10	0	1	1	12	....	....	....	....	....	....	....	....	....	....	....	....	....	....	....	....	....	....
2000-01	St. Petersburg	Russia	34	2	4	6	20	....	....	....	....	....	....	....	....	....	....	....	....	....	....	....	....	....	....
2001-02	Guelph Storm	OHL	53	19	40	59	54	....	....	....	....	....	....	....	....	....	9	2	8	10	8	....	....	....	....
2002-03	St. Petersburg	Russia	10	1	1	2	16	....	....	....	....	....	....	....	....	....	....	....	....	....	....	....	....	....	....
	Ak Bars Kazan	Russia	10	0	0	0	8	....	....	....	....	....	....	....	....	....	5	0	0	0	4	....	....	....	....
2003-04	**NY Rangers**	**NHL**	**25**	**2**	**5**	**7**	**14**	**0**	**1**	**0**	**33**	**6.1**	**–4**	**1**	**0.0**	**20:08**	....	....	....	....	....	....	....	....	....
	Hartford	AHL	43	5	9	14	50	....	....	....	....	....	....	....	....	....	16	0	5	5	18	....	....	....	....
2004-05	Hartford	AHL	13	2	1	3	10	....	....	....	....	....	....	....	....	....	....	....	....	....	....	....	....	....	....
	St. Petersburg	Russia	35	5	3	8	24	....	....	....	....	....	....	....	....	....	....	....	....	....	....	....	....	....	....
2005-06	**NY Rangers**	**NHL**	**77**	**6**	**19**	**25**	**58**	**4**	**0**	**2**	**102**	**5.9**	**1**	**1**	**0.0**	**20:33**	**4**	**0**	**1**	**1**	**0**	**0**	**0**	**0**	**17:50**
	Russia	Olympics	8	0	1	1	4	....	....	....	....	....	....	....	....	....	....	....	....	....	....	....	....	....	....
2006-07	**NY Rangers**	**NHL**	**66**	**2**	**12**	**14**	**44**	**1**	**1**	**0**	**75**	**2.7**	**–8**	**1**	**0.0**	**20:02**	**10**	**0**	**5**	**5**	**8**	**0**	**0**	**0**	**19:30**
2007-08	**NY Rangers**	**NHL**	**82**	**5**	**15**	**20**	**43**	**1**	**0**	**0**	**131**	**3.8**	**5**	**0**	**0.0**	**20:27**	**10**	**0**	**3**	**3**	**4**	**0**	**0**	**0**	**19:52**
2008-09	**Columbus**	**NHL**	**82**	**9**	**25**	**34**	**81**	**5**	**1**	**0**	**167**	**5.4**	**1**	**1**	**100.0**	**23:31**	**4**	**0**	**0**	**0**	**0**	**0**	**0**	**0**	**23:16**
2009-10	**Columbus**	**NHL**	**80**	**6**	**26**	**32**	**49**	**3**	**0**	**2**	**149**	**4.0**	**–7**	**3**	**33.3**	**23:31**	....	....	....	....	....	....	....	....	....
	Russia	Olympics	4	0	2	2	2	....	....	....	....	....	....	....	....	....	....	....	....	....	....	....	....	....	....
2010-11	**Columbus**	**NHL**	**80**	**7**	**20**	**27**	**32**	**1**	**0**	**0**	**128**	**5.5**	**–12**	**2**	**50.0**	**22:42**	....	....	....	....	....	....	....	....	....
	NHL Totals		**492**	**37**	**122**	**159**	**321**	**15**	**3**	**4**	**785**	**4.7**		**9**	**33.3**	**21:46**	**28**	**0**	**9**	**9**	**12**	**0**	**0**	**0**	**19:56**

Signed as a free agent by **St. Petersburg** (Russia), November 11, 2004. Traded to **Columbus** by **NY Rangers** with Christian Backman for Nikolai Zherdev and Dan Fritsche, July 2, 2008.

UMBERGER, R.J.

(UHM-buhr-guhr, AHR-JAY) **CBJ**

Center. Shoots left. 6'2", 220 lbs. Born, Pittsburgh, PA, May 3, 1982. Vancouver's 1st choice, 16th overall, in 2001 Entry Draft.

Season	Club	League	GP	G	A	Pts	PIM	PP	SH	GW	S	%	+/-	TF	F%	Min	GP	G	A	Pts	PIM	PP	SH	GW	Min
1997-98	Plum Mustangs	High-PA	26	*60	*56	*116	....	....	....	....	....	....	....	....	....	....	....	....	....	....	....	....	....	....	....
1998-99	USNTDP	USHL	5	2	2	4	0	....	....	....	....	....	....	....	....	....	....	....	....	....	....	....	....	....	....
	USNTDP	NAHL	50	21	21	42	32	....	....	....	....	....	....	....	....	....	....	....	....	....	....	....	....	....	....
99-2000	USNTDP	U-18	6	1	0	1	2	....	....	....	....	....	....	....	....	....	....	....	....	....	....	....	....	....	....
	USNTDP	USHL	57	33	35	68	20	....	....	....	....	....	....	....	....	....	....	....	....	....	....	....	....	....	....
2000-01	Ohio State	CCHA	32	14	23	37	18	....	....	....	....	....	....	....	....	....	....	....	....	....	....	....	....	....	....
2001-02	Ohio State	CCHA	37	18	21	39	31	....	....	....	....	....	....	....	....	....	....	....	....	....	....	....	....	....	....
2002-03	Ohio State	CCHA	43	26	27	53	16	....	....	....	....	....	....	....	....	....	....	....	....	....	....	....	....	....	....
2003-04			DID NOT PLAY																						
2004-05	Philadelphia	AHL	80	21	44	65	36	....	....	....	....	....	....	....	....	....	21	3	7	10	12	....	....	....	....
2005-06	**Philadelphia**	**NHL**	**73**	**20**	**18**	**38**	**18**	**5**	**0**	**2**	**138**	**14.5**	**9**	**163**	**50.3**	**13:14**	**5**	**1**	**0**	**1**	**2**	**0**	**0**	**0**	**11:15**
	Philadelphia	AHL	8	3	7	10	8	....	....	....	....	....	....	....	....	....	....	....	....	....	....	....	....	....	....
2006-07	**Philadelphia**	**NHL**	**81**	**16**	**12**	**28**	**41**	**2**	**2**	**1**	**134**	**11.9**	**–32**	**535**	**44.5**	**14:32**	....	....	....	....	....	....	....	....	....
2007-08	**Philadelphia**	**NHL**	**74**	**13**	**37**	**50**	**19**	**4**	**0**	**3**	**173**	**7.5**	**0**	**117**	**38.5**	**17:52**	**17**	**10**	**5**	**15**	**10**	**1**	**0**	**2**	**16:51**
2008-09	**Columbus**	**NHL**	**82**	**26**	**20**	**46**	**53**	**9**	**0**	**2**	**234**	**11.1**	**–10**	**841**	**48.0**	**18:46**	**4**	**3**	**0**	**3**	**0**	**2**	**0**	**0**	**16:22**
2009-10	**Columbus**	**NHL**	**82**	**23**	**32**	**55**	**40**	**8**	**1**	**4**	**221**	**10.4**	**–16**	**704**	**52.8**	**19:10**	....	....	....	....	....	....	....	....	....
2010-11	**Columbus**	**NHL**	**82**	**25**	**32**	**57**	**38**	**8**	**3**	**3**	**220**	**11.4**	**3**	**220**	**50.5**	**19:13**	....	....	....	....	....	....	....	....	....
	NHL Totals		**474**	**123**	**151**	**274**	**209**	**36**	**6**	**15**	**1120**	**11.0**		**2580**	**48.5**	**17:12**	**26**	**14**	**5**	**19**	**12**	**3**	**0**	**2**	**15:42**

CCHA All-Rookie Team (2001) • CCHA Rookie of the Year (2001) • CCHA First All-Star Team (2003) • NCAA West Second All-American Team (2003)

• Missed entire 2003-04 season due to contract dispute. Traded to **NY Rangers** by **Vancouver** with Martin Grenier for Martin Rucinsky, March 9, 2004. Signed as a free agent by **Philadelphia**, June 16, 2004. Traded to **Columbus** by **Philadelphia** with Philadelphia's 4th round choice (Drew Olson) in 2008 Entry Draft for Colorado's 1st round choice (previously acquired, Philadelphia selected Luca Sbisa) in 2008 Entry Draft and Columbus's 3rd round choice (Marc-Andre Bourdon) in 2008 Entry Draft, June 20, 2008.

UPSHALL, Scottie

(UHP-shuhl, SKAW-tee) **FLA**

Left wing. Shoots left. 6', 200 lbs. Born, Fort McMurray, Alta., October 7, 1983. Nashville's 1st choice, 6th overall, in 2002 Entry Draft.

Season	Club	League	GP	G	A	Pts	PIM	PP	SH	GW	S	%	+/-	TF	F%	Min	GP	G	A	Pts	PIM	PP	SH	GW	Min
1998-99	Fort McMurray	AMHL	28	62	40	102	100	....	....	....	....	....	....	....	....	....	....	....	....	....	....	....	....	....	....
99-2000	Fort McMurray	AJHL	52	26	26	52	65	....	....	....	....	....	....	....	....	....	....	....	....	....	....	....	....	....	....
2000-01	Kamloops Blazers	WHL	70	42	45	87	111	....	....	....	....	....	....	....	....	....	4	0	2	2	10	....	....	....	....
2001-02	Kamloops Blazers	WHL	61	32	51	83	139	....	....	....	....	....	....	....	....	....	4	1	2	3	21	....	....	....	....
2002-03	**Nashville**	**NHL**	**8**	**1**	**0**	**1**	**0**	**0**	**0**	**0**	**6**	**16.7**	**2**	**2**	**0.0**	**8:42**	....	....	....	....	....	....	....	....	....
	Kamloops Blazers	WHL	42	25	31	56	111	....	....	....	....	....	....	....	....	....	6	0	2	2	34	....	....	....	....
	Milwaukee	AHL	2	1	0	1	2	....	....	....	....	....	....	....	....	....	6	0	0	0	2	....	....	....	....
2003-04	**Nashville**	**NHL**	**7**	**0**	**1**	**1**	**0**	**0**	**0**	**0**	**6**	**0.0**	**–2**	**8**	**37.5**	**9:11**	....	....	....	....	....	....	....	....	....
	Milwaukee	AHL	31	13	11	24	42	....	....	....	....	....	....	....	....	....	8	3	0	3	4	....	....	....	....
2004-05	Milwaukee	AHL	62	19	27	46	108	....	....	....	....	....	....	....	....	....	5	2	2	4	8	....	....	....	....
2005-06	**Nashville**	**NHL**	**48**	**8**	**16**	**24**	**34**	**1**	**0**	**2**	**72**	**11.1**	**14**	**11**	**45.5**	**10:26**	**2**	**0**	**0**	**0**	**0**	**0**	**0**	**0**	**11:57**
	Milwaukee	AHL	23	17	16	33	44	....	....	....	....	....	....	....	....	....	14	6	10	16	20	....	....	....	....
2006-07	**Nashville**	**NHL**	**14**	**2**	**1**	**3**	**18**	**0**	**0**	**2**	**27**	**7.4**	**–1**	**0**	**0.0**	**10:28**	....	....	....	....	....	....	....	....	....
	Milwaukee	AHL	5	0	1	1	6	....	....	....	....	....	....	....	....	....	....	....	....	....	....	....	....	....	....
	Philadelphia	**NHL**	**18**	**6**	**7**	**13**	**8**	**1**	**1**	**2**	**60**	**10.0**	**4**	**18**	**44.4**	**18:05**	....	....	....	....	....	....	....	....	....
2007-08	**Philadelphia**	**NHL**	**61**	**14**	**16**	**30**	**74**	**3**	**0**	**1**	**128**	**10.9**	**2**	**7**	**28.6**	**13:20**	**17**	**3**	**4**	**7**	***44**	**1**	**0**	**1**	**13:57**
2008-09	**Philadelphia**	**NHL**	**55**	**7**	**14**	**21**	**63**	**2**	**0**	**0**	**126**	**5.6**	**5**	**10**	**10.0**	**13:13**	....	....	....	....	....	....	....	....	....
	Phoenix	**NHL**	**19**	**8**	**5**	**13**	**26**	**3**	**0**	**1**	**66**	**12.1**	**2**	**9**	**44.4**	**18:35**	....	....	....	....	....	....	....	....	....
2009-10	**Phoenix**	**NHL**	**49**	**18**	**14**	**32**	**50**	**2**	**0**	**4**	**119**	**15.1**	**5**	**17**	**41.2**	**15:03**	....	....	....	....	....	....	....	....	....
2010-11	**Phoenix**	**NHL**	**61**	**16**	**11**	**27**	**42**	**2**	**0**	**2**	**144**	**11.1**	**5**	**19**	**21.1**	**13:27**	....	....	....	....	....	....	....	....	....
	Columbus	**NHL**	**21**	**6**	**1**	**7**	**10**	**0**	**0**	**0**	**47**	**12.8**	**–12**	**6**	**66.7**	**15:46**	....	....	....	....	....	....	....	....	....
	NHL Totals		**361**	**86**	**86**	**172**	**325**	**14**	**1**	**14**	**801**	**10.7**		**107**	**35.5**	**13:33**	**19**	**3**	**4**	**7**	**44**	**1**	**0**	**1**	**13:44**

WHL All-Rookie Team (2001) • WHL Rookie of the Year (2001) • CHL All-Rookie Team (2001) • Canadian Major Junior Rookie of the Year (2001) • WHL West Second All-Star Team (2002)

• Missed majority of 2003-04 due to knee injury vs. Phoenix, December 22, 2003. Traded to **Philadelphia** by **Nashville** with Ryan Parent and Nashville's 1st (later traded back to Nashville – Nashville selected Jonathon Blum) and 3rd (later traded to Washington – Washington selected Phil Desimone) round choices in 2007 Entry Draft for Peter Forsberg, February 15, 2007. Traded to **Phoenix** by **Philadelphia** with Philadelphia's 2nd round choice (Lucas Lessio) in 2011 Entry Draft for Daniel Carcillo, March 4, 2009. Traded to **Columbus** by **Phoenix** with Sami Lepisto for Rostislav Klesla and Dane Byers, February 28, 2011. Signed as a free agent by **Florida**, July 1, 2011.

URBOM, Alexander

(OOR-bohm, al-ehx-AN-duhr) **N.J.**

Defense. Shoots left. 6'5", 215 lbs. Born, Stockholm, Sweden, December 20, 1990. New Jersey's 3rd choice, 73rd overall, in 2009 Entry Draft.

Season	Club	League	GP	G	A	Pts	PIM	PP	SH	GW	S	%	+/-	TF	F%	Min	GP	G	A	Pts	PIM	PP	SH	GW	Min
2005-06	Djurgarden U18	Swe-U18	2	0	0	0	0	....	....	....	....	....	....	....	....	....	....	....	....	....	....	....	....	....	....
2006-07	Djurgarden U18	Swe-U18	31	6	11	17	36	....	....	....	....	....	....	....	....	....	3	0	1	1	2	....	....	....	....
2007-08	Djurgarden U18	Swe-U18	7	2	6	8	6	....	....	....	....	....	....	....	....	....	5	1	0	1	2	....	....	....	....
	Djurgarden Jr.	Swe-Jr.	39	3	8	11	54	....	....	....	....	....	....	....	....	....	7	0	1	1	2	....	....	....	....
2008-09	Djurgarden Jr.	Swe-Jr.	16	5	6	11	45	....	....	....	....	....	....	....	....	....	....	....	....	....	....	....	....	....	....
	Djurgarden	Sweden	28	0	0	0	2	....	....	....	....	....	....	....	....	....	....	....	....	....	....	....	....	....	....
	Djurgarden U18	Swe-U18	....	....	....	....	....	....	....	....	....	....	....	....	....	....	5	1	0	1	2	....	....	....	....
2009-10	Brandon	WHL	66	12	21	33	87	....	....	....	....	....	....	....	....	....	15	4	3	7	17	....	....	....	....

Season	Club	League	GP	G	A	Pts	PIM	PP	SH	GW	S	%	+/-	TF	F%	Min	GP	G	A	Pts	PIM	PP	SH	GW	Min
					Regular Season												Playoffs								
2010-11	**New Jersey**	**NHL**	**8**	**1**	**0**	**1**	**0**	**0**	**0**	**1**	**5**	**20.0**	**–2**	**0**	**0.0**	**12:35**	....	....	....	....	....	....	....	....	....
	Albany Devils	AHL	72	2	21	23	64	....	....	....	....	....	....	....	....	....	....	....	....	....	....	....	....	....	....
	NHL Totals		**8**	**1**	**0**	**1**	**0**	**0**	**0**	**1**	**5**	**20.0**		**0**	**0.0**	**12:35**	....	....	....	....	....	....	....	....	....

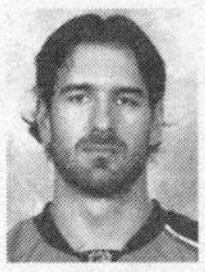

VALABIK, Boris

(vuh-LA-bihk, BOHR-ihs) **PIT**

Defense. Shoots left. 6'7", 245 lbs. Born, Nitra, Czech., February 14, 1986. Atlanta's 1st choice, 10th overall, in 2004 Entry Draft.

Season	Club	League	GP	G	A	Pts	PIM	PP	SH	GW	S	%	+/-	TF	F%	Min	GP	G	A	Pts	PIM	PP	SH	GW	Min
2002-03	HKM Nitra Jr.	Slovak-Jr.	46	2	12	14	145	....	....	....	....	....	....	....	....	....	....	....	....	....	....	....	....	....	....
2003-04	Kitchener Rangers	OHL	68	3	13	16	278	....	....	....	....	....	....	....	....	....	5	0	0	0	8	....	....	....	....
2004-05	Kitchener Rangers	OHL	43	0	4	4	231	....	....	....	....	....	....	....	....	....	15	0	0	0	56	....	....	....	....
2005-06	Kitchener Rangers	OHL	52	1	9	10	216	....	....	....	....	....	....	....	....	....	5	0	2	2	14	....	....	....	....
2006-07	Chicago Wolves	AHL	50	2	7	9	184	....	....	....	....	....	....	....	....	....	8	0	1	1	37	....	....	....	....
2007-08	**Atlanta**	**NHL**	**7**	**0**	**0**	**0**	**42**	**0**	**0**	**0**	**5**	**0.0**	**–2**	**0**	**0.0**	**16:42**	....	....	....	....	....	....	....	....	....
	Chicago Wolves	AHL	58	1	7	8	229	....	....	....	....	....	....	....	....	....	24	3	1	4	71	....	....	....	....
2008-09	**Atlanta**	**NHL**	**50**	**0**	**5**	**5**	**132**	**0**	**0**	**0**	**16**	**0.0**	**–14**	**0**	**0.0**	**15:15**	....	....	....	....	....	....	....	....	....
	Chicago Wolves	AHL	11	1	2	3	21	....	....	....	....	....	....	....	....	....	....	....	....	....	....	....	....	....	....
2009-10	**Atlanta**	**NHL**	**23**	**0**	**2**	**2**	**36**	**0**	**0**	**0**	**22**	**0.0**	**2**	**0**	**0.0**	**13:14**	....	....	....	....	....	....	....	....	....
	Chicago Wolves	AHL	6	0	0	0	10	....	....	....	....	....	....	....	....	....	....	....	....	....	....	....	....	....	....
2010-11	Chicago Wolves	AHL	49	0	9	9	165	....	....	....	....	....	....	....	....	....	....	....	....	....	....	....	....	....	....
	Providence Bruins	AHL	10	0	2	2	24	....	....	....	....	....	....	....	....	....	....	....	....	....	....	....	....	....	....
	NHL Totals		**80**	**0**	**7**	**7**	**210**	**0**	**0**	**0**	**43**	**0.0**		**0**	**0.0**	**14:47**	....	....	....	....	....	....	....	....	....

OHL All-Rookie Team (2004) • Canadian Major Junior All-Rookie Team (2004)

• Missed majority of 2009-10 due to ankle injury in practice, October 5, 2009 and knee injury at Washington, February 5, 2010. Traded to **Boston** by **Atlanta** with Rich Peverley for Blake Wheeler and Mark Stuart, February 18, 2011. Signed as a free agent by **Pittsburgh**, July 3, 2011.

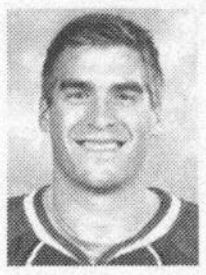

VAN DER GULIK, David

(VAN DUHR-GOO-lihk, DAY-vihd) **COL**

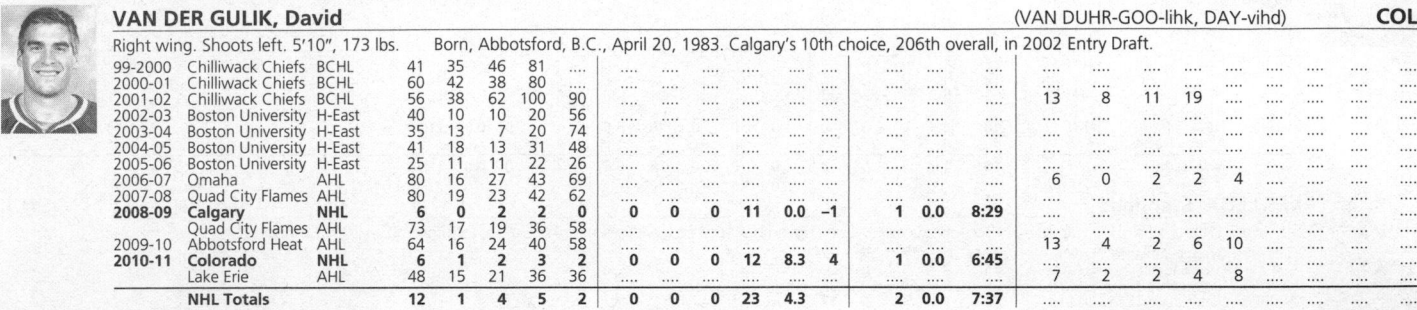

Right wing. Shoots left. 5'10", 173 lbs. Born, Abbotsford, B.C., April 20, 1983. Calgary's 10th choice, 206th overall, in 2002 Entry Draft.

Season	Club	League	GP	G	A	Pts	PIM	PP	SH	GW	S	%	+/-	TF	F%	Min	GP	G	A	Pts	PIM	PP	SH	GW	Min
99-2000	Chilliwack Chiefs	BCHL	41	35	46	81	....	....	....	....	....	....	....	....	....	....	....	....	....	....	....	....	....	....	....
2000-01	Chilliwack Chiefs	BCHL	60	42	38	80	....	....	....	....	....	....	....	....	....	....	....	....	....	....	....	....	....	....	....
2001-02	Chilliwack Chiefs	BCHL	56	38	62	100	90	....	....	....	....	....	....	....	....	....	13	8	11	19	....	....	....	....	....
2002-03	Boston University	H-East	40	10	10	20	56	....	....	....	....	....	....	....	....	....	....	....	....	....	....	....	....	....	....
2003-04	Boston University	H-East	35	13	7	20	74	....	....	....	....	....	....	....	....	....	....	....	....	....	....	....	....	....	....
2004-05	Boston University	H-East	41	18	13	31	48	....	....	....	....	....	....	....	....	....	....	....	....	....	....	....	....	....	....
2005-06	Boston University	H-East	25	11	11	22	26	....	....	....	....	....	....	....	....	....	....	....	....	....	....	....	....	....	....
2006-07	Omaha	AHL	80	16	27	43	69	....	....	....	....	....	....	....	....	....	6	0	2	2	4	....	....	....	....
2007-08	Quad City Flames	AHL	80	19	23	42	62	....	....	....	....	....	....	....	....	....	....	....	....	....	....	....	....	....	....
2008-09	**Calgary**	**NHL**	**6**	**0**	**2**	**2**	**0**	**0**	**0**	**0**	**11**	**0.0**	**–1**	**1**	**0.0**	**8:29**	....	....	....	....	....	....	....	....	....
	Quad City Flames	AHL	73	17	19	36	58	....	....	....	....	....	....	....	....	....	....	....	....	....	....	....	....	....	....
2009-10	Abbotsford Heat	AHL	64	16	24	40	58	....	....	....	....	....	....	....	....	....	13	4	2	6	10	....	....	....	....
2010-11	**Colorado**	**NHL**	**6**	**1**	**2**	**3**	**2**	**0**	**0**	**0**	**12**	**8.3**	**4**	**1**	**0.0**	**6:45**	....	....	....	....	....	....	....	....	....
	Lake Erie	AHL	48	15	21	36	36	....	....	....	....	....	....	....	....	....	7	2	2	4	8	....	....	....	....
	NHL Totals		**12**	**1**	**4**	**5**	**2**	**0**	**0**	**0**	**23**	**4.3**		**2**	**0.0**	**7:37**	....	....	....	....	....	....	....	....	....

Hockey East All-Rookie Team (2003)

Signed as a free agent by **Colorado**, July 2, 2010.

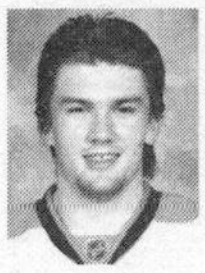

van RIEMSDYK, James

(VAN REEMZ-dighk, JAYMZ) **PHI**

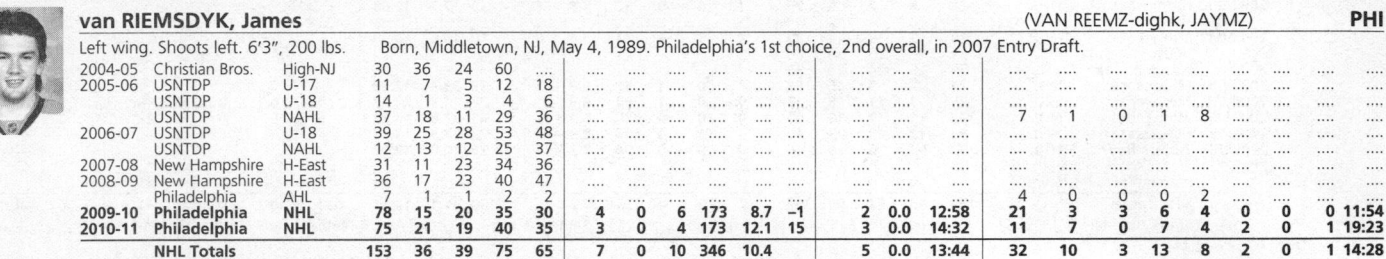

Left wing. Shoots left. 6'3", 200 lbs. Born, Middletown, NJ, May 4, 1989. Philadelphia's 1st choice, 2nd overall, in 2007 Entry Draft.

Season	Club	League	GP	G	A	Pts	PIM	PP	SH	GW	S	%	+/-	TF	F%	Min	GP	G	A	Pts	PIM	PP	SH	GW	Min
2004-05	Christian Bros.	High-NJ	30	36	24	60	....	....	....	....	....	....	....	....	....	....	....	....	....	....	....	....	....	....	....
2005-06	USNTDP	U-17	11	7	5	12	18	....	....	....	....	....	....	....	....	....	....	....	....	....	....	....	....	....	....
	USNTDP	U-18	14	1	3	4	6	....	....	....	....	....	....	....	....	....	....	....	....	....	....	....	....	....	....
	USNTDP	NAHL	37	18	11	29	36	....	....	....	....	....	....	....	....	....	7	1	0	1	8	....	....	....	....
2006-07	USNTDP	U-18	39	25	28	53	48	....	....	....	....	....	....	....	....	....	....	....	....	....	....	....	....	....	....
	USNTDP	NAHL	12	13	12	25	37	....	....	....	....	....	....	....	....	....	....	....	....	....	....	....	....	....	....
2007-08	New Hampshire	H-East	31	11	23	34	36	....	....	....	....	....	....	....	....	....	....	....	....	....	....	....	....	....	....
2008-09	New Hampshire	H-East	36	17	23	40	47	....	....	....	....	....	....	....	....	....	....	....	....	....	....	....	....	....	....
	Philadelphia	AHL	7	1	1	2	2	....	....	....	....	....	....	....	....	....	4	0	0	0	2	....	....	....	....
2009-10	**Philadelphia**	**NHL**	**78**	**15**	**20**	**35**	**30**	**4**	**0**	**6**	**173**	**8.7**	**–1**	**2**	**0.0**	**12:58**	**21**	**3**	**3**	**6**	**4**	**0**	**0**	**0**	**11:54**
2010-11	**Philadelphia**	**NHL**	**75**	**21**	**19**	**40**	**35**	**3**	**0**	**4**	**173**	**12.1**	**15**	**3**	**0.0**	**14:32**	**11**	**7**	**0**	**7**	**4**	**2**	**0**	**1**	**19:23**
	NHL Totals		**153**	**36**	**39**	**75**	**65**	**7**	**0**	**10**	**346**	**10.4**		**5**	**0.0**	**13:44**	**32**	**10**	**3**	**13**	**8**	**2**	**0**	**1**	**14:28**

Hockey East All-Rookie Team (2008) • Hockey East Second All-Star Team (2009)

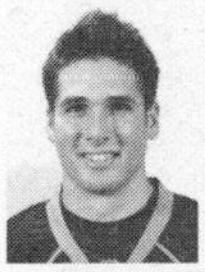

VANDE VELDE, Chris

(VAN-deh VEHLD, KRIHS) **EDM**

Center. Shoots left. 6'2", 190 lbs. Born, Moorhead, MN, March 15, 1987. Edmonton's 5th choice, 97th overall, in 2005 Entry Draft.

Season	Club	League	GP	G	A	Pts	PIM	PP	SH	GW	S	%	+/-	TF	F%	Min	GP	G	A	Pts	PIM	PP	SH	GW	Min
2003-04	Moorhead Spuds	High-MN	29	19	24	43	....	....	....	....	....	....	....	....	....	....	....	....	....	....	....	....	....	....	....
2004-05	Moorhead Spuds	High-MN	30	35	32	67	28	....	....	....	....	....	....	....	....	....	....	....	....	....	....	....	....	....	....
	Lincoln Stars	USHL	7	1	4	5	0	....	....	....	....	....	....	....	....	....	4	0	2	2	0	....	....	....	....
2005-06	Lincoln Stars	USHL	56	16	20	36	70	....	....	....	....	....	....	....	....	....	9	1	3	4	10	....	....	....	....
2006-07	North Dakota	WCHA	38	3	6	9	37	....	....	....	....	....	....	....	....	....	....	....	....	....	....	....	....	....	....
2007-08	North Dakota	WCHA	43	15	17	32	38	....	....	....	....	....	....	....	....	....	....	....	....	....	....	....	....	....	....
2008-09	North Dakota	WCHA	43	18	17	35	69	....	....	....	....	....	....	....	....	....	....	....	....	....	....	....	....	....	....
2009-10	North Dakota	WCHA	42	16	25	41	22	....	....	....	....	....	....	....	....	....	....	....	....	....	....	....	....	....	....
2010-11	**Edmonton**	**NHL**	**12**	**0**	**2**	**2**	**12**	**0**	**0**	**0**	**16**	**0.0**	**–6**	**159**	**52.8**	**17:17**	....	....	....	....	....	....	....	....	....
	Oklahoma City	AHL	67	12	4	16	45	....	....	....	....	....	....	....	....	....	6	1	0	1	6	....	....	....	....
	NHL Totals		**12**	**0**	**2**	**2**	**12**	**0**	**0**	**0**	**16**	**0.0**		**159**	**52.8**	**17:17**	....	....	....	....	....	....	....	....	....

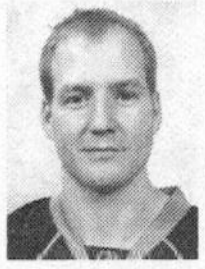

VANDERMEER, Jim

(VAN-duhr-meer, JIHM) **S.J.**

Defense. Shoots left. 6'1", 215 lbs. Born, Caroline, Alta., February 21, 1980.

Season	Club	League	GP	G	A	Pts	PIM	PP	SH	GW	S	%	+/-	TF	F%	Min	GP	G	A	Pts	PIM	PP	SH	GW	Min
1997-98	Red Deer	AMHL	26	4	8	12	51	....	....	....	....	....	....	....	....	....	....	....	....	....	....	....	....	....	....
	Red Deer Rebels	WHL	35	0	3	3	55	....	....	....	....	....	....	....	....	....	2	0	0	0	0	....	....	....	....
1998-99	Red Deer Rebels	WHL	70	5	23	28	258	....	....	....	....	....	....	....	....	....	9	0	1	1	24	....	....	....	....
99-2000	Red Deer Rebels	WHL	71	8	30	38	221	....	....	....	....	....	....	....	....	....	4	0	1	1	16	....	....	....	....
2000-01	Red Deer Rebels	WHL	72	21	44	65	180	....	....	....	....	....	....	....	....	....	22	3	13	16	43	....	....	....	....
2001-02	Philadelphia	AHL	74	1	13	14	88	....	....	....	....	....	....	....	....	....	5	0	2	2	14	....	....	....	....
2002-03	**Philadelphia**	**NHL**	**24**	**2**	**1**	**3**	**27**	**0**	**0**	**0**	**22**	**9.1**	**9**	**0**	**0.0**	**13:42**	**8**	**0**	**1**	**1**	**9**	**0**	**0**	**0**	**12:42**
	Philadelphia	AHL	48	4	8	12	122	....	....	....	....	....	....	....	....	....	....	....	....	....	....	....	....	....	....
2003-04	**Philadelphia**	**NHL**	**23**	**3**	**2**	**5**	**25**	**0**	**0**	**1**	**24**	**12.5**	**–5**	**0**	**0.0**	**15:47**	....	....	....	....	....	....	....	....	....
	Philadelphia	AHL	26	1	6	7	120	....	....	....	....	....	....	....	....	....	....	....	....	....	....	....	....	....	....
	Chicago	**NHL**	**23**	**2**	**10**	**12**	**58**	**1**	**1**	**0**	**37**	**5.4**	**–6**	**1**	**100.0**	**22:03**	....	....	....	....	....	....	....	....	....
2004-05	Norfolk Admirals	AHL	52	3	10	13	164	....	....	....	....	....	....	....	....	....	....	....	....	....	....	....	....	....	....
2005-06	**Chicago**	**NHL**	**76**	**6**	**18**	**24**	**116**	**2**	**0**	**1**	**93**	**6.5**	**–2**	**1**	**100.0**	**21:47**	....	....	....	....	....	....	....	....	....
2006-07	**Chicago**	**NHL**	**46**	**1**	**6**	**7**	**53**	**0**	**0**	**0**	**50**	**2.0**	**–3**	**0**	**0.0**	**17:50**	....	....	....	....	....	....	....	....	....
2007-08	**Chicago**	**NHL**	**26**	**2**	**7**	**9**	**44**	**1**	**0**	**0**	**23**	**8.7**	**3**	**0**	**0.0**	**19:37**	....	....	....	....	....	....	....	....	....
	Philadelphia	**NHL**	**28**	**1**	**5**	**6**	**27**	**1**	**0**	**0**	**26**	**3.8**	**–1**	**0**	**0.0**	**19:34**	....	....	....	....	....	....	....	....	....
	Calgary	**NHL**	**21**	**0**	**2**	**2**	**39**	**0**	**0**	**0**	**23**	**0.0**	**4**	**0**	**0.0**	**19:44**	**7**	**0**	**0**	**0**	**4**	**0**	**0**	**0**	**16:18**
2008-09	**Calgary**	**NHL**	**45**	**1**	**6**	**7**	**108**	**0**	**0**	**0**	**31**	**3.2**	**1**	**0**	**0.0**	**16:01**	**6**	**0**	**1**	**1**	**4**	**0**	**0**	**0**	**16:33**
2009-10	**Phoenix**	**NHL**	**62**	**4**	**8**	**12**	**60**	**0**	**0**	**1**	**64**	**6.3**	**3**	**0**	**0.0**	**17:41**	....	....	....	....	....	....	....	....	....
2010-11	**Edmonton**	**NHL**	**62**	**2**	**12**	**14**	**74**	**0**	**0**	**0**	**57**	**3.5**	**–15**	**0**	**0.0**	**18:12**	....	....	....	....	....	....	....	....	....
	NHL Totals		**436**	**24**	**77**	**101**	**631**	**5**	**1**	**3**	**450**	**5.3**		**2**	**100.0**	**18:34**	**21**	**0**	**2**	**2**	**17**	**0**	**0**	**0**	**15:00**

WHL East First All-Star Team (2001) • Canadian Major Junior Humanitarian Player of the Year (2001)

Signed as a free agent by **Philadelphia**, December 21, 2000. Traded to **Chicago** by **Philadelphia** with the rights to Colin Fraser and Los Angeles' 2nd round choice (previously acquired, Chicago selected Bryan Bickell) in 2004 Entry Draft for Alex Zhamnov and Washington's 4th round choice (previously acquired, Philadelphia selected R.J. Anderson) in 2004 Entry Draft, February 19, 2004. Traded to **Philadelphia** by **Chicago** for Ben Eager, December 18, 2007. Traded to **Calgary** by **Philadelphia** for Calgary's 3rd round choice (Adam Morrison) in 2009 Entry Draft, February 20, 2008. Traded to **Phoenix** by **Calgary** for Brandon Prust, June 27. 2009. Traded to **Edmonton** by **Phoenix** for Patrick O'Sullivan, June 30, 2010. Signed as a free agent by **San Jose**, July 1, 2011.

			Regular Season															Playoffs								
Season	Club	League	GP	G	A	Pts	PIM	PP	SH	GW	S	%	+/-	TF	F%	Min	GP	G	A	Pts	PIM	PP	SH	GW	Min

VANEK, Thomas — (VAN-ehk, TAW-muhs) — **BUF**

Left wing. Shoots right. 6'2", 205 lbs. Born, Vienna, Austria, January 19, 1984. Buffalo's 1st choice, 5th overall, in 2003 Entry Draft.

Season	Club	League	GP	G	A	Pts	PIM	PP	SH	GW	S	%	+/-	TF	F%	Min	GP	G	A	Pts	PIM	PP	SH	GW	Min
99-2000	Sioux Falls	USHL	35	15	18	33	12	....	....	....	....	....	....	....	....	....	3	0	1	1	0	....	....	....	....
2000-01	Sioux Falls	USHL	20	19	10	29	15	....	....	....	....	....	....	....	....	....	8	5	4	9	2	....	....	....	....
2001-02	Sioux Falls	USHL	53	46	45	91	54	....	....	....	....	....	....	....	....	....	3	0	0	0	9	....	....	....	....
2002-03	U. of Minnesota	WCHA	45	31	31	62	60	....	....	....	....	....	....	....	....	....	....	....	....	....	....	....	....	....	....
2003-04	U. of Minnesota	WCHA	38	26	25	51	72	....	....	....	....	....	....	....	....	....	....	....	....	....	....	....	....	....	....
2004-05	Rochester	AHL	74	42	26	68	62	....	....	....	....	....	....	....	....	....	5	2	3	5	10	....	....	....	....
2005-06	**Buffalo**	**NHL**	81	25	23	48	72	11	0	4	204	12.3	–11	23	21.7	14:44	10	2	0	2	6	2	0	0	10:45
2006-07	**Buffalo**	**NHL**	82	43	41	84	40	15	0	5	237	18.1	*47	39	28.2	16:47	16	6	4	10	10	1	0	2	16:27
2007-08	**Buffalo**	**NHL**	82	36	28	64	64	19	0	9	240	15.0	–5	13	46.2	16:51	....	....	....	....	....	....	....	....	....
2008-09	**Buffalo**	**NHL**	73	40	24	64	44	*20	2	5	211	19.0	–1	6	16.7	17:12	....	....	....	....	....	....	....	....	....
2009-10	**Buffalo**	**NHL**	71	28	25	53	42	10	0	6	182	15.4	9	9	22.2	16:46	3	2	1	3	2	0	0	0	13:38
2010-11	**Buffalo**	**NHL**	80	32	41	73	24	11	0	5	238	13.4	2	26	30.8	17:21	7	5	0	5	0	4	0	0	17:10
	NHL Totals		469	204	182	386	286	86	2	34	1312	15.5		116	28.4	16:36	36	15	5	20	18	7	0	2	14:46

USHL First All-Star Team (2002) • USHL MVP (2002) • WCHA All-Rookie Team (2003) • WCHA Second All-Star Team (2003, 2004) • WCHA Rookie of the Year (2003) • NCAA Championship All-Tournament Team (2003) • NCAA Championship Tournament MVP (2003) • NCAA West Second All-American Team (2004) • AHL All-Rookie Team (2005) • NHL Second All-Star Team (2007)
Played in NHL All-Star Game (2009)

VASYUNOV, Alexander — (vahs-YUH-nawv, al-EHX-AN-duhr) — **N.J.**

Left wing. Shoots right. 6'1", 205 lbs. Born, Yaroslavl, USSR, April 22, 1988. New Jersey's 2nd choice, 58th overall, in 2006 Entry Draft.

Season	Club	League	GP	G	A	Pts	PIM	PP	SH	GW	S	%	+/-	TF	F%	Min	GP	G	A	Pts	PIM	PP	SH	GW	Min
2004-05	Yaroslavl 2	Russia-3	28	10	2	12	6	....	....	....	....	....	....	....	....	....	....	....	....	....	....	....	....	....	....
2005-06	Yaroslavl 2	Russia-3	29	29	6	35	14	....	....	....	....	....	....	....	....	....	....	....	....	....	....	....	....	....	....
	Yaroslavl	Russia	2	0	0	0	2	....	....	....	....	....	....	....	....	....	....	....	....	....	....	....	....	....	....
2006-07	Yaroslavl 2	Russia-3	30	16	9	25	52	....	....	....	....	....	....	....	....	....	....	....	....	....	....	....	....	....	....
	Yaroslavl	Russia	17	0	0	0	4	....	....	....	....	....	....	....	....	....	....	....	....	....	....	....	....	....	....
2007-08	Yaroslavl	Russia	22	4	0	4	4	....	....	....	....	....	....	....	....	....	16	2	0	2	2	....	....	....	....
2008-09	Yaroslavl	Rus-KHL	2	0	0	0	0	....	....	....	....	....	....	....	....	....	....	....	....	....	....	....	....	....	....
	Lowell Devils	AHL	69	15	13	28	12	....	....	....	....	....	....	....	....	....	....	....	....	....	....	....	....	....	....
2009-10	Lowell Devils	AHL	68	16	22	38	10	....	....	....	....	....	....	....	....	....	5	2	2	4	0	....	....	....	....
2010-11	**New Jersey**	**NHL**	18	1	4	5	0	0	0	0	18	5.6	0	0	0.0	11:29	....	....	....	....	....	....	....	....	....
	Albany Devils	AHL	50	8	17	25	11	....	....	....	....	....	....	....	....	....	....	....	....	....	....	....	....	....	....
	NHL Totals		18	1	4	5	0	0	0	0	18	5.6		0	0.0	11:29									

VEILLEUX, Stephane — (VAY-oo, STEH-fan) — **N.J.**

Left wing. Shoots left. 6'1", 190 lbs. Born, Beauceville, Que., November 16, 1981. Minnesota's 4th choice, 93rd overall, in 2001 Entry Draft.

Season	Club	League	GP	G	A	Pts	PIM	PP	SH	GW	S	%	+/-	TF	F%	Min	GP	G	A	Pts	PIM	PP	SH	GW	Min
1997-98	Beauce-Amiante	QAAA	21	20	17	37	....	....	....	....	....	....	....	....	....	....	1	0	0	0	0	....	....	....	....
	Levis-Lauzon	QAAA	14	3	5	8	....	....	....	....	....	....	....	....	....	....	6	1	3	4	2	....	....	....	....
1998-99	Victoriaville Tigres	QMJHL	65	6	13	19	35	....	....	....	....	....	....	....	....	....	....	....	....	....	....	....	....	....	....
99-2000	Victoriaville Tigres	QMJHL	22	1	4	5	17	....	....	....	....	....	....	....	....	....	....	....	....	....	....	....	....	....	....
	Val-d'Or Foreurs	QMJHL	50	14	28	42	100	....	....	....	....	....	....	....	....	....	....	....	....	....	....	....	....	....	....
2000-01	Val-d'Or Foreurs	QMJHL	68	48	67	115	90	....	....	....	....	....	....	....	....	....	21	15	18	33	42	....	....	....	....
2001-02	Houston Aeros	AHL	77	13	22	35	113	....	....	....	....	....	....	....	....	....	14	2	4	6	20	....	....	....	....
2002-03	**Minnesota**	**NHL**	38	3	2	5	23	1	0	0	52	5.8	–6	13	7.7	12:08	....	....	....	....	....	....	....	....	....
	Houston Aeros	AHL	29	8	4	12	43	....	....	....	....	....	....	....	....	....	23	7	11	18	12	....	....	....	....
2003-04	**Minnesota**	**NHL**	19	2	8	10	20	1	1	1	37	5.4	0	10	40.0	14:20	....	....	....	....	....	....	....	....	....
	Houston Aeros	AHL	64	13	25	38	66	....	....	....	....	....	....	....	....	....	2	1	1	2	4	....	....	....	....
2004-05	Houston Aeros	AHL	59	15	24	39	35	....	....	....	....	....	....	....	....	....	....	....	....	....	....	....	....	....	....
2005-06	**Minnesota**	**NHL**	71	7	9	16	63	0	0	1	87	8.0	–13	33	33.3	12:58	....	....	....	....	....	....	....	....	....
2006-07	**Minnesota**	**NHL**	75	7	11	18	47	0	0	3	84	8.3	3	32	21.9	12:17	5	0	0	0	4	0	0	0	12:40
2007-08	**Minnesota**	**NHL**	77	11	7	18	61	0	0	0	136	8.1	–13	45	37.8	14:32	6	0	0	0	27	0	0	0	15:43
2008-09	**Minnesota**	**NHL**	81	13	10	23	40	0	0	1	146	8.9	–17	22	27.3	15:48	....	....	....	....	....	....	....	....	....
2009-10	**Tampa Bay**	**NHL**	77	3	6	9	48	0	0	0	94	3.2	–14	25	40.0	12:17	....	....	....	....	....	....	....	....	....
2010-11	Blues Espoo	Finland	25	1	6	7	18	....	....	....	....	....	....	....	....	....	....	....	....	....	....	....	....	....	....
	HC Ambri-Piotta	Swiss	7	0	0	0	4	....	....	....	....	....	....	....	....	....	11	0	1	1	31	....	....	....	....
	NHL Totals		438	46	53	99	302	2	2	4	636	7.2		180	31.1	13:31	11	0	0	0	31	0	0	0	14:20

Signed as a free agent by **Tampa Bay**, July 7, 2009. Signed as a free agent by **Espoo** (Finland), October 15, 2010. Signed as a free agrent by **Ambri-Piotta** (Swiss), January 23, 2011. Signed as a free agent by **New Jersey**, July 30, 2011.

VERMETTE, Antoine — (vuhr-MEHT, AN-twuhn) — **CBJ**

Center. Shoots left. 6'1", 199 lbs. Born, St-Agapit, Que., July 20, 1982. Ottawa's 3rd choice, 55th overall, in 2000 Entry Draft.

Season	Club	League	GP	G	A	Pts	PIM	PP	SH	GW	S	%	+/-	TF	F%	Min	GP	G	A	Pts	PIM	PP	SH	GW	Min
1997-98	Quebec Select	QAHA	19	11	20	31	36	....	....	....	....	....	....	....	....	....	....	....	....	....	....	....	....	....	....
	Levis-Lauzon	QAAA	8	1	1	2	4	....	....	....	....	....	....	....	....	....	1	0	0	0	0	....	....	....	....
1998-99	Quebec Remparts	QMJHL	57	9	17	26	32	....	....	....	....	....	....	....	....	....	13	0	0	0	2	....	....	....	....
99-2000	Victoriaville Tigres	QMJHL	71	30	41	71	87	....	....	....	....	....	....	....	....	....	6	0	1	1	6	....	....	....	....
2000-01	Victoriaville Tigres	QMJHL	71	57	62	119	102	....	....	....	....	....	....	....	....	....	9	4	6	10	14	....	....	....	....
2001-02	Victoriaville Tigres	QMJHL	4	0	2	2	6	....	....	....	....	....	....	....	....	....	22	10	16	26	10	....	....	....	....
2002-03	Binghamton	AHL	80	34	28	62	57	....	....	....	....	....	....	....	....	....	14	2	9	11	10	....	....	....	....
2003-04	**Ottawa**	**NHL**	57	7	7	14	16	0	1	0	63	11.1	5	100	44.0	11:59	4	0	1	1	4	0	0	0	11:35
	Binghamton	AHL	3	0	0	0	6	....	....	....	....	....	....	....	....	....	....	....	....	....	....	....	....	....	....
2004-05	Binghamton	AHL	78	28	45	73	36	....	....	....	....	....	....	....	....	....	6	1	4	5	10	....	....	....	....
2005-06	**Ottawa**	**NHL**	82	21	12	33	44	1	6	4	123	17.1	17	537	57.9	12:35	10	2	0	2	4	0	0	1	15:00
2006-07	**Ottawa**	**NHL**	77	19	20	39	52	2	3	2	151	12.6	–2	834	53.0	15:42	20	2	3	5	6	0	0	0	16:20
2007-08	**Ottawa**	**NHL**	81	24	29	53	51	4	3	3	175	13.7	3	1217	56.7	17:35	4	0	0	0	4	0	0	0	20:33
2008-09	**Ottawa**	**NHL**	62	9	19	28	42	2	0	0	141	6.4	–12	771	58.4	18:03	....	....	....	....	....	....	....	....	....
	Columbus	**NHL**	17	7	6	13	8	1	1	1	33	21.2	5	341	56.3	19:29	4	0	0	0	10	0	0	0	16:47
2009-10	**Columbus**	**NHL**	82	27	38	65	32	6	2	1	156	17.3	2	1573	54.2	20:09	....	....	....	....	....	....	....	....	....
2010-11	**Columbus**	**NHL**	82	19	28	47	60	3	1	3	183	10.4	0	1540	55.6	18:49	....	....	....	....	....	....	....	....	....
	NHL Totals		540	133	159	292	305	19	17	14	1025	13.0		6913	55.5	16:39	42	4	4	8	28	0	0	1	16:00

AHL All-Rookie Team (2003)

• Missed majority of 2001-02 due to neck injury in Team Canada Jr. Selection Camp, June 3, 2001. Traded to **Columbus** by **Ottawa** for Pascal Leclaire and Columbus' 2nd round choice (Robin Lehner) in 2009 Entry Draft, March 4, 2009.

VERNACE, Michael — (vuhr-NAYS, MIGH-kuhl) — **T.B.**

Defense. Shoots left. 6', 216 lbs. Born, Toronto, Ont., May 26, 1986. San Jose's 6th choice, 201st overall, in 2004 Entry Draft.

Season	Club	League	GP	G	A	Pts	PIM	PP	SH	GW	S	%	+/-	TF	F%	Min	GP	G	A	Pts	PIM	PP	SH	GW	Min
2003-04	Bramalea Blues	OPJHL	33	3	12	15	16	....	....	....	....	....	....	....	....	....	....	....	....	....	....	....	....	....	....
	Brampton	OHL	2	1	1	2	0	....	....	....	....	....	....	....	....	....	11	2	3	5	8	....	....	....	....
2004-05	Brampton	OHL	68	12	38	50	42	....	....	....	....	....	....	....	....	....	6	2	4	6	4	....	....	....	....
2005-06	Brampton	OHL	68	10	62	72	54	....	....	....	....	....	....	....	....	....	11	1	5	6	6	....	....	....	....
2006-07	Albany River Rats	AHL	30	1	11	12	35	....	....	....	....	....	....	....	....	....	....	....	....	....	....	....	....	....	....
	Arizona Sundogs	CHL	24	3	11	14	20	....	....	....	....	....	....	....	....	....	....	....	....	....	....	....	....	....	....
2007-08	Lake Erie	AHL	79	3	26	29	59	....	....	....	....	....	....	....	....	....	....	....	....	....	....	....	....	....	....
2008-09	**Colorado**	**NHL**	12	0	0	0	8	0	0	0	9	0.0	–5	0	0.0	19:39	....	....	....	....	....	....	....	....	....
	Lake Erie	AHL	65	3	14	17	52	....	....	....	....	....	....	....	....	....	....	....	....	....	....	....	....	....	....
2009-10	Chicago Wolves	AHL	47	2	10	12	29	....	....	....	....	....	....	....	....	....	....	....	....	....	....	....	....	....	....
	Hamilton	AHL	15	0	1	1	23	....	....	....	....	....	....	....	....	....	18	0	4	4	8	....	....	....	....
2010-11	**Tampa Bay**	**NHL**	10	0	1	1	2	0	0	0	6	0.0	–2	0	0.0	8:42	....	....	....	....	....	....	....	....	....
	Norfolk Admirals	AHL	68	7	21	28	60	....	....	....	....	....	....	....	....	....	6	0	2	2	8	....	....	....	....
	NHL Totals		22	0	1	1	10	0	0	0	15	0.0		0	0.0	14:41									

OHL All-Rookie Team (2005)

• Rights traded to **Colorado** by **San Jose** for Colorado's 6th round choice (Patrick Zackrisson) in 2007 Entry Draft, June 1, 2006. Signed as a free agent by **Atlanta**, July 30, 2009. Traded to **San Jose** by **Atlanta** with Brett Sterling and Atlanta's 7th round choice (Lee Moffie) in 2010 Entry Draft for future considerations, June 23, 2010. Signed as a free agent by **Tampa Bay**, July 29, 2010.

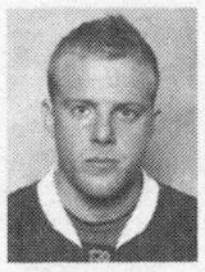

VERSTEEG, Kris (vuhr-STEEG, KRIHS) FLA

Right wing. Shoots right. 5'10", 182 lbs. Born, Lethbridge, Alta., May 13, 1986. Boston's 4th choice, 134th overall, in 2004 Entry Draft.

			Regular Season														Playoffs								
Season	Club	League	GP	G	A	Pts	PIM	PP	SH	GW	S	%	+/-	TF	F%	Min	GP	G	A	Pts	PIM	PP	SH	GW	Min
2002-03	Lethbridge	WHL	57	8	10	18	32	....	....	....	....	....	....	....	....	....	....	....	....	....	....	....	....	....	....
2003-04	Lethbridge	WHL	68	16	33	49	85	....	....	....	....	....	....	....	....	....	....	....	....	....	....	....	....	....	....
2004-05	Lethbridge	WHL	68	22	30	52	68	....	....	....	....	....	....	....	....	....	5	0	1	1	4	....	....	....	....
2005-06	Kamloops Blazers	WHL	14	6	6	12	24	....	....	....	....	....	....	....	....	....	....	....	....	....	....	....	....	....	....
	Red Deer Rebels	WHL	57	10	26	36	103	....	....	....	....	....	....	....	....	....	....	....	....	....	....	....	....	....	....
	Providence Bruins	AHL	13	2	4	6	13	....	....	....	....	....	....	....	....	....	3	0	0	0	6	....	....	....	....
2006-07	Providence Bruins	AHL	43	22	27	49	19	....	....	....	....	....	....	....	....	....	....	....	....	....	....	....	....	....	....
	Norfolk Admirals	AHL	27	4	19	23	20	....	....	....	....	....	....	....	....	....	2	0	0	0	2	....	....	....	....
2007-08	**Chicago**	**NHL**	**13**	**2**	**2**	**4**	**6**	**0**	**0**	**0**	**21**	**9.5**	**-1**	**3**	**66.7**	**15:52**	....	....	....	....	....	....	....	....	....
	Rockford IceHogs	AHL	56	18	31	49	174	....	....	....	....	....	....	....	....	....	12	6	5	11	6	....	....	....	....
2008-09	**Chicago**	**NHL**	**78**	**22**	**31**	**53**	**55**	**6**	**4**	**3**	**139**	**15.8**	**15**	**266**	**46.6**	**17:02**	**17**	**4**	**8**	**12**	**22**	**3**	**0**	**0**	**16:14**
2009-10♦	**Chicago**	**NHL**	**79**	**20**	**24**	**44**	**35**	**4**	**3**	**4**	**184**	**10.9**	**8**	**183**	**42.1**	**15:44**	**22**	**6**	**8**	**14**	**14**	**0**	**0**	**2**	**17:13**
2010-11	**Toronto**	**NHL**	**53**	**14**	**21**	**35**	**29**	**5**	**0**	**0**	**128**	**10.9**	**-13**	**77**	**52.0**	**18:56**	....	....	....	....	....	....	....	....	....
	Philadelphia	**NHL**	**27**	**7**	**4**	**11**	**24**	**1**	**1**	**0**	**52**	**13.5**	**4**	**53**	**43.4**	**15:22**	**11**	**1**	**5**	**6**	**12**	**0**	**0**	**0**	**15:00**
	NHL Totals		**250**	**65**	**82**	**147**	**149**	**16**	**8**	**7**	**524**	**12.4**		**582**	**45.7**	**16:47**	**50**	**11**	**21**	**32**	**48**	**3**	**0**	**2**	**16:24**

NHL All-Rookie Team (2009)

Traded to **Chicago** by **Boston** with future considerations for Brandon Bochenski, February 3, 2007. Traded to **Toronto** by **Chicago** with Bill Sweatt for Viktor Stalberg, Chris Didomenico and Phillipe Paradis, June 30, 2010. Traded to **Philadelphia** by **Toronto** for Philadelphia's 1st (Stuart Percy) and 3rd (Josh Leivo) round choices in 2011 Entry Draft, February 14, 2011. Traded to **Florida** by **Philadelphia** for a 2nd round choice in 2012 or 2013 Entry Draft and a 3rd round choice in 2012 Entry Draft, July 1, 2011.

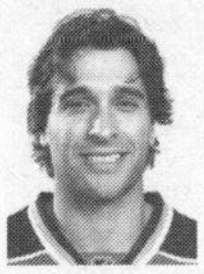

VESCE, Ryan (veks-KEE, RIGH-uhn)

Center. Shoots right. 5'8", 175 lbs. Born, Lloyd Harbor, NY, April 7, 1982.

			Regular Season														Playoffs								
Season	Club	League	GP	G	A	Pts	PIM	PP	SH	GW	S	%	+/-	TF	F%	Min	GP	G	A	Pts	PIM	PP	SH	GW	Min
2000-01	Cornell Big Red	ECAC	33	7	20	27	10	....	....	....	....	....	....	....	....	....	....	....	....	....	....	....	....	....	....
2001-02	Cornell Big Red	ECAC	35	10	20	30	10	....	....	....	....	....	....	....	....	....	....	....	....	....	....	....	....	....	....
2002-03	Cornell Big Red	ECAC	36	19	26	45	16	....	....	....	....	....	....	....	....	....	....	....	....	....	....	....	....	....	....
2003-04	Cornell Big Red	ECAC	27	10	16	26	14	....	....	....	....	....	....	....	....	....	....	....	....	....	....	....	....	....	....
2004-05	Rogle	Sweden-2	43	20	25	45	51	....	....	....	....	....	....	....	....	....	....	....	....	....	....	....	....	....	....
2005-06	Springfield	AHL	80	18	49	67	50	....	....	....	....	....	....	....	....	....	....	....	....	....	....	....	....	....	....
2006-07	Binghamton	AHL	80	16	35	51	51	....	....	....	....	....	....	....	....	....	....	....	....	....	....	....	....	....	....
2007-08	HIFK Helsinki	Finland	56	26	18	44	42	....	....	....	....	....	....	....	....	....	7	1	2	3	2	....	....	....	....
2008-09	**San Jose**	**NHL**	**10**	**0**	**0**	**0**	**4**	**0**	**0**	**0**	**11**	**0.0**	**-2**	**64**	**46.9**	**9:45**	....	....	....	....	....	....	....	....	....
	Worcester Sharks	AHL	67	24	47	71	28	....	....	....	....	....	....	....	....	....	12	3	7	10	22	....	....	....	....
2009-10	**San Jose**	**NHL**	**9**	**3**	**2**	**5**	**0**	**0**	**0**	**1**	**20**	**15.0**	**-1**	**50**	**50.0**	**10:57**	....	....	....	....	....	....	....	....	....
	Worcester Sharks	AHL	35	14	16	30	20	....	....	....	....	....	....	....	....	....	6	3	1	4	0	....	....	....	....
2010-11	Nizhny Novgorod	Rus-KHL	51	25	23	48	18	....	....	....	....	....	....	....	....	....	....	....	....	....	....	....	....	....	....
	NHL Totals		**19**	**3**	**2**	**5**	**4**	**0**	**0**	**1**	**31**	**9.7**		**114**	**48.2**	**10:19**	....	....	....	....	....	....	....	....	....

Signed as a free agent by **Rogle** (Sweden), August, 2004. Signed as a free agent by **Ottawa**, July 17, 2006. Signed as a free agent by **HIFK Helsinki** (Finland), July 17, 2007. Signed as a free agent by **San Jose**, August 13, 2008. Signed as a free agent by **Nizhny Novgorod** (Russia-KHL), June 28, 2010.

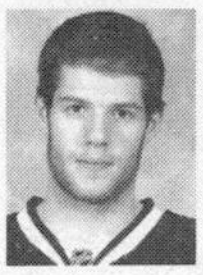

VINCOUR, Tomas (VIHN-tsoh-oor, TAW-mahsh) DAL

Center. Shoots right. 6'2", 199 lbs. Born, Brno, Czechoslovakia, November 19, 1990. Dallas' 4th choice, 129th overall, in 2009 Entry Draft.

			Regular Season														Playoffs								
Season	Club	League	GP	G	A	Pts	PIM	PP	SH	GW	S	%	+/-	TF	F%	Min	GP	G	A	Pts	PIM	PP	SH	GW	Min
2004-05	Brno U17	CzR-U17	42	23	13	36	36	....	....	....	....	....	....	....	....	....	....	....	....	....	....	....	....	....	....
2005-06	Brno U17	CzR-U17	21	13	14	27	77	....	....	....	....	....	....	....	....	....	....	....	....	....	....	....	....	....	....
	Brno Jr.	CzRep-Jr.	28	8	10	18	61	....	....	....	....	....	....	....	....	....	....	....	....	....	....	....	....	....	....
	Brno	CzRep-2	1	0	0	0	0	....	....	....	....	....	....	....	....	....	....	....	....	....	....	....	....	....	....
2006-07	Brno U17	CzR-U17	1	0	0	0	0	....	....	....	....	....	....	....	....	....	2	0	2	2	0	....	....	....	....
	Brno Jr.	CzRep-Jr.	41	15	24	39	58	....	....	....	....	....	....	....	....	....	....	....	....	....	....	....	....	....	....
	Brno	CzRep-2	4	0	1	1	0	....	....	....	....	....	....	....	....	....	....	....	....	....	....	....	....	....	....
2007-08	Edmonton	WHL	65	16	23	39	36	....	....	....	....	....	....	....	....	....	....	....	....	....	....	....	....	....	....
2008-09	Edmonton	WHL	49	17	19	36	23	....	....	....	....	....	....	....	....	....	....	....	....	....	....	....	....	....	....
2009-10	Edmonton	WHL	33	17	9	26	31	....	....	....	....	....	....	....	....	....	....	....	....	....	....	....	....	....	....
	Vancouver Giants	WHL	24	12	10	22	17	....	....	....	....	....	....	....	....	....	15	7	6	13	8	....	....	....	....
2010-11	**Dallas**	**NHL**	**24**	**1**	**1**	**2**	**4**	**0**	**0**	**0**	**26**	**3.8**	**-5**	**4**	**75.0**	**9:26**	....	....	....	....	....	....	....	....	....
	Texas Stars	AHL	44	5	7	12	10	....	....	....	....	....	....	....	....	....	6	0	1	1	4	....	....	....	....
	NHL Totals		**24**	**1**	**1**	**2**	**4**	**0**	**0**	**0**	**26**	**3.8**		**4**	**75.0**	**9:26**	....	....	....	....	....	....	....	....	....

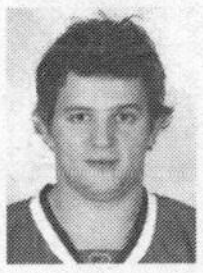

VISHNEVSKIY, Ivan (vihsh-NEHV-skee, ee-VAHN)

Defense. Shoots left. 6', 193 lbs. Born, Barnaul, USSR, February 18, 1988. Dallas' 1st choice, 27th overall, in 2006 Entry Draft.

			Regular Season														Playoffs								
Season	Club	League	GP	G	A	Pts	PIM	PP	SH	GW	S	%	+/-	TF	F%	Min	GP	G	A	Pts	PIM	PP	SH	GW	Min
2003-04	Lada Togliatti 2	Russia-3	16	0	0	0	10	....	....	....	....	....	....	....	....	....	....	....	....	....	....	....	....	....	....
2004-05	Lada Togliatti 2	Russia-3	STATISTICS NOT AVAILABLE																						
2005-06	Rouyn-Noranda	QMJHL	54	13	35	48	57	....	....	....	....	....	....	....	....	....	5	2	1	3	2	....	....	....	....
2006-07	Rouyn-Noranda	QMJHL	60	14	37	51	90	....	....	....	....	....	....	....	....	....	16	5	8	13	8	....	....	....	....
2007-08	Rouyn-Noranda	QMJHL	45	17	28	45	50	....	....	....	....	....	....	....	....	....	17	0	6	6	16	....	....	....	....
2008-09	**Dallas**	**NHL**	**3**	**0**	**2**	**2**	**2**	**0**	**0**	**0**	**9**	**0.0**	**1**	**0**	**0.0**	**19:33**	....	....	....	....	....	....	....	....	....
	Peoria Rivermen	AHL	67	6	13	19	28	....	....	....	....	....	....	....	....	....	5	0	2	2	2	....	....	....	....
2009-10	**Dallas**	**NHL**	**2**	**0**	**0**	**0**	**0**	**0**	**0**	**0**	**4**	**0.0**	**-2**	**0**	**0.0**	**16:39**	....	....	....	....	....	....	....	....	....
	Texas Stars	AHL	51	8	16	24	18	....	....	....	....	....	....	....	....	....	....	....	....	....	....	....	....	....	....
	Chicago Wolves	AHL	28	2	10	12	10	....	....	....	....	....	....	....	....	....	14	0	6	6	4	....	....	....	....
2010-11	Rockford IceHogs	AHL	46	5	10	15	26	....	....	....	....	....	....	....	....	....	....	....	....	....	....	....	....	....	....
	NHL Totals		**5**	**0**	**2**	**2**	**2**	**0**	**0**	**0**	**13**	**0.0**		**0**	**0.0**	**18:23**	....	....	....	....	....	....	....	....	....

QMJHL All-Rookie Team (2006) • QMJHL Second All-Star Team (2008)

Traded to **Atlanta** by **Dallas** with Dallas' 4th round choice (Ivan Telegin) in 2010 Entry Draft for Kari Lehtonen, February 9, 2010. Traded to **Chicago** by **Atlanta** with Winnipeg/Atlanta's 2nd round choice (Adam Clendening) in the 2011 Entry Draft for Andrew Ladd, July 1, 2010.

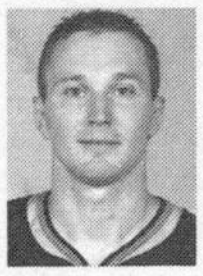

VISNOVSKY, Lubomir (vihsh-NAWV-skee, LOO-boh-mihr) ANA

Defense. Shoots left. 5'10", 197 lbs. Born, Topolcany, Czech., August 11, 1976. Los Angeles' 4th choice, 118th overall, in 2000 Entry Draft.

			Regular Season														Playoffs								
Season	Club	League	GP	G	A	Pts	PIM	PP	SH	GW	S	%	+/-	TF	F%	Min	GP	G	A	Pts	PIM	PP	SH	GW	Min
1994-95	Bratislava	Slovakia	36	11	12	23	10	....	....	....	....	....	....	....	....	....	9	1	3	4	2	....	....	....	....
1995-96	Bratislava	Slovakia	35	8	6	14	22	....	....	....	....	....	....	....	....	....	13	1	5	6	2	....	....	....	....
1996-97	Bratislava	Slovakia	44	11	12	23	....	....	....	....	....	....	....	....	....	....	2	0	1	1	....	....	....	....	....
	Bratislava	EuroHL	6	3	1	4	2	....	....	....	....	....	....	....	....	....	2	0	0	0	6	....	....	....	....
1997-98	Bratislava	Slovakia	36	7	9	16	16	....	....	....	....	....	....	....	....	....	11	2	4	6	8	....	....	....	....
	Bratislava	EuroHL	6	1	0	1	4	....	....	....	....	....	....	....	....	....	....	....	....	....	....	....	....	....	....
	Slovakia	Olympics	3	0	0	0	2	....	....	....	....	....	....	....	....	....	....	....	....	....	....	....	....	....	....
1998-99	Bratislava	Slovakia	40	9	10	19	31	....	....	....	....	....	....	....	....	....	10	5	5	10	0	....	....	....	....
	Bratislava	EuroHL	6	0	3	3	4	....	....	....	....	....	....	....	....	....	....	....	....	....	....	....	....	....	....
99-2000	Bratislava	Slovakia	52	21	24	45	38	....	....	....	....	....	....	....	....	....	8	5	3	8	16	....	....	....	....
2000-01	**Los Angeles**	**NHL**	**81**	**7**	**32**	**39**	**36**	**3**	**0**	**3**	**105**	**6.7**	**16**	**0**	**0.0**	**16:58**	**8**	**0**	**0**	**0**	**0**	**0**	**0**	**0**	**13:57**
2001-02	**Los Angeles**	**NHL**	**72**	**4**	**17**	**21**	**14**	**1**	**0**	**2**	**95**	**4.2**	**-5**	**0**	**0.0**	**16:15**	**4**	**0**	**1**	**1**	**0**	**0**	**0**	**0**	**8:22**
	Slovakia	Olympics	3	1	2	3	0	....	....	....	....	....	....	....	....	....	....	....	....	....	....	....	....	....	....
2002-03	**Los Angeles**	**NHL**	**57**	**8**	**16**	**24**	**28**	**1**	**0**	**1**	**85**	**9.4**	**2**	**0**	**0.0**	**19:20**	....	....	....	....	....	....	....	....	....
2003-04	**Los Angeles**	**NHL**	**58**	**8**	**21**	**29**	**26**	**5**	**0**	**0**	**114**	**7.0**	**8**	**0**	**0.0**	**24:02**	....	....	....	....	....	....	....	....	....
2004-05	Bratislava	Slovakia	43	13	25	38	40	....	....	....	....	....	....	....	....	....	14	2	10	12	10	....	....	....	....
2005-06	**Los Angeles**	**NHL**	**80**	**17**	**50**	**67**	**50**	**10**	**0**	**3**	**152**	**11.2**	**7**	**1**	**100.0**	**23:16**	....	....	....	....	....	....	....	....	....
	Slovakia	Olympics	6	1	1	2	2	....	....	....	....	....	....	....	....	....	....	....	....	....	....	....	....	....	....
2006-07	**Los Angeles**	**NHL**	**69**	**18**	**40**	**58**	**26**	**8**	**0**	**0**	**159**	**11.3**	**1**	**6**	**33.3**	**24:27**	....	....	....	....	....	....	....	....	....
2007-08	**Los Angeles**	**NHL**	**82**	**8**	**33**	**41**	**34**	**3**	**0**	**1**	**153**	**5.2**	**-18**	**8**	**12.5**	**23:00**	....	....	....	....	....	....	....	....	....
2008-09	**Edmonton**	**NHL**	**50**	**8**	**23**	**31**	**30**	**5**	**0**	**1**	**86**	**9.3**	**6**	**0**	**0.0**	**23:01**	....	....	....	....	....	....	....	....	....

			Regular Season														Playoffs								
Season	Club	League	GP	G	A	Pts	PIM	PP	SH	GW	S	%	+/-	TF	F%	Min	GP	G	A	Pts	PIM	PP	SH	GW	Min
2009-10	**Edmonton**	**NHL**	**57**	**10**	**22**	**32**	**16**	**4**	**0**	**1**	**78**	**12.8**	**–4**	**0**	**0.0**	**20:45**	....	....	....	....	....	....	....	....	....
	Slovakia	Olympics	7	2	1	3	0	....	....	....	....	....	....	....	....	....	....	....	....	....	....	....	....	....	....
	Anaheim	**NHL**	**16**	**5**	**8**	**13**	**4**	**1**	**0**	**1**	**53**	**9.4**	**–6**	**0**	**0.0**	**26:00**	....	....	....	....	....	....	....	....	....
2010-11	**Anaheim**	**NHL**	**81**	**18**	**50**	**68**	**24**	**5**	**0**	**4**	**152**	**11.8**	**18**	**0**	**0.0**	**24:18**	**6**	**0**	**3**	**3**	**2**	**0**	**0**	**0**	**21:21**
	NHL Totals		**703**	**111**	**312**	**423**	**288**	**46**	**0**	**17**	**1232**	**9.0**		**15**	**26.7**	**21:37**	**18**	**0**	**4**	**4**	**2**	**0**	**0**	**0**	**15:11**

NHL All-Rookie Team (2001) • NHL Second All-Star Team (2011)

Played in NHL All-Star Game (2007)

Signed as a free agent by **Bratislava** (Slovakia), September 27, 2004. Traded to **Edmonton** by **Los Angeles** for Jarret Stoll and Matt Greene, June 29, 2008. Traded to **Anaheim** by **Edmonton** for Ryan Whitney and Anaheim's 6th round choice (Brandon Davidson) in 2010 Entry Draft, March 3, 2010.

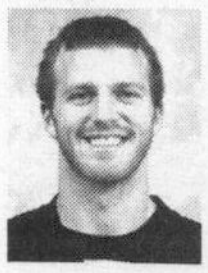

VITALE, Joe

(vih-TA-lee, JOH) **PIT**

Center. Shoots right. 5'11", 205 lbs. Born, St. Louis, MO, August 20, 1985. Pittsburgh's 7th choice, 195th overall, in 2005 Entry Draft.

Season	Club	League	GP	G	A	Pts	PIM	PP	SH	GW	S	%	+/-	TF	F%	Min	GP	G	A	Pts	PIM	PP	SH	GW	Min
2003-04	St. Louis Jr. Blues	CSJHL	43	21	29	50	42	....	....	....	....	....	....	....	....	....	....	....	....	....	....	....	....	....	....
2004-05	Sioux Falls	USHL	53	11	20	31	62	....	....	....	....	....	....	....	....	....	....	....	....	....	....	....	....	....	....
2005-06	Northeastern	H-East	31	8	8	16	71	....	....	....	....	....	....	....	....	....	....	....	....	....	....	....	....	....	....
2006-07	Northeastern	H-East	35	7	9	16	54	....	....	....	....	....	....	....	....	....	....	....	....	....	....	....	....	....	....
2007-08	Northeastern	H-East	37	12	23	35	75	....	....	....	....	....	....	....	....	....	....	....	....	....	....	....	....	....	....
2008-09	Northeastern	H-East	40	7	20	27	68	....	....	....	....	....	....	....	....	....	....	....	....	....	....	....	....	....	....
	Wilkes-Barre	AHL	5	2	2	4	2	....	....	....	....	....	....	....	....	....	12	0	0	0	12	....	....	....	....
2009-10	Wilkes-Barre	AHL	74	6	26	32	70	....	....	....	....	....	....	....	....	....	4	0	2	2	0	....	....	....	....
2010-11	**Pittsburgh**	**NHL**	**9**	**1**	**1**	**2**	**13**	**0**	**0**	**0**	**13**	**7.7**	**–1**	**64**	**56.3**	**10:34**	....	....	....	....	....	....	....	....	....
	Wilkes-Barre	AHL	60	9	21	30	64	....	....	....	....	....	....	....	....	....	11	3	3	6	18	....	....	....	....
	NHL Totals		**9**	**1**	**1**	**2**	**13**	**0**	**0**	**0**	**13**	**7.7**		**64**	**56.3**	**10:34**	....	....	....	....	....	....	....	....	....

Hockey East Second All-Star Team (2008)

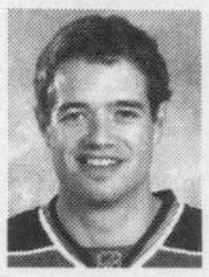

VLASIC, Marc-Edouard

(vih-LASH-ihc, MAHRK-EHD-wahrd) **S.J.**

Defense. Shoots left. 6'1", 200 lbs. Born, Montreal, Que., March 30, 1987. San Jose's 2nd choice, 35th overall, in 2005 Entry Draft.

Season	Club	League	GP	G	A	Pts	PIM	PP	SH	GW	S	%	+/-	TF	F%	Min	GP	G	A	Pts	PIM	PP	SH	GW	Min
2003-04	Quebec Remparts	QMJHL	41	1	9	10	4	....	....	....	....	....	....	....	....	....	5	0	1	1	0	....	....	....	....
2004-05	Quebec Remparts	QMJHL	70	5	25	30	33	....	....	....	....	....	....	....	....	....	13	2	7	9	2	....	....	....	....
2005-06	Quebec Remparts	QMJHL	66	16	57	73	57	....	....	....	....	....	....	....	....	....	23	5	24	29	10	....	....	....	....
2006-07	**San Jose**	**NHL**	**81**	**3**	**23**	**26**	**18**	**2**	**0**	**0**	**66**	**4.5**	**13**	**0**	**0.0**	**22:12**	**11**	**0**	**1**	**1**	**2**	**0**	**0**	**0**	**22:52**
2007-08	**San Jose**	**NHL**	**82**	**2**	**12**	**14**	**24**	**1**	**0**	**0**	**72**	**2.8**	**–12**	**0**	**0.0**	**21:37**	**13**	**0**	**1**	**1**	**0**	**0**	**0**	**0**	**24:39**
	Worcester Sharks	AHL	1	0	2	2	0	....	....	....	....	....	....	....	....	....	....	....	....	....	....	....	....	....	....
2008-09	**San Jose**	**NHL**	**82**	**6**	**30**	**36**	**42**	**3**	**0**	**1**	**104**	**5.8**	**15**	**0**	**0.0**	**23:54**	**6**	**0**	**1**	**1**	**0**	**0**	**0**	**0**	**20:39**
2009-10	**San Jose**	**NHL**	**64**	**3**	**13**	**16**	**33**	**1**	**0**	**0**	**74**	**4.1**	**21**	**0**	**0.0**	**22:05**	**15**	**0**	**3**	**3**	**4**	**0**	**0**	**0**	**21:53**
2010-11	**San Jose**	**NHL**	**80**	**4**	**14**	**18**	**18**	**0**	**0**	**2**	**116**	**3.4**	**14**	**0**	**0.0**	**20:52**	**18**	**0**	**3**	**3**	**4**	**0**	**0**	**0**	**21:45**
	NHL Totals		**389**	**18**	**92**	**110**	**135**	**7**	**0**	**3**	**432**	**4.2**		**0**	**0.0**	**22:08**	**63**	**0**	**9**	**9**	**10**	**0**	**0**	**0**	**22:29**

NHL All-Rookie Team (2007)

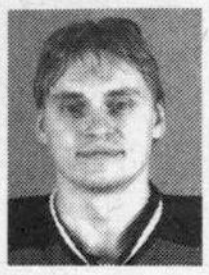

VOLCHENKOV, Anton

(vohl-chen-KAHF, AN-tawn) **N.J.**

Defense. Shoots left. 6'1", 225 lbs. Born, Moscow, USSR, February 25, 1982. Ottawa's 1st choice, 21st overall, in 2000 Entry Draft.

Season	Club	League	GP	G	A	Pts	PIM	PP	SH	GW	S	%	+/-	TF	F%	Min	GP	G	A	Pts	PIM	PP	SH	GW	Min
99-2000	HK Moscow 2	Russia-3	6	0	1	1	10	....	....	....	....	....	....	....	....	....	....	....	....	....	....	....	....	....	....
	HK Moscow	Russia-2	30	2	9	11	36	....	....	....	....	....	....	....	....	....	....	....	....	....	....	....	....	....	....
2000-01	Krylja Sovetov	Russia-2	34	3	4	7	56	....	....	....	....	....	....	....	....	....	....	....	....	....	....	....	....	....	....
2001-02	Krylja Sovetov 2	Russia-3	1	0	0	0	0	....	....	....	....	....	....	....	....	....	....	....	....	....	....	....	....	....	....
	Krylja Sovetov	Russia	47	4	16	20	50	....	....	....	....	....	....	....	....	....	3	0	0	0	29	....	....	....	....
2002-03	**Ottawa**	**NHL**	**57**	**3**	**13**	**16**	**40**	**0**	**0**	**0**	**75**	**4.0**	**–4**	**0**	**0.0**	**15:30**	**17**	**1**	**1**	**2**	**4**	**0**	**0**	**1**	**13:31**
2003-04	**Ottawa**	**NHL**	**19**	**1**	**2**	**3**	**8**	**0**	**0**	**0**	**15**	**6.7**	**1**	**0**	**0.0**	**13:04**	**5**	**0**	**0**	**0**	**6**	**0**	**0**	**0**	**11:52**
2004-05	Binghamton	AHL	69	10	35	45	62	....	....	....	....	....	....	....	....	....	6	0	3	3	0	....	....	....	....
2005-06	**Ottawa**	**NHL**	**75**	**4**	**13**	**17**	**53**	**0**	**0**	**0**	**82**	**4.9**	**21**	**0**	**0.0**	**18:03**	**9**	**0**	**4**	**4**	**8**	**0**	**0**	**0**	**13:53**
	Russia	Olympics	8	0	0	0	2	....	....	....	....	....	....	....	....	....	....	....	....	....	....	....	....	....	....
2006-07	**Ottawa**	**NHL**	**78**	**1**	**18**	**19**	**67**	**0**	**0**	**0**	**85**	**1.2**	**37**	**0**	**0.0**	**21:17**	**20**	**2**	**4**	**6**	**24**	**0**	**0**	**1**	**23:19**
2007-08	**Ottawa**	**NHL**	**67**	**1**	**14**	**15**	**55**	**0**	**0**	**1**	**71**	**1.4**	**14**	**0**	**0.0**	**20:31**	**4**	**0**	**1**	**1**	**2**	**0**	**0**	**0**	**17:11**
2008-09	**Ottawa**	**NHL**	**68**	**2**	**8**	**10**	**36**	**0**	**0**	**1**	**79**	**2.5**	**–10**	**0**	**0.0**	**20:08**	....	....	....	....	....	....	....	....	....
2009-10	**Ottawa**	**NHL**	**64**	**4**	**10**	**14**	**38**	**0**	**0**	**0**	**69**	**5.8**	**2**	**0**	**0.0**	**20:41**	**6**	**0**	**2**	**2**	**4**	**0**	**0**	**0**	**22:30**
	Russia	Olympics	4	0	1	1	2	....	....	....	....	....	....	....	....	....	....	....	....	....	....	....	....	....	....
2010-11	**New Jersey**	**NHL**	**57**	**0**	**8**	**8**	**36**	**0**	**0**	**0**	**65**	**0.0**	**3**	**0**	**0.0**	**18:06**	....	....	....	....	....	....	....	....	....
	NHL Totals		**485**	**16**	**86**	**102**	**333**	**0**	**0**	**2**	**541**	**3.0**		**0**	**0.0**	**19:04**	**61**	**3**	**12**	**15**	**48**	**0**	**0**	**2**	**17:47**

• Missed majority of 2003-04 due to shoulder injury vs. Boston, December 8, 2003. Signed as a free agent by **New Jersey**, July 1, 2010.

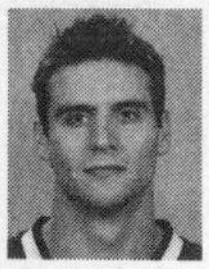

VOLPATTI, Aaron

(vohl-PA-tee, AIR-uhn) **VAN**

Left wing. Shoots left. 6', 215 lbs. Born, Revelstoke, B.C., May 30, 1985.

Season	Club	League	GP	G	A	Pts	PIM	PP	SH	GW	S	%	+/-	TF	F%	Min	GP	G	A	Pts	PIM	PP	SH	GW	Min
2003-04	Vernon Vipers	BCHL	55	1	4	5	134	....	....	....	....	....	....	....	....	....	....	....	....	....	....	....	....	....	....
2004-05	Vernon Vipers	BCHL	57	6	12	18	106	....	....	....	....	....	....	....	....	....	....	....	....	....	....	....	....	....	....
2005-06	Vernon Vipers	BCHL	25	6	8	14	39	....	....	....	....	....	....	....	....	....	....	....	....	....	....	....	....	....	....
2006-07	Brown U.	ECAC	23	5	2	7	39	....	....	....	....	....	....	....	....	....	....	....	....	....	....	....	....	....	....
2007-08	Brown U.	ECAC	31	4	6	10	28	....	....	....	....	....	....	....	....	....	....	....	....	....	....	....	....	....	....
2008-09	Brown U.	ECAC	32	6	6	12	54	....	....	....	....	....	....	....	....	....	....	....	....	....	....	....	....	....	....
2009-10	Brown U.	ECAC	37	17	15	32	*115	....	....	....	....	....	....	....	....	....	....	....	....	....	....	....	....	....	....
	Manitoba Moose	AHL	8	1	1	2	17	....	....	....	....	....	....	....	....	....	5	1	0	1	21	....	....	....	....
2010-11	**Vancouver**	**NHL**	**15**	**1**	**1**	**2**	**16**	**0**	**0**	**0**	**6**	**16.7**	**–1**	**0**	**0.0**	**6:50**	....	....	....	....	....	....	....	....	....
	Manitoba Moose	AHL	53	2	9	11	74	....	....	....	....	....	....	....	....	....	12	1	2	3	36	....	....	....	....
	NHL Totals		**15**	**1**	**1**	**2**	**16**	**0**	**0**	**0**	**6**	**16.7**		**0**	**0.0**	**6:50**	....	....	....	....	....	....	....	....	....

Signed as a free agent by **Vancouver**, March 22, 2010.

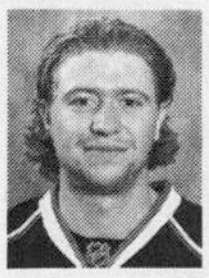

VORACEK, Jakub

(VOHR-rah-chehk, YA-kuhb) **PHI**

Right wing. Shoots left. 6'2", 214 lbs. Born, Kladno, Czech., August 15, 1989. Columbus' 1st choice, 7th overall, in 2007 Entry Draft.

Season	Club	League	GP	G	A	Pts	PIM	PP	SH	GW	S	%	+/-	TF	F%	Min	GP	G	A	Pts	PIM	PP	SH	GW	Min
2002-03	HC Kladno U17	CzR-U17	2	1	1	2	2	....	....	....	....	....	....	....	....	....	2	1	1	2	0	....	....	....	....
2003-04	HC Kladno U17	CzR-U17	52	30	24	54	26	....	....	....	....	....	....	....	....	....	2	0	0	0	2	....	....	....	....
2004-05	HC Kladno U17	CzR-U17	30	23	39	62	44	....	....	....	....	....	....	....	....	....	7	5	4	9	14	....	....	....	....
	HC Kladno Jr.	CzRep-Jr.	16	5	7	12	6	....	....	....	....	....	....	....	....	....	1	1	0	1	2	....	....	....	....
2005-06	HC Kladno U17	CzR-U17	....	....	....	....	....	....	....	....	....	....	....	....	....	....	2	1	3	4	31	....	....	....	....
	HC Kladno Jr.	CzRep-Jr.	46	21	38	59	54	....	....	....	....	....	....	....	....	....	6	7	4	11	2	....	....	....	....
	HC Rabat Kladno	CzRep	1	0	0	0	0	....	....	....	....	....	....	....	....	....	....	....	....	....	....	....	....	....	....
2006-07	Halifax	QMJHL	59	23	63	86	26	....	....	....	....	....	....	....	....	....	12	7	17	24	6	....	....	....	....
2007-08	Halifax	QMJHL	53	33	68	101	42	....	....	....	....	....	....	....	....	....	15	5	13	18	14	....	....	....	....
2008-09	**Columbus**	**NHL**	**80**	**9**	**29**	**38**	**44**	**0**	**0**	**1**	**101**	**8.9**	**11**	**3**	**0.0**	**12:40**	**4**	**0**	**1**	**1**	**8**	**0**	**0**	**0**	**12:06**
2009-10	**Columbus**	**NHL**	**81**	**16**	**34**	**50**	**26**	**4**	**0**	**1**	**154**	**10.4**	**–7**	**6**	**33.3**	**15:37**	....	....	....	....	....	....	....	....	....
2010-11	**Columbus**	**NHL**	**80**	**14**	**32**	**46**	**26**	**2**	**0**	**2**	**183**	**7.7**	**–3**	**65**	**36.9**	**16:58**	....	....	....	....	....	....	....	....	....
	NHL Totals		**241**	**39**	**95**	**134**	**96**	**6**	**0**	**4**	**438**	**8.9**		**74**	**35.1**	**15:05**	**4**	**0**	**1**	**1**	**8**	**0**	**0**	**0**	**12:06**

QMJHL All-Rookie Team (2007) • QMJHL Rookie of the Year (2007) • QMJHL Second All-Star Team (2008)

Traded to **Philadelphia** by **Columbus** with Columbus's 1st (Sean Couturier) and 3rd (Nick Cousins) round choices in 2011 Entry Draft for Jeff Carter, June 23, 2011.

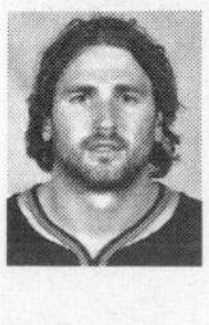

VOROS, Aaron

(VOH-ruhs, AIR-ruhn)

Center. Shoots left. 6'4", 215 lbs. Born, Vancouver, B.C., July 2, 1981. New Jersey's 10th choice, 229th overall, in 2001 Entry Draft.

Season	Club	League	GP	G	A	Pts	PIM	PP	SH	GW	S	%	+/-	TF	F%	Min	GP	G	A	Pts	PIM	PP	SH	GW	Min
99-2000	Victoria Salsa	BCHL	58	14	21	35	285	....	....	....	....	....	....	....	....	....	....	....	....	....	....	....	....	....	....
2000-01	Victoria Salsa	BCHL	57	34	34	68	196	....	....	....	....	....	....	....	....	....	30	16	15	31	....	....	....	....	....
2001-02	Alaska	CCHA	37	18	12	30	*101	....	....	....	....	....	....	....	....	....	....	....	....	....	....	....	....	....	....
2002-03	Alaska	CCHA	16	2	5	7	42	....	....	....	....	....	....	....	....	....	....	....	....	....	....	....	....	....	....
2003-04	Alaska	CCHA	36	16	8	24	*132	....	....	....	....	....	....	....	....	....	....	....	....	....	....	....	....	....	....
	Albany River Rats	AHL	9	2	1	3	14	....	....	....	....	....	....	....	....	....	....	....	....	....	....	....	....	....	....
2004-05	Albany River Rats	AHL	71	11	17	28	220	....	....	....	....	....	....	....	....	....	....	....	....	....	....	....	....	....	....

			Regular Season														Playoffs								
Season	Club	League	GP	G	A	Pts	PIM	PP	SH	GW	S	%	+/-	TF	F%	Min	GP	G	A	Pts	PIM	PP	SH	GW	Min
2005-06	Albany River Rats	AHL	73	16	14	30	180	....	....	....	....	....	....	....	....	....	....	....	....	....	....	....	....	....	....
2006-07	Lowell Devils	AHL	39	9	8	17	111	....	....	....	....	....	....	....	....	....	....	....	....	....	....	....	....	....	....
	Houston Aeros	AHL	19	2	3	5	58	....	....	....	....	....	....	....	....	....	....	....	....	....	....	....	....	....	....
2007-08	**Minnesota**	**NHL**	**55**	**7**	**7**	**14**	**141**	**0**	**0**	**1**	**52**	**13.5**	**–7**	**15**	**20.0**	**9:11**	**5**	**1**	**0**	**1**	**16**	**0**	**0**	**0**	**10:39**
	Houston Aeros	AHL	12	4	4	8	46	....	....	....	....	....	....	....	....	....	....	....	....	....	....	....	....	....	....
2008-09	**NY Rangers**	**NHL**	**54**	**8**	**8**	**16**	**122**	**3**	**0**	**1**	**66**	**12.1**	**–9**	**10**	**40.0**	**11:11**	**4**	**0**	**0**	**0**	**14**	**0**	**0**	**0**	**6:51**
2009-10	**NY Rangers**	**NHL**	**41**	**3**	**4**	**7**	**89**	**1**	**0**	**0**	**22**	**13.6**	**–2**	**6**	**50.0**	**6:09**	....	....	....	....	....	....	....	....	....
2010-11	**Anaheim**	**NHL**	**12**	**0**	**0**	**0**	**43**	**0**	**0**	**0**	**8**	**0.0**	**–4**	**3**	**66.7**	**5:33**	....	....	....	....	....	....	....	....	....
	Syracuse Crunch	AHL	2	0	0	0	5	....	....	....	....	....	....	....	....	....	....	....	....	....	....	....	....	....	....
	Toronto Marlies	AHL	26	3	4	7	61	....	....	....	....	....	....	....	....	....	....	....	....	....	....	....	....	....	....
	NHL Totals		**162**	**18**	**19**	**37**	**395**	**4**	**0**	**2**	**148**	**12.2**		**34**	**35.3**	**8:49**	**9**	**1**	**0**	**1**	**30**	**0**	**0**	**0**	**8:58**

CCHA All-Rookie Team (2002)

• Missed majority of 2002-03 due to leg surgery, January 30, 2003. Traded to **Minnesota** by **New Jersey** for Minnesota's 7th round choice (Jean-Sebastien Berube) in 2008 Entry Draft, February 28, 2007. Signed as a free agent by **NY Rangers**, July 1, 2008. Traded to **Anaheim** by **NY Rangers** with Ryan Hillier for Steve Eminger, July 9, 2010. Traded to **Toronto** by **Anaheim** for future considerations, February 15, 2011. • Missed majority of 2010-11 due to eye injury at Vancouver, December 8, 2010.

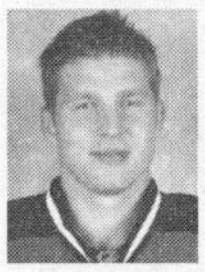

VRANA, Petr (vuh-RA-nuh, PEE-tuhr) N.J.

Center. Shoots left. 5'10", 190 lbs. Born, Sternberk, Czech., March 29, 1985. New Jersey's 2nd choice, 42nd overall, in 2003 Entry Draft.

Season	Club	League	GP	G	A	Pts	PIM	PP	SH	GW	S	%	+/-	TF	F%	Min	GP	G	A	Pts	PIM	PP	SH	GW	Min
2001-02	HC Havirov Jr.	CzRep-Jr.	38	11	12	23	....	....	....	....	....	....	....	....	....	....	....	....	....	....	....	....	....	....	....
	HC Femax Havirov	CzRep	6	0	0	0	4	....	....	....	....	....	....	....	....	....	....	....	....	....	....	....	....	....	....
2002-03	Halifax	QMJHL	72	37	46	83	32	....	....	....	....	....	....	....	....	....	24	5	15	20	12	....	....	....	....
2003-04	Halifax	QMJHL	48	13	25	38	56	....	....	....	....	....	....	....	....	....	....	....	....	....	....	....	....	....	....
2004-05	Halifax	QMJHL	60	16	35	51	77	....	....	....	....	....	....	....	....	....	12	10	4	14	12	....	....	....	....
2005-06	Albany River Rats	AHL	74	12	23	35	91	....	....	....	....	....	....	....	....	....	....	....	....	....	....	....	....	....	....
2006-07	Lowell Devils	AHL	61	13	19	32	44	....	....	....	....	....	....	....	....	....	....	....	....	....	....	....	....	....	....
2007-08	Lowell Devils	AHL	80	20	41	61	64	....	....	....	....	....	....	....	....	....	....	....	....	....	....	....	....	....	....
2008-09	**New Jersey**	**NHL**	**16**	**1**	**0**	**1**	**2**	**0**	**0**	**0**	**6**	**16.7**	**–4**	**36**	**41.7**	**6:54**	....	....	....	....	....	....	....	....	....
	Lowell Devils	AHL	14	5	4	9	6	....	....	....	....	....	....	....	....	....	....	....	....	....	....	....	....	....	....
2009-10	Vitkovice	CzRep	39	7	6	13	10	....	....	....	....	....	....	....	....	....	16	3	3	6	8	....	....	....	....
2010-11	Vitkovice	CzRep	42	15	14	29	24	....	....	....	....	....	....	....	....	....	16	9	2	11	20	....	....	....	....
	NHL Totals		**16**	**1**	**0**	**1**	**2**	**0**	**0**	**0**	**6**	**16.7**		**36**	**41.7**	**6:54**	....	....	....	....	....	....	....	....	....

QMJHL All-Rookie Team (2003) • QMJHL Rookie of the Year (2003)

Signed as a free agent by **Vitkovice** (CzRep), June 1, 2009.

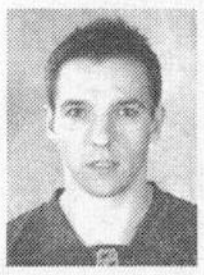

VRBATA, Radim (vuhr-BA-tuh, RA-dihm) PHX

Right wing. Shoots right. 6'1", 197 lbs. Born, Mlada Boleslav, Czech., June 13, 1981. Colorado's 10th choice, 212th overall, in 1999 Entry Draft.

Season	Club	League	GP	G	A	Pts	PIM	PP	SH	GW	S	%	+/-	TF	F%	Min	GP	G	A	Pts	PIM	PP	SH	GW	Min
1997-98	Ml. Boleslav Jr.	CzRep-Jr.	35	42	31	73	4	....	....	....	....	....	....	....	....	....	....	....	....	....	....	....	....	....	....
1998-99	Hull Olympiques	QMJHL	54	22	38	60	16	....	....	....	....	....	....	....	....	....	23	6	13	19	6	....	....	....	....
99-2000	Hull Olympiques	QMJHL	58	29	45	74	26	....	....	....	....	....	....	....	....	....	15	3	9	12	8	....	....	....	....
2000-01	Shawinigan	QMJHL	55	56	64	120	67	....	....	....	....	....	....	....	....	....	10	4	7	11	4	....	....	....	....
	Hershey Bears	AHL	....	....	....	....	....	....	....	....	....	....	....	....	....	....	1	0	1	1	2	....	....	....	....
2001-02	**Colorado**	**NHL**	**52**	**18**	**12**	**30**	**14**	**6**	**0**	**3**	**112**	**16.1**	**7**	**8**	**37.5**	**14:32**	**9**	**0**	**0**	**0**	**0**	**0**	**0**	**0**	**13:05**
	Hershey Bears	AHL	20	8	14	22	8	....	....	....	....	....	....	....	....	....	....	....	....	....	....	....	....	....	....
2002-03	**Colorado**	**NHL**	**66**	**11**	**19**	**30**	**16**	**3**	**0**	**4**	**171**	**6.4**	**0**	**14**	**50.0**	**13:55**	....	....	....	....	....	....	....	....	....
	Carolina	**NHL**	**10**	**5**	**0**	**5**	**2**	**3**	**0**	**0**	**44**	**11.4**	**–7**	**15**	**46.7**	**19:00**	....	....	....	....	....	....	....	....	....
2003-04	**Carolina**	**NHL**	**80**	**12**	**13**	**25**	**24**	**4**	**0**	**2**	**195**	**6.2**	**–10**	**21**	**38.1**	**13:42**	....	....	....	....	....	....	....	....	....
2004-05	Liberec	CzRep	45	18	21	39	91	....	....	....	....	....	....	....	....	....	12	3	2	5	0	....	....	....	....
2005-06	**Carolina**	**NHL**	**16**	**2**	**3**	**5**	**6**	**1**	**0**	**0**	**38**	**5.3**	**0**	**3**	**33.3**	**12:37**	....	....	....	....	....	....	....	....	....
	Chicago	**NHL**	**45**	**13**	**21**	**34**	**16**	**5**	**0**	**0**	**147**	**8.8**	**4**	**6**	**50.0**	**15:43**	....	....	....	....	....	....	....	....	....
2006-07	**Chicago**	**NHL**	**77**	**14**	**27**	**41**	**26**	**5**	**0**	**2**	**215**	**6.5**	**–4**	**12**	**33.3**	**16:53**	....	....	....	....	....	....	....	....	....
2007-08	**Phoenix**	**NHL**	**76**	**27**	**29**	**56**	**14**	**7**	**3**	**5**	**246**	**11.0**	**6**	**19**	**36.8**	**18:12**	....	....	....	....	....	....	....	....	....
2008-09	**Tampa Bay**	**NHL**	**18**	**3**	**3**	**6**	**8**	**1**	**0**	**0**	**41**	**7.3**	**–1**	**3**	**33.3**	**14:13**	....	....	....	....	....	....	....	....	....
	BK Mlada Boleslav	CzRep	11	5	3	8	18	....	....	....	....	....	....	....	....	....	....	....	....	....	....	....	....	....	....
	Liberec	CzRep	7	7	2	9	2	....	....	....	....	....	....	....	....	....	3	0	1	1	2	....	....	....	....
2009-10	**Phoenix**	**NHL**	**82**	**24**	**19**	**43**	**24**	**7**	**0**	**4**	**266**	**9.0**	**6**	**8**	**25.0**	**16:13**	**7**	**2**	**2**	**4**	**4**	**1**	**0**	**1**	**15:42**
2010-11	**Phoenix**	**NHL**	**79**	**19**	**29**	**48**	**20**	**10**	**0**	**2**	**240**	**7.9**	**5**	**7**	**28.6**	**16:22**	**4**	**2**	**3**	**5**	**0**	**1**	**0**	**0**	**19:55**
	NHL Totals		**601**	**148**	**175**	**323**	**170**	**52**	**3**	**22**	**1715**	**8.6**		**116**	**38.8**	**15:42**	**20**	**4**	**5**	**9**	**4**	**2**	**0**	**1**	**15:22**

QMJHL First All-Star Team (2001)

Traded to **Carolina** by **Colorado** for Bates Battaglia, March 11, 2003. Signed as a free agent by **Liberec** (CzRep), September 4, 2004. Traded to **Chicago** by **Carolina** for Chicago's 4th round choice (later traded to St. Louis - St. Louis selected Cade Fairchild) in 2007 Entry Draft, December 29, 2005. Traded to **Phoenix** by **Chicago** for Kevyn Adams, August 11, 2007. Signed as a free agent by **Tampa Bay**, July 1, 2008. • Assigned to **Mlada Boleslav** (CzRep) by **Tampa Bay**, December 9, 2008. • Loaned to **Liberec** (CzRep) by **Mlada Boleslav** (CzRep), January 29, 2009. Traded to **Phoenix** by **Tampa Bay** for Todd Fedoruk and David Hale, July 21, 2009.

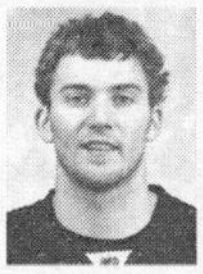

WAGNER, Steve (WAG-nuhr, STEEV)

Defense. Shoots left. 6'2", 200 lbs. Born, Grand Rapids, MN, March 6, 1984.

Season	Club	League	GP	G	A	Pts	PIM	PP	SH	GW	S	%	+/-	TF	F%	Min	GP	G	A	Pts	PIM	PP	SH	GW	Min
2002-03	Des Moines	USHL	14	0	1	1	17	....	....	....	....	....	....	....	....	....	....	....	....	....	....	....	....	....	....
	Tri-City Storm	USHL	27	0	5	5	52	....	....	....	....	....	....	....	....	....	3	1	0	1	0	....	....	....	....
2003-04	Tri-City Storm	USHL	43	3	19	22	52	....	....	....	....	....	....	....	....	....	9	0	4	4	13	....	....	....	....
2004-05	Minnesota State	WCHA	37	1	9	10	40	....	....	....	....	....	....	....	....	....	....	....	....	....	....	....	....	....	....
2005-06	Minnesota State	WCHA	38	5	11	16	53	....	....	....	....	....	....	....	....	....	....	....	....	....	....	....	....	....	....
2006-07	Minnesota State	WCHA	38	6	23	29	63	....	....	....	....	....	....	....	....	....	....	....	....	....	....	....	....	....	....
	Peoria Rivermen	AHL	14	1	2	3	8	....	....	....	....	....	....	....	....	....	....	....	....	....	....	....	....	....	....
2007-08	**St. Louis**	**NHL**	**24**	**2**	**6**	**8**	**8**	**1**	**0**	**0**	**25**	**8.0**	**–4**	**0**	**0.0**	**18:29**	....	....	....	....	....	....	....	....	....
	Peoria Rivermen	AHL	23	5	7	12	16	....	....	....	....	....	....	....	....	....	....	....	....	....	....	....	....	....	....
2008-09	**St. Louis**	**NHL**	**22**	**2**	**2**	**4**	**18**	**0**	**0**	**0**	**16**	**12.5**	**–5**	**0**	**0.0**	**15:38**	....	....	....	....	....	....	....	....	....
	Peoria Rivermen	AHL	47	6	16	22	38	....	....	....	....	....	....	....	....	....	7	1	3	4	4	....	....	....	....
2009-10	Peoria Rivermen	AHL	46	3	12	15	20	....	....	....	....	....	....	....	....	....	....	....	....	....	....	....	....	....	....
	Wilkes-Barre	AHL	20	1	6	7	10	....	....	....	....	....	....	....	....	....	4	0	1	1	2	....	....	....	....
2010-11	Wilkes-Barre	AHL	69	5	23	28	43	....	....	....	....	....	....	....	....	....	12	3	1	4	2	....	....	....	....
	NHL Totals		**46**	**4**	**8**	**12**	**26**	**1**	**0**	**0**	**41**	**9.8**		**0**	**0.0**	**17:07**	....	....	....	....	....	....	....	....	....

Signed as a free agent by **St. Louis**, March 20, 2007. Traded to **Pittsburgh** by **St. Louis** for Nathan Guenin, February 11, 2010.

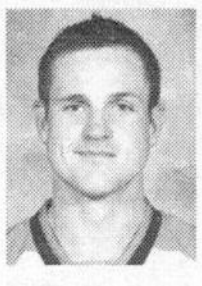

WALKER, Matt (WAH-kuhr, MAT) PHI

Defense. Shoots right. 6'4", 215 lbs. Born, Beaverlodge, Alta., April 7, 1980. St. Louis' 3rd choice, 83rd overall, in 1998 Entry Draft.

Season	Club	League	GP	G	A	Pts	PIM	PP	SH	GW	S	%	+/-	TF	F%	Min	GP	G	A	Pts	PIM	PP	SH	GW	Min
1996-97	Grand Prairie	AAHA	68	22	62	74	186	....	....	....	....	....	....	....	....	....	....	....	....	....	....	....	....	....	....
1997-98	Portland	WHL	64	2	13	15	124	....	....	....	....	....	....	....	....	....	16	0	0	0	21	....	....	....	....
1998-99	Portland	WHL	64	1	10	11	151	....	....	....	....	....	....	....	....	....	4	0	1	1	6	....	....	....	....
99-2000	Portland	WHL	38	2	7	9	97	....	....	....	....	....	....	....	....	....	....	....	....	....	....	....	....	....	....
	Kootenay Ice	WHL	31	4	19	23	53	....	....	....	....	....	....	....	....	....	21	5	13	18	24	....	....	....	....
2000-01	Worcester IceCats	AHL	61	4	8	12	131	....	....	....	....	....	....	....	....	....	11	0	0	0	6	....	....	....	....
	Peoria Rivermen	ECHL	8	1	0	1	70	....	....	....	....	....	....	....	....	....	....	....	....	....	....	....	....	....	....
2001-02	Worcester IceCats	AHL	49	2	11	13	164	....	....	....	....	....	....	....	....	....	3	0	0	0	8	....	....	....	....
2002-03	**St. Louis**	**NHL**	**16**	**0**	**1**	**1**	**38**	**0**	**0**	**0**	**13**	**0.0**	**0**	**1**	**100.0**	**11:09**	....	....	....	....	....	....	....	....	....
	Worcester IceCats	AHL	40	1	8	9	58	....	....	....	....	....	....	....	....	....	....	....	....	....	....	....	....	....	....
2003-04	**St. Louis**	**NHL**	**14**	**0**	**1**	**1**	**25**	**0**	**0**	**0**	**8**	**0.0**	**0**	**0**	**0.0**	**11:23**	**4**	**0**	**0**	**0**	**0**	**0**	**0**	**0**	**9:43**
	Worcester IceCats	AHL	4	0	1	1	7	....	....	....	....	....	....	....	....	....	....	....	....	....	....	....	....	....	....
2004-05	Worcester IceCats	AHL	20	2	4	6	44	....	....	....	....	....	....	....	....	....	....	....	....	....	....	....	....	....	....
2005-06	**St. Louis**	**NHL**	**54**	**0**	**2**	**2**	**79**	**0**	**0**	**0**	**59**	**0.0**	**–7**	**0**	**0.0**	**14:15**	....	....	....	....	....	....	....	....	....
2006-07	**St. Louis**	**NHL**	**48**	**0**	**5**	**5**	**72**	**0**	**0**	**0**	**34**	**0.0**	**7**	**0**	**0.0**	**15:15**	....	....	....	....	....	....	....	....	....
	Peoria Rivermen	AHL	2	0	1	1	0	....	....	....	....	....	....	....	....	....	....	....	....	....	....	....	....	....	....
2007-08	**St. Louis**	**NHL**	**43**	**1**	**1**	**2**	**61**	**0**	**0**	**0**	**47**	**2.1**	**–3**	**0**	**0.0**	**15:54**	....	....	....	....	....	....	....	....	....
2008-09	**Chicago**	**NHL**	**65**	**1**	**13**	**14**	**79**	**0**	**0**	**0**	**83**	**1.2**	**7**	**0**	**0.0**	**16:38**	**17**	**0**	**2**	**2**	**14**	**0**	**0**	**0**	**15:21**
2009-10	**Tampa Bay**	**NHL**	**66**	**2**	**3**	**5**	**90**	**0**	**0**	**0**	**54**	**3.7**	**–11**	**0**	**0.0**	**16:09**	....	....	....	....	....	....	....	....	....

Season	Club	League	Regular Season GP	G	A	Pts	PIM	PP	SH	GW	S	%	+/-	TF	F%	Min	Playoffs GP	G	A	Pts	PIM	PP	SH	GW	Min
2010-11	**Philadelphia**	**NHL**	**4**	**0**	**0**	**0**	**4**	**0**	**0**	**0**	**3**	**0.0**	**0**	**0**	**0.0**	**11:38**									
	Adirondack	AHL	11	0	2	2	8																		
	NHL Totals		**310**	**4**	**26**	**30**	**448**	**0**	**0**	**0**	**301**	**1.3**		**1**	**100.0**	**15:13**	**21**	**0**	**2**	**2**	**14**	**0**	**0**	**0**	**14:17**

• Missed majority of 2003-04 due to groin injury in training camp, September 23, 2003. Signed as a free agent by **Chicago**, July 7, 2008. Signed as a free agent by **Tampa Bay**, July 1, 2009. Traded to **Philadelphia** by **Tampa Bay** with Tampa Bay's 4th round choice (Marcel Noebels) in 2011 Entry Draft for Simon Gagne, July 19, 2010. • Missed majority of 2010-11 due to hip injury in pre-season.

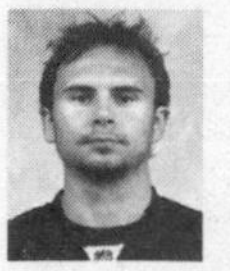

WALLACE, Tim

(WAHL-uhs, TIHM) **NYI**

Right wing. Shoots right. 6'1", 207 lbs. Born, Anchorage, AK, August 6, 1984.

Season	Club	League	GP	G	A	Pts	PIM	PP	SH	GW	S	%	+/-	TF	F%	Min	GP	G	A	Pts	PIM	PP	SH	GW	Min
2002-03	U. of Notre Dame	CCHA	40	6	5	11	28																		
2003-04	U. of Notre Dame	CCHA	39	3	8	11	10																		
2004-05	U. of Notre Dame	CCHA	38	5	9	14	20																		
2005-06	U. of Notre Dame	CCHA	36	11	12	23	28																		
2006-07	Wilkes-Barre	AHL	32	5	9	14	39										11	1	1	2	2				
	Wheeling Nailers	ECHL	19	6	11	17	23																		
2007-08	Wilkes-Barre	AHL	74	12	14	26	82										23	2	6	8	21				
2008-09	**Pittsburgh**	**NHL**	**16**	**0**	**2**	**2**	**7**	**0**	**0**	**0**	**17**	**0.0**	**2**	**3**	**66.7**	**8:07**									
	Wilkes-Barre	AHL	58	11	8	19	51										7	0	2	2	2				
2009-10	**Pittsburgh**	**NHL**	**1**	**0**	**0**	**0**	**0**	**0**	**0**	**0**	**0**	**0.0**	**0**	**0**	**0.0**	**5:50**									
	Wilkes-Barre	AHL	78	27	14	41	61										4	0	0	0	2				
2010-11	**Pittsburgh**	**NHL**	**7**	**0**	**0**	**0**	**5**	**0**	**0**	**0**	**1**	**0.0**	**–3**	**3**	**100.0**	**8:03**									
	Wilkes-Barre	AHL	62	20	17	37	61										10	1	4	5	6				
	NHL Totals		**24**	**0**	**2**	**2**	**12**	**0**	**0**	**0**	**18**	**0.0**		**6**	**83.3**	**8:00**									

Signed as a free agent by **Pittsburgh**, May 29, 2007.

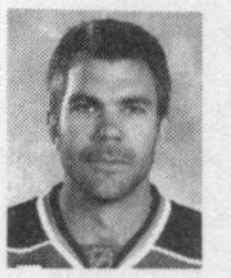

WALLIN, Niclas

(WAHL-ihn, NIHK-luhs)

Defense. Shoots left. 6'3", 220 lbs. Born, Boden, Sweden, February 20, 1975. Carolina's 3rd choice, 97th overall, in 2000 Entry Draft.

Season	Club	League	GP	G	A	Pts	PIM	PP	SH	GW	S	%	+/-	TF	F%	Min	GP	G	A	Pts	PIM	PP	SH	GW	Min
1994-95	Bodens IK	Swe-Jr.	30	2	13	15	125																		
	Bodens IK	Sweden-2	13	0	0	0	0										2	0	0	0	0				
1995-96	Bodens IK	Swe-Jr.	2	2	2	4	0																		
	Bodens IK	Sweden-2	30	2	7	9	26										2	0	1	1	2				
1996-97	Brynas IF Gavle	Sweden	47	1	1	2	14																		
1997-98	Brynas IF Gavle	Sweden	44	2	3	5	57										3	0	1	1	4				
1998-99	Brynas IF Gavle	Sweden	46	2	4	6	52										14	0	1	1	8				
99-2000	Brynas IF Gavle	Sweden	48	7	9	16	73										11	2	1	3	14				
	Brynas IF Gavle	EuroHL	5	1	1	2	10																		
2000-01	**Carolina**	**NHL**	**37**	**2**	**3**	**5**	**21**	**0**	**0**	**0**	**19**	**10.5**	**–11**	**0**	**0.0**	**14:57**	**3**	**0**	**0**	**0**	**2**	**0**	**0**	**0**	**19:10**
	Cincinnati	IHL	8	1	2	3	4										3	0	0	0	2				
2001-02	**Carolina**	**NHL**	**52**	**1**	**2**	**3**	**36**	**0**	**0**	**0**	**33**	**3.0**	**1**	**0**	**0.0**	**12:12**	**23**	**2**	**1**	**3**	**12**	**0**	**0**	**2**	**15:26**
2002-03	**Carolina**	**NHL**	**77**	**2**	**8**	**10**	**71**	**0**	**0**	**2**	**69**	**2.9**	**–19**	**0**	**0.0**	**16:12**									
2003-04	**Carolina**	**NHL**	**57**	**3**	**7**	**10**	**51**	**0**	**0**	**0**	**74**	**4.1**	**–8**	**0**	**0.0**	**18:40**									
2004-05	Lulea HF	Sweden	39	6	7	13	89										3	0	1	1	6				
2005-06♦	**Carolina**	**NHL**	**50**	**4**	**4**	**8**	**42**	**0**	**0**	**0**	**44**	**9.1**	**2**	**0**	**0.0**	**16:50**	**25**	**1**	**4**	**5**	**14**	**0**	**0**	**1**	**16:39**
2006-07	**Carolina**	**NHL**	**67**	**2**	**8**	**10**	**48**	**0**	**0**	**0**	**76**	**2.6**	**–2**	**0**	**0.0**	**18:33**									
2007-08	**Carolina**	**NHL**	**66**	**2**	**6**	**8**	**54**	**0**	**0**	**0**	**60**	**3.3**	**–18**	**1**	**0.0**	**18:08**									
2008-09	**Carolina**	**NHL**	**64**	**2**	**8**	**10**	**42**	**0**	**0**	**1**	**53**	**3.8**	**–1**	**1**	**0.0**	**16:16**	**18**	**0**	**0**	**0**	**4**	**0**	**0**	**0**	**13:46**
2009-10	**Carolina**	**NHL**	**47**	**0**	**5**	**5**	**26**	**0**	**0**	**0**	**50**	**0.0**	**–5**	**1**	**0.0**	**17:47**									
	San Jose	**NHL**	**23**	**0**	**2**	**2**	**23**	**0**	**0**	**0**	**22**	**0.0**	**0**	**0**	**0.0**	**16:23**	**6**	**0**	**0**	**0**	**2**	**0**	**0**	**0**	**11:17**
2010-11	**San Jose**	**NHL**	**74**	**3**	**5**	**8**	**46**	**0**	**0**	**0**	**86**	**3.5**	**0**	**0**	**0.0**	**15:50**	**18**	**1**	**3**	**4**	**10**	**0**	**0**	**1**	**16:35**
	NHL Totals		**614**	**21**	**58**	**79**	**460**	**0**	**0**	**3**	**586**	**3.6**		**3**	**0.0**	**16:37**	**93**	**4**	**8**	**12**	**44**	**0**	**0**	**4**	**15:31**

Signed as a free agent by **Lulea** (Sweden), September 19, 2004. Traded to **San Jose** by **Carolina** with Carolina's 5th round choice (Cody Ferriero) in 2010 Entry Draft for Buffalo's 2nd round choice (previously acquired, Carolina selected Mark Alt) in 2010 Entry Draft, February 7, 2010.

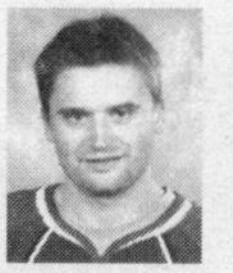

WALTER, Ben

(WAHL-tuhr, BEHN) **CGY**

Center. Shoots left. 6', 185 lbs. Born, Beaconsfield, Que., May 11, 1984. Boston's 5th choice, 160th overall, in 2004 Entry Draft.

Season	Club	League	GP	G	A	Pts	PIM	PP	SH	GW	S	%	+/-	TF	F%	Min	GP	G	A	Pts	PIM	PP	SH	GW	Min
2000-01	Langley Hornets	BCHL	50	8	22	30	19																		
2001-02	Langley Hornets	BCHL	50	29	47	76	29																		
2002-03	U. Mass-Lowell	H-East	35	5	12	17	12																		
2003-04	U. Mass-Lowell	H-East	36	18	16	34	18																		
2004-05	U. Mass-Lowell	H-East	36	*26	13	39	28																		
2005-06	**Boston**	**NHL**	**6**	**0**	**0**	**0**	**4**	**0**	**0**	**0**	**6**	**0.0**	**2**	**32**	**53.1**	**11:49**									
	Providence Bruins	AHL	62	16	25	41	33										3	2	0	2	2				
2006-07	**Boston**	**NHL**	**4**	**0**	**0**	**0**	**0**	**0**	**0**	**0**	**0**	**0.0**	**0**	**24**	**41.7**	**6:11**									
	Providence Bruins	AHL	73	24	43	67	58										13	4	4	8	6				
2007-08	**NY Islanders**	**NHL**	**8**	**1**	**0**	**1**	**0**	**1**	**0**	**0**	**6**	**16.7**	**–1**	**33**	**30.3**	**6:05**									
	Bridgeport	AHL	68	20	46	66	31																		
2008-09	**NY Islanders**	**NHL**	**4**	**0**	**0**	**0**	**0**	**0**	**0**	**0**	**2**	**0.0**	**–2**	**43**	**41.9**	**10:58**									
	Bridgeport	AHL	65	20	30	50	10										5	1	4	5	2				
2009-10	**New Jersey**	**NHL**	**2**	**0**	**0**	**0**	**2**	**0**	**0**	**0**	**0**	**0.0**	**0**	**6**	**33.3**	**5:48**									
	Lowell Devils	AHL	78	22	36	58	26										5	1	1	2	2				
2010-11	Lake Erie	AHL	77	23	47	70	24										7	3	2	5	4				
	NHL Totals		**24**	**1**	**0**	**1**	**6**	**1**	**0**	**0**	**14**	**7.1**		**138**	**41.3**	**8:19**									

Hockey East Second All-Star Team (2005)

Traded to **NY Islanders** by **Boston** with Boston's 2nd round choice (later traded to Columbus – Columbus selected Kevin Lynch) in 2009 Entry Draft for Petteri Nokelainen, September 11, 2007. Traded to **New Jersey** by **NY Islanders** with future considerations for Tony Romano, June 30, 2009. Signed as a free agent by **Colorado**, July 7, 2010. Signed as a free agent by **Calgary**, July 2, 2011.

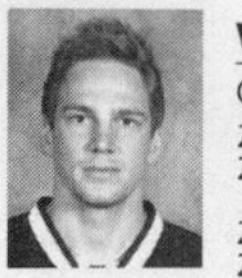

WANDELL, Tom

(VAHN-dehl, TAWM) **DAL**

Center. Shoots left. 6'1", 197 lbs. Born, Sodertalje, Sweden, January 29, 1987. Dallas' 5th choice, 146th overall, in 2005 Entry Draft.

Season	Club	League	GP	G	A	Pts	PIM	PP	SH	GW	S	%	+/-	TF	F%	Min	GP	G	A	Pts	PIM	PP	SH	GW	Min
2002-03	Sodertalje SK U18	Swe-U18	13	8	7	15	6																		
2003-04	Sodertalje SK U18	Swe-U18	6	5	7	12	6										2	0	0	0	0				
	Sodertalje SK Jr.	Swe-Jr.	33	7	15	22	14										2	0	0	0	0				
2004-05	Sodertalje SK Jr.	Swe-Jr.	5	1	2	3	4																		
2005-06	Sodertalje SK Jr.	Swe-Jr.	41	19	20	39	45										4	1	0	1	2				
	Sodertalje SK	Sweden	6	0	0	0	0																		
	Sodertalje SK	Sweden-Q	1	1	0	1	0																		
2006-07	Assat Pori Jr.	Fin-Jr.	4	1	1	2	0																		
	Assat Pori	Finland	50	6	6	12	20																		
2007-08	Iowa Stars	AHL	53	10	9	19	16																		
	Idaho Steelheads	ECHL	3	3	0	3	2																		
2008-09	Timra IK	Sweden	51	15	26	41	26										7	0	4	4	0				
	Dallas	**NHL**	**14**	**1**	**2**	**3**	**4**	**0**	**0**	**0**	**23**	**4.3**	**–1**	**113**	**51.3**	**11:09**									
2009-10	**Dallas**	**NHL**	**50**	**5**	**10**	**15**	**14**	**0**	**0**	**3**	**85**	**5.9**	**2**	**486**	**44.0**	**13:52**									
2010-11	**Dallas**	**NHL**	**75**	**7**	**2**	**9**	**14**	**0**	**0**	**1**	**94**	**7.4**	**–5**	**435**	**43.7**	**11:45**									
	NHL Totals		**139**	**13**	**14**	**27**	**32**	**0**	**0**	**4**	**202**	**6.4**		**1034**	**44.7**	**12:27**									

• Assigned to **Timra** (Sweden) by **Dallas**, July 24, 2008 .

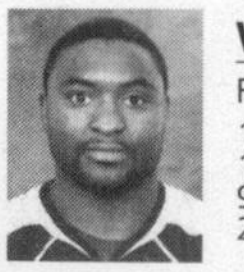

WARD, Joel

(WOHRD, JOHL) **WSH**

Right wing. Shoots right. 6'1", 218 lbs. Born, Toronto, Ont., December 2, 1980.

Season	Club	League	GP	G	A	Pts	PIM	PP	SH	GW	S	%	+/-	TF	F%	Min	GP	G	A	Pts	PIM	PP	SH	GW	Min
1997-98	Owen Sound	OHL	47	8	4	12	14										11	1	1	2	5				
1998-99	Owen Sound	OHL	58	19	16	35	23										16	2	4	6	0				
99-2000	Owen Sound	OHL	63	23	20	43	51																		
2000-01	Owen Sound	OHL	67	26	36	62	45										5	2	4	6	4				
	Long Beach	WCHL	....	....	....	....	....										8	0	0	0	0				
2001-02	U. of P.E.I.	CIS	22	13	14	27	16																		

			Regular Season														Playoffs								
Season	Club	League	GP	G	A	Pts	PIM	PP	SH	GW	S	%	+/-	TF	F%	Min	GP	G	A	Pts	PIM	PP	SH	GW	Min
2002-03	U. of P.E.I.	CIS	19	11	15	26	24																		
2003-04	U. of P.E.I.	CIS	27	14	24	38	42																		
2004-05	U. of P.E.I.	CIS	28	16	28	44	42																		
2005-06	Houston Aeros	AHL	66	8	14	22	34										8	4	2	6	4				
2006-07	**Minnesota**	**NHL**	**11**	**0**	**1**	**1**	**0**	**0**	**0**	**0**	**12**	**0.0**	**0**	**1**	**0.0**	**7:42**									
	Houston Aeros	AHL	64	9	14	23	45																		
2007-08	Houston Aeros	AHL	79	21	20	41	47										4	0	2	2	0				
2008-09	**Nashville**	**NHL**	**79**	**17**	**18**	**35**	**29**	**3**	**2**	**2**	**133**	**12.8**	**1**	**46**	**43.5**	**16:01**									
2009-10	**Nashville**	**NHL**	**71**	**13**	**21**	**34**	**18**	**3**	**1**	**1**	**134**	**9.7**	**–5**	**81**	**38.3**	**17:33**	**6**	**2**	**2**	**4**	**2**	**0**	**1**	**0**	**19:54**
2010-11	**Nashville**	**NHL**	**80**	**10**	**19**	**29**	**42**	**5**	**0**	**4**	**157**	**6.4**	**–1**	**168**	**48.8**	**17:04**	**12**	**7**	**6**	**13**	**6**	**2**	**0**	**1**	**20:25**
	NHL Totals		**241**	**40**	**59**	**99**	**89**	**11**	**3**	**7**	**436**	**9.2**		**296**	**44.9**	**16:26**	**18**	**9**	**8**	**17**	**8**	**2**	**1**	**1**	**20:15**

Signed as a free agent by **Houston** (AHL), December 4, 2005. Signed as a free agent by **Minnesota**, September 27, 2006. Signed as a free agent by **Nashville**, July 14, 2008. Signed as a free agent by **Washington**, July 1, 2011.

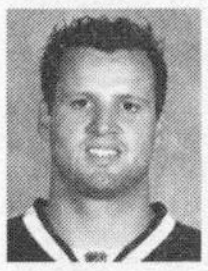

WATHIER, Francis

(waw-TEE-ay, FRAN-sihs)

Left wing. Shoots left. 6'4", 208 lbs. Born, St Isidore, Ont., December 7, 1984. Dallas' 8th choice, 185th overall, in 2003 Entry Draft.

2001-02	Hull Olympiques	QMJHL	63	1	3	4	68										12	1	2	3	30				
2002-03	Hull Olympiques	QMJHL	72	9	18	27	143										20	1	6	7	20				
2003-04	Gatineau	QMJHL	51	9	16	25	127										15	0	2	2	23				
2004-05	Gatineau	QMJHL	67	15	20	35	96										10	0	2	2	8				
2005-06	Iowa Stars	AHL	11	0	1	1	26																		
2006-07	Iowa Stars	AHL	57	14	3	17	78										12	0	4	4	25				
	Idaho Steelheads	ECHL	17	4	9	13	31										7	1	1	2	4				
2007-08	Iowa Stars	AHL	19	2	3	5	17																		
2008-09	Iowa Chops	AHL	77	6	10	16	127																		
2009-10	**Dallas**	**NHL**	**5**	**0**	**0**	**0**	**5**	**0**	**0**	**0**	**4**	**0.0**	**0**	**1**	**100.0**	**5:18**									
	Texas Stars	AHL	76	19	21	40	101										24	2	6	8	18				
2010-11	**Dallas**	**NHL**	**3**	**0**	**0**	**0**	**0**	**0**	**0**	**0**	**0**	**0.0**	**–2**	**0**	**0.0**	**3:55**									
	Texas Stars	AHL	68	19	16	35	78										6	0	0	0	4				
	NHL Totals		**8**	**0**	**0**	**0**	**5**	**0**	**0**	**0**	**4**	**0.0**		**1**	**100.0**	**4:47**									

• Missed majority of 2005-06 and 2007-08 due to recurring shoulder injury.

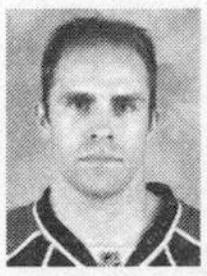

WEAVER, Mike

(WEE-vuhr, MIGHK) **FLA**

Defense. Shoots right. 5'9", 186 lbs. Born, Bramalea, Ont., May 2, 1978.

1995-96	Bramalea Blues	OPJHL	48	10	39	49	103																		
1996-97	Michigan State	CCHA	39	0	7	7	46																		
1997-98	Michigan State	CCHA	44	4	22	26	68																		
1998-99	Michigan State	CCHA	42	1	6	7	54																		
99-2000	Michigan State	CCHA	26	0	7	7	20																		
2000-01	Orlando	IHL	68	0	8	8	34										16	0	2	2	8				
2001-02	**Atlanta**	**NHL**	**16**	**0**	**1**	**1**	**10**	**0**	**0**	**0**	**9**	**0.0**	**0**	**0**	**0.0**	**13:54**									
	Chicago Wolves	AHL	58	2	8	10	67										25	1	3	4	21				
2002-03	**Atlanta**	**NHL**	**40**	**0**	**5**	**5**	**20**	**0**	**0**	**0**	**21**	**0.0**	**–5**	**0**	**0.0**	**18:38**									
	Chicago Wolves	AHL	33	2	2	4	32										9	0	3	3	4				
2003-04	**Atlanta**	**NHL**	**1**	**0**	**0**	**0**	**0**	**0**	**0**	**0**	**0**	**0.0**	**–1**	**0**	**0.0**	**8:28**									
	Chicago Wolves	AHL	78	3	14	17	89										9	2	2	4	20				
2004-05	Manchester	AHL	79	1	22	23	61										6	0	1	1	0				
2005-06	**Los Angeles**	**NHL**	**53**	**0**	**9**	**9**	**14**	**0**	**0**	**0**	**21**	**0.0**	**–3**	**0**	**0.0**	**15:03**									
2006-07	**Los Angeles**	**NHL**	**39**	**3**	**6**	**9**	**16**	**1**	**0**	**1**	**22**	**13.6**	**–4**	**3**	**66.7**	**15:20**									
	Manchester	AHL	7	1	3	4	2																		
2007-08	**Vancouver**	**NHL**	**55**	**0**	**1**	**1**	**33**	**0**	**0**	**0**	**33**	**0.0**	**1**	**1**	**0.0**	**14:02**									
2008-09	**St. Louis**	**NHL**	**58**	**0**	**7**	**7**	**12**	**0**	**0**	**0**	**36**	**0.0**	**–3**	**0**	**0.0**	**17:16**	**4**	**0**	**0**	**0**	**0**	**0**	**0**	**0**	**17:02**
2009-10	**St. Louis**	**NHL**	**77**	**1**	**9**	**10**	**29**	**0**	**0**	**0**	**33**	**3.0**	**10**	**2**	**50.0**	**16:58**									
2010-11	**Florida**	**NHL**	**82**	**2**	**11**	**13**	**34**	**0**	**0**	**1**	**53**	**3.8**	**1**	**0**	**0.0**	**20:48**									
	NHL Totals		**421**	**6**	**49**	**55**	**168**	**1**	**0**	**2**	**228**	**2.6**		**6**	**50.0**	**17:00**	**4**	**0**	**0**	**0**	**0**	**0**	**0**	**0**	**17:02**

OPJHL Defenseman of the Year (1996) • CCHA All-Tournament Team (1997) • CCHA First All-Star Team (1999, 2000) • CCHA Best Defensive Defenseman Award (1999, 2000) • NCAA West Second All-American Team (1999, 2000)

Signed as a free agent by **Atlanta**, June 15, 2000. Signed as a free agent by **Los Angeles**, July 16, 2004. Signed as a free agent by **Pittsburgh**, August 8, 2007. Claimed on waivers by **Vancouver** from **Pittsburgh**, October 2, 2007. Signed as a free agent by **St. Louis**, July 10, 2008. Signed as a free agent by **Florida**, August 3, 2010.

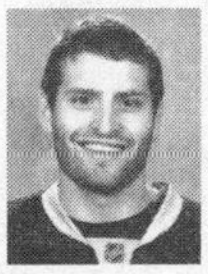

WEBER, Mike

(WEH-buhr, MIGHK) **BUF**

Defense. Shoots left. 6'2", 211 lbs. Born, Pittsburgh, PA, December 16, 1987. Buffalo's 3rd choice, 57th overall, in 2006 Entry Draft.

2002-03	Jr. Penguins	EmJHL	28	4	11	15	109										3	0	0	0	20				
2003-04	Windsor Spitfires	OHL	65	0	2	2	49																		
2004-05	Windsor Spitfires	OHL	68	2	6	8	132										11	0	1	1	18				
2005-06	Windsor Spitfires	OHL	68	5	21	26	181										7	0	0	0	12				
2006-07	Windsor Spitfires	OHL	30	3	16	19	86																		
	Barrie Colts	OHL	30	3	12	15	86										7	0	6	6	10				
2007-08	**Buffalo**	**NHL**	**16**	**0**	**3**	**3**	**14**	**0**	**0**	**0**	**12**	**0.0**	**12**	**0**	**0.0**	**16:41**									
	Rochester	AHL	59	1	13	14	178																		
2008-09	**Buffalo**	**NHL**	**7**	**0**	**0**	**0**	**19**	**0**	**0**	**0**	**2**	**0.0**	**–3**	**0**	**0.0**	**14:10**									
	Portland Pirates	AHL	42	1	7	8	94																		
2009-10	Portland Pirates	AHL	80	5	16	21	153										4	1	0	1	14				
2010-11	**Buffalo**	**NHL**	**58**	**4**	**13**	**17**	**69**	**0**	**0**	**0**	**53**	**7.5**	**13**	**0**	**0.0**	**16:54**	**7**	**0**	**1**	**1**	**6**	**0**	**0**	**0**	**15:51**
	NHL Totals		**81**	**4**	**16**	**20**	**102**	**0**	**0**	**0**	**67**	**6.0**		**0**	**0.0**	**16:37**	**7**	**0**	**1**	**1**	**6**	**0**	**0**	**0**	**15:51**

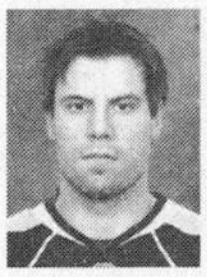

WEBER, Shea

(WEH-buhr, SHAY) **NSH**

Defense. Shoots right. 6'4", 234 lbs. Born, Sicamous, B.C., August 14, 1985. Nashville's 4th choice, 49th overall, in 2003 Entry Draft.

2001-02	Sicamous Eagles	KIJHL	47	9	33	42	87																		
	Kelowna Rockets	WHL	5	0	0	0	0																		
2002-03	Kelowna Rockets	WHL	70	2	16	18	167										19	1	4	5	26				
2003-04	Kelowna Rockets	WHL	60	12	20	32	126										17	3	14	17	16				
2004-05	Kelowna Rockets	WHL	55	12	29	41	95										18	9	8	17	25				
2005-06	**Nashville**	**NHL**	**28**	**2**	**8**	**10**	**42**	**2**	**0**	**1**	**46**	**4.3**	**8**	**0**	**0.0**	**17:00**	**4**	**2**	**0**	**2**	**8**	**1**	**0**	**0**	**14:12**
	Milwaukee	AHL	46	12	15	27	49										14	6	5	11	16				
2006-07	**Nashville**	**NHL**	**79**	**17**	**23**	**40**	**60**	**6**	**0**	**2**	**152**	**11.2**	**13**	**0**	**0.0**	**19:23**	**5**	**0**	**3**	**3**	**2**	**0**	**0**	**0**	**21:41**
2007-08	**Nashville**	**NHL**	**54**	**6**	**14**	**20**	**49**	**5**	**0**	**2**	**152**	**3.9**	**–6**	**0**	**0.0**	**19:30**	**6**	**1**	**3**	**4**	**6**	**0**	**0**	**0**	**19:30**
2008-09	**Nashville**	**NHL**	**81**	**23**	**30**	**53**	**80**	**10**	**1**	**4**	**251**	**9.2**	**1**	**0**	**0.0**	**23:58**									
2009-10	**Nashville**	**NHL**	**78**	**16**	**27**	**43**	**36**	**7**	**0**	**3**	**222**	**7.2**	**0**	**0**	**0.0**	**23:10**	**6**	**2**	**1**	**3**	**4**	**0**	**0**	**0**	**24:27**
	Canada	Olympics	7	2	4	6	2																		
2010-11	**Nashville**	**NHL**	**82**	**16**	**32**	**48**	**56**	**6**	**1**	**3**	**254**	**6.3**	**7**	**0**	**0.0**	**25:19**	**12**	**3**	**2**	**5**	**8**	**2**	**0**	**0**	**27:58**
	NHL Totals		**402**	**80**	**134**	**214**	**323**	**36**	**2**	**15**	**1077**	**7.4**		**0**	**0.0**	**22:06**	**33**	**8**	**9**	**17**	**28**	**3**	**0**	**0**	**23:10**

WHL West Second All-Star Team (2004) • Memorial Cup All-Star Team (2004) • WHL West First All-Star Team (2005) • Canadian Major Junior Second All-Star Team (2005) • Olympic All-Star Team (2010) • NHL First All-Star Team (2011)

Played in NHL All-Star Game (2009, 2011)

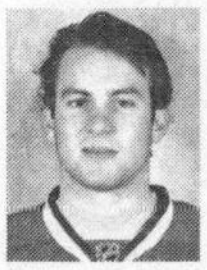

WEBER, Yannick

(WEH-buhr, YAH-nihk) **MTL**

Defense. Shoots right. 5'11", 193 lbs. Born, Morges, Switz., September 23, 1988. Montreal's 5th choice, 73rd overall, in 2007 Entry Draft.

2003-04	SC Bern Jr.	Swiss-Jr.	32	2	3	5	39										8	2	0	2	8				
2004-05	SC Bern Jr.	Swiss-Jr.	37	5	4	9	62										5	0	0	0	22				
2005-06	SC Bern Future Jr.	Swiss-Jr.	17	1	6	7	46																		
	SC Langenthal	Swiss-2	28	3	0	3	8																		
2006-07	SC Bern Future Jr.	Swiss-Jr.	1	0	0	0	2																		
	Kitchener Rangers	OHL	51	13	28	41	42										9	3	6	9	8				

Season	Club	League	Regular Season														Playoffs								
			GP	G	A	Pts	PIM	PP	SH	GW	S	%	+/-	TF	F%	Min	GP	G	A	Pts	PIM	PP	SH	GW	Min
2007-08	Kitchener Rangers	OHL	59	20	35	55	79	....	....	....	....	....	....	....	....	....	17	4	13	17	24	....	....	....	....
2008-09	Montreal	NHL	3	0	1	1	2	0	0	0	6	0.0	–1	0	0.0	15:06	3	1	1	2	0	0	0	0	13:36
	Hamilton	AHL	68	16	28	44	42	....	....	....	....	....	....	....	....	....	2	0	1	1	10	....	....	....	....
2009-10	Montreal	NHL	5	0	0	0	4	0	0	0	2	0.0	–5	0	0.0	13:53	....	....	....	....	....	....	....	....	....
	Hamilton	AHL	65	7	25	32	58	....	....	....	....	....	....	....	....	....	....	....	....	....	....	....	....	....	....
	Switzerland	Olympics	5	0	0	0	6	....	....	....	....	....	....	....	....	....	3	0	0	0	2	....	....	....	....
2010-11	Montreal	NHL	41	1	10	11	14	0	0	0	63	1.6	0	0	0.0	16:34	3	2	0	2	0	1	0	0	8:46
	Hamilton	AHL	15	8	4	12	10	....	....	....	....	....	....	....	....	....	....	....	....	....	....	....	....	....	....
	NHL Totals		49	1	11	12	20	0	0	0	71	1.4		0	0.0	16:12	6	3	1	4	0	1	0	0	11:11

OHL Second All-Star Team (2008) • AHL All-Rookie Team (2009)

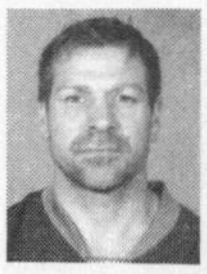

WEIGHT, Doug

(WAYT, DUHG)

Center. Shoots left. 5'11", 202 lbs. Born, Warren, MI, January 21, 1971. NY Rangers' 2nd choice, 34th overall, in 1990 Entry Draft.

Season	Club	League	GP	G	A	Pts	PIM	PP	SH	GW	S	%	+/-	TF	F%	Min	GP	G	A	Pts	PIM	PP	SH	GW	Min
1988-89	Bloomfield Jets	NAHL	34	26	53	79	105	....	....	....	....	....	....	....	....	....	....	....	....	....	....	....	....	....	....
1989-90	Lake Superior	CCHA	46	21	48	69	44	....	....	....	....	....	....	....	....	....	....	....	....	....	....	....	....	....	....
1990-91	Lake Superior	CCHA	42	29	46	75	86	....	....	....	....	....	....	....	....	....	....	....	....	....	....	....	....	....	....
	NY Rangers	NHL	....	....	....	....	....	....	....	....	....	....	....	....	....	....	1	0	0	0	0	0	0	0	....
1991-92	NY Rangers	NHL	53	8	22	30	23	0	0	2	72	11.1	–3	....	....	....	7	2	2	4	0	1	0	0	....
	Binghamton	AHL	9	3	14	17	2	....	....	....	....	....	....	....	....	....	4	1	4	5	6	....	....	....	....
1992-93	NY Rangers	NHL	65	15	25	40	55	3	0	1	90	16.7	4	....	....	....	....	....	....	....	....	....	....	....	....
	Edmonton	NHL	13	2	6	8	10	0	0	0	35	5.7	–2	....	....	....	....	....	....	....	....	....	....	....	....
1993-94	Edmonton	NHL	84	24	50	74	47	4	1	1	188	12.8	–22	....	....	....	....	....	....	....	....	....	....	....	....
1994-95	Rosenheim	Germany	8	2	3	5	18	....	....	....	....	....	....	....	....	....	....	....	....	....	....	....	....	....	....
	Edmonton	NHL	48	7	33	40	69	1	0	1	104	6.7	–17	....	....	....	....	....	....	....	....	....	....	....	....
1995-96	Edmonton	NHL	82	25	79	104	95	9	0	2	204	12.3	–19	....	....	....	....	....	....	....	....	....	....	....	....
1996-97	Edmonton	NHL	80	21	61	82	80	4	0	2	235	8.9	1	....	....	....	12	3	8	11	8	0	0	0	....
1997-98	Edmonton	NHL	79	26	44	70	69	9	0	4	205	12.7	1	....	....	....	12	2	7	9	14	2	0	1	....
	United States	Olympics	4	0	2	2	2	....	....	....	....	....	....	....	....	....	....	....	....	....	....	....	....	....	....
1998-99	Edmonton	NHL	43	6	31	37	12	1	0	0	79	7.6	–8	853	49.5	19:51	4	1	1	2	15	0	0	0	14:43
99-2000	Edmonton	NHL	77	21	51	72	54	3	1	4	167	12.6	6	1588	50.4	20:35	5	3	2	5	4	2	0	1	21:05
2000-01	Edmonton	NHL	82	25	65	90	91	8	0	3	188	13.3	12	1514	51.3	22:08	6	1	5	6	17	0	0	0	22:45
2001-02	St. Louis	NHL	61	15	34	49	40	3	0	1	131	11.5	20	1123	49.2	19:48	10	1	1	2	4	1	0	1	16:26
	United States	Olympics	6	0	3	3	4	....	....	....	....	....	....	....	....	....	....	....	....	....	....	....	....	....	....
2002-03	St. Louis	NHL	70	15	52	67	52	7	0	3	182	8.2	–6	1048	50.4	20:23	7	5	8	13	2	*5	0	1	22:26
2003-04	St. Louis	NHL	75	14	51	65	37	6	0	5	198	7.1	–3	1115	50.4	20:25	5	2	1	3	6	1	1	0	19:24
2004-05	Frankfurt Lions	Germany	7	6	9	15	26	....	....	....	....	....	....	....	....	....	11	2	10	12	8	....	....	....	....
2005-06	St. Louis	NHL	47	11	33	44	50	7	0	1	123	8.9	–11	638	49.8	22:17	....	....	....	....	....	....	....	....	....
	♦ Carolina	NHL	23	4	9	13	25	2	0	0	52	7.7	–6	256	46.1	17:35	23	3	13	16	20	2	0	0	15:27
	United States	Olympics	6	0	3	3	4	....	....	....	....	....	....	....	....	....	....	....	....	....	....	....	....	....	....
2006-07	St. Louis	NHL	82	16	43	59	56	5	0	3	123	13.0	10	1025	47.7	18:17	....	....	....	....	....	....	....	....	....
2007-08	St. Louis	NHL	29	4	7	11	12	0	0	0	47	8.5	4	289	49.5	16:11	....	....	....	....	....	....	....	....	....
	Anaheim	NHL	38	6	8	14	20	2	0	1	49	12.2	0	325	45.2	13:25	5	0	1	1	4	0	0	0	7:39
2008-09	NY Islanders	NHL	53	10	28	38	55	5	0	0	96	10.4	–15	679	45.1	18:17	....	....	....	....	....	....	....	....	....
2009-10	NY Islanders	NHL	36	1	16	17	8	0	0	0	61	1.6	–1	152	45.4	15:51	....	....	....	....	....	....	....	....	....
2010-11	NY Islanders	NHL	18	2	7	9	10	1	0	0	26	7.7	–3	110	51.8	17:32	....	....	....	....	....	....	....	....	....
	NHL Totals		1238	278	755	1033	970	80	2	34	2655	10.5		10715	49.4	19:21	97	23	49	72	94	14	1	4	17:07

CCHA First All-Star Team (1991) • NCAA West Second All-American Team (1991) • King Clancy Memorial Trophy (2011)

Played in NHL All-Star Game (1996, 1998, 2001, 2003)

Traded to **Edmonton** by **NY Rangers** for Esa Tikkanen, March 17, 1993. Traded to **St. Louis** by **Edmonton** with Michel Riesen for Marty Reasoner, Jochen Hecht and Jan Horacek, July 1, 2001. Signed as a free agent by **Frankfurt** (Germany), February 11, 2005. Traded to **Carolina** by **St. Louis** with Erkki Rajamaki for Jesse Boulerice, Mike Zigomanis, the rights to Magnus Kahnberg, Carolina's 1st round choice (later traded to New Jersey - New Jersey selected Matthew Corrente) in 2006 Entry Draft, Toronto's 4th round choice (previously acquired, St. Louis selected Reto Berra) in 2006 Entry Draft and Chicago's 4th round choice (previously acquired, St. Louis selected Cade Fairchild) in 2007 Entry Draft, January 30, 2006. Signed as a free agent by **St. Louis**, July 2, 2006. Traded to **Anaheim** by **St. Louis** with Michal Birner and St. Louis' 7th round choice (later traded to Los Angeles, later traded back to St. Louis - St. Louis selected Paul Karpowich) in 2008 Entry Draft for Andy McDonald, December 14, 2007. Signed as a free agent by **NY Islanders**, July 2, 2008. • Missed majority of 2009-10 due to various injuries. • Missed majority of 2010-11 due to recurring back injury. • Officially announced his retirement, May 26, 2011.

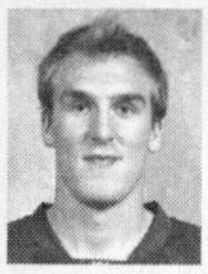

WEISE, Dale

(WIHGS, DAYL) **NYR**

Right wing. Shoots right. 6'2", 210 lbs. Born, Winnipeg, Man., August 5, 1988. NY Rangers' 5th choice, 111th overall, in 2008 Entry Draft.

Season	Club	League	GP	G	A	Pts	PIM	PP	SH	GW	S	%	+/-	TF	F%	Min	GP	G	A	Pts	PIM	PP	SH	GW	Min
2005-06	Swift Current	WHL	53	4	14	18	57	....	....	....	....	....	....	....	....	....	4	0	0	0	2	....	....	....	....
2006-07	Swift Current	WHL	67	18	25	43	94	....	....	....	....	....	....	....	....	....	6	0	1	1	8	....	....	....	....
2007-08	Swift Current	WHL	53	29	22	51	84	....	....	....	....	....	....	....	....	....	12	7	6	13	20	....	....	....	....
2008-09	Hartford	AHL	74	11	12	23	64	....	....	....	....	....	....	....	....	....	6	3	1	4	2	....	....	....	....
2009-10	Hartford	AHL	73	28	22	50	114	....	....	....	....	....	....	....	....	....	....	....	....	....	....	....	....	....	....
2010-11	NY Rangers	NHL	10	0	0	0	19	0	0	0	9	0.0	–1	0	0.0	6:30	....	....	....	....	....	....	....	....	....
	Connecticut	AHL	47	18	20	38	73	....	....	....	....	....	....	....	....	....	5	2	1	3	8	....	....	....	....
	NHL Totals		10	0	0	0	19	0	0	0	9	0.0		0	0.0	6:30	....	....	....	....	....	....	....	....	....

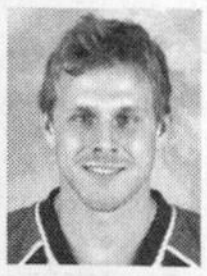

WEISS, Stephen

(WIGHS, STEE-vehn) **FLA**

Center. Shoots left. 5'11", 185 lbs. Born, Toronto, Ont., April 3, 1983. Florida's 1st choice, 4th overall, in 2001 Entry Draft.

Season	Club	League	GP	G	A	Pts	PIM	PP	SH	GW	S	%	+/-	TF	F%	Min	GP	G	A	Pts	PIM	PP	SH	GW	Min
1997-98	Tor. Young Nats	MTHL	48	51	58	109	....	....	....	....	....	....	....	....	....	....	....	....	....	....	....	....	....	....	....
1998-99	North York	OPJHL	35	15	22	37	10	....	....	....	....	....	....	....	....	....	....	....	....	....	....	....	....	....	....
99-2000	Plymouth Whalers	OHL	64	24	42	66	35	....	....	....	....	....	....	....	....	....	23	8	18	26	18	....	....	....	....
2000-01	Plymouth Whalers	OHL	62	40	47	87	45	....	....	....	....	....	....	....	....	....	18	7	16	23	10	....	....	....	....
2001-02	Florida	NHL	7	1	1	2	0	1	0	0	15	6.7	0	107	52.3	16:14	....	....	....	....	....	....	....	....	....
	Plymouth Whalers	OHL	46	25	45	70	69	....	....	....	....	....	....	....	....	....	6	2	7	9	13	....	....	....	....
2002-03	Florida	NHL	77	6	15	21	17	0	0	2	87	6.9	–13	1065	46.3	14:17	....	....	....	....	....	....	....	....	....
2003-04	Florida	NHL	50	12	17	29	10	3	0	2	82	14.6	–10	799	44.9	17:42	....	....	....	....	....	....	....	....	....
	San Antonio	AHL	10	6	3	9	14	....	....	....	....	....	....	....	....	....	....	....	....	....	....	....	....	....	....
2004-05	San Antonio	AHL	62	15	23	38	38	....	....	....	....	....	....	....	....	....	....	....	....	....	....	....	....	....	....
	Chicago Wolves	AHL	18	7	9	16	12	....	....	....	....	....	....	....	....	....	18	2	7	9	17	....	....	....	....
2005-06	Florida	NHL	41	9	12	21	22	5	0	1	74	12.2	–2	514	49.6	15:15	....	....	....	....	....	....	....	....	....
2006-07	Florida	NHL	74	20	28	48	28	10	0	1	176	11.4	–1	1182	45.9	17:07	....	....	....	....	....	....	....	....	....
2007-08	Florida	NHL	74	13	29	42	40	4	0	4	132	9.8	14	1198	51.2	17:35	....	....	....	....	....	....	....	....	....
2008-09	Florida	NHL	78	14	47	61	22	4	1	4	154	9.1	19	1277	50.9	17:48	....	....	....	....	....	....	....	....	....
2009-10	Florida	NHL	80	28	32	60	40	12	0	2	180	15.6	–7	1551	52.4	20:00	....	....	....	....	....	....	....	....	....
2010-11	Florida	NHL	76	21	28	49	49	3	2	1	172	12.2	–9	1279	53.9	20:06	....	....	....	....	....	....	....	....	....
	NHL Totals		557	124	209	333	228	42	3	17	1072	11.6		8972	49.8	17:37	....	....	....	....	....	....	....	....	....

OHL All-Rookie Team (2000)

• Loaned to **Chicago** (AHL) by **San Antonio** (AHL) for cash, March 8, 2005.

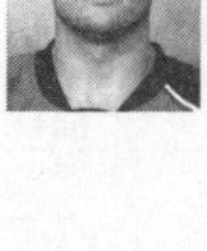

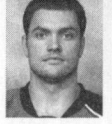

WELCH, Noah

(WEHLCH, NOH-uh)

Defense. Shoots left. 6'4", 215 lbs. Born, Brighton, MA, August 26, 1982. Pittsburgh's 2nd choice, 54th overall, in 2001 Entry Draft.

Season	Club	League	GP	G	A	Pts	PIM	PP	SH	GW	S	%	+/-	TF	F%	Min	GP	G	A	Pts	PIM	PP	SH	GW	Min
99-2000	St. Sebastian's	High-MA	26	4	11	15	35	....	....	....	....	....	....	....	....	....	....	....	....	....	....	....	....	....	....
	Eastern-Mass	MBAHL	4	0	3	3	6	....	....	....	....	....	....	....	....	....	....	....	....	....	....	....	....	....	....
2000-01	St. Sebastian's	High-MA	30	11	20	31	37	....	....	....	....	....	....	....	....	....	....	....	....	....	....	....	....	....	....
2001-02	Harvard Crimson	ECAC	27	5	6	11	56	....	....	....	....	....	....	....	....	....	....	....	....	....	....	....	....	....	....
2002-03	Harvard Crimson	ECAC	34	6	22	28	70	....	....	....	....	....	....	....	....	....	....	....	....	....	....	....	....	....	....
2003-04	Harvard Crimson	ECAC	34	6	13	19	58	....	....	....	....	....	....	....	....	....	....	....	....	....	....	....	....	....	....
2004-05	Harvard Crimson	ECAC	34	6	12	18	*86	....	....	....	....	....	....	....	....	....	....	....	....	....	....	....	....	....	....
2005-06	Pittsburgh	NHL	5	1	3	4	2	0	0	0	5	20.0	0	0	0.0	17:24	....	....	....	....	....	....	....	....	....
	Wilkes-Barre	AHL	77	9	20	29	99	....	....	....	....	....	....	....	....	....	11	1	0	1	18	....	....	....	....
2006-07	Pittsburgh	NHL	22	1	1	2	22	0	0	0	14	7.1	1	0	0.0	13:34	....	....	....	....	....	....	....	....	....
	Wilkes-Barre	AHL	27	5	16	21	24	....	....	....	....	....	....	....	....	....	....	....	....	....	....	....	....	....	....
	Florida	NHL	2	1	0	1	2	0	0	0	4	25.0	3	0	0.0	18:08	....	....	....	....	....	....	....	....	....
	Rochester	AHL	11	2	4	6	21	....	....	....	....	....	....	....	....	....	6	0	2	2	12	....	....	....	....
2007-08	Florida	NHL	4	0	0	0	7	0	0	0	0	0.0	1	0	0.0	8:04	....	....	....	....	....	....	....	....	....

			Regular Season														Playoffs								
Season	Club	League	GP	G	A	Pts	PIM	PP	SH	GW	S	%	+/-	TF	F%	Min	GP	G	A	Pts	PIM	PP	SH	GW	Min
2008-09	Florida	NHL	23	1	1	2	11	0	0	0	11	9.1	-5	0	0.0	6:38									
	Rochester	AHL	7	0	3	3	10																		
	Tampa Bay	NHL	17	0	0	0	14	0	0	0	11	0.0	-4	0	0.0	16:45									
2009-10	Chicago Wolves	AHL	37	1	4	5	33										14	0	2	2	10				
2010-11	Atlanta	NHL	2	0	0	0	0	0	0	0	1	0.0	-1	0	0.0	17:33									
	Chicago Wolves	AHL	50	2	11	13	65																		
	NHL Totals		75	4	5	9	58	0	0	0	46	8.7		0	0.0	12:21									

ECAC All-Rookie Team (2002) • ECAC Second All-Star Team (2002, 2003) • NCAA East Second All-American Team (2003) • ECAC First All-Star Team (2005) • NCAA East First All-American Team (2005)

Traded to **Florida** by **Pittsburgh** for Gary Roberts, February 27, 2007. • Missed remainder of 2007-08 due to shoulder injury at Montreal, October 16, 2007. Traded to **Tampa Bay** by **Florida** with Florida's 3rd round choice (later traded to Detroit – Detroit selected Andrej Nestrasil) in 2009 Entry Draft for Steve Eminger, March 4, 2009. Signed as a free agent by **Atlanta**, July 13, 2009. • Missed majority of 2009-10 due to recurring knee injury. • Transferred to **Winnipeg** after **Atlanta** franchise relocated, June 21, 2011.

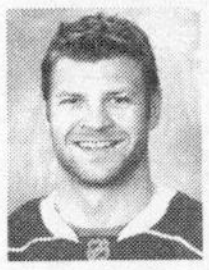

WELLER, Craig
(WEHL-uhr, KRAIG)

Right wing. Shoots right. 6'4", 220 lbs. Born, Calgary, Alta., January 17, 1981. St. Louis' 6th choice, 167th overall, in 2000 Entry Draft.

Season	Club	League	GP	G	A	Pts	PIM	PP	SH	GW	S	%	+/-	TF	F%	Min	GP	G	A	Pts	PIM	PP	SH	GW	Min
1997-98	Calgary Flames	AMHL	33	2	10	12	65										3	0	1	1	2				
1998-99	Calgary Canucks	AJHL	49	4	14	18	80										13	0	1	1	10				
99-2000	Calgary Canucks	AJHL	53	3	14	17	100										4	0	0	0	4				
2000-01	U. Minn-Duluth	WCHA	6	0	1	1	0																		
	Kootenay Ice	WHL	30	1	5	6	40										11	0	2	2	26				
2001-02	Kootenay Ice	WHL	69	5	13	18	127										22	3	7	10	27				
2002-03	Hartford	AHL	11	0	0	0	8										2	0	0	0	0				
	Charlotte	ECHL	48	3	11	14	84																		
2003-04	Hartford	AHL	68	5	9	14	86										16	2	2	4	30				
2004-05	Hartford	AHL	76	10	9	19	182										6	0	1	1	6				
2005-06	Hartford	AHL	80	12	21	33	152										13	2	3	5	44				
2006-07	Hartford	AHL	56	11	6	17	96										4	0	0	0	4				
2007-08	Phoenix	NHL	59	3	8	11	80	0	0	1	72	4.2	-7	2	0.0	10:23									
2008-09	Minnesota	NHL	36	1	2	3	47	1	0	0	27	3.7	-3	5	0.0	6:57									
2009-10	Houston Aeros	AHL	5	0	1	1	7																		
	Providence Bruins	AHL	55	4	10	14	62																		
	Chicago Wolves	AHL	14	0	3	3	21										4	0	0	0	4				
2010-11	Cardiff Devils	Britain	41	16	32	52	52																		
	NHL Totals		95	4	10	14	127	1	0	1	99	4.0		7	0.0	9:05									

WHL West Second All-Star Team (2002)

• Left **University of Minnesota-Duluth** (WCHA) and signed as a free agent by **Kootenay** (WHL), January 7, 2001. Signed as a free agent by **NY Rangers**, July 11, 2002. Signed as a free agent by **Phoenix**, July 19, 2007. Signed as a free agent by **Minnesota**, July 1, 2008. • Missed majority of 2008-09 due to various injuries and as a healthy reserve. Traded to **Boston** by **Minnesota** with Alexander Fallstrom and Minnesota's 2nd round choice (Alexander Khokhlachev) in 2011 Entry Draft for Chuck Kobasew, October 18, 2009. Traded to **Florida** by **Boston** with Byron Bitz and Tampa Bay's 2nd round choice (previously acquired, Florida selected Alexander Petrovic) in 2010 Entry Draft for Dennis Seidenberg and Matt Bartkowski, March 3, 2010. Signed as a free agent by **Cardiff** (Britain), November 1, 2010.

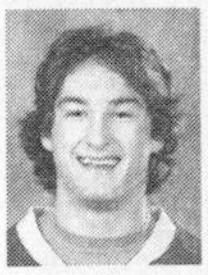

WELLMAN, Casey
(WEHL-man, KAY-see) **MIN**

Center. Shoots right. 6', 186 lbs. Born, Brentwood, CA, October 18, 1987.

Season	Club	League	GP	G	A	Pts	PIM	PP	SH	GW	S	%	+/-	TF	F%	Min	GP	G	A	Pts	PIM	PP	SH	GW	Min
2006-07	Cedar Rapids	USHL	50	6	13	19	30										6	1	2	3	0				
2007-08	Cedar Rapids	USHL	59	22	23	45	30										3	1	1	2	4				
2008-09	Massachusetts	H-East	39	11	22	33	32																		
2009-10	Massachusetts	H-East	36	23	22	45	38																		
	Minnesota	NHL	12	1	3	4	0	0	0	0	18	5.6	-2	32	53.1	12:03									
2010-11	Minnesota	NHL	15	1	1	2	4	0	0	1	20	5.0	-1	16	50.0	10:39									
	Houston Aeros	AHL	42	14	21	35	14										24	6	5	11	6				
	NHL Totals		27	2	4	6	4	0	0	1	38	5.3		48	52.1	11:16									

Hockey East All-Rookie Team (2009)

Signed as a free agent by **Minnesota**, March 16, 2010.

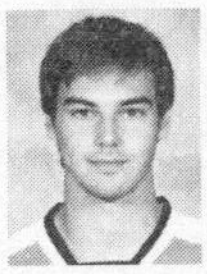

WELLWOOD, Eric
(WEHL-wud, AIR-ihk) **PHI**

Left wing. Shoots left. 5'11", 180 lbs. Born, Windsor, Ont., March 6, 1990. Philadelphia's 5th choice, 172nd overall, in 2009 Entry Draft.

Season	Club	League	GP	G	A	Pts	PIM	PP	SH	GW	S	%	+/-	TF	F%	Min	GP	G	A	Pts	PIM	PP	SH	GW	Min
2006-07	Tecumseh Chiefs	ON-Jr.B	34	10	10	20	33																		
	Windsor Spitfires	OHL	23	2	5	7	0																		
2007-08	Windsor Spitfires	OHL	68	9	7	16	12										5	0	0	0	2				
2008-09	Windsor Spitfires	OHL	61	16	18	34	12										20	10	11	21	12				
2009-10	Windsor Spitfires	OHL	65	31	37	68	36										19	4	6	10	6				
2010-11	Philadelphia	NHL	3	0	1	1	2	0	0	0	8	0.0	1	0	0.0	13:25									
	Adirondack	AHL	73	16	12	28	24																		
	NHL Totals		3	0	1	1	2	0	0	0	8	0.0		0	0.0	13:25									

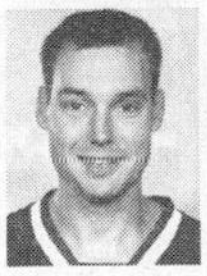

WELLWOOD, Kyle
(WEHL-wud, KIGHL)

Center. Shoots right. 5'10", 181 lbs. Born, Windsor, Ont., May 16, 1983. Toronto's 6th choice, 134th overall, in 2001 Entry Draft.

Season	Club	League	GP	G	A	Pts	PIM	PP	SH	GW	S	%	+/-	TF	F%	Min	GP	G	A	Pts	PIM	PP	SH	GW	Min
1998-99	Tecumseh	ON-Jr.B	51	22	41	63	12																		
99-2000	Belleville Bulls	OHL	65	14	37	51	14										16	3	7	10	6				
2000-01	Belleville Bulls	OHL	68	35	*83	*118	24										10	3	16	19	4				
2001-02	Belleville Bulls	OHL	28	16	24	40	4																		
	Windsor Spitfires	OHL	26	14	21	35	0										16	12	12	24	0				
2002-03	Windsor Spitfires	OHL	57	41	59	100	0										7	5	9	14	0				
2003-04	Toronto	NHL	1	0	0	0	0	0	0	0	1	0.0	-1	13	30.8	7:56									
	St. John's	AHL	76	20	35	55	6																		
2004-05	St. John's	AHL	80	38	49	87	20										5	2	2	4	2				
2005-06	Toronto	NHL	81	11	34	45	14	3	0	0	117	9.4	0	593	56.3	12:47									
2006-07	Toronto	NHL	48	12	30	42	0	7	0	2	99	12.1	3	291	56.4	16:38									
2007-08	Toronto	NHL	59	8	13	21	0	5	0	1	57	14.0	-12	325	54.8	12:39									
2008-09	Vancouver	NHL	74	18	9	27	4	10	0	3	94	19.1	2	621	57.5	13:48	10	1	5	6	0	0	0	0	15:05
2009-10	Vancouver	NHL	75	14	11	25	12	3	0	2	98	14.3	6	725	53.8	13:52	12	2	5	7	0	1	0	0	15:44
2010-11	Mytischi	Rus-KHL	25	5	3	8	2																		
	San Jose	NHL	35	5	8	13	0	0	0	0	50	10.0	10	132	49.2	13:41	18	1	6	7	0	0	0	0	13:49
	NHL Totals		373	68	105	173	30	28	0	8	516	13.2		2700	55.3	13:45	40	4	16	20	0	1	0	0	14:43

OHL First All-Star Team (2001) • Canadian Major Junior Sportsman of the Year (2003)

Claimed on waivers by **Vancouver** from **Toronto**, June 25, 2008. Signed as a free agent by **Mytischi** (Russia-KHL), October 4, 2010. Signed as a free agent by **St. Louis**, January 17, 2011. Claimed on waivers by **San Jose** from **St. Louis**, January 18, 2011.

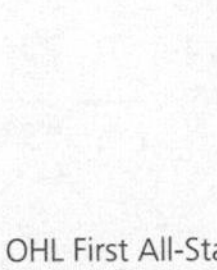

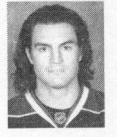

WESTGARTH, Kevin
(WEHST-garth, KEH-vihn) **L.A.**

Right wing. Shoots right. 6'4", 228 lbs. Born, Amherstburg, Ont., February 7, 1984.

Season	Club	League	GP	G	A	Pts	PIM	PP	SH	GW	S	%	+/-	TF	F%	Min	GP	G	A	Pts	PIM	PP	SH	GW	Min
2003-04	Princeton	ECAC	25	3	3	6	48																		
2004-05	Princeton	ECAC	29	4	3	7	36																		
2005-06	Princeton	ECAC	29	10	13	23	36																		
2006-07	Princeton	ECAC	33	8	16	24	40																		
	Manchester	AHL	14	1	2	3	44																		
2007-08	Manchester	AHL	69	6	6	12	191										4	0	0	0	6				
2008-09	Los Angeles	NHL	9	0	0	0	9	0	0	0	1	0.0	1	1	0.0	5:02									
	Manchester	AHL	65	4	6	10	165																		
2009-10	Manchester	AHL	76	11	14	25	180										6	1	0	1	10				
2010-11	Los Angeles	NHL	56	0	3	3	105	0	0	0	20	0.0	-6	4	50.0	5:26	6	0	2	2	14	0	0	0	6:15
	NHL Totals		65	0	3	3	114	0	0	0	21	0.0		5	40.0	5:23	6	0	2	2	14	0	0	0	6:15

Signed as a free agent by **Los Angeles**, March 16, 2007.

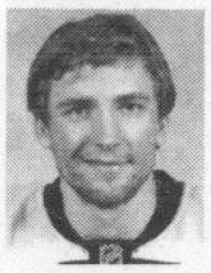

WHEELER, Blake

(WEE-luhr, BLAYK) **WPG**

Right wing. Shoots right. 6'5", 205 lbs. Born, Robbinsdale, MN, August 31, 1986. Phoenix's 1st choice, 5th overall, in 2004 Entry Draft.

			Regular Season														Playoffs								
Season	Club	League	GP	G	A	Pts	PIM	PP	SH	GW	S	%	+/-	TF	F%	Min	GP	G	A	Pts	PIM	PP	SH	GW	Min
2002-03	Breck Mustangs	High-MN	26	15	27	42																			
2003-04	Team Northwest	UMEHL	24	5	6	11																			
	Breck Mustangs	High-MN	27	39	50	89	34										3	6	5	11	0				
2004-05	Green Bay	USHL	58	19	28	47	43																		
2005-06	U. of Minnesota	WCHA	39	9	14	23	41																		
2006-07	U. of Minnesota	WCHA	44	18	20	38	42																		
2007-08	U. of Minnesota	WCHA	44	15	20	35	72																		
2008-09	**Boston**	**NHL**	**81**	**21**	**24**	**45**	**46**	**3**	**2**	**3**	**150**	**14.0**	**36**	**34**	**38.2**	**13:41**	**8**	**0**	**0**	**0**	**0**	**0**	**0**	**0**	**12:08**
2009-10	**Boston**	**NHL**	**82**	**18**	**20**	**38**	**53**	**3**	**1**	**2**	**159**	**11.3**	**–4**	**27**	**48.2**	**15:47**	**13**	**1**	**5**	**6**	**6**	**0**	**0**	**0**	**14:14**
2010-11	**Boston**	**NHL**	**58**	**11**	**16**	**27**	**32**	**0**	**0**	**2**	**101**	**10.9**	**8**	**136**	**38.2**	**15:12**									
	Atlanta	**NHL**	**23**	**7**	**10**	**17**	**14**	**0**	**0**	**0**	**78**	**9.0**	**2**	**12**	**0.0**	**18:53**									
	NHL Totals		**244**	**57**	**70**	**127**	**145**	**6**	**3**	**7**	**488**	**11.7**		**209**	**37.3**	**15:15**	**21**	**1**	**5**	**6**	**6**	**0**	**0**	**0**	**13:26**

USHL All-Rookie Team (2005)

Signed as a free agent by **Boston**, July 1, 2008. Traded to **Atlanta** by **Boston** with Mark Stuart for Rich Peverley and Boris Valabik, February 18, 2011. • Transferred to **Winnipeg** after **Atlanta** franchise relocated, June 21, 2011.

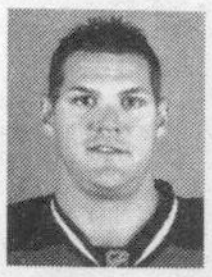

WHITE, Colin

(WIGHT, KAW-lihn) **S.J.**

Defense. Shoots left. 6'4", 215 lbs. Born, New Glasgow, N.S., December 12, 1977. New Jersey's 5th choice, 49th overall, in 1996 Entry Draft.

			Regular Season														Playoffs								
Season	Club	League	GP	G	A	Pts	PIM	PP	SH	GW	S	%	+/-	TF	F%	Min	GP	G	A	Pts	PIM	PP	SH	GW	Min
1994-95	Laval Titan	QMJHL	7	0	1	1	32																		
	Hull Olympiques	QMJHL	5	0	1	1	4										12	0	0	0	23				
1995-96	Hull Olympiques	QMJHL	62	2	8	10	303										18	0	4	4	42				
1996-97	Hull Olympiques	QMJHL	63	3	12	15	297										14	3	12	15	65				
1997-98	Albany River Rats	AHL	76	3	13	16	235										13	0	0	0	55				
1998-99	Albany River Rats	AHL	77	2	12	14	265										5	0	1	1	8				
99-2000♦	**New Jersey**	**NHL**	**21**	**2**	**1**	**3**	**40**	**0**	**0**	**1**	**29**	**6.9**	**3**	**0**	**0.0**	**14:45**	**23**	**1**	**5**	**6**	**18**	**0**	**0**	**1**	**14:25**
	Albany River Rats	AHL	52	5	21	26	176																		
2000-01	**New Jersey**	**NHL**	**82**	**1**	**19**	**20**	**155**	**0**	**0**	**1**	**114**	**0.9**	**32**	**0**	**0.0**	**19:06**	**25**	**0**	**3**	**3**	**42**	**0**	**0**	**0**	**16:45**
2001-02	**New Jersey**	**NHL**	**73**	**2**	**3**	**5**	**133**	**0**	**0**	**0**	**81**	**2.5**	**6**	**0**	**0.0**	**20:06**	**6**	**0**	**0**	**0**	**2**	**0**	**0**	**0**	**21:50**
2002-03♦	**New Jersey**	**NHL**	**72**	**5**	**8**	**13**	**98**	**0**	**0**	**1**	**81**	**6.2**	**19**	**0**	**0.0**	**19:41**	**24**	**0**	**5**	**5**	**29**	**0**	**0**	**0**	**22:02**
2003-04	**New Jersey**	**NHL**	**75**	**2**	**11**	**13**	**96**	**0**	**0**	**0**	**61**	**3.3**	**10**	**0**	**0.0**	**21:02**	**5**	**0**	**0**	**0**	**4**	**0**	**0**	**0**	**19:40**
2004-05			DID NOT PLAY																						
2005-06	**New Jersey**	**NHL**	**73**	**3**	**14**	**17**	**91**	**1**	**0**	**1**	**60**	**5.0**	**–2**	**0**	**0.0**	**21:48**	**4**	**0**	**0**	**0**	**4**	**0**	**0**	**0**	**17:39**
2006-07	**New Jersey**	**NHL**	**69**	**0**	**8**	**8**	**69**	**0**	**0**	**0**	**47**	**0.0**	**–8**	**0**	**0.0**	**22:28**	**7**	**0**	**0**	**0**	**6**	**0**	**0**	**0**	**21:16**
2007-08	**New Jersey**	**NHL**	**57**	**2**	**8**	**10**	**26**	**0**	**0**	**1**	**27**	**7.4**	**–5**	**0**	**0.0**	**19:40**	**5**	**0**	**0**	**0**	**6**	**0**	**0**	**0**	**20:27**
2008-09	**New Jersey**	**NHL**	**71**	**1**	**17**	**18**	**46**	**0**	**0**	**0**	**68**	**1.5**	**18**	**1**	**0.0**	**19:01**	**7**	**0**	**1**	**1**	**6**	**0**	**0**	**0**	**19:46**
2009-10	**New Jersey**	**NHL**	**81**	**2**	**10**	**12**	**46**	**0**	**0**	**0**	**47**	**4.3**	**8**	**0**	**0.0**	**20:04**	**5**	**1**	**0**	**1**	**8**	**0**	**0**	**0**	**18:56**
2010-11	**New Jersey**	**NHL**	**69**	**0**	**6**	**6**	**48**	**0**	**0**	**0**	**50**	**0.0**	**–2**	**0**	**0.0**	**18:51**									
	NHL Totals		**743**	**20**	**105**	**125**	**848**	**1**	**0**	**5**	**665**	**3.0**		**1**	**0.0**	**20:01**	**111**	**2**	**14**	**16**	**125**	**0**	**0**	**1**	**18:35**

QMJHL All-Rookie Team (1996) • NHL All-Rookie Team (2001)

Signed as a free agent by **San Jose**, August 3, 2011.

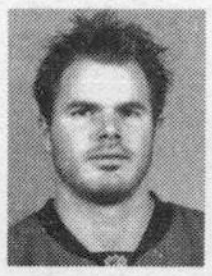

WHITE, Ian

(WIGHT, EE-an) **DET**

Defense. Shoots right. 5'10", 200 lbs. Born, Steinbach, Man., June 4, 1984. Toronto's 6th choice, 191st overall, in 2002 Entry Draft.

			Regular Season														Playoffs								
Season	Club	League	GP	G	A	Pts	PIM	PP	SH	GW	S	%	+/-	TF	F%	Min	GP	G	A	Pts	PIM	PP	SH	GW	Min
99-2000	Eastman Selects	MAHA	32	29	33	62	36																		
2000-01	Swift Current	WHL	69	12	31	43	24																		
2001-02	Swift Current	WHL	70	32	47	79	40										12	4	5	9	12				
2002-03	Swift Current	WHL	64	24	44	68	44										4	0	4	4	0				
2003-04	Swift Current	WHL	43	9	23	32	32										5	1	3	4	8				
	St. John's	AHL	8	0	4	4	2																		
2004-05	St. John's	AHL	78	4	22	26	54										5	0	2	2	2				
2005-06	**Toronto**	**NHL**	**12**	**1**	**5**	**6**	**10**	**0**	**0**	**0**	**21**	**4.8**	**2**	**0**	**0.0**	**19:07**									
	Toronto Marlies	AHL	59	7	30	37	42										5	1	4	5	4				
2006-07	**Toronto**	**NHL**	**76**	**3**	**23**	**26**	**40**	**1**	**0**	**1**	**138**	**2.2**	**8**	**0**	**0.0**	**18:32**									
2007-08	**Toronto**	**NHL**	**81**	**5**	**16**	**21**	**44**	**0**	**0**	**2**	**116**	**4.3**	**–9**	**0**	**0.0**	**18:48**									
2008-09	**Toronto**	**NHL**	**71**	**10**	**16**	**26**	**57**	**2**	**0**	**2**	**158**	**6.3**	**6**	**0**	**0.0**	**22:51**									
2009-10	**Toronto**	**NHL**	**56**	**9**	**17**	**26**	**39**	**2**	**0**	**1**	**130**	**6.9**	**1**	**0**	**0.0**	**23:47**									
	Calgary	**NHL**	**27**	**4**	**8**	**12**	**12**	**1**	**0**	**0**	**43**	**9.3**	**7**	**0**	**0.0**	**20:43**									
2010-11	**Calgary**	**NHL**	**16**	**2**	**4**	**6**	**6**	**1**	**0**	**0**	**34**	**5.9**	**–10**	**0**	**0.0**	**21:44**									
	Carolina	**NHL**	**39**	**0**	**10**	**10**	**12**	**0**	**0**	**0**	**53**	**0.0**	**4**	**0**	**0.0**	**19:19**									
	San Jose	**NHL**	**23**	**2**	**8**	**10**	**8**	**0**	**0**	**0**	**51**	**3.9**	**9**	**0**	**0.0**	**19:56**	**17**	**1**	**8**	**9**	**8**	**1**	**0**	**0**	**20:04**
	NHL Totals		**401**	**36**	**107**	**143**	**228**	**7**	**0**	**6**	**744**	**4.8**		**0**	**0.0**	**20:32**	**17**	**1**	**8**	**9**	**8**	**1**	**0**	**0**	**20:05**

WHL East Second All-Star Team (2002) • WHL East First All-Star Team (2003) • Canadian Major Junior Second All-Star Team (2003)

Traded to **Calgary** by **Toronto** with Matt Stajan, Niklas Hagman and Jamal Mayers for Dion Phaneuf, Fredrik Sjostrom and Keith Aulie, January 31, 2010. Traded to **Carolina** by **Calgary** with Brett Sutter for Anton Babchuk and Tom Kostopoulos, November 17, 2010. Traded to **San Jose** by **Carolina** for San Jose's 2nd round choice in 2012 Entry Draft, February 18, 2011. Signed as a free agent by **Detroit**, July 2, 2011.

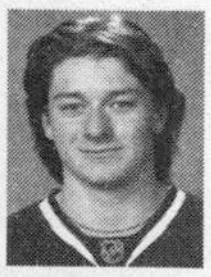

WHITE, Ryan

(WIGHT, RIGH-uhn) **MTL**

Center. Shoots right. 6', 193 lbs. Born, Brandon, Man., March 17, 1988. Montreal's 4th choice, 66th overall, in 2006 Entry Draft.

			Regular Season														Playoffs								
Season	Club	League	GP	G	A	Pts	PIM	PP	SH	GW	S	%	+/-	TF	F%	Min	GP	G	A	Pts	PIM	PP	SH	GW	Min
2003-04	Brandon	MMHL	39	21	41	62	90										11	7	7	14	22				
2004-05	Calgary Hitmen	WHL	63	9	14	23	95										12	2	1	3	26				
2005-06	Calgary Hitmen	WHL	72	20	33	53	121										13	3	4	7	18				
2006-07	Calgary Hitmen	WHL	72	34	55	89	97										18	6	8	14	36				
2007-08	Calgary Hitmen	WHL	68	28	44	72	98										16	6	11	17	8				
2008-09	Hamilton	AHL	80	11	18	29	68										6	3	1	4	9				
2009-10	**Montreal**	**NHL**	**16**	**0**	**2**	**2**	**16**	**0**	**0**	**0**	**5**	**0.0**	**–6**	**10**	**70.0**	**11:09**									
	Hamilton	AHL	62	17	17	34	173										19	4	5	9	47				
2010-11	**Montreal**	**NHL**	**27**	**2**	**3**	**5**	**38**	**0**	**0**	**0**	**30**	**6.7**	**5**	**32**	**40.6**	**8:55**	**7**	**0**	**0**	**0**	**2**	**0**	**0**	**0**	**6:35**
	Hamilton	AHL	33	3	9	12	77										13	2	6	8	37				
	NHL Totals		**43**	**2**	**5**	**7**	**54**	**0**	**0**	**0**	**35**	**5.7**		**42**	**47.6**	**9:45**	**7**	**0**	**0**	**0**	**2**	**0**	**0**	**0**	**6:35**

WHL East First All-Star Team (2007) • WHL East Second All-Star Team (2008)

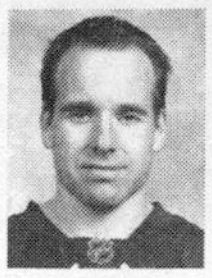

WHITE, Todd

(WIGHT, TAWD)

Center. Shoots left. 5'10", 198 lbs. Born, Kanata, Ont., May 21, 1975.

			Regular Season														Playoffs								
Season	Club	League	GP	G	A	Pts	PIM	PP	SH	GW	S	%	+/-	TF	F%	Min	GP	G	A	Pts	PIM	PP	SH	GW	Min
1991-92	Kanata Valley	CJHL	55	39	49	88	30																		
1992-93	Kanata Valley	CJHL	49	51	87	138	46																		
1993-94	Clarkson Knights	ECAC	33	10	12	22	28																		
1994-95	Clarkson Knights	ECAC	34	13	16	29	44																		
1995-96	Clarkson Knights	ECAC	38	29	43	72	36																		
1996-97	Clarkson Knights	ECAC	37	*38	*36	*74	22																		
1997-98	**Chicago**	**NHL**	**7**	**1**	**0**	**1**	**2**	**0**	**0**	**0**	**3**	**33.3**	**0**												
	Indianapolis Ice	IHL	65	46	36	82	28										5	2	3	5	4				
1998-99	**Chicago**	**NHL**	**35**	**5**	**8**	**13**	**20**	**2**	**0**	**0**	**43**	**11.6**	**–1**	**452**	**46.0**	**13:39**									
	Chicago Wolves	IHL	25	11	13	24	8										10	1	4	5	8				
99-2000	**Chicago**	**NHL**	**1**	**0**	**0**	**0**	**0**	**0**	**0**	**0**	**0**	**0.0**	**0**	**9**	**55.6**	**13:02**									
	Cleveland	IHL	42	21	30	51	32																		
	Philadelphia	**NHL**	**3**	**1**	**0**	**1**	**0**	**0**	**0**	**0**	**4**	**25.0**	**–1**	**25**	**40.0**	**10:29**									
	Philadelphia	AHL	32	19	24	43	12										5	2	1	3	8				
2000-01	**Ottawa**	**NHL**	**16**	**4**	**1**	**5**	**4**	**0**	**0**	**0**	**12**	**33.3**	**5**	**133**	**57.1**	**8:33**	**2**	**0**	**0**	**0**	**0**	**0**	**0**	**0**	**7:29**
	Grand Rapids	IHL	64	22	32	54	20										10	4	4	8	10				
2001-02	**Ottawa**	**NHL**	**81**	**20**	**30**	**50**	**24**	**4**	**0**	**1**	**147**	**13.6**	**12**	**1508**	**50.5**	**18:22**	**12**	**2**	**2**	**4**	**6**	**0**	**0**	**0**	**18:57**
2002-03	**Ottawa**	**NHL**	**80**	**25**	**35**	**60**	**28**	**8**	**1**	**5**	**144**	**17.4**	**19**	**1396**	**50.5**	**17:58**	**18**	**5**	**1**	**6**	**6**	**1**	**1**	**2**	**16:59**
2003-04	**Ottawa**	**NHL**	**53**	**9**	**20**	**29**	**22**	**1**	**1**	**2**	**98**	**9.2**	**12**	**879**	**52.0**	**17:32**	**7**	**1**	**0**	**1**	**4**	**0**	**0**	**0**	**18:04**

			Regular Season														Playoffs								
Season	Club	League	GP	G	A	Pts	PIM	PP	SH	GW	S	%	+/-	TF	F%	Min	GP	G	A	Pts	PIM	PP	SH	GW	Min
2004-05	Sodertalje SK	Sweden	1	0	1	1	4	....	....	....	....	....	....	....	....	....	....	....	....	....	....	....	....	....	....
2005-06	**Minnesota**	**NHL**	**61**	**19**	**21**	**40**	**18**	**5**	**0**	**0**	**109**	**17.4**	**–1**	**886**	**49.1**	**17:12**	....	....	....	....	....	....	....	....	....
2006-07	**Minnesota**	**NHL**	**77**	**13**	**31**	**44**	**24**	**6**	**1**	**1**	**162**	**8.0**	**8**	**1051**	**49.2**	**17:13**	**4**	**0**	**0**	**0**	**0**	**0**	**0**	**0**	**14:18**
2007-08	**Atlanta**	**NHL**	**74**	**14**	**23**	**37**	**36**	**6**	**1**	**4**	**111**	**12.6**	**–12**	**1166**	**46.6**	**18:26**	....	....	....	....	....	....	....	....	....
2008-09	**Atlanta**	**NHL**	**82**	**22**	**51**	**73**	**24**	**12**	**1**	**0**	**150**	**14.7**	**–9**	**1329**	**50.6**	**18:04**	....	....	....	....	....	....	....	....	....
2009-10	**Atlanta**	**NHL**	**65**	**7**	**19**	**26**	**24**	**2**	**0**	**3**	**92**	**7.6**	**–11**	**745**	**53.8**	**15:15**	....	....	....	....	....	....	....	....	....
2010-11	**NY Rangers**	**NHL**	**18**	**1**	**1**	**2**	**2**	**0**	**0**	**0**	**11**	**9.1**	**–2**	**56**	**53.6**	**7:41**	....	....	....	....	....	....	....	....	....
	Connecticut	AHL	9	3	2	5	0	....	....	....	....	....	....	....	....	....	....	....	....	....	....	....	....	....	....
	NHL Totals		**653**	**141**	**240**	**381**	**228**	**46**	**5**	**16**	**1086**	**13.0**		**9635**	**50.0**	**16:49**	**43**	**8**	**3**	**11**	**16**	**1**	**1**	**2**	**17:01**

ECAC Second All-Star Team (1996) • NCAA East Second All-American Team (1996) • ECAC First All-Star Team (1997) • ECAC Player of the Year (1997) • NCAA East First All-American Team (1997) • Garry F. Longman Memorial Trophy (IHL – Rookie of the Year) (1998)

Signed as a free agent by **Chicago**, August 27, 1997. Traded to **Philadelphia** by **Chicago** for future considerations, January 26, 2000. Signed as a free agent by **Ottawa**, July 12, 2000. Signed as a free agent by **Sodertalje** (Sweden), December 21, 2004. Traded to **Minnesota** by **Ottawa** for Colorado's 4th round choice (previously acquired, Ottawa selected Cody Bass) in 2005 Entry Draft, July 30, 2005. Signed as a free agent by **Atlanta**, July 1, 2007. Traded to **NY Rangers** by **Atlanta** for Donald Brashear and Patrick Rissmiller, August 2, 2010. • Missed majority of 2010-11 as a healthy reserve.

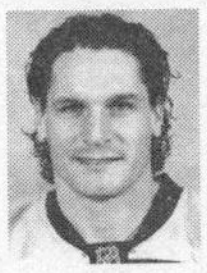

WHITFIELD, Trent

(WHIHT-feeld, TREHNT) **BOS**

Center. Shoots left. 5'11", 209 lbs. Born, Estevan, Sask., June 17, 1977. Boston's 5th choice, 100th overall, in 1996 Entry Draft.

Season	Club	League	GP	G	A	Pts	PIM	PP	SH	GW	S	%	+/-	TF	F%	Min	GP	G	A	Pts	PIM	PP	SH	GW	Min
1993-94	Saskatoon Blazers	SMHL	36	26	22	48	42	....	....	....	....	....	....	....	....	....	....	....	....	....	....	....	....	....	....
	Spokane Chiefs	WHL	5	1	1	2	0	....	....	....	....	....	....	....	....	....	....	....	....	....	....	....	....	....	....
1994-95	Spokane Chiefs	WHL	48	8	17	25	26	....	....	....	....	....	....	....	....	....	11	7	6	13	5	....	....	....	....
1995-96	Spokane Chiefs	WHL	72	33	51	84	75	....	....	....	....	....	....	....	....	....	18	8	10	18	10	....	....	....	....
1996-97	Spokane Chiefs	WHL	58	34	42	76	74	....	....	....	....	....	....	....	....	....	9	5	7	12	10	....	....	....	....
1997-98	Spokane Chiefs	WHL	65	38	44	82	97	....	....	....	....	....	....	....	....	....	18	9	10	19	15	....	....	....	....
1998-99	Portland Pirates	AHL	50	10	8	18	20	....	....	....	....	....	....	....	....	....	....	....	....	....	....	....	....	....	....
	Hampton Roads	ECHL	19	13	12	25	12	....	....	....	....	....	....	....	....	....	4	2	0	2	14	....	....	....	....
99-2000	Portland Pirates	AHL	79	18	35	53	52	....	....	....	....	....	....	....	....	....	3	1	1	2	2	....	....	....	....
	Washington	**NHL**	....	....	....	....	....	....	....	....	....	....	....	....	....	....	**3**	**0**	**0**	**0**	**0**	**0**	**0**	**0**	**5:47**
2000-01	**Washington**	**NHL**	**61**	**2**	**4**	**6**	**35**	**0**	**0**	**0**	**47**	**4.3**	**3**	**520**	**51.9**	**9:39**	**5**	**0**	**0**	**0**	**2**	**0**	**0**	**0**	**7:07**
	Portland Pirates	AHL	19	9	11	20	27	....	....	....	....	....	....	....	....	....	....	....	....	....	....	....	....	....	....
2001-02	**Washington**	**NHL**	**24**	**0**	**1**	**1**	**28**	**0**	**0**	**0**	**15**	**0.0**	**–3**	**189**	**54.0**	**7:06**	....	....	....	....	....	....	....	....	....
	Portland Pirates	AHL	10	4	4	8	8	....	....	....	....	....	....	....	....	....	....	....	....	....	....	....	....	....	....
	NY Rangers	**NHL**	**1**	**0**	**0**	**0**	**0**	**0**	**0**	**0**	**0**	**0.0**	**1**	**18**	**50.0**	**12:44**	....	....	....	....	....	....	....	....	....
	Portland Pirates	AHL	24	10	16	26	16	....	....	....	....	....	....	....	....	....	....	....	....	....	....	....	....	....	....
2002-03	**Washington**	**NHL**	**14**	**1**	**1**	**2**	**6**	**0**	**0**	**1**	**4**	**25.0**	**1**	**124**	**57.3**	**8:30**	**6**	**0**	**0**	**0**	**10**	**0**	**0**	**0**	**11:01**
	Portland Pirates	AHL	64	27	34	61	42	....	....	....	....	....	....	....	....	....	....	....	....	....	....	....	....	....	....
2003-04	**Washington**	**NHL**	**44**	**6**	**5**	**11**	**14**	**0**	**1**	**2**	**38**	**15.8**	**–2**	**598**	**55.4**	**12:48**	....	....	....	....	....	....	....	....	....
	Portland Pirates	AHL	24	8	7	15	22	....	....	....	....	....	....	....	....	....	....	....	....	....	....	....	....	....	....
2004-05	Portland Pirates	AHL	67	17	38	55	75	....	....	....	....	....	....	....	....	....	....	....	....	....	....	....	....	....	....
2005-06	**St. Louis**	**NHL**	**30**	**2**	**5**	**7**	**14**	**1**	**0**	**0**	**41**	**4.9**	**–3**	**330**	**54.6**	**11:56**	....	....	....	....	....	....	....	....	....
	Peoria Rivermen	AHL	41	19	34	53	18	....	....	....	....	....	....	....	....	....	....	....	....	....	....	....	....	....	....
2006-07	Peoria Rivermen	AHL	79	33	45	78	70	....	....	....	....	....	....	....	....	....	....	....	....	....	....	....	....	....	....
2007-08	Peoria Rivermen	AHL	80	22	30	52	51	....	....	....	....	....	....	....	....	....	....	....	....	....	....	....	....	....	....
2008-09	**St. Louis**	**NHL**	**3**	**0**	**1**	**1**	**0**	**0**	**0**	**0**	**4**	**0.0**	**2**	**26**	**73.1**	**11:03**	....	....	....	....	....	....	....	....	....
	Peoria Rivermen	AHL	69	20	30	50	37	....	....	....	....	....	....	....	....	....	7	2	1	3	0	....	....	....	....
2009-10	**Boston**	**NHL**	**16**	**0**	**1**	**1**	**7**	**0**	**0**	**0**	**15**	**0.0**	**–2**	**178**	**57.9**	**11:03**	**4**	**0**	**0**	**0**	**0**	**0**	**0**	**0**	**8:32**
	Providence Bruins	AHL	52	17	26	43	22	....	....	....	....	....	....	....	....	....	....	....	....	....	....	....	....	....	....
2010-11	Providence Bruins	AHL	45	18	18	36	42	....	....	....	....	....	....	....	....	....	....	....	....	....	....	....	....	....	....
	NHL Totals		**193**	**11**	**18**	**29**	**104**	**1**	**1**	**3**	**164**	**6.7**		**1983**	**54.7**	**10:28**	**18**	**0**	**0**	**0**	**12**	**0**	**0**	**0**	**8:31**

WHL West First All-Star Team (1997) • WHL West Second All-Star Team (1998)

Signed as a free agent by **Washington**, September 1, 1998. Claimed on waivers by **NY Rangers** from **Washington**, January 16, 2002. Claimed on waivers by **Washington** from **NY Rangers**, February 1, 2002. Signed as a free agent by **St. Louis**, August 2, 2005. Signed as a free agent by **Boston**, July 13, 2009.

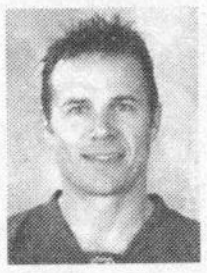

WHITNEY, Ray

(WHIHT-nee, RAY) **PHX**

Left wing. Shoots right. 5'10", 180 lbs. Born, Fort Saskatchewan, Alta., May 8, 1972. San Jose's 2nd choice, 23rd overall, in 1991 Entry Draft.

Season	Club	League	GP	G	A	Pts	PIM	PP	SH	GW	S	%	+/-	TF	F%	Min	GP	G	A	Pts	PIM	PP	SH	GW	Min
1987-88	Ft. Saskatchewan	AMHL	71	80	155	235	119	....	....	....	....	....	....	....	....	....	....	....	....	....	....	....	....	....	....
1988-89	Spokane Chiefs	WHL	71	17	33	50	16	....	....	....	....	....	....	....	....	....	....	....	....	....	....	....	....	....	....
1989-90	Spokane Chiefs	WHL	71	57	56	113	50	....	....	....	....	....	....	....	....	....	6	3	4	7	6	....	....	....	....
1990-91	Spokane Chiefs	WHL	72	67	118	*185	36	....	....	....	....	....	....	....	....	....	15	13	18	*31	12	....	....	....	....
1991-92	Kolner EC	Germany	10	3	6	9	4	....	....	....	....	....	....	....	....	....	....	....	....	....	....	....	....	....	....
	Canada	Nat-Tm	5	1	0	1	6	....	....	....	....	....	....	....	....	....	....	....	....	....	....	....	....	....	....
	San Jose	**NHL**	**2**	**0**	**3**	**3**	**0**	**0**	**0**	**0**	**4**	**0.0**	**–1**	....	....	....	....	....	....	....	....	....	....	....	....
	San Diego Gulls	IHL	63	36	54	90	12	....	....	....	....	....	....	....	....	....	4	0	0	0	0	....	....	....	....
1992-93	**San Jose**	**NHL**	**26**	**4**	**6**	**10**	**4**	**1**	**0**	**0**	**24**	**16.7**	**–14**	....	....	....	....	....	....	....	....	....	....	....	....
	Kansas City	IHL	46	20	33	53	14	....	....	....	....	....	....	....	....	....	12	5	7	12	2	....	....	....	....
1993-94	**San Jose**	**NHL**	**61**	**14**	**26**	**40**	**14**	**1**	**0**	**0**	**82**	**17.1**	**2**	....	....	....	**14**	**0**	**4**	**4**	**8**	**0**	**0**	**0**	....
1994-95	**San Jose**	**NHL**	**39**	**13**	**12**	**25**	**14**	**4**	**0**	**1**	**67**	**19.4**	**–7**	....	....	....	**11**	**4**	**4**	**8**	**2**	**0**	**0**	**1**	....
1995-96	**San Jose**	**NHL**	**60**	**17**	**24**	**41**	**16**	**4**	**2**	**2**	**106**	**16.0**	**–23**	....	....	....	....	....	....	....	....	....	....	....	....
1996-97	**San Jose**	**NHL**	**12**	**0**	**2**	**2**	**4**	**0**	**0**	**0**	**24**	**0.0**	**–6**	....	....	....	....	....	....	....	....	....	....	....	....
	Kentucky	AHL	9	1	7	8	2	....	....	....	....	....	....	....	....	....	....	....	....	....	....	....	....	....	....
	Utah Grizzlies	IHL	43	13	35	48	34	....	....	....	....	....	....	....	....	....	7	3	1	4	6	....	....	....	....
1997-98	**Edmonton**	**NHL**	**9**	**1**	**3**	**4**	**0**	**0**	**0**	**0**	**19**	**5.3**	**–1**	....	....	....	....	....	....	....	....	....	....	....	....
	Florida	**NHL**	**68**	**32**	**29**	**61**	**28**	**12**	**0**	**2**	**156**	**20.5**	**10**	....	....	....	....	....	....	....	....	....	....	....	....
1998-99	**Florida**	**NHL**	**81**	**26**	**38**	**64**	**18**	**7**	**0**	**6**	**193**	**13.5**	**–3**	**144**	**43.8**	**18:20**	....	....	....	....	....	....	....	....	....
99-2000	**Florida**	**NHL**	**81**	**29**	**42**	**71**	**35**	**5**	**0**	**3**	**198**	**14.6**	**16**	**198**	**49.0**	**18:41**	**4**	**1**	**0**	**1**	**4**	**0**	**0**	**0**	**18:13**
2000-01	**Florida**	**NHL**	**43**	**10**	**21**	**31**	**28**	**5**	**0**	**0**	**117**	**8.5**	**–16**	**38**	**39.5**	**17:41**	....	....	....	....	....	....	....	....	....
	Columbus	**NHL**	**3**	**0**	**3**	**3**	**2**	**0**	**0**	**0**	**3**	**0.0**	**–1**	**19**	**36.8**	**20:17**	....	....	....	....	....	....	....	....	....
2001-02	**Columbus**	**NHL**	**67**	**21**	**40**	**61**	**12**	**6**	**0**	**3**	**210**	**10.0**	**–22**	**21**	**47.6**	**20:13**	....	....	....	....	....	....	....	....	....
2002-03	**Columbus**	**NHL**	**81**	**24**	**52**	**76**	**22**	**8**	**2**	**2**	**235**	**10.2**	**–26**	**29**	**44.8**	**21:00**	....	....	....	....	....	....	....	....	....
2003-04	**Detroit**	**NHL**	**67**	**14**	**29**	**43**	**22**	**3**	**1**	**4**	**119**	**11.8**	**7**	**18**	**38.9**	**16:24**	**12**	**1**	**3**	**4**	**4**	**0**	**0**	**1**	**11:56**
2004-05			DID NOT PLAY																						
2005-06♦	**Carolina**	**NHL**	**63**	**17**	**38**	**55**	**42**	**12**	**0**	**2**	**147**	**11.6**	**0**	**13**	**38.5**	**17:11**	**24**	**9**	**6**	**15**	**14**	**5**	**0**	**1**	**14:07**
2006-07	**Carolina**	**NHL**	**81**	**32**	**51**	**83**	**46**	**6**	**0**	**6**	**215**	**14.9**	**–5**	**7**	**28.6**	**18:42**	....	....	....	....	....	....	....	....	....
2007-08	**Carolina**	**NHL**	**66**	**25**	**36**	**61**	**30**	**6**	**0**	**4**	**204**	**12.3**	**–6**	**5**	**60.0**	**18:56**	....	....	....	....	....	....	....	....	....
2008-09	**Carolina**	**NHL**	**82**	**24**	**53**	**77**	**32**	**7**	**0**	**2**	**219**	**11.0**	**2**	**4**	**50.0**	**18:25**	**18**	**3**	**8**	**11**	**4**	**0**	**0**	**1**	**18:36**
2009-10	**Carolina**	**NHL**	**80**	**21**	**37**	**58**	**26**	**7**	**0**	**5**	**171**	**12.3**	**–6**	**9**	**33.3**	**19:09**	....	....	....	....	....	....	....	....	....
2010-11	**Phoenix**	**NHL**	**75**	**17**	**40**	**57**	**24**	**3**	**0**	**1**	**156**	**10.9**	**0**	**100**	**45.0**	**16:57**	**4**	**1**	**2**	**3**	**2**	**1**	**0**	**0**	**19:24**
	NHL Totals		**1147**	**341**	**585**	**926**	**419**	**97**	**5**	**43**	**2669**	**12.8**		**605**	**45.0**	**18:33**	**87**	**19**	**27**	**46**	**38**	**6**	**0**	**4**	**15:36**

WHL West First All-Star Team (1991) • WHL Player of the Year (1991) • Memorial Cup All-Star Team (1991) • George Parsons Trophy (Memorial Cup - Most Sportsmanlike Player) (1991)

Played in NHL All-Star Game (2000, 2003)

Signed as a free agent by **Edmonton**, October 1, 1997. Claimed on waivers by **Florida** from **Edmonton**, November 6, 1997. Traded to **Columbus** by **Florida** with future considerations for Kevyn Adams and Columbus's 4th round choice (Michael Woodford) in 2001 Entry Draft, March 13, 2001. Signed as a free agent by **Detroit**, July 30, 2003. Signed as a free agent by **Carolina**, August 7, 2005. Signed as a free agent by **Phoenix**, July 1, 2010.

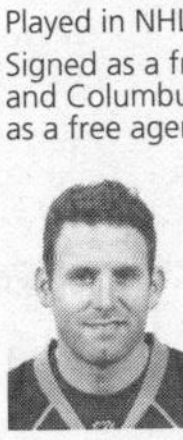

WHITNEY, Ryan

(WHIHT-nee, RIGH-uhn) **EDM**

Defense. Shoots left. 6'3", 210 lbs. Born, Boston, MA, February 19, 1983. Pittsburgh's 1st choice, 5th overall, in 2002 Entry Draft.

Season	Club	League	GP	G	A	Pts	PIM	PP	SH	GW	S	%	+/-	TF	F%	Min	GP	G	A	Pts	PIM	PP	SH	GW	Min
99-2000	Thayer Academy	High-MA	22	5	33	38	....	....	....	....	....	....	....	....	....	....	....	....	....	....	....	....	....	....	....
2000-01	USNTDP	U-18	40	7	23	30	64	....	....	....	....	....	....	....	....	....	....	....	....	....	....	....	....	....	....
	USNTDP	USHL	20	2	8	10	22	....	....	....	....	....	....	....	....	....	....	....	....	....	....	....	....	....	....
2001-02	Boston University	H-East	35	4	17	21	46	....	....	....	....	....	....	....	....	....	....	....	....	....	....	....	....	....	....
2002-03	Boston University	H-East	34	3	10	13	48	....	....	....	....	....	....	....	....	....	....	....	....	....	....	....	....	....	....
2003-04	Boston University	H-East	38	9	16	25	56	....	....	....	....	....	....	....	....	....	....	....	....	....	....	....	....	....	....
	Wilkes-Barre	AHL	....	....	....	....	....	....	....	....	....	....	....	....	....	....	20	1	9	10	6	....	....	....	....
2004-05	Wilkes-Barre	AHL	80	6	35	41	101	....	....	....	....	....	....	....	....	....	11	2	7	9	12	....	....	....	....
2005-06	**Pittsburgh**	**NHL**	**68**	**6**	**32**	**38**	**85**	**2**	**0**	**1**	**113**	**5.3**	**–7**	**1**	**0.0**	**23:50**	....	....	....	....	....	....	....	....	....
	Wilkes-Barre	AHL	9	5	9	14	6	....	....	....	....	....	....	....	....	....	11	1	4	5	8	....	....	....	....
2006-07	**Pittsburgh**	**NHL**	**81**	**14**	**45**	**59**	**77**	**9**	**0**	**2**	**129**	**10.9**	**9**	**5**	**20.0**	**23:56**	**5**	**1**	**1**	**2**	**6**	**1**	**0**	**0**	**22:51**
2007-08	**Pittsburgh**	**NHL**	**76**	**12**	**28**	**40**	**45**	**7**	**1**	**1**	**119**	**10.1**	**–2**	**0**	**0.0**	**22:27**	**20**	**1**	**5**	**6**	**25**	**1**	**0**	**0**	**20:46**

			Regular Season														Playoffs								
Season	Club	League	GP	G	A	Pts	PIM	PP	SH	GW	S	%	+/-	TF	F%	Min	GP	G	A	Pts	PIM	PP	SH	GW	Min
2008-09	Pittsburgh	NHL	28	2	11	13	16	1	0	0	42	4.8	–15	0	0.0	24:34	....	....	....	....	....	....	....	....	....
	Wilkes-Barre	AHL	1	0	1	1	2	....	....	....	....	....	....	....	....	....	....	....	....	....	....	....	....	....	....
	Anaheim	NHL	20	0	10	10	12	0	0	0	29	0.0	1	0	0.0	22:53	13	1	5	6	9	1	0	0	21:34
2009-10	Anaheim	NHL	62	4	24	28	48	3	0	0	107	3.7	–6	1	0.0	24:34	....	....	....	....	....	....	....	....	....
	United States	Olympics	6	0	0	0	0	....	....	....	....	....	....	....	....	....	....	....	....	....	....	....	....	....	....
	Edmonton	NHL	19	3	8	11	22	0	0	1	44	6.8	7	0	0.0	25:23	....	....	....	....	....	....	....	....	....
2010-11	Edmonton	NHL	35	2	25	27	33	0	0	0	43	4.7	13	0	0.0	25:20	....	....	....	....	....	....	....	....	....
	NHL Totals		389	43	183	226	338	22	1	5	626	6.9		7	14.3	23:55	38	3	11	14	40	3	0	0	21:19

Hockey East All-Rookie Team (2002)

Traded to **Anaheim** by **Pittsburgh** for Chris Kunitz and Eric Tangradi, February 26, 2009. Traded to **Edmonton** by **Anaheim** with Anaheim's 6th round choice (Brandon Davidson) in 2010 Entry Draft for Lubomir Visnovsky, March 3, 2010. • Missed majority of 2010-11 due to ankle injury vs. Buffalo, December 28, 2010.

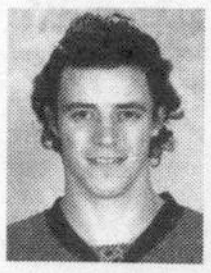

WICK, Roman

(WIHK, ROH-muhn) **OTT**

Right wing. Shoots left. 6'2", 192 lbs. Born, Kloten, Switz., December 30, 1985. Ottawa's 8th choice, 156th overall, in 2004 Entry Draft.

Season	Club	League	GP	G	A	Pts	PIM	PP	SH	GW	S	%	+/-	TF	F%	Min	GP	G	A	Pts	PIM	PP	SH	GW	Min
2000-01	Kloten Flyers Jr.	Swiss-Jr.	26	4	1	5	6	....	....	....	....	....	....	....	....	....	5	1	0	1	2	....	....	....	....
2001-02	Kloten Flyers Jr.	Swiss-Jr.	34	19	27	46	32	....	....	....	....	....	....	....	....	....	8	1	2	3	4	....	....	....	....
2002-03	Kloten Flyers Jr.	Swiss-Jr.	28	29	22	51	68	....	....	....	....	....	....	....	....	....	2	0	1	1	0	....	....	....	....
	Kloten Flyers	Swiss	9	1	0	1	4	....	....	....	....	....	....	....	....	....	1	0	0	0	0	....	....	....	....
2003-04	Kloten Flyers	Swiss	20	1	1	2	6	....	....	....	....	....	....	....	....	....	....	....	....	....	....	....	....	....	....
	Kloten Flyers	Swiss-Q	7	3	1	4	0	....	....	....	....	....	....	....	....	....	....	....	....	....	....	....	....	....	....
	GCK Lions Zurich	Swiss-2	6	4	0	4	6	....	....	....	....	....	....	....	....	....	....	....	....	....	....	....	....	....	....
2004-05	Red Deer Rebels	WHL	66	32	38	70	25	....	....	....	....	....	....	....	....	....	7	1	2	3	6	....	....	....	....
2005-06	Red Deer Rebels	WHL	23	7	10	17	8	....	....	....	....	....	....	....	....	....	....	....	....	....	....	....	....	....	....
	Lethbridge	WHL	38	14	17	31	20	....	....	....	....	....	....	....	....	....	6	4	3	7	6	....	....	....	....
2006-07	Kloten Flyers	Swiss	44	12	11	23	20	....	....	....	....	....	....	....	....	....	11	1	1	2	2	....	....	....	....
2007-08	Kloten Flyers	Swiss	50	12	15	27	46	....	....	....	....	....	....	....	....	....	4	1	2	3	2	....	....	....	....
2008-09	Kloten Flyers	Swiss	45	24	13	37	38	....	....	....	....	....	....	....	....	....	15	5	*10	*15	12	....	....	....	....
2009-10	Kloten Flyers	Swiss	37	15	16	31	8	....	....	....	....	....	....	....	....	....	10	4	6	10	8	....	....	....	....
	Switzerland	Olympics	5	2	3	5	2	....	....	....	....	....	....	....	....	....	....	....	....	....	....	....	....	....	....
2010-11	Ottawa	NHL	7	0	0	0	0	0	0	0	4	0.0	–4	3	33.3	8:38	....	....	....	....	....	....	....	....	....
	Binghamton	AHL	70	20	22	42	28	....	....	....	....	....	....	....	....	....	21	4	5	9	6	....	....	....	....
	NHL Totals		7	0	0	0	0	0	0	0	4	0.0		3	33.3	8:38	....	....	....	....	....	....	....	....	....

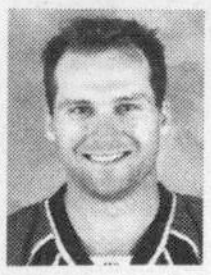

WIDEMAN, Dennis

(WIGHD-muhn, DEH-nihs) **WSH**

Defense. Shoots right. 6', 196 lbs. Born, Kitchener, Ont., March 20, 1983. Buffalo's 9th choice, 241st overall, in 2002 Entry Draft.

Season	Club	League	GP	G	A	Pts	PIM	PP	SH	GW	S	%	+/-	TF	F%	Min	GP	G	A	Pts	PIM	PP	SH	GW	Min
1998-99	Elmira	ON-Jr.B	47	18	30	48	142	....	....	....	....	....	....	....	....	....	....	....	....	....	....	....	....	....	....
99-2000	Sudbury Wolves	OHL	63	10	26	36	64	....	....	....	....	....	....	....	....	....	12	1	2	3	22	....	....	....	....
2000-01	Sudbury Wolves	OHL	25	7	11	18	37	....	....	....	....	....	....	....	....	....	....	....	....	....	....	....	....	....	....
	London Knights	OHL	24	8	8	16	38	....	....	....	....	....	....	....	....	....	5	0	4	4	6	....	....	....	....
2001-02	London Knights	OHL	65	27	42	69	141	....	....	....	....	....	....	....	....	....	12	4	9	13	26	....	....	....	....
2002-03	London Knights	OHL	55	20	27	47	83	....	....	....	....	....	....	....	....	....	14	6	6	12	10	....	....	....	....
2003-04	London Knights	OHL	60	24	41	65	85	....	....	....	....	....	....	....	....	....	15	7	10	17	17	....	....	....	....
2004-05	Worcester IceCats	AHL	79	13	30	43	65	....	....	....	....	....	....	....	....	....	....	....	....	....	....	....	....	....	....
2005-06	St. Louis	NHL	67	8	16	24	83	5	1	1	150	5.3	–31	1	0.0	21:41	....	....	....	....	....	....	....	....	....
	Peoria Rivermen	AHL	12	2	4	6	31	....	....	....	....	....	....	....	....	....	....	....	....	....	....	....	....	....	....
2006-07	St. Louis	NHL	55	5	17	22	44	4	0	1	94	5.3	–7	0	0.0	20:12	....	....	....	....	....	....	....	....	....
	Boston	NHL	20	1	2	3	27	0	0	0	28	3.6	–3	1	0.0	17:20	....	....	....	....	....	....	....	....	....
2007-08	Boston	NHL	81	13	23	36	70	9	0	1	171	7.6	11	0	0.0	25:09	6	0	3	3	0	0	0	0	24:21
2008-09	Boston	NHL	79	13	37	50	34	6	1	2	169	7.7	32	0	0.0	24:39	11	0	7	7	4	0	0	0	24:42
2009-10	Boston	NHL	76	6	24	30	34	2	0	2	146	4.1	–14	0	0.0	23:33	13	1	11	12	4	0	0	0	26:02
2010-11	Florida	NHL	61	9	24	33	33	8	0	1	135	6.7	–26	1	100.0	23:58	....	....	....	....	....	....	....	....	....
	Washington	NHL	14	1	6	7	6	1	0	0	25	4.0	7	0	0.0	24:05	....	....	....	....	....	....	....	....	....
	NHL Totals		453	56	149	205	331	35	2	8	918	6.1		3	33.3	23:09	30	1	21	22	8	0	0	0	25:13

OHL First All-Star Team (2004) • Canadian Major Junior Second All-Star Team (2004)

Signed as a free agent by **St. Louis**, June 30, 2004. Traded to **Boston** by **St. Louis** for Brad Boyes, February 27, 2007. Traded to **Florida** by **Boston** with Boston's 1st round choice (later traded to Los Angeles – Los Angeles selected Derek Forbert) in 2010 Entry Draft and Boston's 3rd round choice (Kyle Rau) in 2011 Entry Draft for Nathan Horton and Gregory Campbell, June 22, 2010. Traded to **Washington** by **Florida** for Jake Hauswirth and Washington's 3rd round choice (Jonathan Racine) in 2011 Entry Draft, February 28, 2011.

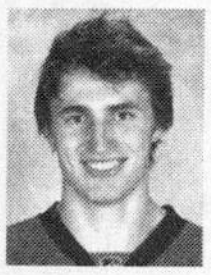

WIERCIOCH, Patrick

(WEER-kawsh, PAT-rihk) **OTT**

Defense. Shoots left. 6'4", 200 lbs. Born, Burnaby, B.C., September 12, 1990. Ottawa's 2nd choice, 42nd overall, in 2008 Entry Draft.

Season	Club	League	GP	G	A	Pts	PIM	PP	SH	GW	S	%	+/-	TF	F%	Min	GP	G	A	Pts	PIM	PP	SH	GW	Min
2006-07	Burnaby Express	BCHL	42	9	16	25	46	....	....	....	....	....	....	....	....	....	14	3	4	7	10	....	....	....	....
2007-08	Omaha Lancers	USHL	40	3	18	21	24	....	....	....	....	....	....	....	....	....	14	2	9	11	22	....	....	....	....
2008-09	U. of Denver	WCHA	36	12	23	35	26	....	....	....	....	....	....	....	....	....	....	....	....	....	....	....	....	....	....
2009-10	U. of Denver	WCHA	39	6	21	27	34	....	....	....	....	....	....	....	....	....	....	....	....	....	....	....	....	....	....
2010-11	Ottawa	NHL	8	0	2	2	4	0	0	0	3	0.0	0	0	0.0	13:54	....	....	....	....	....	....	....	....	....
	Binghamton	AHL	67	4	14	18	25	....	....	....	....	....	....	....	....	....	15	0	1	1	0	....	....	....	....
	NHL Totals		8	0	2	2	4	0	0	0	3	0.0		0	0.0	13:54	....	....	....	....	....	....	....	....	....

WCHA All-Rookie Team (2009) • WCHA Second All-Star Team (2009) • WCHA First All-Star Team (2010) • NCAA West First All-American Team (2010)

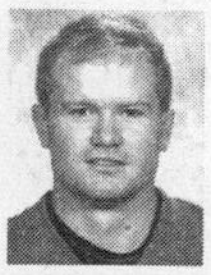

WILLIAMS, Jason

(WIHL-yuhms, JAY-suhn) **PIT**

Center. Shoots right. 5'11", 192 lbs. Born, London, Ont., August 11, 1980.

Season	Club	League	GP	G	A	Pts	PIM	PP	SH	GW	S	%	+/-	TF	F%	Min	GP	G	A	Pts	PIM	PP	SH	GW	Min
1995-96	Mount Brydges	ON-Jr.D	36	31	28	59	18	....	....	....	....	....	....	....	....	....	....	....	....	....	....	....	....	....	....
1996-97	Peterborough	OHL	60	4	8	12	8	....	....	....	....	....	....	....	....	....	10	1	0	1	2	....	....	....	....
1997-98	Peterborough	OHL	55	8	27	35	31	....	....	....	....	....	....	....	....	....	4	0	1	1	2	....	....	....	....
1998-99	Peterborough	OHL	68	26	48	74	42	....	....	....	....	....	....	....	....	....	5	1	2	3	2	....	....	....	....
99-2000	Peterborough	OHL	66	36	37	75	64	....	....	....	....	....	....	....	....	....	5	2	1	3	2	....	....	....	....
2000-01	Detroit	NHL	5	0	3	3	2	0	0	0	7	0.0	1	56	39.3	12:24	2	0	0	0	0	0	0	0	11:45
	Cincinnati	AHL	76	24	45	69	48	....	....	....	....	....	....	....	....	....	1	0	0	0	2	....	....	....	....
2001-02 ♦	Detroit	NHL	25	8	2	10	4	4	0	0	32	25.0	2	208	47.6	10:50	9	0	0	0	2	0	0	0	6:12
	Cincinnati	AHL	52	23	27	50	27	....	....	....	....	....	....	....	....	....	3	0	1	1	6	....	....	....	....
2002-03	Detroit	NHL	16	3	3	6	2	1	0	0	20	15.0	3	78	51.3	10:43	....	....	....	....	....	....	....	....	....
	Grand Rapids	AHL	45	23	22	45	18	....	....	....	....	....	....	....	....	....	15	1	7	8	16	....	....	....	....
2003-04	Detroit	NHL	49	6	7	13	15	0	0	0	44	13.6	1	315	49.2	9:27	3	0	0	0	2	0	0	0	6:11
2004-05	Assat Pori	Finland	43	26	17	43	52	....	....	....	....	....	....	....	....	....	2	1	1	2	4	....	....	....	....
2005-06	Detroit	NHL	80	21	37	58	26	6	0	4	177	11.9	4	29	55.2	14:55	6	1	1	2	6	0	0	0	18:10
2006-07	Detroit	NHL	58	11	15	26	24	3	0	2	111	9.9	7	11	45.5	14:26	....	....	....	....	....	....	....	....	....
	Chicago	NHL	20	4	2	6	20	2	1	0	38	10.5	–6	193	42.5	18:17	....	....	....	....	....	....	....	....	....
2007-08	Chicago	NHL	43	13	23	36	22	6	0	4	101	12.9	–2	15	60.0	16:35	....	....	....	....	....	....	....	....	....
2008-09	Atlanta	NHL	41	7	11	18	8	4	0	2	79	8.9	–9	381	49.1	16:05	....	....	....	....	....	....	....	....	....
	Columbus	NHL	39	12	17	29	16	3	0	2	74	16.2	5	237	40.9	15:38	4	0	1	1	2	0	0	0	14:12
2009-10	Detroit	NHL	44	6	9	15	8	3	0	1	96	6.3	–7	60	50.0	13:32	3	0	0	0	0	0	0	0	8:12
2010-11	Connecticut	AHL	17	4	5	9	10	....	....	....	....	....	....	....	....	....	....	....	....	....	....	....	....	....	....
	Dallas	NHL	27	2	3	5	6	0	0	1	18	11.1	–2	44	40.9	8:07	....	....	....	....	....	....	....	....	....
	NHL Totals		447	93	132	225	153	32	1	16	797	11.7		1627	46.7	13:47	27	1	2	3	12	0	0	0	10:40

Signed as a free agent by **Detroit**, September 18, 2000. Signed as a free agent by **Pori** (Finland), October 18, 2004. Traded to **Chicago** by **Detroit** for Kyle Calder, February 26, 2007. Signed as a free agent by **Atlanta**, July 14, 2008. Traded to **Columbus** by **Atlanta** for Clay Wilson and San Jose's 6th round choice (previously acquired, later traded to Chicago – Chicago selected David Pacan) in 2009 Entry Draft, January 14, 2009. Signed as a free agent by **Detroit**, August 4, 2009. Signed to a PTO (professional tryout) contract by **Connecticut** (AHL), December 26, 2010. Signed as a free agent by **Dallas**, February 12, 2011. Signed as a free agent by **Pittsburgh**, July 26, 2011.

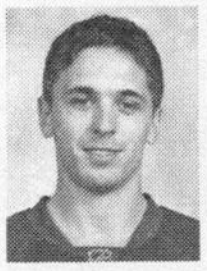

WILLIAMS, Jeremy
(WIHL-yuhms, JAIR-eh-mee)

Right wing. Shoots right. 6', 191 lbs. Born, Regina, Sask., January 26, 1984. Toronto's 5th choice, 220th overall, in 2003 Entry Draft.

Season	Club	League	GP	G	A	Pts	PIM	PP	SH	GW	S	%	+/-	TF	F%	Min	Playoffs GP	G	A	Pts	PIM	PP	SH	GW	Min
2001-02	Swift Current	SMMHL	24	18	23	41	64	....	....	....	....	....	....	....	....	....	....	....	....	....	....	....	....	....	....
	Swift Current	WHL	32	6	7	13	30	....	....	....	....	....	....	....	....	....	12	1	0	1	4	....	....	....	....
2002-03	Swift Current	WHL	72	41	52	93	117	....	....	....	....	....	....	....	....	....	4	1	0	1	6	....	....	....	....
2003-04	Swift Current	WHL	68	*52	49	101	82	....	....	....	....	....	....	....	....	....	5	2	1	3	12	....	....	....	....
	St. John's	AHL	4	0	2	2	0	....	....	....	....	....	....	....	....	....	....	....	....	....	....	....	....	....	....
2004-05	St. John's	AHL	75	16	20	36	24	....	....	....	....	....	....	....	....	....	5	0	0	0	0	....	....	....	....
2005-06	**Toronto**	**NHL**	**1**	**1**	**0**	**1**	**0**	**0**	**0**	**0**	**1**	**100.0**	**0**	**0**	**0.0**	**9:31**	....	....	....	....	....	....	....	....	....
	Toronto Marlies	AHL	55	23	33	56	62	....	....	....	....	....	....	....	....	....	5	1	0	1	6	....	....	....	....
2006-07	**Toronto**	**NHL**	**1**	**1**	**0**	**1**	**0**	**0**	**0**	**0**	**3**	**33.3**	**1**	**1**	**0.0**	**7:18**	....	....	....	....	....	....	....	....	....
	Toronto Marlies	AHL	23	6	9	15	27	....	....	....	....	....	....	....	....	....	....	....	....	....	....	....	....	....	....
2007-08	**Toronto**	**NHL**	**18**	**2**	**0**	**2**	**4**	**0**	**0**	**0**	**16**	**12.5**	**-3**	**4**	**0.0**	**7:20**	....	....	....	....	....	....	....	....	....
	Toronto Marlies	AHL	49	18	15	33	36	....	....	....	....	....	....	....	....	....	....	....	....	....	....	....	....	....	....
2008-09	**Toronto**	**NHL**	**11**	**5**	**2**	**7**	**2**	**0**	**0**	**0**	**21**	**23.8**	**2**	**1**	**0.0**	**13:26**	....	....	....	....	....	....	....	....	....
	Toronto Marlies	AHL	46	27	13	40	29	....	....	....	....	....	....	....	....	....	6	0	1	1	6	....	....	....	....
2009-10	Grand Rapids	AHL	77	32	31	63	55	....	....	....	....	....	....	....	....	....	....	....	....	....	....	....	....	....	....
2010-11	**NY Rangers**	**NHL**	**1**	**0**	**0**	**0**	**0**	**0**	**0**	**0**	**0**	**0.0**	**0**	**0**	**0.0**	**3:43**	....	....	....	....	....	....	....	....	....
	Connecticut	AHL	75	32	23	55	68	....	....	....	....	....	....	....	....	....	6	1	2	3	4	....	....	....	....
	NHL Totals		**32**	**9**	**2**	**11**	**6**	**0**	**0**	**0**	**41**	**22.0**		**6**	**0.0**	**9:23**	....	....	....	....	....	....	....	....	....

WHL East First All-Star Team (2004) • Canadian Major Junior First All-Star Team (2004)

Signed as a free agent by **Detroit**, July 7, 2009. Signed as a free agent by **NY Rangers**, July 12, 2010.

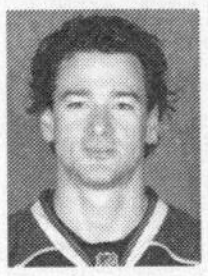

WILLIAMS, Justin
(WIHL-yuhms, JUHS-tihn) **L.A.**

Right wing. Shoots right. 6'1", 188 lbs. Born, Cobourg, Ont., October 4, 1981. Philadelphia's 1st choice, 28th overall, in 2000 Entry Draft.

Season	Club	League	GP	G	A	Pts	PIM	PP	SH	GW	S	%	+/-	TF	F%	Min	Playoffs GP	G	A	Pts	PIM	PP	SH	GW	Min
1997-98	Colborne Colts	OHA-C	36	32	35	67	26	....	....	....	....	....	....	....	....	....	....	....	....	....	....	....	....	....	....
	Cobourg Cougars	OPJHL	17	0	3	3	5	....	....	....	....	....	....	....	....	....	....	....	....	....	....	....	....	....	....
1998-99	Plymouth Whalers	OHL	47	4	8	12	28	....	....	....	....	....	....	....	....	....	7	1	2	3	0	....	....	....	....
99-2000	Plymouth Whalers	OHL	68	37	46	83	46	....	....	....	....	....	....	....	....	....	23	*14	16	*30	10	....	....	....	....
2000-01	**Philadelphia**	**NHL**	**63**	**12**	**13**	**25**	**22**	**0**	**0**	**0**	**99**	**12.1**	**6**	**13**	**53.9**	**12:31**	....	....	....	....	....	....	....	....	....
2001-02	**Philadelphia**	**NHL**	**75**	**17**	**23**	**40**	**32**	**0**	**0**	**1**	**162**	**10.5**	**11**	**16**	**25.0**	**14:27**	**5**	**0**	**0**	**0**	**4**	**0**	**0**	**0**	**16:42**
2002-03	**Philadelphia**	**NHL**	**41**	**8**	**16**	**24**	**22**	**0**	**0**	**2**	**105**	**7.6**	**15**	**16**	**50.0**	**15:57**	**12**	**1**	**5**	**6**	**8**	**0**	**0**	**1**	**14:11**
2003-04	**Philadelphia**	**NHL**	**47**	**6**	**20**	**26**	**32**	**3**	**0**	**1**	**107**	**5.6**	**10**	**38**	**31.6**	**15:30**	....	....	....	....	....	....	....	....	....
	Carolina	**NHL**	**32**	**5**	**13**	**18**	**32**	**1**	**0**	**0**	**96**	**5.2**	**2**	**25**	**36.0**	**18:52**	....	....	....	....	....	....	....	....	....
2004-05	Lulea HF	Sweden	49	14	18	32	61	....	....	....	....	....	....	....	....	....	4	0	1	1	29	....	....	....	....
2005-06♦	**Carolina**	**NHL**	**82**	**31**	**45**	**76**	**60**	**8**	**4**	**4**	**255**	**12.2**	**1**	**17**	**29.4**	**21:08**	**25**	**7**	**11**	**18**	**34**	**0**	**1**	**1**	**21:36**
2006-07	**Carolina**	**NHL**	**82**	**33**	**34**	**67**	**73**	**12**	**2**	**8**	**258**	**12.8**	**-11**	**24**	**37.5**	**20:51**	....	....	....	....	....	....	....	....	....
2007-08	**Carolina**	**NHL**	**37**	**9**	**21**	**30**	**43**	**2**	**0**	**0**	**106**	**8.5**	**2**	**13**	**38.5**	**19:18**	....	....	....	....	....	....	....	....	....
2008-09	**Carolina**	**NHL**	**32**	**3**	**7**	**10**	**9**	**2**	**0**	**0**	**80**	**3.8**	**-9**	**20**	**30.0**	**15:08**	....	....	....	....	....	....	....	....	....
	Los Angeles	**NHL**	**12**	**1**	**3**	**4**	**8**	**1**	**0**	**0**	**28**	**3.6**	**1**	**2**	**50.0**	**17:51**	....	....	....	....	....	....	....	....	....
2009-10	**Los Angeles**	**NHL**	**49**	**10**	**19**	**29**	**39**	**1**	**0**	**1**	**140**	**7.1**	**3**	**11**	**36.4**	**16:23**	**3**	**0**	**1**	**1**	**2**	**0**	**0**	**0**	**11:24**
2010-11	**Los Angeles**	**NHL**	**73**	**22**	**35**	**57**	**59**	**5**	**0**	**3**	**213**	**10.3**	**14**	**14**	**50.0**	**17:15**	**6**	**3**	**1**	**4**	**2**	**1**	**0**	**0**	**16:44**
	NHL Totals		**625**	**157**	**249**	**406**	**431**	**35**	**6**	**20**	**1649**	**9.5**		**209**	**36.8**	**17:15**	**51**	**11**	**18**	**29**	**50**	**1**	**1**	**2**	**18:12**

Played in NHL All-Star Game (2007)

• Missed majority of 2002-03 due to shoulder (November 15, 2002 vs. Carolina) and knee (January 18, 2003 vs. Tampa Bay) injuries. Traded to **Carolina** by **Philadelphia** for Danny Markov, January 20, 2004. Signed as a free agent by **Lulea** (Sweden), September 21, 2004. • Missed majority of 2007-08 due to knee injury at Florida, December 20, 2007. Traded to **Los Angeles** by **Carolina** for Patrick O'Sullivan and Calgary's 2nd round choice (previously acquired, Carolina selected Brian Dumoulin) in 2009 Entry Draft, March 4. 2009.

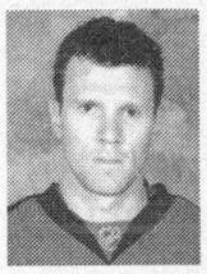

WILLSIE, Brian
(WIHL-see, BRIGH-uhn) **MTL**

Right wing. Shoots right. 6'1", 202 lbs. Born, Belmont, Ont., March 16, 1978. Colorado's 7th choice, 146th overall, in 1996 Entry Draft.

Season	Club	League	GP	G	A	Pts	PIM	PP	SH	GW	S	%	+/-	TF	F%	Min	Playoffs GP	G	A	Pts	PIM	PP	SH	GW	Min
1993-94	Belmont Bombers	ON-Jr.D	13	9	5	14	14	....	....	....	....	....	....	....	....	....	....	....	....	....	....	....	....	....	....
1994-95	St. Thomas Stars	ON-Jr.B	45	35	47	82	47	....	....	....	....	....	....	....	....	....	....	....	....	....	....	....	....	....	....
1995-96	Guelph Storm	OHL	65	13	21	34	18	....	....	....	....	....	....	....	....	....	16	4	2	6	6	....	....	....	....
1996-97	Guelph Storm	OHL	64	37	31	68	37	....	....	....	....	....	....	....	....	....	18	15	4	19	10	....	....	....	....
1997-98	Guelph Storm	OHL	57	45	31	76	41	....	....	....	....	....	....	....	....	....	12	9	5	14	18	....	....	....	....
1998-99	Hershey Bears	AHL	72	19	10	29	28	....	....	....	....	....	....	....	....	....	3	1	0	1	0	....	....	....	....
99-2000	**Colorado**	**NHL**	**1**	**0**	**0**	**0**	**0**	**0**	**0**	**0**	**1**	**0.0**	**0**	**0**	**0.0**	**8:16**	....	....	....	....	....	....	....	....	....
	Hershey Bears	AHL	78	20	39	59	44	....	....	....	....	....	....	....	....	....	12	2	6	8	8	....	....	....	....
2000-01	Hershey Bears	AHL	48	18	23	41	20	....	....	....	....	....	....	....	....	....	12	7	2	9	14	....	....	....	....
2001-02	**Colorado**	**NHL**	**56**	**7**	**7**	**14**	**14**	**2**	**0**	**1**	**66**	**10.6**	**4**	**8**	**12.5**	**11:24**	**4**	**0**	**1**	**1**	**2**	**0**	**0**	**0**	**11:54**
2002-03	**Colorado**	**NHL**	**12**	**0**	**1**	**1**	**15**	**0**	**0**	**0**	**12**	**0.0**	**0**	**7**	**14.3**	**9:36**	**6**	**1**	**0**	**1**	**2**	**0**	**0**	**1**	**10:48**
	Hershey Bears	AHL	59	29	28	57	49	....	....	....	....	....	....	....	....	....	....	....	....	....	....	....	....	....	....
2003-04	**Washington**	**NHL**	**49**	**10**	**5**	**15**	**18**	**1**	**1**	**1**	**85**	**11.8**	**-7**	**46**	**34.8**	**12:42**	....	....	....	....	....	....	....	....	....
2004-05	Ljubljana	Slovenia	2	0	3	3	4	....	....	....	....	....	....	....	....	....	....	....	....	....	....	....	....	....	....
	Ljubljana	Interliga	12	7	6	13	34	....	....	....	....	....	....	....	....	....	....	....	....	....	....	....	....	....	....
	Portland Pirates	AHL	53	23	17	40	47	....	....	....	....	....	....	....	....	....	....	....	....	....	....	....	....	....	....
2005-06	**Washington**	**NHL**	**82**	**19**	**22**	**41**	**77**	**8**	**1**	**2**	**185**	**10.3**	**-19**	**52**	**51.9**	**16:40**	....	....	....	....	....	....	....	....	....
2006-07	**Los Angeles**	**NHL**	**81**	**11**	**10**	**21**	**49**	**2**	**0**	**1**	**131**	**8.4**	**-20**	**201**	**45.3**	**13:23**	....	....	....	....	....	....	....	....	....
2007-08	**Los Angeles**	**NHL**	**53**	**4**	**8**	**12**	**30**	**0**	**0**	**0**	**62**	**6.5**	**-8**	**24**	**58.3**	**10:38**	....	....	....	....	....	....	....	....	....
2008-09	**Colorado**	**NHL**	**42**	**1**	**3**	**4**	**14**	**0**	**0**	**0**	**59**	**1.7**	**-6**	**89**	**33.7**	**11:47**	....	....	....	....	....	....	....	....	....
	Lake Erie	AHL	12	8	6	14	8	....	....	....	....	....	....	....	....	....	....	....	....	....	....	....	....	....	....
2009-10	**Colorado**	**NHL**	**4**	**0**	**0**	**0**	**0**	**0**	**0**	**0**	**2**	**0.0**	**-1**	**18**	**55.6**	**11:05**	....	....	....	....	....	....	....	....	....
	Lake Erie	AHL	75	26	31	57	44	....	....	....	....	....	....	....	....	....	....	....	....	....	....	....	....	....	....
2010-11	**Washington**	**NHL**	**1**	**0**	**1**	**1**	**0**	**0**	**0**	**0**	**0**	**0.0**	**0**	**0**	**0.0**	**6:15**	....	....	....	....	....	....	....	....	....
	Hershey Bears	AHL	76	30	38	68	68	....	....	....	....	....	....	....	....	....	6	2	3	5	6	....	....	....	....
	NHL Totals		**381**	**52**	**57**	**109**	**217**	**13**	**2**	**5**	**603**	**8.6**		**445**	**42.7**	**12:58**	**10**	**1**	**1**	**2**	**4**	**0**	**0**	**1**	**11:14**

OHL First All-Star Team (1998)

Claimed by **Washington** from **Colorado** in Waiver Draft, October 3, 2003. Signed as a free agent by **Ljubljana** (Slovenia), October 8, 2004. Signed as a free agent by **Portland** (AHL), December 15, 2004. Signed as a free agent by **Los Angeles**, July 4, 2006. Signed as a free agent by **Colorado**, July 15, 2008. Signed as a free agent by **Washington**, July 14, 2010. Signed as a free agent by **Montreal**, July 7, 2011.

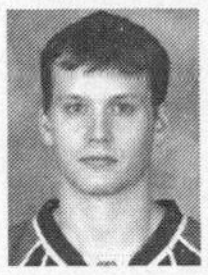

WILSON, Clay
(WIHL-suhn, KLAY) **CGY**

Defense. Shoots left. 6', 195 lbs. Born, Sturgeon Lake, MN, April 5, 1983.

Season	Club	League	GP	G	A	Pts	PIM	PP	SH	GW	S	%	+/-	TF	F%	Min	Playoffs GP	G	A	Pts	PIM	PP	SH	GW	Min
2001-02	Michigan Tech	WCHA	38	4	8	12	18	....	....	....	....	....	....	....	....	....	....	....	....	....	....	....	....	....	....
2002-03	Michigan Tech	WCHA	38	8	17	25	37	....	....	....	....	....	....	....	....	....	....	....	....	....	....	....	....	....	....
2003-04	Michigan Tech	WCHA	37	2	11	13	22	....	....	....	....	....	....	....	....	....	....	....	....	....	....	....	....	....	....
2004-05	Michigan Tech	WCHA	35	3	4	7	42	....	....	....	....	....	....	....	....	....	....	....	....	....	....	....	....	....	....
	Muskegon Fury	UHL	14	3	3	6	2	....	....	....	....	....	....	....	....	....	17	0	2	2	8	....	....	....	....
2005-06	Muskegon Fury	UHL	13	3	9	12	9	....	....	....	....	....	....	....	....	....	....	....	....	....	....	....	....	....	....
	Grand Rapids	AHL	60	10	27	37	40	....	....	....	....	....	....	....	....	....	16	0	3	3	8	....	....	....	....
2006-07	Portland Pirates	AHL	79	9	34	43	52	....	....	....	....	....	....	....	....	....	....	....	....	....	....	....	....	....	....
2007-08	Portland Pirates	AHL	14	3	5	8	6	....	....	....	....	....	....	....	....	....	....	....	....	....	....	....	....	....	....
	Columbus	**NHL**	**7**	**1**	**1**	**2**	**2**	**0**	**0**	**0**	**12**	**8.3**	**3**	**0**	**0.0**	**16:55**	....	....	....	....	....	....	....	....	....
	Syracuse Crunch	AHL	57	11	28	39	29	....	....	....	....	....	....	....	....	....	13	2	5	7	4	....	....	....	....
2008-09	**Columbus**	**NHL**	**5**	**0**	**1**	**1**	**0**	**0**	**0**	**0**	**9**	**0.0**	**-2**	**0**	**0.0**	**9:26**	....	....	....	....	....	....	....	....	....
	Syracuse Crunch	AHL	33	8	12	20	6	....	....	....	....	....	....	....	....	....	....	....	....	....	....	....	....	....	....
	Atlanta	**NHL**	**2**	**0**	**0**	**0**	**0**	**0**	**0**	**0**	**4**	**0.0**	**-1**	**0**	**0.0**	**15:55**	....	....	....	....	....	....	....	....	....
	Chicago Wolves	AHL	37	6	18	24	10	....	....	....	....	....	....	....	....	....	....	....	....	....	....	....	....	....	....
2009-10	**Florida**	**NHL**	**2**	**0**	**0**	**0**	**0**	**0**	**0**	**0**	**0**	**0.0**	**-5**	**0**	**0.0**	**11:07**	....	....	....	....	....	....	....	....	....
	Rochester	AHL	75	14	46	60	58	....	....	....	....	....	....	....	....	....	7	2	0	2	22	....	....	....	....

			Regular Season														Playoffs								
Season	Club	League	GP	G	A	Pts	PIM	PP	SH	GW	S	%	+/-	TF	F%	Min	GP	G	A	Pts	PIM	PP	SH	GW	Min
2010-11	Florida	NHL	15	3	2	5	6	0	0	0	22	13.6	4	0	0.0	14:51	....	....	....	....	....	....	....	....	....
	Rochester	AHL	66	12	36	48	24	....	....	....	....	....	....	....	....	....	....	....	....	....	....	....	....	....	....
	NHL Totals		31	4	4	8	8	0	0	0	47	8.5		0	0.0	14:16	....	....	....	....	....	....	....	....	....

AHL Second All-Star Team (2010)

Signed as a free agent by **Anaheim**, July 11, 2006. Traded to **Columbus** by **Anaheim** with Aaron Rome for Geoff Platt, November 15, 2007. Traded to **Atlanta** by **Columbus** with San Jose's 6th round choice (previously acquired, later traded to Chicago – Chicago selected David Pacan) in 2009 Entry Draft for Jason Williams, January 14, 2009. Signed as a free agent by **Florida**, July 2, 2009. Signed as a free agent by **Calgary**, July 2, 2011.

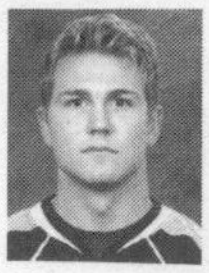

WILSON, Colin

(WIHL-suhn, KAW-lihn) **NSH**

Center. Shoots left. 6'1", 201 lbs. Born, Greenwich, CT, October 20, 1989. Nashville's 1st choice, 7th overall, in 2008 Entry Draft.

Season	Club	League	GP	G	A	Pts	PIM	PP	SH	GW	S	%	+/-	TF	F%	Min	GP	G	A	Pts	PIM	PP	SH	GW	Min
2005-06	USNTDP	U-17	15	9	7	16	2	....	....	....	....	....	....	....	....	....	....	....	....	....	....	....	....	....	....
	USNTDP	U-18	16	2	4	6	8	....	....	....	....	....	....	....	....	....	....	....	....	....	....	....	....	....	....
	USNTDP	NAHL	34	10	11	21	10	....	....	....	....	....	....	....	....	....	2	0	0	0	2	....	....	....	....
2006-07	USNTDP	U-18	41	19	31	50	32	....	....	....	....	....	....	....	....	....	....	....	....	....	....	....	....	....	....
	USNTDP	NAHL	15	11	13	24	21	....	....	....	....	....	....	....	....	....	....	....	....	....	....	....	....	....	....
2007-08	Boston University	H-East	37	12	23	35	22	....	....	....	....	....	....	....	....	....	....	....	....	....	....	....	....	....	....
2008-09	Boston University	H-East	43	17	*38	*55	52	....	....	....	....	....	....	....	....	....	....	....	....	....	....	....	....	....	....
2009-10	Nashville	NHL	35	8	7	15	7	1	0	3	58	13.8	–2	124	50.0	15:10	6	0	1	1	0	0	0	0	13:43
	Milwaukee	AHL	40	13	21	34	19	....	....	....	....	....	....	....	....	....	....	....	....	....	....	....	....	....	....
2010-11	Nashville	NHL	82	16	18	34	17	2	0	2	101	15.8	9	228	47.4	13:18	3	0	0	0	0	0	0	0	11:37
	NHL Totals		117	24	25	49	24	3	0	5	159	15.1		352	48.3	13:51	9	0	1	1	0	0	0	0	13:01

Hockey East All-Rookie Team (2008) • Hockey East Rookie of the Year (2008) • Hockey East First All-Star Team (2009) • NCAA East First All-American Team (2009) • NCAA Championship All-Tournament Team (2009)

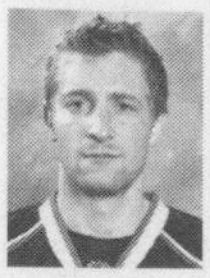

WILSON, Kyle

(WIHL-suhn, KIGHL) **NSH**

Center. Shoots right. 6'2", 205 lbs. Born, Oakville, Ont., December 15, 1984. Minnesota's 12th choice, 272nd overall, in 2004 Entry Draft.

Season	Club	League	GP	G	A	Pts	PIM	PP	SH	GW	S	%	+/-	TF	F%	Min	GP	G	A	Pts	PIM	PP	SH	GW	Min
2000-01	Strathroy Rockets	ON-Jr.B	33	12	17	29	15	....	....	....	....	....	....	....	....	....	5	2	2	4	2	....	....	....	....
2001-02	Strathroy Rockets	ON-Jr.B	53	42	25	67	16	....	....	....	....	....	....	....	....	....	....	....	....	....	....	....	....	....	....
2002-03	Colgate	ECAC	33	4	2	6	15	....	....	....	....	....	....	....	....	....	....	....	....	....	....	....	....	....	....
2003-04	Colgate	ECAC	37	14	17	31	23	....	....	....	....	....	....	....	....	....	....	....	....	....	....	....	....	....	....
2004-05	Colgate	ECAC	30	5	18	23	12	....	....	....	....	....	....	....	....	....	....	....	....	....	....	....	....	....	....
2005-06	Colgate	ECAC	39	*23	18	41	22	....	....	....	....	....	....	....	....	....	....	....	....	....	....	....	....	....	....
2006-07	San Antonio	AHL	7	1	0	1	2	....	....	....	....	....	....	....	....	....	....	....	....	....	....	....	....	....	....
	South Carolina	ECHL	5	3	2	5	4	....	....	....	....	....	....	....	....	....	....	....	....	....	....	....	....	....	....
	Hershey Bears	AHL	54	24	30	54	26	....	....	....	....	....	....	....	....	....	19	7	9	16	8	....	....	....	....
2007-08	Hershey Bears	AHL	80	30	31	61	26	....	....	....	....	....	....	....	....	....	5	0	3	3	2	....	....	....	....
2008-09	Hershey Bears	AHL	80	28	30	58	31	....	....	....	....	....	....	....	....	....	22	3	7	10	2	....	....	....	....
2009-10	Washington	NHL	2	0	2	2	0	0	0	0	1	0.0	1	13	30.8	9:42	....	....	....	....	....	....	....	....	....
	Hershey Bears	AHL	77	24	29	53	23	....	....	....	....	....	....	....	....	....	21	6	6	12	4	....	....	....	....
2010-11	Columbus	NHL	32	4	7	11	12	0	0	0	38	10.5	–3	133	47.4	10:38	....	....	....	....	....	....	....	....	....
	Springfield	AHL	23	12	12	24	2	....	....	....	....	....	....	....	....	....	....	....	....	....	....	....	....	....	....
	NHL Totals		34	4	9	13	12	0	0	0	39	10.3		146	45.9	10:35	....	....	....	....	....	....	....	....	....

ECAC Second All-Star Team (2006)

Signed as a free agent by **San Antonio** (AHL), October 6, 2006. Signed as a free agent by **Washington**, July 5, 2007. Signed as a free agent by **Columbus**, July 2, 2010. Signed as a free agent by **Nashville**, July 5, 2011.

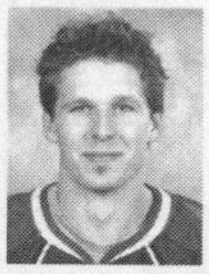

WILSON, Ryan

(WIHL-suhn, RIGH-uhn) **COL**

Defense. Shoots left. 6'1", 207 lbs. Born, Windsor, Ont., February 3, 1987.

Season	Club	League	GP	G	A	Pts	PIM	PP	SH	GW	S	%	+/-	TF	F%	Min	GP	G	A	Pts	PIM	PP	SH	GW	Min
2003-04	St. Michael's	OHL	58	3	22	25	88	....	....	....	....	....	....	....	....	....	18	3	7	10	16	....	....	....	....
2004-05	St. Michael's	OHL	68	13	24	37	149	....	....	....	....	....	....	....	....	....	10	4	5	9	12	....	....	....	....
2005-06	St. Michael's	OHL	64	12	49	61	145	....	....	....	....	....	....	....	....	....	4	1	3	4	12	....	....	....	....
2006-07	Sarnia Sting	OHL	68	17	58	75	136	....	....	....	....	....	....	....	....	....	4	1	3	4	14	....	....	....	....
2007-08	Sarnia Sting	OHL	58	7	64	71	84	....	....	....	....	....	....	....	....	....	9	0	7	7	19	....	....	....	....
2008-09	Quad City Flames	AHL	60	4	16	20	56	....	....	....	....	....	....	....	....	....	....	....	....	....	....	....	....	....	....
	Lake Erie	AHL	8	0	2	2	25	....	....	....	....	....	....	....	....	....	....	....	....	....	....	....	....	....	....
2009-10	Colorado	NHL	61	3	18	21	36	0	0	0	46	6.5	13	0	0.0	16:16	4	0	1	1	0	0	0	0	14:39
	Lake Erie	AHL	3	0	0	0	17	....	....	....	....	....	....	....	....	....	....	....	....	....	....	....	....	....	....
2010-11	Colorado	NHL	67	3	13	16	68	1	0	0	62	4.8	–8	0	0.0	19:48	....	....	....	....	....	....	....	....	....
	NHL Totals		128	6	31	37	104	1	0	0	108	5.6		0	0.0	18:07	4	0	1	1	0	0	0	0	14:39

Signed as a free agent by **Calgary**, July 1, 2008. Traded to **Colorado** by **Calgary** with Lawrence Nycholat and Montreal's 2nd round choice (previously acquired, Colorado selected Stefan Elliott) in 2009 Entry Draft for Jordan Leopold, March 4, 2009.

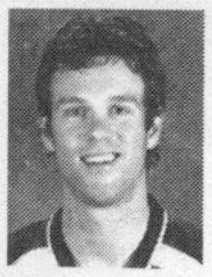

WINCHESTER, Brad

(WIHN-chehs-tuhr, BRAD)

Center/lLeft wing. Shoots left. 6'5", 230 lbs. Born, Madison, WI, March 1, 1981. Edmonton's 2nd choice, 35th overall, in 2000 Entry Draft.

Season	Club	League	GP	G	A	Pts	PIM	PP	SH	GW	S	%	+/-	TF	F%	Min	GP	G	A	Pts	PIM	PP	SH	GW	Min
1997-98	USNTDP	U-17	24	8	5	13	64	....	....	....	....	....	....	....	....	....	....	....	....	....	....	....	....	....	....
	USNTDP	USHL	5	2	1	3	6	....	....	....	....	....	....	....	....	....	....	....	....	....	....	....	....	....	....
	USNTDP	NAHL	40	11	17	28	84	....	....	....	....	....	....	....	....	....	5	1	0	1	8	....	....	....	....
1998-99	USNTDP	U-18	6	0	3	3	6	....	....	....	....	....	....	....	....	....	....	....	....	....	....	....	....	....	....
	USNTDP	USHL	48	14	23	37	103	....	....	....	....	....	....	....	....	....	....	....	....	....	....	....	....	....	....
99-2000	U. of Wisconsin	WCHA	33	9	9	18	48	....	....	....	....	....	....	....	....	....	....	....	....	....	....	....	....	....	....
2000-01	U. of Wisconsin	WCHA	41	7	9	16	71	....	....	....	....	....	....	....	....	....	....	....	....	....	....	....	....	....	....
2001-02	U. of Wisconsin	WCHA	38	14	20	34	38	....	....	....	....	....	....	....	....	....	....	....	....	....	....	....	....	....	....
2002-03	U. of Wisconsin	WCHA	38	10	6	16	58	....	....	....	....	....	....	....	....	....	....	....	....	....	....	....	....	....	....
2003-04	Toronto	AHL	65	13	6	19	85	....	....	....	....	....	....	....	....	....	3	0	0	0	2	....	....	....	....
2004-05	Edmonton	AHL	76	22	18	40	143	....	....	....	....	....	....	....	....	....	....	....	....	....	....	....	....	....	....
2005-06	Edmonton	NHL	19	0	1	1	21	0	0	0	19	0.0	–2	2	100.0	6:05	10	1	2	3	4	0	0	1	9:14
	Hamilton	AHL	40	26	14	40	118	....	....	....	....	....	....	....	....	....	....	....	....	....	....	....	....	....	....
2006-07	Edmonton	NHL	59	4	5	9	86	0	0	0	66	6.1	–10	3	33.3	8:04	....	....	....	....	....	....	....	....	....
2007-08	Dallas	NHL	41	1	2	3	46	0	0	0	36	2.8	–9	2	0.0	7:34	6	0	0	0	8	0	0	0	6:50
	Iowa Stars	AHL	1	0	0	0	2	....	....	....	....	....	....	....	....	....	....	....	....	....	....	....	....	....	....
2008-09	St. Louis	NHL	64	13	8	21	89	5	0	3	82	15.9	–1	20	45.0	12:10	4	0	0	0	10	0	0	0	11:42
	Peoria Rivermen	AHL	13	4	2	6	46	....	....	....	....	....	....	....	....	....	....	....	....	....	....	....	....	....	....
2009-10	St. Louis	NHL	64	3	5	8	108	1	0	0	69	4.3	3	12	25.0	9:04	....	....	....	....	....	....	....	....	....
2010-11	St. Louis	NHL	57	9	5	14	86	3	0	1	67	13.4	–9	7	28.6	10:29	....	....	....	....	....	....	....	....	....
	Anaheim	NHL	19	1	1	2	28	0	0	0	23	4.3	–9	1	0.0	10:28	3	0	0	0	4	0	0	0	5:24
	NHL Totals		323	31	27	58	464	9	0	4	362	8.6		47	36.2	9:28	23	1	2	3	26	0	0	1	8:32

Signed as a free agent by **Dallas**, July 6, 2007. Signed as a free agent by **St. Louis**, July 16, 2008. Traded to **Anaheim** by **St. Louis** for Anaheim's 3rd round choice in 2012 Entry Draft, February 28, 2011.

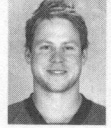

WINCHESTER, Jesse

(WIHN-chehs-tuhr, JEH-see) **OTT**

Center. Shoots right. 6'1", 206 lbs. Born, Long Sault, Ont., October 4, 1983.

Season	Club	League	GP	G	A	Pts	PIM	PP	SH	GW	S	%	+/-	TF	F%	Min	GP	G	A	Pts	PIM	PP	SH	GW	Min
2004-05	Colgate	ECAC	28	2	2	4	22	....	....	....	....	....	....	....	....	....	....	....	....	....	....	....	....	....	....
2005-06	Colgate	ECAC	37	14	22	36	31	....	....	....	....	....	....	....	....	....	....	....	....	....	....	....	....	....	....
2006-07	Colgate	ECAC	37	16	21	37	52	....	....	....	....	....	....	....	....	....	....	....	....	....	....	....	....	....	....
2007-08	Colgate	ECAC	40	8	*29	37	51	....	....	....	....	....	....	....	....	....	....	....	....	....	....	....	....	....	....
	Ottawa	NHL	1	0	0	0	2	0	0	0	1	0.0	0	0	0.0	14:00	....	....	....	....	....	....	....	....	....
2008-09	Ottawa	NHL	76	3	15	18	33	0	0	1	115	2.6	0	199	56.8	10:35	....	....	....	....	....	....	....	....	....
2009-10	Ottawa	NHL	52	2	11	13	22	0	1	0	77	2.6	–1	377	55.4	10:01	6	0	0	0	0	0	0	0	9:38
	Binghamton	AHL	4	2	2	4	0	....	....	....	....	....	....	....	....	....	....	....	....	....	....	....	....	....	....
2010-11	Ottawa	NHL	72	4	9	13	42	0	0	0	118	3.4	–9	545	55.6	10:50	....	....	....	....	....	....	....	....	....
	NHL Totals		201	9	35	44	99	0	1	1	311	2.9		1121	55.8	10:33	6	0	0	0	0	0	0	0	9:38

Signed as a free agent by **Ottawa**, March 24, 2008.

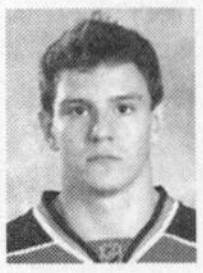

WINGELS, Tommy
(WIHN-guhls, TAW-mee) **S.J.**

Center. Shoots right. 6', 190 lbs. Born, Evanston, IL, April 12, 1988. San Jose's 5th choice, 177th overall, in 2008 Entry Draft.

Season	Club	League	GP	G	A	Pts	PIM	PP	SH	GW	S	%	+/-	TF	F%	Min	GP	G	A	Pts	PIM	PP	SH	GW	Min
2006-07	Cedar Rapids	USHL	47	10	18	28	52	....	....	....	....	....	....	....	....	....	6	3	0	3	6	....	....	....	....
2007-08	Miami U.	CCHA	42	15	14	29	22	....	....	....	....	....	....	....	....	....	....	....	....	....	....	....	....	....	....
2008-09	Miami U.	CCHA	41	11	17	28	66	....	....	....	....	....	....	....	....	....	....	....	....	....	....	....	....	....	....
2009-10	Miami U.	CCHA	44	17	25	42	49	....	....	....	....	....	....	....	....	....	....	....	....	....	....	....	....	....	....
2010-11	**San Jose**	**NHL**	**5**	**0**	**0**	**0**	**0**	**0**	**0**	**0**	**1**	**0.0**	**-1**	**3**	**33.3**	**5:07**	....	....	....	....	....	....	....	....	....
	Worcester Sharks	AHL	69	17	16	33	69	....	....	....	....	....	....	....	....	....	....	....	....	....	....	....	....	....	....
	NHL Totals		**5**	**0**	**0**	**0**	**0**	**0**	**0**	**0**	**1**	**0.0**		**3**	**33.3**	**5:07**	....	....	....	....	....	....	....	....	....

NCAA Championship All-Tournament Team (2009) • CCHA Second All-Star Team (2010)

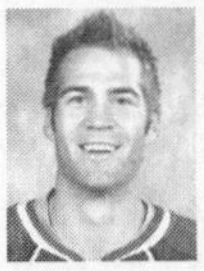

WINNIK, Daniel
(WIHN-ihk, DAN-yehl) **COL**

Center/Left wing. Shoots left. 6'2", 210 lbs. Born, Toronto, Ont., March 6, 1985. Phoenix's 10th choice, 265th overall, in 2004 Entry Draft.

Season	Club	League	GP	G	A	Pts	PIM	PP	SH	GW	S	%	+/-	TF	F%	Min	GP	G	A	Pts	PIM	PP	SH	GW	Min
2002-03	Wexford Raiders	OPJHL	47	20	33	53	70	....	....	....	....	....	....	....	....	....	18	11	11	22	24	....	....	....	....
2003-04	New Hampshire	H-East	38	4	10	14	12	....	....	....	....	....	....	....	....	....	....	....	....	....	....	....	....	....	....
2004-05	New Hampshire	H-East	42	18	22	40	26	....	....	....	....	....	....	....	....	....	....	....	....	....	....	....	....	....	....
2005-06	New Hampshire	H-East	39	15	26	41	44	....	....	....	....	....	....	....	....	....	....	....	....	....	....	....	....	....	....
	San Antonio	AHL	7	1	1	2	8	....	....	....	....	....	....	....	....	....	....	....	....	....	....	....	....	....	....
2006-07	San Antonio	AHL	66	9	12	21	34	....	....	....	....	....	....	....	....	....	....	....	....	....	....	....	....	....	....
	Phoenix	ECHL	5	0	6	6	9	....	....	....	....	....	....	....	....	....	....	....	....	....	....	....	....	....	....
2007-08	**Phoenix**	**NHL**	**79**	**11**	**15**	**26**	**25**	**0**	**0**	**1**	**122**	**9.0**	**-3**	**154**	**42.2**	**14:06**	....	....	....	....	....	....	....	....	....
2008-09	**Phoenix**	**NHL**	**49**	**3**	**4**	**7**	**63**	**0**	**0**	**0**	**66**	**4.5**	**1**	**138**	**37.0**	**13:04**	....	....	....	....	....	....	....	....	....
	San Antonio	AHL	5	0	0	0	4	....	....	....	....	....	....	....	....	....	....	....	....	....	....	....	....	....	....
2009-10	**Phoenix**	**NHL**	**74**	**4**	**15**	**19**	**12**	**0**	**0**	**1**	**83**	**4.8**	**1**	**110**	**45.5**	**13:09**	**7**	**0**	**0**	**0**	**0**	**0**	**0**	**0**	**12:45**
2010-11	**Colorado**	**NHL**	**80**	**11**	**15**	**26**	**35**	**2**	**2**	**1**	**167**	**6.6**	**-2**	**69**	**36.2**	**16:33**	....	....	....	....	....	....	....	....	....
	NHL Totals		**282**	**29**	**49**	**78**	**135**	**2**	**2**	**3**	**438**	**6.6**		**471**	**40.6**	**14:22**	**7**	**0**	**0**	**0**	**0**	**0**	**0**	**0**	**12:45**

Hockey East Second All-Star Team (2006)

Traded to **Colorado** by **Phoenix** for Colorado's 4th round choice in 2012 Entry Draft, June 28, 2010.

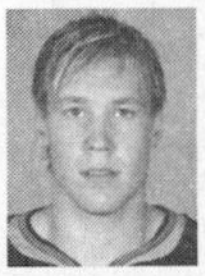

WIRTANEN, Petteri
(WEER-tah-nehn, PEH-tuh-ree) **ANA**

Center. Shoots left. 6'1", 203 lbs. Born, Hyvinkaa, Finland, May 28, 1986. Anaheim's 5th choice, 172nd overall, in 2006 Entry Draft.

Season	Club	League	GP	G	A	Pts	PIM	PP	SH	GW	S	%	+/-	TF	F%	Min	GP	G	A	Pts	PIM	PP	SH	GW	Min
2001-02	Ahmat Jr.	Fin-Jr.	1	1	0	1	2	....	....	....	....	....	....	....	....	....	....	....	....	....	....	....	....	....	....
2002-03	HPK U18	Fin-U18	27	17	12	29	36	....	....	....	....	....	....	....	....	....	2	0	0	0	2	....	....	....	....
	HPK Jr.	Fin-Jr.	2	1	0	1	0	....	....	....	....	....	....	....	....	....	....	....	....	....	....	....	....	....	....
2003-04	HPK U18	Fin-U18	7	2	3	5	10	....	....	....	....	....	....	....	....	....	2	0	0	0	0	....	....	....	....
	HPK Jr.	Fin-Jr.	40	7	11	18	26	....	....	....	....	....	....	....	....	....	....	....	....	....	....	....	....	....	....
2004-05	HPK Jr.	Fin-Jr.	43	14	25	39	42	....	....	....	....	....	....	....	....	....	2	0	0	0	10	....	....	....	....
	HPK Hameenlinna	Finland	8	0	0	0	0	....	....	....	....	....	....	....	....	....	....	....	....	....	....	....	....	....	....
2005-06	Suomi U20	Finland-2	2	2	0	2	2	....	....	....	....	....	....	....	....	....	....	....	....	....	....	....	....	....	....
	HPK Jr.	Fin-Jr.	3	4	2	6	4	....	....	....	....	....	....	....	....	....	....	....	....	....	....	....	....	....	....
	HPK Hameenlinna	Finland	50	8	3	11	24	....	....	....	....	....	....	....	....	....	13	1	0	1	12	....	....	....	....
2006-07	Portland Pirates	AHL	67	7	11	18	40	....	....	....	....	....	....	....	....	....	....	....	....	....	....	....	....	....	....
2007-08	**Anaheim**	**NHL**	**3**	**1**	**0**	**1**	**2**	**0**	**0**	**1**	**1**	**100.0**	**1**	**11**	**45.5**	**4:11**	....	....	....	....	....	....	....	....	....
	Portland Pirates	AHL	78	10	27	37	58	....	....	....	....	....	....	....	....	....	18	0	0	0	14	....	....	....	....
2008-09	Iowa Chops	AHL	78	15	26	41	50	....	....	....	....	....	....	....	....	....	....	....	....	....	....	....	....	....	....
2009-10	HIFK Helsinki	Finland	56	10	17	27	32	....	....	....	....	....	....	....	....	....	6	4	1	5	4	....	....	....	....
2010-11	HIFK Helsinki	Finland	57	12	25	37	40	....	....	....	....	....	....	....	....	....	16	1	5	6	10	....	....	....	....
	NHL Totals		**3**	**1**	**0**	**1**	**2**	**0**	**0**	**1**	**1**	**100.0**		**11**	**45.5**	**4:11**	....	....	....	....	....	....	....	....	....

Signed as a free agent by **HIFK Helsinki** (Finland), July 29, 2009,

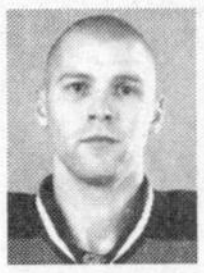

WISEMAN, Chad
(WIGHZ-man, CHAD) **N.J.**

Left wing. Shoots left. 6'1", 205 lbs. Born, Burlington, Ont., March 25, 1981. San Jose's 8th choice, 246th overall, in 2000 Entry Draft.

Season	Club	League	GP	G	A	Pts	PIM	PP	SH	GW	S	%	+/-	TF	F%	Min	GP	G	A	Pts	PIM	PP	SH	GW	Min
1997-98	Burlington	OPJHL	50	28	36	64	31	....	....	....	....	....	....	....	....	....	....	....	....	....	....	....	....	....	....
1998-99	Mississauga	OHL	64	11	25	36	29	....	....	....	....	....	....	....	....	....	....	....	....	....	....	....	....	....	....
99-2000	Mississauga	OHL	68	23	45	68	53	....	....	....	....	....	....	....	....	....	....	....	....	....	....	....	....	....	....
2000-01	Mississauga	OHL	30	15	29	44	22	....	....	....	....	....	....	....	....	....	....	....	....	....	....	....	....	....	....
	Plymouth Whalers	OHL	32	11	16	27	12	....	....	....	....	....	....	....	....	....	19	12	8	20	22	....	....	....	....
2001-02	Cleveland Barons	AHL	76	21	29	50	61	....	....	....	....	....	....	....	....	....	....	....	....	....	....	....	....	....	....
2002-03	**San Jose**	**NHL**	**4**	**0**	**0**	**0**	**4**	**0**	**0**	**0**	**1**	**0.0**	**-2**	**0**	**0.0**	**9:19**	....	....	....	....	....	....	....	....	....
	Cleveland Barons	AHL	77	17	35	52	44	....	....	....	....	....	....	....	....	....	....	....	....	....	....	....	....	....	....
2003-04	**NY Rangers**	**NHL**	**4**	**1**	**0**	**1**	**0**	**0**	**0**	**0**	**3**	**33.3**	**-1**	**0**	**0.0**	**8:49**	....	....	....	....	....	....	....	....	....
	Hartford	AHL	62	25	27	52	45	....	....	....	....	....	....	....	....	....	15	5	6	11	12	....	....	....	....
2004-05	Hartford	AHL	60	17	16	33	74	....	....	....	....	....	....	....	....	....	6	1	1	2	6	....	....	....	....
2005-06	**NY Rangers**	**NHL**	**1**	**0**	**1**	**1**	**4**	**0**	**0**	**0**	**1**	**0.0**	**2**	**0**	**0.0**	**8:47**	**1**	**0**	**0**	**0**	**2**	**0**	**0**	**0**	**6:00**
	Hartford	AHL	69	19	35	54	65	....	....	....	....	....	....	....	....	....	11	3	6	9	22	....	....	....	....
2006-07	Hershey Bears	AHL	48	15	20	35	80	....	....	....	....	....	....	....	....	....	16	2	6	8	16	....	....	....	....
2007-08	Wolfsburg	Germany	28	10	13	23	41	....	....	....	....	....	....	....	....	....	....	....	....	....	....	....	....	....	....
2008-09	Lowell Devils	AHL	23	9	10	19	23	....	....	....	....	....	....	....	....	....	....	....	....	....	....	....	....	....	....
2009-10	Springfield	AHL	67	24	35	59	83	....	....	....	....	....	....	....	....	....	....	....	....	....	....	....	....	....	....
2010-11	Albany Devils	AHL	48	16	28	44	47	....	....	....	....	....	....	....	....	....	....	....	....	....	....	....	....	....	....
	NHL Totals		**9**	**1**	**1**	**2**	**8**	**0**	**0**	**0**	**5**	**20.0**		**0**	**0.0**	**9:02**	**1**	**0**	**0**	**0**	**2**	**0**	**0**	**0**	**6:00**

Traded to **NY Rangers** by **San Jose** for Nils Ekman, August 12, 2003. Signed as a free agent by **Washington**, July 14, 2006. Signed as a free agent by **Wolfsburg** (Germany), July 9, 2007. Signed as a free agent by **New Jersey**, July 17, 2008. • Missed majority of 2007-08 and 2008-09 due to three sports hernia surgeries. Signed as a free agent by **Springfield** (AHL), December 17, 2009. Signed as a free agent by **New Jersey**, July 28, 2010.

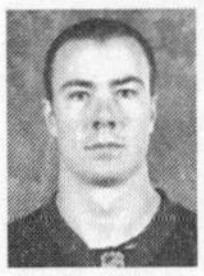

WISHART, Ty
(wih-SHAHRT, TIGH) **NYI**

Defense. Shoots left. 6'4", 222 lbs. Born, Belleville, Ont., May 19, 1988. San Jose's 1st choice, 16th overall, in 2006 Entry Draft.

Season	Club	League	GP	G	A	Pts	PIM	PP	SH	GW	S	%	+/-	TF	F%	Min	GP	G	A	Pts	PIM	PP	SH	GW	Min
2003-04	Comox Valley	Minor-BC	47	26	27	53	48	....	....	....	....	....	....	....	....	....	....	....	....	....	....	....	....	....	....
2004-05	Prince George	WHL	58	1	7	8	41	....	....	....	....	....	....	....	....	....	....	....	....	....	....	....	....	....	....
2005-06	Prince George	WHL	70	5	32	37	68	....	....	....	....	....	....	....	....	....	5	0	0	0	4	....	....	....	....
2006-07	Prince George	WHL	62	11	38	49	59	....	....	....	....	....	....	....	....	....	15	3	8	11	6	....	....	....	....
2007-08	Prince George	WHL	40	12	28	40	34	....	....	....	....	....	....	....	....	....	....	....	....	....	....	....	....	....	....
	Moose Jaw	WHL	32	4	23	27	18	....	....	....	....	....	....	....	....	....	6	1	3	4	2	....	....	....	....
	Worcester Sharks	AHL	5	0	0	0	0	....	....	....	....	....	....	....	....	....	....	....	....	....	....	....	....	....	....
2008-09	**Tampa Bay**	**NHL**	**5**	**0**	**1**	**1**	**0**	**0**	**0**	**0**	**2**	**0.0**	**0**	**0**	**0.0**	**10:07**	....	....	....	....	....	....	....	....	....
	Norfolk Admirals	AHL	61	1	6	7	25	....	....	....	....	....	....	....	....	....	....	....	....	....	....	....	....	....	....
2009-10	Norfolk Admirals	AHL	76	9	23	32	44	....	....	....	....	....	....	....	....	....	....	....	....	....	....	....	....	....	....
2010-11	Norfolk Admirals	AHL	31	4	14	18	33	....	....	....	....	....	....	....	....	....	....	....	....	....	....	....	....	....	....
	NY Islanders	**NHL**	**20**	**1**	**4**	**5**	**10**	**1**	**0**	**0**	**23**	**4.3**	**5**	**0**	**0.0**	**16:49**	....	....	....	....	....	....	....	....	....
	Bridgeport	AHL	20	0	9	9	8	....	....	....	....	....	....	....	....	....	....	....	....	....	....	....	....	....	....
	NHL Totals		**25**	**1**	**5**	**6**	**10**	**1**	**0**	**0**	**25**	**4.0**		**0**	**0.0**	**15:29**	....	....	....	....	....	....	....	....	....

WHL West Second All-Star Team (2007) • WHL East Second All-Star Team (2008)

Traded to **Tampa Bay** by **San Jose** with Matt Carle, San Jose's 1st round choice (later traded to Ottawa, later traded to NY Islanders, later traded to Columbus, later traded to Anaheim - Anaheim selected Kyle Palmieri) in 2009 Entry Draft and San Jose's 4th round choice (James Mullin) in 2010 Entry Draft for Dan Boyle and Brad Lukowich, July 4, 2008. Traded to **NY Islanders** by **Tampa Bay** for Dwayne Roloson, January 2, 2011.

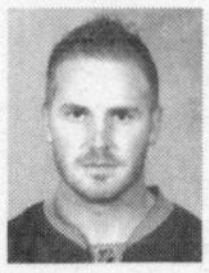

WISNIEWSKI, James

(wihz-NOO-skee, JAYMZ) **CBJ**

Defense. Shoots right. 5'11", 208 lbs. Born, Canton, MI, February 21, 1984. Chicago's 5th choice, 156th overall, in 2002 Entry Draft.

			Regular Season														Playoffs								
Season	Club	League	GP	G	A	Pts	PIM	PP	SH	GW	S	%	+/-	TF	F%	Min	GP	G	A	Pts	PIM	PP	SH	GW	Min
99-2000	Det. Compuware	NAHL	50	5	11	16	67	....	....	....	....	....	....	....	....	....	5	0	3	3	4	....	....	....	....
2000-01	Plymouth Whalers	OHL	53	6	23	29	72	....	....	....	....	....	....	....	....	....	19	3	10	13	34	....	....	....	....
2001-02	Plymouth Whalers	OHL	62	11	25	36	100	....	....	....	....	....	....	....	....	....	6	1	2	3	6	....	....	....	....
2002-03	Plymouth Whalers	OHL	52	18	34	52	60	....	....	....	....	....	....	....	....	....	18	2	10	12	14	....	....	....	....
2003-04	Plymouth Whalers	OHL	50	17	53	70	63	....	....	....	....	....	....	....	....	....	9	3	7	10	8	....	....	....	....
2004-05	Norfolk Admirals	AHL	66	7	18	25	110	....	....	....	....	....	....	....	....	....	5	1	3	4	2	....	....	....	....
2005-06	**Chicago**	**NHL**	**19**	**2**	**5**	**7**	**36**	**0**	**0**	**0**	**25**	**8.0**	**0**	**1**	**0.0**	**15:52**	....	....	....	....	....	....	....	....	....
	Norfolk Admirals	AHL	61	7	28	35	67	....	....	....	....	....	....	....	....	....	4	1	2	3	6	....	....	....	....
2006-07	**Chicago**	**NHL**	**50**	**2**	**8**	**10**	**39**	**0**	**0**	**0**	**55**	**3.6**	**3**	**1**	**0.0**	**19:00**	....	....	....	....	....	....	....	....	....
	Norfolk Admirals	AHL	10	0	6	6	8	....	....	....	....	....	....	....	....	....	....	....	....	....	....	....	....	....	....
2007-08	**Chicago**	**NHL**	**68**	**7**	**19**	**26**	**103**	**1**	**1**	**0**	**82**	**8.5**	**12**	**0**	**0.0**	**17:00**	....	....	....	....	....	....	....	....	....
2008-09	**Chicago**	**NHL**	**31**	**2**	**11**	**13**	**14**	**1**	**0**	**0**	**70**	**2.9**	**6**	**0**	**0.0**	**19:15**	....	....	....	....	....	....	....	....	....
	Rockford IceHogs	AHL	2	3	1	4	0	....	....	....	....	....	....	....	....	....	....	....	....	....	....	....	....	....	....
	Anaheim	**NHL**	**17**	**1**	**10**	**11**	**16**	**0**	**0**	**0**	**19**	**5.3**	**3**	**0**	**0.0**	**20:57**	**12**	**1**	**2**	**3**	**10**	**0**	**0**	**0**	**20:22**
2009-10	**Anaheim**	**NHL**	**69**	**3**	**27**	**30**	**56**	**2**	**0**	**0**	**146**	**2.1**	**–5**	**0**	**0.0**	**24:21**	....	....	....	....	....	....	....	....	....
2010-11	**NY Islanders**	**NHL**	**32**	**3**	**18**	**21**	**18**	**3**	**0**	**0**	**71**	**4.2**	**–18**	**0**	**0.0**	**23:15**	....	....	....	....	....	....	....	....	....
	Montreal	**NHL**	**43**	**7**	**23**	**30**	**20**	**4**	**0**	**2**	**87**	**8.0**	**4**	**0**	**0.0**	**22:43**	**6**	**0**	**2**	**2**	**7**	**0**	**0**	**0**	**22:23**
	NHL Totals		**329**	**27**	**121**	**148**	**302**	**11**	**1**	**2**	**555**	**4.9**		**2**	**0.0**	**20:33**	**18**	**1**	**4**	**5**	**17**	**0**	**0**	**0**	**21:02**

OHL First All-Star Team (2004) • OHL Defenseman of the Year (2004) • Canadian Major Junior First All-Star Team (2004) • Canadian Major Junior Defenseman of the Year (2004)

Traded to **Anaheim** by **Chicago** with Petri Kontiola for Samuel Pahlsson, Logan Stephenson and future considerations, March 4, 2009. Traded to **NY Islanders** by **Anaheim** for NY Islanders' 3rd round choice (Joseph Cramarossa) in 2011 Entry Draft, July 30, 2010. Traded to **Montreal** by **NY Islanders** for Montreal's 2nd round compensatory choice (Johan Sundstrom) in 2011 Entry Draft and future considerations, December 28, 2010. Traded to **Columbus** by **Montreal** for a 5th round choice in 2012 Entry Draft, June 29, 2011.

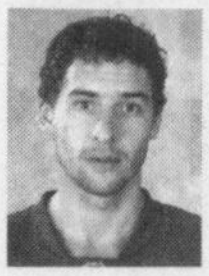

WOLSKI, Wojtek

(VOHL-skee, VOI-tehk) **NYR**

Left wing. Shoots left. 6'3", 215 lbs. Born, Zabrze, Poland, February 24, 1986. Colorado's 1st choice, 21st overall, in 2004 Entry Draft.

2001-02	St. Mike's B's	OPJHL	33	16	33	49	40	....	....	....	....	....	....	....	....	....	....	....	....	....	....	....	....	....	....
2002-03	Brampton	OHL	64	25	32	57	26	....	....	....	....	....	....	....	....	....	11	5	0	5	6	....	....	....	....
2003-04	Brampton	OHL	66	29	41	70	30	....	....	....	....	....	....	....	....	....	12	5	3	8	8	....	....	....	....
2004-05	Brampton	OHL	67	29	44	73	41	....	....	....	....	....	....	....	....	....	6	2	5	7	6	....	....	....	....
2005-06	**Colorado**	**NHL**	**9**	**2**	**4**	**6**	**4**	**2**	**0**	**0**	**9**	**22.2**	**–5**	**4**	**0.0**	**9:44**	**8**	**1**	**3**	**4**	**2**	**0**	**0**	**0**	**12:06**
	Brampton	OHL	56	47	81	128	46	....	....	....	....	....	....	....	....	....	11	7	11	18	4	....	....	....	....
2006-07	**Colorado**	**NHL**	**76**	**22**	**28**	**50**	**14**	**7**	**0**	**2**	**165**	**13.3**	**2**	**3**	**100.0**	**15:31**	....	....	....	....	....	....	....	....	....
2007-08	**Colorado**	**NHL**	**77**	**18**	**30**	**48**	**14**	**4**	**0**	**6**	**158**	**11.4**	**10**	**48**	**50.0**	**15:56**	**7**	**2**	**3**	**5**	**2**	**1**	**0**	**1**	**13:15**
2008-09	**Colorado**	**NHL**	**78**	**14**	**28**	**42**	**28**	**2**	**1**	**3**	**169**	**8.3**	**–13**	**515**	**48.2**	**18:23**	....	....	....	....	....	....	....	....	....
2009-10	**Colorado**	**NHL**	**62**	**17**	**30**	**47**	**21**	**2**	**0**	**4**	**156**	**10.9**	**15**	**23**	**47.8**	**18:57**	....	....	....	....	....	....	....	....	....
	Phoenix	**NHL**	**18**	**6**	**12**	**18**	**6**	**0**	**0**	**1**	**39**	**15.4**	**6**	**13**	**38.5**	**18:01**	**7**	**4**	**1**	**5**	**0**	**1**	**0**	**0**	**17:25**
2010-11	**Phoenix**	**NHL**	**36**	**6**	**10**	**16**	**10**	**0**	**0**	**0**	**57**	**10.5**	**–6**	**24**	**58.3**	**14:41**	....	....	....	....	....	....	....	....	....
	NY Rangers	**NHL**	**37**	**6**	**13**	**19**	**8**	**1**	**0**	**1**	**78**	**7.7**	**12**	**7**	**14.3**	**14:29**	**5**	**1**	**2**	**3**	**0**	**0**	**0**	**0**	**12:16**
	NHL Totals		**393**	**91**	**155**	**246**	**105**	**18**	**1**	**17**	**831**	**11.0**		**637**	**48.0**	**16:31**	**27**	**8**	**9**	**17**	**4**	**2**	**0**	**1**	**13:48**

OHL First All-Star Team (2004) • OHL Second All-Star Team (2006)

Traded to **Phoenix** by **Colorado** for Peter Mueller and Kevin Porter, March 3, 2010. Traded to **NY Rangers** by **Phoenix** for Michael Rozsival, January 10. 2011.

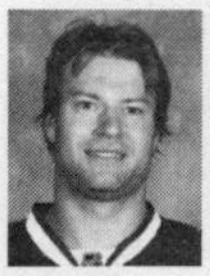

WOYWITKA, Jeff

(WOI-wiht-ka, JEHF)

Defense. Shoots left. 6'3", 227 lbs. Born, Vermilion, Alta., September 1, 1983. Philadelphia's 1st choice, 27th overall, in 2001 Entry Draft.

1998-99	Wainwright	AAHA	26	7	15	22	60	....	....	....	....	....	....	....	....	....	....	....	....	....	....	....	....	....	....
99-2000	Red Deer Rebels	WHL	67	4	12	16	40	....	....	....	....	....	....	....	....	....	4	0	3	3	2	....	....	....	....
2000-01	Red Deer Rebels	WHL	72	7	28	35	113	....	....	....	....	....	....	....	....	....	22	2	8	10	25	....	....	....	....
2001-02	Red Deer Rebels	WHL	72	14	23	37	109	....	....	....	....	....	....	....	....	....	23	2	10	12	22	....	....	....	....
2002-03	Red Deer Rebels	WHL	57	16	36	52	65	....	....	....	....	....	....	....	....	....	23	1	9	10	25	....	....	....	....
2003-04	Philadelphia	AHL	29	0	6	6	51	....	....	....	....	....	....	....	....	....	....	....	....	....	....	....	....	....	....
	Toronto	AHL	53	4	18	22	41	....	....	....	....	....	....	....	....	....	3	0	0	0	2	....	....	....	....
2004-05	Edmonton	AHL	80	6	20	26	84	....	....	....	....	....	....	....	....	....	....	....	....	....	....	....	....	....	....
2005-06	**St. Louis**	**NHL**	**26**	**0**	**2**	**2**	**25**	**0**	**0**	**0**	**23**	**0.0**	**–12**	**0**	**0.0**	**10:38**	....	....	....	....	....	....	....	....	....
	Peoria Rivermen	AHL	53	1	14	15	58	....	....	....	....	....	....	....	....	....	4	0	0	0	4	....	....	....	....
2006-07	**St. Louis**	**NHL**	**34**	**1**	**6**	**7**	**12**	**0**	**0**	**0**	**28**	**3.6**	**4**	**0**	**0.0**	**14:45**	....	....	....	....	....	....	....	....	....
	Peoria Rivermen	AHL	41	0	18	18	20	....	....	....	....	....	....	....	....	....	....	....	....	....	....	....	....	....	....
2007-08	**St. Louis**	**NHL**	**27**	**2**	**6**	**8**	**12**	**0**	**0**	**0**	**25**	**8.0**	**2**	**0**	**0.0**	**16:04**	....	....	....	....	....	....	....	....	....
	Peoria Rivermen	AHL	52	10	20	30	35	....	....	....	....	....	....	....	....	....	....	....	....	....	....	....	....	....	....
2008-09	**St. Louis**	**NHL**	**65**	**3**	**15**	**18**	**57**	**2**	**0**	**1**	**71**	**4.2**	**8**	**0**	**0.0**	**18:29**	**4**	**0**	**0**	**0**	**0**	**0**	**0**	**0**	**18:48**
	Peoria Rivermen	AHL	7	0	7	7	2	....	....	....	....	....	....	....	....	....	....	....	....	....	....	....	....	....	....
2009-10	**Dallas**	**NHL**	**36**	**0**	**3**	**3**	**11**	**0**	**0**	**0**	**44**	**0.0**	**–6**	**0**	**0.0**	**14:06**	....	....	....	....	....	....	....	....	....
2010-11	**Dallas**	**NHL**	**63**	**2**	**9**	**11**	**24**	**1**	**0**	**0**	**72**	**2.8**	**5**	**0**	**0.0**	**17:57**	....	....	....	....	....	....	....	....	....
	NHL Totals		**251**	**8**	**41**	**49**	**141**	**3**	**0**	**1**	**263**	**3.0**		**0**	**0.0**	**16:08**	**4**	**0**	**0**	**0**	**0**	**0**	**0**	**0**	**18:48**

WHL East Second All-Star Team (2002) • WHL East First All-Star Team (2003)

Traded to **Edmonton** by **Philadelphia** with Philadelphia's 1st round choice (Rob Schremp) in 2004 Entry Draft and Philadelphia's 3rd round choice (Danny Syvret) in 2005 Entry Draft for Mike Comrie, December 16, 2003. Traded to **St. Louis** by **Edmonton** with Eric Brewer and Doug Lynch for Chris Pronger, August 2, 2005. Signed as a free agent by **Dallas**, July 7, 2009. • Missed majority of 2009-10 as a healthy reserve.

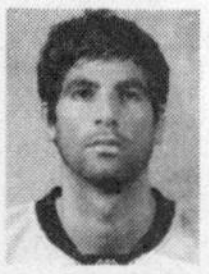

WOZNIEWSKI, Andy

(wuhz-NYOO-skee, AN-dee)

Defense. Shoots left. 6'5", 225 lbs. Born, Buffalo Grove, IL, May 25, 1980.

99-2000	U. Mass-Lowell	H-East	17	1	1	2	8	....	....	....	....	....	....	....	....	....	....	....	....	....	....	....	....	....	....
2000-01	Texas Tornado	NAHL	54	10	34	44	98	....	....	....	....	....	....	....	....	....	8	2	7	9	12	....	....	....	....
2001-02	U. of Wisconsin	WCHA	39	3	13	16	54	....	....	....	....	....	....	....	....	....	....	....	....	....	....	....	....	....	....
2002-03	U. of Wisconsin	WCHA	33	1	7	8	47	....	....	....	....	....	....	....	....	....	....	....	....	....	....	....	....	....	....
2003-04	U. of Wisconsin	WCHA	43	6	8	14	*104	....	....	....	....	....	....	....	....	....	....	....	....	....	....	....	....	....	....
	St. John's	AHL	3	0	1	1	0	....	....	....	....	....	....	....	....	....	....	....	....	....	....	....	....	....	....
2004-05	St. John's	AHL	28	1	4	5	20	....	....	....	....	....	....	....	....	....	....	....	....	....	....	....	....	....	....
2005-06	**Toronto**	**NHL**	**13**	**0**	**1**	**1**	**13**	**0**	**0**	**0**	**6**	**0.0**	**–8**	**0**	**0.0**	**17:55**	....	....	....	....	....	....	....	....	....
	Toronto Marlies	AHL	31	4	11	15	42	....	....	....	....	....	....	....	....	....	....	....	....	....	....	....	....	....	....
2006-07	**Toronto**	**NHL**	**15**	**0**	**2**	**2**	**14**	**0**	**0**	**0**	**10**	**0.0**	**–1**	**0**	**0.0**	**13:55**	....	....	....	....	....	....	....	....	....
	Toronto Marlies	AHL	5	0	3	3	8	....	....	....	....	....	....	....	....	....	....	....	....	....	....	....	....	....	....
2007-08	**Toronto**	**NHL**	**48**	**2**	**7**	**9**	**54**	**0**	**0**	**0**	**34**	**5.9**	**5**	**0**	**0.0**	**14:10**	....	....	....	....	....	....	....	....	....
	Toronto Marlies	AHL	33	7	10	17	26	....	....	....	....	....	....	....	....	....	19	4	5	9	14	....	....	....	....
2008-09	**St. Louis**	**NHL**	**1**	**0**	**0**	**0**	**0**	**0**	**0**	**0**	**0**	**0.0**	**0**	**0**	**0.0**	**6:44**	....	....	....	....	....	....	....	....	....
	Peoria Rivermen	AHL	56	1	16	17	56	....	....	....	....	....	....	....	....	....	....	....	....	....	....	....	....	....	....
	Wilkes-Barre	AHL	18	2	2	4	26	....	....	....	....	....	....	....	....	....	6	1	1	2	2	....	....	....	....
2009-10	**Boston**	**NHL**	**2**	**0**	**0**	**0**	**0**	**0**	**0**	**0**	**1**	**0.0**	**0**	**0**	**0.0**	**9:17**	....	....	....	....	....	....	....	....	....
	Providence Bruins	AHL	68	10	33	43	69	....	....	....	....	....	....	....	....	....	....	....	....	....	....	....	....	....	....
2010-11	EV Zug	Swiss	50	10	13	23	*123	....	....	....	....	....	....	....	....	....	10	1	4	5	6	....	....	....	....
	NHL Totals		**79**	**2**	**10**	**12**	**81**	**0**	**0**	**0**	**51**	**3.9**		**0**	**0.0**	**14:31**	....	....	....	....	....	....	....	....	....

Signed as a free agent by **Toronto**, May 27, 2004. • Missed majority of 2006-07 due to shoulder surgery, October 10, 2006. Signed as a free agent by **St. Louis**, July 17, 2008. Traded to **Pittsburgh** by **St. Louis** for Danny Richmond, March 4, 2009. Signed as a free agent by **Boston**, September 9, 2009. Signed as a free agent by **Zug** (Swiss), May 20, 2010.

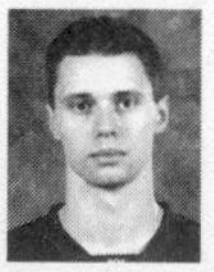

WRIGHT, James

(RIGHT, JAYMZ) **T.B.**

Center. Shoots left. 6'4", 200 lbs. Born, Saskatoon, Sask., March 24, 1990. Tampa Bay's 2nd choice, 117th overall, in 2008 Entry Draft.

2005-06	Sask. Contacts	SMHL	41	13	19	32	43	....	....	....	....	....	....	....	....	....	....	....	....	....	....	....	....	....	....
	Vancouver Giants	WHL	2	0	0	0	2	....	....	....	....	....	....	....	....	....	....	....	....	....	....	....	....	....	....
2006-07	Vancouver Giants	WHL	48	5	7	12	31	....	....	....	....	....	....	....	....	....	14	3	1	4	0	....	....	....	....
2007-08	Vancouver Giants	WHL	60	13	23	36	21	....	....	....	....	....	....	....	....	....	6	1	0	1	2	....	....	....	....
2008-09	Vancouver Giants	WHL	71	21	26	47	54	....	....	....	....	....	....	....	....	....	17	3	7	10	13	....	....	....	....
2009-10	**Tampa Bay**	**NHL**	**48**	**2**	**3**	**5**	**18**	**0**	**0**	**0**	**25**	**8.0**	**–9**	**169**	**45.6**	**11:39**	....	....	....	....	....	....	....	....	....
	Vancouver Giants	WHL	21	6	13	19	17	....	....	....	....	....	....	....	....	....	16	7	9	16	4	....	....	....	....

			Regular Season														Playoffs								
Season	Club	League	GP	G	A	Pts	PIM	PP	SH	GW	S	%	+/-	TF	F%	Min	GP	G	A	Pts	PIM	PP	SH	GW	Min
2010-11	**Tampa Bay**	**NHL**	**1**	**0**	**0**	**0**	**0**	**0**	**0**	**0**	**0**	**0.0**	**–2**	**2**	**0.0**	**4:36**	....	....	....	....	....	....	....	....	....
	Norfolk Admirals	AHL	80	16	31	47	64	....	....	....	....	....	....	....	....	....	6	1	0	1	8	....	....	....	....
	NHL Totals		**49**	**2**	**3**	**5**	**18**	**0**	**0**	**0**	**25**	**8.0**		**171**	**45.0**	**11:30**	....	....	....	....	....	....	....	....	....

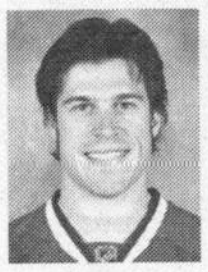

WYMAN, James

(WIGH-muhn, JAYMZ) **T.B.**

Right wing. Shoots right. 6'2", 199 lbs. Born, Edina, MN, February 27, 1986. Montreal's 3rd choice, 100th overall, in 2004 Entry Draft.

Season	Club	League	GP	G	A	Pts	PIM	PP	SH	GW	S	%	+/-	TF	F%	Min	GP	G	A	Pts	PIM	PP	SH	GW	Min
2001-02	Blake Bears	High-MN	26	7	5	12	....	....	....	....	....	....	....	....	....	....	....	....	....	....	....	....	....	....	....
2002-03	Blake Bears	High-MN	28	17	23	40	12	....	....	....	....	....	....	....	....	....	....	....	....	....	....	....	....	....	....
2003-04	Blake Bears	High-MN	27	31	24	55	4	....	....	....	....	....	....	....	....	....	....	....	....	....	....	....	....	....	....
	Team Southwest	UMEHL	24	8	8	16	....	....	....	....	....	....	....	....	....	....	....	....	....	....	....	....	....	....	....
2004-05	Dartmouth	ECAC	33	5	6	11	4	....	....	....	....	....	....	....	....	....	....	....	....	....	....	....	....	....	....
2005-06	Dartmouth	ECAC	28	8	12	20	6	....	....	....	....	....	....	....	....	....	....	....	....	....	....	....	....	....	....
2006-07	Dartmouth	ECAC	33	13	11	24	20	....	....	....	....	....	....	....	....	....	....	....	....	....	....	....	....	....	....
2007-08	Dartmouth	ECAC	29	15	15	30	18	....	....	....	....	....	....	....	....	....	....	....	....	....	....	....	....	....	....
	Hamilton	AHL	8	0	1	1	5	....	....	....	....	....	....	....	....	....	....	....	....	....	....	....	....	....	....
2008-09	Hamilton	AHL	52	6	5	11	8	....	....	....	....	....	....	....	....	....	6	0	1	1	2	....	....	....	....
	Cincinnati	ECHL	15	0	8	8	4	....	....	....	....	....	....	....	....	....	....	....	....	....	....	....	....	....	....
2009-10	**Montreal**	**NHL**	**3**	**0**	**0**	**0**	**0**	**0**	**0**	**0**	**0**	**0.0**	**–2**	**1**	**0.0**	**4:23**	....	....	....	....	....	....	....	....	....
	Hamilton	AHL	76	17	20	37	12	....	....	....	....	....	....	....	....	....	19	1	3	4	2	....	....	....	....
2010-11	Hamilton	AHL	80	18	18	36	36	....	....	....	....	....	....	....	....	....	20	3	5	8	8	....	....	....	....
	NHL Totals		**3**	**0**	**0**	**0**	**0**	**0**	**0**	**0**	**0**	**0.0**		**1**	**0.0**	**4:23**	....	....	....	....	....	....	....	....	....

Signed as a free agent by **Tampa Bay**, July 1, 2011.

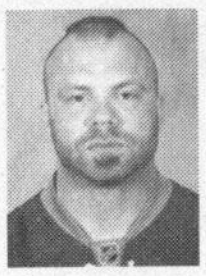

YABLONSKI, Jeremy

(ya-BLAWN-skee, JAIR-eh-mee)

Left wing. Shoots right. 5'11", 239 lbs. Born, Meadow Lake, Sask., March 21, 1980.

Season	Club	League	GP	G	A	Pts	PIM	PP	SH	GW	S	%	+/-	TF	F%	Min	GP	G	A	Pts	PIM	PP	SH	GW	Min
1996-97	Beardy's	SMHL	38	7	3	10	284	....	....	....	....	....	....	....	....	....	....	....	....	....	....	....	....	....	....
1997-98	Edmonton Ice	WHL	47	3	0	3	143	....	....	....	....	....	....	....	....	....	....	....	....	....	....	....	....	....	....
1998-99	Kootenay Ice	WHL	27	1	1	2	77	....	....	....	....	....	....	....	....	....	....	....	....	....	....	....	....	....	....
99-2000	Kootenay Ice	WHL	DID NOT PLAY – INJURED																						
2000-01	Phoenix	WCHL	44	2	1	3	169	....	....	....	....	....	....	....	....	....	....	....	....	....	....	....	....	....	....
2001-02	Idaho Steelheads	WCHL	69	2	1	3	303	....	....	....	....	....	....	....	....	....	....	....	....	....	....	....	....	....	....
2002-03	Peoria Rivermen	ECHL	24	1	2	3	154	....	....	....	....	....	....	....	....	....	....	....	....	....	....	....	....	....	....
	Cincinnati	AHL	9	0	0	0	42	....	....	....	....	....	....	....	....	....	....	....	....	....	....	....	....	....	....
	Worcester IceCats	AHL	20	1	0	1	50	....	....	....	....	....	....	....	....	....	....	....	....	....	....	....	....	....	....
2003-04	Worcester IceCats	AHL	6	0	0	0	19	....	....	....	....	....	....	....	....	....	....	....	....	....	....	....	....	....	....
	St. Louis	**NHL**	**1**	**0**	**0**	**0**	**5**	**0**	**0**	**0**	**1**	**0.0**	**–1**	**0**	**0.0**	**7:53**	....	....	....	....	....	....	....	....	....
	Peoria Rivermen	ECHL	13	0	2	2	62	....	....	....	....	....	....	....	....	....	....	....	....	....	....	....	....	....	....
	Milwaukee	AHL	2	0	0	0	11	....	....	....	....	....	....	....	....	....	....	....	....	....	....	....	....	....	....
2004-05	Milwaukee	AHL	32	3	2	5	116	....	....	....	....	....	....	....	....	....	....	....	....	....	....	....	....	....	....
2005-06	Milwaukee	AHL	30	0	1	1	82	....	....	....	....	....	....	....	....	....	....	....	....	....	....	....	....	....	....
	Idaho Steelheads	ECHL	3	0	1	1	25	....	....	....	....	....	....	....	....	....	....	....	....	....	....	....	....	....	....
2006-07	Idaho Steelheads	ECHL	41	3	3	6	163	....	....	....	....	....	....	....	....	....	....	....	....	....	....	....	....	....	....
2007-08	Binghamton	AHL	76	3	10	13	228	....	....	....	....	....	....	....	....	....	....	....	....	....	....	....	....	....	....
2008-09	Binghamton	AHL	64	1	2	3	215	....	....	....	....	....	....	....	....	....	....	....	....	....	....	....	....	....	....
2009-10	Binghamton	AHL	27	1	0	1	128	....	....	....	....	....	....	....	....	....	....	....	....	....	....	....	....	....	....
2010-11	Bridgeport	AHL	17	0	2	2	48	....	....	....	....	....	....	....	....	....	....	....	....	....	....	....	....	....	....
	NHL Totals		**1**	**0**	**0**	**0**	**5**	**0**	**0**	**0**	**1**	**0.0**		**0**	**0.0**	**7:53**	....	....	....	....	....	....	....	....	....

• Missed majority of 1998-99 and entire 1999-2000 due to concussion in practice, January 3, 1999. Signed as a free agent by **Worcester** (AHL), July 17, 2003. Signed as a free agent by **St. Louis**, December 30, 2003. Claimed on waivers by **Nashville** from **St. Louis**, January 30, 2004. Signed as a free agent by **Binghamton** (AHL), August 9, 2007. Signed as a free agent by **Ottawa**, June 30, 2008. • Missed majority of 2009-10 due to various injuries. Signed as a free agent by **NY Islanders**, July 21, 2010. Signed as a free agent by **Vityaz Chekhov** (Russia-KHL), July 24, 2011.

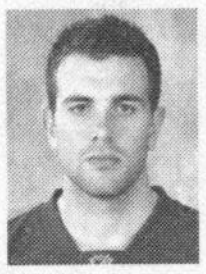

YANDLE, Keith

(Yan-duhl, KEETH) **PHX**

Defense. Shoots left. 6'1", 195 lbs. Born, Boston, MA, September 9, 1986. Phoenix's 3rd choice, 105th overall, in 2005 Entry Draft.

Season	Club	League	GP	G	A	Pts	PIM	PP	SH	GW	S	%	+/-	TF	F%	Min	GP	G	A	Pts	PIM	PP	SH	GW	Min
2004-05	Cushing	High-MA	34	14	40	54	52	....	....	....	....	....	....	....	....	....	....	....	....	....	....	....	....	....	....
2005-06	Moncton Wildcats	QMJHL	66	25	59	84	109	....	....	....	....	....	....	....	....	....	21	6	14	20	36	....	....	....	....
2006-07	**Phoenix**	**NHL**	**7**	**0**	**2**	**2**	**8**	**0**	**0**	**0**	**10**	**0.0**	**0**	**0**	**0.0**	**20:10**	....	....	....	....	....	....	....	....	....
	San Antonio	AHL	69	6	27	33	97	....	....	....	....	....	....	....	....	....	....	....	....	....	....	....	....	....	....
2007-08	**Phoenix**	**NHL**	**43**	**5**	**7**	**12**	**14**	**4**	**0**	**0**	**72**	**6.9**	**–12**	**0**	**0.0**	**14:04**	....	....	....	....	....	....	....	....	....
	San Antonio	AHL	30	1	14	15	80	....	....	....	....	....	....	....	....	....	5	0	0	0	8	....	....	....	....
2008-09	**Phoenix**	**NHL**	**69**	**4**	**26**	**30**	**37**	**1**	**0**	**0**	**118**	**3.4**	**–4**	**0**	**0.0**	**16:37**	....	....	....	....	....	....	....	....	....
2009-10	**Phoenix**	**NHL**	**82**	**12**	**29**	**41**	**45**	**5**	**0**	**2**	**145**	**8.3**	**16**	**0**	**0.0**	**20:14**	**7**	**2**	**3**	**5**	**4**	**1**	**0**	**0**	**17:12**
2010-11	**Phoenix**	**NHL**	**82**	**11**	**48**	**59**	**68**	**3**	**0**	**0**	**199**	**5.5**	**18**	**0**	**0.0**	**24:23**	**4**	**0**	**5**	**5**	**0**	**0**	**0**	**0**	**25:50**
	NHL Totals		**283**	**32**	**112**	**144**	**172**	**13**	**0**	**2**	**544**	**5.9**		**0**	**0.0**	**19:37**	**11**	**2**	**8**	**10**	**4**	**1**	**0**	**0**	**20:20**

QMJHL First All-Star Team (2006) • Canadian Major Junior First All-Star Team (2006) • Canadian Major Junior Defenseman of the Year (2006)
Played in NHL All-Star Game (2011)

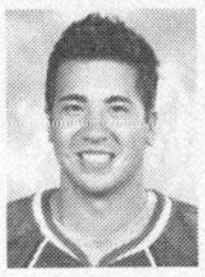

YIP, Brandon

(YIHP, BRAN-duhn) **COL**

Right wing. Shoots right. 6'1", 195 lbs. Born, Vancouver, B.C., April 25, 1985. Colorado's 7th choice, 239th overall, in 2004 Entry Draft.

Season	Club	League	GP	G	A	Pts	PIM	PP	SH	GW	S	%	+/-	TF	F%	Min	GP	G	A	Pts	PIM	PP	SH	GW	Min
2003-04	Coquitlam	BCHL	56	31	38	69	87	....	....	....	....	....	....	....	....	....	4	1	2	3	14	....	....	....	....
2004-05	Coquitlam	BCHL	43	20	42	62	92	....	....	....	....	....	....	....	....	....	7	6	1	7	12	....	....	....	....
2005-06	Boston University	H-East	39	9	22	31	59	....	....	....	....	....	....	....	....	....	....	....	....	....	....	....	....	....	....
2006-07	Boston University	H-East	18	5	6	11	29	....	....	....	....	....	....	....	....	....	....	....	....	....	....	....	....	....	....
2007-08	Boston University	H-East	37	11	12	23	28	....	....	....	....	....	....	....	....	....	....	....	....	....	....	....	....	....	....
2008-09	Boston University	H-East	45	20	23	43	118	....	....	....	....	....	....	....	....	....	....	....	....	....	....	....	....	....	....
2009-10	**Colorado**	**NHL**	**32**	**11**	**8**	**19**	**22**	**4**	**0**	**2**	**65**	**16.9**	**5**	**1**	**0.0**	**14:41**	**6**	**2**	**2**	**4**	**6**	**0**	**0**	**0**	**17:51**
	Lake Erie	AHL	6	2	0	2	4	....	....	....	....	....	....	....	....	....	....	....	....	....	....	....	....	....	....
2010-11	**Colorado**	**NHL**	**71**	**12**	**10**	**22**	**54**	**3**	**1**	**1**	**127**	**9.4**	**–22**	**14**	**35.7**	**13:44**	....	....	....	....	....	....	....	....	....
	NHL Totals		**103**	**23**	**18**	**41**	**76**	**7**	**1**	**3**	**192**	**12.0**		**15**	**33.3**	**14:02**	**6**	**2**	**2**	**4**	**6**	**0**	**0**	**0**	**17:51**

Hockey East All-Rookie Team (2006) • Hockey East Rookie of the Year (2006)
• Missed majority of 2009-10 due to hand injury in pre-season game at St. Louis, September 18, 2009.

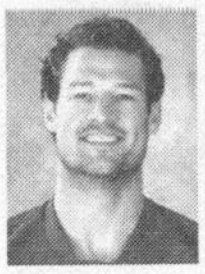

YONKMAN, Nolan

(YAWNK-man, NOH-luhn) **FLA**

Defense. Shoots right. 6'6", 253 lbs. Born, Punnichy, Sask., April 1, 1981. Washington's 5th choice, 37th overall, in 1999 Entry Draft.

Season	Club	League	GP	G	A	Pts	PIM	PP	SH	GW	S	%	+/-	TF	F%	Min	GP	G	A	Pts	PIM	PP	SH	GW	Min
1996-97	Naicam Vikings	SAHA	64	15	23	38	36	....	....	....	....	....	....	....	....	....	....	....	....	....	....	....	....	....	....
	Kelowna Rockets	WHL	4	0	0	0	0	....	....	....	....	....	....	....	....	....	....	....	....	....	....	....	....	....	....
1997-98	Kelowna Rockets	WHL	65	0	2	2	36	....	....	....	....	....	....	....	....	....	7	0	0	0	2	....	....	....	....
1998-99	Kelowna Rockets	WHL	61	1	6	7	129	....	....	....	....	....	....	....	....	....	6	0	0	0	6	....	....	....	....
99-2000	Kelowna Rockets	WHL	71	5	7	12	153	....	....	....	....	....	....	....	....	....	5	0	0	0	8	....	....	....	....
2000-01	Kelowna Rockets	WHL	7	0	1	1	19	....	....	....	....	....	....	....	....	....	....	....	....	....	....	....	....	....	....
	Brandon	WHL	51	6	10	16	94	....	....	....	....	....	....	....	....	....	6	0	1	1	12	....	....	....	....
2001-02	**Washington**	**NHL**	**11**	**1**	**0**	**1**	**4**	**0**	**0**	**0**	**7**	**14.3**	**3**	**0**	**0.0**	**12:44**	....	....	....	....	....	....	....	....	....
	Portland Pirates	AHL	59	4	3	7	116	....	....	....	....	....	....	....	....	....	....	....	....	....	....	....	....	....	....
2002-03	Portland Pirates	AHL	24	1	4	5	40	....	....	....	....	....	....	....	....	....	3	0	1	1	2	....	....	....	....
2003-04	**Washington**	**NHL**	**1**	**0**	**0**	**0**	**0**	**0**	**0**	**0**	**0**	**0.0**	**0**	**0**	**0.0**	**5:00**	....	....	....	....	....	....	....	....	....
	Portland Pirates	AHL	4	0	0	0	11	....	....	....	....	....	....	....	....	....	....	....	....	....	....	....	....	....	....
2004-05	Portland Pirates	AHL	32	0	3	3	68	....	....	....	....	....	....	....	....	....	....	....	....	....	....	....	....	....	....
2005-06	**Washington**	**NHL**	**38**	**0**	**7**	**7**	**86**	**0**	**0**	**0**	**14**	**0.0**	**1**	**0**	**0.0**	**8:13**	....	....	....	....	....	....	....	....	....
	Hershey Bears	AHL	6	0	0	0	15	....	....	....	....	....	....	....	....	....	....	....	....	....	....	....	....	....	....
2006-07	Milwaukee	AHL	77	3	10	13	113	....	....	....	....	....	....	....	....	....	4	0	0	0	2	....	....	....	....
2007-08	Milwaukee	AHL	69	0	7	7	103	....	....	....	....	....	....	....	....	....	6	0	1	1	18	....	....	....	....
2008-09	Milwaukee	AHL	61	3	7	10	80	....	....	....	....	....	....	....	....	....	11	0	0	0	15	....	....	....	....
2009-10	Milwaukee	AHL	76	2	7	9	170	....	....	....	....	....	....	....	....	....	7	0	1	1	2	....	....	....	....

			Regular Season														Playoffs								
Season	Club	League	GP	G	A	Pts	PIM	PP	SH	GW	S	%	+/-	TF	F%	Min	GP	G	A	Pts	PIM	PP	SH	GW	Min
2010-11	**Phoenix**	**NHL**	**16**	**0**	**1**	**1**	**39**	0	0	0	8	0.0	5	0	0.0	12:08	....	....	....	....	....	....	....	....	....
	San Antonio	AHL	56	1	4	5	104	....	....	....	....	....	....	....	....	....	....	....	....	....	....	....	....	....	....
	NHL Totals		**66**	**1**	**8**	**9**	**129**	0	0	0	29	3.4		0	0.0	9:52	....	....	....	....	....	....	....	....	....

• Missed majority of 2002-03 due to abdominal injury in training camp, September 25, 2002. • Missed majority of 2003-04 and 2004-05 due to knee injury vs. Worcester (AHL), October 23, 2003. Signed as a free agent by **Nashville**, July 17, 2006. Signed as a free agent by **Phoenix**, July 3, 2010. Signed as a free agent by **Florida**, July 1, 2011.

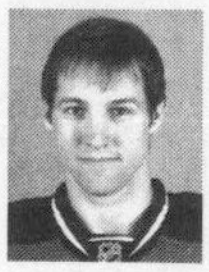

ZAJAC, Travis

(ZAY-jak, TRA-vihs) **N.J.**

Center. Shoots right. 6'3", 200 lbs. Born, Winnipeg, Man., May 13, 1985. New Jersey's 1st choice, 20th overall, in 2004 Entry Draft.

Season	Club	League	GP	G	A	Pts	PIM	PP	SH	GW	S	%	+/-	TF	F%	Min	GP	G	A	Pts	PIM	PP	SH	GW	Min
2002-03	Salmon Arm	BCHL	59	16	36	52	27	....	....	....	....	....	....	....	....	....	11	2	4	6	6	....	....	....	....
2003-04	Salmon Arm	BCHL	59	43	69	112	110	....	....	....	....	....	....	....	....	....	14	10	13	23	10	....	....	....	....
2004-05	North Dakota	WCHA	45	20	19	39	16	....	....	....	....	....	....	....	....	....	....	....	....	....	....	....	....	....	....
2005-06	North Dakota	WCHA	46	18	29	47	20	....	....	....	....	....	....	....	....	....	....	....	....	....	....	....	....	....	....
	Albany River Rats	AHL	2	0	1	1	2	....	....	....	....	....	....	....	....	....	....	....	....	....	....	....	....	....	....
2006-07	**New Jersey**	**NHL**	**80**	**17**	**25**	**42**	**16**	6	0	2	134	12.7	1	904	46.9	16:03	11	1	4	5	4	0	0	0	16:22
2007-08	**New Jersey**	**NHL**	**82**	**14**	**20**	**34**	**31**	5	0	1	155	9.0	-11	1032	51.2	16:44	5	0	1	1	4	0	0	0	13:35
2008-09	**New Jersey**	**NHL**	**82**	**20**	**42**	**62**	**29**	5	1	2	185	10.8	33	1287	53.1	18:39	7	1	3	4	6	0	0	1	17:51
2009-10	**New Jersey**	**NHL**	**82**	**25**	**42**	**67**	**24**	6	0	4	210	11.9	22	1373	52.9	20:13	5	1	1	2	2	0	0	0	21:46
2010-11	**New Jersey**	**NHL**	**82**	**13**	**31**	**44**	**24**	2	1	1	173	7.5	-6	1278	55.3	19:47	....	....	....	....	....	....	....	....	....
	NHL Totals		**408**	**89**	**160**	**249**	**124**	24	2	10	857	10.4		5874	52.2	18:18	28	3	9	12	16	0	0	1	17:12

WCHA All-Rookie Team (2005) • NCAA Championship All-Tournament Team (2005)

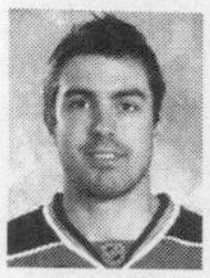

ZALEWSKI, Steven

(zuh-LEH-skee, STEEV) **N.J.**

Center. Shoots left. 6', 195 lbs. Born, Utica, NY, August 20, 1986. San Jose's 5th choice, 153rd overall, in 2004 Entry Draft.

Season	Club	League	GP	G	A	Pts	PIM	PP	SH	GW	S	%	+/-	TF	F%	Min	GP	G	A	Pts	PIM	PP	SH	GW	Min
2003-04	Northwood	High-NY	40	32	34	66	22	....	....	....	....	....	....	....	....	....	....	....	....	....	....	....	....	....	....
2004-05	Clarkson Knights	ECAC	39	12	7	19	60	....	....	....	....	....	....	....	....	....	....	....	....	....	....	....	....	....	....
2005-06	Clarkson Knights	ECAC	35	9	13	22	50	....	....	....	....	....	....	....	....	....	....	....	....	....	....	....	....	....	....
2006-07	Clarkson Knights	ECAC	39	16	18	34	44	....	....	....	....	....	....	....	....	....	....	....	....	....	....	....	....	....	....
2007-08	Clarkson Knights	ECAC	38	21	12	33	34	....	....	....	....	....	....	....	....	....	....	....	....	....	....	....	....	....	....
	Worcester Sharks	AHL	7	2	4	6	0	....	....	....	....	....	....	....	....	....	....	....	....	....	....	....	....	....	....
2008-09	Worcester Sharks	AHL	75	13	26	39	26	....	....	....	....	....	....	....	....	....	12	0	1	1	6	....	....	....	....
2009-10	**San Jose**	**NHL**	**3**	**0**	**0**	**0**	**0**	0	0	0	3	0.0	-2	5	40.0	8:19	....	....	....	....	....	....	....	....	....
	Worcester Sharks	AHL	78	22	40	62	20	....	....	....	....	....	....	....	....	....	11	1	5	6	4	....	....	....	....
2010-11	Worcester Sharks	AHL	50	4	17	21	14	....	....	....	....	....	....	....	....	....	....	....	....	....	....	....	....	....	....
	Albany Devils	AHL	31	11	12	23	14	....	....	....	....	....	....	....	....	....	....	....	....	....	....	....	....	....	....
	NHL Totals		**3**	**0**	**0**	**0**	**0**	0	0	0	3	0.0		5	40.0	8:19	....	....	....	....	....	....	....	....	....

ECAC First All-Star Team (2008)

Traded to **New Jersey** by **San Jose** with Jay Leach for Michael Swift and Patrick Davis, February 9, 2011.

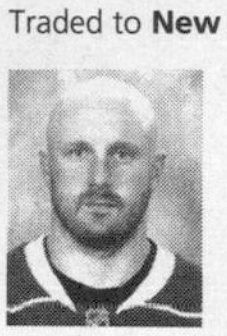

ZANON, Greg

(ZA-nuhn, GREHG) **MIN**

Defense. Shoots left. 5'11", 201 lbs. Born, Burnaby, B.C., June 5, 1980. Ottawa's 6th choice, 156th overall, in 2000 Entry Draft.

Season	Club	League	GP	G	A	Pts	PIM	PP	SH	GW	S	%	+/-	TF	F%	Min	GP	G	A	Pts	PIM	PP	SH	GW	Min
1995-96	Burnaby Beavers	Minor-BC	49	16	27	43	142	....	....	....	....	....	....	....	....	....	....	....	....	....	....	....	....	....	....
1996-97	Victoria Salsa	BCHL	53	4	13	17	124	....	....	....	....	....	....	....	....	....	....	....	....	....	....	....	....	....	....
1997-98	Victoria Salsa	BCHL	59	11	21	32	108	....	....	....	....	....	....	....	....	....	7	0	2	2	10	....	....	....	....
1998-99	South Surrey	BCHL	59	17	54	71	154	....	....	....	....	....	....	....	....	....	....	....	....	....	....	....	....	....	....
99-2000	Nebraska-Omaha	CCHA	42	3	26	29	56	....	....	....	....	....	....	....	....	....	....	....	....	....	....	....	....	....	....
2000-01	Nebraska-Omaha	CCHA	39	12	16	28	64	....	....	....	....	....	....	....	....	....	....	....	....	....	....	....	....	....	....
2001-02	Nebraska-Omaha	CCHA	41	9	16	25	54	....	....	....	....	....	....	....	....	....	....	....	....	....	....	....	....	....	....
2002-03	Nebraska-Omaha	CCHA	32	6	19	25	44	....	....	....	....	....	....	....	....	....	....	....	....	....	....	....	....	....	....
2003-04	Milwaukee	AHL	62	4	12	16	59	....	....	....	....	....	....	....	....	....	22	2	6	8	31	....	....	....	....
2004-05	Milwaukee	AHL	80	2	17	19	59	....	....	....	....	....	....	....	....	....	7	0	1	1	10	....	....	....	....
2005-06	**Nashville**	**NHL**	**4**	**0**	**2**	**2**	**6**	0	0	0	3	0.0	0	0	0.0	17:19	....	....	....	....	....	....	....	....	....
	Milwaukee	AHL	71	8	27	35	55	....	....	....	....	....	....	....	....	....	21	1	7	8	24	....	....	....	....
2006-07	**Nashville**	**NHL**	**66**	**3**	**5**	**8**	**32**	0	0	0	43	7.0	16	0	0.0	17:20	5	0	2	2	2	0	0	0	20:44
	Milwaukee	AHL	2	0	2	2	0	....	....	....	....	....	....	....	....	....	....	....	....	....	....	....	....	....	....
2007-08	**Nashville**	**NHL**	**78**	**0**	**5**	**5**	**24**	0	0	0	38	0.0	-5	0	0.0	18:28	6	0	2	2	4	0	0	0	18:45
2008-09	**Nashville**	**NHL**	**82**	**4**	**7**	**11**	**38**	0	0	1	54	7.4	8	0	0.0	20:51	....	....	....	....	....	....	....	....	....
2009-10	**Minnesota**	**NHL**	**81**	**2**	**13**	**15**	**36**	0	0	0	59	3.4	-10	1	0.0	22:22	....	....	....	....	....	....	....	....	....
2010-11	**Minnesota**	**NHL**	**82**	**0**	**7**	**7**	**48**	0	0	0	55	0.0	-5	0	0.0	21:33	....	....	....	....	....	....	....	....	....
	NHL Totals		**393**	**9**	**39**	**48**	**184**	0	0	1	252	3.6		1	0.0	20:12	11	0	4	4	6	0	0	0	19:39

CCHA First All-Star Team (2001) • NCAA West Second All-American Team (2001, 2002) • CCHA Second All-Star Team (2002)

Signed as a free agent by **Nashville**, July 9, 2004. Signed as a free agent by **Minnesota**, July 1, 2009.

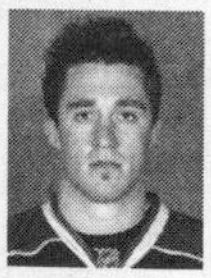

ZEILER, John

(ZIGH-luhr, JAWN)

Right wing. Shoots right. 5'11", 204 lbs. Born, Jefferson Hills, PA, November 21, 1982. Phoenix's 7th choice, 132nd overall, in 2002 Entry Draft.

Season	Club	League	GP	G	A	Pts	PIM	PP	SH	GW	S	%	+/-	TF	F%	Min	GP	G	A	Pts	PIM	PP	SH	GW	Min
99-2000	Pittsburgh	PAHA	27	17	15	32	94	....	....	....	....	....	....	....	....	....	....	....	....	....	....	....	....	....	....
2000-01	Sioux City	USHL	56	8	20	28	45	....	....	....	....	....	....	....	....	....	2	0	0	0	26	....	....	....	....
2001-02	Sioux City	USHL	60	23	27	50	116	....	....	....	....	....	....	....	....	....	12	2	3	5	25	....	....	....	....
2002-03	St. Lawrence	ECAC	37	10	17	27	28	....	....	....	....	....	....	....	....	....	....	....	....	....	....	....	....	....	....
2003-04	St. Lawrence	ECAC	41	8	*28	36	42	....	....	....	....	....	....	....	....	....	....	....	....	....	....	....	....	....	....
2004-05	St. Lawrence	ECAC	38	9	23	32	42	....	....	....	....	....	....	....	....	....	....	....	....	....	....	....	....	....	....
2005-06	St. Lawrence	ECAC	28	13	15	28	28	....	....	....	....	....	....	....	....	....	....	....	....	....	....	....	....	....	....
	San Antonio	AHL	8	0	1	1	10	....	....	....	....	....	....	....	....	....	....	....	....	....	....	....	....	....	....
	Lubbock	CHL	4	2	0	2	16	....	....	....	....	....	....	....	....	....	....	....	....	....	....	....	....	....	....
2006-07	Manchester	AHL	56	12	16	28	70	....	....	....	....	....	....	....	....	....	16	3	2	5	14	....	....	....	....
	Los Angeles	**NHL**	**23**	**1**	**2**	**3**	**22**	0	0	0	12	8.3	-2	22	40.9	8:36	....	....	....	....	....	....	....	....	....
2007-08	**Los Angeles**	**NHL**	**36**	**0**	**1**	**1**	**23**	0	0	0	18	0.0	-6	31	38.7	8:29	....	....	....	....	....	....	....	....	....
	Manchester	AHL	45	6	5	11	40	....	....	....	....	....	....	....	....	....	4	0	2	2	8	....	....	....	....
2008-09	**Los Angeles**	**NHL**	**27**	**0**	**1**	**1**	**42**	0	0	0	3	0.0	-2	5	60.0	6:33	....	....	....	....	....	....	....	....	....
	Manchester	AHL	2	0	1	1	4	....	....	....	....	....	....	....	....	....	....	....	....	....	....	....	....	....	....
2009-10	Manchester	AHL	65	11	9	20	31	....	....	....	....	....	....	....	....	....	16	4	3	7	4	....	....	....	....
2010-11	**Los Angeles**	**NHL**	**4**	**0**	**0**	**0**	**0**	0	0	0	1	0.0	-1	10	50.0	5:36	....	....	....	....	....	....	....	....	....
	Manchester	AHL	69	9	19	28	86	....	....	....	....	....	....	....	....	....	5	1	1	2	4	....	....	....	....
	NHL Totals		**90**	**1**	**4**	**5**	**87**	0	0	0	34	2.9		68	42.6	7:48	....	....	....	....	....	....	....	....	....

ECAC All-Rookie Team (2003)

Signed as a free agent by **San Antonio** (AHL), March 18, 2006. Signed as a free agent by **Los Angeles**, February 17, 2007. • Missed majority of 2008-09 due to pre-season groin injury and as a healthy reserve.

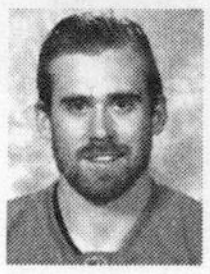

ZETTERBERG, Henrik

(ZEH-tuhr-buhrg, HEHN-rihk) **DET**

Left wing. Shoots left. 5'11", 195 lbs. Born, Njurunda, Sweden, October 9, 1980. Detroit's 4th choice, 210th overall, in 1999 Entry Draft.

Season	Club	League	GP	G	A	Pts	PIM	PP	SH	GW	S	%	+/-	TF	F%	Min	GP	G	A	Pts	PIM	PP	SH	GW	Min
1997-98	Timra IK Jr.	Swe-Jr.	18	9	5	14	4	....	....	....	....	....	....	....	....	....	....	....	....	....	....	....	....	....	....
	Timra IK	Sweden-2	16	1	2	3	4	....	....	....	....	....	....	....	....	....	4	0	1	1	0	....	....	....	....
1998-99	Timra IK	Sweden-2	37	15	13	28	2	....	....	....	....	....	....	....	....	....	4	2	1	3	2	....	....	....	....
99-2000	Timra IK	Sweden-2	32	20	14	34	20	....	....	....	....	....	....	....	....	....	10	10	4	14	4	....	....	....	....
2000-01	Timra IK	Sweden	47	15	31	46	24	....	....	....	....	....	....	....	....	....	....	....	....	....	....	....	....	....	....
2001-02	Timra IK	Sweden	48	10	22	32	20	....	....	....	....	....	....	....	....	....	....	....	....	....	....	....	....	....	....
	Sweden	Olympics	4	0	1	1	0	....	....	....	....	....	....	....	....	....	....	....	....	....	....	....	....	....	....
2002-03	**Detroit**	**NHL**	**79**	**22**	**22**	**44**	**8**	5	1	4	135	16.3	6	401	46.1	16:19	4	1	0	1	0	0	0	0	18:19
2003-04	**Detroit**	**NHL**	**61**	**15**	**28**	**43**	**14**	7	1	2	137	10.9	15	627	45.6	18:15	12	2	2	4	4	0	0	0	17:17
2004-05	Timra IK	Sweden	50	19	31	*50	24	....	....	....	....	....	....	....	....	....	7	6	2	8	2	....	....	....	....
2005-06	**Detroit**	**NHL**	**77**	**39**	**46**	**85**	**30**	17	1	9	270	14.4	29	583	50.3	18:57	6	6	0	6	2	4	0	0	21:43
	Sweden	Olympics	8	3	3	6	0	....	....	....	....	....	....	....	....	....	....	....	....	....	....	....	....	....	....
2006-07	**Detroit**	**NHL**	**63**	**33**	**35**	**68**	**36**	11	1	*10	224	14.7	26	888	52.5	20:50	18	6	8	14	12	3	0	1	22:45
2007-08♦	**Detroit**	**NHL**	**75**	**43**	**49**	**92**	**34**	16	1	7	358	12.0	30	1210	55.0	22:04	22	*13	14	*27	16	4	*2	4	22:36
2008-09	**Detroit**	**NHL**	**77**	**31**	**42**	**73**	**36**	12	2	5	309	10.0	13	1189	53.3	19:53	23	11	13	24	13	4	0	0	22:10

			Regular Season														Playoffs								
Season	Club	League	GP	G	A	Pts	PIM	PP	SH	GW	S	%	+/-	TF	F%	Min	GP	G	A	Pts	PIM	PP	SH	GW	Min
2009-10	Detroit	NHL	74	23	47	70	26	3	0	6	309	7.4	12	1098	49.5	20:04	12	7	8	15	6	2	0	2	20:25
	Sweden	Olympics	4	1	0	1	2	....	....	....	....	....	....	....	....	....	....	....	....	....	....	....	....	....	....
2010-11	Detroit	NHL	80	24	56	80	40	10	0	3	306	7.8	–1	984	52.4	19:35	7	3	5	8	2	1	0	0	21:59
	NHL Totals		586	230	325	555	224	81	7	46	2048	11.2		6980	51.4	19:28	104	49	50	99	55	18	2	7	21:24

Swedish Elite League Rookie of the Year (2001) • NHL All-Rookie Team (2003) • NHL Second All-Star Team (2008) • Conn Smythe Trophy (2008)

Signed as a free agent by **Timra** (Sweden), September 20, 2004.

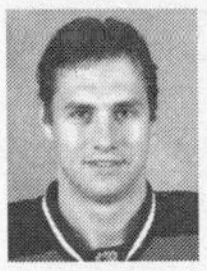

ZHARKOV, Vladimir

(zhar-KAWV, vla-DIH-meer) **N.J.**

Right wing. Shoots left. 6'1", 205 lbs. Born, Elektrostal, USSR, January 10, 1988. New Jersey's 4th choice, 77th overall, in 2006 Entry Draft.

Season	Club	League	GP	G	A	Pts	PIM	PP	SH	GW	S	%	+/-	TF	F%	Min	GP	G	A	Pts	PIM	PP	SH	GW	Min
2004-05	CSKA Moscow 2	Russia-3	STATISTICS NOT AVAILABLE																						
2005-06	CSKA Moscow	Russia	4	0	1	1	4	....	....	....	....	....	....	....	....	....	1	0	0	0	0	....	....	....	....
	CSKA Moscow 2	Russia-3	48	17	22	39	86	....	....	....	....	....	....	....	....	....	....	....	....	....	....	....	....	....	....
2006-07	CSKA Moscow	Russia	47	4	1	5	18	....	....	....	....	....	....	....	....	....	12	0	1	1	2	....	....	....	....
2007-08	CSKA Moscow	Russia	30	5	2	7	6	....	....	....	....	....	....	....	....	....	....	....	....	....	....	....	....	....	....
	CSKA Moscow 2	Russia-3	4	3	4	7	4	....	....	....	....	....	....	....	....	....	12	8	7	15	8	....	....	....	....
2008-09	Lowell Devils	AHL	69	11	23	34	26	....	....	....	....	....	....	....	....	....	....	....	....	....	....	....	....	....	....
2009-10	New Jersey	NHL	40	0	10	10	8	0	0	0	54	0.0	2	4	25.0	11:26	....	....	....	....	....	....	....	....	....
	Lowell Devils	AHL	23	6	15	21	6	....	....	....	....	....	....	....	....	....	....	....	....	....	....	....	....	....	....
2010-11	New Jersey	NHL	38	2	2	4	2	0	0	0	40	5.0	3	6	33.3	11:20	....	....	....	....	....	....	....	....	....
	Albany Devils	AHL	31	8	11	19	19	....	....	....	....	....	....	....	....	....	....	....	....	....	....	....	....	....	....
	NHL Totals		78	2	12	14	10	0	0	0	94	2.1		10	30.0	11:23	....	....	....	....	....	....	....	....	....

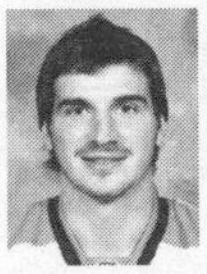

ZHERDEV, Nikolai

(ZHAIR-dehv, NIH-koh-ligh)

Wing. Shoots right. 6'2", 203 lbs. Born, Kiev, USSR, November 5, 1984. Columbus' 1st choice, 4th overall, in 2003 Entry Draft.

Season	Club	League	GP	G	A	Pts	PIM	PP	SH	GW	S	%	+/-	TF	F%	Min	GP	G	A	Pts	PIM	PP	SH	GW	Min
99-2000	Elektrostal 2	Russia-3	21	10	7	17	26	....	....	....	....	....	....	....	....	....	7	0	0	0	0	....	....	....	....
2000-01	Elektrostal	Russia-2	18	5	8	13	12	....	....	....	....	....	....	....	....	....	....	....	....	....	....	....	....	....	....
	Russia	Exhib.	17	10	11	21	17	....	....	....	....	....	....	....	....	....	....	....	....	....	....	....	....	....	....
2001-02	Elektrostal	Russia-2	53	13	15	28	62	....	....	....	....	....	....	....	....	....	....	....	....	....	....	....	....	....	....
	Elektrostal 2	Russia-3	1	1	0	1	4	....	....	....	....	....	....	....	....	....	....	....	....	....	....	....	....	....	....
2002-03	CSKA Moscow	Russia	44	12	12	24	34	....	....	....	....	....	....	....	....	....	....	....	....	....	....	....	....	....	....
2003-04	CSKA Moscow	Russia	20	2	2	4	14	....	....	....	....	....	....	....	....	....	....	....	....	....	....	....	....	....	....
	Columbus	NHL	57	13	21	34	54	5	0	1	137	9.5	–11	9	11.1	16:11	....	....	....	....	....	....	....	....	....
2004-05	CSKA Moscow	Russia	51	19	21	40	62	....	....	....	....	....	....	....	....	....	....	....	....	....	....	....	....	....	....
2005-06	Columbus	NHL	73	27	27	54	50	10	0	0	194	13.9	–13	20	10.0	17:36	....	....	....	....	....	....	....	....	....
	Syracuse Crunch	AHL	2	1	0	1	0	....	....	....	....	....	....	....	....	....	....	....	....	....	....	....	....	....	....
2006-07	Mytischi	Russia	8	2	4	6	10	....	....	....	....	....	....	....	....	....	....	....	....	....	....	....	....	....	....
	Columbus	NHL	71	10	22	32	26	3	0	2	164	6.1	–19	17	23.5	16:13	....	....	....	....	....	....	....	....	....
2007-08	Columbus	NHL	82	26	35	61	34	7	0	3	254	10.2	–9	29	41.4	19:22	....	....	....	....	....	....	....	....	....
2008-09	NY Rangers	NHL	82	23	35	58	39	4	1	3	219	10.5	6	11	9.1	16:50	7	0	0	0	2	0	0	0	12:33
2009-10	Mytischi	Rus-KHL	52	13	26	39	79	....	....	....	....	....	....	....	....	....	4	0	1	1	4	....	....	....	....
2010-11	Philadelphia	NHL	56	16	6	22	22	1	0	1	135	11.9	5	7	28.6	12:51	8	1	2	3	2	0	0	1	11:56
	NHL Totals		421	115	146	261	225	30	1	10	1103	10.4		93	23.7	16:44	15	1	2	3	4	0	0	1	12:13

Signed as a free agent by **CSKA Moscow** (Russia), July 27, 2004. Signed as a free agent by **Mystichi** (Russia), July 20, 2006. Traded to **NY Rangers** by **Columbus** with Dan Fritsche for Fedor Tyutin and Christian Backman, July 2, 2008. Signed as a free agent by **Mytischi** (Russia-KHL), September 16, 2009. Signed as a free agent by **Philadelphia**, July 9, 2010. Signed as a free agent by **Mytischi** (Russia-KHL), August 3, 2011.

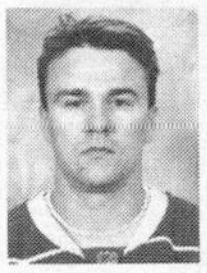

ZIDLICKY, Marek

(zihd-LIH-kee, MAIR-ehk) **MIN**

Defense. Shoots right. 5'11", 190 lbs. Born, Most, Czech., February 3, 1977. NY Rangers' 6th choice, 176th overall, in 2001 Entry Draft.

Season	Club	League	GP	G	A	Pts	PIM	PP	SH	GW	S	%	+/-	TF	F%	Min	GP	G	A	Pts	PIM	PP	SH	GW	Min
1994-95	HC Kladno	CzRep	30	2	2	4	38	....	....	....	....	....	....	....	....	....	11	1	1	2	10	....	....	....	....
1995-96	HC Poldi Kladno	CzRep	37	4	5	9	74	....	....	....	....	....	....	....	....	....	7	1	1	2	8	....	....	....	....
1996-97	HC Poldi Kladno	CzRep	49	5	16	21	60	....	....	....	....	....	....	....	....	....	2	0	0	0	0	....	....	....	....
1997-98	Kladno	CzRep	51	2	13	15	121	....	....	....	....	....	....	....	....	....	....	....	....	....	....	....	....	....	....
1998-99	Kladno	CzRep	50	10	12	22	94	....	....	....	....	....	....	....	....	....	....	....	....	....	....	....	....	....	....
99-2000	HIFK Helsinki	Finland	47	4	16	20	66	....	....	....	....	....	....	....	....	....	9	3	2	5	24	....	....	....	....
	HIFK Helsinki	EuroHL	4	2	2	4	10	....	....	....	....	....	....	....	....	....	1	0	0	0	0	....	....	....	....
2000-01	HIFK Helsinki	Finland	51	12	25	37	146	....	....	....	....	....	....	....	....	....	5	0	1	1	6	....	....	....	....
2001-02	HIFK Helsinki	Finland	56	11	29	40	107	....	....	....	....	....	....	....	....	....	....	....	....	....	....	....	....	....	....
2002-03	HIFK Helsinki	Finland	54	10	37	47	79	....	....	....	....	....	....	....	....	....	4	0	0	0	4	....	....	....	....
2003-04	Nashville	NHL	82	14	39	53	82	9	0	4	143	9.8	–16	0	0.0	20:02	1	0	0	0	0	0	0	0	2:16
2004-05	HIFK Helsinki	Finland	49	11	20	31	91	....	....	....	....	....	....	....	....	....	5	0	3	3	14	....	....	....	....
2005-06	Nashville	NHL	67	12	37	49	82	10	0	1	113	10.6	8	0	0.0	20:04	2	0	1	1	2	0	0	0	15:19
	Czech Republic	Olympics	7	4	1	5	16	....	....	....	....	....	....	....	....	....	....	....	....	....	....	....	....	....	....
2006-07	Nashville	NHL	79	4	26	30	72	2	0	1	114	3.5	8	0	0.0	19:43	5	0	2	2	4	0	0	0	19:19
2007-08	Nashville	NHL	79	5	38	43	63	4	0	0	122	4.1	–5	0	0.0	20:50	6	0	3	3	8	0	0	0	19:04
2008-09	Minnesota	NHL	76	12	30	42	76	10	0	3	147	8.2	–12	0	0.0	22:07	....	....	....	....	....	....	....	....	....
2009-10	Minnesota	NHL	78	6	37	43	67	4	0	3	116	5.2	–16	0	0.0	24:10	....	....	....	....	....	....	....	....	....
	Czech Republic	Olympics	5	0	5	5	2	....	....	....	....	....	....	....	....	....	....	....	....	....	....	....	....	....	....
2010-11	Minnesota	NHL	46	7	17	24	30	3	0	0	53	13.2	–6	0	0.0	21:46	....	....	....	....	....	....	....	....	....
	NHL Totals		507	60	224	284	472	42	0	12	808	7.4		0	0.0	21:13	14	0	6	6	14	0	0	0	17:25

Traded to **Nashville** by **NY Rangers** with Rem Murray and Tomas Kloucek for Mike Dunham, December 12, 2002. Signed as a free agent by **HIFK Helsinki** (Finland), September 17, 2004. Traded to **Minnesota** by **Nashville** for Ryan Jones and Minnesota's 2nd round choice (Charles-Olivier Roussel) in 2009 Entry Draft, July 1, 2008.

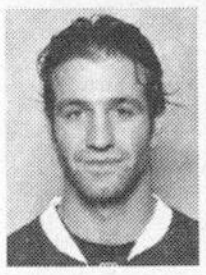

ZIGOMANIS, Mike

(zih-goh-MAN-ihs, MIGHK) **TOR**

Center. Shoots right. 6', 200 lbs. Born, Toronto, Ont., January 17, 1981. Carolina's 2nd choice, 46th overall, in 2001 Entry Draft.

Season	Club	League	GP	G	A	Pts	PIM	PP	SH	GW	S	%	+/-	TF	F%	Min	GP	G	A	Pts	PIM	PP	SH	GW	Min
1996-97	Wexford Raiders	MTHL	40	37	48	85	23	....	....	....	....	....	....	....	....	....	....	....	....	....	....	....	....	....	....
	Wexford Raiders	ON-Jr.A	8	2	5	7	2	....	....	....	....	....	....	....	....	....	....	....	....	....	....	....	....	....	....
1997-98	Kingston	OHL	62	23	51	74	30	....	....	....	....	....	....	....	....	....	12	1	6	7	2	....	....	....	....
1998-99	Kingston	OHL	67	29	56	85	36	....	....	....	....	....	....	....	....	....	5	1	7	8	2	....	....	....	....
99-2000	Kingston	OHL	59	40	54	94	49	....	....	....	....	....	....	....	....	....	5	0	4	4	0	....	....	....	....
2000-01	Kingston	OHL	52	40	37	77	44	....	....	....	....	....	....	....	....	....	....	....	....	....	....	....	....	....	....
2001-02	Lowell	AHL	79	18	30	48	24	....	....	....	....	....	....	....	....	....	5	1	1	2	2	....	....	....	....
2002-03	Carolina	NHL	19	2	1	3	0	1	1	0	19	10.5	–4	147	59.2	9:43	....	....	....	....	....	....	....	....	....
	Lowell	AHL	38	13	18	31	19	....	....	....	....	....	....	....	....	....	....	....	....	....	....	....	....	....	....
2003-04	Carolina	NHL	17	0	3	3	2	0	0	0	13	0.0	–1	108	53.7	8:37	....	....	....	....	....	....	....	....	....
	Lowell	AHL	61	17	35	52	56	....	....	....	....	....	....	....	....	....	....	....	....	....	....	....	....	....	....
2004-05	Lowell	AHL	76	29	31	60	71	....	....	....	....	....	....	....	....	....	11	4	7	11	8	....	....	....	....
2005-06	Carolina	NHL	21	1	0	1	4	0	0	0	16	6.3	1	72	50.0	9:25	....	....	....	....	....	....	....	....	....
	Lowell	AHL	11	6	7	13	19	....	....	....	....	....	....	....	....	....	....	....	....	....	....	....	....	....	....
	St. Louis	NHL	2	0	0	0	0	0	0	0	1	0.0	0	1	100.0	7:39	....	....	....	....	....	....	....	....	....
	Peoria Rivermen	AHL	28	10	18	28	16	....	....	....	....	....	....	....	....	....	4	2	4	6	6	....	....	....	....
2006-07	Phoenix	NHL	75	14	9	23	46	2	1	0	142	9.9	–8	1010	56.2	14:53	....	....	....	....	....	....	....	....	....
2007-08	Phoenix	NHL	33	2	1	3	6	0	0	0	35	5.7	–7	328	59.8	12:24	....	....	....	....	....	....	....	....	....
	San Antonio	AHL	27	10	15	25	14	....	....	....	....	....	....	....	....	....	7	0	5	5	10	....	....	....	....
2008-09 ♦	Pittsburgh	NHL	22	2	4	6	27	0	0	0	23	8.7	–2	251	63.0	11:26	....	....	....	....	....	....	....	....	....
2009-10	Toronto Marlies	AHL	7	0	13	13	0	....	....	....	....	....	....	....	....	....	....	....	....	....	....	....	....	....	....
	Djurgarden	Sweden	27	4	7	11	12	....	....	....	....	....	....	....	....	....	5	0	0	0	8	....	....	....	....
2010-11	Toronto	NHL	8	0	1	1	4	0	0	0	7	0.0	0	40	52.5	6:58	....	....	....	....	....	....	....	....	....
	Toronto Marlies	AHL	64	14	33	47	66	....	....	....	....	....	....	....	....	....	....	....	....	....	....	....	....	....	....
	NHL Totals		197	21	19	40	89	3	2	0	256	8.2		1957	57.5	12:04	....	....	....	....	....	....	....	....	....

• Re-entered NHL Entry Draft. Originally Buffalo's 4th choice, 64th overall, in 1999 Entry Draft.

Traded to **St. Louis** by **Carolina** with Jesse Boulerice, the rights to Magnus Kahnberg, Carolina's 1st round choice (later traded to New Jersey - New Jersey selected Matthew Corrente) in 2006 Entry Draft, Toronto's 4th round choice (previously acquired, St. Louis selected Reto Berra) in 2006 Entry Draft and Chicago's 4th round choice (previously acquired, St. Louis selected Cade Fairchild) in 2007 Entry Draft for Doug Weight and Erkki Rajamaki, January 30, 2006. Signed as a free agent by **Phoenix**, July 21, 2006. Traded to **Pittsburgh** by **Phoenix** for future considerations, October 9, 2008. • Missed majority of 2008-09 due to shoulder surgery. Signed to a PTO (professional tryout) contract by **Toronto** (AHL), October 19, 2009. Signed as a free agent by **Djurgarden** (Sweden), November 10, 2009. Signed as a free agent by **Toronto**, July 15, 2010.

							Regular Season											Playoffs							
Season	Club	League	GP	G	A	Pts	PIM	PP	SH	GW	S	%	+/-	TF	F%	Min	GP	G	A	Pts	PIM	PP	SH	GW	Min

ZUBAREV, Andrei
(ZOO-bah-rehv, AWN-dray)

Defense. Shoots left. 6'1", 210 lbs. Born, Ufa, USSR, March 3, 1987. Atlanta's 7th choice, 187th overall, in 2005 Entry Draft.

Season	Club	League	GP	G	A	Pts	PIM	PP	SH	GW	S	%	+/-	TF	F%	Min	GP	G	A	Pts	PIM	PP	SH	GW	Min
2003-04	Ufa 2	Russia-3			STATISTICS NOT AVAILABLE			....	....	....	....	....		....	....	....		....	....	....	....	....				....
	Ufa	Russia	6	0	1	1	4	....	....	....	....	....		....	....	....		....	....	....	....	....				....
2004-05	Ufa 2	Russia-3	28	2	4	6	32	....	....	....	....	....		....	....	....		....	....	....	....	....				....
	Ufa	Russia	5	0	0	0	4	....	....	....	....	....		....	....	....		....	....	....	....	....				....
2005-06	Ak Bars Kazan	Russia	40	2	11	13	40	....	....	....	....	....		....	....	....		....	....	....	....	....				....
2006-07	Ak Bars Kazan	Russia	20	0	0	0	32	....	....	....	....	....		....	....	....		....	....	....	....	....				....
2007-08	Ak Bars Kazan	Russia	39	4	3	7	86	....	....	....	....	....		....	....	....		2	0	0	0	0				....
2008-09	Mytischi	Rus-KHL	35	0	4	4	65	....	....	....	....	....		....	....	....		7	2	3	5	29				....
2009-10	Mytischi	Rus-KHL	55	7	9	16	58	....	....	....	....	....		....	....	....		4	0	0	0	0				....
2010-11	**Atlanta**	**NHL**	**4**	**0**	**1**	**1**	**4**	**0**	**0**	**0**	**2**	**0.0**	**-4**	**0**	**0.0**	**20:04**	....	....	....	....	....				....
	Chicago Wolves	AHL	51	3	10	13	28	....	....	....	....	....		....	....	....		....	....	....	....	....				....
	NHL Totals		**4**	**0**	**1**	**1**	**4**	**0**	**0**	**0**	**2**	**0.0**		**0**	**0.0**	**20:04**	....	....	....	....	....				....

ZUBOV, Ilya
(ZOO-bahf, IHL-yah)   **OTT**

Center. Shoots left. 6', 211 lbs. Born, Chelyabinsk, USSR, February 14, 1987. Ottawa's 4th choice, 98th overall, in 2005 Entry Draft.

Season	Club	League	GP	G	A	Pts	PIM	PP	SH	GW	S	%	+/-	TF	F%	Min	GP	G	A	Pts	PIM	PP	SH	GW	Min
2003-04	Chelyabinsk	Russia-2	33	7	7	14	16	....	....	....	....	....		....	....	....		8	2	1	3	2				....
2004-05	Chelyabinsk	Russia-2	40	9	8	17	36	....	....	....	....	....		....	....	....		....	....	....	....	....				....
	Chelyabinsk 2	Russia-3	1	0	0	0	0	....	....	....	....	....		....	....	....		....	....	....	....	....				....
2005-06	Spartak 2	Russia-3	1	0	1	1	4	....	....	....	....	....		....	....	....		....	....	....	....	....				....
	Spartak Moscow	Russia	43	4	8	12	12	....	....	....	....	....		....	....	....		3	2	2	4	0				....
2006-07	Mytischi	Russia	16	1	1	2	4	....	....	....	....	....		....	....	....		....	....	....	....	....				....
	Ufa	Russia	26	3	7	10	4	....	....	....	....	....		....	....	....		8	2	3	5	2				....
2007-08	**Ottawa**	**NHL**	**1**	**0**	**0**	**0**	**0**	**0**	**0**	**0**	**0**	**0.0**	**0**	**5**	**40.0**	**14:38**	....	....	....	....	....				....
	Binghamton	AHL	74	15	23	38	18	....	....	....	....	....		....	....	....		....	....	....	....	....				....
2008-09	**Ottawa**	**NHL**	**10**	**0**	**2**	**2**	**0**	**0**	**0**	**0**	**11**	**0.0**	**-1**	**1**	**0.0**	**10:17**	....	....	....	....	....				....
	Binghamton	AHL	63	14	38	52	26	....	....	....	....	....		....	....	....		....	....	....	....	....				....
2009-10	Binghamton	AHL	1	0	0	0	2	....	....	....	....	....		....	....	....		....	....	....	....	....				....
	Ufa	Rus-KHL	25	3	3	6	6	....	....	....	....	....		....	....	....		....	....	....	....	....				....
	CSKA Moscow	Rus-KHL	6	1	0	1	2	....	....	....	....	....		....	....	....		3	1	1	2	2				....
2010-11	CSKA Moscow	Rus-KHL	46	8	21	29	29	....	....	....	....	....		....	....	....		....	....	....	....	....				....
	NHL Totals		**11**	**0**	**2**	**2**	**0**	**0**	**0**	**0**	**11**	**0.0**		**6**	**33.3**	**10:40**	....	....	....	....	....				....

• Loaned to **Ufa** (Russia-KHL) by **Ottawa** for remainder of 2009-10 season, October 20, 2009. Traded to **CSKA Moscow** (Russia-KHL) by **Ufa** (Russia-KHL) with future considerations for Peter Schastlivy. April 3, 2010.

ZUBRUS, Dainius
(ZOO-bruhs, DAYN-ihs)   **N.J.**

Right wing. Shoots left. 6'5", 225 lbs. Born, Elektrenai, USSR, June 16, 1978. Philadelphia's 1st choice, 15th overall, in 1996 Entry Draft.

Season	Club	League	GP	G	A	Pts	PIM	PP	SH	GW	S	%	+/-	TF	F%	Min	GP	G	A	Pts	PIM	PP	SH	GW	Min
1995-96	Pembroke	CJHL	28	19	13	32	73	....	....	....	....	....		....	....	....		....	....	....	....	....				....
	Caledon	ON-Jr.A	7	3	7	10	2	....	....	....	....	....		....	....	....		17	11	12	23	4				....
1996-97	**Philadelphia**	**NHL**	**68**	**8**	**13**	**21**	**22**	**1**	**0**	**2**	**71**	**11.3**	**3**					**19**	**5**	**4**	**9**	**12**	**1**	**0**	**1**	
1997-98	**Philadelphia**	**NHL**	**69**	**8**	**25**	**33**	**42**	**1**	**0**	**5**	**101**	**7.9**	**29**					**5**	**0**	**1**	**1**	**2**	**0**	**0**	**0**	
1998-99	**Philadelphia**	**NHL**	**63**	**3**	**5**	**8**	**25**	**0**	**1**	**0**	**49**	**6.1**	**-5**	**29**	**51.7**	**11:00**		....	....	....	....	....				....
	Montreal	NHL	17	3	5	8	4	0	0	1	31	9.7	-3	2	50.0	16:53		....	....	....	....	....				....
99-2000	Montreal	NHL	73	14	28	42	54	3	0	1	139	10.1	-1	212	39.2	17:37		....	....	....	....	....				....
2000-01	Montreal	NHL	49	12	12	24	30	3	0	0	70	17.1	-7	190	41.1	18:30		....	....	....	....	....				....
	Washington	NHL	12	1	1	2	7	1	0	0	13	7.7	-4	0	0.0	13:05		6	0	0	0	2	0	0	0	17:24
2001-02	Washington	NHL	71	17	26	43	38	4	0	3	138	12.3	5	131	37.4	18:52		....	....	....	....	....				....
2002-03	Washington	NHL	63	13	22	35	43	2	0	0	104	12.5	15	565	50.3	16:26		6	2	2	4	4	1	0	0	21:30
2003-04	Washington	NHL	54	12	15	27	38	6	1	2	115	10.4	-16	916	48.0	19:32		....	....	....	....	....				....
2004-05	Lada Togliatti	Russia	42	8	11	19	85	....	....	....	....	....		....	....	....		10	3	4	7	8				....
2005-06	Washington	NHL	71	23	34	57	84	13	0	5	181	12.7	3	1118	50.3	20:22		....	....	....	....	....				....
2006-07	Washington	NHL	60	20	32	52	50	9	0	4	127	15.7	-16	1096	49.7	19:51		....	....	....	....	....				....
	Buffalo	**NHL**	19	4	4	8	12	1	0	0	31	12.9	-3	69	39.1	18:22		15	0	8	8	8	0	0	0	18:38
2007-08	New Jersey	NHL	82	13	25	38	38	4	0	2	128	10.2	2	144	55.6	15:42		5	0	1	1	8	0	0	0	16:18
2008-09	New Jersey	NHL	82	15	25	40	69	1	0	3	130	11.5	6	923	51.3	15:16		7	0	1	1	10	0	0	0	13:57
2009-10	New Jersey	NHL	51	10	17	27	28	1	0	0	86	11.6	4	400	48.5	16:29		5	1	0	1	8	0	0	1	16:25
2010-11	New Jersey	NHL	79	13	17	30	53	1	0	2	115	11.3	-11	449	56.4	17:09		....	....	....	....	....				....
	NHL Totals		**983**	**189**	**306**	**495**	**637**	**51**	**2**	**34**	**1629**	**11.6**		**6244**	**49.4**	**17:07**		**68**	**8**	**17**	**25**	**54**	**2**	**0**	**2**	**17:36**

Traded to **Montreal** by **Philadelphia** with Philadelphia's 2nd round choice (Matt Carkner) in 1999 Entry Draft and NY Islanders' 6th round choice (previously acquired, Montreal selected Scott Selig) in 2000 Entry Draft for Mark Recchi, March 10, 1999. Traded to **Washington** by **Montreal** with Trevor Linden and New Jersey's 2nd round choice (previously acquired, later traded to Tampa Bay – Tampa Bay selected Andreas Holmqvist) in 2001 Entry Draft for Richard Zednik, Jan Bulis and Washington's 1st round choice (Alexander Perezhogin) in 2001 Entry Draft, March 13, 2001. Signed as a free agent by **Togliatti** (Russia), July 1, 2004. Traded to **Buffalo** by **Washington** with Timo Helbling for Jiri Novotny and Buffalo's 1st round choice (later traded to San Jose - San Jose selected Nicholas Petrecki) in 2007 Entry Draft, February 27, 2007. Signed as a free agent by **New Jersey**, July 3, 2007.

ZUCCARELLO, Mats
(zoo-ka-REHL-oh, MATS)   **NYR**

Left wing. Shoots left. 5'7", 174 lbs. Born, Oslo, Norway, September 1, 1987.

Season	Club	League	GP	G	A	Pts	PIM	PP	SH	GW	S	%	+/-	TF	F%	Min	GP	G	A	Pts	PIM	PP	SH	GW	Min
2003-04	Frisk-Asker U18	Nor-U18	24	23	14	37	44	....	....	....	....	....		....	....	....		2	1	3	4	0				....
	Frisk-Asker Jr.	Norway-Jr.	20	7	14	21	14	....	....	....	....	....		....	....	....		3	0	2	2	0				....
2004-05	Frisk-Asker U18	Nor-U18	12	11	18	29	50	....	....	....	....	....		....	....	....		....	....	....	....	....				....
	Frisk-Asker Jr.	Norway-Jr.	27	19	17	36	16	....	....	....	....	....		....	....	....		5	3	3	6	6				....
	Frisk-Asker IF	Norway	1	0	0	0	0	....	....	....	....	....		....	....	....		....	....	....	....	....				....
2005-06	Frisk Asker IF/NTG	Norway-Jr.	2	7	0	7	0	....	....	....	....	....		....	....	....		2	2	3	5	0				....
	Frisk-Asker Tigers	Norway	21	5	3	8	12	....	....	....	....	....		....	....	....		4	0	0	0	2				....
2006-07	Frisk Asker IF/NTG	Norway-Jr.						....	....	....	....	....		....	....	....		1	3	4	7	2				....
	Frisk-Asker IF	Norway	43	34	25	59	36	....	....	....	....	....		....	....	....		7	4	4	8	2				....
2007-08	Frisk-Asker IF	Norway	33	24	40	64	48	....	....	....	....	....		....	....	....		15	12	15	27	24				....
2008-09	MODO	Sweden	35	12	28	40	38	....	....	....	....	....		....	....	....		....	....	....	....	....				....
2009-10	MODO	Sweden	55	23	41	*64	62	....	....	....	....	....		....	....	....		....	....	....	....	....				....
	Norway	Olympics	4	1	2	3	4	....	....	....	....	....		....	....	....		....	....	....	....	....				....
2010-11	**NY Rangers**	**NHL**	**42**	**6**	**17**	**23**	**4**	**0**	**0**	**2**	**74**	**8.1**	**3**	**15**	**53.3**	**14:10**		**1**	**0**	**0**	**0**	**2**	**0**	**0**	**0**	**7:34**
	Connecticut	AHL	36	13	16	29	16	....	....	....	....	....		....	....	....		2	1	1	2	4				....
	NHL Totals		**42**	**6**	**17**	**23**	**4**	**0**	**0**	**2**	**74**	**8.1**		**15**	**53.3**	**14:10**		**1**	**0**	**0**	**0**	**2**	**0**	**0**	**0**	**7:34**

Signed as a free agent by **NY Rangers**, May 26, 2010.

2010-11
NHL Player of the Week/Month Award Winners

Player of the Week/Month

Period Ending	First Star	Second Star	Third Star
Oct. 17	Tomas Vokoun, Fla.	Marian Hossa, Chi.	Ryan Getzlaf, Ana.
Oct. 24	Rene Bourque, Cgy.	Jaroslav Halak, St.L.	Steven Stamkos, T.B.
Oct. 31	Tim Thomas, Bos.	Joe Thornton, S.J.	Duncan Keith, Chi.
October	**Steven Stamkos,** T.B.	**Tim Thomas,** Bos.	**Chris Stewart,** Col.
Nov. 7	Raffi Torres, Van.	Mathieu Garon, CBJ	Jaroslav Halak, St.L.
Nov. 14	Carey Price, Mtl.	Sidney Crosby, Pit.	Alexander Semin, Wsh.
Nov. 21	Rick Nash, CBJ	John-Michael Liles, Col.	Brian Rafalski, Det.
Nov. 28	Ondrej Pavelec, Atl.	Dustin Byfuglien, Atl.	Sidney Crosby, Pit.
November	**Sidney Crosby,** Pit.	**Carey Price,** Mtl.	**Dustin Byfuglien,** Atl.
Dec. 5	Sidney Crosby, Pit.	Ryan Miller, Buf.	Taylor Hall, Edm.
Dec. 12	Ryane Clowe, S.J.	Marc-Andre Fleury, Pit.	Rick Nash, CBJ
Dec. 19	Matt Duchene, Col.	Tomas Fleischmann, Col.	Eric Staal, Car.
Dec. 26	Dwayne Roloson, NYI	Henrik Zetterberg, Det.	Sidney Crosby, Pit.
December	**Sidney Crosby,** Pit.	**Roberto Luongo,** Van.	**Nicklas Lidstrom,** Det.
Jan. 2	Semyon Varlamov, Wsh.	Shane Doan, Phx.	Nicklas Lidstrom, Det.
Jan. 9	Daniel Sedin, Van.	Jonas Hiller, Ana.	Jose Theodore, Min.
Jan. 16	Jussi Jokinen, Car.	Patrice Bergeron, Bos.	Ilya Bryzgalov, Phx.
Jan. 23	Tim Thomas, Bos.	Steven Stamkos, T.B.	Martin Brodeur, N.J.
Jan. 30	Eric Staal, Car.	Jonathan Quick, L.A.	Michael Grabner, NYI
January	**Patrice Bergeron,** Bos.	**Keith Yandle,** Phx.	**Pekka Rinne,** Nsh.
Feb. 6	Johan Franzen, Det.	Mikael Samuelsson, Van.	Corey Perry, Ana.
Feb. 13	Michael Grabner, NYI	Drew Stafford, Buf.	Ilya Bryzgalov, Phx.
Feb. 20	Antti Niemi, S.J.	Johan Hedberg, N.J.	Ales Hemsky, Edm.
Feb. 27	Phil Kessel, Tor.	Corey Crawford, Chi.	Matt Calvert, CBJ
February	**Jonathan Toews,** Chi.	**Antti Niemi,** S.J.	**Johan Hedberg,** N.J.
Mar. 6	Jarome Iginla, Cgy.	Andrej Sekera, Buf.	Carey Price, Mtl.
Mar. 13	Braden Holtby, Wsh.	Daniel Sedin, Van.	Corey Perry, Ana.
Mar. 20	Joe Pavelski, S.J.	Ray Emery, Ana.	P.K. Subban, Mtl.
Mar. 27	Ryan Miller, Buf.	Corey Perry, Ana.	Henrik Lundqvist, NYR
March	**Corey Perry,** Ana.	**Daniel Sedin,** Van.	**Pekka Rinne,** Nsh.
Apr. 3	Corey Perry, Ana	Jarome Iginla, Cgy.	Jhonas Enroth, Buf.
Apr. 10	Thomas Vanek, Buf.	Vincent Lecavalier, T.B.	Dan Ellis, Ana.

Rookie of the Week/Month

Month	Player
October	Michal Neuvirth, Wsh.
November	Sergei Bobrovsky, Phi.
December	Logan Couture, S.J.
January	Jeff Skinner, Car.
February	Michael Grabner, NYI
March	James Reimer, Tor.

Steven Stamkos (above) of the Tampa Bay Lightning got off to a fast start in 2010-11. He was the NHL scoring leader with 19 points on nine goals and 10 assists during the first ten games of the season and was rewarded with the NHL's first star of the month selection for October.

Toronto's Phil Kessel (right) was named the NHL's first star of the week for the week ending February 27, 2011. Kessel had four goals and four assists in four games that week, including a career-high four points (two goals, two assists) in a 5-4 win over Montreal on February 24.

Montreal's Carey Price (far right) had a record of 8-4-0 during the month of November with a 1.59 goals-against average and a .952 save percentage. He was named the NHL's firs star of the week for the week ending November 14, 2010 and was the league's second star behind Sidney Crosby that month.

NHL Goaltenders

 Craig Anderson

Alex Auld

Richard Bachman

Johan Backlund

Niklas Backstrom

Jonathan Bernier

Martin Biron

Ben Bishop

Brian Boucher

Martin Brodeur

Mike Brodeur

Ilya Bryzgalov

Peter Budaj

Scott Clemmensen

Matt Climie

Ty Conklin

Corey Crawford

John Curry

Yann Danis

Mark Dekanich

Cedrick Desjardins

Jeff Deslauriers

Rick DiPietro

Wade Dubielewicz

Devan Dubnyk

Brian Elliott

Dan Ellis

Ray Emery

Jhonas Enroth

Erik Ersberg

Marc-Andre Fleury

Mathieu Garon

Jean-Sebastien Giguere

Thomas Greiss

Jonas Gustavsson

Jaroslav Halak

Josh Harding

Johan Hedberg

Jonas Hiller

Braden Holtby

Jimmy Howard

Cristobal Huet

Brent Johnson

Chad Johnson

Henrik Karlsson

Nikolai Khabibulin

Anton Khudobin

Miikka Kiprusoff

Jason LaBarbera

Pascal Leclaire

Robin Lehner

Kari Lehtonen

Michael Leighton

David LeNeveu

Henrik Lundqvist

Roberto Luongo

Joey MacDonald

Chris Mason

Steve Mason

Curtis McElhinney

Mike McKenna

Ryan Miller

Al Montoya

Michal Neuvirth

Antti Niemi

Antero Niittymaki

Ondrej Pavelec

Justin Peters

Justin Pogge

Kevin Poulin

Carey Price

Jonathan Quick

Tuukka Rask

Andrew Raycroft

James Reimer

Pekka Rinne

Dwayne Roloson

Dany Sabourin

Curtis Sanford

Cory Schneider

Mike Smith

Jose Theodore

Tim Thomas

Dustin Tokarski

Hannu Toivonen

Marty Turco

Steve Valiquette

Semyon Varlamov

Tomas Vokoun

Cam Ward

2011-12 Goaltender Register

Note: The 2011-12 Goaltender Register lists all active NHL goaltenders, every goaltender drafted in the 2011 Entry Draft, goaltenders on NHL Reserve Lists and other goaltenders.

Trades and roster changes are current as of August 12, 2011.

To calculate a goaltender's goals-against per game average **(Avg)**, divide goals against **(GA)** by minutes played **(Mins)** and multiply this result by **60**.

Abbreviations: GP – games played; **W** – wins; **L** – losses; **O/T** – overtime losses/ties; **Mins** – minutes played; **GA** – goals against; **SO** – shutouts; **Avg** – goals-against-per-game average; ***** – league-leading total ♦ – member of Stanley Cup-winning team.

NHL Player Register begins on page 345.
Prospect Register begins on page 275.
Retired Player Index begins on page 610.
Retired Goaltender Index begins on page 651.
League Abbreviations are listed on page 662.

AITTOKALLIO, Sami   (ay-toh-KAHL-ee-oh, SAHM-ee)   **COL**

Goaltender. Catches left. 6'1", 174 lbs.   Born, Tampere, Finland, August 6, 1992.
(Colorado's 5th choice, 107th overall, in 2010 Entry Draft).

					Regular Season								Playoffs				
Season	Club	League	GP	W	L	O/T	Mins	GA	SO	Avg	GP	W	L	Mins	GA	SO	Avg
2008-09	Ilves Tampere U18	Fin-U18	5	5	0	0	305	9	1	1.77	....	....	....	....	....	....	....
	Ilves Tampere Jr.	Fin-Jr.	13	7	6	0	731	33	1	2.71	....	....	....	....	....	....	....
2009-10	Ilves Tampere	Finland	1	0	0	0	2	0	0	0.00	....	....	....	....	....	....	....
	LeKi Lempaala	Finland-2	2	1	1	0	124	7	0	3.38	....	....	....	....	....	....	....
	Suomi U20	Finland-2	2	1	1	0	120	8	0	4.00	....	....	....	....	....	....	....
	Ilves Tampere U18	Fin-U18	9	6	3	0	542	19	1	2.10	....	....	....	....	....	....	....
	Ilves Tampere Jr.	Fin-Jr.	23	13	9	0	1257	67	2	3.20	9	6	3	504	19	0	2.26
2010-11	Ilves Tampere	Finland	16	5	8	0	790	36	1	2.73	2	0	2	117	5	0	2.57
	Suomi U20	Finland-2	4	2	2	0	196	14	0	4.28	....	....	....	....	....	....	....
	Ilves Tampere Jr.	Fin-Jr.	6	4	2	0	359	14	1	2.34	3	1	2	174	11	0	3.80
	LeKi Lempaala	Finland-2	6	3	3	0	322	20	0	3.73	....	....	....	....	....	....	....

ALLEN, Jake   (A-lehn, JAYK)   **ST.L.**

Goaltender. Catches left. 6'2", 190 lbs.   Born, Fredericton, N.B., August 7, 1990.
(St. Louis' 3rd choice, 34th overall, in 2008 Entry Draft).

					Regular Season								Playoffs				
Season	Club	League	GP	W	L	O/T	Mins	GA	SO	Avg	GP	W	L	Mins	GA	SO	Avg
2006-07	Fredericton	NBPEI					STATISTICS NOT AVAILABLE										
2007-08	St. John's	QMJHL	30	9	12	0	1507	79	2	3.14	4	2	1	128	8	0	3.74
2008-09	Montreal	QMJHL	53	28	25	0	3023	144	3	2.86	10	4	6	585	35	1	3.59
2009-10	Montreal	QMJHL	23	11	11	0	1241	55	1	2.66	....	....	....	....	....	....	....
	Drummondville	QMJHL	22	18	3	0	1271	37	3	1.75	14	9	5	840	34	1	2.43
2010-11	Peoria Rivermen	AHL	47	25	19	3	2805	118	6	2.52	3	0	3	189	12	0	3.80

QMJHL First All-Star Team (2010) • Canadian Major Junior First All-Star Team (2010) • Canadian Major Junior Goaltender of the Year (2010)

ANDERSEN, Frederik   (AHN-duhr-suhn, FREH-duhr-ihk)   **CAR**

Goaltender. Catches left. 6'4", 225 lbs.   Born, Herning, Denmark, October 2, 1989.
(Carolina's 8th choice, 187th overall, in 2010 Entry Draft).

					Regular Season								Playoffs				
Season	Club	League	GP	W	L	O/T	Mins	GA	SO	Avg	GP	W	L	Mins	GA	SO	Avg
2007-08	Herning IK Jr.	Den-Jr.	17	....	....	....	....	....	....	....	....	....	....	....	....	....	....
	Herning IK	Denmark-2	9	....	....	....	....	....	....	....	....	....	....	....	....	....	....
2008-09	Herning IK	Denmark-2	1	....	....	....	....	....	....	....	....	....	....	....	....	....	....
	Herning Blue Fox	Denmark	22	....	....	....	1249	51	1	2.45	....	....	....	....	....	....	....
2009-10	Frederikshavn	Denmark	30	....	....	....	1754	64	6	2.19	10	....	....	607	29	0	2.86
2010-11	Frederikshavn	Denmark	36	....	....	....	1953	81	....	2.49	11	....	....	666	26	....	2.34

ANDERSON, Brandon   (AN-duhr-suhn, BRAN-duhn)   **WSH**

Goaltender. Catches left. 6'1", 170 lbs.   Born, Langley, B.C., July 13, 1992.

					Regular Season								Playoffs				
Season	Club	League	GP	W	L	O/T	Mins	GA	SO	Avg	GP	W	L	Mins	GA	SO	Avg
2008-09	Columbia Valley	KIJHL	33	12	18	0	1879	119	0	3.80	....	....	....	....	....	....	....
	Lethbridge	WHL	5	0	1	0	175	12	0	4.11	1	0	1	60	5	0	5.00
2009-10	Lethbridge	WHL	37	12	19	2	2009	117	0	3.49	....	....	....	....	....	....	....
2010-11	Lethbridge	WHL	59	17	26	12	3282	206	0	3.77	....	....	....	....	....	....	....

Signed as a free agent by **Washington**, September 21, 2010.

ANDERSON, Craig   (AN-duhr-suhn, KRAYG)   **OTT**

Goaltender. Catches left. 6'2", 180 lbs.   Born, Park Ridge, IL, May 21, 1981.
(Chicago's 4th choice, 73rd overall, in 2001 Entry Draft).

					Regular Season								Playoffs				
Season	Club	League	GP	W	L	O/T	Mins	GA	SO	Avg	GP	W	L	Mins	GA	SO	Avg
1997-98	Chicago Jets	MEHL	50	....	....	....	2991	143	2	2.86	....	....	....	....	....	....	....
1998-99	Chicago Freeze	NAHL	14	11	3	0	840	40	0	2.56	....	....	....	....	....	....	....
	Guelph Storm	OHL	21	12	5	1	1006	52	1	3.10	3	0	2	114	9	0	4.74
99-2000	Guelph Storm	OHL	38	12	17	2	1955	117	0	3.59	3	0	1	110	5	0	2.73
2000-01	Guelph Storm	OHL	59	30	19	9	3555	156	3	2.63	4	0	4	240	17	0	4.25
2001-02	Norfolk Admirals	AHL	28	9	13	4	1568	77	2	2.95	1	0	1	21	1	0	2.83
2002-03	**Chicago**	**NHL**	6	0	3	2	270	18	0	4.00	....	....	....	....	....	....	....
	Norfolk Admirals	AHL	32	15	11	5	1795	58	4	1.94	5	2	3	345	15	0	2.61
2003-04	**Chicago**	**NHL**	21	6	14	0	1205	57	1	2.84	....	....	....	....	....	....	....
	Norfolk Admirals	AHL	37	17	20	0	2108	74	3	2.11	5	2	3	327	10	0	1.84
2004-05	Norfolk Admirals	AHL	15	9	4	1	886	27	2	1.83	6	2	4	356	14	0	2.36
2005-06	**Chicago**	**NHL**	29	6	12	4	1554	86	1	3.32	....	....	....	....	....	....	....
2006-07	**Florida**	**NHL**	5	1	1	1	217	8	0	2.21	....	....	....	....	....	....	....
	Rochester	AHL	34	23	10	1	2060	88	1	2.56	6	2	4	376	18	0	2.87
2007-08	Florida	NHL	17	8	8	1	933	33	2	2.23	....	....	....	....	....	....	....
2008-09	**Florida**	**NHL**	31	15	7	5	1636	74	3	2.71	....	....	....	....	....	....	....
2009-10	**Colorado**	**NHL**	71	38	25	7	4235	186	7	2.64	6	2	4	366	16	1	2.62
2010-11	**Colorado**	**NHL**	33	13	15	3	1810	99	0	3.28	....	....	....	....	....	....	....
	Ottawa	**NHL**	18	11	5	1	1055	36	2	2.05	....	....	....	....	....	....	....
	NHL Totals		**231**	**98**	**88**	**24**	**12917**	**599**	**16**	**2.78**	**6**	**2**	**4**	**366**	**16**	**1**	**2.62**

• Re-entered NHL Entry Draft. Originally Calgary's 3rd choice, 77th overall, in 1999 Entry Draft.
OHL First All-Star Team (2001)
Claimed on waivers by **Boston** from **Chicago**, January 19, 2006. Claimed on waivers by **St. Louis** from **Boston**, January 31, 2006. Claimed on waivers by **Chicago** from **St. Louis**, February 3, 2006. Traded to **Florida** by **Chicago** for Florida's 6th round choice (later traded to Tampa Bay - Tampa Bay selected Luke Witkowski in 2008 Entry Draft, June 24, 2006. Signed as a free agent by **Colorado**, July 1, 2009. Traded to **Ottawa** by **Colorado** for Brian Elliott, February 18, 2011.

ANDERSON, J.P.   (AN-duhr-suhn, JAY-PEE)   **S.J.**

Goaltender. Catches right. 5'11", 190 lbs.   Born, Toronto, Ont., April 27, 1992.

					Regular Season								Playoffs				
Season	Club	League	GP	W	L	O/T	Mins	GA	SO	Avg	GP	W	L	Mins	GA	SO	Avg
2008-09	St. Michael's	OHL	26	12	12	0	1409	69	1	2.94	11	6	5	697	29	0	*2.50
2009-10	St. Michael's	OHL	36	23	10	1	2028	88	1	2.60	10	4	5	519	24	0	2.78
2010-11	St. Michael's	OHL	51	*38	10	1	2897	114	*6	*2.36	*20	*15	5	*1223	43	*4	*2.11

OHL Second All-Star Team (2011)
Signed as a free agent by **San Jose**, September 20, 2010.

AUBIN, Jean-Sebastien (oh-BEHN, ZHAWN-suh-BAS-tee-yeh)

Goaltender. Catches right. 5'11", 180 lbs. Born, Montreal, Que., July 19, 1977.
(Pittsburgh's 2nd choice, 76th overall, in 1995 Entry Draft).

			Regular Season								Playoffs						
Season	Club	League	GP	W	L	O/T	Mins	GA	SO	Avg	GP	W	L	Mins	GA	SO	Avg
1993-94	Montreal-Bourassa	QAAA	27	14	13	0	1524	96	1	3.74	4	1	3	222	19	0	5.14
1994-95	Sherbrooke	QMJHL	27	13	10	1	1293	72	1	3.34	3	1	2	186	11	0	3.55
1995-96	Sherbrooke	QMJHL	40	18	14	2	2143	127	0	3.56	4	1	3	174	16	0	5.50
1996-97	Sherbrooke	QMJHL	4	3	1	0	249	8	0	1.93	....	....	....	....	....	....	....
	Moncton Wildcats	QMJHL	23	9	13	0	1311	72	1	3.30	....	....	....	....	....	....	....
	Laval Titan	QMJHL	11	2	6	1	532	41	0	4.62	2	0	2	128	10	0	4.70
1997-98	Syracuse Crunch	AHL	8	2	4	1	380	26	0	4.10	....	....	....	....	....	....	....
	Dayton Bombers	ECHL	21	15	2	2	1177	59	1	3.01	3	1	1	142	4	0	1.69
1998-99	**Pittsburgh**	**NHL**	**17**	**4**	**3**	**6**	**756**	**28**	**2**	**2.22**	....	....	....	....	....	....	....
	Kansas City Blades	IHL	13	5	7	1	751	41	0	3.28	....	....	....	....	....	....	....
99-2000	**Pittsburgh**	**NHL**	**51**	**23**	**21**	**3**	**2789**	**120**	**2**	**2.58**	....	....	....	....	....	....	....
	Wilkes-Barre	AHL	11	2	8	0	538	39	0	4.35	....	....	....	....	....	....	....
2000-01	**Pittsburgh**	**NHL**	**36**	**20**	**14**	**1**	**2050**	**107**	**0**	**3.13**	**1**	**0**	**0**	**1**	**0**	**0**	**0.00**
2001-02	**Pittsburgh**	**NHL**	**21**	**3**	**12**	**1**	**1094**	**65**	**0**	**3.56**	....	....	....	....	....	....	....
2002-03	**Pittsburgh**	**NHL**	**21**	**6**	**13**	**0**	**1132**	**59**	**1**	**3.13**	....	....	....	....	....	....	....
	Wilkes-Barre	AHL	16	8	6	1	919	29	3	1.89	6	3	3	356	12	0	2.02
2003-04	**Pittsburgh**	**NHL**	**22**	**7**	**9**	**0**	**1067**	**53**	**1**	**2.98**	....	....	....	....	....	....	....
	Wilkes-Barre	AHL	13	4	5	2	670	31	0	2.78	....	....	....	....	....	....	....
2004-05	St. John's	AHL	23	12	9	0	1336	64	3	2.87	1	0	0	47	1	0	1.27
2005-06	**Toronto**	**NHL**	**11**	**9**	**0**	**2**	**677**	**25**	**1**	**2.22**	....	....	....	....	....	....	....
	Toronto Marlies	AHL	46	19	18	2	2491	126	2	3.03	5	1	4	359	17	0	2.84
2006-07	**Toronto**	**NHL**	**20**	**3**	**5**	**2**	**804**	**46**	**0**	**3.43**	....	....	....	....	....	....	....
2007-08	**Los Angeles**	**NHL**	**19**	**5**	**6**	**1**	**828**	**44**	**0**	**3.19**	....	....	....	....	....	....	....
	Manchester	AHL	1	0	0	0	9	4	0	27.69	....	....	....	....	....	....	....
	Portland Pirates	AHL	11	6	4	0	645	18	3	1.67	12	9	3	757	29	0	2.30
2008-09	Philadelphia	AHL	23	10	10	1	1252	70	0	3.36	1	0	1	58	1	0	1.03
2009-10	Dusseldorf	Germany	*54	27	25	0	3179	130	2	2.45	3	0	3	174	11	0	3.78
2010-11	Dusseldorf	Germany	48	*29	16	....	2740	128	4	2.80	9	5	4	533	25	*1	2.82
	NHL Totals		**218**	**80**	**83**	**16**	**11197**	**547**	**7**	**2.93**	**1**	**0**	**0**	**1**	**0**	**0**	**0.00**

Signed to a PTO (professional tryout) contract by **St. John's** (AHL), November 13, 2004. Signed as a free agent by **Toronto**, August 18, 2005. Signed as a free agent by **Los Angeles**, August 28, 2007. Traded to **Anaheim** by **Los Angeles** for St. Louis' 7th round choice (previously acquired, later traded back to St. Louis - St. Louis selected Paul Karpowich) in 2008 Entry Draft, February 26, 2008. Signed as a free agent by **Philadelphia**, September 18, 2008. Signed as a free agent by **Dusseldorf** (Germany), July 23, 2009.

AULD, Alex (AWLD, AL-ehx) OTT

Goaltender. Catches left. 6'4", 216 lbs. Born, Cold Lake, Alta., January 7, 1981.
(Florida's 2nd choice, 40th overall, in 1999 Entry Draft).

			Regular Season								Playoffs						
Season	Club	League	GP	W	L	O/T	Mins	GA	SO	Avg	GP	W	L	Mins	GA	SO	Avg
1996-97	Thunder Bay Kings	TBMHL	35	....	....	....	2100	46	10	1.35	....	....	....	....	....	....	....
1997-98	Sturgeon Falls Lynx	NOJHA	11	4	6	0	611	46	0	4.52	....	....	....	....	....	....	....
	North Bay	OHL	6	0	4	0	206	17	0	4.95	....	....	....	....	....	....	....
1998-99	North Bay	OHL	37	9	20	1	1894	106	1	3.36	3	0	3	170	10	0	3.53
99-2000	North Bay	OHL	55	21	26	6	3047	167	2	3.29	6	2	4	375	12	0	*1.92
2000-01	North Bay	OHL	40	22	11	5	2319	98	1	2.54	4	0	4	240	15	0	3.75
2001-02	**Vancouver**	**NHL**	**1**	**1**	**0**	**0**	**60**	**2**	**0**	**2.00**	....	....	....	....	....	....	....
	Columbia Inferno	ECHL	6	3	1	2	375	12	0	1.92	....	....	....	....	....	....	....
	Manitoba Moose	AHL	21	11	9	0	1104	65	1	3.53	1	0	0	20	0	0	0.00
2002-03	**Vancouver**	**NHL**	**7**	**3**	**3**	**0**	**382**	**10**	**1**	**1.57**	**1**	**0**	**0**	**20**	**1**	**0**	**3.00**
	Manitoba Moose	AHL	37	15	19	3	2209	97	3	2.64	....	....	....	....	....	....	....
2003-04	**Vancouver**	**NHL**	**6**	**2**	**2**	**2**	**349**	**12**	**0**	**2.06**	**3**	**1**	**2**	**222**	**9**	**0**	**2.43**
	Manitoba Moose	AHL	40	18	16	4	2329	99	4	2.55	....	....	....	....	....	....	....
2004-05	Manitoba Moose	AHL	50	25	18	4	2764	118	2	2.56	3	0	2	128	7	0	3.29
2005-06	**Vancouver**	**NHL**	**67**	**33**	**26**	**6**	**3859**	**189**	**0**	**2.94**	....	....	....	....	....	....	....
2006-07	**Florida**	**NHL**	**27**	**7**	**13**	**5**	**1471**	**82**	**1**	**3.34**	....	....	....	....	....	....	....
2007-08	**Phoenix**	**NHL**	**9**	**3**	**6**	**0**	**509**	**30**	**1**	**3.54**	....	....	....	....	....	....	....
	San Antonio	AHL	2	1	1	0	119	5	1	2.53	....	....	....	....	....	....	....
	Boston	**NHL**	**23**	**9**	**7**	**5**	**1213**	**47**	**2**	**2.32**	....	....	....	....	....	....	....
2008-09	**Ottawa**	**NHL**	**43**	**16**	**18**	**7**	**2449**	**101**	**1**	**2.47**	....	....	....	....	....	....	....
2009-10	**Dallas**	**NHL**	**21**	**9**	**6**	**3**	**1181**	**59**	**0**	**3.00**	....	....	....	....	....	....	....
	NY Rangers	**NHL**	**3**	**0**	**1**	**0**	**119**	**5**	**0**	**2.52**	....	....	....	....	....	....	....
2010-11	**Montreal**	**NHL**	**16**	**6**	**2**	**2**	**749**	**33**	**0**	**2.64**	....	....	....	....	....	....	....
	NHL Totals		**223**	**89**	**84**	**30**	**12341**	**570**	**6**	**2.77**	**4**	**1**	**2**	**242**	**10**	**0**	**2.48**

Traded to **Vancouver** by **Florida** for Vancouver's 2nd round compensatory choice (later traded to New Jersey – New Jersey selected Tuomas Pihlman) in 2001 Entry Draft and Vancouver's 3rd round choice (later traded to Atlanta, later traded to Buffalo – Buffalo selected John Adams) in 2002 Entry Draft, May 31, 2001. Traded to **Florida** by **Vancouver** with Todd Bertuzzi and Bryan Allen for Roberto Luongo, Lukas Krajicek and Florida's 6th round choice (Sergei Shirokov) in 2006 Entry Draft, June 23, 2006. Signed as a free agent by **Phoenix**, August 13, 2007. Traded to **Boston** by **Phoenix** for Nate DiCasmirro and Boston's 5th round choice (later traded to Ottawa – Ottawa selected Jeff Costello) in 2009 Entry Draft, December 6, 2007. Signed as a free agent by **Ottawa**, July 1, 2008. Traded to **Dallas** by **Ottawa** for San Jose's 6th round choice (previously acquired, Ottawa selected Mark Stone) in 2010 Entry Draft, July 8, 2009. Claimed on waivers by **NY Rangers** from **Dallas**, February 27, 2010. Signed as a free agent by **Montreal**, July 1, 2010. Signed as a free agent by **Ottawa**, July 1, 2011.

BACASHIHUA, Jason (buh-KAH-shoo-wuh, JAY-suhn) PHI

Goaltender. Catches left. 5'11", 177 lbs. Born, Dearborn Heights, MI, September 20, 1982.
(Dallas' 1st choice, 26th overall, in 2001 Entry Draft).

			Regular Season								Playoffs						
Season	Club	League	GP	W	L	O/T	Mins	GA	SO	Avg	GP	W	L	Mins	GA	SO	Avg
99-2000	Chicago Freeze	NAHL	41	20	19	2	2432	118	2	2.91	2	0	2	103	12	0	6.97
2000-01	Chicago Freeze	NAHL	39	24	14	0	2246	121	1	3.23	3	1	2	190	12	0	3.79
2001-02	Plymouth Whalers	OHL	46	26	12	7	2688	105	*5	2.34	6	2	4	360	15	0	2.50
	Utah Grizzlies	AHL	1	0	1	0	61	3	0	2.97	....	....	....	....	....	....	....
2002-03	Utah Grizzlies	AHL	39	18	18	2	2245	118	3	3.15	1	0	1	59	2	0	2.05
2003-04	Utah Grizzlies	AHL	39	13	19	5	2234	99	3	2.66	....	....	....	....	....	....	....
2004-05	Worcester IceCats	AHL	35	18	13	1	1909	80	2	2.51	....	....	....	....	....	....	....
2005-06	**St. Louis**	**NHL**	**19**	**4**	**10**	**1**	**966**	**52**	**0**	**3.23**	....	....	....	....	....	....	....
	Peoria Rivermen	AHL	15	9	4	0	820	36	2	2.63	....	....	....	....	....	....	....
2006-07	**St. Louis**	**NHL**	**19**	**3**	**7**	**3**	**894**	**47**	**0**	**3.15**	....	....	....	....	....	....	....
	Peoria Rivermen	AHL	20	5	10	4	1139	55	1	2.90	....	....	....	....	....	....	....
2007-08	Peoria Rivermen	AHL	4	1	3	0	208	11	0	3.17	....	....	....	....	....	....	....
	Johnstown Chiefs	ECHL	1	1	0	0	65	4	0	3.70	....	....	....	....	....	....	....
	Lake Erie Monsters	AHL	19	5	11	2	1074	60	1	3.35	....	....	....	....	....	....	....
2008-09	Lake Erie Monsters	AHL	39	13	21	3	2255	104	2	2.77	....	....	....	....	....	....	....
2009-10	Hershey Bears	AHL	22	17	3	1	1258	52	1	2.48	....	....	....	....	....	....	....
2010-11	Lake Erie Monsters	AHL	42	23	16	3	2466	94	4	2.29	2	1	1	118	5	0	2.54
	NHL Totals		**38**	**7**	**17**	**4**	**1860**	**99**	**0**	**3.19**	....	....	....	....	....	....	....

Traded to **St. Louis** by **Dallas** for Shawn Belle, June 25, 2004. Traded to **Colorado** by **St. Louis** for future considerations, November 8, 2007. Signed as a free agent by **Hershey** (AHL), July 31, 2009. Signed as a free agent by **Colorado**, July 2, 2010. Signed as a free agent by **Philadelphia**, July 19, 2011.

BACHMAN, Richard (BAWK-mahn, RIH-chuhrd) DAL

Goaltender. Catches left. 5'10", 170 lbs. Born, Salt Lake City, UT, July 25, 1987.
(Dallas' 3rd choice, 120th overall, in 2006 Entry Draft).

			Regular Season								Playoffs						
Season	Club	League	GP	W	L	O/T	Mins	GA	SO	Avg	GP	W	L	Mins	GA	SO	Avg
2004-05	Cushing	High-MA	28	....	....	....	1498	53	3	1.89	....	....	....	....	....	....	....
	Boston Jr. Bruins	EmJHL	25	....	....	....	....	....	....	....	....	....	....	....	....	....	....
2005-06	Cushing	High-MA	30	....	....	....	1598	60	4	2.25	....	....	....	....	....	....	....
	Boston Jr. Bruins	EmJHL	....	31	1	2	....	....	....	1.69	....	....	....	....	....	....	....
2006-07	Chicago Steel	USHL	7	2	5	0	359	29	0	4.85	....	....	....	....	....	....	....
	Cedar Rapids	USHL	26	14	10	2	1565	78	4	2.99	6	4	1	329	7	*2	*1.28
2007-08	Colorado College	WCHA	35	25	9	1	2103	65	4	1.85	....	....	....	....	....	....	....
2008-09	Colorado College	WCHA	35	14	11	10	2073	91	3	2.63	....	....	....	....	....	....	....
2009-10	Texas Stars	AHL	8	4	4	0	446	16	1	2.15	....	....	....	....	....	....	....
	Idaho Steelheads	ECHL	35	22	7	4	2028	77	*4	*2.28	8	6	2	492	13	1	1.59
2010-11	**Dallas**	**NHL**	**1**	**0**	**0**	**0**	**10**	**0**	**0**	**0.00**	....	....	....	....	....	....	....
	Texas Stars	AHL	55	28	19	5	3191	117	6	2.20	6	2	4	394	15	0	2.29
	NHL Totals		**1**	**0**	**0**	**0**	**10**	**0**	**0**	**0.00**	....	....	....	....	....	....	....

WCHA All-Rookie Team (2008) • WCHA First All-Star Team (2008) • WCHA Rookie of the Year (2008) • WCHA Player of the Year (2008) • NCAA West First All-American Team (2008) • NCAA Rookie of the Year (2008)

BACKLUND, Johan (BAHK-luhnd, YOH-han) PHI

Goaltender. Catches left. 6'2", 198 lbs. Born, Skelleftea, Sweden, July 24, 1981.

			Regular Season								Playoffs						
Season	Club	League	GP	W	L	O/T	Mins	GA	SO	Avg	GP	W	L	Mins	GA	SO	Avg
2005-06	Leksands IF	Sweden	32	....	....	....	1843	81	1	2.64	....	....	....	....	....	....	....
2006-07	Timra IK	Sweden	*49	....	....	....	2835	106	*6	2.24	7	....	....	444	16	0	2.16
2007-08	Timra IK	Sweden	47	....	....	....	2794	107	6	2.30	11	....	....	662	27	1	2.45
2008-09	Timra IK	Sweden	*49	....	....	....	*2840	121	*4	2.56	5	....	....	317	18	0	3.41
2009-10	**Philadelphia**	**NHL**	**1**	**0**	**1**	**0**	**40**	**2**	**0**	**3.00**	**1**	**0**	**0**	**1**	**0**	**0**	**0.00**
	Adirondack	AHL	41	21	17	2	2451	114	2	2.79	....	....	....	....	....	....	....
2010-11	Adirondack	AHL	33	10	19	3	1900	104	0	3.28	....	....	....	....	....	....	....
	NHL Totals		**1**	**0**	**1**	**0**	**40**	**2**	**0**	**3.00**	**1**	**0**	**0**	**1**	**0**	**0**	**0.00**

Signed as a free agent by **Philadelphia**, March 26, 2009.

BACKSTROM, Niklas (BAK-struhm, NIHK-luhs) MIN

Goaltender. Catches left. 6'1", 189 lbs. Born, Helsinki, Finland, February 13, 1978.

			Regular Season								Playoffs						
Season	Club	League	GP	W	L	O/T	Mins	GA	SO	Avg	GP	W	L	Mins	GA	SO	Avg
1994-95	HIFK Helsinki U18	Fin-U18					STATISTICS NOT AVAILABLE										
1995-96	HIFK Helsinki U18	Fin-U18	12	....	....	....	699	44	....	3.77	4	....	....	203	9	....	2.66
1996-97	HIFK Helsinki Jr.	Fin-Jr.	21	....	....	....	1243	57	....	2.75	....	....	....	....	....	....	....
	PiTa Helsinki	Finland-2	8	....	....	....	390	24	....	3.69	....	....	....	....	....	....	....
	HIFK Helsinki	Finland	2	0	0	0	30	3	0	5.85	....	....	....	....	....	....	....
1997-98	HIFK Helsinki Jr.	Fin-Jr.	14	7	7	0	847	42	....	2.98	....	....	....	....	....	....	....
	Hermes Kokkola	Finland-2	9	4	3	1	468	23	1	2.95	....	....	....	....	....	....	....
1998-99	HIFK Helsinki	Finland	16	9	5	1	923	26	1	*1.69	....	....	....	....	....	....	....
	HIFK Helsinki Jr.	Fin-Jr.	15	7	7	1	898	45	1	3.01	....	....	....	....	....	....	....
99-2000	HIFK Helsinki	Finland	4	0	4	0	155	17	0	6.58	....	....	....	....	....	....	....
	FPS Forssa	Finland-2	22	13	8	1	1320	50	1	2.27	3	1	2	178	8	0	2.69
2000-01	SaiPa	Finland	49	22	24	3	2826	120	2	2.55	....	....	....	....	....	....	....
2001-02	AIK Solna	Sweden	40	....	....	....	2186	111	1	3.05	....	....	....	....	....	....	....
	AIK Solna	Sweden-Q	9	....	....	....	543	20	0	2.21	....	....	....	....	....	....	....
2002-03	Karpat Oulu	Finland	36	16	8	9	2136	77	4	2.16	*15	7	8	*990	33	1	2.00
2003-04	Karpat Oulu	Finland	43	24	8	0	2572	87	7	2.03	*15	*9	6	*927	36	1	2.33
2004-05	Karpat Oulu	Finland	47	27	10	10	2819	102	7	2.17	*12	*10	2	720	15	*3	*1.25
2005-06	Karpat Oulu	Finland	51	*32	9	10	3077	86	*10	*1.68	4	3	1	195	6	0	1.84
	Finland	Olympics					DID NOT PLAY – SPARE GOALTENDER										
2006-07	**Minnesota**	**NHL**	**41**	**23**	**8**	**6**	**2227**	**73**	**5**	***1.97**	**5**	**1**	**4**	**297**	**11**	**0**	**2.22**
2007-08	**Minnesota**	**NHL**	**58**	**33**	**13**	**8**	**3409**	**131**	**4**	**2.31**	**6**	**2**	**4**	**361**	**17**	**0**	**2.83**
2008-09	**Minnesota**	**NHL**	**71**	**37**	**24**	**8**	**4088**	**159**	**8**	**2.33**	....	....	....	....	....	....	....
2009-10	**Minnesota**	**NHL**	**60**	**26**	**23**	**8**	**3489**	**158**	**2**	**2.72**	....	....	....	....	....	....	....
	Finland	Olympics	2	1	0	0	110	2	1	*1.09	....	....	....	....	....	....	....
2010-11	**Minnesota**	**NHL**	**51**	**22**	**23**	**5**	**2978**	**132**	**3**	**2.66**	....	....	....	....	....	....	....
	NHL Totals		**281**	**141**	**91**	**35**	**16191**	**653**	**22**	**2.42**	**11**	**3**	**8**	**658**	**28**	**0**	**2.55**

MBNA Roger Crozier Saving Grace Award (2007) • William M. Jennings Trophy (2007) (shared with Manny Fernandez)

Played in NHL All-Star Game (2009)

Signed as a free agent by **Minnesota**, June 1, 2006.

BARULIN, Konstantin (bah-ROO-lihn, KAWN-stan-tihn) ST.L.

Goaltender. Catches left. 6'2", 200 lbs. Born, Karaganda, USSR, September 4, 1984.
(St. Louis' 3rd choice, 84th overall, in 2003 Entry Draft).

			Regular Season								Playoffs						
Season	Club	League	GP	W	L	O/T	Mins	GA	SO	Avg	GP	W	L	Mins	GA	SO	Avg
2001-02	Gazovik Tyumen	Russia-2	4	....	....	....	190	15	0	4.73	....	....	....	....	....	....	....
2002-03	Gazovik Tyumen	Russia-2	41	....	....	....	2361	67	5	1.70	....	....	....	....	....	....	....
2003-04	Gazovik Tyumen	Russia-2	11	....	....	....	663	24	....	2.17	....	....	....	....	....	....	....
	SKA St. Petersburg	Russia	1	....	....	....	1	0	0	0.00	....	....	....	....	....	....	....
	St. Petersburg 2	Russia-3	11	....	....	....	668	24	1	2.15	....	....	....	....	....	....	....
2004-05	Gazovik Tyumen	Russia-2	30	....	....	....	1773	59	6	2.00	3	....	....	136	9	0	3.97
2005-06	Spartak Moscow	Russia	36	....	....	....	2102	75	2	2.14	2	....	....	104	4	0	2.30
2006-07	Mytischi	Russia	26	....	....	....	1249	45	1	2.16	1	....	....	48	3	0	3.76
2007-08	Mytischi	Russia	11	....	....	....	434	20	0	2.77	....	....	....	....	....	....	....
2008-09	CSKA Moscow	Rus-KHL	41	....	....	....	2443	100	2	2.46	2	....	....	100	9	0	5.40
2009-10	CSKA Moscow	Rus-KHL	45	....	....	....	2277	80	3	2.11	3	....	....	136	10	0	4.43
2010-11	Mytischi	Rus-KHL	28	....	....	....	1505	48	6	*1.91	*22	....	....	*1286	44	2	2.05

BENNETT, Brett (BEHN-eht, BREHT) PHX

Goaltender. Catches left. 6'1", 185 lbs. Born, Buffalo, NY, March 8, 1988.
(Phoenix's 4th choice, 130th overall, in 2006 Entry Draft).

			Regular Season								Playoffs						
Season	Club	League	GP	W	L	O/T	Mins	GA	SO	Avg	GP	W	L	Mins	GA	SO	Avg
2003-04	Det. Honeybaked	MWEHL	31	....	....	....	....	....	....	....	....	....	....	....	....	....	....
2004-05	USNTDP	U-17	14	10	6	1	930	41	0	2.65	....	....	....	....	....	....	....
	USNTDP	NAHL	23	10	7	1	1217	56	1	2.76	10	7	3	598	20	3	2.01
2005-06	USNTDP	U-18	12	7	2	0	593	24	0	2.43	....	....	....	....	....	....	....
	USNTDP	NAHL	5	3	0	0	238	5	0	1.26	....	....	....	....	....	....	....
2006-07	Boston University	H-East	1	1	0	0	60	1	0	1.00	....	....	....	....	....	....	....
2007-08	Boston University	H-East	31	16	10	3	1780	78	*3	2.63	....	....	....	....	....	....	....
2008-09	Indiana Ice	USHL	*54	*35	17	2	*3110	134	*4	2.59	*13	*9	4	*789	31	*1	*2.36
2009-10	U. of Wisconsin	WCHA	14	8	6	0	765	36	1	2.82	....	....	....	....	....	....	....
2010-11	U. of Wisconsin	WCHA	13	5	5	3	775	34	1	2.63	....	....	....	....	....	....	....

BERNIER, Jonathan (BAIRN-yay, JAWN-ah-thuhn) L.A.

Goaltender. Catches left. 5'11", 186 lbs. Born, Laval, Que., August 7, 1988.
(Los Angeles' 1st choice, 11th overall, in 2006 Entry Draft).

			Regular Season								Playoffs						
Season	Club	League	GP	W	L	O/T	Mins	GA	SO	Avg	GP	W	L	Mins	GA	SO	Avg
2003-04	Laval Regents	QAAA	27	16	4	0	1329	62	2	2.80	3	1	2	180	5	0	1.70
2004-05	Lewiston	QMJHL	23	7	12	3	1353	67	0	2.97	1	0	0	20	0	0	0.00
2005-06	Lewiston	QMJHL	54	27	26	0	3241	146	2	2.70	6	2	4	359	17	1	2.84
2006-07	Lewiston	QMJHL	37	26	10	0	2186	94	2	2.58	17	*16	1	1025	40	1	2.34
2007-08	**Los Angeles**	**NHL**	**4**	**1**	**3**	**0**	**238**	**16**	**0**	**4.03**	....	....	....	....	....	....	....
	Lewiston	QMJHL	34	18	15	0	2024	92	0	2.73	6	2	4	348	17	0	2.93
	Manchester	AHL	3	1	1	1	184	5	0	1.63	3	0	3	195	9	0	2.76
2008-09	Manchester	AHL	54	23	24	4	3101	124	5	2.40	....	....	....	....	....	....	....
2009-10	**Los Angeles**	**NHL**	**3**	**3**	**0**	**0**	**185**	**4**	**1**	**1.30**	....	....	....	....	....	....	....
	Manchester	AHL	58	30	21	6	3424	116	*9	2.03	16	10	6	996	30	*3	*1.81
2010-11	**Los Angeles**	**NHL**	**25**	**11**	**8**	**3**	**1378**	**57**	**3**	**2.48**	....	....	....	....	....	....	....
	NHL Totals		**32**	**15**	**11**	**3**	**1801**	**77**	**4**	**2.57**	....	....	....	....	....	....	....

QMJHL Second All-Star Team (2007) • Canadian Major Junior Second All-Star Team (2007) • AHL First All-Star Team (2010) • Aldege "Baz" Bastien Award (AHL – Outstanding Goaltender) (2010)

BERRA, Reto (BAIR-uh, REH-toh) ST.L.

Goaltender. Catches left. 6'4", 209 lbs. Born, Bulach, Switz., January 3, 1987.
(St. Louis' 6th choice, 106th overall, in 2006 Entry Draft).

			Regular Season								Playoffs						
Season	Club	League	GP	W	L	O/T	Mins	GA	SO	Avg	GP	W	L	Mins	GA	SO	Avg
2004-05	GCK Zurich Jr.	Swiss-Jr.	22	....	....	....	....	....	....	....	....	....	....	....	....	....	....
	GCK Lions Zurich	Swiss-2	3	....	....	....	180	12	0	4.00	....	....	....	....	....	....	....
	EHC Dubendorf	Swiss-3					STATISTICS NOT AVAILABLE										
2005-06	GCK Zurich Jr.	Swiss-Jr.	23	....	....	....	....	....	....	....	....	....	....	....	....	....	....
	GCK Lions Zurich	Swiss-2	15	....	....	....	835	51	1	3.56	....	....	....	....	....	....	....
	ZSC Lions Zurich	Swiss	2	0	1	0	90	6	0	3.99	....	....	....	....	....	....	....
2006-07	Switzerland U20	Swiss-2	3	0	3	0	179	13	0	4.69	....	....	....	....	....	....	....
	GCK Lions Zurich	Swiss-2	6	4	2	0	359	18	0	3.01	....	....	....	....	....	....	....
	ZSC Lions Zurich	Swiss	2	1	0	0	78	4	0	3.08	4	0	3	188	9	0	2.87
2007-08	HC Davos	Swiss	16	9	7	0	966	44	0	2.73	....	....	....	....	....	....	....
2008-09	EV Zug	Swiss	6	1	5	0	368	17	0	2.77	....	....	....	....	....	....	....
	SCL Tigers Langnau	Swiss	2	1	1	0	120	9	0	4.50	....	....	....	....	....	....	....
	HC Davos	Swiss	8	3	4	0	445	20	0	2.70	4	3	1	216	5	0	1.39
2009-10	EHC Biel-Bienne	Swiss	40	16	20	0	2319	130	3	3.36	10	3	7	582	33	0	3.40
	EHC Biel-Bienne	Swiss-Q	....	....	....	....	....	....	....	....	7	4	3	419	20	0	2.86
2010-11	EHC Biel-Bienne	Swiss	41	17	24	0	2452	122	3	2.99	....	....	....	....	....	....	....

BERUBE, Jean-Francois (beh-ROO-bay, ZHAWN-fran-SWUH) L.A.

Goaltender. Catches left. 6'1", 170 lbs. Born, Repentigny, Que., July 13, 1991.
(Los Angeles' 4th choice, 95th overall, in 2009 Entry Draft).

			Regular Season								Playoffs						
Season	Club	League	GP	W	L	O/T	Mins	GA	SO	Avg	GP	W	L	Mins	GA	SO	Avg
2007-08	Laurentides	QAAA	10	0	6	1	511	35	0	4.11	....	....	....	....	....	....	....
	Lachute Stars	QueAA					STATISTICS NOT AVAILABLE										
2008-09	Montreal	QMJHL	20	6	9	0	1059	51	1	2.89	1	0	0	20	1	0	3.00
2009-10	Montreal	QMJHL	45	17	23	0	2394	121	1	3.03	7	3	4	449	18	0	2.40
	Manchester	AHL	3	2	1	0	180	11	0	3.67	....	....	....	....	....	....	....
2010-11	Montreal	QMJHL	50	32	7	8	2935	127	3	2.60	10	6	4	623	29	*2	2.79

BESKOROWANY, Tyler (behs-koor-WAH-nee, TIGH-luhr) DAL

Goaltender. Catches left. 6'4", 208 lbs. Born, Sudbury, Ont., April 28, 1990.
(Dallas' 1st choice, 59th overall, in 2008 Entry Draft).

			Regular Season								Playoffs						
Season	Club	League	GP	W	L	O/T	Mins	GA	SO	Avg	GP	W	L	Mins	GA	SO	Avg
2006-07	Valley East Cobras	GNML	32	....	....	....	1443	80	1	3.33	7	....	....	410	22	2	3.22
2007-08	Owen Sound	OHL	35	12	19	3	2021	136	0	4.04	....	....	....	....	....	....	....
2008-09	Owen Sound	OHL	37	11	12	10	2160	131	1	3.64	1	0	1	27	5	0	11.16
2009-10	Kingston	OHL	62	29	25	4	3461	203	1	3.52	7	3	4	424	23	0	3.26
2010-11	Texas Stars	AHL	18	7	8	1	978	42	1	2.58	1	0	0	20	1	0	3.00
	Idaho Steelheads	ECHL	20	10	5	4	1149	45	1	2.35	....	....	....	....	....	....	....

BINNINGTON, Jordan (BIHN-ihng-tuhn, JOHR-duhn) ST.L.

Goaltender. Catches left. 6'2", 158 lbs. Born, Richmond Hill, Ont., July 11, 1993.
(St. Louis' 4th choice, 88th overall, in 2011 Entry Draft).

			Regular Season								Playoffs						
Season	Club	League	GP	W	L	O/T	Mins	GA	SO	Avg	GP	W	L	Mins	GA	SO	Avg
2008-09	Vaughan Kings	GTHL	....	34	15	....	....	....	....	2.18	....	....	....	....	....	....	....
	Dixie Beehives	ON-Jr.A	1	0	1	0	59	3	0	3.04	....	....	....	....	....	....	....
2009-10	Owen Sound	OHL	22	6	10	2	1068	78	0	4.38	....	....	....	....	....	....	....
2010-11	Owen Sound	OHL	46	27	12	5	2596	132	1	3.05	7	4	2	355	19	0	3.21

Memorial Cup All-Star Team (2011)

BIRON, Martin (BEE-rawn, MAHR-tihn) NYR

Goaltender. Catches left. 6'2", 180 lbs. Born, Lac-St-Charles, Que., August 15, 1977.
(Buffalo's 2nd choice, 16th overall, in 1995 Entry Draft).

			Regular Season								Playoffs						
Season	Club	League	GP	W	L	O/T	Mins	GA	SO	Avg	GP	W	L	Mins	GA	SO	Avg
1993-94	Trois-Rivieres	QAAA	23	14	8	1	1412	80	1	3.40	2	1	1	112	7	0	3.73
1994-95	Beauport Harfangs	QMJHL	56	29	16	9	3199	132	3	*2.48	16	8	7	903	37	*4	2.46
1995-96	Beauport Harfangs	QMJHL	55	29	17	7	3207	152	1	2.84	*19	*12	7	1135	64	0	3.38
	Buffalo	**NHL**	**3**	**0**	**2**	**0**	**119**	**10**	**0**	**5.04**	....	....	....	....	....	....	....
1996-97	Beauport Harfangs	QMJHL	18	6	10	1	935	62	1	3.98	....	....	....	....	....	....	....
	Hull Olympiques	QMJHL	16	11	4	1	972	43	2	2.66	6	3	1	326	19	0	3.50
1997-98	South Carolina	ECHL	2	0	1	1	86	3	0	2.09	....	....	....	....	....	....	....
	Rochester	AHL	41	14	18	6	2312	113	*5	2.93	4	1	3	239	16	0	4.01
1998-99	**Buffalo**	**NHL**	**6**	**1**	**2**	**1**	**281**	**10**	**0**	**2.14**	....	....	....	....	....	....	....
	Rochester	AHL	52	36	13	3	3129	108	*6	*2.07	*20	12	8	1167	42	1	*2.16
99-2000	**Buffalo**	**NHL**	**41**	**19**	**18**	**2**	**2229**	**90**	**5**	**2.42**	....	....	....	....	....	....	....
	Rochester	AHL	6	6	0	0	344	12	1	2.09	....	....	....	....	....	....	....
2000-01	**Buffalo**	**NHL**	**18**	**7**	**7**	**1**	**918**	**39**	**2**	**2.55**	....	....	....	....	....	....	....
	Rochester	AHL	4	3	1	0	239	4	1	1.00	....	....	....	....	....	....	....
2001-02	**Buffalo**	**NHL**	**72**	**31**	**28**	**10**	**4085**	**151**	**4**	**2.22**	....	....	....	....	....	....	....
2002-03	**Buffalo**	**NHL**	**54**	**17**	**28**	**6**	**3170**	**135**	**4**	**2.56**	....	....	....	....	....	....	....
2003-04	**Buffalo**	**NHL**	**52**	**26**	**18**	**5**	**2972**	**125**	**2**	**2.52**	....	....	....	....	....	....	....
2004-05								DID NOT PLAY									
2005-06	**Buffalo**	**NHL**	**35**	**21**	**8**	**3**	**1934**	**93**	**1**	**2.89**	....	....	....	....	....	....	....
2006-07	**Buffalo**	**NHL**	**19**	**12**	**4**	**1**	**1066**	**54**	**0**	**3.04**	....	....	....	....	....	....	....
	Philadelphia	**NHL**	**16**	**6**	**8**	**2**	**935**	**47**	**0**	**3.02**	....	....	....	....	....	....	....
2007-08	**Philadelphia**	**NHL**	**62**	**30**	**20**	**9**	**3539**	**153**	**5**	**2.59**	**17**	**9**	**8**	**1049**	**52**	**1**	**2.97**
2008-09	**Philadelphia**	**NHL**	**55**	**29**	**19**	**5**	**3177**	**146**	**2**	**2.76**	**6**	**2**	**4**	**375**	**16**	**1**	**2.56**
2009-10	**NY Islanders**	**NHL**	**29**	**9**	**14**	**4**	**1634**	**89**	**1**	**3.27**	....	....	....	....	....	....	....
	Bridgeport	AHL	2	1	1	0	124	7	0	3.40	....	....	....	....	....	....	....
2010-11	**NY Rangers**	**NHL**	**17**	**8**	**6**	**0**	**928**	**33**	**0**	**2.13**	....	....	....	....	....	....	....
	NHL Totals		**479**	**216**	**182**	**49**	**26987**	**1175**	**26**	**2.61**	**23**	**11**	**12**	**1424**	**68**	**2**	**2.87**

QMJHL All-Rookie Team (1995) • Canadian Major Junior First All-Star Team (1995) • Canadian Major Junior Goaltender of the Year (1995) • AHL First All-Star Team (1999) • Harry "Hap" Holmes Memorial Award (AHL – fewest goals against) (1999) (shared with Tom Draper) • Aldege "Baz" Bastien Memorial Award (AHL – Outstanding Goaltender) (1999)

Traded to **Philadelphia** by **Buffalo** for Philadelphia's 2nd round choice (T.J. Brennan) in 2007 Entry Draft, February 27, 2007. Signed as a free agent by **NY Islanders**, July 22, 2009. Signed as a free agent by **NY Rangers**, July 1, 2010.

BISHOP, Ben (BIH-shuhp, BEHN) ST.L.

Goaltender. Catches left. 6'7", 215 lbs. Born, Denver, CO, November 21, 1986.
(St. Louis' 3rd choice, 85th overall, in 2005 Entry Draft).

			Regular Season								Playoffs						
Season	Club	League	GP	W	L	O/T	Mins	GA	SO	Avg	GP	W	L	Mins	GA	SO	Avg
2003-04	St.L. AAA Blues	MAHL	11	8	1	2	660	19	1	1.73	....	....	....	....	....	....	....
	St.L. AAA Blues	Exhib.	26	15	7	4	1480	62	3	2.51	....	....	....	....	....	....	....
2004-05	Texas Tornado	NAHL	45	*35	8	0	2577	83	5	1.93	*11	*9	2	*660	30	0	2.73
2005-06	University of Maine	H-East	31	21	8	2	1788	68	0	2.28	....	....	....	....	....	....	....
2006-07	University of Maine	H-East	34	21	9	2	1907	68	3	2.14	....	....	....	....	....	....	....
2007-08	University of Maine	H-East	34	13	18	3	1972	80	2	2.43	....	....	....	....	....	....	....
	Peoria Rivermen	AHL	5	2	2	1	302	12	0	2.38	....	....	....	....	....	....	....
2008-09	**St. Louis**	**NHL**	**6**	**1**	**1**	**1**	**245**	**12**	**0**	**2.94**	....	....	....	....	....	....	....
	Peoria Rivermen	AHL	33	15	16	1	1898	89	1	2.81	....	....	....	....	....	....	....
2009-10	Peoria Rivermen	AHL	48	23	18	4	2793	129	0	2.77	....	....	....	....	....	....	....
2010-11	**St. Louis**	**NHL**	**7**	**3**	**4**	**0**	**369**	**17**	**1**	**2.76**	....	....	....	....	....	....	....
	Peoria Rivermen	AHL	35	17	14	2	2043	87	2	2.55	1	0	1	59	2	0	2.04
	NHL Totals		**13**	**4**	**5**	**1**	**614**	**29**	**1**	**2.83**	....	....	....	....	....	....	....

Hockey East All-Rookie Team (2006) • Hockey East Second All-Star Team (2008)

BOBKOV, Igor (bawb-KAWF, EE-gohr) ANA

Goaltender. Catches left. 6'4", 192 lbs. Born, Surgut, USSR, January 2, 1991.
(Anaheim's 4th choice, 76th overall, in 2009 Entry Draft).

			Regular Season								Playoffs						
Season	Club	League	GP	W	L	O/T	Mins	GA	SO	Avg	GP	W	L	Mins	GA	SO	Avg
2008-09	Magnitogorsk 2	Russia-3	9	....	....	....	....	24	....	....	....	....	....	....	....	....	....
2009-10	Magnitogorsk Jr.	Russia-Jr.	14	....	....	....	665	30	2	2.71	2	....	....	59	3	0	3.05
2010-11	London Knights	OHL	21	4	10	0	1048	72	0	4.12	3	0	0	29	2	0	4.14
	Syracuse Crunch	AHL	2	2	0	0	120	7	0	3.51	....	....	....	....	....	....	....

BOBROVSKY, Sergei (bawb-RAWF-skee, SAIR-gay) PHI

Goaltender. Catches left. 6'2", 190 lbs. Born, Novokuznetsk, USSR, September 20, 1988.

			Regular Season								Playoffs						
Season	Club	League	GP	W	L	O/T	Mins	GA	SO	Avg	GP	W	L	Mins	GA	SO	Avg
2006-07	Novokuznetsk	Russia	8	....	....	....	280	13	0	2.78	....	....	....	....	....	....	....
2007-08	Novokuznetsk	Russia	24	....	....	....	1153	57	1	2.97	....	....	....	....	....	....	....
2008-09	Novokuznetsk	Rus-KHL	32	....	....	....	1636	69	1	2.53	....	....	....	....	....	....	....
2009-10	Novokuznetsk	Rus-KHL	35	....	....	....	1964	89	1	2.72	....	....	....	....	....	....	....
2010-11	**Philadelphia**	**NHL**	**54**	**28**	**13**	**8**	**3017**	**130**	**0**	**2.59**	**6**	**0**	**2**	**186**	**10**	**0**	**3.23**
	NHL Totals		**54**	**28**	**13**	**8**	**3017**	**130**	**0**	**2.59**	**6**	**0**	**2**	**186**	**10**	**0**	**3.23**

Signed as a free agent by **Philadelphia**, May 6, 2010.

BOUCHER, Brian (BOO-shay, BRIGH-uhn) CAR

Goaltender. Catches left. 6'2", 200 lbs. Born, Woonsocket, RI, January 2, 1977.
(Philadelphia's 1st choice, 22nd overall, in 1995 Entry Draft).

			Regular Season								Playoffs						
Season	Club	League	GP	W	L	O/T	Mins	GA	SO	Avg	GP	W	L	Mins	GA	SO	Avg
1993-94	Mount St. Charles	High-RI	15	*14	0	1	*504	*8	*9	*0.57	4	*4	0	*180	*6	*1	*1.20
1994-95	Wexford Raiders	ON-Jr.A	8	....	....	....	425	23	0	3.25	....	....	....	....	....	....	....
	Tri-City Americans	WHL	35	17	11	2	1969	108	1	3.29	13	6	5	795	50	0	3.77
1995-96	Tri-City Americans	WHL	55	33	19	2	3183	181	1	3.41	11	6	5	653	37	*2	3.40
1996-97	Tri-City Americans	WHL	41	10	24	6	2458	149	1	3.64	....	....	....	....	....	....	....
1997-98	Philadelphia	AHL	34	16	12	3	1901	101	0	3.19	2	0	0	30	1	0	1.95
1998-99	Philadelphia	AHL	36	20	8	5	2061	89	2	2.59	16	9	7	947	45	0	2.85
99-2000	**Philadelphia**	**NHL**	**35**	**20**	**10**	**3**	**2038**	**65**	**4**	***1.91**	**18**	**11**	**7**	**1183**	**40**	**1**	**2.03**
	Philadelphia	AHL	1	0	0	1	65	3	0	2.77	....	....	....	....	....	....	....
2000-01	**Philadelphia**	**NHL**	**27**	**8**	**12**	**5**	**1470**	**80**	**1**	**3.27**	**1**	**0**	**0**	**37**	**3**	**0**	**4.86**
2001-02	**Philadelphia**	**NHL**	**41**	**18**	**16**	**4**	**2295**	**92**	**2**	**2.41**	**2**	**0**	**1**	**88**	**2**	**0**	**1.36**
2002-03	**Phoenix**	**NHL**	**45**	**15**	**20**	**8**	**2544**	**128**	**0**	**3.02**	....	....	....	....	....	....	....
2003-04	**Phoenix**	**NHL**	**40**	**10**	**19**	**10**	**2364**	**108**	**5**	**2.74**	....	....	....	....	....	....	....
2004-05	HV 71 Jonkoping	Sweden	4	....	....	....	235	13	0	3.32	....	....	....	....	....	....	....
2005-06	**Phoenix**	**NHL**	**11**	**3**	**6**	**0**	**512**	**33**	**0**	**3.87**	....	....	....	....	....	....	....
	San Antonio	AHL	6	2	3	0	345	8	0	1.39	....	....	....	....	....	....	....
	Calgary	**NHL**	**3**	**1**	**2**	**0**	**182**	**15**	**0**	**4.95**	....	....	....	....	....	....	....
2006-07	**Chicago**	**NHL**	**15**	**1**	**10**	**3**	**827**	**45**	**1**	**3.26**	....	....	....	....	....	....	....
	Columbus	**NHL**	**3**	**1**	**1**	**0**	**142**	**9**	**0**	**3.80**	....	....	....	....	....	....	....
2007-08	Philadelphia	AHL	42	23	16	1	2288	94	4	2.47	....	....	....	....	....	....	....
	San Jose	**NHL**	**5**	**3**	**1**	**1**	**238**	**7**	**1**	**1.76**	**1**	**0**	**0**	**2**	**0**	**0**	**0.00**
2008-09	**San Jose**	**NHL**	**22**	**12**	**6**	**3**	**1291**	**47**	**2**	**2.18**	....	....	....	....	....	....	....
2009-10	**Philadelphia**	**NHL**	**33**	**9**	**18**	**3**	**1742**	**80**	**1**	**2.76**	**12**	**6**	**6**	**656**	**27**	**1**	**2.47**
	Adirondack	AHL	1	1	0	0	60	2	0	2.00	....	....	....	....	....	....	....
2010-11	**Philadelphia**	**NHL**	**34**	**18**	**10**	**4**	**1885**	**76**	**0**	**2.42**	**9**	**4**	**4**	**422**	**22**	**0**	**3.13**
	NHL Totals		**314**	**119**	**131**	**44**	**17530**	**785**	**17**	**2.69**	**43**	**21**	**18**	**2388**	**94**	**2**	**2.36**

WHL West Second All-Star Team (1996) • WHL West First All-Star Team (1997) • WHL Goaltender of the Year (1997) • NHL All-Rookie Team (2000)

Traded to **Phoenix** by **Philadelphia** with Nashville's 3rd round choice (previously acquired, Phoenix selected Joe Callahan) in 2002 Entry Draft for Michal Handzus and Robert Esche, June 12, 2002. Signed as a free agent by **Jonkoping** (Sweden), October 20, 2004. Traded to **Calgary** by **Phoenix** with Mike Leclerc for Steve Reinprecht and Philippe Sauve, February 2, 2006. Signed as a free agent by **Chicago**, September 24, 2006. Claimed on waivers by **Columbus** from **Chicago**, February 27, 2007. Signed as a free agent by **Philadelphia** (AHL), July 23, 2007. Signed as a free agent by **San Jose**, February 26, 2008. Signed as a free agent by **Philadelphia**, July 1, 2009. Signed as a free agent by **Carolina**, July 1, 2011.

BRITTAIN, Sam (brih-TAYN, SAM) FLA

Goaltender. Catches left. 6'3", 215 lbs. Born, Calgary, Alta., May 10, 1992.
(Florida's 8th choice, 92nd overall, in 2010 Entry Draft).

			Regular Season								Playoffs						
Season	Club	League	GP	W	L	O/T	Mins	GA	SO	Avg	GP	W	L	Mins	GA	SO	Avg
2008-09	Calgary Buffaloes	AMHL	26	14	9	3	1542	67	....	2.61	15	11	4	901	45	....	3.00
	Canmore Eagles	AJHL	3	1	2	0	179	9	0	3.02	....	....	....	....	....	....	....
2009-10	Canmore Eagles	AJHL	52	23	19	8	3065	167	2	3.27	9	5	4	559	28	0	3.01
2010-11	U. of Denver	WCHA	33	19	9	5	1998	76	1	2.28	....	....	....	....	....	....	....

WCHA All-Rookie Team (2011)

BRODEUR, Martin (broh-DUHR, MAHR-tihn) N.J.

Goaltender. Catches left. 6'2", 215 lbs. Born, Montreal, Que., May 6, 1972.
(New Jersey's 1st choice, 20th overall, in 1990 Entry Draft).

			Regular Season								Playoffs						
Season	Club	League	GP	W	L	O/T	Mins	GA	SO	Avg	GP	W	L	Mins	GA	SO	Avg
1988-89	Montreal-Bourassa	QAAA	27	13	12	1	1580	98	0	3.72	3	0	3	210	14	0	3.99
1989-90	St-Hyacinthe Laser	QMJHL	42	23	12	2	2331	156	0	4.02	12	5	7	680	46	0	4.06
1990-91	St-Hyacinthe Laser	QMJHL	52	22	22	4	2946	162	2	3.30	4	0	4	232	16	0	4.14
1991-92	St-Hyacinthe Laser	QMJHL	48	27	14	4	2846	161	2	3.39	5	2	3	317	14	0	2.65
	New Jersey	**NHL**	**4**	**2**	**1**	**0**	**179**	**10**	**0**	**3.35**	**1**	**0**	**1**	**32**	**3**	**0**	**5.63**
1992-93	Utica Devils	AHL	32	14	13	5	1952	131	0	4.03	4	1	3	258	18	0	4.19
1993-94	**New Jersey**	**NHL**	**47**	**27**	**11**	**8**	**2625**	**105**	**3**	**2.40**	**17**	**8**	**9**	**1171**	**38**	**1**	**1.95**
1994-95 ♦	**New Jersey**	**NHL**	**40**	**19**	**11**	**6**	**2184**	**89**	**3**	**2.45**	***20**	***16**	**4**	***1222**	**34**	***3**	***1.67**
1995-96	**New Jersey**	**NHL**	**77**	**34**	**30**	**12**	***4433**	**173**	**6**	**2.34**	....	....	....	....	....	....	....
1996-97	**New Jersey**	**NHL**	**67**	**37**	**14**	**13**	**3838**	**120**	***10**	***1.88**	**10**	**5**	**5**	**659**	**19**	**2**	***1.73**
1997-98	**New Jersey**	**NHL**	**70**	***43**	**17**	**8**	**4128**	**130**	**10**	**1.89**	**6**	**2**	**4**	**366**	**12**	**0**	**1.97**
1998-99	**New Jersey**	**NHL**	***70**	***39**	**21**	**10**	***4239**	**162**	**4**	**2.29**	**7**	**3**	**4**	**425**	**20**	**0**	**2.82**
99-2000 ♦	**New Jersey**	**NHL**	**72**	***43**	**20**	**8**	**4312**	**161**	**6**	**2.24**	***23**	***16**	**7**	***1450**	**39**	**2**	***1.61**
2000-01	**New Jersey**	**NHL**	**72**	***42**	**17**	**11**	**4297**	**166**	**9**	**2.32**	***25**	**15**	**10**	***1505**	**52**	***4**	**2.07**
2001-02	**New Jersey**	**NHL**	***73**	**38**	**26**	**9**	***4347**	**156**	**4**	**2.15**	**6**	**2**	**4**	**381**	**9**	**1**	**1.42**
	Canada	Olympics	5	*4	0	1	300	9	0	*1.80	....	....	....	....	....	....	....
2002-03 ♦	**New Jersey**	**NHL**	**73**	***41**	**23**	**9**	**4374**	**147**	***9**	**2.02**	***24**	***16**	**8**	***1491**	**41**	***7**	**1.65**
2003-04	**New Jersey**	**NHL**	***75**	***38**	**26**	**11**	***4555**	**154**	***11**	**2.03**	**5**	**1**	**4**	**298**	**13**	**0**	**2.62**
2004-05							Did not play										
2005-06	**New Jersey**	**NHL**	**73**	***43**	**23**	**7**	**4365**	**187**	**5**	**2.57**	**9**	**5**	**4**	**533**	**20**	**1**	**2.25**
	Canada	Olympics	4	2	2	0	239	8	0	2.01	....	....	....	....	....	....	....
2006-07	**New Jersey**	**NHL**	***78**	***48**	**23**	**7**	***4697**	**171**	***12**	**2.18**	**11**	**5**	**6**	**688**	**28**	**1**	**2.44**
2007-08	**New Jersey**	**NHL**	***77**	**44**	**27**	**6**	***4635**	**168**	**4**	**2.17**	**5**	**1**	**4**	**301**	**16**	**0**	**3.19**
2008-09	**New Jersey**	**NHL**	**31**	**19**	**9**	**3**	**1814**	**73**	**5**	**2.41**	**7**	**3**	**4**	**427**	**17**	**1**	**2.39**
2009-10	**New Jersey**	**NHL**	***77**	***45**	**25**	**6**	***4499**	**168**	***9**	**2.24**	**5**	**1**	**4**	**299**	**15**	**0**	**3.01**
	Canada	Olympics	2	1	1	0	124	6	0	2.90	....	....	....	....	....	....	....
2010-11	**New Jersey**	**NHL**	**56**	**23**	**26**	**3**	**3116**	**127**	**6**	**2.45**	....	....	....	....	....	....	....
	NHL Totals		**1132**	**625**	**350**	**137**	**66637**	**2467**	**116**	**2.22**	**181**	**99**	**82**	**11248**	**376**	**23**	**2.01**

QMJHL All-Rookie Team (1990) • QMJHL Second All-Star Team (1992) • NHL All-Rookie Team (1994) • Calder Memorial Trophy (1994) • NHL Second All-Star Team (1997, 1998, 2006, 2008) • William M. Jennings Trophy (1997) (shared with Mike Dunham) • William M. Jennings Trophy (1998, 2004, 2010) • NHL First All-Star Team (2003, 2004, 2007) • William M. Jennings Trophy (2003) (tied with Roman Cechmanek/Robert Esche) • Vezina Trophy (2003, 2004, 2007, 2008)

Played in NHL All-Star Game (1996, 1997, 1998, 1999, 2000, 2001, 2003, 2004, 2007)

• Scored a goal in playoffs vs. Montreal, April 17, 1997. • Missed majority of 2008-09 due to elbow injury vs. Atlanta, November 1, 2008.

BRODEUR, Mike (broh-DUHR, MIGHK)

Goaltender. Catches left. 6'2", 190 lbs. Born, Calgary, Alta., March 30, 1983.
(Chicago's 7th choice, 211th overall, in 2003 Entry Draft).

			Regular Season								Playoffs						
Season	Club	League	GP	W	L	O/T	Mins	GA	SO	Avg	GP	W	L	Mins	GA	SO	Avg
2000-01	Calgary Flames	AMHL	21	11	8	3	1231	54	1	2.63	10	6	4	620	31	0	3.00
2001-02	Camrose Kodiaks	AJHL	24	13	9	1	1299	65	1	2.91	....	....	....	....	....	....	....
2002-03	Camrose Kodiaks	AJHL	48	28	16	2	2570	113	2	2.64	21	16	5	1378	48	4	2.09
2003-04	Moose Jaw	WHL	41	23	12	5	2385	84	5	2.11	10	6	4	624	18	1	*1.73
2004-05	Norfolk Admirals	AHL	1	0	1	0	39	4	0	6.17	....	....	....	....	....	....	....
	Greenville Grrrowl	ECHL	35	19	15	1	2081	93	2	2.68	5	2	3	302	10	1	1.98
2005-06	Greenville Grrrowl	ECHL	24	14	8	2	1466	63	1	2.58	....	....	....	....	....	....	....
2006-07	Norfolk Admirals	AHL	10	4	3	0	495	28	0	3.39	1	0	0	8	2	0	14.17
	Augusta Lynx	ECHL	2	2	0	0	120	4	1	2.00	....	....	....	....	....	....	....
	Toledo Storm	ECHL	5	3	2	0	300	10	2	2.00	....	....	....	....	....	....	....
2007-08	Rockford IceHogs	AHL	8	2	3	0	341	16	0	2.81	....	....	....	....	....	....	....
	Pensacola Ice Pilots	ECHL	26	10	9	5	1504	71	1	2.83	....	....	....	....	....	....	....
2008-09	Rochester	AHL	38	18	13	4	2127	87	2	2.45	....	....	....	....	....	....	....
	Augusta Lynx	ECHL	8	2	4	1	457	23	1	3.02	....	....	....	....	....	....	....
2009-10	**Ottawa**	**NHL**	**3**	**3**	**0**	**0**	**180**	**3**	**1**	**1.00**	....	....	....	....	....	....	....
	Binghamton	AHL	36	13	13	2	1881	96	2	3.06	....	....	....	....	....	....	....
2010-11	**Ottawa**	**NHL**	**4**	**0**	**1**	**0**	**97**	**7**	**0**	**4.33**	....	....	....	....	....	....	....
	Binghamton	AHL	9	3	5	0	466	23	0	2.96	....	....	....	....	....	....	....
	Elmira Jackals	ECHL	4	3	1	0	232	10	1	2.59	....	....	....	....	....	....	....
	NHL Totals		**7**	**3**	**1**	**0**	**277**	**10**	**1**	**2.17**	....	....	....	....	....	....	....

Signed as a free agent by **Ottawa**, July 1, 2009.

BROSSOIT, Laurent (BRAH-sah, LAWR-ehnt) CGY

Goaltender. Catches left. 6'3", 200 lbs. Born, Port Alberni, B.C., March 23, 1993.
(Calgary's 5th choice, 164th overall, in 2011 Entry Draft).

			Regular Season								Playoffs						
Season	Club	League	GP	W	L	O/T	Mins	GA	SO	Avg	GP	W	L	Mins	GA	SO	Avg
2008-09	Valley West Hawks	BCMML					Statistics not available										
	Edmonton	WHL	1	0	0	0	37	5	0	8.11	....	....	....	....	....	....	....
2009-10	Cowichan Valley	BCHL	21	10	8	0	999	61	2	3.66	5	1	3	259	17	0	3.93
	Edmonton	WHL	2	0	1	0	86	4	0	2.79	....	....	....	....	....	....	....
2010-11	Edmonton	WHL	34	13	12	2	1664	92	2	3.32	2	0	2	117	7	0	3.59

BRUST, Barry (BRUHST, BAIR-ree)

Goaltender. Catches left. 6'2", 216 lbs. Born, Swan River, Man., August 8, 1983.
(Minnesota's 4th choice, 73rd overall, in 2002 Entry Draft).

			Regular Season								Playoffs						
Season	Club	League	GP	W	L	O/T	Mins	GA	SO	Avg	GP	W	L	Mins	GA	SO	Avg
99-2000	Swan Valley	MJHL	19	10	9	0	1140	67	0	3.50	....	....	....	....	....	....	....
2000-01	Spokane Chiefs	WHL	16	4	6	1	778	42	0	3.24	....	....	....	....	....	....	....
2001-02	Spokane Chiefs	WHL	60	28	21	10	3542	152	1	2.57	11	6	5	678	23	0	2.04
2002-03	Spokane Chiefs	WHL	*59	22	32	4	*3385	195	0	3.46	11	4	7	722	37	0	3.07
2003-04	Spokane Chiefs	WHL	27	10	13	2	1504	75	0	2.99	....	....	....	....	....	....	....
	Calgary Hitmen	WHL	25	12	8	3	1448	54	2	2.24	7	3	4	457	15	2	1.97
2004-05	Reading Royals	ECHL	42	27	9	4	2413	79	4	1.96	8	4	4	481	14	2	1.74
2005-06	Manchester	AHL	35	19	14	1	1971	89	2	2.71	5	2	2	279	17	1	3.66
	Reading Royals	ECHL	6	3	3	0	361	18	0	3.00	....	....	....	....	....	....	....
2006-07	**Los Angeles**	**NHL**	**11**	**2**	**4**	**1**	**486**	**30**	**0**	**3.70**	....	....	....	....	....	....	....
	Manchester	AHL	18	9	7	0	951	38	2	2.40	5	2	1	199	6	0	1.81
2007-08	Houston Aeros	AHL	43	24	16	3	2380	90	4	2.27	3	1	2	202	6	1	1.78
2008-09	Houston Aeros	AHL	28	9	9	3	1548	65	0	2.52	....	....	....	....	....	....	....
2009-10	Houston Aeros	AHL	15	6	6	0	756	31	1	2.46	....	....	....	....	....	....	....
	Florida Everblades	ECHL	16	9	3	2	882	33	0	2.24	....	....	....	....	....	....	....
2010-11	Binghamton	AHL	52	29	19	2	2986	126	7	2.53	6	2	3	330	19	0	3.45
	NHL Totals		**11**	**2**	**4**	**1**	**486**	**30**	**0**	**3.70**	....	....	....	....	....	....	....

WHL West First All-Star Team (2002) • Harry "Hap" Holmes Memorial Award (AHL – fewest goals against) (2008) (shared with Nolan Schaefer)

Signed as a free agent by **Los Angeles**, June 10, 2004. Signed as a free agent by **Minnesota**, July 6, 2008. Signed as a free agent by **Binghamton** (AHL), July 21, 2010.

BRYZGALOV, Ilya (breez-GAH-lahf, IHL-yah) PHI

Goaltender. Catches left. 6'3", 213 lbs. Born, Togliatti, USSR, June 22, 1980.
(Anaheim's 2nd choice, 44th overall, in 2000 Entry Draft).

			Regular Season								Playoffs						
Season	Club	League	GP	W	L	O/T	Mins	GA	SO	Avg	GP	W	L	Mins	GA	SO	Avg
1996-97	Lada Togliatti 2	Russia-3	5	....	....	....	....	....	....	....	....	....	....	....	....	....	....
1997-98	Lada Togliatti 2	Russia-3	8	....	....	....	....	28	....	....	....	....	....	....	....	....	....
1998-99	Lada Togliatti 2	Russia-4	20	....	....	....	....	43	....	....	....	....	....	....	....	....	....
99-2000	Spartak Moscow	Russia-2	10	....	....	....	500	21	....	2.52	....	....	....	....	....	....	....
	Lada Togliatti 2	Russia-3	2	....	....	....	....	5	....	....	....	....	....	....	....	....	....
	Lada Togliatti	Russia	14	....	....	....	796	18	3	1.36	7	....	....	407	10	1	1.47
2000-01	Lada Togliatti	Russia	34	....	....	....	1992	61	8	1.84	5	....	....	249	8	0	1.93
2001-02	**Anaheim**	**NHL**	**1**	**0**	**0**	**0**	**32**	**1**	**0**	**1.88**	....	....	....	....	....	....	....
	Cincinnati	AHL	45	20	16	4	2399	99	4	2.48	....	....	....	....	....	....	....
	Russia	Olympics					Did not play – spare goaltender										
2002-03	Cincinnati	AHL	54	12	26	9	3020	142	1	2.82	....	....	....	....	....	....	....
2003-04	**Anaheim**	**NHL**	**1**	**1**	**0**	**0**	**60**	**2**	**0**	**2.00**	....	....	....	....	....	....	....
	Cincinnati	AHL	*64	27	25	10	*3748	145	6	2.32	9	5	4	536	27	1	3.02
2004-05	Cincinnati	AHL	36	17	13	1	2007	87	4	2.60	7	3	3	314	13	0	2.48
2005-06	**Anaheim**	**NHL**	**31**	**13**	**12**	**1**	**1575**	**66**	**1**	**2.51**	**11**	**6**	**4**	**659**	**16**	***3**	***1.46**
	Russia	Olympics	1	0	1	0	60	5	0	5.00	....	....	....	....	....	....	....
2006-07 ♦	**Anaheim**	**NHL**	**27**	**10**	**8**	**6**	**1509**	**62**	**1**	**2.47**	**5**	**3**	**1**	**267**	**10**	**0**	**2.25**
2007-08	**Anaheim**	**NHL**	**9**	**2**	**3**	**1**	**447**	**19**	**0**	**2.55**	....	....	....	....	....	....	....
	Phoenix	**NHL**	**55**	**26**	**22**	**5**	**3167**	**128**	**3**	**2.43**	....	....	....	....	....	....	....
2008-09	**Phoenix**	**NHL**	**65**	**26**	**31**	**6**	**3760**	**187**	**3**	**2.98**	....	....	....	....	....	....	....
2009-10	**Phoenix**	**NHL**	**69**	**42**	**20**	**6**	**4084**	**156**	**8**	**2.29**	**7**	**3**	**4**	**419**	**24**	**0**	**3.44**
	Russia	Olympics	2	0	1	0	101	3	0	1.78	....	....	....	....	....	....	....
2010-11	**Phoenix**	**NHL**	**68**	**36**	**20**	**10**	**4060**	**168**	**7**	**2.48**	**4**	**0**	**4**	**234**	**17**	**0**	**4.36**
	NHL Totals		**326**	**156**	**116**	**35**	**18694**	**789**	**23**	**2.53**	**27**	**12**	**13**	**1579**	**67**	**3**	**2.55**

NHL Second All-Star Team (2010)

Claimed on waivers by **Phoenix** from **Anaheim**, November 17, 2007. Traded to **Philadelphia** by **Phoenix** for Matt Clackson, Philadelphia's 3rd round choice in 2012 Entry Draft and future considerations, June 7, 2011.

BUDAJ, Peter (BOO-digh, PEE-tuhr) MTL

Goaltender. Catches left. 6'1", 200 lbs. Born, Banska Bystrica, Czech., September 18, 1982.
(Colorado's 1st choice, 63rd overall, in 2001 Entry Draft).

			Regular Season								Playoffs						
Season	Club	League	GP	W	L	O/T	Mins	GA	SO	Avg	GP	W	L	Mins	GA	SO	Avg
99-2000	St. Michael's	OHL	34	6	18	1	1676	112	1	4.01	....	....	....	....	....	....	....
2000-01	St. Michael's	OHL	37	17	12	3	1996	95	3	2.86	11	6	4	621	26	1	2.51
2001-02	St. Michael's	OHL	42	26	9	5	2329	89	2	*2.29	12	5	6	621	34	*1	3.29
2002-03	Hershey Bears	AHL	28	10	10	2	1467	65	2	2.66	1	0	0	6	2	0	20.81
2003-04	Hershey Bears	AHL	46	17	20	6	2574	120	3	2.80	....	....	....	....	....	....	....
2004-05	Hershey Bears	AHL	59	29	25	2	3356	148	5	2.65	....	....	....	....	....	....	....
2005-06	**Colorado**	**NHL**	**34**	**14**	**10**	**6**	**1803**	**86**	**2**	**2.86**	....	....	....	....	....	....	....
	Slovakia	Olympics	3	2	1	0	179	6	0	2.01	....	....	....	....	....	....	....
2006-07	**Colorado**	**NHL**	**57**	**31**	**16**	**6**	**3199**	**143**	**3**	**2.68**	....	....	....	....	....	....	....
2007-08	**Colorado**	**NHL**	**35**	**16**	**10**	**4**	**1912**	**82**	**0**	**2.57**	**3**	**0**	**0**	**108**	**6**	**0**	**3.33**
2008-09	**Colorado**	**NHL**	**56**	**20**	**29**	**5**	**3232**	**154**	**2**	**2.86**	....	....	....	....	....	....	....
2009-10	**Colorado**	**NHL**	**15**	**5**	**5**	**2**	**728**	**32**	**1**	**2.64**	**1**	**0**	**0**	**9**	**1**	**0**	**6.67**
	Slovakia	Olympics					Did not play – spare goaltender										
2010-11	**Colorado**	**NHL**	**45**	**15**	**21**	**4**	**2439**	**130**	**1**	**3.20**	....	....	....	....	....	....	....
	NHL Totals		**242**	**101**	**91**	**27**	**13313**	**627**	**9**	**2.83**	**4**	**0**	**0**	**117**	**7**	**0**	**3.59**

OHL Second All-Star Team (2002)

Signed as a free agent by **Montreal**, July 1, 2011.

BUNZ, Tyler (BUHNZ, TIGH-luhr) EDM

Goaltender. Catches left. 6'2", 199 lbs. Born, Regina, Sask., February 11, 1992.
(Edmonton's 7th choice, 121st overall, in 2010 Entry Draft).

			Regular Season								Playoffs						
Season	Club	League	GP	W	L	O/T	Mins	GA	SO	Avg	GP	W	L	Mins	GA	SO	Avg
2007-08	St. Albert	AMHL	24	11	9	4	1503	80	....	3.19	4	2	2	240	16	....	4.00
	Medicine Hat	WHL	1	1	0	0	60	3	0	3.00	....	....	....	....	....	....	....
2008-09	Medicine Hat	WHL	22	9	6	1	1007	58	0	3.46	2	0	1	73	6	0	4.93
2009-10	Medicine Hat	WHL	57	31	19	5	3214	156	2	2.91	12	6	6	720	35	0	2.92
2010-11	Medicine Hat	WHL	56	35	13	8	3350	138	3	2.47	10	4	6	566	28	1	2.97

WHL East Second All-Star Team (2011)

CAMPBELL, Jack (KAM-behl, JAK) DAL

Goaltender. Catches left. 6'2", 182 lbs. Born, Port Huron, MI, January 9, 1992.
(Dallas' 1st choice, 11th overall, in 2010 Entry Draft).

			Regular Season								Playoffs						
Season	Club	League	GP	W	L	O/T	Mins	GA	SO	Avg	GP	W	L	Mins	GA	SO	Avg
2007-08	Det. Honeybaked	MWEHL	12	8	2	2	630	24	2	2.06	....	....	....	....	....	....	....
	Det. Honeybaked	Minor-MI	25	20	4	1	....	....	....	....	....	....	....	....	....	....	....
2008-09	USNTDP	NAHL	21	14	6	1	1262	53	1	2.52	....	....	....	....	....	....	....
	USNTDP	U-17	7	6	0	1	394	7	3	1.07	....	....	....	....	....	....	....
	USNTDP	U-18	7	7	0	0	421	12	2	1.71	....	....	....	....	....	....	....
2009-10	USNTDP	USHL	11	6	3	1	569	21	1	2.21	....	....	....	....	....	....	....
	USNTDP	U-18	25	16	9	0	1469	54	3	2.21	....	....	....	....	....	....	....
2010-11	Windsor Spitfires	OHL	45	24	14	4	2447	155	0	3.80	18	9	9	1124	70	2	3.74

CANN, Trevor (KAN, TREH-vuhr) COL

Goaltender. Catches left. 5'11", 199 lbs. Born, Oakville, Ont., March 30, 1989.
(Colorado's 3rd choice, 49th overall, in 2007 Entry Draft).

			Regular Season								Playoffs						
Season	Club	League	GP	W	L	O/T	Mins	GA	SO	Avg	GP	W	L	Mins	GA	SO	Avg
2005-06	Peterborough	OHL	20	16	2	0	1176	52	1	2.65	1	0	0	35	3	0	5.14
2006-07	Peterborough	OHL	*62	23	32	5	3565	219	0	3.69	....	....	....	....	....	....	....
2007-08	Peterborough	OHL	51	20	28	3	2976	178	2	3.59	5	1	4	317	21	0	3.97
2008-09	Peterborough	OHL	10	5	5	0	545	28	1	3.08	....	....	....	....	....	....	....
	London Knights	OHL	42	30	10	1	2482	104	5	2.51	13	9	4	805	38	0	2.83
2009-10	Lake Erie Monsters	AHL	13	3	6	1	671	40	1	3.58	....	....	....	....	....	....	....
	Tulsa Oilers	CHL	18	11	6	1	1088	51	0	2.81	....	....	....	....	....	....	....
2010-11	Lake Erie Monsters	AHL	7	2	3	0	350	20	0	3.43	....	....	....	....	....	....	....
	Tulsa Oilers	CHL	26	13	9	3	1390	79	0	3.41	7	4	3	353	17	0	2.89

CANNATA, Joe (ka-NA-tuh, JOH) VAN

Goaltender. Catches left. 6'1", 200 lbs. Born, Wakefield, MA, January 2, 1990.
(Vancouver's 6th choice, 173rd overall, in 2009 Entry Draft).

			Regular Season								Playoffs						
Season	Club	League	GP	W	L	O/T	Mins	GA	SO	Avg	GP	W	L	Mins	GA	SO	Avg
2007-08	USNTDP	NAHL	5	3	1	1	307	12	0	2.35	....	....	....	....	....	....	....
	USNTDP	U-18	28	13	13	2	1474	64	1	2.61	....	....	....	....	....	....	....
2008-09	Merrimack College	H-East	23	7	11	4	1353	53	2	2.35	....	....	....	....	....	....	....
2009-10	Merrimack College	H-East	24	10	13	1	1362	69	2	3.04	....	....	....	....	....	....	....
2010-11	Merrimack College	H-East	*39	25	10	4	2252	93	1	2.48	....	....	....	....	....	....	....

CARROZZI, Chris (ka-ROH-zee, KRIHS) WPG

Goaltender. Catches left. 6'3", 195 lbs. Born, Ottawa, Ont., March 2, 1990.
(Atlanta's 6th choice, 154th overall, in 2008 Entry Draft).

			Regular Season								Playoffs						
Season	**Club**	**League**	**GP**	**W**	**L**	**O/T**	**Mins**	**GA**	**SO**	**Avg**	**GP**	**W**	**L**	**Mins**	**GA**	**SO**	**Avg**
2005-06	Nepean Raiders	Minor-ON	23	....	....	....	....	42	4	1.82	....	....	....	....	....	....	....
2006-07	St. Michael's	OHL	25	6	7	2	1130	81	0	4.30	....	....	....	....	....	....	....
2007-08	St. Michael's	OHL	47	25	18	2	2505	115	*4	2.75	4	0	4	240	18	0	4.50
2008-09	St. Michael's	OHL	47	27	14	3	2715	133	2	2.94	2	0	0	33	3	0	5.52
2009-10	St. Michael's	OHL	37	19	10	5	2089	82	*5	2.36	8	5	2	448	16	1	*2.14
2010-11	Chicago Wolves	AHL	1	0	1	0	65	6	0	5.55	....	....	....	....	....	....	....
	Gwinnett	ECHL	47	16	20	6	2546	137	2	3.23	....	....	....	....	....	....	....

OHL First All-Star Team (2010)

CARRUTH, Mac (kair-UHTH, MAK) CHI

Goaltender. Catches left. 6'3", 174 lbs. Born, Salt Lake City, UT, March 25, 1992.
(Chicago's 10th choice, 191st overall, in 2010 Entry Draft).

			Regular Season								Playoffs						
Season	**Club**	**League**	**GP**	**W**	**L**	**O/T**	**Mins**	**GA**	**SO**	**Avg**	**GP**	**W**	**L**	**Mins**	**GA**	**SO**	**Avg**
2008-09	Wenatchee Wild	NAHL	26	18	7	1	1462	74	1	3.04	5	2	2	232	15	0	3.88
2009-10	Wenatchee Wild	NAHL	16	11	4	0	866	35	1	2.42	....	....	....	....	....	....	....
	Portland	WHL	26	14	9	1	1427	81	1	3.41	11	5	4	614	39	0	3.81
2010-11	Portland	WHL	48	31	13	1	2729	140	1	3.08	*21	13	8	*1251	62	1	2.97

CHEVERIE, Marc (sheh-VEH-ree, MAHRK) FLA

Goaltender. Catches left. 6'3", 183 lbs. Born, Cole Harbour, N.S., February 22, 1987.
(Florida's 6th choice, 193rd overall, in 2006 Entry Draft).

			Regular Season								Playoffs						
Season	**Club**	**League**	**GP**	**W**	**L**	**O/T**	**Mins**	**GA**	**SO**	**Avg**	**GP**	**W**	**L**	**Mins**	**GA**	**SO**	**Avg**
2003-04	Dartmouth	NSMHL	....	19	4	2	1521	76	1	2.99	....	....	....	....	....	....	....
2004-05	Notre Dame	SMHL	25	....	....	....	....	....	....	2.25	....	....	....	....	....	....	....
2005-06	Nanaimo Clippers	BCHL	46	23	9	0	2032	86	4	2.54	....	....	....	....	....	....	....
2006-07	Nanaimo Clippers	BCHL	34	21	9	2	2015	104	3	3.10	....	....	....	....	....	....	....
2007-08	U. of Denver	WCHA	5	1	0	0	141	4	0	1.70	....	....	....	....	....	....	....
2008-09	U. of Denver	WCHA	40	23	12	5	2383	93	4	2.34	....	....	....	....	....	....	....
2009-10	U. of Denver	WCHA	35	*24	6	3	2044	71	*6	*2.08	....	....	....	....	....	....	....
2010-11	Rochester	AHL	15	2	7	1	675	44	0	3.91	....	....	....	....	....	....	....
	Cincinnati	ECHL	30	13	9	5	1695	88	3	3.11	....	....	....	....	....	....	....

WCHA Second All-Star Team (2009) • WCHA First All-Star Team (2010) • WCHA Player of the Year (2010) • NCAA West First All-American Team (2010)

CLEMMENSEN, Scott (KLEH-mehn-sehn, SKAWT) FLA

Goaltender. Catches left. 6'3", 205 lbs. Born, Des Moines, IA, July 23, 1977.
(New Jersey's 7th choice, 215th overall, in 1997 Entry Draft).

			Regular Season								Playoffs						
Season	**Club**	**League**	**GP**	**W**	**L**	**O/T**	**Mins**	**GA**	**SO**	**Avg**	**GP**	**W**	**L**	**Mins**	**GA**	**SO**	**Avg**
1995-96	Dubuque	USHL	20	10	7	1	1082	62	0	3.44	....	....	....	....	....	....	....
1996-97	Des Moines	USHL	36	22	9	2	2042	111	1	3.26	4	1	2	200	9	1	2.70
1997-98	Boston College	H-East	37	24	9	4	2205	102	*4	2.78	....	....	....	....	....	....	....
1998-99	Boston College	H-East	*42	26	12	4	*2507	120	1	2.87	....	....	....	....	....	....	....
99-2000	Boston College	H-East	29	19	7	0	1610	59	*5	2.20	....	....	....	....	....	....	....
2000-01	Boston College	H-East	*39	*30	7	2	*2312	82	3	2.13	....	....	....	....	....	....	....
2001-02	**New Jersey**	**NHL**	**2**	**0**	**0**	**0**	**20**	**1**	**0**	**3.00**	....	....	....	....	....	....	....
	Albany River Rats	AHL	29	5	19	4	1677	92	0	3.29	....	....	....	....	....	....	....
2002-03	Albany River Rats	AHL	47	12	24	8	2694	119	1	2.65	....	....	....	....	....	....	....
2003-04	**New Jersey**	**NHL**	**4**	**3**	**1**	**0**	**238**	**4**	**2**	**1.01**	....	....	....	....	....	....	....
	Albany River Rats	AHL	22	5	12	4	1309	67	0	3.07	....	....	....	....	....	....	....
2004-05	Albany River Rats	AHL	46	13	25	5	2645	124	2	2.81	....	....	....	....	....	....	....
2005-06	**New Jersey**	**NHL**	**13**	**3**	**4**	**2**	**627**	**35**	**0**	**3.35**	**1**	**0**	**0**	**7**	**0**	**0**	**0.00**
	Albany River Rats	AHL	1	0	1	0	59	5	0	5.05	....	....	....	....	....	....	....
2006-07	**New Jersey**	**NHL**	**6**	**1**	**1**	**2**	**305**	**16**	**0**	**3.15**	....	....	....	....	....	....	....
	Lowell Devils	AHL	1	1	0	0	60	0	1	0.00	....	....	....	....	....	....	....
2007-08	**Toronto**	**NHL**	**3**	**1**	**1**	**0**	**154**	**10**	**0**	**3.90**	....	....	....	....	....	....	....
	Toronto Marlies	AHL	40	23	14	2	2363	96	1	2.44	17	8	9	992	50	0	3.02
2008-09	**New Jersey**	**NHL**	**40**	**25**	**13**	**1**	**2356**	**94**	**2**	**2.39**	....	....	....	....	....	....	....
	Lowell Devils	AHL	12	6	5	1	707	40	0	3.39	....	....	....	....	....	....	....
2009-10	**Florida**	**NHL**	**23**	**9**	**8**	**2**	**1215**	**59**	**1**	**2.91**	....	....	....	....	....	....	....
2010-11	**Florida**	**NHL**	**31**	**8**	**11**	**7**	**1696**	**74**	**1**	**2.62**	....	....	....	....	....	....	....
	NHL Totals		**122**	**50**	**39**	**14**	**6611**	**293**	**6**	**2.66**	**1**	**0**	**0**	**7**	**0**	**0**	**0.00**

NCAA Championship All-Tournament Team (2001)

Signed as a free agent by **Toronto**, July 6, 2007. Signed as a free agent by **New Jersey**, July 10, 2008. Signed as a free agent by **Florida**, July 1, 2009.

CLERMONT, Maxime (KLAIR-mawnt, max-EEM) N.J.

Goaltender. Catches left. 6'1", 195 lbs. Born, Montreal, Que., December 31, 1991.
(New Jersey's 4th choice, 174th overall, in 2010 Entry Draft).

			Regular Season								Playoffs						
Season	**Club**	**League**	**GP**	**W**	**L**	**O/T**	**Mins**	**GA**	**SO**	**Avg**	**GP**	**W**	**L**	**Mins**	**GA**	**SO**	**Avg**
2006-07	Crabtree Draveurs	QAAA	26	10	11	2	1436	74	1	3.09	3	0	2	95	10	0	6.31
2007-08	Gatineau	QMJHL	29	13	7	0	1285	62	1	2.89	3	0	1	56	3	0	3.20
2008-09	Gatineau	QMJHL	49	25	20	0	2665	143	1	3.22	2	0	0	10	1	0	5.99
2009-10	Gatineau	QMJHL	59	24	31	0	3354	157	4	2.81	11	4	6	635	38	0	3.59
2010-11	Gatineau	QMJHL	48	28	10	5	2659	113	4	2.55	*21	11	10	*1325	49	1	2.22

CLIMIE, Matt (KLIGH-mee, MAT) VAN

Goaltender. Catches left. 6'3", 194 lbs. Born, Leduc, Alta., February 11, 1983.

			Regular Season								Playoffs						
Season	**Club**	**League**	**GP**	**W**	**L**	**O/T**	**Mins**	**GA**	**SO**	**Avg**	**GP**	**W**	**L**	**Mins**	**GA**	**SO**	**Avg**
2002-03	Truro Bearcats	MJrHL	STATISTICS NOT AVAILABLE														
2003-04	Truro Bearcats	MJrHL	45	30	10	0	2731	119	0	2.61	....	....	....	....	....	....	....
2004-05	Bemidji State	CHA	21	12	5	1	1167	35	4	*1.80	....	....	....	....	....	....	....
2005-06	Bemidji State	CHA	18	8	7	2	1065	48	1	2.70	....	....	....	....	....	....	....
2006-07	Bemidji State	CHA	29	11	10	5	*1666	84	*2	*3.03	....	....	....	....	....	....	....
2007-08	Bemidji State	CHA	27	14	8	3	1529	55	*5	*2.16	....	....	....	....	....	....	....
	Iowa Stars	AHL	6	1	4	1	346	23	0	....	....	....	....	....	....	....	....
2008-09	**Dallas**	**NHL**	**3**	**2**	**1**	**0**	**185**	**9**	**0**	**2.92**	....	....	....	....	....	....	....
	Idaho Steelheads	ECHL	42	27	12	1	2404	92	4	2.30	4	0	4	199	8	0	2.41
	Houston Aeros	AHL	....	....	....	....	....	....	....	....	5	1	1	191	6	0	1.88
2009-10	**Dallas**	**NHL**	**1**	**0**	**1**	**0**	**60**	**5**	**0**	**5.00**	....	....	....	....	....	....	....
	Texas Stars	AHL	43	21	17	3	2539	104	3	2.46	15	7	6	885	40	0	2.71
2010-11	**Phoenix**	**NHL**	**1**	**0**	**0**	**0**	**32**	**1**	**0**	**1.88**	....	....	....	....	....	....	....
	San Antonio	AHL	55	26	22	3	3040	134	3	2.64	....	....	....	....	....	....	....
	NHL Totals		**5**	**2**	**2**	**0**	**277**	**15**	**0**	**3.25**	....	....	....	....	....	....	....

CHA Second All-Star Team (2008)

Signed as a free agent by **Dallas**, March 20, 2008. Signed as a free agent by **Phoenix**, July 3, 2010. Signed as a free agent by **Vancouver**, July 7, 2011.

COLEMAN, Gerald (KOHL-man, JAIR-uhld)

Goaltender. Catches left. 6'4", 214 lbs. Born, Romeoville, IL, April 3, 1985.
(Tampa Bay's 5th choice, 224th overall, in 2003 Entry Draft).

			Regular Season								Playoffs						
Season	**Club**	**League**	**GP**	**W**	**L**	**O/T**	**Mins**	**GA**	**SO**	**Avg**	**GP**	**W**	**L**	**Mins**	**GA**	**SO**	**Avg**
99-2000	Chicago	MEHL	26	....	....	....	1560	65	0	2.50	....	....	....	....	....	....	....
2000-01	USNTDP	U-17	9	3	0	4	527	26	0	2.96	....	....	....	....	....	....	....
	USNTDP	NAHL	36	8	23	1	1859	132	0	4.26	....	....	....	....	....	....	....
2001-02	USNTDP	U-18	13	8	1	3	667	38	1	3.42	....	....	....	....	....	....	....
	USNTDP	USHL	2	1	1	0	76	4	0	3.15	....	....	....	....	....	....	....
	USNTDP	NAHL	22	5	14	2	1263	75	0	3.56	....	....	....	....	....	....	....
2002-03	London Knights	OHL	26	6	9	3	1074	59	1	3.30	....	....	....	....	....	....	....
2003-04	London Knights	OHL	33	24	8	0	1852	68	*5	2.20	8	5	2	442	19	1	2.58
2004-05	London Knights	OHL	38	*32	2	2	2224	63	*8	*1.70	8	7	1	454	13	0	*1.72
2005-06	**Tampa Bay**	**NHL**	**2**	**0**	**0**	**1**	**43**	**2**	**0**	**2.79**	....	....	....	....	....	....	....
	Springfield Falcons	AHL	43	14	21	3	2413	156	2	3.88	....	....	....	....	....	....	....
2006-07	Springfield Falcons	AHL	3	2	1	0	179	6	0	2.01	....	....	....	....	....	....	....
	Johnstown Chiefs	ECHL	17	7	9	0	914	52	0	3.41	....	....	....	....	....	....	....
	Portland Pirates	AHL	11	4	5	0	603	29	0	2.89	....	....	....	....	....	....	....
2007-08	Portland Pirates	AHL	18	8	7	1	968	47	2	2.91	1	0	0	39	4	0	6.09
	Augusta Lynx	ECHL	9	2	5	0	500	22	0	2.64	....	....	....	....	....	....	....
2008-09	Worcester Sharks	AHL	3	0	2	0	112	6	0	3.23	....	....	....	....	....	....	....
	Phoenix	ECHL	4	2	1	1	244	6	1	1.48	....	....	....	....	....	....	....
	Trenton Devils	ECHL	40	27	8	2	2322	92	3	2.38	3	1	2	246	15	0	3.66
2009-10	Lowell Devils	AHL	3	1	2	0	182	13	0	4.28	....	....	....	....	....	....	....
	Trenton Devils	ECHL	28	11	9	7	1563	94	0	3.61	....	....	....	....	....	....	....
2010-11	Alaska Aces	ECHL	47	*30	15	1	2737	100	*4	*2.19	12	11	1	729	21	*3	1.73
	NHL Totals		**2**	**0**	**0**	**1**	**43**	**2**	**0**	**2.79**	....	....	....	....	....	....	....

ECHL Second All-Star Team (2009)

Traded to **Anaheim** by **Tampa Bay** with Tampa Bay's 1st round choice (later traded to Minnesota - Minnesota selected Colton Gillies) in 2007 Entry Draft for Shane O'Brien and Colorado's 3rd round choice (previously acquired, Tampa Bay selected Luca Cunti) in 2007 Entry Draft, February 24, 2007. Signed as a free agent by **New Jersey**, July 31, 2009.

CONKLIN, Ty (KAWN-klihn, TIGH) DET

Goaltender. Catches left. 6'1", 192 lbs. Born, Anchorage, AK, March 30, 1976.

			Regular Season								Playoffs						
Season	**Club**	**League**	**GP**	**W**	**L**	**O/T**	**Mins**	**GA**	**SO**	**Avg**	**GP**	**W**	**L**	**Mins**	**GA**	**SO**	**Avg**
1995-96	Green Bay	USHL	30	....	....	....	1727	82	1	2.85	....	....	....	....	....	....	....
1996-97	Alaska Anchorage	WCHA	DID NOT PLAY – FRESHMAN														
	Green Bay	USHL	30	19	7	1	1609	86	1	3.21	17	8	9	980	56	1	3.43
1997-98	New Hampshire	H-East	DID NOT PLAY – TRANSFERRED COLLEGES														
1998-99	New Hampshire	H-East	22	18	3	1	1338	41	0	*1.84	....	....	....	....	....	....	....
99-2000	New Hampshire	H-East	*37	*22	8	6	*2194	91	2	2.49	....	....	....	....	....	....	....
2000-01	New Hampshire	H-East	34	17	12	5	2048	70	*5	*2.05	....	....	....	....	....	....	....
2001-02	**Edmonton**	**NHL**	**4**	**2**	**0**	**0**	**148**	**4**	**0**	**1.62**	....	....	....	....	....	....	....
	Hamilton Bulldogs	AHL	37	13	12	8	2043	89	1	2.61	7	4	2	416	18	0	2.60
2002-03	Hamilton Bulldogs	AHL	38	19	13	3	2140	91	4	2.55	17	9	6	1024	38	1	2.23
2003-04	**Edmonton**	**NHL**	**38**	**17**	**14**	**4**	**2086**	**84**	**1**	**2.42**	....	....	....	....	....	....	....
2004-05	Wolfsburg	Germany	11	....	....	....	623	31	0	2.99	7	....	....	414	11	2	1.59
2005-06	**Edmonton**	**NHL**	**18**	**8**	**5**	**1**	**922**	**43**	**1**	**2.80**	**1**	**0**	**1**	**6**	**1**	**0**	**10.00**
	Hamilton Bulldogs	AHL	3	1	2	0	152	8	0	3.17	....	....	....	....	....	....	....
	Hartford Wolf Pack	AHL	2	1	0	1	130	5	0	2.31	....	....	....	....	....	....	....
2006-07	**Columbus**	**NHL**	**11**	**2**	**3**	**2**	**491**	**27**	**0**	**3.30**	....	....	....	....	....	....	....
	Syracuse Crunch	AHL	19	3	12	3	1085	60	0	3.32	....	....	....	....	....	....	....
	Buffalo	**NHL**	**5**	**1**	**2**	**0**	**227**	**13**	**0**	**3.44**	....	....	....	....	....	....	....
2007-08	**Pittsburgh**	**NHL**	**33**	**18**	**8**	**5**	**1866**	**78**	**2**	**2.51**	....	....	....	....	....	....	....
	Wilkes-Barre	AHL	18	11	7	0	1058	39	2	2.21	....	....	....	....	....	....	....
2008-09	**Detroit**	**NHL**	**40**	**25**	**11**	**2**	**2246**	**94**	**6**	**2.51**	**1**	**0**	**0**	**20**	**0**	**0**	**0.00**
2009-10	**St. Louis**	**NHL**	**26**	**10**	**10**	**2**	**1451**	**60**	**4**	**2.48**	....	....	....	....	....	....	....
2010-11	**St. Louis**	**NHL**	**25**	**8**	**8**	**4**	**1285**	**69**	**2**	**3.22**	....	....	....	....	....	....	....
	NHL Totals		**200**	**91**	**61**	**20**	**10722**	**472**	**16**	**2.64**	**2**	**0**	**1**	**26**	**1**	**0**	**2.31**

USHL Second All-Star Team (1996) • Hockey East All-Rookie Team (1999) • Hockey East Second All-Star Team (1999) • Hockey East First All-Star Team (2000, 2001) • Hockey East Player of the Year (2000) (co-winner - Mike Mottau) • NCAA East Second All-American Team (2000) • NCAA East First All-American Team (2001)

• Left **Alaska-Anchorage** (WCHA) and returned to **Green Bay** (USHL), November 14, 1996. Signed as a free agent by **Edmonton**, April 18, 2001. Signed as a free agent by **Wolfsburg** (Germany), January 25, 2005. • Loaned to **Hartford** (AHL) by **Edmonton**, March 8, 2006. Signed as a free agent by **Columbus**, July 6, 2006. Traded to **Buffalo** by **Columbus** for Buffalo's 5th round choice (later traded to Dallas - Dallas selected Michael Neal) in 2007 Entry Draft, February 27, 2007. Signed as a free agent by **Pittsburgh**, July 19, 2007. Signed as a free agent by **Detroit**, July 1, 2008. Signed as a free agent by **St. Louis**, July 1, 2009. Signed as a free agent by **Detroit**, July 20, 2011.

CORBEIL, Mathieu (kawr-BAY, MA-tyew) CBJ

Goaltender. Catches left. 6'6", 197 lbs. Born, Montreal, Que., September 27, 1991.
(Columbus' 5th choice, 102nd overall, in 2010 Entry Draft).

			Regular Season								Playoffs						
Season	**Club**	**League**	**GP**	**W**	**L**	**O/T**	**Mins**	**GA**	**SO**	**Avg**	**GP**	**W**	**L**	**Mins**	**GA**	**SO**	**Avg**
2007-08	Mtl. Predateurs	QAAA	27	3	21	0	1296	109	1	5.04	2	0	1	95	9	0	5.70
2008-09	Halifax	QMJHL	24	3	14	0	1094	81	0	4.44	....	....	....	....	....	....	....
2009-10	Halifax	QMJHL	50	8	39	0	2692	172	0	3.83	....	....	....	....	....	....	....
2010-11	Saint John	QMJHL	15	13	1	1	914	33	0	2.17	....	....	....	....	....	....	....

COURCHAINE, Adam (KOOR-shayn, A-duhm) BOS

Goaltender. Catches left. 6'2", 181 lbs. Born, Calgary, Alta., February 20, 1989.

			Regular Season								Playoffs						
Season	**Club**	**League**	**GP**	**W**	**L**	**O/T**	**Mins**	**GA**	**SO**	**Avg**	**GP**	**W**	**L**	**Mins**	**GA**	**SO**	**Avg**
2006-07	Orleans Blues	CJHL	39	19	11	7	2285	119	1	3.12	6	2	4	362	16	0	2.65
2007-08	Ottawa 67's	OHL	48	17	25	4	2813	152	2	3.24	4	0	4	158	12	0	4.56
	Providence Bruins	AHL	3	2	0	0	144	4	0	1.67	....	....	....	....	....	....	....
2008-09	Ottawa 67's	OHL	30	13	11	2	1520	83	2	3.28	5	2	3	280	14	*1	3.00
	Providence Bruins	AHL	1	0	1	0	60	3	0	3.00	....	....	....	....	....	....	....
2009-10	Sarnia Sting	OHL	27	8	16	2	1520	89	1	3.51	....	....	....	....	....	....	....
	Erie Otters	OHL	21	12	8	0	1200	58	2	2.90	2	0	2	120	9	0	4.50
2010-11	Reading Royals	ECHL	1	0	0	0	7	4	0	33.26	....	....	....	....	....	....	....
	Alaska Aces	ECHL	28	17	7	2	1585	63	*4	2.39	1	1	0	60	2	0	2.00

Signed as a free agent by **Boston**, September 30, 2007.

COUSINEAU, Marco (KOO-zih-noh, MAHR-koh) ANA

Goaltender. Catches left. 6', 195 lbs. Born, St.Lazare, Que., November 9, 1989.
(Anaheim's 6th choice, 83rd overall, in 2008 Entry Draft).

			Regular Season								Playoffs						
Season	Club	League	GP	W	L	O/T	Mins	GA	SO	Avg	GP	W	L	Mins	GA	SO	Avg
2006-07	Baie-Comeau	QMJHL	23	4	12	0	1015	71	0	4.20	1	0	0	10	2	0	11.88
2007-08	Baie-Comeau	QMJHL	58	34	19	0	3227	151	4	2.81	5	1	4	306	11	0	*2.16
2008-09	Baie-Comeau	QMJHL	34	9	25	0	1878	115	1	3.67	....	....	....	....	....	....	....
	Drummondville	QMJHL	16	12	4	0	919	36	0	2.35	17	*13	3	1009	41	0	2.44
2009-10	P.E.I. Rocket	QMJHL	25	10	14	0	1442	77	1	3.20	....	....	....	....	....	....	....
	Saint John	QMJHL	20	15	5	0	1218	48	3	2.36	21	14	7	1222	57	2	2.80
2010-11	Elmira Jackals	ECHL	44	21	16	5	2470	133	0	3.23	4	1	3	251	8	0	1.91

QMJHL Second All-Star Team (2008)

CRAWFORD, Corey (KRAW-fohrd, KOH-ree) CHI

Goaltender. Catches left. 6'2", 200 lbs. Born, Montreal, Que., December 31, 1984.
(Chicago's 2nd choice, 52nd overall, in 2003 Entry Draft).

			Regular Season								Playoffs						
Season	Club	League	GP	W	L	O/T	Mins	GA	SO	Avg	GP	W	L	Mins	GA	SO	Avg
2000-01	Gatineau Intrepide	QAAA	21	17	3	1	1260	40	2	1.92	....	....	....	....	....	....	....
2001-02	Moncton Wildcats	QMJHL	38	9	20	3	1863	116	1	3.74	....	....	....	....	....	....	....
2002-03	Moncton Wildcats	QMJHL	50	24	17	6	2855	130	2	2.73	6	2	3	303	20	0	3.97
2003-04	Moncton Wildcats	QMJHL	54	*35	15	3	3019	132	2	2.62	*20	*13	6	*1170	42	0	2.15
2004-05	Moncton Wildcats	QMJHL	51	28	16	6	2942	121	*5	2.47	12	6	6	725	33	*1	2.73
2005-06	**Chicago**	**NHL**	**2**	**0**	**0**	**1**	**86**	**5**	**0**	**3.49**	....	....	....	....	....	....	....
	Norfolk Admirals	AHL	48	22	23	1	2734	134	1	2.94	1	0	0	17	1	0	3.49
2006-07	Norfolk Admirals	AHL	60	38	20	2	3467	164	1	2.84	6	2	4	363	20	0	3.31
2007-08	**Chicago**	**NHL**	**5**	**1**	**2**	**0**	**224**	**8**	**1**	**2.14**	....	....	....	....	....	....	....
	Rockford IceHogs	AHL	55	29	19	5	3028	143	3	2.83	12	7	5	741	27	0	2.19
2008-09	Rockford IceHogs	AHL	47	22	20	3	2686	116	2	2.59	2	0	2	117	5	0	2.57
	Chicago	**NHL**	....	....	....	....	....	....	....	....	**1**	**0**	**0**	**16**	**1**	**0**	**3.75**
2009-10	**Chicago**	**NHL**	**1**	**0**	**1**	**0**	**59**	**3**	**0**	**3.05**	....	....	....	....	....	....	....
	Rockford IceHogs	AHL	45	24	16	2	2521	112	1	2.67	4	0	4	216	13	0	3.61
2010-11	**Chicago**	**NHL**	**57**	**33**	**18**	**6**	**3337**	**128**	**4**	**2.30**	**7**	**3**	**4**	**435**	**16**	**1**	**2.21**
	NHL Totals		**65**	**34**	**21**	**7**	**3706**	**144**	**5**	**2.33**	**8**	**3**	**4**	**451**	**17**	**1**	**2.26**

QMJHL Second All-Star Team (2004, 2005) • NHL All-Rookie Team (2011)

CURRY, John (KUH-ree, JAWN)

Goaltender. Catches left. 5'11", 185 lbs. Born, Shorewood, MN, February 27, 1984.

			Regular Season								Playoffs						
Season	Club	League	GP	W	L	O/T	Mins	GA	SO	Avg	GP	W	L	Mins	GA	SO	Avg
2003-04	Boston University	H-East	1	0	0	0	5	0	0	0.00	....	....	....	....	....	....	....
2004-05	Boston University	H-East	33	18	11	3	1950	64	3	1.97	....	....	....	....	....	....	....
2005-06	Boston University	H-East	37	*24	8	4	2166	81	3	2.24	....	....	....	....	....	....	....
2006-07	Boston University	H-East	36	17	10	8	2154	72	*7	2.01	....	....	....	....	....	....	....
2007-08	Wilkes-Barre	AHL	40	24	12	3	2343	87	3	2.23	23	14	9	1358	64	1	2.83
	Las Vegas	ECHL	6	4	1	0	342	16	0	2.81	....	....	....	....	....	....	....
	Wheeling Nailers	ECHL	1	0	1	0	60	4	0	4.00	....	....	....	....	....	....	....
2008-09	**Pittsburgh**	**NHL**	**3**	**2**	**1**	**0**	**150**	**6**	**0**	**2.40**	....	....	....	....	....	....	....
	Wilkes-Barre	AHL	50	33	15	1	2996	119	4	2.38	7	4	3	393	22	0	3.36
2009-10	**Pittsburgh**	**NHL**	**1**	**0**	**1**	**0**	**24**	**5**	**0**	**12.50**	....	....	....	....	....	....	....
	Wilkes-Barre	AHL	46	23	19	2	2657	127	1	2.87	3	0	3	176	9	0	3.07
2010-11	Wilkes-Barre	AHL	41	23	13	0	2239	91	2	2.44	....	....	....	....	....	....	....
	NHL Totals		**4**	**2**	**2**	**0**	**174**	**11**	**0**	**3.79**	....	....	....	....	....	....	....

NCAA East Second All-American Team (2006) • NCAA East First All-American Team (2007) • AHL All-Rookie Team (2008) • Harry "Hap" Holmes Memorial Award (AHL – fewest goals against) (2011) (shared with Brad Thiessen)

Signed as a free agent by **Pittsburgh**, July 13, 2007.

DALTON, Matt (DAWL-tuhn, MAT)

Goaltender. Catches left. 6'1", 189 lbs. Born, Clinton, Ont., July 4, 1986.

			Regular Season								Playoffs						
Season	Club	League	GP	W	L	O/T	Mins	GA	SO	Avg	GP	W	L	Mins	GA	SO	Avg
2005-06	Bozeman Icedogs	NAHL	39	33	5	1	2315	63	*9	*1.63	11	9	2	658	17	2	1.55
2006-07	Des Moines	USHL	*53	*27	15	9	*3030	143	*5	2.83	*8	6	2	*540	14	1	1.56
2007-08	Bemidji State	CHA	5	1	3	0	233	12	1	3.09	....	....	....	....	....	....	....
2008-09	Bemidji State	CHA	31	*19	11	1	1861	68	2	2.19	....	....	....	....	....	....	....
2009-10	Providence Bruins	AHL	6	0	4	1	331	18	0	3.26	....	....	....	....	....	....	....
	Reading Royals	ECHL	46	22	20	4	2735	158	1	3.47	16	*10	6	955	48	0	3.02
2010-11	Providence Bruins	AHL	16	7	9	0	862	46	2	3.20	....	....	....	....	....	....	....
	Reading Royals	ECHL	33	20	11	1	1970	94	3	2.86	7	3	4	420	22	1	3.15

CHA Second All-Star Team (2009)

Signed as a free agent by **Boston**, April 22, 2009.

DANIS, Yann (DA-nihs, YAN) EDM

Goaltender. Catches left. 6', 185 lbs. Born, Lafontaine, Que., June 21, 1981.

			Regular Season								Playoffs						
Season	Club	League	GP	W	L	O/T	Mins	GA	SO	Avg	GP	W	L	Mins	GA	SO	Avg
99-2000	St-Jerome	QJHL	STATISTICS NOT AVAILABLE														
	Cornwall Colts	CJHL	26	....	....	....	1367	71	0	3.12	....	....	....	....	....	....	....
2000-01	Brown U.	ECAC	12	2	8	1	667	40	0	3.60	....	....	....	....	....	....	....
2001-02	Brown U.	ECAC	24	11	10	2	1451	45	3	1.86	....	....	....	....	....	....	....
2002-03	Brown U.	ECAC	*34	15	14	5	*2074	80	5	2.31	....	....	....	....	....	....	....
2003-04	Brown U.	ECAC	30	15	11	4	1821	55	*5	*1.81	....	....	....	....	....	....	....
	Hamilton Bulldogs	AHL	2	2	0	0	120	3	1	1.50	1	0	0	12	0	0	0.00
2004-05	Hamilton Bulldogs	AHL	53	28	17	6	3075	120	5	2.34	4	0	4	237	13	0	3.29
2005-06	**Montreal**	**NHL**	**6**	**3**	**2**	**0**	**312**	**14**	**1**	**2.69**	....	....	....	....	....	....	....
	Hamilton Bulldogs	AHL	39	17	17	3	2242	111	0	2.97	....	....	....	....	....	....	....
2006-07	Hamilton Bulldogs	AHL	44	23	14	5	2540	119	1	2.81	1	1	0	54	1	0	1.12
2007-08	Hamilton Bulldogs	AHL	38	11	19	4	2064	113	0	3.28	....	....	....	....	....	....	....
2008-09	**NY Islanders**	**NHL**	**31**	**10**	**17**	**3**	**1760**	**84**	**2**	**2.86**	....	....	....	....	....	....	....
	Bridgeport	AHL	10	7	3	0	611	23	0	2.26	....	....	....	....	....	....	....
2009-10	**New Jersey**	**NHL**	**12**	**3**	**2**	**1**	**467**	**16**	**0**	**2.06**	....	....	....	....	....	....	....
2010-11	Amur Khabarovsk	Rus-KHL	31	....	....	....	1652	84	2	3.05	....	....	....	....	....	....	....
	NHL Totals		**49**	**16**	**21**	**4**	**2539**	**114**	**3**	**2.69**	....	....	....	....	....	....	....

ECAC Second All-Star Team (2002, 2003) • ECAC First All-Star Team (2004) • ECAC Goaltender of the Year (2004) • ECAC Player of the Year (2004) • NCAA East First All-American Team (2004)

Signed as a free agent by **Montreal**, March 19, 2004. Signed as a free agent by **NY Islanders**, July 2, 2008. Signed as a free agent by **New Jersey**, July 10, 2009. Signed as a free agent by **Khabarovsk** (Russia-KHL), July 27, 2010. Signed as a free agent by **Edmonton**, July 4, 2011.

DARLING, Scott (DAHR-lihng, SKAWT) PHX

Goaltender. Catches left. 6'6", 220 lbs. Born, Lemont, IL, December 22, 1988.
(Phoenix's 7th choice, 153rd overall, in 2007 Entry Draft).

			Regular Season								Playoffs						
Season	Club	League	GP	W	L	O/T	Mins	GA	SO	Avg	GP	W	L	Mins	GA	SO	Avg
2005-06	Chicago Y.A.	MWEHL	2	0	2	0	120	10	0	5.00	....	....	....	....	....	....	....
	North Iowa	NAHL	8	2	4	0	405	28	0	4.15	....	....	....	....	....	....	....
2006-07	Capital District	EJHL	22	9	9	3	1243	70	1	3.38	....	....	....	....	....	....	....
	North Iowa	NAHL	1	0	0	0	15	3	0	12.00	....	....	....	....	....	....	....
2007-08	Indiana Ice	USHL	42	27	10	2	2391	121	1	3.04	3	1	2	179	11	0	3.69
2008-09	University of Maine	H-East	27	10	14	3	1566	72	*3	2.76	....	....	....	....	....	....	....
2009-10	University of Maine	H-East	27	15	6	3	1511	78	0	3.10	....	....	....	....	....	....	....
2010-11	Louisiana	SPHL	30	6	22	0	1598	102	0	3.83	....	....	....	....	....	....	....

DEKANICH, Mark (DEHK-ihn-ihch, MAHRK) CBJ

Goaltender. Catches left. 6'2", 190 lbs. Born, N. Vancouver, B.C., May 10, 1986.
(Nashville's 3rd choice, 146th overall, in 2006 Entry Draft).

			Regular Season								Playoffs						
Season	Club	League	GP	W	L	O/T	Mins	GA	SO	Avg	GP	W	L	Mins	GA	SO	Avg
2003-04	Coquitlam Express	BCHL	30	13	15	1	1647	89	2	3.24	....	....	....	....	....	....	....
2004-05	Colgate	ECAC	5	1	1	0	162	5	0	1.85	....	....	....	....	....	....	....
2005-06	Colgate	ECAC	36	18	11	6	2126	81	4	2.29	....	....	....	....	....	....	....
2006-07	Colgate	ECAC	36	15	17	4	2136	83	1	2.33	....	....	....	....	....	....	....
2007-08	Colgate	ECAC	*41	18	16	6	*2389	86	*6	2.16	....	....	....	....	....	....	....
2008-09	Milwaukee	AHL	30	15	10	2	1663	58	1	2.09	....	....	....	....	....	....	....
2009-10	Milwaukee	AHL	49	27	16	4	2804	109	4	2.33	7	3	4	408	19	1	2.79
	Cincinnati	ECHL	2	2	0	0	125	1	1	0.48	....	....	....	....	....	....	....
2010-11	**Nashville**	**NHL**	**1**	**0**	**0**	**0**	**50**	**3**	**0**	**3.60**	....	....	....	....	....	....	....
	Milwaukee	AHL	43	23	12	5	2500	84	4	2.02	....	....	....	....	....	....	....
	NHL Totals		**1**	**0**	**0**	**0**	**50**	**3**	**0**	**3.60**	....	....	....	....	....	....	....

ECAC First All-Star Team (2006) • ECAC Second All-Star Team (2007)

Signed as a free agent by **Columbus**, July 1, 2011.

DELMAS, Peter (DEHL-mas, PEE-tuhr) MTL

Goaltender. Catches left. 6'2", 190 lbs. Born, Alliston, Ont., February 16, 1990.
(Colorado's 2nd choice, 61st overall, in 2008 Entry Draft).

			Regular Season								Playoffs						
Season	Club	League	GP	W	L	O/T	Mins	GA	SO	Avg	GP	W	L	Mins	GA	SO	Avg
2006-07	Lewiston	QMJHL	34	23	10	....	1983	93	3	2.81	....	....	....	....	....	....	....
2007-08	Lewiston	QMJHL	34	17	17	....	1987	94	0	2.84	....	....	....	....	....	....	....
2008-09	Lewiston	QMJHL	38	9	27	....	2090	146	0	4.19	2	0	2	75	15	0	11.96
2009-10	Quebec Remparts	QMJHL	27	15	9	....	1459	76	1	3.15	....	....	....	....	....	....	....
	Halifax	QMJHL	14	5	7	....	771	44	0	3.42	....	....	....	....	....	....	....
2010-11	Halifax	QMJHL	2	0	2	0	117	8	0	4.10	....	....	....	....	....	....	....
	Hamilton Bulldogs	AHL	2	1	0	1	125	4	0	1.92	....	....	....	....	....	....	....
	Wichita Thunder	CHL	5	0	3	1	272	22	0	4.85	....	....	....	....	....	....	....
	Wheeling Nailers	ECHL	24	15	6	2	1417	48	3	2.03	15	8	6	804	42	0	3.13

QMJHL All-Rookie Team (2007) • Canadian Major Junior Rookie All-Star Team (2007)

Signed as a free agent by **Montreal**, July 5, 2011.

DESJARDINS, Cedrick (deh-ZHAHR-dai, SEH-DRIHK) COL

Goaltender. Catches left. 6', 192 lbs. Born, Edmundston, N.B., September 30, 1985.

			Regular Season								Playoffs						
Season	Club	League	GP	W	L	O/T	Mins	GA	SO	Avg	GP	W	L	Mins	GA	SO	Avg
2002-03	Coaticook	QJHL	STATISTICS NOT AVAILABLE														
	Rimouski Oceanic	QMJHL	23	1	19	0	1239	109	0	5.28	....	....	....	....	....	....	....
2003-04	Rimouski Oceanic	QMJHL	20	8	11	0	1119	72	0	3.86	1	0	0	14	0	0	0.00
2004-05	Rimouski Oceanic	QMJHL	44	*30	7	4	2439	120	2	2.95	13	*12	1	*767	34	*1	2.66
2005-06	Quebec Remparts	QMJHL	41	28	10	0	2254	111	*5	2.95	*23	14	9	*1413	60	1	2.55
2006-07	Hamilton Bulldogs	AHL	3	0	2	0	142	7	0	2.96	....	....	....	....	....	....	....
	Cincinnati	ECHL	45	24	19	1	2648	112	4	2.54	....	....	....	....	....	....	....
2007-08	Hamilton Bulldogs	AHL	12	4	3	2	572	29	0	3.04	....	....	....	....	....	....	....
	Cincinnati	ECHL	22	16	4	2	1285	41	*5	1.91	16	11	4	947	29	1	*1.83
2008-09	Hamilton Bulldogs	AHL	30	16	12	0	1718	73	4	2.55	....	....	....	....	....	....	....
2009-10	Hamilton Bulldogs	AHL	47	29	9	4	2576	86	6	*2.00	10	6	4	596	26	1	2.62
2010-11	**Tampa Bay**	**NHL**	**2**	**2**	**0**	**0**	**120**	**2**	**0**	**1.00**	....	....	....	....	....	....	....
	Norfolk Admirals	AHL	24	15	6	1	1391	60	1	2.59	....	....	....	....	....	....	....
	NHL Totals		**2**	**2**	**0**	**0**	**120**	**2**	**0**	**1.00**	....	....	....	....	....	....	....

Memorial Cup All-Star Team (2006) • Hap Emms Memorial Trophy (Memorial Cup - Top Goaltender) (2006) • ECHL All-Rookie-Team (2007) • ECHL Playoff MVP (2009) • AHL Second All-Star Team (2010) • Harry "Hap" Holmes Memorial Award (AHL – fewest goals against) (2010) (shared with Curtis Sanford)

Signed as a free agent by **Hamilton** (AHL), July 26, 2006. Signed as a free agent by **Montreal**, July 3, 2008. Traded to **Tampa Bay** by **Montreal** for Karri Ramo, August 16, 2010. Signed as a free agent by **Colorado**, July 8, 2011.

DESLAURIERS, Jeff (duh-LAW-ree-yay, JEHF) ANA

Goaltender. Catches right. 6'4", 200 lbs. Born, St-Jean-Richelieu, Que., May 15, 1984.
(Edmonton's 2nd choice, 31st overall, in 2002 Entry Draft).

			Regular Season								Playoffs						
Season	Club	League	GP	W	L	O/T	Mins	GA	SO	Avg	GP	W	L	Mins	GA	SO	Avg
2000-01	Gatineau Intrepide	QAAA	22	10	9	2	1194	61	2	3.07	2	1	0	125	6	0	2.89
2001-02	Chicoutimi	QMJHL	51	28	20	1	2909	170	1	3.51	4	0	3	197	20	0	6.11
2002-03	Chicoutimi	QMJHL	48	18	24	1	2583	164	0	3.81	4	0	4	240	15	0	3.75
2003-04	Chicoutimi	QMJHL	50	21	20	6	2701	129	1	2.87	18	10	8	956	50	1	3.14
2004-05	Edmonton	AHL	22	6	13	2	1258	62	0	2.96	....	....	....	....	....	....	....
	Greenville Grrrowl	ECHL	11	7	3	1	673	26	1	2.32	....	....	....	....	....	....	....
2005-06	Hamilton Bulldogs	AHL	13	4	7	0	666	35	0	3.15	....	....	....	....	....	....	....
	Greenville Grrrowl	ECHL	6	2	4	0	335	17	0	3.05	....	....	....	....	....	....	....
2006-07	Wilkes-Barre	AHL	40	22	12	3	2231	92	4	2.47	....	....	....	....	....	....	....
2007-08	Springfield Falcons	AHL	57	26	23	5	3045	147	0	2.90	....	....	....	....	....	....	....
2008-09	**Edmonton**	**NHL**	**10**	**4**	**3**	**0**	**540**	**30**	**0**	**3.33**	....	....	....	....	....	....	....
	Springfield Falcons	AHL	5	1	4	0	286	13	0	2.73	....	....	....	....	....	....	....
2009-10	**Edmonton**	**NHL**	**48**	**16**	**28**	**4**	**2798**	**152**	**3**	**3.26**	....	....	....	....	....	....	....
2010-11	Oklahoma City	AHL	35	17	13	4	1945	91	3	2.81	....	....	....	....	....	....	....
	NHL Totals		**58**	**20**	**31**	**4**	**3338**	**182**	**3**	**3.27**	....	....	....	....	....	....	....

QMJHL All-Rookie Team (2002)

Signed as a free agent by **Anaheim**, July 12, 2011.

DiPIETRO, Rick (dee-pee-EHT-roh, RIHK) NYI

Goaltender. Catches right. 6'1", 190 lbs. Born, Winthrop, MA, September 19, 1981.
(NY Islanders' 1st choice, 1st overall, in 2000 Entry Draft).

			Regular Season								Playoffs						
Season	Club	League	GP	W	L	O/T	Mins	GA	SO	Avg	GP	W	L	Mins	GA	SO	Avg
1997-98	USNTDP	U-17	10	6	4	0	800	31	0	2.33	....	....	....	....	....	....	....
	USNTDP	USHL	3	0	2	0	117	8	0	4.09	....	....	....	....	....	....	....
	USNTDP	NAHL	30	13	12	0	1602	85	1	3.18	3	2	1	179	7	1	2.35
	St. Sebastian's	High-MA					STATISTICS NOT AVAILABLE										
1998-99	USNTDP	U-18	16	9	5	1	1027	46	....	2.69	....	....	....	....	....	....	....
	USNTDP	USHL	30	22	6	1	1733	67	3	2.32	....	....	....	....	....	....	....
99-2000	Boston University	H-East	29	18	5	5	1790	73	2	2.45	....	....	....	....	....	....	....
2000-01	**NY Islanders**	**NHL**	**20**	**3**	**15**	**1**	**1083**	**63**	**0**	**3.49**	....	....	....	....	....	....	....
	Chicago Wolves	IHL	14	4	5	2	778	44	0	3.39	....	....	....	....	....	....	....
2001-02	Bridgeport	AHL	59	*30	22	7	3472	134	4	2.32	20	12	8	*1270	45	*3	2.13
2002-03	**NY Islanders**	**NHL**	**10**	**2**	**5**	**2**	**585**	**29**	**0**	**2.97**	**1**	**0**	**0**	**15**	**0**	**0**	**0.00**
	Bridgeport	AHL	34	16	10	8	2044	73	3	2.14	5	2	3	299	10	1	2.01
2003-04	**NY Islanders**	**NHL**	**50**	**23**	**18**	**5**	**2844**	**112**	**5**	**2.36**	**5**	**1**	**4**	**303**	**11**	**1**	**2.18**
	Bridgeport	AHL	2	0	2	0	119	3	0	1.51	....	....	....	....	....	....	....
2004-05							DID NOT PLAY										
2005-06	**NY Islanders**	**NHL**	**63**	**30**	**24**	**5**	**3572**	**180**	**1**	**3.02**	....	....	....	....	....	....	....
	United States	Olympics	4	1	3	0	237	9	0	2.28	....	....	....	....	....	....	....
2006-07	**NY Islanders**	**NHL**	**62**	**32**	**19**	**9**	**3627**	**156**	**5**	**2.58**	**4**	**1**	**3**	**236**	**13**	**0**	**3.31**
2007-08	**NY Islanders**	**NHL**	**63**	**26**	**28**	**7**	**3707**	**174**	**3**	**2.82**	....	....	....	....	....	....	....
2008-09	**NY Islanders**	**NHL**	**5**	**1**	**3**	**0**	**256**	**15**	**0**	**3.52**	....	....	....	....	....	....	....
2009-10	**NY Islanders**	**NHL**	**8**	**2**	**5**	**0**	**462**	**20**	**1**	**2.60**	....	....	....	....	....	....	....
	Bridgeport	AHL	4	1	2	0	199	11	0	3.31	....	....	....	....	....	....	....
2010-11	**NY Islanders**	**NHL**	**26**	**8**	**14**	**4**	**1533**	**88**	**1**	**3.44**	....	....	....	....	....	....	....
	NHL Totals		**307**	**127**	**131**	**33**	**17669**	**837**	**16**	**2.84**	**10**	**2**	**7**	**554**	**24**	**1**	**2.60**

Hockey East Second All-Star Team (2000) • Hockey East Rookie of the Year (2000)

Played in NHL All-Star Game (2008)

• Missed majority of 2008-09 and 2009-10 due to arthroscopic knee surgery, October 31, 2008.

DOMINGUE, Louis (doh-MIHN-gay, LOO-ee) PHX

Goaltender. Catches right. 6'3", 191 lbs. Born, St-Hyacinthe, Que., March 6, 1992.
(Phoenix's 5th choice, 138th overall, in 2010 Entry Draft).

			Regular Season								Playoffs						
Season	Club	League	GP	W	L	O/T	Mins	GA	SO	Avg	GP	W	L	Mins	GA	SO	Avg
2007-08	Lac St-Louis Lions	QAAA	35	22	9	0	1732	90	2	3.12	13	8	2	761	33	1	2.60
2008-09	Moncton Wildcats	QMJHL	12	5	5	0	621	26	0	2.51	....	....	....	....	....	....	....
2009-10	Moncton Wildcats	QMJHL	22	11	9	0	1196	56	1	2.81	....	....	....	....	....	....	....
	Quebec Remparts	QMJHL	19	9	8	0	1017	43	2	2.54	9	3	5	455	33	0	4.35
2010-11	Quebec Remparts	QMJHL	57	37	12	3	3033	134	2	2.65	18	11	6	996	41	1	2.47

DUBIELEWICZ, Wade (DOO-bih-wihtz, WAYD)

Goaltender. Catches left. 5'10", 180 lbs. Born, Invermere, B.C., January 30, 1979.

			Regular Season								Playoffs						
Season	Club	League	GP	W	L	O/T	Mins	GA	SO	Avg	GP	W	L	Mins	GA	SO	Avg
1997-98	Trail Smoke Eaters	BCHL	41	....	....	....	2225	118	0	3.18	....	....	....	....	....	....	....
1998-99	Trail Smoke Eaters	BCHL					STATISTICS NOT AVAILABLE										
	Chilliwack Chiefs	BCHL	14	10	4	0	834	....	0	....	....	....	....	....	....	....	....
99-2000	U. of Denver	WCHA	13	3	5	1	596	27	1	2.72	....	....	....	....	....	....	....
2000-01	U. of Denver	WCHA	29	12	9	3	1542	59	2	2.30	....	....	....	....	....	....	....
2001-02	U. of Denver	WCHA	24	20	4	0	1431	41	2	*1.72	....	....	....	....	....	....	....
2002-03	U. of Denver	WCHA	19	9	8	2	1060	43	3	2.43	....	....	....	....	....	....	....
2003-04	**NY Islanders**	**NHL**	**2**	**1**	**0**	**1**	**105**	**3**	**0**	**1.71**	....	....	....	....	....	....	....
	Bridgeport	AHL	33	20	8	5	1959	45	9	*1.38	3	2	1	181	11	0	3.64
2004-05	Bridgeport	AHL	43	18	23	1	2539	113	1	2.67	....	....	....	....	....	....	....
2005-06	**NY Islanders**	**NHL**	**7**	**2**	**3**	**0**	**310**	**15**	**0**	**2.90**	....	....	....	....	....	....	....
	Bridgeport	AHL	46	20	21	2	2575	134	3	3.12	7	3	4	435	16	0	2.21
2006-07	**NY Islanders**	**NHL**	**8**	**4**	**1**	**0**	**379**	**13**	**0**	**2.06**	**1**	**0**	**1**	**59**	**4**	**0**	**4.07**
	Bridgeport	AHL	40	22	12	5	2405	108	2	2.69	....	....	....	....	....	....	....
2007-08	**NY Islanders**	**NHL**	**20**	**9**	**9**	**1**	**1132**	**51**	**0**	**2.70**	....	....	....	....	....	....	....
	Bridgeport	AHL	2	1	1	0	124	5	0	2.42	....	....	....	....	....	....	....
2008-09	Ak Bars Kazan	Rus-KHL	21	....	....	....	1236	58	0	2.82	....	....	....	....	....	....	....
	Columbus	**NHL**	**3**	**1**	**2**	**0**	**169**	**10**	**0**	**3.55**	....	....	....	....	....	....	....
2009-10	**Minnesota**	**NHL**	**3**	**1**	**1**	**0**	**101**	**5**	**0**	**2.97**	....	....	....	....	....	....	....
	Houston Aeros	AHL	32	12	14	1	1564	71	0	2.72	....	....	....	....	....	....	....
2010-11	Kolner Haie	Germany	12	2	8	....	722	47	0	3.90	....	....	....	....	....	....	....
	NHL Totals		**43**	**18**	**16**	**2**	**2196**	**97**	**0**	**2.65**	**1**	**0**	**1**	**59**	**4**	**0**	**4.07**

WCHA Second All-Star Team (2001, 2003) • WCHA First All-Star Team (2002) • AHL All-Rookie Team (2004) • AHL Second All-Star Team (2004) • Dudley "Red" Garrett Memorial Award (AHL - Rookie of the Year) (2004) • Harry "Hap" Holmes Memorial Award (AHL - fewest goals against) (2004) (shared with Dieter Kochan)

Signed as a free agent by **NY Islanders**, May 25, 2003. Signed as a free agent by **Kazan** (Russia-KHL), June 25, 2008. Signed as a free agent by **NY Islanders**, January 15, 2009. Claimed on waivers by **Columbus** from **NY Islanders**, January 17, 2009. Signed as a free agent by **Minnesota**, July 17, 2009. Signed as a free agent by **Koln** (Germany), September 30, 2010.

DUBNYK, Devan (DOOB-nihk, DEH-vuhn) EDM

Goaltender. Catches left. 6'6", 202 lbs. Born, Regina, Sask., May 4, 1986.
(Edmonton's 1st choice, 14th overall, in 2004 Entry Draft).

			Regular Season								Playoffs						
Season	Club	League	GP	W	L	O/T	Mins	GA	SO	Avg	GP	W	L	Mins	GA	SO	Avg
2000-01	Calgary Bruins	CBHL	14	....	....	....	815	39	2	3.10	....	....	....	....	....	....	....
2001-02	Calgary Bruins	CBHL	18	7	9	2	1105	68	1	3.69	....	....	....	....	....	....	....
	Titaanit Kotka Jr.	Fin-Jr.	5	5	0	0	300	7	....	1.40	....	....	....	....	....	....	....
	Kamloops Blazers	WHL	3	1	1	0	143	13	0	5.44	....	....	....	....	....	....	....
2002-03	Kamloops Blazers	WHL	26	12	8	1	1278	66	2	3.10	....	....	....	....	....	....	....
2003-04	Kamloops Blazers	WHL	44	20	18	5	2532	106	6	2.51	4	1	3	245	12	0	2.94
2004-05	Kamloops Blazers	WHL	*65	23	34	7	3699	166	6	2.69	6	2	4	362	22	0	3.65
2005-06	Kamloops Blazers	WHL	54	27	26	1	3207	136	1	2.54	....	....	....	....	....	....	....
2006-07	Wilkes-Barre	AHL	4	2	1	0	204	10	0	2.94	....	....	....	....	....	....	....
	Stockton Thunder	ECHL	43	24	11	7	2529	108	2	2.56	6	2	4	395	18	0	2.73
2007-08	Springfield Falcons	AHL	33	9	17	0	1772	92	0	3.12	....	....	....	....	....	....	....
2008-09	Springfield Falcons	AHL	*62	18	41	2	*3635	180	3	2.97	....	....	....	....	....	....	....
2009-10	**Edmonton**	**NHL**	**19**	**4**	**10**	**2**	**1075**	**64**	**0**	**3.57**	....	....	....	....	....	....	....
	Springfield Falcons	AHL	33	13	17	2	1985	100	0	3.02	....	....	....	....	....	....	....
2010-11	**Edmonton**	**NHL**	**35**	**12**	**13**	**8**	**2061**	**93**	**2**	**2.71**	....	....	....	....	....	....	....
	NHL Totals		**54**	**16**	**23**	**10**	**3136**	**157**	**2**	**3.00**	....	....	....	....	....	....	....

Canadian Major Junior Scholastic Player of the Year (2004)

DUCHESNE, Jeremy (DOO-shayn, JAIR-eh-mee)

Goaltender. Catches left. 6', 201 lbs. Born, Silver Spring, MD, October 17, 1986.
(Philadelphia's 3rd choice, 119th overall, in 2005 Entry Draft).

			Regular Season								Playoffs						
Season	Club	League	GP	W	L	O/T	Mins	GA	SO	Avg	GP	W	L	Mins	GA	SO	Avg
2002-03	St-Francois Blizzard	QAAA	26	7	11	5	1341	75	0	3.35	....	....	....	....	....	....	....
2003-04	Victoriaville Tigres	QMJHL	17	3	8	1	870	60	0	4.14	....	....	....	....	....	....	....
2004-05	Victoriaville Tigres	QMJHL	15	2	9	0	711	41	2	*3.46	....	....	....	....	....	....	....
	Halifax	QMJHL	18	12	0	2	921	23	3	*1.50	12	8	4	723	33	*1	2.74
2005-06	Halifax	QMJHL	55	25	29	0	3175	185	4	3.50	11	5	6	626	34	1	3.26
2006-07	Halifax	QMJHL	28	12	15	0	1580	97	1	3.68	....	....	....	....	....	....	....
	Val-d'Or Foreurs	QMJHL	24	13	10	0	1356	66	1	2.92	*18	11	7	*1157	56	0	2.90
2007-08	Philadelphia	AHL	2	1	0	0	80	6	0	4.50	....	....	....	....	....	....	....
	Dayton Bombers	ECHL	31	13	13	5	1838	91	1	2.97	....	....	....	....	....	....	....
2008-09	Mississippi	ECHL	13	3	7	2	718	57	1	4.77	....	....	....	....	....	....	....
	South Carolina	ECHL	5	2	2	0	206	17	0	4.94	....	....	....	....	....	....	....
2009-10	**Philadelphia**	**NHL**	**1**	**0**	**0**	**0**	**17**	**1**	**0**	**3.53**	....	....	....	....	....	....	....
	Adirondack	AHL	5	1	4	0	263	13	1	2.97	....	....	....	....	....	....	....
	Kalamazoo Wings	ECHL	19	9	4	5	1162	62	1	3.20	....	....	....	....	....	....	....
2010-11	St-Georges	QNAHL	22	16	3	2	1309	62	1	2.84	....	....	....	....	....	....	....
	NHL Totals		**1**	**0**	**0**	**0**	**17**	**1**	**0**	**3.53**	....	....	....	....	....	....	....

Signed as a free agent by **St-Georges** (QNAHL), September 10, 2010.

EHELECHNER, Patrick (eh-heh-LEHCH-nuhr, PAT-rihk) PIT

Goaltender. Catches left. 6'2", 176 lbs. Born, Rosenheim, West Germany, September 23, 1984.
(San Jose's 5th choice, 139th overall, in 2003 Entry Draft).

			Regular Season								Playoffs						
Season	Club	League	GP	W	L	O/T	Mins	GA	SO	Avg	GP	W	L	Mins	GA	SO	Avg
2000-01	Jung. Mannheim	German-4	40	....	....	....	2423	171	2	4.23	....	....	....	....	....	....	....
2001-02	EV Landshut	German-3	2	....	....	....	130	6	0	2.77	....	....	....	....	....	....	....
	Hannover	Germany	8	....	....	....	475	24	0	3.03	....	....	....	....	....	....	....
2002-03	ESC Wedemark	German-4					STATISTICS NOT AVAILABLE										
	Hannover	Germany	4	....	....	....	162	16	0	5.90	....	....	....	....	....	....	....
2003-04	Sudbury Wolves	OHL	56	22	26	6	3089	148	3	2.87	7	2	4	390	14	2	2.15
2004-05	Sudbury Wolves	OHL	51	23	21	4	2997	128	3	2.56	10	4	5	497	29	0	3.50
2005-06	Adler Mannheim	Germany	1	....	....	....	59	5	0	5.02	....	....	....	....	....	....	....
	Fuchse Duisburg	Germany	26	....	....	....	1243	75	2	3.62	....	....	....	....	....	....	....
2006-07	Fuchse Duisburg	Germany	6	....	....	....	244	28	0	6.89	....	....	....	....	....	....	....
2007-08	Nurnberg	Germany	15	10	4	0	820	37	0	2.71	2	0	0	17	1	0	3.57
2008-09	Nurnberg	Germany	7	4	3	....	428	15	0	2.10	....	....	....	....	....	....	....
2009-10	Nurnberg	Germany	49	25	22	....	2848	123	1	2.59	4	1	3	286	12	0	2.52
2010-11	Nurnberg	Germany	46	21	24	....	2710	131	2	2.90	2	0	2	118	6	0	3.06

OHL Second All-Star Team (2004)

Signed as a free agent by **Mannheim** (Germany), April 25, 2005. Traded to **Pittsburgh** by **San Jose** with Nils Ekman for Carolina's 2nd round choice (previously acquired, later traded to Philadelphia - Philadelphia selected Kevin Marshall) in 2007 Entry Draft, July 20, 2006. Signed as a free agent by **Nurnberg** (Germany), April 25, 2007.

EIDSNESS, Brad (IGHD-nehz, BRAD) BUF

Goaltender. Catches left. 6', 190 lbs. Born, Chestermere, Alta., June 2, 1989.
(Buffalo's 4th choice, 139th overall, in 2007 Entry Draft).

			Regular Season								Playoffs						
Season	Club	League	GP	W	L	O/T	Mins	GA	SO	Avg	GP	W	L	Mins	GA	SO	Avg
2005-06	Okotoks Oilers	AJHL	4	3	1	0	238	4	2	1.01	....	....	....	....	....	....	....
	UFA Bisons	AMHL	18	12	4	2	1046	45	....	2.58	8	5	3	512	14	....	1.64
2006-07	Okotoks Oilers	AJHL	48	24	18	2	2658	127	4	2.87	16	8	8	1010	46	1	2.73
2007-08	Okotoks Oilers	AJHL	37	29	4	4	2264	80	3	2.12	9	4	5	547	25	0	2.74
2008-09	North Dakota	WCHA	41	*24	12	0	2441	104	1	2.56	....	....	....	....	....	....	....
2009-10	North Dakota	WCHA	*41	*24	10	4	*2388	84	3	2.11	....	....	....	....	....	....	....
2010-11	North Dakota	WCHA	7	2	2	1	323	22	0	4.09	....	....	....	....	....	....	....

WCHA All-Rookie Team (2009) • WCHA Second All-Star Team (2010)

ELLIOTT, Brian (EHL-lee-awt, BRIGH-uhn) ST.L.

Goaltender. Catches left. 6'3", 201 lbs. Born, Newmarket, Ont., April 9, 1985.
(Ottawa's 9th choice, 291st overall, in 2003 Entry Draft).

			Regular Season								Playoffs						
Season	Club	League	GP	W	L	O/T	Mins	GA	SO	Avg	GP	W	L	Mins	GA	SO	Avg
2002-03	Ajax Axemen	OPJHL	39	....	....	....	2097	135	0	3.86	....	....	....	....	....	....	....
2003-04	U. of Wisconsin	WCHA	6	3	3	0	336	12	0	2.14	....	....	....	....	....	....	....
2004-05	U. of Wisconsin	WCHA	9	6	2	1	467	9	3	1.16	....	....	....	....	....	....	....
2005-06	U. of Wisconsin	WCHA	35	*27	5	3	2128	55	*8	*1.55	....	....	....	....	....	....	....
2006-07	U. of Wisconsin	WCHA	36	15	17	2	2053	72	*5	2.10	....	....	....	....	....	....	....
	Binghamton	AHL	8	3	4	0	425	30	0	4.24	....	....	....	....	....	....	....
2007-08	**Ottawa**	**NHL**	**1**	**1**	**0**	**0**	**60**	**1**	**0**	**1.00**	....	....	....	....	....	....	....
	Binghamton	AHL	44	18	19	1	2394	112	2	2.81	....	....	....	....	....	....	....
2008-09	**Ottawa**	**NHL**	**31**	**16**	**8**	**3**	**1667**	**77**	**1**	**2.77**	....	....	....	....	....	....	....
	Binghamton	AHL	30	18	8	1	1691	65	2	2.31	....	....	....	....	....	....	....
2009-10	**Ottawa**	**NHL**	**55**	**29**	**18**	**4**	**3038**	**130**	**5**	**2.57**	**4**	**1**	**2**	**203**	**14**	**0**	**4.14**
2010-11	**Ottawa**	**NHL**	**43**	**13**	**19**	**8**	**2293**	**122**	**3**	**3.19**	....	....	....	....	....	....	....
	Colorado	**NHL**	**12**	**2**	**8**	**1**	**690**	**44**	**0**	**3.83**	....	....	....	....	....	....	....
	NHL Totals		**142**	**61**	**53**	**16**	**7748**	**374**	**9**	**2.90**	**4**	**1**	**2**	**203**	**14**	**0**	**4.14**

WCHA Second All-Star Team (2006, 2007) • NCAA West First All-American Team (2006) • NCAA Championship All-Tournament Team (2006)

Traded to **Colorado** by **Ottawa** for Craig Anderson, February 18, 2011. Signed as a free agent by **St. Louis**, July 1, 2011.

ELLIS, Dan (EHL-ihs, DAN) ANA

Goaltender. Catches left. 6'1", 191 lbs. Born, Saskatoon, Sask., June 19, 1980.
(Dallas' 2nd choice, 60th overall, in 2000 Entry Draft).

			Regular Season								Playoffs						
Season	Club	League	GP	W	L	O/T	Mins	GA	SO	Avg	GP	W	L	Mins	GA	SO	Avg
1998-99	Newmarket	OPJHL	28	24	3	1	1670	63	3	2.25							
99-2000	Omaha Lancers	USHL	55	*34	16	4	*3274	123	*11	*2.25	4	1	3	238	10	0	2.52
2000-01	Nebraska-Omaha	CCHA	40	21	14	3	2285	95	2	2.49							
2001-02	Nebraska-Omaha	CCHA	40	20	15	4	2405	97	3	2.42							
2002-03	Nebraska-Omaha	CCHA	39	11	21	5	2211	117	3	3.18							
2003-04	**Dallas**	**NHL**	**1**	**1**	**0**	**0**	**60**	**3**	**0**	**3.00**							
	Utah Grizzlies	AHL	20	5	14	0	1130	55	2	2.92							
	Idaho Steelheads	ECHL	23	13	8	1	1334	57	2	2.56	*16	*13	3	*966	30	*3	*1.86
2004-05	Hamilton Bulldogs	AHL	31	10	19	0	1774	82	1	2.77							
2005-06	Iowa Stars	AHL	34	16	13	1	1857	86	2	2.78							
2006-07	Iowa Stars	AHL	55	30	21	1	3194	148	4	2.78	12	6	6	679	35	0	3.09
2007-08	**Nashville**	**NHL**	**44**	**23**	**10**	**3**	**2229**	**87**	**6**	**2.34**	**6**	**2**	**4**	**357**	**15**	**0**	**2.52**
2008-09	**Nashville**	**NHL**	**35**	**11**	**19**	**4**	**1965**	**96**	**3**	**2.93**							
2009-10	**Nashville**	**NHL**	**31**	**15**	**13**	**1**	**1715**	**77**	**1**	**2.69**							
2010-11	**Tampa Bay**	**NHL**	**31**	**13**	**7**	**6**	**1679**	**82**	**2**	**2.93**							
	Anaheim	**NHL**	**13**	**8**	**3**	**1**	**729**	**29**	**0**	**2.39**	**1**	**0**	**1**	**41**	**4**	**0**	**5.85**
	NHL Totals		**155**	**71**	**52**	**15**	**8377**	**374**	**12**	**2.68**	**7**	**2**	**5**	**398**	**19**	**0**	**2.86**

USHL First All-Star Team (2000) • USHL Goaltender of the Year (2000) • USHL Player of the Year (2000) • CCHA Second All-Star Team (2002) • ECHL Playoff MVP (2004)

Signed as a free agent by **Nashville**, July 5, 2007. Traded to **Montreal** by **Nashville** with Dustin Boyd and future considerations for Sergei Kostitsyn and future considerations, June 29, 2010. Signed as a free agent by **Tampa Bay**, July 1, 2010. Traded to **Anaheim** by **Tampa Bay** for Curtis McElhinney, February 24, 2011.

EMERY, Ray (EH-muhr-ee, RAY)

Goaltender. Catches left. 6'2", 196 lbs. Born, Cayuga, Ont., September 28, 1982.
(Ottawa's 4th choice, 99th overall, in 2001 Entry Draft).

			Regular Season								Playoffs						
Season	Club	League	GP	W	L	O/T	Mins	GA	SO	Avg	GP	W	L	Mins	GA	SO	Avg
1998-99	Dunnville Terriers	ON-Jr.C	22	3	19	0	1320	140	0	6.37							
99-2000	Welland Cougars	ON-Jr.B	23	13	10	1	1323	62	1	2.68							
	Sault Ste. Marie	OHL	16	9	3	0	716	36	1	3.02	15	8	7	884	33	*3	2.24
2000-01	Sault Ste. Marie	OHL	52	18	29	2	2938	174	1	3.55							
2001-02	Sault Ste. Marie	OHL	*59	*33	17	9	*3477	158	4	2.73	6	2	4	360	19	*1	3.17
2002-03	**Ottawa**	**NHL**	**3**	**1**	**0**	**0**	**85**	**2**	**0**	**1.41**							
	Binghamton	AHL	50	27	17	6	2924	118	*7	2.42	14	8	6	848	40	*2	2.83
2003-04	**Ottawa**	**NHL**	**3**	**2**	**0**	**0**	**126**	**5**	**0**	**2.38**							
	Binghamton	AHL	53	21	23	7	3109	128	3	2.47	2	0	2	120	6	0	3.01
2004-05	Binghamton	AHL	51	28	18	5	2993	132	0	2.65	6	2	4	409	14	0	2.05
2005-06	**Ottawa**	**NHL**	**39**	**23**	**11**	**4**	**2168**	**102**	**3**	**2.82**	**10**	**5**	**5**	**604**	**29**	**0**	**2.88**
2006-07	**Ottawa**	**NHL**	**58**	**33**	**16**	**6**	**3351**	**138**	**5**	**2.47**	***20**	***13**	**7**	***1249**	**47**	***3**	**2.26**
2007-08	**Ottawa**	**NHL**	**31**	**12**	**13**	**4**	**1689**	**88**	**0**	**3.13**							
	Binghamton	AHL	2	1	1	0	120	6	0	3.00							
2008-09	Mytischi	Rus-KHL	36	....	....	....	2070	73	2	2.12	7	....	....	419	13	1	1.86
2009-10	**Philadelphia**	**NHL**	**29**	**16**	**11**	**1**	**1684**	**74**	**3**	**2.64**							
	Adirondack	AHL	1	0	1	0	59	2	0	2.03							
2010-11	**Anaheim**	**NHL**	**10**	**7**	**2**	**0**	**527**	**20**	**0**	**2.28**	**6**	**2**	**3**	**319**	**17**	**0**	**3.20**
	Syracuse Crunch	AHL	5	4	1	0	303	10	0	1.98							
	NHL Totals		**173**	**94**	**53**	**15**	**9630**	**429**	**11**	**2.67**	**36**	**20**	**15**	**2172**	**93**	**3**	**2.57**

OHL First All-Star Team (2002) • Canadian Major Junior First All-Star Team (2002) • Canadian Major Junior Goaltender of the Year (2002) • AHL All-Rookie Team (2003)

Signed as a free agent by **Mytischi** (Russia-KHL), July 9, 2008. Signed as a free agent by **Philadelphia** June 10, 2009. Signed as a free agent by **Anaheim**, February 7, 2011.

ENDRAS, Dennis (EHN-dras, DEHN-his) MIN

Goaltender. Catches left. 6', 167 lbs. Born, Immenstadt, West Germany, July 14, 1985.

			Regular Season								Playoffs						
Season	Club	League	GP	W	L	O/T	Mins	GA	SO	Avg	GP	W	L	Mins	GA	SO	Avg
2003-04	Bayreuth Tigers	German-3	26	....	....	....	1395	76	1	3.27							
2004-05	Augsburg	Germany	2	....	....	....	120	3	1	1.50							
	Bayreuth Tigers	German-3	17	....	....	....	996	70	0	4.22							
2005-06	Augsburg	Germany	5	....	....	....	145	14	0	5.79							
	EV Landsberg 2000	German-3	20	....	....	....	1185	39	1	1.97	8	....	....	498	10	2	1.21
2006-07	Frankfurt Lions	Germany	2	....	....	....	122	6	0	2.96							
	EV Landsberg 2000	German-2	42	....	....	....	2483	124	1	3.00							
2007-08	EV Landsberg 2000	German-2	29	....	....	....	1728	83	0	2.88							
	Ravensburg	German-2	20	....	....	....	1146	58	0	3.04	4	....	....	242	13	0	3.23
2008-09	Augsburg	Germany	50	26	24	....	2933	149	6	3.05	4	1	3	240	10	0	2.50
2009-10	Augsburg	Germany	52	28	24	....	3036	166	2	3.28	*14	8	6	*838	33	*1	2.36
2010-11	Augsburg	Germany	46	19	26	....	2673	140	1	3.14							

Signed as a free agent by **Minnesota**, July 7, 2010. • Assigned to **Augsburg** (Germany) by **Minnesota**, October 9, 2010.

ENGREN, Atte (EHN-grehn, AH-tay) NSH

Goaltender. Catches left. 6'1", 186 lbs. Born, Rauma, Finland, February 19, 1988.
(Nashville's 9th choice, 204th overall, in 2007 Entry Draft).

			Regular Season								Playoffs						
Season	Club	League	GP	W	L	O/T	Mins	GA	SO	Avg	GP	W	L	Mins	GA	SO	Avg
2004-05	Lukko Rauma U18	Fin-U18	10	....	....	....	603	22	0	2.19							
2005-06	Lukko Rauma U18	Fin-U18	16	....	....	....	966	44	0	2.73							
	Lukko Rauma Jr.	Fin-Jr.	11	....	....	....	637	30	0	2.83	9	....	....	509	27	0	3.18
2006-07	Lukko Rauma Jr.	Fin-Jr.	38	....	....	....	2277	115	1	3.03							
	Suomi U20	Finland-2	2	....	....	....	100	7	0	4.20							
2007-08	Hokki Kajaani	Finland-2	1	0	0	0	15	4	0	15.70							
	Lukko Rauma	Finland	1	0	1	0	59	3	0	3.04							
	Lukko Rauma Jr.	Fin-Jr.	31	14	13	0	1791	89	1	2.98	2	2	0	120	3	0	1.50
2008-09	TPS Turku Jr.	Fin-Jr.	4	3	1	0	240	11	0	2.75							
	Kiekko-Vantaa	Finland-2	5	3	2	0	264	9	0	2.05							
	TPS Turku	Finland	6	1	4	1	317	17	1	3.22							
2009-10	TuTo Turku	Finland-2	1	1	0	0	60	1	1	1.00	2	....	....	59	3	0	3.05
	TPS Turku	Finland	35	15	13	1	1778	78	2	2.63	8	7	1	494	15	1	1.82
2010-11	TPS Turku	Finland	51	10	25	13	2914	137	4	2.82							
	Milwaukee	AHL	4	2	2	0	247	10	0	2.43							

ENO, Nick (EE-noh, NIHK) BUF

Goaltender. Catches left. 6'3", 193 lbs. Born, Howell, MI, February 12, 1989.
(Buffalo's 7th choice, 187th overall, in 2007 Entry Draft).

			Regular Season								Playoffs						
Season	Club	League	GP	W	L	O/T	Mins	GA	SO	Avg	GP	W	L	Mins	GA	SO	Avg
2005-06	Howell	High-MI	25	....	....	....	1020	52	5	2.29							
2006-07	Green Mountain	EJHL	25	9	14	2	1398	84	1	3.60							
2007-08	Bowling Green	CCHA	22	12	10	0	1269	59	0	2.79							
2008-09	Bowling Green	CCHA	7	0	5	0	328	25	0	4.58							
2009-10	Bowling Green	CCHA	27	5	13	4	1343	74	0	3.30							
2010-11	Bowling Green	CCHA	18	4	10	1	960	50	0	3.12							

CCHA All-Rookie Team (2008)

ENROTH, Jhonas (EHN-rawth, YOH-nuhs) BUF

Goaltender. Catches left. 5'10", 166 lbs. Born, Stockholm, Sweden, June 25, 1988.
(Buffalo's 2nd choice, 46th overall, in 2006 Entry Draft).

			Regular Season								Playoffs						
Season	Club	League	GP	W	L	O/T	Mins	GA	SO	Avg	GP	W	L	Mins	GA	SO	Avg
2003-04	Huddinge IK U18	Swe-U18	6	....	....	....	324	15	0	2.77							
2004-05	Huddinge IK Jr.	Swe-Jr.	19	....	....	....	1144	49	3	2.57	3	....	....	186	6	1	1.93
	Huddinge IK U18	Swe-U18	2	....	....	....	125	5	0	2.40							
	Huddinge IK	Sweden-2	2	....	....	....	51	6	0	6.95							
2005-06	Sodertalje SK Jr.	Swe-Jr.	39	....	....	....	2378	86	1	2.17	4	....	....	243	9	0	2.22
	Sodertalje SK U18	Swe-U18	2	....	....	....	120	5	0	2.50							
2006-07	Sodertalje SK Jr.	Swe-Jr.	3	....	....	....	180	4	0	1.33							
	Sodertalje SK	Sweden-2	33	....	....	....	1938	57	3	1.76							
2007-08	Sodertalje SK Jr.	Swe-Jr.	1	....	....	....	59	4	0	4.05							
	Sodertalje SK	Sweden	27	....	....	....	1578	56	2	*2.13							
2008-09	Portland Pirates	AHL	58	26	23	6	3424	157	3	2.75	5	1	4	264	10	1	2.27
2009-10	**Buffalo**	**NHL**	**1**	**0**	**1**	**0**	**58**	**4**	**0**	**4.14**							
	Portland Pirates	AHL	48	28	18	1	2781	110	5	2.37							
2010-11	**Buffalo**	**NHL**	**14**	**9**	**2**	**2**	**769**	**35**	**1**	**2.73**	**1**	**0**	**0**	**17**	**1**	**0**	**3.53**
	Portland Pirates	AHL	41	20	17	2	2393	111	0	2.78	4	1	2	217	10	0	2.77
	NHL Totals		**15**	**9**	**3**	**2**	**827**	**39**	**1**	**2.83**	**1**	**0**	**0**	**17**	**1**	**0**	**3.53**

ERSBERG, Erik (AIRZH-buhrg, AIR-ihk)

Goaltender. Catches left. 6', 165 lbs. Born, Sala, Sweden, March 8, 1982.

			Regular Season								Playoffs						
Season	Club	League	GP	W	L	O/T	Mins	GA	SO	Avg	GP	W	L	Mins	GA	SO	Avg
99-2000	Vasteras IK U18	Swe-U18	1	....	....	....	60	2	0	2.00	2	....	....	119	10	0	5.02
	Vasteras IK Jr.	Swe-Jr.	16	....	....	....	885	36	0	2.44							
2000-01	Vasteras	Sweden-4	33	....	....	....	....	....	....	1.48							
2001-02	Vasteras Jr.	Swe-Jr.	....	....	....	....	....	....	....	....	2	....	....	118	11	0	5.61
	Vasteras	Sweden-3	37	....	....	....	....	....	....	....							
2002-03	Vasteras	Sweden-2	32	....	....	....	1920	91	1	2.84							
2003-04	Vasteras	Sweden-2	32	....	....	....	1850	79	3	2.56							
2004-05	Vasteras	Sweden-2	37	....	....	....	2189	76	3	2.08	5	....	....	308	8	2	1.56
2005-06	VIK Vasteras HK	Sweden-2	2	....	....	....	118	4	0	2.02							
	HV 71 Jonkoping	Sweden	10	....	....	....	602	18	2	1.79	2	....	....	79	4	0	3.05
	HV 71 Jr.	Swe-Jr.	1	....	....	....	60	1	0	1.00							
2006-07	HV 71 Jonkoping	Sweden	41	....	....	....	2455	98	4	2.39	14	....	....	834	39	0	2.81
2007-08	**Los Angeles**	**NHL**	**14**	**6**	**5**	**3**	**799**	**33**	**2**	**2.48**							
	Manchester	AHL	30	10	13	2	1540	75	1	2.92							
2008-09	**Los Angeles**	**NHL**	**28**	**8**	**11**	**5**	**1477**	**65**	**0**	**2.64**							
2009-10	**Los Angeles**	**NHL**	**11**	**4**	**3**	**2**	**551**	**22**	**0**	**2.40**	**1**	**0**	**0**	**13**	**2**	**0**	**9.23**
2010-11	Manchester	AHL	2	1	1	0	119	4	0	2.02							
	Ufa	Rus-KHL	18	....	....	....	991	35	4	2.12	20	....	....	1118	36	3	1.93
	NHL Totals		**53**	**18**	**19**	**10**	**2827**	**120**	**2**	**2.55**	**1**	**0**	**0**	**13**	**2**	**0**	**9.23**

Signed as a free agent by **Los Angeles**, May 31, 2007. Signed as a free agent by **Ufa** (Russia-KHL), October 26, 2010.

FALLON, Joe (FA-luhn, JOH)

Goaltender. Catches left. 6'3", 190 lbs. Born, Bemidji, MN, February 1, 1985.
(Chicago's 9th choice, 167th overall, in 2005 Entry Draft).

			Regular Season								Playoffs						
Season	Club	League	GP	W	L	O/T	Mins	GA	SO	Avg	GP	W	L	Mins	GA	SO	Avg
2001-02	Rochester	USHL	27	7	16	1	1484	93	0	3.76							
2002-03	Cedar Rapids	USHL	42	20	15	6	2495	108	2	2.60	7	3	4	426	21	0	2.96
2003-04	Cedar Rapids	USHL	42	25	13	2	2370	108	4	2.73	4	1	3	237	9	0	2.28
2004-05	U. of Vermont	ECAC	32	17	10	4	1932	63	5	1.96							
2005-06	U. of Vermont	H-East	33	14	14	5	1931	65	6	2.02							
2006-07	U. of Vermont	H-East	34	17	14	3	1997	62	6	*1.86							
2007-08	U. of Vermont	H-East	33	15	13	5	1942	77	*3	2.38							
2008-09	Rockford IceHogs	AHL	2	0	0	0	63	1	0	0.95							
	Fresno Falcons	ECHL	13	8	4	1	747	32	1	2.57							
	Gwinnett	ECHL	22	10	10	1	1246	67	1	3.23							
2009-10	Rockford IceHogs	AHL	29	15	10	1	1545	68	1	2.64							
	Peoria Rivermen	AHL	10	4	6	0	532	31	0	3.50							
2010-11	Las Vegas	ECHL	27	18	8	1	1620	67	2	2.48							
	San Antonio	AHL	13	3	7	0	667	33	1	2.97							

ECAC All-Rookie Team (2005) • ECAC Rookie of the Year (2005)

Traded to **St. Louis** by **Chicago** with Daryl Boyle for Hannu Toivonen and Danny Richmond, March 1, 2010. Signed as a free agent by **San Antonio** (AHL), August 16, 2010.

FLEURY, Marc-Andre (fluh-REE, MAHRK-AWN-dray) PIT

Goaltender. Catches left. 6'2", 180 lbs. Born, Sorel, Que., November 28, 1984.
(Pittsburgh's 1st choice, 1st overall, in 2003 Entry Draft).

			Regular Season								Playoffs						
Season	Club	League	GP	W	L	O/T	Mins	GA	SO	Avg	GP	W	L	Mins	GA	SO	Avg
99-2000	Charles-Lemoyne	QAAA	15	4	9	0	780	36	1	2.77							
2000-01	Cape Breton	QMJHL	35	12	13	2	1705	115	0	4.05	2	0	1	32	4	0	7.50
2001-02	Cape Breton	QMJHL	55	26	14	8	3043	141	2	2.78	16	9	7	1003	55	0	3.29
2002-03	Cape Breton	QMJHL	51	17	24	6	2889	162	2	3.36	4	0	4	228	17	0	4.47
2003-04	**Pittsburgh**	**NHL**	**21**	**4**	**14**	**2**	**1154**	**70**	**1**	**3.64**							
	Cape Breton	QMJHL	10	8	1	1	606	20	0	1.98	4	1	3	251	13	0	3.10
	Wilkes-Barre	AHL	....	....	....	....	....	....	....	....	2	0	1	92	6	0	3.90
2004-05	Wilkes-Barre	AHL	54	26	19	4	3029	127	5	2.52	4	0	2	151	11	0	4.36
2005-06	**Pittsburgh**	**NHL**	**50**	**13**	**27**	**6**	**2809**	**152**	**1**	**3.25**							
	Wilkes-Barre	AHL	12	10	2	0	727	19	0	1.57	5	2	3	311	18	0	3.48
2006-07	**Pittsburgh**	**NHL**	**67**	**40**	**16**	**9**	**3905**	**184**	**5**	**2.83**	**5**	**1**	**4**	**287**	**18**	**0**	**3.76**
2007-08	**Pittsburgh**	**NHL**	**35**	**19**	**10**	**2**	**1857**	**72**	**4**	**2.33**	***20**	***14**	**6**	***1251**	**41**	***3**	**1.97**
	Wilkes-Barre	AHL	5	3	2	0	297	7	0	1.42							
2008-09♦	**Pittsburgh**	**NHL**	**62**	**35**	**18**	**7**	**3641**	**162**	**4**	**2.67**	***24**	***16**	**8**	***1447**	**63**	**0**	**2.61**
2009-10	**Pittsburgh**	**NHL**	**67**	**37**	**21**	**6**	**3798**	**168**	**1**	**2.65**	**13**	**7**	**6**	**798**	**37**	**1**	**2.78**
	Canada	Olympics	DID NOT PLAY – SPARE GOALTENDER														
2010-11	**Pittsburgh**	**NHL**	**65**	**36**	**20**	**5**	**3695**	**143**	**3**	**2.32**	**7**	**3**	**4**	**405**	**17**	**1**	**2.52**
	NHL Totals		**367**	**184**	**126**	**37**	**20859**	**951**	**19**	**2.74**	**69**	**41**	**28**	**4188**	**176**	**5**	**2.52**

QMJHL Second All-Star Team (2003)

Played in NHL All-Star Game (2011)

FORSBERG, Anton (FORZ-buhrg, AN-tawn) CBJ

Goaltender. Catches left. 6'2", 176 lbs. Born, Harnosand, Sweden, November 27, 1992.
(Columbus' 6th choice, 188th overall, in 2011 Entry Draft).

			Regular Season								Playoffs						
Season	Club	League	GP	W	L	O/T	Mins	GA	SO	Avg	GP	W	L	Mins	GA	SO	Avg
2007-08	Harnosand Jr.	Swe-Jr.	9	....	....	....	....	....	....	....							
	Harnosand	Sweden-3	1	....	....	....	20	2	0	6.00							
2008-09	MODO U18	Swe-U18	12	....	....	....	619	34	0	3.29	5	....	....	225	11	1	2.93
2009-10	MODO U18	Swe-U18	9	....	....	....	538	26	0	2.90	2	....	....	120	5	0	2.50
	MODO Jr.	Swe-Jr.	21	....	....	....	1183	73	1	3.70	3	....	....	177	7	0	2.37
2010-11	MODO Jr.	Swe-Jr.	33	....	....	....	1942	94	3	2.90	6	....	....	358	17	0	2.85
	AIK Harnosand	Sweden-3	1	....	....	....	59	5	0	5.11							

FOSTER, Brian (FAW-stuhr, BRIGH-uhn) FLA

Goaltender. Catches left. 6'1", 155 lbs. Born, Pembroke, NH, February 4, 1987.
(Florida's 6th choice, 161st overall, in 2005 Entry Draft).

			Regular Season								Playoffs						
Season	**Club**	**League**	**GP**	**W**	**L**	**O/T**	**Mins**	**GA**	**SO**	**Avg**	**GP**	**W**	**L**	**Mins**	**GA**	**SO**	**Avg**
2003-04	N.H. Jr. Monarchs	EJHL					STATISTICS NOT AVAILABLE										
2004-05	N.H. Jr. Monarchs	EJHL	41	30	6	4	2339	....	3	2.51	....	....	....	....	....	....	....
2005-06	Des Moines	USHL	26	12	9	3	1516	71	0	2.81	1	0	0	12	0	0	0.00
2006-07	New Hampshire	H-East	7	2	2	0	298	11	2	2.21	....	....	....	....	....	....	....
2007-08	New Hampshire	H-East	6	2	2	2	372	19	0	3.06	....	....	....	....	....	....	....
2008-09	New Hampshire	H-East	35	19	11	4	2080	93	*3	2.68	....	....	....	....	....	....	....
2009-10	New Hampshire	H-East	*38	17	14	7	*2297	114	0	2.98	....	....	....	....	....	....	....
2010-11	Bossier-Shreve.	CHL	20	9	9	1	1124	60	0	3.20	....	....	....	....	....	....	....
	Cincinnati	ECHL	19	11	6	1	1098	42	2	2.30	4	1	3	292	11	0	2.26

Hockey East First All-Star Team (2010) • NCAA East Second All-American Team (2010)

Signed as a free agent by **Rochester** (AHL), August 25, 2010. • Loaned to **Bossier-Shreverport** (CHL) by **Rochester** (AHL), October 6, 2010.

FRAZEE, Jeff (FRAY-zee, JEHF) N.J.

Goaltender. Catches left. 6', 195 lbs. Born, Edina, MN, May 13, 1987.
(New Jersey's 2nd choice, 38th overall, in 2005 Entry Draft).

			Regular Season								Playoffs						
Season	**Club**	**League**	**GP**	**W**	**L**	**O/T**	**Mins**	**GA**	**SO**	**Avg**	**GP**	**W**	**L**	**Mins**	**GA**	**SO**	**Avg**
2001-02	Holy Angels	High-MN	6	6	0	0	....	....	....	....	....	....	....	....	....	....	....
2002-03	Holy Angels	High-MN	16	14	1	1	....	....	....	....	....	....	....	....	....	....	....
2003-04	USNTDP	U-17	16	9	3	0	781	31	....	2.38	....	....	....	....	....	....	....
	USNTDP	NAHL	25	14	8	3	1463	71	3	2.91	....	....	....	....	....	....	....
2004-05	USNTDP	U-18	24	....	....	....	1309	59	3	2.71	....	....	....	....	....	....	....
	USNTDP	NAHL	9	8	1	0	500	18	1	2.16	....	....	....	....	....	....	....
2005-06	U. of Minnesota	WCHA	12	6	3	2	660	26	2	2.36	....	....	....	....	....	....	....
2006-07	U. of Minnesota	WCHA	20	14	3	1	1148	45	1	2.35	....	....	....	....	....	....	....
2007-08	U. of Minnesota	WCHA	14	6	7	0	798	39	1	2.93	....	....	....	....	....	....	....
	Lowell Devils	AHL	1	0	1	0	40	3	0	4.50	....	....	....	....	....	....	....
2008-09	Lowell Devils	AHL	58	28	22	6	3407	149	4	2.62	....	....	....	....	....	....	....
	Trenton Devils	ECHL	5	2	2	0	272	12	0	2.65	4	2	2	271	10	0	2.22
2009-10	Lowell Devils	AHL	31	14	16	0	1778	83	1	2.80	....	....	....	....	....	....	....
2010-11	Albany Devils	AHL	33	11	15	3	1842	89	2	2.90	....	....	....	....	....	....	....

GARON, Mathieu (gah-ROHN, MA-tyew) T.B.

Goaltender. Catches right. 6'1", 206 lbs. Born, Chandler, Que., January 9, 1978.
(Montreal's 2nd choice, 44th overall, in 1996 Entry Draft).

			Regular Season								Playoffs						
Season	**Club**	**League**	**GP**	**W**	**L**	**O/T**	**Mins**	**GA**	**SO**	**Avg**	**GP**	**W**	**L**	**Mins**	**GA**	**SO**	**Avg**
1993-94	Jonquiere Elites	QAAA	17	0	13	0	834	88	0	6.33	....	....	....	....	....	....	....
1994-95	Jonquiere Elites	QAAA	27	13	13	1	1554	94	0	3.63	9	6	2	467	26	0	3.34
1995-96	Victoriaville Tigres	QMJHL	51	18	27	0	2716	189	1	4.17	12	7	4	676	38	1	3.37
1996-97	Victoriaville Tigres	QMJHL	53	29	18	3	3026	148	*6	2.93	6	2	4	330	23	0	4.18
1997-98	Victoriaville Tigres	QMJHL	47	27	18	2	2802	125	5	2.68	6	2	4	345	22	0	3.82
1998-99	Fredericton	AHL	40	14	22	2	2222	114	3	3.08	6	1	1	208	12	0	3.47
99-2000	Quebec Citadelles	AHL	53	17	28	3	2884	149	2	3.10	1	0	0	20	3	0	8.82
2000-01	**Montreal**	**NHL**	**11**	**4**	**5**	**1**	**589**	**24**	**2**	**2.44**	....	....	....	....	....	....	....
	Quebec Citadelles	AHL	31	16	13	1	1768	86	1	2.92	8	4	4	459	22	1	2.88
2001-02	**Montreal**	**NHL**	**5**	**1**	**4**	**0**	**261**	**19**	**0**	**4.37**	....	....	....	....	....	....	....
	Quebec Citadelles	AHL	50	21	15	12	2988	136	2	2.73	3	0	3	198	12	0	3.63
2002-03	**Montreal**	**NHL**	**8**	**3**	**5**	**0**	**482**	**16**	**2**	**1.99**	....	....	....	....	....	....	....
	Hamilton Bulldogs	AHL	20	15	2	2	1150	34	4	1.77	....	....	....	....	....	....	....
2003-04	**Montreal**	**NHL**	**19**	**8**	**6**	**2**	**1003**	**38**	**0**	**2.27**	**1**	**0**	**0**	**12**	**0**	**0**	**0.00**
2004-05	Manchester	AHL	52	32	14	4	2969	105	8	2.12	6	2	4	285	17	0	3.58
2005-06	**Los Angeles**	**NHL**	**63**	**31**	**26**	**3**	**3446**	**185**	**4**	**3.22**	....	....	....	....	....	....	....
2006-07	**Los Angeles**	**NHL**	**32**	**13**	**10**	**6**	**1779**	**79**	**2**	**2.66**	....	....	....	....	....	....	....
2007-08	**Edmonton**	**NHL**	**47**	**26**	**18**	**1**	**2658**	**118**	**4**	**2.66**	....	....	....	....	....	....	....
2008-09	**Edmonton**	**NHL**	**15**	**6**	**8**	**0**	**815**	**43**	**0**	**3.17**	....	....	....	....	....	....	....
	♦ **Pittsburgh**	**NHL**	**4**	**2**	**1**	**0**	**206**	**10**	**0**	**2.91**	**1**	**0**	**0**	**24**	**0**	**0**	**0.00**
2009-10	**Columbus**	**NHL**	**35**	**12**	**9**	**6**	**1771**	**83**	**2**	**2.81**	....	....	....	....	....	....	....
2010-11	**Columbus**	**NHL**	**36**	**10**	**14**	**6**	**1938**	**88**	**3**	**2.72**	....	....	....	....	....	....	....
	NHL Totals		**275**	**116**	**106**	**25**	**14948**	**703**	**19**	**2.82**	**2**	**0**	**0**	**36**	**0**	**0**	**0.00**

QMJHL All-Rookie Team (1996) • QMJHL Defensive Rookie of the Year (1996) • QMJHL First All-Star Team (1998) • Canadian Major Junior First All-Star Team (1998) • Canadian Major Junior Goaltender of the Year (1998)

Traded to **Los Angeles** by **Montreal** with San Jose's 3rd round choice (previously acquired, Los Angeles selected Paul Baier) in 2004 Entry Draft for Radek Bonk and Cristobal Huet, June 26, 2004. Signed as a free agent by **Edmonton**, July 3, 2007. Traded to **Pittsburgh** by **Edmonton** for Dany Sabourin, Ryan Stone and Pittsburgh's 4th round choice (Tobias Rieder) in 2011 Entry Draft, January 17, 2009. Signed as a free agent by **Columbus**, July 1, 2009. Signed as a free agent by **Tampa Bay**, July 1, 2011.

GAYDUCHENKO, Sergei (gay-doo-CHEHN-koh, SAIR-gay) FLA

Goaltender. Catches left. 6'5", 222 lbs. Born, Kiev, USSR, June 6, 1989.
(Florida's 8th choice, 202nd overall, in 2007 Entry Draft).

			Regular Season								Playoffs						
Season	**Club**	**League**	**GP**	**W**	**L**	**O/T**	**Mins**	**GA**	**SO**	**Avg**	**GP**	**W**	**L**	**Mins**	**GA**	**SO**	**Avg**
2006-07	Yaroslavl 2	Russia-3	23	....	....	....	1180	57	3	2.90	....	....	....	....	....	....	....
2007-08	Novokuznetsk 2	Russia-3	2	....	....	....	....	5	....	....	....	....	....	....	....	....	....
	Novokuznetsk	Russia	11	....	....	....	533	27	0	3.04	....	....	....	....	....	....	....
2008-09	Yaroslavl 2	Russia-3					STATISTICS NOT AVAILABLE										
	Yaroslavl	Rus-KHL	3	....	....	....	185	6	0	1.95	....	....	....	....	....	....	....
2009-10	Yaroslavl	Rus-KHL	20	....	....	....	1091	44	0	2.42	....	....	....	....	....	....	....
2010-11	CSKA Moscow	Rus-KHL	23	....	....	....	1201	58	1	2.90	....	....	....	....	....	....	....
	CSKA Jr.	Russia-Jr.	7	....	....	....	332	21	1	3.80	15	....	....	872	28	2	1.93

GERBER, Martin (GUHR-buhr, MAHR-tihn)

Goaltender. Catches left. 6', 205 lbs. Born, Burgdorf, Switz., September 3, 1974.
(Anaheim's 10th choice, 232nd overall, in 2001 Entry Draft).

			Regular Season								Playoffs						
Season	**Club**	**League**	**GP**	**W**	**L**	**O/T**	**Mins**	**GA**	**SO**	**Avg**	**GP**	**W**	**L**	**Mins**	**GA**	**SO**	**Avg**
1996-97	SC Langnau	Swiss-2	38	....	....	....	2286	121	0	3.18	8	....	....	488	29	0	3.57
1997-98	SC Langnau	Swiss-2	40	....	....	....	2430	141	2	3.48	16	....	....	961	42	0	2.62
1998-99	SC Langnau	Swiss	42	....	....	....	2521	203	1	4.83	11	....	....	664	50	0	4.52
99-2000	SC Langnau	Swiss	44	....	....	....	2652	161	3	3.64	6	....	....	360	13	*2	*2.17
2000-01	SCL Tigers Langnau	Swiss	*44	....	....	....	2671	114	3	2.56	5	....	....	319	7	1	1.32
2001-02	Farjestad	Sweden	44	....	....	....	2664	87	*4	*1.96	*10	....	....	*657	18	*2	*1.64
	Switzerland	Olympics	3	1	1	1	158	4	0	1.52	....	....	....	....	....	....	....
2002-03	**Anaheim**	**NHL**	**22**	**6**	**11**	**3**	**1203**	**39**	**1**	**1.95**	**2**	**0**	**0**	**20**	**1**	**0**	**3.00**
	Cincinnati	AHL	1	1	0	0	60	2	0	2.00	....	....	....	....	....	....	....
2003-04	**Anaheim**	**NHL**	**32**	**11**	**12**	**4**	**1698**	**64**	**2**	**2.26**	....	....	....	....	....	....	....
2004-05	SCL Tigers Langnau	Swiss	20	6	10	4	1220	59	0	2.90	....	....	....	....	....	....	....
	Farjestad	Sweden	30	20	6	4	1827	58	4	1.90	*15	9	6	*900	36	1	2.40
2005-06 ♦	**Carolina**	**NHL**	**60**	**38**	**14**	**6**	**3493**	**162**	**3**	**2.78**	**6**	**1**	**1**	**221**	**13**	**1**	**3.53**
	Switzerland	Olympics	3	1	2	0	160	11	1	4.13	....	....	....	....	....	....	....
2006-07	**Ottawa**	**NHL**	**29**	**15**	**9**	**3**	**1599**	**74**	**1**	**2.78**	....	....	....	....	....	....	....
2007-08	**Ottawa**	**NHL**	**57**	**30**	**18**	**4**	**3197**	**145**	**2**	**2.72**	**4**	**0**	**4**	**238**	**14**	**0**	**3.53**
2008-09	**Ottawa**	**NHL**	**14**	**4**	**9**	**1**	**839**	**40**	**1**	**2.86**	....	....	....	....	....	....	....
	Binghamton	AHL	14	6	7	0	783	38	1	2.91	....	....	....	....	....	....	....
	Toronto	**NHL**	**12**	**6**	**5**	**0**	**706**	**38**	**0**	**3.23**	....	....	....	....	....	....	....
2009-10	Mytischi	Rus-KHL	30	....	....	....	1750	64	2	2.19	....	....	....	....	....	....	....
2010-11	**Edmonton**	**NHL**	**3**	**3**	**0**	**0**	**185**	**4**	**0**	**1.30**	....	....	....	....	....	....	....
	Oklahoma City	AHL	42	20	16	4	2472	107	4	2.60	6	2	3	335	10	1	1.79
	NHL Totals		**229**	**113**	**78**	**21**	**12920**	**566**	**10**	**2.63**	**12**	**1**	**5**	**479**	**28**	**1**	**3.51**

• Scored a goal in playoffs vs. Martigny (Swiss-2), February 27, 1997. Traded to **Carolina** by **Anaheim** for Tomas Malec and Carolina's 3rd round choice (Kyle Klubertanz) in 2004 Entry Draft, June 18, 2004. Signed as a free agent by **Langnau** (Swiss), September 17, 2004. Signed as a free agent by **Farjestad** (Sweden), November 7, 2004. Signed as a free agent by **Ottawa**, July 1, 2006. Claimed on waivers by **Toronto** from **Ottawa**, March 4, 2009. Signed as a free agent by **Mytischi** (Russia-KHL), July 21, 2009. Signed as a free agent by **Edmonton**, August 6, 2010.

GIBSON, Christopher (GIHB-suhn, KRIHS-tuh-fuhr) L.A.

Goaltender. Catches left. 6'1", 191 lbs. Born, Karkkila, Finland, December 27, 1992.
(Los Angeles' 1st choice, 49th overall, in 2011 Entry Draft).

			Regular Season								Playoffs						
Season	**Club**	**League**	**GP**	**W**	**L**	**O/T**	**Mins**	**GA**	**SO**	**Avg**	**GP**	**W**	**L**	**Mins**	**GA**	**SO**	**Avg**
2008-09	Notre Dame	SMHL	18	16	1	0	1049	46	1	2.63	6	6	0	360	11	1	1.83
2009-10	Chicoutimi	QMJHL	29	8	19	0	1592	93	2	3.50	4	0	4	230	13	0	3.39
2010-11	Chicoutimi	QMJHL	37	14	15	8	2235	90	4	2.42	4	0	4	219	19	0	5.20

QMJHL First All-Star Team (2011)

GIBSON, John (GIHB-suhn, JAWN) ANA

Goaltender. Catches left. 6'3", 206 lbs. Born, Pittsburgh, PA, July 14, 1993.
(Anaheim's 2nd choice, 39th overall, in 2011 Entry Draft).

			Regular Season								Playoffs						
Season	**Club**	**League**	**GP**	**W**	**L**	**O/T**	**Mins**	**GA**	**SO**	**Avg**	**GP**	**W**	**L**	**Mins**	**GA**	**SO**	**Avg**
2009-10	USNTDP	USHL	18	7	9	0	1023	63	0	3.69	....	....	....	....	....	....	....
	USNTDP	U-17	6	3	1	1	335	16	0	2.87	....	....	....	....	....	....	....
	USNTDP	U-18	2	2	0	0	120	4	0	2.00	....	....	....	....	....	....	....
2010-11	USNTDP	USHL	17	9	4	3	983	39	1	2.38	....	....	....	....	....	....	....
	USNTDP	U 18	23	15	7	0	1255	56	0	2.68	....	....	....	....	....	....	....

GIGUERE, Jean-Sebastien (zhih-GAIR, ZHAWN-suh-BAS-t'yehn) COL

Goaltender. Catches left. 6'1", 202 lbs. Born, Montreal, Que., May 16, 1977.
(Hartford's 1st choice, 13th overall, in 1995 Entry Draft).

			Regular Season								Playoffs						
Season	**Club**	**League**	**GP**	**W**	**L**	**O/T**	**Mins**	**GA**	**SO**	**Avg**	**GP**	**W**	**L**	**Mins**	**GA**	**SO**	**Avg**
1992-93	Laval-Laurentides	QAAA	25	12	11	2	1498	76	0	3.02	11	6	5	654	38	0	3.49
1993-94	Verdun	QMJHL	26	13	7	2	1288	69	1	3.21	1	0	0	29	2	0	4.14
1994-95	Halifax	QMJHL	47	14	27	5	2762	181	2	3.93	7	3	4	418	17	1	*2.44
1995-96	Halifax	QMJHL	55	26	23	2	3236	185	1	3.43	6	1	5	357	24	0	4.04
1996-97	**Hartford**	**NHL**	**8**	**1**	**4**	**0**	**394**	**24**	**0**	**3.65**	....	....	....	....	....	....	....
	Halifax	QMJHL	50	28	19	3	3009	169	2	3.37	16	9	7	954	58	0	3.65
1997-98	Saint John Flames	AHL	31	16	10	3	1758	72	2	2.46	10	5	3	536	27	0	3.02
1998-99	**Calgary**	**NHL**	**15**	**6**	**7**	**1**	**860**	**46**	**0**	**3.21**	....	....	....	....	....	....	....
	Saint John Flames	AHL	39	18	16	3	2145	123	3	3.44	7	3	2	304	21	0	4.14
99-2000	**Calgary**	**NHL**	**7**	**1**	**3**	**1**	**330**	**15**	**0**	**2.73**	....	....	....	....	....	....	....
	Saint John Flames	AHL	41	17	17	3	2243	114	0	3.05	3	0	3	178	9	0	3.03
2000-01	**Anaheim**	**NHL**	**34**	**11**	**17**	**5**	**2031**	**87**	**4**	**2.57**	....	....	....	....	....	....	....
	Cincinnati	AHL	23	12	7	2	1306	53	0	2.43	....	....	....	....	....	....	....
2001-02	**Anaheim**	**NHL**	**53**	**20**	**25**	**6**	**3127**	**111**	**4**	**2.13**	....	....	....	....	....	....	....
2002-03	**Anaheim**	**NHL**	**65**	**34**	**22**	**6**	**3775**	**145**	**8**	**2.30**	**21**	**15**	**6**	**1407**	**38**	**5**	***1.62**
2003-04	**Anaheim**	**NHL**	**55**	**17**	**31**	**6**	**3210**	**140**	**3**	**2.62**	....	....	....	....	....	....	....
2004-05	Hamburg Freezers	Germany	6	....	....	....	301	12	0	2.39	2	....	....	100	7	0	4.20
2005-06	**Anaheim**	**NHL**	**60**	**30**	**15**	**11**	**3381**	**150**	**2**	**2.66**	**6**	**3**	**3**	**318**	**18**	**0**	**3.40**
2006-07 ♦	**Anaheim**	**NHL**	**56**	**36**	**10**	**8**	**3245**	**122**	**4**	**2.26**	**18**	***13**	**4**	**1067**	**35**	**1**	**1.97**
2007-08	**Anaheim**	**NHL**	**58**	**35**	**17**	**6**	**3310**	**117**	**4**	**2.12**	**6**	**2**	**4**	**358**	**19**	**0**	**3.18**
2008-09	**Anaheim**	**NHL**	**46**	**19**	**18**	**6**	**2458**	**127**	**2**	**3.10**	**1**	**0**	**0**	**17**	**0**	**0**	**0.00**
2009-10	**Anaheim**	**NHL**	**20**	**4**	**8**	**5**	**1108**	**58**	**1**	**3.14**	....	....	....	....	....	....	....
	Toronto	**NHL**	**15**	**6**	**7**	**2**	**915**	**38**	**2**	**2.49**	....	....	....	....	....	....	....
2010-11	**Toronto**	**NHL**	**33**	**11**	**11**	**4**	**1633**	**78**	**0**	**2.87**	....	....	....	....	....	....	....
	NHL Totals		**525**	**231**	**195**	**67**	**29777**	**1258**	**34**	**2.53**	**52**	**33**	**17**	**3167**	**110**	**6**	**2.08**

QMJHL Second All-Star Team (1997) • AHL All-Rookie Team (1998) • Harry "Hap" Holmes Memorial Award (AHL – fewest goals against) (1998) (shared with Tyler Moss) • Conn Smythe Trophy (2003)

Played in NHL All-Star Game (2009)

• Transferred to **Carolina** after **Hartford** franchise relocated, June 25, 1997. Traded to **Calgary** by **Carolina** with Andrew Cassels for Gary Roberts and Trevor Kidd, August 25, 1997. Traded to **Anaheim** by **Calgary** for Anaheim's 2nd round choice (later traded to Washington – Washington selected Matt Pettinger) in 2000 Entry Draft, June 10, 2000. Signed as a free agent by **Hamburg** (Germany), January 31, 2005. Traded to **Toronto** by **Anaheim** for Vesa Toskala and Jason Blake, January 31, 2010. Signed as a free agent by **Colorado**, July 1, 2011.

GOTHBERG, Zane (GAWTH-buhrg, ZAYN) BOS

Goaltender. Catches left. 6'1", 177 lbs. Born, Grand Forks, ND, August 20, 1992.
(Boston's 6th choice, 165th overall, in 2010 Entry Draft).

			Regular Season								Playoffs						
Season	**Club**	**League**	**GP**	**W**	**L**	**O/T**	**Mins**	**GA**	**SO**	**Avg**	**GP**	**W**	**L**	**Mins**	**GA**	**SO**	**Avg**
2007-08	Thief River Falls	High-MN	....	14	12	0	....	....	....	2.15	....	....	....	....	....	....	....
2008-09	Thief River Falls	High-MN	27	20	5	2	1354	....	4	1.49	....	....	....	....	....	....	....
2009-10	Team Great Plains	UMHSEL	5	0	4	0	250	32	0	7.68	....	....	....	....	....	....	....
	Thief River Falls	High-MN	28	18	8	1	1434	51	3	1.84	....	....	....	....	....	....	....
2010-11	Fargo Force	USHL	23	14	8	0	1318	49	2	2.23	1	0	1	55	3	0	3.25

• Signed Letter of Intent to attend **University of North Dakota** (WCHA) in fall of 2011.

GRAHAME, John (GRAY-uhm, JAWN)

Goaltender. Catches left. 6'3", 220 lbs. Born, Denver, CO, August 31, 1975.
(Boston's 7th choice, 229th overall, in 1994 Entry Draft).

			Regular Season								Playoffs						
Season	Club	League	GP	W	L	O/T	Mins	GA	SO	Avg	GP	W	L	Mins	GA	SO	Avg
1993-94	Sioux City	USHL	20	....	....	....	1200	73	0	3.70	....	....	....	....	....	....	....
1994-95	Lake Superior State	CCHA	28	16	7	3	1616	75	2	2.79	....	....	....	....	....	....	....
1995-96	Lake Superior State	CCHA	29	21	4	2	1558	66	2	2.54	....	....	....	....	....	....	....
1996-97	Lake Superior State	CCHA	37	19	13	4	2197	134	3	3.66	....	....	....	....	....	....	....
1997-98	Providence Bruins	AHL	55	15	31	4	3053	164	3	3.22	....	....	....	....	....	....	....
1998-99	Providence Bruins	AHL	48	*37	9	1	2771	134	3	2.90	19	*15	4	*1209	48	1	2.38
99-2000	**Boston**	**NHL**	**24**	**7**	**10**	**5**	**1344**	**55**	**2**	**2.46**	....	....	....	....	....	....	....
	Providence Bruins	AHL	27	11	13	2	1528	86	1	3.38	13	10	3	839	35	0	2.50
2000-01	**Boston**	**NHL**	**10**	**3**	**4**	**0**	**471**	**28**	**0**	**3.57**	....	....	....	....	....	....	....
	Providence Bruins	AHL	16	4	7	3	893	47	0	3.16	17	8	9	1043	46	2	2.65
2001-02	**Boston**	**NHL**	**19**	**8**	**7**	**2**	**1079**	**52**	**1**	**2.89**	....	....	....	....	....	....	....
2002-03	**Boston**	**NHL**	**23**	**11**	**9**	**2**	**1352**	**61**	**1**	**2.71**	....	....	....	....	....	....	....
	Tampa Bay	**NHL**	**17**	**6**	**5**	**4**	**914**	**34**	**2**	**2.23**	**1**	**0**	**1**	**111**	**2**	**0**	**1.08**
2003-04 ♦	**Tampa Bay**	**NHL**	**29**	**18**	**9**	**1**	**1688**	**58**	**1**	**2.06**	**1**	**0**	**0**	**34**	**2**	**0**	**3.53**
2004-05							DID NOT PLAY										
2005-06	**Tampa Bay**	**NHL**	**57**	**29**	**22**	**1**	**3152**	**161**	**5**	**3.06**	**4**	**1**	**3**	**188**	**15**	**0**	**4.79**
	United States	Olympics	1	0	0	1	60	3	0	3.00	....	....	....	....	....	....	....
2006-07	**Carolina**	**NHL**	**28**	**10**	**13**	**2**	**1515**	**72**	**0**	**2.85**	....	....	....	....	....	....	....
2007-08	**Carolina**	**NHL**	**17**	**5**	**7**	**1**	**848**	**53**	**0**	**3.75**	....	....	....	....	....	....	....
	Albany River Rats	AHL	7	4	3	0	415	21	0	3.04	....	....	....	....	....	....	....
2008-09	Omsk	Rus-KHL	20	9	10	0	1195	57	3	2.86	....	....	....	....	....	....	....
2009-10	Adirondack	AHL	12	2	10	0	717	34	0	2.84	....	....	....	....	....	....	....
	Lake Erie Monsters	AHL	14	4	7	3	837	48	0	3.44	....	....	....	....	....	....	....
2010-11	Lake Erie Monsters	AHL	34	19	12	2	2009	80	1	2.39	5	2	3	303	13	0	2.58
	NHL Totals		**224**	**97**	**86**	**18**	**12363**	**574**	**12**	**2.79**	**6**	**1**	**4**	**333**	**19**	**0**	**3.42**

Traded to **Tampa Bay** by **Boston** for Tampa Bay's 4th round choice (later traded to San Jose – San Jose selected Jason Churchill) in 2004 Entry Draft, January 13, 2003. Signed as a free agent by **Carolina**, July 1, 2006. Signed as a free agent by **Omsk** (Russia-KHL), May 17, 2008. Signed to a PTO (professional tryout) contract by **Adirondack** (AHL), December 13, 2009. Signed as a free agent by **Colorado**, March 3, 2010.

GREISS, Thomas (GRIGHS, TAW-muhs) S.J.

Goaltender. Catches left. 6'1", 210 lbs. Born, Straubing, West Germany, January 29, 1986.
(San Jose's 2nd choice, 94th overall, in 2004 Entry Draft).

			Regular Season								Playoffs						
Season	Club	League	GP	W	L	O/T	Mins	GA	SO	Avg	GP	W	L	Mins	GA	SO	Avg
2001-02	EV Fussen Jr.	Ger-Jr.					STATISTICS NOT AVAILABLE										
2002-03	Koln Jr.	Ger-Jr.	25	....	....	....	1613	58	0	2.16	3	1	2	180	8	1	2.67
2003-04	Koln Jr.	Ger-Jr.	24	....	....	....	1286	56	....	2.61	....	....	....	....	....	....	....
	Kolner Haie	Germany	1	....	....	....	20	4	0	12.00	....	....	....	....	....	....	....
2004-05	Kolner Haie	Germany	8	....	....	....	459	16	0	2.09	....	....	....	....	....	....	....
	Regensburg	German-2	1	....	....	....	60	2	0	2.00	2	....	....	56	2	0	2.14
2005-06	Kolner Haie	Germany	27	....	....	....	1560	64	1	2.46	9	....	....	533	27	*1	3.04
	Germany	Olympics	1	0	1	0	60	5	0	5.00	....	....	....	....	....	....	....
2006-07	Worcester Sharks	AHL	43	26	15	2	2555	111	0	2.61	3	0	3	172	12	0	4.18
	Fresno Falcons	ECHL	3	1	2	0	180	7	0	2.34	....	....	....	....	....	....	....
2007-08	**San Jose**	**NHL**	**3**	**0**	**1**	**1**	**129**	**7**	**0**	**3.26**	....	....	....	....	....	....	....
	Worcester Sharks	AHL	41	18	21	2	2424	125	0	3.09	....	....	....	....	....	....	....
2008-09	Worcester Sharks	AHL	57	30	24	2	3346	138	1	2.47	12	6	6	742	30	2	2.43
2009-10	**San Jose**	**NHL**	**16**	**7**	**4**	**1**	**782**	**35**	**0**	**2.69**	**1**	**0**	**0**	**40**	**2**	**0**	**3.00**
	Germany	Olympics	3	0	3	0	179	15	0	5.03	....	....	....	....	....	....	....
2010-11	Brynas IF Gavle	Sweden	32	....	....	....	1850	90	2	2.92	5	....	....	317	18	0	3.40
	NHL Totals		**19**	**7**	**5**	**2**	**911**	**42**	**0**	**2.77**	**1**	**0**	**0**	**40**	**2**	**0**	**3.00**

• Assigned to **Brynas** (Sweden) by **San Jose**, October 21, 2010.

GRUBAUER, Philipp (groo-BAHW-uhr, FIHL-ihp) WSH

Goaltender. Catches left. 6', 170 lbs. Born, Rosenheim, Germany, November 25, 1991.
(Washington's 3rd choice, 112th overall, in 2010 Entry Draft).

			Regular Season								Playoffs						
Season	Club	League	GP	W	L	O/T	Mins	GA	SO	Avg	GP	W	L	Mins	GA	SO	Avg
2006-07	Rosenheim Jr.	Ger-Jr.	6	....	....	....	354	49	....	8.32	3	....	....	180	12	....	4.00
2007-08	Rosenheim Jr.	Ger-Jr.	23	....	....	....	1288	71	....	3.31	3	....	....	181	8	....	2.65
	Rosenheim	German-3	5	....	....	....	307	14	1	2.74	7	....	....	420	12	....	1.71
2008-09	Belleville Bulls	OHL	17	7	8	0	947	62	1	3.93	1	0	0	56	4	0	4.26
2009-10	Belleville Bulls	OHL	31	10	14	5	1717	90	5	3.14	....	....	....	....	....	....	....
	Windsor Spitfires	OHL	19	13	1	2	1011	40	2	2.37	18	*16	2	1094	49	0	2.69
2010-11	Kingston	OHL	38	22	13	3	2239	135	2	3.62	....	....	....	....	....	....	....

GUSTAFSSON, Johan (GUHS-tahf-suhn, YOH-han) MIN

Goaltender. Catches left. 6'2", 202 lbs. Born, Koping, Sweden, February 28, 1992.
(Minnesota's 5th choice, 159th overall, in 2010 Entry Draft).

			Regular Season								Playoffs						
Season	Club	League	GP	W	L	O/T	Mins	GA	SO	Avg	GP	W	L	Mins	GA	SO	Avg
2006-07	IFK Arboga IK	Sweden-2	4	....	....	....	201	22	0	6.55	....	....	....	....	....	....	....
2007-08	Kopings HC	Sweden-4					STATISTICS NOT AVAILABLE										
2008-09	Farjestad U18	Swe-U18	27	....	....	....	1581	47	5	1.78	4	....	....	228	14	0	3.68
2009-10	Farjestad U18	Swe-U18	10	....	....	....	600	34	1	3.40	7	....	....	417	22	0	3.16
	Farjestad	Sweden	3	....	....	....	136	9	0	3.96	....	....	....	....	....	....	....
	Skare BK	Sweden-3	26	....	....	....	1553	74	2	2.86	....	....	....	....	....	....	....
2010-11	VIK Vasteras HK Jr.	Swe-Jr.	7	....	....	....	424	20	1	2.83	....	....	....	....	....	....	....
	VIK Vasteras HK	Sweden-2	28	....	....	....	1632	64	2	2.35	....	....	....	....	....	....	....

GUSTAVSSON, Jonas (GUHS-tahv-suhn, YOH-nuhs) TOR

Goaltender. Catches left. 6'3", 192 lbs. Born, Danderyd, Sweden, October 24, 1984.

			Regular Season								Playoffs						
Season	Club	League	GP	W	L	O/T	Mins	GA	SO	Avg	GP	W	L	Mins	GA	SO	Avg
2000-01	AIK Solna U18	Swe-U18	12	....	....	....	667	42	1	3.78	....	....	....	....	....	....	....
2001-02	AIK Solna U18	Swe-U18	8	....	....	....	439	13	2	1.78	4	....	....	239	12	0	3.01
2002-03	AIK Solna Jr.	Swe-Jr.	21	....	....	....	1261	69	0	3.28	4	....	....	198	9	0	2.72
2003-04	AIK Solna Jr.	Swe-Jr.	9	....	....	....	505	24	0	2.85	....	....	....	....	....	....	....
	AIK Solna	Sweden-2	1	....	....	....	20	1	0	2.95	....	....	....	....	....	....	....
2004-05	AIK Solna Jr.	Swe-Jr.	10	....	....	....	557	32	0	3.45	....	....	....	....	....	....	....
	AIK Solna	Sweden-3	22	....	....	....	1270	32	4	1.51	....	....	....	....	....	....	....
2005-06	AIK Solna Jr.	Swe-Jr.	5	....	....	....	258	14	0	3.26	....	....	....	....	....	....	....
	AIK Solna	Sweden-2	6	....	....	....	351	14	0	2.39	....	....	....	....	....	....	....
2006-07	AIK IF Solna	Sweden-2	23	....	....	....	1269	59	2	2.79	....	....	....	....	....	....	....
2007-08	Skare BK	Sweden-3	6	....	....	....	368	16	0	2.61	....	....	....	....	....	....	....
	Farjestad	Sweden	20	....	....	....	1102	44	2	2.40	10	....	....	517	31	0	3.60
2008-09	Farjestad	Sweden	42	....	....	....	2475	81	3	*1.96	13	....	....	819	14	*5	*1.03
2009-10	**Toronto**	**NHL**	**42**	**16**	**15**	**9**	**2340**	**112**	**1**	**2.87**	....	....	....	....	....	....	....
	Sweden	Olympics	1	1	0	0	60	2	0	2.00	....	....	....	....	....	....	....
2010-11	**Toronto**	**NHL**	**23**	**6**	**13**	**2**	**1242**	**68**	**0**	**3.29**	....	....	....	....	....	....	....
	Toronto Marlies	AHL	5	3	1	1	263	5	0	1.14	....	....	....	....	....	....	....
	NHL Totals		**65**	**22**	**28**	**11**	**3582**	**180**	**1**	**3.02**	....	....	....	....	....	....	....

Signed as a free agent by **Toronto**, July 7, 2009.

HACKETT, Matt (HA-keht, MA-thew) MIN

Goaltender. Catches left. 6'2", 180 lbs. Born, London, Ont., March 7, 1990.
(Minnesota's 2nd choice, 77th overall, in 2009 Entry Draft).

			Regular Season								Playoffs						
Season	Club	League	GP	W	L	O/T	Mins	GA	SO	Avg	GP	W	L	Mins	GA	SO	Avg
2006-07	London Jr. Knights	Minor-ON	38	28	7	3	....	52	20	1.39	6	5	1	....	12	2	2.00
	St. Catharines	ON-Jr.B	16	7	7	0	902	63	0	4.19	....	....	....	....	....	....	....
	Windsor Spitfires	OHL	7	0	7	0	429	36	0	5.04	....	....	....	....	....	....	....
2007-08	Windsor Spitfires	OHL	4	1	1	0	130	10	0	4.61	....	....	....	....	....	....	....
	Plymouth Whalers	OHL	18	6	9	1	978	56	0	3.44	1	0	0	16	0	0	0.00
2008-09	Plymouth Whalers	OHL	55	34	15	3	3036	154	2	3.04	11	6	5	638	32	*1	3.01
2009-10	Plymouth Whalers	OHL	56	33	18	3	3165	138	4	2.62	8	3	4	429	24	0	3.36
2010-11	Houston Aeros	AHL	45	23	16	4	2552	101	2	2.37	*24	*14	10	*1465	61	1	2.50

OHL Second All-Star Team (2010)

HALAK, Jaroslav (HA-lak, YAHR-roh-slav) ST.L.

Goaltender. Catches left. 5'11", 185 lbs. Born, Bratislava, Czech., May 13, 1985.
(Montreal's 11th choice, 271st overall, in 2003 Entry Draft).

			Regular Season								Playoffs						
Season	Club	League	GP	W	L	O/T	Mins	GA	SO	Avg	GP	W	L	Mins	GA	SO	Avg
2001-02	Bratislava Jr.	Slovak-Jr.	22	....	....	....	1257	41	0	1.96	6	6	0	353	7	2	1.19
2002-03	Bratislava Jr.	Slovak-Jr.	20	13	3	3	1200	41	1	2.02	....	....	....	....	....	....	....
2003-04	Bratislava Jr.	Slovak-Jr.	29	....	....	....	1694	51	....	1.81	....	....	....	....	....	....	....
	HK 91 Senica	Slovak-2	21	....	....	....	1240	54	....	2.61	....	....	....	....	....	....	....
	Bratislava	Slovakia	12	....	....	....	650	18	0	1.66	1	....	....	45	6	0	8.00
2004-05	Lewiston	QMJHL	47	24	17	4	2697	125	4	2.78	8	4	4	460	27	0	3.52
2005-06	Hamilton Bulldogs	AHL	13	7	6	0	786	30	3	2.29	....	....	....	....	....	....	....
	Long Beach	ECHL	20	11	4	2	1026	35	2	2.05	4	2	2	252	13	0	3.10
2006-07	**Montreal**	**NHL**	**16**	**10**	**6**	**0**	**912**	**44**	**2**	**2.89**	....	....	....	....	....	....	....
	Hamilton Bulldogs	AHL	28	16	11	0	1618	54	6	*2.00	....	....	....	....	....	....	....
2007-08	**Montreal**	**NHL**	**6**	**2**	**1**	**1**	**285**	**10**	**1**	**2.11**	**2**	**0**	**1**	**77**	**3**	**0**	**2.34**
	Hamilton Bulldogs	AHL	28	15	10	2	1630	57	2	2.10	....	....	....	....	....	....	....
2008-09	**Montreal**	**NHL**	**34**	**18**	**14**	**1**	**1931**	**92**	**1**	**2.86**	**1**	**0**	**0**	**20**	**0**	**0**	**0.00**
2009-10	**Montreal**	**NHL**	**45**	**26**	**13**	**5**	**2630**	**105**	**5**	**2.40**	**18**	**9**	**9**	**1013**	**43**	**0**	**2.55**
	Slovakia	Olympics	7	3	4	0	423	17	1	2.41	....	....	....	....	....	....	....
2010-11	**St. Louis**	**NHL**	**57**	**27**	**21**	**7**	**3294**	**136**	**7**	**2.48**	....	....	....	....	....	....	....
	NHL Totals		**158**	**83**	**55**	**14**	**9052**	**387**	**16**	**2.57**	**21**	**9**	**10**	**1110**	**46**	**0**	**2.49**

AHL All-Rookie Team (2007)

Traded to **St. Louis** by **Montreal** for Lars Eller and Ian Schultz, June 17, 2010.

HARDING, Josh (HAHR-dihng, JAWSH) MIN

Goaltender. Catches right. 6'1", 197 lbs. Born, Regina, Sask., June 18, 1984.
(Minnesota's 2nd choice, 38th overall, in 2002 Entry Draft).

			Regular Season								Playoffs						
Season	Club	League	GP	W	L	O/T	Mins	GA	SO	Avg	GP	W	L	Mins	GA	SO	Avg
2000-01	Reg. Pat Cdns.	SMHL	36	17	13	0	2106	96	2	2.75	3	1	2	170	11	0	3.88
2001-02	Regina Pats	WHL	42	27	13	1	2389	95	*4	2.39	6	2	4	326	16	0	2.95
2002-03	Regina Pats	WHL	57	18	25	13	*3384	155	3	2.75	5	1	4	320	13	0	2.44
2003-04	Regina Pats	WHL	28	12	14	2	1664	67	2	2.42	....	....	....	....	....	....	....
	Brandon	WHL	27	13	11	3	1612	65	5	2.42	11	5	6	660	36	0	3.27
2004-05	Houston Aeros	AHL	42	21	16	3	2388	80	4	2.01	2	0	2	119	8	0	4.03
2005-06	**Minnesota**	**NHL**	**3**	**2**	**1**	**0**	**185**	**8**	**1**	**2.59**	....	....	....	....	....	....	....
	Houston Aeros	AHL	38	29	8	0	2215	99	2	2.68	8	4	4	476	30	0	3.79
2006-07	**Minnesota**	**NHL**	**7**	**3**	**2**	**1**	**361**	**7**	**1**	**1.16**	....	....	....	....	....	....	....
	Houston Aeros	AHL	38	17	16	4	2270	94	1	2.48	....	....	....	....	....	....	....
2007-08	**Minnesota**	**NHL**	**29**	**11**	**15**	**2**	**1571**	**77**	**1**	**2.94**	**1**	**0**	**0**	**20**	**0**	**0**	**0.00**
2008-09	**Minnesota**	**NHL**	**19**	**3**	**9**	**1**	**870**	**32**	**0**	**2.21**	....	....	....	....	....	....	....
2009-10	**Minnesota**	**NHL**	**25**	**9**	**12**	**0**	**1300**	**66**	**1**	**3.05**	....	....	....	....	....	....	....
2010-11	**Minnesota**	**NHL**					DID NOT PLAY – INJURED										
	NHL Totals		**83**	**28**	**39**	**4**	**4287**	**190**	**4**	**2.66**	**1**	**0**	**0**	**20**	**0**	**0**	**0.00**

WHL East Second All-Star Team (2002) • WHL East First All-Star Team (2003) • WHL Goaltender of the Year (2003) • WHL Player of the Year (2003) • Canadian Major Junior Second All-Star Team (2003)

• Missed 2010-11 due to knee injury in pre-season at St. Louis, September 24, 2010.

HEDBERG, Johan (HEHD-buhrg, YOH-han) N.J.

Goaltender. Catches left. 6', 190 lbs. Born, Stockholm, Sweden, May 5, 1973.
(Philadelphia's 8th choice, 218th overall, in 1994 Entry Draft).

			Regular Season								Playoffs						
Season	Club	League	GP	W	L	O/T	Mins	GA	SO	Avg	GP	W	L	Mins	GA	SO	Avg
1992-93	Leksands IF	Sweden	10	....	....	....	600	24	....	2.40	....	....	....	....	....	....	....
1993-94	Leksands IF	Sweden	17	....	....	....	1020	48	....	2.82	....	....	....	....	....	....	....
1994-95	Leksands IF	Sweden	17	....	....	....	986	58	....	3.53	....	....	....	....	....	....	....
1995-96	Leksands IF	Sweden	34	....	....	....	2013	95	....	2.83	4	....	....	240	13	....	3.25
1996-97	Leksands IF	Sweden	38	....	....	....	2260	95	3	2.52	8	....	....	581	18	1	1.86
1997-98	Detroit Vipers	IHL	16	7	2	2	726	32	1	2.64	....	....	....	....	....	....	....
	Baton Rouge	ECHL	2	1	1	0	100	7	0	4.20	....	....	....	....	....	....	....
	Manitoba Moose	IHL	14	8	4	1	745	32	1	2.58	2	0	2	105	6	0	3.40
	Sweden	Olympics					DID NOT PLAY – SPARE GOALTENDER										
1998-99	Leksands IF	Sweden	*48	....	....	....	*2940	140	0	2.86	4	....	....	255	15	0	3.53
99-2000	Kentucky	AHL	33	18	9	5	1973	88	3	2.68	5	3	2	311	10	1	1.93
2000-01	Manitoba Moose	IHL	46	23	13	7	2697	115	1	2.56	....	....	....	....	....	....	....
	Pittsburgh	**NHL**	**9**	**7**	**1**	**1**	**545**	**24**	**0**	**2.64**	**18**	**9**	**9**	**1123**	**43**	**2**	**2.30**
2001-02	**Pittsburgh**	**NHL**	**66**	**25**	**34**	**7**	**3877**	**178**	**6**	**2.75**	....	....	....	....	....	....	....
	Sweden	Olympics	1	1	0	0	60	1	0	1.00	....	....	....	....	....	....	....
2002-03	**Pittsburgh**	**NHL**	**41**	**14**	**22**	**4**	**2410**	**126**	**1**	**3.14**	....	....	....	....	....	....	....
2003-04	**Vancouver**	**NHL**	**21**	**8**	**6**	**2**	**1098**	**46**	**3**	**2.51**	**2**	**1**	**1**	**98**	**4**	**0**	**2.45**
	Manitoba Moose	AHL	2	0	2	0	125	9	0	4.32	....	....	....	....	....	....	....
2004-05	Leksands IF	Sweden-2	21	....	....	....	1274	45	1	2.12	....	....	....	....	....	....	....
2005-06	**Dallas**	**NHL**	**19**	**12**	**4**	**1**	**1079**	**48**	**0**	**2.67**	....	....	....	....	....	....	....
2006-07	**Atlanta**	**NHL**	**21**	**9**	**4**	**2**	**1057**	**51**	**0**	**2.89**	**2**	**0**	**2**	**117**	**5**	**0**	**2.56**
2007-08	**Atlanta**	**NHL**	**36**	**14**	**15**	**3**	**1927**	**111**	**1**	**3.46**	....	....	....	....	....	....	....
2008-09	**Atlanta**	**NHL**	**33**	**13**	**12**	**3**	**1717**	**100**	**0**	**3.49**	....	....	....	....	....	....	....
2009-10	**Atlanta**	**NHL**	**47**	**21**	**16**	**6**	**2632**	**115**	**3**	**2.62**	....	....	....	....	....	....	....
2010-11	**New Jersey**	**NHL**	**34**	**15**	**12**	**2**	**1717**	**68**	**3**	**2.38**	....	....	....	....	....	....	....
	NHL Totals		**327**	**138**	**126**	**31**	**18059**	**867**	**17**	**2.88**	**22**	**10**	**12**	**1338**	**52**	**2**	**2.33**

• Rights traded to **San Jose** by **Philadelphia** for San Jose's 7th round choice (Pavel Kasparik) in 1999 Entry Draft, August 6, 1998. Traded to **Pittsburgh** by **San Jose** with Bobby Dollas for Jeff Norton, March 12, 2001. Traded to **Vancouver** by **Pittsburgh** for Vancouver's 2nd round choice (Alex Goligoski) in 2004 Entry Draft, August 25, 2003. Signed as a free agent by **Leksands** (Sweden-2), August 1, 2004. Signed as a free agent by **Dallas**, August 5, 2005. Signed as a free agent by **Atlanta**, July 1, 2006. Signed as a free agent by **New Jersey**, July 1, 2010.

HEEMSKERK, Thomas (HEEMZ-kuhrk, TAW-muhs) S.J.

Goaltender. Catches left. 6', 195 lbs. Born, Chilliwack, B.C., April 11, 1990.

			Regular Season								Playoffs						
Season	**Club**	**League**	**GP**	**W**	**L**	**O/T**	**Mins**	**GA**	**SO**	**Avg**	**GP**	**W**	**L**	**Mins**	**GA**	**SO**	**Avg**
2006-07	Fraser Valley Bruins	BCMML	20	....	....	....	1125	68	1	3.31	....	....	....	....	....	....	....
2007-08	Kootenay Ice	WHL	27	15	4	3	1379	61	1	2.65	....	....	....	....	....	....	....
2008-09	Kootenay Ice	WHL	18	7	6	4	978	47	0	2.88	....	....	....	....	....	....	....
	Everett Silvertips	WHL	27	9	15	2	1481	82	2	3.32	5	1	4	306	22	0	4.31
2009-10	Everett Silvertips	WHL	42	24	12	4	2415	94	4	2.34	2	1	1	146	9	0	3.70
2010-11	Moose Jaw	WHL	65	36	21	6	3841	188	2	2.94	6	2	4	357	15	2	2.52

Signed as a free agent by **San Jose**, September 29, 2009.

HELENIUS, Riku (heh-lehn-NEE-uhs, REE-koo) T.B.

Goaltender. Catches left. 6'3", 211 lbs. Born, Palkane, Finland, March 1, 1988.
(Tampa Bay's 1st choice, 15th overall, in 2006 Entry Draft).

			Regular Season								Playoffs						
Season	**Club**	**League**	**GP**	**W**	**L**	**O/T**	**Mins**	**GA**	**SO**	**Avg**	**GP**	**W**	**L**	**Mins**	**GA**	**SO**	**Avg**
2004-05	Ilves Tampere U18	Fin-U18	16	....	....	....	903	30	3	1.99	5	....	....	295	15	0	3.05
	Ilves Tampere Jr.	Fin-Jr.	2	....	....	....	86	4	0	2.77	....	....	....	....	....	....	....
2005-06	Suomi U20	Finland-2	1	....	....	....	60	3	0	3.00	....	....	....	....	....	....	....
	Ilves Tampere U18	Fin-U18	2	....	....	....	120	2	0	1.00	5	....	....	300	13	0	2.60
	Ilves Tampere Jr.	Fin-Jr.	26	....	....	....	1565	70	4	2.68	2	....	....	135	7	0	3.11
2006-07	Ilves Tampere Jr.	Fin-Jr.	2	2	0	0	120	4	0	2.00	....	....	....	....	....	....	....
2007-08	Seattle	WHL	41	22	12	6	2358	95	3	2.42	9	4	5	534	24	0	2.70
2008-09	**Tampa Bay**	**NHL**	**1**	**0**	**0**	**0**	**7**	**0**	**0**	**0.00**	....	....	....	....	....	....	....
	Norfolk Admirals	AHL	25	9	15	0	1388	63	1	2.72	....	....	....	....	....	....	....
	Augusta Lynx	ECHL	8	3	4	1	463	34	0	4.41	....	....	....	....	....	....	....
	Mississippi	ECHL	3	1	1	1	184	7	0	2.28	....	....	....	....	....	....	....
	Elmira Jackals	ECHL	....	....	....	....	....	....	....	....	2	0	1	87	10	0	6.91
2009-10	Norfolk Admirals	AHL	12	5	7	0	719	33	0	2.75	....	....	....	....	....	....	....
	Sodertalje SK	Sweden	9	....	....	....	545	22	0	2.42	....	....	....	....	....	....	....
	Sodertalje SK	Sweden-Q	9	....	....	....	548	25	1	2.74	....	....	....	....	....	....	....
2010-11	Sodertalje SK	Sweden	18	....	....	....	911	46	0	3.03	....	....	....	....	....	....	....
	Sodertalje SK	Sweden-Q	5	....	....	....	198	7	0	2.23	....	....	....	....	....	....	....
	NHL Totals		**1**	**0**	**0**	**0**	**7**	**0**	**0**	**0.00**	....	....	....	....	....	....	....

• Assigned to **Sodertalje** (Sweden) by **Tampa Bay**, January 24, 2010.

HELLBERG, Magnus (HEHL-buhrg, MAG-nuhs) NSH

Goaltender. Catches left. 6'5", 185 lbs. Born, Uppsala, Sweden, April 4, 1991.
(Nashville's 1st choice, 38th overall, in 2011 Entry Draft).

			Regular Season								Playoffs						
Season	**Club**	**League**	**GP**	**W**	**L**	**O/T**	**Mins**	**GA**	**SO**	**Avg**	**GP**	**W**	**L**	**Mins**	**GA**	**SO**	**Avg**
2007-08	Arlanda U18	Swe-U18	11	....	....	....	....	....	....	....	....	....	....	....	....	....	....
	Arlanda Jr.	Swe-Jr.	1	....	....	....	....	....	....	8.00	....	....	....	....	....	....	....
2008-09	Arlanda U18	Swe-U18	33	....	....	....	1979	103	2	3.12	....	....	....	....	....	....	....
	Wings HC Arlanda	Sweden-3	2	....	....	....	119	7	0	3.52	....	....	....	....	....	....	....
2009-10	Almtuna Jr.	Swe-Jr.	22	....	....	....	1339	44	2	1.97	....	....	....	....	....	....	....
	IF Vallentuna BK	Sweden-3	1	....	....	....	24	3	0	7.57	....	....	....	....	....	....	....
2010-11	IFK Kumla IK	Sweden-3	3	....	....	....	179	6	0	2.01	....	....	....	....	....	....	....
	Almtuna	Sweden-2	31	....	....	....	1790	61	5	2.04	5	....	....	277	15	0	3.24

HILLER, Jonas (HIHL-uhr, YOH-nuhs) ANA

Goaltender. Catches right. 6'2", 194 lbs. Born, Felben Wellhausen, Switz., February 12, 1982.

			Regular Season								Playoffs						
Season	**Club**	**League**	**GP**	**W**	**L**	**O/T**	**Mins**	**GA**	**SO**	**Avg**	**GP**	**W**	**L**	**Mins**	**GA**	**SO**	**Avg**
2000-01	HC Davos	Swiss	1	0	0	0	9	0	0	0.00	....	....	....	....	....	....	....
2001-02	HC Davos	Swiss					Did not play										
2002-03	HC Davos	Swiss					Did not play										
2003-04	Lausanne HC	Swiss	21	....	....	....	1161	64	1	3.31	....	....	....	....	....	....	....
	Chaux-de-Fonds	Swiss-2	1	0	1	0	60	4	0	4.00	....	....	....	....	....	....	....
	Lausanne HC	Swiss-Q	....	....	....	....	....	....	....	....	4	4	0	251	7	0	1.67
2004-05	HC Davos	Swiss	43	26	12	4	2519	95	*8	2.26	*15	12	3	*932	34	0	*2.19
2005-06	HC Davos	Swiss	*44	23	16	5	*2676	110	3	2.47	15	9	6	900	45	1	3.00
2006-07	HC Davos	Swiss	*44	*28	16	0	*2656	115	3	2.60	*19	*12	7	*1138	39	3	2.05
2007-08	**Anaheim**	**NHL**	**23**	**10**	**7**	**1**	**1223**	**42**	**0**	**2.06**	....	....	....	....	....	....	....
	Portland Pirates	AHL	6	3	2	1	370	13	0	2.11	....	....	....	....	....	....	....
2008-09	**Anaheim**	**NHL**	**46**	**23**	**15**	**1**	**2486**	**99**	**4**	**2.39**	**13**	**7**	**6**	**807**	**30**	***2**	**2.23**
2009-10	**Anaheim**	**NHL**	**59**	**30**	**23**	**4**	**3338**	**152**	**2**	**2.73**	....	....	....	....	....	....	....
	Switzerland	Olympics	5	2	3	0	316	13	0	2.47	....	....	....	....	....	....	....
2010-11	**Anaheim**	**NHL**	**49**	**26**	**16**	**3**	**2672**	**114**	**5**	**2.56**	....	....	....	....	....	....	....
	NHL Totals		**177**	**89**	**61**	**9**	**9719**	**407**	**11**	**2.51**	**13**	**7**	**6**	**807**	**30**	**2**	**2.23**

Signed as a free agent by **Anaheim**, May 25, 2007.

Played in NHL All-Star Game (2011)

HOLTBY, Braden (HOHLT-bee, BRAY-duhn) WSH

Goaltender. Catches left. 6'1", 209 lbs. Born, Lloydminster, Sask., September 16, 1989.
(Washington's 5th choice, 93rd overall, in 2008 Entry Draft).

			Regular Season								Playoffs						
Season	**Club**	**League**	**GP**	**W**	**L**	**O/T**	**Mins**	**GA**	**SO**	**Avg**	**GP**	**W**	**L**	**Mins**	**GA**	**SO**	**Avg**
2005-06	Saskatoon Blazers	SMHL					Statistics not available										
	Saskatoon Blades	WHL	1	0	1	0	59	4	0	4.07	....	....	....	....	....	....	....
2006-07	Saskatoon Blades	WHL	51	17	29	3	2725	146	0	3.21	....	....	....	....	....	....	....
2007-08	Saskatoon Blades	WHL	*64	25	29	8	3632	172	1	2.84	....	....	....	....	....	....	....
2008-09	Saskatoon Blades	WHL	*61	40	16	4	*3571	156	6	2.62	7	3	4	414	16	0	2.32
2009-10	Hershey Bears	AHL	37	25	8	2	2146	83	2	2.32	3	2	1	200	12	0	3.60
	South Carolina	ECHL	12	7	2	3	712	35	0	2.95	....	....	....	....	....	....	....
2010-11	**Washington**	**NHL**	**14**	**10**	**2**	**2**	**736**	**22**	**2**	**1.79**	....	....	....	....	....	....	....
	Hershey Bears	AHL	30	17	10	2	1785	68	5	2.29	6	2	4	359	18	0	3.01
	NHL Totals		**14**	**10**	**2**	**2**	**736**	**22**	**2**	**1.79**	....	....	....	....	....	....	....

WHL East First All-Star Team (2009)

HONZIK, David (HAWN-zihk, DAY-vihd) VAN

Goaltender. Catches left. 6'3", 209 lbs. Born, Milevsko, Czech Republic, August 9, 1993.
(Vancouver's 2nd choice, 71st overall, in 2011 Entry Draft).

			Regular Season								Playoffs						
Season	**Club**	**League**	**GP**	**W**	**L**	**O/T**	**Mins**	**GA**	**SO**	**Avg**	**GP**	**W**	**L**	**Mins**	**GA**	**SO**	**Avg**
2008-09	Karlovy Vary U17	CzR-U17	32	....	....	....	1762	78	1	2.66	2	....	....	129	10	0	4.65
2009-10	Karlovy Vary U18	CzR-U18	38	....	....	....	2174	95	2	2.62	3	....	....	190	8	0	2.53
	Karlovy Vary Jr.	CzRep-Jr.	1	....	....	....	60	1	0	1.00	....	....	....	....	....	....	....
2010-11	Victoriaville Tigres	QMJHL	36	17	12	1	1781	105	1	3.54	9	5	4	548	30	0	3.28

HOWARD, Jimmy (HOW-uhrd, JIHM-ee) DET

Goaltender. Catches left. 6', 210 lbs. Born, Syracuse, NY, March 26, 1984.
(Detroit's 1st choice, 64th overall, in 2003 Entry Draft).

			Regular Season								Playoffs						
Season	**Club**	**League**	**GP**	**W**	**L**	**O/T**	**Mins**	**GA**	**SO**	**Avg**	**GP**	**W**	**L**	**Mins**	**GA**	**SO**	**Avg**
2001-02	USNTDP	U-18	19	15	4	1	1170	37	4	1.90	....	....	....	....	....	....	....
	USNTDP	USHL	8	4	3	0	425	14	0	1.98	....	....	....	....	....	....	....
	USNTDP	NAHL	8	3	4	0	381	25	0	3.93	....	....	....	....	....	....	....
2002-03	University of Maine	H-East	21	14	6	0	1151	47	3	2.45	....	....	....	....	....	....	....
2003-04	University of Maine	H-East	23	14	4	3	1364	27	*6	*1.19	....	....	....	....	....	....	....
2004-05	University of Maine	H-East	*39	*19	13	7	*2310	74	*6	1.92	....	....	....	....	....	....	....
2005-06	**Detroit**	**NHL**	**4**	**1**	**2**	**0**	**201**	**10**	**0**	**2.99**	....	....	....	....	....	....	....
	Grand Rapids	AHL	38	27	6	2	2140	92	2	2.58	13	5	7	763	44	0	3.46
2006-07	Grand Rapids	AHL	49	21	21	3	2776	125	6	2.70	7	3	4	434	14	0	*1.93
2007-08	**Detroit**	**NHL**	**4**	**0**	**2**	**0**	**197**	**7**	**0**	**2.13**	....	....	....	....	....	....	....
	Grand Rapids	AHL	54	21	28	2	3097	146	2	2.83	....	....	....	....	....	....	....
2008-09	**Detroit**	**NHL**	**1**	**0**	**1**	**0**	**59**	**4**	**0**	**4.07**	....	....	....	....	....	....	....
	Grand Rapids	AHL	45	21	18	4	2644	112	4	2.54	10	4	6	598	24	0	2.41
2009-10	**Detroit**	**NHL**	**63**	**37**	**15**	**10**	**3740**	**141**	**3**	**2.26**	**12**	**5**	**7**	**720**	**33**	**1**	**2.75**
2010-11	**Detroit**	**NHL**	**63**	**37**	**17**	**5**	**3615**	**168**	**2**	**2.79**	**11**	**7**	**4**	**673**	**28**	**0**	**2.50**
	NHL Totals		**135**	**75**	**37**	**15**	**7812**	**330**	**5**	**2.53**	**23**	**12**	**11**	**1393**	**61**	**1**	**2.63**

Hockey East All-Rookie Team (2003) • Hockey East Rookie of the Year (2003) • Hockey East First All-Star Team (2004) • NCAA East Second All-American Team (2004) • AHL All-Rookie Team (2006) • NHL All-Rookie Team (2010)

HUET, Cristobal (hew-AY, KRIHS-toh-bahl) CHI

Goaltender. Catches left. 6'1", 206 lbs. Born, St. Martin d'Heres, France, September 3, 1975.
(Los Angeles' 9th choice, 214th overall, in 2001 Entry Draft).

			Regular Season								Playoffs						
Season	**Club**	**League**	**GP**	**W**	**L**	**O/T**	**Mins**	**GA**	**SO**	**Avg**	**GP**	**W**	**L**	**Mins**	**GA**	**SO**	**Avg**
1997-98	CSG Grenoble	France					Statistics not available										
	France	Olympics	2	1	1	0	120	5	0	2.50	....	....	....	....	....	....	....
1998-99	HC Lugano	Swiss	21	....	....	....	1275	58	1	2.73	10	....	....	628	18	1	*1.72
99-2000	HC Lugano	Swiss	31	....	....	....	1886	50	*8	*1.59	13	....	....	783	29	0	2.22
2000-01	HC Lugano	Swiss	39	....	....	....	2365	77	*6	*1.95	*18	....	....	*1141	39	2	2.05
2001-02	HC Lugano	Swiss	39	....	....	....	2313	107	*4	2.78	1	0	1	60	3	0	3.00
	France	Olympics	3	0	2	1	179	10	0	3.36	....	....	....	....	....	....	....
	France	WC-B	5	4	1	0	299	5	2	1.00	....	....	....	....	....	....	....
2002-03	**Los Angeles**	**NHL**	**12**	**4**	**4**	**1**	**541**	**21**	**1**	**2.33**	....	....	....	....	....	....	....
	Manchester	AHL	30	16	8	5	1784	68	1	2.29	1	0	1	30	4	0	8.08
2003-04	**Los Angeles**	**NHL**	**41**	**10**	**16**	**10**	**2199**	**89**	**3**	**2.43**	....	....	....	....	....	....	....
2004-05	Adler Mannheim	Germany	36	....	....	....	2001	93	1	2.79	*14	....	....	*850	40	2	2.82
2005-06	**Montreal**	**NHL**	**36**	**18**	**11**	**4**	**2103**	**77**	**7**	**2.20**	**6**	**2**	**4**	**386**	**15**	**0**	**2.33**
	Hamilton Bulldogs	AHL	4	0	4	0	237	15	0	3.79	....	....	....	....	....	....	....
2006-07	**Montreal**	**NHL**	**42**	**19**	**16**	**3**	**2286**	**107**	**2**	**2.81**	....	....	....	....	....	....	....
2007-08	**Montreal**	**NHL**	**39**	**21**	**12**	**6**	**2278**	**97**	**2**	**2.55**	....	....	....	....	....	....	....
	Washington	**NHL**	**13**	**11**	**2**	**0**	**771**	**21**	**2**	**1.63**	**7**	**3**	**4**	**451**	**22**	**0**	**2.93**
2008-09	**Chicago**	**NHL**	**41**	**20**	**15**	**4**	**2351**	**99**	**3**	**2.53**	**3**	**1**	**2**	**130**	**7**	**0**	**3.23**
2009-10 ♦	**Chicago**	**NHL**	**48**	**26**	**14**	**4**	**2731**	**114**	**4**	**2.50**	**1**	**0**	**0**	**20**	**0**	**0**	**0.00**
2010-11	Fribourg	Swiss	41	17	23	....	2451	117	4	2.86	4	0	4	213	18	0	5.07
	NHL Totals		**272**	**129**	**90**	**32**	**15260**	**625**	**24**	**2.46**	**17**	**6**	**10**	**987**	**44**	**0**	**2.67**

Played in NHL All-Star Game (2007)

Traded to **Montreal** by **Los Angeles** with Radek Bonk for Mathieu Garon and San Jose's 3rd round choice (previously acquired, Los Angeles selected Piaul Baier) in 2004 Entry Draft, June 26, 2004. Signed as a free agent by **Mannheim** (Germany), September 14, 2004. Traded to **Washington** by **Montreal** for Anaheim's 2nd round choice (previously acquired, later traded to Atlanta – Atlanta selected Jeremy Morin) in 2009 Entry Draft, February 26, 2008. Signed as a free agent by **Chicago**, July 1, 2008. • Assigned to **Fribourg** (Swiss) by **Chicago**, September 27, 2010.

HUTCHINSON, Michael (HUH-chihn-suhn, MIGH-kuhl) BOS

Goaltender. Catches right. 6'3", 185 lbs. Born, Barrie, Ont., March 2, 1990.
(Boston's 3rd choice, 77th overall, in 2008 Entry Draft).

			Regular Season								Playoffs						
Season	**Club**	**League**	**GP**	**W**	**L**	**O/T**	**Mins**	**GA**	**SO**	**Avg**	**GP**	**W**	**L**	**Mins**	**GA**	**SO**	**Avg**
2005-06	Markham Majors	GTHL	34	....	....	....	1530	69	9	2.02	....	....	....	....	....	....	....
2006-07	Orangeville	OPJHL	8	1	4	0	289	24	0	4.99	....	....	....	....	....	....	....
	Barrie Colts	OHL	14	8	3	0	768	27	0	2.11	1	1	0	45	1	0	1.33
2007-08	Barrie Colts	OHL	32	12	15	4	1826	92	1	3.02	8	4	4	500	22	1	2.64
2008-09	Barrie Colts	OHL	38	15	20	1	2146	108	5	3.02	3	0	2	112	10	0	5.37
2009-10	London Knights	OHL	46	32	12	2	2667	127	3	2.86	12	7	5	686	47	0	4.11
2010-11	Providence Bruins	AHL	28	13	10	1	1476	77	1	3.13	....	....	....	....	....	....	....
	Reading Royals	ECHL	18	9	5	4	1049	50	1	2.86	....	....	....	....	....	....	....

HUTTON, Carter (HUH-tuhn, KAR-tuhr)

Goaltender. Catches left. 6'1", 195 lbs. Born, Thunder Bay, Ont., December 19, 1985.

			Regular Season								Playoffs						
Season	**Club**	**League**	**GP**	**W**	**L**	**O/T**	**Mins**	**GA**	**SO**	**Avg**	**GP**	**W**	**L**	**Mins**	**GA**	**SO**	**Avg**
2005-06	F-Wm. North Stars	SIJHL	36	33	1	0	2053	63	10	1.84	15	12	3	928	36	2	2.33
2006-07	U. Mass-Lowell	H-East	19	3	10	5	1097	52	1	2.84	....	....	....	....	....	....	....
2007-08	U. Mass-Lowell	H-East	20	7	11	2	1187	49	2	2.48	....	....	....	....	....	....	....
2008-09	U. Mass-Lowell	H-East	19	9	8	1	1106	38	*3	2.06	....	....	....	....	....	....	....
2009-10	U. Mass-Lowell	H-East	27	13	12	2	1614	55	*4	*2.04	....	....	....	....	....	....	....
	Adirondack	AHL	4	1	2	1	244	11	0	2.71	....	....	....	....	....	....	....
2010-11	Worcester Sharks	AHL	22	11	7	2	1174	59	2	3.01	....	....	....	....	....	....	....

Hockey East Second All-Star Team (2010)

Signed to an ATO (amateur tryout) contract by **Adirondack** (AHL), March 20, 2010. Signed as a free agent by **San Jose**, June 1, 2010.

IILAHTI, Jonathan (ee-eh-LAH-tee, JAWN-ah-thuhn) VAN

Goaltender. Catches left. 6', 167 lbs. Born, Vaasa, Finland, April 27, 1992.
(Vancouver's 4th choice, 175th overall, in 2010 Entry Draft).

			Regular Season								Playoffs						
Season	**Club**	**League**	**GP**	**W**	**L**	**O/T**	**Mins**	**GA**	**SO**	**Avg**	**GP**	**W**	**L**	**Mins**	**GA**	**SO**	**Avg**
2007-08	Sport Vaasa U18	Fin-U18	2	0	2	0	119	8	0	4.03	....	....	....	....	....	....	....
2008-09	Blues Espoo U18	Fin-U18	19	9	10	0	1096	63	0	3.45	2	0	2	98	9	0	5.51
2009-10	Blues Espoo U18	Fin-U18	21	15	5	0	1176	47	1	2.40	11	5	6	667	31	1	2.79
	Blues Espoo Jr.	Fin-Jr.	14	8	6	0	832	37	1	2.67	....	....	....	....	....	....	....
2010-11	Suomi U20	Finland-2	2	0	1	0	112	7	0	3.75	....	....	....	....	....	....	....
	Blues Espoo Jr.	Fin-Jr.	18	13	5	0	1044	48	0	2.76	....	....	....	....	....	....	....
	Kiekko-Laser Oulu	Finland-2	6	1	5	0	359	23	0	3.84	....	....	....	....	....	....	....

IRVING, Leland (UHR-vihng, LEE-land) CGY

Goaltender. Catches left. 6', 175 lbs. Born, Barrhead, Alta., April 11, 1988.
(Calgary's 1st choice, 26th overall, in 2006 Entry Draft).

			Regular Season								Playoffs						
Season	Club	League	GP	W	L	O/T	Mins	GA	SO	Avg	GP	W	L	Mins	GA	SO	Avg
2002-03	Spruce Grove	AMBHL	....	11	11	4	1559	94	....	3.62	....	....	....	....	....	....	....
2003-04	Spruce Grove	RAMHL	19	....	....	....	1017	44	1	2.60	....	....	....	....	....	....	....
	Everett Silvertips	WHL	1	0	0	0	8	0	0	0.00	....	....	....	....	....	....	....
2004-05	Everett Silvertips	WHL	23	9	7	1	1132	35	2	1.86	....	....	....	....	....	....	....
2005-06	Everett Silvertips	WHL	*67	37	22	4	*3791	121	4	1.91	12	8	4	747	21	3	1.69
2006-07	Everett Silvertips	WHL	48	34	9	3	2802	87	*11	1.86	12	6	5	639	30	0	2.82
2007-08	Everett Silvertips	WHL	56	27	24	3	3258	133	4	2.45	3	0	3	139	10	0	4.30
2008-09	Quad City Flames	AHL	47	24	18	2	2658	99	1	2.23	....	....	....	....	....	....	....
2009-10	Abbotsford Heat	AHL	35	14	17	2	1850	85	1	2.76	1	0	1	14	3	0	12.97
	Victoria	ECHL	8	2	4	2	490	25	0	3.06	....	....	....	....	....	....	....
2010-11	Abbotsford Heat	AHL	*61	30	24	2	*3437	132	*8	2.30	....	....	....	....	....	....	....

WHL West Second All-Star Team (2006, 2007)

JANUS, Jaroslav (YA-nuhs, YAHR-roh-slav) T.B.

Goaltender. Catches left. 6'1", 189 lbs. Born, Presov, Czechoslovakia, September 21, 1989.
(Tampa Bay's 6th choice, 162nd overall, in 2009 Entry Draft).

			Regular Season								Playoffs						
Season	Club	League	GP	W	L	O/T	Mins	GA	SO	Avg	GP	W	L	Mins	GA	SO	Avg
2003-04	Presov U18	Svk-U18	14	....	....	....	....	....	....	....	....	....	....	....	....	....	....
2004-05	PHK Presov U18	Svk-U18	34	....	....	....	1743	53	3	1.82	....	....	....	....	....	....	....
	PHK Presov Jr.	Slovak-Jr.	1	....	....	....	60	7	0	7.00	1	....	....	23	1	0	2.61
2005-06	Bratislava U18	Svk-U18	37	....	....	....	1913	92	2	2.89	8	....	....	486	19	0	2.34
	Bratislava Jr.	Slovak-Jr.	13	....	....	....	609	25	0	2.46	....	....	....	....	....	....	....
2006-07	Bratislava U18	Svk-U18	35	....	....	....	2010	84	1	2.51	....	....	....	....	....	....	....
	Bratislava Jr.	Slovak-Jr.	24	....	....	....	1355	49	4	2.17	1	....	....	33	4	0	7.28
2007-08	Erie Otters	OHL	48	13	29	3	2740	201	0	4.40	....	....	....	....	....	....	....
2008-09	Erie Otters	OHL	49	25	20	4	2818	152	3	3.24	5	1	4	285	20	*1	4.21
2009-10	Erie Otters	OHL	13	7	4	2	770	36	0	2.81	....	....	....	....	....	....	....
	Norfolk Admirals	AHL	13	7	6	0	783	27	1	2.07	....	....	....	....	....	....	....
2010-11	Norfolk Admirals	AHL	9	2	5	1	478	29	0	3.64	....	....	....	....	....	....	....
	Florida Everblades	ECHL	27	12	13	0	1491	76	0	3.06	....	....	....	....	....	....	....

JOHNSON, Brent (JAWN-suhn, BREHNT) PIT

Goaltender. Catches left. 6'3", 199 lbs. Born, Farmington, MI, March 12, 1977.
(Colorado's 5th choice, 129th overall, in 1995 Entry Draft).

			Regular Season								Playoffs						
Season	Club	League	GP	W	L	O/T	Mins	GA	SO	Avg	GP	W	L	Mins	GA	SO	Avg
1993-94	Det. Compuware	NAHL	18	....	....	....	1024	49	1	3.52	....	....	....	....	....	....	....
1994-95	Owen Sound	OHL	18	3	9	1	904	75	0	4.98	....	....	....	....	....	....	....
1995-96	Owen Sound	OHL	58	24	28	1	3211	243	1	4.54	6	2	4	371	29	0	4.69
1996-97	Owen Sound	OHL	50	20	28	1	2798	201	1	4.31	4	0	4	253	24	0	5.69
1997-98	Worcester IceCats	AHL	42	14	15	7	2240	119	0	3.19	6	3	2	332	19	0	3.43
1998-99	**St. Louis**	**NHL**	**6**	**3**	**2**	**0**	**286**	**10**	**0**	**2.10**	....	....	....	....	....	....	....
	Worcester IceCats	AHL	49	22	22	4	2925	146	2	2.99	4	1	3	238	12	0	3.02
99-2000	Worcester IceCats	AHL	58	24	27	5	3319	161	3	2.91	9	4	5	561	23	1	2.46
2000-01	**St. Louis**	**NHL**	**31**	**19**	**9**	**2**	**1744**	**63**	**4**	**2.17**	**2**	**0**	**1**	**62**	**2**	**0**	**1.94**
2001-02	**St. Louis**	**NHL**	**58**	**34**	**20**	**4**	**3491**	**127**	**5**	**2.18**	**10**	**5**	**5**	**590**	**18**	**3**	**1.83**
2002-03	**St. Louis**	**NHL**	**38**	**16**	**13**	**5**	**2042**	**84**	**2**	**2.47**	....	....	....	....	....	....	....
	Worcester IceCats	AHL	2	0	1	1	125	8	0	3.84	....	....	....	....	....	....	....
2003-04	**St. Louis**	**NHL**	**10**	**4**	**3**	**1**	**493**	**20**	**1**	**2.43**	....	....	....	....	....	....	....
	Worcester IceCats	AHL	8	2	2	2	365	14	0	2.30	....	....	....	....	....	....	....
	Phoenix	**NHL**	**8**	**1**	**6**	**1**	**486**	**21**	**0**	**2.59**	....	....	....	....	....	....	....
2004-05							DID NOT PLAY										
2005-06	**Washington**	**NHL**	**26**	**9**	**12**	**1**	**1413**	**81**	**1**	**3.44**	....	....	....	....	....	....	....
2006-07	**Washington**	**NHL**	**30**	**6**	**15**	**7**	**1644**	**99**	**0**	**3.61**	....	....	....	....	....	....	....
2007-08	**Washington**	**NHL**	**19**	**7**	**8**	**2**	**1032**	**46**	**0**	**2.67**	....	....	....	....	....	....	....
	Hershey Bears	AHL	1	0	1	0	59	3	0	3.04	....	....	....	....	....	....	....
2008-09	**Washington**	**NHL**	**21**	**12**	**6**	**2**	**1131**	**53**	**0**	**2.81**	....	....	....	....	....	....	....
2009-10	**Pittsburgh**	**NHL**	**23**	**10**	**6**	**1**	**1108**	**51**	**0**	**2.76**	**1**	**0**	**0**	**31**	**1**	**0**	**1.94**
2010-11	**Pittsburgh**	**NHL**	**23**	**13**	**5**	**3**	**1297**	**47**	**1**	**2.17**	**1**	**0**	**0**	**34**	**4**	**0**	**7.06**
	NHL Totals		**293**	**134**	**105**	**29**	**16167**	**702**	**14**	**2.61**	**14**	**5**	**6**	**717**	**25**	**3**	**2.09**

Traded to **St. Louis** by **Colorado** for San Jose's 3rd round choice (previously acquired, Colorado selected Rick Berry) in 1997 Entry Draft, May 30, 1997. Traded to **Phoenix** by **St. Louis** for Mike Sillinger, March 4, 2004. Signed as a free agent by **Vancouver**, September 1, 2005. Claimed on waivers by **Washington** from **Vancouver**, October 4, 2005. Signed as a free agent by **Pittsburgh**, July 21, 2009.

JOHNSON, Chad (JAWN-suhn, CHAD) NYR

Goaltender. Catches left. 6'3", 198 lbs. Born, Calgary, Alta., June 10, 1986.
(Pittsburgh's 4th choice, 125th overall, in 2006 Entry Draft).

			Regular Season								Playoffs						
Season	Club	League	GP	W	L	O/T	Mins	GA	SO	Avg	GP	W	L	Mins	GA	SO	Avg
2002-03	Calgary Buffaloes	AMHL	....	8	8	2	1145	62	....	3.25	1	0	1	60	3	0	3.00
2003-04	Brooks Bandits	AJHL	31	6	20	3	1782	117	0	3.94	....	....	....	....	....	....	....
2004-05	Brooks Bandits	AJHL	43	25	16	2	2505	109	2	2.61	119	4	5	493	....	....	....
2005-06	Alaska	CCHA	18	6	7	4	985	42	0	2.56	....	....	....	....	....	....	....
2006-07	Alaska	CCHA	19	5	6	2	1002	52	1	3.11	....	....	....	....	....	....	....
2007-08	Alaska	CCHA	7	0	6	0	357	20	0	3.36	....	....	....	....	....	....	....
2008-09	Alaska	CCHA	35	14	16	5	2062	57	6	*1.66	....	....	....	....	....	....	....
2009-10	**NY Rangers**	**NHL**	**5**	**1**	**2**	**1**	**281**	**11**	**0**	**2.35**	....	....	....	....	....	....	....
	Hartford Wolf Pack	AHL	47	24	18	2	2649	112	3	2.54	....	....	....	....	....	....	....
2010-11	**NY Rangers**	**NHL**	**1**	**0**	**0**	**0**	**20**	**2**	**0**	**6.00**	....	....	....	....	....	....	....
	Connecticut Whale	AHL	40	16	19	3	2271	103	2	2.72	....	....	....	....	....	....	....
	NHL Totals		**6**	**1**	**2**	**1**	**301**	**13**	**0**	**2.59**	....	....	....	....	....	....	....

AJHL South Division First All-Star Team (2005) • CCHA First All-Star Team (2009) • CCHA Rookie of the Year (2009) • NCAA West Second All-American Team (2009)

Traded to **NY Rangers** by **Pittsburgh** for Pittsburgh's 5th round choice (previously acquired, Pittsburgh selected Andy Bathgate) in 2009 Entry Draft, June 27, 2009.

JONES, Martin (JOHNZ, MAR-tihn) L.A.

Goaltender. Catches left. 6'4", 193 lbs. Born, North Vancouver, B.C., January 10, 1990.

			Regular Season								Playoffs						
Season	Club	League	GP	W	L	O/T	Mins	GA	SO	Avg	GP	W	L	Mins	GA	SO	Avg
2006-07	Calgary Hitmen	WHL	18	9	4	3	1029	52	0	3.03	....	....	....	....	....	....	....
2007-08	Calgary Hitmen	WHL	27	18	8	1	1529	54	1	2.12	5	2	1	250	12	0	2.88
2008-09	Calgary Hitmen	WHL	55	*45	5	4	3295	114	*7	2.08	18	14	4	1095	34	2	1.86
2009-10	Calgary Hitmen	WHL	48	36	11	1	2851	105	*8	*2.21	*23	*16	7	*1401	55	*2	*2.36
2010-11	Manchester	AHL	39	23	12	1	2187	82	4	2.25	4	2	1	213	9	0	2.54
	Ontario Reign	ECHL	1	1	0	0	64	4	0	3.76	....	....	....	....	....	....	....

WHL East Second All-Star Team (2009) • WHL East First All-Star Team (2010) • WHL Goaltender of the Year (2010) • Canadian Major Junior Second All-Star Team (2010) • Memorial Cup All-Star Team (2010) • Hap Emms Memorial Trophy (Memorial Cup – Top Goaltender) (2010)

Signed as a free agent by **Los Angeles**, October 2, 2008.

KANGAS, Alex (KANG-uhs, AL-ehx) WPG

Goaltender. Catches left. 6'2", 175 lbs. Born, Rochester, MN, May 28, 1987.
(Atlanta's 4th choice, 135th overall, in 2006 Entry Draft).

			Regular Season								Playoffs						
Season	Club	League	GP	W	L	O/T	Mins	GA	SO	Avg	GP	W	L	Mins	GA	SO	Avg
2001-02	Rochester Century	High-MN	3	3	0	0	....	3	2	1.00	....	....	....	....	....	....	....
2002-03	Rochester Century	High-MN	27	17	9	0	....	50	6	1.76	....	....	....	....	....	....	....
2003-04	Rochester Century	High-MN	28	15	12	1	....	59	3	2.08	....	....	....	....	....	....	....
2004-05	Rochester Century	High-MN	30	23	4	3	....	55	7	1.86	....	....	....	....	....	....	....
2005-06	Sioux Falls	USHL	29	20	6	3	1733	62	3	2.15	6	4	2	359	17	0	2.84
2006-07	Indiana Ice	USHL	46	19	19	5	2467	136	1	3.31	7	6	1	434	18	0	2.49
2007-08	U. of Minnesota	WCHA	31	12	10	9	1967	65	0	1.98	....	....	....	....	....	....	....
2008-09	U. of Minnesota	WCHA	36	17	11	6	2019	94	3	2.79	....	....	....	....	....	....	....
2009-10	U. of Minnesota	WCHA	33	16	15	1	1934	84	1	2.61	....	....	....	....	....	....	....
2010-11	U. of Minnesota	WCHA	9	2	5	0	453	28	0	3.71	....	....	....	....	....	....	....

USHL All-Rookie Team (2006)

KARLSSON, Henrik (KARL-suhn, HEHN-rihk) CGY

Goaltender. Catches left. 6'5", 215 lbs. Born, Stockholm, Sweden, November 27, 1983.

			Regular Season								Playoffs						
Season	Club	League	GP	W	L	O/T	Mins	GA	SO	Avg	GP	W	L	Mins	GA	SO	Avg
2000-01	Hammarby U18	Swe-U18	2	....	....	....	120	7	0	3.50	....	....	....	....	....	....	....
	Hammarby Jr.	Swe-Jr.	13	....	....	....	706	56	0	4.76	....	....	....	....	....	....	....
2001-02	Hammarby Jr.	Swe-Jr.	23	....	....	....	1356	97	1	4.29	....	....	....	....	....	....	....
2002-03	Botkyrka	Sweden-3	....	....	....	....	....	....	....	2.58	....	....	....	....	....	....	....
2003-04	Botkyrka	Sweden-3	21	....	....	....	....	....	....	2.49	6	....	....	236	15	0	3.82
2004-05	Olofstroms IK	Sweden-3	1	....	....	....	60	0	1	0.00	....	....	....	....	....	....	....
	IK Oskarshamn	Sweden-2	11	....	....	....	613	25	1	2.45	2	....	....	109	7	0	3.87
2005-06	IK Oskarshamn	Sweden-2	1	....	....	....	40	3	0	4.54	....	....	....	....	....	....	....
2006-07	Hammarby Jr.	Swe-Jr.	1	....	....	....	59	2	0	2.04	....	....	....	....	....	....	....
	Hammarby	Sweden-2	35	....	....	....	1893	111	1	3.52	....	....	....	....	....	....	....
2007-08	Hammarby	Sweden-2	29	....	....	....	1692	109	1	3.86	....	....	....	....	....	....	....
	Malmo	Sweden-2	3	....	....	....	180	8	0	2.67	....	....	....	....	....	....	....
2008-09	Malmo	Sweden-2	32	....	....	....	1888	77	4	2.45	....	....	....	....	....	....	....
	Sodertalje SK	Sweden	7	....	....	....	410	17	0	2.49	....	....	....	....	....	....	....
	Sodertalje SK	Sweden-Q	8	....	....	....	483	16	0	1.99	....	....	....	....	....	....	....
2009-10	Farjestad	Sweden	34	....	....	....	1934	79	3	2.45	....	....	....	....	....	....	....
2010-11	**Calgary**	**NHL**	**17**	**4**	**5**	**6**	**838**	**36**	**0**	**2.58**	....	....	....	....	....	....	....
	NHL Totals		**17**	**4**	**5**	**6**	**838**	**36**	**0**	**2.58**	....	....	....	....	....	....	....

Signed as a free agent by **San Jose**, August 12, 2009. Signed as a free agent by **Riga** (Russia-KHL), June 14, 2010. Traded to **Calgary** by **San Jose** for Calgary's 6th round choice (Konrad Abeltshauser) in 2010 Entry Draft, June 25, 2010.

KARPOWICH, Paul (KAHR-puh-wihch, PAWL) ST.L.

Goaltender. Catches left. 6'2", 195 lbs. Born, Thunder Bay, Ont., October 25, 1988.
(St. Louis' 10th choice, 185th overall, in 2008 Entry Draft).

			Regular Season								Playoffs						
Season	Club	League	GP	W	L	O/T	Mins	GA	SO	Avg	GP	W	L	Mins	GA	SO	Avg
2004-05	Thunder Bay Kings	Minor-ON	38	25	7	3	2057	103	2	3.00	....	....	....	....	....	....	....
2005-06	Thunder Bay Kings	Minor-ON	42	29	8	3	2280	91	6	2.39	....	....	....	....	....	....	....
2006-07	Brooks Bandits	AJHL	18	6	6	2	1010	59	0	3.51	2	1	0	92	8	0	5.21
2007-08	Wellington Dukes	OPJHL	22	15	3	2	1202	43	3	2.15	13	9	4	771	35	1	2.72
2008-09	Clarkson Knights	ECAC	27	7	14	4	1516	72	1	2.85	....	....	....	....	....	....	....
2009-10	Clarkson Knights	ECAC	31	8	19	4	1744	101	0	3.48	....	....	....	....	....	....	....
2010-11	Clarkson Knights	ECAC	35	15	18	2	2007	102	1	3.05	....	....	....	....	....	....	....

KASDORF, Jason (KAZ-dawrf, JAY-suhn) WPG

Goaltender. Catches left. 6'4", 187 lbs. Born, Winnipeg, Man., May 18, 1992.
(Winnipeg's 6th choice, 157th overall, in 2011 Entry Draft).

			Regular Season								Playoffs						
Season	Club	League	GP	W	L	O/T	Mins	GA	SO	Avg	GP	W	L	Mins	GA	SO	Avg
2008-09	Wpg. Thrashers	MMHL	44	....	....	....	1032	36	4	2.09	....	....	....	....	....	....	....
2009-10	Portage Terriers	MJHL	....	19	10	5	2094	89	2	2.55	....	....	....	....	....	....	....
2010-11	Portage Terriers	MJHL	34	24	10	0	2018	85	2	2.53	16	10	5	930	34	2	2.19

• Signed Letter of Intent to attend **R.P.I.** (ECAC) in fall of 2012.

KHABIBULIN, Nikolai (khah-bee-BOO-lihn, NIH-koh-ligh) EDM

Goaltender. Catches left. 6'1", 206 lbs. Born, Sverdlovsk, USSR, January 13, 1973.
(Winnipeg's 8th choice, 204th overall, in 1992 Entry Draft).

			Regular Season								Playoffs						
Season	Club	League	GP	W	L	O/T	Mins	GA	SO	Avg	GP	W	L	Mins	GA	SO	Avg
1988-89	Sverdlovsk	USSR	1	....	....	....	3	0	0	0.00	....	....	....	....	....	....	....
1989-90	Luch Sverdlovsk	USSR-2					STATISTICS NOT AVAILABLE										
1990-91	Nizhny Tagil	USSR-3	10	....	....	....	....	....	....	....	....	....	....	....	....	....	....
	Sverdlovsk	USSR-Q	2	....	....	....	....	7	....	....	....	....	....	....	....	....	....
1991-92	CSKA Moscow 2	CIS-3	11	....	....	....	....	....	....	....	....	....	....	....	....	....	....
	CSKA Moscow	CIS	2	....	....	....	34	2	0	3.53	....	....	....	....	....	....	....
	Russia	Olympics					DID NOT PLAY – SPARE GOALTENDER										
1992-93	CSKA Moscow	CIS	13	....	....	....	491	27	....	3.29	....	....	....	....	....	....	....
	Serov	CIS-2	18	....	....	....	....	....	....	....	....	....	....	....	....	....	....
1993-94	CSKA Moscow	CIS	46	....	....	....	2625	116	....	2.65	....	....	....	....	....	....	....
	Russian Penguins	IHL	12	2	7	2	639	47	0	4.41	....	....	....	....	....	....	....
1994-95	Springfield Indians	AHL	23	9	9	3	1240	80	0	3.87	....	....	....	....	....	....	....
	Winnipeg	**NHL**	**26**	**8**	**9**	**4**	**1339**	**76**	**0**	**3.41**	....	....	....	....	....	....	....
1995-96	**Winnipeg**	**NHL**	**53**	**26**	**20**	**3**	**2914**	**152**	**2**	**3.13**	**6**	**2**	**4**	**359**	**19**	**0**	**3.18**
1996-97	**Phoenix**	**NHL**	**72**	**30**	**33**	**6**	**4091**	**193**	**7**	**2.83**	**7**	**3**	**4**	**426**	**15**	**1**	**2.11**

1997-98	**Phoenix**	**NHL**	**70**	**30**	**28**	**10**	**4026**	**184**	**4**	**2.74**	**4**	**2**	**1**	**185**	**13**	**0**	**4.22**
1998-99	**Phoenix**	**NHL**	**63**	**32**	**23**	**7**	**3657**	**130**	**8**	**2.13**	**7**	**3**	**4**	**449**	**18**	**0**	**2.41**
99-2000	Long Beach	IHL	33	21	11	1	1936	59	5	*1.83	5	2	3	321	15	0	2.81
2000-01	**Tampa Bay**	**NHL**	**2**	**1**	**1**	**0**	**123**	**6**	**0**	**2.93**	....	....	....	....	....	....	....
2001-02	**Tampa Bay**	**NHL**	**70**	**24**	**32**	**10**	**3896**	**153**	**7**	**2.36**	....	....	....	....	....	....	....
	Russia	Olympics	6	3	2	1	*359	14	*1	2.34	....	....	....	....	....	....	....
2002-03	**Tampa Bay**	**NHL**	**65**	**30**	**22**	**11**	**3787**	**156**	**4**	**2.47**	**10**	**5**	**5**	**644**	**26**	**0**	**2.42**
2003-04 ♦	**Tampa Bay**	**NHL**	**55**	**28**	**19**	**7**	**3274**	**127**	**3**	**2.33**	**23**	***16**	**7**	**1401**	**40**	***5**	**1.71**
2004-05	Ak Bars Kazan	Russia	24	....	....	....	1457	40	5	1.65	2	....	....	118	6	0	3.04
2005-06	**Chicago**	**NHL**	**50**	**17**	**26**	**6**	**2815**	**157**	**0**	**3.35**	....	....	....	....	....	....	....
	Russia	Olympics					DID NOT PLAY – INJURED										
2006-07	**Chicago**	**NHL**	**60**	**25**	**26**	**5**	**3425**	**163**	**1**	**2.86**	....	....	....	....	....	....	....
2007-08	**Chicago**	**NHL**	**50**	**23**	**20**	**6**	**2892**	**127**	**2**	**2.63**	....	....	....	....	....	....	....
2008-09	**Chicago**	**NHL**	**42**	**25**	**8**	**7**	**2467**	**96**	**3**	**2.33**	**15**	**8**	**6**	**881**	**43**	**0**	**2.93**
2009-10	**Edmonton**	**NHL**	**18**	**7**	**9**	**2**	**1089**	**55**	**0**	**3.03**	....	....	....	....	....	....	....
2010-11	**Edmonton**	**NHL**	**47**	**10**	**32**	**4**	**2701**	**153**	**2**	**3.40**	....	....	....	....	....	....	....
	NHL Totals		**743**	**316**	**308**	**88**	**42496**	**1928**	**43**	**2.72**	**72**	**39**	**31**	**4345**	**174**	**6**	**2.40**

James Gatschene Memorial Trophy (IHL – MVP) (2000) (co-winner - Frederic Chabot)

Played in NHL All-Star Game (1998, 1999, 2002, 2003)

• Transferred to **Phoenix** after **Winnipeg** franchise relocated, July 1, 1996. • Missed 1999-2000 NHL season and majority of 2000-01 after failing to come to contract terms with **Phoenix**. Signed as a free agent by **Long Beach** (IHL) with **Phoenix** retaining NHL rights, January 14, 2000. Traded to **Tampa Bay** by **Phoenix** with Stan Neckar for Mike Johnson, Paul Mara, Ruslan Zainullin and NY Islanders' 2nd round choice (previously acquired, Phoenix selected Matthew Spiller) in 2001 Entry Draft, March 5, 2001. Signed as a free agent by **Kazan** (Russia), November 8, 2004. Signed as a free agent by **Chicago**, August 5, 2005. Signed as a free agent by **Edmonton**, July 1, 2009.

KHUDOBIN, Anton (khuh-DAW-bihn, AN-tawn) BOS

Goaltender. Catches left. 5'11", 203 lbs. Born, Ust-Kamenogorsk, USSR, May 7, 1986.
(Minnesota's 11th choice, 206th overall, in 2004 Entry Draft).

			Regular Season								Playoffs						
Season	**Club**	**League**	**GP**	**W**	**L**	**O/T**	**Mins**	**GA**	**SO**	**Avg**	**GP**	**W**	**L**	**Mins**	**GA**	**SO**	**Avg**
2003-04	Magnitogorsk 2	Russia-3	38	....	....	....	....	80	....	....	....	....	....	....	....	....	....
2004-05	Magnitogorsk	Russia	4	....	....	....	133	0	1	0.00	....	....	....	....	....	....	....
	Magnitogorsk 2	Russia-3	27	....	....	....	....	52	....	....	....	....	....	....	....	....	....
2005-06	Saskatoon Blades	WHL	44	23	13	3	2362	114	4	2.90	10	4	6	685	32	0	2.80
2006-07	Magnitogorsk	Russia	16	....	....	....	618	28	0	2.72	3	....	....	26	1	0	2.30
2007-08	Houston Aeros	AHL	12	2	2	1	482	16	1	1.99	....	....	....	....	....	....	....
	Texas Wildcatters	ECHL	27	20	1	4	1549	51	3	*1.98	9	5	4	547	20	1	2.19
2008-09	Houston Aeros	AHL	10	3	6	1	512	26	0	3.04	17	8	8	890	40	2	2.70
	Florida Everblades	ECHL	33	18	10	1	1706	77	4	2.71	....	....	....	....	....	....	....
2009-10	**Minnesota**	**NHL**	**2**	**2**	**0**	**0**	**69**	**1**	**0**	**0.87**	....	....	....	....	....	....	....
	Houston Aeros	AHL	40	14	19	4	2247	91	4	2.43	....	....	....	....	....	....	....
2010-11	**Minnesota**	**NHL**	**4**	**2**	**1**	**0**	**189**	**5**	**1**	**1.59**	....	....	....	....	....	....	....
	Houston Aeros	AHL	34	19	12	1	1883	81	1	2.58	....	....	....	....	....	....	....
	Providence Bruins	AHL	16	9	4	1	901	36	1	2.40	....	....	....	....	....	....	....
	NHL Totals		**6**	**4**	**1**	**0**	**258**	**6**	**1**	**1.40**	....	....	....	....	....	....	....

ECHL First All-Star Team (2008) • ECHL Goaltender of the Year (2008)

Traded to **Boston** by **Minnesota** for Jeff Penner and Mikko Lehtonen, February 28, 2011.

KILLEEN, Patrick (kih-LEEN, PAT-rihk) PIT

Goaltender. Catches left. 6'4", 194 lbs. Born, Almonte, Ont., April 15, 1990.
(Pittsburgh's 3rd choice, 180th overall, in 2008 Entry Draft).

			Regular Season								Playoffs						
Season	**Club**	**League**	**GP**	**W**	**L**	**O/T**	**Mins**	**GA**	**SO**	**Avg**	**GP**	**W**	**L**	**Mins**	**GA**	**SO**	**Avg**
2005-06	Ott. Valley Titans	Minor-ON	36	....	....	....	1620	74	6	2.05	....	....	....	....	....	....	....
2006-07	Ottawa Jr. Sens	CJHL	7	5	1	0	376	20	0	3.19	....	....	....	....	....	....	....
	Brampton Battalion	OHL	8	1	3	0	304	29	0	5.72	....	....	....	....	....	....	....
2007-08	Brampton Battalion	OHL	34	20	9	2	1959	90	1	2.76	....	....	....	....	....	....	....
2008-09	Brampton Battalion	OHL	34	19	11	2	1916	91	2	2.85	2	0	0	26	4	0	9.27
2009-10	Brampton Battalion	OHL	*63	23	25	13	*3693	149	*5	2.42	11	4	7	664	38	0	3.43
2010-11	Wilkes-Barre	AHL	2	0	0	0	19	2	0	6.38	....	....	....	....	....	....	....
	Wheeling Nailers	ECHL	40	19	16	2	2233	107	3	2.87	5	1	2	247	11	0	2.68

KINKAID, Keith (kihn-KAID, KEETH) N.J.

Goaltender. Catches left. 6'3", 180 lbs. Born, Farmingville, NY, July 4, 1989.

			Regular Season								Playoffs						
Season	**Club**	**League**	**GP**	**W**	**L**	**O/T**	**Mins**	**GA**	**SO**	**Avg**	**GP**	**W**	**L**	**Mins**	**GA**	**SO**	**Avg**
2007-08	Des Moines	USHL	15	4	9	2	844	48	0	3.41	....	....	....	....	....	....	....
2008-09	St. Louis Bandits	NAHL	40	*30	5	4	2393	71	*7	*1.78	*12	*10	2	*728	14	*3	*1.15
2009-10	Union College	ECAC	25	12	8	3	1478	61	1	2.48	....	....	....	....	....	....	....
2010-11	Union College	ECAC	*38	25	10	3	*2266	75	3	1.99	....	....	....	....	....	....	....

ECAC All-Rookie Team (2010)

Signed as a free agent by **New Jersey**, April 18, 2011.

KIPRUSOFF, Miikka (KIHP-roo-sawf, MEE-kah) CGY

Goaltender. Catches left. 6'1", 184 lbs. Born, Turku, Finland, October 26, 1976.
(San Jose's 5th choice, 116th overall, in 1995 Entry Draft).

			Regular Season								Playoffs						
Season	**Club**	**League**	**GP**	**W**	**L**	**O/T**	**Mins**	**GA**	**SO**	**Avg**	**GP**	**W**	**L**	**Mins**	**GA**	**SO**	**Avg**
1993-94	TPS Turku Jr.	Fin-Jr.	35	20	9	5	2101	100	0	2.85	6	3	3	369	26	0	4.23
1994-95	TPS Turku Jr.	Fin-Jr.	31	13	14	4	1896	92	2	2.91	....	....	....	....	....	....	....
	Kiekko-67 Turku	Finland-2	1	0	1	0	60	6	0	6.00	....	....	....	....	....	....	....
	TPS Turku	Finland	4	3	1	0	240	12	0	3.00	2	2	0	120	7	0	3.50
1995-96	TPS Turku Jr.	Fin-Jr.	3	1	2	0	180	9	0	3.00	....	....	....	....	....	....	....
	Kiekko-67 Turku	Finland-2	5	5	0	0	300	7	1	1.40	....	....	....	....	....	....	....
	TPS Turku	Finland	12	5	3	1	550	38	0	4.14	3	0	1	113	4	0	2.12
1996-97	AIK Solna	Sweden	42	....	....	....	2440	93	3	2.29	7	....	....	420	22	0	3.14
1997-98	AIK Solna	Sweden	43	....	....	....	2517	111	1	2.65	....	....	....	....	....	....	....
	AIK Solna	Sweden-Q	9	....	....	....	540	15	2	1.67	....	....	....	....	....	....	....
1998-99	TPS Turku	Finland	39	26	6	6	2259	70	4	1.86	10	9	1	580	15	3	1.55
99-2000	Kentucky	AHL	47	23	19	4	2759	114	3	2.48	5	1	3	239	13	0	3.27
2000-01	**San Jose**	**NHL**	**5**	**2**	**1**	**0**	**154**	**5**	**0**	**1.95**	**3**	**1**	**1**	**149**	**5**	**0**	**2.01**
	Kentucky	AHL	36	19	9	6	2038	76	2	2.24	....	....	....	....	....	....	....
2001-02	**San Jose**	**NHL**	**20**	**7**	**6**	**3**	**1037**	**43**	**2**	**2.49**	**1**	**0**	**0**	**8**	**0**	**0**	**0.00**
	Cleveland Barons	AHL	4	4	0	0	242	7	0	1.73	....	....	....	....	....	....	....
2002-03	**San Jose**	**NHL**	**22**	**5**	**14**	**0**	**1199**	**65**	**1**	**3.25**	....	....	....	....	....	....	....
2003-04	**Calgary**	**NHL**	**38**	**24**	**10**	**4**	**2301**	**65**	**4**	***1.69**	***26**	**15**	**11**	***1655**	**51**	***5**	**1.85**
2004-05	Timra IK	Sweden	46	....	....	....	2719	97	5	2.14	6	....	....	356	13	0	2.19
2005-06	**Calgary**	**NHL**	**74**	**42**	**20**	**11**	***4380**	**151**	***10**	***2.07**	**7**	**3**	**4**	**428**	**16**	**0**	**2.24**
	Finland	Olympics					DID NOT PLAY – INJURED										
2006-07	**Calgary**	**NHL**	**74**	**40**	**24**	**9**	**4419**	**181**	**7**	**2.46**	**6**	**2**	**4**	**384**	**18**	**0**	**2.81**
2007-08	**Calgary**	**NHL**	**76**	**39**	**26**	**10**	**4398**	**197**	**2**	**2.69**	**7**	**2**	**4**	**336**	**18**	**1**	**3.21**
2008-09	**Calgary**	**NHL**	***76**	***45**	**24**	**5**	***4418**	**209**	**4**	**2.84**	**6**	**2**	**4**	**324**	**19**	**0**	**3.52**
2009-10	**Calgary**	**NHL**	**73**	**35**	**28**	**10**	**4235**	**163**	**4**	**2.31**	....	....	....	....	....	....	....
	Finland	Olympics	5	3	2	0	250	11	1	2.64	....	....	....	....	....	....	....
2010-11	**Calgary**	**NHL**	**71**	**37**	**24**	**6**	**4156**	**182**	**6**	**2.63**	....	....	....	....	....	....	....
	NHL Totals		**529**	**276**	**177**	**58**	**30697**	**1261**	**40**	**2.46**	**56**	**25**	**28**	**3284**	**127**	**6**	**2.32**

NHL First All-Star Team (2006) • Vezina Trophy (2006)

Played in NHL All-Star Game (2007)

Traded to **Calgary** by **San Jose** for Calgary's 2nd round choice (Marc-Edouard Vlasic) in 2005 Entry Draft, November 16, 2003. Signed as a free agent by **Timra** (Sweden), September 20, 2004.

KNAPP, Connor (NAP, KAW-nuhr) BUF

Goaltender. Catches left. 6'6", 222 lbs. Born, New York, NY, May 1, 1990.
(Buffalo's 5th choice, 164th overall, in 2009 Entry Draft).

			Regular Season								Playoffs						
Season	**Club**	**League**	**GP**	**W**	**L**	**O/T**	**Mins**	**GA**	**SO**	**Avg**	**GP**	**W**	**L**	**Mins**	**GA**	**SO**	**Avg**
2005-06	Buffalo Saints	Minor-NY	26	....	....	....	1326	64	5	2.46	....	....	....	....	....	....	....
2006-07	Bos. Jr. Bruins	EmJHL	23	*22	1	0	1340	37	3	*1.66	5	5	0	290	6	*2	*1.24
2007-08	Bos. Jr. Bruins	EJHL	....	14	7	2	1307	....	....	1.92	....	....	....	....	....	....	....
2008-09	Miami U.	CCHA	23	13	5	3	1350	47	2	2.09	....	....	....	....	....	....	....
2009-10	Miami U.	CCHA	20	10	4	4	1127	37	4	1.97	....	....	....	....	....	....	....
2010-11	Miami U.	CCHA	17	8	5	4	976	33	2	2.03	....	....	....	....	....	....	....

CCHA All-Rookie Team (2009)

KOSHECHKIN, Vasily (KOH-shech-kihn, va-SEE-lee) T.B.

Goaltender. Catches left. 6'5", 225 lbs. Born, Togliatti, USSR, March 27, 1983.
(Tampa Bay's 9th choice, 233rd overall, in 2002 Entry Draft).

			Regular Season								Playoffs						
Season	**Club**	**League**	**GP**	**W**	**L**	**O/T**	**Mins**	**GA**	**SO**	**Avg**	**GP**	**W**	**L**	**Mins**	**GA**	**SO**	**Avg**
1998-99	Lada Togliatti 2	Russia-4	8	....	....	....	....	8	....	....	....	....	....	....	....	....	....
99-2000	Lada Togliatti 2	Russia-3	18	....	....	....	....	20	....	....	....	....	....	....	....	....	....
2000-01	Lada Togliatti 2	Russia-3					STATISTICS NOT AVAILABLE										
2001-02	Lada Togliatti 2	Russia-3					STATISTICS NOT AVAILABLE										
2002-03	Lada Togliatti 2	Russia-3					STATISTICS NOT AVAILABLE										
	Kirovo-Chepetsk	Russia-2	10	....	....	....	613	14	3	1.37	....	....	....	....	....	....	....
	Almetjevsk	Russia-2	14	....	....	....	675	29	1	2.58	....	....	....	....	....	....	....
2003-04	Lada Togliatti 2	Russia-3	13	....	....	....	....	19	1	....	3	....	....	....	....	....	....
	Lada Togliatti	Russia	8	....	....	....	247	10	0	2.43	1	....	....	40	3	0	4.50
2004-05	Lada Togliatti	Russia	4	....	....	....	121	5	0	2.47	....	....	....	....	....	....	....
2005-06	Lada Togliatti	Russia	41	....	....	....	2375	63	9	1.59	8	....	....	474	20	1	2.53
2006-07	Lada Togliatti	Russia	42	....	....	....	2430	82	5	2.02	3	....	....	179	13	0	4.35
2007-08	Ak Bars Kazan	Russia	19	....	....	....	990	45	0	2.73	....	....	....	....	....	....	....
2008-09	Lada Togliatti	Rus-KHL	43	....	....	....	2404	67	8	1.67	5	....	....	280	9	1	1.93
2009-10	Lada Togliatti	Rus-KHL	*23	....	....	....	1304	46	*2	2.12	....	....	....	....	....	....	....
	Magnitogorsk	Rus-KHL	*26	....	....	....	1536	47	*6	1.84	9	....	....	535	18	1	2.02
2010-11	Cherepovets	Rus-KHL	32	....	....	....	1809	88	2	2.92	6	....	....	327	12	0	2.20

KOSKINEN, Mikko (KAWS-kih-nehn, MEE-koh) NYI

Goaltender. Catches left. 6'6", 202 lbs. Born, Vantaa, Finland, July 18, 1988.
(NY Islanders' 3rd choice, 31st overall, in 2009 Entry Draft).

			Regular Season								Playoffs						
Season	**Club**	**League**	**GP**	**W**	**L**	**O/T**	**Mins**	**GA**	**SO**	**Avg**	**GP**	**W**	**L**	**Mins**	**GA**	**SO**	**Avg**
2004-05	Blues-T U18	Fin-U18	21	....	....	....	1138	67	0	3.53	....	....	....	....	....	....	....
2005-06	Blues Espoo U18	Fin-U18	3	....	....	....	142	12	0	5.07	....	....	....	....	....	....	....
2006-07	Kiekko-Vantaa Jr.	Fin-Jr.	27	16	8	0	1567	62	3	2.37	....	....	....	....	....	....	....
2007-08	Blues Espoo Jr.	Fin-Jr.	20	12	4	0	1176	45	2	2.30	2	0	2	81	7	0	5.18
	Blues Espoo	Finland	1	1	0	0	60	0	1	0.00	....	....	....	....	....	....	....
2008-09	Blues Espoo Jr.	Fin-Jr.	9	9	0	0	545	15	2	1.65	....	....	....	....	....	....	....
	Blues Espoo	Finland	33	17	9	7	1921	61	1	1.91	14	6	8	856	37	0	2.59
2009-10	Bridgeport	AHL	2	1	1	0	123	5	0	2.45	3	1	1	147	7	0	2.85
	Utah Grizzlies	ECHL	6	6	0	0	360	15	0	2.50	4	2	1	172	10	0	3.49
2010-11	**NY Islanders**	**NHL**	**4**	**2**	**1**	**0**	**208**	**15**	**0**	**4.33**	....	....	....	....	....	....	....
	Bridgeport	AHL	36	12	21	1	2063	120	0	3.49	....	....	....	....	....	....	....
	NHL Totals		**4**	**2**	**1**	**0**	**208**	**15**	**0**	**4.33**	....	....	....	....	....	....	....

KOVAR, Jakub (KOH-vahr, YA-kuhb) PHI

Goaltender. Catches left. 6', 176 lbs. Born, Pisek, Czech., July 19, 1988.
(Philadelphia's 7th choice, 109th overall, in 2006 Entry Draft).

			Regular Season								Playoffs						
Season	**Club**	**League**	**GP**	**W**	**L**	**O/T**	**Mins**	**GA**	**SO**	**Avg**	**GP**	**W**	**L**	**Mins**	**GA**	**SO**	**Avg**
2004-05	IHC Pisek U17	CzR-U17	40	....	....	....	2298	137	4	3.58	....	....	....	....	....	....	....
2005-06	C. Budejovice Jr.	CzRep-Jr.	19	....	....	....	1048	39	2	2.23	5	....	....	304	8	0	1.58
2006-07	C. Budejovice Jr.	CzRep-Jr.	38	....	....	....	2231	77	3	2.07	3	....	....	160	16	0	6.00
2007-08	Oshawa Generals	OHL	16	12	3	0	917	48	0	3.14	....	....	....	....	....	....	....
	Windsor Spitfires	OHL	20	14	3	3	1194	68	1	3.42	4	1	2	188	13	0	4.15
2008-09	C. Budejovice	CzRep	25	....	....	....	1355	63	0	2.79	....	....	....	....	....	....	....
2009-10	C. Budejovice	CzRep	17	....	....	....	879	36	1	2.46	....	....	....	....	....	....	....
	HC Tabor	CzRep-2	13	....	....	....	758	32	1	2.53	5	....	....	300	18	0	3.60
2010-11	C. Budejovice	CzRep	52	....	....	....	3134	129	4	2.47	6	....	....	368	11	1	1.79

KRAHN, Brent (KRAWN, BREHNT)

Goaltender. Catches left. 6'4", 232 lbs. Born, Winnipeg, Man., April 2, 1982.
(Calgary's 1st choice, 9th overall, in 2000 Entry Draft).

			Regular Season								Playoffs						
Season	Club	League	GP	W	L	O/T	Mins	GA	SO	Avg	GP	W	L	Mins	GA	SO	Avg
1997-98	Pembina Valley	MMMHL	22	20	0	1	1265	40	3	1.90	2	2	0	120	2	1	1.00
1998-99	Pembina Valley	MMMHL	13	10	3	0	770	30	2	2.34	....	....	....	....	....	....	....
99-2000	Calgary Hitmen	WHL	39	33	6	0	2315	92	4	2.38	5	2	2	266	13	0	2.93
2000-01	Calgary Hitmen	WHL	37	22	10	3	2087	104	1	2.99	....	....	....	....	....	....	....
2001-02	Calgary Hitmen	WHL	18	8	6	2	1033	61	0	3.54	2	1	1	119	6	0	3.03
2002-03	Calgary Hitmen	WHL	23	11	10	2	1343	72	2	3.22	....	....	....	....	....	....	....
	Seattle	WHL	5	5	0	0	302	9	2	1.79	15	9	6	960	38	2	2.38
2003-04	San Antonio	AHL	14	3	7	1	715	41	0	3.44	....	....	....	....	....	....	....
	Lowell	AHL	7	2	3	0	344	15	0	2.62	....	....	....	....	....	....	....
	Las Vegas	ECHL	14	7	5	2	828	36	0	2.61	....	....	....	....	....	....	....
2004-05	Lowell	AHL	35	20	11	2	1998	83	6	2.49	1	0	0	1	0	0	0.00
2005-06	Omaha	AHL	57	26	20	9	3241	135	3	2.50	....	....	....	....	....	....	....
2006-07	Omaha	AHL	28	14	12	0	1564	63	2	2.42	1	0	1	59	3	0	3.06
2007-08	Quad City Flames	AHL	14	6	6	2	795	33	0	2.49	....	....	....	....	....	....	....
2008-09	**Dallas**	**NHL**	**1**	**0**	**0**	**0**	**20**	**3**	**0**	**9.00**	....	....	....	....	....	....	....
	Chicago Wolves	AHL	13	6	6	0	738	26	2	2.11	....	....	....	....	....	....	....
	Las Vegas	ECHL	6	1	4	1	342	23	0	4.04	....	....	....	....	....	....	....
2009-10	Texas Stars	AHL	22	17	4	0	1246	38	5	1.83	11	7	4	628	26	0	2.48
2010-11	Texas Stars	AHL	12	6	6	0	675	36	1	3.20	....	....	....	....	....	....	....
	NHL Totals		**1**	**0**	**0**	**0**	**20**	**3**	**0**	**9.00**	....	....	....	....	....	....	....

Signed as a free agent by **Dallas**, September 24, 2008.

KUEMPER, Darcy (KEHM-puhr, DAHR-see) MIN

Goaltender. Catches left. 6'4", 205 lbs. Born, Saskatoon, Sask., May 5, 1990.
(Minnesota's 5th choice, 161st overall, in 2009 Entry Draft).

			Regular Season								Playoffs						
Season	Club	League	GP	W	L	O/T	Mins	GA	SO	Avg	GP	W	L	Mins	GA	SO	Avg
2006-07	Sask. Contacts	SMHL	25	8	14	3	1489	87	1	3.51	4	1	3	200	19	0	5.70
	Spokane Chiefs	WHL	....	....	....	....	....	....	....	....	1	0	0	0	0	0	0.00
2007-08	Saskatoon Blazers	SMHL	26	15	7	4	1578	62	1	2.36	13	7	6	781	34	1	2.61
2008-09	Red Deer Rebels	WHL	55	21	25	8	3167	156	3	2.96	....	....	....	....	....	....	....
2009-10	Houston Aeros	AHL	4	2	1	0	199	8	0	2.41	....	....	....	....	....	....	....
	Red Deer Rebels	WHL	61	28	23	4	3234	147	3	2.73	2	0	2	61	6	0	5.90
2010-11	Red Deer Rebels	WHL	62	*45	12	5	3685	114	*13	*1.86	7	4	3	403	19	0	2.83

WHL East Second All-Star Team (2010) • WHL East First All-Star Team (2011) • Canadian Major Junior Goaltender of the Year (2011)

LaBARBERA, Jason (luh-BAHR-buhr-ah, JAY-suhn) PHX

Goaltender. Catches left. 6'3", 230 lbs. Born, Burnaby, B.C., January 18, 1980.
(NY Rangers' 3rd choice, 66th overall, in 1998 Entry Draft).

			Regular Season								Playoffs						
Season	Club	League	GP	W	L	O/T	Mins	GA	SO	Avg	GP	W	L	Mins	GA	SO	Avg
1995-96	Prince George	Minor-BC	31	....	....	....	1860	83	0	2.68	....	....	....	....	....	....	....
1996-97	Tri-City Americans	WHL	2	1	0	0	63	4	0	3.81	....	....	....	....	....	....	....
	Portland	WHL	9	5	1	1	443	18	0	2.44	....	....	....	....	....	....	....
1997-98	Portland	WHL	23	18	4	0	1305	72	1	3.31	....	....	....	....	....	....	....
1998-99	Portland	WHL	51	18	23	9	2991	170	4	3.41	4	0	4	252	19	0	4.52
99-2000	Portland	WHL	34	8	24	2	2005	123	1	3.68	....	....	....	....	....	....	....
	Spokane Chiefs	WHL	21	12	6	2	1146	50	0	2.62	9	6	1	435	18	1	2.48
2000-01	**NY Rangers**	**NHL**	**1**	**0**	**0**	**0**	**10**	**0**	**0**	**0.00**	....	....	....	....	....	....	....
	Hartford Wolf Pack	AHL	4	1	1	0	156	12	0	4.61	....	....	....	....	....	....	....
	Charlotte Checkers	ECHL	35	18	10	7	2100	112	1	3.20	2	1	1	143	5	0	2.09
2001-02	Hartford Wolf Pack	AHL	20	7	11	1	1058	55	0	3.12	....	....	....	....	....	....	....
	Charlotte Checkers	ECHL	13	9	3	1	744	29	0	2.34	4	2	2	212	12	0	3.39
2002-03	Hartford Wolf Pack	AHL	46	18	17	6	2452	105	2	2.57	2	0	2	117	6	0	3.07
2003-04	**NY Rangers**	**NHL**	**4**	**1**	**2**	**0**	**198**	**16**	**0**	**4.85**	....	....	....	....	....	....	....
	Hartford Wolf Pack	AHL	59	34	9	9	3393	90	*13	1.59	16	11	5	1043	30	*3	*1.73
2004-05	Hartford Wolf Pack	AHL	53	31	16	2	2937	90	6	1.84	4	1	3	238	9	0	2.27
2005-06	**Los Angeles**	**NHL**	**29**	**11**	**9**	**2**	**1433**	**69**	**1**	**2.89**	....	....	....	....	....	....	....
	Manchester	AHL	3	1	1	1	185	10	0	3.25	....	....	....	....	....	....	....
2006-07	Manchester	AHL	*62	*39	20	1	*3619	133	*7	2.21	13	6	7	824	38	1	2.77
2007-08	**Los Angeles**	**NHL**	**45**	**17**	**23**	**2**	**2421**	**121**	**1**	**3.00**	....	....	....	....	....	....	....
2008-09	**Los Angeles**	**NHL**	**19**	**5**	**8**	**4**	**995**	**47**	**2**	**2.83**	....	....	....	....	....	....	....
	Vancouver	**NHL**	**9**	**3**	**2**	**2**	**451**	**20**	**0**	**2.66**	....	....	....	....	....	....	....
2009-10	**Phoenix**	**NHL**	**17**	**8**	**5**	**1**	**928**	**33**	**0**	**2.13**	....	....	....	....	....	....	....
2010-11	**Phoenix**	**NHL**	**17**	**7**	**6**	**3**	**883**	**48**	**2**	**3.26**	....	....	....	....	....	....	....
	NHL Totals		**141**	**52**	**55**	**14**	**7319**	**354**	**6**	**2.90**	....	....	....	....	....	....	....

AHL First All-Star Team (2004, 2007) • Aldege "Baz" Bastien Memorial Award (AHL - Outstanding Goaltender) (2004, 2007) • Les Cunningham Award (AHL - MVP) (2004) • Harry "Hap" Holmes Memorial Trophy (AHL - fewest goals against) (2005) (shared with Steve Valiquette) • Harry "Hap" Holmes Memorial Trophy (AHL - fewest goals against) (2007)

Signed as a free agent by **Los Angeles**, August 2, 2005. Traded to **Vancouver** by **Los Angeles** for Vancouver's 7th round choice (later traded to Atlanta – Atlanta selected Jordan Samuels-Thomas) in 2009 Entry Draft, December 30, 2008. Signed as a free agent by **Phoenix**, July 1, 2009.

LACK, Eddie (LAK, EH-dee) VAN

Goaltender. Catches left. 6'4", 187 lbs. Born, Norrtalje, Sweden, January 5, 1988.

			Regular Season								Playoffs						
Season	Club	League	GP	W	L	O/T	Mins	GA	SO	Avg	GP	W	L	Mins	GA	SO	Avg
2004-05	Djurgarden U18	Swe-U18	9	....	....	....	527	21	1	2.39	3	....	....	140	6	0	2.57
	Djurgarden Jr.	Swe-Jr.	1	....	....	....	60	6	0	6.00	....	....	....	....	....	....	....
2005-06	Djurgarden Jr.	Swe-Jr.	23	....	....	....	1400	49	3	2.10	....	....	....	....	....	....	....
2006-07	Leksands IF Jr.	Swe-Jr.	30	....	....	....	1782	85	0	2.86	....	....	....	....	....	....	....
	Leksands IF	Sweden-2	3	....	....	....	137	7	0	3.06	....	....	....	....	....	....	....
2007-08	Leksands IF Jr.	Swe-Jr.	18	....	....	....	1077	47	4	2.62	3	....	....	179	8	0	2.68
	Leksands IF	Sweden-2	26	....	....	....	1530	50	4	1.96	....	....	....	....	....	....	....
2008-09	Leksands IF Jr.	Swe-Jr.	2	....	....	....	120	4	1	2.00	....	....	....	....	....	....	....
	Leksands IF	Sweden-2	38	....	....	....	2260	78	4	2.07	....	....	....	....	....	....	....
2009-10	Brynas IF Gavle Jr.	Swe-Jr.	6	....	....	....	359	21	0	....	....	....	....	....	....	....	....
	Brynas IF Gavle	Sweden	14	....	....	....	809	36	0	2.67	2	....	....	79	2	0	1.53
2010-11	Manitoba Moose	AHL	53	28	21	4	3135	118	5	2.26	12	6	5	752	25	2	1.99

AHL All-Rookie Team (2011)

Signed as a free agent by **Vancouver**, April 6, 2010.

LALIME, Patrick (lah-LEEM, PAT-rihk)

Goaltender. Catches left. 6'3", 192 lbs. Born, St-Bonaventure, Que., July 7, 1974.
(Pittsburgh's 6th choice, 156th overall, in 1993 Entry Draft).

			Regular Season								Playoffs						
Season	Club	League	GP	W	L	O/T	Mins	GA	SO	Avg	GP	W	L	Mins	GA	SO	Avg
1990-91	Abitibi Forestiers	QAAA	26	9	17	0	1595	151	0	5.81	....	....	....	....	....	....	....
1991-92	Shawinigan	QMJHL	6	1	2	0	271	25	0	5.54	....	....	....	....	....	....	....
1992-93	Shawinigan	QMJHL	44	10	26	5	2468	192	0	4.67	....	....	....	....	....	....	....
1993-94	Shawinigan	QMJHL	48	22	20	2	2718	188	1	4.15	5	1	3	223	25	0	6.73
1994-95	Hampton Roads	ECHL	26	15	7	3	1470	82	2	3.35	....	....	....	....	....	....	....
	Cleveland	IHL	23	7	10	4	1230	91	0	4.44	....	....	....	....	....	....	....
1995-96	Cleveland	IHL	41	20	12	7	2314	149	0	3.86	....	....	....	....	....	....	....
1996-97	**Pittsburgh**	**NHL**	**39**	**21**	**12**	**2**	**2058**	**101**	**3**	**2.94**	....	....	....	....	....	....	....
	Cleveland	IHL	14	6	6	2	834	45	1	3.24	....	....	....	....	....	....	....
1997-98	Grand Rapids	IHL	31	10	10	9	1749	76	2	2.61	1	0	1	77	4	0	3.11
1998-99	Kansas City Blades	IHL	*66	*39	20	4	*3789	190	2	3.01	3	1	2	179	6	1	2.01
99-2000	**Ottawa**	**NHL**	**38**	**19**	**14**	**3**	**2038**	**79**	**3**	**2.33**	....	....	....	....	....	....	....
2000-01	**Ottawa**	**NHL**	**60**	**36**	**19**	**5**	**3607**	**141**	**7**	**2.35**	**4**	**0**	**4**	**251**	**10**	**0**	**2.39**
2001-02	**Ottawa**	**NHL**	**61**	**27**	**24**	**8**	**3583**	**148**	**7**	**2.48**	**12**	**7**	**5**	**778**	**18**	**4**	***1.39**
2002-03	**Ottawa**	**NHL**	**67**	**39**	**20**	**7**	**3943**	**142**	**8**	**2.16**	**18**	**11**	**7**	**1122**	**34**	**1**	**1.82**
2003-04	**Ottawa**	**NHL**	**57**	**25**	**23**	**7**	**3324**	**127**	**5**	**2.29**	**7**	**3**	**4**	**398**	**13**	**0**	**1.96**
2004-05								DID NOT PLAY									
2005-06	**St. Louis**	**NHL**	**31**	**4**	**18**	**8**	**1699**	**103**	**0**	**3.64**	....	....	....	....	....	....	....
	Peoria Rivermen	AHL	14	6	6	1	798	38	1	2.86	....	....	....	....	....	....	....
2006-07	**Chicago**	**NHL**	**12**	**4**	**6**	**1**	**645**	**33**	**1**	**3.07**	....	....	....	....	....	....	....
	Norfolk Admirals	AHL	4	3	1	0	241	10	0	2.49	....	....	....	....	....	....	....
2007-08	**Chicago**	**NHL**	**32**	**16**	**12**	**2**	**1828**	**86**	**1**	**2.82**	....	....	....	....	....	....	....
2008-09	**Buffalo**	**NHL**	**24**	**5**	**13**	**3**	**1297**	**67**	**0**	**3.10**	....	....	....	....	....	....	....
2009-10	**Buffalo**	**NHL**	**16**	**4**	**8**	**2**	**854**	**40**	**0**	**2.81**	....	....	....	....	....	....	....
	Portland Pirates	AHL	2	0	1	1	124	6	0	2.91	....	....	....	....	....	....	....
2010-11	**Buffalo**	**NHL**	**7**	**0**	**5**	**0**	**365**	**18**	**0**	**2.96**	....	....	....	....	....	....	....
	NHL Totals		**444**	**200**	**174**	**48**	**25241**	**1085**	**35**	**2.58**	**41**	**21**	**20**	**2549**	**75**	**5**	**1.77**

NHL All-Rookie Team (1997) • IHL First All-Star Team (1999)

Played in NHL All-Star Game (2003)

• Rights traded to **Anaheim** by **Pittsburgh** for Sean Pronger, March 24, 1998. Traded to **Ottawa** by **Anaheim** for Ted Donato and the rights to Antti-Jussi Niemi, June 18, 1999. Traded to **St. Louis** by **Ottawa** for St. Louis' 4th round choice (Ilya Zubov) in 2005 Entry Draft, June 27, 2004. Signed as a free agent by **Chicago**, July 1, 2006. Signed as a free agent by **Buffalo**, July 1, 2008. • Officially announced his retirement, July 20, 2011.

LAMOUREUX, Jean-Phillippe (LA-muh-roo, ZHAWN-fihl-EEP)

Goaltender. Catches left. 5'10", 165 lbs. Born, Grand Forks, ND, August 20, 1984.

			Regular Season								Playoffs						
Season	Club	League	GP	W	L	O/T	Mins	GA	SO	Avg	GP	W	L	Mins	GA	SO	Avg
2001-02	Lincoln Stars	USHL	31	20	8	1	1758	66	6	2.25	....	....	....	....	....	....	....
2002-03	Lincoln Stars	USHL	34	22	7	4	1968	71	4	2.16	4	4	0	228	6	0	1.58
2003-04	Lincoln Stars	USHL	50	22	23	3	2874	134	3	2.80	....	....	....	....	....	....	....
2004-05	North Dakota	WCHA	18	7	8	2	1043	38	0	2.19	....	....	....	....	....	....	....
2005-06	North Dakota	WCHA	14	5	7	0	734	32	1	2.61	....	....	....	....	....	....	....
2006-07	North Dakota	WCHA	*37	*21	12	4	*2184	88	3	2.42	....	....	....	....	....	....	....
2007-08	North Dakota	WCHA	*42	*27	11	4	*2508	73	*6	*1.75	....	....	....	....	....	....	....
2008-09	Alaska Aces	ECHL	51	*33	16	2	3071	117	*8	2.29	*21	*15	6	*1263	41	*4	*1.95
2009-10	Portland Pirates	AHL	31	14	12	2	1750	87	2	2.98	4	0	3	207	10	0	2.90
2010-11	Abbotsford Heat	AHL	19	8	4	3	953	35	2	2.20	....	....	....	....	....	....	....
	Utah Grizzlies	ECHL	20	11	7	1	1157	48	3	2.49	....	....	....	....	....	....	....

ECHL Goaltender of the Year (2009)

Signed as a free agent by **Buffalo**, July 30, 2009. Signed as a free agent by **Calgary**, July 22, 2010.

LARSSON, Daniel (LAR-suhn, DAN-yehl) DET

Goaltender. Catches left. 6', 180 lbs. Born, Boden, Sweden, February 7, 1986.
(Detroit's 4th choice, 92nd overall, in 2006 Entry Draft).

			Regular Season								Playoffs						
Season	Club	League	GP	W	L	O/T	Mins	GA	SO	Avg	GP	W	L	Mins	GA	SO	Avg
2002-03	Lulea HF U18	Swe-U18	12	....	....	....	731	50	0	4.10	....	....	....	....	....	....	....
2003-04	Lulea HF Jr.	Swe-Jr.	4	....	....	....	239	12	0	3.01	....	....	....	....	....	....	....
	Bodens IK	Sweden-2	1	....	....	....	20	1	0	3.00	....	....	....	....	....	....	....
2004-05	Bodens IK	Sweden-2	28	....	....	....	1514	97	1	3.84	....	....	....	....	....	....	....
2005-06	Hammarby Jr.	Swe-Jr.	9	....	....	....	548	24	1	2.63	....	....	....	....	....	....	....
	Hammarby	Sweden-2	36	....	....	....	2001	90	0	2.70	....	....	....	....	....	....	....
2006-07	Djurgarden	Sweden	24	....	....	....	1259	53	3	2.53	....	....	....	....	....	....	....
2007-08	Djurgarden	Sweden	46	....	....	....	2721	104	6	2.29	5	....	....	295	13	0	2.64
2008-09	Grand Rapids	AHL	40	22	12	2	2152	99	5	2.76	....	....	....	....	....	....	....
2009-10	Grand Rapids	AHL	53	23	24	2	2840	135	1	2.85	....	....	....	....	....	....	....
2010-11	HV 71 Jonkoping	Sweden	45	....	....	....	2728	115	2	2.53	2	....	....	116	5	0	2.58

Signed as a free agent by **Jonkoping** (Sweden), May 19, 2010.

LAWSON, Nathan (LAW-suhn, NAY-thuhn) MTL

Goaltender. Catches left. 6'2", 203 lbs. Born, Calgary, Alta., September 29, 1983.

			Regular Season								Playoffs						
Season	Club	League	GP	W	L	O/T	Mins	GA	SO	Avg	GP	W	L	Mins	GA	SO	Avg
2004-05	Alaska Anchorage	WCHA	27	7	15	3	1482	82	1	3.32	....	....	....	....	....	....	....
2005-06	Alaska Anchorage	WCHA	21	4	11	3	1063	61	1	3.44	....	....	....	....	....	....	....
2006-07	Alaska Anchorage	WCHA	27	10	15	2	1523	77	0	3.03	....	....	....	....	....	....	....
2007-08	Phoenix	ECHL	5	3	2	0	279	14	1	3.01	....	....	....	....	....	....	....
	Utah Grizzlies	ECHL	24	14	7	1	1390	67	1	2.89	10	5	4	543	26	2	2.87
2008-09	Bridgeport	AHL	31	19	9	2	1723	62	2	2.16	2	0	2	123	8	0	3.89
	Utah Grizzlies	ECHL	3	2	0	0	158	6	0	2.28	....	....	....	....	....	....	....
2009-10	Bridgeport	AHL	36	16	16	3	2121	89	1	2.52	1	0	0	46	2	0	2.63
2010-11	**NY Islanders**	**NHL**	**10**	**1**	**4**	**2**	**384**	**26**	**0**	**4.06**	....	....	....	....	....	....	....
	Bridgeport	AHL	16	6	5	4	953	46	0	2.90	....	....	....	....	....	....	....
	NHL Totals		**10**	**1**	**4**	**2**	**384**	**26**	**0**	**4.06**	....	....	....	....	....	....	....

AHL All-Rookie Team (2009)

Signed as a free agent by **NY Islanders**, March 2, 2008. Signed as a free agent by **Montreal**, July 5, 2011.

LECLAIRE, Pascal (luh-KLAIR, pas-KAL)

Goaltender. Catches left. 6'2", 202 lbs. Born, Repentigny, Que., November 7, 1982.
(Columbus' 1st choice, 8th overall, in 2001 Entry Draft).

			Regular Season								Playoffs						
Season	Club	League	GP	W	L	O/T	Mins	GA	SO	Avg	GP	W	L	Mins	GA	SO	Avg
1997-98	Cap-d-Madeleine	QAAA	26	6	17	3	1580	127	0	4.90	....	....	....	....	....	....	....
1998-99	Halifax	QMJHL	33	19	11	1	1828	96	2	3.15	1	0	0	17	2	0	7.20
99-2000	Halifax	QMJHL	31	16	8	4	1729	103	1	3.57	5	1	2	198	12	0	3.64
2000-01	Halifax	QMJHL	35	14	16	5	2111	126	1	3.58	2	0	2	109	10	0	5.49
2001-02	Montreal Rocket	QMJHL	45	15	23	4	2513	138	1	3.29	7	3	4	441	15	0	*2.04
2002-03	Syracuse Crunch	AHL	36	8	21	3	1886	112	0	3.56	....	....	....	....	....	....	....
2003-04	**Columbus**	**NHL**	**2**	**0**	**2**	**0**	**119**	**7**	**0**	**3.53**	....	....	....	....	....	....	....
	Syracuse Crunch	AHL	44	21	16	3	2447	125	2	3.06	3	1	2	142	12	0	5.07
2004-05	Syracuse Crunch	AHL	14	5	6	3	845	33	2	2.34	....	....	....	....	....	....	....
2005-06	**Columbus**	**NHL**	**33**	**11**	**15**	**3**	**1804**	**97**	**0**	**3.23**	....	....	....	....	....	....	....
	Syracuse Crunch	AHL	7	3	3	0	340	16	1	2.82	5	2	3	288	11	1	2.29
2006-07	**Columbus**	**NHL**	**24**	**6**	**15**	**2**	**1315**	**65**	**1**	**2.97**	....	....	....	....	....	....	....
2007-08	**Columbus**	**NHL**	**54**	**24**	**17**	**6**	**2986**	**112**	**9**	**2.25**	....	....	....	....	....	....	....
2008-09	**Columbus**	**NHL**	**12**	**4**	**6**	**1**	**674**	**43**	**0**	**3.83**	....	....	....	....	....	....	....
2009-10	**Ottawa**	**NHL**	**34**	**12**	**14**	**2**	**1745**	**93**	**0**	**3.20**	**3**	**1**	**2**	**211**	**10**	**0**	**2.84**
2010-11	**Ottawa**	**NHL**	**14**	**4**	**7**	**1**	**763**	**36**	**0**	**2.83**	....	....	....	....	....	....	....
	Binghamton	AHL	1	0	0	1	65	2	0	1.85	....	....	....	....	....	....	....
	NHL Totals		**173**	**61**	**76**	**15**	**9406**	**453**	**10**	**2.89**	**3**	**1**	**2**	**211**	**10**	**0**	**2.84**

• Missed majority of 2008-09 due to ankle injury vs. Minnesota, October 25, 2008. Traded to **Ottawa** by **Columbus** with Columbus' 2nd round choice (Robin Lehner) in 2009 Entry Draft for Antoine Vermette, March 4, 2009.

LEE, Michael (LEE, MIGH-kuhl) PHX

Goaltender. Catches left. 6'1", 185 lbs. Born, Fargo, ND, October 5, 1990.
(Phoenix's 3rd choice, 91st overall, in 2009 Entry Draft).

			Regular Season								Playoffs						
Season	Club	League	GP	W	L	O/T	Mins	GA	SO	Avg	GP	W	L	Mins	GA	SO	Avg
2006-07	Roseau Rams	High-MN	12	12	0	0	612	9	6	0.75	....	....	....	....	....	....	....
2007-08	Roseau Rams	High-MN	29	27	2	0	1482	32	12	1.10	1	0	0	16	0	0	0.00
2008-09	Fargo Force	USHL	48	26	15	4	2745	110	3	2.40	10	7	3	546	24	*1	2.64
2009-10	St. Cloud State	WCHA	26	12	9	3	1477	69	2	2.80	....	....	....	....	....	....	....
2010-11	St. Cloud State	WCHA	32	12	14	4	1879	86	1	2.75	....	....	....	....	....	....	....

USHL All-Rookie Team (2009) • USHL Goaltender of the Year (2009)

LEGACE, Manny (LEH-gah-see, MAN-ee)

Goaltender. Catches left. 5'10", 200 lbs. Born, Toronto, Ont., February 4, 1973.
(Hartford's 5th choice, 188th overall, in 1993 Entry Draft).

			Regular Season								Playoffs						
Season	Club	League	GP	W	L	O/T	Mins	GA	SO	Avg	GP	W	L	Mins	GA	SO	Avg
1987-88	Alliston Hornets	ON-Jr.C	16	7	9	0	960	83	0	5.17	....	....	....	....	....	....	....
1988-89	Vaughan Raiders	ON-Jr.B	23	....	....	....	1303	92	1	4.24	....	....	....	....	....	....	....
1989-90	Vaughan Raiders	ON-Jr.B	21	8	11	1	1180	89	1	4.53	....	....	....	....	....	....	....
	Thornhill	ON-Jr.B	8	3	3	2	480	30	0	3.75	....	....	....	....	....	....	....
1990-91	Niagara Falls	OHL	30	13	11	2	1515	107	0	4.24	4	1	1	119	10	0	5.04
1991-92	Niagara Falls	OHL	43	21	16	3	2384	143	0	3.60	14	8	5	791	56	0	4.25
1992-93	Niagara Falls	OHL	48	22	19	3	2630	171	0	3.90	4	0	4	240	18	0	4.50
1993-94	Canada	Nat-Tm	16	8	6	0	859	36	2	2.51	....	....	....	....	....	....	....
1994-95	Springfield Indians	AHL	39	12	17	6	2169	128	2	3.54	....	....	....	....	....	....	....
1995-96	Springfield Falcons	AHL	37	20	12	4	2196	83	*5	*2.27	4	1	3	220	18	0	4.91
1996-97	Springfield Falcons	AHL	36	17	14	5	2119	107	1	3.03	12	9	3	745	25	*2	2.01
	Richmond	ECHL	3	2	1	0	157	8	0	3.05	....	....	....	....	....	....	....
1997-98	Springfield Falcons	AHL	6	4	2	0	345	16	0	2.78	....	....	....	....	....	....	....
	Las Vegas Thunder	IHL	41	18	16	4	2106	111	1	3.16	4	1	3	237	16	0	4.05
1998-99	**Los Angeles**	**NHL**	**17**	**2**	**9**	**2**	**899**	**39**	**0**	**2.60**	....	....	....	....	....	....	....
	Long Beach	IHL	33	22	8	1	1796	67	2	2.24	6	4	2	338	9	0	*1.60
99-2000	**Detroit**	**NHL**	**4**	**4**	**0**	**0**	**240**	**11**	**0**	**2.75**	....	....	....	....	....	....	....
	Manitoba Moose	IHL	42	17	18	5	2409	104	2	2.59	2	0	2	141	7	0	2.97
2000-01	**Detroit**	**NHL**	**39**	**24**	**5**	**5**	**2136**	**73**	**2**	**2.05**	....	....	....	....	....	....	....
2001-02 ♦	**Detroit**	**NHL**	**20**	**10**	**6**	**2**	**1117**	**45**	**1**	**2.42**	**1**	**0**	**0**	**11**	**1**	**0**	**5.45**
2002-03	**Detroit**	**NHL**	**25**	**14**	**5**	**4**	**1406**	**51**	**0**	**2.18**	....	....	....	....	....	....	....
2003-04	**Detroit**	**NHL**	**41**	**23**	**10**	**5**	**2325**	**82**	**3**	**2.12**	**4**	**2**	**2**	**220**	**8**	**0**	**2.18**
2004-05	Voskresensk	Russia	2	....	....	....	89	10	0	6.73	....	....	....	....	....	....	....
2005-06	**Detroit**	**NHL**	**51**	**37**	**8**	**3**	**2905**	**106**	**7**	**2.19**	**6**	**2**	**4**	**408**	**18**	**0**	**2.65**
	Grand Rapids	AHL	1	1	0	0	60	2	0	2.00	....	....	....	....	....	....	....
2006-07	**St. Louis**	**NHL**	**45**	**23**	**15**	**5**	**2522**	**109**	**5**	**2.59**	....	....	....	....	....	....	....
2007-08	**St. Louis**	**NHL**	**66**	**27**	**25**	**8**	**3666**	**147**	**5**	**2.41**	....	....	....	....	....	....	....
2008-09	**St. Louis**	**NHL**	**29**	**13**	**9**	**2**	**1452**	**77**	**0**	**3.18**	....	....	....	....	....	....	....
	Peoria Rivermen	AHL	23	14	7	1	1290	43	3	2.00	7	3	4	429	18	0	2.52
2009-10	Chicago Wolves	AHL	6	2	2	1	317	17	1	3.21	....	....	....	....	....	....	....
	Carolina	**NHL**	**28**	**10**	**7**	**5**	**1472**	**69**	**1**	**2.81**	....	....	....	....	....	....	....
2010-11	Iserlohn Roosters	Germany	40	17	22	....	2323	97	3	2.51	....	....	....	....	....	....	....
	NHL Totals		**365**	**187**	**99**	**41**	**20140**	**809**	**24**	**2.41**	**11**	**4**	**6**	**639**	**27**	**0**	**2.54**

OHL First All-Star Team (1993) • AHL First All-Star Team (1996) • Harry ''Hap'' Holmes Memorial Award (AHL – fewest goals against) (1996) (shared with Scott Langkow) • Aldege "Baz" Bastien Memorial Award (AHL – Outstanding Goaltender) (1996)

Played in NHL All-Star Game (2008)

• Rights transferred to **Carolina** after **Hartford** franchise relocated, June 25, 1997. Traded to **Los Angeles** by **Carolina** for future considerations, July 31, 1998. Signed as a free agent by **Detroit**, August 9, 1999. Claimed on waivers by **Vancouver** from **Detroit**, September 30, 1999. Claimed on waivers by **Detroit** from **Vancouver**, October 13, 1999. Signed as a free agent by **Voskresensk** (Russia), December 20, 2004. Signed as a free agent by **St. Louis**, August 8, 2006. Signed to a PTO (professional tryout) contract by **Chicago** (AHL), October 12, 2009. Signed as a free agent by **Carolina**, November 9, 2009. Signed as a free agent by **Iserlohn** (Germany), October 13, 2010.

LEGGIO, David (LEH-JEE-oh, DAY-vihd) BUF

Goaltender. Catches left. 6', 180 lbs. Born, Buffalo, NY, July 31, 1984.

			Regular Season								Playoffs						
Season	Club	League	GP	W	L	O/T	Mins	GA	SO	Avg	GP	W	L	Mins	GA	SO	Avg
2003-04	Capital District	EJHL	42	25	10	6	....	....	4	2.80	....	....	....	....	....	....	....
2004-05	Clarkson Knights	ECAC	5	2	1	0	182	9	0	2.97	....	....	....	....	....	....	....
2005-06	Clarkson Knights	ECAC	23	11	9	3	1446	62	1	2.57	....	....	....	....	....	....	....
2006-07	Clarkson Knights	ECAC	37	24	7	5	2167	78	2	2.16	....	....	....	....	....	....	....
2007-08	Clarkson Knights	ECAC	38	22	12	4	2211	81	5	2.20	....	....	....	....	....	....	....
	Binghamton	AHL	1	0	1	0	30	2	0	4.06	....	....	....	....	....	....	....
2008-09	Albany River Rats	AHL	1	0	1	0	60	7	0	7.00	....	....	....	....	....	....	....
	Florida Everblades	ECHL	39	27	7	3	2284	86	4	2.26	11	6	5	734	30	0	2.45
2009-10	TPS Turku	Finland	30	12	13	3	1598	78	1	2.93	7	5	2	419	11	1	1.57
2010-11	Portland Pirates	AHL	36	22	12	0	1993	93	3	2.80	9	5	4	510	27	0	3.18

ECAC Second All-Star Team (2008)

Signed as a free agent by **Turku** (Finland), June 4, 2009. Signed as a free agent by **Buffalo**, November 12, 2010.

LEHNER, Robin (LEH-nuhr, RAW-bihn) OTT

Goaltender. Catches left. 6'4", 224 lbs. Born, Goteborg, Sweden, July 24, 1991.
(Ottawa's 3rd choice, 46th overall, in 2009 Entry Draft).

			Regular Season								Playoffs						
Season	Club	League	GP	W	L	O/T	Mins	GA	SO	Avg	GP	W	L	Mins	GA	SO	Avg
2007-08	Frolunda U18	Swe-U18	19	....	....	....	1147	34	6	1.78	4	....	....	243	15	0	3.70
2008-09	Frolunda U18	Swe-U18	2	....	....	....	117	5	0	2.56	7	....	....	438	19	0	2.60
	Frolunda Jr.	Swe-Jr.	22	....	....	....	1318	67	1	3.05	1	....	....	58	3	0	3.08
2009-10	Sault Ste. Marie	OHL	47	27	13	3	2574	120	*5	2.80	5	1	4	279	20	0	4.30
	Binghamton	AHL	2	2	0	0	120	6	0	3.00	....	....	....	....	....	....	....
2010-11	**Ottawa**	**NHL**	**8**	**1**	**4**	**0**	**341**	**20**	**0**	**3.52**	....	....	....	....	....	....	....
	Binghamton	AHL	22	10	8	2	1246	56	3	2.70	19	*14	4	1112	39	*3	2.10
	NHL Totals		**8**	**1**	**4**	**0**	**341**	**20**	**0**	**3.52**	....	....	....	....	....	....	....

Jack A. Butterfield Trophy (AHL – Playoff MVP) (2011)

LEHTONEN, Kari (LEH-tuh-nehn, KAH-ree) DAL

Goaltender. Catches left. 6'4", 215 lbs. Born, Helsinki, Finland, November 16, 1983.
(Atlanta's 1st choice, 2nd overall, in 2002 Entry Draft).

			Regular Season								Playoffs						
Season	Club	League	GP	W	L	O/T	Mins	GA	SO	Avg	GP	W	L	Mins	GA	SO	Avg
1998-99	Jokerit U18	Fin-U18	2	....	....	....	....	....	....	....	4	2	2	240	7	0	1.75
99-2000	Jokerit Helsinki Jr.	Fin-Jr.	33	21	9	3	1974	86	2	2.61	12	9	3	758	14	4	1.11
2000-01	Jokerit U18	Fin-U18	....	....	....	....	....	....	....	....	6	....	....	....	....	....	....
	Jokerit Helsinki Jr.	Fin-Jr.	31	20	9	1	1799	71	3	2.37	1	0	1	54	4	0	4.44
	Jokerit Helsinki	Finland	4	3	1	0	189	6	0	1.90	....	....	....	....	....	....	....
2001-02	Jokerit Helsinki Jr.	Fin-Jr.	6	5	1	0	360	11	1	1.83	....	....	....	....	....	....	....
	Jokerit Helsinki	Finland	23	13	5	2	1242	37	4	1.79	11	8	2	623	18	3	1.73
2002-03	Jokerit Helsinki	Finland	45	23	14	6	2634	87	5	1.98	10	6	4	626	17	2	1.63
2003-04	**Atlanta**	**NHL**	**4**	**4**	**0**	**0**	**240**	**5**	**1**	**1.25**	....	....	....	....	....	....	....
	Chicago Wolves	AHL	39	20	14	2	2192	88	3	2.41	10	6	4	663	23	1	2.08
2004-05	Chicago Wolves	AHL	57	38	17	2	3378	128	5	2.27	16	10	6	983	28	2	*1.71
2005-06	**Atlanta**	**NHL**	**38**	**20**	**15**	**0**	**2166**	**106**	**2**	**2.94**	....	....	....	....	....	....	....
2006-07	**Atlanta**	**NHL**	**68**	**34**	**24**	**9**	**3934**	**183**	**4**	**2.79**	**2**	**0**	**2**	**118**	**11**	**0**	**5.59**
2007-08	**Atlanta**	**NHL**	**48**	**17**	**22**	**5**	**2707**	**131**	**4**	**2.90**	....	....	....	....	....	....	....
	Chicago Wolves	AHL	2	2	0	0	124	4	0	1.93	....	....	....	....	....	....	....
2008-09	**Atlanta**	**NHL**	**46**	**19**	**22**	**3**	**2624**	**134**	**3**	**3.06**	....	....	....	....	....	....	....
2009-10	**Dallas**	**NHL**	**12**	**6**	**4**	**0**	**663**	**31**	**0**	**2.81**	....	....	....	....	....	....	....
	Chicago Wolves	AHL	4	1	1	2	247	11	0	2.67	....	....	....	....	....	....	....
2010-11	**Dallas**	**NHL**	**69**	**34**	**24**	**11**	**4119**	**175**	**3**	**2.55**	....	....	....	....	....	....	....
	NHL Totals		**285**	**134**	**111**	**28**	**16453**	**765**	**17**	**2.79**	**2**	**0**	**2**	**118**	**11**	**0**	**5.59**

AHL Second All-Star Team (2005)

• Missed majority of 2009-10 due to off-season back surgery. Traded to **Dallas** by **Atlanta** for Ivan Vishnevskiy and Dallas' 4th round choice (Ivan Telegin) in 2010 Entry Draft, February 9, 2010.

LEIGHTON, Michael (LAY-tohn, MIGH-kuhl) PHI

Goaltender. Catches left. 6'3", 186 lbs. Born, Petrolia, Ont., May 19, 1981.
(Chicago's 5th choice, 165th overall, in 1999 Entry Draft).

			Regular Season								Playoffs						
Season	Club	League	GP	W	L	O/T	Mins	GA	SO	Avg	GP	W	L	Mins	GA	SO	Avg
1997-98	Petrolia Jets	ON-Jr.B	30	....	....	....	1583	87	2	3.30	....	....	....	....	....	....	....
1998-99	Windsor Spitfires	OHL	28	4	15	9	1390	112	0	4.83	3	0	1	81	10	0	7.43
99-2000	Windsor Spitfires	OHL	42	17	17	2	2272	118	1	3.12	12	5	6	617	32	0	3.11
2000-01	Windsor Spitfires	OHL	54	32	13	5	3035	138	2	2.73	9	4	5	519	27	1	3.12
2001-02	Norfolk Admirals	AHL	52	27	16	8	3114	111	6	2.14	4	1	2	238	8	0	2.02
2002-03	**Chicago**	**NHL**	**8**	**2**	**3**	**2**	**447**	**21**	**1**	**2.82**	....	....	....	....	....	....	....
	Norfolk Admirals	AHL	36	18	13	5	2184	91	4	2.50	4	3	1	240	7	1	1.75
2003-04	**Chicago**	**NHL**	**34**	**6**	**18**	**8**	**1988**	**99**	**2**	**2.99**	....	....	....	....	....	....	....
	Norfolk Admirals	AHL	18	10	7	1	1081	33	1	1.83	4	2	1	212	2	2	0.57
2004-05	Norfolk Admirals	AHL	41	20	16	3	2319	78	7	2.02	....	....	....	....	....	....	....
2005-06	Rochester	AHL	40	15	22	1	2318	124	2	3.21	....	....	....	....	....	....	....
2006-07	Portland Pirates	AHL	16	8	6	1	962	37	2	2.31	....	....	....	....	....	....	....
	Nashville	**NHL**	**1**	**0**	**0**	**0**	**20**	**2**	**0**	**6.00**	....	....	....	....	....	....	....
	Philadelphia	**NHL**	**4**	**2**	**2**	**0**	**195**	**12**	**0**	**3.69**	....	....	....	....	....	....	....
	Philadelphia	AHL	5	2	0	2	270	7	0	1.56	....	....	....	....	....	....	....
2007-08	**Carolina**	**NHL**	**3**	**1**	**1**	**0**	**158**	**7**	**0**	**2.66**	....	....	....	....	....	....	....
	Albany River Rats	AHL	58	28	25	4	3451	121	*7	2.10	7	3	4	510	10	*2	*1.18
2008-09	**Carolina**	**NHL**	**19**	**6**	**7**	**2**	**1029**	**50**	**0**	**2.92**	....	....	....	....	....	....	....
2009-10	**Carolina**	**NHL**	**7**	**1**	**4**	**0**	**350**	**25**	**0**	**4.29**	....	....	....	....	....	....	....
	Philadelphia	**NHL**	**27**	**16**	**5**	**2**	**1449**	**60**	**1**	**2.48**	**14**	**8**	**3**	**757**	**31**	***3**	***2.46**
2010-11	**Philadelphia**	**NHL**	**1**	**1**	**0**	**0**	**60**	**4**	**0**	**4.00**	**2**	**0**	**1**	**70**	**4**	**0**	**3.43**
	Adirondack	AHL	30	14	12	3	1783	66	5	2.22	....	....	....	....	....	....	....
	NHL Totals		**104**	**35**	**40**	**14**	**5696**	**280**	**4**	**2.95**	**16**	**8**	**4**	**827**	**35**	**3**	**2.54**

AHL All-Rookie Team (2002) • AHL First All-Star Team (2008) • Aldege "Baz" Bastien Memorial Award (AHL – Outstanding Goaltender) (2008)

Traded to **Buffalo** by **Chicago** for Milan Bartovic, October 4, 2005. Signed as a free agent by **Anaheim**, July 13, 2006. Claimed on waivers by **Nashville** from **Anaheim**, November 27, 2006. Claimed on waivers by **Philadelphia** from **Nashville**, January 11, 2007. Claimed on waivers by **Montreal** from **Philadelphia**, February 27, 2007. Traded to **Carolina** by **Montreal** for Carolina's 7th round choice (Scott Kishel) in 2007 Entry Draft, June 23, 2007. Claimed on waivers by **Philadelphia** from **Carolina**, December 15, 2009.

LeNEVEU, David (LEH-neh-voo, DAY-vihd)

Goaltender. Catches left. 6'1", 190 lbs. Born, Fernie, B.C., May 23, 1983.
(Phoenix's 3rd choice, 46th overall, in 2002 Entry Draft).

			Regular Season								Playoffs						
Season	Club	League	GP	W	L	O/T	Mins	GA	SO	Avg	GP	W	L	Mins	GA	SO	Avg
99-2000	Fernie Ghostriders	AWHL	22	15	2	0	1140	48	0	2.49	....	....	....	....	....	....	....
2000-01	Nanaimo Clippers	BCHL	41	....	....	....	2330	127	6	3.29	....	....	....	....	....	....	....
2001-02	Cornell Big Red	ECAC	14	11	2	1	842	21	2	*1.50	....	....	....	....	....	....	....
2002-03	Cornell Big Red	ECAC	32	*28	3	1	1946	39	*9	*1.20	....	....	....	....	....	....	....
2003-04	Springfield Falcons	AHL	38	16	19	3	2217	102	1	2.76	....	....	....	....	....	....	....
2004-05	Utah Grizzlies	AHL	48	11	32	3	2702	132	0	2.93	....	....	....	....	....	....	....
2005-06	**Phoenix**	**NHL**	**15**	**3**	**8**	**2**	**814**	**44**	**0**	**3.24**	....	....	....	....	....	....	....
	San Antonio	AHL	28	10	16	2	1646	80	2	2.92	....	....	....	....	....	....	....
2006-07	**Phoenix**	**NHL**	**6**	**2**	**1**	**0**	**233**	**15**	**0**	**3.86**	....	....	....	....	....	....	....
	San Antonio	AHL	37	13	20	2	2101	104	2	2.97	....	....	....	....	....	....	....
2007-08	San Antonio	AHL	21	9	7	3	1172	52	1	2.66	....	....	....	....	....	....	....
	Hartford Wolf Pack	AHL	13	8	3	2	786	24	1	1.83	4	1	3	266	11	0	2.48
2008-09	Iowa Chops	AHL	46	20	19	6	2627	129	0	2.95	....	....	....	....	....	....	....
2009-10	Salzburg	Austria	43	....	....	....	2467	106	2	2.58	9	6	2	....	....	....	2.17
2010-11	**Columbus**	**NHL**	**1**	**0**	**0**	**0**	**20**	**2**	**0**	**6.00**	....	....	....	....	....	....	....
	Springfield Falcons	AHL	42	16	21	2	2426	120	0	2.97	....	....	....	....	....	....	....
	NHL Totals		**22**	**5**	**9**	**2**	**1067**	**61**	**0**	**3.43**	....	....	....	....	....	....	....

ECAC All-Rookie Team (2002) • ECAC First All-Star Team (2003) • ECAC Goaltender of the Year (2003) • ECAC Player of the Year (2003) (co-winner - Christopher Higgins) • NCAA East First All-American Team (2003)

Traded to **NY Rangers** by **Phoenix** with Josh Gratton, Fredrik Sjostrom and Phoenix's 5th round choice (Roman Horak) in 2009 Entry Draft for Marcel Hossa and Al Montoya, February 26, 2008. Signed as a free agent by **Anaheim**, July 7, 2008. Signed as a free agent by **Salzburg** (Austria), August 7, 2009. Signed as a free agent by **Columbus**, July 7, 2010.

LEVASSEUR, Jean-Philippe (leh-VAH-soor, ZHAWN-fihl-EEP)

Goaltender. Catches right. 6'1", 205 lbs. Born, Victoriaville, Que., January 15, 1987.
(Anaheim's 6th choice, 197th overall, in 2005 Entry Draft).

			Regular Season								Playoffs						
Season	Club	League	GP	W	L	O/T	Mins	GA	SO	Avg	GP	W	L	Mins	GA	SO	Avg
2002-03	Magog	QAAA	28	15	10	1	1563	71	3	2.73	....	....	....	....	....	....	....
2003-04	Magog	QAAA	24	12	11	2	1424	86	0	3.62	13	7	5	762	35	0	2.80
	Rouyn-Noranda	QMJHL	3	0	2	1	184	14	0	4.57	....	....	....	....	....	....	....
2004-05	Rouyn-Noranda	QMJHL	29	8	14	3	1393	89	0	3.83	3	0	0	48	3	0	3.76
2005-06	Rouyn-Noranda	QMJHL	58	*35	19	0	3125	178	2	3.42	5	1	4	297	16	0	3.23
2006-07	Rouyn-Noranda	QMJHL	58	*31	21	0	3118	182	1	3.50	15	8	6	852	51	0	3.59
2007-08	Portland Pirates	AHL	10	4	5	1	600	25	1	2.50	....	....	....	....	....	....	....
	Augusta Lynx	ECHL	29	10	11	2	1527	76	1	2.99	1	0	1	59	2	0	2.02
2008-09	Iowa Chops	AHL	41	13	18	4	2217	115	0	3.11	....	....	....	....	....	....	....
2009-10	Springfield Falcons	AHL	25	8	16	1	1438	86	1	3.59	....	....	....	....	....	....	....
	Laredo Bucks	CHL	16	10	3	3	986	38	0	2.31	....	....	....	....	....	....	....
	Bakersfield	ECHL	5	2	3	0	298	18	0	3.63	6	3	3	368	16	1	2.61
2010-11	Syracuse Crunch	AHL	45	13	23	3	2449	123	5	3.01	....	....	....	....	....	....	....

LIEUWEN, Nathan (l'YEW-uhn, NAY-thun) BUF

Goaltender. Catches left. 6'5", 189 lbs. Born, Abbotsford, B.C., August 8, 1991.
(Buffalo's 5th choice, 167th overall, in 2011 Entry Draft).

			Regular Season								Playoffs						
Season	Club	League	GP	W	L	O/T	Mins	GA	SO	Avg	GP	W	L	Mins	GA	SO	Avg
2007-08	Westside Warriors	BCHL	13	9	2	0	710	23	0	1.94	3	0	2	139	10	0	4.32
	Kootenay Ice	WHL	3	1	1	0	184	10	0	3.26	....	....	....	....	....	....	....
2008-09	Kootenay Ice	WHL	37	14	12	2	1915	94	3	2.95	....	....	....	....	....	....	....
2009-10	Kootenay Ice	WHL	26	10	10	0	1244	64	0	3.09	3	0	1	125	4	0	1.92
2010-11	Kootenay Ice	WHL	55	33	16	4	3098	144	3	2.79	19	*16	3	1178	44	*3	*2.24

LINDBACK, Anders (LIHND-bak, AN-duhrs) NSH

Goaltender. Catches left. 6'6", 205 lbs. Born, Gavle, Sweden, May 3, 1988.
(Nashville's 7th choice, 207th overall, in 2008 Entry Draft).

			Regular Season								Playoffs						
Season	Club	League	GP	W	L	O/T	Mins	GA	SO	Avg	GP	W	L	Mins	GA	SO	Avg
2003-04	Brynas U18	Swe-U18	3	....	....	....	178	13	0	4.38	....	....	....	....	....	....	....
2004-05	Brynas U18	Swe-U18	49	....	....	....	2940	108	7	2.20	....	....	....	....	....	....	....
2005-06	Brynas U18	Swe-U18	11	....	....	....	666	36	2	3.24	....	....	....	....	....	....	....
	Brynas IF Gavle Jr.	Swe-Jr.	5	....	....	....	257	7	2	1.64	....	....	....	....	....	....	....
2006-07	Brynas IF Gavle Jr.	Swe-Jr.	36	....	....	....	2143	81	5	2.27	3	....	....	180	6	0	2.00
2007-08	Almtuna	Sweden-2	18	....	....	....	1034	53	0	3.07	....	....	....	....	....	....	....
2008-09	Brynas IF Gavle Jr.	Swe-Jr.	3	....	....	....	179	7	0	2.35	....	....	....	....	....	....	....
	Brynas IF Gavle	Sweden	24	....	....	....	1332	57	1	2.57	3	....	....	177	7	0	2.37
2009-10	Timra IK	Sweden	42	....	....	....	2537	104	3	2.46	5	....	....	306	15	0	2.94
2010-11	**Nashville**	**NHL**	**22**	**11**	**5**	**2**	**1131**	**49**	**2**	**2.60**	**1**	**0**	**0**	**13**	**0**	**0**	**0.00**
	Milwaukee	AHL	4	2	2	0	241	11	0	2.73	....	....	....	....	....	....	....
	NHL Totals		**22**	**11**	**5**	**2**	**1131**	**49**	**2**	**2.60**	**1**	**0**	**0**	**13**	**0**	**0**	**0.00**

LUNDQVIST, Henrik (LUHND-kvihst, HEHN-rihk) NYR

Goaltender. Catches left. 6'1", 195 lbs. Born, Are, Sweden, March 2, 1982.
(NY Rangers' 7th choice, 205th overall, in 2000 Entry Draft).

			Regular Season								Playoffs						
Season	Club	League	GP	W	L	O/T	Mins	GA	SO	Avg	GP	W	L	Mins	GA	SO	Avg
1998-99	V.Frolunda Jr.	Swe-Jr.	35	....	....	....	2100	95	0	2.73	....	....	....	....	....	....	....
99-2000	V.Frolunda Jr.	Swe-Jr.	30	....	....	....	1726	73	0	2.54	5	4	1	300	7	2	1.40
2000-01	V.Frolunda U18	Swe-U18	2	....	....	....	120	5	0	2.50	3	2	1	182	5	0	1.62
	V.Frolunda Jr.	Swe-Jr.	19	....	....	....	1140	50	2	2.64	....	....	....	....	....	....	....
	IF Molndal Hockey	Sweden-2	7	....	....	....	420	29	0	4.22	....	....	....	....	....	....	....
	V.Frolunda	Sweden	4	....	....	....	190	11	0	3.47	....	....	....	....	....	....	....
2001-02	V.Frolunda	Sweden	20	....	....	....	1152	52	2	2.71	8	8	0	489	18	*2	2.21
	V.Frolunda Jr.	Swe-Jr.	1	1	0	0	60	4	0	4.00	....	....	....	....	....	....	....
2002-03	V.Frolunda	Sweden	28	....	....	....	1650	40	*6	*1.45	12	....	....	739	26	*2	2.11
	V.Frolunda Jr.	Swe-Jr.	1	1	0	0	60	4	0	4.00	....	....	....	....	....	....	....
2003-04	V.Frolunda	Sweden	*48	....	....	....	*2897	105	7	2.17	10	....	....	610	20	0	1.97
2004-05	Frolunda	Sweden	44	*33	8	3	2642	79	*6	*1.79	*14	*12	2	854	15	*6	*1.05
2005-06	**NY Rangers**	**NHL**	**53**	**30**	**12**	**9**	**3112**	**116**	**2**	**2.24**	**3**	**0**	**3**	**177**	**13**	**0**	**4.41**
	Sweden	Olympics	6	5	1	0	360	14	0	2.33	....	....	....	....	....	....	....
2006-07	**NY Rangers**	**NHL**	**70**	**37**	**22**	**8**	**4109**	**160**	**5**	**2.34**	**10**	**6**	**4**	**637**	**22**	**1**	**2.07**
2007-08	**NY Rangers**	**NHL**	**72**	**37**	**24**	**10**	**4305**	**160**	***10**	**2.23**	**10**	**5**	**5**	**608**	**26**	**1**	**2.57**
2008-09	**NY Rangers**	**NHL**	**70**	**38**	**25**	**7**	**4153**	**168**	**3**	**2.43**	**7**	**3**	**4**	**380**	**19**	**1**	**3.00**
2009-10	**NY Rangers**	**NHL**	**73**	**35**	**27**	**10**	**4204**	**167**	**4**	**2.38**	....	....	....	....	....	....	....
	Sweden	Olympics	3	2	1	0	179	4	*2	1.34	....	....	....	....	....	....	....
2010-11	**NY Rangers**	**NHL**	**68**	**36**	**27**	**5**	**4007**	**152**	***11**	**2.28**	**5**	**1**	**4**	**346**	**13**	**0**	**2.25**
	NHL Totals		**406**	**213**	**137**	**49**	**23890**	**923**	**35**	**2.32**	**35**	**15**	**20**	**2148**	**93**	**3**	**2.60**

NHL All-Rookie Team (2006)

Played in NHL All-Star Game (2009, 2011)

LUNDSTROM, Niklas (LOOND-struhm, NIHK-luhs) ST.L.

Goaltender. Catches left. 6'2", 187 lbs. Born, Varmdo, Sweden, January 10, 1993.
(St. Louis' 6th choice, 132nd overall, in 2011 Entry Draft).

			Regular Season								Playoffs						
Season	Club	League	GP	W	L	O/T	Mins	GA	SO	Avg	GP	W	L	Mins	GA	SO	Avg
2008-09	AIK IF Solna U18	Swe-U18	8	....	....	....	465	18	0	2.32	....	....	....	....	....	....	....
2009-10	AIK IF Solna U18	Swe-U18	16	....	....	....	963	39	3	2.43	2	....	....	117	3	0	1.54
	AIK IF Solna Jr.	Swe-Jr.	17	....	....	....	939	46	3	2.94	3	....	....	190	7	0	2.22
	AIK IF Solna	Sweden-2	1	....	....	....	34	1	0	1.79	....	....	....	....	....	....	....
2010-11	AIK IF Solna U18	Swe-U18	1	....	....	....	60	3	0	3.00	6	....	....	388	16	0	2.47
	AIK IF Solna Jr.	Swe-Jr.	22	....	....	....	1260	64	1	3.05	....	....	....	....	....	....	....
	AIK IF Solna	Sweden	1	....	....	....	47	5	0	6.34	....	....	....	....	....	....	....
	Lindlovens IF	Sweden-3	2	....	....	....	128	5	0	2.35	....	....	....	....	....	....	....

LUONGO, Roberto (loo-WAHN-goh, roh-BUHR-toh) VAN

Goaltender. Catches left. 6'3", 208 lbs. Born, Montreal, Que., April 4, 1979.
(NY Islanders' 1st choice, 4th overall, in 1997 Entry Draft).

			Regular Season								Playoffs						
Season	Club	League	GP	W	L	O/T	Mins	GA	SO	Avg	GP	W	L	Mins	GA	SO	Avg
1994-95	Montreal-Bourassa	QAAA	25	10	14	0	1465	94	0	3.85	....	....	....	....	....	....	....
1995-96	Val-d'Or Foreurs	QMJHL	23	6	11	4	1201	74	0	3.70	3	0	1	68	5	0	4.41
1996-97	Val-d'Or Foreurs	QMJHL	60	32	21	2	3305	171	2	3.10	13	8	5	777	44	0	3.40
1997-98	Val-d'Or Foreurs	QMJHL	54	27	20	5	3046	157	*7	3.09	*17	*14	3	*1020	37	*2	*2.18
1998-99	Val-d'Or Foreurs	QMJHL	21	6	10	2	1177	77	1	3.93	....	....	....	....	....	....	....
	Acadie-Bathurst	QMJHL	22	14	7	1	1341	74	0	3.31	*23	*16	6	*1400	64	0	2.74
99-2000	**NY Islanders**	**NHL**	**24**	**7**	**14**	**1**	**1292**	**70**	**1**	**3.25**	....	....	....	....	....	....	....
	Lowell	AHL	26	10	12	4	1517	74	1	2.93	6	3	3	359	18	0	3.01
2000-01	**Florida**	**NHL**	**47**	**12**	**24**	**7**	**2628**	**107**	**5**	**2.44**	....	....	....	....	....	....	....
	Louisville Panthers	AHL	3	1	2	0	178	10	0	3.38	....	....	....	....	....	....	....
2001-02	**Florida**	**NHL**	**58**	**16**	**33**	**4**	**3030**	**140**	**4**	**2.77**	....	....	....	....	....	....	....
2002-03	**Florida**	**NHL**	**65**	**20**	**34**	**7**	**3627**	**164**	**6**	**2.71**	....	....	....	....	....	....	....
2003-04	**Florida**	**NHL**	**72**	**25**	**33**	**14**	**4252**	**172**	**7**	**2.43**	....	....	....	....	....	....	....
2004-05							DID NOT PLAY										
2005-06	**Florida**	**NHL**	***75**	**35**	**30**	**9**	**4305**	**213**	**4**	**2.97**	....	....	....	....	....	....	....
	Canada	Olympics	2	1	1	0	119	3	0	1.51	....	....	....	....	....	....	....
2006-07	**Vancouver**	**NHL**	**76**	**47**	**22**	**6**	**4490**	**171**	**5**	**2.29**	**12**	**5**	**7**	**847**	**25**	**0**	**1.77**
2007-08	**Vancouver**	**NHL**	**73**	**35**	**29**	**9**	**4233**	**168**	**6**	**2.38**	....	....	....	....	....	....	....
2008-09	**Vancouver**	**NHL**	**54**	**33**	**13**	**7**	**3181**	**124**	**9**	**2.34**	**10**	**6**	**4**	**618**	**26**	**1**	**2.52**
2009-10	**Vancouver**	**NHL**	**68**	**40**	**22**	**4**	**3899**	**167**	**4**	**2.57**	**12**	**6**	**6**	**707**	**38**	**0**	**3.22**
	Canada	Olympics	5	5	0	0	308	9	1	1.76	....	....	....	....	....	....	....
2010-11	**Vancouver**	**NHL**	**60**	***38**	**15**	**7**	**3590**	**126**	**4**	**2.11**	***25**	**15**	**10**	**1427**	**61**	***4**	**2.56**
	NHL Totals		**672**	**308**	**269**	**75**	**38527**	**1622**	**55**	**2.53**	**59**	**32**	**27**	**3599**	**150**	**5**	**2.50**

NHL Second All-Star Team (2004, 2007) • William M. Jennings Trophy (2011) (shared with Cory Schneider)

Played in NHL All-Star Game (2004, 2007, 2009)

Traded to **Florida** by **NY Islanders** with Olli Jokinen for Mark Parrish and Oleg Kvasha, June 24, 2000. Traded to **Vancouver** by **Florida** with Lukas Krajicek and Florida's 6th round choice (Sergei Shirokov) in 2006 Entry Draft for Todd Bertuzzi, Bryan Allen and Alex Auld, June 23, 2006.

MacDONALD, Joey (MAK-DAWN-uhld, JOH-ee) DET

Goaltender. Catches left. 6', 197 lbs. Born, Pictou, N.S., February 7, 1980.

			Regular Season								Playoffs						
Season	Club	League	GP	W	L	O/T	Mins	GA	SO	Avg	GP	W	L	Mins	GA	SO	Avg
1997-98	Halifax	QMJHL	17	3	12	0	816	54	0	3.97	3	1	2	140	15	0	6.43
1998-99	Peterborough	OHL	47	22	15	2	2483	123	3	2.97	3	0	2	145	13	0	5.38
99-2000	Peterborough	OHL	48	20	15	6	2641	125	2	2.84	5	1	4	280	16	1	3.43
2000-01	Peterborough	OHL	57	25	21	7	3284	161	1	2.94	7	3	4	426	18	0	2.54
2001-02	Toledo Storm	ECHL	38	12	15	7	2084	100	1	2.88	....	....	....	....	....	....	....
	Cincinnati	AHL	....	....	....	....	....	....	....	....	1	0	1	84	3	0	2.14
2002-03	Grand Rapids	AHL	25	14	6	0	1337	49	3	2.20	1	0	0	8	1	0	7.95
2003-04	Grand Rapids	AHL	39	22	12	3	2249	74	6	1.97	1	0	1	40	4	0	6.04
2004-05	Grand Rapids	AHL	*66	34	29	2	*3755	143	5	2.29	....	....	....	....	....	....	....
2005-06	Grand Rapids	AHL	32	17	9	2	1745	91	2	3.13	....	....	....	....	....	....	....
	Toledo Storm	ECHL	1	1	0	0	60	1	0	1.00	....	....	....	....	....	....	....
2006-07	**Detroit**	**NHL**	**8**	**1**	**5**	**1**	**468**	**27**	**0**	**3.46**	....	....	....	....	....	....	....
	Grand Rapids	AHL	2	1	1	0	123	6	0	2.93	....	....	....	....	....	....	....
	Boston	**NHL**	**7**	**2**	**2**	**1**	**358**	**16**	**0**	**2.68**	....	....	....	....	....	....	....
2007-08	**NY Islanders**	**NHL**	**2**	**0**	**1**	**1**	**120**	**6**	**0**	**3.00**	....	....	....	....	....	....	....
	Bridgeport	AHL	38	16	19	2	2266	109	2	2.89	....	....	....	....	....	....	....
2008-09	**NY Islanders**	**NHL**	**49**	**14**	**26**	**6**	**2792**	**157**	**1**	**3.37**	....	....	....	....	....	....	....
2009-10	**Toronto**	**NHL**	**6**	**1**	**4**	**0**	**319**	**17**	**0**	**3.20**	....	....	....	....	....	....	....
	Toronto Marlies	AHL	36	14	19	3	2112	112	2	3.18	....	....	....	....	....	....	....
2010-11	**Detroit**	**NHL**	**15**	**5**	**5**	**3**	**721**	**31**	**1**	**2.58**	....	....	....	....	....	....	....
	Grand Rapids	AHL	20	10	9	1	1164	54	1	2.78	....	....	....	....	....	....	....
	NHL Totals		**87**	**23**	**43**	**12**	**4778**	**254**	**2**	**3.19**							

Harry "Hap" Holmes Memorial Award (AHL – fewest goals against) (2003) (shared with Marc Lamothe)

Signed as a free agent by **Detroit**, December 21, 2001. Claimed on waivers by **Boston** from **Detroit**, February 24, 2007. Signed as a free agent by **NY Islanders**, July 7, 2007. Signed as a free agent by **Toronto**, August 10, 2009. Traded to **Anaheim** by **Toronto** for Anaheim's 7th round choice (Max Everson) in 2011 Entry Draft, March 3, 2010. Signed as a free agent by **Detroit**, July 6, 2010.

MacINTYRE, Drew (MAK-ihn-tighr, DROO) BUF

Goaltender. Catches left. 6'1", 190 lbs. Born, Charlottetown, P.E.I., June 24, 1983.
(Detroit's 2nd choice, 121st overall, in 2001 Entry Draft).

			Regular Season								Playoffs						
Season	Club	League	GP	W	L	O/T	Mins	GA	SO	Avg	GP	W	L	Mins	GA	SO	Avg
1998-99	Trenton Sting	OPJHL	20	....	....	....	1173	71	2	3.63	....	....	....	....	....	....	....
99-2000	Sherbrooke	QMJHL	24	10	7	2	1254	67	0	3.21	....	....	....	....	....	....	....
2000-01	Sherbrooke	QMJHL	48	17	22	3	2552	139	4	3.27	4	0	4	238	19	0	4.78
2001-02	Sherbrooke	QMJHL	55	15	34	3	3008	201	1	3.98	....	....	....	....	....	....	....
2002-03	Sherbrooke	QMJHL	*61	31	24	5	*3515	161	2	2.75	12	5	7	767	52	0	4.07
2003-04	Toledo Storm	ECHL	11	6	4	0	574	25	0	2.61	....	....	....	....	....	....	....
2004-05	Grand Rapids	AHL	24	7	8	0	1049	47	1	2.69	....	....	....	....	....	....	....
	Toledo Storm	ECHL	2	0	1	0	87	6	0	4.12	....	....	....	....	....	....	....
2005-06	Grand Rapids	AHL	13	8	4	0	681	33	0	2.91	5	3	1	260	7	0	1.62
	Toledo Storm	ECHL	33	24	7	2	1981	68	2	*2.06	6	5	1	360	12	0	2.00
2006-07	Manitoba Moose	AHL	41	24	12	2	2290	83	3	2.17	11	4	6	633	21	1	1.99
2007-08	**Vancouver**	**NHL**	**2**	**0**	**1**	**0**	**61**	**3**	**0**	**2.95**	....	....	....	....	....	....	....
	Manitoba Moose	AHL	46	25	18	2	2736	106	2	2.32	1	1	0	31	2	0	3.93
2008-09	Milwaukee	AHL	55	*34	15	4	3180	122	4	2.30	11	7	4	655	18	1	*1.65
2009-10	Chicago Wolves	AHL	41	20	17	2	2246	95	3	2.54	5	1	2	228	11	1	2.90
2010-11	Chicago Wolves	AHL	20	12	5	1	1135	55	0	2.91	....	....	....	....	....	....	....
	Hamilton Bulldogs	AHL	21	12	6	2	1241	39	1	1.89	20	11	9	1289	42	1	1.95
	NHL Totals		**2**	**0**	**1**	**0**	**61**	**3**	**0**	**2.95**							

AHL Second All-Star Team (2008, 2009)

• Missed majority of 2003-04 due to thigh injury in practice, December 27, 2003. Traded to **Vancouver** by **Detroit** for future considerations, September 12, 2006. Signed as a free agent by **Nashville**, July 1, 2008. Signed as a free agent by **Atlanta**, July 6, 2009. Traded to **Montreal** by **Atlanta** for Brett Festerling, February 28, 2011. Signed as a free agent by **Buffalo**, July 7, 2011.

MAHALAK, Matt (muh-HA-lehk, MAT) CAR

Goaltender. Catches left. 6'2", 182 lbs. Born, Toledo, OH, January 22, 1993.
(Carolina's 5th choice, 163rd overall, in 2011 Entry Draft).

			Regular Season								Playoffs						
Season	Club	League	GP	W	L	O/T	Mins	GA	SO	Avg	GP	W	L	Mins	GA	SO	Avg
2008-09	Culver Academy	High-IN	22	10	9	3	....	....	....	2.51	....	....	....	....	....	....	....
2009-10	Youngstown	USHL	31	9	17	3	1767	125	0	4.24	....	....	....	....	....	....	....
2010-11	Plymouth Whalers	OHL	21	8	8	4	1053	54	1	3.08	2	0	1	80	4	0	3.00

MANNINO, Peter (ma-NEE-noh, PE-tuhr) WPG

Goaltender. Catches right. 6'1", 195 lbs. Born, Farmington Hills, MI, February 17, 1984.

			Regular Season								Playoffs						
Season	Club	League	GP	W	L	O/T	Mins	GA	SO	Avg	GP	W	L	Mins	GA	SO	Avg
2001-02	Pittsburgh Forge	NAHL	11	....	....	....	....	....	....	....	....	....	....	....	....	....	....
2002-03	Pittsburgh Forge	NAHL	45	....	....	....	....	....	....	....	....	....	....	....	....	....	....
2003-04	Tri-City Storm	USHL	38	26	7	0	1988	70	5	*2.11	7	4	1	334	12	*1	2.15
2004-05	U. of Denver	WCHA	21	16	4	1	1224	46	*5	2.25	....	....	....	....	....	....	....
2005-06	U. of Denver	WCHA	22	12	8	1	1241	56	1	2.71	....	....	....	....	....	....	....
2006-07	U. of Denver	WCHA	18	8	6	2	1021	39	3	2.29	....	....	....	....	....	....	....
2007-08	U. of Denver	WCHA	40	25	14	1	2302	87	*6	2.27	....	....	....	....	....	....	....
2008-09	**NY Islanders**	**NHL**	**3**	**1**	**1**	**0**	**133**	**10**	**0**	**4.51**	....	....	....	....	....	....	....
	Bridgeport	AHL	34	17	12	2	1959	96	1	2.94	3	1	2	189	10	0	3.18
	Utah Grizzlies	ECHL	9	4	3	2	549	25	0	2.73	....	....	....	....	....	....	....
2009-10	Chicago Wolves	AHL	38	26	5	1	2026	79	2	2.34	12	6	5	653	34	2	3.12
2010-11	**Atlanta**	**NHL**	**2**	**0**	**0**	**0**	**73**	**5**	**0**	**4.11**	....	....	....	....	....	....	....
	Chicago Wolves	AHL	42	16	17	4	2232	116	0	3.12	....	....	....	....	....	....	....
	NHL Totals		**5**	**1**	**1**	**0**	**206**	**15**	**0**	**4.37**	....	....	....	....	....	....	....

Signed as a free agent by **NY Islanders**, July 3, 2008. Signed as a free agent by **Atlanta**, July 6, 2009. • Transferred to **Winnipeg** after **Atlanta** franchise relocated, June 21, 2011.

MARKSTROM, Jacob (MAHRK-struhm, JAY-kawb) FLA

Goaltender. Catches left. 6'3", 178 lbs. Born, Gavle, Sweden, January 31, 1990.
(Florida's 1st choice, 31st overall, in 2008 Entry Draft).

			Regular Season								Playoffs						
Season	Club	League	GP	W	L	O/T	Mins	GA	SO	Avg	GP	W	L	Mins	GA	SO	Avg
2006-07	Brynas U18	Swe-U18	13	....	....	....	789	27	0	2.05	3	....	....	193	6	1	1.86
	Brynas IF Gavle Jr.	Swe-Jr.	1	....	....	....	65	3	0	2.77	1	....	....	25	4	0	9.76
2007-08	Brynas U18	Swe-U18	1	....	....	....	60	3	0	3.00	....	....	....	....	....	....	....
	Brynas IF Gavle Jr.	Swe-Jr.	22	....	....	....	1320	44	2	2.00	....	....	....	....	....	....	....
	Brynas IF Gavle	Sweden	7	....	....	....	423	22	0	3.12	....	....	....	....	....	....	....
	Brynas IF Gavle	Sweden-Q	9	....	....	....	505	15	2	1.78	....	....	....	....	....	....	....
2008-09	Brynas IF Gavle	Sweden	35	....	....	....	1992	79	3	2.38	1	....	....	59	2	0	2.02
2009-10	Brynas IF Gavle	Sweden	43	....	....	....	2542	85	*5	*2.01	4	....	....	224	12	0	3.21
	Brynas IF Gavle Jr.	Swe-Jr.	....	....	....	....	....	....	....	....	2	....	....	119	6	0	3.03
2010-11	**Florida**	**NHL**	**1**	**0**	**1**	**0**	**40**	**2**	**0**	**3.00**	....	....	....	....	....	....	....
	Rochester	AHL	37	16	20	1	2174	108	1	2.98	....	....	....	....	....	....	....
	NHL Totals		**1**	**0**	**1**	**0**	**40**	**2**	**0**	**3.00**	....	....	....	....	....	....	....

MASON, Chris (MAY-sohn, KRIHS) WPG

Goaltender. Catches left. 6', 195 lbs. Born, Red Deer, Alta., April 20, 1976.
(New Jersey's 7th choice, 122nd overall, in 1995 Entry Draft).

			Regular Season								Playoffs						
Season	Club	League	GP	W	L	O/T	Mins	GA	SO	Avg	GP	W	L	Mins	GA	SO	Avg
1992-93	Red Deer	AMHL	20	....	....	....	1280	76	0	3.35	....	....	....	....	....	....	....
1993-94	Victoria Cougars	WHL	5	1	4	0	237	27	0	6.84	....	....	....	....	....	....	....
1994-95	Prince George	WHL	44	8	30	1	2288	192	1	5.03	....	....	....	....	....	....	....
1995-96	Prince George	WHL	59	16	37	1	3289	236	1	4.31	....	....	....	....	....	....	....
1996-97	Prince George	WHL	50	19	24	4	2851	172	2	3.62	15	9	6	938	44	*1	2.81
1997-98	Cincinnati	AHL	47	13	19	7	2368	136	0	3.45	....	....	....	....	....	....	....
1998-99	**Nashville**	**NHL**	**3**	**0**	**0**	**0**	**69**	**6**	**0**	**5.22**	....	....	....	....	....	....	....
	Milwaukee	IHL	34	15	12	6	1901	92	1	2.90	....	....	....	....	....	....	....
99-2000	Milwaukee	IHL	53	20	21	8	2952	137	2	2.78	3	1	2	252	11	0	2.62
2000-01	**Nashville**	**NHL**	**1**	**0**	**1**	**0**	**59**	**2**	**0**	**2.03**	....	....	....	....	....	....	....
	Milwaukee	IHL	37	17	14	5	2226	87	5	2.35	4	1	3	239	12	0	3.02
2001-02	Milwaukee	AHL	48	17	21	7	2755	116	2	2.53	....	....	....	....	....	....	....
2002-03	San Antonio	AHL	50	25	18	6	2914	122	1	2.51	3	0	3	195	9	0	2.77
2003-04	**Nashville**	**NHL**	**17**	**4**	**4**	**1**	**744**	**27**	**1**	**2.18**	....	....	....	....	....	....	....
	Milwaukee	AHL	1	1	0	0	60	2	0	2.00	....	....	....	....	....	....	....
2004-05	Valerengen IF Oslo	Norway	20	....	....	....	1204	36	1	1.79	11	....	....	657	22	1	2.01
2005-06	**Nashville**	**NHL**	**23**	**12**	**5**	**1**	**1227**	**52**	**2**	**2.54**	**5**	**1**	**4**	**296**	**17**	**0**	**3.45**
2006-07	**Nashville**	**NHL**	**40**	**24**	**11**	**4**	**2342**	**93**	**5**	**2.38**	....	....	....	....	....	....	....
2007-08	**Nashville**	**NHL**	**51**	**18**	**22**	**6**	**2692**	**130**	**4**	**2.90**	....	....	....	....	....	....	....
2008-09	**St. Louis**	**NHL**	**57**	**27**	**21**	**7**	**3215**	**129**	**6**	**2.41**	**4**	**0**	**4**	**256**	**10**	**0**	**2.34**
2009-10	**St. Louis**	**NHL**	**61**	**30**	**22**	**8**	**3512**	**148**	**2**	**2.53**	....	....	....	....	....	....	....
2010-11	**Atlanta**	**NHL**	**33**	**13**	**13**	**3**	**1682**	**95**	**1**	**3.39**	....	....	....	....	....	....	....
	NHL Totals		**286**	**128**	**99**	**30**	**15542**	**682**	**21**	**2.63**	**9**	**1**	**8**	**552**	**27**	**0**	**2.93**

Signed as a free agent by **Anaheim**, June 27, 1997. Traded to **Nashville** by **Anaheim** with Marc Moro for Dominic Roussel, October 5, 1998. Signed as a free agent by **Florida**, August 20, 2002. Claimed by **Nashville** from **Florida** in Waiver Draft, October 3, 2003. Signed as a free agent by **Oslo** (Norway), November 30, 2004. Traded to **St. Louis** by **Nashville** for NY Rangers' 4th round choice (previously acquired, later traded back to NY Rangers – NY Rangers selected Dale Weise) in 2008 Entry Draft, June 20, 2008. Signed as a free agent by **Atlanta**, July 1, 2010. • Transferred to **Winnipeg** after **Atlanta** franchise relocated, June 21, 2011.

MASON, Steve (MAY-sohn, STEEV) CBJ

Goaltender. Catches right. 6'4", 211 lbs. Born, Oakville, Ont., May 29, 1988.
(Columbus' 2nd choice, 69th overall, in 2006 Entry Draft).

			Regular Season								Playoffs						
Season	Club	League	GP	W	L	O/T	Mins	GA	SO	Avg	GP	W	L	Mins	GA	SO	Avg
2003-04	Oakville Rangers	Minor-ON	27	....	....	....	1209	41	5	1.58	....	....	....	....	....	....	....
2004-05	Grimsby	ON-Jr.C	45	....	....	....	2800	....	6	1.75	....	....	....	....	....	....	....
2005-06	Petrolia Jets	ON-Jr.B	9	6	3	0	522	22	1	2.53	5	3	2	348	9	0	1.55
	London Knights	OHL	12	5	3	0	497	22	0	2.66	4	0	1	150	7	0	2.80
2006-07	London Knights	OHL	*62	*45	13	4	*3733	199	2	3.20	16	9	7	931	54	0	3.48
2007-08	London Knights	OHL	26	19	4	3	1569	73	2	2.79	....	....	....	....	....	....	....
	Kitchener Rangers	OHL	16	13	3	0	961	33	1	2.06	5	5	0	313	10	1	1.92
2008-09	**Columbus**	**NHL**	**61**	**33**	**20**	**7**	**3664**	**140**	***10**	**2.29**	**4**	**0**	**4**	**239**	**17**	**0**	**4.27**
	Syracuse Crunch	AHL	3	2	1	0	184	5	0	1.63	....	....	....	....	....	....	....
2009-10	**Columbus**	**NHL**	**58**	**20**	**26**	**9**	**3201**	**163**	**5**	**3.06**	....	....	....	....	....	....	....
2010-11	**Columbus**	**NHL**	**54**	**24**	**21**	**7**	**3027**	**153**	**3**	**3.03**	....	....	....	....	....	....	....
	NHL Totals		**173**	**77**	**67**	**23**	**9892**	**456**	**18**	**2.77**	**4**	**0**	**4**	**239**	**17**	**0**	**4.27**

OHL First All-Star Team (2007) • OHL Second All-Star Team (2008) • NHL All-Rookie Team (2009) • NHL Second All-Star Team (2009) • Calder Memorial Trophy (2009)

MATTSSON, Johan (MAT-suhn, YOH-han) CHI

Goaltender. Catches left. 6'3", 200 lbs. Born, Huddinge, Sweden, April 25, 1992.
(Chicago's 11th choice, 211th overall, in 2011 Entry Draft).

			Regular Season								Playoffs						
Season	Club	League	GP	W	L	O/T	Mins	GA	SO	Avg	GP	W	L	Mins	GA	SO	Avg
2008-09	Sodertalje SK U18	Swe-U18	23	....	....	....	1291	66	1	3.06	4	....	....	240	17	0	4.25
	Sodertalje SK Jr.	Swe-Jr.	1	....	....	....	60	3	0	3.00	....	....	....	....	....	....	....
	Sodertalje SK	Sweden-Q	1	....	....	....	25	3	0	7.20	....	....	....	....	....	....	....
2009-10	Sodertalje SK U18	Swe-U18	12	....	....	....	720	31	2	2.58	2	....	....	118	8	0	4.08
	Sodertalje SK Jr.	Swe-Jr.	20	....	....	....	1156	72	1	3.74	....	....	....	....	....	....	....
2010-11	Sodertalje SK Jr.	Swe-Jr.	26	....	....	....	1559	68	0	2.62	2	....	....	119	10	0	5.04

MAYER, Robert (MAY-uhr, RAW-buhrt) MTL

Goaltender. Catches left. 6'1", 200 lbs. Born, Havirov, Czech., October 9, 1989.

			Regular Season								Playoffs						
Season	Club	League	GP	W	L	O/T	Mins	GA	SO	Avg	GP	W	L	Mins	GA	SO	Avg
2005-06	ESV Kaufbeuren	German-2	3	....	....	....	....	....	....	....	....	....	....	....	....	....	....
2006-07	ESV Kaufbeuren	German-2	7	....	....	....	....	....	....	....	....	....	....	....	....	....	....
	Kloten Flyers	Swiss	1	0	0	0	10	1	0	6.00	....	....	....	....	....	....	....
2007-08	Saint John	QMJHL	32	16	11	0	1669	105	2	3.77	2	0	0	65	5	0	4.61
2008-09	Saint John	QMJHL	57	26	28	0	3155	169	2	3.21	4	0	3	204	16	0	4.70
2009-10	Hamilton Bulldogs	AHL	1	0	0	1	65	2	0	1.85	1	0	0	37	3	0	4.83
	Cincinnati	ECHL	31	19	10	1	1750	82	2	2.81	9	6	1	508	13	*3	*1.54
2010-11	Hamilton Bulldogs	AHL	21	9	10	2	1215	62	0	3.06	....	....	....	....	....	....	....

Signed as a free agent by **Montreal**, September 25, 2008.

McCOLLUM, Thomas (muh-KAW-luhm, TAW-muhs) DET

Goaltender. Catches left. 6'2", 210 lbs. Born, Amherst, NY, December 7, 1989.
(Detroit's 1st choice, 30th overall, in 2008 Entry Draft).

			Regular Season								Playoffs						
Season	Club	League	GP	W	L	O/T	Mins	GA	SO	Avg	GP	W	L	Mins	GA	SO	Avg
2005-06	Wheatfield Blades	EmJHL	24	2	19	3	1448	109	1	4.52	....	....	....	....	....	....	....
2006-07	Guelph Storm	OHL	55	26	18	10	3158	126	*5	2.39	4	0	4	233	17	0	4.38
2007-08	Guelph Storm	OHL	51	25	17	6	2978	124	*4	2.50	10	5	5	596	19	1	1.91
2008-09	Guelph Storm	OHL	31	17	10	4	1859	69	*3	2.23	....	....	....	....	....	....	....
	Brampton Battalion	OHL	23	17	6	0	1333	43	*4	1.94	*21	13	8	*1284	62	*1	2.90
2009-10	Grand Rapids	AHL	32	10	16	2	1741	101	0	3.48	....	....	....	....	....	....	....
	Toledo Walleye	ECHL	4	2	1	0	188	14	0	4.48	....	....	....	....	....	....	....
2010-11	**Detroit**	**NHL**	**1**	**0**	**0**	**0**	**15**	**3**	**0**	**12.00**	....	....	....	....	....	....	....
	Grand Rapids	AHL	22	6	12	2	1152	64	1	3.33	....	....	....	....	....	....	....
	Toledo Walleye	ECHL	23	11	9	2	1305	60	3	2.76	....	....	....	....	....	....	....
	NHL Totals		**1**	**0**	**0**	**0**	**15**	**3**	**0**	**12.00**	....	....	....	....	....	....	....

OHL Second All-Star Team (2009)

McELHINNEY, Curtis (MAK-IHL-ehn-ee, KUHR-this) PHX

Goaltender. Catches left. 6'2", 193 lbs. Born, London, Ont., May 23, 1983.
(Calgary's 9th choice, 176th overall, in 2002 Entry Draft).

			Regular Season								Playoffs						
Season	Club	League	GP	W	L	O/T	Mins	GA	SO	Avg	GP	W	L	Mins	GA	SO	Avg
2000-01	Notre Dame	SJHL					STATISTICS NOT AVAILABLE										
2001-02	Colorado College	WCHA	9	6	0	1	441	15	1	2.04	....	....	....	....	....	....	....
2002-03	Colorado College	WCHA	*37	*25	6	5	*2147	85	*4	2.37	....	....	....	....	....	....	....
2003-04	Colorado College	WCHA	19	10	6	1	1015	41	2	2.42	....	....	....	....	....	....	....
2004-05	Colorado College	WCHA	26	*21	4	1	1550	58	2	2.24	....	....	....	....	....	....	....
2005-06	Omaha	AHL	33	9	14	2	1621	68	3	2.52	....	....	....	....	....	....	....
2006-07	Omaha	AHL	57	35	17	1	3181	113	*7	2.13	5	2	3	311	11	0	2.12
2007-08	**Calgary**	**NHL**	**5**	**0**	**2**	**0**	**150**	**5**	**0**	**2.00**	....	....	....	....	....	....	....
	Quad City Flames	AHL	41	20	18	2	2320	88	3	2.28	....	....	....	....	....	....	....
2008-09	**Calgary**	**NHL**	**14**	**1**	**6**	**1**	**518**	**31**	**0**	**3.59**	**1**	**0**	**0**	**34**	**1**	**0**	**1.76**
2009-10	**Calgary**	**NHL**	**10**	**3**	**4**	**0**	**502**	**27**	**0**	**3.23**	....	....	....	....	....	....	....
	Anaheim	**NHL**	**10**	**5**	**1**	**2**	**521**	**24**	**0**	**2.76**	....	....	....	....	....	....	....
2010-11	**Anaheim**	**NHL**	**21**	**6**	**9**	**1**	**996**	**57**	**2**	**3.43**	....	....	....	....	....	....	....
	Ottawa	**NHL**	**7**	**3**	**4**	**0**	**399**	**17**	**0**	**2.56**	....	....	....	....	....	....	....
	NHL Totals		**67**	**18**	**26**	**4**	**3086**	**161**	**2**	**3.13**	**1**	**0**	**0**	**34**	**1**	**0**	**1.76**

WCHA First All-Star Team (2003, 2005) • NCAA West Second All-American Team (2003) • NCAA West First All-American Team (2005) • AHL Second All-Star Team (2007)

Traded to **Anaheim** by **Calgary** for Vesa Toskala, March 3, 2010. Traded to **Tampa Bay** by **Anaheim** for Dan Ellis, February 24, 2011. Claimed on waivers by **Ottawa** from **Tampa Bay**, February 28, 2011. Signed as a free agent by **Phoenix**, July 4, 2011.

McKENNA, Mike (mih-KEHN-ah, MIGHK) OTT

Goaltender. Catches right. 6'3", 195 lbs. Born, St. Louis, MO, April 11, 1983.
(Nashville's 4th choice, 172nd overall, in 2002 Entry Draft).

			Regular Season								Playoffs						
Season	Club	League	GP	W	L	O/T	Mins	GA	SO	Avg	GP	W	L	Mins	GA	SO	Avg
2001-02	St. Lawrence	ECAC	20	7	10	1	1121	59	0	3.16	....	....	....	....	....	....	....
2002-03	St. Lawrence	ECAC	15	1	7	2	618	38	0	3.69	....	....	....	....	....	....	....
2003-04	St. Lawrence	ECAC	27	9	10	3	1475	60	3	2.44	....	....	....	....	....	....	....
2004-05	St. Lawrence	ECAC	35	15	17	2	2022	92	3	2.73	....	....	....	....	....	....	....
2005-06	Norfolk Admirals	AHL	7	4	2	1	388	25	0	3.86	....	....	....	....	....	....	....
	Las Vegas	ECHL	25	19	2	1	1383	49	1	2.13	4	1	1	173	9	0	3.12
2006-07	Milwaukee	AHL	1	0	0	0	11	3	0	15.72	....	....	....	....	....	....	....
	Omaha	AHL	2	0	1	0	96	6	0	3.74	....	....	....	....	....	....	....
	Las Vegas	ECHL	38	27	4	7	2258	83	5	*2.21	6	3	3	358	15	0	2.51
2007-08	Portland Pirates	AHL	41	24	13	1	2269	103	3	2.72	6	2	4	320	18	0	3.38
2008-09	**Tampa Bay**	**NHL**	**15**	**4**	**8**	**1**	**776**	**46**	**1**	**3.56**	....	....	....	....	....	....	....
	Norfolk Admirals	AHL	24	11	10	1	1315	65	1	2.97	....	....	....	....	....	....	....
2009-10	Lowell Devils	AHL	50	24	17	6	2891	119	3	2.47	5	1	4	317	17	0	3.22
2010-11	Albany Devils	AHL	39	14	20	2	2062	124	1	3.61	....	....	....	....	....	....	....
	New Jersey	**NHL**	**2**	**0**	**1**	**0**	**118**	**6**	**0**	**3.05**	....	....	....	....	....	....	....
	NHL Totals		**17**	**4**	**9**	**1**	**894**	**52**	**1**	**3.49**	....	....	....	....	....	....	....

ECHL Second All-Star Team (2007)

Signed as a free agent by **Tampa Bay**, February 3, 2009. Signed as a free agent by **Lowell** (AHL), October 7, 2009. Signed as a free agent by **New Jersey**, February 10, 2010. Signed as a free agent by **Ottawa**, July 8, 2011.

MICHALEK, Stephen (MIGH-KUHL-ehk, STEE-vehn) MIN

Goaltender. Catches . 6'2", 196 lbs. Born, Hartford, CT, August 6, 1993.
(Minnesota's 5th choice, 161st overall, in 2011 Entry Draft).

			Regular Season								Playoffs						
Season	Club	League	GP	W	L	O/T	Mins	GA	SO	Avg	GP	W	L	Mins	GA	SO	Avg
2009-10	Loomis Chaffee	High-CT	35	....	....	....	1121	106	....	....	....	....	....	....	....	....	....
2010-11	Loomis Chaffee	High-CT	23	2	19	2	1203	91	....	3.95	....	....	....	....	....	....	....
	Boston Little Bruins	Minor-MA					STATISTICS NOT AVAILABLE										

• Signed Letter of Intent to attend **Harvard University** (ECAC) in fall of 2011.

MILLAN, Kieran (MIH-luhn, KEER-uhn) COL

Goaltender. Catches left. 6', 190 lbs. Born, Edmonton, Alta., August 31, 1989.
(Colorado's 5th choice, 124th overall, in 2009 Entry Draft).

			Regular Season								Playoffs						
Season	Club	League	GP	W	L	O/T	Mins	GA	SO	Avg	GP	W	L	Mins	GA	SO	Avg
2006-07	Spruce Grove	AJHL	32	20	7	4	1883	82	3	2.61	4	2	2	200	10	1	3.00
2007-08	Spruce Grove	AJHL	43	21	12	8	2391	121	1	3.04	15	8	7	931	34	1	2.19
2008-09	Boston University	H-East	35	29	2	3	2073	67	3	1.94	....	....	....	....	....	....	....
2009-10	Boston University	H-East	32	16	16	0	1869	98	1	3.15	....	....	....	....	....	....	....
2010-11	Boston University	H-East	36	16	10	8	2127	95	1	2.68	....	....	....	....	....	....	....

Hockey East All-Rookie Team (2009) • Hockey East Second All-Star Team (2009, 2011) • Hockey East Rookie of the Year (2009) • NCAA Rookie of the Year (2009) • NCAA Championship All-Tournament Team (2009)

MILLER, Ryan (MIH-luhr, RIGH-uhn) BUF

Goaltender. Catches left. 6'2", 175 lbs. Born, East Lansing, MI, July 17, 1980.
(Buffalo's 7th choice, 138th overall, in 1999 Entry Draft).

			Regular Season								Playoffs						
Season	Club	League	GP	W	L	O/T	Mins	GA	SO	Avg	GP	W	L	Mins	GA	SO	Avg
1997-98	Soo Indians	NAHL	37	21	14	0	2113	82	3	2.33	2	0	2	158	7	0	2.66
1998-99	Soo Indians	NAHL	47	31	14	1	2711	104	8	2.30	4	2	2	218	10	1	2.76
99-2000	Michigan State	CCHA	26	16	5	3	1525	39	*8	*1.53	....	....	....	....	....	....	....
2000-01	Michigan State	CCHA	40	*31	5	4	2447	54	*10	*1.32	....	....	....	....	....	....	....
2001-02	Michigan State	CCHA	40	26	9	5	2411	71	*8	*1.77	....	....	....	....	....	....	....
2002-03	**Buffalo**	**NHL**	**15**	**6**	**8**	**1**	**912**	**40**	**1**	**2.63**	....	....	....	....	....	....	....
	Rochester	AHL	47	23	18	5	2817	110	2	2.34	3	1	2	190	13	0	4.11
2003-04	**Buffalo**	**NHL**	**3**	**0**	**3**	**0**	**178**	**15**	**0**	**5.06**	....	....	....	....	....	....	....
	Rochester	AHL	60	27	25	7	3579	132	5	2.21	14	7	7	857	26	2	1.82
2004-05	Rochester	AHL	63	*41	17	4	3741	153	8	2.45	9	5	4	547	24	0	2.63
2005-06	**Buffalo**	**NHL**	**48**	**30**	**14**	**3**	**2862**	**124**	**1**	**2.60**	**18**	**11**	**7**	**1123**	**48**	**1**	**2.56**
	Rochester	AHL	2	1	1	0	120	5	0	2.50	....	....	....	....	....	....	....
2006-07	**Buffalo**	**NHL**	**63**	**40**	**16**	**6**	**3692**	**168**	**2**	**2.73**	**16**	**9**	**7**	**1029**	**38**	**0**	**2.22**
2007-08	**Buffalo**	**NHL**	**76**	**36**	**27**	**10**	**4474**	**197**	**3**	**2.64**	....	....	....	....	....	....	....
2008-09	**Buffalo**	**NHL**	**59**	**34**	**18**	**6**	**3443**	**145**	**5**	**2.53**	....	....	....	....	....	....	....
2009-10	**Buffalo**	**NHL**	**69**	**41**	**18**	**8**	**4047**	**150**	**5**	**2.22**	**6**	**2**	**4**	**384**	**15**	**0**	**2.34**
	United States	Olympics	6	5	1	0	355	8	1	1.35	....	....	....	....	....	....	....
2010-11	**Buffalo**	**NHL**	**66**	**34**	**22**	**8**	**3829**	**165**	**5**	**2.59**	**7**	**3**	**4**	**410**	**20**	**2**	**2.93**
	NHL Totals		**399**	**221**	**126**	**42**	**23437**	**1004**	**22**	**2.57**	**47**	**25**	**22**	**2946**	**121**	**3**	**2.46**

CCHA Second All-Star Team (2000) • CCHA First All-Star Team (2001, 2002) • CCHA Player of the Year (2001, 2002) • NCAA West First All-American Team (2001, 2002) • Hobey Baker Memorial Award (Top U.S. Collegiate Player) (2001) • AHL First All-Star Team (2005) • Aldege "Baz" Bastien Memorial Award (AHL – Outstanding Goaltender) (2005) • NHL First All-Star Team (2010) • NHL Foundation Award (2010) • Vezina Trophy (2010) • Olympic All-Star Team (2010) • Olympics – Best Goaltender (2010) • Olympics – MVP (2010)

Played in NHL All-Star Game (2007)

MISSIAEN, Jason (MIHS-ee-ehn, JAY-suhn) NYR

Goaltender. Catches left. 6'8", 220 lbs. Born, Chatham, Ont., April 25, 1990.
(Montreal's 3rd choice, 116th overall, in 2008 Entry Draft).

			Regular Season								Playoffs						
Season	Club	League	GP	W	L	O/T	Mins	GA	SO	Avg	GP	W	L	Mins	GA	SO	Avg
2004-05	Dresden Jr. Kings	ON-Jr.C	16	11	4	1	919	47	1	3.07	....	....	....	....	....	....	....
2005-06	Dresden Jr. Kings	ON-Jr.C	26	13	8	2	1560	76	1	2.93	....	....	....	....	....	....	....
	Petrolia Jets	ON-Jr.B	1	0	0	0	14	0	0	0.00	1	0	0	2	0	0	0.00
2006-07	Peterborough	OHL	12	1	7	0	559	48	0	5.15	....	....	....	....	....	....	....
2007-08	Peterborough	OHL	22	8	8	1	1134	62	1	3.28	....	....	....	....	....	....	....
2008-09	Peterborough	OHL	38	12	21	2	2221	141	1	3.81	4	0	4	241	17	0	4.23
2009-10	Peterborough	OHL	59	27	29	3	3358	206	1	3.68	4	0	4	238	11	0	2.77
2010-11	Baie-Comeau	QMJHL	53	10	33	8	3026	168	1	3.33	....	....	....	....	....	....	....

Signed as a free agent by **NY Rangers**, March 24, 2011.

MODIG, Mattias (moh-DIHG, mat-TEE-uhs) PIT

Goaltender. Catches left. 6', 163 lbs. Born, Lulea, Sweden, April 1, 1987.
(Anaheim's 7th choice, 121st overall, in 2007 Entry Draft).

			Regular Season								Playoffs						
Season	Club	League	GP	W	L	O/T	Mins	GA	SO	Avg	GP	W	L	Mins	GA	SO	Avg
2002-03	Lulea HF U18	Swe-U18	2	....	....	....	120	4	0	2.00	....	....	....	....	....	....	....
2003-04	Lulea HF U18	Swe-U18	14	....	....	....	854	30	2	2.11	7	....	....	449	14	0	1.87
	Lulea HF Jr.	Swe-Jr.	2	....	....	....	66	2	0	1.81	....	....	....	....	....	....	....
2004-05	Lulea HF U18	Swe-U18	2	....	....	....	120	4	0	2.00	....	....	....	....	....	....	....
	Lulea HF Jr.	Swe-Jr.	14	....	....	....	819	42	2	3.08	5	....	....	306	16	0	3.14
2005-06	Lulea HF Jr.	Swe-Jr.	19	....	....	....	1154	42	1	2.18	3	....	....	175	10	0	3.43
	Lulea HF	Sweden	2	....	....	....	66	3	0	2.74	....	....	....	....	....	....	....
2006-07	Lulea HF Jr.	Swe-Jr.	2	....	....	....	120	7	0	3.50	....	....	....	....	....	....	....
	Lulea HF	Sweden	32	....	....	....	1636	69	1	2.53	1	....	....	20	1	0	3.00
2007-08	Lulea HF Jr.	Swe-Jr.	5	....	....	....	297	14	0	2.83	....	....	....	....	....	....	....
	Lulea HF	Sweden	13	....	....	....	696	41	1	3.53	....	....	....	....	....	....	....
2008-09	Lulea HF	Sweden	40	....	....	....	2268	85	*4	2.25	4	....	....	238	13	0	3.28
2009-10	Lulea HF	Sweden	34	....	....	....	1925	80	2	2.49	....	....	....	....	....	....	....
2010-11	Wheeling Nailers	ECHL	9	3	6	0	495	27	0	3.27	....	....	....	....	....	....	....

Traded to **Pittsburgh** by **Anaheim** for Montreal's 6th round choice (previously acquired, Anaheim selected Kevin Lind) in 2010 Entry Draft, May 28, 2010.

MONTOYA, Al (mawn-TOI-uh, AL) NYI

Goaltender. Catches left. 6'2", 195 lbs. Born, Chicago, IL, February 13, 1985.
(NY Rangers' 1st choice, 6th overall, in 2004 Entry Draft).

			Regular Season								Playoffs						
Season	Club	League	GP	W	L	O/T	Mins	GA	SO	Avg	GP	W	L	Mins	GA	SO	Avg
99-2000	Loyola Academy	High-MN	28	12	13	3	1685	56	1	2.01	....	....	....	....	....	....	....
2000-01	Texas Tornado	NAHL	15	10	3	0	780	38	0	2.92	1	1	0	60	2	0	2.00
	United States	Nat-Tm	2	2	0	0	120	4	0	2.00	....	....	....	....	....	....	....
2001-02	USNTDP	U-17	10	5	5	0	570	24	0	2.53	....	....	....	....	....	....	....
	USNTDP	NAHL	24	6	11	4	1344	79	0	3.53	....	....	....	....	....	....	....
2002-03	U. of Michigan	CCHA	*43	*30	10	3	*2547	99	4	2.33	....	....	....	....	....	....	....
2003-04	U. of Michigan	CCHA	*40	*26	12	2	*2340	87	6	2.23	....	....	....	....	....	....	....
2004-05	U. of Michigan	CCHA	*40	*30	7	3	*2359	99	3	2.52	....	....	....	....	....	....	....
2005-06	Hartford Wolf Pack	AHL	40	23	9	1	2094	91	2	2.61	5	2	1	257	8	1	1.87
	Charlotte Checkers	ECHL	2	1	1	0	123	8	0	3.92	....	....	....	....	....	....	....
2006-07	Hartford Wolf Pack	AHL	48	27	17	0	2556	98	6	2.30	7	3	4	391	20	1	3.07
2007-08	Hartford Wolf Pack	AHL	31	16	8	3	1704	72	0	2.54	....	....	....	....	....	....	....
	San Antonio	AHL	14	8	6	0	789	34	1	2.59	1	0	1	59	4	0	4.04
2008-09	**Phoenix**	**NHL**	**5**	**3**	**1**	**0**	**259**	**9**	**1**	**2.08**	....	....	....	....	....	....	....
	San Antonio	AHL	29	7	17	2	1562	84	0	3.23	....	....	....	....	....	....	....
2009-10	San Antonio	AHL	14	4	7	1	771	34	0	2.65	....	....	....	....	....	....	....
2010-11	**NY Islanders**	**NHL**	**20**	**9**	**5**	**5**	**1154**	**46**	**1**	**2.39**	....	....	....	....	....	....	....
	San Antonio	AHL	21	11	8	0	1130	60	0	3.19	....	....	....	....	....	....	....
	NHL Totals		**25**	**12**	**6**	**5**	**1413**	**55**	**2**	**2.34**	....	....	....	....	....	....	....

CCHA All-Rookie Team (2003) • NCAA West Second All-American Team (2004)

Traded to **Phoenix** by **NY Rangers** with Marcel Hossa for Josh Gratton, David LeNeveu, Fredrik Sjostrom and Phoenix's 5th round choice (Roman Horak) in 2009 Entry Draft, February 26, 2008. Traded to **NY Islanders** by **Phoenix** for NY Islanders' 6th round choice (Andrew Fritsch) in 2011 Entry Draft, February 9, 2011.

MRAZEK, Petr (M'RAZ-ihk, PEH-tuhr) DET

Goaltender. Catches left. 6', 170 lbs. Born, Ostrava, Czechoslovakia, February 14, 1992.
(Detroit's 5th choice, 141st overall, in 2010 Entry Draft).

			Regular Season								Playoffs						
Season	Club	League	GP	W	L	O/T	Mins	GA	SO	Avg	GP	W	L	Mins	GA	SO	Avg
2006-07	HC Vitkovice U17	CzR-U17	23	....	....	....	1273	51	2	2.40	9	....	....	486	15	1	1.85
2007-08	HC Vitkovice U17	CzR-U17	34	....	....	....	1974	81	4	2.46	3	....	....	179	8	0	2.68
	HC Vitkovice Steel	CzRep	1	....	....	....	24	4	0	10.00	....	....	....	....	....	....	....
2008-09	HC Vitkovice U17	CzR-U17	28	....	....	....	1601	53	5	1.99	4	....	....	193	3	2	0.93
	HC Vitkovice Jr.	CzRep-Jr.	13	....	....	....	795	33	0	2.49	1	....	....	60	1	0	1.00
2009-10	Ottawa 67's	OHL	30	12	9	1	1562	78	2	3.00	8	4	4	451	18	0	2.39
2010-11	Ottawa 67's	OHL	52	33	15	3	3089	146	4	2.84	4	0	3	224	21	0	5.63

MUNROE, Scott (muhn-ROH, SKAWT) PIT

Goaltender. Catches left. 6'2", 210 lbs. Born, Moose Jaw, Sask., January 20, 1982.

			Regular Season								Playoffs						
Season	Club	League	GP	W	L	O/T	Mins	GA	SO	Avg	GP	W	L	Mins	GA	SO	Avg
2002-03	AL-Huntsville	CHA	20	11	6	1	1049	49	1	2.80	....	....	....	....	....	....	....
2003-04	AL-Huntsville	CHA	17	5	9	1	891	47	0	3.16	....	....	....	....	....	....	....
2004-05	AL-Huntsville	CHA	31	16	10	4	1805	69	3	2.29	....	....	....	....	....	....	....
2005-06	AL-Huntsville	CHA	31	17	11	2	1813	91	0	3.01	....	....	....	....	....	....	....
	Philadelphia	AHL	2	0	2	0	119	7	0	3.54	....	....	....	....	....	....	....
2006-07	Philadelphia	AHL	40	15	19	2	2298	117	2	3.05	....	....	....	....	....	....	....
2007-08	Philadelphia	AHL	36	18	8	2	1779	68	4	2.29	12	5	7	784	29	*2	2.22
2008-09	Philadelphia	AHL	56	31	19	4	3271	134	4	2.46	3	0	3	180	12	0	4.01
2009-10	Bridgeport	AHL	40	19	16	3	2310	97	3	2.52	3	0	3	110	10	0	5.46
2010-11	Nizhnekamsk	Rus-KHL	31	....	....	....	1366	69	1	3.03	1	....	....	47	4	0	5.08

CHA All-Rookie Team (2003) • CHA Rookie of the Year (2003)

Signed as a free agent by **Philadelphia** (AHL), March 18, 2006. Signed as a free agent by **NY Islanders**, July 2, 2009. Signed as a free agent by **Nizhnekamsk** (Russia-KHL), May 7, 2010.

MURPHY, Mike (MUHR-fee, MIGHK) CAR

Goaltender. Catches left. 5'11", 172 lbs. Born, Kingston, Ont., January 15, 1989.
(Carolina's 4th choice, 165th overall, in 2008 Entry Draft).

			Regular Season								Playoffs						
Season	Club	League	GP	W	L	O/T	Mins	GA	SO	Avg	GP	W	L	Mins	GA	SO	Avg
2004-05	Kingston Predators	Minor-ON	25	....	....	....	1120	34	4	1.41	....	....	....	....	....	....	....
2005-06	Kingston	OPJHL	33	16	13	2	....	102	3	3.30	4	0	3	174	19	0	6.55
	Belleville Bulls	OHL	3	1	1	0	93	9	0	5.81	....	....	....	....	....	....	....
2006-07	Belleville Bulls	OHL	18	8	6	2	995	61	0	3.68	....	....	....	....	....	....	....
2007-08	Belleville Bulls	OHL	49	36	7	4	2942	110	3	*2.24	*19	*14	4	*1085	42	1	2.32
2008-09	Belleville Bulls	OHL	54	40	9	4	3169	110	5	*2.08	17	10	7	1007	43	0	2.56
2009-10	Albany River Rats	AHL	20	10	9	0	1109	52	2	2.81	....	....	....	....	....	....	....
2010-11	Charlotte Checkers	AHL	39	21	11	3	2159	91	2	2.53	14	7	7	817	35	1	2.57

OHL First All-Star Team (2008, 2009) • Canadian Major Junior Second All-Star Team (2008) • Canadian Major Junior First All-Star Team (2009) • Canadian Major Junior Goaltender of the Year (2009)

NABOKOV, Evgeni (na-BAW-kahv, ehv-GEH-nee) NYI

Goaltender. Catches left. 6', 200 lbs. Born, Ust-Kamenogorsk, USSR, July 25, 1975.
(San Jose's 9th choice, 219th overall, in 1994 Entry Draft).

			Regular Season								Playoffs						
Season	Club	League	GP	W	L	O/T	Mins	GA	SO	Avg	GP	W	L	Mins	GA	SO	Avg
1991-92	Ust-Kamenogorsk	CIS	1	....	....	....	20	1	0	3.00	....	....	....	....	....	....	....
1992-93	Ust-Kam'gorsk 2	CIS-2	19	....	....	....	....	....	....	....	....	....	....	....	....	....	....
	Ust-Kamenogorsk	CIS	4	....	....	....	109	5	0	2.75	....	....	....	....	....	....	....
1993-94	Ust-Kamenogorsk	CIS	11	....	....	....	539	29	....	3.23	....	....	....	....	....	....	....
1994-95	Dynamo Moscow	CIS	24	....	....	....	1326	40	3	1.81	13	....	....	806	30	2	2.23
1995-96	Dynamo Moscow	CIS	39	....	....	....	2008	67	5	2.00	....	....	....	....	....	....	....
1996-97	Dynamo Moscow	Russia	27	....	....	....	1588	56	2	2.11	4	....	....	255	12	0	2.82
	Dynamo Moscow 2	Russia-3	1	....	....	....	....	2	....	....	....	....	....	....	....	....	....
1997-98	Kentucky	AHL	33	10	21	2	1866	122	0	3.92	1	0	0	23	1	0	2.59
1998-99	Kentucky	AHL	43	26	14	1	2429	106	5	2.62	11	6	5	599	30	*2	3.00
99-2000	**San Jose**	**NHL**	**11**	**2**	**2**	**1**	**414**	**15**	**1**	**2.17**	**1**	**0**	**0**	**20**	**0**	**0**	**0.00**
	Kentucky	AHL	2	1	1	0	120	3	1	1.50	....	....	....	....	....	....	....
	Cleveland	IHL	20	12	4	3	1164	52	0	2.68	....	....	....	....	....	....	....
2000-01	**San Jose**	**NHL**	**66**	**32**	**21**	**7**	**3700**	**135**	**6**	**2.19**	**4**	**1**	**3**	**218**	**10**	**1**	**2.75**
2001-02	**San Jose**	**NHL**	**67**	**37**	**24**	**5**	**3901**	**149**	**7**	**2.29**	**12**	**7**	**5**	**712**	**31**	**0**	**2.61**
2002-03	**San Jose**	**NHL**	**55**	**19**	**28**	**8**	**3227**	**146**	**3**	**2.71**	....	....	....	....	....	....	....
2003-04	**San Jose**	**NHL**	**59**	**31**	**19**	**8**	**3456**	**127**	**9**	**2.20**	**17**	**10**	**7**	**1052**	**30**	**3**	**1.71**
2004-05	Magnitogorsk	Russia	14	....	....	....	808	27	3	2.00	5	....	....	307	13	0	2.53
2005-06	**San Jose**	**NHL**	**45**	**16**	**19**	**7**	**2575**	**133**	**1**	**3.10**	**1**	**0**	**0**	**12**	**1**	**0**	**5.00**
	Russia	Olympics	7	4	2	0	359	8	3	1.34	....	....	....	....	....	....	....
2006-07	**San Jose**	**NHL**	**50**	**25**	**16**	**4**	**2778**	**106**	**7**	**2.29**	**11**	**6**	**5**	**701**	**26**	**1**	**2.23**
2007-08	**San Jose**	**NHL**	***77**	***46**	**21**	**8**	**4561**	**163**	**6**	**2.14**	**13**	**6**	**7**	**853**	**31**	**1**	**2.18**
2008-09	**San Jose**	**NHL**	**62**	**41**	**12**	**8**	**3686**	**150**	**7**	**2.44**	**6**	**2**	**4**	**362**	**17**	**0**	**2.82**
2009-10	**San Jose**	**NHL**	**71**	**44**	**16**	**10**	**4194**	**170**	**3**	**2.43**	**15**	**8**	**7**	**890**	**38**	**1**	**2.56**
	Russia	Olympics	3	2	1	0	144	10	0	4.16	....	....	....	....	....	....	....
2010-11	SKA St. Petersburg	Rus-KHL	22	....	....	....	1230	62	2	3.02	....	....	....	....	....	....	....
	NHL Totals		**563**	**293**	**178**	**66**	**32492**	**1294**	**50**	**2.39**	**80**	**40**	**38**	**4820**	**184**	**7**	**2.29**

NHL All-Rookie Team (2001) • Calder Memorial Trophy (2001) • NHL First All-Star Team (2008)

Played in NHL All-Star Game (2001, 2008)

• Scored a goal vs. Vancouver, March 10, 2002. Signed as a free agent by **Magnitogorsk** (Russia), December 2, 2004. Signed as a free agent by **St. Petersburg** (Russia-KHL), July 7, 2010. Signed as a free agent by **Detroit**, January 20, 2011. Claimed on waivers by **NY Islanders** from **Detroit**, January 22, 2011. • Suspended by **NY Islanders** for failing to report to team after waiver claim, January 25, 2011.

NAGLE, Pat (NAY-guhl, PAT) T.B.

Goaltender. Catches left. 6'3", 182 lbs. Born, Bloomfield, MI, September 21, 1987.

			Regular Season								Playoffs						
Season	Club	League	GP	W	L	O/T	Mins	GA	SO	Avg	GP	W	L	Mins	GA	SO	Avg
2006-07	St. Louis Bandits	NAHL	36	24	12	0	2136	81	1	2.28	11	9	1	662	26	0	2.36
2007-08	Ferris State	CCHA	16	8	7	0	867	38	1	2.63	....	....	....	....	....	....	....
2008-09	Ferris State	CCHA	22	7	11	3	1246	59	0	2.84	....	....	....	....	....	....	....
2009-10	Ferris State	CCHA	26	12	10	3	1496	53	1	2.13	....	....	....	....	....	....	....
2010-11	Ferris State	CCHA	37	18	14	5	2193	74	3	2.02	....	....	....	....	....	....	....

Signed as a free agent by **Tampa Bay**, March 22, 2011.

NEUVIRTH, Michal (NOI-vihrt, MIGHK-ahl) WSH

Goaltender. Catches left. 6'1", 190 lbs. Born, Usti nad Labem, Czech., March 23, 1988.
(Washington's 3rd choice, 34th overall, in 2006 Entry Draft).

			Regular Season								Playoffs						
Season	Club	League	GP	W	L	O/T	Mins	GA	SO	Avg	GP	W	L	Mins	GA	SO	Avg
2003-04	Sparta U17	CzR-U17	55	....	....	....	3137	96	5	1.84	3	....	....	180	13	0	4.33
2004-05	Sparta U17	CzR-U17	20	....	....	....	1178	49	3	2.50	8	....	....	482	17	0	2.12
	Sparta Jr.	CzRep-Jr.	10	....	....	....	501	20	1	2.40	....	....	....	....	....	....	....
2005-06	Sparta Jr.	CzRep-Jr.	42	....	....	....	2516	82	5	1.96	3	....	....	179	9	0	3.02
2006-07	Plymouth Whalers	OHL	41	26	8	4	2223	86	4	*2.32	*18	*14	4	*1080	44	0	*2.44
2007-08	Plymouth Whalers	OHL	10	5	4	1	600	26	0	2.60	....	....	....	....	....	....	....
	Windsor Spitfires	OHL	8	6	1	1	482	17	0	2.12	....	....	....	....	....	....	....
	Oshawa Generals	OHL	15	6	2	6	844	57	0	4.05	9	7	2	507	21	0	2.49
2008-09	**Washington**	**NHL**	**5**	**2**	**1**	**0**	**220**	**11**	**0**	**3.00**	....	....	....	....	....	....	....
	Hershey Bears	AHL	17	9	5	2	1001	45	1	2.70	*22	*16	6	*1346	43	*4	1.92
	South Carolina	ECHL	13	6	7	0	762	29	2	2.28	....	....	....	....	....	....	....
2009-10	**Washington**	**NHL**	**17**	**9**	**4**	**0**	**872**	**40**	**0**	**2.75**	....	....	....	....	....	....	....
	Hershey Bears	AHL	22	15	6	0	1231	46	1	2.24	*18	*14	4	*1133	39	1	2.07
2010-11	**Washington**	**NHL**	**48**	**27**	**12**	**4**	**2689**	**110**	**4**	**2.45**	**9**	**4**	**5**	**590**	**23**	**1**	**2.34**
	NHL Totals		**70**	**38**	**17**	**4**	**3781**	**161**	**4**	**2.55**	**9**	**4**	**5**	**590**	**23**	**1**	**2.34**

OHL Second All-Star Team (2007) • Jack A. Butterfield Trophy (AHL – Playoff MVP) (2009)

NIEMI, Antti (nee-YEH-mee, AN-tee) S.J.

Goaltender. Catches left. 6'2", 215 lbs. Born, Vantaa, Finland, August 29, 1983.

			Regular Season								Playoffs						
Season	Club	League	GP	W	L	O/T	Mins	GA	SO	Avg	GP	W	L	Mins	GA	SO	Avg
2000-01	Kiekko-Vantaa Jr.	Fin-Jr.	4							6.86							
2001-02	Kiekko-Vantaa	Finland-2	24								3						
2002-03	Kiekko-Vantaa	Finland-2					364	16	0	2.63							
2003-04	Kiekko-Vantaa	Finland-2	19				1048	47	1	2.52	3			187	13	0	4.17
	Kiekko-Vantaa Jr.	Fin-Jr.	19				1095	58	2	3.18							
2004-05	Kiekko-Vantaa	Finland-2	38				2261	95	1	2.52	3			187	13	0	4.17
2005-06	Pelicans Lahti	Finland	40	12	17	8	2263	103	3	2.73							
2006-07	Pelicans Lahti	Finland	48	18	21	7	2780	119	3	2.57	6	2	4	371	9	1	1.46
2007-08	Pelicans Lahti	Finland	49	26	14	6	2778	109	4	2.35	6	2	3	327	21	0	3.85
2008-09	**Chicago**	**NHL**	**3**	**1**	**1**	**1**	**141**	**8**	**0**	**3.40**							
	Rockford IceHogs	AHL	38	18	14	3	2095	85	2	2.43	2	0	2	115	7	0	3.65
2009-10 ♦	**Chicago**	**NHL**	**39**	**26**	**7**	**4**	**2190**	**82**	**7**	**2.25**	***22**	***16**	**6**	***1322**	**58**	**2**	**2.63**
2010-11	**San Jose**	**NHL**	**60**	**35**	**18**	**6**	**3524**	**140**	**6**	**2.38**	**18**	**8**	**9**	**1044**	**56**	**0**	**3.22**
	NHL Totals		**102**	**62**	**26**	**11**	**5855**	**230**	**13**	**2.36**	**40**	**24**	**15**	**2366**	**114**	**2**	**2.89**

Signed as a free agent by **Chicago**, May 5, 2008. Signed as a free agent by **San Jose**, September 2, 2010.

NIITTYMAKI, Antero (nih-tih-MA-kee, AN-tehr-oh) S.J.

Goaltender. Catches left. 6'1", 210 lbs. Born, Turku, Finland, June 18, 1980.
(Philadelphia's 7th choice, 168th overall, in 1998 Entry Draft).

			Regular Season								Playoffs						
Season	Club	League	GP	W	L	O/T	Mins	GA	SO	Avg	GP	W	L	Mins	GA	SO	Avg
1997-98	TPS Turku U18	Fin-U18	12								1	1	0	60	1	0	1.00
	TPS Turku Jr.	Fin-Jr.	19	10	8	1	1131	34		1.80	4	3	1	220	7	0	1.91
1998-99	TPS Turku Jr.	Fin-Jr.	35	27	8	0	2095	60	3	1.72	6	3	3	362	14	0	2.32
99-2000	TPS Turku Jr.	Fin-Jr.	1	1	0	0	60	1	0	1.00	1	0	1	60	5	0	5.00
	TPS Turku	Finland	32	23	6	3	1899	68	3	2.15	8	6	2	453	13	0	1.72
2000-01	TPS Turku Jr.	Fin-Jr.									2	1	1	120	4	1	2.00
	TPS Turku	Finland	21	10	5	1	1112	46	2	2.48							
2001-02	TPS Turku	Finland	27	16	8	1	1498	46	3	1.84	4	2	2	295	11	0	2.24
2002-03	Philadelphia	AHL	40	14	21	2	2283	98	0	2.58							
2003-04	**Philadelphia**	**NHL**	**3**	**3**	**0**	**0**	**180**	**3**	**0**	**1.00**							
	Philadelphia	AHL	49	24	13	6	2728	92	7	2.02	12	6	6	796	24	0	1.81
2004-05	Philadelphia	AHL	58	33	21	4	3453	119	6	2.07	*21	*15	5	*1269	37	*3	1.75
2005-06	**Philadelphia**	**NHL**	**46**	**23**	**15**	**6**	**2690**	**133**	**2**	**2.97**	**2**	**0**	**0**	**73**	**5**	**0**	**4.11**
	Finland	Olympics	6	5	1	0	359	8	3	1.34							
2006-07	**Philadelphia**	**NHL**	**52**	**9**	**29**	**9**	**2943**	**166**	**0**	**3.38**							
2007-08	**Philadelphia**	**NHL**	**28**	**12**	**9**	**2**	**1424**	**69**	**1**	**2.91**							
2008-09	**Philadelphia**	**NHL**	**32**	**15**	**8**	**6**	**1805**	**83**	**1**	**2.76**							
2009-10	**Tampa Bay**	**NHL**	**49**	**21**	**18**	**5**	**2657**	**127**	**1**	**2.87**							
	Finland	Olympics	DID NOT PLAY – SPARE GOALTENDER														
2010-11	**San Jose**	**NHL**	**24**	**12**	**7**	**3**	**1414**	**64**	**0**	**2.72**	**2**	**1**	**0**	**91**	**1**	**0**	**0.66**
	NHL Totals		**234**	**95**	**86**	**31**	**13113**	**645**	**5**	**2.95**	**4**	**1**	**0**	**164**	**6**	**0**	**2.20**

Jack A. Butterfield Trophy (AHL – Playoff MVP) (2005) • Olympic All-Star Team (2006) • Olympics – Best Goaltender (2006) • Olympics – MVP (2006)

Signed as a free agent by **Tampa Bay**, July 10, 2009. Signed as a free agent by **San Jose**, July 1, 2010.

NILSSON, Anders (NIHL-suhn, AN-duhrz) NYI

Goaltender. Catches left. 6'5", 220 lbs. Born, Lulea, Sweden, March 19, 1990.
(NY Islanders' 4th choice, 62nd overall, in 2009 Entry Draft).

			Regular Season								Playoffs						
Season	Club	League	GP	W	L	O/T	Mins	GA	SO	Avg	GP	W	L	Mins	GA	SO	Avg
2004-05	Lulea HF Jr.	Swe-Jr.	1				24	4	0	9.90							
2007-08	Lulea HF U18	Swe-U18	11				625	31	0	2.97							
	Lulea HF Jr.	Swe-Jr.	16				898	31	2	2.07	1			60	6	0	6.00
2008-09	Lulea HF Jr.	Swe-Jr.	37				2199	75	4	2.05	6			357	14	1	2.35
	Lulea HF	Sweden	1				28	0	0	0.00							
	Kalix Ungdoms HC	Sweden-3	1				59	3	0	3.05							
2009-10	Lulea HF Jr.	Swe-Jr.	4				244	12	0	2.95							
	Lulea HF	Sweden	27				1383	61	2	2.65							
2010-11	Lulea HF	Sweden	31				1876	60	6	*1.92	13			827	27	0	1.96

ORTIO, Joni (OHR-tee-oh, YOH-nee) CGY

Goaltender. Catches left. 6'1", 181 lbs. Born, Turku, Finland, April 16, 1991.
(Calgary's 5th choice, 171st overall, in 2009 Entry Draft).

			Regular Season								Playoffs						
Season	Club	League	GP	W	L	O/T	Mins	GA	SO	Avg	GP	W	L	Mins	GA	SO	Avg
2007-08	TuTo Turku U18	Fin-U18	7	1	6	0	392	34	0	5.20							
	TuTo Turku Jr.	Fin-Jr.	5	1	3	0	302	16	0	3.18							
2008-09	TPS Turku U18	Fin-U18	1	1	0	0	60	4	0	4.00							
	TPS Turku Jr.	Fin-Jr.	26	18	8	0	1573	69	1	2.63	12	6	6	716	23	0	1.93
2009-10	Suomi U20	Finland-2	5	3	2	0	312	11	0	2.12							
	TuTo Turku	Finland-2	9	5	4	0	546	27	0	2.96							
	TPS Turku Jr.	Fin-Jr.	16	8	6	0	935	45	1	2.89							
	TPS Turku	Finland	3	1	0	0	108	8	0	4.45							
2010-11	TPS Turku	Finland	15	2	7	3	730	38	1	3.12							
	Abbotsford Heat	AHL	1	0	1	0	60	6	0	6.03							

OSGOOD, Chris (AWS-gud, KRIHS)

Goaltender. Catches left. 5'10", 180 lbs. Born, Peace River, Alta., November 26, 1972.
(Detroit's 3rd choice, 54th overall, in 1991 Entry Draft).

			Regular Season								Playoffs						
Season	Club	League	GP	W	L	O/T	Mins	GA	SO	Avg	GP	W	L	Mins	GA	SO	Avg
1988-89	Medicine Hat	AMHL	26				1441	88	0	3.66							
1989-90	Medicine Hat	WHL	57	24	28	2	3094	228	0	4.42	3	0	3	173	17	0	5.91
1990-91	Medicine Hat	WHL	46	23	18	3	2630	173	2	3.95	12	7	5	712	42	0	3.54
1991-92	Medicine Hat	WHL	15	10	3	0	819	44	0	3.22							
	Brandon	WHL	16	3	10	1	890	60	1	4.04							
	Seattle	WHL	21	12	7	1	1217	65	1	3.20	15	9	6	904	51	0	3.38
1992-93	Adirondack	AHL	45	19	19	4	2438	159	0	3.91	1	0	1	59	2	0	2.03
1993-94	**Detroit**	**NHL**	**41**	**23**	**8**	**5**	**2206**	**105**	**2**	**2.86**	**6**	**3**	**2**	**307**	**12**	**1**	**2.35**
	Adirondack	AHL	4	3	1	0	239	13	0	3.26							
1994-95	**Detroit**	**NHL**	**19**	**14**	**5**	**0**	**1087**	**41**	**1**	**2.26**	**2**	**0**	**0**	**68**	**2**	**0**	**1.76**
	Adirondack	AHL	2	1	1	0	120	6	0	3.00							
1995-96	**Detroit**	**NHL**	**50**	***39**	**6**	**5**	**2933**	**106**	**5**	**2.17**	**15**	**8**	**7**	**936**	**33**	**2**	**2.12**
1996-97 ♦	**Detroit**	**NHL**	**47**	**23**	**13**	**9**	**2769**	**106**	**6**	**2.30**	**2**	**0**	**0**	**47**	**2**	**0**	**2.55**
1997-98 ♦	**Detroit**	**NHL**	**64**	**33**	**20**	**11**	**3807**	**140**	**6**	**2.21**	***22**	***16**	**6**	***1361**	**48**	**2**	**2.12**
1998-99	**Detroit**	**NHL**	**63**	**34**	**25**	**4**	**3691**	**149**	**3**	**2.42**	**6**	**4**	**2**	**358**	**14**	**1**	**2.35**
99-2000	**Detroit**	**NHL**	**53**	**30**	**14**	**8**	**3148**	**126**	**6**	**2.40**	**9**	**5**	**4**	**547**	**18**	**2**	**1.97**
2000-01	**Detroit**	**NHL**	**52**	**25**	**19**	**4**	**2834**	**127**	**1**	**2.69**	**6**	**2**	**4**	**365**	**15**	**1**	**2.47**
2001-02	**NY Islanders**	**NHL**	**66**	**32**	**25**	**6**	**3743**	**156**	**4**	**2.50**	**7**	**3**	**4**	**392**	**17**	**0**	**2.60**
2002-03	**NY Islanders**	**NHL**	**37**	**17**	**14**	**4**	**1993**	**97**	**2**	**2.92**							
	St. Louis	**NHL**	**9**	**4**	**3**	**2**	**532**	**27**	**2**	**3.05**	**7**	**3**	**4**	**417**	**17**	**1**	**2.45**
2003-04	**St. Louis**	**NHL**	**67**	**31**	**25**	**8**	**3861**	**144**	**3**	**2.24**	**5**	**1**	**4**	**287**	**12**	**0**	**2.51**
2004-05			DID NOT PLAY														
2005-06	**Detroit**	**NHL**	**32**	**20**	**6**	**5**	**1846**	**85**	**2**	**2.76**							
	Grand Rapids	AHL	3	2	1	0	180	10	0	3.34							
2006-07	**Detroit**	**NHL**	**21**	**11**	**3**	**6**	**1161**	**46**	**0**	**2.38**							
2007-08 ♦	**Detroit**	**NHL**	**43**	**27**	**9**	**4**	**2409**	**84**	**4**	***2.09**	**19**	***14**	**4**	**1160**	**30**	***3**	***1.55**
2008-09	**Detroit**	**NHL**	**46**	**26**	**9**	**8**	**2663**	**137**	**2**	**3.09**	**23**	**15**	**8**	**1406**	**47**	***2**	**2.01**
2009-10	**Detroit**	**NHL**	**23**	**7**	**9**	**4**	**1252**	**63**	**1**	**3.02**							
2010-11	**Detroit**	**NHL**	**11**	**5**	**3**	**2**	**629**	**29**	**0**	**2.77**							
	NHL Totals		**744**	**401**	**216**	**95**	**42564**	**1768**	**50**	**2.49**	**129**	**74**	**49**	**7651**	**267**	**15**	**2.09**

WHL East Second All-Star Team (1991) • NHL Second All-Star Team (1996) • William M. Jennings Trophy (1996) (shared with Mike Vernon) • William M. Jennings Trophy (2008) (shared with Dominik Hasek)

Played in NHL All-Star Game (1996, 2008)

• Scored a goal while with Medicine Hat (WHL), January 3, 1991. • Scored a goal vs. Hartford, March 6, 1996. Claimed by **NY Islanders** from **Detroit** in Waiver Draft, September 28, 2001. Traded to **St. Louis** by **NY Islanders** with NY Islanders' 3rd round choice (Konstantin Barulin) in 2003 Entry Draft for Justin Papineau and St. Louis' 2nd round choice (Jeremy Colliton) in 2003 Entry Draft, March 11, 2003. Signed as a free agent by **Detroit**, August 8, 2005. • Officially announced his retirement, July 19, 2011.

OUELLETTE, Martin (OO-leht, MAHR-tihn) CBJ

Goaltender. Catches left. 6'2", 173 lbs. Born, Saint-Jerome, Que., December 30, 1991.
(Columbus' 8th choice, 184th overall, in 2010 Entry Draft).

			Regular Season								Playoffs						
Season	Club	League	GP	W	L	O/T	Mins	GA	SO	Avg	GP	W	L	Mins	GA	SO	Avg
2008-09	Kimball Union	High-NH	16							2.93							
2009-10	Kimball Union	High-NH	29	21	6	2	1461	45		1.61							
2010-11	University of Maine	H-East	9	3	3	2	490	26	1	3.18							

OWUYA, Mark (oh-WUH-yuh, MAHRK) TOR

Goaltender. Catches left. 6'2", 198 lbs. Born, Stockholm, Sweden, July 18, 1989.

			Regular Season								Playoffs						
Season	Club	League	GP	W	L	O/T	Mins	GA	SO	Avg	GP	W	L	Mins	GA	SO	Avg
2005-06	Djurgarden U18	Swe-U18	7				390	17	1	2.62	3			120	5	0	2.50
2006-07	Djurgarden U18	Swe-U18	6				317	10	0	1.89	1			26	4	0	9.15
	Djurgarden Jr.	Swe-Jr.	12				722	22	3	1.83							
2007-08	Djurgarden Jr.	Swe-Jr.	21				1218	58	1	2.86							
	Djurgarden	Sweden	1				25	2	0	4.75							
	Malarh/Bre Hockey	Sweden-3	7				430	17	0	2.37							
2008-09	Almtuna	Sweden-2	40				2415	91	4	2.26	6			361	12	1	1.99
	Djurgarden Jr.	Swe-Jr.									5			342	12	1	2.11
2009-10	Orebro HK	Sweden-2	24				1341	85	0	3.80							
	Mora IK	Sweden-2	5				300	17	0	3.39	1			37	1	0	1.64
2010-11	Djurgarden Jr.	Swe-Jr.	1				60	1	0	1.00							
	Boras HC	Sweden-2	2				121	4	0	1.98							
	Djurgarden	Sweden	32				1848	67	2	2.18	7			433	12	*2	1.66

Signed as a free agent by **Toronto**, April 28, 2011.

PALMER, Joe (PAHL-muhr, JOH) CHI

Goaltender. Catches left. 6'2", 200 lbs. Born, Yorkville, NY, February 19, 1988.
(Chicago's 6th choice, 96th overall, in 2006 Entry Draft).

			Regular Season								Playoffs						
Season	Club	League	GP	W	L	O/T	Mins	GA	SO	Avg	GP	W	L	Mins	GA	SO	Avg
2003-04	Syracuse Jr. Stars	EmJHL	31				1147	69	1	3.61	6			368	19	0	3.10
	USNTDP	U-17	1	0	0	0	11	2	0	10.91							
2004-05	USNTDP	U-17	8	6	1	1	495	22	0	2.67							
	USNTDP	NAHL	19	10	8	1	1020	56	0	3.29							
2005-06	USNTDP	U-18	33	16	14	3	1900	99	0	3.13							
	USNTDP	NAHL	14	13	1	0	776	22	1	1.70							
2006-07	Ohio State	CCHA	34	15	15	4	1968	97	1	2.96							
2007-08	Ohio State	CCHA	34	10	19	4	1980	103	1	3.12							
2008-09	Ohio State	CCHA	3	0	2	1	122	11	0	5.40							
2009-10	Texas Brahmas	CHL	32	13	10	4	1786	82	*3	2.75	3	0	1	117	4	0	2.06
2010-11	Toledo Walleye	ECHL	28	10	14	1	1496	104	0	4.17							

Signed as a free agent by **Rockford** (AHL), July 29, 2010. • Assigned to **Texas** (CHL) by **Rockford** (AHL), December 11, 2010.

PASQUALE, Edward (pas-KWAHL-ee, EHD-wuhrd) WPG

Goaltender. Catches left. 6'3", 215 lbs. Born, Toronto, Ont., November 20, 1990.
(Atlanta's 4th choice, 117th overall, in 2009 Entry Draft).

			Regular Season								Playoffs						
Season	Club	League	GP	W	L	O/T	Mins	GA	SO	Avg	GP	W	L	Mins	GA	SO	Avg
2005-06	Tor. Red Wings	GTHL	53				2385	98	5	1.84							
2006-07	Wellington Dukes	OPJHL	18	13	3	2	1091	35	1	1.92							
	Belleville Bulls	OHL	7	4	1	0	367	19	0	3.11							
2007-08	Belleville Bulls	OHL	10	4	4	2	558	27	1	2.90							
	Saginaw Spirit	OHL	13	8	5	0	661	39	0	3.54	2	0	1	97	5	0	3.09
2008-09	Saginaw Spirit	OHL	*61	32	21	6	*3536	178	0	3.02	8	4	4	530	34	0	3.85
2009-10	Saginaw Spirit	OHL	51	27	17	5	2898	153	1	3.17	6	2	4	361	14	0	2.33
2010-11	Chicago Wolves	AHL	24	11	11	1	1372	67	1	2.93							
	Gwinnett	ECHL	12	7	4	0	715	44	0	3.69							

PATTERSON, Kent (PA-tuhr-suhn, KEHNT) COL

Goaltender. Catches left. 6', 184 lbs. Born, St. Louis Park, MN, September 15, 1989.
(Colorado's 6th choice, 113th overall, in 2007 Entry Draft).

			Regular Season								Playoffs						
Season	Club	League	GP	W	L	O/T	Mins	GA	SO	Avg	GP	W	L	Mins	GA	SO	Avg
2004-05	Blake Bears	High-MN	14	9	4	1	673	27		2.05							
2005-06	Blake Bears	High-MN	25	14	8	2	1249	66		2.70							
2006-07	Cedar Rapids	USHL	29	20	5	3	1710	83	2	2.91	1	0	1	41	6	0	8.78
2007-08	Cedar Rapids	USHL	20	10	6	1	1110	46	1	2.49							
2008-09	U. of Minnesota	WCHA	7	0	2	1	231	9	0	2.34							
2009-10	U. of Minnesota	WCHA	8	2	4	1	406	21	0	3.10							
2010-11	U. of Minnesota	WCHA	30	14	9	6	1724	73	0	2.54							

USHL All-Rookie Team (2007) • WCHA Second All-Star Team (2011)

PAVELEC, Ondrej (pah-vah-LEK, AWN-dray) WPG

Goaltender. Catches left. 6'3", 220 lbs. Born, Kladno, Czech., August 31, 1987.
(Atlanta's 2nd choice, 41st overall, in 2005 Entry Draft).

			Regular Season								Playoffs						
Season	Club	League	GP	W	L	O/T	Mins	GA	SO	Avg	GP	W	L	Mins	GA	SO	Avg
2003-04	HC Kladno U17	CzR-U17	38	....	....	....	2079	77	3	2.22	2	....	....	67	7	0	6.27
2004-05	HC Kladno Jr.	CzRep-Jr.	39	....	....	....	2218	85	7	2.30	10	....	....	587	24	1	2.45
	HK LEV Slany	CzRep-3	1	....	....	....	60	4	0	4.00							
2005-06	Cape Breton	QMJHL	47	27	18	0	2578	108	3	2.51	9	4	5	507	19	0	*2.25
2006-07	Cape Breton	QMJHL	43	28	11	0	2335	98	1	*2.52	16	11	5	970	37	*2	*2.29
2007-08	**Atlanta**	**NHL**	**7**	**3**	**3**	**0**	**347**	**18**	**0**	**3.11**							
	Chicago Wolves	AHL	52	33	16	3	3033	140	2	2.77	*24	*16	8	*1438	56	*2	2.34
2008-09	**Atlanta**	**NHL**	**12**	**3**	**7**	**0**	**599**	**36**	**0**	**3.61**							
	Chicago Wolves	AHL	40	18	20	2	2417	104	3	2.58							
2009-10	**Atlanta**	**NHL**	**42**	**14**	**18**	**7**	**2317**	**127**	**2**	**3.29**							
	Czech Republic	Olympics	DID NOT PLAY – SPARE GOALTENDER														
2010-11	**Atlanta**	**NHL**	**58**	**21**	**23**	**9**	**3225**	**147**	**4**	**2.73**							
	Chicago Wolves	AHL	1	0	1	0	58	3	0	3.10							
	NHL Totals		**119**	**41**	**51**	**16**	**6488**	**328**	**6**	**3.03**							

QMJHL All-Rookie Team (2006) • QMJHL First All-Star Team (2006, 2007) • QMJHL Defensive Rookie of the Year (2006)

• Transferred to **Winnipeg** after **Atlanta** franchise relocated, June 21, 2011.

PEARCE, Jordan (PEERS-JOHR-dahn) DET

Goaltender. Catches left. 6'1", 195 lbs. Born, Anchorage, AK, October 10, 1986.

			Regular Season								Playoffs						
Season	Club	League	GP	W	L	O/T	Mins	GA	SO	Avg	GP	W	L	Mins	GA	SO	Avg
2004-05	Lincoln Stars	USHL	38	22	10	4	2227	114	0	3.07	2	0	1	69	7	0	6.06
2005-06	U. of Notre Dame	CCHA	9	4	4	0	442	24	1	3.25							
2006-07	U. of Notre Dame	CCHA	3	2	1	0	180	6	1	2.01							
2007-08	U. of Notre Dame	CCHA	*43	23	15	4	*2558	87	2	2.04							
2008-09	U. of Notre Dame	CCHA	*39	*30	6	3	*2326	65	8	1.68							
	Grand Rapids	AHL	1	0	1	0	59	5	0	5.11							
2009-10	Grand Rapids	AHL	5	1	2	0	236	15	0	3.82							
	Toledo Walleye	ECHL	37	15	16	2	2047	124	2	3.63	4	1	3	247	16	0	3.88
2010-11	Grand Rapids	AHL	44	20	15	5	2452	118	1	2.89							
	Toledo Walleye	ECHL	8	3	4	1	451	31	1	4.13							

Signed as a free agent by **Detroit**, April 10, 2009.

PECHURSKI, Alexander (puh-CHUHR-skee, al-ehx-AN-duhr) PIT

Goaltender. Catches left. 6', 190 lbs. Born, Magnitogorsk, USSR, June 4, 1990.
(Pittsburgh's 2nd choice, 150th overall, in 2008 Entry Draft).

			Regular Season								Playoffs						
Season	Club	League	GP	W	L	O/T	Mins	GA	SO	Avg	GP	W	L	Mins	GA	SO	Avg
2007-08	Magnitogorsk 2	Russia-3	27	....	....	....	....	62	....	....							
	Magnitogorsk	Russia	1	....	....	....	1	0	0	0.00							
2008-09	Magnitogorsk 2	Russia-3	20	....	....	....	....	54	....	....							
2009-10	Magnitogorsk	Rus-KHL	1	....	....	....	30	3	0	6.00							
	Magnitogorsk Jr.	Russia-Jr.	5	....	....	....	299	14	0	2.81							
	Pittsburgh	**NHL**	**1**	**0**	**0**	**0**	**36**	**1**	**0**	**1.67**							
	Tri-City Americans	WHL	27	13	10	1	1403	61	4	2.61	7	1	2	305	15	0	2.95
2010-11	Tri-City Americans	WHL	3	2	0	1	184	11	0	3.60							
	Mississippi	CHL	37	17	14	2	2030	103	1	3.04							
	NHL Totals		**1**	**0**	**0**	**0**	**36**	**1**	**0**	**1.67**							

PERHONEN, Samu (PAIR-hoh-nehn, SA-moo) EDM

Goaltender. Catches left. 6'5", 184 lbs. Born, Jamsankoski, Finland, March 7, 1993.
(Edmonton's 4th choice, 62nd overall, in 2011 Entry Draft).

			Regular Season								Playoffs						
Season	Club	League	GP	W	L	O/T	Mins	GA	SO	Avg	GP	W	L	Mins	GA	SO	Avg
2008-09	JyP Jyvaskyla U18	Fin-U18	1	1	0	0	60	0	1	0.00							
2009-10	JyP Jyvaskyla U18	Fin-U18	13	5	5	0	745	41	1	3.30							
	JyP Jyvaskyla Jr.	Fin-Jr.	1	0	1	0	26	2	0	4.67							
2010-11	Suomi U20	Finland-2	1	0	1	0	59	3	0	3.04							
	JyP Jyvaskyla Jr.	Fin-Jr.	29	16	11	0	1659	75	2	2.71	12	8	4	736	30	2	2.45

PETERS, Justin (PEE-tuhrz, JUHS-tihn) CAR

Goaltender. Catches left. 6'1", 205 lbs. Born, Blyth, Ont., August 30, 1986.
(Carolina's 2nd choice, 38th overall, in 2004 Entry Draft).

			Regular Season								Playoffs						
Season	Club	League	GP	W	L	O/T	Mins	GA	SO	Avg	GP	W	L	Mins	GA	SO	Avg
2001-02	Huron-Perth	Minor-ON	17	11	2	4	810	32	1	1.89	13	9	4	285	30	1	2.31
2002-03	St. Michael's	OHL	23	6	10	1	1052	54	0	3.08	7	1	0	126	4	0	1.90
2003-04	St. Michael's	OHL	53	30	16	6	3149	139	4	2.65	18	10	8	1109	37	4	2.00
2004-05	St. Michael's	OHL	58	23	23	5	3150	146	3	2.78	10	4	4	524	25	0	2.86
2005-06	St. Michael's	OHL	20	10	6	3	1174	75	0	3.83							
	Plymouth Whalers	OHL	35	19	15	1	2073	95	1	2.75	13	6	7	789	42	0	3.19
2006-07	Albany River Rats	AHL	34	10	18	0	1765	96	1	3.26							
	Florida Everblades	ECHL	1	0	0	1	65	6	0	5.54							
2007-08	Albany River Rats	AHL	11	7	3	0	645	29	0	2.70							
	Florida Everblades	ECHL	31	18	10	2	1846	79	1	2.57							
2008-09	Albany River Rats	AHL	56	19	30	4	3178	153	4	2.89							
2009-10	**Carolina**	**NHL**	**9**	**6**	**3**	**0**	**488**	**23**	**0**	**2.83**							
	Albany River Rats	AHL	47	26	18	2	2763	117	1	2.54	8	4	4	509	29	0	3.42
2010-11	**Carolina**	**NHL**	**12**	**3**	**5**	**1**	**648**	**43**	**0**	**3.98**							
	NHL Totals		**21**	**9**	**8**	**1**	**1136**	**66**	**0**	**3.49**							

PETTERSSON-WENTZEL, Fredrik PEH-tuhr-suhn-WEHNT-zuhl, FREH-drik WPG

Goaltender. Catches left. 6'1", 170 lbs. Born, Uppsala, Sweden, July 23, 1991.
(Atlanta's 4th choice, 128th overall, in 2010 Entry Draft).

			Regular Season								Playoffs						
Season	Club	League	GP	W	L	O/T	Mins	GA	SO	Avg	GP	W	L	Mins	GA	SO	Avg
2008-09	Almtuna U18	Swe-U18	25	....	....	....	1457	59	3	2.43							
	Almtuna Jr.	Swe-Jr.	1	....	....	....	29	0	0	0.00							
2009-10	Almtuna Jr.	Swe-Jr.	5	....	....	....	299	10	2	2.01							
	Nykopings HK	Sweden-3	1	....	....	....	60	3	0	3.00							
	Almtuna	Sweden-2	47	....	....	....	2746	88	7	1.92	5	....	....	311	11	0	2.12
2010-11	Almtuna	Sweden-2	16	....	....	....	939	46	0	2.94							
	Timra IK	Sweden	14	....	....	....	730	33	0	2.71							

PHILLIPS, Brad (FIHL-ihps , BRAD) PHI

Goaltender. Catches left. 6'2", 163 lbs. Born, Allen Park, MI, April 22, 1989.
(Philadelphia's 7th choice, 182nd overall, in 2007 Entry Draft).

			Regular Season								Playoffs						
Season	Club	League	GP	W	L	O/T	Mins	GA	SO	Avg	GP	W	L	Mins	GA	SO	Avg
2004-05	Det. Honeybaked	MWEHL	38	32	3	3	....	50	10	1.32							
2005-06	USNTDP	U-17	13	8	5	0	610	28	....	2.75							
	USNTDP	NAHL	21	12	6	3	1261	51	0	2.43	4	1	3	254	12	0	2.83
2006-07	USNTDP	U-18	12	7	1	2	706	29	0	2.46							
	USNTDP	NAHL	11	8	3	0	660	24	2	2.18	1	0	1	60	3	0	3.00
2007-08	U. of Notre Dame	CCHA	5	4	1	0	275	7	1	1.53							
2008-09	U. of Notre Dame	CCHA	DID NOT PLAY – INJURED														
2009-10	U. of Notre Dame	CCHA	10	2	3	3	559	23	1	2.47							
2010-11	Bloomington	CHL	30	12	7	5	1589	63	0	2.38	3	0	2	136	7	0	3.08

• Missed 2008-09 due to pre-season knee injury.

PICKARD, Calvin (pih-KARD, KAL-vihn) COL

Goaltender. Catches left. 6', 197 lbs. Born, Moncton, N.B., April 15, 1992.
(Colorado's 2nd choice, 49th overall, in 2010 Entry Draft).

			Regular Season								Playoffs						
Season	Club	League	GP	W	L	O/T	Mins	GA	SO	Avg	GP	W	L	Mins	GA	SO	Avg
2007-08	Winnipeg Wild	MMHL	40	....	....	....	....	....	....	1.91							
2008-09	Seattle	WHL	47	23	16	5	2694	137	3	3.05	5	1	4	297	15	0	3.03
2009-10	Seattle	WHL	*62	16	34	12	*3688	190	3	3.09							
2010-11	Seattle	WHL	*68	27	33	8	*4013	225	1	3.36							

WHL West First All-Star Team (2010) • WHL West Second All-Star Team (2011)

PICKARD, Chet (PIH-kuhrd, CHEHT) NSH

Goaltender. Catches left. 6'2", 206 lbs. Born, Moncton, N.B., November 29, 1989.
(Nashville's 2nd choice, 18th overall, in 2008 Entry Draft).

			Regular Season								Playoffs						
Season	Club	League	GP	W	L	O/T	Mins	GA	SO	Avg	GP	W	L	Mins	GA	SO	Avg
2004-05	Wpg. Monarchs	MMHL	22	....	....	....	1264	55	2	2.61							
2005-06	Tri-City Americans	WHL	26	9	9	1	1270	62	3	2.93							
2006-07	Tri-City Americans	WHL	29	17	10	1	1577	75	1	2.85	1	0	0	20	1	0	3.00
2007-08	Tri-City Americans	WHL	*64	*46	12	4	*3779	146	2	2.32	16	11	5	1010	30	*3	1.78
2008-09	Tri-City Americans	WHL	50	35	12	3	2947	112	6	2.28	11	6	5	650	37	0	3.41
2009-10	Milwaukee	AHL	36	14	16	3	2024	96	1	2.85	1	0	0	12	1	0	5.08
2010-11	Milwaukee	AHL	7	1	4	1	365	18	0	2.96							
	Cincinnati	ECHL	29	9	14	3	1506	85	1	3.39							

WHL West First All-Star Team (2008, 2009) • WHL Goaltender of the Year (2008, 2009) • Canadian Major Junior First All-Star Team (2008) • Canadian Major Junior Goaltender of the Year (2008)

PIELMEIER, Timo (PEEL-migh-uhr, TEE-moh) ANA

Goaltender. Catches left. 6', 170 lbs. Born, Deggendorf, West Germany, July 7, 1989.
(San Jose's 3rd choice, 83rd overall, in 2007 Entry Draft).

			Regular Season								Playoffs						
Season	Club	League	GP	W	L	O/T	Mins	GA	SO	Avg	GP	W	L	Mins	GA	SO	Avg
2004-05	Mannheimer ERC	German-5	1	....	....	....	....	....	....	8.15							
	Mannheim Jr.	Ger-Jr.	10	....	....	....	568	33	....	3.49							
2005-06	Koln Jr.	Ger-Jr.	8	....	....	....	459	52	....	6.79	2	....	....	100	17	....	10.20
2006-07	Koln Jr.	Ger-Jr.	20	....	....	....	1159	77	....	3.99	6	....	....	370	17	....	2.76
2007-08	St. John's	QMJHL	50	23	26	0	2719	133	1	2.94	5	0	3	231	22	0	5.71
2008-09	Shawinigan	QMJHL	43	29	11	0	2407	106	2	2.64	*18	12	5	1021	47	0	2.76
2009-10	Bakersfield	ECHL	57	27	22	5	3251	178	0	3.29	4	1	3	247	14	0	3.39
2010-11	**Anaheim**	**NHL**	**1**	**0**	**0**	**0**	**40**	**5**	**0**	**7.50**							
	Syracuse Crunch	AHL	37	16	17	1	1942	100	1	3.09							
	Elmira Jackals	ECHL	2	1	0	1	125	7	0	3.37							
	NHL Totals		**1**	**0**	**0**	**0**	**40**	**5**	**0**	**7.50**							

Traded to **Anaheim** by **San Jose** with Nick Bonino and future considerations for Travis Moen and Kent Huskins, March 4, 2009.

PITTON, Bryan (PIH-tuhn, BRIGH-uhn)

Goaltender. Catches left. 6'3", 204 lbs. Born, Mississauga, Ont., January 26, 1988.
(Edmonton's 3rd choice, 133rd overall, in 2006 Entry Draft).

			Regular Season								Playoffs						
Season	Club	League	GP	W	L	O/T	Mins	GA	SO	Avg	GP	W	L	Mins	GA	SO	Avg
2003-04	Brampton Battalion	Minor-ON	31	....	....	....	1375	58	3	1.87							
2004-05	Wellington Dukes	OPJHL	....	24	7	3	....	....	2	2.93							
2005-06	Brampton Battalion	OHL	24	16	4	0	1293	74	0	3.43	2	0	0	45	5	0	6.67
2006-07	Brampton Battalion	OHL	61	26	29	4	3494	208	0	3.57	4	0	4	270	15	0	3.33
2007-08	Brampton Battalion	OHL	39	22	13	2	2153	91	*4	2.54	5	1	4	333	10	0	*1.80
	Springfield Falcons	AHL	1	0	0	0	12	1	0	4.88							
2008-09	Stockton Thunder	ECHL	34	9	19	3	1949	110	0	3.39	3	1	2	144	12	0	5.01
2009-10	Springfield Falcons	AHL	8	2	6	0	458	36	0	4.71							
	Stockton Thunder	ECHL	22	9	9	3	1242	59	1	2.85	4	2	1	247	7	1	1.70
2010-11	Oklahoma City	AHL	8	3	2	1	447	23	0	3.09							
	Stockton Thunder	ECHL	34	18	10	4	1886	91	1	2.90	1	0	1	20	3	0	9.00

PLANTE, Tyler (PLAWNT, TIGH-luhr) FLA

Goaltender. Catches left. 6'3", 191 lbs. Born, Milwaukee, WI, April 16, 1987.
(Florida's 2nd choice, 32nd overall, in 2005 Entry Draft).

			Regular Season								Playoffs						
Season	Club	League	GP	W	L	O/T	Mins	GA	SO	Avg	GP	W	L	Mins	GA	SO	Avg
2003-04	Brandon	WHL	2	0	0	1	58	2	0	2.08							
2004-05	Brandon	WHL	48	34	11	2	2832	122	6	2.58	*24	*13	11	*1408	69	0	2.94
2005-06	Brandon	WHL	60	25	24	9	3414	189	2	3.32	6	2	4	360	18	0	3.00
2006-07	Brandon	WHL	54	30	14	9	3215	145	4	2.71	11	6	5	659	37	0	3.37
2007-08	Rochester	AHL	25	6	16	1	1451	86	0	3.56							
	Florida Everblades	ECHL	10	4	5	1	598	28	1	2.81							
2008-09	Rochester	AHL	19	5	10	1	904	49	0	3.25							
	Dayton Bombers	ECHL	19	6	11	1	1076	60	0	3.35							
2009-10	Rochester	AHL	27	12	12	1	1487	66	3	2.66	7	3	3	346	14	0	2.43
2010-11	Rochester	AHL	35	13	17	2	1942	101	1	3.12							

WHL Rookie of the Year (2005) • Canadian Major Junior All-Rookie Team (2005)

POGGE, Justin — (POH-gee, JUHS-tihn) — PHX

Goaltender. Catches left. 6'3", 204 lbs. Born, Ft. McMurray, Alta., April 22, 1986.
(Toronto's 1st choice, 90th overall, in 2004 Entry Draft).

			Regular Season								Playoffs						
Season	**Club**	**League**	**GP**	**W**	**L**	**O/T**	**Mins**	**GA**	**SO**	**Avg**	**GP**	**W**	**L**	**Mins**	**GA**	**SO**	**Avg**
2002-03	Summerland Sting	KIJHL	30	....	....	....	1761	91	0	3.13	....	....	....	....	....	....	....
2003-04	Prince George	WHL	44	17	18	2	2271	107	3	2.83	....	....	....	....	....	....	....
2004-05	Prince George	WHL	24	10	9	2	1198	56	4	2.80	....	....	....	....	....	....	....
	Calgary Hitmen	WHL	29	14	12	3	1727	66	2	2.29	12	7	5	742	24	1	1.94
2005-06	Calgary Hitmen	WHL	54	38	10	6	3237	93	*11	*1.72	13	7	6	802	34	2	2.54
2006-07	Toronto Marlies	AHL	48	19	25	2	2812	142	3	3.03	....	....	....	....	....	....	....
2007-08	Toronto Marlies	AHL	41	26	10	4	2415	94	4	2.34	4	1	1	172	6	0	2.09
2008-09	**Toronto**	**NHL**	**7**	**1**	**4**	**1**	**372**	**27**	**0**	**4.35**	....	....	....	....	....	....	....
	Toronto Marlies	AHL	53	26	21	5	3155	142	0	2.70	5	2	3	304	16	0	3.15
2009-10	San Antonio	AHL	23	12	7	3	1332	57	1	2.57	....	....	....	....	....	....	....
	Bakersfield	ECHL	9	6	2	0	491	22	1	2.69	....	....	....	....	....	....	....
	Albany River Rats	AHL	4	1	0	2	199	8	0	2.41	....	....	....	....	....	....	....
2010-11	Charlotte Checkers	AHL	48	22	18	4	2617	136	0	3.12	4	1	1	155	12	0	4.65
	NHL Totals		**7**	**1**	**4**	**1**	**372**	**27**	**0**	**4.35**	....	....	....	....	....	....	....

WHL East First All-Star Team (2006) • WHL Goaltender of the Year (2006) • WHL Player of the Year (2006) • Canadian Major Junior First All-Star Team (2006) • Canadian Major Junior Goaltender of the Year (2006)

Traded to **Anaheim** by **Toronto** for Anaheim's 6th round choice (Dennis Robertson) in 2011 Entry Draft, August 10, 2009. Traded to **Carolina** by **Anaheim** with Boston's 4th round choice (previously acquired, Carolina selected Justin Shugg) in 2010 Entry Draft for Aaron Ward, March 3, 2010. Signed as a free agent by **Phoenix**, July 27, 2011.

POULIN, Kevin — (POO-lihn, KEH-vihn) — NYI

Goaltender. Catches left. 6'2", 211 lbs. Born, Montreal, Que., April 12, 1990.
(NY Islanders' 10th choice, 126th overall, in 2008 Entry Draft).

			Regular Season								Playoffs						
Season	**Club**	**League**	**GP**	**W**	**L**	**O/T**	**Mins**	**GA**	**SO**	**Avg**	**GP**	**W**	**L**	**Mins**	**GA**	**SO**	**Avg**
2005-06	C.C. Lemoyne	QAAA	27	13	8	2	1440	71	1	2.96	7	4	3	373	16	1	2.57
2006-07	Victoriaville Tigres	QMJHL	24	10	6	0	1220	68	0	3.34	2	0	0	42	5	0	7.20
2007-08	Victoriaville Tigres	QMJHL	52	18	24	0	2734	168	0	3.69	6	2	4	279	27	0	5.80
2008-09	Victoriaville Tigres	QMJHL	39	18	19	0	2273	120	1	3.17	4	0	4	249	18	0	4.34
2009-10	Victoriaville Tigres	QMJHL	54	*35	16	0	3105	136	*7	2.63	16	10	6	971	46	0	2.84
2010-11	**NY Islanders**	**NHL**	**10**	**4**	**2**	**1**	**491**	**20**	**0**	**2.44**	....	....	....	....	....	....	....
	Bridgeport	AHL	15	10	5	0	903	33	2	2.19	....	....	....	....	....	....	....
	NHL Totals		**10**	**4**	**2**	**1**	**491**	**20**	**0**	**2.44**	....	....	....	....	....	....	....

QMJHL Second All-Star Team (2010)

PRICE, Carey — (PRIGHS, KAIR-ee) — MTL

Goaltender. Catches left. 6'3", 219 lbs. Born, Vancouver, B.C., August 16, 1987.
(Montreal's 1st choice, 5th overall, in 2005 Entry Draft).

			Regular Season								Playoffs						
Season	**Club**	**League**	**GP**	**W**	**L**	**O/T**	**Mins**	**GA**	**SO**	**Avg**	**GP**	**W**	**L**	**Mins**	**GA**	**SO**	**Avg**
2002-03	Williams Lake	Minor-BC	18	....	....	....	1050	48	1	2.70	....	....	....	....	....	....	....
	Tri-City Americans	WHL	1	0	0	0	20	2	0	6.00	....	....	....	....	....	....	....
2003-04	Tri-City Americans	WHL	28	8	9	3	1362	54	1	2.38	8	5	3	470	19	0	2.43
2004-05	Tri-City Americans	WHL	63	24	31	8	3712	145	8	2.34	5	1	4	324	12	0	2.22
2005-06	Tri-City Americans	WHL	55	21	25	6	3072	147	3	2.87	5	1	4	302	12	0	2.39
2006-07	Tri-City Americans	WHL	46	30	13	1	2722	111	3	2.45	6	2	4	348	17	0	2.93
	Hamilton Bulldogs	AHL	2	1	1	0	117	3	0	1.53	*22	*15	6	*1314	45	*2	2.06
2007-08	**Montreal**	**NHL**	**41**	**24**	**12**	**3**	**2413**	**103**	**3**	**2.56**	**11**	**5**	**6**	**648**	**30**	**2**	**2.78**
	Hamilton Bulldogs	AHL	10	6	4	0	581	26	1	2.69	....	....	....	....	....	....	....
2008-09	**Montreal**	**NHL**	**52**	**23**	**16**	**10**	**3036**	**143**	**1**	**2.83**	**4**	**0**	**4**	**219**	**15**	**0**	**4.11**
2009-10	**Montreal**	**NHL**	**41**	**13**	**20**	**5**	**2358**	**109**	**0**	**2.77**	**4**	**0**	**1**	**135**	**8**	**0**	**3.56**
2010-11	**Montreal**	**NHL**	**72**	***38**	**28**	**6**	**4206**	**165**	**8**	**2.35**	**7**	**3**	**4**	**455**	**16**	**1**	**2.11**
	NHL Totals		**206**	**98**	**76**	**24**	**12013**	**520**	**12**	**2.60**	**26**	**8**	**15**	**1457**	**69**	**3**	**2.84**

WHL West First All-Star Team (2007) • WHL Goaltender of the Year (2007) • Canadian Major Junior First All-Star Team (2007) • Canadian Major Junior Goaltender of the Year (2007) • Jack A. Butterfield Trophy (AHL - Playoff MVP) (2007) • NHL All-Rookie Team (2008)

Played in NHL All-Star Game (2009, 2011)

QUICK, Jonathan — (KWIHK, JAWN-ah-thuhn) — L.A.

Goaltender. Catches left. 6'1", 212 lbs. Born, Milford, CT, January 21, 1986.
(Los Angeles' 4th choice, 72nd overall, in 2005 Entry Draft).

			Regular Season								Playoffs						
Season	**Club**	**League**	**GP**	**W**	**L**	**O/T**	**Mins**	**GA**	**SO**	**Avg**	**GP**	**W**	**L**	**Mins**	**GA**	**SO**	**Avg**
2002-03	Avon Old Farms	High-CT	13	8	5	0	780	38	0	2.92	....	....	....	....	....	....	....
2003-04	Avon Old Farms	High-CT	21	20	1	0	1260	26	2	1.71	....	....	....	....	....	....	....
2004-05	Avon Old Farms	High-CT	27	25	2	0	1413	27	9	1.14	....	....	....	....	....	....	....
2005-06	Massachusetts	H-East	17	4	10	1	905	45	0	2.98	....	....	....	....	....	....	....
2006-07	Massachusetts	H-East	37	19	12	5	2224	80	3	2.16	....	....	....	....	....	....	....
2007-08	**Los Angeles**	**NHL**	**3**	**1**	**2**	**0**	**141**	**9**	**0**	**3.83**	....	....	....	....	....	....	....
	Manchester	AHL	19	11	8	0	1085	42	3	2.32	1	0	1	59	1	0	1.02
	Reading Royals	ECHL	38	23	11	3	2257	105	1	2.79	....	....	....	....	....	....	....
2008-09	**Los Angeles**	**NHL**	**44**	**21**	**18**	**2**	**2495**	**103**	**4**	**2.48**	....	....	....	....	....	....	....
	Manchester	AHL	14	6	5	2	827	37	0	2.68	....	....	....	....	....	....	....
2009-10	**Los Angeles**	**NHL**	**72**	**39**	**24**	**7**	**4258**	**180**	**4**	**2.54**	**6**	**2**	**4**	**360**	**21**	**0**	**3.50**
	United States	Olympics				DID NOT PLAY – SPARE GOALTENDER											
2010-11	**Los Angeles**	**NHL**	**61**	**35**	**22**	**3**	**3591**	**134**	**6**	**2.24**	**6**	**2**	**4**	**380**	**20**	**1**	**3.16**
	NHL Totals		**180**	**96**	**66**	**12**	**10485**	**426**	**14**	**2.44**	**12**	**4**	**8**	**740**	**41**	**1**	**3.32**

Hockey East Second All-Star Team (2007) • NCAA East Second All-American Team (2007)

RAMO, Karri — (RAH-moh, KAH-ree) — MTL

Goaltender. Catches left. 6', 215 lbs. Born, Asikkala, Finland, July 1, 1986.
(Tampa Bay's 7th choice, 191st overall, in 2004 Entry Draft).

			Regular Season								Playoffs						
Season	**Club**	**League**	**GP**	**W**	**L**	**O/T**	**Mins**	**GA**	**SO**	**Avg**	**GP**	**W**	**L**	**Mins**	**GA**	**SO**	**Avg**
2002-03	K-Reipas U18	Fin-U18	19	12	3	2	1013	47	0	2.78	4	2	2	182	11	0	3.62
2003-04	Pelicans Lahti U18	Fin-U18	3	3	0	0	180	7	0	2.33	5	2	2	268	10	0	2.24
	Pelicans Lahti Jr.	Fin-Jr.	18	5	9	2	960	53	0	3.31	2	2	0	120	1	1	0.50
	Pelicans Lahti	Finland	3	0	2	0	138	10	0	4.34	....	....	....	....	....	....	....
2004-05	Pelicans Lahti Jr.	Fin-Jr.	21	10	5	6	1269	36	6	1.70	4	1	3	206	16	0	4.66
	Pelicans Lahti	Finland	26	4	12	4	1267	84	1	3.98	....	....	....	....	....	....	....
2005-06	Haukat Jarvenpaa	Finland-2	1	....	....	....	60	5	0	5.00	....	....	....	....	....	....	....
	Suomi U20	Finland-2	3	....	....	....	183	12	0	3.93	....	....	....	....	....	....	....
	HPK Hameenlinna	Finland	24	7	8	7	1359	49	2	2.16	3	2	1	204	5	1	1.46
2006-07	**Tampa Bay**	**NHL**	**2**	**0**	**0**	**0**	**70**	**4**	**0**	**3.43**	....	....	....	....	....	....	....
	Springfield Falcons	AHL	45	15	24	1	2432	127	1	3.13	....	....	....	....	....	....	....
2007-08	**Tampa Bay**	**NHL**	**22**	**7**	**11**	**3**	**1269**	**64**	**0**	**3.03**	....	....	....	....	....	....	....
	Norfolk Admirals	AHL	6	2	4	0	342	19	0	3.33	....	....	....	....	....	....	....
2008-09	**Tampa Bay**	**NHL**	**24**	**4**	**10**	**7**	**1312**	**80**	**0**	**3.66**	....	....	....	....	....	....	....
	Norfolk Admirals	AHL	26	7	14	4	1507	95	0	3.78	....	....	....	....	....	....	....
2009-10	Omsk	Rus-KHL	44	....	....	....	2582	91	4	2.11	3	....	....	158	8	0	3.04
2010-11	Omsk	Rus-KHL	44	....	....	....	2593	85	5	1.97	14	....	....	891	32	1	2.16
	NHL Totals		**48**	**11**	**21**	**10**	**2651**	**148**	**0**	**3.35**	....	....	....	....	....	....	....

Signed as a free agent by **Omsk** (Russia-KHL), June 23, 2009. Traded to **Montreal** by **Tampa Bay** for Cedrick Desjardins, August 16, 2010.

RASK, Tuukka — (RASK, TU-kah) — BOS

Goaltender. Catches left. 6'3", 169 lbs. Born, Savonlinna, Finland, March 10, 1987.
(Toronto's 1st choice, 21st overall, in 2005 Entry Draft).

			Regular Season								Playoffs						
Season	**Club**	**League**	**GP**	**W**	**L**	**O/T**	**Mins**	**GA**	**SO**	**Avg**	**GP**	**W**	**L**	**Mins**	**GA**	**SO**	**Avg**
2003-04	Ilves Tampere U18	Fin-U18	9	4	3	2	533	25	0	2.81	....	....	....	....	....	....	....
	Ilves Tampere Jr.	Fin-Jr.	30	12	10	7	1767	65	2	2.21	3	1	2	178	6	0	2.02
2004-05	Ilves Tampere Jr.	Fin-Jr.	26	17	3	4	1517	47	2	1.86	10	9	1	619	9	6	0.87
	Ilves Tampere	Finland	4	0	1	1	201	15	0	4.46	....	....	....	....	....	....	....
2005-06	Ilves Tampere Jr.	Fin-Jr.	1	....	....	....	60	2	0	2.00	....	....	....	....	....	....	....
	Suomi U20	Finland-2	3	....	....	....	179	6	0	2.01	....	....	....	....	....	....	....
	Ilves Tampere	Finland	30	12	8	7	1724	60	2	2.09	3	0	3	180	7	0	2.33
2006-07	Suomi U20	Finland-2	1	0	1	0	58	4	0	4.14	....	....	....	....	....	....	....
	Ilves Tampere	Finland	49	18	18	10	2872	114	3	2.38	7	2	5	397	20	0	3.02
2007-08	**Boston**	**NHL**	**4**	**2**	**1**	**1**	**184**	**10**	**0**	**3.26**	....	....	....	....	....	....	....
	Providence Bruins	AHL	45	27	13	2	2570	100	1	2.33	10	6	4	605	22	*2	2.18
2008-09	**Boston**	**NHL**	**1**	**1**	**0**	**0**	**60**	**0**	**1**	**0.00**	....	....	....	....	....	....	....
	Providence Bruins	AHL	57	33	20	4	3340	139	4	2.50	16	9	7	977	36	0	2.21
2009-10	**Boston**	**NHL**	**45**	**22**	**12**	**5**	**2562**	**84**	**5**	***1.97**	**13**	**7**	**6**	**829**	**36**	**0**	**2.61**
2010-11 ♦	**Boston**	**NHL**	**29**	**11**	**14**	**2**	**1594**	**71**	**2**	**2.67**	....	....	....	....	....	....	....
	NHL Totals		**79**	**36**	**27**	**8**	**4400**	**165**	**8**	**2.25**	**13**	**7**	**6**	**829**	**36**	**0**	**2.61**

Traded to **Boston** by **Toronto** for Andrew Raycroft, June 24, 2006.

RAYCROFT, Andrew — (RAY-krawft, AN-droo) — DAL

Goaltender. Catches left. 6'1", 178 lbs. Born, Belleville, Ont., May 4, 1980.
(Boston's 4th choice, 135th overall, in 1998 Entry Draft).

			Regular Season								Playoffs						
Season	**Club**	**League**	**GP**	**W**	**L**	**O/T**	**Mins**	**GA**	**SO**	**Avg**	**GP**	**W**	**L**	**Mins**	**GA**	**SO**	**Avg**
1996-97	Wellington Dukes	ON-Jr.A	27	....	....	....	1402	92	0	3.94	....	....	....	....	....	....	....
1997-98	Sudbury Wolves	OHL	33	8	16	5	1802	125	0	4.16	2	0	1	90	8	0	5.33
1998-99	Sudbury Wolves	OHL	45	17	22	5	2528	173	1	4.11	3	0	2	96	13	0	8.13
99-2000	Kingston	OHL	*61	33	20	5	3340	191	0	3.43	5	1	4	300	21	0	4.20
2000-01	**Boston**	**NHL**	**15**	**4**	**6**	**0**	**649**	**32**	**0**	**2.96**	....	....	....	....	....	....	....
	Providence Bruins	AHL	26	8	14	4	1459	82	1	3.37	....	....	....	....	....	....	....
2001-02	**Boston**	**NHL**	**1**	**0**	**0**	**1**	**65**	**3**	**0**	**2.77**	....	....	....	....	....	....	....
	Providence Bruins	AHL	56	25	24	6	3317	142	4	2.57	2	0	2	119	5	0	2.52
2002-03	**Boston**	**NHL**	**5**	**2**	**3**	**0**	**300**	**12**	**0**	**2.40**	....	....	....	....	....	....	....
	Providence Bruins	AHL	39	23	10	3	2255	94	1	2.50	4	1	3	264	6	1	*1.36
2003-04	**Boston**	**NHL**	**57**	**29**	**18**	**9**	**3420**	**117**	**3**	**2.05**	**7**	**3**	**4**	**447**	**16**	**1**	**2.15**
2004-05	Tappara Tampere	Finland	11	4	5	2	657	32	1	2.92	3	0	2	104	11	0	6.36
2005-06	**Boston**	**NHL**	**30**	**8**	**19**	**2**	**1619**	**100**	**0**	**3.71**	....	....	....	....	....	....	....
	Providence Bruins	AHL	1	1	0	0	64	3	0	2.80	....	....	....	....	....	....	....
2006-07	**Toronto**	**NHL**	**72**	**37**	**25**	**9**	**4108**	**205**	**2**	**2.99**	....	....	....	....	....	....	....
2007-08	**Toronto**	**NHL**	**19**	**2**	**9**	**5**	**965**	**63**	**1**	**3.92**	....	....	....	....	....	....	....
2008-09	**Colorado**	**NHL**	**31**	**12**	**16**	**0**	**1722**	**90**	**0**	**3.14**	....	....	....	....	....	....	....
2009-10	**Vancouver**	**NHL**	**21**	**9**	**5**	**1**	**967**	**39**	**1**	**2.42**	**1**	**0**	**0**	**25**	**1**	**0**	**2.40**
2010-11	**Dallas**	**NHL**	**19**	**8**	**5**	**0**	**847**	**40**	**2**	**2.83**	....	....	....	....	....	....	....
	NHL Totals		**270**	**111**	**106**	**27**	**14662**	**701**	**9**	**2.87**	**8**	**3**	**4**	**472**	**17**	**1**	**2.16**

OHL First All-Star Team (2000) • Canadian Major Junior First All-Star Team (2000) • Canadian Major Junior Goaltender of the Year (2000) • NHL All-Rookie Team (2004) • Calder Memorial Trophy (2004)

Signed as a free agent by **Tappara Tampere** (Finland), January 17, 2005. Traded to **Toronto** by **Boston** for Tuukka Rask, June 24, 2006. Signed as a free agent by **Colorado**, July 1, 2008. Signed as a free agent by **Vancouver**, July 6, 2009. Signed as a free agent by **Dallas**, July 1, 2010.

REIMER, James — (RIGH-muhr, JAYMZ) — TOR

Goaltender. Catches left. 6'2", 220 lbs. Born, Morweena, Man., March 15, 1988.
(Toronto's 3rd choice, 99th overall, in 2006 Entry Draft).

			Regular Season								Playoffs						
Season	**Club**	**League**	**GP**	**W**	**L**	**O/T**	**Mins**	**GA**	**SO**	**Avg**	**GP**	**W**	**L**	**Mins**	**GA**	**SO**	**Avg**
2003-04	Interlake Lightning	MMHL	27	....	....	....	....	....	1	2.85	....	....	....	....	....	....	....
2004-05	Interlake Lightning	MMHL	37	....	....	....	....	....	4	2.11	....	....	....	....	....	....	....
2005-06	Red Deer Rebels	WHL	34	7	18	3	1709	80	0	2.81	....	....	....	....	....	....	....
2006-07	Red Deer Rebels	WHL	60	26	23	7	3339	148	3	2.66	7	3	4	417	27	0	3.88
2007-08	Red Deer Rebels	WHL	30	8	15	4	1668	76	1	2.73	....	....	....	....	....	....	....
2008-09	Toronto Marlies	AHL	3	1	2	0	183	10	0	3.28	....	....	....	....	....	....	....
	Reading Royals	ECHL	22	10	7	3	1236	68	0	3.30	....	....	....	....	....	....	....
	South Carolina	ECHL	6	6	0	0	363	8	2	1.32	8	4	3	497	18	1	2.17
2009-10	Toronto Marlies	AHL	26	14	8	2	1520	57	1	2.25	....	....	....	....	....	....	....
2010-11	**Toronto**	**NHL**	**37**	**20**	**10**	**5**	**2080**	**90**	**3**	**2.60**	....	....	....	....	....	....	....
	Toronto Marlies	AHL	15	9	5	1	858	37	3	2.59	....	....	....	....	....	....	....
	NHL Totals		**37**	**20**	**10**	**5**	**2080**	**90**	**3**	**2.60**	....	....	....	....	....	....	....

ECHL Playoff MVP (2009)

RICHARDS, Alec (RIH-chuhrds, ALEHK) CHI

Goaltender. Catches left. 6'4", 210 lbs. Born, Robbinsdale, MN, June 29, 1987.

			Regular Season								Playoffs						
Season	Club	League	GP	W	L	O/T	Mins	GA	SO	Avg	GP	W	L	Mins	GA	SO	Avg
2003-04	Breck Mustangs	High-MN	....	19	1	1	....	....	....	1.70							
2004-05	Breck Mustangs	High-MN	....	15	2	2	....	....	....	1.90							
	Indiana Ice	USHL	4	1	2	1	241	14	0	3.47							
2005-06	Yale	ECAC	29	8	15	3	1686	85	1	3.02							
2006-07	Yale	ECAC	26	9	15	2	1518	79	0	3.12							
2007-08	Yale	ECAC	11	3	4	0	563	19	1	2.02							
2008-09	Yale	ECAC	25	19	5	1	1458	50	4	2.06							
2009-10	Rockford IceHogs	AHL	6	3	2	0	307	16	0	3.12							
	Toledo Walleye	ECHL	34	17	12	5	2004	112	1	3.35							
2010-11	Rockford IceHogs	AHL	44	17	21	1	2369	114	2	2.89							

Signed as a free agent by **Chicago**, June 8, 2009.

RINNE, Pekka (RIH-neh, PEH-kuh) NSH

Goaltender. Catches left. 6'5", 209 lbs. Born, Kempele, Finland, November 3, 1982.
(Nashville's 10th choice, 258th overall, in 2004 Entry Draft).

			Regular Season								Playoffs						
Season	Club	League	GP	W	L	O/T	Mins	GA	SO	Avg	GP	W	L	Mins	GA	SO	Avg
2000-01	Karpat Oulu Jr.	Fin-Jr.	20	9	4	5	1148	63	0	3.29							
2001-02	Karpat Oulu Jr.	Fin-Jr.	30	19	7	3	1724	61	3	2.12	3	1	2	184	10	1	3.26
2002-03	Karpat Oulu Jr.	Fin-Jr.	25	14	8	3	1479	48	5	1.95	4	1	3	238	7	0	1.76
	Karpat Oulu	Finland	1	0	1	0	60	7	0	7.00							
2003-04	Karpat Oulu	Finland	14	5	4	4	824	41	0	2.99	2	1	0	22	0	0	0.00
	Hokki Kajaani	Finland-2	8	5	2	1	463	16	2	2.07							
2004-05	Karpat Oulu	Finland	10	8	0	1	571	16	0	1.68							
2005-06	Nashville	NHL	2	1	1	0	63	4	0	3.81							
	Milwaukee	AHL	51	30	18	2	2960	139	2	2.82	14	10	4	734	35	3	2.86
2006-07	Milwaukee	AHL	29	15	7	6	1670	65	3	2.34	4	0	4	247	12	0	2.91
2007-08	Nashville	NHL	1	0	0	0	29	0	0	0.00							
	Milwaukee	AHL	*65	*36	24	3	*3840	158	5	2.47	6	2	4	358	15	1	2.51
2008-09	Nashville	NHL	52	29	15	4	2999	119	7	2.38							
2009-10	Nashville	NHL	58	32	16	5	3246	137	7	2.53	6	2	4	358	16	0	2.68
2010-11	Nashville	NHL	64	33	22	9	3789	134	6	2.12	12	6	6	748	32	0	2.57
	NHL Totals		177	95	54	18	10126	394	20	2.33	18	8	10	1106	48	0	2.60

NHL Second All-Star Team (2011)

RIOPEL, Nic (ree-OH-pehl, NIHK)

Goaltender. Catches left. 6', 172 lbs. Born, St-Pie de Bagot, Que., February 20, 1989.
(Philadelphia's 3rd choice, 142nd overall, in 2009 Entry Draft).

			Regular Season								Playoffs						
Season	Club	League	GP	W	L	O/T	Mins	GA	SO	Avg	GP	W	L	Mins	GA	SO	Avg
2006-07	Moncton Wildcats	QMJHL	37	17	12	0	1914	107	1	3.35	4	1	3	185	16	0	5.19
2007-08	Moncton Wildcats	QMJHL	47	15	29	0	2662	135	1	3.04							
2008-09	Moncton Wildcats	QMJHL	*59	*43	15	0	*3487	117	5	*2.01	10	5	5	620	21	*2	*2.03
2009-10	Moncton Wildcats	QMJHL	25	19	5	0	1455	50	3	*2.06	*21	*16	4	*1291	46	*3	*2.14
	Adirondack	AHL	10	4	6	0	573	32	0	3.35							
2010-11	Adirondack	AHL	11	3	7	0	591	35	1	3.55							
	Greenville	ECHL	38	24	12	2	2301	107	2	2.79	7	4	3	436	18	0	2.48

QMJHL All-Rookie Team (2009) • QMJHL First All-Star Team (2009) • Canadian Major Junior Second All-Star Team (2009)

ROLLHEISER, Grant (rohl-HIGH-zuhr, GRANT) TOR

Goaltender. Catches left. 6'4", 195 lbs. Born, Chilliwak, B.C., July 24, 1989.
(Toronto's 7th choice, 158th overall, in 2008 Entry Draft).

			Regular Season								Playoffs						
Season	Club	League	GP	W	L	O/T	Mins	GA	SO	Avg	GP	W	L	Mins	GA	SO	Avg
2006-07	Nelson Leafs	KIJHL	35	25	8	0	1990	110	2	3.32	15	9	6	907	35	2	2.31
2007-08	Trail Smoke Eaters	BCHL	46	19	26	0	2557	136	2	3.19	3	0	3	159	13	0	4.90
2008-09	Boston University	H-East	12	6	4	1	648	23	1	2.13							
2009-10	Boston University	H-East	7	2	1	3	389	22	0	3.39							
2010-11	Boston University	H-East	5	2	2	0	241	16	0	3.98							

ROLOSON, Dwayne (ROH-loh-suhn, DWAYN) T.B.

Goaltender. Catches left. 6'1", 170 lbs. Born, Simcoe, Ont., October 12, 1969.

			Regular Season								Playoffs						
Season	Club	League	GP	W	L	O/T	Mins	GA	SO	Avg	GP	W	L	Mins	GA	SO	Avg
1984-85	Simcoe Penguins	ON-Jr.C	3	....	....	....	100	21	0	12.60							
1985-86	Simcoe Rams	ON-Jr.C	1	....	....	....	60	6	0	6.00							
1986-87	Norwich	ON-Jr.C	19	....	....	....	1091	55	0	*3.03							
1987-88	Belleville Bobcats	ON-Jr.B	21	9	6	1	1070	60	*2	3.36							
1988-89	Thorold	ON-Jr.B	27	15	6	4	1490	82	0	3.30							
1989-90	Thorold	ON-Jr.B	30	18	8	1	1683	108	0	3.85							
1990-91	U. Mass-Lowell	H-East	15	5	9	0	823	63	0	4.59							
1991-92	U. Mass-Lowell	H-East	12	3	8	0	660	52	0	4.73							
1992-93	U. Mass-Lowell	H-East	*39	20	17	2	*2342	150	0	3.84							
1993-94	U. Mass-Lowell	H-East	*40	*23	10	7	*2305	106	0	2.76							
1994-95	Saint John Flames	AHL	46	16	21	8	2734	156	1	3.42	5	1	4	298	13	0	2.61
1995-96	Saint John Flames	AHL	67	*33	22	11	4026	190	1	2.83	16	10	6	1027	49	1	2.86
1996-97	Calgary	NHL	31	9	14	3	1618	78	1	2.89							
	Saint John Flames	AHL	8	6	2	0	481	22	1	2.75							
1997-98	Calgary	NHL	39	11	16	8	2205	110	0	2.99							
	Saint John Flames	AHL	4	3	0	1	245	8	0	1.96							
1998-99	Buffalo	NHL	18	6	8	2	911	42	1	2.77	4	1	1	139	10	0	4.32
	Rochester	AHL	2	2	0	0	120	4	0	2.00							
99-2000	Buffalo	NHL	14	1	7	3	677	32	0	2.84							
2000-01	Worcester IceCats	AHL	52	*32	15	5	*3127	113	*6	*2.17	11	6	5	697	23	1	1.98
2001-02	Minnesota	NHL	45	14	20	7	2506	112	5	2.68							
2002-03	Minnesota	NHL	50	23	16	8	2945	98	4	2.00	11	5	6	579	25	0	2.59
2003-04	Minnesota	NHL	48	19	18	11	2847	89	5	1.88							
2004-05	Lukko Rauma	Finland	34	20	10	4	2048	70	4	2.05	9	4	5	512	18	2	2.11
2005-06	Minnesota	NHL	24	6	17	1	1361	68	1	3.00							
	Edmonton	NHL	19	8	7	4	1163	47	1	2.42	18	12	5	1160	45	1	2.33
2006-07	Edmonton	NHL	68	27	34	6	3932	180	4	2.75							
2007-08	Edmonton	NHL	43	15	17	5	2340	119	0	3.05							
2008-09	Edmonton	NHL	63	28	24	9	3597	166	1	2.77							
2009-10	NY Islanders	NHL	50	23	18	7	2897	145	1	3.00							
2010-11	NY Islanders	NHL	20	6	13	1	1206	53	0	2.64							
	Tampa Bay	NHL	34	18	12	4	1993	85	4	2.56	17	10	6	982	41	1	2.51
	NHL Totals		566	214	241	79	32198	1424	28	2.65	50	28	18	2860	121	2	2.54

Hockey East First All-Star Team (1994) • Hockey East Player of the Year (1994) • NCAA East First All-American Team (1994) • AHL First All-Star Team (2001) • Aldege "Baz" Bastien Memorial Award (AHL – Outstanding Goaltender) (2001) • MBNA/Mastercard Roger Crozier Saving Grace Award (2004)

Played in NHL All-Star Game (2004)

Signed as a free agent by **Calgary**, July 4, 1994. Signed as a free agent by **Buffalo**, July 15, 1998. Claimed by **Columbus** from **Buffalo** in Expansion Draft, June 23, 2000. Signed as a free agent by **St. Louis**, July 14, 2000. Signed as a free agent by **Minnesota**, July 2, 2001. Signed as a free agent by **Rauma** (Finland), October 18, 2004. Traded to **Edmonton** by **Minnesota** for Edmonton's 1st round choice (later traded to Los Angeles - Los Angeles selected Trevor Lewis) in 2006 Entry Draft and Edmonton's 3rd round chocie (later traded to Atlanta - Atlanta selected Spencer Machacek) in 2007 Entry Draft, March 8, 2006. Signed as a free agent by **NY Islanders**, July 1, 2009. Traded to **Tampa Bay** by **NY Islanders** for Ty Wishart, January 2, 2011.

ROSEN, Cody (ROH-zehn, KOH-dee) NYI

Goaltender. Catches left. 5'11", 180 lbs. Born, Kingston, Ont., September 27, 1990.
(NY Islanders' 6th choice, 185th overall, in 2010 Entry Draft).

			Regular Season								Playoffs						
Season	Club	League	GP	W	L	O/T	Mins	GA	SO	Avg	GP	W	L	Mins	GA	SO	Avg
2008-09	Kingston	ON-Jr.A	18	14	3	1	1055	51	3	2.90							
2009-10	Clarkson Knights	ECAC	1	0	0	0	20	3	0	9.00							
2010-11	Clarkson Knights	ECAC	3	0	1	0	93	3	0	1.94							

ROY, Olivier (WAH, oh-LIHV-ee-ay) EDM

Goaltender. Catches left. 6', 180 lbs. Born, Amqui, Que., July 12, 1991.
(Edmonton's 7th choice, 133rd overall, in 2009 Entry Draft).

			Regular Season								Playoffs						
Season	Club	League	GP	W	L	O/T	Mins	GA	SO	Avg	GP	W	L	Mins	GA	SO	Avg
2006-07	Ecole Notre Dame	QAAA	27	15	8	0	1459	65	2	2.67	4	2	1	206	13	0	3.79
2007-08	Cape Breton	QMJHL	47	27	15	0	2428	116	4	2.87	11	5	6	707	30	1	2.55
2008-09	Cape Breton	QMJHL	54	35	13	0	2935	137	3	2.80	11	7	4	740	30	0	2.43
2009-10	Cape Breton	QMJHL	54	32	21	0	3156	138	5	2.62	5	1	4	311	19	0	3.66
	Springfield Falcons	AHL	3	1	1	0	140	6	0	2.57							
2010-11	Acadie-Bathurst	QMJHL	45	29	13	2	2604	121	2	2.79	3	0	2	106	12	0	6.88

QMJHL All-Rookie Team (2008)

RYNNAS, Jussi (RIH-nuhs, YEW-see) TOR

Goaltender. Catches left. 6'5", 212 lbs. Born, Pori, Finland, May 22, 1987.

			Regular Season								Playoffs						
Season	Club	League	GP	W	L	O/T	Mins	GA	SO	Avg	GP	W	L	Mins	GA	SO	Avg
2006-07	Assat Pori Jr.	Fin-Jr.	23	....	....	....	....	....	....	4.20							
2007-08	Assat Pori Jr.	Fin-Jr.	27	....	....	....	....	....	....	2.90							
2008-09	Assat Pori	Finland	DID NOT PLAY – SPARE GOALTENDER														
	Sport Vaasa	Finland-2	1	....	....	....	....	....	....	6.00							
	Kiekko-Vantaa	Finland-2	7	....	....	....	....	....	....	3.99							
2009-10	Assat Pori	Finland	31	14	13	1	1717	71	2	2.48							
2010-11	Toronto Marlies	AHL	30	10	15	3	1660	75	2	2.71							

Signed as a free agent by **Toronto**, April 23, 2010.

SABOURIN, Dany (SA-boo-rihn, DA-nee) WSH

Goaltender. Catches left. 6'4", 208 lbs. Born, Val-d'Or, Que., September 2, 1980.
(Calgary's 5th choice, 108th overall, in 1998 Entry Draft).

			Regular Season								Playoffs						
Season	Club	League	GP	W	L	O/T	Mins	GA	SO	Avg	GP	W	L	Mins	GA	SO	Avg
1996-97	Amos Forestiers	QAAA	24	6	16	0	1440	107	0	4.48							
1997-98	Sherbrooke	QMJHL	37	15	15	2	1907	128	1	4.03							
1998-99	Sherbrooke	QMJHL	30	8	13	2	1477	102	1	4.14	1	0	1	49	2	0	2.43
	Saint John Flames	AHL	....	....	....	....	....	....	....	....	1	0	1	57	4	0	4.19
99-2000	Sherbrooke	QMJHL	55	25	22	5	3067	181	1	3.54	5	1	4	324	18	0	3.33
2000-01	Saint John Flames	AHL	1	1	0	0	40	0	0	0.00							
	Johnstown Chiefs	ECHL	19	4	9	1	903	56	0	3.72	1	0	0	40	2	0	3.00
2001-02	Johnstown Chiefs	ECHL	27	14	10	1	1539	84	0	3.28	3	0	2	137	5	0	2.18
2002-03	Saint John Flames	AHL	41	15	17	4	2220	100	4	2.70							
2003-04	Calgary	NHL	4	0	3	0	169	10	0	3.55							
	Lowell	AHL	14	5	7	2	821	39	0	2.85							
	Las Vegas	ECHL	10	6	3	1	613	24	0	2.35	1	0	1	58	2	0	2.07
2004-05	Wilkes-Barre	AHL	20	8	8	2	1029	38	1	2.22							
	Wheeling Nailers	ECHL	27	19	6	1	1579	44	5	*1.67							
2005-06	Pittsburgh	NHL	1	0	1	0	21	4	0	11.43							
	Wilkes-Barre	AHL	49	30	14	4	2943	111	4	*2.26	6	2	4	362	13	1	2.15
2006-07	Vancouver	NHL	9	2	4	1	480	21	0	2.63	2	0	0	14	1	0	4.29
	Manitoba Moose	AHL	2	1	1	0	119	4	1	2.01							
2007-08	Pittsburgh	NHL	24	10	9	1	1242	57	2	2.75							
2008-09	Pittsburgh	NHL	19	6	8	2	989	47	0	2.85							
	Springfield Falcons	AHL	13	5	6	2	795	42	0	3.17							
2009-10	Providence Bruins	AHL	56	28	27	0	3278	146	3	2.67							
2010-11	Hershey Bears	AHL	23	14	9	0	1299	53	2	2.45							
	NHL Totals		57	18	25	4	2901	139	2	2.87	2	0	0	14	1	0	4.29

AHL First All-Star Team (2006) • Aldege "Baz" Bastien Memorial Award (AHL – Outstanding Goaltender) (2006)

Signed as a free agent by **Pittsburgh**, August 10, 2005. Claimed on waivers by **Vancouver** from **Pittsburgh**, October 4, 2006. Signed as a free agent by **Pittsburgh**, July 1, 2007. Traded to **Edmonton** by **Pittsburgh** with Ryan Stone and Pittsburgh's 4th round choice Tobias Rieder) in 2011 Entry Draft for Mathieu Garon, January 17, 2009. Signed as a free agent by **Boston**, July 7, 2009. Signed as a free agent by **Washington**, July 2, 2010.

SALAK, Alexander (SAL-ak, al-EHX-AN-duhr) CHI

Goaltender. Catches left. 6'1", 189 lbs. Born, Strakonice, Czech., January 5, 1987.

			Regular Season								Playoffs						
Season	Club	League	GP	W	L	O/T	Mins	GA	SO	Avg	GP	W	L	Mins	GA	SO	Avg
2006-07	Jokipojat Joensuu	Finland-2	35	....	....	....	....	....	....	2.81							
2007-08	TPS Turku	Finland	31	7	12	6	1757	76	1	2.59							
2008-09	TPS Turku	Finland	52	20	20	9	2981	119	4	2.40	8	4	4	489	16	0	1.96
2009-10	Florida	NHL	2	0	1	0	67	6	0	5.37							
	Rochester	AHL	48	29	14	0	2557	123	1	2.89	2	0	1	69	5	0	4.37
2010-11	Farjestad	Sweden	32	....	....	....	1857	61	*7	1.97	9	....	....	562	22	0	2.35
	NHL Totals		2	0	1	0	67	6	0	5.37							

Signed as a free agent by **Florida**, May 29, 2009. • Loaned to **Farjestad** (Sweden) by **Florida**, August 8, 2010. Traded to **Chicago** by **Florida** with Michael Frolik for Jack Skille, Hugh Jessiman and David Pacan, February 9, 2011.

SANFORD, Curtis (SAN-fohrd, KUHR-this) CBJ

Goaltender. Catches left. 5'11", 185 lbs. Born, Owen Sound, Ont., October 5, 1979.

			Regular Season								Playoffs						
Season	**Club**	**League**	**GP**	**W**	**L**	**O/T**	**Mins**	**GA**	**SO**	**Avg**	**GP**	**W**	**L**	**Mins**	**GA**	**SO**	**Avg**
1994-95	Wiarton Wolves	ON-Jr.C	18	....	....	....	949	98	0	6.20	....	....	....	....	....	....	....
1995-96	Collingwood Blues	ON-Jr.A	21	....	....	....	2128	74	0	3.54	....	....	....	....	....	....	....
1996-97	Owen Sound	OHL	19	4	8	1	847	77	0	5.45	....	....	....	....	....	....	....
	Owen Sound	ON-Jr.B	6	....	....	....	360	28	0	4.68	....	....	....	....	....	....	....
1997-98	Owen Sound	OHL	30	13	10	2	1542	114	1	4.44	9	4	4	456	30	1	3.95
1998-99	Owen Sound	OHL	56	30	16	5	2998	191	2	3.82	16	9	7	960	58	0	3.63
99-2000	Owen Sound	OHL	53	18	26	6	3124	198	1	3.80	....	....	....	....	....	....	....
	Missouri	UHL	6	3	1	0	237	6	0	1.52	....	....	....	....	....	....	....
	Rochester	AHL	....	....	....	....	....	....	....	....	1	0	0	14	1	0	4.25
2000-01	Worcester IceCats	AHL	5	3	0	1	237	16	0	4.06	....	....	....	....	....	....	....
	Peoria Rivermen	ECHL	27	15	7	4	1511	48	3	*1.91	14	9	4	813	28	*2	2.07
2001-02	Worcester IceCats	AHL	9	5	4	0	537	22	0	2.46	....	....	....	....	....	....	....
	Peoria Rivermen	ECHL	24	13	8	2	1418	58	1	2.45	....	....	....	....	....	....	....
2002-03	**St. Louis**	**NHL**	**8**	**5**	**1**	**0**	**397**	**13**	**1**	**1.96**	....	....	....	....	....	....	....
	Worcester IceCats	AHL	41	18	14	8	2317	93	3	2.41	3	0	3	179	8	0	2.68
2003-04	Worcester IceCats	AHL	43	20	16	3	2367	84	5	2.13	9	4	5	569	24	0	2.53
2004-05	Worcester IceCats	AHL	50	19	25	2	2743	123	2	2.69	....	....	....	....	....	....	....
2005-06	**St. Louis**	**NHL**	**34**	**13**	**13**	**5**	**1830**	**81**	**3**	**2.66**	....	....	....	....	....	....	....
	Peoria Rivermen	AHL	6	4	2	0	358	11	2	1.84	....	....	....	....	....	....	....
2006-07	**St. Louis**	**NHL**	**31**	**8**	**12**	**5**	**1492**	**79**	**0**	**3.18**	....	....	....	....	....	....	....
	Peoria Rivermen	AHL	2	1	1	0	119	5	0	2.52	....	....	....	....	....	....	....
2007-08	**Vancouver**	**NHL**	**16**	**4**	**3**	**1**	**679**	**32**	**0**	**2.83**	....	....	....	....	....	....	....
2008-09	**Vancouver**	**NHL**	**19**	**7**	**8**	**0**	**973**	**42**	**1**	**2.59**	....	....	....	....	....	....	....
	Manitoba Moose	AHL	16	7	3	3	865	25	2	1.73	1	0	1	43	1	0	1.40
2009-10	Hamilton Bulldogs	AHL	41	23	11	3	2230	79	4	2.13	9	5	4	565	19	2	2.02
2010-11	Hamilton Bulldogs	AHL	40	22	13	2	2274	73	5	*1.93	....	....	....	....	....	....	....
	NHL Totals		**108**	**37**	**37**	**11**	**5371**	**247**	**5**	**2.76**	....	....	....	....	....	....	....

ECHL Second All-Star Team (2001) • Harry "Hap" Holmes Memorial Award (AHL – fewest goals against) (2010) (shared with Cedrick Desjardins) • AHL Second All-Star Team (2011)

Signed as a free agent by **St. Louis**, October 1, 2000. Signed as a free agent by **Vancouver**, July 2, 2007. Signed as a free agent by **Montreal**, July 20, 2009. Signed as a free agent by **Columbus**, July 1, 2011.

SATERI, Harri (SA-teh-ree, HAR-ree) S.J.

Goaltender. Catches left. 6'1", 210 lbs. Born, Toijala, Finland, December 29, 1989.
(San Jose's 3rd choice, 106th overall, in 2008 Entry Draft).

			Regular Season								Playoffs						
Season	**Club**	**League**	**GP**	**W**	**L**	**O/T**	**Mins**	**GA**	**SO**	**Avg**	**GP**	**W**	**L**	**Mins**	**GA**	**SO**	**Avg**
2005-06	HPK U18	Fin-U18	27	....	....	....	1515	66	5	2.61	2	....	....	118	10	0	5.08
	HPK Jr.	Fin-Jr.	1	....	....	....	50	3	0	3.60	....	....	....	....	....	....	....
2006-07	Tappara U18	Fin-U18	2	....	....	....	119	4	0	2.02	....	....	....	....	....	....	....
	Tappara Jr.	Fin-Jr.	23	....	....	....	1346	59	2	2.63	10	....	....	614	31	0	3.03
2007-08	Tappara Jr.	Fin-Jr.	34	13	17	0	2048	102	1	2.99	3	0	3	178	8	0	2.70
2008-09	Suomi U20	Finland-2	4	2	2	0	247	12	0	2.91	....	....	....	....	....	....	....
2009-10	Tappara Tampere	Finland	49	21	22	4	2836	129	2	2.73	9	4	5	572	27	0	2.83
2010-11	Tappara Tampere	Finland	37	9	19	8	2147	106	2	2.96	....	....	....	....	....	....	....
	Worcester Sharks	AHL	7	1	3	1	351	15	0	2.56	....	....	....	....	....	....	....

SCHAEFER, Nolan (SHAY-fuhr, NOH-luhn)

Goaltender. Catches right. 6'2", 200 lbs. Born, Regina, Sask., January 15, 1980.
(San Jose's 4th choice, 166th overall, in 2000 Entry Draft).

			Regular Season								Playoffs						
Season	**Club**	**League**	**GP**	**W**	**L**	**O/T**	**Mins**	**GA**	**SO**	**Avg**	**GP**	**W**	**L**	**Mins**	**GA**	**SO**	**Avg**
1996-97	Yorkton Mallers	SMHL	36	....	....	....	1854	132	0	4.27	....	....	....	....	....	....	....
1997-98	Yorkton Mallers	SMHL	5	....	....	....	239	17	0	4.25	....	....	....	....	....	....	....
	Nipawin Hawks	SJHL	21	12	4	3	1080	42	*3	*2.33	....	....	....	....	....	....	....
1998-99	Nipawin Hawks	SJHL	46	....	....	....	2478	165	0	3.60	....	....	....	....	....	....	....
99-2000	Providence College	H-East	14	6	5	1	778	42	0	3.24	....	....	....	....	....	....	....
2000-01	Providence College	H-East	25	15	8	2	1529	63	3	2.47	....	....	....	....	....	....	....
2001-02	Providence College	H-East	*35	11	18	5	*2062	113	0	3.29	....	....	....	....	....	....	....
2002-03	Providence College	H-East	25	13	8	2	1440	71	0	2.96	....	....	....	....	....	....	....
2003-04	Cleveland Barons	AHL	27	14	9	3	1592	62	2	2.34	9	4	5	573	24	0	2.51
	Fresno Falcons	ECHL	12	5	5	0	654	34	1	3.12	....	....	....	....	....	....	....
2004-05	Cleveland Barons	AHL	43	17	23	1	2418	110	3	2.73	....	....	....	....	....	....	....
2005-06	**San Jose**	**NHL**	**7**	**5**	**1**	**0**	**352**	**11**	**1**	**1.88**	....	....	....	....	....	....	....
	Cleveland Barons	AHL	36	12	21	2	2058	118	2	3.44	....	....	....	....	....	....	....
2006-07	Worcester Sharks	AHL	16	5	8	3	921	43	0	2.80	....	....	....	....	....	....	....
	Hershey Bears	AHL	3	0	3	0	162	10	0	3.70	....	....	....	....	....	....	....
	Wilkes-Barre	AHL	15	9	5	0	804	30	1	2.24	11	5	6	699	32	0	2.75
2007-08	Houston Aeros	AHL	34	19	13	0	1980	68	6	*2.06	2	0	2	117	4	0	2.05
2008-09	Houston Aeros	AHL	51	26	17	5	2711	114	1	2.52	4	1	1	148	11	0	4.46
2009-10	CSKA Moscow	Rus-KHL	22	....	....	....	1107	49	1	2.66	1	....	....	44	2	0	2.73
2010-11	Providence Bruins	AHL	30	9	16	1	1604	83	0	3.11	....	....	....	....	....	....	....
	Hershey Bears	AHL	10	4	4	2	607	24	0	2.37	....	....	....	....	....	....	....
	NHL Totals		**7**	**5**	**1**	**0**	**352**	**11**	**1**	**1.88**	....	....	....	....	....	....	....

Hockey East Second All-Star Team (2001) • NCAA East Second All-American Team (2001) • Harry "Hap" Holmes Memorial Award (AHL – fewest goals against) (2008) (shared with Barry Brust)

Traded to **Pittsburgh** by **San Jose** for Pittsburgh's 7th round choice (Justin Braun) in 2007 Entry Draft, February 27, 2007. Signed as a free agent by **Minnesota**, July 3, 2007. Signed as a free agent by **CSKA Moscow** (Russia-KHL), August 4, 2009. Signed as a free agent by **Boston**, July 5, 2010. • Loaned to **Hershey** (AHL) by **Boston** (Providence-AHL), March 5, 2011.

SCHNEIDER, Cory (SHNIGH-duhr, KOHR-ee) VAN

Goaltender. Catches left. 6'2", 195 lbs. Born, Marblehead, MA, March 18, 1986.
(Vancouver's 1st choice, 26th overall, in 2004 Entry Draft).

			Regular Season								Playoffs						
Season	**Club**	**League**	**GP**	**W**	**L**	**O/T**	**Mins**	**GA**	**SO**	**Avg**	**GP**	**W**	**L**	**Mins**	**GA**	**SO**	**Avg**
2002-03	Andover	High-MA	23	13	7	2	1385	39	3	1.69	....	....	....	....	....	....	....
2003-04	Andover	High-MA	24	17	5	2	1336	32	6	1.42	....	....	....	....	....	....	....
	USNTDP	U-18	10	9	1	0	559	15	1	1.61	....	....	....	....	....	....	....
	USNTDP	NAHL	2	2	0	0	120	6	0	3.00	....	....	....	....	....	....	....
2004-05	Boston College	H-East	18	13	1	4	1102	35	1	1.90	....	....	....	....	....	....	....
2005-06	Boston College	H-East	*39	*24	13	2	*2362	83	*8	2.11	....	....	....	....	....	....	....
2006-07	Boston College	H-East	*42	*29	12	1	*2517	90	6	2.15	....	....	....	....	....	....	....
2007-08	Manitoba Moose	AHL	36	21	12	2	2054	78	3	2.28	6	1	4	375	12	0	1.92
2008-09	**Vancouver**	**NHL**	**8**	**2**	**4**	**1**	**355**	**20**	**0**	**3.38**	....	....	....	....	....	....	....
	Manitoba Moose	AHL	40	28	10	1	2324	79	5	*2.04	*22	14	7	1315	47	0	2.15
2009-10	**Vancouver**	**NHL**	**2**	**0**	**1**	**0**	**79**	**5**	**0**	**3.80**	....	....	....	....	....	....	....
	Manitoba Moose	AHL	60	35	23	2	*3557	149	4	2.51	6	2	4	366	19	0	3.12
2010-11	**Vancouver**	**NHL**	**25**	**16**	**4**	**2**	**1372**	**51**	**1**	**2.23**	**5**	**0**	**0**	**163**	**7**	**0**	**2.58**
	NHL Totals		**35**	**18**	**9**	**3**	**1806**	**76**	**1**	**2.52**	**5**	**0**	**0**	**163**	**7**	**0**	**2.58**

Hockey East All-Rookie Team (2005) (co-winners - Kevin Regan and Peter Vetri) • Hockey East Second All-Star Team (2006) • NCAA East First All-American Team (2006) • AHL First All-Star Team (2009) • Harry "Hap" Holmes Memorial Award (AHL – fewest goals against) (2009) (shared with Karl Goehring) • Aldege "Baz" Bastien Memorial Award (AHL – Outstanding Goaltender) (2009) • William M. Jennings Trophy (2011) (shared with Roberto Luongo)

SCRIVENS, Ben (SKRIH-vehnz, BEHN) TOR

Goaltender. Catches left. 6'2", 192 lbs. Born, Spruce Grove, Alta., September 11, 1986.

			Regular Season								Playoffs						
Season	**Club**	**League**	**GP**	**W**	**L**	**O/T**	**Mins**	**GA**	**SO**	**Avg**	**GP**	**W**	**L**	**Mins**	**GA**	**SO**	**Avg**
2004-05	Drayton Valley	AJHL	1	0	1	0	59	3	0	3.03	....	....	....	....	....	....	....
	Calgary Canucks	AJHL	16	7	3	3	857	43	1	3.01	....	....	....	....	....	....	....
2005-06	Spruce Grove	AJHL	45	27	12	2	2469	100	3	2.43	13	9	4	777	37	*2	2.86
2006-07	Cornell Big Red	ECAC	12	3	6	2	574	22	1	2.30	....	....	....	....	....	....	....
2007-08	Cornell Big Red	ECAC	35	*19	12	3	1965	66	4	*2.02	....	....	....	....	....	....	....
2008-09	Cornell Big Red	ECAC	36	*22	10	4	2153	65	*7	*1.81	....	....	....	....	....	....	....
2009-10	Cornell Big Red	ECAC	34	*21	9	4	*2018	63	*7	*1.87	....	....	....	....	....	....	....
2010-11	Toronto Marlies	AHL	33	13	12	5	1929	75	2	2.33	....	....	....	....	....	....	....
	Reading Royals	ECHL	13	10	3	0	779	29	0	2.23	3	0	1	107	9	0	5.04

ECAC Second All-Star Team (2009) • ECAC First All-Star Team (2010) • NCAA East First All-American Team (2010)

Signed as a free agent by **Toronto**, April 28, 2010.

SEXSMITH, Tyson (SEHX-smihth, TIGH-suhn) S.J.

Goaltender. Catches left. 5'11", 210 lbs. Born, Calgary, Alta., March 19, 1989.
(San Jose's 4th choice, 91st overall, in 2007 Entry Draft).

			Regular Season								Playoffs						
Season	**Club**	**League**	**GP**	**W**	**L**	**O/T**	**Mins**	**GA**	**SO**	**Avg**	**GP**	**W**	**L**	**Mins**	**GA**	**SO**	**Avg**
2004-05	Olds Grizzlys	AJHL					STATISTICS NOT AVAILABLE										
	Medicine Hat	WHL	1	0	0	0	4	0	0	0.00	....	....	....	....	....	....	....
	Vancouver Giants	WHL	2	1	0	0	80	4	0	3.00	....	....	....	....	....	....	....
2005-06	Vancouver Giants	WHL	11	6	3	1	547	21	1	2.30	....	....	....	....	....	....	....
2006-07	Vancouver Giants	WHL	51	31	12	8	3047	91	10	*1.79	22	14	7	1339	40	*4	*1.79
2007-08	Vancouver Giants	WHL	62	43	11	8	3678	116	*9	*1.89	10	6	4	658	20	0	1.82
2008-09	Vancouver Giants	WHL	52	39	9	4	3109	117	6	2.26	17	10	7	1150	36	1	1.88
2009-10	Worcester Sharks	AHL	13	4	6	1	716	47	1	3.94	....	....	....	....	....	....	....
	Kalamazoo Wings	ECHL	2	2	0	0	120	5	0	2.50	....	....	....	....	....	....	....
2010-11	Worcester Sharks	AHL	6	2	3	1	367	18	0	2.94	....	....	....	....	....	....	....
	Stockton Thunder	ECHL	17	10	3	3	1029	47	1	2.74	4	1	2	222	11	0	2.98

WHL West Second All-Star Team (2008)

SHANTZ, David (SHAWNTS, DAY-vihd)

Goaltender. Catches left. 6'1", 202 lbs. Born, Burlington, Ont., May 5, 1986.
(Florida's 2nd choice, 37th overall, in 2004 Entry Draft).

			Regular Season								Playoffs						
Season	**Club**	**League**	**GP**	**W**	**L**	**O/T**	**Mins**	**GA**	**SO**	**Avg**	**GP**	**W**	**L**	**Mins**	**GA**	**SO**	**Avg**
2002-03	Thorold	ON-Jr.B	36	30	3	3	2107	63	8	1.79	....	....	....	....	....	....	....
2003-04	Mississauga	OHL	43	21	18	3	2483	120	1	2.90	*24	12	12	*1449	49	*5	2.03
2004-05	Mississauga	OHL	27	10	11	3	1524	72	0	2.83	2	0	1	80	2	0	1.50
2005-06	Peterborough	OHL	49	31	14	3	2946	141	2	2.87	*19	*16	3	*1239	54	1	2.62
2006-07	Rochester	AHL	2	1	1	0	120	9	0	4.51	....	....	....	....	....	....	....
	Florida Everblades	ECHL	23	13	7	1	1338	66	0	2.96	1	0	0	20	1	0	3.00
2007-08	Rochester	AHL	14	1	10	1	780	53	0	4.07	....	....	....	....	....	....	....
	Florida Everblades	ECHL	20	11	5	3	1101	47	0	2.56	2	0	1	77	3	0	2.33
2008-09	Rochester	AHL	12	3	6	2	690	30	1	2.61	....	....	....	....	....	....	....
	Elmira Jackals	ECHL	11	5	4	1	645	31	1	2.88	....	....	....	....	....	....	....
	Dayton Bombers	ECHL	23	10	9	3	1326	69	1	3.12	....	....	....	....	....	....	....
2009-10	Abbotsford Heat	AHL	32	15	10	4	1813	83	1	2.75	13	6	6	762	34	1	2.68
	Victoria	ECHL	28	18	5	4	1585	76	2	2.88	....	....	....	....	....	....	....
2010-11	Victoria	ECHL	*54	25	24	3	*3130	145	3	2.78	12	7	5	746	30	1	2.41

OHL All-Rookie Team (2004) • Canadian Major Junior All-Rookie Team (2004)

Signed as a free agent by **Abbotsford** (AHL), September 14, 2009.

SIMILA, Petteri (sih-MIH-la, PEH-tuhr-ree) MTL

Goaltender. Catches left. 6'6", 189 lbs. Born, Oulu, Finland, April 9, 1990.
(Montreal's 8th choice, 211th overall, in 2009 Entry Draft).

			Regular Season								Playoffs						
Season	**Club**	**League**	**GP**	**W**	**L**	**O/T**	**Mins**	**GA**	**SO**	**Avg**	**GP**	**W**	**L**	**Mins**	**GA**	**SO**	**Avg**
2006-07	Karpat Oulu U18	Fin-U18	15	7	5	0	826	46	0	3.34	....	....	....	....	....	....	....
2007-08	Karpat Oulu U18	Fin-U18	12	4	3	0	738	35	0	2.84	3	0	2	162	9	0	3.33
2008-09	Karpat Oulu Jr.	Fin-Jr.	18	7	9	0	980	58	0	3.55	....	....	....	....	....	....	....
2009-10	Niagara Ice Dogs	OHL	11	1	4	3	550	38	0	4.15	....	....	....	....	....	....	....
2010-11	KalPa Kuopio	Finland	1	0	0	0	25	3	0	7.15	....	....	....	....	....	....	....
	SaPKo Savonlinna	Finland-2	4	2	2	0	245	11	0	2.71	....	....	....	....	....	....	....
	KalPa Kuopio Jr.	Fin-Jr.	33	15	17	0	1878	100	3	3.19	....	....	....	....	....	....	....

SIMPSON, Kent (SIHMP-suhn, KEHNT) CHI

Goaltender. Catches left. 6'2", 190 lbs. Born, Edmonton, Alta., March 26, 1992.
(Chicago's 4th choice, 58th overall, in 2010 Entry Draft).

			Regular Season								Playoffs						
Season	**Club**	**League**	**GP**	**W**	**L**	**O/T**	**Mins**	**GA**	**SO**	**Avg**	**GP**	**W**	**L**	**Mins**	**GA**	**SO**	**Avg**
2007-08	AMC Bulldogs	Minor-AB	....	4	10	6	1126	93	....	4.96	....	....	....	....	....	....	....
	Everett Silvertips	WHL	1	0	0	0	29	1	0	2.07	....	....	....	....	....	....	....
2008-09	Everett Silvertips	WHL	27	8	11	4	1451	93	1	3.85	....	....	....	....	....	....	....
2009-10	Everett Silvertips	WHL	34	22	9	1	1938	73	1	2.26	5	2	3	298	13	1	2.62
2010-11	Everett Silvertips	WHL	53	21	20	9	3132	145	2	2.78	....	....	....	....	....	....	....

SMITH, Jeremy (SMIHTH, JAIR-eh-mee) NSH

Goaltender. Catches left. 6', 173 lbs. Born, Dearborn, MI, April 13, 1989.
(Nashville's 2nd choice, 54th overall, in 2007 Entry Draft).

			Regular Season								Playoffs						
Season	**Club**	**League**	**GP**	**W**	**L**	**O/T**	**Mins**	**GA**	**SO**	**Avg**	**GP**	**W**	**L**	**Mins**	**GA**	**SO**	**Avg**
2005-06	Det. Compuware	MWEHL	13	5	6	0	696	31	0	2.67	....	....	....	....	....	....	....
	Det. Compuware	Exhib.	3	2	1	0	178	8	0	2.70	....	....	....	....	....	....	....
	Plymouth Whalers	OHL	5	0	2	0	111	11	0	5.95	....	....	....	....	....	....	....
2006-07	Plymouth Whalers	OHL	34	23	6	1	1901	82	4	2.59	3	2	0	149	8	0	3.22
2007-08	Plymouth Whalers	OHL	40	23	13	4	2431	116	3	2.86	4	0	4	224	29	0	7.77
2008-09	Plymouth Whalers	OHL	17	3	9	2	901	72	0	4.80	....	....	....	....	....	....	....
	Niagara Ice Dogs	OHL	26	12	9	3	1488	79	1	3.19	12	5	7	724	45	*1	3.73
2009-10	Milwaukee	AHL	1	0	0	0	5	0	0	0.00	....	....	....	....	....	....	....
	Cincinnati	ECHL	42	23	15	2	2468	108	2	2.63	*17	9	8	*988	44	1	2.67
2010-11	Milwaukee	AHL	28	16	8	2	1513	57	2	2.26	13	7	6	843	32	0	2.28
	Cincinnati	ECHL	1	0	0	1	65	3	0	2.78	....	....	....	....	....	....	....

ECHL Playoff MVP (2010) (co-winner - Robert Mayer)

SMITH, Mike (SMIHTH, MIGHK) PHX

Goaltender. Catches left. 6'4", 215 lbs. Born, Kingston, Ont., March 22, 1982.
(Dallas' 5th choice, 161st overall, in 2001 Entry Draft).

			Regular Season								Playoffs						
Season	Club	League	GP	W	L	O/T	Mins	GA	SO	Avg	GP	W	L	Mins	GA	SO	Avg
1998-99	Kingston	OPJHL	16	....	....	....	906	53	0	3.51	....	....	....	....	....	....	....
99-2000	Kingston	OHL	15	4	5	0	666	42	0	3.78	....	....	....	....	....	....	....
2000-01	Kingston	OHL	3	0	0	2	136	8	0	3.53	....	....	....	....	....	....	....
	Sudbury Wolves	OHL	43	22	13	7	2571	108	3	2.52	12	7	5	735	26	2	*2.12
2001-02	Sudbury Wolves	OHL	53	19	28	5	3082	157	3	3.06	5	1	4	302	15	0	2.98
2002-03	Utah Grizzlies	AHL	11	5	5	0	614	33	0	3.23	....	....	....	....	....	....	....
	Lexington	ECHL	27	11	10	4	1553	66	1	2.55	2	0	1	93	8	0	5.14
2003-04	Utah Grizzlies	AHL	21	8	11	0	1186	56	2	2.83	....	....	....	....	....	....	....
2004-05	Houston Aeros	AHL	45	19	17	3	2408	97	5	2.42	3	1	2	181	4	0	1.33
2005-06	Iowa Stars	AHL	50	25	19	6	2998	125	3	2.50	7	3	4	417	19	0	2.74
2006-07	**Dallas**	**NHL**	**23**	**12**	**5**	**2**	**1213**	**45**	**3**	**2.23**	....	....	....	....	....	....	....
2007-08	**Dallas**	**NHL**	**21**	**12**	**9**	**0**	**1172**	**48**	**2**	**2.46**	....	....	....	....	....	....	....
	Tampa Bay	**NHL**	**13**	**3**	**10**	**0**	**774**	**36**	**1**	**2.79**	....	....	....	....	....	....	....
2008-09	**Tampa Bay**	**NHL**	**41**	**14**	**18**	**9**	**2471**	**108**	**2**	**2.62**	....	....	....	....	....	....	....
2009-10	**Tampa Bay**	**NHL**	**42**	**13**	**18**	**7**	**2273**	**117**	**2**	**3.09**	....	....	....	....	....	....	....
2010-11	**Tampa Bay**	**NHL**	**22**	**13**	**6**	**1**	**1202**	**58**	**1**	**2.90**	**3**	**1**	**1**	**120**	**2**	**0**	**1.00**
	Norfolk Admirals	AHL	5	1	4	0	296	9	1	1.83	....	....	....	....	....	....	....
	NHL Totals		**162**	**67**	**66**	**19**	**9105**	**412**	**11**	**2.71**	**3**	**1**	**1**	**120**	**2**	**0**	**1.00**

NHL All-Rookie Team (2007)

Traded to **Tampa Bay** by **Dallas** with Jussi Jokinen, Jeff Halpern and Dallas' 4th round choice (later traded to Minnesota, later traded to Edmonton – Edmonton selected Kyle Bigos) in 2009 Entry Draft for Brad Richards and Johan Holmqvist, February 26, 2008. Signed as a free agent by **Phoenix**, July 1, 2011.

SOBERG, Steffen (SOH-buhrg, STEH-fan) WSH

Goaltender. Catches left. 5'11", 165 lbs. Born, Oslo, Norway, August 6, 1993.
(Washington's 1st choice, 117th overall, in 2011 Entry Draft).

			Regular Season								Playoffs						
Season	Club	League	GP	W	L	O/T	Mins	GA	SO	Avg	GP	W	L	Mins	GA	SO	Avg
2007-08	Manglerud Jr.	Norway-Jr.	2	....	....	....	80	2	1	1.50	....	....	....	....	....	....	....
2008-09	Manglerud U17	Nor-U17	25	....	....	....	1503	81	0	3.23	6	....	....	340	11	0	1.94
	Manglerud Jr.	Norway-Jr.	3	....	....	....	150	6	0	2.39	....	....	....	....	....	....	....
2009-10	Manglerud U17	Nor-U17	1	....	....	....	60	1	0	1.00	3	....	....	180	3	1	1.00
	Manglerud 2	Norway-2	17	....	....	....	947	55	1	3.48	....	....	....	....	....	....	....
	Manglerud	Norway	3	0	3	0	132	8	0	3.65	4	1	1	143	5	0	2.09
2010-11	Manglerud Jr.	Norway-Jr.	3	....	....	....	180	7	0	2.33	1	....	....	70	4	0	3.42
	Manglerud 2	Norway-2	2	....	....	....	120	6	0	3.00	....	....	....	....	....	....	....
	Manglerud	Norway	27	5	21	0	1538	107	0	4.17	....	....	....	....	....	....	....

SPARKS, Garret (SPARKS, GAIR-eht) TOR

Goaltender. Catches . 6'2", 200 lbs. Born, Elmhurst, IL, June 28, 1993.
(Toronto's 8th choice, 190th overall, in 2011 Entry Draft).

			Regular Season								Playoffs						
Season	Club	League	GP	W	L	O/T	Mins	GA	SO	Avg	GP	W	L	Mins	GA	SO	Avg
2008-09	Team Illinois	T1EHL	18	9	6	2	854	51	0	3.05	....	....	....	....	....	....	....
2009-10	Chicago Mission	T1EHL	27	19	7	2	1392	51	3	1.98	....	....	....	....	....	....	....
2010-11	Guelph Storm	OHL	19	8	6	1	972	59	0	3.64	....	....	....	....	....	....	....

STAJCER, Scott (STA-chuhr, SKAWT) NYR

Goaltender. Catches left. 6'3", 196 lbs. Born, Cambridge, Ont., June 14, 1991.
(NY Rangers' 5th choice, 140th overall, in 2009 Entry Draft).

			Regular Season								Playoffs						
Season	Club	League	GP	W	L	O/T	Mins	GA	SO	Avg	GP	W	L	Mins	GA	SO	Avg
2006-07	Mississauga Rebels	GTHL	39	....	....	....	1755	81	6	2.07	....	....	....	....	....	....	....
2007-08	Owen Sound	ON-Jr.B	32	8	21	2	1862	130	0	3.90	....	....	....	....	....	....	....
	Owen Sound	OHL	6	1	3	1	306	22	0	4.31	....	....	....	....	....	....	....
2008-09	Owen Sound	OHL	35	15	15	5	1969	117	0	3.57	4	0	3	211	20	0	5.70
2009-10	Owen Sound	OHL	55	21	23	6	3042	186	1	3.67	....	....	....	....	....	....	....
2010-11	Owen Sound	OHL	14	10	3	0	782	38	1	2.92	13	8	4	688	32	0	2.79

STALOCK, Alex (STAY-lahk, AL-ehx) S.J.

Goaltender. Catches left. 6', 185 lbs. Born, St. Paul, MN, July 28, 1987.
(San Jose's 3rd choice, 112th overall, in 2005 Entry Draft).

			Regular Season								Playoffs						
Season	Club	League	GP	W	L	O/T	Mins	GA	SO	Avg	GP	W	L	Mins	GA	SO	Avg
2003-04	South St. Paul	High-MN	31	23	7	1	....	....	....	2.20	....	....	....	....	....	....	....
2004-05	Cedar Rapids	USHL	32	19	9	3	1801	82	1	2.73	9	7	2	582	14	*1	*1.44
2005-06	Cedar Rapids	USHL	44	*28	13	3	2641	112	4	2.54	8	3	5	472	25	0	3.18
2006-07	U. Minn-Duluth	WCHA	23	5	14	3	1364	76	1	3.34	....	....	....	....	....	....	....
2007-08	U. Minn-Duluth	WCHA	36	13	17	6	2170	85	3	2.35	....	....	....	....	....	....	....
2008-09	U. Minn-Duluth	WCHA	*42	21	13	8	*2534	90	*5	*2.13	....	....	....	....	....	....	....
2009-10	Worcester Sharks	AHL	*61	*39	19	2	3534	155	4	2.63	11	6	5	683	26	0	2.28
2010-11	**San Jose**	**NHL**	**1**	**1**	**0**	**0**	**30**	**0**	**0**	**0.00**	....	....	....	....	....	....	....
	Worcester Sharks	AHL	41	19	17	4	2397	105	0	2.63	....	....	....	....	....	....	....
	NHL Totals		**1**	**1**	**0**	**0**	**30**	**0**	**0**	**0.00**	....	....	....	....	....	....	....

USHL Playoff MVP (2005) • USHL First All-Star Team (2006) • USHL Goaltender of the Year (2006) • WCHA All-Rookie Team (2007) • WCHA First All-Star Team (2009) • NCAA West First All-American Team (2009) • AHL All-Rookie Team (2010)

TALBOT, Cameron (TAL-buht, KAM-ruhn) NYR

Goaltender. Catches left. 6'3", 205 lbs. Born, Caledonia, Ont., June 5, 1987.

			Regular Season								Playoffs						
Season	Club	League	GP	W	L	O/T	Mins	GA	SO	Avg	GP	W	L	Mins	GA	SO	Avg
2005-06	Hamilton	OPJHL	35	21	13	1	2046	87	1	2.55	14	8	6	903	52	1	3.46
2006-07	Hamilton	OPJHL	28	19	5	2	1644	57	1	2.08	19	13	6	1243	51	0	2.46
2007-08	AL-Huntsville	CHA	13	1	10	0	583	45	0	4.63	....	....	....	....	....	....	....
2008-09	AL-Huntsville	CHA	24	2	16	3	1320	65	1	2.95	....	....	....	....	....	....	....
2009-10	AL-Huntsville	CHA	*33	12	18	3	*1958	85	1	2.61	....	....	....	....	....	....	....
	Hartford Wolf Pack	AHL	1	0	0	0	19	3	0	9.70	....	....	....	....	....	....	....
2010-11	Connecticut Whale	AHL	22	11	9	2	1308	62	2	2.84	1	0	1	38	2	0	3.13
	Greenville	ECHL	2	1	0	1	122	5	0	2.46	....	....	....	....	....	....	....

Signed as a free agent by **NY Rangers**, March 30, 2010.

TARKKI, Iiro (TAHR-kee, EE-roh) ANA

Goaltender. Catches . 6'2", 191 lbs. Born, Rauma, Finland, July 1, 1985.

			Regular Season								Playoffs						
Season	Club	League	GP	W	L	O/T	Mins	GA	SO	Avg	GP	W	L	Mins	GA	SO	Avg
2002-03	Lukko Rauma Jr.	Fin-Jr.	20	....	....	....	....	4.15	....	....	....	....	....	....	....	....	....
2003-04	Lukko Rauma Jr.	Fin-Jr.	34	....	....	....	....	....	....	3.74	....	....	....	....	....	....	....
	Suomi U20	Finland-2	1	....	....	....	....	....	....	0.94	....	....	....	....	....	....	....
2004-05	Lukko Rauma	Finland	1	....	....	....	20	0	0	0.00	....	....	....	....	....	....	....
2005-06	Lukko Rauma	Finland	6	....	....	....	....	....	....	....	....	....	....	....	....	....	....
2006-07	SaPKo Savonlinna	Finland-2	21	....	....	....	....	....	....	3.84	....	....	....	....	....	....	....
	SaiPa	Finland	2	....	....	....	120	7	0	3.50	....	....	....	....	....	....	....
2007-08	SaiPa	Finland	40	....	....	....	2330	94	4	2.42	....	....	....	....	....	....	....
2008-09	SaiPa	Finland	48	14	27	6	2753	129	1	2.81	3	....	....	189	8	0	1.80
2009-10	Blues Espoo	Finland	54	22	22	9	3228	131	2	2.44	3	....	....	219	7	0	1.91
2010-11	Blues Espoo	Finland	55	20	20	14	3218	112	5	2.09	18	10	8	1098	40	3	2.19

Signed as a free agent by **Anaheim**, May 6, 2011.

TAYLOR, Daniel (TAY-luhr, DAN-yehl)

Goaltender. Catches left. 5'11", 179 lbs. Born, Plymouth, England, April 28, 1986.
(Los Angeles' 8th choice, 221st overall, in 2004 Entry Draft).

			Regular Season								Playoffs						
Season	Club	League	GP	W	L	O/T	Mins	GA	SO	Avg	GP	W	L	Mins	GA	SO	Avg
2002-03	Cumberland Grads	CJHL	23	13	3	1	1009	41	1	2.44	6	3	3	432	17	0	2.36
2003-04	Guelph Storm	OHL	26	16	4	3	1462	66	0	2.71	3	1	1	159	9	0	3.40
2004-05	Guelph Storm	OHL	31	13	14	3	1821	80	2	2.64	1	0	1	59	4	0	4.07
2005-06	Kingston	OHL	57	32	15	6	3319	172	3	3.11	....	....	....	....	....	....	....
2006-07	Bakersfield	ECHL	17	7	7	2	969	70	0	4.33	....	....	....	....	....	....	....
	Wheeling Nailers	ECHL	1	0	0	1	62	4	0	3.86	....	....	....	....	....	....	....
	Texas Wildcatters	ECHL	2	0	1	0	74	2	0	1.61	....	....	....	....	....	....	....
2007-08	**Los Angeles**	**NHL**	**1**	**0**	**0**	**0**	**20**	**2**	**0**	**6.00**	....	....	....	....	....	....	....
	Manchester	AHL	23	13	5	2	1275	51	4	2.40	....	....	....	....	....	....	....
	Reading Royals	ECHL	5	3	0	0	182	8	0	2.63	13	7	6	815	38	1	2.80
2008-09	Manchester	AHL	15	7	4	2	744	33	0	2.66	....	....	....	....	....	....	....
2009-10	Syracuse Crunch	AHL	9	2	4	0	397	24	0	3.63	....	....	....	....	....	....	....
	Gwinnett	ECHL	37	18	13	5	2181	126	1	3.47	....	....	....	....	....	....	....
2010-11	Springfield Falcons	AHL	4	2	2	0	230	9	0	2.35	....	....	....	....	....	....	....
	Hamburg Freezers	Germany	28	14	14	....	1679	81	1	2.90	....	....	....	....	....	....	....
	NHL Totals		**1**	**0**	**0**	**0**	**20**	**2**	**0**	**6.00**	....	....	....	....	....	....	....

Signed to a PTO (professional tryout) contract by **Springfield** (AHL), October, 2010. Signed as a free agent by **Hamburg** (Germany), November 14, 2010.

THEODORE, Jose (THEE-uh-dohr, joh-SAY) FLA

Goaltender. Catches right. 5'11", 185 lbs. Born, Laval, Que., September 13, 1976.
(Montreal's 2nd choice, 44th overall, in 1994 Entry Draft).

			Regular Season								Playoffs						
Season	Club	League	GP	W	L	O/T	Mins	GA	SO	Avg	GP	W	L	Mins	GA	SO	Avg
1990-91	Richelieu	QAHA	42	....	....	....	2520	80	0	1.90	....	....	....	....	....	....	....
1991-92	Richelieu Riverains	QAAA	24	9	13	2	1440	96	0	3.99	5	2	3	295	26	0	5.28
1992-93	St-Jean Lynx	QMJHL	33	12	14	2	1775	111	0	3.75	3	0	3	175	11	0	3.77
1993-94	St-Jean Lynx	QMJHL	57	20	28	6	3230	196	0	3.64	5	1	4	296	18	0	3.65
1994-95	St-Jean Lynx	QMJHL	14	5	8	1	833	67	0	4.83	....	....	....	....	....	....	....
	Hull Olympiques	QMJHL	*43	*27	14	1	*2521	126	5	3.00	*21	*15	6	*1267	59	*1	2.79
	Fredericton	AHL	....	....	....	....	....	....	....	....	1	0	1	60	3	0	3.00
1995-96	**Montreal**	**NHL**	**1**	**0**	**0**	**0**	**9**	**1**	**0**	**6.67**	....	....	....	....	....	....	....
	Hull Olympiques	QMJHL	48	33	11	2	2809	158	0	3.38	5	2	3	300	20	0	4.00
1996-97	**Montreal**	**NHL**	**16**	**5**	**6**	**2**	**821**	**53**	**0**	**3.87**	**2**	**1**	**1**	**168**	**7**	**0**	**2.50**
	Fredericton	AHL	26	12	12	0	1469	87	0	3.55	....	....	....	....	....	....	....
1997-98	Fredericton	AHL	53	20	23	8	3053	145	2	2.85	4	1	3	237	13	0	3.28
	Montreal	**NHL**	....	....	....	....	....	....	....	....	**3**	**0**	**1**	**120**	**1**	**0**	**0.50**
1998-99	**Montreal**	**NHL**	**18**	**4**	**12**	**0**	**913**	**50**	**1**	**3.29**	....	....	....	....	....	....	....
	Fredericton	AHL	27	12	13	2	1609	77	2	2.87	13	8	5	694	35	1	3.03
99-2000	**Montreal**	**NHL**	**30**	**12**	**13**	**2**	**1655**	**58**	**5**	**2.10**	....	....	....	....	....	....	....
2000-01	**Montreal**	**NHL**	**59**	**20**	**29**	**5**	**3298**	**141**	**2**	**2.57**	....	....	....	....	....	....	....
	Quebec Citadelles	AHL	3	3	0	0	180	9	0	3.00	....	....	....	....	....	....	....
2001-02	**Montreal**	**NHL**	**67**	**30**	**24**	**10**	**3864**	**136**	**7**	**2.11**	**12**	**6**	**6**	**686**	**35**	**0**	**3.06**
2002-03	**Montreal**	**NHL**	**57**	**20**	**31**	**6**	**3419**	**165**	**2**	**2.90**	....	....	....	....	....	....	....
2003-04	**Montreal**	**NHL**	**67**	**33**	**28**	**5**	**3961**	**150**	**6**	**2.27**	**11**	**4**	**7**	**678**	**27**	**1**	**2.39**
2004-05	Djurgarden	Sweden	17	....	....	....	1024	42	0	2.46	12	....	....	728	27	0	2.23
2005-06	**Montreal**	**NHL**	**38**	**17**	**15**	**5**	**2114**	**122**	**0**	**3.46**	....	....	....	....	....	....	....
	Colorado	**NHL**	**5**	**1**	**3**	**1**	**296**	**15**	**0**	**3.04**	**9**	**4**	**5**	**573**	**29**	**0**	**3.04**
2006-07	**Colorado**	**NHL**	**33**	**13**	**15**	**1**	**1748**	**95**	**0**	**3.26**	....	....	....	....	....	....	....
2007-08	**Colorado**	**NHL**	**53**	**28**	**21**	**3**	**3028**	**123**	**3**	**2.44**	**10**	**4**	**6**	**514**	**27**	**0**	**3.15**
	Lake Erie Monsters	AHL	1	0	1	0	60	3	0	3.02	....	....	....	....	....	....	....
2008-09	**Washington**	**NHL**	**57**	**32**	**17**	**5**	**3287**	**157**	**2**	**2.87**	**2**	**0**	**1**	**97**	**6**	**0**	**3.71**
2009-10	**Washington**	**NHL**	**47**	**30**	**7**	**7**	**2586**	**121**	**1**	**2.81**	**2**	**0**	**1**	**81**	**5**	**0**	**3.70**
2010-11	**Minnesota**	**NHL**	**32**	**15**	**11**	**3**	**1793**	**81**	**1**	**2.71**	....	....	....	....	....	....	....
	NHL Totals		**580**	**260**	**232**	**55**	**32792**	**1468**	**30**	**2.69**	**51**	**19**	**28**	**2917**	**137**	**1**	**2.82**

QMJHL Second All-Star Team (1995, 1996) • NHL Second All-Star Team (2002) • MBNA Roger Crozier Saving Grace Award (2002) • Vezina Trophy (2002) • Hart Memorial Trophy (2002) • Bill Masterton Memorial Trophy (2010)

Played in NHL All-Star Game (2002, 2004)

• Scored a goal vs. NY Islanders, January 2, 2001. Signed as a free agent by **Djurgarden** (Sweden), December 20, 2004. Traded to **Colorado** by **Montreal** for David Aebischer, March 8, 2006. Signed as a free agent by **Washington**, July 1, 2008. Signed as a free agent by **Minnesota**, October 2, 2010. Signed as a free agent by **Florida**, July 1, 2011.

THIESSEN, Brad (THEE-suhn, BRAD) PIT

Goaltender. Catches left. 6', 180 lbs. Born, Aldergrove, B.C., March 19, 1986.

			Regular Season								Playoffs						
Season	Club	League	GP	W	L	O/T	Mins	GA	SO	Avg	GP	W	L	Mins	GA	SO	Avg
2003-04	Penticton Panthers	BCHL	42	13	17	1	2131	122	2	3.44	....	....	....	....	....	....	....
2004-05	Penticton Vees	BCHL	26	7	18	1	1492	86	1	3.46	....	....	....	....	....	....	....
	Prince George	BCHL	10	5	4	0	561	31	0	3.31	3	1	1	158	9	0	3.42
2005-06	Prince George	BCHL	36	14	17	4	2058	99	5	2.89	....	....	....	....	....	....	....
	Merritt	BCHL	13	8	4	0	754	36	2	2.87	6	3	3	261	16	1	3.68
2006-07	Northeastern	H-East	33	11	17	5	1985	82	4	2.48	....	....	....	....	....	....	....
2007-08	Northeastern	H-East	37	16	17	3	2180	96	2	2.64	....	....	....	....	....	....	....
2008-09	Northeastern	H-East	*41	25	12	4	*2496	88	*3	2.12	....	....	....	....	....	....	....
2009-10	Wilkes-Barre	AHL	30	14	14	1	1763	72	4	2.45	....	....	....	....	....	....	....
	Wheeling Nailers	ECHL	12	8	3	0	674	30	1	2.67	....	....	....	....	....	....	....
2010-11	Wilkes-Barre	AHL	46	*35	8	1	2567	83	7	1.94	12	6	6	720	20	2	*1.67

Hockey East First All-Star Team (2009) • Hockey East Player of the Year (2009) • NCAA East First All-American Team (2009) • AHL First All-Star Team (2011) • Harry ''Hap'' Holmes Memorial Award (AHL – fewest goals against) (2011) (shared with John Curry) • Aldege "Baz" Bastien Award (AHL – Outstanding Goaltender) (2011)

Signed as a free agent by **Pittsburgh**, April 8, 2009.

THOMAS, Tim (TAW-mas, TIHM) BOS

Goaltender. Catches left. 5'11", 201 lbs. Born, Flint, MI, April 15, 1974.
(Quebec's 11th choice, 217th overall, in 1994 Entry Draft).

			Regular Season								Playoffs						
Season	Club	League	GP	W	L	O/T	Mins	GA	SO	Avg	GP	W	L	Mins	GA	SO	Avg
1992-93	Davison High	High-MI	27	....	....	....	1580	87	....	3.30	....	....	....	....	....	....	....
1993-94	U. of Vermont	ECAC	*33	15	12	6	1864	94	0	3.03	....	....	....	....	....	....	....
1994-95	U. of Vermont	ECAC	34	18	13	2	2010	90	*4	*2.69	....	....	....	....	....	....	....
1995-96	U. of Vermont	ECAC	37	*26	7	4	*2254	88	*3	*2.34	....	....	....	....	....	....	....
1996-97	U. of Vermont	ECAC	36	22	11	3	2158	101	2	2.81	....	....	....	....	....	....	....
1997-98	Birmingham Bulls	ECHL	6	4	1	1	360	13	1	2.17	....	....	....	....	....	....	....
	Houston Aeros	IHL	1	0	1	0	59	4	0	4.01	....	....	....	....	....	....	....
	HIFK Helsinki	Finland	18	13	4	1	1034	28	2	1.62	9	9	0	551	14	3	1.52
1998-99	Hamilton Bulldogs	AHL	15	6	8	0	837	45	0	3.23	....	....	....	....	....	....	....
	HIFK Helsinki	Finland	14	8	3	3	833	31	2	2.23	11	7	4	658	25	0	2.28
99-2000	Detroit Vipers	IHL	36	10	21	3	2020	120	1	3.56	....	....	....	....	....	....	....
2000-01	AIK Solna	Sweden	43	....	....	....	2542	105	3	2.48	5	....	....	299	20	0	4.01
2001-02	Karpat Oulu	Finland	32	15	12	5	1937	79	4	2.44	3	1	2	180	12	0	4.00
2002-03	**Boston**	**NHL**	**4**	**3**	**1**	**0**	**220**	**11**	**0**	**3.00**	....	....	....	....	....	....	....
	Providence Bruins	AHL	35	18	12	5	2049	98	1	2.87	....	....	....	....	....	....	....
2003-04	Providence Bruins	AHL	43	20	16	6	2544	78	9	1.84	2	0	2	84	10	0	7.13
2004-05	Jokerit Helsinki	Finland	54	34	13	7	3266	86	15	1.58	12	8	4	720	22	0	1.83
2005-06	**Boston**	**NHL**	**38**	**12**	**13**	**10**	**2187**	**101**	**1**	**2.77**	....	....	....	....	....	....	....
	Providence Bruins	AHL	26	15	11	0	1515	57	1	2.26	....	....	....	....	....	....	....
2006-07	**Boston**	**NHL**	**66**	**30**	**29**	**4**	**3619**	**189**	**3**	**3.13**	....	....	....	....	....	....	....
2007-08	**Boston**	**NHL**	**57**	**28**	**19**	**6**	**3342**	**136**	**3**	**2.44**	**7**	**3**	**4**	**430**	**19**	**0**	**2.65**
2008-09	**Boston**	**NHL**	**54**	**36**	**11**	**7**	**3259**	**114**	**5**	***2.10**	**11**	**7**	**4**	**680**	**21**	**1**	***1.85**
2009-10	**Boston**	**NHL**	**43**	**17**	**18**	**8**	**2442**	**104**	**5**	**2.56**	....	....	....	....	....	....	....
	United States	Olympics	1	0	0	0	12	1	0	5.21							
2010-11 ♦	**Boston**	**NHL**	**57**	**35**	**11**	**9**	**3364**	**112**	**9**	***2.00**	***25**	***16**	**9**	***1542**	**51**	***4**	***1.98**
	NHL Totals		**319**	**161**	**102**	**44**	**18433**	**767**	**26**	**2.50**	**43**	**26**	**17**	**2652**	**91**	**5**	**2.06**

ECAC First All-Star Team (1995, 1996) • ECAC Goaltender of the Year (1996) • NCAA East Second All-American Team (1995) • NCAA East First All-American Team (1996) • NHL First All-Star Team (2009, 2011) • William M. Jennings Trophy (2009) (shared with Manny Fernandez) • Vezina Trophy (2009, 2011) • Conn Smythe Trophy (2011)

Played in NHL All-Star Game (2008, 2009, 2011)

• Rights transferred to **Colorado** after **Quebec** franchise relocated, June 21, 1995. Signed as a free agent by **Edmonton**, June 4, 1998. Signed as free agent by **Solna** (Sweden), July 26. 2000. Signed as a free agent by **Boston**, August 8, 2002. Signed as a free agent by **Jokerit Helsinki** (Finland), May 17, 2004.

TOIVONEN, Hannu (TOI-voh-nuhn, HA-noo)

Goaltender. Catches left. 6'2", 200 lbs. Born, Kalvola, Finland, May 18, 1984.
(Boston's 1st choice, 29th overall, in 2002 Entry Draft).

			Regular Season								Playoffs						
Season	Club	League	GP	W	L	O/T	Mins	GA	SO	Avg	GP	W	L	Mins	GA	SO	Avg
2000-01	HPK U18	Fin-U18	....	....	....	....	....	....	....	....	....	....	....	....	....	....	....
2001-02	HPK U18	Fin-U18	5	4	1	0	277	14	0	3.03	....	....	....	....	....	....	....
	HPK Jr.	Fin-Jr.	31	15	12	4	1877	103	2	3.29	7	3	4	440	31	0	4.23
2002-03	HPK Jr.	Fin-Jr.	6	3	3	0	359	20	0	3.34	....	....	....	....	....	....	....
	HPK Hameenlinna	Finland	24	16	2	4	1432	54	2	2.26	2	1	1	117	3	1	1.53
2003-04	Providence Bruins	AHL	36	15	16	4	2162	83	2	2.30	....	....	....	....	....	....	....
2004-05	Providence Bruins	AHL	54	29	18	3	3017	103	7	2.05	17	10	7	1038	42	0	2.43
2005-06	**Boston**	**NHL**	**20**	**9**	**5**	**4**	**1163**	**51**	**1**	**2.63**	....	....	....	....	....	....	....
2006-07	**Boston**	**NHL**	**18**	**3**	**9**	**1**	**894**	**63**	**0**	**4.23**	....	....	....	....	....	....	....
	Providence Bruins	AHL	27	13	13	1	1618	64	2	2.37	13	6	7	742	36	0	2.91
2007-08	**St. Louis**	**NHL**	**23**	**6**	**10**	**5**	**1202**	**69**	**0**	**3.44**	....	....	....	....	....	....	....
	Peoria Rivermen	AHL	11	6	4	0	627	33	0	3.16	....	....	....	....	....	....	....
2008-09	Ilves Tampere	Finland	52	19	23	9	2913	130	3	2.68	3	1	2	198	6	1	1.82
2009-10	Peoria Rivermen	AHL	26	11	11	3	1516	69	0	2.73	....	....	....	....	....	....	....
	Rockford IceHogs	AHL	6	1	4	0	296	17	0	3.44	1	0	0	20	1	0	3.00
2010-11	Rockford IceHogs	AHL	49	21	16	4	2463	119	3	2.90	....	....	....	....	....	....	....
	NHL Totals		**61**	**18**	**24**	**10**	**3259**	**183**	**1**	**3.37**	....	....	....	....	....	....	....

Traded to **St. Louis** by **Boston** for Carl Soderberg, July 23, 2007. Signed as a free agent by **Ilves Tampere** (Finland), July 15, 2008. Signed as a free agent by **St. Louis**, July 9, 2009. Traded to **Chicago** by **St. Louis** with Danny Richmond for Joe Fallon and Daryl Boyle, March 1, 2010.

TOKARSKI, Dustin (toh-KAHR-skee, DUHS-tihn) T.B.

Goaltender. Catches left. 5'11", 198 lbs. Born, Humboldt, Sask., September 16, 1989.
(Tampa Bay's 3rd choice, 122nd overall, in 2008 Entry Draft).

			Regular Season								Playoffs						
Season	Club	League	GP	W	L	O/T	Mins	GA	SO	Avg	GP	W	L	Mins	GA	SO	Avg
2006-07	Spokane Chiefs	WHL	30	13	11	2	1674	78	2	2.80	6	2	4	364	17	0	2.80
2007-08	Spokane Chiefs	WHL	45	30	10	3	2543	87	6	2.05	*21	*16	5	*1352	31	*3	*1.38
2008-09	Spokane Chiefs	WHL	54	34	18	2	3264	107	*7	*1.97	12	7	5	812	23	1	*1.70
2009-10	**Tampa Bay**	**NHL**	**2**	**0**	**0**	**0**	**44**	**3**	**0**	**4.09**	....	....	....	....	....	....	....
	Norfolk Admirals	AHL	55	27	25	3	3319	139	4	2.51	....	....	....	....	....	....	....
2010-11	Norfolk Admirals	AHL	46	21	20	4	2691	119	2	2.65	6	2	4	355	13	1	2.19
	NHL Totals		**2**	**0**	**0**	**0**	**44**	**3**	**0**	**4.09**	....	....	....	....	....	....	....

Memorial Cup All-Star Team (2008) • Hap Emms Memorial Trophy (Memorial Cup - Top Goaltender) (2008) • Stafford Smythe Memorial Trophy (Memorial Cup - MVP) (2008) • WHL West Second All-Star Team (2009)

TORDJMAN, Josh (TOHRJ-man, JAWSH)

Goaltender. Catches left. 6'1", 156 lbs. Born, Montreal, Que., January 11, 1985.

			Regular Season								Playoffs						
Season	Club	League	GP	W	L	O/T	Mins	GA	SO	Avg	GP	W	L	Mins	GA	SO	Avg
2002-03	Valleyfield Braves	QJHL	STATISTICS NOT AVAILABLE														
	Victoriaville Tigres	QMJHL	10	4	3	0	432	24	1	3.33	2	0	1	112	12	0	6.44
2003-04	Victoriaville Tigres	QMJHL	42	10	24	4	2177	143	2	3.94	....	....	....	....	....	....	....
2004-05	Victoriaville Tigres	QMJHL	56	22	28	4	3185	171	5	3.22	7	3	4	435	24	0	3.31
2005-06	Victoriaville Tigres	QMJHL	31	13	17	0	1792	106	2	3.55	....	....	....	....	....	....	....
	Moncton Wildcats	QMJHL	25	18	6	0	1427	55	2	*2.31	21	*15	5	1238	48	*2	2.33
2006-07	San Antonio	AHL	37	15	18	2	2114	91	1	2.58	....	....	....	....	....	....	....
	Phoenix	ECHL	9	4	4	0	480	25	0	3.12	....	....	....	....	....	....	....
2007-08	San Antonio	AHL	43	22	14	4	2466	109	1	2.65	6	3	3	357	11	1	1.85
2008-09	**Phoenix**	**NHL**	**2**	**0**	**2**	**0**	**118**	**8**	**0**	**4.07**	....	....	....	....	....	....	....
	San Antonio	AHL	51	25	22	2	2921	127	6	2.61	....	....	....	....	....	....	....
2009-10	San Antonio	AHL	45	20	22	2	2537	125	1	2.96	....	....	....	....	....	....	....
2010-11	Houston Aeros	AHL	8	4	1	0	393	16	0	2.44	1	0	0	26	3	0	6.82
	Bakersfield	ECHL	35	16	16	3	2033	97	3	2.86	....	....	....	....	....	....	....
	NHL Totals		**2**	**0**	**2**	**0**	**118**	**8**	**0**	**4.07**	....	....	....	....	....	....	....

QMJHL Second All-Star Team (2006) • Yanick Dupre Memorial Award (AHL – Outstanding Humanitarian Contribution) (2010)

Signed as a free agent by **Phoenix**, July 2, 2006. Signed as a free agent by **Houston** (AHL), September 7, 2010. • Loaned to **Bakersfield** (ECHL) by **Houston** (AHL), October 12, 2010.

TUOHIMAA, Frans (too-OH-hay-ma, FRANZ) EDM

Goaltender. Catches left. 6'2", 178 lbs. Born, Helsinki, Finland, August 19, 1991.
(Edmonton's 9th choice, 182nd overall, in 2011 Entry Draft).

			Regular Season								Playoffs						
Season	Club	League	GP	W	L	O/T	Mins	GA	SO	Avg	GP	W	L	Mins	GA	SO	Avg
2007-08	HIFK Helsinki U18	Fin-U18	22	11	8	0	1251	55	3	2.64	2	0	1	71	13	0	10.98
	HIFK Helsinki Jr.	Fin-Jr.	1	0	0	0	17	3	0	10.71	....	....	....	....	....	....	....
2008-09	HIFK Helsinki U18	Fin-U18	13	12	1	0	780	20	4	1.54	8	7	1	478	14	2	1.76
	HIFK Helsinki Jr.	Fin-Jr.	18	4	13	0	983	65	0	3.97	....	....	....	....	....	....	....
2009-10	Suomi U20	Finland-2	1	0	1	0	60	3	0	3.01	....	....	....	....	....	....	....
	HIFK Helsinki Jr.	Fin-Jr.	20	14	5	0	1144	55	2	2.89	12	7	5	696	31	1	2.67
2010-11	Jokerit Helsinki Jr.	Fin-Jr.	37	24	13	0	2183	78	6	2.14	7	3	4	425	21	0	2.97

TURCO, Marty (TUHR-koh, MAHR-tee)

Goaltender. Catches left. 5'11", 184 lbs. Born, Sault Ste. Marie, Ont., August 13, 1975.
(Dallas' 4th choice, 124th overall, in 1994 Entry Draft).

			Regular Season								Playoffs						
Season	Club	League	GP	W	L	O/T	Mins	GA	SO	Avg	GP	W	L	Mins	GA	SO	Avg
1993-94	Cambridge	ON-Jr.B	34	19	10	3	1973	114	0	3.47	....	....	....	....	....	....	....
1994-95	U. of Michigan	CCHA	37	*27	7	1	2063	95	1	2.76	....	....	....	....	....	....	....
1995-96	U. of Michigan	CCHA	*42	*34	7	1	*2335	84	*5	*2.16	....	....	....	....	....	....	....
1996-97	U. of Michigan	CCHA	*41	*33	4	4	*2296	87	*4	*2.27	....	....	....	....	....	....	....
1997-98	U. of Michigan	CCHA	*45	*33	10	1	*2640	95	4	2.16	....	....	....	....	....	....	....
1998-99	Michigan K-Wings	IHL	54	24	17	10	3127	136	1	2.61	5	2	3	300	14	0	2.80
99-2000	Michigan K-Wings	IHL	60	23	27	*7	3399	139	*7	2.45	....	....	....	....	....	....	....
2000-01	**Dallas**	**NHL**	**26**	**13**	**6**	**1**	**1266**	**40**	**3**	***1.90**	....	....	....	....	....	....	....
2001-02	**Dallas**	**NHL**	**31**	**15**	**6**	**2**	**1519**	**53**	**2**	**2.09**	....	....	....	....	....	....	....
2002-03	**Dallas**	**NHL**	**55**	**31**	**10**	**10**	**3203**	**92**	**7**	***1.72**	**12**	**6**	**6**	**798**	**25**	**0**	**1.88**
2003-04	**Dallas**	**NHL**	**73**	**37**	**21**	**13**	**4359**	**144**	**9**	**1.98**	**5**	**1**	**4**	**325**	**18**	**0**	**3.32**
2004-05	Djurgarden	Sweden	6	....	....	....	356	12	1	2.02	....	....	....	....	....	....	....
2005-06	**Dallas**	**NHL**	**68**	**41**	**19**	**5**	**3910**	**166**	**3**	**2.55**	**5**	**1**	**4**	**319**	**18**	**0**	**3.39**
	Canada	Olympics	DID NOT PLAY – SPARE GOALTENDER														
2006-07	**Dallas**	**NHL**	**67**	**38**	**20**	**5**	**3764**	**140**	**6**	**2.23**	**7**	**3**	**4**	**509**	**11**	**3**	***1.30**
2007-08	**Dallas**	**NHL**	**62**	**32**	**21**	**6**	**3629**	**140**	**3**	**2.31**	**18**	**10**	**8**	**1152**	**40**	**1**	**2.08**
2008-09	**Dallas**	**NHL**	**74**	**33**	**31**	**10**	**4327**	**203**	**3**	**2.81**	....	....	....	....	....	....	....
2009-10	**Dallas**	**NHL**	**53**	**22**	**20**	**11**	**3088**	**140**	**4**	**2.72**	....	....	....	....	....	....	....
2010-11	**Chicago**	**NHL**	**29**	**11**	**11**	**3**	**1631**	**82**	**1**	**3.02**	....	....	....	....	....	....	....
	NHL Totals		**538**	**273**	**165**	**66**	**30696**	**1200**	**41**	**2.35**	**47**	**21**	**26**	**3103**	**112**	**4**	**2.17**

CCHA Rookie of the Year (1995) • NCAA Championship All-Tournament Team (1996, 1998) • CCHA First All-Star Team (1997) • NCAA West First All-American Team (1997) • CCHA Second All-Star Team (1998) • NCAA Championship Tournament MVP (1998) • Garry F. Longman Memorial Trophy (IHL – Rookie of the Year) (1999) • MBNA Roger Crozier Saving Grace Award (2001, 2003) • NHL Second All-Star Team (2003) • NHL Foundation Award (2006)

Played in NHL All-Star Game (2003, 2004, 2007)

Signed as a free agent by **Djurgarden** (Sweden), November 13, 2004. Signed as a free agent by **Chicago**, August 2, 2010.

VALIQUETTE, Steve (val-ih-KEHT, STEEV)

Goaltender. Catches left. 6'6", 210 lbs. Born, Etobicoke, Ont., August 20, 1977.
(Los Angeles' 8th choice, 190th overall, in 1996 Entry Draft).

			Regular Season								Playoffs						
Season	Club	League	GP	W	L	O/T	Mins	GA	SO	Avg	GP	W	L	Mins	GA	SO	Avg
1993-94	Burlington	OPJHL	30	....	....	....	1663	112	1	4.04	....	....	....	....	....	....	....
1994-95	Rayside-Balfour	NOJHA	2	0	2	0	89	12	0	8.09	....	....	....	....	....	....	....
	Smiths Falls Bears	CJHL	21	10	8	3	1275	75	0	3.53	....	....	....	....	....	....	....
	Sudbury Wolves	OHL	4	2	0	0	138	6	0	2.61	....	....	....	....	....	....	....
1995-96	Sudbury Wolves	OHL	39	13	16	2	1887	123	0	3.91	....	....	....	....	....	....	....
1996-97	Sudbury Wolves	OHL	*61	21	29	7	3311	232	1	4.20	....	....	....	....	....	....	....
	Dayton Bombers	ECHL	3	1	0	0	89	6	0	4.03	2	1	1	118	5	0	2.54
1997-98	Sudbury Wolves	OHL	14	5	7	1	807	50	0	3.72	....	....	....	....	....	....	....
	Erie Otters	OHL	28	16	7	3	1525	65	3	2.56	7	3	4	468	15	1	1.92
1998-99	Lowell	AHL	1	0	1	0	59	3	0	3.05	....	....	....	....	....	....	....
	Hampton Roads	ECHL	31	18	7	3	1713	84	1	2.94	2	0	1	60	7	0	7.00
99-2000	**NY Islanders**	**NHL**	**6**	**2**	**0**	**0**	**193**	**6**	**0**	**1.87**	....	....	....	....	....	....	....
	Lowell	AHL	14	8	5	0	727	36	0	2.97	....	....	....	....	....	....	....
	Providence Bruins	AHL	1	1	0	0	60	3	0	3.00	....	....	....	....	....	....	....
	Trenton Titans	ECHL	12	5	6	1	692	36	1	3.12	....	....	....	....	....	....	....
2000-01	Springfield Falcons	AHL	20	7	10	1	1066	54	0	3.04	....	....	....	....	....	....	....
2001-02	Bridgeport	AHL	20	10	5	1	1071	45	2	2.52	1	0	0	18	1	0	3.30
2002-03	Bridgeport	AHL	34	15	14	3	1962	86	2	2.63	4	3	1	253	9	0	2.13
2003-04	**Edmonton**	**NHL**	**1**	**0**	**0**	**0**	**14**	**2**	**0**	**8.57**	....	....	....	....	....	....	....
	Toronto	AHL	35	14	14	5	2064	89	2	2.59	....	....	....	....	....	....	....
	NY Rangers	**NHL**	**2**	**1**	**1**	**0**	**120**	**6**	**0**	**3.00**	....	....	....	....	....	....	....
	Hartford Wolf Pack	AHL	7	2	4	1	400	15	1	2.25	1	0	0	11	0	0	0.00
2004-05	Hartford Wolf Pack	AHL	35	19	11	1	1900	56	7	*1.77	2	1	1	118	4	0	2.03
2005-06	Yaroslavl	Russia	45	....	....	....	2734	89	4	1.95	8	....	....	458	23	0	3.01
2006-07	**NY Rangers**	**NHL**	**3**	**1**	**2**	**0**	**115**	**6**	**0**	**3.13**	....	....	....	....	....	....	....
	Hartford Wolf Pack	AHL	30	17	12	0	1694	66	2	2.34	....	....	....	....	....	....	....
2007-08	**NY Rangers**	**NHL**	**13**	**5**	**3**	**3**	**686**	**25**	**2**	**2.19**	....	....	....	....	....	....	....
2008-09	**NY Rangers**	**NHL**	**15**	**5**	**5**	**2**	**823**	**39**	**1**	**2.84**	**2**	**0**	**0**	**40**	**0**	**0**	**0.00**
2009-10	**NY Rangers**	**NHL**	**6**	**2**	**3**	**0**	**305**	**19**	**1**	**3.74**	....	....	....	....	....	....	....
	Hartford Wolf Pack	AHL	11	4	5	1	547	34	0	3.73	....	....	....	....	....	....	....
2010-11	CSKA Moscow	Rus-KHL	35	....	....	....	1897	93	2	2.94	....	....	....	....	....	....	....
	NHL Totals		**46**	**16**	**14**	**5**	**2256**	**103**	**4**	**2.74**	**2**	**0**	**0**	**40**	**0**	**0**	**0.00**

Harry "Hap" Holmes Memorial Trophy (AHL - fewest goals against) (2005) (shared with Jason LaBarbera)

Signed as a free agent by **NY Islanders**, August 18, 1998. Signed as a free agent by **Edmonton**, July 20, 2003. Claimed by **Florida** from **Edmonton** in Waiver Draft, October 3, 2003. Claimed on waivers by **Edmonton** from **Florida**, October 9, 2003. Traded to **NY Rangers** by **Edmonton** with Dwight Helminen and Edmonton's 2nd round compensatory choice (Dane Byers) in 2004 Entry Draft for Petr Nedved and Jussi Markkanen, March 3, 2004. Signed as a free agent by **Yaroslavl** (Russia), April 26, 2005. Signed as a free agent by **NY Rangers**, July 1, 2006. Signed as a free agent by **CSKA Moscow** (Russia-KHL), July 15, 2010.

VARLAMOV, Semyon (vahr-LA-mawv, sehm-YAWN) COL

Goaltender. Catches left. 6'2", 209 lbs. Born, Kuybyshev, USSR, April 27, 1988.
(Washington's 2nd choice, 23rd overall, in 2006 Entry Draft).

			Regular Season								Playoffs						
Season	Club	League	GP	W	L	O/T	Mins	GA	SO	Avg	GP	W	L	Mins	GA	SO	Avg
2004-05	Yaroslavl 2	Russia-3	8	....	....	....	369	15	1	2.43	....	....	....	....	....	....	....
2005-06	Yaroslavl 2	Russia-3	33	....	....	....	1782	60	8	2.02	....	....	....	....	....	....	....
2006-07	Yaroslavl 2	Russia-3	2	....	....	....	120	3	0	1.50	....	....	....	....	....	....	....
	Yaroslavl	Russia	33	....	....	....	1936	70	3	2.17	6	....	....	368	18	0	2.94
2007-08	Yaroslavl	Russia	44	....	....	....	2592	106	3	2.45	*16	....	....	*924	25	*5	1.62
2008-09	**Washington**	**NHL**	**6**	**4**	**0**	**1**	**329**	**13**	**0**	**2.37**	**13**	**7**	**6**	**759**	**32**	***2**	**2.53**
	Hershey Bears	AHL	27	19	7	1	1551	62	2	2.40	....	....	....	....	....	....	....
2009-10	**Washington**	**NHL**	**26**	**15**	**4**	**6**	**1527**	**65**	**2**	**2.55**	**6**	**3**	**3**	**349**	**14**	**0**	**2.41**
	Hershey Bears	AHL	3	3	0	0	185	6	0	1.95	....	....	....	....	....	....	....
	Russia	Olympics	DID NOT PLAY – SPARE GOALTENDER														
2010-11	**Washington**	**NHL**	**27**	**11**	**9**	**5**	**1560**	**58**	**2**	**2.23**	....	....	....	....	....	....	....
	Hershey Bears	AHL	3	2	1	0	179	10	0	3.36	....	....	....	....	....	....	....
	NHL Totals		**59**	**30**	**13**	**12**	**3416**	**136**	**4**	**2.39**	**19**	**10**	**9**	**1108**	**46**	**2**	**2.49**

Traded to **Colorado** by **Washington** for Colorado's 1st round choice in 2012 Entry Draft and Colorado's 2nd round choice in 2012 or 2013 Entry Draft, July 1, 2011.

VISENTIN, Mark (vih-SEHN-tihn, MAHRK) PHX

Goaltender. Catches left. 6'2", 201 lbs. Born, Hamilton, Ont., August 7, 1992.
(Phoenix's 2nd choice, 27th overall, in 2010 Entry Draft).

			Regular Season								Playoffs						
Season	Club	League	GP	W	L	O/T	Mins	GA	SO	Avg	GP	W	L	Mins	GA	SO	Avg
2007-08	Halton Hurricanes	Minor-ON	44	....	....	....	1980	98	3	2.22	....	....	....	....	....	....	....
2008-09	Niagara Ice Dogs	OHL	23	5	11	3	1099	78	2	4.26	....	....	....	....	....	....	....
2009-10	Niagara Ice Dogs	OHL	55	24	26	5	3209	160	7	2.99	5	1	4	305	18	0	3.54
2010-11	Niagara Ice Dogs	OHL	46	30	9	6	2714	114	4	2.52	14	9	5	823	35	1	2.55

OHL First All-Star Team (2011)

VOKOUN, Tomas (voh-KOON, TAW-mas) WSH

Goaltender. Catches right. 6', 195 lbs. Born, Karlovy Vary, Czech., July 2, 1976.
(Montreal's 11th choice, 226th overall, in 1994 Entry Draft).

			Regular Season								Playoffs						
Season	Club	League	GP	W	L	O/T	Mins	GA	SO	Avg	GP	W	L	Mins	GA	SO	Avg
1993-94	HC Kladno	CzRep	1	0	0	0	20	2	0	6.01	....	....	....	....	....	....	....
1994-95	HC Kladno	CzRep	26	....	....	....	1368	70	....	3.07	5	....	....	240	19	....	4.75
1995-96	Wheeling	ECHL	35	20	10	2	1912	117	0	3.67	7	4	3	436	19	0	2.61
	Fredericton	AHL	....	....	....	....	....	....	....	....	1	0	1	59	4	0	4.09
1996-97	**Montreal**	**NHL**	**1**	**0**	**0**	**0**	**20**	**4**	**0**	**12.00**	....	....	....	....	....	....	....
	Fredericton	AHL	47	12	26	7	2645	154	2	3.49	....	....	....	....	....	....	....
1997-98	Fredericton	AHL	31	13	13	2	1735	90	0	3.11	....	....	....	....	....	....	....
1998-99	**Nashville**	**NHL**	**37**	**12**	**18**	**4**	**1954**	**96**	**1**	**2.95**	....	....	....	....	....	....	....
	Milwaukee	IHL	9	3	2	4	539	22	1	2.45	2	0	2	149	8	0	3.22
99-2000	**Nashville**	**NHL**	**33**	**9**	**20**	**1**	**1879**	**87**	**1**	**2.78**	....	....	....	....	....	....	....
	Milwaukee	IHL	7	5	2	0	364	17	0	2.80	....	....	....	....	....	....	....
2000-01	**Nashville**	**NHL**	**37**	**13**	**17**	**5**	**2088**	**85**	**2**	**2.44**	....	....	....	....	....	....	....
2001-02	**Nashville**	**NHL**	**29**	**5**	**14**	**4**	**1471**	**66**	**2**	**2.69**	....	....	....	....	....	....	....
2002-03	**Nashville**	**NHL**	**69**	**25**	**31**	**11**	**3974**	**146**	**3**	**2.20**	....	....	....	....	....	....	....
2003-04	**Nashville**	**NHL**	**73**	**34**	**29**	**10**	**4221**	**178**	**3**	**2.53**	**6**	**2**	**4**	**356**	**12**	**1**	**2.02**
2004-05	Znojmo	CzRep	27	....	....	....	1599	69	3	2.59	....	....	....	....	....	....	....
	HIFK Helsinki	Finland	19	11	4	4	1149	35	2	1.83	4	0	3	205	12	0	3.51
2005-06	**Nashville**	**NHL**	**61**	**36**	**18**	**7**	**3601**	**160**	**4**	**2.67**	....	....	....	....	....	....	....
	Czech Republic	Olympics	7	3	4	0	342	14	1	2.46	....	....	....	....	....	....	....
2006-07	**Nashville**	**NHL**	**44**	**27**	**12**	**4**	**2601**	**104**	**5**	**2.40**	**5**	**1**	**4**	**324**	**16**	**0**	**2.96**
2007-08	**Florida**	**NHL**	**69**	**30**	**29**	**8**	**4031**	**180**	**4**	**2.68**	....	....	....	....	....	....	....
2008-09	**Florida**	**NHL**	**59**	**26**	**23**	**6**	**3324**	**138**	**6**	**2.49**	....	....	....	....	....	....	....
2009-10	**Florida**	**NHL**	**63**	**23**	**28**	**11**	**3695**	**157**	**7**	**2.55**	....	....	....	....	....	....	....
	Czech Republic	Olympics	5	3	2	0	304	9	0	1.78	....	....	....	....	....	....	....
2010-11	**Florida**	**NHL**	**57**	**22**	**28**	**5**	**3224**	**137**	**6**	**2.55**	....	....	....	....	....	....	....
	NHL Totals		**632**	**262**	**267**	**76**	**36083**	**1538**	**44**	**2.56**	**11**	**3**	**8**	**680**	**28**	**1**	**2.47**

Played in NHL All-Star Game (2004, 2008)

Claimed by **Nashville** from **Montreal** in Expansion Draft, June 26, 1998. Signed as a free agent by **Znojmo** (CzRep), September 6, 2004. Signed as a free agent by **HIFK Helsinki** (Finland), December 20, 2004. Traded to **Florida** by **Nashville** for Detroit's 2nd round choice (previously acquired, Nashville selected Nick Spaling) in 2007 Entry Draft and Florida's 1st (later traded to NY Islanders – NY Islanders selected Joshua Bailey) and 2nd (later traded to NY Islanders – NY Islanders selected Aaron Ness) round choices in 2008 Entry Draft, June 22, 2007. Signed as a free agent by **Washington**, July 2, 2011.

VOLDEN, Lars (VOHL-duhn, LARZ) BOS

Goaltender. Catches left. 6'3", 198 lbs. Born, Oslo, Norway, July 26, 1992.
(Boston's 6th choice, 181st overall, in 2011 Entry Draft).

			Regular Season								Playoffs						
Season	Club	League	GP	W	L	O/T	Mins	GA	SO	Avg	GP	W	L	Mins	GA	SO	Avg
2007-08	Manglerud Jr.	Norway-Jr.	11	....	....	....	527	15	0	1.71	3	....	....	180	9	0	3.01
2008-09	Stavanger Oilers 2	Norway-2	17	....	....	....	948	37	1	2.34	....	....	....	....	....	....	....
2009-10	Stavanger Oilers 2	Norway-2	15	....	....	....	899	33	3	2.20	....	....	....	....	....	....	....
	Stavanger Oilers	Norway	10	4	5	0	479	25	0	3.13	1	0	0	17	0	0	0.00
2010-11	Blues Espoo Jr.	Fin-Jr.	24	14	9	0	1435	66	0	2.76	13	8	5	789	33	0	2.51

WARD, Cam (WOHRD, KAM) CAR

Goaltender. Catches left. 6'1", 185 lbs. Born, Saskatoon, Sask., February 29, 1984.
(Carolina's 1st choice, 25th overall, in 2002 Entry Draft).

			Regular Season								Playoffs						
Season	Club	League	GP	W	L	O/T	Mins	GA	SO	Avg	GP	W	L	Mins	GA	SO	Avg
1998-99	Sherwood Park	Minor-AB	24	13	7	4	1403	85	0	3.64	....	....	....	....	....	....	....
99-2000	Sherwood Park	AMHL	20	9	5	1	1194	71	0	3.57	7	4	3	262	22	0	3.57
2000-01	Sherwood Park	AMHL	25	14	6	3	1449	70	0	2.90	....	....	....	....	....	....	....
	Red Deer Rebels	WHL	1	1	0	0	60	0	1	0.00	....	....	....	....	....	....	....
2001-02	Red Deer Rebels	WHL	46	30	11	4	2695	102	1	*2.27	*23	14	9	*1503	52	*2	2.08
2002-03	Red Deer Rebels	WHL	57	*40	13	2	3367	118	5	2.10	*23	14	9	*1407	49	3	2.09
2003-04	Red Deer Rebels	WHL	56	31	16	8	3338	114	4	2.05	19	10	9	1199	37	3	1.85
2004-05	Lowell	AHL	50	27	17	3	2829	94	6	1.99	11	5	6	664	28	2	2.53
2005-06 ♦	**Carolina**	**NHL**	**28**	**14**	**8**	**2**	**1484**	**91**	**0**	**3.68**	***23**	***15**	**8**	***1320**	**47**	**2**	**2.14**
	Lowell	AHL	2	0	2	0	118	5	0	2.54	....	....	....	....	....	....	....
2006-07	**Carolina**	**NHL**	**60**	**30**	**21**	**6**	**3422**	**167**	**2**	**2.93**	....	....	....	....	....	....	....
2007-08	**Carolina**	**NHL**	**69**	**37**	**25**	**5**	**3930**	**180**	**4**	**2.75**	....	....	....	....	....	....	....
2008-09	**Carolina**	**NHL**	**68**	**39**	**23**	**5**	**3928**	**160**	**6**	**2.44**	**18**	**8**	**10**	**1101**	**49**	***2**	**2.67**
2009-10	**Carolina**	**NHL**	**47**	**18**	**23**	**5**	**2651**	**119**	**0**	**2.69**	....	....	....	....	....	....	....
2010-11	**Carolina**	**NHL**	***74**	**37**	**26**	**10**	***4318**	**184**	**4**	**2.56**	....	....	....	....	....	....	....
	NHL Totals		**346**	**175**	**126**	**33**	**19733**	**901**	**16**	**2.74**	**41**	**23**	**18**	**2421**	**96**	**4**	**2.38**

WHL East First All-Star Team (2002, 2004) • Canadian Major Junior Second All-Star Team (2002) • WHL East Second All-Star Team (2003) • WHL Goaltender of the Year (2002, 2004) • WHL Player of the Year (2004) • Canadian Major Junior First All-Star Team (2004) • Canadian Major Junior Goaltender of the Year (2004) • AHL All-Rookie Team (2005) • Conn Smythe Trophy (2006)

Played in NHL All-Star Game (2011)

WEDGEWOOD, Scott (WEHJ-wud, SKAWT) N.J.

Goaltender. Catches left. 6'1", 190 lbs. Born, Etobicoke, Ont., August 14, 1992.
(New Jersey's 2nd choice, 84th overall, in 2010 Entry Draft).

			Regular Season								Playoffs						
Season	Club	League	GP	W	L	O/T	Mins	GA	SO	Avg	GP	W	L	Mins	GA	SO	Avg
2007-08	Miss. Senators	GTHL	29	....	....	....	1305	63	2	2.17	....	....	....	....	....	....	....
2008-09	Plymouth Whalers	OHL	6	0	2	0	158	12	0	4.56	3	0	1	26	2	0	4.62
2009-10	Plymouth Whalers	OHL	18	5	9	0	938	51	2	3.26	4	1	1	116	4	0	2.07
2010-11	Plymouth Whalers	OHL	55	28	18	2	3046	152	2	2.99	10	4	6	606	33	0	3.27

WEIMAN, Tyler (WIGH-muhn, TIGH-luhr)

Goaltender. Catches left. 5'11", 180 lbs. Born, Saskatoon, Sask., June 5, 1984.
(Colorado's 6th choice, 164th overall, in 2002 Entry Draft).

			Regular Season								Playoffs						
Season	Club	League	GP	W	L	O/T	Mins	GA	SO	Avg	GP	W	L	Mins	GA	SO	Avg
99-2000	Ft. Saskatchewan	AMBHL	21	15	4	2	1239	60	0	2.91	....	....	....	....	....	....	....
2000-01	Tri-City Americans	WHL	44	10	25	4	2466	155	0	3.77	....	....	....	....	....	....	....
2001-02	Tri-City Americans	WHL	47	18	17	6	2494	149	2	3.58	5	1	4	301	14	0	2.79
2002-03	Tri-City Americans	WHL	55	16	35	2	3129	211	1	4.05	....	....	....	....	....	....	....
2003-04	Tri-City Americans	WHL	54	23	21	7	3023	136	1	2.70	5	1	2	233	11	0	2.83
2004-05	Colorado Eagles	CHL	44	*33	6	5	2630	79	*8	*1.80	*13	*8	4	*744	32	1	2.58
2005-06	Lowell	AHL	14	6	6	1	844	36	0	2.56	....	....	....	....	....	....	....
	San Diego Gulls	ECHL	32	14	12	3	1797	84	1	2.81	4	0	4	251	15	0	3.59
2006-07	Albany River Rats	AHL	54	27	22	3	3047	152	2	2.99	5	1	4	294	17	0	3.47
2007-08	**Colorado**	**NHL**	**1**	**0**	**0**	**0**	**16**	**0**	**0**	**0.00**	....	....	....	....	....	....	....
	Lake Erie Monsters	AHL	31	9	19	1	1769	98	2	3.32	....	....	....	....	....	....	....
2008-09	Lake Erie Monsters	AHL	44	21	20	2	2559	105	*8	2.46	....	....	....	....	....	....	....
2009-10	Lake Erie Monsters	AHL	43	21	18	3	2538	105	3	2.48	....	....	....	....	....	....	....
2010-11	Manitoba Moose	AHL	29	15	10	2	1717	75	1	2.62	4	1	2	160	8	0	3.01
	NHL Totals		**1**	**0**	**0**	**0**	**16**	**0**	**0**	**0.00**	....	....	....	....	....	....	....

Signed as a free agent by **Vancouver**, July 12, 2010.

WESLOSKY, Jase (wehs-LAWZ-kee, JAYS) NYI

Goaltender. Catches left. 6'2", 170 lbs. Born, St. Albert, Alta., August 14, 1988.
(NY Islanders' 5th choice, 108th overall, in 2006 Entry Draft).

			Regular Season								Playoffs						
Season	Club	League	GP	W	L	O/T	Mins	GA	SO	Avg	GP	W	L	Mins	GA	SO	Avg
2004-05	St. Albert Blues	EMHA	....	13	3	2	1043	38	....	2.19	....	....	....	....	....	....	....
2005-06	Sherwood Park	AJHL	41	9	18	8	2123	110	2	3.11	....	....	....	....	....	....	....
2006-07	St. Cloud State	WCHA	6	5	1	0	359	16	1	2.67	....	....	....	....	....	....	....
2007-08	St. Cloud State	WCHA	33	16	13	2	1901	67	3	2.11	....	....	....	....	....	....	....
2008-09	St. Cloud State	WCHA	33	16	13	2	1889	85	2	2.70	....	....	....	....	....	....	....
2009-10	Bemidji State	CHA	DID NOT PLAY – TRANSFERRED COLLEGES														
2010-11	Idaho Steelheads	ECHL	20	7	6	3	1102	54	0	2.94	....	....	....	....	....	....	....
	Ontario Reign	ECHL	4	2	1	0	210	7	0	2.00	....	....	....	....	....	....	....

• Ruled academically ineligible by **St. Cloud State**, August 25, 2009.

WILCOX, Adam (WIHL-cawx, A-duhm) T.B.

Goaltender. Catches left. 6', 175 lbs. Born, South St. Paul, MN, November 26, 1992.
(Tampa Bay's 4th choice, 178th overall, in 2011 Entry Draft).

			Regular Season								Playoffs						
Season	Club	League	GP	W	L	O/T	Mins	GA	SO	Avg	GP	W	L	Mins	GA	SO	Avg
2009-10	South St. Paul	High-MN	23	11	11	0	1119	73	0	3.33	2	1	1	102	8	0	4.00
2010-11	Green Bay	USHL	24	16	6	1	1420	52	1	2.20	2	1	0	88	1	0	0.68

• Signed Letter of Intent to attend **University of Minnesota** (WCHA) in fall of 2011.

YORK, Allen (YOHRK, AL-ihn) CBJ

Goaltender. Catches left. 6'4", 190 lbs. Born, Wetaskiwin, Alta., June 17, 1989.
(Columbus' 6th choice, 158th overall, in 2007 Entry Draft).

			Regular Season								Playoffs						
Season	Club	League	GP	W	L	O/T	Mins	GA	SO	Avg	GP	W	L	Mins	GA	SO	Avg
2006-07	Camrose Kodiaks	AJHL	32	23	4	0	1661	60	2	2.17	22	16	6	1391	46	4	1.98
2007-08	Camrose Kodiaks	AJHL	....	24	5	3	2005	75	3	2.24	....	....	....	....	....	....	....
2008-09	RPI Engineers	ECAC	16	5	10	0	913	46	1	3.02	....	....	....	....	....	....	....
2009-10	RPI Engineers	ECAC	33	14	12	4	1935	82	1	2.54	....	....	....	....	....	....	....
2010-11	RPI Engineers	ECAC	34	18	11	4	2051	74	2	2.17	....	....	....	....	....	....	....
	Springfield Falcons	AHL	4	3	1	0	206	7	1	2.04	....	....	....	....	....	....	....

ECAC Second All-Star Team (2010)

ZATKOFF, Jeff (ZAT-kawf, JEHF) L.A.

Goaltender. Catches left. 6'1", 170 lbs. Born, Detroit, MI, June 9, 1987.
(Los Angeles' 4th choice, 74th overall, in 2006 Entry Draft).

			Regular Season								Playoffs						
Season	Club	League	GP	W	L	O/T	Mins	GA	SO	Avg	GP	W	L	Mins	GA	SO	Avg
2004-05	Sioux City	USHL	24	13	6	3	1271	54	1	2.55	2	0	0	68	10	0	8.88
2005-06	Miami U.	CCHA	20	14	5	1	1217	41	3	2.02	....	....	....	....	....	....	....
2006-07	Miami U.	CCHA	26	14	8	3	1542	58	1	2.26	....	....	....	....	....	....	....
2007-08	Miami U.	CCHA	36	27	8	1	2161	62	3	*1.72	....	....	....	....	....	....	....
2008-09	Manchester	AHL	3	1	2	0	182	7	0	2.31	....	....	....	....	....	....	....
	Ontario Reign	ECHL	37	17	15	3	2164	107	1	2.97	7	3	4	418	26	0	3.73
2009-10	Manchester	AHL	22	10	9	0	1170	57	2	2.92	....	....	....	....	....	....	....
2010-11	Manchester	AHL	45	20	17	5	2508	112	3	2.68	5	1	3	253	16	0	3.80

CCHA Second All-Star Team (2008)

Late Additions to Player Register

FREE AGENT SIGNINGS

HANNAN, Scott   *(see page 423 for data panel)*   **CGY**
Defense   Signed as a free agent by **Calgary**, August 13, 2011.

LeNEVEU, David   *(see page 597 for data panel)*   **EDM**
Goaltender   Signed as a free agent by **Oklahome City** (AHL), August 12, 2011.

WOYWITKA, Jeff   *(see page 576 for data panel)*   **MTL**
Defense   Signed as a free agent by **Montreal**, August 15, 2011.

DECEASED

RYPIEN, Rick   *(see page 525 for data panel)*   **WPG**
Died August 15, 2011.

HOCKEY OPERATIONS/FRONT OFFICE ADDITIONS

GRANATO, Don   **USA HOCKEY**
Named by **USA Hockey** as Co-Head Coach, US National Team Development Program, August 15, 2011.

TAYLOR, Karl   **VAN**
Hired by **Vancouver** as Assistant Coach, Chicago Wolves (AHL), August 11, 2011.

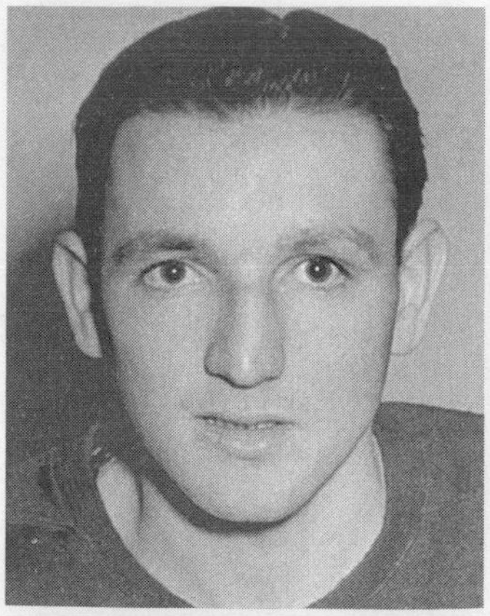
Sid Abel

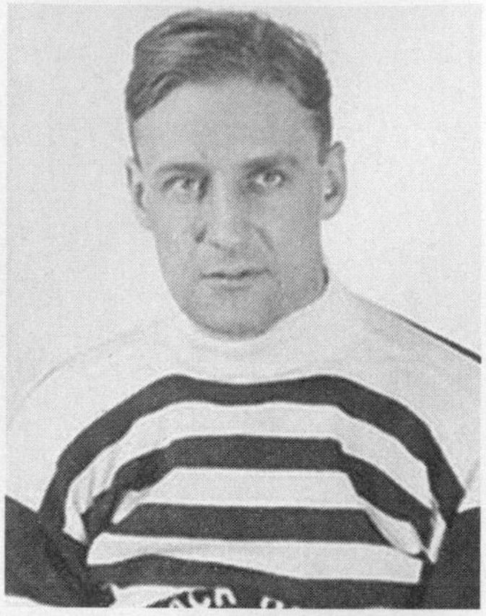
Stew Adams

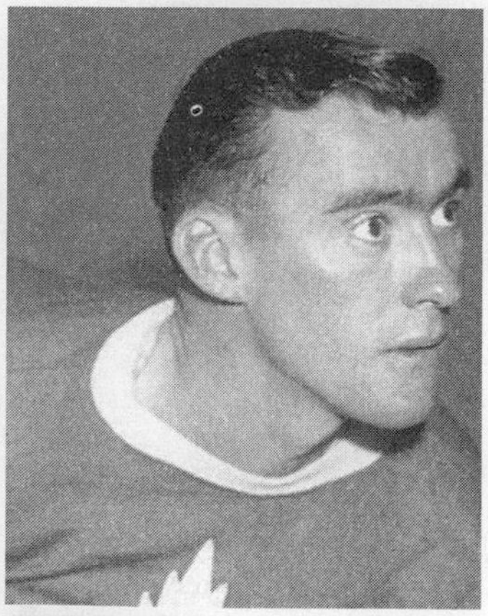
Murray Armstrong

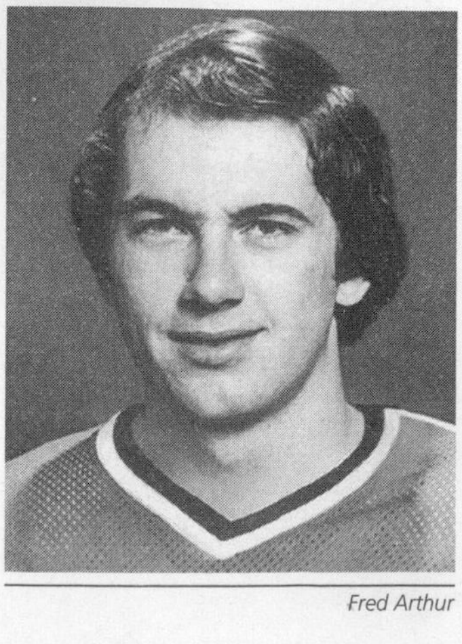
Fred Arthur

Retired NHL Player Index

Abbreviations: Teams/Cities: – **Ana**. – Anaheim; **Atl**. – Atlanta; **Bos**. – Boston; **Bro**. – Brooklyn; **Buf**. – Buffalo; **Cgy**. – Calgary; **Cal**. – California; **Car**. – Carolina; **Chi**. – Chicago; **Cle**. – Cleveland; **Col**. – Colorado; **CBJ** – Columbus; **Dal**. – Dallas; **Det**. – Detroit; **Edm**. – Edmonton; **Fla**. – Florida; **Ham**. – Hamilton; **Hfd**. – Hartford; **K.C**. – Kansas City; **L.A**. – Los Angeles; **Min**. – Minnesota; **Mtl**. – Montreal; **Mtl.M**. – Montreal Maroons; **Mtl.W**. – Montreal Wanderers; **Nsh**. – Nashville; **N.J**. – New Jersey; **NYA** – NY Americans; **NYI** – NY Islanders; **NYR** – New York Rangers; **Oak**. – Oakland; **Ott**. – Ottawa; **Phi**. – Philadelphia; **Phx**. – Phoenix; **Pit**. – Pittsburgh; **Que**. – Quebec; **St.L**. – St. Louis; **S.J**. – San Jose; **T.B**. – Tampa Bay; **Tor**. – Toronto; **Van**. – Vancouver; **Wsh**. – Washington; **Wpg**. – Winnipeg

A – assists; **G** – goals; **GP** – games played; **PIM** – penalties in minutes; **TP** – total points.
• – deceased. Assists not recorded during 1917-18 season ‡ – Remains active in other leagues.

NHL Seasons – A player or goaltender who does not play in a regular season but who does appear in that year's playoffs is credited with an NHL Season in this Index. Total seasons are rounded off to the nearest full season.

			Regular Schedule					Playoffs							
Name	NHL Teams	NHL Seasons	GP	G	A	TP	PIM	GP	G	A	TP	PIM	NHL Cup Wins	First NHL Season	Last NHL Season
A															
Aalto, Antti	Ana.	4	151	11	17	28	52	4	0	0	0	2	....	1997-98	2000-01
Abbott, Reg	Mtl.	1	3	0	0	0	0	....	....	....	....	....	....	1952-53	1952-53
• Abel, Clarence	NYR, Chi.	8	333	19	18	37	359	38	1	1	2	58	2	1926-27	1933-34
Abel, Gerry	Det.	1	1	0	0	0	0	....	....	....	....	....	....	1966-67	1966-67
• Abel, Sid	Det., Chi.	14	612	189	283	472	376	97	28	30	58	79	3	1938-39	1953-54
Abgrall, Dennis	L.A.	1	13	0	2	2	4	....	....	....	....	....	....	1975-76	1975-76
‡ Abid, Ramzi	Phx., Pit., Atl., Nsh.	4	68	14	16	30	78	2	0	0	0	0	....	2002-03	2006-07
Abrahamsson, Thommy	Hfd.	1	32	6	11	17	16	....	....	....	....	....	....	1980-81	1980-81
Achtymichuk, Gene	Mtl., Det.	4	32	3	5	8	2	....	....	....	....	....	....	1951-52	1958-59
Acomb, Doug	Tor.	1	2	0	1	1	0	....	....	....	....	....	....	1969-70	1969-70
Acton, Keith	Mtl., Min., Edm., Phi., Wsh., NYI	15	1023	226	358	584	1172	66	12	21	33	88	1	1979-80	1993-94
• Adam, Douglas	NYR	1	4	0	1	1	0	....	....	....	....	....	....	1949-50	1949-50
Adam, Russ	Tor.	1	8	1	2	3	11	....	....	....	....	....	....	1982-83	1982-83
‡ Adams, Bryan	Atl.	2	11	0	1	1	2	....	....	....	....	....	....	1999-00	2000-01
Adams, Greg	Phi., Hfd., Wsh., Edm., Van., Que., Det.	10	545	84	143	227	1173	43	2	11	13	153	....	1980-81	1989-90
Adams, Greg	N.J., Van., Dal., Phx., Fla.	17	1056	355	388	743	326	81	20	22	42	16	....	1984-85	2000-01
• Adams, Jack	Tor., Ott.	7	173	83	32	115	366	10	2	0	2	13	2	1917-18	1926-27
Adams, John	Mtl.	1	42	6	12	18	11	3	0	0	0	0	....	1940-41	1940-41
Adams, Kevyn	Tor., CBJ, Fla., Car., Phx., Chi.	10	540	59	77	136	317	67	2	2	4	39	1	1997-98	2007-08
• Adams, Stew	Chi., Tor.	4	95	9	26	35	60	11	3	3	6	14	....	1929-30	1932-33
Adduono, Rick	Bos., Atl.	2	4	0	0	0	2	....	....	....	....	....	....	1975-76	1979-80
Afanasenkov, Dmitry	T.B., Phi.	5	227	27	27	54	52	28	1	3	4	8	1	2000-01	2006-07
Affleck, Bruce	St.L., Van., NYI	7	280	14	66	80	86	8	0	0	0	0	....	1974-75	1983-84
Agnew, Jim	Van., Hfd.	6	81	0	1	1	257	4	0	0	0	6	....	1986-87	1992-93
Ahern, Fred	Cal., Cle., Col.	4	146	31	30	61	130	2	0	1	1	2	....	1974-75	1977-78
• Ahlin, Rudy	Chi.	1	1	0	0	0	0	....	....	....	....	....	....	1937-38	1937-38
Ahola, Peter	L.A., Pit., S.J., Cgy.	3	123	10	17	27	137	6	0	0	0	2	....	1991-92	1993-94
Ahrens, Chris	Min.	6	52	0	3	3	84	1	0	0	0	0	....	1972-73	1977-78
• Ailsby, Lloyd	NYR	1	3	0	0	0	2	....	....	....	....	....	....	1951-52	1951-52
Aitken, Brad	Pit., Edm.	2	14	1	3	4	25	....	....	....	....	....	....	1987-88	1990-91
Aitken, Johnathan	Bos., Chi.	2	44	0	1	1	70	....	....	....	....	....	....	1999-00	2003-04
Aivazoff, Micah	Det., Edm., NYI	3	92	4	6	10	46	....	....	....	....	....	....	1993-94	1995-96
Alatalo, Mika	Phx.	2	152	17	29	46	58	5	0	0	0	2	....	1999-00	2000-01
Albelin, Tommy	Que., N.J., Cgy.	18	952	44	211	255	417	81	7	15	22	22	2	1987-88	2005-06
• Albright, Clint	NYR	1	59	14	5	19	19	....	....	....	....	....	....	1948-49	1948-49
Aldcorn, Gary	Tor., Det., Bos.	5	226	41	56	97	78	6	1	2	3	4	....	1956-57	1960-61
Aldridge, Keith	Dal.	1	4	0	0	0	0	....	....	....	....	....	....	1999-00	1999-00
Alexander, Claire	Tor., Van.	4	155	18	47	65	36	16	2	4	6	4	....	1974-75	1977-78
• Alexandre, Art	Mtl.	2	11	0	2	2	8	4	0	0	0	0	....	1931-32	1932-33
Alexeev, Nikita	T.B., Chi.	3	159	20	17	37	28	11	1	0	1	0	....	2001-02	2006-07
Allan, Jeff	Cle.	1	4	0	0	0	2	....	....	....	....	....	....	1977-78	1977-78
Allen, Bobby	Edm., Bos.	3	51	0	3	3	12	....	....	....	....	....	....	2002-03	2007-08
Allen, Chris	Fla.	2	2	0	0	0	2	....	....	....	....	....	....	1997-98	1998-99
• Allen, George	NYR, Chi., Mtl.	8	339	82	115	197	179	41	9	10	19	32	....	1938-39	1946-47
Allen, Keith	Det.	2	28	0	4	4	8	5	0	0	0	0	1	1953-54	1954-55
Allen, Peter	Pit.	1	8	0	0	0	8	....	....	....	....	....	....	1995-96	1995-96
• Allen, Viv	NYA	1	6	0	1	1	0	....	....	....	....	....	....	1940-41	1940-41
Alley, Steve	Hfd.	2	15	3	3	6	11	3	0	1	1	0	....	1979-80	1980-81
Allison, Dave	Mtl.	1	3	0	0	0	12	....	....	....	....	....	....	1983-84	1983-84
Allison, Jamie	Cgy., Chi., CBJ, Nsh., Fla.	10	372	7	23	30	639	....	....	....	....	....	....	1994-95	2005-06
Allison, Jason	Wsh., Bos., L.A., Tor.	12	552	154	331	485	441	25	7	18	25	14	....	1993-94	2005-06
Allison, Mike	NYR, Tor., L.A.	10	499	102	166	268	630	82	9	17	26	135	....	1980-81	1989-90
Allison, Ray	Hfd., Phi.	7	238	64	93	157	223	12	2	3	5	20	....	1979-80	1986-87
• Allum, Bill	NYR	1	1	0	1	1	0	....	....	....	....	....	....	1940-41	1940-41
• Amadio, Dave	Det., L.A.	3	125	5	11	16	163	16	1	2	3	18	....	1957-58	1968-69
Ambroziak, Peter	Buf.	1	12	0	1	1	0	....	....	....	....	....	....	1994-95	1994-95
Amodeo, Mike	Wpg.	1	19	0	0	0	2	....	....	....	....	....	....	1979-80	1979-80
Amonte, Tony	NYR, Chi., Phx., Phi., Cgy.	16	1174	416	484	900	752	99	22	33	55	56	....	1990-91	2006-07
• Anderson, Bill	Bos.	1	....	....	....	....	....	1	0	0	0	0	....	1942-43	1942-43
Anderson, Dale	Det.	1	13	0	0	0	6	2	0	0	0	0	....	1956-57	1956-57
Anderson, Doug	Mtl.	1	....	....	....	....	....	2	0	0	0	0	....	1952-53	1952-53
Anderson, Earl	Det., Bos.	3	109	19	19	38	22	5	0	1	1	0	....	1974-75	1976-77
Anderson, Glenn	Edm., Tor., NYR, St.L.	16	1129	498	601	1099	1120	225	93	121	214	442	6	1980-81	1995-96
Anderson, Jim	L.A.	1	7	1	2	3	2	....	....	....	....	....	....	1967-68	1967-68
Anderson, John	Tor., Que., Hfd.	12	814	282	349	631	263	37	9	18	27	2	....	1977-78	1988-89
Anderson, Murray	Wsh.	1	40	0	1	1	68	....	....	....	....	....	....	1974-75	1974-75
Anderson, Perry	St.L., N.J., S.J.	10	400	50	59	109	1051	36	2	1	3	161	....	1981-82	1991-92
Anderson, Ron	Det., L.A., St.L., Buf.	5	251	28	30	58	146	5	0	0	0	4	....	1967-68	1971-72
Anderson, Ron	Wsh.	1	28	9	7	16	8	....	....	....	....	....	....	1974-75	1974-75
Anderson, Russ	Pit., Hfd., L.A.	9	519	22	99	121	1086	10	0	3	3	28	....	1976-77	1984-85
Anderson, Shawn	Buf., Que., Wsh., Phi.	8	255	11	51	62	117	19	1	1	2	16	....	1986-87	1994-95
• Anderson, Tom	Det., NYA, Bro.	8	319	62	127	189	180	16	2	7	9	8	....	1934-35	1941-42
Andersson, Erik	Cgy.	1	12	2	1	3	8	....	....	....	....	....	....	1997-98	1997-98
Andersson, Kent-Erik	Min., NYR	7	456	72	103	175	78	50	4	11	15	4	....	1977-78	1983-84
Andersson, Mikael	Buf., Hfd., T.B., Phi., NYI	15	761	95	169	264	134	25	2	7	9	10	....	1985-86	1999-00
‡ Andersson, Niklas	Que., NYI, S.J., Nsh., Cgy.	6	164	29	53	82	85	....	....	....	....	....	....	1992-93	2000-01
Andersson, Peter	Wsh., Que.	3	172	10	41	51	81	7	0	2	2	2	....	1983-84	1985-86
Andersson, Peter	NYR, Fla.	2	47	6	13	19	20	....	....	....	....	....	....	1992-93	1993-94
Andrascik, Steve	NYR	1	....	....	....	....	....	1	0	0	0	0	....	1971-72	1971-72
Andrea, Paul	NYR, Pit., Cal., Buf.	4	150	31	49	80	10	....	....	....	....	....	....	1965-66	1970-71
• Andrews, Lloyd	Tor.	4	53	8	5	13	10	2	0	0	0	0	1	1921-22	1924-25
Andreychuk, Dave	Buf., Tor., N.J., Bos., Col., T.B.	23	1639	640	698	1338	1125	162	43	54	97	162	1	1982-83	2005-06
Andrievski, Alexander	Chi.	1	1	0	0	0	0	....	....	....	....	....	....	1992-93	1992-93
Andruff, Ron	Mtl., Col.	5	153	19	36	55	54	2	0	0	0	0	....	1974-75	1978-79
Andrusak, Greg	Pit., Tor.	5	28	0	6	6	16	15	1	0	1	8	....	1993-94	1999-00
Angelstad, Mel	Wsh.	1	2	0	0	0	2	....	....	....	....	....	....	2003-04	2003-04
Angotti, Lou	NYR, Chi., Phi., Pit., St.L.	10	653	103	186	289	228	65	8	8	16	17	....	1964-65	1973-74
Anholt, Darrel	Chi.	1	1	0	0	0	0	....	....	....	....	....	....	1983-84	1983-84
• Anslow, Hub	NYR	1	2	0	0	0	0	....	....	....	....	....	....	1947-48	1947-48
Antonovich, Mike	Min., Hfd., N.J.	5	87	10	15	25	37	....	....	....	....	....	....	1975-76	1983-84
Antoski, Shawn	Van., Phi., Pit., Ana.	8	183	3	5	8	599	36	1	3	4	74	....	1990-91	1997-98
• Apps, Syl	Tor.	10	423	201	231	432	56	69	25	29	54	8	3	1936-37	1947-48
Apps, Syl	NYR, Pit., L.A.	10	727	183	423	606	311	23	5	5	10	23	....	1970-71	1979-80
Arbour, Al	Det., Chi., Tor., St.L.	16	626	12	58	70	617	86	1	8	9	92	4	1953-54	1970-71
• Arbour, Amos	Mtl., Ham., Tor.	6	113	52	20	72	77	....	....	....	....	....	....	1918-19	1923-24
• Arbour, Jack	Det., Tor.	2	47	5	1	6	56	....	....	....	....	....	....	1926-27	1928-29
Arbour, John	Bos., Pit., Van., St.L.	5	106	1	9	10	149	5	0	0	0	0	....	1965-66	1971-72
• Arbour, Ty	Pit., Chi.	5	207	28	28	56	112	11	2	0	2	6	....	1926-27	1930-31
Archambault, Michel	Chi.	1	3	0	0	0	0	....	....	....	....	....	....	1976-77	1976-77
Archibald, Dave	Min., NYR, Ott., NYI	8	323	57	67	124	139	5	0	1	1	0	....	1987-88	1996-97
Archibald, Jim	Min.	3	16	1	2	3	45	....	....	....	....	....	....	1984-85	1986-87

			Regular Schedule					Playoffs					NHL	First	Last
Name	NHL Teams	NHL Seasons	GP	G	A	TP	PIM	GP	G	A	TP	PIM	Cup Wins	NHL Season	NHL Season
Areshenkoff, Ron	Edm.	1	4	0	0	0	0	....	....	....	....	....	....	1979-80	1979-80
Arkhipov, Denis	Nsh., Chi.	5	352	56	82	138	128	....	....	....	....	....	....	2000-01	2006-07
Armstrong, Bill	Phi.	1	1	0	1	1	0	....	....	....	....	....	....	1990-91	1990-91
• Armstrong, Bob	Bos.	12	542	13	86	99	671	42	1	7	8	28	....	1950-51	1961-62
Armstrong, Chris	Min., Ana.	2	7	0	1	1	0	....	....	....	....	....	....	2000-01	2003-04
Armstrong, Derek	NYI, Ott., NYR, L.A., St.L.	14	477	72	149	221	355	....	....	....	....	....	....	1993-94	2009-10
Armstrong, George	Tor.	21	1187	296	417	713	721	110	26	34	60	52	4	1949-50	1970-71
• Armstrong, Murray	Tor., NYA, Bro., Det.	8	270	67	121	188	72	30	4	6	10	2	....	1937-38	1945-46
• Armstrong, Norm	Tor.	1	7	1	1	2	2	....	....	....	....	....	....	1962-63	1962-63
Armstrong, Tim	Tor.	1	11	1	0	1	6	....	....	....	....	....	....	1988-89	1988-89
Arnason, Chuck	Mtl., Atl., Pit., K.C., Col., Cle., Min., Wsh.	8	401	109	90	199	122	9	2	4	6	4	....	1971-72	1978-79
‡ Arnason, Tyler	Chi., Ott., Col.	7	487	88	157	245	140	13	2	3	5	2	....	2001-02	2008-09
Arniel, Scott	Wpg., Buf., Bos.	11	730	149	189	338	599	34	3	3	6	39	....	1981-82	1991-92
Arthur, Fred	Hfd., Phi.	3	80	1	8	9	49	4	0	0	0	2	....	1980-81	1982-83
• Arundel, John	Tor.	1	3	0	0	0	9	....	....	....	....	....	....	1949-50	1949-50
Arvedson, Magnus	Ott., Van.	7	434	100	125	225	241	52	3	8	11	34	....	1997-98	2003-04
• Ashbee, Barry	Bos., Phi.	5	284	15	70	85	291	17	0	4	4	22	1	1965-66	1973-74
• Ashby, Don	Tor., Col., Edm.	6	188	40	56	96	40	12	1	0	1	4	....	1975-76	1980-81
Ashton, Brent	Van., Col., N.J., Min., Que., Det., Wpg., Bos., Cgy.	14	998	284	345	629	635	85	24	25	49	70	....	1979-80	1992-93
Ashworth, Frank	Chi.	1	18	5	4	9	2	....	....	....	....	....	....	1946-47	1946-47
• Asmundson, Oscar	NYR, Det., St.L., NYA, Mtl.	5	111	11	23	34	30	9	0	2	2	4	1	1932-33	1937-38
Astashenko, Kaspars	T.B.	2	23	1	2	3	8	....	....	....	....	....	....	1999-00	2000-01
Astley, Mark	Buf.	3	75	4	19	23	92	2	0	0	0	0	....	1993-94	1995-96
• Atanas, Walt	NYR	1	49	13	8	21	40	....	....	....	....	....	....	1944-45	1944-45
Atcheynum, Blair	Ott., St.L., Nsh., Chi.	5	196	27	33	60	36	23	1	3	4	8	....	1992-93	2000-01
• Atkinson, Steve	Bos., Buf., Wsh.	6	302	60	51	111	104	1	0	0	0	0	....	1968-69	1974-75
Attwell, Bob	Col.	2	22	1	5	6	0	....	....	....	....	....	....	1979-80	1980-81
Attwell, Ron	St.L., NYR	1	22	1	7	8	8	....	....	....	....	....	....	1967-68	1967-68
Aubin, Norm	Tor.	2	69	18	13	31	30	1	0	0	0	0	....	1981-82	1982-83
‡ Aubin, Serge	Col., CBJ, Atl.	7	374	44	64	108	361	22	0	1	1	10	....	1998-99	2005-06
Aubry, Pierre	Que., Det.	5	202	24	26	50	133	20	1	1	2	32	....	1980-81	1984-85
Aubuchon, Ossie	Bos., NYR	2	50	20	12	32	4	6	1	0	1	0	....	1942-43	1943-44
Audet, Philippe	Det.	1	4	0	0	0	0	....	....	....	....	....	....	1998-99	1998-99
Audette, Donald	Buf., L.A., Atl., Dal., Mtl., Fla.	15	735	260	249	509	584	73	21	27	48	46	....	1989-90	2003-04
• Auge, Les	Col.	1	6	0	3	3	4	....	....	....	....	....	....	1980-81	1980-81
Augusta, Patrik	Tor., Wsh.	2	4	0	0	0	0	....	....	....	....	....	....	1993-94	1998-99
‡ Aulin, Jared	L.A.	1	17	2	2	4	0	....	....	....	....	....	....	2002-03	2002-03
• Aurie, Larry	Det.	12	489	147	129	276	279	24	6	9	15	10	2	1927-28	1938-39
Awrey, Don	Bos., St.L., Mtl., Pit., NYR, Col.	16	979	31	158	189	1065	71	0	18	18	150	2	1963-64	1978-79
‡ Axelsson, P.J.	Bos.	11	797	103	184	287	276	54	4	3	7	24	....	1997-98	2008-09
• Ayres, Vern	NYA, Mtl.M., St.L., NYR	6	211	6	11	17	350	....	....	....	....	....	....	1930-31	1935-36

B

Babando, Pete	Bos., Det., Chi., NYR	6	351	86	73	159	194	17	3	3	6	6	1	1947-48	1952-53
Babcock, Bobby	Wsh.	2	2	0	0	0	2	....	....	....	....	....	....	1990-91	1992-93
Babe, Warren	Min.	3	21	2	5	7	23	2	0	0	0	0	....	1987-88	1990-91
‡ Babenko, Yuri	Col.	1	3	0	0	0	0	....	....	....	....	....	....	2000-01	2000-01
Babin, Mitch	St.L.	1	8	0	0	0	0	....	....	....	....	....	....	1975-76	1975-76
Baby, John	Cle., Min.	2	26	2	8	10	26	....	....	....	....	....	....	1977-78	1978-79
Babych, Dave	Wpg., Hfd., Van., Phi., L.A.	19	1195	142	581	723	970	114	21	41	62	113	....	1980-81	1998-99
Babych, Wayne	St.L., Pit., Que., Hfd.	9	519	192	246	438	498	41	7	9	16	24	....	1978-79	1986-87
Baca, Jergus	Hfd.	2	10	0	2	2	14	....	....	....	....	....	....	1990-91	1991-92
‡ Backman, Christian	St.L., NYR, CBJ	6	302	23	56	79	182	13	0	2	2	16	....	2002-03	2008-09
Backman, Mike	NYR	3	18	1	6	7	18	10	2	2	4	2	....	1981-82	1983-84
• Backor, Pete	Tor.	1	36	4	5	9	6	....	....	....	....	....	1	1944-45	1944-45
Backstrom, Ralph	Mtl., L.A., Chi.	17	1032	278	361	639	386	116	27	32	59	68	6	1956-57	1972-73
• Bailey, Ace	Tor.	8	313	111	82	193	472	21	3	4	7	12	1	1926-27	1933-34
• Bailey, Bob	Tor., Det., Chi.	5	150	15	21	36	207	15	0	4	4	22	....	1953-54	1957-58
• Bailey, Garnet	Bos., Det., St.L., Wsh.	10	568	107	171	278	633	15	2	4	6	28	2	1968-69	1977-78
Bailey, Reid	Phi., Tor., Hfd.	4	40	1	3	4	105	16	0	2	2	25	....	1980-81	1983-84
Baillargeon, Joel	Wpg., Que.	3	20	0	2	2	31	....	....	....	....	....	....	1986-87	1988-89
Baird, Ken	Cal.	1	10	0	2	2	15	....	....	....	....	....	....	1971-72	1971-72
Baker, Bill	Mtl., Col., St.L., NYR	3	143	7	25	32	175	6	0	0	0	0	....	1980-81	1982-83
Baker, Jamie	Que., Ott., S.J., Tor.	10	404	71	79	150	271	25	5	4	9	42	....	1989-90	1998-99
Bakovic, Peter	Van.	1	10	2	0	2	48	....	....	....	....	....	....	1987-88	1987-88
Bala, Chris	Ott.	1	6	0	1	1	0	....	....	....	....	....	....	2001-02	2001-02
‡ Balastik, Jaroslav	CBJ	2	74	13	11	24	30	....	....	....	....	....	....	2005-06	2006-07
Balderis, Helmut	Min.	1	26	3	6	9	2	....	....	....	....	....	....	1989-90	1989-90
• Baldwin, Doug	Tor., Det., Chi.	3	24	0	1	1	8	....	....	....	....	....	....	1945-46	1947-48
‡ Balej, Jozef	Mtl., NYR, Van.	2	18	1	5	6	4	....	....	....	....	....	....	2003-04	2005-06
Balfour, Earl	Tor., Chi.	7	288	30	22	52	78	26	0	3	3	4	1	1951-52	1960-61
• Balfour, Murray	Mtl., Chi., Bos.	8	306	67	90	157	393	40	9	10	19	45	1	1956-57	1964-65
Ball, Terry	Phi., Buf.	4	74	7	19	26	26	....	....	....	....	....	....	1967-68	1971-72
Balmochnykh, Maxim	Ana.	1	6	0	1	1	2	....	....	....	....	....	....	1999-00	1999-00
• Balon, Dave	NYR, Mtl., Min., Van.	14	776	192	222	414	607	78	14	21	35	109	2	1959-60	1972-73
Baltimore, Bryon	Edm.	1	2	0	0	0	4	....	....	....	....	....	....	1979-80	1979-80
Baluik, Stan	Bos.	1	7	0	0	0	2	....	....	....	....	....	....	1959-60	1959-60
Bancroft, Steve	Chi., S.J.	2	6	0	1	1	2	....	....	....	....	....	....	1992-93	2001-02
Bandura, Jeff	NYR	1	2	0	1	1	0	....	....	....	....	....	....	1980-81	1980-81
Banham, Frank	Ana., Phx.	4	32	9	2	11	16	....	....	....	....	....	....	1996-97	2002-03
Banks, Darren	Bos.	2	20	2	2	4	73	....	....	....	....	....	....	1992-93	1993-94
‡ Bannister, Drew	T.B., Edm., Ana., NYR	6	164	5	25	30	161	12	0	0	0	30	....	1995-96	2001-02
Barahona, Ralph	Bos.	2	6	2	2	4	0	....	....	....	....	....	....	1990-91	1991-92
• Barbe, Andy	Tor.	1	1	0	0	0	2	....	....	....	....	....	....	1950-51	1950-51
Barber, Bill	Phi.	12	903	420	463	883	623	129	53	55	108	109	2	1972-73	1983-84
Barber, Don	Min., Wpg., Que., S.J.	4	115	25	32	57	64	11	4	4	8	10	....	1988-89	1991-92
• Barilko, Bill	Tor.	5	252	26	36	62	456	47	5	7	12	104	4	1946-47	1950-51
‡ Barinka, Michal	Chi.	2	34	0	2	2	26	....	....	....	....	....	....	2003-04	2005-06
Barkley, Doug	Chi., Det.	6	253	24	80	104	382	30	0	9	9	63	....	1957-58	1965-66
Barlow, Bob	Min.	2	77	16	17	33	10	6	2	2	4	6	....	1969-70	1970-71
Barnaby, Matthew	Buf., Pit., T.B., NYR, Col., Chi., Dal.	14	834	113	187	300	2562	62	7	15	22	170	....	1992-93	2006-07
• Barnes, Blair	L.A.	1	1	0	0	0	0	....	....	....	....	....	....	1982-83	1982-83
Barnes, Norm	Phi., Hfd.	5	156	6	38	44	178	12	0	0	0	8	....	1976-77	1981-82
Barnes, Ryan	Det.	1	2	0	0	0	0	....	....	....	....	....	....	2003-04	2003-04
Barnes, Stu	Wpg., Fla., Pit., Buf., Dal.	16	1136	261	336	597	438	116	30	32	62	24	....	1991-92	2007-08
‡ Barney, Scott	L.A., Atl.	3	27	5	6	11	4	....	....	....	....	....	....	2002-03	2005-06
Baron, Murray	Phi., St.L., Mtl., Phx., Van.	15	988	35	94	129	1309	73	2	8	10	78	....	1989-90	2003-04
Baron, Normand	Mtl., St.L.	2	27	2	0	2	51	3	0	0	0	22	....	1983-84	1985-86
Barr, Dave	Bos., NYR, St.L., Hfd., Det., N.J., Dal.	13	614	128	204	332	520	71	12	10	22	70	....	1981-82	1993-94
Barrault, Doug	Min., Fla.	2	4	0	0	0	2	....	....	....	....	....	....	1992-93	1993-94
Barrett, Fred	Min., L.A.	13	745	25	123	148	671	44	0	2	2	60	....	1970-71	1983-84
Barrett, John	Det., Wsh., Min.	8	488	20	77	97	604	16	2	2	4	50	....	1980-81	1987-88
Barrie, Doug	Pit., Buf., L.A.	3	158	10	42	52	268	....	....	....	....	....	....	1968-69	1971-72
Barrie, Len	Phi., Fla., Pit., L.A.	7	184	19	45	64	290	8	1	0	1	8	....	1989-90	2000-01
Barry, Ed	Bos.	1	19	1	3	4	2	....	....	....	....	....	....	1946-47	1946-47
• Barry, Marty	NYA, Bos., Det., Mtl.	12	509	195	192	387	231	43	15	18	33	34	2	1927-28	1939-40
Barry, Ray	Bos.	1	18	1	2	3	6	....	....	....	....	....	....	1951-52	1951-52
‡ Bartecko, Lubos	St.L., Atl.	5	257	46	65	111	107	12	1	1	2	2	....	1998-99	2002-03
Bartel, Robin	Cgy., Van.	2	41	0	1	1	14	6	0	0	0	16	....	1985-86	1986-87
Bartlett, Jim	Mtl., NYR, Bos.	5	191	34	23	57	273	2	0	0	0	0	....	1954-55	1960-61
• Barton, Cliff	Pit., Phi., NYR	3	85	10	9	19	22	....	....	....	....	....	....	1929-30	1939-40
Bartos, Peter	Min.	1	13	4	2	6	6	....	....	....	....	....	....	2000-01	2000-01
‡ Bartovic, Milan	Buf., Chi.	3	50	3	14	17	26	....	....	....	....	....	....	2002-03	2005-06
Bashkirov, Andrei	Mtl.	3	30	0	3	3	0	....	....	....	....	....	....	1998-99	2000-01
Bassen, Bob	NYI, Chi., St.L., Que., Dal., Cgy.	15	765	88	144	232	1004	93	9	15	24	134	....	1985-86	1999-00
Bast, Ryan	Phi.	1	2	0	1	1	0	....	....	....	....	....	....	1998-99	1998-99
Bates, Shawn	Bos., NYI	10	465	72	126	198	266	29	3	4	7	19	....	1997-98	2007-08
Bathe, Frank	Det., Phi.	9	224	3	28	31	542	27	1	3	4	42	....	1974-75	1983-84
Bathgate, Andy	NYR, Tor., Det., Pit.	17	1069	349	624	973	624	54	21	14	35	76	1	1952-53	1970-71
Bathgate, Frank	NYR	1	2	0	0	0	2	....	....	....	....	....	....	1952-53	1952-53
‡ Battaglia, Bates	Car., Col., Wsh., Tor.	9	580	80	118	198	385	42	5	16	21	28	....	1997-98	2007-08
• Batters, Jeff	St.L.	2	16	0	0	0	28	....	....	....	....	....	....	1993-94	1994-95
Batyrshin, Ruslan	L.A.	1	2	0	0	0	6	....	....	....	....	....	....	1995-96	1995-96

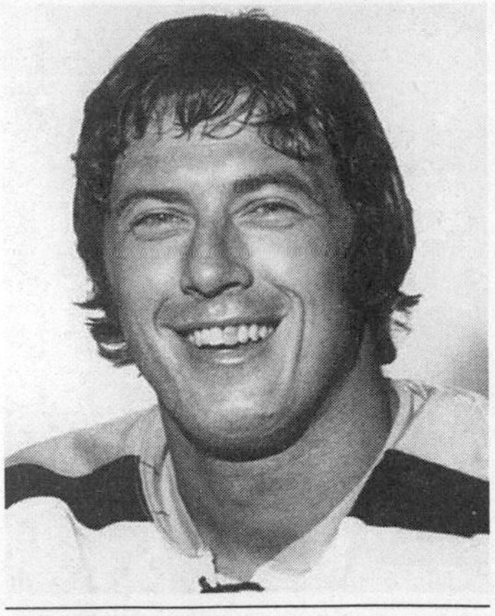

Don Awrey

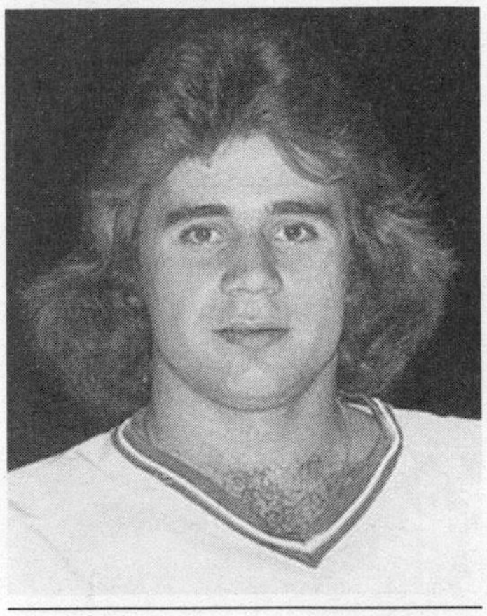

John Baby

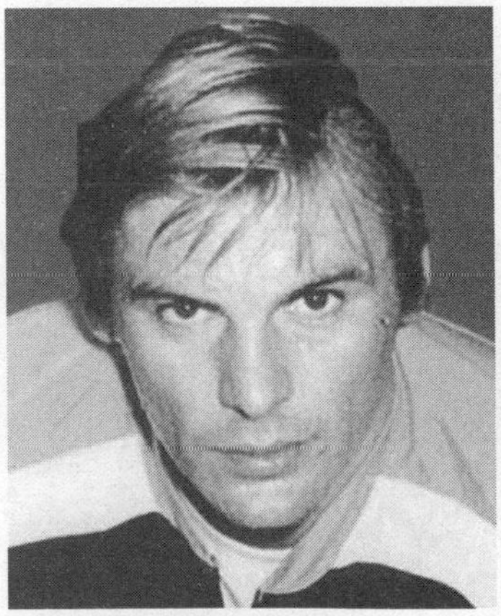

Garnet Bailey

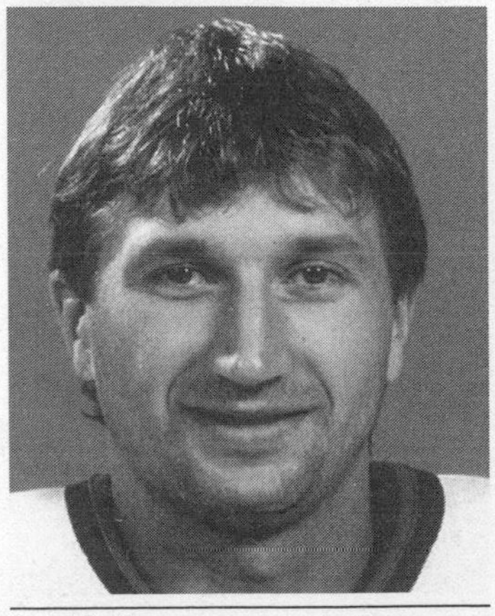

Sergei Bautin

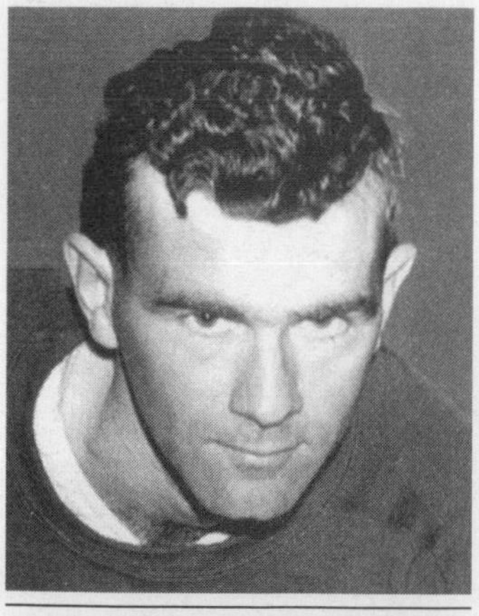

Lin Bend

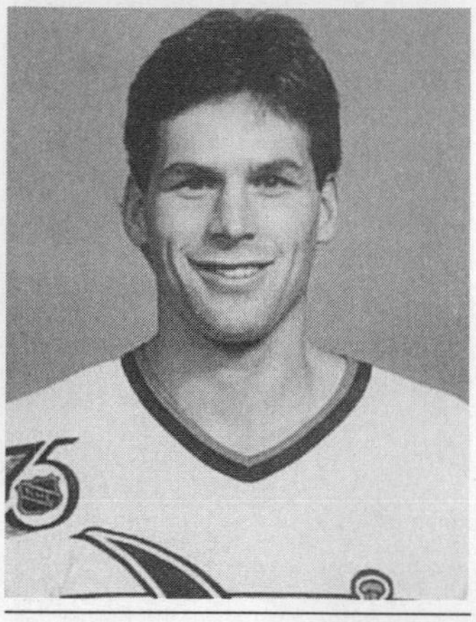

Perry Berezan

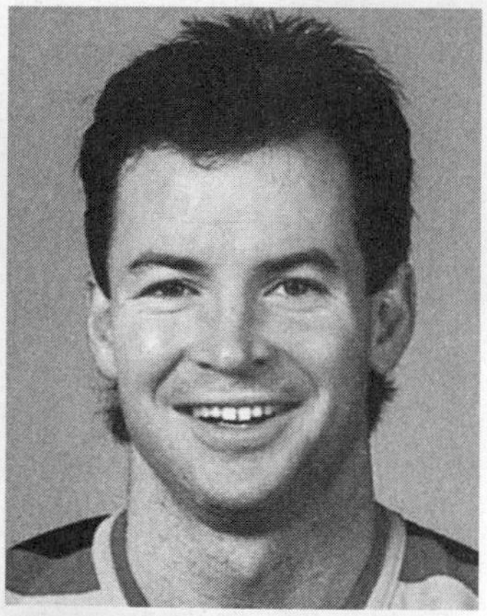

Ken Berry

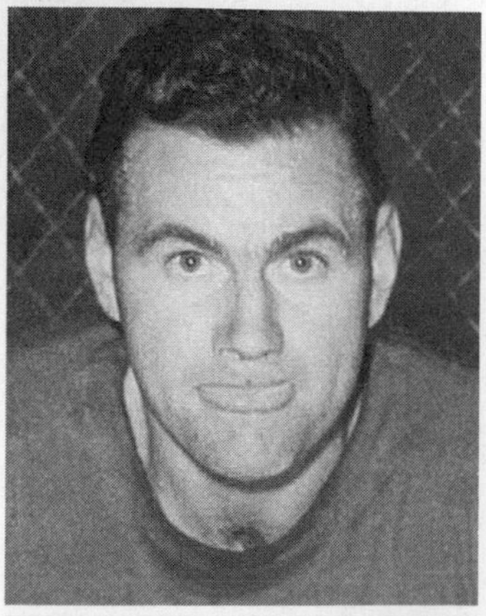

Mickey Blake

			Regular Schedule					Playoffs							
Name	NHL Teams	NHL Seasons	GP	G	A	TP	PIM	GP	G	A	TP	PIM	NHL Cup Wins	First NHL Season	Last NHL Season
• Bauer, Bobby	Bos.	9	327	123	137	260	36	48	11	8	19	6	2	1936-37	1951-52
Baumgartner, Ken	L.A., NYI, Tor., Ana., Bos.	12	696	13	41	54	2244	51	1	2	3	106	....	1987-88	1998-99
Baumgartner, Mike	K.C.	1	17	0	0	0	0	....	....	....	....	....	....	1974-75	1974-75
Baun, Bob	Tor., Oak., Det.	17	964	37	187	224	1493	96	3	12	15	171	4	1956-57	1972-73
Bautin, Sergei	Wpg., Det., S.J.	3	132	5	25	30	176	6	0	0	0	2	....	1992-93	1995-96
Bawa, Robin	Wsh., Van., S.J., Ana.	4	61	6	1	7	60	1	0	0	0	0	....	1989-90	1993-94
Baxter, Paul	Que., Pit., Cgy.	8	472	48	121	169	1564	40	0	5	5	162	....	1979-80	1986-87
Beadle, Sandy	Wpg.	1	6	1	0	1	2	....	....	....	....	....	....	1980-81	1980-81
Beaton, Frank	NYR	2	25	1	1	2	43	....	....	....	....	....	....	1978-79	1979-80
• Beattie, Red	Bos., Det., NYA	9	334	62	85	147	137	24	4	2	6	8	....	1930-31	1938-39
Beaudin, Norm	St.L., Min.	2	25	1	2	3	4	....	....	....	....	....	....	1967-68	1970-71
‡ Beaudoin, Eric	Fla.	3	53	3	8	11	41	....	....	....	....	....	....	2001-02	2003-04
Beaudoin, Serge	Atl.	1	3	0	0	0	0	....	....	....	....	....	....	1979-80	1979-80
Beaudoin, Yves	Wsh.	3	11	0	0	0	5	....	....	....	....	....	....	1985-86	1987-88
Beaufait, Mark	S.J.	1	5	1	0	1	0	....	....	....	....	....	....	1992-93	1992-93
Beck, Barry	Col., NYR, L.A.	10	615	104	251	355	1016	51	10	23	33	77	....	1977-78	1989-90
Beckett, Bob	Bos.	4	68	7	6	13	18	....	....	....	....	....	....	1956-57	1963-64
Bedard, James	Chi.	2	22	1	1	2	8	....	....	....	....	....	....	1949-50	1950-51
Beddoes, Clayton	Bos.	2	60	2	8	10	57	....	....	....	....	....	....	1995-96	1996-97
‡ Bednar, Jaroslav	L.A., Fla.	3	102	10	25	35	30	3	0	0	0	0	....	2001-02	2003-04
Bednarski, John	NYR, Edm.	4	100	2	18	20	114	1	0	0	0	17	....	1974-75	1979-80
‡ Beech, Kris	Wsh., Pit., Nsh., CBJ, Van.	7	198	25	42	67	113	....	....	....	....	....	....	2000-01	2007-08
Beers, Bob	Bos., T.B., Edm., NYI	8	258	28	79	107	225	21	1	1	2	22	....	1989-90	1996-97
Beers, Eddy	Cgy., St.L.	5	250	94	116	210	256	41	7	10	17	47	....	1981-82	1985-86
• Behling, Dick	Det.	2	5	1	0	1	2	....	....	....	....	....	....	1940-41	1942-43
• Beisler, Frank	NYA	2	2	0	0	0	0	....	....	....	....	....	....	1936-37	1939-40
Bekar, Derek	St.L., L.A., NYI	3	11	0	0	0	6	....	....	....	....	....	....	1999-00	2003-04
Belanger, Alain	Tor.	1	9	0	1	1	6	....	....	....	....	....	....	1977-78	1977-78
Belanger, Francis	Mtl.	1	10	0	0	0	29	....	....	....	....	....	....	2000-01	2000-01
Belanger, Jesse	Mtl., Fla., Van., Edm., NYI	8	246	59	76	135	56	12	0	3	3	2	1	1991-92	2000-01
Belanger, Ken	Tor., NYI, Bos., L.A.	11	248	11	12	23	695	12	1	0	1	16	....	1994-95	2005-06
Belanger, Roger	Pit.	1	44	3	5	8	32	....	....	....	....	....	....	1984-85	1984-85
Belisle, Danny	NYR	1	4	2	0	2	0	....	....	....	....	....	....	1960-61	1960-61
Beliveau, Jean	Mtl.	20	1125	507	712	1219	1029	162	79	97	176	211	10	1950-51	1970-71
• Bell, Billy	Mtl.W., Mtl., Ott.	6	66	3	2	5	14	5	0	0	0	0	1	1917-18	1923-24
Bell, Bruce	Que., St.L., NYR, Edm.	5	209	12	64	76	113	34	3	5	8	41	....	1984-85	1989-90
• Bell, Huddy	NYR	1	1	0	1	1	0	....	....	....	....	....	....	1946-47	1946-47
Bell, Joe	NYR	2	62	8	9	17	18	....	....	....	....	....	....	1942-43	1946-47
Belland, Neil	Van., Pit.	6	109	13	32	45	54	21	2	9	11	23	....	1981-82	1986-87
Bellefeuille, Blake	CBJ	2	5	0	1	1	0	....	....	....	....	....	....	2001-02	2002-03
• Bellefeuille, Pete	Tor., Det.	4	92	26	4	30	58	....	....	....	....	....	....	1925-26	1929-30
• Bellemer, Andy	Mtl.M.	1	15	0	0	0	0	....	....	....	....	....	....	1932-33	1932-33
Bellows, Brian	Min., Mtl., T.B., Ana., Wsh.	17	1188	485	537	1022	718	143	51	71	122	143	1	1982-83	1998-99
• Bend, Lin	NYR	1	8	3	1	4	2	....	....	....	....	....	....	1942-43	1942-43
‡ Benda, Jan	Wsh.	1	9	0	3	3	6	....	....	....	....	....	....	1997-98	1997-98
Bennett, Adam	Chi., Edm.	3	69	3	8	11	69	....	....	....	....	....	....	1991-92	1993-94
Bennett, Bill	Bos., Hfd.	2	31	4	7	11	65	....	....	....	....	....	....	1978-79	1979-80
Bennett, Curt	St.L., NYR, Atl.	10	580	152	182	334	347	21	1	1	2	57	....	1970-71	1979-80
Bennett, Frank	Det.	1	7	0	1	1	2	....	....	....	....	....	....	1943-44	1943-44
Bennett, Harvey	Pit., Wsh., Phi., Min., St.L.	5	268	44	46	90	347	4	0	0	0	2	....	1974-75	1978-79
• Bennett, Max	Mtl.	1	1	0	0	0	0	....	....	....	....	....	....	1935-36	1935-36
Bennett, Rick	NYR	3	15	1	1	2	13	....	....	....	....	....	....	1989-90	1991-92
Benning, Brian	St.L., L.A., Phi., Edm., Fla.	11	568	63	233	296	963	48	3	20	23	74	....	1984-85	1994-95
Benning, Jim	Tor., Van.	9	605	52	191	243	461	7	1	1	2	2	....	1981-82	1989-90
• Benoit, Joe	Mtl.	5	185	75	69	144	94	11	6	3	9	11	1	1940-41	1946-47
Benson, Bill	NYA, Bro.	2	67	11	25	36	35	....	....	....	....	....	....	1940-41	1941-42
• Benson, Bobby	Bos.	1	8	0	1	1	4	....	....	....	....	....	....	1924-25	1924-25
• Bentley, Doug	Chi., NYR	13	566	219	324	543	217	23	9	8	17	12	....	1939-40	1953-54
• Bentley, Max	Chi., Tor., NYR	12	646	245	299	544	179	51	18	27	45	14	3	1940-41	1953-54
• Bentley, Reg	Chi.	1	11	1	2	3	2	....	....	....	....	....	....	1942-43	1942-43
Benysek, Ladislav	Edm., Min.	4	161	3	12	15	74	....	....	....	....	....	....	1997-98	2002-03
Beraldo, Paul	Bos.	2	10	0	0	0	4	....	....	....	....	....	....	1987-88	1988-89
Beranek, Josef	Edm., Phi., Van., Pit.	9	531	118	144	262	398	57	5	8	13	24	....	1991-92	2000-01
Berard, Bryan	NYI, Tor., NYR, Bos., Chi., CBJ	10	619	76	247	323	500	20	2	8	10	10	....	1996-97	2007-08
Berehowsky, Drake	Tor., Pit., Edm., Nsh., Van., Phx.	13	549	37	112	149	848	22	1	3	4	30	....	1990-91	2003-04
Berenson, Red	Mtl., NYR, St.L., Det.	17	987	261	397	658	305	85	23	14	37	49	1	1961-62	1977-78
Berenzweig, Bubba	Nsh.	4	37	3	7	10	14	....	....	....	....	....	....	1999-00	2002-03
Berezan, Perry	Cgy., Min., S.J.	9	378	61	75	136	279	31	4	7	11	34	....	1984-85	1992-93
Berezin, Sergei	Tor., Phx., Mtl., Chi., Wsh.	7	502	160	126	286	54	52	13	17	30	6	....	1996-97	2002-03
‡ Berg, Aki	L.A., Tor.	9	606	15	70	85	374	54	1	7	8	47	....	1995-96	2005-06
Berg, Bill	NYI, Tor., NYR, Ott.	10	546	55	67	122	488	61	3	4	7	34	....	1988-89	1998-99
• Bergdinon, Fred	Bos.	1	2	0	0	0	0	....	....	....	....	....	....	1925-26	1925-26
Bergen, Todd	Phi.	1	14	11	5	16	4	17	4	9	13	8	....	1984-85	1984-85
Berger, Mike	Min.	2	30	3	1	4	67	....	....	....	....	....	....	1987-88	1988-89
Bergeron, Michel	Det., NYI, Wsh.	5	229	80	58	138	165	....	....	....	....	....	....	1974-75	1978-79
Bergeron, Yves	Pit.	2	3	0	0	0	0	....	....	....	....	....	....	1974-75	1976-77
Bergevin, Marc	Chi., NYI, Hfd., T.B., Det., St.L., Pit., Van.	20	1191	36	145	181	1090	80	3	6	9	52	....	1984-85	2003-04
Bergkvist, Stefan	Pit.	2	7	0	0	0	9	4	0	0	0	2	....	1995-96	1996-97
Bergland, Tim	Wsh., T.B.	5	182	17	26	43	75	26	2	2	4	22	....	1989-90	1993-94
Bergloff, Bob	Min.	1	2	0	0	0	5	....	....	....	....	....	....	1982-83	1982-83
Berglund, Bo	Que., Min., Phi.	3	130	28	39	67	40	9	2	0	2	6	....	1983-84	1985-86
‡ Berglund, Christian	N.J., Fla.	3	86	11	16	27	42	3	0	0	0	2	....	2001-02	2003-04
• Bergman, Gary	Det., Min., K.C.	12	838	68	299	367	1249	21	0	5	5	20	....	1964-65	1975-76
Bergman, Thommie	Det.	6	246	21	44	65	243	7	0	2	2	2	....	1972-73	1979-80
Bergqvist, Jonas	Cgy.	1	22	2	5	7	10	....	....	....	....	....	....	1989-90	1989-90
• Berlinguette, Louis	Mtl., Mtl.M., Pit.	8	193	45	33	78	129	11	0	5	5	9	....	1917-18	1925-26
Bernier, Serge	Phi., L.A., Que.	7	302	78	119	197	234	5	1	1	2	0	....	1968-69	1980-81
Berry, Bob	Mtl., L.A.	8	541	159	191	350	344	26	2	6	8	6	....	1968-69	1976-77
Berry, Brad	Wpg., Min., Dal.	8	241	4	28	32	323	13	0	1	1	16	....	1985-86	1993-94
Berry, Doug	Col.	2	121	10	33	43	25	....	....	....	....	....	....	1979-80	1980-81
Berry, Fred	Det.	1	3	0	0	0	0	....	....	....	....	....	....	1976-77	1976-77
Berry, Ken	Edm., Van.	4	55	8	10	18	30	....	....	....	....	....	....	1981-82	1988-89
Berry, Rick	Col., Pit., Wsh.	4	197	2	13	15	314	....	....	....	....	....	....	2000-01	2003-04
Berti, Adam	Chi.	1	2	0	0	0	0	....	....	....	....	....	....	2007-08	2007-08
Bertrand, Eric	N.J., Atl., Mtl.	2	15	0	0	0	4	....	....	....	....	....	....	1999-00	2000-01
Berube, Craig	Phi., Tor., Cgy., Wsh., NYI	17	1054	61	98	159	3149	89	3	1	4	211	....	1986-87	2002-03
• Besler, Phil	Bos., Chi., Det.	2	30	1	4	5	18	....	....	....	....	....	....	1935-36	1938-39
• Bessone, Pete	Det.	1	6	0	1	1	6	....	....	....	....	....	....	1937-38	1937-38
Bethel, John	Wpg.	1	17	0	2	2	4	....	....	....	....	....	....	1979-80	1979-80
Betik, Karel	T.B.	1	3	0	2	2	2	....	....	....	....	....	....	1998-99	1998-99
Bets, Maxim	Ana.	1	3	0	0	0	0	....	....	....	....	....	....	1993-94	1993-94
• Bettio, Sam	Bos.	1	44	9	12	21	32	....	....	....	....	....	....	1949-50	1949-50
Beukeboom, Jeff	Edm., NYR	14	804	30	129	159	1890	99	3	16	19	197	4	1985-86	1998-99
Beverley, Nick	Bos., Pit., NYR, Min., L.A., Col.	11	502	18	94	112	156	7	0	1	1	0	....	1966-67	1979-80
‡ Bezina, Goran	Phx.	1	3	0	0	0	2	....	....	....	....	....	....	2003-04	2003-04
Bialowas, Dwight	Atl., Min.	4	164	11	46	57	46	....	....	....	....	....	....	1973-74	1976-77
Bialowas, Frank	Tor.	1	3	0	0	0	12	....	....	....	....	....	....	1993-94	1993-94
Bianchin, Wayne	Pit., Edm.	7	276	68	41	109	137	3	0	1	1	6	....	1973-74	1979-80
Bicanek, Radim	Ott., Chi., CBJ	7	122	1	11	12	62	7	0	0	0	8	....	1994-95	2001-02
‡ Bicek, Jiri	N.J.	4	62	6	7	13	29	7	0	0	0	0	1	2000-01	2003-04
Bidner, Todd	Wsh.	1	12	2	1	3	7	....	....	....	....	....	....	1981-82	1981-82
Biggs, Don	Min., Phi.	2	12	2	0	2	8	....	....	....	....	....	....	1984-85	1989-90
Bignell, Larry	Pit.	2	20	0	3	3	2	3	0	0	0	2	....	1973-74	1974-75
• Bilodeau, Gilles	Que.	1	9	0	1	1	25	....	....	....	....	....	....	1979-80	1979-80
• Bionda, Jack	Tor., Bos.	4	93	3	9	12	113	11	0	1	1	14	....	1955-56	1958-59
‡ Biron, Mathieu	NYI, T.B., Fla., Wsh.	6	253	12	32	44	177	....	....	....	....	....	....	1999-00	2005-06
‡ Bisaillon, Sebastien	Edm.	1	2	0	0	0	0	....	....	....	....	....	....	2006-07	2006-07
Bishai, Mike	Edm.	1	14	0	2	2	19	....	....	....	....	....	....	2003-04	2003-04
Bissett, Tom	Det.	1	5	0	0	0	0	....	....	....	....	....	....	1990-91	1990-91
Bjugstad, Scott	Min., Pit., L.A.	9	317	76	68	144	144	9	0	1	1	2	....	1983-84	1991-92
Black, James	Hfd., Min., Dal., Buf., Chi., Wsh.	11	352	58	57	115	84	13	2	1	3	4	....	1989-90	2000-01
• Black, Steve	Det., Chi.	2	113	11	20	31	77	13	0	0	0	13	1	1949-50	1950-51
Blackburn, Bob	NYR, Pit.	3	135	8	12	20	105	6	0	0	0	4	....	1968-69	1970-71
Blackburn, Don	Bos., Phi., NYR, NYI, Min.	6	185	23	44	67	87	12	3	0	3	10	....	1962-63	1972-73
• Blade, Hank	Chi.	2	24	2	3	5	2	....	....	....	....	....	....	1946-47	1947-48

			Regular Schedule					Playoffs							
Name	NHL Teams	NHL Seasons	GP	G	A	TP	PIM	GP	G	A	TP	PIM	NHL Cup Wins	First NHL Season	Last NHL Season
Bladon, Tom	Phi., Pit., Edm., Wpg., Det.	9	610	73	197	270	392	86	8	29	37	70	2	1972-73	1980-81
● Blaine, Garry	Mtl.	1	1	0	0	0	0	....	....	....	....	....	....	1954-55	1954-55
● Blair, Andy	Tor., Chi.	9	402	74	86	160	323	38	6	6	12	32	1	1928-29	1936-37
● Blair, Chuck	Tor.	1	1	0	0	0	0	....	....	....	....	....	....	1948-49	1948-49
Blair, Dusty	Tor.	1	2	0	0	0	0	....	....	....	....	....	....	1950-51	1950-51
Blaisdell, Mike	Det., NYR, Pit., Tor.	9	343	70	84	154	166	6	1	2	3	10	....	1980-81	1988-89
● Blake, Bob	Bos.	1	12	0	0	0	0	....	....	....	....	....	....	1935-36	1935-36
● Blake, Mickey	Mtl.M., St.L., Tor.	3	10	1	1	2	4	....	....	....	....	....	....	1932-33	1935-36
Blake, Rob	L.A., Col., S.J.	20	1270	240	537	777	1679	146	26	47	73	166	1	1989-90	2009-10
● Blake, Toe	Mtl.M., Mtl.	14	577	235	292	527	272	58	25	37	62	23	3	1934-35	1947-48
‡ Blatny, Zdenek	Atl., Bos.	3	25	3	0	3	8	....	....	....	....	....	....	2002-03	2005-06
● Blight, Rick	Van., L.A.	7	326	96	125	221	170	5	0	5	5	2	....	1975-76	1982-83
● Blinco, Russ	Mtl.M., Chi.	6	268	59	66	125	24	19	3	3	6	4	1	1933-34	1938-39
Block, Ken	Van.	1	1	0	0	0	0	....	....	....	....	....	....	1970-71	1970-71
Bloemberg, Jeff	NYR	4	43	3	6	9	25	7	0	3	3	5	....	1988-89	1991-92
Blomqvist, Timo	Wsh., N.J.	5	243	4	53	57	293	13	0	0	0	24	....	1981-82	1986-87
Blomsten, Arto	Wpg., L.A.	3	25	0	4	4	8	....	....	....	....	....	....	1993-94	1995-96
Bloom, Mike	Wsh., Det.	3	201	30	47	77	215	....	....	....	....	....	....	1974-75	1976-77
Blouin, Sylvain	NYR, Mtl., Min.	6	115	3	4	7	336	....	....	....	....	....	....	1996-97	2002-03
Blum, John	Edm., Bos., Wsh., Det.	8	250	7	34	41	610	20	0	2	2	27	....	1982-83	1989-90
Bodak, Bob	Cgy., Hfd.	2	4	0	0	0	29	....	....	....	....	....	....	1987-88	1989-90
Boddy, Gregg	Van.	5	273	23	44	67	263	3	0	0	0	0	....	1971-72	1975-76
Bodger, Doug	Pit., Buf., S.J., N.J., L.A., Van.	16	1071	106	422	528	1007	47	6	18	24	25	....	1984-85	1999-00
● Bodnar, Gus	Tor., Chi., Bos.	12	667	142	254	396	207	32	4	3	7	10	2	1943-44	1954-55
Boehm, Ron	Oak.	1	16	2	1	3	10	....	....	....	....	....	....	1967-68	1967-68
● Boesch, Garth	Tor.	4	197	9	28	37	205	34	2	5	7	18	3	1946-47	1949-50
Boguniecki, Eric	Fla., St.L., Pit., NYI	7	178	34	42	76	105	9	1	3	4	2	....	1999-00	2006-07
Boh, Rick	Min.	1	8	2	1	3	4	....	....	....	....	....	....	1987-88	1987-88
Bohonos, Lonny	Van., Tor.	4	83	19	16	35	22	9	3	6	9	2	....	1995-96	1998-99
Boikov, Alexandre	Nsh.	2	10	0	0	0	15	....	....	....	....	....	....	1999-00	2000-01
● Boileau, Marc	Det.	1	54	5	6	11	8	....	....	....	....	....	....	1961-62	1961-62
Boileau, Patrick	Wsh., Det., Pit.	5	48	5	11	16	26	....	....	....	....	....	....	1996-97	2003-04
● Boileau, Rene	NYA	1	7	0	0	0	0	....	....	....	....	....	....	1925-26	1925-26
Boimistruck, Fred	Tor.	2	83	4	14	18	45	....	....	....	....	....	....	1981-82	1982-83
‡ Bois, Danny	Ott.	1	1	0	0	0	7	....	....	....	....	....	....	2006-07	2006-07
Boisvert, Serge	Tor., Mtl.	5	46	5	7	12	8	23	3	7	10	4	1	1982-83	1987-88
Boivin, Claude	Phi., Ott.	4	132	12	19	31	364	....	....	....	....	....	....	1991-92	1994-95
Boivin, Leo	Tor., Bos., Det., Pit., Min.	19	1150	72	250	322	1192	54	3	10	13	59	....	1951-52	1969-70
Boland, Mike	Phi.	1	2	0	0	0	0	....	....	....	....	....	....	1974-75	1974-75
Boland, Mike	K.C., Buf.	2	23	1	2	3	29	3	1	0	1	2	....	1974-75	1978-79
Boldirev, Ivan	Bos., Cal., Chi., Atl., Van., Det.	16	1052	361	505	866	507	48	13	20	33	14	1	1969-70	1984-85
Bolduc, Danny	Det., Cgy.	3	102	22	19	41	33	1	0	0	0	0	....	1978-79	1983-84
Bolduc, Michel	Que.	2	10	0	0	0	6	....	....	....	....	....	....	1981-82	1982-83
● Boll, Buzz	Tor., NYA, Bro., Bos.	12	437	133	130	263	148	31	7	3	10	13	....	1932-33	1943-44
Bolonchuk, Larry	Van., Wsh.	4	74	3	9	12	97	....	....	....	....	....	....	1972-73	1977-78
● Bolton, Hugh	Tor.	8	235	10	51	61	221	17	0	5	5	14	1	1949-50	1956-57
Bombardir, Brad	N.J., Min., Nsh.	7	356	8	46	54	127	16	0	1	1	2	1	1997-98	2003-04
Bonar, Dan	L.A.	3	170	25	39	64	208	14	3	4	7	22	....	1980-81	1982-83
Bondra, Peter	Wsh., Ott., Atl., Chi.	16	1081	503	389	892	761	80	30	26	56	60	....	1990-91	2006-07
Bonin, Brian	Pit., Min.	2	12	0	0	0	0	3	0	0	0	0	....	1998-99	2000-01
Bonin, Marcel	Det., Bos., Mtl.	9	454	97	175	272	336	50	11	14	25	51	4	1952-53	1961-62
‡ Bonk, Radek	Ott., Mtl., Nsh.	14	969	194	303	497	581	73	12	15	27	42	....	1994-95	2008-09
Bonni, Ryan	Van.	1	3	0	0	0	0	....	....	....	....	....	....	1999-00	1999-00
Bonsignore, Jason	Edm., T.B.	4	79	3	13	16	34	....	....	....	....	....	....	1994-95	1998-99
Bonvie, Dennis	Edm., Chi., Pit., Bos., Ott., Col.	9	92	1	2	3	311	1	0	0	0	0	....	1994-95	2003-04
Boo, Jim	Min.	1	6	0	0	0	22	....	....	....	....	....	....	1977-78	1977-78
● Boone, Buddy	Bos.	2	34	5	3	8	28	22	2	1	3	25	....	1956-57	1957-58
● Boothman, George	Tor.	2	58	17	19	36	18	5	2	1	3	2	....	1942-43	1943-44
‡ Bootland, Darryl	Det., NYI	3	32	1	2	3	85	....	....	....	....	....	....	2003-04	2007-08
Bordeleau, Christian	Mtl., St.L., Chi.	4	205	38	65	103	82	19	4	7	11	17	1	1968-69	1971-72
Bordeleau, J.P.	Chi.	10	519	97	126	223	143	48	3	6	9	12	....	1969-70	1979-80
Bordeleau, Paulin	Van.	3	183	33	56	89	47	5	2	1	3	0	....	1973-74	1975-76
‡ Bordeleau, Sebastien	Mtl., Nsh., Min., Phx.	7	251	37	61	98	118	5	0	0	0	2	....	1995-96	2001-02
Borotsik, Jack	St.L.	1	1	0	0	0	0	....	....	....	....	....	....	1974-75	1974-75
Borsato, Luciano	Wpg.	5	203	35	55	90	113	7	1	0	1	4	....	1990-91	1994-95
Borschevsky, Nikolai	Tor., Cgy., Dal.	4	162	49	73	122	44	31	4	9	13	4	....	1992-93	1995-96
Boschman, Laurie	Tor., Edm., Wpg., N.J., Ott.	14	1009	229	348	577	2265	57	8	13	21	140	....	1979-80	1992-93
Bossy, Mike	NYI	10	752	573	553	1126	210	129	85	75	160	38	4	1977-78	1986-87
● Bostrom, Helge	Chi.	4	96	3	3	6	58	13	0	0	0	16	....	1929-30	1932-33
Botell, Mark	Phi.	1	32	4	10	14	31	....	....	....	....	....	....	1981-82	1981-82
Bothwell, Tim	NYR, St.L., Hfd.	11	502	28	93	121	382	49	0	3	3	56	....	1978-79	1988-89
Botterill, Jason	Dal., Atl., Cgy., Buf.	6	88	5	9	14	89	....	....	....	....	....	....	1997-98	2003-04
Botting, Cam	Atl.	1	2	0	1	1	0	....	....	....	....	....	....	1975-76	1975-76
Boucha, Henry	Det., Min., K.C., Col.	6	247	53	49	102	157	....	....	....	....	....	....	1971-72	1976-77
Bouchard, Butch	Mtl.	15	785	49	144	193	863	113	11	21	32	121	4	1941-42	1955-56
● Bouchard, Dick	NYR	1	1	0	0	0	0	....	....	....	....	....	....	1954-55	1954-55
● Bouchard, Edmond	Mtl., Ham., NYA, Pit.	8	211	19	21	40	117	....	....	....	....	....	....	1921-22	1928-29
Bouchard, Joel	Cgy., Nsh., Dal., Phx., N.J., NYR, Pit., NYI	11	364	22	53	75	264	....	....	....	....	....	....	1994-95	2005-06
Bouchard, Pierre	Mtl., Wsh.	12	595	24	82	106	433	76	3	10	13	56	5	1970-71	1981-82
● Boucher, Billy	Mtl., Bos., NYA	7	213	93	38	131	409	14	3	0	3	17	1	1921-22	1927-28
● Boucher, Bobby	Mtl.	1	11	1	0	1	0	2	0	0	0	0	1	1923-24	1923-24
● Boucher, Clarence	NYA	2	47	2	2	4	133	....	....	....	....	....	....	1926-27	1927-28
● Boucher, Frank	Ott., NYR	14	557	160	263	423	119	55	16	20	36	12	2	1921-22	1943-44
● Boucher, George	Ott., Mtl.M., Chi.	15	449	117	87	204	838	28	5	3	8	88	4	1917-18	1931-32
Boucher, Philippe	Buf., L.A., Dal., Pit.	16	748	94	206	300	702	65	4	10	14	39	1	1992-93	2008-09
‡ Bouck, Tyler	Dal., Phx., Van.	5	91	4	8	12	93	2	0	0	0	0	....	2000-01	2006-07
Boudreau, Bruce	Tor., Chi.	8	141	28	42	70	46	9	2	0	2	0	....	1976-77	1985-86
Boudrias, Andre	Mtl., Min., Chi., St.L., Van.	12	662	151	340	491	216	34	6	10	16	12	....	1963-64	1975-76
Boughner, Barry	Oak., Cal.	2	20	0	0	0	11	....	....	....	....	....	....	1969-70	1970-71
Boughner, Bob	Buf., Nsh., Pit., Cgy., Car., Col.	10	630	15	57	72	1382	65	0	12	12	67	....	1995-96	2005-06
‡ Boumedienne, Josef	N.J., T.B., Wsh.	3	47	4	12	16	36	....	....	....	....	....	....	2001-02	2003-04
Bourbonnais, Dan	Hfd.	2	59	3	25	28	11	....	....	....	....	....	....	1981-82	1983-84
Bourbonnais, Rick	St.L.	3	71	9	15	24	29	4	0	1	1	0	....	1975-76	1977-78
● Bourcier, Conrad	Mtl.	1	6	0	0	0	0	....	....	....	....	....	....	1935-36	1935-36
● Bourcier, Jean	Mtl.	1	9	0	1	1	0	....	....	....	....	....	....	1935-36	1935-36
● Bourdon, Luc	Van.	2	36	2	0	2	24	....	....	....	....	....	....	2006-07	2007-08
● Bourgeault, Leo	Tor., NYR, Ott., Mtl.	8	307	24	20	44	334	24	1	1	2	18	1	1926-27	1934-35
Bourgeois, Charlie	Cgy., St.L., Hfd.	7	290	16	54	70	788	40	2	3	5	194	....	1981-82	1987-88
Bourne, Bob	NYI, L.A.	14	964	258	324	582	605	139	40	56	96	108	4	1974-75	1987-88
Bourque, Phil	Pit., NYR, Ott.	12	477	88	111	199	516	56	13	12	25	107	2	1983-84	1995-96
Bourque, Raymond	Bos., Col.	22	1612	410	1169	1579	1141	214	41	139	180	171	1	1979-80	2000-01
Boutette, Pat	Tor., Hfd., Pit.	10	756	171	282	453	1354	46	10	14	24	109	....	1975-76	1984-85
Boutilier, Paul	NYI, Bos., Min., NYR, Wpg.	8	288	27	83	110	358	41	1	9	10	45	1	1981-82	1988-89
Bowen, Jason	Phi., Edm.	6	77	2	6	8	109	....	....	....	....	....	....	1992-93	1997-98
Bowler, Bill	CBJ	1	9	0	2	2	8	....	....	....	....	....	....	2000-01	2000-01
Bowman, Kirk	Chi.	3	88	11	17	28	19	7	1	0	1	0	....	1976-77	1978-79
● Bowman, Ralph	Ott., St.L., Det.	7	274	8	17	25	260	22	2	2	4	6	2	1933-34	1939-40
● Bownass, Jack	Mtl., NYR	4	80	3	8	11	58	....	....	....	....	....	....	1957-58	1961-62
Bowness, Rick	Atl., Det., St.L., Wpg.	7	173	18	37	55	191	5	0	0	0	2	....	1975-76	1981-82
● Boyd, Bill	NYR, NYA	4	138	15	7	22	72	10	0	0	0	4	1	1926-27	1929-30
● Boyd, Irwin	Bos., Det.	4	96	10	10	20	30	5	0	1	1	4	....	1931-32	1943-44
Boyd, Randy	Pit., Chi., NYI, Van.	8	257	20	67	87	328	13	0	2	2	26	....	1981-82	1988-89
Boyer, Wally	Tor., Chi., Oak., Pit.	7	365	54	105	159	163	15	1	3	4	0	....	1965-66	1971-72
Boyer, Zac	Dal.	2	3	0	0	0	0	2	0	0	0	0	....	1994-95	1995-96
Boyko, Darren	Wpg.	1	1	0	0	0	0	....	....	....	....	....	....	1988-89	1988-89
Bozek, Steve	L.A., Cgy., St.L., Van., S.J.	11	641	164	167	331	309	58	12	11	23	69	....	1981-82	1991-92
Bozon, Philippe	St.L.	4	144	16	25	41	101	19	2	0	2	31	....	1991-92	1994-95
● Brackenborough, John	Bos.	1	7	0	0	0	0	....	....	....	....	....	....	1925-26	1925-26
Brackenbury, Curt	Que., Edm., St.L.	4	141	9	17	26	226	2	0	0	0	0	....	1979-80	1982-83
● Bradley, Bart	Bos.	1	1	0	0	0	0	....	....	....	....	....	....	1949-50	1949-50
Bradley, Brian	Cgy., Van., Tor., T.B.	13	651	182	321	503	528	13	3	7	10	16	....	1985-86	1997-98
Bradley, Lyle	Cal., Cle.	2	6	1	0	1	2	....	....	....	....	....	....	1973-74	1976-77
Brady, Neil	N.J., Ott., Dal.	5	89	9	22	31	95	....	....	....	....	....	....	1989-90	1993-94
Bragnalo, Rick	Wsh.	4	145	15	35	50	46	....	....	....	....	....	....	1975-76	1978-79
Brandner, Christoph	Min.	1	35	4	5	9	8	....	....	....	....	....	....	2003-04	2003-04

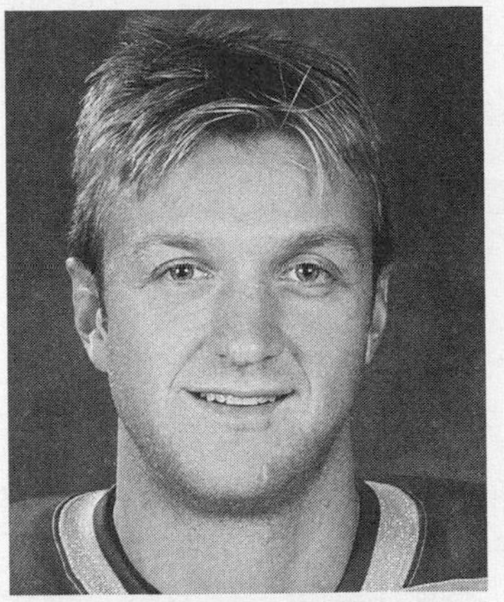
Rob Blake

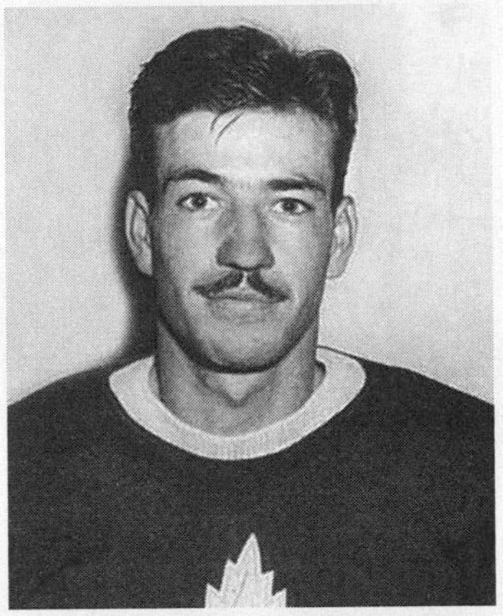
Garth Boesch

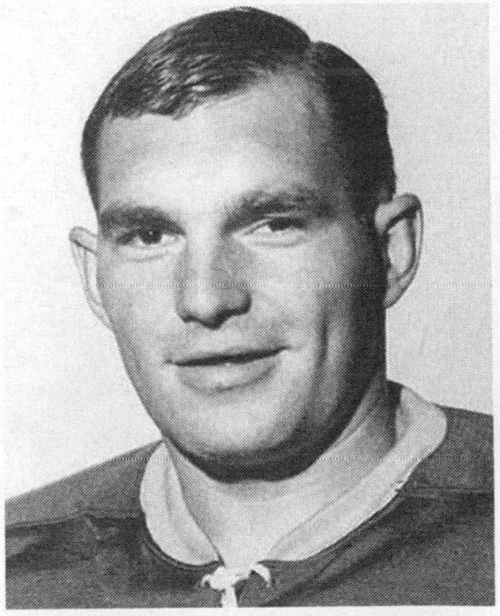
Andre Boudrais

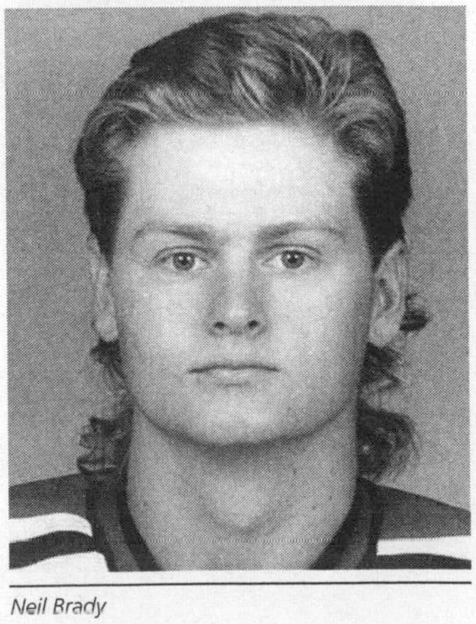
Neil Brady

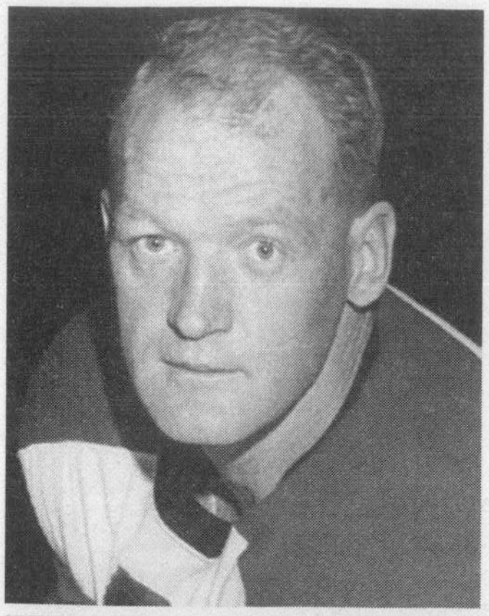

Andy Branigan

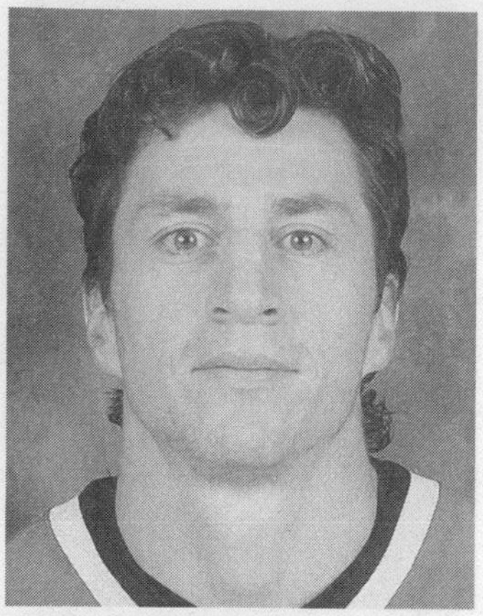

Rod Brind'Amour

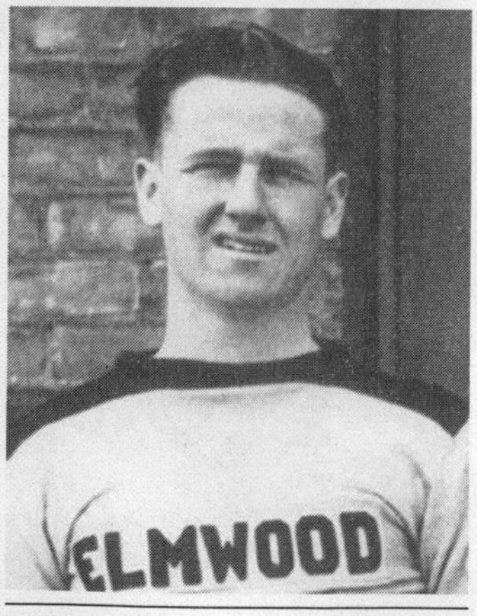

George Brown

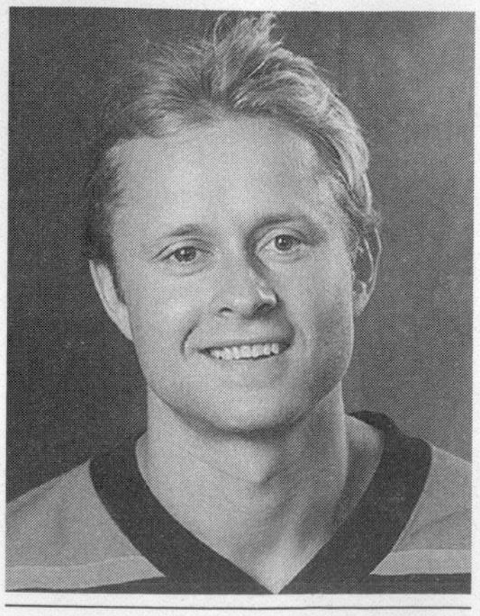

Valeri Bure

Name	NHL Teams	NHL Seasons	Regular Schedule GP	G	A	TP	PIM	Playoffs GP	G	A	TP	PIM	NHL Cup Wins	First NHL Season	Last NHL Season
• Branigan, Andy	NYA, Bro.	2	27	1	2	3	31	....	....	....	....	....	....	1940-41	1941-42
Brasar, Per-Olov	Min., Van.	5	348	64	142	206	33	13	1	2	3	0	....	1977-78	1981-82
‡ Brashear, Donald	Mtl., Van., Phi., Wsh., NYR	16	1025	85	120	205	2634	60	3	6	9	121	....	1993-94	2009-10
• Brayshaw, Russ	Chi.	1	43	5	9	14	24	....	....	....	....	....	....	1944-45	1944-45
Breault, Francis	L.A.	3	27	2	4	6	42	....	....	....	....	....	....	1990-91	1992-93
Breitenbach, Ken	Buf.	3	68	1	13	14	49	8	0	1	1	4	....	1975-76	1978-79
‡ Bremberg, Fredrik	Edm.	1	8	0	0	0	2	....	....	....	....	....	....	1998-99	1998-99
‡ Brendl, Pavel	Phi., Car., Phx.	4	78	11	11	22	16	2	0	0	0	0	....	2001-02	2005-06
Brennan, Dan	L.A.	2	8	0	1	1	9	....	....	....	....	....	....	1983-84	1985-86
• Brennan, Doug	NYR	3	123	9	7	16	152	16	1	0	1	21	1	1931-32	1933-34
‡ Brennan, Kip	L.A., Atl., Ana., NYI	5	61	1	1	2	222	....	....	....	....	....	....	2001-02	2007-08
Brennan, Rich	Col., S.J., NYR, L.A., Nsh., Bos.	6	50	2	6	8	33	....	....	....	....	....	....	1996-97	2002-03
• Brennan, Tom	Bos.	2	12	2	2	4	2	....	....	....	....	....	....	1943-44	1944-45
Brenneman, John	Chi., NYR, Tor., Det., Oak.	5	152	21	19	40	46	....	....	....	....	....	1	1964-65	1968-69
• Bretto, Joe	Chi.	1	3	0	0	0	4	....	....	....	....	....	....	1944-45	1944-45
• Brewer, Carl	Tor., Det., St.L.	12	604	25	198	223	1037	72	3	17	20	146	3	1957-58	1979-80
Brickley, Andy	Phi., Pit., N.J., Bos., Wpg.	11	385	82	140	222	81	17	1	4	5	4	....	1982-83	1993-94
• Briden, Archie	Bos., Det., Pit.	2	71	9	5	14	56	....	....	....	....	....	....	1926-27	1929-30
Bridgman, Mel	Phi., Cgy., N.J., Det., Van.	14	977	252	449	701	1625	125	28	39	67	298	....	1975-76	1988-89
• Briere, Michel	Pit.	1	76	12	32	44	20	10	5	3	8	17	....	1969-70	1969-70
Brigley, Travis	Cgy., Col.	3	55	3	6	9	16	....	....	....	....	....	....	1997-98	2003-04
‡ Brimanis, Aris	Phi., NYI, Ana., St.L.	7	113	2	12	14	57	....	....	....	....	....	....	1993-94	2003-04
Brind'Amour, Rod	St.L., Phi., Car.	21	1484	452	732	1184	1100	159	51	60	111	97	1	1988-89	2009-10
Brindley, Doug	Tor.	1	3	0	0	0	0	....	....	....	....	....	....	1970-71	1970-71
• Brink, Milt	Chi.	1	5	0	0	0	0	....	....	....	....	....	....	1936-37	1936-37
Brisebois, Patrice	Mtl., Col.	18	1009	98	322	420	623	98	9	23	32	76	1	1990-91	2008-09
Brisson, Gerry	Mtl.	1	4	0	2	2	4	....	....	....	....	....	....	1962-63	1962-63
Britz, Greg	Tor., Hfd.	3	8	0	0	0	4	....	....	....	....	....	....	1983-84	1986-87
• Broadbent, Punch	Ott., Mtl.M., NYA	11	303	121	51	172	564	23	4	6	10	60	4	1918-19	1928-29
Brochu, Stephane	NYR	1	1	0	0	0	0	....	....	....	....	....	....	1988-89	1988-89
Broden, Connie	Mtl.	3	6	2	1	3	2	7	0	1	1	0	2	1955-56	1957-58
Brooke, Bob	NYR, Min., N.J.	7	447	69	97	166	520	34	9	9	18	59	....	1983-84	1989-90
Brooks, Alex	N.J.	1	19	0	1	1	4	....	....	....	....	....	....	2006-07	2006-07
Brooks, Gord	St.L., Wsh.	3	70	7	18	25	37	....	....	....	....	....	....	1971-72	1974-75
• Brophy, Bernie	Mtl.M., Det.	3	62	4	4	8	25	2	0	0	0	2	1	1925-26	1929-30
Brossart, Willie	Phi., Tor., Wsh.	6	129	1	14	15	88	1	0	0	0	0	....	1970-71	1975-76
Broten, Aaron	Col., N.J., Min., Que., Tor., Wpg.	12	748	186	329	515	441	34	7	18	25	40	....	1980-81	1991-92
Broten, Neal	Min., Dal., N.J., L.A.	17	1099	289	634	923	569	135	35	63	98	77	1	1980-81	1996-97
Broten, Paul	NYR, Dal., St.L.	7	322	46	55	101	264	38	4	6	10	18	....	1989-90	1995-96
Brousseau, Paul	Col., T.B., Fla.	4	26	1	3	4	29	....	....	....	....	....	....	1995-96	2000-01
• Brown, Adam	Det., Chi., Bos.	10	391	104	113	217	378	26	2	4	6	14	1	1941-42	1951-52
Brown, Arnie	Tor., NYR, Det., NYI, Atl.	12	681	44	141	185	738	22	0	6	6	23	....	1961-62	1973-74
Brown, Brad	Mtl., Chi., NYR, Min., Buf.	7	330	2	27	29	747	11	0	0	0	16	....	1996-97	2003-04
Brown, Cam	Van.	1	1	0	0	0	7	....	....	....	....	....	....	1990-91	1990-91
• Brown, Connie	Det.	5	73	15	24	39	12	14	2	3	5	0	1	1938-39	1942-43
‡ Brown, Curtis	Buf., S.J., Chi.	13	736	129	171	300	398	87	14	15	29	58	....	1994-95	2007-08
Brown, Dave	Phi., Edm., S.J.	14	729	45	52	97	1789	80	2	3	5	209	1	1982-83	1995-96
Brown, Doug	N.J., Pit., Det.	15	854	160	214	374	210	109	23	23	46	26	2	1986-87	2000-01
• Brown, Fred	Mtl.M.	1	19	1	0	1	0	9	0	0	0	0	....	1927-28	1927-28
Brown, George	Mtl.	3	79	6	22	28	34	7	0	0	0	2	....	1936-37	1938-39
• Brown, Gerry	Det.	2	23	4	5	9	2	12	2	1	3	4	....	1941-42	1945-46
Brown, Greg	Buf., Pit., Wpg.	4	94	4	14	18	86	6	0	1	1	4	....	1990-91	1994-95
Brown, Harold	NYR	1	13	2	1	3	2	....	....	....	....	....	....	1945-46	1945-46
Brown, Jeff	Que., St.L., Van., Hfd., Car., Tor., Wsh.	13	747	154	430	584	498	87	20	45	65	59	....	1985-86	1997-98
Brown, Jim	L.A.	1	3	0	1	1	5	....	....	....	....	....	....	1982-83	1982-83
Brown, Keith	Chi., Fla.	16	876	68	274	342	916	103	4	32	36	184	....	1979-80	1994-95
Brown, Kevin	L.A., Hfd., Car., Edm.	6	64	7	9	16	28	1	0	0	0	0	....	1994-95	1999-00
Brown, Larry	NYR, Det., Phi., L.A.	9	455	7	53	60	180	35	0	4	4	10	....	1969-70	1977-78
Brown, Mike	Van., Ana., Chi.	4	34	1	2	3	130	....	....	....	....	....	....	2000-01	2005-06
Brown, Rob	Pit., Hfd., Chi., Dal., L.A.	11	543	190	248	438	599	54	12	14	26	45	....	1987-88	1999-00
Brown, Sean	Edm., Bos., N.J., Van.	9	436	14	43	57	907	9	0	0	0	37	....	1996-97	2005-06
• Brown, Stan	NYR, Det.	2	48	8	2	10	18	2	0	0	0	0	....	1926-27	1927-28
Brown, Wayne	Bos.	1	....	....	....	....	....	4	0	0	0	2	....	1953-54	1953-54
• Browne, Cecil	Chi.	1	13	2	0	2	4	....	....	....	....	....	....	1927-28	1927-28
Brownschidle, Jack	St.L., Hfd.	9	494	39	162	201	151	26	0	5	5	18	....	1977-78	1985-86
• Brownschidle, Jeff	Hfd.	2	7	0	1	1	2	....	....	....	....	....	....	1981-82	1982-83
Brubaker, Jeff	Hfd., Mtl., Cgy., Tor., Edm., NYR, Det.	8	178	16	9	25	512	2	0	0	0	27	....	1979-80	1988-89
Bruce, David	Van., St.L., S.J.	8	234	48	39	87	338	3	0	0	0	2	....	1985-86	1993-94
• Bruce, Gordie	Bos.	3	28	4	9	13	13	7	2	3	5	4	....	1940-41	1945-46
• Bruce, Morley	Ott.	4	71	8	3	11	27	3	0	0	0	2	2	1917-18	1921-22
Brule, Steve	N.J., Col.	2	2	0	0	0	0	1	0	0	0	0	1	1999-00	2002-03
Brumwell, Murray	Min., N.J.	7	128	12	31	43	70	2	0	0	0	2	....	1980-81	1987-88
Brunet, Benoit	Mtl., Dal., Ott.	13	539	101	161	262	229	54	5	20	25	32	1	1988-89	2001-02
• Bruneteau, Eddie	Det.	7	180	40	42	82	35	31	7	6	13	0	....	1940-41	1948-49
• Bruneteau, Mud	Det.	11	411	139	138	277	80	77	23	14	37	22	3	1935-36	1945-46
• Brydge, Bill	Tor., Det., NYA	9	368	26	52	78	506	2	0	0	0	4	....	1926-27	1935-36
Brydges, Paul	Buf.	1	15	2	2	4	6	....	....	....	....	....	....	1986-87	1986-87
• Brydson, Glenn	Mtl.M., St.L., NYR, Chi.	8	299	56	79	135	203	11	0	0	0	8	....	1930-31	1937-38
• Brydson, Gord	Tor.	1	8	2	0	2	8	....	....	....	....	....	....	1929-30	1929-30
‡ Brylin, Sergei	N.J.	13	765	129	179	308	273	109	15	19	34	32	3	1994-95	2007-08
Bubla, Jiri	Van.	5	256	17	101	118	202	6	0	0	0	7	....	1981-82	1985-86
• Buchanan, Al	Tor.	2	4	0	1	1	2	....	....	....	....	....	....	1948-49	1949-50
• Buchanan, Bucky	NYR	1	2	0	0	0	0	....	....	....	....	....	....	1948-49	1948-49
Buchanan, Jeff	Col.	1	6	0	0	0	6	....	....	....	....	....	....	1998-99	1998-99
Buchanan, Mike	Chi.	1	1	0	0	0	0	....	....	....	....	....	....	1951-52	1951-52
Buchanan, Ron	Bos., St.L.	2	5	0	0	0	0	....	....	....	....	....	....	1966-67	1969-70
Buchberger, Kelly	Edm., Atl., L.A., Phx., Pit.	18	1182	105	204	309	2297	97	10	15	25	129	2	1986-87	2003-04
Bucyk, John	Det., Bos.	23	1540	556	813	1369	497	124	41	62	103	42	2	1955-56	1977-78
Bucyk, Randy	Mtl., Cgy.	2	19	4	2	6	8	2	0	0	0	0	....	1985-86	1987-88
• Buhr, Doug	K.C.	1	6	0	2	2	4	....	....	....	....	....	....	1974-75	1974-75
• Bukovich, Tony	Det.	2	17	7	3	10	6	6	0	1	1	0	....	1943-44	1944-45
‡ Bulis, Jan	Wsh., Mtl., Van.	9	552	96	149	245	268	35	3	3	6	14	....	1997-98	2006-07
Bullard, Mike	Pit., Cgy., St.L., Phi., Tor.	11	727	329	345	674	703	40	11	18	29	44	....	1980-81	1991-92
• Buller, Hy	Det., NYR	5	188	22	58	80	215	....	....	....	....	....	....	1943-44	1953-54
Bulley, Ted	Chi., Wsh., Pit.	8	414	101	113	214	704	29	5	5	10	24	....	1976-77	1983-84
Burakovsky, Robert	Ott.	1	23	2	3	5	6	....	....	....	....	....	....	1993-94	1993-94
• Burch, Billy	Ham., NYA, Bos., Chi.	11	390	137	61	198	255	2	0	0	0	0	....	1922-23	1932-33
• Burchell, Fred	Mtl.	2	4	0	0	0	2	....	....	....	....	....	....	1950-51	1953-54
Burdon, Glen	K.C.	1	11	0	2	2	0	....	....	....	....	....	....	1974-75	1974-75
Bure, Pavel	Van., Fla., NYR	12	702	437	342	779	484	64	35	35	70	74	....	1991-92	2002-03
Bure, Valeri	Mtl., Cgy., Fla., St.L., Dal.	10	621	174	226	400	221	22	0	7	7	16	....	1994-95	2003-04
Bureau, Marc	Cgy., Min., T.B., Mtl., Phi.	11	567	55	83	138	327	50	5	7	12	46	....	1989-90	1999-00
Burega, Bill	Tor.	1	4	0	1	1	4	....	....	....	....	....	....	1955-56	1955-56
• Burke, Eddie	Bos., NYA	4	106	29	20	49	55	....	....	....	....	....	....	1931-32	1934-35
• Burke, Marty	Mtl., Pit., Ott., Chi.	11	494	19	47	66	560	31	2	4	6	44	2	1927-28	1937-38
• Burmister, Roy	NYA	3	67	4	3	7	2	....	....	....	....	....	....	1929-30	1931-32
Burnett, Garrett	Ana.	1	39	1	2	3	184	....	....	....	....	....	....	2003-04	2003-04
Burnett, Kelly	NYR	1	3	1	0	1	0	....	....	....	....	....	....	1952-53	1952-53
• Burns, Bobby	Chi.	3	20	1	0	1	8	....	....	....	....	....	....	1927-28	1929-30
Burns, Charlie	Det., Bos., Oak., Pit., Min.	11	749	106	198	304	252	31	5	4	9	6	....	1958-59	1972-73
Burns, Gary	NYR	2	11	2	2	4	18	5	0	0	0	2	....	1980-81	1981-82
• Burns, Norm	NYR	1	11	0	4	4	2	....	....	....	....	....	....	1941-42	1941-42
Burns, Robin	Pit., K.C.	5	190	31	38	69	139	....	....	....	....	....	....	1970-71	1975-76
Burr, Shawn	Det., T.B., S.J.	16	878	181	259	440	1069	91	16	19	35	95	....	1984-85	1999-00
Burridge, Randy	Bos., Wsh., L.A., Buf.	13	706	199	251	450	458	107	18	34	52	103	....	1985-86	1997-98
Burrows, Dave	Pit., Tor.	10	724	29	135	164	373	29	1	5	6	25	....	1971-72	1980-81
• Burry, Bert	Ott.	1	4	0	0	0	0	....	....	....	....	....	....	1932-33	1932-33
Burt, Adam	Hfd., Car., Phi., Atl.	13	737	37	115	152	961	21	0	1	1	8	....	1988-89	2000-01
Burton, Cummy	Det.	3	43	0	2	2	21	3	0	0	0	0	....	1955-56	1958-59
Burton, Nelson	Wsh.	2	8	1	0	1	21	....	....	....	....	....	....	1977-78	1978-79
• Bush, Eddie	Det.	2	26	4	6	10	40	11	1	6	7	23	....	1938-39	1941-42
Buskas, Rod	Pit., Van., L.A., Chi.	11	556	19	63	82	1294	18	0	3	3	45	....	1982-83	1992-93
Busniuk, Mike	Phi.	2	143	3	23	26	297	25	2	5	7	34	....	1979-80	1980-81
Busniuk, Ron	Buf.	2	6	0	3	3	13	....	....	....	....	....	....	1972-73	1973-74
• Buswell, Walt	Det., Mtl.	8	368	10	40	50	164	24	2	1	3	10	....	1932-33	1939-40
Butcher, Garth	Van., St.L., Que., Tor.	14	897	48	158	206	2302	50	6	5	11	122	....	1981-82	1994-95

Name	NHL Teams	NHL Seasons	Regular Schedule GP	G	A	TP	PIM	Playoffs GP	G	A	TP	PIM	NHL Cup Wins	First NHL Season	Last NHL Season
‡ Butenschon, Sven	Pit., Edm., NYI, Van.	8	140	2	12	14	86	4	0	0	0	0	....	1997-98	2005-06
● Butler, Dick	Chi.	1	7	2	0	2	0	....	....	....	....	....	....	1947-48	1947-48
Butler, Jerry	NYR, St.L., Tor., Van., Wpg.	11	641	99	120	219	515	48	3	3	6	79	....	1972-73	1982-83
Butsayev, Viacheslav	Phi., S.J., Ana., Fla., Ott., T.B.	6	132	17	26	43	133	....	....	....	....	....	....	1992-93	1999-00
Butsayev, Yuri	Det., Atl.	4	99	10	4	14	28	....	....	....	....	....	....	1999-00	2002-03
Butters, Bill	Min.	2	72	1	4	5	77	....	....	....	....	....	....	1977-78	1978-79
Buttrey, Gord	Chi.	1	10	0	0	0	0	....	....	....	....	....	....	1943-44	1943-44
Buynak, Gord	St.L.	1	4	0	0	0	2	....	....	....	....	....	....	1974-75	1974-75
Buzek, Petr	Dal., Atl., Cgy.	6	157	9	22	31	94	....	....	....	....	....	....	1997-98	2002-03
Byakin, Ilja	Edm., S.J.	2	57	8	25	33	44	....	....	....	....	....	....	1993-94	1994-95
Byce, John	Bos.	3	21	2	3	5	6	8	2	0	2	2	....	1989-90	1991-92
● Byers, Gord	Bos.	1	1	0	1	1	0	....	....	....	....	....	....	1949-50	1949-50
● Byers, Jerry	Min., Atl., NYR	4	43	3	4	7	15	....	....	....	....	....	....	1972-73	1977-78
Byers, Lyndon	Bos., S.J.	10	279	28	43	71	1081	37	2	2	4	96	....	1983-84	1992-93
● Byers, Mike	Tor., Phi., L.A., Buf.	4	166	42	34	76	39	4	0	1	1	0	....	1967-68	1971-72
‡ Bykov, Dmitri	Det.	1	71	2	10	12	43	4	0	0	0	0	....	2002-03	2002-03
Bylsma, Dan	L.A., Ana.	9	429	19	43	62	184	16	0	1	1	2	....	1995-96	2003-04
Byram, Shawn	NYI, Chi.	2	5	0	0	0	14	....	....	....	....	....	....	1990-91	1991-92

C

Name	NHL Teams	NHL Seasons	GP	G	A	TP	PIM	GP	G	A	TP	PIM	NHL Cup Wins	First NHL Season	Last NHL Season
● Caffery, Jack	Tor., Bos.	3	57	3	2	5	22	10	1	0	1	4	....	1954-55	1957-58
Caffery, Terry	Chi., Min.	2	14	0	0	0	0	1	0	0	0	0	....	1969-70	1970-71
● Cahan, Larry	Tor., NYR, Oak., L.A.	13	666	38	92	130	700	29	1	1	2	38	....	1954-55	1970-71
● Cahill, Charles	Bos.	2	32	0	1	1	4	....	....	....	....	....	....	1925-26	1926-27
● Cain, Francis	Mtl.M., Tor.	2	61	4	0	4	35	....	....	....	....	....	....	1924-25	1925-26
● Cain, Herb	Mtl.M., Mtl., Bos.	13	570	206	194	400	178	67	16	13	29	13	2	1933-34	1945-46
Cairns, Don	K.C., Col.	2	9	0	1	1	2	....	....	....	....	....	....	1975-76	1976-77
Cairns, Eric	NYR, NYI, Fla., Pit.	10	457	10	32	42	1182	16	0	0	0	28	....	1996-97	2006-07
‡ Cajanek, Petr	St.L.	4	269	46	107	153	144	7	0	2	2	4	....	2002-03	2006-07
Calder, Eric	Wsh.	2	2	0	0	0	0	....	....	....	....	....	....	1981-82	1982-83
‡ Calder, Kyle	Chi., Phi., Det., L.A., Ana.	10	590	114	180	294	309	18	2	1	3	10	....	1999-00	2009-10
‡ Caldwell, Ryan	NYI, Phx.	2	4	0	0	0	4	....	....	....	....	....	....	2005-06	2007-08
● Calladine, Norm	Bos.	3	63	19	29	48	8	....	....	....	....	....	....	1942-43	1944-45
Callander, Drew	Phi., Van.	4	39	6	2	8	7	....	....	....	....	....	....	1976-77	1979-80
Callander, Jock	Pit., T.B.	5	109	22	29	51	116	22	3	8	11	12	1	1987-88	1992-93
Callighen, Brett	Edm.	3	160	56	89	145	132	14	4	6	10	8	....	1979-80	1981-82
● Callighen, Patsy	NYR	1	36	0	0	0	32	9	0	0	0	0	1	1927-28	1927-28
Caloun, Jan	S.J., CBJ	3	24	8	6	14	2	....	....	....	....	....	....	1995-96	2000-01
Camazzola, James	Chi.	2	3	0	0	0	0	....	....	....	....	....	....	1983-84	1986-87
Camazzola, Tony	Wsh.	1	3	0	0	0	4	....	....	....	....	....	....	1981-82	1981-82
Cameron, Al	Det., Wpg.	6	282	11	44	55	356	7	0	1	1	2	....	1975-76	1980-81
● Cameron, Billy	Mtl., NYA	2	39	0	0	0	2	2	0	0	0	0	1	1923-24	1925-26
Cameron, Craig	Det., St.L., Min., NYI	9	552	87	65	152	196	27	3	1	4	17	....	1966-67	1975-76
Cameron, Dave	Col., N.J.	3	168	25	28	53	238	....	....	....	....	....	....	1981-82	1983-84
● Cameron, Harry	Tor., Ott., Mtl.	6	128	88	51	139	189	11	5	4	9	16	2	1917-18	1922-23
● Cameron, Scotty	NYR	1	35	8	11	19	0	....	....	....	....	....	....	1942-43	1942-43
Campbell, Bryan	L.A., Chi.	5	260	35	71	106	74	22	3	4	7	2	....	1967-68	1971-72
Campbell, Colin	Pit., Col., Edm., Van., Det.	11	636	25	103	128	1292	45	4	10	14	181	....	1974-75	1984-85
‡ Campbell, Darcy	CBJ	1	1	0	0	0	0	....	....	....	....	....	....	2006-07	2006-07
● Campbell, Dave	Mtl.	1	2	0	0	0	0	....	....	....	....	....	....	1920-21	1920-21
Campbell, Don	Chi.	1	17	1	3	4	8	....	....	....	....	....	....	1943-44	1943-44
● Campbell, Earl	Ott., NYA	3	76	6	3	9	14	1	0	0	0	6	....	1923-24	1925-26
Campbell, Jim	Ana., St.L., Mtl., Chi., Fla., T.B.	9	285	61	75	136	268	14	8	3	11	18	....	1995-96	2005-06
Campbell, Scott	Wpg., St.L.	3	80	4	21	25	243	....	....	....	....	....	....	1979-80	1981-82
Campbell, Wade	Wpg., Bos.	6	213	9	27	36	305	10	0	0	0	20	....	1982-83	1987-88
● Campeau, Tod	Mtl.	3	42	5	9	14	16	1	0	0	0	0	....	1943-44	1948-49
Campedelli, Dom	Mtl.	1	2	0	0	0	0	....	....	....	....	....	....	1985-86	1985-86
Capuano, Dave	Pit., Van., T.B., S.J.	4	104	17	38	55	56	6	1	1	2	5	....	1989-90	1993-94
Capuano, Jack	Tor., Van., Bos.	3	6	0	0	0	0	....	....	....	....	....	....	1989-90	1991-92
● Carbol, Leo	Chi.	1	6	0	1	1	4	....	....	....	....	....	....	1942-43	1942-43
Carbonneau, Guy	Mtl., St.L., Dal.	19	1318	260	403	663	820	231	38	55	93	161	3	1980-81	1999-00
‡ Card, Mike	Buf.	1	4	0	0	0	0	....	....	....	....	....	....	2006-07	2006-07
Cardin, Claude	St.L.	1	1	0	0	0	0	....	....	....	....	....	....	1967-68	1967-68
Cardwell, Steve	Pit.	3	53	9	11	20	35	4	0	0	0	2	....	1970-71	1972-73
● Carey, George	Que., Ham., Tor.	5	72	21	12	33	20	....	....	....	....	....	....	1919-20	1923-24
Carkner, Terry	NYR, Que., Phi., Det., Fla.	13	858	42	188	230	1588	54	1	9	10	48	....	1986-87	1998-99
Carleton, Wayne	Tor., Bos., Cal.	7	278	55	73	128	172	18	2	4	6	14	1	1965-66	1971-72
Carlin, Brian	L.A.	1	5	1	0	1	0	....	....	....	....	....	....	1971-72	1971-72
Carlson, Jack	Min., St.L.	6	236	30	15	45	417	25	1	2	3	72	....	1978-79	1986-87
Carlson, Kent	Mtl., St.L., Wsh.	5	113	7	11	18	148	8	0	0	0	13	....	1983-84	1988-89
Carlson, Steve	L.A.	1	52	9	12	21	23	4	1	1	2	7	....	1979-80	1979-80
Carlsson, Anders	N.J.	3	104	7	26	33	34	3	1	0	1	2	....	1986-87	1988-89
Carlyle, Randy	Tor., Pit., Wpg.	17	1055	148	499	647	1400	69	9	24	33	120	....	1976-77	1992-93
Carnback, Patrik	Mtl., Ana.	4	154	24	38	62	122	....	....	....	....	....	....	1992-93	1995-96
Carney, Keith	Buf., Chi., Phx., Ana., Van., Min.	16	1018	45	183	228	904	91	3	19	22	67	....	1991-92	2007-08
● Caron, Alain	Oak., Mtl.	2	60	9	13	22	18	....	....	....	....	....	....	1967-68	1968-69
Carpenter, Bob	Wsh., NYR, L.A., Bos., N.J.	18	1178	320	408	728	919	140	21	38	59	136	1	1981-82	1998-99
● Carpenter, Ed	Que., Ham.	2	45	10	5	15	41	....	....	....	....	....	....	1919-20	1920-21
Carr, Gene	St.L., NYR, L.A., Pit., Atl.	8	465	79	136	215	365	35	5	8	13	66	....	1971-72	1978-79
● Carr, Lorne	NYR, NYA, Tor.	13	580	204	222	426	132	53	10	9	19	13	2	1933-34	1945-46
Carr, Red	Tor.	1	5	0	1	1	2	....	....	....	....	....	....	1943-44	1943-44
Carriere, Larry	Buf., Atl., Van., L.A., Tor.	7	367	16	74	90	462	27	0	3	3	42	....	1972-73	1979-80
● Carrigan, Gene	NYR, Det., St.L.	3	37	2	1	3	13	4	0	0	0	0	....	1930-31	1934-35
Carroll, Billy	NYI, Edm., Det.	7	322	30	54	84	113	71	6	12	18	18	4	1980-81	1986-87
● Carroll, George	Mtl.M., Bos.	1	16	0	0	0	11	....	....	....	....	....	....	1924-25	1924-25
Carroll, Greg	Wsh., Det., Hfd.	2	131	20	34	54	44	....	....	....	....	....	....	1978-79	1979-80
Carruthers, Dwight	Det., Phi.	2	2	0	0	0	0	....	....	....	....	....	....	1965-66	1967-68
● Carse, Bill	NYR, Chi.	4	124	28	43	71	38	13	3	2	5	0	....	1938-39	1941-42
● Carse, Bob	Chi., Mtl.	5	167	32	55	87	52	10	0	2	2	2	....	1939-40	1947-48
● Carson, Bill	Tor., Bos.	4	159	54	24	78	156	11	3	0	3	14	1	1926-27	1929-30
● Carson, Frank	Mtl.M., NYA, Det.	7	248	42	48	90	166	27	0	2	2	9	1	1925-26	1933-34
● Carson, Gerry	Mtl., NYR, Mtl.M.	6	261	12	11	23	205	22	0	0	0	12	1	1928-29	1936-37
Carson, Jimmy	L.A., Edm., Det., Van., Hfd.	10	626	275	286	561	254	55	17	15	32	22	....	1986-87	1995-96
Carson, Lindsay	Phi., Hfd.	7	373	66	80	146	524	49	4	10	14	56	....	1981-82	1987-88
Carter, Anson	Wsh., Bos., Edm., NYR, L.A., Van., CBJ, Car.	10	674	202	219	421	229	24	8	5	13	4	....	1996-97	2006-07
Carter, Billy	Mtl., Bos.	3	16	0	0	0	6	....	....	....	....	....	....	1957-58	1961-62
Carter, John	Bos., S.J.	8	244	40	50	90	201	31	7	5	12	51	....	1985-86	1992-93
Carter, Ron	Edm.	1	2	0	0	0	0	....	....	....	....	....	....	1979-80	1979-80
● Carveth, Joe	Det., Bos., Mtl.	11	504	150	189	339	81	69	21	16	37	28	2	1940-41	1950-51
Cashman, Wayne	Bos.	17	1027	277	516	793	1041	145	31	57	88	250	2	1964-65	1982-83
Casselman, Mike	Fla.	1	3	0	0	0	0	....	....	....	....	....	....	1995-96	1995-96
Cassels, Andrew	Mtl., Hfd., Cgy., Van., CBJ, Wsh.	16	1015	204	528	732	410	21	4	7	11	8	....	1989-90	2005-06
Cassidy, Bruce	Chi.	6	36	4	13	17	10	1	0	0	0	0	....	1983-84	1989-90
Cassidy, Tom	Pit.	1	26	3	4	7	15	....	....	....	....	....	....	1977-78	1977-78
Cassolato, Tony	Wsh.	3	23	1	6	7	4	....	....	....	....	....	....	1979-80	1981-82
Caufield, Jay	NYR, Min., Pit.	7	208	5	8	13	759	17	0	0	0	42	2	1986-87	1992-93
Cavallini, Gino	Cgy., St.L., Que.	9	593	114	159	273	507	74	14	19	33	66	....	1984-85	1992-93
Cavallini, Paul	Wsh., St.L., Dal.	10	564	56	177	233	750	69	8	27	35	114	....	1986-87	1995-96
● Cavanagh, Tom	S.J.	2	18	1	2	3	4	....	....	....	....	....	....	2007-08	2008-09
Ceresino, Ray	Tor.	1	12	1	1	2	2	....	....	....	....	....	....	1948-49	1948-49
Cernik, Frantisek	Det.	1	49	5	4	9	13	....	....	....	....	....	....	1984-85	1984-85
Chabot, John	Mtl., Pit., Det.	8	508	84	228	312	85	33	6	20	26	2	....	1983-84	1990-91
● Chad, John	Chi.	3	80	15	22	37	29	10	0	1	1	2	....	1939-40	1945-46
● Chalmers, Chick	NYR	1	1	0	0	0	0	....	....	....	....	....	....	1953-54	1953-54
Chalupa, Milan	Det.	1	14	0	5	5	6	....	....	....	....	....	....	1984-85	1984-85
● Chamberlain, Murph	Tor., Mtl., Bro., Bos.	12	510	100	175	275	769	66	14	17	31	96	2	1937-38	1948-49
Chambers, Shawn	Min., Wsh., T.B., N.J., Dal.	13	625	50	185	235	364	94	7	26	33	72	2	1987-88	1999-00
Champagne, Andre	Tor.	1	2	0	0	0	0	....	....	....	....	....	....	1962-63	1962-63
Chapdelaine, Rene	L.A.	3	32	0	2	2	32	....	....	....	....	....	....	1990-91	1992-93
● Chapman, Art	Bos., NYA	10	438	62	176	238	140	26	1	5	6	9	....	1930-31	1939-40
Chapman, Blair	Pit., St.L.	7	402	106	125	231	158	25	4	6	10	15	....	1976-77	1982-83
Chapman, Brian	Hfd.	1	3	0	0	0	29	....	....	....	....	....	....	1990-91	1990-91
Charbonneau, Jose	Mtl., Van.	4	71	9	13	22	67	11	1	0	1	8	....	1987-88	1994-95
Charbonneau, Stephane	Que.	1	2	0	0	0	0	....	....	....	....	....	....	1991-92	1991-92

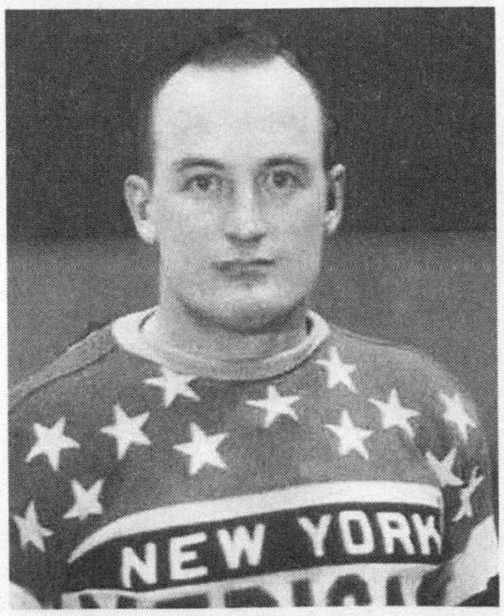

Eddie Burke

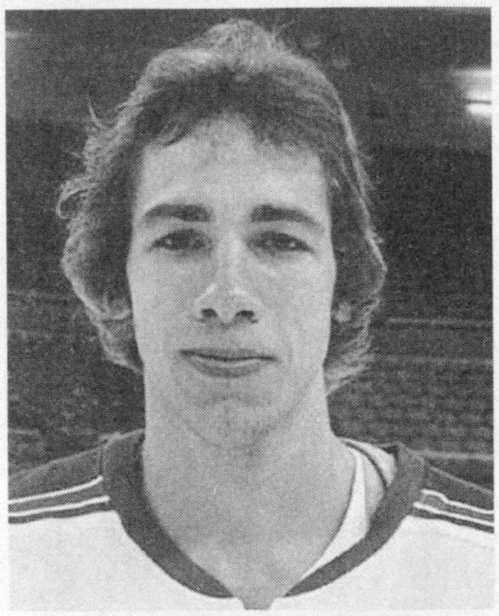
Brett Callighen

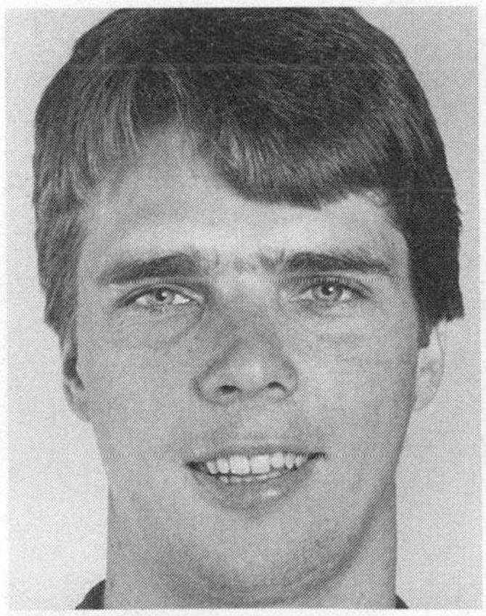
Dave Cameron

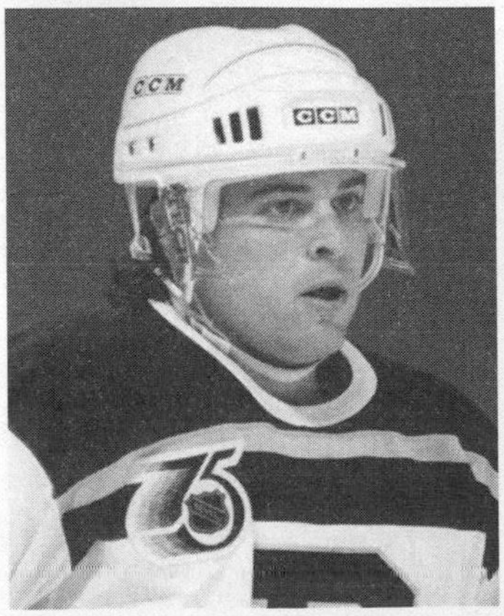

Jack Capuano

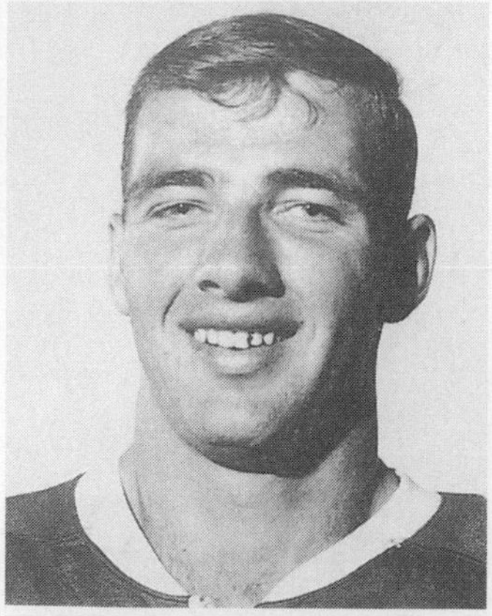

Wayne Carleton

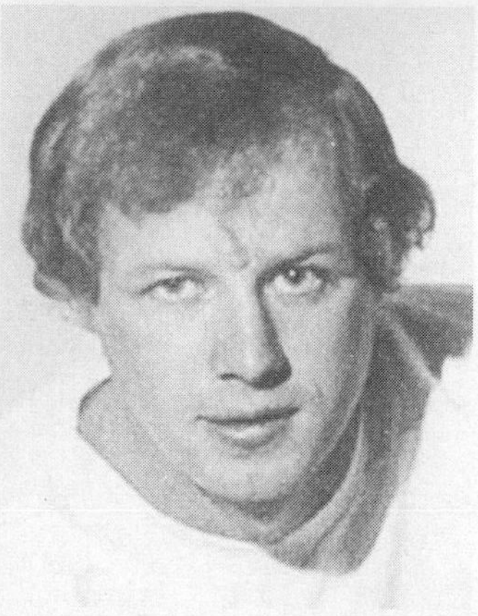

Wayne Cashman

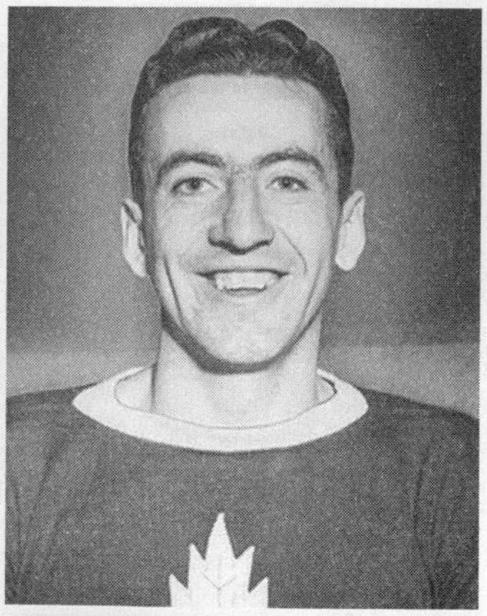

Jack Church

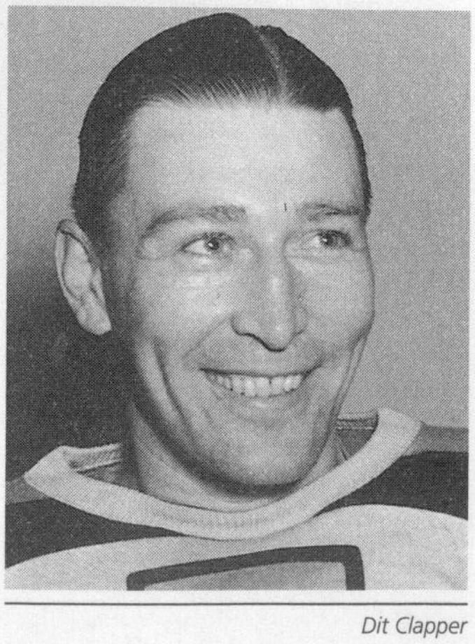

Dit Clapper

			Regular Schedule					Playoffs							
Name	NHL Teams	NHL Seasons	GP	G	A	TP	PIM	GP	G	A	TP	PIM	NHL Cup Wins	First NHL Season	Last NHL Season
Charlebois, Bob	Min.	1	7	1	0	1	0	....	....	....	....	....	....	1967-68	1967-68
Charlesworth, Todd	Pit., NYR	6	93	3	9	12	47	....	....	....	....	....	....	1983-84	1989-90
Charron, Eric	Mtl., T.B., Wsh., Cgy.	8	130	2	7	9	127	6	0	0	0	8	....	1992-93	1999-00
Charron, Guy	Mtl., Det., K.C., Wsh.	12	734	221	309	530	146	....	....	....	....	....	....	1969-70	1980-81
Chartier, Dave	Wpg.	1	1	0	0	0	0	....	....	....	....	....	....	1980-81	1980-81
Chartrand, Brad	L.A.	5	215	25	25	50	122	11	1	1	2	8	....	1999-00	2003-04
Chartraw, Rick	Mtl., L.A., NYR, Edm.	10	420	28	64	92	399	75	7	9	16	80	4	1974-75	1983-84
Chase, Kelly	St.L., Hfd., Tor.	11	458	17	36	53	2017	27	1	1	2	100	....	1989-90	1999-00
Chasse, Denis	St.L., Wsh., Wpg., Ott.	4	132	11	14	25	292	7	1	7	8	23	....	1993-94	1996-97
Chebaturkin, Vladimir	NYI, St.L., Chi.	5	62	2	7	9	52	3	0	0	0	2	....	1997-98	2001-02
• Check, Lude	Det., Chi.	2	27	6	2	8	4	....	....	....	....	....	....	1943-44	1944-45
Chelios, Chris	Mtl., Chi., Det., Atl.	26	1651	185	763	948	2891	266	31	113	144	423	3	1983-84	2009-10
Chernoff, Mike	Min.	1	1	0	0	0	0	....	....	....	....	....	....	1968-69	1968-69
Chernomaz, Rich	Col., N.J., Cgy.	7	51	9	7	16	18	....	....	....	....	....	....	1981-82	1991-92
Cherry, Dick	Bos., Phi.	3	145	12	10	22	45	4	1	0	1	4	....	1956-57	1969-70
Cherry, Don	Bos.	1	....	....	....	....	....	1	0	0	0	0	....	1954-55	1954-55
Chervyakov, Denis	Bos.	1	2	0	0	0	2	....	....	....	....	....	....	1992-93	1992-93
• Chevrefils, Real	Bos., Det.	8	387	104	97	201	185	30	5	4	9	20	....	1951-52	1958-59
• Chiasson, Steve	Det., Cgy., Hfd., Car.	13	751	93	305	398	1107	63	16	19	35	119	....	1986-87	1998-99
Chibirev, Igor	Hfd.	2	45	7	12	19	2	....	....	....	....	....	....	1993-94	1994-95
Chicoine, Dan	Cle., Min.	3	31	1	2	3	12	1	0	0	0	0	....	1977-78	1979-80
Chinnick, Rick	Min.	2	4	0	2	2	0	....	....	....	....	....	....	1973-74	1974-75
Chipperfield, Ron	Edm., Que.	2	83	22	24	46	34	....	....	....	....	....	....	1979-80	1980-81
Chisholm, Art	Bos.	1	3	0	0	0	0	....	....	....	....	....	....	1960-61	1960-61
Chisholm, Colin	Min.	1	1	0	0	0	0	....	....	....	....	....	....	1986-87	1986-87
• Chisholm, Lex	Tor.	2	54	10	8	18	19	3	1	0	1	0	....	1939-40	1940-41
‡ Chistov, Stanislav	Ana., Bos.	3	196	19	42	61	116	21	4	2	6	8	....	2002-03	2006-07
Chorney, Marc	Pit., L.A.	4	210	8	27	35	209	7	0	1	1	2	....	1980-81	1983-84
Chorske, Tom	Mtl., N.J., Ott., NYI, Wsh., Cgy., Pit.	11	596	115	122	237	225	50	5	12	17	10	1	1989-90	1999-00
‡ Chouinard, Eric	Mtl., Phi., Min.	4	90	11	11	22	16	....	....	....	....	....	....	2000-01	2005-06
• Chouinard, Gene	Ott.	1	8	0	0	0	0	....	....	....	....	....	....	1927-28	1927-28
Chouinard, Guy	Atl., Cgy., St.L.	10	578	205	370	575	120	46	9	28	37	12	....	1974-75	1983-84
Chouinard, Marc	Ana., Min., Van.	6	320	37	41	78	123	15	1	0	1	0	....	2000-01	2006-07
Christian, Dave	Wpg., Wsh., Bos., St.L., Chi.	15	1009	340	433	773	284	102	32	25	57	27	....	1979-80	1993-94
Christian, Jeff	N.J., Pit., Phx.	5	18	2	2	4	17	....	....	....	....	....	....	1991-92	1997-98
Christie, Mike	Cal., Cle., Col., Van.	7	412	15	101	116	550	2	0	0	0	0	....	1974-75	1980-81
‡ Christie, Ryan	Dal., Cgy.	2	7	0	0	0	0	....	....	....	....	....	....	1999-00	2001-02
Christoff, Steve	Min., Cgy., L.A.	5	248	77	64	141	108	35	16	12	28	25	....	1979-80	1983-84
Chrystal, Bob	NYR	2	132	11	14	25	112	....	....	....	....	....	....	1953-54	1954-55
Chubarov, Artem	Van.	5	228	25	33	58	40	27	0	4	4	4	....	1999-00	2003-04
Church, Brad	Wsh.	1	2	0	0	0	0	....	....	....	....	....	....	1997-98	1997-98
• Church, Jack	Tor., Bro., Bos.	5	130	4	19	23	154	25	1	1	2	18	....	1938-39	1945-46
Churla, Shane	Hfd., Cgy., Min., Dal., L.A., NYR	11	488	26	45	71	2301	78	5	7	12	282	....	1986-87	1996-97
Chychrun, Jeff	Phi., L.A., Pit., Edm.	8	262	3	22	25	744	19	0	2	2	65	1	1986-87	1993-94
Chynoweth, Dean	NYI, Bos.	9	241	4	18	22	667	6	0	0	0	26	....	1988-89	1997-98
Chyzowski, Dave	NYI, Chi.	6	126	15	16	31	144	2	0	0	0	0	....	1989-90	1996-97
Ciavaglia, Peter	Buf.	2	5	0	0	0	0	....	....	....	....	....	....	1991-92	1992-93
‡ Cibak, Martin	T.B.	3	154	5	18	23	60	11	0	1	1	0	1	2001-02	2005-06
Ciccarelli, Dino	Min., Wsh., Det., T.B., Fla.	19	1232	608	592	1200	1425	141	73	45	118	211	....	1980-81	1998-99
Ciccone, Enrico	Min., Wsh., T.B., Chi., Car., Van., Mtl.	9	374	10	18	28	1469	13	1	0	1	48	....	1991-92	2000-01
Cichocki, Chris	Det., N.J.	4	68	11	12	23	27	....	....	....	....	....	....	1985-86	1988-89
‡ Ciernik, Ivan	Ott., Wsh.	5	89	12	14	26	32	2	0	1	1	6	....	1997-98	2003-04
Cierny, Jozef	Edm.	1	1	0	0	0	0	....	....	....	....	....	....	1993-94	1993-94
• Ciesla, Hank	Chi., NYR	4	269	26	51	77	87	6	0	2	2	0	....	1955-56	1958-59
Ciger, Zdeno	N.J., Edm., NYR, T.B.	7	352	94	134	228	101	13	2	6	8	4	....	1990-91	2001-02
Cimellaro, Tony	Ott.	1	2	0	0	0	0	....	....	....	....	....	....	1992-93	1992-93
Cimetta, Rob	Bos., Tor.	4	103	16	16	32	66	1	0	0	0	15	....	1988-89	1991-92
Cirella, Joe	Col., N.J., Que., NYR, Fla., Ott.	15	828	64	211	275	1446	38	0	13	13	98	....	1981-82	1995-96
Cirone, Jason	Wpg.	1	3	0	0	0	2	....	....	....	....	....	....	1991-92	1991-92
Cisar, Marian	Nsh.	3	73	13	17	30	57	....	....	....	....	....	....	1999-00	2001-02
Clackson, Kim	Pit., Que.	2	106	0	8	8	370	8	0	0	0	70	....	1979-80	1980-81
• Clancy, King	Ott., Tor.	16	592	136	147	283	914	55	8	8	16	88	3	1921-22	1936-37
Clancy, Terry	Oak., Tor.	4	93	6	6	12	39	....	....	....	....	....	....	1967-68	1972-73
• Clapper, Dit	Bos.	20	833	228	246	474	462	82	13	17	30	50	3	1927-28	1946-47
Clark, Dan	NYR	1	4	0	1	1	6	....	....	....	....	....	....	1978-79	1978-79
Clark, Dean	Edm.	1	1	0	0	0	0	....	....	....	....	....	....	1983-84	1983-84
Clark, Gordie	Bos.	2	8	0	1	1	0	1	0	0	0	0	....	1974-75	1975-76
• Clark, Nobby	Bos.	1	5	0	0	0	0	....	....	....	....	....	....	1927-28	1927-28
Clark, Wendel	Tor., Que., NYI, T.B., Det., Chi.	15	793	330	234	564	1690	95	37	32	69	201	....	1985-86	1999-00
Clarke, Bobby	Phi.	15	1144	358	852	1210	1453	136	42	77	119	152	2	1969-70	1983-84
‡ Clarke, Dale	St.L.	1	3	0	0	0	0	....	....	....	....	....	....	2000-01	2000-01
‡ Clarke, Noah	L.A., N.J.	4	21	3	1	4	4	....	....	....	....	....	....	2003-04	2007-08
‡ Classen, Greg	Nsh.	3	90	7	10	17	48	....	....	....	....	....	....	2000-01	2002-03
• Cleghorn, Odie	Mtl., Pit.	10	181	95	34	129	142	12	7	2	9	5	1	1918-19	1927-28
• Cleghorn, Sprague	Ott., Tor., Mtl., Bos.	10	259	83	55	138	538	21	4	3	7	26	2	1918-19	1927-28
Clement, Bill	Phi., Wsh., Atl., Cgy.	11	719	148	208	356	383	50	5	3	8	26	2	1971-72	1981-82
Cline, Bruce	NYR	1	30	2	3	5	10	....	....	....	....	....	....	1956-57	1956-57
Clippingdale, Steve	L.A., Wsh.	2	19	1	2	3	9	1	0	0	0	0	....	1976-77	1979-80
Cloutier, Real	Que., Buf.	6	317	146	198	344	119	25	7	5	12	20	....	1979-80	1984-85
Cloutier, Rejean	Det.	2	5	0	2	2	2	....	....	....	....	....	....	1979-80	1981-82
Cloutier, Roland	Det., Que.	3	34	8	9	17	2	....	....	....	....	....	....	1977-78	1979-80
Cloutier, Sylvain	Chi.	1	7	0	0	0	0	....	....	....	....	....	....	1998-99	1998-99
• Clune, Wally	Mtl.	1	5	0	0	0	6	....	....	....	....	....	....	1955-56	1955-56
Clymer, Ben	T.B., Wsh.	7	438	52	77	129	367	16	0	2	2	6	1	1999-00	2006-07
Coalter, Gary	Cal., K.C.	2	34	2	4	6	2	....	....	....	....	....	....	1973-74	1974-75
Coates, Steve	Det.	1	5	1	0	1	24	....	....	....	....	....	....	1976-77	1976-77
Cochrane, Glen	Phi., Van., Chi., Edm.	10	411	17	72	89	1556	18	1	1	2	31	....	1978-79	1988-89
Coffey, Paul	Edm., Pit., L.A., Det., Hfd., Phi., Chi., Car., Bos.	21	1409	396	1135	1531	1802	194	59	137	196	264	4	1980-81	2000-01
Coflin, Hugh	Chi.	1	31	0	3	3	33	....	....	....	....	....	....	1950-51	1950-51
Cole, Danton	Wpg., T.B., N.J., NYI, Chi.	7	318	58	60	118	125	1	0	0	0	0	1	1989-90	1995-96
Colley, Kevin	NYI	1	16	0	0	0	52	....	....	....	....	....	....	2005-06	2005-06
Colley, Tom	Min.	1	1	0	0	0	2	....	....	....	....	....	....	1974-75	1974-75
Collings, Norm	Mtl.	1	1	0	1	1	0	....	....	....	....	....	....	1934-35	1934-35
Collins, Bill	Min., Mtl., Det., St.L., NYR, Phi., Wsh.	11	768	157	154	311	415	18	3	5	8	12	....	1967-68	1977-78
Collins, Gary	Tor.	1	....	....	....	....	....	2	0	0	0	0	....	1958-59	1958-59
‡ Collins, Rob	NYI	1	8	1	1	2	0	....	....	....	....	....	....	2005-06	2005-06
Collyard, Bob	St.L.	1	10	1	3	4	4	....	....	....	....	....	....	1973-74	1973-74
• Colman, Michael	S.J.	1	15	0	1	1	32	....	....	....	....	....	....	1991-92	1991-92
• Colville, Mac	NYR	9	353	71	104	175	130	40	9	10	19	14	1	1935-36	1946-47
• Colville, Neil	NYR	12	464	99	166	265	213	46	7	19	26	32	1	1935-36	1948-49
Colwill, Les	NYR	1	69	7	6	13	16	....	....	....	....	....	....	1958-59	1958-59
Comeau, Rey	Mtl., Atl., Col.	9	564	98	141	239	175	9	2	1	3	8	....	1971-72	1979-80
Comrie, Paul	Edm.	1	15	1	2	3	4	....	....	....	....	....	....	1999-00	1999-00
Conacher, Brian	Tor., Det.	5	155	28	28	56	84	12	3	2	5	21	1	1961-62	1971-72
• Conacher, Charlie	Tor., Det., NYA	12	459	225	173	398	523	49	17	18	35	49	1	1929-30	1940-41
Conacher, Jim	Det., Chi., NYR	8	328	85	117	202	91	19	5	2	7	4	....	1945-46	1952-53
• Conacher, Lionel	Pit., NYA, Mtl.M., Chi.	12	498	80	105	185	882	35	2	2	4	34	2	1925-26	1936-37
Conacher, Pat	NYR, Edm., N.J., L.A., Cgy., NYI	13	521	63	76	139	235	67	11	10	21	40	1	1979-80	1995-96
Conacher, Pete	Chi., NYR, Tor.	6	229	47	39	86	57	7	0	0	0	0	....	1951-52	1957-58
• Conacher, Roy	Bos., Det., Chi.	11	490	226	200	426	90	42	15	15	30	14	2	1938-39	1951-52
• Conn, Red	NYA	2	96	9	28	37	22	....	....	....	....	....	....	1933-34	1934-35
Conn, Rob	Chi., Buf.	2	30	2	5	7	20	....	....	....	....	....	....	1991-92	1995-96
• Connelly, Bert	NYR, Chi.	3	87	13	15	28	37	14	1	0	1	0	1	1934-35	1937-38
Connelly, Wayne	Mtl., Bos., Min., Det., St.L., Van.	10	543	133	174	307	156	24	11	7	18	4	....	1960-61	1971-72
Connor, Cam	Mtl., Edm., NYR	5	89	9	22	31	256	20	5	0	5	6	1	1978-79	1982-83
• Connor, Harry	Bos., NYA, Ott.	4	134	16	5	21	149	10	0	0	0	2	....	1927-28	1930-31
• Connors, Bob	NYA, Det.	3	78	17	10	27	110	2	0	0	0	10	....	1926-27	1929-30
Conroy, Al	Phi.	3	114	9	14	23	156	....	....	....	....	....	....	1991-92	1993-94
Contini, Joe	Col., Min.	3	68	17	21	38	34	2	0	0	0	0	....	1977-78	1980-81
Convery, Brandon	Tor., Van., L.A.	4	72	9	19	28	36	5	0	0	0	2	....	1995-96	1998-99
• Convey, Eddie	NYA	3	36	1	1	2	33	....	....	....	....	....	....	1930-31	1932-33
• Cook, Bill	NYR	11	474	229	138	367	386	46	13	11	24	68	2	1926-27	1936-37
• Cook, Bob	Van., Det., NYI, Min.	4	72	13	9	22	22	....	....	....	....	....	....	1970-71	1974-75
• Cook, Bud	Bos., Ott., St.L.	3	50	5	4	9	22	....	....	....	....	....	....	1931-32	1934-35
• Cook, Bun	NYR, Bos.	11	473	158	144	302	444	46	15	3	18	50	2	1926-27	1936-37

Name	NHL Teams	NHL Seasons	GP	G	A	TP	PIM	GP	G	A	TP	PIM	NHL Cup Wins	First NHL Season	Last NHL Season
• Cook, Lloyd	Bos.	1	4	0	1	0								1924-25	1924-25
• Cook, Tom	Chi., Mtl.M.	9	349	77	98	175	184	24	2	4	6	19	1	1929-30	1937-38
• Cooper, Carson	Bos., Mtl., Det.	8	294	110	57	167	111	7	0	0	0	2	....	1924-25	1931-32
Cooper, David	Tor.	3	30	3	7	10	24							1996-97	2000-01
Cooper, Ed	Col.	2	49	8	7	15	46							1980-81	1981-82
Cooper, Hal	NYR	1	8	0	0	0	2							1944-45	1944-45
• Cooper, Joe	NYR, Chi.	11	420	30	66	96	442	35	3	5	8	58	....	1935-36	1946-47
• Copp, Bobby	Tor.	2	40	3	9	12	26							1942-43	1950-51
‡ Corazzini, Carl	Bos., Chi.	2	19	2	1	3	2							2003-04	2006-07
• Corbeau, Bert	Mtl., Ham., Tor.	10	258	63	49	112	629	9	2	2	4	38	....	1917-18	1926-27
• Corbet, Rene	Que., Col., Cgy., Pit.	8	362	58	74	132	420	53	7	6	13	52	1	1993-94	2000-01
Corbett, Mike	L.A.	1	....	...	...	...	...	2	0	1	1	2	....	1967-68	1967-68
Corcoran, Norm	Bos., Det., Chi.	4	29	1	3	4	21	4	0	0	0	6	....	1949-50	1955-56
• Corkum, Bob	Buf., Ana., Phi., Phx., L.A., N.J., Atl.	12	720	97	103	200	281	62	7	7	14	24	....	1989-90	2001-02
• Cormier, Roger	Mtl.	1	1	0	0	0	0							1925-26	1925-26
Cornforth, Mark	Bos.	1	6	0	0	0	4							1995-96	1995-96
Corrigan, Chuck	Tor., NYA	2	19	2	2	4	2							1937-38	1940-41
• Corrigan, Chuck	Tor., NYA	10	594	152	195	347	698	17	2	3	5	20	....	1967-68	1977-78
Corrigan, Mike	L.A., Van., Pit.	1	8	0	1	1	6							2001-02	2001-02
Corrinet, Chris	Wsh.	1	3	0	1	1	0							1953-54	1953-54
• Corriveau, Andre	Mtl.	9	280	48	40	88	310	29	5	7	12	50	....	1985-86	1993-94
Corriveau, Yvon	Wsh., Hfd., S.J.	4	77	14	11	25	20	14	0	1	1	4	....	2000-01	2003-04
‡ Corso, Daniel	St.L., Atl.	19	1156	273	420	693	2357	140	38	49	87	291	....	1985-86	2003-04
Corson, Shayne	Mtl., Edm., St.L., Tor., Dal.	2	51	2	10	12	41							1979-80	1980-81
Cory, Ross	Wpg.	3	64	8	6	14	29	3	0	1	1	4	....	1975-76	1978-79
Cossette, Jacques	Pit.	3	15	3	5	11	4	6	2	2	4	2	1	1947-48	1949-50
• Costello, Les	Tor.	4	162	13	19	32	54	5	0	0	0	2	....	1953-54	1956-57
Costello, Murray	Chi., Bos., Det.	2	12	2	4	2	0							1983-84	1985-86
Costello, Rich	Tor.	1	12	1	0	1	0							1924-25	1924-25
• Cotch, Charlie	Ham., Tor.	10	696	103	190	293	383	67	9	15	24	44	....	1979-80	1988-89
Cote, Alain	Que.	9	119	2	18	20	124	11	0	2	2	26	....	1985-86	1993-94
Cote, Alain	Bos., Wsh., Mtl., T.B., Que.	1	8	0	0	0	4							2005-06	2005-06
‡ Cote, Jean-Philippe	Mtl.	6	105	1	2	3	377							1995-96	2000-01
Cote, Patrick	Dal., Nsh., Edm.	3	15	0	0	4	0	14	3	2	5	0	....	1982-83	1984-85
Cote, Ray	Edm.	4	156	1	6	7	411	3	0	0	0	0	....	2006-07	2009-10
Cote, Riley	Phi.	19	1171	122	313	435	545	102	11	22	33	62	....	1984-85	2002-03
• Cote, Sylvain	Hfd., Wsh., Tor., Chi., Dal.	12	503	101	103	204	419	43	4	9	13	46	1	1925-26	1936-37
• Cotton, Baldy	Pit., Tor., NYA	3	19	2	0	2	3							1917-18	1920-21
• Coughlin, Jack	Tor., Que., Mtl., Ham.	4	47	4	5	9	138	3	1	0	1	2	....	1979-80	1985-86
Coulis, Tim	Wsh., Min.	1	7	0	1	1	4							2006-07	2006-07
‡ Coulombe, Patrick	Van.	1	28	0	0	0	103							1930-31	1930-31
Coulson, D'arcy	Phi.	11	465	30	82	112	543	49	4	5	9	61	2	1931-32	1941-42
• Coulter, Art	Chi., NYR	3	26	5	5	10	11							1985-86	1987-88
Coulter, Neal	NYI	1	2	0	0	0	0							1933-34	1933-34
• Coulter, Thomas	Chi.	16	968	428	435	863	255	147	64	63	127	47	10	1963-64	1978-79
Cournoyer, Yvan	Mtl.	3	44	7	13	20	10	1	0	0	0	0	....	1984-85	1986-87
Courteau, Yves	Cgy., Hfd.	3	44	7	13	20	10							1991-92	1992-93
Courtenay, Ed	S.J.	17	1048	367	432	799	1465	156	39	70	109	262	1	1983-84	1999-00
• Courtnall, Geoff	Bos., Edm., Wsh., St.L., Van.	16	1029	297	447	744	557	129	39	44	83	83	....	1983-84	1998-99
Courtnall, Russ	Tor., Mtl., Min., Dal., Van., NYR, L.A.	3	33	1	2	3	16							1995-96	1997-98
Courville, Larry	Van.	10	244	33	21	54	478	19	1	1	2	39	1	1917-18	1926-27
• Coutu, Billy	Mtl., Ham., Bos.	10	385	86	70	156	89	45	9	7	16	4	1	1944-45	1953-54
Couture, Gerry	Det., Mtl., Chi.	8	309	48	56	104	184	23	1	5	6	15	1	1928-29	1935-36
• Couture, Rosie	Chi., Mtl.	3	33	4	5	9	4							1988-89	1991-92
Couturier, Sylvain	L.A.	3	70	5	6	11	43	8	0	0	0	9	1	1973-74	1975-76
Cowick, Bruce	Phi., Wsh., St.L.	2	78	7	12	19	52							1994-95	1995-96
Cowie, Rob	L.A.	13	549	195	353	548	143	64	12	34	46	22	2	1934-35	1946-47
• Cowley, Bill	St.L., Bos.	8	319	47	49	96	128	10	0	1	1	4	....	1926-27	1933-34
• Cox, Danny	Tor., Ott., Det., NYR	8	235	14	31	45	713	5	1	0	1	18	....	1984-85	1991-92
Coxe, Craig	Van., Cgy., St.L., S.J.	9	423	71	97	168	550	26	2	2	4	49	....	1990-91	2001-02
Craig, Mike	Min., Dal., Tor., S.J.	1	5	0	0	0	10							1996-97	1996-97
Craighead, John	Tor.	3	98	11	18	29	28							1991-92	1993-94
Craigwell, Dale	S.J.	6	140	7	36	43	50							1965-66	1975-76
Crashley, Bart	Det., K.C., L.A.	18	1071	266	493	759	524	118	27	43	70	64	....	1982-83	1999-00
• Craven, Murray	Det., Phi., Hfd., Van., Chi., S.J.	7	246	71	71	142	72	11	0	1	1	8	....	1979-80	1986-87
Crawford, Bob	St.L., Hfd., NYR, Wsh.	2	16	1	3	4	6							1980-81	1982-83
Crawford, Bobby	Col., Det.	13	548	38	140	178	202	66	3	13	16	36	2	1937-38	1949-50
• Crawford, Jack	Bos.	2	26	2	1	3	29	1	0	0	0	0	....	1989-90	1991-92
Crawford, Lou	Bos.	6	176	19	31	50	229	20	1	2	3	44	....	1981-82	1986-87
Crawford, Marc	Van.	2	38	10	8	18	117	2	1	3	9	1	....	1917-18	1918-19
• Crawford, Rusty	Ott., Tor.	14	708	187	216	403	1077	61	11	14	25	137	....	1983-84	1996-97
Creighton, Adam	Buf., Chi., NYI, T.B., St.L.	12	616	140	174	314	223	51	11	13	24	20	....	1948-49	1959-60
Creighton, Dave	Bos., Tor., Chi., NYR	1	11	0	1	1	2							1930-31	1930-31
• Creighton, Jimmy	Det.	2	85	6	8	14	37							1974-75	1975-76
Cressman, Dave	Min.	1	4	0	0	0	0							1956-57	1956-57
Cressman, Glen	Mtl.	11	536	67	134	201	135	110	15	28	43	40	2	1965-66	1976-77
Crisp, Terry	Bos., St.L., NYI, Phi.	1	9	0	1	1	4							1989-90	1989-90
Cristofoli, Ed	Mtl.	1	16	0	0	0	4							1937-38	1937-38
• Croghan, Maurice	Mtl.M.	8	475	55	68	123	218	27	6	2	8	32	....	1977-78	1984-85
Crombeen, Mike	Cle., St.L., Hfd.	7	292	3	18	21	877	32	1	0	1	38	....	1988-89	1994-95
Cronin, Shawn	Wsh., Wpg., Phi., S.J.	12	659	34	97	131	684	47	2	4	6	62	....	1993-94	2005-06
Cross, Cory	T.B., Tor., NYR, Edm., Pit., Det.	1	21	0	0	0	10							1930-31	1930-31
• Crossett, Stan	Phi.														
Crossman, Doug	Chi., Phi., L.A., NYI, Hfd., Det., T.B., St.L.	14	914	105	359	464	534	97	12	39	51	105	....	1980-81	1993-94
Croteau, Gary	L.A., Det., Cal., K.C., Col.	12	684	144	175	319	143	11	3	2	5	8	....	1968-69	1979-80
Crowder, Bruce	Bos., Pit.	4	243	47	51	98	156	31	8	4	12	41	....	1981-82	1984-85
Crowder, Keith	Bos., L.A.	10	662	223	271	494	1354	85	14	22	36	218	....	1980-81	1989-90
Crowder, Troy	N.J., Det., L.A., Van.	7	150	9	7	16	433	4	0	0	0	22	....	1987-88	1996-97
Crowe, Phil	L.A., Phi., Ott., Nsh.	6	94	4	5	9	173	3	0	0	0	16	....	1993-94	1999-00
Crowley, Mike	Ana.	3	67	5	15	20	44							1997-98	2000-01
Crowley, Ted	Hfd., Col., NYI	2	34	2	4	6	12							1993-94	1998-99
Crozier, Greg	Pit.	1	1	0	0	0	0							2000-01	2000-01
Crozier, Joe	Tor.	1	5	0	3	3	2							1959-60	1959-60
• Crutchfield, Nels	Mtl.	1	41	5	5	10	20	2	0	1	1	22	....	1934-35	1934-35
Culhane, Jim	Hfd.	1	6	0	1	1	4							1989-90	1989-90
Cullen, Barry	Tor., Det.	5	219	32	52	84	111	6	0	0	0	0	....	1955-56	1959-60
Cullen, Brian	Tor., NYR	7	326	56	100	156	92	19	3	0	3	2	....	1954-55	1960-61
Cullen, David	Phx., Min.	2	19	0	0	0	6							2000-01	2001-02
Cullen, John	Pit., Hfd., Tor., T.B.	11	621	187	363	550	898	53	12	22	34	58	....	1988-89	1998-99
Cullen, Ray	NYR, Det., Min., Van.	6	313	92	123	215	120	20	3	10	13	2	....	1965-66	1970-71
Cummins, Barry	Cal.	1	36	1	2	3	39							1973-74	1973-74
Cummins, Jim	Det., Phi., T.B., Chi., Phx., Mtl., Ana., NYI, Col.	12	511	24	36	60	1538	37	1	2	3	43	....	1991-92	2003-04
Cunneyworth, Randy	Buf., Pit., Wpg., Hfd., Chi., Ott.	16	866	189	225	414	1280	45	7	7	14	61	....	1980-81	1998-99
Cunningham, Bob	NYR	2	4	0	1	1	0							1960-61	1961-62
• Cunningham, Jim	Phi.	1	1	0	0	0	4							1977-78	1977-78
• Cunningham, Les	NYA, Chi.	2	60	7	19	26	21	1	0	0	0	4	....	1936-37	1939-40
Cupolo, Bill	Bos.	1	47	11	13	24	10	7	1	2	3	0	....	1944-45	1944-45
Curran, Brian	Bos., NYI, Tor., Buf., Wsh.	10	381	7	33	40	1461	24	0	1	1	122	....	1983-84	1993-94
Currie, Dan	Edm., L.A.	4	22	2	1	3	4							1990-91	1993-94
Currie, Glen	Wsh., L.A.	8	326	39	79	118	100	12	1	3	4	4	....	1979-80	1987-88
Currie, Hugh	Mtl.	1	1	0	0	0	0							1950-51	1950-51
Currie, Tony	St.L., Van., Hfd.	8	290	92	119	211	83	16	4	12	16	14	....	1977-78	1984-85
• Curry, Floyd	Mtl.	11	601	105	99	204	147	91	23	17	40	38	4	1947-48	1957-58
Curtale, Tony	Cgy.	1	2	0	0	0	0							1980-81	1980-81
Curtis, Paul	Mtl., L.A., St.L.	4	185	3	34	37	161	5	0	0	0	4	....	1969-70	1972-73
Cushenan, Ian	Chi., Mtl., NYR, Det.	5	129	3	11	14	134							1956-57	1963-64
Cusson, Jean	Oak.	1	2	0	0	0	0							1967-68	1967-68
‡ Cutta, Jakub	Wsh.	3	6	0	0	0	6							2000-01	2003-04
Cyr, Denis	Cgy., Chi., St.L.	6	193	41	43	84	36	4	0	0	0	0	....	1980-81	1985-86
Cyr, Paul	Buf., NYR, Hfd.	9	470	101	140	241	623	24	4	6	10	31	....	1982-83	1991-92
Czerkawski, Mariusz	Bos., Edm., NYI, Mtl., Tor.	12	745	215	220	435	274	42	8	7	15	18	....	1993-94	2005-06

D

| ‡ Dackell, Andreas | Ott., Mtl. | 8 | 613 | 91 | 159 | 250 | 162 | 44 | 5 | 5 | 10 | 10 | .... | 1996-97 | 2003-04 |

Riley Cote

Bill Cowley

Jack Crawford

Joe Crozier

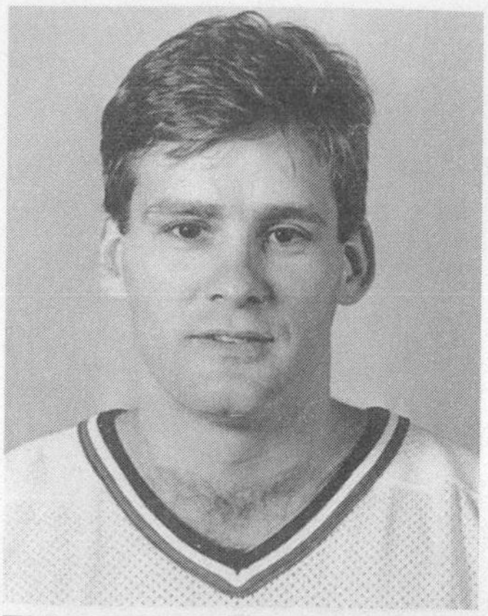

Paul Cyr

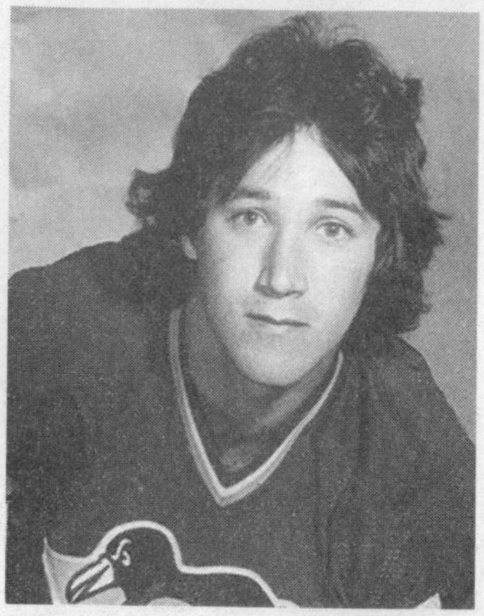

Kim Davis

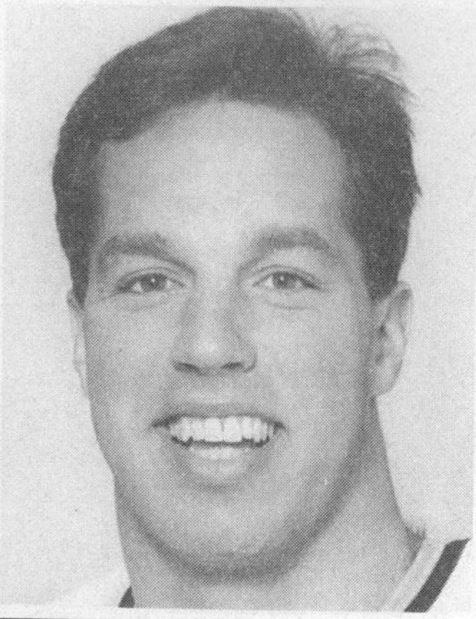

Dale DeGray

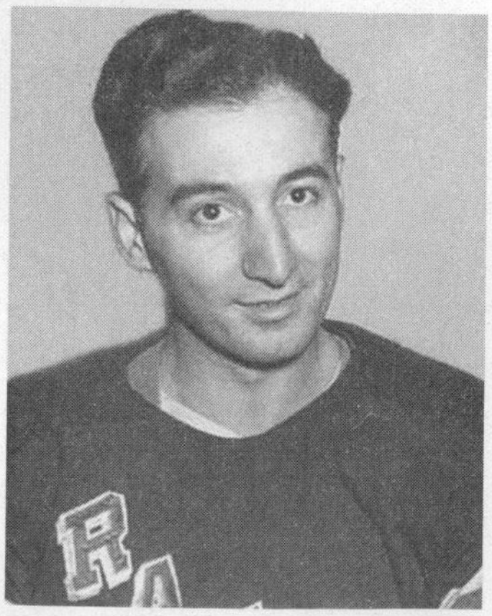

Ab DeMarco

Name	NHL Teams	NHL Seasons	Regular Schedule					Playoffs					NHL Cup Wins	First NHL Season	Last NHL Season
			GP	G	A	TP	PIM	GP	G	A	TP	PIM			
Dagenais, Pierre	N.J., Fla., Mtl.	5	142	35	23	58	58	8	0	1	1	6	....	2000-01	2005-06
Dahl, Kevin	Cgy., Phx., Tor., CBJ	8	188	7	22	29	153	16	0	2	2	12	....	1992-93	2000-01
Dahlen, Ulf	NYR, Min., Dal., S.J., Chi., Wsh.	14	966	301	354	655	230	85	15	25	40	12	....	1987-88	2002-03
Dahlin, Kjell	Mtl.	3	166	57	59	116	10	35	6	11	17	6	1	1985-86	1987-88
‡ Dahlman, Toni	Ott.	2	22	1	1	2	0	....	....	....	....	....	....	2001-02	2002-03
Dahlquist, Chris	Pit., Min., Cgy., Ott.	11	532	19	71	90	488	39	4	7	11	30	....	1985-86	1995-96
● Dahlstrom, Cully	Chi.	8	342	88	118	206	58	29	6	8	14	4	1	1937-38	1944-45
Daigle, Alain	Chi.	6	389	56	50	106	122	17	0	1	1	0	....	1974-75	1979-80
Daigle, Alexandre	Ott., Phi., T.B., NYR, Pit., Min.	10	616	129	198	327	186	12	0	2	2	2	....	1993-94	2005-06
Daigneault, J.J.	Van., Phi., Mtl., St.L., Pit., Ana., NYI, Nsh., Phx., Min.	16	899	53	197	250	687	99	5	26	31	100	1	1984-85	2000-01
Dailey, Bob	Van., Phi.	9	561	94	231	325	814	63	12	34	46	105	....	1973-74	1981-82
● Daley, Frank	Det.	1	5	0	0	0	0	2	0	0	0	0	....	1928-29	1928-29
Daley, Pat	Wpg.	2	12	1	0	1	13	....	....	....	....	....	....	1979-80	1980-81
Dalgarno, Brad	NYI	10	321	49	71	120	332	27	2	4	6	37	....	1985-86	1995-96
‡ Dallman, Kevin	Bos., St.L., L.A.	3	154	8	23	31	45	....	....	....	....	....	....	2005-06	2007-08
Dallman, Marty	Tor.	2	6	0	1	1	0	....	....	....	....	....	....	1987-88	1988-89
Dallman, Rod	NYI, Phi.	4	6	1	0	1	26	1	0	1	1	0	....	1987-88	1991-92
● Dame, Bunny	Mtl.	1	34	2	5	7	4	....	....	....	....	....	....	1941-42	1941-42
● Damore, Hank	NYR	1	4	1	0	1	2	....	....	....	....	....	....	1943-44	1943-44
Damphousse, Vincent	Tor., Edm., Mtl., S.J.	18	1378	432	773	1205	1190	140	41	63	104	144	1	1986-87	2003-04
Dandenault, Mathieu	Det., Mtl.	13	868	68	135	203	516	83	3	8	11	24	3	1995-96	2008-09
Daneyko, Ken	N.J.	20	1283	36	142	178	2519	175	5	17	22	296	3	1983-84	2002-03
Daniels, Jeff	Pit., Fla., Hfd., Car., Nsh.	12	425	17	26	43	83	41	3	5	8	2	1	1990-91	2002-03
Daniels, Kimbi	Phi.	2	27	1	2	3	4	....	....	....	....	....	....	1990-91	1991-92
Daniels, Scott	Hfd., Phi., N.J.	6	149	8	12	20	667	1	0	0	0	0	....	1992-93	1998-99
Danton, Mike	N.J., St.L.	3	87	9	5	14	182	5	1	0	1	2	....	2000-01	2003-04
Daoust, Dan	Mtl., Tor.	8	522	87	167	254	544	32	7	5	12	83	....	1982-83	1989-90
Darby, Craig	Mtl., NYI, Phi., N.J.	9	196	21	35	56	32	....	....	....	....	....	....	1994-95	2003-04
Dark, Michael	St.L.	2	43	5	6	11	14	....	....	....	....	....	....	1986-87	1987-88
● Darragh, Harold	Pit., Phi., Bos., Tor.	8	308	68	49	117	50	16	1	3	4	4	1	1925-26	1932-33
● Darragh, Jack	Ott.	6	121	66	46	112	113	11	3	0	3	9	3	1917-18	1923-24
David, Richard	Que.	3	31	4	4	8	10	1	0	0	0	0	....	1979-80	1982-83
● Davidson, Bob	Tor.	12	491	94	160	254	398	79	5	17	22	76	2	1934-35	1945-46
● Davidson, Gord	NYR	2	51	3	6	9	8	....	....	....	....	....	....	1942-43	1943-44
Davidson, Matt	CBJ	3	56	5	7	12	28	....	....	....	....	....	....	2000-01	2002-03
‡ Davidsson, Johan	Ana., NYI	2	83	6	9	15	16	1	0	0	0	0	....	1998-99	1999-00
● Davie, Bob	Bos.	3	41	0	1	1	25	....	....	....	....	....	....	1933-34	1935-36
● Davies, Buck	NYR	1	....	....	....	....	....	1	0	0	0	0	....	1947-48	1947-48
● Davis, Bob	Det.	1	3	0	0	0	0	....	....	....	....	....	....	1932-33	1932-33
Davis, Kim	Pit., Tor.	4	36	5	7	12	51	4	0	0	0	0	....	1977-78	1980-81
● Davis, Lorne	Mtl., Chi., Det., Bos.	6	95	8	12	20	20	18	3	1	4	10	1	1951-52	1959-60
Davis, Mal	Det., Buf.	6	100	31	22	53	34	7	1	0	1	0	....	1978-79	1985-86
● Davison, Murray	Bos.	1	1	0	0	0	0	....	....	....	....	....	....	1965-66	1965-66
Davydov, Evgeny	Wpg., Fla., Ott.	4	155	40	39	79	120	11	2	2	4	2	....	1991-92	1994-95
Daw, Jeff	Col.	1	1	0	1	1	0	....	....	....	....	....	....	2001-02	2001-02
Dawe, Jason	Buf., NYI, Mtl., NYR	8	366	86	90	176	162	22	4	3	7	18	....	1993-94	2001-02
● Dawes, Bob	Tor., Mtl.	4	32	2	7	9	6	10	0	0	0	2	1	1946-47	1950-51
● Day, Hap	Tor., NYA	14	581	86	116	202	601	53	4	7	11	56	1	1924-25	1937-38
Day, Joe	Hfd., NYI	3	72	1	10	11	87	....	....	....	....	....	....	1991-92	1993-94
Daze, Eric	Chi.	11	601	226	172	398	176	37	5	7	12	8	....	1994-95	2005-06
de Vries, Greg	Edm., Nsh., Col., NYR, Ott., Atl.	13	878	48	146	194	780	111	8	14	22	91	1	1995-96	2008-09
Dea, Billy	NYR, Det., Chi., Pit.	8	397	67	54	121	44	11	2	1	3	6	....	1953-54	1970-71
● Deacon, Don	Det.	3	30	6	4	10	6	2	2	1	3	0	....	1936-37	1939-40
Deadmarsh, Adam	Que., Col., L.A.	10	567	184	189	373	819	105	26	40	66	100	1	1994-95	2003-04
Deadmarsh, Butch	Buf., Atl., K.C.	5	137	12	5	17	155	4	0	0	0	17	....	1970-71	1974-75
Dean, Barry	Col., Phi.	3	165	25	56	81	146	....	....	....	....	....	....	1976-77	1978-79
Dean, Kevin	N.J., Atl., Dal., Chi.	7	331	7	48	55	138	16	2	2	4	2	1	1994-95	2000-01
Debenedet, Nelson	Det., Pit.	2	46	10	4	14	13	....	....	....	....	....	....	1973-74	1974-75
DeBlois, Lucien	NYR, Col., Wpg., Mtl., Que., Tor.	15	993	249	276	525	814	52	7	6	13	38	1	1977-78	1991-92
Debol, Dave	Hfd.	2	92	26	26	52	4	3	0	0	0	0	....	1979-80	1980-81
DeBrusk, Louie	Edm., T.B., Phx., Chi.	11	401	24	17	41	1161	15	2	0	2	10	....	1991-92	2002-03
DeFauw, Brad	Car.	1	9	3	0	3	2	....	....	....	....	....	....	2002-03	2002-03
Defazio, Dean	Pit.	1	22	0	2	2	28	....	....	....	....	....	....	1983-84	1983-84
DeGray, Dale	Cgy., Tor., L.A., Buf.	5	153	18	47	65	195	13	1	3	4	28	....	1985-86	1989-90
● Delisle, Jonathan	Mtl.	1	1	0	0	0	0	....	....	....	....	....	....	1998-99	1998-99
Delisle, Xavier	T.B., Mtl.	2	16	3	2	5	6	....	....	....	....	....	....	1998-99	2000-01
● Delmonte, Armand	Bos.	1	1	0	0	0	0	....	....	....	....	....	....	1945-46	1945-46
‡ Delmore, Andy	Phi., Nsh., Buf., CBJ	7	283	43	58	101	105	20	6	2	8	16	....	1998-99	2005-06
Delorme, Gilbert	Mtl., St.L., Que., Det., Pit.	9	541	31	92	123	520	56	1	9	10	56	....	1981-82	1989-90
Delorme, Ron	Col., Van.	9	524	83	83	166	667	25	1	2	3	59	....	1976-77	1984-85
Delory, Val	NYR	1	1	0	0	0	0	....	....	....	....	....	....	1948-49	1948-49
Delparte, Guy	Col.	1	48	1	8	9	18	....	....	....	....	....	....	1976-77	1976-77
Delvecchio, Alex	Det.	24	1549	456	825	1281	383	121	35	69	104	29	3	1950-51	1973-74
● DeMarco, Ab	Chi., Tor., Bos., NYR	7	209	72	93	165	53	11	3	0	3	2	....	1938-39	1946-47
DeMarco, Ab	NYR, St.L., Pit., Van., L.A., Bos.	9	344	44	80	124	75	25	1	2	3	17	....	1969-70	1978-79
● Demers, Tony	Mtl., NYR	6	83	20	22	42	23	2	0	0	0	0	....	1937-38	1943-44
‡ Demitra, Pavol	Ott., St.L., L.A., Min., Van.	16	847	304	464	768	284	94	23	36	59	34	....	1993-94	2009-10
Dempsey, Nathan	Tor., Chi., L.A., Bos.	8	260	21	67	88	120	6	0	2	2	0	....	1996-97	2006-07
Denis, Jean-Paul	NYR	2	10	0	2	2	2	....	....	....	....	....	....	1946-47	1949-50
Denis, Lulu	Mtl.	2	3	0	1	1	0	....	....	....	....	....	....	1949-50	1950-51
● Denneny, Corb	Tor., Ham., Chi.	9	176	103	42	145	148	6	1	0	1	7	2	1917-18	1927-28
● Denneny, Cy	Ott., Bos.	12	328	248	85	333	301	25	16	2	18	23	5	1917-18	1928-29
Dennis, Norm	St.L.	4	12	3	0	3	11	5	0	0	0	2	....	1968-69	1971-72
● Denoird, Gerry	Tor.	1	17	0	1	1	0	....	....	....	....	....	....	1922-23	1922-23
DePalma, Larry	Min., S.J., Pit.	7	148	21	20	41	408	3	0	0	0	6	....	1985-86	1993-94
Derlago, Bill	Van., Tor., Bos., Wpg., Que.	9	555	189	227	416	247	13	5	0	5	8	....	1978-79	1986-87
● Desaulniers, Gerard	Mtl.	3	8	0	2	2	4	....	....	....	....	....	....	1950-51	1953-54
Descoteaux, Matthieu	Mtl.	1	5	1	1	2	4	....	....	....	....	....	....	2000-01	2000-01
● Desilets, Joffre	Mtl., Chi.	5	192	37	45	82	57	7	1	0	1	7	....	1935-36	1939-40
Desjardins, Eric	Mtl., Phi.	17	1143	136	439	575	757	168	23	57	80	93	1	1988-89	2005-06
Desjardins, Martin	Mtl.	1	8	0	2	2	2	....	....	....	....	....	....	1989-90	1989-90
● Desjardins, Vic	Chi., NYR	2	87	6	15	21	27	16	0	0	0	0	....	1930-31	1931-32
Deslauriers, Jacques	Mtl.	1	2	0	0	0	0	....	....	....	....	....	....	1955-56	1955-56
Deuling, Jarrett	NYI	2	15	0	1	1	11	....	....	....	....	....	....	1995-96	1996-97
Devereaux, Boyd	Edm., Det., Phx., Tor.	11	627	67	112	179	205	27	3	4	7	4	1	1997-98	2008-09
Devine, Kevin	NYI	1	2	0	1	1	8	....	....	....	....	....	....	1982-83	1982-83
● Dewar, Tom	NYR	1	9	0	2	2	4	....	....	....	....	....	....	1943-44	1943-44
● Dewsbury, Al	Det., Chi.	9	347	30	78	108	365	14	1	5	6	16	1	1946-47	1955-56
Deziel, Michel	Buf.	1	....	....	....	....	....	1	0	0	0	0	....	1974-75	1974-75
● Dheere, Marcel	Mtl.	1	11	1	2	3	2	5	0	0	0	6	....	1942-43	1942-43
Diachuk, Edward	Det.	1	12	0	0	0	19	....	....	....	....	....	....	1960-61	1960-61
● Dick, Harry	Chi.	1	12	0	1	1	12	....	....	....	....	....	....	1946-47	1946-47
● Dickens, Ernie	Tor., Chi.	6	278	12	44	56	98	13	0	0	0	4	1	1941-42	1950-51
Dickenson, Herb	NYR	2	48	18	17	35	10	....	....	....	....	....	....	1951-52	1952-53
Diduck, Gerald	NYI, Mtl., Van., Chi., Hfd., Phx., Tor., Dal.	17	932	56	156	212	1612	114	8	16	24	212	....	1984-85	2000-01
Dietrich, Don	Chi., N.J.	2	28	0	7	7	10	....	....	....	....	....	....	1983-84	1985-86
● Dill, Bob	NYR	2	76	15	15	30	135	....	....	....	....	....	....	1943-44	1944-45
● Dillabough, Bob	Det., Bos., Pit., Oak.	9	283	32	54	86	76	17	3	0	3	0	....	1961-62	1969-70
● Dillon, Cecil	NYR, Det.	10	453	167	131	298	105	43	14	9	23	14	1	1930-31	1939-40
Dillon, Gary	Col.	1	13	1	1	2	29	....	....	....	....	....	....	1980-81	1980-81
Dillon, Wayne	NYR, Wpg.	4	229	43	66	109	60	3	0	1	1	0	....	1975-76	1979-80
DiMaio, Rob	NYI, T.B., Phi., Bos., NYR, Car., Dal.	17	894	106	171	277	840	62	7	9	16	40	....	1988-89	2005-06
‡ Dimitrakos, Niko	S.J., Phi.	4	158	24	38	62	95	20	1	8	9	10	....	2002-03	2006-07
Dineen, Bill	Det., Chi.	5	323	51	44	95	122	37	1	1	2	18	2	1953-54	1957-58
● Dineen, Gary	Min.	1	4	0	1	1	0	....	....	....	....	....	....	1968-69	1968-69
Dineen, Gord	NYI, Min., Pit., Ott.	13	528	16	90	106	695	40	1	7	8	68	....	1982-83	1994-95
Dineen, Kevin	Hfd., Phi., Car., Ott., CBJ	19	1188	355	405	760	2229	59	23	18	41	127	....	1984-85	2002-03
Dineen, Peter	L.A., Det.	2	13	0	2	2	13	....	....	....	....	....	....	1986-87	1989-90
Dingman, Chris	Cgy., Col., Car., T.B.	8	385	15	19	34	769	52	2	5	7	100	2	1997-98	2005-06
● Dinsmore, Chuck	Mtl.M.	4	100	6	2	8	50	8	1	0	1	2	1	1924-25	1929-30
Dionne, Gilbert	Mtl., Phi., Fla.	6	223	61	79	140	108	39	10	12	22	34	1	1990-91	1995-96
Dionne, Marcel	Det., L.A., NYR	18	1348	731	1040	1771	600	49	21	24	45	17	....	1971-72	1988-89
‡ DiPietro, Paul	Mtl., Tor., L.A.	6	192	31	49	80	96	31	11	10	21	10	1	1991-92	1996-97
Dirk, Robert	St.L., Van., Chi., Ana., Mtl.	9	402	13	29	42	786	39	0	1	1	56	....	1987-88	1995-96

Name	NHL Teams	NHL Seasons	Regular Schedule GP	G	A	TP	PIM	Playoffs GP	G	A	TP	PIM	NHL Cup Wins	First NHL Season	Last NHL Season
‡ Divisek, Tomas	Phi.	2	5	1	0	1	0	....	....	....	....	....	....	2000-01	2001-02
Djoos, Per	Det., NYR	3	82	2	31	33	58	....	....	....	....	....	....	1990-91	1992-93
Doak, Gary	Det., Bos., Van., NYR	16	789	23	107	130	908	78	2	4	6	121	1	1965-66	1980-81
Dobbin, Brian	Phi., Bos.	5	63	7	8	15	61	2	0	0	0	17	....	1986-87	1991-92
Dobson, Jim	Min., Col., Que.	4	12	0	0	0	6	....	....	....	....	....	....	1979-80	1983-84
● Doherty, Fred	Mtl.	1	1	0	0	0	0	....	....	....	....	....	....	1918-19	1918-19
Doig, Jason	Wpg., Phx., NYR, Wsh.	7	158	6	18	24	285	6	0	1	1	6	....	1995-96	2003-04
Dollas, Bobby	Wpg., Que., Det., Ana., Edm., Pit., Ott., Cgy., S.J.	16	646	42	96	138	467	47	2	1	3	41	....	1983-84	2000-01
Dome, Robert	Pit., Cgy.	3	53	7	7	14	12	....	....	....	....	....	....	1997-98	2002-03
‡ Domenichelli, Hnat	Hfd., Cgy., Atl., Min.	7	267	52	61	113	104	....	....	....	....	....	....	1996-97	2002-03
Domi, Tie	Tor., NYR, Wpg.	16	1020	104	141	245	3515	98	7	12	19	238	....	1989-90	2005-06
Donaldson, Gary	Chi.	1	1	0	0	0	0	....	....	....	....	....	....	1973-74	1973-74
Donatelli, Clark	Min., Bos.	2	35	3	4	7	39	2	0	0	0	0	....	1989-90	1991-92
Donato, Ted	Bos., NYI, Ott., Ana., Dal., St.L., L.A., NYR	13	796	150	197	347	396	58	8	10	18	22	....	1991-92	2003-04
● Donnelly, Babe	Mtl.M.	1	34	0	1	1	14	2	0	0	0	0	....	1926-27	1926-27
Donnelly, Dave	Bos., Chi., Edm.	5	137	15	24	39	150	5	0	0	0	0	....	1983-84	1987-88
Donnelly, Gord	Que., Wpg., Buf., Dal.	12	554	28	41	69	2069	26	0	2	2	61	....	1983-84	1994-95
Donnelly, Mike	NYR, Buf., L.A., Dal., NYI	11	465	114	121	235	255	47	12	12	24	30	....	1986-87	1996-97
Donovan, Shean	S.J., Col., Atl., Pit., Cgy., Bos., Ott.	15	951	112	129	241	705	49	6	6	12	39	....	1994-95	2009-10
‡ Dopita, Jiri	Phi., Edm.	2	73	12	21	33	19	....	....	....	....	....	....	2001-02	2002-03
● Doran, John	NYA, Det., Mtl.	5	98	5	10	15	110	3	0	0	0	0	....	1933-34	1939-40
● Doran, Lloyd	Det.	1	24	3	2	5	10	....	....	....	....	....	....	1946-47	1946-47
● Doraty, Ken	Chi., Tor., Det.	5	103	15	26	41	24	15	7	2	9	2	....	1926-27	1937-38
Dore, Andre	NYR, St.L., Que.	7	257	14	81	95	261	23	1	2	3	32	....	1978-79	1984-85
Dore, Daniel	Que.	2	17	2	3	5	59	....	....	....	....	....	....	1989-90	1990-91
Dorey, Jim	Tor., NYR	4	232	25	74	99	553	11	0	2	2	40	....	1968-69	1971-72
Dorion, Dan	N.J.	2	4	1	1	2	2	....	....	....	....	....	....	1985-86	1987-88
Dornhoefer, Gary	Bos., Phi.	14	787	214	328	542	1291	80	17	19	36	203	2	1963-64	1977-78
● Dorohoy, Eddie	Mtl.	1	16	0	0	0	6	....	....	....	....	....	....	1948-49	1948-49
Douglas, Jordy	Hfd., Min., Wpg.	6	268	76	62	138	160	6	0	0	0	4	....	1979-80	1984-85
● Douglas, Kent	Tor., Oak., Det.	7	428	33	115	148	631	19	1	3	4	33	3	1962-63	1968-69
● Douglas, Les	Det.	4	52	6	12	18	8	10	3	2	5	2	1	1940-41	1946-47
Doull, Doug	Bos., Wsh.	2	37	0	1	1	151	....	....	....	....	....	....	2003-04	2005-06
Douris, Peter	Wpg., Bos., Ana., Dal.	11	321	54	67	121	80	27	3	5	8	14	....	1985-86	1997-98
Dowd, Jim	N.J., Van., NYI, Cgy., Edm., Min., Mtl., Chi., Col., Phi.	16	728	71	168	239	390	99	9	17	26	50	1	1991-92	2007-08
Downey, Aaron	Bos., Chi., Dal., St.L., Mtl., Det.	9	243	8	10	18	494	5	0	0	0	8	1	1999-00	2008-09
● Downie, Dave	Tor.	1	11	0	1	1	2	....	....	....	....	....	....	1932-33	1932-33
Doyon, Mario	Chi., Que.	3	28	3	4	7	16	....	....	....	....	....	....	1988-89	1990-91
Drake, Dallas	Det., Wpg., Phx., St.L.	15	1009	177	300	477	885	90	14	19	33	79	1	1992-93	2007-08
● Draper, Bruce	Tor.	1	1	0	0	0	0	....	....	....	....	....	....	1962-63	1962-63
● Drillon, Gordie	Tor., Mtl.	7	311	155	139	294	56	50	26	15	41	10	1	1936-37	1942-43
Driscoll, Peter	Edm.	2	60	3	8	11	97	3	0	0	0	0	....	1979-80	1980-81
Driver, Bruce	N.J., NYR	15	922	96	390	486	670	108	10	40	50	64	1	1983-84	1997-98
Drolet, Rene	Phi., Det.	2	2	0	0	0	0	....	....	....	....	....	....	1971-72	1974-75
Droppa, Ivan	Chi.	2	19	0	1	1	14	....	....	....	....	....	....	1993-94	1995-96
● Drouillard, Clarence	Det.	1	10	0	1	1	0	....	....	....	....	....	....	1937-38	1937-38
Drouin, Jude	Mtl., Min., NYI, Wpg.	12	666	151	305	456	346	72	27	41	68	33	....	1968-69	1980-81
Drouin, P.C.	Bos.	1	3	0	0	0	0	....	....	....	....	....	....	1996-97	1996-97
● Drouin, Polly	Mtl.	7	160	23	50	73	80	5	0	1	1	5	....	1934-35	1940-41
Druce, John	Wsh., Wpg., L.A., Phi.	10	531	113	126	239	347	53	17	6	23	38	....	1988-89	1997-98
Druken, Harold	Van., Car., Tor.	5	146	27	36	63	36	4	0	1	1	0	....	1999-00	2003-04
Drulia, Stan	T.B.	3	126	15	27	42	52	....	....	....	....	....	....	1992-93	2000-01
● Drummond, Jim	NYR	1	2	0	0	0	0	....	....	....	....	....	....	1944-45	1944-45
● Drury, Herb	Pit., Phi.	6	213	24	13	37	203	4	1	1	2	0	....	1925-26	1930-31
Drury, Ted	Cgy., Hfd., Ott., Ana., NYI, CBJ	8	414	41	52	93	367	14	1	0	1	4	....	1993-94	2000-01
‡ Dube, Christian	NYR	2	33	1	1	2	4	3	0	0	0	0	....	1996-97	1998-99
Dube, Gilles	Mtl., Det.	2	12	1	2	3	2	2	0	0	0	0	1	1949-50	1953-54
Dube, Norm	K.C.	2	57	8	10	18	54	....	....	....	....	....	....	1974-75	1975-76
Duberman, Justin	Pit.	1	4	0	0	0	0	....	....	....	....	....	....	1993-94	1993-94
Dubinsky, Steve	Chi., Cgy., Nsh., St.L.	10	375	25	45	70	164	10	1	0	1	14	....	1993-94	2002-03
● Duchesne, Gaetan	Wsh., Que., Min., S.J., Fla.	14	1028	179	254	433	617	84	14	13	27	97	....	1981-82	1994-95
Duchesne, Steve	L.A., Phi., Que., St.L., Ott., Det.	16	1113	227	525	752	824	121	16	61	77	96	1	1986-87	2001-02
Dudley, Rick	Buf., Wpg.	6	309	75	99	174	292	25	7	2	9	69	....	1972-73	1980-81
Duerden, Dave	Fla.	1	2	0	0	0	0	....	....	....	....	....	....	1999-00	1999-00
Duff, Dick	Tor., NYR, Mtl., L.A., Buf.	18	1030	283	289	572	743	114	30	49	79	78	6	1954-55	1971-72
Dufour, Luc	Bos., Que., St.L.	3	167	23	21	44	199	18	1	0	1	32	....	1982-83	1984-85
Dufour, Marc	NYR, L.A.	3	14	1	0	1	2	....	....	....	....	....	....	1963-64	1968-69
Dufresne, Donald	Mtl., T.B., L.A., St.L., Edm.	9	268	6	36	42	258	34	1	3	4	47	1	1988-89	1996-97
● Duggan, John	Ott.	1	27	0	0	0	0	2	0	0	0	0	....	1925-26	1925-26
Duggan, Ken	Min.	1	1	0	0	0	0	....	....	....	....	....	....	1987-88	1987-88
Duguay, Ron	NYR, Det., Pit., L.A.	12	864	274	346	620	582	89	31	22	53	118	....	1977-78	1988-89
● Duguid, Lorne	Mtl.M., Det., Bos.	6	135	9	15	24	57	4	1	0	1	6	....	1931-32	1936-37
● Dukowski, Duke	Chi., NYA, NYR	5	200	16	30	46	172	6	0	0	0	6	....	1926-27	1933-34
● Dumart, Woody	Bos.	16	772	211	218	429	99	88	12	15	27	23	2	1935-36	1953-54
Dunbar, Dale	Van., Bos.	2	2	0	0	0	2	....	....	....	....	....	....	1985-86	1988-89
● Duncan, Art	Det., Tor.	5	156	18	16	34	225	5	0	0	0	4	....	1926-27	1930-31
Duncan, Iain	Wpg.	4	127	34	55	89	149	11	0	3	3	6	....	1986-87	1990-91
Duncanson, Craig	L.A., Wpg., NYR	7	38	5	4	9	61	....	....	....	....	....	....	1985-86	1992-93
Dundas, Rocky	Tor.	1	5	0	0	0	14	....	....	....	....	....	....	1989-90	1989-90
● Dunlap, Frank	Tor.	1	15	0	1	1	2	....	....	....	....	....	....	1943-44	1943-44
Dunlop, Blake	Min., Phi., St.L., Det.	11	550	130	274	404	172	40	4	10	14	18	....	1973-74	1983-84
Dunn, Dave	Van., Tor.	3	184	14	41	55	313	10	1	1	2	41	....	1973-74	1975-76
Dunn, Richie	Buf., Cgy., Hfd.	12	483	36	140	176	314	36	3	15	18	24	....	1977-78	1988-89
Dupere, Denis	Tor., Wsh., St.L., K.C., Col.	8	421	80	99	179	66	16	1	0	1	0	....	1970-71	1977-78
Dupont, Andre	NYR, St.L., Phi., Que.	13	800	59	185	244	1986	140	14	18	32	352	2	1970-71	1982-83
Dupont, Jerome	Chi., Tor.	6	214	7	29	36	468	20	0	2	2	56	....	1981-82	1986-87
‡ DuPont, Micki	Cgy., Pit., St.L.	4	23	1	3	4	12	....	....	....	....	....	....	2001-02	2007-08
Dupont, Norm	Mtl., Wpg., Hfd.	5	256	55	85	140	52	13	4	2	6	0	....	1979-80	1983-84
● Dupre, Yanick	Phi.	3	35	2	0	2	16	....	....	....	....	....	....	1991-92	1995-96
● Durbano, Steve	St.L., Pit., K.C., Col.	6	220	13	60	73	1127	5	0	2	2	8	....	1972-73	1978-79
Duris, Vitezslav	Tor.	2	89	3	20	23	62	3	0	1	1	2	....	1980-81	1982-83
Dusablon, Benoit	NYR	1	3	0	0	0	2	....	....	....	....	....	....	2003-04	2003-04
Dussault, Norm	Mtl.	4	206	31	62	93	47	7	3	1	4	0	....	1947-48	1950-51
● Dutton, Red	Mtl.M., NYA	10	449	29	67	96	871	18	1	0	1	33	....	1926-27	1935-36
● Dvorak, Miroslav	Phi.	3	193	11	74	85	51	18	0	2	2	6	....	1982-83	1984-85
Dwyer, Gordie	T.B., NYR, Mtl.	5	108	0	5	5	394	....	....	....	....	....	....	1999-00	2003-04
Dwyer, Mike	Col., Cgy.	4	31	2	6	8	25	1	1	0	1	0	....	1978-79	1981-82
● Dyck, Henry	NYR	1	1	0	0	0	0	....	....	....	....	....	....	1943-44	1943-44
● Dye, Babe	Tor., Ham., Chi., NYA	11	271	201	47	248	221	10	2	0	2	11	1	1919-20	1930-31
Dykhuis, Karl	Chi., Phi., T.B., Mtl.	12	644	42	91	133	495	62	8	10	18	50	....	1991-92	2003-04
Dykstra, Steve	Buf., Edm., Pit., Hfd.	5	217	8	32	40	545	1	0	0	0	2	....	1985-86	1989-90
● Dyte, Jack	Chi.	1	27	1	0	1	31	....	....	....	....	....	....	1943-44	1943-44
Dziedzic, Joe	Pit., Phx.	3	130	14	14	28	131	21	1	3	4	23	....	1995-96	1998-99

E

Name	NHL Teams	NHL Seasons	Regular Schedule GP	G	A	TP	PIM	Playoffs GP	G	A	TP	PIM	NHL Cup Wins	First NHL Season	Last NHL Season
Eagles, Mike	Que., Chi., Wpg., Wsh.	16	853	74	122	196	928	44	2	6	8	34	....	1982-83	1999-00
Eakin, Bruce	Cgy., Det.	4	13	2	2	4	4	....	....	....	....	....	....	1981-82	1985-86
Eakins, Dallas	Wpg., Fla., St.L., Phx., NYR, Tor., NYI, Cgy.	10	120	0	9	9	208	5	0	0	0	4	....	1992-93	2001-02
Eastwood, Mike	Tor., Wpg., Phx., NYR, St.L., Chi., Pit.	13	783	87	149	236	354	97	8	11	19	64	....	1991-92	2003-04
Eatough, Jeff	Buf.	1	1	0	0	0	0	....	....	....	....	....	....	1981-82	1981-82
Eaves, Mike	Min., Cgy.	8	324	83	143	226	80	43	7	10	17	14	....	1978-79	1985-86
Eaves, Murray	Wpg., Det.	8	57	4	13	17	9	4	0	1	1	2	....	1980-81	1989-90
Ecclestone, Tim	St.L., Det., Tor., Atl.	11	692	126	233	359	344	48	6	11	17	76	....	1967-68	1977-78
Edberg, Rolf	Wsh.	3	184	45	58	103	24	....	....	....	....	....	....	1978-79	1980-81
● Eddolls, Frank	Mtl., NYR	8	317	23	43	66	114	31	0	2	2	10	1	1944-45	1951-52
Edestrand, Darryl	St.L., Phi., Pit., Bos., L.A.	10	455	34	90	124	404	42	3	9	12	57	....	1967-68	1978-79
Edmundson, Garry	Mtl., Tor	3	43	4	6	10	49	11	0	1	1	8	....	1951-52	1960-61
Edur, Tom	Col., Pit.	2	158	17	70	87	67	....	....	....	....	....	....	1976-77	1977-78
● Egan, Pat	NYA, Bro., Det., Bos., NYR	11	554	77	153	230	776	46	9	4	13	48	....	1939-40	1950-51
Egeland, Allan	T.B.	3	17	0	0	0	16	....	....	....	....	....	....	1995-96	1997-98
Egers, Jack	NYR, St.L., Wsh.	7	284	64	69	133	154	32	5	6	11	32	....	1969-70	1975-76

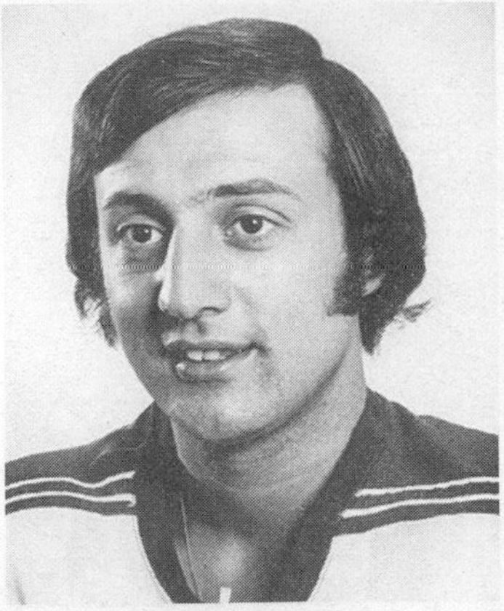

Ab DeMarco

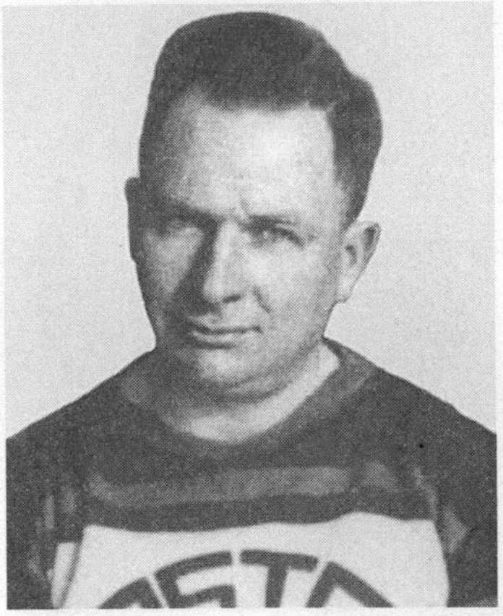

Cy Denneny

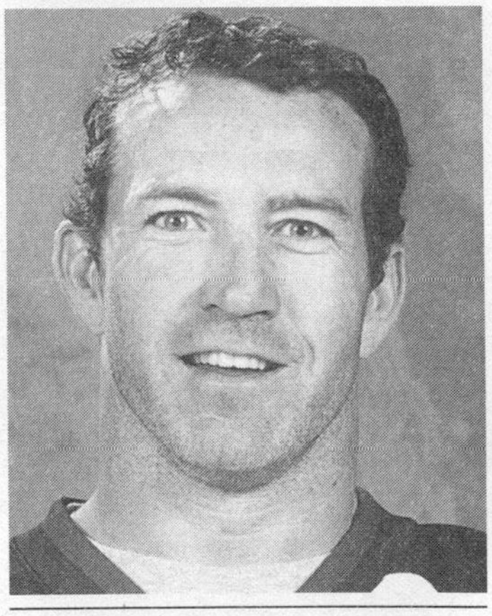

Kevin Dineen

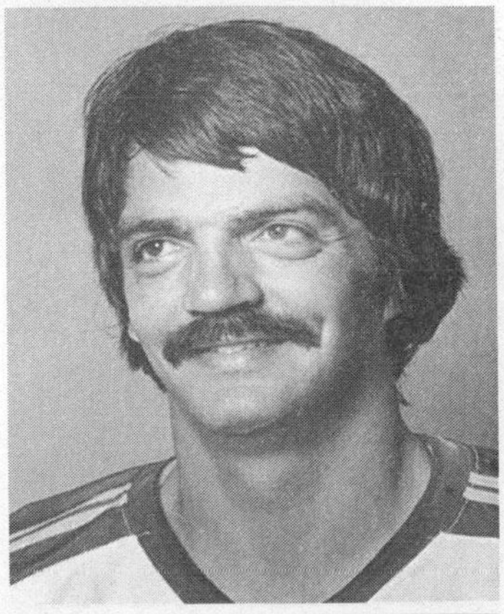

Denis Dupere

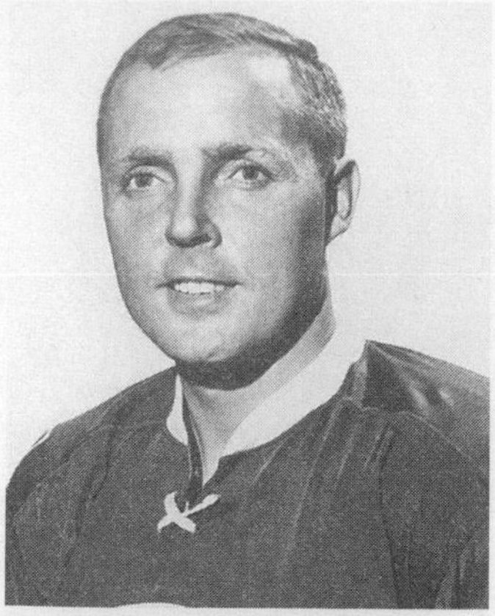

Aut Erickson

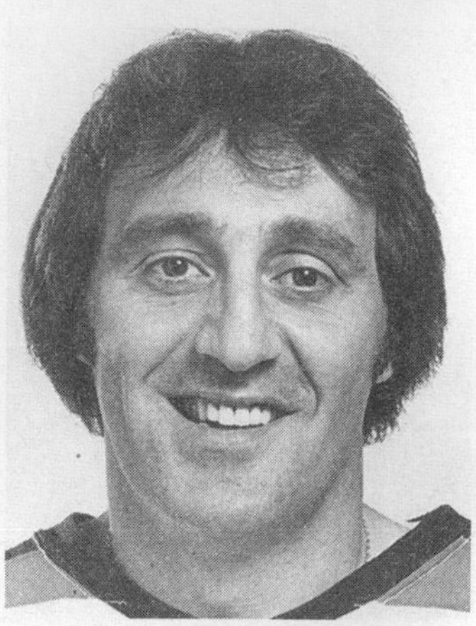

Phil Esposito

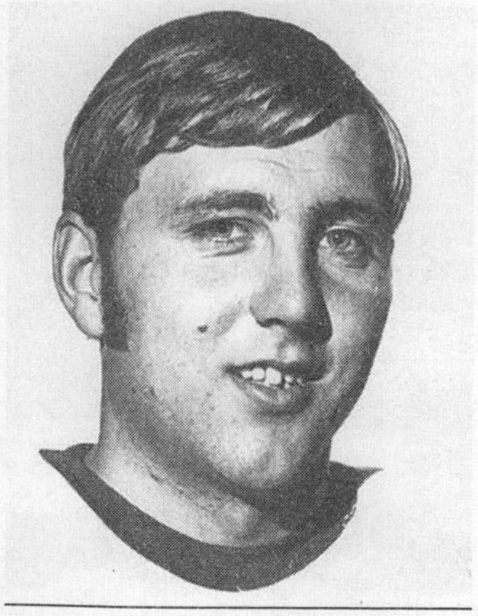

Bob Falkenberg

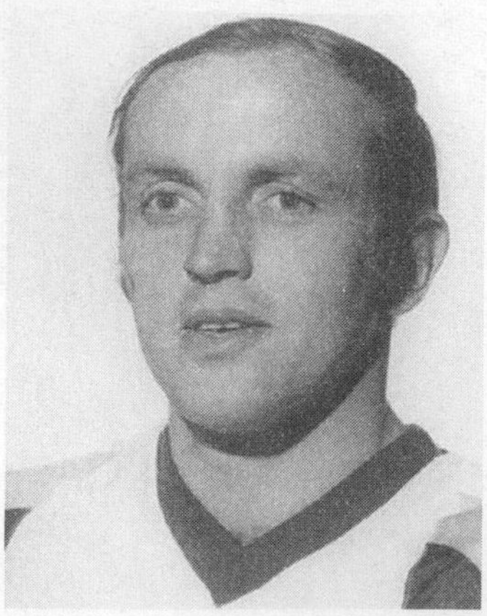

Norm Ferguson

Name	NHL Teams	NHL Seasons	Regular Schedule					Playoffs					NHL Cup Wins	First NHL Season	Last NHL Season
			GP	G	A	TP	PIM	GP	G	A	TP	PIM			
• Ehman, Gerry	Bos., Det., Tor., Oak., Cal.	9	429	96	118	214	100	41	10	10	20	12	1	1957-58	1970-71
Eisenhut, Neil	Van., Cgy.	2	16	1	3	4	21	....	....	....	....	....	....	1993-94	1994-95
Eklund, Pelle	Phi., Dal.	9	594	120	335	455	109	66	10	36	46	8	....	1985-86	1993-94
‡ Ekman, Nils	T.B., S.J., Pit.	5	264	60	91	151	188	28	2	5	7	16	....	1999-00	2006-07
Eldebrink, Anders	Van., Que.	2	55	3	11	14	29	14	0	0	0	10	....	1981-82	1982-83
Elich, Matt	T.B.	2	16	1	1	2	0	....	....	....	....	....	....	1999-00	2000-01
Elik, Bo	Det.	1	3	0	0	0	0	....	....	....	....	....	....	1962-63	1962-63
Elik, Todd	L.A., Min., Edm., S.J., St.L., Bos.	8	448	110	219	329	453	52	15	27	42	48	....	1989-90	1996-97
Ellett, Dave	Wpg., Tor., N.J., Bos., St.L.	16	1129	153	415	568	985	116	11	46	57	87	....	1984-85	1999-00
• Elliott, Fred	Ott.	1	43	2	0	2	6	....	....	....	....	....	....	1928-29	1928-29
Ellis, Ron	Tor.	16	1034	332	308	640	207	70	18	8	26	20	1	1963-64	1980-81
‡ Ellison, Matt	Chi., Phi.	3	43	3	11	14	19	....	....	....	....	....	....	2003-04	2006-07
Elomo, Miika	Wsh.	1	2	0	1	1	2	....	....	....	....	....	....	1999-00	1999-00
Eloranta, Kari	Cgy., St.L.	5	267	13	103	116	155	26	1	7	8	19	....	1981-82	1986-87
Eloranta, Mikko	Bos., L.A.	4	264	32	44	76	186	7	1	1	2	2	....	1999-00	2002-03
Elynuik, Pat	Wpg., Wsh., T.B., Ott.	9	506	154	188	342	459	20	6	9	15	25	....	1987-88	1995-96
• Emberg, Eddie	Mtl.	1	....	....	....	....	....	2	1	0	1	0	....	1944-45	1944-45
Emerson, Nelson	St.L., Wpg., Hfd., Car., Chi., Ott., Atl., L.A.	12	771	195	293	488	575	40	7	15	22	33	....	1990-91	2001-02
Emma, David	N.J., Bos., Fla.	5	34	5	6	11	2	....	....	....	....	....	....	1992-93	2000-01
Emmons, Gary	S.J.	1	3	1	0	1	0	....	....	....	....	....	....	1993-94	1993-94
Emmons, John	Ott., T.B., Bos.	3	85	2	4	6	64	....	....	....	....	....	....	1999-00	2001-02
• Emms, Hap	Mtl.M., NYA, Det., Bos.	10	320	36	53	89	311	14	0	0	0	12	....	1926-27	1937-38
Endean, Craig	Wpg.	1	2	0	1	1	0	....	....	....	....	....	....	1986-87	1986-87
Endicott, Shane	Pit.	2	45	1	2	3	47	....	....	....	....	....	....	2001-02	2005-06
Engblom, Brian	Mtl., Wsh., L.A., Buf., Cgy.	11	659	29	177	206	599	48	3	9	12	43	2	1976-77	1986-87
Engele, Jerry	Min.	3	100	2	13	15	162	2	0	1	1	0	....	1975-76	1977-78
English, John	L.A.	1	3	1	3	4	4	1	0	0	0	0	....	1987-88	1987-88
Ennis, Jim	Edm.	1	5	1	0	1	10	....	....	....	....	....	....	1987-88	1987-88
• Erickson, Aut	Bos., Chi., Tor., Oak.	7	226	7	24	31	182	7	0	0	0	2	1	1959-60	1969-70
Erickson, Bryan	Wsh., L.A., Pit., Wpg.	9	351	80	125	205	141	14	3	4	7	7	....	1983-84	1993-94
Erickson, Grant	Bos., Min.	2	6	1	0	1	0	....	....	....	....	....	....	1968-69	1969-70
Eriksson, Peter	Edm.	1	20	3	3	6	24	....	....	....	....	....	....	1989-90	1989-90
Eriksson, Roland	Min., Van.	3	193	48	95	143	26	2	1	0	1	0	....	1976-77	1978-79
Eriksson, Thomas	Phi.	5	208	22	76	98	107	19	0	3	3	12	....	1980-81	1985-86
Erixon, Jan	NYR	10	556	57	159	216	167	58	7	7	14	16	....	1983-84	1992-93
Errey, Bob	Pit., Buf., S.J., Det., Dal., NYR	15	895	170	212	382	1005	99	13	16	29	109	2	1983-84	1997-98
Esau, Len	Tor., Que., Cgy., Edm.	4	27	0	10	10	24	....	....	....	....	....	....	1991-92	1994-95
Esposito, Phil	Chi., Bos., NYR	18	1282	717	873	1590	910	130	61	76	137	138	2	1963-64	1980-81
• Evans, Chris	Tor., Buf., St.L., Det., K.C.	5	241	19	42	61	143	12	1	1	2	8	....	1969-70	1974-75
Evans, Daryl	L.A., Wsh., Tor.	6	113	22	30	52	25	11	5	8	13	12	....	1981-82	1986-87
Evans, Doug	St.L., Wpg., Phi.	8	355	48	87	135	502	22	3	4	7	38	....	1985-86	1992-93
• Evans, Jack	NYR, Chi.	14	752	19	80	99	989	56	2	2	4	97	1	1948-49	1962-63
Evans, Kevin	Min., S.J.	2	9	0	1	1	44	....	....	....	....	....	....	1990-91	1991-92
Evans, Paul	Tor.	2	11	1	1	2	21	2	0	0	0	0	....	1976-77	1977-78
Evans, Paul	Phi.	3	103	14	25	39	34	1	0	0	0	0	....	1978-79	1982-83
Evans, Shawn	St.L., NYI	2	9	1	0	1	2	....	....	....	....	....	....	1985-86	1989-90
• Evans, Stewart	Det., Mtl.M., Mtl.	8	367	28	49	77	425	26	0	0	0	20	1	1930-31	1938-39
Evason, Dean	Wsh., Hfd., S.J., Dal., Cgy.	13	803	139	233	372	1002	55	9	20	29	132	....	1983-84	1995-96
Ewen, Todd	St.L., Mtl., Ana., S.J.	11	518	36	40	76	1911	26	0	0	0	87	1	1986-87	1996-97
Ezinicki, Bill	Tor., Bos., NYR	9	368	79	105	184	713	40	5	8	13	87	3	1944-45	1954-55

F

Name	NHL Teams	NHL Seasons	GP	G	A	TP	PIM	GP	G	A	TP	PIM	NHL Cup Wins	First NHL Season	Last NHL Season
Fahey, Jim	S.J., N.J.	4	92	1	24	25	67	2	0	0	0	0	....	2002-03	2006-07
Fahey, Trevor	NYR	1	1	0	0	0	0	....	....	....	....	....	....	1964-65	1964-65
Fairbairn, Bill	NYR, Min., St.L.	11	658	162	261	423	173	54	13	22	35	42	....	1968-69	1978-79
Fairchild, Kelly	Tor., Dal., Col.	4	34	2	3	5	6	....	....	....	....	....	....	1995-96	2001-02
Falkenberg, Bob	Det.	5	54	1	5	6	26	....	....	....	....	....	....	1966-67	1971-72
Falloon, Pat	S.J., Phi., Ott., Edm., Pit.	9	575	143	179	322	141	66	11	7	18	16	....	1991-92	1999-00
Farkas, Jeff	Tor., Atl.	4	11	0	2	2	6	5	1	0	1	0	....	1999-00	2002-03
• Farrant, Walt	Chi.	1	1	0	0	0	0	....	....	....	....	....	....	1943-44	1943-44
Farrell, Mike	Wsh., Nsh.	3	13	0	0	0	2	....	....	....	....	....	....	2001-02	2003-04
Farrish, Dave	NYR, Que., Tor.	7	430	17	110	127	440	14	0	2	2	24	....	1976-77	1983-84
Fashoway, Gordie	Chi.	1	13	3	2	5	14	....	....	....	....	....	....	1950-51	1950-51
Fast, Brad	Car.	1	1	1	0	1	0	....	....	....	....	....	....	2003-04	2003-04
‡ Fata, Drew	NYI	2	8	1	1	2	9	1	0	0	0	0	....	2006-07	2007-08
‡ Fata, Rico	Cgy., NYR, Pit., Atl., Wsh.	8	230	27	36	63	104	....	....	....	....	....	....	1998-99	2006-07
Faubert, Mario	Pit.	7	231	21	90	111	292	10	2	2	4	6	....	1974-75	1981-82
Faulkner, Alex	Tor., Det.	3	101	15	17	32	15	12	5	0	5	2	....	1961-62	1963-64
Fauss, Ted	Tor.	2	28	0	2	2	15	....	....	....	....	....	....	1986-87	1987-88
Faust, Andre	Phi.	2	47	10	7	17	14	....	....	....	....	....	....	1992-93	1993-94
Feamster, Dave	Chi.	4	169	13	24	37	154	33	3	5	8	61	....	1981-82	1984-85
Featherstone, Glen	St.L., Bos., NYR, Hfd., Cgy.	9	384	19	61	80	939	28	0	2	2	103	....	1988-89	1996-97
Featherstone, Tony	Oak., Cal., Min.	3	130	17	21	38	65	2	0	0	0	0	....	1969-70	1973-74
Federko, Bernie	St.L., Det.	14	1000	369	761	1130	487	91	35	66	101	83	....	1976-77	1989-90
‡ Fedorov, Fedor	Van., NYR	3	18	0	2	2	14	....	....	....	....	....	....	2002-03	2005-06
‡ Fedorov, Sergei	Det., Ana., CBJ, Wsh.	18	1248	483	696	1179	839	183	52	124	176	133	3	1990-91	2008-09
Fedotov, Anatoli	Wpg., Ana.	2	4	0	2	2	0	....	....	....	....	....	....	1992-93	1993-94
Fedyk, Brent	Det., Phi., Dal., NYR	10	470	97	112	209	308	16	3	2	5	12	....	1987-88	1998-99
Felix, Chris	Wsh.	4	35	1	12	13	10	2	0	1	1	0	....	1987-88	1990-91
Felsner, Brian	Chi.	1	12	1	3	4	12	....	....	....	....	....	....	1997-98	1997-98
Felsner, Denny	St.L.	4	18	1	4	5	6	10	2	3	5	2	....	1991-92	1994-95
Feltrin, Tony	Pit., NYR	4	48	3	3	6	65	....	....	....	....	....	....	1980-81	1985-86
Fenton, Paul	Hfd., NYR, L.A., Wpg., Tor., Cgy., S.J.	8	411	100	83	183	198	17	4	1	5	27	....	1984-85	1991-92
Fenyves, David	Buf., Phi.	9	206	3	32	35	119	11	0	0	0	9	....	1982-83	1990-91
Ference, Brad	Fla., Phx., Cgy.	6	250	4	30	34	565	....	....	....	....	....	....	1999-00	2006-07
Fergus, Tom	Bos., Tor., Van.	12	726	235	346	581	499	65	21	17	38	48	....	1981-82	1992-93
Ferguson, Craig	Mtl., Cgy., Fla.	5	27	1	1	2	6	....	....	....	....	....	....	1993-94	1999-00
Ferguson, George	Tor., Pit., Min.	12	797	160	238	398	431	86	14	23	37	44	....	1972-73	1983-84
• Ferguson, John	Mtl.	8	500	145	158	303	1214	85	20	18	38	260	5	1963-64	1970-71
• Ferguson, Lorne	Bos., Det., Chi.	8	422	82	80	162	193	31	6	3	9	24	....	1949-50	1958-59
Ferguson, Norm	Oak., Cal.	4	279	73	66	139	72	10	1	4	5	7	....	1968-69	1971-72
Ferguson, Scott	Edm., Ana., Min.	7	218	7	14	21	310	11	0	0	0	8	....	1997-98	2005-06
Ferland, Jonathan	Mtl.	1	7	1	0	1	2	....	....	....	....	....	....	2005-06	2005-06
Ferner, Mark	Buf., Wsh., Ana., Det.	6	91	3	10	13	51	....	....	....	....	....	....	1986-87	1994-95
Ferraro, Chris	NYR, Pit., Edm., NYI, Wsh.	6	74	7	9	16	57	....	....	....	....	....	....	1995-96	2001-02
Ferraro, Peter	NYR, Pit., Bos., Wsh.	6	92	9	15	24	58	2	0	0	0	0	....	1995-96	2001-02
Ferraro, Ray	Hfd., NYI, NYR, L.A., Atl., St.L.	18	1258	408	490	898	1288	68	21	22	43	54	....	1984-85	2001-02
Fetisov, Viacheslav	N.J., Det.	9	546	36	192	228	656	116	2	26	28	147	2	1989-90	1997-98
Fibiger, Jesse	S.J.	1	16	0	0	0	2	....	....	....	....	....	....	2002-03	2002-03
Fidler, Mike	Cle., Min., Hfd., Chi.	7	271	84	97	181	124	....	....	....	....	....	....	1976-77	1982-83
• Field, Wilf	NYA, Bro., Mtl., Chi.	6	219	17	25	42	151	2	0	0	0	2	....	1936-37	1944-45
Fielder, Guyle	Chi., Det., Bos.	4	9	0	0	0	2	6	0	0	0	2	....	1950-51	1957-58
‡ Filewich, Jonathan	Pit.	1	5	0	0	0	0	....	....	....	....	....	....	2007-08	2007-08
Filimonov, Dmitri	Ott.	1	30	1	4	5	18	....	....	....	....	....	....	1993-94	1993-94
Fillion, Bob	Mtl.	7	327	42	61	103	84	33	7	4	11	10	2	1943-44	1949-50
• Fillion, Marcel	Bos.	1	1	0	0	0	0	....	....	....	....	....	....	1944-45	1944-45
• Filmore, Tommy	Det., NYA, Bos.	4	117	15	12	27	33	....	....	....	....	....	....	1930-31	1933-34
• Finkbeiner, Lloyd	NYA	1	2	0	0	0	0	....	....	....	....	....	....	1940-41	1940-41
Finley, Jeff	NYI, Phi., Wpg., Phx., NYR, St.L.	15	708	13	70	83	457	52	1	6	7	38	....	1987-88	2003-04
Finn, Steven	Que., T.B., L.A.	12	725	34	78	112	1724	23	0	4	4	39	....	1985-86	1996-97
• Finney, Sid	Chi.	3	59	10	7	17	4	7	0	2	2	0	....	1951-52	1953-54
• Finnigan, Ed	St.L., Bos.	2	15	1	1	2	2	....	....	....	....	....	....	1934-35	1935-36
• Finnigan, Frank	Ott., Tor., St.L.	14	553	115	88	203	407	38	6	9	15	22	2	1923-24	1936-37
Fiorentino, Peter	NYR	1	1	0	0	0	0	....	....	....	....	....	....	1991-92	1991-92
Fischer, Jiri	Det.	6	305	11	49	60	295	38	4	3	7	55	1	1999-00	2005-06
Fischer, Patrick	Phx.	1	27	4	6	10	24	....	....	....	....	....	....	2006-07	2006-07
Fischer, Ron	Buf.	2	18	0	7	7	6	....	....	....	....	....	....	1981-82	1982-83
• Fisher, Alvin	Tor.	1	9	1	0	1	4	....	....	....	....	....	....	1924-25	1924-25
Fisher, Craig	Phi., Wpg., Fla.	4	12	0	0	0	2	....	....	....	....	....	....	1989-90	1996-97
Fisher, Dunc	NYR, Bos., Det.	7	275	45	70	115	104	21	4	4	8	14	....	1947-48	1958-59
• Fisher, Joe	Det.	4	65	8	12	20	13	12	2	1	3	6	1	1939-40	1942-43
Fitchner, Bob	Que.	2	78	12	20	32	59	3	0	0	0	10	....	1979-80	1980-81
Fitzgerald, Rusty	Pit.	2	25	2	2	4	12	5	0	0	0	4	....	1994-95	1995-96
Fitzgerald, Tom	NYI, Fla., Col., Nsh., Chi., Tor., Bos.	17	1097	139	190	329	776	78	7	12	19	90	....	1988-89	2005-06

Name	NHL Teams	NHL Seasons	Regular Schedule					Playoffs					NHL Cup Wins	First NHL Season	Last NHL Season
			GP	G	A	TP	PIM	GP	G	A	TP	PIM			
Fitzpatrick, Rory	Mtl., St.L., Nsh., Buf., Van., Phi.	10	287	10	25	35	201	20	1	5	6	22	....	1995-96	2007-08
Fitzpatrick, Ross	Phi.	4	20	5	2	7	0	....	....	....	....	....	....	1982-83	1985-86
Fitzpatrick, Sandy	NYR, Min.	2	22	3	6	9	8	12	0	0	0	0	....	1964-65	1967-68
Flaman, Fern	Bos., Tor.	17	910	34	174	208	1370	63	4	8	12	93	1	1944-45	1960-61
Flatley, Pat	NYI, NYR	14	780	170	340	510	686	70	18	15	33	75	....	1983-84	1996-97
Fleming, Gerry	Mtl.	2	11	0	0	0	42	....	....	....	....	....	....	1993-94	1994-95
• Fleming, Reggie	Mtl., Chi., Bos., NYR, Phi., Buf.	12	749	108	132	240	1468	50	3	6	9	106	1	1959-60	1970-71
Flesch, John	Min., Pit., Col.	4	124	18	23	41	117	....	....	....	....	....	....	1974-75	1979-80
Fletcher, Steven	Mtl., Wpg.	2	3	0	0	0	5	1	0	0	0	5	....	1987-88	1988-89
• Flett, Bill	L.A., Phi., Tor., Atl., Edm.	11	689	202	215	417	501	52	7	16	23	42	1	1967-68	1979-80
Fleury, Theoren	Cgy., Col., NYR, Chi.	15	1084	455	633	1088	1840	77	34	45	79	116	1	1988-89	2002-03
Flichel, Todd	Wpg.	3	6	0	1	1	4	....	....	....	....	....	....	1987-88	1989-90
Flinn, Ryan	L.A.	3	31	1	0	1	84	....	....	....	....	....	....	2001-02	2005-06
Flockhart, Rob	Van., Min.	5	55	2	5	7	14	1	1	0	1	2	....	1976-77	1980-81
Flockhart, Ron	Phi., Pit., Mtl., St.L., Bos.	9	453	145	183	328	208	19	4	6	10	14	....	1980-81	1988-89
Floyd, Larry	N.J.	2	12	2	3	5	9	....	....	....	....	....	....	1982-83	1983-84
Focht, Dan	Phx., Pit.	3	82	2	6	8	145	1	0	1	1	0	....	2001-02	2003-04
• Fogarty, Bryan	Que., Pit., Mtl.	6	156	22	52	74	119	....	....	....	....	....	....	1989-90	1994-95
• Fogolin, Lee	Det., Chi.	9	427	10	48	58	575	28	0	2	2	30	1	1947-48	1955-56
Fogolin, Lee	Buf., Edm.	13	924	44	195	239	1318	108	5	19	24	173	2	1974-75	1986-87
Folco, Peter	Van.	1	2	0	0	0	0	....	....	....	....	....	....	1973-74	1973-74
Foley, Gerry	Tor., NYR, L.A.	4	142	9	14	23	99	9	0	1	1	2	....	1954-55	1968-69
Foley, Rick	Chi., Phi., Det.	3	67	11	26	37	180	4	0	1	1	4	....	1970-71	1973-74
Foligno, Mike	Det., Buf., Tor., Fla.	15	1018	355	372	727	2049	57	15	17	32	185	....	1979-80	1993-94
Folk, Bill	Det.	2	12	0	0	0	4	....	....	....	....	....	....	1951-52	1952-53
Fontaine, Len	Det.	2	46	8	11	19	10	....	....	....	....	....	....	1972-73	1973-74
Fontas, Jon	Min.	2	2	0	0	0	0	....	....	....	....	....	....	1979-80	1980-81
Fonteyne, Val	Det., NYR, Pit.	13	820	75	154	229	26	59	3	10	13	8	....	1959-60	1971-72
Fontinato, Lou	NYR, Mtl.	9	535	26	78	104	1247	21	0	2	2	42	....	1954-55	1962-63
‡ Forbes, Colin	Phi., T.B., Ott., NYR, Wsh.	9	311	33	28	61	213	13	1	0	1	16	....	1996-97	2005-06
Forbes, Dave	Bos., Wsh.	6	363	64	64	128	341	45	1	4	5	13	....	1973-74	1978-79
Forbes, Mike	Bos., Edm.	3	50	1	11	12	41	....	....	....	....	....	....	1977-78	1981-82
Forey, Connie	St.L.	1	4	0	0	0	2	....	....	....	....	....	....	1973-74	1973-74
• Forsey, Jack	Tor.	1	19	7	9	16	10	3	0	1	1	0	....	1942-43	1942-43
• Forslund, Gus	Ott.	1	48	4	9	13	2	....	....	....	....	....	....	1932-33	1932-33
Forslund, Tomas	Cgy.	2	44	5	11	16	12	....	....	....	....	....	....	1991-92	1992-93
Forsyth, Alex	Wsh.	1	1	0	0	0	0	....	....	....	....	....	....	1976-77	1976-77
Fortier, Dave	Tor., NYI, Van.	4	205	8	21	29	335	20	0	2	2	33	....	1972-73	1976-77
Fortier, Marc	Que., Ott., L.A.	6	212	42	60	102	135	....	....	....	....	....	....	1987-88	1992-93
Fortin, Jean-Francois	Wsh.	3	71	1	4	5	42	....	....	....	....	....	....	2001-02	2003-04
Fortin, Ray	St.L.	3	92	2	6	8	33	6	0	0	0	8	....	1967-68	1969-70
Foster, Corey	N.J., Phi., Pit., NYI	4	45	5	6	11	24	3	0	0	0	4	....	1988-89	1996-97
Foster, Dwight	Bos., Col., N.J., Det.	10	541	111	163	274	420	35	5	12	17	4	....	1977-78	1986-87
• Foster, Herb	NYR	2	6	1	0	1	5	....	....	....	....	....	....	1940-41	1947-48
• Foster, Yip	NYR, Bos., Det.	4	83	3	2	5	32	....	....	....	....	....	....	1929-30	1934-35
Fotiu, Nick	NYR, Hfd., Cgy., Phi., Edm.	13	646	60	77	137	1362	38	0	4	4	67	....	1976-77	1988-89
• Fowler, Jimmy	Tor.	3	135	18	29	47	39	18	0	3	3	2	....	1936-37	1938-39
Fowler, Tom	Chi.	1	24	0	1	1	18	....	....	....	....	....	....	1946-47	1946-47
Fox, Greg	Atl., Chi., Pit.	8	494	14	92	106	637	44	1	9	10	67	....	1977-78	1984-85
Fox, Jim	L.A.	9	578	186	293	479	143	22	4	8	12	0	....	1980-81	1989-90
Foy, Matt	Min.	3	56	6	7	13	48	1	0	0	0	0	....	2005-06	2007-08
• Foyston, Frank	Det.	2	64	17	7	24	32	....	....	....	....	....	....	1926-27	1927-28
Frampton, Bob	Mtl.	1	2	0	0	0	0	3	0	0	0	0	....	1949-50	1949-50
Franceschetti, Lou	Wsh., Tor., Buf.	10	459	59	81	140	747	44	3	2	5	111	....	1981-82	1991-92
Francis, Bobby	Det.	1	14	2	0	2	0	....	....	....	....	....	....	1982-83	1982-83
Francis, Ron	Hfd., Pit., Car., Tor.	23	1731	549	1249	1798	979	171	46	97	143	95	2	1981-82	2003-04
• Fraser, Archie	NYR	1	3	0	1	1	0	....	....	....	....	....	....	1943-44	1943-44
• Fraser, Charles	Ham.	1	1	0	0	0	0	....	....	....	....	....	....	1923-24	1923-24
Fraser, Curt	Van., Chi., Min.	12	704	193	240	433	1306	65	15	18	33	198	....	1978-79	1989-90
• Fraser, Gord	Chi., Det., Mtl., Pit., Phi.	5	144	24	12	36	224	2	1	0	1	6	....	1926-27	1930-31
• Fraser, Harvey	Chi.	1	21	5	4	9	0	....	....	....	....	....	....	1944-45	1944-45
Fraser, Iain	NYI, Que., Dal., Edm., Wpg., S.J.	5	94	23	23	46	31	4	0	0	0	0	....	1992-93	1996-97
Fraser, Scott	Mtl., Edm., NYR	3	72	16	15	31	24	11	1	1	2	0	....	1995-96	1998-99
Frawley, Dan	Chi., Pit.	6	273	37	40	77	674	1	0	0	0	0	....	1983-84	1988-89
Freadrich, Kyle	T.B.	2	23	0	1	1	75	....	....	....	....	....	....	1999-00	2000-01
• Fredrickson, Frank	Det., Bos., Pit.	5	161	39	34	73	206	10	2	3	5	24	....	1926-27	1930-31
Freer, Mark	Phi., Ott., Cgy.	7	124	16	23	39	61	....	....	....	....	....	....	1986-87	1993-94
• Frew, Irv	Mtl.M., St.L., Mtl.	3	96	2	5	7	146	4	0	0	0	6	....	1933-34	1935-36
Friday, Tim	Det.	1	23	0	3	3	6	....	....	....	....	....	....	1985-86	1985-86
Fridgen, Dan	Hfd.	2	13	2	3	5	2	....	....	....	....	....	....	1981-82	1982-83
Friedman, Doug	Edm., Nsh.	2	18	0	1	1	34	....	....	....	....	....	....	1997-98	1998-99
‡ Friesen, Jeff	S.J., Ana., N.J., Wsh., Cgy.	12	893	218	298	516	488	84	18	15	33	48	1	1994-95	2006-07
Friest, Ron	Min.	3	64	7	7	14	191	6	1	0	1	7	....	1980-81	1982-83
Frig, Len	Chi., Cal., Cle., St.L.	7	311	13	51	64	479	14	2	1	3	0	....	1972-73	1979-80
‡ Fritsch, Jamie	Phi.	1	1	0	0	0	0	....	....	....	....	....	....	2008-09	2008-09
‡ Fritz, Mitch	NYI	1	20	0	0	0	42	....	....	....	....	....	....	2008-09	2008-09
‡ Frogren, Jonas	Tor.	1	41	1	6	7	28	....	....	....	....	....	....	2008-09	2008-09
• Frost, Harry	Bos.	1	4	0	0	0	0	1	0	0	0	0	1	1938-39	1938-39
Frycer, Miroslav	Que., Tor., Det., Edm.	8	415	147	183	330	486	17	3	8	11	16	....	1981-82	1988-89
• Fryday, Bob	Mtl.	2	5	1	0	1	0	....	....	....	....	....	....	1949-50	1951-52
Ftorek, Robbie	Det., Que., NYR	8	334	77	150	227	262	19	9	6	15	28	....	1972-73	1984-85
Fullan, Larry	Wsh.	1	4	1	0	1	0	....	....	....	....	....	....	1974-75	1974-75
Funk, Michael	Buf.	2	9	0	2	2	0	....	....	....	....	....	....	2006-07	2007-08
Fusco, Mark	Hfd.	2	80	3	12	15	42	....	....	....	....	....	....	1983-84	1984-85
Fussey, Owen	Wsh.	1	4	0	1	1	0	....	....	....	....	....	....	2003-04	2003-04

G

Name	NHL Teams	NHL Seasons	GP	G	A	TP	PIM	GP	G	A	TP	PIM	NHL Cup Wins	First NHL Season	Last NHL Season
Gadsby, Bill	Chi., NYR, Det.	20	1248	130	438	568	1539	67	4	23	27	92	....	1946-47	1965-66
Gaetz, Link	Min., S.J.	3	65	6	8	14	412	....	....	....	....	....	....	1988-89	1991-92
Gage, Jody	Det., Buf.	6	68	14	15	29	26	....	....	....	....	....	....	1980-81	1991-92
• Gagne, Art	Mtl., Bos., Ott., Det.	6	228	67	33	100	257	11	2	1	3	20	....	1926-27	1931-32
Gagne, Paul	Col., N.J., Tor., NYI	8	390	110	101	211	127	....	....	....	....	....	....	1980-81	1989-90
Gagne, Pierre	Bos.	1	2	0	0	0	0	....	....	....	....	....	....	1959-60	1959-60
Gagner, Dave	NYR, Min., Dal., Tor., Cgy., Fla., Van.	15	946	318	401	719	1018	57	22	26	48	64	....	1984-85	1998-99
Gagnon, Germain	Mtl., NYI, Chi., K.C.	5	259	40	101	141	72	19	2	3	5	2	....	1971-72	1975-76
• Gagnon, Johnny	Mtl., Bos., NYA	10	454	120	141	261	295	32	12	12	24	37	1	1930-31	1939-40
Gagnon, Sean	Phx., Ott.	3	12	0	1	1	34	....	....	....	....	....	....	1997-98	2000-01
Gainey, Bob	Mtl.	16	1160	239	262	501	585	182	25	48	73	151	5	1973-74	1988-89
Gainey, Steve	Dal., Phx.	4	33	0	2	2	34	....	....	....	....	....	....	2000-01	2005-06
• Gainor, Dutch	Bos., NYR, Ott., Mtl.M.	7	246	51	56	107	129	22	2	1	3	14	2	1927-28	1934-35
Galanov, Maxim	NYR, Pit., Atl., T.B.	4	122	8	12	20	44	1	0	0	0	0	....	1997-98	2000-01
Galarneau, Michel	Hfd.	3	78	7	10	17	34	....	....	....	....	....	....	1980-81	1982-83
• Galbraith, Percy	Bos., Ott.	8	347	29	31	60	224	31	4	7	11	24	1	1926-27	1933-34
• Gallagher, John	Mtl.M., Det., NYA	7	205	14	19	33	153	24	2	3	5	27	1	1930-31	1938-39
Gallant, Gerard	Det., T.B.	11	615	211	269	480	1674	58	18	21	39	178	....	1984-85	1994-95
Galley, Garry	L.A., Wsh., Bos., Phi., Buf., NYI	17	1149	125	475	600	1218	89	7	23	30	119	....	1984-85	2000-01
Gallimore, Jamie	Min.	1	2	0	0	0	0	....	....	....	....	....	....	1977-78	1977-78
• Gallinger, Don	Bos.	5	222	65	88	153	89	23	5	5	10	19	....	1942-43	1947-48
‡ Gamache, Simon	Atl., Nsh., St.L., Tor.	4	48	6	7	13	18	....	....	....	....	....	....	2002-03	2007-08
Gamble, Dick	Mtl., Chi., Tor.	8	195	41	41	82	66	14	1	2	3	4	1	1950-51	1966-67
Gambucci, Gary	Min.	2	51	2	7	9	9	....	....	....	....	....	....	1971-72	1973-74
Ganchar, Perry	St.L., Mtl., Pit.	4	42	3	7	10	36	7	3	1	4	0	....	1983-84	1988-89
Gans, Dave	L.A.	2	6	0	0	0	2	....	....	....	....	....	....	1982-83	1985-86
Gardiner, Bruce	Ott., T.B., CBJ, N.J.	6	312	34	54	88	263	21	1	4	5	8	....	1996-97	2001-02
• Gardiner, Herb	Mtl., Chi.	3	108	10	9	19	52	9	0	1	1	16	....	1926-27	1928-29
Gardner, Bill	Chi., Hfd.	9	380	73	115	188	68	45	3	8	11	17	....	1980-81	1988-89
• Gardner, Cal	NYR, Tor., Chi., Bos.	12	696	154	238	392	517	61	7	10	17	20	2	1945-46	1956-57
Gardner, Dave	Mtl., St.L., Cal., Cle., Phi.	7	350	75	115	190	41	....	....	....	....	....	....	1972-73	1979-80
Gardner, Paul	Col., Tor., Pit., Wsh., Buf.	10	447	201	201	402	207	16	2	6	8	14	....	1976-77	1985-86
Gare, Danny	Buf., Det., Edm.	13	827	354	331	685	1285	64	25	21	46	195	....	1974-75	1986-87
Gariepy, Ray	Bos., Tor.	2	36	1	6	7	43	....	....	....	....	....	....	1953-54	1955-56
• Garland, Scott	Tor., L.A.	3	91	13	24	37	115	7	1	2	3	35	....	1975-76	1978-79
Garner, Rob	Pit.	1	1	0	0	0	0	....	....	....	....	....	....	1982-83	1982-83
Garpenlov, Johan	Det., S.J., Fla., Atl.	10	609	114	197	311	276	44	10	9	19	22	....	1990-91	1999-00
• Garrett, Red	NYR	1	23	1	1	2	18	....	....	....	....	....	....	1942-43	1942-43

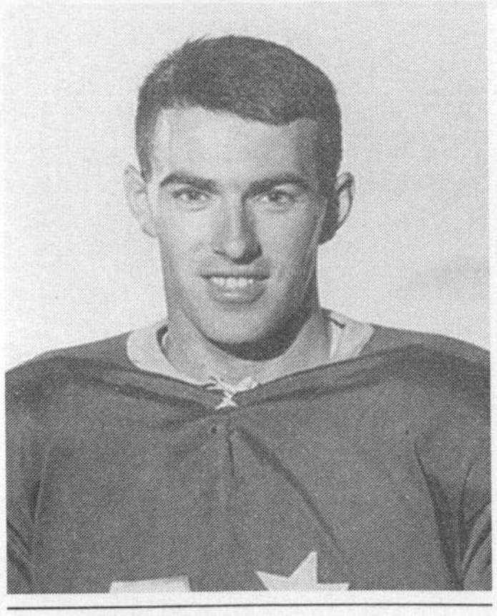
Sandy Fitzpatrick

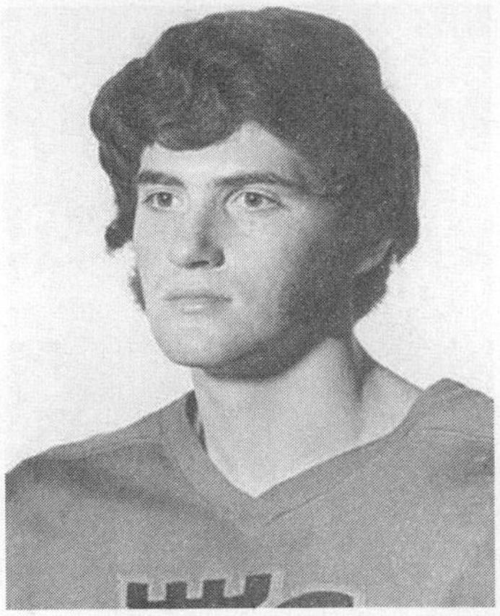
Peter Folco

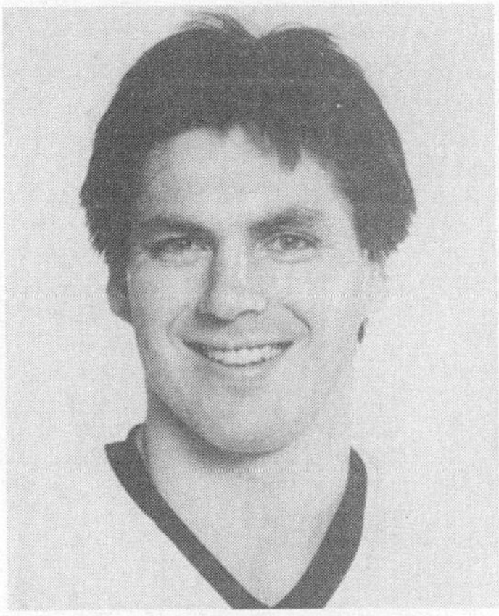
Dan Frawley

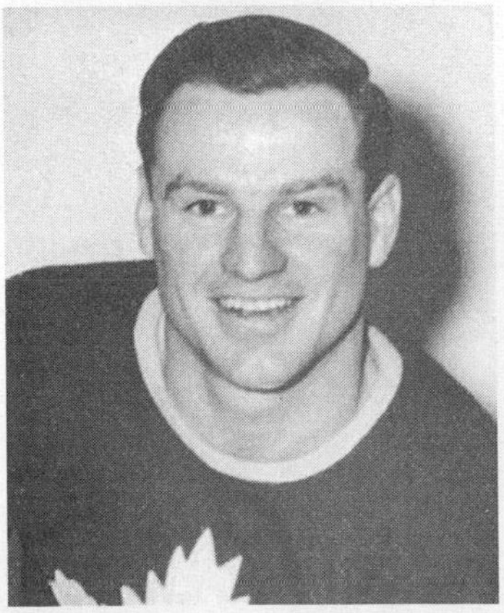
Cal Gardner

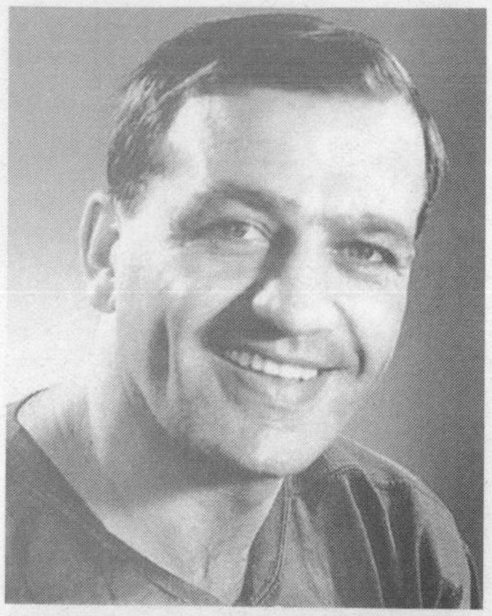

Bernie Geoffrion

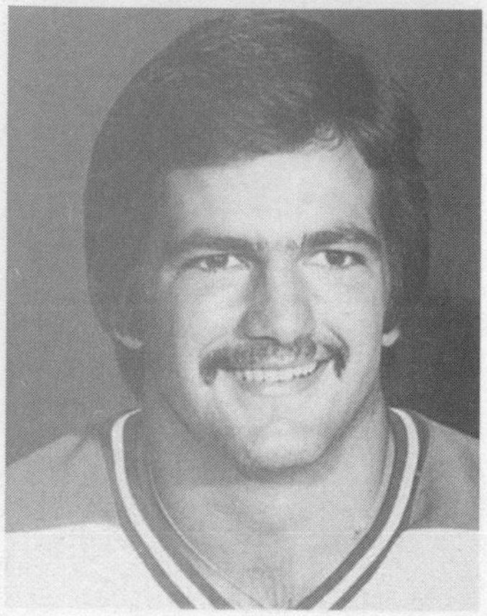

Danny Geoffrion

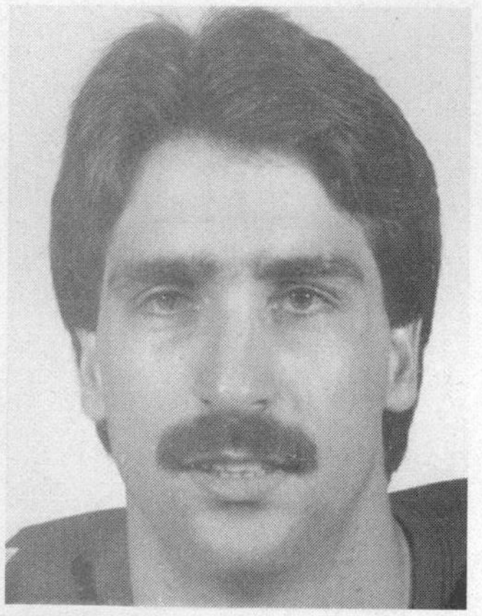

John Gibson

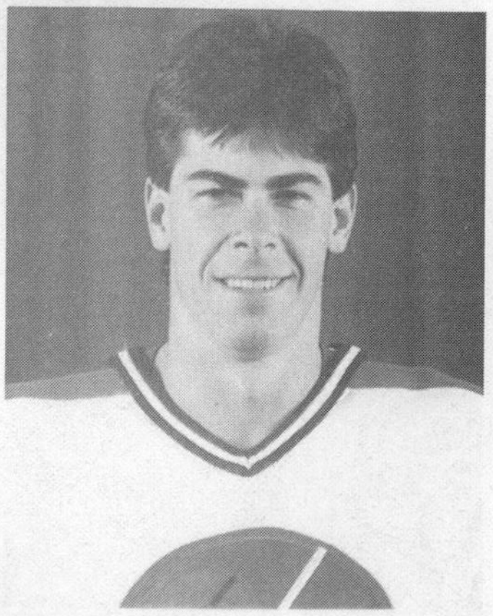

Randy Gilhen

			Regular Schedule					Playoffs							
Name	NHL Teams	NHL Seasons	GP	G	A	TP	PIM	GP	G	A	TP	PIM	NHL Cup Wins	First NHL Season	Last NHL Season
Gartner, Mike	Wsh., Min., NYR, Tor., Phx.	19	1432	708	627	1335	1159	122	43	50	93	125	....	1979-80	1997-98
• Gassoff, Bob	St.L.	4	245	11	47	58	866	9	0	1	1	16	....	1973-74	1976-77
Gassoff, Brad	Van.	4	122	19	17	36	163	3	0	0	0	0	....	1975-76	1978-79
Gatzos, Steve	Pit.	4	89	15	20	35	83	1	0	0	0	0	....	1981-82	1984-85
Gaudreau, Rob	S.J., Ott.	4	231	51	54	105	69	14	2	0	2	0	....	1992-93	1995-96
Gaudreault, Armand	Bos.	1	44	15	9	24	27	7	0	2	2	8	....	1944-45	1944-45
• Gaudreault, Leo	Mtl.	3	67	8	4	12	30	....	....	....	....	....	....	1927-28	1932-33
Gaul, Mike	Col., CBJ	2	3	0	0	0	4	....	....	....	....	....	....	1998-99	2000-01
Gaulin, Jean-Marc	Que.	4	26	4	3	7	8	1	0	0	0	0	....	1982-83	1985-86
Gaume, Dallas	Hfd.	1	4	1	1	2	0	....	....	....	....	....	....	1988-89	1988-89
• Gauthier, Art	Mtl.	1	13	0	0	0	0	1	0	0	0	0	....	1926-27	1926-27
Gauthier, Daniel	Chi.	1	5	0	0	0	0	....	....	....	....	....	....	1994-95	1994-95
Gauthier, Denis	Cgy., Phx., Phi., L.A.	10	554	17	60	77	748	12	0	2	2	23	....	1997-98	2008-09
• Gauthier, Fern	NYR, Mtl., Det.	6	229	46	50	96	35	22	5	1	6	7	....	1943-44	1948-49
‡ Gauthier, Gabe	L.A.	2	8	0	0	0	2	....	....	....	....	....	....	2006-07	2007-08
Gauthier, Jean	Mtl., Phi., Bos.	10	166	6	29	35	150	14	1	3	4	22	1	1960-61	1969-70
Gauthier, Luc	Mtl.	1	3	0	0	0	2	....	....	....	....	....	....	1990-91	1990-91
Gauvreau, Jocelyn	Mtl.	1	2	0	0	0	0	....	....	....	....	....	....	1983-84	1983-84
Gavey, Aaron	T.B., Cgy., Dal., Min., Tor., Ana.	9	360	41	50	91	272	19	1	2	3	14	....	1995-96	2005-06
Gavin, Stew	Tor., Hfd., Min.	13	768	130	155	285	584	66	14	20	34	75	....	1980-81	1992-93
Geale, Bob	Pit.	1	1	0	0	0	2	....	....	....	....	....	....	1984-85	1984-85
• Gee, George	Chi., Det.	9	551	135	183	318	345	41	6	13	19	32	1	1945-46	1953-54
Geldart, Gary	Min.	1	4	0	0	0	5	....	....	....	....	....	....	1970-71	1970-71
Gelinas, Martin	Edm., Que., Van., Car., Cgy., Fla., Nsh.	19	1273	309	351	660	820	147	23	33	56	120	1	1988-89	2007-08
Gendron, Jean-Guy	NYR, Bos., Mtl., Phi.	14	863	182	201	383	701	42	7	4	11	47	....	1955-56	1971-72
Gendron, Martin	Wsh., Chi.	3	30	4	2	6	10	....	....	....	....	....	....	1994-95	1997-98
• Geoffrion, Bernie	Mtl., NYR	16	883	393	429	822	689	132	58	60	118	88	6	1950-51	1967-68
Geoffrion, Danny	Mtl., Wpg.	3	111	20	32	52	99	2	0	0	0	7	....	1979-80	1981-82
• Geran, Gerry	Mtl.W., Bos.	2	37	5	1	6	6	....	....	....	....	....	....	1917-18	1925-26
• Gerard, Eddie	Ott.	6	128	50	48	98	108	11	4	0	4	17	3	1917-18	1922-23
Germain, Eric	L.A.	1	4	0	1	1	13	1	0	0	0	4	....	1987-88	1987-88
Germyn, Carsen	Cgy.	2	4	0	0	0	0	....	....	....	....	....	....	2005-06	2006-07
Gernander, Ken	NYR	3	12	2	3	5	6	15	0	0	0	0	....	1995-96	2003-04
• Getliffe, Ray	Bos., Mtl.	10	393	136	137	273	250	45	9	10	19	30	2	1935-36	1944-45
Giallonardo, Mario	Col.	2	23	0	3	3	6	....	....	....	....	....	....	1979-80	1980-81
Gibbs, Barry	Bos., Min., Atl., St.L., L.A.	13	797	58	224	282	945	36	4	2	6	67	....	1967-68	1979-80
Gibson, Don	Van.	1	14	0	3	3	20	....	....	....	....	....	....	1990-91	1990-91
Gibson, Doug	Bos., Wsh.	3	63	9	19	28	0	1	0	0	0	0	....	1973-74	1977-78
Gibson, John	L.A., Tor., Wpg.	3	48	0	2	2	120	....	....	....	....	....	....	1980-81	1983-84
• Giesebrecht, Gus	Det.	4	135	27	51	78	13	17	2	3	5	0	....	1938-39	1941-42
Giffin, Lee	Pit.	2	27	1	3	4	9	....	....	....	....	....	....	1986-87	1987-88
Gilbert, Ed	K.C., Pit.	3	166	21	31	52	22	....	....	....	....	....	....	1974-75	1976-77
Gilbert, Greg	NYI, Chi., NYR, St.L.	15	837	150	228	378	576	133	17	33	50	162	3	1981-82	1995-96
Gilbert, Jeannot	Bos.	2	9	0	1	1	4	....	....	....	....	....	....	1962-63	1964-65
Gilbert, Rod	NYR	18	1065	406	615	1021	508	79	34	33	67	43	....	1960-61	1977-78
Gilbertson, Stan	Cal., St.L., Wsh., Pit.	6	428	85	89	174	148	3	1	1	2	2	....	1971-72	1976-77
Gilchrist, Brent	Mtl., Edm., Min., Dal., Det., Nsh.	15	792	135	170	305	400	90	17	14	31	48	1	1988-89	2002-03
Giles, Curt	Min., NYR, St.L.	14	895	43	199	242	733	103	6	16	22	118	....	1979-80	1992-93
Gilhen, Randy	Hfd., Wpg., Pit., L.A., NYR, T.B., Fla.	11	457	55	60	115	314	33	3	2	5	26	1	1982-83	1995-96
Gill, Todd	Tor., S.J., St.L., Det., Phx., Col., Chi.	19	1007	82	272	354	1214	103	7	30	37	193	....	1984-85	2002-03
Gillen, Don	Phi., Hfd.	2	35	2	4	6	22	....	....	....	....	....	....	1979-80	1981-82
• Gillie, Farrand	Det.	1	1	0	0	0	0	....	....	....	....	....	....	1928-29	1928-29
Gillies, Clark	NYI, Buf.	14	958	319	378	697	1023	164	47	47	94	287	4	1974-75	1987-88
Gillis, Jere	Van., NYR, Que., Buf., Phi.	9	386	78	95	173	230	19	4	7	11	9	....	1977-78	1986-87
Gillis, Mike	Col., Bos.	6	246	33	43	76	186	27	2	5	7	10	....	1978-79	1983-84
Gillis, Paul	Que., Chi., Hfd.	11	624	88	154	242	1498	42	3	14	17	156	....	1982-83	1992-93
Gilmour, Doug	St.L., Cgy., Tor., N.J., Chi., Buf., Mtl.	20	1474	450	964	1414	1301	182	60	128	188	235	1	1983-84	2002-03
Gingras, Gaston	Mtl., Tor., St.L.	10	476	61	174	235	161	52	6	18	24	20	1	1979-80	1988-89
Girard, Bob	Cal., Cle., Wsh.	5	305	45	69	114	140	....	....	....	....	....	....	1975-76	1979-80
Girard, Jonathan	Bos.	5	150	10	34	44	46	3	0	1	1	2	....	1998-99	2002-03
Girard, Kenny	Tor.	3	7	0	1	1	2	....	....	....	....	....	....	1956-57	1959-60
• Giroux, Art	Mtl., Bos., Det.	3	54	6	4	10	14	2	0	0	0	0	....	1932-33	1935-36
Giroux, Larry	St.L., K.C., Det., Hfd.	7	274	15	74	89	333	5	0	0	0	4	....	1973-74	1979-80
Giroux, Pierre	L.A.	1	6	1	0	1	17	....	....	....	....	....	....	1982-83	1982-83
‡ Giroux, Raymond	NYI, N.J.	4	38	0	13	13	22	4	0	0	0	0	....	1999-00	2003-04
‡ Giuliano, Jeff	L.A.	2	101	3	10	13	40	....	....	....	....	....	....	2005-06	2007-08
Gladney, Bob	L.A., Pit.	2	14	1	5	6	4	....	....	....	....	....	....	1982-83	1983-84
Gladu, Jean-Paul	Bos.	1	40	6	14	20	2	7	2	2	4	0	....	1944-45	1944-45
Glennie, Brian	Tor., L.A.	10	572	14	100	114	621	32	0	1	1	66	....	1969-70	1978-79
Glennon, Matt	Bos.	1	3	0	0	0	2	....	....	....	....	....	....	1991-92	1991-92
Globke, Rob	Fla.	3	46	1	1	2	8	....	....	....	....	....	....	2005-06	2007-08
Gloeckner, Lorry	Det.	1	13	0	2	2	6	....	....	....	....	....	....	1978-79	1978-79
Gloor, Dan	Van.	1	2	0	0	0	0	....	....	....	....	....	....	1973-74	1973-74
• Glover, Fred	Det., Chi.	5	92	13	11	24	62	8	0	0	0	0	1	1948-49	1952-53
Glover, Howie	Chi., Det., NYR, Mtl.	5	144	29	17	46	101	11	1	2	3	2	....	1958-59	1968-69
Glynn, Brian	Cgy., Min., Edm., Ott., Van., Hfd.	10	431	25	79	104	410	57	6	10	16	40	....	1987-88	1996-97
‡ Goc, Sascha	N.J., T.B.	2	22	0	0	0	4	....	....	....	....	....	....	2000-01	2001-02
Godden, Ernie	Tor.	1	5	1	1	2	6	....	....	....	....	....	....	1981-82	1981-82
• Godfrey, Warren	Bos., Det.	16	786	32	125	157	752	52	1	4	5	42	....	1952-53	1967-68
Godin, Eddy	Wsh.	2	27	3	6	9	12	....	....	....	....	....	....	1977-78	1978-79
• Godin, Sam	Ott., Mtl.	3	83	4	3	7	36	....	....	....	....	....	....	1927-28	1933-34
Godynyuk, Alexander	Tor., Cgy., Fla., Hfd.	7	223	10	39	49	224	....	....	....	....	....	....	1990-91	1996-97
• Goegan, Pete	Det., NYR, Min.	11	383	19	67	86	365	33	1	3	4	61	....	1957-58	1967-68
Goertz, Dave	Pit.	1	2	0	0	0	2	....	....	....	....	....	....	1987-88	1987-88
• Goldham, Bob	Tor., Chi., Det.	12	650	28	143	171	400	66	3	14	17	53	5	1941-42	1955-56
Goldmann, Erich	Ott.	1	1	0	0	0	0	....	....	....	....	....	....	1999-00	1999-00
• Goldsworthy, Bill	Bos., Min., NYR	14	771	283	258	541	793	40	18	19	37	30	....	1964-65	1977-78
• Goldsworthy, Leroy	NYR, Det., Chi., Mtl., Bos., NYA	10	336	66	57	123	79	24	1	0	1	4	1	1928-29	1938-39
Goldup, Glenn	Mtl., L.A.	9	291	52	67	119	303	16	4	3	7	22	....	1973-74	1981-82
• Goldup, Hank	Tor., NYR	6	202	63	80	143	97	26	5	1	6	6	1	1939-40	1945-46
Golubovsky, Yan	Det., Fla.	4	56	1	7	8	32	....	....	....	....	....	....	1997-98	2000-01
Goneau, Daniel	NYR	3	53	12	3	15	14	....	....	....	....	....	....	1996-97	1999-00
• Gooden, Bill	NYR	2	53	9	11	20	15	....	....	....	....	....	....	1942-43	1943-44
Goodenough, Larry	Phi., Van.	6	242	22	77	99	179	22	3	15	18	10	1	1974-75	1979-80
• Goodfellow, Ebbie	Det.	14	557	134	190	324	511	45	8	8	16	65	3	1929-30	1942-43
Gordiouk, Viktor	Buf.	2	26	3	8	11	0	....	....	....	....	....	....	1992-93	1994-95
• Gordon, Fred	Det., Bos.	2	81	8	7	15	68	2	0	0	0	0	....	1926-27	1927-28
Gordon, Jack	NYR	3	36	3	10	13	0	9	1	1	2	7	....	1948-49	1950-51
Gordon, Robb	Van.	1	4	0	0	0	2	....	....	....	....	....	....	1998-99	1998-99
‡ Goren, Lee	Bos., Fla., Van.	5	67	5	4	9	44	5	0	0	0	5	....	2000-01	2006-07
Gorence, Tom	Phi., Edm.	6	303	58	53	111	89	37	9	6	15	47	....	1978-79	1983-84
Goring, Butch	L.A., NYI, Bos.	16	1107	375	513	888	102	134	38	50	88	32	4	1969-70	1984-85
Gorman, Dave	Atl.	1	3	0	0	0	0	....	....	....	....	....	....	1979-80	1979-80
• Gorman, Ed	Ott., Tor.	4	111	14	6	20	108	8	0	0	0	2	1	1924-25	1927-28
Gosselin, Benoit	NYR	1	7	0	0	0	33	....	....	....	....	....	....	1977-78	1977-78
Gosselin, David	Nsh.	2	13	2	1	3	11	....	....	....	....	....	....	1999-00	2001-02
Gosselin, Guy	Wpg.	1	5	0	0	0	6	....	....	....	....	....	....	1987-88	1987-88
Gotaas, Steve	Pit., Min.	3	49	6	9	15	53	3	0	1	1	5	....	1987-88	1990-91
• Gottselig, Johnny	Chi.	16	589	176	195	371	203	43	13	13	26	18	2	1928-29	1944-45
Gould, Bobby	Atl., Cgy., Wsh., Bos.	11	697	145	159	304	572	78	15	13	28	58	....	1979-80	1989-90
Gould, John	Buf., Van., Atl.	9	504	131	138	269	113	14	3	2	5	4	....	1971-72	1979-80
Gould, Larry	Van.	1	2	0	0	0	0	....	....	....	....	....	....	1973-74	1973-74
Goulet, Michel	Que., Chi.	15	1089	548	604	1152	825	92	39	39	78	110	....	1979-80	1993-94
• Goupille, Red	Mtl.	8	222	12	28	40	256	8	2	0	2	6	....	1935-36	1942-43
Gove, David	Car.	2	2	0	1	1	0	....	....	....	....	....	....	2005-06	2006-07
Govedaris, Chris	Hfd., Tor.	4	45	4	6	10	24	4	0	0	0	2	....	1989-90	1993-94
Goyer, Gerry	Chi.	1	40	1	2	3	4	3	0	0	0	2	....	1967-68	1967-68
Goyette, Phil	Mtl., NYR, St.L., Buf.	16	941	207	467	674	131	94	17	29	46	26	4	1956-57	1971-72
• Graboski, Tony	Mtl.	3	66	6	10	16	24	3	0	0	0	6	....	1940-41	1942-43
• Gracie, Bob	Tor., Bos., NYA, Mtl.M., Mtl., Chi.	9	379	82	109	191	205	33	4	7	11	4	2	1930-31	1938-39
Gradin, Thomas	Van., Bos.	9	677	209	384	593	298	42	17	25	42	20	....	1978-79	1986-87
Graham, Dirk	Min., Chi.	12	772	219	270	489	917	90	17	27	44	92	....	1983-84	1994-95
• Graham, Leth	Ott., Ham.	6	27	3	0	3	0	1	0	0	0	0	1	1920-21	1925-26
Graham, Pat	Pit., Tor.	3	103	11	17	28	136	4	0	0	0	2	....	1981-82	1983-84
Graham, Rod	Bos.	1	14	2	1	3	7	....	....	....	....	....	....	1974-75	1974-75
• Graham, Ted	Chi., Mtl.M., Det., St.L., Bos., NYA	9	346	14	25	39	300	24	3	1	4	30	....	1927-28	1936-37

			Regular Schedule					Playoffs							
Name	NHL Teams	NHL Seasons	GP	G	A	TP	PIM	GP	G	A	TP	PIM	NHL Cup Wins	First NHL Season	Last NHL Season
Granato, Tony	NYR, L.A., S.J.	13	773	248	244	492	1425	79	16	27	43	141	....	1988-89	2000-01
Grand-Pierre, Jean-Luc	Buf., CBJ, Atl., Wsh.	6	269	7	13	20	311	4	0	0	0	4	....	1998-99	2003-04
Grant, Danny	Mtl., Min., Det., L.A.	13	736	263	273	536	239	43	10	14	24	19	1	1965-66	1978-79
Gratton, Benoit	Wsh., Cgy., Mtl.	6	58	6	10	16	58	....	....	....	....	....	....	1997-98	2003-04
Gratton, Chris	T.B., Phi., Buf., Phx., Col., Fla., CBJ	15	1092	214	354	568	1638	40	8	7	15	82	....	1993-94	2008-09
Gratton, Dan	L.A.	1	7	1	0	1	5	....	....	....	....	....	....	1987-88	1987-88
‡ Gratton, Josh	Phi., Phx.	4	86	3	3	6	294	....	....	....	....	....	....	2005-06	2008-09
Gratton, Norm	NYR, Atl., Buf., Min.	5	201	39	44	83	64	6	0	1	1	2	....	1971-72	1975-76
Gravelle, Leo	Mtl., Det.	5	223	44	34	78	42	17	4	1	5	2	....	1946-47	1950-51
Graves, Adam	Det., Edm., NYR, S.J.	16	1152	329	287	616	1224	125	38	27	65	119	2	1987-88	2002-03
Graves, Hilliard	Cal., Atl., Van., Wpg.	9	556	118	163	281	209	2	0	0	0	0	....	1970-71	1979-80
Graves, Steve	Edm.	3	35	5	4	9	10	....	....	....	....	....	....	1983-84	1987-88
• Gray, Alex	NYR, Tor.	2	50	7	0	7	32	13	1	0	1	0	1	1927-28	1928-29
Gray, Terry	Bos., Mtl., L.A., St.L.	6	147	26	28	54	64	35	5	5	10	22	....	1961-62	1970-71
Green, Mike	Fla., NYR	1	24	1	3	4	4	....	....	....	....	....	....	2003-04	2003-04
• Green, Red	Ham., NYA, Bos., Det.	6	195	59	26	85	290	1	0	0	0	0	1	1923-24	1928-29
Green, Rick	Wsh., Mtl., Det., NYI	15	845	43	220	263	588	100	3	16	19	73	1	1976-77	1991-92
• Green, Shorty	Ham., NYA	4	103	33	20	53	151	....	....	....	....	....	....	1923-24	1926-27
Green, Ted	Bos.	11	620	48	206	254	1029	31	4	8	12	54	1	1960-61	1971-72
Green, Travis	NYI, Ana., Phx., Tor., Bos.	14	970	193	262	455	764	56	10	11	21	60	....	1992-93	2006-07
Greenlaw, Jeff	Wsh., Fla.	6	57	3	6	9	108	2	0	0	0	21	....	1986-87	1993-94
Gregg, Randy	Edm., Van.	10	474	41	152	193	333	137	13	38	51	127	5	1981-82	1991-92
• Greig, Bruce	Cal.	2	9	0	1	1	46	....	....	....	....	....	....	1973-74	1974-75
Greig, Mark	Hfd., Tor., Cgy., Phi.	9	125	13	27	40	90	5	0	1	1	0	....	1990-91	2002-03
Grenier, Lucien	Mtl., L.A.	4	151	14	14	28	18	2	0	0	0	0	....	1968-69	1971-72
Grenier, Martin	Phx., Van., Phi.	4	18	1	0	1	14	....	....	....	....	....	....	2001-02	2006-07
Grenier, Richard	NYI	1	10	1	1	2	2	....	....	....	....	....	....	1972-73	1972-73
Greschner, Ron	NYR	16	982	179	431	610	1226	84	17	32	49	106	....	1974-75	1989-90
Gretzky, Brent	T.B.	2	13	1	3	4	2	....	....	....	....	....	....	1993-94	1994-95
Gretzky, Wayne	Edm., L.A., St.L., NYR	20	1487	894	1963	2857	577	208	122	260	382	66	4	1979-80	1998-99
Grieve, Brent	NYI, Edm., Chi., L.A.	4	97	20	16	36	87	....	....	....	....	....	....	1993-94	1996-97
• Grigor, George	Chi.	1	2	1	0	1	0	1	0	0	0	0	....	1943-44	1943-44
Grimson, Stu	Cgy., Chi., Ana., Det., Hfd., Car., L.A., Nsh.	14	729	17	22	39	2113	42	1	1	2	120	....	1988-89	2001-02
Grisdale, John	Tor., Van.	6	250	4	39	43	346	10	0	1	1	15	....	1972-73	1978-79
Groleau, Francois	Mtl.	3	8	0	1	1	6	....	....	....	....	....	....	1995-96	1997-98
‡ Gron, Stanislav	N.J.	1	1	0	0	0	0	....	....	....	....	....	....	2000-01	2000-01
Gronman, Tuomas	Chi., Pit.	2	38	1	3	4	38	1	0	0	0	0	....	1996-97	1997-98
• Gronsdahl, Lloyd	Bos.	1	10	1	2	3	0	....	....	....	....	....	....	1941-42	1941-42
Gronstrand, Jari	Min., NYR, Que., NYI	5	185	8	26	34	135	3	0	0	0	4	....	1986-87	1990-91
Grosek, Michal	Wpg., Buf., Chi., NYR, Bos.	11	526	84	137	221	509	45	9	11	20	77	....	1993-94	2003-04
• Gross, Lloyd	Tor., NYA, Bos., Det.	3	52	11	5	16	20	1	0	0	0	0	....	1926-27	1934-35
• Grosso, Don	Det., Chi., Bos.	9	336	87	117	204	90	48	15	14	29	63	1	1938-39	1946-47
• Grosvenor, Len	Ott., NYA, Mtl.	6	149	9	11	20	78	4	0	0	0	2	....	1927-28	1932-33
Groulx, Wayne	Que.	1	1	0	0	0	0	....	....	....	....	....	....	1984-85	1984-85
Gruden, John	Bos., Ott., Wsh.	6	92	1	8	9	46	3	0	1	1	0	....	1993-94	2003-04
Gruen, Danny	Det., Col.	3	49	9	13	22	19	....	....	....	....	....	....	1972-73	1976-77
Gruhl, Scott	L.A., Pit.	3	20	3	3	6	6	....	....	....	....	....	....	1981-82	1987-88
Gryp, Bob	Bos., Wsh.	3	74	11	13	24	33	....	....	....	....	....	....	1973-74	1975-76
Guay, Francois	Buf.	1	1	0	0	0	0	....	....	....	....	....	....	1989-90	1989-90
Guay, Paul	Phi., L.A., Bos., NYI	7	117	11	23	34	92	9	0	1	1	12	....	1983-84	1990-91
Guerard, Daniel	Ott.	1	2	0	0	0	0	....	....	....	....	....	....	1994-95	1994-95
Guerard, Stephane	Que.	2	34	0	0	0	40	....	....	....	....	....	....	1987-88	1989-90
Guerin, Bill	N.J., Edm., Bos., Dal., St.L., S.J., NYI, Pit.	18	1263	429	427	856	1660	140	39	35	74	162	2	1991-92	2009-10
Guevremont, Jocelyn	Van., Buf., NYR	9	571	84	223	307	319	40	4	17	21	18	....	1971-72	1979-80
Guidolin, Aldo	NYR	4	182	9	15	24	117	....	....	....	....	....	....	1952-53	1955-56
• Guidolin, Bep	Bos., Det., Chi.	9	519	107	171	278	606	24	5	7	12	35	....	1942-43	1951-52
Guindon, Bobby	Wpg.	1	6	0	1	1	0	....	....	....	....	....	....	1979-80	1979-80
Guolla, Steve	S.J., T.B., Atl., N.J.	6	205	40	46	86	60	....	....	....	....	....	....	1996-97	2002-03
Guren, Miloslav	Mtl.	2	36	1	3	4	16	....	....	....	....	....	....	1998-99	1999-00
Gusarov, Alexei	Que., Col., NYR, St.L.	11	607	39	128	167	313	68	0	14	14	38	1	1990-91	2000-01
Gusev, Sergey	Dal., T.B.	4	89	4	10	14	34	....	....	....	....	....	....	1997-98	2000-01
Gusmanov, Ravil	Wpg.	1	4	0	0	0	0	....	....	....	....	....	....	1995-96	1995-96
Gustafsson, Bengt-Ake	Wsh.	9	629	196	359	555	196	32	9	19	28	16	....	1979-80	1988-89
Gustafsson, Per	Fla., Tor., Ott.	2	89	8	27	35	38	1	0	0	0	0	....	1996-97	1997-98
Gustavsson, Peter	Col.	1	2	0	0	0	0	....	....	....	....	....	....	1981-82	1981-82
Guy, Kevan	Cgy., Van.	6	156	5	20	25	138	5	0	1	1	23	....	1986-87	1991-92

H

Name	NHL Teams	NHL Seasons	GP	G	A	TP	PIM	GP	G	A	TP	PIM	NHL Cup Wins	First NHL Season	Last NHL Season
‡ Haakana, Kari	Edm.	1	13	0	0	0	4	....	....	....	....	....	....	2002-03	2002-03
Haanpaa, Ari	NYI	3	60	6	11	17	37	6	0	0	0	10	....	1985-86	1987-88
Haas, David	Edm., Cgy.	2	7	2	1	3	7	....	....	....	....	....	....	1990-91	1993-94
Habscheid, Marc	Edm., Min., Det., Cgy.	11	345	72	91	163	171	12	1	3	4	13	....	1981-82	1991-92
Hachborn, Len	Phi., L.A.	3	102	20	39	59	29	7	0	3	3	7	....	1983-84	1985-86
Haddon, Lloyd	Det.	1	8	0	0	0	2	1	0	0	0	0	....	1959-60	1959-60
Hadfield, Vic	NYR, Pit.	16	1002	323	389	712	1154	73	27	21	48	117	....	1961-62	1976-77
• Haggarty, Jim	Mtl.	1	5	1	1	2	0	3	2	1	3	0	....	1941-42	1941-42
Haggerty, Sean	Tor., NYI, Nsh.	4	14	1	2	3	4	....	....	....	....	....	....	1995-96	2000-01
• Hagglund, Roger	Que.	1	3	0	0	0	0	....	....	....	....	....	....	1984-85	1984-85
Hagman, Matti	Bos., Edm.	4	237	56	89	145	36	20	5	2	7	6	....	1976-77	1981-82
‡ Hahl, Riku	Col.	3	92	5	8	13	38	34	2	4	6	4	....	2001-02	2003-04
• Haidy, Gord	Det.	1	....	....	....	....	....	1	0	0	0	0	....	1949-50	1949-50
Hajdu, Richard	Buf.	2	5	0	0	0	4	....	....	....	....	....	....	1985-86	1986-87
Hajt, Bill	Buf.	14	854	42	202	244	433	80	2	16	18	70	....	1973-74	1986-87
Hajt, Chris	Edm., Wsh.	2	6	0	0	0	2	....	....	....	....	....	....	2000-01	2003-04
Hakansson, Anders	Min., Pit., L.A.	5	330	52	46	98	141	6	0	0	0	2	....	1981-82	1985-86
• Halderson, Harold	Det., Tor.	1	44	3	2	5	65	....	....	....	....	....	....	1926-27	1926-27
Hale, Larry	Phi.	4	196	5	37	42	90	8	0	0	0	12	....	1968-69	1971-72
Haley, Len	Det.	2	30	2	2	4	14	6	1	3	4	6	....	1959-60	1960-61
Halkidis, Bob	Buf., L.A., Tor., Det., T.B., NYI	11	256	8	32	40	825	20	0	1	1	51	....	1984-85	1995-96
Halko, Steven	Car.	6	155	0	15	15	71	4	0	0	0	2	....	1997-98	2002-03
• Hall, Bob	NYA	1	8	0	0	0	0	....	....	....	....	....	....	1925-26	1925-26
Hall, Del	Cal.	3	9	2	0	2	2	....	....	....	....	....	....	1971-72	1973-74
• Hall, Joe	Mtl.	2	37	15	9	24	235	7	0	1	1	38	....	1917-18	1918-19
Hall, Murray	Chi., Det., Min., Van.	9	164	35	48	83	46	6	0	0	0	0	....	1961-62	1971-72
Hall, Taylor	Van., Bos.	5	41	7	9	16	29	....	....	....	....	....	....	1983-84	1987-88
Hall, Wayne	NYR	1	4	0	0	0	0	....	....	....	....	....	....	1960-61	1960-61
Haller, Kevin	Buf., Mtl., Phi., Hfd., Car., Ana., NYI	13	642	41	97	138	907	64	7	16	23	71	1	1989-90	2001-02
• Halliday, Milt	Ott.	3	67	1	0	1	4	6	0	0	0	0	1	1926-27	1928-29
Hallin, Mats	NYI, Min.	5	152	17	14	31	193	15	1	0	1	13	1	1982-83	1986-87
Halverson, Trevor	Wsh.	1	17	0	4	4	28	....	....	....	....	....	....	1998-99	1998-99
Halward, Doug	Bos., L.A., Van., Det., Edm.	14	653	69	224	293	774	47	7	10	17	113	....	1975-76	1988-89
Hamel, Gilles	Buf., Wpg., L.A.	9	519	127	147	274	276	27	4	5	9	10	....	1980-81	1988-89
• Hamel, Herb	Tor.	1	2	0	0	0	4	....	....	....	....	....	....	1930-31	1930-31
Hamel, Jean	St.L., Det., Que., Mtl.	12	699	26	95	121	766	33	0	2	2	44	....	1972-73	1983-84
• Hamill, Red	Bos., Chi.	12	419	128	94	222	160	24	1	2	3	20	1	1937-38	1950-51
Hamilton, Al	NYR, Buf., Edm.	7	257	10	78	88	258	7	0	0	0	2	....	1965-66	1979-80
Hamilton, Chuck	Mtl., St.L.	2	4	0	2	2	2	....	....	....	....	....	....	1961-62	1972-73
• Hamilton, Jack	Tor.	3	102	28	32	60	20	11	2	1	3	0	....	1942-43	1945-46
‡ Hamilton, Jeff	NYI, Chi., Car., Tor.	5	157	32	45	77	44	....	....	....	....	....	....	2003-04	2008-09
Hamilton, Jim	Pit.	8	95	14	18	32	28	6	3	0	3	0	....	1977-78	1984-85
• Hamilton, Reg	Tor., Chi.	12	424	21	87	108	412	64	3	8	11	46	2	1935-36	1946-47
Hammarstrom, Inge	Tor., St.L.	6	427	116	123	239	86	13	2	3	5	4	....	1973-74	1978-79
Hammond, Ken	L.A., Edm., NYR, Tor., Bos., S.J., Van., Ott.	8	193	18	29	47	290	15	0	0	0	24	....	1984-85	1992-93
Hampson, Gord	Cgy.	1	4	0	0	0	5	....	....	....	....	....	....	1982-83	1982-83
Hampson, Ted	Tor., NYR, Det., Oak., Cal., Min.	12	676	108	245	353	94	35	7	10	17	2	....	1959-60	1971-72
Hampton, Rick	Cal., Cle., L.A.	6	337	59	113	172	147	2	0	0	0	0	....	1974-75	1979-80
Hamr, Radek	Ott.	2	11	0	0	0	0	....	....	....	....	....	....	1992-93	1993-94
Hamway, Mark	NYI	3	53	5	13	18	9	1	0	0	0	0	....	1984-85	1986-87
Handy, Ron	NYI, St.L.	2	14	0	3	3	0	....	....	....	....	....	....	1984-85	1987-88
Hangsleben, Al	Hfd., Wsh., L.A.	3	185	21	48	69	396	....	....	....	....	....	....	1979-80	1981-82
Hankinson, Ben	N.J., T.B.	3	43	3	3	6	45	2	1	0	1	4	....	1992-93	1994-95
Hankinson, Casey	Chi., Ana.	3	18	0	1	1	13	....	....	....	....	....	....	2000-01	2003-04

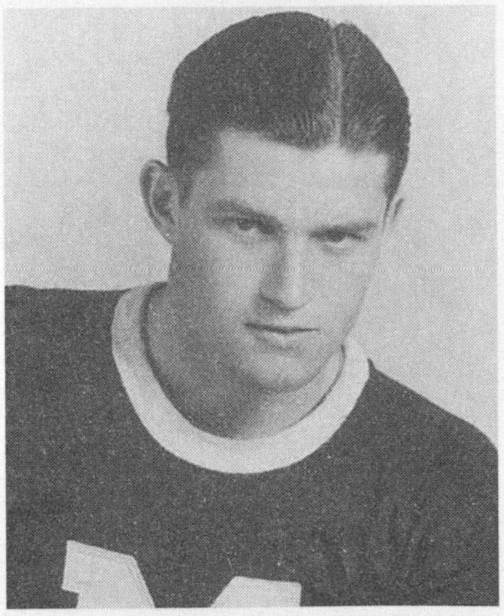

Bob Gracie

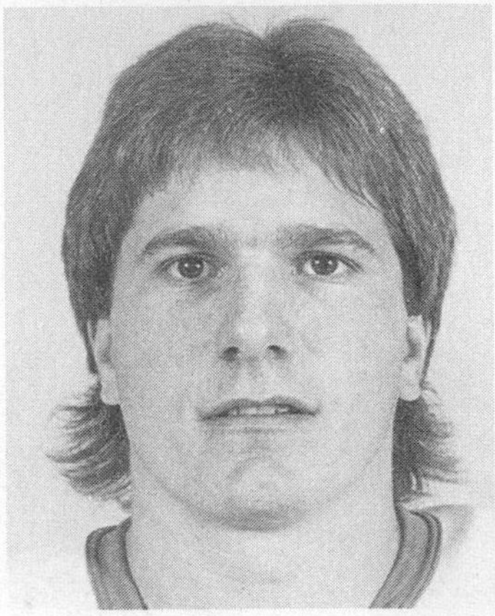

Wayne Groulx

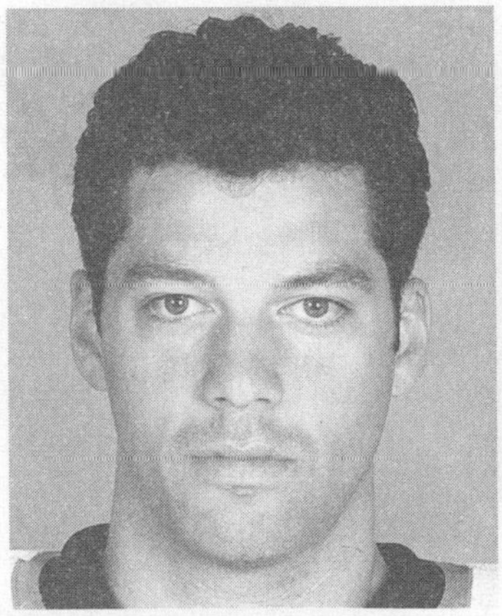

Bill Guerin

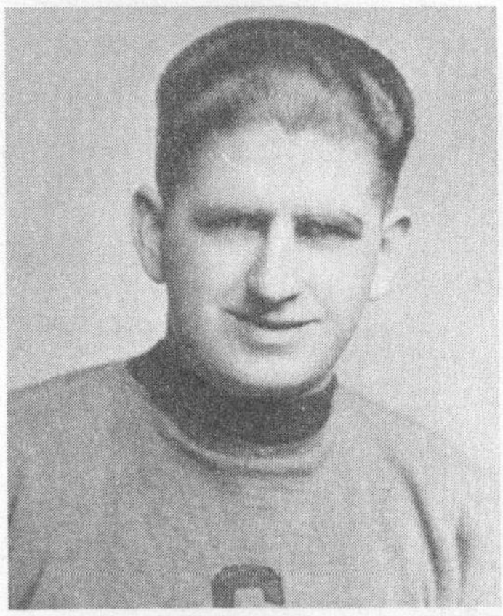

Harold Halderson

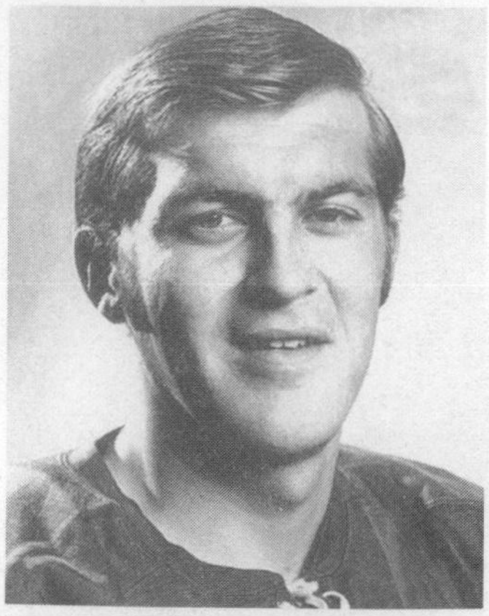

Al Hamilton

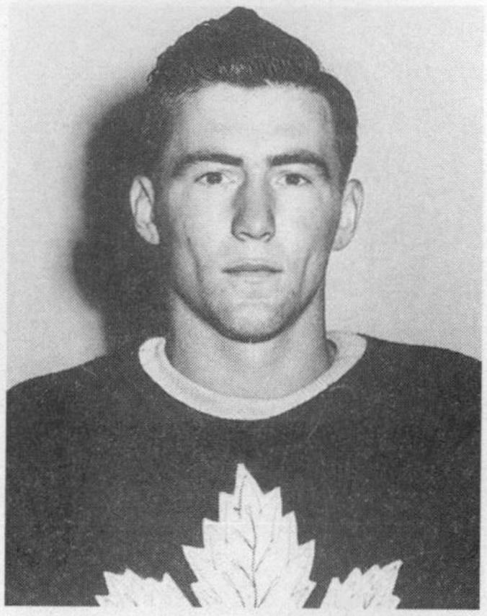

Ray Hannigan

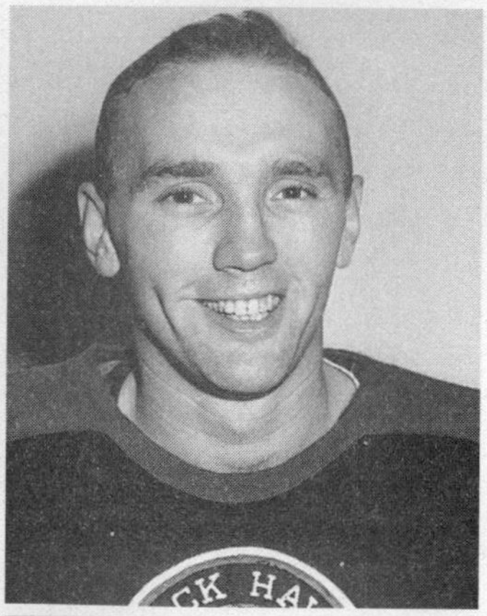

Bob Hassard

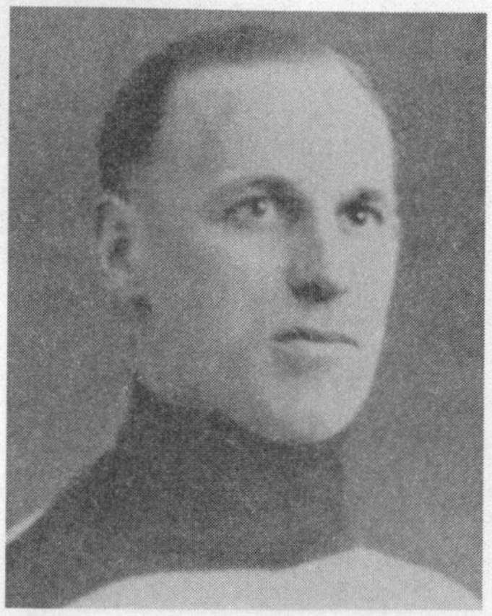

Harry Helman

			Regular Schedule					Playoffs					NHL	First	Last
Name	NHL Teams	NHL Seasons	GP	G	A	TP	PIM	GP	G	A	TP	PIM	Cup Wins	NHL Season	NHL Season
• Hanna, John	NYR, Mtl., Phi.	5	198	6	26	32	206	....	....	....	....	....	....	1958-59	1967-68
Hannan, Dave	Pit., Edm., Tor., Buf., Col., Ott.	16	841	114	191	305	942	63	6	7	13	46	2	1981-82	1996-97
• Hannigan, Gord	Tor.	4	161	29	31	60	117	9	2	0	2	8	....	1952-53	1955-56
• Hannigan, Pat	Tor., NYR, Phi.	5	182	30	39	69	116	11	1	2	3	11	....	1959-60	1968-69
Hannigan, Ray	Tor.	1	3	0	0	0	2	....	....	....	....	....	....	1948-49	1948-49
Hansen, Richie	NYI, St.L.	4	20	2	8	10	4	....	....	....	....	....	....	1976-77	1981-82
Hansen, Tavis	Wpg., Phx.	5	34	2	1	3	16	2	0	0	0	0	....	1994-95	2000-01
Hanson, Dave	Det., Min.	2	33	1	1	2	65	....	....	....	....	....	....	1978-79	1979-80
• Hanson, Emil	Det.	1	7	0	0	0	6	....	....	....	....	....	....	1932-33	1932-33
Hanson, Keith	Cgy.	1	25	0	2	2	77	....	....	....	....	....	....	1983-84	1983-84
• Hanson, Oscar	Chi.	1	8	0	0	0	0	....	....	....	....	....	....	1937-38	1937-38
• Harbaruk, Nick	Pit., St.L.	5	364	45	75	120	273	14	3	1	4	20	....	1969-70	1973-74
Harding, Jeff	Phi.	2	15	0	0	0	47	....	....	....	....	....	....	1988-89	1989-90
Hardy, Joe	Oak., Cal.	2	63	9	14	23	51	4	0	0	0	0	....	1969-70	1970-71
Hardy, Mark	L.A., NYR, Min.	15	915	62	306	368	1293	67	5	16	21	158	....	1979-80	1993-94
Hargreaves, Jim	Van.	2	66	1	7	8	105	....	....	....	....	....	....	1970-71	1972-73
Harkins, Brett	Bos., Fla., CBJ	4	78	6	30	36	22	....	....	....	....	....	....	1994-95	2001-02
Harkins, Todd	Cgy., Hfd.	3	48	3	3	6	78	....	....	....	....	....	....	1991-92	1993-94
Harlock, David	Tor., Wsh., NYI, Atl.	8	212	2	14	16	188	....	....	....	....	....	....	1993-94	2001-02
Harlow, Scott	St.L.	1	1	0	1	1	0	....	....	....	....	....	....	1987-88	1987-88
• Harmon, Glen	Mtl.	9	452	50	96	146	334	53	5	10	15	37	2	1942-43	1950-51
• Harms, John	Chi.	2	44	5	5	10	21	4	3	0	3	2	....	1943-44	1944-45
• Harnott, Walter	Bos.	1	6	0	0	0	2	....	....	....	....	....	....	1933-34	1933-34
Harper, Terry	Mtl., L.A., Det., St.L., Col.	19	1066	35	221	256	1362	112	4	13	17	140	5	1962-63	1980-81
Harrer, Tim	Cgy.	1	3	0	0	0	2	....	....	....	....	....	....	1982-83	1982-83
• Harrington, Hago	Bos., Mtl.	3	72	9	3	12	15	4	1	0	1	2	....	1925-26	1932-33
• Harris, Billy	Tor., Det., Oak., Pit.	13	769	126	219	345	205	62	8	10	18	30	3	1955-56	1968-69
Harris, Billy	NYI, L.A., Tor.	12	897	231	327	558	394	71	19	19	38	48	....	1972-73	1983-84
Harris, Duke	Min., Tor.	1	26	1	4	5	4	....	....	....	....	....	....	1967-68	1967-68
• Harris, Henry	Bos.	1	32	2	4	6	20	....	....	....	....	....	....	1930-31	1930-31
Harris, Hugh	Buf.	1	60	12	26	38	17	3	0	0	0	0	....	1972-73	1972-73
Harris, Ron	Det., Oak., Atl., NYR	11	476	20	91	111	474	28	4	3	7	33	....	1962-63	1975-76
• Harris, Smokey	Bos.	1	6	3	1	4	8	....	....	....	....	....	....	1924-25	1924-25
Harris, Ted	Mtl., Min., Det., St.L., Phi.	12	788	30	168	198	1000	100	1	22	23	230	5	1963-64	1974-75
Harrison, Ed	Bos., NYR	4	194	27	24	51	53	9	1	0	1	2	....	1947-48	1950-51
Harrison, Jim	Bos., Tor., Chi., Edm.	8	324	67	86	153	435	13	1	1	2	43	....	1968-69	1979-80
Hart, Gerry	Det., NYI, Que., St.L.	15	730	29	150	179	1240	78	3	12	15	175	....	1968-69	1982-83
• Hart, Gizzy	Det., Mtl.	3	104	6	8	14	12	8	0	1	1	0	....	1926-27	1932-33
‡ Hartigan, Mark	Atl., CBJ, Ana., Det.	6	102	19	11	30	58	5	0	1	1	4	1	2001-02	2007-08
Hartman, Mike	Buf., Wpg., T.B., NYR	9	397	43	35	78	1388	21	0	0	0	106	1	1986-87	1994-95
Hartsburg, Craig	Min.	10	570	98	315	413	818	61	15	27	42	70	....	1979-80	1988-89
• Harvey, Buster	Min., Atl., K.C., Det.	7	407	90	118	208	131	14	0	2	2	8	....	1970-71	1976-77
• Harvey, Doug	Mtl., NYR, Det., St.L.	20	1113	88	452	540	1216	137	8	64	72	152	6	1947-48	1968-69
Harvey, Hugh	K.C.	2	18	1	1	2	4	....	....	....	....	....	....	1974-75	1975-76
Harvey, Todd	Dal., NYR, S.J., Edm.	11	671	91	132	223	950	68	3	6	9	52	....	1994-95	2005-06
• Hassard, Bob	Tor., Chi.	5	126	9	28	37	22	....	....	....	....	....	1	1949-50	1954-55
Hatcher, Derian	Min., Dal., Det., Phi.	16	1045	80	251	331	1581	133	7	26	33	248	1	1991-92	2007-08
Hatcher, Kevin	Wsh., Dal., Pit., NYR, Car.	17	1157	227	450	677	1392	118	22	37	59	252	....	1984-85	2000-01
Hatoum, Ed	Det., Van.	3	47	3	6	9	25	....	....	....	....	....	....	1968-69	1970-71
Hauer, Brett	Edm., Nsh.	3	37	4	4	8	38	....	....	....	....	....	....	1995-96	2001-02
‡ Havelid, Niclas	Ana., Atl., N.J.	9	628	34	137	171	342	32	0	7	7	4	....	1999-00	2008-09
Hawerchuk, Dale	Wpg., Buf., St.L., Phi.	16	1188	518	891	1409	730	97	30	69	99	67	....	1981-82	1996-97
Hawgood, Greg	Bos., Edm., Phi., Fla., Pit., S.J., Van., Dal.	12	474	60	164	224	426	42	2	8	10	37	....	1987-88	2001-02
Hawkins, Todd	Van., Tor.	3	10	0	0	0	15	....	....	....	....	....	....	1988-89	1991-92
Haworth, Alan	Buf., Wsh., Que.	8	524	189	211	400	425	42	12	16	28	28	....	1980-81	1987-88
Haworth, Gord	NYR	1	2	0	1	1	0	....	....	....	....	....	....	1952-53	1952-53
Hawryliw, Neil	NYI	1	1	0	0	0	0	....	....	....	....	....	....	1981-82	1981-82
Hay, Bill	Chi.	8	506	113	273	386	244	67	15	21	36	62	1	1959-60	1966-67
Hay, Dwayne	Wsh., Fla., T.B., Cgy.	4	79	2	4	6	22	....	....	....	....	....	....	1997-98	2000-01
• Hay, George	Chi., Det.	7	239	74	60	134	84	8	2	3	5	2	....	1926-27	1933-34
Hay, Jim	Det.	3	75	1	5	6	22	9	1	0	1	2	1	1952-53	1954-55
Hayek, Peter	Min.	1	1	0	0	0	0	....	....	....	....	....	....	1981-82	1981-82
Hayes, Chris	Bos.	1	....	....	....	....	....	1	0	0	0	0	....	1971-72	1971-72
• Haynes, Paul	Mtl.M., Bos., Mtl.	11	391	61	134	195	164	24	2	8	10	13	....	1930-31	1940-41
Hayward, Rick	L.A.	1	4	0	0	0	5	....	....	....	....	....	....	1990-91	1990-91
Hazlett, Steve	Van.	1	1	0	0	0	0	....	....	....	....	....	....	1979-80	1979-80
Head, Galen	Det.	1	1	0	0	0	0	....	....	....	....	....	....	1967-68	1967-68
• Headley, Fern	Bos., Mtl.	1	30	1	3	4	10	1	0	0	0	0	....	1924-25	1924-25
Healey, Eric	Bos.	1	2	0	0	0	2	....	....	....	....	....	....	2005-06	2005-06
Healey, Paul	Phi., Tor., NYR, Col.	6	77	6	14	20	44	22	0	2	2	4	....	1996-97	2005-06
Healey, Rich	Det.	1	1	0	0	0	2	....	....	....	....	....	....	1960-61	1960-61
Heaphy, Shawn	Cgy.	1	1	0	0	0	0	....	....	....	....	....	....	1992-93	1992-93
Heaslip, Mark	NYR, L.A.	3	117	10	19	29	110	5	0	0	0	2	....	1976-77	1978-79
Heath, Randy	NYR	2	13	2	4	6	15	....	....	....	....	....	....	1984-85	1985-86
Hebenton, Andy	NYR, Bos.	9	630	189	202	391	83	22	6	5	11	8	....	1955-56	1963-64
Hecl, Radoslav	Buf.	1	14	0	0	0	2	....	....	....	....	....	....	2002-03	2002-03
Hedberg, Anders	NYR	7	465	172	225	397	144	58	22	24	46	31	....	1978-79	1984-85
Hedican, Bret	St.L., Van., Fla., Car., Ana.	17	1039	55	239	294	893	108	4	22	26	108	1	1991-92	2008-09
‡ Hedin, Pierre	Tor.	1	3	0	1	1	0	....	....	....	....	....	....	2003-04	2003-04
‡ Hedstrom, Jonathan	Ana.	2	83	13	14	27	48	3	0	1	1	2	....	2002-03	2005-06
Heerema, Jeff	Car., St.L.	2	32	4	2	6	6	....	....	....	....	....	....	2002-03	2003-04
• Heffernan, Frank	Tor.	1	19	0	1	1	10	....	....	....	....	....	....	1919-20	1919-20
• Heffernan, Gerry	Mtl.	3	83	33	35	68	27	11	3	3	6	8	1	1941-42	1943-44
Heidt, Mike	L.A.	1	6	0	1	1	7	....	....	....	....	....	....	1983-84	1983-84
• Heindl, Bill	Min., NYR	3	18	2	1	3	0	....	....	....	....	....	....	1970-71	1972-73
Heinrich, Lionel	Bos.	1	35	1	1	2	33	....	....	....	....	....	....	1955-56	1955-56
‡ Heins, Shawn	S.J., Pit., Atl.	6	125	4	12	16	154	2	0	0	0	0	....	1998-99	2003-04
Heinze, Steve	Bos., CBJ, Buf., L.A.	12	694	178	158	336	379	69	11	15	26	48	....	1991-92	2002-03
Heiskala, Earl	Phi.	3	127	13	11	24	294	....	....	....	....	....	....	1968-69	1970-71
Heisten, Barrett	NYR	1	10	0	0	0	2	....	....	....	....	....	....	2001-02	2001-02
Helander, Peter	L.A.	1	7	0	1	1	0	....	....	....	....	....	....	1982-83	1982-83
‡ Helbling, Timo	T.B., Wsh.	2	11	0	1	1	8	....	....	....	....	....	....	2005-06	2006-07
Helenius, Sami	Cgy., T.B., Col., Dal., Chi.	6	155	2	4	6	260	1	0	0	0	0	....	1996-97	2002-03
• Heller, Ott	NYR	15	647	55	176	231	465	61	6	8	14	61	2	1931-32	1945-46
• Helman, Harry	Ott.	3	44	1	0	1	7	2	0	0	0	0	1	1922-23	1924-25
‡ Helmer, Bryan	Phx., St.L., Van., Wsh.	7	146	8	18	26	135	6	0	0	0	0	....	1998-99	2008-09
Helminen, Raimo	NYR, Min., NYI	3	117	13	46	59	16	2	0	0	0	0	....	1985-86	1988-89
Hemingway, Colin	St.L.	1	3	0	0	0	0	....	....	....	....	....	....	2005-06	2005-06
• Hemmerling, Tony	NYA	2	22	3	3	6	4	....	....	....	....	....	....	1935-36	1936-37
Henderson, Archie	Wsh., Min., Hfd.	3	23	3	1	4	92	....	....	....	....	....	....	1980-81	1982-83
Henderson, Jay	Bos.	4	33	1	3	4	37	....	....	....	....	....	....	1998-99	2001-02
Henderson, Matt	Nsh., Chi.	2	6	0	1	1	2	....	....	....	....	....	....	1998-99	2001-02
Henderson, Murray	Bos.	8	405	24	62	86	305	41	2	3	5	23	....	1944-45	1951-52
Henderson, Paul	Det., Tor., Atl.	13	707	236	241	477	304	56	11	14	25	28	....	1962-63	1979-80
Hendrickson, Darby	Tor., NYI, Van., Min., Col.	11	518	65	64	129	370	25	3	3	6	6	....	1993-94	2003-04
Hendrickson, John	Det.	3	5	0	0	0	4	....	....	....	....	....	....	1957-58	1961-62
Henning, Lorne	NYI	9	543	73	111	184	102	81	7	7	14	8	2	1972-73	1980-81
Henry, Burke	Chi.	2	39	2	6	8	33	....	....	....	....	....	....	2002-03	2003-04
• Henry, Camille	NYR, Chi., St.L.	14	727	279	249	528	88	47	6	12	18	7	....	1953-54	1969-70
Henry, Dale	NYI	6	132	13	26	39	263	14	1	0	1	19	....	1984-85	1989-90
‡ Hentunen, Jukka	Cgy., Nsh.	1	38	4	5	9	4	....	....	....	....	....	....	2001-02	2001-02
Hepple, Alan	N.J.	3	3	0	0	0	7	....	....	....	....	....	....	1983-84	1985-86
Herbers, Ian	Edm., T.B., NYI	2	65	0	5	5	79	....	....	....	....	....	....	1993-94	1999-00
• Herbert, Jimmy	Bos., Tor., Det.	6	206	83	31	114	253	9	3	0	3	10	....	1924-25	1929-30
• Herchenratter, Art	Det.	1	10	1	2	3	2	....	....	....	....	....	....	1940-41	1940-41
• Hergerts, Fred	NYA	2	20	2	4	6	2	....	....	....	....	....	....	1934-35	1935-36
• Hergesheimer, Phil	Chi., Bos.	4	125	21	41	62	19	6	0	0	0	2	....	1939-40	1942-43
Hergesheimer, Wally	NYR, Chi.	7	351	114	85	199	106	5	1	0	1	0	....	1951-52	1958-59
• Heron, Red	Tor., Bro., Mtl.	4	106	21	19	40	38	21	2	2	4	6	....	1938-39	1941-42
Heroux, Yves	Que.	1	1	0	0	0	0	....	....	....	....	....	....	1986-87	1986-87
‡ Herperger, Chris	Chi., Ott., Atl.	4	169	18	25	43	75	....	....	....	....	....	....	1999-00	2002-03
Herr, Matt	Wsh., Fla., Bos.	4	58	4	5	9	25	....	....	....	....	....	....	1998-99	2002-03
Herter, Jason	NYI	1	1	0	1	1	0	....	....	....	....	....	....	1995-96	1995-96
Hervey, Matt	Wpg., Bos., T.B.	3	35	0	5	5	97	5	0	0	0	6	....	1988-89	1992-93
Hess, Bob	St.L., Buf., Hfd.	8	329	27	95	122	178	4	1	1	2	2	....	1974-75	1983-84

			Regular Schedule					Playoffs					NHL Cup	First NHL	Last NHL
Name	**NHL Teams**	**NHL Seasons**	**GP**	**G**	**A**	**TP**	**PIM**	**GP**	**G**	**A**	**TP**	**PIM**	**Wins**	**Season**	**Season**
Heward, Jamie	Tor., Nsh., NYI, CBJ, Wsh., L.A., T.B.	9	394	38	86	124	221	....	....	....	....	....	....	1995-96	2008-09
• Heximer, Obs	NYR, Bos., NYA	3	84	13	7	20	16	5	0	0	0	2	....	1929-30	1934-35
• Hextall, Bryan	NYR	11	449	187	175	362	227	37	8	9	17	19	1	1936-37	1947-48
Hextall, Bryan	NYR, Pit., Atl., Det., Min.	8	549	99	161	260	738	18	0	4	4	59	....	1962-63	1975-76
Hextall, Dennis	NYR, L.A., Cal., Min., Det., Wsh.	13	681	153	350	503	1398	22	3	3	6	45	....	1967-68	1979-80
• Heyliger, Vic	Chi.	2	33	2	3	5	2	....	....	....	....	....	....	1937-38	1943-44
• Hicke, Bill	Mtl., NYR, Oak., Cal., Pit.	14	729	168	234	402	395	42	3	10	13	41	2	1958-59	1971-72
Hicke, Ernie	Cal., Atl., NYI, Min., L.A.	8	520	132	140	272	407	2	1	0	1	0	....	1970-71	1977-78
Hickey, Greg	NYR	1	1	0	0	0	0	....	....	....	....	....	....	1977-78	1977-78
Hickey, Pat	NYR, Col., Tor., Que., St.L.	10	646	192	212	404	351	55	5	11	16	37	....	1975-76	1984-85
Hicks, Alex	Ana., Pit., S.J., Fla.	5	258	25	54	79	247	15	0	2	2	8	....	1995-96	1999-00
Hicks, Doug	Min., Chi., Edm., Wsh.	9	561	37	131	168	442	18	2	1	3	15	....	1974-75	1982-83
Hicks, Glenn	Det.	2	108	6	12	18	127	....	....	....	....	....	....	1979-80	1980-81
• Hicks, Henry	Mtl.M., Det.	3	96	7	2	9	72	....	....	....	....	....	....	1928-29	1930-31
Hicks, Wayne	Chi., Bos., Mtl., Phi., Pit.	5	115	13	23	36	22	2	0	1	1	2	1	1959-60	1967-68
Hidi, Andre	Wsh.	2	7	2	1	3	9	2	0	0	0	0	....	1983-84	1984-85
Hiemer, Uli	N.J.	3	143	19	54	73	176	....	....	....	....	....	....	1984-85	1986-87
Higgins, Matt	Mtl.	4	57	1	2	3	6	....	....	....	....	....	....	1997-98	2000-01
Higgins, Paul	Tor.	2	25	0	0	0	152	1	0	0	0	0	....	1981-82	1982-83
Higgins, Tim	Chi., N.J., Det.	11	706	154	198	352	719	65	5	8	13	77	....	1978-79	1988-89
Hilbert, Andy	Bos., Chi., Pit., NYI, Min.	8	307	42	62	104	132	10	1	0	1	2	....	2001-02	2009-10
• Hildebrand, Ike	NYR, Chi.	2	41	7	11	18	16	....	....	....	....	....	....	1953-54	1954-55
Hill, Al	Phi.	8	221	40	55	95	227	51	8	11	19	43	....	1976-77	1987-88
Hill, Brian	Hfd.	1	19	1	1	2	4	....	....	....	....	....	....	1979-80	1979-80
• Hill, Mel	Bos., Bro., Tor.	9	324	89	109	198	128	43	12	7	19	18	3	1937-38	1945-46
Hill, Sean	Mtl., Ana., Ott., Car., St.L., Fla., NYI, Min.	17	876	62	236	298	1008	55	5	5	10	42	1	1990-91	2007-08
• Hiller, Dutch	NYR, Det., Bos., Mtl.	9	383	91	113	204	163	48	9	8	17	21	2	1937-38	1945-46
Hiller, Jim	L.A., Det., NYR	2	63	8	12	20	116	2	0	0	0	4	....	1992-93	1993-94
Hillier, Randy	Bos., Pit., NYI, Buf.	11	543	16	110	126	906	28	0	2	2	93	1	1981-82	1991-92
Hillman, Floyd	Bos.	1	6	0	0	0	10	....	....	....	....	....	....	1956-57	1956-57
Hillman, Larry	Det., Bos., Tor., Min., Mtl., Phi., L.A., Buf.	19	790	36	196	232	579	74	2	9	11	30	6	1954-55	1972-73
• Hillman, Wayne	Chi., NYR, Min., Phi.	13	691	18	86	104	534	28	0	3	3	19	1	1960-61	1972-73
Hilworth, John	Det.	3	57	1	1	2	89	....	....	....	....	....	....	1977-78	1979-80
• Himes, Normie	NYA	9	402	106	113	219	127	2	0	0	0	0	....	1926-27	1934-35
Hindmarch, Dave	Cgy.	4	99	21	17	38	25	10	0	0	0	6	....	1980-81	1983-84
Hinote, Dan	Col., St.L.	9	503	38	52	90	383	72	6	9	15	67	1	1999-00	2008-09
Hinse, Andre	Tor.	1	4	0	0	0	0	....	....	....	....	....	....	1967-68	1967-68
Hinton, Dan	Chi.	1	14	0	0	0	16	....	....	....	....	....	....	1976-77	1976-77
Hirsch, Tom	Min.	3	31	1	7	8	30	12	0	0	0	6	....	1983-84	1987-88
• Hirschfeld, Bert	Mtl.	2	33	1	4	5	2	5	1	0	1	0	....	1949-50	1950-51
Hislop, Jamie	Que., Cgy.	5	345	75	103	178	86	28	3	2	5	11	....	1979-80	1983-84
• Hitchman, Lionel	Ott., Bos.	12	417	28	34	62	523	35	2	2	4	73	2	1922-23	1933-34
‡ Hlavac, Jan	NYR, Phi., Van., Car., T.B., Nsh.	6	436	90	134	224	138	11	0	3	3	2	....	1999-00	2007-08
• Hlinka, Ivan	Van.	2	137	42	81	123	28	16	3	10	13	8	....	1981-82	1982-83
‡ Hlinka, Jaroslav	Col.	1	63	8	20	28	16	1	0	0	0	0	....	2007-08	2007-08
Hlushko, Todd	Phi., Cgy., Pit.	6	79	8	13	21	84	3	0	0	0	2	....	1993-94	1998-99
Hocking, Justin	L.A.	1	1	0	0	0	0	....	....	....	....	....	....	1993-94	1993-94
Hodge, Ken	Chi., Bos., NYR	14	881	328	472	800	779	97	34	47	81	120	2	1964-65	1977-78
Hodge, Ken	Min., Bos., T.B.	4	142	39	48	87	32	15	4	6	10	6	....	1988-89	1992-93
Hodgson, Dan	Tor., Van.	4	114	29	45	74	64	....	....	....	....	....	....	1985-86	1988-89
Hodgson, Rick	Hfd.	1	6	0	0	0	6	1	0	0	0	0	....	1979-80	1979-80
Hodgson, Ted	Bos.	1	4	0	0	0	0	....	....	....	....	....	....	1966-67	1966-67
Hoekstra, Cec	Mtl.	1	4	0	0	0	0	....	....	....	....	....	....	1959-60	1959-60
Hoekstra, Ed	Phi.	1	70	15	21	36	6	7	0	1	1	0	....	1967-68	1967-68
Hoene, Phil	L.A.	3	37	2	4	6	22	....	....	....	....	....	....	1972-73	1974-75
• Hoffinger, Val	Chi.	2	28	0	1	1	30	....	....	....	....	....	....	1927-28	1928-29
Hoffman, Mike	Hfd.	3	9	1	3	4	2	....	....	....	....	....	....	1982-83	1985-86
Hoffmeyer, Bob	Chi., Phi., N.J.	6	198	14	52	66	325	3	0	1	1	25	....	1977-78	1984-85
Hofford, Jim	Buf., L.A.	3	18	0	0	0	47	....	....	....	....	....	....	1985-86	1988-89
Hogaboam, Bill	Atl., Det., Min.	8	332	80	109	189	100	2	0	0	0	0	....	1972-73	1979-80
Hoganson, Dale	L.A., Mtl., Que.	7	343	13	77	90	186	11	0	3	3	12	....	1969-70	1981-82
Hoglund, Jonas	Cgy., Mtl., Tor.	7	545	117	145	262	112	59	8	11	19	8	....	1996-97	2002-03
Hogue, Benoit	Buf., NYI, Tor., Dal., T.B., Phx., Bos., Wsh.	15	863	222	321	543	877	92	17	16	33	124	1	1987-88	2001-02
Holan, Milos	Phi., Ana.	3	49	5	11	16	42	....	....	....	....	....	....	1993-94	1995-96
Holbrook, Terry	Min.	2	43	3	6	9	4	6	0	0	0	0	....	1972-73	1973-74
‡ Holden, Josh	Van., Car., Tor.	6	60	5	9	14	16	....	....	....	....	....	....	1998-99	2003-04
Holik, Bobby	Hfd., N.J., NYR, Atl.	18	1314	326	421	747	1423	141	20	39	59	120	2	1990-91	2008-09
‡ Holland, Jason	NYI, Buf., L.A.	7	81	4	5	9	36	1	0	0	0	0	....	1996-97	2003-04
Holland, Jerry	NYR	2	37	8	4	12	6	....	....	....	....	....	....	1974-75	1975-76
• Hollett, Flash	Tor., Ott., Bos., Det.	13	562	132	181	313	358	79	8	26	34	38	2	1933-34	1945-46
Hollinger, Terry	St.L.	2	7	0	0	0	2	....	....	....	....	....	....	1993-94	1994-95
• Hollingworth, Gord	Chi., Det.	4	163	4	14	18	201	3	0	0	0	2	....	1954-55	1957-58
Holloway, Bruce	Van.	1	2	0	0	0	0	....	....	....	....	....	....	1984-85	1984-85
• Holmes, Bill	Mtl., NYA	3	52	6	4	10	35	....	....	....	....	....	....	1925-26	1929-30
Holmes, Chuck	Det.	2	23	1	3	4	10	....	....	....	....	....	....	1958-59	1961-62
• Holmes, Lou	Chi.	2	59	1	4	5	6	2	0	0	0	2	....	1931-32	1932-33
Holmes, Warren	L.A.	3	45	8	18	26	7	....	....	....	....	....	....	1981-82	1983-84
Holmgren, Paul	Phi., Min.	10	527	144	179	323	1684	82	19	32	51	195	....	1975-76	1984-85
‡ Holmqvist, Michael	Ana., Chi.	3	156	18	17	35	72	....	....	....	....	....	....	2003-04	2006-07
• Holota, John	Det.	2	15	2	0	2	0	....	....	....	....	....	....	1942-43	1945-46
Holst, Greg	NYR	3	11	0	0	0	0	....	....	....	....	....	....	1975-76	1977-78
Holt, Gary	Cal., Cle., St.L.	5	101	13	11	24	133	....	....	....	....	....	....	1973-74	1977-78
Holt, Randy	Chi., Cle., Van., L.A., Cgy., Wsh., Phi.	10	395	4	37	41	1438	21	2	3	5	83	....	1974-75	1983-84
• Holway, Albert	Tor., Mtl.M., Pit.	5	112	7	2	9	48	6	0	0	0	0	1	1923-24	1928-29
Holzinger, Brian	Buf., T.B., Pit., CBJ	10	547	93	145	238	339	52	11	18	29	61	....	1994-95	2003-04
Homenuke, Ron	Van.	1	1	0	0	0	0	....	....	....	....	....	....	1972-73	1972-73
Hoover, Ron	Bos., St.L.	3	18	4	0	4	31	8	0	0	0	18	....	1989-90	1991-92
Hopkins, Dean	L.A., Edm., Que.	6	223	23	51	74	306	18	1	5	6	29	....	1979-80	1988-89
Hopkins, Larry	Tor., Wpg.	4	60	13	16	29	26	6	0	0	0	2	....	1977-78	1982-83
Horacek, Tony	Phi., Chi.	5	154	10	19	29	316	2	1	0	1	2	....	1989-90	1994-95
Horava, Miloslav	NYR	3	80	5	17	22	38	2	0	1	1	0	....	1988-89	1990-91
Horbul, Doug	K.C.	1	4	1	0	1	2	....	....	....	....	....	....	1974-75	1974-75
Hordy, Mike	NYI	2	11	0	0	0	7	....	....	....	....	....	....	1978-79	1979-80
• Horeck, Pete	Chi., Det., Bos.	8	426	106	118	224	340	34	6	8	14	43	....	1944-45	1951-52
• Horne, George	Mtl.M., Tor.	3	54	9	3	12	34	4	0	0	0	4	1	1925-26	1928-29
• Horner, Red	Tor.	12	490	42	110	152	1254	71	7	10	17	170	1	1928-29	1939-40
• Hornung, Larry	St.L.	2	48	2	9	11	10	11	0	2	2	2	....	1970-71	1971-72
• Horton, Tim	Tor., NYR, Pit., Buf.	24	1446	115	403	518	1611	126	11	39	50	183	4	1949-50	1973-74
Horvath, Bronco	NYR, Mtl., Bos., Chi., Tor., Min.	9	434	141	185	326	319	36	12	9	21	18	....	1955-56	1967-68
Hospodar, Ed	NYR, Hfd., Phi., Min., Buf.	9	450	17	51	68	1314	44	4	1	5	208	....	1979-80	1987-88
‡ Hossa, Marcel	Mtl., NYR, Phx.	6	237	31	30	61	106	14	2	2	4	10	....	2001-02	2007-08
Hostak, Martin	Phi.	2	55	3	11	14	24	....	....	....	....	....	....	1990-91	1991-92
Hotham, Greg	Tor., Pit.	6	230	15	74	89	139	5	0	3	3	6	....	1979-80	1984-85
Houck, Paul	Min.	3	16	1	2	3	2	....	....	....	....	....	....	1985-86	1987-88
Houda, Doug	Det., Hfd., L.A., Buf., NYI, Ana.	15	561	19	63	82	1104	18	0	3	3	21	....	1985-86	2002-03
Houde, Claude	K.C.	2	59	3	6	9	40	....	....	....	....	....	....	1974-75	1975-76
Houde, Eric	Mtl.	3	30	2	3	5	4	....	....	....	....	....	....	1996-97	1998-99
Hough, Mike	Que., Fla., NYI	14	707	100	156	256	675	44	5	5	10	38	....	1984-85	1998-99
Houlder, Bill	Wsh., Buf., Ana., St.L., T.B., S.J., Nsh.	16	846	59	191	250	412	30	5	6	11	14	....	1987-88	2002-03
Houle, Rejean	Mtl.	11	635	161	247	408	395	90	14	34	48	66	5	1969-70	1982-83
Housley, Phil	Buf., Wpg., St.L., Cgy., N.J., Wsh., Chi., Tor.	21	1495	338	894	1232	822	85	13	43	56	36	....	1982-83	2002-03
Houston, Ken	Atl., Cgy., Wsh., L.A.	9	570	161	167	328	624	35	10	9	19	66	....	1975-76	1983-84
Howard, Jack	Tor.	1	2	0	0	0	0	....	....	....	....	....	....	1936-37	1936-37
Howatt, Garry	NYI, Hfd., N.J.	12	720	112	156	268	1836	87	12	14	26	289	2	1972-73	1983-84
Howe, Gordie	Det., Hfd.	26	1767	801	1049	1850	1685	157	68	92	160	220	4	1946-47	1979-80
Howe, Mark	Hfd., Phi., Det.	16	929	197	545	742	455	101	10	51	61	34	....	1979-80	1994-95
Howe, Marty	Hfd., Bos.	6	197	2	29	31	99	15	1	2	3	9	....	1979-80	1984-85
• Howe, Syd	Ott., Phi., Tor., St.L., Det.	17	698	237	291	528	212	70	17	27	44	10	3	1929-30	1945-46
Howe, Vic	NYR	3	33	3	4	7	10	....	....	....	....	....	....	1950-51	1954-55
Howell, Harry	NYR, Oak., Cal., L.A.	21	1411	94	324	418	1298	38	3	3	6	32	....	1952-53	1972-73
• Howell, Ron	NYR	2	4	0	0	0	0	....	....	....	....	....	....	1954-55	1955-56
Howse, Don	L.A.	1	33	2	5	7	6	2	0	0	0	0	....	1979-80	1979-80

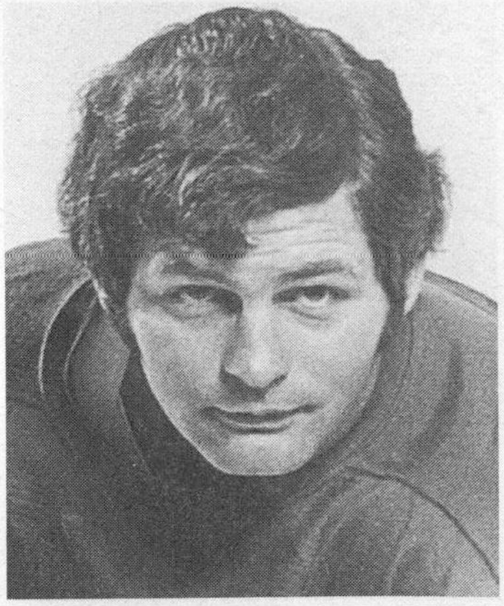

Bryan Hextall Jr

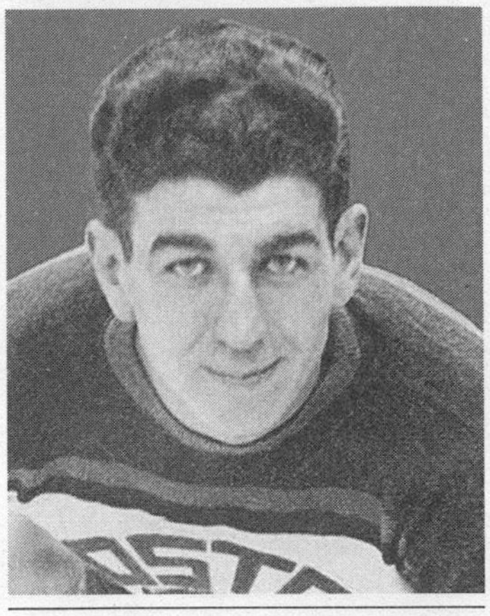

Lionel Hitchman

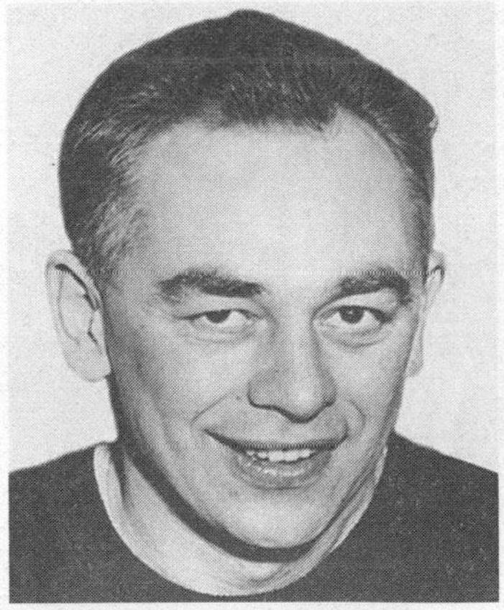

Flash Hollett

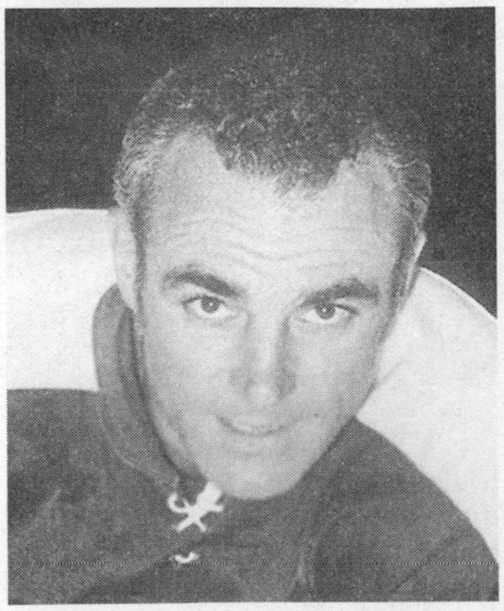

Harry Howell

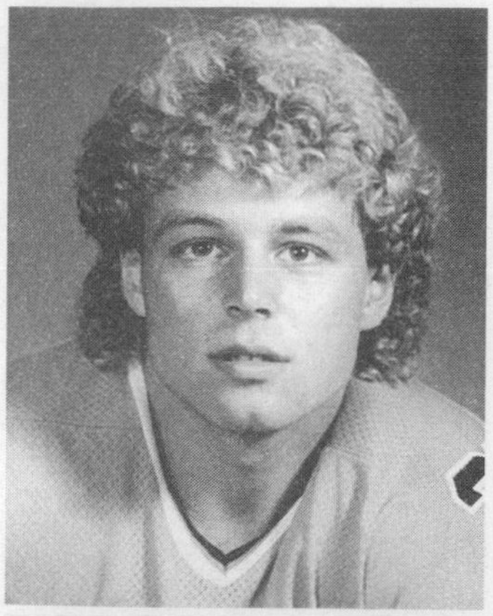
Tim Hrynewich

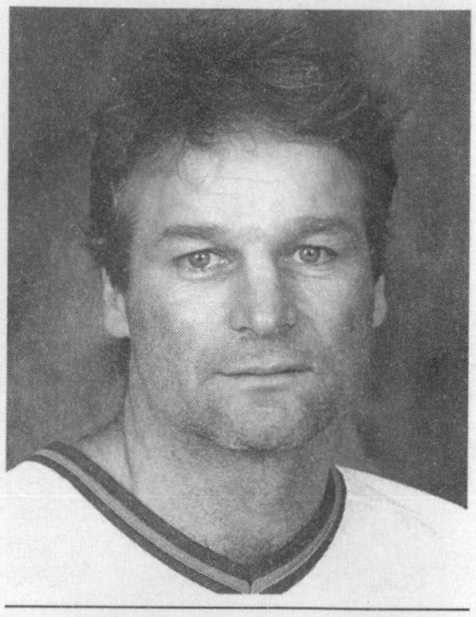
Dale Hunter

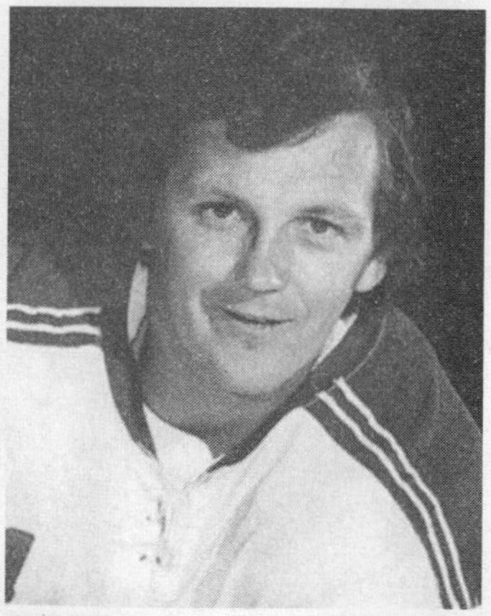
Ted Irvine

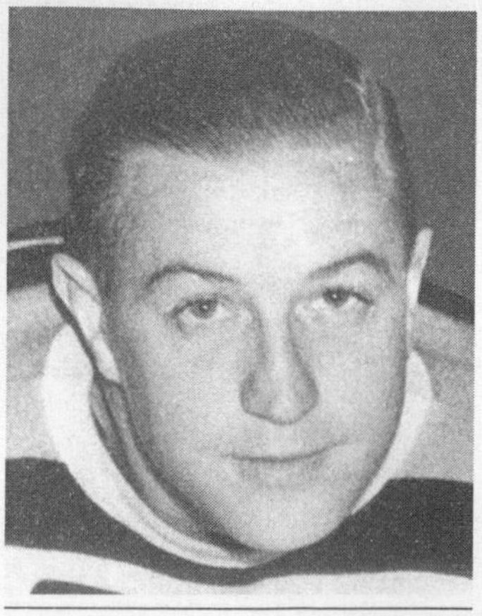
Art Jackson

Name	NHL Teams	NHL Seasons	Regular Schedule GP	G	A	TP	PIM	Playoffs GP	G	A	TP	PIM	NHL Cup Wins	First NHL Season	Last NHL Season
Howson, Scott	NYI	2	18	5	3	8	4	....	....	....	....	....	....	1984-85	1985-86
Hoyda, Dave	Phi., Wpg.	4	132	6	17	23	299	12	0	0	0	17	....	1977-78	1980-81
Hrdina, Jan	Pit., Phx., N.J., CBJ	7	513	101	196	297	341	45	12	14	26	24	....	1998-99	2005-06
Hrdina, Jiri	Cgy., Pit.	5	250	45	85	130	92	46	2	5	7	24	3	1987-88	1991-92
Hrechkosy, Dave	Cal., St.L.	4	140	42	24	66	41	3	1	0	1	2	....	1973-74	1976-77
Hrkac, Tony	St.L., Que., S.J., Chi., Dal., Edm., NYI, Ana., Atl.	13	758	132	239	371	173	41	7	7	14	12	1	1986-87	2002-03
Hrycuik, Jim	Wsh.	1	21	5	5	10	12	....	....	....	....	....	....	1974-75	1974-75
Hrymnak, Steve	Chi., Det.	2	18	2	1	3	4	2	0	0	0	0	....	1951-52	1952-53
Hrynewich, Tim	Pit.	2	55	6	8	14	82	....	....	....	....	....	....	1982-83	1983-84
Huard, Bill	Bos., Ott., Que., Dal., Edm., L.A.	8	223	16	18	34	594	5	0	0	0	2	....	1992-93	1999-00
• Huard, Rolly	Tor.	1	1	1	0	1	0	....	....	....	....	....	....	1930-31	1930-31
‡ Hubacek, Petr	Phi.	1	6	1	0	1	2	....	....	....	....	....	....	2000-01	2000-01
• Huber, Willie	Det., NYR, Van., Phi.	10	655	104	217	321	950	33	5	5	10	35	....	1978-79	1987-88
Hubick, Greg	Tor., Van.	2	77	6	9	15	10	....	....	....	....	....	....	1975-76	1979-80
Huck, Fran	Mtl., St.L.	3	94	24	30	54	38	11	3	4	7	2	....	1969-70	1972-73
Hucul, Fred	Chi., St.L.	5	164	11	30	41	113	6	1	0	1	10	....	1950-51	1967-68
Huddy, Charlie	Edm., L.A., Buf., St.L.	17	1017	99	354	453	785	183	19	66	85	135	5	1980-81	1996-97
Hudson, Dave	NYI, K.C., Col.	6	409	59	124	183	89	2	1	1	2	0	....	1972-73	1977-78
Hudson, Lex	Pit.	1	2	0	0	0	0	2	0	0	0	0	....	1978-79	1978-79
Hudson, Mike	Chi., Edm., NYR, Pit., Tor., St.L., Phx.	9	416	49	87	136	414	49	4	10	14	64	1	1988-89	1996-97
Hudson, Ron	Det.	2	33	5	2	7	2	....	....	....	....	....	....	1937-38	1939-40
Huffman, Kerry	Phi., Que., Ott.	10	401	37	108	145	361	11	0	0	0	2	....	1986-87	1995-96
Huggins, Al	Mtl.M.	1	20	1	1	2	2	....	....	....	....	....	....	1930-31	1930-31
• Hughes, Albert	NYA	2	60	6	8	14	22	....	....	....	....	....	....	1930-31	1931-32
Hughes, Brent	L.A., Phi., St.L., Det., K.C.	8	435	15	117	132	440	22	1	3	4	53	....	1967-68	1974-75
Hughes, Brent	Wpg., Bos., Buf., NYI	8	357	41	39	80	831	29	4	1	5	53	....	1988-89	1996-97
Hughes, Frank	Cal.	1	5	0	0	0	0	....	....	....	....	....	....	1971-72	1971-72
Hughes, Howie	L.A.	3	168	25	32	57	30	14	2	0	2	2	....	1967-68	1969-70
Hughes, Jack	Col.	2	46	2	5	7	104	....	....	....	....	....	....	1980-81	1981-82
• Hughes, James	Det.	1	40	0	1	1	48	....	....	....	....	....	....	1929-30	1929-30
Hughes, John	Van., Edm., NYR	2	70	2	14	16	211	7	0	1	1	16	....	1979-80	1980-81
Hughes, Pat	Mtl., Pit., Edm., Buf., St.L., Hfd.	10	573	130	128	258	646	71	8	25	33	77	3	1977-78	1986-87
Hughes, Ryan	Bos.	1	3	0	0	0	0	....	....	....	....	....	....	1995-96	1995-96
Hulbig, Joe	Edm., Bos.	5	55	4	4	8	16	6	0	1	1	2	....	1996-97	2000-01
Hull, Bobby	Chi., Wpg., Hfd.	16	1063	610	560	1170	640	119	62	67	129	102	1	1957-58	1979-80
Hull, Brett	Cgy., St.L., Dal., Det., Phx.	20	1269	741	650	1391	458	202	103	87	190	73	2	1985-86	2005-06
Hull, Dennis	Chi., Det.	14	959	303	351	654	261	104	33	34	67	30	....	1964-65	1977-78
Hull, Jody	Hfd., NYR, Ott., Fla., T.B., Phi.	16	831	124	137	261	156	69	4	5	9	14	....	1988-89	2003-04
Hulse, Cale	N.J., Cgy., Nsh., Phx., CBJ	10	619	16	79	95	1000	1	0	0	0	0	....	1995-96	2005-06
‡ Huml, Ivan	Bos.	3	49	6	12	18	36	....	....	....	....	....	....	2001-02	2003-04
• Hunt, Fred	NYA, NYR	2	59	15	14	29	6	....	....	....	....	....	....	1940-41	1944-45
‡ Hunt, Jamie	Wsh.	1	1	0	0	0	0	....	....	....	....	....	....	2006-07	2006-07
Hunter, Dale	Que., Wsh., Col.	19	1407	323	697	1020	3565	186	42	76	118	729	....	1980-81	1998-99
Hunter, Dave	Edm., Pit., Wpg.	10	746	133	190	323	918	105	16	24	40	211	3	1979-80	1988-89
Hunter, Mark	Mtl., St.L., Cgy., Hfd., Wsh.	12	628	213	171	384	1426	79	18	20	38	230	1	1981-82	1992-93
Hunter, Tim	Cgy., Que., Van., S.J.	16	815	62	76	138	3146	132	5	7	12	426	1	1981-82	1996-97
Huras, Larry	NYR	1	2	0	0	0	0	....	....	....	....	....	....	1976-77	1976-77
Hurlburt, Bob	Van.	1	1	0	0	0	2	....	....	....	....	....	....	1974-75	1974-75
Hurlbut, Mike	NYR, Que., Buf.	5	29	1	8	9	20	....	....	....	....	....	....	1992-93	1999-00
Hurley, Paul	Bos.	1	1	0	1	1	0	....	....	....	....	....	....	1968-69	1968-69
Hurst, Ron	Tor.	2	64	9	7	16	70	3	0	2	2	4	....	1955-56	1956-57
Huscroft, Jamie	N.J., Bos., Cgy., T.B., Van., Phx., Wsh.	10	352	5	33	38	1065	21	0	1	1	46	....	1988-89	1999-00
Huska, Ryan	Chi.	1	1	0	0	0	0	....	....	....	....	....	....	1997-98	1997-98
‡ Hussey, Matt	Pit., Det.	3	21	2	2	4	2	....	....	....	....	....	....	2003-04	2006-07
Huston, Ron	Cal.	2	79	15	31	46	8	....	....	....	....	....	....	1973-74	1974-75
Hutchinson, Ron	NYR	1	9	0	0	0	0	....	....	....	....	....	....	1960-61	1960-61
Hutchison, Dave	L.A., Tor., Chi., N.J.	10	584	19	97	116	1550	48	2	12	14	149	....	1974-75	1983-84
• Hutton, Bill	Bos., Ott., Phi.	2	64	3	2	5	8	2	0	0	0	0	....	1929-30	1930-31
• Hyland, Harry	Mtl.W., Ott.	1	17	14	2	16	65	....	....	....	....	....	....	1917-18	1917-18
Hynes, Dave	Bos.	2	22	4	0	4	2	....	....	....	....	....	....	1973-74	1974-75
Hynes, Gord	Bos., Phi.	2	52	3	9	12	22	12	1	2	3	6	....	1991-92	1992-93
‡ Hyvonen, Hannes	S.J., CBJ	2	42	4	5	9	22	....	....	....	....	....	....	2001-02	2002-03

I

Name	NHL Teams	NHL Seasons	GP	G	A	TP	PIM	GP	G	A	TP	PIM	NHL Cup Wins	First NHL Season	Last NHL Season
Iafrate, Al	Tor., Wsh., Bos., S.J.	12	799	152	311	463	1301	71	19	16	35	77	....	1984-85	1997-98
‡ Iggulden, Mike	S.J., NYI	2	12	1	4	5	4	....	....	....	....	....	....	2007-08	2008-09
Ignatjev, Victor	Pit.	1	11	0	1	1	6	1	0	0	0	2	....	1998-99	1998-99
Ihnacak, Miroslav	Tor., Det.	3	56	8	9	17	39	1	0	0	0	0	....	1985-86	1988-89
Ihnacak, Peter	Tor.	8	417	102	165	267	175	28	4	10	14	25	....	1982-83	1989-90
Imlach, Brent	Tor.	2	3	0	0	0	0	....	....	....	....	....	....	1965-66	1966-67
‡ Immonen, Jarkko	NYR	2	20	3	5	8	4	....	....	....	....	....	....	2005-06	2006-07
Ingarfield, Earl	NYR, Pit., Oak., Cal.	13	746	179	226	405	239	21	9	8	17	10	....	1958-59	1970-71
Ingarfield, Earl	Atl., Cgy., Det.	2	39	4	4	8	22	2	0	1	1	0	....	1979-80	1980-81
Inglis, Billy	L.A., Buf.	3	36	1	3	4	4	11	1	2	3	4	....	1967-68	1970-71
• Ingoldsby, Jack	Tor.	2	29	5	1	6	15	....	....	....	....	....	....	1942-43	1943-44
• Ingram, Frank	Chi.	3	101	24	16	40	69	11	0	1	1	2	....	1929-30	1931-32
• Ingram, John	Bos.	1	1	0	0	0	0	....	....	....	....	....	....	1924-25	1924-25
• Ingram, Ron	Chi., Det., NYR	4	114	5	15	20	81	2	0	0	0	0	....	1956-57	1964-65
Intranuovo, Ralph	Edm., Tor.	3	22	2	4	6	4	....	....	....	....	....	....	1994-95	1996-97
‡ Irmen, Danny	Min.	1	2	0	0	0	0	....	....	....	....	....	....	2009-10	2009-10
• Irvin, Dick	Chi.	3	94	29	23	52	78	2	2	0	2	4	....	1926-27	1928-29
Irvine, Ted	Bos., L.A., NYR, St.L.	11	724	154	177	331	657	83	16	24	40	115	....	1963-64	1976-77
Irwin, Ivan	Mtl., NYR	5	155	2	27	29	214	5	0	0	0	8	....	1952-53	1957-58
• Isaksson, Ulf	L.A.	1	50	7	15	22	10	....	....	....	....	....	....	1982-83	1982-83
Isbister, Brad	Phx., NYI, Edm., Bos., NYR, Van.	10	541	106	116	222	615	18	1	2	3	33	....	1997-98	2007-08
Issel, Kim	Edm.	1	4	0	0	0	0	....	....	....	....	....	....	1988-89	1988-89

J

Name	NHL Teams	NHL Seasons	GP	G	A	TP	PIM	GP	G	A	TP	PIM	NHL Cup Wins	First NHL Season	Last NHL Season
Jacina, Greg	Fla.	2	14	0	1	1	6	....	....	....	....	....	....	2005-06	2006-07
Jackman, Ric	Dal., Bos., Tor., Pit., Fla., Ana.	7	231	19	58	77	166	7	1	1	2	2	1	1999-00	2006-07
• Jackson, Art	Tor., Bos., NYA	11	468	123	178	301	144	52	8	12	20	29	2	1934-35	1944-45
• Jackson, Busher	Tor., NYA, Bos.	15	633	241	234	475	437	71	18	12	30	53	1	1929-30	1943-44
Jackson, Dane	Van., Buf., NYI	4	45	12	6	18	58	6	0	0	0	10	....	1993-94	1997-98
Jackson, Don	Min., Edm., NYR	10	311	16	52	68	640	53	4	5	9	147	2	1977-78	1986-87
• Jackson, Harold	Chi., Det.	8	219	17	34	51	208	31	1	2	3	33	2	1936-37	1946-47
Jackson, Jack	Chi.	1	48	2	5	7	38	....	....	....	....	....	....	1946-47	1946-47
Jackson, Jeff	Tor., NYR, Que., Chi.	8	263	38	48	86	313	6	1	1	2	16	....	1984-85	1991-92
Jackson, Jim	Cgy., Buf.	4	112	17	30	47	20	14	3	2	5	6	....	1982-83	1987-88
• Jackson, Lloyd	NYA	1	14	1	1	2	0	....	....	....	....	....	....	1936-37	1936-37
• Jackson, Stan	Tor., Bos., Ott.	5	86	9	6	15	75	....	....	....	....	....	1	1921-22	1926-27
Jackson, Walter	NYA, Bos.	4	84	16	11	27	18	....	....	....	....	....	....	1932-33	1935-36
• Jacobs, Paul	Tor.	1	1	0	0	0	0	....	....	....	....	....	....	1918-19	1918-19
Jacobs, Tim	Cal.	1	46	0	10	10	35	....	....	....	....	....	....	1975-76	1975-76
Jakopin, John	Fla., Pit., S.J.	6	113	1	6	7	145	....	....	....	....	....	....	1997-98	2002-03
Jalo, Risto	Edm.	1	3	0	3	3	0	....	....	....	....	....	....	1985-86	1985-86
Jalonen, Kari	Cgy., Edm.	2	37	9	6	15	4	5	1	0	1	0	....	1982-83	1983-84
‡ James, Connor	L.A., Pit.	3	16	1	0	1	2	....	....	....	....	....	....	2005-06	2008-09
James, Gerry	Tor.	5	149	14	26	40	257	15	1	0	1	8	....	1954-55	1959-60
James, Val	Buf., Tor.	2	11	0	0	0	30	3	0	0	0	0	....	1981-82	1986-87
Jamieson, Jim	NYR	1	1	0	1	1	0	....	....	....	....	....	....	1943-44	1943-44
• Jankowski, Lou	Det., Chi.	4	127	19	18	37	15	1	0	0	0	0	....	1950-51	1954-55
Janney, Craig	Bos., St.L., S.J., Wpg., Phx., T.B., NYI	12	760	188	563	751	170	120	24	86	110	53	....	1987-88	1998-99
Janssens, Mark	NYR, Min., Hfd., Ana., NYI, Phx., Chi.	14	711	40	73	113	1422	27	5	1	6	33	....	1987-88	2000-01
Jantunen, Marko	Cgy.	1	3	0	0	0	0	....	....	....	....	....	....	1996-97	1996-97
Jardine, Ryan	Fla.	1	8	0	2	2	2	....	....	....	....	....	....	2001-02	2001-02
Jarrett, Cole	NYI	1	1	0	0	0	0	....	....	....	....	....	....	2005-06	2005-06
Jarrett, Doug	Chi., NYR	13	775	38	182	220	631	99	7	16	23	82	....	1964-65	1976-77
Jarrett, Gary	Tor., Det., Oak., Cal.	7	341	72	92	164	131	11	3	1	4	9	....	1960-61	1971-72
Jarry, Pierre	NYR, Tor., Det., Min.	7	344	88	117	205	142	5	0	1	1	0	....	1971-72	1977-78
Jarvenpaa, Hannu	Wpg.	3	114	11	26	37	83	....	....	....	....	....	....	1986-87	1988-89
‡ Jarventie, Martti	Mtl.	1	1	0	0	0	0	....	....	....	....	....	....	2001-02	2001-02
Jarvi, Iiro	Que.	2	116	18	43	61	58	....	....	....	....	....	....	1988-89	1989-90
Jarvis, Doug	Mtl., Wsh., Hfd.	13	964	139	264	403	263	105	14	27	41	42	4	1975-76	1987-88

Name	NHL Teams	NHL Seasons	Regular Schedule					Playoffs					NHL Cup Wins	First NHL Season	Last NHL Season
			GP	G	A	TP	PIM	GP	G	A	TP	PIM			
• Jarvis, James	Pit., Phi., Tor.	3	112	17	15	32	62	....	....	....	....	....	....	1929-30	1936-37
Jarvis, Wes	Wsh., Min., L.A., Tor.	9	237	31	55	86	98	2	0	0	0	2	....	1979-80	1987-88
‡ Jaspers, Jason	Phx.	3	9	0	1	1	6	....	....	....	....	....	....	2001-02	2003-04
• Javanainen, Arto	Pit.	1	14	4	1	5	2	....	....	....	....	....	....	1984-85	1984-85
Jay, Bob	L.A.	1	3	0	1	1	0	....	....	....	....	....	....	1993-94	1993-94
Jeffrey, Larry	Det., Tor., NYR	8	368	39	62	101	293	38	4	10	14	42	1	1961-62	1968-69
Jelinek, Tomas	Ott.	1	49	7	6	13	52	....	....	....	....	....	....	1992-93	1992-93
Jenkins, Dean	L.A.	1	5	0	0	0	2	....	....	....	....	....	....	1983-84	1983-84
• Jenkins, Roger	Chi., Tor., Mtl., Bos., Mtl.M., NYA	8	325	15	39	54	253	27	1	7	8	12	2	1930-31	1938-39
• Jennings, Bill	Det., Bos.	5	108	32	33	65	45	20	4	4	8	6	....	1940-41	1944-45
Jennings, Grant	Wsh., Hfd., Pit., Tor., Buf.	9	389	14	43	57	804	54	2	1	3	68	2	1987-88	1995-96
Jensen, Chris	NYR, Phi.	6	74	9	12	21	27	....	....	....	....	....	....	1985-86	1991-92
Jensen, David	Min.	3	18	0	2	2	11	....	....	....	....	....	....	1983-84	1985-86
Jensen, David	Hfd., Wsh.	4	69	9	13	22	22	11	0	0	0	2	....	1984-85	1987-88
Jensen, Joe	Car.	1	6	1	0	1	2	....	....	....	....	....	....	2007-08	2007-08
Jensen, Steve	Min., L.A.	7	438	113	107	220	318	12	0	3	3	9	....	1975-76	1981-82
• Jeremiah, Ed	NYA, Bos.	1	15	0	1	1	0	....	....	....	....	....	....	1931-32	1931-32
Jerrard, Paul	Min.	1	5	0	0	0	4	....	....	....	....	....	....	1988-89	1988-89
• Jerwa, Frank	Bos., St.L.	4	81	11	16	27	53	....	....	....	....	....	....	1931-32	1934-35
• Jerwa, Joe	NYR, Bos., NYA	7	234	29	58	87	309	17	2	3	5	16	....	1930-31	1938-39
‡ Jillson, Jeff	S.J., Bos., Buf.	4	140	9	32	41	96	8	0	0	0	0	....	2001-02	2005-06
• Jirik, Jaroslav	St.L.	1	3	0	0	0	0	....	....	....	....	....	....	1969-70	1969-70
• Joanette, Rosario	Mtl.	1	2	0	1	1	4	....	....	....	....	....	....	1944-45	1944-45
Jodzio, Rick	Col., Cle.	1	70	2	8	10	71	....	....	....	....	....	....	1977-78	1977-78
Johannesen, Glenn	NYI	1	2	0	0	0	0	....	....	....	....	....	....	1985-86	1985-86
Johannson, John	N.J.	1	5	0	0	0	0	....	....	....	....	....	....	1983-84	1983-84
• Johansen, Bill	Tor.	1	1	0	0	0	0	....	....	....	....	....	....	1949-50	1949-50
Johansen, Trevor	Tor., Col., L.A.	5	286	11	46	57	282	13	0	3	3	21	....	1977-78	1981-82
Johansson, Andreas	NYI, Pit., Ott., T.B., Cgy., NYR, Nsh.	8	377	81	88	169	190	9	0	0	0	0	....	1995-96	2003-04
Johansson, Bjorn	Cle.	2	15	1	1	2	10	....	....	....	....	....	....	1976-77	1977-78
Johansson, Calle	Buf., Wsh., Tor.	17	1109	119	416	535	519	105	12	43	55	44	....	1987-88	2003-04
Johansson, Jonas	Wsh.	1	1	0	0	0	2	....	....	....	....	....	....	2005-06	2005-06
‡ Johansson, Magnus	Chi., Fla.	1	45	0	14	14	18	....	....	....	....	....	....	2007-08	2007-08
Johansson, Mathias	Cgy., Pit.	1	58	5	10	15	16	....	....	....	....	....	....	2002-03	2002-03
Johansson, Roger	Cgy., Chi.	4	161	9	34	43	163	5	0	1	1	2	....	1989-90	1994-95
Johns, Don	NYR, Mtl., Min.	6	153	2	21	23	76	....	....	....	....	....	....	1960-61	1967-68
Johnson, Allan	Mtl., Det.	4	105	21	28	49	30	11	2	2	4	6	....	1956-57	1962-63
Johnson, Brian	Det.	1	3	0	0	0	5	....	....	....	....	....	....	1983-84	1983-84
• Johnson, Ching	NYR, NYA	12	436	38	48	86	808	61	5	2	7	161	2	1926-27	1937-38
Johnson, Craig	St.L., L.A., Ana., Tor., Wsh.	10	557	75	98	173	260	16	3	2	5	10	....	1994-95	2003-04
• Johnson, Danny	Tor., Van., Det.	3	121	18	19	37	24	....	....	....	....	....	....	1969-70	1971-72
Johnson, Earl	Det.	1	1	0	0	0	0	....	....	....	....	....	1	1953-54	1953-54
Johnson, Greg	Det., Pit., Chi., Nsh.	12	785	145	224	369	345	37	7	6	13	14	....	1993-94	2005-06
Johnson, Jim	NYR, Phi., L.A.	8	302	75	111	186	73	7	0	2	2	2	....	1964-65	1971-72
Johnson, Jim	Pit., Min., Dal., Wsh., Phx.	13	829	29	166	195	1197	51	1	11	12	132	....	1985-86	1997-98
Johnson, Mark	Pit., Min., Hfd., St.L., N.J.	11	669	203	305	508	260	37	16	12	28	10	....	1979-80	1989-90
Johnson, Matt	L.A., Atl., Min.	10	473	23	20	43	1523	16	0	0	0	31	....	1994-95	2003-04
Johnson, Mike	Tor., T.B., Phx., Mtl., St.L.	11	661	129	246	375	315	22	4	3	7	10	....	1996-97	2007-08
Johnson, Norm	Bos., Chi.	3	61	5	20	25	41	14	4	0	4	6	....	1957-58	1959-60
Johnson, Terry	Que., St.L., Cgy., Tor.	9	285	3	24	27	580	38	0	4	4	118	....	1979-80	1987-88
• Johnson, Tom	Mtl., Bos.	17	978	51	213	264	960	111	8	15	23	109	6	1947-48	1964-65
• Johnson, Virgil	Chi.	3	75	1	11	12	27	19	0	3	3	4	1	1937-38	1944-45
Johnsson, Kim	NYR, Phi., Min., Chi.	10	739	67	217	284	406	43	2	10	12	38	....	1999-00	2009-10
Johnston, Bernie	Hfd.	2	57	12	24	36	16	3	0	1	1	0	....	1979-80	1980-81
• Johnston, George	Chi.	4	58	20	12	32	2	....	....	....	....	....	....	1941-42	1946-47
Johnston, Greg	Bos., Tor.	9	187	26	29	55	124	22	2	1	3	12	....	1983-84	1991-92
Johnston, Jay	Wsh.	2	8	0	0	0	13	....	....	....	....	....	....	1980-81	1981-82
Johnston, Joey	Min., Cal., Chi.	6	331	85	106	191	320	....	....	....	....	....	....	1968-69	1975-76
Johnston, Larry	L.A., Det., K.C., Col.	7	320	9	64	73	580	....	....	....	....	....	....	1967-68	1976-77
Johnston, Marshall	Min., Cal.	7	251	14	52	66	58	6	0	0	0	2	....	1967-68	1973-74
Johnston, Randy	NYI	1	4	0	0	0	4	....	....	....	....	....	....	1979-80	1979-80
Johnstone, Eddie	NYR, Det.	10	426	122	136	258	375	55	13	10	23	83	....	1975-76	1986-87
• Johnstone, Ross	Tor.	2	42	5	4	9	14	3	0	0	0	0	1	1943-44	1944-45
‡ Jokela, Mikko	Van.	1	1	0	0	0	0	....	....	....	....	....	....	2002-03	2002-03
• Joliat, Aurele	Mtl.	16	655	270	190	460	771	45	9	13	22	66	3	1922-23	1937-38
• Joliat, Rene	Mtl.	1	1	0	0	0	0	....	....	....	....	....	....	1924-25	1924-25
Joly, Greg	Wsh., Det.	9	365	21	76	97	250	5	0	0	0	8	....	1974-75	1982-83
Joly, Yvan	Mtl.	3	2	0	0	0	0	1	0	0	0	0	....	1979-80	1982-83
Jomphe, Jean-Francois	Ana., Phx., Mtl.	4	111	10	29	39	102	....	....	....	....	....	....	1995-96	1998-99
Jonathan, Stan	Bos., Pit.	8	411	91	110	201	751	63	8	4	12	137	....	1975-76	1982-83
Jones, Bob	NYR	1	2	0	0	0	0	....	....	....	....	....	....	1968-69	1968-69
Jones, Brad	Wpg., L.A., Phi.	6	148	25	31	56	122	9	1	1	2	2	....	1986-87	1991-92
• Jones, Buck	Det., Tor.	4	50	2	2	4	36	12	0	1	1	18	....	1938-39	1942-43
Jones, Jim	Cal.	1	2	0	0	0	0	....	....	....	....	....	....	1971-72	1971-72
Jones, Jimmy	Tor.	3	148	13	18	31	68	19	1	5	6	11	....	1977-78	1979-80
Jones, Keith	Wsh., Col., Phi.	9	491	117	141	258	765	63	12	12	24	120	....	1992-93	2000-01
Jones, Matt	Phx.	3	106	1	10	11	63	....	....	....	....	....	....	2005-06	2007-08
Jones, Ron	Bos., Pit., Wsh.	5	54	1	4	5	31	....	....	....	....	....	....	1971-72	1975-76
Jones, Ty	Chi., Fla.	2	14	0	0	0	19	....	....	....	....	....	....	1998-99	2003-04
‡ Jonsson, Hans	Pit.	4	242	10	38	48	92	27	0	1	1	14	....	1999-00	2002-03
Jonsson, Jorgen	NYI, Ana.	1	81	12	19	31	16	....	....	....	....	....	....	1999-00	1999-00
Jonsson, Kenny	Tor., NYI	10	686	63	204	267	298	19	1	3	4	6	....	1994-95	2003-04
‡ Jonsson, Lars	Phi.	1	8	0	2	2	6	....	....	....	....	....	....	2006-07	2006-07
Jonsson, Tomas	NYI, Edm.	8	552	85	259	344	482	80	11	26	37	97	2	1981-82	1988-89
Joseph, Chris	Pit., Edm., T.B., Van., Phi., Phx., Atl.	14	510	39	112	151	567	31	3	4	7	24	....	1987-88	2000-01
Joseph, Tony	Wpg.	1	2	1	0	1	0	....	....	....	....	....	....	1988-89	1988-89
Joyal, Eddie	Det., Tor., L.A., Phi.	9	466	128	134	262	103	50	11	8	19	18	....	1962-63	1971-72
Joyce, Bob	Bos., Wsh., Wpg.	6	158	34	49	83	90	46	15	9	24	29	....	1987-88	1992-93
Joyce, Duane	Dal.	1	3	0	0	0	0	....	....	....	....	....	....	1993-94	1993-94
• Juckes, Bing	NYR	2	16	2	1	3	6	....	....	....	....	....	....	1947-48	1949-50
Juhlin, Patrik	Phi.	2	56	7	6	13	23	13	1	0	1	2	....	1994-95	1995-96
Julien, Claude	Que.	2	14	0	1	1	25	....	....	....	....	....	....	1984-85	1985-86
Juneau, Joe	Bos., Wsh., Buf., Ott., Phx., Mtl.	13	828	156	416	572	272	112	25	54	79	69	....	1991-92	2003-04
Junker, Steve	NYI	2	5	0	0	0	0	3	0	1	1	0	....	1992-93	1993-94
Jutila, Timo	Buf.	1	10	1	5	6	13	....	....	....	....	....	....	1984-85	1984-85
• Juzda, Bill	NYR, Tor.	9	398	14	54	68	398	42	0	3	3	46	2	1940-41	1951-52

K

Name	NHL Teams	NHL Seasons	GP	G	A	TP	PIM	GP	G	A	TP	PIM	NHL Cup Wins	First NHL Season	Last NHL Season
Kabel, Bob	NYR	2	48	5	13	18	34	....	....	....	....	....	....	1959-60	1960-61
‡ Kaberle, Frantisek	L.A., Atl., Car.	9	523	29	164	193	218	32	4	10	14	10	1	1999-00	2008-09
Kachowski, Mark	Pit.	3	64	6	5	11	209	....	....	....	....	....	....	1987-88	1989-90
Kachur, Ed	Chi.	2	96	10	14	24	35	....	....	....	....	....	....	1956-57	1957-58
Kaese, Trent	Buf.	1	1	0	0	0	0	....	....	....	....	....	....	1988-89	1988-89
‡ Kaigorodov, Alexei	Ott.	1	6	0	1	1	0	....	....	....	....	....	....	2006-07	2006-07
• Kaiser, Vern	Mtl.	1	50	7	5	12	33	2	0	0	0	0	....	1950-51	1950-51
• Kalbfleisch, Walter	Ott., St.L., NYA, Bos.	4	36	0	4	4	32	5	0	0	0	2	....	1933-34	1936-37
• Kaleta, Alex	Chi., NYR	7	387	92	121	213	190	17	1	6	7	2	....	1941-42	1950-51
‡ Kalinin, Dmitri	Buf., NYR, Phx.	9	539	36	126	162	321	37	2	7	9	20	....	1999-00	2008-09
‡ Kallio, Tomi	Atl., CBJ, Phi.	3	140	24	31	55	48	....	....	....	....	....	....	2000-01	2002-03
Kallur, Anders	NYI	6	383	101	110	211	149	78	12	23	35	32	4	1979-80	1984-85
Kamensky, Valeri	Que., Col., NYR, Dal., N.J.	11	637	200	301	501	383	66	25	35	60	72	1	1991-92	2001-02
Kaminski, Kevin	Min., Que., Wsh.	7	139	3	10	13	528	8	0	0	0	52	....	1988-89	1996-97
• Kaminsky, Max	Ott., St.L., Bos., Mtl.M.	4	130	22	34	56	38	4	0	0	0	0	....	1933-34	1936-37
Kaminsky, Yan	Wpg., NYI	2	26	3	2	5	4	2	0	0	0	4	....	1993-94	1994-95
• Kampman, Bingo	Tor.	5	189	14	30	44	287	47	1	4	5	38	1	1937-38	1941-42
Kane, Francis	Det.	1	2	0	0	0	0	....	....	....	....	....	....	1943-44	1943-44
‡ Kanko, Petr	L.A.	1	10	1	0	1	0	....	....	....	....	....	....	2005-06	2005-06
Kannegiesser, Gord	St.L.	2	23	0	1	1	15	....	....	....	....	....	....	1967-68	1971-72
Kannegiesser, Sheldon	Pit., NYR, L.A., Van.	8	366	14	67	81	292	18	0	2	2	10	....	1970-71	1977-78
‡ Kapanen, Niko	Dal., Atl., Phx.	6	397	36	90	126	160	18	5	4	9	22	....	2001-02	2007-08
Kapanen, Sami	Hfd., Car., Phi.	12	831	189	269	458	175	87	13	22	35	22	....	1995-96	2007-08
Karabin, Ladislav	Pit.	1	9	0	0	0	2	....	....	....	....	....	....	1993-94	1993-94
‡ Karalahti, Jere	L.A., Nsh.	3	149	8	19	27	97	17	0	1	1	20	....	1999-00	2001-02
Karamnov, Vitali	St.L.	3	92	12	20	32	65	2	0	0	0	2	....	1992-93	1994-95
Kariya, Paul	Ana., Col., Nsh., St.L.	15	989	402	587	989	399	46	16	23	39	12		1994-95	2009-10

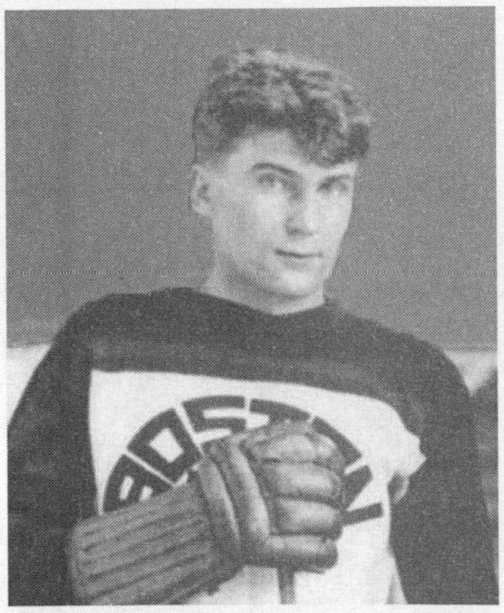
Frank Jerwa

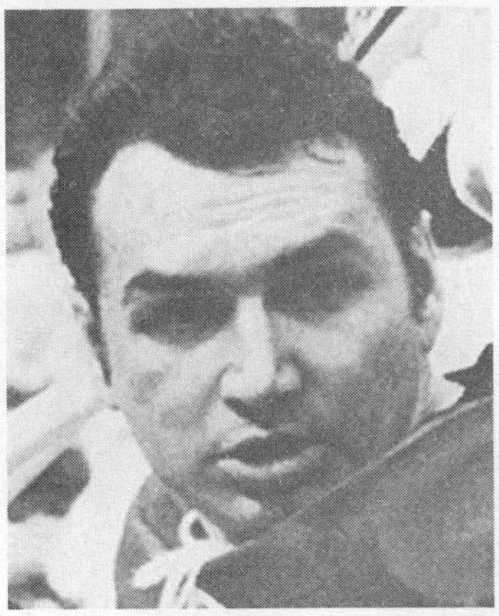
Jaroslav Jirik

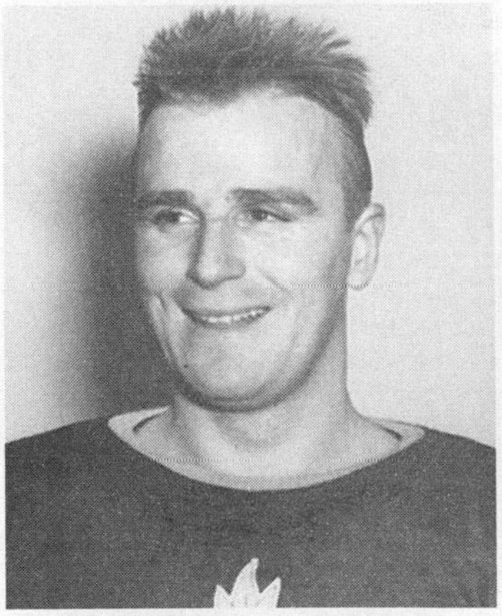
Buck Jones

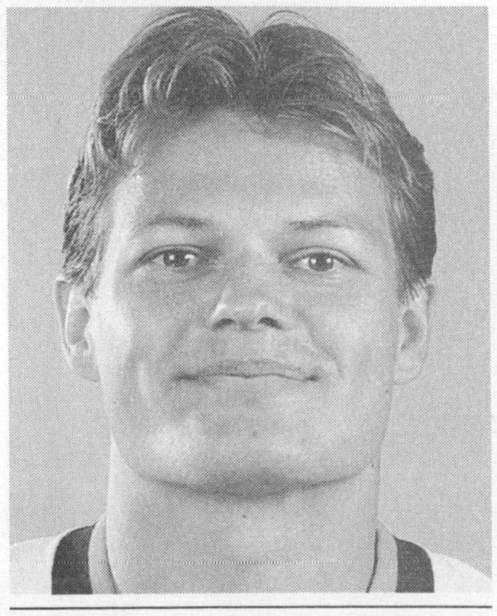
Sami Kapanen

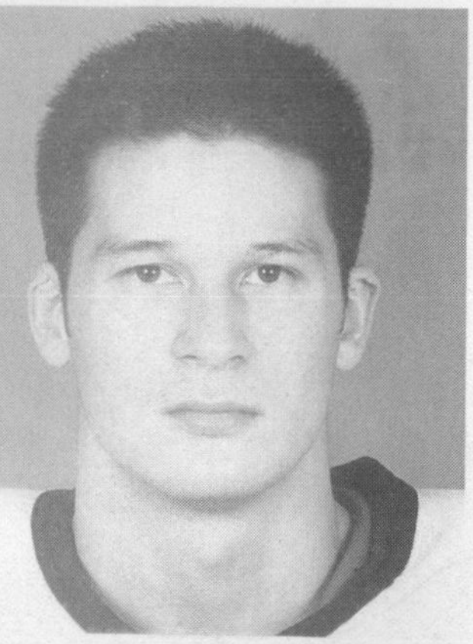

Paul Kariya

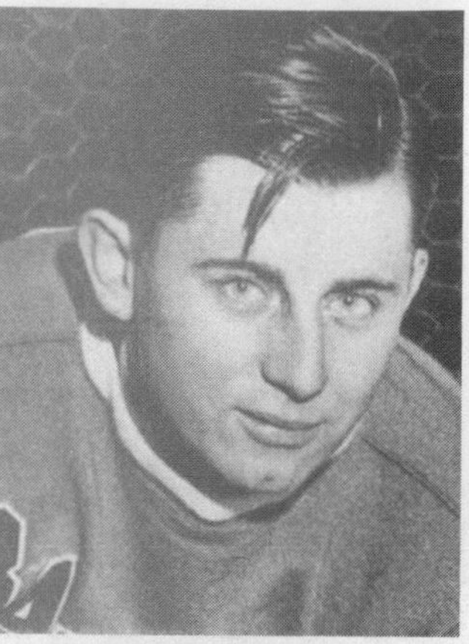

Butch Keeling

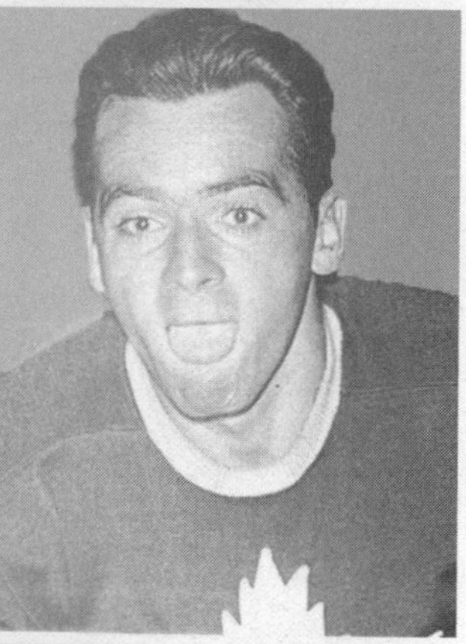

Paul Knox

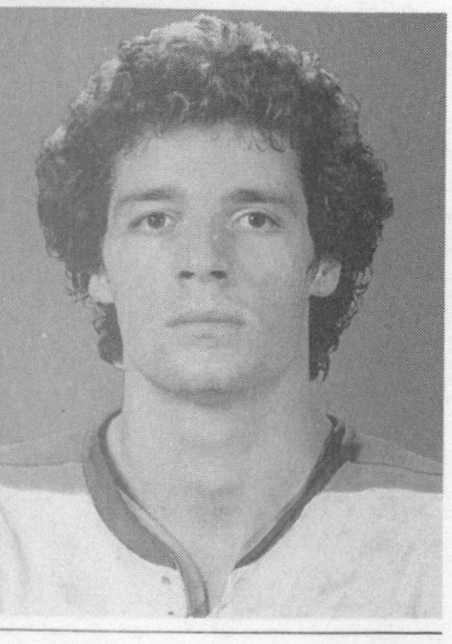

Joe Kowal

			Regular Schedule					Playoffs							
Name	NHL Teams	NHL Seasons	GP	G	A	TP	PIM	GP	G	A	TP	PIM	NHL Cup Wins	First NHL Season	Last NHL Season
Kariya, Steve	Van.	3	65	9	18	27	32	....	....	....	....	....	....	1999-00	2001-02
Karjalainen, Kyosti	L.A.	1	28	1	8	9	12	3	0	1	1	2	....	1991-92	1991-92
Karlander, Al	Det.	4	212	36	56	92	70	4	0	1	1	0	....	1969-70	1972-73
‡ Karlsson, Andreas	Atl., T.B.	5	264	16	35	51	72	6	0	0	0	0	....	1999-00	2007-08
Karpa, Dave	Que., Ana., Car., NYR	12	557	18	80	98	1374	19	1	1	2	39	....	1991-92	2002-03
Karpov, Valeri	Ana.	3	76	14	15	29	32	....	....	....	....	....	....	1994-95	1996-97
Karpovtsev, Alexander	NYR, Tor., Chi., NYI, Fla.	12	596	34	154	188	430	74	4	14	18	52	1	1993-94	2005-06
Kasatonov, Alexei	N.J., Ana., St.L., Bos.	7	383	38	122	160	326	33	4	7	11	40	....	1989-90	1995-96
‡ Kaspar, Lukas	S.J.	2	16	2	2	4	8	....	....	....	....	....	....	2007-08	2008-09
Kasparaitis, Darius	NYI, Pit., Col., NYR	14	863	27	136	163	1379	83	2	10	12	107	....	1992-93	2006-07
Kasper, Steve	Bos., L.A., Phi., T.B.	13	821	177	291	468	554	94	20	28	48	82	....	1980-81	1992-93
Kastelic, Ed	Wsh., Hfd.	7	220	11	10	21	719	8	1	0	1	32	....	1985-86	1991-92
Kaszycki, Mike	NYI, Wsh., Tor.	5	226	42	80	122	108	19	2	6	8	10	....	1977-78	1982-83
‡ Kavanagh, Pat	Van., Phi.	4	14	2	0	2	4	3	0	0	0	2	....	2000-01	2005-06
● Kea, Ed	Atl., St.L.	10	583	30	145	175	508	32	2	4	6	39	....	1973-74	1982-83
Keane, Mike	Mtl., Col., NYR, Dal., St.L., Van.	16	1161	168	302	470	881	220	34	40	74	135	3	1988-89	2003-04
Kearns, Dennis	Van.	10	677	31	290	321	386	11	1	2	3	8	....	1971-72	1980-81
● Keating, Jack	Det.	2	11	3	0	3	4	....	....	....	....	....	....	1938-39	1939-40
● Keating, John	NYA	2	35	5	5	10	17	....	....	....	....	....	....	1931-32	1932-33
Keating, Mike	NYR	1	1	0	0	0	0	....	....	....	....	....	....	1977-78	1977-78
● Keats, Duke	Bos., Det., Chi.	3	82	30	19	49	113	....	....	....	....	....	....	1926-27	1928-29
Keczmer, Dan	Min., Hfd., Cgy., Dal., Nsh.	10	235	8	38	46	212	12	0	1	1	8	....	1990-91	1999-00
Keefe, Sheldon	T.B.	3	125	12	12	24	78	....	....	....	....	....	....	2000-01	2002-03
● Keeling, Butch	Tor., NYR	12	525	157	63	220	331	47	11	11	22	34	1	1926-27	1937-38
Keenan, Larry	Tor., St.L., Buf., Phi.	6	233	38	64	102	28	46	15	16	31	12	....	1961-62	1971-72
Kehoe, Rick	Tor., Pit.	14	906	371	396	767	120	39	4	17	21	4	....	1971-72	1984-85
Kekalainen, Jarmo	Bos., Ott.	3	55	5	8	13	28	....	....	....	....	....	....	1989-90	1993-94
Kelleher, Chris	Bos.	1	1	0	0	0	0	....	....	....	....	....	....	2001-02	2001-02
Keller, Ralph	NYR	1	3	1	0	1	6	....	....	....	....	....	....	1962-63	1962-63
Kellgren, Christer	Col.	1	5	0	0	0	0	....	....	....	....	....	....	1981-82	1981-82
Kelly, Bob	Phi., Wsh.	12	837	154	208	362	1454	101	9	14	23	172	2	1970-71	1981-82
Kelly, Bob	St.L., Pit., Chi.	6	425	87	109	196	687	23	6	3	9	40	....	1973-74	1978-79
Kelly, Dave	Det.	1	16	2	0	2	4	....	....	....	....	....	....	1976-77	1976-77
Kelly, John Paul	L.A.	7	400	54	70	124	366	18	1	1	2	41	....	1979-80	1985-86
● Kelly, Pep	Tor., Chi., Bro.	8	288	74	53	127	105	38	7	6	13	10	....	1934-35	1941-42
● Kelly, Pete	St.L., Det., NYA, Bro.	7	177	21	38	59	68	19	3	1	4	2	2	1934-35	1941-42
Kelly, Red	Det., Tor.	20	1316	281	542	823	327	164	33	59	92	51	8	1947-48	1966-67
Kelly, Steve	Edm., T.B., N.J., L.A., Min.	9	149	9	12	21	83	25	0	0	0	8	1	1996-97	2007-08
● Kemp, Kevin	Hfd.	1	3	0	0	0	4	....	....	....	....	....	....	1980-81	1980-81
● Kemp, Stan	Tor.	1	1	0	0	0	2	....	....	....	....	....	....	1948-49	1948-49
Kenady, Chris	St.L., NYR	2	7	0	2	2	0	....	....	....	....	....	....	1997-98	1999-00
● Kendall, Bill	Chi., Tor.	5	131	16	10	26	28	6	0	0	0	0	1	1933-34	1937-38
Kennedy, Dean	L.A., NYR, Buf., Wpg., Edm.	12	717	26	108	134	1118	36	1	7	8	59	....	1982-83	1994-95
Kennedy, Forbes	Chi., Det., Bos., Phi., Tor.	11	603	70	108	178	988	12	2	4	6	64	....	1956-57	1968-69
‡ Kennedy, Mike	Dal., Tor., NYI	5	145	16	36	52	112	5	0	0	0	9	....	1994-95	1998-99
Kennedy, Sheldon	Det., Cgy., Bos.	8	310	49	58	107	233	24	6	4	10	20	....	1989-90	1996-97
● Kennedy, Ted	Tor.	14	696	231	329	560	432	78	29	31	60	32	5	1942-43	1956-57
● Kenny, Ernest	NYR, Chi.	2	10	0	0	0	18	....	....	....	....	....	....	1930-31	1934-35
Keon, Dave	Tor., Hfd.	18	1296	396	590	986	117	92	32	36	68	6	4	1960-61	1981-82
Kerch, Alexander	Edm.	1	5	0	0	0	2	....	....	....	....	....	....	1993-94	1993-94
Kerr, Alan	NYI, Det., Wpg.	9	391	72	94	166	826	38	5	4	9	70	....	1984-85	1992-93
Kerr, Reg	Cle., Chi., Edm.	6	263	66	94	160	169	7	1	0	1	7	....	1977-78	1983-84
Kerr, Tim	Phi., NYR, Hfd.	13	655	370	304	674	596	81	40	31	71	58	....	1980-81	1992-93
Kesa, Dan	Van., Dal., Pit., T.B.	4	139	8	22	30	66	13	1	0	1	0	....	1993-94	1999-00
Kessell, Rick	Pit., Cal.	5	135	4	24	28	6	....	....	....	....	....	....	1969-70	1973-74
Ketola, Veli-Pekka	Col.	1	44	9	5	14	4	....	....	....	....	....	....	1981-82	1981-82
Ketter, Kerry	Atl.	1	41	0	2	2	58	....	....	....	....	....	....	1972-73	1972-73
Kharin, Sergei	Wpg.	1	7	2	3	5	2	....	....	....	....	....	....	1990-91	1990-91
Kharitonov, Alexander	T.B., NYI	2	71	7	15	22	12	....	....	....	....	....	....	2000-01	2001-02
Khavanov, Alexander	St.L., Tor.	5	348	27	75	102	233	26	5	5	10	18	....	2000-01	2005-06
Khmylev, Yuri	Buf., St.L.	5	263	64	88	152	133	26	8	6	14	24	....	1992-93	1996-97
Khristich, Dmitri	Wsh., L.A., Bos., Tor.	12	811	259	337	596	422	75	15	25	40	41	....	1990-91	2001-02
Kidd, Ian	Van.	2	20	4	7	11	25	....	....	....	....	....	....	1987-88	1988-89
Kiessling, Udo	Min.	1	1	0	0	0	2	....	....	....	....	....	....	1981-82	1981-82
Kilger, Chad	Ana., Wpg., Phx., Chi., Edm., Mtl., Tor.	12	714	107	111	218	363	36	3	2	5	13	....	1995-96	2007-08
Kilrea, Brian	Det., L.A.	2	26	3	5	8	12	....	....	....	....	....	....	1957-58	1967-68
● Kilrea, Hec	Ott., Det., Tor.	15	633	167	129	296	438	48	8	7	15	18	3	1925-26	1939-40
● Kilrea, Ken	Det.	5	91	16	23	39	8	15	2	2	4	4	....	1938-39	1943-44
● Kilrea, Wally	Ott., Phi., NYA, Mtl.M., Det.	9	329	35	58	93	87	25	2	4	6	6	2	1929-30	1937-38
Kimble, Darin	Que., St.L., Bos., Chi.	7	311	23	20	43	1082	23	0	0	0	52	....	1988-89	1994-95
Kindrachuk, Orest	Phi., Pit., Wsh.	10	508	118	261	379	648	76	20	20	40	53	2	1972-73	1981-82
King, Derek	NYI, Hfd., Tor., St.L.	14	830	261	351	612	417	47	4	17	21	24	....	1986-87	1999-00
King, Frank	Mtl.	1	10	1	0	1	2	....	....	....	....	....	....	1950-51	1950-51
‡ King, Jason	Van., Ana.	3	59	12	11	23	8	1	0	0	0	0	....	2002-03	2007-08
King, Kris	Det., NYR, Wpg., Phx., Tor., Chi.	14	849	66	85	151	2030	67	8	5	13	142	....	1987-88	2000-01
King, Steven	NYR, Ana.	3	67	17	8	25	75	....	....	....	....	....	....	1992-93	1995-96
King, Wayne	Cal.	3	73	5	18	23	34	....	....	....	....	....	....	1973-74	1975-76
Kinnear, Geordie	Atl.	1	4	0	0	0	13	....	....	....	....	....	....	1999-00	1999-00
Kinsella, Brian	Wsh.	2	10	0	1	1	0	....	....	....	....	....	....	1975-76	1976-77
● Kinsella, Ray	Ott.	1	14	0	0	0	0	....	....	....	....	....	....	1930-31	1930-31
Kiprusoff, Marko	Mtl., NYI	2	51	0	10	10	12	....	....	....	....	....	....	1995-96	2001-02
● Kirk, Bobby	NYR	1	39	4	8	12	14	....	....	....	....	....	....	1937-38	1937-38
● Kirkpatrick, Bob	NYR	1	49	12	12	24	6	....	....	....	....	....	....	1942-43	1942-43
Kirton, Mark	Tor., Det., Van.	6	266	57	56	113	121	4	1	2	3	7	....	1979-80	1984-85
Kisio, Kelly	Det., NYR, S.J., Cgy.	13	761	229	429	658	768	39	6	15	21	52	....	1982-83	1994-95
Kitchen, Bill	Mtl., Tor.	4	41	1	4	5	40	3	0	1	1	0	....	1981-82	1984-85
● Kitchen, Hobie	Mtl.M., Det.	2	47	5	4	9	58	....	....	....	....	....	1	1925-26	1926-27
Kitchen, Mike	Col., N.J.	8	474	12	62	74	370	2	0	0	0	2	....	1976-77	1983-84
Kjellberg, Patric	Mtl., Nsh., Ana.	6	394	64	96	160	84	10	0	0	0	0	....	1992-93	2002-03
Klassen, Ralph	Cal., Cle., Col., St.L.	9	497	52	93	145	120	26	4	2	6	12	....	1975-76	1983-84
Klatt, Trent	Min., Dal., Phi., Van., L.A.	13	782	143	200	343	307	74	16	9	25	20	....	1991-92	2003-04
Klee, Ken	Wsh., Tor., N.J., Col., Atl., Ana., Phx.	14	934	55	140	195	880	51	2	2	4	50	....	1994-95	2008-09
● Klein, Lloyd	Bos., NYA	8	164	30	24	54	68	5	0	0	0	2	1	1928-29	1937-38
Kleinendorst, Scot	NYR, Hfd., Wsh.	8	281	12	46	58	452	26	2	7	9	40	....	1982-83	1989-90
Klemm, Jon	Que., Col., Chi., Dal., L.A.	15	773	42	100	142	436	105	7	7	14	47	2	1991-92	2007-08
‡ Klepis, Jakub	Wsh.	2	66	4	10	14	36	....	....	....	....	....	....	2005-06	2006-07
Klima, Petr	Det., Edm., T.B., L.A., Pit.	13	786	313	260	573	671	95	28	24	52	83	1	1985-86	1998-99
Klimovich, Sergei	Chi.	1	1	0	0	0	2	....	....	....	....	....	....	1996-97	1996-97
● Klingbeil, Ike	Chi.	1	5	1	2	3	2	....	....	....	....	....	....	1936-37	1936-37
‡ Kloucek, Tomas	NYR, Nsh., Atl.	5	141	2	8	10	250	....	....	....	....	....	....	2000-01	2005-06
● Klukay, Joe	Tor., Bos.	11	566	109	127	236	189	71	13	10	23	23	4	1942-43	1955-56
Kluzak, Gord	Bos.	7	299	25	98	123	543	46	6	13	19	129	....	1982-83	1990-91
● Knibbs, Bill	Bos.	1	53	7	10	17	4	....	....	....	....	....	....	1964-65	1964-65
Knipscheer, Fred	Bos., St.L.	3	28	6	3	9	18	16	2	1	3	6	....	1993-94	1995-96
● Knott, Nick	Bro.	1	14	3	1	4	9	....	....	....	....	....	....	1941-42	1941-42
Knox, Paul	Tor.	1	1	0	0	0	0	....	....	....	....	....	....	1954-55	1954-55
Knutsen, Espen	Ana., CBJ	5	207	30	81	111	105	....	....	....	....	....	....	1997-98	2003-04
Koalska, Matt	NYI	1	3	0	0	0	2	....	....	....	....	....	....	2005-06	2005-06
Kocur, Joe	Det., NYR, Van.	15	820	80	82	162	2519	118	10	12	22	231	3	1984-85	1998-99
Koehler, Greg	Car.	1	1	0	0	0	0	....	....	....	....	....	....	2000-01	2000-01
‡ Kohn, Ladislav	Cgy., Tor., Ana., Atl., Det.	7	186	14	28	42	125	2	0	0	0	5	....	1995-96	2002-03
‡ Koivisto, Tom	St.L.	1	22	2	4	6	10	....	....	....	....	....	....	2002-03	2002-03
Kolanos, Krys	Phx., Edm., Min.	5	136	20	21	41	92	2	0	0	0	6	....	2001-02	2008-09
‡ Kolarik, Pavel	Bos.	2	23	0	0	0	10	....	....	....	....	....	....	2000-01	2001-02
Kolesar, Mark	Tor.	2	28	2	2	4	14	3	1	0	1	2	....	1995-96	1996-97
‡ Kolnik, Juraj	NYI, Fla.	6	240	46	49	95	84	....	....	....	....	....	....	2000-01	2006-07
Kolstad, Dean	Min., S.J.	3	40	1	7	8	69	....	....	....	....	....	....	1988-89	1992-93
‡ Koltsov, Konstantin	Pit.	3	144	12	26	38	50	....	....	....	....	....	....	2002-03	2005-06
Komadoski, Neil	L.A., St.L.	8	502	16	76	92	632	23	0	2	2	47	....	1972-73	1979-80
Komarniski, Zenith	Van., CBJ	3	21	1	1	2	10	....	....	....	....	....	....	1999-00	2003-04
Kondratiev, Maxim	Tor., NYR, Ana.	3	40	1	2	3	24	....	....	....	....	....	....	2003-04	2007-08
Konik, George	Pit.	1	52	7	8	15	26	....	....	....	....	....	....	1967-68	1967-68
Konowalchuk, Steve	Wsh., Col.	14	790	171	225	396	703	52	9	12	21	60	....	1991-92	2005-06
Konroyd, Steve	Cgy., NYI, Chi., Hfd., Det., Ott.	15	895	41	195	236	863	97	10	15	25	99	....	1980-81	1994-95
Konstantinov, Vladimir	Det.	6	446	47	128	175	838	82	5	14	19	107	1	1991-92	1996-97
Kontos, Chris	NYR, Pit., L.A., T.B.	8	230	54	69	123	103	20	11	0	11	12	....	1982-83	1992-93

Name	NHL Teams	NHL Seasons	Regular Schedule GP	G	A	TP	PIM	Playoffs GP	G	A	TP	PIM	NHL Cup Wins	First NHL Season	Last NHL Season
• Kopak, Russ	Bos.	1	24	7	9	16	0	....	....	....	....	....	....	1943-44	1943-44
Korab, Jerry	Chi., Van., Buf., L.A.	15	975	114	341	455	1629	93	8	18	26	201	....	1970-71	1984-85
Kordic, Dan	Phi.	6	197	4	8	12	584	12	1	0	1	22	....	1991-92	1998-99
• Kordic, John	Mtl., Tor., Wsh., Que.	7	244	17	18	35	997	41	4	3	7	131	1	1985-86	1991-92
Korn, Jim	Det., Tor., Buf., N.J., Cgy.	10	597	66	122	188	1801	16	1	2	3	109	....	1979-80	1989-90
Korney, Mike	Det., NYR	4	77	9	10	19	59	....	....	....	....	....	....	1973-74	1978-79
Korolev, Evgeny	NYI	3	42	1	4	5	20	2	0	0	0	0	....	1999-00	2001-02
Korolev, Igor	St.L., Wpg., Phx., Tor., Chi.	12	795	119	227	346	330	41	0	8	8	6	....	1992-93	2003-04
Koroll, Cliff	Chi.	11	814	208	254	462	376	85	19	29	48	67	....	1969-70	1979-80
‡ Korolyuk, Alexander	S.J.	6	296	62	80	142	140	34	6	8	14	18	....	1997-98	2003-04
Kortko, Roger	NYI	2	79	7	17	24	28	10	0	3	3	17	....	1984-85	1985-86
Kostynski, Doug	Bos.	2	15	3	1	4	4	....	....	....	....	....	....	1983-84	1984-85
Kotanen, Dick	NYR	1	1	0	0	0	0	....	....	....	....	....	....	1950-51	1950-51
Kotsopoulos, Chris	NYR, Hfd., Tor., Det.	10	479	44	109	153	827	31	1	3	4	91	....	1980-81	1989-90
Kovalenko, Andrei	Que., Col., Mtl., Edm., Phi., Car., Bos.	9	620	173	206	379	389	33	5	6	11	20	....	1992-93	2000-01
Kowal, Joe	Buf.	2	22	0	5	5	13	2	0	0	0	0	....	1976-77	1977-78
Kozak, Don	L.A., Van.	7	437	96	86	182	480	29	7	2	9	69	....	1972-73	1978-79
Kozak, Les	Tor.	1	12	1	0	1	2	....	....	....	....	....	....	1961-62	1961-62
‡ Kozlov, Viktor	S.J., Fla., N.J., NYI, Wsh.	14	897	198	339	537	248	35	4	8	12	10	....	1994-95	2008-09
‡ Kozlov, Vyacheslav	Det., Buf., Atl.	18	1182	356	497	853	704	118	42	37	79	82	2	1991-92	2009-10
Kraft, Milan	Pit.	4	207	41	41	82	52	8	0	0	0	2	....	2000-01	2003-04
Kraft, Ryan	S.J.	1	7	0	1	1	0	....	....	....	....	....	....	2002-03	2002-03
• Kraftcheck, Stephen	Bos., NYR, Tor.	4	157	11	18	29	83	6	0	0	0	7	....	1950-51	1958-59
Krake, Skip	Bos., L.A., Buf.	7	249	23	40	63	182	10	1	0	1	17	....	1963-64	1970-71
Kravchuk, Igor	Chi., Edm., St.L., Ott., Cgy., Fla.	12	699	64	210	274	251	51	6	15	21	18	....	1991-92	2002-03
Kravets, Mikhail	S.J.	2	2	0	0	0	0	....	....	....	....	....	....	1991-92	1992-93
Krentz, Dale	Det.	3	30	5	3	8	9	2	0	0	0	0	....	1986-87	1988-89
Krestanovich, Jordan	Col.	2	22	0	2	2	6	....	....	....	....	....	....	2001-02	2003-04
Kristek, Jaroslav	Buf.	1	6	0	0	0	4	....	....	....	....	....	....	2002-03	2002-03
Krivokrasov, Sergei	Chi., Nsh., Cgy., Min., Ana.	10	450	86	109	195	288	21	2	0	2	14	....	1992-93	2001-02
• Krol, Joe	NYR, Bro.	3	26	10	4	14	8	....	....	....	....	....	....	1936-37	1941-42
Kromm, Richard	Cgy., NYI	9	372	70	103	173	138	36	2	6	8	22	....	1983-84	1992-93
Kron, Robert	Van., Hfd., Car., CBJ	12	771	144	194	338	119	16	3	2	5	2	....	1990-91	2001-02
Krook, Kevin	Col.	1	3	0	0	0	2	....	....	....	....	....	....	1978-79	1978-79
‡ Kroupa, Vlastimil	S.J., N.J.	5	105	4	19	23	66	20	1	2	3	25	....	1993-94	1997-98
Krulicki, Jim	NYR, Det.	1	41	0	3	3	6	....	....	....	....	....	....	1970-71	1970-71
Krupp, Uwe	Buf., NYI, Que., Col., Det., Atl.	15	729	69	212	281	660	81	6	23	29	86	1	1986-87	2002-03
Kruppke, Gord	Det.	3	23	0	0	0	32	....	....	....	....	....	....	1990-91	1993-94
Kruse, Paul	Cgy., NYI, Buf., S.J.	11	423	38	33	71	1074	28	5	2	7	36	....	1990-91	2000-01
Krushelnyski, Mike	Bos., Edm., L.A., Tor., Det.	14	897	241	328	569	699	139	29	43	72	106	3	1981-82	1994-95
Krutov, Vladimir	Van.	1	61	11	23	34	20	....	....	....	....	....	....	1989-90	1989-90
Krygier, Todd	Hfd., Wsh., Ana.	9	543	100	143	243	533	48	10	7	17	40	....	1989-90	1997-98
Kryskow, Dave	Chi., Wsh., Det., Atl.	4	231	33	56	89	174	12	2	0	2	4	....	1972-73	1975-76
• Kryzanowski, Ed	Bos., Chi.	5	237	15	22	37	65	18	0	1	1	4	....	1948-49	1952-53
Kucera, Frantisek	Chi., Hfd., Van., Phi., CBJ, Pit., Wsh.	9	465	24	95	119	251	12	0	1	1	0	....	1990-91	2001-02
‡ Kudashov, Alexei	Tor.	1	25	1	0	1	4	....	....	....	....	....	....	1993-94	1993-94
Kudelski, Bob	L.A., Ott., Fla.	9	442	139	102	241	218	22	4	4	8	4	....	1987-88	1995-96
‡ Kudroc, Kristian	T.B., Fla.	3	26	2	2	4	38	....	....	....	....	....	....	2000-01	2003-04
• Kuhn, Gord	NYA	1	12	1	1	2	4	....	....	....	....	....	....	1932-33	1932-33
‡ Kukkonen, Lasse	Chi., Phi.	4	159	6	16	22	90	14	0	2	2	6	....	2003-04	2008-09
• Kukulowicz, Aggie	NYR	2	4	1	0	1	0	....	....	....	....	....	....	1952-53	1953-54
Kulak, Stu	Van., Edm., NYR, Que., Wpg.	4	90	8	4	12	130	3	0	0	0	2	....	1982-83	1988-89
Kuleshov, Mikhail	Col.	1	3	0	0	0	0	....	....	....	....	....	....	2003-04	2003-04
• Kullman, Arnie	Bos.	2	13	0	1	1	11	....	....	....	....	....	....	1947-48	1949-50
• Kullman, Eddie	NYR	6	343	56	70	126	298	6	1	0	1	2	....	1947-48	1953-54
Kultanen, Jarno	Bos.	3	102	2	11	13	59	....	....	....	....	....	....	2000-01	2002-03
Kumpel, Mark	Que., Det., Wpg.	6	288	38	46	84	113	39	6	4	10	14	....	1984-85	1990-91
• Kuntz, Alan	NYR	2	45	10	12	22	12	6	1	0	1	2	....	1941-42	1945-46
Kuntz, Murray	St.L.	1	7	1	2	3	0	....	....	....	....	....	....	1974-75	1974-75
‡ Kurka, Tomas	Car.	2	17	3	2	5	2	....	....	....	....	....	....	2002-03	2003-04
Kurri, Jari	Edm., L.A., NYR, Ana., Col.	17	1251	601	797	1398	545	200	106	127	233	123	5	1980-81	1997-98
Kurtenbach, Orland	NYR, Bos., Tor., Van.	13	639	119	213	332	628	19	2	4	6	70	....	1960-61	1973-74
Kurtz, Justin	Van.	1	27	3	5	8	14	....	....	....	....	....	....	2001-02	2001-02
Kurvers, Tom	Mtl., Buf., N.J., Tor., Van., NYI, Ana.	11	659	93	328	421	350	57	8	22	30	68	1	1984-85	1994-95
Kuryluk, Merv	Chi.	1	....	....	....	....	....	2	0	0	0	0	....	1961-62	1961-62
Kushner, Dale	NYI, Phi.	3	84	10	13	23	215	....	....	....	....	....	....	1989-90	1991-92
‡ Kutlak, Zdenek	Bos.	3	16	1	2	3	4	....	....	....	....	....	....	2000-01	2003-04
Kuznetsov, Maxim	Det., L.A.	4	136	2	8	10	137	....	....	....	....	....	....	2000-01	2003-04
Kuznik, Greg	Car.	1	1	0	0	0	0	....	....	....	....	....	....	2000-01	2000-01
Kuzyk, Ken	Cle.	2	41	5	9	14	8	....	....	....	....	....	....	1976-77	1977-78
Kvartalnov, Dmitri	Bos.	2	112	42	49	91	26	4	0	0	0	0	....	1992-93	1993-94
‡ Kvasha, Oleg	Fla., NYI, Phx.	7	493	81	136	217	335	21	1	2	3	8	....	1998-99	2005-06
‡ Kwiatkowski, Joel	Ott., Wsh., Fla., Pit., Atl.	7	282	16	29	45	245	6	0	0	0	2	....	2000-01	2007-08
Kwong, Larry	NYR	1	1	0	0	0	0	....	....	....	....	....	....	1947-48	1947-48
• Kyle, Bill	NYR	2	3	0	3	3	0	....	....	....	....	....	....	1949-50	1950-51
• Kyle, Gus	NYR, Bos.	3	203	6	20	26	362	14	1	2	3	34	....	1949-50	1951-52
Kyllonen, Markku	Wpg.	1	9	0	2	2	2	....	....	....	....	....	....	1988-89	1988-89
Kypreos, Nick	Wsh., Hfd., NYR, Tor.	8	442	46	44	90	1210	34	1	3	4	65	1	1989-90	1996-97
Kyte, Jim	Wpg., Pit., Cgy., Ott., S.J.	13	598	17	49	66	1342	42	0	6	6	94	....	1982-83	1995-96

L

Name	NHL Teams	NHL Seasons	Regular Schedule GP	G	A	TP	PIM	Playoffs GP	G	A	TP	PIM	NHL Cup Wins	First NHL Season	Last NHL Season
Laaksonen, Antti	Bos., Min., Col.	8	483	81	87	168	152	25	1	5	6	6	....	1998-99	2006-07
Labadie, Mike	NYR	1	3	0	0	0	0	....	....	....	....	....	....	1952-53	1952-53
Labatte, Neil	St.L.	2	26	0	2	2	19	....	....	....	....	....	....	1978-79	1981-82
L'Abbe, Moe	Chi.	1	5	0	1	1	0	....	....	....	....	....	....	1972-73	1972-73
Labelle, Marc	Dal.	1	9	0	0	0	46	....	....	....	....	....	....	1996-97	1996-97
• Labine, Leo	Bos., Det.	11	643	128	193	321	730	60	12	11	23	82	....	1951-52	1961-62
Labossiere, Gord	NYR, L.A., Min.	6	215	44	62	106	75	10	2	3	5	28	....	1963-64	1971-72
Labovitch, Max	NYR	1	5	0	0	0	4	....	....	....	....	....	....	1943-44	1943-44
Labraaten, Dan	Det., Cgy.	4	268	71	73	144	47	8	1	0	1	4	....	1978-79	1981-82
Labre, Yvon	Pit., Wsh.	9	371	14	87	101	788	....	....	....	....	....	....	1970-71	1980-81
• Labrie, Guy	Bos., NYR	2	42	4	9	13	16	....	....	....	....	....	....	1943-44	1944-45
Lach, Elmer	Mtl.	14	664	215	408	623	478	76	19	45	64	36	3	1940-41	1953-54
Lachance, Michel	Col.	1	21	0	4	4	22	....	....	....	....	....	....	1978-79	1978-79
Lachance, Scott	NYI, Mtl., Van., CBJ	13	819	31	112	143	567	11	1	2	3	6	....	1991-92	2003-04
Lacombe, Francois	Oak., Buf., Que.	4	78	2	17	19	54	3	1	0	1	0	....	1968-69	1979-80
Lacombe, Normand	Buf., Edm., Phi.	7	319	53	62	115	196	26	5	1	6	49	1	1984-85	1990-91
‡ LaCouture, Dan	Edm., Pit., NYR, Bos., N.J., Car.	9	337	20	25	45	348	6	0	0	0	2	....	1998-99	2008-09
Lacroix, Andre	Phi., Chi., Hfd.	6	325	79	119	198	44	16	2	5	7	0	....	1967-68	1979-80
Lacroix, Daniel	NYR, Bos., Phi., Edm., NYI	7	188	11	7	18	379	16	0	1	1	26	....	1993-94	1999-00
Lacroix, Eric	Tor., L.A., Col., NYR, Ott.	8	472	67	70	137	361	30	1	5	6	25	....	1993-94	2000-01
Lacroix, Pierre	Que., Hfd.	4	274	24	108	132	197	8	0	2	2	10	....	1979-80	1982-83
Ladouceur, Randy	Det., Hfd., Ana.	14	930	30	126	156	1322	40	5	8	13	59	....	1982-83	1995-96
LaFayette, Nathan	St.L., Van., NYR, L.A.	6	187	17	20	37	103	32	2	7	9	8	....	1993-94	1998-99
Laflamme, Christian	Chi., Edm., Mtl., St.L.	8	324	2	45	47	282	9	0	1	1	6	....	1996-97	2003-04
Lafleur, Guy	Mtl., NYR, Que.	17	1126	560	793	1353	399	128	58	76	134	67	5	1971-72	1990-91
• Lafleur, Roland	Mtl.	1	1	0	0	0	0	....	....	....	....	....	....	1924-25	1924-25
LaFontaine, Pat	NYI, Buf., NYR	15	865	468	545	1013	552	69	26	36	62	36	....	1983-84	1997-98
• Laforce, Ernie	Mtl.	1	1	0	0	0	0	....	....	....	....	....	....	1942-43	1942-43
LaForest, Bob	L.A.	1	5	1	0	1	2	....	....	....	....	....	....	1983-84	1983-84
Laforge, Claude	Mtl., Det., Phi.	8	193	24	33	57	82	5	1	2	3	15	....	1957-58	1968-69
Laforge, Marc	Hfd., Edm.	2	14	0	0	0	64	....	....	....	....	....	....	1989-90	1993-94
• Laframboise, Pete	Cal., Wsh., Pit.	4	227	33	55	88	70	9	1	0	1	0	....	1971-72	1974-75
Lafrance, Adie	Mtl.	1	3	0	0	0	2	2	0	0	0	0	....	1933-34	1933-34
• Lafrance, Leo	Mtl., Chi.	2	33	2	0	2	6	....	....	....	....	....	....	1926-27	1927-28
Lafreniere, Jason	Que., NYR, T.B.	5	146	34	53	87	22	15	1	5	6	19	....	1986-87	1993-94
Lafreniere, Roger	Det., St.L.	2	13	0	0	0	4	....	....	....	....	....	....	1962-63	1972-73
Lagace, Jean-Guy	Pit., Buf., K.C.	6	197	9	39	48	251	....	....	....	....	....	....	1968-69	1975-76
Laidlaw, Tom	NYR, L.A.	10	705	25	139	164	717	69	4	17	21	78	....	1980-81	1989-90
Laird, Robbie	Min.	1	1	0	0	0	0	....	....	....	....	....	....	1979-80	1979-80
Lajeunesse, Serge	Det., Phi.	5	103	1	4	5	103	....	....	....	....	....	....	1970-71	1974-75
Lakovic, Sasha	Cgy., N.J.	3	37	0	4	4	118	....	....	....	....	....	....	1996-97	1998-99
• Lalande, Hec	Chi., Det.	4	151	21	39	60	120	....	....	....	....	....	....	1953-54	1957-58
Lalonde, Bobby	Van., Atl., Bos., Cgy.	11	641	124	210	334	298	16	4	2	6	6	....	1971-72	1981-82
• Lalonde, Newsy	Mtl., NYA	6	99	125	41	166	183	7	15	4	19	32	....	1917-18	1926-27

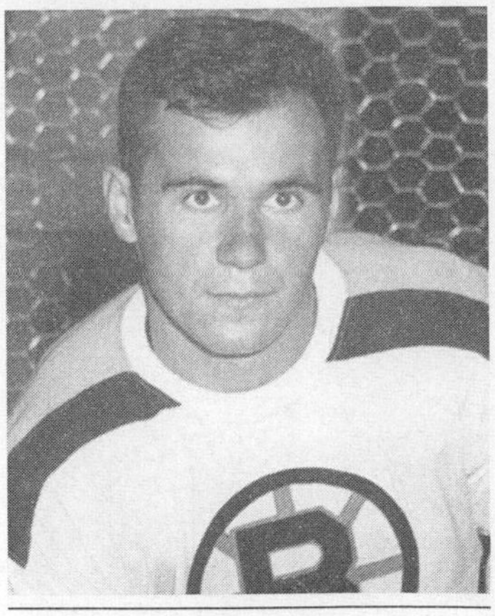
Ed Kryzanowski

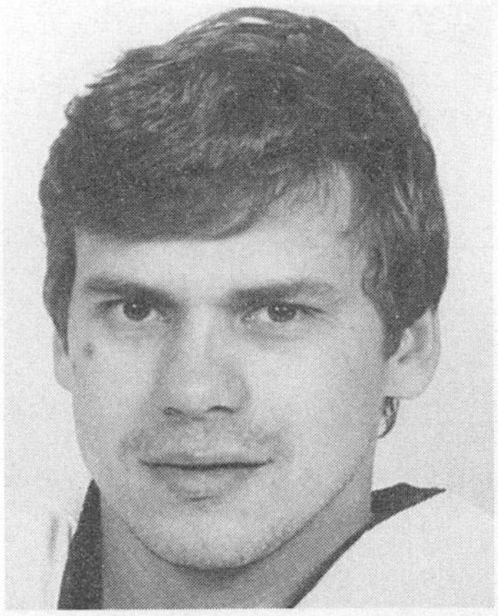
Dmitri Kvartalnov

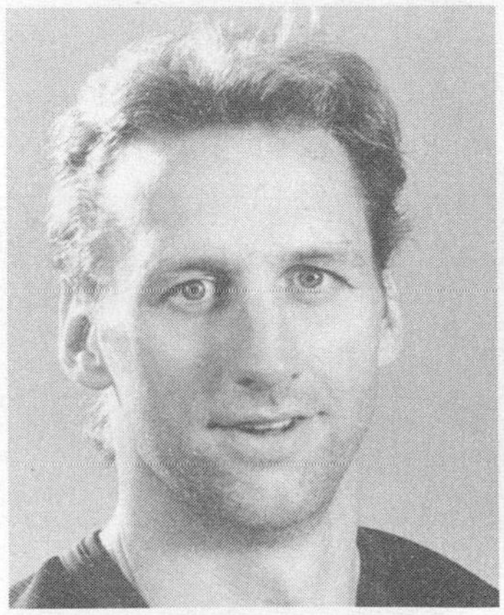
Mike Lalor

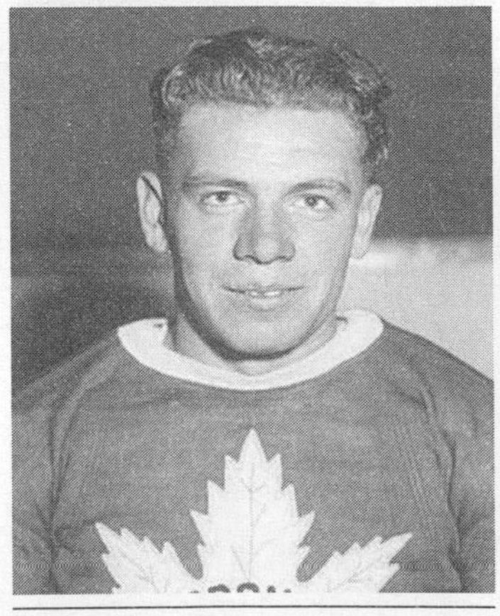
Pete Langelle

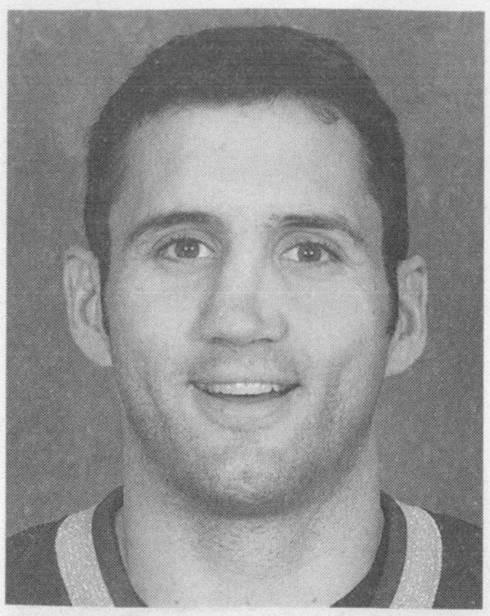

Ian Laperriere

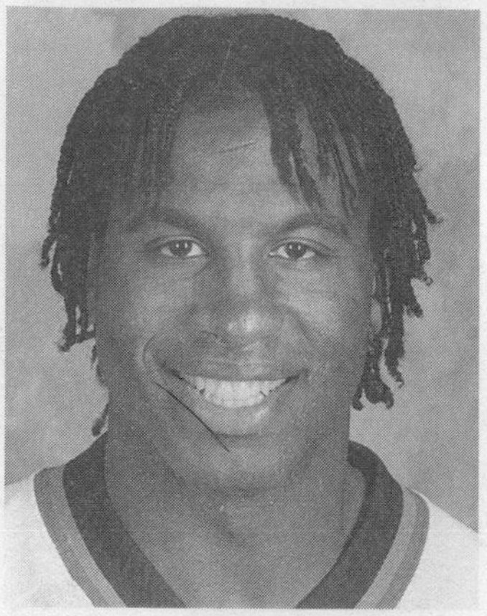

Georges Laraque

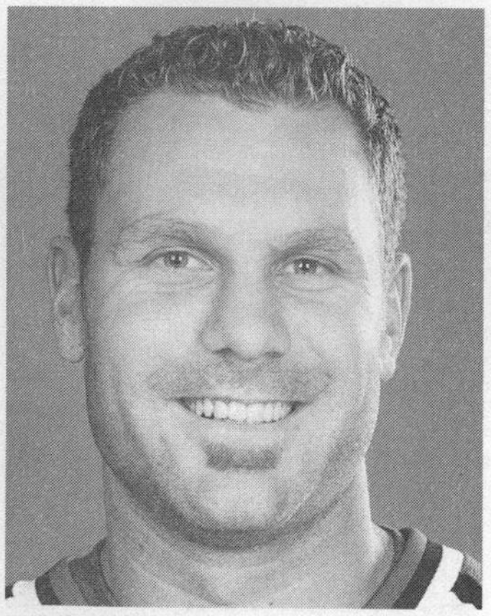

Brad Larsen

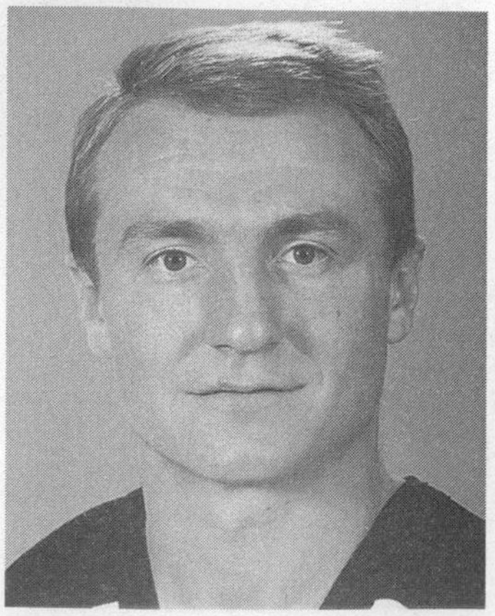

Jere Lehtinen

Name	NHL Teams	NHL Seasons	Regular Schedule GP	G	A	TP	PIM	Playoffs GP	G	A	TP	PIM	NHL Cup Wins	First NHL Season	Last NHL Season
Lalonde, Ron	Pit., Wsh.	7	397	45	78	123	106	....	....	....	....	....	....	1972-73	1978-79
Lalor, Mike	Mtl., St.L., Wsh., Wpg., S.J., Dal.	12	687	17	88	105	677	92	5	10	15	167	1	1985-86	1996-97
• Lamb, Joe	Mtl.M., Ott., NYA, Bos., Mtl., St.L., Det.	11	443	108	101	209	601	18	1	1	2	51	....	1927-28	1937-38
Lamb, Mark	Cgy., Det., Edm., Ott., Phi., Mtl.	11	403	46	100	146	291	70	7	19	26	51	1	1985-86	1995-96
Lambert, Dan	Que.	2	29	6	9	15	22	....	....	....	....	....	....	1990-91	1991-92
Lambert, Denny	Ana., Ott., Nsh., Atl.	8	487	27	66	93	1391	17	0	1	1	28	....	1994-95	2001-02
Lambert, Lane	Det., NYR, Que.	6	283	58	66	124	521	17	2	4	6	40	....	1983-84	1988-89
Lambert, Yvon	Mtl., Buf.	10	683	206	273	479	340	90	27	22	49	67	4	1972-73	1981-82
Lamby, Dick	St.L.	3	22	0	5	5	22	....	....	....	....	....	....	1978-79	1980-81
• Lamirande, Jean-Paul	NYR, Mtl.	4	49	5	5	10	26	8	0	0	0	4	....	1946-47	1954-55
Lammens, Hank	Ott.	1	27	1	2	3	22	....	....	....	....	....	....	1993-94	1993-94
• Lamoureux, Leo	Mtl.	6	235	19	79	98	175	28	1	6	7	16	2	1941-42	1946-47
Lamoureux, Mitch	Pit., Phi.	3	73	11	9	20	59	....	....	....	....	....	....	1983-84	1987-88
‡ Lampman, Bryce	NYR	3	10	0	0	0	2	....	....	....	....	....	....	2003-04	2006-07
Lampman, Mike	St.L., Van., Wsh.	4	96	17	20	37	34	....	....	....	....	....	....	1972-73	1976-77
• Lancien, Jack	NYR	4	63	1	5	6	35	6	0	1	1	2	....	1946-47	1950-51
Landon, Larry	Mtl., Tor.	2	9	0	0	0	2	....	....	....	....	....	....	1983-84	1984-85
‡ Landry, Eric	Cgy., Mtl.	4	68	5	9	14	47	....	....	....	....	....	....	1997-98	2001-02
Lane, Gord	Wsh., NYI	10	539	19	94	113	1228	75	3	14	17	214	4	1975-76	1984-85
• Lane, Myles	NYR, Bos.	3	71	4	1	5	41	11	0	0	0	0	1	1928-29	1933-34
Lang, Robert	L.A., Bos., Pit., Wsh., Det., Chi., Mtl., Phx.	16	989	261	442	703	422	91	18	28	46	24	....	1992-93	2009-10
Langdon, Darren	NYR, Car., Van., Mtl., N.J.	11	521	16	23	39	1251	25	1	0	1	20	....	1994-95	2005-06
Langdon, Steve	Bos.	3	7	0	1	1	2	4	0	0	0	0	....	1974-75	1977-78
• Langelle, Pete	Tor.	4	136	22	51	73	11	39	5	9	14	4	1	1938-39	1941-42
Langevin, Chris	Buf.	2	22	3	1	4	22	....	....	....	....	....	....	1983-84	1985-86
Langevin, Dave	NYI, Min., L.A.	8	513	12	107	119	530	87	2	17	19	106	4	1979-80	1986-87
‡ Langfeld, Josh	Ott., S.J., Bos., Det., Nsh.	6	143	9	23	32	60	1	0	0	0	0	....	2001-02	2007-08
Langlais, Alain	Min.	2	25	4	4	8	10	....	....	....	....	....	....	1973-74	1974-75
Langlois, Albert	Mtl., NYR, Det., Bos.	9	497	21	91	112	488	53	1	5	6	50	3	1957-58	1965-66
• Langlois, Charlie	Ham., NYA, Pit., Mtl.	4	151	22	5	27	189	2	0	0	0	0	....	1924-25	1927-28
Langway, Rod	Mtl., Wsh.	15	994	51	278	329	849	104	5	22	27	97	1	1978-79	1992-93
Lank, Jeff	Phi.	1	2	0	0	0	2	....	....	....	....	....	....	1999-00	1999-00
Lanthier, Jean-Marc	Van.	4	105	16	16	32	29	....	....	....	....	....	....	1983-84	1987-88
• Lanyon, Ted	Pit.	1	5	0	0	0	4	....	....	....	....	....	....	1967-68	1967-68
Lanz, Rick	Van., Tor., Chi.	10	569	65	221	286	448	28	3	8	11	35	....	1980-81	1991-92
Laperriere, Daniel	St.L., Ott.	4	48	2	5	7	27	....	....	....	....	....	....	1992-93	1995-96
Laperriere, Ian	St.L., NYR, L.A., Col., Phi.	17	1083	121	215	336	1956	67	3	10	13	102	....	1993-94	2010-11
Laperriere, Jacques	Mtl.	12	691	40	242	282	674	88	9	22	31	101	6	1962-63	1973-74
Laplante, Darryl	Det.	3	35	0	6	6	10	....	....	....	....	....	....	1997-98	1999-00
Lapointe, Claude	Que., Col., Cgy., NYI, Phi.	14	879	127	178	305	721	34	4	7	11	44	....	1990-91	2003-04
Lapointe, Guy	Mtl., St.L., Bos.	16	884	171	451	622	893	123	26	44	70	138	6	1968-69	1983-84
Lapointe, Martin	Det., Bos., Chi., Ott.	16	991	181	200	381	1417	108	19	24	43	202	2	1991-92	2007-08
• Lapointe, Rick	Det., Phi., St.L., Que., L.A.	11	664	44	176	220	831	46	2	7	9	64	....	1975-76	1985-86
Lappin, Peter	Min., S.J.	2	7	0	0	0	2	....	....	....	....	....	....	1989-90	1991-92
Laprade, Edgar	NYR	10	500	108	172	280	42	18	4	9	13	4	....	1945-46	1954-55
• LaPrairie, Benjamin	Chi.	1	7	0	0	0	0	....	....	....	....	....	....	1936-37	1936-37
Laraque, Georges	Edm., Phx., Pit., Mtl.	12	695	53	100	153	1126	57	4	8	12	72	....	1997-98	2009-10
Larionov, Igor	Van., S.J., Det., Fla., N.J.	14	921	169	475	644	474	150	30	67	97	60	3	1989-90	2003-04
Lariviere, Garry	Que., Edm.	4	219	6	57	63	167	14	0	5	5	8	....	1979-80	1982-83
Larmer, Jeff	Col., N.J., Chi.	5	158	37	51	88	57	5	1	0	1	2	....	1981-82	1985-86
Larmer, Steve	Chi., NYR	15	1006	441	571	1012	532	140	56	75	131	89	1	1980-81	1994-95
• Larochelle, Wildor	Mtl., Chi.	12	474	92	74	166	211	34	6	4	10	24	2	1925-26	1936-37
Larocque, Denis	L.A.	1	8	0	1	1	18	....	....	....	....	....	....	1987-88	1987-88
Larocque, Mario	T.B.	1	5	0	0	0	16	....	....	....	....	....	....	1998-99	1998-99
• Larose, Bonner	Bos.	1	6	0	0	0	0	....	....	....	....	....	....	1925-26	1925-26
Larose, Claude	Mtl., Min., St.L.	16	943	226	257	483	887	97	14	18	32	143	5	1962-63	1977-78
Larose, Claude	NYR	2	25	4	7	11	2	2	0	0	0	0	....	1979-80	1981-82
‡ Larose, Cory	NYR	1	7	0	1	1	4	....	....	....	....	....	....	2003-04	2003-04
Larose, Guy	Wpg., Tor., Cgy., Bos.	6	70	10	9	19	63	4	0	0	0	0	....	1988-89	1994-95
Larouche, Pierre	Pit., Mtl., Hfd., NYR	14	812	395	427	822	237	64	20	34	54	16	2	1974-75	1987-88
Larouche, Steve	Ott., NYR, L.A.	2	26	9	9	18	10	....	....	....	....	....	....	1994-95	1995-96
Larsen, Brad	Col., Atl., Ana.	9	294	19	29	48	134	25	1	3	4	13	....	1997-98	2008-09
• Larson, Norm	NYA, Bro., NYR	3	89	25	18	43	12	....	....	....	....	....	....	1940-41	1946-47
Larson, Reed	Det., Bos., Edm., NYI, Min., Buf.	14	904	222	463	685	1391	32	4	7	11	63	....	1976-77	1989-90
Larter, Tyler	Wsh.	1	1	0	0	0	0	....	....	....	....	....	....	1989-90	1989-90
Latal, Jiri	Phi.	3	92	12	36	48	24	....	....	....	....	....	....	1989-90	1991-92
Latos, James	NYR	1	1	0	0	0	0	....	....	....	....	....	....	1988-89	1988-89
Latreille, Phil	NYR	1	4	0	0	0	2	....	....	....	....	....	....	1960-61	1960-61
Latta, David	Que.	4	36	4	8	12	4	....	....	....	....	....	....	1985-86	1990-91
• Lauder, Martin	Bos.	1	3	0	0	0	2	....	....	....	....	....	....	1927-28	1927-28
Lauen, Mike	Wpg.	1	4	0	1	1	0	....	....	....	....	....	....	1983-84	1983-84
Lauer, Brad	NYI, Chi., Ott., Pit.	9	323	44	67	111	218	34	7	5	12	24	....	1986-87	1995-96
Laughlin, Craig	Mtl., Wsh., L.A., Tor.	8	549	136	205	341	364	33	6	6	12	20	....	1981-82	1988-89
Laughton, Mike	Oak., Cal.	4	189	39	48	87	101	11	3	4	7	0	....	1967-68	1970-71
Laukkanen, Janne	Que., Col., Ott., Pit., T.B.	9	407	22	99	121	335	59	7	9	16	46	....	1994-95	2002-03
Laurence, Don	Atl., St.L.	2	79	15	22	37	14	....	....	....	....	....	....	1978-79	1979-80
Laus, Paul	Fla.	9	530	14	58	72	1702	30	2	7	9	74	....	1993-94	2001-02
LaVallee, Kevin	Cgy., L.A., St.L., Pit.	7	366	110	125	235	85	32	5	8	13	21	....	1980-81	1986-87
LaVarre, Mark	Chi.	3	78	9	16	25	58	1	0	0	0	2	....	1985-86	1987-88
Lavender, Brian	St.L., NYI, Det., Cal.	4	184	16	26	42	174	3	0	0	0	2	....	1971-72	1974-75
Lavigne, Eric	L.A.	1	1	0	0	0	0	....	....	....	....	....	....	1994-95	1994-95
• Laviolette, Jack	Mtl.	1	18	2	1	3	6	2	0	0	0	0	....	1917-18	1917-18
Laviolette, Peter	NYR	1	12	0	0	0	6	....	....	....	....	....	....	1988-89	1988-89
Lavoie, Dominic	St.L., Ott., Bos., L.A.	6	38	5	8	13	32	....	....	....	....	....	....	1988-89	1993-94
Law, Kirby	Phi.	3	9	0	1	1	4	....	....	....	....	....	....	2000-01	2003-04
Lawless, Paul	Hfd., Phi., Van., Tor.	7	239	49	77	126	54	3	0	2	2	2	....	1982-83	1989-90
Lawrence, Mark	Dal., NYI	6	142	18	26	44	115	....	....	....	....	....	....	1994-95	2000-01
• Lawson, Danny	Det., Min., Buf.	5	219	28	29	57	61	16	0	1	1	2	....	1967-68	1971-72
Lawton, Brian	Min., NYR, Hfd., Que., Bos., S.J.	9	483	112	154	266	401	11	1	1	2	12	....	1983-84	1992-93
Laxdal, Derek	Tor., NYI	6	67	12	7	19	88	1	0	2	2	2	....	1984-85	1990-91
• Laycoe, Hal	NYR, Mtl., Bos.	11	531	25	77	102	292	40	2	5	7	39	....	1945-46	1955-56
Lazaro, Jeff	Bos., Ott.	3	102	14	23	37	114	28	3	3	6	32	....	1990-91	1992-93
Leach, Jamie	Pit., Hfd., Fla.	5	81	11	9	20	12	....	....	....	....	....	1	1989-90	1993-94
Leach, Larry	Bos.	3	126	13	29	42	91	7	1	1	2	8	....	1958-59	1961-62
Leach, Reggie	Bos., Cal., Phi., Det.	13	934	381	285	666	387	94	47	22	69	22	1	1970-71	1982-83
Leach, Stephen	Wsh., Bos., St.L., Car., Ott., Phx., Pit.	15	702	130	153	283	978	92	15	11	26	87	....	1985-86	1999-00
Leahy, Patrick	Bos., Nsh.	3	50	4	4	8	19	....	....	....	....	....	....	2003-04	2006-07
Leavins, Jim	Det., NYR	2	41	2	12	14	30	....	....	....	....	....	....	1985-86	1986-87
Lebeau, Patrick	Mtl., Cgy., Fla., Pit.	4	15	3	2	5	6	....	....	....	....	....	....	1990-91	1998-99
Lebeau, Stephan	Mtl., Ana.	7	373	118	159	277	105	30	9	7	16	12	1	1988-89	1994-95
LeBlanc, Fern	Det.	3	34	5	6	11	0	....	....	....	....	....	....	1976-77	1978-79
LeBlanc, J.P.	Chi., Det.	5	153	14	30	44	87	2	0	0	0	0	....	1968-69	1978-79
LeBlanc, John	Van., Edm., Wpg.	7	83	26	13	39	28	1	0	0	0	0	....	1986-87	1994-95
LeBoutillier, Peter	Ana.	2	35	2	1	3	176	....	....	....	....	....	....	1996-97	1997-98
LeBrun, Al	NYR	2	6	0	2	2	4	....	....	....	....	....	....	1960-61	1965-66
Lecaine, Bill	Pit.	1	4	0	0	0	0	....	....	....	....	....	....	1968-69	1968-69
• Leclair, Jackie	Mtl.	3	160	20	40	60	56	20	6	1	7	6	1	1954-55	1956-57
LeClair, John	Mtl., Phi., Pit.	16	967	406	413	819	501	154	42	47	89	94	1	1990-91	2006-07
Leclerc, Mike	Ana., Phx., Cgy.	9	341	64	94	158	288	26	2	9	11	14	....	1996-97	2005-06
Leclerc, Rene	Det.	2	87	10	11	21	105	....	....	....	....	....	....	1968-69	1970-71
Lecuyer, Doug	Chi., Wpg., Pit.	4	126	11	31	42	178	7	4	0	4	15	....	1978-79	1982-83
‡ Ledin, Per	Col.	1	3	0	0	0	2	....	....	....	....	....	....	2008-09	2008-09
Ledingham, Walt	Chi., NYI	3	15	0	2	2	4	....	....	....	....	....	....	1972-73	1976-77
• Leduc, Albert	Mtl., Ott., NYR	10	383	57	35	92	614	28	5	6	11	32	2	1925-26	1934-35
LeDuc, Rich	Bos., Que.	4	130	28	38	66	69	5	0	0	0	9	....	1972-73	1980-81
Ledyard, Grant	NYR, L.A., Wsh., Buf., Dal., Van., Bos., Ott., T.B.	18	1028	90	276	366	766	83	6	12	18	96	....	1984-85	2001-02
• Lee, Bobby	Mtl.	1	1	0	0	0	0	....	....	....	....	....	....	1942-43	1942-43
Lee, Edward	Que.	1	2	0	0	0	5	....	....	....	....	....	....	1984-85	1984-85
Lee, Peter	Pit.	6	431	114	131	245	257	19	0	8	8	4	....	1977-78	1982-83
‡ Leeb, Brad	Van., Tor.	3	5	0	0	0	2	....	....	....	....	....	....	1999-00	2003-04
‡ Leeb, Greg	Dal.	1	2	0	0	0	0	....	....	....	....	....	....	2000-01	2000-01
Leeman, Gary	Tor., Cgy., Mtl., Van., St.L.	14	667	199	267	466	531	36	8	16	24	36	1	1982-83	1996-97
Leetch, Brian	NYR, Tor., Bos.	18	1205	247	781	1028	571	95	28	69	97	36	1	1987-88	2005-06
‡ Lefebvre, Guillaume	Phi., Pit., Bos.	4	39	2	4	6	13	....	....	....	....	....	....	2001-02	2009-10

			Regular Schedule					Playoffs					NHL	First	Last
Name	NHL Teams	NHL Seasons	GP	G	A	TP	PIM	GP	G	A	TP	PIM	Cup Wins	NHL Season	NHL Season
Lefebvre, Patrice	Wsh.	1	3	0	0	0	2	....	....	....	....	....	....	1998-99	1998-99
Lefebvre, Sylvain	Mtl., Tor., Que., Col., NYR	14	945	30	154	184	674	129	4	14	18	101	1	1989-90	2002-03
● Lefley, Bryan	NYI, K.C., Col.	5	228	7	29	36	101	2	0	0	0	0	....	1972-73	1977-78
Lefley, Chuck	Mtl., St.L.	9	407	128	164	292	137	29	5	8	13	10	2	1970-71	1980-81
● Leger, Roger	NYR, Mtl.	5	187	18	53	71	71	20	0	7	7	14	....	1943-44	1949-50
Legge, Barry	Que., Wpg.	3	107	1	11	12	144	....	....	....	....	....	....	1979-80	1981-82
Legge, Randy	NYR	1	12	0	2	2	2	....	....	....	....	....	....	1972-73	1972-73
Lehman, Tommy	Bos., Edm.	3	36	5	5	10	16	....	....	....	....	....	....	1987-88	1989-90
‡ Lehoux, Yanick	Phx.	2	10	2	2	4	6	....	....	....	....	....	....	2005-06	2006-07
Lehtinen, Jere	Dal.	14	875	243	271	514	210	108	27	22	49	12	1	1995-96	2009-10
Lehto, Petteri	Pit.	1	6	0	0	0	4	....	....	....	....	....	....	1984-85	1984-85
Lehtonen, Antero	Wsh.	1	65	9	12	21	14	....	....	....	....	....	....	1979-80	1979-80
‡ Lehtonen, Mikko	Nsh.	1	15	1	2	3	8	....	....	....	....	....	....	2006-07	2006-07
Lehvonen, Henry	K.C.	1	4	0	0	0	0	....	....	....	....	....	....	1974-75	1974-75
Leier, Edward	Chi.	2	16	2	1	3	2	....	....	....	....	....	....	1949-50	1950-51
Leinonen, Mikko	NYR, Wsh.	4	162	31	78	109	71	20	2	11	13	28	....	1981-82	1984-85
Leiter, Bobby	Bos., Pit., Atl.	10	447	98	126	224	144	8	3	0	3	2	....	1962-63	1975-76
Leiter, Ken	NYI, Min.	5	143	14	36	50	62	15	0	6	6	8	....	1984-85	1989-90
Lemaire, Jacques	Mtl.	12	853	366	469	835	217	145	61	78	139	63	8	1967-68	1978-79
Lemay, Moe	Van., Edm., Bos., Wpg.	8	317	72	94	166	442	28	6	3	9	55	1	1981-82	1988-89
Lemelin, Roger	K.C., Col.	4	36	1	2	3	27	....	....	....	....	....	....	1974-75	1977-78
Lemieux, Alain	St.L., Que., Pit.	6	119	28	44	72	38	19	4	6	10	0	....	1981-82	1986-87
Lemieux, Bob	Oak.	1	19	0	1	1	12	....	....	....	....	....	....	1967-68	1967-68
Lemieux, Claude	Mtl., N.J., Col., Phx., Dal., S.J.	21	1215	379	407	786	1777	234	80	78	158	529	4	1983-84	2008-09
Lemieux, Jacques	L.A.	3	19	0	4	4	8	1	0	0	0	0	....	1967-68	1969-70
Lemieux, Jean	Atl., Wsh.	5	204	23	63	86	39	3	1	1	2	0	....	1973-74	1977-78
Lemieux, Jocelyn	St.L., Mtl., Chi., Hfd., N.J., Cgy., Phx.	12	598	80	84	164	740	60	5	10	15	88	....	1986-87	1997-98
Lemieux, Mario	Pit.	18	915	690	1033	1723	834	107	76	96	172	87	2	1984-85	2005-06
● Lemieux, Real	Det., L.A., NYR, Buf.	8	456	51	104	155	262	18	2	4	6	10	....	1966-67	1973-74
Lemieux, Rich	Van., K.C., Atl.	5	274	39	82	121	132	2	0	0	0	0	....	1971-72	1975-76
Lenardon, Tim	N.J., Van.	2	15	2	1	3	4	....	....	....	....	....	....	1986-87	1989-90
● Lepine, Hec	Mtl.	1	33	5	2	7	2	....	....	....	....	....	....	1925-26	1925-26
● Lepine, Pit	Mtl.	13	526	143	98	241	392	41	7	5	12	26	2	1925-26	1937-38
Leroux, Francois	Edm., Ott., Pit., Col.	10	249	3	20	23	577	33	1	3	4	34	....	1988-89	1997-98
Leroux, Gaston	Mtl.	1	2	0	0	0	0	....	....	....	....	....	....	1935-36	1935-36
Leroux, Jean-Yves	Chi.	5	220	16	22	38	146	....	....	....	....	....	....	1996-97	2000-01
Leschyshyn, Curtis	Que., Col., Wsh., Hfd., Car., Min., Ott.	16	1033	47	165	212	669	68	2	6	8	34	1	1988-89	2003-04
● Lesieur, Art	Mtl., Chi.	4	100	4	2	6	50	14	0	0	0	4	1	1928-29	1935-36
‡ Lessard, Junior	Dal., T.B.	3	27	3	1	4	23	....	....	....	....	....	....	2005-06	2007-08
Lessard, Rick	Cgy., S.J.	3	15	0	4	4	18	....	....	....	....	....	....	1988-89	1991-92
Lesuk, Bill	Bos., Phi., L.A., Wsh., Wpg.	8	388	44	63	107	368	9	1	0	1	12	1	1968-69	1979-80
● Leswick, Jack	Chi.	1	37	1	7	8	16	....	....	....	....	....	1	1933-34	1933-34
● Leswick, Pete	NYA, Bos.	2	3	1	0	1	0	....	....	....	....	....	....	1936-37	1944-45
● Leswick, Tony	NYR, Det., Chi.	12	740	165	159	324	900	59	13	10	23	91	3	1945-46	1957-58
Letang, Alan	Dal., Cgy., NYI	3	14	0	0	0	2	....	....	....	....	....	....	1999-00	2002-03
Letowski, Trevor	Phx., Van., CBJ, Car.	9	616	84	117	201	209	17	1	3	4	12	....	1998-99	2007-08
● Levandoski, Joe	NYR	1	8	1	1	2	0	....	....	....	....	....	....	1946-47	1946-47
Leveille, Normand	Bos.	2	75	17	25	42	49	....	....	....	....	....	....	1981-82	1982-83
● Leveque, Guy	L.A.	2	17	2	2	4	21	....	....	....	....	....	....	1992-93	1993-94
Lever, Don	Van., Atl., Cgy., Col., N.J., Buf.	15	1020	313	367	680	593	30	7	10	17	26	....	1972-73	1986-87
Levie, Craig	Wpg., Min., St.L., Van.	6	183	22	53	75	177	16	2	3	5	32	....	1981-82	1986-87
Levins, Scott	Wpg., Fla., Ott., Phx.	5	124	13	20	33	316	....	....	....	....	....	....	1992-93	1997-98
● Levinsky, Alex	Tor., NYR, Chi.	9	367	19	49	68	307	37	2	1	3	26	2	1930-31	1938-39
Levo, Tapio	Col., N.J.	2	107	16	53	69	36	....	....	....	....	....	....	1981-82	1982-83
Lewicki, Danny	Tor., NYR, Chi.	9	461	105	135	240	177	28	0	4	4	8	1	1950-51	1958-59
Lewis, Dale	NYR	1	8	0	0	0	0	....	....	....	....	....	....	1975-76	1975-76
Lewis, Dave	NYI, L.A., N.J., Det.	15	1008	36	187	223	953	91	1	20	21	143	....	1973-74	1987-88
● Lewis, Doug	Mtl.	1	3	0	0	0	0	....	....	....	....	....	....	1946-47	1946-47
● Lewis, Herbie	Det.	11	483	148	161	309	248	38	13	10	23	6	2	1928-29	1938-39
Ley, Rick	Tor., Hfd.	6	310	12	72	84	528	14	0	2	2	20	....	1968-69	1980-81
Liba, Igor	NYR, L.A	1	37	7	18	25	36	2	0	0	0	2	....	1988-89	1988-89
Libby, Jeff	NYI	1	1	0	0	0	0	....	....	....	....	....	....	1997-98	1997-98
Libett, Nick	Det., Pit.	14	982	237	268	505	472	16	6	2	8	2	....	1967-68	1980-81
Licari, Tony	Det.	1	9	0	1	1	0	....	....	....	....	....	....	1946-47	1946-47
Liddington, Bob	Tor.	1	11	0	1	1	2	....	....	....	....	....	....	1970-71	1970-71
Lidster, Doug	Van., NYR, St.L., Dal.	16	897	75	268	343	679	80	6	15	21	64	1	1983-84	1998-99
Lilley, John	Ana.	3	23	3	8	11	13	....	....	....	....	....	....	1993-94	1995-96
Lind, Juha	Dal., Mtl.	3	133	9	13	22	20	15	2	2	4	8	....	1997-98	2000-01
Lindberg, Chris	Cgy., Que.	3	116	17	25	42	47	2	0	1	1	2	....	1991-92	1993-94
Lindbom, Johan	NYR	1	38	1	3	4	28	....	....	....	....	....	....	1997-98	1997-98
Linden, Jamie	Fla.	1	4	0	0	0	17	....	....	....	....	....	....	1994-95	1994-95
Linden, Trevor	Van., NYI, Mtl., Wsh.	19	1382	375	492	867	895	124	34	65	99	104	....	1988-89	2007-08
Lindgren, Lars	Van., Min.	6	394	25	113	138	325	40	5	6	11	20	....	1978-79	1983-84
Lindgren, Mats	Edm., NYI, Van.	8	387	54	74	128	146	24	1	5	6	10	....	1996-97	2003-04
Lindholm, Mikael	L.A.	1	18	2	2	4	2	....	....	....	....	....	....	1989-90	1989-90
Lindros, Brett	NYI	2	51	2	5	7	147	....	....	....	....	....	....	1994-95	1995-96
Lindros, Eric	Phi., NYR, Tor., Dal.	14	760	372	493	865	1398	53	24	33	57	122	....	1992-93	2006-07
Lindsay, Bill	Que., Fla., Cgy., S.J., Mtl., Atl.	13	777	83	141	224	922	42	7	8	15	44	....	1991-92	2003-04
Lindsay, Ted	Det., Chi.	17	1068	379	472	851	1808	133	47	49	96	194	4	1944-45	1964-65
Lindstrom, Willy	Wpg., Edm., Pit.	8	582	161	162	323	200	57	14	18	32	24	2	1979-80	1986-87
‡ Ling, David	Mtl., CBJ	5	93	4	4	8	191	....	....	....	....	....	....	1996-97	2003-04
Linseman, Ken	Phi., Edm., Bos., Tor.	14	860	256	551	807	1727	113	43	77	120	325	1	1978-79	1991-92
‡ Lintner, Richard	Nsh., NYR, Pit.	3	112	8	12	20	54	....	....	....	....	....	....	1999-00	2002-03
Lipuma, Chris	T.B., S.J.	5	72	0	9	9	146	....	....	....	....	....	....	1992-93	1996-97
● Liscombe, Carl	Det.	9	373	137	140	277	117	59	22	19	41	20	1	1937-38	1945-46
● Litzenberger, Ed	Mtl., Chi., Det., Tor.	12	618	178	238	416	283	40	5	13	18	34	4	1952-53	1963-64
Loach, Lonnie	Ott., L.A., Ana.	2	56	10	13	23	29	1	0	0	0	0	....	1992-93	1993-94
● Locas, Jacques	Mtl.	2	59	7	8	15	66	....	....	....	....	....	....	1947-48	1948-49
Lochead, Bill	Det., Col., NYR	6	330	69	62	131	180	7	3	0	3	6	....	1974-75	1979-80
● Locking, Norm	Chi.	2	48	2	6	8	26	....	....	....	....	....	....	1934-35	1935-36
Loewen, Darcy	Buf., Ott.	5	135	4	8	12	211	....	....	....	....	....	....	1989-90	1993-94
Lofthouse, Mark	Wsh., Det.	6	181	42	38	80	73	....	....	....	....	....	....	1977-78	1982-83
Logan, Dave	Chi., Van.	6	218	5	29	34	470	12	0	0	0	10	....	1975-76	1980-81
Logan, Robert	Buf., L.A.	3	42	10	5	15	0	....	....	....	....	....	....	1986-87	1988-89
Loiselle, Claude	Det., N.J., Que., Tor., NYI	13	616	92	117	209	1149	41	4	11	15	58	....	1981-82	1993-94
‡ Lojek, Martin	Fla.	2	5	0	1	1	0	....	....	....	....	....	....	2006-07	2007-08
● Lomakin, Andrei	Phi., Fla.	4	215	42	62	104	92	....	....	....	....	....	....	1991-92	1994-95
Loney, Brian	Van.	1	12	2	3	5	6	....	....	....	....	....	....	1995-96	1995-96
Loney, Troy	Pit., Ana., NYI, NYR	12	624	87	110	197	1091	67	8	14	22	97	2	1983-84	1994-95
Long, Barry	L.A., Det., Wpg.	5	280	11	68	79	250	5	0	1	1	18	....	1972-73	1981-82
● Long, Stan	Mtl.	1	....	....	....	....	....	3	0	0	0	0	....	1951-52	1951-52
Lonsberry, Ross	Bos., L.A., Phi., Pit.	15	968	256	310	566	806	100	21	25	46	87	2	1966-67	1980-81
Loob, Hakan	Cgy.	6	450	193	236	429	189	73	26	28	54	16	1	1983-84	1988-89
Loob, Peter	Que.	1	8	1	2	3	0	....	....	....	....	....	....	1984-85	1984-85
Lorentz, Jim	Bos., St.L., NYR, Buf.	10	659	161	238	399	208	54	12	10	22	30	1	1968-69	1977-78
Lorimer, Bob	NYI, Col., N.J.	10	529	22	90	112	431	49	3	10	13	83	2	1976-77	1985-86
● Lorrain, Rod	Mtl.	6	179	28	39	67	30	11	0	3	3	0	....	1935-36	1941-42
● Loughlin, Clem	Det., Chi.	3	101	8	6	14	77	....	....	....	....	....	....	1926-27	1928-29
● Loughlin, Wilf	Tor.	1	14	0	0	0	2	....	....	....	....	....	....	1923-24	1923-24
Lovsin, Ken	Wsh.	1	1	0	0	0	0	....	....	....	....	....	....	1990-91	1990-91
Low, Reed	St.L., Chi.	5	256	3	16	19	725	....	....	....	....	....	....	2000-01	2006-07
Lowdermilk, Dwayne	Wsh.	1	2	0	1	1	2	....	....	....	....	....	....	1980-81	1980-81
Lowe, Darren	Pit.	1	8	1	2	3	0	....	....	....	....	....	....	1983-84	1983-84
Lowe, Kevin	Edm., NYR	19	1254	84	347	431	1498	214	10	48	58	192	6	1979-80	1997-98
Lowe, Odie	NYR	1	4	1	1	2	0	....	....	....	....	....	....	1949-50	1949-50
● Lowe, Ross	Bos., Mtl.	3	77	6	8	14	82	2	0	0	0	0	....	1949-50	1951-52
● Lowrey, Ed	Ott., Ham.	3	27	2	2	4	6	....	....	....	....	....	....	1917-18	1920-21
● Lowrey, Fred	Mtl.M., Pit.	2	53	1	1	2	10	2	0	0	0	6	....	1924-25	1925-26
● Lowrey, Gerry	Tor., Pit., Phi., Chi., Ott.	6	211	48	48	96	148	2	1	0	1	2	....	1927-28	1932-33
Lowry, Dave	Van., St.L., Fla., S.J., Cgy.	19	1084	164	187	351	1191	111	16	20	36	181	....	1985-86	2003-04
‡ Loyns, Lynn	S.J., Cgy.	3	34	3	2	5	21	....	....	....	....	....	....	2002-03	2005-06
Lucas, Danny	Phi.	1	6	1	0	1	0	....	....	....	....	....	....	1978-79	1978-79
Lucas, Dave	Det.	1	1	0	0	0	0	....	....	....	....	....	....	1962-63	1962-63
Luce, Don	NYR, Det., Buf., L.A., Tor.	13	894	225	329	554	364	71	17	22	39	52	....	1969-70	1981-82
Ludvig, Jan	N.J., Buf.	7	314	54	87	141	418	....	....	....	....	....	....	1982-83	1988-89
Ludwig, Craig	Mtl., NYI, Min., Dal.	17	1256	38	184	222	1437	177	4	25	29	244	2	1982-83	1998-99

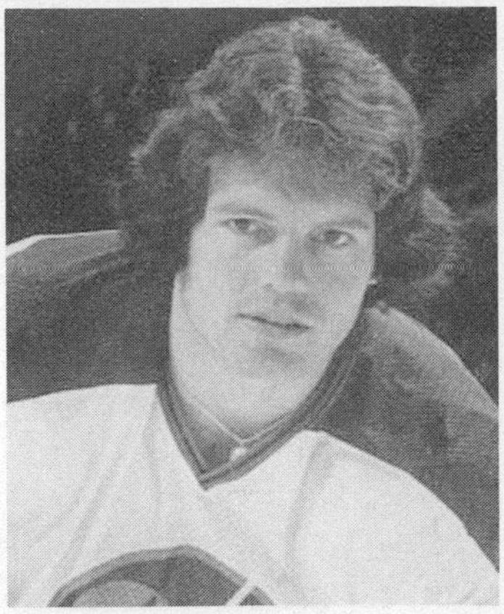

Barry Long

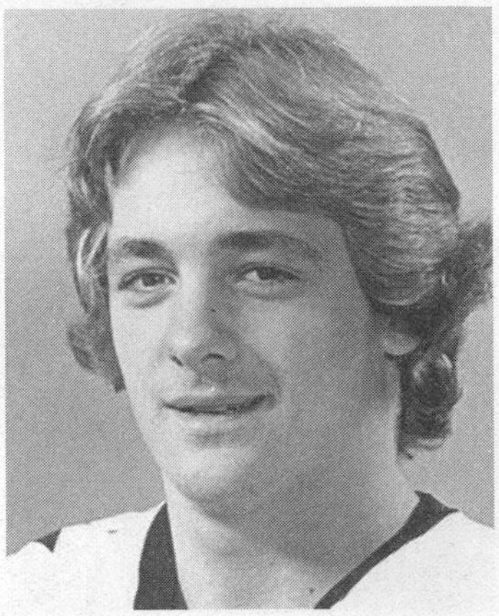

Steve Ludzik

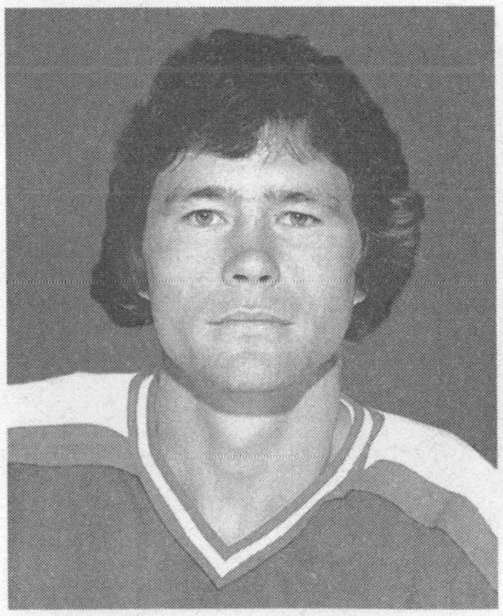

Morris Lukowich

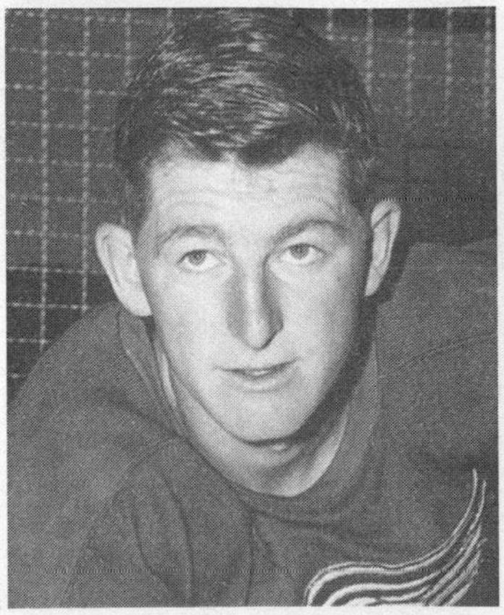

Len Lunde

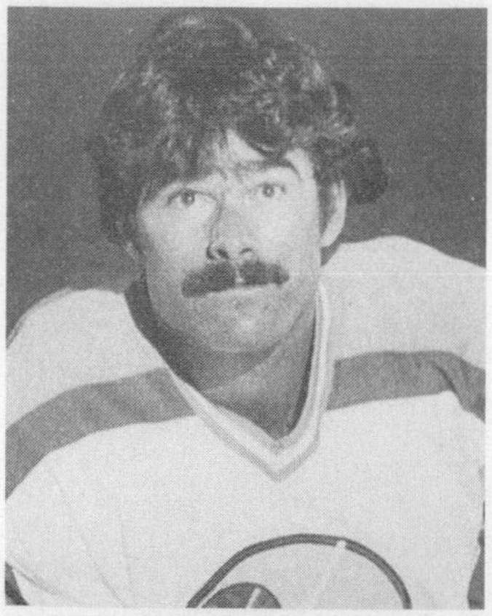

Paul MacLean

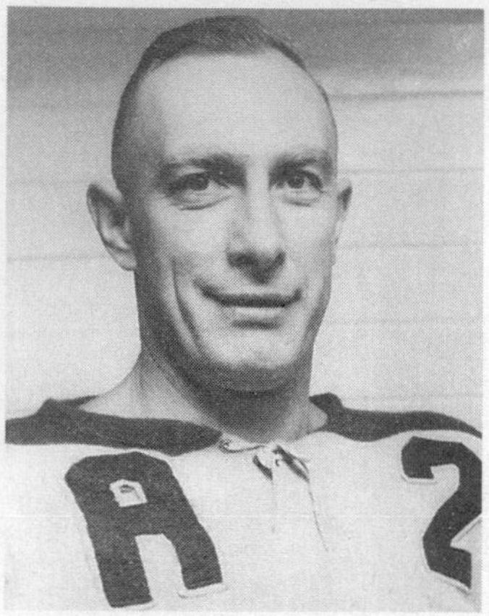

Bud MacPherson

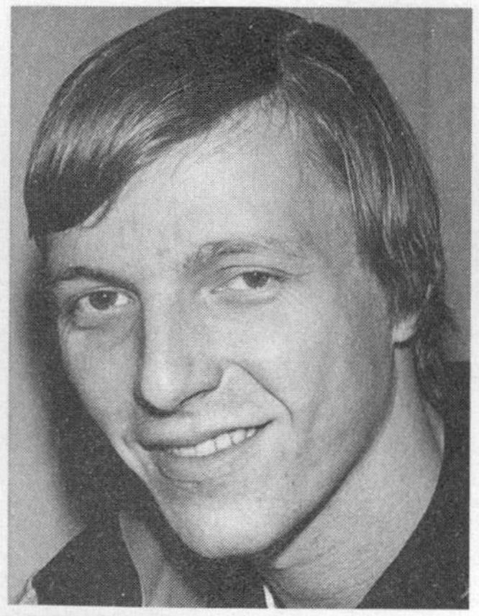

Kris Manery

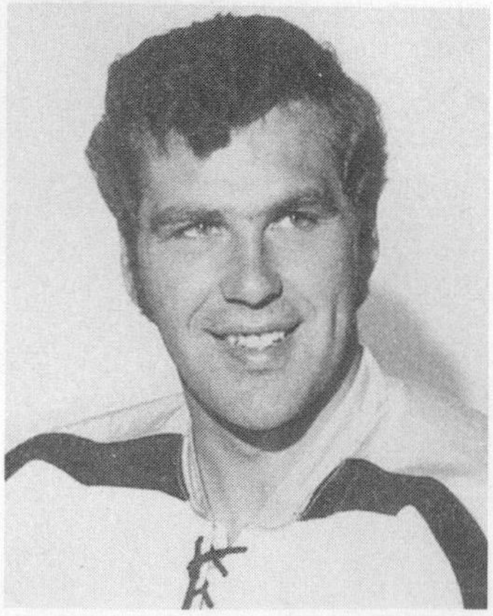

Don Marcotte

Name	NHL Teams	NHL Seasons	Regular Schedule GP	G	A	TP	PIM	Playoffs GP	G	A	TP	PIM	NHL Cup Wins	First NHL Season	Last NHL Season
Ludzik, Steve	Chi., Buf.	9	424	46	93	139	333	44	4	8	12	70	....	1981-82	1989-90
Luhning, Warren	NYI, Dal.	3	29	0	1	1	21	....	....	....	....	....	....	1997-98	1999-00
Lukowich, Bernie	Pit., St.L.	2	79	13	15	28	34	2	0	0	0	0	....	1973-74	1974-75
Lukowich, Morris	Wpg., Bos., L.A.	8	582	199	219	418	584	11	0	2	2	24	....	1979-80	1986-87
Luksa, Charlie	Hfd.	1	8	0	1	1	4	....	....	....	....	....	....	1979-80	1979-80
Lumley, Dave	Mtl., Edm., Hfd.	9	437	98	160	258	680	61	6	8	14	131	2	1978-79	1986-87
Lumme, Jyrki	Mtl., Van., Phx., Dal., Tor.	15	985	114	354	468	620	105	9	35	44	52	....	1988-89	2002-03
Lund, Pentti	Bos., NYR	7	259	44	55	99	40	19	7	5	12	0	....	1946-47	1952-53
Lundberg, Brian	Pit.	1	1	0	0	0	2	....	....	....	....	....	....	1982-83	1982-83
● Lunde, Len	Det., Chi., Min., Van.	8	321	39	83	122	75	20	3	2	5	2	....	1958-59	1970-71
Lundholm, Bengt	Wpg.	5	275	48	95	143	72	14	3	4	7	14	....	1981-82	1985-86
‡ Lundqvist, Joel	Dal.	3	134	7	19	26	56	25	4	5	9	14	....	2006-07	2008-09
Lundrigan, Joe	Tor., Wsh.	2	52	2	8	10	22	....	....	....	....	....	....	1972-73	1974-75
Lundstrom, Tord	Det.	1	11	1	1	2	0	....	....	....	....	....	....	1973-74	1973-74
● Lundy, Pat	Det., Chi.	5	150	37	32	69	31	16	2	2	4	2	....	1945-46	1950-51
‡ Luoma, Mikko	Edm.	1	3	0	1	1	0	....	....	....	....	....	....	2003-04	2003-04
Luongo, Chris	Det., Ott., NYI	5	218	8	23	31	176	....	....	....	....	....	....	1990-91	1995-96
‡ Lupaschuk, Ross	Pit.	1	3	0	0	0	4	....	....	....	....	....	....	2002-03	2002-03
Lupien, Gilles	Mtl., Pit., Hfd.	5	226	5	25	30	416	25	0	0	0	21	2	1977-78	1981-82
● Lupul, Gary	Van.	7	293	70	75	145	243	25	4	7	11	11	....	1979-80	1985-86
● Lyashenko, Roman	Dal., NYR	4	139	14	9	23	55	17	2	1	3	0	....	1999-00	2002-03
Lyle, George	Det., Hfd.	4	99	24	38	62	51	....	....	....	....	....	....	1979-80	1982-83
Lynch, Doug	Edm.	1	2	0	0	0	0	....	....	....	....	....	....	2003-04	2003-04
Lynch, Jack	Pit., Det., Wsh.	7	382	24	106	130	336	....	....	....	....	....	....	1972-73	1978-79
● Lynn, Vic	NYR, Det., Mtl., Tor., Bos., Chi.	11	327	49	76	125	274	47	7	10	17	46	3	1942-43	1953-54
Lyon, Steve	Pit.	1	3	0	0	0	2	....	....	....	....	....	....	1976-77	1976-77
● Lyons, Ron	Bos., Phi.	1	36	2	4	6	27	5	0	0	0	0	....	1930-31	1930-31
Lysak, Brett	Car.	1	2	0	0	0	2	....	....	....	....	....	....	2003-04	2003-04
Lysiak, Tom	Atl., Chi.	13	919	292	551	843	567	76	25	38	63	49	....	1973-74	1985-86

M

Name	NHL Teams	NHL Seasons	Regular Schedule GP	G	A	TP	PIM	Playoffs GP	G	A	TP	PIM	NHL Cup Wins	First NHL Season	Last NHL Season
MacAdam, Al	Phi., Cal., Cle., Min., Van.	12	864	240	351	591	509	64	20	24	44	21	....	1973-74	1984-85
MacDermid, Paul	Hfd., Wpg., Wsh., Que.	14	690	116	142	258	1303	43	5	11	16	116	....	1981-82	1994-95
MacDonald, Blair	Edm., Van.	4	219	91	100	191	65	11	0	6	6	2	....	1979-80	1982-83
MacDonald, Brett	Van.	1	1	0	0	0	0	....	....	....	....	....	....	1987-88	1987-88
‡ MacDonald, Craig	Car., Fla., Bos., Cgy., Chi., T.B., CBJ	8	233	11	24	35	91	7	0	0	0	2	....	1998-99	2008-09
MacDonald, Doug	Buf.	3	11	1	0	1	2	....	....	....	....	....	....	1992-93	1994-95
MacDonald, Jason	NYR	1	4	0	0	0	19	....	....	....	....	....	....	2003-04	2003-04
MacDonald, Kevin	Ott.	1	1	0	0	0	2	....	....	....	....	....	....	1993-94	1993-94
● MacDonald, Kilby	NYR	4	151	36	34	70	47	15	1	2	3	4	1	1939-40	1944-45
MacDonald, Lowell	Det., L.A., Pit.	13	506	180	210	390	92	30	11	11	22	12	....	1961-62	1977-78
MacDonald, Parker	Tor., NYR, Det., Bos., Min.	14	676	144	179	323	253	75	14	14	28	20	....	1952-53	1968-69
MacDougall, Kim	Min.	1	1	0	0	0	0	....	....	....	....	....	....	1974-75	1974-75
MacEachern, Shane	St.L.	1	1	0	0	0	0	....	....	....	....	....	....	1987-88	1987-88
● Macey, Hub	NYR, Mtl.	3	30	6	9	15	0	8	0	0	0	0	....	1941-42	1946-47
MacGregor, Bruce	Det., NYR	14	893	213	257	470	217	107	19	28	47	44	....	1960-61	1973-74
MacGregor, Randy	Hfd.	1	2	1	1	2	2	....	....	....	....	....	....	1981-82	1981-82
MacGuigan, Garth	NYI	2	5	0	1	1	2	....	....	....	....	....	....	1979-80	1983-84
MacInnis, Al	Cgy., St.L.	23	1416	340	934	1274	1511	177	39	121	160	255	1	1981-82	2003-04
MacIntosh, Ian	NYR	1	4	0	0	0	4	....	....	....	....	....	....	1952-53	1952-53
MacIver, Don	Wpg.	1	6	0	0	0	2	....	....	....	....	....	....	1979-80	1979-80
Maciver, Norm	NYR, Hfd., Edm., Ott., Pit., Wpg., Phx.	12	500	55	230	285	350	56	3	11	14	32	....	1986-87	1997-98
MacKasey, Blair	Tor.	1	1	0	0	0	2	....	....	....	....	....	....	1976-77	1976-77
● MacKay, Calum	Det., Mtl.	8	237	50	55	105	214	38	5	13	18	20	1	1946-47	1954-55
MacKay, Dave	Chi.	1	29	3	0	3	26	5	0	1	1	2	....	1940-41	1940-41
● MacKay, Mickey	Chi., Pit., Bos.	4	147	44	19	63	79	11	0	0	0	6	1	1926-27	1929-30
● MacKay, Murdo	Mtl.	4	19	0	3	3	0	15	1	2	3	0	....	1945-46	1948-49
MacKell, Fleming	Tor., Bos.	13	665	149	220	369	562	80	22	41	63	75	2	1947-48	1959-60
● MacKell, Jack	Ott.	2	45	4	2	6	59	2	0	0	0	0	2	1919-20	1920-21
‡ MacKenzie, Aaron	Col.	1	5	0	0	0	0	....	....	....	....	....	....	2008-09	2008-09
MacKenzie, Barry	Min.	1	6	0	1	1	6	....	....	....	....	....	....	1968-69	1968-69
● MacKenzie, Bill	Chi., Mtl.M., NYR, Mtl.	7	264	15	14	29	145	21	1	1	2	11	1	1932-33	1939-40
Mackey, David	Chi., Min., St.L.	6	126	8	12	20	305	3	0	0	0	2	....	1987-88	1993-94
● Mackey, Reg	NYR	1	34	0	0	0	16	1	0	0	0	0	....	1926-27	1926-27
● Mackie, Howie	Det.	2	20	1	0	1	4	8	0	0	0	0	1	1936-37	1937-38
MacKinnon, Paul	Wsh.	5	147	5	23	28	91	....	....	....	....	....	....	1979-80	1983-84
‡ MacLean, Don	L.A., Tor., CBJ, Det., Phx.	6	41	8	5	13	6	3	0	0	0	0	....	1997-98	2006-07
MacLean, John	N.J., S.J., NYR, Dal.	18	1194	413	429	842	1328	104	35	48	83	152	1	1983-84	2001-02
MacLean, Paul	St.L., Wpg., Det.	11	719	324	349	673	968	53	21	14	35	110	....	1980-81	1990-91
MacLeish, Rick	Phi., Hfd., Pit., Det.	14	846	349	410	759	434	114	54	53	107	38	2	1970-71	1983-84
MacLellan, Brian	L.A., NYR, Min., Cgy., Det.	10	606	172	241	413	551	47	5	9	14	42	1	1982-83	1991-92
MacLeod, Pat	Min., S.J., Dal.	4	53	5	13	18	14	....	....	....	....	....	....	1990-91	1995-96
MacMillan, Billy	Tor., Atl., NYI	7	446	74	77	151	184	53	6	6	12	40	....	1970-71	1976-77
MacMillan, Bob	NYR, St.L., Atl., Cgy., Col., N.J., Chi.	11	753	228	349	577	260	31	8	11	19	16	....	1974-75	1984-85
MacMillan, Jeff	Dal.	1	4	0	0	0	0	....	....	....	....	....	....	2003-04	2003-04
MacMillan, John	Tor., Det.	5	104	5	10	15	32	12	0	1	1	2	2	1960-61	1964-65
MacNeil, Al	Tor., Mtl., Chi., NYR, Pit.	11	524	17	75	92	617	37	0	4	4	67	....	1955-56	1967-68
MacNeil, Bernie	St.L.	1	4	0	0	0	0	....	....	....	....	....	....	1973-74	1973-74
MacNeil, Ian	Phi.	1	2	0	0	0	0	....	....	....	....	....	....	2002-03	2002-03
Macoun, Jamie	Cgy., Tor., Det.	16	1128	76	282	358	1208	159	10	32	42	169	2	1982-83	1998-99
● MacPherson, Bud	Mtl.	7	259	5	33	38	233	29	0	3	3	21	1	1948-49	1956-57
● MacSweyn, Ralph	Phi.	5	47	0	5	5	10	8	0	0	0	6	....	1967-68	1971-72
MacTavish, Craig	Bos., Edm., NYR, Phi., St.L.	17	1093	213	267	480	891	193	20	38	58	218	4	1979-80	1996-97
MacWilliam, Mike	NYI	1	6	0	0	0	14	....	....	....	....	....	....	1995-96	1995-96
Madigan, Connie	St.L.	1	20	0	3	3	25	5	0	0	0	4	....	1972-73	1972-73
Madill, Jeff	N.J.	1	14	4	0	4	46	7	0	2	2	8	....	1990-91	1990-91
Magee, Dean	Min.	1	7	0	0	0	4	....	....	....	....	....	....	1977-78	1977-78
Maggs, Darryl	Chi., Cal., Tor.	3	135	14	19	33	54	4	0	0	0	0	....	1971-72	1979-80
Magnan, Marc	Tor.	1	4	0	1	1	5	....	....	....	....	....	....	1982-83	1982-83
● Magnuson, Keith	Chi.	11	589	14	125	139	1442	68	3	9	12	164	....	1969-70	1979-80
Maguire, Kevin	Tor., Buf., Phi.	6	260	29	30	59	782	11	0	0	0	86	....	1986-87	1991-92
Mahaffy, John	Mtl., NYR	3	37	11	25	36	4	1	0	1	1	0	....	1942-43	1944-45
Mahovlich, Frank	Tor., Det., Mtl.	18	1181	533	570	1103	1056	137	51	67	118	163	6	1956-57	1973-74
Mahovlich, Pete	Det., Mtl., Pit.	16	884	288	485	773	916	88	30	42	72	134	4	1965-66	1980-81
Mailhot, Jacques	Que.	1	5	0	0	0	33	....	....	....	....	....	....	1988-89	1988-89
● Mailley, Frank	Mtl.	1	1	0	0	0	0	....	....	....	....	....	....	1942-43	1942-43
Mair, Jim	Phi., NYI, Van.	5	76	4	15	19	49	3	1	2	3	4	....	1970-71	1974-75
● Majeau, Fern	Mtl.	2	56	22	24	46	43	1	0	0	0	0	1	1943-44	1944-45
‡ Majesky, Ivan	Fla., Atl., Wsh.	3	202	8	23	31	234	....	....	....	....	....	....	2002-03	2005-06
Major, Bruce	Que.	1	4	0	0	0	0	....	....	....	....	....	....	1990-91	1990-91
Major, Mark	Det.	1	2	0	0	0	5	....	....	....	....	....	....	1996-97	1996-97
Makarov, Sergei	Cgy., S.J., Dal.	7	424	134	250	384	317	34	12	11	23	8	....	1989-90	1996-97
Makela, Mikko	NYI, L.A., Buf., Bos.	7	423	118	147	265	139	18	3	8	11	14	....	1985-86	1994-95
Maki, Chico	Chi.	15	841	143	292	435	345	113	17	36	53	43	1	1960-61	1975-76
‡ Maki, Tomi	Cgy.	1	1	0	0	0	0	....	....	....	....	....	....	2006-07	2006-07
● Maki, Wayne	Chi., St.L., Van.	6	246	57	79	136	184	2	1	0	1	2	....	1967-68	1972-73
Makkonen, Kari	Edm.	1	9	2	2	4	0	....	....	....	....	....	....	1979-80	1979-80
Malakhov, Vladimir	NYI, Mtl., N.J., NYR, Phi.	13	712	86	260	346	697	75	8	19	27	64	1	1992-93	2005-06
‡ Malec, Tomas	Car., Ott.	4	46	0	2	2	47	....	....	....	....	....	....	2002-03	2006-07
Maley, David	Mtl., N.J., Edm., S.J., NYI	9	466	43	81	124	1043	46	5	5	10	111	1	1985-86	1993-94
Malgunas, Stewart	Phi., Wpg., Wsh., Cgy.	7	129	1	5	6	144	....	....	....	....	....	....	1993-94	1999-00
‡ Malik, Marek	Hfd., Car., Van., NYR, T.B.	13	691	33	135	168	620	65	2	8	10	64	....	1994-95	2008-09
Malinowski, Merlin	Col., N.J., Hfd.	5	282	54	111	165	121	....	....	....	....	....	....	1978-79	1982-83
Malkoc, Dean	Van., Bos., NYI	4	116	1	3	4	299	....	....	....	....	....	....	1995-96	1998-99
Mallette, Troy	NYR, Edm., N.J., Ott., Bos., T.B.	9	456	51	68	119	1226	15	2	2	4	99	....	1989-90	1997-98
‡ Malmivaara, Olli	N.J.	1	2	0	0	0	0	....	....	....	....	....	....	2007-08	2007-08
● Malone, Cliff	Mtl.	1	3	0	0	0	0	....	....	....	....	....	....	1951-52	1951-52
Malone, Greg	Pit., Hfd., Que.	11	704	191	310	501	661	20	3	5	8	32	....	1976-77	1986-87
● Malone, Joe	Mtl., Que., Ham.	7	126	143	32	175	57	9	6	2	8	6	1	1917-18	1923-24
Maloney, Dan	Chi., L.A., Det., Tor.	11	737	192	259	451	1489	40	4	7	11	35	....	1970-71	1981-82
Maloney, Dave	NYR, Buf.	11	657	71	246	317	1154	49	7	17	24	91	....	1974-75	1984-85
Maloney, Don	NYR, Hfd., NYI	13	765	214	350	564	815	94	22	35	57	101	....	1978-79	1990-91
Maloney, Phil	Bos., Tor., Chi.	5	158	28	43	71	16	6	0	0	0	0	....	1949-50	1959-60
Maltais, Steve	Wsh., Min., T.B., Det., CBJ	6	120	9	18	27	53	1	0	0	0	0	....	1989-90	2000-01
Maltby, Kirk	Edm., Det.	16	1072	128	132	260	867	169	16	15	31	149	4	1993-94	2009-10

Name	NHL Teams	NHL Seasons	Regular Schedule GP	G	A	TP	PIM	Playoffs GP	G	A	TP	PIM	NHL Cup Wins	First NHL Season	Last NHL Season
Maluta, Ray	Bos.	2	25	2	3	5	6	2	0	0	0	0	....	1975-76	1976-77
Manastersky, Tom	Mtl.	1	6	0	0	0	11	....	....	....	....	....	....	1950-51	1950-51
● Mancuso, Gus	Mtl., NYR	4	42	7	9	16	17	....	....	....	....	....	....	1937-38	1942-43
Manderville, Kent	Tor., Edm., Hfd., Car., Phi., Pit.	12	646	37	67	104	348	67	3	3	6	44	....	1991-92	2002-03
Mandich, Dan	Min.	4	111	5	11	16	303	7	0	0	0	2	....	1982-83	1985-86
Maneluk, Mike	Phi., Chi., NYR, CBJ	3	85	11	10	21	57	....	....	....	....	....	....	1998-99	2000-01
Manery, Kris	Cle., Min., Van., Wpg.	4	250	63	64	127	91	....	....	....	....	....	....	1977-78	1980-81
Manery, Randy	Det., Atl., L.A.	10	582	50	206	256	415	13	0	2	2	12	....	1970-71	1979-80
Manlow, Eric	Bos., NYI	4	37	2	4	6	8	....	....	....	....	....	....	2000-01	2003-04
Mann, Cameron	Bos., Nsh.	5	93	14	10	24	40	1	0	0	0	0	....	1997-98	2002-03
Mann, Jack	NYR	2	9	3	4	7	0	....	....	....	....	....	....	1943 44	1944 45
Mann, Jimmy	Wpg., Que., Pit.	8	293	10	20	30	895	22	0	0	0	89	....	1979-80	1987-88
Mann, Ken	Det.	1	1	0	0	0	0	....	....	....	....	....	....	1975-76	1975-76
● Mann, Norm	Tor.	3	31	0	3	3	4	2	0	0	0	0	....	1935-36	1940-41
● Manners, Rennison	Pit., Phi.	2	37	3	2	5	14	....	....	....	....	....	....	1929-30	1930-31
‡ Manning, Paul	CBJ	1	8	0	0	0	2	....	....	....	....	....	....	2002-03	2002-03
Manno, Bob	Van., Tor., Det.	8	371	41	131	172	274	17	2	4	6	12	....	1976-77	1984-85
Manson, Dave	Chi., Edm., Wpg., Phx., Mtl., Dal., Tor.	16	1103	102	288	390	2792	112	7	24	31	343	....	1986-87	2001-02
● Manson, Ray	Bos., NYR	2	2	0	1	1	0	....	....	....	....	....	....	1947-48	1948-49
● Mantha, Georges	Mtl.	13	488	89	102	191	148	36	6	2	8	24	2	1928-29	1940-41
Mantha, Moe	Wpg., Pit., Edm., Min., Phi.	12	656	81	289	370	501	17	5	10	15	18	....	1980-81	1991-92
● Mantha, Sylvio	Mtl., Bos.	14	542	63	78	141	671	39	5	5	10	64	3	1923-24	1936-37
‡ Mapletoft, Justin	NYI	2	38	3	6	9	8	2	0	0	0	0	....	2002-03	2003-04
● Maracle, Bud	NYR	1	11	1	3	4	4	4	0	0	0	0	....	1930-31	1930-31
Marcetta, Milan	Tor., Min.	3	54	7	15	22	10	17	7	7	14	4	1	1966-67	1968-69
● March, Mush	Chi.	17	759	153	230	383	540	45	12	15	27	41	2	1928-29	1944-45
Marchinko, Brian	Tor., NYI	4	47	2	6	8	0	....	....	....	....	....	....	1970-71	1973-74
Marchment, Bryan	Wpg., Chi., Hfd., Edm., T.B., S.J., Col., Tor., Cgy.	17	926	40	142	182	2307	83	4	3	7	102	....	1988-89	2005-06
Marcinyshyn, Dave	N.J., Que., NYR	3	16	0	1	1	49	....	....	....	....	....	....	1990-91	1992-93
Marcon, Lou	Det.	3	60	0	4	4	42	....	....	....	....	....	....	1958-59	1962-63
Marcotte, Don	Bos.	15	868	230	254	484	317	132	34	27	61	81	2	1965-66	1981-82
‡ Marha, Josef	Col., Ana., Chi.	6	159	21	32	53	32	....	....	....	....	....	....	1995-96	2000-01
Marini, Hector	NYI, N.J.	5	154	27	46	73	246	10	3	6	9	14	2	1978-79	1983-84
Marinucci, Chris	NYI, L.A.	2	13	1	4	5	2	....	....	....	....	....	....	1994-95	1996-97
● Mario, Frank	Bos.	2	53	9	19	28	24	....	....	....	....	....	....	1941-42	1944-45
● Mariucci, John	Chi.	5	223	11	34	45	308	12	0	3	3	26	....	1940-41	1947-48
‡ Marjamaki, Masi	NYI	1	1	0	0	0	0	....	....	....	....	....	....	2005-06	2005-06
Mark, Gordon	N.J., Edm.	4	85	3	10	13	187	....	....	....	....	....	....	1986-87	1994-95
Markell, John	Wpg., St.L., Min.	4	55	11	10	21	36	....	....	....	....	....	....	1979-80	1984-85
● Marker, Gus	Det., Mtl.M., Tor., Bro.	10	322	64	69	133	133	46	5	7	12	36	1	1932-33	1941-42
Markham, Ray	NYR	1	14	1	1	2	21	7	1	0	1	24	....	1979-80	1979-80
● Markle, Jack	Tor.	1	8	0	1	1	0	....	....	....	....	....	....	1935-36	1935-36
Markov, Danny	Tor., Phx., Car., Phi., Nsh., Det.	9	538	29	118	147	456	81	2	12	14	84	....	1997-98	2006-07
● Marks, Jack	Mtl.W., Tor., Que.	2	7	0	0	0	4	....	....	....	....	....	1	1917-18	1919-20
Marks, John	Chi.	10	657	112	163	275	330	57	5	9	14	60	....	1972-73	1981-82
Markwart, Nevin	Bos., Cgy.	8	309	41	68	109	794	19	1	0	1	33	....	1983-84	1991-92
Marois, Daniel	Tor., NYI, Bos., Dal.	8	350	117	93	210	419	19	3	3	6	28	....	1987-88	1995-96
Marois, Mario	NYR, Van., Que., Wpg., St.L.	15	955	76	357	433	1746	100	4	34	38	182	....	1977-78	1991-92
● Marotte, Gilles	Bos., Chi., L.A., NYR, St.L.	12	808	56	265	321	919	29	3	3	6	26	....	1965-66	1976-77
Marquess, Mark	Bos.	1	27	5	4	9	6	4	0	0	0	0	....	1946-47	1946-47
Marsh, Brad	Atl., Cgy., Phi., Tor., Det., Ott.	15	1086	23	175	198	1241	97	6	18	24	124	....	1978-79	1992-93
Marsh, Gary	Det., Tor.	2	7	1	3	4	4	....	....	....	....	....	....	1967-68	1968-69
Marsh, Peter	Wpg., Chi.	5	278	48	71	119	224	26	1	5	6	33	....	1979-80	1983-84
Marshall, Bert	Det., Oak., Cal., NYR, NYI	14	868	17	181	198	926	72	4	22	26	99	....	1965-66	1978-79
Marshall, Don	Mtl., NYR, Buf., Tor.	19	1176	265	324	589	127	94	8	15	23	14	5	1951-52	1971-72
Marshall, Grant	Dal., CBJ, N.J.	11	700	92	147	239	793	90	6	11	17	95	2	1994-95	2005-06
Marshall, Jason	St.L., Ana., Wsh., Min., S.J.	12	526	16	51	67	1004	43	2	3	5	55	....	1991-92	2005-06
Marshall, Paul	Pit., Tor., Hfd.	4	95	15	18	33	17	1	0	0	0	0	....	1979-80	1982-83
Marshall, Willie	Tor.	4	33	1	5	6	2	....	....	....	....	....	....	1952-53	1958-59
Marson, Mike	Wsh., L.A.	6	196	24	24	48	233	....	....	....	....	....	....	1974-75	1979-80
‡ Martensson, Tony	Ana.	1	6	1	1	2	0	....	....	....	....	....	....	2003-04	2003-04
● Martin, Clare	Bos., Det., Chi., NYR	6	237	12	28	40	78	27	0	2	2	6	1	1941-42	1951-52
Martin, Craig	Wpg., Fla.	2	21	0	1	1	24	....	....	....	....	....	....	1994-95	1996-97
● Martin, Frank	Bos., Chi.	6	282	11	46	57	122	10	0	2	2	2	....	1952-53	1957-58
Martin, Grant	Van., Wsh.	4	44	0	4	4	55	1	1	0	1	2	....	1983-84	1986-87
Martin, Jack	Tor.	1	1	0	0	0	0	....	....	....	....	....	....	1960-61	1960-61
Martin, Matt	Tor.	4	76	0	5	5	71	....	....	....	....	....	....	1993-94	1996-97
● Martin, Pit	Det., Bos., Chi., Van.	17	1101	324	485	809	609	100	27	31	58	56	....	1961-62	1978-79
● Martin, Rick	Buf., L.A.	11	685	384	317	701	477	63	24	29	53	74	....	1971-72	1981-82
● Martin, Ron	NYA	2	94	13	16	29	36	....	....	....	....	....	....	1932-33	1933-34
Martin, Terry	Buf., Que., Tor., Edm., Min.	10	479	104	101	205	202	21	4	2	6	26	....	1975-76	1984-85
Martin, Tom	Tor.	1	3	1	0	1	0	....	....	....	....	....	....	1967-68	1967-68
Martin, Tom	Wpg., Hfd., Min.	6	92	12	11	23	249	4	0	0	0	6	....	1984-85	1989-90
● Martineau, Don	Atl., Min., Det.	4	90	6	10	16	63	....	....	....	....	....	....	1973-74	1976-77
Martini, Darcy	Edm.	1	2	0	0	0	0	....	....	....	....	....	....	1993-94	1993-94
Martins, Steve	Hfd., Car., Ott., T.B., NYI, St.L.	10	267	21	25	46	142	5	0	1	1	0	....	1995-96	2005-06
Martinson, Steve	Det., Mtl., Min.	4	49	2	1	3	244	1	0	0	0	10	....	1987-88	1991-92
Maruk, Dennis	Cal., Cle., Min., Wsh.	14	888	356	522	878	761	34	14	22	36	26	....	1975-76	1988-89
Masnick, Paul	Mtl., Chi., Tor.	6	232	18	41	59	139	33	4	5	9	27	1	1950-51	1957-58
● Mason, Charley	NYR, NYA, Det., Chi.	4	95	7	18	25	44	4	0	1	1	0	....	1934-35	1938-39
● Massecar, George	NYA	3	100	12	11	23	46	....	....	....	....	....	....	1929-30	1931-32
Masters, Jamie	St.L.	3	33	1	13	14	2	2	0	0	0	0	....	1975-76	1978-79
● Masterton, Bill	Min.	1	38	4	8	12	4	....	....	....	....	....	....	1967-68	1967-68
● Mathers, Frank	Tor.	3	23	1	3	4	4	....	....	....	....	....	....	1948-49	1951-52
Mathiasen, Dwight	Pit.	3	33	1	7	8	18	....	....	....	....	....	....	1985-86	1987-88
Mathieson, Jim	Wsh.	1	2	0	0	0	4	....	....	....	....	....	....	1989-90	1989-90
Mathieu, Marquis	Bos.	3	16	0	2	2	14	....	....	....	....	....	....	1998-99	2000-01
Matte, Christian	Col., Min.	5	25	2	3	5	12	....	....	....	....	....	....	1996-97	2000-01
● Matte, Joe	Tor., Ham., Bos., Mtl.	4	68	17	15	32	54	....	....	....	....	....	....	1919-20	1925-26
● Matte, Joe	Det., Chi.	2	24	0	3	3	8	....	....	....	....	....	....	1929-30	1942-43
Matteau, Stephane	Cgy., Chi., NYR, St.L., S.J., Fla.	13	848	144	172	316	742	109	12	22	34	80	1	1990-91	2002-03
Matteucci, Mike	Min.	2	6	0	0	0	4	....	....	....	....	....	....	2000-01	2001-02
Mattiussi, Dick	Pit., Oak., Cal.	4	200	8	31	39	124	8	0	1	1	6	....	1967-68	1970-71
Matvichuk, Richard	Min., Dal., N.J.	14	796	39	139	178	624	123	5	19	24	128	1	1992-93	2006-07
● Matz, Johnny	Mtl.	1	30	2	3	5	0	1	0	0	0	0	....	1924-25	1924-25
Maxner, Wayne	Bos.	2	62	8	9	17	48	....	....	....	....	....	....	1964-65	1965-66
Maxwell, Brad	Min., Que., Tor., Van., NYR	10	612	98	270	368	1292	79	12	49	61	178	....	1977-78	1986-87
Maxwell, Bryan	Min., St.L., Wpg., Pit.	8	331	18	77	95	745	15	1	1	2	86	....	1977-78	1984-85
Maxwell, Kevin	Min., Col., N.J.	3	66	6	15	21	61	16	3	4	7	24	....	1980-81	1983-84
Maxwell, Wally	Tor.	1	2	0	0	0	0	....	....	....	....	....	....	1952-53	1952-53
May, Alan	Bos., Edm., Wsh., Dal., Cgy.	8	393	31	45	76	1348	40	1	2	3	80	....	1987-88	1994-95
May, Brad	Buf., Van., Phx., Col., Ana., Tor., Det.	18	1041	127	161	288	2248	88	4	9	13	112	1	1991-92	2009-10
Mayer, Derek	Ott.	1	17	2	2	4	8	....	....	....	....	....	....	1993-94	1993-94
Mayer, Jim	NYR	1	4	0	0	0	0	....	....	....	....	....	....	1979-80	1979-80
Mayer, Pat	Pit.	1	1	0	0	0	4	....	....	....	....	....	....	1987-88	1987-88
● Mayer, Shep	Tor.	1	12	1	2	3	4	....	....	....	....	....	....	1942-43	1942-43
● Mazur, Eddie	Mtl., Chi.	6	107	8	20	28	120	25	4	5	9	22	1	1950-51	1956-57
Mazur, Jay	Van.	4	47	11	7	18	20	6	0	1	1	8	....	1988-89	1991-92
McAdam, Gary	Buf., Pit., Det., Cgy., Wsh., N.J., Tor.	11	534	96	132	228	243	30	6	5	11	16	....	1975-76	1985-86
● McAdam, Sam	NYR	1	5	0	0	0	0	....	....	....	....	....	....	1930-31	1930-31
McAllister, Chris	Van., Tor., Phi., Col., NYR	7	301	4	17	21	634	9	0	1	1	4	....	1997-98	2003-04
McAlpine, Chris	N.J., St.L., T.B., Atl., Chi., L.A.	8	289	6	24	30	245	28	0	1	1	18	1	1994-95	2002-03
McAmmond, Dean	Chi., Edm., Phi., Cgy., Col., St.L., Ott., NYI, N.J.	17	996	186	262	448	490	46	6	7	13	35	....	1991-92	2009-10
● McAndrew, Hazen	Bro.	1	7	0	1	1	6	....	....	....	....	....	....	1941-42	1941-42
McAneeley, Ted	Cal.	3	158	8	35	43	141	....	....	....	....	....	....	1972-73	1974-75
● McAtee, Jud	Det.	3	46	15	13	28	6	14	2	1	3	0	....	1942-43	1944-45
● McAtee, Norm	Bos.	1	13	0	1	1	0	....	....	....	....	....	....	1946-47	1946-47
● McAvoy, George	Mtl.	1	....	....	....	....	....	4	0	0	0	0	....	1954-55	1954-55
McBain, Andrew	Wpg., Pit., Van., Ott.	11	608	129	172	301	633	24	5	7	12	39	....	1983-84	1993-94
McBain, Jason	Hfd.	2	9	0	0	0	0	....	....	....	....	....	....	1995-96	1996-97
McBain, Mike	T.B.	2	64	0	7	7	22	....	....	....	....	....	....	1997-98	1998-99
McBean, Wayne	L.A., NYI, Wpg.	6	211	10	39	49	168	2	1	1	2	0	....	1987-88	1993-94
● McBride, Cliff	Mtl.M., Tor.	2	2	0	0	0	0	....	....	....	....	....	....	1928-29	1929-30
McBurney, Jim	Chi.	1	1	0	1	1	0	....	....	....	....	....	....	1952-53	1952-53

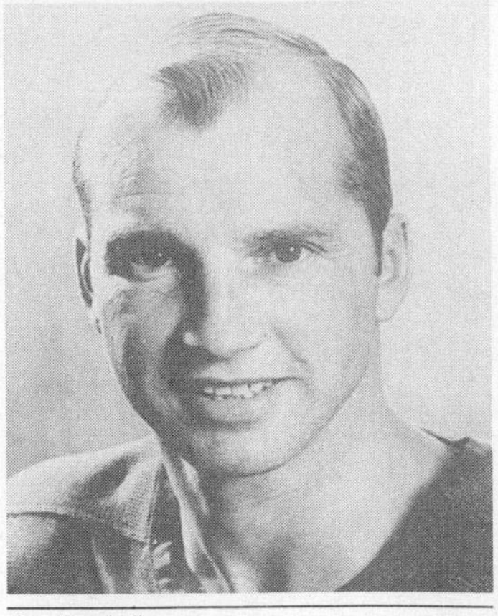

Don Marshall

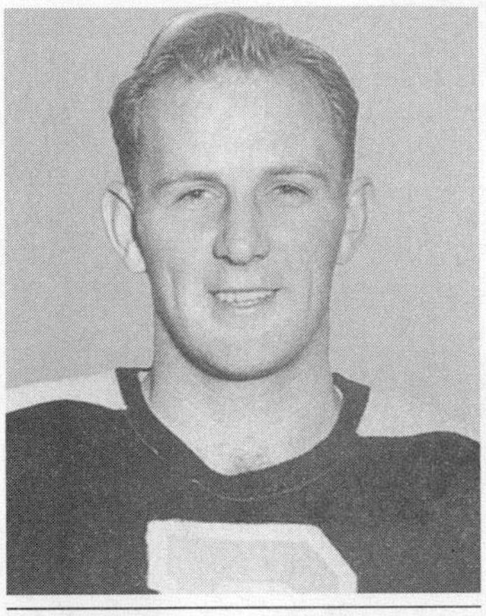

Frank Martin

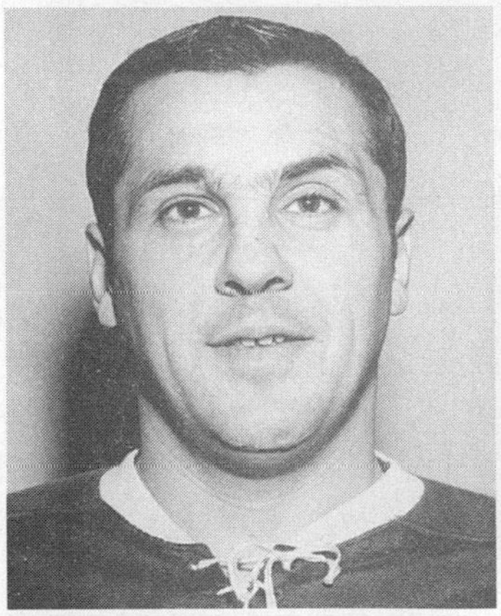

Dick Mattiussi

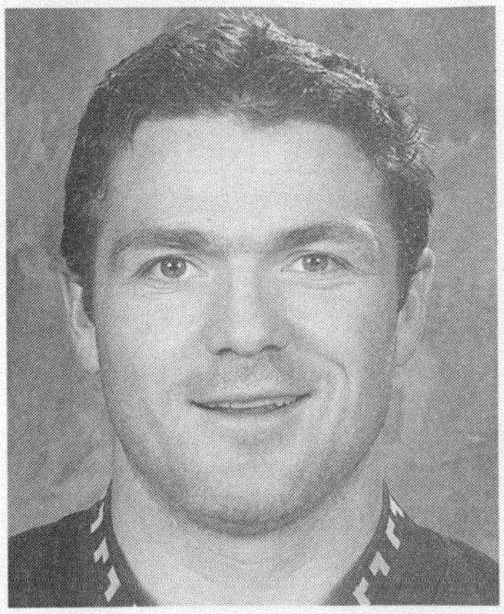

Brad May

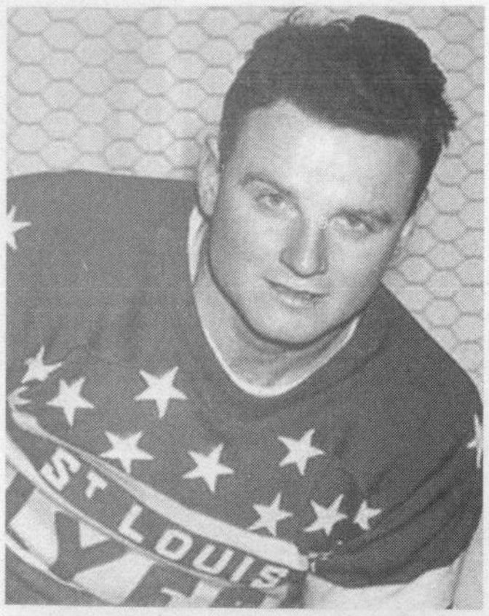

Norm McAtee

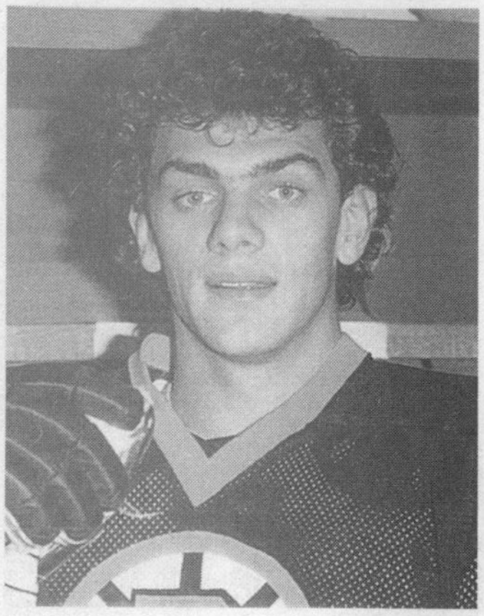

Tom McCarthy

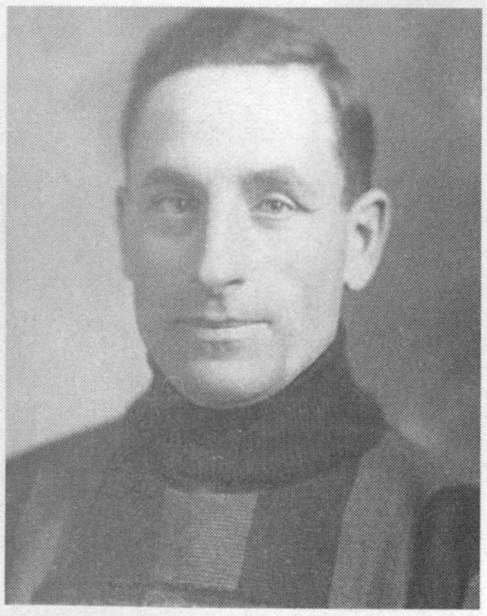

Moylan McDonnell

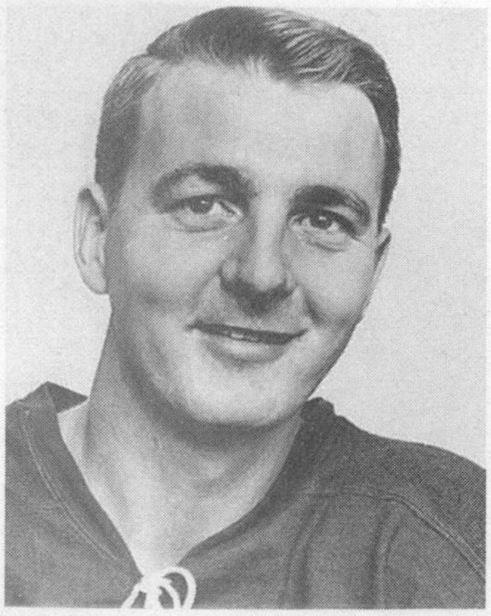

Don McKenney

			Regular Schedule					Playoffs							
Name	NHL Teams	NHL Seasons	GP	G	A	TP	PIM	GP	G	A	TP	PIM	NHL Cup Wins	First NHL Season	Last NHL Season
• McCabe, Stan	Det., Mtl.M.	4	78	9	4	13	49	....	....	....	....	....	....	1929-30	1933-34
• McCaffrey, Bert	Tor., Pit., Mtl.	7	260	43	30	73	202	8	2	1	3	10	1	1924-25	1930-31
McCahill, John	Col.	1	1	0	0	0	0	....	....	....	....	....	....	1977-78	1977-78
• McCaig, Doug	Det., Chi.	7	263	8	21	29	255	7	0	1	1	10	....	1941-42	1950-51
• McCallum, Dunc	NYR, Pit.	5	187	14	35	49	230	10	1	2	3	12	....	1965-66	1970-71
• McCalmon, Eddie	Chi., Phi.	2	39	5	0	5	14	....	....	....	....	....	....	1927-28	1930-31
McCann, Rick	Det.	6	43	1	4	5	6	....	....	....	....	....	....	1967-68	1974-75
McCarthy, Dan	NYR	1	5	4	0	4	4	....	....	....	....	....	....	1980-81	1980-81
McCarthy, Kevin	Phi., Van., Pit.	10	537	67	191	258	527	21	2	3	5	20	....	1977-78	1986-87
McCarthy, Sandy	Cgy., T.B., Phi., Car., NYR, Bos.	11	736	72	76	148	1534	23	0	2	2	61	....	1993-94	2003-04
‡ McCarthy, Steve	Chi., Van., Atl.	8	302	17	38	55	168	....	....	....	....	....	....	1999-00	2007-08
• McCarthy, Thomas	Que., Ham.	2	35	22	7	29	10	....	....	....	....	....	....	1919-20	1920-21
McCarthy, Tom	Det., Bos.	4	60	8	9	17	8	....	....	....	....	....	....	1956-57	1960-61
McCarthy, Tom	Min., Bos.	9	460	178	221	399	330	68	12	26	38	67	....	1979-80	1987-88
• McCartney, Walt	Mtl.	1	2	0	0	0	0	....	....	....	....	....	....	1932-33	1932-33
McCarty, Darren	Det., Cgy.	15	758	127	161	288	1477	174	23	26	49	228	4	1993-94	2008-09
McCaskill, Ted	Min.	1	4	0	2	2	0	....	....	....	....	....	....	1967-68	1967-68
McCauley, Alyn	Tor., S.J., L.A.	9	488	69	97	166	116	52	7	12	19	18	....	1997-98	2006-07
McClanahan, Rob	Buf., Hfd., NYR	5	224	38	63	101	126	34	4	12	16	31	....	1979-80	1983-84
McCleary, Trent	Ott., Bos., Mtl.	4	192	8	15	23	134	....	....	....	....	....	....	1995-96	1999-00
McClelland, Kevin	Pit., Edm., Det., Tor., Wpg.	12	588	68	112	180	1672	98	11	18	29	281	4	1981-82	1993-94
McCord, Bob	Bos., Det., Min., St.L.	7	316	10	58	68	262	14	2	5	7	10	....	1963-64	1972-73
• McCord, Dennis	Van.	1	3	0	0	0	6	....	....	....	....	....	....	1973-74	1973-74
McCormack, John	Tor., Mtl., Chi.	8	311	25	49	74	35	22	1	1	2	0	2	1947-48	1954-55
McCosh, Shawn	L.A., NYR	2	9	1	0	1	6	....	....	....	....	....	....	1991-92	1994-95
McCourt, Dale	Det., Buf., Tor.	7	532	194	284	478	124	21	9	7	16	6	....	1977-78	1983-84
McCreary, Bill	NYR, Det., Mtl., St.L.	8	309	53	62	115	108	48	6	16	22	14	....	1953-54	1970-71
McCreary, Bill	Tor.	1	12	1	0	1	4	....	....	....	....	....	....	1980-81	1980-81
• McCreary, Keith	Mtl., Pit., Atl.	10	532	131	112	243	294	16	0	4	4	6	....	1961-62	1974-75
• McCreedy, John	Tor.	2	64	17	12	29	25	21	4	3	7	16	2	1941-42	1944-45
McCrimmon, Brad	Bos., Phi., Cgy., Det., Hfd., Phx.	18	1222	81	322	403	1416	116	11	18	29	176	1	1979-80	1996-97
McCrimmon, Jim	St.L.	1	2	0	0	0	0	....	....	....	....	....	....	1974-75	1974-75
• McCulley, Bob	Mtl.	1	1	0	0	0	0	....	....	....	....	....	....	1934-35	1934-35
• McCurry, Duke	Pit.	4	148	21	11	32	119	4	0	2	2	2	....	1925-26	1928-29
McCutcheon, Brian	Det.	3	37	3	1	4	7	....	....	....	....	....	....	1974-75	1976-77
McCutcheon, Darwin	Tor.	1	1	0	0	0	2	....	....	....	....	....	....	1981-82	1981-82
McDill, Jeff	Chi.	1	1	0	0	0	0	....	....	....	....	....	....	1976-77	1976-77
McDonagh, Bill	NYR	1	4	0	0	0	2	....	....	....	....	....	....	1949-50	1949-50
McDonald, Ab	Mtl., Chi., Bos., Det., Pit., St.L.	15	762	182	248	430	200	84	21	29	50	42	4	1957-58	1971-72
McDonald, Brian	Chi., Buf.	2	12	0	0	0	29	8	0	0	0	2	....	1967-68	1970-71
• McDonald, Bucko	Det., Tor., NYR	11	446	35	88	123	206	50	6	1	7	24	3	1934-35	1944-45
• McDonald, Butch	Det., Chi.	2	66	8	20	28	2	5	0	2	2	10	....	1939-40	1944-45
McDonald, Gerry	Hfd.	2	8	0	0	0	4	....	....	....	....	....	....	1981-82	1983-84
• McDonald, Jack	Mtl.W., Mtl., Que., Tor.	5	69	26	14	40	30	7	1	3	4	3	....	1917-18	1921-22
McDonald, Jack	NYR	1	43	10	9	19	6	....	....	....	....	....	....	1943-44	1943-44
McDonald, Lanny	Tor., Col., Cgy.	16	1111	500	506	1006	899	117	44	40	84	120	1	1973-74	1988-89
McDonald, Robert	NYR	1	1	0	0	0	0	....	....	....	....	....	....	1943-44	1943-44
McDonald, Terry	K.C.	1	8	0	1	1	6	....	....	....	....	....	....	1975-76	1975-76
‡ McDonell, Kent	CBJ	2	32	1	2	3	36	....	....	....	....	....	....	2002-03	2003-04
McDonnell, Joe	Van., Pit.	3	50	2	10	12	34	....	....	....	....	....	....	1981-82	1985-86
• McDonnell, Moylan	Ham.	1	22	1	2	3	2	....	....	....	....	....	....	1920-21	1920-21
McDonough, Al	L.A., Pit., Atl., Det.	5	237	73	88	161	73	8	0	1	1	2	....	1970-71	1977-78
McDonough, Hubie	L.A., NYI, S.J.	5	195	40	26	66	67	5	1	0	1	4	....	1988-89	1992-93
McDougal, Mike	NYR, Hfd.	4	61	8	10	18	43	....	....	....	....	....	....	1978-79	1982-83
McDougall, Bill	Det., Edm., T.B.	3	28	5	5	10	12	1	0	0	0	0	....	1990-91	1993-94
McEachern, Shawn	Pit., L.A., Bos., Ott., Atl.	14	911	256	323	579	506	97	12	25	37	62	1	1991-92	2005-06
McElmury, Jim	Min., K.C., Col.	5	180	14	47	61	49	....	....	....	....	....	....	1972-73	1977-78
McEwen, Mike	NYR, Col., NYI, L.A., Wsh., Det., Hfd.	12	716	108	296	404	460	78	12	36	48	48	3	1976-77	1987-88
• McFadden, Jim	Det., Chi.	8	412	100	126	226	89	49	10	9	19	30	1	1946-47	1953-54
• McFadyen, Don	Chi.	4	179	12	33	45	77	11	2	2	4	5	1	1932-33	1935-36
McFall, Dan	Wpg.	2	9	0	1	1	0	....	....	....	....	....	....	1984-85	1985-86
• McFarlane, Gord	Chi.	1	2	0	0	0	0	....	....	....	....	....	....	1926-27	1926-27
McGeough, Jim	Wsh., Pit.	4	57	7	10	17	32	....	....	....	....	....	....	1981-82	1986-87
• McGibbon, Irv	Mtl.	1	1	0	0	0	2	....	....	....	....	....	....	1942-43	1942-43
McGill, Bob	Tor., Chi., S.J., Det., NYI, Hfd.	13	705	17	55	72	1766	49	0	0	0	88	....	1981-82	1993-94
• McGill, Jack	Mtl.	3	134	27	10	37	71	3	2	0	2	0	....	1934-35	1936-37
• McGill, Jack	Bos.	4	97	23	36	59	42	27	7	4	11	17	....	1941-42	1946-47
McGill, Ryan	Chi., Phi., Edm.	4	151	4	15	19	391	....	....	....	....	....	....	1991-92	1994-95
McGillis, Dan	Edm., Phi., S.J., Bos., N.J.	9	634	56	182	238	570	64	8	14	22	76	....	1996-97	2005-06
McGregor, Sandy	NYR	1	2	0	0	0	2	....	....	....	....	....	....	1963-64	1963-64
• McGuire, Mickey	Pit.	2	36	3	0	3	6	....	....	....	....	....	....	1926-27	1927-28
McHugh, Mike	Min., S.J.	4	20	1	0	1	16	....	....	....	....	....	....	1988-89	1991-92
McIlhargey, Jack	Phi., Van., Hfd.	8	393	11	36	47	1102	27	0	3	3	68	....	1974-75	1981-82
• McInenly, Bert	Det., NYA, Ott., Bos.	6	166	19	15	34	144	4	0	0	0	2	....	1930-31	1935-36
McInnis, Marty	NYI, Cgy., Ana., Bos.	12	796	170	250	420	330	22	3	2	5	4	....	1991-92	2002-03
McIntosh, Bruce	Min.	1	2	0	0	0	0	....	....	....	....	....	....	1972-73	1972-73
McIntosh, Paul	Buf.	2	48	0	2	2	66	2	0	0	0	7	....	1974-75	1975-76
• McIntyre, Jack	Bos., Chi., Det.	11	499	109	102	211	173	29	7	6	13	4	....	1949-50	1959-60
McIntyre, John	Tor., L.A., NYR, Van.	6	351	24	54	78	516	44	0	6	6	54	....	1989-90	1994-95
McIntyre, Larry	Tor.	2	41	0	3	3	26	....	....	....	....	....	....	1969-70	1972-73
McKay, Doug	Det.	1	....	....	....	....	....	1	0	0	0	0	1	1949-50	1949-50
McKay, Randy	Det., N.J., Dal., Mtl.	15	932	162	201	363	1731	123	20	23	43	123	2	1988-89	2002-03
McKay, Ray	Chi., Buf., Cal.	6	140	2	16	18	102	1	0	0	0	0	....	1968-69	1973-74
McKay, Scott	Ana.	1	1	0	0	0	0	....	....	....	....	....	....	1993-94	1993-94
McKechnie, Walt	Min., Cal., Bos., Det., Wsh., Cle., Tor., Col.	16	955	214	392	606	469	15	7	5	12	7	....	1967-68	1982-83
McKee, Jay	Buf., St.L., Pit.	14	802	21	104	125	622	60	3	6	9	66	....	1995-96	2009-10
McKee, Mike	Que.	1	48	3	12	15	41	....	....	....	....	....	....	1993-94	1993-94
McKegney, Ian	Chi.	1	3	0	0	0	2	....	....	....	....	....	....	1976-77	1976-77
McKegney, Tony	Buf., Que., Min., NYR, St.L., Det., Chi.	13	912	320	319	639	517	79	24	23	47	56	....	1978-79	1990-91
McKendry, Alex	NYI, Cgy.	4	46	3	6	9	21	6	2	2	4	0	1	1977-78	1980-81
McKenna, Sean	Buf., L.A., Tor.	9	414	82	80	162	181	15	1	2	3	2	....	1981-82	1989-90
McKenna, Steve	L.A., Min., Pit., NYR	8	373	18	14	32	824	3	0	1	1	8	....	1996-97	2003-04
McKenney, Don	Bos., NYR, Tor., Det., St.L.	13	798	237	345	582	211	58	18	29	47	10	1	1954-55	1967-68
McKenny, Jim	Tor., Min.	14	604	82	247	329	294	37	7	9	16	10	....	1965-66	1978-79
McKenzie, Brian	Pit.	1	6	1	1	2	4	....	....	....	....	....	....	1971-72	1971-72
McKenzie, Jim	Hfd., Dal., Pit., Wpg., Phx., Ana., Wsh., N.J., Nsh.	15	880	48	52	100	1739	51	0	0	0	38	1	1989-90	2003-04
McKenzie, John	Chi., Det., NYR, Bos.	12	691	206	268	474	917	69	15	32	47	133	2	1958-59	1971-72
McKim, Andrew	Bos., Det.	3	38	1	4	5	6	....	....	....	....	....	....	1992-93	1994-95
• McKinnon, Alex	Ham., NYA, Chi.	5	193	19	11	30	237	....	....	....	....	....	....	1924-25	1928-29
• McKinnon, John	Mtl., Pit., Phi.	6	208	28	11	39	224	2	0	0	0	4	....	1925-26	1930-31
McLaren, Kyle	Bos., S.J.	12	719	46	161	207	671	70	1	13	14	78	....	1995-96	2007-08
McLaren, Steve	St.L.	1	6	0	0	0	25	....	....	....	....	....	....	2003-04	2003-04
McLean, Don	Wsh.	1	9	0	0	0	6	....	....	....	....	....	....	1975-76	1975-76
• McLean, Fred	Que., Ham.	2	8	0	0	0	2	....	....	....	....	....	....	1919-20	1920-21
• McLean, Jack	Tor.	3	67	14	24	38	76	13	2	2	4	8	1	1942-43	1944-45
• McLean, Jeff	S.J.	1	6	1	0	1	0	....	....	....	....	....	....	1993-94	1993-94
• McLellan, John	Tor.	1	2	0	0	0	0	....	....	....	....	....	....	1951-52	1951-52
McLellan, Scott	Bos.	1	2	0	0	0	0	....	....	....	....	....	....	1982-83	1982-83
McLellan, Todd	NYI	1	5	1	1	2	0	....	....	....	....	....	....	1987-88	1987-88
• McLenahan, Rollie	Det.	1	9	2	1	3	10	2	0	0	0	0	....	1945-46	1945-46
McLeod, Al	Det.	1	26	2	2	4	24	....	....	....	....	....	....	1973-74	1973-74
McLeod, Jackie	NYR	5	106	14	23	37	12	7	0	0	0	0	....	1949-50	1954-55
McLlwain, Dave	Pit., Wpg., Buf., NYI, Tor., Ott.	10	501	100	107	207	292	20	0	2	2	2	....	1987-88	1996-97
• McMahon, Mike	Mtl., Bos.	3	57	7	18	25	102	13	1	2	3	30	1	1942-43	1945-46
McMahon, Mike	NYR, Min., Chi., Det., Pit., Buf.	8	224	15	68	83	171	14	3	7	10	4	....	1963-64	1971-72
McManama, Bob	Pit.	3	99	11	25	36	28	8	0	1	1	6	....	1973-74	1975-76
• McManus, Sammy	Mtl.M., Bos.	2	26	0	1	1	8	1	0	0	0	0	1	1934-35	1936-37
McMorrow, Sean	Buf.	1	1	0	0	0	0	....	....	....	....	....	....	2002-03	2002-03
McMurchy, Tom	Chi., Edm.	4	55	8	4	12	65	....	....	....	....	....	....	1983-84	1987-88
• McNab, Max	Det.	4	128	16	19	35	24	25	1	0	1	4	1	1947-48	1950-51
McNab, Peter	Buf., Bos., Van., N.J.	14	954	363	450	813	179	107	40	42	82	20	....	1973-74	1986-87
• McNabney, Sid	Mtl.	1	....	....	....	....	....	5	0	1	1	2	....	1950-51	1950-51
• McNamara, Howard	Mtl.	1	10	1	0	1	4	....	....	....	....	....	....	1919-20	1919-20
• McNaughton, George	Que.	1	1	0	0	0	0	....	....	....	....	....	....	1919-20	1919-20

			Regular Schedule					Playoffs					NHL	First	Last
Name	NHL Teams	NHL Seasons	GP	G	A	TP	PIM	GP	G	A	TP	PIM	Cup Wins	NHL Season	NHL Season
● McNeill, Billy	Det.	6	257	21	46	67	142	4	1	1	2	4	....	1956-57	1963-64
‡ McNeill, Grant	Fla.	1	3	0	0	0	5	....	....	....	....	....	....	2003-04	2003-04
McNeill, Mike	Chi., Que.	2	63	5	11	16	18	....	....	....	....	....	....	1990-91	1991-92
McNeill, Stu	Det.	3	10	1	1	2	2	....	....	....	....	....	....	1957-58	1959-60
McPhee, George	NYR, N.J.	7	115	24	25	49	257	29	5	3	8	69	....	1982-83	1988-89
McPhee, Mike	Mtl., Min., Dal.	11	744	200	199	399	661	134	28	27	55	193	1	1983-84	1993-94
McRae, Basil	Que., Tor., Det., Min., T.B., St.L., Chi.	16	576	53	83	136	2457	78	8	4	12	349	....	1981-82	1996-97
McRae, Chris	Tor., Det.	3	21	1	0	1	122	....	....	....	....	....	....	1987-88	1989-90
McRae, Ken	Que., Tor.	7	137	14	21	35	364	6	0	0	0	4	....	1987-88	1993-94
● McReavy, Pat	Bos., Det.	4	55	5	10	15	4	22	3	3	6	9	1	1938-39	1941-42
McReynolds, Brian	Wpg., NYR, L.A.	3	30	1	5	6	8	....	....	....	....	....	....	1989-90	1993-94
McSheffrey, Bryan	Van., Buf.	3	90	13	7	20	44	....	....	....	....	....	....	1972-73	1974-75
McSorley, Marty	Pit., Edm., L.A., NYR, S.J., Bos.	17	961	108	251	359	3381	115	10	19	29	374	2	1983-84	1999-00
McSween, Don	Buf., Ana.	5	47	3	10	13	55	....	....	....	....	....	....	1987-88	1995-96
McTaggart, Jim	Wsh.	2	71	3	10	13	205	....	....	....	....	....	....	1980-81	1981-82
‡ McTavish, Dale	Cgy.	1	9	1	2	3	2	....	....	....	....	....	....	1996-97	1996-97
McTavish, Gord	St.L., Wpg.	2	11	1	3	4	2	....	....	....	....	....	....	1978-79	1979-80
● McVeigh, Charley	Chi., NYA	9	397	84	88	172	138	4	0	0	0	2	....	1926-27	1934-35
● McVicar, Jack	Mtl.M.	2	88	2	4	6	63	6	0	0	0	2	....	1930-31	1931-32
Meagher, Rick	Mtl., Hfd., N.J., St.L.	12	691	144	165	309	383	62	8	7	15	41	....	1979-80	1990-91
Meehan, Gerry	Tor., Phi., Buf., Van., Atl., Wsh.	10	670	180	243	423	111	10	0	1	1	0	....	1968-69	1978-79
Meeke, Brent	Cal., Cle.	5	75	9	22	31	8	....	....	....	....	....	....	1972-73	1976-77
Meeker, Howie	Tor.	8	346	83	102	185	329	42	6	9	15	50	4	1946-47	1953-54
Meeker, Mike	Pit.	1	4	0	0	0	5	....	....	....	....	....	....	1978-79	1978-79
● Meeking, Harry	Tor., Det., Bos.	3	64	18	12	30	66	9	3	0	3	6	....	1917-18	1926-27
Meger, Paul	Mtl.	6	212	39	52	91	118	35	3	8	11	16	1	1949-50	1954-55
Meighan, Ron	Min., Pit.	2	48	3	7	10	18	....	....	....	....	....	....	1981-82	1982-83
Meissner, Barrie	Min.	2	6	0	1	1	4	....	....	....	....	....	....	1967-68	1968-69
● Meissner, Dick	Bos., NYR	5	171	11	15	26	37	....	....	....	....	....	....	1959-60	1964-65
Melametsa, Anssi	Wpg.	1	27	0	3	3	2	....	....	....	....	....	....	1985-86	1985-86
Melanson, Dean	Buf., Wsh.	2	9	0	0	0	8	....	....	....	....	....	....	1994-95	2001-02
‡ Melichar, Josef	Pit., Car., T.B.	7	349	7	42	49	300	5	0	0	0	2	....	2000-01	2008-09
‡ Melin, Bjorn	Ana.	1	3	1	0	1	0	....	....	....	....	....	....	2006-07	2006-07
Melin, Roger	Min.	2	3	0	0	0	0	....	....	....	....	....	....	1980-81	1981-82
Mellanby, Scott	Phi., Edm., Fla., St.L., Atl.	21	1431	364	476	840	2479	136	24	29	53	220	....	1985-86	2006-07
Mellor, Tom	Det.	2	26	2	4	6	25	....	....	....	....	....	....	1973-74	1974-75
● Melnyk, Gerry	Det., Chi., St.L.	6	269	39	77	116	34	53	6	6	12	6	....	1955-56	1967-68
Melnyk, Larry	Bos., Edm., NYR, Van.	10	432	11	63	74	686	66	2	9	11	127	1	1980-81	1989-90
‡ Meloche, Eric	Pit., Phi.	4	74	9	11	20	36	....	....	....	....	....	....	2001-02	2006-07
Melrose, Barry	Wpg., Tor., Det.	6	300	10	23	33	728	7	0	2	2	38	....	1979-80	1985-86
Menard, Hillary	Chi.	1	1	0	0	0	0	....	....	....	....	....	....	1953-54	1953-54
Menard, Howie	Det., L.A., Chi., Oak.	4	151	23	42	65	87	19	3	7	10	36	....	1963-64	1969-70
Mercredi, Vic	Atl.	1	2	0	0	0	0	....	....	....	....	....	....	1974-75	1974-75
Meredith, Greg	Cgy.	2	38	6	4	10	8	5	3	1	4	4	....	1980-81	1982-83
Merkosky, Glenn	Hfd., N.J., Det.	5	66	5	12	17	22	....	....	....	....	....	....	1981-82	1989-90
● Meronek, Bill	Mtl.	2	19	5	8	13	0	1	0	0	0	0	....	1939-40	1942-43
Merrick, Wayne	St.L., Cal., Cle., NYI	12	774	191	265	456	303	102	19	30	49	30	4	1972-73	1983-84
● Merrill, Horace	Ott.	2	8	0	0	0	3	....	....	....	....	....	1	1917-18	1919-20
Mertzig, Jan	NYR	1	23	0	2	2	8	....	....	....	....	....	....	1998-99	1998-99
Messier, Eric	Col., Fla.	8	406	25	50	75	146	72	3	5	8	22	1	1996-97	2003-04
Messier, Joby	NYR	3	25	0	4	4	24	....	....	....	....	....	....	1992-93	1994-95
Messier, Mark	Edm., NYR, Van.	25	1756	694	1193	1887	1910	236	109	186	295	244	6	1979-80	2003-04
Messier, Mitch	Min.	4	20	0	2	2	11	....	....	....	....	....	....	1987-88	1990-91
Messier, Paul	Col.	1	9	0	0	0	4	....	....	....	....	....	....	1978-79	1978-79
Metcalfe, Scott	Edm., Buf.	3	19	1	2	3	18	....	....	....	....	....	....	1987-88	1989-90
● Metz, Don	Tor.	9	172	20	35	55	42	42	7	8	15	12	5	1938-39	1948-49
● Metz, Nick	Tor.	12	518	131	119	250	149	76	19	20	39	31	4	1934-35	1947-48
‡ Mezei, Branislav	NYI, Fla.	7	240	5	19	24	311	....	....	....	....	....	....	2000-01	2007-08
● Michaluk, Art	Chi.	1	5	0	0	0	0	....	....	....	....	....	....	1947-48	1947-48
Michaluk, John	Chi.	1	1	0	0	0	0	....	....	....	....	....	....	1950-51	1950-51
Michayluk, Dave	Phi., Pit.	3	14	2	6	8	8	7	1	1	2	0	1	1981-82	1991-92
Micheletti, Joe	St.L., Col.	3	158	11	60	71	114	11	1	11	12	10	....	1979-80	1981-82
Micheletti, Pat	Min.	1	12	2	0	2	8	....	....	....	....	....	....	1987-88	1987-88
● Mickey, Larry	Chi., NYR, Tor., Mtl., L.A., Phi., Buf.	11	292	39	53	92	160	9	1	0	1	10	....	1964-65	1974-75
● Mickoski, Nick	NYR, Chi., Det., Bos.	13	703	158	185	343	319	18	1	6	7	6	....	1947-48	1959-60
Middendorf, Max	Que., Edm.	4	13	2	4	6	6	....	....	....	....	....	....	1986-87	1990-91
Middleton, Rick	NYR, Bos.	14	1005	448	540	988	157	114	45	55	100	19	....	1974-75	1987-88
Miehm, Kevin	St.L.	2	22	1	4	5	8	2	0	1	1	0	....	1992-93	1993-94
Migay, Rudy	Tor.	10	418	59	92	151	293	15	1	0	1	20	....	1949-50	1959-60
Mika, Petr	NYI	1	3	0	0	0	0	....	....	....	....	....	....	1999-00	1999-00
‡ Mikhnov, Alexei	Edm.	1	2	0	0	0	0	....	....	....	....	....	....	2006-07	2006-07
Mikita, Stan	Chi.	22	1394	541	926	1467	1270	155	59	91	150	169	1	1958-59	1979-80
Mikkelson, Bill	L.A., NYI, Wsh.	4	147	4	18	22	105	....	....	....	....	....	....	1971-72	1976-77
Mikol, Jim	Tor., NYR	2	34	1	4	5	8	....	....	....	....	....	....	1962-63	1964-65
Mikulchik, Oleg	Wpg., Ana.	3	37	0	3	3	33	....	....	....	....	....	....	1993-94	1995-96
Milbury, Mike	Bos.	12	754	49	189	238	1552	86	4	24	28	219	....	1975-76	1986-87
● Milks, Hib	Pit., Phi., NYR, Ott.	8	317	87	41	128	179	11	0	0	0	2	....	1925-26	1932-33
Millar, Craig	Edm., Nsh., T.B.	5	114	8	14	22	73	....	....	....	....	....	....	1996-97	2000-01
● Millar, Hugh	Det.	1	4	0	0	0	0	1	0	0	0	0	....	1946-47	1946-47
Millar, Mike	Hfd., Wsh., Bos., Tor.	5	78	18	18	36	12	....	....	....	....	....	....	1986-87	1990-91
Millen, Corey	NYR, L.A., N.J., Dal., Cgy.	8	335	90	119	209	236	47	5	7	12	22	....	1989-90	1996-97
Miller, Aaron	Que., Col., L.A., Van.	14	677	25	94	119	422	80	3	9	12	40	....	1993-94	2007-08
● Miller, Bill	Mtl.M., Mtl.	3	95	7	3	10	16	12	0	0	0	0	1	1934-35	1936-37
Miller, Bob	Bos., Col., L.A.	6	404	75	119	194	220	36	4	7	11	27	....	1977-78	1984-85
Miller, Brad	Buf., Ott., Cgy.	6	82	1	5	6	321	....	....	....	....	....	....	1988-89	1993-94
● Miller, Earl	Chi., Tor.	5	109	19	14	33	124	10	1	0	1	6	1	1927-28	1931-32
● Miller, Jack	Chi.	2	17	0	0	0	4	....	....	....	....	....	....	1949-50	1950-51
Miller, Jason	N.J.	3	6	0	0	0	0	....	....	....	....	....	....	1990-91	1992-93
Miller, Jay	Bos., L.A.	7	446	40	44	84	1723	48	2	3	5	243	....	1985-86	1991-92
Miller, Kelly	NYR, Wsh.	15	1057	181	282	463	512	119	20	34	54	65	....	1984-85	1998-99
Miller, Kevin	NYR, Det., Wsh., St.L., S.J., Pit., Chi., NYI, Ott.	13	620	150	185	335	429	61	7	10	17	49	....	1988-89	2003-04
Miller, Kip	Que., Min., S.J., NYI, Chi., Pit., Ana., Wsh.	12	449	74	165	239	105	25	6	11	17	23	....	1990-91	2003-04
Miller, Paul	Col.	1	3	0	3	3	0	....	....	....	....	....	....	1981-82	1981-82
Miller, Perry	Det.	4	217	10	51	61	387	....	....	....	....	....	....	1977-78	1980-81
Miller, Tom	Det., NYI	4	118	16	25	41	34	....	....	....	....	....	....	1970-71	1974-75
Miller, Warren	NYR, Hfd.	4	262	40	50	90	137	6	1	0	1	0	....	1979-80	1982-83
‡ Milley, Norm	Buf., T.B.	4	29	2	4	6	12	....	....	....	....	....	....	2001-02	2005-06
Mills, Craig	Wpg., Chi.	3	31	0	5	5	36	1	0	0	0	0	....	1995-96	1998-99
‡ Milroy, Duncan	Mtl.	1	5	0	1	1	0	....	....	....	....	....	....	2006-07	2006-07
Miner, John	Edm.	1	14	2	3	5	16	....	....	....	....	....	....	1987-88	1987-88
Minor, Gerry	Van.	5	140	11	21	32	173	12	1	3	4	25	....	1979-80	1983-84
Mironov, Boris	Wpg., Edm., Chi., NYR	11	716	76	231	307	891	25	5	11	16	45	....	1993-94	2003-04
Mironov, Dmitri	Tor., Pit., Ana., Det., Wsh.	10	556	54	206	260	568	75	10	26	36	48	1	1991-92	2000-01
Miszuk, John	Det., Chi., Phi., Min.	6	237	7	39	46	232	19	0	3	3	19	....	1963-64	1969-70
Mitchell, Bill	Det.	1	1	0	0	0	0	....	....	....	....	....	....	1963-64	1963-64
● Mitchell, Herb	Bos.	2	44	6	0	6	36	....	....	....	....	....	....	1924-25	1925-26
Mitchell, Jeff	Dal.	1	7	0	0	0	7	....	....	....	....	....	....	1997-98	1997-98
● Mitchell, Red	Chi.	3	83	4	5	9	67	....	....	....	....	....	....	1941-42	1944-45
Mitchell, Roy	Min.	1	3	0	0	0	0	....	....	....	....	....	....	1992-93	1992-93
‡ Modry, Jaroslav	N.J., Ott., L.A., Atl., Dal., Phi.	13	725	49	201	250	510	28	1	5	6	6	....	1993-94	2007-08
● Moe, Bill	NYR	5	261	11	42	53	163	1	0	0	0	0	....	1944-45	1948-49
Moffat, Lyle	Tor., Wpg.	3	97	12	16	28	51	....	....	....	....	....	....	1972-73	1979-80
● Moffat, Ron	Det.	3	37	1	1	2	8	7	0	0	0	0	....	1932-33	1934-35
Moger, Sandy	Bos., L.A.	5	236	41	38	79	212	5	2	2	4	12	....	1994-95	1998-99
Mogilny, Alexander	Buf., Van., N.J., Tor.	16	990	473	559	1032	432	124	39	47	86	58	1	1989-90	2005-06
Moher, Mike	N.J.	1	9	0	1	1	28	....	....	....	....	....	....	1982-83	1982-83
Mohns, Doug	Bos., Chi., Min., Atl., Wsh.	22	1390	248	462	710	1250	94	14	36	50	122	....	1953-54	1974-75
● Mohns, Lloyd	NYR	1	1	0	0	0	0	....	....	....	....	....	....	1943-44	1943-44
‡ Mojzis, Tomas	Van., St.L., Min.	3	17	1	2	3	14	....	....	....	....	....	....	2005-06	2008-09
Mokosak, Carl	Cgy., L.A., Phi., Pit., Bos.	6	83	11	15	26	170	1	0	0	0	0	....	1981-82	1988-89
Mokosak, John	Det.	2	41	0	2	2	96	....	....	....	....	....	....	1988-89	1989-90
Molin, Lars	Van.	3	172	33	65	98	37	19	2	9	11	7	....	1981-82	1983-84
Moller, Mike	Buf., Edm.	7	134	15	28	43	41	3	0	1	1	0	....	1980-81	1986-87
Moller, Randy	Que., NYR, Buf., Fla.	14	815	45	180	225	1692	78	6	16	22	197	....	1981-82	1994-95

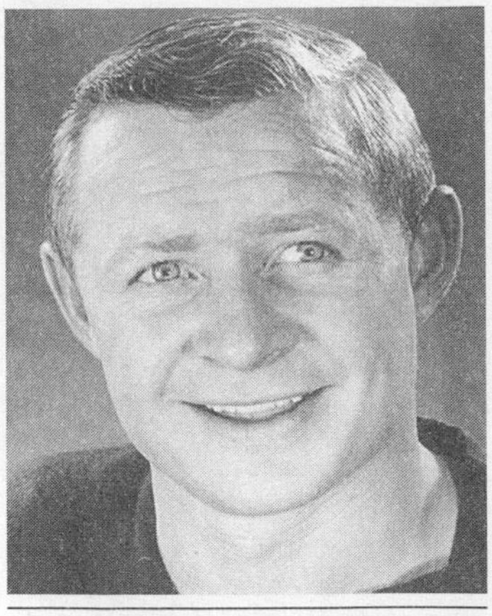
John McKenzie

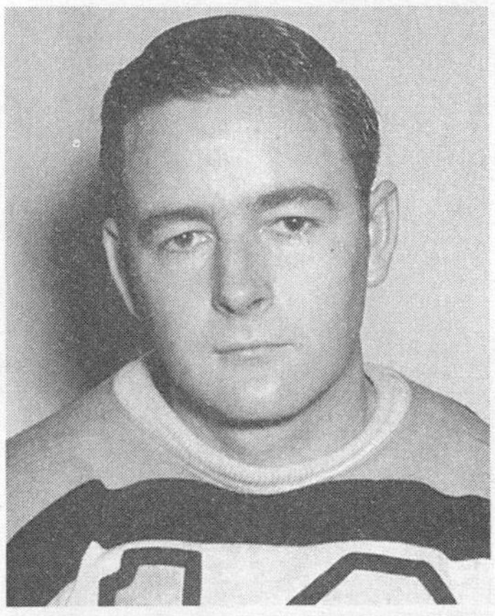
Pat McReavy

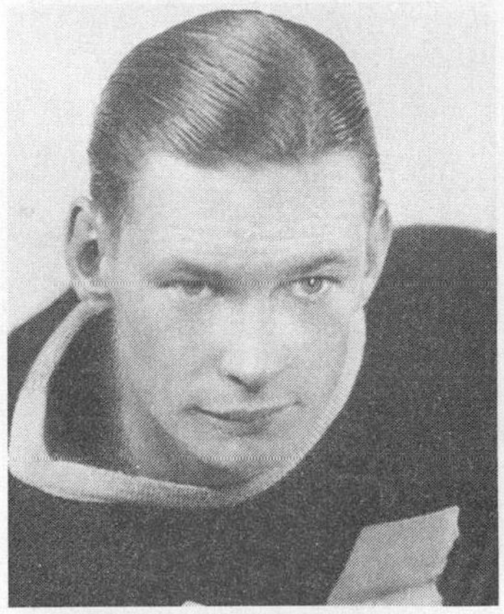
Jack McVicar

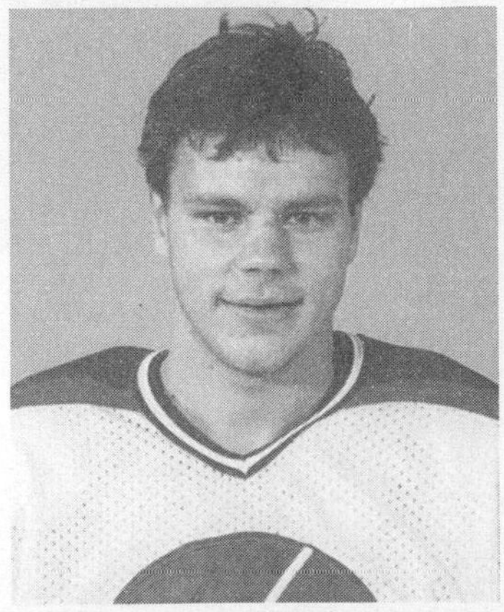
Anssi Melametsa

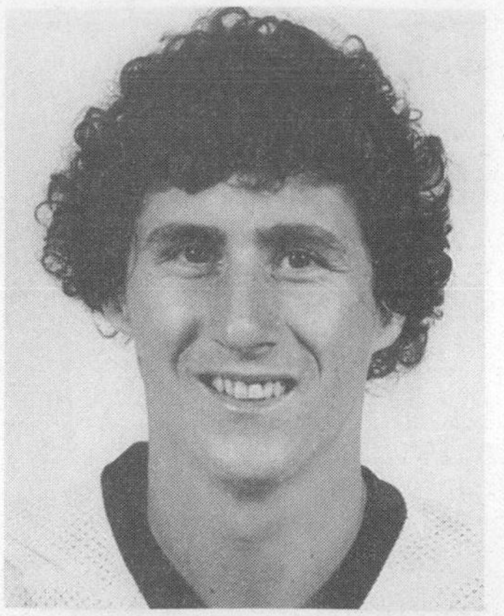

Bob Miller

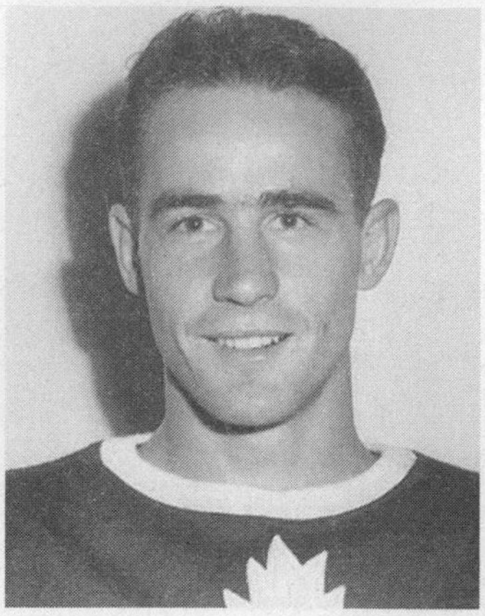

Jim Morrison

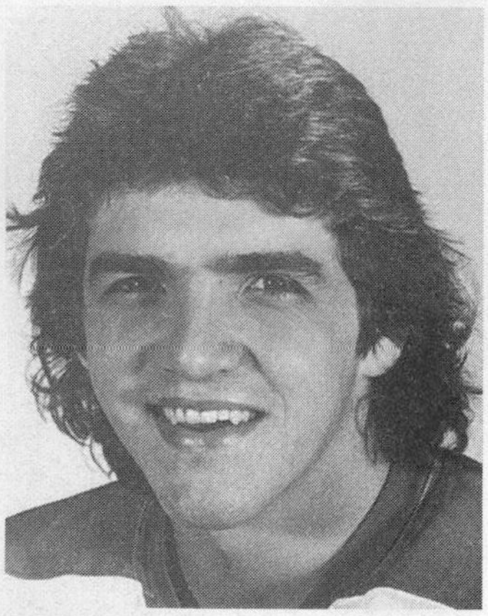

Paul Mulvey

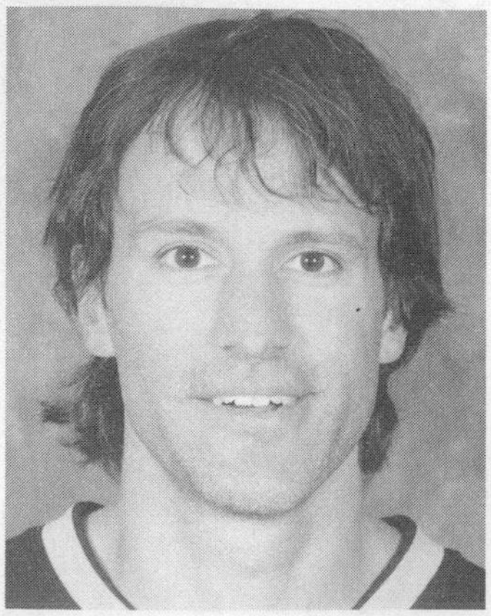

Scott Niedermayer

Name	NHL Teams	NHL Seasons	Regular Schedule					Playoffs					NHL Cup Wins	First NHL Season	Last NHL Season
			GP	G	A	TP	PIM	GP	G	A	TP	PIM			
Molloy, Mitch	Buf.	1	2	0	0	0	10	....	....	....	....	....	....	1989-90	1989-90
• Molyneaux, Larry	NYR	2	45	0	1	1	20	10	0	0	0	8	....	1937-38	1938-39
Momesso, Sergio	Mtl., St.L., Van., Tor., NYR	13	710	152	193	345	1557	119	18	26	44	311	....	1983-84	1996-97
Monahan, Garry	Mtl., Det., L.A., Tor., Van.	12	748	116	169	285	484	22	3	1	4	13	....	1967-68	1978-79
Monahan, Hartland	Cal., NYR, Wsh., Pit., L.A., St.L.	7	334	61	80	141	163	6	0	0	0	4	....	1973-74	1980-81
• Mondou, Armand	Mtl.	12	386	47	71	118	99	32	3	5	8	12	2	1928-29	1939-40
Mondou, Pierre	Mtl.	9	548	194	262	456	179	69	17	28	45	26	3	1976-77	1984-85
• Mongeau, Michel	St.L., T.B.	4	54	6	19	25	10	2	0	1	1	0	....	1989-90	1992-93
Mongrain, Bob	Buf., L.A.	6	81	13	14	27	14	11	1	2	3	2	....	1979-80	1985-86
Monteith, Hank	Det.	3	77	5	12	17	6	4	0	0	0	0	....	1968-69	1970-71
Montgomery, Jim	St.L., Mtl., Phi., S.J., Dal.	6	122	9	25	34	80	8	1	0	1	2	....	1993-94	2002-03
Moore, Barrie	Buf., Edm., Wsh.	3	39	2	6	8	18	....	....	....	....	....	....	1995-96	1999-00
Moore, Dickie	Mtl., Tor., St.L.	14	719	261	347	608	652	135	46	64	110	122	6	1951-52	1967-68
Moore, Steve	Col.	3	69	5	7	12	41	....	....	....	....	....	....	2001-02	2003-04
• Moran, Amby	Mtl., Chi.	2	35	1	1	2	24	....	....	....	....	....	....	1926-27	1927-28
Moran, Ian	Pit., Bos., Ana.	12	489	21	50	71	321	66	1	7	8	24	....	1994-95	2006-07
‡ Moravec, David	Buf.	1	1	0	0	0	0	....	....	....	....	....	....	1999-00	1999-00
More, Jay	NYR, Min., S.J., Phx., Chi., Nsh.	10	406	18	54	72	702	31	0	6	6	45	....	1988-89	1998-99
• Morenz, Howie	Mtl., Chi., NYR	14	550	271	201	472	546	39	13	9	22	58	3	1923-24	1936-37
Moretto, Angelo	Cle.	1	5	1	2	3	2	....	....	....	....	....	....	1976-77	1976-77
Morgan, Gavin	Dal.	1	6	0	0	0	21	....	....	....	....	....	....	2003-04	2003-04
Morgan, Jason	L.A., Cgy., Nsh., Chi., Min.	5	44	2	5	7	18	....	....	....	....	....	....	1996-97	2006-07
• Morin, Pete	Mtl.	1	31	10	12	22	7	1	0	0	0	0	....	1941-42	1941-42
• Morin, Stephane	Que., Van.	5	90	16	39	55	52	....	....	....	....	....	....	1989-90	1993-94
Morisset, Dave	Fla.	1	4	0	0	0	5	....	....	....	....	....	....	2001-02	2001-02
Morissette, Dave	Mtl.	2	11	0	0	0	57	....	....	....	....	....	....	1998-99	1999-00
Moro, Marc	Ana., Nsh., Tor.	4	30	0	0	0	77	....	....	....	....	....	....	1997-98	2001-02
‡ Morozov, Aleksey	Pit.	7	451	84	135	219	98	39	4	5	9	8	....	1997-98	2003-04
• Morris, Bernie	Bos.	1	6	1	0	1	0	....	....	....	....	....	....	1924-25	1924-25
Morris, Jon	N.J., S.J., Bos.	6	103	16	33	49	47	11	1	7	8	25	....	1988-89	1993-94
• Morris, Moe	Tor., NYR	4	135	13	29	42	58	18	4	2	6	16	1	1943-44	1948-49
Morrison, Dave	L.A., Van.	4	39	3	3	6	4	....	....	....	....	....	....	1980-81	1984-85
• Morrison, Don	Det., Chi.	3	112	18	28	46	12	3	0	1	1	0	....	1947-48	1950-51
Morrison, Doug	Bos.	4	23	7	3	10	15	....	....	....	....	....	....	1979-80	1984-85
Morrison, Gary	Phi.	3	43	1	15	16	70	5	0	1	1	2	....	1979-80	1981-82
• Morrison, George	St.L.	2	115	17	21	38	13	3	0	0	0	0	....	1970-71	1971-72
Morrison, Jim	Bos., Tor., Det., NYR, Pit.	12	704	40	160	200	542	36	0	12	12	38	....	1951-52	1970-71
• Morrison, John	NYA	1	18	0	0	0	0	....	....	....	....	....	....	1925-26	1925-26
Morrison, Kevin	Col.	1	41	4	11	15	23	....	....	....	....	....	....	1979-80	1979-80
Morrison, Lew	Phi., Atl., Wsh., Pit.	9	564	39	52	91	107	17	0	0	0	2	....	1969-70	1977-78
Morrison, Mark	NYR	2	10	1	1	2	0	....	....	....	....	....	....	1981-82	1983-84
• Morrison, Rod	Det.	1	34	8	7	15	4	3	0	0	0	0	....	1947-48	1947-48
Morrow, Ken	NYI	10	550	17	88	105	309	127	11	22	33	97	4	1979-80	1988-89
Morrow, Scott	Cgy.	1	4	0	0	0	0	....	....	....	....	....	....	1994-95	1994-95
Morton, Dean	Det.	1	1	1	0	1	2	....	....	....	....	....	....	1989-90	1989-90
Mortson, Gus	Tor., Chi., Det.	13	797	46	152	198	1380	54	5	8	13	68	4	1946-47	1958-59
• Mosdell, Ken	Bro., Mtl., Chi.	16	693	141	168	309	475	80	16	13	29	48	4	1941-42	1958-59
• Mosienko, Bill	Chi.	14	711	258	282	540	121	22	10	4	14	15	....	1941-42	1954-55
Mott, Morris	Cal.	3	199	18	32	50	49	....	....	....	....	....	....	1972-73	1974-75
• Motter, Alex	Bos., Det.	8	255	39	64	103	135	41	3	9	12	41	1	1934-35	1942-43
‡ Motzko, Joe	CBJ, Ana., Wsh., Atl.	5	25	4	2	6	0	3	0	0	0	2	1	2003-04	2008-09
‡ Mowers, Mark	Nsh., Det., Bos., Ana.	7	278	18	44	62	70	3	0	0	0	0	....	1998-99	2007-08
Moxey, Jim	Cal., Cle., L.A.	3	127	22	27	49	59	....	....	....	....	....	....	1974-75	1976-77
Mrozik, Rick	Cgy.	1	2	0	0	0	0	....	....	....	....	....	....	2002-03	2002-03
Muckalt, Bill	Van., NYI, Ott., Min.	5	256	40	57	97	204	5	0	0	0	0	....	1998-99	2002-03
Muir, Bryan	Edm., N.J., Chi., T.B., Col., L.A., Wsh.	11	279	16	37	53	281	29	0	0	0	6	1	1995-96	2006-07
Mulhern, Richard	Atl., L.A., Tor., Wpg.	6	303	27	93	120	217	7	0	3	3	5	....	1975-76	1980-81
Mulhern, Ryan	Wsh.	1	3	0	0	0	0	....	....	....	....	....	....	1997-98	1997-98
Mullen, Brian	Wpg., NYR, S.J., NYI	11	832	260	362	622	414	62	12	18	30	30	....	1982-83	1992-93
Mullen, Joe	St.L., Cgy., Pit., Bos.	17	1062	502	561	1063	241	143	60	46	106	42	3	1979-80	1996-97
Muller, Kirk	N.J., Mtl., NYI, Tor., Fla., Dal.	19	1349	357	602	959	1223	127	33	36	69	153	1	1984-85	2002-03
Muloin, Wayne	Det., Oak., Cal., Min.	3	147	3	21	24	93	11	0	0	0	2	....	1963-64	1970-71
Mulvenna, Glenn	Pit., Phi.	2	2	0	0	0	4	....	....	....	....	....	....	1991-92	1992-93
Mulvey, Grant	Chi., N.J.	10	586	149	135	284	816	42	10	5	15	70	....	1974-75	1983-84
Mulvey, Paul	Wsh., Pit., L.A.	4	225	30	51	81	613	....	....	....	....	....	....	1978-79	1981-82
• Mummery, Harry	Tor., Que., Mtl., Ham.	6	106	33	19	52	226	2	1	1	2	17	....	1917-18	1922-23
Muni, Craig	Tor., Edm., Chi., Buf., Wpg., Pit., Dal.	16	819	28	119	147	775	113	0	17	17	108	3	1981-82	1997-98
• Munro, Dunc	Mtl.M., Mtl.	8	239	28	18	46	172	21	2	2	4	18	1	1924-25	1931-32
• Munro, Gerry	Mtl.M., Tor.	2	34	1	0	1	37	....	....	....	....	....	....	1924-25	1925-26
Murdoch, Bob	Mtl., L.A., Atl., Cgy.	12	757	60	218	278	764	69	4	18	22	92	2	1970-71	1981-82
Murdoch, Bob	Cal., Cle., St.L.	4	260	72	85	157	127	....	....	....	....	....	....	1975-76	1978-79
Murdoch, Don	NYR, Edm., Det.	6	320	121	117	238	155	24	10	8	18	16	....	1976-77	1981-82
• Murdoch, Murray	NYR	11	508	84	108	192	197	55	9	12	21	28	2	1926-27	1936-37
‡ Murley, Matt	Pit., Phx.	3	62	2	7	9	38	....	....	....	....	....	....	2003-04	2007-08
Murphy, Brian	Det.	1	1	0	0	0	0	....	....	....	....	....	....	1974-75	1974-75
‡ Murphy, Curtis	Min.	1	1	0	0	0	0	....	....	....	....	....	....	2002-03	2002-03
Murphy, Gord	Phi., Bos., Fla., Atl.	14	862	85	238	323	668	53	3	16	19	35	....	1988-89	2001-02
Murphy, Joe	Det., Edm., Chi., St.L., S.J., Bos., Wsh.	15	779	233	295	528	810	120	34	43	77	185	1	1986-87	2000-01
Murphy, Larry	L.A., Wsh., Min., Pit., Tor., Det.	21	1615	287	929	1216	1084	215	37	115	152	201	4	1980-81	2000-01
Murphy, Mike	St.L., NYR, L.A.	12	831	238	318	556	514	66	13	23	36	54	....	1971-72	1982-83
Murphy, Rob	Van., Ott., L.A.	7	125	9	12	21	152	4	0	0	0	2	....	1987-88	1993-94
Murphy, Ron	NYR, Chi., Det., Bos.	18	889	205	274	479	460	53	7	8	15	26	2	1952-53	1969-70
• Murray, Allan	NYA	7	271	5	9	14	163	14	0	0	0	10	....	1933-34	1939-40
Murray, Bob	Atl., Van.	4	194	6	16	22	98	10	1	1	2	15	....	1973-74	1976-77
Murray, Bob	Chi.	15	1008	132	382	514	873	112	19	37	56	106	....	1975-76	1989-90
Murray, Chris	Mtl., Hfd., Car., Ott., Chi., Dal.	6	242	16	18	34	550	15	1	0	1	12	....	1994-95	1999-00
Murray, Glen	Bos., Pit., L.A.	16	1009	337	314	651	679	94	20	22	42	66	....	1991-92	2007-08
Murray, Jim	L.A.	1	30	0	2	2	14	....	....	....	....	....	....	1967-68	1967-68
Murray, Ken	Tor., NYI, Det., K.C.	5	106	1	10	11	135	....	....	....	....	....	....	1969-70	1975-76
• Murray, Leo	Mtl.	1	6	0	0	0	2	....	....	....	....	....	....	1932-33	1932-33
Murray, Marty	Cgy., Phi., Car., L.A.	8	261	31	42	73	41	9	0	1	1	4	....	1995-96	2006-07
Murray, Mike	Phi.	1	1	0	0	0	0	....	....	....	....	....	....	1987-88	1987-88
Murray, Pat	Phi.	2	25	3	1	4	15	....	....	....	....	....	....	1990-91	1991-92
Murray, Randy	Tor.	1	3	0	0	0	2	....	....	....	....	....	....	1969-70	1969-70
Murray, Rem	Edm., NYR, Nsh.	9	560	94	121	215	161	62	5	12	17	18	....	1996-97	2005-06
Murray, Rob	Wsh., Wpg., Phx.	8	107	4	15	19	111	9	0	0	0	18	....	1989-90	1998-99
Murray, Terry	Cal., Phi., Det., Wsh.	8	302	4	76	80	199	18	2	2	4	10	....	1972-73	1981-82
Murray, Troy	Chi., Wpg., Ott., Pit., Col.	15	915	230	354	584	875	113	17	26	43	145	1	1981-82	1995-96
Murzyn, Dana	Hfd., Cgy., Van.	14	838	52	152	204	1571	82	9	10	19	166	1	1985-86	1998-99
Musil, Frantisek	Min., Cgy., Ott., Edm.	15	797	34	106	140	1241	42	2	4	6	47	....	1986-87	2000-01
Myers, Hap	Buf.	1	13	0	0	0	6	....	....	....	....	....	....	1970-71	1970-71
Myhres, Brantt	T.B., Phi., S.J., Nsh., Wsh., Bos.	7	154	6	2	8	687	....	....	....	....	....	....	1994-95	2002-03
• Myles, Vic	NYR	1	45	6	9	15	57	....	....	....	....	....	....	1942-43	1942-43
Myrvold, Anders	Col., Bos., NYI, Det.	4	33	0	5	5	12	....	....	....	....	....	....	1995-96	2003-04
N															
‡ Nabokov, Dmitri	Chi., NYI	3	55	11	13	24	28	....	....	....	....	....	....	1997-98	1999-00
Nachbaur, Don	Hfd., Edm., Phi.	8	223	23	46	69	465	11	1	1	2	24	....	1980-81	1989-90
‡ Nagy, Ladislav	St.L., Phx., Dal., L.A.	8	435	115	196	311	358	18	2	2	4	23	....	1999-00	2007-08
Nahrgang, Jim	Det.	3	57	5	12	17	34	....	....	....	....	....	....	1974-75	1976-77
Namestnikov, John	Van., NYI, Nsh.	6	43	0	9	9	24	2	0	0	0	2	....	1993-94	1999-00
Nanne, Lou	Min.	11	635	68	157	225	356	32	4	10	14	8	....	1967-68	1977-78
Nantais, Rich	Min.	3	63	5	4	9	79	....	....	....	....	....	....	1974-75	1976-77
Napier, Mark	Mtl., Min., Edm., Buf.	11	767	235	306	541	157	82	18	24	42	11	2	1978-79	1988-89
Nash, Tyson	St.L., Phx.	7	374	27	37	64	673	23	3	2	5	52	....	1998-99	2005-06
Naslund, Markus	Pit., Van., NYR	15	1117	395	474	869	736	52	14	22	36	56	....	1993-94	2008-09
Naslund, Mats	Mtl., Bos.	9	651	251	383	634	111	102	35	57	92	33	1	1982-83	1994-95
Nasreddine, Alain	Chi., Mtl., NYI, Pit.	5	74	1	4	5	84	....	....	....	....	....	....	1998-99	2007-08
Nattrass, Ralph	Chi.	4	223	18	38	56	308	....	....	....	....	....	....	1946-47	1949-50
Nattress, Ric	Mtl., St.L., Cgy., Tor., Phi.	11	536	29	135	164	377	67	5	10	15	60	1	1982-83	1992-93
Natyshak, Mike	Que.	1	4	0	0	0	0	....	....	....	....	....	....	1987-88	1987-88
Nazarov, Andrei	S.J., T.B., Cgy., Ana., Bos., Phx., Min.	12	571	53	71	124	1409	9	0	0	0	11	....	1993-94	2005-06
Ndur, Rumun	Buf., NYR, Atl.	4	69	2	3	5	137	....	....	....	....	....	....	1996-97	1999-00
Neaton, Pat	Pit.	1	9	1	1	2	12	....	....	....	....	....	....	1993-94	1993-94
Nechayev, Viktor	L.A.	1	3	1	0	1	0	....	....	....	....	....	....	1982-83	1982-83

Name	NHL Teams	NHL Seasons	Regular Schedule GP	G	A	TP	PIM	Playoffs GP	G	A	TP	PIM	NHL Cup Wins	First NHL Season	Last NHL Season
Neckar, Stan	Ott., NYR, Phx., T.B., Nsh.	10	510	12	41	53	316	29	0	3	3	8	1	1994-95	2003-04
Nedomansky, Vaclav	Det., NYR, St.L.	6	421	122	156	278	88	7	3	5	8	0	....	1977-78	1982-83
‡ Nedorost, Andrej	CBJ	3	28	2	3	5	12	....	....	....	....	....	....	2001-02	2003-04
‡ Nedorost, Vaclav	Col., Fla.	3	99	10	10	20	34	....	....	....	....	....	....	2001-02	2003-04
‡ Nedved, Petr	Van., St.L., NYR, Pit., Edm., Phx., Phi.	15	982	310	407	717	708	71	19	23	42	64	....	1990-91	2006-07
Nedved, Zdenek	Tor.	3	31	4	6	10	14	....	....	....	....	....	....	1994-95	1996-97
Needham, Mike	Pit., Dal.	3	86	9	5	14	16	14	2	0	2	4	1	1991-92	1993-94
Neely, Bob	Tor., Col.	5	283	39	59	98	266	26	5	7	12	15	....	1973-74	1977-78
Neely, Cam	Van., Bos.	13	726	395	299	694	1241	93	57	32	89	168	....	1983-84	1995-96
Neilson, Jim	NYR, Cal., Cle.	16	1023	69	299	368	904	65	1	17	18	61	....	1962-63	1977-78
Nelson, Gordie	Tor.	1	3	0	0	0	11	....	....	....	....	....	....	1969-70	1969-70
Nelson, Jeff	Wsh., Nsh.	3	52	3	8	11	20	3	0	0	0	4	....	1994-95	1998-99
Nelson, Todd	Pit., Wsh.	2	3	1	0	1	2	4	0	0	0	0	....	1991-92	1993-94
Nemchinov, Sergei	NYR, Van., NYI, N.J.	11	761	152	193	345	251	105	11	20	31	24	2	1991-92	2001-02
Nemecek, Jan	L.A.	2	7	1	0	1	4	....	....	....	....	....	....	1998-99	1999-00
Nemeth, Steve	NYR	1	12	2	0	2	2	....	....	....	....	....	....	1987-88	1987-88
‡ Nemirovsky, David	Fla.	4	91	16	22	38	42	3	1	0	1	0	....	1995-96	1998-99
Nesterenko, Eric	Tor., Chi.	21	1219	250	324	574	1273	124	13	24	37	127	1	1951-52	1971-72
Nethery, Lance	NYR, Edm.	2	41	11	14	25	14	14	5	3	8	9	....	1980-81	1981-82
Neufeld, Ray	Hfd., Wpg., Bos.	11	595	157	200	357	816	28	8	6	14	55	....	1979-80	1989-90
• Neville, Mike	Tor., NYA	3	65	5	5	10	14	2	0	0	0	0	....	1924-25	1930-31
Nevin, Bob	Tor., NYR, Min., L.A.	18	1128	307	419	726	211	84	16	18	34	24	2	1957-58	1975-76
Newberry, John	Mtl., Hfd.	4	22	0	4	4	6	2	0	0	0	0	....	1982-83	1985-86
Newell, Rick	Det.	2	6	0	0	0	0	....	....	....	....	....	....	1972-73	1973-74
Newman, Dan	NYR, Mtl., Edm.	4	126	17	24	41	63	3	0	0	0	4	....	1976-77	1979-80
• Newman, John	Det.	1	8	1	1	2	0	....	....	....	....	....	....	1930-31	1930-31
Nicholls, Bernie	L.A., NYR, Edm., N.J., Chi., S.J.	18	1127	475	734	1209	1292	118	42	72	114	164	....	1981-82	1998-99
• Nicholson, Al	Bos.	2	19	0	1	1	4	....	....	....	....	....	....	1955-56	1956-57
• Nicholson, Ed	Det.	1	1	0	0	0	0	....	....	....	....	....	....	1947-48	1947-48
• Nicholson, Hickey	Chi.	1	2	1	0	1	0	....	....	....	....	....	....	1937-38	1937-38
Nicholson, Neil	Oak., NYI	4	39	3	1	4	23	2	0	0	0	0	....	1969-70	1977-78
Nicholson, Paul	Wsh.	3	62	4	8	12	18	....	....	....	....	....	....	1974-75	1976-77
Nickulas, Eric	Bos., St.L., Chi.	6	118	15	23	38	82	1	0	0	0	2	....	1998-99	2005-06
Nicolson, Graeme	Bos., Col., NYR	3	52	2	7	9	60	....	....	....	....	....	....	1978-79	1982-83
Nieckar, Barry	Hfd., Cgy., Ana.	4	8	0	0	0	21	....	....	....	....	....	....	1992-93	1997-98
Niedermayer, Scott	N.J., Ana.	18	1263	172	568	740	784	202	25	73	98	155	4	1991-92	2009-10
Niekamp, Jim	Det.	2	29	0	2	2	37	....	....	....	....	....	....	1970-71	1971-72
Nielsen, Chris	CBJ	2	52	6	8	14	8	....	....	....	....	....	....	2000-01	2001-02
Nielsen, Jeff	NYR, Ana., Min.	5	252	20	27	47	70	4	0	0	0	2	....	1996-97	2000-01
Nielsen, Kirk	Bos.	1	6	0	0	0	0	....	....	....	....	....	....	1997-98	1997-98
‡ Niemi, Antti-Jussi	Ana.	2	29	1	1	2	22	....	....	....	....	....	....	2000-01	2001-02
‡ Nieminen, Ville	Col., Pit., Chi., Cgy., NYR, S.J., St.L.	7	385	48	69	117	333	58	8	12	20	99	1	1999-00	2006-07
Nienhuis, Kraig	Bos.	3	87	20	16	36	39	2	0	0	0	14	....	1985-86	1987-88
Nieuwendyk, Joe	Cgy., Dal., N.J., Tor., Fla.	20	1257	564	562	1126	677	158	66	50	116	91	3	1986-87	2006-07
• Nighbor, Frank	Ott., Tor.	13	349	139	98	237	249	20	4	9	13	13	4	1917-18	1929-30
Nigro, Frank	Tor.	2	68	8	18	26	39	3	0	0	0	2	....	1982-83	1983-84
‡ Niinimaa, Janne	Phi., Edm., NYI, Dal., Mtl.	10	741	54	265	319	733	59	3	21	24	60	....	1996-97	2006-07
‡ Nikolishin, Andrei	Hfd., Wsh., Chi., Col.	10	628	93	187	280	270	43	1	17	18	22	....	1994-95	2003-04
Nikulin, Igor	Ana.	1	....	....	....	....	....	1	0	0	0	0	....	1996-97	1996-97
Nilan, Chris	Mtl., NYR, Bos.	13	688	110	115	225	3043	111	8	9	17	541	1	1979-80	1991-92
Nill, Jim	St.L., Van., Bos., Wpg., Det.	9	524	58	87	145	854	59	10	5	15	203	....	1981-82	1989-90
‡ Nilson, Marcus	Fla., Cgy.	9	521	67	101	168	270	34	4	7	11	14	....	1998-99	2007-08
Nilsson, Kent	Atl., Cgy., Min., Edm.	9	553	264	422	686	116	59	11	41	52	14	1	1979-80	1994-95
Nilsson, Ulf	NYR	4	170	57	112	169	85	25	8	14	22	27	....	1978-79	1982-83
‡ Niskala, Janne	T.B.	1	6	1	2	3	6	....	....	....	....	....	....	2008-09	2008-09
Nistico, Lou	Col.	1	3	0	0	0	0	....	....	....	....	....	....	1977-78	1977-78
• Noble, Reg	Tor., Mtl.M., Det.	16	510	168	106	274	916	18	2	2	4	33	3	1917-18	1932-33
Noel, Claude	Wsh.	1	7	0	0	0	0	....	....	....	....	....	....	1979-80	1979-80
Nolan, Brandon	Car.	1	6	0	1	1	0	....	....	....	....	....	....	2007-08	2007-08
• Nolan, Paddy	Tor.	1	2	0	0	0	0	....	....	....	....	....	....	1921-22	1921-22
Nolan, Ted	Det., Pit.	3	78	6	16	22	105	....	....	....	....	....	....	1981-82	1985-86
Nolet, Simon	Phi., K.C., Pit., Col.	10	562	150	182	332	187	34	6	3	9	8	1	1967-68	1976-77
Noonan, Brian	Chi., NYR, St.L., Van., Phx.	12	629	116	159	275	518	71	17	19	36	77	1	1987-88	1998-99
‡ Nordgren, Niklas	Car., Pit.	1	58	4	2	6	34	....	....	....	....	....	....	2005-06	2005-06
Nordmark, Robert	St.L., Van.	4	236	13	70	83	254	7	3	2	5	8	....	1987-88	1990-91
Nordqvist, Jonas	Chi.	1	3	0	2	2	2	....	....	....	....	....	....	2006-07	2006-07
Nordstrom, Peter	Bos.	1	2	0	0	0	0	....	....	....	....	....	....	1998-99	1998-99
Noris, Joe	Pit., St.L., Buf.	3	55	2	5	7	22	....	....	....	....	....	....	1971-72	1973-74
Norris, Dwayne	Que., Ana.	3	20	2	4	6	8	....	....	....	....	....	....	1993-94	1995-96
Norrish, Rod	Min.	2	21	3	3	6	2	....	....	....	....	....	....	1973-74	1974-75
Norstrom, Mattias	NYR, L.A., Dal.	14	903	18	147	165	661	56	2	5	7	54	....	1993-94	2007-08
• Northcott, Baldy	Mtl.M., Chi.	11	446	133	112	245	273	31	8	5	13	14	1	1928-29	1938-39
Norton, Brad	Fla., L.A., Wsh., Ott., Det., S.J.	6	124	3	8	11	287	....	....	....	....	....	....	2001-02	2007-08
Norton, Jeff	NYI, S.J., St.L., Edm., T.B., Fla., Pit., Bos.	15	799	52	332	384	615	65	4	21	25	89	....	1987-88	2001-02
Norwich, Craig	Wpg., St.L., Col.	2	104	17	58	75	60	....	....	....	....	....	....	1979-80	1980-81
Norwood, Lee	Que., Wsh., St.L., Det., N.J., Hfd., Cgy.	12	503	58	153	211	1099	65	6	22	28	171	....	1980-81	1993-94
‡ Novak, Filip	Ott., CBJ	2	17	0	0	0	6	....	....	....	....	....	....	2005-06	2006-07
Novoseltsev, Ivan	Fla., Phx.	5	234	31	44	75	112	....	....	....	....	....	....	1999-00	2003-04
‡ Novotny, Jiri	Buf., Wsh., CBJ	4	189	20	31	51	66	4	0	0	0	0	....	2005-06	2008-09
Novy, Milan	Wsh.	1	73	18	30	48	16	2	0	0	0	0	....	1982-83	1982-83
Nowak, Hank	Pit., Det., Bos.	4	180	26	29	55	161	13	1	0	1	8	....	1973-74	1976-77
‡ Nummelin, Petteri	CBJ, Min.	3	139	9	36	45	34	7	1	2	3	0	....	2000-01	2007-08
Numminen, Teppo	Wpg., Phx., Dal., Buf.	20	1372	117	520	637	513	82	9	14	23	28	....	1988-89	2008-09
Nurminen, Kai	L.A., Min.	2	69	17	11	28	24	....	....	....	....	....	....	1996-97	2000-01
Nykoluk, Mike	Tor.	1	32	3	1	4	20	....	....	....	....	....	....	1956-57	1956-57
‡ Nylander, Michael	Hfd., Cgy., T.B., Chi., Wsh., Bos., NYR	15	920	209	470	679	468	47	12	22	34	14	....	1992-93	2008-09
Nylund, Gary	Tor., Chi., NYI	11	608	32	139	171	1235	24	0	6	6	63	....	1982-83	1992-93
• Nyrop, Bill	Mtl., Min.	4	207	12	51	63	101	35	1	7	8	22	3	1975-76	1981-82
Nystrom, Bob	NYI	14	900	235	278	513	1248	157	39	44	83	236	4	1972-73	1985-86

O

Name	NHL Teams	NHL Seasons	Regular Schedule GP	G	A	TP	PIM	Playoffs GP	G	A	TP	PIM	NHL Cup Wins	First NHL Season	Last NHL Season
Oates, Adam	Det., St.L., Bos., Wsh., Phi., Ana., Edm.	19	1337	341	1079	1420	415	163	42	114	156	66	....	1985-86	2003-04
• Oatman, Russell	Det., Mtl.M., NYR	3	120	20	9	29	100	15	1	0	1	18	....	1926-27	1928-29
O'Brien, Dennis	Min., Col., Cle., Bos.	10	592	31	91	122	1017	34	1	2	3	101	....	1970-71	1979-80
‡ O'Brien, Doug	T.B.	1	5	0	0	0	2	....	....	....	....	....	....	2005-06	2005-06
O'Brien, Ellard	Bos.	1	2	0	0	0	0	....	....	....	....	....	....	1955-56	1955-56
‡ Obsut, Jaroslav	St.L., Col.	2	7	0	0	0	2	....	....	....	....	....	....	2000-01	2001-02
O'Callahan, Jack	Chi., N.J.	7	389	27	104	131	541	32	4	11	15	41	....	1982-83	1988-89
O'Connell, Mike	Chi., Bos., Det.	13	860	105	334	439	605	82	8	24	32	64	....	1977-78	1989-90
• O'Connor, Buddy	Mtl., NYR	10	509	140	257	397	34	53	15	21	36	6	2	1941-42	1950-51
O'Connor, Myles	N.J., Ana.	4	43	3	4	7	69	....	....	....	....	....	....	1990-91	1993-94
Oddleifson, Chris	Bos., Van.	9	524	95	191	286	464	14	1	6	7	8	....	1972-73	1980-81
Odelein, Lyle	Mtl., N.J., Phx., CBJ, Chi., Dal., Fla., Pit.	16	1056	50	202	252	2316	86	5	13	18	209	1	1989-90	2005-06
Odelein, Selmar	Edm.	3	18	0	2	2	35	....	....	....	....	....	....	1985-86	1988-89
Odgers, Jeff	S.J., Bos., Col., Atl.	12	821	75	70	145	2364	47	2	1	3	73	....	1991-92	2002-03
Odjick, Gino	Van., NYI, Phi., Mtl.	12	605	64	73	137	2567	44	4	1	5	142	....	1990-91	2001-02
O'Donnell, Fred	Bos.	2	115	15	11	26	98	5	0	1	1	5	....	1972-73	1973-74
• O'Donoghue, Don	Oak., Cal.	3	125	18	17	35	35	3	0	0	0	0	....	1969-70	1971-72
Odrowski, Gerry	Det., Oak., St.L.	6	309	12	19	31	111	30	0	1	1	16	....	1960-61	1971-72
O'Dwyer, Bill	L.A., Bos.	5	120	9	13	22	108	10	0	0	0	2	....	1983-84	1989-90
O'Flaherty, Gerry	Tor., Van., Atl.	8	438	99	95	194	168	7	2	2	4	6	....	1971-72	1978-79
• O'Flaherty, Peanuts	NYA, Bro.	2	21	5	1	6	0	....	....	....	....	....	....	1940-41	1941-42
Ogilvie, Brian	Chi., St.L.	6	90	15	21	36	29	....	....	....	....	....	....	1972-73	1978-79
• O'Grady, George	Mtl.W.	1	4	0	0	0	0	....	....	....	....	....	....	1917-18	1917-18
Ogrodnick, John	Det., Que., NYR	14	928	402	425	827	260	41	18	8	26	6	....	1979-80	1992-93
Ojanen, Janne	N.J.	4	98	21	23	44	28	3	0	2	2	0	....	1988-89	1992-93
Okerlund, Todd	NYI	1	4	0	0	0	2	....	....	....	....	....	....	1987-88	1987-88
Oksiuta, Roman	Edm., Van., Ana., Pit.	4	153	46	41	87	100	10	2	3	5	0	....	1993-94	1996-97
Olausson, Fredrik	Wpg., Edm., Ana., Pit., Det.	16	1022	147	434	581	450	71	6	23	29	28	1	1986-87	2002-03
Olczyk, Ed	Chi., Tor., Wpg., NYR, L.A., Pit.	16	1031	342	452	794	874	57	19	15	34	57	1	1984-85	1999-00
Oliver, David	Edm., NYR, Ott., Phx., Dal.	9	233	49	49	98	84	10	0	0	0	2	....	1994-95	2005-06
• Oliver, Harry	Bos., NYA	11	463	127	85	212	147	35	10	6	16	24	1	1926-27	1936-37
Oliver, Murray	Det., Bos., Tor., Min.	17	1127	274	454	728	320	35	9	16	25	10	....	1957-58	1974-75

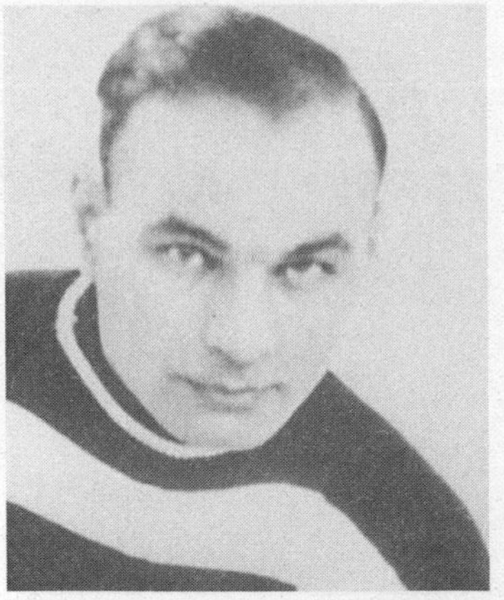

Frank Nighbor

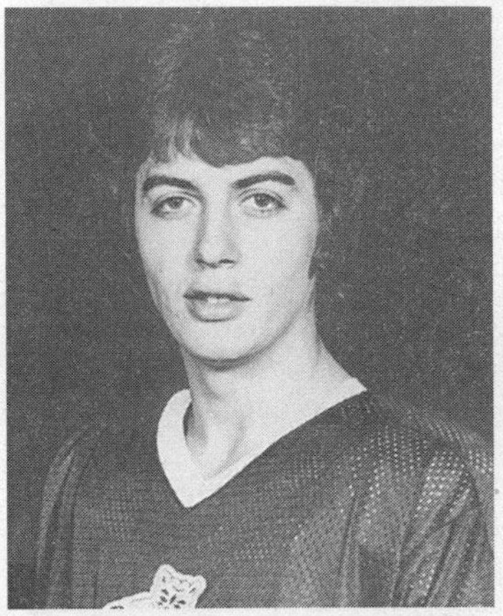

Claude Noel

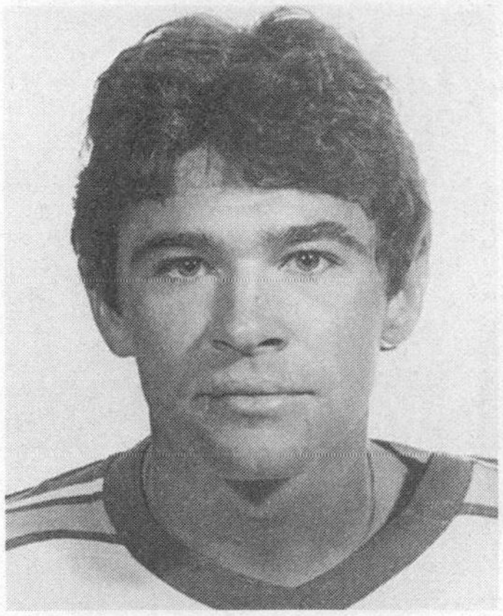

Craig Norwich

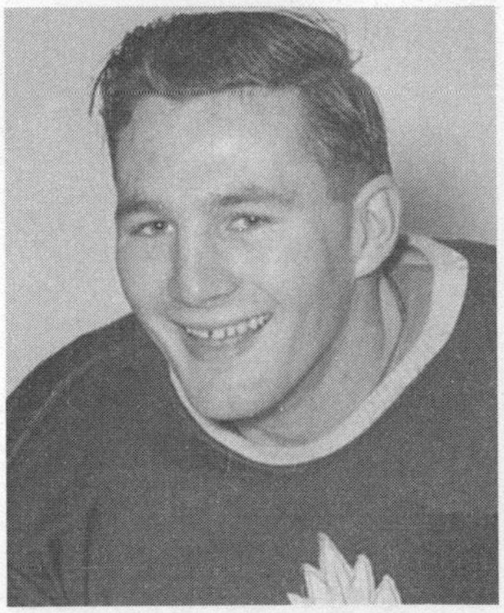

Tom O'Neill

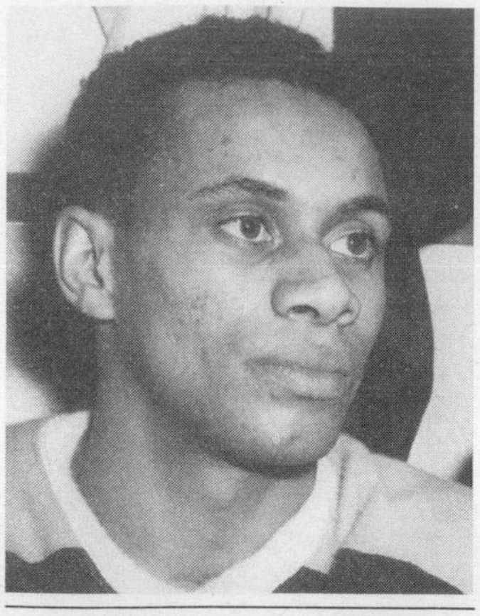
Willie O'Ree

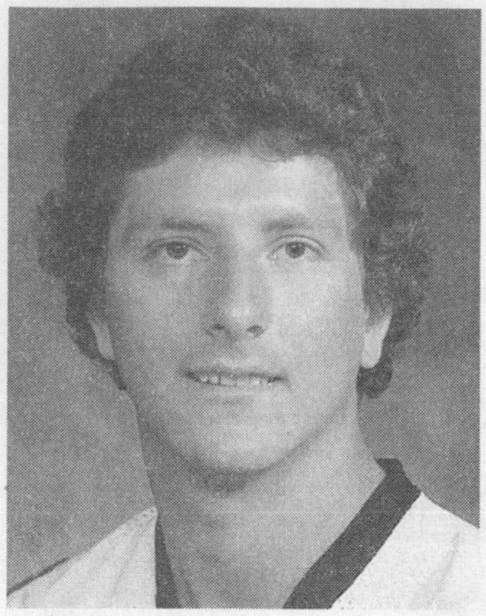
Brad Palmer

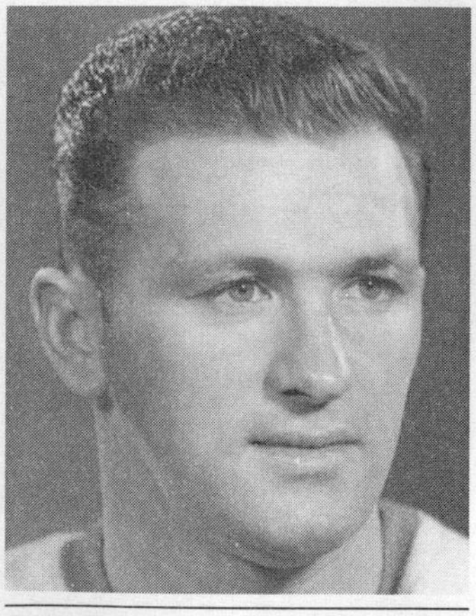
Fern Perreault

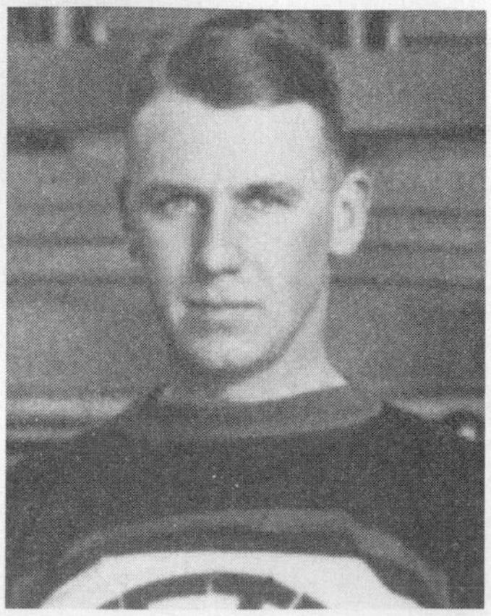
Eric Pettinger

			Regular Schedule					Playoffs							
Name	NHL Teams	NHL Seasons	GP	G	A	TP	PIM	GP	G	A	TP	PIM	NHL Cup Wins	First NHL Season	Last NHL Season
Oliwa, Krzysztof	N.J., CBJ, Pit., NYR, Bos., Cgy.	9	410	17	28	45	1447	32	2	0	2	47	1	1996-97	2005-06
Olmstead, Bert	Chi., Mtl., Tor.	14	848	181	421	602	884	115	16	43	59	101	5	1948-49	1961-62
Olsen, Darryl	Cgy.	1	1	0	0	0	0	....	....	....	....	....	....	1991-92	1991-92
Olson, Dennis	Det.	1	4	0	0	0	0	....	....	....	....	....	....	1957-58	1957-58
Olson, Josh	Fla.	1	5	1	0	1	0	....	....	....	....	....	....	2003-04	2003-04
Olsson, Christer	St.L., Ott.	2	56	4	12	16	24	3	0	0	0	0	....	1995-96	1996-97
‡ Olvecky, Peter	Min., Nsh.	2	32	2	5	7	12	....	....	....	....	....	....	2008-09	2009-10
‡ Olvestad, Jimmie	T.B.	2	111	3	14	17	40	....	....	....	....	....	....	2001-02	2002-03
• O'Neil, Jim	Bos., Mtl.	6	156	6	30	36	109	9	1	1	2	13	....	1933-34	1941-42
O'Neil, Paul	Van., Bos.	2	6	0	0	0	0	....	....	....	....	....	....	1973-74	1975-76
O'Neill, Jeff	Hfd., Car., Tor.	11	821	237	259	496	670	34	9	8	17	37	....	1995-96	2006-07
• O'Neill, Tom	Tor.	2	66	10	12	22	53	4	0	0	0	6	1	1943-44	1944-45
Orban, Bill	Chi., Min.	3	114	8	15	23	67	3	0	0	0	0	....	1967-68	1969-70
O'Ree, Willie	Bos.	2	45	4	10	14	26	....	....	....	....	....	....	1957-58	1960-61
O'Regan, Tom	Pit.	3	61	5	12	17	10	....	....	....	....	....	....	1983-84	1985-86
O'Reilly, Terry	Bos.	14	891	204	402	606	2095	108	25	42	67	335	....	1971-72	1984-85
Orlando, Gates	Buf.	3	98	18	26	44	51	5	0	4	4	14	....	1984-85	1986-87
• Orlando, Jimmy	Det.	6	199	6	25	31	375	36	0	9	9	105	1	1936-37	1942-43
Orleski, Dave	Mtl.	2	2	0	0	0	0	....	....	....	....	....	....	1980-81	1981-82
Orr, Bobby	Bos., Chi.	12	657	270	645	915	953	74	26	66	92	107	2	1966-67	1978-79
Orszagh, Vladimir	NYI, Nsh., St.L.	7	289	54	65	119	194	6	2	0	2	4	....	1997-98	2005-06
Osborne, Keith	St.L., T.B.	2	16	1	3	4	16	....	....	....	....	....	....	1989-90	1992-93
Osborne, Mark	Det., NYR, Tor., Wpg.	14	919	212	319	531	1152	87	12	16	28	141	....	1981-82	1994-95
Osburn, Randy	Tor., Phi.	2	27	0	2	2	0	....	....	....	....	....	....	1972-73	1974-75
O'Shea, Danny	Min., Chi., St.L.	5	369	64	115	179	265	39	3	7	10	61	....	1968-69	1972-73
• O'Shea, Kevin	Buf., St.L.	3	134	13	18	31	85	12	2	1	3	10	....	1970-71	1972-73
Osiecki, Mark	Cgy., Ott., Wpg., Min.	2	93	3	11	14	43	....	....	....	....	....	....	1991-92	1992-93
O'Sullivan, Chris	Cgy., Van., Ana.	5	62	2	17	19	16	....	....	....	....	....	....	1996-97	2002-03
Otevrel, Jaroslav	S.J.	2	16	3	4	7	2	....	....	....	....	....	....	1992-93	1993-94
Otto, Joel	Cgy., Phi.	14	943	195	313	508	1934	122	27	47	74	207	1	1984-85	1997-98
Ouellette, Eddie	Chi.	1	43	3	2	5	11	1	0	0	0	0	....	1935-36	1935-36
Ouellette, Gerry	Bos.	1	34	5	4	9	0	....	....	....	....	....	....	1960-61	1960-61
Owchar, Dennis	Pit., Col.	6	288	30	85	115	200	10	1	1	2	8	....	1974-75	1979-80
• Owen, George	Bos.	5	183	44	33	77	151	21	2	5	7	25	1	1928-29	1932-33
‡ Ozolinsh, Sandis	S.J., Col., Car., Fla., Ana., NYR	15	875	167	397	564	638	137	23	67	90	131	1	1992-93	2007-08
P															
Pachal, Clayton	Bos., Col.	3	35	2	3	5	95	....	....	....	....	....	....	1976-77	1978-79
Paddock, John	Wsh., Phi., Que.	5	87	8	14	22	86	5	2	0	2	0	....	1975-76	1982-83
Paek, Jim	Pit., L.A., Ott.	5	217	5	29	34	155	27	1	4	5	8	2	1990-91	1994-95
Paiement, Rosaire	Phi., Van.	5	190	48	52	100	343	3	3	0	3	0	....	1967-68	1971-72
Paiement, Wilf	K.C., Col., Tor., Que., NYR, Buf., Pit.	14	946	356	458	814	1757	69	18	17	35	185	....	1974-75	1987-88
• Palangio, Pete	Mtl., Det., Chi.	5	71	13	10	23	28	7	0	0	0	0	1	1926-27	1937-38
• Palazzari, Aldo	Bos., NYR	1	35	8	3	11	4	....	....	....	....	....	....	1943-44	1943-44
Palazzari, Doug	St.L.	4	108	18	20	38	23	2	0	0	0	0	....	1974-75	1978-79
Palffy, Ziggy	NYI, L.A., Pit.	12	684	329	384	713	322	24	9	10	19	8	....	1993-94	2005-06
Palmer, Brad	Min., Bos.	3	168	32	38	70	58	29	9	5	14	16	....	1980-81	1982-83
Palmer, Rob	Chi.	3	16	0	3	3	2	....	....	....	....	....	....	1973-74	1975-76
Palmer, Robert	L.A., N.J.	7	320	9	101	110	115	8	1	2	3	6	....	1977-78	1983-84
• Panagabko, Ed	Bos.	2	29	0	3	3	38	....	....	....	....	....	....	1955-56	1956-57
Pandolfo, Jay	N.J.	13	819	99	124	223	154	131	11	22	33	12	2	1996-97	2009-10
Pandolfo, Mike	CBJ	1	3	0	0	0	0	....	....	....	....	....	....	2003-04	2003-04
Pankewicz, Greg	Ott., Cgy.	2	21	0	3	3	22	....	....	....	....	....	....	1993-94	1998-99
Panteleev, Grigori	Bos., NYI	4	54	8	6	14	12	....	....	....	....	....	....	1992-93	1995-96
• Papike, Joe	Chi.	3	20	3	3	6	4	5	0	2	2	0	....	1940-41	1944-45
‡ Papineau, Justin	St.L., NYI	3	81	11	8	19	12	1	0	0	0	0	....	2001-02	2003-04
Pappin, Jim	Tor., Chi., Cal., Cle.	14	767	278	295	573	667	92	33	34	67	101	2	1963-64	1976-77
Paradise, Bob	Min., Atl., Pit., Wsh.	8	368	8	54	62	393	12	0	1	1	19	....	1971-72	1978-79
• Pargeter, George	Mtl.	1	4	0	0	0	0	....	....	....	....	....	....	1946-47	1946-47
Parise, J.P.	Bos., Tor., Min., NYI, Cle.	14	890	238	356	594	706	86	27	31	58	87	....	1965-66	1978-79
Parizeau, Michel	St.L., Phi.	1	58	3	14	17	18	....	....	....	....	....	....	1971-72	1971-72
Park, Brad	NYR, Bos., Det.	17	1113	213	683	896	1429	161	35	90	125	217	....	1968-69	1984-85
Parker, Jeff	Buf., Hfd.	5	141	16	19	35	163	5	0	0	0	26	....	1986-87	1990-91
Parker, Scott	Col., S.J.	8	308	7	14	21	699	5	0	0	0	4	1	1998-99	2007-08
• Parkes, Ernie	Mtl.M.	1	17	0	0	0	2	....	....	....	....	....	....	1924-25	1924-25
Parks, Greg	NYI	3	23	1	2	3	6	2	0	0	0	0	....	1990-91	1992-93
• Parsons, George	Tor.	3	78	12	13	25	20	7	3	2	5	11	....	1936-37	1938-39
‡ Parssinen, Timo	Ana.	1	17	0	3	3	2	....	....	....	....	....	....	2001-02	2001-02
• Pasek, Dusan	Min.	1	48	4	10	14	30	2	1	0	1	0	....	1988-89	1988-89
Pasin, Dave	Bos., L.A.	2	76	18	19	37	50	3	0	1	1	0	....	1985-86	1988-89
Paslawski, Greg	Mtl., St.L., Wpg., Buf., Que., Phi., Cgy.	11	650	187	185	372	169	60	19	13	32	25	....	1983-84	1993-94
‡ Patera, Pavel	Dal., Min.	2	32	2	7	9	8	....	....	....	....	....	....	1999-00	2000-01
Paterson, Joe	Det., Phi., L.A., NYR	9	291	19	37	56	829	22	3	4	7	77	....	1980-81	1988-89
Paterson, Mark	Hfd.	4	29	3	3	6	33	....	....	....	....	....	....	1982-83	1985-86
Paterson, Rick	Chi.	9	430	50	43	93	136	61	7	10	17	51	....	1978-79	1986-87
Patey, Doug	Wsh.	3	45	4	2	6	8	....	....	....	....	....	....	1976-77	1978-79
Patey, Larry	Cal., St.L., NYR	12	717	153	163	316	631	40	8	10	18	57	....	1973-74	1984-85
Patrick, Craig	Cal., St.L., K.C., Wsh.	8	401	72	91	163	61	2	0	1	1	0	....	1971-72	1978-79
Patrick, Glenn	St.L., Cal., Cle.	4	38	2	3	5	72	....	....	....	....	....	....	1973-74	1976-77
Patrick, James	NYR, Hfd., Cgy., Buf.	21	1280	149	490	639	759	117	6	32	38	86	....	1983-84	2003-04
• Patrick, Lester	NYR	1	1	0	0	0	2	....	....	....	....	....	....	1926-27	1926-27
• Patrick, Lynn	NYR	10	455	145	190	335	240	44	10	6	16	22	1	1934-35	1945-46
• Patrick, Muzz	NYR	5	166	5	26	31	133	25	4	0	4	34	1	1937-38	1945-46
Patrick, Steve	Buf., NYR, Que.	6	250	40	68	108	242	12	0	1	1	12	....	1980-81	1985-86
Patterson, Colin	Cgy., Buf.	10	504	96	109	205	239	85	12	17	29	57	1	1983-84	1992-93
Patterson, Dennis	K.C., Phi.	3	138	6	22	28	67	....	....	....	....	....	....	1974-75	1979-80
Patterson, Ed	Pit.	3	68	3	3	6	56	....	....	....	....	....	....	1993-94	1996-97
• Patterson, George	Tor., Mtl., NYA, Bos., Det., St.L.	9	284	51	27	78	218	3	0	0	0	2	....	1926-27	1934-35
• Paul, Butch	Det.	1	3	0	0	0	0	....	....	....	....	....	....	1964-65	1964-65
Paul, Jeff	Col.	1	2	0	0	0	7	....	....	....	....	....	....	2002-03	2002-03
• Paulhus, Rollie	Mtl.	1	33	0	0	0	0	....	....	....	....	....	....	1925-26	1925-26
Pavelich, Mark	NYR, Min., S.J.	7	355	137	192	329	340	23	7	17	24	14	....	1981-82	1991-92
Pavelich, Marty	Det.	10	634	93	159	252	454	91	13	15	28	74	4	1947-48	1956-57
Pavese, Jim	St.L., NYR, Det., Hfd.	8	328	13	44	57	689	36	0	6	6	81	....	1981-82	1988-89
• Payer, Evariste	Mtl.	1	1	0	0	0	0	....	....	....	....	....	....	1917-18	1917-18
Payer, Serge	Fla., Ott.	4	124	7	6	13	49	....	....	....	....	....	....	2000-01	2006-07
Payne, Davis	Bos.	2	22	0	1	1	14	....	....	....	....	....	....	1995-96	1996-97
Payne, Steve	Min.	10	613	228	238	466	435	71	35	35	70	60	....	1978-79	1987-88
Paynter, Kent	Chi., Wsh., Wpg., Ott.	7	37	1	3	4	69	4	0	0	0	10	....	1987-88	1993-94
Peake, Pat	Wsh.	5	134	28	41	69	105	13	2	2	4	20	....	1993-94	1997-98
• Pearson, Mel	NYR, Pit.	5	38	2	6	8	25	....	....	....	....	....	....	1959-60	1967-68
Pearson, Rob	Tor., Wsh., St.L.	6	269	56	54	110	645	33	4	2	6	94	....	1991-92	1996-97
Pearson, Scott	Tor., Que., Edm., Buf., NYI	10	292	56	42	98	615	10	2	0	2	14	....	1988-89	1999-00
Peat, Stephen	Wsh.	4	130	8	2	10	234	....	....	....	....	....	....	2001-02	2005-06
Peca, Michael	Van., Buf., NYI, Edm., Tor., CBJ	14	864	176	289	465	798	97	15	19	34	80	....	1993-94	2008-09
Pedersen, Allen	Bos., Min., Hfd.	8	428	5	36	41	487	64	0	0	0	91	....	1986-87	1993-94
Pederson, Barry	Bos., Van., Pit., Hfd.	12	701	238	416	654	472	34	22	30	52	25	1	1980-81	1991-92
‡ Pederson, Denis	N.J., Van., Phx., Nsh.	8	435	57	71	128	398	27	1	5	6	8	....	1995-96	2002-03
Pederson, Mark	Mtl., Phi., S.J., Det.	5	169	35	50	85	77	2	0	0	0	0	....	1989-90	1993-94
Pederson, Tom	S.J., Tor.	5	240	20	49	69	142	24	1	11	12	10	....	1992-93	1996-97
• Peer, Bert	Det.	1	1	0	0	0	0	....	....	....	....	....	....	1939-40	1939-40
Peirson, Johnny	Bos.	11	545	153	173	326	315	49	10	16	26	26	....	1946-47	1957-58
Pelensky, Perry	Chi.	1	4	0	0	0	5	....	....	....	....	....	....	1983-84	1983-84
Pellerin, Scott	N.J., St.L., Min., Car., Bos., Dal., Phx.	11	536	72	126	198	320	37	1	2	3	26	....	1992-93	2003-04
Pelletier, Roger	Phi.	1	1	0	0	0	0	....	....	....	....	....	....	1967-68	1967-68
Peloffy, Andre	Wsh.	1	9	0	0	0	0	....	....	....	....	....	....	1974-75	1974-75
‡ Peltonen, Ville	S.J., Nsh., Fla.	8	382	52	96	148	119	....	....	....	....	....	....	1995-96	2008-09
Peluso, Mike	Chi., Ott., N.J., St.L., Cgy.	9	458	38	52	90	1951	62	3	4	7	107	1	1989-90	1997-98
Peluso, Mike	Chi., Phi.	2	38	4	2	6	19	....	....	....	....	....	....	2001-02	2003-04
Pelyk, Mike	Tor.	9	441	26	88	114	566	40	0	3	3	41	....	1967-68	1977-78
Penney, Chad	Ott.	1	3	0	0	0	2	....	....	....	....	....	....	1993-94	1993-94
Pennington, Cliff	Mtl., Bos.	3	101	17	42	59	6	....	....	....	....	....	....	1960-61	1962-63
Peplinski, Jim	Cgy.	11	711	161	263	424	1467	99	15	31	46	382	1	1980-81	1994-95
‡ Perezhogin, Alexander	Mtl.	2	128	15	19	34	86	6	1	1	2	4	....	2005-06	2006-07
Perlini, Fred	Tor.	2	8	2	3	5	0	....	....	....	....	....	....	1981-82	1983-84

Name	NHL Teams	NHL Seasons	Regular Schedule GP	G	A	TP	PIM	Playoffs GP	G	A	TP	PIM	NHL Cup Wins	First NHL Season	Last NHL Season
Perreault, Fern	NYR	2	3	0	0	0	0	....	....	....	....	....	....	1947-48	1949-50
Perreault, Gilbert	Buf.	17	1191	512	814	1326	500	90	33	70	103	44	....	1970-71	1986-87
Perreault, Yanic	Tor., L.A., Mtl., Nsh., Phx., Chi.	14	859	247	269	516	402	54	11	19	30	18	....	1993-94	2007-08
‡ Perrin, Eric	T.B., Atl.	4	245	32	72	104	92	18	1	2	3	8	1	2003-04	2008-09
Perrott, Nathan	Nsh., Tor., Dal.	4	89	4	5	9	251	....	....	....	....	....	....	2001-02	2005-06
Perry, Brian	Oak., Buf.	3	96	16	29	45	24	8	1	1	2	4	....	1968-69	1970-71
Persson, Ricard	N.J., St.L., Ott.	7	229	10	44	54	262	26	1	3	4	59	....	1995-96	2001-02
Persson, Stefan	NYI	9	622	52	317	369	574	102	7	50	57	69	4	1977-78	1985-86
‡ Pesonen, Janne	Pit.	1	7	0	0	0	0	....	....	....	....	....	....	2008-09	2008-09
Pesut, George	Cal.	2	92	3	22	25	130	....	....	....	....	....	....	1974-75	1975-76
Peters, Andrew	Buf., N.J.	6	229	4	3	7	650	....	....	....	....	....	....	2003-04	2009-10
• Peters, Frank	NYR	1	43	0	0	0	59	4	0	0	0	2	....	1930-31	1930-31
Peters, Garry	Mtl., NYR, Phi., Bos.	8	311	34	34	68	261	9	2	2	4	31	1	1964-65	1971-72
• Peters, Jimmy	Mtl., Bos., Det., Chi.	9	574	125	150	275	186	60	5	9	14	22	3	1945-46	1953-54
Peters, Jimmy	Det., L.A.	9	309	37	36	73	48	11	0	2	2	2	....	1964-65	1974-75
Peters, Steve	Col.	1	2	0	1	1	0	....	....	....	....	....	....	1979-80	1979-80
Peterson, Brent	Det., Buf., Van., Hfd.	11	620	72	141	213	484	31	4	4	8	65	....	1978-79	1988-89
Peterson, Brent	T.B.	3	56	9	1	10	6	....	....	....	....	....	....	1996-97	1998-99
Petit, Michel	Van., NYR, Que., Tor., Cgy., L.A., T.B., Edm., Phi., Phx.	16	827	90	238	328	1839	19	0	2	2	61	....	1982-83	1997-98
Petrenko, Sergei	Buf.	1	14	0	4	4	0	....	....	....	....	....	....	1993-94	1993-94
‡ Petrov, Oleg	Mtl., Nsh.	8	382	72	115	187	101	20	1	6	7	2	....	1992-93	2002-03
‡ Petrovicky, Robert	Hfd., Dal., St.L., T.B., NYI	8	208	27	38	65	118	2	0	0	0	0	....	1992-93	2000-01
Petrovicky, Ronald	Cgy., NYR, Atl., Pit.	6	342	41	51	92	429	3	0	0	0	2	....	2000-01	2006-07
‡ Petruzalek, Jakub	Car.	1	2	0	1	1	0	....	....	....	....	....	....	2008-09	2008-09
Pettersson, Jorgen	St.L., Hfd., Wsh.	6	435	174	192	366	117	44	15	12	27	4	....	1980-81	1985-86
‡ Pettinen, Tomi	NYI	3	24	0	0	0	18	....	....	....	....	....	....	2002-03	2005-06
• Pettinger, Eric	Bos., Tor., Ott.	3	98	7	12	19	83	4	1	0	1	8	....	1928-29	1930-31
• Pettinger, Gord	NYR, Det., Bos.	8	292	42	74	116	77	47	4	5	9	11	4	1932-33	1939-40
Phair, Lyle	L.A.	3	48	6	7	13	12	1	0	0	0	0	....	1985-86	1987-88
Phillipoff, Harold	Atl., Chi.	3	141	26	57	83	267	6	0	2	2	9	....	1977-78	1979-80
• Phillips, Bill	Mtl.M.	1	27	1	1	2	6	4	0	0	0	2	....	1929-30	1929-30
• Phillips, Charlie	Mtl.	1	17	0	0	0	6	....	....	....	....	....	....	1942-43	1942-43
• Phillips, Merlyn	Mtl.M., NYA	8	302	52	31	83	232	24	5	1	6	19	1	1925-26	1932-33
Picard, Michel	Hfd., S.J., Ott., St.L., Edm., Phi.	9	166	28	42	70	103	5	0	0	0	2	....	1990-91	2000-01
Picard, Noel	Mtl., St.L., Atl.	7	335	12	63	75	616	50	2	11	13	167	1	1964-65	1972-73
Picard, Robert	Wsh., Tor., Mtl., Wpg., Que., Det.	13	899	104	319	423	1025	36	5	15	20	39	....	1977-78	1989-90
Picard, Roger	St.L.	1	15	2	2	4	21	....	....	....	....	....	....	1967-68	1967-68
Pichette, Dave	Que., St.L., N.J., NYR	7	322	41	140	181	348	28	3	7	10	54	....	1980-81	1987-88
Picketts, Hal	NYA	1	48	3	1	4	32	....	....	....	....	....	....	1933-34	1933-34
• Pidhirny, Harry	Bos.	1	2	0	0	0	0	....	....	....	....	....	....	1957-58	1957-58
Pierce, Randy	Col., N.J., Hfd.	8	277	62	76	138	223	2	0	0	0	0	....	1977-78	1984-85
‡ Pihlman, Tuomas	N.J.	3	15	1	1	2	12	....	....	....	....	....	....	2003-04	2006-07
• Pike, Alf	NYR	6	234	42	77	119	145	21	4	2	6	12	1	1939-40	1946-47
‡ Pikkarainen, Ilkka	N.J.	1	31	1	3	4	10	....	....	....	....	....	....	2009-10	2009-10
‡ Pilar, Karel	Tor.	3	90	6	24	30	42	12	1	4	5	12	....	2001-02	2003-04
Pilon, Rich	NYI, NYR, St.L.	14	631	8	69	77	1745	15	0	0	0	50	....	1988-89	2001-02
Pilote, Pierre	Chi., Tor.	14	890	80	418	498	1251	86	8	53	61	102	1	1955-56	1968-69
Pinder, Gerry	Chi., Cal.	3	223	55	69	124	135	17	0	4	4	6	....	1969-70	1971-72
‡ Pineault, Adam	CBJ	1	3	0	0	0	0	....	....	....	....	....	....	2007-08	2007-08
Pirjeta, Lasse	CBJ, Pit.	3	146	23	27	50	50	....	....	....	....	....	....	2002-03	2005-06
‡ Pirnes, Esa	L.A.	1	57	3	8	11	12	....	....	....	....	....	....	2003-04	2003-04
‡ Piros, Kamil	Atl., Fla.	3	28	4	4	8	10	....	....	....	....	....	....	2001-02	2003-04
Pirus, Alex	Min., Det.	4	159	30	28	58	94	2	0	1	1	2	....	1976-77	1979-80
‡ Pisa, Ales	Edm., NYR	2	53	1	3	4	26	....	....	....	....	....	....	2001-02	2002-03
Pitlick, Lance	Ott., Fla.	8	393	16	33	49	298	24	0	2	2	21	....	1994-95	2001-02
• Pitre, Didier	Mtl.	6	127	64	33	97	87	9	2	4	6	19	....	1917-18	1922-23
Pittis, Domenic	Pit., Buf., Edm., Nsh.	7	86	5	11	16	71	3	0	0	0	2	....	1996-97	2003-04
‡ Pivko, Libor	Nsh.	1	1	0	0	0	0	....	....	....	....	....	....	2003-04	2003-04
Pivonka, Michal	Wsh.	13	825	181	418	599	478	95	19	36	55	86	....	1986-87	1998-99
• Plager, Barclay	St.L.	10	614	44	187	231	1115	68	3	20	23	182	....	1967-68	1976-77
Plager, Bill	Min., St.L., Atl.	9	263	4	34	38	294	31	0	2	2	26	....	1967-68	1975-76
Plager, Bob	NYR, St.L.	14	644	20	126	146	802	74	2	17	19	195	....	1964-65	1977-78
Plamondon, Gerry	Mtl.	5	74	7	13	20	10	11	5	2	7	2	1	1945-46	1950-51
Plante, Cam	Tor.	1	2	0	0	0	0	....	....	....	....	....	....	1984-85	1984-85
Plante, Dan	NYI	4	159	9	14	23	135	1	1	0	1	2	....	1993-94	1997-98
Plante, Derek	Buf., Dal., Chi., Phi.	8	450	96	152	248	138	41	6	10	16	18	1	1993-94	2000-01
Plante, Pierre	Phi., St.L., Chi., NYR, Que.	9	599	125	172	297	599	33	2	6	8	51	....	1971-72	1979-80
Plantery, Mark	Wpg.	1	25	1	5	6	14	....	....	....	....	....	....	1980-81	1980-81
Plavsic, Adrien	St.L., Van., T.B., Ana.	8	214	16	56	72	161	13	1	7	8	4	....	1989-90	1996-97
• Plaxton, Hugh	Mtl.M.	1	15	1	2	3	4	....	....	....	....	....	....	1932-33	1932-33
Playfair, Jim	Edm., Chi.	3	21	2	4	6	51	....	....	....	....	....	....	1983-84	1988-89
Playfair, Larry	Buf., L.A.	12	688	26	94	120	1812	43	0	6	6	111	....	1978-79	1989-90
Pleau, Larry	Mtl.	3	94	9	15	24	27	4	0	0	0	0	....	1969-70	1971-72
‡ Pletka, Vaclav	Phi.	1	1	0	0	0	0	....	....	....	....	....	....	2001-02	2001-02
• Pletsch, Charles	Ham.	1	1	0	0	0	0	....	....	....	....	....	....	1920-21	1920-21
Plett, Willi	Atl., Cgy., Min., Bos.	13	834	222	215	437	2572	83	24	22	46	466	....	1975-76	1987-88
‡ Plihal, Tomas	S.J.	3	89	7	9	16	26	4	0	0	0	0	....	2006-07	2008-09
Plumb, Rob	Det.	2	14	3	2	5	2	....	....	....	....	....	....	1977-78	1978-79
Plumb, Ron	Hfd.	1	26	3	4	7	14	....	....	....	....	....	....	1979-80	1979-80
Poapst, Steve	Wsh., Chi., Pit., St.L.	7	307	8	28	36	173	11	0	0	0	0	....	1995-96	2005-06
‡ Pock, Thomas	NYR, NYI	5	118	8	9	17	55	4	0	3	3	4	....	2003-04	2008-09
Pocza, Harvie	Wsh.	2	3	0	0	0	2	....	....	....	....	....	....	1979-80	1981-82
• Poddubny, Walt	Edm., Tor., NYR, Que., N.J.	11	468	184	238	422	454	19	7	2	9	12	....	1981-82	1991-92
Podein, Shjon	Edm., Phi., Col., St.L.	11	699	100	106	206	439	127	14	13	27	132	1	1992-93	2002-03
‡ Podkonicky, Andrej	Fla., Wsh.	2	8	1	0	1	2	....	....	....	....	....	....	2000-01	2003-04
Podloski, Ray	Bos.	1	8	0	1	1	17	....	....	....	....	....	....	1988-89	1988-89
Podollan, Jason	Fla., Tor., L.A., NYI	4	41	1	5	6	19	....	....	....	....	....	....	1996-97	2001-02
Podolsky, Nels	Det.	1	1	0	0	0	0	7	0	0	0	4	....	1948-49	1948-49
Poeschek, Rudy	NYR, Wpg., T.B., St.L.	12	364	6	25	31	817	5	0	0	0	18	....	1987-88	1999-00
• Poeta, Tony	Chi.	1	1	0	0	0	0	....	....	....	....	....	....	1951-52	1951-52
Pohl, John	St.L., Tor.	4	115	17	21	38	24	....	....	....	....	....	....	2003-04	2007-08
• Poile, Bud	Tor., Chi., Det., NYR, Bos.	7	311	107	122	229	91	23	4	5	9	8	1	1942-43	1949-50
Poile, Don	Det.	2	66	7	9	16	12	4	0	0	0	0	....	1954-55	1957-58
• Poirier, Gordie	Mtl.	1	10	0	0	0	0	....	....	....	....	....	....	1939-40	1939-40
‡ Polak, Vojtech	Dal.	2	5	0	0	0	0	....	....	....	....	....	....	2005-06	2006-07
Polanic, Tom	Min.	2	19	0	2	2	53	5	1	1	2	4	....	1969-70	1970-71
• Polich, John	NYR	2	3	0	1	1	0	....	....	....	....	....	....	1939-40	1940-41
Polich, Mike	Mtl., Min.	5	226	24	29	53	57	23	2	1	3	2	1	1976-77	1980-81
Polis, Greg	Pit., St.L., NYR, Wsh.	10	615	174	169	343	391	7	0	2	2	6	....	1970-71	1979-80
Poliziani, Dan	Bos.	1	1	0	0	0	0	3	0	0	0	0	....	1958-59	1958-59
‡ Pollock, Jame	St.L.	1	9	0	0	0	6	....	....	....	....	....	....	2003-04	2003-04
Polonich, Dennis	Det.	8	390	59	82	141	1242	7	1	0	1	19	....	1974-75	1982-83
Pooley, Paul	Wpg.	2	15	0	3	3	0	....	....	....	....	....	....	1984-85	1985-86
Popein, Larry	NYR, Oak.	8	449	80	141	221	162	16	1	4	5	6	....	1954-55	1967-68
Popiel, Poul	Bos., L.A., Det., Van., Edm.	7	224	13	41	54	210	4	1	0	1	4	....	1965-66	1979-80
Popovic, Peter	Mtl., NYR, Pit., Bos.	8	485	10	63	73	291	35	1	4	5	18	....	1993-94	2000-01
• Portland, Jack	Mtl., Bos., Chi.	10	381	15	56	71	323	33	1	3	4	25	1	1933-34	1942-43
Porvari, Jukka	Col., N.J.	2	39	3	9	12	4	....	....	....	....	....	....	1981-82	1982-83
Posa, Victor	Chi.	1	2	0	0	0	2	....	....	....	....	....	....	1985-86	1985-86
Posavad, Mike	St.L.	2	8	0	0	0	0	....	....	....	....	....	....	1985-86	1986-87
Posmyk, Marek	T.B.	2	19	1	2	3	20	....	....	....	....	....	....	1999-00	2000-01
Potomski, Barry	L.A., S.J.	3	68	6	5	11	227	....	....	....	....	....	....	1995-96	1997-98
Potvin, Denis	NYI	15	1060	310	742	1052	1356	185	56	108	164	253	4	1973-74	1987-88
Potvin, Jean	L.A., Phi., NYI, Cle., Min.	11	613	63	224	287	478	39	2	9	11	17	2	1970-71	1980-81
• Potvin, Marc	Det., L.A., Hfd., Bos.	6	121	3	5	8	456	13	0	1	1	50	....	1990-91	1995-96
Poudrier, Daniel	Que.	3	25	1	5	6	10	....	....	....	....	....	....	1985-86	1987-88
Poulin, Daniel	Min.	1	3	1	1	2	2	....	....	....	....	....	....	1981-82	1981-82
Poulin, Dave	Phi., Bos., Wsh.	13	724	205	325	530	482	129	31	42	73	132	....	1982-83	1994-95
Poulin, Patrick	Hfd., Chi., T.B., Mtl.	11	634	101	134	235	299	32	6	2	8	8	....	1991-92	2001-02
Pouzar, Jaroslav	Edm.	4	186	34	48	82	135	29	6	4	10	16	3	1982-83	1986-87
• Powell, Ray	Chi.	1	31	7	15	22	2	....	....	....	....	....	....	1950-51	1950-51
• Powis, Geoff	Chi.	1	2	0	0	0	0	....	....	....	....	....	....	1967-68	1967-68
Powis, Lynn	Chi., K.C.	2	130	19	33	52	25	1	0	0	0	0	....	1973-74	1974-75
Prajsler, Petr	L.A., Bos.	4	46	3	10	13	51	4	0	0	0	0	....	1987-88	1991-92
• Pratt, Babe	NYR, Tor., Bos.	12	517	83	209	292	463	63	12	17	29	90	2	1935-36	1946-47

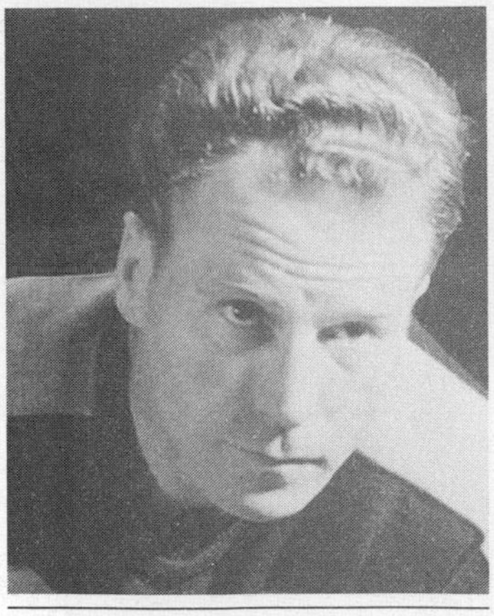

Gord Pettinger

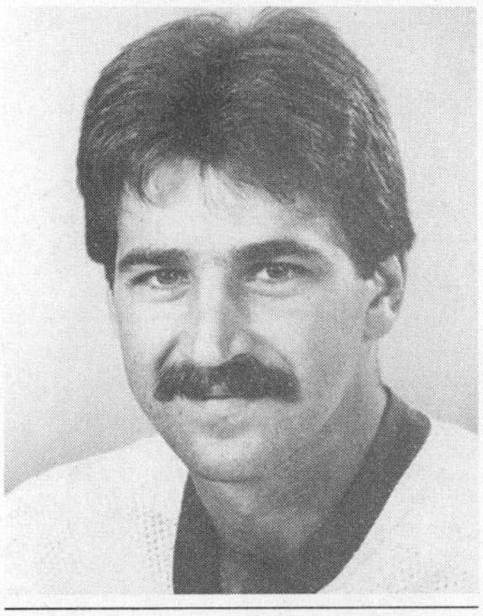

Alex Pirus

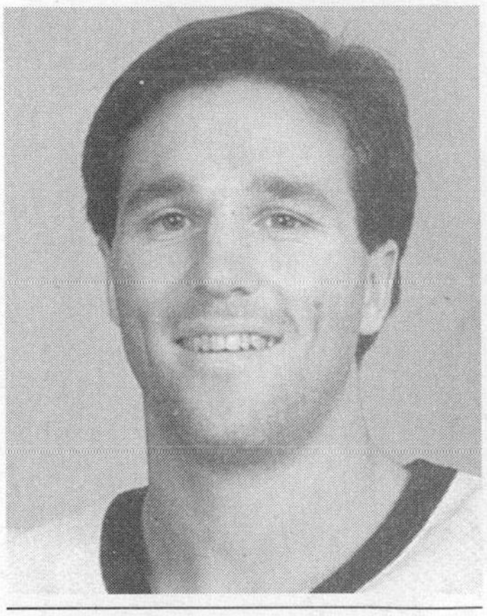

Dave Poulin

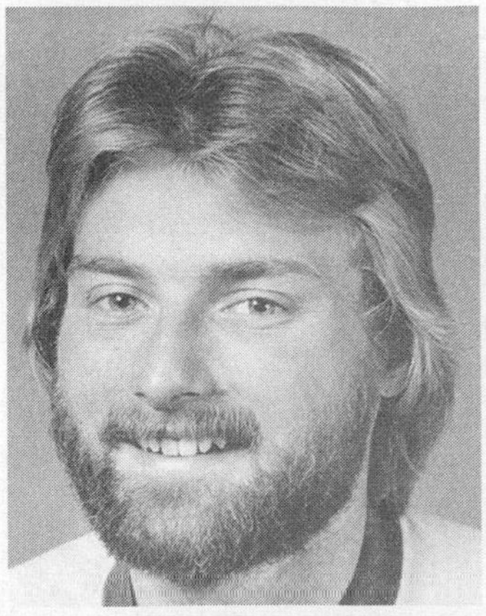

Pat Price

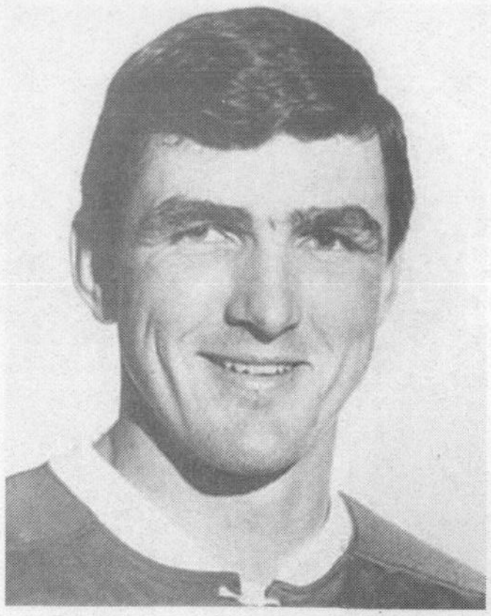

Pat Quinn

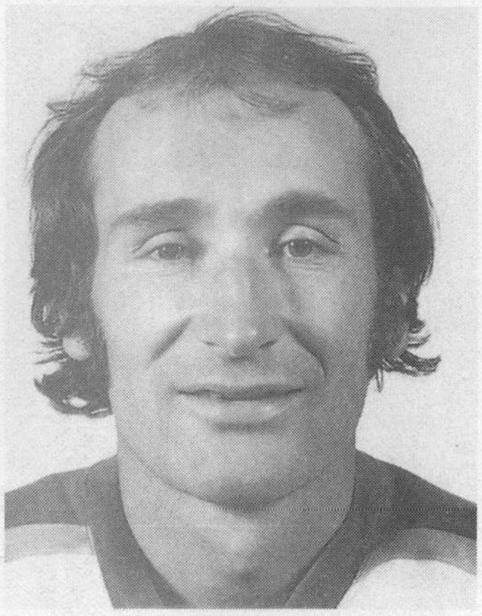

Craig Ramsay

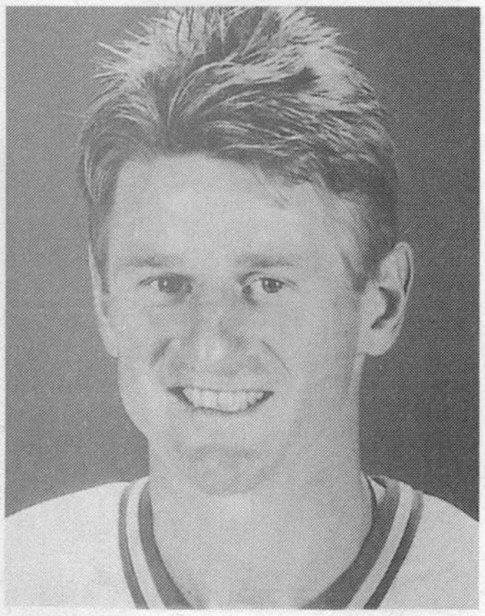

Mark Reeds

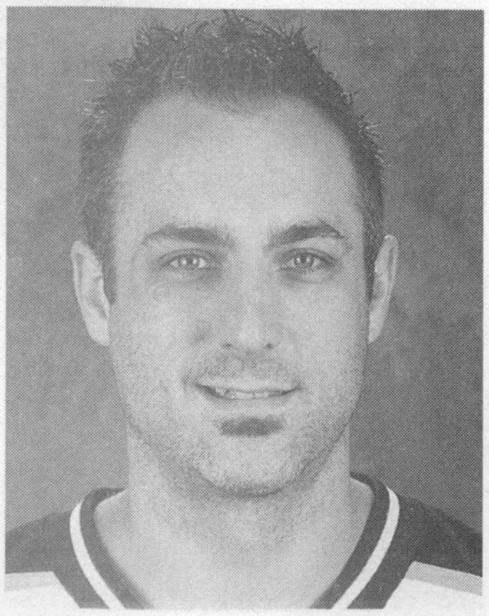

Jamie Rivers

Name	NHL Teams	NHL Seasons	Regular Schedule GP	G	A	TP	PIM	Playoffs GP	G	A	TP	PIM	NHL Cup Wins	First NHL Season	Last NHL Season
• Pratt, Jack	Bos.	2	37	2	0	2	42	4	0	0	0	0	....	1930-31	1931-32
Pratt, Kelly	Pit.	1	22	0	6	6	15	....	....	....	....	....	....	1974-75	1974-75
‡ Pratt, Nolan	Hfd., Car., Col., T.B., Buf.	11	592	9	56	65	537	38	0	1	1	22	1	1996-97	2007-08
Pratt, Tracy	Oak., Pit., Buf., Van., Col., Tor.	10	580	17	97	114	1026	25	0	1	1	62	....	1967-68	1976-77
Prentice, Dean	NYR, Bos., Det., Pit., Min.	22	1378	391	469	860	484	54	13	17	30	38	....	1952-53	1973-74
• Prentice, Eric	Tor.	1	5	0	0	0	4	....	....	....	....	....	....	1943-44	1943-44
Presley, Wayne	Chi., S.J., Buf., NYR, Tor.	12	684	155	147	302	953	83	26	17	43	142	....	1984-85	1995-96
Preston, Rich	Chi., N.J.	8	580	127	164	291	348	47	4	18	22	56	....	1979-80	1986-87
Preston, Yves	Phi.	2	28	7	3	10	4	....	....	....	....	....	....	1978-79	1980-81
Priakin, Sergei	Cgy.	3	46	3	8	11	2	3	0	0	0	0	....	1988-89	1990-91
• Price, Jack	Chi.	3	57	4	6	10	24	4	0	0	0	0	....	1951-52	1953-54
Price, Noel	Tor., NYR, Det., Mtl., Pit., L.A., Atl.	14	499	14	114	128	333	12	0	1	1	8	1	1957-58	1975-76
Price, Pat	NYI, Edm., Pit., Que., NYR, Min.	13	726	43	218	261	1456	74	2	10	12	195	....	1975-76	1987-88
Price, Tom	Cal., Cle., Pit.	5	29	0	2	2	12	....	....	....	....	....	....	1974-75	1978-79
Priestlay, Ken	Buf., Pit.	6	168	27	34	61	63	14	0	0	0	21	1	1986-87	1991-92
• Primeau, Joe	Tor.	9	310	66	177	243	105	38	5	18	23	12	1	1927-28	1935-36
Primeau, Keith	Det., Hfd., Car., Phi.	15	909	266	353	619	1541	128	18	39	57	213	....	1990-91	2005-06
Primeau, Kevin	Van.	1	2	0	0	0	4	....	....	....	....	....	....	1980-81	1980-81
Primeau, Wayne	Buf., T.B., Pit., S.J., Bos., Cgy., Tor.	15	774	69	125	194	789	90	7	14	21	42	....	1994-95	2009-10
• Pringle, Ellie	NYA	1	6	0	0	0	0	....	....	....	....	....	....	1930-31	1930-31
‡ Printz, David	Phi.	2	13	0	0	0	4	....	....	....	....	....	....	2005-06	2006-07
• Probert, Bob	Det., Chi.	16	935	163	221	384	3300	81	16	32	48	274	....	1985-86	2001-02
Prochazka, Martin	Tor., Atl.	2	32	2	5	7	8	....	....	....	....	....	....	1997-98	1999-00
• Prodger, Goldie	Tor., Ham.	6	111	63	29	92	39	....	....	....	....	....	....	1919-20	1924-25
Prokhorov, Vitali	St.L.	3	83	19	11	30	35	4	0	0	0	0	....	1992-93	1994-95
Prokopec, Mike	Chi.	2	15	0	0	0	11	....	....	....	....	....	....	1995-96	1996-97
Pronger, Sean	Ana., Pit., NYR, L.A., Bos., CBJ, Van.	8	260	23	36	59	159	14	0	2	2	8	....	1995-96	2003-04
Pronovost, Andre	Mtl., Bos., Det., Min.	10	556	94	104	198	408	70	11	11	22	58	4	1956-57	1967-68
Pronovost, Jean	Pit., Atl., Wsh.	14	998	391	383	774	413	35	11	9	20	14	....	1968-69	1981-82
Pronovost, Marcel	Det., Tor.	21	1206	88	257	345	851	134	8	23	31	104	5	1949-50	1969-70
Propp, Brian	Phi., Bos., Min., Hfd.	15	1016	425	579	1004	830	160	64	84	148	151	....	1979-80	1993-94
Proulx, Christian	Mtl.	1	7	1	2	3	20	....	....	....	....	....	....	1993-94	1993-94
• Provost, Claude	Mtl.	15	1005	254	335	589	469	126	25	38	63	86	9	1955-56	1969-70
Prpic, Joel	Bos., Col.	3	18	0	3	3	4	....	....	....	....	....	....	1997-98	2000-01
Pryor, Chris	Min., NYI	6	82	1	4	5	122	....	....	....	....	....	....	1984-85	1989-90
Prystai, Metro	Chi., Det.	11	674	151	179	330	231	43	12	14	26	8	2	1947-48	1957-58
• Pudas, Al	Tor.	1	4	0	0	0	0	....	....	....	....	....	....	1926-27	1926-27
Pulford, Bob	Tor., L.A.	16	1079	281	362	643	792	89	25	26	51	126	4	1956-57	1971-72
Pulkkinen, Dave	NYI	1	2	0	0	0	0	....	....	....	....	....	....	1972-73	1972-73
Purinton, Dale	NYR	5	181	4	16	20	578	....	....	....	....	....	....	1999-00	2003-04
• Purpur, Fido	St.L., Chi., Det.	5	144	25	35	60	46	16	1	2	3	4	....	1934-35	1944-45
Purves, John	Wsh.	1	7	1	0	1	0	....	....	....	....	....	....	1990-91	1990-91
‡ Pushkarev, Konstantin	L.A.	2	17	2	3	5	8	....	....	....	....	....	....	2005-06	2006-07
Pushor, Jamie	Det., Ana., Dal., CBJ, Pit., NYR	10	521	14	46	60	648	14	0	1	1	16	1	1995-96	2005-06
• Pusie, Jean	Mtl., NYR, Bos.	5	61	1	4	5	28	7	0	0	0	0	1	1930-31	1935-36
Pyatt, Nelson	Det., Wsh., Col.	7	296	71	63	134	69	....	....	....	....	....	....	1973-74	1979-80

Q

Name	NHL Teams	NHL Seasons	Regular Schedule GP	G	A	TP	PIM	Playoffs GP	G	A	TP	PIM	NHL Cup Wins	First NHL Season	Last NHL Season
• Quackenbush, Bill	Det., Bos.	14	774	62	222	284	95	80	2	19	21	8	....	1942-43	1955-56
Quackenbush, Max	Bos., Chi.	2	61	4	7	11	30	6	0	0	0	4	....	1950-51	1951-52
Quenneville, Joel	Tor., Col., N.J., Hfd., Wsh.	13	803	54	136	190	705	32	0	8	8	22	....	1978-79	1990-91
• Quenneville, Leo	NYR	1	25	0	3	3	10	3	0	0	0	0	....	1929-30	1929-30
• Quilty, John	Mtl., Bos.	4	125	36	34	70	81	13	3	5	8	9	....	1940-41	1947-48
Quinn, Dan	Cgy., Pit., Van., St.L., Phi., Min., Ott., L.A.	14	805	266	419	685	533	65	22	26	48	62	....	1983-84	1996-97
Quinn, Pat	Tor., Van., Atl.	9	606	18	113	131	950	11	0	1	1	21	....	1968-69	1976-77
Quinney, Ken	Que.	3	59	7	13	20	23	....	....	....	....	....	....	1986-87	1990-91
‡ Quint, Deron	Wpg., Phx., N.J., CBJ, Chi., NYI	10	463	46	97	143	166	7	0	2	2	0	....	1995-96	2006-07
Quintal, Stephane	Bos., St.L., Wpg., Mtl., NYR, Chi.	16	1037	63	180	243	1320	52	2	10	12	51	....	1988-89	2003-04
Quintin, Jean-Francois	S.J.	2	22	5	5	10	4	....	....	....	....	....	....	1991-92	1992-93

R

Name	NHL Teams	NHL Seasons	Regular Schedule GP	G	A	TP	PIM	Playoffs GP	G	A	TP	PIM	NHL Cup Wins	First NHL Season	Last NHL Season
‡ Rachunek, Karel	Ott., NYR, N.J.	7	371	22	118	140	227	26	1	7	8	16	....	1999-00	2007-08
Racine, Yves	Det., Phi., Mtl., S.J., Cgy., T.B.	9	508	37	194	231	439	25	5	4	9	37	....	1989-90	1997-98
‡ Radivojevic, Branko	Phx., Phi., Min.	6	393	52	68	120	252	31	2	1	3	36	....	2001-02	2007-08
• Radley, Yip	NYA, Mtl.M.	2	18	0	1	1	13	....	....	....	....	....	....	1930-31	1936-37
‡ Radulov, Igor	Chi.	2	43	9	7	16	22	....	....	....	....	....	....	2002-03	2003-04
Raduns, Nate	Phi.	1	1	0	0	0	0	....	....	....	....	....	....	2008-09	2008-09
Raglan, Herb	St.L., Que., T.B., Ott.	9	343	33	56	89	775	32	3	6	9	50	....	1985-86	1993-94
• Raglan, Rags	Det., Chi.	3	100	4	9	13	52	3	0	0	0	0	....	1950-51	1952-53
Ragnarsson, Marcus	S.J., Phi.	9	632	37	140	177	482	68	2	13	15	60	....	1995-96	2003-04
Raleigh, Don	NYR	10	535	101	219	320	96	18	6	5	11	6	....	1943-44	1955-56
Ralph, Brad	Phx.	1	1	0	0	0	0	....	....	....	....	....	....	2000-01	2000-01
Ramage, Rob	Col., St.L., Cgy., Tor., Min., T.B., Mtl., Phi.	15	1044	139	425	564	2226	84	8	42	50	218	2	1979-80	1993-94
‡ Ramholt, Tim	Cgy.	1	1	0	0	0	0	....	....	....	....	....	....	2007-08	2007-08
• Ramsay, Beattie	Tor.	1	43	0	2	2	10	....	....	....	....	....	....	1927-28	1927-28
Ramsay, Craig	Buf.	14	1070	252	420	672	201	89	17	31	48	27	....	1971-72	1984-85
Ramsay, Les	Chi.	1	11	2	2	4	2	....	....	....	....	....	....	1944-45	1944-45
Ramsey, Mike	Buf., Pit., Det.	18	1070	79	266	345	1012	115	8	29	37	176	....	1979-80	1996-97
Ramsey, Wayne	Buf.	1	2	0	0	0	0	....	....	....	....	....	....	1977-78	1977-78
• Randall, Ken	Tor., Ham., NYA	10	218	68	50	118	533	6	2	1	3	27	2	1917-18	1926-27
Ranheim, Paul	Cgy., Hfd., Car., Phi., Phx.	15	1013	161	199	360	288	36	3	8	11	6	....	1988-89	2002-03
Ranieri, George	Bos.	1	2	0	0	0	0	....	....	....	....	....	....	1956-57	1956-57
Rasmussen, Erik	Buf., L.A., N.J.	9	545	52	76	128	305	52	2	7	9	46	....	1997-98	2006-07
‡ Ratchuk, Peter	Fla.	2	32	1	1	2	10	....	....	....	....	....	....	1998-99	2000-01
Ratelle, Jean	NYR, Bos.	21	1281	491	776	1267	276	123	32	66	98	24	....	1960-61	1980-81
Rathje, Mike	S.J., Phi.	13	768	30	150	180	491	77	9	14	23	51	....	1993-94	2006-07
Rathwell, Jake	Bos.	1	1	0	0	0	0	....	....	....	....	....	....	1974-75	1974-75
Ratushny, Dan	Van.	1	1	0	1	1	2	....	....	....	....	....	....	1992-93	1992-93
Rausse, Errol	Wsh.	3	31	7	3	10	0	....	....	....	....	....	....	1979-80	1981-82
Rautakallio, Pekka	Atl., Cgy.	3	235	33	121	154	122	23	2	5	7	8	....	1979-80	1981-82
Ravlich, Matt	Bos., Chi., Det., L.A.	10	410	12	78	90	364	24	1	5	6	16	....	1962-63	1972-73
Ray, Rob	Buf., Ott.	15	900	41	50	91	3207	55	3	2	5	169	....	1989-90	2003-04
• Raymond, Armand	Mtl.	2	22	0	2	2	10	....	....	....	....	....	....	1937-38	1939-40
• Raymond, Paul	Mtl.	4	76	2	3	5	6	5	0	0	0	2	....	1932-33	1938-39
• Read, Mel	NYR	1	1	0	0	0	0	....	....	....	....	....	....	1946-47	1946-47
‡ Ready, Ryan	Phi.	1	7	0	1	1	0	....	....	....	....	....	....	2005-06	2005-06
• Reardon, Ken	Mtl.	7	341	26	96	122	604	31	2	5	7	62	1	1940-41	1949-50
• Reardon, Terry	Bos., Mtl.	7	193	47	53	100	73	30	8	10	18	12	1	1938-39	1946-47
Reaume, Marc	Tor., Det., Mtl., Van.	9	344	8	43	51	273	21	0	2	2	8	....	1954-55	1970-71
• Reay, Billy	Det., Mtl.	10	479	105	162	267	202	63	13	16	29	43	2	1943-44	1952-53
Redahl, Gord	Bos.	1	18	0	1	1	2	....	....	....	....	....	....	1958-59	1958-59
• Redding, George	Bos.	2	55	3	2	5	23	....	....	....	....	....	....	1924-25	1925-26
Redmond, Craig	L.A., Edm.	5	191	16	68	84	134	3	1	0	1	2	....	1984-85	1988-89
Redmond, Dick	Min., Cal., Chi., St.L., Atl., Bos.	13	771	133	312	445	504	66	9	22	31	27	....	1969-70	1981-82
Redmond, Keith	L.A.	1	12	1	0	1	20	....	....	....	....	....	....	1993-94	1993-94
Redmond, Mickey	Mtl., Det.	9	538	233	195	428	219	16	2	3	5	2	2	1967-68	1975-76
Reeds, Mark	St.L., Hfd.	8	365	45	114	159	135	53	8	9	17	23	....	1981-82	1988-89
Reekie, Joe	Buf., NYI, T.B., Wsh., Chi.	17	902	25	139	164	1326	51	3	4	7	63	....	1985-86	2001-02
• Regan, Bill	NYR, NYA	3	67	3	2	5	67	8	0	0	0	2	....	1929-30	1932-33
• Regan, Larry	Bos., Tor.	5	280	41	95	136	71	42	7	14	21	18	....	1956-57	1960-61
‡ Regehr, Richie	Cgy.	2	20	1	3	4	6	....	....	....	....	....	....	2005-06	2006-07
Regier, Darcy	Cle., NYI	3	26	0	2	2	35	....	....	....	....	....	....	1977-78	1983-84
‡ Regier, Steve	NYI, St.L.	4	26	3	1	4	8	....	....	....	....	....	....	2005-06	2008-09
• Reibel, Dutch	Det., Chi., Bos.	6	409	84	161	245	75	39	6	14	20	4	2	1953-54	1958-59
Reichel, Robert	Cgy., NYI, Phx., Tor.	11	830	252	378	630	388	70	8	23	31	20	....	1990-91	2003-04
Reichert, Craig	Ana.	1	3	0	0	0	0	....	....	....	....	....	....	1996-97	1996-97
‡ Reid, Brandon	Van.	3	13	2	4	6	0	10	0	2	2	0	....	2002-03	2006-07
Reid, Darren	T.B., Phi.	2	21	0	1	1	18	....	....	....	....	....	....	2005-06	2006-07
• Reid, Dave	Tor.	3	7	0	0	0	0	....	....	....	....	....	....	1952-53	1955-56
Reid, Dave	Bos., Tor., Dal., Col.	18	961	165	204	369	253	118	9	26	35	34	2	1983-84	2000-01
Reid, Gerry	Det.	1	....	....	....	....	....	2	0	0	0	2	....	1948-49	1948-49
Reid, Gord	NYA	1	1	0	0	0	2	....	....	....	....	....	....	1936-37	1936-37

Name	NHL Teams	NHL Seasons	Regular Schedule					Playoffs					NHL Cup Wins	First NHL Season	Last NHL Season
			GP	G	A	TP	PIM	GP	G	A	TP	PIM			
● Reid, Reg	Tor.	2	39	1	0	1	4	2	0	0	0	0	....	1924-25	1925-26
Reid, Tom	Chi., Min.	11	701	17	113	130	654	42	1	13	14	49	....	1967-68	1977-78
Reierson, Dave	Cgy.	1	2	0	0	0	2	....	....	....	....	....	....	1988-89	1988-89
● Reigle, Ed	Bos.	1	17	0	2	2	25	....	....	....	....	....	....	1950-51	1950-51
Reinhart, Paul	Atl., Cgy., Van.	11	648	133	426	559	277	83	23	54	77	42	....	1979-80	1989-90
● Reinikka, Ollie	NYR	1	16	0	0	0	0	....	....	....	....	....	....	1926-27	1926-27
Reirden, Todd	Edm., St.L., Atl., Phx.	5	183	11	35	46	181	5	0	1	1	0	....	1998-99	2003-04
● Reise, Leo	Ham., NYA, NYR	8	223	36	29	65	181	6	0	0	0	16	....	1920-21	1929-30
Reise, Leo	Chi., Det., NYR	9	494	28	81	109	399	52	8	5	13	68	2	1945-46	1953-54
Reitz, Erik	Min., NYR	4	48	1	1	2	69	2	0	0	0	0	....	2005-06	2008-09
Renaud, Mark	Hfd., Buf.	5	152	6	50	56	86	....	....	....	....	....	....	1979-80	1983-84
Renberg, Mikael	Phi., T.B., Phx., Tor.	10	661	190	274	464	372	67	16	22	38	42	....	1993-94	2003-04
Reynolds, Bobby	Tor.	1	7	1	1	2	0	....	....	....	....	....	....	1989-90	1989-90
Rheaume, Pascal	N.J., St.L., Chi., Atl., NYR, Phx.	9	318	39	52	91	144	45	3	6	9	27	1	1996-97	2005-06
Ribble, Pat	Atl., Chi., Tor., Wsh., Cgy.	8	349	19	60	79	365	8	0	1	1	12	....	1975-76	1982-83
Ricci, Mike	Phi., Que., Col., S.J., Phx.	16	1099	243	362	605	974	110	23	43	66	77	1	1990-91	2006-07
Rice, Steven	NYR, Edm., Hfd., Car.	8	329	64	61	125	275	2	2	1	3	6	....	1990-91	1997-98
Richard, Henri	Mtl.	20	1256	358	688	1046	928	180	49	80	129	181	11	1955-56	1974-75
● Richard, Jacques	Atl., Buf., Que.	10	556	160	187	347	307	35	5	5	10	34	....	1972-73	1982-83
Richard, Jean-Marc	Que.	2	5	2	1	3	2	....	....	....	....	....	....	1987-88	1989-90
● Richard, Maurice	Mtl.	18	978	544	421	965	1285	133	82	44	126	188	8	1942-43	1959-60
Richard, Mike	Wsh.	2	7	0	2	2	0	....	....	....	....	....	....	1987-88	1989-90
Richards, Todd	Hfd.	2	8	0	4	4	4	11	0	3	3	6	....	1990-91	1991-92
Richards, Travis	Dal.	2	3	0	0	0	2	....	....	....	....	....	....	1994-95	1995-96
Richardson, Dave	NYR, Chi., Det.	4	45	3	2	5	27	....	....	....	....	....	....	1963-64	1967-68
Richardson, Glen	Van.	1	24	3	6	9	19	....	....	....	....	....	....	1975-76	1975-76
Richardson, Ken	St.L.	3	49	8	13	21	16	....	....	....	....	....	....	1974-75	1978-79
Richardson, Luke	Tor., Edm., Phi., CBJ, T.B., Ott.	21	1417	35	166	201	2055	69	0	8	8	130	....	1987-88	2008-09
Richer, Bob	Buf.	1	3	0	0	0	0	....	....	....	....	....	....	1972-73	1972-73
Richer, Stephane	Mtl., N.J., T.B., St.L., Pit.	17	1054	421	398	819	614	134	53	45	98	61	2	1984-85	2001-02
Richer, Stephane	T.B., Bos., Fla.	3	27	1	5	6	20	3	0	0	0	0	....	1992-93	1994-95
Richmond, Steve	NYR, Det., N.J., L.A.	5	159	4	23	27	514	4	0	0	0	12	....	1983-84	1988-89
Richter, Barry	NYR, Bos., NYI, Mtl.	5	151	11	34	45	76	....	....	....	....	....	....	1995-96	2000-01
Richter, Dave	Min., Phi., Van., St.L.	9	365	9	40	49	1030	22	1	0	1	80	....	1981-82	1989-90
Ridley, Mike	NYR, Wsh., Tor., Van.	12	866	292	466	758	424	104	28	50	78	70	....	1985-86	1996-97
‡ Riesen, Michel	Edm.	1	12	0	1	1	4	....	....	....	....	....	....	2000-01	2000-01
Riley, Bill	Wsh., Wpg.	5	139	31	30	61	320	....	....	....	....	....	....	1974-75	1979-80
● Riley, Jack	Det., Mtl., Bos.	4	104	10	22	32	8	4	0	3	3	0	....	1932-33	1935-36
● Riley, Jim	Chi., Det.	1	9	0	2	2	14	....	....	....	....	....	....	1926-27	1926-27
Riopelle, Rip	Mtl.	3	169	27	16	43	73	8	1	1	2	2	....	1947-48	1949-50
Rioux, Gerry	Wpg.	1	8	0	0	0	6	....	....	....	....	....	....	1979-80	1979-80
Rioux, Pierre	Cgy.	1	14	1	2	3	4	....	....	....	....	....	....	1982-83	1982-83
● Ripley, Vic	Chi., Bos., NYR, St.L.	7	278	51	49	100	173	20	4	1	5	10	....	1928-29	1934-35
Risebrough, Doug	Mtl., Cgy.	13	740	185	286	471	1542	124	21	37	58	238	4	1974-75	1986-87
Rissling, Gary	Wsh., Pit.	7	221	23	30	53	1008	5	0	1	1	4	....	1978-79	1984-85
‡ Rita, Jani	Edm., Pit.	4	66	9	5	14	10	....	....	....	....	....	....	2001-02	2005-06
Ritchie, Bob	Phi., Det.	2	29	8	4	12	10	....	....	....	....	....	....	1976-77	1977-78
‡ Ritchie, Byron	Car., Fla., Cgy., Van.	8	324	25	33	58	373	8	0	0	0	10	....	1998-99	2007-08
● Ritchie, Dave	Mtl.W., Ott., Tor., Que., Mtl.	6	58	15	6	21	50	1	0	0	0	0	....	1917-18	1925-26
Ritson, Alex	NYR	1	1	0	0	0	0	....	....	....	....	....	....	1944-45	1944-45
Rittinger, Alan	Bos.	1	19	3	7	10	0	....	....	....	....	....	....	1943-44	1943-44
Rivard, Bob	Pit.	1	27	5	12	17	4	....	....	....	....	....	....	1967-68	1967-68
● Rivers, Gus	Mtl.	3	88	4	5	9	12	16	2	0	2	2	2	1929-30	1931-32
‡ Rivers, Jamie	St.L., NYI, Ott., Bos., Fla., Det., Phx.	11	454	17	49	66	385	15	1	1	2	8	....	1995-96	2006-07
Rivers, Shawn	T.B.	1	4	0	2	2	2	....	....	....	....	....	....	1992-93	1992-93
Rivers, Wayne	Det., Bos., St.L., NYR	7	108	15	30	45	94	....	....	....	....	....	....	1961-62	1968-69
Rizzuto, Garth	Van.	1	37	3	4	7	16	....	....	....	....	....	....	1970-71	1970-71
Roach, Andy	St.L.	1	5	1	2	3	10	....	....	....	....	....	....	2005-06	2005-06
● Roach, Mickey	Tor., Ham., NYA	8	211	77	34	111	54	....	....	....	....	....	....	1919-20	1926-27
Roberge, Mario	Mtl.	5	112	7	7	14	314	15	0	0	0	24	1	1990-91	1994-95
Roberge, Serge	Que.	1	9	0	0	0	24	....	....	....	....	....	....	1990-91	1990-91
● Robert, Claude	Mtl.	1	23	1	0	1	9	....	....	....	....	....	....	1950-51	1950-51
Robert, Rene	Tor., Pit., Buf., Col.	12	744	284	418	702	597	50	22	19	41	73	....	1970-71	1981-82
Roberto, Phil	Mtl., St.L., Det., K.C., Col., Cle.	8	385	75	106	181	464	31	9	8	17	69	1	1969-70	1976-77
Roberts, David	St.L., Edm., Van.	5	125	20	33	53	85	9	0	0	0	16	....	1993-94	1997-98
Roberts, Doug	Det., Oak., Cal., Bos.	10	419	43	104	147	342	16	2	3	5	46	....	1965-66	1974-75
Roberts, Gary	Cgy., Car., Tor., Fla., Pit., T.B.	22	1224	438	472	910	2560	130	32	61	93	332	1	1986-87	2008-09
Roberts, Gordie	Hfd., Min., Phi., St.L., Pit., Bos.	15	1097	61	359	420	1582	153	10	47	57	273	2	1979-80	1993-94
Roberts, Jim	Min.	3	106	17	23	40	33	2	0	0	0	0	....	1976-77	1978-79
Roberts, Jimmy	Mtl., St.L.	15	1006	126	194	320	621	153	20	16	36	160	5	1963-64	1977-78
● Robertson, Fred	Tor., Det.	2	34	1	0	1	35	7	0	0	0	0	1	1931-32	1933-34
Robertson, Geordie	Buf.	1	5	1	2	3	7	....	....	....	....	....	....	1982-83	1982-83
● Robertson, George	Mtl.	2	31	2	5	7	6	....	....	....	....	....	....	1947-48	1948-49
Robertson, Torrie	Wsh., Hfd., Det.	10	442	49	99	148	1751	22	2	1	3	90	....	1980-81	1989-90
Robertsson, Bert	Van., Edm., NYR	4	123	4	10	14	75	5	0	0	0	0	....	1997-98	2000-01
Robidoux, Florent	Chi.	3	52	7	4	11	75	....	....	....	....	....	....	1980-81	1983-84
Robinson, Doug	Chi., NYR, L.A.	7	239	44	67	111	34	11	4	3	7	0	....	1963-64	1970-71
● Robinson, Earl	Mtl.M., Chi., Mtl.	11	417	83	98	181	133	25	5	4	9	0	1	1928-29	1939-40
Robinson, Larry	Mtl., L.A.	20	1384	208	750	958	793	227	28	116	144	211	6	1972-73	1991-92
Robinson, Moe	Mtl.	1	1	0	0	0	0	....	....	....	....	....	....	1979-80	1979-80
‡ Robinson, Nathan	Det., Bos.	2	7	0	0	0	2	....	....	....	....	....	....	2003-04	2005-06
Robinson, Rob	St.L.	1	22	0	1	1	8	....	....	....	....	....	....	1991-92	1991-92
Robinson, Scott	Min.	1	1	0	0	0	2	....	....	....	....	....	....	1989-90	1989-90
Robitaille, Luc	L.A., Pit., NYR, Det.	19	1431	668	726	1394	1177	159	58	69	127	174	1	1986-87	2005-06
Robitaille, Mike	NYR, Det., Buf., Van.	8	382	23	105	128	280	13	0	1	1	4	....	1969-70	1976-77
‡ Robitaille, Randy	Bos., Nsh., L.A., Pit., NYI, Atl., Min., Phi., Ott.	11	531	84	172	256	201	13	1	4	5	8	....	1996-97	2007-08
Roche, Dave	Pit., Cgy., NYI	5	171	15	15	30	334	16	2	7	9	26	....	1995-96	2001-02
● Roche, Des	Mtl.M., Ott., St.L., Mtl., Det.	4	113	20	18	38	44	....	....	....	....	....	....	1930-31	1934-35
● Roche, Earl	Mtl.M., Bos., Ott., St.L., Det.	4	147	25	27	52	48	2	0	0	0	0	....	1930-31	1934-35
Roche, Ernie	Mtl.	1	4	0	0	0	2	....	....	....	....	....	....	1950-51	1950-51
‡ Roche, Travis	Min., Phx.	4	60	6	14	20	24	....	....	....	....	....	....	2000-01	2006-07
Rochefort, Dave	Det.	1	1	0	0	0	0	....	....	....	....	....	....	1966-67	1966-67
Rochefort, Leon	NYR, Mtl., Phi., L.A., Det., Atl., Van.	15	617	121	147	268	93	39	4	4	8	16	2	1960-61	1975-76
Rochefort, Normand	Que., NYR, T.B.	13	598	39	119	158	570	69	7	5	12	82	....	1980-81	1993-94
● Rockburn, Harvey	Det., Ott.	3	94	4	2	6	254	....	....	....	....	....	....	1929-30	1932-33
● Rodden, Eddie	Chi., Tor., Bos., NYR	4	97	6	14	20	60	2	0	1	1	0	....	1926-27	1930-31
Rodgers, Marc	Det.	1	21	1	1	2	10	....	....	....	....	....	....	1999-00	1999-00
Roenick, Jeremy	Chi., Phx., Phi., L.A., S.J.	20	1363	513	703	1216	1463	154	53	69	122	115	....	1988-89	2008-09
‡ Roest, Stacy	Det., Min.	5	244	28	48	76	54	3	0	0	0	0	....	1998-99	2002-03
Rogers, John	Min.	2	14	2	4	6	0	....	....	....	....	....	....	1973-74	1974-75
Rogers, Mike	Hfd., NYR, Edm.	7	484	202	317	519	184	17	1	13	14	6	....	1979-80	1985-86
Rohlicek, Jeff	Van.	2	9	0	0	0	8	....	....	....	....	....	....	1987-88	1988-89
Rohlin, Leif	Van.	2	96	8	24	32	40	5	0	0	0	0	....	1995-96	1996-97
Rohloff, Jon	Bos.	3	150	7	25	32	129	10	1	2	3	8	....	1994-95	1996-97
Rohloff, Todd	Wsh., CBJ	2	75	0	6	6	40	....	....	....	....	....	....	2001-02	2003-04
Rolfe, Dale	Bos., L.A., Det., NYR	9	509	25	125	150	556	71	5	24	29	89	....	1959-60	1974-75
Romanchych, Larry	Chi., Atl.	6	298	68	97	165	102	7	2	2	4	4	....	1970-71	1976-77
Romaniuk, Russell	Wpg., Phi.	5	102	13	14	27	63	2	0	0	0	0	....	1991-92	1995-96
Rombough, Doug	Buf., NYI, Min.	4	150	24	27	51	80	....	....	....	....	....	....	1972-73	1975-76
Rominski, Dale	T.B.	1	3	0	1	1	2	....	....	....	....	....	....	1999-00	1999-00
● Romnes, Doc	Chi., Tor., NYA	10	360	68	136	204	42	43	7	18	25	4	2	1930-31	1939-40
Ronan, Ed	Mtl., Wpg., Buf.	6	182	13	23	36	101	27	4	3	7	16	1	1991-92	1996-97
● Ronan, Skene	Ott.	1	11	0	0	0	6	....	....	....	....	....	....	1918-19	1918-19
Ronning, Cliff	St.L., Van., Phx., Nsh., L.A., Min., NYI	18	1137	306	563	869	453	126	29	57	86	72	....	1985-86	2003-04
Ronnqvist, Jonas	Ana.	1	38	0	4	4	14	....	....	....	....	....	....	2000-01	2000-01
Ronson, Len	NYR, Oak.	2	18	2	1	3	10	....	....	....	....	....	....	1960-61	1968-69
Ronty, Paul	Bos., NYR, Mtl.	8	488	101	211	312	103	21	1	7	8	6	....	1947-48	1954-55
Rooney, Steve	Mtl., Wpg., N.J.	5	154	15	13	28	496	25	3	2	5	86	1	1984-85	1988-89
Root, Bill	Mtl., Tor., St.L., Phi.	6	247	11	23	34	180	22	1	2	3	25	....	1982-83	1987-88
‡ Rosa, Pavel	L.A.	4	36	5	13	18	6	....	....	....	....	....	....	1998-99	2003-04
● Ross, Art	Mtl.W.	1	3	1	0	1	12	....	....	....	....	....	....	1917-18	1917-18
Ross, Jim	NYR	2	62	2	11	13	29	....	....	....	....	....	....	1951-52	1952-53
Rossignol, Roly	Det., Mtl.	3	14	3	5	8	6	1	0	0	0	2	....	1943-44	1945-46
Rossiter, Kyle	Fla., Atl.	3	11	0	1	1	9	....	....	....	....	....	....	2001-02	2003-04
Rota, Darcy	Chi., Atl., Van.	11	794	256	239	495	973	60	14	7	21	147	....	1973-74	1983-84

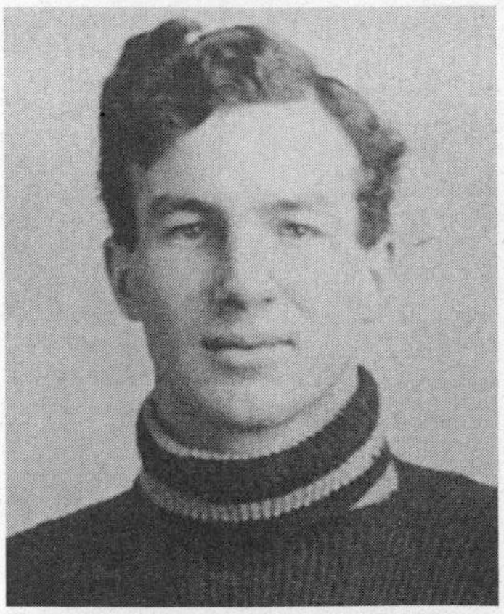

Art Ross

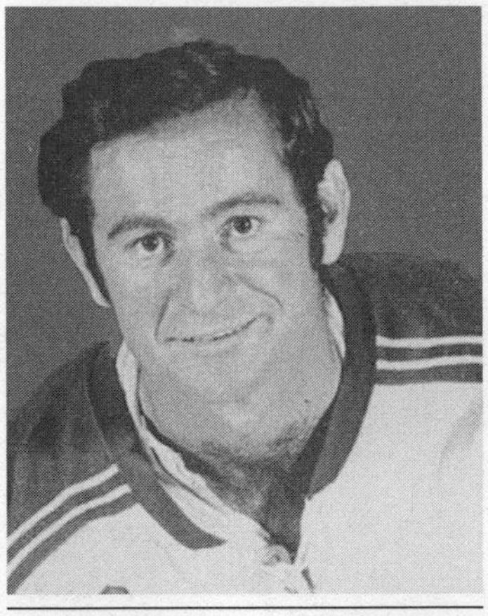

Bobby Rousseau

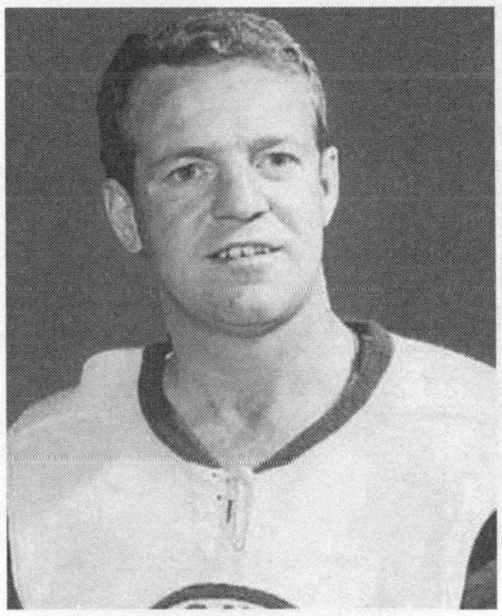

Guy Rousseau

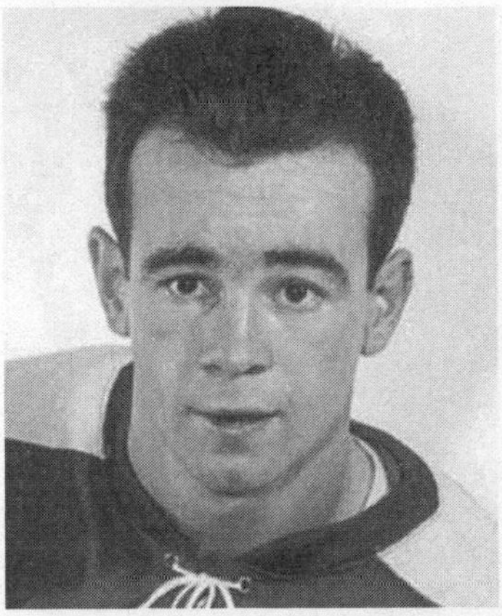

Roland Rousseau

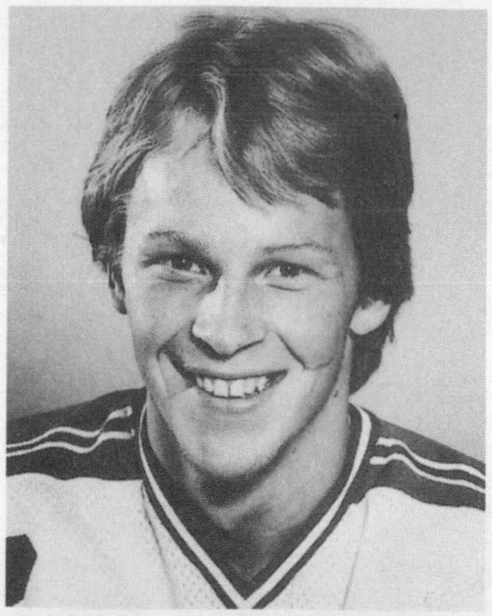

Reijo Ruotsalainen

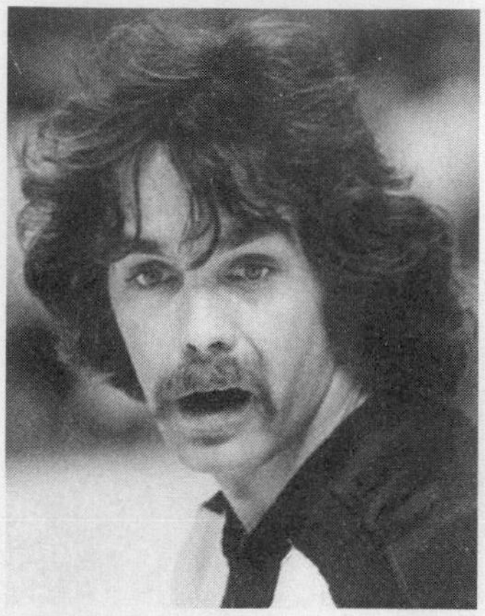

Derek Sanderson

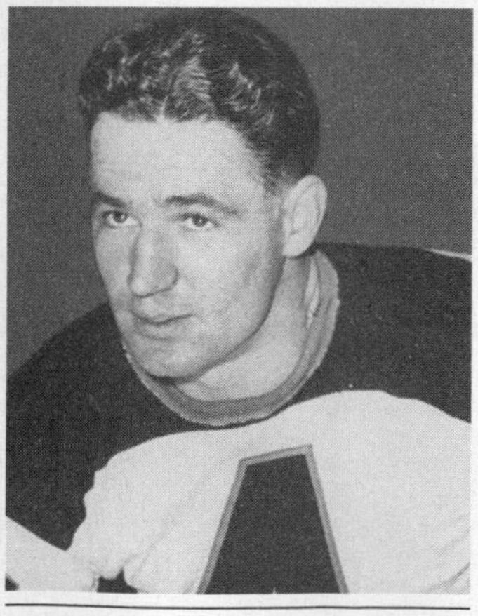

Charlie Sands

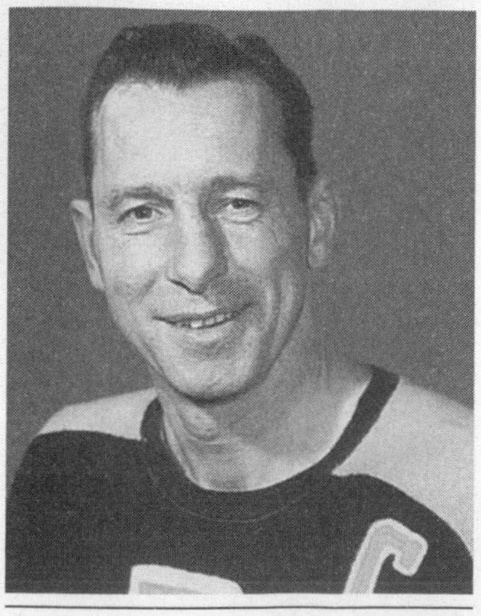

Milt Schmidt

Name	NHL Teams	NHL Seasons	Regular Schedule GP	G	A	TP	PIM	Playoffs GP	G	A	TP	PIM	NHL Cup Wins	First NHL Season	Last NHL Season
Rota, Randy	Mtl., L.A., K.C., Col.	5	212	38	39	77	60	5	0	1	1	0	....	1972-73	1976-77
● Rothschild, Sam	Mtl.M., Pit., NYA	4	100	8	6	14	25	6	0	0	0	0	1	1924-25	1927-28
● Roulston, Rolly	Det.	3	24	0	6	6	10	....	....	....	....	....	1	1935-36	1937-38
Roulston, Tom	Edm., Pit.	5	195	47	49	96	74	21	2	2	4	2	....	1980-81	1985-86
Roupe, Magnus	Phi.	2	40	3	5	8	42	....	....	....	....	....	....	1987-88	1988-89
Rourke, Allan	Car., NYI, Edm.	4	55	1	4	5	31	....	....	....	....	....	....	2003-04	2007-08
Rouse, Bob	Min., Wsh., Tor., Det., S.J.	17	1061	37	181	218	1559	136	7	21	28	198	2	1983-84	1999-00
Rousseau, Bobby	Mtl., Min., NYR	15	942	245	458	703	359	128	27	57	84	69	4	1960-61	1974-75
Rousseau, Guy	Mtl.	2	4	0	1	1	0	....	....	....	....	....	....	1954-55	1956-57
● Rousseau, Roland	Mtl.	1	2	0	0	0	0	....	....	....	....	....	....	1952-53	1952-53
Routhier, Jean-Marc	Que.	1	8	0	0	0	9	....	....	....	....	....	....	1989-90	1989-90
● Rowe, Bobby	Bos.	1	4	1	0	1	0	....	....	....	....	....	....	1924-25	1924-25
Rowe, Mike	Pit.	3	11	0	0	0	11	....	....	....	....	....	....	1984-85	1986-87
● Rowe, Ron	NYR	1	5	1	0	1	0	....	....	....	....	....	....	1947-48	1947-48
Rowe, Tom	Wsh., Hfd., Det.	7	357	85	100	185	615	3	2	0	2	0	....	1976-77	1982-83
Roy, Andre	Bos., Ott., T.B., Pit., Cgy.	11	515	35	33	68	1169	41	1	3	4	98	1	1995-96	2008-09
Roy, Jean-Yves	NYR, Ott., Bos.	4	61	12	16	28	26	....	....	....	....	....	....	1994-95	1997-98
Roy, Stephane	Min.	1	12	1	0	1	0	....	....	....	....	....	....	1987-88	1987-88
Royer, Gaetan	T.B.	1	3	0	0	0	2	....	....	....	....	....	....	2001-02	2001-02
Royer, Remi	Chi.	1	18	0	0	0	67	....	....	....	....	....	....	1998-99	1998-99
● Rozzini, Gino	Bos.	1	31	5	10	15	20	6	1	2	3	6	....	1944-45	1944-45
Rucchin, Steve	Ana., NYR, Atl.	12	735	171	318	489	164	37	9	8	17	12	....	1994-95	2006-07
Rucinski, Mike	Chi.	2	1	0	0	0	0	2	0	0	0	0	....	1987-88	1988-89
Rucinski, Mike	Car.	3	26	0	2	2	10	....	....	....	....	....	....	1997-98	2000-01
‡ Rucinsky, Martin	Edm., Que., Col., Mtl., Dal., NYR, St.L., Van.	16	961	241	371	612	821	37	9	5	14	24	....	1991-92	2007-08
● Ruelle, Bernie	Det.	1	2	1	0	1	0	....	....	....	....	....	....	1943-44	1943-44
Ruff, Jason	St.L., T.B.	2	14	3	3	6	10	....	....	....	....	....	....	1992-93	1993-94
Ruff, Lindy	Buf., NYR	12	691	105	195	300	1264	52	11	13	24	193	....	1979-80	1990-91
Ruhnke, Kent	Bos.	1	2	0	1	1	0	....	....	....	....	....	....	1975-76	1975-76
Rumble, Darren	Phi., Ott., St.L., T.B.	8	193	10	26	36	216	....	....	....	....	....	1	1990-91	2003-04
Rundqvist, Thomas	Mtl.	1	2	0	1	1	0	....	....	....	....	....	....	1984-85	1984-85
● Runge, Paul	Bos., Mtl.M., Mtl.	7	140	18	22	40	57	7	0	0	0	6	....	1930-31	1937-38
Ruotsalainen, Reijo	NYR, Edm., N.J.	7	446	107	237	344	180	86	15	32	47	44	2	1981-82	1989-90
Rupp, Duane	NYR, Tor., Min., Pit.	10	374	24	93	117	220	10	2	2	4	8	....	1962-63	1972-73
Ruskowski, Terry	Chi., L.A., Pit., Min.	10	630	113	313	426	1354	21	1	6	7	86	....	1979-80	1988-89
Russell, Cam	Chi., Col.	10	396	9	21	30	872	44	0	5	5	16	....	1989-90	1998-99
● Russell, Church	NYR	3	90	20	16	36	12	....	....	....	....	....	....	1945-46	1947-48
Russell, Phil	Chi., Atl., Cgy., N.J., Buf.	15	1016	99	325	424	2038	73	4	22	26	202	....	1972-73	1986-87
Ruuttu, Christian	Buf., Chi., Van.	9	621	134	298	432	714	42	4	9	13	49	....	1986-87	1994-95
Ruzicka, Vladimir	Edm., Bos., Ott.	5	233	82	85	167	129	30	4	14	18	2	....	1989-90	1993-94
‡ Ryan, Matt	L.A.	1	12	0	1	1	2	....	....	....	....	....	....	2005-06	2005-06
‡ Ryan, Prestin	Van.	1	1	0	0	0	2	....	....	....	....	....	....	2005-06	2005-06
Ryan, Terry	Mtl.	3	8	0	0	0	36	....	....	....	....	....	....	1996-97	1998-99
Rychel, Warren	Chi., L.A., Tor., Col., Ana.	9	406	38	39	77	1422	70	8	13	21	121	1	1988-89	1998-99
Rycroft, Mark	St.L., Col.	4	226	21	25	46	113	3	0	0	0	2	....	2001-02	2006-07
Rymsha, Andy	Que.	1	6	0	0	0	23	....	....	....	....	....	....	1991-92	1991-92
Ryznar, Jason	N.J.	1	8	0	0	0	2	....	....	....	....	....	....	2005-06	2005-06

S

Name	NHL Teams	NHL Seasons	Regular Schedule GP	G	A	TP	PIM	Playoffs GP	G	A	TP	PIM	NHL Cup Wins	First NHL Season	Last NHL Season
Saarinen, Simo	NYR	1	8	0	0	0	0	....	....	....	....	....	....	1984-85	1984-85
Sabol, Shaun	Phi.	1	2	0	0	0	0	....	....	....	....	....	....	1989-90	1989-90
Sabourin, Bob	Tor.	1	1	0	0	0	2	....	....	....	....	....	....	1951-52	1951-52
Sabourin, Gary	St.L., Tor., Cal., Cle.	10	627	169	188	357	397	62	19	11	30	58	....	1967-68	1976-77
Sabourin, Ken	Cgy., Wsh.	4	74	2	8	10	201	12	0	0	0	34	....	1988-89	1991-92
Sacco, David	Tor., Ana.	3	35	5	13	18	22	....	....	....	....	....	....	1993-94	1995-96
Sacco, Joe	Tor., Ana., NYI, Wsh., Phi.	13	738	94	119	213	421	26	2	0	2	8	....	1990-91	2002-03
Sacharuk, Larry	NYR, St.L.	5	151	29	33	62	42	2	1	1	2	2	....	1972-73	1976-77
‡ Safronov, Kirill	Phx., Atl.	2	35	2	2	4	16	....	....	....	....	....	....	2001-02	2002-03
Saganiuk, Rocky	Tor., Pit.	6	259	57	65	122	201	6	1	0	1	15	....	1978-79	1983-84
Sakic, Joe	Que., Col.	20	1378	625	1016	1641	614	172	84	104	188	78	2	1988-89	2008-09
Saleski, Don	Phi., Col.	9	543	128	125	253	629	82	13	17	30	131	2	1971-72	1979-80
‡ Salmelainen, Tony	Edm., Chi.	2	70	6	12	18	30	....	....	....	....	....	....	2003-04	2006-07
Salming, Borje	Tor., Det.	17	1148	150	637	787	1344	81	12	37	49	91	....	1973-74	1989-90
Salomonsson, Andreas	N.J., Wsh.	2	71	5	9	14	36	4	0	1	1	0	....	2001-02	2002-03
Salovaara, Barry	Det.	2	90	2	13	15	70	....	....	....	....	....	....	1974-75	1975-76
Salvian, Dave	NYI	1	....	....	....	....	....	1	0	1	1	2	....	1976-77	1976-77
Samis, Phil	Tor.	2	2	0	0	0	0	5	0	1	1	2	1	1947-48	1949-50
Sampson, Gary	Wsh.	4	105	13	22	35	25	12	1	0	1	0	....	1983-84	1986-87
Samuelsson, Kjell	NYR, Phi., Pit., T.B.	14	813	48	138	186	1225	123	4	20	24	178	1	1985-86	1998-99
Samuelsson, Martin	Bos.	2	14	0	1	1	2	....	....	....	....	....	....	2002-03	2003-04
Samuelsson, Ulf	Hfd., Pit., NYR, Det., Phi.	16	1080	57	275	332	2453	132	7	27	34	272	2	1984-85	1999-00
Sandelin, Scott	Mtl., Phi., Min.	4	25	0	4	4	2	....	....	....	....	....	....	1986-87	1991-92
Sanderson, Derek	Bos., NYR, St.L., Van., Pit.	13	598	202	250	452	911	56	18	12	30	187	2	1965-66	1977-78
Sanderson, Geoff	Hfd., Car., Van., Buf., CBJ, Phx., Phi., Edm.	17	1104	355	345	700	511	55	9	10	19	32	....	1990-91	2007-08
Sandford, Ed	Bos., Det., Chi.	9	502	106	145	251	355	42	13	11	24	27	....	1947-48	1955-56
Sandlak, Jim	Van., Hfd.	11	549	110	119	229	821	33	7	10	17	30	....	1985-86	1995-96
● Sands, Charlie	Tor., Bos., Mtl., NYR	12	427	99	109	208	58	34	6	6	12	4	1	1932-33	1943-44
Sandstrom, Tomas	NYR, L.A., Pit., Det., Ana.	15	983	394	462	856	1193	139	32	49	81	183	1	1984-85	1998-99
Sandwith, Terran	Edm.	1	8	0	0	0	6	....	....	....	....	....	....	1997-98	1997-98
Sanipass, Everett	Chi., Que.	5	164	25	34	59	358	5	2	0	2	4	....	1986-87	1990-91
‡ Santala, Tommi	Atl., Van.	2	63	2	7	9	46	1	0	0	0	0	....	2003-04	2006-07
‡ Saprykin, Oleg	Cgy., Phx., Ott.	7	325	55	82	137	240	41	4	4	8	18	....	1999-00	2006-07
Sarault, Yves	Mtl., Cgy., Col., Ott., Atl., Nsh.	8	106	10	10	20	51	5	0	0	0	2	....	1994-95	2001-02
Sargent, Gary	L.A., Min.	8	402	61	161	222	273	20	5	7	12	8	....	1975-76	1982-83
Sarner, Craig	Bos.	1	7	0	0	0	0	....	....	....	....	....	....	1974-75	1974-75
‡ Sarno, Peter	Edm., CBJ	2	7	1	0	1	2	....	....	....	....	....	....	2003-04	2005-06
Sarrazin, Dick	Phi.	3	100	20	35	55	22	4	0	0	0	0	....	1968-69	1971-72
Sasakamoose, Fred	Chi.	1	11	0	0	0	6	....	....	....	....	....	....	1953-54	1953-54
Sasser, Grant	Pit.	1	3	0	0	0	0	....	....	....	....	....	....	1983-84	1983-84
‡ Satan, Miroslav	Edm., Buf., NYI, Pit., Bos.	14	1050	363	372	735	464	86	21	33	54	41	1	1995-96	2009-10
Sather, Glen	Bos., Pit., NYR, St.L., Mtl., Min.	10	658	80	113	193	724	72	1	5	6	86	....	1966-67	1975-76
Sauer, Kurt	Ana., Col., Phx.	7	357	5	28	33	250	43	2	1	3	18	....	2002-03	2009-10
Saunders, Bernie	Que.	2	10	0	1	1	8	....	....	....	....	....	....	1979-80	1980-81
Saunders, David	Van.	1	56	7	13	20	10	....	....	....	....	....	....	1987-88	1987-88
● Saunders, Ted	Ott.	1	18	1	3	4	4	....	....	....	....	....	....	1933-34	1933-34
Sauve, Jean-Francois	Buf., Que.	7	290	65	138	203	114	36	9	12	21	10	....	1980-81	1986-87
Savage, Andre	Bos., Phi.	4	66	10	14	24	14	....	....	....	....	....	....	1998-99	2002-03
Savage, Brian	Mtl., Phx., St.L., Phi.	12	674	192	167	359	321	39	3	8	11	12	....	1993-94	2005-06
Savage, Joel	Buf.	1	3	0	1	1	0	....	....	....	....	....	....	1990-91	1990-91
Savage, Reggie	Wsh., Que.	3	34	5	7	12	28	....	....	....	....	....	....	1990-91	1993-94
● Savage, Tony	Bos., Mtl.	1	49	1	5	6	6	2	0	0	0	0	....	1934-35	1934-35
Savard, Andre	Bos., Buf., Que.	12	790	211	271	482	411	85	13	18	31	77	....	1973-74	1984-85
Savard, Denis	Chi., Mtl., T.B.	17	1196	473	865	1338	1336	169	66	109	175	256	1	1980-81	1996-97
Savard, Jean	Chi., Hfd.	3	43	7	12	19	29	....	....	....	....	....	....	1977-78	1979-80
Savard, Serge	Mtl., Wpg.	17	1040	106	333	439	592	130	19	49	68	88	8	1966-67	1982-83
Savoia, Ryan	Pit.	1	3	0	0	0	0	....	....	....	....	....	....	1998-99	1998-99
Sawyer, Kevin	St.L., Bos., Phx., Ana.	6	110	3	3	6	403	....	....	....	....	....	....	1995-96	2002-03
Scamurra, Peter	Wsh.	4	132	8	25	33	59	....	....	....	....	....	....	1975-76	1979-80
Sceviour, Darin	Chi.	1	1	0	0	0	0	....	....	....	....	....	....	1986-87	1986-87
‡ Schaefer, Peter	Van., Ott., Bos.	9	572	99	162	261	200	63	6	18	24	34	....	1998-99	2010-11
● Schaeffer, Butch	Chi.	1	5	0	0	0	6	....	....	....	....	....	....	1936-37	1936-37
Schamehorn, Kevin	Det., L.A.	3	10	0	0	0	17	....	....	....	....	....	....	1976-77	1980-81
‡ Schastlivy, Petr	Ott., Ana.	5	129	18	22	40	30	1	0	0	0	0	....	1999-00	2003-04
Schella, John	Van.	2	115	2	18	20	224	....	....	....	....	....	....	1970-71	1971-72
Scherza, Chuck	Bos., NYR	2	36	6	6	12	35	....	....	....	....	....	....	1943-44	1944-45
Schinkel, Ken	NYR, Pit.	12	636	127	198	325	163	19	7	2	9	4	....	1959-60	1972-73
Schlegel, Brad	Wsh., Cgy.	3	48	1	8	9	10	7	0	1	1	2	....	1991-92	1993-94
Schliebener, Andy	Van.	3	84	2	11	13	74	6	0	0	0	0	....	1981-82	1984-85
Schmautz, Bobby	Chi., Van., Bos., Edm., Col.	13	764	271	286	557	988	84	28	33	61	92	....	1967-68	1980-81
● Schmautz, Cliff	Buf., Phi.	1	56	13	19	32	33	....	....	....	....	....	....	1970-71	1970-71
‡ Schmidt, Chris	L.A.	1	10	0	2	2	5	....	....	....	....	....	....	2002-03	2002-03
● Schmidt, Clarence	Bos.	1	7	1	0	1	2	....	....	....	....	....	....	1943-44	1943-44
Schmidt, Jackie	Bos.	1	45	6	7	13	6	5	0	0	0	0	....	1942-43	1942-43

Name	NHL Teams	NHL Seasons	Regular Schedule GP	G	A	TP	PIM	Playoffs GP	G	A	TP	PIM	NHL Cup Wins	First NHL Season	Last NHL Season
Schmidt, Milt	Bos.	16	776	229	346	575	466	86	24	25	49	60	2	1936-37	1954-55
Schmidt, Norm	Pit.	4	125	23	33	56	73	....	....	....	....	....	....	1983-84	1987-88
Schmidt, Otto	Bos.	1	2	0	0	0	0	....	....	....	....	....	....	1943-44	1943-44
‡ Schnabel, Robert	Nsh.	3	22	0	3	3	34	....	....	....	....	....	....	2001-02	2003-04
● Schnarr, Werner	Bos.	2	26	0	0	0	0	....	....	....	....	....	....	1924-25	1925-26
Schneider, Andy	Ott.	1	10	0	0	0	15	....	....	....	....	....	....	1993-94	1993-94
Schneider, Mathieu	Mtl., NYI, Tor., NYR, L.A., Det., Ana., Atl., Van., Phx.	21	1289	223	520	743	1245	114	11	43	54	155	1	1987-88	2009-10
Schock, Danny	Bos., Phi.	2	20	1	2	3	0	1	0	0	0	0	1	1969-70	1970-71
Schock, Ron	Bos., St.L., Pit., Buf.	15	909	166	351	517	260	55	4	16	20	29	....	1963-64	1977-78
Schoenfeld, Jim	Buf., Det., Bos.	13	719	51	204	255	1132	75	3	13	16	151	....	1972-73	1984-85
Schofield, Dwight	Det., Mtl., St.L., Wsh., Pit., Wpg.	7	211	8	22	30	631	9	0	0	0	55	....	1976-77	1987-88
Schreiber, Wally	Min.	2	41	8	10	18	12	....	....	....	....	....	....	1987-88	1988-89
● Schriner, Sweeney	NYA, Tor.	11	484	201	204	405	148	59	18	11	29	54	2	1934-35	1945-46
Schulte, Paxton	Que., Cgy.	2	2	0	0	0	4	....	....	....	....	....	....	1993-94	1996-97
Schultz, Dave	Phi., L.A., Pit., Buf.	9	535	79	121	200	2294	73	8	12	20	412	2	1971-72	1979-80
‡ Schultz, Jesse	Van.	1	2	0	0	0	0	....	....	....	....	....	....	2006-07	2006-07
Schultz, Ray	NYI	6	45	0	4	4	155	2	0	0	0	2	....	1997-98	2002-03
Schurman, Maynard	Hfd.	1	7	0	0	0	0	....	....	....	....	....	....	1979-80	1979-80
Schutt, Rod	Mtl., Pit., Tor.	8	286	77	92	169	177	22	8	6	14	26	....	1977-78	1985-86
Scissons, Scott	NYI	3	2	0	0	0	0	1	0	0	0	0	....	1990-91	1993-94
Sclisizzi, Enio	Det., Chi.	6	81	12	11	23	26	13	0	0	0	6	1	1946-47	1952-53
● Scott, Ganton	Tor., Ham., Mtl.M.	3	57	1	1	2	0	....	....	....	....	....	....	1922-23	1924-25
● Scott, Laurie	NYA, NYR	2	62	6	3	9	28	....	....	....	....	....	....	1926-27	1927-28
Scott, Richard	NYR	2	10	0	0	0	28	....	....	....	....	....	....	2001-02	2003-04
Scoville, Darrel	Cgy., CBJ	3	16	0	1	1	12	....	....	....	....	....	....	1999-00	2003-04
Scremin, Claudio	S.J.	2	17	0	1	1	29	....	....	....	....	....	....	1991-92	1992-93
Scruton, Howard	L.A.	1	4	0	4	4	9	....	....	....	....	....	....	1982-83	1982-83
Seabrooke, Glen	Phi.	3	19	1	6	7	4	....	....	....	....	....	....	1986-87	1988-89
Secord, Al	Bos., Chi., Tor., Phi.	12	766	273	222	495	2093	102	21	34	55	382	....	1978-79	1989-90
Sedlbauer, Ron	Van., Chi., Tor.	7	430	143	86	229	210	19	1	3	4	27	....	1974-75	1980-81
Seftel, Steve	Wsh.	1	4	0	0	0	2	....	....	....	....	....	....	1990-91	1990-91
Seguin, Dan	Min., Van.	2	37	2	6	8	50	....	....	....	....	....	....	1970-71	1973-74
Seguin, Steve	L.A.	1	5	0	0	0	9	....	....	....	....	....	....	1984-85	1984-85
● Seibert, Earl	NYR, Chi., Det.	15	645	89	187	276	746	66	11	8	19	76	2	1931-32	1945-46
Seiling, Ric	Buf., Det.	10	738	179	208	387	573	62	14	14	28	36	....	1977-78	1986-87
Seiling, Rod	Tor., NYR, Wsh., St.L., Atl.	17	979	62	269	331	601	77	4	8	12	55	....	1962-63	1978-79
Sejba, Jiri	Buf.	1	11	0	2	2	8	....	....	....	....	....	....	1990-91	1990-91
‡ Sejna, Peter	St.L.	4	49	7	4	11	12	....	....	....	....	....	....	2002-03	2006-07
‡ Sekeras, Lubomir	Min., Dal.	4	213	18	53	71	122	15	1	1	2	6	....	2000-01	2003-04
Selby, Brit	Tor., Phi., St.L.	8	350	55	62	117	163	16	1	1	2	8	....	1964-65	1971-72
Self, Steve	Wsh.	1	3	0	0	0	0	....	....	....	....	....	....	1976-77	1976-77
Selivanov, Alex	T.B., Edm., CBJ	7	459	121	114	235	379	13	2	3	5	16	....	1994-95	2000-01
Sellars, Luke	Atl.	1	1	0	0	0	2	....	....	....	....	....	....	2001-02	2001-02
Selmser, Sean	CBJ	1	1	0	0	0	5	....	....	....	....	....	....	2000-01	2000-01
Selwood, Brad	Tor., L.A.	3	163	7	40	47	153	6	0	0	0	4	....	1970-71	1979-80
Semak, Alexander	N.J., T.B., NYI, Van.	6	289	83	91	174	187	8	1	1	2	0	....	1991-92	1996-97
Semchuk, Brandy	L.A.	1	1	0	0	0	2	....	....	....	....	....	....	1992-93	1992-93
Semenko, Dave	Edm., Hfd., Tor.	9	575	65	88	153	1175	73	6	6	12	208	2	1979-80	1987-88
‡ Semenov, Alexei	Edm., Fla., S.J.	6	211	7	26	33	249	8	0	0	0	2	....	2002-03	2008-09
Semenov, Anatoli	Edm., T.B., Van., Ana., Phi., Buf.	8	362	68	126	194	122	49	9	13	22	12	....	1989-90	1996-97
● Senick, George	NYR	1	13	2	3	5	8	....	....	....	....	....	....	1952-53	1952-53
Seppa, Jyrki	Wpg.	1	13	0	2	2	6	....	....	....	....	....	....	1983-84	1983-84
Serafini, Ron	Cal.	1	2	0	0	0	2	....	....	....	....	....	....	1973-74	1973-74
Serowik, Jeff	Tor., Bos., Pit.	3	28	0	6	6	16	....	....	....	....	....	....	1990-91	1998-99
Servinis, George	Min.	1	5	0	0	0	0	....	....	....	....	....	....	1987-88	1987-88
Sevcik, Jaroslav	Que.	1	13	0	2	2	2	....	....	....	....	....	....	1989-90	1989-90
Severson, Cam	Ana., CBJ	3	37	3	0	3	63	1	0	0	0	0	....	2002-03	2005-06
Severyn, Brent	Que., Fla., NYI, Col., Ana., Dal.	7	328	10	30	40	825	8	0	0	0	12	1	1989-90	1998-99
Sevigny, Pierre	Mtl., NYR	4	78	4	5	9	64	3	0	1	1	0	....	1993-94	1997-98
Shack, Eddie	NYR, Tor., Bos., L.A., Buf., Pit.	17	1047	239	226	465	1437	74	6	7	13	151	4	1958-59	1974-75
● Shack, Joe	NYR	2	70	9	27	36	20	....	....	....	....	....	....	1942-43	1944-45
Shafranov, Konstantin	St.L.	1	5	2	1	3	0	....	....	....	....	....	....	1996-97	1996-97
Shakes, Paul	Cal.	1	21	0	4	4	12	....	....	....	....	....	....	1973-74	1973-74
Shaldybin, Yevgeny	Bos.	1	3	1	0	1	0	....	....	....	....	....	....	1996-97	1996-97
Shanahan, Brendan	N.J., St.L., Hfd., Det., NYR	21	1524	656	698	1354	2489	184	60	74	134	279	3	1987-88	2008-09
Shanahan, Sean	Mtl., Col., Bos.	3	40	1	3	4	47	....	....	....	....	....	....	1975-76	1977-78
Shand, Dave	Atl., Tor., Wsh.	8	421	19	84	103	544	26	1	2	3	83	....	1976-77	1984-85
Shank, Daniel	Det., Hfd.	3	77	13	14	27	175	5	0	0	0	22	....	1989-90	1991-92
● Shannon, Chuck	NYA	1	4	0	0	0	2	....	....	....	....	....	....	1939-40	1939-40
Shannon, Darrin	Buf., Wpg., Phx.	10	506	87	163	250	344	45	7	10	17	38	....	1988-89	1997-98
Shannon, Darryl	Tor., Wpg., Buf., Atl., Cgy., Mtl.	13	544	28	111	139	523	29	4	7	11	16	....	1988-89	2000-01
● Shannon, Gerry	Ott., St.L., Bos., Mtl.M.	5	180	23	29	52	80	9	0	1	1	2	....	1933-34	1937-38
Shantz, Jeff	Chi., Cgy., Col.	10	642	72	139	211	341	44	5	8	13	24	....	1993-94	2002-03
Sharifijanov, Vadim	N.J., Van.	3	92	16	21	37	50	4	0	0	0	0	....	1996-97	1999-00
Sharples, Jeff	Det.	3	105	14	35	49	70	7	0	3	3	6	....	1986-87	1988-89
Sharpley, Glen	Min., Chi.	6	389	117	161	278	199	27	7	11	18	24	....	1976-77	1981-82
Shaunessy, Scott	Que.	2	7	0	0	0	23	....	....	....	....	....	....	1986-87	1988-89
Shaw, Brad	Hfd., Ott., Wsh., St.L.	11	377	22	137	159	208	23	4	8	12	6	....	1985-86	1998-99
Shaw, David	Que., NYR, Edm., Min., Bos., T.B.	16	769	41	153	194	906	45	3	9	12	81	....	1982-83	1997-98
● Shay, Norm	Bos., Tor.	2	53	5	3	8	34	....	....	....	....	....	....	1924-25	1925-26
● Shea, Pat	Chi.	1	10	1	0	1	0	....	....	....	....	....	....	1931-32	1931-32
Shearer, Rob	Col.	1	2	0	0	0	0	....	....	....	....	....	....	2000-01	2000-01
Shedden, Doug	Pit., Det., Que., Tor.	8	416	139	186	325	176	....	....	....	....	....	....	1981-82	1990-91
Sheehan, Bobby	Mtl., Cal., Chi., Det., NYR, Col., L.A.	9	310	48	63	111	40	25	4	3	7	8	1	1969-70	1981-82
Sheehy, Neil	Cgy., Hfd., Wsh.	9	379	18	47	65	1311	54	0	3	3	241	....	1983-84	1991-92
Sheehy, Tim	Det., Hfd.	2	27	2	1	3	0	....	....	....	....	....	....	1977-78	1979-80
Shelton, Doug	Chi.	1	5	0	1	1	2	....	....	....	....	....	....	1967-68	1967-68
● Sheppard, Frank	Det.	1	8	1	1	2	0	....	....	....	....	....	....	1927-28	1927-28
Sheppard, Gregg	Bos., Pit.	10	657	205	293	498	243	82	32	40	72	31	....	1972-73	1981-82
● Sheppard, Johnny	Det., NYA, Bos., Chi.	8	308	68	58	126	224	10	0	0	0	0	1	1926-27	1933-34
Sheppard, Ray	Buf., NYR, Det., S.J., Fla., Car.	13	817	357	300	657	212	81	30	20	50	21	....	1987-88	1999-00
● Sherf, John	Det.	5	19	0	0	0	8	8	0	1	1	2	1	1935-36	1943-44
● Shero, Fred	NYR	3	145	6	14	20	137	13	0	2	2	8	....	1947-48	1949-50
● Sherritt, Gordon	Det.	1	8	0	0	0	12	....	....	....	....	....	....	1943-44	1943-44
Sherven, Gord	Edm., Min., Hfd.	5	97	13	22	35	33	3	0	0	0	0	....	1983-84	1987-88
Shevalier, Jeff	L.A., T.B.	3	32	5	9	14	8	....	....	....	....	....	....	1994-95	1999-00
● Shewchuk, Jack	Bos.	6	187	9	19	28	160	20	0	1	1	19	1	1938-39	1944-45
● Shibicky, Alex	NYR	8	324	110	91	201	161	39	12	12	24	12	1	1935-36	1945-46
● Shields, Al	Ott., Phi., NYA, Mtl.M., Bos.	11	459	42	46	88	637	17	0	1	1	14	1	1927-28	1937-38
● Shill, Bill	Bos.	3	79	21	13	34	18	7	1	2	3	2	....	1942-43	1946-47
● Shill, Jack	Tor., Bos., NYA, Chi.	6	160	15	20	35	70	25	1	6	7	23	1	1933-34	1938-39
Shinske, Rick	Cle., St.L.	3	63	5	16	21	10	....	....	....	....	....	....	1976-77	1978-79
Shires, Jim	Det., St.L., Pit.	3	56	3	6	9	32	....	....	....	....	....	....	1970-71	1972-73
‡ Shishkanov, Timofei	Nsh., St.L.	2	24	3	2	5	6	....	....	....	....	....	....	2003-04	2005-06
● Shmyr, Paul	Chi., Cal., Min., Hfd.	7	343	13	72	85	528	34	3	3	6	44	....	1968-69	1981-82
Shoebottom, Bruce	Bos.	4	35	1	4	5	53	14	1	2	3	77	....	1987-88	1990-91
● Shore, Eddie	Bos., NYA	14	550	105	179	284	1047	55	7	12	19	181	2	1926-27	1939-40
● Shore, Hamby	Ott.	1	18	3	8	11	51	....	....	....	....	....	....	1917-18	1917-18
Short, Steve	L.A., Det.	2	6	0	0	0	2	....	....	....	....	....	....	1977-78	1978-79
Shuchuk, Gary	Det., L.A.	5	142	13	26	39	70	20	2	2	4	12	....	1990-91	1995-96
Shudra, Ron	Edm.	1	10	0	5	5	6	....	....	....	....	....	....	1987-88	1987-88
Shutt, Steve	Mtl., L.A.	13	930	424	393	817	410	99	50	48	98	65	5	1972-73	1984-85
Shvidki, Denis	Fla.	4	76	11	14	25	30	....	....	....	....	....	....	2000-01	2003-04
● Siebert, Babe	Mtl.M., NYR, Bos., Mtl.	14	592	140	156	296	982	49	7	5	12	62	2	1925-26	1938-39
Siklenka, Mike	Phi., NYR	2	2	0	0	0	0	....	....	....	....	....	....	2002-03	2003-04
Silk, Dave	NYR, Bos., Det., Wpg.	7	249	54	59	113	271	13	2	4	6	13	....	1979-80	1985-86
Sillinger, Mike	Det., Ana., Van., Phi., T.B., Fla., Ott., CBJ, Phx., St.L.	18	1049	240	308	548	644	43	11	7	18	28	....	1990-91	2003-04
Siltala, Mike	Wsh., NYR	3	7	1	0	1	2	....	....	....	....	....	....	1981-82	1987-88
Siltanen, Risto	Edm., Hfd., Que.	8	562	90	265	355	266	32	6	12	18	30	....	1979-80	1986-87
Sim, Trevor	Edm.	1	3	0	1	1	2	....	....	....	....	....	....	1989-90	1989-90
Simard, Martin	Cgy., T.B.	3	44	1	5	6	183	....	....	....	....	....	....	1990-91	1992-93
Simicek, Roman	Pit., Min.	2	63	7	10	17	59	....	....	....	....	....	....	2000-01	2001-02
Simmer, Charlie	Cal., Cle., L.A., Bos., Pit.	14	712	342	369	711	544	24	9	9	18	32	....	1974-75	1987-88
Simmons, Al	Cal., Bos.	3	11	0	1	1	21	1	0	0	0	0	....	1971-72	1975-76

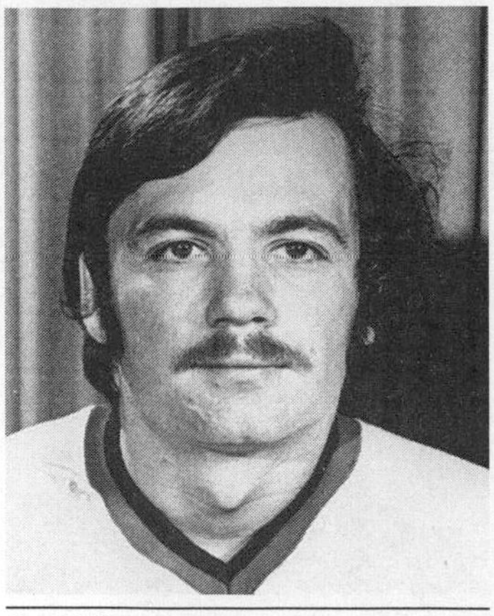
Steve Self

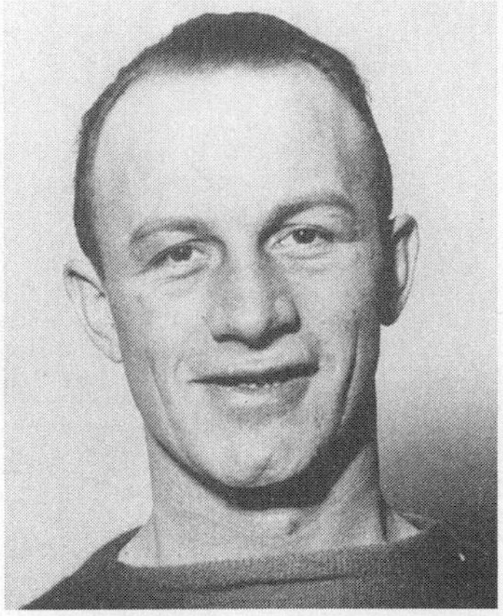
Eddie Shore

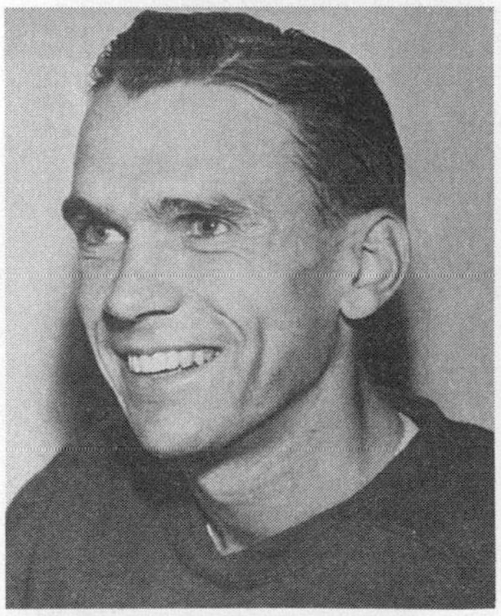
Reg Sinclair

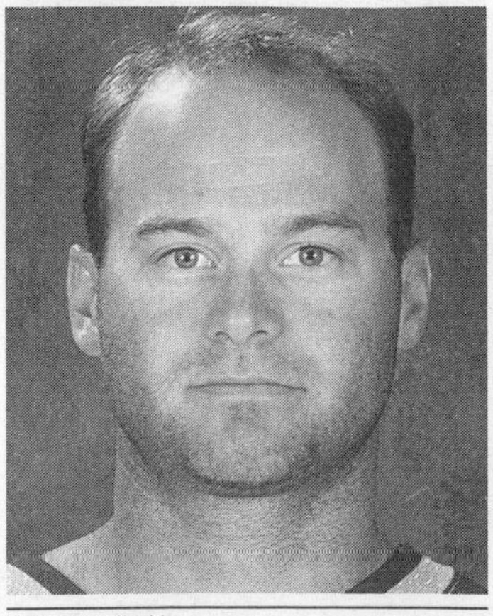
Bryan Smolinski

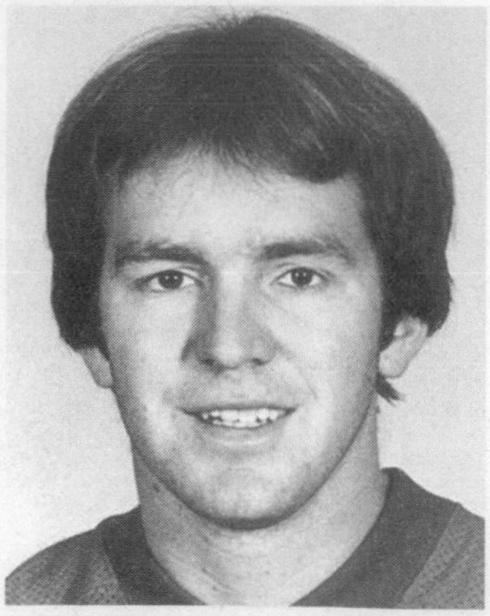

Ted Speers

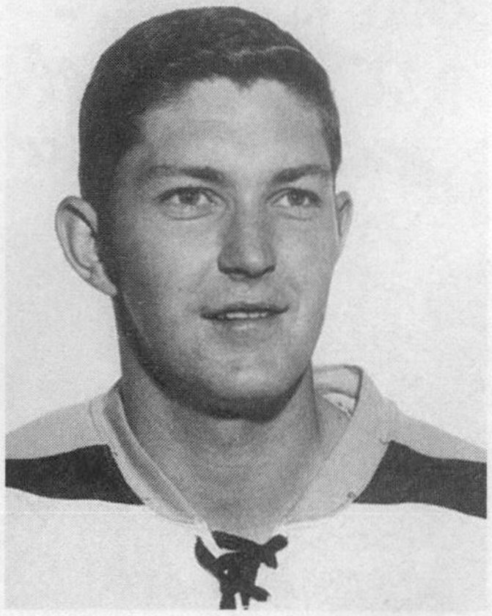

Fred Stanfield

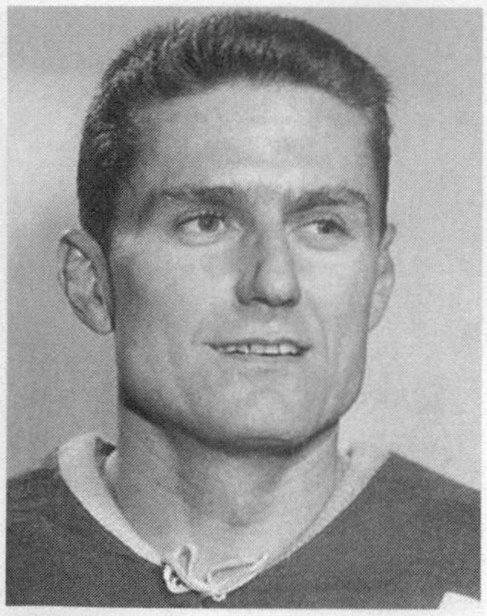

Allan Stanley

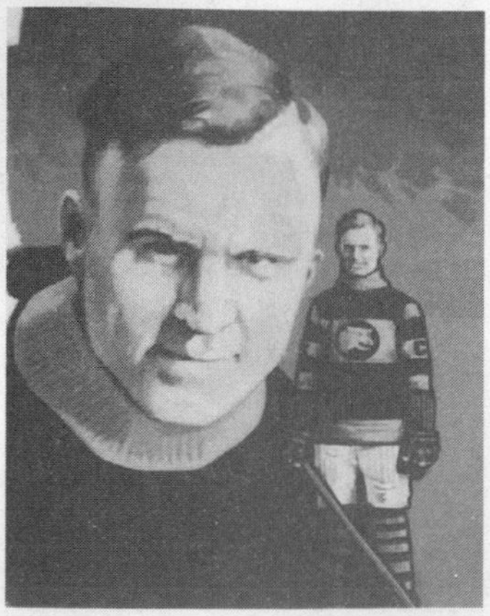

Barney Stanley

			Regular Schedule					Playoffs							
Name	NHL Teams	NHL Seasons	GP	G	A	TP	PIM	GP	G	A	TP	PIM	NHL Cup Wins	First NHL Season	Last NHL Season
‡ Simon, Ben	Atl., CBJ	4	81	3	1	4	47	....	....	....	....	....	....	2001-02	2005-06
‡ Simon, Chris	Que., Col., Wsh., Chi., NYR, Cgy., NYI, Min.	15	782	144	161	305	1824	75	10	7	17	191	1	1992-93	2007-08
• Simon, Cully	Det., Chi.	3	130	4	11	15	121	14	1	0	1	6	1	1942-43	1944-45
Simon, Jason	NYI, Phx.	2	5	0	0	0	34	....	....	....	....	....	....	1993-94	1996-97
• Simon, Thain	Det.	1	3	0	0	0	0	....	....	....	....	....	....	1946-47	1946-47
Simon, Todd	Buf.	1	15	0	1	1	0	5	1	0	1	0	....	1993-94	1993-94
Simonetti, Frank	Bos.	4	115	5	8	13	76	12	0	1	1	8	....	1984-85	1987-88
Simpson, Bobby	Atl., St.L., Pit.	5	175	35	29	64	98	6	0	1	1	2	....	1976-77	1982-83
• Simpson, Cliff	Det.	2	6	0	1	1	0	2	0	0	0	2	....	1946-47	1947-48
Simpson, Craig	Pit., Edm., Buf.	10	634	247	250	497	659	67	36	32	68	56	2	1985-86	1994-95
• Simpson, Joe	NYA	6	228	21	19	40	156	2	0	0	0	0	....	1925-26	1930-31
Simpson, Reid	Phi., Min., N.J., Chi., T.B., St.L., Mtl., Nsh., Pit.	12	301	18	18	36	838	10	0	0	0	31	....	1991-92	2003-04
Simpson, Todd	Cgy., Fla., Phx., Ana., Ott., Chi., Mtl.	10	580	14	63	77	1357	9	0	2	2	10	....	1995-96	2005-06
Sims, Al	Bos., Hfd., L.A.	10	475	49	116	165	286	41	0	2	2	14	....	1973-74	1982-83
Sinclair, Reg	NYR, Det.	3	208	49	43	92	139	3	1	0	1	0	....	1950-51	1952-53
• Singbush, Alex	Mtl.	1	32	0	5	5	15	3	0	0	0	4	....	1940-41	1940-41
Sinisalo, Ilkka	Phi., Min., L.A.	11	582	204	222	426	208	68	21	11	32	6	....	1981-82	1991-92
Siren, Ville	Pit., Min.	5	290	14	68	82	276	7	0	0	0	6	....	1985-86	1989-90
Sirois, Bob	Phi., Wsh.	6	286	92	120	212	42	....	....	....	....	....	....	1974-75	1979-80
Sittler, Darryl	Tor., Phi., Det.	15	1096	484	637	1121	948	76	29	45	74	137	....	1970-71	1984-85
Sivek, Michal	Pit.	1	38	3	3	6	14	....	....	....	....	....	....	2002-03	2002-03
• Sjoberg, Lars-Erik	Wpg.	1	79	7	27	34	48	....	....	....	....	....	....	1979-80	1979-80
Sjodin, Tommy	Min., Dal., Que.	2	106	8	40	48	52	....	....	....	....	....	....	1992-93	1993-94
• Skaare, Bjorn	Det.	1	1	0	0	0	0	....	....	....	....	....	....	1978-79	1978-79
Skalde, Jarrod	N.J., Ana., Cgy., S.J., Chi., Dal., Atl., Phi.	9	115	13	21	34	62	....	....	....	....	....	....	1990-91	2001-02
Skarda, Randy	St.L.	2	26	0	5	5	11	....	....	....	....	....	....	1989-90	1991-92
• Skilton, Raymie	Mtl.W.	1	1	0	0	0	0	....	....	....	....	....	....	1917-18	1917-18
• Skinner, Alf	Tor., Bos., Mtl.M., Pit.	4	71	26	10	36	87	2	0	1	1	9	1	1917-18	1925-26
Skinner, Larry	Col.	4	47	10	12	22	8	2	0	0	0	0	....	1976-77	1979-80
Skolney, Wade	Phi.	1	1	0	0	0	2	....	....	....	....	....	....	2005-06	2005-06
‡ Skopintsev, Andrei	T.B., Atl.	3	40	2	4	6	32	....	....	....	....	....	....	1998-99	2000-01
Skov, Glen	Det., Chi., Mtl.	12	650	106	136	242	413	53	7	7	14	48	3	1949-50	1960-61
‡ Skrbek, Pavel	Pit., Nsh.	3	12	0	0	0	8	....	....	....	....	....	....	1998-99	2001-02
Skriko, Petri	Van., Bos., Wpg., S.J.	9	541	183	222	405	246	28	5	9	14	4	....	1984-85	1992-93
Skrlac, Rob	N.J.	1	8	1	0	1	22	....	....	....	....	....	....	2003-04	2003-04
Skrudland, Brian	Mtl., Cgy., Fla., NYR, Dal.	15	881	124	219	343	1107	164	15	46	61	323	2	1985-86	1999-00
‡ Slaney, John	Wsh., Col., L.A., Phx., Nsh., Pit., Phi.	9	268	22	69	91	99	14	2	1	3	4	....	1993-94	2003-04
• Sleaver, John	Chi.	2	13	1	0	1	6	....	....	....	....	....	....	1953-54	1956-57
‡ Slegr, Jiri	Van., Edm., Pit., Atl., Det., Bos.	11	622	56	193	249	838	42	4	14	18	39	1	1992-93	2005-06
Sleigher, Louis	Que., Bos.	6	194	46	53	99	146	17	1	1	2	64	....	1979-80	1985-86
‡ Sloan, Blake	Dal., CBJ, Cgy.	6	290	11	32	43	162	35	0	2	2	20	1	1998-99	2003-04
Sloan, Tod	Tor., Chi.	13	745	220	262	482	831	47	9	12	21	47	2	1947-48	1960-61
‡ Sloane, David	Phi.	1	1	0	0	0	0	....	....	....	....	....	....	2008-09	2008-09
• Slobodian, Peter	NYA	1	41	3	2	5	54	....	....	....	....	....	....	1940-41	1940-41
• Slowinski, Ed	NYR	6	291	58	74	132	63	16	2	6	8	6	....	1947-48	1952-53
• Sly, Darryl	Tor., Min., Van.	4	79	1	2	3	20	....	....	....	....	....	....	1965-66	1970-71
Smail, Doug	Wpg., Min., Que., Ott.	13	845	210	249	459	602	42	9	2	11	49	....	1980-81	1992-93
• Smart, Alex	Mtl.	1	8	5	2	7	0	....	....	....	....	....	....	1942-43	1942-43
Smedsmo, Dale	Tor.	1	4	0	0	0	0	....	....	....	....	....	....	1972-73	1972-73
Smehlik, Richard	Buf., Atl., N.J.	10	644	49	146	195	415	88	1	14	15	40	1	1992-93	2002-03
• Smillie, Don	Bos.	1	12	2	2	4	4	....	....	....	....	....	....	1933-34	1933-34
Smirnov, Alexei	Ana.	2	52	3	3	6	20	4	0	0	0	2	....	2002-03	2003-04
• Smith, Alex	Ott., Det., Bos., NYA	11	443	41	50	91	645	19	0	2	2	26	1	1924-25	1934-35
• Smith, Art	Tor., Ott.	4	144	15	10	25	249	4	1	1	2	8	....	1927-28	1930-31
Smith, Barry	Bos., Col.	3	114	7	7	14	10	....	....	....	....	....	....	1975-76	1980-81
Smith, Bobby	Min., Mtl.	15	1077	357	679	1036	917	184	64	96	160	245	1	1978-79	1992-93
Smith, Brad	Van., Atl., Cgy., Det., Tor.	9	222	28	34	62	591	20	3	3	6	49	....	1978-79	1986-87
Smith, Brandon	Bos., NYI	4	33	3	4	7	10	....	....	....	....	....	....	1998-99	2002-03
Smith, Brian	Det.	3	61	2	8	10	12	5	0	0	0	0	....	1957-58	1960-61
• Smith, Brian	L.A., Min.	2	67	10	10	20	33	7	0	0	0	0	....	1967-68	1968-69
• Smith, Carl	Det.	1	7	1	1	2	2	....	....	....	....	....	....	1943-44	1943-44
• Smith, Clint	NYR, Chi.	11	483	161	236	397	24	42	10	14	24	2	1	1936-37	1946-47
Smith, D.J.	Tor., Col.	3	45	1	1	2	67	....	....	....	....	....	....	1996-97	2002-03
Smith, Dallas	Bos., NYR	16	890	55	252	307	959	86	3	29	32	128	2	1959-60	1977-78
Smith, Dan	Col., Edm.	3	22	0	0	0	16	....	....	....	....	....	....	1998-99	2005-06
Smith, Dennis	Wsh., L.A.	2	8	0	0	0	4	....	....	....	....	....	....	1989-90	1990-91
Smith, Derek	Buf., Det.	8	335	78	116	194	60	30	9	14	23	13	....	1975-76	1982-83
Smith, Derrick	Phi., Min., Dal.	10	537	82	92	174	373	82	14	11	25	79	....	1984-85	1993-94
• Smith, Des	Mtl.M., Mtl., Chi., Bos.	5	196	22	25	47	236	25	1	4	5	18	1	1937-38	1941-42
• Smith, Don	Mtl.	1	12	1	0	1	6	....	....	....	....	....	....	1919-20	1919-20
• Smith, Don	NYR	1	11	1	1	2	0	1	0	0	0	0	....	1949-50	1949-50
Smith, Doug	L.A., Buf., Edm., Van., Pit.	9	535	115	138	253	624	18	4	2	6	21	....	1981-82	1989-90
Smith, Floyd	Bos., NYR, Det., Tor., Buf.	13	616	129	178	307	207	48	12	11	23	16	....	1954-55	1971-72
Smith, Geoff	Edm., Fla., NYR	10	462	18	73	91	282	13	0	1	1	8	1	1989-90	1998-99
Smith, Glen	Chi.	1	2	0	0	0	0	....	....	....	....	....	....	1950-51	1950-51
• Smith, Glenn	Tor.	1	9	0	0	0	0	....	....	....	....	....	....	1921-22	1921-22
Smith, Gord	Wsh., Wpg.	6	299	9	30	39	284	....	....	....	....	....	....	1974-75	1979-80
Smith, Greg	Cal., Cle., Min., Det., Wsh.	13	829	56	232	288	1110	63	4	7	11	106	....	1975-76	1987-88
• Smith, Hooley	Ott., Mtl.M., Bos., NYA	17	715	200	225	425	1013	54	11	8	19	109	2	1924-25	1940-41
Smith, Jason	N.J., Tor., Edm., Phi., Ott.	15	1008	41	128	169	1099	68	1	10	11	60	....	1993-94	2008-09
• Smith, Ken	Bos.	7	331	78	93	171	49	30	8	13	21	6	....	1944-45	1950-51
Smith, Mark	S.J., Cgy.	7	377	23	47	70	457	24	4	0	4	21	....	2000-01	2007-08
• Smith, Nakina	Det.	1	10	1	2	3	0	....	....	....	....	....	....	1943-44	1943-44
Smith, Nick	Fla.	1	15	0	0	0	0	....	....	....	....	....	....	2001-02	2001-02
Smith, Randy	Min.	2	3	0	0	0	0	....	....	....	....	....	....	1985-86	1986-87
Smith, Rick	Bos., Cal., St.L., Det., Wsh.	11	687	52	167	219	560	78	3	23	26	73	1	1968-69	1980-81
• Smith, Rodger	Pit., Phi.	6	210	20	4	24	172	4	3	0	3	0	....	1925-26	1930-31
Smith, Ron	NYI	1	11	1	1	2	14	....	....	....	....	....	....	1972-73	1972-73
• Smith, Sid	Tor.	12	601	186	183	369	94	44	17	10	27	2	3	1946-47	1957-58
Smith, Stan	NYR	2	9	2	1	3	0	1	0	0	0	0	1	1939-40	1940-41
Smith, Steve	Phi., Buf.	6	18	0	1	1	15	....	....	....	....	....	....	1981-82	1988-89
Smith, Steve	Edm., Chi., Cgy.	16	804	72	303	375	2139	134	11	41	52	288	3	1984-85	2000-01
Smith, Stu	Mtl.	2	4	2	2	4	2	1	0	0	0	0	....	1940-41	1941-42
Smith, Stu	Hfd.	4	77	2	10	12	95	....	....	....	....	....	....	1979-80	1982-83
• Smith, Tommy	Que.	1	10	0	1	1	11	....	....	....	....	....	....	1919-20	1919-20
Smith, Vern	NYI	1	1	0	0	0	0	....	....	....	....	....	....	1984-85	1984-85
Smith, Wayne	Chi.	1	2	1	1	2	2	1	0	0	0	0	....	1966-67	1966-67
‡ Smolenak, Radek	T.B., Chi.	2	7	0	1	1	15	....	....	....	....	....	....	2008-09	2009-10
Smolinski, Bryan	Bos., Pit., NYI, L.A., Ott., Chi., Van., Mtl.	15	1056	274	377	651	606	123	23	29	52	60	....	1992-93	2007-08
Smrek, Peter	St.L., NYR	2	28	2	4	6	18	....	....	....	....	....	....	2000-01	2001-02
Smrke, John	St.L., Que.	3	103	11	17	28	33	....	....	....	....	....	....	1977-78	1979-80
• Smrke, Stan	Mtl.	2	9	0	3	3	0	....	....	....	....	....	....	1956-57	1957-58
Smyl, Stan	Van.	13	896	262	411	673	1556	41	16	17	33	64	....	1978-79	1990-91
• Smylie, Rod	Tor., Ott.	6	74	4	2	6	12	4	0	0	0	2	1	1920-21	1925-26
Smyth, Brad	Fla., L.A., NYR, Nsh., Ott.	6	88	15	13	28	109	....	....	....	....	....	....	1995-96	2002-03
Smyth, Greg	Phi., Que., Cgy., Fla., Tor., Chi.	10	229	4	16	20	783	12	0	0	0	40	....	1986-87	1996-97
Smyth, Kevin	Hfd.	3	58	6	8	14	31	....	....	....	....	....	....	1993-94	1995-96
Snell, Chris	Tor., L.A.	2	34	2	7	9	24	....	....	....	....	....	....	1993-94	1994-95
Snell, Ron	Pit.	2	7	3	2	5	6	....	....	....	....	....	....	1968-69	1969-70
Snell, Ted	Pit., K.C., Det.	2	104	7	18	25	22	....	....	....	....	....	....	1973-74	1974-75
Snepsts, Harold	Van., Min., Det., St.L.	17	1033	38	195	233	2009	93	1	14	15	231	....	1974-75	1990-91
Snow, Sandy	Det.	1	3	0	0	0	2	....	....	....	....	....	....	1968-69	1968-69
Snuggerud, Dave	Buf., S.J., Phi.	4	265	30	54	84	127	12	1	3	4	6	....	1989-90	1992-93
• Snyder, Dan	Atl.	3	49	11	5	16	64	....	....	....	....	....	....	2000-01	2002-03
Sobchuk, Dennis	Det., Que.	2	35	5	6	11	2	....	....	....	....	....	....	1979-80	1982-83
Sobchuk, Gene	Van.	1	1	0	0	0	0	....	....	....	....	....	....	1973-74	1973-74
Solheim, Ken	Chi., Min., Det., Edm.	5	135	19	20	39	34	3	1	1	2	2	....	1980-81	1985-86
Solinger, Bob	Tor., Det.	5	99	10	11	21	19	....	....	....	....	....	....	1951-52	1959-60
• Somers, Art	Chi., NYR	6	222	33	56	89	189	30	1	5	6	20	1	1929-30	1934-35
‡ Somik, Radovan	Phi.	2	113	12	20	32	27	15	2	2	4	10	....	2002-03	2003-04
Sommer, Roy	Edm.	1	3	1	0	1	7	....	....	....	....	....	....	1980-81	1980-81
Songin, Tom	Bos.	3	43	5	5	10	22	....	....	....	....	....	....	1978-79	1980-81

Name	NHL Teams	NHL Seasons	Regular Schedule GP	G	A	TP	PIM	Playoffs GP	G	A	TP	PIM	NHL Cup Wins	First NHL Season	Last NHL Season
Sonmor, Glen	NYR	2	28	2	0	2	21	....	....	....	....	....	....	1953-54	1954-55
Sonnenberg, Martin	Pit., Cgy.	3	63	2	3	5	21	7	0	0	0	0	....	1998-99	2003-04
Sorochan, Lee	Cgy.	2	3	0	0	0	0	....	....	....	....	....	....	1998-99	1999-00
• Sorrell, John	Det., NYA	11	490	127	119	246	100	42	12	15	27	10	2	1930-31	1940-41
Spanhel, Martin	CBJ	2	10	2	0	2	4	....	....	....	....	....	....	2000-01	2001-02
• Sparrow, Emory	Bos.	1	8	0	0	0	4	....	....	....	....	....	....	1924-25	1924-25
• Speck, Fred	Det., Van.	3	28	1	2	3	2	....	....	....	....	....	....	1968-69	1971-72
• Speer, Bill	Pit., Bos.	4	130	5	20	25	79	8	1	0	1	4	1	1967-68	1970-71
Speers, Ted	Det.	1	4	1	1	2	0	....	....	....	....	....	....	1985-86	1985-86
• Spence, Gordon	Tor.	1	3	0	0	0	0	....	....	....	....	....	....	1925-26	1925-26
• Spencer, Brian	Tor., NYI, Buf., Pit.	10	553	80	143	223	634	37	1	5	6	29	....	1969-70	1978-79
• Spencer, Irv	NYR, Bos., Det.	8	230	12	38	50	127	16	0	0	0	8	....	1959-60	1967-68
• Speyer, Chris	Tor., NYA	3	14	0	0	0	0	....	....	....	....	....	....	1923-24	1933-34
Spiller, Matthew	Phx., NYI	3	68	0	2	2	74	....	....	....	....	....	....	2003-04	2007-08
Spring, Corey	T.B.	2	16	1	1	2	12	....	....	....	....	....	....	1997-98	1998-99
Spring, Don	Wpg.	4	259	1	54	55	80	6	0	0	0	10	....	1980-81	1983-84
Spring, Frank	Bos., St.L., Cal., Cle.	5	61	14	20	34	12	....	....	....	....	....	....	1969-70	1976-77
• Spring, Jesse	Ham., Pit., Tor., NYA	6	133	11	4	15	74	2	0	2	2	2	....	1923-24	1929-30
Spruce, Andy	Van., Col.	3	172	31	42	73	111	2	0	2	2	0	....	1976-77	1978-79
‡ Sprukts, Janis	Fla.	2	14	1	2	3	2	....	....	....	....	....	....	2006-07	2008-09
Srsen, Tomas	Edm.	1	2	0	0	0	0	....	....	....	....	....	....	1990-91	1990-91
St. Amour, Martin	Ott.	1	1	0	0	0	2	....	....	....	....	....	....	1992-93	1992-93
‡ St. Jacques, Bruno	Phi., Car., Ana.	4	67	3	7	10	47	....	....	....	....	....	....	2001-02	2005-06
St. Laurent, Andre	NYI, Det., L.A., Pit.	11	644	129	187	316	749	59	8	12	20	48	....	1973-74	1983-84
St. Laurent, Dollard	Mtl., Chi.	12	652	29	133	162	496	92	2	22	24	87	5	1950-51	1961-62
St. Marseille, Frank	St.L., L.A.	10	707	140	285	425	242	88	20	25	45	18	....	1967-68	1976-77
St. Sauveur, Claude	Atl.	1	79	24	24	48	23	2	0	0	0	0	....	1975-76	1975-76
Stackhouse, Ron	Cal., Det., Pit.	12	889	87	372	459	824	32	5	8	13	38	....	1970-71	1981-82
• Stackhouse, Ted	Tor.	1	13	0	0	0	2	1	0	0	0	0	1	1921-22	1921-22
• Stahan, Butch	Mtl.	1	....	....	....	....	....	3	0	1	1	2	....	1944-45	1944-45
Stajduhar, Nick	Edm.	1	2	0	0	0	4	....	....	....	....	....	....	1995-96	1995-96
Staley, Al	NYR	1	1	0	1	1	0	....	....	....	....	....	....	1948-49	1948-49
Stamler, Lorne	L.A., Tor., Wpg.	4	116	14	11	25	16	....	....	....	....	....	....	1976-77	1979-80
Standing, George	Min.	1	2	0	0	0	0	....	....	....	....	....	....	1967-68	1967-68
Stanfield, Fred	Chi., Bos., Min., Buf.	14	914	211	405	616	134	106	21	35	56	10	2	1964-65	1977-78
Stanfield, Jack	Chi.	1	....	....	....	....	....	1	0	0	0	0	....	1965-66	1965-66
• Stanfield, Jim	L.A.	3	7	0	1	1	0	....	....	....	....	....	....	1969-70	1971-72
Stankiewicz, Ed	Det.	2	6	0	0	0	2	....	....	....	....	....	....	1953-54	1955-56
Stankiewicz, Myron	St.L., Phi.	1	35	0	7	7	36	1	0	0	0	0	....	1968-69	1968-69
Stanley, Allan	NYR, Chi., Bos., Tor., Phi.	21	1244	100	333	433	792	109	7	36	43	80	4	1948-49	1968-69
• Stanley, Barney	Chi.	1	1	0	0	0	0	....	....	....	....	....	....	1927-28	1927-28
Stanley, Daryl	Phi., Van.	6	189	8	17	25	408	17	0	0	0	30	....	1983-84	1989-90
Stanowski, Wally	Tor., NYR	10	428	23	88	111	160	60	3	14	17	13	4	1939-40	1950-51
Stanton, Paul	Pit., Bos., NYI	5	295	14	49	63	262	44	2	10	12	66	2	1990-91	1994-95
Stapleton, Brian	Wsh.	1	1	0	0	0	0	....	....	....	....	....	....	1975-76	1975-76
Stapleton, Mike	Chi., Pit., Edm., Wpg., Phx., Atl., NYI, Van.	14	697	71	111	182	342	34	1	0	1	39	....	1986-87	2000-01
Stapleton, Pat	Bos., Chi.	10	635	43	294	337	353	65	10	39	49	38	....	1961-62	1972-73
Starikov, Sergei	N.J.	1	16	0	1	1	8	....	....	....	....	....	....	1989-90	1989-90
• Starr, Harold	Ott., Mtl.M., Mtl., NYR	7	205	6	5	11	186	15	1	0	1	4	....	1929-30	1935-36
• Starr, Wilf	NYA, Det.	4	87	8	6	14	25	7	0	2	2	2	....	1932-33	1935-36
Stasiuk, Vic	Chi., Det., Bos.	14	745	183	254	437	669	69	16	18	34	40	2	1949-50	1962-63
Stastny, Anton	Que.	9	650	252	384	636	150	66	20	32	52	31	....	1980-81	1988-89
Stastny, Marian	Que., Tor.	5	322	121	173	294	110	32	5	17	22	7	....	1981-82	1985-86
Stastny, Peter	Que., N.J., St.L.	15	977	450	789	1239	824	93	33	72	105	123	....	1980-81	1994-95
Staszak, Ray	Det.	1	4	0	1	1	7	....	....	....	....	....	....	1985-86	1985-86
• Steele, Frank	Det.	1	1	0	0	0	0	....	....	....	....	....	....	1930-31	1930-31
Steen, Anders	Wpg.	1	42	5	11	16	22	....	....	....	....	....	....	1980-81	1980-81
Steen, Thomas	Wpg.	14	950	264	553	817	753	56	12	32	44	62	....	1981-82	1994-95
Stefan, Patrik	Atl., Dal.	7	455	64	124	188	158	....	....	....	....	....	....	1999-00	2006-07
Stefaniw, Morris	Atl.	1	13	1	1	2	2	....	....	....	....	....	....	1972-73	1972-73
Stefanski, Bud	NYR	1	1	0	0	0	0	....	....	....	....	....	....	1977-78	1977-78
Stemkowski, Pete	Tor., Det., NYR, L.A.	15	967	206	349	555	866	83	25	29	54	136	1	1963-64	1977-78
Stenlund, Vern	Cle.	1	4	0	0	0	0	....	....	....	....	....	....	1976-77	1976-77
‡ Stephens, Charlie	Col.	2	8	0	2	2	4	....	....	....	....	....	....	2002-03	2003-04
Stephenson, Bob	Hfd., Tor.	1	18	2	3	5	4	....	....	....	....	....	....	1979-80	1979-80
Stephenson, Shay	L.A.	1	2	0	0	0	0	....	....	....	....	....	....	2006-07	2006-07
Stern, Ron	Van., Cgy., S.J.	12	638	75	86	161	2077	43	7	7	14	119	....	1987-88	1999-00
Sterner, Ulf	NYR	1	4	0	0	0	0	....	....	....	....	....	....	1964-65	1964-65
Stevens, John	Phi., Hfd.	5	53	0	10	10	48	....	....	....	....	....	....	1986-87	1993-94
Stevens, Kevin	Pit., Bos., L.A., NYR, Phi.	15	874	329	397	726	1470	103	46	60	106	170	2	1987-88	2001-02
Stevens, Mike	Van., Bos., NYI, Tor.	4	23	1	4	5	29	....	....	....	....	....	....	1984-85	1989-90
• Stevens, Phil	Mtl.W., Mtl., Bos.	3	25	1	0	1	3	....	....	....	....	....	....	1917-18	1925-26
Stevens, Scott	Wsh., St.L., N.J.	22	1635	196	712	908	2785	233	26	92	118	402	3	1982-83	2003-04
‡ Stevenson, Grant	S.J.	1	47	10	12	22	14	5	0	0	0	4	....	2005-06	2005-06
Stevenson, Jeremy	Ana., Nsh., Min., Dal.	9	207	19	19	38	451	21	0	5	5	20	....	1995-96	2005-06
Stevenson, Shayne	Bos., T.B.	3	27	0	2	2	35	....	....	....	....	....	....	1990-91	1992-93
Stevenson, Turner	Mtl., N.J., Phi.	13	644	75	115	190	969	67	6	12	18	66	1	1992-93	2005-06
Stewart, Allan	N.J., Bos.	6	64	6	4	10	243	....	....	....	....	....	....	1985-86	1991-92
Stewart, Bill	Buf., St.L., Tor., Min.	8	261	7	64	71	424	13	1	3	4	11	....	1977-78	1985-86
Stewart, Blair	Det., Wsh., Que.	7	229	34	44	78	326	....	....	....	....	....	....	1973-74	1979-80
Stewart, Bob	Bos., Cal., Cle., St.L., Pit.	9	575	27	101	128	809	5	1	1	2	2	....	1971-72	1979-80
Stewart, Cam	Bos., Fla., Min.	7	202	16	23	39	120	13	1	3	4	9	....	1993-94	2001-02
• Stewart, Gaye	Tor., Chi., Det., NYR, Mtl.	11	502	185	159	344	274	25	2	9	11	16	2	1941-42	1953-54
• Stewart, Jack	Det., Chi.	12	565	31	84	115	765	80	5	14	19	143	2	1938-39	1951-52
Stewart, John	Pit., Atl., Cal.	5	258	58	60	118	158	4	0	0	0	10	....	1970-71	1974-75
Stewart, John	Que.	1	2	0	0	0	0	....	....	....	....	....	....	1979-80	1979-80
‡ Stewart, Karl	Atl., Pit., Chi., T.B.	4	69	2	4	6	68	....	....	....	....	....	....	2003-04	2007-08
Stewart, Ken	Chi.	1	6	1	1	2	2	....	....	....	....	....	....	1941-42	1941-42
• Stewart, Nels	Mtl.M., Bos., NYA	15	650	324	191	515	953	50	9	12	21	47	1	1925-26	1939-40
Stewart, Paul	Que.	1	21	2	0	2	74	....	....	....	....	....	....	1979-80	1979-80
Stewart, Ralph	Van., NYI	7	252	57	73	130	28	19	4	4	8	2	....	1970-71	1977-78
Stewart, Ron	Tor., Bos., St.L., NYR, Van., NYI	21	1353	276	253	529	560	119	14	21	35	60	3	1952-53	1972-73
Stewart, Ryan	Wpg.	1	3	1	0	1	0	....	....	....	....	....	....	1985-86	1985-86
Stienburg, Trevor	Que.	4	71	8	4	12	161	1	0	0	0	0	....	1985-86	1988-89
Stiles, Tony	Cgy.	1	30	2	7	9	20	....	....	....	....	....	....	1983-84	1983-84
Stock, P.J.	NYR, Mtl., Phi., Bos.	7	235	5	21	26	523	8	1	0	1	19	....	1997-98	2003-04
Stoddard, Jack	NYR	2	80	16	15	31	31	....	....	....	....	....	....	1951-52	1952-53
Stojanov, Alek	Van., Pit.	3	107	2	5	7	222	14	0	0	0	21	....	1994-95	1996-97
Stoltz, Roland	Wsh.	1	14	2	2	4	14	....	....	....	....	....	....	1981-82	1981-82
Stone, Steve	Van.	1	2	0	0	0	0	....	....	....	....	....	....	1973-74	1973-74
Storm, Jim	Hfd., Dal.	3	84	7	15	22	44	....	....	....	....	....	....	1993-94	1995-96
Stothers, Mike	Phi., Tor.	4	30	0	2	2	65	5	0	0	0	11	....	1984-85	1987-88
Stoughton, Blaine	Pit., Tor., Hfd., NYR	8	526	258	191	449	204	8	4	2	6	2	....	1973-74	1983-84
Stoyanovich, Steve	Hfd.	1	23	3	5	8	11	....	....	....	....	....	....	1983-84	1983-84
• Strain, Neil	NYR	1	52	11	13	24	12	....	....	....	....	....	....	1952-53	1952-53
‡ Straka, Martin	Pit., Ott., NYI, Fla., L.A., NYR	15	954	257	460	717	360	106	26	44	70	52	....	1992-93	2007-08
Strate, Gord	Det.	3	61	0	0	0	34	....	....	....	....	....	....	1956-57	1958-59
Stratton, Art	NYR, Det., Chi., Pit., Phi.	4	95	18	33	51	24	5	0	0	0	0	....	1959-60	1967-68
‡ Strbak, Martin	L.A., Pit.	1	49	5	11	16	46	....	....	....	....	....	....	2003-04	2003-04
• Strobel, Art	NYR	1	7	0	0	0	0	....	....	....	....	....	....	1943-44	1943-44
Strong, Ken	Tor.	3	15	2	2	4	6	....	....	....	....	....	....	1982-83	1984-85
Stroshein, Garret	Wsh.	1	3	0	0	0	14	....	....	....	....	....	....	2003-04	2003-04
Struch, David	Cgy.	1	4	0	0	0	4	....	....	....	....	....	....	1993-94	1993-94
Strueby, Todd	Edm.	3	5	0	1	1	2	....	....	....	....	....	....	1981-82	1983-84
• Stuart, Billy	Tor., Bos.	7	195	30	20	50	151	12	1	1	2	6	1	1920-21	1926-27
Stuart, Mike	St.L.	2	3	0	0	0	0	....	....	....	....	....	....	2003-04	2005-06
‡ Stumpel, Jozef	Bos., L.A., Fla.	16	957	196	481	677	245	55	6	24	30	24	....	1991-92	2007-08
Stumpf, Bob	St.L., Pit.	1	10	1	1	2	20	....	....	....	....	....	....	1974-75	1974-75
Sturgeon, Peter	Col.	2	6	0	1	1	2	....	....	....	....	....	....	1979-80	1980-81
Stutzel, Mike	Phx.	1	9	0	0	0	0	....	....	....	....	....	....	2003-04	2003-04
‡ Suchy, Radoslav	Phx., CBJ	6	451	13	58	71	104	10	1	1	2	0	....	1999-00	2005-06
‡ Suglobov, Alexander	N.J., Tor.	3	18	1	0	1	4	....	....	....	....	....	....	2003-04	2006-07
Suikkanen, Kai	Buf.	2	2	0	0	0	0	....	....	....	....	....	....	1981-82	1982-83
Sulliman, Doug	NYR, Hfd., N.J., Phi.	11	631	160	168	328	175	16	1	3	4	2	....	1979-80	1989-90
• Sullivan, Barry	Det.	1	1	0	0	0	0	....	....	....	....	....	....	1947-48	1947-48

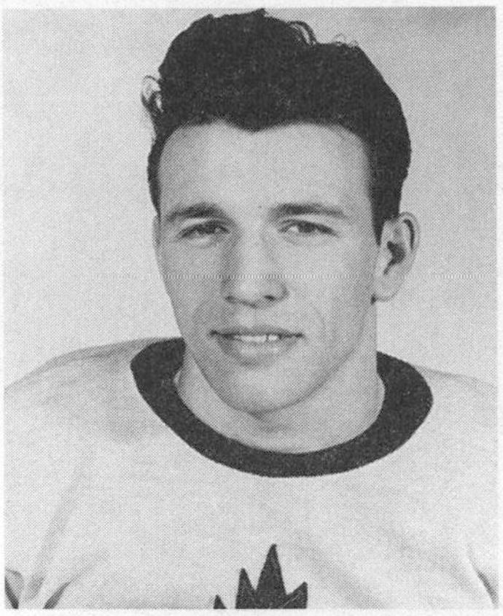

Gaye Stewart

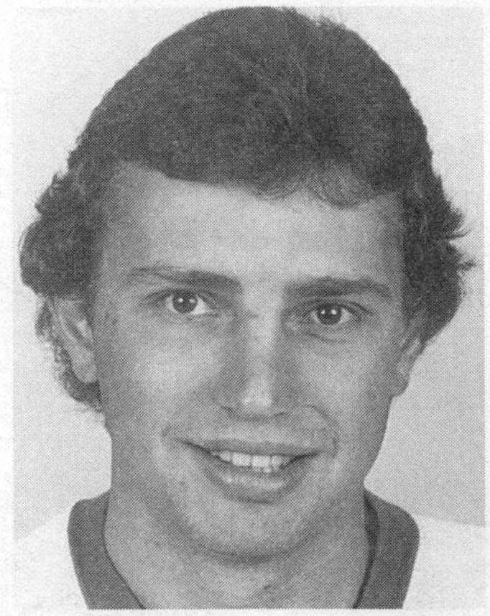

Brent Sutter

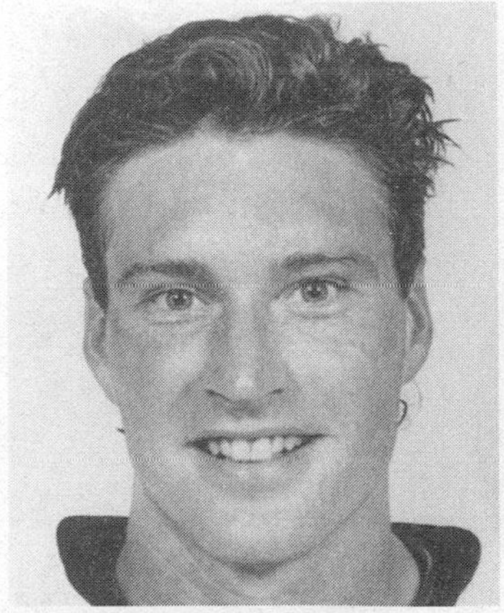

Bob Sweeney

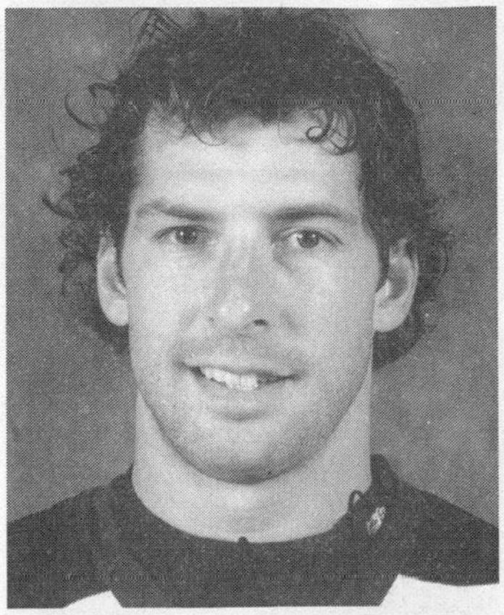

Darryl Sydor

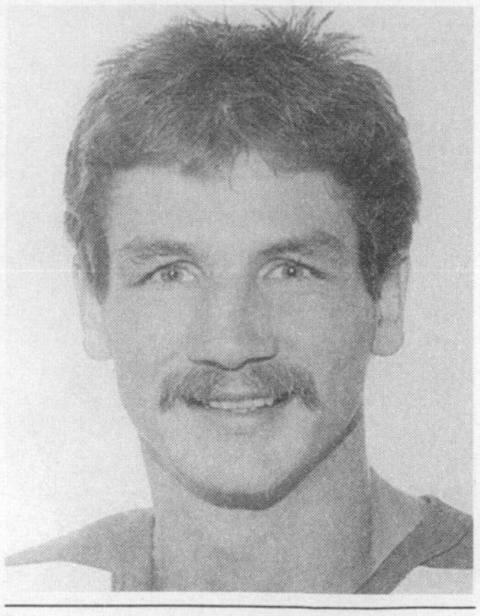

Phil Sykes

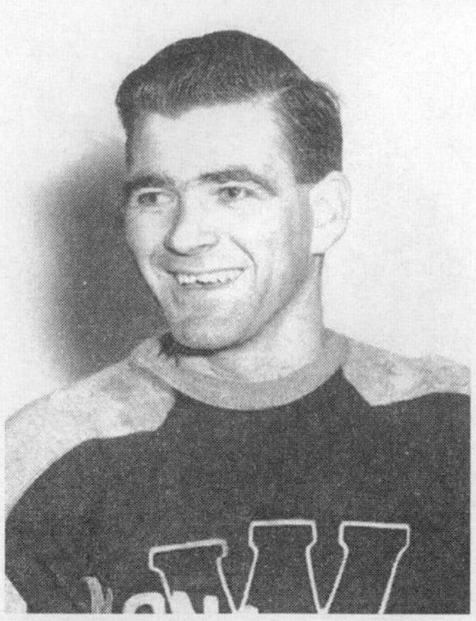

Harry Taylor

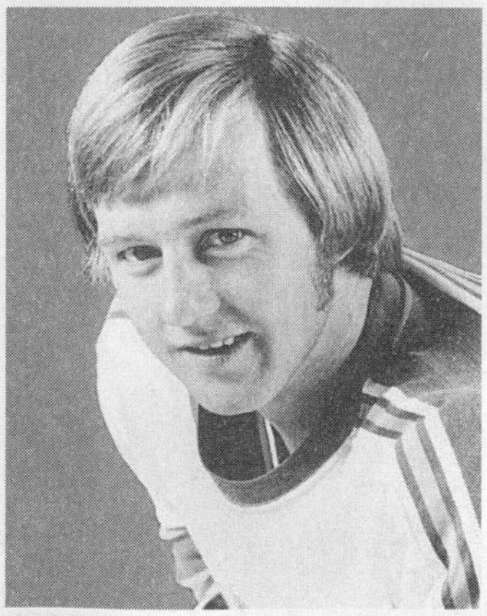

Floyd Thomson

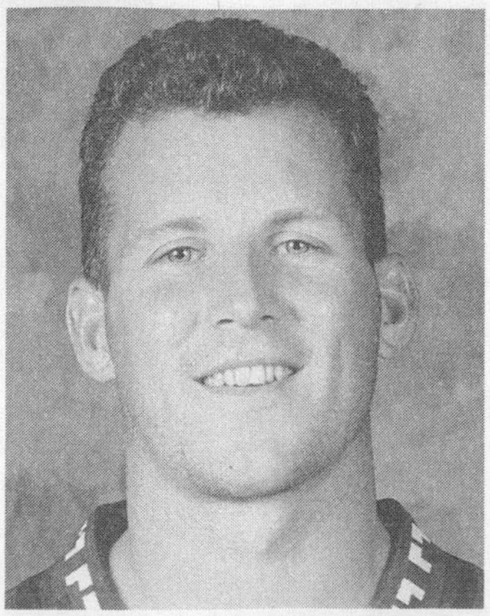

Keith Tkachuk

			Regular Schedule					Playoffs					NHL	First	Last
Name	NHL Teams	NHL Seasons	GP	G	A	TP	PIM	GP	G	A	TP	PIM	Cup Wins	NHL Season	NHL Season
Sullivan, Bob	Hfd.	1	62	18	19	37	18	....	....	....	....	....	....	1982-83	1982-83
Sullivan, Brian	N.J.	1	2	0	1	1	0	....	....	....	....	....	....	1992-93	1992-93
• Sullivan, Frank	Tor., Chi.	4	8	0	0	0	2	....	....	....	....	....	....	1949-50	1955-56
Sullivan, Mike	S.J., Cgy., Bos., Phx.	11	709	54	82	136	203	34	4	8	12	14	....	1991-92	2001-02
Sullivan, Peter	Wpg.	2	126	28	54	82	40	....	....	....	....	....	....	1979-80	1980-81
Sullivan, Red	Bos., Chi., NYR	11	557	107	239	346	441	18	1	2	3	6	....	1949-50	1960-61
Summanen, Raimo	Edm., Van.	5	151	36	40	76	35	10	2	5	7	0	....	1983-84	1987-88
• Summerhill, Bill	Mtl., Bro.	4	72	14	17	31	70	3	0	0	0	2	....	1937-38	1941-42
Sundblad, Niklas	Cgy.	1	2	0	0	0	0	....	....	....	....	....	....	1995-96	1995-96
Sundin, Mats	Que., Tor., Van.	18	1346	564	785	1349	1093	91	38	44	82	74	....	1990-91	2008-09
Sundin, Ronnie	NYR	1	1	0	0	0	0	....	....	....	....	....	....	1997-98	1997-98
‡ Sundstrom, Niklas	NYR, S.J., Mtl.	10	750	117	232	349	256	59	6	22	28	22	....	1995-96	2005-06
Sundstrom, Patrik	Van., N.J.	10	679	219	369	588	349	37	9	17	26	25	....	1982-83	1991-92
Sundstrom, Peter	NYR, Wsh., N.J.	6	338	61	83	144	120	23	3	3	6	8	....	1983-84	1989-90
Suomi, Al	Chi.	1	5	0	0	0	0	....	....	....	....	....	....	1936-37	1936-37
Surma, Damian	Car.	2	2	1	1	2	0	....	....	....	....	....	....	2002-03	2003-04
‡ Surovy, Tomas	Pit.	3	126	27	32	59	71	....	....	....	....	....	....	2002-03	2005-06
‡ Sushinsky, Maxim	Min.	1	30	7	4	11	29	....	....	....	....	....	....	2000-01	2000-01
Suter, Gary	Cgy., Chi., S.J.	17	1145	203	641	844	1349	108	17	56	73	120	1	1985-86	2001-02
Sutherland, Bill	Mtl., Phi., Tor., St.L., Det.	6	250	70	58	128	99	14	2	4	6	0	....	1962-63	1971-72
• Sutherland, Max	Bos.	1	2	0	0	0	0	....	....	....	....	....	....	1931-32	1931-32
Sutter, Brent	NYI, Chi.	18	1111	363	466	829	1054	144	30	44	74	164	2	1980-81	1997-98
Sutter, Brian	St.L.	12	779	303	333	636	1786	65	21	21	42	249	....	1976-77	1987-88
Sutter, Darryl	Chi.	8	406	161	118	279	288	51	24	19	43	26	....	1979-80	1986-87
Sutter, Duane	NYI, Chi.	11	731	139	203	342	1333	161	26	32	58	405	4	1979-80	1989-90
Sutter, Rich	Pit., Phi., Van., St.L., Chi., T.B., Tor.	13	874	149	166	315	1411	78	13	5	18	133	....	1982-83	1994-95
Sutter, Ron	Phi., St.L., Que., NYI, Bos., S.J., Cgy.	19	1093	205	329	534	1352	104	8	32	40	193	....	1982-83	2000-01
Sutton, Ken	Buf., Edm., St.L., N.J., S.J., NYI	11	388	23	80	103	338	32	3	4	7	29	1	1990-91	2001-02
Suzor, Mark	Phi., Col.	2	64	4	16	20	60	....	....	....	....	....	....	1976-77	1977-78
‡ Svartvadet, Per	Atl.	4	247	17	34	51	58	....	....	....	....	....	....	1999-00	2002-03
Svehla, Robert	Fla., Tor.	9	655	68	267	335	649	38	1	14	15	42	....	1994-95	2002-03
Svejkovsky, Jaroslav	Wsh., T.B.	4	113	23	19	42	56	1	0	0	0	2	....	1996-97	1999-00
Svensson, Leif	Wsh.	2	121	6	40	46	49	....	....	....	....	....	....	1978-79	1979-80
Svensson, Magnus	Fla.	2	46	4	14	18	31	....	....	....	....	....	....	1994-95	1995-96
‡ Svitov, Alexander	T.B., CBJ	3	179	13	24	37	223	7	0	0	0	6	....	2002-03	2006-07
‡ Svoboda, Jaroslav	Car., Dal.	4	134	12	17	29	62	25	1	4	5	30	....	2001-02	2005-06
Svoboda, Petr	Mtl., Buf., Phi., T.B.	17	1028	58	341	399	1605	127	4	45	49	140	1	1984-85	2000-01
Svoboda, Petr	Tor.	1	18	1	2	3	10	....	....	....	....	....	....	2000-01	2000-01
Swain, Garry	Pit.	1	9	1	1	2	0	....	....	....	....	....	....	1968-69	1968-69
‡ Swanson, Brian	Edm., Atl.	4	70	4	13	17	16	....	....	....	....	....	....	2000-01	2003-04
Swarbrick, George	Oak., Pit., Phi.	4	132	17	25	42	173	....	....	....	....	....	....	1967-68	1970-71
• Sweeney, Bill	NYR	1	4	1	0	1	0	....	....	....	....	....	....	1959-60	1959-60
Sweeney, Bob	Bos., Buf., NYI, Cgy.	10	639	125	163	288	799	103	15	18	33	197	....	1986-87	1995-96
Sweeney, Don	Bos., Dal.	16	1115	52	221	273	681	108	9	10	19	81	....	1988-89	2003-04
Sweeney, Tim	Cgy., Bos., Ana., NYR	8	291	55	83	138	123	4	0	0	0	2	....	1990-91	1997-98
Sydor, Darryl	L.A., Dal., CBJ, T.B., Pit., St.L.	18	1291	98	409	507	755	155	9	47	56	73	2	1991-92	2009-10
Sykes, Bob	Tor.	1	2	0	0	0	0	....	....	....	....	....	....	1974-75	1974-75
Sykes, Phil	L.A., Wpg.	10	456	79	85	164	519	26	0	3	3	29	....	1982-83	1991-92
Sykora, Michal	S.J., Chi., T.B., Phi.	7	267	15	54	69	185	7	0	1	1	0	....	1993-94	2000-01
‡ Sykora, Petr	N.J., Ana., NYR, Edm., Pit., Min.	14	935	302	375	677	415	115	32	37	69	56	2	1995-96	2009-10
‡ Sykora, Petr	Nsh., Wsh.	2	12	2	2	4	6	....	....	....	....	....	....	1998-99	2005-06
Sylvester, Dean	Buf., Atl.	3	96	21	16	37	32	4	0	0	0	0	....	1998-99	2000-01
• Szura, Joe	Oak.	2	90	10	15	25	30	7	2	3	5	2	....	1967-68	1968-69

T

			Regular Schedule					Playoffs					NHL	First	Last
Name	NHL Teams	NHL Seasons	GP	G	A	TP	PIM	GP	G	A	TP	PIM	Cup Wins	NHL Season	NHL Season
Taft, John	Det.	1	15	0	2	2	4	....	....	....	....	....	....	1978-79	1978-79
Taglianetti, Peter	Wpg., Min., Pit., T.B.	11	451	18	74	92	1106	53	2	8	10	103	2	1984-85	1994-95
Talafous, Dean	Atl., Min., NYR	8	497	104	154	258	163	21	4	7	11	11	....	1974-75	1981-82
• Talakoski, Ron	NYR	2	9	0	1	1	33	....	....	....	....	....	....	1986-87	1987-88
Talbot, Jean-Guy	Mtl., Min., Det., St.L., Buf.	17	1056	43	242	285	1006	150	4	26	30	142	7	1954-55	1970-71
Tallon, Dale	Van., Chi., Pit.	10	642	98	238	336	568	33	2	10	12	45	....	1970-71	1979-80
Tambellini, Steve	NYI, Col., N.J., Cgy., Van.	10	553	160	150	310	105	2	0	1	1	0	1	1978-79	1987-88
Tamer, Chris	Pit., NYR, Atl.	11	644	21	64	85	1183	37	0	8	8	52	....	1993-94	2003-04
Tanabe, David	Car., Phx., Bos.	8	449	30	84	114	245	7	2	1	3	12	....	1999-00	2007-08
Tancill, Chris	Hfd., Det., Dal., S.J.	8	134	17	32	49	54	11	1	1	2	8	....	1990-91	1997-98
Tanguay, Christian	Que.	1	2	0	0	0	0	....	....	....	....	....	....	1981-82	1981-82
Tannahill, Don	Van.	2	111	30	33	63	25	....	....	....	....	....	....	1972-73	1973-74
Tanti, Tony	Chi., Van., Pit., Buf.	11	697	287	273	560	661	30	3	12	15	27	....	1981-82	1991-92
Tapper, Brad	Atl.	3	71	14	11	25	72	....	....	....	....	....	....	2000-01	2002-03
Tardif, Marc	Mtl., Que.	8	517	194	207	401	443	62	13	15	28	75	2	1969-70	1982-83
Tardif, Patrice	St.L., L.A.	2	65	7	11	18	78	....	....	....	....	....	....	1994-95	1995-96
Tarnstrom, Dick	NYI, Pit., Edm., CBJ	5	306	35	105	140	254	17	0	2	2	12	....	2001-02	2007-08
Tatarinov, Mikhail	Wsh., Que., Bos.	4	161	21	48	69	184	....	....	....	....	....	....	1990-91	1993-94
• Tatchell, Spence	NYR	1	1	0	0	0	0	....	....	....	....	....	....	1942-43	1942-43
‡ Taticek, Petr	Fla.	1	3	0	0	0	0	....	....	....	....	....	....	2005-06	2005-06
• Taylor, Billy	Tor., Det., Bos., NYR	7	323	87	180	267	120	33	6	18	24	13	1	1939-40	1947-48
• Taylor, Billy	NYR	1	2	0	0	0	0	....	....	....	....	....	....	1964-65	1964-65
• Taylor, Bob	Bos.	1	8	0	0	0	6	....	....	....	....	....	....	1929-30	1929-30
‡ Taylor, Chris	NYI, Bos., Buf.	8	149	11	21	32	48	2	0	0	0	2	....	1994-95	2003-04
Taylor, Dave	L.A.	17	1111	431	638	1069	1589	92	26	33	59	145	....	1977-78	1993-94
• Taylor, Harry	Tor., Chi.	3	66	5	10	15	30	1	0	0	0	0	1	1946-47	1951-52
Taylor, Mark	Phi., Pit., Wsh.	5	209	42	68	110	73	6	0	0	0	0	....	1981-82	1985-86
• Taylor, Ralph	Chi., NYR	3	99	4	1	5	169	4	0	0	0	10	....	1927-28	1929-30
Taylor, Ted	NYR, Det., Min., Van.	6	166	23	35	58	181	....	....	....	....	....	....	1964-65	1971-72
Taylor, Tim	Det., Bos., NYR, T.B.	13	746	73	94	167	433	89	2	12	14	73	2	1993-94	2006-07
Teal, Jeff	Mtl.	1	6	0	1	1	0	....	....	....	....	....	....	1984-85	1984-85
• Teal, Skip	Bos.	1	1	0	0	0	0	....	....	....	....	....	....	1954-55	1954-55
Teal, Vic	NYI	1	1	0	0	0	0	....	....	....	....	....	....	1973-74	1973-74
Tebbutt, Greg	Que., Pit.	2	26	0	3	3	35	....	....	....	....	....	....	1979-80	1983-84
‡ Tenkrat, Petr	Ana., Nsh., Bos.	3	177	22	30	52	84	....	....	....	....	....	....	2000-01	2006-07
‡ Tenute, Joey	Wsh.	1	1	0	0	0	0	....	....	....	....	....	....	2005-06	2005-06
Tepper, Stephen	Chi.	1	1	0	0	0	0	....	....	....	....	....	....	1992-93	1992-93
Terbenche, Paul	Chi., Buf.	5	189	5	26	31	28	12	0	0	0	0	....	1967-68	1973-74
Terrion, Greg	L.A., Tor.	8	561	93	150	243	339	35	2	9	11	41	....	1980-81	1987-88
Terry, Bill	Min.	1	5	0	0	0	0	....	....	....	....	....	....	1987-88	1987-88
• Tertyshny, Dmitri	Phi.	1	62	2	8	10	30	1	0	0	0	0	....	1998-99	1998-99
Tessier, Orval	Mtl., Bos.	3	59	5	7	12	6	....	....	....	....	....	....	1954-55	1960-61
Tetarenko, Joey	Fla., Ott., Car.	4	73	4	1	5	176	....	....	....	....	....	....	2000-01	2003-04
Tezikov, Alexei	Wsh., Van.	3	30	1	1	2	2	....	....	....	....	....	....	1998-99	2001-02
Theberge, Greg	Wsh.	5	153	15	63	78	73	4	0	1	1	0	....	1979-80	1983-84
Thelin, Mats	Bos.	3	163	8	19	27	107	5	0	0	0	6	....	1984-85	1986-87
Thelven, Michael	Bos.	5	207	20	80	100	217	34	4	10	14	34	....	1985-86	1989-90
Therien, Chris	Phi., Dal.	11	764	29	130	159	585	104	4	10	14	68	....	1994-95	2005-06
Therrien, Gaston	Que.	3	22	0	8	8	12	9	0	1	1	4	....	1980-81	1982-83
Thibaudeau, Gilles	Mtl., NYI, Tor.	5	119	25	37	62	40	8	3	3	6	2	....	1986-87	1990-91
Thibeault, Lorrain	Det., Mtl.	2	5	0	2	2	2	....	....	....	....	....	....	1944-45	1945-46
Thiffault, Leo	Min.	1	....	....	....	....	....	5	0	0	0	0	....	1967-68	1967-68
• Thomas, Cy	Chi., Tor.	1	14	2	2	4	12	....	....	....	....	....	....	1947-48	1947-48
Thomas, Reg	Que.	1	39	9	7	16	6	....	....	....	....	....	....	1979-80	1979-80
Thomas, Scott	Buf., L.A.	3	63	6	4	10	32	12	1	0	1	4	....	1992-93	2000-01
Thomas, Steve	Tor., Chi., NYI, N.J., Ana., Det.	20	1235	421	512	933	1306	174	54	53	107	187	....	1984-85	2003-04
Thomlinson, Dave	St.L., Bos., L.A.	5	42	1	3	4	50	9	3	1	4	4	....	1989-90	1994-95
Thompson, Brent	L.A., Wpg., Phx.	6	121	1	10	11	352	4	0	0	0	4	....	1991-92	1996-97
• Thompson, Cliff	Bos.	2	13	0	1	1	2	....	....	....	....	....	....	1941-42	1948-49
Thompson, Errol	Tor., Det., Pit.	10	599	208	185	393	184	34	7	5	12	11	....	1970-71	1980-81
• Thompson, Ken	Mtl.W.	1	1	0	0	0	0	....	....	....	....	....	....	1917-18	1917-18
• Thompson, Paul	NYR, Chi.	13	582	153	179	332	336	48	11	11	22	54	3	1926-27	1938-39
Thompson, Rocky	Cgy., Fla.	4	25	0	0	0	117	....	....	....	....	....	....	1997-98	2001-02
• Thoms, Bill	Tor., Chi., Bos.	13	548	135	206	341	154	44	6	10	16	6	....	1932-33	1944-45
• Thomson, Bill	Det.	2	9	2	2	4	0	2	0	0	0	0	....	1938-39	1943-44
Thomson, Floyd	St.L.	8	411	56	97	153	341	10	0	2	2	6	....	1971-72	1979-80
Thomson, Jim	Wsh., Hfd., N.J., L.A., Ott., Ana.	7	115	4	3	7	416	1	0	0	0	0	....	1986-87	1993-94
• Thomson, Jimmy	Tor., Chi.	13	787	19	215	234	920	63	2	13	15	135	4	1945-46	1957-58
• Thomson, Rhys	Mtl., Tor.	2	25	0	2	2	38	....	....	....	....	....	....	1939-40	1942-43
Thornbury, Tom	Pit.	1	14	1	8	9	16	....	....	....	....	....	....	1983-84	1983-84

Name	NHL Teams	NHL Seasons	Regular Schedule					Playoffs					NHL Cup Wins	First NHL Season	Last NHL Season
			GP	G	A	TP	PIM	GP	G	A	TP	PIM			
Thornton, Scott	Tor., Edm., Mtl., Dal., S.J., L.A.	17	941	144	141	285	1459	79	13	14	27	82	....	1990-91	2007-08
• Thorsteinson, Joe	NYA	1	4	0	0	0	0	....	....	....	....	....	....	1932-33	1932-33
• Thurier, Fred	NYA, Bro., NYR	3	80	25	27	52	18	....	....	....	....	....	....	1940-41	1944-45
Thurlby, Tom	Oak.	1	20	1	1	2	4	....	....	....	....	....	....	1967-68	1967-68
Thyer, Mario	Min.	1	5	0	0	0	0	1	0	0	0	2	....	1989-90	1989-90
Tibbetts, Billy	Pit., Phi., NYR	3	82	2	8	10	269	....	....	....	....	....	....	2000-01	2002-03
Tichy, Milan	Chi., NYI	3	23	0	5	5	40	....	....	....	....	....	....	1992-93	1995-96
Tidey, Alex	Buf., Edm.	3	9	0	0	0	8	2	0	0	0	0	....	1976-77	1979-80
Tikkanen, Esa	Edm., NYR, St.L., N.J., Van., Fla., Wsh.	15	877	244	386	630	1077	186	72	60	132	275	5	1984-85	1998-99
Tiley, Brad	Phx., Phi.	3	11	0	0	0	0	1	0	0	0	0	....	1997-98	2000-01
Tilley, Tom	St.L.	4	174	4	38	42	89	14	1	3	4	19	....	1988-89	1993-94
‡ Timander, Mattias	Bos., CBJ, NYI, Phi.	8	419	13	57	70	165	23	3	5	8	8	....	1996-97	2003-04
• Timgren, Ray	Tor., Chi.	6	251	14	44	58	70	30	3	9	12	6	2	1948-49	1954-55
‡ Timonen, Jussi	Phi.	1	14	0	4	4	6	....	....	....	....	....	....	2006-07	2006-07
Tinordi, Mark	NYR, Min., Dal., Wsh.	12	663	52	148	200	1514	70	7	11	18	165	....	1987-88	1998-99
Tippett, Dave	Hfd., Wsh., Pit., Phi.	12	721	93	169	262	317	62	6	16	22	34	....	1983-84	1993-94
Titanic, Morris	Buf.	2	19	0	0	0	0	....	....	....	....	....	....	1974-75	1975-76
Titov, German	Cgy., Pit., Edm., Ana.	9	624	157	220	377	311	34	11	12	23	18	....	1993-94	2001-02
‡ Tjarnqvist, Daniel	Atl., Min., Edm., Col.	6	352	18	72	90	130	....	....	....	....	....	....	2001-02	2008-09
‡ Tjarnqvist, Mathias	Dal., Phx.	4	173	13	19	32	60	....	....	....	....	....	....	2003-04	2007-08
Tkachuk, Keith	Wpg., Phx., St.L., Atl.	18	1201	538	527	1065	2219	89	28	28	56	176	....	1991-92	2009-10
Tkaczuk, Daniel	Cgy.	1	19	4	7	11	14	....	....	....	....	....	....	2000-01	2000-01
Tkaczuk, Walt	NYR	14	945	227	451	678	556	93	19	32	51	119	....	1967-68	1980-81
Toal, Mike	Edm.	1	3	0	0	0	0	....	....	....	....	....	....	1979-80	1979-80
Tobler, Ryan	T.B.	1	4	0	0	0	5	....	....	....	....	....	....	2001-02	2001-02
Tocchet, Rick	Phi., Pit., L.A., Bos., Wsh., Phx.	18	1144	440	512	952	2972	145	52	60	112	471	1	1984-85	2001-02
Todd, Kevin	N.J., Edm., Chi., L.A., Ana.	9	383	70	133	203	225	12	3	2	5	16	....	1988-89	1997-98
‡ Tolpeko, Denis	Phi.	1	26	1	5	6	24	....	....	....	....	....	....	2007-08	2007-08
Tomalty, Glenn	Wpg.	1	1	0	0	0	0	....	....	....	....	....	....	1979-80	1979-80
Tomlak, Mike	Hfd.	4	141	15	22	37	103	10	0	1	1	4	....	1989-90	1993-94
Tomlinson, Dave	Tor., Wpg., Fla.	4	42	1	3	4	28	....	....	....	....	....	....	1991-92	1994-95
Tomlinson, Kirk	Min.	1	1	0	0	0	0	....	....	....	....	....	....	1987-88	1987-88
‡ Toms, Jeff	T.B., Wsh., NYI, NYR, Pit., Fla.	8	236	22	33	55	59	1	0	0	0	0	....	1995-96	2002-03
• Tomson, Jack	NYA	3	15	1	1	2	0	2	0	0	0	0	....	1938-39	1940-41
Tonelli, John	NYI, Cgy., L.A., Chi., Que.	14	1028	325	511	836	911	172	40	75	115	200	4	1978-79	1991-92
Tookey, Tim	Wsh., Que., Pit., Phi., L.A.	7	106	22	36	58	71	10	1	3	4	2	....	1980-81	1988-89
Toomey, Sean	Min.	1	1	0	0	0	0	....	....	....	....	....	....	1986-87	1986-87
‡ Toporowski, Shayne	Tor.	1	3	0	0	0	7	....	....	....	....	....	....	1996-97	1996-97
Toppazzini, Jerry	Bos., Chi., Det.	12	783	163	244	407	436	40	13	9	22	13	....	1952-53	1963-64
• Toppazzini, Zellio	Bos., NYR, Chi.	5	123	21	22	43	49	2	0	0	0	0	....	1948-49	1956-57
Torgaev, Pavel	Cgy., T.B.	2	55	6	14	20	20	1	0	0	0	0	....	1995-96	1999-00
Torkki, Jari	Chi.	1	4	1	0	1	0	....	....	....	....	....	....	1988-89	1988-89
Tormanen, Antti	Ott.	1	50	7	8	15	28	....	....	....	....	....	....	1995-96	1995-96
• Touhey, Bill	Mtl.M., Ott., Bos.	7	280	65	40	105	107	2	1	0	1	0	....	1927-28	1933-34
• Toupin, Jacques	Chi.	1	8	1	2	3	0	4	0	0	0	0	....	1943-44	1943-44
• Townsend, Art	Chi.	1	5	0	0	0	0	....	....	....	....	....	....	1926-27	1926-27
Townshend, Graeme	Bos., NYI, Ott.	5	45	3	7	10	28	....	....	....	....	....	....	1989-90	1993-94
Trader, Larry	Det., St.L., Mtl.	4	91	5	13	18	74	3	0	0	0	0	....	1982-83	1987-88
• Trainor, Wes	NYR	1	17	1	2	3	6	....	....	....	....	....	....	1948-49	1948-49
• Trapp, Bob	Chi.	2	82	4	4	8	129	2	0	0	0	4	....	1926-27	1927-28
Trapp, Doug	Buf.	1	2	0	0	0	0	....	....	....	....	....	....	1986-87	1986-87
• Traub, Percy	Chi., Det.	3	130	3	3	6	217	4	0	0	0	6	....	1926-27	1928-29
‡ Traverse, Patrick	Ott., Ana., Bos., Mtl., Dal.	7	279	14	51	65	113	6	0	0	0	2	....	1995-96	2005-06
Trebil, Dan	Ana., Pit., St.L.	5	85	4	4	8	32	10	0	1	1	8	....	1996-97	2000-01
Tredway, Brock	L.A.	1	....	....	....	....	....	1	0	0	0	0	....	1981-82	1981-82
Tremblay, Brent	Wsh.	2	10	1	0	1	6	....	....	....	....	....	....	1978-79	1979-80
Tremblay, Gilles	Mtl.	9	509	168	162	330	161	48	9	14	23	4	4	1960-61	1968-69
• Tremblay, J.C.	Mtl.	13	794	57	306	363	204	108	14	51	65	58	5	1959-60	1971-72
• Tremblay, Marcel	Mtl.	1	10	0	2	2	0	....	....	....	....	....	....	1938-39	1938-39
Tremblay, Mario	Mtl.	12	852	258	326	584	1043	101	20	29	49	187	5	1974-75	1985-86
• Tremblay, Nils	Mtl.	2	3	0	1	1	0	2	0	0	0	0	....	1944-45	1945-46
Tremblay, Yannick	Tor., Atl., Van.	9	390	38	87	125	178	....	....	....	....	....	....	1996-97	2006-07
‡ Trepanier, Pascal	Col., Ana., Nsh.	6	229	12	22	34	252	2	0	0	0	0	....	1997-98	2002-03
Trimper, Tim	Chi., Wpg., Min.	6	190	30	36	66	153	2	0	0	0	2	....	1979-80	1984-85
‡ Tripp, John	NYR, L.A.	2	43	2	7	9	35	....	....	....	....	....	....	2002-03	2003-04
‡ Trnka, Pavel	Ana., Fla.	7	411	14	63	77	323	4	0	1	1	2	....	1997-98	2003-04
Trottier, Bryan	NYI, Pit.	18	1279	524	901	1425	912	221	71	113	184	277	6	1975-76	1993-94
• Trottier, Dave	Mtl.M., Det.	11	446	121	113	234	517	31	4	3	7	39	1	1928-29	1938-39
Trottier, Guy	NYR, Tor.	3	115	28	17	45	37	9	1	0	1	16	....	1968-69	1971-72
Trottier, Rocky	N.J.	2	38	6	4	10	2	....	....	....	....	....	....	1983-84	1984-85
Trudel, Jean-Guy	Phx., Min.	3	5	0	0	0	4	....	....	....	....	....	....	1999-00	2002-03
• Trudel, Lou	Chi., Mtl.	8	306	49	69	118	122	24	1	3	4	4	2	1933-34	1940-41
• Trudell, Rene	NYR	3	129	24	28	52	72	5	0	0	0	2	....	1945-46	1947-48
Tselios, Nikos	Car.	1	2	0	0	0	6	....	....	....	....	....	....	2001-02	2001-02
Tsulygin, Nikolai	Ana.	1	22	0	1	1	8	....	....	....	....	....	....	1996-97	1996-97
Tsygurov, Denis	Buf., L.A.	3	51	1	5	6	45	....	....	....	....	....	....	1993-94	1995-96
Tsyplakov, Vladimir	L.A., Buf.	6	331	69	101	170	90	18	1	2	3	16	....	1995-96	2000-01
Tucker, Darcy	Mtl., T.B., Tor., Col.	14	947	215	261	476	1410	68	10	11	21	81	....	1995-96	2009-10
Tucker, John	Buf., Wsh., NYI, T.B.	12	656	177	259	436	285	31	10	18	28	24	....	1983-84	1995-96
• Tudin, Connie	Mtl.	1	4	0	1	1	4	....	....	....	....	....	....	1941-42	1941-42
Tudor, Rob	Van., St.L.	3	28	4	4	8	19	3	0	0	0	0	....	1978-79	1982-83
Tuer, Allan	L.A., Min., Hfd.	4	57	1	1	2	208	....	....	....	....	....	....	1985-86	1989-90
‡ Tukonen, Lauri	L.A.	2	5	0	0	0	0	....	....	....	....	....	....	2006-07	2007-08
Tuomainen, Marko	Edm., L.A., NYI	4	79	9	9	18	84	1	0	0	0	0	....	1994-95	2001-02
Turcotte, Alfie	Mtl., Wpg., Wsh.	7	112	17	29	46	49	5	0	0	0	0	....	1983-84	1990-91
Turcotte, Darren	NYR, Hfd., Wpg., S.J., St.L., Nsh.	12	635	195	216	411	301	35	6	8	14	12	....	1988-89	1999-00
Turgeon, Pierre	Buf., NYI, Mtl., St.L., Dal., Col.	19	1294	515	812	1327	452	109	35	62	97	36	....	1987-88	2006-07
Turgeon, Sylvain	Hfd., N.J., Mtl., Ott.	12	669	269	226	495	691	36	4	7	11	22	....	1983-84	1994-95
Turlick, Gord	Bos.	1	2	0	0	0	2	....	....	....	....	....	....	1959-60	1959-60
Turnbull, Ian	Tor., L.A., Pit.	10	628	123	317	440	736	55	13	32	45	94	....	1973-74	1982-83
Turnbull, Perry	St.L., Mtl., Wpg.	9	608	188	163	351	1245	34	6	7	13	86	....	1979-80	1987-88
Turnbull, Randy	Cgy.	1	1	0	0	0	2	....	....	....	....	....	....	1981-82	1981-82
• Turner, Bob	Mtl., Chi.	8	478	19	51	70	307	68	1	4	5	44	5	1955-56	1962-63
Turner, Brad	NYI	1	3	0	0	0	0	....	....	....	....	....	....	1991-92	1991-92
Turner, Dean	NYR, Col., L.A.	4	35	1	0	1	59	....	....	....	....	....	....	1978-79	1982-83
• Tustin, Norm	NYR	1	18	2	4	6	0	....	....	....	....	....	....	1941-42	1941-42
• Tuten, Aud	Chi.	2	39	4	8	12	48	....	....	....	....	....	....	1941-42	1942-43
Tutt, Brian	Wsh.	1	7	1	0	1	2	....	....	....	....	....	....	1989-90	1989-90
Tuttle, Steve	St.L.	3	144	28	28	56	12	17	1	6	7	2	....	1988-89	1990-91
Tuzzolino, Tony	Ana., NYR, Bos.	3	9	0	0	0	7	....	....	....	....	....	....	1997-98	2001-02
‡ Tverdovsky, Oleg	Ana., Wpg., Phx., N.J., Car., L.A.	11	713	77	240	317	291	45	0	14	14	6	2	1994-95	2006-07
Tvrdon, Roman	Wsh.	1	9	0	1	1	2	....	....	....	....	....	....	2003-04	2003-04
Twist, Tony	St.L., Que.	10	445	10	18	28	1121	18	1	1	2	22	....	1989-90	1998-99

U V

Name	NHL Teams	NHL Seasons	GP	G	A	TP	PIM	GP	G	A	TP	PIM	NHL Cup Wins	First NHL Season	Last NHL Season
Ubriaco, Gene	Pit., Oak., Chi.	3	177	39	35	74	50	11	2	0	2	4	....	1967-68	1969-70
Ulanov, Igor	Wpg., Wsh., Chi., T.B., Mtl., Edm., NYR, Fla.	14	739	27	135	162	1151	39	1	4	5	84	....	1991-92	2005-06
Ullman, Norm	Det., Tor.	20	1410	490	739	1229	712	106	30	53	83	67	....	1955-56	1974-75
‡ Ulmer, Jeff	NYR	1	21	3	0	3	8	....	....	....	....	....	....	2000-01	2000-01
Ulmer, Layne	NYR	1	1	0	0	0	0	....	....	....	....	....	....	2003-04	2003-04
Unger, Garry	Tor., Det., St.L., Atl., L.A., Edm.	16	1105	413	391	804	1075	52	12	18	30	105	....	1967-68	1982-83
‡ Ustorf, Stefan	Wsh.	2	54	7	10	17	16	5	0	0	0	0	....	1995-96	1996-97
‡ Vaananen, Ossi	Phx., Col., Phi., Van.	7	479	13	55	68	482	20	0	1	1	26	....	2000-01	2008-09
Vachon, Nick	NYI	1	1	0	0	0	0	....	....	....	....	....	....	1996-97	1996-97
Vadnais, Carol	Mtl., Oak., Cal., Bos., NYR, N.J.	17	1087	169	418	587	1813	106	10	40	50	185	2	1966-67	1982-83
‡ Vaic, Lubomir	Van.	2	9	1	1	2	2	....	....	....	....	....	....	1997-98	1999-00
Vail, Eric	Atl., Cgy., Det.	9	591	216	260	476	281	20	5	6	11	6	....	1973-74	1981-82
• Vail, Sparky	NYR	2	50	4	1	5	18	10	0	0	0	2	....	1928-29	1929-30
Vaive, Rick	Van., Tor., Chi., Buf.	13	876	441	347	788	1445	54	27	16	43	111	....	1979-80	1991-92
Valentine, Chris	Wsh.	3	105	43	52	95	127	2	0	0	0	4	....	1981-82	1983-84
Valicevic, Rob	Nsh., L.A., Ana., Dal.	6	193	28	20	48	61	....	....	....	....	....	....	1998-99	2003-04
Valiquette, Jack	Tor., Col.	7	350	84	134	218	79	23	3	6	9	4	....	1974-75	1980-81
Valk, Garry	Van., Ana., Pit., Tor., Chi.	13	777	100	156	256	747	61	6	7	13	79	....	1990-91	2002-03
Vallis, Lindsay	Mtl.	1	1	0	0	0	0	....	....	....	....	....	....	1993-94	1993-94

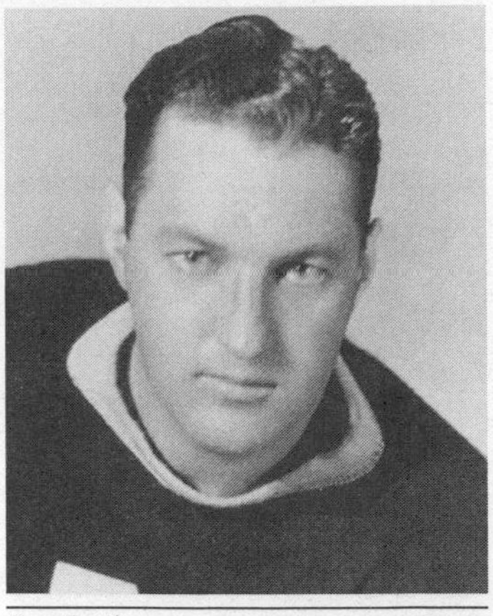
Dave Trottier

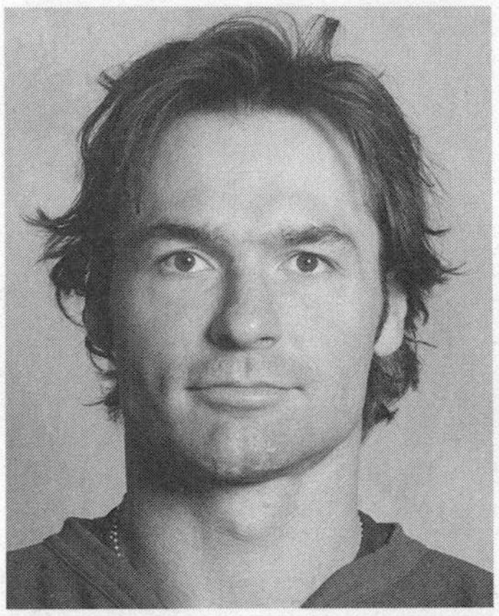
Darcy Tucker

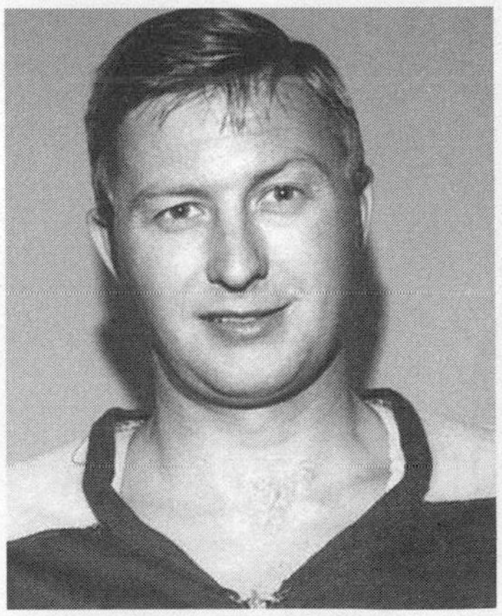
Gord Turlick

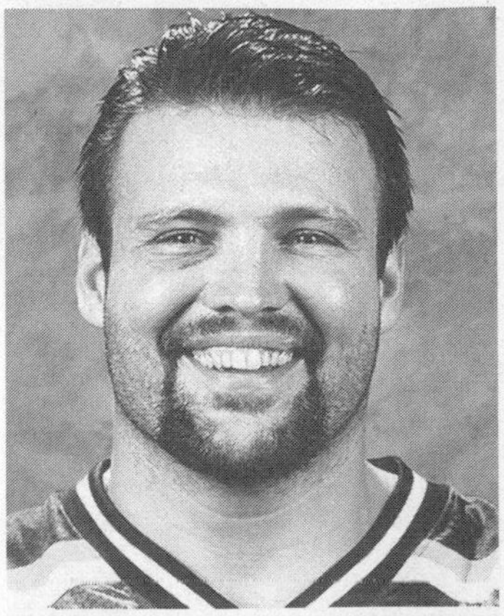
Tony Twist

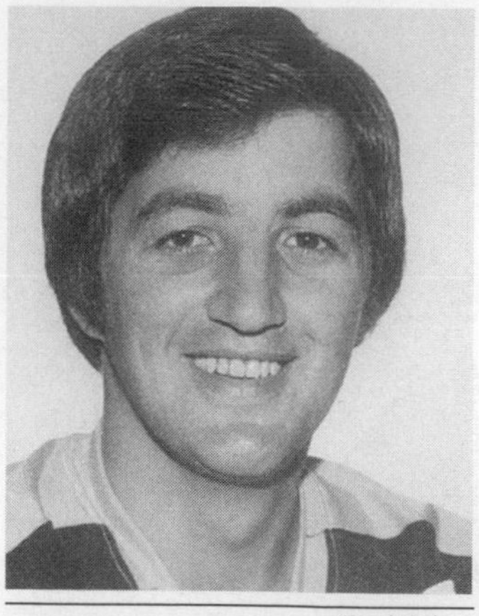

Carol Vadnais

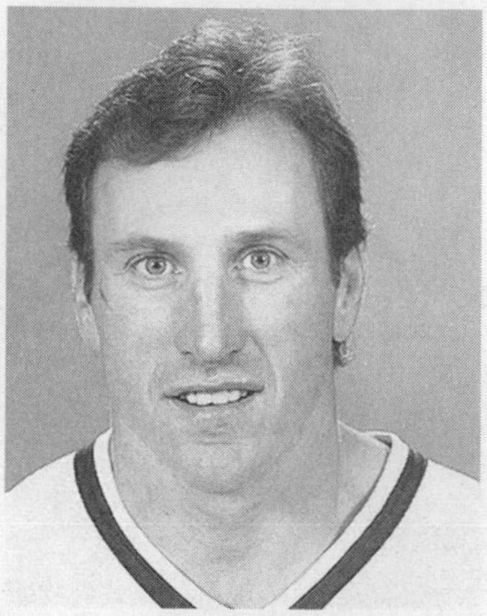

Pat Verbeek

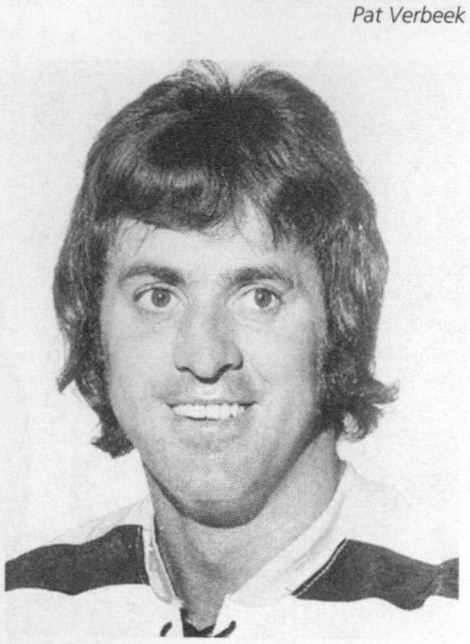

Mike Walton

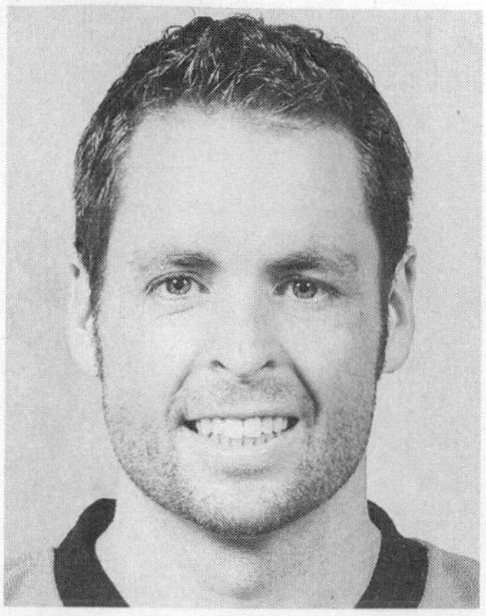

Aaron Ward

			Regular Schedule					Playoffs							
Name	NHL Teams	NHL Seasons	GP	G	A	TP	PIM	GP	G	A	TP	PIM	NHL Cup Wins	First NHL Season	Last NHL Season
Van Allen, Shaun	Edm., Ana., Ott., Dal., Mtl.	13	794	84	185	269	481	61	1	7	8	45	....	1990-91	2003-04
Van Boxmeer, John	Mtl., Col., Buf., Que.	11	588	84	274	358	465	38	5	15	20	37	....	1973-74	1983-84
Van Dorp, Wayne	Edm., Pit., Chi., Que.	6	125	12	12	24	565	27	0	1	1	42	....	1986-87	1991-92
Van Drunen, David	Ott.	1	1	0	0	0	0	....	....	....	....	....	....	1999-00	1999-00
Van Impe, Darren	Ana., Bos., NYR, Fla., NYI, CBJ	9	411	25	90	115	397	33	3	9	12	28	....	1994-95	2002-03
Van Impe, Ed	Chi., Phi., Pit.	11	700	27	126	153	1025	66	1	12	13	131	2	1966-67	1976-77
Van Ryn, Mike	St.L., Fla., Tor.	9	353	30	99	129	260	9	0	0	0	0	....	2000-01	2009-10
VandenBussche, Ryan	NYR, Chi., Pit.	9	310	10	10	20	702	1	0	0	0	0	....	1996-97	2005-06
‡ Vandermeer, Peter	Phx.	1	2	0	0	0	0	....	....	....	....	....	....	2007-08	2007-08
‡ Varada, Vaclav	Buf., Ott.	10	493	58	125	183	410	87	11	19	30	82	....	1995-96	2005-06
Varis, Petri	Chi.	1	1	0	0	0	0	....	....	....	....	....	....	1997-98	1997-98
‡ Varlamov, Sergei	Cgy., St.L.	4	63	8	7	15	26	1	0	0	0	2	....	1997-98	2002-03
Varvio, Jarkko	Dal.	2	13	3	4	7	4	....	....	....	....	....	....	1993-94	1994-95
‡ Vasicek, Josef	Car., Nsh., NYI	7	460	77	106	183	311	37	5	2	7	14	1	2000-01	2007-08
Vasilevski, Alexander	St.L.	2	4	0	0	0	2	....	....	....	....	....	....	1995-96	1996-97
Vasiliev, Alexei	NYR	1	1	0	0	0	2	....	....	....	....	....	....	1999-00	1999-00
‡ Vasiljevs, Herbert	Fla., Atl., Van.	4	51	8	7	15	22	....	....	....	....	....	....	1998-99	2001-02
Vasilyev, Andrei	NYI, Phx.	4	16	2	5	7	6	....	....	....	....	....	....	1994-95	1998-99
Vaske, Dennis	NYI, Bos.	9	235	5	41	46	253	22	0	7	7	16	....	1990-91	1998-99
● Vasko, Moose	Chi., Min.	13	786	34	166	200	719	78	2	7	9	73	1	1956-57	1969-70
Vasko, Rick	Det.	3	31	3	7	10	29	....	....	....	....	....	....	1977-78	1980-81
‡ Vauclair, Julien	Ott.	1	1	0	0	0	2	....	....	....	....	....	....	2003-04	2003-04
Vautour, Yvon	NYI, Col., N.J., Que.	6	204	26	33	59	401	....	....	....	....	....	....	1979-80	1984-85
Vaydik, Greg	Chi.	1	5	0	0	0	0	....	....	....	....	....	....	1976-77	1976-77
Veitch, Darren	Wsh., Det., Tor.	10	511	48	209	257	296	33	4	11	15	33	....	1980-81	1990-91
Velischek, Randy	Min., N.J., Que.	10	509	21	76	97	401	44	2	5	7	32	....	1982-83	1991-92
Vellucci, Mike	Hfd.	1	2	0	0	0	11	....	....	....	....	....	....	1987-88	1987-88
Venasky, Vic	L.A.	7	430	61	101	162	66	21	1	5	6	12	....	1972-73	1978-79
Veneruzzo, Gary	St.L.	2	7	1	1	2	0	9	0	2	2	2	....	1967-68	1971-72
Verbeek, Pat	N.J., Hfd., NYR, Dal., Det.	20	1424	522	541	1063	2905	117	26	36	62	225	1	1982-83	2001-02
Vermette, Mark	Que.	4	67	5	13	18	33	....	....	....	....	....	....	1988-89	1991-92
‡ Vernarsky, Kris	Bos.	2	17	1	0	1	2	....	....	....	....	....	....	2002-03	2003-04
‡ Verot, Darcy	Wsh.	1	37	0	2	2	135	....	....	....	....	....	....	2003-04	2003-04
Verret, Claude	Buf.	2	14	2	5	7	2	....	....	....	....	....	....	1983-84	1984-85
Verstraete, Leigh	Tor.	3	8	0	1	1	14	....	....	....	....	....	....	1982-83	1987-88
Ververgaert, Dennis	Van., Phi., Wsh.	8	583	176	216	392	247	8	1	2	3	6	....	1973-74	1980-81
Vesey, Jim	St.L., Bos.	3	15	1	2	3	7	....	....	....	....	....	....	1988-89	1991-92
Veysey, Sid	Van.	1	1	0	0	0	0	....	....	....	....	....	....	1977-78	1977-78
Vial, Dennis	NYR, Det., Ott.	8	242	4	15	19	794	....	....	....	....	....	....	1990-91	1997-98
Vickers, Steve	NYR	10	698	246	340	586	330	68	24	25	49	58	....	1972-73	1981-82
Vigier, J.P.	Atl.	6	213	23	23	46	97	....	....	....	....	....	....	2000-01	2006-07
Vigneault, Alain	St.L.	2	42	2	5	7	82	4	0	1	1	26	....	1981-82	1982-83
Viitakoski, Vesa	Cgy.	3	23	2	4	6	8	....	....	....	....	....	....	1993-94	1995-96
Vilgrain, Claude	Van., N.J., Phi.	5	89	21	32	53	78	11	1	1	2	17	....	1987-88	1993-94
Vincelette, Dan	Chi., Que.	6	193	20	22	42	351	12	0	0	0	4	....	1986-87	1991-92
Vipond, Pete	Cal.	1	3	0	0	0	0	....	....	....	....	....	....	1972-73	1972-73
Virta, Hannu	Buf.	5	245	25	101	126	66	17	1	3	4	6	....	1981-82	1985-86
Virta, Tony	Min.	1	8	2	3	5	0	....	....	....	....	....	....	2001-02	2001-02
Virtue, Terry	Bos., NYR	2	5	0	0	0	0	....	....	....	....	....	....	1998-99	1999-00
Visheau, Mark	Wpg., L.A.	2	29	1	3	4	107	....	....	....	....	....	....	1993-94	1998-99
‡ Vishnevski, Vitaly	Ana., Atl., Nsh., N.J.	8	552	16	52	68	494	40	0	5	5	18	....	1999-00	2007-08
Vitolinsh, Harijs	Wpg.	1	8	0	0	0	4	....	....	....	....	....	....	1993-94	1993-94
Viveiros, Emanuel	Min.	3	29	1	11	12	6	....	....	....	....	....	....	1985-86	1987-88
‡ Vlasak, Tomas	L.A.	1	10	1	3	4	2	....	....	....	....	....	....	2000-01	2000-01
● Vokes, Ed	Chi.	1	5	0	0	0	0	....	....	....	....	....	....	1930-31	1930-31
Volcan, Mickey	Hfd., Cgy.	4	162	8	33	41	146	....	....	....	....	....	....	1980-81	1983-84
Volchkov, Alexandre	Wsh.	1	3	0	0	0	0	....	....	....	....	....	....	1999-00	1999-00
Volek, David	NYI	6	396	95	154	249	201	15	5	5	10	2	....	1988-89	1993-94
Volmar, Doug	Det., L.A.	4	62	13	8	21	26	2	1	0	1	0	....	1969-70	1972-73
‡ Von Arx, Reto	Chi.	1	19	3	1	4	4	....	....	....	....	....	....	2000-01	2000-01
Von Stefenelli, Phil	Bos., Ott.	2	33	0	5	5	23	....	....	....	....	....	....	1995-96	1996-97
Vopat, Jan	L.A., Nsh.	5	126	11	20	31	70	2	0	1	1	2	....	1995-96	1999-00
Vopat, Roman	St.L., L.A., Chi., Phi.	4	133	6	14	20	253	....	....	....	....	....	....	1995-96	1998-99
Vorobiev, Pavel	Chi.	2	57	10	15	25	38	....	....	....	....	....	....	2003-04	2005-06
Vorobiev, Vladimir	NYR, Edm.	3	33	9	7	16	14	1	0	0	0	0	....	1996-97	1998-99
● Voss, Carl	Tor., NYR, Det., Ott., St.L., NYA, Mtl.M., Chi.	8	261	34	70	104	50	24	5	3	8	0	1	1926-27	1937-38
Vujtek, Vladimir	Mtl., Edm., T.B., Atl., Pit.	6	110	7	30	37	38	....	....	....	....	....	....	1991-92	2002-03
Vukota, Mick	NYI, T.B., Mtl.	11	574	17	29	46	2071	23	0	0	0	73	....	1987-88	1997-98
● Vyazmikin, Igor	Edm.	1	4	1	0	1	0	....	....	....	....	....	....	1990-91	1990-91
‡ Vyborny, David	CBJ	7	543	113	204	317	228	....	....	....	....	....	....	2000-01	2007-08
‡ Vyshedkevich, Sergei	Atl.	2	30	2	5	7	16	....	....	....	....	....	....	1999-00	2000-01

W

Waddell, Don	L.A.	1	1	0	0	0	0	....	....	....	....	....	....	1980-81	1980-81
● Waite, Frank	NYR	1	17	1	3	4	4	....	....	....	....	....	....	1930-31	1930-31
Walker, Gord	NYR, L.A.	4	31	3	4	7	23	....	....	....	....	....	....	1986-87	1989-90
Walker, Howard	Wsh., Cgy.	3	83	2	13	15	133	....	....	....	....	....	....	1980-81	1982-83
● Walker, Jack	Det.	2	80	5	8	13	18	....	....	....	....	....	....	1926-27	1927-28
Walker, Kurt	Tor.	3	71	4	5	9	142	16	0	0	0	34	....	1975-76	1977-78
Walker, Russ	L.A.	2	17	1	0	1	41	....	....	....	....	....	....	1976-77	1977-78
Walker, Scott	Van., Nsh., Car., Wsh.	15	829	151	246	397	1162	30	1	7	8	31	....	1994-95	2009-10
Wall, Bob	Det., L.A., St.L.	8	322	30	55	85	155	22	0	3	3	2	....	1964-65	1971-72
Wallin, Jesse	Det.	4	49	0	2	2	34	....	....	....	....	....	....	1999-00	2002-03
Wallin, Peter	NYR	2	52	3	14	17	14	14	2	6	8	6	....	1980-81	1981-82
‡ Wallin, Rickard	Min., Tor.	3	79	8	11	19	34	....	....	....	....	....	....	2002-03	2009-10
‡ Walser, Derrick	CBJ	4	91	8	21	29	56	....	....	....	....	....	....	2001-02	2006-07
Walsh, Jim	Buf.	1	4	0	1	1	4	....	....	....	....	....	....	1981-82	1981-82
Walsh, Mike	NYI	2	14	2	0	2	4	....	....	....	....	....	....	1987-88	1988-89
Walter, Ryan	Wsh., Mtl., Van.	15	1003	264	382	646	946	113	16	35	51	62	1	1978-79	1992-93
● Walton, Bobby	Mtl.	1	4	0	0	0	0	....	....	....	....	....	....	1943-44	1943-44
Walton, Mike	Tor., Bos., Van., St.L., Chi.	12	588	201	247	448	357	47	14	10	24	45	2	1965-66	1978-79
Walz, Wes	Bos., Phi., Cgy., Det., Min.	13	607	109	151	260	343	32	10	7	17	20	....	1989-90	2007-08
‡ Wanvig, Kyle	Min., T.B.	5	75	6	9	15	94	....	....	....	....	....	....	2002-03	2007-08
Wappel, Gord	Atl., Cgy.	3	20	1	1	2	10	2	0	0	0	4	....	1979-80	1981-82
Ward, Aaron	Det., Car., NYR, Bos., Ana.	15	839	44	107	151	736	95	4	6	10	73	3	1993-94	2009-10
Ward, Dixon	Van., L.A., Tor., Buf., Bos., NYR	10	537	95	129	224	431	62	14	20	34	46	....	1992-93	2002-03
● Ward, Don	Chi., Bos.	2	34	0	1	1	16	....	....	....	....	....	....	1957-58	1959-60
Ward, Ed	Que., Cgy., Atl., Ana., N.J.	8	278	23	26	49	354	....	....	....	....	....	....	1993-94	2000-01
Ward, Jason	Mtl., NYR, L.A., T.B.	8	336	36	45	81	171	12	0	3	3	10	....	1999-00	2008-09
● Ward, Jimmy	Mtl.M., Mtl.	12	527	147	127	274	455	36	4	4	8	26	1	1927-28	1938-39
Ward, Joe	Col.	1	4	0	0	0	2	....	....	....	....	....	....	1980-81	1980-81
‡ Ward, Lance	Fla., Ana.	4	209	4	12	16	391	....	....	....	....	....	....	2000-01	2003-04
Ward, Ron	Tor., Van.	2	89	2	5	7	6	....	....	....	....	....	....	1969-70	1971-72
Ware, Jeff	Tor., Fla.	3	21	0	1	1	12	....	....	....	....	....	....	1996-97	1998-99
Ware, Michael	Edm.	2	5	0	1	1	15	....	....	....	....	....	....	1988-89	1989-90
● Wares, Eddie	NYR, Det., Chi.	9	321	60	102	162	161	45	5	7	12	34	1	1936-37	1946-47
Warner, Bob	Tor.	2	10	1	1	2	4	4	0	0	0	0	....	1975-76	1976-77
Warner, Jim	Hfd.	1	32	0	3	3	10	....	....	....	....	....	....	1979-80	1979-80
Warrener, Rhett	Fla., Buf., Cgy.	12	714	24	82	106	899	101	1	7	8	68	....	1995-96	2007-08
Warriner, Todd	Tor., T.B., Phx., Van., Phi., Nsh.	9	453	65	89	154	249	21	2	1	3	6	....	1994-95	2002-03
● Warwick, Billy	NYR	2	14	3	3	6	16	....	....	....	....	....	....	1942-43	1943-44
● Warwick, Grant	NYR, Bos., Mtl.	9	395	147	142	289	220	16	2	4	6	6	....	1941-42	1949-50
Washburn, Steve	Fla., Van., Phi.	6	93	14	15	29	42	1	0	1	1	0	....	1995-96	2000-01
● Wasnie, Nick	Chi., Mtl., NYA, Ott., St.L.	7	248	57	34	91	176	20	6	3	9	20	2	1927-28	1934-35
Watson, Bill	Chi.	4	115	23	36	59	12	6	0	2	2	0	....	1985-86	1988-89
Watson, Bryan	Mtl., Det., Oak., Pit., St.L., Wsh.	16	878	17	135	152	2212	32	2	0	2	70	1	1963-64	1978-79
Watson, Dave	Col.	2	18	0	1	1	10	....	....	....	....	....	....	1979-80	1980-81
● Watson, Harry	Bro., Det., Tor., Chi.	14	809	236	207	443	150	62	16	9	25	27	5	1941-42	1956-57
Watson, Jim	Det., Buf.	8	221	4	19	23	345	....	....	....	....	....	....	1963-64	1971-72
Watson, Jimmy	Phi.	10	613	38	148	186	492	101	5	34	39	89	2	1972-73	1981-82
Watson, Joe	Bos., Phi., Col.	14	835	38	178	216	447	84	3	12	15	82	2	1964-65	1978-79
● Watson, Phil	NYR, Mtl.	13	590	144	265	409	532	54	10	25	35	67	2	1935-36	1947-48
Watt, Mike	Edm., NYI, Nsh., Car.	5	157	15	26	41	41	....	....	....	....	....	....	1997-98	2002-03
Watters, Tim	Wpg., L.A.	14	741	26	151	177	1289	82	1	5	6	115	....	1981-82	1994-95

Name	NHL Teams	NHL Seasons	Regular Schedule GP	G	A	TP	PIM	Playoffs GP	G	A	TP	PIM	NHL Cup Wins	First NHL Season	Last NHL Season
Watts, Brian	Det.	1	4	0	0	0	0	....	....	....	....	....	....	1975-76	1975-76
Webb, Steve	NYI, Pit.	8	321	5	13	18	532	14	0	0	0	28	....	1996-97	2003-04
• Webster, Aubrey	Phi., Mtl.M.	2	5	0	0	0	0	....	....	....	....	....	....	1930-31	1934-35
• Webster, Don	Tor.	1	27	7	6	13	28	5	0	0	0	12	....	1943-44	1943-44
Webster, John	NYR	1	14	0	0	0	4	....	....	....	....	....	....	1949-50	1949-50
Webster, Tom	Bos., Det., Cal.	5	102	33	42	75	61	1	0	0	0	0	....	1968-69	1979-80
• Weiland, Cooney	Bos., Ott., Det.	11	509	173	160	333	147	45	12	10	22	12	2	1928-29	1938-39
‡ Weinhandl, Mattias	NYI, Min.	4	182	19	37	56	70	5	0	0	0	2	....	2002-03	2006-07
Weinrich, Eric	N.J., Hfd., Chi., Mtl., Bos., Phi., St.L., Van.	17	1157	70	318	388	825	81	6	23	29	67	....	1988-89	2005-06
Weir, Stan	Cal., Tor., Edm., Col., Det.	10	642	139	207	346	183	37	6	5	11	4	....	1972-73	1982-83
Weir, Wally	Que., Hfd., Pit.	6	320	21	45	66	625	23	0	1	1	96	....	1979-80	1984-85
• Wellington, Alex	Que.	1	1	0	0	0	0	....	....	....	....	....	....	1919-20	1919-20
Wells, Chris	Pit., Fla.	5	195	9	20	29	193	3	0	0	0	0	....	1995-96	1999-00
Wells, Jay	L.A., Phi., Buf., NYR, St.L., T.B.	18	1098	47	216	263	2359	114	3	14	17	213	1	1979-80	1996-97
Wensink, John	St.L., Bos., Que., Col., N.J.	8	403	70	68	138	840	43	2	6	8	86	....	1973-74	1982-83
• Wentworth, Cy	Chi., Mtl.M., Mtl.	13	575	39	68	107	355	35	5	6	11	20	1	1927-28	1939-40
Werenka, Brad	Edm., Que., Chi., Pit., Cgy.	7	320	19	61	80	299	19	2	1	3	14	....	1992-93	2000-01
Wesenberg, Brian	Phi.	1	1	0	0	0	5	....	....	....	....	....	....	1998-99	1998-99
Wesley, Blake	Phi., Hfd., Que., Tor.	7	298	18	46	64	486	19	2	2	4	30	....	1979-80	1985-86
Wesley, Glen	Bos., Hfd., Car., Tor.	20	1457	128	409	537	1045	169	15	37	52	141	1	1987-88	2007-08
‡ Westcott, Duvie	CBJ	6	201	11	45	56	299	....	....	....	....	....	....	2001-02	2007-08
Westfall, Ed	Bos., NYI	18	1226	231	394	625	544	95	22	37	59	41	2	1961-62	1978-79
Westlund, Tommy	Car.	4	203	9	13	22	48	25	1	0	1	17	....	1999-00	2002-03
‡ Westrum, Erik	Phx., Min., Tor.	3	27	1	2	3	22	....	....	....	....	....	....	2003-04	2006-07
Wharram, Kenny	Chi.	14	766	252	281	533	222	80	16	27	43	38	1	1951-52	1968-69
• Wharton, Len	NYR	1	1	0	0	0	0	....	....	....	....	....	....	1944-45	1944-45
Wheeldon, Simon	NYR, Wpg.	3	15	0	2	2	10	....	....	....	....	....	....	1987-88	1990-91
• Wheldon, Don	St.L.	1	2	0	0	0	0	....	....	....	....	....	....	1974-75	1974-75
Whelton, Bill	Wpg.	1	2	0	0	0	0	....	....	....	....	....	....	1980-81	1980-81
Whistle, Rob	NYR, St.L.	2	51	7	5	12	16	4	0	0	0	2	....	1985-86	1987-88
White, Bill	L.A., Chi.	9	604	50	215	265	495	91	7	32	39	76	....	1967-68	1975-76
White, Brian	Col.	1	2	0	0	0	0	....	....	....	....	....	....	1998-99	1998-99
White, Moe	Mtl.	1	4	0	1	1	2	....	....	....	....	....	....	1945-46	1945-46
White, Peter	Edm., Tor., Phi., Chi.	9	220	23	37	60	36	19	0	2	2	0	....	1993-94	2003-04
• White, Sherman	NYR	2	4	0	2	2	0	....	....	....	....	....	....	1946-47	1949-50
• White, Tex	Pit., NYA, Phi.	6	203	33	12	45	141	4	0	0	0	4	....	1925-26	1930-31
White, Tony	Wsh., Min.	5	164	37	28	65	104	....	....	....	....	....	....	1974-75	1979-80
Whitelaw, Bob	Det.	2	32	0	2	2	2	8	0	0	0	0	....	1940-41	1941-42
Whitlock, Bob	Min.	1	1	0	0	0	0	....	....	....	....	....	....	1969-70	1969-70
Whyte, Sean	L.A.	2	21	0	2	2	12	....	....	....	....	....	....	1991-92	1992-93
• Wickenheiser, Doug	Mtl., St.L., Van., NYR, Wsh.	10	556	111	165	276	286	41	4	7	11	18	....	1980-81	1989-90
• Widing, Juha	NYR, L.A., Cle.	8	575	144	226	370	208	8	1	2	3	2	....	1969-70	1976-77
Widmer, Jason	NYI, S.J.	3	7	0	1	1	7	....	....	....	....	....	....	1994-95	1996-97
• Wiebe, Art	Chi.	11	414	14	27	41	201	31	1	3	4	10	1	1932-33	1943-44
Wiemer, Jason	T.B., Cgy., Fla., NYI, Min., N.J.	11	726	90	112	202	1420	19	1	0	1	67	....	1994-95	2005-06
Wiemer, Jim	Buf., NYR, Edm., L.A., Bos.	11	325	29	72	101	378	62	5	8	13	63	....	1982-83	1993-94
• Wilcox, Archie	Mtl.M., Bos., St.L.	6	208	8	14	22	158	12	1	0	1	8	....	1929-30	1934-35
Wilcox, Barry	Van.	2	33	3	2	5	15	....	....	....	....	....	....	1972-73	1974-75
• Wilder, Arch	Det.	1	18	0	2	2	2	....	....	....	....	....	....	1940-41	1940-41
Wiley, Jim	Pit., Van.	5	63	4	10	14	8	....	....	....	....	....	....	1972-73	1976-77
Wilkie, Bob	Det., Phi.	2	18	2	5	7	10	....	....	....	....	....	....	1990-91	1993-94
Wilkie, David	Mtl., T.B., NYR	6	167	10	26	36	165	8	1	2	3	14	....	1994-95	2000-01
• Wilkins, Barry	Bos., Van., Pit.	9	418	27	125	152	663	6	0	1	1	4	....	1966-67	1975-76
• Wilkinson, John	Bos.	1	9	0	0	0	6	....	....	....	....	....	....	1943-44	1943-44
Wilkinson, Neil	Min., S.J., Chi., Wpg., Pit.	10	460	16	67	83	813	53	3	6	9	41	....	1989-90	1998-99
Wilks, Brian	L.A.	4	48	4	8	12	27	....	....	....	....	....	....	1984-85	1988-89
Willard, Rod	Tor.	1	1	0	0	0	0	....	....	....	....	....	....	1982-83	1982-83
• Williams, Burr	Det., St.L., Bos.	3	19	0	1	1	28	7	0	0	0	8	....	1933-34	1936-37
Williams, Butch	St.L., Cal.	3	108	14	35	49	131	....	....	....	....	....	....	1973-74	1975-76
Williams, Darryl	L.A.	1	2	0	0	0	10	....	....	....	....	....	....	1992-93	1992-93
Williams, David	S.J., Ana.	4	173	11	53	64	157	....	....	....	....	....	....	1991-92	1994-95
Williams, Fred	Det.	1	44	2	5	7	10	....	....	....	....	....	....	1976-77	1976-77
Williams, Gord	Phi.	2	2	0	0	0	2	....	....	....	....	....	....	1981-82	1982-83
Williams, Sean	Chi.	1	2	0	0	0	4	....	....	....	....	....	....	1991-92	1991-92
Williams, Tiger	Tor., Van., Det., L.A., Hfd.	14	962	241	272	513	3966	83	12	23	35	455	....	1974-75	1987-88
Williams, Tom	NYR, L.A.	8	397	115	138	253	73	29	8	7	15	4	....	1971-72	1978-79
• Williams, Tommy	Bos., Min., Cal., Wsh.	13	663	161	269	430	177	10	2	5	7	2	....	1961-62	1975-76
Willis, Shane	Car., T.B.	5	174	31	43	74	77	2	0	0	0	0	....	1998-99	2003-04
Willson, Don	Mtl.	2	22	2	7	9	0	3	0	0	0	0	....	1937-38	1938-39
‡ Wilm, Clarke	Cgy., Nsh., Tor.	7	455	37	60	97	336	5	0	1	1	2	....	1998-99	2005-06
Wilson, Behn	Phi., Chi.	9	601	98	260	358	1480	67	12	29	41	190	....	1978-79	1987-88
• Wilson, Bert	NYR, St.L., L.A., Cgy.	8	478	37	44	81	646	21	0	2	2	42	....	1973-74	1980-81
Wilson, Bob	Chi.	1	1	0	0	0	0	....	....	....	....	....	....	1953-54	1953-54
Wilson, Carey	Cgy., Hfd., NYR	10	552	169	258	427	314	52	11	13	24	14	....	1983-84	1992-93
• Wilson, Cully	Tor., Mtl., Ham., Chi.	5	127	59	28	87	243	2	1	0	1	6	....	1919-20	1926-27
Wilson, Doug	Chi., S.J.	16	1024	237	590	827	830	95	19	61	80	88	....	1977-78	1992-93
Wilson, Gord	Bos.	1	....	....	....	....	....	2	0	0	0	0	....	1954-55	1954-55
• Wilson, Hub	NYA	1	2	0	0	0	0	....	....	....	....	....	....	1931-32	1931-32
Wilson, Jerry	Mtl.	1	3	0	0	0	2	....	....	....	....	....	....	1956-57	1956-57
Wilson, Johnny	Det., Chi., Tor., NYR	13	688	161	171	332	190	66	14	13	27	11	4	1949-50	1961-62
Wilson, Landon	Col., Bos., Phx., Pit., Dal.	10	375	53	66	119	352	13	1	1	2	20	....	1995-96	2008-09
• Wilson, Larry	Det., Chi.	6	152	21	48	69	75	4	0	0	0	0	1	1949-50	1955-56
Wilson, Mike	Buf., Fla., Pit., NYR	8	336	16	41	57	264	29	0	2	2	15	....	1995-96	2002-03
Wilson, Mitch	N.J., Pit.	2	26	2	3	5	104	....	....	....	....	....	....	1984-85	1986-87
Wilson, Murray	Mtl., L.A.	7	386	94	95	189	162	53	5	14	19	32	4	1972-73	1978-79
Wilson, Rick	Mtl., St.L., Det.	4	239	6	26	32	165	3	0	0	0	0	....	1973-74	1976-77
Wilson, Rik	St.L., Cgy., Chi.	6	251	25	65	90	220	22	0	4	4	23	....	1981-82	1987-88
Wilson, Roger	Chi.	1	7	0	2	2	6	....	....	....	....	....	....	1974-75	1974-75
Wilson, Ron	Tor., Min.	7	177	26	67	93	68	20	4	13	17	8	....	1977-78	1987-88
Wilson, Ron	Wpg., St.L., Mtl.	14	832	110	216	326	415	63	10	12	22	64	....	1979-80	1993-94
• Wilson, Wally	Bos.	1	53	11	8	19	18	1	0	0	0	0	....	1947-48	1947-48
Wing, Murray	Det.	1	1	0	1	1	0	....	....	....	....	....	....	1973-74	1973-74
Winnes, Chris	Bos., Phi.	4	33	1	6	7	6	1	0	0	0	0	....	1990-91	1993-94
Wiseman, Brian	Tor.	1	3	0	0	0	0	....	....	....	....	....	....	1996-97	1996-97
• Wiseman, Eddie	Det., NYA, Bos.	10	456	115	165	280	136	43	10	10	20	16	1	1932-33	1941-42
Wiste, Jim	Chi., Van.	3	52	1	10	11	8	....	....	....	....	....	....	1968-69	1970-71
Witehall, Johan	NYR, Mtl.	3	54	2	5	7	16	....	....	....	....	....	....	1998-99	2000-01
Witherspoon, Jim	L.A.	1	2	0	0	0	2	....	....	....	....	....	....	1975-76	1975-76
Witiuk, Steve	Chi.	1	33	3	8	11	14	....	....	....	....	....	....	1951-52	1951-52
Witt, Brendan	Wsh., Nsh., NYI	14	890	25	96	121	1424	41	4	1	5	44	....	1995-96	2009-10
Woit, Benny	Det., Chi.	7	334	7	26	33	170	41	2	6	8	18	3	1950-51	1956-57
Wojciechowski, Steve	Det.	2	54	19	20	39	17	6	0	1	1	0	....	1944-45	1946-47
Wolanin, Craig	N.J., Que., Col., T.B., Tor.	13	695	40	133	173	894	35	4	6	10	67	1	1985-86	1997-98
Wolf, Bennett	Pit.	3	30	0	1	1	133	....	....	....	....	....	....	1980-81	1982-83
Wong, Mike	Det.	1	22	1	1	2	12	....	....	....	....	....	....	1975-76	1975-76
Wood, Dody	S.J.	5	106	8	10	18	471	....	....	....	....	....	....	1992-93	1997-98
Wood, Randy	NYI, Buf., Tor., Dal.	11	741	175	159	334	603	51	8	9	17	40	....	1986-87	1996-97
• Wood, Robert	NYR	1	1	0	0	0	0	....	....	....	....	....	....	1950-51	1950-51
Woodley, Dan	Van.	1	5	2	0	2	17	....	....	....	....	....	....	1987-88	1987-88
Woods, Paul	Det.	7	501	72	124	196	276	7	0	5	5	4	....	1977-78	1983-84
Woolley, Jason	Wsh., Fla., Pit., Buf., Det.	14	718	68	246	314	430	79	11	36	47	44	....	1991-92	2005-06
Worrell, Peter	Fla., Col.	7	391	19	27	46	1554	4	1	0	1	8	....	1997-98	2003-04
Wortman, Kevin	Cgy.	1	5	0	0	0	2	....	....	....	....	....	....	1993-94	1993-94
‡ Wotton, Mark	Van., Dal.	4	43	3	6	9	25	5	0	0	0	4	....	1994-95	2000-01
• Woytowich, Bob	Bos., Min., Pit., L.A.	8	503	32	126	158	352	24	1	3	4	20	....	1964-65	1971-72
‡ Wren, Bob	Ana., Tor.	3	5	0	0	0	0	1	0	0	0	0	....	1997-98	2001-02
Wright, Jamie	Dal., Cgy., Phi.	6	124	12	20	32	54	5	0	0	0	0	....	1997-98	2002-03
Wright, John	Van., St.L., K.C.	3	127	16	36	52	67	....	....	....	....	....	....	1972-73	1974-75
Wright, Keith	Phi.	1	1	0	0	0	0	....	....	....	....	....	....	1967-68	1967-68
Wright, Larry	Phi., Cal., Det.	5	106	4	8	12	19	....	....	....	....	....	....	1971-72	1977-78
Wright, Tyler	Edm., Pit., CBJ, Ana.	13	613	79	70	149	854	30	3	2	5	40	....	1992-93	2005-06
• Wycherley, Ralph	NYA, Bro.	2	28	4	7	11	6	....	....	....	....	....	....	1940-41	1941-42
• Wylie, Bill	NYR	1	1	0	0	0	0	....	....	....	....	....	....	1950-51	1950-51
Wylie, Duane	Chi.	2	14	3	3	6	2	....	....	....	....	....	....	1974-75	1976-77
Wyrozub, Randy	Buf.	4	100	8	10	18	10	....	....	....	....	....	....	1970-71	1973-74

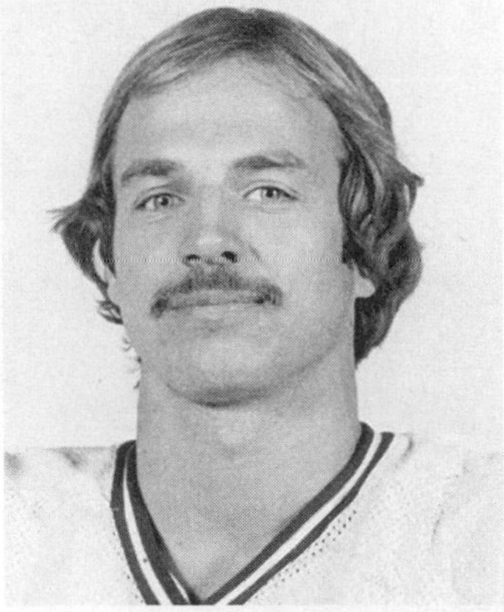

Jim Warner

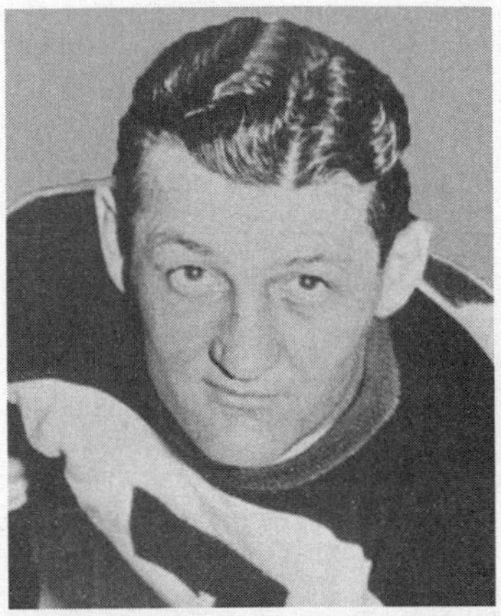

Cooney Weiland

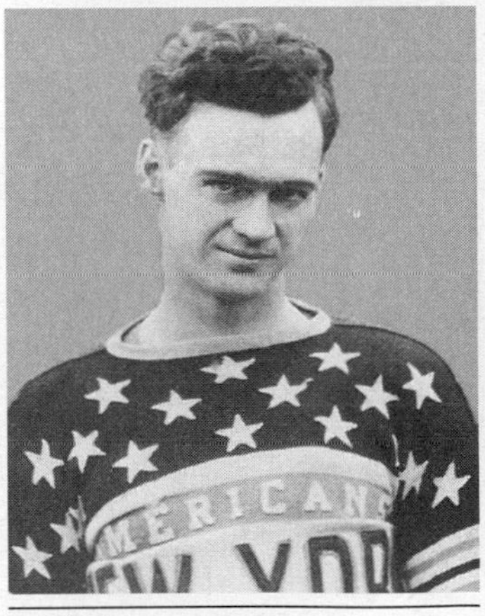

Tex White

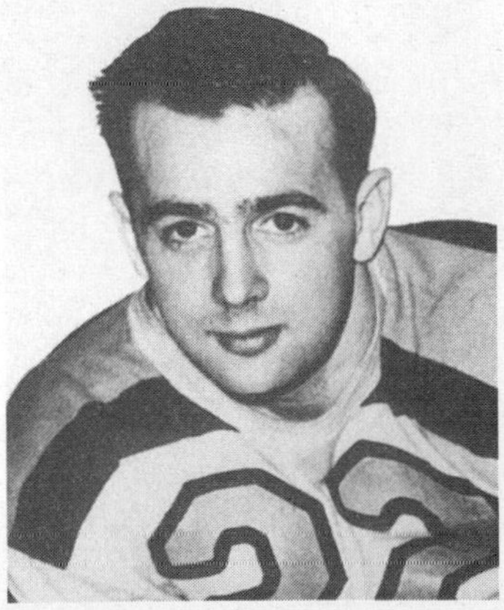

Wally Wilson

Trent Yawney

Sergei Zubov

Y Z

Name	NHL Teams	NHL Seasons	Regular Schedule					Playoffs					NHL Cup Wins	First NHL Season	Last NHL Season
			GP	G	A	TP	PIM	GP	G	A	TP	PIM			
‡ Yachmenev, Vitali	L.A., Nsh.	8	487	83	133	216	88	....					....	1995-96	2002-03
• Yackel, Ken	Bos.	1	6	0	0	0	2	2	0	0	0	2	....	1958-59	1958-59
• Yake, Terry	Hfd., Ana., Tor., St.L., Wsh.	11	403	77	120	197	220	32	4	4	8	36	....	1988-89	2000-01
‡ Yakubov, Mikhail	Chi., Fla.	2	53	2	10	12	20	....					....	2003-04	2005-06
Yakushin, Dmitri	Tor.	1	2	0	0	0	2	....					....	1999-00	1999-00
Yaremchuk, Gary	Tor.	4	34	1	4	5	28	....					....	1981-82	1984-85
Yaremchuk, Ken	Chi., Tor.	6	235	36	56	92	106	31	6	8	14	49	....	1983-84	1988-89
‡ Yashin, Alexei	Ott., NYI	12	850	337	444	781	401	48	11	16	27	24	....	1993-94	2006-07
Yates, Ross	Hfd.	1	7	1	1	2	4	....					....	1983-84	1983-84
Yawney, Trent	Chi., Cgy., St.L.	12	593	27	102	129	783	60	9	17	26	81	....	1987-88	1998-99
• Yegorov, Alexei	S.J.	2	11	3	3	6	2	....					....	1995-96	1996-97
Yelle, Stephane	Col., Cgy., Bos., Car.	14	991	96	169	265	490	171	11	21	32	90	2	1995-96	2009-10
Ylonen, Juha	Phx., T.B., Ott.	6	341	26	76	102	90	15	0	7	7	4	....	1996-97	2001-02
York, Harry	St.L., NYR, Pit., Van.	4	244	29	46	75	99	5	0	0	0	2	....	1996-97	1999-00
York, Jason	Det., Ana., Ott., Nsh., Bos.	13	757	42	187	229	621	34	2	7	9	25	....	1992-93	2006-07
‡ York, Mike	NYR, Edm., NYI, Phi., Phx., CBJ	9	579	127	195	322	135	6	0	2	2	2	....	1999-00	2008-09
• Young, B.J.	Det.	1	1	0	0	0	0	....					....	1999-00	1999-00
Young, Brian	Chi.	1	8	0	2	2	6	....					....	1980-81	1980-81
Young, Bryan	Edm.	2	17	0	0	0	10	....					....	2006-07	2007-08
Young, C.J.	Cgy., Bos.	1	43	7	7	14	32	....					....	1992-93	1992-93
• Young, Doug	Det., Mtl.	10	388	35	45	80	303	28	1	5	6	16	2	1940-41
• Young, Howie	Det., Chi., Van.	8	336	12	62	74	851	19	2	4	6	46	....	1960-61	1970-71
Young, Scott	Hfd., Pit., Que., Col., Ana., St.L., Dal.	17	1181	342	415	757	448	141	44	43	87	64	2	1987-88	2005-06
Young, Tim	Min., Wpg., Phi.	10	628	195	341	536	438	36	7	24	31	27	....	1975-76	1984-85
Young, Warren	Min., Pit., Det.	7	236	72	77	149	472	....					....	1981-82	1987-88
Younghans, Tom	Min., NYR	6	429	44	41	85	373	24	2	1	3	21	....	1976-77	1981-82
Ysebaert, Paul	N.J., Det., Wpg., Chi., T.B.	11	532	149	187	336	217	30	4	3	7	20	....	1988-89	1998-99
Yushkevich, Dmitry	Phi., Tor., Fla., L.A.	11	786	43	182	225	659	72	4	19	23	52	....	1992-93	2002-03
Yzerman, Steve	Det.	22	1514	692	1063	1755	924	196	70	115	185	84	3	1983-84	2005-06
Zabransky, Libor	St.L.	2	40	1	6	7	50	....					....	1996-97	1997-98
Zaharko, Miles	Atl., Chi.	4	129	5	32	37	84	3	0	0	0	0	....	1977-78	1981-82
Zaine, Rod	Pit., Buf.	2	61	10	6	16	25	....					....	1970-71	1971-72
Zalapski, Zarley	Pit., Hfd., Cgy., Mtl., Phi.	12	637	99	285	384	684	48	4	23	27	47	....	1987-88	1999-00
‡ Zalesak, Miroslav	S.J.	2	12	1	2	3	0	....					....	2002-03	2003-04
Zamuner, Rob	NYR, T.B., Ott., Bos.	13	798	139	172	311	467	34	4	5	9	26	....	1991-92	2003-04
Zanussi, Joe	NYR, Bos., St.L.	3	87	1	13	14	46	4	0	1	1	2	....	1974-75	1976-77
Zanussi, Ron	Min., Tor.	5	299	52	83	135	373	17	0	4	4	17	....	1977-78	1981-82
Zavisha, Brad	Edm.	1	2	0	0	0	0	....					....	1993-94	1993-94
‡ Zednik, Richard	Wsh., Mtl., NYI, Fla.	13	745	200	179	379	563	48	16	10	26	41	....	1995-96	2008-09
Zehr, Jeff	Bos.	1	4	0	0	0	2	....					....	1999-00	1999-00
Zeidel, Larry	Det., Chi., Phi.	5	158	3	16	19	198	12	0	1	1	12	1	1951-52	1968-69
Zelepukin, Valeri	N.J., Edm., Phi., Chi.	10	595	117	177	294	527	85	13	13	26	48	1	1991-92	2000-01
Zemlak, Richard	Que., Min., Pit., Cgy.	5	132	2	12	14	587	1	0	0	0	10	....	1986-87	1991-92
• Zeniuk, Ed	Det.	1	2	0	0	0	0	....					....	1954-55	1954-55
Zent, Jason	Ott., Phi.	3	27	3	3	6	13	....					....	1996-97	1998-99
Zetterstrom, Lars	Van.	1	14	0	1	1	2	....					....	1978-79	1978-79
Zettler, Rob	Min., S.J., Phi., Tor., Nsh., Wsh.	14	569	5	65	70	920	14	0	0	0	4	....	1988-89	2001-02
• Zezel, Peter	Phi., St.L., Wsh., Tor., Dal., N.J., Van.	15	873	219	389	608	435	131	25	39	64	83	....	1984-85	1998-99
Zhamnov, Alex	Wpg., Chi., Phi., Bos.	13	807	249	470	719	668	35	6	13	19	18	....	1992-93	2005-06
Zhitnik, Alexei	L.A., Buf., NYI, Phi., Atl.	15	1085	96	375	471	1268	98	9	30	39	168	....	1992-93	2007-08
Zholtok, Sergei	Bos., Ott., Mtl., Edm., Min., Nsh.	10	588	111	147	258	166	45	4	14	18	0	....	1992-93	2003-04
‡ Ziegler, Thomas	T.B.	1	5	0	0	0	0	....					....	2000-01	2000-01
Zinger, Dwayne	Wsh.	1	7	0	1	1	9	....					....	2003-04	2003-04
‡ Zinovjev, Sergei	Bos.	1	10	0	1	1	2	....					....	2003-04	2003-04
‡ Zizka, Tomas	L.A.	2	25	2	6	8	16	....					....	2002-03	2003-04
Zmolek, Doug	S.J., Dal., L.A., Chi.	8	467	11	53	64	905	14	0	1	1	16	....	1992-93	1999-00
Zoborosky, Marty	Chi.	1	1	0	0	0	2	....					....	1944-45	1944-45
Zombo, Rick	Det., St.L., Bos.	12	652	24	130	154	728	60	1	11	12	127	....	1984-85	1995-96
Zubov, Sergei	NYR, Pit., Dal.	16	1068	152	619	771	337	164	24	93	117	62	2	1992-93	2008-09
Zuke, Mike	St.L., Hfd.	8	455	86	196	282	220	26	6	6	12	12	....	1978-79	1985-86
• Zunich, Rudy	Det.	1	2	0	0	0	2	....					....	1943-44	1943-44
‡ Zyuzin, Andrei	S.J., T.B., N.J., Min., Cgy., Chi.	10	496	38	82	120	446	29	2	1	3	30	....	1997-98	2007-08

Retired Players, Goaltenders and Coaches Research Project

Throughout the Retired Players and Retired Goaltenders sections of this book, you will notice many players with a bullet (•) by their names. These players, according to our records, are deceased. The editors recognize that our information on the death dates of NHLers is incomplete. If you have documented information on the passing of any player not marked with a bullet (•) in this edition, we would like to hear from you. We also welcome information on deceased NHL head coaches. Please send this information to:

Retired Player Research Project
c/o NHL Publishing
194 Dovercourt Road
Toronto, Ontario
M6J 3C8   Canada
Fax: 416/531-3939

Many thanks to the following contributors . . .

Tim Bateman, Corey Bryant, Paul R. Carroll, Jr., Bob Duff, Peter Fillman, Ernie Fitzsimmons, Chris Gory, Calvin McLellan, Gary J. Pearce, Martin Schmid, Al Tario, Drew "Whitey" White.

Retired NHL Goaltender Index

Abbreviations: Teams/Cities: – **Ana.** – Anaheim; **Atl.** – Atlanta; **Bos.** – Boston; **Bro.** – Brooklyn; **Buf.** – Buffalo; **Cgy.** – Calgary; **Cal.** – California; **Car.** – Carolina; **Chi.** – Chicago; **Cle.** – Cleveland; **Col.** – Colorado; **CBJ** – Columbus; **Dal.** – Dallas; **Det.** – Detroit; **Edm.** – Edmonton; **Fla.** – Florida; **Ham.** – Hamilton; **Hfd.** – Hartford; **K.C.** – Kansas City; **L.A.** – Los Angeles; **Min.** – Minnesota; **Mtl.** – Montreal; **Mtl.M.** – Montreal Maroons; **Mtl.W.** – Montreal Wanderers; **Nsh.** – Nashville; **N.J.** – New Jersey; **NYA** – NY Americans; **NYI** – NY Islanders; **NYR** – New York Rangers; **Oak.** – Oakland; **Ott.** – Ottawa; **Phi.** – Philadelphia; **Phx.** – Phoenix; **Pit.** – Pittsburgh; **Que.** – Quebec; **St.L.** – St. Louis; **S.J.** – San Jose; **T.B.** – Tampa Bay; **Tor.** – Toronto; **Van.** – Vancouver; **Wsh.** – Washington; **Wpg.** – Winnipeg

Avg. – goals against per 60 minutes played; **GA** – goals agains; **GP** – games played; **Mins** – minutes played; **SO** – shutouts.
● – deceased. § – Forward, defenseman or coach who appeared in goal. For complete career, see Retired Player Index. ‡ – Remains active in other leagues.

NHL Seasons – A player or goaltender who does not play in a regular season but who does appear in that year's playoffs is credited with an NHL Season in this Index. Total seasons are rounded off to the nearest full season.

			Regular Schedule								Playoffs										
Name	NHL Teams	NHL Seasons	GP	W	L	T	Mins	GA	SO	Avg	GP	W	L	T	Mins	GA	SO	Avg	NHL Cup Wins	First NHL Season	Last NHL Season
Abbott, George	Bos.	1	1	0	1	0	60	7	0	7.00	....	....	....	....	....	....	....	....		1943-44	1943-44
Adams, John	Bos., Wsh.	3	22	9	10	1	1180	85	1	4.32	....	....	....	....	....	....	....	....	1	1969-70	1974-75
‡ Aebischer, David	Col., Mtl., Phx.	7	214	106	74	17	12230	513	13	2.52	13	6	5	....	697	24	1	2.07	1	2000-01	2007-08
Aiken, Don	Mtl.	1	1	0	1	0	34	6	0	10.59	....	....	....	....	....	....	....	....		1957-58	1957-58
● Aitkenhead, Andy	NYR	3	106	47	43	16	6570	257	11	2.35	10	6	2	2	608	15	3	1.48	1	1932-33	1934-35
● Almas, Red	Det., Chi.	3	3	0	2	1	180	13	0	4.33	5	1	3	....	263	13	0	2.97		1946-47	1952-53
● Anderson, Lorne	NYR	1	3	1	2	0	180	18	0	6.00	....	....	....	....	....	....	....	....		1951-52	1951-52
Askey, Tom	Ana.	2	7	0	1	2	273	12	0	2.64	1	0	1	....	30	2	0	4.00		1997-98	1998-99
Astrom, Hardy	NYR, Col.	3	83	17	44	12	4456	278	0	3.74	....	....	....	....	....	....	....	....		1977-78	1980-81
Bach, Ryan	L.A.	1	3	0	3	0	108	8	0	4.44	....	....	....	....	....	....	....	....		1998-99	1998-99
Bailey, Scott	Bos.	2	19	6	6	2	965	55	0	3.42	....	....	....	....	....	....	....	....		1995-96	1996-97
Baker, Steve	NYR	4	57	20	20	11	3081	190	3	3.70	14	7	7	....	826	55	0	4.00		1979-80	1982-83
Bales, Mike	Bos., Ott.	4	23	2	15	1	1120	77	0	4.13	....	....	....	....	....	....	....	....		1992-93	1996-97
Bannerman, Murray	Van., Chi.	8	289	116	125	33	16470	1051	8	3.83	40	20	18	....	2322	165	0	4.26		1977-78	1986-87
Baron, Marco	Bos., L.A., Edm.	6	86	34	38	9	4822	292	1	3.63	1	0	1	....	20	3	0	9.00		1979-80	1984-85
Barrasso, Tom	Buf., Pit., Ott., Car., Tor., St.L.	19	777	369	277	86	44180	2385	38	3.24	119	61	54	....	6953	349	6	3.01	2	1983-84	2002-03
● Bassen, Hank	Chi., Det., Pit.	9	156	46	66	31	8759	434	5	2.97	5	1	3	....	274	11	0	2.41		1954-55	1967-68
● Bastien, Baz	Tor.	1	5	0	4	1	300	20	0	4.00	....	....	....	....	....	....	....	....		1945-46	1945-46
● Bauman, Garry	Mtl., Min.	3	35	5	16	6	1719	102	0	3.56	....	....	....	....	....	....	....	....		1966-67	1968-69
Beaupre, Don	Min., Wsh., Ott., Tor.	17	667	268	277	75	37396	2151	17	3.45	72	33	31	....	3943	220	3	3.35		1980-81	1996-97
Beauregard, Stephane	Wpg., Phi.	5	90	19	39	11	4402	268	2	3.65	4	1	3	....	238	12	0	3.03		1989-90	1993-94
‡ Beckford-Tseu, Chris	St.L.	1	1	0	0	0	27	1	0	2.22	....	....	....	....	....	....	....	....		2007-08	2007-08
Bedard, Jim	Wsh.	2	73	17	40	13	4232	278	1	3.94	....	....	....	....	....	....	....	....		1977-78	1978-79
Behrend, Marc	Wpg.	3	39	12	19	3	1991	160	1	4.82	7	1	3	....	312	19	0	3.65		1983-84	1985-86
Belanger, Yves	St.L., Atl., Bos.	6	78	29	33	6	4134	259	2	3.76	....	....	....	....	....	....	....	....		1974-75	1979-80
Belfour, Ed	Chi., S.J., Dal., Tor., Fla.	18	963	484	320	125	55695	2317	76	2.50	161	88	68	....	9945	359	14	2.17	1	1988-89	2006-07
Belhumeur, Michel	Phi., Wsh.	3	65	9	36	7	3306	254	0	4.61	1	0	0	....	10	1	0	6.00		1972-73	1975-76
● Bell, Gordie	Tor., NYR	2	8	3	5	0	480	31	0	3.88	2	1	1	....	120	9	0	4.50		1945-46	1955-56
● Benedict, Clint	Ott., Mtl.M.	13	362	190	143	28	22367	863	57	2.32	28	11	12	5	1707	53	9	1.86	4	1917-18	1929-30
● Bennett, Harvey	Bos.	1	25	10	12	2	1470	103	0	4.20	....	....	....	....	....	....	....	....		1944-45	1944-45
Bergeron, Jean-Claude	Mtl., T.B., L.A.	6	72	21	33	7	3772	232	1	3.69	....	....	....	....	....	....	....	....		1990-91	1996-97
Berkhoel, Adam	Atl.	1	9	2	4	1	473	30	0	3.81	....	....	....	....	....	....	....	....		2005-06	2005-06
Bernhardt, Tim	Cgy., Tor.	4	67	17	36	7	3748	267	0	4.27	....	....	....	....	....	....	....	....		1982-83	1986-87
Berthiaume, Daniel	Wpg., Min., L.A., Bos., Ott.	9	215	81	90	21	11662	714	5	3.67	14	5	9	....	807	50	0	3.72		1985-86	1993-94
Bester, Allan	Tor., Det., Dal.	10	219	73	99	17	11773	786	7	4.01	11	2	6	....	508	37	0	4.37		1983-84	1995-96
● Beveridge, Bill	Det., Ott., St.L., Mtl.M., NYR	9	297	87	166	42	18375	879	18	2.87	5	2	3	....	300	11	0	2.20		1929-30	1942-43
● Bibeault, Paul	Mtl., Tor., Bos., Chi.	7	214	81	107	25	12890	785	10	3.65	20	6	14	....	1237	71	2	3.44		1940-41	1946-47
Bierk, Zac	T.B., Min., Phx.	6	47	9	20	5	2135	113	1	3.18	....	....	....	....	....	....	....	....		1997-98	2003-04
Billington, Craig	N.J., Ott., Bos., Col., Wsh.	15	332	110	149	31	17097	1034	9	3.63	8	0	2	....	213	15	0	4.23		1985-86	2002-03
Binette, Andre	Mtl.	1	1	1	0	0	60	4	0	4.00	....	....	....	....	....	....	....	....		1954-55	1954-55
Binkley, Les	Pit.	5	196	58	94	34	11046	575	11	3.12	7	5	2	....	428	15	0	2.10		1967-68	1971-72
● Bittner, Richard	Bos.	1	1	0	0	1	60	3	0	3.00	....	....	....	....	....	....	....	....		1949-50	1949-50
Blackburn, Dan	NYR	2	63	20	32	4	3499	188	1	3.22	....	....	....	....	....	....	....	....		2001-02	2002-03
Blake, Mike	L.A.	3	40	13	15	5	2117	150	0	4.25	....	....	....	....	....	....	....	....		1981-82	1983-84
Blue, John	Bos., Buf.	3	46	16	18	7	2521	126	1	3.00	2	0	1	....	96	5	0	3.13		1992-93	1995-96
Boisvert, Gilles	Det.	1	3	0	3	0	180	9	0	3.00	....	....	....	....	....	....	....	....		1959-60	1959-60
Bouchard, Dan	Atl., Cgy., Que., Wpg.	14	655	286	232	113	37919	2061	27	3.26	43	13	30	....	2549	147	1	3.46		1972-73	1985-86
● Bourque, Claude	Mtl., Det.	2	62	16	38	8	3830	193	4	3.02	3	1	2	....	188	8	1	2.55		1938-39	1939-40
Boutin, Rollie	Wsh.	3	22	7	10	1	1137	75	0	3.96	....	....	....	....	....	....	....	....		1978-79	1980-81
● Bouvrette, Lionel	NYR	1	1	0	1	0	60	6	0	6.00	....	....	....	....	....	....	....	....		1942-43	1942-43
Bower, Johnny	NYR, Tor.	15	552	250	195	90	32016	1340	37	2.51	74	35	34	....	4378	180	5	2.47	4	1953-54	1969-70
§ ● Branigan, Andy	NYA	1	1	0	0	0	7	0	0	0.00	....	....	....	....	....	....	....	....		1940-41	1940-41
‡ Brathwaite, Fred	Edm., Cgy., St.L., CBJ	9	254	81	99	37	13840	629	15	2.73	1	0	0	0	1	0	0	0.00		1993-94	2003-04
● Brimsek, Frank	Bos., Chi.	10	514	252	182	80	31210	1404	40	2.70	68	32	36	....	4395	186	2	2.54	2	1938-39	1949-50
Brochu, Martin	Wsh., Van., Pit.	3	9	0	5	0	369	22	0	3.58	....	....	....	....	....	....	....	....		1998-99	2003-04
● Broda, Turk	Tor.	14	629	302	224	101	38167	1609	62	2.53	101	60	39	....	6389	211	13	1.98	5	1936-37	1951-52
Broderick, Ken	Min., Bos.	3	27	11	12	1	1464	74	1	3.03	....	....	....	....	....	....	....	....		1969-70	1974-75
Broderick, Len	Mtl.	1	1	1	0	0	60	2	0	2.00	....	....	....	....	....	....	....	....		1957-58	1957-58
Brodeur, Richard	NYI, Van., Hfd.	9	385	131	175	62	21968	1410	6	3.85	33	13	20	....	2009	111	1	3.32		1979-80	1987-88
Bromley, Gary	Buf., Van.	6	136	54	44	28	7427	425	7	3.43	7	2	5	....	360	25	0	4.17		1973-74	1980-81
● Brooks, Art	Tor.	1	4	2	2	0	220	23	0	6.27	....	....	....	....	....	....	....	....		1917-18	1917-18
Brooks, Ross	Bos.	3	54	37	7	6	3047	134	4	2.64	1	0	0	....	20	3	0	9.00		1972-73	1974-75
● Brophy, Frank	Que.	1	21	3	18	0	1249	148	0	7.11	....	....	....	....	....	....	....	....		1919-20	1919-20
Brown, Andy	Det., Pit.	3	62	22	26	9	3373	213	1	3.79	....	....	....	....	....	....	....	....		1971-72	1973-74
Brown, Ken	Chi.	1	1	0	0	0	18	1	0	3.33	....	....	....	....	....	....	....	....		1970-71	1970-71
Brunetta, Mario	Que.	3	40	12	17	1	1967	128	0	3.90	....	....	....	....	....	....	....	....		1987-88	1989-90
Bullock, Bruce	Van.	3	16	3	9	3	927	74	0	4.79	....	....	....	....	....	....	....	....		1972-73	1976-77
Burke, Sean	N.J., Hfd., Car., Van., Phi., Fla., Phx., T.B., L.A.	18	820	324	341	110	46442	2290	38	2.96	38	12	23	....	2151	119	1	3.32		1987-88	2006-07
● Buzinski, Steve	NYR	1	9	2	6	1	560	55	0	5.89	....	....	....	....	....	....	....	....		1942-43	1942-43
Caley, Don	St.L.	1	1	0	0	0	30	3	0	6.00	....	....	....	....	....	....	....	....		1967-68	1967-68
Caprice, Frank	Van.	6	102	31	46	11	5589	391	1	4.20	....	....	....	....	....	....	....	....		1982-83	1987-88
Carey, Jim	Wsh., Bos., St.L.	5	172	79	65	16	9668	416	16	2.58	10	2	5	....	455	35	0	4.62		1994-95	1998-99
Caron, Jacques	L.A., St.L., Van.	5	72	24	29	11	3846	211	2	3.29	12	4	7	....	639	34	0	3.19		1967-68	1973-74
‡ Caron, Sebastien	Pit., Chi., Ana.	4	92	25	47	12	5021	289	4	3.45	....	....	....	....	....	....	....	....		2002-03	2006-07
Carter, Lyle	Cal.	1	15	4	7	0	721	50	0	4.16	....	....	....	....	....	....	....	....		1971-72	1971-72
Casey, Jon	Min., Bos., St.L.	12	425	170	157	55	23255	1246	16	3.21	66	32	31	....	3743	192	3	3.08		1983-84	1996-97
Cassivi, Frederic	Atl., Wsh.	4	13	3	6	1	628	38	0	3.63	....	....	....	....	....	....	....	....		2001-02	2006-07
Cechmanek, Roman	Phi., L.A.	4	212	110	64	28	12085	419	25	2.08	23	9	14	....	1441	56	3	2.33		2000-01	2003-04
Centomo, Sebastien	Tor.	1	1	0	0	0	40	3	0	4.50	....	....	....	....	....	....	....	....		2001-02	2001-02
Chabot, Frederic	Mtl., Phi., L.A.	5	32	4	8	4	1262	62	0	2.95	....	....	....	....	....	....	....	....		1990-91	1998-99
● Chabot, Lorne	NYR, Tor., Mtl., Chi., Mtl.M., NYA	11	412	201	147	62	25411	859	71	2.03	37	13	17	6	2498	64	5	1.54	2	1926-27	1936-37
Chadwick, Ed	Tor., Bos.	6	184	57	92	35	11040	541	14	2.94	....	....	....	....	....	....	....	....		1955-56	1961-62
Champoux, Bob	Det., Cal.	2	17	2	11	3	923	80	0	5.20	1	1	0	....	55	4	0	4.36		1963-64	1973-74
Charpentier, Sebastien	Wsh.	3	26	6	14	1	1350	66	0	2.93	....	....	....	....	....	....	....	....		2001-02	2003-04
Cheevers, Gerry	Tor., Bos.	13	418	230	102	74	24394	1174	26	2.89	88	53	34	....	5396	242	8	2.69	2	1961-62	1979-80
Cheveldae, Tim	Det., Wpg., Bos.	9	340	149	136	37	19172	1116	10	3.49	25	9	15	....	1418	71	2	3.00		1988-89	1996-97
Chevrier, Alain	N.J., Wpg., Chi., Pit., Det.	6	234	91	100	14	12202	845	2	4.16	16	9	7	....	1013	44	0	2.61		1985-86	1990-91
‡ Chiodo, Andy	Pit.	1	8	3	4	1	486	28	0	3.46	....	....	....	....	....	....	....	....		2003-04	2003-04
Chouinard, Mathieu	L.A.	1	1	0	0	0	3	0	0	0.00	....	....	....	....	....	....	....	....		2003-04	2003-04
§ ● Clancy, King	Ott., Tor.	2	2	0	0	0	3	1	0	20.00	....	....	....	....	....	....	....	....		1924-25	1931-32
§ ● Cleghorn, Odie	Pit.	1	1	1	0	0	60	2	0	2.00	....	....	....	....	....	....	....	....		1925-26	1925-26
§ ● Cleghorn, Sprague	Ott., Mtl.	2	2	0	0	0	5	0	0	0.00	....	....	....	....	....	....	....	....		1918-19	1921-22

				Regular Schedule								Playoffs										
	Name	NHL Teams	NHL Seasons	GP	W	L	T	Mins	GA	SO	Avg	GP	W	L	T	Mins	GA	SO	Avg	NHL Cup Wins	First NHL Season	Last NHL Season
	Clifford, Chris	Chi.	2	2	0	0	0	24	0	0	0.00	....	....	....	....	....	....	....	....		1984-85	1988-89
	Cloutier, Dan	NYR, T.B., Van., L.A.	10	351	139	142	37	18927	874	15	2.77	25	10	13	0	1361	75	0	3.31		1997-98	2007-08
	Cloutier, Jacques	Buf., Chi., Que.	12	255	82	102	24	12826	778	3	3.64	8	1	5	....	413	18	1	2.62		1981-82	1993-94
•	Colvin, Les	Bos.	1	1	0	1	0	60	4	0	4.00	....	....	....	....	....	....	....	....		1948-49	1948-49
§ •	Conacher, Charlie	Tor., Det.	3	4	0	0	0	10	0	0	0.00	....	....	....	....	....	....	....	....		1932-33	1938-39
•	Connell, Alec	Ott., Det., NYA, Mtl.M.	12	417	193	156	67	26050	830	81	1.91	21	8	5	8	1309	26	4	1.19	2	1924-25	1936-37
	Corsi, Jim	Edm.	1	26	8	14	3	1366	83	0	3.65	....	....	....	....	....	....	....	....		1979-80	1979-80
•	Courteau, Maurice	Bos.	1	6	2	4	0	360	33	0	5.50	....	....	....	....	....	....	....	....		1943-44	1943-44
	Cousineau, Marcel	Tor., NYI, L.A.	4	26	4	10	1	1047	51	1	2.92	....	....	....	....	....	....	....	....		1996-97	1999-00
	Cowley, Wayne	Edm.	1	1	0	1	0	57	3	0	3.16	....	....	....	....	....	....	....	....		1993-94	1993-94
•	Cox, Abbie	Mtl.M., NYA, Det., Mtl.	3	5	1	1	2	263	11	0	2.51	....	....	....	....	....	....	....	....		1929-30	1935-36
	Craig, Jim	Atl., Bos., Min.	3	30	11	10	7	1588	100	0	3.78	....	....	....	....	....	....	....	....		1979-80	1983-84
	Crha, Jiri	Tor.	2	69	28	27	11	3942	261	0	3.97	5	0	4	....	186	21	0	6.77		1979-80	1980-81
•	Crozier, Roger	Det., Buf., Wsh.	14	518	206	197	70	28567	1446	30	3.04	32	14	16	....	1789	82	1	2.75		1963-64	1976-77
•	Cude, Wilf	Phi., Bos., Chi., Mtl., Det.	10	282	100	132	49	17586	798	24	2.72	19	7	11	1	1257	51	1	2.43		1930-31	1940-41
	Cutts, Don	Edm.	1	6	1	2	1	269	16	0	3.57	....	....	....	....	....	....	....	....		1979-80	1979-80
•	Cyr, Claude	Mtl.	1	1	0	0	0	20	1	0	3.00	....	....	....	....	....	....	....	....		1958-59	1958-59
	Dadswell, Doug	Cgy.	2	27	8	8	3	1346	99	0	4.41	....	....	....	....	....	....	....	....		1986-87	1987-88
	Dafoe, Byron	Wsh., L.A., Bos., Atl.	12	415	171	170	56	23478	1051	26	2.69	27	10	16	....	1686	65	3	2.31		1992-93	2003-04
	D'Alessio, Corrie	Hfd.	1	1	0	0	0	11	0	0	0.00	....	....	....	....	....	....	....	....		1992-93	1992-93
	Daley, Joe	Pit., Buf., Det.	4	105	34	44	19	5836	326	3	3.35	....	....	....	....	....	....	....	....		1968-69	1971-72
•	Damore, Nick	Bos.	1	1	1	0	0	60	3	0	3.00	....	....	....	....	....	....	....	....		1941-42	1941-42
	D'Amour, Marc	Cgy., Phi.	2	16	2	4	2	579	32	0	3.32	....	....	....	....	....	....	....	....		1985-86	1988-89
	Damphousse, Jean-Fr.	N.J.	1	6	1	3	0	294	12	0	2.45	....	....	....	....	....	....	....	....		2001-02	2001-02
§ •	Darragh, Jack	Ott.	1	1	0	0	0	2	0	0	0.00	....	....	....	....	....	....	....	....		1919-20	1919-20
	Daskalakis, Cleon	Bos.	3	12	3	4	1	506	41	0	4.86	....	....	....	....	....	....	....	....		1984-85	1986-87
	Davidson, John	St.L., NYR	10	301	123	124	39	17109	1004	7	3.52	31	16	14	....	1862	77	1	2.48		1973-74	1982-83
	Decourcy, Bob	NYR	1	1	0	1	0	29	6	0	12.41	....	....	....	....	....	....	....	....		1947-48	1947-48
	Defelice, Norm	Bos.	1	10	3	5	2	600	30	0	3.00	....	....	....	....	....	....	....	....		1956-57	1956-57
	DeJordy, Denis	Chi., L.A., Mtl., Det.	12	316	124	128	51	17798	929	15	3.13	18	6	9	....	946	55	0	3.49	1	1960-61	1973-74
	DelGuidice, Matt	Bos.	2	11	2	5	1	434	28	0	3.87	....	....	....	....	....	....	....	....		1990-91	1991-92
	Denis, Marc	Col., CBJ, T.B., Mtl.	11	349	112	179	31	19526	982	16	3.02	....	....	....	....	....	....	....	....		1996-97	2008-09
	DeRouville, Philippe	Pit.	2	3	1	2	0	171	9	0	3.16	....	....	....	....	....	....	....	....		1994-95	1996-97
	Desjardins, Gerry	L.A., Chi., NYI, Buf.	10	331	122	153	44	19014	1042	12	3.29	35	15	15	....	1874	108	0	3.46		1968-69	1977-78
	DesRochers, Patrick	Phx., Car.	2	11	2	6	1	540	33	0	3.67	....	....	....	....	....	....	....	....		2001-02	2002-03
•	Dickie, Bill	Chi.	1	1	1	0	0	60	3	0	3.00	....	....	....	....	....	....	....	....		1941-42	1941-42
	Dion, Connie	Det.	2	38	23	11	4	2280	119	1	3.13	5	1	4	....	300	17	0	3.40		1943-44	1944-45
	Dion, Michel	Que., Wpg., Pit.	6	227	60	118	32	12695	898	2	4.24	5	2	3	....	304	22	0	4.34		1979-80	1984-85
	Divis, Reinhard	St.L.	4	28	6	9	3	1212	67	0	3.32	1	0	0	....	18	0	0	0.00		2001-02	2005-06
•	Dolson, Dolly	Det.	3	93	35	41	17	5820	192	16	1.98	2	0	2	0	120	7	0	3.50		1928-29	1930-31
	Dopson, Rob	Pit.	1	2	0	0	0	45	3	0	4.00	....	....	....	....	....	....	....	....		1993-94	1993-94
	Dowie, Bruce	Tor.	1	2	0	1	0	72	4	0	3.33	....	....	....	....	....	....	....	....		1983-84	1983-84
	Draper, Tom	Wpg., Buf., NYI	6	53	19	23	5	2807	173	1	3.70	7	3	4	....	433	19	1	2.63		1988-89	1995-96
	Dryden, Dave	NYR, Chi., Buf., Edm.	9	203	66	76	31	10424	555	9	3.19	3	0	2	....	133	9	0	4.06		1961-62	1979-80
	Dryden, Ken	Mtl.	8	397	258	57	74	23352	870	46	2.24	112	80	32	....	6846	274	10	2.40	6	1970-71	1978-79
	Duffus, Parris	Phx.	1	1	0	0	0	29	1	0	2.07	....	....	....	....	....	....	....	....		1996-97	1996-97
	Dumas, Michel	Chi.	3	8	2	1	2	362	24	0	3.98	1	0	0	....	19	1	0	3.16		1974-75	1976-77
	Dunham, Mike	N.J., Nsh., NYR, Atl., NYI	10	394	141	178	44	21653	989	19	2.74	....	....	....	....	....	....	....	....		1996-97	2006-07
	Dupuis, Bob	Edm.	1	1	0	1	0	60	4	0	4.00	....	....	....	....	....	....	....	....		1979-80	1979-80
•	Durnan, Bill	Mtl.	7	383	208	112	62	22945	901	34	2.36	45	27	18	....	2871	99	2	2.07	2	1943-44	1949-50
	Dyck, Ed	Van.	3	49	8	28	5	2453	178	1	4.35	....	....	....	....	....	....	....	....		1971-72	1973-74
	Edwards, Don	Buf., Cgy., Tor.	10	459	208	155	74	26181	1449	16	3.32	42	16	21	....	2302	132	1	3.44		1976-77	1985-86
	Edwards, Gary	St.L., L.A., Cle., Min., Edm., Pit.	13	286	88	125	51	16002	973	10	3.65	11	5	4	....	537	34	0	3.80		1968-69	1981-82
	Edwards, Marv	Pit., Tor., Cal.	4	61	15	34	7	3467	218	2	3.77	....	....	....	....	....	....	....	....		1968-69	1973-74
•	Edwards, Roy	Chi., Det., Pit.	8	236	97	88	38	13109	637	12	2.92	4	0	3	....	206	11	0	3.20	1	1960-61	1973-74
	Eklund, Brian	T.B.	1	1	0	1	0	58	3	0	3.10	....	....	....	....	....	....	....	....		2005-06	2005-06
	Eliot, Darren	L.A., Det., Buf.	5	89	25	41	12	4931	377	1	4.59	1	0	0	....	40	7	0	10.50		1984-85	1988-89
	Ellacott, Ken	Van.	1	12	2	3	4	555	41	0	4.43	....	....	....	....	....	....	....	....		1982-83	1982-83
	Erickson, Chad	N.J.	1	2	1	1	0	120	9	0	4.50	....	....	....	....	....	....	....	....		1991-92	1991-92
‡	Esche, Robert	Phx., Phi.	8	186	78	64	22	10139	464	10	2.75	25	13	11	....	1405	64	1	2.73		1998-99	2006-07
	Esposito, Tony	Mtl., Chi.	16	886	423	306	151	52585	2563	76	2.92	99	45	53	....	6017	308	6	3.07	1	1968-69	1983-84
	Essensa, Bob	Wpg., Det., Edm., Phx., Van., Buf.	12	446	173	176	47	24215	1270	18	3.15	16	4	9	....	864	51	0	3.54		1988-89	2001-02
•	Evans, Claude	Mtl., Bos.	2	5	1	2	1	260	16	0	3.69	....	....	....	....	....	....	....	....		1954-55	1957-58
	Exelby, Randy	Mtl., Edm.	2	2	0	1	0	63	5	0	4.76	....	....	....	....	....	....	....	....		1988-89	1989-90
	Fankhouser, Scott	Atl.	2	23	4	12	2	1180	65	0	3.31	....	....	....	....	....	....	....	....		1999-00	2000-01
	Farr, Rocky	Buf.	3	19	2	6	3	722	42	0	3.49	....	....	....	....	....	....	....	....		1972-73	1974-75
	Favell, Doug	Phi., Tor., Col.	12	373	123	153	69	20771	1096	18	3.17	21	6	15	....	1270	66	1	3.12		1967-68	1978-79
	Fernandez, Manny	Dal., Min., Bos.	13	325	143	123	35	18580	775	15	2.50	11	3	4	....	571	19	0	2.00		1994-95	2008-09
	Fichaud, Eric	NYI, Nsh., Car., Mtl.	6	95	22	47	10	4799	251	2	3.14	....	....	....	....	....	....	....	....		1995-96	2000-01
	Finley, Brian	Nsh., Bos.	3	4	0	2	0	166	13	0	4.70	....	....	....	....	....	....	....	....		2002-03	2006-07
	Fiset, Stephane	Que., Col., L.A., Mtl.	13	390	164	153	44	21785	1114	16	3.07	14	1	7	....	563	37	0	3.94	1	1989-90	2001-02
	Fitzpatrick, Mark	L.A., NYI, Fla., T.B., Chi., Car.	12	329	113	136	49	18329	953	8	3.12	9	0	3	....	289	23	0	4.78		1988-89	1999-00
	Flaherty, Wade	S.J., NYI, T.B., Fla., Nsh.	11	120	27	56	9	5941	348	5	3.51	7	2	3	....	377	31	0	4.93		1991-92	2002-03
•	Forbes, Jake	Tor., Ham., NYA, Phi.	13	210	85	114	11	12922	594	19	2.76	2	0	2	0	120	7	0	3.50		1919-20	1932-33
	Ford, Brian	Que., Pit.	2	11	3	7	0	580	61	0	6.31	....	....	....	....	....	....	....	....		1983-84	1984-85
	Foster, Norm	Bos., Edm.	2	13	7	4	0	623	34	0	3.27	....	....	....	....	....	....	....	....		1990-91	1991-92
	Fountain, Mike	Van., Car., Ott.	4	11	2	6	0	483	28	1	3.48	....	....	....	....	....	....	....	....		1996-97	2000-01
•	Fowler, Hec	Bos.	1	7	1	6	0	409	42	0	6.16	....	....	....	....	....	....	....	....		1924-25	1924-25
	Francis, Emile	Chi., NYR	6	95	31	52	11	5660	355	1	3.76	....	....	....	....	....	....	....	....		1946-47	1951-52
•	Franks, Jimmy	Det., NYR, Bos.	4	42	12	23	7	2520	181	1	4.31	1	0	1	....	30	2	0	4.00	1	1936-37	1943-44
•	Frederick, Ray	Chi.	1	5	0	4	1	300	22	0	4.40	....	....	....	....	....	....	....	....		1954-55	1954-55
	Friesen, Karl	N.J.	1	4	0	2	1	130	16	0	7.38	....	....	....	....	....	....	....	....		1986-87	1986-87
	Froese, Bob	Phi., NYR	8	242	128	72	20	13451	694	13	3.10	18	3	9	....	830	55	0	3.98		1982-83	1989-90
	Fuhr, Grant	Edm., Tor., Buf., L.A., St.L., Cgy.	19	868	403	295	114	48945	2756	25	3.38	150	92	50	....	8834	430	6	2.92	5	1981-82	1999-00
	Fukufuji, Yutaka	L.A.	1	4	0	3	0	96	7	0	4.38	....	....	....	....	....	....	....	....		2006-07	2006-07
	Gage, Joaquin	Edm.	3	23	4	12	1	1076	67	0	3.74	....	....	....	....	....	....	....	....		1994-95	2000-01
	Gagnon, Dave	Det.	1	2	0	1	0	35	6	0	10.29	....	....	....	....	....	....	....	....		1990-91	1990-91
•	Gamble, Bruce	NYR, Bos., Tor., Phi.	10	327	110	150	46	18442	988	22	3.21	5	0	4	....	206	25	0	7.28		1958-59	1971-72
	Gamble, Troy	Van.	4	72	22	29	9	3804	229	1	3.61	4	1	3	....	249	16	0	3.86		1986-87	1991-92
•	Gardiner, Bert	NYR, Mtl., Chi., Bos.	6	144	49	68	27	8760	554	3	3.79	9	4	5	....	647	20	0	1.85		1935-36	1943-44
•	Gardiner, Charlie	Chi.	7	316	112	152	52	19687	664	42	2.02	21	12	6	3	1472	35	5	1.43	1	1927-28	1933-34
•	Gardner, George	Det., Van.	5	66	16	30	6	3313	207	0	3.75	....	....	....	....	....	....	....	....		1965-66	1971-72
	Garner, Tyrone	Cgy.	1	3	0	2	0	139	12	0	5.18	....	....	....	....	....	....	....	....		1998-99	1998-99
‡	Garnett, Michael	Atl.	1	24	10	7	4	1271	73	2	3.45	....	....	....	....	....	....	....	....		2005-06	2005-06
	Garrett, John	Hfd., Que., Van.	6	207	68	91	37	11763	837	1	4.27	9	4	3	....	461	33	0	4.30		1979-80	1984-85
	Gatherum, Dave	Det.	1	3	2	0	1	180	3	1	1.00	....	....	....	....	....	....	....	....	1	1953-54	1953-54
	Gauthier, Paul	Mtl.	1	1	0	0	1	70	2	0	1.71	....	....	....	....	....	....	....	....		1937-38	1937-38
	Gauthier, Sean	S.J.	1	1	0	0	0	3	0	0	0.00	....	....	....	....	....	....	....	....		1998-99	1998-99
•	Gelineau, Jack	Bos., Chi.	4	143	46	64	33	8580	447	7	3.13	4	1	2	....	260	7	1	1.62		1948-49	1953-54
	Giacomin, Ed	NYR, Det.	13	609	289	209	96	35633	1672	54	2.82	65	29	35	....	3838	180	1	2.81		1965-66	1977-78
	Gilbert, Gilles	Min., Bos., Det.	14	416	192	143	60	23677	1290	18	3.27	32	17	15	....	1919	97	3	3.03		1969-70	1982-83
	Gill, Andre	Bos.	1	5	3	2	0	270	13	1	2.89	....	....	....	....	....	....	....	....		1967-68	1967-68
•	Goodman, Paul	Chi.	3	52	23	20	9	3240	117	6	2.17	3	0	3	....	187	10	0	3.21	1	1937-38	1940-41
	Gordon, Scott	Que.	2	23	2	16	0	1082	101	0	5.60	....	....	....	....	....	....	....	....		1989-90	1990-91
	Gosselin, Mario	Que., L.A., Hfd.	9	241	91	107	14	12857	801	6	3.74	32	16	15	....	1816	99	0	3.27		1983-84	1993-94
	Goverde, David	L.A.	3	5	1	4	0	278	29	0	6.26	....	....	....	....	....	....	....	....		1991-92	1993-94
	Grahame, Ron	Bos., L.A., Que.	4	114	50	43	15	6472	409	5	3.79	4	2	1	....	202	7	0	2.08		1977-78	1980-81
•	Grant, Benny	Tor., NYA, Bos.	6	52	17	27	4	3036	188	4	3.72	....	....	....	....	....	....	....	....		1928-29	1943-44

Name	NHL Teams	NHL Seasons	Regular Schedule GP	W	L	T	Mins	GA	SO	Avg	Playoffs GP	W	L	T	Mins	GA	SO	Avg	NHL Cup Wins	First NHL Season	Last NHL Season
Grant, Doug	Det., St.L.	7	77	27	34	8	4199	280	2	4.00	....	....	....	....	....	....	....	....		1973-74	1979-80
Gratton, Gilles	St.L., NYR	2	47	13	18	9	2299	154	0	4.02	....	....	....	....	....	....	....	....		1975-76	1976-77
Gray, Gerry	Det., NYI	2	8	1	5	1	440	35	0	4.77	....	....	....	....	....	....	....	....		1970-71	1972-73
Gray, Harrison	Det.	1	1	0	1	0	40	5	0	7.50	....	....	....	....	....	....	....	....		1963-64	1963-64
Greenlay, Mike	Edm.	1	2	0	0	0	20	4	0	12.00	....	....	....	....	....	....	....	....		1989-90	1989-90
Guenette, Steve	Pit., Cgy.	5	35	19	16	0	1958	122	1	3.74	....	....	....	....	....	....	....	....		1986-87	1990-91
Gustafson, Derek	Min.	2	5	1	3	0	265	10	0	2.26	....	....	....	....	....	....	....	....		2000-01	2001-02
Hackett, Jeff	NYI, S.J., Chi., Mtl., Bos., Phi.	15	500	166	244	56	28125	1361	26	2.90	12	3	7	....	610	36	0	3.54		1988-89	2003-04
● Hainsworth, George	Mtl., Tor.	11	465	246	145	74	29087	937	94	1.93	52	22	25	5	3486	112	8	1.93	2	1926-27	1936-37
Hall, Glenn	Det., Chi., St.L.	19	906	407	326	163	53484	2222	84	2.49	115	49	65	....	6899	320	6	2.78	2	1951-52	1970-71
Hamel, Pierre	Tor., Wpg.	4	69	13	41	7	3766	276	0	4.40	....	....	....	....	....	....	....	....		1974-75	1980-81
Hanlon, Glen	Van., St.L., NYR, Det.	14	477	167	202	61	26037	1561	13	3.60	35	11	15	....	1756	92	4	3.14		1977-78	1990-91
Harrison, Paul	Min., Tor., Pit., Buf.	7	109	28	59	9	5806	408	2	4.22	4	0	1	....	157	9	0	3.44		1975-76	1981-82
‡ Hasek, Dominik	Chi., Buf., Det., Ott.	16	735	389	223	95	42837	1572	81	2.20	119	65	49	....	7318	246	14	2.02	2	1990-91	2007-08
‡ Hauser, Adam	L.A.	1	1	0	0	0	51	6	0	7.06	....	....	....	....	....	....	....	....		2005-06	2005-06
Hayward, Brian	Wpg., Mtl., Min., S.J.	11	357	143	156	37	20025	1242	8	3.72	37	11	18	....	1803	104	0	3.46		1982-83	1992-93
Head, Don	Bos.	1	38	9	26	3	2280	158	2	4.16	....	....	....	....	....	....	....	....		1961-62	1961-62
Healy, Glenn	L.A., NYI, NYR, Tor.	15	437	166	190	47	24256	1361	13	3.37	37	13	15	....	1930	108	0	3.36	1	1985-86	2000-01
Hebert, Guy	St.L., Ana., NYR	10	491	191	222	56	27889	1307	28	2.81	14	4	7	....	744	33	1	2.66		1991-92	2000-01
● Hebert, Sammy	Tor., Ott.	2	4	2	1	0	200	19	0	5.70	....	....	....	....	....	....	....	....	1	1917-18	1923-24
Heinz, Rick	St.L., Van.	5	49	14	19	5	2356	159	2	4.05	1	0	0	....	8	1	0	7.50		1980-81	1984-85
Henderson, John	Bos.	2	46	15	15	15	2688	113	5	2.52	2	0	2	....	120	8	0	4.00		1954-55	1955-56
● Henry, Gord	Bos.	4	3	1	2	0	180	5	1	1.67	5	0	4	....	283	21	0	4.45		1948-49	1952-53
● Henry, Jim	NYR, Chi., Bos.	9	406	161	173	70	24355	1166	28	2.87	29	11	18	....	1741	81	2	2.79		1941-42	1954-55
Herron, Denis	Pit., K.C., Mtl.	14	462	146	203	76	25608	1579	10	3.70	15	5	10	....	901	50	0	3.33		1972-73	1985-86
Hextall, Ron	Phi., Que., NYI	13	608	296	214	69	34750	1723	23	2.97	93	47	43	....	5456	276	2	3.04		1986-87	1998-99
● Highton, Hec	Chi.	1	24	10	14	0	1440	108	0	4.50	....	....	....	....	....	....	....	....		1943-44	1943-44
§ ● Himes, Normie	NYA	2	2	0	1	0	79	3	0	2.28	....	....	....	....	....	....	....	....		1927-28	1928-29
Hirsch, Corey	NYR, Van., Wsh., Dal.	7	108	34	45	14	5775	301	4	3.13	6	2	3	....	338	21	0	3.73		1992-93	2002-03
Hnilicka, Milan	NYR, Atl., L.A.	5	121	29	67	13	6509	359	5	3.31	....	....	....	....	....	....	....	....		1999-00	2003-04
Hodge, Charlie	Mtl., Oak., Van.	14	358	150	125	61	20573	925	24	2.70	16	7	8	....	804	32	2	2.39	6	1954-55	1970-71
Hodson, Kevin	Det., T.B.	6	71	17	18	10	2910	134	4	2.76	1	0	0	....	1	0	0	0.00	2	1995-96	2002-03
Hoffort, Bruce	Phi.	2	9	4	0	3	368	22	0	3.59	....	....	....	....	....	....	....	....		1989-90	1990-91
Hoganson, Paul	Pit.	1	2	0	1	0	57	7	0	7.37	....	....	....	....	....	....	....	....		1970-71	1970-71
Hogosta, Goran	NYI, Que.	2	22	5	12	3	1208	83	1	4.12	....	....	....	....	....	....	....	....		1977-78	1979-80
Holden, Mark	Mtl., Wpg.	4	8	2	2	1	372	25	0	4.03	....	....	....	....	....	....	....	....		1981-82	1984-85
Holland, Ken	Hfd., Det.	2	4	0	2	1	206	17	0	4.95	....	....	....	....	....	....	....	....		1980-81	1983-84
Holland, Rob	Pit.	2	44	11	22	9	2513	171	1	4.08	....	....	....	....	....	....	....	....		1979-80	1980-81
● Holmes, Hap	Tor., Det.	4	103	39	54	10	6510	264	17	2.43	2	1	1	0	120	7	0	3.50	1	1917-18	1927-28
‡ Holmqvist, Johan	NYR, T.B., Dal.	5	99	48	34	9	5264	262	3	2.99	6	2	4	....	370	18	0	2.92		2000-01	2007-08
‡ Holt, Chris	NYR, St.L.	2	2	0	0	0	29	0	0	0.00	....	....	....	....	....	....	....	....		2005-06	2008-09
§ ● Horner, Red	Tor.	2	2	0	0	0	3	1	0	20.00	....	....	....	....	....	....	....	....		1928-29	1931-32
Houle, Martin	Phi.	1	1	0	0	0	2	1	0	30.00	....	....	....	....	....	....	....	....		2006-07	2006-07
Hrivnak, Jim	Wsh., Wpg., St.L.	5	85	34	30	3	4217	262	0	3.73	....	....	....	....	....	....	....	....		1989-90	1993-94
Hrudey, Kelly	NYI, L.A., S.J.	15	677	271	265	88	38084	2174	17	3.43	85	36	46	....	5163	283	0	3.29		1983-84	1997-98
Hurme, Jani	Ott., Fla.	4	76	29	25	11	4041	176	6	2.61	....	....	....	....	....	....	....	....		1999-00	2002-03
Ing, Peter	Tor., Edm., Det.	4	74	20	37	9	3941	266	1	4.05	....	....	....	....	....	....	....	....		1989-90	1993-94
Inness, Gary	Pit., Phi., Wsh.	7	162	58	61	27	8710	494	2	3.40	9	5	4	....	540	24	0	2.67		1973-74	1980-81
Irbe, Arturs	S.J., Dal., Van., Car.	13	568	218	236	79	32066	1513	33	2.83	51	23	27	....	2981	142	1	2.86		1991-92	2003-04
Ireland, Randy	Buf.	1	2	0	0	0	30	3	0	6.00	....	....	....	....	....	....	....	....		1978-79	1978-79
Irons, Robbie	St.L.	1	1	0	0	0	3	0	0	0.00	....	....	....	....	....	....	....	....		1968-69	1968-69
● Ironstone, Joe	Ott., NYA, Tor.	3	2	0	0	1	110	3	1	1.64	....	....	....	....	....	....	....	....		1924-25	1927-28
Jablonski, Pat	St.L., T.B., Mtl., Phx., Car.	8	128	28	62	18	6634	413	1	3.74	4	0	0	....	139	6	0	2.59		1989-90	1997-98
Jackson, Doug	Chi.	1	6	2	3	1	360	42	0	7.00	....	....	....	....	....	....	....	....		1947-48	1947-48
Jackson, Percy	Bos., NYA, NYR	4	7	1	3	1	392	26	0	3.98	....	....	....	....	....	....	....	....		1931-32	1935-36
Jaks, Pauli	L.A.	1	1	0	0	0	40	2	0	3.00	....	....	....	....	....	....	....	....		1994-95	1994-95
Janaszak, Steve	Min., Col.	2	3	0	1	1	160	15	0	5.63	....	....	....	....	....	....	....	....		1979-80	1981-82
Janecyk, Bob	Chi., L.A.	6	110	43	47	13	6250	432	2	4.15	3	0	3	....	184	10	0	3.26		1983-84	1988-89
§ ● Jenkins, Roger	NYA	1	1	0	1	0	30	7	0	14.00	....	....	....	....	....	....	....	....		1938-39	1938-39
Jensen, Al	Det., Wsh., L.A.	7	179	95	53	18	9974	557	8	3.35	12	5	5	....	598	32	0	3.21		1980-81	1986-87
Jensen, Darren	Phi.	2	30	15	10	1	1496	95	2	3.81	....	....	....	....	....	....	....	....		1984-85	1985-86
Johnson, Bob	St.L., Pit.	2	24	9	9	1	1059	66	0	3.74	....	....	....	....	....	....	....	....		1972-73	1974-75
Johnston, Eddie	Bos., Tor., St.L., Chi.	16	592	234	257	80	34216	1852	32	3.25	18	7	10	....	1023	57	1	3.34	2	1962-63	1977-78
Joseph, Curtis	St.L., Edm., Tor., Det., Phx., Cgy.	19	943	454	352	96	54054	2516	51	2.79	133	63	66	....	8106	327	16	2.42		1989-90	2008-09
Junkin, Joe	Bos.	1	1	0	0	0	8	0	0	0.00	....	....	....	....	....	....	....	....		1968-69	1968-69
Kaarela, Jari	Col.	1	5	2	2	0	220	22	0	6.00	....	....	....	....	....	....	....	....		1980-81	1980-81
Kamppuri, Hannu	N.J.	1	13	1	10	1	645	54	0	5.02	....	....	....	....	....	....	....	....		1984-85	1984-85
● Karakas, Mike	Chi., Mtl.	8	336	114	169	53	20614	1002	28	2.92	23	11	12	0	1434	72	3	3.01	1	1935-36	1945-46
Keans, Doug	L.A., Bos.	9	210	96	64	26	11388	666	4	3.51	9	2	6	....	432	34	0	4.72		1979-80	1987-88
● Keenan, Don	Bos.	1	1	0	1	0	60	4	0	4.00	....	....	....	....	....	....	....	....		1958-59	1958-59
‡ Keetley, Matt	Cgy.	1	1	0	0	0	9	0	0	0.00	....	....	....	....	....	....	....	....		2007-08	2007-08
● Kerr, Dave	Mtl.M., NYA, NYR	11	427	203	148	75	26639	954	51	2.15	40	18	19	3	2616	76	8	1.74	1	1930-31	1940-41
Kidd, Trevor	Cgy., Car., Fla., Tor.	12	387	140	162	52	21426	1014	19	2.84	10	3	5	....	550	36	1	3.93		1991-92	2003-04
King, Scott	Det.	2	2	0	0	0	61	3	0	2.95	....	....	....	....	....	....	....	....		1990-91	1991-92
Kleisinger, Terry	NYR	1	4	0	2	0	191	14	0	4.40	....	....	....	....	....	....	....	....		1985-86	1985-86
Klymkiw, Julian	NYR	1	1	0	0	0	19	2	0	6.32	....	....	....	....	....	....	....	....		1958-59	1958-59
Knickle, Rick	L.A.	2	14	7	6	0	706	44	0	3.74	....	....	....	....	....	....	....	....		1992-93	1993-94
Kochan, Dieter	T.B., Min.	4	21	1	11	1	849	56	0	3.96	....	....	....	....	....	....	....	....		1999-00	2002-03
‡ Kolesnik, Vitali	Col.	1	8	3	3	0	370	20	0	3.24	....	....	....	....	....	....	....	....		2005-06	2005-06
Kolzig, Olaf	Wsh., T.B.	17	719	303	297	87	41671	1885	35	2.71	45	20	24	....	2799	100	6	2.14		1989-90	2008-09
Konstantinov, Evgeny	T.B.	2	2	0	0	0	21	1	0	2.86	....	....	....	....	....	....	....	....		2000-01	2002-03
Kuntar, Les	Mtl.	1	6	2	2	0	302	16	0	3.18	....	....	....	....	....	....	....	....		1993-94	1993-94
Kurt, Gary	Cal.	1	16	1	7	5	838	60	0	4.30	....	....	....	....	....	....	....	....		1971-72	1971-72
Labbe, Jean-Francois	NYR, CBJ	3	15	3	6	0	628	36	0	3.44	....	....	....	....	....	....	....	....		1999-00	2002-03
Labrecque, Patrick	Mtl.	1	2	0	1	0	98	7	0	4.29	....	....	....	....	....	....	....	....		1995-96	1995-96
Lacher, Blaine	Bos.	2	47	22	16	4	2636	123	4	2.80	5	1	4	....	283	12	0	2.54		1994-95	1995-96
‡ LaCosta, Dan	CBJ	2	4	2	0	0	169	4	1	1.42	....	....	....	....	....	....	....	....		2007-08	2008-09
● Lacroix, Frenchy	Mtl.	2	5	1	4	0	280	16	0	3.43	....	....	....	....	....	....	....	....		1925-26	1926-27
LaFerriere, Rick	Col.	1	1	0	0	0	20	1	0	3.00	....	....	....	....	....	....	....	....		1981-82	1981-82
LaForest, Mark	Det., Phi., Tor., Ott.	6	103	25	54	4	5032	354	2	4.22	2	1	0	....	48	1	0	1.25		1985-86	1993-94
Lajeunesse, Simon	Ott.	1	1	0	0	0	24	0	0	0.00	....	....	....	....	....	....	....	....		2001-02	2001-02
Lamothe, Marc	Chi., Det.	2	4	2	1	1	241	13	0	3.24	....	....	....	....	....	....	....	....		1999-00	2003-04
‡ Langkow, Scott	Wpg., Phx., Atl.	4	20	3	12	1	943	68	0	4.33	....	....	....	....	....	....	....	....		1995-96	1999-00
● Larocque, Michel	Mtl., Tor., Phi., St.L.	11	312	160	89	45	17615	978	17	3.33	14	6	6	....	759	37	1	2.92	4	1973-74	1983-84
Larocque, Michel	Chi.	1	3	0	2	0	152	9	0	3.55	....	....	....	....	....	....	....	....		2000-01	2000-01
‡ Lasak, Jan	Nsh.	2	6	0	4	0	267	18	0	4.04	....	....	....	....	....	....	....	....		2001-02	2002-03
Laskoski, Gary	L.A.	2	59	19	27	5	2942	228	0	4.65	....	....	....	....	....	....	....	....		1982-83	1983-84
Laxton, Gord	Pit.	4	17	4	9	0	800	74	0	5.55	....	....	....	....	....	....	....	....		1975-76	1978-79
LeBlanc, Ray	Chi.	1	1	1	0	0	60	1	0	1.00	....	....	....	....	....	....	....	....		1991-92	1991-92
§ ● Leduc, Albert	Mtl.	1	1	0	0	0	2	1	0	30.00	....	....	....	....	....	....	....	....		1931-32	1931-32
Legris, Claude	Det.	2	4	0	1	1	91	4	0	2.64	....	....	....	....	....	....	....	....		1980-81	1981-82
● Lehman, Hugh	Chi.	2	48	20	24	4	3047	136	6	2.68	2	0	1	1	120	10	0	5.00		1926-27	1927-28
Lemelin, Reggie	Atl., Cgy., Bos.	15	507	236	162	63	28006	1613	12	3.46	59	23	25	....	3119	186	2	3.58		1978-79	1992-93
Lenarduzzi, Mike	Hfd.	2	4	1	1	1	189	10	0	3.17	....	....	....	....	....	....	....	....		1992-93	1993-94
Lessard, Mario	L.A.	6	240	92	97	39	13529	843	9	3.74	20	6	12	....	1136	83	0	4.38		1978-79	1983-84
Levasseur, Jean-Louis	Min.	1	1	0	1	0	60	7	0	7.00	....	....	....	....	....	....	....	....		1979-80	1979-80
§ ● Levinsky, Alex	Tor.	1	1	0	0	0	1	1	0	60.00	....	....	....	....	....	....	....	....		1931-32	1931-32
● Lindbergh, Pelle	Phi.	5	157	87	49	15	9150	503	7	3.30	23	12	10	....	1214	63	3	3.11		1981-82	1985-86

Name	NHL Teams	NHL Seasons	Regular Schedule GP	W	L	T	Mins	GA	SO	Avg	Playoffs GP	W	L	T	Mins	GA	SO	Avg	NHL Cup Wins	First NHL Season	Last NHL Season
• Lindsay, Bert	Mtl.W., Tor.	2	20	6	14	0	1238	118	0	5.72	....	....	....	....	....	....	....	....		1917-18	1918-19
Little, Neil	Phi.	2	2	0	2	0	93	6	0	3.87	....	....	....	....	....	....	....	....		2001-02	2003-04
Littman, David	Buf., T.B.	3	3	0	2	0	141	14	0	5.96	....	....	....	....	....	....	....	....		1990-91	1992-93
Liut, Mike	St.L., Hfd., Wsh.	13	664	294	271	74	38215	2221	25	3.49	67	29	32	....	3814	215	2	3.38		1979-80	1991-92
Lockett, Ken	Van.	2	55	13	15	8	2348	131	2	3.35	1	0	1	....	60	6	0	6.00		1974-75	1975-76
• Lockhart, Howard	Tor., Que., Ham., Bos.	5	59	16	41	0	3413	287	1	5.05	....	....	....	....	....	....	....	....		1919-20	1924-25
LoPresti, Pete	Min., Edm.	6	175	43	102	20	9858	668	5	4.07	2	0	2	....	77	6	0	4.68		1974-75	1980-81
• LoPresti, Sam	Chi.	2	74	30	38	6	4530	236	4	3.13	8	3	5	....	530	17	1	1.92		1940-41	1941-42
Lorenz, Danny	NYI	3	8	1	5	0	357	25	0	4.20	....	....	....	....	....	....	....	....		1990-91	1992-93
Loustel, Ron	Wpg.	1	1	0	1	0	60	10	0	10.00	....	....	....	....	....	....	....	....		1980-81	1980-81
Low, Ron	Tor., Wsh., Det., Que., Edm., N.J.	11	382	102	203	38	20502	1463	4	4.28	7	1	6	....	452	29	0	3.85		1972-73	1984-85
Lozinski, Larry	Det.	1	30	6	11	7	1459	105	0	4.32	....	....	....	....	....	....	....	....		1980-81	1980-81
• Lumley, Harry	Det., NYR, Chi., Tor., Bos.	16	803	330	329	142	48044	2206	71	2.75	76	29	47	....	4778	198	7	2.49	1	1943-44	1959-60
MacKenzie, Shawn	N.J.	1	4	0	1	0	130	15	0	6.92	....	....	....	....	....	....	....	....		1982-83	1982-83
Madeley, Darrin	Ott.	3	39	4	23	5	1928	140	0	4.36	....	....	....	....	....	....	....	....		1992-93	1994-95
Malarchuk, Clint	Que., Wsh., Buf.	10	338	141	130	45	19030	1100	12	3.47	15	2	9	....	781	56	0	4.30		1981-82	1991-92
Maneluk, George	NYI	1	4	1	1	0	140	15	0	6.43	....	....	....	....	....	....	....	....		1990-91	1990-91
Maniago, Cesare	Tor., Mtl., NYR, Min., Van.	15	568	190	257	97	32569	1773	30	3.27	36	15	21	....	2247	100	3	2.67		1960-61	1977-78
‡ Maracle, Norm	Det., Atl.	5	66	14	33	8	3430	177	1	3.10	2	0	0	....	58	3	0	3.10		1997-98	2001-02
‡ Markkanen, Jussi	Edm., NYR	5	128	43	47	15	6610	297	7	2.70	7	3	3	....	374	14	1	2.25		2001-02	2006-07
Marois, Jean	Tor., Chi.	2	3	1	2	0	180	15	0	5.00	....	....	....	....	....	....	....	....		1943-44	1953-54
Martin, Seth	St.L.	1	30	8	10	7	1552	67	1	2.59	2	0	0	....	73	5	0	4.11		1967-68	1967-68
Mason, Bob	Wsh., Chi., Que., Van.	8	145	55	65	16	7988	500	1	3.76	5	2	3	....	369	12	1	1.95		1983-84	1990-91
Mattsson, Markus	Wpg., Min., L.A.	4	92	21	46	14	5007	343	6	4.11	....	....	....	....	....	....	....	....		1979-80	1983-84
May, Darrell	St.L.	2	6	1	5	0	364	31	0	5.11	....	....	....	....	....	....	....	....		1985-86	1987-88
Mayer, Gilles	Tor.	4	9	2	6	1	540	24	0	2.67	....	....	....	....	....	....	....	....		1949-50	1955-56
• McAuley, Ken	NYR	2	96	17	64	15	5740	537	1	5.61	....	....	....	....	....	....	....	....		1943-44	1944-45
McCartan, Jack	NYR	2	12	2	7	3	680	42	1	3.71	....	....	....	....	....	....	....	....		1959-60	1960-61
• McCool, Frank	Tor.	2	72	34	31	7	4320	242	4	3.36	13	8	5	....	807	30	4	2.23	1	1944-45	1945-46
McDuffe, Peter	St.L., NYR, K.C., Det.	5	57	11	36	6	3207	218	0	4.08	1	0	1	....	60	7	0	7.00		1971-72	1975-76
McGrattan, Tom	Det.	1	1	0	0	0	8	1	0	7.50	....	....	....	....	....	....	....	....		1947-48	1947-48
McKay, Ross	Hfd.	1	1	0	0	0	35	3	0	5.14	....	....	....	....	....	....	....	....		1990-91	1990-91
McKenzie, Bill	Det., K.C., Col.	6	91	18	49	13	4776	326	2	4.10	....	....	....	....	....	....	....	....		1973-74	1979-80
McKichan, Steve	Van.	1	1	0	0	0	20	2	0	6.00	....	....	....	....	....	....	....	....		1990-91	1990-91
McLachlan, Murray	Tor.	1	2	0	1	0	25	4	0	9.60	....	....	....	....	....	....	....	....		1970-71	1970-71
McLean, Kirk	N.J., Van., Car., Fla., NYR	16	612	245	262	72	35090	1904	22	3.26	68	34	34	....	4189	198	6	2.84		1985-86	2000-01
McLelland, Dave	Van.	1	2	1	1	0	120	10	0	5.00	....	....	....	....	....	....	....	....		1972-73	1972-73
McLennan, Jamie	NYI, St.L., Min., Cgy., NYR, Fla.	11	254	80	109	36	13834	617	13	2.68	5	0	2	....	134	7	0	3.13		1993-94	2006-07
McLeod, Don	Det., Phi.	2	18	3	10	1	879	74	0	5.05	....	....	....	....	....	....	....	....		1970-71	1971-72
McLeod, Jim	St.L.	1	16	6	6	4	880	44	0	3.00	....	....	....	....	....	....	....	....		1971-72	1971-72
McNamara, Gerry	Tor.	2	7	2	2	1	323	14	0	2.60	....	....	....	....	....	....	....	....		1960-61	1969-70
• McNeil, Gerry	Mtl.	8	276	119	105	52	16535	649	28	2.36	35	17	18	....	2284	72	5	1.89	3	1947-48	1957-58
McRae, Gord	Tor.	5	71	30	22	10	3799	221	1	3.49	8	2	5	....	454	22	0	2.91		1972-73	1977-78
McVicar, Rob	Van.	1	1	0	0	0	3	0	0	0.00	....	....	....	....	....	....	....	....		2005-06	2005-06
Melanson, Roland	NYI, Min., L.A., N.J., Mtl.	11	291	129	106	33	16452	995	6	3.63	23	4	9	....	801	59	0	4.42	3	1980-81	1991-92
Meloche, Gilles	Chi., Cal., Cle., Min., Pit.	18	788	270	351	131	45401	2756	20	3.64	45	21	19	....	2464	143	2	3.48		1970-71	1987-88
Micalef, Corrado	Det.	5	113	26	59	15	5794	409	2	4.24	3	0	0	....	49	8	0	9.80		1981-82	1985-86
Michaud, Alfie	Van.	1	2	0	1	0	69	5	0	4.35	....	....	....	....	....	....	....	....		1999-00	1999-00
Michaud, Olivier	Mtl.	1	1	0	0	0	18	0	0	0.00	....	....	....	....	....	....	....	....		2001-02	2001-02
Middlebrook, Lindsay	Wpg., Min., N.J., Edm.	4	37	3	23	6	1845	152	0	4.94	....	....	....	....	....	....	....	....		1979-80	1982-83
• Millar, Al	Bos.	1	6	1	4	1	360	25	0	4.17	....	....	....	....	....	....	....	....		1957-58	1957-58
Millen, Greg	Pit., Hfd., St.L., Que., Chi., Det.	14	604	215	284	89	35377	2281	17	3.87	59	27	29	....	3383	193	0	3.42		1978-79	1991-92
• Miller, Joe	NYA, NYR, Pit., Phi.	4	127	24	87	16	7871	383	16	2.92	3	2	1	0	180	3	1	1.00	1	1927-28	1930-31
Minard, Mike	Edm.	1	1	1	0	0	60	3	0	3.00	....	....	....	....	....	....	....	....		1999-00	1999-00
Mio, Eddie	Edm., NYR, Det.	7	192	64	73	30	10428	705	4	4.06	17	9	7	....	986	63	0	3.83		1979-80	1985-86
• Mitchell, Mike	Tor.	3	22	10	9	0	1190	88	0	4.44	....	....	....	....	....	....	....	....	1	1919-20	1921-22
Moffat, Mike	Bos.	3	19	7	7	2	979	70	0	4.29	11	6	5	....	663	38	0	3.44		1981-82	1983-84
Moog, Andy	Edm., Bos., Dal., Mtl.	18	713	372	209	88	40151	2097	28	3.13	132	68	57	....	7452	377	4	3.04	3	1980-81	1997-98
• Moore, Alfie	NYA, Chi., Det.	4	21	7	14	0	1290	81	1	3.77	3	1	2	....	180	7	0	2.33	1	1936-37	1939-40
Moore, Robbie	Phi., Wsh.	2	6	3	1	1	257	8	2	1.87	5	3	2	....	268	18	0	4.03		1978-79	1982-83
Morissette, Jean-Guy	Mtl.	1	1	0	1	0	36	4	0	6.67	....	....	....	....	....	....	....	....		1963-64	1963-64
Morrison, Mike	Edm., Ott., Phx.	2	29	11	7	3	1226	67	0	3.28	....	....	....	....	....	....	....	....		2005-06	2006-07
Moss, Tyler	Cgy., Car., Van.	4	30	6	16	1	1496	81	0	3.25	....	....	....	....	....	....	....	....		1997-98	2002-03
• Mowers, Johnny	Det.	4	152	65	61	26	9350	399	15	2.56	32	19	13	....	2000	85	2	2.55	1	1940-41	1946-47
Mrazek, Jerome	Phi.	1	1	0	0	0	6	1	0	10.00	....	....	....	....	....	....	....	....		1975-76	1975-76
§ • Mummery, Harry	Que., Ham.	2	4	2	1	0	192	20	0	6.25	....	....	....	....	....	....	....	....		1919-20	1921-22
‡ Munro, Adam	Chi.	2	17	4	10	3	927	51	1	3.30	....	....	....	....	....	....	....	....		2003-04	2005-06
§ • Munro, Dunc	Mtl.M.	1	1	0	0	0	2	0	0	0.00	....	....	....	....	....	....	....	....		1924-25	1924-25
• Murphy, Hal	Mtl.	1	1	1	0	0	60	4	0	4.00	....	....	....	....	....	....	....	....		1952-53	1952-53
• Murray, Mickey	Mtl.	1	1	0	1	0	60	4	0	4.00	....	....	....	....	....	....	....	....		1929-30	1929-30
Muzzatti, Jason	Cgy., Hfd., NYR, S.J.	5	62	13	25	10	3014	167	1	3.32	....	....	....	....	....	....	....	....		1993-94	1997-98
Myllys, Jarmo	Min., S.J.	4	39	4	27	1	1846	161	0	5.23	....	....	....	....	....	....	....	....		1988-89	1991-92
Mylnikov, Sergei	Que.	1	10	1	7	2	568	47	0	4.96	....	....	....	....	....	....	....	....		1989-90	1989-90
Myre, Phil	Mtl., Atl., St.L., Phi., Col., Buf.	14	439	149	198	76	25220	1482	14	3.53	12	6	5	....	747	41	1	3.29		1969-70	1982-83
Naumenko, Gregg	Ana.	1	2	0	1	0	70	7	0	6.00	....	....	....	....	....	....	....	....		2000-01	2000-01
Newton, Cam	Pit.	2	16	4	7	1	814	51	0	3.76	....	....	....	....	....	....	....	....		1970-71	1972-73
‡ Noronen, Mika	Buf., Van.	5	71	23	32	6	3652	163	3	2.68	....	....	....	....	....	....	....	....		2000-01	2005-06
‡ Norrena, Fredrik	CBJ	3	100	35	45	11	5235	243	5	2.79	....	....	....	....	....	....	....	....		2006-07	2008-09
Norris, Jack	Bos., Chi., L.A.	4	58	20	25	4	3119	202	2	3.89	....	....	....	....	....	....	....	....		1964-65	1970-71
Nurminen, Pasi	Atl.	3	125	48	54	12	7059	338	5	2.87	....	....	....	....	....	....	....	....		2001-02	2003-04
Oleschuk, Bill	K.C., Col.	4	55	7	28	10	2835	188	1	3.98	....	....	....	....	....	....	....	....		1975-76	1979-80
• Olesevich, Dan	NYR	1	1	0	0	1	29	2	0	4.14	....	....	....	....	....	....	....	....		1961-62	1961-62
O'Neill, Mike	Wpg., Ana.	4	21	0	9	2	855	61	0	4.28	....	....	....	....	....	....	....	....		1991-92	1996-97
Ouellet, Maxime	Phi., Wsh., Van.	3	12	2	6	2	663	34	1	3.08	....	....	....	....	....	....	....	....		2000-01	2005-06
Ouimet, Ted	St.L.	1	1	0	1	0	60	2	0	2.00	....	....	....	....	....	....	....	....		1968-69	1968-69
Pageau, Paul	L.A.	1	1	0	1	0	60	8	0	8.00	....	....	....	....	....	....	....	....		1980-81	1980-81
• Paille, Marcel	NYR	7	107	32	52	22	6342	362	2	3.42	....	....	....	....	....	....	....	....		1957-58	1964-65
Palmateer, Mike	Tor., Wsh.	8	356	149	138	52	20131	1183	17	3.53	29	12	17	....	1765	89	2	3.03		1976-77	1983-84
Pang, Darren	Chi.	3	81	27	35	7	4252	287	0	4.05	6	1	3	....	250	18	0	4.32		1984-85	1988-89
Parent, Bernie	Bos., Phi., Tor.	13	608	271	198	121	35136	1493	54	2.55	71	38	33	....	4302	174	6	2.43	2	1965-66	1978-79
Parent, Bob	Tor.	2	3	0	2	0	160	15	0	5.63	....	....	....	....	....	....	....	....		1981-82	1982-83
Parent, Rich	St.L., T.B., Pit.	4	32	7	11	5	1561	82	1	3.15	....	....	....	....	....	....	....	....		1997-98	2000-01
Parro, Dave	Wsh.	4	77	21	36	10	4015	274	2	4.09	....	....	....	....	....	....	....	....		1980-81	1983-84
Passmore, Steve	Edm., Chi., L.A.	6	93	23	44	12	5045	235	2	2.79	3	0	2	....	138	6	0	2.61		1998-99	2003-04
§ • Patrick, Lester	NYR	1	....	....	....	....	....	....	....	....	1	1	0	0	46	1	0	1.30	1	1927-28	1927-28
‡ Patzold, Dimitri	S.J.	1	3	0	0	0	44	4	0	5.45	....	....	....	....	....	....	....	....		2007-08	2007-08
Peeters, Pete	Phi., Bos., Wsh.	13	489	246	155	51	27699	1424	21	3.08	71	35	35	....	4200	232	2	3.31		1978-79	1990-91
Pelletier, Jean-Marc	Phi., Phx.	3	7	1	4	0	354	23	0	3.90	....	....	....	....	....	....	....	....		1998-99	2003-04
Pelletier, Marcel	Chi., NYR	2	8	1	6	0	395	32	0	4.86	....	....	....	....	....	....	....	....		1950-51	1962-63
Penney, Steve	Mtl., Wpg.	5	91	35	38	12	5194	313	1	3.62	27	15	12	....	1604	72	4	2.69		1983-84	1987-88
• Perreault, Bob	Mtl., Det., Bos.	3	31	8	16	7	1827	103	3	3.38	....	....	....	....	....	....	....	....		1955-56	1962-63
Pettie, Jim	Bos.	3	21	9	7	2	1157	71	1	3.68	....	....	....	....	....	....	....	....		1976-77	1978-79
Pietrangelo, Frank	Pit., Hfd.	7	141	46	59	6	7141	490	1	4.12	12	7	5	....	713	34	1	2.86	1	1987-88	1993-94
• Plante, Jacques	Mtl., NYR, St.L., Tor., Bos.	18	837	437	246	145	49533	1964	82	2.38	112	71	36	....	6651	237	14	2.14	6	1952-53	1972-73
• Plasse, Michel	St.L., Mtl., K.C., Pit., Col., Que.	11	299	92	136	54	16760	1058	2	3.79	4	1	2	....	195	9	1	2.77	1	1970-71	1981-82
§ • Plaxton, Hugh	Mtl.M.	1	1	0	1	0	57	5	0	5.26	....	....	....	....	....	....	....	....		1932-33	1932-33
‡ Popperle, Tomas	CBJ	1	2	0	0	0	45	1	0	1.33	....	....	....	....	....	....	....	....		2006-07	2006-07
Potvin, Felix	Tor., NYI, Van., L.A., Bos.	13	635	266	260	85	36765	1694	32	2.76	72	35	37	....	4435	195	8	2.64		1991-92	2003-04

Name	NHL Teams	NHL Seasons	Regular Schedule								Playoffs								NHL Cup Wins	First NHL Season	Last NHL Season
			GP	W	L	T	Mins	GA	SO	Avg	GP	W	L	T	Mins	GA	SO	Avg			
Pronovost, Claude	Bos., Mtl.	2	3	1	1	0	120	7	1	3.50	....	....	....	....	....	....	....	....		1955-56	1958-59
‡ Prusek, Martin	Ott., CBJ	4	57	31	12	4	2898	114	3	2.36	1	0	0	....	40	1	0	1.50		2001-02	2005-06
Puppa, Daren	Buf., Tor., T.B.	15	429	179	161	54	23819	1204	19	3.03	16	4	9	....	786	51	0	3.89		1985-86	1999-00
Pusey, Chris	Det.	1	1	0	0	0	40	3	0	4.50	....	....	....	....	....	....	....	....		1985-86	1985-86
Racicot, Andre	Mtl.	5	68	26	23	8	3357	196	2	3.50	4	0	1	....	31	4	0	7.74	1	1989-90	1993-94
Racine, Bruce	St.L.	1	11	0	3	0	230	12	0	3.13	1	0	0	....	1	0	0	0.00		1995-96	1995-96
Ram, Jamie	NYR	1	1	0	0	0	27	0	0	0.00	....	....	....	....	....	....	....	....		1995-96	1995-96
Ranford, Bill	Bos., Edm., Wsh., T.B., Det.	15	647	240	279	76	35936	2042	15	3.41	53	28	25	....	3110	159	4	3.07	2	1985-86	1999-00
Raymond, Alain	Wsh.	1	1	0	1	0	40	2	0	3.00	....	....	....	....	....	....	....	....		1987-88	1987-88
• Rayner, Chuck	NYA, Bro., NYR	10	424	138	208	77	25491	1294	25	3.05	18	9	9	....	1135	46	1	2.43		1940-41	1952-53
Reaugh, Daryl	Edm., Hfd.	3	27	8	9	1	1246	72	1	3.47	....	....	....	....	....	....	....	....		1984-85	1990-91
Reddick, Pokey	Wpg., Edm., Fla.	6	132	46	58	16	7162	443	0	3.71	4	0	2	....	168	10	0	3.57	1	1986-87	1993-94
§ • Redding, George	Bos.	1	1	0	0	0	11	1	0	5.45	....	....	....	....	....	....	....	....		1924-25	1924-25
Redquest, Greg	Pit.	1	1	0	0	0	13	3	0	13.85	....	....	....	....	....	....	....	....		1977-78	1977-78
Reece, Dave	Bos.	1	14	7	5	2	777	43	2	3.32	....	....	....	....	....	....	....	....		1975-76	1975-76
Reese, Jeff	Tor., Cgy., Hfd., T.B., N.J.	11	174	53	65	17	8667	529	5	3.66	11	3	5	....	515	35	0	4.08		1987-88	1998-99
Resch, Glenn	NYI, Col., N.J., Phi.	14	571	231	224	82	32279	1761	26	3.27	41	17	17	....	2044	85	2	2.50	1	1973-74	1986-87
• Rheaume, Herb	Mtl.	1	31	10	20	1	1889	92	0	2.92	....	....	....	....	....	....	....	....		1925-26	1925-26
Rhodes, Damian	Tor., Ott., Atl.	10	309	99	140	48	17339	820	12	2.84	13	5	7	....	741	27	0	2.19		1990-91	2001-02
Ricci, Nick	Pit.	4	19	7	12	0	1087	79	0	4.36	....	....	....	....	....	....	....	....		1979-80	1982-83
Richardson, Terry	Det., St.L.	5	20	3	11	0	906	85	0	5.63	....	....	....	....	....	....	....	....		1973-74	1978-79
Richter, Mike	NYR	15	666	301	258	73	38183	1840	24	2.89	76	41	33	....	4514	202	9	2.68	1	1988-89	2002-03
Ridley, Curt	NYR, Van., Tor.	6	104	27	47	16	5498	355	1	3.87	2	0	2	....	120	8	0	4.00		1974-75	1980-81
Riendeau, Vincent	Mtl., St.L., Det., Bos.	8	184	85	65	20	10423	573	5	3.30	25	11	12	....	1277	71	1	3.34		1987-88	1994-95
Riggin, Dennis	Det.	2	18	6	10	2	999	52	1	3.12	....	....	....	....	....	....	....	....		1959-60	1962-63
Riggin, Pat	Atl., Cgy., Wsh., Bos., Pit.	9	350	153	120	52	19872	1135	11	3.43	25	8	13	....	1336	72	0	3.23		1979-80	1987-88
Ring, Bob	Bos.	1	1	0	0	0	33	4	0	7.27	....	....	....	....	....	....	....	....		1965-66	1965-66
Rivard, Fern	Min.	4	55	9	27	11	2865	190	2	3.98	....	....	....	....	....	....	....	....		1968-69	1974-75
• Roach, John Ross	Tor., NYR, Det.	14	492	219	204	68	30444	1246	58	2.46	29	12	14	3	1901	60	7	1.89	1	1921-22	1934-35
• Roberts, Moe	Bos., NYA, Chi.	4	10	3	5	0	501	31	0	3.71	....	....	....	....	....	....	....	....		1925-26	1951-52
• Robertson, Earl	Det., NYA, Bro.	6	190	60	95	34	11820	575	16	2.92	15	7	7	....	995	29	2	1.75	1	1936-37	1941-42
• Rollins, Al	Tor., Chi., NYR	9	430	141	205	83	25723	1192	28	2.78	13	6	7	....	755	30	0	2.38	1	1949-50	1959-60
Romano, Roberto	Pit., Bos.	6	126	46	63	8	7111	471	4	3.97	....	....	....	....	....	....	....	....		1982-83	1993-94
Rosati, Mike	Wsh.	1	1	1	0	0	28	0	0	0.00	....	....	....	....	....	....	....	....		1998-99	1998-99
Roussel, Dominic	Phi., Wpg., Ana., Edm.	8	205	77	70	23	10665	555	7	3.12	1	0	0	....	23	0	0	0.00		1991-92	2000-01
Roy, Patrick	Mtl., Col.	19	1029	551	315	131	60235	2546	66	2.54	247	151	94	....	15209	584	23	2.30	4	1984-85	2002-03
Rudkowsky, Cody	St.L.	1	1	1	0	0	30	0	0	0.00	....	....	....	....	....	....	....	....		2002-03	2002-03
• Rupp, Pat	Det.	1	1	0	1	0	60	4	0	4.00	....	....	....	....	....	....	....	....		1963-64	1963-64
Rutherford, Jim	Det., Pit., Tor., L.A.	13	457	151	227	59	25895	1576	14	3.65	8	2	5	....	440	28	0	3.82		1970-71	1982-83
• Rutledge, Wayne	L.A.	3	82	28	37	9	4325	241	2	3.34	8	2	4	....	378	20	0	3.17		1967-68	1969-70
St. Croix, Rick	Phi., Tor.	8	130	49	54	18	7295	451	2	3.71	11	4	6	....	562	29	1	3.10		1977-78	1984-85
St. Laurent, Sam	N.J., Det.	5	34	7	12	4	1572	92	1	3.51	1	0	0	....	10	1	0	6.00		1985-86	1989-90
Salo, Tommy	NYI, Edm., Col.	10	526	210	225	73	30436	1296	37	2.55	22	5	16	....	1369	58	0	2.54		1994-95	2003-04
§ • Sands, Charlie	Mtl.	1	1	0	0	0	25	5	0	12.00	....	....	....	....	....	....	....	....		1939-40	1939-40
Sands, Mike	Min.	2	6	0	5	0	302	26	0	5.17	....	....	....	....	....	....	....	....		1984-85	1986-87
Sarjeant, Geoff	St.L., S.J.	2	8	1	2	1	291	20	0	4.12	....	....	....	....	....	....	....	....		1994-95	1995-96
Sauve, Bob	Buf., Det., Chi., N.J.	13	420	182	154	54	23711	1377	8	3.48	34	15	16	....	1850	95	4	3.08		1976-77	1988-89
Sauve, Philippe	Col., Cgy., Phx., Bos.	3	32	10	14	3	1616	93	0	3.45	....	....	....	....	....	....	....	....		2003-04	2006-07
• Sawchuk, Terry	Det., Bos., Tor., L.A., NYR	21	971	447	330	172	57194	2389	103	2.51	106	54	48	....	6290	266	12	2.54	4	1949-50	1969-70
• Schaefer, Joe	NYR	2	2	0	2	0	86	8	0	5.58	....	....	....	....	....	....	....	....		1959-60	1960-61
Schafer, Paxton	Bos.	1	3	0	0	0	77	6	0	4.68	....	....	....	....	....	....	....	....		1996-97	1996-97
Schwab, Corey	N.J., T.B., Van., Tor.	8	147	42	63	13	7476	360	6	2.89	3	0	0	....	40	0	0	0.00	1	1995-96	2003-04
‡ Schwarz, Marek	St.L.	3	6	0	2	0	125	9	0	4.32	....	....	....	....	....	....	....	....		2006-07	2008-09
Scott, Ron	NYR, L.A.	5	28	8	13	4	1450	91	0	3.77	1	0	0	....	32	4	0	7.50		1983-84	1989-90
Scott, Travis	L.A.	1	1	0	0	0	25	3	0	7.20	....	....	....	....	....	....	....	....		2000-01	2000-01
Sevigny, Richard	Mtl., Que.	9	176	80	54	20	9485	507	5	3.21	4	0	3	....	208	13	0	3.75	1	1978-79	1986-87
Sharples, Scott	Cgy.	1	1	0	0	1	65	4	0	3.69	....	....	....	....	....	....	....	....		1991-92	1991-92
§ • Shields, Al	NYA	1	2	0	0	0	41	9	0	13.17	....	....	....	....	....	....	....	....		1931-32	1931-32
Shields, Steve	Buf., S.J., Ana., Bos., Fla., Atl.	10	246	80	104	40	13630	606	10	2.67	25	9	16	....	1445	74	1	3.07		1995-96	2005-06
Shtalenkov, Mikhail	Ana., Edm., Phx., Fla.	7	190	62	82	19	9966	480	8	2.89	4	0	3	....	211	10	0	2.84		1993-94	1999-00
Shulmistra, Richard	N.J., Fla.	2	2	1	1	0	122	3	0	1.48	....	....	....	....	....	....	....	....		1997-98	1999-00
Sidorkiewicz, Peter	Hfd., Ott., N.J.	8	246	79	128	27	13884	832	8	3.60	15	5	10	....	912	55	0	3.62		1987-88	1997-98
Sigalet, Jordan	Bos.	1	1	0	0	0	1	0	0	0.00	....	....	....	....	....	....	....	....		2005-06	2005-06
• Simmons, Don	Bos., Tor., NYR	11	249	101	101	41	14555	701	20	2.89	24	13	11	....	1436	62	3	2.59	3	1956-57	1968-69
Simmons, Gary	Cal., Cle., L.A.	4	107	30	57	15	6162	366	5	3.56	1	0	0	....	20	1	0	3.00		1974-75	1977-78
Skidmore, Paul	St.L.	1	2	1	1	0	120	6	0	3.00	....	....	....	....	....	....	....	....		1981-82	1981-82
Skorodenski, Warren	Chi., Edm.	5	35	12	11	4	1732	100	2	3.46	2	0	0	....	33	6	0	10.91		1981-82	1987-88
Skudra, Peter	Pit., Buf., Bos., Van.	6	146	51	47	20	7162	326	6	2.73	3	0	1	....	116	6	0	3.10		1997-98	2002-03
• Smith, Al	Tor., Pit., Det., Buf., Hfd., Col.	10	233	74	99	36	12752	735	10	3.46	6	1	4	....	317	21	0	3.97		1965-66	1980-81
Smith, Billy	L.A., NYI	18	680	305	233	105	38431	2031	22	3.17	132	88	36	....	7645	348	5	2.73	4	1971-72	1988-89
Smith, Gary	Tor., Oak., Cal., Chi., Van., Min., Wsh., Wpg.	14	532	173	261	74	29619	1675	26	3.39	20	5	13	....	1153	62	1	3.23		1965-66	1979-80
• Smith, Normie	Mtl.M., Det.	8	199	81	83	35	12357	479	17	2.33	12	9	2	0	820	18	3	1.32	2	1931-32	1944-45
Sneddon, Bob	Cal.	1	5	0	2	0	225	21	0	5.60	....	....	....	....	....	....	....	....		1970-71	1970-71
Snow, Garth	Que., Phi., Van., Pit., NYI	12	368	135	147	44	19837	925	16	2.80	20	9	8	....	1040	48	1	2.77		1993-94	2005-06
Soderstrom, Tommy	Phi., NYI	5	156	45	69	19	8189	496	10	3.63	....	....	....	....	....	....	....	....		1992-93	1996-97
Soetaert, Doug	NYR, Wpg., Mtl.	12	284	110	104	42	15583	1030	6	3.97	5	1	2	....	180	14	0	4.67	1	1975-76	1986-87
Soucy, Christian	Chi.	1	1	0	0	0	3	0	0	0.00	....	....	....	....	....	....	....	....		1993-94	1993-94
• Spooner, Red	Pit.	1	1	0	1	0	60	6	0	6.00	....	....	....	....	....	....	....	....		1929-30	1929-30
§ • Spring, Jesse	Ham.	1	1	0	0	0	2	0	0	0.00	....	....	....	....	....	....	....	....		1924-25	1924-25
‡ Stana, Rastislav	Wsh.	1	6	1	2	0	211	11	0	3.13	....	....	....	....	....	....	....	....		2003-04	2003-04
Staniowski, Ed	St.L., Wpg., Hfd.	10	219	67	104	21	12075	818	2	4.06	8	1	6	....	428	28	0	3.93		1975-76	1984-85
§ • Starr, Harold	Mtl.M.	1	1	0	0	0	3	0	0	0.00	....	....	....	....	....	....	....	....		1931-32	1931-32
Stauber, Robb	L.A., Buf.	4	62	21	23	9	3295	209	1	3.81	4	3	1	....	240	16	0	4.00		1989-90	1994-95
Stefan, Greg	Det.	9	299	115	127	30	16333	1068	5	3.92	30	12	17	....	1681	99	1	3.53		1981-82	1989-90
• Stein, Phil	Tor.	1	1	0	0	1	70	2	0	1.71	....	....	....	....	....	....	....	....		1939-40	1939-40
‡ Stephan, Tobias	Dal.	2	11	1	3	2	499	29	0	3.49	....	....	....	....	....	....	....	....		2007-08	2008-09
• Stephenson, Wayne	St.L., Phi., Wsh.	10	328	146	103	49	18343	937	14	3.06	26	11	12	....	1522	79	2	3.11	1	1971-72	1980-81
• Stevenson, Doug	NYR, Chi.	3	8	2	6	0	480	39	0	4.88	....	....	....	....	....	....	....	....		1944-45	1945-46
• Stewart, Charles	Bos.	3	77	30	41	5	4742	194	10	2.45	....	....	....	....	....	....	....	....		1924-25	1926-27
Stewart, Jim	Bos.	1	1	0	1	0	20	5	0	15.00	....	....	....	....	....	....	....	....		1979-80	1979-80
Storr, Jamie	L.A., Car.	10	219	85	86	23	11512	488	16	2.54	5	0	3	....	182	11	0	3.63		1994-95	2003-04
• Stuart, Herb	Det.	1	3	1	2	0	180	5	0	1.67	....	....	....	....	....	....	....	....		1926-27	1926-27
Sylvestri, Don	Bos.	1	3	0	0	2	102	6	0	3.53	....	....	....	....	....	....	....	....		1984-85	1984-85
Tabaracci, Rick	Pit., Wpg., Wsh., Cgy., T.B., Atl., Col.	11	286	93	125	30	15255	760	15	2.99	17	4	12	....	1025	53	0	3.10		1988-89	1999-00
Takko, Kari	Min., Edm.	6	142	37	71	14	7317	475	1	3.90	4	0	1	....	109	7	0	3.85		1985-86	1990-91
Tallas, Robbie	Bos., Chi.	6	99	28	42	10	5069	246	3	2.91	....	....	....	....	....	....	....	....		1995-96	2000-01
Tanner, John	Que.	3	21	2	11	5	1084	65	1	3.60	....	....	....	....	....	....	....	....		1989-90	1991-92
Tataryn, Dave	NYR	1	2	1	1	0	80	10	0	7.50	....	....	....	....	....	....	....	....		1976-77	1976-77
Taylor, Bobby	Phi., Pit.	5	46	15	17	6	2268	155	0	4.10	....	....	....	....	....	....	....	....	1	1971-72	1975-76
‡ Tellqvist, Mikael	Tor., Phx., Buf.	6	113	45	41	10	6034	303	6	3.01	....	....	....	....	....	....	....	....		2002-03	2008-09
• Teno, Harvey	Det.	1	5	2	3	0	300	15	0	3.00	....	....	....	....	....	....	....	....		1938-39	1938-39
Terreri, Chris	N.J., S.J., Chi., NYI	14	406	151	172	43	22369	1143	9	3.07	29	12	12	....	1523	86	0	3.39	2	1986-87	2000-01
Thibault, Jocelyn	Que., Col., Mtl., Chi., Pit., Buf.	14	586	238	238	75	32892	1508	39	2.75	18	4	11	....	848	50	0	3.54		1993-94	2007-08
Thomas, Wayne	Mtl., Tor., NYR	9	243	103	93	34	13768	766	10	3.34	15	6	8	....	849	50	1	3.53		1972-73	1980-81
• Thompson, Tiny	Bos., Det.	12	553	284	194	75	34175	1183	81	2.08	44	20	24	0	2974	93	7	1.88	1	1928-29	1939-40
§ Toppazzini, Jerry	Bos.	1	1	0	0	0	1	0	0	0.00	....	....	....	....	....	....	....	....		1960-61	1960-61
Torchia, Mike	Dal.	1	6	3	2	1	327	18	0	3.30	....	....	....	....	....	....	....	....		1994-95	1994-95
‡ Toskala, Vesa	S.J., Tor., Cgy.	8	266	129	82	30	14767	679	13	2.76	11	6	5	....	686	28	1	2.45		2001-02	2009-10

Name	NHL Teams	NHL Seasons	Regular Schedule								Playoffs								NHL Cup Wins	First NHL Season	Last NHL Season
			GP	W	L	T	Mins	GA	SO	Avg	GP	W	L	T	Mins	GA	SO	Avg			
Trefilov, Andrei	Cgy., Buf., Chi.	7	54	12	25	4	2663	153	2	3.45	1	0	0	....	5	0	0	0.00		1992-93	1998-99
Tremblay, Vincent	Tor., Pit.	5	58	12	26	8	2785	223	1	4.80	....									1979-80	1983-84
Tucker, Ted	Cal.	1	5	1	1	1	177	10	0	3.39	....									1973-74	1973-74
Tugnutt, Ron	Que., Edm., Ana., Mtl., Ott., Pit., CBJ, Dal.	16	537	186	239	62	29486	1497	26	3.05	25	9	13	....	1482	56	3	2.27		1987-88	2003-04
Turek, Roman	Dal., St.L., Cgy.	8	328	159	115	43	19095	734	27	2.31	22	12	9	....	1342	50	0	2.24	1	1996-97	2003-04
• Turner, Joe	Det.	1	1	0	0	1	70	3	0	2.57	....									1941-42	1941-42
Underhill, Matt	Chi.	1	1	0	1	0	61	4	0	3.93	....									2003-04	2003-04
Vachon, Rogie	Mtl., L.A., Det., Bos.	16	795	355	291	127	46298	2310	51	2.99	48	23	23	....	2876	133	2	2.77	3	1966-67	1981-82
Vanbiesbrouck, John	NYR, Fla., Phi., NYI, N.J.	20	882	374	346	119	50475	2503	40	2.98	71	28	38	....	3969	177	5	2.68		1981-82	2001-02
Veisor, Mike	Chi., Hfd., Wpg.	10	139	41	62	26	7806	532	5	4.09	4	0	2	....	180	15	0	5.00		1973-74	1983-84
Vernon, Mike	Cgy., Det., S.J., Fla.	19	781	385	273	92	44449	2206	27	2.98	138	77	56	....	8214	367	6	2.68	2	1982-83	2001-02
• Vezina, Georges	Mtl.	9	190	103	81	5	11592	633	13	3.28	13	10	3	0	780	35	2	2.69	1	1917-18	1925-26
Villemure, Gilles	NYR, Chi.	10	205	100	64	29	11581	542	13	2.81	14	5	5	....	656	32	0	2.93		1963-64	1976-77
Waite, Jimmy	Chi., S.J., Phx.	11	106	28	41	12	5253	293	4	3.35	6	0	3	....	211	14	0	3.98		1988-89	1998-99
Wakaluk, Darcy	Buf., Min., Dal., Phx.	8	191	67	75	21	9756	524	9	3.22	8	4	2	....	364	18	0	2.97		1988-89	1996-97
Wakely, Ernie	Mtl., St.L.	7	113	41	42	17	6244	290	8	2.79	10	2	6	....	509	37	1	4.36	2	1962-63	1971-72
Wall, Michael	Ana.	1	4	2	2	0	202	10	0	2.97	....									2006-07	2006-07
• Walsh, Flat	Mtl.M., NYA	7	108	48	43	16	6641	256	12	2.31	8	2	4	2	570	16	2	1.68	1	1926-27	1932-33
Wamsley, Rick	Mtl., St.L., Cgy., Tor.	13	407	204	131	46	23123	1287	12	3.34	27	7	18	....	1397	81	0	3.48	1	1980-81	1992-93
Watt, Jim	St.L.	1	1	0	0	0	20	2	0	6.00	....									1973-74	1973-74
Weekes, Kevin	Fla., Van., NYI, T.B., Car., NYR, N.J.	11	348	105	163	39	18837	903	19	2.88	9	3	3	....	468	15	2	1.92		1997-98	2008-09
Weeks, Steve	NYR, Hfd., Van., NYI, L.A., Ott.	14	290	111	119	33	15879	989	5	3.74	12	3	5	....	486	27	0	3.33		1980-81	1992-93
Wetzel, Carl	Det., Min.	2	7	1	4	1	301	22	0	4.39	....									1964-65	1967-68
Whitmore, Kay	Hfd., Van., Bos., Cgy.	9	155	60	64	16	8596	508	4	3.55	4	0	2	....	174	13	0	4.48		1988-89	2001-02
Wilkinson, Derek	T.B.	4	22	3	12	3	933	57	0	3.67	....									1995-96	1998-99
Willis, Jordan	Dal.	1	1	0	1	0	19	1	0	3.16	....									1995-96	1995-96
Wilson, Dunc	Phi., Van., Tor., NYR, Pit.	10	287	80	150	33	15851	988	8	3.74	....									1969-70	1978-79
• Wilson, Lefty	Det., Tor., Bos.	3	3	0	0	1	81	1	0	0.74	....									1953-54	1957-58
• Winkler, Hal	NYR, Bos.	2	75	35	26	14	4739	126	21	1.60	10	2	3	5	640	18	2	1.69		1926-27	1927-28
Wolfe, Bernie	Wsh.	4	120	20	61	21	6104	424	1	4.17	....									1975-76	1978-79
Wood, Alex	NYA	1	1	0	1	0	70	3	0	2.57	....									1936-37	1936-37
Worsley, Gump	NYR, Mtl., Min.	21	861	335	352	150	50183	2407	43	2.88	70	40	26	....	4084	189	5	2.78	4	1952-53	1973-74
• Worters, Roy	Pit., NYA, Mtl.	12	484	171	229	83	30175	1143	67	2.27	11	3	6	2	690	24	3	2.09		1925-26	1936-37
• Worthy, Chris	Oak., Cal.	3	26	5	10	4	1326	98	0	4.43	....									1968-69	1970-71
Wregget, Ken	Tor., Phi., Pit., Cgy., Det.	17	575	225	248	53	31663	1917	9	3.63	56	28	25	....	3341	160	3	2.87	1	1983-84	1999-00
Yeats, Matthew	Wsh.	1	5	1	3	0	258	13	0	3.02	....									2003-04	2003-04
‡ Yeremeyev, Vitali	NYR	1	4	0	4	0	212	16	0	4.53	....									2000-01	2000-01
§ • Young, Doug	Det.	1	1	0	0	0	21	1	0	2.86	....									1933-34	1933-34
Young, Wendell	Van., Phi., Pit., T.B.	10	187	59	86	12	9410	618	2	3.94	2	0	1	....	99	6	0	3.64	2	1985-86	1994-95
‡ Zaba, Matt	NYR	1	1	0	0	0	34	2	0	3.53	....									2009-10	2009-10
Zanier, Mike	Edm.	1	3	1	1	1	185	12	0	3.89	....									1984-85	1984-85

Red Almas

Paul Goodman

Markus Mattsson

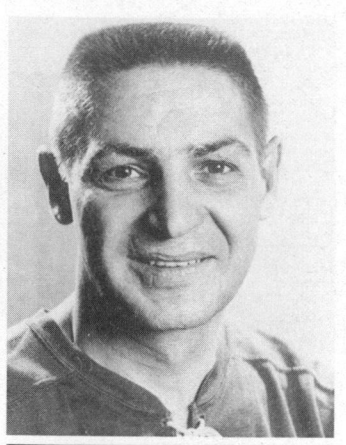

Terry Sawchuk

Wilf Cude

Glen Hanlon

Mike Palmateer

Rick Wamsley

Hockey Hall of Fame and U.S. Hockey Hall of Fame 2011 Inductees and Award Winners

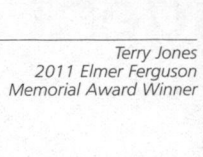

*Terry Jones
2011 Elmer Ferguson
Memorial Award Winner*

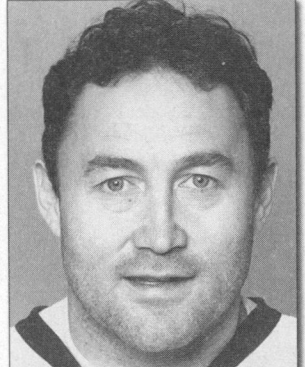

*Ed Belfour
Hockey Hall of Fame
2011 Inductee*

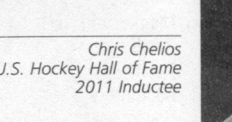

*Joe Nieuwendyk
Hockey Hall of Fame
2011 Inductee*

*Chris Chelios
U.S. Hockey Hall of Fame
2011 Inductee*

*Mickey Redmond
2011 Foster Hewitt
Memorial Award Winner*

*Mike "Doc" Emrick
U.S. Hockey Hall of Fame
2011 Inductee*

*Ed Snider
U.S. Hockey Hall of Fame
2011 Inductee*

*Doug Gilmour
Hockey Hall of Fame
2011 Inductee*

*Gary Suter
U.S. Hockey Hall of Fame
2011 Inductee*

*Mark Howe
Hockey Hall of Fame
2011 Inductee*

*Keith Tkachuk
U.S. Hockey Hall of Fame
2011 Inductee*

Free Agent Signing Register, 2011

SIGNING DATE	POS.	PLAYER	SIGNED BY	PREVIOUS ORGANIZATION
July 1 —	G	Alex Auld	Ottawa	Montreal
—	LW	Darcy Hordichuk	Edmonton	Florida
—	D	Cam Barker	Edmonton	Minnesota
—	D	Andy Greene	New Jersey	New Jersey
—	D	Jonathan Ericcson	Detroit	Detroit
—	RW	Jakub Voracek	Philadelphia	Philadelphia
—	C	Ryan Potulny	Washington	Ottawa
—	LW	Erik Cole	Montreal	Carolina
—	D	Roman Hamrlik	Washington	Montreal
—	C	Marty Reasoner	NY Islanders	Florida
—	RW	Joel Ward	Washington	Nashville
—	RW	Steve Sullivan	Pittsburgh	Nashville
—	D	Mike Commodore	Detroit	Columbus
—	G	Peter Budaj	Montreal	Colorado
—	C	Mike Rupp	NY Rangers	Pittsburgh
—	G	Brian Boucher	Carolina	Philadelphia
—	C	Jiri Tlusty	Carolina	Carolina
—	C	Marcel Goc	Florida	Nashville
—	D	Jan Hejda	Colorado	Columbus
—	LW	Vernon Fiddler	Dallas	Phoenix
—	LW	Daniel Carcillo	Chicago	Philadelphia
—	C	Boyd Gordon	Phoenix	Washington
—	RW	Mark Mancari	Vancouver	Buffalo
—	RW	Radek Dvorak	Dallas	Winnipeg
—	D	Adam Pardy	Dallas	Calgary
—	G	Semyon Varlamov	Colorado	Colorado
—	G	Johan Hedberg	New Jersey	New Jersey
—	C	Maxime Talbot	Philadelphia	Pittsburgh
—	RW	Radim Vrbata	Phoenix	Phoenix
—	D	Ed Jovanovski	Florida	Phoenix
—	D	Andreas Lilja	Philadelphia	Anaheim
—	LW	Scottie Upshall	Florida	Columbus
—	D	Sean O'Donnell	Chicago	Philadelphia
—	RW	Jamal Mayers	Chicago	San Jose
—	LW	Andrew Brunette	Chicago	Minnesota
—	C	Cody McCormick	Buffalo	Buffalo
—	D	Chris Butler	Calgary	Calgary
—	C	Jeff Halpern	Washington	Montreal
—	G	Mike Smith	Phoenix	Tampa Bay
—	LW	Raffi Torres	Phoenix	Vancouver
—	RW	Matt D'Agostini	St. Louis	St. Louis
—	G	Mathieu Garon	Tampa Bay	Columbus
—	G	Jose Theodore	Florida	Minnesota
—	LW	Ben Eager	Edmonton	San Jose
—	RW	Michael Ryder	Dallas	Boston
—	C	Jake Dowell	Dallas	Chicago
—	C	Tim Brent	Carolina	Toronto
—	LW	Ville Leino	Buffalo	Philadelphia
—	RW	Adam Cracknell	St. Louis	St. Louis
—	LW	Marco Sturm	Vancouver	Washington
—	LW	Alexei Ponikarovsky	Carolina	Los Angeles
—	D	Sheldon Souray	Dallas	Edmonton
—	D	Jim Vandermeer	San Jose	Edmonton
—	LW	Tomas Fleischmann	Florida	Colorado
—	LW	Benoit Pouliot	Boston	Montreal
—	G	Anton Khudobin	Boston	Boston
—	C	Eric Belanger	Edmonton	Phoenix
—	C	Chuck Kobasew	Colorado	Minnesota
—	G	Brian Elliott	St. Louis	Colorado
—	RW	Francis Lessard	Ottawa	Ottawa
—	RW	Patrick Eaves	Detroit	Detroit
—	LW	Drew Miller	Detroit	Detroit
—	RW	James Wyman	Tampa Bay	Montreal
—	G	J.S. Giguere	Colorado	Toronto
—	C	Andrew Joudrey	Columbus	Washington
—	C	Nicholas Drazenovic	Columbus	St. Louis
—	G	Curtis Sanford	Columbus	Montreal
—	G	Mark Dekanich	Columbus	Nashville
—	D	Nolan Yonkman	Florida	Phoenix
—	D	Sami Salo	Vancouver	Vancouver
—	C	Trent Whitfield	Boston	Boston

SIGNING DATE	POS.	PLAYER	SIGNED BY	PREVIOUS ORGANIZATION
—	C	Michal Handzus	San Jose	Los Angeles
—	D	Corey Potter	Edmonton	Pittsburgh
—	LW	Sean Bergenheim	Florida	Tampa Bay
—	LW	Ruslan Fedotenko	NY Rangers	NY Rangers
—	RW	Colin McDonald	Pittsburgh	Edmonton
July 2 —	C	Brad Richards	NY Rangers	Dallas
—	D	Matt Gilroy	Tampa Bay	NY Rangers
—	LW	Justin Soryal	Carolina	NY Rangers
—	RW	Anthony Stewart	Carolina	Atlanta
—	D	Clay Wilson	Calgary	Florida
—	C	Ben Walter	Calgary	Colorado
—	RW	Matt Bradley	Florida	Washington
—	C	Tim Connolly	Toronto	Buffalo
—	LW	Simon Gagne	Los Angeles	Tampa Bay
—	C	Alexandre Bolduc	Phoenix	Vancouver
—	D	Richard Petiot	Tampa Bay	Edmonton
—	D	Ian White	Detroit	San Jose
—	G	Tomas Vokoun	Washington	Florida
—	D	Kent Huskins	St. Louis	San Jose
—	RW	Andrew Gordon	Anaheim	Washington
—	D	Nolan Baumgartner	Vancouver	Vancouver
—	LW	Tanner Glass	Winnipeg	Vancouver
—	D	Derek Meech	Winnipeg	Detroit
—	C	Jed Ortmeyer	Minnesota	Minnesota
July 3 —	D	Boris Valabik	Pittsburgh	Boston
—	RW	Niclas Bergfors	Nashville	Florida
—	LW	Josh Green	Edmonton	Anaheim
—	C	Steve Pinizzotto	Vancouver	Washington
July 4 —	C	Aaron Gagnon	Winnipeg	Dallas
—	C	Rick Rypien	Winnipeg	Vancouver
—	D	Randy Jones	Winnipeg	Tampa Bay
—	D	Danny Richmond	Washington	Toronto
—	D	Mike Weber	Buffalo	Buffalo
—	LW	Brett Sterling	St. Louis	Pittsburgh
—	D	Tyler Eckford	Phoenix	New Jersey
—	G	Curtis McElhinney	Phoenix	Ottawa
—	RW	Guillaume Desbiens	Calgary	Vancouver
—	D	Anton Babchuk	Calgary	Calgary
—	LW	Alexandre Giroux	Columbus	Edmonton
—	D	Theo Peckham	Edmonton	Edmonton
July 5 —	C	Trevor Smith	Tampa Bay	Columbus
—	C	Scott Nichol	St. Louis	San Jose
—	LW	Andrew Ladd	Winnipeg	Winnipeg
—	G	Ben Bishop	St. Louis	St. Louis
—	C	Zenon Konopka	Ottawa	NY Islanders
—	RW	Zack Stortini	Nashville	Edmonton
—	C	Kyle Wilson	Nashville	Columbus
—	D	Bryan Rodney	Anaheim	Carolina
—	G	Nathan Lawson	Montreal	NY Islanders
—	C	Jeff Taffe	Minnesota	Chicago
—	C	Darroll Powe	Minnesota	Minnesota
—	D	Marc Methot	Columbus	Columbus
—	C	Andrew Ebbett	Vancouver	Phoenix
—	LW	Clarke MacArthur	Toronto	Toronto
—	D	Keith Yandle	Phoenix	Phoenix
—	D	Tomas Kaberle	Carolina	Boston
—	D	Alexandre Picard	Pittsburgh	Montreal
—	D	Garnet Exelby	Detroit	Chicago
—	D	Logan Pyett	Detroit	Detroit
—	RW	Chris Conner	Detroit	Pittsburgh
—	C	Tyler Bozak	Toronto	Toronto
—	RW	Jamie Tardif	Boston	Detroit
—	C	Josh Hennessy	Boston	Ottawa
July 6 —	RW	Jamie Langenbrunner	St. Louis	Dallas
—	C	Jason Arnott	St. Louis	Washington
—	C	Colton Gillies	Minnesota	Minnesota
—	LW	Jean-Francois Jacques	Anaheim	Edmonton
—	C	Tom Pyatt	Tampa Bay	Montreal
—	D	Radek Martinek	Columbus	NY Islanders
—	RW	Erik Condra	Ottawa	Ottawa
—	G	Leland Irving	Calgary	Calgary

SIGNING DATE	POS.	PLAYER	SIGNED BY	PREVIOUS ORGANIZATION
–	RW	Matt Watkins	Phoenix	Phoenix
–	D	Dean Arsene	Phoenix	St. Louis
–	D	Nathan Oystrick	Phoenix	St. Louis
–	D	Matt Pelech	San Jose	Calgary
–	D	Thomas Greiss	San Jose	San Jose
July 7	D	Colin Stuart	Buffalo	Buffalo
–	LW	Derek Whitmore	Buffalo	Buffalo
–	G	Drew MacIntyre	Buffalo	Montreal
–	RW	Brian Willsie	Montreal	Washington
–	G	Matt Climie	Vancouver	Phoenix
–	D	Alexander Sulzer	Vancouver	Florida
–	D	Matt Lashoff	Toronto	Toronto
–	C	Philippe Dupuis	Toronto	Colorado
–	RW	Brian McGrattan	Anaheim	Anaheim
–	C	Chris Mueller	Nashville	Nashville
–	C	Cal O'Reilly	Nashville	Nashville
–	C	Nick Spaling	Nashville	Nashville
–	RW	Matt Halischuk	Nashville	Nashville
–	C	Mike Santorelli	Florida	Florida
–	RW	Wayne Simmonds	Philadelphia	Philadelphia
–	LW	Alexandre Picard	Tampa Bay	Phoenix
–	C	Ryan Shannon	Tampa Bay	Ottawa
July 8	RW	Mark Parrish	Ottawa	Buffalo
–	C	Artem Anisimov	NY Rangers	NY Rangers
–	D	Michael Sauer	NY Rangers	NY Rangers
–	C	Sergei Kostitsyn	Nashville	Nashville
–	G	Mike McKenna	Ottawa	New Jersey
–	D	Alec Martinez	Los Angeles	Los Angeles
–	G	Cedrick Desjardins	Colorado	Tampa Bay
–	C	Evan Brophey	Colorado	Chicago
–	D	Derek Joslin	Carolina	Carolina
–	C	Brodie Dupont	Nashville	Nashville
–	RW	Ben Guite	San Jose	Columbus
–	C	Benn Ferriero	San Jose	San Jose
July 9	D	Mike Lundin	Minnesota	Tampa Bay
–	D	Ryan Wilson	Colorado	Colorado
–	C	Kevin Porter	Colorado	Colorado
July 10	LW	Viktor Stalberg	Chicago	Chicago
July 11	C	Christian Hanson	Washington	Toronto
–	G	Joey MacDonald	Detroit	Detroit
–	D	Lee Sweatt	Ottawa	Vancouver
–	RW	Dan Sexton	Anaheim	Anaheim
–	D	Tim Conboy	Ottawa	Buffalo
–	LW	Dane Byers	Columbus	Phoenix
–	G	Alec Richards	Chicago	Chicago
–	LW	Rob Klinkhammer	Chicago	Chicago
July 12	C	Mike Zigomanis	Toronto	Toronto
–	G	Jeff Deslauriers	Anaheim	Edmonton
–	C	Dustin Jeffrey	Pittsburgh	Pittsburgh
–	RW	Eric Godard	Dallas	Pittsburgh
–	LW	Patrick Rissmiller	Colorado	Florida
–	LW	T.J. Galiardi	Colorado	Colorado
July 13	C	Ryan White	Montreal	Montreal
–	C	Cody Bass	Columbus	Ottawa
–	C	Brad Richardson	Los Angeles	Los Angeles
–	C	Mathieu Perreault	Washington	Washington
–	D	Derek Smith	Calgary	Ottawa
–	C	Brandon Sutter	Carolina	Carolina
–	D	Shane O'Brien	Colorado	Nashville
July 14	RW	Bobby Butler	Ottawa	Ottawa
–	D	Matt Smaby	Anaheim	Tampa Bay
–	C	Darryl Boyce	Toronto	Toronto
–	RW	Mike Duco	Vancouver	Vancouver
–	C	Jeremy Colliton	NY Islanders	NY Islanders
–	D	Brendan Mikkelson	Calgary	Calgary
–	C	Bracken Kearns	Florida	Phoenix
–	RW	Cam Janssen	New Jersey	St. Louis
July 15	C	Chris Durno	Carolina	Tampa Bay
–	D	Karl Alzner	Washington	Washington
–	RW	Francois Bouchard	Washington	Washington
–	C	Brett Sutter	Carolina	Carolina
–	D	Bobby Sanguinetti	Carolina	Carolina

SIGNING DATE	POS.	PLAYER	SIGNED BY	PREVIOUS ORGANIZATION
–	D	Sami Lepisto	Chicago	Columbus
–	LW	Michael Frolik	Chicago	Chicago
–	D	Scott Jackson	Tampa Bay	Tampa Bay
–	C	Trevor Lewis	Los Angeles	Los Angeles
–	G	Jeff Zatkoff	Los Angeles	Los Angeles
–	D	Patrick Mullen	Los Angeles	Los Angeles
–	D	Andrew Campbell	Los Angeles	Los Angeles
–	C	David Meckler	Los Angeles	Los Angeles
–	LW	Rich Clune	Los Angeles	Los Angeles
–	C	Marc-Andre Cliché	Los Angeles	Los Angeles
–	C	Nick Bonino	Anaheim	Anaheim
–	C	Brendan Morrison	Calgary	Calgary
–	C	Travis Turnbull	Buffalo	Buffalo
–	D	Dennis Persson	Buffalo	Buffalo
–	C	Ryan O'Marra	Edmonton	Edmonton
–	D	Taylor Chorney	Edmonton	Edmonton
–	D	Dylan Reese	NY Islanders	NY Islanders
–	D	Ty Wishart	NY Islanders	NY Islanders
–	C	Michael Haley	NY Islanders	NY Islanders
July 16	LW	Patrick Maroon	Anaheim	Anaheim
July 18	RW	Ryan Reaves	St. Louis	St. Louis
–	D	Mathieu Carle	Anaheim	Anaheim
–	RW	Kenndal McArdle	Winnipeg	Winnipeg
–	C	Ben Maxwell	Winnipeg	Winnipeg
–	RW	Spencer Machacek	Winnipeg	Winnipeg
–	D	Arturs Kulda	Winnipeg	Winnipeg
–	C	Riley Holzapfel	Winnipeg	Winnipeg
–	D	Brett Festerling	Winnipeg	Winnipeg
–	RW	Blake Wheeler	Winnipeg	Winnipeg
July 19	RW	Raymond Sawada	Dallas	Dallas
–	RW	Joey Crabb	Toronto	Toronto
–	C	Jason Jaffray	Winnipeg	Anaheim
–	C	Marc Pouliot	Phoenix	Phoenix
–	C	Kyle Chipchura	Phoenix	Anaheim
–	LW	Brett Maclean	Phoenix	Phoenix
–	C	Andrew Murray	San Jose	Columbus
–	C	Andrew Cogliano	Anaheim	Anaheim
–	LW	Matt Ellis	Buffalo	Buffalo
–	D	Andrej Sekera	Buffalo	Buffalo
–	C	Jon Kalinski	Philadelphia	Philadelphia
–	G	Jason Bacashihua	Philadelphia	Colorado
–	C	Steven Stamkos	Tampa Bay	Tampa Bay
July 20	G	Ty Conklin	Detroit	St. Louis
–	RW	Teddy Purcell	Tampa Bay	Tampa Bay
–	LW	Lauri Korpikoski	Phoenix	Phoenix
–	C	Mark Bell	Anaheim	Kloten (Swiss)
July 21	C	Brandon Dubinsky	NY Rangers	NY Rangers
–	G	Jhonas Enroth	Buffalo	Buffalo
–	G	Jordan Pearce	Detroit	Detroit
July 22	D	Josh Gorges	Montreal	Montreal
July 23	C	Vinny Prospal	Columbus	NY Rangers
July 25	D	Steve Eminger	NY Rangers	NY Rangers
July 26	RW	Byron Bitz	Vancouver	Florida
–	C	Jason Williams	Pittsburgh	Dallas
July 27	G	Justin Pogge	Phoenix	Carolina
–	RW	Ryan Callahan	NY Rangers	NY Rangers
July 28	RW	Jannik Hansen	Vancouver	Vancouver
July 29	D	Tyler Sloan	Nashville	Washington
–	LW	Zach Parise	New Jersey	New Jersey
Aug. 2	LW	Blake Comeau	NY Islanders	NY Islanders
Aug. 3	LW	Kaspars Daugavins	Ottawa	Ottawa
–	D	Colin White	San Jose	New Jersey
–	D	Shea Weber	Nashville	Nashville
Aug. 5	C	Patrick O'Sullivan	Phoenix	Minnesota
Aug. 8	RW	Sean Backman	NY Islanders	Dallas
–	D	Danny Syvret	St. Louis	Philadelphia
–	D	Jack Hillen	Nashville	NY Islanders
–	LW	Ryan Russell	Columbus	Columbus
Aug. 9	LW	Michael Ryan	Buffalo	Philadelphia
–	C	Paul Szczechura	Buffalo	Tampa Bay
Aug. 10	RW	Viktor Tikhonov	Phoenix	Phoenix
Aug. 11	D	Marc-Andre Gragnani	Buffalo	Buffalo

Trade Register, 2010-11

AUGUST, 2010

1 – Atlanta traded C **Todd White** to NY Rangers for LW **Donald Brashear** and LW **Patrick Rissmiller**.

3 – St. Louis traded D **T.J. Fast** to Florida for RW **Graham Mink**.

5 – Nashville traded C **Mike Santorelli** to Florida for Florida's 4th-round choice (LW **Josh Shalla**) in the 2011 Entry Draft.

16 – Montreal traded G **Cedrick Desjardins** to Tampa Bay for G **Karri Ramo**.

27 – Toronto traded RW **Alex Berry** and LW **Stefano Giliati** to Tampa Bay for D **Matt Lashoff**.

SEPTEMBER, 2010

1 – Atlanta traded D **Grant Lewis** to Nashville for RW **Ian McKenzie**.

OCTOBER, 2010

5 – Vancouver traded D **Shane O'Brien** and RW **Dan Gendur** to Nashville for D **Ryan Parent** and RW **Jonas Andersson**.

6 – Vancouver traded LW **Darcy Hordichuk** to Florida for LW **Andrew Peters**.

7 – Vancouver traded D **Sean Zimmerman** to Florida for D **Nathan Paetsch**.

NOVEMBER, 2010

11 – Montreal traded D **Ryan O'Byrne** to Colorado for LW **Michael Bournival**.

11 – NY Rangers traded LW **Dane Byers** to Columbus for C **Chad Kolarik**.

17 – Calgary traded D **Ian White** and LW **Brett Sutter** to Carolina for D **Anton Babchuk** and RW **Tom Kostopoulos**.

21 – Philadelphia traded RW **David Laliberte** and LW **Patrick Maroon** to Anaheim for C **Rob Bordson** and D **Danny Syvret**.

23 – NY Rangers traded D **Nigel Williams** to Anaheim for D **Stu Bickel**.

23 – Anaheim traded C **Ryan Carter** to Carolina for C **Stefan Chaput** and RW **Matt Kennedy**.

29 – Colorado traded D **Colby Cohen** to Boston for D **Matt Hunwick**.

30 – Colorado traded D **Scott Hannan** to Washington for LW **Tomas Fleischmann**.

DECEMBER, 2010

9 – Tampa Bay traded LW **Juraj Simek** to Boston for C **Levi Nelson**.

9 – Boston traded LW **Jeff LoVecchio** and RW **Jordan Knackstedt** to Florida for D **Sean Zimmerman** and future considerations.

11 – Boston traded LW **Marco Sturm** to Los Angeles for future considerations.

28 – NY Islanders traded D **James Wisniewski** to Montreal for Montreal's 2nd-round compensatory choice (C **Johan Sundstrom**) in the 2011 Entry Draft and a conditional choice in 2012.

31 – Montreal traded C **Maxim Lapierre** to Anaheim for D **Brett Festerling** and Anaheim's 5th-round choice (later traded back to Anaheim) in the 2012 Entry Draft.

JANUARY, 2011

1 – Tampa Bay traded D **Ty Wishart** to NY Islanders for G **Dwayne Roloson**.

4 – Anaheim traded C **Trevor Smith** to Columbus for D **Nate Guenin**.

7 – New Jersey traded RW **Jamie Langenbrunner** to Dallas for a for Dallas's 3rd-round choice (C **Blake Coleman**) in the 2011 Entry Draft and future considerations.

10 – Phoenix traded LW **Wojtek Wolski** to NY Rangers for D **Michal Rozsival**.

13 – Dallas traded LW **Fabian Brunnstrom** to Toronto for C **Mikhail Stefanovich**.

18 – Atlanta traded LW **Ben Eager** to San Jose for San Jose's 5th-round choice (later traded to Winnipeg – Winnipeg selected RW **Austen Brassard**) in the 2011 Entry Draft.

FEBRUARY, 2011

9 – Anaheim traded RW **Joffrey Lupul** and D **Jake Gardiner** to Toronto for D **Francois Beauchemin**.

9 – Chicago traded RW **Jack Skille**, RW **Hugh Jessiman** and C **David Pacan** to Florida for LW **Michael Frolik** and G **Alexander Salak**.

9 – Phoenix traded G **Al Montoya** to NY Islanders for NY Islanders' 6th-round choice (D **Andrew Fritsch**) in the 2011 Entry Draft.

9 – San Jose traded C **Steven Zalewski** and D **Jay Leach** to New Jersey for RW **Patrick Davis** and C **Michael Swift**.

10 – Ottawa traded C **Mike Fisher** to Nashville for Nashville's 1st-round choice (RW **Stefan Noesen**) in the 2011 Entry Draft and a conditional choice in 2012.

14 – Toronto traded RW **Kris Versteeg** to Philadelphia for Philadelphia's 1st- and 3rd-round choices (LW **Josh Salla** and LW **Josh Leivo**) in the 2011 Entry Draft.

15 – Anaheim traded LW **Aaron Voros** to Toronto for future considerations.

15 – Ottawa traded C **Chris Kelly** to Boston for Boston's 2nd-round choice (C **Shane Prince**) in the 2011 Entry Draft.

15 – Anaheim traded D **Paul Mara** to Montreal for a 5th-round choice in the 2012 Entry Draft.

17 – Ottawa traded LW **Jarkko Ruutu** to Anaheim for Phoenix's 6th-round choice (previously acquired – Ottawa selected LW **Max McCormick**) in the 2011 Entry Draft.

18 – Colorado traded G **Craig Anderson** to Ottawa for G **Brian Elliott**.

18 – Atlanta traded C **Rich Peverley** and D **Boris Valabik** to Boston for RW **Blake Wheeler** and D **Mark Stuart**.

18 – Toronto traded D **Tomas Kaberle** to Boston for C **Joe Colborne**, Boston's 1st-round choice (later traded to Anaheim – Anaheim selected RW **Rickard Rakell**) in the 2011 Entry Draft and Boston's 2nd-round choice (later traded to Colorado) in 2012 Entry Draft.

18 – San Jose traded D **Derek Joslin** to Carolina for future considerations.

18 – Carolina traded D **Ian White** to San Jose for San Jose's 2nd-round choice in the 2012 Entry Draft.

18 – St. Louis traded D **Eric Brewer** to Tampa Bay for D **Brock Beukeboom** and Tampa Bay's 3rd-round choice (G **Jordan Binnington**) in the 2011 Entry Draft.

19 – Colorado traded D **Kevin Shattenkirk**, RW **Chris Stewart** and Colorado's 2nd-round choice (RW **Ty Rattie**) in 2011 Entry Draft to St. Louis for D **Erik Johnson**, C **Jay McClement** and St. Louis's 1st round choice (D **Duncan Siemens**) in 2011 Entry Draft.

.21 – Dallas traded D **Matt Niskanen** and LW **James Neal** to Pittsburgh for D **Alex Goligoski**.

24 – Anaheim traded G **Curtis McElhinney** to Tampa Bay for G **Dan Ellis**.

24 – Ottawa traded RW **Alex Kovalev** to Pittsburgh for Pittsburgh's 7th round choice (C **Ryan Dzingel**) in the 2011 Entry Draft.

24 – Florida traded LW **Cory Stillman** to Carolina for C **Ryan Carter** and Carolina's 5th-round choice (later traded to Florida, later traded to Winnipeg, later traded to San Jose – San Jose selected C **Sean Kuraly**) in the 2011 Entry Draft.

24 – Atlanta traded D **Brent Sopel** and LW **Nigel Dawes** to Montreal for C **Ben Maxwell** and Atlanta/Winnipeg's 4th-round choice (D **Josiah Didier**) in the 2011 Entry Draft.

25 – Nashville traded D **Alexander Sulzer** to Florida for a conditional 7th-round choice in the 2012 Entry Draft.

26 – Florida traded D **Bryan McCabe** to NY Rangers for LW **Tim Kennedy** and NY Rangers' 3rd-round choice (RW **Logan Shaw**) in the 2011 Entry Draft.

27 – Anaheim traded RW **David Laliberte** and C **Stefan Chaput** to Boston for RW **Brian McGrattan** and D **Sean Zimmerman**.

27 – St. Louis traded RW **Brad Boyes** to Buffalo for Buffalo's 2nd-round choice (D **Joel Edmundson**) in the 2011 Entry Draft.

28 – Anaheim traded C **Maxim Lapierre** and C **MacGregor Sharp** to Vancouver for C **Joel Perrault** and Vancouver's 3rd-round choice in the 2012 Entry Draft.

28 – Atlanta traded RW **Niclas Bergfors** and LW **Patrick Rissmiller** to Florida for RW **Radek Dvorak** and Carolina's 5th-round choice in the 2011 Entry Draft (previously acquired, later traded to San Jose – San Jose selected C **Sean Kuraly**).

28 – Atlanta traded G **Drew MacIntyre** to Montreal for D **Brett Festerling**.

28 – Atlanta traded LW **Fredrik Modin** to Calgary for Calgary's 7th-round choice (later traded to San Jose – San Jose selected C **Colin Blackwell**) in 2011 Entry Draft.

28 – Boston traded D **Jeff Penner** and RW **Mikko Lehtonen** to Minnesota for G **Anton Khudobin**.

28 – Carolina traded LW **Sergei Samsonov** to Florida for D **Bryan Allen**.

28 – Chicago traded C **Ryan Potulny** and Chicago's 2nd-round choice (later traded to Detroit – Detroit selected D **Xavier Ouellet**) in the 2011 Entry Draft to Ottawa for D **Chris Campoli** and a conditional 7th-round choice in 2012.

28 – Colorado traded D **Kevin Montgomery** to Edmonton for D **Shawn Belle**.

28 – Columbus traded D **Rostislav Klesla** and LW **Dane Byers** to Phoenix for LW **Scottie Upshall** and D **Sami Lepisto**.

28 – Columbus traded LW **Tom Sestito** to Philadelphia for C **Michael Chaput** and RW **Greg Moore**.

28 – Edmonton traded RW **Dustin Penner** to Los Angeles for D **Colten Teubert**, Los Angeles' 1st-round choice (D **Oscar Klefborn**) in the 2011 Entry Draft and a conditional 3rd-round choice in 2012.

28 – Florida traded D **Dennis Wideman** to Washington for C **Jake Hauswirth** and Washington's 3rd-round choice (D **Jonathan Racine**) in the 2011 Entry Draft.

28 – Florida traded LW **Chris Higgins** to Vancouver for D **Evan Oberg** and Vancouver's 3rd-round choice in the 2013 Entry Draft.

28 – Florida traded D **Bryan Allen** to Carolina for LW **Sergei Samsonov**.

28 – New Jersey traded C **Jason Arnott** to Washington for C **David Steckel** and Washington's 2nd-round choice in the 2012 Entry Draft.

28 – St. Louis traded LW **Brad Winchester** to Anaheim for Anaheim's 3rd-round choice in the 2012 Entry Draft.

28 – Toronto traded C **John Mitchell** to NY Rangers for the Rangers' 7th-round choice in the 2012 Entry Draft.

MARCH, 2011

1 – Minnesota traded RW **Petr Kalus** to Columbus for future considerations.

MAY, 2011

8 – NY Rangers traded C **Ethan Werek** to Phoenix for C **Oscar Lindberg**.

JUNE, 2011

1 – NY Rangers traded LW **Roman Horak**, NY Rangers' 2nd round choice (C **Markus Granlund**) in 2011 Entry Draft and Washington's 2nd round choice (previously acquired, Calgary selected D **Tyler Wotherspoon**) in 2011 Entry Draft to Calgary for D **Tim Erixon** and Calgary's 5th round choice (RW **Shane McColgan**) in 2011 Entry Draft.

2 – Nashville traded LW **Taylor Stefishen** to Washington for future considerations.

7 – Phoenix traded the rights to G **Ilya Bryzgalov** to Philadelphia for LW **Matt Clackson**, Philadelphia's 3rd round choice in the 2012 Entry Draft and future considerations.

16 – Minnesota traded D **Maxim Noreau** to New Jersey for D **David McIntyre**.

23 – Columbus traded RW **Jakub Voracek** and Columbus's 1st (C **Sean Couturier**) and 3rd (C **Nick Cousins**) round choices in 2011 Entry Draft to Philadelphia for C **Jeff Carter**.

23 – Los Angeles traded C **Brayden Schenn**, RW **Wayne Simmonds** and a 2nd round choice in 2012 Entry Draft to Philadelphia for C **Mike Richards** and F **Rob Bordson**.

24 – Colorado traded D **John-Michael Liles** to Toronto for Boston's 2nd round choice (previously acquired) in 2012 Entry Draft.

24 – Chicago traded RW **Troy Brouwer** to Washington for Washington's 1st round choice (LW **Phillip Danault**) in 2011 Entry Draft.

24 – Minnesota traded D **Brent Burns** and a 2nd round choice in 2012 Entry Draft to San Jose for RW **Devin Setoguchi**, F **Charlie Coyle** and San Jose's 1st round choice (C **Zack Phillips**) in 2011 Entry Draft.

24 – Chicago traded D **Brian Campbell** to Florida for C **Rostislav Olesz.**

25 – Tampa Bay traded C **Marc Pouliot** to Phoenix for Phoenix's 7th round choice (C **Matthew Peca**) in 2011 Entry Draft.

25 – NY Islanders traded D **Bruno Gervais** to Tampa Bay for future considerations

25 – NY Rangers traded C **Evgeny Grachev** to St. Louis for St. Louis's 3rd round choice (C **Steven Fogarty**) in 2011 Entry Draft.

25 – Buffalo traded D **Chris Butler** and C **Paul Byron** to Calgary for D **Robyn Regehr**, RW **Ales Kotalik** and Calgary's 2nd round choice in 2012 Entry Draft.

25 – Columbus traded LW **Nikita Filatov** to Ottawa for Ottawa's 3rd round choice (C **Thomas Tynan**) in 2011 Entry Draft.

26 – Edmonton traded C **Colin Fraser** and a 7th round choice in 2012 Entry Draft to Los Angeles for LW **Ryan Smyth**.

27 – Philadelphia traded LW **Darrol Powe** to Minnesota for a 3rd round choice in 2013 Entry Draft.

27 – Chicago traded C **Tomas Kopecky** to Florida for future considerations.

28 – Vancouver traded D **Christian Ehrhoff** to NY Islanders for a 4th round choice in 2012 Entry Draft.

29 – Montreal traded D **James Wisniewski** to Columbus for future considerations.

29 – NY Islanders traded D **Christian Ehrhoff** to Buffalo for Buffalo's 4th round choice in 2012 Entry Draft.

29 – Buffalo traded the D **Steve Montador** to Chicago for future considerations.

JULY, 2011

1 – Philadelphia traded the rights to RW **Kris Versteeg** to Florida for a 2nd round choice in 2012 or 2013 Entry Draft and a 3rd round choice in 2012 Entry Draft.

1 – Washington traded the rights to G **Semyon Varlamov** to Colorado for Colorado's 1st round choice in 2012 Entry Draft and Colorado's 3rd round choice in 2012 or 2013 Entry Draft.

1 – Edmonton traded D **Kurtis Foster** to Anaheim for D **Andy Sutton**.

3 – Toronto traded D **Brett Lebda**, LW **Robert Slaney** and future considerations to Nashville for D **Cody Franson**, C **Matthew Lombardi** and future considerations.

3 – Minnesota traded RW **Martin Havlat** to San Jose for RW **Dany Heatley**.

5 – Carolina traded D **Joe Corvo** to Boston for Boston's 4th round choice in 2012 Entry Draft.

7 – Columbus traded RW **Michael Blunden** to Montreal for C **Ryan Russell**.

8 – Winnipeg traded RW **Danick Paquette** and a 4th round choice in 2012 Entry Draft to Washington for RW **Eric Fehr**.

8 – Florida traded LW **Mike Duco** to Vancouver for LW **Sergei Shirokov**.

9 – Florida traded LW **Kenndal McArdle** to Winnipeg for C **Angelo Esposito**.

9 – Calgary traded D **Keith Seabrook** to Florida for D **Jordan Henry**.

12 – Edmonton traded C **Andrew Cogliano** to Anaheim for a 2nd round choice in 2013 Entry Draft.

12 – New Jersey traded LW **Pierre-Luc Letourneau-Leblond** to Calgary for Calgary's 5th round choice in 2012 Entry Draft.

15 – Anaheim traded D **Mark Mitera** to Montreal for D **Mathieu Carle**.

28 – New Jersey traded C **Brian Rolston** to NY Islanders for RW **Trent Hunter**.

AUGUST, 2011

7 – Minnesota traded C **James Sheppard** to San Jose for San Jose's 3rd-round choice in the 2013 Entry Draft.

Trades and free agent signings after Aug. 12, 2011 are listed on page 609.

League Abbreviations

AHA ....Alberta Amateur Hockey Association
AAHL ....Alaska Amateur Hockey League
AASHA...............Alaska All-Stars Hockey Association
ACHA ....American Collegiate Hockey Association
ACHL ....Atlantic Coast Hockey League
AFHL ....American Frontier Hockey League
AH ....Atlantic Hockey
AHL ....American Hockey League
AJHL ....Alberta Junior Hockey League
ALIH ....Asia League Ice Hockey
Alpenliga ....Alpenliga (Austria, Italy, Slovenia 1994-1999)
AMHA ....Alberta Minor Hockey Association
AMBHL ....Alberta Major Bantam Hockey League
AMHL ....Alberta Midget AAA Hockey League
AUAA...............Atlantic University Athletic Association
AtJHL ....Atlantic Junior Hockey League
AWHL ....American West Hockey League
AYHL ....Atlantic Youth Hockey League
BCAHA ....British Columbia Amateur Hockey Association
BCHL ....British Columbia (Junior) Hockey League (also BCJHL)
BCMML ....British Columbia Major Midget League
CABHL ....Central Alberta Bantam Hockey League
CBHL ....Calgary Bantam Hockey League
CCHA ....Central Collegiate Hockey Association
CEGEP ....Quebec College Prep
CHA...............College Hockey America
CHL ....Central Hockey League
CIS.................Commonwealth of Independent States
CIS.................Canadian Interuniversity Sport
CJHL ....Central Junior A Hockey League
CMHA.............Calgary Minor Hockey Association
ColHL.............Colonial Hockey League
CSHL.............Central States Hockey League
CSJHL ....Central States Junior Hockey League
CWUAA ....Canadian Western University Athletic Association
ECAC ....Eastern College Athletic Conference
ECACHL ....ECAC Hockey League
ECHL ....East Coast Hockey League
EEHL ....Eastern European Hockey League
EJHL...............Eastern Junior Hockey League
EMHA.............Edmonton Minor Hockey Association
EmJHL.............Empire Junior B Hockey League
EuroHL...........European Hockey League
Exhib. ....Exhibition Games, Series or Season
GLHL...............Great Lakes Hockey League
GNML.............Greater North Midget League
GPAC.............Great Plains Athletic Conference
GTHL ....Greater Toronto Hockey League
H-East.............Hockey East
HJHL ....Heritage Junior Hockey League
High-XX ....High School (state/province)
IEHL...............Internationale Eishockey Liga
IHL.................International Hockey League
KIJHL ....Kootenay International Junior B Hockey League
LCJHL.............Little Caesar's Junior Hockey League
MAAC.............Metro Atlantic Athletic Conference
MAHA.............Manitoba Amateur Hockey Association
MAHL ....Mid America Hockey League
MBAHL ....Metropolitan Boston Amateur Hockey League
MBHL ....Metropolitan Boston Hockey League
MEHL.............Midwest Elite Hockey League
Metro-HL ....Metro Hockey League
MIAC.............Minnesota Intercollegiate Athletic Conference
Minor-XX ....Minor/Youth hockey (state/province)
MJHL ....Manitoba Junior Hockey League
MJrHL ....Maritime Junior A Hockey League
MMBHL ....Manitoba Major Bantam Hockey League
MMHL ....Manitoba Midget AAA Hockey League
MMHL ....Michigan Minor Hockey League
MMMHL ....Manitoba Minor Midget Hockey League
MNHL ....Michigan National Hockey League
MtJHL ....Metropolitan Junior Hockey League (New York)
MTJHL.............Metropolitan Toronto Junior Hockey League
MTHL.............Metro Toronto Hockey League

MWEHL ....Midwest Elite Hockey League
NAHL..............North American Hockey League (Tier I Junior)
NAJHL..............North American Junior Hockey League
Nat-Team ....National Team (also Nt.-Team)
NBAHA ....New Brunswick Amateur Hockey Association
NBMHL...........New Brunswick Midget Hockey League
NBPEI............New Brunswick Prince Edward Island Midget Hockey League
NCAA ....National Collegiate Athletic Association
NCHA ....Northern Collegiate Hockey Association
NEJHL ....New England Junior Hockey League
NFAHA...........Newfoundland Amateur Hockey Association
NHL ....National Hockey League
NJCAA.............National Junior Collegiate Athletic Association
NOBHL............Northern Ontario Bantam Hockey League
NOHA ....Northern Ontario Hockey Association
NOJHA............Northern Ontario Junior Hockey Association
NOJHL ....Northern Ontario Junior Hockey League
NSBHL............Nova Scotia Bantam Hockey League
NSMHL ....Nova Scotia Midget AAA Hockey League
NTHL ....North Texas Hockey League
NWJHL ....Northwest Junior B Hockey League
NYJHL............New York Junior Hockey League
OCJHL............Ontario Central Junior A Hockey League
OHA ....Ontario Hockey Association
OHL ....Ontario Hockey League
OJHL-B............Ontario Junior B Hockey Leagues
OMJHL............Ontario Major Junior Hockey League
OPJHL ....Ontario Provincial Junior A Hockey League
OUAA ....Ontario Universities Athletic Association
PAHA.............Pennsylvania Amateur Hockey Association
PCJHL ....Pacific Coast Junior Hockey League
PEIHA ....Prince Edward Island Hockey Association
PIJHL..............Pacific International Junior Hockey League
QAA ....Quebec Junior AA
QAAA ....Quebec Midget AAA Hockey League
QAHA ....Quebec Amateur Hockey Association
QJHL ....Quebec Junior Hockey League
QMJHL ....Quebec Major Junior Hockey League
QNAHL ....(Quebec) North American Hockey League
Q-RHL............(Quebec) Richelieu Elite Hockey League
QSPHL ....Quebec Semi-Pro Hockey League
RAMHL ....Rural Alberta Midget Hockey League
RMJHL ....Rocky Mountain Junior Hockey League
SAHA.............Saskatchewan Amateur Hockey Association
SAMHL ....Southern Alberta Midget Hockey League
SBHL ....Saskatchewan Bantam Hockey League
SCAHA............Southern California Amateur Hockey Association
SIJHL ....Superior International Junior Hockey League
SJHL..............Saskatchewan Junior Hockey League
SMBHL............Saskatchewan Major Bantam Hockey League
SMHL.............Saskatchewan Midget AAA Hockey League
SMMHL...........Saskatchewan Minor Midget Hockey League
SPHL ....Southern Professional Hockey League
SSJHL..............South Saskatchewan Junior B Hockey League
SSMHL............South Saskatchewan Minor Hockey League
SunHL............Sunshine Hockey League
T1EHL............Tier 1 Elite Hockey League
TBAHA...........Thunder Bay Amateur Hockey Association
TBJHL..............Thunder Bay Junior Hockey League
TBMHL...........Thunder Bay Midget Hockey League
U-17..............Under 17
U-18..............Under 18
UHL ....United Hockey League
UMEHL ....Upper Midwest Elite Hockey League
UMHSEL ....Upper Midwest High School Elite League
USAHA ....United States Amateur Hockey Association
USHL ....United States (Junior A) Hockey League
VIJHL ....Vancouver Island Junior Hockey League
WCHA ....Western Collegiate Hockey Association
WCHL ....West Coast Hockey League
WHL ....Western Hockey League
WNYHA ....Western New York Hockey Association
WPHL ....Western Professional Hockey League
WSJHL ....Western States Junior Hockey League

NHL Goal of the Year

Edmonton's Jordan Eberle wasted no time making an impact. His first goal, in his NHL debut versus Calgary on October 7, 2010, was a spectacular effort in which he took a long pass off the boards, jumped over the stick of a Flames defenseman and hoisted a backhander over goalie Miikka Kiprusoff. After tabulating Facebook fan voting, Eberle's effort was named NHL Goal of the Year and celebrated at the NHL Awards show in Las Vegas.

Contributors

The NHL Official Guide & Record Book is produced with the help of many. **Special thanks to:** Manny Almela, Dave Andjelic, Joe Babik (ECHL), Pam Baranski, John Batchelor, Guy Belair, Bob Borgen, Minako Borgen, Scott Bowley, Chris Brooks, John Bullman, Craig Campbell, Hugh Campbell, Paul Cannata, Jason Chaimovitch (AHL), Betty Chmilar, Des Christopher, Frank Cirone, Al Clark, Ken Coleman, Keith Davidson, Kim Davis, Pat Dennehy, Jason Farris, Dave Fischer (USA Hockey), Brent Fisher, Ernie Fitzsimmons, Cory Flett (WHL), Jon Frape, John Gardner, George Georgeopoulos, Stu Hackel, Curtis Hall, Kristian Hanson, Tiffany Harris, Hockey Hall of Fame, www.hockey-reference.com, www.hockeydb.com, Marlene Hoffmann, Bob Howe, Dane Jackson, Peter Jagla, Karl Jahnke (QMJHL), Allan Johnson, Alex Joseph, Jacques Henri, Karson Kaebel, Bruce Kirby, Edward Krajewski (ECAC), Igor Kuperman, Doug Langan, Keegan Lowe, Joanne Mahura, Sam Malkin, Liz Malone, Jim Mancuso, Jean-Patrice Martel, Kelly Masse, Chris Masters, Bob McAfee, Lori McDonald, Herb Morell (OHL), Bryan Morrison, Jeff Nash (Hockey Canada), NCAA Conference and School Sports Information Departments, NHL Broadcasters' Association, NHL Central Registry, www.nhlgms.com, NHL Officiating, NHL Players' Association, Blair Noel, Glenn Odebralski, Jim Parcels, John Paulson, Martine Pettem (Hockey Canada), Natasha Phillipson, Fred Pletsch (CCHA), www.pointstreak.com, Cale Politoski, Phil Pritchard, Pearl Rajwanth, Alex Riazanov, George Richards, Rita Rocys, Rob Rogers, David Rourke (AH), Della Ruopp, Martin Schmid, Darlene Shaw, Allie Skelly, Susan Snow, SIHR, Peter Souris (Hockey East), Doug Spencer (WCHA), Brian Strong, Kyle Tapp, Greg Thompson, Lesley Turcotte, Mike Vallescuro, Greg Walters, Jesse Watts (WHL), Courtney Welsh (USA Hockey), Jake Wesolek (U.S. National Team Development Program), Alex Whalen, Damon White, Paul Wilkinson (OPJHL).

Photo Credits

Hockey Hall of Fame: Various Collections.
Getty Images: Graig Abel (Abelimages), Claus Andersen, Scott Audette, Joel Auerbach, Brian Babineau, Steve Babineau, Al Bello, Bruce Bennett, Paul Bereswill, Andrew D. Bernstein, Frederick Breedon, S. Brinegar, Rob Carr, Kevin C. Cox, Andy Devlin, Melchior DiGiacomo, Elsa, Greg Fiume, Gregg Forwerck, Noah Graham, Jeff Gross, Norm Hall, Harry How, Craig Jones, Andy King, Francois Lacasse, Nick Laham, Rich Lam, S. Levy, Phillip MacCallum, Andy Marlin, Ronald Martinez, Juan Ocampo, Christian Petersen, Dave Reginek, Mike Ridewood, Andre Ringuette, Debra Robinson, John Russell, Jamie Sabau, Dave Sanford, Eliot J. Schechter, Gregory Shamus, Bill Smith, Rick Stewart, Mike Stobe, Jeff Vinnick, Bill Wippert.
Additional NHL team photographers: Chase Agnello-Dean, Doug Benc, Mark Buckner, Scott Cunningham, Glenn James, Bruce Kluckhohn, Mitchell Layton, Michael Martin, MSG Photo Department, Olivier Samson-Arcand, Gregory Shamus, Don Smith, Gerry Thomas, Rocky Widner.

Special thanks to Bruce Bennett, Paul Michinard, Getty Images

Researchers and historians: contact the Society for International Hockey Research (www.sihrhockey.org) and/or Hockey Reference (www.hockey-reference.com).

THREE STAR SELECTION...

NHL OFFICIAL GUIDE
IS PLEASED TO OFFER...

1.

THE NHL OFFICIAL GUIDE & RECORD BOOK
The NHL's authoritative information source. 80th year in print. 664 pages. The "Bible of Hockey". Read worldwide. This is the book issued to reporters, broadcasters, scouts and general managers.

2.

THE NHL YEARBOOK
200-page, full-color magazine with features on each club. Award winners, All-Stars and special statistics.

3.

THE NHL RULE BOOK
Larger format for 2011-12. Coil bound, new diagrams and tables. Combines complete playing rules, with the NHL officiating casebook. Plus rink dimensions and officials' signals.

Free Book List with each order.